Pocket Oxford Spanish Dictionary
Diccionario Oxford Compact

Diccionario Oxford Compact

Tercera edición

Español ---> Inglés
Inglés ---> Español

Dirección editorial
Nicholas Rollin
Carol Styles Carvajal
Jane Horwood

Pocket Oxford Spanish Dictionary

Third edition

Spanish ·····> English
English ·····> Spanish

Chief editors
Nicholas Rollin
Carol Styles Carvajal
Jane Horwood

OXFORD
UNIVERSITY PRESS

OXFORD
UNIVERSITY PRESS

Great Clarendon Street, Oxford OX2 6DP

Oxford University Press is a department of the University of Oxford.
It furthers the University's objective of excellence in research, scholarship,
and education by publishing worldwide in

Oxford New York

Auckland Cape Town Dar es Salaam Hong Kong Karachi
Kuala Lumpur Madrid Melbourne Mexico City Nairobi
New Delhi Shanghai Taipei Toronto

With offices in
Argentina Austria Brazil Chile Czech Republic France Greece
Guatemala Hungary Italy Japan South Korea Poland Portugal
Singapore Switzerland Thailand Turkey Ukraine Vietnam

Oxford is a registered trade mark of Oxford University Press
in the UK and in certain other countries

Published in the United States
by Oxford University Press Inc., New York

British Library Cataloguing in Publication Data

Data available

Library of Congress Cataloging in Publication Data

Data available

ISBN 978-0-19-861072-4
ISBN 978-0-19-861073-1 (Spanish cover edition for Spain)
ISBN 978-0-19-860733-5 (Spanish cover edition for USA)

7

Designed by Information Design Unit, Newport Pagnell
Typeset in Nimrod, Arial and Meta by Tradespools
Printed in Great Britain by Clays Ltd, St Ives plc

Preface / Prólogo

This new edition of the *Pocket Oxford Spanish Dictionary* has been revised and updated to meet the needs of both the general and school user. New words and phrases reflect scientific and technological innovations, as well as changes in politics, culture, and society.

Combining the authority of the *Oxford Spanish Dictionary* with the convenience of a smaller format and quick-access layout, this easy-to-use pocket dictionary is the ideal reference tool for all those requiring quick and reliable answers to their translation questions. It provides clear guidance on selecting the most appropriate translation, numerous examples to help with problems of usage and construction, and precise information on grammar, style, and pronunciation.

Included as special features are an A–Z guide to the culture of Spanish-speaking countries; a calendar of traditions, festivals, and holidays; a guide to letter writing, including sample letters and practical tips about key differences between Spanish and English letter styles and layout; information on text messaging and a glossary explaining grammatical terms used in the dictionary.

Geared to the needs of a wide range of users, from the student at intermediate level and above to the enthusiastic tourist or business professional, the *Pocket Oxford Spanish Dictionary* is an invaluable practical resource for learners of Spanish at the start of the twenty-first century.

Esta nueva edición del *Diccionario Oxford Compact* ha sido exhaustivamente revisada y actualizada a fin de satisfacer las necesidades tanto del usuario en general como del escolar. Nuevas palabras y frases reflejan las novedades producidas en el campo científico y técnico como también los cambios que se han experimentado en el plano político, cultural y social.

Al combinarse la autoridad del *Gran Diccionario Oxford* con la comodidad del formato más pequeño y un diseño de acceso rápido, este diccionario es un instrumento ideal de referencia para todos aquellos que necesiten una respuesta rápida y fiable para las preguntas que surjan al traducir. Proporciona una guía clara para seleccionar la traducción más apropiada, incluye numerosos ejemplos que ayudan con los problemas de uso y construcción, como también información precisa sobre gramática, estilo y pronunciación.

Como característica relevante, se incluyen una lista desde la A a la Z de la vida y cultura estadounidenses y británicas, y un calendario con los días festivos, fiestas y tradiciones en estos países. Además contiene una guía para la redacción de cartas, con datos prácticos sobre las diferencias fundamentales entre el español y el inglés en cuanto al estilo y composición de una carta, y también un glosario con los términos gramaticales usados en el diccionario. Se incluye una sección sobre mensajes de texto por primera vez.

El *Diccionario Oxford Compact* ha sido preparado teniendo en cuenta las necesidades de una gran variedad de usuarios, y es un inapreciable instrumento práctico de trabajo para los que aprenden el inglés a comienzos del siglo veintiuno.

List of contributors / Lista de colaboradores

Chief Editors/Dirección editorial
Nicholas Rollin
Carol Styles Carvajal
Jane Horwood

Data input/Entrada de datos
Anne McConnell
Marianne Selby-Smith
Anna Cotgreave
Sara Hawker

Días festivos, fiestas y tradiciones en EEUU y Gran Bretaña
La vida y cultura anglosajonas desde la 'A' a la 'Z'

Traditions, festivals and holidays in the Hispanic world
A–Z of Hispanic life and culture

Penelope Isaac
Carol Styles Carvajal
Stephen Curtis

Valerie Grundy
Ana Cristina Llompart
Josephine Grundy
Mónica Bossons

Spanish Grammar
John Butt

Gramática inglesa
Nicholas Rollin
Carmen Fernández Marsden

Contents / Índice

Proprietary names / Marcas registradas

This dictionary includes some words which have, or are asserted to have, proprietary status as trademarks or otherwise. Their inclusion does not imply that they have acquired for legal purposes a non-proprietary or general significance, nor is any other judgment implied concerning their legal status. In cases where the editorial staff have some evidence that a word has proprietary status, this is indicated in the entry for that word by the symbol ®, but no judgment concerning the legal status of such words is made or implied thereby.

Este diccionario incluye palabras que constituyen, o se afirma que constituyen, marcas registradas o nombres comerciales. Su inclusión no significa que a efectos legales hayan dejado de tener ese carácter, ni supone un pronunciamiento respecto de su situación legal.

Cuando al editor le consta que una palabra es una marca registrada o un nombre comercial, esto se indica por medio del símbolo ®, lo que tampoco supone un pronunciamiento acerca de la situación legal de esa palabra.

Structure of a Spanish–English entry

Headword •————— **acertijo** *m* riddle, puzzle
Vocablo cabeza de
artículo

Variant form of •——— **achichincle, achichinque** *mf* (Méx fam &
headword pey) hanger-on (colloq & pej)
Variante del vocablo
cabeza de artículo

acomodar [A1] *vt* **1** (adaptar, amoldar) to adapt •—— **Sense divisions**
2 ⟨*huésped*⟩ to put ... up **3** **(a)** (AmL) (arreglar) to **Divisiones**
arrange; (poner) to put **(b)** (fam) ⟨*persona*⟩ (en correspondientes a las
puesto): **su tío lo acomodó en su sección** his uncle distintas acepciones
fixed him up with a job in his department

acomplejado -da *adj*: **es muy** ∼ he's full of
complexes; **está** ∼ **por su gordura** he has a
complex about being fat
A change of part of •——— ■ *m,f*: **es un** ∼ he's a mass of complexes
speech within an entry **acomplejar** [A1] *vt* to give ... a complex
is marked by a box ■ ■ **acomplejarse** *v pron* to get a complex
Todo cambio de categoría
gramatical dentro de una
entrada se indica con el
símbolo ■

acondicionar [A1] *vt* **(a)** ⟨*vivienda/local*⟩ to •—— **Part of speech**
equip, fit out **(b)** (Col) ⟨*carro*⟩ to soup up Función gramatical
aconsejable *adj* advisable

Irregular plural form •——— **acusetas** *mf* (*pl* ∼), **acusete -ta** *m,f* (fam)
Plurales irregulares tattletale (AmE colloq), telltale (BrE colloq)

adecuar [A1] *or* [A18] *vt* ∼ **algo A algo** to •—— **Every verb has a**
adapt sth ᴛᴏ sth **reference to the verb**
 tables on p. 1003
 Cada verbo se remite a
 la tabla de
 conjugaciones en la
 página 1003

The use of ser or estar •——— **agarrado¹ -da** *adj* **(a)** [ꜱᴇʀ] (fam) (tacaño)
with adjectives is tightfisted (colloq) **(b)** [ᴇꜱᴛᴀʀ] (CS fam) (enamorado)
marked when necessary in love
El uso de ser o estar con ■ *m,f* (fam) (tacaño) skinflint (colloq), tightwad (AmE
adjetivos se indica donde colloq)
es necesario

águila *f‡* **(a)** (ave) eagle; **ser un** ∼ to be very •—— **The part of speech** *f‡*
sharp **(b)** (Méx) (de moneda) ≈ heads (*pl*); **¿**∼ **o** **indicates a feminine**
sol? heads or tails? **noun that takes the**
 masculine article in
 the singular
 La función gramatical
 f‡ indica un sustantivo
 femenino usado con el
 artículo masculino en el
 singular

Structure of a Spanish–English entry

Pronominal verb •———— ■ **apretujarse** *v pron* to squash *o* squeeze
Verbo pronominal together

aprobación *f* (de proyecto de ley, moción) ———• **Sense indicators**
passing; (de préstamo, acuerdo, plan) approval, Indicadores semánticos
endorsement; (de actuación, conducta) approval

Field labels •———— **arco** *m* 1 (Arquit) arch; (Anat) arch; (Mat) arc; ~
Indicadores de campo **de triunfo** triumphal arch; ~ **iris** rainbow
semántico 2 (AmL) (en fútbol) goal 3 (a) (Arm, Dep) bow (b)
(de violín) bow

arete *m* (Col, Méx) earring ———————• **Regional labels**
armario *m* (a) (para ropa — mueble) wardrobe; Indicadores de uso
(— empotrado) closet (AmE), wardrobe (BrE) (b) (de regional
cocina) cupboard; (de cuarto de baño) cabinet

Stylistic labels •———— **armatoste** *m* (fam) huge great thing (colloq)
Indicadores de estilo

ascendencia *f* (a) (linaje) descent, ancestry; ———• **Examples**
es de ~ francesa he is of French descent (b) Ejemplos
(origen) origin(s); **su ~ humilde** her humble
origins

Idioms and proverbs •———— **ascua** *f‡* ember; **estar en/tener a algn en ~s**
appear in bold italics (fam) to be on/to keep sb on tenterhooks
Los modismos y los **aspereza** *f* 1 (a) (de superficie, piel) roughness
proverbios aparecen en **(b)** (de sabor) sharpness; (de voz, clima) harshness
negritas cursivas 2 (parte áspera): **usar papel de lija para quitar las**
~s use sandpaper to remove any roughness;
limar ~s to smooth things over

aviso *m* 1 (a) (notificación) notice; ❺ **aviso al** ———• ❺ **indicates the use of**
público notice to the public; **dio ~ a la policía** he **the headword in**
notified *o* informed the police ... **signs, notices,**
warnings, etc
El símbolo ❺ indica el
uso del vocablo cabeza
de artículo en letreros,
anuncios, advertencias,
etc.

Universally valid translation(s) followed by regional alternative(s)
Traducción universalmente válida seguida de alternativas regionales

balancín *m* (de niños) seesaw, teeter-totter (AmE)
balompié *m* soccer, football (BrE)

defensa *f* ⬚1 **(a)** (protección) defense*; **salir en ~ de algn** to come to sb's defense; **actuó en ~ propia** he acted in self-defense; **~ DE algo/algn** defense* or sth/sb; **~ personal** self-defense* **(b)** (Dep) defense* ⬚2 **(a) Defensa** *f* the Defense Department (AmE), the Ministry of Defence (BrE) **(b) defensas** *fpl* (Biol, Med) defenses* (*pl*) **(c) defensa** *mf* (jugador) defender

• Si una traducción va seguida de un asterisco (*), la grafía que se ofrece es la norteamericana. La versión británica se encuentra como variante del vocablo en la parte Inglés-Español
An asterisk (*) following a translation shows an American English spelling. The British spelling is given in the English-Spanish section as a variant of the word concerned

Words often used with the headword, shown to help select the correct translation for each context
Palabras que suelen acompañar al vocablo cabeza de artículo y que ayudan a elegir la traducción que corresponde a cada contexto

bancario -ria *adj* ‹*interés/préstamo*› bank (*before n*); ‹*sector*› banking (*before n*)
bañar [A1] *vt* ⬚1 ‹*niño/enfermo*› to bath, give ... a bath ⬚2 ‹*pulsera/cubierto*› to plate
bifurcarse [A2] *v pron* «*camino*» to fork, diverge (frml); «*vía férrea*» to diverge

bancario -ria *adj* ‹*interés/préstamo*› bank (*before n*); ‹*sector*› banking (*before n*)

• Nouns modified by an adjective
Sustantivos calificados por un adjetivo

bañar [A1] *vt* ⬚1 ‹*niño/enfermo*› to bath, give ... a bath ⬚2 ‹*pulsera/cubierto*› to plate

• Objects of a verb
Complementos de un verbo

bifurcarse [A2] *v pron* «*camino*» to fork, diverge (frml); «*vía férrea*» to diverge

• Subjects of a verb appear in double angled parentheses
Los posibles sujetos de un verbo aparecen entre paréntesis angulares dobles

The sign ≈ is used to indicate approximate equivalence
El símbolo ≈ indica un equivalente aproximado en la lengua de destino

canciller *m* **(a)** (jefe de estado) chancellor **(b)** (AmS) (ministro) ≈ Secretary of State (*in US*), ≈ Foreign Secretary (*in UK*)

Grammatical constructions in which the headword commonly occurs are indicated by small capitals
Las construcciones gramaticales en las que suele aparecer el vocablo cabeza de artículo se destacan mediante versalitas

■ **cansarse** *v pron* (a) (fatigarse) to tire oneself out; **se le cansa la vista** her eyes get tired (b) (aburrirse) to get bored; ~**se DE algo/algn** to get tired OF sth/sb, get bored WITH sth/sb, ~**se DE hacer algo** to get tired OF doing sth

carnet /kar'ne/ *m* (*pl* -**nets**) ▶ CARNÉ
ceder [E1] *vt* ⓵ (a) ⟨*derecho*⟩ to transfer, assign; ⟨*territorio*⟩ to cede; ⟨*puesto/título*⟩ (voluntariamente) to hand over; (a la fuerza) to give up; ~ **el poder** to hand over power; **me cedió el asiento** he let me have his seat; ▶ PASO 1B (b) ⟨*balón/pelota*⟩ to pass

• An arrow directs the user to another entry with the same meaning or to where a compound, idiomatic expression, or other useful expression is to be found
Se utiliza una flecha para remitir al usuario a una variante sinónima o a otro artículo donde aparece un compuesto, un modismo u otro uso de interés

'ver tb' directs the user to a headword where additional information is to be found
'ver tb' remite al usuario a otro artículo donde se hallará información complementaria

chiva *f* ⓵ (AmL) (barba) goatee ⓶ (Col) (bus) rural *o* country bus ⓷ (Col period) (primicia) scoop, exclusive ⓸ (Chi fam) (mentira) cock-and-bull story (colloq); *ver tb* CHIVO ⓹ **chivas** *fpl* (Méx fam) (cachivaches) junk (colloq)

Estructura del artículo Inglés–Español

Vocablo cabeza de artículo
Headword

alligator /'æləgeɪtər ‖ 'ælɪgeɪtə(r)/ *n* aligátor *m*

all: ~**-important** /'ɔːlɪm'pɔːrtn̩t ‖ ,ɔːlɪm'pɔːtn̩t/ *adj* de suma importancia; ~**-night** /'ɔːl'naɪt/ *adj* ⟨*party/show*⟩ que dura toda la noche; ⟨*café/store*⟩ que está abierto toda la noche

• Nombres compuestos
Compounds

La transcripción fonética aparece inmediatamente después del vocablo cabeza de artículo [ver página xxi]
Pronunciation is shown immediately after the headword [see p. xxi]

allocate /'æləkeɪt/ *vt* asignar; (distribute) repartir; **$3 million has been ~d for research** se han destinado tres millones de dólares a la investigación

Variante del vocablo •——— **amoeba**, (AmE also) **ameba** /əˈmiːbə/ n ameba
cabeza de artículo   f, amiba f
Variant form of a
headword

answer¹ /ˈænsər ‖ ˈɑːnsə(r)/ n 🔟 (a) (reply)   ——• **Divisiones**
respuesta f, contestación f; in ∼ to your question   **correspondientes a**
para contestar tu pregunta **(b)** (response): her ∼   **las distintas**
to his rudeness was to ignore it respondió a su   **acepciones**
grosería ignorándola; **Britain's** ∼ **to Elvis Presley**   Sense divisions
el Elvis Presley británico 🔢 **(a)** (in exam, test,
quiz) respuesta f **(b)** (solution) solución f; ∼ TO sth
solución DE algo

Los verbos con •——— **answer²** vt 🔟 **(a)** (reply to) ⟨person/letter⟩
partícula aparecen al   contestar ...
final del artículo   ■ **answer back** 🔟 [v + adv] (rudely) contestar
correspondiente   🔢 [v + o + adv] to ∼ sb back contestarle mal or
Phrasal verbs appear at   de mala manera a algn
the end of the root word   ■ **answer for** [v + prep + o] (accept responsibility
entry   for) ⟨conduct/consequences⟩ responder de; **his**
                               parents have a lot to ∼ **for** sus padres tienen
                               mucha culpa

appreciate /əˈpriːʃieɪt/ vt **(a)** (value) ⟨food/   ——• **Todo cambio de**
novel⟩ apreciar **(b)** (be grateful for) agradecer* **(c)**   **categoría gramatical**
(understand) ⟨danger/difficulties⟩ darse* cuenta de;   **de un verbo se indica**
I ∼ that, but ... lo comprendo, pero ...   **con el símbolo ■**
■ ∼ vi «shares/property» (re)valorizarse*   A change of part of
                                                        speech of a verb is
                                                        marked by a box ■

Función gramatical •——— **approximate** /əˈprɑːksəmət ‖ əˈprɒksɪmət/
Part of speech   **adj** aproximado
                        approximately /əˈprɑːksəmətli
                        ‖ əˈprɒksɪmətli/ **adv** aproximadamente

artery /ˈɑːrtəri ‖ ˈɑːtəri/ n (pl **-ries**) arteria f   ——• **Inflexiones**
auditorium /ˈɔːdəˈtɔːriəm ‖ ˌɔːdɪˈtɔːriəm/ n (pl   **irregulares**
-riums or **-ria** /-riə/) auditorio m   Irregular inflections

El comparativo y el •——— **baggy** /ˈbægi/ adj **-gier, -giest** ancho, guango
superlativo del adjetivo   (Méx)
Comparative and
superlative forms of an
adjective

Estructura del artículo Inglés–Español

bang² *vt* **(a)** (strike) golpear **(b)** (slam): he ~ed the door dio un portazo (fam)
■ ~ *vi* **(a)** (strike) to ~ ON sth golpear algo; to ~ INTO sth darse* CONTRA algo **(b)** (slam) «*door*» cerrarse* de un golpe

— **Las construcciones gramaticales en las que suele aparecer el vocablo cabeza de artículo se destacan mediante versalitas**
Grammatical constructions in which the headword commonly occurs are indicated by small capitals

Fórmulas que demuestran el comportamiento sintáctico de cada verbo con partícula. Señalan las posibles combinaciones de verbo [v], adverbio [adv], preposición [prep] y complemento [o]
Syntactical pattern of phrasal verbs, showing the possible combinations of verb [v], adverb [adv], preposition [prep], and object [o]

■ **bear out** [v + o + adv, v + adv + o] «*theory*» confirmar
■ **bear up** [v + adv]: she bore up well under the strain sobrellevó muy bien la situación

beg /beg/ **-gg-** *vt* ⬛1 «*money/food*» pedir*, mendigar* ⬛2 (fml) **(a)** (entreat) «*person*» suplicarle* a, rogarle* a **(b)** (ask for) «*forgiveness*» suplicar*, rogar*
■ ~ *vi* «*beggar*» pedir*, mendigar*; to ~ for mercy pedir* *or* suplicar* clemencia

— **Un asterisco señala los verbos de conjugación irregular en la traducción al español**
An asterisk indicates an irregular verb in the translation

Indicadores semánticos
Sense indicators

belief /bə'liːf ‖ bɪ'liːf/ *n* **(a)** (conviction, opinion) creencia *f* **(b)** (confidence) ~ IN sb/sth confianza *f* *or* fe *f* EN algn/algo **(c)** (Relig) fe *f*

belt¹ /belt/ *n* ⬛1 (Clothing) cinturón *m* ⬛2 (Mech Eng) correa *f*

— **Indicadores de campo semántico**
Field labels

Indicadores de uso regional
Regional labels

Biro®, **biro** /'baɪrəʊ ‖ 'baɪərəʊ/ *n* (*pl* **biros**) (BrE) bolígrafo *m*, birome *f* **(RPl)**, esfero *m* (Col), lápiz *m* de pasta (Chi), boli *m* (Esp fam)

Estructura del artículo Inglés–Español

bitch /bɪtʃ/ n **1** (female dog) perra f **2** (spiteful woman) (AmE vulg, BrE sl) bruja f (fam), arpía f (fam), cabrona f (Esp, Méx vulg)

• **Indicadores de estilo**
Stylistic labels

Ejemplos
Examples

bounce² n **(a)** (action) rebote m, pique m (AmL) **(b)** (springiness, vitality): **this shampoo puts the ~ back into your hair** este champú les da nueva vida a sus cabellos; **she's full of ~** es una persona llena de vida

breath /breθ/ n aliento m; **to have bad ~** tener* mal aliento; **to take a ~** aspirar, inspirar; **take a deep ~** respire hondo; **out of ~** sin aliento; **to hold one's ~** contener* la respiración; **to take sb's ~ away** dejar a algn sin habla

• **Los modismos y los proverbios aparecen en negritas cursivas**
Idioms and proverbs appear in bold italics

El símbolo ⑤ indica el uso del vocablo cabeza de artículo en letreros, anuncios, advertencias, etc.
⑤ indicates the use of the headword in signs, notices, warnings, etc

2 [v + o + adv] **to ~ sb back** contestarle mal or de mala manera a algn
■ **answer for** [v + prep + o] (accept responsibility

dump¹ /dʌmp/ n **1** (place for waste) vertedero m (de basura), basural m (AmL), tiradero m (Méx) ...

• **Traducción universalmente válida seguida de alternativas regionales**
Universal Spanish translation followed by regional alternatives

Palabras que suelen acompañar al vocablo cabeza de artículo y que ayudan a elegir la traducción que corresponde a cada contexto
Words often used with the headword, shown to help select the correct translation for each context

ease² vt **1 (a)** (relieve) ‹pain› calmar, aliviar; ‹tension› hacer* disminuir, aliviar; ‹burden› aligerar; **to ~ sb's mind** tranquilizar* a algn **(b)** (make easier) ‹situation› paliar; ‹transition› facilitar; **to ~ the way for sth** preparar el terreno para algo
■ **ease off** [v + adv] «rain» amainar; «pain» aliviarse, calmarse; «pressure/traffic» disminuir*
efficient /ɪ'fɪʃənt/ adj ‹person/system› eficiente; ‹machine/engine› de buen rendimiento

ease² vt **1 (a)** (relieve) ‹pain› calmar, aliviar; ‹tension› hacer* disminuir, aliviar; ‹burden› aligerar; **to ~ sb's mind** tranquilizar* a algn **(b)** (make easier) ‹situation› paliar; ‹transition› facilitar; **to ~ the way for sth** preparar el terreno para algo

• **Complementos de un verbo**
Objects of a verb

■ **ease off** [v + adv] «rain» amainar; «pain» aliviarse, calmarse; «pressure/traffic» disminuir*

• **Los posibles sujetos de un verbo aparecen entre paréntesis angulares dobles**
Subjects of a verb appear in double angled brackets

efficient /ɪ'fɪʃənt/ adj ‹person/system› eficiente; ‹machine/engine› de buen rendimiento

• **Sustantivos calificados por un adjetivo**
Nouns modified by an adjective

Estructura del artículo Inglés–Español

Inland Revenue /'ɪnlənd/ *n* (in UK) the ~ ~
≈ Hacienda, ≈ la Dirección General Impositiva
(*en RPl*), ≈ Impuestos Internos (*en Chi*)

**El símbolo ≈ indica
un equivalente
aproximado en la
lengua de destino**
The sign ≈ is used to
indicate approximate
equivalence

**Se utiliza una flecha
para remitir al usuario a
una variante sinónima o
a otro artículo donde
aparece un compuesto,
un modismo u otro uso
de interés**
An arrow directs the user
to another entry with the
same meaning or to
where a compound,
idiomatic expression, or
other useful expression is
to be found

inmost /'ɪnməʊst/ *adj* ▶ INNERMOST
jersey /'dʒərzi ‖ 'dʒɜːzi/ *n* (*pl* **-seys**) ① (a)
(sports shirt) camiseta *f* (b) (Tex) jersey *m* (c) (BrE)
▶ SWEATER ② **Jersey** (la isla de) Jersey

jetsam /'dʒetsəm/ *n* echazón *f*; *see also* FLOTSAM

**'see also' remite al
usuario a otro artículo
donde se hallará
información
complementaria**
'see also' directs the
user to a headword
where additional
information is to be
found

The pronunciation of Spanish

Symbols used in this dictionary

The pronunciation of Spanish words is directly represented by their written form and therefore phonetic transcriptions have only been supplied for loan words which retain their original spelling.

Consonants and semi-vowels

Symbol	Example	Approximation
/b/	**boca** /'boka/ **vaso** /'baso/	English *b* in bin but without the aspiration that follows it.
/β/	**cabo** /'kaβo/ **ave** /'aβe/	Very soft *b*, produced with the lips hardly meeting.
/d/	**dolor** /do'lor/	English *d* in *den*.
/ð/	**cada** /'kaða/	English *th* in *rather*.
/f/	**fino** /'fino/	English *f* in *feat*.
/g/	**gota** /'gota/	English *g* in *goat*.
/ɤ/	**pago** /'paɤo/ **largo** /'larɤo/	Very soft continuous sound, not punctuated like /g/.
/ʝ/	**mayo** /'maʝo/ **llave** /'ʝaβe/	English *y* in *yet*. For regional variants see points 7 and 14 of **General Rules of Spanish Pronunciation** on page xviii.
/j/	**tiene** /'tjene/	English *y* in *yet*.
/k/	**cama** /'kama/ **cuna** /'kuna/ **quiso** /'kiso/ **kilo** /'kilo/	English *c* in *cap* but without the aspiration that follows it.
/l/	**lago** /'laɤo/	English *l* in *lid*.

Symbol	Example	Approximation
/m/	**mono** /'mono/	English *m* in *most*.
/n/	**no** /no/	English *n* in *nib*.
/ŋ/	banco /'baŋko/	English *ng* in *song*.
/ɲ/	**año** /'aɲo/	Like *gn* in French *soigné*, similar to the *ni* in *onion*.
/p/	**peso** /'peso/	English *p* in *spin*.
/r/	**aro** /'aro/ **árbol** /'arβol/	A single flap with a curved tongue against the palate.
/rr/	**rato** /'rrato/ **parra** /'parra/	A rolled 'r' as found in some Scottish accents.
/s/	**asa** /'asa/ **celo** /'selo/ **cinco** /'siŋko/ **azote** /a'sote/	Latin-American Spanish — English *s* in stop.
/θ/	**celo** /'θelo/ **cinco** /'θiŋko/ **azote** /a'θote/	European Spanish — English *th* in *thin*.
/t/	**todo** /'toðo/	English *t* in *step*.
/tʃ/	**chapa** /'tʃapa/	English *ch* in *church*.
/w/	**cuatro** /'kwatro/	English *w*.
/x/	**jota** /'xota/ **general** /xene'ral/ **gigante** /xi'ɤante/	*ch* in *Scottish loch*.
/z/	**desde** /'dezðe/	English *s* in *is*.

The pronunciation of Spanish

Vowels

None of the five Spanish vowels corresponds exactly to an English vowel.

Symbol	Example	Approximation
/a/	**casa** /'kasa/	Shorter than *a* in *father*.
/e/	**seco** /'seko/	English *e* in *pen*.
/i/	**fin** /fin/	Between English *ee* in *seen* and *i* in *sin*.
/o/	**oro** /'oro/	Shorter than English *o* in *rose*.
/u/	**uña** /'uɲa/	Between English *oo* in *boot* and *oo* in *foot*.

The stress mark

When phonetic transcriptions of Spanish headwords are given in the dictionary, the symbol ' precedes the syllable that carries the stress:

footing /'futin/

For information about where other words should be stressed, see the section **Stress** on the next page.

General rules of Spanish pronunciation

Consonants

1 The letters *b* and *v* are pronounced in exactly the same way: /b/ when at the beginning of an utterance or after *m* or *n* (**barco** /'barko/, **vaca** /'baka/, **ambos** /'ambos/), and /β/ in all other contexts (**rabo** /'rraβo/, **ave** /'aβe/, **árbol** /'arβol/).

2 *C* is pronounced /k/ when followed by a consonant other than *h* or by *a*, *o* or *u* (**acto** /'akto/, **casa** /'kasa/, **coma** /'koma/). When it is followed by *e* or

i, it is pronounced /s/ in Latin America and parts of southern Spain and /θ/ in the rest of Spain (**cero** /'sero/, /'θero/; **cinco** /'siŋko/, /'θiŋko/).

3 *D* is pronounced /d/ when it occurs at the beginning of an utterance or after *n* or *l* (**digo** /'diɣo/, **anda** /'anda/) and /ð/ in all other contexts (**hada** /'aða/, **arde** /'arðe/). It is often not pronounced at all at the end of a word (**libertad** /liβer'ta(ð)/, **Madrid** /ma'ðri(ð)/).

4 *G* is pronounced /x/ when followed by *e* or *i* (**gitano** /xi'tano/, **auge** /'awxe/). When followed by *a*, *o*, *u*, *ue* or *ui* it is pronounced /g/ if at the beginning of an utterance or after *n* (**gato** /'gato/, **gula** /'gula/, **tango** /'taŋgo/, **guiso** /'giso/) and /ɣ/ in all other contexts (**hago** /'aɣo/, **trague** /'traɣe/). Note that the *u* is not pronounced in the combinations *gue* and *gui*, unless it is written with a diaeresis (**paragüero** /para'ɣwero/, **agüita** /a'ɣwita/).

5 *H* is mute in Spanish, (**huevo** /'weβo/, **almohada** /almo'aða/) except in the combination *ch*, which is pronounced /tʃ/ (**chico** /'tʃiko/, **leche** /'letʃe/).

6 *J* is always pronounced /x/ (**jamón** /xa'mon/, **jefe** /'xefe/).

7 The pronunciation of *ll* varies greatly throughout the Spanish-speaking world.

a It is pronounced rather like the *y* in English *yes* by the majority of speakers, who do not distinguish between the pronunciation of *ll* and that of *y* (e.g. between *haya* and *halla*). The sound is pronounced slightly more emphatically when at the beginning of an utterance.

b In some areas, particularly Bolivia, parts of Chile, Peru and Castile in Spain, the distinction between *ll* and *y* has been preserved. In these areas *ll* is pronounced similarly to *lli* in *million*.

c In the River Plate area *ll* is pronounced /ʒ/ (as in English *measure*), sometimes tending toward /ʃ/ (as in *shop*).

8 *Ñ* is always pronounced /ɲ/.

9 *Q* is pronounced /k/, and the *u* that always follows it is silent (**quema** /ˈkema/, **quiso** /ˈkiso/).

10 *R* is pronounced /r/ when it occurs between vowels or in syllable-final position (**aro** /ˈaro/, **barco** /ˈbarko/, **cantar** /kanˈtar/). It is pronounced /rr/ when in initial position (**rama** /ˈrrama/). The double consonant *rr* is always pronounced /rr/.

11 *S* is pronounced /s/ but it is aspirated by speakers in many regions when it occurs in syllable-final position (**hasta** /ˈahta/, **los cuatro** /lohˈkwatro/). In other regions it is voiced when followed by a voiced consonant (**mismo** /ˈmɪzmo/, **los dos** /lozˈðos/).

12 *V* see 1 above.

13 *X* is pronounced /ks/, although there is a marked tendency to render it as /s/ before consonants (**extra** /ˈekstra/, /ˈestra/).

In some words derived from Nahuatl and other Indian languages it is pronounced /x/ (**México** /ˈmexiko/) and in others it is pronounced /s/ (**Xochimilco** /sotʃiˈmilko/).

14 When followed by a vowel within the same syllable *y* is pronounced rather like the *y* in English *yes* (slightly more emphatically when at the beginning of an utterance). In the River Plate area it is pronounced /ʒ/ (as in English *measure*), sometimes tending toward /ʃ/ (as in *shop*).

As the conjunction *y* and in syllable-final position, *y* is pronounced /i/.

15 *Z* is pronounced /s/ in Latin America and parts of southern Spain and /θ/ in the rest of Spain.

Stress

When no phonetic transcription is given for a Spanish headword, the following rules determine where it should be stressed:

1 If there is no written accent:

a a word is stressed on the penultimate syllable if it ends in a vowel, or in *n* or *s*:
arma /ˈarma/
ponen /ˈponen/
mariposas /mariˈposas/

b words which end in a consonant other than *n* or *s* are stressed on the last syllable:
cantar /kanˈtar/
delantal /delanˈtal/
maguey /maˈɣei/

2 If a word is not stressed in accordance with the above rules, the written accent indicates the syllable where the emphasis is to be placed:
balcón /balˈkon/
salí /saˈli/
carácter /kaˈrakter/

It should be noted that unstressed vowels have the same quality as stressed vowels and are not noticeably weakened as they are in

English. For example, there is no perceptible difference between any of the e's in *entenderé* or between the a's in *Panamá*.

Combinations of vowels

A combination of a strong vowel (*a, e* or *o*) and a weak vowel (*i* or *u*) or of two weak vowels forms a diphthong and is therefore pronounced as one syllable. The stress falls on the strong vowel if there is one. In a combination of two weak vowels, it falls on the second element:

cuando /ˈkwando/ *stressed on the* /a/
aula /ˈawla/ *stressed on the* /a/
viudo /ˈbjuðo/ *stressed on the* /u/

A combination of two strong vowels does not form a diphthong and the vowels retain their separate values. They count as two separate syllables for the purposes of applying the above rules on stress:

faena /faˈena/ *stressed on the* /e/
polea /poˈlea/ *stressed on the* /e/

La pronunciación del inglés

La transcripción fonética que sigue a cada palabra cabeza de artículo corresponde a la pronunciación norteamericana de uso más extendido en los Estados Unidos.

Se ha incluido la pronunciación británica (precedida por el símbolo ‖) únicamente en aquellos casos en que esta difiere sustancialmente de la pronunciación norteamericana. Ejemplo:

address[1] /ˈædres ‖ əˈdres/
induce /ɪnˈduːs ‖ ɪnˈdjuːs/

Se reconoce la validez de muchas variantes regionales, tanto norteamericanas como británicas, pero estas no se han incluido por razones de espacio.

Los símbolos empleados en las transcripciones son los del Alfabeto Fonético Internacional (AFI). Estos se enumeran a continuación, seguidos de un ejemplo y una breve aproximación o descripción del sonido que representan. Estas descripciones no siguen criterios fonéticos estrictos.

Consonantes y semivocales

Símbolo	Ejemplo	Aproximación
/b/	**bat** /bæt/	Sonido más explosivo que el de una *b* inicial española.
/d/	**dig** /dɪg/	Sonido más explosivo que el de una *d* inicial española.
/dʒ/	**jam** /dʒæm/	Similar a una *ch* pero más cercano al sonido inicial de *Giuseppe* en italiano.
/f/	**fit** /fɪt/	Como la *f* española.
/g/	**good** /gʊd/	Sonido más explosivo que el de una *g* inicial española.

Símbolo	Ejemplo	Aproximación
/h/	**hat** /hæt/	Sonido de aspiración más suave que la *j* española, articulado como si se estuviera intentando empañar un espejo con el aliento.
/hw/	**wheel** /hwiːl/	Una /w/ con la aspiración de la /h/ (muchos hablantes no distinguen entre /hw/ y /w/ y pronuncian *whale* de la misma manera que *wail*).
/j/	**yes** /jes/	Como la *y* española en *yema* y *yo* (excepto en el español rioplatense).

La pronunciación del inglés

Símbolo	Ejemplo	Aproximación
/k/	**cat** /kæt/	Sonido más explosivo que el de una c española en *cama* o *acto*.
/l/	**lid** /lɪd/	Como la l española.
/l̩/	**tidal** /'taɪdl̩/	l alargada y resonante.
/m/	**mat** /mæt/	Como la m española.
/n/	**nib** /nɪb/	Como la n española.
/n̩/	**threaten** /'θretn̩/	n alargada y resonante.
/ŋ/	**sing** /sɪŋ/	Como la n española en *banco* o *anca*.
/p/	**pet** /pet/	Sonido más explosivo que el de una p española.
/r/	**rat** /ræt/	Entre la r y la rr españolas, pronunciado con la punta de la lengua curvada hacia atrás y sin llegar a tocar el paladar.
/s/	**sip** /sɪp/	Como la s española.
/ʃ/	**ship** /ʃɪp/	Sonido similar al de la interjección *¡sh!*, utilizada para pedir silencio (ver también /tʃ/).
/t/	**tip** /tɪp/	Sonido más explosivo que el de una t española.
/tʃ/	**chin** /tʃɪn/	Como la ch española.
/θ/	**thin** /θɪn/	Como la c o la z del español europeo en *cinco* o *zapato*.
/ð/	**the** /ðə/	Sonido similar a una d intervocálica española como la de *cada* o *modo*.
/v/	**van** /væn/	Sonido sonoro que se produce con los incisivos superiores sobre el labio inferior.
/w/	**win** /wɪn/	Similar al sonido inicial de *huevo*.
/x/	**loch** /lɑːx/	Como la j española.
/z/	**zip** /zɪp/	s sonora (con zumbido).
/ʒ/	**vision** /'vɪʒən/	Sonido similar al de la y o la ll del español rioplatense en *yo* o *llave*, o al de la j francesa en *je* (ver también /dʒ/).

Vocales y diptongos

El símbolo : indica que la vocal precedente es larga

Símbolo	Ejemplo	Aproximación
/ɑː/	**father** /'fɑːðər/	Sonido más largo que el de una a española.
/æ/	**fat** /fæt/	Sonido que se obtiene al pronunciar una a española con los labios en la posición de pronunciar una e.
/ʌ/	**cup** /kʌp/	Sonido más breve que la a española y que se pronuncia en la parte posterior de la boca.

La pronunciación del inglés

Símbolo	Ejemplo	Aproximación
/e/	met /met/	Sonido parecido a la e española en *mesa*.
/ə/	abet /ə'bet/	Sonido similar al de la e francesa en *je* (ver también /əʊ/).
/ɜ:/	fur /fɜ:r/	Sonido que se obtiene al pronunciar una e española con los labios en la posición de pronunciar una o.
/ɪ/	bit /bɪt/	Sonido más breve que el de la i española.
/i:/	beat /bi:t/	Sonido más largo que el de la i española.
/i/	very /'veri/	Sonido similar al de la i española en *papi*.
/ɔ:/	paw /pɔ:/	Sonido más largo que el de la o española.
/u:/	boot /bu:t/	Sonido más largo que el de una u española.
/ʊ/	book /bʊk/	Sonido más breve que el de la u española.
/aɪ/	fine /faɪn/	Como ai en las palabras españolas *aire*, *baile*.
/aʊ/	now /naʊ/	Como au en las palabras españolas *pausa*, *flauta*.
/eɪ/	fate /feɪt/	Como ei en las palabras españolas *peine*, *aceite*.

Símbolo	Ejemplo	Aproximación
/əʊ/	goat /gəʊt/	Como una o pronunciada sin redondear demasiado los labios.
/ɔɪ/	boil /bɔɪl/	Como oy en *voy*, *coypu*.
/uə/	sexual /'sekʃuəl/	Como una u pronunciada sin redondear demasiado los labios y seguida de una /ə/.

Símbolos adicionales utilizados en la transcripción de sonidos vocálicos británicos

Símbolo	Ejemplo	Aproximación
/ɒ/	dog /dɒg/	Similar a una o española.
/eə/	fair /feə(r)/	Como una e española seguida de /ə/.
/ɪə/	near /nɪə(r)/	Como una i española seguida de /ə/.
/ʊə/	tour /tʊə(r)/	Como una u española pronunciada sin redondear demasiado los labios y seguida de /ə/.

Acentuación

El símbolo ' precede a la sílaba sobre la cual recae el acento tónico primario:
ago /ə'gəʊ/
dinosaur /'daɪnəsɔ:r/

El símbolo , precede a la sílaba sobre la cual recae el acento tónico secundario:
blackmailer /'blæk,meɪlər/

Abbreviations and labels / Abreviaturas e indicadores

adjetivo	adj	adjective	Correspondencia	Corresp	Correspondence
adjetivo invariable	adj inv	invariable adjective	numerable	count	countable
Administración	Adm	Administration	Costa Rica	CR	Costa Rica
adverbio	adv	adverb	uso criticado	crit	criticized usage
Espacio	Aerosp	Aerospace	Cono Sur	CS	Southern Cone
Agricultura	Agr	Agriculture	Cuba	Cu	Cuba
América Central	AmC	Central America	Cocina	Culin	Cookery
inglés norteamericano	AmE	American English	anticuado	dated	dated
América Latina	AmL	Latin America	artículo definido	def art	definite article
América del Sur	AmS	South America	Odontología	Dent	Dentistry
Anatomía	Anat	Anatomy	Deporte	Dep	Sport
Andes	Andes	Andes	Derecho	Der	Law
anticuado	ant	dated	dialecto	dial	dialect
Antropología	Anthrop	Anthropology	Ecuador	Ec	Ecuador
arcaico	arc, arch	archaic	Comunidad Europea	EC	European Community
Arqueología	Archeol	Archeology	Ecología	Ecol	Ecology
Arquitectura	Archit	Architecture	Economía	Econ	Economics
argot	arg	slang	Educación	Educ	Education
Argentina	Arg	Argentina	Electricidad	Elec	Electricity
Armas	Arm	Arms	Electrónica	Electrón, Electron	Electronics
Arqueología	Arqueol	Archeology	enfático	enf	emphatic
Arquitectura	Arquit	Architecture	Ingeniería	Eng	Engineering
artículo	art	article	Equitación	Equ	Equestrianism
Arte	Arte, Art	Art	especialmente	esp	especially
Astrología	Astrol	Astrology	España	Esp	Spain
Astronomía	Astron	Astronomy	Espacio	Espac	Aerospace
Audio	Audio	Audio	Espectáculos	Espec	Entertainment
Automovilismo	Auto	Cars	eufemismo	euf, euph	euphemism
Aviación	Aviac, Aviat	Aviation	excepto	exc	excluding
			femenino	f	feminine
Biblia	Bib	Bible	véase página ix	f‡	see page ix
Biología	Biol	Biology	familiar	fam	colloquial
Bolivia	Bol	Bolivia	Farmacología	Farm	Pharmacology
Botánica	Bot	Botany	Ferrocarriles	Ferr	Railways
inglés británico	BrE	British English	Filosofía	Fil	Philosophy
causativo	caus	causative	Finanzas	Fin	Finance
Química	Chem	Chemistry	Física	Fís	Physics
Chile	Chi	Chile	Fisco	Fisco	Tax
Cine	Cin	Cinema	Fisiología	Fisiol	Physiology
Ingeniería civil	Civil Eng	Civil Engineering	Fotografía	Fot	Photography
Indumentaria	Clothing	Clothing	femenino plural	fpl	feminine plural
Cocina	Coc	Cookery	frase hecha	fr hecha	set phrase
Colombia	Col	Colombia	formal	frml	formal
familiar	colloq	colloquial	Juegos	Games	Games
Comercio	Com	Business	generalmente	gen	generally
Informática	Comput	Computing	Geografía	Geog	Geography
conjunción	conj	conjunction	Geología	Geol	Geology
Construcción	Const	Building	gerundio	ger	gerund

Gobierno	**Gob, Govt**	Government
Historia	**Hist**	History
Horticultura	**Hort**	Horticulture
humorístico	**hum**	humorous
Imprenta e Industria editorial	**Impr**	Printing and Publishing
artículo indefinido	**indef art**	indefinite article
Indumentaria	**Indum**	Clothing
Informática	**Inf**	Computing
Ingeniería	**Ing**	Engineering
interjección	**interj**	exclamation
irónico	**iró, iro**	ironical
lenguaje periodístico	**journ**	journalese
Periodismo	**Journ**	Journalism
Juegos	**Jueg**	Games
Relaciones Laborales	**Lab Rel**	Labor Relations
Derecho	**Law**	Law
Ocio	**Leisure**	Leisure
lenguaje infantil	**leng infantil**	used to or by children
Lingüística	**Ling**	Linguistics
Literatura	**Lit**	Literature
literario	**liter**	literary
locución	**loc**	phrase
locución adjetiva	**loc adj**	adjectival phrase
locución adverbial	**loc adv**	adverbial phrase
locución preposicional	**loc prep**	prepositional phrase
masculino	**m**	masculine
Márketing	**Marketing**	Marketing
Matemáticas	**Mat, Math**	Mathematics
Mecánica	**Mec, Mech Eng**	Mechanical Engineering
Medicina	**Med**	Medicine
Metalurgia	**Metal, Metall**	Metallurgy
Meteorología	**Meteo**	Meteorology
México	**Méx**	Mexico
masculino y femenino	**mf**	masculine and feminine
masculino, femenino	**m, f**	masculine, feminine
Militar	**Mil**	Military
Minería	**Min**	Mining
Mitología	**Mit**	Mythology
masculino plural	**mpl**	masculine plural
Música	**Mús, Mus**	Music
Mitología	**Myth**	Mythology
nombre, sustantivo	**n**	noun
Náutica	**Náut, Naut**	Nautical
negativo	**neg**	negative
Ocultismo	**Occult**	Occult
Ocio	**Ocio**	Leisure
Odontología	**Odont**	Dentistry
Óptica	**Ópt, Opt**	Optics
Panamá	**Pan**	Panama
Paraguay	**Par**	Paraguay
participio pasado	**past p**	past participle
peyorativo	**pej**	pejorative
Perú	**Per**	Peru
lenguaje periodístico	**period**	journalese
Periodismo	**Period**	Journalism
peyorativo	**pey**	pejorative
Farmacología	**Pharm**	Pharmacology
Filosofía	**Phil**	Philosophy
Fotografía	**Phot**	Photography
Física	**Phys**	Physics
Fisiología	**Physiol**	Physiology
plural	**pl**	plural
sustantivo plural	**pl n**	plural noun
poético	**poet**	poetic
Política	**Pol**	Politics
Correo	**Post**	Post
participio pasado	**pp**	past participle
prefijo	**pref**	prefix
preposición	**prep**	preposition
participio presente	**pres p**	present participle
Imprenta	**Print**	Printing
pronombre	**pron**	pronoun
pronombre demostrativo	**pron dem**	demonstrative pronoun
pronombre personal	**pron pers**	personal pronoun
pronombre relativo	**pron rel**	relative pronoun
Psicología	**Psic, Psych**	Psychology
Industria editorial	**Publ**	Publishing
Química	**Quím**	Chemistry
marca registrada	**®**	registered trademark
Radio	**Rad**	Radio
Ferrocarriles	**Rail**	Railways
recíproco	**recipr**	reciprocal
reflexivo	**refl**	reflexive
Religión	**Relig**	Religion
Relaciones Laborales	**Rels Labs**	Labor Relations
Río de la Plata	**RPI**	River Plate area
inglés de Escocia	**Scot**	Scottish English
Servicios Sociales	**Servs Socs**	Social Administration
singular	**sing**	singular
argot	**sl**	slang
Servicios Sociales	**Soc Adm**	Social Administration
Sociología	**Sociol**	Sociology
Deporte	**Sport**	Sport

Abbreviations and labels /Abreviaturas e indicadores

sufijo	**suf, suff**	suffix	Uruguay	**Ur**	Uruguay
Tauromaquia	**Taur**	Bullfighting	verbo	**v**	verb
Fisco	**Tax**	Tax	verbo auxiliar	**v aux**	auxiliary verb
también	**tb**	also	verbo	**vb**	verb
Teatro	**Teatr**	Theater	Venezuela	**Ven**	Venezuela
Tecnología	**Tec, Tech**	Technology	Veterinaria	**Vet, Vet Sci**	Veterinary Science
lenguaje técnico	**téc, tech**	technical language	verbo intransitivo	**vi**	intransitive verb
Telecomunica- ciones	**Telec**	Telecommunica- tions	Video	**Video**	Video
			verbo impersonal	**v impers**	impersonal verb
Textiles	**Tex**	Textiles	Vinicultura	**Vin**	Wine
Teatro	**Theat**	Theater	verbo modal	**v mod**	modal verb
Turismo	**Tourism**	Tourism	verbo pronominal	**v pron**	pronominal verb
Transporte	**Transp**	Transport	verbo transitivo	**vt**	transitive verb
Televisión	**TV**	Television	vulgar	**vulg**	vulgar
no numerable	**uncount**	uncountable	Zoología	**Zool**	Zoology

Aa

A, a *f* (*pl* **aes**) (*read as* /a/) *the letter* A, a
a *prep*

■ **Nota** La preposición *a* suele emplearse precedida de ciertos verbos como *empezar, ir, oler, sonar* etc, en cuyo caso *ver bajo el respectivo verbo*. No se traduce cuando introduce el complemento directo de persona (ser humano, pronombres personales que lo representan, como *quien, alguien, algún* etc) o un nombre con un objeto o animal personalizado: *amo a mi patria* = I love my country, *paseo a mi perro* = I walk my dog. En los casos en que precede al artículo definido *el* para formar la contracción *al*, ver bajo la siguiente entrada, donde también se encontrarán otros ejemplos y usos de *a*.

1 **(a)** (indicando dirección) to; **voy a México/la tienda** I'm going to Mexico/to the shop; **voy a casa** I'm going home; **se cayó al río** she fell into the river **(b)** (indicando posición): **estaban sentados a la mesa** they were sitting at the table; **a orillas del Ebro** on the banks of the Ebro; **se sentó al sol** he sat in the sun; **se sentó a mi derecha** he sat down on my right **(c)** (indicando distancia): **a diez kilómetros de aquí** ten kilometers from here
2 **(a)** (señalando hora, momento) at; **a las ocho** at eight o'clock; **a la hora de comer** at lunch time; **¿a qué hora vengo?** what time shall I come?; **a mediados de abril** in mid-April; **al día siguiente** the next *o* following day **(b)** (señalando fecha): **hoy estamos a lunes/a 20** today is Monday/it's the 20th today **(c)** **al + INF**: **se cayó al bajar del tren** she fell as she was getting off the train; **al enterarse de la noticia** when he learnt *o* on learning the news **(d)** (indicando distancia en el tiempo): **a escasos minutos de su llegada** (después) a few minutes after she arrived; (antes) a few minutes before she arrived; **de lunes a viernes** (from) Monday to Friday
3 (en relaciones de proporción, equivalencia): **tres veces al día** three times a day; **sale a 100 euros cada uno** it works out at 100 euros each; **a 100 kilómetros por hora** (at) 100 kilometers per hour; **nos ganaron cinco a tres** they beat us five three *o* (AmE) five to three
4 (indicando modo, medio, estilo): **a pie/a caballo** on foot/on horseback; **a crédito** on credit; **funciona a pilas** it runs on batteries; **a mano** by hand; **a rayas** striped; **vestirse a lo punk** to wear punk clothes
5 **(a)** (introduciendo el complemento directo de persona): **¿viste a José?** did you see José?; **no he leído a Freud** I haven't read (any) Freud **(b)** (introduciendo el complemento indirecto) to; **le escribió una carta a su padre** he wrote a letter to his father, he wrote his father a letter; **dáselo a ella** give it to her; **le enseña español a mis hijos** she teaches my children English; **le echó (la) llave a la puerta** she locked the door **(c)** (indicando procedencia): **se lo compré a una gitana** I bought it from *o* (colloq) off a gipsy

abadía *f* (monasterio) abbey; (dignidad) abbacy
abajo *adv* **1** **(a)** (lugar, parte): **aquí ~** down

here; **en el estante de ~** (el siguiente) on the shelf below; (el último) on the bottom shelf; **más ~** further down; **por ~** underneath; **la parte de ~** the bottom (part) **(b)** (en un edificio) downstairs; **los vecinos de ~** (en una escala, jerarquía): **del jefe para ~** from the boss down *o* downward(s); **de 20 años para ~** 20 or under
2 (expresando dirección, movimiento) down; **calle/escaleras ~** down the street/stairs; **tire hacia ~** pull down *o* downward(s); **desde ~** from below
3 **abajo de** (AmL) under; **~ de la cama** under the bed
4 (en interjecciones) down with; **¡~ la dictadura!** down with the dictatorship!

abalanzarse [A4] *v pron*: **se abalanzaron hacia las salidas** they rushed toward(s) the exits; **~ SOBRE algn/algo** to leap ON sb/sth

abandonado -da *adj* **1** [ESTAR] (deshabitado) deserted **2** [ESTAR] ‹niño/perro/coche› abandoned **3** [ESTAR] (desatendido, descuidado) ‹jardín/parque› neglected

abandonar [A1] *vt* **1** **(a)** (frml) ‹lugar› to leave **(b)** ‹familia/bebé› to leave, abandon; ‹marido/amante› to leave; ‹coche/barco› to abandon; **los abandonó a su suerte** he abandoned them to their fate
2 ‹fuerzas› to desert
3 **(a)** ‹actividad/propósito/esperanza› to give up; **~ los estudios** to drop out of school/college **(b)** (Dep) ‹carrera/partido› to retire from, pull out of
■ **~** *vi* (Dep) **(a)** (en carrera, competición) to pull out **(b)** (en ajedrez) to resign; (en boxeo, lucha) to concede defeat
■ **abandonarse** *v pron* **1** (entregarse) **~se A algo** ‹a vicios/placeres› to abandon oneself TO sth **2** (en el aspecto personal) to let oneself go

abandono *m* **1** **(a)** (de una persona) abandonment; **~ del hogar** desertion **2** (Dep) (antes de la carrera, competición) withdrawal; (iniciada la carrera, competición) retirement; (en ajedrez) resignation **3** (descuido, desatención) neglect

abanicar [A2] *vt/vi* to fan
■ **abanicarse** *v pron* to fan oneself

abanico *m* (utensilio) fan

abaratar [A1] *vt* ‹precios/costos› to reduce; ‹producto› to make ... cheaper, reduce the price of
■ **abaratarse** *v pron* «costos» to drop, come down; «producto» to become cheaper, come down in price

abarcar [A2] *vt* **(a)** ‹temas/materias› to cover; ‹superficie/territorio› span, cover; ‹siglos/generaciones› to span; **la conversación abarcó varios temas** the conversation ranged over many topics **(b)** (dar abasto con) ‹trabajos/actividades› to cope with; **quien mucho abarca poco aprieta** you shouldn't bite off more than you can chew **(c)** (con los brazos, la mano) to encircle

abarrotado -da adj crammed, packed; ~ DE algo ‹de gente› packed o crammed WITH sth

abarrotar [A1] vt ‹sala/teatro› to pack

abarrotería f (Méx) grocery store (AmE), grocer's (shop) (BrE)

abarrotero -ra m,f (Chi, Méx) (tendero) storekeeper (AmE), shopkeeper (BrE)

abarrotes mpl (AmL exc RPl) (comestibles) groceries (pl); (tienda) grocery store (AmE), grocer's (shop) (BrE)

abastecedor -dora m,f supplier

abastecer [E3] vt to supply; ~ a algn DE algo to supply sb with sth
■ **abastecerse** v pron ~se DE algo (obtener) to obtain sth; (almacenar) to stock up WITH sth

abastecimiento m supply

abasto m (a) (aprovisionamiento) supply; no dar ~: no dan ~ con el trabajo they can't cope with all the work (b) (provisiones) tb ~s mpl basic provisions (pl) (esp foodstuffs)

abatible adj ‹respaldo› reclining (before n); (hacia adelante) folding (before n)

abatido -da adj [ESTAR] (deprimido, triste) depressed; (desanimado) downhearted, dispirited

abatir [I1] vt [1] (derribar) ‹pájaro/avión› to bring down; ‹muro/edificio› to knock down; ‹árbol› to fell; **fue abatido a tiros** he was gunned down [2] (deprimir, entristecer): **la enfermedad lo abatió mucho** his illness made him feel very low; **no te dejes ~ por las preocupaciones** don't let your worries get you down [3] ‹asiento› to recline
■ **abatirse** v pron [1] (deprimirse) to get depressed [2] (frml) ~se SOBRE algo/algn «pájaro/avión» to swoop down ON sth/sb; «desgracia» to befall sth/sb (frml); **el caos se abatió sobre el país** the country was plunged into chaos

abdicación f abdication

abdicar [A2] vi «soberano» to abdicate; ~ EN algn to abdicate IN FAVOR OF sb
■ ~ vt ‹trono/corona› to give up, abdicate

abdomen m abdomen

abdominal adj abdominal
■ m sit-up

abecedario m alphabet

abedul m birch

abeja f bee; ~ obrera/reina worker/queen bee

abejorro m bumblebee

aberración f (disparate, extravío) outrage; **robarle a un ciego es una ~** stealing from sb who's blind is outrageous

abertura f (en general) opening; (agujero) hole; (rendija) gap; (corte, tajo) slit

abeto m fir (tree)

abierto¹ -ta adj [1] (a) ‹ventana/boca› open; **está ~** it's open; **con los ojos muy ~s** with eyes wide open; **un sobre ~** an unsealed envelope; **los espacios ~s de la ciudad** the city's open spaces (b) [ESTAR] ‹válvula› open; **dejaste la llave ~** you left the faucet (AmE) o (BrE) tap running (c) (desabrochado) undone ‹herida› open; ‹madera/ costura› split [2] [ESTAR] ‹comercio/museo› open [3] (Ling) ‹vocal› open [4] (a) [SER] (espontáneo) open (b) (receptivo) open-minded; ~ A algo open TO sth [5] (manifiesto, directo) open

abierto² m (Dep) (tournament)

abismante adj (Andes) ‹valentía› extraordinary; ‹belleza› breathtaking; ‹cifra/ cantidad› staggering

abismo m abyss; **hay un profundo ~ entre ellos** there's a deep rift between them

ablandar [A1] vt (a) ‹cera/cuero› to soften; ‹carne› to tenderize (b) ‹persona› to soften; ‹corazón› to melt
■ **ablandarse** v pron (a) «cera/cuero» to soften (b) «persona» to soften up; «mirada» to soften

abnegación f self-denial, abnegation (frml)

abnegado -da adj self-sacrificing, selfless

abofetear [A1] vt to slap

abogacía f law; **ejercer la ~** to practice law

abogado -da m,f (en general) lawyer, solicitor (in UK); (ante un tribunal superior) attorney (in US), barrister (in UK); ~ **defensor** defense lawyer (AmE), defence counsel (BrE); ~ **del diablo** devil's advocate

abolición f abolition

abolir [I32] vt to abolish

abolladura f dent

abollar [A1] vt ‹coche/cacerola› to dent
■ **abollarse** v pron to get dented

abombado -da adj [1] ‹superficie› convex; ‹techo› domed [2] (AmL fam) (atontado) dopey (colloq), dozy (colloq) [3] (AmS) (en mal estado) ‹alimento›: **esta carne está abombada** this meat has gone bad o (BrE) is off

abombarse [A1] v pron (AmS) to go bad, go off

abominable adj abominable

abominar [A1] vt to detest, abominate (frml)

abonado -da m,f (del teléfono, a revista) subscriber; (del gas) consumer, customer; (a espectáculo, transporte) season-ticket holder

abonar [A1] vt [1] ‹tierra/campo› to fertilize [2] (a) (frml) (pagar) ‹cantidad/honorarios› to pay; **el cheque se lo ~án en caja** you can cash the check at the cash desk (b) (depositar) to credit; **hemos abonado la cantidad en su cuenta** we have credited your account with the amount (c) (Andes, Méx) (dar a cuenta) to give ... on account
■ **abonarse** v pron ~se A algo ‹a espectáculo› to buy a season ticket FOR sth; ‹a revista› to subscribe TO sth

abono m [1] (Agr) fertilizer [2] (para espectáculos, transporte) season ticket [3] (frml) (a) (pago) payment (b) (en una cuenta) credit (c) (Andes, Méx) (cuota) installment*

abordar [A1] vt [1] (a) (encarar) ‹problema› to tackle, deal with (b) (plantear) ‹tema/asunto› to raise [2] (persona) to approach; (agresivamente) to accost [3] (Méx) «pasajero» ‹barco/avión› to board; ‹automóvil› to get into
■ ~ vi (Méx) (subir a bordo) to board

aborigen adj aboriginal, indigenous
■ mf aborigine, aboriginal

aborrecer [E3] *vt* **(a)** ⟨*persona/actividad*⟩ to detest, loathe **(b)** ⟨*crías*⟩ to reject

aborrecible *adj* loathsome, detestable

abortar [A1] *vi* (Med) (de forma espontánea) to have a miscarriage, miscarry; (de forma provocada) to have an abortion, abort
■ ~ *vt* ⟨*maniobra/aterrizaje*⟩ to abort

aborto *m* (Med) (espontáneo) miscarriage; (provocado) abortion

abotagado -da *adj* ⟨*cara*⟩ swollen; ⟨*cuerpo*⟩ bloated

abotonar [A1] *vt* to button up, do up
■ **abotonarse** *v pron* ⟨*chaqueta/camisa*⟩ to button up, do up

abrasador -dora *adj* burning (*before n*)

abrasar [A1] *vt* **(a)** (quemar) to burn; **murieron abrasados** they were burned to death **(b)** «*bebida*» to scald, burn; «*comida*» to burn
■ ~ *vi* «*sol*» to burn, scorch
■ **abrasarse** *v pron* «*bosque*» to be burned (down); «*planta*» to get scorched; **nos abrasábamos bajo el sol** we were sweltering under the sun

abrasivo -va *adj/m* abrasive

abrazar [A4] *vt* ⟨*persona*⟩ to hug; (con más sentimiento) to embrace; **abrázame fuerte** hold me tight
■ **abrazarse** *v pron* (*recípr*) to hug each other; (con más sentimiento) to embrace each other; **~se A algn/algo** to hold on *o* cling TO sb/sth

abrazo *m* hug; (con más sentimiento) embrace; **me dio un ~** he gave me a hug, he hugged/embraced me; **dale un ~ de mi parte** give my love to her; **un ~, Miguel** (en cartas) best wishes, Miguel, regards, Miguel; (más íntimo) love, Miguel

abrebotellas *m* (*pl* ~) bottle opener

abrecartas *m* (*pl* ~) letter opener

abrelatas *m* (*pl* ~) can opener, tin opener (BrE)

abreviar [A1] *vt* ⟨*permanencia/visita*⟩ to cut short; ⟨*plazo*⟩ to shorten; ⟨*texto/artículo*⟩ to abridge; ⟨*palabra*⟩ to abbreviate
■ ~ *vi*: **abreviando ... in short ...**

abreviatura *f* abbreviation

abridor *m* (de botellas) bottle opener; (de latas) can opener, tin opener (BrE)

abrigado -da *adj* **(a)** [ESTAR] ⟨*lugar*⟩ sheltered **(b)** [ESTAR] ⟨*persona*⟩: **¿estás bien ~ con esas mantas?** are you warm enough with those blankets?; **está demasiado ~** he has too many clothes on; **iba bien ~** he was wrapped up warm **(c)** [SER] (RPl, Ven) ⟨*ropa*⟩ warm

abrigador -dora *adj* [SER] (Andes, Méx) ⟨*ropa*⟩ warm

abrigar [A3] *vt* **1** (con ropa) to wrap ... up warm; **el pañuelo me abriga el cuello** the scarf keeps my neck warm **2** ⟨*idea/esperanza*⟩ to cherish; ⟨*sospecha/duda*⟩ to harbor*, entertain
■ ~ *vi* «*ropa*» to be warm
■ **abrigarse** *v pron* (*refl*) to wrap up warm

abrigo *m* **1** **(a)** (prenda) coat **(b)** (calor que brinda la ropa): **necesita más ~** she needs to be wrapped up more warmly; **con una manta no tengo suficiente ~** I'm not warm enough with one blanket; **ropa de ~** warm clothes **2** (refugio,

protección) shelter; **al ~ de la lluvia/los árboles** sheltered from the rain/under the trees; **al ~ de la lumbre** by the fireside

abril *m* April; *para ejemplos ver* ENERO

abrillantar [A1] *vt* to polish

abrir [I33] *vt* **1** (en general) to open; ⟨*paraguas*⟩ to open, put up; ⟨*mapa*⟩ to open out, unfold; ⟨*cortinas*⟩ to open, draw back; ⟨*persianas*⟩ to raise, pull up; ⟨*cremallera*⟩ to undo
2 ⟨*llave/gas*⟩ to turn on; ⟨*válvula*⟩ to open; ⟨*cerradura*⟩ to unlock
3 **(a)** ⟨*zanja/túnel*⟩ to dig; ⟨*agujero*⟩ to make **(b)** (fam) ⟨*paciente*⟩ to open ... up (colloq)
4 **(a)** ⟨*comercio/museo*⟩ (para el quehacer diario) to open; (inaugurar) to open (up); **¿a qué hora abren la taquilla?** what time does the box office open? **(b)** ⟨*carretera/aeropuerto*⟩ to open; ⟨*frontera*⟩ to open (up)
5 **(a)** (iniciar) ⟨*cuenta bancaria*⟩ to open; ⟨*negocio*⟩ to start, set up; ⟨*suscripción*⟩ to take out; ⟨*investigación*⟩ to begin, set up I **no han abierto la matrícula aún** registration hasn't begun yet; **~ fuego** to open fire **(b)** ⟨*acto/debate/baile*⟩ to open **(c)** ⟨*desfile/cortejo*⟩ to head, lead **(d)** ⟨*paréntesis/comillas*⟩ to open
6 ⟨*apetito*⟩ to whet
■ **abrirse** *v pron* **1** **(a)** «*puerta/ventana*» to open; **~se A algo** ⟨*jardín/corredor*⟩ to open ONTO sth **(b)** «*flor/almeja*» to open; «*paracaídas*» to open
2 (*refl*) ⟨*chaqueta/cremallera*⟩ to undo
3 **(a)** «*porvenir*» to lie ahead; «*perspectivas*» to open up; **con este descubrimiento se abren nuevos horizontes** this discovery opens up new horizons **(b)** «*período/era*» to begin

abrochar [A1] *vt* ⟨*chaqueta/botón*⟩ to fasten, do up; ⟨*collar/cinturón de seguridad*⟩ to fasten
■ **abrocharse** *v pron* ⟨*chaqueta/botón*⟩ to fasten, do up; ⟨*collar/cinturón de seguridad*⟩ to fasten

abrumador -dora *adj* **(a)** ⟨*victoria/mayoría*⟩ overwhelming **(b)** ⟨*trabajo/tarea*⟩ exhausting

abrumar [A1] *vt* to overwhelm; **~ a algn CON algo** ⟨*con problemas/quejas*⟩ to wear sb out WITH sth; **la ~on con sus atenciones** she was overwhelmed by their kindness

abrupto -ta *adj* **(a)** ⟨*camino/pendiente*⟩ steep; ⟨*terreno*⟩ rough **(b)** ⟨*tono*⟩ abrupt **(c)** ⟨*cambio/descenso*⟩ abrupt, sudden

absentismo *m* (Esp) absenteeism; **~ escolar** (Esp) truancy, absenteeism

absolución *f* **(a)** (Relig) absolution **(b)** (Der) acquittal

absolutamente *adv* totally, absolutely; **no se ve ~ nada** you can't see a thing; **~ nadie** not a soul; **¿estás segura? — ~** are you sure? — absolutely *o* I'm positive

absoluto -ta *adj* **1** ⟨*monarca/poder*⟩ absolute **2** **(a)** (total) total, absolute, complete; **tengo la absoluta certeza** I am absolutely convinced **(b)** **en absoluto** (*loc adv*): **¿te gustó? — en ~** did you like it? — no, not at all; **no lo consentiré en ~** there is absolutely no way I will agree to it

absolver [E11] *vt* **(a)** (Relig) to absolve **(b)** (Der) ⟨*acusado*⟩ to acquit, find ... not guilty

absorbente *adj* **1** ⟨*esponja/papel*⟩ absorbent **2** ⟨*persona*⟩ demanding; ⟨*hobby/tarea*⟩ time-consuming; ⟨*profesión*⟩ demanding

absorber [E1] vt (a) ⟨líquido/ruido/calor⟩ to absorb (b) ⟨tiempo⟩ to occupy, take up; ⟨recursos/energía⟩ to absorb

absorción f (de líquido, calor, ruido) absorption

absorto -ta adj engrossed, absorbed

abstemio -mia adj teetotal
■ m,f teetotaler*

abstención f abstention

abstencionismo m abstentionism

abstenerse [E27] v pron (a) (en votación) to abstain (b) (frml) (no hacer): ~ DE hacer algo to refrain FROM doing sth (c) (privarse de): ~ del alcohol to avoid alcohol

abstinencia f abstinence

abstracto -ta adj abstract

abstraerse [E23] v pron ~se DE algo ⟨de pensamiento/preocupación⟩ to block out FROM sth

abstraído -da adj: estar ~ en algo to be absorbed in sth; lo noté como ~ he seemed rather preoccupied

absuelto -ta pp: ▶ ABSOLVER

absurdo -da adj absurd, ridiculous

abuchear [A1] vt to boo

abucheo m booing

abuelito -ta m,f (m) grandpa (colloq), granddad (colloq); (f) grandma (colloq), granny (colloq)

abuelo -la m,f 1 (pariente) (m) grandfather; (f) grandmother; mis ~s my grandparents; ¡cuéntaselo a tu abuela! (fam) pull the other one! (colloq) 2 (fam) (persona mayor) (m) old man, old guy (colloq); (f) old woman, old lady; ¡oiga ~! hey, granddad! (colloq)

abultado -da adj (a) ⟨ojos/vientre⟩ bulging; ⟨labios⟩ thick; ⟨cartera⟩ bulging (b) (abundante) ⟨deuda/suma⟩ enormous, huge (c) (exagerado) ⟨cifra/cantidad⟩ inflated

abultar [A1] vi (a) (formar un bulto) to make a bulge (b) (ocupar lugar) to be bulky
■ ~ vt ⟨cifras/resultados⟩ to inflate

abundancia f 1 (gran cantidad) abundance; la ~ de peces the abundance of fish; hay comida en ~ there's an abundance of food; darse en ~ to be plentiful 2 (riqueza): tiempos de ~ times of plenty; viven en la ~ they're well-off; nadar en la ~ to be rolling in money (colloq)

abundante adj ⟨reservas/cosecha⟩ plentiful, abundant; la pesca es ~ the fishing is good; aguas ~s en especies marinas waters which abound in marine life

abundar [A1] vi (a) (existir en gran número o cantidad) ⟨especie/mineral⟩ to be abundant (b) (tener mucho) ~ EN algo to abound o be rich IN sth

aburrido -da adj 1 [ESTAR] ⟨persona⟩ (a) (sin entretenimiento) bored; estoy muy ~ I'm bored stiff (b) (harto) fed up; ~ DE algo tired OF sth, fed up WITH sth; ~ DE hacer algo tired OF doing sth 2 [SER] ⟨película/persona⟩ boring; ⟨trabajo⟩ boring, tedious
■ m,f bore

aburridor -dora adj (AmL) ▶ ABURRIDO 2

aburrimiento m (a) (estado) boredom (b) (cosa aburrida): ¡qué ~! what a bore!

aburrir [I1] vt to bore
■ **aburrirse** v pron (a) (por falta de entretenimiento)

to get bored (b) (hartarse) ~se DE algo/algn to get tired OF o fed up WITH sth/sb; ~se DE hacer algo to get tired of doing sth

abusador -dora adj (aprovechado) ⟨comerciante⟩ opportunist; ¡qué ~ eres! you really take advantage of the situation!
■ m,f: estos comerciantes son unos ~es these shopkeepers really take advantage; es un ~ con sus padres he takes advantage of his parents

abusar [A1] vi 1 (a) (aprovecharse): es muy hospitalaria pero no abuses she's very hospitable but don't take advantage of her; ~ DE algo ⟨de autoridad/posición/generosidad⟩ to abuse sth; no quisiera ~ de su amabilidad I don't want to impose ~ (on you); ~ DE algn ⟨de padres/amigo⟩ to take advantage OF sb (b) (sexualmente) ~ DE algn to sexually abuse sb 2 (usar en exceso): abusa de los tranquilizantes he takes too many tranquilizers; no se debe ~ del alcohol alcohol should be drunk in moderation

abusivo -va adj ⟨precio/interés⟩ outrageous

abuso m (a) (uso excesivo) abuse; ~ de autoridad abuse of authority; el ~ en la bebida excessive drinking; ~s deshonestos indecent assault; ~ sexual infantil child abuse (b) (de hospitalidad, generosidad): espero no lo considere un ~ I hope you don't think it an imposition; ¡qué ~ de confianza! (fam) what a nerve! (colloq) (c) (injusticia) outrage; ¡esto es un ~! this is outrageous!; prestarse a ~s to lay itself open to abuse

abusón -sona adj/m,f (Esp, Méx fam) ▶ ABUSADOR

acá adv 1 (en el espacio) here; ¡ven ~! come here!; ya viene para ~ he's on his way over; nos pasamos el día de ~ para allá we spent the whole day going to and fro; un poquito más ~ a little closer o nearer (to me) 2 (en el tiempo): del verano (para) ~ since the summer

acabado¹ -da adj [ESTAR] (a) ⟨trabajo⟩ finished; son todos productos muy bien ~s they are all well-finished products (b) ⟨persona⟩ finished

acabado² m finish

acabar [A1] vi 1 (a) ⟨⟨reunión/película⟩⟩ to finish, end; ⟨⟨persona⟩⟩ to finish; ⟨⟨novios⟩⟩ to split up; ya casi acabo I've nearly finished (b) (en un estado, situación) to end up; acabó en la cárcel he ended up in jail; (+ compl) acabamos cansadísimos by the end we were exhausted; ese chico va a ~ mal that boy will come to no good; la película acabó bien the movie had a happy ending; ~án aceptándolo o por aceptarlo they'll end up accepting it; ~ DE algo to end up AS sth; acabó de camarero he ended up (working) as a waiter (c) (rematar) ~ EN algo to end IN sth 2 acabar con (a) ~ CON algo (terminar) ⟨con libro/tarea⟩ to finish WITH sth; ⟨con bombones/bebidas⟩ to finish off sth; ⟨con salud/carrera⟩ to ruin sth; ⟨con sueldo/herencia⟩ to fritter AWAY sth; ⟨con abuso/problema⟩ to put an end to sth (b) (fam) ~ CON algn (pelearse) to finish WITH sb; (matar) to do away WITH sb (colloq); este niño va a ~ conmigo this child will be the death of me 3 acabar de (a) (terminar) ~ DE hacer algo to finish doing sth; cuando acabes de leerlo when you've finished reading it (b) (para referirse a acción reciente): acaba de salir she's just gone out; acababa de meterme en la cama cuando … I had

just got into bed when ... **(c)** (llegar a): **no acabo de entenderlo** I just don't understand; **no acababa de gustarle** she wasn't totally happy about it
■ ～ *vt* ⟨*trabajo/libro*⟩ to finish; ⟨*curso/carrera*⟩ to finish, complete

■ **acabarse** *v pron* ⃞1 (terminarse) «*provisiones/comida*» to run out; «*problema*» to be over; «*reunión/fiesta/curso*» to end; «*proyecto*» to finish, come to an end; «*año*» to come to an end; **se nos acabó el café** we ran out of coffee; **se le ～on las fuerzas** he ran out of energy; **un trabajo que no se acaba nunca** a never-ending *o* an endless task; **¡esto se acabó!** that's it!
⃞2 (*enf*) (comer) to finish (up)

acabose *m* (fam): **¡esto es el ～!** this is the end *o* limit! (colloq)

academia *f* **(a)** (sociedad) academy **(b)** (Educ) school; **～ de conductores** *or* (AmL) **choferes** driving school; **～ de idiomas** language school

académico -ca *adj* ⟨*estudios/año*⟩ academic (*before n*); ⟨*estilo/lenguaje*⟩ academic
■ *m,f* academician

acalorado -da *adj* ⃞1 [SER] ⟨*discusión/riña*⟩ heated ⃞2 [ESTAR] ⟨*persona*⟩ (enfadado) worked up; (con calor) hot

acalorarse [A1] *v pron* (enfadarse) to get worked up; (sofocarse) to get hot

acampada *f* camp; **ir de ～** to go camping

acampanado -da *adj* ⟨*falda/pantalones*⟩ flared

acampante *mf* camper

acampar [A1] *vi* to camp

acantilado *m* cliff

acaparador -dora *adj* (egoísta) selfish, greedy; (posesivo) possessive
■ *m,f* **(a)** (de productos) hoarder **(b)** (persona egoísta) selfish person

acaparar [A1] *vt* **(a)** ⟨*productos/existencias*⟩ to hoard, stockpile **(b)** ⟨*interés/atención*⟩ to capture; **el trabajo acapara todo su tiempo** work takes up all his time

acaramelado -da *adj* **(a)** ⟨*pareja*⟩: **estaban ～s** they were hugging and kissing **(b)** ⟨*voz*⟩ sugary **(c)** (Coc) toffee-coated; ⟨*molde*⟩ coated with caramel

acariciar [A1] *vt* ⟨*persona*⟩ to caress; ⟨*mejilla/pelo*⟩ to stroke, caress; ⟨*perro/gato*⟩ to stroke

acarrear [A1] *vt* **(a)** ⟨*problema*⟩ to give rise to, lead to; **esto le acarreó problemas** this caused her problems **(b)** ⟨*materiales/paquetes*⟩ to carry

acaso *adv* ⃞1 (en preguntas): **¿～ no te lo dije?** I told you, didn't I?; **¿～ tengo yo la culpa?** is it my fault? ⃞2 (*en locs*) **por si acaso** just in case; **si acaso** (quizás) maybe, perhaps; (en caso de que) if

acatar [A1] *vt* ⟨*leyes/orden*⟩ to obey, comply with

acatarrado -da *adj*: **estar ～** to have a cold

acatarrarse [A1] *v pron* (resfriarse) to catch a cold

acceder [E1] *vi* ⃞1 (consentir) to agree; **～ A algo** to agree TO sth ⃞2 (entrar) **～ A algo** gain access TO sth; (Inf) to access sth

accesible *adj* **(a)** ⟨*lugar*⟩ accessible; ⟨*persona*⟩ approachable; ⟨*precio*⟩ affordable **(b)** ⟨*novela/lenguaje*⟩ accessible

acceso *m* ⃞1 **(a)** (a un lugar) access; **rutas de ～**

approach roads **(b)** (a persona, información) access **(c)** (Inf) access ⃞2 (a curso) entrance; **pruebas de ～** entrance examinations; **curso de ～** preparatory course

accesorio *m* accessory (Cin, Teatr) prop; **～s del vestir** accessories; **～s de baño** bathroom fittings

accidentado -da *adj* ⃞1 **(a)** ⟨*viaje*⟩ eventful; ⟨*historia*⟩ turbulent; ⟨*carrera/pasado*⟩ checkered* (*before n*); ⟨*vida*⟩ troubled **(b)** ⟨*terreno*⟩ rough, rugged; ⟨*costa*⟩ broken ⃞2 ⟨*persona*⟩ hurt, injured
■ *m,f*: **llevaron a los ～s al hospital** those injured *o* hurt in the accident were taken to hospital

accidental *adj* ⟨*encuentro*⟩ chance (*before n*), accidental; ⟨*circunstancias*⟩ coincidental

accidente *m* ⃞1 (percance) accident; **tener** *or* **sufrir un ～** to have an accident; **～ aéreo** plane crash; **～ de circulación/tráfico** traffic *o* road accident; **～ laboral** industrial accident ⃞2 (hecho fortuito) coincidence; **por ～** by chance ⃞3 (del terreno) unevenness; **～ geográfico** geographical feature

acción *f* ⃞1 (acto, hecho) act; **acciones dignas de elogio** praiseworthy acts *o* actions; **hacer una buena ～** to do a good deed; **～ de gracias** thanksgiving ⃞2 **(a)** (actividad) action; **poner algo en ～** to put sth into action; **novela de ～** adventure story; **una película llena de ～** an action-packed movie *o* (BrE) film **(b)** (Mil) action **(c)** (Cin, Lit) (trama) action, plot ⃞3 **(a)** (Der) action, lawsuit **(b)** (Fin) share; **acciones** shares, stock ⃞4 (Per) (de una rifa) ticket

accionar [A1] *vt* ⟨*palanca*⟩ to pull; ⟨*mecanismo/dispositivo*⟩ activate, trigger

accionista *mf* stockholder, shareholder

acebo *m* holly; (árbol) holly tree

acechar [A1] *vt* ⟨*enemigo/presa*⟩ to lie in wait for; **el peligro que nos acecha** the danger that lies ahead of us

acecho *m*: **al ～** lying in wait

aceite *m* oil; **～ lubricante** lubricating oil; **～ de oliva/girasol** olive/sunflower oil; **～ de ricino** castor oil

aceitera *f* (Tec) oilcan; (Coc) cruet

aceitoso -sa *adj* oily

aceituna *f* olive; **～s rellenas/sin hueso** stuffed/pitted olives

aceitunado -da *adj* olive (*before n*)

aceleración *f* acceleration

acelerado -da *adj* ⟨*curso*⟩ intensive, crash (*before n*); **a paso ～** at a brisk pace

acelerador *m* (Auto) accelerator

acelerar [A1] *vt* **(a)** ⟨*coche/motor*⟩: **aceleró el coche** (en marcha) he accelerated; (sin desplazarse) he revved the engine *o* car (up) **(b)** ⟨*proceso/cambio*⟩ to speed up; ⟨*paso*⟩ to quicken
■ **～** *vi* **(a)** (Auto) to accelerate **(b)** (fam) (darse prisa) to hurry (up)

acelgas *fpl* Swiss chard

acento *m* **(a)** (Ling) (tilde) accent; (de intensidad) stress, accent **(b)** (énfasis) emphasis **(c)** (dejo, pronunciación) accent; **tiene ～ francés** he has a French accent

acentuado -da *adj* **(a)** ⟨*palabra/sílaba*⟩ accented **(b)** ⟨*diferencia/cambio*⟩ marked, distinct

acentuar [A18] vt (a) (Ling) (al hablar) to stress, accent; (al escribir) to accent (b) (intensificar, hacer resaltar) to accentuate, emphasize
■ **acentuarse** v pron ⟨diferencias/problemas⟩ to become accentuated

acepción f sense, meaning

aceptable adj acceptable, passable

aceptación f (a) (éxito) success; **de gran ~ entre los jóvenes** very popular o successful with young people (b) (acción) acceptance

aceptar [A1] vt ⟨excusas/invitación/cargo⟩ to accept; ⟨términos/condiciones⟩ to agree to; **aceptan cheques** they take checks; **aceptó venir** she agreed to come; **no acepto que me digas eso** I won't have you saying that to me

acequia f irrigation ditch o channel

acera f sidewalk (AmE), pavement (BrE)

acerca de loc prep about

acercamiento m (entre posturas, países) rapprochement; (entre personas): **ese incidente produjo un ~ entre ellos** that incident brought them closer together

acercar [A2] vt **1** (a) (aproximar) to bring ... closer o nearer; **~on la mesa a la puerta** they moved the table closer o nearer to the door; **acercó las manos al fuego** he held his hands closer to the fire; **¿puedes ~me ese libro?** can you pass o give me that book? (b) (unir) ⟨posturas/países⟩ to bring ... closer **2** (llevar): **me acercó a la parada** she gave me a ride (AmE) o (BrE) lift to the bus stop
■ **acercarse** v pron (a) (aproximarse) to approach, to get closer o nearer; **acércate más** (acercándose al hablante) come o get closer o nearer; (alejándose del hablante) go o get closer o nearer; **se le ~on dos policías** two policemen came up to o approached him (b) ⟨amigos/países⟩ to draw o come closer together (c) ⟨hora/momento⟩ to draw near, approach; **ahora que se acerca la Navidad** now that Christmas is coming

acero m (Metal) steel; **~ inoxidable** stainless steel

acérrimo -ma adj ⟨partidario/defensor⟩ staunch; ⟨enemigo⟩ bitter

acertado -da adj ⟨comentario⟩ pertinent; ⟨solución/elección⟩ good

acertante adj winning (before n)
■ m,f winner

acertar [A5] vt ⟨respuesta/resultado⟩ to get ... right; **a ver si aciertas quién es** see if you can guess who it is
■ vi **1** (a) (dar, pegar): **~le A algo** to hit sth; **tiró pero no le acertó** he shot at it but (he) missed (b) (atinar) to be right; **acertaste con el regalo** your present was perfect **2** (lograr) **~ A hacer algo** to manage to do sth

acertijo m riddle, puzzle

acetona f (Quím) acetone; (quitaesmaltes) nail-polish remover

achacar [A2] vt: **~le la culpa a algn** to lay o put the blame on sb

achaques mpl ailments (pl); **mis acostumbrados ~** my usual aches and pains

achatar [A1] vt to flatten

achicar [A2] vt **1** (a) ⟨chaqueta/vestido⟩ to take in (b) ⟨persona⟩ to intimidate, daunt **2** ⟨agua⟩ to bail out
■ **achicarse** v pron (a) (de tamaño) to shrink (b) (amilanarse) to be intimidated, be daunted

achicharrante adj (fam) ⟨sol⟩ scorching; **hizo un calor ~** it was scorching

achicharrar [A1] vt (fam) (a) ⟨carne/comida⟩ to burn ... to a cinder (colloq) (b) «sol» ⟨planta⟩ to scorch; **hace un sol que te achicharra** the sun is scorching hot
■ **achicharrarse** v pron (fam) (a) «persona» to fry (colloq); «planta» to get scorched (b) «carne/comida» to be burned to a crisp (colloq)

achichincle, achichinque mf (Méx fam & pey) hanger-on (colloq & pej)

achicopalar [A1] vt (Col, Méx fam) to intimidate
■ **achicopalarse** v pron (Col, Méx fam) to feel intimidated

achicoria f chicory

achinado -da adj ⟨ojos⟩ slanting

achiote m (AmL) annatto

achispado -da adj (fam) tipsy (colloq)

achuras fpl (RPl) offal

acicalarse [A1] v pron to dress up, get dressed up

acicate m (a) (estímulo) incentive (b) (espuela) spur

acidez f (Quím) acidity; (Med) (en el estómago) acidity; (en el esófago) heartburn

ácido¹ -da adj (a) ⟨sabor⟩ acid; ⟨fruta⟩ acid, tart, sharp; ⟨vino⟩ sharp (b) ⟨carácter/tono⟩ acid, caustic

ácido² m (a) (Quím) acid (b) (arg) (droga) acid (sl)

acierta, aciertas, etc ▶ ACERTAR

acierto m (a) (decisión correcta) good decision, good o wise move (b) (respuesta correcta) correct answer

acitronar [A1] vt (Méx) to fry ... until golden brown

aclamación f acclaim

aclamar [A1] vt to acclaim, applaud

aclaración f explanation; **quisiera hacer una ~** I'd like to make one thing clear

aclarado m (Esp) rinse

aclarar [A1] v impers (a) (amanecer): **aclara temprano** it gets light early; **cuando nos levantamos estaba aclarando** dawn o day was breaking when we got up (b) (escampar) to clear up
■ **~ vi** (a) «día» (empezar) to break, dawn (b) «tiempo/día» (escampar) to clear up
■ **~ vt 1** (quitar color a) to lighten

②〈*ideas*〉 to get ... straight; 〈*duda*〉 to clear up, clarify; **quiero ∼ que** ... I want to make it clear that ...

③ (Esp) 〈*ropa/vajilla*〉 to rinse

■ **aclararse** *v pron* ① **∼se la voz** to clear one's throat

② (Esp fam) (entender) to understand; **a ver si nos aclaramos** let's see if we can sort things out *o* get things straight

aclimatarse [A1] *v pron* to acclimatize, get *o* become acclimatized

acné *m or f* acne

acobardar [A1] *vt* 〈*persona*〉 to unnerve, intimidate

■ **acobardarse** *v pron* to lose one's nerve; **∼se ante el peligro** to lose one's nerve in the face of danger

acogedor -dora *adj* 〈*casa/habitación*〉 cozy*, welcoming; 〈*ambiente*〉 warm, friendly

acoger [E6] *vt* **(a)** 〈*huérfano/anciano*〉 to take in; 〈*refugiado*〉 to accept, admit **(b)** 〈*propuesta/ persona*〉 to receive; **acogieron la noticia con satisfacción** the news was well received

■ **acogerse** *v pron* **∼se a algo** 〈*a la ley*〉 to have recourse *o* sth; 〈*a un régimen*〉 to opt FOR sth

acogida *f* **(a)** (de persona) welcome; (de noticia, propuesta) reception **(b)** (de huérfano) taking in; (de refugiado) acceptance

acolchar, acolchonar [A1] *vt* 〈*bata/tela*〉 to quilt; 〈*pared/puerta*〉 to pad

acomedido -da *adj* (Chi, Méx, Per) obliging, helpful

acomedirse [I14] *v pron* (Méx) to offer to help

acometer [E1] *vi* to attack; **∼ CONTRA algo/ algn** to attack sth/sb

acomodado -da *adj* ① 〈*familia/gente*〉 well-off, well-to-do; **de posición acomodada** well-off, well-to-do ② (CS, Méx fam) (que tiene palanca): **estar ∼** to have contacts *o* connections

acomodador -dora *m,f* (*m*) usher; (*f*) usherette

acomodar [A1] *vt* ① (adaptar, amoldar) to adapt ② 〈*huésped*〉 to put ... up ③ **(a)** (AmL) (arreglar) to arrange; (poner) to put **(b)** (fam) 〈*persona*〉 (en puesto): **su tío lo acomodó en su sección** his uncle fixed him up with a job in his department

■ **acomodarse** *v pron* **(a)** (ponerse cómodo) to make oneself comfortable **(b)** (adaptarse, amoldarse): **∼se a algo** to adapt TO sth **(c)** (AmL) (arreglarse) 〈*ropa/anteojos*〉 to adjust

acompañado -da *adj* accompanied; **bien/mal ∼** in good/bad company; **vino ∼ de un amigo** he came with a friend

acompañamiento *m* **(a)** (Mús) accompaniment **(b)** (Coc) accompaniment; **¿con qué ∼ lo quiere?** what would you like it served with?

acompañar [A1] *vt* ① **(a)** (a un lugar) to go with, accompany (frml); **acompáñalo hasta la puerta** see him to the door, see him out; **la acompañé a su casa** I walked her home; **¿me acompañas?** will you come with me? **(b)** (hacer compañía) to keep ... company **(c)** (Mús) to accompany ② (frml) (adjuntar) to enclose; **acompañado de un certificado médico** accompanied by a medical certificate

acomplejado -da *adj*: **es muy ∼** he's full of complexes; **está ∼ por su gordura** he has a complex about being fat

■ *m,f*: **es un ∼** he's a mass of complexes

acomplejar [A1] *vt* to give ... a complex

■ **acomplejarse** *v pron* to get a complex

acondicionador *m* **(a)** *tb* **∼ de pelo** (hair) conditioner **(b)** **∼ de aire** air conditioner

acondicionamiento *m* fitting-out

acondicionar [A1] *vt* **(a)** 〈*vivienda/local*〉 to equip, fit out **(b)** (Col) 〈*carro*〉 to soup up

aconsejable *adj* advisable

aconsejar [A1] *vt* to advise; **∼le a algn hacer algo/que haga algo** to advise sb to do sth; **has sido mal aconsejado** you've been given bad advice; **necesito que alguien me aconseje** I need some advice

acontecer [E3] *vi* (en *3ª pers*) (frml) to take place, occur (frml); **los sucesos acontecidos ayer** the events which took place *o* occurred yesterday;

■ *m*: **el diario ∼** everyday events *o* occurrences

acontecimiento *m* event; **adelantarse a los ∼s** to jump the gun

acoplar [A1] *vt* **(a)** 〈*piezas*〉 to fit *o* put together **(b)** (Elec) to connect **(c)** (Ferr) to couple

acorazado *m* battleship

acordar [A10] *vt* 〈*términos*〉 to agree; 〈*precio/ fecha*〉 to agree (on)

■ **∼** *vi* (Andes) (recordar) **∼le a algn DE hacer algo/ que haga algo** to remind sb to do sth

■ **acordarse** *v pron* to remember; **si mal no me acuerdo** if I remember right; **∼se DE algo/algn** to remember sb/sth; **no quiero ni ∼me** I don't even want to think about it; **∼se DE hacer algo** (de una acción que hay/había que realizar) to remember to do sth; (de una acción que ya se realizó) to remember *o* recall doing sth; **se acordó de haberlo visto allí** she remembered *o* recalled seeing him there; **∼se (DE) QUE** ... to remember THAT ...

acorde *adj* (en armonía) 〈*sonidos*〉 harmonious; **colores ∼s** colors that go *o* blend well together; **con un salario ∼** with a salary to match; **∼ CON** *or* **A algo** appropriate TO sth, in keeping WITH sth

■ *m* (Mús) chord

acordeón *m* ① (Mús) accordion ② (Méx fam) (para un examen) crib

acordeonista *mf* accordionist

acordonar [A1] *vt* **(a)** 〈*lugar*〉 to cordon off **(b)** 〈*zapatos*〉 to lace (up)

acorralar [A1] *vt* **(a)** 〈*animal/fugitivo*〉 to corner **(b)** 〈*ganado*〉 to round up

acortar [A1] *vt* 〈*falda/vestido*〉 to shorten; 〈*texto/artículo*〉 to cut, shorten; 〈*vacaciones/ permanencia*〉 to cut short; 〈*película/carrera*〉 to reduce the length of; 〈*distancia*〉 to reduce; **∼ camino** to take a short cut

■ **acortarse** *v pron* to get shorter

acosar [A1] *vt* **(a)** 〈*persona*〉 to hound; (sexualmente) to harass; **me ∼on con preguntas** they plagued *o* bombarded me with questions **(b)** 〈*presa*〉 to hound, pursue relentlessly

acosijar [A1] *vt* (Méx) to badger, pester

acoso *m* **(a)** (de persona) hounding, harassment; **∼ sexual** sexual harassment **(b)** (de presa) hounding, relentless pursuit

acostar [A10] vt ⟨persona⟩ to put ... to bed
■ **acostarse** v pron (a) (irse a dormir) to go to bed
(b) (tenderse, tumbarse) to lie down; **~se boca
abajo** to lie face down (c) (tener relaciones sexuales)
to go to bed together, sleep together; **~se CON
algn** to go to bed WITH sb, sleep WITH sb

acostumbrado -da adj (a) (habituado): **está
mal ~** he's got into bad habits; **~ A algo/hacer
algo** used TO sth/doing sth; **estamos ~s a cenar
temprano** we're used to having dinner early; **está
~ a que le sirvan** he's used to being served (b)
(habitual) customary, usual

acostumbrar [A1] vt **~ a algn A algo/hacer
algo** to get sb used TO sth/doing sth
■ **~** vi: **~ A hacer algo** to be accustomed TO doing
sth, be in the habit OF doing sth
■ **acostumbrarse** v pron **~se A algo/algn** to
get used TO sth/sb; **~se A hacer algo** to get used
TO doing sth

acotación f (en texto) marginal note,
annotation

acotamiento m (Méx) shoulder (AmE), hard
shoulder (BrE)

acrecentar [A5] vt to increase
■ **acrecentarse** v pron to increase, grow

acreditado -da adj (a) ⟨establecimiento/
marca⟩ reputable, well-known (b) ⟨diplomático/
periodista⟩ accredited; ⟨agente/representante⟩
authorized, official

acreditar [A1] vt **1** ⟨diplomático/periodista⟩ to
accredit; ⟨representante⟩ to authorize **2** (frml) (a)
(probar, avalar) ⟨pago⟩ to prove; **este libro lo
acredita como un gran pensador** this book
confirms him as a great thinker (b) (dar renombre):
con la calidad que lo acredita with the quality for
which it's renowned **3** (Fin) to credit

acreedor -dora m,f creditor

acribillar [A1] vt (a) (llenar de agujeros): **lo ~on
a balazos** they riddled him with bullets (b)
(asediar): **me ~on a preguntas** they fired a barrage
of questions at me

acrílico m acrylic

acristalar [A1] vt to glaze

acrobacia f (arte) acrobatics; **hacer ~s** to
perform acrobatics; **~ aérea** aerobatics

acróbata mf acrobat

acta f. (de reunión) minutes (pl); **levantar (el) ~**
to take (the) minutes; **~ de defunción** (Col, Méx,
Ven) entry in the register of deaths; **~ de
matrimonio/nacimiento** (Méx) marriage/birth
certificate; **~ notarial** notarial deed

actitud f (disposición) attitude; **adoptar una ~
firme** (con algn) to be firm (with sb)

activar [A1] vt (a) (agilizar) ⟨proceso/crecimiento⟩
to speed up; ⟨economía/producción⟩ to stimulate;
⟨circulación⟩ to stimulate; ⟨negociaciones⟩ to give
fresh impetus to (b) (poner en funcionamiento)
⟨alarma⟩ to activate, trigger; ⟨dispositivo⟩ to
activate; ⟨máquina⟩ to set ... in motion
■ **activarse** v pron «alarma» to go off;
«dispositivo» to start working

actividad f activity; **un volcán en ~** an active
volcano

activista mf activist

activo¹ -va adj active

activo² m assets (pl)

acto m **1** (a) (acción) act; **morir en ~ de
servicio** «soldado» to die on active service;
«policía/bombero» to die in the course of one's
duty; **~ sexual** sexual act (frml) (b) (en locs) **acto
seguido** immediately after; **en el acto** ⟨morir⟩
instantly; ⟨acudir⟩ immediately; **lo despidieron
en el ~** he was fired on the spot **2** (a)
(ceremonia) ceremony (b) (Teatr) act

actor m actor

actriz f actress

actuación f (a) (acción) action (b) (Cin, Dep,
Teatr) performance; **la ~ es pésima** the acting is
appalling (c) (conducta) conduct (d) (recital, sesión)
performance, concert

actual adj ⟨ley/situación/dirección⟩ present,
current; **en el Chile ~** in present-day Chile; **en el
mundo ~** in the modern world, in today's world

actualidad f (a) (tiempo presente): **en la ~**
currently, at present; **la ~ cubana** the current
situation in Cuba (b) (de tema, noticia) topicality;
las noticias de ~ today's (o this week's etc) news;
un tema de ~ (period) a topical subject; **sucesos
de ~** current affairs

actualizar [A4] vt ⟨salarios/pensiones/
legislación⟩ to bring ... up to date; ⟨información/
manual⟩ to update; (Inf) ⟨software⟩ to upgrade

actualmente adv (hoy en día) nowadays; (en
este momento) at present; **se encuentra ~ en
Suecia** she is currently in Sweden, she is in
Sweden at present

actuar [A18] vi (a) «persona» (obrar) to act;
forma de ~ behavior* (b) «medicamento» to
work, act (c) «actor» to act; «torero» to
perform; **¿quién actúa en esa película?** who's in
the movie?

acuarela f watercolor*

acuario m aquarium

Acuario m (signo) Aquarius; **es (de) ~** he's an
Aquarius o Aquarian
■ mf (persona) tb **acuario** Aquarian, Aquarius

acuático -ca adj aquatic

acuatizaje m: landing on water

acuatizar [A4] vi to land on water

acuchillar [A1] vt «persona» to stab

acudir [I1] vi **1** (frml) (ir) to go; (venir) to come;
nadie acudió en su ayuda nobody went/came to
his aid; **~ A algo** ⟨a cita⟩ to arrive FOR sth; ⟨a
reunión⟩ to attend sth; **la policía acudió al lugar
de los hechos** the police arrived at the scene (of
the incident) **2** (recurrir) **~ A algn** to turn TO sb;
no tenía a quien ~ he had nobody to turn to

acueducto m aqueduct

acuerdo m (a) (arreglo, pacto) agreement; **llegar
a un ~** to reach an agreement; **~ de paz** peace
agreement o (frml) accord (b) **estar de ~** to agree;
ponerse de ~ to come to o reach an agreement;
estar de ~ EN algo to agree ON something; **estar
de ~ CON algn/algo** to agree WITH sb/sth;
¿mañana a las ocho? — de ~ (indep) tomorrow
at eight? — OK o all right (c) **de ~ con** or **a** in
accordance with

acuesta, acuestas, etc ▶ ACOSTAR

acumulación f accumulation

acumular [A1] vt ⟨riquezas/poder⟩ to
accumulate; ⟨experiencia⟩ to gain

■ **acumularse** *v pron* «*trabajo*» to pile up, mount up; «*intereses*» to accumulate; «*deudas*» to mount up; «*polvo*» to accumulate

acunar [A1] *vt* to rock

acuñar [A1] *vt* ‹*moneda*› to mint; ‹*frase/palabra*› to coin

acuoso -sa *adj* watery

acupuntura *f* acupuncture

acupunturista *mf* acupuncturist

acurrucarse [A2] *v pron* to curl up

acusación *f* **(a)** (imputación) accusation **(b)** (Der) charge

acusado -da *m,f*: **el/la ~** the accused, the defendant

acusador -dora *adj* accusing, accusatory (frml); **una mirada ~a** an accusing look
■ *m,f* prosecuting attorney (AmE), prosecuting counsel (BrE)

acusar [A1] *vt* **1 (a)** (culpar) to accuse; **~ a algn DE algo** to accuse sb OF sth; **me acusan de haber mentido** they accuse me of lying **(b)** (Der) **~ a algn DE algo** to charge sb WITH sth **(c)** (fam) (delatar) to tell on (colloq) **2** (reconocer): **~ recibo de algo** (Corresp) to acknowledge receipt of sth

acusetas *mf* (*pl* **~**)**, acusete -ta** *m,f* (fam) tattletale (AmE colloq), telltale (BrE colloq)

acústica *f* (ciencia) acoustics; (de local) acoustics (*pl*)

acústico -ca *adj* acoustic

adaptable *adj* adaptable

adaptación *f* **(a)** (proceso) adaptation, adjustment **(b)** (cosa adaptada) adaptation; **la ~ cinematográfica** the screen version

adaptador *m* adaptor

adaptar [A1] *vt* ‹*cortinas/vestido*› to alter; ‹*habitación*› to convert; ‹*pieza/motor*› to adapt; ‹*obra/novela*› to adapt; (Inf) to convert
■ **adaptarse** *v pron* to adapt; **~se A algo/hacer algo** to adapt TO sth/doing sth; **un coche que se adapta a cualquier terreno** a car which is well suited to any terrain

a. de C. (= **antes de Cristo**) BC, before Christ

adecentar [A1] *vt* ‹*habitación*› to tidy up

adecuado -da *adj* **(a)** (apropiado) ‹*vestido/regalo*› suitable; ‹*momento*› right; ‹*medios*› adequate; **la persona adecuada para el cargo** the right person for the job **(b)** (aceptable) adequate

adecuar [A1] *or* [A18] *vt* **~ algo A algo** to adapt sth TO sth

adefesio *m* (cosa) eyesore; (persona): **es un ~** he's so ugly; **ir hecho un ~** to look a sight *o* fright (colloq)

adelantado -da *adj* **1 (a)** (desarrollado) ‹*país*› advanced **(b)** (aventajado): **va muy ~ en sus estudios** he is doing very well in his studies; **va ~ para su edad** he's advanced for his age **2** [ESTAR] ‹*reloj*› fast **3** (Com, Fin): **pago ~** payment in advance; **por ~** in advance **4** (avanzado): **las obras están muy adelantadas** construction is already well underway; **vamos bastante ~s** we're quite far ahead with it **5** (Dep) ‹*pase*› forward

adelantamiento *m* passing maneuver (AmE), overtaking manoeuvre (BrE)

adelantar [A1] *vt* **1 (a)** ‹*fecha/viaje*› to bring forward **(b)** ‹*pieza/ficha*› to move ... forward **2** (sobrepasar) to overtake, pass **3 (a)** ‹*reloj*› to put ... forward **(b)** ‹*balón*› to pass ... forward **(c)** ‹*trabajo*› to get on with **4** (conseguir) to gain; **con llorar no adelantas nada** crying won't get you anywhere
■ **~** *vi* **1 (a)** (avanzar) to make progress **(b)** «*reloj*» to gain **2** (Auto) to pass, overtake (BrE)
■ **adelantarse** *v pron* **1 (a)** (avanzar) to move forward **(b)** (ir delante) to go ahead; **se adelantó para comprar las entradas** she went (on) ahead to buy the tickets **2 (a)** «*cosecha*» to be early; «*verano/frío*» to arrive early **(b)** «*reloj*» to gain **3** (anticiparse): **se adelantó a su época** he was ahead of his time; **~se a los acontecimientos** to jump the gun; **yo iba a pagar, pero él se me adelantó** I was going to pay, but he beat me to it

adelante *adv* **1** (en el espacio) **(a)** (expresando dirección, movimiento) forward; **para/hacia ~** forward; **seguir ~** to go on; **¡~!** (*como interj*) (autorizando la entrada) come in!; (ordenando marchar) forward! **(b)** (lugar, posición): **se sentó ~** (en coche) she sat in front; (en clase, cine) she sat at the front; **más ~ la calle se bifurca** further on, the road forks; **la parte de ~** the front **2** (en el tiempo): **más ~** later; **(de ahora) en ~** from now on; **de hoy en ~** as of *o* from today **3 adelante de** (*loc prep*) (AmL) in front of

adelanto *m* **1** (avance) step forward; **los ~s de la ciencia** the advances of science **2** (del sueldo) advance; (depósito) deposit **3** (en el tiempo): **llegó con un poco de ~** he/she/it arrived slightly early

adelgazamiento *m* slimming

adelgazante *adj* weight-reducing (*before n*), slimming (*before n*) (BrE)

adelgazar [A4] *vt* ‹*caderas/cintura*› to slim down; ‹*kilos*› to lose
■ **~** *vi* to lose weight

ademán *m* (expresión) expression; (movimiento, gesto) gesture; **hizo ~ de levantarse** he made as if to get up

además *adv* **1 (a)** (también) as well, too; **~ habla ruso** she speaks Russian as well *o* too **(b)** (lo que es más) what's more **(c)** (por otra parte) anyway, besides; **~ ¿a mí qué me importa?** anyway, what do I care? **2 además de** besides, apart from; **~ de hacerte mal, engorda** besides *o* apart from being bad for you, it's also fattening; **~ de hacerlos, los diseña** he designs them as well as making them

adentro *adv* **1 (a)** (expresando dirección, movimiento): **vamos para ~** let's go in **(b)** (lugar, parte) inside; **ven aquí ~** come in here **(b)** (lugar, parte) inside; [*European Spanish prefers* DENTRO *in many of these examples*] **¡qué calor hace aquí ~!** it's so hot in here!; **¿comemos ~?** shall we eat indoors *o* inside?; **la parte de ~** the inside **2 adentro de** (AmL), in inside

adentros *mpl*: **dije para mis ~** I said to myself; **se rió para sus ~s** he chuckled to himself

adepto -ta *adj*: **ser ~ A algo** ‹*a secta*› to be a follower OF sth; ‹*a partido*› to be a supporter OF sth
■ *m,f* (de secta) follower; (de partido) supporter

aderezar [A4] *vt* ‹guiso› to season; ‹ensalada› to dress

aderezo *m* (de guiso) seasoning; (de ensalada) dressing

adherencia *f* (a) (acción) adherence (b) (Auto) grip, roadholding (c) (Med) adhesion

adherente *adj* adhesive

adherir [I11] *vt* to stick
■ **adherirse** *v pron* (a) (pegarse) to stick (b) (unirse) ~**se** A **algo** ‹a propuesta/causa› to give one's support TO sth; ‹a movimiento/partido› to join sth

adhesión *f* (a) (a una superficie) adhesion (b) (apoyo) support (c) (a una organización) joining

adhesivo¹ -va *adj* adhesive, sticky

adhesivo² *m* (sustancia) adhesive; (lámina, estampa) sticker

adicción *f* addiction; ~ **a la heroína** heroin addiction

adición *f* (a) (Mat) addition (b) (RPl) (cuenta) check (AmE), bill (BrE)

adicional *adj* additional

adicto -ta *adj* (a la bebida, la droga) addicted; ~ A **algo** addicted TO sth
■ *m,f* addict; **los** ~**s a la cocaína** cocaine addicts

adiestrar [A1] *vt* to train

adinerado -da *adj* wealthy, moneyed

adiós *m/interj* (al despedirse) goodbye, bye (colloq); (al pasar) hello; ▶ DECIR² *vt* 3B

aditivo *m* additive

adivinanza *f* riddle; **jugar a las** ~**s** to play at guessing riddles

adivinar [A1] *vt* (a) (por conjeturas, al azar) to guess (b) (por magia) to foretell, predict
■ ~ *vi* to guess

adivino -na *m,f* fortune-teller

adjetivo *m* adjective

adjudicación *f* (a) (de premio, contrato) awarding; (de viviendas) allocation (b) (en subasta) sale

adjudicar [A2] *vt* (a) ‹premio/contrato› to award; ‹vivienda› to allot, allocate (b) (en subasta): **le** ~**on la alfombra al anticuario** the carpet was sold to *o* went to the antique dealer; **¡adjudicado!** sold!

adjuntar [A1] *vt* to enclose

adjunto -ta *adj* (a) ‹director› deputy (before *n*); **profesor** ~ associate professor (AmE), senior lecturer (BrE) (b) ‹lista/copia› enclosed, attached

ADM *fpl* (= **armas de destrucción masiva**) WMD

administración *f* ⑴ (a) (de empresa, bienes) management (b) (Pol) administration; ~ **pública** civil service ⑵ (a) (conjunto de personas) management (b) (oficina, departamento) administration

administrador -dora *m,f* (de empresa) manager, administrator; (de bienes) administrator

administrar [A1] *vt* (a) ‹empresa/bienes› to manage, administer (frml) (b) (frml) (dar) ‹sacramentos/medicamento› to give
■ **administrarse** *v pron*: ~**se bien/mal** to manage one's money well/badly

administrativo -va *adj* administrative
■ *m,f* administrative assistant (*o* officer *etc*); (con funciones más rutinarias) clerk

admirable *adj* admirable

admiración *f* (a) (respeto) admiration (b) (sorpresa) amazement

admirador -dora *m,f* (a) (de persona) admirer, fan (b) (hum) (pretendiente) admirer (hum)

admirar [A1] *vt* (a) (respetar) ‹persona/cualidad› to admire (b) (contemplar) to admire (c) (sorprender) to amaze
■ **admirarse** *v pron* ~**se** DE **algo** to be amazed AT *o* ABOUT sth

admisible *adj* ‹comportamiento› admissible, acceptable; ‹excusa› acceptable

admisión *f* admission; **examen** *or* **prueba de** ~ entrance examination *o* test

admitir [I1] *vt* ① (a) (aceptar) to accept; **Ⓢ se admiten tarjetas de crédito** we take *o* accept credit cards (b) (permitir) to allow (c) (reconocer) to admit ② (dar cabida a) «local» to hold

ADN *m* (= **ácido desoxirribonucleico**) DNA

adobar [A1] *vt* ‹carne/pescado› (condimentar) to marinade; (para conservar) to pickle; (para curar) to cure

adobe *m* adobe

adobo *m* (condimento) marinade; (para conservar) pickle

adoctrinar [A1] *vt* to indoctrinate

adolecer [E3] *vi* ~ DE **algo** ‹de enfermedad/defecto› to suffer FROM sth

adolescencia *f* adolescence; **durante su** ~ (when he was) in his teens, in adolescence (frml)

adolescente *adj* adolescent; **tiene dos hijos** ~**s** she has two teenage *o* adolescent children
■ *mf* (en contextos no técnicos) teenager; (Med, Psic) adolescent

adolorido -da *adj* (esp AmL) ▶ DOLORIDO A

adonde *adv* where; **el lugar** ~ **se dirigían** the place where *o* to which they were going

adónde *adv* where

adondequiera *adv*: ~ **que vayas** wherever you go

adopción *f* adoption

adoptar [A1] *vt* (a) ‹actitud/costumbre› to adopt; ‹decisión/medida/posición› to take (b) ‹niño/nacionalidad› to adopt

adoptivo -va *adj* (a) ‹hijo› adopted; ‹padres› adoptive (b) ‹patria/país› adopted

adoquín *m* (a) (de piedra) paving stone; (ovalado) cobblestone (b) (Per) (helado) Popsicle® (AmE), ice lolly (BrE)

adorable *adj* adorable

adoración *f* **(a)** (de persona) adoration **(b)** (de deidad) adoration, worship

adorar [A1] *vt* **(a)** ⟨*persona/cosa*⟩ to adore **(b)** ⟨*deidad*⟩ to worship, adore

adormecer [E3] *vt* **(a)** ⟨*persona*⟩ to make ... sleepy *o* drowsy; ⟨*sentidos*⟩ to numb, dull **(b)** ⟨*pierna/mano*⟩ to numb
■ **adormecerse** *v pron* to fall asleep, doze off

adormecimiento *m* **(a)** (somnolencia) sleepiness, drowsiness **(b)** (de un miembro) numbness

adormilarse [A1] *v pron* to doze

adornar [A1] *vt* **(a)** ⟨*habitación/sombrero/ comida*⟩ to decorate **(b)** ⟨*relato/discurso*⟩ to embellish **(c)** «*flores/banderas*» to adorn
■ **adornarse** *v pron* (*refl*) ⟨*cabeza/pelo*⟩ to adorn

adorno *m* **(a)** (objeto) ornament; **los ∼s de Navidad** the Christmas decorations **(b)** (decoración) adornment; **de ∼** for decoration

adosado -da *adj* ∼ **A algo** fixed **TO** sth; ▶ CASA 1A

adosar [A1] *vt* **(a)** ⟨*armario/escritorio*⟩ ∼ **algo A algo** to fix sth **TO** sth **(b)** (Méx) ⟨*documento*⟩ to enclose, attach

adquiera, adquirió, etc ▶ ADQUIRIR

adquirir [I13] *vt* ⟨*casa/coche*⟩ to acquire, obtain; (comprar) to purchase, buy; ⟨*conocimientos/ colección/fortuna*⟩ to acquire; ⟨*fama*⟩ to attain, achieve; ⟨*experiencia*⟩ to gain; ∼ **malas costumbres** to get into bad habits

adquisición *f* acquisition; (compra) purchase

adquisitivo -va *adj* purchasing

adrede *adv* on purpose, deliberately

adrenalina *f* adrenaline

aduana *f* customs; **libre de derechos de ∼** duty free

aduanero -ra *adj* customs (*before n*)
■ *m,f* customs officer

adulación *f* flattery

adulador -dora *adj* flattering
■ *m,f* flatterer

adular [A1] *vt* to flatter

adulterar [A1] *vt* ⟨*alimento/vino*⟩ to adulterate; ⟨*información*⟩ to falsify

adulterio *m* adultery

adulto -ta *adj* **(a)** ⟨*persona/animal*⟩ adult (*before n*) **(b)** ⟨*reacción/opinión*⟩ adult
■ *m,f* adult

adusto -ta *adj* ⟨*persona/expresión*⟩ austere, severe; ⟨*paisaje*⟩ bleak, harsh

advenedizo -za *adj* upstart (*before n*)
■ *m,f* social climber

adverbio *m* adverb

adversario -ria *adj* opposing (*before n*)
■ *m,f* opponent, adversary

adversidad *f* adversity; **en la ∼** in adversity

adverso -sa *adj* ⟨*circunstancias/resultado*⟩ adverse

advertencia *f* warning; **que les sirva de ∼** let it be a warning to them

advertir [I11] *vt* **(a)** (avisar) to warn; **¡te lo advierto!** I'm warning you!; ∼**le A algn DE algo** to warn sb ABOUT sth; **le advertí que tuviera cuidado** I warned him to be careful; **te advierto que no me sorprendió nada** I must say I wasn't at all surprised **(b)** (notar) to notice

adviento *m* Advent

advierta, advirtió, etc ▶ ADVERTIR

adyacente *adj* adjacent

aéreo -rea *adj* ⟨*vista*⟩ aerial; ⟨*tráfico*⟩ air (*before n*)

aerobic /e'roβik/ *m*, (Méx) **aerobics** *mpl* aerobics

aerodeslizador *m* (Náut) hovercraft

aerodinámica *f* aerodynamics

aerodinámico -ca *adj* aerodynamic

aeródromo *m* aerodrome, airfield

aeroespacial *adj* aerospace (*before n*)

aerograma *m* aerogram, air (mail) letter

aerolínea *f* airline

aeromodelismo *m* model airplane making

aeromozo -za *m,f* (AmL) flight attendant

aeronáutica *f* **(a)** (ciencia) aeronautics **(b)** (RPI) (aviación militar) air force

aeronáutico -ca *adj* aeronautic, aeronautical

aeronave *f* **(a)** (globo dirigible) airship **(b)** (frml) (avión) airliner, aircraft

aeroplano *m* (ant) airplane, aeroplane (BrE)

aeropuerto *m* airport

aerosol *m* aerosol, spray can

afable *adj* affable

afán *m* ⟦1⟧ **(a)** (anhelo) eagerness; **su ∼ de aventuras** his thirst for adventure; **∼ DE hacer algo** eagerness **TO** do sth; **su ∼ de agradar** their eagerness to please; **tiene ∼ de aprender** she's eager to learn **(b)** (empeño) effort ⟦2⟧ (Col fam) (prisa) hurry

afanado -da *adj* ⟦1⟧ [ESTAR] ⟨*persona*⟩ busy ⟦2⟧ [ESTAR] (Col, Per fam) (con prisa) in a hurry

afanarse [A1] *v pron* (esforzarse) to work, toil; **∼se EN** *or* **POR hacer algo** to strive **TO** do sth

afear [A1] *vt* **(a)** ⟨*persona*⟩ to make ... look ugly; ⟨*paisaje*⟩ to spoil **(b)** ⟨*conducta*⟩ to criticize
■ **afearse** *v pron* to lose one's looks

afectación *f* affectation

afectado -da *adj* **(a)** ⟨*gestos/acento*⟩ affected **(b)** ⟨*área/órgano*⟩ affected; **está afectado de una grave enfermedad** (frml) he is suffering from a serious disease

afectar [A1] *vt* ⟦1⟧ **(a)** (tener efecto en) to affect; **esto nos afecta a todos** this affects us all **(b)** (afligir) to affect (frml); **la noticia lo afectó mucho** the news upset him terribly ⟦2⟧ (fingir) ⟨*admiración/indiferencia*⟩ to affect, feign

afectísimo -ma *adj* (Corresp) (frml): **suyo ∼** yours truly

afectivo -va *adj* emotional

afecto *m* (cariño) affection; **tenerle ∼ a algn** to be fond of sb; **tomarle ∼ a algn** to grow fond of sb

afectuoso -sa *adj* ⟨*persona*⟩ affectionate; **recibe un ∼ saludo** (Corresp) with warm *o* kind regards

afeitadora *f* shaver, electric razor

afeitar [A1] *vt* ⟨*persona/cabeza*⟩ to shave; ⟨*barba*⟩ to shave off
■ **afeitarse** *v pron* (*refl*) to shave; **se afeitó la barba** he shaved off his beard

afeminado -da adj effeminate

aferrarse [A1] v pron: ~se A algo/algn to cling (ON) TO sth/sb

affmo. affma. (Corresp) (frml) = **afectísimo, -ma**

Afganistán m Afghanistan

afgano -na adj/m,f Afghan

afianzar [A4] vt ⟨posición/postura⟩ to consolidate
■ **afianzarse** v pron «prestigio/sistema» to become consolidated

afiche m (esp AmL) poster

afición f (a) (inclinación, gusto) love, liking; ~ a la lectura/música love of reading/music (b) (pasatiempo) hobby (c) (Dep, Taur): la ~ the fans (pl)

aficionado -da adj [SER] (a) (entusiasta) ~ A algo fond OF o keen ON sth (b) (no profesional) amateur
■ m,f (a) (entusiasta) enthusiast; **para los** ~s **al bricolaje** for do-it-yourself enthusiasts; **un** ~ **a la música** a music lover; **los** ~s **al tenis/fútbol** tennis/football fans (b) (no profesional) amateur

aficionarse [A1] v pron ~se A algo to become interested IN sth

afilado -da adj [1] (a) ⟨borde/cuchillo⟩ sharp (b) ⟨nariz⟩ pointed; ⟨rasgos⟩ sharp; ⟨dedos⟩ long [2] (mordaz) ⟨lengua⟩ sharp; ⟨pluma⟩ biting

afilar [A1] vt ⟨navaja/cuchillo⟩ to sharpen, hone

afiliación f affiliation

afiliado -da m,f member

afiliarse [A1] v pron ~se A algo ⟨a partido/sindicato⟩ to become a member OF sth, to join sth; ⟨a sistema⟩ to join sth

afín adj ⟨temas/lenguas⟩ related; ⟨culturas/ideologías⟩ similar; ⟨intereses⟩ common; **ideas afines a las nuestras** ideas which have a lot in common with our own

afinación f tuning

afinar [A1] vt [1] (a) ⟨instrumento⟩ to tune (b) ⟨coche⟩ to tune up; ⟨motor⟩ to tune [2] ⟨punta⟩ to sharpen

afinidad f (entre personas, caracteres) affinity; **no tengo ninguna** ~ **con él** I have nothing in common with him

afirmación f (declaración) statement, assertion; (respuesta positiva) affirmation

afirmar [A1] vt [1] (aseverar) to state, declare, assert (frml); **no lo afirmó ni lo negó** she neither confirmed nor denied it [2] ⟨escalera⟩ to steady
■ ~ vi: **afirmó con la cabeza** he nodded
■ **afirmarse** v pron (físicamente) to steady oneself; ~se EN algo/algn to hold ON to sth/sb

afirmativo -va adj ⟨respuesta/frase⟩ affirmative

afligido -da adj distressed

afligir [I7] vt (a) (afectar) to afflict (b) (apenar) to upset
■ **afligirse** v pron to get upset

aflojar [A1] vt [1] ⟨cinturón/tornillo⟩ to loosen; ⟨cuerda/riendas⟩ to slacken; ⟨presión/tensión⟩ to ease; ⟨marcha/paso⟩ to slow [2] (fam) ⟨dinero⟩ to hand over [3] (AmL) ⟨motor⟩ to run in
■ ~ vi «tormenta» to ease off; «fiebre/viento» to drop; «calor» to let up; «tensión/presión» to ease off

■ **aflojarse** v pron (a) (refl) ⟨cinturón⟩ to loosen (b) «tornillo/tuerca» to come o work loose

afónico -ca adj: **estar** ~ to have lost one's voice; **quedarse** ~ to lose one's voice

afortunadamente adv fortunately, luckily

afortunado adj ⟨persona⟩ lucky, fortunate; ⟨encuentro/coincidencia⟩ happy, fortunate; **una elección poco afortunada** a rather unfortunate choice

África f♱ tb **el** ~ Africa

África del Sur f♱ South Africa

africano -na adj/m,f African

afrikaans m Afrikaans

afrikaner adj/mf (pl **-ners**) Afrikaner

afrodisíaco¹ -ca adj aphrodisiac

afrodisíaco² m aphrodisiac

afrontar [A1] vt ⟨problema/responsabilidad⟩ to face up to; ⟨desafío/peligro⟩ to face

afuera adv [1] (a) (expresando dirección, movimiento) outside; **ven aquí** ~ come out here; **¡**~**!** get out of here! (b) (lugar, parte) outside; [European Spanish prefers FUERA in many of these examples] **aquí** ~ **se está muy bien** it's really nice out here; **comimos** ~ (en el jardín) we ate outside o outdoors; (en un restaurante) we ate out; **por** ~ **es rojo** it's red on the outside [2] (esp AmL): **¿qué haces** ~ **de la cama?** what are you doing out of bed?; ~ **del edificio** outside the building

afueras fpl: **las** ~ the outskirts

agachar [A1] vt ⟨cabeza⟩ to lower
■ **agacharse** v pron (a) (ponerse en cuclillas) to crouch down; (inclinarse) to bend down (b) (AmL fam) (rebajarse) to eat humble pie o (AmE) crow (colloq)

agallas fpl (fam) (valor) guts (pl) (colloq); **con** ~s gutsy (colloq); **hay que tener** ~s it takes guts (colloq)

agarrado¹ -da adj (a) [SER] (fam) (tacaño) tightfisted (colloq) (b) [ESTAR] (CS fam) (enamorado) in love
■ m,f (fam) (tacaño) skinflint (colloq), tightwad (AmE colloq)

agarrado² adv: **bailar** ~ to dance closely

agarrar [A1] vt [1] (sujetar) to grab, get hold of; **me agarró del brazo** (para apoyar) she took hold of my arm; (con violencia, rapidez) she grabbed me by the arm [2] (esp AmL) ⟨objeto⟩ (tomar) to take; (atajar) to catch; **agarra un papel y toma nota** get a piece of paper and take this down [3] (AmL) (pescar, atrapar) to catch; **si lo agarro, lo mato** if I get o lay my hands on him, I'll kill him [4] (esp AmL) (adquirir) ⟨resfriado/pulmonía⟩ to catch; ⟨costumbre/vicio⟩ to pick up; ⟨ritmo⟩ to get into; ⟨velocidad⟩ to gather, pick up; ~**le cariño a algn** to grow fond of sb; **le agarró asco** he got sick of it; **le he agarrado odio** I've come to hate him [5] (AmL) (entender) ⟨indirecta/chiste⟩ to get
■ ~ vi [1] (asir, sujetar): **toma, agarra** here, hold this; **agarra por ahí** take hold of that part [2] «planta/injerto» to take; «tornillo» to grip, catch; «ruedas» to grip; «tinte» to take
■ **agarrarse** v pron [1] (asirse) to hold on; **agárrate bien** or **fuerte** hold on tight; ~se A or DE algo to hold on TO sth; **iban agarrados del brazo** they were walking along arm in arm

2 ⟨dedo/manga⟩ to catch; **me agarré el dedo en el cajón** I caught my finger in the drawer **3** (esp AmL) ⟨resfriado/pulmonía⟩ to catch; ~**se una borrachera** to get drunk; ~**se un disgusto/ una rabieta** to get upset/into a temper **4** (AmL fam) (pelearse) to get into a fight; **se** ~**on a patadas** they started kicking each other; ~**se con** algn to have a set-to with sb (colloq)

agarre *m* (de neumático) grip; (de coche) roadholding

agarrotar [A1] *vt* ⟨piernas/músculos⟩ to make ... stiff

■ **agarrotarse** *v pron* **(a)** «manos/músculos» to stiffen up; **tengo las manos agarrotadas** my hands are stiff **(b)** «motor/máquina» to seize up

agazaparse [A1] *v pron* «animal» to crouch; «persona» to crouch (down)

agencia *f* (oficina) office; (sucursal) branch; ~ **de colocaciones** employment agency *o* bureau (*generally for domestic staff*); ~ **de prensa** *or* **de noticias** press *o* news agency; ~ **de viajes** travel agent's, travel agency; ~ **matrimonial** marriage bureau

agenda *f* (libreta) appointment book (AmE), diary (BrE); (programa) agenda; ~ **de bolsillo** pocket diary; ~ **de trabajo** engagement book

agente *mf* **1** (Com, Fin) agent; ~ **de bolsa** stockbroker; ~ **de publicidad** advertising agent; ~ **de seguros** insurance broker; ~ **de viajes** travel agent **2** (frml) (funcionario) employee; ~ **de policía** police officer; ~ **de tráfico** *or* (Arg, Méx) **de tránsito** ≈ traffic policeman (*in US*), ≈ traffic warden (*in UK*); ~ **secreto** secret agent

ágil *adj* ⟨persona/movimiento⟩ agile; ⟨estilo/ programa⟩ lively

agilidad *f* (de persona) agility; (de estilo) liveliness

agilizar [A4] *vt* ⟨gestiones/proceso⟩ to speed up; ⟨pensamiento⟩ to sharpen; ⟨ritmo/presentación⟩ to make ... livelier *o* more dynamic

agitación *f* **(a)** (nerviosismo) agitation **(b)** (de calle, ciudad) bustle

agitado -da *adj* **(a)** ⟨mar⟩ rough, choppy **(b)** ⟨día/vida⟩ hectic, busy **(c)** ⟨persona⟩ worked up, agitated

agitador -dora *m,f* (persona) agitator

agitar [A1] *vt* **(a)** ⟨líquido/botella⟩ to shake **(b)** ⟨brazo/pañuelo⟩ to wave; ⟨alas⟩ to flap

■ **agitarse** *v pron* **(a)** «mar» to get rough; «barca» to toss; «toldo» to flap **(b)** (inquietarse) to get worked up

aglomeración *f* **(a)** (de gente): **se produjo una** ~ **a la entrada** people crowded at the entrance; **para evitar las aglomeraciones** to avoid crowding; **las aglomeraciones urbanas** the built-up urban areas **(b)** (de tráfico) buildup

aglomerarse [A1] *v pron* to crowd (together)

agnóstico -ca *adj/m,f* agnostic

agobiado -da *adj* [ESTAR] ~ **DE** algo ⟨de trabajo⟩ snowed under with sth; ⟨de deudas⟩ overwhelmed with sth; **estaba agobiada con tantos problemas** she was weighed down by all those problems

agobiante, agobiador -dora *adj* ⟨trabajo/ día⟩ exhausting; ⟨calor⟩ stifling; **es una carga** ~ **para él** it's/he's/she's a terrible burden on him

agobiar [A1] *vt* «problemas/responsabilidad»

to weigh *o* get ... down; «calor» to oppress, get ... down; **te agobia con tanta amabilidad** she smothers you with kindness; **este niño me agobia** this child is too much for me

agobio *m*: **una sensación de** ~ a sense of oppression

agonía *f* **(a)** (de moribundo) death throes (*pl*) **(b)** (sufrimiento) suffering

agonizar [A4] *vi* «persona» to be dying, be in the throes of death; «imperio/régimen» to be in its death throes

agosto *m* August; *para ejemplos ver* ENERO; *hacer su* ~ to make a fortune, to make a killing (colloq)

agotado -da *adj* **(a)** [ESTAR] ⟨recursos⟩ exhausted; ⟨edición⟩ sold out; ⟨pila⟩ dead, flat; ❺ **agotadas todas las localidades** sold out **(b)** [ESTAR] ⟨persona⟩ exhausted

agotador -dora *adj* exhausting

agotamiento *m* exhaustion

agotar [A1] *vt* **(a)** ⟨recursos⟩ to exhaust, use up; ⟨pila⟩ to wear out, run down; ⟨mina/tierra⟩ to exhaust **(b)** (cansar) ⟨persona⟩ to tire ... out, wear ... out

■ **agotarse** *v pron* **(a)** «existencias/reservas» to run out, be used up; «pila» to run down; «mina/tierra» to become exhausted; «edición» to sell out; **se me está agotando la paciencia** my patience is running out **(b)** «persona» to wear *o* tire oneself out

agraciado -da *adj* ⟨persona/figura⟩ attractive; **es muy poco** ~ he's not very attractive

agradable *adj* ⟨persona⟩ pleasant, nice; ⟨carácter⟩ pleasant; ⟨día/velada⟩ enjoyable, nice; ⟨sensación/efecto⟩ pleasant, pleasing; ⟨sabor/olor⟩ pleasant, nice; ~ **a la vista** pleasing to the eye

agradar [A1] *vi* (frml): **¿le agrada este, señora?** is this one to your liking, madam? (frml); **la idea no me agrada** the idea doesn't appeal to me; **le agrada verlo contento** it gives her pleasure to see him happy; **me** ~**ía mucho verlos allí** I would be very pleased to see you there

■ ~ *vt* to please

agradecer [E3] *vt* **(a)** (sentir gratitud por) ⟨ayuda/ amabilidad⟩ to appreciate, to be grateful for; ~**le algo a** algn to be grateful to sb for sth; **le** ~**ía (que) me llamara** (frml) I would appreciate it if you would call me (frml) **(b)** (dar las gracias por) to thank; ~**le algo a** algn to thank sb for sth; **¡y así es como me lo agradece!** and this is all the thanks I get!

agradecido -da *adj* ⟨persona⟩ grateful; **estar** ~ to be grateful; **¡qué poco** ~ **eres!** you're so ungrateful!

agradecimiento *m* gratitude; **demostrar** ~ to show gratitude; **en** ~ **por todo lo que ha hecho** in appreciation of all you have done

agradezca, agradezcas, etc ▶ AGRADECER

agrado *m* (frml): **espero que sea de su** ~ I hope this is to your liking; **con sumo** ~ gladly; **tuve el** ~ **de verla** I had the pleasure of seeing her

agrandar [A1] *vt* **(a)** ⟨casa⟩ to extend; ⟨agujero/pozo⟩ to make ... larger *o* bigger; ⟨fotocopia⟩ to enlarge, blow up; ⟨vestido⟩ to let out **(b)** (exagerar) to exaggerate

■ **agrandarse** *v pron* «agujero/bulto» to grow larger, get bigger

agrario -ria adj ‹sector/política› agricultural (before n); ‹sociedad› agrarian

agravante adj aggravating
■ f or m (Der) aggravating factor o circumstance; **con la ∼ de que estaba borracho** what makes it even worse is that he was drunk

agravar [A1] vt to make … worse, aggravate
■ **agravarse** v pron «problema/situación» to become worse, worsen; «enfermo» to deteriorate, get worse

agredir [I32] vt (frml) to attack, assault

agregar [A3] vt (añadir) to add; **∼ algo A algo** to add sth TO sth

agresión f aggression; **una ∼ brutal** a brutal attack

agresividad f aggressiveness

agresivo -va adj aggressive

agresor -sora adj ‹ejército› attacking (before n); ‹país› aggressor (before n)
■ m,f (país, ejército) aggressor; (persona) attacker, assailant (frml)

agreste adj ‹terreno/camino› rough; ‹paisaje› rugged; ‹vegetación/animal› wild

agriarse [A1 or A17] v pron «leche/vino» to turn o go sour; «persona» to become bitter o embittered

agrícola adj ‹técnicas› agricultural, farming (before n)

agricultor -tora m,f farmer

agricultura f agriculture

agridulce adj bittersweet; (Coc) sweet-and-sour

agrietarse [A1] v pron «tierra/pared» to crack; «piel» to chap, become chapped

agringado -da adj (AmL fam & pey) ‹persona› Americanized; ‹acento/costumbres› (norteamericanizado) Americanized; (extranjero) foreign

agrio, agria adj (a) ‹manzana› sour, tart; ‹naranja/limón› sour, sharp (b) ‹tono/persona› sour, sharp; ‹disputa› bitter

agriparse [A1] v pron (Andes) to get the flu (AmE), to get flu (BrE); **está agripado** he has (the) flu

agronomía f agronomy

agrónomo -ma m,f agronomist

agrupación f ① (grupo) group; (asociación) association; **∼ coral** choral group, choir ② (acción) grouping (together)

agrupar [A1] vt (a) (formar grupos) to put … into groups, to group (b) (reunir) ‹organizaciones/partidos› to bring together
■ **agruparse** v pron (a) (formar un grupo) «niños/policías» to gather; «partidos» to come together (b) (dividirse en grupos) to get into groups

agua f ① ① water; **∼ de lluvia/mar** rainwater/seawater; **∼ corriente/destilada** running/distilled water; **∼ de colonia** eau de cologne; **∼ dulce** fresh water; **∼ mineral** mineral water; **∼ mineral con gas/sin gas** sparkling/still mineral water; **∼ oxigenada** peroxide, hydrogen peroxide (tech); **∼ potable/salada** drinking/salt water; **como ∼ para**

chocolate (Méx fam) furious; **estar con el ∼ al cuello** to be up to one's neck; **estar más claro que el ∼** to be (patently) obvious; **hacérsele ∼ la boca a algn** (AmL): **se me hizo ∼ la boca** it made my mouth water; **ser ∼ pasada** to be a thing of the past; **∼ que no has de beber déjala correr** if you're not interested, don't spoil things for me/for other people; **nunca digas de esta ∼ no beberé** you never know when the same thing might happen to you
② (lluvia) rain
③ (AmC, Andes) (infusión) herb tea (AmE), herbal tea (BrE); **∼ de menta** mint tea
④ **aguas** fpl (a) ‹de mar, río› waters (pl) (b) ‹de balneario, manantial› waters (pl); **tomar las ∼s** to take the waters; **∼s termales** thermal waters (pl)

aguacate m ‹árbol› avocado; ‹fruto› avocado (pear)

aguacero m downpour

aguado -da adj ① ‹leche/vino› watered-down; ‹sopa› watery, thin; ‹café› weak; ‹salsa› thin ② (AmC, Méx fam) (aburrido) [ESTAR] ‹fiesta/película› boring, dull; [SER] ‹persona› boring, dull

aguafiestas mf (pl ∼) (fam) wet blanket (colloq), party pooper (AmE colloq)

aguafuerte m (grabado) etching

aguaitar [A1] vt (AmS fam) (espiar) to spy on; (vigilar) to keep an eye on
■ ∼ vi (AmS fam) (espiar) to snoop (colloq); (mirar) to have a look

aguanieve f sleet

aguantador -dora adj (AmL) ① (fam) (resistente) ‹tela/ropa/zapatos› hard-wearing; ‹coche› sturdy ② (fam) (a) (paciente, tolerante): **es muy ∼** he puts up with a lot (colloq) (b) (del dolor, sufrimiento) tough (colloq)

aguantar [A1] vt ① ‹dolor/sufrimiento› to bear, endure; **aguanto bien el calor** I can take the heat; **no tengo por qué ∼ esto** I don't have to put up with this; **este calor no hay quien lo aguante** this heat is unbearable; **no sabes ∼ una broma** you can't take a joke; **no los aguanto** I can't stand them; **no puedo ∼ este dolor de muelas** this toothache's unbearable
② ‹peso/carga› to support, bear; ‹presión› to withstand (b) (durar): **estas botas ∼án otro invierno** these boots will last (me/you/him) another winter
③ (sostener) to hold
④ (contener, reprimir) ‹risa/lágrimas› to hold back; **∼ la respiración** to hold one's breath
■ ∼ vi: **¡ya no aguanto más!** I can't take any more!; **no creo que este clavo aguante** I don't think this nail will hold
■ **aguantarse** v pron ① (conformarse, resignarse): **me tendré que ∼** I'll just have to put up with it; **si no le gusta, que se aguante** if he doesn't like it, he can lump it (colloq)
② (euf) (reprimirse, contenerse): **no me pude ∼ y me puse a llorar** I couldn't contain myself and burst into tears; **aguántate un poquito que ya llegamos** just hold o hang on a minute, we'll soon be there

3 (AmL fam) (esperarse) to hang on (colloq)

aguar [A16] *vt* **(a)** ‹*leche/vino*› to water down **(b)** (fam) (estropear) to put a damper on (colloq)

■ **aguarse** *v pron* (fam) to be spoiled

aguardar [A1] *vt* ‹*persona*› to wait for; ‹*acontecimiento*› to await

■ ~ *vi* «*noticia/destino*» to await; **les aguardaba una sorpresa** there was a surprise in store for them

aguardiente *m* eau-de-vie (*clear brandy distilled from fermented fruit juice*)

aguarrás *m* turpentine, turps (colloq)

aguayo *m* (Bol) *multicolored cloth*

agudeza *f* **1 (a)** (de voz, sonido) high pitch **(b)** (de dolor — duradero) intensity; (— momentáneo) sharpness **2** (perspicacia) sharpness; (de sentido, instinto) keenness, sharpness **3** (comentario ingenioso) witty comment

agudizar [A4] *vt* ‹*sensación*› to heighten; ‹*crisis/conflicto*› to make worse; ‹*instinto*› to heighten; ‹*sentido*› to sharpen

■ **agudizarse** *v pron* «*sensación*» to heighten; «*dolor*» to get worse; «*crisis*» to worsen; «*instinto*» to become heightened; «*sentido*» to become sharper

agudo -da *adj* **1 (a)** ‹*filo/punta*› sharp **(b)** ‹*ángulo*› acute **2 (a)** ‹*voz/sonido*› high-pitched; ‹*nota*› high **(b)** ‹*dolor*› (duradero) intense, acute; (momentáneo) sharp **(c)** ‹*crisis*› severe **(d)** ‹*aumento/descenso*› sharp **3 (a)** (perspicaz) ‹*persona*› quick-witted, sharp; ‹*comentario*› shrewd **(b)** (gracioso) ‹*comentario/persona*› witty **(c)** ‹*sentido/instinto*› sharp

agüero *m*: **ser de mal/buen** ~ (presagio) to be a bad/good omen; (causa) to bring bad/good luck

agüevado -da *adj* (AmC fam) [**ESTAR**] upset

aguijón *m* **(a)** (vara) goad **(b)** (Zool) sting

águila *f* ⚥ **(a)** (ave) eagle; **ser un** ~ to be very sharp **(b)** (Méx) (de moneda) ≈ heads (*pl*); **¿~ o sol?** heads or tails?

aguileño -ña *adj* ‹*nariz*› aquiline

aguinaldo *m* **1 (a)** (propina) Christmas bonus (AmE), Christmas box (BrE) **(b)** (paga extra) *extra month's salary paid at Christmas*, Christmas bonus (AmE) **2** (Col, Ven) (canción) ≈ Christmas carol

aguja *f* **(a)** (de coser, tejer) needle; (para inyecciones) needle; (de tocadiscos) stylus, needle; (de instrumento) needle; (de balanza) pointer, needle; (de reloj) hand; **buscar una** ~ **en un pajar** to look for a needle in a haystack (Inf) pin

agujereado -da *adj*: **está** ~ it has holes in it

agujerear [A1] *vt* (hacer agujeros en) to make holes in; (atravesar) to pierce

agujero *m* hole; **hacerse** ~**s en las orejas** to have one's ears pierced

agujeta *f* **1** (Méx) (de zapato) (shoe) lace **2 agujetas** *fpl* (Esp) stiffness; **tengo** ~**s en las piernas** my legs are stiff

aguzar [A4] *vt* to sharpen; **aguzó el oído** he pricked up his ears

ah *interj* (expresando sorpresa, lástima, asentimiento) oh!

ahí *adv* **1 (a)** (en el espacio) there; ~ **está/viene** there he is/here he comes; ~ **arriba/abajo** up/down there; ~ **mismo** *or* (AmL) **nomás** *or* (Méx)

mero right *o* just there **(b) por ahí** somewhere; **debe estar por** ~ it must be around somewhere; **fue a dar una vuelta por** ~ she went off for a walk; **se fue por** ~ she went that way; **yo he estado por** ~ I've been around there; **tendrá unos 35 años o por** ~ he must be 35 or thereabouts **2 (a)** (refiriéndose a un lugar figurado): ~ **está el truco/problema** that's the secret/problem; **de** ~ **a la drogadicción solo hay un paso** from there it's just a short step to becoming a drug addict; *hasta* ~ *llego yo* that's as far as I'm prepared to go **(b) de ahí: de** ~ **mi sorpresa** hence my surprise; **de** ~ **que hayan fracasado** that is why they failed; **de** ~ **a que venga es otra cosa** whether or not he actually comes is another matter **3** (en el tiempo) then; **de** ~ **en adelante** from then on; ~ **mismo** there and then

ahijado -da *m,f* (por bautizo) (*m*) godson; (*f*) goddaughter; **mis** ~**s** my godchildren

ahogado -da *adj* **1** (en agua): **dos niños resultaron** ~**s** two children were drowned; **morir** ~ (en agua) to drown; (asfixiarse) to suffocate; (atragantarse) to choke to death **2** ‹*llanto/grito*› stifled **3** (Méx fam) (borracho) blind *o* rolling drunk (colloq)

ahogador *m* (Chi, Méx) (Auto) choke

ahogar [A3] *vt* **1 (a)** ‹*persona/animal*› (en agua) to drown; (asfixiar) to suffocate **(b)** ‹*motor*› to flood **2 (a)** ‹*palabras/voz*› to drown (out); ‹*llanto/grito*› to stifle **(b)** ‹*penas*› to drown

■ **ahogarse** *v pron* **(a)** «*persona/animal*» (en agua) to drown; (asfixiarse) to suffocate; (atragantarse) to choke **(b)** «*motor*» to flood

ahogo *m* breathlessness; **tiene** ~**s** he gets out of breath

ahora *adv* **1 (a)** (en el momento presente) now; ~ **que lo pienso** now I come to think of it; **la juventud de** ~ young people today; **hasta** ~ so far, up to now; **de** ~ **en adelante** from now on; **por** ~ for the time being; **por** ~ **va todo bien** everything's going all right so far **(b)** (inmediatamente, pronto): ~ **mismo** right now *o* away; ~ **te lo muestro** I'll show it to you in a minute *o* second *o* moment; ¡~ **voy!** I'm coming!; ¡**hasta** ~! (esp Esp) see you soon! **(c)** (hace un momento) a moment ago **2 ahora bien** (*indep*) however

ahorcar [A2] *vt* to hang

■ **ahorcarse** *v pron* (*refl*) to hang oneself

ahorita *adv* (esp AmL fam) **(a)** (en este momento) just *o* right now **(b)** (inmediatamente, pronto): ~ **te lo doy** I'll give it to you in a second *o* moment **(c)** (hace un momento) a moment ago

ahorrador -dora *adj* thrifty; **no soy muy** ~**a** I'm not very good at saving (money)

■ *m,f* saver, investor

ahorrante *mf* (Chi) saver, investor

ahorrar [A1] *vt* **1** ‹*dinero/energía/agua*› to save; ‹*tiempo*› to save **2** (evitar) ‹*molestia/viaje*› (+ *me/te/le etc*) to save, spare

■ ~ *vi* to save

■ **ahorrarse** *v pron* (*enf*) **(a)** ‹*dinero*› to save (oneself) **(b)** (evitarse) ‹*molestia/viaje*› to save oneself

ahorrista *mf* (RPl, Ven) saver, investor

ahorro *m* **(a)** (acción) saving **(b) ahorros** *mpl* (cantidad) savings (*pl*)

ahuecar [A2] *vt* (a) ⟨*tronco/calabaza*⟩ to hollow out; ⟨*mano*⟩ to cup (b) ⟨*almohadón*⟩ to plump up; ⟨*pelo*⟩ to give volume to

ahumado *adj* (a) (Coc) smoked (b) ⟨*cristal*⟩ smoked; ⟨*gafas*⟩ tinted

ahumar [A23] *vt* (a) ⟨*jamón/pescado*⟩ to smoke (b) ⟨*paredes/techo*⟩ to blacken

ahuyentar [A1] *vt* (a) (hacer huir) ⟨*ladrón/animal*⟩ to frighten off *or* away (b) (mantener a distancia) ⟨*fiera/mosquitos*⟩ to keep … away

aimará *adj* Aymara
■ *mf* Aymara Indian

airbag /'erbag/ *f* airbag

aire *m* **1** (a) air; sintió que le faltaba el ~ she felt as if she was going to suffocate; salir a tomar el ~ to go outside for a breath of fresh air; al ~ libre outdoors, in the open air; ~ acondicionado air-conditioning; con ~ acondicionado air-conditioned; a mi/tu/su ~: ellos salen en grupo, yo prefiero ir a mi ~ they go out in a group, I prefer doing my own thing (colloq); quedar en el ~: todo quedó en el ~ everything was left up in the air; saltar *or* volar por los ~s to explode, blow up; **2** (viento) wind; (corriente) draft (AmE), draught (BrE) **3** (Rad, TV): salir al ~ to go on the air **4** (a) (aspecto) air; tiene un ~ aristocrático she has an aristocratic air; la protesta tomó ~s de revuelta the protest began to look like a revolt; darse ~s (de grandeza) to put on *o* give oneself airs (b) (parecido) resemblance; tienen un ~ they look a little alike; ~ de familia family resemblance

airear [A1] *vt* (a) (ventilar) to air (b) (hacer público) ⟨*asunto*⟩ to air (c) ⟨*masa/tierra*⟩ to aerate
■ **airearse** *v pron* (a) «*persona*» to get some (fresh) air (b) «*manta/abrigo*» to air; para que se airee el cuarto to let some air into the room

aislado -da *adj* (a) (alejado) remote, isolated (b) (sin comunicación) cut off; quedar ~ to be cut off; vive ~ del mundo he's cut himself off from the world (c) ⟨*caso*⟩ isolated (d) (Elec) insulated

aislamiento *m* (a) (en general) isolation (b) (Elec) insulation

aislante *adj* insulating, insulation (*before n*)
■ *m* insulator

aislar [A19] *vt* (a) (apartar, separar) ⟨*enfermo*⟩ to isolate, keep in isolation; ⟨*preso*⟩ to place … in solitary confinement; ⟨*virus*⟩ to isolate (b) (dejar sin communicación) ⟨*lugar*⟩ to cut off (c) (Elec) to insulate
■ **aislarse** *v pron* (*refl*) to cut oneself off

ajado -da *adj* ⟨*ropa*⟩ worn; ⟨*manos*⟩ wrinkly; ⟨*piel*⟩ wrinkled

ajedrecista *mf* chess player

ajedrez *m* (juego) chess; (tablero y fichas) chess set

ajeno -na *adj* [SER] (a) (que no corresponde, pertenece): mis ideales le son totalmente ~s my ideals are completely alien to him; aquel ambiente me era ~ that environment was alien *o* foreign to me; por razones ajenas a nuestra voluntad for reasons beyond our control (b) (que pertenece, corresponde a otro): conduce un coche ~ he drives someone else's car; por el bien ~ for the good of others; las desgracias ajenas other people's misfortunes

ajetreado -da *adj* hectic, busy

ajetreo *m* hustle and bustle; un día de mucho ~ a hectic day

ají *m* (a) (chile) chili* (b) (Andes) (salsa) chili* sauce (c) (RPl) (pimiento) pepper

ajo *m* (Coc) garlic; un diente de ~ a clove of garlic

ajonjolí *m* sesame

ajuar *m* (de novia) trousseau; (de bebé) layette

ajustado -da *adj* (a) (ceñido) tight; me queda muy ~ it's too tight (for me) (b) ⟨*presupuesto*⟩ tight

ajustar [A1] *vt* **1** (a) (apretar) to tighten (up) (b) ⟨*volumen/temperatura*⟩ to adjust; ~ la entrada de agua to regulate the flow of water (c) ⟨*retrovisor/asiento/cinturón de seguridad*⟩ to adjust (d) (encajar) ⟨*piezas*⟩ to fit **2** (en costura) to take in **3** (a) ⟨*gastos/horarios*⟩ ~ algo A algo to adapt sth TO sth (b) ⟨*sueldos/precios*⟩ to adjust **4** (concertar) to fix, set **5** ⟨*cuentas*⟩ (sacar el resultado de) to balance; (saldar) to settle
■ ~ *vi* to fit
■ **ajustarse** *v pron* **1** (*refl*) ⟨*cinturón de seguridad*⟩ to adjust **2** ⟨*piezas*⟩ to fit

al *contraction of* A *and* EL

ala *f* ♗ **1** (de ave, de avión) wing; ~ delta (deporte) hang gliding; (aparato) hang glider; cortarle las ~s a algn to clip sb's wings; darle ~s a algn: si le das ~s, luego no podrás controlarlo if you let him have his own way, you won't be able to control him later **2** (de sombrero) brim **3** (a) (de edificio) wing (b) (facción) wing (c) (flanco) flank, wing (d) (Dep) (posición) wing
■ *mf* ♗ (jugador) wing, winger

alabanza *f* praise; digno de ~ praiseworthy

alabar [A1] *vt* to praise

alacena *f* larder

alacrán *m* scorpion

alambrada *f* (valla) wire fence; (material) wire fencing

alambrado *m* (AmL) (a) (acción) fencing in/off (b) (valla) wire fence

alambrar [A1] *vt* to fence in/off

alambre *m* (hilo metálico) wire; ~ de púas barbed wire, barbwire (AmE)

alameda *f* (avenida) tree-lined avenue; (terreno con álamos) poplar grove

álamo *m* poplar

alarde *m* show, display; hacer ~ de fuerza to show off strength

alardear [A1] *vi* ~ DE algo to boast ABOUT *o* OF sth; alardea de tener dinero she boasts about being well-off

alargado -da *adj* ⟨*forma*⟩ elongated; ⟨*hoja*⟩ elongate

alargador *m* extension cord (AmE), extension lead (BrE)

alargar [A3] *vt* **1** (a) ⟨*vestido/pantalón*⟩ to let down, lengthen; ⟨*manguera/cable*⟩ to lengthen, extend; ⟨*riendas/soga*⟩ to let out; ⟨*paso*⟩ to lengthen (b) ⟨*cuento/discurso*⟩ to drag out; ⟨*vacaciones/plazo*⟩ to extend; puede ~le la vida it could prolong her life **2** (a) (extender) ⟨*mano/brazo*⟩ to hold out (b) (alcanzar) ~le algo A algn to hand *o* give *o* pass sth TO sb

■ **alargarse** *v pron* «*cara/sombra*» to get longer; «*días*» to grow longer; «*reunión/fiesta*» to go on

alarido *m* (de miedo) shriek; (de dolor) scream

alarma *f* $\boxed{1}$ (ante peligro) alarm; **dar la voz de ~** to sound *o* raise the alarm $\boxed{2}$ (dispositivo) alarm; **~ contra robos/incendios** burglar/fire alarm

alarmante *adj* alarming

alarmar [A1] *vt* to alarm

■ **alarmarse** *v pron* to be alarmed

alba *f*: (del día) dawn, daybreak; **al rayar el ~** (liter) at the break of day (liter); **al** *or* **con el ~** at the crack of dawn

albacora *f* (atún) albacore; (pez espada) (Chi) swordfish

albahaca *f* basil

albanés¹ -nesa *adj/m,f* Albanian

albanés² *m* (idioma) Albanian

Albania *f* Albania

albañil *m* (constructor) builder; (que coloca ladrillos) bricklayer

albaricoque *m* (Esp) apricot

albaricoquero *m* (Esp) apricot tree

albedrío *m* (free) will; **lo hizo a su ~** he did it of his own free will; **lo dejo a tu libre ~** I leave it entirely up to you

alberca *f* **(a)** (embalse) reservoir **(b)** (Méx) (piscina) swimming pool **(c)** (Col) (lavadero) sink (*for washing clothes*) **(d)** (Bol, Per) (comedero) trough

albergar [A3] *vt* ‹*personas*› to house, accommodate; ‹*biblioteca/exposición*› to house

■ **albergarse** *v pron* **(a)** (hospedarse) to lodge **(b)** (refugiarse) to shelter, take refuge

albergue *m* **(a)** (alojamiento) lodging, accommodations (*pl*) (AmE); **darle ~ a algn** to take sb in **(b)** (hostal) hostel; **~ juvenil** youth hostel **(c)** (en la montaña) refuge, shelter; (para vagabundos, mendigos) shelter

albino -na *adj/m,f* albino

albóndiga *f* meatball

albornoz *m* bathrobe

alborotado -da *adj* $\boxed{1}$ **(a)** (nervioso) agitated; (animado, excitado) excited **(b)** (ruidoso) noisy, rowdy; (amotinado) riotous $\boxed{2}$ ‹*mar*› rough; ‹*pelo*› untidy, disheveled*

alborotador -dora *adj* rowdy, noisy

■ *m,f* troublemaker

alborotar [A1] *vi* to make a racket

■ **~** *vt* **(a)** (agitar) to agitate, get ... agitated; (excitar) to get ... excited **(b)** ‹*muchedumbre*› to stir up

■ **alborotarse** *v pron* **(a)** (agitarse) to get agitated *o* upset; (excitarse) to get excited **(b)** (amotinarse) to riot

alboroto *m* **(a)** (agitación, nerviosismo) agitation; (excitación) excitement **(b)** (ruido) racket **(c)** (disturbio, jaleo) disturbance, commotion; (motín) riot

álbum *m* **(a)** (de fotos, sellos) album; (libro de historietas) comic book **(b)** (disco) album

alcachofa *f* **(a)** (Bot, Coc) artichoke **(b)** (de ducha) shower head; (de regadera) sprinkler (AmE), rose (BrE)

alcahuete -ta *m,f* **(a)** (ant) (mediador) procurer (arch) **(b)** (CS fam) (chismoso) gossip (colloq); (soplón) tattletale (AmE colloq), telltale (BrE colloq)

alcahuetear [A1] *vi* **(a)** (hacer de mediador) to act as a go-between, to procure **(b)** (Andes fam) (tapar): **les alcahuetea las travesuras** he lets them get away with all kinds of things; **le alcahuetea las mentiras** she covers up for him when he lies **(c)** (CS fam) (chismear) to gossip (colloq)

■ **~** *vt* (fam) (delatar) to tell *o* snitch on (colloq)

alcalde -desa *m,f* $\boxed{1}$ (Gob) mayor

$\boxed{2}$ **alcaldesa** *f* (mujer del alcalde) mayoress

alcance *m* **(a)** (de persona) reach; **fuera del ~ de los niños** out of reach of children; **está fuera de mi ~** it is beyond my means **(b)** (de arma, emisora) range; **misiles de largo ~** long-range missiles **(c)** (de ley, proyecto) scope; (de declaración, noticia) implications (*pl*) **(d)** (*en locs*) **al alcance de** within reach of; **precios al ~ de su bolsillo** prices to suit your pocket; **un lujo que no está a mi ~** a luxury I can't afford

alcancía *f* (AmL) (de niño) piggy bank; (para colectas) collection box

alcanfor *m* camphor

alcantarilla *f* (cloaca) sewer; (sumidero) drain

alcantarillado *m* sewer system, drains (*pl*)

alcanzar [A4] *vt* $\boxed{1}$ **(a)** ‹*persona*› (llegar a la altura de) to catch up with, to catch ... up (BrE); (pillar, agarrar) to catch; **lo alcancé en la curva** I caught up with him on the bend; **¡a que no me alcanzas!** I bet you can't catch me! (colloq) **(b)** (en tarea, estatura) to catch up with

$\boxed{2}$ (llegar a) ‹*lugar*› to reach, get to; ‹*temperatura/nivel/edad*› to reach; **casi no alcanzo el tren** I almost missed the train; **estos árboles alcanzan una gran altura** these trees can reach *o* grow to a great height; **~ la mayoría de edad** to come of age

$\boxed{3}$ (conseguir, obtener) ‹*objetivo/éxito*› to achieve; ‹*acuerdo*› to reach

$\boxed{4}$ (acercar, pasar) **~le algo a algn** to pass sb sth, to pass sth ᴛᴏ sb

■ **~** *vi* $\boxed{1}$ (llegar con la mano) to reach; **hasta donde alcanzaba la vista** as far as the eye could see; **~ a hacer algo** to manage to do sth

$\boxed{2}$ (ser suficiente) «*comida/provisiones*» to be enough; **el sueldo no le alcanza** he can't manage on his salary

alcaparra *f* caper

alcaucil *m* (RPl) artichoke

alcázar *m* (fortaleza) fortress; (palacio) palace

alcista *adj* ‹*tendencia*› upward; ‹*mercado*› bull (*before n*)

alcoba *f* bedroom, bedchamber (liter)

alcohol *m* $\boxed{1}$ (Quím) alcohol; (Farm) *tb* **~ de 90 (grados)** rubbing alcohol (AmE), surgical spirit (BrE) $\boxed{2}$ (bebida) alcohol, drink

alcoholemia *f*: **hacerle la prueba de la ~ a algn** to breathalyze sb

alcohólico -ca *adj* alcoholic; **bebida no alcohólica** nonalcoholic drink

■ *m,f* alcoholic

alcoholímetro *m* Breathalyzer®, drunkometer (AmE)

alcoholismo *m* alcoholism

alcornoque *m* **(a)** (árbol) cork oak **(b)** (fam) (persona) idiot

aldaba *f* (llamador) doorknocker; (cerrojo) latch

aldea *f* small village, hamlet

aldeano -na *adj* village (*before n*)
■ *m,f* villager

alebrestarse [A1] *v pron* (a) (Col, Méx) (alterarse, agitarse) to get worked up, agitated (b) (Ven fam) (animarse) to get excited; (excesivamente) to get overexcited

alegación *f* declaration, statement

alegar [A3] *vt* (a) ⟨*motivos/causas*⟩ to cite; ⟨*razones*⟩ to put forward; ⟨*ignorancia/defensa propia*⟩to plead; ⟨*inmunidad diplomática*⟩ to claim; **alegó que no lo sabía** she claimed not to know
■ ~ *vi* (AmL) (a) (discutir) to argue; ~ DE algo to argue ABOUT sth (b) (protestar) to complain; ~ POR algo to complain ABOUT sth

alegata *f* (Méx) argument

alegato *m* (a) (exposición) statement, declaration (b) (Der) (escrito) submission (c) (Andes) (discusión) argument

alegrar [A1] *vt* (a) (hacer feliz) ⟨*persona*⟩ to make ... happy; **me alegra saberlo** I'm glad *o* pleased to hear it (b) (animar) ⟨*persona*⟩ to cheer up; ⟨*fiesta*⟩ to liven up; ⟨*habitación*⟩ to brighten up; **¡alegra esa cara!** cheer up!
■ **alegrarse** *v pron* (a) (ponerse feliz, contento): **me alegro mucho por ti** I'm really happy for you; **se alegró muchísimo cuando lo vio** she was really happy when she saw him; **¡cuánto me alegro!** I'm so happy *o* pleased!; **está mucho mejor — me alegro** she's much better — I'm glad (to hear that); **~se CON algo** to be glad *o* pleased ABOUT sth; **me alegro de verte** it's good *o* nice to see you; **me alegro de que todo haya salido bien** I'm glad *o* pleased that everything went well (b) (animarse) to cheer up (c) (por el alcohol) to get tipsy (colloq)

alegre *adj* (a) ⟨*persona/carácter*⟩ happy, cheerful; ⟨*color*⟩ bright; ⟨*fiesta/música*⟩ lively; **su habitación es muy ~** her room is nice and bright; **es muy ~** she's very cheerful, she's a very happy person (b) [ESTAR] (por el alcohol) tipsy (colloq)

alegría *f* (dicha, felicidad) happiness, joy; **¡qué ~ verte!** it's great to see you!; **saltar de ~** to jump for joy

alejado -da *adj* (a) ⟨*lugar*⟩ remote (b) (distanciado) ⟨*persona*⟩: **hace tiempo que está ~ de la política** he's been away from *o* out of politics for some time; **está ~ de su familia** he's estranged from his family

alejar [A1] *vt* (a) (poner lejos, más lejos) to move ... (further) away; **~ algo/a algn DE algo/algn** to move sth/sb away FROM sth/sb (b) (distanciar) **~ a algn DE algn** to distance sb FROM sb (c) ⟨*dudas/ temores*⟩ to dispel
■ **alejarse** *v pron* to move away; (caminando) to walk away; **no se alejen demasiado** don't go too far; **se alejó de su familia** he drifted apart from his family; **necesito ~me de todo** I need to get away from everything

aleluya *interj* halleluja!

alemán¹ -mana *adj/m,f* German

alemán² *m* (idioma) German

Alemania *f* Germany

alentador -dora *adj* encouraging

alentar [A5] *vt* (a) ⟨*persona*⟩ to encourage; ⟨*jugador/equipo*⟩ to cheer ... on (b) ⟨*esperanza/ ilusión*⟩ to cherish

alergia *f* allergy; **le produce ~** she's allergic to it; **~ A algo** allergy TO sth; **tiene ~ a la penicilina** he's allergic to penicillin

alérgico -ca *adj* (a) [SER] ⟨*persona*⟩ allergic; **~ A algo** allergic TO sth (b) ⟨*afección/reacción*⟩ allergic

alerta *adj* alert; **estar ~** (tener cuidado) to be alert; (estar en guardia) to be on the alert; **mantener el oído ~** to keep one's ears open
■ *f*: **dar la (voz de) ~** to raise the alarm; **en estado de ~** on alert

alertar [A1] *vt* **~ a algn DE algo** to alert sb TO sth

aleta *f* (a) (de pez) fin; (de foca) flipper (b) (para natación) flipper (c) (de la nariz) wing

aletargado -da *adj* lethargic, drowsy

aletargar [A3] *vt* ⟨*persona*⟩ to make ... feel lethargic *o* drowsy

aletear [A1] *vi* «*pájaro/gallina*» to flap its wings; «*mariposa*» to flutter its wings

alfabético -ca *adj* alphabetical

alfabetización *f* teaching of basic literacy; **campaña de ~** literacy campaign

alfabetizar [A4] *vt* (a) (Educ) to teach ... to read and write (b) ⟨*sistema/fichero*⟩ to put ... in alphabetical order, to alphabetize (frml)

alfabeto *m* alphabet

alfajor *m*: *type of candy or cake varying from region to region*

alfalfa *f* alfalfa, lucerne (BrE)

alfarería *f* pottery

alfarero -ra *m,f* potter

alféizar *m* sill; **el ~ de la ventana** the windowsill

alférez *m* second lieutenant

alfil *m* bishop

alfiler *m* (en costura) pin; (broche) brooch, pin; **~ de corbata** tiepin; **~ de gancho** (CS, Ven) *or* (Col) **de nodriza** safety pin

alfombra *f* (a) (suelta) rug; (más grande) carpet (b) (AmL) (de pared a pared) carpet

alfombrado -da *adj* carpeted

alfombrar [A1] *vt* to carpet

alfombrilla *f* **1** (de coche) mat; (de baño) bath mat; **~ para ratón** (Inf) mouse mat **2** (Med) *type of measles*

alforja *f* (para caballerías) saddlebag; (sobre el hombro) knapsack

alga *f⚥* (en el mar) seaweed; (en agua dulce) weed, waterweed; (nombre genérico) alga

algarroba *f* carob (bean)

algarrobo *m* carob (tree)

álgebra *f⚥* algebra

álgido -da *adj* ⟨*punto/momento*⟩ culminating (*before n*), decisive

algo¹ *pron* **(a)** something; (en frases interrogativas, condicionales, etc) anything; (esperando respuesta afirmativa) something; **quiero decirte ∼** I want to tell you something; **si llegara a pasarle ∼** if anything happened to her; **¿quieres ∼ de beber?** do you want something *o* anything to drink?; **por ∼ será** there must be some *o* a reason; **le va a dar ∼** he'll have a fit; **o ∼ así** or something like that; **eso ya es ∼** at least that's something; **sé ∼ de francés** I know some French; **¿queda ∼ de pan?** is there any bread left? **(b)** (en aproximaciones): **serán las once y ∼** it must be some time after eleven; **pesa tres kilos y ∼** it weighs three kilos and a bit

algo² *adv* a little, slightly; **está ∼ nublado** it's a bit cloudy; **es ∼ grande para ti** it's a bit too big for you

algodón *m* ⟨1⟩ (Bot, Tex) cotton ⟨2⟩ (Farm) **(a)** (material) *tb* **∼ hidrófilo** cotton (AmE), cotton wool (BrE) **(b)** (trozo) piece of cotton (AmE), piece of cotton wool (BrE); **∼ de azúcar** cotton candy (AmE), candy floss (BrE)

algodonal, algodonar *m* cotton field

algodonero -ra *adj* cotton (*before n*)
■ *m,f* (agricultor) cotton planter *o* farmer; (vendedor) cotton dealer

alguacil -cila *m,f* **(a)** (agente de autoridad) sheriff **(b)** (de tribunal de justicia) bailiff (AmE), constable (BrE)

alguien *pron* somebody, someone; (en frases interrogativas, condicionales, etc) anybody, anyone; (esperando respuesta afirmativa) somebody, someone; **∼ con experiencia** somebody *o* someone with experience; **¿ha llamado ∼?** has anybody *o* anyone called?; **si ∼ preguntara** if anybody *o* anyone should ask

algún *adj*: apocopated form of ALGUNO *used before masculine singular nouns*

alguno¹ -na *adj* ⟨1⟩ (delante del n) **(a)** (indicando uno indeterminado) some; **algún día** some *o* one day; **en algún lugar** somewhere **(b)** (en frases interrogativas, condicionales, etc) any; **¿tocas algún instrumento?** do you play any instruments?; **si tienes algún problema** if there's any problem, if you have any problems **(c)** (indicando cantidad indeterminada): **esto tiene alguna importancia** this is of some importance; **hace ∼s años** some years ago, a few years ago; **me quedan tres tazas y algún plato** I have three cups and one or two plates; **escribió algún que otro artículo** he wrote one or two articles ⟨2⟩ (detrás del n) (con valor negativo): **esto no lo afectará en modo ∼** this won't affect it in the slightest *o* at all

alguno² -na *pron* **(a)** (cosa, persona indeterminada) one; **∼ de nosotros** one of us; **siempre hay ∼ que no está conforme** there's always someone who doesn't agree **(b)** (en frases interrogativas, condicionales, etc): **buscaba una guía ¿tiene alguna?** I was looking for a guide, do you have one *o* any?; **si tuviera ∼** if I had one **(c)** (una cantidad indeterminada — de personas) some (people); (— de cosas) some; **∼s creen que fue así** some (people) believe that was the case; **he visto algunas** I've seen some; **he tenido ∼ que otro** I've had one or two

alhaja *f* **(a)** (joya) piece of jewelry* **(b)** (persona) gem, treasure

alhajero *m*, **alhajera** *f* (AmL) jewel case

alharaca *f* fuss; **hacer ∼s** to make a fuss

alhelí *m* wallflower

aliado -da *adj* allied
■ *m,f* (Hist, Pol) ally; **los A∼s** the Allies

alianza *f* **(a)** (pacto, unión) alliance; **la A∼ Atlántica** the Atlantic Alliance **(b)** (anillo) wedding ring

aliarse [A17] *v pron* to join forces; **∼se CON algn** to form an alliance WITH sb, ally oneself WITH sb

alias *adv* alias
■ *m* (*pl* **∼**) alias

alicaído -da *adj* low, down in the dumps (colloq)

alicate *m*, **alicates** *mpl* (Tec) pliers (*pl*); (para uñas) nail clippers (*pl*); (para cutícula) cuticle clippers (*pl*)

aliciente *m* incentive

aliento *m* ⟨1⟩ **(a)** (respiración, aire) breath; **sin ∼** out of breath, breathless **(b)** (aire espirado) breath; **mal ∼** bad breath ⟨2⟩ (ánimo, valor): **dar ∼ a algn** to encourage sb

aligerar [A1] *vt* **(a)** ⟨carga⟩ to lighten; **∼ a algn DE algo** to relieve sb OF sth **(b)** (acelerar): **∼ el paso** to quicken one's pace

alijo *m* consignment

alimaña *f* pest; **∼s** vermin

alimentación *f* **(a)** (nutrición, comida) diet; **la ∼ integral va ganando adeptos** health food *o* (BrE) wholefood is growing in popularity **(b)** (de máquina, motor) fuel supply

alimentar [A1] *vt* ⟨1⟩ ⟨persona/animal⟩ to feed ⟨2⟩ **(a)** ⟨ilusión/esperanza⟩ to nurture, cherish; ⟨ego⟩ to boost **(b)** ⟨odio/pasión⟩ to fuel ⟨3⟩ ⟨máquina/motor⟩ to feed; ⟨caldera⟩ to stoke
■ **∼** *vi* to be nourishing
■ **alimentarse** *v pron* ⟨persona/animal⟩ to feed oneself; **∼se CON** *or* **DE algo** to live ON sth

alimenticio -cia, alimentario -ria *adj* **(a)** ⟨industria⟩ food (*before n*); **productos ∼s** foodstuffs; **hábitos ∼s** eating habits **(b)** ⟨valor⟩ nutritional; ⟨comida/plato⟩ nutritious, nourishing

alimento *m* ⟨1⟩ (frml) (comida) food, nourishment; **la leche es un ∼ completo** milk is a complete food; **∼s naturales** health food; ⟨2⟩ (valor nutritivo): **no tiene ∼ ninguno** it has no nutritional value; **de mucho ∼** very nutritious

alineación *f* ⟨1⟩ **(a)** (Dep) (de equipo) lineup; (de jugador) selection **(b)** (puesta en fila) lining up ⟨2⟩ (Pol, Tec) alignment

alinear [A1] *vt* ⟨1⟩ ⟨equipo/jugador⟩ to select, pick ⟨2⟩ **(a)** (poner en fila, línea) to line up **(b)** (Tec) to align, line up
■ **alinearse** *v pron* ⟨tropa⟩ to fall in; ⟨niños/presos⟩ to line up

aliñar [A1] *vt* ⟨ensalada⟩ to dress; ⟨carne/pescado⟩ to season

aliño *m* (para ensalada) dressing; (para otros alimentos) seasoning

alioli *m* (mayonesa) garlic mayonnaise; (salsa) garlic and olive oil vinaigrette

alisar [A1] *vt* ⟨colcha/papel⟩ to smooth out; ⟨pared/superficie⟩ to smooth down ⋯⋗

■ **alisarse** *v pron* (*refl*) **(a)** ⟨*vestido/falda*⟩ to smooth out **(b)** ⟨*pelo*⟩ (con la mano) to smooth down; (quitar los rizos) to straighten

alistamiento *m* (acción) enlistment, recruitment; (soldados alistados) call-up, draft (AmE)

alistarse [A1] *v pron* **(a)** (Mil) to enlist, join up; ~ **en el ejército** to join the army **(b)** (AmL) (prepararse) to get ready

alivianar *vt* [A1] (AmL) to lighten

aliviar [A1] *vt* ⟨*dolor*⟩ to relieve, soothe; ⟨*síntomas*⟩ to relieve; ⟨*tristeza/pena*⟩ to alleviate; ⟨*persona*⟩ to make … feel better

■ **aliviarse** *v pron* **(a)** «*dolor*» to let up **(b)** «*persona*» to get better

alivio *m* relief; **¡qué ~!** what a relief!

aljibe *m* **(a)** (pozo) well; (depósito de agua) cistern, tank **(b)** (Per) (cárcel) dungeon

allá *adv* **1** **(a)** (en el espacio): **ya vamos para ~** we're on our way (over); ~ **en América** over in America; **lo pusiste muy ~** you've put it too far away; **¡~ voy!** here I come/go! **(b)** (*en locs*) **más allá** further away; **más allá de** (más lejos que) beyond; (aparte de) over and above; ~ **tú/él** that's your/his lookout *o* problem (colloq) **2** (en el tiempo): ~ **por los años 40** back in the forties; ~ **para enero** sometime in January

allanamiento *m* **(a)** (AmL) (con autorización judicial) raid; **orden de ~** search warrant **(b)** (Esp, Méx) (sin autorización judicial) breaking and entering

allanar [A1] *vt* **1** **(a)** (AmL) «*autoridad/policía*» to raid **(b)** (Esp, Méx) «*delincuente*» to break into **2** ⟨*problemas*⟩ to solve, resolve; ⟨*obstáculo*⟩ to remove, overcome; ⟨*terreno*⟩ to level out; ~*(le)* **el terreno a** *algn* to smooth the way *o* path for sb

allegado -da *adj* close; **mis amigos y parientes más ~s** my close family and friends

■ *m,f* (amigo, pariente): **los ~s del difunto** those closest to the deceased; **un ~ de la familia** a close friend of the family

allí *adv* there; ~ **arriba/dentro** up/in there; ~ **donde estés/vayas** wherever you are/go

alma *f* **1** (espíritu) soul; **tener ~ de niño** to be a child at heart; ~ **mía** *or* **mi ~** (*como apelativo*) my love; **con toda el ~** *or* **mi/tu/su ~** with all my/your/his/ heart; **del ~: su amigo del ~** his bosom friend; **en el ~: lo siento en el ~** I'm really *o* terribly sorry; **te lo agradezco en el ~** I can't tell you how grateful I am; **llegarle a** *algn* **al ~: aquellas palabras me llegaron al ~** (me conmovieron) I was deeply touched by those words; (me dolieron) I was deeply hurt by those words; **me/le parte el ~** it breaks my/his heart **2** (persona) soul; **ni un ~ viviente** not a living soul; **ser ~s gemelas** to be soul mates; **ser un ~ bendita** *or* **de Dios** to be a kind soul

almacén *m* **(a)** (depósito) warehouse **(b)** (CS) (de comestibles) grocery store (AmE), grocer's (shop) (BrE) **(c)** (AmC, Col, Ven) (de ropa, etc) store (AmE), shop (BrE) **(d)** (de mayorista) wholesaler's **(e) almacenes** *mpl* department store

almacenamiento *m* storage; ~ **de datos** data storage

almacenar [A1] *vt* ⟨*mercancías/datos*⟩ to store

almanaque *m* (calendario — de escritorio) almanac, desk calendar; (— de pared) calendar

almeja *f* clam

almendra *f* **(a)** (fruta) almond **(b)** (centro) kernel

almendro *m* almond tree

almíbar *m* syrup

almibarar [A1] *vt* ⟨*fruta*⟩ to preserve … in syrup; ⟨*pastel*⟩ to soak … in syrup

almidón *m* starch

almidonar [A1] *vt* to starch

almirante *m* admiral

almohada *f* pillow; **consultarlo con la ~** to sleep on it

almohadilla *f* **1** (para alfileres) pincushion; (para entintar) ink pad; (para sellos) damper **2** (para sentarse) cushion; (en béisbol) bag

almohadón *m* (cuadrado, redondo) cushion; (cilíndrico) bolster; (en la iglesia) kneeler

almorranas *fpl* (fam) piles (*pl*)

almorzar [A11] *vi* **(a)** (a mediodía) to have lunch **(b)** (en algunas regiones) (a media mañana) to have a mid-morning snack

■ ~ *vt* **(a)** (a mediodía) to have … for lunch **(b)** (en algunas regiones) (a media mañana) to have … mid-morning

almuerza, almuerzas, etc ▶ ALMORZAR

almuerzo *m* **(a)** (a mediodía) lunch **(b)** (en algunas regiones) (a media mañana) mid-morning snack

aló *interj* (AmS excl RPl) (al contestar el teléfono) hello?

alocado -da *adj* (irresponsable, imprudente) crazy, wild; (irreflexivo, impetuoso) rash, impetuous; (despistado) scatterbrained

■ *m,f* (imprudente) crazy *o* reckless fool; (irreflexivo) rash fool; (despistado) scatterbrain

alojado -da *m,f* (Chi) guest; **pieza de ~s** guestroom

alojamiento *m* accommodations (*pl*) (AmE), accommodation (BrE); **nos dio ~** he put us up

alojar [A1] *vt* **1** **(a)** (en hotel): **los hemos alojado en el hotel Plaza** we've booked them into the Plaza Hotel; **el hotel en el que estaban alojados** the hotel where they were staying **(b)** (en casa particular) to put … up **2** (albergar) ⟨*evacuados/refugiados*⟩ to house

■ **alojarse** *v pron* **(a)** (hospedarse) to stay **(b)** «*proyectil/bala*» to lodge

alondra *f* lark

alpaca *f* **1** (Zool, Tex) alpaca; **lana de ~** alpaca (wool) **2** (Metal) nickel silver, German silver

alpargata *f* espadrille

Alpes *mpl*: **los ~** the Alps

alpinismo *m* mountaineering, (mountain) climbing

alpinista *mf* mountaineer, (mountain) climber

alpino -na *adj* Alpine

alpiste *m* (semillas) birdseed

alquilar [A1] *vt* **1** (dar en alquiler) ⟨*casa/local*⟩ to rent (out), let (BrE); ⟨*televisor*⟩ to rent; ⟨*coche/bicicleta*⟩ to rent (out) (AmE), to hire out (BrE) **2** (tomar en alquiler) ⟨*casa/local/televisor*⟩ to rent; ⟨*coche/bicicleta/disfraz*⟩ to rent (AmE), to hire (BrE)

alquiler *m* **(a)** (renta — de apartamento) rent; (— de televisor, bicicleta) rental **(b)** (acción de alquilar — una casa) renting, letting (BrE); (— un televisor) rental; (— un coche, disfraz) rental (AmE), hire (BrE);

se dedica al ~ de coches he's in the car-rental (AmE) *o* (BrE) car-hire business; **contrato de ~** tenancy agreement; **coches de ~** rental (AmE) *o* (BrE) hire cars

alquitrán *m* tar

alrededor *adv* (a) (en torno) around; **a mi ~** around me (b) **alrededor de** (*loc prep*) (en torno a) around; (aproximadamente) around, about

alrededores *mpl* (a) (barrios periféricos, extrarradio de ciudad) outskirts (*pl*); (otras localidades): surroundings (*pl*) (b) (de edificio, calle) surrounding area; **en los ~ de la iglesia** in the area around the church

alta *f⚕* **1** (Med) discharge; **dar el ~ a** *or* **dar de ~ a un enfermo** to discharge a patient **2** (Fisco, Servs Socs): **los dieron de ~ en la Seguridad Social** they registered them with Social Security

altanero -ra *adj* arrogant, haughty

altar *m* altar

altavoz *m* (Audio) loudspeaker; (megáfono) megaphone

alteración *f* (a) (de plan, texto) change, alteration (b) (de hechos, verdad) distortion (c) (del orden, de la paz) disturbance; (agitación) agitation ; **~ del orden público** breach of the peace

alterado -da *adj* [ESTAR] ⟨persona⟩ upset

alterar [A1] *vt* **1** (a) ⟨plan/texto⟩ to change, alter (b) ⟨hechos/verdad⟩ to distort (c) ⟨alimento⟩ to make ... go off, turn ... bad **2** (perturbar) (a) ⟨paz⟩ to disturb; **~ el orden público** to cause a breach of the peace (b) ⟨persona⟩ to upset
■ **alterarse** *v pron* **1** «*alimentos*» to go off, go bad **2** «*pulso/respiración*» to become irregular; «*color*» to change **3** «*persona*» to get upset

altercado *m* argument

alternar [A1] *vt* **~ algo CON algo** to alternate sth WITH sth; **alternamos la gimnasia con el tenis** we alternate gymnastics with tennis
■ ~ *vi* «*persona*» to socialize; **~ CON algn** to mix WITH sb
■ **alternarse** *v pron* to take turns

alternativa *f* (opción) alternative; **la ~ es clara** the choice is clear

alternativo -va *adj* ⟨medicina/prensa/música⟩ alternative

Alteza *mf* (tratamiento) Highness; **sí, (su) ~** yes, your Highness

altibajos *mpl* (a) (cambios bruscos) ups and downs (*pl*) (b) (del terreno) undulations (*pl*)

altillo *m* (desván) attic; (en habitación) (sleeping) loft

altiplanicie *f*, **altiplano** *m* high plateau, high plain; **el altiplano boliviano** the Bolivian altiplano

altiro *adv* (Chi fam) right away, immediately

altitud *f* altitude

altivo -va *adj* (arrogante) arrogant, haughty; (noble, orgulloso) proud

alto¹ -ta *adj* **1** (a) [SER] ⟨persona/edificio/árbol⟩ tall; ⟨pared/montaña⟩ high; **una blusa de cuello ~** a high-necked blouse (b) [ESTAR]: **¡qué ~ estás!** haven't you grown!; **está tan alta como yo** she's as tall as me now **2** (indicando posición, nivel) (a) [SER] high; **los techos eran muy ~s** the rooms had very high ceilings (b) [ESTAR]: **el río está muy ~** the river

is very high; **la marea está alta** it's high tide; **los pisos más ~s** the top floors; **salgan con los brazos en ~** come out with your hands in the air; **con la moral bastante alta** in pretty high spirits; **en lo ~ de la montaña** high up on the mountainside; **en lo ~ del árbol** high up in the tree; **por todo lo ~** in style **3** (en cantidad, calidad) high; **el alto nivel de contaminación** the high level of pollution; **productos de alta calidad** high-quality products; **tirando por lo ~** at the most **4** (a) [ESTAR] (en intensidad) ⟨volumen/televisión⟩ loud; **pon la radio más alta** turn the radio up (b) **en alto** *or* **en voz alta** aloud, out loud **5** (*delante del n*) (a) (en importancia, trascendencia) ⟨ejecutivo/funcionario⟩ high-ranking, top; **conversaciones de ~ nivel** high-level talks (b) ⟨ideales/opinión⟩ high; **un ~ sentido del deber** a strong sense of duty (c) (en nombres compuestos) **alta burguesía** *f* upper-middle classes (*pl*); **alta costura** *f* haute couture; **alta fidelidad** *f* high fidelity, hi-fi; **alta mar** *f*: **en alta mar** on the high seas; **flota/pesca de alta mar** deep-sea fleet/fishing; **alta sociedad** *f* high society; **alta tensión** *f* high tension *o* voltage; **~ cargo** *m* (puesto) high-ranking position; (persona) high-ranking official; **~ mando** *m* high-ranking officer

alto² *adv* **1** ⟨volar/subir⟩ high **2** ⟨hablar⟩ loud, loudly; **habla más ~** speak up a little

alto³ *interj* halt!; **¡~ el fuego!** cease fire!

alto⁴ *m* **1** (a) (altura) **de alto** high; **tiene tres metros de ~** it's three meters high (b) (en terreno) high ground; **construido en un ~** built on high ground **2** (a) (parada, interrupción): **hacer un ~** to stop; **~ el fuego** (Esp) (Mil) cease-fire (b) (Méx) (Auto): **pasarse al ~** (un semáforo) to run the red light (AmE), to jump the lights (BrE); (un stop) to go through the stop sign

altoparlante *m* (AmL) ▶ ALTAVOZ

altruismo *m* altruism

altruista *adj* altruistic
■ *mf* altruist

altura *f* **1** (de persona, edificio, techo) height; **el muro tiene un metro de ~** the wall is one meter high **2** (indicando posición) height; **ponlos a la misma ~** put them at the same height; **a la ~ de los ojos** at eye level; **estar/ponerse a la ~ de algo/algn**: **para ponernos a la ~ de la competencia** to put ourselves on a par with our competitors; **estar a la ~ de las circunstancias** to rise to the occasion; **no está a la ~ de su predecesor** he doesn't match up to his predecessor **3** (a) (Aviac, Geog) (altitud) altitude; **a 2.240 metros de ~** at an altitude of 2,240 meters (b) **de altura** (pesquero/flota) deep-sea (*before n*); ⟨remolcador⟩ oceangoing (*before n*) **4** (en sentido horizontal): **¿a qué ~ de Serrano vive?** how far up Serrano do you live?; **cuando llegamos a la ~ de la plaza** when we reached the square **5** (en sentido temporal): **a estas ~s ya debe haber llegado** he should have arrived by now; **¡a estas ~s me vienes con eso!** you wait till now to bring this to me!; **a estas ~s del año** this late on in the year; **a esas ~s ya no me importaba** by that stage I didn't mind **6** (Mús) pitch

alturado -da *adj* (Per) calm

alubia *f* (haricot) bean

alucinación *f* hallucination

alucinado -da *adj* (fam): **los dejó a todos ∼s** she left everybody stunned

alucinante *adj* (a) (Med) hallucinatory (b) (Esp, Méx fam) (increíble) amazing (colloq), mind-boggling (colloq)

alucinar [A1] *vi* to hallucinate

alud *m* (de nieve) avalanche; (de tierra) landslide, landslip

aludir [I1] *vi* (a) (sin nombrar) **∼ A** algn/algo to refer TO sb/sth, allude TO sb/sth; **se sintió aludido** he thought we were referring to him; **no se dio por aludido** he didn't take the hint (b) (mencionar) **∼ A** algn/algo to refer TO sb/sth, mention sb/sth

alumbrado *m* lighting

alumbramiento *m* (frml) birth

alumbrar [A1] *vt* (iluminar) to light, illuminate; **está muy mal alumbrado** it's very poorly lit; **alumbra este rincón** shine the light in this corner ■ **∼** *vi* «*sol*» to be bright; «*lámpara/bombilla*» to give off light

aluminio *m* aluminum (AmE), aluminium (BrE)

alumnado *m* (de colegio) students (*pl*) (AmE), pupils (*pl*) (BrE); (de universidad) students (*pl*)

alumno -na *m,f* (de colegio) pupil; (de universidad) student; **∼ interno** boarder

alunizar [A4] *vi* to land on the moon

alusión *f* **∼** (**A** algo/algn) allusion *o* reference (TO sth/sb); **hacer ∼ a** algo/a algn to make reference *o* an allusion to sth/sb

alverjilla *f* (AmL) sweet pea

alza *f⁺* rise; **el ∼ de los precios** the rise in prices; **en ∼** «*intereses/precios*» rising (*before n*); **una escritora en ∼** an up-and-coming writer; **estar en ∼** to be on the rise

alzado -da *adj* (a) (Andes, Ven fam) (levantisco): **la servidumbre anda medio alzada** the servants have been rather uppity lately (colloq); **un chiquillo ∼ a** cocky little brat (colloq) (b) (Méx, Ven fam) (altivo) stuck-up (colloq)

alzamiento *m* uprising

alzar [A4] *vt* 1 (levantar) (a) «*brazo/cabeza/voz*» to raise; **alzó al niño para que viera el desfile** she lifted the little boy up so he could see the parade; **alzó la mirada** she looked up (b) (AmL) «*bebé*» to pick up 2 «*edificio/monumento*» to erect 3 (Méx) (poner en orden) «*juguetes*» to pick up; «*cuarto/ casa*» to clean (up) ■ **alzarse** *v pron* (sublevarse) to rise up; **∼se en armas** to take up arms

ama *f⁺* (a) (de bebé) *tb* **∼ de leche** *or* **de cría** wet nurse (b) (de niño mayor) nanny (c) **∼ de casa/de llaves** housewife/housekeeper; *ver tb* AMO

amabilidad *f* (a) (cualidad) kindness (b) (gesto): **tuvo la ∼ de invitarnos** she was kind enough to invite us; **¿tendría la ∼ de cerrar la puerta?** would you be so kind as to close the door?; **tenga la ∼ de esperar aquí** would you mind waiting here?

amable *adj* (a) «*persona/gesto*» kind; **es muy ∼ de su parte** that's very kind of you; **¿sería tan ∼ de ...?** would you be so kind as to ...? (b) (AmS) «*rato/velada*» pleasant

amablemente *adv* kindly

amado -da *adj* dear, beloved ■ *m,f* love, sweetheart

amadrinar [A1] *vt* «*niño*» to be godmother to; «*boda*» to act as MADRINA at; «*barco*» to launch, christen

amaestrar [A1] *vt* «*animales*» to train

amago *m*: **tuvo un ∼ de infarto** he had a mild heart attack; **un ∼ de revuelta** a threat of revolt; **hacer un ∼** (Dep) to make a feint

amainar [A1] *vi* «*lluvia*» to ease up *o* off, abate; «*temporal/viento*» to die down, abate

amamantar [A1] *vt/vi* «*mujer*» to breastfeed; «*animal*» to suckle

amanecer¹ [E3] *v impers*: **¿a qué hora amanece?** what time does it get light?; **amanecía cuando partieron** dawn was breaking when they left ■ **∼** *vi* (+ *compl*) (a) «*persona*»: **amaneció con fiebre** he woke up with a temperature; **amanecieron bailando** they were still dancing at dawn (b) (aparecer por la mañana): **amaneció nublado** it was cloudy first thing in the morning; **todo amaneció cubierto de nieve** in the morning everything was covered in snow ■ **amanecerse** *v pron* (Chi, Méx) to stay up all night

amanecer² *m* dawn, daybreak; **al ∼** at dawn *o* at daybreak

amanerado -da *adj* (afectado) affected, mannered; (afeminado) (fam) mannered, camp (colloq)

amansar [A1] *vt* «*caballo*» to break in; «*fiera*» to tame ■ **amansarse** *v pron* «*fiera*» to become tame; «*caballo*» to quiet (AmE) *o* (BrE) quieten down

amante *mf* lover

amañar [A1] *vt* (fam) «*elecciones*» to rig; «*partido/pelea*» to fix; «*carnet/documento*» to tamper with; «*informe*» to alter, doctor (*esp AmE*); «*excusa/historia*» to dream *o* cook up, concoct ■ **amañarse** *v pron* 1 *tb* **amañárselas** (ingeniarse) to manage 2 (Col, Ven) (acostumbrarse) to settle in

amapola *f* poppy

amar [A1] *vt* to love ■ **amarse** *v pron* (recípr) to love each other

amarga *f* (Col) beer

amargado -da *adj* bitter, embittered ■ *m,f* bitter *o* embittered person

amargar [A3] *vt* «*ocasión/día*» to spoil; «*persona*» to make ... bitter ■ **amargarse** *v pron* to become bitter; **no te amargues la existencia** (fam) don't get all uptight about it

amargo -ga *adj* 1 (a) «*fruta/sabor*» bitter (b) (sin azúcar) unsweetened, without sugar 2 «*experiencia/recuerdo*» bitter, painful

amargor *m* bitterness

amargura *f* bitterness; **con ~** bitterly

amarillento -ta *adj* yellowish

amarillista *adj* (Period) (pey): **prensa ~** sensationalist *o* yellow press

amarillo¹ -lla *adj* 1 ⟨color/blusa⟩ yellow; **el semáforo estaba (en) ~** the light was yellow (AmE), the lights were (on) amber (BrE) 2 **(a)** ⟨piel⟩ (de raza oriental) yellow **(b)** ⟨piel/cara⟩ (por enfermedad) yellow, jaundiced

amarillo² *m* yellow

amarra *f* mooring rope; **~s** moorings (*pl*); **echar (las) ~s** to moor

amarradero *m* **(a)** (poste) bollard; (argolla) mooring ring **(b)** (lugar) berth, slip (AmE)

amarrado -da *adj* (Col, Méx, Ven fam) stingy (colloq), tightfisted (colloq)

amarrar [A1] *vt* **(a)** ⟨embarcación⟩ to moor; ⟨animal/persona⟩ to tie up; **le ~on las manos** they tied his hands together; **~ algo/a algn A algo** to tie sth/sb TO sth **(b)** (AmL exc RPl) ⟨zapatos/cordones⟩ to tie; ⟨paquete⟩ to tie ... up
■ **amarrarse** *v pron* (AmL exc RPl) ⟨zapatos/cordones⟩ to tie up, do up; ⟨pelo⟩ to tie up

amarrete -ta *adj* (AmS fam) stingy (colloq), tightfisted (colloq)
■ *m,f* (AmS fam) scrooge (colloq), skinflint (colloq)

amasar [A1] *vt* 1 ⟨pan⟩ to knead; ⟨yeso/argamasa⟩ to mix 2 ⟨fortuna/riquezas⟩ to amass

amateur /amaˈter/ *adj/mf* (*pl* **-teurs**) amateur

amazona *f* (Mit) Amazon; (Equ) horsewoman

Amazonas *m*: **el ~** the Amazon

amazónico -ca *adj* Amazonian, Amazon (*before n*)

ámbar *m* **(a)** (piedra) amber **(b)** (color) amber

ambición *f* ambition

ambicionar [A1] *vt* to aspire to

ambicioso -sa *adj* ambitious; (codicioso) overambitious

ambidextro -tra *adj* ambidextrous
■ *m,f* ambidextrous person

ambientación *f* **(a)** (de obra, película) atmosphere **(b)** (de persona) adjustment

ambientador *m* air freshener

ambiental *adj* environmental

ambientar [A1] *vt* **(a)** ⟨obra/película⟩ to set **(b)** ⟨fiesta/local⟩ to give ... some atmosphere
■ **ambientarse** *v pron* to adjust, adapt

ambiente *m* **(a)** (entorno físico, social, cultural) environment; **crecí en un ~ rural** I grew up in a rural environment; **se encuentra realmente en su ~** he's really in his element; **había una cierta tensión en el ~** there was a feeling of tension in the air **(b)** (creado por la decoración, arquitectura, la gente) atmosphere; **un ~ de camaradería/de fiesta** a friendly/festive atmosphere **(c)** (animación) life

ambigüedad *f* ambiguity

ambiguo -gua *adj* ambiguous

ámbito *m* **(a)** (campo, círculo) sphere, field **(b)** (alcance) scope, range; **el ~ (de aplicación) de la ley** the scope of the law

ambo *m* (CS) (two-piece) suit

ambos -bas *adj pl* both; **a ~ lados** on both sides

■ *pron pl* both; **~ aceptaron la propuesta** they both accepted the proposal; **~ me gustan** I like both of them

ambulancia *f* ambulance

ambulanciero -ra *m,f* **(m)** ambulance man; **(f)** ambulance woman; **los ~s** the ambulance crew

ambulante *adj* traveling* (*before n*); **biblioteca ~** bookmobile (AmE), mobile library (BrE)

ambulatorio¹ -ria *adj* outpatient (*before n*)

ambulatorio² *m* (Esp) outpatients' department

ameba *f* amoeba

amén *m* amen; **~ de ...** as well as ...

amenaza *f* threat; **no me vengas con ~s** don't threaten me; **~ de bomba/muerte** bomb/death threat

amenazador -dora, amenazante *adj* threatening, menacing

amenazar [A4] *vt* **(a)** «persona» to threaten; **nos amenazó con llamar a la policía** he threatened to call the police **(b)** (dar indicios de): **esas nubes amenazan lluvia** those clouds look threatening
■ **~** *vi*: **~ CON hacer algo** to threaten to do sth
■ **~** *v impers* (Meteo): **amenaza tormenta** there's a storm brewing; **amenaza lluvia** it's threatening to rain

amenizar [A4] *vt* ⟨conversación/discurso⟩ to make ... more enjoyable; **la fiesta fue amenizada por un payaso** a clown provided the entertainment for the party

ameno -na *adj* pleasant, enjoyable

América *f* 1 (continente) America; **hacerse la ~** to make a fortune, get rich; **~ Central** Central America; **~ del Norte** *or* **Septentrional** North America; **~ del Sur** *or* **Meridional** South America; **~ Latina** Latin America 2 (Esp) (Estados Unidos) America, the States (*pl*)

americana *f* jacket

americanismo *m* Americanism

americano -na *adj/m,f* American

amerindio -dia *adj/m,f* American Indian, Amerindian

ameritado -da *adj* (AmL) meritorious (frml)

ameritar [A1] *vt* (AmL) to deserve

ametralladora *f* machine gun

ametrallar [A1] *vt* to machine-gun

amianto *m* asbestos

amiba *f* amoeba

amigable *adj* ⟨persona⟩ friendly; ⟨trato⟩ friendly, amicable; **un tono poco ~** a rather unfriendly manner

amígdalas *fpl* tonsils (*pl*)

amigdalitis *f* tonsillitis

amigo -ga *adj*: **son/se hicieron muy ~s** they are/they became good friends; **hacerse ~ de algn** to become friends with sb; **es muy ~ mío** he's a close friend of mine; **un país ~** a friendly country; **es muy ~ de contradecir** he's a great one for contradicting people (colloq); **no es amiga de las fiestas** she's not keen on parties
■ *m,f* friend; **un ~ mío** a friend of mine; **somos íntimos ~s** we're very close friends; **¡un momento, ~!** now, just a minute, pal *o* buddy (AmE) *o* (BrE) mate! (colloq)

a

amigote *m* (fam) crony (colloq & pej), buddy (AmE colloq), mate (BrE colloq)

amilanar [A1] *vt* to daunt
■ **amilanarse** *v pron* to be daunted

amistad *f* (a) (entre personas, países) friendship; **entabló** *or* **hizo** ~ **con ella** he struck up a friendship with her (b) **amistades** *fpl* (amigos) friends (*pl*)

amistoso -sa *adj* ⟨consejo/palmadita/charla⟩ friendly; ⟨partido⟩ friendly (*before n*)

amnesia *f* amnesia

amnistía *f* amnesty

amnistiado -da *m,f*: person pardoned under an amnesty

amnistiar [A17] *vt* ⟨persona⟩ to grant an amnesty to; ⟨delito⟩ to amnesty

amo, ama *m,f* (de animal, criado) (*m*) master; (*f*) mistress; **son los ~s del pueblo** they own the whole village; *ver tb* AMA

amoblar [A10] *vt* (CS) ▶ AMUEBLAR

amoldable *adj* adaptable

amoldar [A1] *vt* to adjust
■ **amoldarse** *v pron* to adapt; ~**se A algo** ⟨a un trabajo/una situación⟩ to adjust TO sth; **estos zapatos todavía no se me han amoldado al pie** I haven't broken these shoes in yet

amonestación *f* (reprimenda) warning; (en fútbol) caution, booking

amonestar [A1] *vt* (reprender) to reprimand, admonish (frml); (en fútbol) to caution, book

amoníaco *m* ammonia

amontonar [A1] *vt* (a) (apilar) to pile ... up (b) (juntar) to accumulate
■ **amontonarse** *v pron* ⟨personas⟩ to gather *o* crowd together; ⟨objetos/trabajo⟩ to pile up

amor *m* [1] (a) (sentimiento) love; ~ **no correspondido** unrequited love; ~ **a primera vista** love at first sight; ~ **al prójimo/a la patria** love for one's neighbor/one's country; ~ **propio** pride, self-esteem; **un gran ~ a la vida/a los animales** a great love of life/animals; **por ~ al arte** (fam) just for the fun of it; **por (el) ~ de Dios** (mendigando) for the love of God; (expresando irritación) for God's sake! (b) (el acto sexual): **hacer el ~ a/con algn** to make love to/with sb (c) (persona, cosa amada) love; ~ **mío** *or* **mi** ~ my darling, my love (d) (esmero, dedicación): **hacer algo con** ~ to do sth lovingly
[2] (fam) (persona encantadora) darling (colloq), dear (colloq)

amoral *adj* amoral

amoratado -da *adj* (de frío) blue; (por un golpe) ⟨piernas/brazos⟩ bruised; **ojo** ~ black eye

amordazar [A4] *vt* ⟨persona⟩ to gag; ⟨perro⟩ to muzzle

amorío *m* love affair

amoroso -sa *adj* (a) (AmL) ⟨persona/casa⟩ lovely (b) ⟨vida⟩ love (*before n*); **sus relaciones amorosas** his relationships

amortajar [A1] *vt* to shroud

amortiguador *m* shock absorber

amortiguar [A16] *vt* ⟨golpe⟩ to cushion, absorb; ⟨sonido⟩ to muffle

amortizable *adj* redeemable

amortización *f* (de inversión) recovery; (de préstamo) repayment; (de bonos, hipoteca) redemption

amortizar [A4] *vt* (a) ⟨compra⟩ to recoup the cost of (b) (recuperar) ⟨inversión⟩ to recoup, recover (c) (pagar) ⟨deuda⟩ to repay, amortize (frml); ⟨valores/hipoteca⟩ to redeem

amotinado -da *adj* ⟨soldado/ejército⟩ rebel (*before n*), insurgent (*before n*); ⟨pueblo/ciudadanos⟩ rebellious, insurgent (*before n*)
■ *m,f* insurgent

amotinar [A1] *vt* ⟨tropa⟩ to incite ... to mutiny *o* rebellion; ⟨población/pueblo⟩ to incite ... to rebellion
■ **amotinarse** *v pron* «soldados/oficiales» to mutiny, rebel; «población civil» to rise up

amparar [A1] *vt* (a) (proteger) to protect; **¡que Dios nos ampare!** may the Lord help us! (b) (ofrecer refugio) to shelter, give shelter to
■ **ampararse** *v pron* (a) ~**se EN algo** ⟨en la ley⟩ to seek protection IN sth; **se amparó en su inmunidad diplomática** he used his diplomatic immunity to protect himself (b) (resguardarse) ~**se DE** *or* **CONTRA algo** to shelter FROM sth

amparo *m* (a) (protección) protection (b) (refugio) refuge; **dar** ~ **a algn** to give sb refuge

amperio *m* amp, ampere (frml)

ampliación *f* (a) (de local, carretera) extension; (de negocio) expansion (b) (Com, Fin): ~ **de capital/de personal** an increase in capital/in the number of staff (c) (de conocimientos, vocabulario) widening (d) (de plazo, período) extension (e) (Fot) enlargement

ampliar [A17] *vt* (a) ⟨local/carretera⟩ to extend; ⟨negocio⟩ to expand (b) ⟨capital/personal⟩ to increase (c) ⟨conocimientos/vocabulario⟩ to increase; ⟨explicación⟩ to expand (on); ⟨campo de acción⟩ to widen, broaden; **para** ~ **sus estudios** to further her studies (d) ⟨plazo/período⟩ to extend (e) ⟨fotografía⟩ to enlarge, blow up

amplificador *m* amplifier

amplificar [A2] *vt* to amplify

amplio -plia *adj* (a) ⟨calle/valle/margen⟩ wide; ⟨casa⟩ spacious; ⟨vestido/abrigo⟩ loose-fitting; ⟨sonrisa⟩ broad (b) ⟨criterio/sentido⟩ broad; **por amplia mayoría** by a large majority; **una amplia gama de colores** a wide range of colors (c) ⟨garantías/programa⟩ comprehensive

amplitud *f* (a) (de calle, margen) width; (de casa) spaciousness; (de vestido) looseness (b) (de miras, criterios) range; (de facultades, garantías) extent; **la** ~ **de sus conocimientos** the breadth *o* depth of his knowledge (c) (Fís) amplitude

ampolla *f* [1] (por quemadura, rozamiento) blister [2] (con medicamento) ampoule (frml), vial (AmE), phial (BrE)

ampolleta *f* (Chi) light bulb

amputar [A1] *vt* ⟨brazo/pierna⟩ to amputate

amueblar [A1] *vt* to furnish; **casa amueblada/sin** ~ furnished/unfurnished house

amuleto *m* charm, amulet

anacardo *m* cashew (nut)

anaconda *f* anaconda

anacrónico -ca *adj* anachronistic

anacronismo *m* anachronism

ánade *mf* duck

anafe, anafre *m* (Chi, Méx) portable stove

anagrama *m* anagram

anal *adj* anal

anales *mpl* annals (*pl*)

analfabetismo *m* illiteracy

analfabeto -ta *adj* illiterate

■ *m,f* **(a)** (que no sabe leer) illiterate (person) **(b)** (fam & pey) (ignorante) ignoramus (colloq & pej)

analgésico *m* analgesic, painkiller

análisis *m* (*pl* ~) analysis; **hacerse un ~ de sangre** to have a blood test

analista *mf* analyst

analítico -ca *adj* analytic

analizar [A4] *vt* **(a)** (examinar) to analyze*, examine **(b)** (Med, Quím) to analyze* **(c)** (Ling) to parse

■ **analizarse** *v pron* to undergo *o* have analysis

analogía *f* analogy

ananá *m* (*pl* **-nás**) (RPl) pineapple

anaquel *m* shelf

anaranjado -da *adj* orangish (AmE), orangey (BrE)

anarquía *f* anarchy

anárquico -ca *adj* anarchic

anarquismo *m* anarchism

anarquista *adj* anarchist (*before n*)

■ *mf* anarchist

anarquizar [A4] *vt* to cause chaos *o* anarchy in

anatomía *f* anatomy

anatómico -ca *adj* **(a)** (Anat) anatomical **(b)** ⟨asiento/respaldo⟩ anatomically designed

anca *f⸣* (de animal) haunch; **~s de rana** frogs' legs; **llevar a algn en ~s** (AmL) to take sb on the crupper

ancestral *adj* ⟨costumbre⟩ ancient; ⟨temor⟩ primitive, ancient

ancestro *m* ancestor

ancho¹ -cha *adj* **1** **(a)** ⟨camino/río/mueble⟩ wide; **a todo lo ~ de la carretera** right across the road; **a lo ~** breadthways *o* (BrE) widthways **(b)** ⟨manos/cara/espalda⟩ broad; **es ~ de espaldas** he's broad-shouldered **(c)** ⟨ropa⟩ loose-fitting, loose; **me queda ~ de cintura** it's too big around the waist for me **2** (cómodo, tranquilo): **allí estaremos más ~s** (Esp) we'll have more room there; **estar/sentirse/ponerse a sus anchas** to be/feel/make oneself at home

ancho² *m* width; **¿cuánto mide de ~?** how wide is it?; **tiene 6 metros de ~** it's 6 meters wide

anchoa *f* anchovy

anchura *f* **(a)** (de camino, río, mueble) width **(b)** (medida): **~ de caderas** hip measurement

ancianato *m* (Col, Ven) old people's home

anciano -na *adj* elderly

■ *m,f* **(m)** elderly man; **(f)** elderly woman

ancla *f⸣* anchor; **echar el ~** to drop anchor; **levar ~s** to weigh anchor

anclar [A1] *vt/vi* to anchor

andadera *f* (Méx, Ven) ▶ ANDADOR 1

andador *m* **1** **(a)** (con ruedas) baby walker **(b)** **andadores** *mpl* (arnés) baby harness, reins (*pl*) **2** (para ancianos) Zimmer® frame

Andalucía *f* Andalusia

andaluz -luza *adj/m,f* Andalusian

andamio *m*: *tb* **~s** scaffolding

andanzas *fpl* adventures (*pl*)

andar¹ [A24] *vi* **1** **(a)** (esp Esp) (caminar) to walk; **¿has venido andando?** did you come on foot?, did you walk? **(b)** (AmL): **~ a caballo/en bicicleta** to ride (a horse/a bicycle) **(c)** (*en imperativo*) (AmS) (ir): **anda a comprar el periódico** go and buy the newspaper

2 (marchar, funcionar) to work; **el coche anda de maravilla** the car's running *o* (BrE) going like a dream

3 (+ *compl*) **(a)** (estar) to be; **¿cómo andas?** how are you?, how's it going? (colloq); **¿quién anda por ahí?** who's there?; **anda en Londres** he's in London; **anda buscando pelea** he's out for *o* he's looking for a fight; **me anda molestando** (AmL fam) he keeps bothering me **(b)** **~ CON algn** (juntarse) to mix WITH sb; (salir con) to go out WITH sb; **dime con quién andas y te diré quién eres** a man is known by the company he keeps **(c)** **~ DETRÁS DE** *or* **TRAS** algn/algo (buscar, perseguir) to be AFTER sb/sth

4 (rondar): **~á por los 60 (años)** he must be around *o* about 60

5 **~ CON** algo (esp AmL fam) ⟨con revólver/dinero⟩ to carry sth; ⟨con traje/sombrero⟩ to wear sth

6 (en exclamaciones) **(a)** (expresando sorpresa, incredulidad): **¡anda! ¡qué casualidad!** good heavens! what a coincidence!; **¡anda! ¡mira quién está aquí!** well, well! look who's here! **(b)** (expresando irritación, rechazo): **¡anda! ¡déjame en paz!** oh, leave me alone!; **¡anda! ¡se me ha vuelto a olvidar!** damn! I've forgotten it again! (colloq) **(c)** (instando a hacer algo): **préstamelo, anda** go on, lend it to me!; **¡ándale** (Méx) *or* (Col) **ándele que llegamos tarde!** come on, we'll be late! (colloq)

■ **~** *vt* **1** (caminar) to walk

2 (AmC) (llevar): **no ando dinero** I don't have any money on me; **siempre ando shorts** I always wear shorts

■ **andarse** *v pron* **1** **~se CON** algo: **ese no se anda con bromas** he's not one to joke; **ándate con cuidado** take care, be careful

2 (*en imperativo*) (AmL) (irse): **ándate de aquí** get out of here; **ándate luego** get going, get a move on (colloq)

andar² *m*, **andares** *mpl* gait, walk

andarivel *m* **(a)** (AmL) (cable) ferry cable **(b)** (AmS) (en una piscina — carril) lane; (— soga) lane divider

andas *fpl* portable platform (*used in religious processions*); **llevar a algn en ~** (CS) to carry sb on one's shoulders

ándele, ándale *interj*: ▶ ANDAR¹ 6B, C

andén *m* **(a)** (en estación) platform **(b)** (AmC, Col) (acera) sidewalk (AmE), pavement (BrE)

Andes *mpl*: **los ~** the Andes

andinismo *m* (AmL) mountaineering, mountain climbing, climbing

andinista *mf* (AmL) mountaineer, mountain climber, climber

andino -na *adj* Andean

andrajo *m* rag

andrajoso -sa *adj* ragged

anduve, anduviste, etc ▶ ANDAR

anécdota *f* anecdote

anecdótico -ca adj (a) ⟨relato⟩ anecdotal (b) ⟨interés/valor⟩ incidental

anegar [A3] vt to flood
■ **anegarse** v pron «campo/terreno» to be flooded

anemia f anemia*

anémico -ca adj anemic*
■ m,f anemic person

anestesia f (proceso) anesthesia*; (droga) anesthetic*; **bajo los efectos de la ~** under (the) anesthetic; **lo operaron con ~** he was operated on under (an) anesthetic; **sin ~** without an anesthetic

anestesiar [A1] vt ⟨encía/dedo⟩ to anesthetize*; **me ~on** they gave me an anesthetic

anestesista mf anesthetist*

anexo¹ -xa adj (a) ⟨edificio/local⟩ joined, annexed (b) ⟨cláusula⟩ added, appended (frml); ⟨documento⟩ (en informe) attached; (en carta) enclosed

anexo² m (a) (edificio) annex* (b) (documento — en informe) appendix; (— en carta) enclosure (c) (Chi) (del teléfono) extension

anfetamina f amphetamine

anfibio¹ -bia adj amphibious; **avión ~** seaplane

anfibio² m amphibian

anfiteatro m (Arquit) amphitheater*; (Geol) natural amphitheater*; (en la universidad) lecture hall

anfitrión -triona m,f (m) host; (f) hostess

ánfora f⁺ (cántaro) amphora

angas (Andes, Méx fam): **por ~ o por mangas, nunca estás trabajando** for one reason or another, you're never working; **por ~ o por mangas tengo que salir** I have to go out whether I like it or not

ángel m (a) (Relig) angel; **~ guardián** or **de la guarda** guardian angel; **que sueñes con los angelitos** sweet dreams; **pobre angelito** poor little darling (b) (encanto) charm; **tener ~** to be charming

angelical adj angelic

angelito m (AmL) dead child; ver tb ÁNGEL

angina f ①(Arg, Col, Ven) (de la garganta) inflammation of the palate, tonsils and/or pharynx ②tb **~ de pecho** angina (pectoris)

anginas fpl (a) (Esp, Méx) (inflamación) throat infection (b) (Méx, Ven) (amígdalas) tonsils (pl)

anglicano -na adj/m,f Episcopalian (in US and Scotland), Anglican (in UK)

anglicismo m Anglicism

angloparlante adj English-speaking

Angola f Angola

angoleño -leña adj/m,f Angolan

angora f angora

angosto -ta adj ⟨calle/cama⟩ narrow; ⟨falda⟩ tight

anguila f eel

angular adj angular

ángulo m (Mat) angle; (rincón, esquina) corner; (punto de vista) angle; **~ recto** right angle

anguloso -sa adj angular

angustia f (a) (congoja) anguish, distress; **gritos de ~** anguished cries (b) (desasosiego) anxiety; **vive con la ~ de que...** she's constantly worried that... (c) (Psic) anxiety

angustiado -da adj (a) (acongojado) distressed (b) (preocupado) worried, anxious; **vive angustiada** she lives in a constant state of anxiety

angustiar [A1] vt (a) (acongojar) to distress (b) (preocupar) to worry, make ... anxious
■ **angustiarse** v pron (acongojarse) to get distressed, get upset; (preocuparse) to get worried, become anxious

angustioso -sa adj ⟨situación⟩ distressing; ⟨mirada/grito⟩ anguished

anhelante adj (liter) ⟨mirada⟩ longing (before n); **esperaba ~ su regreso** she longed o she yearned for his return; **con voz ~** in a voice full of longing

anhelar [A1] vt (liter) ⟨fama/poder⟩ to yearn for, to long for; **~ hacer algo** to long to do sth, yearn to do sth; **anhelaba que su hijo fuera feliz** his greatest wish was for his son to be happy

anhelo m (liter) wish, desire; **mi mayor ~** my greatest wish

anhídrido m anhydride; **~ carbónico** carbon dioxide

anidar [A1] vi «aves» to nest

aniego m (Per) flood

anilla f (a) (de cortina, llavero) ring; (de puro) band; (de lata) ringpull; (de ave) ring (b) **anillas** fpl (Dep) rings (pl)

anillo m ①(sortija) ring; **~ de boda/compromiso** wedding/engagement ring; **como ~ al dedo** (fam) ⟨sentar/quedar⟩ to suit down to the ground; ⟨venir⟩ to come in very handy (colloq) ②(aro, arandela) ring; (de columna) annulet; (en árbol) ring

ánima f⁺ (liter) (alma) soul

animación f ①(bullicio, actividad) activity; **un bar con mucha ~** a very lively bar ②(de una velada) entertainment ③(Cin) animation

animado -da adj ①(a) ⟨fiesta/ambiente⟩ lively; ⟨conversación/discusión⟩ lively, animated (b) (optimista, con ánimo) cheerful, in good spirits ②(impulsado) **~ DE** or **POR algo** inspired o motivated BY sth

animador -dora m,f (a) (de programa) (m) presenter, host; (f) presenter, hostess (b) **animadora** f (de equipo) cheerleader

animal adj ①⟨instinto⟩ animal (before n) ②(fam) (a) (estúpido) stupid (b) (grosero) rude, uncouth
■ m (a) (Zool) animal; **~ doméstico** (de granja) domestic animal; (mascota) pet (b) (fam) (persona — violenta) brute, animal; (— grosera) lout

animar [A1] vt ①(a) (alentar) to encourage; (levantar el espíritu) to cheer ... up; **tu visita lo animó mucho** your visit cheered him up a lot; **~ a algn A hacer algo** or **A que haga algo** to

· ·

AmC	América Central	Arg	Argentina	Cu	Cuba	Per	Perú
AmL	América Latina	Bol	Bolivia	Ec	Ecuador	RPI	Río de la Plata
AmS	América del Sur	Chi	Chile	Esp	España	Ur	Uruguay
Andes	Región andina	CS	Cono Sur	Méx	México	Ven	Venezuela

encourage sb to do sth **(b)** ‹*fiesta/reunión*› to liven up; **el vino empezaba a ∼los** the wine was beginning to liven them up **(c)** (con luces, colores) to brighten up

2 ‹*programa*› to present, host

3 (impulsar) to inspire

■ **animarse** *v pron* **(a)** (alegrarse, cobrar vida) «*fiesta/reunión*» to liven up, warm up; «*persona*» to liven up **(b)** (cobrar ánimos) to cheer up; **si me animo a salir te llamo** if I feel like going out, I'll call you **(c)** (atreverse): **¿quién se anima a decírselo?** who's going to be brave enough to tell him?; **no me animo a saltar** I can't bring myself to jump; **al final me animé a confesárselo** I finally plucked up the courage to tell her

anímicamente *adv* emotionally

anímico -ca *adj*: **su estado ∼** her state of mind

ánimo *m* 1 **(a)** (espíritu): **no estoy con el ∼ para bromas** I'm not in the mood for jokes; **tu visita le levantó el ∼** your visit cheered her up; **con el ∼ por el suelo** in very low spirits, feeling very down-hearted; **apaciguar los ∼s** to calm everyone down; **hacerse el ∼ de hacer algo** to bring oneself to do sth **(b)** (aliento, coraje) encouragement; **darle ∼(s) a algn** (animar) to encourage sb; (con aplausos, gritos) to cheer sb on; **¡∼, que ya falta poco para llegar!** come on! it's not far now!; **no tengo ∼(s) de** *or* **para nada** I don't feel up to anything

2 **(a)** (intención, propósito) intention; **lo dije sin ∼ de ofender** I meant no offense, no offense intended (colloq) **(b)** (mente, pensamiento) mind

animosidad *f* animosity, hostility; **∼ CONTRA algn** animosity *o* hostility TOWARD(S) sb

aniquilar [A1] *vt* ‹*enemigo/población*› to annihilate, wipe out; ‹*defensas/instalaciones*› to destroy

anís *m* **(a)** (Bot) (planta) anise; (semilla) aniseed **(b)** (licor) anisette

aniversario *m* anniversary

ano *m* anus

anoche *adv* last night

anochecer¹ [E3] *v impers* to get dark

■ **anochecerse** *v pron* (Chi, Méx) to stay up till really late

anochecer² *m* nightfall; **al ∼** at nightfall

anomalía *f* anomaly

anonadado -da *adj* dumbfounded, speechless

anonimato *m* anonymity; **salir del ∼** to rise from obscurity

anónimo -ma *adj* anonymous

anorak /ano'rak/ *m* parka (AmE), anorak (BrE)

anorexia *f* anorexia

anoréxico -ca *adj/m,f* anorexic

anormal *adj* abnormal

■ *mf* (fam) idiot

anormalidad *f* abnormality

anotación *f* **(a)** (nota) note **(b)** (AmL) (en fútbol) goal; (en fútbol americano) touchdown; (en básquetbol) point

anotador -dora *m,f* (AmL) (en fútbol) scorer, goalscorer; (en fútbol americano, básquetbol) scorer

anotar [A1] *vt* 1 **(a)** (tomar nota de) ‹*dirección/*

nombre› to make a note of **(b)** ‹*texto*› to annotate **(c)** (RPl) ▶ APUNTAR *vt* 1B 2 (aml) ‹*gol/tanto*› to score

■ **anotarse** *v pron* 1 (AmL) ‹*gol/tanto*› to score 2 (RPl) (inscribirse) ▶ APUNTARSE A

anquilosado -da *adj* **(a)** ‹*articulación*› (atrofiado) ankylosed; (entumecido) stiff **(b)** ‹*ideas/economía*› stagnant

anquilosarse [A1] *v pron* **(a)** «*miembro/articulación*» (atrofiarse) to ankylose; (entumecerse) to get stiff **(b)** «*ideas/economía*» to stagnate

ansia *f* 1 **(a)** (avidez, deseo): **con ∼** ‹*comer/beber*› eagerly; **∼ DE algo** ‹*de paz/libertad*› longing FOR sth, yearning FOR sth; ‹*de poder*› thirst FOR sth, craving FOR sth; **sentir ∼ de hacer algo** to long *o* yearn to do sth; **sus ∼s de aprender** her eagerness to learn **(b)** (Psic) anxiety **(c) ansias** *fpl* (Col, Ven fam) (náuseas) nausea

ansiar [A17] *vt* (liter) ‹*libertad/poder*› to long for, yearn for; **∼ hacer algo** to long to do sth

ansiedad *f* **(a)** (preocupación) anxiety; **con ∼** anxiously **(b)** (Med, Psic) anxiety

ansioso -sa *adj* **(a)** (deseoso) eager; **está ∼ por saberlo** he's eager *o* (colloq) dying to know; **estoy ∼ de verlos** I can't wait to see them **(b)** [SER] (fam) (voraz) greedy

antagónico -ca *adj* conflicting

antagonismo *m* antagonism

antagonista *adj* antagonistic

■ *mf* antagonist

antártico -ca *adj* Antarctic

Antártida *f*: **la ∼** Antarctica, the Antarctic

ante *prep* 1 **(a)** (frml) (delante de) before; **ante el juez** before the judge **(b)** (frente a): **∼ la gravedad de la situación** in view of the seriousness of the situation; **iguales ∼ la ley** equal in the eyes of the law; **nos hallamos ∼ un problema** we are faced with a problem 2 **ante todo** (primero) first and foremost; (sobre todo) above all

■ *m* (cuero) suede

anteanoche *adv* the night before last

anteayer *adv* the day before yesterday

antebrazo *m* forearm

antecedente *m* 1 **(a)** (precedente) precedent; **no hay ningún ∼ de la enfermedad en mi familia** there's no history of the illness in my family **(b)** (causa) cause; **estar/poner a algn en ∼s** to be/put sb in the picture 2 (Fil, Ling) antecedent 3 **antecedentes** *mpl* (historial) background, record; **∼s penales** (criminal) record

anteceder [E1] *vt* to precede, come before; **∼ A algo** to come BEFORE sth, precede sth

antecesor -sora *m,f* (predecesor) predecessor; (antepasado) ancestor

antecomedor *m* (Méx) breakfast room

antelación *f*: **con ∼** ‹*reservar/pagar*› in advance; ‹*avisar/salir*› in plenty of time; **saqué la entrada con un mes de ∼** I got the ticket one month in advance; **llegó con dos días de ∼** she arrived two days early; **con ∼ a su boda** prior to her wedding

antemano: **de ∼** (*loc adv*) in advance

antena *f* 1 (de radio, televisión, coche) antenna (AmE), aerial (BrE); **en ∼** on the air; **∼ colectiva** ···⁝

communal antenna o aerial; **∼ de radar** radar dish; **∼ parabólica** satellite dish; **∼ repetidora** relay mast ② (Zool) antenna

antenoche *adv* (AmL) the night before last

anteojo *m* (a) (telescopio) telescope (b) **anteojos** *mpl* (esp AmL) ▶ GAFAS

antepasado -da *adj* ⟨año/semana⟩ before last ■ *m,f* ancestor

antepenúltimo -ma *adj* (delante del *n*) third from last, antepenultimate (frml) ■ *m,f*: **fue el ∼ en la carrera** he came third from last on the race; **es el ∼ en la lista** he's third from bottom on the list

anteponer [E22] *vt* **∼ algo A algo** (poner delante) to put sth BEFORE *o* IN FRONT OF sth; (dar preferencia) to put sth BEFORE sth

anteproyecto *m* draft; **∼ de ley** bill

anterior *adj* (a) (en el tiempo) previous; **el día ∼** the previous day, the day before; **en épocas ∼es** in earlier times; **∼ A algo** prior *to* sth (b) (en un orden) previous, preceding; **el capítulo ∼ a este** the previous chapter (c) (en el espacio) front (*before n*); **la parte ∼** the front (part); **las patas ∼es** the forelegs *o* front legs

anterioridad *f* (frml) anteriority (frml); **con ∼** (antes) before, previously; (con antelación) beforehand, in advance; **con ∼ a algo** before sth, prior to sth

antes *adv* ① (a) (con anterioridad) before; **lo compré el día ∼** I bought it the day before; **lo ∼ posible** as soon as possible (b) (más temprano) earlier; **no pude llegar ∼** I couldn't arrive earlier (c) (*en locs*) **antes de** before; **∼ de Jesucristo** before Christ, BC; **no van a llegar ∼ de dos horas** they won't be here for two hours; **le daré la respuesta ∼ de una semana** I will give you my reply within a week; **∼ de lo esperado** earlier than expected; **∼ DE hacer algo** before doing sth; **∼ (de) que me olvide** before I forget; **no se lo des ∼ (de) que yo lo vea** don't give it to him until I've seen it (d) (en el espacio) before ② (en tiempos pasados) before, in the past; **ya no es el mismo de ∼** he's not the same person any more ③ (a) (indicando orden, prioridad) first; **∼ que nada** first of all; **yo estaba ∼** I was here first (b) (indicando preferencia): **¡∼ me muero!** I'd rather *o* sooner die!; **cualquier cosa ∼ que eso** anything but that

antiabortista *mf* antiabortionist

antiaborto *adj inv* antiabortion (*before n*)

antiaéreo -rea *adj* antiaircraft (*before n*)

antialérgico -ca *adj* antiallergenic

antibalas *adj inv* bulletproof

antibiótico *m* antibiotic

anticiclón *m* anticyclone

anticipación *f* (antelación): **con (mucha) ∼** (well) in advance; **con un mes de ∼** a month in advance

anticipado -da *adj* ⟨pago⟩ advance (*before n*); ⟨elecciones⟩ early; **por ∼** in advance

anticipar [A1] *vt* (a) ⟨viaje/elecciones⟩ to move up (AmE), to bring forward (BrE) (b) ⟨dinero/ sueldo⟩ to advance; **¿nos podría ∼ de qué se trata?** could you give us an idea of what it is about? ■ **anticiparse** *v pron* (a) «verano/lluvias» to be

o come early (b) (adelantarse): **se anticipó a su tiempo** he was ahead of his time; **no nos anticipemos a los acontecimientos** let's not jump the gun

anticipo *m* (a) (del sueldo, dinero) advance (b) (pago inicial) down payment

anticoncepción *f* contraception, birth control

anticonceptivo¹ -va *adj* contraceptive (*before n*); **métodos ∼s** methods of contraception

anticonceptivo² *m* contraceptive

anticongelante *adj/m* antifreeze

anticuado -da *adj* old-fashioned ■ *m,f*: **eres un ∼** you're so old-fashioned

anticuario -ria *m,f* (a) (persona) antique dealer (b) **anticuario** *m* (tienda) antique shop

anticucho *m* (Bol, Chi, Per) kebab

anticuerpo *m* antibody

antidemocrático -ca *adj* (poco democrático) undemocratic; (opuesto a la democracia) antidemocratic

antideportivo -va *adj* unsportsmanlike

antideslizante *adj* ⟨superficie/suela⟩ nonslip; ⟨neumático/freno⟩ antiskid (*before n*)

antidisturbios *adj inv* riot (*before n*)

antídoto *m* antidote

antiestético -ca *adj* unsightly

antifaz *m* mask

antigripal *adj* ⟨vacuna⟩ flu (*before n*) ■ *m* flu remedy

antiguamente *adv* in the past, in the old days

antigüedad *f* (a) (de monumento, objeto) age; **esas ruinas tienen varios siglos de ∼** those ruins are several centuries old (b) (en el trabajo) seniority (c) (objeto) antique; **tienda de ∼es** antique shop (d) (época): **en la ∼** in ancient times

antiguo -gua *adj* ① (a) (viejo) ⟨ciudad/libro⟩ old; ⟨ruinas/civilización⟩ ancient; ⟨mueble/ lámpara⟩ antique, old; ⟨coche⟩ vintage, old; ⟨costumbre/tradición⟩ old; **el A∼ Testamento** the Old Testament (b) (veterano) old, long-standing (c) (*en locs*) **a la antigua** in an old-fashioned way; **chapado a la antigua** old-fashioned; **de** *or* **desde antiguo** from time immemorial ② (delante del *n*) (de antes) old (*before n*), former (*before n*); **la antigua capital del Brasil** the former capital of Brazil ③ (anticuado) old-fashioned

antiguos *mpl*: **los ∼** the ancients

antihéroe *m* antihero

antihigiénico -ca *adj* unhygienic

antiincendios *adj inv* firefighting (*before n*)

antiinflamatorio *m* anti-inflammatory

antillano -na *adj/m,f* West Indian

Antillas *fpl*: **las ∼** the West Indies

antílope *m* antelope

antimanchas *adj inv* stain-resistant

antimisil *adj* antiballistic (*before n*) ■ *m* antiballistic missile

antimonárquico -ca *adj* antimonarchical, antimonarchist (*before n*) ■ *m,f* antimonarchist

antinatural *adj* unnatural

antioxidante *adj* (Quím) antioxidant (*before n*); ⟨pintura⟩ antirust (*before n*)

antipatía f dislike, antipathy; **tomarle ～ a algo/algn** to take a dislike to sth/sb

antipático -ca adj **(a)** ⟨persona⟩ unpleasant; **¡qué tipo más ～!** what a horrible man! **(b)** (fam) ⟨tarea⟩: **esto de planchar es de lo más ～** ironing is such a drag (colloq)
■ m,f: **es un ～** he's really unpleasant

antipatriótico -ca adj unpatriotic

antipedagógico -ca adj pedagogically unsound

antiperspirante m antiperspirant

antípodas fpl: **las ～** the antipodes

antirreglamentario -ria adj (Dep): **una jugada antirreglamentaria** a foul; **estaba en posición antirreglamentaria** (period) he was offside

antirrobo m antitheft device

antisemita adj anti-Semitic
■ mf anti-Semite

antiséptico m antiseptic

antisocial adj antisocial
■ mf (Andes period) delinquent

antiterrorista adj antiterrorist (before n)

antítesis f (pl ～) antithesis

antivirus m antivirus software

antojarse [A1] v pron (+ me/te/le etc): **se me antojó una cerveza** I felt like (having) a beer; **de embarazada se me antojaban las uvas** when I was pregnant, I had a craving for grapes; **hace lo que se le antoja** he does as he pleases; **porque no se me antoja** because I don't feel like it

antojitos mpl (Méx) typical Mexican snacks, usually bought at street stands

antojo m **(a)** (capricho) whim; **tiene que hacerlo todo a su ～** she has to do everything her own way; **maneja al marido a su ～** she has her husband twisted around her little finger **(b)** (de embarazada) craving **(c)** (en la piel) birthmark

antología f anthology; **de ～** (muy bueno) excellent, fantastic (colloq); (muy malo) terrible

antorcha f torch

antro m (local sórdido) dive (colloq)

antropología f anthropology

antropólogo -ga m,f anthropologist

anual adj **(a)** ⟨cuota/asamblea⟩ annual, yearly; ⟨interés/dividendo⟩ annual; **cinco mil euros ～es** five thousand euros a year **(b)** ⟨planta⟩ annual

anualidad f (inversión) annuity; (cuota anual) annual payment (o subscription etc)

anuario m yearbook

anudar [A1] vt ⟨cordón/corbata⟩ to tie
■ **anudarse** v pron (refl) ⟨corbata/pañuelo⟩ to tie

anulación f (de contrato, viaje) cancellation; (de matrimonio) annulment; (de sentencia) quashing, overturning; **protestó la ～ del gol** he protested when the goal was disallowed

anular vt **(a)** ⟨contrato/viaje⟩ to cancel; ⟨matrimonio⟩ to annul; ⟨fallo/sentencia⟩ to quash, overturn; ⟨resultado⟩ to declare ... null and void; ⟨tanto/gol⟩ to disallow **(b)** ⟨cheque⟩ (destruir) to cancel; (dar orden de no pagar) to stop
■ m finger ring

anunciador -dora m,f, **anunciante** mf advertiser

anunciar [A1] vt **(a)** ⟨noticia/decisión⟩ to

announce, make ... public; ⟨lluvias/tormentas⟩ to forecast **(b)** (frml) ⟨persona⟩ to announce **(c)** ⟨producto⟩ to advertise, promote

anuncio m **(a)** (de noticia) announcement; (presagio) sign, omen **(b)** (en periódico) advertisement, ad (colloq); (en televisión) commercial; **～s clasificados** or **por palabras** classified advertisements (pl)

anverso m obverse

anzuelo m hook; **morder** or **tragarse el ～** to swallow o take the bait

añadir [I1] vt to add

añejo -ja adj ⟨vino/queso⟩ mature; ⟨costumbre⟩ old, ancient

añicos mpl: **hacerse ～** to shatter; **tiró el florero y lo hizo ～** he knocked the vase over and smashed it to smithereens

año m **1** (período) year; **los ～s 50** the 50s; **el ～ pasado** last year; **una vez al ～** once a year; **hace ～s que no lo veo** I haven't seen him for o in years; **el ～ de la pera** or **de Maricastaña** (fam): **ese peinado es del ～ de la pera** that hairstyle went out with the ark (colloq), that hairstyle is really old-fashioned; **un disco del ～ de la pera** a record that's really ancient; **～ bisiesto** leap year; **～ fiscal** fiscal year (AmE), tax year (BrE); **～ luz** light year; **A～ Nuevo** New Year
2 (indicando edad): **soltero, de 30 ～s de edad** single, 30 years old o (frml) 30 years of age; **¿cuántos ～s tienes?** how old are you?; **tengo 14 ～s** I'm 14 (years old); **hoy cumple 29 ～s** she's 29 today; **ya debe de tener sus añitos** he must be getting on (a bit); **quitarse ～s: se quita ～s** she's older than she admits o says
3 (curso) year; **～ académico/escolar** academic/ school year

añoranza f yearning; **siente ～ de** or **por su país** he yearns for his country

añorar [A1] vt ⟨patria/tranquilidad⟩ to yearn for; ⟨persona⟩ to miss

aorta f aorta

apabullante adj ⟨victoria/éxito⟩ resounding (before n), overwhelming; ⟨rapidez/habilidad⟩ incredible, extraordinary; ⟨personalidad⟩ overpowering

apabullar [A1] vt (vencer) to overwhelm, crush; (dejar confuso) to overwhelm

apache adj Apache (before n)
■ mf Apache

apachurrar [A1] vt (AmL fam) to squash

apacible adj ⟨carácter/persona⟩ calm, placid; ⟨vida⟩ quiet, peaceful; ⟨clima⟩ mild; ⟨mar⟩ calm; ⟨viento⟩ gentle

apaciguar [A16] vt ⟨ánimos⟩ to pacify; ⟨persona⟩ to calm ... down, to pacify
■ **apaciguarse** v pron «persona» to calm down; «mar» to become calm; «temporal/ viento» to abate, die down

apadrinar [A1] vt ⟨niño⟩ to be godfather o godparent to; ⟨boda⟩ to act as PADRINO at; ⟨artista/novillero⟩ to sponsor, be patron to; ⟨político/idea/candidatura⟩ to support, back; ⟨barco⟩ to launch, christen

apagado -da adj **1** ⟨persona⟩ [SER] spiritless, lifeless; [ESTAR] subdued **2 (a)** ⟨sonido⟩ muffled **(b)** ⟨color⟩ muted, dull **3 (a)** (no encendido): **la** ···⊱

a

televisión/luz **está apagada** the TV/light is off; **el horno está** ~ the oven is switched off; **con el motor** ~ with the engine off **(b)** ⟨volcán⟩ extinct

apagar [A3] vt ⟨luz/televisión/motor⟩ to turn off, switch off; ⟨cigarrillo/fuego⟩ to put out; ⟨vela/cerilla⟩ to put out; (soplando) to blow out
■ **apagarse** v pron «luz/fuego/vela» to go out

apagón m power cut, blackout

apalabrar [A1] vt: **lo había apalabrado pero no llegué a firmar nada** it was all arranged o fixed but I never actually signed anything; **ya tengo apalabrado a un albañil** (fam) I've already fixed up with a builder

apalancar [A2] vt **(a)** (para levantar) to jack up (AmE), to lever up (BrE) **(b)** (para abrir) to force open

apalear [A1] vt **(a)** ⟨persona/alfombra⟩ to beat; ⟨árbol⟩ to beat the branches of **(b)** ⟨arena/carbón⟩ to shovel

apanar [A1] vt (Andes) ▶ EMPANAR

apantallar [A1] vt **1** (Méx) (impresionar) to impress **2** (RPI) (abanicar) to fan

apañar [A1] vt **1** (fam) ⟨elecciones⟩ to fix (colloq), to rig **2** (AmS fam) (encubrir) to cover up for
■ **apañarse** v pron (Esp fam) ▶ ARREGLARSE 4

apapachar [A1] vt (Cu, Méx fam) (abrazar) to cuddle; (acariciar) to stroke, caress

apapacho m (Cu, Méx fam) (abrazo) cuddle; (caricia) caress

aparador m **(a)** (mueble) sideboard **(b)** (AmL exc CS) (vitrina) store window (AmE), shop window (BrE)

aparato m **1** **(a)** (máquina): **uno de esos** ~s **para hacer pasta** one of those pasta machines; ~s **eléctricos** electrical appliances **(b)** (de televisión) set; (de radio) receiver **(c)** (dispositivo) device; ~ **ortopédico** surgical appliance; ~ **auditivo** hearing aid **(d)** (Odont) tb ~s braces (pl) **(e)** (teléfono) telephone; **ponerse al** ~ to come to the phone **2** (para gimnasia) piece of apparatus; **los** ~s the apparatus, the equipment **3** (Aviac) (avión) aircraft **4** (estructura, sistema) machine; **el** ~ **del partido** the party machine; ~ **circulatorio/digestivo/respiratorio** circulatory/digestive/respiratory system

aparatoso -sa adj ⟨gesto⟩ flamboyant; ⟨sombrero⟩ showy, flamboyant; ⟨caída/accidente⟩ spectacular, dramatic

aparcamiento m (Esp) **(a)** (acción) parking **(b)** (lugar — en ciudad) parking lot (AmE), car park (BrE); (— en carretera) rest area o stop (AmE), lay-by (BrE); ~ **disuasorio** (Esp) overflow parking lot (AmE) o car park (BrE)

aparcar [A2] vt/vi (Esp) to park; ~ **en doble fila** to double-park

aparear [A1] vt ⟨animales⟩ to mate; ⟨objetos⟩ to match, pair up
■ **aparearse** v pron to mate

aparecer [E3] vi **1** **(a)** «síntoma/mancha» to appear **(b)** «objeto perdido» to turn up; **hizo** ~ **un ramo de flores** he produced a bouquet of flowers **(c)** (en documento) to appear; **mi nombre aparece en la lista** my name appears on the list **(d)** ⟨revista/libro⟩ to come out **2** «persona» **(a)** (fam) (llegar) to appear, turn up **(b)** (fam) (dejarse ver) to appear, show up (colloq) **(c)** (en película, televisión) to appear
■ **aparecerse** v pron **(a)** «fantasma/aparición» ~se A algn to appear TO sb **(b)** (AmL fam) «persona» to turn up; **¡no te vuelvas a** ~ **por aquí!** don't you dare show up round here again!

aparejar [A1] vt ⟨caballos⟩ (para montar) to saddle; (a carro) to harness

aparejo m (de caballo) tack; (de pesca) tackle; (polea) block and tackle

aparentar [A1] vt **(a)** (fingir) ⟨indiferencia/interés⟩ to feign; **quiere** ~ **que no le importa** he's trying to make out he's not bothered about it **(b)** (parecer): **no aparentas la edad que tienes** you don't look your age
■ ~ vi «persona» to show off; **solo por** ~ just for show **(b)** «regalo/joya» to look impressive

aparente adj **1** (que parece real) ⟨timidez/interés⟩ apparent (before n); **la** ~ **victoria se tornó en derrota** what had seemed like victory turned into defeat **2** (obvio, palpable) apparent, obvious

apariencia f appearance; **un hombre de** ~ **fuerte** a strong-looking man; **a juzgar por las** ~s judging by appearances; **guardar las** ~s to keep up appearances; **las** ~s **engañan** appearances can be deceptive

apartado¹ -da adj **(a)** ⟨zona/lugar⟩ isolated **(b)** ⟨persona⟩: **se mantuvo** ~ **de la vida pública** he stayed out of public life; **vive** ~ **de la familia** he has little to do with his family

apartado² m **1** (Corresp) tb ~ **de correos** or ~ **postal** post office box, P.O. Box **2** (de artículo, capítulo) section

apartamento m apartment

apartar [A1] vt **1** **(a)** (alejar) to move ... away; **sus amigos lo** ~on **del buen camino** his friends led him astray; **apartó los ojos** he averted his eyes **(b)** ⟨obstáculo⟩ to move, move ... out of the way **(c)** (frml) (de un cargo) to remove **(d)** (separar) to separate **2** (guardar, reservar) to set aside; **aparta un poco de comida para él** put a bit of food aside for him
■ **apartarse** v pron (refl) **(a)** (despejar el camino) to stand aside **(b)** (alejarse, separarse): **apártate de ahí** get/come away from there; **no se aparta de mi lado** he never leaves her side; **¡apártate de mi vista!** get out of my sight!; **se apartó de su familia** she drifted away from her family; **nos estamos apartando del tema** we're getting off the subject

aparte adv **1** (a un lado, por separado): **pon las verduras** ~ put the vegetables to o on one side; **¿me lo podría envolver** ~? could you wrap it separately?; **lo llamó** ~ **y lo reprendió** she called him aside and reprimanded him; **bromas** ~ joking aside; ~ **de** (excepto) apart from; (además

de) as well as; ~ **de eso me encuentro bien** apart
from that I'm all right; ~ **de hacerlos, los diseña**
she designs them as well as making them
2 (además) as well; (por otra parte) anyway,
besides
■ *adj inv*: **esto merece un capítulo** ~ this deserves
a separate chapter; **es un caso** ~ he's a special
case

apasionado -da *adj* ⟨*amor/persona*⟩
passionate; ⟨*discurso*⟩ impassioned
■ *m,f* enthusiast

apasionante *adj* ⟨*obra*⟩ exciting, enthralling;
⟨*tema*⟩ fascinating

apasionar [A1] *vi*: **le apasiona la música** she
has a passion for music; **no es un tema que me
apasione** the subject doesn't exactly fascinate me

apatía *f* apathy

apático -ca *adj* apathetic

apátrida *mf* (a) (sin patria) stateless person (b)
(RPI) (que no ama a su país) unpatriotic person

apearse [A1] *v pron* (frml) (bajarse) to get off,
alight (frml); ~ **DE algo** ⟨*de un tren/caballo/una
bicicleta*⟩ to get **OFF** sth

apechugar [A3] *vi* (fam) to grin and bear it
(colloq), to put up with it (colloq); ~ **con las
consecuencias** to put up with *o* suffer the
consequences

apedrear [A1] *vt* (a) (tirar piedras a) to throw
stones at (b) (matar a pedradas) to stone (to death)

apego *m* ~ **A algo/algn** attachment **TO** sth/sb;
tenerle ~ **a algn/algo** to be attached **TO** sb/sth; **les
tiene poco** ~ **a las cosas materiales** he attaches
little importance to material things

apelación *f* appeal

apelar [A1] *vi* (a) (Der) to appeal; ~ **ante el
Tribunal Supremo** to appeal to the Supreme Court
(b) (invocar, recurrir a) ~ **A algo/algn** to appeal **TO**
sth/sb

apelativo *m* (a) (sobrenombre) name (b) (Ling)
form of address; **un** ~ **cariñoso** a term of
endearment

apellido *m* surname, last name (AmE); ~ **de
soltera/de casada** maiden/married name

apelmazarse [A4] *v pron* (a) «*arroz/pasta*»
to stick together (b) «*colchón/cojín*» to go
lumpy; «*lana*» to get *o* become matted

apenar [A1] *vt* to sadden
■ **apenarse** *v pron* **1** (entristecerse): **se sintió
apenado por su muerte** he was saddened by her
death; **se apenó mucho cuando lo supo** he was
very upset *o* sad when he learned of it **2** (AmL
exc CS) (sentir vergüenza) to be embarrassed

apenas *adv* (a) (a duras penas) hardly; ~
podíamos oírlo we could hardly hear him; **hace**
~ **dos horas** only two hours ago (b) (no bien): ~
había llegado cuando ... no sooner had he
arrived than ... (c) (Méx, Ven fam) (recién): ~ **el
lunes la podré ir a ver** I won't be able to go and
see her until Monday; ~ **va por la página 10** he's
only on page 10
■ *conj* (esp AmL) (en cuanto) as soon as

apendejarse [A1] *v pron* (AmL exc CS fam)
(volverse estúpido) to go soft in the head (colloq)

apéndice *m* (a) (del intestino) appendix; (de otro
miembro) appendage; **lo operaron del** ~ his
appendix was removed (b) (de texto, documento)
appendix

apendicitis *f* appendicitis

apergaminado -da *adj* ⟨*papel*⟩
parchment-like; ⟨*piel*⟩ leathery; ⟨*cara*⟩ wizened

aperitivo *m* (a) (bebida) aperitif; **nos invitaron a
tomar el** ~ they invited us for drinks before
lunch (*o* dinner *etc*) (b) (comida) snack, appetizer

apersonarse [A1] *v pron* (a) (comparecer) to
appear (b) (Col) (encargarse) ~ **DE algo** to take
charge **OF** sth, take sth in hand (c) (CS, Ven fam)
(presentarse) to appear in person

apertura *f* **1** (a) (de caja, sobre, cuenta) opening
(b) (inauguración) opening; **la sesión de** ~ the
opening session (c) (de curso, año académico)
beginning, start (d) (Fot) aperture **2** (actitud
abierta) openness; (proceso) opening-up

apestado -da *adj* (a) (con la peste): **gente
apestada** plague victims (b) ⟨*lugar*⟩: ~ **de
turistas** crawling *o* infested with tourists

apestar [A1] *vi* (fam) to stink (colloq); ~ **A algo**
to stink *o* reek **OF** sth (colloq)
■ ~ *vt* (fam) to stink out (colloq)

apetecer [E3] *vi* (esp Esp): **me apetece un
helado/pasear** I feel like an ice-cream/going for a
walk; **haz lo que te apetezca** do whatever you
like

apetecible *adj* ⟨*manjar*⟩ appetizing,
mouthwatering; ⟨*puesto*⟩ desirable

apetito *m* appetite; **no tengo** ~ I don't feel
hungry, I'm not hungry; **tiene buen** ~ he has a
good appetite; **esta caminata me ha abierto el** ~
this walk has given me an appetite

apetitoso -sa *adj* ⟨*plato/manjar*⟩ appetizing,
mouthwatering

apiadarse [A1] *v pron* ~ **DE algn** to take pity
on sb

apiario *m* (AmL) apiary

apicultura *f* beekeeping, apiculture (tech)

apilar [A1] *vt* to pile up, put ... into a pile

apiñarse [A1] *v pron* «*gente*» to crowd
together

apio *m* celery

apiolarse [A1] *v pron* (RPI fam) to wise up
(colloq)

apisonadora *f* road roller, steamroller

apisonar [A1] *vt* (con apisonadora) to roll,
steamroll; (con pisón) to tamp

aplacar [A2] *vt* (a) ⟨*ira*⟩ to soothe; **supo** ~ **los
ánimos** she was able to calm people down (b)
⟨*sed*⟩ to quench; ⟨*hambre*⟩ to satisfy; ⟨*dolor*⟩ to
soothe

aplanadora *f* (AmL) road roller, steamroller

aplanar [A1] *vt* (con niveladora) to level; (con
apisonadora) to roll

aplastante *adj* ⟨*mayoría*⟩ overwhelming;
⟨*victoria/derrota*⟩ overwhelming, crushing;
⟨*lógica*⟩ devastating

aplastar [A1] *vt* **1** (a) (algo blando) to squash;
(algo duro) to crush (b) (hacer puré) ⟨*plátanos/
papas*⟩ to mash **2** (a) ⟨*rebelión*⟩ to crush, quash
(b) ⟨*rival*⟩ to crush, overwhelm; (moralmente) to
devastate

aplaudir [I1] *vt* to applaud
■ ~ *vi* to applaud, clap

aplauso *m* (a) (ovación) applause; **un** ~ **para** ... ···⟶

a round of applause for ...; **fuertes ～s** loud applause **(b)** (elogio) praise; **ser digno de ～** to be commendable *o* praiseworthy

aplazamiento *m* **(a)** (de reunión — antes de iniciarse) postponement; (— una vez iniciada) adjournment **(b)** (de pago) deferment

aplazar [A4] *vt* ⒈ **(a)** 〈*viaje*〉 to postpone, put off **(b)** 〈*juicio/reunión*〉 (antes de iniciarse) to postpone; (una vez iniciado) to adjourn **(c)** 〈*pago*〉 to defer ⒉ (RPl, Ven) 〈*estudiante*〉 to fail

aplazo *m* (RPl) fail

aplicable *adj* applicable

aplicación *f* ⒈ **(a)** (frml) (de crema) application (frml); (de pintura, barniz) coat, application (frml) **(b)** (de sanción) imposition; (de técnica, método) application; (de plan, medida) implementation ⒉ (uso práctico) application, use ⒊ (Col, Ven) (solicitud) application ⒋ (Inf) application

aplicado -da *adj* 〈*ciencias/tecnología*〉 applied (*before n*); 〈*estudiante*〉 diligent, hard-working

aplicar [A2] *vt* ⒈ (frml) 〈*pomada/maquillaje/ barniz*〉 to apply (frml) ⒉ 〈*sanción*〉 to impose; 〈*descuento*〉 to allow; **el acuerdo se aplica solo a los afiliados** the agreement only applies to members ⒊ 〈*método/sistema*〉 to put into practice ■ **～** *vi* (Col, Ven) to apply; **～ a un puesto/una beca** to apply for a job/a scholarship ■ **aplicarse** *v pron* to apply oneself

aplique, appliqué *m* **(a)** (lámpara) wall light **(b)** (adorno — en mueble) overlay; (— en prenda) appliqué

aplomo *m* composure

apocado -da *adj* **(a)** [SER] (de poco carácter) timid **(b)** [ESTAR] (deprimido) depressed, down (colloq)

apocalipsis *m* apocalypse

apocarse [A2] *v pron:* **se apocó** she lost all her self-confidence; **no se apoca ante** *or* **por nada** nothing intimidates *o* daunts him

apócope *f or m* apocope; (vocablo) apocopated form

apodar [A1] *vt* to nickname, call

apoderado -da *m,f* **(a)** (Der) proxy, representative; **nombrar a algn ～** to give sb power of attorney **(b)** (de deportista) agent, manager

apoderarse [A1] *v pron* **～ DE algo** 〈*de ciudad/ fortaleza*〉 to seize sth, take sth; **se apoderó del control de la empresa** he took control of the company

apodo *m* nickname

apogeo *m* height

apolillado -da *adj* 〈*ropa*〉 moth-eaten; 〈*madera*〉 worm-eaten; 〈*ideas*〉 antiquated, fusty

apolillarse [A1] *v pron* «*ropa*» to get moth-eaten; «*madera*» to get infested with woodworm

apolítico -ca *adj* apolitical

apología *f* apologia (frml); **hizo ～ del terrorismo** he made a statement (*o* speech *etc*) justifying terrorism

apoltronarse [A1] *v pron* (en asiento) to settle oneself

aporrear [A1] *vt* 〈*puerta/mesa*〉 to bang *o* hammer on; 〈*persona*〉 (fam) to beat

aportación *f* **(a)** (contribución) contribution **(b)** (de socio) investment

aportar [A1] *vt* **(a)** (contribuir) 〈*dinero/tiempo/ idea*〉 to contribute **(b)** «*socio*» to invest ■ **～** *vi* (RPl) (a la seguridad social) to pay contributions

aporte *m* **(a)** (esp AmL) ▶ APORTACIÓN **(b)** (RPl) (a la seguridad social) social security contribution, ≈ National Insurance contribution (*in UK*)

aposento *m* (arc o hum) (habitación) chamber (dated)

apostar [A10] *vt* to bet; **te apuesto una cerveza** I bet you a beer; **～ algo POR algo/algn** to bet sth ON sth/sb ■ **～** *vi* to bet; **～ a las carreras** to bet on the horses; **te apuesto (a) que gana** I bet (you) he wins ■ **apostarse** *v pron* **(a)** (*recípr*): **se ～on una comida** they bet a meal on it **(b)** (*enf*) to bet

apóstol *m* (Relig) apostle

apostolado *m* (Relig) ministry, preaching

apostólico -ca *adj* apostolic

apóstrofo *m* apostrophe

apoteósico -ca *adj* tremendous

apoteosis *f* (a) (exaltación) apotheosis; **cuando salió en escena aquello fue la ～** (fam) the audience went wild when she came on stage (colloq) **(b)** (Teatr) finale

apoyabrazos *m* (*pl* **～**) armrest

apoyacabezas *m* (*pl* **～**) headrest

apoyar [A1] *vt* ⒈ (hacer descansar) **～ (algo EN algo)** to rest (sth ON sth); **apóyalo contra la pared** lean it against the wall ⒉ **(a)** (respaldar) 〈*propuesta/persona*〉 to back, support **(b)** 〈*teoría*〉 to support, bear out ■ **apoyarse** *v pron* ⒈ (para sostenerse, descansar) **～se EN algo** to lean on sth ⒉ (basarse, fundarse) **～se EN algo** to be based on sth

apoyo *m* support; **～ A algo** support FOR sth

apreciable *adj* 〈*cambio/mejoría*〉 appreciable, substantial; 〈*suma/cantidad*〉 considerable, substantial

apreciación *f* ⒈ **(a)** (percepción, enfoque) interpretation **(b)** (juicio) appraisal, assessment ⒉ (aprecio, valoración) appreciation; **～ musical** musical appreciation

apreciado -da *adj* 〈*amigo*〉 valued; **su piel es muy apreciada** its fur is highly prized

apreciar [A1] *vt* ⒈ 〈*persona*〉 to be fond of ⒉ 〈*interés/ayuda/arte*〉 to appreciate ⒊ (percibir, observar) to see; **para ～ la magnitud de los daños** in order to appreciate the extent of the damage

aprecio *m* (estima) esteem; **siente gran ～ por él** she holds him in great esteem; **goza del ～ de sus compañeros** she is highly regarded by her colleagues

apremiante *adj* 〈*necesidad*〉 pressing, urgent

apremiar [A1] *vt* (presionar): **me están apremiando para que lo termine** they are putting pressure on me to get it finished; **estamos apremiados de tiempo** we are pushed for *o* short of time ■ **～** *vi* to be urgent; **el tiempo apremia** time is getting on *o* is pressing

aprender [E1] *vi/vt* to learn; **～ A hacer algo** to learn to do sth

■ **aprenderse** *v pron* (*enf*) ⟨*lección/parte*⟩ to learn; **me la aprendí de memoria** I learnt it by heart

aprendiz -diza *m,f* apprentice, trainee; **es ~ de mecánico** he's an apprentice mechanic

aprendizaje *m* (a) (proceso) learning (b) (período como aprendiz) apprenticeship, training period

aprensión *f* (a) (preocupación, miedo) apprehension (b) (asco) squeamishness; **me da ~ ver sangre** I get squeamish at the sight of blood

aprensivo -va *adj*: **es muy ~** he's such a worrier

apresar [A1] *vt* ⟨*nave*⟩ to seize, arrest; ⟨*delincuente*⟩ to capture, catch (b) «*animal*» ⟨*presa*⟩ to capture, catch

aprestarse [A1] *v pron* (*refl*) **~se PARA algo/ A hacer algo** to prepare *o* get ready FOR sth/to do sth

apresurado -da *adj* (a) ⟨*despedida*⟩ quick, hurried; ⟨*visita*⟩ rushed, hurried (b) ⟨*decisión*⟩ rushed, hasty; ⟨*respuesta/comentario*⟩ hasty

apresurar [A1] *vt* (a) (meter prisa a) to hurry (b) (acelerar) ⟨*proceso/cambio*⟩ to speed up; ⟨*paso*⟩ to quicken

■ **apresurarse** *v pron*: **¡apresúrate!** hurry up!; **no nos apresuremos demasiado** let's not be hasty; **se apresuró a defenderla** he hastened *o* rushed to her defense

apretado -da *adj* ⟨1⟩ (a) (ajustado) tight; **me queda muy ~** it is too tight for me (b) (sin dinero): **andamos** *or* **estamos algo ~s** we're a little short of money (colloq) (c) (apretujado) cramped ⟨2⟩ ⟨*calendario/programa*⟩ tight; ⟨*victoria*⟩ narrow ⟨3⟩ (fam) (tacaño) tight (colloq), tightfisted (colloq)

apretar [A5] *vt* ⟨1⟩ (a) ⟨*botón*⟩ to press, push; ⟨*acelerador*⟩ to put one's foot on, press; ⟨*gatillo*⟩ to pull, squeeze (b) ⟨*nudo/tapa/tornillo*⟩ to tighten; ⟨*puño/mandíbulas*⟩ to clench; **apreté los dientes** I gritted my teeth

⟨2⟩ (a) (apretujar): **apretó al niño contra su pecho** he clasped *o* clutched the child to his breast; **me apretó el brazo con fuerza** he squeezed *o* gripped my arm firmly (b) (presionar) to put pressure on

■ **~** *vi* ⟨1⟩ «*ropa/zapatos*» (+ *me/te/le etc*) to be too tight; **el vestido le aprieta** the dress is too tight for her

⟨2⟩ (hacer presión) to press down (*o* in *etc*)

■ **apretarse** *v pron* to squeeze *o* squash together

apretón *m* (abrazo) hug; **se dieron un ~ de manos** they shook hands

apretujado -da *adj* cramped; **tuvimos que comer todos ~s** we had to eat all squashed together round the table

apretujar [A1] *vt* (fam): **no me apretujes, que me haces daño** don't squeeze me so hard, you're hurting me; **me ~on mucho en el tren** I got squashed on the train

■ **apretujarse** *v pron* to squash *o* squeeze together

aprieta, aprietas, etc ▶ APRETAR

aprieto *m* ▶ APURO 2

aprisa *adv* ▶ DEPRISA

aprisionar [A1] *vt* to trap

aprobación *f* (de proyecto de ley, moción) passing; (de préstamo, acuerdo, plan) approval, endorsement; (de actuación, conducta) approval

aprobado *m* (Educ) pass

aprobar [A10] *vt* ⟨1⟩ ⟨*proyecto de ley/moción*⟩ to pass; ⟨*préstamo/acuerdo/plan*⟩ to approve, sanction; ⟨*actuación/conducta*⟩ to approve of ⟨2⟩ (Educ) to pass

■ **~** *vi* «*estudiante*» to pass

aprontarse [A1] *v pron* (CS) (*refl*) to get ready

apropiado -da *adj* suitable; **el discurso fue muy ~ a la ocasión** the speech was very fitting for the occasion; **no era el momento ~** it wasn't the right moment

apropiarse [A1] *v pron* **~ (de) algo** to take *o* (frml) appropriate sth

aprovechable *adj* usable

aprovechado -da *adj* ⟨1⟩ (oportunista) opportunistic; **no seas ~** don't take advantage (of the situation) ⟨2⟩ ⟨*estudiante*⟩ hardworking

■ *m,f* opportunist

aprovechar [A1] *vt* (a) ⟨*tiempo/espacio/ talento*⟩ to make the most of; **dinero/tiempo bien aprovechado** money/time well spent; **es espacio mal aprovechado** it's a waste of space (b) ⟨*oportunidad*⟩ to take advantage of; **aprovecho la ocasión para decirles que …** I would like to take this opportunity to tell you that … (c) (usar) to use; **no tira nada, todo lo aprovecha** she doesn't throw anything away, she makes use of everything

■ **~** *vi*: **aproveché para venir a verte** I thought I'd take the opportunity to come and see you; **¡que aproveche!** enjoy your meal, bon appétit; **aprovechen ahora, que son jóvenes** make the most of it now, while you're young

■ **aprovecharse** *v pron* (a) (abusar) **~se DE algo/algn** to take advantage OF sth/sb, to exploit sth/sb (b) (abusar sexualmente) **~se DE algn** ⟨*de una mujer*⟩ to take advantage of sb; ⟨*de un niño*⟩ to abuse sb

aprovisionar [A1] *vt* ⟨*buque/tropas*⟩ to provision, to supply … with provisions

■ **aprovisionarse** *v pron* **~se DE algo** to stock up WITH sth

aproximado -da *adj* ⟨*cálculo/traducción/idea*⟩ rough (*before n*); ⟨*costo/velocidad*⟩ estimated (*before n*)

aproximar [A1] *vt* (a) (acercar): **aproximó la mesa a la ventana** she moved (*o* brought *etc*) the table over to the window (b) ⟨*países*⟩ to bring … closer together

■ **aproximarse** *v pron* (a) (acercarse) «*fecha/ persona/vehículo*» to approach; **se aproximó a mí** she came up to me (b) **~se A algo** ⟨*a la realidad/ una cifra*⟩ to come close *TO* sth

aprueba, apruebas, etc ▶ APROBAR

aptitud *f* flair; **tener ~ para los idiomas** to have a flair for languages; **carece de ~es para el ballet** she shows no talent for ballet

apto -ta *adj* [SER] **~ PARA algo** suitable FOR sth; **no es ~ para el cargo** he's not suitable *o* right for the job; **~ para el servicio militar** fit for military service; **no ~ para el consumo** not fit for consumption

apuesta *f* bet; **le hice una ~** I had a bet with him

apuesta, apuestas, etc ▶ APOSTAR

apuesto -ta *adj* (liter) ⟨*hombre/figura*⟩ handsome

apunamiento *m* (AmS) altitude *o* mountain sickness

apunarse [A1] *v pron* (AmS) to get altitude *o* mountain sickness

apuntalar [A1] *vt* ‹*edificio/túnel*› to shore up, brace; ‹*cimientos*› to underpin

apuntar [A1] *vt* ⬚1 **(a)** (tomar nota de) to make a note of, note down **(b)** (para excursión, actividad) to put ... down
⬚2 (señalar, indicar) to point at; **no la apuntes con el dedo** don't point (your finger) at her
■ ~ *vi* **(a)** (con arma) to aim; **preparen ... apunten ... ¡fuego!** ready ... take aim ... fire!; **le apuntó con una pistola** she pointed/aimed a gun at him **(b)** (indicar, señalar) to point
■ **apuntarse** *v pron* **(a)** (inscribirse) ~se A *or* EN algo ‹*a curso*› to enroll* ON sth; ‹*a clase*› to sign up FOR sth; **me apunté para ir a la excursión** I put my name down for the outing; **~se al paro** (Esp) to register as unemployed, to sign on (BrE colloq) **(b)** (obtener) ‹*tanto*› to score; ‹*victoria*› to chalk up, achieve

apunte *m* ⬚1 **(a)** (nota) note **(b) apuntes** *mpl* (Educ) notes (*pl*); (texto preparado) handout; **tomar** *or* (CS) **sacar ~s** to take notes ⬚2 **(a)** (Art) sketch; (Lit) outline **(b)** (AmL) (Teatr, TV) sketch ⬚3 (Com) entry

apuñalar [A1] *vt* to stab

apurado -da *adj* ⬚1 (avergonzado) embarrassed ⬚2 (AmL) (con prisa) in a hurry; **andaba ~** he was in a hurry; **a las apuradas** (RPI fam) in a rush ⬚3 (en apuros): **se vio muy ~ para contestar las preguntas** he was hard put to answer the questions; **si te encuentras ~,** dímelo if you run into any difficulties, let me know ⬚4 **(a)** (agobiado) **~ de trabajo** overwhelmed with work **(b)** (escaso) **~ DE algo** ‹*de dinero/tiempo*› short OF sth

apurar [A1] *vt* ⬚1 ‹*copa/botella*›: **apuró la cerveza y se fue** he finished (off) his beer and left ⬚2 (meter prisa): **nos están apurando para que lo terminemos** they're pushing us to finish it; **no me apures** (AmL) don't hurry *o* rush me
■ ~ *vi* (Chi) (+ *me/te/le etc*) (urgir): **no me apura** I'm not in a hurry for it
■ **apurarse** *v pron* ⬚1 (preocuparse) to worry ⬚2 (AmL) (darse prisa) to hurry; **¡apúrate!** hurry up!

apuro *m* ⬚1 (vergüenza): **¡qué ~!** how embarrassing!; **me daba ~ pedirle dinero** I was too embarrassed to ask him for money ⬚2 (aprieto, dificultad) predicament; **estar/verse en ~s** to be/find oneself in a predicament *o* tight spot; **me sacó del ~** he got me out of trouble; **me puso en un ~** she put me in a real predicament; **pasaron muchos ~s** they had an uphill struggle *o* they went through a lot ⬚3 (AmL) (prisa) rush; **esto tiene ~** this is urgent

aquel, aquella *adj dem* (*pl* **aquellos, aquellas**) that; (*pl*) those

aquél, aquélla *pron dem* (*pl* **aquéllos, aquéllas**) [*The written accent may be omitted when there is no risk of confusion with the adjective*] **(a)** (refiriéndose a cosa) that one; (*pl*) those; **ese no, ~** *or* **aquel** not that one, the *o* that other one **(b)** (refiriéndose a persona): **todo ~** *or* **aquel que lo necesite** (frml) anyone *o* (frml) any person needing it; **el cuento de ~** *or* **aquel que ...** the story about the man who ...

aquello *pron dem* (neutro): **¿qué es ~ que se ve allá?** what's that over there?; **~ que te dije el otro día** what I told you the other day

aquí *adv* ⬚1 (en el espacio) here; **está ~ dentro** it's in here; **~ mismo** right here; **no soy de ~** I'm not from these parts *o* from around here; **pase por ~** come this way; **viven por ~** they live around here; **el agua me llegaba hasta ~** the water came up to here; **dando vueltas de ~ para allá** going to and fro *o* from one place to another ⬚2 (en el tiempo): **de ~ al 2015** from now until 2015; **de ~ en adelante** from now on; **de ~ a un año** a year from now

ara *f* ⬚ (altar) altar; (piedra consagrada) altar stone

árabe *adj* **(a)** ‹*país/plato*› Arab; ‹*escritura/manuscritos*› Arabic **(b)** (Hist) (de Arabia) Arabian; (de los moros) Moorish
■ *mf* **(a)** (de país árabe) Arab **(b)** (Hist) (de Arabia) Arabian; (moro) Moor
■ *m* (idioma) Arabic

Arabia Saudí, Arabia Saudita *f* Saudi Arabia

arado *m* plow* (AmE), plough (BrE)

arancel *m* (tarifa) tariff; (impuesto) duty

arancelario -ria *adj* customs (*before n*)

arándano *m* blueberry

arandela *f* washer

araña *f* (Zool) spider

arañar [A1] *vt/vi* to scratch

arañazo *m* scratch

arar [A1] *vt/vi* to plow (AmE), to plough (BrE)

araucano -na *adj/m,f* Araucanian

arbitraje *m* **(a)** (en fútbol, boxeo) refereeing; (en tenis, béisbol) umpiring (b) (Der, Rels Labs) (acción) arbitration; (resolución) decision, judgment

arbitrar [A1] *vt/vi* **(a)** (en fútbol, boxeo) to referee; (en tenis, béisbol) to umpire **(b)** (en conflicto, disputa) to arbitrate

arbitrario -ria *adj* arbitrary

árbitro -tra *m,f* **(a)** (en fútbol, boxeo) referee; (en tenis, béisbol) umpire; **los ~s de la moda** the arbiters of fashion **(b)** (en conflicto) arbitrator

árbol *m* (Bot) tree; **~ de Navidad** *or* (Andes) **de Pascua** Christmas tree; **~ genealógico** family tree; **los ~es no dejan ver el bosque** you can't see the forest (AmE) *o* (BrE) wood for the trees

arbolado -da *adj* ‹*terreno*› wooded; ‹*calle*› tree-lined (*before n*)

arboleda *f* grove

arbusto *m* shrub, bush

arca *f* ⬚1 (cofre) chest; **el A~ de Noé** Noah's Ark ⬚2 **arcas** *fpl* (de institución) coffers (*pl*)

arcada *f* 1 (Med): **tener** ∼**s** to retch; **me provocó** ∼**s** it made me retch 2 (Arquit) arcade; (de puente) arch

arcaico -ca *adj* archaic

arcángel *m* archangel

arce *m* maple

arcén *m* shoulder (AmE), hard shoulder (BrE)

archidiócesis *f* (*pl* ∼) archdiocese

archiduque -quesa *m,f* (*m*) archduke; (*f*) archduchess

archipiélago *m* archipelago

archivador *m* (mueble) filing cabinet; (carpeta) ring binder, file

archivar [A1] *vt* ⟨documentos⟩ to file; ⟨investigación/asunto⟩ (por un tiempo) to shelve; (para siempre) to close the file on

archivo *m* (a) (local) archive; (conjunto de documentos) *tb* ∼**s** archives (*pl*), archive; **los** ∼**s de la policía** the police files *o* records (b) (Inf) file

arcilla *f* clay

arco *m* 1 (Arquit) arch; (Anat) arch; (Mat) arc; ∼ **de triunfo** triumphal arch; ∼ **iris** rainbow 2 (AmL) (en fútbol) goal 3 (a) (Arm, Dep) bow (b) (de violín) bow

arcón *m* large chest

arder [E1] *vi* 1 (quemarse) to burn 2 (estar muy caliente) to be boiling (hot); **estar que arde** «*persona*» to be fuming; **la cosa está que arde** things have reached boiling point 3 (escocer) «*herida/ojos*» to sting, smart

ardid *m* trick, ruse

ardiente *adj* ⟨defensor⟩ ardent; ⟨deseo⟩ ardent, burning; ⟨amante⟩ passionate

ardilla *f* squirrel

ardor *m* (dolor) burning; (escozor) smarting; ∼ **de estómago** heartburn

ardoroso -sa *adj* ardent

arduo -dua *adj* arduous

área *f* area; ∼ **chica** *or* **pequeña** goal area; ∼ **de castigo** penalty area; ∼ **de servicio** service area, services (*pl*)

arena *f* 1 (Const, Geol) sand; ∼ **movediza** quicksand 2 (palestra) arena; **en la** ∼ **política** in the political arena

arenoso -sa *adj* ⟨playa/terreno⟩ sandy

arenque *m* herring; ∼ **ahumado** kipper

arepa *f*: cornmeal roll

arete *m* (Col, Méx) earring

argamasa *f* mortar

Argel *m* Algiers

Argelia *f* Algeria

argelino -na *adj/m,f* Algerian

Argentina *f*: *tb* **la** ∼ Argentina

argentino -na *adj* ⟨gobierno/presidente⟩ Argentine (*before n*); ⟨escritor/música⟩ Argentinian

■ *m,f* Argentinian

argolla *f* ring; ∼ **de compromiso/de matrimonio** (AmL) engagement/wedding ring; **tener** ∼ (AmC fam) to have contacts (colloq)

argot *m* (*pl* **-gots**) slang

argüendero -ra *m,f* (Méx fam) gossip

arguir [I19] *vt* to argue

■ ∼*vi* «*hechos*» to point to

argumentación *f* line of argument (frml)

argumentar [A1] *vt* to argue

argumento *m* (a) (razón) argument (b) (Cin, Lit) plot, story line

aria *f* aria

aridez *f* aridity, dryness

árido -da *adj* arid, dry

Aries *m* (signo, constelación) Aries; **es (de)** ∼ she's an Aries *o* an Arian

■ *mf* (*pl* ∼) (persona) *tb* **aries** Aries, person born under (the sign of) Aries

arisco -ca *adj* (a) (huraño) ⟨persona⟩ unfriendly, unsociable; ⟨animal⟩ unfriendly (b) [ESTAR] (Méx fam) (enojado) upset, angry

arista *f* (Mat) edge; (de viga) arris; (de bóveda) groin; (en montañismo) arête, ridge

aristocracia *f* aristocracy

aristócrata *mf* aristocrat

aristocrático -ca *adj* aristocratic

aritmética *f* arithmetic

aritmético -ca *adj* arithmetic

arma *f* (a) (Arm, Mil) weapon; ∼ **nuclear** nuclear weapon; ∼ **blanca** any sharp instrument used as a weapon; ∼ **de fuego** firearm; ∼**s de destrucción masiva** weapons of mass destruction; **deponer las** ∼**s** to lay down one's arms; **no llevaba** ∼**s** he wasn't carrying a weapon; **ser un** ∼ **de doble filo** to be a double-edged sword (b) (instrumento, medio) weapon

armada *f* navy

armadillo *m* armadillo

armado -da *adj* ⟨lucha/persona⟩ armed; ∼ DE *or* CON **algo** armed WITH sth

armador -dora *m,f* shipowner

armadura *f* 1 (Hist, Mil) armor** 2 (Const) framework

armamentista *adj* arms (*before n*)

armamento *m* armaments (*pl*)

armar [A1] *vt* 1 (a) (Mil) ⟨ciudadanos/país⟩ to arm, supply ... with arms (b) (equipar) ⟨embarcación⟩ to fit out, equip 2 (a) ⟨estantería/reloj⟩ to assemble; ⟨tienda/carpa⟩ to pitch, put up (b) (AmL) ⟨rompecabezas⟩ to do, piece together (c) (Col, RPl) ⟨cigarro⟩ to roll 3 (fam) ⟨alboroto/ruido/lío⟩ to make; ∼ **jaleo** to kick up *o* make a racket (colloq); ∼ **un escándalo** to kick up a fuss; ∼**la** (fam): **¡buena la has armado!** you've really done it now! (colloq)

■ **armarse** *v pron* 1 (a) (Mil) to arm oneself (b) ∼**se DE algo** ⟨de armas/herramientas⟩ to arm oneself WITH sth; ∼**se de paciencia** to be patient; ∼**se de valor** to pluck up courage 2 (a) (fam) «*pelea/discusión*» to break out; **¡qué jaleo se armó!** there was a real commotion (b) (fam) «*persona*»: **me armé un lío/una confusión** I got into a mess (colloq)

armario *m* (a) (para ropa — mueble) wardrobe; (— empotrado) closet (AmE), wardrobe (BrE) (b) (de cocina) cupboard; (de cuarto de baño) cabinet

armatoste *m* (fam) huge great thing (colloq)

armazón *m or f* 1 (Const) skeleton; (de avión) airframe; (de barco, mueble) frame; (de gafas) frames (*pl*) 2 (de obra literaria) framework, outline

Armenia *f* Armenia

armenio¹ -nia *adj/m,f* Armenian

armenio² *m* (idioma) Armenian

armisticio *m* armistice

armonía *f* harmony

armónica *f* harmonica, mouth organ

armónico -ca *adj* **(a)** (Mús) harmonic **(b)** (armonioso) harmonious

armonioso -sa *adj* harmonious

armonizar [A4] *vt* **(a)** (Mús) to harmonize **(b)** ‹*tendencias/opiniones*› to reconcile, harmonize; ‹*diferencias*› to reconcile
▪ ~ *vi* «*estilos/colores*» to blend in, harmonize; ~ CON algo «*color/estilo*» to blend (in) WITH sth

arnés *m* (para niño) baby reins (*pl*); (Dep) harness; (arreos) harness

aro *m* **(a)** (Jueg) hoop **(b)** (Arg, Chi) (para el lóbulo) earring; (en forma de aro) hooped earring **(c)** (de servilleta) napkin ring

aroma *m* (de flores) scent, perfume; (del café, de hierbas) aroma; (del vino) bouquet

aromaterapia *f* aromatherapy

aromático -ca *adj* aromatic

arpa *f⚥* harp

arpegio *m* arpeggio

arpillera *f* sacking, hessian, burlap (AmE)

arpista *mf* harpist

arpón *m* harpoon; ~ **submarino** speargun

arquear [A1] *vt* ‹*espalda*› to arch; ‹*cejas*› to raise, arch; ‹*estante*› to bow, bend
▪ **arquearse** *v pron* «*estante*» to sag, bend; «*persona*» to arch one's back

arqueología *f* archaeology

arqueológico -ca *adj* archaeological

arqueólogo -ga *m,f* archaeologist

arquero *m* ⓵ (Hist, Mil) archer ⓶ (AmL) (en fútbol) goalkeeper

arquetipo *m* archetype

arquitecto -ta *m,f* architect

arquitectónico -ca *adj* architectural

arquitectura *f* architecture

arrabal *m* poor quarter *o* area

arraigado -da *adj* ‹*costumbre*› deeply rooted, deep-rooted; ‹*vicio*› deeply entrenched

arraigar [A3] *vi* ‹*costumbre*» to become rooted, take root; «*vicio*» to become entrenched; «*planta*» to take root
▪ **arraigarse** *v pron* «*costumbres/ideas*» to take root; «*persona*» to settle

arrancar [A2] *vt* ⓵ ‹*hoja de papel*› to tear out; ‹*etiqueta*› to tear off; ‹*botón/venda*› to pull off; ‹*planta*› to pull up; ‹*flor*› to pick; ‹*diente/pelo*› to pull out; **le arrancó el bolso** he snatched her bag ⓶ ‹*confesión/declaración*› to extract ⓷ ‹*motor/coche*› to start
▪ ~ *vi* «*motor/vehículo*» to start
▪ **arrancarse** *v pron* ⓵ (*refl*) ‹*pelo/diente*› to pull out; ‹*piel/botón*› to pull off ⓶ (Chi fam) (huir) to run away

arranque *m* **(a)** (Auto, Mec) starting mechanism; **tengo problemas con el** ~ I have problems starting the car **(b)** (arrebato) ~ DE algo fit OF sth

arrasar [A1] *vi* ~ CON algn ‹*con contrincante*› to demolish sb; ‹*con enemigo*› to destroy sb; **nuestro equipo volvió a** ~ our team swept to victory again; ~ CON algo: **la inundación arrasó**

con las cosechas the flood devastated the crops; ~on con toda la comida they polished off all the food (colloq)
▪ ~ *vt* ‹*zona*› to devastate; ‹*edificio*› to destroy

arrastrar [A1] *vt* ⓵ **(a)** (por el suelo) to drag **(b)** ‹*remolque/caravana*› to tow **(c)** (llevar consigo): **arrastró todo a su paso** it swept away everything in its path; **la corriente lo arrastraba mar adentro** the current was carrying him out to sea ⓶ **(a)** ‹*problema/enfermedad*›: **arrastra esa tos desde el invierno** that cough of hers has been dragging on since the winter; **vienen arrastrando el problema desde hace años** they've been dragging out the problem for years **(b)** (atraer) to draw; **se dejan** ~ **por la moda** they are slaves to fashion
▪ ~ *vi* «*mantel/cortina*» to trail along the ground
▪ **arrastrarse** *v pron* **(a)** (por el suelo) «*persona*» to crawl; «*culebra*» to slither **(b)** (humillarse) to grovel, crawl

arrastre *m* **(a)** (acción) dragging; **estar para el** ~ (fam) to be done in (colloq) **(b)** (CS fam) (atractivo) appeal

arre *interj* (a un caballo) gee up!, giddy up!

arrear [A1] *vt* **(a)** ‹*ganado*› to drive, herd; ‹*caballerías*› to spur, urge on **(b)** (AmL fam) ‹*gente*› to chivy* (colloq), to hurry ... along **(c)** (AmL fam) (llevar) ~ CON algo/algn to cart sth/sb off (colloq)

arrebatador -dora *adj* ‹*belleza*› breathtaking; ‹*sonrisa*› dazzling; ‹*mirada*› captivating

arrebatar [A1] *vt* (quitar) to snatch

arrebato *m* **(a)** (arranque) ~ DE algo fit OF sth; **le dio un** ~ he flew into a rage **(b)** (éxtasis) ecstasy, rapture

arrechar [A1] *vt* **(a)** (AmL vulg) (excitar sexualmente) to turn ... on (colloq) **(b)** (AmL fam) (enojar) to bug (colloq)
▪ **arrecharse** *v pron* **(a)** (AmL vulg) (sexualmente) «*persona*» to get horny (sl); «*animal*» to come in (AmE) *o* (BrE) on heat **(b)** (AmL fam) (enfurecerse) to get furious

arrecho -cha *adj* ⓵ **(a)** (AmL vulg) (sexualmente excitado) ‹*persona*› horny (sl), turned-on (colloq); ‹*animal*› in heat (AmE), on heat (BrE) **(b)** (Col, Ven fam) (valiente) gutsy (colloq) ⓶ (AmL fam) (enojado) furious, mad (AmE colloq) ⓷ (AmC, Ven fam) (difícil) tough

arrecife *m* reef

arreglado -da *adj* ⓵ **(a)** (limpio, ordenado) tidy **(b)** (ataviado) smartly turned out, smart ⓶ (AmL fam) ‹*partido/elecciones*› fixed (colloq)

arreglar [A1] *vt* ⓵ **(a)** ‹*aparato/reloj*› to mend, fix; ‹*zapatos*› to mend, repair; ‹*falda/vestido*› to alter; ‹*calle*› to repair; **el dentista me está arreglando la boca** (fam) the dentist is fixing my teeth (colloq); **esto te** ~**á el estómago** (fam) this'll sort your stomach out (colloq) ⓶ **(a)** ‹*casa/habitación*› (ordenar) to straighten up, to tidy (up) (BrE); (hacer arreglos en) to do up (colloq) **(b)** (preparar, organizar): **ve arreglando a los niños ¿quieres?** can you start getting the children ready? (colloq); **tengo todo arreglado para el viaje** I've got everything ready for the trip; **un amigo me está arreglando los papeles** a friend is sorting out the papers for me; ~ **una entrevista** to arrange an interview **(c)** (disponer) ⟨*flores/ muebles*⟩ to arrange

3 (solucionar) ⟨*situación*⟩ to sort out; ⟨*asunto*⟩ to settle, sort out; **lo quiso ~ diciendo que …** she tried to put things right by saying that …

■ **arreglarse** *v pron* **1** (*refl*) (ataviarse): **tarda horas en ~se** she takes hours to get ready; **no te arregles tanto** you don't need to get so dressed up; **sabe ~se** she knows how to make herself look good

2 ⟨*pelo/manos*⟩ **(a)** (*refl*) to do **(b)** (*caus*): **tengo que ~me el pelo** I must have my hair done **3** (solucionarse) «*situación/asunto*» to get sorted out

4 (fam) (amañarse): **ya me ~é para volver a casa** I'll make my own way home; **la casa es pequeña pero nos arreglamos** it's a small house, but we manage; *arreglárselas* (fam) to manage; **no sé cómo se las arreglan** I don't know how they manage; **arréglatelas como puedas** sort *o* work it out as best you can; **ya me las ~é** I'll manage, I'll be OK

5 «*día/tiempo*» to get better, clear up

arreglo *m* **1** **(a)** (reparación) repair; **hacerle ~s a algo** to carry out repairs on sth; **la casa necesita algunos ~s** the house needs some work done on it; *no tiene ~* «*reloj/máquina*» it's beyond repair; «*persona*» he/she is a hopeless case **(b)** (de ropa) alteration **(c)** (Mús) *tb ~* **musical** musical arrangement **2** (acuerdo) arrangement, agreement

arrellanarse [A1] *v pron:* **se arrellanó en el sofa** he settled himself into the sofa

arremangarse [A3] *v pron* ▶ REMANGARSE

arremeter [E1] *vi* (embestir) to charge; (atacar) to attack; ~ **CONTRA algo/algn** (acometer) to charge AT sth/sb; (atacar, criticar) to attack sth/sb

arremolinarse [A1] *v pron* «*agua/hojas*» to swirl; «*personas/animales*» to mill around

arrendador -dora *m,f* (*m*) landlord, lessor (frml); (*f*) landlady, lessor (frml)

arrendamiento *m* **(a)** (de casa) renting, letting (BrE); (de tierras, local) renting, leasing; **contrato de ~** tenancy agreement **(b)** (de otra cosa — por el propietario) renting (out); (— por el que la recibe) renting **(c)** (precio — de casa, local) rent; (— de otra cosa) rental

arrendar [A5] *vt* **1** (Der) **(a)** (dar en arriendo) ⟨*casa*⟩ to rent (out), let (BrE); ⟨*local/tierras*⟩ to rent (out), lease **(b)** (tomar en arriendo) ⟨*casa*⟩ to rent; ⟨*local/tierras*⟩ to rent, lease **(c)** (contratar) ⟨*servicios*⟩ to hire **2** (Andes) ⟨*coche/bicicleta*⟩ (dar en arriendo) to rent (out) (AmE), to hire out (BrE); (tomar en arriendo) to rent (AmE), to hire (BrE); **❸ se arriendan coches** cars for rent (AmE), car hire (BrE)

arrendatario -ria *m,f* (de propiedad) lessee, tenant; (de contrata) contractor

arrepentido -da *adj* ⟨*pecador*⟩ repentant; **estaba ~ de lo que había hecho** he was sorry for *o* feeling remorse for what he had done; **estoy ~ de haberlo dicho** I regret having said it

arrepentimiento *m* remorse, repentance

arrepentirse [I11] *v pron* **(a)** (lamentar) to be sorry; ~ DE **algo** to regret sth; ~ DE **hacer algo** to regret doing sth **(b)** (cambiar de idea) to change one's mind

arrepienta, arrepintió, etc ▶ ARREPENTIRSE

arrestar [A1] *vt* to arrest

arresto *m* (Der, Mil) **(a)** (detención) arrest; **bajo ~** under arrest **(b)** (prisión) detention

arriar [A17] *vt* ⟨*bandera/vela*⟩ to lower

arriba *adv* **1** **(a)** (lugar, parte): **ahí/aquí ~** up there/here; **en el estante de ~** (el siguiente) on the shelf above; (el último) on the top shelf; **ponlo un poco más ~** put it a little higher up; **la parte de ~** the top (part); ~ **del ropero** (AmL) on top of the wardrobe; ~ **de la cocina está el baño** (AmL) the bathroom is above the kitchen; **de ~ abajo:** **me miró de ~ abajo** he looked me up and down; **limpiar la casa de ~ abajo** to clean the house from top to bottom **(b)** (en edificio) upstairs; **los vecinos de ~** the people upstairs **(c)** (en escala, jerarquía) above; **órdenes de ~** orders from above; **las puntuaciones de 80 para ~** scores of 80 or over

2 (expresando dirección, movimiento): **corrió escaleras ~** he ran upstairs; **calle ~** up the street; **miró hacia ~** he looked up

3 (en interjecciones) **(a)** (expresando aprobación): **¡~ la democracia!** long live democracy! **(b)** (expresando estímulo) come on!; (llamando a levantarse) get up!

arribista *adj* socially ambitious
■ *mf* arriviste, social climber

arriendo *m* (esp Andes) ▶ ARRENDAMIENTO

arriesgado -da *adj* ⟨*acción/empresa*⟩ risky, hazardous; ⟨*persona*⟩ brave, daring

arriesgar [A3] *vt* **(a)** ⟨*vida/dinero*⟩ to risk **(b)** ⟨*opinión*⟩ to venture
■ **arriesgarse** *v pron:* **¿nos arriesgamos?** shall we risk it *o* take a chance?; **~se A hacer algo** to risk doing sth

arrimar [A1] *vt* (acercar) to move/bring … closer; **arrimó la cama a *or* contra la pared** he pushed *o* moved the bed up against the wall
■ **arrimarse** *v pron* **1** (*refl*) (acercarse): **se arrimó mucho a la orilla** he went too close to the edge; **arrímate al fuego** come (up) closer to the fire; **se arrimó a *or* contra la pared** he moved up against the wall; **~se A algn** to move closer TO sb; (buscando calor, abrigo) to snuggle up TO sb **2** (Méx, Ven fam) (en casa de algn): **se ~on en mi casa** they came to live *o* stay with me, they dumped themselves on me (pey)

arrinconado -da *adj* **(a)** (bloqueado) blocked in, boxed in **(b)** (acorralado, acosado) cornered **(c)** (arrumbado) lying around

arrinconar [A1] *vt* **(a)** (poner en rincón) to put … in a corner **(b)** (acosar, acorralar) to corner **(c)** (marginar) to exclude **(d)** (arrumbar) to leave, dump (colloq)

arroba *f* **1** (en dirección electrónica) at, at sign **2** (Hist) **(a)** (medida de peso) *unit of weight of about 14 kg* **(b)** (medida de capacidad) *unit of liquid measure of about 15 l*

arrocero -ra *adj* ⟨*cultivo/producción*⟩ rice (*before n*); ⟨*región*⟩ rice-growing (*before n*)
■ *m,f* rice grower

arrodillarse [A1] *v pron* to kneel (down)

arrogancia *f* arrogance; **con ~** arrogantly

arrogante *adj* arrogant, haughty

arrojar [A1] *vt* **1** **(a)** (tirar) to throw; (Aviac) ⋯⋮

a

‹*bomba*› to drop **(b)** ‹*lava*› to spew (out); ‹*humo*› to belch out; ‹*luz*› to shed ② (vomitar) to bring up, throw up
■ **arrojarse** *v pron* (*refl*) to throw oneself; ~**se** SOBRE algo/algn «*persona*» to throw oneself ONTO sth/sb; «*perro/tigre*» to pounce ON sth/sb
arrollador -dora *adj* **(a)** ‹*éxito/mayoría/ victoria*› overwhelming **(b)** ‹*fuerza/ataque*› devastating **(c)** ‹*personalidad/elocuencia*› overpowering
arrollar [A1] *vt* **(a)** «*vehículo*» to run over; «*muchedumbre/agua/viento*» to sweep o carry away **(b)** (derrotar, vencer) to crush, overwhelm
arropar [A1] *vt* ‹*niño/enfermo*› (abrigar) to wrap … up; (en la cama) to tuck … in
■ **arroparse** *v pron* (abrigarse) to wrap up warm; (en la cama) to pull the covers up
arroyo *m* **(a)** (riachuelo) stream **(b)** (cuneta) gutter **(c)** (AmC) (torrentera) gully **(d)** (Méx) (Auto) slow lane
arroz *m* rice; ~ a la cubana *rice with fried egg, plantain and tomato sauce*; ~ con leche rice pudding; ~ integral brown rice
arrozal *m* ricefield, paddy
arruga *f* (en piel) wrinkle, line; (en tela, papel) crease
arrugado -da *adj* ‹*persona/manos/piel*› wrinkled; ‹*ropa*› wrinkled (AmE), creased (BrE); ‹*papel*› crumpled
arrugar [A3] *vt* ‹*piel*› to wrinkle; ‹*tela*› to wrinkle (AmE), to crease (BrE); ‹*papel*› to crumple; ‹*ceño*› to knit; ‹*nariz*› to wrinkle; ‹*cara*› to screw up; **arrugó el entrecejo** he frowned
■ **arrugarse** *v pron* **(a)** «*persona/piel*» to become wrinkled **(b)** (por acción del agua) «*piel/ manos*» to shrivel up, go wrinkled **(c)** «*tela*» to wrinkle o get wrinkled (AmE), to crease o get creased (BrE); «*papel*» to crumple
arruinar [A1] *vt* to ruin
■ **arruinarse** *v pron* to be ruined
arrullo *m* (de palomas) cooing; (para adormecer) lullaby
arrumbar [A1] *vt* ▶ ARRINCONAR C, D
arsenal *m* **(a)** (Mil) arsenal; **un ~ de datos** a mine of information **(b)** (Esp) (Náut) navy yard (AmE), naval dockyard (BrE)
arsénico *m* arsenic
arte (*gen m en el singular y f en el plural*) ① (Art) art; **el ~ por el ~** art for art's sake; **no trabajo por amor al ~** (hum) I'm not working for the good of my health (hum); **~s gráficas** graphic arts; (*como*) *por ~ de magia* as if by magic ② (habilidad, destreza) art; **el ~ de la conversación** the art of conversation; **tiene ~ para arreglar flores** she has a flair o gift for flower arranging
artefacto *m* (instrumento) artifact; (dispositivo) device; **~s de baño** (CS) bathroom fixtures (*pl*), sanitary ware (frml); **un raro ~** a contraption
arteria *f* artery
arterial *adj* arterial
artesa *f* trough

artesanal *adj*: **de fabricación ~** ‹*muebles*› handcrafted; ‹*queso*› farmhouse; **productos ~es** handicrafts, craftwork
artesanía *f* **(a)** (actividad) handicraft; **una ~** a piece of craftwork; **objetos de ~** craftwork, handicrafts **(b)** **artesanías** *fpl* (AmL) (productos) crafts (*pl*), craftwork; **mercado de ~s** craft market
artesano -na *m,f* (*m*) craftsman, artisan; (*f*) craftswoman, artisan
ártico -ca *adj* Arctic
Ártico *m*: **el ~** (región) the Arctic; (océano) the Arctic Ocean
articulación *f* ① **(a)** (Anat, Mec) joint **(b)** (organización) organization, coordination ② (Ling) articulation
articulado -da *adj* articulated
articular [A1] *vt* (Tec, Ling) to articulate
articulista *mf* feature writer, columnist
artículo *m* ① (Com): **~s del hogar/de consumo** household/consumer goods; **~ de primera necesidad** essential item, essential; **~s de escritorio** stationery; **~s de tocador** toiletries; **~s de punto** knitwear ② **(a)** (en periódico, revista) article; **~ de fondo** editorial, leader (BrE) **(b)** (de ley) article ③ (Ling) article
artífice *mf* **(a)** (responsable, autor): **fue el ~ del secuestro** he planned the kidnapping; **el ~ de esta victoria** the architect of this victory **(b)** (artista) (*m*) craftsman, artisan; (*f*) craftswoman, artisan
artificial *adj* ‹*flor/satélite/sonrisa*› artificial; ‹*fibra*› man-made, artificial
artificio *m* **(a)** (artimaña) trick, artful device **(b)** (afectación) affectation **(c)** (artilugio) device
artillería *f* artillery
artilugio *m* **(a)** (aparato) device, contraption **(b)** **artilugios** *mpl* (de oficio) equipment
artimaña *f* trick
artista *mf* **(a)** (Arte) artist **(b)** (actor) actor; (actriz) actress; (cantante, músico) artist; **una ~ de cine** a movie star (AmE) o (BrE) film star
artístico -ca *adj* artistic
artritis *f* arthritis
arveja *f* (AmL) pea
arvejilla, arverjilla *f* (RPI) sweet pea
arzobispado *m* archbishopric
arzobispal *adj* ‹*sede/comisión*› archiepiscopal (frml)
arzobispo *m* archbishop
as *m* ace
asa *f♣* (asidero) handle
asadera *f* (RPI) roasting pan o dish o tin
asadero *m* (Coc) griddle
asado¹ -da *adj* ① **(a)** ‹*carne/pollo*› (en horno) roast (*before n*); (con espetón) spit-roast (*before n*); (a la parrilla) barbecued, grilled **(b)** ‹*castaña/papa*› roast (*before n*); ‹*papa con piel*› baked ② (fam) [ESTAR] (acalorado) roasting (colloq)

· ·

asado² *m* **(a)** (al horno) roast; ~ **de cordero** roast lamb **(b)** (AmL) (a la parrilla) barbecued meat **(c)** (AmL) (reunión) barbecue

asador¹ *m* (espetón) spit; (aparato — de espetones) rotisserie; (— de parrilla) barbecue

asador² -dora *m,f* (RPl) cook (*person who cooks the meat at a barbecue*)

asalariado -da *adj* wage-earning (*before n*)
■ *m,f* wage *o* salary earner

asaltante *mf* **(a)** (ladrón) robber **(b)** (atacante) attacker; **los ~s de la embajada** those who stormed the embassy

asaltar [A1] *vt* **(a)** (atracar) ‹*banco/tienda*› to hold up, rob; ‹*persona*› to rob, mug **(b)** (tomar por asalto) ‹*ciudad/embajada*› to storm **(c)** (atacar) to attack, assault **(d)** «*idea*» to strike; **me asaltó una duda** I was struck *o* seized by a sudden doubt

asalto *m* [1] **(a)** (atraco — a banco, tienda) holdup, robbery; (— a persona) mugging; **un ~ a mano armada** an armed robbery *o* raid **(b)** (ataque) attack, assault; **tomar algo por ~** to take sth by storm [2] (en boxeo) round; (en esgrima) bout

asamblea *f* **(a)** (reunión) meeting **(b)** (cuerpo) assembly

asar [A1] *vt* **(a)** ‹*carne/pollo*› (en horno) to roast; (a la parrilla) to grill; (en espetón) to spit-roast **(b)** ‹*castaña/papa*› to roast; ‹*papa con piel*› to bake
■ **asarse** *v pron* **(a)** (en horno) to roast **(b)** (fam) (de calor) to roast (colloq)

asbesto *m* asbestos

ascendencia *f* **(a)** (linaje) descent, ancestry; **es de ~ francesa** he is of French descent **(b)** (origen) origin(s); **su ~ humilde** her humble origins

ascendente *adj* ‹*movimiento/tendencia*› upward; ‹*astro/marea*› rising

ascender [E8] *vi* [1] (frml) «*temperatura/precios*» to rise; «*globo*» to rise, ascend (frml); «*escalador/alpinista*» to climb, to ascend (frml) [2] (frml) «*gastos/pérdidas*» ~ **A algo** TO sth [3] «*empleado/oficial*» to be promoted; **ascendió rápidamente en su carrera** he advanced rapidly in his career; ~ **al trono** to ascend the throne
■ ~ *vt* ‹*empleado/oficial*› to promote

ascendiente *mf* (antepasado) ancestor

Ascensión *f*: **la ~** the Ascension

ascenso *m* **(a)** (de temperatura, precios) rise **(b)** (a montaña) ascent; **una industria en ~** a growing industry **(c)** (de empleado, equipo, oficial) promotion

ascensor *m* elevator (AmE), lift (BrE)

ascensorista *mf* elevator operator (AmE), lift attendant (BrE)

asco *m* **(a)** (repugnancia): **¡qué ~!** how revolting!, how disgusting!; **me dio ~** it made me feel sick; **poner cara de ~** to make *o* (BrE) pull a face; **tanta corrupción da ~** all this corruption is sickening **(b)** (fam) (cosa repugnante, molesta): **tienen la casa que es un ~** their house is like a pigsty; **el parque está hecho un ~** the park is in a real state (colloq); **¡qué ~ de tiempo!** what foul *o* lousy weather!

ascua *f*: ember; **estar en/tener a algn en ~s** (fam) to be on/to keep sb on tenterhooks

aseado -da *adj* (limpio) clean; (arreglado) neat, tidy

asear [A1] *vt* (limpiar) to clean; (arreglar) to straighten (up), to tidy up (BrE)
■ **asearse** *v pron* (refl) (lavarse) to wash; (arreglarse) to straighten *o* (BrE) tidy oneself up

asediar [A1] *vt* **(a)** (Mil) ‹*ciudad*› to lay siege to, besiege; ‹*ejército*› to surround, besiege **(b)** (acosar) ‹*persona*› to besiege

asegurado -da *adj* insured; **tengo el coche ~ a todo riesgo** I have fully comprehensive insurance for the car
■ *m,f* (persona que contrata el seguro) policy-holder; (persona asegurada): **el ~/la asegurada** the insured

asegurador -dora *adj* ‹*compañía*› insurance (*before n*)
■ *mf* **(a)** (persona) insurer **(b) aseguradora** *f* (compañía) insurance company

asegurar [A1] *vt* [1] **(a)** (prometer) to assure; **te lo aseguro** I assure you; **asegura no haberlo visto** she maintains that she did not see **(b)** (garantizar) ‹*funcionamiento/servicio*› to guarantee [2] (Com, Fin) ‹*persona/casa*› to insure; **aseguró el coche a todo riesgo** she took out fully comprehensive insurance for *o* on the car [3] **(a)** (sujetar, fijar) ‹*puerta/estante*› to secure **(b)** ‹*edificio/entrada*› to secure, make … secure
■ **asegurarse** *v pron* [1] **(a)** (cerciorarse) to make sure **(b)** (garantizarse, procurarse): **con ese gol se ~on el triunfo** by scoring that goal they guaranteed themselves victory [2] (Com, Fin) to insure oneself

asemejar [A1] *vt* **(a)** (hacer parecido) to make … (look) like **(b)** (comparar) to compare, liken
■ **asemejarse** *v pron* **(a)** ‹*personas*› to be *o* look alike; «*objetos*» to be similar; ~**se A algo/algn** to resemble sth/sb, look like sth/sb

asentado -da *adj* **(a)** [ESTAR] (situado): **el pueblo está ~ a orillas de un río** the village lies *o* is situated on the banks of a river **(b)** [ESTAR] (establecido) ‹*creencia/tradición*› deep-rooted, deeply rooted; ‹*persona*› settled (in) **(c)** [SER] (esp AmL) (maduro, juicioso) mature

asentamiento *m* settlement

asentar [A5] *vt* [1] ‹*campamento*› to set up; ‹*damnificados/refugiados*› to place [2] **(a)** ‹*objeto*› to place carefully (*o* firmly *etc*) **(b)** ‹*conocimientos/postura*› to consolidate [3] (Com, Fin) to enter
■ **asentarse** *v pron* [1] «*café/polvo/terreno*» to settle [2] (estar situado) «*ciudad/edificio*» to be situated, be built [3] (a) (establecerse) to settle **(b)** (esp AmL) (adquirir madurez) to settle down

asentir [I11] *vi* to agree, consent; **asintió con la cabeza** she nodded

aseo *m* (limpieza) cleanliness; ~ **personal** personal hygiene; ❺ **aseos** rest room (AmE), toilets (BrE)

asequible *adj* ‹*precio*› affordable, reasonable; ‹*meta*› attainable, achievable; ‹*proyecto*› feasible; ‹*persona*› approachable; ‹*obra/estilo*› accessible

aserradero *m* sawmill

aserrar [A5] *vt* to saw

aserrín *m* (esp AmL) sawdust

aserrío *m* (Col, Ec) sawmill

aserruchar [A1] *vt* (Chi) to saw

asesinar [A1] *vt* to murder; (por razones políticas) to assassinate

asesinato *m* murder; (por razones políticas) assassination

asesino -na *adj* ‹instinto/odio› murderous, homicidal; ‹animal› killer (*before n*)
■ *m,f* murderer; (por razones políticas) assassin; ~ a sueldo hired killer; ~ en serie serial killer

asesor -sora *adj* ‹consejo› advisory; ‹arquitecto/ingeniero› consultant (*before n*)
■ *m,f* advisor*, consultant

asesoramiento *m* advice

asesorar [A1] *vt* to advise
■ **asesorarse** *v pron* ~se CON algn to consult sb

asesoría *f* consultancy; ~ fiscal/jurídica tax/legal consultancy

asestar [A1] *vt*: me asestó una puñalada/un puñetazo he stabbed/punched me

asexuado -da *adj* asexual

asfaltado -da *adj* asphalt (*before n*), asphalted

asfaltar [A1] *vt* to asphalt

asfalto *m* asphalt

asfixia *f* (a) (Med) asphyxia, suffocation (b) (fam) (agobio) suffocation

asfixiante *adj* (a) ‹gas/humo› asphyxiating (*before n*) (b) (fam) ‹calor› suffocating, stifling; ‹ambiente/relación› oppressive, stifling

asfixiar [A1] *vt* (a) (ahogar) to asphyxiate, suffocate; murió asfixiado he died of asphyxiation o suffocation (b) (agobiar) to suffocate, stifle
■ **asfixiarse** *v pron* (a) (ahogarse) to be asphyxiated, to suffocate; (por obstrucción de la tráquea) to choke to death; me asfixiaba de calor (fam) I was suffocating in the heat (b) (fam) (agobiarse) to suffocate, feel stifled

así¹ *adj inv* like that; no seas ~ don't be like that; con gente ~ yo no me meto I don't mix with people like that; yo soy ~ that's the way I am; ~ es la vida (fr hecha) that's life; es un tanto ~ de hojas it's about that many pages; esperamos horas ¿no es ~? we waited for hours, didn't we?; tanto es ~ que ... so much so that ...

así² *adv* [1] (de ese modo) like this; (de ese modo) like that; ¿por qué me tratas ~? why are you treating me like this?; no le hables ~ don't talk to him like that; ¡~ cualquiera! that's cheating! (colloq & hum); ~ es como pasó this is how it happens; no te pongas ~ don't get so worked up; ~ me podré comprar lo que quiera that way I'll be able to buy whatever I want; ~ es that's right; ¿está bien ~ o quieres más? is that enough, or do you want some more?; y ~ sucesivamente and so on
[2] ¡~ de fácil! it's as easy as that; ~ de alto/grueso this high/thick
[3] (en locs) así así (fam) so-so; así como así just like that; ¡así me gusta! (fr hecha) that's what I like to see!; así nomás (AmL) just like that; así pues so; así que (por lo tanto) so; así y todo even so; por así decirlo so to speak

Asia *f‡* Asia

asiático -ca *adj/m,f* Asian, Asiatic

asidero *m* (a) (asa) handle (b) (punto de sujeción) hand (hold); sin ~s en la realidad with no grip on reality

asiduo -dua *adj* (a) (persistente) ‹estudiante/lector› assiduous; ‹admirador› devoted (b) (frecuente) ‹cliente› regular, frequent
■ *m,f* regular

asiento *m* [1] (a) (para sentarse) seat; ~ anatómico anatomically designed seat; por favor, tome ~ (frml) please take a seat (frml) (b) (de bicicleta) saddle (c) (de silla) seat (d) (base, estabilidad) base [2] (en contabilidad) entry

asignación *f* [1] (a) (de tarea, función) assignment (b) (de fondos, renta) allocation, assignment [2] (sueldo) wages (*pl*); (paga) allowance [3] (AmC) (Educ) homework

asignar [A1] *vt* (a) (dar, adjudicar) ‹renta/función/tarea› to assign; ‹valor› to ascribe; ‹fondos/parcela› to allocate; me ~on la vacante I was appointed to the post; le ~on una beca he was awarded a grant (b) (destinar) ‹persona› to assign; ~ a algn A algo to assign sb TO sth

asignatura *f* subject; ~ pendiente (Educ) subject which one has to retake; (asunto sin resolver) unresolved matter

asilado -da *m,f* inmate; ~ político political refugee (who has been granted asylum)

asilar [A1] *vt* (a) (acoger) ‹anciano/huérfano› to take ... into care; ‹refugiado› to grant ... asylum (b) (internar) to put ... in a home
■ **asilarse** *v pron* «anciano/huérfano» to take refuge; «refugiado» to seek asylum

asilo *m* [1] (Servs Socs) home, institution; (para vagabundos, mujeres maltratadas) shelter; ~ de ancianos or de la tercera edad old people's home [2] (Pol) asylum; pedir ~ político to seek political asylum

asimétrico -ca *adj* asymmetric

asimilación *f* assimilation

asimilar [A1] *vt* [1] ‹alimentos/ideas/cultura› to assimilate [2] (en boxeo) ‹golpes› to take, soak up (colloq)

asimismo *adv* (a) (también) also (b) (igualmente) likewise

asir [I10] *vt* (liter) to seize, grasp; ~ a algn DE or POR algo: la asió de un brazo he seized o grasped her arm
■ **asirse** *v pron* (liter) ~se DE or A algo: se asió a la cuerda she grabbed (hold of) o seized the rope; caminaban asidos de la mano they walked hand in hand

asistencia *f* [1] (presencia) attendance; ~ A algo attendance AT sth [2] (ayuda) assistance; prestarle ~ a algn to give sb assistance; ~ en carretera breakdown service; ~ médica (servicio) medical care; (atención médica) medical attention; ~ pública (en CS) municipal health service (*esp for emergencies*); ~ técnica after-sales service [3] (Dep) assist

asistencial *adj* welfare (*before n*)

asistenta *f* (Esp) cleaning lady o woman

asistente *mf* [1] (ayudante) assistant; ~ social social worker [2] (frml) los ~s (a una reunión) those present; (a un espectáculo) the audience

asistido -da *adj* assisted

asistir [I1] *vi* (estar presente) ~ A algo ‹a reunión/acto/clases› to attend sth; asistió a una sola clase he only came/went to one class; ~ a misa to go to o attend Mass
■ ~ *vt* (frml) (ayudar): en el consulado lo ~án you will receive assistance at the consulate (frml); ~ a los pobres to care for the poor

asma *f‡* asthma

asmático -ca *adj/m,f* asthmatic

asno *m* (Zool) donkey; (tonto) (fam) dimwit (colloq)

asociación *f* association; **∼ de ideas** association of ideas

asociado -da *adj* associate (*before n*)
■ *m,f* (Com) associate; (de club, asociación) member

asociar [A1] *vt* ⟨*ideas/palabras*⟩ to associate; **∼ algo/a algn CON algo/algn** to associate sth/sb WITH sth/sb; **no logro ∼la con nada** I can't place her
■ **asociarse** *v pron* (a) «*empresas/comerciantes*» to collaborate; **∼se CON algn** to go into partnership WITH sb (b) «*hechos/factores*» to combine (c) (a grupo, club) **∼se A algo** to become a member OF sth

asolar [A1 *or* A10] *vt* «*guerra/huracán/sequía*» to devastate

asoleada *f* (Andes) (de una persona): **pegarse una ∼** (fam) to sunbathe

asoleado -da *adj* sunny

asolear [A1] *vt* (exponer al sol) ⟨*ropa*⟩ to hang ... out in the sun; ⟨*uvas*⟩ to dry ... in the sun
■ **asolearse** *v pron* (AmL) to sunbathe

asomar [A1] *vi* to show; **empiezan a ∼ los primeros brotes** the first shoots begin to show *o* appear
■ **∼** *vt* ⟨*cabeza*⟩: **asomó la cabeza por la ventanilla** she stuck her head out of the window; **abrió la puerta y asomó la cabeza** she opened the door and stuck her head out/in
■ **asomarse** *v pron*: **∼se POR algo** to lean out OF sth; **se asomó a la ventana** she looked out of the window; **se ∼on al balcón** they came out onto the balcony

asombrar [A1] *vt* to amaze, astonish; **me asombró su reacción** I was astonished *o* taken aback by his reaction
■ **asombrarse** *v pron* to be astonished *o* amazed; **se asombró con los resultados** she was amazed *o* astonished at the results; **yo ya no me asombro por nada** nothing surprises me any more

asombro *m* astonishment; **no salía de su ∼** he couldn't get over his surprise

asombroso -sa *adj* amazing, astonishing

asonante *adj* assonant

asorocharse [A1] *v pron* (a) (Chi, Per) (por la altura) to get mountain *o* altitude sickness (b) (Chi) (por calor, vergüenza) to flush

aspa *f*⚇ (de molino) sail; (de ventilador) blade; (cruz) cross

aspaviento *m*: **deja de hacer ∼s** stop getting in such a flap

aspecto *m* **1** (a) (de persona, lugar) look, appearance; **un hombre de ∼ distinguido** a distinguished-looking man; **¿qué ∼ tiene?** what does he look like?; **a juzgar por su ∼** judging by the look of her; **tiene mal ∼** «*persona*» she doesn't look well; «*cosa*» it doesn't look nice (b) (de problema, asunto): **no me gusta el ∼ que van tomando las cosas** I don't like the way things are going *o* looking **2** (rasgo, faceta) aspect; **en ese ∼ tienes razón** in that respect you're right

aspereza *f* **1** (a) (de superficie, piel) roughness (b) (de sabor) sharpness; (de voz, clima) harshness **2** (parte áspera): **usar papel de lija para quitar las ∼s** use sandpaper to remove any roughness; **limar ∼s** to smooth things over

áspero -ra *adj* **1** ⟨*superficie/piel*⟩ rough; ⟨*tela*⟩ coarse **2** (a) ⟨*sabor*⟩ sharp (b) ⟨*voz/sonido/clima*⟩ harsh **3** (a) (en el trato) abrupt, surly (b) ⟨*discusión*⟩ acrimonious

aspersor *m* sprinkler

aspiración *f* **1** (deseo, ambición) aspiration **2** (Fisiol) inhalation; (Ling) aspiration; (Mús) breath

aspiradora *f*, **aspirador** *m* (electrodoméstico) vacuum cleaner; **pasé la ∼ por la habitación** I vacuumed *o* (BrE) hoovered the bedroom

aspirante *mf*: **las ∼s al título** the contenders for the title; **ocho ∼s al puesto de redactor** eight candidates *o* applicants for the post of editor

aspirar [A1] *vi* **1** (desear, pretender) **∼ A algo/hacer algo** to aspire TO sth/do sth **2** (a) «*aparato*» to suck; «*aspiradora*» to pick up (b) (Fisiol) to breathe in (c) (AmL) (pasar la aspiradora) to vacuum, hoover (BrE)
■ **∼** *vt* (a) «*aparato*» to suck up *o* in; «*aspiradora*» to pick up (b) (Fisiol) to inhale (c) (Ling) to aspirate

aspirina *f* aspirin

asqueante *adj* sickening, nauseating

asquear [A1] *vt* (dar asco a) to sicken; (aburrir, hartar): **está asqueado de todo** he's fed up with everything (colloq)

asqueroso -sa *adj* **1** (a) ⟨*libro/película*⟩ digusting, filthy (b) ⟨*olor/comida/costumbre*⟩ disgusting, revolting (c) (sucio) filthy **2** (lascivo): **¡viejo ∼!** you dirty old man!

asquiento -ta *adj* (AmL) ▶ ASQUEROSO 1

asta *f* (a) (de bandera) flagpole; **con la bandera a media ∼** with the flag at half-mast (b) (cuerno) horn (c) (de lanza, flecha) shaft

astabandera *f* (Méx) flagpole

asterisco *m* asterisk

asteroide *m* asteroid

astigmatismo *m* astigmatism

astilla *f* (a) (fragmento) chip; (de madera, hueso) splinter; **se me metió una ∼ en el dedo** I have a splinter in my finger (b) **astillas** *fpl* (para el fuego) kindling

astillarse [A1] *v pron* «*madera/hueso*» to splinter; «*piedra*» to chip

astillero *m* shipyard

astracán *m* astrakhan

astringente *adj* ⟨*loción*⟩ astringent; ⟨*alimento/medicamento*⟩ binding (*before n*)
■ *m* astringent

astro *m* (Astrol, Astron) heavenly body; (Espec) star

astrología *f* astrology

astrólogo -ga *m,f* astrologist

astronauta *mf* astronaut

astronomía *f* astronomy

astronómico -ca *adj* astronomical

astrónomo -ma *m,f* astronomer

astucia *f* (a) (cualidad — de sagaz) astuteness, shrewdness; (— de ladino) (pey) craftiness, cunning; **la ∼ del zorro** the slyness of a fox (b) (ardid) trick, ploy

astuto -ta *adj* (sagaz) shrewd, astute; (ladino) (pey) crafty, sly, cunning

a

asueto *m* time off; **tomarse un día de** ∼ to take a day off

asumir [I1] *vt* 1 (a) ⟨cargo/tarea/responsabilidad⟩ to take on, assume (frml); ⟨riesgo⟩ to take (b) (adoptar) ⟨actitud⟩ to assume (frml) (c) (aceptar) to come to terms with 2 (AmL) (suponer) to assume

asunceno -na, asunceño -ña *adj* of/from Asunción
■ *m,f* person from Asunción

Asunción *f* (Geog) Asunción

asunto *m* (a) (cuestión, problema) matter; ∼**s de negocios** business matters; ∼**s exteriores** (Esp) foreign affairs; **un** ∼ **muy delicado** a very delicate matter *o* issue; **está implicado en un** ∼ **de drogas** he's mixed up in something to do with drugs; **no es** ∼ **mío/tuyo** it's none of my/your business (b) (pey) (relación amorosa) affair

asustado -da *adj* (atemorizado) frightened; (preocupado) worried

asustar [A1] *vt* to frighten; **me asustó cuando se puso tan serio** he gave me a fright when he went all serious
■ **asustarse** *v pron* to get frightened; **me asusté cuando vi que no estaba allí** I got a fright *o* I got worried when I saw he wasn't there; **no se asuste, no es nada grave** there's no need to worry, it's nothing serious

atacante *mf* attacker, assailant (frml)

atacar [A2] *vt* to attack

atado *m* (a) (de ropa) bundle (b) (CS) (de espinacas, zanahorias) bunch; **ser un** ∼ **de nervios** (CS) to be a bundle of nerves (c) (RPl) (de cigarrillos) pack (AmE), packet (BrE)

ataduras *fpl* ties (*pl*)

atajada *f* (CS) save

atajador -dora *m,f* (Méx) (*m*) ballboy; (*f*) ballgirl

atajar [A1] *vt* 1 (a) (AmL) (agarrar) ⟨pelota⟩ to catch (b) (Esp) (interceptar) ⟨pase/pelota⟩ to intercept 2 (a) ⟨golpe/puñetazo⟩ to parry, block (b) ⟨persona⟩ (agarrar) to stop, catch; (interrumpir, detener) to stop 3 ⟨enfermedad/problema⟩ to keep … in check; ⟨incendio⟩ to contain; ⟨rumor⟩ to quell

atajo *m* short cut

atañer [E7] *vi* (*en 3ª pers*) to concern; **por lo que a mí atañe** as far as I'm concerned

ataque *m* 1 (a) (Dep, Mil) attack; ∼ **aéreo** air strike (b) (verbal) attack 2 (Med) attack; ∼ **de asma** asthma attack; ∼ **al corazón** heart attack; ∼ **epiléptico** epileptic fit; **me dio un** ∼ **de nervios** I got into a panic; **un** ∼ **de risa** a fit of hysterics

atar [A1] *vt* 1 (a) ⟨caja/paquete⟩ to tie; **le até el pelo con una cinta** I tied her hair back with a ribbon (b) ⟨persona/caballo⟩ to tie … up; ⟨cabra⟩ to tether; **lo** ∼**on de pies y manos** they bound him hand and foot; **ató al perro a un poste** she tied the dog to a lamppost 2 ⟨trabajo/hijos⟩ to tie … down

■ **atarse** *v pron* (refl) ⟨zapatos/cordones⟩ to tie up, do up; ⟨pelo⟩ to tie up

atarantado -da *adj* (a) (Col, Méx, Per fam) (por golpe) dazed, stunned (b) (Méx, Per fam) (confundido) in a spin, dazed (c) (Chi fam) (precipitado) harum-scarum (colloq)

atarantar [A1] *vt* (Col, Méx, Per fam): **con tantas preguntas me** ∼**on** they made my head spin with all their questions; **el golpe lo atarantó** the blow left him dazed
■ **atarantarse** *v pron* (a) (Col, Méx, Per fam) (aturdirse, confundirse) to get flustered, get in a dither (b) (Chi fam) (precipitarse): **no te atarantes** don't rush into it (colloq)

atardecer¹ [E3] *v impers* to get dark

atardecer² *m* dusk; **al** ∼ at dusk

atareado -da *adj* busy

atascar [A2] *vt* (a) ⟨cañería⟩ to block (b) (Méx) ⟨motor⟩ to stall
■ **atascarse** *v pron* 1 (a) «cañería/fregadero» to block, get blocked (b) «tráfico» to get snarled up 2 (a) «mecanismo» to jam, seize up (b) (Méx) «motor» to stall

atasco *m* (a) (de tráfico) traffic jam; (en proceso) holdup, delay (b) (en tubería) blockage

ataúd *m* coffin

ateísmo *m* atheism

atemorizar [A4] *vt* (liter) ⟨persona⟩ to frighten, intimidate; ⟨barrio/población⟩ to terrorize

Atenas *f* Athens

atención¹ *f* 1 (a) (concentración) attention; **pon/presta** ∼ **a esto** pay attention to this; **con** ∼ attentively (b) **llamar la** ∼: **se viste así para llamar la** ∼ he dresses like that to attract attention (to himself); **una chica que llama la** ∼ a very striking girl; **me llamó la** ∼ **que estuviera sola** I was surprised she was alone; **llamarle la** ∼ **a algn** (reprenderlo) to reprimand sb (frml), to give sb a talking to 2 (a) (en hotel, tienda) service; 🟒 **horario de atención al público** (en banco) hours of business; (en oficina pública) opening hours (b) (cortesía): **nos colmaron de atenciones** we were showered with attention *o* (BrE) attentions; **no tuvo ninguna** ∼ **con ella a pesar de su hospitalidad** he didn't show the slightest appreciation despite her hospitality

atención² *interj* (a) (para que se atienda) attention; **¡**∼**, por favor!** (your) attention, please! (b) (para avisar de peligro) look out!, watch out!

atender [E8] *vi* (a) (prestar atención) to pay attention; ∼ **A algo/algn** to pay attention TO sth/sb (b) (cumplir con) ∼ **A algo** ⟨a compromisos/gastos/obligaciones⟩ to meet sth (c) (prestar un servicio): **el doctor no atiende los martes** the doctor does not see anyone on Tuesdays; **en esa tienda atienden muy mal** the service is very bad in that store
■ ∼ *vt* 1 (a) ⟨paciente⟩: **¿qué médico la atiende?** which doctor usually sees you?; **los atendieron enseguida en el hospital** they were seen immediately at the hospital; **no tiene quien lo**

atienda he has no one to look after him **(b)** ⟨*cliente*⟩ to attend to, see to; (en tienda) to serve; ¿la están atendiendo? are you being served? **(c)** ⟨*asunto*⟩ to deal with; ⟨*llamada*⟩ to answer; ⟨*demanda*⟩ to meet ▣ ⟨*consejo/advertencia*⟩ to listen to ■ **atenderse** *v pron* (AmL): ¿con qué médico se atiende? which doctor usually sees you?

atenerse [E27] *v pron* **(a)** (ajustarse, someterse) ~ A algo ⟨*a las reglas*⟩ to abide BY *o* comply WITH sth; ⟨*a las órdenes*⟩ to obey sth; ⟨*a las consecuencias*⟩ to live with *o* abide BY sth; no sé a qué atenerme I don't know where I stand **(b)** (limitarse): si nos atenemos a lo que dijeron ellos ... if we go by what they said ...; aténgase a los hechos confine yourself to the facts

atentado *m* **(a)** (ataque): un ~ terrorista a terrorist attack; un ~ contra el presidente an assassination attempt on the president **(b)** (afrenta) ~ CONTRA *or* A algo ⟨*a honor/dignidad*⟩ affront TO sth; un ~ contra la moral an offense against decency

atentamente *adv* **(a)** ⟨*escuchar/mirar*⟩ attentively, carefully **(b)** (amablemente) thoughtfully, kindly; lo saluda ~ (Corresp) sincerely (AmE), yours faithfully/sincerely (BrE)

atentar [A1] *vi*: ~on contra su vida they made an attempt on her life; ~ contra la seguridad del Estado to threaten national security

atento -ta *adj* ▢ **(a)** (que presta atención) ⟨*alumno/público*⟩ attentive; estar ~ (A algo) to pay attention (TO sth) **(b)** (alerta): estáte ~ y avísame si viene alguien stay alert and let me know if anyone comes; estar ~ A algo to be on the alert FOR sth ▢ **(a)** (amable) ⟨*esposo/anfitrión/camarero*⟩ attentive; ser ~ CON algn to be kind TO sb **(b)** (cortés) courteous

atenuante *adj* extenuating ■ *m or f* mitigating factor, extenuating circumstance

atenuar [A18] *vt* **(a)** (disminuir, moderar) ⟨*luz*⟩ to dim; ⟨*color*⟩ to tone down; deberías ~ el tono de tus críticas you should tone down your criticism **(b)** (Der) ⟨*responsabilidad*⟩ to reduce, lessen

ateo, atea *adj* atheistic ■ *m,f* atheist

aterrador -dora *adj* terrifying

aterrar [A1] *vt* ⟨*persona*⟩ to terrify; le aterra la idea she's terrified at the thought

aterrizaje *m* landing; un ~ forzoso an emergency landing

aterrizar [A4] *vi* to land, touch down

aterrorizado -da *adj* terrified

aterrorizar [A4] *vt* to terrorize

atesorar [A1] *vt* ⟨*dinero*⟩ to amass

atestado -da *adj* packed, crammed; ~ DE algo packed *o* crammed full OF sth; el salón estaba ~ (de gente) the hall was packed *o* crammed (with people)

atestiguar [A16] *vt* **(a)** (Der) to testify **(b)** (probar) to bear witness to

atiborrar [A1] *vt* ~ algo/a algn DE algo to stuff sth/sb WITH sth; atiborrado de gente packed *o* jam-packed with people ■ **atiborrarse** *v pron* ~se DE algo to stuff oneself WITH sth

ático *m* **(a)** (apartamento) top-floor apartment *o* (BrE) flat; (de lujo) penthouse; (de techo bajo) garret (AmE), attic flat (BrE) **(b)** (desván) attic, loft (BrE)

atienda, atiendas, etc ▶ ATENDER

atinado -da *adj* ⟨*respuesta/comentario*⟩ pertinent, spot-on (colloq); ⟨*decisión/medida*⟩ sensible, wise; ⟨*solución*⟩ sensible

atinar [A1] *vi*: ~ en el blanco to hit the target; ¡atinaste! you're dead right!; no atiné a decir nada I couldn't say a word; ~ CON algo ⟨*con solución/respuesta*⟩ to hit ON *o* UPON sth, come up WITH sth; atinaste con el regalo the gift you got him/her was perfect; no atinaba con la calle I couldn't find the street

atizador *m* poker

atizar [A4] *vt* ⟨*fuego*⟩ to poke

Atlántico *m*: el (océano) ~ the Atlantic (Ocean)

Atlántida *f*: la ~ Atlantis

atlas *m* (*pl* ~) atlas

atleta *mf* athlete

atlético -ca *adj* **(a)** ⟨*club/competición*⟩ athletics (*before n*) **(b)** ⟨*figura*⟩ athletic

atletismo *m* athletics

atmósfera *f* atmosphere

atmosférico -ca *adj* atmospheric

atole *m* (Méx) hot corn *o* maize drink

atolladero *m* **(a)** (lugar cenagoso) mire **(b)** (aprieto, apuro) predicament, awkward situation

atolondrado -da *adj* **(a)** [SER] (impetuoso) rash, impetuous; (despistado) scatterbrained **(b)** [ESTAR] (por golpe) dazed, stunned ■ *m,f* scatterbrain

atolondrar [A1] *vt* **(a)** (confundir) to fluster **(b)** «*golpe*» to daze, stun ■ **atolondrarse** *v pron* **(a)** (confundirse) to get flustered **(b)** (precipitarse): no te atolondres, piénsalo bien don't rush into it, think it over carefully

atómico -ca *adj* atomic

atomizador *m* spray, atomizer

átomo *m* atom

atónito -ta *adj* astonished, amazed; se quedó mirándola ~ he stared at her in amazement

atontado -da *adj* (por golpe, asombro) stunned, dazed; (distraído): contesta, que estás medio ~ answer me, you're in a daze; *ver tb* ATONTAR

atontar [A1] *vt* «*golpe*» to stun, daze; estas pastillas me atontan these pills make me groggy; la televisión los atonta television turns them into vegetables *o* zombies

atorar [A1] *vt* ▢ (esp AmL) ⟨*cañería*⟩ to block (up) ▢ (Méx) (sujetar): atoramos la puerta con una silla we jammed the door shut/open with a chair; atóralo con este alambre secure it with this bit of wire ■ **atorarse** *v pron* (esp AmL) **(a)** (atragantarse) to choke **(b)** «*cañería*» to get blocked; «*puerta/cajón*» to jam; (+ *me/te/le etc*) se me atoró el cierre my zipper got stuck; se le atoró el chicle en la garganta the chewing gum got stuck in her throat

atormentar [A1] *vt* «*persona*» (físicamente) to torture; (mentalmente) to torment ■ **atormentarse** *v pron* (*refl*) to torment oneself

atornillar [A1] *vt* to screw on (*o* down *etc*)

atorrante _adj_ (a) (Andes, CS fam) (holgazán) lazy; (desaseado) scruffy (b) (Bol, RPl fam) (sinvergüenza) crooked (c) (Col, Per fam) (pesado, cargante): **no seas ~** don't be such a pain in the neck (colloq)
■ _mf_ (a) (Andes, CS fam) (vagabundo) tramp; (holgazán) good-for-nothing, layabout; (desaseado) slob (colloq) (b) (Bol, RPl fam) (sinvergüenza): **es un ~** he's a bit of a crook (colloq) (c) (Col, Per fam) (pesado, cargante) pain in the neck (colloq)

atosigar [A3] _vt_ (importunar) to pester, hassle (colloq); (presionar) to pressure (AmE), to pressurize (BrE)

atrabancado -da _adj_ (Méx fam) (precipitado) rash, reckless

atracador -dora _m,f_ (de banco) bank robber, raider (journ); (de persona) mugger

atracar [A2] _vi_ «_barco_» to dock, berth
■ **~** _vt_ (asaltar) ‹_banco_› to hold up; ‹_persona_› to mug

atracción _f_ attraction; **la ~ más concurrida** the most popular attraction; **una ~ turística** a tourist attraction; **las atracciones están en la playa** the funfair is on the beach; **siente una gran ~ por ella** he feels strongly attracted to her

atraco _m_ (a banco) robbery, raid (journ); (a persona) mugging; **~ a mano armada** armed robbery _o_ (journ) raid

atracón _m_ (fam): **se dio un ~ de paella** he stuffed himself with paella (colloq)

atractivo¹ -va _adj_ attractive

atractivo² _m_ (a) (encanto) charm, attractiveness; **tiene mucho ~** she's very charming; **el mayor ~ de la ciudad** the city's main attraction _o_ appeal (b) (interés) appeal; **para mí viajar no tiene ningún ~** travel holds no appeal to me

atraer [E23] _vt_ (a) (Fís) to attract (b) (traer, hacer venir) to attract; **un truco para ~ al público** a gimmick to attract the public (c) (cautivar, gustar): **se siente atraído por ella** he feels attracted to her; **no me atrae la idea** the idea doesn't attract me _o_ appeal to me (d) ‹_atención/miradas_› to attract
■ **atraerse** _v pron_ (a) (ganarse) ‹_amistad_› to gain; ‹_interés_› to attract (b) (recípr) to attract (each other)

atragantarse [A1] _v pron_ (al tragar) to choke; **se le atragantó una espina** he choked on a fish bone

atraiga, atrajo, etc ▶ ATRAER

atrancar [A2] _vt_ ‹_cañería_› to block (up); ‹_puerta/ventana_› to bar
■ **atrancarse** _v pron_ (a) «_cañería_» to get blocked (b) (fam) «_persona_» (en tarea) to get stuck

atrapar [A1] _vt_ to catch

atrás _adv_ ⓵ (en el espacio) (a) (expresando dirección) back; **muévelo para** _or_ **hacia ~** move it back; **da un paso ~** take one step back (b) ¡**~!** (_como interj_) get back! (c) (lugar, parte): **está allí ~** it's back there; **me senté ~** (en coche) I sat in the back; (en clase, cine) I sat at the back; **la parte de ~** the back; **me estaba quedando ~** I was getting left behind; **dejamos ~ la ciudad** we left the city behind us; **estar hasta ~** (Méx fam) to be as high as a kite (colloq)

⓶ (en el tiempo): **sucedió tres años ~** it happened three years ago; **había sucedido tres años ~** it had happened three years earlier _o_ before
③ **atrás de** (_loc prep_) (AmL) behind

atrasado -da _adj_ ⓵ (a) [ESTAR] ‹_reloj_› slow (b) (con respecto a lo esperado): **está muy ~ en los estudios** he's really behind in his studies; **el proyecto está ~** the project is behind schedule; **el tren llegó/salió ~** (AmL) the train arrived/left late; **apúrate que voy ~** (AmL) hurry up, I'm late
⓶ (acumulado, pasado): **tengo mucho sueño ~** I have a lot of sleep to catch up on; **tengo trabajo ~** I'm behind with my work; **todas las cuotas atrasadas** all outstanding payments; **un ejemplar ~** a back number _o_ issue
③ (a) (anticuado, desfasado) ‹_ideas/persona_› old-fashioned (b) ‹_país/pueblo_› backward

atrasar [A1] _vt_ (a) ‹_reloj_› to put back (b) ‹_reunión/viaje_› to postpone, put back
■ **~** _vi_ ‹_reloj_› to lose time
■ **atrasarse** _v pron_ ⓵ (a) «_reloj_» to lose time; **se me ha atrasado 15 minutos** it's 15 minutes slow (b) (esp AmL) (llegar tarde) «_avión/tren_» to be late, be delayed; «_persona_» to be late ⓶ (a) (en estudios, trabajo, pagos) to fall behind, get behind (b) «_país/industria_» to fall behind

atraso _m_ (a) (de país, ideas) backwardness (b) (esp AmL) (retraso) delay; **perdona el ~** I'm sorry about the delay; **salió con unos minutos de ~** it left a few minutes late; **viene con una hora de ~** it's (running) an hour late

atravesado -da _adj_ (cruzado): **el piano estaba ~ en el pasillo** the piano was stuck (_o_ placed _etc_) across the corridor; **un árbol/camión ~ en la carretera** a tree lying across/a truck blocking the road

atravesar [A5] _vt_ ⓵ (a) ‹_río/frontera_› to cross; **atravesó el río a nado** she swam across the river (b) «_bala/espada_» to go through; **le atravesó la pierna** it went through his leg (c) ‹_crisis/período_› to go through ⓶ (colocar) to put ... across
■ **atravesarse** _v pron_: **se nos atravesó un camión** a truck crossed right in front of us; **se me atravesó una espina en la garganta** I got a fish bone stuck in my throat

atraviesa, atraviesas, etc ▶ ATRAVESAR

atrayente _adj_ appealing

atreverse [E1] _v pron_ to dare; **¡anda, atrévete!** go on then, I dare you (to); **no me atrevo a decírselo** I daren't tell him; **¿cómo te atreves a pegarle?** how dare you hit him?; **¿a que conmigo no te atreves?** I bet you wouldn't dare take me on

atrevido -da _adj_ (a) (insolente) sassy (AmE colloq), cheeky (BrE colloq) (b) (osado) ‹_escote/persona_› daring; ‹_chiste_› risqué; ‹_diseño_› bold (c) (valiente) brave

atrevimiento _m_ nerve

atribuir [I20] _vt_ (a) **~ algo A algn/algo** to attribute sth to sb/sth; **le atribuyen algo que no dijo** they attribute words to him which he did not say; **le atribuyen propiedades curativas** it is held _o_ believed to have healing powers (b) ‹_funciones/poder_› to confer
■ **atribuirse** _v pron_ (refl) (a) ‹_éxito/autoría_› to claim (b) ‹_poderes/responsabilidad_› to assume

atributo *m* (cualidad) attribute, quality; (símbolo) insignia

atril *m* (para partituras) music stand; (para libros) lectern

atrincherar [A1] *vt* to entrench

■ **atrincherarse** *v pron* to entrench oneself

atrocidad *f* (cualidad) atrocity; (acto) atrocity; ¡qué ~! how atrocious! *o* how awful!

atrofiarse [A1] *v pron* to atrophy

atropellado -da *adj*: ¡qué ~ eres! you always do things in such a rush!

atropellar [A1] *vt* (a) «*coche/camión*» to knock ... down; (pasando por encima) to run ... over (b) ⟨*libertades/derechos*⟩ to violate, ride roughshod over

■ **atropellarse** *v pron* (a) (al hablar, actuar) to rush (b) (*recípr*) (empujarse): salieron corriendo, atropellándose unos a otros they came running out, pushing and shoving as they went

atropello *m* (abuso) outrage; ~ DE *or* A algo violation OF sth

atroz *adj* atrocious

atte. (Corresp) (= **atentamente**): lo saluda ~ sincerely yours (AmE), yours sincerely/faithfully (BrE)

atuendo *m* (frml) outfit

atún *m* tuna (fish)

aturdimiento *m* (perplejidad) bewilderment; (por golpe, noticia) daze

aturdir [I1] *vt* (a) «*música/ruido*»: la música te aturdía the music was deafening; este ruido me aturde I can't think straight with this noise (b) (dejar perplejo) to bewilder, confuse (c) «*golpe/noticia/suceso*» to stun, daze

■ **aturdirse** *v pron* (confundirse) to get confused *o* flustered; (por golpe, noticia) to be stunned *o* dazed

audacia *f* (valor) courage, daring; (osadía) boldness, audacity

audaz *adj* (valiente) brave, courageous; (osado) daring, bold

audición *f* [1] (facultad de oír) hearing [2] (prueba) audition [3] (RPl) (Rad) program*

audiencia *f* [1] (cita) audience; pedir ~ to seek an audience [2] (Der) (a) (tribunal) court (b) (sesión) hearing [3] (espectadores, oyentes) audience; un programa de mucha ~ a program with a large audience; horas de máxima/mayor ~ peak viewing/prime time

audífono *m* (a) (para sordos) hearing aid, deaf-aid (BrE) (b) (de radio) earphone (c) **audífonos** *mpl* (AmL) headphones (*pl*)

audiolibro *m* audiobook

audiomensajería *f* voice mail

audiovisual *adj* audiovisual

■ *m* audiovisual presentation

auditar [A1] *vt* to audit

auditivo -va *adj* (a) ⟨*nervio/conducto*⟩ auditory (b) ⟨*problemas*⟩ hearing (*before n*)

auditor -tora *m,f* (a) (persona) auditor (b) **auditora** *f* (empresa) auditors (*pl*), firm of auditors

auditoría *f* audit

auditorio *m* (público) audience; (sala) auditorium

auge *m* (a) (punto culminante) peak; en el ~ de su carrera at the peak *o* height of his career (b)

(aumento): la comida vegetariana está en ~ vegetarian food is on the increase; un período de ~ económico a period of economic growth

augurar [A1] *vt* ⟨*futuro*⟩ to predict, foretell

augurio *m* (presagio): sus ~s no se cumplieron his predictions did not come true; es un ~ de mala suerte it's (a sign of) bad luck *o* a bad omen

aula *f̣* (a) (en escuela) classroom (b) (en universidad) lecture (*o* seminar *etc*) room; ~ magna main lecture theater* *o* hall

aullar [A23] *vi* «*lobo/viento*» to howl

aullido *m* howl; los ~s del perro the howling of the dog

aumentar [A1] *vt* (a) (en general) to increase; ⟨*precio/sueldo*⟩ to increase, raise (b) (Opt) to magnify

■ ~ *vi* «*temperatura/presión*» to rise; «*velocidad*» to increase; «*precio/producción/valor*» to increase, rise; ~á el frío it will become colder; ~ DE algo ⟨*de volumen/tamaño*⟩ to increase IN sth; aumentó de peso he put on *o* gained weight

aumento *m* (a) (incremento) rise, increase; ~ de peso increase in weight; ~ de temperatura rise in temperature; ~ de precio price rise *o* increase; ~ de sueldo salary increase, pay raise (AmE), pay rise (BrE) (b) (Opt) magnification; lentes de mucho ~ glasses with very strong lenses

aun *adv* even; ni ~ trabajando 12 horas al día (not) even if we worked 12 hours a day; ~ así, creo que ... even so, I think ...; ni ~ así me quedaría even then I wouldn't stay

aún *adv* [1] (todavía) (a) (en frases afirmativas *o* interrogativas) still; ~ falta un mes there's still a month to go; ¿~ estás aquí? are you still here? (b) (en frases negativas) yet; ~ no ha llamado she hasn't called yet [2] (en comparaciones) even

aunar [A23] *vt* ⟨*ideas*⟩ to combine

■ **aunarse** *v pron* to unite, come together

aunque *conj* [1] (a pesar de que) (a) (refiriéndose a hechos) although; ~ no estaba bien fue a trabajar although he wasn't well he went to work (b) (respondiendo a una objeción) (+ *subjuntivo*): es millonario, ~ no lo parezca he's a millionaire though he may not look it; ~ no lo creas ... believe it or not ... [2] (refiriéndose a posibilidades, hipótesis) (+ *subjuntivo*) even if; iré ~ llueva I'll go even if it rains

au pair /o'per/ *mf* (*pl* **-pairs**) au pair

aura *f̣* (halo) aura

aureola *f* (a) (Relig) halo, aureole (liter) (b) (de gloria, fama) aura (c) (Astron) aureole, corona (d) (CS) (de mancha) ring

auricular *m* (a) (del teléfono) receiver (b) **auriculares** *mpl* (Audio) headphones (*pl*), earphones (*pl*)

aurora *f* dawn

auscultar [A1] *vt* to auscultate (tech); el médico me auscultó the doctor listened to my chest (with a stethoscope)

ausencia *f* (a) (de persona) absence; brillar por su ~ to be conspicuous by one's absence; el orden brilla por su ~ there's a distinct lack of order (b) (no existencia) lack, absence (c) (frml) (inasistencia) absence

ausentarse [A1] *v pron* (fml) to go away; pidió permiso para ∼ un momento he asked to leave the room (*o class etc*)

ausente *adj* [ESTAR] (a) (no presente) absent; todos los alumnos ∼s all those pupils who are absent (b) (distraído) ⟨*persona*⟩ distracted; ⟨*mirada/expresión*⟩ absent (*before n*)

ausentismo *m* absenteeism; ∼ escolar absenteeism, truancy

auspiciar [A1] *vt* (a) (patrocinar) ⟨*exposición/función*⟩ to back, sponsor (b) (propiciar, facilitar) to foster, promote

austeridad *f* austerity

austero -ra *adj* ⟨*vida/costumbres/estilo*⟩ austere; es ∼ en el comer he is frugal in his eating habits

austral *adj* southern

Australia *f* Australia

australiano -na *adj/m,f* Australian

Austria *f*. Austria

austriaco -ca, austríaco -ca *adj/m,f* Austrian

autenticar [A2] *vt* (a) ⟨*firma/documento*⟩ to authenticate (b) (RPl) ⟨*fotocopia*⟩ to attest

autenticidad *f* authenticity

auténtico -ca *adj* (a) ⟨*cuadro*⟩ genuine, authentic; ⟨*perla/piel*⟩ real; ⟨*documento*⟩ authentic (b) ⟨*interés/cariño/persona*⟩ genuine (c) ⟨*pesadilla/catástrofe*⟩ (*delante del n*) real (*before n*)

autista *adj* autistic

auto *m* [1] (esp CS) (Auto) car, automobile (AmE); ∼ de carrera (CS) racing car; autitos chocadores (RPl) bumper cars [2] (Lit, Teatr) play

autoabastecerse [E3] *v pron* to be self-sufficient; ∼ DE *or* EN algo to be self-sufficient IN sth

autoadhesivo -va *adj* self-adhesive

autobiografía *f* autobiography

autobomba *m* (RPl) water tender, fire engine

autobús *m* bus; ∼ de dos pisos double-decker bus; ∼ de línea (inter-city) bus

autocar *m* (Esp) bus, coach (BrE)

autocine *m* drive-in

autocross *m* autocross

autóctono -na *adj* ⟨*flora/fauna*⟩ indigenous, native; el elefante es ∼ de la India the elephant is indigenous *o* native to India

autodefensa *f* self-defence

autodeterminación *f* self-determination

autodidacta *mf* self-taught person, autodidact (fml)

autodisciplina *f* self-discipline

auto-escuela, autoescuela *f* driving school

autoestop *m* ▶ AUTOSTOP

autoestopista *mf* hitchhiker

autogol *m* own goal

autografiar [A17] *vt* to autograph

autógrafo *m* autograph

autómata *m* automaton

automático¹ -ca *adj* automatic; es ∼, se sienta a ver la tele y se queda dormido (fam) it happens every time, he sits down in front of the TV and falls asleep

automático² *m* (a) (Fot) self-timer; (Elec) circuit breaker, trip switch (b) (cierre) snap fastener (AmE), press stud (BrE)

automatizado -da *adj* automated

automatizar [A4] *vt* to automate

automedicación *f* self-medication

automercado *m* (AmC) supermarket

automotor¹ -triz *adj* (fml) ⟨*vehículo/industria*⟩ motor (*before n*)

automotor² *m* (Ferr) railcar (*diesel or electric motor unit*)

automóvil *m* car, automobile (AmE)

automovilismo *m* motoring; ∼ deportivo motor racing

automovilista *mf* motorist

automovilístico -ca *adj* ⟨*carrera*⟩ motor (*before n*); ⟨*accidente*⟩ car (*before n*)

autonomía *f* [1] (a) (independencia) autonomy; (Pol) autonomy, self-government; obran con ∼ they act autonomously (b) (en Esp, comunidad autónoma) autonomous *or* self-governing region [2] (Aviac, Náut) range

autonómico -ca *adj* (a) (independiente) autonomous (b) ⟨*presidente/elecciones*⟩ (en Esp) regional

autónomo -ma *adj* (a) ⟨*departamento/entidad*⟩ autonomous (b) (Pol) (en Esp) ⟨*región*⟩ autonomous (c) ⟨*trabajador*⟩ self-employed; ⟨*fotógrafo/periodista*⟩ freelance
■ *m,f* (trabajador) self-employed worker *o* person; (fotógrafo, periodista) freelancer

autopista *f* expressway (AmE), motorway (BrE); ∼ de peaje *or* (Méx) de cuota turnpike (road) (AmE), toll motorway (BrE); la ∼ de la información (Inf) the information superhighway

autopsia *f* autopsy, post mortem; hacerle la ∼ a algn to perform an autopsy *o* a post mortem on sb

autor -tora *m,f* (a) (de libro, poema) author, writer; (de canción) writer; (de obra teatral) playwright (b) (de delito) perpetrator (fml); el ∼ del gol the goalscorer

autoridad *f* [1] (a) (poder, competencia) authority (b) (persona, institución): la máxima ∼ en el ministerio the top official in the ministry; se entregó a las ∼es she gave herself up to the authorities [2] (experto) authority; una ∼ en la materia an authority on the subject

autoritario -ria *adj* authoritarian

autorización *f* authorization (fml); los menores necesitan la ∼ paterna minors need their parents' consent; no tiene ∼ de sus padres he doesn't have his parents' permission

autorizado -da *adj* ⟨*fuente/portavoz*⟩ official; ⟨*distribuidor*⟩ authorized, official; ⟨*opinión*⟩ expert (*before n*)

autorizar [A4] *vt* **(a)** ⟨*manifestación/ documento/firma*⟩ to authorize; ⟨*aumento/pago/ obra*⟩ to authorize, approve **(b)** ⟨*persona*⟩: **¿quién te autorizó?** who gave you permission?; **lo autoricé para recibir el pago** I authorized him to receive the payment; **me autorizó para salir** he gave me permission to go out; **eso no te autoriza a** *or* **para hablarme así** that doesn't give you the right to talk to me like that

autorretrato *m* self-portrait

autoservicio *m* (tienda) supermarket; (restaurante) self-service restaurant, cafeteria

autostop, auto-stop /auto'(e)stop/ *m* hitchhiking; **hacer** ~ to hitchhike

autosuficiencia *f* self-sufficiency

autosuficiente *adj* **(a)** (Econ) self-sufficient **(b)** (presumido) smug, self-satisfied

autovagón *m* (Per) railcar

autovía *f* divided highway (AmE), dual carriageway (BrE)

auxiliar¹ *adj* **(a)** ⟨*profesor*⟩ assistant (*before n*); ⟨*personal/elementos*⟩ auxiliary (*before n*) **(b)** ⟨*servicios*⟩ auxiliary **(c)** (Tec) auxiliary **(d)** (Inf) peripheral
■ *mf* **(a)** (persona) assistant; ~ **de vuelo** flight attendant **(b)** **auxiliar** *f* (RPl) (Auto) spare tire

auxiliar² [A1] *vt* to help

auxilio *m* (a) (ayuda) help; **pedir** ~ to ask for help; ~ **en carretera** breakdown *o* recovery service; **acudieron en** ~ **de las víctimas** they went to the aid of the victims **(b)** (RPl) (grúa) recovery *o* breakdown truck

Av. *f* (= **Avenida**) Ave.

aval *m* (Com, Fin) guarantee; (respaldo) backing, support; (recomendación) reference

avalancha *f* avalanche

avalar [A1] *vt* (Com, Fin) ⟨*documento*⟩ to guarantee; ⟨*persona/préstamo*⟩ to guarantee, act as guarantor for

avaluar [A18] *vt* (AmL) to value

avalúo *m* (AmL) valuation

avance *m* **(a)** (adelanto) advance; **un** ~ **en este campo** an advance *o* a step forward in this field **(b)** (movimiento) advance; (Mil) advance; (Dep) move forward

avanzado -da *adj* advanced; **de avanzada edad** of advanced years, advanced in years; **a horas tan avanzadas** at such a late hour

avanzar [A4] *vi* **(a)** «*persona/tráfico*» to advance, move forward **(b)** «*ciencia/medicina*» to advance **(c)** «*cinta/rollo*» to wind on **(d)** «*persona*» (en los estudios, el trabajo) to make progress; «*negociaciones/proyecto*» to progress **(e)** «*tiempo*» to draw on
■ ~ *vt* **(a)** (adelantarse) to move forward, advance **(b)** (mover) to move ... forward, advance

avaricia *f* avarice; **la** ~ **rompe el saco** if you're too greedy you end up with nothing

avaricioso -sa, avariento -ta *adj* greedy, avaricious
■ *m,f* greedy *o* avaricious person

avaro -ra *adj* miserly
■ *m,f* miser

avasallador -dora, avasallante *adj* **(a)** ⟨*persona/actitud*⟩ domineering, overbearing **(b)** ⟨*triunfo*⟩ resounding (*before n*)

Avda. *f* (= **Avenida**) Ave.

ave *f‡* bird; ~ **de corral** fowl; ~ **de mal agüero** bird of ill omen; ~ **rapaz** *or* **de rapiña** (Zool) bird of prey; (persona) shark

AVE *m* (= **Alta Velocidad Española**) high-speed train

avecinarse [A1] *v pron* to approach

avejentado -da *adj*: **está muy** ~ he's aged a lot; **un rostro** ~ an old face

avejentar [A1] *vt* to age, make ... look older

avellana *f* hazelnut

avellano *m* hazel

Avemaría *f‡* (Relig) Hail Mary; (Mús) Ave Maria

avena *f* oats (*pl*)

avenida *f* **(a)** (calle) avenue, boulevard **(b)** (de río) freshet, flood

avenido -da *adj*: **bien** ~ well-matched; **es una pareja mal avenida** they don't get on well as a couple

avenirse [I31] *v pron* **(a)** (ponerse de acuerdo) ~**se EN algo** to agree ON sth **(b)** (llevarse bien) ~**se CON algn** to get on WITH sb

aventajado -da *adj* outstanding, excellent

aventajar [A1] *vt* (estar por delante de) to be ahead of; (adelantarse) to overtake, get ahead of

aventar [A5] *vt* **(a)** (Col, Méx, Per) ⟨*pelota/ piedra*⟩ to throw; **le aventé un sopapo** (fam) I smacked *o* (BrE) thumped him (colloq) **(b)** (Méx) (empujar) to push
■ **aventarse** *v pron* **(a)** (Méx fam) (atreverse) to dare; ~**se A hacer algo** to dare to do sth **(b)** (*refl*) (Col, Méx) (arrojarse, tirarse) to throw oneself; **se aventó al agua** he dived into the water

aventón *m* (Méx) (fam) lift; **darle** ~ **a algn** to give sb a lift *o* ride; **pedir** ~ to hitch *o* thumb a lift; **ir de** ~ to go hitching

aventura *f* **(a)** (suceso extraordinario) adventure **(b)** (empresa arriesgada) venture **(c)** (relación amorosa — pasajera) fling; (— ilícita) affair

aventurado -da *adj* risky, hazardous

aventurar [A1] *vt* ⟨*opinión*⟩ to venture, put forward; ⟨*conjetura*⟩ to hazard
■ **aventurarse** *v pron* to venture; **me** ~**ía a decir que ...** I would go so far as to say that ...

aventurero -ra *adj* adventurous
■ *m,f* adventurer

avergonzado -da *adj* **(a)** (por algo reprensible) ashamed; ~ **POR** *or* **DE algo** ashamed OF sth **(b)** (en situación embarazosa) embarrassed

avergonzar [A13] *vt* **(a)** (por algo reprensible): **¿no te avergüenza salir así a la calle?** aren't you ashamed to go out looking like that? **(b)** (en situación embarazosa) to embarrass; **me avergüenza decírselo** I'm embarrassed to tell him
■ **avergonzarse** *v pron* to be ashamed (of oneself); ~**se DE algo** to be ashamed OF sth; **se avergonzó de haberle mentido** she was ashamed of herself for having lied to him

avergüenza, avergüenzas, etc ▶ AVERGONZAR

avería *f* (Auto, Mec) breakdown

averiado -da *adj* [ESTAR] ⟨*coche/máquina*⟩ broken down; ⟨*ascensor/teléfono*⟩ out of order

averiarse [A17] *v pron* to break down
averiguación *f* inquiry
averiguar [A16] *vt* to find out
■ ~ *vi* (Méx) to quarrel, argue; *averiguárselas* (Méx) to manage
aversión *f* aversion
avestruz *m* ostrich
aviación *f* (civil) aviation; (Mil) air force
aviador -dora *m,f* (Aviac, Mil) pilot
avícola *adj* poultry (*before n*)
avicultura *f* poultry farming
avidez *f* eagerness, avidity; **lee con** ~ he reads avidly
ávido -da *adj* ~ DE algo ⟨*de noticias/aventuras*⟩ eager FOR sth; ⟨*de poder*⟩ hungry FOR sth
avinagrar [A1] *vt* ⟨*vino*⟩ to make ... taste vinegary; ⟨*carácter*⟩ to make ... sour *o* bitter
■ **avinagrarse** *v pron* «*vino*» to turn *o* go vinegary; «*persona*» to become bitter *o* sour
avión *m* (Aviac) plane, aircraft (frml), airplane (AmE), aeroplane (BrE); **viajar en** ~ to fly; ❸ **por avión** (Corresp) air mail; ~ **a chorro** *or* **a reacción** jet (plane); ~ **de combate/de pasajeros** fighter/passenger plane
avionazo *m* (Méx) plane crash
avioneta *f* light aircraft
avisar [A1] *vt* (a) (notificar): **¿por qué no me avisaste que venías?** why didn't you let me know you were coming?; **nos han avisado que...** they've notified us that... (b) (Esp, Méx) (llamar) to call; ~ **al médico** to call the doctor (c) (advertir) to warn; **quedas** *or* **estás avisado** you've been warned
■ ~ *vi*: **llegó sin** ~ she showed up without any prior warning *o* unexpectedly; **avísame cuando acabes** let me know when you've finished; ~ **a algn** DE **algo** to let sb know ABOUT sth
aviso *m* ①⃞ (a) (notificación) notice; ❸ **aviso al público** notice to the public; **dio** ~ **a la policía** he notified *o* informed the police; **sin previo** ~ without prior warning; **último** ~ **para los pasajeros ...** last call for passengers ... (b) (advertencia) warning; **poner sobre** ~ **a algn** to warn sb (c) (Cin, Teatr) bell (d) (Taur) warning ②⃞ (AmL) (anuncio, cartel) advertisement, ad
avispa *f* wasp
avispado -da *adj* (fam) sharp, bright
avispero *m* (nido) wasps' nest
avivar [A1] *vt* ⟨*fuego*⟩ to get ... going; ⟨*color*⟩ to make ... brighter; ⟨*pasión/deseo*⟩ to arouse; ⟨*dolor*⟩ to intensify
■ **avivarse** *v pron* (a) «*fuego*» to revive, flare up; «*debate*» to come alive, liven up (b) (AmL fam) (despabilarse) to wise up (colloq)
axila *f* (Anat) armpit, axilla (tech)
axilar *adj* underarm (*before n*)
ay *interj* (a) (expresando — dolor) ow!, ouch!; (— susto, sobresalto) oh! (b) (expresando aflicción) oh dear! (c) (expresando amenaza): **¡~ del que se atreva!** woe betide anyone who tries it!
ayer *adv* (refiriéndose al día anterior) yesterday; ~ **hizo un mes** a month ago yesterday; ~ **por** *or* (esp Am) **en la mañana** yesterday morning; **antes de** ~ the day before yesterday; **el periódico de** ~ yesterday's paper
ayuda *f* (asistencia) help; **nadie acudió en su** ~

nobody went to his aid; ~**s para la inversión** incentives for investment; **ha sido de gran** ~ it has been a great help
ayudante *mf* assistant; ~ **de cátedra** assistant professor (AmE), (junior) lecturer (BrE); ~ **de cocina** kitchen assistant
ayudar [A1] *vt* to help; ~ **al prójimo** to help one's neighbor; **¿te ayudo?** do you need any help?; **vino a ~me** she came to help me out; **ayúdame a poner la mesa** help me (to) set the table
■ ~ *vi* to help; **¿puedo** ~ **en algo?** can I do anything to help?
ayunar [A1] *vi* to fast
ayunas: en ~ (*loc adv*): **estoy en** ~ I haven't eaten anything; **debe tomarse en** ~ it should be taken on an empty stomach
ayuno *m* fast, fasting
ayuntamiento *m* (corporación) town/city council; (edificio) town/city hall
azabache *m* jet; **negro como el** ~ jet black
azada *f* hoe
azadón *m* mattock
azafata *f* ①⃞ (a) (en avión) flight attendant, air hostess; ~ **de tierra** ground stewardess (b) (en programa, concurso) hostess; ~ **de congresos** conference hostess ②⃞ (Per) (bandeja) tray
azafate *m* (AmS) tray
azafrán *m* saffron
azahar *m* (del naranjo) orange blossom; (del limonero) lemon blossom
azar *m* (a) (casualidad) chance; **dejar algo al** ~ to trust sth to chance; **al** ~ at random (b) **azares** *mpl* (vicisitudes) ups and downs (*pl*), vicissitudes (*pl*)
azaroso -sa *adj* ⟨*viaje*⟩ hazardous; ⟨*proyecto*⟩ risky; ⟨*vida*⟩ eventful
Azerbaiyán, Azerbaiján *m* Azerbaijan, Azerbaidzhan
azerbaiyaní *adj/mf* Azerbaijani, Azeri
■ *m* (idioma) Azerbaijani
azorado -da *adj* (a) (turbado) embarrassed (b) (Col, Méx, RPl) (asombrado) amazed, astonished
azorar [A1] *vt* (turbar) to embarrass
■ **azorarse** *v pron* to get embarrassed
azotador *m* (Méx) caterpillar
azotaina *f* (fam) spanking
azotar [A1] *vt* ①⃞ (con látigo) to whip, flog ②⃞ (Méx) ⟨*puerta*⟩ to slam
azote *m* ①⃞ (látigo) whip, lash; (latigazo) lash (b) (fam) (a un niño): **te voy a dar unos** ~**s** I'm going to spank you ②⃞ (calamidad) scourge
azotea *f* terrace roof, flat roof
azteca *adj/mf* Aztec
azúcar *m or f* sugar; **el nivel de** ~ **en la sangre** the blood-sugar level; **chicle sin** ~ sugar-free gum; ~ **blanca** white sugar; ~ **en terrones** *or* (RPl) **pancitos** sugar lumps *o* cubes (*pl*); ~ **glasé** *or* (Méx) **glas** confectioners sugar (AmE), icing sugar (BrE); ~ **lustre/morena** castor*/brown sugar
azucarar [A1] *vt* ⟨*café/leche*⟩ to add sugar to; ⟨*fruta*⟩ to sprinkle ... with sugar
azucarera *f* (a) (AmL) (recipiente) sugar bowl (b) (fábrica) sugar refinery

azucarero¹ -ra *adj* ⟨*industria*⟩ sugar (*before n*); ⟨*zona*⟩ sugar-producing (*before n*)

azucarero² *m* sugar bowl

azucena *f* Madonna lily, Annunciation lily

azufre *m* sulfur*

azul *adj/m* blue; **de un** ～ **intenso** deep blue; ～ **verdoso (a)** *m* greenish blue **(b)** *adj inv* (*before n*) greenish-blue; ～ **cielo** *or* **celeste (a)** *m* sky

blue **(b)** *adj inv* sky-blue (*before n*); ～ **marino (a)** *m* navy blue **(b)** *adj inv* navy blue, navy-blue (*before n*)

azulado -da *adj* bluish

azulejo *m* (glazed ceramic) tile

azuzar [A4] *vt* **(a)** ⟨*perros*⟩ to sic; ～**le los perros a algn** to set the dogs on sb **(b)** ⟨*persona*⟩ to egg … on

B b

B, b *f* (*read as* /be ('larva)/) *the letter* B, b

baba *f* **(a)** (de niño) dribble, drool (AmE) **(b)** (de adulto) saliva; **caérsele a algn la** ～ **por** *or* **con algn** to drool over sb **(c)** (de perro, caballo) slobber; (de caracol) slime

babear [A1] *vi* **(a)** «*persona*» to dribble, drool (AmE) **(b)** «*animal*» to slaver, slobber

babero *m* bib

babor *m* port; **a** ～ to port

babosa *f* slug

babosada *f* (AmL fam) drivel; **decir** ～**s** to talk drivel

baboso -sa *adj* **1** (con babas) slimy **2** (AmL fam) (estúpido) ⟨*persona*⟩ dim (colloq); ⟨*libro/ espectáculo*⟩ ridiculous
■ *m,f* (AmL fam) (tonto) dimwit (colloq)

babucha *f* (zapatilla) slipper

baca *f* roof-rack, luggage-rack

bacalao *m* cod, codfish (AmE); ～ **seco** salt cod

bacenilla *f* (Col, Ven) chamber pot

bache *m* **(a)** (Auto) pothole **(b)** (Aviac) air pocket **(c)** (mal momento) bad time *o* (BrE) patch

bachillerato *m* **(a)** (educación secundaria) *secondary education and the qualification obtained,* ≈ high school diploma (*in US*) **(b)** (Per) (licenciatura) bachelor's degree

bacinica *f* (AmL exc RPl fam) chamber pot, potty (colloq)

bacteria *f* bacterium; ～**s** bacteria (*pl*)

badén *m* **(a)** (vado) ford **(b)** (montículo) road hump **(c)** (depresión) dip

bádminton /ˈbaðminton/ *m* badminton

baffle /ˈbafle/, **bafle** *m* (altavoz) speaker, loudspeaker

bagaje *m*: ～ **cultural** (de persona) cultural knowledge; (de un pueblo) cultural heritage

bagatela *f* (alhaja) trinket; (adorno) knickknack

bah *interj* (expresando — desprecio) huh!, bah!; (— conformidad) oh well!

bahía *f* bay

bailaor -laora *m,f* flamenco dancer

bailar [A1] *vi* **1** (Mús) to dance; **salir a** ～ to go out dancing; **la sacó a** ～ he asked her to dance **2** «*trompo/peonza*» to spin **3** (fam) (quedar grande) (+ *me/te/le etc*): **estos zapatos me bailan** these shoes are too big for me (colloq)
■ ～ *vt* to dance; ～ **un tango** to (dance a) tango

bailarín -rina *m,f* dancer; **primer** ～ leading dancer; **primera bailarina** prima ballerina

baile *m* **(a)** (acción) dancing; **abrir el** ～ to start the dancing **(b)** (arte, composición, fiesta) dance; ～ **de disfraces/máscaras** fancy-dress/masked ball

baja *f* **1** (descenso) fall, drop; **una** ～ **en los precios** a fall *o* drop in prices; **la** ～ **de las tasas de interés** the cut in interest rates; **tendencia a la** ～ downward trend **2 (a)** (Esp) (Rels Labs) (permiso) sick leave; (certificado) medical certificate; **está (dado) de** ～ he's off sick *o* on sick leave; ～ **por maternidad** (Esp) maternity leave **(b)** (Dep): **el equipo tiene varias** ～**s** the team is missing several regulars **(c)** (Mil) (muerte) loss, casualty **3** (en entidad): **darse de** ～ (en club) to cancel one's membership, leave; (en partido) to resign, leave; (Mil) (cese) discharge; **dar de** ～ to discharge

bajada *f* **1** (acción) descent; **durante la** ～ **on** the way down; **tuvo una** ～ **de tensión** his blood pressure dropped; ～ **de bandera** (en taxi) minimum fare **2 (a)** (pendiente) slope; **una** ～ **muy empinada** a very steep slope **(b)** (camino): **la** ～ **a la playa es muy empinada** the path (*o* road *etc*) down to the beach is very steep

bajamar *f* low tide

bajar [A1] *vi* **1 (a)** «*ascensor/persona*» (alejándose) to go down; (acercándose) to come down; ～ **por las escaleras** to go/come down the stairs; **ya bajo** I'll be right down **(b)** (apearse) ～ **DE algo** ⟨*de tren/avión*⟩ to get off sth; ⟨*de coche*⟩ to get out **OF** sth; ⟨*de caballo/bicicleta*⟩ to get off sth **(c)** (Dep) «*equipo*» to go down **2 (a)** «*marea*» to go out **(b)** «*fiebre/tensión*» to go down, drop; «*hinchazón*» to go down; «*temperatura*» to fall, drop **(c)** «*precio/valor*» to fall; «*calidad*» to deteriorate; «*popularidad*» to diminish; ～ **de precio** to go down in price
■ ～ *vt* **1** ⟨*escalera/cuesta*⟩ to go down **2** ⟨*brazo/mano*⟩ to put down, lower **3 (a)** ～ **algo (DE algo)** ⟨*de armario/estante*⟩ to get sth down (**FROM** sth); ⟨*del piso de arriba*⟩ (traer) to bring sth down (**FROM** sth); (llevar) to take sth down (**TO** sth) **(b)** ～ **a algn DE algo** ⟨*de mesa/ caballo*⟩ to get sb off sth **4 (a)** ⟨*persiana/telón*⟩ to lower; ⟨*ventanilla*⟩ to open **(b)** ⟨*cremallera*⟩ to undo **5** ⟨*precio*⟩ to lower; ⟨*fiebre*⟩ to bring down; ⟨*volumen*⟩ to turn down; ⟨*voz*⟩ to lower **6** (Inf) to download   ⋯

■ **bajarse** v pron [1] (apearse) ~**se** DE algo ⟨de tren/autobús⟩ to get off sth; ⟨de coche⟩ to get out OF sth; ⟨de caballo/bicicleta⟩ to get off sth; ⟨de pared/árbol⟩ to get down off sth [2] ⟨pantalones⟩ to take down; ⟨falda⟩ to pull down

bajativo m (CS) liqueur, digestif

bajío m (a) (zona poco profunda) shallows (pl); (banco de arena) sandbank (b) (AmL) (terreno bajo) low-lying area

bajista mf bass player, bassist

bajo¹ -ja adj [1] [SER] ⟨persona⟩ short [2] (a) [SER] ⟨techo⟩ low; ⟨tierras⟩ low-lying (b) [ESTAR] ⟨lámpara/cuadro/nivel⟩ low; **la marea está baja** the tide is out; **están ~s de moral** their morale is low; **está ~ de defensas** his defenses are low [3] (a) ⟨calificación/precio/temperatura⟩ low; ~ **en nicotina y alquitrán** low in nicotine and tar; ~ **en calorías** low-calorie; **de baja calidad** poor-quality (b) ⟨volumen/luz⟩ low; **en voz baja** quietly, in a low voice [4] (grave) ⟨tono/voz⟩ deep, low [5] (vil) ⟨acción/instinto⟩ low, base; **los ~s fondos** the underworld

bajo² adv (a) ⟨volar/pasar⟩ low (b) ⟨hablar/cantar⟩ softly, quietly; **¡habla más ~!** keep your voice down!
■ m [1] (a) (planta baja) first (AmE) o (BrE) ground floor (b) **los bajos** (CS) the first (AmE) o (BrE) ground floor [2] (contrabajo) (double) bass
■ prep under; ~ **techo** under cover, indoors; **tres grados ~ cero** three degrees below zero; ~ **juramento** under oath

bajón m (fam) (a) (descenso fuerte) sharp drop o fall (b) (de ánimo) depression

bajorrelieve m bas-relief

bala f [1] (Arm) (de pistola, rifle) bullet; (de cañón) cannon ball; ~ **de fogueo** blank (round o cartridge); ~ **de goma/plástico** rubber/plastic bullet; **a prueba de ~s** bulletproof; **una ~ perdida** a stray bullet; **como (una) ~** ⟨salir/entrar⟩ like a shot (colloq) [2] (AmL) (Dep) shot; **lanzamiento de ~** shot put

balaca f (Col) (a) (Indum) hair-band (b) (Dep) sweatband, headband

balacera f (AmL) shooting

balada f ballad

balance m [1] (a) (resumen, valoración) assessment, evaluation; **hacer ~** DE algo to take stock OF sth, to evaluate sth (b) (resultado) result, outcome [2] (Com, Fin) (cálculo, cómputo) balance; (documento) balance sheet; (de cuenta) balance

balancear [A1] vt [1] ⟨paquetes/carga⟩ to balance [2] ⟨pierna/brazo⟩ to swing; ⟨barco⟩ to rock
■ **balancearse** v pron (a) «árbol/ramas» to sway; «objeto colgante» to swing (b) «barco» to rock

balanceo m (de hamaca) swinging; (de árboles) swaying; (de barco) rocking

balancín m (de niños) seesaw, teeter-totter (AmE)

balanza f scales (pl); (de dos platillos) scales (pl),

balance; ~ **comercial/de pagos** balance of trade/ of payments; **poner en la ~** to weigh (AmE), to weigh up (BrE)

balar [A1] vi to bleat, baa

balazo m (Arm) (tiro) shot; (herida) bullet wound; **recibió un ~** he was shot

balboa m balboa (Panamanian unit of currency)

balbucear [A1] vt to stammer
■ ~ vi «adulto» to mutter, mumble; «bebé» to babble

balbuceo m (de adulto) mumbling, muttering; (de bebé) babble

balcón m balcony

balde m [1] (cubo) bucket, pail; **caer como un ~ de agua fría** to come as a complete shock [2] (en locs) **de balde** ⟨trabajar/viajar⟩ for nothing, for free; **en balde** in vain

baldío¹ -día adj (a) (sin cultivar): **terreno ~** waste land (b) ⟨esfuerzo⟩ vain, useless

baldío² m (a) (terreno sin cultivar) area of waste land (b) (Bol, Méx, RPl) (solar) piece o plot of land, vacant lot (AmE)

baldosa f floor tile; **suelo de ~s** tiled floor

baldosín m tile

balear [A1] vt (AmL) to shoot; **murió baleado** he was shot dead

baleo m (AmL) shooting

balero m (Méx, RPl) (juguete) cup-and-ball toy

balido m bleat, baa

balín m (perdigón) pellet; (bala pequeña) shot

balística f ballistics

baliza f (a) (boya) buoy; (señal fija) marker (b) (Aviac) beacon

ballena f (Zool) whale

ballenato m whale calf

ballenero -ra m,f (a) (persona) whaler (b) **ballenero** m (barco) whaleboat, whaler

ballet /ba'le/ m (pl **-llets**) ballet

balneario m [1] (de baños medicinales) spa [2] (AmL) (núcleo residencial) seaside resort, (holiday) resort

balompié m soccer, football (BrE)

balón m (a) (Dep) ball (b) (recipiente) cylinder; ~ **de oxígeno** oxygen cylinder

baloncesto m basketball

balonmano m handball

balonvolea m volleyball

balsa f (embarcación) raft; ~ **inflable/salvavidas** inflatable/life raft

bálsamo m (a) (Farm, Med) balsam, balm (b) (Chi) (para el pelo) conditioner

baluarte m bastion

bambalina f (Teatr) drop (curtain); **entre ~s** behind the scenes

bambolearse v pron «persona/árbol/torre» to sway; «objeto colgante» to swing; «barco/tren» to rock; «avión/ascensor» to lurch

bambú m (pl **-búes** or **-bús**) bamboo

banal adj banal

banana ⋯⟶ barba ⋯ ⋯

banana f (Per, RPl) banana
bananal, bananar m (AmL) banana plantation
bananero¹ -ra adj (AmL) banana (*before n*)
bananero² m (AmL) banana tree
banano m (árbol) banana tree; (fruta) (AmC, Col) banana
banca f ⓵ **la** ~ (sector) banking; (bancos) the banks ⓶ (AmL) **(a)** (asiento) bench; (pupitre) desk **(b)** (Dep) (asiento) bench; (jugadores) substitutes (*pl*)
bancario -ria adj ⟨interés/préstamo⟩ bank (*before n*); ⟨sector⟩ banking (*before n*)
bancarrota f bankruptcy; **en** ~ bankrupt; **ir a la** ~ to go bankrupt
banco m ⓵ **(a)** (de parque) bench; (de iglesia) pew; (de barca) thwart; (pupitre) (Chi) desk **(b)** (de carpintero) workbench ⓶ (Com, Fin) bank; (de órganos, sangre) bank; (de información) bank; ~ **de datos** data base o bank; ~ **de esperma** o **semen** sperm bank ⓷ (de peces) shoal; (bajío) bar, bank; ~ **de arena** sandbank
banda f ⓵ (en la cintura, cruzando el pecho) sash; (franja, lista) band; (para pelo) (Méx) hair-band; (en brazo) armband; ~ **de frecuencias** frequency band; ~ **sonora** (Cin) sound track; ~ **ancha** broad band; ~ **transportadora** (Méx) conveyor belt ⓶ (de barco) side; (en billar) cushion; (en fútbol, rugby) touchline; **saque de** ~ (en fútbol) throw-in; (en rugby) put-in ⓷ **(a)** (de delincuentes) gang; **(b)** (Mús) band
bandada f (de pájaros) flock; (de peces) shoal
bandazo m: **dar** ~**s** «*equipaje*» to move about; «*coche*» to swerve about
bandeja f tray; **servirle algo a algn en** ~ to hand sb sth on a platter (AmE) o (BrE) plate
bandera f **(a)** (de nación, club) flag; (de regimiento) colors* (*pl*); **izar la** ~ to run up o raise the flag; **arriar la** ~ to lower o strike the flag **(b)** (para señales) flag, pennant; ~ **ajedrezada** or **a cuadros** checkered* flag **(c)** (de taxi): **bajar la** ~ to start the meter **(d)** (Inf) flag
banderilla f (Taur) banderilla (*barbed dart stuck into the bull's neck*)
banderillero m banderillero (*person who sticks the banderillas into the bull's neck*)
banderín m (banderita triangular) pennant; (Dep) flag
banderola f (enseña) banderole
bandido -da m,f (delincuente) bandit; (granuja) crook; (pícaro) rascal
bando m ⓵ (edicto) edict ⓶ (facción) side, camp; **están en** ~**s contrarios** they're on opposing sides
bandolera f (cinturón) Sam Browne (belt); (para cartuchos) bandolier; **en** ~ slung across one's shoulder
bandolero -ra m,f bandit
bandoneón m: *type of accordion*
banjo /'bandʒo/ m banjo
banqueta f **(a)** (taburete) stool; (para los pies) footstool **(b)** (Méx) (acera) sidewalk (AmE), pavement (BrE)
banquete m banquet; ~ **de bodas/de gala** wedding/gala reception
banquillo m **(a)** (Der): **el** ~ (de los acusados) the dock **(b)** (Dep) bench

banquina f (RPl) (en autopista) shoulder (AmE), hard shoulder (BrE); (cuneta) ditch
bañado -da adj (Bol, RPl) ~ **EN algo** (en sangre/ sudor) covered WITH sth; ⟨en lágrimas⟩ bathed IN sth; ~ **en oro/plata** gold-plated/silver-plated
bañador m (Esp) (de mujer) bathing suit (esp AmE), swimming costume (BrE); (de hombre) swimming trunks
bañar [A1] vt ⓵ ⟨niño/enfermo⟩ to bath, give ... a bath ⓶ ⟨pulsera/cubierto⟩ to plate
■ **bañarse** v pron (refl) **(a)** (en bañera) to have o take a bath, to bathe (AmE) **(b)** (en mar, río) to swim, bathe
bañera f bath, bathtub
bañero -ra m,f (RPl) lifeguard
bañista mf bather
baño m

■ **Nota** Con referencia al cuarto de baño de una casa particular, el inglés americano emplea normalmente *bathroom*. El inglés británico emplea *toilet*, *lavatory* o (coloquialmente) *loo*. Cuando se habla de los servicios de un edificio público, el inglés americano utiliza *washroom*, *restroom*, *men's room* o *ladies' room*. El inglés británico emplea the *Gents*, the *ladies*, o the *toilets*. En la calle y en los parques públicos se emplea *public toilets*, o en inglés británico más formal, *public conveniences*.

⓵ (en bañera) bath; (en mar, río) swim; **darse un** ~ to have a bath/to go for a swim; ~ **de sangre** bloodbath; ~**s públicos** public baths (*pl*); ~ **turco** Turkish bath ⓶ **(a)** (bañera) bath **(b)** (esp AmL) (en casa privada) bathroom (AmE), toilet (BrE); (en edificio público) restroom (AmE), toilet (BrE); ~ **público** (AmL) public toilet ⓷ (de metal) plating
baptista adj Baptist (*before n*)
■ mf Baptist
baqueta f **(a)** (Arm) ramrod **(b)** (Mús) drumstick
baquiano -na m,f (AmL) guide
bar m (local) bar; (mueble) liquor cabinet (AmE), drinks cabinet (BrE)
baraja f deck o (BrE) pack (of cards)
barajar [A1] vt ⓵ ⟨cartas⟩ to shuffle ⓶ ⟨nombres/posibilidades⟩ to consider, look at; ⟨cifras⟩ to talk about, mention
baranda, (Esp) **barandilla** f (de balcón) rail; (de escalera) handrail, banister
barata f ⓵ (Chi) (cucaracha) cockroach ⓶ (Méx) (liquidación) sale
baratija f (alhaja) trinket; (adorno) knickknack
barato¹ -ta adj **(a)** ⟨vestido/restaurante/viaje⟩ cheap, low-priced **(b)** (como adv) ⟨costar/comprar⟩ cheap
barato² adv ⟨comer/vivir⟩ cheaply; **se compra más** ~ **en el mercado** you can get things cheaper in the market
barba f **(a)** (de quien se la afeita) stubble; **una** ~ **de dos días** two days' growth of stubble **(b)** (de quien se la deja) beard; **dejarse (la)** ~ to grow a beard; **un hombre con** ~ a man with a beard; **hacerle la** ~ **a algn** (Méx fam) to suck up to sb (colloq) **(c)** (mentón, barbilla) chin

barbacoa *f* (a) (parrilla) barbecue; (carne) barbecued meat (b) (Méx) *meat roasted in an oven dug in the earth*

barbaridad *f* (a) (acto atroz) atrocity (b) (disparate): **pagar tanto es una** ~ it's madness to pay that much; **lo que hiciste/dijiste es una** ~ what you did/said is outrageous; **es capaz de cualquier** ~ he's quite capable of doing something really terrible *o* stupid; **¡qué** ~**!** good heavens!; **una** ~ (fam) ‹*comer*› like a horse; ‹*fumar*› like a chimney; ‹*pagar/costar*› a fortune

barbarie *f* (de tribu, pueblo) barbarism, savagery; (brutalidad) barbarity

barbarismo *m* (extranjerismo) loan word, borrowing; (solecismo) barbarism

bárbaro¹ -ra *adj* [1] (Hist) barbarian [2] (bruto): **el muy** ~ **la hizo llorar** the brute made her cry; **no seas** ~, **no se lo digas** don't be crass *o* cruel, don't tell him [3] (fam) (como intensificador) ‹*casa/coche*› fantastic; **tengo un hambre bárbara** I'm starving

bárbaro² *adv* (fam): **lo pasamos** ~ we had a fantastic time (colloq)

bárbaro³ -ra *m,f* [1] (Hist) Barbarian [2] (fam) (bruto) lout, thug

barbecho *m* (estado): **dejar la tierra en** ~ to leave the land fallow; **estar en** ~ (CS) to be in preparation

barbería *f* barber's (shop)

barbero¹ *m* barber

barbero² -ra *m,f* (Méx fam) toady

barbilampiño *adj*: **un hombre** ~ a man with a light beard

barbilla *f* chin

barbitúrico *m* barbiturate

barbudo *m* bearded man, man with a beard

barca *f* boat; ~ **de remos** rowboat (AmE), rowing boat (BrE)

barcaza *f* (en canales, ríos) barge; (entre barco y tierra) lighter

barco *m* (Náut) boat; (grande) ship, vessel (frml); **un viaje en** ~ a journey by sea (*o* river *etc*); **ir/viajar en** ~ to go/travel by boat/ship; ~ **de guerra** warship; ~ **de vapor** steamboat, steamer; ~ **de vela** sailing boat, sailboat (AmE)

barda *f* (Méx) (de cemento) wall; (de madera) fence

barítono -na *adj/m* baritone

barman /'barman/ *m* (*pl* **-mans**) barman, bartender (AmE)

barniz *m* (a) (para madera) varnish (b) (de cultura, educación) veneer; ~ **de** *or* **para las uñas** nail polish, nail varnish (esp BrE)

barnizar [A4] *vt* to varnish

barómetro *m* barometer

barón *m* (título nobiliario) baron; (de organización) influential member

baronesa *f* baroness

barquero -ra (*m*) boatman; (*f*) boatwoman

barquilla *f* (de globo) basket, carriage; (Náut) log

barquillo *m* (galleta) wafer; (cono) ice-cream cone *o* (BrE) cornet

barra *f* [1] (a) (de armario) rail; (para cortinas) rod, pole; (de bicicleta) crossbar (b) (de oro, jabón, chocolate) bar; (de turrón, helado) block; (de desodorante) stick; (de pan) (Esp, Méx) stick, French loaf; ~ **de labios** lipstick [2] (a) (banda, franja) bar (b) (Mús) bar (line) (c) (signo de puntuación) oblique, slash [3] (para ballet, gimnasia) bar; ~ **fija** horizontal bar; ~**s asimétricas/paralelas** asymmetric/parallel bars (*pl*) [4] (de bar, cafetería) bar [5] (AmL fam) (a) (de hinchas, seguidores) supporters (*pl*) (b) (de amigos) gang (colloq) [6] (Inf): ~ **de herramientas** toolbar

barrabasada *f* (fam) prank; **hacer** ~**s** to play pranks

barraca *f* (a) (puesto) stall; (caseta) booth (b) (Mil) barrack hut (c) (casa) adobe house (*typical of Valencia and Murcia*) (d) (CS) (de materiales de construcción) builders merchant *o* yard

barranca *f*, **barranco** *m* gully; (más profundo) ravine

barrena *f* (punzón) gimlet; (taladro, perforadora) drill

barrenar [A1] *vt* (perforar) to drill; (volar) ‹*roca*› to blast

barrendero -ra *m,f* road sweeper, street cleaner

barreno *m* (barrena) drill; (para explosivo) shot hole

barrer [E1] *vt* [1] ‹*suelo/cocina*› to sweep [2] (a) (arrastrar) to sweep away (b) ‹*rival*› to thrash, trounce
■ ~ *vi* [1] (con escoba) to sweep [2] (arrasar) «*equipo/candidato*» to sweep to victory; ~ **con** algo ‹*con premios/medallas*› to walk off WITH sth; **la inundación barrió con todo** the flood swept everything away; **barrió con todos los premios** she walked off with all the prizes
■ **barrerse** *v pron* (Méx) «*vehículo*» to skid; (en fútbol, béisbol) to slide

barrera *f* barrier; ~ **de peaje** toll barrier; ~ **generacional** generation gap; ~ **idiomática** language barrier

barriada *f* (a) (barrio) area, district (*often poor or working-class*) (b) (AmL) (barrio marginal) slum area, shantytown

barrial *m* (AmL) quagmire

barricada *f* barricade

barriga *f* (fam) (vientre) belly (colloq), tummy (colloq); **dolor de** ~ bellyache (colloq), tummy ache (colloq); **echar** ~ to develop a paunch *o* (colloq) gut

barrigón -gona *adj* (fam): **se está volviendo barrigona** she's getting a bit of a belly *o* tummy (colloq); **un viejo** ~ an old man with a paunch

barril *m* barrel; (de pólvora, cerveza) keg; **ser un** ~ **sin fondo** (AmL fam) to be a bottomless pit (colloq)

barrio *m* (a) (zona) neighborhood*; **la gente del** ~ people in the neighborhood, local people; **el mercado del** ~ the local market; ~ **alto** (Chi) smart neighborhood; ~ **chino** (Esp) red-light district; ~ **espontáneo** (AmC) shantytown; ~**s bajos** poor neighborhoods (*pl*); ~ **de invasión** (Col) shantytown (b) (de las afueras) suburb

barriobajero -ra *adj* (pey) common (pej)

barrizal *m* quagmire, muddy area

barro *m* (lodo) mud; (Art) clay, earthenware (*before n*)

barroco -ca *adj* ‹*estilo*› baroque; (recargado) overelaborate

barrote *m* (de celda, ventana) bar; (en carpintería) crosspiece

bartola *f*: *echarse a la* ~ (fam) (estar sin trabajar) to laze about

bártulos *mpl* (fam) gear (colloq), stuff (colloq)

barullo *m* (alboroto) racket (colloq), ruckus (AmE); (desorden) muddle, mess

basar [A1] *vt* ⟨*teoría/idea*⟩ ~ *algo* EN *algo* to base sth ON sth
■ **basarse** *v pron* (a) «*persona*» ~*se* EN *algo*: ¿en qué te basas para decir eso? and what basis *o* grounds do you have for saying that?; **se basó en esos datos** he based his argument (*o* theory *etc*) on that information (b) «*teoría/creencia/idea/opinión*» ~*se* EN *algo* to be based ON sth

báscula *f* scales (*pl*); ~ *de baño* bathroom scales

base *f* **1** (a) (parte inferior) base (b) *tb* ~ *de maquillaje* foundation
2 (a) (fundamento) basis; **la** ~ **de una buena salud** the basis of good health; **tengo suficiente** ~ **para asegurar eso** I have sufficient grounds to claim that; **sentar las** ~**s de algo** to lay the foundations of sth; **tomar algo como** ~ to take sth as a starting point (b) (conocimientos básicos): **tiene una sólida** ~ **científica** he has a sound grounding in science; **llegó al curso sin ninguna** ~ he didn't have the basics when he began the course; ~ *de datos* database
3 (*en locs*) **a base de: un régimen a** ~ **de verdura** a vegetable-based diet; **vive a** ~ **de pastillas** he lives on pills
4 (centro de operaciones) base; ~ *aérea/naval/militar* air/naval/military base
5 **bases** *fpl* (de concurso) rules (*pl*)
6 (a) (en béisbol) base (b) **base** *mf* (en baloncesto) guard

básica *f* (Esp) primary *o* elementary education

básico -ca *adj* (a) (fundamental, esencial) basic; **alimento** ~ staple food (b) ⟨*requisito*⟩ essential, fundamental

basílica *f* basilica

basket, básquet *m* basketball

básquetbol, basquetbol *m* (AmL) basketball

basquetbolista *mf* (AmL) basketball player

bastante *adj* (a) (suficiente) enough; ~**s vasos/** ~ *vino* enough glasses/wine (b) (cantidad considerable) plenty of, quite a lot of; **había** ~ **gente/**~**s coches** there were plenty of people/cars
■ *pron* **1** (suficiente) enough; **ya tenemos** ~**s** we already have enough **2** (demasiado): **deja** ~ **que desear** it leaves rather a lot to be desired
■ *adv* **1** (suficientemente) enough; **no te has esforzado** ~ you haven't tried hard enough **2** (considerablemente) (*con verbos*) quite a lot; (*con adjetivos, adverbios*) quite; **le gusta bastante** she likes him quite a lot; **me pareció** ~ **agradable/aburrido** I thought he was quite pleasant/rather boring

bastar [A1] *vi* to be enough; **¿basta con esto?** will this be enough?; **basta con marcar el 101** just dial 101; **¡basta ya!** that's enough!; (+ *me/te/le etc*) **me basta con tu palabra** your word is good enough for me

bastardilla *f* italic type, italics (*pl*)

bastardo -da *adj* (a) (ilegítimo) illegitimate (b) (innoble) base
■ *m,f* bastard

bastidor *m* (Teatr) wing; *entre* ~*es* behind the scenes

basto -ta *adj* coarse

bastón *m* (para caminar) walking stick, cane; (en desfiles) baton; (de esquí) ski stick *o* pole

basura *f* (a) (recipiente) garbage *o* trash can (AmE), dustbin (BrE); **echar** *or* **tirar algo a la** ~ to throw sth in the garbage *o* trash (can) *o* dustbin (b) (desechos) garbage (AmE), trash (AmE), rubbish (BrE); (en sitios públicos) litter; **sacar la** ~ to take out the garbage *o* trash *o* rubbish (c) (fam) (porquería) trash (AmE colloq), rubbish (BrE colloq)

basural *m* (AmL) ▶ BASURERO B

basurero -ra *m,f* **1** (persona) garbage collector (AmE), dustman (BrE) **2** (a) **basurero** *m* (vertedero) garbage dump (AmE), rubbish dump *o* tip (BrE) (b) (recipiente) (Chi, Méx) trash can (AmE), dustbin (BrE)

bata *f* (para estar en casa) dressing gown, robe; (de médico) white coat; (de colegio) work coat (AmE), overall (BrE)

batahola *f* (esp AmL fam) racket, din, ruckus (AmE)

batalla *f* battle; **librar** ~ to do battle; ~ *campal* pitched battle; **de** ~ (fam) ⟨*zapatos/abrigo*⟩ everyday (*before n*)

batallar [A1] *vi* (a) (luchar) to battle; ~ CON *algn/algo* (lidiar) to battle WITH sb/sth (b) (Mil) to fight

batallón *m* (Mil) battalion

batata *f* sweet potato, yam

bate *m* (en béisbol, cricket) bat

batea *f* (a) (bandeja) tray (b) (AmL) (recipiente) shallow pan *o* tray (*for washing*)

bateador -dora *m,f* (en béisbol, softbol) batter; (en cricket) batsman

batear [A1] *vi* to bat
■ ~ *vt* to hit

batería *f* **1** (Auto) battery; **se me descargó la** ~ my battery went dead (AmE) *o* (BrE) flat **2** (a) (Mús) drums (*pl*), drum kit (b) **batería** *mf* drummer

baterista *mf* (AmL) drummer

batido *m* (de leche) (milk) shake; (para panqueques) (AmL) batter

batidor *m* (a) (manual) whisk, beater; (eléctrico) mixer, blender (b) **batidora** *f* (máquina eléctrica) mixer, blender

batir [I1] *vt* **1** ⟨*huevos*⟩ to beat, whisk; ⟨*crema/nata*⟩ to whip; ⟨*mantequilla*⟩ to churn **2** ⟨*marca/récord*⟩ to break; ⟨*enemigo/rival*⟩ to beat **3** (a) ⟨*ala*⟩ to beat, flap (b) ~ *palmas* to clap
■ **batirse** *v pron* **1** (enfrentarse): ~*se a* *or* **en duelo** to fight a duel **2** (Méx) (ensuciarse) to get dirty; **llegó todo batido de lodo** he arrived all covered in mud

batracio *m* batrachian

batuta *f* baton; *llevar la* ~ (fam) to be the boss (colloq)

baúl *m* (arca) chest; (de viaje) trunk; (del coche, carro) (Col, Ven, RPl) trunk (AmE), boot (BrE)

bautismo *m* (de bebé) baptism, christening; (de adulto) baptism

bautizar [A4] *vt* (a) (Relig) ⟨*bebé*⟩ to baptize, ···⋮

christen; ⟨adulto⟩ to baptize; **la ~ron con el nombre de Ana** she was christened Ana **(b)** ⟨barco⟩ to name

bautizo m **(a)** (de bebé) christening, baptism; (de adulto) baptism; (fiesta) christening party **(b)** (de barco) naming, launching

bayeta f **(a)** (para limpiar) cloth **(b)** (Bol, Col) (tela) baize

bayoneta f bayonet

bazar m **(a)** (mercado oriental) bazaar **(b)** (tienda) hardware store (often selling a wide range of electrical goods and toys)

bazo m spleen

bazofia f (fam) (comida) crap (colloq); (libro, película) garbage (AmE colloq), rubbish (BrE colloq)

bazooka /ba'suka, ba'θuka/, **bazuca** f bazooka

be f: name of the letter b, often called BE LARGA or GRANDE to distinguish it from v

beato -ta adj (Relig) blessed; (piadoso) pious; (santurrón) (pey) excessively devout

bebe -ba m,f (RPl, Per) baby

bebé m baby; **~ probeta** test-tube baby

bebedero m (paraje) watering hole; (recipiente) trough; (para personas) (CS, Méx) drinking fountain

bebedor -dora m,f drinker; **un ~ empedernido** a hardened drinker

beber [E1] vt/vi to drink; **¿quieres ~ algo?** do you want something to drink?; **~ a sorbos** to sip; **si bebes no conduzcas** don't drink and drive; **~ a la salud de algn** to drink to sb's health; **~ POR algn/algo** to drink TO sb/sth
■ **beberse** v pron (enf) to drink up; **nos bebimos la botella entera** we drank the whole bottle

bebida f (líquido) drink, beverage (frml); (vicio) drink

bebido -da adj [ESTAR] (borracho) drunk

beca f (ayuda económica) grant; (que se otorga por méritos) scholarship

becado -da m,f (AmL) ▶ BECARIO

becar [A2] vt (dar ayuda económica) to give o (frml) award a grant to; (dar beca por méritos) to give o (frml) award a scholarship to

becario -ria m,f recipient of a grant; (por méritos) scholarship holder, scholar

becerro -rra m,f calf, young bull; (piel) calfskin

bedel mf ≈ porter

beduino -na adj/m,f bedouin

beige, (Esp) **beis** /beɪs, beis/ adj inv/m beige

béisbol, (Méx) **beisbol** m baseball

belén m nativity scene, crib, crèche (AmE)

Belén m Bethlehem

belga adj/mf Belgian

Bélgica f Belgium

bélico -ca adj ⟨conflicto/material⟩ military; **preparativos ~s** preparations for war

belicosidad f aggressiveness

belicoso -sa adj ⟨pueblo⟩ warlike; ⟨persona/ carácter⟩ bellicose, belligerent

beligerante adj belligerent; **los países ~s** the belligerent o warring nations

bellaco -ca m,f (fam & hum) rogue (colloq & hum)

belleza f **(a)** (cualidad) beauty **(b)** (mujer bella) beauty **(c)** (cosa bella): **este paisaje es una ~** this is beautiful countryside

bello -lla adj **(a)** ⟨mujer/paisaje/poema⟩ (liter) beautiful; **ser una bella persona** to be a good person **(b)** (Art) **bellas artes** fine art

bellota f acorn

bemba f (AmL fam) thick lips (pl)

bemol adj flat; **si ~** B flat

bencina f (a) (Quím) benzine, petroleum ether **(b)** (Andes) (gasolina) gasoline (AmE), petrol (BrE)

bencinera f (Andes) filling station, gas station (AmE), petrol station (BrE)

bencinero -ra m,f (Andes) filling station attendant

bendecir [I25] vt to bless; **¡que Dios te bendiga!** God bless you!; **~ la mesa** to say grace

bendice, etc ▶ BENDECIR

bendición f **(a)** (Relig) blessing, benediction **(b)** (aprobación) blessing; (regalo divino) godsend

bendiga, bendijo, etc ▶ BENDECIR

bendito -ta adj **(a)** (Relig) blessed; **¡~ sea Dios!** (expresando contrariedad) good God o grief!; (expresando alivio) thank God! **(b)** ⟨agua/pan⟩ holy
■ m,f simple soul

benedictino -na adj/m,f Benedictine

benefactor -tora m,f benefactor

beneficencia f (caridad) charity; **asociación/ obra de ~** charitable organization/work

beneficiar [A1] vt (favorecer) to benefit, to be of benefit to; **esto beneficia a ambas partes** this benefits both sides; **salir beneficiado con algo** to be better off with sth
■ **beneficiarse** v pron to benefit; **~se CON/DE algo** to benefit FROM sth

beneficiario -ria m,f beneficiary; (de cheque) payee

beneficio m **(a)** (Com, Fin) profit; **producir** or **reportar ~s** to yield o bring returns o profits **(b)** (ventaja, bien) benefit; **a ~ de** in aid of; **en ~ de todos** in the interests of everyone

beneficioso -sa adj beneficial

benéfico -ca adj ⟨influencia⟩ benign, beneficial; ⟨espectáculo⟩ charity (before n), benefit (before n)

beneplácito m approval

benevolencia f (indulgencia) leniency, indulgence; (bondad) kindness, benevolence (frml)

benevolente, benévolo -la adj (indulgente) lenient, indulgent; (bondadoso) kind, benevolent (frml)

bengala f flare

benignidad f (del clima) mildness; (de tumor) benignancy

benigno -na *adj* ‹clima/invierno› mild; ‹tumor› benign

benjamín -mina *m,f* (*m*) youngest son, (*f*) youngest daughter

beodo -da *adj* (frml o hum) inebriated (frml or hum)
■ *m,f* (frml o hum) drunkard, toper (liter o hum)

berberecho *m* cockle

berenjena *f* eggplant (AmE), aubergine (BrE)

Berlín *m* Berlin

berlinés -nesa *adj* of/from Berlin
■ *m,f* Berliner

berma *f* (Andes) (de asfalto) shoulder (AmE), hard shoulder (BrE); (de tierra) verge

bermudas *fpl or mpl* Bermuda shorts (*pl*)

Bermudas *fpl*: las ~ Bermuda; el triángulo de las ~ the Bermuda Triangle

berrear [A1] *vi* «becerro/ciervo» to bellow

berrido *m* (de becerro, ciervo) bellow

berrinche *m* (fam) tantrum; le dio un *or* (Méx) hizo un ~ he threw *o* had a tantrum

berro *m* watercress

besar [A1] *vt* to kiss
■ **besarse** *v pron* (recípr) to kiss (each other)

beso *m* kiss; darle un ~ a algn to give sb a kiss

bestia *adj* (fam) (a) (grosero) rude (b) (violento, brusco): ¡qué hombre más ~! ha vuelto a pegarle what a brute *o* an animal! he's hit her again
■ *f* beast; ~ salvaje *or* feroz wild animal
■ *mf* (persona violenta) animal, brute

bestial *adj* (fam) (muy grande): tengo un hambre ~ I'm starving; hace un frío ~ it's incredibly cold

best-seller /bes'seler/ *m* (*pl* **-llers**) best-seller

besugo *m* (Coc, Zool) red bream

besuquear [A1] *vt* (fam) to smother … with kisses
■ **besuquearse** *v pron* (recípr) (fam) to neck (colloq)

betabel *m* (Méx) beet, beetroot (BrE)

betún *m* (para calzado) shoe polish; dales ~ a esos zapatos give those shoes a polish

bianual *adj* biannual

biberón *m* (baby's *o* feeding) bottle; hay que darle el ~ I have to give the baby his bottle *o* feed

biblia *f* bible; La B~ the Bible

bíblico -ca *adj* biblical

bibliografía *f* (en libro, informe) bibliography; (para curso) booklist

biblioteca *f* (a) (institución, lugar) library; ~ pública/de consulta public/reference library (b) (colección) book collection (c) (mueble) bookshelves (*pl*), bookcase

bibliotecario -ria *m,f* librarian

bicameral *adj* bicameral (frml)

bicampeón -peona *m,f* twice champion

bicarbonato *m* bicarbonate

bicentenario *m* bicentenary

bíceps *m* (*pl* ~) biceps

bicho *m* [1] (fam) (a) (insecto) bug (colloq), creepy-crawly (colloq) (b) (animal) animal, creature; me picó *or* (Esp) ha picado un ~ I've

been bitten by something [2] (fam) (persona) nasty piece of work (colloq); ~ raro weirdo (colloq); todo ~ viviente everyone

bici *f* (fam) bike (colloq)

bicicleta *f* bicycle; va en ~ al trabajo she cycles to work; ¿sabes montar *or* (AmL) andar en ~? can you ride a bicycle?; ~ de carreras/ ejercicio/montaña racing/exercise/mountain bike

bicimoto *m* (Méx) moped

bicolor *adj* two-colored*

bidé, bidet /bi'ðe/ *m* bidet

bidón *m* (a) (para gasolina, agua) can; (más grande) jerry can (b) (barril) barrel

bien¹ *adj inv* [1] [ESTAR] (de salud, en general) well; sentirse *or* encontrarse ~ to feel well; ¿cómo estás? — muy ~, gracias how are you? — (I'm) very well, thank you; ¡qué ~ estás! you look really well!; ¡tú no estás ~ de la cabeza! you are not right in the head
[2] [ESTAR] (a) (cómodo, agradable): ¿vas ~ ahí atrás? are you all right in the back?; se está ~ a la sombra it's nice in the shade; la casa está muy ~ the house is very nice (b) [ESTAR] (correcto, adecuado) right; la fecha/el reloj está ~ the date/ the clock is right; ¿está ~ así? is this all right?; si te parece ~ if that's all right with you; el cuadro no queda ~ ahí the picture doesn't look right there (c) (suficiente): estar *or* andar ~ de algo to be all right for sth; ¿estamos ~ de aceite? are we all right for oil?; ya está ~ that's enough
[3] [ESTAR] (a) (en calidad) good; ¿lo has leído? está muy ~ have you read it? it's very good (b) (fam) (sexualmente atractivo) good-looking, attractive
[4] (fam) (a) (de buena posición social) ‹familia/gente› well-to-do (b) ‹barrio› well-to-do, posh (BrE)

bien² *adv* [1] (a) (de manera satisfactoria) ‹dormir/ funcionar/cantar› well; no le fue ~ en Alemania things didn't work out for her in Germany (b) (correctamente) well; habla muy ~ inglés she speaks English very well *o* very good English; ¡~ hecho/dicho! well done/said!; pórtate ~ behave yourself; hiciste ~ en decírselo you were right to tell him; siéntate ~ sit properly (c) (de manera agradable) ‹oler/saber› good
[2] (a) (a fondo, completamente) well, properly; ~ cocido well *o* properly cooked; ¿cerraste ~? did you lock the door properly?; ~ sabes que … you know perfectly well that … (b) (con cuidado, atención) ‹escuchar/mirar› carefully
[3] (a) (como intensificador) (muy) very; canta ~ mal he sings really badly; ~ entrada la noche very late at night; ¿estás ~ seguro? are you positive? (b) (en locs) más bien rather; no bien as soon as; si bien although
■ *interj*: ¡(muy) ~! well done!, (very) good!; ¡qué ~! great!
■ *conj*: ~ … o … either … or …; se puede subir ~ a pie o a caballo you can go up either on foot or on horseback

bien³ *m* [1] (Fil) good; el ~ y el mal good and evil; hacer el ~ to do good deeds; un hombre de ~ a good man
[2] (a) (beneficio, bienestar) good; es por mi/tu ~ it's for my/your own good (b) hacer bien (+ me/te/le etc): esto te hará ~ this will do you good
[3] (en calificaciones escolares) grade of between 6 and 6.9 on a scale of 1-10 ⋯⟶

4 **bienes** *mpl* (a) (Com) goods; ~es de consumo consumer goods (b) (Der) property; le dejó todos sus ~es she left him everything she owned; ~es inmuebles *or* raíces real estate, property (BrE); ~es muebles personal property, goods and chattels; ~es públicos public property

bienal *adj* biennial

bienaventurado -da *adj* blessed

bienestar *m* well-being, welfare; estado de ~ social welfare state; ~ social social welfare

bienhablado -da *adj* well-spoken

bienintencionado -da *adj* well-meaning, well-intentioned

bienvenida *f* welcome; darle la ~ a algn to welcome sb

bienvenido -da *adj* welcome; ser ~ to be welcome

bies *m*: al ~ on the cross

bife *m* (CS) (Coc) steak

bifocal *adj* bifocal

bifurcación *f* (en carretera) fork; (en la vía férrea) junction

bifurcarse [A2] *v pron* «*camino*» to fork, diverge (frml); «*vía férrea*» to diverge

bigamia *f* bigamy

bígamo -ma *adj* bigamous
■ *m,f* bigamist

bigote *m* **1** (de persona) *tb* ~s mustache*; **2** (de gato, ratón) whisker

bigotudo -da, (Méx) **bigotón -tona** *adj* (fam): un hombre ~ a man with a big mustache*

bigudí *m* (*pl* **-díes -dis**) curler, roller

bikini *m or* (RPl) *f* bikini

bilateral *adj* bilateral

bilingüe *adj* bilingual

bilis *f* (Fisiol) bile

billar *m* (con tres bolas) billiards; (con 16 bolas) pool; (con 22 bolas) snooker

billete *m* **1** (Fin) bill (esp AmE), note (BrE) **2** (de lotería, rifa, de transporte) ticket; sacar/pagar un ~ to get/pay for a ticket; ~ de ida y vuelta (Esp) round-trip ticket (AmE), return (ticket) (BrE); ~ sencillo *or* de ida (Esp) one-way ticket, single (ticket) (BrE)

billetera *f*, **billetero** *m* wallet, billfold (AmE); (con monedero) change purse (AmE), purse (BrE)

billetero -ra *m,f* (Méx, Ven) lottery ticket vendor

billón *m* trillion

bimensual *adj* (dos veces al mes) twice-monthly, fortnightly (BrE)

bimestral *adj* (cada dos meses) bimonthly; (que dura dos meses) two-month (*before n*)

bimestre *m* (period of) two months; (pago) bimonthly payment

bimotor *m* twin-engined aircraft

binario -ria *adj* binary

bingo *m* (juego) bingo; (sala) bingo hall

binoculares, (Col, Ven) **binóculos** *mpl* binoculars (*pl*)

biodegradable *adj* biodegradable

biodiversidad *f* biodiversity

biografía *f* biography

biográfico -ca *adj* biographical

biógrafo -fa *m,f* biographer

biología *f* biology

biológico -ca *adj* (Biol) biological; «*verduras*» organic

biólogo -ga *m,f* biologist

biombo *m* folding screen

biopsia *f* biopsy

bioquímica *f* biochemistry

bioquímico -ca *adj* biochemical
■ *m,f* biochemist

bióxido *m* dioxide

bip *m* (a) (sonido) pip, beep (b) (Méx) (aparato) pager, beeper, bleeper (BrE)

bipartidismo *m* two-party system

bípedo *m* biped

biplaza *m* two-seater

biquini *m* bikini

birlar [A1] *vt* (fam) to swipe (colloq), to pinch (BrE colloq)

Birmania *f* Burma

birmano¹ -na *adj/m,f* Burmese; los ~s the Burmese

birmano² *m* (idioma) Burmese

birome *f* (RPl) ballpoint pen, Biro®

birrete *m* (a) cap (*worn by lawyers, professors, etc*) (b) (birreta) biretta

bis *m* encore

bisabuelo -la *m, f* (*m*) great-grandfather; (*f*) great-grandmother; mis ~s my great-grandparents

bisagra *f* hinge

biselar [A1] *vt* to bevel

bisexual *adj/mf* bisexual

bisexualidad *f* bisexuality

bisiesto *adj*: 1992 fue (año) ~ 1992 was a leap year

bisne *m* (AmC fam) hustling (colloq), black marketeering

bisnieto -ta *m, f* (*m*) great-grandson; (*f*) great-granddaughter; mis ~s my great-grandchildren

bisonte *m* bison

bisoñé *m* toupee, hairpiece

bisoño -ña *adj* inexperienced; soldados ~s raw recruits

bistec /bi'stek/ *m* (*pl* **-tecs**) steak, beefsteak

bisturí *m* scalpel

bisutería *f* costume *o* imitation jewelry*

bit *m* (*pl* **bits**) (Inf) bit

bividí /biβi'ði/ *m* (Per) undershirt (AmE), vest (BrE)

bizantino -na *adj* (Hist) Byzantine

bizco -ca *adj* cross-eyed
■ *m,f* cross-eyed person

bizcocho *m* (pastel) sponge (cake); (galleta) sponge finger

blanca *f* **1** (Mús) half note (AmE), minim (BrE) **2** (en dominó) blank; (en ajedrez) white piece **3** (Esp fam) (dinero): estar sin *or* no tener ~ to be broke (colloq)

Blancanieves Snow White

blanco¹ -ca *adj* **1** (a) «*color/vestido/pelo*» white; en ~ «*cheque/página*» blank; rellenar los espacios en ~ fill in the blanks; me quedé en ~

my mind went blank **(b)** (pálido) [SER]
fair-skinned, pale-skinned; [ESTAR] white; **estoy
muy ~** I'm very white *o* pale **2** ⟨*persona/raza*⟩
white **3** ⟨*vino*⟩ white
■ *m,f* white person

blanco² *m* **1** (color) white; **en ~ y negro** black
and white **2** (Dep, Jueg) (objeto) target; (centro)
bullseye; **tirar al ~** to shoot at the target; **dar en
el ~** to hit the target/bullseye **3** (vino) white
(wine)

blancura *f* whiteness

blandir [I1] *vt* to brandish, wave

blando -da *adj* **1 (a)** ⟨*carne*⟩ tender; ⟨*queso/
mantequilla*⟩ soft; **ponerse ~** to go soft **(b)**
⟨*cama/madera/agua*⟩ soft; **un cepillo de cerdas
blandas** a soft brush **2** ⟨*carácter*⟩ (débil) weak;
(poco severo) soft

blandura *f* **1** (en general) softness; (de la carne)
tenderness **2** (falta de severidad) leniency; **trata a
sus alumnos con demasiada ~** she's too lenient
with *o* too soft on her pupils

blanqueador *m* (para visillos) whitener; (lejía)
(Col, Méx) bleach

blanquear [A1] *vt* **(a)** ⟨*ropa*⟩ to bleach; ⟨*pared*⟩
to whitewash **(b)** ⟨*dinero*⟩ to launder

blanqueo *m* **(a)** (de paredes) whitewashing **(b)**
(de dinero) laundering

blasfemia *f* blasphemy

blindado -da *adj* ⟨*coche*⟩ armor-plated*,
armored*; ⟨*puerta*⟩ reinforced

blindar [A1] *vt* ⟨*barco/coche*⟩ to armor-plate*;
⟨*puerta*⟩ to reinforce

bloc *m* (*pl* **blocs**) (de papel) pad; **~ de notas**
note *o* writing pad

blof *m* (Col, Méx) bluff

blofear [A1] *vi* (Col, Méx) **(a)** (en el juego) to bluff
(b) (fam) (alardear) to show off

bloque *m* **1** (de piedra, hormigón) block
2 (edificio) block; **un ~ de departamentos** (AmL)
or (Esp) **pisos** an apartment block, a block of flats
(BrE) **3** (Inf) block **4** (fuerza política) bloc; **en ~**
(*loc adv*) en bloc, en masse

bloquear [A1] *vt* **1 (a)** ⟨*camino/entrada/
salida*⟩ to block; **estamos bloqueados por un
camión** there's a truck blocking our way **(b)** (Mil)
to blockade **2** ⟨*cuenta/fondos*⟩ to freeze, block
■ **bloquearse** *v pron* **1** «*mecanismo*» to jam;
«*frenos*» to jam, lock on; «*ruedas*» to lock
2 «*negociaciones*» to reach deadlock

bloqueo *m* (de ciudad) blockade, siege; (de puerto)
blockade; (Dep) block

bluff /bluf/ *m* (*pl* **bluffs**) **(a)** (Jueg) bluff **(b)**
(fam) (fanfarronería): **es puro ~** he's all talk (colloq)

blusa *f* blouse

blusón *m* loose shirt *o* blouse

blvar. *m* (= **bulevar**) Blvd (*in US*)

Bº = **Banco**

boa *f* (Zool) boa

bobada *f* (cosa boba) silly thing; **deja de hacer
~s** stop being so stupid *o* silly; **deja de decir ~s**
stop talking nonsense

bobina *f* **(a)** (de hilo) reel **(b)** (Auto, Elec) coil

bobo -ba *adj* (fam) silly
■ *m,f* (fam) fool

boca *f* **1 (a)** (Anat, Zool) mouth **(b)** (*en locs*)
boca abajo/arriba ⟨*dormir/echarse*⟩ on one's

stomach/back; **puso los naipes ~ arriba** she laid
the cards face up; **en boca de: la pregunta que
anda en ~ de todos los niños** the question which
is on every child's lips; **el escándalo andaba en
~ de todos** the scandal was common knowledge;
por boca de from; **lo supe por ~ de su hermana** I
heard it from his sister; **a pedir de ~** just fine;
hacerle el ~ a ~ a algn to give sb the kiss of life;
hacérsele la ~ agua a algn (Esp): **se le hacía la ~
agua mirando los pasteles** looking at the cakes
made her mouth water; **quedarse con la ~
abierta** to be dumbfounded *o* (colloq) flabbergasted
2 (de buzón) slot; (de túnel) mouth, entrance; (de
puerto) entrance; (de vasija, botella) rim; **~ de
incendios** fire hydrant, fireplug (AmE); **~ del
estómago** (fam) pit of the stomach; **~ de metro** *or*
(RPI) **subte** subway entrance (AmE), underground
o tube station entrance (BrE)

bocacalle *f*: entrance to a street; **la primera ~
a la derecha** the first turning on the right

bocadillo *m* **1** (Esp) (emparedado) roll **2** (Col,
Ven) (dulce) guava jelly

bocado *m* **(a)** (de comida) bite; **de un ~ in** one
bite; **no ha probado ~** she hasn't had a bite to
eat **(b)** (comida ligera) snack

bocajarro: a ~ (*loc adv*) **(a)** ⟨*disparar*⟩ at
point-blank range **(b)** ⟨*decir/preguntar*⟩
point-blank

bocamanga *f* cuff

bocanada *f* (de humo, aliento) puff, mouthful;
(ráfaga) gust, blast

bocatoma *f* (Andes) water inlet

boceto *m* (dibujo) sketch; (de proyecto) outline

bochar [A1] *vt* **(a)** (RPI fam) ⟨*sugerencia/
propuesta*⟩ to squash (colloq) **(b)** (RPI arg) (en
examen) ⟨*estudiante*⟩ to fail, to flunk (AmE colloq)

bochas *fpl* (RPI) (Jueg) bowls

bochinche *m* (esp AmL fam) **(a)** (riña, pelea)
fight, brawl **(b)** (barullo, alboroto) racket (colloq),
ruckus (AmE colloq), row (BrE colloq) **(c)** (confusión,
lío) muddle, mess (colloq)

bochinchear [A1] *vi* (AmL fam) to fight

bochinchero -ra *adj* (AmL fam) rowdy

bochorno *m* **1** (calor) sultry *o* muggy weather
2 (vergüenza) embarrassment; **¡qué ~!** how
embarrassing!

bochornoso -sa *adj* **1** ⟨*tiempo*⟩ sultry,
muggy; ⟨*calor*⟩ sticky; **hacía un día ~** it was a
close *o* muggy day **2** ⟨*espectáculo/situación*⟩
embarrassing

bocina *f* **1** (de coche) horn; (de fábrica) hooter,
siren; (de faro) foghorn **2** (AmL) (auricular) receiver
3 (Méx) (Audio) loudspeaker

bocio *m* goiter*

boda *f* wedding; **~s de oro/plata** (de matrimonio)
golden/silver wedding anniversary; (de
organización) golden/silver jubilee

bodega *f* **1 (a)** (Vin) (fábrica) winery; (almacén)
wine cellar; (tienda) wine merchant's, wine shop
(b) (taberna) bar **(c)** (en casa) cellar **2 (a)** (AmC,
Per, Ven) (tienda de comestibles) grocery store (AmE),
grocer's (BrE) **(b)** (AmL exc RPI) (depósito) store,
warehouse

bodegón *m* **1** (Art) still life **2** (casa de comidas)
inn

bodeguero -ra *m,f* **1** (Vin) (productor) ⋯❖

wine-producer $\boxed{2}$ **(a)** (AmC, Per, Ven) (tendero)
shopkeeper **(b)** (AmL exc RPl) (de un depósito)
warehouseman

bodrio *m* (fam): **es un** ~ it is garbage (AmE) *o*
(BrE) rubbish (colloq)

bofetada *f*, **bofetón** *m* slap; **le di** *or* **pegué
una** ~ I slapped him (in the face)

boga *f*: **estar en** ~ to be in fashion *o* in vogue

Bogotá *m* Bogotá

bogotano -na *adj* of/from Bogotá

bohemio -mia *adj* **(a)** ⟨*vida/artista*⟩ bohemian
(b) (de Bohemia) Bohemian
■ *m,f* bohemian

bohío *m* (AmC, Col, Ven) hut

boicot /boj'kot/ *m* (*pl* **-cots**) boycott

boicotear [A1] *vt* to boycott

boina *f* beret

boite /bwat/ *f* night club

bol *m* bowl

bola *f* $\boxed{1}$ (cuerpo redondo) ball; (de helado) scoop;
(Dep) ball; (de petanca) boule; (canica) (Col, Per)
marble; ~ **de cristal** crystal ball; ~ **de nieve**
snowball; ~ **de partido/de set** match/set point
$\boxed{2}$ **bolas** *fpl* (fam: en algunas regiones vulg)
(testículos) balls (*pl*) (colloq *or* vulg); **estar en** ~**s**
(fam *or* vulg) to be stark naked (colloq); **hacerse** ~**s**
con algo (Méx) to get in a mess over sth
$\boxed{3}$ (fam) (mentira) lie, fib (colloq); **me metió una** ~
he told me a fib; **contar/decir** ~**s** to fib (colloq), to
tell fibs (colloq)
$\boxed{4}$ (Méx fam) (montón): **una** ~ **de** loads of (colloq)

bolchevique *adj/mf* Bolshevik

boleador -dora *m,f* $\boxed{1}$ (Méx) (lustrabotas)
bootblack $\boxed{2}$ (en las pampas) *person who uses bolas
to catch cattle*

boleadoras *fpl* bolas

bolear [A1] *vi* (Col) to knock up, knock a ball
about
■ ~ *vt* (Méx) to polish, shine

bolera *f* bowling alley

bolero¹ *m* $\boxed{1}$ (Mús) bolero $\boxed{2}$ (Indum) bolero
jacket/top

bolero² -ra *m,f* (Méx) bootblack

boleta *f* **(a)** (AmL) (en rifa) ticket **(b)** (CS) (de
multa) ticket **(c)** (CS) (recibo) receipt **(d)** (Col)
(entrada) ticket; ~ **de calificaciones** (Méx) school
report, report card (AmE); ~ **de depósito** (RPl)
deposit slip (AmE), paying-in slip (BrE); ~
electoral (Méx, RPl) ballot paper

boletaje *m* (Méx, Per) tickets (*pl*)

boletería *f* (AmL) (de teatro, cine) box office; (de
estación, estadio) ticket office

boletín *m* bulletin; ~ **de calificaciones** *or* **notas**
school report, report card (AmE)

boleto *m* (de lotería, rifa) ticket; (de quinielas) (Esp)
coupon; (de tren, autobús) (AmL) ticket; ~ **de ida**
(AmL) one-way ticket, single (ticket) (BrE); ~ **de
ida y vuelta** (AmL) round trip (ticket) (AmE),
return (ticket) (BrE); ~ **de viaje redondo** (Méx)
round trip (ticket) (AmE), return (ticket) (BrE)

boli *m* (Esp fam) ballpoint pen, Biro® (BrE)

boliche *m* $\boxed{1}$ **(a)** (en petanca) jack **(b)** (juguete)
cup-and-ball toy **(c)** (Col) (bolo) tenpin $\boxed{2}$ (Méx)
(juego) bowling, ten pin bowling (BrE); (lugar)
bowling alley $\boxed{3}$ **(a)** (CS) (tienda pequeña) (fam)
small store (AmE), small shop (BrE) **(b)** (Bol, RPl)
(taberna) bar

bolígrafo *m* ballpoint pen, Biro®

bolillo *m* (en pasamanería) bobbin; **encaje de** ~**s**
bobbin lace

bolita *f* (AmS) (Jueg) marble; **jugar a las** ~**s** to
play marbles

bolívar *m* bolivar (*Venezuelan unit of currency*)

Bolivia *f* Bolivia

boliviano -na *adj/m,f* Bolivian

bollo *m* (Coc) bun; **ser un** ~ (RPl fam) to be a
piece of cake (colloq)

bolo *m* **(a)** (palo) skittle, tenpin **(b) bolos** *mpl*
(juego) bowling, ten pin bowling (BrE); **jugar a los**
~**s** to play skittles, to go bowling

bolsa *f* $\boxed{1}$ **(a)** (en general) bag; ~ **de plástico/de
la compra** plastic/shopping bag; ~ **de (la) basura**
garbage *o* trash bag (AmE), rubbish bag *o* bin
liner (BrE); **una** ~ **de patatas fritas** (Esp) a bag of
chips (AmE), a packet *o* bag of crisps (BrE); ~ **de
agua caliente** hot-water bottle **(b)** (Méx) (bolso)
handbag, purse (AmE)
$\boxed{2}$ **(a)** (de marsupial) pouch **(b)** scrotum **(c)** (Méx)
(bolsillo) pocket
$\boxed{3}$ (de aire, gas, agua) pocket
$\boxed{4}$ (Econ, Fin) *tb* B~ *or* ~ **de valores** stock
exchange, stock market; **jugar a la** ~ to play the
market; **se cotizará en** ~ it will be listed on the
stock exchange; ~ **de empleo** (Col) employment
agency; ~ **de trabajo** *job vacancies and place
where they are advertised*

bolsear [A1] *vt* **(a)** (Méx fam) (robar): **me** ~**on en
el camión** I had my pocket picked on the bus **(b)**
(Chi fam) ⟨*comida/cigarillos*⟩ ~**le algo** A algn to
scrounge sth FROM *o* OFF sb

bolsillo *m* pocket; **de** ~ ⟨*calculadora/
diccionario*⟩ pocket (*before n*); **meterse a algn en
el** ~ to get sb eating out of one's hand

bolso *m* (de mujer) (Esp) handbag, purse (AmE); ~
de mano (de viaje) (overnight) bag; (de mujer) (Esp)
handbag, purse (AmE); ~ **de viaje** (overnight) bag

boludo -da *adj* (Col, RPl, Ven vulg) (imbécil): **es tan**
~ he's such a jerk (colloq) *o* (vulg) prick
■ *m,f* (Col, RPl, Ven vulg) asshole (AmE vulg),
dickhead (BrE vulg)

bomba *f* $\boxed{1}$ **(a)** (Arm, Mil) bomb; **lanzar/arrojar**
~**s** to drop bombs; **poner una** ~ to plant a bomb;
~ **atómica** atom *o* atomic bomb; ~ **de tiempo**
time bomb; ~ **lacrimógena** tear gas canister; **caer
como una** ~ «*noticia*» to come as a bombshell
(b) (notición) big news **(c)** (en fútbol americano) bomb
$\boxed{2}$ (Tec) pump; ~ **de aire** air pump; ~ **de agua** water
pump $\boxed{3}$ (Andes, Ven) (gasolinera) gas station (AmE),
petrol station (BrE) $\boxed{4}$ (Chi) (vehículo) fire engine,
fire truck (AmE); (estación) fire station

AmC	América Central	Arg	Argentina	Cu	Cuba	Per	Perú
AmL	América Latina	Bol	Bolivia	Ec	Ecuador	RPl	Río de la Plata
AmS	América del Sur	Chi	Chile	Esp	España	Ur	Uruguay
Andes	Región andina	CS	Cono Sur	Méx	México	Ven	Venezuela

bombacha _f_ **(a)** (CS) (de gaucho) baggy trousers (_pl_) **(b)** (RPl) (de mujer) panties (_pl_), knickers (_pl_) (BrE)

bombardear [A1] _vt_ (desde avión) to bomb; (con artillería) to bombard, shell; **me ~on a preguntas** they bombarded me with questions

bombardeo _m_ (desde aviones) bombing; (con artillería) bombardment, shelling

bombardero _m_ bomber

bombazo _m_ ☐1 (Méx) (explosión) bomb explosion ☐2 (fam) (noticia) bombshell

bombear [A1] _vt_ to pump

bombero _mf_, **bombero -ra** _m,f_ (de incendios) (_m_) firefighter, fireman; (_f_) firefighter; **llamar a los ~s** to call the fire department (AmE) _o_ (BrE) brigade; **cuerpo de ~s** fire department (AmE) _o_ (BrE) brigade

bombilla _f_ ☐1 (Esp) (Elec) light bulb ☐2 (para el mate) _tube through which mate tea is drunk_

bombillo _m_ (AmC, Col, Ven) light bulb

bombín _m_ ☐1 (Indum) derby (AmE), bowler hat (BrE) ☐2 (para inflar) pump

bombita _f_ (RPl) (Elec) light bulb

bombo _m_ ☐1 (Mús) (instrumento) bass drum; (músico) bass drummer; **tengo la cabeza como un ~** my head's about to explode; **con ~s y platillos** _or_ (Esp) **a ~ y platillo** with a great fanfare; **darle ~ a algo** to give sth a lot of hype (colloq) ☐2 (de sorteo) drum

bombón _m_ **(a)** (confite) chocolate **(b)** (fam) (persona) stunner (colloq) **(c)** (Méx) (malvavisco) marshmallow

bombona _f_ gas cylinder _o_ canister

bombonería _f_ candy store (AmE), sweet shop (BrE)

bonachón -chona _adj_ (fam) (amable) good-natured, kind
■ _m,f_ (fam) (persona amable) good-natured _o_ kind person

bonaerense _adj_: _of/from the province of Buenos Aires_

bonche _m_ ☐1 (AmC, Col fam) (riña) fight; (contienda) contest ☐2 (Ven fam) (fiesta) party, rave-up (BrE sl)

bondad _f_ **(a)** (afabilidad, generosidad) goodness, kindness; **¿tendría la ~ de cerrar la puerta?** (frml) would you mind closing the door? **(b)** (del clima) mildness

bondadoso -sa _adj_ kind, kindhearted, kindly

bongó, bongo _m_ bongo

boniato _m_ sweet potato

bonificación _f_ **(a)** (aumento, beneficio) bonus **(b)** (descuento) discount

bonito¹ -ta _adj_ pretty; ‹canción/apartamento› nice, lovely

bonito² _m_ tuna, bonito

bono _m_ (vale) voucher; (Econ, Fin) bond

boquera _f_ cold sore

boquerón _m_ anchovy

boquete _m_ hole

boquiabierto -ta _adj_: **quedarse ~** to be speechless _o_ dumbfounded

boquilla _f_ (de instrumento musical) mouthpiece; (de pipa) stem; (para cigarrillos) cigarette holder

borbotón _m_ gush; **a borbotones** ‹hervir› fiercely; ‹salir› «sangre/agua» to gush out

borda _f_ gunwale, rail; **echar** _or_ **tirar algo por la ~** to throw sth overboard

bordado¹ -da _adj_ ‹mantel/sábana› embroidered

bordado² _m_ embroidery

bordar [A1] _vt_ ‹sábana/blusa› to embroider; **lo bordó a mano** she embroidered it by hand

borde _m_ (de mesa, cama, acantilado) edge; (de moneda, taza, vaso) rim; **llenó el vaso hasta el ~** she filled the glass to the brim; **al ~ de algo** ‹de la guerra/locura› on the brink of sth; ‹de las lágrimas/del caos/de la ruina› on the verge of sth; **al ~ de la muerte** on the point of death

bordear [A1] _vt_ **(a)** (seguir el borde de) ‹costa› to go along; ‹isla› to go around **(b)** (estar a lo largo del borde): **un camino bordeado de álamos** a road lined with poplars

bordillo _m_ curb (AmE), kerb (BrE)

bordo _m_: **a ~** on board; **subir a ~** to go aboard _o_ on board

borgoña _m_ (Vin) Burgundy, burgundy

borra _f_ (sedimento — del café) dregs; (— del vino) lees (_pl_), sediment

borrachera _f_: **pegarse** _or_ (Esp) **cogerse** _or_ (esp AmL) **agarrarse una ~** to get drunk

borracho -cha _adj_ **(a)** [ESTAR] drunk **(b)** [SER]: **es muy ~** he is a drunkard _o_ a heavy drinker
■ _m,f_ drunk; (habitual) drunkard, drunk

borrador _m_ ☐1 (de redacción, carta) rough draft; (de contrato, proyecto) draft; (de dibujo) sketch; **lo hice en ~** I did a rough draft ☐2 (para la pizarra) eraser (AmE), board rubber (BrE)

borraja _f_ borage

borrar [A1] _vt_ **(a)** ‹palabra/dibujo› (con goma) to rub out, erase; (con líquido corrector) to white out, tippex out (BrE); ‹pizarra› to clean; ‹huellas digitales› to wipe off **(b)** ‹cassette/disquete› to erase, wipe **(c)** (Inf) ‹archivo› delete; ‹pantalla› to clear **(d)** ‹recuerdos/imagen› to blot out
■ **borrarse** _v pron_ «inscripción/letrero» to fade; **se borró con la lluvia** the rain washed it away _o_ off

borrasca _f_ **(a)** (área de bajas presiones) area of low pressure **(b)** (tormenta) squall

borrascoso -sa _adj_ ‹viento› squally; ‹tiempo› stormy, squally

borrego -ga _m,f_ (cordero) lamb; (oveja) sheep

borrón _m_ (mancha) inkblot; (mancha borroneada) smudge; **~ y cuenta nueva** let's make a fresh start

borronear [A1] _vt_ to smudge

borroso -sa _adj_ ‹foto/imagen› blurred; ‹inscripción› worn; ‹contorno› indistinct, blurred

boscoso -sa _adj_ wooded

bosque _m_ wood; (más grande) forest, woods (_pl_); (terreno) woodland; **~ ecuatorial** _or_ **pluvial** (equatorial) rainforest

bosquejar [A1] _vt_ (Art) to sketch, make a sketch of; ‹idea/proyecto› to outline, sketch out

bosquejo _m_ (Art) sketch; (de novela) outline

bostezar [A4] _vi_ to yawn

bostezo _m_ yawn

bota _f_ ☐1 (calzado) boot; **~s de caña alta/de** ⸱⸱⸱▸

b

media caña knee-high/calf-length boots; ~s de
agua rubber boots, wellingtons (BrE); ~s de
esquí/montar ski/riding boots ⟨2⟩ (para vino) small
wineskin

botadero *m* (Andes) *tb* ~ de basura garbage
dump (AmE), rubbish dump *o* tip (BrE)

botado -da *adj* [ESTAR] (AmS exc RPl fam) **(a)**
(barato) dirt cheap (colloq) **(b)** (fácil) dead easy
(colloq)

botadura *f* launching

botana *f* (Méx) snack, appetizer

botánico -ca *adj* botanical

botar [A1] *vt* ⟨1⟩ ⟨barco⟩ to launch
⟨2⟩ ⟨pelota⟩ to bounce
⟨3⟩ (AmL exc RPl) (tirar) to throw … out; **no lo botes
al suelo** don't throw it on the ground; **bótalo a la
basura** chuck *o* throw it out (colloq); ~ **el dinero**
to throw your money away
⟨4⟩ (AmL exc RPl fam) **(a)** (echar — de lugar) to throw
… out (colloq); (— de trabajo) to fire (colloq), to sack
(BrE colloq) **(b)** (abandonar) ⟨novio/novia⟩ to chuck
(colloq), to ditch (colloq); ⟨marido/esposa⟩ to leave;
el tren nos dejó botados we missed the train
⟨5⟩ (AmL exc RPl) (derribar) ⟨puerta/árbol⟩ to
knock down; ⟨botella/taza⟩ to knock over; **no
empujes que me botas** stop pushing, you're going
to knock me over
⟨6⟩ (AmL exc RPl) (perder) ⟨aceite/gasolina⟩ to leak
■ ~ *vi* (Esp) «pelota» to bounce
■ **botarse** *v pron* (AmL exc CS fam) **(a)** (apresurarse)
to rush **(b)** (arrojarse) to jump

botarate *mf* **(a)** (fam) (irresponsable)
irresponsible fool **(b)** (AmL exc RPl) (derrochador)
spendthrift

bote *m* ⟨1⟩ (Náut) boat; ~ de *or* a remos rowboat
(AmE), rowing boat (BrE); ~ salvavidas lifeboat
⟨2⟩ (recipiente — de lata) tin; (— de vidrio, plástico)
storage jar; (— de cerveza) (Esp) can; (— de
mermelada) (Esp) jar; **el** ~ **de la basura** (Méx) the
trash can (AmE), the rubbish bin (BrE); **de** ~ **en**
~ packed ⟨3⟩ (de pelota) bounce; **dio dos** ~**s** it
bounced twice

botella *f* bottle; **una** ~ **de vino** (recipiente) a wine
bottle; (con contenido) a bottle of wine; **cerveza de
o en** ~ bottled beer

botica *f* (en algunas regiones ant) (farmacia)
pharmacy

botijo *m*: *drinking jug with spout*

botillería *f* (Chi) liquor store (AmE), off licence
(BrE)

botín *m* ⟨1⟩ (bota corta) ankle boot; (de bebé)
bootee; (de futbolista) (CS) boot ⟨2⟩ (de guerra)
plunder, booty; (de ladrones) haul, loot

botiquín *m* **(a)** (armario — para medicinas)
medicine chest *o* cabinet; (— para colonias, jabón,
etc) bathroom cabinet **(b)** (maletín) *tb* ~ de
primeros auxilios first-aid kit

botón *m* ⟨1⟩ (Indum) button; ~ de presión (AmL)
snap fastener (AmE), press stud (BrE) ⟨2⟩ (de
mecanismo) button; **el** ~ **del volumen** the volume
control ⟨3⟩ (AmL) (insignia) badge, button (AmE)
⟨4⟩ (de flor) bud

botones *mf* (*pl* ~) (de hotel) bellboy; (de oficina)
(*m*) office boy; (*f*) office girl

bouquet /bu'ke/ *m* (*pl* **-quets**) **(a)** (del vino)
bouquet **(b)** (ramillete) bouquet

boutique /bu'tik/ *f* boutique

bóveda *f* ⟨1⟩ (Arquit) vault; ~ de seguridad (AmL)
bank vault ⟨2⟩ (RPl) (sepulcro) tomb

bovino -na *adj* bovine

bowling /'boulin/ *m* **(a)** (deporte) tenpins (AmE),
tenpin bowling (BrE) **(b)** (lugar) bowling alley

box /boks/ *m* (AmL) (boxeo) boxing

boxeador -dora *m,f* boxer

boxear [A1] *vi* to box

boxeo *m* boxing

boya *f* (Náut) buoy; (en pesca) float

boyante *adj* ⟨situación/economía⟩ buoyant

bozal *m* (de perro) muzzle; (de caballo) halter

bozo *m* down (on upper lip)

bracero -ra *m,f* temporary farm worker

bragas *fpl* (Esp) (de mujer) panties (*pl*), knickers
(*pl*) (BrE)

braguero *m* truss

bragueta *f* fly, flies (*pl*)

braille /'brajle/ *adj* braille (before n)
■ *m* braille

bramante *m* twine, string

bramar [A1] *vi* «toro/ciervo» to bellow;
«elefante» to trumpet

bramido *m* (de toro, ciervo) bellowing; (de elefante)
trumpeting; **dio un** ~ it bellowed/trumpeted

branquia *f* gill

brasa *f* ember; **carne/pescado a la(s)** ~**(s)**
charcoal-grilled meat/fish

brasero *m* (de carbón — para interiores) small
brazier; (— para la intemperie) brazier; (eléctrico)
electric heater

brasier *m* (Col, Méx, Ven) bra

Brasil *m*: *tb* **el** ~ Brazil

brasileño -ña, (AmL) **brasilero -ra** *adj/m,f*
Brazilian

bravío -vía *adj* ⟨toro⟩ fierce, wild; ⟨potro⟩ wild,
unmanageable

bravo¹ -va *adj* **(a)** [SER] ⟨toro/perro⟩ fierce; *ver
tb* TORO **(b)** [ESTAR] ⟨mar⟩ rough **(c)** [ESTAR]
(AmL fam) (enojado) angry

bravo² *interj* (expresando aprobación) well done!,
good job! (AmE); (tras actuación) bravo!

bravucón -cona *adj* (fam) bragging (before n)

bravuconada *f* piece of bravado; ~**s** bravado

braza *f* (Esp) (en natación) breaststroke; **nadar a**
~ to swim (the) breaststroke

brazada *f* (al nadar) stroke

brazalete *m* **(a)** (pulsera — de una pieza) bangle,
bracelet; (— de eslabones) bracelet **(b)** (de tela)
armband

brazo *m* ⟨1⟩ (Anat) arm; (parte superior) upper
arm; **llevaba una cesta al** ~ she had a basket on
one arm; **caminar/ir del** ~ to walk arm in arm;
llevaba al niño en ~**s** he was carrying the child
in his arms; **cruzado de** ~**s: no te quedes ahí
cruzado de** ~**s** don't just stand/sit there (doing
nothing); **dar el** *or* **a torcer** to give in; **no dio el** *or*
su ~ **a torcer** he didn't let them/her twist his
arm
⟨2⟩ (de sillón) arm; (de tocadiscos) arm; (de grúa) jib;
(de río) branch, channel; ~ **de gitano** (Coc) jelly
roll (AmE), swiss roll (BrE); ~ **de mar** inlet, sound
⟨3⟩ **brazos** *mpl* (trabajadores) hands (*pl*)

brea *f* pitch, tar

brebaje *m* potion; **un** ~ **mágico** a magic potion

brecha *f* (en muro) breach, opening; (en la frente, cabeza) gash; ~ **generacional** generation gap

bretel *m* (CS) strap

bretón¹ -tona *adj/m,f* Breton

bretón² *m* (idioma) Breton

breva *f* (Bot) early fig, black fig

breve *adj* (frml) brief, short; ⟨*viaje/distancia*⟩ short; **dentro de ~s momentos** in a few moments; **sea usted ~, por favor** please be brief; **en ~** shortly, soon

brevedad *f* (a) (de discurso, texto) brevity (b) (frml) (prontitud): **con la mayor ~** *or* **a la ~ posible** as soon as possible *o* (frml) at your earliest convenience

brevete *m* (Per) driver's license (AmE), driving licence (BrE)

bribón -bona *m,f* (fam) rascal (colloq), scamp (colloq)

bricolaje, bricolage *m* do-it-yourself, DIY

brida *f* bridle

briega *f* (Col) hard work, struggle

brigada *f* (Mil) brigade; (de policía) squad; ~ **de explosivos** bomb squad; ~ **antidroga** *or* **de estupefacientes** drug squad; ~ **de salvamento** rescue team

brillante *adj* (a) ⟨*luz/estrella/color*⟩ bright; ⟨*zapatos/metal/pelo*⟩ shiny; ⟨*pintura*⟩ gloss (*before n*); ⟨*papel*⟩ glossy; ⟨*tela*⟩ with a sheen (b) ⟨*escritor/porvenir*⟩ brilliant; ⟨*mente*⟩ great; **su actuación fue ~** she performed brilliantly
■ *m* (diamante) diamond; **un anillo de ~s** a diamond ring

brillar [A1] *vi* (a) «*sol/luz*» to shine; «*estrella*» to shine, sparkle; «*zapatos/suelo/metal*» to shine, gleam; «*diamante/ojos*» to sparkle (b) (destacarse) «*persona*» to shine
■ ~ *vt* (Col) to polish

brillo *m* (a) (en general) shine; (de estrella) brightness, brilliance; (de diamante, ojos) sparkle; (de tela) sheen; **darle ~ al suelo** to polish the floor; **fotos con ~** gloss finish photos; **dale un poco de ~** (TV) turn the brightness up a bit (b) (esplendor, lucimiento) splendor*; **sin ~** ⟨*discurso/interpretación*⟩ dull (c) (para labios) lip gloss; (para uñas) clear nail polish

brilloso -sa *adj* (AmL) shiny

brincar [A2] *vi* «*niño*» to jump up and down; «*cordero*» to gambol, skip around; «*liebre*» to hop; ~ **de alegría** to jump for joy
■ ~ *vt* (Méx) ⟨*valla/obstáculo*⟩ to jump

brinco *m* jump, leap, bound; **pegó** *or* **dio un ~ del susto** (fam) he jumped with fright

brindar [A1] *vi* to drink a toast; ~ **POR algn/algo** to drink a toast TO sb/sth
■ ~ *vt* (frml) (proporcionar) to give; **le brindó su apoyo** she gave him her support
■ **brindarse** *v pron* (frml) **~se A hacer algo** to offer *o* volunteer to do sth; **se brindó a acompañarme** he offered *o* volunteered to accompany me

brindis *m* (*pl* ~) toast; **hacer un ~ por algn** to drink a toast to sb

brío *m* (a) (ánimo, energía) spirit; **luchó con ~** he fought with great spirit *o* determination (b) (de caballo) spirit

brioso -sa *adj* ⟨*caballo*⟩ spirited

brisa *f* breeze

británico -ca *adj* British
■ *m,f* British person, Briton; **los ~s** the British, British people

brizna *f* (hebra) strand; (de hierba) blade

briznar [A1] *v impers* (Ven) to drizzle

broca *f* (drill) bit

brocado *m* brocade

brocha *f* (de pintor) paintbrush, brush; (de afeitar) shaving brush; (en cosmética) blusher brush

broche *m* (a) (joya) brooch (b) (de collar, monedero) clasp; ~ **de presión** (AmL) snap fastener (AmE), press stud (BrE) (c) (Méx, Ur) (para el pelo) barrette (AmE), hair slide (BrE) (d) (Arg) (grapa) staple

brocheta *f* (aguja) brochette, skewer; (plato) kebab

brócoli *m* broccoli

broma *f* joke; **hacerle** *or* **gastarle una ~ a algn** to play a (practical) joke on sb; **déjate de ~s** stop kidding around (colloq); **no estoy para ~s** I'm not in the mood for jokes; **~s aparte** joking apart; **lo dije de** *or* **en ~** I was joking; **ni en ~** no way (colloq)

bromear [A1] *vi* to joke

bromista *adj*: **es muy ~** he's always joking; **¡qué ~ eres!** you're such a joker
■ *mf* joker

bromuro *m* bromide

bronca *f* ① (a) (fam) (disputa, lío) row; **armar** *or* **montar una ~** to kick up a fuss (colloq); **buscar ~** to look for trouble *o* a fight (b) (alboroto, bullicio) racket (colloq) ② (esp Esp fam) (regañina) scolding, telling off (colloq); **echarle la ~ a algn** to tell sb off (colloq) ③ (AmL fam) (rabia): **está con una ~** he's furious; **me da mucha ~** it really gets to *o* bugs me (colloq); **tenerle ~ a algn** to have it in for sb (colloq)

bronce *m* (a) (para estatuas, cañones) bronze; **una medalla de ~** a bronze medal (b) (AmL) (para llamadores, placas) brass

bronceado¹ -da *adj* tanned, suntanned

bronceado² *m* (de la piel) tan, suntan; (Metal) bronzing

bronceador *m* suntan lotion

broncear [A1] *vt* ⟨*piel*⟩ to tan
■ **broncearse** *v pron* to get a tan *o* a suntan

bronconeumonía *f* bronchopneumonia

bronquio *m* bronchial tube

bronquitis *f* bronchitis

brotar [A1] *vi* (a) «*planta*» to sprout, come up; «*hoja*» to appear, sprout; «*flor*» to come out (b) «*sarampión/grano*» to appear
■ **brotarse** *v pron* (AmL) to come out in spots

brote *m* (a) (Bot) shoot; **echar ~s** to sprout, put out shoots (b) (de violencia, enfermedad) outbreak (c) (Col) (sarpullido) rash

bruces: de ~ (*loc adv*) face down; **se cayó de ~** he fell flat on his face

brujería *f* witchcraft

brujo -ja *adj* (a) ⟨*ojos/amor*⟩ bewitching (b) (AmC, Méx fam) (sin dinero) broke (colloq)
■ *m,f* (*m*) warlock; (*f*) witch

brújula *f* compass

bruma *f* (marina) (sea) mist; (del alba) mist

brumoso -sa *adj* misty
bruñir [I9] *vt* to polish
brusco -ca *adj* (a) ⟨movimiento/cambio⟩ abrupt, sudden; ⟨subida/descenso⟩ sharp, sudden (b) ⟨carácter/modales⟩ rough; ⟨tono/gesto⟩ brusque, abrupt; ⟨respuesta⟩ curt, brusque
Bruselas *f* Brussels
brusquedad *f* (a) (en el trato) roughness; **con ~** ⟨hablar/actuar⟩ abruptly (b) (de movimiento) abruptness, suddenness; **frenó con ~** he braked sharply
brutal *adj* ⟨crimen⟩ brutal; ⟨atentado⟩ savage
brutalidad *f* brutality, savageness
bruto -ta *adj* ⚊1⚊ ⟨persona⟩ (a) (ignorante) ignorant (b) (violento, brusco): **¡qué ~!** what a brute! ⚊2⚊ ⟨peso/sueldo⟩ gross; **en ~** ⟨diamante⟩ uncut; ⟨mineral⟩ crude
■ *m,f* (a) (ignorante) ignorant person (b) (persona violenta) brute, animal
bucal *adj* ⟨lesión⟩ mouth (before n); ⟨antiséptico/higiene⟩ oral (before n)
buceador -dora *m,f* diver
bucear [A1] *vi* to swim underwater, to dive
buceo *m* underwater swimming, diving
buchaca *f* (Col) pocket
buche *m* ⚊1⚊ (a) (de aves) crop (b) (de otros animales) maw ⚊2⚊ (Med, Odont): **hacer ~s con algo** to rinse one's mouth out with sth
bucle *m* (a) (en el pelo) ringlet (b) (Inf) loop
bucólico -ca *adj* bucolic, pastoral
budín *m* (a) (dulce) pudding (b) (salado) pie
budismo *m* Buddhism
budista *adj/mf* Buddhist
buen *adj* ▶ BUENO¹
buenaventura *f* (a) (buena suerte) good fortune (b) (futuro): **me dijo/leyó la ~** she told my fortune
buen mozo, -na moza *adj* ⟨hombre⟩ good-looking, handsome; ⟨mujer⟩ attractive, good-looking
bueno¹ -na *adj* [BUEN *is used before masculine singular nouns*]
⚊1⚊ [SER] (a) ⟨hotel/producto/trabajo⟩ good; **ropa buena** good-quality clothes; **la buena mesa** good cooking (b) ⟨remedio/método⟩ good; **es ~ para la gripe/los dolores de cabeza** it's good for the flu/headaches (c) ⟨médico/alumno⟩ good; **un buen padre/amigo** he's a good father/friend; **es muy buena en francés** she's very good at French; **es buena para los negocios** she's got a good head for business (d) (amable, bondadoso) good, kind; **fueron muy ~s conmigo** they were very good o kind to me (e) (conveniente, correcto) good; **no es buena hora** it's not a good time; **no es ~ comer tanto** it isn't good to eat so much; **es ~ para la salud** it's good for your health; **su inglés es ~** her English is good
⚊2⚊ (a) (agradable) nice; **hace muy buen tiempo** the weather is nice (en general) **ser ~** to be good, be nice; (en particular) **estar ~** to be good, be nice; **el guacamole es buenísimo** guacamole is

really good; **esta sopa está muy buena** this soup is very good (c) (favorable) ⟨oferta/crítica⟩ good; **una buena noticia** a piece of good news
⚊3⚊ [ESTAR] (a) (en buen estado) ⟨leche/pescado⟩ fresh; **esta leche no está buena** this milk is off o sour (b) (fam) (sexualmente atractivo): **está buenísimo** he's really gorgeous
⚊4⚊ (saludable, sano) ⟨costumbre/alimentación⟩ good; **estar en buena forma** to be in good shape
⚊5⚊ (a) (en fórmulas, saludos) good; **¡~s días!** good morning; **¡buenas tardes!** (temprano) good afternoon; (más tarde) good evening; **¡buenas noches!** (al llegar) good evening; (al despedirse) good night; **¡buen viaje!** have a good trip!; **¡buen provecho!** enjoy your meal (b) ⟨delante de n⟩ (uso enfático) ⟨susto⟩ terrible; **una buena cantidad** a fair amount; **un buen día** one day (c) **¡qué ~!** (AmL) great (d) **de buenas a primeras** suddenly; **por las buenas** willingly
■ *m,f* (a) (hum o leng infantil) (en películas, cuentos) goody (colloq); **los ~s y los malos** the good guys and the bad guys (colloq) (b) (bonachón, buenazo): **el ~ de Juan/la buena de Pilar** good old Juan/Pilar
bueno² *interj* ⚊1⚊ (a) (expresando — duda) well; (— conformidad) OK (colloq), all right; **¿un café? — bueno** coffee? — OK o all right (b) (expresando resignación): **~, otra vez será** never mind, maybe next time (c) (expresando irritación): **~, se acabó ¡a la cama!** right, that's it, bed!; **¡y ~! ¿qué querías que hiciera?** (RPl) well, what did you expect me to do? ⚊2⚊ (Méx) (al contestar el teléfono) **¡~!** hello
Buenos Aires *m* Buenos Aires
buey *m* (Agr, Zool) ox
■ *adj* (Méx fam) dumb (colloq)
búfalo¹ -la *adj* (AmC fam) great (colloq), fantastic (colloq)
búfalo² *m* buffalo
bufanda *f* scarf
bufar [A1] *vi* to snort
bufet /bu'fe/, **bufé** *m* ⚊1⚊ (Coc) buffet ⚊2⚊ (Andes) (aparador) sideboard
bufete *m* (Der) (despacho) lawyer's office; (negocio) legal practice, law firm
bufido *m* snort
bufón *m* (Hist) jester; (gracioso) (fam) clown (colloq)
buhardilla *f* (a) (desván) attic (b) (apartamento) attic apartment (AmE) o (BrE) room (c) (ventana) dormer window
búho *m* owl
buitre *m* vulture
bujía *f* (a) (Auto) spark plug (b) (AmC) (Elec) light bulb
bula *f* (Relig) bull; **~ papal** papal bull
bulbo *m* bulb
bulevar *m* boulevard
Bulgaria *f* Bulgaria
búlgaro¹ -ra *adj/m,f* Bulgarian
búlgaro² *m* (idioma) Bulgarian
bulín *m* ⚊1⚊ (RPl fam) (a) (de soltero) bachelor pad

(b) (vivienda): **se compraron un bulincito** they bought a little place of their own (colloq) **2** (Per) (burdel) brothel

bulla *f* (ruido) racket (colloq), ruckus (AmE colloq); (actividad) bustle; **armar** *or* **meter** ~ to make a racket, to create a ruckus

bullanguero -ra *adj* (fam) ⟨persona⟩ fun-loving; ⟨música/ambiente⟩ lively

bullicio *m* **(a)** (ruido) noise, racket (colloq) **(b)** (actividad): **el ~ de la gran ciudad** the hustle and bustle of the city

bullicioso -sa *adj* noisy

bullir [I9] *vi*: **la calle bullía de gente** the street was teeming *o* swarming with people; **el lugar bullía de actividad** the place was a hive of activity

bulto *m* **1** **(a)** (cuerpo, forma) shape; **vi un ~ que se movía** I saw a shape moving; **escurrir el ~** (fam) (en el trabajo) to duck out; (en entrevista) to dodge the issue **(b)** (volumen): **hace mucho/poco ~** it is/isn't very bulky **2** (Med) lump **3** **(a)** (maleta, bolsa) piece of luggage; **~ de mano** piece *o* item of hand baggage *o* luggage; **cargada de ~s** laden with packages (*o* bags *etc*) **(b)** (Col, Méx) (saco) sack

búnker /'buŋker/ *m* (*pl* **-kers**) bunker

buñuelo *m* fritter

BUP /bup/ *m* (en Esp) = **Bachillerato Unificado Polivalente**

buque *m* ship, vessel; **~ cisterna/de guerra** tanker/warship

burbuja *f* (de gas, aire) bubble; **una bebida con/ sin ~s** a fizzy/still drink

burbujear [A1] *vi* **(a)** «champán/agua mineral» to fizz **(b)** (al hervir) to bubble

burdel *m* brothel

burdeos *adj inv* (color) burgundy

burdo -da *adj* **(a)** ⟨persona/modales⟩ coarse **(b)** ⟨mentira⟩ blatant; ⟨imitación⟩ crude; ⟨excusa⟩ flimsy **(c)** ⟨paño/tela⟩ rough, coarse

burgués -guesa *adj* (Hist) bourgeois; (de clase media) middle-class; (pey) bourgeois (pej)
■ *m,f* **(a)** (Hist) bourgeois **(b)** (persona de clase media) member of the middle class; (pey) bourgeois

burguesía *f* (Hist) bourgeoisie; (clase media) middle class, middle classes (*pl*); (pey) bourgeoisie

burla *f* **(a)** (mofa): **hacerle ~ a algn** to make fun of sb, to mock sb **(b)** (atropello): **esto es una ~ del reglamento** this makes a mockery of the regulations

burladero *m*: *barrier behind which the bullfighter takes refuge*

burlar [A1] *vt* **(a)** ⟨medidas de seguridad⟩ to evade, get around; **~on la vigilancia de la policía** they slipped past the police **(b)** ⟨enemigo⟩ to outwit
■ **burlarse** *v pron* **~se DE algo/algn** to make fun OF sth/sb

burlesco -ca *adj* ⟨género⟩ burlesque; ⟨espectáculo⟩ comic

burlete *m* draft* excluder

burlón -lona *adj* **(a)** (de mofa) ⟨actitud/tono⟩ mocking; ⟨risa⟩ sardonic, derisive **(b)** (de broma) ⟨actitud⟩ joking, teasing

buró *m* **(a)** (escritorio) writing desk, bureau (BrE) **(b)** (Méx) (mesa de noche) bedside table

burocracia *f* bureaucracy

burócrata *mf* **(a)** (pey) bureaucrat (pej) **(b)** (Méx) (funcionario) civil servant, official

burocrático -ca *adj* **(a)** (pey) ⟨trámite/ proceso⟩ bureaucratic **(b)** (Méx) ⟨empleado/ jerarquía⟩ government (*before n*), state (*before n*)

burrada *f* (fam) (necedad, barbaridad): **decir ~s** to talk nonsense *o* drivel; **¿cómo pudiste hacer semejante ~?** how could you do such a stupid thing?

burro¹ -rra *adj* **(a)** (fam) (ignorante) stupid, dumb (AmE colloq), thick (BrE colloq) **(b)** (fam) (obstinado, cabezón) pigheaded (colloq)
■ *m,f* **1** (Zool) (asno) (*m*) donkey; (*f*) female donkey, jenny; **trabajar como un ~** to slog one's guts out **2** (fam) **(a)** (ignorante) idiot **(b)** (cabezón, obstinado) stubborn mule, obstinate pig (colloq)

burro² *m* **(a)** (en carpintería) sawhorse; (en herrería) workbench **(b)** (Méx) (para planchar) ironing board; (caballete) trestle; (escalera) stepladder

bursátil *adj* stock market *o* exchange (*before n*)

bus *m* (Auto, Transp) bus; (Inf) bus

busca *f* (búsqueda) search; **en ~ de algo** in search of sth; **salieron en su ~** they set out to look for him
■ *m* (Esp fam) pager, beeper (AmE), bleeper (BrE)

buscador¹ -dora *m,f*: **~ de oro** gold prospector; **~ de tesoros** treasure hunter

buscador² *m* (Inf) search engine

buscapleitos *mf* (*pl* **~**) (fam) troublemaker

buscar [A2] *vt* **1** **(a)** (intentar encontrar) to look for; ⟨fama/fortuna⟩ to seek; **te buscan en la portería** someone is asking for you at reception **(b)** (en libro, lista) to look up; **busca el número en la guía** look up the number in the directory **2** **(a)** (recoger) to collect, pick up; **fui a ~lo al aeropuerto** (para traerlo — en coche) I went to pick him up from the airport; (— en tren, a pie) I went to meet him at the airport; **vengo a ~ mis cosas** I've come to collect *o* pick up my things **(b)** (conseguir) to get; **yo le busqué trabajo** I found him a job; **fue a ~ un médico/un taxi** he went to get a doctor/a taxi; **¿qué buscas con eso?** what are you trying to achieve by that?
■ **~** *vi* to look; **busca en el cajón** look *o* have a look in the drawer
■ **buscarse** *v pron* **1** (intentar encontrar) to look for **2** ⟨problemas⟩ to ask for; **no quiero ~me complicaciones/problemas** I don't want any trouble; **tú te lo has buscado** you've brought it on yourself, it serves you right; **buscársela(s)** (fam): **te la estás buscando** you're asking for trouble, you're asking for it (colloq)

buseta *f* (Col, Ven) small bus

búsqueda *f* **~** (DE algo/algn) search (FOR sth/ sb)

busto *m* bust

butaca *f* **(a)** (con respaldo) (esp Esp) armchair; (sin respaldo) (esp AmL) stool **(b)** (en teatro, cine) seat; **~ de patio** (Esp) orchestra (AmE) *o* (BrE) stall seat

buzo *m* **1** (Náut) diver **2** (Indum) **(a)** (Chi, Per) (para hacer ejercicio) track suit **(b)** (Col) (suéter de

cuello alto) turtleneck sweater (AmE), polo-neck
jumper (BrE) **(c)** (Arg, Col) (camiseta) sweatshirt **(d)**
(Ur) (jersey) sweater, jumper (BrE)
buzón *m* (en la calle) postbox, mailbox (AmE),

letter-box (BrE); (en una casa) mailbox (AmE),
letter-box (BrE); **echar una carta al** *or* **en el** ~ to
mail (AmE) *o* (BrE) post a letter
byte *m* /'bait/ byte

Cc

C, c *f* (*read as* /se/ *or* (Esp) /θe/) *the letter* C, c
c/ (= **calle**) St, Rd
C *m* (= **centígrado** *or* **Celsius**) C, Centigrade,
Celsius
cabales *mpl*: **no está en sus** ~ he's not in his
right mind
cabalgar [A3] *vi* (liter) «*jinete*» to ride
cabalgata *f* (desfile) parade; **la** ~ **de los Reyes
Magos** the Epiphany parade *o* procession
caballa *f* mackerel
caballerango *m* (Méx) groom
caballería *f* (Mil) cavalry
caballeriza *f* (edificio) stable; (caballos) stable,
stables (*pl*)
caballero *m* **(a)** (en general) gentleman; **es todo
un** ~ he's a perfect gentleman; **sección de** ~**s**
men's department; **¿en qué puedo servirle,** ~?
how can I help you, sir?; **⑤ caballeros** Men *o*
Gentlemen *o* Gents **(b)** (Hist) knight
caballeroso -sa *adj* gentlemanly, gallant
caballete *m* (para mesa) trestle; (para lienzo,
pizarra) easel; (de moto) kickstand; (del tejado) ridge
caballito *m* **(a)** (juguete — que se mece) rocking
horse; (— con palo) hobbyhorse; ~ **de mar** sea
horse; *ver tb* CABALLO **(b) caballitos** *mpl*
(carrusel) carousel, merry-go-round
caballo¹ -lla *adj* (AmC fam) (estúpido) stupid
caballo² *m* **1 (a)** (Equ, Zool) horse; **montar** *or*
(AmL) **andar a** ~ to ride (a horse); **dieron un
paseo a** ~ they went for a ride (on horseback);
~ **de carga/de tiro** packhorse/carthorse; ~ **de
carreras** racehorse; **a** ~ **entre ...** halfway between
...; **llevar a algn a** ~ to give sb a piggyback **(b)**
(en ajedrez) knight; (en naipes) ≈ queen (*in a
Spanish pack of cards*) **(c)** (Méx) (en gimnasia)
horse **2** (Auto, Fís, Mec) *tb* ~ **de vapor** (metric)
horsepower
cabaña *f* (choza) cabin, shack
cabaré, cabaret /kaβa're/ *m* (*pl* **-rets**)
cabaret
cabeceada *f* **(a)** (AmL) ▶ CABEZADA **(b)** (CS)
(Dep) header
cabecear [A1] *vi* **(a)** «*persona*» to nod off **(b)**
«*caballo*» to toss its head; «*barco*» to pitch
■ ~ *vt* ‹*balón*› to head
cabecera *f* **(a)** (de la cama) headboard **(b)** (de
una mesa) head, top **(c)** (de una manifestación) head,
front
cabecero *m* headboard
cabecilla *mf* ringleader
cabellera *f* **(a)** (melena) hair **(b)** (de un cometa)
tail

cabello *m* hair; ~**s de ángel** (fideos) vermicelli
caber [E15] *vi* **1 (a)** (en un lugar) to fit; **no cabe
en la caja** it won't fit in the box; **no cabemos los
cuatro** there isn't room for all four of us; **en esta
botella caben diez litros** this bottle holds ten
liters; **no** ~ **en sí de alegría** to be beside oneself
with joy **(b)** (pasar) to fit, go; ~ **POR algo** to go
THROUGH sth **(c)** «*falda/zapatos*» to fit; **estos
pantalones ya no me caben** these trousers don't
fit me any more
2 (*en 3ª pers*) (frml) (ser posible): **cabe la
posibilidad de que haya perdido el tren** he may
have missed the train; **no cabe duda de que ...**
there is no doubt that ...; **cabría decir que ...** it
could be said that ...; **es, si cabe, aún mejor** it is
even better, if such a thing is possible; *dentro de
lo que cabe* all things considered
3 (Mat): **17 entre 5 cabe a 3 y sobran 2** 5 into 17
goes 3 times and 2 over
cabestrillo *m* sling; **llevaba el brazo en** ~ he
had his arm in a sling
cabeza *f* **1 (a)** (Anat) head; **de la** ~ **a los pies**
from head to toe *o* foot; **me duele la** ~ I've got a
headache; **marcó de** ~ he scored with a header;
pararse en la *or* **de** ~ (AmL) to do a headstand; ~
rapada skinhead **(b)** (medida) head; **me saca una**
~ he's a head taller than me **(c)** (pelo) hair; **me
lavé la** ~ I washed my hair **(d)** (inteligencia): **usa la**
~ use your head; **¡qué poca** ~**!** have you/has he
no sense? **(e)** (mente): **¡que** ~ **la mía!** what a
memory!; **tú estás mal de la** ~ you're out of your
mind; **se me ha ido de la** ~ it's gone right out of
my head; **se le ha metido en la** ~ **que ...** she's got
it into her head that ...; **no se me pasó por la** ~
it didn't cross my mind; ~ **de chorlito** *mf* (fam)
scatterbrain (colloq); **írsele a algn la** ~ to feel
dizzy; **levantar** ~ (fam) (superar problemas) to get
back on one's feet; *perder la* ~: **no perdamos la**
~ let's not panic *o* lose our heads; **perdió la** ~
por esa mujer he lost his head over that woman;
quitarle a algn algo de la ~ to get sth out of sb's
head; *romperse la* ~ (fam) (preocuparse) to rack
one's brains; (lastimarse) to break one's neck
(colloq); *subírsele a algn a la* ~ «*vino/éxito*» to go
to one's head; *tener la* ~ *llena de pájaros* (fam) to
have one's head in the clouds
2 (a) (individuo): **por** ~ each, a head **(b)** (de
ganado) head; **50** ~**s de ganado** 50 head of cattle
3 (primer lugar, delantera): **estamos a la** ~ **del
sector** we are the leading company in this sector;
a la ~ **de la manifestación** at the front *o* head of
the demonstration; **el equipo va en** ~ **de la
clasificación** the team is at the top of the
division; ~ **de familia** head of the family; ~ **de
serie** seed

4 **(a)** (de alfiler, clavo, fósforo) head **(b)** (de misil) warhead
5 (Audio, Video) head
6 (de plátanos) hand, bunch; ~ **de ajo** bulb of garlic

cabezada f (movimiento) nod; **iba dormido, dando ~s** his head kept nodding in his sleep; **dar** or **echar una ~** (fam) to have a nap (colloq)

cabezal m **1** **(a)** (almohada) bolster **(b)** (de sillón) headrest **(c)** (AmL) (de cama) headboard/footboard **2** (AmL) (terminal) terminal **3** (Audio, Video) head

cabezazo m **(a)** (golpe): **se dio un ~ en el estante** he hit o banged his head on the shelf **(b)** (Dep) header

cabezón -zona adj **(a)** (fam) (terco) pigheaded (colloq) **(b)** (fam) (de cabeza grande): **¡qué ~ es!** what a big head he has! **(c)** ‹vino› heady
■ m,f (fam): **¡eres un ~!** you're so pigheaded! (colloq)

cabezota adj/mf ▶ CABEZÓN A, B

cabezudo¹ -da adj (de cabeza grande): **es ~** he has a very big head

cabezudo² m: carnival figure with a large head

cabida f (capacidad de recipiente, estadio, teatro) capacity; **solo hay ~ para diez pasajeros** there's only room o space for ten passengers; **el estadio puede dar ~ a 100.000 personas** the stadium can hold 100,000 people

cabina f **1** **(a)** (vestuario) cubicle, stall (AmE) **(b)** (de laboratorio de idiomas, estudio de radio) booth; **~ telefónica** telephone booth o (BrE) box **2** **(a)** (de camión, grúa) cab **(b)** (Aviac) (para pilotos — en avión grande) flight deck; (— en avión pequeño) cockpit; (para pasajeros) cabin

cabizbajo -ja adj (alicaído) downcast; **caminaba ~** he walked along, head bowed

cable m (Elec, Telec) cable

cablevisión f (esp AmL) cable television

cabo m **1** (Geog) cape **2** **(a)** (Mil) corporal **(b)** (en remo) stroke **3** (extremo) end; **al ~ de** after; **de ~ a rabo** (fam) from beginning to end; **llevar a ~** ‹misión› to carry out; **lleva a ~ una excelente labor** he does an excellent job

cabra f goat; **estar como una ~** (fam) to be completely nuts (colloq)

cabrá, cabré, etc ▶ CABER

cabreado -da adj (fam) furious, mad (colloq)

cabrear [A1] vt (fam) (enfadar) to make ... mad (colloq), to piss ... off (sl)
■ **cabrearse** v pron (fam) (enojarse) to get mad (colloq)

cabreo m (fam) (enojo, irritación): **¡qué ~ tiene!** he's in a foul o a terrible mood! (colloq); **agarrarse un ~** to get mad (colloq), to hit the roof (colloq)

cabría, etc ▶ CABER

cabriola f: **hacer ~s** ‹niño› to caper o jump around; ‹caballo› to buck, prance around

cabritas fpl (Chi) popcorn

cabrito m (Zool) kid

cabro -bra adj (Chi fam): **es muy ~ para eso** he's too young for that
■ m,f (Chi fam) (niño) kid (colloq)

cabrón¹ -brona adj (Esp, Méx vulg): **el muy ~/la muy cabrona** the bastard o (AmE) son of a bitch (vulg)/the bitch (vulg)
■ m,f (Esp, Méx vulg) (m) bastard (vulg), son of a bitch (AmE vulg); (f) bitch (vulg)

cabrón² m (vulg) (cornudo) cuckold; (proxeneta) (Andes fam o vulg) pimp, ponce (BrE)

cabús m (Méx) caboose (AmE), guard's van (BrE)

caca f (fam o leng infantil): **hacer ~** to go to the bathroom (AmE) o (BrE) toilet (euph), to do a poop (AmE) o (BrE) pooh (used to or by children); **hacerse ~** to mess oneself; **el niño se hizo ~** the baby dirtied his diaper (AmE) o (BrE) nappy (colloq); ~ **de perro** dog mess; **¡no toques eso!** ¡~! don't touch that, it's dirty!

cacahuete, cacahuate m peanut, monkey nut; **me/te/le importa un (reverendo) ~** (Méx fam) I/you/he couldn't give a damn (colloq)

cacao m **1** **(a)** (Coc) (polvo, bebida) cocoa **(b)** (Bot) (planta) cacao; (semillas) cocoa beans (pl) **(c)** (Esp) (para los labios) lipsalve **2** (fam) (jaleo) ruckus (AmE), to-do (BrE); **¡qué ~ se armó!** all hell broke loose (colloq)

cacarear [A1] vi **(a)** «gallo» to crow; «gallina» to cluck **(b)** (fam) (presumir) to brag

cacatúa f (Zool) cockatoo

cacería f (de zorro, jabalí) hunt; (de conejo, perdiz) shoot; **ir de ~** to go hunting/shooting

cacerola f saucepan, pan

cachalote m sperm whale

cachapa f (Ven) corn-based pancake

cachar [A1] vt **(a)** (AmL fam) ‹pelota› to catch; ‹persona›: **la caché del brazo** I caught o grabbed her by the arm **(b)** (AmL fam) (sorprender, pillar) to catch **(c)** (RPl fam) (gastar una broma) to kid (colloq) **(d)** (Andes fam) (enterarse) to get (colloq)

cacharrería f (Col) hardware store, ironmonger's (BrE)

cacharro m **(a)** (de cocina) pot **(b)** (fam) (cachivache) thing; (coche viejo) jalopy (AmE), old banger (BrE colloq); (aparato) gadget

cachaza f (bebida) type of rum

cachear [A1] vt **1** (fam) (registrar) to frisk, search **2** (AmL) (Taur) to gore

cachemir m, **cachemira** f cashmere

cachetada f (AmL) slap

cachete m **1** (mejilla) (esp AmL) cheek; (nalga) (CS fam) cheek **2** (esp Esp) (bofetada) slap

cachetear [A1] vt (AmL) to slap

cachetón -tona adj (Andes, Méx fam) (carrilludo) chubby-cheeked

cachimba f pipe; **fumar ~** to smoke a pipe

cachiporra f (palo) billy club (AmE), truncheon (BrE)

cachito m **1** (Méx) (de lotería) one twentieth of a lottery ticket; ver tb CACHO 1 **2** (Ven) (Coc) croissant

cachivache m (fam) (trasto inútil) piece of junk; **tiró todos los ~s que tenía** she threw out all her old junk (colloq)

cacho m **1** (fam) (pedazo) bit **2** **(a)** (AmS) (cuerno) horn **(b)** (Andes) (juego) poker dice; (cubilete) shaker

cachondearse [A1] v pron (Esp fam) ~ **DE algn/algo** to make fun **OF** sb/sth

cachondeo *m* (Esp fam): **estar de** ∼ to be joking; **se lo toma a** ∼ he treats it as a joke

cachondo -da *adj* (fam) **(a)** (Esp) (divertido) funny **(b)** (Esp, Méx) (sexualmente) hot (colloq), horny (sl)

cachorro -rra *m,f* (de perro) puppy, pup; (de león) cub

cachucha *f* (Col, Méx, Ven) (Indum) cap

cacillo *m* (cacerola) small saucepan; (cucharón) ladle

cacique *m* (Hist) chief, cacique; (Pol) local political boss; (hombre poderoso) tyrant

caco *m* (fam) burglar

cactus (*pl* ∼), **cacto** *m* cactus

cada *adj inv* [1] **(a)** (con énfasis en el individuo o cosa particular) each; (con énfasis en la totalidad del conjunto) every; **los ganadores de** ∼ **grupo** the winners from each group; **hay un bar en** ∼ **esquina** ther's a bar in every corner; ∼ **día** every day, each day; **¿**∼ **cuánto viene?** how often does she come?; **hay cinco para** ∼ **uno** there are five each; **cuestan $25** ∼ **uno** they cost $25 each; ∼ **uno** *or* **cual sabe qué es lo que más le conviene** everyone *o* each individual knows what's best for him or her; ∼ **vez que viene** every time *o* whenever he comes **(b)** (delante de numeral) every; ∼ **dos días** every two days, every other day; **siete de** ∼ **diez** seven out of (every) ten [2] (indicando progresión): ∼ **vez más rápido** faster and faster; **lo hace** ∼ **vez mejor** she's getting better all the time; ∼ **vez más gente** more and more people; ∼ **vez menos tiempo** less and less time

cadalso *m* (patíbulo) scaffold; (horca) gallows (*pl*)

cadáver *m* (de persona) corpse; (de animal) carcass

cadavérico -ca *adj* cadaverous, ghastly

caddie, caddy /'kaði/ *mf* (*pl* **-dies**) caddy

cadena *f* [1] **(a)** (de eslabones) chain; (para la nieve) (snow) chain; ∼ **antirrobo** bicycle lock; ∼ **perpetua** life imprisonment **(b)** (del wáter) chain; **tirar de la** ∼ to flush the toilet [2] **(a)** (de hechos, fenómenos) chain; **una larga** ∼ **de atentados** a long series of attacks; ∼ **de fabricación** *or* **producción** production line; ∼ **de montañas** mountain range *o* chain; **en** ∼ ‹*transmisión*› simultaneous; **una choque en** ∼ a pileup **(b)** (de hoteles, supermercados) chain; ∼ **de radiodifusión** radio network [3] (TV) channel

cadencia *f* cadence

cadeneta *f* (labor) chain stitch; (de papel) paper chain

cadera *f* hip

cadete *m* (Mil, Náut) cadet

caducar [A2] *vi* **(a)** ‹*carné/pasaporte*› to expire; **el plazo caduca el 17 de enero** the closing date (*for enrollment, etc*) is January 17; **estar caducado** to be out of date; ‹*yogurt*› to be past

its sell-by date/use-by date **(b)** ‹*medicamento*› to expire (frml); ❸ **caduca a los tres meses** use within three months

caduco -ca *adj* **(a)** ‹*hoja*› deciduous **(b)** ‹*teoría/costumbres/valores*› outdated

caer [E16] *vi* [1] (de una altura) to fall; (de posición vertical) to fall over; **el coche cayó por un precipicio** the car went over a cliff; **cayó muerto allí mismo** he dropped down dead on the spot; **cayó en el mar** it came down in the sea; ∼ **parado** (AmL) to land on one's feet; **dejar** ∼ **algo** ‹*objeto*› to drop sth; ‹*indirecta*› to drop sth; **dejó** ∼ **la noticia que …** she let drop the news that … [2] **(a)** ‹*chaparrón/nevada*›: **cayó un chaparrón** it poured down; **cayó una fuerte nevada** it snowed heavily; **el rayo cayó cerca** the lightning struck nearby **(b)** ‹*noche*› to fall; **al** ∼ **la tarde/noche** at sunset *o* dusk/nightfall [3] **(a)** (pender) ‹*cortinas/falda*› to hang **(b)** ‹*terreno*› to drop; ∼ **en pendiente** to slope down [4] (en error, trampa): **no caigas en ese error** don't make that mistake; **todos caímos (en la trampa)** we all fell for it; **cayó en la tentación de mirar** she succumbed to the temptation to look; ∼ **muy bajo** to stoop very low [5] (fam) (entender, darse cuenta): **¡ah, ya caigo!** (ya entiendo) oh, now I get it! (ya recuerdo) oh, now I remember; **no caigo** I'm not sure what (*o* who *etc*) you mean; **no caí en que tú no tenías llave** I didn't realize *o* (fam) I didn't click that you didn't have keys [6] (en un estado): ∼ **en el olvido** to sink into oblivion; ∼ **enfermo** to fall ill [7] ‹*gobierno/ciudad*› to fall; ‹*soldado*› (morir) to fall, die [8] ‹*precios/temperatura*› to fall, drop [9] **(a)** (sentar): **el pescado me cayó mal** the fish didn't agree with me; **le cayó muy mal que no la invitaran** she was very upset about not being invited **(b)** ‹*persona*›: **tu primo me cae muy bien** I really like your cousin; **me cae muy mal** (fam) I can't stand him (colloq); **¿qué tal te cayó?** what did you think of him? [10] ‹*cumpleaños/festividad*› to fall on; **¿el 27 en qué (día) cae?** what day's the 27th?

■ **caerse** *v pron* **(a)** (de una altura) to fall; (de posición vertical) to fall over, to fall over; **me caí por las escaleras** I fell down the stairs; ∼**se del caballo/de la cama** to fall off one's horse/out of bed; **está que se cae de cansancio** (fam) she's dead on her feet (colloq) **(b)** **caérsele algo A algn**: **oiga, se le cayó un guante** excuse me, you dropped your glove; **no se te vaya a** ∼ don't drop it; **se me cayó de las manos** it slipped out of my hands; **se me están cayendo las medias** my stockings are falling down **(c)** (desprenderse) ‹*diente*› to fall out; ‹*hojas*› to fall off; ‹*botón*› to come off, fall off; **se le empieza a** ∼ **el pelo** he's started to lose his hair

café *adj* (gen inv) (AmC, Chi, Méx) (marrón) brown; **ojos** ∼(**s**) brown eyes
■ *m* [1] (cultivo, bebida) coffee; **me sirvió un** ∼ he gave me a cup of coffee, he gave me a coffee

(BrE); **~ cerrero** (Col) large strong black coffee; **~
con leche** (bebida) regular coffee (AmE), white
coffee (BrE); **~ cortado** *coffee with a dash of milk*;
~ expreso espresso; **~ instantáneo** *o* **soluble**
instant coffee; **~ natural/torrefacto** light roast/
high roast coffee; **~ negro** (AmL) *or* (Chi) **puro** *or*
(Col) **tinto** *or* (Esp) **solo** black coffee
[2] (cafetería) café; **~ bar** café
[3] (AmC, Chi, Méx) (marrón) brown
cafeína *f* caffeine
cafetal *m* coffee plantation
cafetera *f* (a) (para hacer café) coffee maker;
(para servir café) coffeepot; ***estar como una* ~** (fam)
to be off one's rocker *o* head (colloq) (b) (fam)
(coche viejo) old heap (colloq)
cafetería *f* (café) café; (en museo, fábrica)
cafeteria
cafetero -ra *adj* ⟨*industria/finca*⟩ coffee
(*before n*); ⟨*país*⟩ coffee-producing (*before n*),
coffee-growing (*before n*); **ser muy ~** to be a real
coffee addict
■ *m,f* coffee planter *o* grower
cafeto *m* coffee tree
caficultor -tora *m,f* (Col) coffee grower
cagar [A3] *vi* (vulg) (defecar) to have a shit (vulg)
■ **cagarse** *v pron* (vulg) to shit oneself (vulg)
caída *f* [1] (en general) fall; **sufrir una ~**
⟨*persona*⟩ to have a fall; **~ libre** free fall; **la ~
del gobierno** the fall of the government; **la ~ del
cabello** hair loss [2] (de tela, falda): **necesitas una
tela con más ~** you need a heavier material;
tiene buena ~ it hangs well [3] (descenso) **~ DE**
algo ⟨*del dólar/de los precios/de la demanda*⟩ fall
IN sth; ⟨*de temperatura/voltaje*⟩ drop IN sth; **~ de
agua** waterfall
caído¹ -da *adj* [1] (a) (en el suelo) fallen (b)
⟨*pechos*⟩ drooping, sagging; **tener los hombros ~s**
to be round-shouldered (c) (en la guerra): **soldados
~s en combate** soldiers who fell in combat
[2] (Col) ⟨*vivienda*⟩ dilapidated, run-down
caído² *m*: **los ~s** the fallen
caiga, caigas, etc ▶ CAER
caimán *m* (Zool) caiman, cayman, alligator
Cairo *m*: **el ~** Cairo
caja *f* [1] (a) (recipiente) box; **una ~ de fósforos**
(con fósforos) a box of matches; (vacía) a matchbox;
una ~ de vino a crate of wine; **~ de cambios**
gearbox; **~ de herramientas** toolbox; **~ de música**
music box; **~ de resonancia** (Mús) soundbox; **~
de seguridad** safe-deposit box, safety deposit box;
~ fuerte safe, strongbox; **~ negra** (Aviat) black
box; **~ tonta** (fam) goggle box (colloq) (de reloj)
case, casing (c) (Mús) (de violín, guitarra) soundbox;
(tambor) drum (d) (fam) (ataúd) coffin
[2] (Com) (a) (lugar — en banco) window; (— en
supermercado) checkout; (— en tienda, restaurante)
cash desk, till (b) (máquina) *tb* **~ registradora**
till, cash register (c) (dinero) cash; **hicimos una ~
de medio millón** we took half a million pesos
(*etc*); **~ de ahorros** savings bank; **hacer (la) ~** to
cash up
cajero -ra *m,f* (en tienda) cashier; (en banco)
teller, cashier; (en supermercado) check out
operator; **~ automático** *or* **permanente** cash
dispenser, automated teller machine (AmE), ATM
(AmE)
cajeta *f* (Méx) caramel topping/filling

cajetilla *f* pack (AmE), packet (BrE)
cajón *m* [1] (a) (en mueble) drawer (b) (caja
grande) *tb* **~ de embalaje** crate; (para mudanzas)
packing case (c) (AmL) (ataúd) coffin, casket (AmE)
[2] (Méx) (en un estacionamiento) parking space
cajuela *f* (Méx) trunk (AmE), boot (BrE)
cal *f* lime
cala *f* (a) (ensenada) cove (b) (Náut) hold
calabacín *m*, (Méx) **calabacita** *f* zucchini
(AmE), courgette (BrE)
calabaza *f* (fruto — redondo) pumpkin; (—
alargado) squash
calabozo *m* (en comisaría, cárcel) cell; (en cuartel)
guardroom; (Hist) dungeon
calada *f* (Esp fam) (de cigarro) drag (sl), puff
(colloq)
caladero *m* fishing ground
calado -da *adj* [1] (empapado) [ESTAR] soaked,
drenched [2] ⟨*jersey/tela*⟩ openwork (*before n*)
calamar *m* squid; **~es a la romana** squid fried
in batter
calambre *m* (a) (espasmo) cramp; **me ha dado
un ~ en el pie** I have a cramp (AmE) *o* (BrE) I've
got cramp in my foot (b) (sacudida eléctrica)
electric shock; **me dio un ~** I got an electric
shock
calamidad *f* (a) (desastre, desgracia) disaster,
calamity; **¡las ~es que ha pasado!** the terrible
things he's gone through! (b) (persona inútil)
disaster (colloq)
calar [A1] *vt* [1] ⟨*líquido*⟩ (empapar) to soak;
(atravesar) to soak through; **el agua me caló los
calcetines** water soaked through my socks
[2] (fam) ⟨*persona/intenciones*⟩ to rumble (colloq),
to suss ... out (BrE colloq) [3] ⟨*barco*⟩ to draw
[4] (Esp) ⟨*coche/motor*⟩ to stall
■ **~** *vi* [1] ⟨*moda*⟩ to catch on; ⟨*costumbre/
filosofía*⟩ to take root [2] ⟨*zapatos/tienda de
campaña*⟩ to leak, let water in
■ **calarse** *v pron* [1] (empaparse) to get soaked, get
drenched [2] (Esp) ⟨*coche/motor*⟩ to stall
calavera¹ *f* [1] (Anat) skull [2] (Méx) (Auto)
taillight
calavera² *m* (fam) rake
calcado -da *adj* (a) [SER] (fam): **ser ~ a algn**
to be the spitting image of sb (colloq); **ser ~ a
algo** to be exactly the same as sth (b) [ESTAR]
(fam): **están ~s** one is a carbon copy of the other;
está ~ del de Serra it's a straight copy of Serra's
calcar [A2] *vt* (a) ⟨*dibujo/mapa*⟩ to trace (b)
(plagiar) to copy
calceta *f* (labor) knitting; **hacer ~** to knit
calcetín *m* sock
calcinar [A1] *vt* (a) (abrasar) ⟨*fuego*⟩ to burn;
cadáveres calcinados charred bodies (b) (Quím) to
calcine
calcio *m* calcium
calco *m* (copia) exact replica
calcomanía *f* transfer, decal (AmE)
calculador -dora *adj* calculating
calculadora *f* calculator
calcular [A1] *vt* [1] (a) (Mat) to calculate, work
out; **calculé mal la distancia** I miscalculated the
distance (b) (evaluar) ⟨*pérdidas/gastas*⟩ to estimate
(c) (conjeturar) to reckon, to guess (esp AmE); **yo le
calculo unos sesenta años** I reckon *o* guess he's ···⊹·

about sixty **(d)** (imaginar) to imagine **2** (planear)
to work out; **lo tenía todo calculado** he had it all
worked out

cálculo m **1** (Mat) **(a)** (operación) calculation;
según mis ∼s according to my calculations; **hizo
un ∼ aproximado** she made a rough estimate; **∼
mental** mental arithmetic **(b)** (disciplina) calculus
2 (plan): **eso no entraba en mis ∼s** I hadn't
allowed for that in my plans o calculations; **le
fallaron los ∼s** things didn't work out as he had
planned; **un error de ∼** a miscalculation **3** (Med)
stone, calculus (tech)

caldear [A1] vt ⟨habitación/local⟩ to heat, heat
... up
■ **caldearse** v pron **(a)** «habitación/local» to
warm up, heat up **(b)** (enardecerse): **se estaban
empezando a ∼ los ánimos** feelings started to
run high

caldera f **(a)** (industrial, de calefacción) boiler **(b)**
(caldero) caldron*, copper (BrE)

calderilla f change, small o loose change

caldero m caldron*, copper (BrE)

caldo m (Coc) clear soup; (con arroz, etc) soup;
(para cocinar) stock; (salsa de asado, etc) juices (pl);
∼ de pollo chicken stock

calé adj gypsy (before n)
■ mf gypsy

calefacción f heating; **∼ a gas** gas heating;
∼ central central heating

caleidoscopio m kaleidoscope

calendario m **(a)** (en general) calendar; **∼ de
taco** tear-off calendar; **∼ escolar** school calendar
(b) (programa) schedule; **tiene un ∼ muy apretado**
she has a very tight schedule

calentador m **(a)** (para agua) (water) heater;
(estufa) heater **(b) calentadores** mpl (Dep,
Indum) legwarmers (pl)

calentamiento m **(a)** (Dep) warm-up **(b)** (Fís)
warming; **∼ global** or **del planeta** global warming

calentar [A5] vt **1** **(a)** ⟨agua/comida⟩ to heat
(up); ⟨habitación⟩ to heat **(b)** ⟨motor/coche⟩ to
warm up **(c)** (Dep): **∼ los músculos** to warm up
2 (AmL fam) (enojar) to make ... mad (colloq)
■ vi: **¡cómo calienta hoy el sol!** the sun's really
hot today!; **esta estufa casi no calienta** this heater
is hardly giving off any heat
■ **calentarse** v pron **1** **(a)** «horno/plancha» to
heat up; «habitación» to warm up, get warm **(b)**
«motor/coche» (al arrancar) to warm up; (en exceso)
to overheat
2 (vulg) (excitarse sexualmente) to get turned on
(colloq)
3 «debate» to become heated; **los ánimos se
∼on** tempers flared
4 (AmL fam) (enojarse) to get mad (colloq)

calentura f **(a)** (fiebre) temperature **(b)** (en la
boca) cold sore

calesita f (Per, RPl) merry-go-round, carousel

caleta f (ensenada) cove

calibrar [A1] vt **(a)** ⟨arma/tubo⟩ to calibrate
(b) ⟨consecuencias/situación⟩ to weigh up

calibre m caliber*; **de ∼ 22** 22 caliber; **de
grueso ∼** ⟨arma/proyectil⟩ large-bore; ⟨error⟩
(AmL) serious

calidad f **1** (de producto, servicio) quality; **un
artículo de primera ∼** a top-quality product;
productos de mala ∼ poor-quality products; **∼ de**

vida quality of life **2** (condición): **asistió en ∼ de
observador** he attended as an observer; **en su ∼
de presidente** in his capacity as president

cálido -da adj **(a)** (Meteo) hot **(b)** ⟨acogida/
bienvenida⟩ warm **(c)** ⟨color/tono⟩ warm

calidoscopio m kaleidoscope

calienta, etc ▶ CALENTAR

caliente adj **1** ⟨agua/comida/horno⟩ hot; **aquí
estaremos más calentas** we'll be warmer here;
tomó la decisión en ∼ she made the decision in
the heat of the moment **2** (fam) (sexualmente) hot
(colloq), horny (sl)

caliento ▶ CALENTAR

califa m caliph

calificación f **(a)** (Educ) grade (AmE), mark
(BrE) **(b)** (descripción) description **(c)** (de película)
rating

calificado -da adj (esp AmL) ⟨mano de obra⟩
skilled; ⟨profesional⟩ qualified

calificar [A2] vt **1** **∼ algo/a algn DE algo**
(describir) to describe sth/sb as sth; (categorizar) to
label sth/sb AS sth **2** (Educ) **(a)** ⟨examen⟩ to
grade (AmE), to mark (BrE); ⟨alumno⟩ to give a
grade (AmE) o (BrE) mark to **(b)** (habilitar) «título/
diploma»: **∼ a algn PARA hacer algo** to qualify sb
TO do sth **3** (Ling) to qualify

California f California

californiano -na adj/m,f Californian

caligrafía f (arte) calligraphy; (de persona)
writing, handwriting

calipso m **(a)** (Mús) calypso **(b) de color ∼**
deep turquoise

cáliz m **(a)** (Relig) chalice **(b)** (Bot) calyx

caliza f limestone

calizo -za adj ⟨tierra⟩ limy; **piedra caliza**
limestone

callado -da adj **(a)** [ESTAR] (silencioso) quiet;
estuvo ∼ durante toda la reunión he kept quiet
throughout the whole meeting; **lo escucharon ∼s**
they listened to him quietly **(b)** [SER] (poco
hablador) quiet

callampa f (Chi) **(a)** (hongo) mushroom **(b)**
(vivienda) shanty (dwelling) **(c) callampas** fpl
(poblaciones marginales) shantytown

callar [A1] vi to be quiet, shut up (colloq); **no
pude hacerlo ∼** I couldn't get him to be quiet;
hacer ∼ a la oposición to silence the opposition
■ **∼** vt **(a)** ⟨secreto/información⟩ to keep ... quiet
(b) (AmL) ⟨persona⟩ to get ... to be quiet, to shut
... up (colloq)
■ **callarse** v pron **(a)** (guardar silencio) to be quiet;
¡cállate! be quiet!, shut up! (colloq); **cuando entró
todos se ∼on** when he walked in everyone went
quiet o stopped talking; **la próxima vez no me ∼é**
next time I'll say something **(b)** (no decir)
⟨noticia⟩ to keep ... quiet, keep ... to oneself

calle f **1** (vía) street; **∼ ciega** (Andes, Ven) dead
end, cul-de-sac (BrE); **∼ de dirección única** or (Col)
de una vía one-way street; **∼ peatonal** pedestrian
street; **hoy no he salido a la ∼** I haven't been out
today; **el film saldrá a la ∼ mañana** the book
comes out tomorrow; **el hombre de la ∼** the man
in the street; **el lenguaje de la ∼** colloquial
language; **echar a algn a la ∼** to throw sb out (on
the street); **en la ∼** ⟨estar/quedar⟩ (en la ruina)
penniless; (sin vivienda) homeless; (sin trabajo) out of
work

2 (Esp) (en atletismo, natación) lane; (en golf) fairway

callejear [A1] *vi* to hang around the streets (colloq)

callejero¹ -ra *adj* ‹riña/venta/músico› street (*before n*); ‹perro› stray (*before n*)

callejero² *m* (Esp) street map o plan

callejón *m* alley, narrow street; ~ sin salida (calle) dead end, blind alley; (situación) dead end

callejuela *f* narrow street

callista *mf* chiropodist

callo *m* **(a)** (en los dedos del pie) corn; (en la planta del pie, en las manos) callus; (en una fractura) callus **(b) callos** *mpl* (Esp) (Coc) tripe

callosidad *f* callus

calma *f* calm; con ~ calmly; **mantener la** ~ to keep calm; **tómatelo con** ~ take it easy; **no hay que perder la** ~ the thing is not to lose your cool; **el mar está en** ~ the sea is calm; **¡~, por favor!** (en situación peligrosa) please, keep calm! *o* don't panic!; (en discusión acalorada) calm down, please!

calmante *m* (para dolores) painkiller; (para los nervios) tranquilizer

calmar [A1] *vt* **(a)** (tranquilizar) ‹persona› to calm … down; ‹nervios› to calm; **esto calmó los ánimos** this eased the tension **(b)** (aliviar) ‹dolor› to relieve, ease; ‹sed› to quench; ‹hambre› to take the edge off
■ **calmarse** *v pron* **(a)** «persona» to calm down **(b)** «mar» to become calm

calmo -ma *adj* (esp AmL) calm

caló *m* gypsy slang

calor *m* [*Use of the feminine gender, although common in some areas, is generally considered to be archaic or non-standard*] **1 (a)** (Fis, Meteo) heat; **hace** ~ it's hot; **hacía un** ~ **agobiante** the heat was stifling *o* suffocating **(b)** (sensación): **tener** ~ to be hot; **pasamos un** ~ **horrible** it was terribly hot; **entrar en** ~ to get warm; **esta chaqueta me da mucho** ~ I feel very hot in this jacket; **al** ~ **del fuego** by the fireside **2** (afecto) warmth **3 calores** *mpl* (de la menopausia) hot flashes (*pl*) (AmE), hot flushes (*pl*) (BrE)

caloría *f* calorie

calumnia *f* (oral) defamation, slander; (escrita) libel; **levantaron** ~s **contra la institución** they spread slanderous rumors about the institution

calumniar [A1] *vt* (por escrito) to libel; (oralmente) to slander

caluroso -sa *adj* **(a)** ‹día/clima› hot **(b)** ‹acogida/aplauso› warm; **recibe un** ~ **saludo** (Corresp) best wishes

calva *f* (cabeza sin pelo) bald head; (parte sin pelo) bald patch

calvicie *f* baldness

calvo -va *adj* ‹persona› bald; **quedarse** ~ to go bald
■ *m,f* bald person

calza *f* **1 (a)** (cuña) chock **(b)** (Col) (en una muela) filling; **2 calzas** *fpl* (Ind, arc) hose (*pl*), breeches (*pl*)

calzada *f* (camino) road; (de calle) road; (de autopista) side, carriageway

calzado *m* (frml) footwear (frml)

calzador *m* shoehorn

calzar [A4] *vt* **1 (a)** ‹persona› (proveerla de

calzado) to provide … with shoes; (ponerle los zapatos): **calzó a los niños** she put the children's shoes on **(b)** (llevar): **calzo (un) 39** I take (a) size 39, I'm a 39; **calzaba zapatillas de deporte** he was wearing training shoes **2** ‹rueda› to chock, wedge a block under **3** (Col) ‹muela› to fill
■ **calzarse** *v pron* (refl) **(a)** (ponerse los zapatos) to put one's shoes on **(b)** ‹zapato› to put on

calzoncillos *mpl*, **calzoncillo** *m* underpants, shorts (*pl*) (AmE), pants (*pl*) (BrE); ~ **largos** long underwear, long johns (*pl*) (colloq)

calzones *mpl*, **calzón** *m* **1 (a)** (antiguos) long underwear, long johns (*pl*) (colloq) **(b)** (AmS) (modernos) panties (*pl*), knickers (*pl*) (BrE) **2 calzón** *m* (Esp) (para deporte) shorts (*pl*)

cama *f* (para dormir) bed; **hacer** *or* (AmL) **tender la** ~ to make the bed; **¡métete en la** ~! get into bed!; **guardar** ~ to stay in bed; **está en** ~ she's in bed; ~ **camarote** (AmL) bunk bed; ~ **doble** *or* **de matrimonio** *or* (AmL) **de dos plazas** double bed; ~ **individual** *or* (AmL) **de una plaza** single bed; ~ **solar** sunbed; **caer en** ~ to fall ill

camada *f* (Zool) litter; (de ladrones, sinvergüenzas) (pey) gang

camaleón *m* chameleon

cámara *f* **1 (a)** (arc) (aposento) chamber (frml) **(b)** (recinto): ~ **acorazada** *or* **blindada** strongroom, vault; ~ **de descompresión** decompression chamber; ~ **de gas** gas chamber; ~ **frigorífica** cold store **2** (Gob, Pol): **C~ de los Diputados** Chamber of Deputies; **C~ de los Comunes/de los Lores** House of Commons/of Lords; **C~ de Representantes** House of Representatives **3** (Com, Fin) association; ~ **de comercio** chamber of commerce **4** (aparato) camera; **en** *or* (Esp) **a** ~ **lenta** in slow motion; ~ **de cine** film camera; ~ **de video** *or* (Esp) **vídeo** video camera; ~ **fotográfica** camera

camarada *mf* **(a)** (de partido político) comrade **(b)** (de colegio) school friend; (de trabajo) colleague

camaradería *f* camaraderie, comradeship

camarero -ra *m,f* **1** (esp Esp) (en bar, restaurante) (*m*) waiter; (*f*) waitress; (detrás de mostrador) (*m*) barman, bartender (AmE); (*f*) barmaid, bartender (AmE) **2 (a)** (en hotel) (*m*) bellboy; (*f*) maid **(b)** (Transp) (*m*) steward; (*f*) stewardess

camarín *m* (CS) **(a)** (Teatr) dressing room **(b)** (en vestuarios) changing cubicle **(c) camarines** *mpl* (Chi) (Dep) changing rooms (*pl*), locker rooms (*pl*)

camarógrafo -fa *m,f* (*m*) cameraman; (*f*) camerawoman

camarón *m* (crustáceo — pequeño) shrimp; (— más grande) shrimp (AmE), prawn (BrE)

camarote *m* cabin

cambalache *m* **(a)** (fam) (trueque) swap (colloq); **hacer** ~s to swap (colloq) **(b)** (RPl fam & pey) (tienda) thrift store (AmE), junk shop (BrE)

cambiante *adj* ‹tiempo› changeable, unsettled; ‹persona/carácter› moody, temperamental

cambiar [A1] *vt* **1 (a)** (alterar, modificar) ‹horario/imagen/persona› to change **(b)** (de lugar, posición): ~ **los muebles de lugar** to move the furniture around; **cambié las flores de florero** I put the flowers in a different vase **(c)** (reemplazar) ····⊹

⟨pieza/fecha/sábanas⟩ to change; **le cambió la pila al reloj** she changed the battery in the clock; **∼le el nombre a algo** to change the name of sth ⟨niño/bebé⟩ to change **(e)** (Fin) to change; **cambié 100 libras a** or (Esp) **en dólares** I changed 100 pounds into dollars

2 (canjear) ⟨sellos/estampas⟩ to swap, to trade (esp AmE); **∼ algo POR algo** ⟨sellos/estampas⟩ to swap o (esp AmE) trade sth FOR sth; ⟨compra⟩ to exchange o change sth FOR sth; **¿quieres que te cambie el lugar?** do you want me to swap o change places with you?

■ **vi (a)** ⟨ciudad/persona⟩ to change; **∼ para peor** to change for the worse; **le está cambiando la voz** his voice is breaking **(b)** (Auto) to change gear **(c)** (hacer transbordo) to change; **∼ de avión/tren** to change planes/train **(d)** **∼ DE algo** ⟨de tema/canal/color⟩ to change sth; **∼ de idea** to change one's mind; **∼ de sentido** to make (AmE) o (BrE) do a U-turn

■ **cambiarse** v pron **(a)** (refl) (de ropa) to change, get changed **(b)** (refl) ⟨camisa/nombre/peinado⟩ to change; **∼se DE algo** ⟨de camisa/zapatos⟩ to change sth; **me cambié de sitio** I changed places; **∼se de casa** to move house; **cámbiate de camisa** change your shirt **(c)** **∼se POR algn** to change places WITH sb **(d)** (recípr) ⟨sellos/estampas⟩ to swap, to trade (esp AmE) **(e)** (CS) (mudarse de casa) to move

cambio m **1** **(a)** (alteración) change; **∼ DE algo** ⟨de planes/domicilio⟩ change OF sth; **un ∼ de aire(s)** or **ambiente** a change of scene **(b)** (Auto) gearshift (AmE), gear change (BrE); **un coche con cinco ∼s** (AmL) a car with a five-speed gearbox; **∼ de sentido** U-turn
2 **(a)** (canje) exchange; **❺ no se admiten cambios** goods cannot be exchanged **(b)** (en locs) **a cambio (de)** in exchange (for), in return (for); **en cambio: el viaje en autobús es agotador, en ∼ en tren es muy agradable** the bus journey is exhausting; by train however o on the other hand is very pleasant
3 **(a)** (Fin) (de moneda extranjera) exchange; **∼ de divisas** foreign exchange; **¿a cómo está el ∼?** what's the exchange rate?; **❺ cambio** bureau de change, change **(b)** (diferencia) change; **me ha dado mal el ∼** he's given me the wrong change **(c)** (dinero suelto) change

cambista mf moneychanger
cambur m (Ven) (fruta) banana
camelia f camellia
camello m **1** (Zool) camel **2** **camello** mf (arg) (traficante) pusher (sl), dealer (colloq)
camellón m (Méx) (en la calle) traffic island
camelo m (fam) (timo) con (colloq); (mentira) lie
camerino m **(a)** (Teatr) dressing room **(b)** **camerinos** mpl (Col) (Dep) changing rooms (pl)
camilla f (de lona) stretcher; (con ruedas) trolley, gurney (AmE); (en un consultorio) couch
camillero -ra m,f stretcher-bearer
caminante mf hiker; (liter) traveler*
caminar [A1] vi **1** (andar) to walk; **salieron a**

∼ they went out for a walk; **podemos ir caminando** we can walk, we can go on foot; **∼ HACIA algo** ⟨hacia meta/fin⟩ to move TOWARD(S) sth **2** (AmL) ⟨reloj/motor⟩ to work; **el asunto va caminando** (fam) things are moving (colloq)
■ **∼** vt ⟨distancia⟩ to walk

caminata f long walk; (en el campo) long walk, hike; **después de darme semejante ∼** after walking o (colloq) trekking all that way

camino m **1** (en general) road; (de tierra) track; (sendero) path; **∼ vecinal** minor road (built and maintained by local council)
2 **(a)** (ruta, dirección) way; **saberse el ∼** to know the way; **me salieron al ∼** ⟨asaltantes⟩ they blocked my path o way; ⟨amigos⟩ they came out to meet me; **este es el mejor ∼ a seguir** this is the best course to follow; **el ∼ a la fama** the road o path to fame; **se abrió ∼ entre la espesura** she made her way through the dense thickets; **abrirse ∼ en la vida** to get on in life; **buen/mal ∼**: **este niño va por mal ∼** this boy's heading for trouble; **ibas por buen ∼ pero te equivocaste** you were on the right track but you made a mistake; **llevar a algn por mal ∼** to lead sb astray **(b)** (trayecto, viaje): **el ∼ de regreso** the return journey; **se pusieron en ∼** they set off; **todavía nos quedan dos horas de ∼** we still have two hours to go **(c)** (en locs) **camino de/a ...** on my/his/her way to ...; **ir ∼ de algo**: **una tradición que va ∼ de desaparecer** a tradition which looks set to disappear; **de camino on the way; pilla de ∼** it's on the way; **me queda de ∼** I pass it on my way; **de ∼ a la estación** on the way to the station; **en camino** on the way; **deben estar ya en ∼** they must be on their way already; **por el camino** on the way; **a mitad de** or **a medio ∼** halfway through

camión m **(a)** (de carga) truck, lorry (BrE); (contenido) truckload; **∼ cisterna** tanker; **∼ de la basura** garbage truck (AmE), dustcart (BrE); **∼ de mudanzas** moving van (AmE), removal van (BrE) **(b)** (AmC, Méx) (autobús) bus

camionero -ra m,f truck driver, lorry driver (BrE); (conductor de autobús) (AmC, Méx) bus driver
camioneta f **(a)** (furgoneta) van; (camión pequeño) light truck, pickup truck **(b)** (AmL) (coche familiar) station wagon (AmE), estate car (BrE)
camisa f shirt; **en mangas de ∼** in shirtsleeves; **∼ de fuerza** straitjacket; **cambiar de ∼** to change sides
camiseta f **(a)** (prenda interior) undershirt (AmE), vest (BrE) **(b)** (prenda exterior) T-shirt; (de fútbol) shirt, jersey (AmE); (sin mangas) jersey (AmE), vest (BrE)
camisón m nightdress
camomila f camomile, chamomile
camorra f (fam) (bronca, riña) fight; **armar ∼** to start a fight; **buscar ∼** to look for a fight (colloq)
camorrero -ra adj/mf (Col, CS) ▸ CAMORRISTA
camorrista adj (fam) (pendenciero): **no seas ∼** stop being a troublemaker
■ mf troublemaker (colloq)

AmC Central America	Arg Argentina	Cu Cuba	Per Peru
AmL Latin America	Bol Bolivia	Ec Ecuador	RPI River Plate Area
AmS South America	Chi Chile	Esp Spain	Ur Uruguay
Andes Andean Region	CS Southern Cone	Méx Mexico	Ven Venezuela

camote *m* (Bot) (Andes, Méx) (batata) sweet potato; **hacerse** ~ (Méx fam) to get in a muddle (colloq)

campamento *m* camp; **nos fuimos a Bariloche de** ~ we went camping in Bariloche

campana *f* **(a)** (de iglesia, colegio) bell; **oía las** ~s I could hear the bells ringing; **tocar la** ~ to ring the bell; **¿ya ha sonado la** ~? has the bell gone yet? **(b)** (de chimenea) hood; (de cocina) extractor hood

campanada *f* **(a)** (de campana) chime, stroke; (de reloj) stroke; **el reloj dio 12** ~s the clock struck 12 **(b)** (fam) (sorpresa): **la noticia fue una** ~ the news came like a bolt from the blue (colloq); **dar la** ~ to cause a stir

campanario *m* bell tower, belfry

campanazo *m* (AmL) ▶ CAMPANADA

campanilla *f* **(a)** (campana pequeña) small bell, hand bell **(b)** (Anat) uvula **(c)** (Bot) campanula, bellflower

campante *adj*: **se quedó tan** ~ he didn't bat an eyelash (AmE) o (BrE) eyelid; **nosotros muertos de miedo y él tan** ~ we were scared stiff but he was as cool as a cucumber

campaña *f* campaign; ~ **electoral** electoral o election campaign; ~ **publicitaria** advertising campaign; **hacer una** ~ to run o conduct a campaign

campechano -na *adj* (sin complicaciones) straightforward; (bondadoso) good-natured

campeón -peona *adj* champion (before n)
■ *m,f* champion; **el** ~ **del mundo** the world champion

campeonato *m* championship

cámper *f* (Chi, Méx) camper (van)

campera *f* **(a)** (RPl) (chaqueta) jacket **(b) camperas** *fpl* (Esp) (botas) cowboy boots

campero *m* (Col) (Auto) jeep

campesino -na *adj* (vida/costumbre) rural, country (before n); (modales/aspecto) peasant-like
■ *m,f* (persona del campo) country person; (con connotaciones de pobreza) peasant; **son** ~s they are country people o folk; **los obreros y los** ~s the manual workers and the agricultural workers

campestre *adj* (escena/vida) rural, country (before n); (casa/club) country (before n)

camping /'kampin/ *m* (pl **-pings**) **(a)** (actividad) camping; **irse de** ~ to go camping **(b)** (lugar) campsite, campground (AmE)

campiña *f* countryside; **la** ~ **inglesa** the English countryside

campista *mf* camper

campo *m* **1** (zona no urbana) country; (paisaje) countryside; **la gente del** ~ the country people; **el** ~ **se ve precioso** the countryside looks beautiful; ~ **a través** or **a** ~ **traviesa** (caminar/ir) cross-country
2 (zona agraria) land; (terreno) field; **trabajar el** ~ to work the land; **las faenas del** ~ farm work; **los** ~s **de cebada** the field of barley; ~ **de aterrizaje** landing field; ~ **de batalla** battlefield; ~ **de minas** minefield; ~ **petrolífero** oilfield
3 (Dep) (de fútbol) field, pitch (BrE); (de golf) course; **jugar en** ~ **propio/contrario** to play at home/away; ~ **a través** cross-country running; ~ **de tiro** firing range

4 (ámbito, área de acción) field; **el** ~ **de la informática** the field of computing
5 (campamento) camp; ~ **de concentración/de refugiados** concentration/refugee camp

camposanto *m* (liter) graveyard, cemetery

campus *m* (pl ~) campus

camuflaje *m* camouflage

camuflar [A1] *vt* (tanques/contrabando) to camouflage; (intenciones) to disguise
■ **camuflarse** *v pron* «persona» to camouflage oneself; «animal» to camouflage itself

cana¹ *f* **1** (pelo) gray* hair, white hair; **echar una** ~ **al aire** to let one's hair down (colloq)
2 (AmS arg) (cárcel) slammer (sl), nick (BrE colloq)
3 (RPl arg) (cuerpo de policía): **la** ~ the cops (pl) (colloq)

cana² *mf* (RPl arg) (agente) cop (colloq)

Canadá *m*: tb **el** ~ Canada

canadiense *adj/mf* Canadian

canal *m* **1** (Náut) (cauce artificial) canal; (Agr, Ing) channel; ~ **de la Mancha** English Channel; ~ **de Panamá** Panama Canal; ~ **de San Lorenzo** St Lawrence Seaway **2** **(a)** (Rad, Telec, TV) channel; **cambia de** ~ change o switch channels **(b)** (medio) channel
■ *f* or *m* (canalón) gutter; (ranura) groove

canalizar [A4] *vt* to channel

canalla *mf* (fam) (bribón, granuja) swine (colloq)

canallada *f* (fam): **¡qué** ~! what a rotten o mean thing to do (colloq)

canalón *m* (Esp) gutter

canapé *m* **1** (Coc) canapé **2** (sofá) couch

Canarias *fpl*: tb **las (Islas)** ~ the Canaries, the Canary Islands

canario¹ -ria *adj* of/from the Canary Islands
■ *m,f* (de las Canarias) person from the Canary Islands

canario² *m* (Zool) canary

canasta *f* **(a)** (para la compra) basket **(b)** (AmL) (en rifa) hamper **(c)** (en baloncesto) basket; **meter una** ~ to make o score a basket **(d)** (Jueg) canasta

canastilla *f* layette

canasto *m* basket (gen large and with a lid)

cancel *m* (contrapuerta) inner door; (tabique) (Col, Méx) partition; (biombo) (Méx) folding screen

cancelación *f* **1** (suspensión) cancellation **2** (liquidación) payment

cancelar [A1] *vt* **(a)** (reunión/viaje/pedido) to cancel **(b)** (deuda) to settle, pay off; (cuenta) to pay

cáncer *m* (Med) cancer; **tiene (un)** ~ **de mama** she has breast cancer

Cáncer *m* (signo) Cancer; **es (de)** ~ he's a Cancer o Cancerian
■ *mf* (persona) tb **cáncer** Cancerian, Cancer

cancha *f* **1** **(a)** (Dep) (de baloncesto, frontón, squash, tenis) court; (de fútbol, rugby) (AmL) field, pitch; (BrE) (de golf) (CS) course; (de polo) (AmL) field; (de esquí) (CS) slope **(b)** (Chi) (Aviac) tb ~ **de aterrizaje** runway **2** (AmL fam) (desenvoltura): **un político con mucha** ~ a politician with a great deal of experience, a seasoned politician

canchita *f* (Per) popcorn

canciller m (a) (jefe de estado) chancellor (b) (AmS) (ministro) ≈ Secretary of State (in US), ≈ Foreign Secretary (in UK)

cancillería f (a) (de embajada) chancery, chancellery (b) (AmS) (ministerio) ≈ State Department (in US), ≈ Foreign Office (in UK)

canción f song; ~ de cuna lullaby; ~ nacional (Chi) national anthem

candado m (cerradura) padlock; está cerrada con ~ it is padlocked

candela f (a) (fuego) fire; ¿tienes ~? (fam) have you got a light? (b) (vela) candle

candelabro m candelabra

candelero m candlestick; estar en el ~ to be in the limelight

candente adj (a) ⟨hierro⟩ red-hot (b) ⟨tema⟩ burning

candidato -ta m,f candidate; ~ a la presidencia presidential candidate; los ~s al puesto de ... the applicants for the post of ...; presentarse como ~ para algo (Pol) to run (AmE) o (BrE) stand for sth

candidatura f (a) (propuesta) candidacy, candidature (b) (Esp) (lista) list of candidates

cándido -da adj naive

candil m oil lamp

candilejas fpl footlights (pl)

candor m innocence, naivety

caneca f (Col) (papelera) wastebasket, waste-paper basket (BrE); (cubo de la basura) garbage o trash can (AmE), dustbin (BrE)

canela f (Bot, Coc) cinnamon; ~ en polvo/en rama ground/stick cinnamon

canelón m (a) (Const) gutter (b) canelones mpl cannelloni

cangrejo m (de mar) crab; (de río) crayfish

canguro m [1] (Zool) kangaroo [2] (a) (anorak) cagoule (b) (para llevar a un niño) sling [3] (Esp) **canguro** mf babysitter; **hacer de ~** to babysit

caníbal mf (antropófago) cannibal

canica f marble

caniche mf /ka'nitʃe, ka'niʃ/ poodle

canijo -ja adj [1] (fam) (pequeño) tiny, puny (hum or pej) [2] (Méx fam) (terco) stubborn, pig-headed (colloq)

canilla f (a) (RPI) (grifo) faucet (AmE), tap (BrE); cerrar la ~ to turn off the faucet o tap (b) (bobina) bobbin

canillita mf (Bol, CS) newspaper vendor o seller

canino m (Odont) canine (tooth); (Zool) canine

canjear [A1] vt to exchange

cannabis m cannabis

cano -na adj white

canoa f canoe

canódromo m greyhound stadium, dog track (colloq)

canon m [1] (norma) rule, canon (frml) [2] (Mús) canon

canónico -ca adj canonical, canonic

canonizar [A4] vt to canonize

canoso -sa adj ⟨persona⟩ gray-haired*, white-haired; ⟨pelo/barba⟩ gray*, white

cansado -da adj [1] [ESTAR] (a) (fatigado) tired; ~s de tanto caminar tired from so much walking; tienes cara de ~ you look tired; en un tono ~ in

a weary tone of voice (b) (aburrido) ~ DE algo/ hacer algo tired OF sth/doing sth [2] [SER] ⟨viaje/ trabajo⟩ tiring

cansador -dora adj (AmS) tiring

cansancio m tiredness; me caigo de ~ I'm absolutely worn out o exhausted

cansar [A1] vt (a) (fatigar) to tire, tire ... out; le cansa la vista it makes her eyes tired, it strains her eyes (b) (aburrir): ¿no te cansa oír la misma música? don't you get tired of listening to the same music?
■ ~ vi (a) (fatigar) to be tiring (b) (aburrir) to get tiresome
■ **cansarse** v pron (a) (fatigarse) to tire oneself out; se le cansa la vista her eyes get tired (b) (aburrirse) to get bored; ~se DE algo/algn to get tired OF sth/sb, get bored WITH sth/sb, ~se DE hacer algo to get tired OF doing sth

cantábrico -ca adj Cantabrian

Cantábrico m: el (mar) ~ the Bay of Biscay

cantante adj singing (before n)
■ mf singer

cantar [A1] vt ⟨canción⟩ to sing
■ ~ vi [1] (a) (Mús) to sing ⟨pájaro⟩ to sing; «gallo» to crow; «cigarra/grillo» to chirp, chirrup [2] (fam) (confesar) to talk (colloq)
■ m poem (gen set to music)

cántara f churn

cantarín -rina, (CS) **cantarino -na** adj ⟨voz/ tono/risa⟩ singsong; ⟨fuente/aguas⟩ (liter) babbling

cántaro m pitcher, jug; llover a ~s to pour with rain

cantautor -tora m,f singer-songwriter

cante m (Mús) Andalusian folk song; ~ flamenco flamenco (singing)

cantera f (de piedra) quarry

cántico m canticle

cantidad f (a) (volumen) quantity, amount (b) (suma de dinero) sum, amount (c) (número) number; la ~ de cartas recibidas the number of letters received (d) (volumen impresionante): había ~ de turistas there were lots of tourists; ¡qué ~ de gente/de comida había! there were so many people/there was so much food!; tenemos ~ or ~es there have lots o tons (colloq); cualquier ~ de (AmS) lots of, loads of (colloq)

cantimplora f water bottle, canteen

cantina f [1] (a) (en estación) buffet, cafeteria; (en universidad) refectory; (en fábrica) canteen (b) (AmL exc RPI) (bar) bar (c) (RPI) (restaurante italiano) trattoria [2] (Col) (para la leche) churn

cantinela f: siempre la misma ~ always the same old story (o thing etc)

cantinflear [A1] vi (fam) to babble

canto m [1] (Mús) (acción, arte) singing; (canción) chant [2] (de pájaro) song; (del gallo) crowing [3] (Lit) (canción) hymn [4] (borde, filo) edge; colocó el ladrillo de ~ he lay the brick on its side [5] (Geol) tb ~ rodado (roca) boulder; (guijarro) pebble

cantor -tora adj singing (before n)
■ m,f (cantante) singer

canturrear [A1] vi to sing softly to oneself
■ ~ vt to sing ... softly to oneself

canuto m (tubo) document tube

caña f (a) (planta) reed (b) (tallo del bambú, azúcar)

cane; **muebles de** ∼ cane furniture; ∼ **de azúcar** sugar cane **(c)** (de pescar) rod **(d)** (de la bota) leg; **botas de media** ∼ calf-length boots

cañada f **(a)** (Geog) gully; (más profunda) ravine **(b)** (AmL) (arroyo) stream

cáñamo m (planta) cannabis plant, hemp; (tela) canvas

cañaveral m (de juncos) reedbed; (de cañas de azúcar) (Col) sugar-cane plantation

cañería f (tubo) pipe; (conjunto de tubos) piping, pipes (pl)

cañero -ra adj (AmL) (Agr) sugarcane (before n)

cañizal m reedbed

caño m (conducto) pipe; (de una fuente) spout; (grifo) (Per) faucet (AmE), tap (BrE)

cañón m **(a)** (Arm) (arma) cannon; (de una escopeta, pistola) barrel **(b)** (valle) canyon; **el Gran C**∼ **del Colorado** the Grand Canyon **(c)** (de pluma) quill

cañonazo m (Arm, Mil) cannonshot; **una salva de 21** ∼**s** a 21-gun salute

caoba f **(a)** (árbol) mahogany tree (madera) mahogany **(b)** (de) color ∼ mahogany

caos m chaos; **será un verdadero** ∼ there'll be absolute chaos

caótico -ca adj chaotic

capa f ⓵ **(a)** (en general) layer; **una** ∼ **de nieve** a layer o carpet of snow; **la** ∼ **de ozono** the ozone layer; **lleva el pelo cortado en** or (Esp) **a** ∼**s** she has layered hair **(b)** (de barniz, pintura) coat **(c)** (estrato) stratum; **las** ∼**s de la sociedad** the social strata ⓶ **(a)** (Indum) cloak, cape; ∼ **de agua** raincape **(b)** (Taur) cape

capacidad f ⓵ **(a)** (competencia) ability **(b)** (potencial) capacity; **su gran** ∼ **de trabajo** her great capacity for work; ∼ **DE** or **PARA hacer algo** ability o capacity to do sth **(c)** (Der) capacity ⓶ (cupo) capacity

capacitado -da adj ∼ **PARA algo/hacer algo** qualified FOR sth/to do sth

capacitar [A1] vt (formar) to prepare; (profesionalmente) ∼ **algn PARA algo** to qualify sb FOR sth; ∼ **algn PARA hacer algo** to qualify o entitle sb to do sth
■ **capacitarse** v pron (formarse) to train; (obtener un título) to qualify, become qualified

capar [A1] vt ⓵ (castrar) to castrate ⓶ (Col fam) ∼ **clase** to play hooky (esp AmE colloq), to skive off (school) (BrE colloq)

caparazón m or f shell

capataz mf (m) foreman; (f) forewoman

capaz adj **(a)** (competente) capable, able **(b)** (de una hazaña) capable; **es** ∼ **de grandes logros** he's capable of great things; **¿te sientes** ∼ **de enfrentarte con ella?** do you feel able to face her?; **¿a qué no eres** ∼ **de saltar esto?** I bet you can't jump over this; **es (muy)** ∼ **de irse sin pagar** he's quite capable of leaving without paying

capazo m (cesta) basket; (para un niño) portacrib® (AmE), carrycot (BrE)

capea f: amateur bullfight using young bulls

capear [A1] vt ⓵ (Taur) to make passes at (with the cape) ⓶ (Chi fam) (trabajo) to skip, to skive off (BrE colloq); ∼ **clase** to play hooky (esp AmE colloq), to skive off (school) (BrE colloq)

capellán m chaplain

Caperucita Roja Little Red Riding Hood

caperuza f **(a)** (Indum) pointed hood **(b)** (de un bolígrafo) top, cap

capicúa adj palindromic (frml); **era un número** ∼ the number read the same both ways

capilar adj **(a)** (loción) hair (before n) **(b)** (vaso/tubo) capillary (before n)
■ m capillary

capilla f chapel; ∼ **ardiente** funeral chapel

capital adj (importancia) cardinal, prime; (influencia) seminal (frml); (obra) key, seminal (frml)
■ m **(a)** (Com, Fin) capital **(b)** (recursos, riqueza) resources (pl)
■ f (de país) capital; (de provincia) provincial capital, ≈ county seat (in US), ≈ county town (in UK); **Valencia** ∼ the city of Valencia

capitalino -na adj (AmL) of/from the capital
■ m,f (AmL) inhabitant of the capital

capitalismo m capitalism

capitalista adj capitalist (before n)
■ mf capitalist

capitán -tana m,f ⓵ **(a)** (del ejército) captain; (de la Fuerza Aérea) captain (AmE), flight lieutenant (BrE) **(b)** (Náut) (de transatlántico, carguero) captain, master; (de buque de pesca) skipper **(c)** (Aviac) captain ⓶ (Dep) captain

capitel m capital

capítulo m (de libro) chapter; (de serie) episode

capó m hood (AmE), bonnet (BrE)

capón adj castrated
■ m (gallo) capon

caporal m (Méx) foreman, charge hand (BrE)

capot /ka'po/ m hood (AmE), bonnet (BrE)

capota f (de automóvil) convertible top; (de cochecito de bebé) canopy, hood

capote m ⓵ **(a)** (capa) cloak; (de militar, torero) cape ⓶ (Méx) (Auto) hood (AmE), bonnet (BrE)

capricho m ⓵ (antojo) whim, caprice (liter); **le consienten todos los** ∼**s** they indulge his every whim; **se lo compró por puro** ∼ he bought it on a whim; **entran y salen a** ∼ they come in and go out at will o as they please ⓶ (Mús) capriccio

caprichoso -sa adj (a) (inconstante) (carácter/ persona) capricious; (tiempo/moda) changeable **(b)** (difícil, exigente) fussy
■ m,f: **es un** ∼ (es inconstante) he's always changing his mind; (es difícil, exigente) he's so fussy

Capricornio m (signo, constelación) Capricorn; **es (de)** ∼ she's a Capricorn
■ mf (persona) tb **capricornio** Capricornean, Capricorn

cápsula f **(a)** (Farm, Espac) capsule **(b)** (Audio) cartridge

captar [A1] vt **(a)** (atención/interés) to capture; (clientes) to win, gain; (partidarios/empleados) to attract, recruit **(b)** (sentido/matiz) to grasp; (significado/indirecta) to get **(c)** (emisora/señal) to pick up, receive

captura f (de delincuente, enemigo, animal) capture; (de un alijo) seizure; (en pesca) catch

capturar [A1] vt (delincuente/enemigo/animal) to capture; (alijo) to seize, confiscate; (peces) to catch

capucha f hood

capuchón m (de pluma, bolígrafo) top, cap; (Indum) hood

capullo m (a) (Bot) bud (b) (Zool) cocoon

caqui adj inv/m khaki

cara f [1] (a) (Anat) face; **dímelo a la ~** say it to my face; **se le rio en la ~** she laughed in his face; **mírame a la ~** look at me (b) (en locs) **cara a cara** face to face; **de cara: el sol me da de ~** the sun is in my eyes; **se puso de ~ a la pared** she turned to face the wall, she turned her face to the wall; **dar la ~:** **nunca da la ~** he never does his own dirty work; **dar la ~ por algn** to stand up for sb; **echarle algo en ~ a algn** to throw sth back in sb's face; **romperle la ~ a algn** (fam) to smash sb's face in (colloq)

[2] (a) (expresión): **no pongas esa ~ que no es para tanto** don't look like that, it's not that bad; **alegra esa ~** cheer up; **le cambió la ~ cuando ...** her face changed when ...; **poner ~ de bueno** to play o act the innocent; **poner ~ de asco** to make o (BrE) pull a face; **andaba con/puso ~ larga** (fam) he had/he pulled a long face (b) (aspecto) look; **tiene ~ de cansado** he looks tired; **tienes mala ~** you don't look well; **¡qué buena ~ tiene la comida!** the food looks delicious!

[3] (a) (Mat) face (b) (de disco, papel) side; **~ o cruz** or (Arg) **ceca** or (Andes, Ven) **sello** heads or tails; **lo echaron a ~ o cruz** they tossed for it [4] (fam) (frescura, descaro) nerve (colloq), cheek (BrE colloq); **¡qué ~ (más dura) tienes!** you have some nerve!

■ mf: tb **~ dura** (fam) (persona) sassy devil (AmE colloq), cheeky swine (BrE colloq)

carabina f (a) (Arm) carbine (b) (Esp fam) (acompañante): **ir de ~** to play gooseberry (colloq)

carabinero -ra m,f (a) (policía) (m) police officer, policeman; (f) police officer, policewoman (b) (agente fronterizo) border guard (c) **carabineros** mpl (institución) police (force); (policía fronteriza) border police

Caracas f Caracas

caracol m (a) (Zool) (de mar) winkle; (de tierra) snail (b) (AmL) (concha) conch

caracola f conch

carácter m (pl -racteres) (a) (en general) character; **tenemos un ~ muy distinto** we have very different characters; **el restaurante tiene mucho ~** the restaurant has lots of character; **una persona de ~ fuerte** a person of strong character; **una persona de buen ~ a** good-natured person; **un ~ abierto** an open nature; **tener mal ~** to have a (bad) temper (b) (índole, naturaleza) nature; **una visita de ~ oficial** a visit of an official nature; **heridas de ~ leve** (period) minor wounds (c) (Biol) characteristic (d) (Col, Méx) (personaje) character

característica f (a) (rasgo) feature, characteristic (b) (RPl) (Telec) exchange code

característico -ca adj characteristic

caracterizar [A4] vt [1] (distinguir) to characterize; **con la franqueza que lo caracteriza** with his characteristic frankness [2] (describir) to portray, depict [3] (Teatr) (encarnar) to play, portray

■ **caracterizarse** v pron: **~se POR algo** «enfermedad/región/raza» to be characterized BY sth; «persona» to be noted FOR sth

caradura adj (fam) sassy (AmE colloq), cheeky (BrE colloq)

■ mf (fam) sassy devil (AmE colloq), cheeky swine (BrE colloq)

■ f (fam) nerve (colloq), cheek (BrE colloq)

carajillo m (café) coffee with brandy or similar

carajito -ta m,f (Ven fam) (niño) kid (colloq)

caramba interj (expresando — sorpresa) good heavens!; (— disgusto) dammit! (colloq)

carámbano m icicle

carambola f (a) (en billar) carom (AmE), cannon (BrE) (b) (fam) (casualidad): **fue de ~** it was pure chance (c) (Méx) (choque múltiple) pileup

caramelo m (a) (golosina) candy (AmE), sweet (BrE); **un ~ de menta** a mint (b) (azúcar fundida) caramel

carantoña f (Esp fam) caress

caraota f (Ven) bean

caraqueño -ña adj of/from Caracas

carátula f (a) (de disco) jacket (AmE), sleeve (BrE); (de video) case (b) (Méx) (de reloj) face, dial (c) (máscara) mask

caravana f [1] (a) (de tráfico — retención) backup (AmE) tailback (BrE); (— hilera) convoy; **ir en ~** to drive in (a) convoy (b) (remolque) trailer (AmE), caravan (BrE) [2] (Méx) (reverencia) bow

carbohidrato m carbohydrate

carbón m (a) (mineral) coal; **negro como el ~** as black as coal (b) (vegetal) charcoal

carboncillo m charcoal; **dibujo al ~** charcoal drawing

carbonilla f (a) (polvo de carbón) cinders (pl) (b) (RPl) (Art) charcoal

carbonizarse [A4] v pron (a) «edificio/muebles» to be reduced to ashes; **los cuerpos carbonizados de las víctimas** the victims' charred remains (b) (Quím) to carbonize

carbono m carbon

carburador m carburetor*

carburante m fuel

carburar [A1] vi (a) «motor» to carburet (b) (fam) (funcionar) «electrodoméstico/coche» to work

■ vt (Andes) «motor» to tune

carca adj (fam) old-fashioned, fuddy-duddy (colloq)

■ mf old fogey (colloq)

carcacha f (Andes, Méx fam) (auto viejo) wreck (colloq), old heap (colloq); (otro aparato) contraption (colloq)

carcajada f guffaw; **soltar una ~** to give a guffaw, to burst out laughing; **reírse a ~s** to roar with laughter

AmC	América Central	Arg	Argentina	Cu	Cuba
AmL	América Latina	Bol	Bolivia	Ec	Ecuador
AmS	América del Sur	Chi	Chile	Esp	España
Andes	Región andina	CS	Cono Sur	Méx	México

Per	Perú
RPl	Río de la Plata
Ur	Uruguay
Ven	Venezuela

carcasa *f* **(a)** (armazón, estructura) frame; (de aparato) casing; (de barca) hulk **(b)** (esqueleto de animal) skeleton

cárcel *f* (prisión) prison, jail; **la metieron en la ∼** she was put in prison

carcelero -ra *m,f* jailer

carcoma *f* (Zool) woodworm

carcomer [E1] *vt* **(a)** «*carcoma*» to eat away (at); **el marco está carcomido** the frame is worm-eaten **(b)** «*salud*» to undermine; **la envidia lo carcomía** he was eaten up with envy

cardar [A1] *vt* **(a)** ⟨*lana*⟩ to card **(b)** ⟨*pelo*⟩ to backcomb, tease
■ **cardarse** *v pron* (*refl*) to backcomb

cardenal *m* **1** (Relig) cardinal **2** (fam) (moretón) bruise

cardíaco, cardiaco -ca *adj* heart (*before n*), cardiac (tech); **enfermos ∼s** heart patients

cárdigan *m* (*pl* **-gans**) cardigan

cardiólogo -ga *m,f* cardiologist

cardo *m* (Bot) thistle

carecer [E3] *vi* (frml) **∼ DE algo** to lack sth; **carece de interés** it is lacking in interest, it lacks interest; **carece de valor** it's worthless

carencia *f* **(a)** (escasez) lack, shortage; **∼ de recursos financieros** lack of financial resources **(b)** (Med) deficiency; **∼ de vitamina A** vitamin A deficiency

carente *adj* (frml): **lugares ∼s de interés** places which are of no interest; **niños ∼s de cariño** children lacking affection

careo *n* confrontation (*in court*)

carero -ra *adj* (fam) ⟨*comerciante*⟩ pricey (colloq)

carestía *f* (costo elevado) high cost; **la ∼ de la vida** the high cost of living

careta *f* mask

carey *m* (Zool) hawksbill turtle; (material) tortoiseshell

carga *f* **1** **(a)** (de barco, avión) cargo; (de camión) load; (de tren) freight; ✆ **zona de carga y descarga** loading and unloading only **(b)** (peso) load; **no lleves tanta ∼** don't carry such a heavy load **2** **(a)** (de escopeta, cañón) charge **(b)** (de bolígrafo, pluma) refill; (de lavadora) load **3** (Elec) (de cuerpo) charge; (de circuito) load **4** (responsabilidad) burden; **es una ∼ para la familia** he is a burden to his family **5** **(a)** (de tropas, policía) charge; **¡a la ∼!** charge! **(b)** (Dep) *tb* **∼ defensiva** blitz

cargada *f* (RPl fam) practical joke

cargaderas *fpl* (Col) suspenders (*pl*) (AmE), braces (*pl*) (BrE)

cargado -da *adj* **1** **(a)** (con peso): **iba muy cargada** she had a lot to carry; **∼ DE algo** ⟨*de regalos*⟩ laden WITH sth; ⟨*de paquetes/maletas*⟩ loaded down WITH sth; **∼ de deudas** heavily in debt; **un árbol ∼ de fruta** a tree laden with fruit; **∼ de trabajo** overloaded with work **(b)** ⟨*ambiente/atmósfera*⟩ (bochornoso) heavy, close; (con humo, olores desagradables) stuffy; (tenso) strained, tense **(c)** ⟨*café*⟩ strong **2** **∼ de hombros** *or* **de espaldas** with bowed shoulders

cargador *m* **(a)** (Arm) clip, magazine **(b)** (de pilas, baterías) battery charger

cargamento *m* (de camión) load; (de barco, avión) cargo; (de tren) freight

cargante *adj* **(a)** (CS fam) (antipático) unpleasant, horrible (colloq) **(b)** (Esp fam) annoying

cargar [A3] *vt* **1** **(a)** ⟨*barco/avión/camión*⟩ to load; **∼on la camioneta de cajas** they loaded the van with boxes; **no cargues tanto el coche** don't put so much in the car **(b)** ⟨*pistola/escopeta*⟩ to load; ⟨*pluma/encendedor*⟩ to fill; ⟨*cámara*⟩ to load, put a film in **(c)** (Elec) to charge **2** **(a)** ⟨*mercancías*⟩ to load **(b)** ⟨*combustible*⟩ to fuel; **tengo que ∼ nafta** (RPl) I have to fill up with gasoline (AmE) *o* (BrE) petrol **(c)** (Inf) to load **3** (de obligaciones) **∼ a algn DE algo** to burden sb WITH sth; **me ∼on la culpa** they put *o* laid the blame on me **4** **(a)** ⟨*paquetes/bolsas*⟩ to carry; ⟨*niño*⟩ (AmL) to carry **(b)** (AmL exc RPl) ⟨*armas*⟩ to carry **(c)** (Ven fam) (llevar puesto) to wear; (tener consigo): **cargo las llaves** I have the keys **5** (a una cuenta) to charge **6** (Méx fam) (matar) to kill
■ **∼** *vi* **1** **∼ CON algo** ⟨*con bulto*⟩ to carry sth; **tiene que ∼ con todo el peso de la casa** she has to shoulder all the responsibility for the household **2** **∼ CONTRA algn** «*tropas/policía*» to charge ON *o* AT sb **3** «*batería*» to charge **4** (fam) (fastidiar): **me cargan los fanfarrones** I can't stand show-offs
■ **cargarse** *v pron* **1** **(a)** «*pilas/flash*» to charge; «*partícula*» to become charged **(b)** **∼se DE algo** ⟨*de bolsas/equipaje*⟩ to load oneself down WITH sth; ⟨*de responsabilidades*⟩ to take on a lot OF sth; ⟨*de deudas*⟩ to saddle oneself WITH sth **2** **(a)** (fam) (matar) to kill **(b)** (Esp fam) ⟨*motor*⟩ to wreck; ⟨*jarrón*⟩ to smash

cargo *m* **1** (puesto) post, position (frml); (de presidente, ministro) office; **tener un ∼ público** to hold public office; **un ∼ de responsabilidad** a responsible job *o* post **2** (responsabilidad, cuidado): **los niños están a mi ∼** the children are in my care; **estar a ∼ de algo** to be in charge of sth; **los gastos corren a ∼ de la empresa** expenses will be paid *o* met by the company; **hacerse ∼** ⟨*de puesto/tarea*⟩ to take charge of sth; ⟨*de gastos*⟩ to take care of sth; **me da ∼ de conciencia** I feel guilty **3** **(a)** (Com, Fin) charge; **sin ∼** free of charge **(b)** (Der) charge

cargoso -sa *adj* (CS, Per fam) annoying

cargue *m* (Col, Ven) loading; ✆ **zona de cargue y descargue** loading and unloading only

carguero *m* freighter, cargo ship

Caribe *m*: **el (mar) ∼** the Caribbean (Sea)

caribeño -ña *adj* Caribbean
■ *m,f*: person from the Caribbean region

caribú *m* caribou

caricatura *f* (dibujo) caricature

caricaturizar [A4] *vt* to caricature

caricia *f* caress; **hacer ∼s** to caress; **le hizo una ∼ al perro** she stroked the dog

caridad *f* charity; **vivir de la ∼** to live on charity; **por ∼** for pity's sake

caries *f* (*pl* **∼**) **(a)** (proceso) tooth decay, caries (*pl*) (tech) **(b)** (cavidad) cavity

cariño *m* **(a)** (afecto) affection; **les tengo mucho** ⋯⟶

c

~ I am very fond of them; **te ha tomado mucho** ~ he's become very fond of you; **~s por tu casa/ a tu mujer** (AmL) (send my) love to your family/ your wife; **~s, Beatriz** (en cartas) (AmL) love, Beatriz **(b)** (caricia): **le hice un cariñito al niño** I gave the little boy a cuddle (*o* kiss *etc*) **(c)** (como apelativo) dear, honey, love (BrE)

cariñoso -sa *adj* ⟨persona⟩ affectionate; ⟨bienvenida⟩ warm; **un ~ saludo de mi parte** regards

carioca *adj* of/from Rio de Janeiro

carisma *m* charisma

carismático -ca *adj* charismatic

caritativo -va *adj* charitable; **una organización con fines ~s** a charitable organization

cariz *m*: **el ~ que están tomando las cosas** the way things are going *o* developing; **la situación está tomando mal ~** the situation is beginning to look bad

carmín *adj inv* carmine

■ *m* **(a)** (para labios) lipstick **(b)** (color) carmine

carnada *f* bait

carnal *adj* ⟨amor/deseo⟩ carnal

■ *m* (Méx arg) pal (colloq), buddy (AmE colloq), mate (BrE colloq)

carnaval *m* (fiesta) carnival

carne *f* 1 **(a)** (de mamífero, ave) meat; (de pescado) flesh; **~ de cerdo** *or* (Chi, Per) **chancho** *or* (Ven) **cochino** *or* (Méx) **puerco** pork; **~ de cordero** lamb; **~ de ternera** veal; **~ de vaca** *or* (AmC, Col, Méx, Ven) **res** beef; **~ molida** *or* (Esp, RPl) **picada** ground beef (AmE), mince (BrE) **(b)** (de fruta) flesh 2 (de una persona) flesh; **es ~ de mi ~** he's my flesh and blood; **tenía la herida en ~ viva** her wound was raw; **(de) color ~** flesh-colored*; **en ~ y hueso** in the flesh; **me pone la ~ de gallina** it gives me goose pimples (colloq)

carné *m* identity card; **sacar el ~** to have one's identity (*o* membership *etc*) card issued; **~ de conducir** driver's license (AmE), driving licence (BrE); **~ de estudiante** student card; **~ de identidad** identity card; **~ de socio** (de club, mutual) membership card; (de biblioteca) library card

carnear [A1] *vt* (CS) to slaughter

■ **~** *vi* (CS) to slaughter a cow (*o* lamb *etc*)

carnecería *f* butcher's shop (*o* stall *etc*)

cárneo -nea *adj* (CS) meat (*before n*)

carnero *m* ram

carnet /kar'ne/ *m* (*pl* **-nets**) ▶ CARNÉ

carnicería *f* **(a)** (tienda) butcher's shop (*o* stall *etc*) **(b)** (fam) (matanza) slaughter

carnicero -ra *m,f* **(a)** (vendedor) butcher **(b)** (fam & pey) (cirujano) butcher (colloq & pej)

carnitas *fpl* (Méx) pieces of barbecued pork (*pl*)

carnívoro¹ -ra *adj* carnivorous, meat-eating

carnívoro² *m* carnivore

caro¹ -ra *adj* **(a)** ⟨coche/entrada/ciudad⟩ expensive; **la vida está muy cara** everything costs so much nowadays **(b)** (como adv): **me costó muy ~** I had to pay a lot of money for it; **pagarás ~ tu error** you'll pay dearly for your mistake

caro² *adv*: **vender ~** to charge a lot; *ver tb* CARO¹ B

carpa *f* 1 **(a)** (de circo) big top; (para actuaciones) marquee **(b)** (AmL) (para acampar) tent 2 (Zool) carp

carpeta *f* (para documentos, dibujos) folder; **~ de anillos** *or* (Esp) **anillas** *or* (RPl) **ganchos** ring binder

carpintería *f* **(a)** (taller) carpenter's workshop; (actividad) carpentry **(b)** (de construcción, casa) woodwork; **~ metálica** metalwork

carpintero -ra *m,f* carpenter

carraca *f* **(a)** (matraca) rattle **(b)** (fam) (trasto) wreck (colloq))

carraspear [A1] *vi* to clear one's throat

carraspera *f*: **tener ~** to have a rough throat

carrasposo -sa *adj* **(a)** ⟨garganta⟩ rough **(b)** (Col) ⟨superficie⟩ rough

carrera *f* 1 (Dep) (competición) race; **~ de caballos** horse race; **la ~ de los 100 metros vallas** the 100 meters hurdles; **te echo una ~** I'll race you; **~ de armamentos** arms race; **~ contra reloj** (Dep) time trial; **~ de fondo** long-distance race; **~ de postas** *o* **relevos** relay race 2 (fam) (corrida): **darse** *or* **pegarse una ~** to run as fast as one can; **me fui de una ~ a su casa** I raced *o* rushed round to her house (colloq); **a la(s) ~(s)** in a rush 3 **(a)** (Educ) degree course; **está haciendo la ~ de Derecho** he's doing a degree in law **(b)** (profesión, trayectoria) career; **un diplomático de ~** a career diplomat; **~ media/superior** *three-year/ five-year university course* 4 (en la media) run, ladder (BrE); (en el pelo) (Col, Ven) part (AmE), parting (BrE)

carrerear [A1] *vt* (Méx fam) to push (colloq)

carrerilla *f*: **se lo saben de ~** they know it (off) by heart; **me lo dijo de ~** he reeled it off parrot-fashion; **coger ~** (Esp) to take a run-up

carreta *f* (con toldo) wagon; (sin toldo) cart

carrete *m* (de hilo, cinta) spool, reel (BrE); (de película) film; (de caña de pescar) reel

carretear [A1] *vi* (AmL) (Aviac) to taxi

carretela *f* (Chi) cart

carretera *f* road; **~ de circunvalación** bypass, beltway (AmE), ring road (BrE); **~ nacional** ≈highway (*in US*), ≈A-road (*in UK*)

carretilla *f* 1 (de mano) wheelbarrow 2 (CS) (quijada) jaw, jawbone

carricoche *m* covered wagon

carril *m* **(a)** (Auto) lane; **~ bus** bus lane; **~ de adelantamiento** overtaking lane, fast lane; **~ de bicicletas** cycleway, cycle path **(b)** (Ferr) rail **(c)** (AmL) (Dep) lane

carrillo *m* cheek

carriola *f* (Méx) baby carriage (AmE), baby buggy (BrE)

carrito *m* **(a)** (para el equipaje) trolley; (en supermercado) shopping cart (AmE), trolley (BrE); (de la compra) shopping trolley *o* (AmE) cart; **~ chocón** (Méx, Ven) bumper car **(b)** (mesita de servir) trolley

carro *m* 1 **(a)** (carreta) cart; **un ~ de tierra** a cartload of earth; **~ de combate** tank **(b)** (AmL exc CS) (Auto) car, automobile (AmE); **~ bomba** (Col) car bomb; **~ loco** (Andes) bumper car; **~ sport** (AmL exc CS) sports car; **~ de bomberos** (Andes, Méx) fire engine **(c)** (Chi, Méx) (vagón) coach, carriage (BrE); ~ **comedor/dormitorio** (Méx) dining/sleeping car **(d)** (Hist) (romano) chariot ②(de máquina de escribir) carriage

carrocería *f* (de automóvil) bodywork

carroña *f* **(a)** (de animal muerto) carrion **(b)** (gente despreciable) riffraff (+ *sing or pl vb*)

carroza *f* **(a)** (coche de caballos) carriage **(b)** (de carnaval) float **(c)** (Chi, Ur) (coche fúnebre) hearse

carruaje *m* carriage

carrusel *m* **(a)** (para diapositivas) carousel, slide tray **(b)** (para niños) merry-go-round, carousel (AmE)

carta *f* ① (Corresp) letter; ¿hay ~ **para mí?** are there any letters for me?; **echar una ~ al correo** to mail (esp AmE) *o* (esp BrE) post a letter; ~ **adjunta** *or* **explicatoria** covering letter; ~ **blanca** carte blanche; ~ **certificada** registered letter; ~ **de amor** love letter; ~ **de recomendación** reference, letter of recommendation; ~ **urgente** special-delivery letter
② (naipe) card; **jugar a las** ~s to play cards; **dar las** ~s to deal the cards; **echarle las** ~s *a algn* to tell sb's fortune; **poner las** ~s **sobre la mesa** to put *o* lay one's cards on the table
③ (en restaurante) menu; **comer a la** ~ to eat à la carte; ~ **de vinos** wine list

cartearse [A1] *v pron*: **nos carteamos durante años** we wrote to each other *o* corresponded for years; ~ **CON** *algn* to correspond **WITH** sb

cartel *m* (de publicidad, propaganda) poster; (letrero) sign; ~ **luminoso** neon sign; **lleva dos meses en** ~ «*obra/película*» it has been on for two months; **de** ~ «*cantante/actor*» famous; «*torero*» star (*before n*)

cartelera *f* **(a)** (Cin, Teatr) publicity board; **la película sigue en** ~ the movie is still on *o* still showing; **la obra estuvo en** ~ **durante cuatro años** the play ran for four years **(b)** (en el periódico) listings (*pl*); ~ **de espectáculos** entertainment guide **(c)** (AmL) (tablón de anuncios) bulletin board (AmE), notice board (BrE)

cárter *m* (del cigüeñal) crankcase, sump; (del embrague) housing

cartera *f* ① **(a)** (billetera) wallet, billfold (AmE) **(b)** (para documentos) document case, briefcase; (de colegial) satchel; (de cobrador) money bag; (de cartero) sack, bag **(c)** (AmS) (bolso de mujer) purse (AmE), handbag (BrE) ② (Com, Fin) portfolio

carterear [A1] *vt* (Chi): **me** ~**on en la micro** my handbag was picked on the bus

carterista *mf* pickpocket

cartero (*m*) mailman (AmE), postman (BrE); (*f*) mailwoman (AmE), postwoman (BrE)

cartílago *m* cartilage

cartilla *f* **(a)** (para aprender a leer) reader, primer **(b)** (libreta) book; ~ **de ahorros** passbook, savings book; ~ **de racionamiento** ration book

cartón *m* **(a)** (material) cardboard; ~ **ondulado** corrugated cardboard; ~ **piedra** papier-mâché **(b)** (de cigarrillos, leche) carton; (de huevos) tray

cartoné *m*: **en** ~ hardback

cartuchera *f* ① **(a)** (estuche — para cartuchos) cartridge clip; (— para pistola) holster **(b)** (cinturón — para cartuchos) cartridge belt; (— para pistola) gun belt ② (RPl) (de escolar) pencil case

cartucho *m* cartridge

cartuja *f* charterhouse, monastery

cartulina *f* card

casa *f* ① **(a)** (vivienda) house; **cambiarse de** ~ to move house; **casita del perro** kennel; ~ **adosada** *or* **pareada** semi-detached *o* terraced house; **C**~ **Blanca** White House; ~ **de acogida** refuge; ~ **de huéspedes** boardinghouse; ~ **de socorro** first-aid post; ~ **de vecinos** *or* (Méx) **de vecindad** tenement house; **C**~ **Real** Royal Household; ~ **refugio** refuge *o* hostel for battered women; ~ **rodante** (CS) trailer (AmE), caravan (BrE) **(b)** (hogar) home; **a los 18 años se fue de** ~ *or* (AmL) **de la** ~ she left home at 18; **no está nunca en** ~ *or* (AmL) **en la** ~ he's never (at) home; **está en casa de Ana** she's (over) at Ana's (house); ¿**por qué no pasas por** ~ *or* (AmL) **por la** ~? why don't you drop in?; **de** *or* **para andar por** ~ ‹*vestido*› for wearing around the house; ‹*definición/terminología*› crude, rough; **echar** *or* **tirar la** ~ **por la ventana** to push the boat out
② **(a)** (empresa) company, firm (BrE); **una** ~ **de discos** a record company; ~ **de cambios** bureau de change **(b)** (bar, restaurante): **especialidad de la** ~ house specialty (AmE), speciality of the house (BrE); **invita la** ~ it's on the house
③ (Dep): **perdieron en** ~ they lost at home

casabe *m* (Col, Ven) cassava bread

casaca *f* (chaqueta) jacket; (Equ) riding jacket

casado -da *adj* married; **está** ~ **con una japonesa** he's married to a Japanese woman
■ *m,f* (*m*) married man; (*f*) married woman; **los recién** ~s the newlyweds

casamiento *m* (unión) marriage; (boda) wedding

casar [A1] *vt* «*cura/juez*» to marry
■ ~ *vi* **(a)** (encajar) «*dibujos*» to match up; «*piezas*» to fit together; «*cuentas*» to match, tally **(b)** (armonizar) «*colores/estilos*» to go together; ~ **CON** *algo* to go well **WITH** sth
■ **casarse** *v pron* to get married; ~**se por la Iglesia** to get married in church; **se casó con un abogado** she married a lawyer; ~**se en segundas nupcias** to marry again, to remarry

cascabel *m* **(a)** (campanita) bell **(b)** (Chi) (sonajero) rattle
■ *f* (Zool) rattlesnake

cascada *f* (Geog) waterfall, cascade

cascajo *m* (fam) ① (trasto viejo) wreck (colloq) ② (Col) (Const) piece of gravel

cascanueces *m* (*pl* ~) (a pair of) nutcrackers

cascar [A2] *vt* ‹*nuez/huevo*› to crack; ‹*taza*› to chip
■ **cascarse** *v pron* «*huevo*» to crack; «*taza*» to chip

cáscara *f* (de huevo, nuez) shell; (del queso) rind; (de naranja, limón) peel, rind; (de plátano, papa) skin; (de manzana) peel

cascarilla *f* (de cacao) roasted cacao husks (*pl*) (used in infusions); (de cereal) husk

cascarón *m* (de huevo, nuez) shell

cascarrabias *adj inv* (fam) cantankerous, grumpy
■ *mf* (*pl* ~) grouch (colloq)

casco *m* ① **(a)** (para la cabeza) helmet; ~ **protector** (de obrero) safety helmet; (de motorista) crash helmet **(b) cascos** *mpl* (Audio) ⋯❖

headphones (*pl*) **2** (Equ, Zool) hoof **3** (Náut) hull **4** (a) (de ciudad): ~ **antiguo** old quarter; ~ **urbano** urban area, built-up area (b) (RPI) (de estancia) farmhouse and surrounding buildings **5** (Col) (gajo) segment **6** (Esp, Méx) (envase) bottle

cascote *m* piece of rubble; ~**s** rubble

caserío *m* (poblado) hamlet; (finca) (Esp) farmhouse

casero -ra *adj* (a) ⟨*vino/flan*⟩ homemade; ⟨*reparación*⟩ amateur; ⟨*trabajo*⟩ domestic (b) ⟨*persona*⟩ home-loving
■ *m,f* **1** (a) (propietario) (*m*) landlord; (*f*) landlady (b) (cuidador) caretaker **2** (Chi) (cliente) customer; (vendedor) storekeeper (AmE), stallholder

caseta *f* (a) (en la playa, de guardia etc) hut (b) (en exposición) stand (c) (para perro) kennel (d) (en fútbol) dugout

casete *m or f* (cinta) cassette; ~ **digital** digital audio tape
■ *m* (Esp) (grabador) cassette recorder/player

casi *adv* **1** (cerca de) almost, nearly; ~ **me caigo** I nearly fell over **2** (en frases negativas): ~ **no se le oía** you could hardly hear him; ~ **nunca** hardly ever; **no nos queda** ~ **nada de pan** there's hardly any bread left; **¿pudiste dormir? —** ~ **nada** did you manage to sleep? — hardly at all; ~ **no vengo** I almost didn't come **3** (expresando una opinión tentativa): ~ **sería mejor venderlo** maybe it would be better to sell it

casilla *f* **1** (para cartas, llaves) pigeonhole; ~ **postal** *or* **de correo** (CS, Per) post office box, P.O. Box **2** (en ajedrez, crucigrama) square; (en formulario) box **3** (a) (de guardia, sereno) hut (b) (de perro) kennel (c) (Méx) (de votación) polling booth

casillero *m* (a) (mueble) set of pigeonholes; (compartimento) pigeonhole (b) (CS) (en formulario) box

casino *m* **1** (de juego) casino **2** (club social) club

casitas *fpl* (Chi fam & euf) (baño) bathroom (euph)

caso *m* **1** (situación, coyuntura) case; **en esos** ~**s** in cases like that; **yo en tu caso** ... if I were you ...; **en último** ~ if it comes to it, if the worst comes to the worst; **en el mejor de los** ~ at (the very) best; **en el peor de los** ~**s te multarán** the worst they can do is fine you; **eso no venía al** ~ that had nothing to do with what we were talking about; **pongamos por** ~ **que** ... let's assume that ...; **en** ~ **de incendio** in case of fire; **en** ~ **contrario** otherwise; **en cualquier** ~ in any case; **en tal** ~ in that case, in such a case (frml); **en todo** ~ **dijo que llamaría** in any case she said she'd ring; **llegado el** ~ if it comes to it; **según el** ~ as appropriate; *no hay/hubo caso* (AmL fam) it is no good *o* no use/it was no good *o* no use **2** (Der, Med) case; **ser un** ~ **perdido** (fam) to be a hopeless case (colloq) **3** (atención): **hacerle** ~ A **algn** to pay attention TO sb, take notice OF sb; **hacer** ~ DE **algo** to pay attention TO sth, to take notice OF sth; **hacer** ~ **omiso de algo** to ignore sth

caspa *f* dandruff

casquillo *m* (a) (de bala, cartucho) case (b) (portalámparas) lampholder, bulbholder; (de bombilla): ~ **de rosca/bayoneta** screw-in/bayonet fitting

cassette /ka'set/ *m or f* ▶ CASETE

casta *f* caste; **de** ~ ⟨*toro*⟩ thoroughbred; ⟨*torero*⟩ top-class

castaña *f* (fruto) chestnut; ~ **de Indias** horse chestnut; ~ **de Pará** (RPI) Brazil nut; ~ **pilonga** dried chestnut

castañetear [A1] *vi*: **me castañetean los dientes** my teeth are chattering

castaño¹ -ña *adj* ⟨*pelo*⟩ chestnut; ⟨*ojos*⟩ brown

castaño² *m* (a) (Bot) chestnut tree; ~ **de Indias** horse chestnut (b) (color) chestnut

castañuela *f* castanet

castellano¹ -na *adj* (de Castilla) Castilian; (español) Spanish
■ *m,f* (persona) Castilian

castellano² *m* (idioma — de Castilla) Castilian; (— español) Spanish

castidad *f* chastity

castigar [A3] *vt* (a) (en general) to punish; **fueron castigados con la pena máxima** they received the maximum sentence (b) ⟨*niño*⟩ (a quedarse en el colegio) to keep ... in detention; (a quedarse en casa) to keep ... in as a punishment, to ground (esp AmE colloq); **lo** ~**on sin postre** as a punishment he was made to go without dessert

castigo *m* punishment; ~ **corporal** corporal punishment; **les impusieron** ~**s severos** they were severely punished; **levantar un** ~ to lift a punishment

Castilla *f* Castile

castillo *m* castle; ~ **de arena** sandcastle; *construir* ~**s en el aire** to build castles in the air

castizo -za *adj* (a) (puro, tradicional) ⟨*estilo/costumbre*⟩ traditional (b) (típicamente castellano): **un lenguaje muy** ~ very pure Castilian/Spanish

casto -ta *adj* chaste

castor *m* beaver

castrar [A1] *vt* ⟨*caballo*⟩ to geld; ⟨*toro/hombre*⟩ to castrate; ⟨*gato*⟩ to neuter

casual *adj* chance (*before n*)

casualidad *f* chance; **por** (**pura**) ~ by (sheer) chance; **si por** ~ **la ves** if you happen to see her; **¿no tendrás su dirección por** ~? you wouldn't (happen to) have her address by any chance?; **¡qué** ~! what a coincidence!; **da la** ~ **de que** ... as it happens ...

cataclismo *m* natural disaster, cataclysm (frml)

catacumbas *fpl* catacombs (*pl*)

catador -dora *m,f* taster

catalán¹ -lana *adj/m,f* Catalan

catalán² *m* (idioma) Catalan

catalejo *m* (ant) telescope, spyglass

catalizador *m* (Auto) catalytic converter

catalogar [A3] *vt* **(a)** (en un catálogo) to catalog (AmE), to catalogue (BrE); (en una lista) to record, list **(b)** (considerar) to class

catálogo *m* (Art, Com) catalog (AmE), catalogue (BrE); **compra por** ~ mail-order shopping

Cataluña *f* Catalonia

catamarán *m* catamaran

cataplasma *f* poultice, cataplasm (tech)

catapulta *f* catapult

catapultar [A1] *vt* to catapult

catar [A1] *vt* ‹vino› to taste

catarata *f* **(a)** (Geog) waterfall; **las ~s del Iguazú** Iguaçú Falls **(b)** (Med) cataract

catarro *m* **(a)** (resfriado) cold; **pescarse** *or* (esp Esp) **coger un** ~ to catch a cold **(b)** (inflamación) catarrh

catastro *m* (censo) cadastre, land registry; (impuesto) property tax

catástrofe *f* catastrophe, disaster

catastrófico -ca *adj* catastrophic, disastrous

catear [A1] *vt* ⟦1⟧ (Esp arg) (suspender) to fail ⟦2⟧ **(a)** (Chi) (Min) to prospect **(b)** (Méx) (registrar) ‹persona› to frisk; ‹vivienda› to search

catecismo *m* catechism

cátedra *f* (en universidad) professorship, chair; (en colegio) post of head of department

catedral *f* cathedral

catedrático -ca *m,f* (de universidad) professor; (en colegio) head of department

categoría *f* **(a)** (grupo) category; ~ **gramatical** part of speech; **hotel de primera** ~ first-class hotel **(b)** (calidad): **de** ~ ‹actor/espectáculo/revista› first-rate; **un periódico de poca** ~ a second-rate newspaper; **el hotel de más** ~ the finest *o* best hotel **(c)** (estatus): **tiene** ~ **de embajador** he has ambassadorial status; **gente de cierta** ~ people of some standing

categórico -ca *adj* ‹respuesta› categorical

cateo *m* (Chi, Méx) (cacheo) body search

catequesis *f*: *teaching of the catechism*

catire -ra *adj* (Ven) (de piel blanca) fair-skinned; (de pelo rubio) fair, fair-haired
■ *m,f* (Ven) (de piel blanca) fair-skinned person; (de pelo rubio) fair-haired person

catita *f* (CS) budgerigar

catolicismo *m* Catholicism

católico -ca *adj* **(a)** (Relig) Catholic; **es** ~ he's a Catholic **(b)** (ortodoxo) orthodox
■ *m,f* Catholic

catorce *adj inv/m/pron* fourteen; *para ejemplos ver* CINCO

catre *m* **(a)** (cama — plegable) folding bed; (— de campaña) camp bed **(b)** (CS) (armazón) bedstead

catsup *m* ketchup, catsup (AmE)

cauce *m* **(a)** (Geog) bed; **el río se salió de su** ~ the river burst its banks; **desviaron el** ~ **del arroyo** they changed the course of the stream **(b)** (rumbo, vía): **desvió la conversación hacia otros** ~s he steered the conversation onto another tack; **seguir los** ~s **establecidos** to go through the normal channels

cauchera *f* (Col) (tirachinas) (fam) slingshot (AmE), catapult (BrE)

caucho *m* **(a)** (sustancia) rubber; (árbol) (Col) rubber tree **(b)** (neumático) (Ven) tire*; (gomita) (Col) rubber band, elastic band (BrE)

caudal *m* **(a)** (de un fluido) volume of flow; **el río tiene muy poco** ~ the water level is very low **(b)** (riqueza) fortune **(c)** (abundancia) wealth; **un** ~ **de conocimientos** a wealth of knowledge

caudaloso -sa *adj* ‹río› large

caudillo *m* (líder) leader; **el C~** *title used to refer to General Franco*

causa *f* ⟦1⟧ (motivo) cause; **la** ~ **de todas mis desgracias** the cause of *o* the reason for all my misfortunes; **se enfadó sin** ~ **alguna** she got annoyed for no reason at all *o* for no good reason; **a** *or* **por** ~ **de** because of ⟦2⟧ (ideal) cause; **una** ~ **perdida** a lost cause ⟦3⟧ (Der) (pleito) lawsuit; (proceso) trial

causante *adj*: **los factores** ~s **de la crisis** the factors which caused the crisis
■ *mf* (causa) cause; **la** ~ **de todas mis desgracias** the cause of all my misfortunes

causar [A1] *vt* ‹daños/problema/sufrimiento› to cause; ‹indignación› to cause, arouse; ‹alarma› to cause, provoke; ‹placer› to give; **le causó mucha pena** it made him very sad; **me causó muy buena impresión** I was very impressed with her

cautela *f* caution; **con** ~ cautiously

cauteloso -sa *adj* [SER] ‹persona› cautious

cautivador -dora *adj* captivating

cautivar [A1] *vt* (atraer) to captivate

cautiverio *m* captivity

cautivo -va *adj/m,f* captive

cauto -ta *adj* careful, cautious

cava *f* cellar
■ *m* cava (sparkling wine)

cavar [A1] *vt* **(a)** ‹fosa/zanja› to dig; ‹pozo› to sink **(b)** ‹tierra› to hoe

caverna *f* cave, cavern

cavernícola *adj* (Hist) cave-dwelling; **un hombre** ~ a caveman
■ *mf* (Hist) cave dweller

caviar *m* caviar

cavidad *f* cavity

cavilar [A1] *vi* to ponder, think deeply; **después de mucho** ~ after much thought *o* deliberation

cayena *f* cayenne (pepper)

cayera, cayese, etc ▶ CAER

caza *f* **(a)** (para subsistir) hunting; (como deporte — caza mayor) hunting; (— caza menor) shooting; **ir de** ~ to go hunting/shooting; ~ **del tesoro** treasure hunt; ~ **furtiva** poaching; **salieron a la** ~ **del ladrón** they set off in pursuit of the thief; **dar** ~ **a algn** (perseguir) to pursue *o* chase sb; (alcanzar) to catch sb **(b)** (animales) game
■ *m* fighter

cazabombardero *m* fighter-bomber

cazador -dora *m,f* hunter; ~ **furtivo** poacher

cazadora *f* (Esp) (Indum) jacket

cazamariposas *m* (*pl* ~) butterfly net

cazar [A4] *vt* **(a)** (para subsistir) to hunt; (como deporte—caza mayor) to hunt; (— caza menor) to shoot **(b)** ‹mariposas› to catch **(c)** (fam) (conseguir, atrapar): **ha cazado un millonario/buen empleo** she's landed herself a millionaire/good job ···⧽

■ ~ *vi* to hunt; (con fusil) to shoot; **salimos a ~** we went out hunting/shooting

cazo *m* (cacerola) small saucepan; (cucharón) ladle

cazuela *f* casserole

cazurro -rra *adj* (fam) (huraño) sullen, surly; (obstinado) stubborn, pig-headed (colloq)
■ *m,f* (fam) (huraño) sullen *o* surly person; (obstinado) stubborn *o* (colloq) pig-headed person

c.c. (= **centímetros cúbicos**) cc

CD *m* (= **compact disc**) CD

CD-ROM *m* (= **compact disc read-only memory**) CD-ROM

ce *f. name of the letter* c

CE *f* (a) (= **Comisión Europea**) EC (b) (= **Comunidad Europea**) EC

cebada *f* barley

cebar [A1] *vt* 1 ⟨animal⟩ to fatten ... up 2 ⟨anzuelo/cepo⟩ to bait 3 (CS) ⟨mate⟩ to prepare (*and serve*)

cebo *m* (a) (en pesca, caza) bait (b) (Arm) primer

cebolla *f* onion

cebolleta *f*, **cebollino** *m* (a) (con tallo verde) scallion (AmE), spring onion (BrE) (b) (hierba) chive

cebra *f* zebra

cebú *m* (*pl* **-bús** *or* **-búes**) zebu

cecear [A1] *vi* (a) (Ling) *to pronounce the Spanish* [/s/] *as* [θ] (b) (como defecto) to lisp

ceceo *m* (a) (Ling) *pronunciation of the Spanish* [/s/] *as* [θ] (b) (como defecto) lisp

cedazo *m* sieve

ceder [E1] *vt* 1 (a) ⟨derecho⟩ to transfer, assign; ⟨territorio⟩ to cede; ⟨puesto/título⟩ (voluntariamente) to hand over; (a la fuerza) to give up; **~ el poder** to hand over power; **me cedió el asiento** he let me have his seat; ▶ PASO 1B (b) ⟨balón/pelota⟩ to pass 2 (prestar) ⟨jugador⟩ to loan
■ ~ *vi* 1 (cejar) to give way; **no cedió ni un ápice** she didn't give *o* yield an inch; **cedió en su empeño** she gave up the undertaking; **~ A algo** to give in TO sth 2 «⟨fiebre/lluvia/viento/dolor⟩» to ease off 3 «⟨muro/puente/cuerda⟩» to give way; «⟨zapatos/muelle⟩» to give

cedro *m* cedar

cédula *f* (Fin) bond, warrant; **~ de identidad** identity card

cegador -dora *adj* blinding

cegar [A7] *vt* 1 (a) (deslumbrar) to blind (b) (ofuscar) to blind; **cegado por los celos** blinded by jealousy 2 ⟨conducto/cañería⟩ to block

ceguera *f* blindness

ceja *f* (a) (Anat) eyebrow; **arquear las ~s** to raise one's eyebrows (b) (Mús) capo

cejilla *f* capo

celador -dora *m,f* (a) (en museo, biblioteca) security guard (b) (AmL) (en la cárcel) prison guard (AmE), prison warder (BrE) (c) (en hospital) orderly, porter

celda *f* cell

celebración *f* celebration

celebrar [A1] *vt* 1 (a) ⟨éxito/cumpleaños/festividad⟩ to celebrate (b) (liter) ⟨belleza/valor/hazaña⟩ to celebrate (liter) (c) ⟨chiste/ocurrencia⟩

to laugh at 2 (frml) (alegrarse) to be delighted at, be very pleased at; **celebro su éxito** I'm delighted to hear about your success 3 (a) (frml) ⟨reunión/elecciones/juicio⟩ to hold; ⟨partido⟩ to play (b) ⟨misa⟩ to say, celebrate; ⟨boda⟩ to perform
■ ~ *vi* «⟨sacerdote⟩» to say *o* celebrate mass

célebre *adj* (a) (famoso) famous, celebrated (b) (Col) ⟨mujer⟩ elegant

celebridad *f* (fama) fame; (persona) celebrity

celeste *adj* 1 (del cielo) heavenly, celestial 2 ⟨ojos⟩ blue; ⟨pintura/vestido⟩ (claro) light *o* pale blue; (intenso) sky-blue (*before n*)
■ *m* (claro) light *o* pale blue; (intenso) sky blue

celestial *adj* (a) (Relig) celestial (b) ⟨placer⟩ heavenly

célibe *adj/mf* celibate

celo *m* 1 (esmero, fervor) zeal 2 (Zool) (a) (de los machos) rut (b) (de las hembras) heat; **estar en ~** to be in season, to be in heat (AmE) *o* (BrE) on heat 3 **celos** *mpl* jealousy; **tener ~s DE algn** to be jealous OF sb; **darle ~s a algn** to make sb jealous 4 (Esp) (cinta adhesiva) Scotch® tape (AmE), Sellotape® (BrE)

celofán *m* cellophane

celoso -sa *adj* (a) ⟨marido/novia⟩ jealous; **estar ~ DE algn** to be jealous OF sb (b) (diligente, esmerado) conscientious, zealous

celta *adj* Celtic
■ *mf* (persona) Celt
■ *m* (Ling) Celtic

célula *f* cell

celular *adj* cellular
■ *m* (a) (AmL) (teléfono) cell phone (AmE), mobile (BrE) (b) (Esp) (furgoneta para presos) patrol wagon (AmE), police van (BrE)

celulitis *f* (gordura) cellulite; (inflamación) cellulitis

cementerio *m* cemetery; (junto a una iglesia) graveyard; **~ de coches** salvage *o* wrecker's yard (AmE), scrapyard (BrE)

cemento *m* (a) (Const, Odont) cement; **~ armado** reinforced concrete (b) (AmL) (pegamento) glue, adhesive

cena *f* dinner, supper; (formal, fuera de casa) dinner; **¿qué hay de ~?** what's for dinner *o* supper?; **~ de gala** banquet

cenagal *m* (barrizal) bog, mire

cenar [A1] *vi* to have dinner *o* supper; (en algunas regiones del Reino Unido) to have tea; **nos invitaron a ~** they invited us for *o* to dinner; **salimos a ~** we went out for dinner
■ ~ *vt* ⟨tortilla/pescado⟩ to have ... for dinner *o* supper

cencerro *m* cowbell

cenefa *f* (en ropa, sábanas) border; (en techos, muros) frieze

cenicero *m* ashtray

cenicienta *f* drudge; **la C~** Cinderella

cenit *m* zenith

ceniza *f* ash

censo *m* 1 (a) (de población) census (b) (Esp) *tb* **~ electoral** electoral roll *o* register 2 (Der, Fin) charge; (sobre una finca) ground rent

censor -sora *m,f* (a) (Cin, Period) censor (b) (crítico) critic (c) (Der, Fin) *tb* **~ de cuentas** auditor

censura *f* **(a)** (reprobación) censure (frml), condemnation **(b)** (de libros, películas) censorship

censurar [A1] *vt* **(a)** (reprobar) to censure (frml), to condemn **(b)** ⟨*libro/película*⟩ to censor, ⟨*escena/párrafo*⟩ to cut, censor

centavo *m* **(a)** (en AmL) *hundredth part of many currencies*; **estar sin un** ∼ to be penniless **(b)** (del dólar) cent

centella *f* (rayo) flash of lightning; (chispa) spark; **como una** ∼ like greased lightning

centelleante *adj* ⟨*estrella*⟩ twinkling; ⟨*luz/ joya*⟩ sparkling; ⟨*ojos*⟩ blazing

centellear [A1] *vi* «*luz/joya*» to sparkle, «*estrella*» to twinkle

centena *f*: **una** ∼ a hundred; **unidades, decenas y** ∼**s** units, tens and hundreds

centenar *m*: **un** ∼ **de personas** a hundred or so people; ∼**es de cartas** hundreds of letters

centenario *m* centenary, centennial (AmE)

centeno *m* rye

centésima *f* hundredth; **en una** ∼ **de segundo** in a fraction of a second

centésimo *m* (Fís, Mat) hundredth

centígrado -da *adj* centigrade, Celsius

centigramo *m* centigram

centímetro *m* centimeter*

céntimo *m*: *hundredth part of the euro, the former Spanish peseta, the Venezuelan bolívar and the Paraguayan guaraní*; **no tener un** ∼ to be penniless *o* (colloq) broke; **no vale ni un** ∼ it's totally worthless

centinela *mf* (Mil) guard, sentry; (no militar) lookout; **estar de** ∼ (Mil) to be on sentry duty

centolla *f*, **centollo** *m* spider crab

centrado -da *adj* (equilibrado) stable, well-balanced; (en un trabajo, lugar) settled

central *adj* central
■ *f* head office; ∼ **telefónica** telephone exchange; ∼ **hidroeléctrica/nuclear** hydroelectric/nuclear power station

centralista *adj/mf* centralist

centralita *f* switchboard

centralizar [A4] *vt* to centralize

centrar [A1] *vt* **(a)** ⟨*imagen*⟩ to center* **(b)** (Dep) to center* **(c)** ⟨*atención/investigación/ esfuerzos*⟩ **algo EN algo** to focus sth ON sth
■ ∼ *vi* (Dep) to center*, cross
■ **centrarse** *v pron* ∼**se EN algo** «*investigación/ atención/esfuerzos*» to focus *o* center* ON sth

céntrico -ca *adj* ⟨*área/calle*⟩ central; **un bar** ∼ a downtown bar (AmE), a bar in the centre of town (BrE)

centrifugado *m* spin

centrifugar [A3] *vt* **(a)** ⟨*ropa*⟩ to spin **(b)** (Tec) to centrifuge

centrista *adj/mf* centrist

centro *m* **(a)** (en general) center*; ∼ **ciudad/ urbano** downtown (AmE), city/town centre (BrE); **ser el** ∼ **de atención** to be the center of attention; **se convirtió en el** ∼ **de interés** it became the focus of attention; ∼ **turístico** tourist resort *o* center; ∼ **comercial** shopping mall (AmE), shopping centre (BrE); ∼ **de llamadas** call center (AmE) *o* centre (BrE); ∼ **de planificación familiar** family planning clinic **(b)** (en fútbol) cross, center*
■ *mf* (jugador) center*; ∼ **delantero** center* forward

Centroamérica *f* Central America

centroamericano -na *adj/m,f* Central American

centrocampista *mf* midfield player

ceñido -da *adj* tight; **me queda muy** ∼ it's very tight on me

ceñir [I15] *vt*: **esa falda te ciñe demasiado** that skirt is too tight for you; **el vestido le ceñía el talle** the dress clung to her waist
■ **ceñirse** *v pron* ∼**se A algo** ⟨*a las reglas*⟩ to adhere TO *o* (colloq) stick TO sth; ∼**se al tema** to keep to the subject

ceño *m*: **arrugó el** ∼ he frowned; **me miró con el** ∼ **fruncido** she frowned at me

cepa *f* (Bot) stump; (Vin) stock (*of a vine*)

cepillar [A1] *vt* **(a)** ⟨*ropa/dientes/pelo*⟩ to brush **(b)** ⟨*madera*⟩ to plane
■ **cepillarse** *v pron* (*refl*) ⟨*ropa*⟩ to brush; ⟨*dientes*⟩ to brush, clean

cepillo *m* **1** (para ropa, zapatos, pelo) brush; (para suelo) scrubbing brush; **lleva el pelo cortado al** ∼ he has a crew cut; ∼ **de dientes/uñas** toothbrush/nailbrush **2** (de carpintería) plane **3** (en la iglesia) collection box (*o* plate *etc*)

cepo *m* (trampa) trap; (Auto) wheel clamp; (Hist) stocks (*pl*)

cera *f* (para velas) wax; (para pisos, muebles) wax polish; (de abejas) beeswax; (de los oídos) wax; **le di** ∼ **al suelo** I polished the floor

cerámica *f* (arte) ceramics, pottery; (pieza) piece of pottery

cerca *adv* **(a)** (en el espacio) near, close; ∼ **DE algo/algn** near sth/sb; **¿hay algún banco** ∼? is there a bank nearby *o* close by?; **está por aquí** ∼ it's near here (somewhere); **mirar algo/a algn de** ∼ to look at sth/sb close up *o* close to; **seguir algo de** ∼ to follow sth closely **(b)** (en el tiempo) close; **los exámenes estaban** ∼ the exams were close; **estás tan** ∼ **de lograrlo** you're so close to achieving it; **serán** ∼ **de las dos** it must be nearly 2 o'clock **(c)** (indicando aproximación): ∼ **de** almost, nearly
■ *f* (de alambre, madera) fence; (de piedra) wall

cercado *m* **(a)** (de alambre, madera) fence; (de piedra) wall **(b)** (terreno) enclosure **(c)** (Per) (distrito) district

cercanía *f* **1** (en el espacio) closeness, proximity; (en el tiempo) proximity, imminence **2 cercanías** *fpl*: **Madrid y sus** ∼**s** Madrid and its environs; **en las** ∼**s del aeropuerto** in the vicinity of the airport

cercano -na *adj* **1** **(a)** (en el espacio) nearby, neighboring*; ∼ **A algo** near sth, close to sth; **el C**∼ **Oriente** the Near East **(b)** (en el tiempo) close, near; **en fecha cercana** soon; ∼ **A algo** close TO sth **2** ⟨*pariente/amigo*⟩ close

cercar [A2] *vt* **(a)** ⟨*campo/terreno*⟩ to enclose, surround; (con valla) to fence in **(b)** ⟨*persona*⟩ to surround **(c)** (Mil) ⟨*ciudad*⟩ to besiege; ⟨*enemigo*⟩ to surround

cerciorarse *v pron* ∼**se DE algo** to make certain OF sth

cerco *m* **(a)** (asedio) siege **(b)** (de una mancha) ring **(c)** (AmL) (valla) fence; (seto) hedge

cerda *f* **(a)** (animal) sow **(b)** (fam) (mujer — sucia) slob (colloq); (— despreciable) bitch (sl) **(c)** (pelo) bristle

cerdo m **(a)** (animal) pig, hog (AmE) **(b)** (carne) pork **(c)** (fam) (hombre — sucio) slob (colloq); (— despreciable) bastard (sl), swine (colloq)

cereal m cereal

cereales mpl (Esp) (para desayunar) cereal

cerebral adj ‹actividad/tumor/derrame› brain (before n); ‹persona› cerebral

cerebro m **(a)** (Anat) brain; **lavarle el ~ a algn** to brainwash sb **(b)** (persona) brains; **el ~ de la operación** the brains behind the operation

ceremonia f ceremony; **no andemos con ~s** let's not stand on ceremony

cereza f (fruta) cherry

cerezo m cherry tree

cerilla f **1** (esp Esp) (fósforo) match **2** (de los oídos) wax

cerillo m (esp AmC, Méx) match

cernícalo m (Zool) kestrel

cero m **(a)** (Fís, Mat) zero; (en números de teléfono) zero (AmE), oh (BrE); **~ coma cinco** zero point five; **empezar** or **partir de ~** to start from scratch; **ser un ~ a la izquierda** to be useless **(b)** (en fútbol, rugby) zero (AmE), nil (BrE); (en tenis) love; **ganan por tres a ~** they're winning three-zero (AmE) o (BrE) three-nil **(c)** (Educ) zero, nought (BrE)

cerquillo m (AmL) (flequillo) bangs (pl) (AmE), fringe (BrE)

cerrado -da adj **1** **(a)** ‹puerta/ventana/ojos/boca› closed, shut; ‹mejillones/almejas› closed; ‹sobre/carta› sealed; ‹puño› clenched; ‹cortinas› drawn, closed; **estaba ~ con llave** it was locked **(b)** ‹válvula› closed, shut off; ‹grifo/llave› turned off **2** ‹tienda/restaurante/museo› closed, shut **3** ‹espacio/recinto› enclosed; ‹curva› sharp **4** ‹acento/dialecto› broad **5** ‹persona› (poco comunicativo) uncommunicative; **está ~ a todo cambio** his mind is closed to change; **~ a influencias externas** shut off from outside influence

cerradura f lock; ▶ OJO

cerrajería f locksmith's shop

cerrajero -ra m,f locksmith

cerrar [A5] vt **1** **(a)** ‹puerta/ventana› to close, shut; ‹ojos/boca› to close, shut; **cierra la puerta con llave** lock the door **(b)** ‹botella› to put the top on/cork in; ‹frasco› to put the lid on; ‹sobre› to seal **(c)** ‹paraguas/abanico/mano› to close; ‹libro› to close, shut; ‹puño› to clench **(d)** ‹cortinas› to close, draw; ‹persianas› to lower, pull down; ‹abrigo› to fasten, button up; ‹cremallera› to do ... up **(e)** ‹grifo/agua/gas› to turn off; ‹válvula› to close, shut off **2** **(a)** ‹fábrica/comercio/oficina› (en el quehacer diario) to close; (definitivamente) to close (down) **(b)** ‹aeropuerto/carretera/frontera› to close **3** **(a)** ‹cuenta bancaria› to close **(b)** ‹caso/juicio› to close **(c)** ‹acuerdo/negociación› to finalize **(d)** ‹acto/debate› to bring ... to an end
■ **~** vi **1** (hablando de puerta, ventana): **cierra, que hace frío** close o shut the door (o window etc), it's cold; **¿cerraste con llave?** did you lock up?

2 «puerta/ventana/cajón» to close, shut
3 «comercio/oficina» (en el quehacer diario) to close, shut; (definitivamente) to close (down)
■ **cerrarse** v pron **1** **(a)** «puerta/ventana» to shut, close; **la puerta se cerró de golpe** the door slammed shut **(b)** «ojos» to close; **se le cerraban los ojos** his eyes were closing **(c)** «flor/almeja» to close up **(d)** «herida» to heal (up) **2** (refl) ‹abrigo› to fasten, button up; ‹cremallera› to do ... up **3** «acto/debate/jornada» to end

cerrazón m (terquedad) stubbornness; (mentalidad poco flexible) blinkered attitude

cerro m (Geog) hill

cerrojo m bolt; **echar el ~** to bolt the door

certamen m competition, contest

certero -ra adj **(a)** ‹tiro› accurate; ‹golpe› well-aimed **(b)** ‹juicio› sound; ‹respuesta› good

certeza, certidumbre f certainty; **no lo sé con ~** I'm not sure, I don't know for sure

certificado¹ -da adj ‹paquete/carta› registered; **mandé la carta certificada** I sent the letter by registered mail

certificado² m certificate

certificar [A2] vt to certify

cervatillo m fawn

cerveza f beer; **~ tirada** o **de barril** draft beer (AmE), draught beer (BrE); **~ rubia** lager; **~ negra** dark beer

cesante adj [ESTAR] (Chi) (sin empleo) unemployed; **quedó ~** he lost his job
■ mf (Chi) (sin empleo) unemployed person

cesantía f (desempleo) (Chi) unemployment; (despido) (RPI frml) dismissal; (pago) (Col) severance pay

cesar [A1] vi **1** (parar) to stop; **~ DE hacer algo** to stop doing sth; **sin ~** incessantly **2** (frml o period) (dimitir): **cesó en su cargo** she left her post, she resigned

cesárea f cesarean* (section); **le tuvieron que hacer una ~** she had to have a cesarean

cese m (frml o period) **(a)** (interrupción) cessation (frml); **el ~ de hostilidades** the cessation of hostilities; **~ del fuego** (AmL) ceasefire **(b)** (renuncia) resignation

césped m **(a)** (planta) grass; (extensión) lawn, grass; **🟢 prohibido pisar el césped** keep off the grass **(b)** (Dep) field, pitch (BrE); (en tenis) (AmL) grass

cesta f **(a)** (recipiente) basket; **~ de Navidad** Christmas hamper; **~ punta** (deporte) pelota; (canasta) basket (for playing pelota) **(b)** (esp AmL) (en baloncesto) basket

cesto m **(a)** (esp Esp) (recipiente) basket; **el ~ de la ropa sucia** the laundry basket **(b)** (esp AmL) (en baloncesto) basket

cetro m scepter*

CFC m (= **clorofluorocarbono**) CFC

cg. (= **centigramo**) cg

AmC	América Central	Arg	Argentina	Cu	Cuba
AmL	América Latina	Bol	Bolivia	Ec	Ecuador
AmS	América del Sur	Chi	Chile	Esp	España
Andes	Región andina	CS	Cono Sur	Méx	México

Per	Perú
RPI	Río de la Plata
Ur	Uruguay
Ven	Venezuela

Ch, ch *f (read as* /tʃe/ *or* /se 'atʃe/ *or* (Esp) /θe 'atʃe/) *combination traditionally considered as a separate letter in the Spanish alphabet*

chabacano¹ -na *adj* ‹*ropa/decoración*› gaudy, tasteless; ‹*espectáculo/persona*› vulgar; ‹*chiste/ cuento*› coarse, tasteless

chabacano² *m* (Méx) (árbol) apricot tree; (fruta) apricot

chabola *f* (Esp) **(a)** (en los suburbios) shack, shanty dwelling **(b) chabolas** *fpl* shantytown

chabolismo *m* (Esp): **para resolver la cuestión del ~** in order to find a solution to the shanty town problem

chacal *m* jackal

chacarero -ra *m,f* (CS, Per) farmer (*who works a* CHACRA)

cháchara *f* [1] (fam) (conversación) chatter; **se pasa la mañana de ~** she spends the whole morning chattering [2] (Méx) (objeto de poca importancia) piece of junk; **un cajón lleno de ~s** a drawer's full of junk

chacharear [A1] *vi* (fam) to chatter

Chaco *m*: *tb* **el Gran ~** *region of scrub and swamp plains covering parts of Paraguay, Bolivia and Argentina*

chacra *f* (CS, Per) (granja) small farm; (casa) farmhouse

chafar [A1] *vt* (fam) **(a)** ‹*peinado*› to flatten; ‹*plátano/pulpa*› to mash; ‹*huevos*› to break; ‹*ajo*› to crush **(b)** ‹*vestido/falda*› to wrinkle (AmE), to crumple (BrE)
■ **chafarse** *v pron* to get squashed

chal *m* shawl, wrap

chala *f* **(a)** (RPI) (Bot) corn husk **(b)** (Chi) (Indum) sandal

chalado -da *adj* (fam) [ESTAR] crazy (colloq), nuts (colloq)
■ *m,f* nutter (colloq)

chale *interj* (Méx fam) you're kidding! (colloq)

chalé *m* ▶ CHALET

chaleca *f* (Chi) cardigan

chaleco *m* (de traje) vest (AmE), waistcoat (BrE); (jersey sin mangas) sleeveless sweater; (acolchado) body warmer; (chaqueta de punto) (CS) cardigan; **~ antibalas** bulletproof vest; **~ de fuerza** straitjacket; **~ salvavidas** lifejacket; *a* **~** (Méx) no matter what

chalet /tʃa'le/ *m* (*pl* **-lets**) (en urbanización) house; (en el campo) cottage; (en la montaña) chalet; (en la playa) villa

chalote *m*, **chalota** *f* shallot, scallion (AmE)

chalupa *f* [1] (barca) skiff; (canoa) (AmL) small canoe [2] (Méx) (Coc) stuffed tortilla

chamaco -ca *m,f* (Méx fam) (muchacho) kid (colloq), youngster (colloq)

chamagoso -sa *adj* (Méx fam) dirty, filthy

chamarra *f* (chaqueta) jacket

chamba *f* [1] (Méx, Per, Ven fam) (trabajo) work; (empleo) job; (lugar) work [2] (Col) **(a)** (zanja) ditch **(b)** (herida) wound, gash

chambear [A1] *vi* (Méx, Per fam) to work

chambón -bona *adj* (AmL) clumsy, klutzy (AmE colloq)

chambonada *f* (AmL fam) botch (colloq)

chamizo *m* [1] **(a)** (leña quemada) charred log **(b)** (Col) (ramas secas) *tb* **~s** brushwood [2] (choza) thatched hut

chamo -ma *m,f* (Ven fam) (niño, muchacho) kid (colloq)

champán *m*, **champaña** *m or f* champagne

champiñón *m* mushroom

champú *m* (*pl* **-pús** *or* **-púes**) shampoo

champurrear [A1] *vt* (CS) ▶ CHAPURREAR

chamuscar [A2] *vt* to scorch, singe; **madera chamuscada** charred wood
■ **chamuscarse** *v pron*: **~se el pelo** to singe one's hair

chamuyar [A1] *vi* (RPI fam) to chatter
■ **~** *vt* (RPI fam) to mutter

chan *m* (AmC) mountain guide

chancaca *f* **(a)** (Andes) (melaza) brown sugarloaf **(b)** (Per) (dulce de maíz) maize cake

chancar [A2] *vt* [1] (Andes) (triturar) to crush, grind [2] (Per arg) (estudiar) to cram (colloq)

chance *f or m* (AmL) (oportunidad) chance; **dar ~ a algn** to give sb the chance; **tiene pocas ~s de ganar** he doesn't have *o* stand much chance of winning

chancear [A1] *vi* (Col fam) to joke, kid around (colloq)
■ **chancearse** *v pron* **~se DE algn** to make fun *or* sb

chanchada *f* (AmL fam) **(a)** (porquería, suciedad) mess **(b)** (acción indigna) dirty trick (colloq); **hacerle una ~ a algn** to play a dirty trick on sb

chanchería *f* (AmL) pork butcher's shop

chanchito *m* (fam) [1] (Andes, CS) (Zool) woodlouse [2] (CS) (alcancía) piggy bank

chancho¹ -cha *adj* (AmL fam) (sucio) filthy, gross (colloq); (miserable, ruin) mean
■ *m,f* **(a)** (Zool) pig **(b)** (fam) (persona sucia) dirty *o* filthy pig (colloq)

chancho² *m* (Chi, Per) (Coc) *tb* **carne de ~** pork

chanchullero -ra *adj* (fam) shady (colloq), crooked (colloq)
■ *m,f* (fam) racket (colloq)

chanchullo *m* (fam) racket (colloq), fiddle (BrE colloq)

chancla *f* (sandalia) thong (AmE), flip-flop (BrE); (pantufla) (Col) slipper

chancleta *f* (sandalia) thong (AmE), flip-flop (BrE)

chándal *m* (*pl* **-dals**) (Esp) tracksuit

changador *m* (RPI) porter

changarro *m* (Méx) small store

chango -ga *m,f* (Méx) monkey

changuito® *m* (Arg) (para las compras) shopping cart (AmE), shopping trolley (BrE); (para el bebé) stroller (AmE), pushchair (BrE)

chanquetes *mpl* whitebait (*pl*)

chanta *adj* (RPI arg) (informal) unreliable; (mentiroso) deceitful
■ *mf* (RPI arg) (informal) unreliable person; (mentiroso) liar

chantaje *m* blackmail; **le hacen ~** he is being blackmailed

chantajear [A1] *vt* to blackmail

chantajista *mf* blackmailer

chantillí, chantilly /ʃanti'ʝi, tʃanti'ʝi/ *m*: *tb* crema ~ *f* whipped cream, chantilly

chao *interj* (fam) bye (colloq), bye-bye (colloq)

chapa *f* **1** (a) (plancha — de metal) sheet; (— de madera) panel (b) (lámina de madera) veneer (c) (carrocería) bodywork **2** (a) (distintivo) badge; (de policía) shield (AmE), badge (BrE); (con el nombre) nameplate; (de perro) identification disc *o* tag (b) (RPI) (de matrícula) license plate (AmE), numberplate (BrE) **3** (de botella) cap, top **4** (AmL) (cerradura) lock **5 chapas** *fpl* (AmL fam) (en las mejillas): **le salieron ~s** (por vergüenza) her cheeks flushed (red); (por el aire fresco) her cheeks were red **6** (AmC fam) (joya) earring; (dentadura postiza) false teeth (*pl*)

chapado -da *adj* ⟨metal⟩ plated; **un reloj ~ en oro** a gold-plated watch

chaparrastroso -sa *adj* (Méx fam) scruffy

chaparro -rra *adj* (AmL fam) short, squat; **quedarse ~** to stop growing
■ *m,f* (AmL fam) shorty (colloq), titch (colloq)

chaparrón *m* (Meteo) downpour, cloudburst

chape *m* (Chi) (trenza) braid (AmE), plait (BrE); (pelo atado) bunch

chapetes *mpl* (Méx) ▶ CHAPA 5

chapista *mf* panel beater

chapopote *m* (Méx) (alquitrán) tar; (asfalto) asphalt

chapotear [A1] *vi* (en agua) splash (around); (en barro) squelch (around)

chapucero -ra *adj* ⟨persona⟩ sloppy, slapdash; ⟨trabajo/reparación⟩ botched
■ *m,f*: **es un ~** his work is very slapdash

chapulín *m* (AmC, Méx) (Zool) locust

chapurrear [A1] *vt* (fam): **~ el inglés** to speak broken *o* poor English

chapuza *f* (fam) (trabajo mal hecho) botched job (colloq), botch (colloq)

chapuzón *m* dip; **darse un ~** to have a dip

chaquet (*pl* **-quets**), **chaqué** *m* morning coat

chaqueta *f* **1** (Indum) jacket; **~ de punto** cardigan **2** (Col) (Odont) crown

chaquetón *m* three-quarter length coat

charanga *f* brass band; (militar) military band

charango *m* small five-stringed guitar

charca *f* pond, pool

charco *m* (a) puddle, pool (b) **el ~** (fam) (océano Atlántico) the Atlantic, the Pond (colloq & hum)

charcutería *f* delicatessen, charcuterie (AmE)

charla *f* (a) (conversación) chat; **estábamos de ~** we were having a chat (b) (conferencia) talk

charlar [A1] *vi* to chat, talk

charlatán -tana *adj* (fam) talkative
■ *m,f* (fam) (a) (parlanchín) chatterbox (colloq) (b) (vendedor) dishonest hawker; (curandero) charlatán

charlestón *m* charleston

charme /ʃarm/ *m* charm

charol *m* **1** (barniz) lacquer; (cuero) patent leather; **zapatos de ~** patent leather shoes **2** (Col, Per) (bandeja) tray

charola *f* (Bol, Méx, Per) tray

charqui *m* (AmS) charqui, jerked beef

charrasquear [A1] *vt* **1** (AmL) ⟨guitarra⟩ to strum **2** (Méx) ⟨persona⟩ to stab

charrería *f* (Méx) *the culture of horsemanship and rodeo riding*

charretera *f* epaulette

charro -rra *adj* **1** (fam) (de mal gusto) gaudy, garish **2** (en Méx) ⟨tradiciones/música⟩ of/relating to the CHARRO
■ *m,f* (en Méx) (jinete) (*m*) horseman, cowboy; (*f*) horsewoman, cowgirl

chárter *adj inv* charter (*before n*)
■ *m* charter (flight)

chasco *m* (decepción) disappointment, let-down (colloq); **me llevé un ~** I felt let down

chasis, chasís *m* (*pl* ~) (Auto) chassis; (Fot) plateholder

chasquear [A1] *vt* (a) ⟨lengua⟩ to click; ⟨dedos⟩ to click, snap (b) ⟨látigo⟩ to crack

chasquido *m* (a) (de la lengua) click; (de los dedos) click, snap (b) (de látigo) crack; (de rama seca) crack, snap

chasquilla *f* (Chi) bangs (*pl*) (AmE), fringe (BrE)

chat *m* chat room

chatarra *adj inv* (Méx): **comida ~** junk food; **productos ~** cheap goods
■ *f* (Metal) scrap (metal); **el coche es pura ~** the car is just a heap of scrap

chatarrero -ra *m,f* scrap merchant

chatel -tela *m,f* (AmC fam) (*m*) little boy; (*f*) little girl

chato -ta *adj* (a) ⟨nariz⟩ snub (*before n*) (b) (Per fam) (bajo) short (c) (AmS) ⟨nivel⟩ low; ⟨obra⟩ pedestrian

chaucha *f* (RPI) (Bot, Coc) French bean

chauvinismo /tʃoβi'nismo/ *m* chauvinism

chauvinista /tʃoβi'nista/ *adj* chauvinistic
■ *mf* chauvinist

chaval -vala *m,f* (esp Esp fam) (niño) kid (colloq), youngster

chavalo -la *m,f* (AmC, Méx) ▶ CHAVAL

chavo -va *adj* (Méx fam) young
■ *m,f* (Méx) (a) (fam) (muchacho) guy (colloq); (muchacha) girl (b) (como apelativo) kid (colloq)

chayote *m* (planta, fruto) chayote, mirliton

che *interj* (RPI fam): **no te hagas el bobo, ~** come on, don't act the innocent; **~, Marta, ¿qué tal?** hey Marta, how are you?; **¡pero ~! ¡cómo le dijiste eso!** for Heaven's sake! whatever made you tell her that?

checar [A2] *vt* (Méx) (a) (revisar, mirar) to check; **me chequé la presión** (Med) I had my blood pressure checked; **¿por qué no vas a que te chequen?** why don't you go for a checkup? (b) (verificar) to check (c) (vigilar) to check up on

checo¹ -ca *adj/m,f* Czech

checo² *m* (idioma) Czech

checoslovaco -ca *adj/m,f* (Hist) Czechoslovakian, Czechoslovak

Checoslovaquia *f* (Hist) Czechoslovakia

chef /ʃef, tʃef/ *m* chef

chele -la *adj* (AmC) (de piel) light-skinned; (de pelo) blond-haired

chelín *m* shilling

chelista *mf* cellist

chelo *m* cello

cheque *m* check (AmE), cheque (BrE); **pagar con**

~ to pay by check; **un ~ a nombre de** ... a check made out to *o* made payable to ...; **~ bancario** *o* (AmL) **de gerencia** banker's draft; **~ cruzado/en blanco** crossed/blank check*; **~ de viaje** *or* **de viajero** traveler's check (AmE), traveller's cheque (BrE); **~ sin fondos** bad *o* (frml) dishonored* check*

chequear [A1] *vt* **1** (revisar, verificar) to check; **~ algo CON algo** to check sth AGAINST sth **2** (AmL) ⟨*equipaje*⟩ to check in
■ **chequearse** *v pron* **(a)** (Col, Ven) (Aviac) to check in **(b)** (Ven) (Med) to have a checkup

chequeo *m* **(a)** (Med) checkup; (para entrar en el ejército, a trabajar) medical; **someterse a un ~ médico** to have a medical/a checkup **(b)** (control, inspección) check; **mostradores de ~ de tiquetes** (Col) check-in desks

chequera *f* checkbook (AmE), chequebook (BrE)

chévere *adj* (AmL exc CS fam) great (colloq), fantastic (colloq); **¡qué ~!** that's great!

chic /ʃik, tʃik/ *adj inv* chic, fashionable
■ *m* chic; **tiene ~** she's very chic

chica *f* (fam) maid; *ver tb* CHICO

chicanero -ra *adj* (Andes, Méx) tricky, crafty

chicano -na *adj/m,f* Chicano

chicha *f* **1** **(a)** (bebida alcohólica) *alcoholic drink made from fermented maize, also called* CHICHA BRUJA; **~ andina** *alcoholic drink made with corn flour and pineapple juice*; **~ de manzana/uva** *alcoholic drink made from apple/grape juice* **(b)** (bebida sin alcohol) *cold drink made with maize or fruit* **2** (AmC vulg) (teta) tit (sl)

chícharo *m* (esp Méx) pea

chicharra *f* **(a)** (Zool) cicada **(b)** (timbre) buzzer

chicharrón *m* piece of crackling; **chicharrones** cracklings (*pl*) (AmE), pork scratchings (*pl*) (BrE)

chiche *adj* (AmC fam) dead easy (colloq)
■ *m* **1** (juguete) (CS fam) toy; (adorno) (Chi) trinket **2** (AmC fam) (pecho) tit (sl)

chichi *f* (Méx fam) (de mujer) tit (sl); (de animal) teat

chicho -cha *adj* (Méx fam) **(a)** (bonito) nice, neat (AmE colloq) **(b)** ⟨*persona*⟩: **es muy chicha para los deportes** she's brilliant at sport (colloq)

chichón *m* swelling *o* bump on the head

chicle, chiclé *m* chewing gum

chiclero -ra *m,f* **1** (Méx) (vendedor) street vendor (*selling chewing gum, candy, etc*) **2** (AmC) (Agr) rubber tapper

chico -ca *adj* (esp AmL) **(a)** (joven) young; **cuando éramos ~s** when we were little (colloq) **(b)** (bajo) small **(c)** (pequeño) small
■ *m,f* **1** **(a)** (niño) (*m*) boy; (*f*) girl **(b)** (hijo) (*m*) son, boy; (*f*) daughter, girl **(c)** (joven) (*m*) guy (colloq), boy (colloq), bloke (BrE colloq); (*f*) girl; **unos ~s** (varones) some boys; (varones y hembras) some boys and girls **(d)** (empleado joven) (*m*) boy; (*f*) girl **(e)** (como apelativo): **¡~! ¿tú por aquí?** well, well! what brings you here? **2** **chico** *m* (AmL) (en billar) frame; (en bolos) game

chicoria *f* chicory

chicotazo *m* (AmL) whipping

chicote *m* (fam) (AmL) (látigo) whip

chicotear [A1] *vt* (AmL) to whip

chifa *m* (Per fam) Chinese (restaurant)

chifla *f* whistling, catcalls (*pl*)

chiflado -da *adj* (fam) crazy (colloq), mad (BrE); **estar ~ POR algo/algn** to be crazy *o* mad ABOUT sth/sb (colloq)
■ *m,f* (fam) nutter (colloq)

chiflar [A1] *vt* ⟨*actor/cantante*⟩ to whistle at (*as sign of disapproval*), ≈to boo
■ ~ *vi* **1** (silbar) to whistle **2** (fam) (gustar mucho): **le chiflan los coches** he's crazy about cars (colloq)
■ **chiflarse** *v pron* (fam) **~se POR algo/algn** to be crazy ABOUT sth/sb (colloq)

chihuahua *mf* chihuahua

chiíta *adj* Shiite
■ *mf* Shiite

chilaba *f* djellaba

chilango -ga *adj* (Méx) of/from Mexico City

chilaquiles *mpl* (Méx) *corn tortilla in tomato and chili sauce*

chile *m* **1** (AmC, Méx) (Bot, Coc) chili, hot pepper; **~ con carne** chili con carne **2** (AmC fam) (chiste) joke

Chile *m* Chile

chilear [A1] *vi* (AmC fam) to tell jokes

chileno -na *adj/m,f* Chilean

chilicote *m* (AmS) cricket

chillar [A1] *vi* **(a)** ⟨*pájaro*⟩ to screech; ⟨*cerdo*⟩ to squeal; ⟨*ratón*⟩ to squeak **(b)** ⟨*persona*⟩ to shout, yell (colloq); (de dolor, miedo) to scream; **~se A algn** to yell *o* shout AT sb **(c)** ⟨*bebé/niño*⟩ (llorar) to scream

chillido *m* **(a)** (de ave) screech; (de cerdo) squeal; (de ratón) squeak **(b)** (grito) shout, yell; (de dolor, miedo) scream, shriek

chillón -llona *adj* (fam) ⟨*voz*⟩ shrill, piercing; ⟨*color*⟩ loud

chilote *m* (AmC) baby sweetcorn

chiltoma *f* (AmC) sweet pepper

chimbo -ba *adj* **(a)** (Col fam) (falsificado) ⟨*perfume*⟩ fake (*before n*); ⟨*whisky/grabación*⟩ bootleg (*before n*); **un cheque ~** a dud check (colloq) **(b)** (Ven arg) (malo) lousy (colloq)

chimbomba *f* (AmC) balloon

chimenea *f* **1** **(a)** (de casa) chimney; (de locomotora, fábrica) smokestack (AmE), chimney (BrE) **(b)** (de volcán) vent **2** (hogar) fireplace

chimpancé *mf* chimpanzee

chimpún *m* (Per) football boot

china *f* **(a)** (piedra) pebble, small stone **(b)** (Esp) (porcelana) porcelain

China *f*: *tb* **la ~** China

chinamo *m* (AmC fam) (en feria) stall; (bar) small bar

chinchar [A1] *vt* (fam) to pester (colloq)

chinche *adj* (fam) (pesado) irritating; (quisquilloso): **es muy ~** he's a real nit-picker
■ *f or m* **1** (insecto) bedbug **2** (RPl fam) (mal humor) bad mood
■ *mf* **(a)** (fam) (pesado) nuisance, pain in the neck (colloq) **(b)** (fam) (quisquilloso) nit-picker (colloq)
■ *f* (en algunas regiones *m*) (clavito) thumbtack (AmE), drawing pin (BrE)

chincheta *f* (Esp) thumbtack (AmE), drawing pin (BrE)

chinchilla *f* chinchilla

chin-chin *interj* (fam) cheers!

chinchorro *m* (Col, Ven) (hamaca) hammock

chinchulines *mpl* (Bol, RPl) chitterlings (*pl*)

chincol *m* (Chi) (pájaro) crown sparrow

chinela *f* (pantufla) slipper; (chancla) (AmC) thong (AmE), flip-flop (BrE)

chingada *f* (Méx vulg): **está pa' la ~** he's/she's had it (colloq); **¡vete a la ~!** screw you! (vulg); **la casa estaba en la ~** the house was in the middle of nowhere (colloq); **¡hijo de la ~!** you son-of-a-bitch! (sl)

chingadera *f* (Méx vulg) trash (colloq), crap (sl)

chingar [A3] *vi* (a) (esp Méx vulg) (copular) to screw (vulg), to fuck (vulg) (b) (Méx vulg) (molestar): **te lo dijo para ~ nada más** he only said it to annoy you; **¡deja de ~!** stop being such a pain in the ass! (vulg); **¡no chingues!** (no digas) you're kidding! (colloq)
■ **~** *vt* (a) (AmL vulg) (en sentido sexual) to fuck (vulg), to screw (vulg) (b) (Méx vulg) (jorobar) to screw (vulg); **~la: ¡no la chingues!** (Méx vulg) shit! (vulg)
■ **chingarse** *v pron* [1] (a) (*enf*) (AmL vulg) (en sentido sexual) to fuck (vulg), to screw (vulg) (b) (esp Méx vulg) (jorobarse): **creyó que ganaría pero se chingó** he thought he'd win but he got a shock; **se chingó el motor** the engine's had it (colloq); **estamos chingados** we're in deep shit (vulg) [2] (Méx vulg) (a) (aguantarse): **si no te gusta, te chingas** if you don't like it, tough (colloq) (b) (robar) to rip ... off (colloq)

chingaste *m* (AmC) coffee grounds (*pl*)

chingo¹ -ga *adj* (AmC fam) (desnudo) stark naked (colloq)
■ *m,f* (Ven fam) snub-nosed person

chingo² *m* (Méx fam o vulg): **un ~ de** loads of (colloq); **me costó un ~** it cost me a bundle *o* (BrE) packet (colloq)

chingón -gona *adj* (Méx vulg) ⟨partido/película⟩ fantastic (colloq); ⟨persona⟩ cool (sl)

chingue *m* (Chi) (a) (Zool) skunk (b) (fam) (persona hedionda) smelly person

chinguear [A1] *vi/vt* (AmC) ▶ CHINGAR

chinita *f* (Chi) ladybug (AmE), ladybird (BrE)

chino¹ -na *adj* [1] (de la China) Chinese [2] (Méx) ⟨pelo⟩ curly
■ *m,f* [1] (de la China) (*m*) Chinese man; (*f*) Chinese woman; **los ~s** the Chinese [2] (a) (Arg, Per) (mestizo) mestizo, person of mixed Amerindian and European parentage (b) (Col fam) (joven) kid (colloq)

chino² *m* [1] (idioma) Chinese; **me suena a ~** it's all Greek to me [2] (Méx) (pelo rizado) curly hair; (para rizar el pelo) curler, roller [3] (Per fam) (tienda) convenience store, corner shop (BrE)

chip *m* (*pl* **chips**) (a) (Inf) chip (b) (papa frita) potato chip (AmE), crisp (BrE) (c) (Arg) (pancito) bridge roll

chipirón *m* small cuttlefish

chipote *m* (Méx fam) bump, lump

Chipre *f* Cyprus

chipriota *adj/mf* Cypriot

chiqueado *adj* (Méx fam) spoilt

chiquear [A1] *vt* (Méx fam) to spoil

chiquero *m* (AmL) (pocilga) pigpen (AmE), pigsty (BrE)

chiquilín -lina *adj* (AmL fam) (infantil) childish; **ser ~** to be childish, to act like a kid (colloq)
■ *m,f* (fam) (persona infantil) (AmL) big kid (colloq); (niño) (Ur) kid (colloq)

chiquillada *f*: **se pelearon por una ~** they fought over something really silly

chiquillo -lla *adj*: **no seas ~** don't be childish
■ *m,f* kid (colloq)

chiquito¹ -ta, chiquitito -ta *adj* (esp AmL fam) small

chiquito² -ta *m,f* (esp AmL fam) (niño) (*m*) little boy; (*f*) little girl

chiribita *f* (a) (chispa) spark (b) **chiribitas** *fpl* (en la vista) spots in front of the eyes; **los ojos le hacían ~s** his eyes glowed

chirigota *f* (fam) (broma) joke; **estar de ~** to be kidding around (colloq)

chirimiri *m* fine drizzle

chirimoya *f* custard apple

chiripa *f* [1] (fam) (casualidad) fluke; **de** *or* **por ~** (fam) by sheer luck, by a fluke [2] (Ven) (a) (insecto) cockroach (b) (palmera) palm

chirla *f* (Coc, Zool) baby clam

chirona *f* (Esp fam) can (AmE sl), nick (BrE sl)

chiros *mpl* (Col) rags (*pl*)

chirriar [A17] *vi* «puerta/gozne» to squeak, creak; «frenos/neumáticos» to screech

chirrido *m* (de puerta) squeaking, creaking; (de frenos, neumáticos) screech, screeching

chis, chist *interj* shush!, ssh!

chisme *m* (a) (chismorreo) piece of gossip; **~s** gossip, tittle-tattle (colloq); **contar ~s** to gossip (b) (Esp, Méx fam) (trasto, cacharro) thing, thingamajig (colloq); **un cuarto lleno de ~s** a room full of junk *o* stuff (colloq)

chismear, chismorrear [A1] *vi* (fam) to gossip

chismorreo *m* (fam) gossip, tittle-tattle (colloq)

chismoso -sa *adj* gossipy (colloq)
■ *m,f* gossip, scandalmonger (colloq)

chispa *f* [1] (a) (del fuego) spark; **está/están que echa/echan ~s** (fam) he's/they're hopping mad (colloq) (b) (Auto, Elec) spark [2] (fam) (pizca) little bit [3] (gracia, ingenio) wit; **tener ~** to be witty
■ *adj inv* (Esp fam) tipsy (colloq)

chisparse [A1] *v pron* (Méx) to come loose

chispazo *m* (Elec, Tec) spark

chispeante *adj* (a) ⟨leña/fuego⟩ crackling (b) ⟨lenguaje/personalidad⟩ witty; ⟨ingenio⟩ lively, sparkling (c) ⟨ojos⟩ (de alegría) sparkling; (de ira) flashing

chispear [A1] *vi* (a) «leña» to spark (b) (Elec) to spark, give off sparks
■ **~** *v impers* (fam) (lloviznar) to spit, spot

chispero *m* (AmC) (encendedor) (fam) lighter; (Auto) spark plug

chisporrotear [A1] *vi* «*leña/fuego*» to spark, crackle; «*aceite*» to spit, splutter; «*carne/pescado*» to sizzle

chistar [A1] *vi*: **¡y sin ∼!** and not another word!; **no chistó** he didn't say a word

chiste *m* **(a)** (*cuento gracioso*) joke; **contar** *or* (Col) **echar un ∼** to tell a joke; **∼ picante** *or* **verde** *or* (Bol, Méx) **colorado** dirty joke **(b)** (Bol, CS, Méx) (*broma*) joke; **hacerle un ∼ a algn** to play a joke *o* trick on sb; **me lo dijo en ∼** he was joking **(c)** (Col, Méx fam) (*gracia*): **el ∼ está en hacerlo rápido** the idea *o* point is to do it quickly; **tener su ∼** (Méx) to be tricky **(d) chistes** *mpl* (RPl) (*historietas*) comic strips (*pl*), funnies (*pl*) (AmE colloq)

chistera *f* top hat

chistoso -sa *adj* funny, amusing
■ *m,f* comic, joker

chiva *f* [1] (AmL) (*barba*) goatee [2] (Col) (*bus*) rural *o* country bus [3] (Col period) (*primicia*) scoop, exclusive [4] (Chi fam) (*mentira*) cock-and-bull story (colloq); *ver tb* CHIVO [5] **chivas** *fpl* (Méx fam) (*cachivaches*) junk (colloq)

chivarse [A1] *v pron* (Esp fam) to tell; (a la policía) to squeal (sl)

chivatazo *m* (Esp fam) tip-off (colloq); **les dieron el ∼** they were tipped off

chivato¹ -ta *m,f* (Esp, Ven fam) **(a)** (*informador*) informer, stool pigeon (colloq) **(b)** (*acusetas*) tattletale (AmE colloq), telltale (BrE colloq)

chivato² *m* (Esp fam) (*dispositivo sonoro*) bleeper (colloq); (*luz piloto*) pilot light

chivearse [A1] *v pron* (Méx) (fam) (*turbarse*) to get embarrassed

chivo -va *m,f* [1] **(a)** (*cría de la cabra*) kid **(b)** (Ven) (*cabra*) goat; *ver tb* CHIVA [2] **(a) chivo** *m* (AmL) (*macho cabrío*) billy goat **(b) ∼ expiatorio** scapegoat

chocado -da *adj* (AmL fam) smashed up (colloq); (*superficialmente*) dented

chocante *adj* **(a)** (*que causa impresión*): **su reacción me pareció ∼** I was shocked *o* taken aback by her reaction, his reaction shocked me **(b)** (*en cuestiones morales*) shocking **(c)** (Col, Méx, Ven) (*desagradable*) unpleasant

chocar [A2] *vi* [1] **(a)** (*colisionar*) to crash; (*entre sí*) to collide; **∼ de frente** to collide *o* crash head-on; **∼ CON** *or* **CONTRA algo** «*vehículo*» to crash *o* run INTO sth; (*con otro en marcha*) to collide WITH sth; **el balón chocó contra el poste** the ball hit the goalpost; **∼ CON algn** «*persona*» to run INTO sb; (*con otra en movimiento*) to collide WITH sth **(b)** (*entrar en conflicto*) **∼ CON algn** to clash WITH sb **(c)** **∼ CON algo** «*con problema/obstáculo*» to come up AGAINST sth
[2] **(a)** (*extrañar*): **me chocó que no me lo dijera** I was surprised that he hadn't told me **(b)** (*escandalizar*) to shock; **me chocó su lenguaje** I was shocked by her language
[3] (Col, Méx, Ven fam) (*irritar, molestar*) to annoy, bug (colloq)
■ **∼** *vt* **(a)** «*copas*» to clink; **¡chócala!** (fam) put it there! (colloq), give me five! (colloq) **(b)** (AmL) «*vehículo*» (*que se conduce*) to crash; (*de otra persona*) to run into
■ **chocarse** *v pron* (Col) [1] (*en vehículo*) to have a crash *o* an accident

[2] (fam) (*molestarse*) to get annoyed

chochada *f* (AmC fam) silly little thing (colloq)

chochear [A1] *vi* (fam) **(a)** «*anciano*» to be gaga (colloq) **(b)** (*sentir adoración*) **∼ POR algn** to dote ON sb

chocho -cha *adj* (fam) **(a)** 〈*viejo*〉 gaga (colloq) **(b)** (fam) (*encantado*): **está ∼ con su hijita** he dotes on his daughter; **se quedó ∼ con el regalo** he was delighted with his present

choclo *m* [1] (CS, Per) (*mazorca*) corn cob; (*granos*) sweet corn; (*cultivo*) corn (AmE), maize (BrE) [2] (Méx fam) (Indum) brogue

chocolate *m* [1] **(a)** (*para comer*) chocolate; **∼ blanco/con leche** white/milk chocolate; **∼ negro** plain chocolate, dark chocolate; **(b)** (AmL) chocolate; **sirvieron unos ∼s con el café** they gave us chocolates with our coffee **(c)** (*bebida*) hot chocolate [2] (Esp arg) (*hachís*) dope (sl), pot (colloq)

chocolatería *f* (*cafetería*) *café serving hot chocolate as a speciality*

chocolatina *f*, (RPl) **chocolatín** *m* chocolate bar

chocoyo *m* (AmC) parakeet

chofer *m*, (Esp) **chófer** *mf* **(a)** (*asalariado – de coche particular*) chauffeur; (*– de transporte colectivo*) driver **(b)** (*persona que maneja*) driver

cholga *f* (Chi) mussel

chollo *m* (Esp fam) (*trabajo fácil*) cushy job *o* number (colloq); (*ganga*) steal (colloq), bargain

chomba *f* (*sin botones*) (Chi) sweater; (*con botones*) (Arg) polo shirt

chompa *f* (*chaqueta*) (Col, Ec) jacket; (*suéter*) (Bol, Per) sweater

chompipe *m* (AmC, Méx) turkey

choncho -cha *adj* (Méx fam) 〈*problema/situación*〉 serious **(b)** 〈*persona*〉 hefty (colloq), big

chongo *m* (Méx) (*moño*) bun

chopo *m* (Bot) black poplar

choque *m* **(a)** (*de vehículos*) crash, collision; **∼ múltiple** pile-up; **∼ frontal** (Auto) head-on collision; (*enfrentamiento*) head-on confrontation **(b)** (*conflicto*) clash **(c)** (*sorpresa, golpe*) shock

chorear [A1] *vt* (fam) [1] (CS, Per) (*robar*) to swipe (colloq) [2] (Chi) **(a)** (*aburrir*): **esto me choreó** I'm fed up with this (colloq) **(b)** (*molestar, enojar*) to annoy
■ **chorearse** *v pron* (fam) [1] (CS) (*robarse*) to swipe (colloq) [2] (Chi) **(a)** (fam) (*aburrirse*) to get bored, get fed up (colloq) **(b)** (*molestarse, enojarse*) to get annoyed

choreto -ta *adj* (Ven fam) crooked

chorito *m* (Chi) baby mussel

chorizar [A4] *vt* (Esp fam) to swipe

chorizo *m* (*embutido curado*) chorizo (*highly-seasoned pork sausage*); (*salchicha*) (RPl) sausage

chorlito *m* plover

choro *m* (Chi, Per) [1] (Coc, Zool) mussel [2] (fam) (*delincuente*) crook (colloq)

chorrada *f* (Esp fam) **(a)** (*estupidez*): **decir ∼s** to talk drivel *o* twaddle (colloq) **(b)** (*cosa insignificante*) little thing

chorrear [A1] *vi* to drip; **estaba chorreando** (*muy mojado*) it was dripping wet; **chorreando de sudor** dripping with sweat; **la sangre le chorreaba de la nariz** blood was pouring from his nose

■ ~ *vt* **1** (AmL fam) (manchar): **chorreado de café** covered in coffee stains **2** (Col, RPl arg) (robar) to swipe (colloq)
■ **chorrearse** *v pron* (*refl*) (CS, Per fam) (mancharse): **cuidado con ~te** mind you don't get it all over yourself
chorrillo *m* (Méx fam) diarrhea*, the runs (colloq)
chorro *m* **1** (de agua) stream, jet; (de vapor, gas) jet; **un chorrito de agua** a trickle of water; **a ~** ⟨*motor/avión*⟩ jet (*before n*); **el agua salía a ~s** water gushed out **2** (AmC, Ven) (llave) faucet (AmE), tap (BrE) **3** (Méx fam) (cantidad): **¡qué ~ de gente!** what a lot of people!; **~s de dinero** loads of money (colloq); **me gusta un ~ salir** I really love going out
chotis *m* schottische
chovinismo *m* chauvinism
chovinista *adj/mf* chauvinist
choza *f* hut, shack
christmas /'krismas/ *m* (*pl* ~) (Esp) Christmas card
chubasco *m* heavy shower
chubasquero *m* slicker (AmE), cagoule (BrE)
chuchería *f* **(a)** (alhaja) trinket; (adorno) knickknack **(b)** (dulce) tidbit (AmE), titbit (BrE)
chucho -cha *m,f* **1** (Esp fam) (perro) mongrel **2** **chucho** *m* (RPl fam) (escalofrío) shiver; **tengo ~s de frío** I have the shivers (colloq)
chueca *f* (Chi) (juego) *game similar to hockey, and the stick with which it's played*
chueco¹ -ca *adj* **1** (AmL) (torcido) crooked, askew **2** (Chi, Méx fam) (deshonesto) ⟨*persona*⟩ crooked (colloq); ⟨*documento*⟩ false; ⟨*elecciones*⟩ rigged
■ *m,f* (Chi, Méx fam) (deshonesto): **es un ~** he's crooked (colloq)
chueco² *adv* (AmL fam) **(a)** (torcido): **camina/ escribe ~** he can't walk/write straight **(b)** ⟨*jugar/pelear*⟩ dirty (colloq)
chufa *f* tiger nut, earth almond
chuico *m* (Chi) demijohn
chulear [A1] *vt* **1** (Arg fam) (provocar) to needle (colloq) **2** (Méx fam) (piropear) to compliment; ⟨*vestido/peinado*⟩ to make nice comments about **3** (Col) (con un signo) to check (AmE), to tick (BrE)
chuleta *f* **1** (Coc) chop; **~ de cordero** lamb chop **2** (Esp arg) (para copiar) crib (colloq) **3** (Chi fam) (patilla) sideburn
chulla *mf* (Ec) (quiteño) *person from Quito*
chulo¹ -la *adj* **1** (fam) (bonito) **(a)** (Esp, Méx) ⟨*vestido/casa*⟩ neat (AmE colloq), lovely (BrE) **(b)** (Méx) ⟨*hombre*⟩ good-looking, cute (esp AmE); ⟨*mujer*⟩ pretty, cute (esp AmE) **2** (Esp fam) (bravucón) nervy (AmE colloq), cocky (BrE colloq) **3** (Chi fam) (de mal gusto) tacky (colloq)
■ *m,f* (Esp fam) (bravucón) flashy type
chulo² *m* (Esp fam) **1** (proxeneta) pimp **2** (Col) (Zool) black vulture **3** (Col) (signo) check mark (AmE), tick (BrE)
chumero -ra *m,f* (AmC) apprentice
chunche *m* (AmC) (fam) (cosa) thing, thingamajig (colloq)
chuño *m* (CS) (fécula de papa) potato flour
chupachups® *m* (*pl* ~) (Esp) lollipop

chupada *f* (fam) (de helado) lick; (de cigarrillo) puff; **le dio unas ~s a la pipa** he puffed on his pipe a few times
chupado -da *adj* **1** [ESTAR] (fam) (flaco) skinny **2** [ESTAR] (Esp fam) (fácil) dead easy (colloq) **3** [ESTAR] (AmL fam) (borracho) plastered (colloq) **4** **(a)** [ESTAR] (Chi, Per) (inhibido) withdrawn **(b)** [SER] (Chi, Per fam) (tímido) shy
chupalla *f* (Chi) straw hat
chupamedias *mf* (*pl* ~) (CS, Ven fam) bootlicker (colloq)
chupar [A1] *vt* **(a)** (extraer) ⟨*sangre/savia*⟩ to suck **(b)** ⟨*biberón/chupete*⟩ to suck (on); ⟨*naranja/caramelo*⟩ to suck; ⟨*pipa/cigarrillo*⟩ to puff on **(c)** (AmL fam) (beber) to drink
■ ~ *vi* **(a)** «*bebé/cría*» to suckle **(b)** (AmL fam) (beber) to booze (colloq)
■ **chuparse** *v pron* ⟨*dedo*⟩ to suck
chupeta *f* (Col) lollipop
chupete *m* **1** **(a)** (de bebé) pacifier (AmE), dummy (BrE) **(b)** (CS) (del biberón) nipple (AmE), teat (BrE) **2** (Chi, Per) (golosina) lollipop **3** (Chi) (Auto) choke
chupetín *m* (RPl) lollipop
chupón *m* **(a)** (AmL) ► CHUPETE 1A **(b)** (Méx) (del biberón) nipple (AmE), teat (BrE) **(c)** (Col) (chupada) lick
churrasquería *f* (AmS) steak house
churro *m* **1** (Coc) *strip of fried dough* **2** (Esp fam) (chapuza) botched job
churrusco *m* (Col) (Zool) caterpillar; (cepillo) bottle brush
chusco -ca *adj* **1** (gracioso) ⟨*persona/humor*⟩ earthy **2** (Chi, Per fam & pey) **(a)** (ordinario) ⟨*persona*⟩ common (- pej); ⟨*perro*⟩ mongrel; ⟨*barrio/lugar*⟩ plebeian (- pej) **(b)** ⟨*mujer*⟩ loose (colloq)
chusma *f* rabble (*pl*), plebs (*pl*) (colloq)
chuspa *f* (Col) (para lápices) pencil case; (para gafas) glasses case
chutar [A1] *vi* (Dep) to shoot
chute *m* (Dep) shot
chutear [A1] *vt/vi* (CS) to shoot
chuza *f* (Méx) (Dep) (jugada) strike; (marca) mark
chuzo *adj* (CS fam) ⟨*pelo*⟩ dead straight (colloq); ⟨*persona*⟩ hopeless (colloq)
■ *m:* **llover a ~s** (fam) to pour (down with rain)
Cía. *f* (= **Compañía**) Co
cianuro *m* cyanide
ciática *f* sciatica
cibercafé *m* cybercafe
ciberespacio *m* (Inf) cyberspace
cibernética *f* cybernetics
cicatero -ra *adj* (fam) tightfisted (colloq)
■ *m,f* (fam) skinflint (colloq)
cicatriz *f* scar; **la herida le dejó ~** the wound left her with a scar
cicatrizar [A4] *vi*, **cicatrizarse** [A4] *v pron* to heal (up), cicatrize (tech)
cicerone *mf* (liter) guide, cicerone (liter)
ciclismo *m* cycling, biking (colloq)
ciclista *adj* cycle (*before n*)
■ *mf* cyclist

ciclo *m* **(a)** (de fenómenos, sucesos) cycle **(b)** (de películas) season; (de conferencias) series **(c)** (Educ): **el primer ~** primary school

ciclocross *m* cyclo-cross; **bicicleta de ~** mountain bike

ciclomotor *m* moped

ciclón *m* cyclone

ciclovía *f* (Col) cycle path

cicuta *f* hemlock

ciego -ga *adj* **1 (a)** (invidente) blind; **es ~ de nacimiento** he was born blind; **se quedó ~** he went blind; **anduvimos a ciegas por el pasillo** we groped our way along the corridor **(b)** (ante una realidad) **estar ~ A algo** to be blind ⊤o sth **(c)** (ofuscado) blind; **~ de ira** blind with fury **2** ‹fe/ obediencia› blind **3** ‹conducto/cañería› blocked; ■ *m,f* (invidente) (*m*) blind man; (*f*) blind woman; **los ~s** the blind

cielo *m* **1** (firmamento) sky; **~ cubierto** overcast sky; **a ~ abierto** (Min) opencast (*before n*); **este dinero me viene como caído del ~** this money is a godsend **2** (Relig) **(a) el ~** (Paraíso) heaven; **ir al ~** to go to heaven; **ganarse el ~** to earn oneself a place in heaven **(b)** (como interj): **¡~s!** (good) heavens! **3** (techo) ceiling **~ raso** ceiling **4 (a)** (aplicado a personas) angel **(b)** (como apelativo) sweetheart, darling; **¡mi ~!** my darling

ciempiés *m* (*pl* **~**) centipede

cien *adj inv/pron* a/one hundred; **~ mil** a/one hundred thousand; **es ~ por ~ algodón** (esp Esp) it's a hundred percent cotton
■ *m*: **el ~** (number) one hundred

ciénaga *f* swamp

ciencia *f* **(a)** (rama del saber) science; (saber, conocimiento) knowledge, learning; **~ ficción** science fiction; **a ~ cierta** for sure, for certain **(b) ciencias** *fpl* (Educ) science; **C~s Empresariales/de la Información** Business/Media Studies; **C~s Políticas/de la Educación** Politics/ Education

cieno *m* silt, mud

científico -ca *adj* scientific
■ *m,f* scientist

ciento *adj/pron* (delante de otro número) a/one hundred; **~ dos** a/one hundred and two; *para ejemplos ver* QUINIENTOS
■ *m* **(a)** (número): **~s de libros** hundreds of books; **vinieron a ~s** they came in the (AmE) *o* (BrE) in their hundreds **(b) por ciento** percent; **cien por ~** a hundred percent

cierra, cierras, etc ▶ CERRAR

cierre *m* **1** (acción) **(a)** (de fábrica, empresa, hospital) closure **(b)** (de establecimiento) closing **(c)** (de frontera) closing **(d)** (de emisión) end, close **(e)** (Fin) close **2 (a)** (de bolso, pulsera) clasp, fastener; (de puerta, ventana) lock **(b)** (cremallera) zipper (AmE), zip (BrE); **~ metálico** (en tienda) metal shutter *o* grille; **~ relámpago** (CS, Per) zipper (AmE), zip (BrE)

cierro ▶ CERRAR

cierto -ta *adj* **1** (verdadero) true; **no hay nada de ~ en ello** there is no truth in it; **una cosa es cierta** one thing's certain; **¡ah!, es ~** oh yes, of course; **parece más joven, ¿no es ~?** he looks younger, doesn't he *o* don't you think?; **estabas en lo ~** you were right; **lo ~ es que ...** the fact is

that ...; **si bien es ~ que ...** while *o* although it's true to say that ...; **por ~** (a propósito) by the way, incidentally
2 (delante del n) (que no se especifica, define) certain; **cierta clase de gente** a certain kind of people; **de cierta edad** of a certain age; **en cierta ocasión** on one occasion; **en ~ modo** in some ways; **hasta ~ punto** up to a point; **durante un ~ tiempo** for a while

ciervo -va *m,f* (especie) deer; (macho) stag; (hembra) hind

cifra *f* **1 (a)** (dígito) figure; **un número de cinco ~s** a five-figure number **(b)** (número, cantidad) number; **la ~ de muertos** the number of dead, the death toll (period) **(c)** (de dinero) figure, sum **2** (clave) code, cipher; **en ~** in code

cifrar [A1] *vt* **1 (a)** ‹mensaje/carta› to write ... in code, encode (frml) **(b)** (Inf) to encrypt **2** ‹esperanza› to place, pin

cigala *f* crawfish, crayfish

cigarra *f* cicada

cigarrería *f* (Andes) tobacco shop (AmE), tobacconist's (BrE)

cigarrillo *m* cigarette; **~ con filtro** filter tipped cigarette

cigarro *m* (puro) cigar; (cigarrillo) cigarette

cigüeña *f* stork

cigüeñal *m* crankshaft

cilantro *m* coriander

cilindrada *f*, **cilindraje** *m* cubic capacity

cilíndrico -ca *adj* cylindrical

cilindro *m* cylinder; **un motor de cuatro ~s** a four-cylinder engine

cima *f* (de montaña) top, summit; (de árbol) top; (de profesión) top; (de carrera) peak, height; **está en la ~ de su carrera** she is at the peak of her career

cimarra *f* (Chi): **hacer la ~** to play hooky (esp AmE colloq); to skive off (school) (BrE colloq)

cimentar [A1] *or* [A5] *vt* **(a)** ‹edificio› to lay the foundations of **(b)** (consolidar) to consolidate, strengthen **(c)** (basar) **~ algo EN algo** to base sth ON sth

cimientos *mpl* foundations (*pl*); **poner los ~ de algo** to lay the foundations of sth

cinc *m* ▶ ZINC

cincel *m* (de escultor, albañil) chisel; (de orfebre) graver

cincelar [A1] *vt* ‹piedra› to chisel, carve; ‹metal› to engrave

cinco *adj inv/pron* five; [nótese que algunas frases requieren el uso del número ordinal 'fifth' en inglés] **noventa y ~** ninety-five; **quinientos ~** five hundred and five; **la fila ~** row five, the fifth row; **vinimos los ~** the five of us came; **somos ~** there are five of us; **entraron de ~ en ~** they went in five at a time; **tiene ~ años** she's five (years old); **son las ~ de la mañana** it's five (o'clock) in the morning; **las ocho y ~** five after (AmE) *o* (BrE) past eight; **~ para las dos** (AmL exc RPl) five to two; *ver tb* MENOS *prep* 2 B; **hoy estamos a ~** today is the fifth
■ *m* **1** (número) (number) five; **el ~ de corazones** the five of hearts
2 (Per) (momento) moment

cincuenta *adj inv/m/pron* fifty; **los (años) ~** *or* **la década de los ~** the fifties; **tiene unos ~** ···✧

cincuentón ⋯⋗ cítrico

años she's about 50 years old; ~ **y tantos/pico** fifty-odd, fifty something; **la página** ~ page fifty; **el** ~ **aniversario** the fiftieth anniversary
cincuentón -tona *adj* (fam): **es** ~ he's in his fifties
■ *m,f* (fam): **una cincuentona** a woman in her fifties
cine *m* **(a)** (arte, actividad) cinema; **el** ~ **francés** French cinema; **actor de** ~ movie *o* film actor; **hacer** ~ to make movies *o* films **(b)** (local) movie house *o* theater (AmE), cinema (BrE); **¿vamos al** ~**?** shall we go to the movies (AmE) *o* (BrE) cinema?; ~ **de barrio** local movie theater (AmE), local cinema (BrE); ~ **de estreno** *movie theater where new releases are shown*
cineasta *mf* filmmaker, moviemaker (AmE)
cineclub, cine-club *m* film club
cinéfilo -la *m,f* movie buff, cinema buff (BrE)
cinematografía *f* cinematography
cinematográfico -ca *adj* movie (*before n*), film (BrE) (*before n*)
cínico -ca *adj* cynical
■ *m,f* cynic
cinismo *m* cynicism
cinta *f* **(a)** (para adornar, envolver) ribbon; ~ **adhesiva** (en papelería) adhesive tape; (Med) sticking plaster; ~ **durex®** (AmL excl CS) *or* (AmL) **scotch®** *or* (Col) **pegante** Scotch tape® (AmE), Sellotape® (BrE); ~ **métrica** tape measure; ~ **negra** (Méx) *mf* (Dep) black belt; ~ **transportadora** conveyor belt **(b)** (en gimnasia rítmica) ribbon; (en carreras) tape **(c)** (Audio, Video) tape; ~ **virgen** blank tape; ~ **de video** *or* (Esp) **vídeo** videotape
cintura *f* (de persona, prenda) waist; **me tomó de la** ~ he grabbed me round the waist; **me queda grande de** ~ it's too big for me round the waist
cinturilla *f* waistband
cinturón *m* **(a)** (Indum) belt; ~ **de castidad** chastity belt; ~ **de seguridad** seat belt, safety belt; ~ **negro/verde** (Dep) black/green belt **(b)** (de ciudad) belt; **el** ~ **industrial** the industrial belt
ciprés *m* cypress
circo *m* (Espec, Hist) circus
circuito *m* **(a)** (pista) track, circuit; (de circo, exposición) circuit **(b)** (Elec, Electrón) circuit
circulación *f* **(a)** (en general) circulation; **tener mala** ~ to have poor circulation **(b)** (movimiento) movement; (Auto) traffic
circular¹ *adj* circular; **de forma** ~ circular
■ *f* circular
circular² [A1] *vi* **(a)** «*sangre/savia*» to circulate, flow; «*agua/corriente*» to flow **(b)** «*transeúnte/peatón*» to walk; (referido al tráfico): **circulan por la izquierda** they drive on the left **(c)** «*autobús/tren*» (estar de servicio) to run, operate **(d)** «*dinero/billete/sello*» to be in circulation **(e)** «*noticia/rumor/memo*» to circulate, go around
■ ~ *vt* to circulate
circulatorio -ria *adj* circulation (*before n*)
círculo *m* **(a)** (en general) circle; **coloca las mesas en** ~ arrange the tables in a circle; **en**

(los) ~**s teatrales** in theatrical circles; **C**~ **Polar Antártico/Ártico** Antarctic/Arctic Circle; ~ **vicioso** vicious circle **(b)** (asociación) society; ~ **de Bellas Artes** Fine Arts Association *o* Society
circuncisión *f* circumcision
circundante *adj* surrounding (*before n*)
circunferencia *f* **(a)** (Mat) circle; **dibujar una** ~ to draw a circle **(b)** (perímetro) circumference; **tiene 1 km de** ~ it has a circumference of 1 km
circunscripción *f* (distrito) district
circunstancia *f* **1** (particularidad): **si por alguna** ~ **no puede ir** if for any reason you cannot go; **se da la** ~ **de que ...** as it happens ...; **bajo ninguna** ~ under no circumstances **2 circunstancias** *fpl* (situación) circumstances (*pl*); **dadas las** ~**s** given the circumstances; **debido a sus** ~**s familiares** due to her family situation
cirio *m* candle
cirrosis *f* cirrhosis
ciruela *f* (Bot, Coc) plum; ~ **pasa** *or* (CS) **seca** prune
ciruelo *m* plum tree
cirugía *f* surgery; **hacerse la** ~ **estética/plástica** to have cosmetic/plastic surgery
cirujano -na *m,f* surgeon; ~ **dentista** dental surgeon
Cisjordania *f* the West Bank
cisma *m* (Rel) schism; (en partido) split
cisne *m* (Zool) swan
cisterna *f* (depósito) tank; (subterránea) cistern; (del retrete) cistern
cistitis *f* cystitis
cita *f* **1** **(a)** (con profesional) appointment; **pedir** ~ to make an appointment; **concertar una** ~ to arrange an appointment **(b)** (con novio, amigo): **tengo una** ~ **con mi novio/con un amigo** I have a date with my boyfriend/I'm going out with a friend; **faltó a la** ~ he didn't show up (colloq); ~**s por computadora** *or* (Esp) **ordenador** computer dating **2** (en texto, discurso) quote; **una** ~ **de Cervantes** a quotation *o* quote from Cervantes
citadino -na *adj* (AmL) urban, city (*before n*)
■ *m,f* **(a)** (AmL) (ciudadano) city dweller **(b)** (Méx) (defeño) inhabitant of México City
citar [A1] *vt* **1** **(a)** (dar una cita) «*doctor/jefe de personal*» to give ... an appointment; **estar citado con algn** to have an appointment with sb **(b)** (convocar): **nos citó a todos a una reunión** she called us all to a meeting **(c)** (Der) to summon; ~ **a algn como testigo** to call sb as a witness **2** **(a)** (mencionar) to mention **(b)** «*escritor/pasaje*» to quote
■ **citarse** *v pron* ~**se con** algn to arrange to meet sb; **se** ~**on en la plaza** (*recípr*) they arranged to meet in the square
citófono *m* (Andes) internal phone system
citología *f* (análisis) smear test
cítrico¹ -ca *adj* citrus (*before n*)
cítrico² *m* citrus

AmC	América Central	Arg	Argentina	Cu	Cuba	Per	Perú
AmL	América Latina	Bol	Bolivia	Ec	Ecuador	RPI	Río de la Plata
AmS	América del Sur	Chi	Chile	Esp	España	Ur	Uruguay
Andes	Región andina	CS	Cono Sur	Méx	México	Ven	Venezuela

ciudad *f* town; (de mayor tamaño) city; **❺ centro ciudad** town *o* city center; **~ balneario** (AmL) coastal resort; **C~ del Vaticano/de México** Vatican/Mexico City; **~ dormitorio** bedroom community (AmE), dormitory town (BrE); **~ perdida** (Méx) shantytown; **~ satélite** satellite town; **~ universitaria** university campus

ciudadanía *f* **(a)** (nacionalidad) citizenship **(b)** (conjunto de ciudadanos) citizenry (frml), citizens (*pl*)

ciudadano -na *adj* ⟨*vida*⟩ city (*before n*); **la inseguridad ciudadana** the lack of safety in towns *o* cities; **es un deber ~** it's the duty of every citizen
■ *m,f* (habitante) citizen

cívico -ca *adj* **(a)** ⟨*deberes/derechos*⟩ civic **(b)** ⟨*acto*⟩ public-spirited, civic-minded

civil *adj* **(a)** ⟨*derechos/responsabilidades*⟩ civil **(b)** (no religioso) civil; **casarse por lo ~** *or* (Per, RPl, Ven) **sólo por ~** *or* (Chi, Méx) **por el ~** to be married in a civil ceremony (AmE), to have a registry office wedding (BrE) **(c)** (no militar) civilian (*before n*); **iba (vestido) de ~** he was in civilian clothes
■ *mf* **(a)** (persona no militar) civilian **(b)** (Esp) (guardia civil) Civil Guard

civilización *f* civilization

civilizado -da *adj* civilized

civilizar [A4] *vt* ⟨*país/pueblo*⟩ to civilize; ⟨*persona*⟩ to teach ... to behave properly
■ **civilizarse** *v pron* «*pueblo*» to become civilized; «*persona*» to learn to behave properly

civismo *m* public-spiritedness

cizaña *f* darnel

clamar [A1] *vi* ~ CONTRA algo to protest AGAINST sth; ~ POR algo to clamor* FOR sth, cry out FOR sth
■ ~ *vt*: ~ **venganza** to cry out for vengeance

clamor *m* clamor*

clamoroso -sa *adj* ⟨*acogida*⟩ rousing (*before n*); ⟨*ovación*⟩ rapturous, thunderous; ⟨*éxito*⟩ resounding (*before n*)

clan *m* clan

clandestinidad *f* secrecy, secret nature; **trabajar en la ~** to work underground; **pasar a la ~** to go underground

clandestino -na *adj* ⟨*reunión/relación*⟩ clandestine, secret; ⟨*periódico*⟩ underground
■ *m,f* (fam) illegal immigrant

claqué *m* tap (dancing); **bailar ~** to tap dance

claqueta *f* clapperboard

clara *f* **(a)** *tb* **~ de huevo** (egg) white **(b)** (Esp) (bebida) shandy

claraboya *f* skylight

clarear [A1] *v impers* **(a)** (amanecer): **estaba clareando** it was getting light *o* day was breaking **(b)** (Meteo): **comenzó a ~** the sky/the clouds began to clear
■ ~ *vi* «*pelo*» to go gray*/white

clarete *m* (rosado) rosé; (tinto) claret

claridad *f* **(a)** (luz) light **(b)** (luminosidad) brightness **(c)** (de explicación, imagen, sonido) clarity; **con ~** clearly

clarificar [A2] *vt* to clarify

clarín *m* bugle

clarinete *m* clarinet

clarinetista *mf* clarinetist

clarividente *adj* (que adivina el futuro) clairvoyant; (perspicaz) discerning, clear-sighted
■ *mf* clairvoyant

claro¹ -ra *adj* **(a)** (luminoso) ⟨*cielo/habitación*⟩ bright **(b)** (pálido) ⟨*color/verde/azul*⟩ light, pale; ⟨*piel*⟩ fair; **tiene los ojos ~s** she has blue/green/ gray eyes **(c)** ⟨*salsa/sopa*⟩ thin **(d)** ⟨*agua/sonido*⟩ clear; ⟨*ideas/explicación/instrucciones*⟩ clear; ⟨*situación/postura*⟩ clear; **tener algo ~** to be clear about sth; **¿está ~?** is that clear?; **quiero dejar (en) ~ que** ... I want to make it clear that ...; *sacar algo en* **~** *de algo* to make sense of sth **(e)** (evidente) clear, obvious; **está ~ que** ... it is clear *o* obvious that ...; **a no ser, ~ está, que esté mintiendo** unless, of course, he's lying

claro² *adv* **1** ⟨*ver*⟩ clearly; **voy a hablarte ~** I'm not going to beat around *o* about the bush; **me lo dijo muy ~** he made it very quite clear (to me) **2** (*indep*) (en exclamaciones de asentimiento) of course
■ *m* **(a)** (en bosque) clearing; (en pelo, barba) bald patch **(b)** (Meteo) sunny spell *o* period

clase *f* **1** (tipo) kind, sort, type; **distintas ~s de arroz** different kinds of rice
2 (Transp, Sociol) class; **viajar en segunda ~** to travel (in) second class; **~ económica** *or* **turista** economy *o* tourist class; **~ ejecutiva** *or* **preferente** business class; **~ alta/baja/media** upper/lower/ middle class; **~ dirigente** *or* **dominante** ruling class; **~ obrera** working class
3 (a) (distinción, elegancia) class; **tiene ~** she has class **(b)** (categoría): **productos de primera ~** top-quality products
4 (Educ) **(a)** (lección) class; **~s de conducir** *or* **manejar** driving lessons; **dictar ~** ⟨(DE algo)⟩ (AmL frml) to lecture (IN sth); **dar ~** *or* (Chi) **hacer ~s** ⟨(DE algo)⟩ «*profesor*» to teach (sth); **da ~s de piano** (Esp) she has piano lessons; **~ particular** private class *o* lesson **(b)** (grupo de alumnos) class **(c)** (aula — en escuela) classroom; (— en universidad) lecture hall *o* room

clásico¹ -ca *adj* **(a)** ⟨*lengua/mundo*⟩ classical; ⟨*decoración/estilo/ropa*⟩ classical **(b)** ⟨*método*⟩ standard, traditional; ⟨*error/malentendido/caso*⟩ classic

clásico² *m* **(a)** (obra) classic **(b)** (AmL) (Dep) traditional big game

clasificación *f* **1** (de documentos, animales, plantas) classification; (de cartas) sorting **2** (de película) certificate **3 (a)** (Dep) (para una etapa posterior) qualification; **partido de ~** qualifying match **(b)** (tabla) placings (*pl*); (puesto) position, place; **quinto en la ~ final del rally** fifth in the final placings for the rally

clasificador *m* **(a)** (carpeta) ring binder **(b)** (de una máquina) sorter **(c)** (mueble) filing cabinet

clasificar [A2] *vt* **(a)** ⟨*documentos/datos*⟩ to sort, put in order; ⟨*cartas*⟩ to sort **(b)** ⟨*planta/ animal/elemento*⟩ to classify **(c)** ⟨*hotel*⟩ to class, rank; ⟨*fruta*⟩ to class; ⟨*persona*⟩ to class, rank
■ **clasificarse** *v pron* (Dep) **(a)** (para etapa posterior) to qualify; **~ para la final** to qualify for the final **(b)** (en tabla, carrera): **se clasificó en sexto lugar** he finished in sixth place

clasista *adj* ⟨*actitud/sociedad*⟩ classist; ⟨*persona*⟩ class-conscious

c

claustro *m* (a) (Arquit, Relig) cloister (b) (Educ) (de universidad) senate; (de colegio) staff; (reunión) senate/staff meeting

claustrofobia *f* claustrophobia; **siento ∼ allí dentro** I get claustrophobia in there

cláusula *f* clause

clausura *f* (a) (de congreso, festival) closing ceremony; **de ∼** ⟨*ceremonia/discurso*⟩ closing (*before n*) (b) (de local) closure

clausurar [A1] *vt* (a) ⟨*congreso/sesión*⟩ «*acto/ discurso*» to bring ... to a close; «*persona*» to close (b) ⟨*local/estadio*⟩ to close ... down

clavada *f* (Méx) (en natación) dive

clavadista *mf* (Méx) diver

clavado¹ **-da** *adj* **1** (a) **∼ EN algo** ⟨*puñal/ tachuela/espina*⟩ stuck in sth; ⟨*estaca*⟩ driven INTO sth (b) (fijo): **con la vista clavada en un punto** staring at a point, with his gaze fixed on a point; **se quedó ∼ en el lugar** he was rooted to the spot **2** (fam) (a) (idéntico) **ser ∼ A algn** «*persona*» to be the spitting image of sb (colloq); **ser ∼ A algo** «*objeto*» to be identical TO sth (b) (en punto): **llegó a las cinco clavadas** he arrived on the dot of five (colloq)

clavado² *m* (AmL) dive

clavar [A1] *vt* **1** (a) **∼ algo EN algo** ⟨*clavo*⟩ to hammer sth INTO sth; ⟨*puñal/cuchillo*⟩ to stick sth IN sth; ⟨*estaca*⟩ to drive INTO sth; **me clavó los dientes/las uñas** he sank his teeth/dug his nails into me (b) ⟨*cartel/estante*⟩ to put up (*with nails, etc*) (c) ⟨*ojos/vista*⟩ to fix ... on **2** (fam) (a) (cobrar caro) to rip ... off (colloq); **nos ∼on $10,000** they stung us for $10,000 (b) (CS) (engañar) to cheat (c) (Méx) (robar) to swipe (colloq), to filch (colloq)

■ **clavarse** *v pron* **1** (a) ⟨*aguja*⟩ to stick ... into one's finger (*o thumb etc*); **me clavé una espina en el dedo** I got a thorn in my finger (b) (*refl*) ⟨*cuchillo/puñal*⟩: **se clavó el puñal en el pecho** he plunged the dagger into his chest **2** (CS fam) **∼se CON algo** (por no poder venderlo) to get stuck WITH sth (colloq); (por ser mala compra): **se clavó con el auto que compró** the car turned out to be a bad buy **3** (Méx) (Dep) to dive

clave *adj* (*pl ∼ or* **-ves**) key (*before n*); **un factor ∼** a key factor

■ *f* (a) (código) code; **en ∼** in code; **∼ de acceso** (Inf) password (b) (de problema, misterio) key (c) (Mús) clef; **∼ de fa/sol** bass/treble clef

■ *m* harpsichord

clavel *m* carnation

clavicordio *m* clavichord

clavícula *f* collarbone, clavicle (tech)

clavija *f* (a) (Mec) pin (b) (Elec) (enchufe) plug; (de enchufe) pin (c) (de guitarra) tuning peg

clavo *m* (a) (Tec) nail; **dar en el ∼** to hit the nail on the head (b) (Med) pin (c) (en montañismo) piton (d) (Bot, Coc) *tb* **∼ de olor** clove

claxon /'klakson/ *m* (*pl* **-xons**) horn; **tocar el ∼** to sound *o* blow one's horn, to honk

clemencia *f* mercy, clemency (frml)

clementina *f* clementine

cleptómano -na *m,f* kleptomaniac

clérigo -ga *m,f* **1** (en el clero protestante) (*m*)

clergyman, cleric; (*f*) clergywoman, cleric **2** **clérigo** *m* (en el clero católico) clergyman, priest

clero *m* clergy

clic *m* (*pl* **clics**) click; (al romperse algo) snap; **hacer doble ∼** (Inf) to double-click

cliché *m* (a) (expresión, idea) cliché (b) (de multicopista) stencil; (Impr) plate; (Fot) negative

cliente -ta *m,f* (de tienda, restaurante) customer; (de empresa, abogado) client; (de hotel) guest; (en taxi) fare, customer; **∼ habitual** regular customer (*o* client *etc*)

clientela *f* (de tienda, restaurante) clientele, customers (*pl*); (de hotel) guests (*pl*); (de abogado) clients (*pl*)

clima *m* (a) (Meteo) climate (b) (ambiente) atmosphere; **un ∼ festivo** a festive atmosphere; **el ∼ económico** the economic climate

climatizado -da *adj* ⟨*local/casa*⟩ air-conditioned; ⟨*piscina*⟩ heated

clímax *m* (*pl* **∼**) climax

clínica *f* private hospital *o* clinic; **∼ dental** dental office (AmE), dental surgery (BrE); **∼ de reposo** convalescent *o* rest home

clínico -ca *adj* ⟨*ensayo*⟩ clinical (*before n*); ▶ HOSPITAL
■ *m,f* (RPl) general practitioner

clip *m* (*pl* **clips**) **1** (a) (sujetapapeles) paperclip (b) (para el pelo) bobby pin (AmE), hairgrip (BrE) (c) (cierre) clip; **aretes** *or* **pendientes de ∼** clip-on earrings **2** (Video) (pop) video

cloaca *f* **1** (alcantarilla) sewer **2** (de ave, reptil) cloaca

clon *m* clone

clonar [A1] *vt* to clone

cloro *m* (Quím) chlorine; (lejía) (AmC, Chi) bleach

clorofila *f* chlorophyll

clorofluorocarbono *m* chlorofluorocarbon, CFC

cloroformo *m* chloroform

clóset *m* (*pl* **-sets**) (AmL exc RPl) (en dormitorio) built-in closet (AmE), fitted *o* built-in wardrobe (BrE)

clotch /'klotʃ/ *m* ▶ CLUTCH

clown /'klaun/ *m* (*pl* **clowns**) clown

club *m* (*pl* **clubs** *or* **-es**) club; **∼ juvenil** youth club; **∼ nocturno** nightclub

clueca *adj* broody

clutch /'klʊtʃ/ *m* (AmC, Col, Méx, Ven) clutch

cm. (= **centímetro**) cm.

coacción *f* coercion; **bajo ∼** under duress

coaccionar [A1] *vt* to coerce

coagular [A1] *vt* to clot, coagulate
■ **coagularse** *v pron* to clot, coagulate

coágulo *m* clot

coalición *f* coalition; **gobierno de ∼** coalition government

coartada *f* alibi

coartar [A1] *vt* ⟨*persona*⟩ to inhibit; ⟨*libertad/ voluntad*⟩ to restrict

coba *f* (Ven arg) (mentira, engaño) lie; **darle ∼ a algn** (adular) (Esp, Méx, Ven fam) to suck up to sb (colloq)

cobarde *adj* cowardly
■ *mf* coward

cobardía *f* cowardice; **fue una** ~ it was an act of cowardice

cobaya *f*, **cobayo** *m* guinea pig

cobertizo *m* shed

cobertura *f* **(a)** (de seguro) cover **(b)** (Period, Rad, TV) coverage; ~ **informativa** news coverage

cobija *f* (AmL) **(a)** (manta) blanket **(b) cobijas** *fpl* (ropa de cama) bedclothes (*pl*)

cobijar [A1] *vt* ⟨persona⟩ (proteger) to shelter; (hospedar) to give ... shelter, take ... in
■ **cobijarse** *v pron* to shelter, take shelter

cobijo *m* shelter; **darle** ~ **a algn** to shelter sb

cobra *f* cobra

cobrador -dora *m,f* (a domicilio) collector; (de autobús) bus conductor

cobrar [A1] *vt* ⓵ **(a)** ⟨precio/suma/intereses⟩ to charge; **nos cobran 30.000 pesos de alquiler** they charge us 30,000 pesos in rent; ~ **algo POR algo/hacer algo** to charge sth FOR sth/doing sth; **vino a** ~ **el alquiler** she came for the rent *o* to collect the rent; **¿me cobra estas cervezas?** can I pay for these beers, please?; **me cobró el vino dos veces** he charged me twice for the wine **(b)** ⟨sueldo⟩ to earn; ⟨pensión⟩ to draw; **cobra 2.000 euros al mes** he earns/draws 2,000 euros a month; **todavía no hemos cobrado junio** we still haven't been paid for June **(c)** ⟨deuda⟩ to recover; **nunca llegó a** ~ **esas facturas** he never received payment for those bills **(d)** ⟨cheque⟩ to cash
⓶ **(a)** (Chi) (pedir): **le cobré los libros que le presté** I asked him to give back the books I'd lent him **(b)** (Chi) ⟨gol/falta⟩ to give
⓷ (adquirir) ⟨fuerzas⟩ to gather; ~ **fama/importancia** become famous/important
⓸ (period) ⟨vidas/víctimas⟩ to claim
■ ~ *vi* **(a)** ~ **POR algo/hacer algo** to charge FOR sth/doing sth; **¿me cobra, por favor?** can you take for this, please?, can I pay, please?; **llámame por** ~ (Chi, Méx) call collect (AmE), reverse the charges (BrE) **(b)** (recibir el sueldo) to be paid
■ **cobrarse** *v pron* **(a)** (recibir dinero): **tenga, cóbrese** here you are; **cóbrese las cervezas** can you take for the beers, please? **(b)** (period) ⟨vidas/víctimas⟩ to claim

cobre *m* (Metal, Quím) copper

cobrizo -za *adj* coppery, copper-colored*

cobro *m* **(a)** (de cheque) cashing; (de sueldo, pensión): **para el** ~ **de la pensión** in order to collect your pension **(b)** (Telec): **llamó a** ~ **revertido** she called collect (AmE), she reversed the charges (BrE)

coca *f* (Bot) coca; (cocaína) (arg) coke (sl)

cocaína *f* cocaine

cocainómano -na *m,f* cocaine addict

cocaví *m* (Chi) things to eat

cocer [E10] *vt* **(a)** (Coc) (cocinar) to cook; (hervir) to boil; ~ **algo a fuego lento** to simmer sth, cook sth over a low heat **(b)** ⟨ladrillos/cerámica⟩ to fire
■ **cocerse** *v pron* ⓵ «verduras/arroz» (hacerse) to cook; (hervir) to boil; **tardan unos 15 minutos en** ~**se** they take about 15 minutes to cook ⓶ (Chi) «bebé» to have a diaper (AmE) *o* (BrE) nappy rash

coche *m* **(a)** (Auto) car, auto (AmE), automobile (AmE); **nos llevó en** ~ **a la estación** he drove us to the station; ~ **bomba** car bomb; ~ **de bomberos** fire engine, fire truck (AmE); ~ **de carreras**

racing car; ~ **de choque** bumper car; ~ **fúnebre** hearse **(b)** (Ferr) car (AmE), carriage (BrE); ~ **cama** *or* (CS) **dormitorio** sleeper, sleeping car **(c)** (de bebé) baby carriage (AmE), pram (BrE); (en forma de sillita) stroller (AmE), pushchair (BrE) **(d)** (carruaje) coach, carriage; ~ **de caballos** carriage

cochera *f* **(a)** (para autobuses) depot, garage; **las** ~**s** the depot **(b)** (garaje) (Esp, Méx) garage

cochinada *f* (fam) **(a)** (suciedad) filth **(b)** (palabra, acción): **¡no digas esas** ~**s!** don't use such filthy language!; **eso es una** ~ that's a disgusting thing to do **(c)** (mala pasada) dirty trick

cochino -na *adj* **(a)** (fam) (sucio) ⟨persona/manos⟩ filthy **(b)** (fam) (indecoroso) ⟨persona⟩ disgusting; ⟨revista/película⟩ dirty (colloq) **(c)** (Chi) (Dep, Jueg) (violento) dirty (colloq); (tramposo): **es muy** ~ he's a terrible cheat
■ *m,f* **(a)** (Zool) pig, hog (AmE) **(b)** (fam) (persona sucia) filthy pig (colloq), slob (colloq)

cocido¹ -da *adj* **(a)** (hervido) ⟨huevos/verduras⟩ boiled **(b)** (CS) (no crudo) cooked; **muy/poco** ~ well done/rare **(c)** ⟨arcilla⟩ fired

cocido² *m* **(a)** (Esp) stew (*made with meat and chickpeas*) **(b)** (Col, Ven) stew (*made with meat, plantains and cassava*)

cociente *m* quotient

cocina *f* **(a)** (habitación) kitchen **(b)** (aparato) stove, cooker (BrE); ~ **de** *or* **a gas** gas stove *o* (BrE) cooker; ~ **eléctrica** electric stove *o* (BrE) cooker **(c)** (arte) cookery; (gastronomía) cuisine; **libro de** ~ cookbook, cookery book (BrE); **la** ~ **casera** home cooking

cocinar [A1] *vt/vi* to cook; **¿quién cocina en tu casa?** who does the cooking in your house?

cocinero -ra *m,f* cook

cocineta *f* (Méx) (cocina) kitchenette

cocinilla *f* camp stove (AmE), camping stove (BrE)

cocktail /'koktel/ *m* (*pl* -**tails**) ▶ CÓCTEL

coco *m* **(a)** (Bot, Coc) coconut **(b)** (fam) (cabeza) head; **está mal del** ~ he's off his head (colloq) **(c)** (fam) (fantasma, espantajo) boogeyman (AmE), bogeyman (BrE)

cocoa *f* (AmL) cocoa

cocodrilo *m* crocodile

cocol *m* (Méx) (bizcocho) cookie (*covered in sesame seeds*)

cocotero *m* coconut palm

cóctel *m* (*pl* -**teles** *or* -**tels**) **(a)** (bebida) cocktail; ~ **de frutas** (AmC, Col) fruit salad, fruit cocktail; ~ **de gambas** (Esp) shrimp (AmE) *o* (BrE) prawn cocktail; ~ **Molotov** Molotov cocktail **(b)** (fiesta) cocktail party

cocuyo *m* **(a)** (AmL) (insecto) firefly **(b)** (Col, Ven) (Auto) parking light (AmE), sidelight (BrE)

codazo *m*: **darle un** ~ **a algn** (leve) to nudge sb; (fuerte) to elbow sb; **se abrió camino a** ~**s** he elbowed his way through

codearse [A1] *v pron* ~ **CON algn** to rub shoulders WITH sb

codera *f* (Indum) elbow patch

codicia *f* (avaricia) greed, avarice

codiciar [A1] *vt* to covet

codicioso -sa *adj* ⟨persona/mirada⟩ covetous, greedy
■ *m,f* covetous *o* greedy person

codificar [A2] vt **(a)** ⟨leyes/normas⟩ to codify **(b)** (Inf) ⟨información⟩ to code **(c)** (Ling) ⟨mensaje⟩ to encode

código m **(a)** (de signos) code; ~ **barrado** or **de barras** bar code; ~ **postal** zipcode (AmE), postcode (BrE) **(b)** (de leyes, normas) code; ~ **de la circulación** Highway Code

codillo m **(a)** (Zool) elbow **(b)** (Coc) knuckle

codo¹ -da adj (Méx fam) tightfisted (colloq)

codo² m elbow; ~ **con** or **a** ~ side by side; **empinar el** ~ (fam) to prop up the bar; **hablar (hasta) por los** ~**s** (fam) to talk nineteen to the dozen (colloq)

codorniz f quail

coeficiente m (Mat) coefficient; ~ **intelectual** or **de inteligencia** IQ, intelligence quotient

coexistir [I1] vi to coexist

cofia f cap

cofradía f (Relig) brotherhood

cofre m **(a)** (joyero) jewel case, jewelry* box **(b)** (arcón) chest **(c)** (Méx) (capó) hood (AmE), bonnet (BrE)

coger [E6] vt **1** (esp Esp) **(a)** (tomar) to take; **lo cogió del brazo** she took him by the arm; **coge un folleto** pick up o take a leaflet **(b)** (quitar) to take; **siempre me está cogiendo los lápices** she's always taking my pencils **(c)** ⟨flores/fruta⟩ to pick **(d)** (levantar) to pick up; **coge esa revista del suelo** pick that magazine up off the floor; **no cogen el teléfono** (Esp) they're not answering the phone **2** (atrapar) (esp Esp) **(a)** ⟨ladrón/pelota⟩ to catch **(b)** ⟨pescado/liebre⟩ to catch **(c)** (descubrir) to catch; **lo cogieron robando** he was caught stealing **(d)** ⟨toro⟩ to gore **3** **(a)** ⟨tren/autobús/taxi⟩ to catch, take **(b)** ⟨calle/camino⟩ to take **4** (Esp fam) (obtener) ⟨billete/entrada⟩ to get; ~ **hora para el médico** to make an appointment to see the doctor; ~ **sitio** to save a place **(b)** (aceptar) ⟨dinero/trabajo/casa⟩ to take **(c)** (admitir) ⟨alumnos/solicitudes⟩ to take **5** (esp Esp) (adquirir) **(a)** ⟨enfermedad⟩ to catch; ⟨insolación⟩ to get; **vas a** ~ **frío** you'll catch cold **(b)** ⟨acento⟩ to pick up; ⟨costumbre/vicio⟩ to pick up; **le cogí cariño** I got quite fond of him **6** (esp Esp) (captar) **(a)** ⟨sentido/significado⟩ to get **(b)** ⟨emisora⟩ to pick up, get **7** (Méx, RPl, Ven vulg) to screw (vulg), to fuck (vulg) ■ ~ vi **1** (esp Esp) ⟨planta⟩ to take; ⟨tinte/permanente⟩ to take **2** (Méx, RPl, Ven vulg) to screw (vulg), to fuck (vulg) ■ **cogerse** v pron (esp Esp) **(a)** (agarrarse, sujetarse) to hold on; **cógete de la barandilla** hold on to the railing **(b)** (recípr): **se cogieron de la mano** they held hands

cogida f (Taur) goring; **sufrió una** ~ he was gored

cognac m brandy

cogollo m (de lechuga, col) heart; (de hinojo) bulb

cogote m (fam) (nuca) scruff of the neck; (cuello) (AmL) neck

cohabitar [A1] vi (frml) to cohabit (frml), to live together

coherencia f **(a)** (congruencia) coherence, logic; **con** ~ coherently o logically **(b)** (consecuencia) consistency; **actuar con** ~ to be consistent **(c)** (Fís) coherence

coherente adj **(a)** (congruente) ⟨discurso/razonamiento⟩ coherent, logical **(b)** (consecuente) ⟨actitud⟩ consistent; **una mujer** ~ a woman who acts according to her beliefs

cohesión f **(a)** (de ideas, pensamientos) coherence **(b)** (en grupo) cohesion, unity

cohete m **1** (Espac, Mil) rocket **2** **cohetes** mpl fireworks (pl)

cohibido -da adj (tímido) shy; (inhibido) inhibited; (incómodo) awkward

cohibir [I22] vt **(a)** to inhibit; **su presencia me cohíbe** I feel inhibited in front of him **(b)** (hacer sentir incómodo): **hablar en público lo cohíbe** he feels awkward about speaking in public ■ **cohibirse** v pron **(a)** (inhibirse) to feel inhibited **(b)** (sentirse incómodo) to feel awkward

coincidencia f **(a)** (casualidad) coincidence; **se dio la** ~ **de que él también estaba allá** by coincidence o chance he was there too; **¡que** ~! what a coincidence! **(b)** (de opiniones) agreement

coincidir [I1] vi **(a)** «fechas/sucesos/líneas» to coincide; «dibujos» to match up; «versiones/resultados» to coincide, match up, tally; ~ **con algo** to coincide (o match up etc) with sth **(b)** (en opiniones, gustos): **coinciden en sus gustos** they share the same tastes; **todos coincidieron en que ... everyone agreed that ...**; ~ **con algn** to agree with sb **(c)** (en un lugar): **a veces coincidimos en el supermercado** we sometimes see each other in the supermarket

coito m intercourse, coitus (frml)

cojear [A1] vi **(a)** (por herida, dolor) to limp; (permanentemente) to be lame; **entró cojeando** he limped o hobbled in **(b)** «silla/mesa» to wobble **(c)** (fam) «explicación/definición» to fall short

cojera f limp

cojín m cushion

cojo -ja adj **(a)** ⟨persona/animal⟩ lame; **está** ~ **del pie derecho** he's lame in his right leg; **andar a la pata coja** or (Méx) **brincar de cojito** (fam) to hop **(b)** ⟨mesa/silla⟩ wobbly **(c)** (fam) ⟨razonamiento⟩ shaky, weak ■ m,f lame person

cojones mpl (vulg) (testículos) balls (pl) (sl o vulg); **estar hasta los** ~ (vulg) to be pissed off (sl); **tener** ~ (vulg) to have guts (colloq), to have balls (sl)

col f (Esp, Méx) cabbage; ~ **de Bruselas** Brussels sprout

cola f **1** (Zool) tail; ~ **de caballo** (en el pelo) ponytail **(b)** (de vestido) train; (de frac) tails (pl) **(c)** (de avión, cometa) tail **(d)** (RPl fam) (nalgas) bottom (colloq) **2** (fila) line (AmE), queue (BrE); **hacer** ~ to line up (AmE), to queue (up) (BrE); **pónganse a la** ~

por favor please join the (end of the) line *o* queue; **brincarse la ~** (Méx) to jump the line *o* queue; **a la ~ del pelotón** at the tail end of the group

3 **(a)** (*pegamento*) glue; **~ de contacto** superglue **(b)** (*bebida*) Coke®, cola

4 (Ven) (Auto): **pedir ~** to hitchhike; **darle la ~ a algn** to give sb a lift *o* a ride

colaboración *f* collaboration; **en ~ con algn/ algo** in collaboration with sb/sth

colaborador -dora *m,f* (*en revista*) contributor; (*en tarea*) collaborator

colaborar [A1] *vi* to collaborate; **~ CON algn** to collaborate WITH sb; **~ con dinero** to contribute some money; **~ EN algo** ‹*en proyecto/ tarea*› to collaborate ON sth; ‹*en revista*› to contribute TO sth

colada *f* (Esp) (*lavado*) laundry, washing

coladera *f* **(a)** (Méx) (*sumidero*) drain **(b)** (Col) ▶ COLADOR

colador *m* (*para té*) tea strainer; (*para pastas, verduras*) colander

colapso *m* **(a)** (Med) collapse; **sufrió un ~** he collapsed **(b)** (*paralización*) standstill

colar [A10] *vt* **(a)** ‹*verdura/pasta*› to strain, drain; ‹*caldo/té*› to strain **(b)** ‹*billete falso*› to pass

■ **~** *vi* (fam) «*cuento/historia*»: **no va a ~** it won't wash (colloq)

■ **colarse** *v pron* (fam) **(a)** (*en cola*) to jump the line (AmE) *o* (BrE) queue **(b)** (*entrar a hurtadillas*) to sneak in; (*en cine, autobús*) to sneak in without paying (colloq); (*en fiesta*) to gatecrash

colcha *f* bedspread

colchón *m* (*de cama*) mattress; **~ de muelles** sprung mattress

colchoneta *f* (*de playa*) air bed, Lilo® (BrE); (*de gimnasia*) mat; (*de cama*) (Méx) comforter (AmE), duvet (BrE)

colección *f* collection

coleccionar [A1] *vt* to collect

coleccionista *mf* collector

colecta *f* (*de donativos*) collection; **hacer una ~** (*para comprar un regalo*) to have a collection; (*con fines caritativos*) to collect

colectar [A1] *vt* to collect

colectivero -ra *m,f* (*de autobús*) (Arg) bus driver

colectividad *f* group, community; **en ~** collectively

colectivo¹ -va *adj* collective

colectivo² *m* **(a)** (*period*) (*agrupación*) group **(b)** (Andes) (*taxi*) collective taxi (*with a fixed route and fare*) **(c)** (Arg) (*autobús*) bus **(d)** (Per, Ur) (*para regalo*) collection

colega *mf* **(a)** (*de profesión*) colleague **(b)** (*homólogo*) counterpart **(c)** (fam) (*amigo*) buddy (AmE), mate (BrE colloq)

colegiado -da *m,f* (*profesional*) member (*of a professional association*)

colegial -giala *m,f* (*de colegio*) (*m*) schoolboy; (*f*) schoolgirl; **los ~es** (the) schoolchildren

colegiatura *f* (Méx) school fees (*pl*)

colegio *m* **(a)** (Educ) school; **los niños están en el ~** the children are at school; **un ~ de monjas** convent school; **un ~ de curas** a Catholic boys'

school; **~ privado** *or* **de pago** fee-paying *o* private school; **~ electoral** electoral college; **~ estatal** *or* **público** public school (AmE), state school (BrE) **(b)** (*de profesionales*): **C~ de Abogados** ≈ Bar Association; **C~ Oficial de Médicos** ≈ Medical Association

colegir [I8] *vt* to deduce

cólera *m* cholera

■ *f* rage, anger

colérico -ca *adj* **(a)** [ESTAR] (*furioso*) furious **(b)** [SER] (*malhumorado*) quick-tempered

colesterol *m* cholesterol

coleta *f* ponytail; (*de torero*) braid (AmE), ponytail (BrE)

coletazo *m* **(a)** (*con la cola*) thrash of the tail; **dar ~s** to thrash about **(b)** (Auto): **el coche dio un ~** the rear of the car skidded

coletilla *f* tag

colgado -da *adj*: **dejar a algn ~** (*dejarlo en la estacada*) to leave sb in the lurch; *ver tb* COLGAR

colgante *adj* hanging; ▶ PUENTE 1

■ *m* pendant

colgar [A8] *vt* **(a)** ‹*cuadro*› to hang, put up; ‹*lámpara*› to put up; ‹*ropa lavada*› to hang (out); **~ algo DE algo** to hang sth ON sth; **el abrigo estaba colgado de un gancho** the coat was hanging on a hook **(b)** (*ahorcar*) to hang **(c)** ‹*teléfono/auricular*› to put down; **tienen el teléfono mal colgado** their phone is off the hook

■ **~** *vi* **(a)** (*pender*) to hang; **colgaba del techo** it was hanging from the ceiling; **el vestido me cuelga de un lado** my dress is hanging down on one side **(b)** (Telec) to hang up; **no cuelgue, por favor** hold the line please, please hold; **me colgó** he hung up on me

■ **colgarse** *v pron* (refl) **1** **(a)** (*ahorcarse*) to hang oneself **(b)** (*agarrarse, suspenderse*): **no te cuelgues de ahí** don't hang off there; **no te cuelgues de mí** don't cling on to me; **se pasa colgada del teléfono** (fam) she spends her time on the phone

2 (Chi, Méx) (Elec): **~se del suministro eléctrico** to tap into the electricity supply

colibrí *m* hummingbird

cólico *m* colic

coliflor *f or* (RPl) *m* cauliflower

colilla *f* (*de cigarrillo*) cigarette end *o* butt

colina *f* hill

colirio *m* eye drops (*pl*)

colisión *f* **(a)** (*de trenes, aviones*) collision, crash; **~ en cadena** pileup **(b)** (*conflicto*) conflict, clash

colitis *f* colitis

collado *m* (*colina*) hill; (*entre montañas*) pass

collage /ko'laʒ/ *m* (*pl* **-llages**) collage

collar *m* **(a)** (*alhaja*) necklace; **~ de perlas** string of pearls **(b)** (*para animales*) collar **(c)** (*plumaje*) collar, ruff

colleras *fpl* (Chi) (*gemelos*) cuff links (*pl*)

colmado -da *adj* ‹*cucharada*› heaped; *ver tb* COLMAR

colmar [A1] *vt* **(a)** ‹*vaso/cesta*› to fill … to the brim **(b)** ‹*deseos/aspiraciones*› to fulfill* **(c)** ‹*paciencia*› to stretch … to the limit; **~ a algn DE algo** ‹*de atenciones*› to lavish sth on sb; ‹*de regalos*› to shower sb WITH sth

colmena *f* beehive

colmillo *m* (de persona) eyetooth, canine (tech); (de elefante, jabalí, morsa) tusk; (de perro, lobo) fang, canine

colmo *m*: el ∼ de la vagancia the height of laziness; para ∼ de desgracias to top *o* cap it all; sería el ∼ que ... it would be too much if ...; ¡esto es el ∼! this is the limit *o* the last straw!

colocación *f* (a) (empleo) job; buscar ∼ to look for a job (b) (acción) positioning, placing; (de losas, alfombra) laying

colocado -da *adj* **1** (en un trabajo): está muy bien ∼ he has a very good job; ya está ∼ he's found a job **2** (Esp) (a) (fam) (borracho) plastered (colloq) (b) (arg) (con drogas) stoned (colloq)

colocar [A2] *vt* **1** (a) (en lugar) to place, put; ‹losas/alfombra› to lay; ‹cuadro› to hang; ‹bomba› to plant (b) (Com, Fin) ‹acciones› to place; ‹dinero› to place, invest **2** ‹persona› (a) (en lugar) to put (b) (en trabajo) to get ... a job
■ **colocarse** *v pron* (a) (situarse, ponerse): se colocó a mi lado she stood/sat beside me (b) (en trabajo) to get a job

colocho -cha *m,f* (AmC) (a) (persona) curly-haired person (b) **colocho** *m* (rizo) curl

Colombia *f* Colombia

colombiano -na *adj/m,f* Colombian

colón *m* colon (*Costa Rican and Salvadoran unit of currency*)

Colón (Hist) Columbus; **Cristóbal** ∼ Christopher Columbus

colonia *f* **1** (a) (Hist, Pol, Zool, Biol) colony (b) (de viviendas) residential development; ∼ militar housing estate (*for service families*); ∼ penal (Per) penal colony (c) (Méx) (barrio) quarter, district (d) (campamento) camp; ∼ de vacaciones holiday camp **2** (perfume) (eau de) cologne

colonial *adj* colonial

colonialismo *m* colonialism

colonización *f* colonization

colonizador -dora *m,f* colonizer

colonizar [A4] *vt* to colonize

colono *m* (a) (inmigrante) colonist (b) (Agr) (en tierras baldías) settler; (en tierras arrendadas) tenant farmer

coloquial *adj* colloquial

coloquio *m* (a) (debate) discussion, talk; (simposio) (AmL) colloquium, symposium; conferencia ∼ talk (*followed by discussion*) (b) (Lit) dialogue

color *m* (a) color*; ¿de qué ∼ es? what color is it?; cambiar de ∼ to change color; un sombrero de un ∼ oscuro/claro a dark/light hat; las de ∼ amarillo the yellow ones; ilustraciones a todo ∼ full color illustrations; cintas de ∼es colored ribbons; fotos en ∼es *or* (Esp) en ∼ color photos; sin distinción de credo ni ∼ regardless of creed or color; una chica de ∼ (euf) a colored girl (dated); tomar ∼ ‹pollo› to brown; ‹cebolla frita/pastel› to turn golden-brown; ‹fruta› to ripen; ‹piel› to become tanned; ponerse ∼ de hormiga (AmL) to start looking pretty grim; subido de ∼ (chiste) risqué (b) **colores** *mpl* (lápices) colored* pencils (*pl*), crayons (*pl*)

colorado¹ -da *adj* (a) red; ponerse ∼ to blush, turn red, go red (BrE) (b) (Méx fam) ‹chiste› risqué

colorado² *m* red

colorante *m* coloring*; ❸ no contiene colorantes no artificial colors

colorear [A1] *vt* (Art) to color*; ∼ algo DE algo to color* sth IN sth

colorete *m* blusher, rouge

colorido *m* colors* (*pl*); un desfile de gran ∼ a very colorful parade

colosal *adj* ‹estatua/obra/fortuna› colossal; ‹ambiente/idea› (fam) great (colloq)

coloso *m* (estatua) colossus; (gigante) giant

columna *f* (a) (Arquit) column, pillar (b) (Anat) *tb* ∼ VERTEBRAL spine, backbone (c) (Impr, Period, Mil) column

columnista *mf* columnist

columpiar [A1] *vt* to push (*on a swing*)
■ **columpiarse** *v pron* (refl) to swing

columpio *m* (a) (Jueg, Ocio) swing (b) (sofá de jardín) couch hammock

colza *f* rape, colza; aceite de ∼ rapeseed oil

coma *m* (Med) coma; entrar en (estado de) ∼ to go into a coma
■ *f* (a) (Ling) comma; ▶ PUNTO 1B (b) (Mat) point

comadre *f*: godmother of one's child *or* mother of one's godchild

comadreja *f* (mustélido) weasel

comadrona *f* midwife

comal *m* (Méx) ceramic dish *or* metal hotplate for cooking TORTILLAS 2

comandante *mf* (a) (en el ejército) major; (en las fuerzas aéreas) squadron leader (AmE), squadron leader (BrE); ∼ en jefe commander in chief (b) (oficial al mando) commanding officer (c) (Aviac) captain

comando *m* **1** (a) (grupo de combate) commando group; ∼ terrorista terrorist cell *o* squad (b) (AmL) (mando militar) command **2** (Inf) command

comarca *f* region

comarcal *adj* regional

comba *f* (a) (de viga, cable) sag; (de pared) bulge (b) (Esp) (Jueg) jump rope (AmE), skipping rope (BrE); saltar la ∼ to jump rope (AmE), to skip (BrE)

combarse [A1] *v pron* ‹viga/cable› to sag; ‹pared› to bulge; ‹disco› to warp

combate *m* (a) (Mil) combat; zona de ∼ combat zone; avión de ∼ fighter plane (b) (en boxeo) fight

combatiente *mf* combatant (frml); antiguo *or* ex ∼ veteran

combatir [I1] *vi* ‹soldado/ejército› to fight
■ ∼ *vt* ‹enemigo/enfermedad/fuego› to fight, to combat (frml); ‹proyecto/propuesta› to fight; ‹frío› to fight off

combativo -va *adj* (a) (luchador) spirited, combative; espíritu ∼ fighting spirit (b) (agresivo) combative

combi® *f* (Méx, Per, RPl) VW® van, combi (van) (BrE)

combinación *f* (a) (de colores, sabores) combination (b) (de caja fuerte) combination (c) (Mat) permutation (d) (Indum) slip (e) (Transp) connection

combinado *m* (a) (bebida) cocktail (b) (Andes period) (Dep) team, line-up (journ)

combinar [A1] *vt* (a) (en general) to combine

(b) ⟨*colores*⟩ to put together; ⟨*ropa*⟩ to coordinate; ~ **el rojo con el violeta** to put red and purple together

■ ~ *vi* ⟨*colores/ropa*⟩ to go together; ~ **con** algo to go **with** sth

combustible *adj* combustible
■ *m* (Fís, Quím) combustible; (Transp) (carburante) fuel

combustión *f* combustion

comedero *m* (Agr) (para el ganado) feeding trough

comedia *f* **(a)** (Teatr) (obra) play; (cómica) comedy; ~ **musical** musical **(b)** (serie cómica) comedy series **(c)** (telenovela) soap (opera); (radionovela) radio serial

comediante -ta *m,f* **(a)** (Teatr) (*m*) actor; (*f*) actress **(b)** (farsante) fraud

comedido -da *adj* **(a)** (moderado) moderate, restrained **(b)** (AmL) (atento) obliging, well-meaning

comedor *m* **(a)** (sala — en casa, hotel) dining room; (— en colegio, universidad) dining hall, refectory; (— en fábrica, empresa) canteen, cafeteria **(b)** (muebles) dining-room furniture

comedura de coco *f* (Esp fam) **(a)** (lavado de cerebro): **la tele es una ~ de ~** TV just tries to brainwash you **(b)** (preocupación): **tener una ~ de ~** to worry nonstop

comentar [A1] *vt* **(a)** ⟨*suceso/película*⟩ to talk about, discuss; ⟨*obra/poema*⟩ to comment on **(b)** (mencionar) to mention; (hacer una observación) to remark on; **comentó que ...** he remarked that ... **(c)** (CS) (Rad, TV) ⟨*partido*⟩ to commentate on

comentario *m* ⟨1⟩ **(a)** (observación) comment; **hacer un ~** to make a comment; **fue un ~ de mal gusto** it was a tasteless remark; **sin ~(s)** no comment **(b)** (mención): **no hagas ningún ~ sobre esto** don't mention this **(c)** (análisis) commentary; **~ de texto** textual analysis ⟨2⟩ (Rad, TV) commentary

comentarista *mf* commentator

comenzar [A6] *vt* to begin, commence (fml)
■ ~ *vi* to begin; **al ~ el día** at the beginning of the day; **~ haciendo algo/por hacer algo** to begin **by** doing sth; **~ a hacer algo** to start doing *o* to do sth; **~on a disparar** they started firing *o* to fire; **~ por algo** to begin **with** sth

comer [E1] *vi* **(a)** (en general) to eat; **no tengo ganas de ~** I'm not hungry; **este niño no me come nada** (fam) this child won't eat anything (colloq); **dar(le) de ~ a algn** (en la boca) to spoonfeed sb; **darle de ~ al gato/al niño** to feed the cat/the kid; **salir a ~ (fuera)** to go out for a meal, to eat out; **¿qué hay de ~?** (a mediodía) what's for lunch?; (por la noche) what's for dinner *o* supper? **(b)** (esp Esp, Méx) (almorzar) to have lunch; **nos invitaron a ~** they asked us to lunch **(c)** (esp AmL) (cenar) to have dinner

■ ~ *vt* **(a)** ⟨*fruta/verdura/carne*⟩ to eat; **¿puedo ~ otro?** can I have another one?; **no tienen qué ~** they don't have anything to eat **(b)** (fam) (hacer desaparecer) ▶ **COMERSE** 3 **(c)** (en ajedrez, damas) to take

■ **comerse** *v pron* ⟨1⟩ **(a)** (al escribir) ⟨*acento/palabra*⟩ to leave off; ⟨*línea/párrafo*⟩ to miss out **(b)** (al hablar) ⟨*letra*⟩ to leave off; ⟨*palabra*⟩ to swallow

⟨2⟩ (enf) ⟨*comida*⟩ to eat; **cómetelo todo** eat it all up; **~se las uñas** to bite one's nails

⟨3⟩ (fam) (hacer desaparecer) **(a)** «*acido/óxido*» to eat away (at); «*polilla/ratón*» to eat away (at) **(b)** «*inflación/alquiler*» ⟨*sueldo/ahorros*⟩ to eat away at

comercial *adj* **(a)** ⟨*zona/operación/carta*⟩ business (*before n*); **una firma ~** a company; **el déficit ~** the trade deficit; ▶ **GALERÍA, CENTRO (b)** ⟨*película/arte*⟩ commercial
■ *m* **(a)** (anuncio) commercial, advert (BrE) **(b)** (CS) (Educ) business school

comercializar [A4] *vt* ⟨*producto*⟩ to market; ⟨*lugar/deporte*⟩ to commercialize
■ **comercializarse** *v pron* to become commercialized

comerciante *mf* **(a)** (dueño de tienda) storekeeper (AmE), shopkeeper (BrE); (negociante) dealer, trader **(b)** (mercenario) money-grubber (colloq)

comerciar [A1] *vi* to trade, do business; **~ en algo** to trade *o* deal in sth

comercio *m* **(a)** (actividad) trade; **el ~ de armas** the arms trade; **el mundo del ~** the world of commerce **(b)** (tiendas): **hoy cierra el ~** the stores (AmE) *o* (BrE) shops are closed today **(c)** (tienda) store (AmE), shop (BrE)

comestible *adj* edible

comestibles *mpl* food; **tienda de ~** grocery store (AmE), grocer's (shop) (BrE)

cometa *m* comet
■ *f* kite; **hacer volar una ~** *or* (RPl) **remontar una ~** to fly a kite

cometer [E1] *vt* ⟨*crimen/delito/pecado*⟩ to commit; ⟨*error/falta*⟩ to make

cometido *m* **(a)** (tarea, deber) task, mission **(b)** (Chi) (actuación) performance

comezón *f* (Med) itching, itch; **tenía ~ en la espalda** his back was itching

comic /'komik/, **cómic** *m* (*pl* **-mics**) (esp Esp) (tira ilustrada) comic strip; (revista) comic

comicios *mpl* elections (*pl*)

cómico -ca *adj* ⟨*actor/género/obra*⟩ comedy (*before n*); ⟨*situación/mueca*⟩ comical, funny
■ *m,f* (actor) comedy actor, comic actor; (humorista) comedian, comic

comida *f* **(a)** (en general) food; **~ para perros** dog food; **~ basura/rápida** junk/fast food **(b)** (ocasión en que se come) meal; **la ~ fuerte del día** the main meal of the day; **¿quién hace la ~ en tu casa?** who does the cooking in your house?; **todavía no he hecho la ~** I still haven't cooked the meal **(c)** (esp Esp, Méx) (almuerzo) lunch **(d)** (esp AmL) (cena) dinner, supper; (en algunas regiones del Reino Unido) tea

comidilla *f*: **ser la ~ del pueblo** to be the talk of the town

comience, comienza, etc ▶ **COMENZAR**

comienzo *m* beginning; **al ~** at first, in the beginning; **dar ~** to begin; **dar ~ a algo** «*persona*» to begin sth; «*ceremonia/acto*» to mark the beginning of sth; **el proyecto está en sus ~s** the project is still in its early stages

comillas *fpl* quotation marks (*pl*), inverted commas (BrE) (*pl*); **poner algo entre ~** to put sth in quotation marks *o* in inverted commas

comilona *f* (fam) feast (colloq); **nos dimos una ~** we had a blowout

comino m (Bot, Coc) cumin

comisaría f (edificio) tb ~ **de policía** (police) station

comisario m (a) (de policía) captain (AmE), superintendent (BrE) (b) (delegado) commissioner

comisión f (a) (delegación, organismo) committee; **C~ Europea** European Commission (b) (Com) commission; **trabajar a ~** to work on a commission basis

comisionado -da m,f commissioner

comisionista mf commission agent

comiso m (Col) packed lunch

comisura f (de los labios) corner

comité m (junta) committee; **~ de redacción** editorial board o committee

comitiva f (a) (séquito) procession; **~ fúnebre** funeral procession, cortège (b) (grupo) delegation

como prep (a) (en calidad de) as; **quiero hablarte ~ amigo** I want to speak to you as a friend (b) (con el nombre de) as; **se la conoce ~ 'flor de luz'** it's known as 'flor de luz' (c) (en comparaciones, contrastes) like; **uno ~ el tuyo** one like yours; **¡no hay nada ~ un buen coñac!** there's nothing like a good brandy!; **es ~ para echarse a llorar** it's enough to make you want to cry (d) (en locs) **así como** (frml) as well as; **como mucho/poco** at (the) most/at least; **como ser** (CS) such as, for example; **como si** (+ subj) as if, as though
■ conj (a) (de la manera que) as; **tal ~ había prometido** just as he had promised; **~ era de esperar** as was to be expected; **no me gustó ~ lo dijo** I didn't like the way she said it; **(tal y) ~ están las cosas** as things stand; **hazlo ~ quieras/~ mejor puedas** do it any way you like/as best as you can; **no voy — ~ quieras** I'm not going — please yourself (b) (puesto que) as, since; **~ era temprano, fui a dar una vuelta** as it was early, I went for a walk (c) (si) (+ subj) if; **~ te pille ... si** I catch you ...
■ adv (expresando aproximación) about; **está ~ a cincuenta kilómetros** it's about fifty kilometers away; **un sabor ~ a almendras** a kind of almondy taste

cómo adv (a) (de qué manera) how; **¿~ estás?** how are you?; **¿~ es tu novia?** what's your girlfriend like?; **¿~ es de grande?** how big is it?; **¿~ te llamas?** what's your name? (b) (por qué) why, how come (colloq); **¿~ no me lo dijiste antes?** why didn't you tell me before? (c) (al solicitar que se repita algo) sorry?, pardon?; **¿~ dijo?** sorry, what did you say? (d) (en exclamaciones) **¡~ llueve!** it's really raining!; **¡~ comes!** the amount you eat!; **¡~! ¿no te lo han dicho?** what! haven't they told you? (e) (en locs) **¿a cómo ...?: ¿a ~ están los tomates?** (fam) how much are the tomatoes?; **¿a ~ estamos hoy?** (AmL) what's the date today?; **¡cómo no!** of course!; **¿cómo que ...?: ¿~ que no fuiste tú?** what do you mean it wasn't you?; **aquí no está — ¿~ que no?** it isn't here — what do you mean it isn't there?

cómoda f chest of drawers

comodidad f ① (a) (confort) comfort; **la ~ del**

hogar the comfort of home (b) (conveniencia) convenience; **por ~** for the sake of convenience (c) (holgazanería): **no lo hace por ~** he doesn't do it because he's lazy ② **comodidades** fpl (aparatos, servicios) comforts (pl)

comodín m (a) (Jueg) (mono) joker; (otra carta) wild card (b) (Inf) wild card

cómodo -da adj (a) (confortable) comfortable, comfy (colloq); **ponte ~** make yourself comfortable (b) (conveniente, fácil) ⟨horario/sistema⟩ convenient; **esa es una actitud muy cómoda** that's a very easy attitude to take (c) (holgazán) lazy, idle

compact disc /kompakˈðis(k)/ m (pl **-discs**) (disco) compact disc, CD; (aparato) compact disc player, CD player

compacto -ta adj (a) ⟨tejido⟩ close; ⟨estructura/coche⟩ compact (b) ⟨muchedumbre⟩ dense

compadecer [E3] vt to feel sorry for
■ **compadecerse** v pron (apiadarse) **~se DE algn** to take pity ON sb; **~se de sí mismo** to feel sorry for oneself

compadre m (a) (padrino) godfather of one's child or father of one's godchild (b) (esp AmL fam) (amigo) buddy (AmE colloq), mate (BrE colloq)

compaginar [A1] vt ⟨actividades/soluciones⟩ to combine; **compagina el trabajo con los estudios** she combines work with studying
■ vi (a) (combinar) to go together (b) (llevarse bien) to get on; **~ CON algn** to get on well WITH sb

compañerismo m comradeship

compañero -ra m,f (a) (en actividad): **un ~ de equipo** a fellow team member; **fuimos ~s de universidad** we were at college together; **~ de clase/de trabajo** classmate/workmate (b) (pareja sentimental, en juegos) partner; (de guante, calcetín) (fam) pair (c) (Pol) comrade

compañía f ① (acompañamiento) company; **llegó en ~ de sus abogados** he arrived accompanied by his lawyers; **hacerle ~ a algn** to keep sb company; **andar en malas ~s** to keep bad company ② (empresa) company, firm; **~ de seguros** insurance company; **~ de teatro** theater* company; **Ⓢ Muñoz y Compañía** Muñoz and Co. ③ (Mil) company

comparable adj comparable; **~ A or CON** comparable TO o WITH

comparación f comparison; **hacer una ~** to make a comparison; **en ~ a or con el año pasado** compared to o with last year; **no tienen ni punto de ~** you cannot even begin to compare them

comparar [A1] vt to compare; **~ algo/a algn A or CON algo/algn** to compare sth/sb TO o WITH sth/sb; **no puede ni ~se al otro** it doesn't even compare at all to o with the other one
■ vi to make a comparison, to compare

comparecer [E3] vi to appear (in court)

compartimento, compartimiento m compartment

compartir [I1] vt to share; **~ algo CON algn** to share sth WITH sb

compás *m* **1** (Mús) **(a)** (ritmo) time, meter (esp AmE); **marcar/llevar el ~** to beat/keep time; **perder el ~** to get out of time; **se movía al ~ de la música** she moved in time to the music **(b)** (división) measure (AmE), bar (BrE); **~ de dos por cuatro** two-four time; **~ mayor/menor** four-four/ two-four time **2** (Mat, Náut) (instrumento) compass

compasión *f* pity, compassion; **lo hace por ~** he does it out of compassion

compasivo -va *adj* compassionate

compatible *adj* compatible

compatriota *m,f* *(m)* fellow countryman, compatriot; *(f)* fellow countrywoman, compatriot

compendio *m* (libro) textbook, coursebook; (resumen) summary, compendium (BrE)

compenetrarse [A1] *v pron* **~ CON algo** ⟨*con ideas/objetivos*⟩ to identify WITH sth; **~ CON algn** to have a good relationship WITH sb; (en trabajo) to work well WITH sb; **se han compenetrado a la perfección** they understand each other perfectly

compensación *f* (contrapartida) compensation; **en ~** by way of compensation; **en ~ por algo** in compensation for sth

compensar [A1] *vi*: **no compensa hacer un viaje tan largo** it's not worth making such a long journey; **no me compensa** it's not worth my while
■ **~** *vt* **1** **(a)** (contrarrestar) ⟨*pérdida/deficiencia*⟩ to compensate for, make up for; ⟨*efecto*⟩ to offset; **su entusiasmo compensa su falta de experiencia** his enthusiasm makes up for his lack of experience **(b)** ⟨*persona*⟩ **~ a algn POR algo** ⟨*por pérdidas/ retraso*⟩ to compensate sb FOR sth; **lo ~on con $2.000 por los daños** he was awarded $2,000 compensation in damages **2** ⟨*cheque*⟩ to clear
■ **compensarse** *v pron* «*fuerzas*» (recípr) to compensate each other, cancel each other out

competencia *f* **1** **(a)** (pugna) competition, rivalry; **hacerse la ~** to be rivals *o* in competition; **hacerle la ~ a algn** to compete with sb **(b)** (persona, entidad) competition; **la ~ se nos adelantó** the competition got in first **(c)** (AmL) (certamen) competition **2** **(a)** (de juez, tribunal) competence; **este asunto no es de mi ~** I have no authority *o* say in this matter **(b)** (habilidad, aptitud) competence, ability; **falta de ~** incompetence

competente *adj* competent

competición *f* (Esp) **(a)** (rivalidad): **espíritu de ~** competitive spirit **(b)** (certamen) competition

competidor -dora *m,f* competitor, rival

competir [I14] *vi* **(a)** (pugnar, luchar) to compete; **~ CON** *or* **CONTRA algn** **(POR algo)** to compete WITH *o* AGAINST sb (FOR sth) **(b)** (estar al mismo nivel): **los dos modelos compiten en calidad** the two models rival each other in quality

competitividad *f* competitiveness

competitivo -va *adj* competitive

compilar [A1] *vt* to compile

compinche *m,f* (compañero) (fam) buddy (AmE colloq), mate (BrE colloq); (cómplice en crimen) partner in crime

complacer [E3] *vt* to please
■ **complacerse** *v pron* **~se EN algo** to take pleasure IN sth

complaciente *adj* indulgent

complejidad *f* complexity

complejo¹ -ja *adj* complex

complejo² *m* **(a)** (de edificios) complex; **~ deportivo/industrial** sports/industrial complex **(b)** (Psic) complex; **tiene ~ porque es bajito** he's got a complex about being short; **~ de culpa** *or* **culpabilidad** guilt complex; **~ de inferioridad/ superioridad** inferiority/superiority complex

complementar [A1] *vt* to complement
■ **complementarse** *v pron* (recípr) to complement each other

complementario -ria *adj* **(a)** ⟨*personalidades/ángulos/colores*⟩ complementary **(b)** (adicional) additional

complemento *m* **(a)** (Ling, Mat) complement; **~ directo/indirecto** direct/indirect object **(b)** (acompañamiento) accompaniment **(c)** **complementos** *mpl* (Auto, Indum) accessories *(pl)*

completar [A1] *vt* **(a)** (terminar) to finish, complete **(b)** (AmL) ⟨*cuestionario/impreso*⟩ to complete, fill out *o* in

completo -ta *adj* **1** **(a)** (entero) complete; **las obras completas de Neruda** the complete works of Neruda **(b)** (total, absoluto) complete, total; **lo olvidé por ~** I completely forgot about it **(c)** (exhaustivo) ⟨*explicación*⟩ detailed; ⟨*obra/ diccionario*⟩ comprehensive; ⟨*tesis/ensayo*⟩ thorough **(d)** ⟨*deportista/actor*⟩ complete, very versatile **2** (lleno) ⟨*vagón/hotel*⟩ full; **⑤ completo** (en hostal) no vacancies; (en taquilla) sold out

complexión *f* constitution

complicación *f* **(a)** (contratiempo, dificultad) complication **(b)** (cualidad) complexity **(c)** (esp AmL) (implicación) involvement

complicado -da *adj* **(a)** ⟨*problema/sistema/ situación*⟩ complicated, complex **(b)** ⟨*carácter*⟩ complex; ⟨*persona*⟩ complicated **(c)** ⟨*diseño/ adorno*⟩ elaborate

complicar [A2] *vt* **(a)** ⟨*situación/problema/ asunto*⟩ to complicate, make … complicated **(b)** (implicar) ⟨*persona*⟩ to involve, get … involved
■ **complicarse** *v pron* **(a)** «*situación/problema/ asunto*» to get complicated; «*enfermedad*»: **se le complicó con un problema respiratorio** he developed respiratory complications; ▸ VIDA 2 **(b)** (implicarse) **~se EN algo** to get involved IN sth

cómplice *m,f* accomplice; **~ EN algo** accomplice TO sth

complicidad *f* complicity

compló, complot *m* (*pl* **-plots**) plot, conspiracy

compondré, compondría, etc ▸ COMPONER

componente *m* **(a)** (de sustancia) constituent (part), component (part); (de equipo, comisión) member **(b)** (Tec) component

componer [E22] *vt* **(a)** (constituir) ⟨*jurado/ equipo/plantilla*⟩ to make up; **el tren estaba compuesto por ocho vagones** the train was made up of eight cars **(b)** ⟨*sinfonía/canción/verso*⟩ to compose **(c)** (esp AmL) (arreglar) ⟨*reloj/radio/ zapatos*⟩ to repair **(d)** (AmL) ⟨*hueso*⟩ to set
■ **~** *vi* to compose
■ **componerse** *v pron* **1** (estar formado) **~se DE algo** to be made up OF sth, to consist OF sth; **un** ···▸

conjunto compuesto de falda y chaqueta an outfit consisting of a skirt and a jacket ② (esp AmL fam) «*persona*» to get better

comportamiento *m* (a) (conducta) behavior*; **mal ~** bad behavior (b) (Mec) performance

comportarse [A1] *v pron* to behave; **~ mal** to behave badly, misbehave

composición *f* composition

compositor -tora *m,f* composer

compostura *f* (a) (circunspección) composure; **guardar la ~** to maintain *o* keep one's composure (b) (CS) (arreglo) repair

compota *f* compote

compra *f* (a) (acción): **ir de ~s** to go shopping; **hacer las ~s** *or* (Esp) **la ~** to do the shopping; **~ por teléfono** teleshopping (b) (cosa comprada) buy, purchase (fml); **fue una buena ~** it was a good buy

comprador -dora *m,f* buyer, purchaser (fml)

comprar [A1] *vt* (a) ‹*casa/regalo/comida*› to buy, purchase (fml); **~le algo A algn** (a quien lo vende) to buy sth FROM sb; (a quien lo recibe) to buy sth FOR sb (b) (fam) (sobornar) to buy (colloq)

comprender [E1] *vt* ① (a) (entender) to understand, comprehend (fml); **nadie me comprende** nobody understands me (b) (darse cuenta) to realize, understand; **comprendió que lo habían engañado** he realized that he had been tricked ② (abarcar, contener) «*libro*» to cover; «*factura/precio*» to include
■ **~** *vi* (entender) to understand; **hacerse ~** to make oneself understood

comprensible *adj* understandable

comprensión *f* understanding; **capacidad de ~** comprehension; **~ auditiva** listening comprehension

comprensivo -va *adj* understanding

compresa *f* (a) (Med) compress (b) (Esp) *tb* **~ higiénica** sanitary napkin (AmE) *o* (BrE) towel

comprimido *m* (Farm) pill, tablet

comprimir [I1] *vt* to compress

comprobación *f* (a) (acción) verification, checking (b) (Col) (examen) test

comprobante *m* proof; **~ de pago** proof of payment

comprobar [A10] *vt* (a) (verificar) ‹*operación/resultado/funcionamiento*› to check (b) (demostrar) to prove (c) (darse cuenta) to realize (d) «*hecho*» (confirmar) to confirm

comprometedor -dora *adj* compromising

comprometer [E1] *vt* (a) (poner en un apuro) to compromise (b) ‹*vida/libertad*› to jeopardize, threaten (c) (obligar) **~ a algn A algo** to commit sb TO sth; **esto no me compromete a nada** this does not commit me to anything
■ **comprometerse** *v pron* (a) (dar su palabra) **~se A hacer algo** to promise to do sth; **me he comprometido para salir esta noche** I've arranged to go out tonight (b) «*autor/artista*» to commit oneself politically (c) «*novios*» to get engaged; **~se CON algn** to get engaged TO sb

comprometido -da *adj* [SER] ‹*asunto/situación*› awkward, delicate (b) [SER] ‹*cine/escritor*› politically committed (c) [ESTAR] (para casarse) engaged; **~ CON algn** engaged TO sb

compromiso *m* (a) (moral, financiero)

commitment; **adquirir un ~ con algn** to make a commitment to sb; **sin ~ alguno** without obligation; **los invitó por ~** she felt obliged to invite them; **yo con ellos no tengo ningún ~** I'm under no obligation to them (b) (cita) engagement; **~s sociales** social engagements *o* commitments (c) (de matrimonio) engagement (d) (acuerdo) agreement; (con concesiones recíprocas) compromise; **llegaron a un ~** they came to *o* reached an agreement/a compromise (e) (apuro) awkward situation; **me puso en un ~** he put me in an awkward position

compuesto -ta *adj* ‹*oración/número/flor*› compound (*before n*); *ver tb* COMPONER

compungido -da *adj* (arrepentido) remorseful, contrite; (triste) sad

compuse, compuso, etc ▶ COMPONER

computadora *f*, **computador** *m* (esp AmL) computer; **~ personal/de escritorio** *or* **mesa** personal/desktop computer

computerizar [A4] *vt* to computerize

comulgar [A3] *vi* (Relig) to receive *o* take communion

común *adj* (a) ‹*intereses/características*› common (*before n*); ‹*amigo*› mutual (b) (*en locs*) **de común acuerdo** by common consent; **de ~ acuerdo con algn** in agreement with sb; **en común** ‹*esfuerzo/regalo*› joint (*before n*); **no tenemos nada en ~** we have nothing in common (c) (corriente, frecuente) common; **es un nombre muy ~** it's a very common name; **un modelo fuera de lo ~** a very unusual model; **~ y corriente** (normal, nada especial) ordinary

comuna *f* (a) (de convivencia) commune (b) (CS, Per) (municipio) town, municipality (fml)

comunal *adj* (a) (de todos) communal (b) (CS, Per) (del municipio) town (*before n*), municipal

comunicación *f* (a) (enlace) link; **~ vía satélite** satellite link (b) (contacto) contact; **ponerse en ~ con algn** to get in contact *o* in touch with sb (c) (por teléfono): **se ha cortado la ~** I've/we've been cut off (d) (entendimiento, relación) communication *o* **comunicaciones** *fpl* (por carretera, teléfono, etc) communications (*pl*)

comunicado *m* communiqué; **~ de prensa** press release

comunicar [A2] *vt* ① (fml) (a) (informar) to inform; **~le algo A algn** to inform sb OF sth (b) (AmL) (por teléfono) ‹*persona*› to put ... through ② (transmitir) (a) ‹*entusiasmo/miedo*› to convey, communicate (b) ‹*conocimientos*› to impart, pass on; ‹*información*› to convey, communicate; ‹*idea*› to put across (c) ‹*fuerza/calor*› to transmit ③ ‹*habitaciones/ciudades*› to connect, link; **un barrio bien comunicado** an area easily accessible by road/well served by public transport; **~ algo CON algo** to connect sth WITH sth
■ **~** *vi* ① «*habitaciones*» to be connected ② (Esp) «*teléfono*» to be busy (AmE) *o* (BrE) engaged; **está comunicando** it's busy *o* engaged
■ **comunicarse** *v pron* ① (a) (recípr) (relacionarse) to communicate; **~ por señas** to communicate using sign language; **~se CON algn** to communicate WITH sb (b) (ponerse en contacto) **~se CON algn** to get in touch *o* in contact WITH sb ② «*habitaciones/ciudades/lagos*» (recípr) to be connected; **~se CON algo** to be connected TO sth

comunicativo -va *adj* communicative

comunidad *f* community; **C~** (Económica) Europea European (Economic) Community

comunión *f* (Relig) communion; **hacer la primera ~** to make one's first Holy Communion

comunismo *m* communism

comunista *adj/mf* communist

comunitario -ria *adj* (a) ‹bienes› communal; ‹espíritu/trabajo› community (*before n*) (b) (de la CE) EC (*before n*), Community (*before n*)

con *prep* (a) (en general) with; **vive ~ su novio** she lives with her boyfriend; **¡~ mucho gusto!** with pleasure!; **córtalo ~ la tijera** cut it with the scissor; **amaneció ~ fiebre** he woke up with a temperature; **hablar ~ algn** to talk to sb; **está casada ~ mi primo** she's married to my cousin; **portarse mal ~ algn** to behave badly toward(s) sb; **tener paciencia ~ algn** to be patient with sb; **pan ~ mantequilla** bread and butter; **¿vas a ir ~ ese vestido?** are you going in that dress? (b) (indicando una relación de causa): **¿cómo vamos a ir ~ esta lluvia?** how can we go in this rain?; **ella se lo ofreció, ~ lo que** *or* **lo cual me puso a mí en un aprieto** she offered it to him, which put me in an awkward position; **~ lo tarde que es, ya se debe haber ido** it's really late, he should have gone by now (c) **~ + INF: ~ llorar no se arregla nada** crying won't solve anything; **~ llamarlo por teléfono ya cumples** as long as you call him, that should do; **me contento ~ que apruebes** as long as you pass I'll be happy; ▶ TAL *adv* 2 (d) (AmL) (indicando el agente, destinatario): **me peino ~ Gerardo** Gerardo does my hair; **se estuvo quejando ~migo** she was complaining to me

cóncavo -va *adj* concave

concebir [I14] *vt* ⟨1⟩ (Biol) to conceive ⟨2⟩ ‹plan/idea› to conceive ⟨3⟩ (entender, imaginar): **no concibe la vida sin él** she can't conceive of life without him; **yo concibo la amistad de modo distinto** I have a different conception of friendship
■ **~** *vi* to conceive

conceder [E1] *vt* ⟨1⟩ (a) ‹premio/beca› to give, award; ‹descuento/préstamo› to give; ‹privilegio/favor/permiso› to grant; **nos concedió una entrevista** she agreed to give us an interview; **¿me podría ~ unos minutos?** could you spare me a few minutes? (b) ‹importancia/valor› to give ⟨2⟩ (admitir, reconocer) to admit, acknowledge

concejal -jala *m,f* town/city councilor*

concejero -ra *m,f* (AmL) town/city councilor*

concejo *m* council

concentración *f* (a) (Psic, Quim) concentration; **falta de ~** lack of concentration (b) (acumulación) concentration (c) (Pol) rally, mass meeting

concentrado¹ -da *adj* concentrated (*before n*)

concentrado² -da *m* (de verdura, tomate) concentrate; **~ de carne** meat extract

concentrar [A1] *vt* (a) ‹solución/caldo› to make ... more concentrated (b) ‹esfuerzos› to concentrate; ‹atención› to focus (c) (congregar) ‹multitud/tropas› to assemble, bring ... together
■ **concentrarse** *v pron* (a) (Psic) to concentrate; **~se EN algo** to concentrate ON sth (b) (reunirse) to assemble, gather together

concéntrico -ca *adj* concentric

concepción *f* (Biol) conception

concepto *m* (a) (idea): **el ~ de la libertad** the concept of freedom; **tener un ~ equivocado de algo/algn** to have a mistaken idea of sth/sb; **tengo (un) mal ~ de su trabajo** I have a very low opinion of her work; **bajo** *or* **por ningún ~** on no account (b) (Com, Fin): **en** *or* **por ~ de** in respect of

conceptuoso -sa *adj* (CS) (amable, elogioso): **una conceptuosa felicitación** warm congratulations

concerniente *adj* **~ A algo** concerning sth; **en lo ~ a este problema** as far as this problem is concerned

concernir [I12] *vi* (en *3ª pers*) to concern; **~ A algn** to concern sb; **por lo que a mí concierne** as far as I'm concerned; **en lo que concierne a su pedido** with regard to your order

concertar [A5] *vt* ‹cita/entrevista› to arrange, set up; ‹plan› to arrange; ‹precio› to agree (on)

concertista *mf* soloist; **~ de piano** concert pianist

concesión *f* (a) (de premios) awarding; (de préstamo) granting (b) (en una postura) concession; **hacer concesiones** to make concessions (c) (Com) dealership, concession, franchise

concesionario *m* dealer, concessionaire

concha *f* (a) (de moluscos) shell; **~ nácar** (Méx) *or* (Chi) **de perla** mother-of-pearl (b) (carey) tortoise shell (c) (Teatr) prompt box (d) (Ven) (cáscara — de verduras, fruta) skin; (— del queso) rind; (— del pan) crust; (— de nueces) shell

cónchale *interj* (Ven fam) good heavens!

concho *m* (Chi) (a) (del vino) lees (*pl*); (del café) dregs (*pl*) (b) (fam) (parte final) end, last bit (c) **conchos** *mpl* (restos) leftovers (*pl*)

conciencia *f* (a) (en moral) conscience; **tener la ~ tranquila** to have a clear *o* clean conscience; **tener la ~ sucia** to have a bad *o* guilty conscience; **me remuerde la ~** my conscience is pricking me; **no siente ningún cargo de ~** she feels no remorse; **hacer algo a ~** to do something conscientiously (b) (conocimiento) awareness; **tener/tomar ~ de algo** to be/become aware of sth

concienciar [A1] *vt* (Esp) ▶ CONCIENTIZAR

concientizar [A4] *vt* (esp AmL) ‹población/sociedad› to make ... aware; **~ a algn DE algo** to raise sb's consciousness ABOUT *o* awareness OF sth
■ **concientizarse** *v pron* (esp AmL) **~se DE algo** to become aware OF sth

concienzudo -da *adj* ‹trabajador/estudiante› conscientious; ‹estudio/repaso/análisis› thorough, painstaking

concierto *m* (Mús) (a) (obra) concerto (b) (función) concert, recital

conciliación *f* conciliation

conciliar [A1] *vt* ⟨1⟩ (a) ‹personas› to conciliate (b) ‹ideas› to reconcile; ‹actividades› to combine ⟨2⟩ ‹sueño›: **~ el sueño** to get to sleep

concilio *m* council

conciso -sa *adj* concise

conciudadano -na *m,f* fellow citizen

concluir [I20] *vt* (a) (fml) (terminar) ‹obras› to complete, finish; ‹trámite› to complete; ‹acuerdo/ ···⟩

tratado⟩ to conclude **(b)** (frml) (deducir) to conclude, come to the conclusion; ∼ algo DE algo to conclude sth FROM sth

■ ∼ *vi* (frml) **(a)** «*congreso/negociaciones*» to end, conclude; **el plazo concluyó el día 17** the time limit expired on the 17th **(b)** «*persona*» ∼ DE hacer algo to finish doing sth

conclusión *f* **(a)** (terminación) completion **(b)** (deducción) conclusion; **saqué la** ∼ **de que** ... I came to the conclusion that ...; **puedes sacar tus propias conclusiones** you can draw your own conclusions; **en** ∼ (en suma) in short; (en consecuencia) so

concluyente *adj* ⟨*razón/respuesta/prueba*⟩ conclusive; **fue** ∼ **al responder** he answered categorically

concordante *adj* concordant (frml), concurrent

concordar [A10] *vi* **(a)** (Ling) to agree; ∼ CON algo to agree WITH sth **(b)** «*cifras*» to tally; «*versiones*» to agree, coincide; ∼ CON algo ⟨*con documento/versión*⟩ to coincide WITH sth; **su comportamiento no concuerda con sus principios** his behavior is not in keeping with his principles

concordato *m* concordat

concretamente *adv* (específicamente) specifically; **vive en Wisconsin,** ∼ **en Madison** he lives in Wisconsin, in Madison to be precise

concretar [A1] *vt* **(a)** (concertar) ⟨*fecha/precio*⟩ to fix, set **(b)** (precisar, definir) to be specific about; **no concretamos nada** we didn't settle on anything definite

■ ∼ *vi*: **a ver si concretas** try and be more specific; **llámame para** ∼ give me a call to arrange the details

■ **concretarse** *v pron* to become a reality

concreto¹ -ta *adj* **(a)** (específico) ⟨*política/solución/acusación*⟩ concrete, specific; ⟨*motivo/ejemplo/pregunta*⟩ specific; ⟨*fecha/hora*⟩ definite; ⟨*caso*⟩ particular; ⟨*lugar*⟩ specific, particular; **en tu caso** ∼ in your particular case; **en** ∼ specifically; **en una zona en** ∼ in a particular o specific area; **no sé nada en** ∼ I don't know anything definite **(b)** (no abstracto) concrete

concreto² *m* (AmL) concrete; ∼ **armado** reinforced concrete

concubina *f* concubine

concuñado -da *m,f*: **mi** ∼ my wife's brother-in-law; **mi concuñada** my husband's sister-in-law

concurrido -da *adj* **(a)** [ESTAR] (con mucha gente) ⟨*discoteca/local*⟩ busy, crowded; ⟨*concierto/exposición*⟩ well-attended **(b)** [SER] (frecuentado) popular

concursante *mf* (en concurso) competitor, contestant; (para empleo) candidate

concursar [A1] *vi* (en concurso) to take part; (para puesto) to compete (*through interviews and competitive examinations*)

concurso *m* **(a)** (certamen) competition; **presentarse a un** ∼ to take part in a competition; ∼ **de belleza** beauty contest o (esp AmE) pageant;

∼ **hípico** show jumping competition **(b)** (para puestos, vacantes) *selection process involving interviews and competitive examinations* **(c)** (TV) (de preguntas y respuestas) quiz show; (de juegos y pruebas) game show **(d)** (licitación) tender; **sacar algo a** ∼ to put sth out to tender

condado *m* (división territorial) county

conde -desa *m,f* (en Gran Bretaña) (*m*) earl; (*f*) countess; (en otros países) (*m*) count; (*f*) countess

condecoración *f* decoration

condecorar [A1] *vt* to decorate

condena *f* **(a)** (Der) sentence; **está cumpliendo su** ∼ he is serving his sentence **(b)** (reprobación) ∼ DE or A algo condemnation OF sth

condenado -da *adj* **(a)** (destinado) ∼ A algo doomed TO sth **(b)** (obligado) ∼ A hacer algo condemned o forced to do sth **(c)** (fam) (expresando irritación) wretched (colloq), damn (colloq)

■ *m,f* **(a)** (Der) convicted person; **el** ∼ **a muerte** the condemned man **(b)** (Relig): **los** ∼**s** the damned; **como (un)** ∼ (fam) ⟨*correr*⟩ like hell (colloq); ⟨*work*⟩ like mad

condenar [A1] *vt* **(a)** (Der) to sentence, condemn; ∼ **a algn A algo** to sentence sb TO sth; ∼ **a algn a muerte** to sentence sb to death; **lo** ∼**on por robo** he was convicted of o found guilty of robbery **(b)** (reprobar, censurar) to condemn

condensación *f* condensation

condensar [A1] *vt* to condense

■ **condensarse** *v pron* to condense

condesa *f* countess

condescendiente *adj* **(a)** ⟨*actitud/respuesta*⟩ (con aires de superioridad) condescending **(b)** (comprensivo) understanding

condición *f* [1] (requisito) condition; **sin condiciones** unconditionally; **a** ∼ *or* **con la** ∼ **de que** on condition (that); **acepto con una** ∼ I accept on one condition; **me puso una** ∼ she made one condition

[2] **(a)** (calidad, situación): **en su** ∼ **de sacerdote** as a priest; **en su** ∼ **de jefe de la delegación** in his capacity as head of the delegation **(b)** (naturaleza) condition; **la** ∼ **humana** the human condition

[3] **condiciones** *fpl* **(a)** (estado, circunstancias) conditions (*pl*); **condiciones de trabajo/vida** working/living conditions; **estar en perfectas condiciones** «*coche/mueble*» to be in perfect condition; «*persona*» to be in good shape; **estar en condiciones de hacer algo** (de ayudar,exigir) to be in a position to do sth; (de correr, viajar, jugar) to be fit to do sth **(b)** (aptitudes) talent; **tener condiciones para algo** (para la música, el arte) to have a talent for sth; (para un trabajo) to be suited for sth

condicional *adj* conditional

condicionar [A1] *vt* **(a)** (determinar) to condition, determine **(b)** (supeditar) ∼ **algo A algo** to make sth conditional ON sth

condimentar [A1] *vt* to season

condimento *m*: **el comino es un** ∼ cumin is a

condiment; **le falta** ~ it needs some seasoning; **los ~s usados en la cocina india** the herbs and spices used in Indian cooking

condominio *m* **(a)** (propiedad) joint ownership, joint control **(b)** (Pol) (territorio) condominium **(c)** (AmL) (edificio) condominium (esp AmE), block of flats (BrE)

condón *m* condom

cóndor *m* condor

conducción *f* **(a)** (Elec, Fís) conduction **(b)** (esp Esp) (Auto) driving **(c)** (AmL) (de programa) presentation; **está a cargo de la ~ del programa** he's in charge of presenting the program **(d)** (Arg) (cúpula) leadership

conducir [16] *vi* **(a)** (llevar) ~ A algo «*camino/ sendero*» to lead TO sth; **esa actitud no conduce a nada** that attitude won't achieve anything *o* (colloq) won't get us anywhere; **a qué conduce eso?** what's the point of that? **(b)** (esp Esp) (Auto) to drive; ~ **por la izquierda** to drive on the left
■ ~ *vt* **(a)** (guiar, dirigir) to lead; ~ **a algn A algo** to lead sb TO sth; ~ **a algn ANTE algn** to take sb BEFORE sb **(b)** (AmL) ‹*programa*› to host, present; ‹*debate*› to chair **(c)** (esp Esp) ‹*vehículo*› to drive **(d)** ‹*electricidad/calor*› to conduct

conducta *f* behavior*, conduct; **mala ~** bad behavior, misconduct (frml)

conducto *m* **(a)** (Anat) duct, tube **(b)** (Tec) (canal, tubo) pipe, tube

conductor¹ -tora *adj* conductive; **materiales ~es de la electricidad** materials which conduct electricity
■ *m,f* **(a)** (de vehículo) driver **(b)** (AmL) (de programa) host

conductor² *m* (Elec, Fís) conductor

conduje, condujiste, etc ▶ CONDUCIR

conduzca, conduzcas, etc ▶ CONDUCIR

conectar [A1] *vt* **(a)** ‹*cables/aparatos*› to connect (up); ‹*luz/gas/teléfono*› to connect **(b)** (relacionar) ‹*hechos/sucesos*› to connect, link **(c)** (AmL) (poner en contacto) ~ **a algn CON algn** to put sb in touch *o* in contact WITH sb
■ ~ *vi* **(a)** (Rad, TV) ~ **CON algn/algo** to go over TO sb/sth **(b)** (empalmar) to connect, link up **(c)** (llevarse bien, entenderse) to get along *o* on well **(d)** (AmL) ~ **CON algo** «*vuelo/tren*» to connect WITH sth; **conectamos con el vuelo a Lima** we took a connecting flight to Lima

conecte *mf* **(a)** (Méx arg) (traficante) (drug) dealer **(b)** (AmC fam) (contacto) friend on the inside (colloq)

conector *m* connector

conejera *f* (madriguera) burrow; (para crianza) (rabbit) hutch

conejillo de Indias *m* guinea pig

conejo -ja *m,f* (Zool) rabbit

conexión *f* **(a)** (Elec) connection; ~ **a tierra** ground (AmE), earth (BrE); ~ **a la red** connection to the mains **(b)** (relación entre hechos, etc) connection **(c)** (Transp) connection; **perdí la ~ con Roma** I missed my connection to Rome **(d) conexiones** *fpl* (AmL) (amistades) connections (*pl*), contacts (*pl*)

confabularse [A1] *v pron* ~ (**CONTRA algn**) to plot *o* conspire (AGAINST sb)

confección *f* **(a)** (de trajes) tailoring; (de

vestidos) dressmaking; **industria de la ~** clothing industry; **de ~** ready-to-wear, off-the-peg **(b)** (de lista) drawing-up

confeccionar [A1] *vt* ‹*falda/vestido*› to make (up); ‹*artefactos*› to make; ‹*lista*› to draw up

confederación *f* confederation

conferencia *f* **(a)** (charla — formal) lecture; (— más informal) talk; **dar una ~ SOBRE algo** to give a lecture/talk ON sth **(b)** (reunión) conference; ~ **de prensa** press conference **(c)** (Esp) (Telec) long distance call; **poner una ~** to make *o* (AmE) place a long-distance call; ~ **a cobro revertido** collect call (AmE), reverse charge call (BrE)

conferenciante, (AmL) **conferencista** *mf* lecturer

conferir [I11] *vt* (frml *o* liter) **(a)** ‹*honor/ dignidad/responsabilidad*› to confer **(b)** ‹*prestigio*› to confer; ‹*encanto*› to lend; **la barba le confería un aire distinguido** the beard lent him an air of distinction

confesar [A5] *vt* **(a)** (Relig) ‹*pecado*› to confess; **el cura que la confiesa** the priest who hears her confession **(b)** ‹*sentimiento/ignorancia/delito*› to confess; ‹*error*› to admit
■ ~ *vi* **(a)** (Relig) to hear confession **(b)** (admitir culpabilidad) to confess, make a confession
■ **confesarse** *v pron* **(a)** (Relig) to go to confession; ~**se DE algo** to confess sth; ~**se CON algn** (Relig) to go to sb for confession; (hacer confidencias) to open up one's heart to sb **(b)** (declararse) (+ *compl*) to confess to being, admit to being

confesión *f* confession

confesionario *m* confessional

confesor *m* confessor

confeti *m* confetti

confiable *adj* (esp AmL) **(a)** ‹*estadísticas*› reliable **(b)** ‹*persona*› (cumplidor) reliable, dependable; (honesto) trustworthy

confiado -da *adj* **(a)** (SER) (crédulo) trusting **(b)** [ESTAR] (seguro): **está muy ~ en que lo van a llevar** he's convinced they're going to take him; **no estés tan ~** don't get over-confident

confianza *f* **(a)** (fe) confidence; **ella me inspira ~** I feel I can trust her; **lo considero digno de toda ~** he has my complete trust; ~ **EN algn/algo** confidence IN sb/sth; **tiene ~ en sí misma** she is self-confident; **había puesto toda mi ~ en él** I had put all my trust *o* faith in him; **de ~** ‹*persona*› trustworthy, reliable; ‹*producto*› reliable; ‹*puesto/ posición*› of trust; **nombró a alguien de su ~** he appointed someone he trusted **(b)** (intimidad): **tenemos mucha ~** we are close friends; **no les des tanta(s) ~(s)** don't let them be so familiar with you; **estamos en ~** we're among friends; **te lo digo en ~** I'm telling you in confidence; **tratar a algn con ~** to be friendly with sb

confianzudo -da *adj* (esp AmL fam) forward

confiar [A17] *vi* **(a)** (tener fe) ~ **EN algn/algo** to trust sb/sth; **no confío en ella** I don't trust her; **confiamos en su discreción** we rely *o* depend on your discretion **(b)** (estar seguro) ~ **EN algo** to be confident or sth; ~ **en la victoria** to be confident of victory; **confiamos en poder llevarlo a cabo** we are confident that we can do it; **confiemos en que venga** let's hope she comes ···⫸

■ ~ *vt* ~**le algo** A **algn** ⟨*secreto*⟩ to confide sth TO sb; ⟨*trabajo*/*responsabilidad*⟩ to entrust sb with sth

■ **confiarse** *v pron* **(a)** (hacerse ilusiones) to be overconfident; **no te confíes demasiado** don't get overconfident *o* too confident **(b)** (desahogarse, abrirse) ~**se** A **algn** to confide IN sb

confidencia *f* secret, confidence (*frml*); **hacer una ~ a algn** to tell sb a secret

confidencial *adj* confidential

confidente *mf* **(a)** (amigo) (*m*) confidant; (*f*) confidante **(b)** (de la policía) informer

configurar [A1] *vt* to configure

confinamiento *m* confinement

confinar [A1] *vt* ~ **a algn** A **algo** ⟨*a hospital*/*a calabozo*⟩ to put sb INTO sth; ⟨*a casa*⟩ to confine sb TO sth; ⟨*a isla*⟩ to banish sb TO sth; **la parálisis lo confinó a una silla de ruedas** he was confined to a wheelchair because of paralysis

confirmación *f* [1] (de noticia, de pasaje) confirmation [2] (Relig) confirmation; **hacer la ~** to be confirmed

confirmar [A1] *vt* to confirm; **la excepción que confirma la regla** the exception that proves the rule

confiscar [A2] *vt* **(a)** ⟨*contrabando*/*armas*⟩ to confiscate, seize **(b)** (para uso del estado) to requisition

confitería *f* **(a)** (tienda) patisserie, cake shop (*also selling sweets*) **(b)** (Bol, RPl) (salón de té) tearoom

confitura *f* preserve, jam

conflictivo -va *adj* **(a)** (problemático) ⟨*situación*⟩ difficult; ⟨*época*⟩ troubled; **una zona conflictiva** a trouble spot **(b)** (polémico) ⟨*tema*/*persona*⟩ controversial

conflicto *m* **(a)** (enfrentamiento) conflict; **estar en ~** to be in conflict; **entrar en ~ con algn**/**algo** to come into conflict with sb/sth **(b)** (Psic) conflict **(c)** (apuro) difficult situation

confluir [I20] *vi* **(a)** «*calles*/*ríos*» to converge, meet; «*corrientes*/*ideologías*» to come together, merge **(b)** «*grupos*/*personas*» to congregate, come together

conformar [A1] *vt* **(a)** (contentar) ⟨*persona*⟩ to satisfy **(b)** ⟨*cheque*⟩ to authorize payment of

■ **conformarse** *v pron* **(a)** (contentarse) ~**se** CON **algo** to be satisfied WITH sth; **no se conforma con nada** he's never satisfied; **tuvo que** ~**se con lo que tenía** he had to make do with what he had **(b)** (*esp AmL*) (resignarse): **no tienes más remedio que** ~**te** you'll just have to accept it *o* to resign yourself to it; **no se puede** ~ she can't get over it

conforme *adj* [ESTAR] **(a)** (satisfecho) satisfied, happy; ~ CON **algo**/**algn** satisfied *o* happy WITH sth/sb **(b)** (de acuerdo): **¡~!** agreed!, fine!; **estoy ~ en que se haga así** I agree that it should be done like that; ~ A **algo** in accordance WITH sth (*frml*) **(c)** (en regla) in order

■ *conj* as; ~ **se entra, está a mano izquierda** it's on the left as you go in

conformidad *f* **(a)** (aprobación) consent, approval **(b)** (*esp AmL*) (resignación) resignation

conformista *adj*/*mf* conformist

confort /kom'for/ *m* comfort; **apartamento todo ~** well-appointed *o* fully equipped apartment

confortable *adj* comfortable

confortar [A1] *vt* to reassure, comfort

confrontación *f* **(a)** (enfrentamiento) confrontation **(b)** (de textos) comparison

confrontar [A1] *vt* **(a)** ⟨*textos*/*versiones*⟩ to compare **(b)** ⟨*testigos*/*equipos*⟩ to bring ... face to face; ⟨*ejércitos*⟩ to bring ... into conflict **(c)** ⟨*dificultad*/*peligro*⟩ to confront, face

■ **confrontarse** *v pron* ~**se** CON **algo** to face up to sth

confundir [I1] *vt* **(a)** (por error) ⟨*fechas*/*datos*⟩ to confuse, get ... mixed *o* muddled up; ⟨*personas*⟩ to confuse, mix up; ~ **algo**/**a algn** CON **algo**/**algn** to mistake sth/sb FOR sth/sb; **me confundió con mi hermana** he mistook me for my sister **(b)** (desconcertar) to confuse **(c)** (turbar) to embarrass

■ **confundirse** *v pron* **(a)** (equivocarse) to make mistakes/a mistake; **me confundí de calle** I got the wrong street **(b)** (desconcertarse) to get confused

confusión *f* **(a)** (en general) confusion; **para que no haya confusiones** to avoid any confusion **(b)** (turbación) embarrassment, confusion

confuso -sa *adj* **(a)** ⟨*idea*/*texto*/*explicación*⟩ confused; ⟨*recuerdo*⟩ confused, hazy; ⟨*imagen*⟩ blurred, hazy; ⟨*información*⟩ confused **(b)** (turbado) embarrassed, confused

congelado -da *adj* **(a)** ⟨*alimentos*⟩ frozen **(b)** (Med) frostbitten; *ver tb* CONGELAR

congelador *m* (en el refrigerador) freezer compartment; (independiente) freezer, deepfreeze

congelar [A1] *vt* to freeze

■ **congelarse** *v pron* **(a)** «*agua*/*lago*» to freeze **(b)** (Med): **se le congeló el pie** he got frostbite in his foot **(c)** (tener mucho frío) to be freezing; **me estoy congelando** I'm freezing!

congeniar [A1] *vi* to get along (*esp AmE*), to get on (*esp BrE*); ~ CON **algn** to get on WITH sb

congénito -ta *adj* congenital

congestión *f* congestion

congestionado -da *adj* **(a)** (Med) congested **(b)** ⟨*cara*⟩ flushed **(c)** ⟨*calle*/*área*⟩ congested

congestionarse [A1] *v pron* **(a)** «*cara*» to become flushed **(b)** (Med) to become congested *o* blocked **(c)** «*calle*/*área*» to become congested

conglomerado *m* conglomeration

conglomerarse [A1] *v pron* to conglomerate

congratular [A1] *vt* (*frml*) to congratulate; ~ **a algn** POR **algo** to congratulate sb on sth

■ **congratularse** *v pron* ~**se** DE *or* POR **algo** (alegrarse) to be pleased ABOUT sth, congratulate oneself ON sth (*frml*)

congregar [A3] *vt* to bring together

■ **congregarse** *v pron* to assemble, gather

congreso *m* [1] (reunión) conference, congress [2] **Congreso** (Gob, Pol) **(a)** (asamblea) Parliament; (in US) Congress; **C~ de los Diputados** (Esp) Chamber of Deputies (*lower chamber of Spanish Parliament*) **(b)** (edificio) Parliament (*o* Congress *etc*) building

congrio *m* (Coc, Zool) conger eel

congruente *adj* (coherente) coherent; **ser ~ con algo** to be consistent with sth

cónico -ca *adj* ⟨*pieza*/*forma*⟩ conical, conic (tech); ⟨*sección*⟩ conic

conífera *f* conifer

conjetura f conjecture, speculation; **hacer ~s** to surmise, conjecture (frml); **son simples ~s** that's pure conjecture o speculation

conjugar [A3] vt (Ling) to conjugate

conjunción f (a) (Ling, Astron) conjunction (b) (unión) combination; **en ~ con** in conjunction with

conjuntivitis f conjunctivitis

conjunto¹ -ta adj ⟨esfuerzo/acción⟩ joint *before n*

conjunto² m (a) (de objetos, obras) collection; (de personas) group; **en su ~** (referido a — obra, exposición) as a whole; (— comité, partido) as a group; **~ residencial** residential complex (b) (Mús) tb **~ musical** (de música clásica) ensemble; (de música popular) pop group (c) (Indum) (de pulóver y chaqueta) twinset; (de prendas en general) outfit; **un ~ de chaqueta y pantalón** matching jacket and trousers; **hacer ~ con algo** to go well with sth (d) (Mat) set

conjura, conjuración f conspiracy, plot

conjurar [A1] vi to conspire, plot

conjuro m (fórmula mágica) spell

conllevar [A1] vt (a) (en 3ª pers) (comportar, implicar) to entail; **conlleva mucha responsabilidad** it entails a great deal of responsibility (b) ⟨desgracia/enfermedad⟩ to bear
■ **~** vi (Ven) **~ A algo** to lead TO sth

conmemoración f commemoration; **en ~ de** in commemoration of

conmemorar [A1] vt to commemorate

conmemorativo adj commemorative; **un monumento ~** a memorial

conmigo pron pers with me; **vino ~** she came with me; **estoy furiosa ~ misma** I'm furious with myself; **ha sido muy bueno ~** he's been very good to me

conmoción f (a) (Med) tb **~ cerebral** concussion (b) (trastorno, agitación): **la noticia produjo una ~ familiar** the news shocked the whole family (c) (Geol) shock

conmocionar [A1] vt to shake

conmovedor -dora adj moving, touching

conmover [E9] vt (a) (emocionar) to move (b) (inducir a piedad) to move ... to pity
■ **conmoverse** v pron (enternecerse, emocionarse) to be moved

conmutar [A1] vt (Der) ⟨pena⟩ to commute

connotación f connotation

cono m (figura) cone; **el C~ Sur** the Southern Cone (*Argentina, Chile, Paraguay and Uruguay*)

conocedor -dora m,f connoisseur, expert

conocer [E3] vt **1** ⟨persona⟩ to know; (por primera vez) to meet; ⟨ciudad/país⟩ to know; **¿conoces a Juan?** do you know/have you met Juan?; **te conocía de oídas** he'd heard of you; **lo conozco de nombre** I know the name; **~ a algn de vista** to know sb by sight; **es de todos conocido** he's well known; **quiero que conozcas a mi novio** I want you to meet my boyfriend; **nunca llegué a ~lo bien** I never really got to know him; **¿conoces Irlanda?** do you know Ireland? o have you been to Ireland?; **quiere ~ mundo** she wants to see the world; **me encantaría ~ tu país** I'd love to visit your country

2 (estar familiarizado con, dominar) ⟨tema/autor/obra⟩ to know, be familiar with; ⟨lengua⟩ to speak, know

3 (a) (saber de la existencia de) to know, know of; **conocían sus actividades** they knew o about his activities **(b)** dar a **~** (frml) ⟨noticia/resultado⟩ to announce; ⟨identidad/intenciones⟩ to reveal; **darse a ~** «*persona*» to make oneself known; **intentó no darse a ~** he tried to keep his identity a secret

4 (reconocer) to recognize*; **te conocí por la voz** I knew it was you by your voice

5 (impers) (notar): **se conoce que no están en casa** they don't seem to be in; **se conoce que ya llevaba algún tiempo enfermo** apparently he'd been ill for some time
■ **~** vi (saber) **~ DE algo** ⟨de tema/materia⟩ to know ABOUT sth
■ **conocerse** v pron **1** (recípr) (tener cierta relación con) to know each other; (por primera vez) to meet; (aprender cómo se es) to get to know each other

2 (refl) **(a)** (aprender cómo se es) to get to know oneself **(b)** (saber cómo se es) to know oneself

conocido -da adj **(a)** (famoso) ⟨actor/cantante⟩ famous, well-known **(b)** ⟨cara/voz⟩ familiar **(c)** ⟨hecho/nombre⟩ well-known; **más ~ como ...** better known as ...
■ m,f acquaintance

conocimiento m **(a)** (saber) knowledge; **tiene algunos ~s de inglés** he has some knowledge of English; **poner algo en ~ de algn** to inform sb of sth; **tener ~ de algo** to be aware of sth **(b)** (sentido) consciousness; **perder/recobrar el ~** to lose/regain consciousness; **estar sin ~** to be unconscious

conozca, conozco, etc ▶ CONOCER

conque conj so; **~ ya lo sabes** so now you know

conquista f **(a)** (de territorio, pueblo) conquest; **la C~** (Hist) the Spanish conquest (*of America*) **(b)** (logro) achievement **(c)** (fam) (amorosa) conquest

conquistador -dora adj ⟨ejército⟩ conquering
■ m,f **(a)** (Hist) conqueror; (en la conquista de América) conquistador **(b)** (fam) (en el amor) (m) lady-killer; (f) femme fatale

conquistar [A1] vt **(a)** ⟨territorio/pueblo/montaña⟩ to conquer; ⟨mercado⟩ to capture **(b)** ⟨victoria/título⟩ to win; ⟨éxito/fama⟩ to achieve **(c)** ⟨simpatía/respeto⟩ to win; ⟨persona/público⟩ to captivate; ⟨corazón⟩ to capture; **acabó conquistándola** he won her heart in the end

consagrado -da adj **(a)** (Relig) consecrated **(b)** ⟨artista⟩ acclaimed **(c)** ⟨costumbre/procedimiento⟩ established

consagrar [A1] vt **(a)** (Relig) to consecrate **(b)** **~ algo A algo/algn** ⟨monumento/edificio⟩ to dedicate sth TO sth/sb; ⟨vida/tiempo/esfuerzo⟩ to dedicate o devote sth TO sth/sb; ⟨programa/publicación⟩ to devote sth TO sth/sb **(c)** (establecer) ⟨artista/profesional⟩ to establish; **la película que la consagró como actriz** the movie that established her as an actress
■ **consagrarse** v pron (refl) (dedicarse) **~se A algo/algn** to devote oneself TO sth/sb

consciencia f ▶ CONCIENCIA B

consciente adj **(a)** [ESTAR] (Med) conscious ⋯❖

conscripto ···❖ consistencia

(c) (de problema, hecho) **ser** or (Chi, Méx) **estar** ~ **DE algo** to be aware o conscious OF sth **(c)** [SER] (sensato) sensible; (responsable) responsible

conscripto m (AmL) conscript

consecuencia f consequence; **atenerse a las** ~**s** to accept the consequences; **esto trajo como** ~ **su renuncia** this resulted in his resignation; **a** ~ **de** as a result of; **en** ~ (fml) (por consiguiente) consequently, as a result; (actuar/obrar) accordingly

consecuente adj consistent; **hay que ser** ~ you have to be consistent; **es** ~ **con sus ideas** she acts according to her beliefs (o principles etc)

consecutivo -va adj consecutive

conseguir [I30] vt (objetivo/fin/resultado) to achieve, obtain; (entrada/permiso/empleo) to get; (medalla/título) to win; **si lo intentas, al final lo** ~**ás** if you try, you'll succeed in the end; **la película consiguió un gran éxito** the film was a great success; ~ **hacer algo** to manage to do sth; **no consigo entenderlo** I can't work it out; **conseguí que me lo prestara** I got him to lend it to me

consejero -ra m,f **(a)** (asesor) adviser **(b)** (Adm, Com) director **(c)** (en embajada) counselor*

consejo m **(a)** (recomendación) piece of advice; **te voy a dar un** ~ let me give you some advice o a piece of advice; **me pidió** ~ he asked me for advice o asked (for) my advice; **sus** ~**s son siempre acertados** she always gives good advice **(b)** (organismo) council, board; ~ **de administración** board of directors; ~ **de guerra** court-martial; ~ **de ministros** (grupo) cabinet; (reunión) cabinet meeting; **C**~ **de Europa** Council of Europe; **C**~ **de Seguridad** Security Council

consenso m consensus; **por** ~ by general consent o assent

consentido -da adj spoiled
■ m,f: **es un** ~ he's spoiled

consentimiento m (autorización) consent

consentir [I11] vt **(a)** (permitir, tolerar) to allow; **¡no te consiento que me hables así!** I won't have you speak to me like that; **se lo consiente todo** he's allowed to do whatever he likes **(b)** (mimar) (niño) to spoil
■ ~ vi: ~ **EN algo** to consent o agree TO sth

conserje mf **(a)** (de establecimiento público) superintendent (AmE), caretaker (BrE) **(b)** (de colegio) custodian (AmE), caretaker (BrE) **(c)** (de hotel) receptionist

conserjería f reception

conserva f: **latas de** ~ cans o (BrE) tins of food; **piña en** ~ canned o (BrE) tinned pineapple; ~**s** canned o (BrE) tinned food

conservación f **(a)** (de alimentos) preserving **(b)** (Ecol) conservation **(c)** (de monumentos, obras de arte) preservation

conservador -dora adj conservative
■ m,f **(a)** (Pol) conservative **(b)** (de museo) curator

conservante m preservative

conservar [A1] vt **(a)** (mantener, preservar) (alimentos) to preserve; (sabor/calor) to retain; (tradiciones/costumbres) to preserve; (amigo/cargo) to keep; (naturaleza) to conserve; **conservo buenos recuerdos suyos** I have good memories of him; ~ **la calma** to keep calm; ~ **la línea** to keep one's figure **(b)** (guardar) (cartas/fotografías) to keep
■ **conservarse** v pron **(a)** «alimentos» to keep **(b)** (perdurar) «restos/tradiciones» to survive **(c)** «persona» (+ compl) to keep; **se conserva joven** she keeps herself young; **está muy bien conservada** she's very well preserved

conservatorio m conservatory, conservatoire

considerable adj considerable

consideración f consideration; **tomar algo en** ~ to take sth into consideration o account; **por** ~ **a su familia** out of consideration for his family; **en** ~ **a sus méritos** in recognition of her merits; **la trataron sin ninguna** ~ they treated her most inconsiderately; **¡qué falta de** ~! how thoughtless!; **de** ~ serious

considerado -da adj [SER] considerate; **ser** ~ **CON algn** to be considerate TOWARD(s) sb

considerar [A1] vt (asunto/posibilidad/oferta) to consider; (ventajas/consecuencias) to weigh up, consider; **considerando que ha estado enfermo** considering (that) he's been ill; **tenemos que** ~ **que ...** we must take into account that ...; **eso se considera de mala educación** that's considered bad manners; **está muy bien considerado** he is very highly regarded
■ **considerarse** v pron «persona» (juzgarse) to consider oneself; **se considera afortunado** he considers himself (to be) lucky

consiga, consigas, etc ▶ CONSEGUIR

consigna f **(a)** (eslogan) slogan **(b)** (para equipaje) baggage room (AmE), left-luggage (office) (BrE); ~ **automática** (coin-operated o automatic) luggage locker (AmE) o (BrE) left-luggage locker

consignar [A1] vt **1** (depositar) **(a)** (mercancías) to consign **(b)** (equipaje) to check (AmE), to place o deposit ... in left luggage (BrE) **(c)** (Der) to pay ... into court **(d)** (Col) (dinero/cheques) to deposit **2** (fml) (hecho/dato) to record **3** (fml) (enviar) (paquete/carga) to dispatch **4** (fml) (asignar) to allocate **5** (Méx) (Der) (presunto delincuente) to bring ... before the authorities

consigo pron pers (con él) with him; (con ella) with her; (con uno) with you o one; (con usted, ustedes) with you; **no está satisfecho** ~ **mismo** he's not happy with himself; **traigan** ~ **todo lo necesario** bring everything you'll need with you; **hablaba** ~ **misma** she was talking to herself

consigo, consigues, etc ▶ CONSEGUIR

consiguiente adj resulting (before n), consequent (before n) (fml); **por** ~ consequently

consistencia f **(a)** (de mezcla, masa) consistency; **tomar** ~ to thicken **(b)** (de teoría, argumento) soundness; **un argumento sin** ~ a flimsy argument

---

AmC América Central	Arg Argentina	Cu Cuba	Per Perú
AmL América Latina	Bol Bolivia	Ec Ecuador	RPI Río de la Plata
AmS América del Sur	Chi Chile	Esp España	Ur Uruguay
Andes Región andina	CS Cono Sur	Méx México	Ven Venezuela

consistente adj (a) ‹salsa/líquido› thick; ‹masa› solid (b) ‹argumentación/tesis› sound (c) (Andes, Méx) ‹conducta› consistent; ‹persona› ▶ CONSECUENTE

consistir [I1] vi (a) (expresando composición) ~ EN algo to consist OF sth; **el mobiliario consistía en una cama y una silla** the furniture consisted of a bed and a chair (b) (expresando naturaleza): **¿en qué consiste el juego?** what does the game involve?; ~ EN hacer algo to involve o entail doing sth (c) (radicar) ~ EN algo to lie in sth; **en eso consiste su gracia** that is where its charm lies

consola f (a) (mueble) console table (b) (panel de controles) console

consolar [A10] vt to console, comfort; **si en algo te consuela** if it's any consolation to you
■ **consolarse** v pron (refl): **me consuelo pensando que ...** I take comfort o I find some consolation in the thought that ...

consolidar [A1] vt (a) ‹situación/posición/acuerdo› to consolidate; ‹amistad› to strengthen (b) ‹deuda/préstamo› to consolidate
■ **consolidarse** v pron «situación/acuerdo» to be consolidated; «amistad/relación» to grow stronger

consomé m consommé

consonante f consonant

conspiración f conspiracy, plot

conspirador -dora m,f conspirator

conspirar [A1] vi to conspire, plot

constancia f [1] (perseverancia) perseverance [2] (prueba) proof; **dejar ~ DE algo** (en registro, acta) to record sth (in writing); (verbalmente) to state sth; (atestiguar) to prove sth

constante adj (a) (continuo) constant (b) (perseverante) ‹persona› persevering
■ f (a) (Mat) constant (b) (característica) constant feature (c) **constantes** fpl (Med) tb ~s vitales vital signs (pl)

constar [A1] vi (a) (figurar) ~ EN algo ‹en acta/documento› to be stated o recorded IN sth; ‹en archivo/catálogo› to be listed IN sth; ‹en libro/texto› to appear IN sth (b) (quedar claro): **que conste que yo no fui** it certainly wasn't me; **yo nunca dije eso, que conste** just to set the record straight, I never actually said that; **eso me consta** I am sure of that (c) **hacer ~ algo** (manifestar) to state sth; (por escrito) to register sth, to put sth on record (d) (estar compuesto de) ~ DE algo to consist of sth

constelación f constellation

consternación f consternation, dismay

consternar [A1] vt to fill ... with dismay

constipación f (esp AmL) constipation

constipado¹ -da adj (a) (resfriado) **está muy ~** he has a bad cold (b) (AmL) (estreñido) constipated

constipado² m cold

constiparse [A1] v pron to catch a cold

constitución f (a) (establecimiento) setting-up (b) (Pol) (de país) constitution (c) (complexión) constitution; **un hombre de ~ fuerte** a man with a strong constitution

constitucional adj constitutional

constituir [I20] vt (frml) (a) (componer, formar) to

make up, constitute (b) (ser, representar) to represent, constitute (frml); **esta acción no constituye delito** this action does not constitute a crime (c) (crear) ‹comisión/compañía› to set up, establish

construcción f (a) (acción) construction, building; **en ~** under construction; **obrero de la ~** building o construction worker (b) (edificio, estructura) construction (c) (Ling) construction

constructivo -va adj constructive

constructor -tora m,f (a) (Const) builder, building contractor (b) **constructora** f construction company, building firm

construir [I20] vt (a) ‹edificio/barco/sociedad› to build (b) ‹figura/frases/oraciones› to construct

construya, etc ▶ CONSTRUIR

consuegro -gra m,f (m) father-in-law of one's son or daughter; (f) mother-in-law of one's son or daughter

consuelo m consolation, comfort

cónsul mf consul

consulado m (oficina) consulate; (cargo) consulship

consulta f (a) (pregunta, averiguación): **¿te puedo hacer una ~?** can I ask you something?; **de ~** ‹biblioteca/libro› reference (before n) (b) (Med) (entrevista) consultation; (consultorio) office (AmE), practice (AmE), surgery (BrE); **¿a qué horas tiene ~s el Dr. Sosa?** what are Dr Sosa's office hours (AmE) o (BrE) surgery times?; ~ **a domicilio** home o house visit

consultar [A1] vt ‹persona/obra› to consult; ‹dato/duda› to look up; ~ **algo CON algn** to consult sb ABOUT sth
■ ~ vi: ~ **CON algn** to consult sb

consultor -tora m,f consultant

consultorio m (a) (de médico, dentista) office (AmE), practice (AmE), surgery (BrE); (de abogado) office (b) (consultoría) consultancy; ~ **sentimental** (en revista) problem page; (en la radio) phone-in (about personal problems)

consumición f (esp Esp) (bebida) drink; ~ **mínima** minimum charge

consumido -da adj [ESTAR] (por enfermedad, hambre) emaciated; ver tb CONSUMIR

consumidor -dora m,f consumer

consumir [I1] vt (a) (frml) ‹comida/bebida› to eat/drink, consume (frml) (b) ‹gasolina/energía/producto› to consume, use; ‹tiempo› to take up (c) ‹salud› to ruin (d) (destruir) «fuego/llamas» to consume; «envidia/celos»: **la envidia la consumía** she was consumed by o with envy
■ **consumirse** v pron (a) «enfermo/anciano» to waste away; **se consumía de pena** she was being consumed by grief (b) «vela/cigarrillo» to burn down (c) «líquido» to reduce

consumismo m consumerism

consumo m consumption; ~ **mínimo** (AmL) minimum charge; **el ~ de drogas** drug-taking

contabilidad f (a) (ciencia) accounting (b) (profesión) accountancy (c) (cuentas) accounts (pl), books (pl); **lleva la ~** she does the accounts o the books

contabilizar [A4] vt (en contabilidad) to enter; (contar) to count

contable mf (Esp) accountant

contactar [A1] *vi* ~ CON algn to contact sb, get in touch WITH sb
■ ~ *vt* to contact
contacto *m* (a) (entre dos cuerpos) contact; **entrar en** ~ to come into contact; **hacer** ~ to make contact (b) (comunicación) contact; **estar/ponerse en** ~ **con algn** to be/get in touch *o* contact with sb (c) (entrevista, reunión) encounter (d) (persona, conocido) contact (e) (Auto) ignition (f) (Méx) (Elec) socket, power point
contado¹ -da *adj* few; **en contadas ocasiones** on (a) very few occasions; **salimos con los minutos** ~s we left with only a few minutes to spare
contado² *m* (a) **al** ~ *or* (Col) **de** ~ ⟨pago/precio⟩ cash (before n); ⟨pagar⟩ (in) cash; **lo compré al** ~ I paid cash for it, I paid for it in cash (b) (Col) (cuota, plazo) installment*
contador¹ *m* (a) (de luz, de gas) meter; (taxímetro) meter, taximeter (b) (AmL) (ábaco) abacus
contador² -dora *m,f* (AmL) accountant; ~ **público** (AmL) certified public (AmE) *o* (BrE) chartered accountant
contagiar [A1] *vt* ⟨enfermedad⟩ to pass on, transmit (tech); ⟨persona⟩ to infect; **me contagió la gripe** she passed her flu on to me; **no te acerques que te voy a** ~ don't come near or I'll give it to you
■ **contagiarse** *v pron* (a) «persona/animal» to become infected; **se ha contagiado de mí** she has caught it from me (b) «enfermedad» to be transmitted; «manía/miedo» to spread; **se contagia con facilidad** it is very contagious; **se contagió de la enfermedad** she caught the disease
contagioso -sa *adj* (a) (por contacto — directo) contagious; (— indirecto) infectious (b) ⟨risa/alegría⟩ infectious
contaminación *f* (del mar, aire) pollution; (de agua potable, comida) contamination; (por radioactividad) contamination; ~ **acústica** noise pollution
contaminante *m* pollutant, contaminant
contaminar [A1] *vt* ⟨mar/atmósfera⟩ to pollute; ⟨agua potable/comida⟩ to contaminate; (por radioactividad) to contaminate
contar [A10] *vt* (a) ⟨dinero/votos/días⟩ to count; **eran 6 sin** ~ **al conductor** there were 6 of them not counting the driver; **y eso sin** ~ **las horas extras** and that's without including overtime; **lo cuento entre mis amigos** I consider him (to be) one of my friends
[2] ⟨cuento/chiste/secreto⟩ to tell; **no se lo cuentes a nadie** don't tell anyone; **es muy largo de** ~ it's a long story; **¿qué cuentas (de nuevo)?** (fam) how're things? (colloq)
■ ~ *vi* [1] (en general) to count; ~ **con los dedos** to count on one's fingers; **¿este trabajo cuenta para la nota final?** does this piece of work count toward(s) the final grade?; **ella no cuenta para nada** what she says (o thinks etc) doesn't count for anything
[2] **contar con** (a) ⟨persona/ayuda/discreción⟩ to count on, rely on; **cuento contigo para la fiesta** I'm counting o relying on you being at the party; **sin** ~ **con que ...** without taking into account that ... (b) (prever) to expect; **no contaba con que hiciera tan mal tiempo** I wasn't expecting the

weather to be so bad (c) (frml) (tener) to have; **cuenta con 10 años de experiencia** she has 10 years of experience
■ **contarse** *v pron* (a) (frml) (estar incluido): **me cuento entre sus partidarios** I count myself as one of their supporters; **su novela se cuenta entre las mejores** his novel is among the best (b) **¿qué te cuentas?** how's it going? (colloq)
contemplación *f* [1] (observación) contemplation [2] **contemplaciones** *fpl* (miramientos): **tienes demasiadas contemplaciones con él** you're too soft on him; **lo echaron sin contemplaciones** they threw him out without ceremony
contemplar [A1] *vt* (a) ⟨paisaje/cuadro⟩ to gaze at, contemplate (b) ⟨posibilidad/idea⟩ to consider, contemplate
contemporáneo -nea *adj* contemporary; **ser** ~ DE algn to be a contemporary OF sb, be contemporary WITH sb
■ *m,f* contemporary
contenedor *m* container; (para basuras) bin, container; (para escombros) Dumpster® (AmE), skip (BrE); ~ **de recogida de vidrio** bottle bank
contener [E27] *vt* (a) «recipiente/producto/libro» to contain (b) (parar, controlar) ⟨infección/epidemia⟩ to contain; ⟨tendencia⟩ to curb; ⟨respiración⟩ to hold; ⟨risa/lágrimas⟩ to contain (frml), to hold back; ⟨invasión/revuelta⟩ to contain
■ **contenerse** *v pron* (refl) to contain oneself; **no se pudo** ~ **más** he could contain himself no longer
contenido *m* (de recipiente, producto, mezcla) contents; (de libro, carta) content
contentar [A1] *vt* to please; **¡qué difícil de** ~ **eres!** you're so hard to please!
■ **contentarse** *v pron* ~**se** CON algo to be satisfied WITH sth; **se contenta con muy poco** he's easy to please
contento -ta *adj* [ESTAR] (a) (feliz, alegre) happy; **se puso muy** ~ **al oír que venías** he was very happy to hear you were coming; ~ CON algo/algn happy WITH sth/sb (b) (satisfecho) pleased; **estamos** ~**s con la nueva secretaria** we're pleased with the new secretary; **no** ~ **con que le prestara el coche ...** not content *o* satisfied with me lending him the car ...
conteo *m* (Andes, Ven) count
contestación *f* (respuesta) answer, reply
contestador -dora *adj* (CS fam) ▶ CONTESTÓN
contestador automático *m* answering machine
contestar [A1] *vt* ⟨pregunta/teléfono⟩ to answer; ⟨carta⟩ to answer, reply to; **me contestó que no** he said no
■ ~ *vi* (a) (a pregunta, al teléfono) to answer; (a carta, invitación) to answer, reply; **no contesta nadie** (Telec) there's no answer (b) (insolentarse) to answer back
contestón -tona *adj* (fam): **es muy** ~ he's always answering back
contexto *m* context
contigo *pron pers* with you; **¿puedo ir** ~**?** can I go with you?; **en paz** ~ **misma** at peace with yourself; **ha sido muy amable** ~ she's been very kind to you
contiguo -gua *adj* adjoining

continental *adj* continental

continente *m* (Geog) continent

continuación *f* **(a)** (acción) continuation **(b)** (de calle) continuation **(c)** (de novela) sequel; (de serie) next part *o* episode **(d) a continuación** next, then; **a ∼ de** after, following

continuamente *adv* (con frecuencia, repetidamente) continually, constantly; (sin interrupción) continuously

continuar [A18] *vt* to continue
■ ∼ *vi* «*guerra/espectáculo/vida*» to continue; **si las cosas continúan así** if things go on *o* continue like this; **❺ continuará** to be continued; **la película continúa en cartelera** the movie is still showing; **∼ CON algo** to continue WITH sth; **continuó diciendo que ...** she went on to say that ...

continuidad *f* continuity

continuo -nua *adj* **(a)** (sin interrupción) «*dolor*» constant; «*movimiento/sonido*» continuous, constant; «*lucha*» continual **(b)** (frecuente) «*llamadas/viajes*» continual, constant

contonearse [A1] *v pron* to swing one's hips

contorno *m* **(a)** (forma) outline **(b)** (de árbol, columna) girth; **medir el ∼ de cintura** to take the waist measurement **(c)** (de ciudad) surrounding area

contorsión *f* contortion; **hacer contorsiones** to contort one's body

contorsionista *mf* contortionist

contra *prep* against; **lo puso ∼ la pared** he put it against the wall; **nos estrellamos ∼ un árbol** we crashed into a tree; **dos ∼ uno** two against one; **yo estoy en ∼** I'm against it; **40 votos en ∼** 40 votes against; **en ∼ de** (opuesto a) against; (contrariamente a) contrary to
■ *f* **(a)** (esp AmL fam) (dificultad) snag; **llevarle la ∼ a algn** to contradict sb **(b)** (Col) (antídoto) antidote **(c)** (Pol, Hist) (grupo): **la ∼ the Contras** (*pl*)
■ *mf* (individuo) Contra rebel
■ *m* ▶ PRO

contraatacar [A2] *vi* to counterattack

contraataque *m* counterattack

contrabajo *m* (instrumento) double bass; (cantante) basso profundo
■ *mf* double-bass player

contrabandista *mf* smuggler

contrabando *m* **(a)** (actividad) smuggling; **∼ de armas** gunrunning; **pasaba relojes de ∼** he smuggled watches **(b)** (mercancías) smuggled goods (*pl*), contraband

contracción *f* contraction

contracorriente *f* crosscurrent; **ir a ∼** «*barco*» to go against the current; «*nadador*» to swim against the current; «*diseñador/escritor*» to go *o* swim against the tide

contradecir [I24] *vt* «*persona/argumento*» to contradict
■ **contradecirse** *v pron* **(a)** «*persona*» to contradict oneself **(b)** (recípr) «*afirmaciones/órdenes*» to contradict each other, be contradictory; **∼se CON algo** to conflict WITH sth, contradict sth

contradicción *f* contradiction; **eso está en ∼ con lo que predica** that is a contradiction of what he advocates

contradictorio -ria *adj* contradictory

contraer [E23] *vt* **1** (frml) **(a)** «*enfermedad*» to contract (frml), to catch **(b)** «*obligación/deudas*» to contract (frml); «*compromiso*» to make; **∼ matrimonio con algn** to marry sb **2 (a)** «*músculo*» to contract, tighten; «*facciones/cara*» to contort **(b)** «*metal/material*» to cause ... to contract
■ **contraerse** *v pron* to contract

contrafuerte *m* (Arquit) buttress

contraincendios *adj inv* fire-prevention (*before n*)

contraindicado -da *adj* «*remedio/preparado*» contraindicated (tech)

contralto *m,f* (*f*) (en coro) alto; (solista) contralto; (*m*) countertenor

contraluz *m or f* back light; **a ∼** against the light

contramano: el coche venía a ∼ (en calle de dirección única) the car was coming the wrong way down the street; (por el lado contrario) the car was on the wrong side of the road

contraofensiva *f* counteroffensive

contraparte *f* (Andes) opposing party

contrapartida *f* **(a)** (compensación) compensation; (contraste) contrast; **como ∼** in contrast **(b)** (Com) balancing entry

contrapelo: cepillar a ∼ «*tela*» to brush ... against the nap; «*pelo*» to brush ... the wrong way

contrapesar [A1] *vt* to counterbalance

contrapeso *m* (del ascensor) counterweight; (de equilibrista) balancing pole; **siéntate al otro lado para hacer ∼** sit on the other side to balance it

contraportada *f* (de libro, revista) back cover; (de periódico) back page

contraposición *f* comparison; **en ∼ a** *or* **con algo** in comparison to *o* with sth

contraproducente *adj* counterproductive

contrapunto *m* counterpoint

contrariado -da *adj* (disgustado) upset; (enojado) annoyed

contrariar [A17] *vt* (disgustar) to upset; (enojar) to annoy

contrariedad *f* **(a)** (dificultad, problema) setback, hitch; **nos surgió una ∼** something came up; **¡qué ∼!** how annoying! **(b)** (disgusto) annoyance, vexation (frml)

contrario -ria *adj* **1** (opuesto) «*opiniones/intereses*» conflicting; «*dirección/lado*» opposite; «*equipo*» opposing; «*bando*» opposite; **yo pienso lo ∼** I think the opposite; **mientras no se demuestre lo ∼** until proven otherwise; **sería ∼ a mis intereses** it would be against *o* (frml) contrary to my interests; ▶ SENTIDO² 4
2 (en locs) **al contrario** on the contrary; **al ∼ de su hermano ...** unlike his brother, ...; **de lo contrario** or else, otherwise; **por el contrario** on the contrary; **en el sur, por el ∼, el clima es seco** the south, on the other hand, has a dry climate; **todo lo contrario** quite the opposite; **llevarle la contraria a algn** to contradict sb
■ *m,f* opponent

contrarreloj *adj* «*carrera/etapa*» timed; **a ∼** against the clock

contrarrestar [A1] *vt* to counteract

contrasentido *m* contradiction in terms

contraseña f (Mil) watchword, password; (Teatr, Cin) stub; (Inf) password

contrastar [A1] vi ~ CON algo to contrast WITH sth
■ ~ vt ~ algo CON algo to contrast sth WITH sth

contraste m contrast; **hacer** ~ **con algo** to contrast with sth; **en** ~ **con algo** in contrast to sth

contrata f contract

contratar [A1] vt **(a)** ⟨empleado/obrero⟩ to hire, take on; ⟨artista/deportista⟩ to sign up; ⟨servicios⟩ to contract **(b)** (Const) ⟨ejecución de una obra⟩ to put ... out to contract

contratiempo m ⟨problema⟩ setback, hitch; ⟨accidente⟩ mishap; **sufrir** or **tener un** ~ to have a setback/a mishap

contratista mf contractor

contrato m contract; ~ **de alquiler** rental agreement; ~ **de compraventa/de trabajo** contract of sale and purchase/of employment

contravenir [I31] vt to contravene

contraventana f shutter

contravía (Col): **ir en** ~ to drive the wrong way down the road; **un carro que venía en** ~ an oncoming car

contribución f ⟨colaboración, donación⟩ contribution; (Fisco) tax

contribuir [I20] vi **(a)** (en general) to contribute; **contribuyó con 10 euros** he contributed 10 euros; ~ A **algo** to contribute TO sth **(b)** (Fisco) to pay taxes

contribuyente mf taxpayer

contrincante mf opponent

control m ① (en general) control; **bajo** ~ under control; **sin** ~ out of control; **perdí el** ~ I lost control (of myself); **hacerse con el** ~ **de algo** to gain control of sth; **lleva el** ~ **de los gastos** she keeps a check on the money that is spent; ~ **de (la) natalidad** birth control; ~ **de calidad** quality control o check; ~ **de pasaportes** passport control; ~ **remoto** remote control ② (en carretera, rally) checkpoint ③ **(a)** (Educ) test **(b)** (Med) check-up; ~ **antidoping** dope test, drug test

controlador -dora m,f controller; ~ **aéreo** or **de vuelo** air traffic controller

controlar [A1] vt ① ⟨nervios/impulsos/persona⟩ to control; ⟨incendio⟩ to bring ... under control; **controlamos la situación** we are in control of the situation; **pasaron a** ~ **la empresa** they took control of the company ② ⟨inflación/proceso⟩ to monitor; ⟨persona⟩ to keep a check on; ~ **el peso/la línea** to watch one's weight/one's waistline; **controlé el tiempo que me llevó** I timed how long it took me ③ (regular) ⟨presión/inflación⟩ to control
■ **controlarse** v pron (dominarse) to control oneself; (vigilar) ⟨peso/colesterol⟩ to check, monitor

controversia f controversy

controversial adj (Ven) ▶ CONTROVERTIDO

controvertido -da adj [SER] ⟨persona/tema⟩ controversial

contundente adj **(a)** ⟨objeto/instrumento⟩ blunt; ⟨golpe⟩ severe, heavy **(b)** ⟨argumento/respuesta⟩ forceful; ⟨prueba⟩ convincing; ⟨fracaso/victoria⟩ resounding (before n); **fue** ~ **en sus declaraciones** he was categorical in his statements

conurbano m (Arg): **el** ~ the suburbs (pl)

convalecencia f convalescence

convaleciente adj convalescent

convalidar [A1] vt ⟨estudios/título⟩ to validate, recognize

convencer [E2] vt **(a)** (de hecho, idea) to convince; **no se dejó** ~ she wouldn't be convinced; **la convencí de que estaba equivocada** I convinced her that she was wrong **(b)** (para hacer algo) to persuade; **no pude** ~**lo de que** or **para que me prestara dinero** I couldn't persuade him to lend me any money **(c)** (en frases negativas) (satisfacer): **no me convence del todo la idea** I'm not absolutely sure about the idea; **su explicación no convenció a nadie** his explanation wasn't at all convincing
■ **convencerse** v pron to be convinced; **¿te convenciste?** are you convinced?; ~**se DE algo** to accept sth; **¿te convences de que tenía razón?** do you believe o accept I was right?

convención f convention

convencional adj conventional

convenenciero -ra m,f (Méx fam) user (colloq)

convenible adj ⟨solución⟩ suitable; ⟨precio⟩ reasonable

conveniencia f **(a)** (interés, provecho): **solo piensa en su propia** ~ he only thinks of his own interests; **lo hizo por** ~ she only did it because it was in her own interest; **se casó por** ~ it was a marriage of convenience **(b)** (comodidad) convenience **(c)** (de proyecto, acción) advisability

conveniente adj **(a)** (cómodo) convenient **(b)** (aconsejable, provechoso) advisable; **sería** ~ **que guardaras cama** it would be advisable for you to stay in bed

convenio m agreement

convenir [I31] vi **(a)** (ser aconsejable): **no conviene que nos vean juntos** we'd better not be seen together; **convendría que descansaras** it would be a good idea if you rest; **no te conviene venderlo** it's not worth your while selling it; **no le conviene que eso se sepa** it's not in his interest for anybody to know that **(b)** (venir bien): **el jueves no me conviene** Thursday's no good for me; **te convendría tomarte unas vacaciones** it would do you good to take a vacation ② (acordar) ~ EN **algo** ⟨en fecha/precio⟩ to agree (ON) sth
■ ~ vt ⟨precio/fecha⟩ to agree (on); **a la hora convenida** at the agreed o (frml) appointed time

conventillo m (CS) tenement; **esta oficina es un** ~ (fam) this office is a hotbed of gossip

convento m convent

convergente adj convergent

conversación f **(a)** (charla) conversation;

trabar ∼ **con algn** to strike up a conversation with sb; **no tiene** ∼ she has no conversation **(b) conversaciones** *fpl* (negociaciones) talks (*pl*)

conversador -dora *adj* chatty
■ *m,f* conversationalist

conversar [A1] *vi* **(a)** (hablar) to talk **(b)** (esp AmL) (charlar) to chat, gab (AmE colloq); **conversé largo rato con ella** I had a long chat with her

conversión *f* conversion

convertible *m* (AmL) convertible

convertir [I11] *vt* ⓵ **(a)** (transformar) ∼ **algo/a algn EN algo** to turn sth/sb INTO sth **(b)** (a una religión) to convert; ∼ **a algn A algo** to convert sb TO sth **(c)** ⟨*medida/peso*⟩ ∼ **algo EN algo** to convert sth INTO sth ⓶ (period) (Dep) to score
■ **convertirse** *v pron* **(a)** (transformarse) ∼**se EN algo** to turn INTO sth **(b)** (a una religión) to convert, be converted; ∼**se A algo** to convert TO sth

convicción *f* **(a)** (convencimiento) conviction; **tengo la** ∼ **de que lo sabe** I'm certain *o* convinced he knows it **(b)** (persuasión) persuasion; **poder de** ∼ powers of persuasion **(c) convicciones** *fpl* (ideas, creencias) convictions (*pl*)

convicto -ta *m,f* prisoner, convict

convidado -da *m,f* guest

convidar [A1] *vt* **(a)** (invitar) to invite; ∼ **a algn A algo** ⟨*a una boda/fiesta*⟩ to invite sb TO sth; **nos** ∼**on a unas copas** they invited us for a few drinks; ∼ **a algn a cenar** to invite sb to *o* for dinner **(b)** (AmL) (ofrecer) to offer; ∼ **a algn CON algo** *or* (Chi, Méx) ∼ **algo A algn** to offer sth TO sb, offer sb sth

convincente *adj* convincing

convivencia *f* (de etnias, sectas) coexistence; (de individuos): **la** ∼ **pone el amor a prueba** living together puts love to the test

convivir [I1] *vi* ⟨*personas*⟩ to live together; ⟨*ideologías/etnias*⟩ to coexist; ∼ **CON algn** to live WITH sb

convocar [A2] *vt* ⟨*huelga/elecciones*⟩ to call; ⟨*manifestación*⟩ to organize; ⟨*concurso/certamen*⟩ to announce; ⟨*reunión/asamblea*⟩ to call, convene (frml); ∼ **a algn A algo** to summon sb TO sth

convocatoria *f* **(a)** (llamamiento a huelga, elecciones) call; **la** ∼ **de huelga** the strike call **(b)** (anuncio — para una reunión) notification; (— de exámenes, concursos) official announcement **(c)** (Esp) (Educ) (período de exámenes): **la** ∼ **de junio** the June exams

convoy *m* (de barcos, camiones) convoy; (Ferr) (period) train

convulsión *f* (Med) convulsion

convulsionar [A1] *vt* to throw … into confusion

conyugal *adj* (frml) marital, conjugal (frml); **problemas** ∼**es** marital problems

cónyuge *mf* (frml) spouse (frml); **los** ∼**s** the married couple

coñac, coñá *m* brandy, cognac

coñazo *m* **(a)** (Esp fam *o* vulg) (persona o cosa pesada) pain (in the neck) (colloq); **dar el** ∼ (fam) to be a pain (colloq) **(b)** (Col, Ven fam) (golpe) blow

coño *m* (vulg) (de la mujer) cunt (vulg), beaver (AmE sl), fanny (BrE sl)

cooperación *f* cooperation

cooperador -dora *adj* cooperative, helpful

cooperar [A1] *vi* to cooperate; ∼ **CON algn** to cooperate WITH sb; ∼ **en la lucha contra el cáncer** to work together in the fight against cancer

cooperante *mf* (Esp) aid worker

cooperativa *f* (asociación) cooperative; (tienda) company store

coordinación *f* coordination

coordinado -da *adj* coordinate

coordinador -dora *m,f* **(a)** (organizador) coordinator **(b) coordinadora** *f* coordinating committee

coordinar [A1] *vt* ⟨*movimientos/actividades/ropa*⟩ to coordinate; **no lograba** ∼ **las ideas** he couldn't speak/think coherently
■ ∼ *vi* ⟨⟨*colores*⟩⟩ to match, go together

copa *f* ⓵ **(a)** (para vino) glass (*with a stem*); (para postres) parfait dish; (para helado) sundae dish; ∼ **de champán/coñac** champagne/brandy glass; ∼ **de vino** wineglass **(b)** (contenido) drink; **vamos a tomar una(s)** ∼**(s)** let's go for a drink ⓶ (Dep) cup ⓷ **(a)** (de árbol) top, crown **(b)** (de un sostén) cup **(c)** (de sombrero) crown ⓸ **copas** *fpl* (en naipes) *a suit in a Spanish pack of cards*

Copenhague *m* Copenhagen

copeo *m* (fam): **ir/estar de** ∼ to go/be out drinking; **fuimos de** ∼ **por los pubs del barrio** we went barhopping around the area (AmE), we went on a pub crawl around the area (BrE colloq)

copera *f* (AmS) hostess

coperacha *f* (Méx fam) (recaudación) kitty (colloq), collection; (contribución) contribution; **hacer una** ∼ to get up a collection (AmE colloq), to have a whip round (BrE colloq)

copetín *m* (RPl) aperitif

copia *f* copy; **saqué dos** ∼**s** I made two copies

copiadora *f* photocopier, copier

copiar [A1] *vt* to copy; **copió el artículo a máquina** he typed out a copy of the article; **le copia todo al hermano** he copies his brother in everything; **le copié la respuesta a Ana** I copied the answer from Ana
■ ∼ *vi* to copy

copihue *m* Chile-bells (*national flower of Chile*)

copiloto *mf* (Aviac) copilot; (Auto) co-driver

copión -piona *m,f* (fam) copycat (colloq)

copioso -sa *adj* ⟨*cosecha/comida*⟩ abundant, plentiful; ⟨*nevada/lluvia*⟩ heavy; ⟨*información/ejemplos*⟩ copious; ⟨*llamadas*⟩ numerous

copla *f* **(a)** (Lit) stanza **(b)** (Mús) popular folk song

copo *m* (de nieve) flake, snowflake; (de algodón) ball; ∼**s de avena** rolled oats (*pl*); ∼**s de maíz** cornflakes (*pl*)

coproducción *f* coproduction, joint production

copucha *f* (Chi fam) (rumor, chisme) rumor*; (curiosidad) nosiness (colloq)

copuchar [A1] *vi* (Chi fam) (conversar) to chat (colloq); (curiosear) to nose around (colloq)

cópula *f* **(a)** (Biol, Zool) copulation **(b)** (Ling) copula

copular [A1] *vi* to copulate

copulativo -va *adj* copulative

copyright /kopi'rraj(t)/ *m* (*pl* **-rights**) copyright

coqueta *f* (a) (chica que flirtea) flirt, coquette (liter); (presumida) vain girl/woman; **eres una ~** you are so vain (b) (mueble) dressing table

coquetear [A1] *vi* to flirt; **~ CON algn** to flirt WITH sb

coqueto -ta *adj* (a) (en el arreglo personal): **es muy coqueta** she's very concerned about her appearance (b) ‹casa/dormitorio› cute, sweet (c) ‹sonrisa/mirada/mujer› flirtatious, coquettish (liter)

coraje *m* (a) (valor) courage (b) (fam) (desfachatez) nerve; **¡qué ~!** what a lot of nerve! (AmE), what a nerve! (BrE)

coral *adj* choral
■ *m* (Zool) coral; **color ~** coral (*before n*), coral-colored*
■ *f* (Mús) (coro) choir

Corán *m*: **el ~** the Koran

coraza *f* (a) (armadura) cuirasse (b) (de tortuga) shell

corazón *m* [1] (a) (en general) heart; **sufre del ~** she has heart trouble; **es un hombre de buen/ gran~** he's very kind-hearted/big-hearted; **no tener ~** to be heartless (colloq); **con todo mi ~** with all my heart; **de (todo) ~** sincerely; **le partió el ~** it broke her heart; **tener un ~ de oro/de piedra** to have a heart of gold/of stone (b) (apelativo cariñoso) (fam) sweetheart (colloq) [2] (a) (de manzana, pera) core; (de alcachofa) heart (b) (de ciudad, área) heart [3] (en naipes) (a) (carta) heart (b) **corazones** *mpl* (palo) hearts (*pl*)

corazonada *f* hunch; **tuve la ~ de que ibas a venir** I had a hunch o feeling you'd come

corbata *f* (Indum) tie, necktie (AmE); **hay que ir de ~** you have to wear a tie; **~ de lazo** or (AmL) **de moño** or (Chi) **de humita** bow tie

corbatín *m* bow tie

corchete *m* (a) (Impr) square bracket (b) (en costura) hook and eye (c) (Chi) (para sujetar papeles) staple

corchetear [A1] *vt* (Chi) to staple

corchetera *f* (Chi) stapler

corcho *m* cork; (para pescar, nadar) float

corcholata *f* (Méx) bottle top

corcovear [A1] *vi* to buck

cordel *m* (a) (fino) cord, string (b) (Chi) (cuerda) rope; **saltar al ~** to jump rope (AmE), to skip (BrE)

cordero *m* (a) (cría) lamb (b) (carne — de cordero) lamb; (— de oveja) mutton (c) (piel) lambskin (d) (fam) (persona dócil): **ser un corderito** to be as good as gold

corderoy *m* (AmS) corduroy

cordial *adj* (frml) (amistoso) cordial, friendly; ‹ambiente› congenial; **recibe un ~ saludo** (Corresp) (kindest) regards

cordialidad *f* (frml) cordiality

cordillera *f* (mountain) range; **la ~ de los Andes** the Andes

cordillerano -na *adj* (AmL) Andean, mountain (*before n*)

córdoba *m* cordoba (*Nicaraguan unit of currency*)

cordón *m* [1] (a) (cuerda) cord; **~ umbilical**

umbilical cord (b) (de zapatos) shoelace, lace (c) (Elec) cord (d) (de personas) cordon; **~ policial** police cordon [2] (a) (CS) (de cerros) chain (b) (RPl) (de la vereda) curb (AmE), kerb (BrE)

cordura *f* (Psic) sanity; (sensatez) good sense; **obrar con ~** to act sensibly

Corea *f* Korea

coreano -na *adj/m,f* Korean

corear [A1] *vt* ‹consignas/insultos› to chant, chorus; ‹marcha/estrofa› to sing ... in unison

coreografía *f* choreography

coreógrafo -fa *m,f* choreographer

corista *f* (en revista musical) chorus girl

cornada *f* (golpe) thrust (*with the horns*); (herida) wound (*caused by a bull's horn*); **darle una ~ a algn** to gore sb

córnea *f* cornea

córner *m* (*pl* **-ners**) corner (kick); **lanzar un ~** to take a corner

corneta *f* (a) (Mús) (sin llaves) bugle; (con llaves) cornet (b) (Ven) (Auto) horn

cornetista *mf* (de corneta sin llaves) bugler; (de corneta con llaves) cornet player

cornisa *f* (Arquit) cornice

corno *m* (Mús) horn; **~ inglés** English horn (AmE), cor anglais (BrE)

cornudo -da *m,f* (fam) (*m*) deceived husband; (*f*) deceived wife

coro *m* (a) (conjunto vocal) choir; (en revista musical) chorus line; **a ~** ‹repetir› together, in unison; ‹cantar› in chorus, together (b) (composición) chorus (c) (Arquit) choir

corola *f* corolla

corona *f* [1] (a) (de soberano) crown (b) (institución): **la ~** the Crown (c) (de flores) crown, wreath; (para funerales) wreath (d) (Astron) corona [2] (moneda) crown [3] (Odont) crown

coronación *f* (a) (de soberano) coronation (b) (culminación) culmination

coronar [A1] *vt* (a) ‹soberano› to crown; **lo ~on rey** he was crowned king (b) ‹montaña/ cima› to reach the top of (c) (en damas) to crown

coronel -nela *m,f* (en el ejército) colonel; (en las fuerzas aéreas) ≈ Colonel (*in US*), ≈ Group Captain (*in UK*)

coronilla *f* crown (of the head); **estar hasta la ~** (**de algo/algn**) (fam) to be fed up to the back teeth (with sth/sb) (colloq)

coronta *f* (Chi, Per) *tb* **~ de choclo** stripped corn cob

coroto *m* (a) (Col, Ven fam) (trasto) piece of junk (colloq); **recoge tus ~s** get your things o stuff together (b) (Ven) (poder político) (political) power

corpiño *m* (chaleco) bodice; (del vestido) bodice; (prenda interior) (RPl) brassière

corporación *f* (Com, Fin) corporation

corporal *adj* ‹trabajo› physical; ‹necesidades› bodily (*before n*); ‹castigo› corporal (*before n*)

corpulento -ta *adj* ‹persona/animal› hefty, burly; ‹árbol› solid, sturdy

corpus *m* (*pl* **~**) corpus

Corpus, Corpus Christi Corpus Christi

corral *m* (a) (en granja) yard, farmyard (b) (para ganado) corral (c) *tb* **corralito** (para niños) playpen

corralón *m* (a) (Méx) (de la policía) car pound

(b) (Per) (terreno baldío) piece of waste land (*sometimes with shanty dwellings*) **(c)** (Arg) (Const) lumberyard

correa *f* **(a)** (tira) strap; (cinturón) belt; (de perro) leash; ~ **de reloj** watchband (AmE), watchstrap (BrE) **(b)** (Mec) belt; ~ **del ventilador** fan belt

corrección *f* 1 **(a)** (buenos modales)**: es un hombre de una gran** ~ he is very well-mannered *o* correct; **vestir con** ~ to dress correctly *o* properly **(b)** (honestidad) correctness **(c)** (propiedad)**: habla el francés con** ~ he speaks French well *o* correctly 2 (de exámenes, errores) correction; ~ **de pruebas** proofreading

correccional *f or* (Esp) *m*: *tb* ~ **de menores** reformatory (AmE), detention centre (BrE)

correctamente *adv* **(a)** (sin errores) correctly **(b)** (con cortesía) politely **(c)** (honestamente) honorably

correcto -ta *adj* **(a)** (educado) correct, polite; (honesto) honest **(b)** (respuesta/solución) correct, right **(c)** (funcionamiento/procedimiento) correct

corrector¹ -tora *m,f* (de exámenes) marker; ~ **de pruebas** proofreader

corrector² *m*: ~ **ortográfico** (Inf) spell checker

corredor¹ -dora *m,f* 1 (Dep) runner; (ciclista) cyclist; ~ **de coches** racing driver; ~ **de fondo** long-distance runner 2 **(a)** (agente) agent; ~ **de Bolsa** stockbroker; ~ **de bienes raíces** *or* (Esp) de fincas real estate broker (AmE), estate agent (BrE) **(b)** (RPl) (viajante) sales representative

corredor² *m* (Arquit, Geog, Pol) corridor

corregir [I8] *vt* (en general) to correct; (modales) to improve, mend; (examen/prueba) to correct; (puntuar) to grade (AmE), to mark (BrE)

■ **corregirse** *v pron* **(a)** (en el comportamiento) to change *o* mend one's ways **(b)** (refl) (al hablar) to correct oneself; **un defecto físico que se corrige solo** a defect which corrects itself

correlación *f* correlation

correntoso -sa *adj* (CS) fast-flowing

correo *m* **(a)** mail, post (BrE); **envíamelo por** ~ mail (AmE) *o* (BrE) post it to me; **echar una carta al** ~ to mail (AmE) *o* (BrE) post a letter; ~ **aéreo** air mail; ~ **certificado** *o* (Col, Ur) recomendado registered mail; ~ **electrónico** e-mail, electronic mail; ~ **urgente** special delivery; **de** ~**s** (servicio/huelga) postal (*before n*) **(b)** (tren) mail train **(c)** (oficina) *tb* **C**~**s** (Esp) post office **(d)** (mensajero) messenger

correoso -sa *adj* tough, leathery

correr [E1] *vi* 1 **(a)** (en general) to run; **bajó/subió las escaleras corriendo** she ran down/up the stairs; **salieron corriendo del banco** they ran out of the bank; **echó a** ~ he started to run **(b)** (Auto, Dep) (piloto/conductor) to race 2 **(a)** (apresurarse): **¡corre, ponte los zapatos!** hurry *o* quick, put your shoes on!; **no corras tanto que te equivocarás** don't do it so quickly, you'll only make mistakes ; **corrí a llamarte** I rushed to call you; **me tengo que ir corriendo** I have to rush off **(b)** (fam) (vehículo) to go fast; (conductor) to drive fast 3 **(a)** (carretera/río) to run; (agua) to run; (sangre) to flow; **corría una brisa suave** there was a gentle breeze **(b)** (rumor)**: corre el rumor/la voz de que** ... there is a rumor going around that ...

4 (pasar, transcurrir): **corría el año 1973 cuando** ... it was 1973 when ...; **con el** ~ **de los años** as time went/goes by; **¡cómo corre el tiempo!** how time flies!

5 (hacerse cargo) ~ **CON** algo (con gastos) to pay sth; (con organización) to be responsible FOR sth

■ *vt* 1 **(a)** (Dep) (maratón) to run **(b)** (Auto, Dep) (prueba/gran premio) to race in 2 (exponerse a): **corres el riesgo de perderlo** you run the risk of losing it; **aquí no corres peligro** you're safe here 3 **(a)** (botón/ficha/silla) to move; (cortina) (cerrar) to draw, close; (abrir) to open, pull back; **corre el cerrojo** bolt the door **(b)** (Inf) (texto) to scroll

■ **correrse** *v pron* 1 **(a)** (silla/cama)» to move; «pieza/carga» to shift **(b)** (fam) «persona» to move up *o* over 2 **(a)** (tinta) to run; «rímel/maquillaje» to run, smudge; **se me corrió el rímel** my mascara ran **(b)** (AmL) «media» to ladder

correspondencia *f* **(a)** (relación por correo) correspondence; (cartas) mail, post (BrE); **mantener** ~ **con** algn to correspond with sb **(b)** (equivalencia) correspondence

corresponder [E1] *vi* 1 **(a)** (en un reparto): **le corresponde la mitad de la herencia** he's entitled to half the inheritance; **la parte que te corresponde** your part *o* share **(b)** (incumbir): **te corresponde a ti preparar el informe** it's your job to prepare the report; **el lugar que le corresponde** his rightful place **(c)** (en 3ª pers) (ser adecuado): **debe disculparse, como corresponde** he must apologize, as is right and proper (frml); **según corresponda** as appropriate 2 (encajar, cuadrar): **su aspecto corresponde a la descripción** his appearance fits *o* matches the description; **el texto no corresponde a la foto** the text doesn't belong with *o* match the photograph 3 ~ **A** algo (a un favor) to return sth; (a amabilidad/generosidad) to repay sth

■ *vt* (favor/atención) to return; **un amor no correspondido** an unrequited love

correspondiente *adj* **(a)** (en general) corresponding (*before n*); **la etiqueta** ~ the corresponding label; **los números** ~**s a cada página** the numbers corresponding to each page **(b)** (propio) own; **viene con su** ~ **caja** it comes with its own box **(c)** (pertinente) relevant; **rellene el impreso** ~ complete the relevant form

corresponsal *mf* (Period, Rad, TV) correspondent; ~ **extranjero/de guerra** foreign/war correspondent

corretear [A1] *vi* (correr) to run around

■ *vt* 1 (esp AmL) (perseguir) to chase, pursue 2 (RPl) (Com) to wholesale

corrida *f* 1 (Taur) bullfight 2 (Chi) (serie) series; (fila) row; (de bebidas) round

corrido *m*: Mexican folk song

corriente *adj* 1 (que se da con frecuencia) common; (normal, no extraño) usual, normal; **es un error muy** ~ it's a very common mistake; **lo** ~ **es pagar al contado** the normal thing is to pay cash; **un tipo normal y** ~ an ordinary guy; ~ **y moliente** (fam) ordinary, run-of-the-mill 2 **(a)** (en curso) (mes/año) current **(b)** al corriente: **estoy al** ~ **en los pagos** I'm up to date with the payments; **empezó con retraso pero se** ···⫶

ha puesto al ~ she started late but she has caught up; **mantener a algn al ~ de algo** to keep sb informed about sth

■ *f* **(a)** (de agua) current; **~s marinas** ocean currents; **dejarse llevar por la ~** to go along with the crowd; **seguirle la ~ a algn** to humor* sb **(b)** (de aire) draft (AmE), draught (BrE) **(c)** (Elec) current; **me dio (la) ~** I got a shock *o* an electric shock; **se cortó la ~** there was a power cut

corro *m* **(a)** (círculo) circle, ring; **hacer un ~** to stand/sit in a circle; **se formó un ~ a su alrededor** a circle of people formed around her **(b)** (Jueg): **jugar al ~** to play a singing game standing in a ring

corroborar [A1] *vt* to corroborate

corroer [E13] *vt* ⟨metal⟩ to corrode; ⟨mármol⟩ to erode

corromper [E1] *vt* **(a)** ⟨persona/lengua/ sociedad⟩ to corrupt **(b)** ⟨materia orgánica⟩ to rot
■ **corromperse** *v pron* **(a)** «costumbres/ persona/lengua» to become corrupted **(b)** «materia orgánica» to rot

corrompido -da *adj* **(a)** ⟨persona/sociedad⟩ corrupt **(b)** ⟨materia orgánica⟩ rotten

corrosión *f* corrosion

corrosivo -va *adj* ⟨sustancia/acción⟩ corrosive

corrupción *f* **(a)** (de moral, persona, lengua) corruption; **~ de menores** corruption of minors **(b)** (de materia) decay

corrupto -ta *adj* corrupt

corsé, corset /kor'se/ *m* (*pl* **-sets**) corset

cortacésped *m* lawnmower

cortada *f* **(a)** (Col, Méx) (herida) cut; **hacerse una ~** to cut oneself **(b)** (RPl) (calle sin salida) no through road

cortado¹ -da *adj* **1** ⟨persona⟩ **(a)** [ESTAR] (Chi, Esp) (turbado, avergonzado) embarrassed **(b)** [ESTAR] (Esp, CS) (aturdido) stunned; **me quedé ~ con su respuesta** I was stunned by her reply **(c)** [SER] (Esp) (tímido) shy **2** [ESTAR] **(a)** ⟨calle/carretera⟩ closed, closed off **(b)** ⟨película⟩ cut **3** **(a)** [ESTAR] ⟨mayonesa/salsa⟩ separated; **la leche está cortada** the milk is curdled *o* off **(b)** ⟨café⟩ with a dash of milk

cortado² *m* expresso with a dash of milk

cortante *adj* **(a)** ⟨instrumento/objeto⟩ sharp **(b)** ⟨viento⟩ biting **(c)** ⟨respuesta/tono⟩ sharp

cortaplumas *m or f* (*pl* **~**) penknife

cortar [A1] *vt* **1** (dividir) ⟨cuerda/pastel⟩ to cut, chop; ⟨asado⟩ to carve; ⟨leña/madera⟩ to chop; ⟨baraja⟩ to cut; **~ algo por la mitad** to cut sth in half *o* in two; **~ algo en rodajas/en cuadritos** to slice/dice sth; **~ algo en trozos** to cut sth into pieces
2 (quitar, separar) ⟨rama/punta/pierna⟩ to cut off; ⟨árbol⟩ to cut down, chop down; ⟨flores⟩ to pick; **me cortó un trozo de melón** she cut me a piece of melon
3 (hacer más corto) ⟨pelo/uñas⟩ to cut; ⟨césped/ pasto⟩ to mow; ⟨seto⟩ to cut; ⟨rosal⟩ to cut back; ⟨texto⟩ to cut down

4 (en costura) ⟨falda/vestido⟩ to cut out
5 (interrumpir) **(a)** ⟨agua/gas/luz/teléfono⟩ to cut off; ⟨película/programa⟩ to interrupt **(b)** ⟨calle⟩ «policía/obreros» to close, block off; «manifestantes» to block; **me cortó el paso** he stood in my way
6 (censurar, editar) ⟨película⟩ to cut; ⟨escena/ diálogo⟩ to cut (out)
7 ⟨frío⟩: **el frío me cortó los labios** my lips were chapped *o* cracked from the cold weather
■ **~** *vi* **1** ⟨cuchillo/tijeras⟩ to cut
2 **(a)** (Cin): **¡corten! cut! (b)** (CS) (por teléfono) to hang up; **no me cortes** don't hang up on me **(c)** (en naipes) to cut

■ **cortarse** *v pron* **1** (interrumpirse) «proyección/ película» to stop; «llamada/gas» to get cut off; **se cortó la luz** there was a power cut; **se me cortó la respiración** I could hardly breathe
2 **(a)** (refl) (hacerse un corte) to cut oneself; ⟨brazo/cara⟩ to cut; **me corté un dedo** I cut my finger **(b)** (refl) ⟨uñas/pelo⟩ to cut; **se corta el pelo ella misma** she cuts her own hair **(c)** (caus) ⟨pelo⟩ to have ... cut; **tengo que ~me el pelo** I have to have my hair cut **(d)** ⟨piel/labios⟩ to crack, become chapped
3 (cruzarse) «líneas/calles» to cross
4 «leche» to curdle; «mayonesa/salsa» to separate
5 (Chi, Esp) «persona» (turbarse, aturdirse) to get embarrassed

cortaúñas *m* (*pl* **~**) nail clippers (*pl*)

corte *m* **1** (en general) cut; **se hizo un ~ en la cabeza** he cut his head; **~ de pelo** haircut; **~ a (la) navaja** razor cut; **un ~ de luz** a power cut; **tuvimos varios ~s de agua** the water was cut off several times; **~ de digestión** stomach cramp; **~ publicitario** (RPl) commercial break
2 **(a)** (de tela) length, length of material **(b)** (en costura) cut; **un traje de buen ~** a well-made *o* well-cut suit; **~ y confección** dressmaking
3 (Esp fam) (vergüenza) embarrassment; **me da ~ ir sola** I'm embarrassed to go by myself; **¡qué ~!** how embarrassing!
4 (RPl fam) (atención): **darle ~ a algn** to take notice of sb
■ *f* **(a)** (del rey) court **(b)** (esp AmL) (Der) Court of Appeal; **C~ Suprema (de Justicia)** (AmL) Supreme Court **(c) las Cortes** *fpl* (Pol) (en Esp) Parliament, the legislative assembly

cortejo *m* (de rey) retinue, entourage; (de ministro) entourage; **~ fúnebre** funeral procession *o* (frml) cortege

cortés *adj* polite, courteous

cortesía *f* **(a)** (urbanidad, amabilidad) courtesy, politeness; **la trató con ~** he was polite to her; **tuvo la ~ de invitarnos** she was kind enough to invite us **(b)** **de cortesía** ⟨entrada⟩ complimentary; ⟨visita⟩ courtesy (*before n*)

corteza *f* (de árbol) bark; (del pan) crust; (del queso) rind; (de naranja, limón) peel, rind; **la ~ terrestre** the earth's crust

cortijo *m* (en Esp) (finca) country estate; (casa) country house

cortina *f* curtain, drape (AmE); ~ **de ducha** shower curtain; ~ **de humo** smokescreen

cortisona *f* cortisone

corto¹ -ta *adj* ⬚1 **(a)** (en longitud) ⟨*calle/río*⟩ short; **de manga corta** short-sleeved; **el vestido le quedó** ~ the dress is too short for her now; **iba vestida de** ~ she was wearing a short dress/skirt **(b)** (en duración) ⟨*película/curso/viaje*⟩ short; ⟨*visita/conversación*⟩ short, brief; **a la corta o a la larga** sooner or later ⬚2 (escaso, insuficiente): **un niño de corta edad** a very young child; ~ **de vista** near-sighted, shortsighted (BrE); **andar** ~ **de tiempo** to be pressed for time ⬚3 (fam) (poco inteligente) stupid; ~ **de entendederas** *or* **alcances** dim, dense (colloq)

corto² *m* (Cin) **(a)** (cortometraje) short (movie *o* film) **(b) cortos** *mpl* (Col, Méx, Ven) (de película) trailer

cortocircuito *m* short circuit; **hacer** ~ to short-circuit

cortometraje *m* short (movie *o* film)

cosa *f* ⬚1 (en general) thing; **cualquier** ~ anything; **¿alguna otra** ~? anything else?; **pon cada** ~ **en su lugar** put everything in its place; **entre una(s)** ~**(s) y otra(s)** ... what with one thing and another ...; **¡qué** ~**s dices!** really, what a thing to say!; **dime una** ~ ... tell me something ...; **tengo que contarte una** ~ there's something I have to tell you; **fue** ~ **fácil** it was easy; **se enfada por cualquier** ~ he gets angry over the slightest thing; **si por cualquier** ~ **no puedes venir** if you can't come for any reason; **por una** ~ **o por otra** for one reason or another; **esto no es** ~ **de risa/broma** this is no laughing matter/no joke ⬚2 **cosas** *fpl* (pertenencias) things (*pl*); **mis** ~**s de deporte** my sports things ⬚3 (situación, suceso): **así están las** ~**s** that's how things are *o* stand; **la** ~ **se pone fea** things are starting to get unpleasant; **¿cómo (te) van las** ~**s?** how are things?; **son** ~**s de la vida** that's life!; **¡qué** ~ **más extraña!** how strange *o* funny! ⬚4 **(a)** (fam) (ocurrencia): **¡tienes cada** ~! the things you come up (AmE) *o* (BrE) out with!; **esto es** ~ **de tu padre** this is your father's doing *o* idea **(b)** (comportamiento típico): **son** ~**s de niños** children are like that; **son** ~**s de Ana** that's one of Ana's little ways ⬚5 (asunto): **no es** ~ **tuya** it's none of your business; **no te preocupes, eso es** ~ **mía** don't worry, I'll handle it ⬚6 (*en locs*) **cosa de** (AmS fam) so as to; ~ **de terminarlo** so as to finish it; **cosa que** (AmS fam) so that; ~ **que no me olvide** so that I don't forget; **no sea cosa que: llévate el paraguas, no sea** ~ **que llueva** take your umbrella just in case; **átalo, no sea** ~ **que se escape** tie it up so that it doesn't get away; **ser** ~ **de** ... (fam): **es** ~ **de unos minutos** it'll (only) take a couple of minutes; **es** ~ **de intentarlo** you just have to give it a go

cosecha *f* **(a)** (acción, época) harvest; **un vino de la** ~ **del 99** a 1999 vintage wine **(b)** (producto) crop

cosechador -dora *m,f* **(a)** (persona) harvester **(b) cosechadora** *f* (máquina) combine (harvester)

cosechar [A1] *vt* **(a)** (recoger) ⟨*cereales*⟩ to

harvest; ⟨*legumbres*⟩ to pick **(b)** (Esp) (cultivar) ⟨*cereales/patatas*⟩ to grow **(c)** ⟨*aplausos/premios/honores*⟩ to win; ⟨*éxitos*⟩ to achieve
■ ~ *vi* to harvest

coser [E1] *vt* **(a)** ⟨*dobladillo*⟩ to sew; ⟨*botón*⟩ to sew on; ⟨*agujero*⟩ to sew (up); **cóselo a máquina** sew it on the machine **(b)** ⟨*herida*⟩ to stitch
■ ~ *vi* to sew

cosmético¹ -ca *adj* cosmetic (*before n*)

cosmético² *m* cosmetic

cósmico -ca *adj* cosmic

cosmopolita *adj/mf* cosmopolitan

cosmos *m* cosmos

cosquillas *fpl*: **hacerle** ~ **a algn** to tickle sb; **tener** ~ to be ticklish

costa *f* ⬚1 (Geog) (del mar — área) coast; (— perfil) coastline; **una** ~ **muy accidentada** a very rugged coastline; **la** ~ **atlántica** the Atlantic coast ⬚2 (*en locs*) **a costa de: lo terminó a** ~ **de muchos sacrificios** he had to make a lot of sacrifices to finish it; **a** ~ **mía/de los demás** at my/other people's expense; **a toda costa** at all costs ⬚3 **costas** *fpl* (Der) costs (*pl*)

costado *m* side; **pasar de** ~ to go through sideways; **duerme de** ~ she sleeps on her side

costal *m* sack, bag

costanera *f* (CS) (de río) riverside path (*o* road *etc*); (del mar) promenade; (de lago) lakeside path (*o* road *etc*)

costar [A10] *vt* **(a)** (en dinero) to cost; **¿cuánto me** ~**á arreglarlo?** how much will it cost to fix it? **(b)** (en perjuicios): **el atentado que le costó la vida** the attack in which he lost his life; **le costó el puesto** it cost him his job **(c)** (en esfuerzo): **me costó mucho trabajo** it took me a lot of hard work; **cuesta abrirlo** it's hard to open; **me cuesta trabajo creerlo** I find it hard *o* difficult to believe
■ ~ *vi* **(a)** (en dinero) to cost; **el reloj me costó caro** the watch cost a lot **(b)** (resultar perjudicial): **esto te va a** ~ **caro** you're going to pay dearly for this **(c)** (resultar difícil): **cuesta un poco acostumbrarse** it's not easy to get used to; **no te cuesta nada intentarlo** it won't do you any harm to give it a try; **la física le cuesta** he finds physics difficult; **me costó dormirme** I had trouble getting to sleep

Costa Rica *f* Costa Rica

costarricense *adj/mf* Costa Rican

costarriqueño -ña *adj/m,f* Costa Rican

coste *m* (Esp) ▶ COSTO

costear [A1] *vt* (financiar) to finance
■ **costearse** *v pron* (*refl*) (financiarse): **yo me costeé el viaje** I paid for the trip myself

costeño -ña *adj* coastal
■ *m,f*: **los** ~**s** people from coastal regions

costero -ra *adj* ⟨*camino/pueblo*⟩ coastal

costilla *f* **(a)** (Anat) rib **(b)** (AmS) (chuleta — de vaca) T-bone steak; (— de cerdo, cordero) chop

costipado -da *adj/m* ▶ CONSTIPADO

costo *m* (Com, Econ, Fin) cost; **de bajo** ~ low-cost, budget; **precio de** ~ cost price; **al** ~ at cost price; ~ **de (la) vida** cost of living

costoso -sa *adj* ⟨*casa/coche/joya*⟩ expensive **(b)** ⟨*error*⟩ costly **(c)** ⟨*trabajo/tarea*⟩ difficult

costra *f* **(a)** (de herida) scab **(b)** (de suciedad) layer, coating

costumbre *f* **(a)** (de individuo) habit; **tenía (la)** **~ de madrugar** he was in the habit of getting up early; **agarró la ~ de ...** she got into the habit of ...; **hacer algo por ~** to do sth out of habit; **a la hora de ~** at the usual time; **como de ~** as usual; **se quejó menos que de ~** he complained less than he usually does **(b)** (de país, pueblo) custom

costura *f* **(a)** (acción) sewing **(b)** (puntadas) seam

costurera *f* seamstress

costurero *m* (caja, estuche) workbox; (canasta) sewing basket; **~ de viaje** sewing kit

cotejar [A1] *vt* ⟨documentos⟩ to compare; ⟨información/respuesta⟩ to collate; **~ algo CON algo** to check sth AGAINST sth

cotelé *m* (Chi) corduroy

cotidiano -na *adj* daily; ⟨vida⟩ everyday, daily

cotilla *mf* (Esp fam) gossip (colloq)

cotillear [A1] *vi* (Esp fam) to gossip

cotilleo *m* (Esp fam) gossip

cotización *f* **(a)** (de moneda) value; (de acciones, valores, producto) price; **su ~ llegó a 500 pesos** it reached 500 pesos **(b)** (Andes) (evaluación) valuation; (presupuesto) estimate

cotizado -da *adj* sought-after

cotizar [A4] *vt* **(a)** (Fin) ⟨acciones⟩ to quote; **las acciones se cotizan a 525 pesos** the shares are quoted at 525 pesos; **la libra se cotizó a 1,58 euros** the pound stood at 1.58 euros **(b)** (Andes) ⟨cuadro/joyas⟩ to value; ⟨obra/reparación⟩ to give an estimate for

coto *m* (Dep, Ecol) reserve; **~ de caza/pesca** game/fishing preserve

cotorra *f* **(a)** (Zool) (loro) parrot **(b)** (fam) (persona) chatterbox (colloq)

cototo *m* (Chi fam) bump (*on the head*)

cottolengo /koto'leŋgo/ *m* (RPI) (para ancianos) old people's home; (para niños) children's home; (para drogadictos, desamparados, etc) shelter, refuge

cotufas *fpl* (Ven) (maíz tostado) popcorn

COU /kou/ *m* (en Esp) = **Curso de Orientación Universitaria**

courier /ku'rje(r)/ *mf* courier

coya *mf*: indian from the Andean region of Bolivia, Peru and the NW of Argentina

coyote *m* (Zool) coyote

coyuntura *f* (Anat) joint

coz *f* kick; **dar coces** to kick

crac *m* (*pl* **cracs**) **(a)** (sonido) crack, snap **(b)** (Fin) crash

crack *m* (*pl* **cracks**) (droga) crack

cráneo *m* skull, cranium (tech)

cráter *m* crater

crawl /krol/ *m*: *tb* **estilo ~** crawl, front crawl

crayón *m* (Méx, RPI) wax crayon

creación *f* **(a)** (en general) creation **(b)** (Relig) **la C~** the Creation

creador -dora *adj* creative

■ *m,f* **(a)** (en general) creator; **~es de moda** fashion designers **(b)** (Relig) **el C~** the Creator

crear [A1] *vt* to create; ⟨producto⟩ to develop; ⟨institución/comisión/fondo⟩ to set up; ⟨fama/prestigio⟩ to bring; ⟨reputación⟩ to earn; **crea muchos problemas** it causes *o* creates a lot of problems; **no quiero ~ falsas expectativas** I don't want to raise false hopes

■ **crearse** *v pron* ⟨problema⟩ to create ... for oneself; ⟨enemigos⟩ to make

creatividad *f* creativity

creativo -va *adj* creative

crecer [E3] *vi* **1** **(a)** «ser vivo/pelo/uñas» to grow; **dejarse ~ la barba** to grow a beard **(b)** (criarse) to grow up; **crecieron en un pueblo** they grew up in a village **2** **(a)** «río» to rise; «ciudad» to grow; «luna» to wax **(b)** «sentimiento/interés» to grow; «rumor» to spread **(c)** «economía» to grow; **el número de desempleados ha crecido** the number of unemployed has risen **(d)** (en importancia, sabiduría) **~ EN algo** to grow IN sth

creces: **pagar con ~ un error** to pay dearly for a mistake; **superar algo con ~** ⟨nivel/previsiones⟩ to far exceed sth

crecida *f* **(a)** (subida de nivel): **el río experimentó una fuerte ~** the river level rose sharply **(b)** (desbordamiento): **las ~s del Paraná** the flooding of the Paraná

creciente *adj* **(a)** ⟨interés/necesidad⟩ increasing **(b)** (Astron): **luna ~** waxing moon

crecimiento *m* growth; **una industria en ~** a growth industry; **durante el ~** while they are growing

credibilidad *f* credibility

crédito *m* **1** **(a)** (en negocio) credit; **tengo ~ aquí** they let me have credit here; **a ~** on credit **(b)** (cuenta) account **(c)** (préstamo) loan; **~ hipotecario** mortgage loan **2** (credibilidad): **fuentes dignas de ~** reliable sources; **no di ~ a sus palabras** I doubted his words (frml) **3** (Cin, TV, Educ) credit

credo *m* creed

crédulo -la *adj* credulous, gullible

creencia *f* belief

creer [E13] *vi* **(a)** (tener fe, aceptar como verdad) to believe; **~ EN algo/algn** to believe in sth/sb; **¿me crees?** do you believe me? **(b)** (pensar, juzgar) to think; **¿tú crees?** do you think so?; **no creo** I don't think so; **no creas, es bastante difícil** believe me, it's quite hard

■ **~** *vt* **(a)** (dar por cierto) to believe; **hay que verlo para ~lo** it has to be seen to be believed; **aunque no lo creas** believe it or not; **¡no lo puedo ~!** I don't believe it!; **¡ya lo creo!** of course! **(b)** (pensar, juzgar) to think; **creo que sí/creo que no** I think so/I don't think so; **creo que va a llover** I think it's going to rain; **no la creo capaz** I do not think she is capable; **se cree que el incendio fue provocado** the fire is thought to have been started deliberately; **no lo creí necesario** I didn't think it necessary; **no creo que pueda ir** I doubt if *o* I don't think I'll be able to go; **creí oír un ruido** I thought I heard a noise; **creo recordar que ...** I seem to remember that ...

■ **creerse** *v pron* **(a)** (enf) (con ingenuidad) to believe; **eso nadie se lo cree** no one believes that **(b)** (con arrogancia) to think; **se cree muy listo** he thinks he's really clever; **¿quién se ~á que es?** who does he think he is? **(c)** (CS fam) (estimarse superior) to think one is special (*o* great *etc*) **(d)** (Méx) (fiarse) **~se DE algn** to trust sb

creído -da adj [SER] (engreído) conceited

crema f (a) (plato dulce) type of custard (b) (esp AmL) (de la leche) cream; ~ **batida** whipped cream; ~ **agria** or **ácida** (AmL) sour o soured cream; ~ **chantilly** or **chantillí** (AmL) whipped cream (with sugar, vanilla and egg white); ~ **doble/líquida** (AmL) double/single cream; ~ **pastelera** crème pâtissière, confectioner's custard (c) (sopa) cream (d) (en cosmética) cream; ~ **bronceadora** suntan lotion o cream; ~ **de afeitar** shaving cream; ~ **de calzado** (Esp) shoe cream; ~ **hidratante** moisturizer, moisturizing cream
■ adj inv cream; (de) color ~ cream, cream-colored

cremallera f (a) (Indum) zipper (AmE), zip (BrE) (b) (Mec, Tec) rack

cremar [A1] vt to cremate

crematorio m crematorium

cremoso -sa adj ‹salsa› creamy; ‹queso› soft, creamy

crep m (pl **creps**), (Méx) **crepa** f crepe

crepe /krep/ m or f (Coc) crepe

crepé m (Tex) crepe

crepería f creperie

crepúsculo m (del anochecer) twilight; (del amanecer) dawn light

crespo¹ -pa adj (rizado) (AmL) curly; (muy rizado) frizzy

crespo² m (AmL) curl

cresta f (a) (Zool) crest; (de gallo) comb (b) (de ola, monte) crest

cretino -na adj cretinous
■ m,f cretin

creyente adj: es muy ~ she has a strong faith
■ mf believer; los no ~s the nonbelievers

creyera, creyese, etc ▶ CREER

cría f (a) (crianza) rearing, raising; (para la reproducción) breeding (b) (Zool) (camada) litter; (nidada) brood (c) (animal): una ~ de ciervo a baby deer

criadero m farm; ~ **de pollos/de truchas** poultry/trout farm; ~ **de perros** kennel (AmE), kennels (BrE); ~ **de ostras** oyster bed

criado -da m,f (m) servant; (f) servant, maid

criador -dora m,f breeder

crianza f ⑴ (Agr) raising, rearing; (para la reproducción) breeding ⑵ (de niños) upbringing

criar [A17] vt ⑴ ‹niño› (a) (cuidar, educar) to bring up, raise (b) (amamantar) to breast-feed; **criado con biberón** bottle-fed ⑵ (a) ‹ganado› to raise, rear; (para la reproducción) to breed (b) ‹pollos/pavos› to breed
■ **criarse** v pron to grow up; **me crié en el campo** I grew up in the country; **me crié con mi abuela** I was brought up by my grandmother

criatura f (a) (niño — pequeño) child; (— recién nacido) baby (b) (cosa creada) creature

criba f (a) (instrumento) sieve (b) (proceso de selección): **la primera** ~ the first stage of the selection process; **hicimos una** ~ **de las solicitudes** we went through the applications

cribar [A1] vt to sieve, sift

cricket /'krike(t)/ m cricket

crimen m (delito grave) serious crime; (asesinato) murder; ~ **de guerra** war crime; ~ **pasional**

crime of passion; **es un** ~ **tirar esta comida** it's a crime to throw away this food; **¡qué** ~**!** it's wicked o criminal

criminal adj/mf criminal

criminalidad f (a) (cualidad) criminality (b) (número de crímenes) crime

criminalista adj criminal (before n)
■ mf criminal lawyer

crin f (a) (del caballo) tb ~**es** mane (b) (pelo de caballo) horsehair (c) (esparto) esparto grass

crío, cría (esp Esp fam) m,f kid (colloq)

criollo -lla adj (a) (Hist) Creole (b) (AmL) (por oposición a extranjero) Venezuelan (o Peruvian etc); ‹plato/artesanía/cocina› national
■ m,f (a) (Hist) Creole (of European descent born in a Spanish American colony) (b) (AmL) (nativo) Venezuelan (o Peruvian etc)

cripta f crypt

criquet m (Dep) cricket

crisantemo m chrysanthemum

crisis f (pl ~) (a) (en general) crisis; ~ **nerviosa** nervous breakdown (b) (period) (remodelación ministerial) tb ~ **de Gobierno** cabinet reshuffle

crismas m (pl ~) (Esp) Christmas card

crispar [A1] vt (a) (contraer): **con la expresión crispada por el dolor** his face tensed/contorted with pain (b) (exasperar) to infuriate; **me crispa los nervios** it really irritates me o gets on my nerves
■ **crisparse** v pron ‹‹rostro/expresión›› to tense up; ‹‹persona›› to get irritated

cristal m ① (a) (vidrio fino) crystal; ~ **de roca** rock crystal; ~ **tallado** or (AmL) **cortado** cut glass (b) (lente) lens ② (Esp) (vidrio) glass; (trozo) piece of glass; (de ventana) pane; **puerta de** ~ glass door; ~**es rotos** pieces of glass; **limpiar los** ~**s** to clean the windows; ~ **delantero** (Esp) windshield (AmE), windscreen (BrE); ~ **trasero** (Esp) rear windshield (AmE), rear windscreen (BrE)

cristalera f (Esp) (a) (mueble) display cabinet, dresser (b) (escaparate) shop window (c) (puertas) French windows (pl), French doors (pl) (AmE); (ventanas) windows (pl)

cristalería f (objetos) glassware; (juego) set of glasses

cristalero -ra m,f (Esp) (persona que instala) glazier

cristalino -na adj crystalline

cristalizar [A4] vi/vt to crystallize

cristiandad f Christendom

cristianismo m Christianity

cristianizar [A4] vt to Christianize

cristiano -na adj/m,f Christian; **¿eres** ~**?** are you a Christian?; ~ **renacido** born-again Christian

Cristo Christ; **antes/después de** ~ before Christ o BC/AD

criterio m (a) (norma, principio) criterion; **tenemos que unificar** ~**s** we have to agree on our criteria (b) (capacidad para juzgar, discernir) discernment (frml), judgment*; **lo dejo a tu** ~ I leave that to your discretion; **no tiene** ~ he has no common sense (c) (opinión, juicio) opinion

crítica f (a) (ataque, censura) criticism; **fue objeto de numerosas** ~**s** she was the object of a lot of criticism (b) (reseña) review; (ensayo) critique; **la** ···⊹

película recibió muy buenas ∼s the movie had very good reviews; **la** ∼ **(los críticos)** the critics (*pl*); ∼ **literaria** literary criticism

criticar [A2] *vt* **(a)** (censurar) to criticize **(b)** (Art, Espec, Lit) ⟨*libro/película*⟩ to review
■ ∼ *vi* to gossip, backbite

crítico -ca *adj* critical
■ *m,f* critic

criticón -cona *adj* (fam & pey) critical, hypercritical
■ *m,f* (fam & pey) faultfinder

Croacia *f* Croatia

croar [A1] *vi* to croak

croata *adj* Croatian, Croat
■ *mf* Croat; **los** ∼**s** the Croats, Croatian people

crochet /kro'tʃe/ *m* crochet; **hacer** ∼ to crochet

croissant /krwa'san/ *m* (*pl* **-ssants**) croissant

crol *m* (Dep) crawl

cromo *m* **(a)** (metal) chromium, chrome **(b)** (Esp) (estampa) picture card, sticker

cromosoma *m* chromosome

crónica *f* **(a)** (Period) report, article; (Rad, TV) report; ∼ **deportiva/de sociedad** sport(s)/society page (*o* section *etc*) **(b)** (Hist) chronicle

crónico -ca *adj* chronic

cronista *mf* **(a)** (esp AmL) (periodista) journalist, reporter; ∼ **de radio** radio broadcaster **(b)** (Hist) chronicler

cronograma *m* timescale, time line

cronología *f* chronology

cronológico -ca *adj* chronological

cronometrar [A1] *vt* to time

cronómetro *m* (Tec) chronometer; (Dep) stopwatch

croqueta *f* croquette

croquis *m* (*pl* ∼) sketch

cross /kros/ *m* **(a)** (deporte — en atletismo) cross-country running; (— en motociclismo) motocross **(b)** (carrera — a pie) cross country, cross-country race; (— en moto) motocross race

cruce *m* **1** **(a)** (acción) crossing **(b)** (de calles) crossroads; **⊗ cruce peligroso** dangerous junction; ∼ **peatonal** *or* **de peatones** pedestrian crossing **(c)** (Telec): **hay un** ∼ **en las líneas** there's a crossed line **2** (Agr, Biol) cross

cruceiro *m* (Hist) (unidad monetaria) cruzeiro

crucero *m* **(a)** (viaje) cruise; **hizo un** ∼ **por el Caribe** he went on a Caribbean cruise **(b)** (barco de guerra) cruiser **(c)** (Méx) (de carreteras) crossroads; (Ferr) grade crossing (AmE), level crossing (BrE)

crucial *adj* crucial

crucificar [A2] *vt* to crucify

crucifijo *m* crucifix

crucigrama *m* crossword, crossword puzzle

cruda *f* (AmC, Méx fam) hangover

crudeza *f* harshness; (del clima) severity, harshness

crudo -da *adj* **1** [ESTAR] ⟨*carne/verduras/ pescado*⟩ (sin cocinar) raw; (poco hecho) underdone **2** [SER] **(a)** ⟨*invierno/clima*⟩ severe, harsh **(b)** ⟨*lenguaje/imágenes/realidad*⟩ harsh

cruel *adj* cruel; **ser** ∼ **con algn** to be cruel to sb

crueldad *f* cruelty; **eso es una** ∼ that's cruel; ∼ **mental** mental cruelty

crujido *m* **(a)** (de tablas, muelles, ramas) creaking **(b)** (de papel, hojas secas) rustling; (de seda) rustle **(c)** (de los nudillos, las rodillas) cracking **(d)** (de la grava, nieve) crunching **(e)** (de los dientes) grinding

crujiente *adj* ⟨*galletas/tostadas*⟩ crunchy; ⟨*pan*⟩ crusty

crujir [I1] *vi* **(a)** «*tabla/muelles/ramas*» to creak; «*hojas secas*» to rustle **(b)** «*nudillos/ rodillas*» to crack **(c)** «*grava/nieve*» to crunch **(d)** «*galletas/tostadas*» to be crunchy **(e)** «*dientes*»: **le crujen los dientes** he grinds his teeth

crustáceo *m* crustacean

cruz *f* **1** **(a)** (figura) cross; **ponte con los brazos en** ∼ stand with your arms stretched out to the sides; **la C**∼ (Relig) the Cross; ∼ **gamada** swastika; **la C**∼ **Roja** the Red Cross **(b)** (ornamento, condecoración) cross **2** (de moneda) reverse; **cara o** ∼ heads or tails

cruzada *f* crusade

cruzado -da *adj* **1** **(a)** (atravesado): **había un árbol** ∼ **en la carretera** there was a tree lying across the road **(b)** ⟨*abrigo/chaqueta*⟩ double-breasted **2** ⟨*cheque*⟩ crossed; *ver tb* CRUZAR

cruzar [A4] *vt* **1** (atravesar) ⟨*calle/mar/puente*⟩ to cross **2** ⟨*piernas*⟩ to cross; ⟨*brazos*⟩ to cross, fold **3** **(a)** ⟨*cheque*⟩ to cross **(b)** (tachar) to cross out **(c)** ⟨*palabras/saludos*⟩ to exchange **4** (llevar al otro lado) to take (*o* carry *etc*) ... across **5** ⟨*animales/plantas*⟩ to cross
■ ∼ *vi* (atravesar) to cross; ∼**on por el puente** they went across the bridge
■ **cruzarse** *v pron* **1** (*recípr*) **(a)** «*caminos/ líneas*» to intersect, meet **(b)** (en viaje, camino): **nos cruzamos en el camino** we met *o* passed each other on the way; **nuestras cartas se han debido de** ∼ our letters must have crossed in the post; ∼**se CON algn** to see *o* pass sb **2** (interponerse): **se me cruzó una moto** a motorcycle pulled out in front of him; **se me cruzó otro corredor** another runner cut in front of me

cta. (= **cuenta**) a/c

cuaderno *m* (de ejercicios) exercise book; (de notas) notebook; ∼ **(de) borrador** rough notebook; ∼ **de espiral** *o* (Chi) **de anillos** spiral-bound notebook

cuadra *f* **(a)** (Equ) stable, stables (*pl*) **(b)** (AmL) (distancia entre dos esquinas) block

cuadrado¹ -da *adj* **1** **(a)** (de forma) square **(b)** (Mat) ⟨*metro/centímetro*⟩ square (*before n*); **2**

---

m² ∼s (*read as: dos metros cuadrados*) m² (*léase: two square meters*) **2** [ESTAR] (fam) (fornido) well-built, big, hefty (colloq) **3** [SER] (AmL fam) (cerrado de mente) inflexible

cuadrado² *m* square; **25 elevado al** ∼ **25** squared

cuadrar [A1] *vi* **(a)** «*cuentas*» to tally, balance **(b)** «*declaraciones/testimonias*» to tally; ∼ CON **algo** to fit in WITH sth, tally WITH sth **(c)** (Ven) (para una cita) ∼ CON **algn** to arrange to meet sb; ∼ **PARA hacer algo** to arrange to do sth
■ **cuadrarse** *v pron* **(a)** «*soldado*» to stand to attention **(b)** «*caballo/toro*» to stand stock-still **(c)** (Col, Ven fam) (estacionarse) to park

cuadriculado -da *adj* ‹*papel*› squared; **mapa** ∼ grid map

cuadrilátero *m* **(a)** (Mat) quadrilateral **(b)** (period) (de boxeo) ring

cuadrilla *f* **(a)** (Taur) cuadrilla (*team of matador's assistants*) **(b)** (de obreros) team, gang; (de soldados) squad; (de maleantes) gang

cuadro *m* **1** **(a)** (Art) (pintura) painting; (grabado, reproducción) picture **(b)** (Teatr) scene **(c)** (gráfico) table, chart **2** **(a)** (cuadrado) square, check; **tela a** ∼s checked material; **zanahorias cortadas en cuadritos** diced carrots **(b)** (tablero) board, panel; ∼ **de mandos** or **instrumentos** (Auto) dashboard; (Aviac) instrument panel **(c)** (de bicicleta) frame **3** (en organización): **los** ∼s **directivos del partido** the top party officials; **los** ∼s **superiores de la empresa** the company's senior management; ∼s **de mando** (Mil) commanders (*pl*)

cuadrúpedo -da *adj/m* quadruped (*before n*)

cuádruple, cuádruplo *m*: **esta cifra es el** ∼ **de la que esperábamos** this figure is four times what we expected

cuajada *f* junket, curd

cuajar [A1] *vi* **1** **(a)** «*leche*» to curdle; «*flan/ yogur*» to set **(b)** «*nieve*» to settle **2** **(a)** «*ideología*» to be accepted; «*plan/proyecto*» to come off; «*moda*» to catch on, take off **(b)** «*persona*» to fit in
■ ∼ *vt* ‹*leche*› to curdle

cuajo *m* **1** (sustancia) rennet **2** (raíz): **arrancar algo de** ∼ ‹*planta*› to pull sth out by the roots; ‹*vicio/corrupción*› to root out (completely)

cual *pron* **1** **(a)** **el/la** ∼/**los/las** ∼**es** (hablando de personas) (*sujeto*) who; (*complemento*) who, whom (frml); (hablando de cosas) which; **mis vecinos, a los** ∼**es no conocía** my neighbors who I didn't know *o* (frml) whom I did not know; **el motivo por el** ∼ **lo hizo** the reason why he did it; **según lo** ∼ ... by which ...; **dos de los** ∼**es** two of whom/which **(b)** **lo** ∼ which; **por lo** ∼ as a result, therefore; **con lo** ∼ so **2** (en locs) **cada cual** everyone, everybody; **sea cual sea** or **fuera** or **fuere** whatever

cuál *pron* (uno en particular) which; (uno en general) what; **¿**∼ **quieres?** which (one) do you want?; **¿y** ∼ **es el problema?** so, what's the problem?
■ *adj* (esp AmL): **¿a** ∼ **colegio vas?** what *o* which school do you go to?

cualidad *f* quality

cualificado -da *adj* (Esp) ▶ CALIFICADO

cualificar [A2] *vt* (Esp) ▶ CALIFICAR 2 B

cualquier *adj*: *apocopated form of* CUALQUIERA *used before nouns*

cualquiera¹ (*pl* **cualesquiera** or (crit) **cualquiera**) *adj* [*see also note under* CUALQUIER] any; **en cualquier momento** (at) any time; **cualquier cosa/persona** anything/anyone; **en cualquier lado** anywhere; **de cualquier forma que se haga** whichever way you do it; **lo voy a hacer de** ∼ **forma** I'm going to do it anyway; **es un mercenario** ∼ he's nothing but a mercenary
■ *pron* (refiriéndose – a dos personas o cosas) either (of them); (– a más de dos personas) anybody, anyone; (– a más de dos cosas) any one; **¿cuál de los dos?** — **cualquiera** which one? — either (of them); **pregúntaselo a** ∼ ask anybody *o* anyone (you like); ∼ **que elijas estará bien** whichever (one) you choose *o* any one you choose will be fine

cualquiera² *mf*: **un** ∼ a nobody; **una** ∼ a floozy *o* (BrE) tart (colloq & pey)

cuando *conj* **(a)** (con valor temporal) when; **ven** ∼ **quieras** come when *o* whenever you like; ∼ **se mejore** when she gets better; **ahora es** ∼ **me viene mejor** now is the best time for me **(b)** (si) if; **será verdad** ∼ **él lo dice** it must be true if he says so **(c)** (en locs) **cada cuando** (esp AmL) every so often; **de vez en cuando** from time to time, every so often

cuándo *adv* when; **¿de** ∼ **es esa foto?** when was that photo taken?; **¿desde** ∼ **lo sabes?** how long have you known?; **¿desde** ∼**?** since when?; **¡∼ no!** (AmL) as usual!

cuantificar [A2] *vt* ‹*valor/daños/pérdidas*› to quantify, assess

cuantioso -sa *adj* substantial

cuanto¹ *adv* **(a)** (tanto como) as much as; **grita** ∼ **quieras** shout as much as you like **(b)** (*como conj*): ∼ **más/menos seamos, mejor** the more/ the fewer of us there are, the better; ∼ **antes empecemos, más pronto terminaremos** the sooner we begin, the sooner we'll finish **(c)** (en locs) **cuanto antes** as soon as possible; **en cuanto** (tan pronto como) as soon as; **en cuanto a** (en lo que concierne) as for, as regards

cuanto² -ta *adj*: **llévate** ∼s **discos quieras** take as many records as you want *o* like; **unos** ∼s **amigos** a few friends; **tiene** ∼ **libro hay sobre el tema** she has every book there is on the subject
■ *pron*: **le di todo** ∼ **tenía** I gave her everything I had; **fuimos solo unos** ∼s only a few of us went

cuánto¹ *adv* **(a)** (en preguntas) how much **(b)** (uso indirecto): **si supieras** ∼ **la quiero/lo siento** if you knew how much I love her/how sorry I am

cuánto² -ta *adj* **(a)** (en preguntas) (*sing*) how much; (*pl*) how many; **¿**∼ **café queda?** how much coffee is there left?; **¿**∼ **alumnos tienes?** how many students do you have?; **¿**∼s **años tienes?** how old are you?; **¿**∼ **tiempo tardarás?** how long will you take? **(b)** (uso indirecto) (*sing*) how much; (*pl*) how many; **no sé** ∼ **dinero/**∼s **libros tengo** I don't know how much money/how many books I have **(c)** (en exclamaciones): **¡**∼ **vino!** what a lot of wine!; **¡**∼ **tiempo sin verte!** I haven't seen you for ages! (colloq)
■ *pron* **1** (en preguntas) **(a)** (*sing*) how much; (*pl*) how many; **¿**∼ **pesas?** how much do you weigh?; **¿**∼ **mides?** how tall are you?; **¿**∼s **quieres?** how many do you want?; **¿a** ∼ **estamos hoy?** what's the date today? **(b)** (referido a tiempo) how long; **¿**∼ **falta para llegar?** how long before we get there? ···❖

c

(c) (referido a precios, dinero) how much; ¿~ **cuesta?** how much is it?; ¿~ **es?** how much is that (altogether?)

2 (uso indirecto): **pregúntale** ~ **va a demorar** ask her how long she'll be; **no sé** ~ **puede costar/**~**s tiene** I don't know how much it might cost/how many she has

3 (en exclamaciones): **¡**~ **has tardado!** it's taken you a long time!

cuarenta adj inv/pron/m forty; *para ejemplos ver* CINCUENTA; **cantarle las** ~ **a algn** to give sb a piece of one's mind

cuarentena f (aislamiento) quarantine

cuarentón -tona m,f (fam) person in his/her forties

Cuaresma f Lent

cuarta f (Auto) fourth (gear); **mete la** ~ put it in fourth

cuartel m **(a)** (Mil) barracks (*sing o pl*); ~ **de bomberos** (RPl) fire station, fire house (AmE); ~ **general** headquarters (*sing o pl*) **(b)** (tregua): **no dieron** ~ **a los rebeldes** they showed no mercy to the rebels; **una lucha sin** ~ a merciless fight

cuartelada f, **cuartelazo** m putsch, military uprising

cuarteto m (Mús) quartet

cuarto¹ -ta adj/pron fourth; **la cuarta parte** a quarter; *para ejemplos ver* QUINTO

cuarto² m 1 (habitación) room; (dormitorio) room, bedroom; ~ **de baño** bathroom; ~ **de estar** living room, parlor (AmE), sitting room (BrE); ~ **de (los) huéspedes** guest room, spare room; ~ **trastero** lumber room, junk room

2 **(a)** (cuarta parte) quarter; **un** ~ **de kilo** a quarter (of a) kilo; **un** ~ **de pollo** a quarter chicken; ~ **creciente/menguante** first/last quarter; ~**s de final** quarterfinals (*pl*) **(b)** (en expresiones de tiempo) quarter; **un** ~ **de hora** a quarter of an hour; **la una y** ~ **(a)** quarter after (AmE) *o* (BrE) past one, one fifteen; **es un** ~ **para las dos** *or* (Esp, RPl) **son las dos menos** ~ it is a quarter to two

cuarzo m quartz

cuate mf (Méx) **(a)** (mellizo) twin **(b)** (fam) (amigo) pal (colloq) **(c)** (fam) (tipo, tipa) (m) guy (colloq); (f) woman

cuatrapearse [A1] v pron (Méx) «aparato» to break; «planes» to fall through

cuatrero -ra m,f rustler

cuatrillizo -za m,f quadruplet, quad

cuatro adj inv/pron four; **¿llueve?** — **no, solo son** ~ **gotas** is it raining? no, it's just a drop or two; **le escribí** ~ **líneas** I wrote him a couple of lines; *para más ejemplos ver tb* CINCO

■ m **(a)** (número) (number) four; *para ejemplos ver* CINCO **(b)** (Ven) (guitarra) four-stringed guitar

cuatrocientos -tas adj/pron four hundred; *para ejemplos ver* QUINIENTOS

cuba f **(a)** (barril) barrel, cask; **estar como una** ~ (fam) to be plastered (colloq) **(b)** (tina) tub, vat

Cuba f Cuba

cubalibre m (de ron) rum and coke; (de ginebra) gin and coke

cubano -na adj/m,f Cuban

cubertería f cutlery; **una** ~ **de plata** a set of silver cutlery

cubeta f **(a)** (Fot, Quím) tray; (de paredes más altas) tank **(b)** (para hielo) ice tray **(c)** (barril) keg, small cask **(d)** (Méx) (balde) bucket

cúbico -ca adj cubic; **2m³** (*read as: dos metros cúbicos*) 2m³ (*léase: two cubic meters*)

cubierta f 1 **(a)** (funda) cover; (de libro) cover, sleeve **(b)** (Auto) tire* 2 (Náut) (en barco) deck; **salir a** ~ to go up on deck

cubierto¹ -ta adj ‹cielo› overcast, cloudy; *ver tb* CUBRIR

cubierto² m 1 **(a)** (pieza) piece of cutlery; **los** ~**s de plata** the silver cutlery **(b)** (servicio de mesa) place setting; **pon otro** ~ can you set another place? 2 (en locs) **a cubierto: ponerse a** ~ **de la lluvia** to take cover *o* to shelter from the rain

cubilete m **(a)** (vaso) beaker; (para dados) shaker, cup **(b)** (Col) (sombrero) top hat

cubitera f (bandeja) ice tray; (cubo) ice bucket

cubo m 1 (Esp) bucket; ~ **de (la) basura** (de la cocina) garbage can (AmE), (kitchen) bin (BrE); (de edificio) garbage can (AmE), rubbish bin (BrE) 2 **(a)** (cuerpo geométrico) cube; **cubito de hielo** ice cube; **cubito de caldo** stock cube **(b)** (Mat) cube; **elevar un número al** ~ to cube a number

cubrecama m bedspread

cubrir [I33] vt **(a)** (en general) to cover; ~ **algo DE algo** to cover sth WITH sth; **cubrí al niño con una manta** I covered the child with a blanket **(b)** ‹demanda/necesidad› to meet **(c)** ‹plaza/vacante› to fill

■ **cubrirse** v pron 1 **(a)** (refl) (taparse) to cover oneself; ‹cara› to cover; (ponerse el sombrero) to put one's hat on **(c)** (protegerse) to take cover **(d)** (contra riesgo) to cover oneself 2 (llenarse): **las calles se habían cubierto de nieve** the streets were covered with snow

cucaracha f (Zool) cockroach

cuchara f spoon; ~ **de postre** dessertspoon; ~ **sopera** *or* **de sopa** soup spoon

cucharada f spoonful; ~ **sopera** ≈ tablespoonful

cucharadita f teaspoon, teaspoonful

cucharilla, cucharita f (Coc) teaspoon

cucharón m ladle

cucheta f (RPl) trundle bed, truckle bed

cuchichear [A1] vi (fam) to whisper

cuchilla f **(a)** (de segadora, batidora, cuchillo) blade; (de arado) coulter, share **(b)** tb ~ **de afeitar** (hoja) razor blade; (maquinilla) razor

cuchillada f, **cuchillazo** m **(a)** (golpe) stab; **le dio una** ~ she stabbed him **(b)** (herida) stab wound

cuchillo m knife; ~ **de cocina** kitchen knife

cuchitril m hole (colloq), hovel

cucho -cha m,f 1 (Col fam) **(a)** (padre) dad (colloq); (madre) mom (AmE colloq), mum (BrE colloq) **(b)** (profesor) teacher **(c)** (viejecito) (m) old guy (colloq); (f) old girl (colloq) 2 (Chi fam) (gato) puss (colloq)

cuclillas fpl: **en** ~ squatting, crouching; **ponerse en** ~ to squat

cuco m 1 (Zool) cuckoo 2 (Esp) (de bebé) Moses basket 3 (CS, Per leng infantil) bogeyman

cucú m cuckoo

cucurucho *m* **(a)** (de papel, cartón) cone; (de barquillo) cone **(b)** (helado) cone, cornet (BrE) **(c)** (capirote) hood, pointed hat

cuece, cuecen, etc ▶ COCER

cuello *m* **(a)** (Anat) neck; **le cortaron el ～** they slit *o* cut his throat **(b)** (de botella) neck; **～ de botella** (Auto) bottleneck **(c)** (de prenda de vestir) collar; **sin ～** collarless **(d)** (escote) neck; **～ alto** *or* **vuelto** *or* (AmL) **tortuga** turtleneck (AmE), polo neck (BrE); **～ de pico** V neck; **～ redondo** round neck

cuenca *f* **(a)** (Geog, Geol) basin **(b)** (del ojo) socket

cuenco *m* (recipiente) bowl

cuenta *f*

■ **Nota** Cuando la frase *darse cuenta* va seguida de una oración subordinada introducida por *de que*, en el español latinoamericano existe cierta tendencia a omitir la preposición *de* en el lenguaje coloquial: *se dio cuenta que no iba a convencerla* = he realized (that) he wasn't going to convince her

1 **(a)** (operación, cálculo) calculation, sum; **hacer una ～** to do a calculation *o* sum; **saca la ～** add it up, work it out; **hacer** *o* **sacar ～s** to do some calculations; *a fin de* **～s** after all **(b)** **cuentas** *fpl* (contabilidad): **yo llevo las ～s del negocio** I do the accounts for the business, I handle the money side of the business (colloq); **ella se ocupa de las ～s de la casa** she pays all the bills and looks after the money **(c)** (cómputo) count; **llevar/perder la ～** to keep/lose count; **～ atrás** countdown; *más de la* **～**too much

2 **(a)** (factura) bill; **¿nos trae la ～, por favor?** could we have the check (AmE) *o* (BrE) bill, please?; **la ～ del gas** the gas bill; **a cuenta** on account; **entregó $2.000 a ～** she gave me/him/them $2,000 on account; **este dinero es a ～ de lo que te debo** this money is to go toward(s) what I owe you **(b)** (Com, Fin) (en banco, comercio) account; **abrir/cerrar/liquidar una ～** to open/close/to settle an account; **～ corriente/de ahorro(s)** current/savings account

3 **cuentas** *fpl* (explicaciones): **no tengo por qué darte ～s** I don't have to explain *o* justify myself to you; **dar** *or* **rendir ～s de algo** to account for sth; *en resumidas* **～s** in short

4 (cargo, responsabilidad): **los gastos corren por ～ de la empresa** the expenses are covered *o* paid by the company; **se instaló por su ～** she set up (in business) on her own; **trabaja por ～ propia** she's self-employed

5 **darse ～ (de algo)** (comprender) to realize (sth); (notar) to notice (sth); **se da ～ de todo** she's aware of everything that's going on (around her); **date ～ de que es imposible** you must realize (that) it's impossible; **tener algo en ～** to bear sth in mind; **ten en ～ que es joven** bear in mind that he's young; **sin tener en ～ los gastos** without taking the expenses into account; **tomar algo en ～** to take sth into consideration

6 (de collar, rosario) bead

cuenta, cuentas, etc ▶ CONTAR

cuentagotas *m* (*pl* **～**) dropper

cuentakilómetros *m* (*pl* **～**) (de distancia recorrida) odometer (AmE), mileometer (BrE); (de velocidad) speedometer

cuentero -ra *adj* (Méx, RPl fam) **(a)** (mentiroso): **ser ～** to be a fibber (colloq) **(b)** (chismoso) gossipy

cuentista *adj* **(a)** (fam) (exagerado): **no seas ～, que no duele tanto** don't exaggerate, it doesn't hurt that much **(b)** (fantasioso): **ser ～** to be a fibber (colloq)
■ *mf* **(a)** (Lit) short-story writer **(b)** (fam) (exagerado): **no te fíes de ese ～, es puro teatro** don't fall for his playacting, he's just putting it on **(c)** (fantasioso) fibber (colloq)

cuento *m* **(a)** (narración corta) short story; (para niños) story, tale; **cuéntame un ～** tell me a story; **～ de hadas** fairy story, fairy tale; *venir a* **～**: *eso no viene a* **～** that doesn't come into it; **sin venir a ～** for no reason at all **(b)** (chiste) joke, story **(c)** (fam) (mentira, excusa) story (colloq); **no me vengas con ～s** I'm not interested in your excuses *o* stories **(d)** (fam) (exageración): **todo ese llanto es puro ～** all that crying is just put on; **eso es un ～ chino** what a load of baloney; **el ～ del tío** a con trick

cuento ▶ CONTAR

cuerda *f* **1** **(a)** (gruesa) rope; (delgada) string; **～ floja** (Espec) tightrope **(b)** (Jueg) jump rope (AmE), skipping rope (BrE); **saltar a la ～** to jump rope (AmE), to skip (BrE) **(c)** (para tender ropa) washing line, clothes line **(d)** (de arco) bowstring **2** (Mús) **(a)** (de guitarra, violín) string **(b)** **cuerdas** *fpl* (instrumentos) strings (*pl*); **～s vocales** vocal chords (*pl*) **3** (de reloj, juguete): **un juguete de ～** a clockwork toy; **le dio ～ al despertador** she wound up the alarm clock

cuerdo -da *adj* [ESTAR] sane; **no está ～** he is insane

cuerno *m* **(a)** (de toro) horn; (de caracol) feeler; (de ciervo) antler; **irse al ～** (fam) «*plan*» to fall through; «*fiesta*» to be ruined *o* spoiled; **ponerle los ～s a algn** (fam) to be unfaithful to sb **(b)** (Mús) horn

cuero *adj* (Méx fam) gorgeous (colloq)
■ *m* **(a)** (piel) leather; (sin curtir) skin, hide; **chaqueta de ～** leather jacket; **～ de chancho** (AmL) pigskin; **～ de vaca** cowhide; **en ～s** (*vivos*) (fam) (desnudo) stark naked (colloq); **ser un ～** (Chi, Méx fam) «*mujer*» she's a real stunner (colloq); «*hombre*» he's a real hunk (colloq)

cuerpo *m* **1** **(a)** (Anat) body; **el ～ humano** the human body; **retrato/espejo de ～ entero** full-length portrait/mirror; **～ a ～** hand-to-hand **(b)** (cadáver) body, corpse **(c)** (Fís) (objeto) body, object **2** (conjunto de personas, de ideas, normas) body; **～ de bomberos** fire department (AmE), fire brigade (BrE); **～ de policía** police force; **～ diplomático** diplomatic corps **3** (consistencia, densidad): **de mucho ～** ‹*tela*› heavy; ‹*vino*› full-bodied

cuervo *m* raven; (como nombre genérico) crow

cuesco *m* (Bot) stone

cuesta *f* **(a)** (pendiente) slope; **una ～ muy pronunciada** a very steep slope **ir ～ arriba** to go uphill; **iba corriendo ～ abajo** I was running downhill **(b)** a cuestas: **llevar algo a ～s** to carry sth on one's shoulders/back; **echarse algo a ～s** ‹*carga/bulto*› to put sth on one's back; ‹*problema*› to burden oneself with sth

cuesta, cuestan, etc ▶ COSTAR

cuestión *f* **(a)** (tema, problema) question, matter; **cuestiones de derecho internacional** matters *o*

questions of international law; **llegar al fondo de la ~** to get to the heart of the matter **(b)** (*en locs*) **en cuestión** in question; **en cuestión de** in a matter of; **la cuestión es ...** the thing is ...; **la ~ es divertirnos** the main thing is to enjoy ourselves; **ser cuestión de** to be a matter of; **todo es ~ de ...** it's just a question of ...

cuestionar [A1] *vt* to question

cuestionario *m* (encuesta) questionnaire; (Educ) question paper, questions (*pl*)

cuete *m* ⟨1⟩ (Méx, RPI fam) (borrachera): **agarrar un ~** to get plastered (colloq) ⟨2⟩ (AmL fam) (petardo) firecracker ⟨3⟩ (Per fam) (pistola) shooter (colloq), rod (sl) ⟨4⟩ (Méx) (Coc) braising steak

cueva *f* cave

cueza, cuezan, etc ► COCER

cuidado¹ -da *adj* ⟨*presentación*⟩ meticulous, careful; ⟨*aspecto*⟩ impeccable; ⟨*dicción*⟩ precise

cuidado² *m* **(a)** (precaución): **tener ~** to be careful; **lo envolvió con mucho ~** she wrapped it very carefully; **¡~ con el escalón!** mind the step!; **~ con lo que haces** watch o be careful what you do ; **de ~** (fam) ⟨*problema/herida*⟩ serious **(b)** (atención) care; **pone mucho ~ en su trabajo** he takes a great deal of care over his work **(c)** (de niños, enfermos): **no tiene experiencia en el ~ de los niños** he has no experience of looking after children; **estar al ~ de algn/algo** (cuidar) to look after sb/sth; (ser cuidado por) to be in sb's care **(d)** **cuidados** *mpl* (Med) attention, care, treatment; **necesita los ~s de una enfermera** she needs to be looked after by a nurse; **~s intensivos** intensive care **(e)** (preocupación): **pierde ~** (AmL) don't worry; **me tiene sin ~** I'm not worried
■ *interj* be careful!, watch out!

cuidador -dora *m,f* (de niños) baby sitter (AmE), childminder (BrE); (de animales) zookeeper; (Esp) (de discapacitados) carer

cuidadoso -sa *adj* **(a)** ⟨*persona*⟩ careful; **~ CON algo** careful WITH sth **(b)** ⟨*búsqueda/investigación*⟩ careful, thorough

cuidar [A1] *vt* **(a)** ⟨*juguetes/plantas/casa*⟩ to look after; ⟨*niño*⟩ to look after, take care of; ⟨*enfermo*⟩ to care for, look after **(b)** ⟨*estilo/apariencia*⟩ to take care over; **debes ~ la ortografía** you must take care over your spelling
■ ~ *vi* **~ DE algo/algn** to take care OF sth/sb; **~ré de que no les falte nada** I'll make sure they have everything they need
■ **cuidarse** *v pron* (*refl*) to take care of oneself, look after oneself; **¡cuídate!** take care!; **se cuidó bien de no volver por ahí** he made very sure he didn't go back there; **cuídate de decir algo que te comprometa** take care not to say something which might compromise you

cuije *mf* (Méx) office junior

culantro *m* (fam) coriander

culata *f* **(a)** (de escopeta, revólver) butt; (de cañón) breech **(b)** (de motor) cylinder head

culebra *f* (Zool) snake

culebrón *m* (fam) soap opera, soap (colloq)

culinario -ria *adj* culinary (frml)

culminación *f* **(a)** (de carrera, negociaciones) culmination; (de fiesta) climax **(b)** (realización) fulfillment*

culminante *adj*: **punto ~** (de carrera) peak, high point; (de historia, película) climax; (de negociaciones) crucial stage

culminar [A1] *vi* (llegar al clímax): **la novela culmina cuando ...** the novel reaches its climax when ...; **~ EN** *or* **CON algo** to culminate IN sth

culo *m* (fam: en algunas regiones vulg) **(a)** (nalgas) backside (colloq), butt (AmE colloq), bum (BrE colloq), ass (AmE vulg), arse (BrE vulg); **te voy a pegar en el ~** I'm going to spank o smack you **(b)** (de vaso, botella) bottom

culpa *f* **(a)** (responsabilidad) fault; **yo no tengo la ~** it's not my fault; **echarle la ~ a algn** (de algo) to blame sb o put the blame on sb (for sth); **llegó tarde por ~ del tráfico** he arrived late because of the traffic **(b)** (falta, pecado) sin

culpabilidad *f* (Der,Psic) guilt

culpable *adj* [SER] ⟨*persona*⟩ guilty; **sentirse ~ de algo** to feel guilty about sth; **ser ~ de algo** to be to blame for sth; (Der) to be guilty of sth
■ *mf* (de delito) culprit **(b)** (de problema, situación): **tú eres el ~ de todo esto** this is all your fault, you're to blame for all this

culpar [A1] *vt* to blame; **~ a algn DE algo** to blame sb FOR sth, blame sth ON sb

cultivable *adj* cultivable

cultivado -da *adj* cultivated

cultivar [A1] *vt* **(a)** ⟨*campo/tierras*⟩ to cultivate, farm; ⟨*plantas*⟩ to grow, cultivate **(b)** ⟨*bacterias/perlas*⟩ to culture **(c)** ⟨*amistad*⟩ to cultivate; ⟨*inteligencia/memoria*⟩ to develop; ⟨*artes/interés*⟩ to encourage

cultivo *m* **(a)** (de tierra) farming, cultivation; (de plantas, frutas) growing, cultivation; **~ intensivo** intensive farming **(b)** (cosa cultivada) crop; **~s de secano** dry-farmed crops **(c)** (Biol, Med) (acción) culturing; (producto) culture **(d)** (de las artes) promotion, encouragement

culto¹ -ta *adj* **(a)** ⟨*persona/pueblo*⟩ educated, cultured **(b)** (Ling) ⟨*palabra*⟩ learned; ⟨*literatura/música*⟩ highbrow

culto² *m* **(a)** (adoración, creencia) worship; **rendir ~ a algo/algn** to worship sth/sb; **libertad de ~(s)** freedom of worship **(b)** (interés obsesivo) cult; **el ~ del dinero** the cult of money

cultura *f* **(a)** (civilización) culture **(b)** (conocimientos, ilustración): **una persona de gran ~** a very well-educated o cultured person; **~ general/musical** general/musical knowledge; **la ~ popular** popular culture

cultural *adj* cultural; **un acto ~** a cultural event; **bajo nivel ~** low standard of general education

culturismo *m* bodybuilding

cumbre *f* **(a)** (de montaña) top **(b)** (apogeo) height; **en la ~ del éxito** at the height of his success **(c)** (Pol) summit (meeting)

cumpleañero -ra *m,f* (fam) (*m*) birthday boy (colloq); (*f*) birthday girl (colloq)

cumpleaños *m* (*pl* ∼) **(a)** (aniversario) birthday; **¡feliz ∼!** happy birthday!; **¿qué vas a hacer el día de tu ∼?** what are you going to do on your birthday? **(b)** (fiesta) birthday party

cumplido¹ -da *adj* [SER] **(a)** (atento, cortés) polite **(b)** (considerado) thoughtful **(c)** (Col) (puntual) punctual; *ver tb* CUMPLIR

cumplido² *m*: **hacerle un ∼ a algn** to pay sb a compliment; **una visita de ∼** a duty *o* courtesy call; **la invitó por ∼** he invited her because he felt he ought to

cumplidor -dora *adj* reliable

cumplimiento *m* [1] **(a)** (de ley, norma) performance; **falleció en el ∼ del deber** he died in the line of duty; **en ∼ con lo dispuesto por la legislación vigente** in compliance with current legislation; **la ley es de obligado ∼ para todas las empresas** the law is binding on all companies (frml) **(b)** (logro): **esto favorecerá el ∼ de nuestros objetivos** this will help to achieve our objectives [2] (elogio, piropo) ▶ CUMPLIDO²

cumplir [I1] *vt* [1] **(a)** (ejecutar) ‹*orden*› to carry out; ‹*ley*› to obey; **la satisfacción del deber cumplido** the satisfaction of having done one's duty **(b)** ‹*promesa/palabra*› to keep; ‹*compromiso*› to honor*, fulfill*; ‹*obligación/ contrato*› to fulfill* **(c)** (alcanzar) ‹*objetivo/ ambición*› to achieve; ‹*requisitos*› fulfill*; **¡misión cumplida!** mission accomplished **(d)** (desempeñar) ‹*papel*› to perform, fulfill*
[2] ‹*condena/sentencia*› to serve; ‹*servicio militar*› to do
[3] ‹*años/meses*›: **mañana cumple 20 años** she'll be 20 tomorrow; **¡que cumplas muchos más!** many happy returns!; **mañana cumplimos 20 años de casados** (AmL) tomorrow we'll have been married 20 years

■ ∼ *vi* **(a)** ∼ **CON algo** ‹*con obligación*› to fulfill* sth, satisfy sth; ‹*con tarea*› to carry out sth; ‹*con trámite*› to comply WITH sth; ‹*con requisito/ condición*› to fulfill* sth; **cumple con su deber** he does his duty **(b)** (con una obligación social): **nos invitó solo por ∼** she only invited us because she felt she ought to; **con los Lara ya hemos cumplido** we've done our bit as far as the Laras are concerned (colloq)

■ **cumplirse** *v pron* **(a)** «*deseo/predicción*» to come true; «*ambición*» to be realized, be fulfilled **(b)** «*plazo*»: **mañana se cumple el plazo para pagar el impuesto** tomorrow is the last day for paying the tax; **hoy se cumple el primer aniversario de ...** today marks the first anniversary of ...

cuna *f* **(a)** (tradicional) cradle; (cama con barandas) crib (AmE), cot (BrE); (portabebé) portacrib (AmE), carrycot (BrE) **(b)** (liter) (lugar de nacimiento) birthplace

cuncho *m* (Col) (poso — del café) grounds (*pl*); (— del vino) lees (*pl*)

cuncuna *f* (Chi) (Zool) caterpillar

cundir [I1] *vi* **(a)** «*rumor*» to spread; «*miedo*» to grow; **¡que no cunda el pánico!** don't panic!; **cundió la alarma** there was widespread alarm **(b)** (rendir) «*detergente/lana*» to go a long way; **hoy no me ha cundido el trabajo** I haven't got much work done today

cuneta *f* **(a)** (en carretera) ditch **(b)** (Chi) (de calle) curb (AmE), kerb (BrE)

cuña *f* [1] **(a)** (pieza triangular) wedge; **en ∼** in a V-formation *o* wedge formation **(b)** (Col) (muesca) groove [2] (CS fam) ▶ PALANCA 2

cuñado -da *m,f* **(a)** (pariente político) (*m*) brother-in-law; (*f*) sister-in-law; **mis ∼s** (solo varones) my brothers-in-law; (varones y mujeres) my brothers and sisters-in-law **(b)** (Per fam) (compañero) buddy (AmE colloq), mate (BrE colloq)

cuño *m* (troquel) die; (sello) stamp; **de nuevo ∼** ‹*palabra*› newly-coined (*before n*)

cuota *f* **(a)** (de club, asociación) membership fees (*pl*); (de sindicato) dues (*pl*); ∼ **inicial** deposit, down payment **(b)** (AmL) (plazo) installment*, payment; (parte proporcional) quota; ∼**s de producción** production quotas **(c)** (Méx) (Auto) toll

cupe ▶ CABER

Cupido *m* Cupid

cupiera, cupiese, etc ▶ CABER

cupimos, cupisteis, etc ▶ CABER

cupo *m* **(a)** (cantidad establecida) quota **(b)** (AmL) (capacidad) room; **una sala con ∼ para 300 personas** a hall with room for 300 people **(c)** (AmL) (plaza) place

cupo, cupiste, etc ▶ CABER

cupón *m* **(a)** (vale) coupon, voucher **(b)** (Esp) (de lotería) ticket

cúpula *f* (Arquit) dome, cupola

cura *m* (sacerdote) priest; **se metió de** *or* **a ∼** he became a priest
■ *f* **(a)** (curación, tratamiento) cure; **tener/no tener ∼** to be curable/incurable; ∼ **de urgencias** first aid **(b)** (vendaje) dressing; (curita) (Col) Band-Aid® (AmE), (sticking) plaster (BrE)

curable *adj* curable

curación *f* **(a)** (tratamiento) treatment **(b)** (recuperación—de enfermo) recovery; (— de herida) healing

curado -da *adj* [1] ‹*jamón/carne*› cured; ‹*cuero/ piel*› tanned [2] (fam) (borracho) plastered (colloq)

curandero -ra *m,f* (en medicina popular) folk healer; (hechicero) witch doctor; (charlatán) (pey) quack doctor (pej)

curar [A1] *vt* [1] **(a)** (poner bien) ‹*enfermo/ enfermedad*› to cure; ‹*herida*› to heal **(b)** (tratar) ‹*enfermo/enfermedad*› to treat; ‹*herida*› (desinfectar) to clean; (vendar) to dress [2] ‹*jamón/ pescado*› to cure; ‹*cuero/piel*› to tan
■ **curarse** *v pron* «*enfermo*» to recover, get better; «*herida*» to heal up; ∼**se DE algo** to get over sth

curda *mf* (RPl fam) (borracho) soak (colloq)

curiosear [A1] *vi* **(a)** (fisgonear) to pry; ∼ **en la vida ajena** to pry into other people's affairs; **estaba curioseando en mis cajones** he was going *o* looking through my drawers **(b)** (por las tiendas, en una biblioteca) to browse

curiosidad *f* (cualidad) curiosity; **por ∼** out of curiosity; **siente mucha ∼** he is very curious; **tengo ∼ por saberlo** I'm curious to know; **están muertos de ∼** they are dying to see him (*o* to know *etc*)

curioso -sa *adj* [1] (interesante, extraño) curious, ⋯⟶

strange, odd **2** **(a)** [SER] (inquisitivo) inquisitive; (entrometido) (pey) nosy* (colloq) **(b)** [ESTAR] (interesado) curious
■ *m,f* **(a)** (espectador) onlooker **(b)** (fam) (fisgón) busybody (colloq)

curita *f* (AmL) Band-Aid® (AmE), (sticking) plaster (BrE)

currículo *m* (Educ) curriculum

curriculum, currículum *m* (*pl* **-lums**) **(a)** (antecedentes) *tb* ~ **vitae** curriculum vitae, CV **(b)** (Educ) curriculum

curry /'kurri/ *m* (*pl* **-rries**) (polvo) curry powder; (plato) curry; **pollo al** ~ curried chicken

cursar [A1] *vt* (estudiar): **cursa segundo** (año) she is in her second year; **cursó estudios de Derecho** she did *o* studied *o* (BrE) read Law

cursi *adj* (fam) ⟨objeto⟩ corny, twee (BrE); ⟨idea⟩ sentimental, twee (BrE); ⟨decoración⟩ chichi; ⟨persona⟩ affected;
■ *mf* (fam): **es un** ~ he's so affected *o* (BrE) twee

cursillo *m* **(a)** (curso corto) short course; ~ **de natación** swimming lessons **(b)** (ciclo de conferencias) series of lectures

cursiva *f* italics (*pl*)

curso *m* **1** (Educ) **(a)** (año académico) year; **está en (el) tercer** ~ he's in the third year; **el** ~ **escolar/universitario** the academic year **(b)** (de inglés, mecanografía) course; ~ **intensivo** crash *o* intensive course; **C~ de Orientación Universitaria** (en Esp) pre-university course; ~ **por correspondencia** correspondence course **2** **(a)** (transcurso, desarrollo) course; **dejar que algo siga su** ~ to let sth take its course **(b)** (de río) course **3** (circulación): **monedas de** ~ **legal** legal tender, legal currency

cursor *m* cursor

curtido -da *adj* ⟨rostro/piel⟩ weather-beaten; ⟨manos⟩ hardened

curul *f* (Col, Méx) (Pol) seat

curva *f* **(a)** (línea) curve **(b)** (en camino, carretera) curve; (más pronunciada) bend; **una** ~ **cerrada** a sharp bend **(c)** (Dep) curveball **(c)** **curvas** *fpl* (de una mujer) curves (*pl*); **con** ~**s** curvaceous

curvo -va *adj* curved

cúspide *f* **(a)** (de montaña) top, summit; (de pirámide) top, apex **(b)** (de fama, poder) height, pinnacle **(c)** (de organización) leadership

custodia *f* custody; **le otorgaron la** ~ **de los hijos** she was granted custody of the children

cusuco *m* (AmC) armadillo

cutáneo -nea *adj* skin (*before n*), cutaneous (tech)

cutícula *f* cuticle

cutis *m* (*pl* ~) skin

cuy *m* (AmS) guinea pig

cuye *m* (Chi) guinea pig

cuyo -ya *adj* whose; **un amigo** ~**s hijos van a ese colegio** a friend whose children go to that school; **vocablos** ~ **uso es extendido** words which are in widespread use, **en** ~ **caso** in which case

C.V. *m* (= **curriculum vitae**) CV

Dd

D, d *f* (*read as* /de/) *the letter* D, d

D. = **Don**

dactilar *adj* finger (*before n*); ▶ HUELLA A

dactilografía *f* typing, typewriting

dactilógrafo -fa *m,f* typist

dado¹ -da *adj* **1** (determinado) given; **en un momento** ~ at a given moment **2** (*como conj*) given; **dadas las circunstancias** given *o* in view of the circumstances; ~ **que** given that **3** [SER] (proclive) ~ **A algo/hacer algo** given TO sth/doing sth

dado² *m* **1** (Jueg) dice, die (frml); **jugar a los** ~**s** to play dice **2** (Arquit) dado

daga *f* dagger

dalia *f* dahlia

daltónico -ca *adj* color-blind*
■ *m,f*: **los** ~**s** people suffering from color-blindness*

daltonismo *m* color-blindness*

dama *f* **1** (frml) (señora) lady; ~**s y caballeros** ladies and gentlemen; ~ **de honor** (de novia) bridesmaid; (de reina) lady-in-waiting **2** (figura —

en damas) king; (— en ajedrez, en naipes) queen **3** **damas** *fpl* (juego) checkers (AmE), draughts (BrE); **jugar a las** ~**s** to play checkers *o* draughts

damasco *m* **1** (Tex) damask **2** (AmS) (fruta) apricot; (árbol) apricot tree

Damasco *m* Damascus

damnificado -da *m,f* (frml) victim

danés -nesa *adj* Danish
■ *m,f* **(a)** (persona) (*m*) Dane, Danish man; (*f*) Dane, Danish woman **(b)** **danés** *m* (idioma) Danish

danza *f* dance; ~ **moderna** modern dance

danzar [A4] *vi* (frml) (bailar) to dance

danzarín -rina *adj*: **es muy** ~ he loves dancing
■ *m,f* dancer

dañar [A1] *vt* (en general) to damage; ⟨salud/ organismo⟩ to be bad for
■ **dañarse** *v pron* **1** (en general) to be/get damaged; ⟨salud⟩ to damage **2** (Col, Ven) **(a)** «carne/comida» to rot, go bad **(b)** «carro» to break down; «aparato» to break

dañino -na *adj* [SER] ⟨planta/sustancia⟩ harmful; ~ **PARA algo** harmful TO sth

daño m **(a)** (dolor físico): **hacerse** ∼ to hurt oneself; **me he hecho** ∼ **en la espalda** I've hurt my back; **hacerle** ∼ **a algn** «*persona*» to hurt sb; **el picante me hace** ∼ hot, spicy food doesn't agree with me **(b)** (destrozo) damage; **sufrir** ∼**s** to be damaged, to suffer damage **(c)** ∼**s y perjuicios** damages (*pl*)

dar [A25] *vt*

I ⌷1⌷ **(a)** (entregar) to give; **dale las llaves a Pedro** give the keys to Pedro; **déme un kilo de peras** can I have a kilo of pears?; ▶ CONOCER *vt* 3 B, ENTENDER *vt* ⌷1⌷ «*cartas/mano*» to give **⌷2⌷ (a)** (donar, regalar) «*sangre/limosna*» to give; **me dio su reloj** she gave me her watch **(b)** (proporcionar) «*fuerzas/valor/esperanza*» to give; «*información/idea*» to give

⌷3⌷ (a) (conferir, aportar) «*sabor/color/forma*» to give **(b)** (aplicar) «*mano de pintura/barniz*» to give **(c)** «*sedante/masaje*» to give

⌷4⌷ (conceder) «*prórroga/permiso*» to give; **el dentista me dio hora para el miércoles** I have an appointment with the dentist on Wednesday; **nos dieron un premio** we won *o* got a prize

⌷5⌷ (a) (expresar, decir) «*parecer/opinón*» to give; **¿le diste las gracias?** did you thank him?, did you say thank you?; **dales saludos** give/send them my regards; **tuve que** ∼**le la noticia** I was the one who had to break the news to him **(b)** (señalar, indicar): **me da ocupado** *or* (Esp) **comunicando** the line's busy *o* (BrE) engaged; **el reloj dio las cinco** the clock struck five

II ⌷1⌷ **(a)** (producir) «*fruto/flor*» to bear; «*dividendos*» to pay; **un negocio que da mucho dinero** a business which makes a lot of money **(b)** (AmL) (alcanzar hasta): **da 150 kilómetros por hora** it can do *o* go 150 kilometres an hour; **venía a todo lo que daba** it was travelling at full speed; **ponen la radio a todo lo que da** they turn the radio on full blast

⌷2⌷ (causar, provocar) «*placer/susto*» to give; «*problemas*» to cause; ∼ **trabajo** to be hard work; **el calor le dio sueño/sed** the heat made him sleepy/thirsty

III ⌷1⌷ **(a)** (presentar) «*concierto*» to give; **¿qué dan esta noche en la tele?** what's on TV tonight? (colloq); **¿dónde están dando esa película?** where's that film showing?

⌷2⌷ (a) «*fiesta/conferencia*» to give; «*baile/banquete*» to hold; «*discurso*» (AmL) to make **(b)** (CS) «*examen*» to take *o* (BrE) sit; *ver tb* CLASE 4

IV (realizar la acción que se indica) «*grito*» to give; ∼ **un paso atrás** to take a step back; **dame un beso** give me a kiss; *ver tb* GOLPE, PASEO, VUELTA, ETC

V (considerar) ∼ **algo/a algn POR algo: lo dieron por muerto** they gave him up for dead; **ese tema lo doy por sabido** I'm assuming you've already covered that topic; **¡dalo por hecho!** consider it done!

■ ∼ *vi*

I ⌷1⌷ **dar a** «*puerta*» to give onto, open onto; «*ventana/balcón*» to look onto, give onto; «*fachada/frente*» to face

⌷2⌷ (ser suficiente, alcanzar) ∼ **PARA algo/algn** to be enough FOR sth/sb; **no me dio (el) tiempo** I didn't have time; ∼ **de sí** «*zapatos/jersey*» to stretch

⌷3⌷ (arrojar un resultado): **el análisis le dio positivo** her test was positive; **¿cuánto da la cuenta?** what does it come to?; **a mí me dio 247** I made it (to be) 247

⌷4⌷ (importar): **da lo mismo** it doesn't matter; **¡qué**

más da! what does it matter!; **¿qué más da?** what difference does it make?; **me da igual** I don't mind

⌷5⌷ (en naipes) to deal

II ⌷1⌷ **(a)** (pegar, golpear): ∼**le A algn** to hit sb; (como castigo) to smack sb; **dale al balón** kick the ball; **el balón dio en el poste** the ball hit the post **(b)** (acertar) to hit; ∼ **en el blanco** to hit the target

⌷2⌷ (accionar, mover) ∼**le A algo** «*a botón/tecla*» to press sth; «*a interruptor*» to flick sth; «*a manivela/volante*» to turn sth

⌷3⌷ dar con (encontrar) «*persona*» to find; «*solución*» to hit upon, find; «*palabra*» to come up with

⌷4⌷ (hablando de manías, ocurrencias) ∼**le a algn POR hacer algo** «*por pintar/cocinar*» to take to doing sth; **le ha dado por decir que …** he's started saying that …

⌷5⌷ «*sol/luz*»: **aquí da el sol toda la mañana** you get the sun all morning here; **la luz le daba de lleno en los ojos** the light was shining right in his eyes

■ **darse** *v pron*

I ⌷1⌷ (producirse) «*fruta/trigo*» to grow **⌷2⌷** (presentarse) «*oportunidad/ocasión*» to arise **⌷3⌷** (resultar) (+ *me/te/le etc*): **se le dan los idiomas** she's good at languages

II (a) (refl) (realizar lo que se indica) «*ducha/banquete*» to have; **dárselas de algo: se las da de valiente/de que sabe mucho** he likes to make out he's brave/he knows a lot; **dárselas de listo** to act smart **(b)** (golpearse, pegarse): **se dio con el martillo en el dedo** he hit his finger with the hammer; **se dieron contra un árbol** they crashed into a tree; **se dio** ∼ **un golpe en la rodilla** he hit his knee

III (considerarse) ∼**se POR algo: con eso me** ∼**ía por satisfecha** I'd be quite happy with that; *ver tb* ALUDIR A, ENTERADO 1

dardo m **(a)** (Jueg) dart; **jugar a los** ∼**s** to play darts **(b)** (arma) small spear

datar [A1] *vi* to date; **data del siglo XII** it dates from the 12th century; **data de hace muchos años** it goes back many years

dátil m (Bot) date

dativo m (Ling) dative

dato m **(a)** (elemento de información) piece of information; **no dispongo de todos los** ∼**s** I don't have all the information; ∼**s personales** personal details (*pl*) **(b) datos** mpl (Inf) data (*pl*), information

d. de C. (= **después de Jesucristo**) AD

de[1] *prep* ⌷1⌷ **(a)** (pertenencia, posesión): **la casa** ∼ ∼ **mis padres** my parents' house; **el rey** ∼ **Francia** the king of France; **no es** ∼ **él** it isn't his; **es un amigo** ∼ **mi hijo** he's a friend of my son's; **un estudiante** ∼ **quinto año** a fifth-year student; **la tapa** ∼ **la cacerola** the saucepan lid; **un avión** ∼ **Mexair** a Mexair plane **(b)** (con un nombre en aposición) of; **la ciudad** ∼ **Lima** the city of Lima; **el aeropuerto** ∼ **Barajas** Barajas airport; **el mes** ∼ **enero** the month of January

⌷2⌷ (a) (procedencia, origen, tiempo) from; **es** ∼ **Bogotá** she's/she comes from Bogotá; **una carta** ∼ **Julia** a letter from Julia; **un amigo** ∼ **la infancia** a childhood friend; **la literatura** ∼ **ese período** the literature of *o* from that period; ∼ **aquí a tu casa** from here to your house **(b)** (material, contenido, composición): **son** ∼ **plástico** they're (made of) ⋯✦

plastic; **una mesa ∼ caoba** a mahogany table; **un vaso ∼ agua** a glass of water; **un millón ∼ dólares** a million dollars **(c)** (causa, modo): **murió ∼ viejo** he died of old age; **∼ tanto gritar** from shouting so much; **verde ∼ envidia** green with envy; **temblando ∼ miedo** trembling with fear; **∼ memoria** by heart; **lo tumbó ∼ un golpe** he knocked him down with one blow **(d)** (en oraciones pasivas) by; **un poema ∼ Neruda** a poem by Neruda; **rodeada ∼ árboles** surrounded by trees **3 (a)** (cualidades, características): **de gran inteligencia** of great intelligence; **objetos ∼ mucho valor** objects of great value; **¿∼ qué color lo quiere?** what color do you want it?; **tiene cara ∼ aburrido** he looks bored; **una botella ∼ un litro** a liter bottle; **la chica ∼ azul** the girl in blue **(b)** (al definir, especificar): **el botón ∼ abajo** the bottom button; **tiene dos metros ∼ ancho** it's two meters wide; **es fácil de pronunciar** it's easy to pronounce; **uno ∼ los míos** one of mine; **el mayor ∼ los Soto** the eldest of the Soto children **4 (a)** (con cifras): **pagan un interés ∼l 15%** they pay 15% interest *o* interest at 15% **(b)** (en comparaciones de cantidad) than; **más ∼ £100** more than *o* over £100; **pesa menos ∼ un kilo** it weighs less than *o* under a kilo; **un número mayor/menor ∼ 29** a number over/under 29 **(c)** (con un superlativo): **es el más caro ∼ todos** it's the most expensive one; **la ciudad más grande ∼l mundo** the biggest city in the world **(d)** (refiriéndose a una parte del día): **∼ día/noche** during the day/at night; **∼ madrugada** early in the morning **5 (a)** (en calidad de) as; **trabaja ∼ secretaria** she works as a secretary; **hace ∼ rey en la obra** he plays (the part of) a king in the play **(b)** (en expresiones de estado, actividad): **∼ mal humor** in a bad mood; **estamos ∼ fiesta** we're having a party **(c)** (indicando uso, destino, finalidad): **el cepillo ∼ la ropa** the clothes brush; **copas ∼ vino** wine glasses; **ropa ∼ cama** bed clothes; **dales algo ∼ comer** give them something to eat; **¿qué hay ∼ postre?** what's for dessert? **6** (con sentido condicional): **∼ haberlo sabido** if I had known, had I known; **∼ no ser así** otherwise

de² *f: name of the letter* d

dé ▶ DAR

deambular [A1] *vi* to wander around *o* about

debajo *adv* **1** [*Latin American Spanish also uses* ABAJO *in many of these examples*] underneath; **no hay nada ∼** there's nothing underneath; **el que está ∼** the one below, the next one down **2 debajo de** (*loc prep*) under, underneath; **∼ del coche** under *o* underneath the car; **∼ del agua** underwater; **por ∼ de la puerta** under the door; **temperaturas por ∼ de lo normal** temperatures below average

debate *m* debate; (más informal) discussion

debatir [I1] *vt* to debate; (más informal) to discuss

debe *m* debit

deber¹ [E1] *vt* ⟨*dinero/favor/explicación*⟩ to owe; **te debo las entradas de ayer** I owe you for the tickets from yesterday

■ **∼** *v aux* **1** (expresando obligación): **debemos trabajar más** we must work harder; **no debes usarlo** you must not use it; **∼ías** *or* **debías habérselo dicho** you ought to have *o* you should have told her; **no se debe mentir** you mustn't tell lies; **no ∼ías haberlo dejado solo** you shouldn't have left him alone **2** (expresando suposición, probabilidad): **deben (de) ser más de las cinco** it must be after five o'clock; **deben (de) haber salido** they must have gone out; **debe (de) estar enamorado** she/he must be in love; **no deben (de) saber la dirección** they probably don't know the address; **no les debe (de) interesar** they can't be interested

■ **deberse** *v pron* **1** (tener su causa en) **∼se** A **algo** to be due TO sth; **se debe a que no estudia** it's due to the fact that she doesn't study; **¿a qué se debe este escándalo?** what's all this racket about?

2 ⟨*persona*⟩ (tener obligaciones hacia) **∼se** A **algn** to have a duty TO sb

deber² *m* **1** (obligación) duty; **cumplió con su ∼** he carried out *o* did his duty **2 deberes** *mpl* (tarea escolar) homework, assignment (AmE)

debido -da *adj* **(a)** (apropiado): **a su ∼ tiempo** in due course; **tratar a algn con el ∼ respeto** to show due respect to sb; **tomó las debidas precauciones** she took the necessary precautions; **como es ∼** ⟨*sentarse/comer*⟩ properly; ⟨*comida/regalo*⟩ proper; **más de lo ∼** too much **(b)** (en locs) **debido a** owing to, on account of; **debido a que** owing to the fact that

débil *adj* **(a)** ⟨*persona/economía/gobierno*⟩ weak **(b)** ⟨*sonido/voz*⟩ faint; ⟨*moneda/argumento*⟩ weak; ⟨*excusa*⟩ feeble, lame; ⟨*luz*⟩ dim, faint; ⟨*sílaba/vocal*⟩ unstressed, weak

debilidad *f* weakness; **siento una gran ∼** I feel terribly debilitated *o* weak; **se aprovechan de su ∼** they take advantage of his weak character; **tener ∼ por algn/algo** to have a soft spot for sb/a weakness for sth

debilitar [A1] *vt* to weaken

■ **debilitarse** *v pron* **(a)** ⟨*persona*⟩ to become weak; ⟨*salud*⟩ to deteriorate; ⟨*voluntad*⟩ to weaken **(b)** ⟨*sonido*⟩ to get *o* become faint/fainter **(c)** ⟨*economía*⟩ to grow *o* become weak/weaker

débito *m* debit; **∼ bancario** (AmL) direct debit, direct billing (AmE)

debutante *mf* (Dep, Espec) player or artist *making his/her public debut*

debutar [A1] *vi* to make one's debut

década *f* decade; **la ∼ de los ochenta** the eighties

decadencia *f* **(a)** (proceso) decline **(b)** (estado) decadence

decadente *adj* **(a)** ⟨*moral/costumbres*⟩ decadent **(b)** ⟨*salud*⟩ declining

decaer [E16] *vi* **(a)** ⟨*ánimo/fuerzas*⟩ to flag; ⟨*enfermo*⟩ to deteriorate; ⟨*interés/popularidad*⟩ to wane **(b)** ⟨*barrio/restaurante*⟩ to go downhill; ⟨*calidad/prestigio*⟩ to decline **(c)** ⟨*imperio/civilización*⟩ to decay, decline

AmC	Central America	Arg	Argentina	Cu	Cuba	Per	Peru
AmL	Latin America	Bol	Bolivia	Ec	Ecuador	RPI	River Plate Area
AmS	South America	Chi	Chile	Esp	Spain	Ur	Uruguay
Andes	Andean Region	CS	Southern Cone	Méx	Mexico	Ven	Venezuela

decaído -da *adj* [ESTAR] low, down (colloq)

decálogo *m* decalogue

decano -na *m,f* (de una facultad) dean; (de una profesión, un grupo) senior member

decapitar [A1] *vt* to behead, decapitate

decatlón *m* decathlon

decena *f*: unidades, ~s y centenas (Mat) units, tens and hundreds; **una ~ de personas** about ten people; **~s de personas lo presenciaron** dozens *o* scores of people witnessed it

decencia *f* decency

decenio *m* decade

decente *adj* **(a)** (honrado, decoroso) decent, respectable **(b)** (aceptable) ‹sueldo/vivienda› decent, reasonable **(c)** [ESTAR] (de apariencia aceptable) respectable

decepción *f* disappointment, letdown (colloq); **me llevé una gran ~** I was very disappointed

decepcionado -da *adj* disappointed; **estar ~ con algo/de algn** to be disappointed with sth/sb

decepcionante *adj* disappointing

decepcionar [A1] *vt* to disappoint; **la película me decepcionó** I was disappointed with the movie

decidido -da *adj* **(a)** [SER] ‹persona/tono› (resuelto, enérgico) decisive, determined **(b)** [ESTAR] **~ A hacer algo** determined *o* resolved to do sth

decidir [I1] *vt* **1** **(a)** (tomar una determinación) to decide; **decidí comprarlo** I decided to buy it **(b)** ‹persona› to make ... decide; **lo que me decidió** what made me decide **2** ‹asunto› to settle; ‹resultado› to decide

■ **~** *vi* to decide; **tiene que ~ entre los dos** she has to choose *o* decide between the two; **~ SOBRE algo** to decide ON sth

■ **decidirse** *v pron* to decide, to make up one's mind; **~se A hacer algo** to decide to do sth; **~se POR algo** to decide ON sth

décima *f* (de segundo, grado) tenth; **tiene 39 y tres ~s** his temperature is 39.3 (degrees)

decimal *m* (número) decimal (number)

décimo¹ -ma *adj/pron* tenth; *para ejemplos ver* QUINTO; **la décima parte** a tenth

décimo² ** *m* **(a) (partitivo) tenth **(b)** (de lotería) *tenth share in a lottery ticket*

decir¹ *m*: **¿cientos de personas? — bueno, es un ~** hundreds of people? — well, figuratively speaking

decir² [I24] *vt* **1** **(a)** ‹palabra/frase/poema› to say; ‹mentira/verdad› to tell; [para ejemplos con complemento indirecto ver división 2] **no digas estupideces** don't talk nonsense!; **¿eso lo dices por mí?** are you referring to me?; **¡no lo dirás en serio!** you can't be serious!; **dijo que sí con la cabeza** he nodded; **no se dice 'andé', se dice 'anduve'** it isn't 'andé', it's 'anduve'; **¡eso no se dice!** you mustn't say that!; **¿cómo se dice 'amor' en ruso?** how do you say 'love' in Russian?; **¿lo encontró? — dice que sí/no** did he find it? — he says he did/he didn't **(b)** **decir misa** to say mass

2 ~le algo A algn to tell sb sth; **voy a ~le a papá que ...** I'm going to tell Dad ...; **¡ya te lo decía yo!** I told you so!

3 (a) (expresando órdenes, deseos, advertencias): **¡porque lo digo yo!** because I say so!; **harás lo que yo diga** you'll do as I say; **dice que llames**

cuando llegues she says (you are) to phone when you get there; **dijo que tuviéramos cuidado** she said to be careful; **diles que empiecen** tell them to start; **le dije que no lo hiciera** I told him not to do it **(b)** **~(le) adiós (a algn)** to say goodbye (to sb)

4 (a) (opinar, pensar) to think; **¿y los padres qué dicen?** what do her parents think of it?, how do her parents feel about it?; **¡quién lo hubiera dicho!** who would have thought *o* believed it?; **es muy fácil — si tú lo dices ...** it's very easy — if you say so ... **(b)** (sugerir, comunicar): **el tiempo lo dirá** time will tell; **¿te dice algo ese nombre?** does that name mean anything to you?

5 **querer decir** «palabra/persona» to mean; **¿qué quieres ~ con eso?** what do you mean by that?

6 (*en locs*) **a decir verdad** to tell you the truth, to be honest; **como quien dice** so to speak; **es decir** that is; **¡he dicho!** that's that *o* final!; **ni que decir tiene ...** it goes without saying that ...; **¡no me digas!** no!, you're kidding *o* joking! (colloq); **por así decirlo** so to speak; **el qué dirán** (fam) what other people (might) think; *ver tb* DICHO¹

■ **~** *vi* **(a)** (invitando a hablar): **papá — dime, hijo** dad — yes, son?; **quería pedirle un favor — usted dirá** I wanted to ask you a favor — certainly, go ahead **(b)** (Esp) (al contestar el teléfono): **¿diga?** *or* **¿dígame?** hello?

■ **decirse** *v pron* **(a)** (*refl*) to say ... to oneself **(b)** (*recípr*) to say .... to each other; **se decían secretos al oído** they were whispering secrets to each other

decisión *f* **(a)** (acción) decision; **tomar una ~** to make a decision; **su ~ de marcharse** her decision to leave **(b)** (cualidad) decisiveness, decision; **una mujer con ~** a woman of decision **(c)** (AmL) (en boxeo): **ganó por ~** he won on points *o* by a decision

decisivo -va *adj* ‹fecha/voto/resultado› crucial, decisive; ‹prueba› conclusive; ‹papel› decisive

declaración *f* **1** **(a)** (afirmación) declaration; **una ~ de amor** a declaration of love **(b)** (a la prensa, en público) statement; **hacer una ~** to issue a statement **(c)** (proclamación) declaration; **~ de guerra** declaration of war **2** (Der) statement, testimony; **el policía me tomó ~** the policeman took my statement; **prestar ~ como testigo** to give evidence, to testify; **~ del impuesto sobre la renta** income tax return

declarado -da *adj* declared, professed

declarar [A1] *vt* **1** **(a)** (manifestar) ‹apoyo/oposición/intención› to declare, state; **le declaró su amor** he declared his love to her **(b)** (proclamar) ‹guerra/independencia› to declare; **el jurado lo declaró inocente** the jury found him not guilty **2** **(a)** (en la aduana) to declare **(b)** (Fisco) ‹bienes/ingresos› to declare

■ **~** *vi* to give evidence, testify; **~ como testigo** to give evidence, to testify

■ **declararse** *v pron* **1** **(a)** (manifestarse) to declare oneself; **~se en quiebra** to declare oneself bankrupt; **~se culpable/inocente** to plead guilty/not guilty; **~se en huelga** to go on strike **(b)** (confesar amor): **se le declaró** he declared himself *o* his love to her

2 «incendio/epidemia» to break out

declinación f (Ling) declension

declinar [A1] vt (a) ⟨invitación/oferta/honor⟩ to turn down, decline (frml) (b) (Ling) to decline

declive m (a) (de una superficie) slope, incline (frml); **terreno en** ~ sloping ground (b) (decadencia) decline

decolaje m (AmL) take-off

decolar [A1] vi (AmL) to take off

decoración f (a) (de pasteles, platos) decoration; (de habitación) decor; (de árbol de Navidad) (AmL) decoration (b) (interiorismo) tb ~ **de interiores** interior decoration

decorado m set

decorador -dora m,f: tb ~ **de interiores** interior decorator

decorar [A1] vt to decorate

decorativo -va adj decorative

decoro m (pudor, respeto) decorum

decoroso -sa adj decent, respectable

decrecer [E3] vi (a) «afición/interés» to wane, decrease; «importancia» to decline (b) «número/cantidad» to decline, fall (c) «aguas» to drop, fall

decreciente adj decreasing (before n)

decrépito -ta adj decrepit

decretar [A1] vt to order, decree (frml)

decreto m decree

dedal m thimble

dedicación f dedication

dedicar [A2] vt (a) (consagrar) ~ **algo A algo/ hacer algo** ⟨tiempo/esfuerzos⟩ to devote sth TO sth/doing sth; **dedicó su vida a la ciencia/ayudar a los pobres** she devoted her life to science/to helping the poor (b) (ofrendar, ofrecer) ⟨obra/ canción⟩ to dedicate

■ **dedicarse** v pron (a) (consagrarse) ~**se A algo/ hacer algo** to devote oneself TO sth/doing sth (b) (tener cierta ocupación, profesión): **¿a qué se dedica tu padre?** what does your father do?; **se dedica a la investigación** she does research; **se dedica a pintar en sus ratos libres** she spends her free time painting

dedicatoria f dedication

dedillo m: **conocer algo al** ~ to know sth like the back of one's hand; **sabía la lección al** ~ I knew the lesson (off) by heart

dedo m (de mano, guante) finger; (del pie) toe; **señalar con el** ~ to point; ~ **anular/(del) corazón** ring/middle finger; ~ **gordo** (fam) (del pie) big toe; (de la mano) thumb; ~ **índice** forefinger, index finger; ~ **meñique** little finger; ~ **pulgar** thumb; **a** ~ (fam): **ir a** ~ to hitchhike, hitch (colloq); **recorrió Europa a** ~ she hitchhiked around Europe; **hacer** ~ (fam) to hitchhike, hitch (colloq); **poner el** ~ **en la llaga** to hit o touch a raw nerve; **señalar a algn con el** ~ (literal) to point at sb; (culpar) to point the finger at sb

deducción f deduction

deducible adj ❶ (que se puede inferir) deducible ❷ (Com, Fin) deductible

deducir [I6] vt ❶ (inferir) to deduce; ~ **algo DE algo** to deduce sth FROM sth ❷ (descontar) to deduct

deduje, deduzca, etc ▶ DEDUCIR

defecto m (a) (en un sistema) fault, flaw, defect;

~ **de fábrica** manufacturing fault o defect (b) (de una persona) fault, shortcoming; ~ **físico** physical handicap

defectuoso -sa adj faulty, defective

defender [E8] vt to defend; ⟨intereses⟩ to protect; ~ **a algo/algn DE algo/algn** to defend sth/ sb AGAINST sth/sb

■ **defenderse** v pron (a) (refl) (contra una agresión) to defend o protect oneself; (Der) to defend oneself; ~**se DE algo/algn** to defend oneself AGAINST sth/sb (b) (fam) (arreglárselas) to get by (colloq); **me defiendo bastante bien en francés** I can get by quite well in French

defensa f ❶ (a) (protección) defense*; **salir en** ~ **de algn** to come to sb's defense; **actuó en** ~ **propia** he acted in self-defense; ~ **DE algo/algn** defense* OF sth/sb; ~ **personal** self-defense* (b) (Dep) defense* ❷ (a) **Defensa** f the Defense Department (AmE), the Ministry of Defence (BrE) (b) **defensas** fpl (Biol, Med) defenses* (pl) (c) **defensa** mf (jugador) defender

defensivo -va adj ⟨arma/actitud/táctica⟩ defensive; **estar/ponerse a la defensiva** to be/get on the defensive

defensor -sora adj (a) ⟨ejército⟩ defending (before n) (b) (Der) ⟨abogado⟩ defense* (before n)

■ m,f (a) (Mil) defender (b) (de una causa) champion (c) (Der) defense counsel (AmE), defence lawyer (BrE)

defeño -ña m,f (Méx) person from the DISTRITO FEDERAL

deferencia f (frml) deference; **por** ~ **a algn/ algo** out of o in deference to sb/sth

deficiencia f (a) (defecto) fault (b) (insuficiencia alimentaria, inmunológica) deficiency

deficiente adj poor, inadequate; ⟨salud⟩ poor; ~ **EN algo** deficient IN sth

■ mf (persona) tb ~ **mental** mentally subnormal person

■ m (calificación) poor

déficit m (pl ~ or **-cits**) (a) (Com, Fin) deficit (b) (en la producción) shortfall; (de lluvias) shortage

defienda, defiendas, etc ▶ DEFENDER

definición f (de palabra, postura) definition

definido -da adj clearly-defined

definir [I1] vt to define

definitivamente adv ⟨resolver/rechazar⟩ once and for all; ⟨quedarse/instalarse⟩ permanently, for good

definitivo -va adj ⟨texto/solución/respuesta⟩ definitive; ⟨cierre⟩ permanent, definitive; **ya es** ~ **que no viene** he's definitely not coming

deforestación f deforestation

deforestar [A1] vt to deforest

deformación f (a) (en general) distortion (b) (Anat, Med) deformity

deformar [A1] vt (a) (en general) to distort (b) (Anat, Med) to deform

■ **deformarse** v pron (a) (en general) to become distorted (b) (Anat, Med) to become deformed

deforme adj deformed

defraudar [A1] vt (a) (decepcionar) to disappoint (b) (estafar) to defraud; **defraudó al fisco** he evaded his taxes

defunción f (frml) death; Ⓢ **cerrado por defunción** closed owing to bereavement

degenerado -da *adj/m,f* degenerate

degenerar [A1] *vi* to degenerate; ~ **EN algo** to degenerate INTO sth

degollar [A12] *vt* ⟨*persona/animal*⟩: **lo ~on** they slit his/its throat

degradante *adj* degrading

degradar [A1] *vt* **(a)** (Mil) to demote **(b)** (envilecer) to degrade **(c)** (empeorar) ⟨*calidad/valor*⟩ to diminish
■ **degradarse** *v pron* «*persona*» to demean oneself, degrade oneself

dehesa *f* **(a)** (terreno) meadow, pasture **(b)** (hacienda) farm

dejación *f* (AmC, Chi) ▶ DEJADEZ

dejadez *f* **(a)** (en el aseo personal) slovenliness **(b)** (en tarea, trabajo) laziness, slackness

dejado -da *adj* **(a)** (en aseo personal, aspecto) slovenly **(b)** (en tarea, trabajo) slack, lazy

dejar [A1] *vt*
I **1** **(a)** (en lugar determinado) to leave; **lo dejé en recepción** I left it in reception; **dejó a los niños en el colegio** she dropped the children (off) at school; ~ **un recado** to leave a message; ~ **propina** to leave a tip; **deja ese cuchillo** put that knife down; **déjala, ella no tuvo la culpa** leave her alone, it wasn't her fault; ~ **mucho que desear** to leave a great deal to be desired **(b)** (olvidar) ⟨*dinero/objeto*⟩to leave; **¡déjalo!** forget it! **(c)** (como herencia) to leave
2 **(a)** ⟨*mancha/huella/sabor*⟩ to leave **(b)** ⟨*ganancia*⟩ to produce; **el negocio dejó pérdidas** the business made a loss
3 (abandonar) ⟨*novia/marido*⟩ to leave; ⟨*familia*⟩ to leave, abandon; ⟨*trabajo*⟩ to give up, leave; ⟨*lugar*⟩ to leave; **quiere ~ el ballet** he wants to give up ballet dancing
4 (+ *compl*) (en cierto estado) to leave; **dejé la ventana abierta** I left the window open; **me dejó esperando afuera** she left me waiting outside; **¡déjame en paz!** leave me alone!; **me dejó en 1.000 pesos** he let me have it for 1,000 pesos; ▶ LADO 3
5 **(a)** (posponer) leave; **no lo dejes para después, hazlo ahora** don't put it off *o* leave it until later, do it now **(b)** (reservar, guardar) ⟨*espacio/margen/comida*⟩ to leave
II (permitir) ~**a algo/algn hacer algo** to let sth/sb do sth; **déjalo entrar** let it/him in; **deja correr el agua** let the water run; **¿me dejas ir?** will you let me go?; ~ **que algo/algn haga algo** to let sb/sth do sth; **déjame que te ayude** let me help you; ▶ CAER 1, PASO 1B
■ ~ *vi* ~ **DE hacer algo** to stop doing sth; ~ **de fumar** to give up *o* to stop smoking; **no dejes de escribirme** make sure you write to me
■ **dejarse** *v pron* **1** **(a)** (abandonarse) to let oneself go **(b)** ~**se hacer algo: se deja dominar por la envidia** he lets his feelings of envy get the better of him; **se deja influir fácilmente** he's easily influenced; ~**se llevar por la música** to let oneself be carried along by the music; ~**se estar** (AmL); (descuidarse) to be careless; (abandonarse) to let oneself go
2 ⟨*barba/bigote*⟩ to grow
3 ~**se DE hacer algo** to stop doing sth; **déjate de lamentarte** stop complaining
4 (esp Esp fam) (olvidar) to leave

deje *m* ▶ DEJO A

dejo *m* **(a)** (acento) (slight) accent, lilt **(b)** (de una bebida, comida) aftertaste; ~ **A algo** slight taste OF sth **(c)** (de arrogancia, ironía) touch, hint **(d)** (impresión, sensación): **me quedó un ~ triste** I was left with a feeling of sadness

del: contraction of DE and EL

delantal *m* (para cocinar) apron; (de escolar) pinafore

delante *adv* **1** (lugar, parte) [*Latin American Spanish also uses* ADELANTE *in many of these examples*]: **yo voy ~** I'll go ahead *o* in front; **no te pongas ~** don't stand in front of me; **lo tengo aquí ~** I have it right here; **el asiento de ~** the front seat; **la parte de ~** the front; **el pasajero de ~** the passenger in the front **2** **delante de** (*loc prep*) in front of

delantera *f* **(a)** (en general) lead; **llevar/tomar la ~** to be in/to take the lead **(b)** (Dep) (de equipo) forwards (*pl*), forward line

delantero -ra *adj* ⟨*asiento/rueda*⟩ front (*before n*) **(b)** (Dep) ⟨*línea/posición*⟩ forward (*before n*), offensive (*before n*) (AmE)
■ *m,f* (Dep) forward; ~ **forward center*** forward

delatar [A1] *vt* «*persona*» (acusar) to denounce, inform on
■ **delatarse** *v pron* (*refl*) to give oneself away

delator -tora *adj* **(a)** ⟨*prueba/arma*⟩ incriminating **(b)** ⟨*mirada/sonrisa*⟩ revealing
■ *m,f* informer

delegación *f* **1** (grupo) delegation **2** (de poderes) delegation **3** **(a)** (Méx) (comisaría) police station **(b)** (Esp) (oficina local) regional *o* local office

delegado *m,f* (representante) delegate; ~ **de curso** student representative

delegar [A3] *vt* to delegate; ~ **algo EN algn** to delegate sth TO sb
■ ~ *vi* to delegate

deleitar [A1] *vt* to delight
■ **deleitarse** *v pron* ~**se haciendo algo** to delight IN doing sth, enjoy doing sth

deleite *m* delight

deletrear [A1] *vt* to spell

delfín *m* (Zool) dolphin

delgado -da *adj* **(a)** ⟨*persona/piernas*⟩ (esbelto) slim; (flaco) thin **(b)** ⟨*tela/lámina/pared*⟩ thin; ⟨*hilo*⟩ fine, thin

deliberado -da *adj* deliberate

delicadeza *f* **1** (cuidado, suavidad) gentleness; **con mucha ~** very gently **2** (tacto, discreción) tact; **fue una falta de ~** it was tactless of him (*o* you *etc*) **(b)** (gesto amable): **fue una ~ de su parte traerme** it was very kind of him to bring me; **ni siquiera tuvo la ~ de informarme** he didn't even have the courtesy to inform me

delicado -da *adj* **1** (fino) ⟨*rasgos/manos*⟩ delicate; ⟨*sabor*⟩ delicate, subtle; ⟨*lenguaje/modales*⟩ refined **2** **(a)** (que requiere cuidados) ⟨*cerámica/cristal*⟩ fragile; ⟨*tela*⟩ delicate; ⟨*piel*⟩ sensitive **(b)** ⟨*salud/estómago*⟩ delicate; ⟨*corazón*⟩ weak **3** ⟨*asunto/cuestión/tema*⟩ delicate, sensitive; ⟨*situación*⟩ delicate, tricky **4** **(a)** (melindroso) delicate, fussy **(b)** (susceptible) touchy

delicia *f* delight; **ser una ~** to be delicious

delicioso -sa *adj* ⟨*comida/bebida/sabor*⟩ delicious; ⟨*tiempo*⟩ delightful

delimitar [A1] *vt* **(a)** ⟨*terreno/espacio*⟩ to demarcate (frml), to delimit (frml) **(b)** ⟨*poderes/responsabilidades*⟩ to define, specify

delincuencia *f* crime, delinquency (frml); ∼ **juvenil** juvenile delinquency

delincuente *mf* criminal; ∼ **común** common criminal; ∼ **juvenil** juvenile delinquent

delinear [A1] *vt* **(a)** ⟨*dibujo/plano*⟩ to outline, draft; ⟨*contorno*⟩ to delineate **(b)** ⟨*programa/proyecto*⟩ to formulate, draw up

delinquir [I3] *vi* to commit a criminal offense*

delirar [A1] *vi* (Med) to be delirious; **la fiebre lo hacía** ∼ the fever made him delirious

delirio *m* (Med) delirium; ∼**s de grandeza** *mpl* delusions of grandeur (*pl*)

delito *m* crime, offense*; ∼ **ambiental** environmental crime; ∼ **informático** computer crime

delta *m* (Geog) delta
■ *f* (letra griega) delta

demacrado -da *adj* (pálido) haggard, drawn; (delgado) emaciated

demagogia *f* demagogy, demagoguery

demagogo -ga *m,f* demagogue, demagog (AmE)

demanda *f* **1** (Com) demand; **tiene mucha** ∼ it's in great demand **2 (a)** (Der) lawsuit; **presentar una** ∼ **contra algn** to bring a lawsuit against sb **(b)** (petición) request; **accedí a su** ∼ I agreed to his request

demandado -da *m,f* defendant

demandante *mf* plaintiff

demandar [A1] *vt* **1** (Der) to sue **2** (AmL) (requerir) to require

demarcar [A2] to demarcate

demás *adj inv* (delante del n): **los** ∼ **estudiantes** the rest of the *o* the remaining students
■ *pron* **1 (a) lo** ∼ the rest; **todo lo** ∼ everything else **(b)** (en locs) **por lo demás** apart from that, otherwise; **por demás** extremely **2 los/las** ∼ (referido a cosas) the rest, the others; (referido a personas) the rest, everybody else; **me dio uno y se quedó con los** ∼ he gave me one and kept the rest *o* the others; **los** ∼ **han terminado** the rest (of them) have finished, everybody else has finished

demasía: **en** ∼ ⟨*beber/comer*⟩ to excess; **todo alimento, tomado en** ∼, **es perjudicial** any food, when eaten in excess, can be harmful

demasiado¹ -da *adj* (delante del n): ∼ **dinero** too much money; **había** ∼**s coches** there were too many cars; **hace** ∼ **calor** it's too hot
■ *pron*: **es** ∼ it's too much; **somos** ∼**s** there are too many of us; **hizo** ∼ **s** she made too many

demasiado² *adv* **1** ⟨*pequeño/caliente/caro*⟩ too; **fue un esfuerzo** ∼ **grande para él** it was too much of an effort for him **2** ⟨*comer/hablar/preocuparse*⟩ too much; ⟨*trabajar*⟩ too hard

demencia *f* dementia

demente *adj* insane

■ *mf* insane person

democracia *f* democracy

demócrata *mf* democrat

democratacristiano -na *adj/m,f* Christian Democrat

democrático -ca *adj* democratic

demografía *f* demography

demográfico -ca *adj* demographic, population (before n)

demoledor -dora *adj* **(a)** ⟨*máquina*⟩ demolition (before n) **(b)** ⟨*ataque/crítica*⟩ devastating

demoler [E9] *vt* **(a)** ⟨*edificio*⟩ to demolish, pull down **(b)** ⟨*mito/teoría*⟩ (fam) to debunk, demolish

demonio *m* **1** (diablo) devil **2** (fam) (uso expletivo): **¡cómo** ∼**s lo hizo!** how on earth did he do it?; **¿qué** ∼**s** … **?** what the hell … ? (colloq); **¡**∼**(s)!** (expresando enfado) damn! it takes me 3; (expresando sorpresa) goodness!, heavens!

demora *f* **1** (esp AmL) (retraso) delay; **perdón por la** ∼ I'm sorry I'm late; ∼ **EN hacer algo** delay IN doing sth; **sin** ∼ without delay **2** (Náut) bearing

demorar [A1] *vt* **(a)** (AmL) (tardar): **demoró tres horas en llegar** he took *o* it took him three hours to arrive **(b)** (AmL) (retrasar) ⟨*viaje/decisión*⟩ to delay
■ ∼ *vi* (AmL): **¡no demores!** don't be long!
■ **demorarse** *v pron* (AmL) **(a)** (tardar cierto tiempo): **¡qué poco te demoraste!** that didn't take you very long; **me demoro 3 horas** it takes me 3 hours **(b)** (tardar demasiado) to be *o* take too long; ∼**se EN hacer algo** to take a long time TO do sth

demoroso -sa *adj* (Bol, Chi) ⟨*persona/vehículo*⟩ slow; ⟨*trabajo*⟩ time-consuming

demostración *f* demonstration; (de teorema) proof

demostrar [A10] *vt* **1** ⟨*verdad/teorema*⟩ to prove, demonstrate; ⟨*ignorancia*⟩ to show, prove; **ha demostrado ser muy capaz** he's shown himself to be very able; ∼ **que algo es/no es cierto** to prove sth right/wrong **2 (a)** ⟨*interés/sentimiento*⟩ to show **(b)** ⟨*funcionamiento/método*⟩ to demonstrate

demostrativo -va *adj* **(a)** ⟨*ejemplo*⟩ illustrative **(b)** ⟨*adjetivo/pronombre*⟩ demonstrative **(c)** (AmL) ⟨*persona/carácter*⟩ demonstrative

denantes *adv* (Chi fam) a moment ago, just now

denegar [A7] *vt* (frml) ⟨*permiso/autorización*⟩ to refuse; ⟨*petición*⟩ to turn down; ⟨*recurso*⟩ (Der) to refuse

dengue *m* (Med) dengue fever

denigrante *adj* degrading, humiliating

denigrar [A1] *vt* **(a)** (hablar mal de) to denigrate **(b)** (degradar) to degrade

denominar [A1] *vt* (frml) **(a)** (dar nombre a) to call; **el denominado efecto invernadero** the so-called greenhouse effect **(b)** (con carácter oficial) to designate

denotar [A1] *vt* **(a)** (frml) (demostrar, indicar) to show, denote (frml); **sus modales denotan una esmerada educación** her manners are the sign of an impeccable upbringing **(b)** (Ling) to denote

densidad *f* density; (de vegetación, niebla) thickness, denseness

denso -sa *adj* dense

dentado -da *adj* ‹filo› serrated; **una rueda dentada** a gearwheel, a cogwheel

dentadura *f* teeth (*pl*); ~ **postiza** false teeth (*pl*), dentures (*pl*)

dental *adj* dental

dentera *f* (sensación): **darle** ~ **a algn** to set sb's teeth on edge

dentífrico *m* toothpaste

dentista *mf* dentist

dentística *f* (Chi) dentistry, dental surgery

dentro *adv* **1** (lugar, parte) [*Latin American Spanish also uses* ADENTRO *in this sense*] inside; **aquí/ahí** ~ in here/there; **el perro duerme** ~ the dog sleeps indoors; **por** ~ on the inside; **la parte de** ~ the inside **2** ‹dentro de **(a)** (en el espacio) in, inside; ~ **del edificio** in *o* inside the building **(b)** (en el tiempo) in; ~ **de dos semanas** in two weeks' time **(c)** (de límites, posibilidades) within; ~ **de nuestras posibilidades** within our means

denuncia *f* **1** (de robo, asesinato) report; **hizo la** ~ **del robo del coche** he reported the theft of his car; **presentar una** ~ to make a formal complaint **2** (crítica pública) denunciation

denunciar [A1] *vt* **1** ‹robo/asesinato/persona› to report **2** (condenar públicamente) to denounce, condemn

Dep., Dept. (= **Departamento**) Dept

departamento *m* **1** **(a)** (de empresa, institución) department **(b)** (provincia, distrito) department **2** (AmL) (apartamento) apartment (esp AmE), flat (BrE)

dependencia *f* **1** (condición) dependence; ~ DE algo dependence ON sth **2** **dependencias** *fpl* (edificios) buildings (*pl*); (salas) rooms (*pl*)

depender [E1] *vi* **(a)** «resultado/solución» to depend; ~ DE algo/algn to depend ON sth/sb **(b)** «persona» ~ DE algn/algo to be dependent ON sb/sth

dependiente -ta *m,f* salesclerk (AmE), shop assistant (BrE)

depilación *f* (con cera) waxing; (con crema) hair-removal, depilation (frml); (de cejas) plucking

depilar [A1] *vt* ‹piernas/axilas› to wax (*o* shave *etc*); ‹cejas› to pluck
■ **depilarse** *v pron*: ~**se las piernas** to shave (*o* wax *etc*) one's legs; (*caus*) to have one's legs waxed

deplorable *adj* deplorable

deportar [A1] *vt* to deport

deporte *m* sport; **no practican ningún** ~ they don't play *o* do any sport(s); **hace** ~ **para estar en forma** she does sports (AmE) *o* (BrE) some sport to keep fit; ~ **acuático/de invierno** water/winter sport

deportista *adj* sporty; **fue muy** ~ **en su juventud** he was a keen sportsman in his youth;
■ *mf* (*m*) sportsman (*f*) sportswoman

deportividad *f* sportsmanship

deportivo¹ -va *adj* **(a)** ‹club/centro› sports (*before n*) **(b)** ‹ropa› (para deporte) sports (*before n*); (informal) sporty, casual

deportivo² *m* sports car

depositar [A1] *vt* **1** (frml) **(a)** (colocar) to place, deposit (frml) **(b)** (dejar) to leave, deposit (frml) **2** (Fin) ‹dinero› to deposit; (en cuenta corriente) (AmL) to deposit, pay in (BrE)

depósito *m* **1** **(a)** (almacén) warehouse; ~ **de armas** arms depot; ~ **de cadáveres** morgue, mortuary (BrE) **(b)** (tanque) tank; ~ **de gasolina** gas tank (AmE), petrol tank (BrE) **2** (sedimento) deposit, sediment; (yacimiento) deposit **3** (Fin) **(a)** (AmL) (en una cuenta) deposit **(b)** (garantía) deposit

depravado -da *m,f* degenerate

depreciarse [A1] *v pron* to depreciate, fall in value

depredador¹ -dora *adj* (Zool) ‹animal/ave› predatory

depredador² *m* predator

depresión *f* depression

deprimente *adj* depressing

deprimido -da *adj* depressed

deprimir [I1] *vt* to depress
■ **deprimirse** *v pron* to get/become depressed

deprisa *adv* fast; **trabajar más** ~ to work faster; **¡~! escóndelo** quick! hide it

depurado -da *adj* ‹lenguaje/estilo› polished, refined; ‹gusto› refined

depuradora *f* **(a)** (de aguas residuales) sewage treatment plant **(b)** (en piscina) filter system

depurar [A1] *vt* **1** **(a)** ‹agua› to purify, treat; ‹aguas residuales› to treat **(b)** ‹sangre› to cleanse **2** **(a)** ‹organización/partido› to purge **(b)** ‹lenguaje/estilo› to polish, refine

derecha *f* **1** **(a)** (lado derecho) right; **la primera calle a la** ~ the first street on the right; **dobla a la** ~ turn right; **por la** ~ ‹conducir/caminar› on the right; **mantenga su** ~ keep to the right **(b)** (mano derecha) right hand **2** (Pol): **la** ~ **the Right**; **un político de** ~ *or* (Esp) ~**s** a right-wing politician

derecho¹ -cha *adj* **1** ‹mano/ojo/zapato› right; ‹lado› right, right-hand; **el ángulo superior** ~ the top right-hand corner; **queda a mano derecha** it's on the right-hand side *o* on the right **2** **(a)** (recto) straight; **ese cuadro no está** ~ that picture isn't straight; **siéntate** ~ sit up straight **(b)** (fam) (justo, honesto) honest, straight

derecho² *adv* straight; **siga todo** ~ go *o* keep straight on

derecho³ *m* **1** **(a)** (facultad, privilegio) right; ~**s humanos** human rights (*pl*); **estás en tu** ~ you're within your rights; ~ **A algo** right TO sth; **el** ~ **al voto** the right to vote; **tengo** ~ **a saber** I have a *o* the right to know; **esto da** ~ **a participar** this entitles you to participate; **¡no hay** ~**!** (fam) it's not fair! **(b)** (Com, Fin) tax; ~**s de aduana** customs duties (*pl*); ~**s de autor** royalties; ~ **de matrícula** registration fee; ~ **de reproducción** copyright **2** (Der) law **3** (de prenda) right side, outside; (de tela) right side, face; **póntelo al** ~ put it on properly *o* right side out

deriva *f*: **a la** ~ adrift

derivar [A1] *vi* **(a)** (proceder) ~ DE algo   ···⟊

d

«*palabra*» to derive FROM sth, come FROM sth; «*problema/situación*» to arise FROM sth **(b)** (traer como consecuencia) ~ EN algo to result IN sth, lead TO sth
■ ~ *vt* (Med) (AmL) ~ **a algn a un especialista** to refer sb to a specialist
■ **derivarse** *v pron* (proceder) ~se DE algo «*palabra*» to be derived FROM sth, come FROM sth; «*problema/situación*» to arise FROM sth

dermatólogo -ga *m,f* dermatologist

derogar [A3] *vt* to abolish, repeal

derramar [A1] *vt* **(a)** ‹*agua/leche/azúcar*› to spill; ‹*cuentas/sangre*› to shed **(b)** ‹*lentejas/botones*› to spill, scatter
■ **derramarse** *v pron* **(a)** «*tinta/leche*» to spill; «*corriente*» to pour out **(b)** «*cuentas/botones*» to scatter, spread

derrame *m* **(a)** (Med): **tengo un ~ en el ojo** I have a burst blood vessel in my eye; ~ **cerebral** brain hemorrhage* **(b)** (de líquido) spillage

derrapar [A1] *vi* «*vehículo*» to skid; «*embrague*» to slip; «*llantas*» to spin

derredor: al/en ~ (*loc adv*) around

derretir [I14] *vt* ‹*mantequilla/helado*› to melt; ‹*hielo/nieve*› to melt, thaw
■ **derretirse** *v pron* «*mantequilla/helado*» to melt; «*nieve/hielo*» to thaw, melt

derribar [A1] *vt* **(a)** ‹*edificio/muro*› to demolish, knock down; ‹*puerta*› to break down **(b)** ‹*avión*› to shoot down, bring down **(c)** ‹*persona*› to floor, knock ... down; ‹*novillo*› to knock ... over **(d)** «*viento*» to bring down **(e)** ‹*gobierno*› to overthrow, topple

derrocar [A2] *vt* to overthrow, topple

derrochador -dora *adj*: **es muy ~** he's a real spendthrift
■ *m,f* squanderer, spendthrift

derrochar [A1] *vt* (malgastar) ‹*dinero*› to squander, waste; ‹*electricidad/agua*› to waste
■ ~ *vi* to throw money away, to squander money

derroche *m* (de dinero, bienes) waste

derrota *f* (Dep, Mil) defeat

derrotado -da *adj* **(a)** ‹*ejército*› defeated; ‹*equipo/contrincante*› defeated, beaten **(b)** (desesperanzado) despondent

derrotar [A1] *vt* ‹*ejército/partido*› to defeat; ‹*equipo/contrincante*› to defeat, beat

derrotista *adj/mf* defeatist

derruido -da *adj* ‹*casa*› ruined; **medio ~** virtually in ruins

derrumbamiento *m* collapse

derrumbar [A1] *vt* ‹*casa/edificio*› to demolish, pull down
■ **derrumbarse** *v pron* **(a)** «*edificio*» to collapse **(b)** «*persona*» to go to pieces; «*esperanzas/ilusiones*» to be shattered, collapse

desabastecimiento, (Méx) **desabasto** *m* shortage of supplies (*o* food *etc*)

desabotonarse [A1] *v pron* **(a)** «*prenda*» to come undone **(b)** (*refl*) «*persona*» ‹*camisa/abrigo*› to unbutton, undo

desabrido -da *adj* (comida) tasteless, bland

desabrigado -da *adj* ‹*lugar*› exposed; **estás muy ~** you're not wearing warm enough clothes

desabrochar [A1] *vt* ‹*prenda/zapatos/pulsera*› to undo; **¿me desabrochas?** can you undo me? (colloq)
■ **desabrocharse** *v pron* **(a)** «*prenda*» to come undone **(b)** (*refl*) «*persona*» ‹*camisa/abrigo*› to undo

desaconsejar [A1] *vt* to advise against

desacostumbrarse [A1] *v pron* to get out of the habit; ~ **A hacer algo** to get out of the habit OF doing sth; **se desacostumbró al tráfico de la ciudad** she forgot what city traffic was like

desacreditar [A1] *vt* to discredit
■ **desacreditarse** *v pron* (*refl*) to discredit oneself, damage one's reputation

desactivar [A1] *vt* ‹*bomba/explosivo*› to defuse, deactivate

desacuerdo *m* disagreement; ~ **CON algo/algn** disagreement WITH sth/sb

desadaptado -da *adj*: **un niño ~** a child who has problems settling in *o* adjusting; **sentirse ~** to feel unsettled

desafiante *adj* ‹*gesto/palabras*› defiant

desafiar [A17] *vt* **(a)** ‹*persona*› to challenge; ~ **a algn A algo/hacer algo** to challenge sb TO sth/do sth **(b)** ‹*peligro/muerte*› to defy

desafilado -da *adj* blunt

desafinado -da *adj* out of tune

desafinar [A1] *vi* «*instrumento*» to be out of tune; «*músico/cantante*» to be off key *o* out of tune

desafío *m* (reto) challenge; (al peligro, a la muerte) defiance

desaforado -da *m,f*: **como un ~** ‹*correr*› hell for leather; ‹*gritar*› at the top of one's voice

desafortunado -da *adj* **(a)** (desdichado) ‹*persona*› unlucky; ‹*suceso*› unfortunate **(b)** (desacertado) ‹*medidas/actuación*› unfortunate

desagradable *adj* unpleasant; ‹*respuesta/comentario*› unkind

desagradar [A1] *vt*: **me desagrada el calor/tener que decírselo** I don't like the heat/having to tell her

desagradecido -da *adj* ‹*persona*› ungrateful; ‹*trabajo/tarea*› thankless

desagrado *m* displeasure; **lo hizo con ~** she did it reluctantly *o* unwillingly

desagüe *m* **(a)** (de lavabo, lavadora) wastepipe; (de patio, azotea) drain **(b)** (acción) drainage

desahogado -da *adj* ‹*posición económica/vida*› comfortable; ‹*casa/habitación*› uncluttered, spacious

desahogar [A3] *vt* ‹*penas/ira*› to give vent to
■ **desahogarse** *v pron* to let off steam ; **se desahogó dándole patadas a la rueda** he vented his anger (*o* frustration *etc*) by kicking the wheel; ~**se CON algn** to pour one's heart out to sb

desahogo *m* **(a)** (alivio) relief; **llorar le servirá de ~** crying will make him feel better **(b)** (con ~) comfortably; **vivir con ~** to be comfortably off

desahuciar [A1] *vt* ⟦1⟧ ‹*enfermo*› to declare ... terminally ill ⟦2⟧ **(a)** ‹*inquilino*› to evict **(b)** (Chi) ‹*empleado*› (despedir) to dismiss; (notificar el despido) to give ... notice

desaire *m* snub, slight; **hacerle un ~ a algn** to snub *o* slight sb

desalentador -dora *adj* disheartening, discouraging

desalentar [A5] *vt* to discourage, dishearten

desaliento *m* dejection, despondency

desaliñado -da *adj* slovenly

desalojar [A1] *vt* **(a)** ⟨*edificio/recinto*⟩ «*ocupantes*» to vacate; «*policía/juez*» to clear **(b)** ⟨*residentes*⟩ to evacuate; ⟨*inquilino*⟩ (esp AmL) to evict

desamarrar [A1] *vt* (AmL exc RPl) ⟨*embarcación*⟩ to cast off; ⟨*zapatos/paquete*⟩ to undo, untie; ⟨*animal/persona*⟩ to untie
■ **desamarrarse** *v pron* (AmL exc RPl)
[1] «*paquete/zapatos*» to come undone; « *bultos/ barco*» to come untied [2] (*refl*) «*persona*» to get free; «*animal*» to get loose *o* free

desamparado -da *adj* ⟨*niño/anciano*⟩ defenseless*; ⟨*lugar*⟩ bleak, unprotected

desamparo *m* neglect

desangrarse *v pron* to bleed to death

desanimado -da *adj* discouraged, dispirited

desanimar [A1] *vt* to discourage
■ **desanimarse** *v pron* to become disheartened *o* discouraged

desánimo *m* dejection, despondency

desaparecer [E3] *vi* «*persona/objeto*» to disappear; «*dolor/síntoma/cicatriz*» to disappear, go; «*costumbre*» to disappear, die out; «*mancha*» to come out
■ **desaparecerse** *v pron* (Andes) to disappear

desaparecido -da *adj* **(a)** (que no se encuentra) missing **(b)** (period) (muerto) late (*before n*), deceased (frml)
■ *m,f* **(a)** (en un accidente) missing person **(b)** (Pol): los ～s the disappeared *o* those who have disappeared

desaparición *f* disappearance; una especie en vías de ～ an endangered species

desapercibido -da *adj*: pasar ～ to go unnoticed

desaprovechar [A1] *vt* ⟨*oportunidad*⟩ to waste; ⟨*tiempo/comida*⟩ to waste

desarmable *adj* ⟨*mueble/mecanismo*⟩ which can be dismantled *o* taken apart

desarmado -da *adj* ⟨*policía/criminal*⟩ unarmed

desarmador *m* (Méx) **(a)** (herramienta) screwdriver **(b)** (bebida) screwdriver

desarmar [A1] *vt* [1] ⟨*mueble/mecanismo*⟩ to dismantle; ⟨*carpa*⟩ (AmL) to take down; ⟨*rifle/ motor*⟩ to strip (down); ⟨*rompecabezas*⟩ to take ... to pieces, break up; ⟨*juguete/maqueta*⟩ to take ... apart [2] **(a)** (quitar armas) to disarm **(b)** (dejar sin argumentos) to disarm

desarme *m* disarmament

desarrollado -da *adj* developed; un niño muy/poco ～a a well-developed/an underdeveloped child

desarrollar [A1] *vt* [1] (en general) to develop [2] **(a)** (exponer) ⟨*teoría/tema*⟩ to explain **(b)** (llevar a cabo) ⟨*actividad/labor*⟩ to carry out
■ **desarrollarse** *v pron* [1] (en general) to develop [2] «*acto/entrevista/escena*» to take place

desarrollo *m* development; países en vías de ～ developing countries; según el ～ de los acontecimientos according to how things develop

desastrado -da *adj* ⟨*persona*⟩ scruffy, untidy; ⟨*habitación/trabajo*⟩ untidy

desastre *m* disaster; **como cantante es un ～** he's a hopeless singer; **tienes la habitación hecha un ～** your room is a shambles; **vas hecha un ～** you look a real mess (colloq)

desastroso -sa *adj* disastrous

desatado -da *adj*: estar ～ ⟨*perro*⟩ to be loose; ⟨*cordón/nudo*⟩ to be undone

desatar [A1] *vt* **(a)** ⟨*nudo/lazo*⟩ to untie, undo **(b)** ⟨*persona*⟩ to untie; ⟨*perro*⟩ to let ... loose
■ **desatarse** *v pron* **(a)** «*nudo/cordones*» to come undone *o* untied; «*perro/caballo*» to get loose **(b)** (*refl*) «*persona*» to untie oneself; ⟨*cordones/zapatos*⟩ to untie, undo

desatascador *m* (instrumento) plunger; (producto) nitric acid (*o* caustic soda *etc*) (*used to clear blocked drains*)

desatascar [A2] *vt* ⟨*cañería/fregadero*⟩ to unblock, clear
■ **desatascarse** *v pron* «*cañería/fregadero*» to unblock; «*carretera*» to clear

desatender [E8] *vt* **(a)** ⟨*trabajo/familia*⟩ to neglect **(b)** ⟨*tienda/mostrador*⟩ to leave ... unattended

desatento -ta *adj* **(a)** [SER] (desconsiderado) thoughtless, inconsiderate **(b)** [ESTAR] (distraído) inattentive

desatornillador *m* (AmC, Chi) screwdriver

desatornillar [A1] *vt* to unscrew

desautorizar [A4] *vt* **(a)** (restar autoridad a) ⟨*persona*⟩ to undermine the authority of; ⟨*declaraciones*⟩ to disavow (frml) **(b)** (retirar la autorización para) ⟨*marcha/huelga*⟩ to ban

desayunar [A1] *vt* to have ... for breakfast; ¿qué desayunaste? what did you have for breakfast?
■ ～ *vi* to have breakfast
■ **desayunarse** *v pron* (AmL) (tomar el desayuno) to have breakfast; ～se CON algo to have sth FOR breakfast

desayuno *m* breakfast; **tomar el ～** to have breakfast

desbarajuste *m* (fam) mess; un ～ económico an economic mess *o* chaos

desbaratar [A1] *vt* **(a)** ⟨*planes*⟩ to spoil, ruin; ⟨*sistema*⟩ to disrupt **(b)** (Méx) ⟨*papeles*⟩ to jumble (up), muddle (up); ⟨*mecanismo*⟩ to ruin, destroy
■ **desbaratarse** *v pron* **(a)** «*plan*» to be ruined, be spoiled; «*sistema*» to be disrupted, break down **(b)** (Méx) «*papeles*» to get jumbled up, get muddled (up); «*mecanismo*» to break, get broken

desbarrancarse [A2] *v pron* to go over a sheer drop

desbloquear [A1] *vt* **(a)** ⟨*carretera/entrada*⟩ to clear; ⟨*mecanismo*⟩ to release, free **(b)** ⟨*negociaciones/diálogo*⟩ to break the deadlock in **(c)** (Com, Fin) ⟨*cuenta*⟩ to unfreeze

desbocado -da *adj* **(a)** ⟨*caballo*⟩ runaway (*before n*) **(b)** ⟨*cuello/escote*⟩ loose, wide

desbocarse [A2] *v pron* ⟨*caballo*⟩ to bolt

desbordante *adj* ⟨*entusiasmo/júbilo*⟩ boundless; **está ～ de entusiasmo** he's bursting with enthusiasm

desbordarse [A1] *v pron* **(a)** «*río/canal*» to burst its banks **(b)** «*vaso/cubo*» to overflow **(c)** «*multitud*» to get out of hand, get out of control

descabellado -da *adj* crazy, ridiculous

descafeinado -da *adj* decaffeinated

descalabro *m* **(a)** (desastre) disaster **(b)** (Mil) defeat

descalificación *f* (Dep) disqualification

descalificar [A2] *vt* «*deportista/equipo*» to disqualify

descalzarse [A4] *v pron* to take off one's shoes

descalzo -za *adj* «*pie*» bear; «*persona*» barefoot

descaminado -da *adj*: andar ∼ to be on the wrong track

descampado *m* **(a)** (terreno) area *o* piece of open ground *o* land **(b)** al descampado (AmS) «*dormir*» in the open (air)

descansado -da *adj* **(a)** [ESTAR] «*persona*» rested, refreshed **(b)** [SER] «*actividad/trabajo*» easy, undemanding; «*vida*» quiet, peaceful

descansar [A1] *vt* **(a)** (de actividad, trabajo) to rest, have a rest; sin ∼ without a break; ∼ DE algo to have a rest *o* break FROM sth **(b)** (yacer) to lie; que en paz descanse God rest his soul ∎ ∼ *vt* ∼ la vista to rest one's eyes, to give one's eyes a rest; ∼ la mente to give one's mind a rest

descansillo *m* (Esp) landing

descanso *m* **1** **(a)** (reposo) rest **(b)** (en trabajo, colegio) break; sin ∼ without a break **(c)** (Mil): estar en posición de ∼ to be standing at ease **2** (intervalo) (Dep) half time; (Teatr) interval **3** (alivio, tranquilidad) relief **4** (AmL) (rellano) landing

descapotable *adj/m* convertible

descarado -da *adj* «*persona/actitud*» brazen, shameless; es muy ∼ he has a lot of nerve

descarga *f* **1** (de mercancías) unloading **2** (Elec) discharge; una ∼ eléctrica an electric shock **3** (de arma) shot, discharge (frml); (de conjunto de armas) volley

descargar [A3] *vt* **1** «*vehículo/mercancías*» to unload **2** **(a)** «*pistola*» (extraer las balas) to unload; (disparar) to fire, discharge (frml); la pistola está descargada the pistol is not loaded **(b)** «*tiro*» to fire; «*golpe*» to deal, land **3** (Inf) to download **4** «*ira/agresividad*» to vent; «*preocupaciones/ tensiones*» to relieve ∎ ∼ *v impers* «*aguacero*» to pour down; «*temporal*» to break ∎ **descargarse** *v pron* **1** (Elec) «*pila*» to run down; «*batería*» to go dead *o* flat **2** «*tormenta*» to break; «*lluvias*» to come down, fall

descaro *m* audacity, nerve (colloq); ¡qué ∼! what a nerve!

descarriado -da *adj*: hoy día la juventud anda descarriada the youth of today has lost its way; ▶ OVEJA

descarrilamiento *m* derailment

descarrilar [A1] *vi* to derail, be derailed

∎ **descarrilarse** *v pron* (AmL) to derail, be derailed

descartar [A1] *vt* to rule out

descascararse [A1] *vpron* «*pared/pintura*» to peel; «*taza/plato*» to chip

descendencia *f* descendants (*pl*)

descendente *adj* «*curva/línea*» downward; «*escala*» descending

descender [E8] *vi* **1** **(a)** «*temperatura/ nivel*» to fall, drop **(b)** (frml) (desde una altura) «*avión*» to descend; «*persona*» to descend (frml), to come/go down **2** (en clasificación) to go down **3** (proceder) ∼ DE algn to be descended FROM sb

descendiente *mf* descendant

descenso *m* **1** **(a)** (de temperatura, nivel) fall, drop; (de precios) fall **(b)** (desde una altura) descent **2** (Dep) relegation

descentrado -da *adj* **(a)** «*eje/rueda*» off-center* **(b)** «*persona*» disoriented, disorientated (BrE)

descentralizar [A4] *vt* to decentralize

descifrar [A1] *vt* **(a)** «*mensaje*» to decode, decipher; «*escritura/jeroglífico/código*» to decipher **(b)** «*misterio/enigma*» to work out, figure out

descodificador *m* decoder

descolgar [A8] *vt* **(a)** «*cuadro/cortina*» to take down **(b)** «*teléfono*» to pick up; dejar el teléfono descolgado to leave the phone off the hook ∎ **descolgarse** *v pron* **1** (por una cuerda) to lower oneself **2** (en carrera) to pull away, break away

descollar [A10] *vi* to be outstanding

descolorido -da *adj* «*tela/papel*» faded

descomponer [E22] *vt* **1** «*alimento/cadáver*» to rot, cause ... to decompose *o* rot **2** (esp AmL) «*máquina/aparato*» to break; «*peinado*» to mess up **3** «*persona*» **(a)** (producir malestar) «*color*» to make ... queasy **(b)** (producir diarrea) to give ... diarrhea* ∎ **descomponerse** *v pron* **1** «*luz*» to split; «*sustancia*» to break down, separate **2** «*cadáver/alimento*» to rot, decompose (frml) **3** (esp AmL) «*máquina/aparato*» to break down **4** «*persona*» (sentir malestar) to feel sick; (del estómago) to have an attack of diarrhea* **6** (CS) «*tiempo*» to become unsettled; «*día*» to cloud over

descompuesto -ta *adj* **1** «*alimento*» rotten, decomposed (frml); «*cadáver*» decomposed **2** «*expresión*» changed, altered **3** (esp AmL) [ESTAR] «*máquina/aparato*» broken; «*teléfono*» out of order **4** estar ∼ (indispuesto) to feel sick; (del estómago) to have diarrhea*/an upset stomach

descompuse, descompuso, etc ▶ DESCOMPONER

desconcertado -da *adj* disconcerted; quedarse ∼ to be taken aback

desconcertante *adj* disconcerting

desconcertar [A5] *vt* to disconcert; su respuesta me desconcertó I was disconcerted by her reply

desconchado *m* (en taza, plato) chip; (en pared) *place where plaster or paint has come off*

desconcharse [A1] *v pron* «*taza/plato*» to chip, get chipped; «*pared/piel*» to peel

desconcierto *m*: su llamada los llenó de ∼ they were disconcerted by his call; el ∼ reinante the prevailing atmosphere of uncertainty

desconectar [A1] *vt* ⟨*alarma/teléfono*⟩ to disconnect; ⟨*calefacción*⟩ to switch off, turn off; ∼ algo DE algo to disconnect sth FROM sth
■ **desconectarse** *v pron* «*aparato*» to switch *o* turn off

desconfiado -da *adj* (receloso) distrustful; (suspicaz) suspicious

desconfianza *f* distrust, suspicion

desconfiar [A17] *vi* ∼ DE algn to mistrust sb, to distrust sb; ∼ DE algo ⟨*de motivos*⟩ to mistrust sth; ⟨*de honestidad*⟩ to doubt sth

descongelante *m* deicer

descongelar [A1] *vt* ⟨*refrigerador*⟩ to defrost; ⟨*alimentos*⟩ to defrost, thaw
■ **descongelarse** *v pron* «*refrigerador*» to defrost; «*alimentos*» to defrost, thaw

descongestionar [A1] *vt* to clear

desconocer [E3] *vt* (a) (no conocer): por razones que desconocemos for reasons unknown to us; desconocía este hecho I was unaware of this fact (b) (no reconocer): te desconocí I didn't recognize you

desconocido -da *adj* (en general) unknown; un cantante ∼ an unknown singer; una persona desconocida a stranger
■ *m,f* (no conocido) stranger

desconocimiento *m* ignorance

desconsiderado -da *adj* thoughtless, inconsiderate

desconsolado -da *adj* estar ∼ POR algo to be heartbroken OVER sth; lloraba ∼ he cried inconsolably

desconsuelo *m* grief, despair

descontado *adj*: eso dalo por ∼ you can be sure of that; doy por ∼ que vendrás a cenar I'm assuming that you're coming to dinner

descontaminar [A1] *vt* ⟨*alimentos/cultivos*⟩ to decontaminate; ⟨*atmósfera*⟩ to clean up

descontar [A10] *vt* 1 (a) (rebajar): me descontó el 15% he gave me a 15% discount (b) (restar) ⟨*gastos/impuestos*⟩ to deduct, take off; ⟨*horas*⟩ to deduct 2 (exceptuar): si descontamos a Pedro/los domingos … if we don't count Pedro/Sundays … 3 ⟨*letra/pagaré*⟩ to discount

descontento¹ -ta *adj* [ESTAR] dissatisfied; ∼ CON algo/algn unhappy *o* dissatisfied WITH sth/sb

descontento² *m* discontent

descontrolado -da *adj* out of control

descontrolarse [A1] *v pron* to get out of control

desconvocar [A2] *vt* to call off

descorazonar [A1] *vt* to dishearten, discourage

descorchar [A1] *vt* to uncork, open

descorrer [E1] *vt* ⟨*cortinas*⟩ to draw (back); ⟨*cerrojo*⟩ to draw back

descortés *adj* ⟨*persona*⟩ impolite, ill-mannered; ⟨*comportamiento*⟩ rude, impolite

descortesía *f* (a) (acto descortés) discourtesy (b) (cualidad) rudeness, impoliteness

descoserse [E1] *v pron* «*prenda/costura*» to come unstitched

descosido -da *adj* ⟨*dobladillo/costura*⟩ unstitched

descremado -da *adj* skimmed

describir [I34] *vt* to describe

descripción *f* description

descriptivo -va *adj* descriptive

descrito -ta *pp*: ▶ DESCRIBIR

descuartizar [A4] *vt* (a) ⟨*res*⟩ to quarter (b) «*asesino*» to chop … (up) into pieces

descubierto -ta *adj* 1 ⟨*piscina/terraza*⟩ open-air, outdoor (*before n*); ⟨*carroza*⟩ open-top 2 ⟨*cielos*⟩ clear 3 al descubierto: quedar al ∼ «*planes/escándalo*» to come to light; han puesto al ∼ sus chanchullos his shady dealings have been exposed; girar al *or* en ∼ (Com, Fin) to overdraw

descubridor -dora *m,f* discoverer

descubrimiento *m* discovery

descubrir [I33] *vt* 1 ⟨*tierras/oro/artista*⟩ to discover 2 (a) (enterarse de, averiguar) ⟨*razón/solución*⟩ to discover, find out; ⟨*complot/engaño*⟩ to uncover; ⟨*fraude*⟩ to detect (b) ⟨*persona escondida*⟩ to find, track down (c) ⟨*culpable*⟩ find … out (d) (delatar) to give … away 3 (a) ⟨*estatua/placa*⟩ to unveil (b) (revelar) ⟨*planes/intenciones*⟩ to reveal

descuento *m* 1 (a) (rebaja) discount; hacen un ∼ del 15% they give a 15% discount (b) (del sueldo) deduction 2 (Dep) injury time 3 (de letra, pagaré) discount

descuidado -da *adj* (a) [SER] (negligente) careless; (en el vestir) sloppy (b) [ESTAR] (desatendido) neglected

descuidar [A1] *vt* ⟨*negocio/jardín*⟩ to neglect
■ ∼ *vi*: descuide, yo me ocuparé de eso don't worry, I'll see to that
■ **descuidarse** *v pron* (a) (no prestar atención, distraerse): se descuidó un momento y el perro se le escapó his attention strayed for a moment and the dog ran off; si te descuidas, te roban if you don't watch out, they'll rob you; como te descuides, te van a quitar el puesto if you don't look out, they'll take your job from you (b) (en el aspecto físico) to neglect one's appearance

descuido *m* (a) (distracción): en un ∼ el niño se le escapó she took her eyes off the child for a moment and he ran off; basta el más pequeño ∼ the smallest lapse of concentration is enough (b) (error) slip; (omisión) oversight

desde *prep* 1 (en el tiempo) since; ∼ entonces/ ∼ que se casó since then/since he got married; ¿∼ cuándo trabajas aquí? how long have you been working here?; ∼ el primer momento right from the start; no los veo ∼ hace meses I haven't seen them for months; ∼ el 15 hasta el 30 from the 15th to *o* until the 30th 2 (en el espacio) from; ∼ aquí/allá from here/there; ¿∼ dónde tengo que leer? where do I have to read from?; ∼ la página 12 hasta la 20 from page 12 (up) to page 20 3 (en escalas, jerarquías) from; blusas ∼ 12 euros blouses from 12 euros.

desdén *m* disdain, scorn

desdeñable *adj* insignificant

desdeñar [A1] *vt* (a) (menospreciar) to scorn (b) ⟨pretendiente⟩ to spurn

desdeñoso -sa *adj* disdainful

desdicha *f* (desgracia) misfortune; (infelicidad) unhappiness

desdichado -da *adj* (a) (infeliz) unhappy (b) [SER] ⟨día⟩ ill-fated; **ser ~ en amores** to be unlucky in love
■ *m,f*: **es un pobre ~** he's a poor unfortunate wretch

desdoblar [A1] *vt* ⟨servilleta/pañuelo⟩ to unfold
■ **desdoblarse** *v pron* to divide into two, split into two

deseable *adj* desirable

desear [A1] *vt* 1 ⟨suerte/éxito/felicidad⟩ to wish; **te deseo un feliz viaje** I hope you have a good trip 2 (querer): **un embarazo no deseado** an unwanted pregnancy; **las tan deseadas vacaciones** the long-awaited holidays; **lo que más deseo es …** my greatest wish is …; **si tú lo deseas** if you want to; **~ía una respuesta ahora** I would like a reply now; **está deseando verte** he's really looking forward to seeing you; **¿desea que se lo envuelva?** (frml) would you like me to wrap it for you? 3 ⟨persona⟩ to desire, want

desechable *adj* disposable

desechar [A1] *vt* (a) ⟨ayuda/propuesta⟩ to reject; ⟨idea/plan⟩ (rechazar) to reject; (renunciar a) to drop, give up (b) ⟨restos/residuos⟩ to throw away o out; ⟨ropa⟩ to throw out

desecho *m* waste

desembarcar [A2] *vi* (de barco, avión) ⟨pasajeros⟩ to disembark; ⟨tropas⟩ to land, disembark
■ **~** *vt* ⟨mercancías⟩ to unload; ⟨pasajeros⟩ to disembark; (en emergencia) to evacuate

desembocadura *f* mouth, estuary

desembocar [A2] *vi* **~ EN algo** ⟨en mar/río⟩ to flow INTO sth; ⟨en calle⟩ to come out ONTO sth; ⟨en plaza⟩ to come out INTO sth

desembolsar [A1] *vt* to spend, pay out

desembolso *m* expenditure; (gasto inicial) outlay

desempacar [A2] *vt/vi* (esp AmL) to unpack

desempaquetar [A1] *vt* to unwrap

desempatar [A1] *vi* (a) (Dep) to break the tie (AmE), to break the deadlock (BrE) (b) (en una votación) to break the deadlock

desempate *m* (a) (Dep): **el ~ se produjo en el minuto 36** the breakthrough came in the 36th minute; **un partido de ~ a decider**; **~ a penaltys** penalty shoot-out (b) (en concurso) tiebreak, tiebreaker; (en una votación) run-off

desempeñar [A1] *vt* (a) (Teatr) ⟨papel⟩ to play (b) ⟨funciones⟩ to carry out, perform; ⟨cargo⟩ to hold
■ **desempeñarse** *v pron* (AmL): **se desempeña bien en su trabajo** she does her job well; **se desempeñó muy bien** she did o managed very well

desempleado -da *m,f*: **un ~** someone who is out of work o unemployed; **los ~s** the unemployed

desempleo *m* (a) (situación) unemployment (b) (subsidio) unemployment benefit

desencadenar [A1] *vt* (a) ⟨crisis/protesta/reacción⟩ to trigger (b) ⟨perro⟩ to unleash; ⟨preso⟩ to unchain
■ **desencadenarse** *v pron* «explosión/reacción» to be triggered off; «guerra» to break out; «tempestad» to break

desencajado -da *adj* (a) ⟨pieza⟩ out of position (b) ⟨mandíbula/rótula⟩ dislocated (c) (alterado) shaken

desencajar [A1] *vt* (a) (Mec) to knock out of position (b) ⟨mandíbula/rótula⟩ to dislocate
■ **desencajarse** *v pron* (a) «pieza» (Mec) to be knocked/come out of position (b) «mandíbula/rótula» to become/get dislocated

desencaminado -da *adj* (AmL) ▶ DESCAMINADO

desencanto *m* disillusionment, disenchantment

desenchufar [A1] *vt* to unplug, disconnect

desenfadado -da *adj* (a) (seguro de sí mismo) self-assured, confident; (sin inhibiciones) uninhibited (b) ⟨estilo/moda/actitud⟩ free-and-easy, carefree

desenfocado -da *adj* out of focus

desenganchar [A1] *vt* ⟨caballos/remolque⟩ to unhitch; ⟨vagones⟩ to uncouple

desengañar [A1] *vt* (decepcionar) to disillusion; (sacar del engaño, error) to get … to face the facts
■ **desengañarse** *v pron* (a) (decepcionarse) **~se DE algo** to become disillusioned WITH o ABOUT sth (b) (salir del engaño, error) to stop fooling oneself

desengaño *m* disappointment; **llevarse un ~** to be disappointed; **un ~ amoroso** an unhappy love affair

desenlace *m* (de película, libro) ending; (de aventura) outcome

desenredar [A1] *vt* ⟨pelo/lana⟩ to untangle, disentangle; ⟨lío⟩ to straighten out, sort out
■ **desenredarse** *v pron* (refl) ⟨pelo⟩ to get the knots out of

desenrollar [A1] *vt* ⟨alfombra/póster⟩ to unroll; ⟨persiana⟩ to let down; ⟨ovillo/cuerda⟩ to unwind

desenroscar [A2] *vt* to unscrew

desentenderse [E8] *v pron* **~ DE algo** ⟨de un asunto⟩ to wash one's hands OF sth; **se desentiende de los hijos** he doesn't take an interest in the children

desenterrar [A5] *vt* ⟨cadáver⟩ to exhume, dig up; ⟨ruinas/tesoro⟩ to unearth, dig up

desentonar [A1] *vi* (a) (Mús) to go out of tune o off key (b) ⟨color⟩ to clash (c) «atuendo/comentario» to be out of place

desentrenado -da *adj* out of condition o training

desenvoltura *f* self-assurance

desenvolver [E11] *vt* to unwrap, open
■ **desenvolverse** *v pron* (a) (manejarse) to get by, manage; **se desenvuelve muy bien en inglés** she gets by very well in English; **se desenvolvió bien en la entrevista** she managed the interview all right (b) (en situaciones difíciles) to cope (c) «hechos/sucesos» to develop

desenvuelto -ta *adj* ⟨*persona*⟩ self-assured, confident

deseo *m* **(a)** (anhelo) wish; **formular un** ∼ to make a wish **(b)** (apetito sexual) desire

desequilibrado -da *adj* ⟨*rueda/mecanismo*⟩ out of balance; ⟨*persona*⟩ unbalanced

desequilibrar [A1] *vt* **(a)** ⟨*embarcación/ vehículo*⟩ to unbalance, make ... unbalanced; ⟨*persona*⟩ (físicamente) to throw ... off balance; (mentalmente) to unbalance **(b)** ⟨*fuerzas/poder*⟩ to upset the balance of
■ **desequilibrarse** *v pron* «*ruedas/mecanismo*» to get out of balance

desequilibrio *m* **(a)** (desigualdad) imbalances **(b)** (Psic) unbalanced state of mind

desertar [A1] *vi* (Mil) to desert; (de partido) to defect

desértico -ca *adj* ⟨*zona/clima*⟩ desert (*before n*)

desertización *f* desertification

desertor -tora *m,f* (Mil) deserter; (de un partido) defector

desesperación *f* **(a)** (angustia) desperation; **con** ∼ ⟨*luchar/gritar*⟩ desperately; ⟨*mirar/ suplicar*⟩ despairingly; ⟨*llorar*⟩ bitterly; **de** ∼ out of desperation **(b)** (desesperanza) despair

desesperado -da *adj* desperate

desesperante *adj* **(a)** (exasperante) exasperating **(b)** (angustioso) distressing

desesperar [A1] *vt* to drive ... to distraction *o* despair
■ ∼ *vi* to despair, give up hope
■ **desesperarse** *v pron* to become exasperated

desestabilizar [A4] *vt* to destabilize

desfachatez *f* audacity, nerve (colloq)

desfalco *m* embezzlement

desfallecer [E3] *vi* **(a)** (flaquear) «*persona*» to become weak; «*fuerzas*» to fade, fail; «*ánimos*» to flag; **lucharon sin** ∼ they fought tirelessly **(b)** (desmayarse) to faint, pass out

desfasado -da *adj* ⟨*ideas/persona*⟩ old-fashioned

desfase *m* (falta de correspondencia): **hay un** ∼ **entre su madurez física y su desarollo mental** his physical maturity is out of step with his intellectual development; ∼ **de horario** jetlag

desfavorable *adj* unfavorable*; **el tiempo nos ha sido** ∼ we had unfavorable weather conditions

desfigurado -da *adj* disfigured

desfigurar [A1] *vt* **1** «*quemaduras/cicatriz*» ⟨*persona*⟩ to disfigure **2** ⟨*hechos*⟩ to distort, twist; ⟨*realidad*⟩ to distort

desfiladero *m* (barranco) ravine, narrow gorge; (puerto) narrow pass

desfilar [A1] *vi* **(a)** «*soldados*» to parade **(b)** «*manifestantes*» to march; **la manifestación desfiló por la Gran Vía** the demonstration passed along the Gran Vía **(c)** «*modelo*» to parade up and down the catwalk

desfile *m* (de carrozas) parade, procession; (Mil) parade, march past; ∼ **de modelos** fashion show

desgajar [A1] *vt* ∼ **algo DE algo** ⟨*rama*⟩ to break *o* snap sth OFF sth; ⟨*páginas*⟩ to tear *o* rip sth OUT OF sth

■ **desgajarse** *v pron* «*rama*» to break off, snap off

desgana *f* **(a)** (inapetencia) lack of appetite **(b)** (falta de entusiasmo): **con** *or* **a** ∼ ⟨*trabajar*⟩ half-heartedly; ⟨*obedecer*⟩ reluctantly

desganado -da *adj* **(a)** (inapetente): **me siento** ∼ I'm not hungry **(b)** (apático) lethargic

desgano *m* (AmL) ▶ DESGANA

desgarbado -da *adj* ⟨*persona/aspecto*⟩ gangling, gawky; ⟨*movimientos/andar*⟩ ungainly

desgarrador -dora *adj* heartbreaking, heartrending

desgarrar [A1] *vt* **(a)** ⟨*vestido/papel*⟩ to tear, rip **(b)** ⟨*corazón*⟩ to break
■ **desgarrarse** *v pron* **(a)** «*vestido/camisa*» to tear, rip **(b)** (Med) to tear

desgarro *m* (de ligamento, músculo): **sufrió un** ∼ she tore a muscle

desgastar [A1] *vt* **(a)** (gastar) ⟨*suelas/ropa*⟩ to wear out; ⟨*roca*⟩ to wear away, erode **(b)** (debilitar) to wear ... down
■ **desgastarse** *v pron* **(a)** (gastarse) «*ropa*» to wear out; «*roca*» to wear away; «*tacón*» to wear down **(b)** «*persona*» to wear oneself out; «*relación*» to grow stale

desgaste *m* **(a)** (de ropa, suelas) wear; (de rocas) erosion, wearing away **(b)** (debilitamiento físico) debilitation

desgracia *f* **(a)** (desdicha, infortunio) misfortune; **tiene la** ∼ **de ser ciego** he has the misfortune to be blind; **caer en** ∼ to fall from favor **(b)** **por desgracia** (indep) unfortunately

desgraciado -da *adj* **(a)** [SER] (infeliz) unhappy **(b)** [SER] (desafortunado) ⟨*viaje*⟩ ill-fated **(c)** (desacertado) ⟨*elección/coincidencia*⟩ unfortunate, unwise
■ *m,f* **1** (desdichado) wretch **2** (persona vil) swine (colloq)

desgravación *f* tax exemption (AmE), tax relief (BrE)

desgravar [A1] *vt* **(a)** ⟨*gastos/suma*⟩ to claim tax exemption on (AmE), to claim tax relief on (BrE) **(b)** ⟨*producto/importación*⟩ to eliminate the tax *o* duty on
■ ∼ *vi* to be tax-deductible

desguazar [A4] *vt* to scrap

deshabitado -da *adj* ⟨*región*⟩ uninhabited; ⟨*edificio*⟩ empty, unoccupied

deshacer [E18] *vt* **1** **(a)** ⟨*costura/bordado*⟩ to unpick **(b)** ⟨*nudo/lazo/trenza*⟩ to undo; ⟨*ovillo*⟩ to unwind
2 **(a)** (desarmar, desmontar) ⟨*maqueta/mecanismo*⟩ to take ... apart; ⟨*paquete*⟩ to undo, unwrap **(b)** ⟨*cama*⟩ (para cambiarla) to strip; (desordenar) to mess up; ⟨*maleta*⟩ to unpack
3 **(a)** (derretir) ⟨*nieve/helado*⟩ to melt **(b)** (desmenuzar) to break up **(c)** (en líquido) to dissolve
4 ⟨*acuerdo/trato*⟩ to break; ⟨*noviazgo*⟩ to break off; ⟨*planes/compromiso*⟩ to cancel
■ **deshacerse** *v pron* **1** «*dobladillo/costura*» to come undone *o* unstitched; «*nudo/trenza/ moño*» to come undone; «*peinado*» to get messed up, be ruined
2 **(a)** (desintegrarse) to disintegrate **(b)** «*nieve/ helado*» to melt **(c)** (en líquido) to dissolve

3 ~se EN algo: ~se en llanto to dissolve into tears; me deshice en cumplidos I went out of my way to be complimentary

4 deshacerse de (a) (librarse de) to get rid of (b) (desprenderse de) to part with

deshaga, deshagas, etc ▶ DESHACER

deshecho -cha adj [ESTAR] (a) (cansado, agotado) exhausted (b) (destrozado moralmente) shattered, devastated (c) (estropeado) ruined

deshelar [A5] vt ⟨cañería⟩ to thaw out, unfreeze; ⟨nevera/congelador⟩ to defrost; ⟨parabrisas⟩ to deice

■ **deshelarse** v pron «nieves» to thaw, melt; «río/lago» to thaw; «relaciones» to thaw

desheredar [A1] vt to disinherit

deshice, deshiciera, etc ▶ DESHACER

deshidratarse [A1] v pron to become dehydrated

deshielo m (a) (de ríos, nieves) thaw; agua de ~ meltwater (b) (de relaciones) thaw, thawing-out

deshizo ▶ DESHACER

deshojar [A1] vt ⟨flor⟩ to pull the petals off; ⟨cuaderno⟩ to tear o rip the pages out of

deshonesto -ta adj (a) (tramposo, mentiroso) dishonest (b) (indecente) ⟨proposiciones⟩ improper, indecent

deshonor m ▶ DESHONRA A

deshonra f (a) (vergüenza) disgrace; ese chico es una ~ para su familia that boy is a disgrace to his family (b) (pérdida de la honra) dishonor*

deshonrar [A1] vt ⟨familia/patria⟩ to dishonor*, disgrace; ⟨mujer⟩ to dishonor*

deshonroso -sa adj dishonorable*, disgraceful

deshora: a ~(s) off hours (AmE), out of hours (BrE)

deshuesar [A1] vt **1** (a) ⟨aceitunas⟩ to pit (b) ⟨pollo⟩ to bone **2** (Méx) ⟨coche/barco⟩ to scrap

desidia f (a) (apatía) slackness, indolence (frml) (b) (desaseo) slovenliness

desierto¹ -ta adj ⟨lugar⟩ deserted

desierto² m desert

designar [A1] vt **1** (frml) (elegir) (a) ⟨persona⟩ to appoint, designate (frml) (b) ⟨lugar/fecha⟩ to fix, set; (con carácter oficial) to designate **2** (frml) (denominar) to designate (frml)

designio m plan

desigual adj **1** (a) (diferente) uneven; las mangas quedaron ~es one sleeve turned out longer (o wider etc) than the other (b) (desequilibrado) ⟨lucha⟩ unequal; ⟨fuerzas⟩ unevenly-matched **2** (irregular) ⟨terreno/superficie⟩ uneven; ⟨letra⟩ uneven, irregular; ⟨calidad⟩ variable, varying (before n); ⟨rendimiento⟩ inconsistent, erratic

desigualdad f **1** (a) (diferencia) inequality (b) (desequilibrio) inequality, disparity **2** (de superficie) unevenness

desilusión f (decepción) disappointment; se llevó una ~ she was disappointed

desilusionado -da adj (decepcionado) disappointed

desilusionar [A1] vt to disappoint

■ **desilusionarse** v pron (decepcionarse) to be disappointed; (perder las ilusiones) to become disillusioned

desinfectante m disinfectant

desinfectar [A1] vt to disinfect

desinflar [A1] vt ⟨globo/balón/neumático⟩ to let the air out of, to deflate, let down (esp BrE)

■ **desinflarse** v pron to deflate, go down

desinformación f disinformation, misleading information

desinformar [A1] vt to misinform

desinhibido -da adj uninhibited

desintegrarse [A1] v pron to disintegrate, break up; «familia» to break up

desinterés m (falta de interés) lack of interest; (altruismo) unselfishness

desinteresado -da adj ⟨consejo/ayuda⟩ disinterested; ⟨persona⟩ selfless

desintoxicación f detoxification

desintoxicarse [A2] v pron to undergo detoxification

desistir [I1] vi to give up; ~ DE algo ⟨de propósito⟩ to give up sth, desist FROM sth (frml); ⟨de demanda/derecho⟩ to relinquish sth; ~ DE hacer algo to give up doing sth

desleal adj [SER] disloyal; ~ CON or A algn/algo disloyal TO sb/sth

desligarse [A3] v pron (a) (librarse) ~se DE algo ⟨de obligaciones⟩ to free oneself OF sth; ⟨de compromiso⟩ to get out OF sth (b) (apartarse) ~se DE algo/algn to cut oneself off FROM sth/sb

desliz m (error, falta) slip; (al hablar) gaffe, faux pas

deslizador m (Méx) (ala delta) hang glider

deslizar [A4] vt (hacer resbalar) to slip, slide

■ **deslizarse** v pron (a) «patinador/bailarines» to glide; «esquiador» to ski, slide; «serpiente» to slither, glide; ~se POR algo to slide down sth; se deslizó por la cuerda he slid down the rope (b) «barco/cisne» to glide; ~se SOBRE algo to glide OVER sth (c) «cajón/argollas de cortina» to slide (d) «agua/arroyo» to flow gently (e) (escurrirse, escaparse) to slip away

deslocalizar [A4] vt ⟨puestos de trabajo⟩ to relocate (to reduce production costs)

deslucido -da adj ⟨actuación/desfile⟩ dull, lackluster*; ⟨colores/paredes⟩ faded, drab; ⟨plata⟩ tarnished

deslumbrante, deslumbrador -dora adj ⟨luz⟩ blinding; ⟨belleza⟩ dazzling, stunning

deslumbrar [A1] vt to dazzle

desmadrarse [A1] v pron (fam) «persona» to go wild (colloq)

desmán m (exceso, abuso) outrage, excess

desmanchar [A1] vt (AmL) to get the stains out of

desmandarse [A1] *v pron* «*niños/tropas*» to get out of control *o* hand

desmano: a ∼ (*loc adv*) ⟨*estar/quedar*⟩ out of the way; **me pilla a ∼** it's out of my way

desmantelar [A1] *vt* to dismantle; ⟨*coche*⟩ to strip

desmarcarse [A2] *v pron* (Dep) to slip the coverage (AmE), to slip one's marker (BrE)

desmayado -da *adj* ⟨*persona*⟩ unconscious (*from having fainted*)

desmayarse [A1] *v pron* to faint

desmayo *m* **(a)** (Med) faint; **sufrir un ∼** to faint **(b)** sin ∼ ⟨*luchar/trabajar*⟩ resolutely, tirelessly

desmedido -da *adj* excessive; **le han dado una importancia desmedida** they have attributed too much importance to it

desmejorado -da *adj* **(a)** (de salud): **lo encontré muy ∼** he didn't look at all well to me **(b)** (de atractivo): **está desmejorada** she's lost her looks

desmemoriado -da *adj* forgetful, absent-minded

desmentir [I11] *vt* ⟨*noticia/rumor*⟩ to deny; ⟨*acusación*⟩ to deny, refute

desmenuzar [A4] *vt* ⟨*pescado*⟩ to flake; ⟨*pollo*⟩ to shred; ⟨*pan*⟩ to crumble

desmigajarse [A1] *v pron* to crumble

desmilitarizar [A4] *vt* to demilitarize

desmontable *adj* **(a)** (desarmable) ⟨*mecanismo/mueble*⟩ which can be dismantled *o* taken apart **(b)** (separable) ⟨*forro/pieza*⟩ detachable, removable

desmontar [A1] *vt* **(a)** (desarmar) ⟨*mueble/mecanismo*⟩ to dismantle, take apart; ⟨*tienda de campaña*⟩ to take down **(b)** (separar) ⟨*forro/pieza*⟩ to detach, remove

■ ∼ *vi* «*jinete*» to dismount

desmoralizar [A4] *vt* to demoralize, dishearten

■ **desmoralizarse** *v pron* to get demoralized *o* disheartened, to lose heart

desmoronarse [A1] *v pron* **(a)** «*muro/edificio*» to collapse; «*imperio/sociedad*» to crumble, collapse **(b)** «*fe/moral*» to crumble; «*persona*» to go to pieces

desnatado -da *adj* (Esp) skimmed

desnaturalizado -da *adj* **(a)** ⟨*aceite/vino*⟩ denatured **(b)** ⟨*madre*⟩ unnatural

desnivel *m* ⓵ (en superficie) **(a)** (irregularidad) unevenness, irregularity; **es un terreno lleno de ∼es** it is a very uneven piece of land; **un ∼ entre la cocina y el comedor** a difference in floor level between the kitchen and the dining room **(b)** (inclinación, pendiente) slope, incline (frml) **(c)** (depresión) drop (*in the level of the ground*) ⓶ (diferencia) difference, disparity

desnivelado -da *adj* **(a)** (irregular) ⟨*terreno*⟩ uneven **(b)** (fuera de nivel): **la mesa está desnivelada** the table isn't level

desnucarse [A2] *v pron* to break one's neck

desnuclearizar [A4] *vt* to denuclearize; **zona desnuclearizada** nuclear-free zone

desnudar [A1] *vt* (desvestir) to undress

■ **desnudarse** *v pron* (*refl*) (desvestirse) to undress, take one's clothes off; **∼se de (la) cintura para arriba** to strip to the waist

desnudez *f* (de persona) nakedness, nudity

desnudo¹ -da *adj* **(a)** (sin ropa) ⟨*persona*⟩ naked; **nadar ∼** to swim in the nude; **totalmente ∼** stark naked; **∼ de la cintura para arriba** naked to the waist **(b)** (descubierto) ⟨*hombros/brazos/torso*⟩ bare

desnudo² ∼ *m* (Art) nude

desnutrido -da *adj* malnourished, undernourished

desobedecer [E3] *vt/vi* to disobey

desobediente *adj* disobedient

desocupado -da *adj* ⓵ (vacío, libre) ⟨*casa/habitación*⟩ unoccupied, vacant; ⟨*asiento/baño*⟩ free ⓶ (desempleado) unemployed

desodorante *m* deodorant; **∼ en barra** stick deodorant; **∼ ambiental** (CS) air freshener

desolado -da *adj* ⓵ ⟨*paisaje/campos*⟩ desolate; ⟨*ciudad*⟩ devastated ⓶ (afligido) desolated, devastated

desolador -dora *adj* ⓵ (devastador) ⟨*tormenta/epidemia*⟩ devastating ⓶ (triste, penoso) ⟨*noticia*⟩ devastating; ⟨*espectáculo*⟩ distressing

desollar [A10] *vt* ⟨*animal*⟩ to skin, flay

desorbitado -da *adj* **(a)** ⟨*precios*⟩ exorbitant, astronomical **(b)** **con los ojos ∼s** with her/his eyes popping out of her/his head (colloq)

desorden *m* ⓵ **(a)** (de persona, cuarto, cajón) untidiness, mess (colloq); **perdona el ∼** sorry about the mess; **en ∼** ⟨*salir/entrar*⟩ in a disorderly fashion; **todo estaba en ∼** everything was in disorder *o* in a mess **(b)** (confusión) disorder ⓶ **desórdenes** *mpl* (disturbios) disturbances (*pl*), disorder

desordenado -da *adj* ⓵ **(a)** ⟨*persona/habitación*⟩ untidy, messy (colloq); **tengo la casa toda desordenada** my house is in a mess *o* is very untidy **(b)** [ESTAR] ⟨*naipes/hojas*⟩ out of order ⓶ ⟨*vida*⟩ disorganized

desordenar [A1] *vt* ⟨*mesa/habitación*⟩ to make ... untidy, mess up (colloq); ⟨*naipes/hojas*⟩ to get ... out of order

desorganización *f* lack of organization

desorganizado -da *adj* disorganized

desorientado -da *adj* disoriented, disorientated (BrE)

desorientar [A1] *vt* to confuse

■ **desorientarse** *v pron* to lose one's bearings, become disoriented

despabilado -da *adj* ▶ ESPABILADO

despabilar [A1] *vt* ▶ ESPABILAR

despachar [A1] *vt* ⓵ **(a)** ⟨*asunto/tarea/*⟩ to take care of, deal with; ⟨*correspondencia*⟩ to deal with, attend to **(b)** ⟨*carta/paquete*⟩ to send; ⟨*mercancías*⟩ (por barco) to ship; (por avión, tren) to send, dispatch ⓶ (Com) (en tienda) to serve, deal with

■ ∼ *vi* (Com) «*dependiente*» to serve

despacho *m* ⓵ **(a)** (oficina) office; (estudio) study **(b)** (mobiliario) office furniture ⓶ (envío) dispatch, despatch ⓷ (comunicado) communiqué; (Mil) dispatch; (Period) report

despacio *adv* ⓵ (lentamente) slowly ⓶ (CS) (en voz baja) quietly, softly; (sin hacer ruido) quietly

despampanante *adj* (fam) stunning (colloq)

desparpajo *m* (desenvoltura) self-confidence; (desfachatez) audacity, nerve (colloq)

desparramado -da adj (esparcido) scattered; (derramado) spilt

desparramar [A1] vt ⟨líquido/azúcar⟩ to spill; ⟨botones/monedas⟩ to spill, scatter; ⟨papeles/juguetes⟩ to scatter

■ **desparramarse** v pron «líquido/azúcar» to spill; «botones/monedas» to scatter, spill

despavorido -da adj terrified, petrified

despecho m spite; **por ~** out of spite

despectivo -va adj ⟨trato/gesto/actitud⟩ contemptuous; ⟨tono⟩ disparaging; ⟨término⟩ pejorative, derogatory

despedazar [A4] vt (a) (cortar en trozos) to cut ... into pieces (b) ⟨presa⟩ to tear ... to pieces o shreds

despedida f (a) (acción) goodbye, farewell (liter) (b) (celebración) farewell party; **regalo de ~** a farewell gift; **~ de soltera/soltero** hen/stag night o party

despedir [I14] vt 1 (decir adiós): **vinieron a ~me al aeropuerto** they came to see me off at the airport 2 (del trabajo) to dismiss, fire (colloq); (por reducción de personal) to lay off 3 ⟨olor⟩ to give off; ⟨humo/vapor⟩ to emit, give off; **salir despedido** «corcho/pelota»» to shoot out; **el conductor salió despedido del asiento** the driver was thrown out of his seat

■ **despedirse** v pron (decir adiós) to say goodbye; **~se DE algn** to say goodbye TO sb

despegar [A3] vt ⟨etiqueta/esparadrapo⟩ to remove, peel off; ⟨piezas/ensambladura⟩ to get ... unstuck o apart; **no despegó los labios** she didn't say a word

■ **~** vi «avión» to take off; «cohete» to lift off, be launched

■ **despegarse** v pron «sello/etiqueta» to come unstuck, peel off; «esparadrapo/empapelado» to come off

despegue m (de avión) takeoff; (de cohete) launch, lift-off

despeinado -da adj ⟨pelo/melena⟩ unkempt, disheveled*; **estar ~** to have one's hair in a mess

despeinar [A1] vt: **~ a algn** to mess up sb's hair

■ **despeinarse** v pron to mess one's hair up

despejado -da adj 1 (Meteo) ⟨día/cielo⟩ clear 2 (libre, vacío) ⟨carretera/camino⟩ clear 3 (a) ⟨persona⟩ clearheaded; ⟨mente⟩ clear (b) [ESTAR] (sobrio) sober

despejar [A1] vt 1 (a) (desocupar, desalojar) to clear (b) ⟨nariz⟩ to unblock, clear; **el paseo me despejó** the walk cleared my head 2 ⟨balón⟩ (en fútbol) to clear; (en fútbol americano) to punt

■ **~** vi (en fútbol) to clear; (en fútbol americano) to punt

■ **~** v impers (Meteo) to clear up

■ **despejarse** v pron (espabilarse) to wake (oneself) up; (desembotarse) to clear one's head; «borracho» to sober up

despellejar [A1] vt ⟨animal⟩ to skin

■ **despellejarse** v pron to peel; **se me despellejó la nariz** my nose peeled

despelote m (AmL fam) (caos, lío) shambles (colloq)

despenalizar [A4] vt to legalize, decriminalize

despensa f larder, pantry

despeñadero m cliff, precipice

despeñarse [A1] v pron to go over a cliff (o precipice etc)

desperdiciar [A1] vt ⟨comida/papel/tela⟩ to waste; ⟨oportunidad⟩ to miss, waste

desperdicio m (a) (de comida, papel) waste (b) **desperdicios** mpl (residuos) scraps (pl)

desperdigado -da adj scattered

desperezarse [A4] v pron to stretch

desperfecto m (a) (daño) damage (b) (defecto) flaw

despertador m alarm clock; **poner el ~** to set the alarm

despertar [A5] vt (a) ⟨persona⟩ to wake, wake ... up (b) ⟨sentimientos/pasiones⟩ to arouse; ⟨apetito⟩ to whet; ⟨recuerdos⟩ to evoke; ⟨interés⟩ to awaken, stir up

■ **~** vi (del sueño) to wake (up); (de la anestesia) to come round

■ **despertarse** v pron (del sueño) to wake (up)

despiadado -da adj ⟨persona⟩ ruthless, heartless; ⟨ataque/crítica⟩ savage, merciless

despida, despidas, etc ▶ DESPEDIR

despido m dismissal; (por falta de trabajo) redundancy, layoff

despierta, despiertas, etc ▶ DESPERTAR

despierto -ta adj (a) [ESTAR] (del sueño) awake (b) [SER] ⟨persona/mente⟩ bright, alert

despilfarrar [A1] vi to waste o squander money

■ **~** vt to squander, waste

despilfarro m waste

despistado -da adj (a) [SER] vague, absentminded; **soy muy ~ para los nombres** I never remember names (b) **estar ~** to be miles away (colloq) o daydreaming; (desorientado, confuso) to be bewildered o lost

■ m,f scatterbrain (colloq)

despistar [A1] vt (a) (desorientar, confundir) to confuse (b) ⟨perseguidor⟩ to shake off; ⟨sabueso⟩ to throw ... off the scent

■ **despistarse** v pron (confundirse) to get confused o muddled; (distraerse) to lose concentration

despiste m (a) (distracción) absentmindedness; **fue un ~** it was a lapse of concentration (b) (equivocación) slip, mistake

desplazamiento m 1 (movimiento) movement, displacement 2 (frml) (traslado, viaje) trip; **gastos de ~** traveling expenses

desplazar [A4] vt 1 (frml) (mover, correr) to move; (Inf) to scroll 2 (suplantar, relegar) ⟨persona⟩ to displace; **~ A algo** to take the place OF sth

■ **desplazarse** v pron (frml) (trasladarse, moverse) «animal» to move around; «avión/barco» to travel, go; «persona» to get around

desplegar [A7] vt 1 (a) ⟨alas⟩ to spread; ⟨mapa⟩ to open out, spread out; ⟨velas⟩ to unfurl (b) (demostrar) ⟨talento/ingenio⟩ to display; (emplear) ⟨encantos/poder⟩ to use (c) (llevar a cabo) ⟨campaña⟩ to mount; ⟨esfuerzo⟩ to make 2 (Mil) ⟨tropas/misiles⟩ to deploy

■ **desplegarse** v pron (Mil) to deploy

despliegue m 1 (de tropas, recursos) deployment 2 (de riqueza, sabiduría) display

desplomarse [A1] *v pron* «*persona/edificio*» to collapse

desplumar [A1] *vt* (a) ⟨*ave*⟩ to pluck (b) (fam) ⟨*persona*⟩ to fleece (colloq)

despoblación *f* depopulation; ~ **forestal** (Esp) deforestation

despoblado -da *adj* **1** (sin habitantes) deserted, uninhabited; (subpoblado) underpopulated, sparsely populated **2** ⟨*cejas*⟩ thin, sparse

despojar [A1] *vt* (frml) ~ A algn DE algo ⟨*de privilegios/poderes*⟩ to divest sb OF sth (frml); ⟨*de título/posesiones*⟩ to dispossess (frml) o strip sb OF sth
■ **despojarse** *v pron* (frml o liter) ~se DE algo ⟨*de ropa*⟩ to remove sth; ⟨*de bienes*⟩ to relinquish sth

despojos *mpl* (a) (restos) remains (*pl*) (b) (presa, botín) spoils (*pl*), loot (c) (de aves) head, wings, feet and giblets; (de reses) head, feet and offal

desportillado -da *adj* chipped

desposeído -da *m,f*: **los ~s** the destitute, the dispossessed

déspota *mf* tyrant, despot

despótico -ca *adj* despotic, tyrannical

despotricar [A2] *vi* (fam) ~ (CONTRA algo/algn) to rant and rave (ABOUT sth/sb)

despreciable *adj* (a) ⟨*persona/conducta*⟩ despicable, contemptible (b) no/nada ~ ⟨*suma/número*⟩ not inconsiderable, significant

despreciar [A1] *vt* (a) (menospreciar) ⟨*persona*⟩ to look down on; (profundamente) to despise (b) (rechazar) ⟨*oferta/ayuda*⟩ to reject

despreciativo -va *adj* disdainful

desprecio *m* (a) (menosprecio) disdain; (más intenso) contempt; **me miró con ~** she gave me a disdainful o scornful look (b) (indiferencia por el peligro, la vida) disregard (c) (desaire) snub, slight; **hacerle un ~ a algn** to snub o slight sb

desprender [E1] *vt* (soltar, separar) ⟨*teja*⟩ to dislodge; ⟨*etiqueta*⟩ to detach
■ **desprenderse** *v pron* **1** «*teja*» to come loose; «*botón*» to come off; «*retina*» to become detached; ~se DE algo to come away FROM sth **2** (renunciar, entregar) ~se DE algo ⟨*de posesiones*⟩ to part WITH sth

desprendido -da *adj* [SER] generous, open-handed; *ver tb* DESPRENDER

desprendimiento *m* detachment; ~ **de retina** detachment of the retina; ~ **de tierras** landslide

despreocupado -da *adj* (a) (sin preocupaciones) ⟨*vida*⟩ carefree (b) (descuidado) negligent (c) (indiferente) unworried

despreocuparse [A1] *v pron* (a) ▶ DESENTENDERSE (b) (dejar de preocuparse): **despreocúpate de todo** don't worry about anything

desprestigiar [A1] *vt* to discredit
■ **desprestigiarse** *v pron* «*persona/producto/empresa*» to lose prestige

desprestigio *m* (a) (pérdida de prestigio) loss of prestige; **ir en ~ de algo/algn** to bring discredit on o upon sth/sb (b) (falta de prestigio) bad reputation

desprevenido -da *adj*: **estar ~** to be unprepared o unready; **pillar a algn ~** «*pregunta*» to catch sb unawares o off guard; «*lluvia*» to catch sb by surprise

desprolijo -ja *adj* (CS) (a) [ESTAR] ⟨*trabajo*⟩ untidy, messy (b) [SER] ⟨*persona*⟩ careless

desproporción *f* disparity, disproportion

desproporcionado -da *adj* out of proportion

desprovisto -ta *adj* ~ DE algo lacking IN sth

después *adv* **1** (a) (más tarde) later; **para ~** for later (b) (en una serie de sucesos) then, afterward(s); ~ **no lo he vuelto a ver** I haven't seen him since then (c) (*en locs*) **después de** after; ~ **de Cristo** AD; ~ DE hacer algo after doing sth; **después de todo** after all; **después (de) que** after; (refiriéndose al futuro) once, when; ~ **(de) que todos se hayan ido** once o when everybody has left; **después que** after **2** (en el espacio): **bájate dos paradas ~** get off two stops further on; **hay una casa y ~ está el colegio** there is a house and then you come to the school; **está justo ~ del puente** it's just past the bridge

despuntado -da *adj* blunt

despuntar [A1] *vt* to blunt
■ ~ *vi* (a) «*día*» to break, dawn; **al ~ el día** at daybreak (b) «*flor*» to bud; «*plantas*» to sprout (c) «*persona*» ~ EN algo to excel AT o IN sth

desquiciado -da *adj* ⟨*mundo/persona*⟩ crazy; **tengo los nervios ~s** my nerves are in tatters

desquiciante *adj* maddening, infuriating

desquicio *m* (RPl fam) chaos

desquitarse [A1] *v pron* to get even; **lo hizo para ~ de él** she did it to get even with him; ~ CON algn/algo to take it out on sb/sth

destacado -da *adj* **1** ⟨*profesional/artista*⟩ prominent, distinguished; ⟨*actuación*⟩ outstanding **2** [ESTAR] ⟨*tropas*⟩ stationed

destacar [A2] *vt* **1** (recalcar, subrayar) to emphasize, stress **2** (realzar) ⟨*belleza/figura*⟩ to enhance; ⟨*color/plano*⟩ to bring out **3** (a) (Mil) ⟨*tropas*⟩ to post (b) ⟨*periodista/fotógrafo*⟩ to send
■ ~ *vi* to stand out; ~ EN algo to excel AT o IN sth

destajo *m* (Com, Rels Labs) piecework; **trabajar a ~** to do piecework

destapado -da *adj* (sin tapa) ⟨*olla*⟩ uncovered; **dejó la botella destapada** he left the top off the bottle (b) (en la cama): **siempre duerme ~** he always sleeps with the covers thrown back

destapador *m* (AmL) bottle opener

destapar [A1] *vt* **1** (a) ⟨*botella/caja*⟩ to open, take the top/lid off; ⟨*olla*⟩ to uncover, take the lid off (b) (descubrir) ⟨*mueble*⟩ to uncover; ⟨*escándalo*⟩ to uncover (c) (en la cama) to pull the covers off **2** (AmL) ⟨*cañería/inodoro*⟩ to unblock
■ **destaparse** *v pron* (refl) **1** (en la cama) to throw the covers o bedclothes off **2** «*nariz/oídos*» to unblock

destaponar [A1] *vt* ⟨*cañería*⟩ to unblock

destartalado -da *adj* (fam) ⟨*coche*⟩ beat-up (AmE colloq), clapped-out (BrE colloq); ⟨*mueble*⟩ shabby; ⟨*casa*⟩ ramshackle, rundown

destellar [A1] *vi* «*brillante/joya*» to sparkle, glitter; «*estrella*» to twinkle, sparkle

destello *m* (de estrella) twinkle, sparkle; (de brillante, joya) sparkle, glitter

destemplado -da adj [1] ⟨persona⟩: **estoy ~** (con fiebre) I have a slight fever; (indispuesto) I'm feeling off-color*; [2] **(a)** ⟨instrumento/voz/tono⟩ discordant **(b)** ⟨nervios⟩ frayed

destemplar [A1] vt [1] ⟨guitarra/violín⟩ to make ... go out of tune [2] ⟨ánimos/nervios⟩ to fray [3] (AmL) ⟨dientes⟩ to set ... on edge

desteñir [I15] vi ⟨prenda/color⟩ to run; (decolorarse) to fade
■ **desteñirse** v pron to run; (decolorarse) to fade

desternillarse [A1] v pron (fam): **~ de risa** to split one's sides (laughing) (colloq)

desterrado -da m,f exile

desterrar [A5] vt ⟨persona⟩ to exile, banish (liter)

destiempo: **a ~** ⟨marchar⟩ out of step; ⟨tocar⟩ out of time; **habló a ~** she picked the wrong moment to say it

destierro m exile, banishment

destilar [A1] vt **(a)** ⟨alcohol/petróleo⟩ to distill*; ⟨hulla/madera⟩ to char **(b)** (rezumar) to ooze

destilería f distillery

destinado -da adj [1] **(a)** (predestinado): **~ a triunfar/al fracaso** destined to succeed/to fail **(b)** (dirigido, asignado): **~ A** algn ⟨carta/paquete⟩ addressed TO sb; ⟨víveres⟩ intended FOR sb; ⟨libro/novela⟩ aimed AT sb; **las cajas destinadas a Montevideo** the boxes destined for Montevideo; **los aviones ~s a este fin** the planes used for this purpose [2] **(a)** ⟨militar⟩: **~ en Ceuta** stationed in Ceuta **(b)** ⟨funcionario/diplomático⟩: **ahora está ~ en Lima** now he's been posted to Lima

destinar [A1] vt [1] ⟨funcionario/militar⟩ to post, send, assign [2] (asignar un fin): **destinó todos sus ahorros a pagar las deudas** she used all her savings to pay her debts; **~on el dinero a la investigación** the money was used for research; **~on parte de los fondos a este fin** they earmarked part of the funds for this purpose

destinatario -ria m,f (de carta, paquete) addressee; (de giro, transferencia) payee

destino m [1] (sino) fate [2] **(a)** (de avión, autobús) destination; **con ~ a Roma** ⟨vuelo/tren⟩ to Rome; ⟨pasajero⟩ traveling to Rome; ⟨carga⟩ destined for Rome; **salieron con ~ a Lima** they set off for Lima **(b)** (puesto) posting, assignment [3] (uso, fin) use

destituir [I20] vt (frml) (despedir) to dismiss

destornillador m screwdriver

destornillar [A1] vt to unscrew

destreza f skill; **con gran ~** very skillfully

destronar [A1] vt ⟨rey⟩ to dethrone, depose; ⟨líder/campeón⟩ to depose, topple

destrozar [A4] vt **(a)** (romper, deteriorar) ⟨zapatos⟩ to ruin; ⟨cristal/jarrón⟩ to smash; ⟨juguete⟩ to pull ... apart; ⟨coche⟩ to wreck; ⟨libro⟩ to pull apart **(b)** ⟨felicidad/matrimonio/vida⟩ to wreck, destroy; ⟨corazón⟩ to break; **tiene los nervios destrozados** he's a nervous wreck

■ **destrozarse** v pron **(a)** (romperse) ⟨zapatos⟩ to be ruined; ⟨jarrón/cristal⟩ to smash **(b)** ⟨estómago/hígado⟩ to ruin

destrozo m: tb **~s** damage

destrucción f destruction

destructivo -va adj destructive

destructor m destroyer

destruir [I20] vt **(a)** ⟨documentos/pruebas⟩ to destroy; ⟨ciudad⟩ to destroy; ⟨medio ambiente⟩ to damage (echar por tierra) ⟨reputación⟩ to ruin; ⟨plan⟩ to wreck; ⟨esperanzas⟩ to dash, shatter

desubicado -da adj (AmS) **(a)** [ESTAR] (desplazado) out of position **(b)** [ESTAR] (desorientado) confused, disoriented **(c)** [SER] (en cuestiones sociales): **es tan ~** he just doesn't have a clue (colloq)

desuso m disuse; **caer en ~** to fall into disuse

desvaído -da adj ⟨color⟩ faded, washed-out; ⟨persona⟩ colorless*, insipid

desvalido -da m,f helpless person

desvalijar [A1] vt **(a)** ⟨casa/tienda⟩ to strip ... bare **(b)** ⟨persona⟩ (robar) to rob; (en juego) (fam) to clean ... out (colloq)

desván m attic, loft

desvanecerse [E3] v pron **(a)** ⟨humo/nubes/niebla⟩ to clear, disperse; ⟨dudas/temores/sospechas⟩ to vanish, be dispelled; ⟨fantasma/visión⟩ to disappear, vanish **(b)** ⟨color⟩ to fade

desvariar [A17] vi (Med) to be delirious; (decir tonterías) to talk nonsense, rave

desvelado -da adj: **estoy ~** I can't sleep

desvelar [A1] vt [1] ⟨persona⟩ to keep ... awake, stop ... from sleeping [2] (Esp) ▶ DEVELAR
■ **desvelarse** v pron (perder el sueño): **me desvelé anoche** I couldn't sleep last night

desvelo m [1] (insomnio) sleeplessness [2] **desvelos** mpl (esfuerzos) efforts (pl), pains (pl)

desvencijado -da adj ⟨silla/cama⟩ rickety; ⟨coche⟩ dilapidated, beat-up (AmE colloq), clapped-out (BrE colloq)

desventaja f disadvantage; **en ~** at a disadvantage

desvergonzado -da m,f: **ser un ~** (impúdico) to have no shame; (descarado) to be very impertinent

desvestir [I14] vt to undress
■ **desvestirse** v pron to undress, get undressed; **~se de la cintura para arriba** to strip to the waist

desviación f **(a)** (en general) diversion **(b)** (Med) curvature **(c)** (alejamiento) **~ DE algo** deviation FROM sth

desviar [A17] vt ⟨tráfico/vuelo/fondos⟩ to divert; ⟨río⟩ to alter the course of; ⟨golpe/pelota⟩ to deflect, parry; **~ la conversación** to change the subject; **desvió la mirada** he looked away
■ **desviarse** v pron [1] ⟨carretera⟩ to branch off; ⟨vehículo⟩ to turn off; **la conversación se desvió hacia otros temas** the conversation turned to other things [2] ⟨persona⟩ **~se DE algo** ⟨de ruta⟩ to deviate FROM sth; ⟨de tema⟩ to get off sth

desvincularse [A1] *v pron* ~**se** DE **algn/algo** to dissociate oneself FROM sth/sb; **está desvinculado de la política** he is no longer involved in politics

desvío *m* **(a)** (por obras) diversion, detour (AmE); **tomar un** ~ to make a detour **(b)** (Esp) (salida, carretera) exit

desvivirse [I1] *v pron* ~ POR **algn** to be completely devoted TO sb; ~ **POR hacer algo** to go out of one's way to do sth

detallado -da *adj ⟨factura/cuenta⟩* itemized; *⟨estudio/descripción⟩* detailed

detallar [A1] *vt* to detail

detalle *m* **1** **(a)** (pormenor) detail; **entrar en** ~**s** to go into details; **describir algo con todo** ~ to describe sth in great detail **(b)** (elemento decorativo) detail **2** **(a)** (pequeño regalo) little gift **(b)** (Esp, Méx) (atención, gesto) nice (o thoughtful *etc*) gesture; **tener un** ~ **CON algn** to do sth nice FOR sb **3** (Com) **al detalle** retail

detallista *adj* (minucioso) precise, meticulous

detectar [A1] *vt* to detect

detective *mf* detective

detector *m* detector; ~ **de mentiras/metales** lie/metal detector

detención *f* **1** (arresto) arrest; (encarcelamiento) detention **2** ▶ DETENIMIENTO

detener [E27] *vt* **1** (parar) *⟨vehículo/máquina⟩* to stop; *⟨trámite/proceso⟩* to halt; *⟨hemorragia⟩* to stop, staunch **2** (arrestar) to arrest; (encarcelar) to detain; **¡queda usted detenido!** you're under arrest!

■ **detenerse** *v pron* **(a)** (pararse) *«vehículo/ persona»* to stop; ~**se** A **hacer algo** to stop to do sth **(b)** (tomar mucho tiempo) ~**se** EN **algo: no nos detengamos demasiado en los detalles** let's not spend too much time discussing the details

detenido -da *adj* **(a)** *⟨vehículo/tráfico⟩* held up **(b)** *⟨investigación/estudio⟩* detailed, thorough **(c)** [ESTAR] *⟨persona⟩* under arrest; (por período más largo) in custody

■ *m,f* person under arrest; (durante un período más largo) detainee, person held in custody

detenimiento *m*: **con** ~ carefully *o* in detail

detergente *m* **(a)** (para ropa) laundry detergent (AmE), washing powder (BrE) **(b)** (Bol, CS) (para vajilla) dishwashing liquid (AmE), washing-up liquid (BrE)

deteriorado -da *adj ⟨mercancías⟩* damaged; *⟨edificio⟩* dilapidated, run down; *⟨mueble/cuadro⟩* in bad condition

deteriorar [A1] *vt ⟨relaciones/salud/situación⟩* to cause ... to deteriorate

■ **deteriorarse** *v pron* *«relaciones/salud/ situación»* to deteriorate, worsen; *«mercancías»* to get damaged

deterioro *m* **(a)** (de edificio, muebles) deterioration, wear **(b)** (empeoramiento) deterioration, worsening

determinación *f* (cualidad) determination, resolve; (decisión) decision; **tomar una** ~ to make a decision

determinado -da *adj ⟨fecha/lugar⟩* certain; **en determinadas circunstancias** in certain circumstances; **una determinada dosis** a particular dosage

determinante *adj ⟨causa⟩* main (*before n*); *⟨factor⟩* deciding (*before n*)

determinar [A1] *vt* **1** (establecer, precisar) **(a)** *«ley/contrato»* to state; *«persona»* to determine **(b)** (por deducción) to establish, determine **2** (motivar) to cause, bring about

detestar [A1] *vt* to hate, detest

detiene, detienes, etc ▶ DETENER

detonación *f* **(a)** (ruido) explosion; (acción) detonation **(b)** (Auto) (de motor) backfire

detonador *m* detonator

detonar [A1] *vi* to detonate, explode

detrás *adv* **1** (lugar, parte) [*Latin American Spanish also uses* ATRÁS *in this sense*]: **iba corriendo** ~ he ran along behind; **las cajas de** ~ the boxes at the back; **por** ~ *⟨abrocharse⟩* at the back; *⟨atacar⟩* from behind **2** **detrás de** (*loc prep*) ~ **de la puerta** behind the door; ~ **de mí/ti** behind me/you; **un cigarrillo** ~ **de otro** one cigarette after another

detuve, detuvo, etc ▶ DETENER

deuda *f* **(a)** (Com, Fin) debt; **pagar una** ~ to pay (off) a debt; **contraer una** ~ to run up *o* (frml) contract a debt; ~ **pública** public debt (AmE), national debt (BrE) **(b)** (compromiso moral): **estoy en** ~ **con usted** I am indebted to you

deudor -dora *adj* debtor (*before n*)

■ *m,f* debtor

devaluación *f* devaluation

devaluar [A18] *vt* to devalue

■ **devaluarse** *v pron* *«moneda»* to fall; *«terrenos/propiedad»* to depreciate, fall in value

devanar [A1] *vt ⟨hilo/lana/alambre⟩* to wind

devaneo *m* **(a)** (amorío) affair; (pasajero) fling **(b)** (pasatiempo frívolo) idle pursuit

devastador -dora *adj* devastating

devastar [A1] *vt* to devastate

develar [A1] *vt* (AmL) *⟨secreto⟩* to reveal, disclose; *⟨misterio⟩* to uncover; *⟨monumento/ placa⟩* to unveil

devoción *f* devotion; **siente** ~ **por sus hijos** she's devoted to her children

devolución *f* (de artículo) return; (de dinero) refund

devolver [E11] *vt* **1** **(a)** (restituir) *⟨objeto prestado⟩* to return, give back; *⟨dinero⟩* to give back, pay back; *⟨envase⟩* to return; *⟨objeto comprado⟩* to bring/take ... back; **devuélvelo a su lugar** put it back in its place; ~**le algo** A **algn** to return sth TO sb; *⟨dinero⟩* to give *o* pay sth back TO sb; **me devolvieron los documentos** I got my papers back; **el teléfono me devolvía las monedas** the telephone kept rejecting my coins; **la operación le devolvió la vista** the operation restored his sight **(b)** *⟨refugiado⟩* to return, send back **(c)** (Fin) *⟨letra⟩* to return **2** (corresponder) *⟨visita/favor⟩* to return **3** (vomitar) to bring up, throw up (colloq)

■ ~ *vi* to bring up; **tengo ganas de** ~ I feel sick

■ **devolverse** *v pron* (AmL exc RPl) (regresar) to go/come/turn back

devorar [A1] *vt* *«animal»* to devour; *«persona»* to devour, wolf down (colloq); ~ **a algn con los ojos** *or* **la mirada** to devour sb with one's eyes (colloq); **fue devorado por las llamas** it was consumed by the flames

devoto -ta adj ⟨persona⟩ devout; ⟨lugar/obra⟩ devotional
■ m,f **(a)** (Relig) ~ **DE** algn devotee OF sb **(b)** (aficionado) ~ **DE** algo/algn devotee OF sth/admirer of sb

devuelva, devuelvas, etc ▶ DEVOLVER

DF m (en Méx) = **Distrito Federal**

di ▶ DAR, DECIR

día m ⓵ **(a)** (en general) day; **todos los** ~**s** every day; ~ **a** ~ day by day; **de** or **durante el** ~ during the day; **el** ~ **anterior** the day before, the previous day; **el** ~ **siguiente** the next o the following day; **trabaja doce horas por** ~ she works twelve hours a day; **un** ~ **sí y otro no** or (AmL) ~ **(de) por medio** every other day, on alternate days; **dentro de quince** ~**s** in two weeks o (BrE) a fortnight; **cada** ~ every day; **buenos** ~**s** or (RPl) **buen** ~ good morning; **al** ~: **una vez al** ~ once a day; **estoy al** ~ **en los pagos** I'm up to date with the payments; **poner algo al** ~ to bring sth up to date; **ponerse al** ~ **con algo** (con noticias) to get up to date with sth; (con trabajo) to catch up on sth; **mantenerse al** ~ to keep up to date; **de un** ~ **para otro** overnight; **hoy en** ~ nowadays, these days **(b)** (fecha): **¿qué** ~ **es hoy?** what day is it today?; **empieza el** ~ **dos** it starts on the second; **el** ~ **de Año Nuevo** New Year's Day; ~ **de los enamorados** (St) Valentine's Day; ~ **de los inocentes** December 28, ≈ April Fool's Day; ~ **de Reyes** Epiphany; ~ **festivo** or (AmL) **feriado** public holiday; ~ **laborable** working day; ~ **libre** (sin trabajo) day off; (sin compromisos) free day
⓶ **(a)** (tiempo indeterminado) day; **algún** ~ one day; **lo haremos otro** ~ we'll do it some other time; **un** ~ **de estos** one of these days; **¡hasta otro** ~! so long!, see you!; **el** ~ **menos pensado** when you least expect it **(b)** **días** mpl (vida, tiempo) days (pl); **tiene los** ~**s contados** his days are numbered; **hasta nuestros** ~**s** (up) to the present day

diabetes f diabetes

diabético -ca adj/m,f diabetic

diablo m ⓵ (demonio) devil; **como (el** or **un)** ~ like crazy o mad (colloq); **del** ~ or **de mil** ~**s** (fam) devilish (colloq); **está de un humor de mil** ~**s** she's in a devil of a mood (colloq); **donde el** ~ **perdió el poncho** (AmS fam) (en un lugar — aislado) in the back of beyond; (— lejano) miles away (colloq); **mandar algo/a algn al** ~ (fam) to pack sth in/to tell sb to go to hell (colloq) ⓶ (fam) (uso expletivo): **¿cómo/dónde/qué/quién** ~**s ...?** how/where/what/who the hell ... ? (colloq)

diablura f (fam) prank

diabólico -ca adj (del diablo) diabolic, satanic; ⟨persona⟩ evil; ⟨plan/intenciones⟩ devilish, fiendish

diadema f (para el pelo) hair-band; (corona) crown, diadem; (media corona) tiara

diafragma m (Anat, Fot, Med) diaphragm

diagnosticar [A2] vt to diagnose

diagnóstico m diagnosis

diagonal f **(a)** (Mat) diagonal **(b)** (en fútbol americano) endzone

diagrama m diagram

dial m (Rad, Tec) dial; (del teléfono) dial

dialecto m dialect

dialogar [A3] vi to talk; ~ **CON** algn to talk TO sb

diálogo m **(a)** (conversación) conversation; (Lit) dialogue, dialog (AmE) **(b)** (Pol, Rels Labs) talks (pl), negotiations (pl)

diamante m **(a)** (piedra) diamond; **un anillo de** ~**s** a diamond ring **(b)** (Dep) diamond **(c)** **diamantes** mpl (en naipes) diamonds (pl)

diámetro m diameter

diana f ⓵ (Mil) reveille ⓶ (Dep, Jueg) (objeto) target; (para dardos) dartboard; (centro) bull's-eye

diapasón m (para afinar) tuning fork; (de instrumento de cuerda) fingerboard

diapositiva f slide, transparency

diariero -ra m,f (CS) newspaper vendor

diario -ria adj **(a)** (de todos los días) ⟨tarea/clases⟩ daily; ⟨gastos⟩ everyday, day-to-day **(b)** (por día): **trabaja cuatro horas diarias** she works four hours a day **(c)** (en locs) **a diario** every day; **de diario** ⟨ropa/vajilla⟩ everyday (before n); **para diario** for everyday (use)
■ m ⓵ (periódico) newspaper; ~ **mural** (Chi) bulletin board (AmE), notice board (BrE) ⓶ (libro personal) diary, journal (AmE) ⓷ (Méx, Col, Ven) (gastos cotidianos): **el** ~ day-to-day expenses

diarrea f diarrhea*

dibujante mf (m) draftsman*; (f) draftswoman*; (de cómics) comic book artist, strip cartoonist

dibujar [A1] vt/vi to draw; ~ **a mano alzada** to draw freehand

dibujo m **(a)** (arte) drawing; **clase de** ~ drawing class; ~ **lineal** line drawing **(b)** (representación) drawing; **un** ~ **al carboncillo** a charcoal drawing; ~**s animados** cartoons (pl) **(c)** (estampado) pattern

diccionario m dictionary; ~ **bilingüe** bilingual dictionary; ~ **de sinónimos** dictionary of synonyms, ≈ thesaurus

dice, dices, etc ▶ DECIR

dicha f **(a)** (felicidad) happiness; **¡qué** ~ **verlos a todos reunidos!** what a joy to see you all together!; **¡qué** ~**!** **dejó de llover** (AmL fam) fantastic o wonderful! it's stopped raining! **(b)** (suerte) good luck, good fortune; **nunca es tarde si la** ~ **es buena** better late than never

dicharachero -ra adj (que habla mucho) chatty (colloq), talkative; (gracioso) witty

dicho¹ -cha pp [ver tb DECIR²]: ~ **esto, se fue** having said this, he left; **con eso queda todo** ~ that says it all; ~ **de otro modo** to put it another way, in other words; ~ **sea de paso** incidentally, by the way; **y** ¡~**! y hecho!** and in diez minutos estaba listo and, sure enough, ten minutes later there it was
■ adj dem (frml): **en dichas ciudades ...** in these cities ...; **dicha información** that information; ~**s documentos** (en escrito, documento) the above o (frml) said documents

dicho² m saying

dichoso -sa adj ⓵ (feliz) happy; (afortunado) fortunate, lucky ⓶ (delante del n) (fam) (maldito) blessed (colloq), damn (sl)

diciembre m December; para ejemplos ver ENERO

diciendo ▶ DECIR

dictado *m* dictation; **nos hizo un ~** she gave us a dictation; **escribir al ~** to take dictation

dictador -dora *m,f* dictator

dictadura *f* dictatorship

dictar [A1] *vt* **(a)** ⟨*carta/texto*⟩ to dictate **(b)** ⟨*leyes/medidas*⟩ to announce; ⟨*sentencia*⟩ to pronounce, pass **(c)** ⟨*acción/tendencia/moda*⟩ to dictate **(d)** (AmL) ⟨*clase/curso/conferencia*⟩ to give ■ **~** *vi* to dictate

didáctico -ca *adj* ⟨*juguete/programa*⟩ educational; ⟨*poema/exposición*⟩ didactic

diecinueve *adj inv/m/pron* nineteen; *para ejemplos ver* CINCO

dieciocho *adj inv/m/pron* eighteen; *para ejemplos ver* CINCO

dieciséis *adj inv/m/pron* sixteen; *para ejemplos ver* CINCO

diecisiete *adj inv/m/pron* seventeen; *para ejemplos ver* CINCO

diente *m* **(a)** (Anat, Zool) tooth; **lavarse** *or* **cepillarse los ~s** to clean *o* brush one's teeth; **~ de leche** milk tooth; *daba ~ con ~* my/his teeth were chattering; *hablar* or *murmurar entre ~s* to mutter (under one's breath) **(b)** (de engranaje, sierra) tooth; (de tenedor) prong, tine; **~ de ajo** clove of garlic

diera, dieras, etc ▶ DAR

diéresis *f* (*pl* **~**) diaeresis

diese, dieses, etc ▶ DAR

diestra *f* (liter *o* period) right hand; *a ~ y siniestra* left and right (AmE), left, right and centre (BrE)

diestro¹ -tra *adj* **(a)** (frml) ⟨*mano*⟩ right; ⟨*persona*⟩ right-handed **(b)** (hábil) ⟨*persona/jugada*⟩ skillful*

diestro² *m* matador, bullfighter; *a ~ y siniestro* (Esp) left and right (AmE), left, right and centre (BrE)

dieta *f* ⟦1⟧ (alimentación, régimen) diet; **ponerse a ~** to go on a diet ⟦2⟧ **(a)** (para viajes) allowance **(b)** (de parlamentario) salary

diez *adj inv/m/pron* ten; *para ejemplos ver* CINCO

difamar [A1] *vt* (por escrito) to libel, defame (frml); (oralmente) to slander, defame (frml)

difamatorio -ria *adj* ⟨*palabras/discurso*⟩ slanderous; ⟨*artículo/carta*⟩ libelous*

diferencia *f* **(a)** (disparidad) difference; **la ~ de precio** the difference in price; **a ~ del marido, ella es encantadora** unlike her husband, she's really charming **(b)** (distinción) distinction; **hacer una ~** to make a distinction **(c)** (desacuerdo) difference; **resolver sus** (*or* **mis** *etc*) **~s** to resolve one's differences **(d)** (resto) difference, **yo pagué la ~** I paid the difference

diferenciar [A1] *vt* ⟨*colores/sonidos*⟩ to tell the difference between, differentiate between

■ **diferenciarse** *v pron:* **¿en qué se diferencia esta especie?** what makes this species different?; **no se diferencian en nada** there's no difference between them; **~se DE algo/algn** to differ FROM sth/sb; **solo se diferencia del otro en** *or* **por el precio** the only difference between this one and the other one is the price

diferente *adj* **(a)** (distinto) different; **ser ~ A** *or* **DE algn/algo** to be different FROM sb/sth **(b)** (*en pl, delante del n*) ⟨*motivos/soluciones/maneras*⟩ various; **nos vimos en ~s ocasiones** we've met on several occasions

diferido: **una transmisión en ~** a prerecorded broadcast

difícil *adj* ⟦1⟧ **(a)** ⟨*problema/situación*⟩ difficult; ⟨*examen*⟩ hard, difficult; **me fue muy ~ decírselo** it was very hard *o* difficult for me to tell him; **es ~ de hacer/entender** it's difficult *o* hard to do/understand **(b)** ⟨*persona/carácter*⟩ difficult ⟦2⟧ (poco probable) unlikely; **va a ser ~ que acepte** it's unlikely that he'll accept; **veo ~ que gane** I doubt it she'll win

dificultad *f* difficulty; **respira con ~** he has difficulty breathing; **tiene ~es en hacerse entender** she has difficulty in making herself understood; **me pusieron muchas ~es para entrar** they made it very hard for me to get in; **meterse en ~es** to get into difficulties

dificultar [A1] *vt* to make ... difficult

dificultoso -sa *adj* difficult, problematic

difteria *f* diphtheria

difundir [I1] *vt* ⟨*noticia/rumor*⟩ to spread; ⟨*ideas/doctrina*⟩ to spread, disseminate; ⟨*cultura*⟩ to disseminate; ⟨*comunicado*⟩ to issue; (por radio) to disseminate; **muy difundidas** very widespread

difunto -ta *adj* (frml) late (*before n*), deceased (frml); **su ~ marido** her late husband ■ *m,f* (frml) deceased (frml)

difusión *f* (de noticia, rumor) spreading; (de ideas, doctrina, cultura) spreading, diffusion (frml); **los medios de ~** the media

difuso -sa *adj* ⟨*luz*⟩ dim, diffused; ⟨*idea/conocimientos*⟩ vague

diga, digas, etc ▶ DECIR

digerir [I11] *vt* to digest

digestión *f* digestion; **hacer la ~** to let one's food go down

digestivo -va *adj* ⟨*aparato*⟩ digestive

digital *adj* **(a)** (dactilar) finger (*before n*), digital (frml) **(b)** ⟨*aparato/sonido*⟩ digital

dignarse [A1] *v pron* **~ (A) hacer algo** to condescend *o* deign TO sth

dignatario -ria *m,f* dignitary

dignidad *f* **(a)** (cualidad) dignity **(b)** (título) rank; (cargo) position

digno -na *adj* ⟦1⟧ **(a)** ⟨*persona/actitud*⟩ honorable* **(b)** ⟨*sueldo*⟩ decent, living (*before n*); ⟨*vivienda*⟩ decent ⟦2⟧ (merecedor) **~ DE algo/algn** worthy OF sth/sb; **una persona digna de admiración** a person worthy of admiration; **una medida digna de elogio** a praiseworthy measure; **un espectáculo ~ de verse** a show worth seeing

dije *adj* (Chi fam) **(a)** (agradable) nice, lovely **(b)** (bondadoso) kind ■ *m* charm

dije, dijera, etc ▶ DECIR

dilapidar [A1] *vt* to squander

dilatado -da *adj* ⟨*pupila/conducto*⟩ dilated

dilatarse [A1] *v pron* ⟦1⟧ «*cuerpo/metal*» to expand; «*corazón*» to expand, dilate; «*pupila*» to dilate; «*embarazada*» to dilate ⟦2⟧ **(a)** (prolongarse) to be prolonged **(b)** (diferirse) to be postponed, be put off ⟦3⟧ (Méx, Ven) ▶ DEMORARSE B

dilema *m* (disyuntiva) dilemma

diligencia *f* **(a)** (aplicación) diligence,

conscientiousness; **con** ~ diligently **(b)** (gestión):
tengo que hacer unas ~s I have some business
to attend to

diligente adj (trabajador) diligent, conscientious

diluir [I20] vt ‹líquido› to dilute; ‹pintura› to
thin (down); ‹sólido› to dissolve

diluviar [A1] vi to pour (with rain)

diluvio m (lluvia) heavy rain, deluge; (inundación)
flood; **el D~ Universal** the Flood

diluyente m thinner

dimensión f **1** **(a)** (Fís, Mat) dimension; **una
figura en tres dimensiones** a three-dimensional
figure **(b) dimensiones** fpl (tamaño)
dimensions (pl); **de enormes dimensiones** huge,
enormous **2** (alcance, magnitud — de problema)
magnitude, scale; (— de tragedia) scale

diminutivo m diminutive

diminuto -ta adj tiny, minute

dimisión f resignation

dimitir [I1] vi to resign; ~ **DE algo** to resign
FROM sth

dimos ▶ DAR

Dinamarca f Denmark

dinamarqués -quesa adj/m,f ▶ DANÉS

dinámico -ca adj dynamic

dinamita f dynamite

dinamitar [A1] vt to dynamite

dínamo, dinamo m or (Esp) f dynamo

dinastía f dynasty

dineral m fortune, huge amount of money

dinero m money; **estar escaso de** ~ to be short
of money; **gente de** ~ well-off o wealthy people;
hacer ~ to make money; ~ **de bolsillo** pocket
money; ~ **(en) efectivo** cash; ~ **suelto** change; ~
contante y sonante (fam) hard cash

dinosaurio m dinosaur

dio ▶ DAR

diócesis f diocese

dioptría f diopter*; **¿cuántas ~s tiene?** what's
your correction o gradation?

dios, diosa m,f **1** (Mit) (m) god; (f) goddess
2 Dios m (Relig) God; **el D~ de los musulmanes**
the Muslim God; **gracias a D~** thank God o
heaven; **si D~ quiere** God willing; **te lo juro por
D~** I swear to God; **¡por (el) amor de D~!** for
God's sake o for heaven's sake!; **que D~ te
bendiga** God bless you; **¡D~ me libre!** God o
heaven forbid!; **¡sabe D~!** God knows!; **¡vaya por
D~!** oh dear!; **¡por D~!** for God's o heaven's
sake!; **¡D~ mío!** or **¡D~ santo!** (expresando angustia)
my God!, oh God!; (expresando sorpresa) (good)
God!; **como D~ manda**: **un coche como D~
manda** a real o a proper car; **pórtate como D~
manda** behave properly; **hacer algo a la buena de
D~** to do sth any which way (AmE) o (BrE) any
old how

diploma m diploma, certificate

diplomacia f **1** (Pol) (carrera) diplomacy;
(cuerpo) diplomatic corps **2** (tacto) diplomacy, tact

diplomado -da adj qualified; ~ **en peluquería**
qualified hairdresser

diplomarse [A1] v pron **(a)** (AmL) (obtener un
título universitario) to graduate; ~ **DE/EN algo** to
graduate AS/IN sth **(b)** (obtener otro título) to obtain
a diploma (o certificate etc)

diplomático -ca adj **1** (Pol) ‹carrera/
pasaporte› diplomatic **2** (en el trato) diplomatic,
tactful
■ m,f diplomat

diptongo m diphthong

diputación f **(a)** (delegación) deputation,
delegation **(b)** (Gob) (en Esp) council

diputado -da m,f deputy, ≈representative (in
US), ≈member of parliament (in UK)

dique m dike*

diré, dirá, etc ▶ DECIR

dirección f **1** (señas) address
2 (sentido, rumbo) direction; **ellos venían en** ~
contraria they were coming the other way o from
the opposite direction; **¿en qué** ~ **iba?** which
way was he heading o going?; **señal de** ~
prohibida no-entry sign; ~ **obligatoria** one way
only
3 (Auto) (mecanismo) steering; ~ **asistida**
power-assisted steering, power steering
4 (Adm) **(a)** (cargo — en escuela) principalship
(AmE), headship (BrE); (— en empresa) post o
position of manager **(b)** (cuerpo directivo — de
empresa) management; (— de periódico) editorial
board; (— de prisión) authorities (pl); (— de partido)
leadership **(c)** (oficina — en escuela) principal's
office (AmE), headmaster's/headmistress's office
(BrE); (— en empresa) manager's/director's office;
(— en periódico) editorial office

direccional f (Col, Méx) turn signal (AmE),
indicator (BrE)

directamente adv (derecho) straight; (sin
intermediarios) directly

directiva f **1** (de empresa) board (of directors);
(de partido) executive committee, leadership
2 (directriz) guideline

directo -ta adj **1** ‹vuelo› direct, nonstop;
‹ruta/acceso› direct; ‹tren› direct, through (before
n) **2** (Rad, TV): **en** ~ live **3** ‹lenguaje/pregunta›
direct; ‹respuesta› straight; ‹persona› direct,
straightforward

director -tora m,f **(a)** (de escuela) (m) head
teacher, principal (AmE), headmaster (BrE); (f)
head teacher, principal (AmE), headmistress (BrE);
(de periódico, revista) editor (in chief); (de hospital)
administrator; (de prisión) warden (AmE), governor
(BrE) **(b)** (Com) (gerente) manager; (miembro de junta
directiva) director, executive; ~ **gerente** managing
director **(c)** (Cin, Teatr) director; ~ **de orquesta**
conductor

directorio m (AmL exc CS) (guía telefónica)
telephone directory, directory

directriz f (Mat) directrix; (guía) guideline,
principle; (instrucción) directive

dirigente mf (de partido, país) leader

dirigible *m* airship, dirigible

dirigir [I7] *vt* ☐ **(a)** ⟨*empresa*⟩ to manage, run; ⟨*periódico/revista*⟩ to run, edit; ⟨*investigación/tesis*⟩ to supervise; ⟨*debate*⟩ to lead, chair; ⟨*tráfico*⟩ to direct **(b)** ⟨*obra/película*⟩ to direct; ⟨*orquesta*⟩ to conduct
☐ **(a)** ~ algo a algn ⟨*mensaje/carta*⟩ to address sth to sb; ⟨*críticas*⟩ to direct sth to sb; **la pregunta iba dirigida a usted** the question was meant for you; **no me dirigió la palabra** he didn't say a word to me **(b)** ~ algo hacia *or* a algo/algn ⟨*telescopio*⟩ to point sth toward(s) sth/sb; ⟨*pistola*⟩ to point sth toward(s) sth/sb; ~ **la mirada hacia** *or* **a algo/algn** to look at sth/sb; **dirigió sus pasos hacia la esquina** he walked toward(s) the corner
☐ (encaminar) ~ algo a hacer algo ⟨*esfuerzos*⟩ to channel sth into doing sth; ⟨*energía/atención*⟩ to direct sth toward(s) doing sth
■ **dirigirse** *v pron* ☐ (encaminarse): ~se hacia algo to head for sth
☐ ~se a algn (oralmente) to speak *o* talk to sb; (por escrito) to write to sb

discado *m* (AmL) dialing*; ~ **automático** *or* **directo** (AmL) direct dialing*

discapacitado -da *m,f* disabled person, handicapped person

discar [A2] *vt/vi* (AmL) to dial

disciplina *f* discipline; **mantener la** ~ to keep *o* maintain discipline

discípulo -la *m,f* disciple

disco *m* ☐ **(a)** (Audio) record; **grabar un** ~ to make a record; **poner un** ~ to put on a record; ~ **compacto** CD, compact disc; ~ **de larga duración** album, LP; ~ **volador** (CS) flying saucer **(b)** (Inf) disk; ~ **duro** hard disk; ~ **flexible** *or* **floppy** floppy disk ☐ **(a)** (Dep) discus **(b)** (Anat) disk*; (Auto, Mec) disk **(c)** (del teléfono) dial ☐ (señal de tráfico) (road) sign

disconforme *adj* **(a)** (no satisfecho) dissatisfied; ~ con algo/algn dissatisfied with sth/sb **(b)** (en desacuerdo) ~ con algo in disagreement with sth

discontinuo -nua *adj* ⟨*línea*⟩ broken; ⟨*sonido*⟩ intermittent

discordante *adj* (Mús) discordant; ⟨*opiniones/versiones*⟩ conflicting

discordia *f* discord

discoteca *f* **(a)** (local) discotheque **(b)** (colección de discos) record collection **(c)** (AmC) (tienda) record store *o* shop

discreción *f* ☐ **(a)** (tacto, mesura) tact, discretion **(b)** (reserva) discretion ☐ **a discreción** ⟨*comer/beber*⟩ as much as you (*o* we *etc*) like; **esto queda a** ~ **del juez** this is left to the discretion of the judge

discreto -ta *adj* **(a)** ⟨*persona/carácter/comportamiento*⟩ discreet **(b)** ⟨*color/vestido*⟩ discreet **(c)** ⟨*cantidad/sueldo/actuación*⟩ modest

discriminación *f* discrimination

discriminar [A1] *vt* **(a)** ⟨*persona/colectividad*⟩ to discriminate against **(b)** (distinguir) to differentiate, distinguish

disculpa *f* apology; **me debe una** ~ she owes me an apology; **un error que no tiene** ~ an inexcusable error; **pedir(le)** ~s **(a algn) por algo** to apologize (to sb) for sth

disculpar [A1] *vt* **(a)** ⟨*error/falta/comportamiento*⟩ to forgive, excuse; **le disculpó la indiscreción** he forgave her her indiscretion; **disculpa mi tardanza** I am sorry I'm late **(b)** ⟨*persona*⟩ to make excuses for; **su madre siempre lo está disculpando** his mother's always making excuses for him
■ ~ *vi*: **disculpe, no lo volveré a hacer** I'm sorry *o* (frml) I apologize, I won't do it again
■ **disculparse** *v pron* to apologize; ~se con algn to apologize to sb

discurso *m* speech; **pronunciar un** ~ to give *o* make a speech

discusión *f* **(a)** (de asunto, tema) discussion **(b)** (altercado, disputa) argument

discutible *adj* debatable

discutido -da *adj* controversial

discutir [I1] *vt* **(a)** (debatir) ⟨*problema/asunto*⟩ to discuss; ⟨*proyecto de ley*⟩ to debate, discuss **(b)** (cuestionar) ⟨*derecho/afirmación*⟩ to question, challenge
■ ~ *vi* to argue, quarrel; **discutió de política con su padre** he argued with his father about politics; ~ por algo to argue about sth; ~le a algn to argue with sb

disecar [A2] *vt* **(a)** ⟨*animal muerto*⟩ (para estudiarlo) to dissect; (para conservarlo) to stuff **(b)** ⟨*planta*⟩ to preserve

disección *f* dissection

diseccionar [A1] *vt* to dissect

diseminado -da *adj* scattered; **los pueblos** ~s **por la región** the villages scattered throughout the region; **los hoteles están muy** ~s the hotels are very spread out

diseminarse [A1] *v pron* «*personas*» to scatter, disperse; «*ideas/cultura*» to spread

diseñador -dora *m,f* designer; ~ **de moda(s)** fashion designer

diseñar [A1] *vt* ⟨*moda/mueble/máquina*⟩ to design; ⟨*parque/edificio*⟩ to design, plan

diseño *m* design; ~ **de moda** fashion design; **blusas de** ~ **francés** French-designed blouses; **ropa de** ~ designer clothes

disforzarse [A11] *v pron* (Per fam) to clown around

disfraz *m* **(a)** (Indum) (para jugar, fiestas) costume, fancy dress outfit (BrE); (para engañar) disguise; **una fiesta de disfraces** a costume *o* (BrE) fancy dress party **(b)** (simulación) front

disfrazar [A4] *vt* **(a)** ~ a algn de algo (para fiesta) to dress sb up as sth; (para engañar) to disguise sb as sth **(b)** (disimular, ocultar) ⟨*sentimiento/verdad*⟩ to conceal, hide; ⟨*voz/escritura/intención*⟩ to disguise
■ **disfrazarse** *v pron* **(a)** (por diversión) to dress up; ~se de algo/algn to dress up as sth/sb **(b)** (para engañar) to disguise oneself; ~se de algo/algn to disguise oneself as sth/sb, dress up as sth/sb

disfrutar [A1] *vi* **(a)** (divertirse) to enjoy oneself, have fun; ~ con/de algo to enjoy sth; ~ haciendo algo to enjoy doing sth **(b)** (tener) ~ de algo ⟨*de privilegio/derecho/buena salud*⟩ to enjoy, have
■ ~ *vt* ⟨*viaje/espectáculo*⟩ to enjoy; ⟨*beneficio/derecho*⟩ to have, enjoy

disgregarse [A3] v pron (a) «grupo/familia» to break up, split up; «multitud/manifestantes» to break up, disperse (b) (Tec) to disintegrate

disgustado -da adj [ESTAR] upset

disgustar [A1] vt: me disgustó mucho que me mintiera I was very upset that he lied to me; me disgusta tener que decírselo I don't like having to tell her
■ **disgustarse** v pron to get upset

disgusto m ① (sufrimiento, pesar): tiene un ~ tremendo he's very upset; me ha dado muchos ~s he's given me lots of upset o heartache; lo hizo a ~ she did it reluctantly ② (discusión) argument, quarrel

disidente mf (que discrepa) dissident; (escindido) member of a splinter o breakaway group

disimulado -da adj (a) (disfrazado, oculto) disguised; un mal ~ descontento ill-concealed displeasure (b) (discreto) discreet; sé más ~ be more discreet
■ m,f: me vio pero se hizo el ~ he saw me but he pretended he hadn't

disimular [A1] vt (a) «alegría/rabia/dolor» to hide, conceal (b) «defecto/imperfección» to hide, disguise

disimulo m: con ~ without anyone noticing; sin ~ openly

disiparse [A1] v pron «nubes/niebla» to clear; «temores/sospechas» to be dispelled; «ilusiones» to vanish, disappear

dislexia f dyslexia

disléxico -ca adj/m,f dyslexic

dislocado -da adj «articulación» dislocated

dislocarse [A2] v pron «articulación» to dislocate

disminución f decrease, fall; (de temperatura) drop; (de tarifa) reduction

disminuido -da m,f: ~ psíquico/físico mentally/physically handicapped person

disminuir [I20] vi (menguar) «número/cantidad» to decrease, fall; «precios/temperaturas» to drop, fall; «dolor» to diminish, lessen
■ ~ vt (reducir) «gastos/producción» to cut back on; «impuestos» to cut; «velocidad/número/cantidad» to reduce

disolución f (a) (de contrato, matrimonio) annulment; (de organización, del parlamento) dissolution (b) (de manifestación) breaking up (c) (Quím) (acción) dissolving

disolvente m solvent; (de pintura) thinner

disolver [E11] vt (a) «matrimonio/contrato» to annul; «parlamento/organización» to dissolve (b) «manifestación/reunión» to break up (c) (en líquido) to dissolve (d) (Med) to dissolve, break up
■ **disolverse** v pron «manifestación/reunión» to break up; «azúcar/aspirina» to dissolve

disonante adj (Mús) dissonant; «voz» discordant; «colores» clashing

dispar adj (a) (irregular) uneven (b) (diferente) different, disparate (frml)

disparado -da adj (fam): salir ~ (irse de prisa) to shoot off (colloq); con el choque salió ~ del asiento the impact catapulted him from his seat; ver tb DISPARAR

disparador m (de arma) trigger; (Fot) shutter release; (de reloj) escapement

disparar [A1] vi (a) (con arma) to shoot, fire; ~ al aire to fire o shoot into the air; ~ a matar to shoot to kill; le disparó por la espalda he shot him in the back; ~ a quemarropa o a bocajarro to fire at point-blank range; ~ CONTRA algn to shoot o fire AT sb (b) (Dep) to shoot
■ ~ vt ① (a) «arma/flecha» to shoot, fire; «tiro/proyectil» to fire; le ~on un tiro en la nuca they shot him in the back of the head (b) (Dep): disparó el balón a portería he shot at goal ② (Méx fam) (pagar) to buy
■ **dispararse** v pron ① (a) «arma» to go off (b) (refl): se disparó un tiro en la sien he shot himself in the head ② (fam) «precio» to shoot up, rocket

disparatado -da adj «acto/proyecto/idea» crazy, ludicrous; «gasto/precio» outrageous, ridiculous

disparate m (a) (acción insensata, cosa absurda): hacer ~s to do stupid things; decir ~s to make foolish remarks; es un ~ casarse tan joven it's crazy to get married so young; temo que haga algún ~ I'm afraid he might do something crazy (b) (fam) (cantidad exagerada) ridiculous (o crazy etc) amount

disparo m shot

dispensar [A1] vt ① «honor» to give, accord (frml); «acogida» to give, extend (frml); «ayuda/protección» to give, afford (frml); «asistencia médica» to give; «medicamentos» to dispense; le ~on un caluroso recibimiento he was given o (frml) extended a warm reception ② (a) (eximir) a algn DE algo to exempt sb FROM sth; la ~on de asistir a misa she was excused from attending mass (b) (perdonar) to forgive
■ ~ vi to forgive; dispense, por favor excuse me

dispersar [A1] vt (a) «manifestantes/multitud/enemigo» to disperse (b) «rayos» to scatter, diffuse; «niebla/humo» to clear, disperse
■ **dispersarse** v pron (a) «manifestantes/manifestación/multitud» to disperse (b) «rayos» to diffuse, scatter; «niebla/humo» to disperse, clear

disperso -sa adj (diseminado) scattered, dispersed (frml)

displicente adj (indiferente) indifferent, blasé; (frío) disdainful

disponer [E22] vt ① (frml) (establecer, ordenar) «ley» to provide (frml), to stipulate (frml); «rey» to decree; «general/juez» to order ② (frml) (colocar, arreglar) to arrange, set out, lay out
■ ~ vi: ~ DE algo «de tiempo/ayuda» to have sth; con los recursos de que dispongo with the means available to me o at my disposal
■ **disponerse** v pron (frml) mientras se disponían a tomar el tren as they were about to catch the train; la tropa se dispuso a atacar the troops prepared to attack

disponible adj available; «tiempo» free (before n), available; cuando estés ~ when you're free

disposición f ① (norma) regulation ② (a) (actitud) disposition (b) (talento) aptitude (c) (inclinación, voluntad) willingness ③ (a) (de un bien) disposal (b) a ~ de algn «coche/chofer» at sb's disposal; estoy a tu ~ para lo que sea I'm here to help if you need anything; **será puesto a ∼ del juez** he will appear before the judge; **puso su casa a mí ∼** he offered me his house

dispositivo *m* $\boxed{1}$ (mecanismo) mechanism; (aparato) device $\boxed{2}$ (frml) (destacamento): **un fuerte ∼ policial/militar** a large police/military presence

dispuesto -ta *adj* (a) (preparado) ready (b) (con voluntad) willing; **∼ A hacer algo** prepared to do sth

dispuse, dispuso, etc ▶ DISPONER

disputa *f* (a) (discusión, pelea) quarrel, argument (b) (combate) fight (c) (controversia) dispute

disputar [A1] *vt* (a) **∼le algo A algn** ⟨título⟩ to challenge sb for sth; **le disputaban su derecho a la herencia** they contested his right to the inheritance (b) ⟨partido⟩ to play; ⟨combate⟩ to fight

■ **disputarse** *v pron*: **se disputan el primer puesto** they are competing for first place

disquete, disquette /dis'kete/ *m* diskette, floppy disk

distancia *f* (a) (distance; **la ∼ que separa dos puntos** the distance between two points; **¿a qué ∼ está Londres?** how far is it to London?, **se situó a ∼ de un metro** she stood a meter away; ▶ LLAMADA (b) (en locs) **a distancia: se situó a ∼ para verlo en conjunto** she stood back to see it as a whole; **se veía a ∼** one could see it from a distance; **mantenerse a ∼** to keep at a distance; **en la distancia** in the distance; ▶ EDUCACIÓN 1, ENSEÑANZA B

distanciado -da *adj* (afectivamente): **estamos algo distanciadas** we're not as close as we were

distanciar [A1] *vt* (a) (espaciar) to space ... out (b) (en lo afectivo) «amigos/familiares» to make ... drift apart; **∼ a algn DE algn** to distance sb FROM sb

■ **distanciarse** *v pron* (a) (en el espacio) **∼se DE algo** to get far FROM sth (b) (en lo afectivo) (recípr) to grow o drift apart; (refl) **∼se DE algn** to distance oneself FROM sb

distante *adj* distant

distar [A1] *vi* (en 3ª pers) (estar a): **el colegio dista unos dos kilómetros de su casa** the school is about two kilometers from her house

diste, etc ▶ DAR

distinción *f* (a) (diferencia) distinction; **hacer una ∼** to make a distinction; **sin ∼ de raza o credo** regardless of race or creed; **no hago distinciones con nadie** I don't give anyone preferential treatment (b) (elegancia) distinction, elegance (c) (honor, condecoración) award

distinguido -da *adj* ⟨escritor/actor/aire⟩ distinguished; ⟨alumno⟩ outstanding

distinguir [I2] *vt* $\boxed{1}$ (a) (diferenciar) to distinguish (b) (caracterizar) to characterize $\boxed{2}$ (percibir) ⟨figura/sonido⟩ to make out $\boxed{3}$ (con medalla, honor) to honor*

■ **distinguirse** *v pron* (destacarse): **∼se POR algo** «persona» to distinguish oneself BY sth; «producto» to be distinguished BY sth

distintivo¹ -va *adj* ⟨rasgo/característica⟩ distinctive

distintivo² *m* (insignia) emblem; (símbolo) sign

distinto -ta *adj* $\boxed{1}$ (diferente) different; **ser ∼ A** *or* **DE algo/algn** to be different FROM o TO o (AmE)

THAN sth/sb; **estas/te encuentro ∼** you look different $\boxed{2}$ (en pl, delante del n) (varios) several, various

distorsionar [A1] *vt* to distort

distracción *f* (a) (entretenimiento) entertainment (b) (descuido): **en un momento de ∼se la robaron** she took her eye off it for a moment and someone stole it; **la más mínima ∼ puede ser fatal** the slightest lapse of concentration could be fatal (c) (de fondos) embezzlement

distraer [E23] *vt* ⟨persona/atención⟩ to distract; **∼ a algn DE algo** ⟨de trabajo/estudios⟩ to distract sb FROM sth ⟨de preocupaciones⟩ to take sb's mind OFF sth (b) (entretener) ⟨persona⟩ to keep ... entertained

■ **distraerse** *v pron* (a) (despistarse, descuidarse) to get distracted (b) (entretenerse): **se distraen viendo la televisión** they pass the time watching television; **se distrae con cualquier cosa** she doesn't need much to keep amused

distraído -da *adj* (a) [SER] ⟨persona⟩ absentminded, vague (b) **estaba/iba ∼** he was miles away (colloq)

distribución *f* (a) (reparto — de dinero, víveres) distribution; (— de tareas) allocation (b) (de producto, película) distribution (c) (disposición, división) layout, arrangement (d) (Auto) valve-operating gear

distribuidor¹ -dora *m,f* (Com) distributor

distribuidor² *m* (Auto, Mec) distributor

distribuidora *f* (empresa) distributor, distribution company

distribuir [I20] *vt* (a) ⟨dinero/víveres/panfletos⟩ to hand out, distribute; ⟨ganancias⟩ to distribute; ⟨tareas⟩ to allocate, assign; ⟨carga/peso⟩ to distribute, spread (b) ⟨producto/película⟩ to distribute (c) «canal/conducto» ⟨agua⟩ to distribute (d) (disponer) to lay out (e) (dividir) to divide ... up; **los distribuyeron en tres grupos** they divided them (up) into three groups

■ **distribuirse** *v pron* (refl) to divide up

distrito *m* district

Distrito Federal *m* Federal District (including Mexico City)

disturbio *m* (a) (perturbación del orden) disturbance (b) **disturbios** *mpl* (motín) riot, disturbances (journ)

disuadir [I1] *vt* to deter, discourage; **∼ A algn DE algo/DE que haga algo** to dissuade sb FROM sth/doing sth

disuasión *f* (Mil, Pol) deterrence

disuasivo -va, disuasorio -ria *adj* ⟨tono/ palabras⟩ dissuasive, discouraging; ⟨efecto⟩ deterrent; ⟨medida⟩ designed to act as a deterrent

disuelto -ta *pp* ▶ DISOLVER

diurético *m* diuretic

diurno -na *adj* day (before n); **clases diurnas** daytime classes

diva *f* diva, prima donna; **ver tb** DIVO

divagación *f* digression

divagar [A3] *vi* (a) (desviarse del tema) to digress (b) (hablar sin sentido) to ramble

diván *m* couch

diversidad *f* diversity

diversificar [A2] vt ⟨actividades/métodos⟩ to diversify; ⟨inversión/producción⟩ to diversify
■ **diversificarse** v pron to diversify

diversión f **(a)** (esparcimiento) fun **(b)** (espectáculo, juego): **aquí hay pocas diversiones** there isn't much to do here

diverso -sa adj **1** (variado, diferente): **su obra es muy diversa** his work is very diverse; **seres de diversa naturaleza** various types of creatures; **ha desempeñado las más diversas actividades** she has engaged in a very wide range of activities **2** (pl) (varios) various, several

divertido -da adj **(a)** (que interesa, divierte) ⟨espectáculo/fiesta⟩ fun, enjoyable; ⟨momento/situación⟩ entertaining; **es un tipo muy ~** he's a really fun guy, he's really fun to be with **(b)** (gracioso) funny

divertir [I11] vt to amuse
■ **divertirse** v pron (entretenerse) to amuse oneself; (pasarlo bien) to have fun, enjoy oneself; **¡que te diviertas!** have fun!, enjoy yourself!; **nos divertimos mucho en la fiesta** we had a really good time at the party

dividendo m dividend

dividir [I11] vt **(a)** (partir) to divide; **lo dividió en partes iguales** he divided it (up) into equal portions **(b)** (repartir) to divide, share (out) **(c)** (enemistar) ⟨partido/familia⟩ to divide
■ **~** vi (Mat) to divide
■ **dividirse** v pron ⟨célula⟩ to split; ⟨grupo/partido⟩ to split up; ⟨camino/río⟩ to divide **(b)** **~ EN algo** ⟨obra/período⟩ to be divided INTO sth **(c)** (repartirse) to divide up, share out

divierta, divirtió, etc ▶ DIVERTIR

divinidad f **(a)** (deidad) deity, god **(b)** (cualidad) divinity **(c)** (fam) (preciosidad) delight

divinizar [A4] vt to deify

divino -na adj divine

divisa f **1** (Com, Fin) currency; **la fuga de ~s** the flight of capital; **una fuente de ~s** a source of foreign currency **2** (emblema) emblem, insignia

divisar [A1] vt ⟨tierra/barco⟩ to sight, make out; **a lo lejos se divisaba un poblado** they (or he etc) could make out a village in the distance

divisible adj **~ POR algo** divisible BY sth

división f (en general) division; **hacer una ~** (Mat) to do a division

divisor m divisor

divisorio -ria adj dividing (before n)

divo -va m,f (estrella) celebrity, star; (con actitud soberbia) prima donna; ver tb DIVA

divorciado -da adj divorced
■ m,f (m) divorcé (esp AmE), divorcee (esp BrE); (f) divorcée (esp AmE), divorcee (esp BrE)

divorciarse [A1] v pron to get divorced; **~se DE algn** to divorce sb, get divorced FROM sb

divorcio m (Der) divorce

divulgar [A3] vt ⟨noticia/información⟩ to spread, circulate; ⟨secreto/plan⟩ to divulge; ⟨cultura⟩ to spread, disseminate
■ **divulgarse** v pron to spread

dizque, diz que adv (AmL) **(a)** (según parece) apparently **(b)** (expresando escepticismo): **esta ~ democracia** this so-called democracy; **estaban allí, ~ trabajando** they were there, supposedly working

Dn. = **Don**

Dña. = **Doña**

do m (nota) C; (en solfeo) do, doh (BrE); **~ de pecho** high C, top C

dobladillo m hem

doblar [A1] vt **1** ⟨camisa/papel⟩ to fold; ⟨brazo/vara⟩ to bend **2** ⟨esquina⟩ to turn, go around; ⟨cabo⟩ to round **3** (aumentar al doble) ⟨oferta/apuesta/capital⟩ to double; (tener el doble que): **la dobla en edad** he's twice her age **4** ⟨actor⟩ (en banda sonora) to dub; (en escena) to double for; ⟨película⟩ to dub; **doblada al castellano** dubbed into Spanish
■ **~** vi **1** (torcer, girar) «persona» to turn; «camino» to bend, turn; **dobla a la izquierda** turn left **2** «campanas» to toll
■ **doblarse** v pron **1** «rama/alambre» to bend **2** «precios/población» to double

doble¹ adj **1** ⟨whisky/flor/puerta⟩ double; ⟨café⟩ large; ⟨costura/hilo/consonante⟩ double; **lo veo todo ~** I'm seeing double; **cerrar con ~ llave** to double-lock; **tiene ~ sentido** it has a double meaning; **calle de ~ sentido** two-way street; **~ crema** f (Méx) double cream; **~ fondo** m false bottom; **~ ve** or **~ u** f: name of the letter W; **~ ventana** f double glazing **2** (Andes, Ven fam) ⟨persona⟩ two-faced

doble² m **1** (Mat): **los precios aumentaron el ~** prices doubled; **tardó el ~** she took twice as long; **el ~ de tres es seis** two threes are six; **el ~ QUE algn/algo** twice as much AS sb/sth; **el ~ de largo/rápido** twice as long/quick **2** **(a)** (en béisbol) double **(b)** **dobles** mpl (en tenis) doubles **3** **doble** mf (actor, actriz) stand-in, double; (en escenas peligrosas) (m) stuntman; (f) stuntwoman; (persona parecida) (fam) double

doblez m **1** (en tela, papel) fold **2** **doblez** m or f (falsedad) deceitfulness

doce adj inv/m/pron twelve; **son las ~ de la noche** it's twelve o'clock, it's midnight; **para más ejemplos ver tb** CINCO

docena f dozen; **una ~ de huevos** a dozen eggs; **media ~** half a dozen

dócil adj ⟨niño/comportamiento⟩ meek, docile; ⟨perro/caballo⟩ docile, well-trained; ⟨pelo⟩ manageable

doctor -tora m,f doctor; **~ en derecho** Doctor of Law

doctorado m doctorate, PhD

doctorarse [A1] v pron to earn o get one's doctorate, do one's PhD

doctrina f (ideología) doctrine; (enseñanza) teaching

documentación f **1** (de persona) papers (pl); (de vehículo, envío) documents (pl), documentation (frml) **2** (información) information, data (pl)

AmC	Central America	Arg	Argentina	Cu	Cuba	Per	Peru
AmL	Latin America	Bol	Bolivia	Ec	Ecuador	RPI	River Plate Area
AmS	South America	Chi	Chile	Esp	Spain	Ur	Uruguay
Andes	Andean Region	CS	Southern Cone	Méx	Mexico	Ven	Venezuela

documental *adj* **(a)** (Cin, TV) ⟨*programa/serie*⟩ documentary (*before n*) **(b)** (Der) ⟨*prueba*⟩ documentary
■ *m* documentary

documentar [A1] *vt* ① ⟨*trabajo/hipótesis/ solicitud*⟩ to document ② (Méx) ⟨*equipaje*⟩ to check in
■ **documentarse** *v pron* ① (informarse) to do research ② (Méx) ⟨*pasajero*⟩ to check in

documento *m* (Adm, Der, Inf) document; ~ adjunto (Corresp) enclosed document; (Inf) attachment

dogma *m* dogma

dogmático -ca *adj* dogmatic

dólar *m* dollar

dolencia *f* ailment, complaint

doler [E9] *vi* **(a)** ⟨*inyección/herida/brazo*⟩ to hurt; **no duele nada** it doesn't hurt at all; (+ *me/ te/le etc*) **le dolió mucho** it hurt a lot; **le duele una muela/la cabeza** she has (a) toothache/a headache; **me dolía el estómago** I had (a) stomachache; **me duele la garganta** I have a sore throat; **me duelen los pies** my feet ache; **me duele todo (el cuerpo)** I ache all over **(b)** (apenar) (+ *me/ te/le etc*): **me duele tener que decirte esto** I'm sorry to have to tell you this; **me dolió muchísimo lo que me dijo** I was deeply hurt by what he said

dolido -da *adj* hurt; **estar ~ POR algo** to be hurt AT sth

dolor *m* **(a)** (físico) pain; **sentía mucho ~** he was in a lot of pain; **tener ~ de muelas/cabeza/ garganta** to have a toothache/a headache/a sore throat **(b)** (pena, tristeza) pain, grief

dolorido -da *adj* **(a)** (físicamente): **estoy toda dolorida** I'm aching all over; **tengo el brazo muy ~** I've got a very sore arm **(b)** (afligido) hurt

doloroso -sa *adj* **(a)** ⟨*tratamiento/enfermedad*⟩ painful **(b)** ⟨*decisión/momento/recuerdo*⟩ painful; ⟨*separación/espectáculo*⟩ distressing, upsetting

domador -dora *m,f* (de fieras) tamer; (de caballos) horsebreaker, broncobuster (AmE)

domar [A1] *vt* **(a)** ⟨*fieras*⟩ to tame; ⟨*caballo*⟩ to break in **(b)** (fam) ⟨*niño*⟩ to bring o get ... under control **(c)** (fam) ⟨*zapatos*⟩ to break in

domesticado -da *adj* tame, domesticated

domesticar [A2] *vt* to domesticate

doméstico -ca *adj* ① ⟨*vida/problemas/ servicio*⟩ domestic; ⟨*gastos*⟩ household; **tareas domésticas** housework ② ⟨*vuelo*⟩ domestic

domiciliar [A1] *vt* (Esp) ⟨*pago/letras*⟩ to pay ... by direct debit o (AmE) direct billing; ⟨*sueldo*⟩ to have ... paid direct into one's bank account
■ **domiciliarse** *v pron* (frml) (residir) to reside (frml), to be domiciled (frml)

domicilio *m* (frml) address; **en su ~ particular** at his home address; **sin ~ fijo** of no fixed abode (frml); **Pat Lee, con ~ en Londres** Pat Lee currently living in London

dominante *adj* ① **(a)** ⟨*color/tendencia*⟩ predominant, dominant; ⟨*opinión*⟩ prevailing (*before n*); ⟨*cultura*⟩ dominant **(b)** (Biol, Mús, Astrol) dominant ② ⟨*persona*⟩ domineering

dominar [A1] *vt* **(a)** (controlar) ⟨*nación/territorio/ persona*⟩ to dominate; ⟨*pasión/cólera*⟩ to control; ⟨*vehículo/caballo*⟩ to control; **dominado por la ambición/los celos** ruled by ambition/consumed by jealousy **(b)** ⟨*idioma*⟩ to have a good command of; ⟨*tema/asignatura*⟩ to know ... very well **(c)** (abarcar con la vista): **desde allí se domina toda la bahía** there's a view over the whole bay from there
■ ~ *vi* ⟨*color/tendencia*⟩ to predominate; ⟨*opinión*⟩ to prevail; ⟨*equipo*⟩ to dominate
■ **dominarse** *v pron* ⟨*persona*⟩ to restrain o control oneself

domingo *m* (día) Sunday; (Relig) Sabbath; **traje de ~** Sunday best; **~ de Pascua** *or* **de Resurrección** Easter Sunday; **~ de Ramos** Palm Sunday; *para más ejemplos ver* LUNES

dominicano -na *adj/m,f* (Geog) Dominican

dominio *m* ① **(a)** (control) control; **perdió el ~ de sí mismo** he lost his self-control **(b)** (de idioma, tema) command; **ser del ~ público** to be public knowledge ② **(a)** (Hist, Pol) dominion **(b)** **dominios** *mpl* (colonias) dominions (*pl*) ③ (Inf) domain

dominó *m* (*pl* **-nós**) **(a)** (juego) dominoes; **jugar** *or* (Esp, RPl) **al ~** to play dominoes **(b)** (ficha) domino

don *m* ① **(a)** (liter) (dádiva) gift **(b)** (talento) talent, gift; **el ~ de la palabra** the gift of speech; **~ de gentes** ability to get on well with people; **~ de mando** leadership qualities (*pl*) ② (tratamiento de cortesía) ≈ Mr; **buenos días ~ Miguel** good morning Mr López; **ser un ~ nadie** to be a nobody

dona *f* (Méx) (Coc) doughnut, donut (AmE)

donación *f* donation

donador -dora *m,f*, **donante** *mf* donor

donar [A1] *vt* ⟨*bienes/dinero*⟩ to donate, give; ⟨*sangre*⟩ to give, donate; ⟨*órganos*⟩ to donate

donativo *m* donation

doncella *f* **(a)** (arc) (virgen) maiden (liter) **(b)** (ant) (criada) maid

donde *conj* where; **la ciudad ~ se conocieron** the city where they met; **siéntate ~ quieras** sit wherever o where you like; **déjalo ~ sea** leave it anywhere; **de ~ se deduce que ...** from which it can be deduced that ...; **la ventana por ~ había entrado** the window through which he had got in
■ *prep* (esp AmL, en algunas regiones crit): **ve ~ tu hermana y dile que ...** (a su casa) go over to your sister's and tell her ...; (al lugar donde está ella) go and tell your sister ...

dónde *adv* ① where; **¿~ está?** where is it?; **¿de ~ es?** where is he from?; **¿por ~ quieres ir?** which way do you want to go? ② (Chi, Méx, Per) (cómo) how; **¡~ íbamos a imaginar que ...!** how were we to imagine that ...!

dondequiera *adv*: **~ QUE** wherever

donjuán *m* (tenorio) womanizer, Don Juan

doña *f* (tratamiento de cortesía) ≈ Mrs/Ms; **~ Cristina Fuentes** Mrs/Ms Cristina Fuentes

dopado -da *adj* [ESTAR] drugged

dopar [A1] *vt* ⟨*enfermo*⟩ to drug, dope (colloq); ⟨*caballo*⟩ to dope
■ **doparse** *v pron* (refl) to take drugs

doping *m* (Equ) doping; (Dep) drug-taking

dorada *f* gilthead (bream)

dorado¹ -da *adj* **(a)** ⟨*botón/galones*⟩ gold; ⟨*pintura*⟩ gold, gold-colored*; ⟨*cabello*⟩ (liter) golden **(b)** ⟨*época*⟩ golden

dorado² *m* (acción) gilding; (capa) gilt

dorar [A1] *vt* ‹marco/porcelana› to gild; (Coc) ‹cebolla/papas› to brown
■ **dorarse** *v pron* (Coc) to brown

dormida *f* (AmL) sleep

dormido -da *adj* **(a)** (durmiendo) asleep; **estar/quedarse** ~ to be/to fall asleep **(b)** (sin sensibilidad): **tengo la pierna dormida** my leg's gone to sleep (colloq); *ver tb* DORMIR

dormilón -lona *adj* (fam): **es muy** ~ he's a real sleepyhead (colloq)
■ *m,f* (fam) (persona) sleepyhead (colloq)

dormir [I16] *vi* to sleep; **no dormí nada** I didn't sleep a wink; **dormimos en un hotel** we spent the night in a hotel; **durmió de un tirón** she slept right through (the night); **se fue a** ~ **temprano** he went off to bed early, he had an early night; ~ *a pierna suelta* (fam) to sleep the sleep of the dead; ~ *como un lirón* or *tronco* to sleep like a log (colloq)
■ ~ *vt* **(a)** (hacer dormir) ‹niño/bebé› to get … off to sleep; **sus clases me duermen** his classes send o put me to sleep **(b)** (anestesiar) ‹persona› to put to sleep, put out (colloq); **todavía tengo este lado dormido** this side is still numb **(c)** ~ **la siesta** to have a siesta o nap
■ **dormirse** *v pron* **(a)** (conciliar el sueño) to fall asleep; (lograr conciliar el sueño) to get to sleep; **casi me duermo en la clase** I almost fell asleep o (colloq) dropped off in class **(b)** (no despertarse) to oversleep, sleep in (AmE) **(c)** «pierna/brazo» (+ *me/te/le etc*) «se me durmió el pie» my foot went to sleep (colloq) **(d)** (fam) (distraerse, descuidarse): **no te duermas** don't waste any time

dormitar [A1] *vi* to doze, snooze (colloq)

dormitorio *m* (en casa) bedroom; (en colegio, cuartel) dormitory

dorso *m* **(a)** (de un papel) back; **al** ~ ‹ver› overleaf; ‹escribir› on the back **(b)** (de la mano, animal) back

dos *adj inv/m/pron* two; **lo hicimos entre los** ~ we did it between the two of us; **sujétalo con las** ~ **manos** hold it with both hands; **llamó** ~ **veces** he called twice; **caminaban de** ~ **en** ~ they walked in pairs; **entraron de** ~ **en** ~ they came in two at a time o two by two; ~ **puntos** colon; **en un** ~ **por tres** in a flash; *para más ejemplos ver* CINCO

doscientos¹ -tas *adj/pron* two hundred; *para ejemplos ver* QUINIENTOS

doscientos² *m* (number) two hundred

dosel *m* (de cama) canopy; (de trono, púlpito) baldachin

dosificar [A2] *vt* ‹medicamento› to dose

dosis *f* (*pl* ~) dose

dotado -da *adj* ‹persona› gifted; **estar** ~ **DE algo** «persona» to be blessed WITH sth; «cocina/oficina» to be equipped WITH sth

dotar [A1] *vt* **(a)** (frml) ‹institución/organismo› ~ **(A) algo DE** or **CON algo** ‹de fondos› to provide sth WITH sth; ‹de técnica/maquinaria› to equip sth WITH sth; ‹de poderes› to invest sth WITH sth **(b)** «naturaleza/Dios» ~ **a algn DE** or **CON algo** to endow o bless sb WITH sth

dote *f* 1 (de novia) dowry 2 **dotes** *fpl*: ~s **para el canto** a talent for singing; ~s **de mando** leadership qualities

doy ▶ DAR

Dr. *m* (= **Doctor**) Dr

Dra. *f* (= **Doctora**) Dr

dracma *m* drachma

dragar [A3] *vt* ‹río› to dredge; ‹minas› to sweep for

dragón *m* (Mit) dragon

drama *m* drama; **hacer un** ~ **de algo** (fam) to make a big deal out of sth

dramático -ca *adj* dramatic; **un autor** ~ a playwright o dramatist

dramatismo *m* dramatic quality o character

dramatización *f* dramatization

dramaturgo -ga *m,f* dramatist, playwright

drástico -ca *adj* drastic

driblar, driblear [A1] *vt* to dribble past o around

drible *m* dribble

droga *f* drug; ~s **duras/blandas** hard/soft drugs

drogadicción *f* (drug) addiction

drogadicto -ta *adj* addicted to drugs
■ *m,f* drug addict

drogar [A3] *vt* to drug
■ **drogarse** *v pron* (refl) to take drugs

drogata *mf* (fam) junkie (colloq)

drogodependiente *adj* (frml) drug-dependent
■ *mf* (frml) drug addict

droguería *f* **(a)** (Esp) (tienda) *store selling cleaning materials and other household goods* **(b)** (Col) (farmacia) drugstore (AmE), chemist's (BrE) **(c)** (RPl) (de productos químicos) pharmaceutical wholesaler's

dromedario *m* dromedary

dual *adj/m* dual

Dublín *m* Dublin

dublinés -nesa *m,f* Dubliner

ducado *m* (título) dukedom; (territorio) duchy, dukedom

ducha *f* shower; **darse una** ~ to take o (BrE) have a shower

ducharse [A1] *v pron* (refl) to take o (BrE) have a shower

ducto *m* **(a)** (Méx) (de gas, petróleo) pipeline **(b)** (Ur) (para la basura) garbage chute (AmE), rubbish chute (BrE) **(c)** (Col, Ven) (de ventilación) duct, shaft

duda *f* 1 (interrogante, sospecha) doubt; **expuso sus** ~s **sobre …** he expressed his reservations about …; **tengo unas** ~s **para consultar** I have a few points I'd like to check; **me ha surgido una** ~ there's something I'm not sure about; **¿tienen alguna** ~? are there any queries o questions?; **nunca tuve la menor** ~ **de que tenía razón** I never doubted that he was right; **fuera de (toda)** ~ beyond (all) doubt; **de eso no cabe la menor** ~ there's absolutely no doubt about that; **lo pongo en** ~ I doubt it; **sin** ~ or **sin lugar a** ~s undoubtedly; **sin** ~ **ya te lo habrás preguntado** no doubt you'll have already asked yourself that question; **para salir de** ~s just to be doubly sure 2 (estado de incertidumbre, indecisión): **ahora me has hecho entrar en (la)** ~ now you've made me wonder; **a ver si puedes sacarme de la** ~ do you

dudar [A1] *vt* to doubt; **dudo que la haya terminado** I doubt if *o* whether he's finished it
■ ~ *vi*: **duda entre comprar y alquilar** she can't make up her mind whether to buy or rent; ~ **EN hacer algo** to hesitate to do sth; ~ **DE algo/algn** to doubt sth/sb

dudoso -sa *adj* **(a)** (incierto) doubtful; **lo veo** ~ I doubt it **(b)** (cuestionable) dubious **(c)** (indeciso) hesitant, undecided

duela *f* (Méx) (del suelo) floorboard

duele, duelen, etc ▶ DOLER

duelo *m* ⓵ (dolor) sorrow, grief; (luto) mourning; **estar de** ~ to be in mourning ⓶ (desafío) duel; **retar a** ~ to challenge … to a duel; **batirse en** ~ to fight a duel; ~ **a muerte** duel to the death

duende *m* **(a)** (en cuentos) goblin, imp **(b)** (espíritu) spirit *(which inhabits a house or room)*

dueño -ña *adj* ⓵ [SER] (libre) ~ **DE hacer algo** free to do sth, at liberty to do sth (frml) ⓶ [SER] (indicando control): **ser** ~ **DE algo** to be in control of sth; **hacerse** ~ **DE algo** to gain control of sth
■ *m,f* **(a)** (de casa, pensión) (*m*) owner, landlord; (*f*) owner, landlady; (de negocio) (*m*) owner, proprietor; (*f*) owner, proprietress; ~ **de casa** (AmL) (propietario) householder; (en fiesta) (*m*) host; (*f*) hostess **(b)** (de perro) owner

duerma, duermas, etc ▶ DORMIR

dulce *adj* **(a)** ⟨fruta/vino⟩ sweet; **prefiero lo** ~ **l** prefer sweet things **(b)** ⟨agua⟩ fresh; **pez de agua** ~ freshwater fish **(c)** ⟨persona⟩ gentle, kind; ⟨sonrisa/voz⟩ sweet; ⟨música⟩ soft, sweet
■ *m* **(a)** (AmL exc RPl) (golosina) candy (AmE), sweet (BrE) **(b)** (RPl) (mermelada) jam; ~ **de leche** caramel spread *(made by boiling down milk and sugar)* **(c)** (AmC) (azúcar) *type of sugarloaf* **(d) dulces** *mpl* (cosas dulces) sweet things (*pl*)

dulcificar [A2] *vt* ⟨persona⟩ to mellow; ⟨vejez⟩ to make … more pleasant
■ **dulcificarse** *v pron* «carácter/persona» to mellow, soften

dulzor *m* sweetness, sweet taste

dulzura *f* sweetness; **habló con** ~ she spoke kindly *o* gently; **los trata con mucha** ~ she's very sweet *o* gentle with them

duna *f* dune

dúo *m* **(a)** (composición) duet, duo **(b)** (de músicos, instrumentos) duo; **a** ~ ⟨contestar⟩ in unison; **lo cantaron a** ~ they sang it as a duet

duodécimo -ma *adj/pron* twelfth

dúplex *m* (*pl* ~) **(a)** (apartamento) duplex apartment, maisonette (BrE) **(b)** (Méx) (casa) semi-detached house

duplicado¹ -da *adj* duplicated; **por** ~ in duplicate

duplicado² *m* copy, duplicate

duplicar [A2] *vt* ⟨documento/llave⟩ to copy, duplicate
■ **duplicarse** *v pron* «número» to double

duplo *m*: **el** ~ **de dos es cuatro** two times two is four

duque *m* duke

duquesa *f* duchess

duración *f* **(a)** (de película, acto, curso) length, duration **(b)** (de pila, bombilla) life; **pila de larga** ~ long-life battery; ▶ DISCO 1A

duradero -ra *adj* ⟨amistad/recuerdo⟩ lasting *(before n)*; ⟨ropa/zapatos⟩ hardwearing, longwearing (AmE)

durante *prep* (en el transcurso de) during; (cuando se especifica la duración) for; ~ **1980** during *o* in 1980; **gobernó el país** ~ **casi dos décadas** she governed the country for almost two decades; **los precios aumentaron un 0,3%** ~ **el mes de diciembre** prices rose by 0.3% in December; ~ **todo el invierno** throughout the winter

durar [A1] *vi* **(a)** «reunión/guerra/relación» to last; **¿cuánto dura la película?** how long is the film? **(b)** «coche/zapatos» to last **(c)** (Col, Ven) ▶ DEMORAR A
■ **durarse** *v pron* (Ven) ▶ DEMORARSE

durazno *m* (esp AmL) (fruto) peach; (árbol) peach tree

durex® *m* (AmL) Scotch tape® (AmE), Sellotape® (BrE)

dureza *f* ⓵ (en general) hardness; (de la carne) toughness ⓶ **(a)** (severidad, inflexibilidad) harshness; **nos trataban con** ~ they treated us harshly; **fue castigado con** ~ he was severely punished **(b)** (en el deporte) roughness

durmiera, durmió, etc ▶ DORMIR

duro¹ -ra *adj* ⓵ (en general) hard; ⟨carne⟩ tough; ⟨pan⟩ stale; **las peras están duras** the pears aren't ripe ⓶ ⟨luz/voz⟩ harsh; ⟨facciones⟩ hard, harsh ⓷ **(a)** (severo, riguroso) harsh; ⟨juego⟩ rough, hard; **fuiste demasiado** ~ **con él** you were too hard on him; **una postura más dura** a tougher line **(b)** (difícil, penoso) ⟨trabajo/vida⟩ hard, tough; **fue un golpe muy** ~ it was a very hard blow

duro² *adv* (esp AmL) ⟨trabajar/estudiar/llover⟩ hard; ⟨hablar⟩ (Col, Ven) loudly

duro³ *m* (en España) (Hist) five-peseta coin

E e

E, e *f* (*pl* **es**) *(read as* /e/*) the letter* E, e

e *conj* [*used instead of* Y *before* I- *or* HI-] and

E. (= **Este**) E, East

EAU *mpl* (= **Emiratos Árabes Unidos**) UAE

ebanista *mf* cabinetmaker

ébano *m* ebony

ebrio, ebria *adj* (frml) inebriated (frml), drunk

ebullición f (a) (Coc, Fís): **entrar en ~** to come to the boil; **punto de ~** boiling point (b) (agitación) turmoil

eccema m eczema

echado -da adj (acostado): **está ~ en el sofá** he's lying down on the sofa

echador -dora adj (Méx fam) boastful
■ m,f (Méx fam) boaster (colloq)

echar [A1] vt
I ⓵ (a) (lanzar, tirar) to throw; **lo eché a la basura** I threw it out o away; **echó la moneda al aire** he tossed the coin; **~on el ancla/la red** they cast anchor/their net; **echó la cabeza hacia atrás** she threw her head back; **~ algo a perder** to ruin sth; **~ de menos algo/a algn** to miss sth/sb (b) **echar abajo** ⟨edificio⟩ to pull down; ⟨gobierno⟩ to bring down; ⟨proyecto⟩ to destroy; ⟨esperanzas⟩ to dash; ⟨moral⟩ to undermine; ⟨puerta/valla⟩ to break ... down
⓶ (expulsar) ⟨persona⟩ (de trabajo) to fire (colloq), to sack (BrE colloq); (de bar, casa) to throw ... out; (de colegio) to expel
⓷ ⟨carta⟩ to mail (AmE), to post (BrE)
⓸ (a) (pasar, correr) ⟨cortinas⟩ to pull, draw; **échale (la) llave** lock it; **¿echaste el cerrojo?** did you bolt the door? (b) (mover): **lo echó para atrás/a un lado** she pushed (o moved etc) it backward(s)/to one side
⓹ (a) (expeler, despedir) ⟨olor/humo/chispas⟩ to give off (b) (producir) ⟨hojas⟩ to sprout; **ya está echando flores** it's flowering already
II ⓵ (a) (poner) ⟨leña/carbón⟩ to put; ⟨gasolina⟩ to put in; **¿le echas azúcar al café?** do you take sugar in your coffee? (b) (servir, dar) to give; **échame un poco de vino** can you give me a little wine? (c) ⟨trago⟩ to have
⓶ (a) ⟨sermón/discurso⟩ (fam) (+ me/te/le etc) to give; **le echó una maldición** she put a curse on him (b) (fam) ⟨condena/multa⟩ (+ me/te/le etc): **~le la culpa a algn** to put o lay the blame on sb
⓷ (fam) (calcular) (+ me/te/le etc): **¿cuántos años me echas?** how old do you think I am?; **de aquí a tu casa échale una hora** it's o it takes about an hour from here to your house
⓸ (Esp fam) (dar, exhibir) ⟨programa/película⟩ to show
■ **echarse** v pron ⓵ (a) (tirarse, arrojarse) to throw oneself; **me eché al suelo** I threw myself to the ground; **~se de cabeza al agua** to dive into the water; **~se a perder** «comida» to go bad, go off (BrE); «cosecha/proyecto/plan» to be ruined (b) (tumbarse, acostarse) to lie down (c) (apartarse, moverse) (+ compl): **se echó a un lado** she moved to one side; **échate un poco para allá** move over that way a bit; **~se atrás** to back out
⓶ (a) (ponerse) ⟨crema/bronceador⟩ to put on (b) ⟨cigarrillo⟩ to have (c) (Esp fam) ⟨novio/novia⟩: **se ha echado novia** he's found o got himself a girlfriend (d) (Méx fam) (beberse) to drink
⓷ (Méx fam) (romper) to break
⓸ (Col fam) (tardar) ⟨horas/días⟩ to take
⓹ (empezar) **~se a** to start o begin to, start o

begin; **se echó a correr** he started to run o started running; **las palomas se ~on a volar** the doves flew off

echarpe m shawl, stole

ecléctico -ca adj/m,f eclectic

eclesiástico -ca adj ecclesiastical, church (before n)

eclipse m eclipse

eco m (Fís) echo; **la cueva tiene ~** there's an echo in the cave; **hacer ~** to echo

ecografía f ultrasound scan

ecología f ecology

ecológico -ca adj ⟨problema/estudio⟩ ecological; ⟨daño/desastre⟩ environmental; ⟨producto⟩ eco-friendly, environmentally friendly; ⟨cultivo/agricultura⟩ organic

ecologismo m environmentalism, conservationism

ecologista adj ecology (before n), environmentalist (before n)
■ mf ecologist, environmentalist

economato m (a) (de empresa) company store (b) (Mil) PX (AmE), NAAFI shop (BrE)

economía f (a) (ciencia) economics (b) (de país) economy; **~ de (libre) mercado** (free) market economy (c) (ahorro): **hacer ~s** to economize (d) (de persona, familia) finances (pl)

económico -ca adj ⓵ ⟨crisis/situación⟩ economic (before n); ⟨problema/independencia⟩ financial ⓶ (a) ⟨piso/comida⟩ cheap; ⟨restaurante/hotel⟩ cheap, inexpensive (b) (que gasta poco) ⟨motor⟩ economical; ⟨persona⟩ thrifty

economista mf economist

economizar [A4] vt ⟨tiempo⟩ to save; ⟨combustible/recursos⟩ to economize on, save
■ ~ vi to economize, save money

ecosistema m ecosystem

ecu, ECU /'eku/ m (= **Unidad Monetaria Europea**) ECU

ecuación f equation

ecuador m ⓵ (línea) equator ⓶ **Ecuador** (país) Ecuador

ecuatorial adj equatorial

ecuatoriano -na adj/m,f Ecuadorean

eczema m eczema

edad f ⓵ (de persona, árbol) age; **tienen la misma ~** they are the same age; **un joven de unos quince años de ~** a boy of about fifteen; **¿qué ~ tiene?** how old is he?; **aún no tiene la ~ suficiente** he's still not old enough ...; **de ~ madura** or **de mediana ~** middle-aged; **una persona de ~** an elderly person; **niños en ~ escolar** children of school age; **estar en la ~ del pavo** to be at that awkward age ⓶ (Hist) (época) age, period; **la E~ de bronce/de hierro/de piedra** the Bronze/Iron/Stone Age; **la E~ media** the Middle Ages (pl)

edema m edema*

Edén m: **el ~** (the Garden of) Eden

edición f ⓵ (Impr, Period) (tirada) edition; (acción)

AmC	América Central	Arg	Argentina	Cu	Cuba	Per	Perú
AmL	América Latina	Bol	Bolivia	Ec	Ecuador	RPI	Río de la Plata
AmS	América del Sur	Chi	Chile	Esp	España	Ur	Uruguay
Andes	Región andina	CS	Cono Sur	Méx	México	Ven	Venezuela

publication; ~ **de bolsillo** pocket edition;
Ediciones Rivera Rivera Publications [2] (Rad, TV)
program*, edition

edificado -da adj built-up

edificar [A2] vt/vi to build

edificio m building

Edimburgo m Edinburgh

editar [A1] vt [1] (publicar) ‹libro/revista› to
publish [2] (modificar) ‹película/grabación/texto› to
edit; (Inf) to edit

editor -tora adj publishing (before n)
■ m,f (que publica) publisher; (que revisa, modifica)
editor

editorial adj ‹casa/actividad› publishing
(before n); ‹puesto/decisión› editorial
■ f (empresa) publishing company o house
■ m (en periódico) editorial, leading article

edredón m eiderdown, comforter (AmE); (que se
usa sin mantas) duvet, continental quilt (BrE)

educación f [1] (enseñanza) education; (para la
convivencia) upbringing; ~ **a distancia**
correspondence courses (pl), distance learning;
~ **física** physical education; ~ **general básica** (en
Esp) primary education; ~ **para adultos** adult
education; ~ **primaria/secundaria/superior**
primary/secondary/higher education; ~
universitaria university education, college
education (AmE); ~ **vocacional** (AmS) careers
guidance [2] (modales) manners (pl); **es una falta
de** ~ it's rude, it's bad manners

educado -da adj polite, well-mannered

educador -dora m,f (frml) teacher, educator
(frml)

educar [A2] vt [1] (a) (Educ) to educate, teach
(b) (para la convivencia) ‹hijos› to bring up;
‹ciudadanos› to educate [2] ‹oído/voz› to train
■ **educarse** v pron (hacer los estudios) to be
educated

educativo -va adj ‹programa/juego›
educational; ‹establecimiento› educational,
teaching (before n); ‹sistema› education (before n)

edulcorante m sweetener

EEUU or **EE.UU.** (= **Estados Unidos**) USA

efe f: name of the letter f

efectista adj theatrical, dramatic

efectividad f (eficacia) effectiveness

efectivo¹ -va adj ‹remedio/medio/castigo›
effective; **hacer** ~ ‹cheque› to cash; ‹pago› to
make

efectivo² m (Fin) cash; **pagar en** ~ to pay cash

efecto m [1] (a) (resultado, consecuencia) effect;
hacer ~ to take effect; **un calmante de** ~
inmediato a fast-acting painkiller; **mecanismo de**
~ **retardado** delayed-action mechanism; **bajo los**
~**s del alcohol** under the influence of alcohol; ~
dos mil (Inf) millennium bug; ~ **invernadero**
greenhouse effect; ~ **óptico** optical illusion; ~
secundario side effect; ~**s especiales** special
effects; ~**s sonoros** sound effects (b) **en efecto** in
fact; (así es) indeed
[2] (impresión): **su conducta causó mal** ~ his
behavior made a bad impression o (colloq) didn't
go down well; **no sé qué** ~ **le causaron mis
palabras** I don't know what effect my words had
on him

[3] (Dep) (desvío) swerve; (movimiento rotatorio) spin;
le dio a la bola con ~ she put some spin on the
ball

[4] ~**s personales** personal effects (pl)

efectuar [A18] vt (frml) ‹maniobra/redada› to
carry out, execute (frml); ‹pago› to make; ‹viaje/
cambio› to make; ‹disparo› to fire; **el tren** ~**á su
salida a las 10.50** the train will depart at 10:50

efervescente adj ‹pastilla› effervescent;
‹bebida› sparkling, fizzy (colloq)

eficacia f **(a)** (de acción, remedio) effectiveness,
efficacy (frml) **(b)** (eficiencia) efficiency

eficaz adj **(a)** ‹fórmula/remedio› effective,
efficacious (frml) **(b)** (eficiente) efficient

eficiencia f efficiency

eficiente adj efficient

efigie f (cuadro) image, picture; (estatua) statue,
effigy

efímero -ra adj ephemeral

efusivo -va adj ‹temperamento/recibimiento›
effusive; ‹persona› demonstrative; ‹recibimiento›
warm

EGB f (en Esp) = **Educación General
Básica**

egipcio -cia adj/m,f Egyptian

Egipto m Egypt

ego m ego

egocéntrico -ca adj egocentric,
self-centered*

egoísmo m selfishness, egotism

egoísta adj selfish, egotistic
■ mf (Psic) egotist; **es una** ~ she is very selfish

egresado -da adj (AmL): **los alumnos** ~**s** (de
universidad) the graduates; (de colegio) the high
school graduates (AmE), the school leavers (BrE)
■ m,f (AmL) (de universidad) graduate; (de colegio)
high school graduate (AmE), school leaver (BrE)

egresar [A1] vi (AmL) (de universidad) to
graduate; (de colegio) to graduate from high school
(AmE), to leave school (o college etc) (BrE)
■ ~ vt (Andes) (Fin) to withdraw, take out

egreso m (AmL) (de universidad) graduation; (de
colegio) graduation (AmE)

eh interj **(a)** (para llamar la atención) hey! **(b)**
(expresando amenaza, advertencia) eh?, huh?, OK? **(c)**
(contestando una pregunta) eh?, what?

Ej., ej. (read as por ejemplo) eg

eje m [1] (a) (Astron, Fís, Mat) axis (b) (Auto, Mec)
(barra) axle [2] (de asunto, política) core, central
theme

ejecución f [1] (de persona) execution [2] (a)
(de plan) implementation; (de orden) carrying out
(b) (Mús) performance

ejecutar [A1] vt [1] ‹condenado/reo› to execute
[2] ‹plan› to implement, carry out; ‹orden/
trabajo› to carry out; ‹sentencia› to execute,
enforce; ‹ejercicio/salto› to perform; ‹sinfonía/
himno nacional› to play, perform

ejecutivo¹ -va adj ‹función/comisión›
executive
■ m,f (Bot, Com) executive

ejecutivo² m (Gob) executive

ejemplar adj ‹conducta/vida/castigo›
exemplary; ‹trabajador/padre› model (before n)
■ m **(a)** (de libro, documento) copy **(b)** (Bot, Zool)
specimen

ejemplarizador -dora *adj* (Chi, Per) exemplary

ejemplo *m* example; **dar (el) ∼** to set an example; **pongamos por ∼ el caso de Elena** let's take Elena's case as an example; **por ejemplo** for example

ejercer [E2] *vt* **1** **(a)** ⟨*profesión*⟩ to practice*; **∼ la abogacía** to practice law **(b)** ⟨*derecho*⟩ to exercise **2** ⟨*influencia/poder/presión*⟩ to exert ■ **∼** *vi* «*abogado/médico*» to practice*; **es maestra pero no ejerce** she's a teacher but she doesn't practice her profession

ejercicio *m* **1** (actividad física) exercise; **hacer ∼** to exercise **2** (Educ) **(a)** (trabajo de práctica) exercise **(b)** (prueba, examen) test, exam **3** (de profesión) practice **4** (Mil) exercise, maneuver*

ejercitar [A1] *vt* **1** ⟨*músculo/dedos/memoria*⟩ to exercise **2** ⟨*caballos*⟩ to train; ⟨*tropa*⟩ to drill, train; ⟨*alumnos*⟩ to train

ejército *m* army; **∼ del aire** air force; **∼ de tierra** army

ejidal *adj* (en Méx) cooperative (*before n*)

ejidatario -ria *m,f* (en Méx) member of a cooperative

ejido *m* (en Méx) (sistema) *system of communal or cooperative farming*; (sociedad) cooperative; (terreno) *land belonging to a cooperative*

ejote *m* (Méx) green bean

el (*pl* **los**), **la** (*pl* **las**) *art* [*the masculine article* EL *is also used before feminine nouns which begin with accented* A *or* HA, *e.g.* EL AGUA PURA, EL HADA MADRINA] **1** **(a)** (en general) the; **la Tierra** the Earth **(b)** (con sustantivos en sentido genérico): **odio el pescado** I hate fish; **así es la vida** that's life; **(nosotros) los mexicanos** we Mexicans; **¿ya vas a la escuela?** do you go to school yet? **(c)** (refiriéndose a algo que se conoce o se está definiendo): **en la calle Solís** in Solís street; **las tuyas** yours; **el último** the last one; **el estúpido del marido** that stupid husband of hers

2 **(a)** **el +** DE: **la del sombrero** the one with the hat; **el de las nueve** the nine o'clock one; **el de mi hijo** my son's **(b)** **el +** QUE: **las que yo vi** the ones I saw; **los que estén cansados**; those who are tired, anyone who's tired; **la que te guste** whichever you like

3 (en expresiones de tiempo): **ocurrió el domingo** it happened last Sunday; **mi cumpleaños es el 28 de mayo** my birthday's on May 28; **el mes pasado** last month; **toda la mañana** all morning; **a las ocho** at eight o'clock

4 (cada): **$80 el metro/kilo** $80 a meter/a kilo, $80 per kilo/meter

5 (con fracciones, porcentajes, números): **la mitad/la cuarta parte del dinero** half the money/a quarter of the money; **el 20% de ...** 20% of ...

6 (con partes del cuerpo, prendas de vestir, artículos personales, etc): **tenía las manos en los bolsillos** she had her hands in her pockets; **¡te cortaste el pelo!** you've had your hair cut!; **tiene los ojos azules** he has blue eyes

7 **(a)** (con apellidos acompañados de título, adjetivos, etc): **el señor Ortiz/la doctora Vidal** Mr Ortiz/Doctor Vidal; **los Ortega** the Ortegas **(b)** (con algunos nombres geográficos): **en la India** in India; ▶ ÁFRICA, ARGENTINA, ETC

él *pron pers* **(a)** (como sujeto) he; **¿quién se lo va a decir? — él** who's going to tell her? — he is; **lo**

hizo **∼ mismo** he did it himself; **fue ∼** it was him **(b)** (en comparaciones, con preposiciones) him; (refiriéndose a cosas) it; **llegué antes que ∼** I arrived before him *o* before he did; **con/para ∼** with/for him; **son de ∼** they're his

elaboración *f* (de producto, vino) production, making; (de pan) baking, making

elaborado -da *adj* elaborate

elaborar [A1] *vt* **1** ⟨*producto/vino*⟩ to produce, make; ⟨*pan*⟩ to bake, make **2** ⟨*plan/teoría*⟩ to devise, draw up; ⟨*informe/estudio*⟩ to prepare, write

elasticidad *f* (de material) elasticity; (de horario) flexibility

elástico¹ -ca *adj* ⟨*membrana/cinta*⟩ elastic; ⟨*medias/venda*⟩ elastic, stretch (*before n*); ⟨*horario*⟩ flexible

elástico² *m* **(a)** (material) elastic; (cordón) piece of elastic; (en géneros de punto) rib, ribbing **(b)** (Chi) (goma) rubber band

ele *f*: *name of the letter* l

elección *f* **(a)** (acción de escoger) choice; **llévate tres, a tu ∼** take *o* choose any three **(b)** (Pol) (de candidato) election **(c)** **elecciones** *fpl* (Pol) election; **convocar elecciones** to call an election

elector -tora *m,f* (Pol) voter, elector

electorado *m* electorate

electoral *adj* ⟨*campaña/discurso*⟩ election (*before n*)

electricidad *f* electricity

electricista *mf* electrician

eléctrico -ca *adj* ⟨*tren/motor/luz*⟩ electric; ⟨*instalación/aparato*⟩ electrical; ⟨*carga*⟩ electrical, electric

electrocardiograma *m* electrocardiogram

electrocutar [A1] *vt* to electrocute ■ **electrocutarse** *v pron* to be electrocuted

electrodoméstico *m* electrical appliance

electrón *m* electron

electrónica *f* electronics

electrónico -ca *adj* electronic

elefante -ta *m,f* elephant

elegancia *f* **(a)** (en el vestir) smartness, elegance; (garbo, gracilidad) elegance; (de barrio, restaurante) smartness **(b)** (de estilo) elegance

elegante *adj* **1** **(a)** ⟨*moda/vestido*⟩ elegant, smart; **iba muy ∼** he was very well *o* very smartly dressed **(b)** ⟨*barrio/restaurante/fiesta*⟩ smart **2** ⟨*estilo/frase*⟩ elegant, polished

elegir [I8] *vt* **(a)** (escoger) to choose; **me dieron a ∼** I was given a *o* the choice **(b)** (por votación) to elect

elemental *adj* **(a)** (esencial) ⟨*norma/principio*⟩ fundamental **(b)** (básico) ⟨*curso/nivel/texto*⟩ elementary; ⟨*conocimientos/nociones*⟩ rudimentary, basic

elemento *m* **(a)** (en general) element; **se siente en su ∼** he's in his element; **los ∼s** (fuerzas naturales) the elements **(b)** (persona): **un ∼ pernicioso** a bad influence; **∼s subversivos** subversive elements; **es un ∼ de cuidado** (Esp fam & pey) he's a nasty piece of work **(c)** (RPl) (tipo de gente) crowd

elepé *m* album, LP

elevado -da *adj* **1** ⟨*terreno/montaña*⟩ high; ⟨*edificio*⟩ tall, high **2** **(a)** ⟨*cantidad*⟩ large;

⟨*precio/impuestos*⟩ high; ⟨*pérdidas*⟩ heavy, substantial **(b)** ⟨*categoría/calidad/posición*⟩ high **(c)** ⟨*ideas/pensamientos*⟩ noble, elevated; ⟨*estilo*⟩ lofty, elevated

elevador *m* (montacargas) hoist; (ascensor) (Méx) elevator (AmE), lift (BrE)

elevar [A1] *vt* ⓵ (frml) **(a)** (levantar) ⟨*objeto*⟩ to raise, lift **(b)** ⟨*espíritu/mente*⟩ to uplift **(c)** ⟨*muro/ nivel*⟩ to raise, make ... higher ⓶ (frml) **(a)** (aumentar) ⟨*precios/impuestos*⟩ to raise, increase; ⟨*nivel de vida*⟩ to raise **(b)** ⟨*voz/tono*⟩ to raise
■ **elevarse** *v pron* ⓵ (tomar altura) «*avión/ cometa*» to climb, gain height; «*globo*» to rise, gain height ⓶ (frml) (aumentar) «*temperatura*» to rise; «*precios/impuestos*» to rise, increase; «*tono/voz*» to rise ⓷ (frml) (ascender): **la cifra se elevaba ya al 13%** the figure had already reached 13%

elige, elija, etc ▶ ELEGIR

eliminación *f* elimination; (de residuos) disposal

eliminar [A1] *vt* **(a)** ⟨*obstáculo*⟩ to remove; ⟨*párrafo*⟩ to delete, remove **(b)** ⟨*candidato*⟩ to eliminate; (Dep) to eliminate, knock out **(c)** (euf) (matar) to eliminate (euph), to get rid of (euph) **(d)** ⟨*residuos*⟩ to dispose of **(e)** ⟨*toxinas/grasas*⟩ to eliminate

eliminatoria *f* (en torneo) qualifying round; (para carrera) heat; (certamen) qualifying competition

eliminatorio -ria *adj* ⟨*examen/fase*⟩ qualifying (*before n*), preliminary (*before n*)

elite /e'lit/, **élite** /'elite e'lit/ *f* elite, élite

elitista *adj* ⟨*sociedad/actitud*⟩ elitist; ⟨*colegio/ club*⟩ exclusive

elixir *m* **(a)** (Mit) elixir **(b)** (Esp) (Farm) mouthwash

ella *pron pers* **(a)** (como sujeto) she; **¿quién lo va a hacer? — ella** who's going to do it? — she is; **lo hizo ~ misma** she did it herself; **fue ~** it was her **(b)** (en comparaciones, con preposiciones) her; (referido a cosas) it; **salí después que ~** I left after her *o* after she did; **con/para ~** with/for her; **son de ~** they're hers

ello *pron pers* it; **ya que estamos en ~** while we're at it; **todo ~ exquisitamente presentado** all beautifully presented; **para ello hay que obtener un permiso** (frml) you need a permit for this

ellos, ellas *pron pers pl* **(a)** (como sujeto) they; **lo hicieron ~ mismos** they did it themselves; **fueron ellas** it was them **(b)** (en comparaciones, con preposiciones) them; **llegué antes que ~** I arrived before them *o* before they did; **con/para ~/ellas** with/for them; **son de ~** they're theirs, they belong to them

elocuencia *f* eloquence; **con ~** eloquently

elocuente *adj* eloquent

elogiar [A1] *vt* to praise

elogio *m* praise; **digno de ~** praiseworthy

elote *m* (mazorca) (AmC, Méx) corncob, ear of corn (AmE); (granos) (Méx) corn (AmE), sweetcorn (BrE)

El Salvador *m* El Salvador

eludir [I1] *vt* **(a)** ⟨*problema/compromiso/pago*⟩ to evade, avoid **(b)** ⟨*persona*⟩ to avoid

emancipación *f* emancipation

emancipado -da *adj* emancipated

embadurnar [A1] *vt* **~ algo DE algo** to smear sth WITH sth
■ **embadurnarse** *v pron* (*refl*) **~se DE algo** to plaster *o* smear oneself WITH sth

embajada *f* (sede, delegación) embassy; (cargo) ambassadorship

embajador -dora *m,f* (Adm, Pol) ambassador

embalaje *m* ⓵ (acción) packing; (envoltura) packaging, wrapping ⓶ (Col) (Dep) sprint

embalar [A1] *vt* to pack

embaldosar [A1] *vt* to tile

embalsamar [A1] *vt* to embalm

embalse *m* (depósito) reservoir

embarazada *adj* pregnant; **(se) quedó ~** she got *o* became pregnant; **está ~ de dos meses** she's two months pregnant; **la dejó ~** he got her pregnant
■ *f* pregnant woman

embarazo *m* (Med) pregnancy

embarazoso -sa *adj* embarrassing, awkward

embarcación *f* (frml) vessel (frml), craft (frml)

embarcadero *m* (atracadero) jetty; (para mercancías) wharf

embarcar [A2] *vi* (Aviac) to board; (Náut) to embark, board
■ **~** *vt* ⓵ ⟨*mercancías/equipaje*⟩ to load ⓶ (Ven) to let ... down
■ **embarcarse** *v pron* **(a)** «*pasajero*» (en barco) to board, embark; (en tren, avión) to board, get on; **se ~on para América** they set sail for America **(b)** (en asunto, negocio) **~se EN algo** to embark ON sth

embargar [A3] *vt* ⟨*bienes*⟩ to seize, to sequestrate (frml); ⟨*vehículo*⟩ to impound

embargo *m* ⓵ **(a)** (Der) (incautación, decomiso) seizure, sequestration (frml) **(b)** (Mil, Pol) embargo ⓶ **sin embargo: sin ~, tiene algunas desventajas** however *o* nevertheless, it has some disadvantages; **sin ~, ayer no decías eso** you weren't saying that yesterday, though; **tiene de todo y sin embargo se queja** he has everything and yet he still complains

embarrada *f* (AmS fam) (metida de pata) blunder, boo-boo (colloq)

embarrar [A1] *vt* to cover ... in mud; **~la** (AmS fam) to mess up (AmE colloq), to mess things up (BrE colloq)
■ **embarrarse** *v pron* «*persona*» to get covered in mud; ⟨*prenda/ropa*⟩ to get...muddy

embaucador -dora *adj* deceitful
■ *m,f* trickster

embaucar [A2] *vt* to trick, con (colloq)

embeber [E1] *vt* **(a)** (en líquido) ⟨*bizcocho/ esponja*⟩ to soak **(b)** «*secante/toalla*» ⟨*líquido*⟩ to soak up **(c)** ⟨*tela*⟩ to gather in
■ **~** *vi* to shrink
■ **embeberse** *v pron* **(a)** (enfrascarse) **~se EN algo** to become wrapped up *o* absorbed IN sth **(b)** (imbuirse) **~se DE algo** to become imbued WITH sth (frml)

embelesado -da *adj* spellbound

embelesar [A1] *vt* to captivate

embellecer [E3] *vt* ⟨*persona*⟩ to make ... beautiful; ⟨*campiña/ciudad*⟩ to beautify, improve the appearance of

embestida f charge

embestir [I14] vi to charge; ~ **CONTRA algo/algn** to charge AT sth/sb
■ ~ vt «*toro*» to charge (at)

embetunar [A1] vt [1] ⟨*zapatos*⟩ to polish, put polish on [2] (CS) (ensuciar) to get … dirty

emblema m emblem

embobado -da adj spellbound; **la miraban** ~**s** they were watching her open-mouthed; **está** ~ **con ella** he's besotted with her

embolador -dora m,f (Col) bootblack

embolar [A1] vt [1] (RPl arg) (fastidiar) to bug (colloq), to piss … off (sl) [2] (Col) ⟨*zapatos*⟩ to shine, polish
■ **embolarse** v pron (AmC fam) to get plastered (colloq)

embolia f embolism

embolsarse [A1] v pron ⟨*dinero ajeno*⟩ to pocket; ⟨*premio*⟩ to collect, receive; ⟨*ganancia*⟩ to make

embonar [A1] vi (Méx) ⟨*tubos/ventana/piezas*⟩ to fit; ~ **CON algo** to fit in WITH sth

emborrachar [A1] vt «*bebida*» to make … drunk; «*persona*» to get … drunk
■ **emborracharse** v pron to get drunk

emborronar [A1] vt (manchar) to smudge; (con tinta) to make blots on, to blot
■ **emborronarse** v pron to smudge, get smudged

emboscada f ambush

emboscar [A2] vt to ambush

embotado -da adj ⟨*punta/filo*⟩ dull, blunt; **estoy totalmente** ~ my brain's seized up, I can't take in any more

embotar [A1] vt ⟨*mente/sentidos*⟩ to dull

embotellado -da adj (a) ⟨*agua/vino*⟩ bottled (b) ⟨*calle/tráfico*⟩ jammed solid

embotellamiento m (del tráfico) traffic jam

embotellar [A1] vt to bottle

embragar [A3] vi to engage the clutch

embrague m clutch

embriagado -da adj (frml) (borracho) inebriated (frml)

embriagador -dora adj ⟨*vino*⟩ heady; ⟨*sensación*⟩ (liter) intoxicating (liter)

embriagarse [A3] v pron (frml) (con alcohol) to become intoxicated (frml)

embriaguez f (borrachera) drunkness

embrión m (Biol) embryo

embrollar [A1] vt (a) ⟨*hilo/madeja*⟩ to tangle (up) (b) (confundir) ⟨*situación*⟩ to complicate; ⟨*persona*⟩ to muddle, confuse (c) (implicar) ~ **a algn EN algo** to embroil sb IN sth, get sb involved IN sth
■ **embrollarse** v pron ⟨*hilo/madeja*⟩ to get tangled; «*situación*» to get confused o muddled; «*persona*» to get muddled, to get mixed up (colloq)

embrollo m (de hilos, cables) tangle; (de callejuelas,

pasillos) maze; (situación confusa) muddle, mess; **el argumento es un** ~ the plot is extremely involved o complicated

embromado -da adj [1] [ESTAR] (AmS fam) (enfermo, delicado) in a bad way; **tiene un pie** ~ she has a bad foot [2] (AmS fam) ⟨*situación*⟩ tricky; ⟨*problema*⟩ thorny

embromar [A1] vt (AmS fam) (a) (molestar) to pester (b) (estropear) ⟨*aparato*⟩ to ruin (colloq); ⟨*plan*⟩ to ruin, spoil (c) (perjudicar): **la guerra nos embromó a todos** we all suffered because of the war; **¡me embromaste!** now you've really landed me in it! (colloq)
■ **embromarse** v pron (AmS fam) (a) (jorobarse): **que se embrome por estúpido** it serves him right for being so stupid; **si no te gusta, te embromas** if you don't like it, tough! (b) (hacerse daño) to hurt oneself; ⟨*rodilla/hígado*⟩ to screw up (AmE colloq), to do … in (BrE colloq) (c) (enfermarse) to get ill (colloq) (d) «*aparato/frenos*» to go wrong

embrujado -da adj [ESTAR] ⟨*persona*⟩ bewitched; ⟨*casa/lugar*⟩ haunted

embrujar [A1] vt (a) (hechizar) to bewitch, put … under a spell (b) (fascinar, enamorar) to bewitch

embrujo m (a) (hechizo) spell; (maleficio) curse (b) (encanto, atractivo) magic, enchantment

embrutecer [E3] vt «*trabajo*» to stultify; «*televisión*» to make … mindless

embudo m funnel

embuste m tall story, story (colloq)

embustero -ra adj: **¡qué niño más** ~! what a little fibber (colloq)
■ m,f fibber (colloq), liar

embutido m (salchicha) sausage; (fiambre) cold meat

eme f: name of the letter m

emergencia f emergency

emerger [E6] vi (a) «*submarino*» to surface (b) «*persona*» to emerge (c) (sobresalir) to emerge

emigración f (de personas) emigration; (de animales) migration

emigrante adj/mf emigrant

emigrar [A1] vi «*persona*» to emigrate; «*animal*» to migrate

eminencia f (a) (personalidad) expert (b) (frml) (Relig) Eminence (frml)

eminente adj eminent

Emiratos Árabes Unidos mpl United Arab Emirates

emisario -ria m,f emissary

emisión f (a) (Tec) emission (b) (Fin) issue (c) (Rad, TV) (acción) broadcasting; (programa) (frml) program*, broadcast

emisor m (aparato) transmitter

emisora f (Rad) radio station

emitir [I1] vt ⟨*sonido/luz/señal*⟩ to emit, give out; ⟨*acciones/sellos/comunicado*⟩ to issue; ⟨*programa*⟩ to broadcast; ⟨*película*⟩ to show; ⟨*veredicto*⟩ to deliver, announce; ⟨*voto*⟩ to cast

AmC	Central America	Arg	Argentina	Cu	Cuba
AmL	Latin America	Bol	Bolivia	Ec	Ecuador
AmS	South America	Chi	Chile	Esp	Spain
Andes	Andean Region	CS	Southern Cone	Méx	Mexico

Per	Peru
RPl	River Plate Area
Ur	Uruguay
Ven	Venezuela

emoción f (sentimiento) emotion; (expectación, excitación) excitement; ¡qué ∼! how exciting!

emocionado -da adj (conmovido) moved; (entusiasmado) excited

emocional adj emotional

emocionante adj (conmovedor) moving; (excitante, apasionado) exciting

emocionar [A1] vt to move, affect
■ **emocionarse** v pron (conmoverse) to be moved; (entusiasmarse) to get excited

emotivo -va adj ‹desarrollo/mundo/persona› emotional; ‹acto/discurso› moving, emotional

empacar [A2] vt (a) (empaquetar) to pack (b) ‹algodón/heno› to bale (c) (AmL) ‹maleta› to pack
■ ∼ vi to pack

empachar [A1] vt (fam) (indigestar) to give ... an upset stomach
■ **empacharse** v pron (fam) (indigestarse) ∼se DE algo to get an upset stomach FROM sth

empacho m (fam) (indigestión): agarrarse un ∼ to get o have an upset stomach

empadronarse [A1] v pron to register

empalagar [A3] vt: los bombones me empalagan chocolates are too sweet o sickly for my taste
■ ∼ vi ‹licor/dulce› to be too sweet o sickly; ‹estilo/sentimentalismo› to be cloying

empalagoso -sa adj ‹tarta/licor› sickly; ‹persona/sonrisa› sickly sweet, cloying

empalizada f palisade

empalmar [A1] vt ‹cuerdas/películas/cintas› to splice; ‹cables› to connect
■ ∼ vi ‹líneas/carreteras› to converge, meet

empalme m (de cables) connection; (de cuerdas) splice; (de carreteras, líneas) junction

empanada f (a) (AmL) (individual) pasty, pie (b) (Esp) (grande) pie

empanadilla f (Esp) tuna/meat pasty

empanar [A1], (Méx) **empanizar** [A4] vt to coat ... in breadcrumbs

empantanado -da adj ‹camino/campo› swampy

empantanarse [A1] v pron «camino/campo» to become swamped; «coche» to get bogged down

empañar [A1] vt ‹vidrio/espejo› to steam o mist up
■ **empañarse** v pron «vidrio/espejo» to steam o mist up

empapar [A1] vt (a) (embeber) ‹esponja/toalla/galleta› to soak (b) (mojar mucho) ‹persona› to soak, drench
■ **empaparse** v pron (mojarse mucho) «persona/zapatos/ropa» to get soaking wet

empapelar [A1] vt ‹habitación/pared› to wallpaper, paper

empaque m ⓵ (Col, Méx, Ven) (Tec) seal; (de llave de agua) washer ⓶ (Col) (acción de empaquetar) packing; (de regalo) wrapping

empaquetar [A1] vt (embalar) to pack

emparedado m sandwich

emparejar [A1] vt ⓵ ‹personas› to pair ... off; ‹calcetines/zapatos› to pair up ⓶ ‹pelo› to make ... even; ‹dobladillo› to even up; ‹pared/suelo› to level, make ... level; ‹montones/pilas› to make ... the same height

emparejarse v pron (a) (formar parejas) to pair off (b) (nivelarse) to level off, even up

emparentado -da adj [ESTAR] related; ∼ con algn related TO sb

empastar [A1] vt ‹diente/muela› to fill

empaste m (Odont) filling; (Chi) (pasta) filler

empatar [A1] vi ⓵ (a) (durante un partido) to draw level, equalize; (como resultado) to tie, draw (BrE); ∼on a dos they tied two-two (AmE), it was a two-all draw (BrE); **van empatados** they're equal o level at the moment (b) (en una votación) to tie ⓶ (Col, Ven) «listones/piezas» to fit together
■ ∼ vt (a) (Ven) (amarrar) to tie o join ... together (b) (Col, Per, Ven) ‹cables/tubos› to connect

emparatarse v pron (Ven) (a) (unirse) «calles/líneas» to join, meet (up); «huesos» to knit together (b) (fam) «pareja» to get together (colloq), to start going out together

empate m ⓵ (a) (en partido, certamen) tie (AmE), draw (BrE); **terminó con ∼ a cero** it finished in a scoreless tie (AmE) o (BrE) goalless draw; **el gol del ∼** the equalizer o (AmE) the tying goal (b) (en una votación) tie ⓶ (Col, Per, Ven) (unión — en carpintería) joint; (— de tubos, cables) connection ⓷ (Ven fam) (novio) boyfriend; (novia) girlfriend

empecinado -da adj (esp AmL) (terco) stubborn; (determinado) determined

empecinarse [A1] v pron (obstinarse) to get an idea into one's head; (empeñarse) to persist

empedernido -da adj ‹bebedor/fumador› hardened, inveterate; ‹jugador› compulsive; ‹solterón› confirmed

empedrado m (de adoquines) paving; (de piedras irregulares) cobbled paving

empedrar [A5] vt to pave

empeine m instep

empellón m shove; **se abrió paso a empellones** she shoved her way through

empeñado -da adj ⓵ (a) (resuelto) determined; **está ∼ en hacerlo** he's determined to do it (b) (obstinado): **está ∼ en que nos quedemos** he's insistent that we should stay ⓶ (endeudado) in debt

empeñar [A1] vt (a) ‹joyas/pertenencias› to pawn, hock (colloq) (b) ‹palabra› to give
■ **empeñarse** v pron ⓵ (endeudarse) to get o go into debt ⓶ ∼se EN hacer algo (esforzarse) to strive to do sth (frml), to make an effort to do sth; (proponerse) to be determined to do sth; (obstinarse) to insist ON doing sth

empeño m (a) (afán) determination; (esfuerzo) effort; **estudiar con ∼** to study hard; **pondré todo mi ∼** I will do my best (b) (obstinación) ∼ EN algo insistence ON sth (c) (intento, empresa) undertaking, endeavour*

empeñoso -sa adj (AmL) hard-working

empeoramiento m (de la salud) deterioration, worsening; (del tiempo, de una situación) worsening

empeorar [A1] vi «salud» to deteriorate, get worse; «tiempo/situación» to get worse, worsen
■ ∼ vt to make ... worse

emperador m (soberano) emperor

emperatriz f empress

empezar [A6] *vi* **1** «*película/conferencia/invierno*» to begin, start; **empezó a nevar** it started to snow *o* snowing **2** «*persona*» to start; **volver a ~** to start again; **todo es cuestión de ~** it'll be fine once we/you get started; **no sé por dónde ~** I don't know where to begin; **vamos a ~ por ti** let's start with you; **~ A hacer algo** to start doing sth, start to do sth; **empezó diciendo que ...** she started *o* began by saying that ...; **empezó trabajando de mecánico** he started out as a mechanic; **empecemos por estudiar el contexto histórico** let's start by looking at the historical context **3** **para empezar** first of all, to start with
■ **~** *vt* **(a)** «*tarea/actividad*» to start **(b)** «*frasco/mermelada*» to start, open

empiece, empieza *etc* ▶ EMPEZAR

empinado -da *adj* «*calle/pendiente*» steep

empinar [A1] *vt* «*bota/botella/vaso*» to raise
■ **empinarse** *v pron* (de puntillas) to stand on tiptoe

emplasto *m* **(a)** (Farm, Med) dressing **(b)** (fam) (cosa blanda, pegajosa) sticky mess (colloq)

empleada *f* maid; **~ de planta** (Méx) live-in maid; **~ doméstica** *or* **de servicio** (frml) maid, domestic servant (frml); *ver tb* EMPLEADO

empleado -da *m,f* **(a)** (trabajador) employee; **una nómina de 300 ~s** a staff of 300; **~ público** civil servant **(b)** (en oficina) office *o* clerical worker; (en banco) bank clerk, teller; (en tienda) (AmL) clerk (AmE), shop assistant (BrE)

empleador -dora *m,f* employer

emplear [A1] *vt* **1** **(a)** «*empresa/organización*» to employ **(b)** (colocar) «*hijo/sobrino*» to fix ... up with a job **2** (usar) «*energía/imaginación/material*» to use
■ **emplearse** *v pron* (esp AmL) to get a job

empleo *m* **1** **(a)** (trabajo) employment; **la creación de ~** job creation **(b)** (puesto) job; **está sin ~** she's out of work **2** (uso) use; **Ⓢ modo de empleo** instructions for use

emplomadura *f* (RPl) filling

emplomar [A1] *vt* (RPl) to fill

empobrecer [E3] *vt* «*población/tierra/lenguaje*» to impoverish
■ **empobrecerse** *v pron* «*país/lenguaje/vocabulario*» to become impoverished

empobrecimiento *m* impoverishment

empollar [A1] *vi* **1** «*gallina*» to brood **2** (Esp fam) «*estudiante*» to cram (colloq), to swot (BrE colloq)
■ **~** *vt* **1** «*huevos*» to hatch, sit on **2** (Esp fam) «*lección*» to cram (colloq), to swot up (on) (BrE colloq)

empollón -llona *m,f* (Esp fam & pey) grind (AmE colloq), swot (BrE colloq & pej)

empolvarse [A1] *v pron* (refl) «*nariz/cara*» to powder

empotrado -da *adj* «*mueble*» built-in, fitted (*before n*); «*periodista*» embedded

empotrarse [A1] *v pron*: **el coche se empotró en el muro** the car crashed into the wall

emprendedor -dora *adj* enterprising

emprender [E1] *vt* «*viaje*» to embark on; «*proyecto/aventura*» to undertake; «*ataque/ofensiva*» to launch; **~ la marcha** to set out; **~ el regreso** to begin one's return journey

empresa *f* **1** (compañía) company, firm (BrE); **~ pública** public sector company **2** (tarea, labor) venture, undertaking

empresario -ria *m,f* **(a)** (Com, Fin) (*m*) businessman; (*f*) businesswoman; **~ de pompas fúnebres** undertaker **(b)** (Teatr) impresario **(c)** (en boxeo) promoter

empujar [A1] *vt* **(a)** «*coche/columpio*» to push; **¡empújame!** give me a push! **(b)** (incitar, presionar) to spur ... on; (obligar) to force **(c)** (Tec) to drive
■ **~** *vi* **(a)** (hacer presión) to push **(b)** (dar empellones) to push, shove

empuje *m* (dinamismo) drive

empujón *m* **(a)** (empellón) shove, push; **abrió la puerta de un ~** he pushed the door open; **abrirse paso a (los) empujones** to shove one's way through **(b)** (fam) (para animar, incitar) prod (colloq); **voy a darle un ~ al asunto** I'm going to push things along a bit (colloq)

empuñadura *f* (de espada) hilt; (de daga, navaja) handle; (de bastón, paraguas) handle

empuñar [A1] *vt* «*arma/espada*» to take up; «*bastón/palo*» to brandish

en *prep* **1** (en expresiones de lugar) **(a)** (refiriéndose a ciudad, edificio): **viven ~ París/~ el número diez/~ un hotel** they live in Paris/at number ten/in a hotel; **~ el último piso** on the top floor; **está ~ la calle Goya** it's on *o* (BrE) in Goya Street; **~ casa** at home **(b)** (dentro de) in; **~ una caja** in a box **(c)** (sobre) on; **~ una silla** on a chair; **se le nota ~ la cara** you can see it in his face **2** (expresando circunstancias, ambiente) in; **~ peligro** in danger **3** **(a)** (indicando tema, especialidad): **un experto ~ la materia** an expert on the subject; **doctor ~ derecho** Doctor of Law **(b)** (indicando proporción, precio): **~ un diez por ciento** by ten per cent; **~ dólares** in dollars **4** **(a)** (indicando estado, manera) in; **~ malas condiciones** in bad condition; **~ llamas** in flames, on fire **(b)** (en forma de): **termina ~ punta** it's pointed; **colóquense ~ círculo** get into *o* in a circle **(c)** (con medios de transporte) by; **ir ~ taxi** to go by taxi; **fueron ~ bicicleta** they cycled, they went on their bikes; **dimos una vuelta ~ coche** we went for a ride in the car **5** **(a)** (indicando el material): **~ seda natural** in natural silk; **una escultura ~ bronce** a bronze (sculpture) **(b)** (indicando el modo de presentación *o* expresión) in; **~ azul/ruso** in blue/Russian **6** (con expresiones de tiempo): **~ verano** in (the) summer; **~ varias ocasiones** on several occasions; **~ la mañana/noche** (esp AmL) in the morning/at night **7** **(a)** (seguido de construcción verbal): **no hay nada de malo ~ lo que hacen** there's nothing wrong in what they're doing; **fui el último ~ salir** I was the last to leave **(b)** (con complementos de persona): **no sé qué ve ~ ella** I don't know what he sees in her

enagua *f*, **enaguas** *fpl* **(a)** (prenda interior) petticoat, underskirt **(b)** (AmC) (falda) skirt

enamorado -da *adj* [ESTAR] in love; **~ DE algn** in love WITH sb; **están muy ~s** they are very much in love
■ *m,f* lover; **una pareja de ~s** two lovers; **vino con su ~** (Bol, Per) she came with her boyfriend; **es un ~ de su profesión** he loves his work

enamoramiento *m* infatuation

enamorar [A1] *vt* to make ... fall in love, get ... to fall in love
■ **enamorarse** *v pron* to fall in love; ~**se DE algo/algn** to fall in love WITH sth/sb

enano -na *m,f* (de proporciones normales) midget; (de cabeza más grande) dwarf; (en los cuentos) dwarf
■ *adj* ⟨especie/planta⟩ dwarf (*before n*); ⟨ración⟩ (fam) minute, tiny

encabezado *m* (Chi, Méx) headline

encabezamiento *m* (a) (en carta — saludo) opening; (— dirección, fecha) heading (b) (en ficha, documento) heading

encabezar [A4] *vt* **1** ⟨artículo/escrito⟩ to head **2** (a) ⟨liga/clasificación/lista⟩ to head, be at the top of; ⟨carrera/movimiento/revolución⟩ to lead (b) ⟨delegación/comité⟩ to head, lead

encabritarse [A1] *v pron* «caballo» to rear up

encachado -da *adj* (Chi fam) (a) (bonito) ⟨ropa/lugar⟩ lovely, nice; ⟨persona⟩ attractive (b) (arreglado) well-dressed (c) (entretenido) ⟨historia⟩ entertaining

encadenar [A1] *vt* ⟨prisionero/bicicleta⟩ to chain (up)

encajar [A1] *vt* **1** (meter, colocar) to fit **2** (esp AmL fam) (endilgar): **me ~on a mí el trabajito** I got saddled *o* landed with the job (colloq); **le encaja los hijos a la suegra** she dumps the kids on her mother-in-law (colloq); **les ~on tres goles** they put three goals past them
■ ~ *vi* (a) «pieza/cajón» to fit; **no encaja bien** it doesn't fit it properly; **las piezas ~on** the pieces fitted together (b) (corresponder, cuadrar) «⟨hechos/descripción⟩» to fit; **no encaja con la decoración** it doesn't fit in with the decor

encaje *m* (Indum) lace; **pañuelo de ~** lace handkerchief

encajonar [A1] *vt* (en lugar estrecho) ~ **algo/a algn EN algo** to cram *o* pack sth/sb INTO sth; **me ~on el coche** my car *o* I got boxed in

encalar [A1] *vt* to whitewash

encalillarse [A1] *v pron* (Chi fam) to get into debt

encallar [A1] *vi* to run aground

encallecido -da *adj* ⟨manos⟩ callused

encamar [A1] *vt* (Méx) to confine ... to bed

encaminado -da *adj*: **el proyecto va bien ~** the project is shaping up well *o* is going well; **iba bien ~** he was on the right track; **medidas encaminadas a reducir ...** measures designed to reduce *o* aimed at reducing ...

encaminar [A1] *vt* (a) ⟨intereses/esfuerzos⟩ to direct, channel (b) ⟨estudiante/niño⟩ to point ... in the right direction
■ **encaminarse** *v pron* (liter) ~**se HACIA algo (a)** «persona» (dirigirse a) to head FOR/TOWARD(S) sth; (emprender el camino) to set off FOR/TOWARD(S) sth (b) «esfuerzos» to be aimed AT sth, be directed TOWARD(S) sth

encandilar [A1] *vt* (a) «luz» to dazzle (b) (asombrar, pasmar) to dazzle

encanecer [E3] *vi* to (go) gray*

encantado -da *adj* **1** (a) (muy contento) delighted; **estoy ~ de haber venido** I am delighted *o* very glad that I came (b) (en fórmulas de cortesía): ~ **de conocerla** pleased to meet you; **le presento al Señor Ruiz — encantado** let me introduce you to Mr Ruiz — how do you do; ~ **de poder ayudarte** I'm glad to be/to have been of help **2** ⟨bosque/castillo⟩ enchanted

encantador -dora *adj* ⟨persona/lugar⟩ charming, delightful
■ *m,f* magician; ~ **de serpientes** snake charmer

encantar [A1] *vi* (+ *me/te/le etc*): **me encantó la obra** I really enjoyed the play; **me ~ía que me acompañaras** I'd love you to come with me
■ ~ *vt* to cast *o* put a spell on, bewitch

encanto *m* **1** (a) (atractivo) charm; **sabe utilizar sus ~s** she knows how to use her charms; **su sencillez es su mayor ~** its most appealing feature is its simplicity (b) (fam) (maravilla): **¡qué ~ de hombre!** what a lovely *o* charming man!; **tienen un jardín que es un ~** they have a lovely garden **2** (a) (hechizo) spell; **como por ~** as if by magic (b) (Ven fam) (fantasma) ghost

encapotado -da *adj* overcast, cloudy

encapricharse [A1] *v pron*: **se ha encaprichado con esa moto** he's really taken a liking *o* (BrE) a fancy to that motorbike; ~ **CON** *or* (Esp) **DE algn** to fall for sb (colloq)

encarado -da *adj* (Esp, Méx): **mal ~** (enojado) bad-tempered; (de mal aspecto) nasty-looking

encaramarse [A1] *v pron* ~ **A** *or* **EN algo** ⟨a árbol/valla⟩ to climb up; ⟨a taburete⟩ to climb on to

encarar [A1] *vt* **1** (enfocar) ⟨tarea⟩ to approach; (afrontar) ⟨desgracia/problema⟩ to face up to; ⟨futuro⟩ to face **2** (AmL) ⟨persona⟩ to stand up to
■ **encararse** *v pron* ~**se CON algn** to face up to *o* stand up to sb

encarcelar [A1] *vt* to imprison, jail

encarecer [E3] *vt* (hacer más caro): **el envase encarece el producto** the container makes the product more expensive; ~**á los alquileres** it will push rents up
■ **encarecerse** *v pron* «precios» to increase, rise; «productos/vida» to become more expensive

encargado -da *adj* ~ **DE algo/hacer algo** responsible FOR sth/doing sth, in charge OF sth/doing sth
■ *m,f* (a) (de negocio) manager, person in charge (b) (de tarea): **tú serás el ~ de avisarles** it will be your responsibility to tell them

encargar [A3] *vt* **1** (a) ~**le algo A algn** ⟨tarea⟩ to entrust sb WITH sth; **me encargó una botella de whisky escocés** she asked me to buy *o* get her a bottle of Scotch (b) ~ **a algn QUE haga algo** to ask sb to do sth **2** ⟨mueble/paella/libro⟩ to order; ⟨informe/cuadro⟩ to commission
■ **encargarse** *v pron* ~**se DE algo/algn** to take care OF sth/sb; **me tuve que ~ del asunto** I had to take charge of the matter

encargo *m* (a) (recado, pedido): **¿te puedo hacer unos ~s?** could you buy *o* get a few things for me?; **mi hijo está haciendo un ~** my son is out on *o* is running an errand (b) (Com) order; **los hacemos por ~** we make them to order (c) (cargo, misión) job, assignment

encariñarse [A1] *v pron* ∼ CON algo/algn to grow fond OF sth/sb

encarnación *f* incarnation

encarnado -da *adj* ⟨1⟩ ⟨color/vestido⟩ red ⟨2⟩ ⟨uña⟩ ingrowing

encarnarse [A1] *v pron* **(a)** (Relig) to become incarnate **(b)** ⟨uña⟩ to become ingrown

encarrilar [A1] *vt* ⟨trabajo/asunto⟩ to direct; ⟨persona⟩ to guide, give guidance to

encasillar [A1] *vt* to class, categorize, pigeonhole

encauzar [A4] *vt* to channel; ∼ algo HACIA algo to channel sth INTO sth

encefalograma *m* encephalogram

enceguecedor -dora *adj* (AmL) blinding

enceguecer [E3] *vt* (AmL) to blind

■ **enceguecerse** *v pron* (AmL) (por la luz) to be blinded; (de ira) to become furious

encendedor *m* lighter

encender [E8] *vt* **(a)** ⟨cigarrillo/hoguera/vela⟩ to light; ⟨fósforo⟩ to strike, light **(b)** ⟨luz/calefacción⟩ to switch on, turn on; ⟨motor⟩ to start; no dejes el televisor encendido don't leave the television on

■ ∼ *vi* «fósforo» to light; «leña» to catch light; «luz/radio» to come on

■ **encenderse** *v pron* «aparato/luz» to come on; «fósforo/piloto» to light; «leña» to catch light

encendido *m* ignition

enceradora *f* polisher

encerar [A1] *vt* to polish, wax

encerrado -da *adj*: está ∼ en su habitación he's shut away *o* shut up in his room; se quedó ∼ en el cuarto de baño he got locked in the bathroom; siguen ∼s en la universidad they are still occupying the university; oler a ∼ (AmL) to be stuffy

encerrar [A5] *vt* ⟨1⟩ ⟨ganado⟩ to shut up, pen; ⟨perro⟩ to shut ... in; ⟨persona⟩ (en cárcel, calabozo) to lock up; me encerró en mi habitación he shut me *o* locked me in my room; me dejaron encerrada en la oficina I got locked in the office ⟨2⟩ ⟨conllevar⟩ ⟨peligro/riesgo⟩ to involve, entail

■ **encerrarse** *v pron* (refl) (en habitación) to shut oneself in; (en fábrica, universidad) «obreros/estudiantes» to lock oneself in

encerrona *f* (trampa) trap

encestar [A1] *vi* to score (a basket)

enchapar [A1] *vt* (de metal) to plate; (de madera) to veneer

encharcarse [A2] *v pron* «terreno/zona» to become waterlogged *o* flooded; «agua» to form a pool/pools

enchastrar [A1] *vt* (RPl fam) ⟨ropa/cocina⟩ to make a mess of

■ **enchastrarse** *v pron* (RPl fam) to get dirty

enchastre *m* (RPl fam) mess

enchilada *f* enchilada (tortilla with a meat or cheese filling, served with a tomato and chili sauce)

enchilado¹ -da *adj* (Méx) (Coc) seasoned with chili

enchilado² *m* stew (with chili)

enchilar [A1] *vt* (Méx) (Coc) to add chili to

■ **enchilarse** *v pron* (Méx) (comiendo): ya me enchilé my mouth's burning; con este plato me enchilo this dish is too hot for me

enchinar [A1] *vt* (Méx) to perm

■ **enchinarse** *v pron* (Méx): se me enchina la piel I come out in goose bumps *o* goose pimples

enchuecar [A2] *vt* (AmL fam) ⟨metal⟩ to bend; ⟨madera/lámina⟩ to warp; ⟨cara/boca⟩ to twist; ⟨cuadro⟩ to tilt

■ **enchuecarse** *v pron* (Chi fam) «metal» to bend, get bent; «madera/lámina» to warp; «cara/boca» to become twisted

enchufado -da *adj* (fam): está ∼ he knows all the right people; estar ∼ con ... to be well in with ... (colloq)

enchufar [A1] *vt* ⟨1⟩ (fam) ⟨radio/televisión⟩ to plug in ⟨2⟩ (fam) ⟨persona⟩: me enchufó en la empresa he set me up with a job in the company (colloq)

enchufe *m* ⟨1⟩ **(a)** (Elec) (macho) plug; (hembra) socket, power point (BrE) **(b)** (del teléfono) socket, point (BrE) ⟨2⟩ (Esp fam) (influencia): necesitas algún ∼ you need to have connections; por ∼ by pulling some strings

encía *f* gum

enciclopedia *f* encyclopedia

encienda, enciendas, etc ▶ ENCENDER

encierra, encierras, etc ▶ ENCERRAR

encierro *m* **(a)** (en fábrica, universidad) sit-in **(b)** (reclusión): salió de su ∼ después de ocho meses she emerged after being holed up for eight months **(c)** (Taur) (conducción) *running of bulls through the streets*; (toros) *bulls to be used in a bullfight*

encima *adv* ⟨1⟩ (en el espacio): le puso una piedra ∼ he put a stone on it; no llevo dinero ∼ I don't have any money on me; se tiró el café ∼ she spilled the coffee over herself; se me vino el armario ∼ the cupboard came down on top of me ⟨2⟩ (además): y ∼ se queja! and then she goes and complains!; y ∼ no me lo devolvió and on top of that, he didn't give it back!

⟨3⟩ (en locs) encima de: ∼ de la mesa on the table; ∼ del armario on top of the cupboard; llevaba un chal ∼ de la chaqueta she wore a shawl over her jacket; viven ∼ de la tienda they live over *o* above the shop; ∼ de caro es feo not only is it expensive, it's also ugly; por encima over; saltó por ∼ he jumped over it; le eché un vistazo por ∼ I just looked over it quickly; una limpieza por ∼ a quick clean; por encima de above; por ∼ de la media above average; por ∼ de todo above everything; volaban por ∼ de las nubes/del pueblo they flew above the clouds/over the town; está por ∼ del jefe de sección she's above the head of department; quitarse algo de ∼ ⟨problema/tarea⟩ to get sth out of the way; quitarse a algn de ∼ to get rid of sb

encimar [A1] *vt* **(a)** (Col) (regalar): **me encimó dos más** she gave me two extra **(b)** (Méx, RPl) ⟨*cajas/libros*⟩ to stack up

encina *f* holm oak, ilex

encinta *adj* ▶ EMBARAZADA

enclenque *adj* **(a)** ⟨*persona*⟩ (enfermizo) sickly; (delgado) weak, weedy (colloq) **(b)** ⟨*estructura*⟩ rickety

encoger [E6] *vi* to shrink
■ ∼ *vt* **(a)** ⟨*ropa*⟩ to shrink **(b)** ⟨*piernas*⟩ to tuck … in; **encogió el cuerpo de miedo** he shrank back in fear
■ **encogerse** *v pron* ☐1 «*ropa/tela*» to shrink ☐2 «*persona*» **(a)** (físicamente): ∼**se de hombros** to shrug one's shoulders; **caminar encogido** to walk with one's shoulders hunched **(b)** (por la edad) to shrink, get shorter **(c)** (acobardarse) to be intimidated

encomendería *f* (Per) grocery store (AmE), grocer's shop (BrE)

encomendero *m* (Per) (tendero) grocer

encomienda *f* (AmL) (Corresp) package (AmE), parcel (BrE)

encontrar [A10] *vt* ☐1 **(a)** (buscando) ⟨*casa/trabajo/persona*⟩ to find; **no encontré entradas para el teatro** I couldn't get tickets for the theater; **no le encuentro lógica** I can't see the logic in it **(b)** (casualmente) ⟨*cartera/billete*⟩ to find, come across **(c)** (descubrir) ⟨*falta/error*⟩ to find, spot; ⟨*cáncer/quiste*⟩ to find, discover **(d)** ⟨*obstáculo/dificultad*⟩ to meet (with), encounter ☐2 (+ *compl*): **te encuentro muy cambiado** you look very different; **lo encuentro ridículo** I find it ridiculous; **¿cómo encontraste el país?** how did the country seem to you?
■ **encontrarse** *v pron* ☐1 (por casualidad) ∼**se CON algn** to meet sb, bump INTO sb (colloq) ☐2 (*recípr*) **(a)** (reunirse) to meet; (por casualidad) to meet, bump into each other (colloq) **(b)** «*carreteras/líneas*» to meet ☐3 (*enf*) (inesperadamente) ⟨*billete/cartera*⟩ to find, come across; **me encontré con que todos se habían ido** I found they had all gone ☐4 (fml) (estar) to be; **me encuentro mejor** I am feeling better; **el hotel se encuentra cerca de la estación** the hotel is (located) near the station

encorvado -da *adj*: **anda** ∼ he walks with a stoop

encorvarse [A1] *v pron* to develop a stoop

encrespar [A1] *vt* ⟨*pelo*⟩ to make … go curly; ⟨*mar*⟩ to make … rough o choppy
■ **encresparse** *v pron* «*pelo*» to curl, go curly; «*mar*» to get rough o choppy

encrucijada *f* crossroads

encuadernación *f* **(a)** (cubierta) binding **(b)** (acción) book binding

encuadernador -dora *m,f* bookbinder

encuadernar [A1] *vt* to bind

encuadrar [A1] *vt* **(a)** (clasificar) to class, classify **(b)** (Cin, Fot, TV) to frame, center*

encubrir [I33] *vt* **(a)** ⟨*delincuente*⟩ to harbor* **(b)** ⟨*delito*⟩ to cover up; **siempre lo está encubriendo** she's always covering up for him **(c)** ⟨*temor/verdad/problema*⟩ to mask

encuclillarse [A1] *v pron* to squat (down)

encuentra, encuentras, etc ▶ ENCONTRAR

encuentro *m* **(a)** (acción) meeting, encounter; **una secretaria le salió al** ∼ he was met by a secretary **(b)** (Dep) (period) game

encuerarse [A1] *v pron* (*refl*) (AmL fam) (desnudarse) to strip off (colloq), get undressed; (en el escenario) to strip

encuesta *f* **(a)** (sondeo) survey; ∼ **de opinión** opinion poll **(b)** (investigación) inquiry

encuestado -da *m,f*: **el 50% de los** ∼**s** 50% of those polled

encumbrar [A1] *vt* (Chi) ⟨*volantín*⟩ to fly

endeble *adj* weak; ⟨*salud*⟩ delicate, poor

endemoniado -da *adj* **(a)** (inaguantable) ⟨*niño/asunto*⟩ wretched (before *n*); ⟨*genio/humor*⟩ foul, wicked **(b)** (poseído del demonio) possessed (by the devil)

enderezar [A4] *vt* **(a)** (destorcer) ⟨*clavo*⟩ to straighten **(b)** (poner vertical) ⟨*poste/espalda*⟩ to straighten; ⟨*planta*⟩ to stake; ⟨*barco*⟩ to right **(c)** ⟨*persona*⟩ to straighten … out
■ **enderezarse** *v pron* (ponerse derecho) «*persona*» to stand up straight, straighten up; «*árbol*» to straighten up

endeudado -da *adj* in debt; ∼ **CON algn** indebted TO sb

endeudarse [A1] *v pron* to get (oneself) into debt; ∼ **CON algn** to get into debt WITH sb

endiablado -da *adj* **(a)** (malo) ⟨*carácter/genio*⟩ terrible; **¡este** ∼ **niño!** this wretched child! **(b)** (peligroso) ⟨*velocidad*⟩ reckless, dangerous

endibia *f* endive, chicory (BrE)

endilgar [A3] *vt* (fam): **nos endilgó un sermón** he lectured us; **me** ∼**on el trabajito** I got saddled o landed with the job (colloq); **me endilgó a los niños** she dumped the kids on me (colloq)

endivia *f* endive, chicory (BrE)

endrogarse [A3] *v pron* (Méx) to get into debt

endulzar [A4] *vt* **(a)** ⟨*café*⟩ to sweeten **(b)** ⟨*tono/respuesta*⟩ to soften; ⟨*vida/vejez*⟩ to brighten up; ⟨*carácter*⟩ to mellow

endurecer [E3] *vt* ☐1 (en general) to harden ☐2 ⟨*persona/carácter*⟩ (volver insensible) to harden; (fortalecer) to toughen … up; **ese corte te endurece las facciones** that haircut makes you look harsher
■ **endurecerse** *v pron* **(a)** (en general) to harden; «*pan*» to go stale **(b)** «*persona/carácter*» (volverse insensible) to harden; (fortalecerse) to toughen up **(c)** «*facciones*» to become harder o harsher

ene *f*: *name of the letter* n

eneldo *m* dill

enemigo -ga *adj* **(a)** ⟨*tropas/soldados/país*⟩ enemy (before *n*) **(b)** ser ∼ DE algo to be against sth; **era enemiga de pegarles a los niños** she was against hitting children
■ *m,f* enemy

enemistad *f* enmity

enemistado -da *adj*: **están** ∼**s** they're at odds (with each other); **quedó** ∼ **con ellos** she fell out with them

enemistar [A1] *vt* ⟨*dos facciones/países*⟩ to make enemies of; ∼ **un país con otro** to turn one country against the other; **ella los enemistó** she turned them against each other ⋯⫶⋯

■ **enemistarse** *v pron* to fall out; ~**se con** algn (**por** algo) to fall out with algn (**over** sth)

energético -ca *adj* ‹crisis/política/recursos› energy (*before n*); ‹alimento› energy-giving, fuel (*before n*) (AmE)

energía *f* **1** (Fís) energy; ~ **nuclear/solar** nuclear/solar power **2** **(a)** (vigor, empuje) energy; **protestar con** ~ to protest vigorously; **está lleno de** ~ he's very energetic **(b)** (firmeza) firmness

enérgico -ca *adj* **(a)** (físicamente) energetic **(b)** (firme, resuelto) ‹carácter› forceful; ‹protesta/ ataque› vigorous; ‹medidas› firm, strong; ‹negativa/rechazo› flat, firm

enero *m* January; **a principios de** ~ at the beginning of January; **a mediados de** ~ in the middle of January, in mid-January; **el tres de** ~ the third of January, January the third, January third (AmE); **en (el mes de)** ~ in (the month of) January; **Lima, 8 de** ~ **de 1987** (Corresp) Lima, January 8 o January 8th, 1987

enfadado -da *adj* (esp Esp) angry; (en menor grado) annoyed; **están** ~**s** they've fallen out; **está** ~ **contigo** he's angry/annoyed with you

enfadar [A1] *vt* (esp Esp) (enojar) to anger, make ... angry; (en menor grado) to annoy

■ **enfadarse** *v pron* (esp Esp) **(a)** (enojarse) to get angry, get mad (esp AmE colloq); (en menor grado) to get annoyed, get cross (BrE colloq); ~**se con** algn to get angry/annoyed with sb **(b)** «novios» to fall out

enfado *m* (esp Esp) anger; (menos serio) annoyance

énfasis *m* emphasis; **poner** ~ **en algo** to stress o emphasize sth

enfático -ca *adj* emphatic

enfatizar [A4] *vt* to emphasize, stress

enfermar [A1] *vi* to fall ill, get sick (AmE)

■ **enfermarse** *v pron* **(a)** (esp AmL) (caer enfermo) to fall ill, get sick (AmE); ~**se del estómago** to develop stomach trouble **(b)** (CS euf) (menstruar) to get one's period

enfermedad *f* illness; **contraer una** ~ to contract an illness/a disease (frml); **después de una larga** ~ after a long illness; **está con permiso por** ~ he's off sick; ~**es de la piel** skin diseases; ~ **mental** mental illness; ~ **nerviosa** nervous disorder

enfermería *f* **1** (sala) infirmary, sickbay **2** (carrera) nursing

enfermero -ra *m,f* nurse; ~ **jefe** ≈ head nurse (AmE), ≈ charge nurse (BrE)

enfermizo -za *adj* unhealthy, sickly; **de aspecto** ~ unhealthy-looking

enfermo -ma *adj* (Med) ill, sick; **gravemente** ~ seriously ill; **está** ~ **del corazón** he has heart trouble; **está enferma de los nervios** she suffers with her nerves; **se puso** ~ he fell o got ill, he got sick (AmE); **poner** ~ **a** algn (fam) to get on sb's nerves (colloq), to get sb (colloq) **(b)** (CS euf) (con la menstruación): **estoy enferma** I've got my period, it's the time of the month (euph)

■ *m,f* (en hospital) patient; **quiere cuidar** ~**s** she wants to care for sick people o the sick; ~**s del corazón** people with heart trouble; ~**s de cáncer** cancer sufferers

enfocar [A2] *vt* **1** ‹objeto/persona› (con cámara, prismáticos) to focus on; **los** ~**on con la linterna** they shone the torch on them **2** **(a)** (Fot, Ópt) ‹telescopio/cámara› to focus **(b)** ‹tema/asunto› to approach, look at

enfoque *m* **(a)** (Fot, Ópt) (acción) focusing*; (efecto) focus **(b)** (de asunto) approach; **todo depende del** ~ **que se le dé** everything depends on the way you look at it; ~ **de algo** approach **to** sth

enfrentamiento *m* clash; ~ **bélico** military confrontation

enfrentar [A1] *vt* **1** ‹problema/peligro/ realidad› to confront, face up to; ‹futuro› to face **2** **(a)** ‹contrincantes/opositores› to bring ... face to face **(b)** (enemistar) to bring ... into conflict

■ **enfrentarse** *v pron* **(a)** (hacer frente a) ~**se con** algn ‹con rival/enemigo› to confront sb; ~**se a algo** ‹a dificultades/peligros› to face sth; ‹a realidad/responsabilidad› to face up to sth **(b)** (recípr) «equipos/atletas» to meet; «tropas/ oponentes» to clash

enfrente *adv* **1** (al otro lado de una calle, etc) opposite; ~ **de mí/del parque** opposite me/the park **2** (delante) in front; ~ **de algo** in front of sth

enfriamiento *m* **(a)** (catarro) chill **(b)** (de amor, entusiasmo, relaciones) cooling (off)

enfriar [A17] *vt* **(a)** ‹alimento› to cool; (en el refrigerador) to chill, cool **(b)** ‹entusiasmo/relación› to cool, cause ... to cool

■ ~ *vi*: **no dejes** ~ **el café** don't let your coffee go o get cold; **deja** ~ **el motor** let the engine cool down; **ponlo a** ~ put it in the refrigerator to chill

■ **enfriarse** *v pron* **1** **(a)** ‹comida/bebida› (ponerse — demasiado frío) to get cold, go cold; (— lo suficientemente frío) to cool down **(b)** «manos» to get cold **(c)** «entusiasmo/relaciones» to cool (off) **2** (tomar frío) to catch o get cold; (resfriarse) to catch a cold, catch a chill

enfurecer [E3] *vt* to infuriate, make ... furious

■ **enfurecerse** *v pron* to fly into a rage, get furious

enfurecido -da *adj* [ESTAR] ‹persona› furious

enfurruñarse [A1] *v pron* (fam) to go into a sulk (colloq), to get into a huff (colloq)

enganchar [A1] *vt* **(a)** ‹cable/cadena› to hook **(b)** ‹remolque› to hitch up, attach; ‹caballos› to harness; ‹vagón› to couple, attach **(c)** ‹pez› to hook

■ **engancharse** *v pron* **(a)** (quedar prendido) to get caught; **se me enganchó la media en el clavo** my tights got caught on the nail **(b)** (fam) (hacerse adicto) ~**se (a** algo) to get hooked (on sth)

enganche *m* **1** (pieza, mecanismo) (Auto) towing hook; (Ferr) coupling **2** (Esp) (de la luz, del teléfono) connection **3** (Méx) (Fin) down payment

engañar [A1] *vt* **(a)** (hacer errar en el juicio) to deceive, mislead; **me engañó la vista** my eyes deceived me; **tú a mí no me engañas** you can't fool me; **lo engañó haciéndole creer que ...** she deceived him into thinking that ...; ~ **a** algn **para que haga algo** to trick sb **into** doing sth **(b)** (estafar, timar) to cheat, con (colloq) **(c)** (ser infiel a) to be unfaithful to, cheat on

■ **engañarse** *v pron* (refl) (mentirse) to deceive oneself, kid oneself (colloq)

engaño *m* **(a)** (mentira) deception **(b)** (timo, estafa) swindle, con (colloq) **(c)** (ardid) ploy, trick

engañoso -sa *adj* ‹*palabras*› deceitful; ‹*apariencias*› deceptive

engarce *m* setting

engarzar [A4] *vt* **1** ‹*piedra*/*brillante*› to set **2** (Col, Ven) (enganchar) to hook
■ **engarzarse** *v pron* (Col) (engancharse) to get caught

engatusar [A1] *vt* to sweet-talk; ~ **a algn** PARA QUE **haga algo** to sweet-talk sb INTO doing sth

engendrar [A1] *vt* ‹*hijos*› to father; ‹*odio*/ *sospecha*› to breed, engender (fml)

engendro *m* **(a)** (feto) fetus* **(b)** (criatura malformada) malformed creature **(c)** (creación monstruosa) freak, monster

engentado -da *adj* (Méx) dazed, confused

engomado -da *adj* ‹*etiqueta*› gummed, self-adhesive; ‹*sobre*› gummed, self-sealing

engordar [A1] *vt* **(a)** (aumentar) to put on, gain **(b)** (cebar) to fatten (up) **(c)** ‹*cifras*/*estadísticas*› to swell
■ ~ *vi* **(a)** «*persona*» to put on *o* gain weight; «*animales*» to fatten **(b)** «*alimentos*» to be fattening

engorroso -sa *adj* ‹*problema*› complicated, thorny; ‹*situación*› awkward, difficult; ‹*asunto*› trying, tiresome

engranaje *m* **1** (Mec) gear assembly (*o* mechanism *etc*), gears (*pl*); **el** ~ **del reloj** the cogs of the watch **2** (de partido, sociedad) machinery

engrandecer [E3] *vt* (ennoblecer) to ennoble (fml)

engrapadora *f* (AmL) stapler

engrapar [A1] *vt* (AmL) to staple

engrasado *m* lubrication, greasing

engrasar [A1] *vt* **(a)** (Auto, Mec) (con grasa) to grease, lubricate; (con aceite) to oil, lubricate **(b)** (Coc) ‹*molde*› to grease

engreído -da *adj* **(a)** (vanidoso) conceited, bigheaded (colloq) **(b)** (Per) (mimado) spoiled*
■ *m,f* **(a)** (vanidoso) bighead (colloq) **(b)** (Per) (mimado) spoiled brat

engrupir [I1] *vt* (CS fam) to fool (colloq)

engullir [I9] *vt* to bolt (down)

enhebrar [A1] *vt* ‹*aguja*› to thread; ‹*perlas*› to string

enhorabuena *f* congratulations (*pl*); **darle la** ~ **a algn** to congratulate sb
■ *interj* congratulations!

enigma *m* enigma, mystery

enigmático -ca *adj* enigmatic, mysterious

enjabonar [A1] *vt* to soap
■ **enjabonarse** *v pron* (*refl*) to soap oneself; ~**se las manos** to soap one's hands

enjambre *m* (Zool) swarm

enjaular [A1] *vt* ‹*pájaro*/*fiera*› to cage, put ... in a cage

enjuagar [A3] *vt* ‹*boca*/*ropa*/*vajilla*› to rinse; ‹*palangana*/*cubo*› to swill out
■ **enjuagarse** *v pron* (*refl*) to wash off the soap; ~**se el pelo** to rinse one's hair

enjuague *m* **(a)** (acción de enjuagar) rinse **(b)** (AmL) (para el pelo) conditioner **(c)** ~ **bucal** mouthwash

enjugar [A3] *vt* (liter) ‹*lágrimas*/*sudor*› to wipe away

■ **enjugarse** *v pron* (*refl*) (liter) ‹*lágrimas*› to wipe away; ‹*frente*› to mop, wipe

enlace *m* **(a)** (conexión, unión) link **(b)** (de vías, carreteras) intersection, junction **(c)** *tb* ~ **matrimonial** marriage **(d)** (persona) liaison; ~ **sindical** (Esp) shop steward, union rep

enlatado¹ -da *adj* ‹*alimentos*› canned, tinned (BrE) **(b)** ‹*música*/*programa*› canned **(c)** (Inf) ‹*programa*› stored

enlatado² *m* **1** (proceso) canning **2** (AmL pey) (TV) poor-quality program

enlazar [A4] *vt* **1** **(a)** ‹*ciudades*› to link (up); ‹*ideas*/*temas*› to link, connect **(b)** ‹*cintas*› to tie ... together **2** (Col, RPl) ‹*res*/*caballo*› to lasso, rope (AmE) **3** (Méx fml) (casar) to marry
■ ~ *vi* ~ CON **algo** «*tren*/*vuelo*» to connect WITH sth; «*carretera*» to link up WITH sth

enlistarse [A1] *v pron* (AmC, Col, Ven) to enlist, join up

enloquecedor -dora *adj* ‹*dolor*› excruciating; **el ruido era** ~ the noise was enough to drive you crazy

enloquecer [E3] *vt* to drive ... crazy *o* mad
■ ~ *vi* (perder el juicio) to go crazy *o* mad; **enloqueció de celos** he was driven crazy *o* insane with jealousy

enlozado -da *adj* (AmL) ‹*cacerola*› enameled*; ‹*fuente*› glazed

enmarañado -da *adj* **(a)** ‹*pelo*/*lana*› tangled **(b)** (complicado, confuso) complicated, involved

enmarcar [A2] *vt* ‹*lámina*/*foto*› to frame

enmascarado -da *adj* masked
■ *m,f* (*m*) masked man; (*f*) masked woman

enmendar [A5] *vt* ‹*conducta*› to improve, amend (fml); ‹*actitud*› to change; ‹*error*› to amend, rectify
■ **enmendarse** *v pron* (*refl*) to mend one's ways

enmienda *f* amendment

enmohecer [E3] *vt* ‹*ropa*› to make ... moldy*; ‹*metal*› to rust
■ **enmohecerse** *v pron* «*ropa*/*pan*/*queso*» to become moldy*; «*metal*» to rust, become rusty

enmoquetar [A1] *vt* (Esp) to carpet

enmudecer [E3] *vi* to fall silent

ennegrecer [E3] *vt* (poner negro) to blacken; (oscurecer) to darken
■ **ennegrecerse** *v pron* **(a)** (ponerse negro) to go black **(b)** (ponerse oscuro) «*cielo*/*nubes*» to darken, go dark; «*plata*» to tarnish

enojadizo -za *adj* (esp AmL) irritable, touchy

enojado -da *adj* (esp AmL) angry, mad (esp AmE colloq); (en menor grado) annoyed, cross (BrE colloq); **está** ~ **contigo** he's angry/annoyed with you; **están** ~**s** they've fallen out

enojar [A1] *vt* (esp AmL) to make ... angry; (en menor grado) to annoy
■ **enojarse** *v pron* (esp AmL) to get angry, get mad (esp AmE colloq); (en menor grado) to get annoyed, get cross (BrE colloq); ~**se** CON **algn** to get angry/annoyed WITH sb

enojo *m* (esp AmL) anger; (menos serio) annoyance; **¿ya se te pasó el** ~**?** are you still angry/annoyed?

enojón -jona *adj* (Chi, Méx fam) irritable, touchy

enojoso -sa adj (esp AmL) (violento) awkward; (aburrido) tedious, tiresome

enorgullecer [E3] vt: **mi hijo me enorgullece** I am proud of my son
■ **enorgullecerse** v pron to be proud; **no es para ~se** it's nothing to be proud of; **~se DE algo** to take pride in sth

enorme adj ‹edificio/animal/suma› huge, enormous; ‹zona› vast, huge; **sentí una pena ~** I felt tremendously sad

enraizado -da adj ‹prejuicio› deep-seated, deep-rooted; ‹tradición› deeply rooted

enrarecido -da adj **(a)** ‹atmósfera/aire› rarefied **(b)** ‹ambiente/relaciones› strained, tense

enredadera f creeper, climbing plant

enredado -da adj ① ‹lana/cuerda› tangled; ‹pelo› tangled, knotted; ‹asunto/idea› complicated ② **(a)** (involucrado) ~ **EN algo** mixed up IN sth **(b)** (fam) (en lío amoroso) ~ **CON algn** involved WITH sb

enredar [A1] vt **(a)** ‹cuerdas/cables› to get ... tangled up, tangle up **(b)** (embarullar) ‹persona› to muddle ... up, confuse; ‹asunto/situación› to complicate **(c)** (fam) (involucrar) ~ **a algn EN algo** to get sb mixed up o caught up IN sth
■ ~ vi (fam) **(a)** (intrigar) to make trouble, stir up trouble **(b)** (Esp) (molestar) to fidget; ~ **CON algo** to fiddle (around) WITH sth
■ **enredarse** v pron ① ‹‹lana/cuerda›› to get tangled, become entangled; ‹‹pelo›› to get tangled o knotted; ‹‹planta›› to twist itself around ② (fam) **(a)** (en lío amoroso) ~se **CON algn** to get involved WITH sb **(b)** (involucrarse) ~se **EN algo** to get mixed up o involved IN sth **(c)** (fam) (embarullarse) to get mixed up, get muddled up

enredo m **(a)** (de hilos) tangle; (en el pelo) tangle, knot **(b)** (embrollo) mess; **tengo un ~ en las cuentas ...** my accounts are in a terrible mess **(c)** (fam) (lío amoroso) affair

enrejado m (de verja, balcón) railing, railings (pl); (rejilla) grating, grille; (para plantas) trellis

enrevesado -da adj complicated

enrielar [A1] vt ▶ ENCARRILAR

enriquecer [E3] vt ① ‹país/población› to make ... rich ② ‹espíritu/lengua/alimento› to enrich
■ **enriquecerse** v pron ① (hacerse rico) to get rich ② ‹cultura/relación/lengua› to be enriched

enrojecer [E3] vt ‹rostro/mejillas› to redden, make ... go red; ‹pelo› to turn ... red, make ... go red
■ ~ vi (liter) (ruborizarse) to redden, blush; (de ira, rabia) to go red in the face
■ **enrojecerse** v pron ‹‹rostro/mejillas›› to redden, blush; ‹‹pelo›› to go o turn red; ‹‹cielo›› to turn red

enrolarse [A1] v pron to enlist, join up; ~ **en la marina** to enlist in o join the navy; ~ **en un partido** to join a party

enrollado -da adj ① **(a)** ‹papel› rolled up **(b)** ‹cable› coiled (up) ② (Esp) (fam) **estar ~ CON algn** to have a thing (going) WITH sb (colloq); **están ~s** they've got sth going between them (colloq)

(c) estar ~ CON algo ‹con exámenes/preparativos› wrapped up IN sth **(c)** (arg) (en la onda) ‹persona/música/coche› cool (sl) ③ (Ven fam) (preocupado) uptight (colloq), freaked out (sl)

enrollar [A1] vt ① ‹papel/persiana› to roll up; ‹cable/manguera› to coil; ~ **el hilo en el carrete** wind the thread onto the spool ② (Esp arg) ‹persona› (confundir) to confuse, get ... confused; (en asunto) to involve, get ... involved
■ **enrollarse** v pron ① ‹‹papel›› to roll up; ‹‹cuerda/cable›› to coil up; **la cadena se enrolló en la rueda** the chain wound itself around the wheel ② (Esp fam) **(a)** (hablar mucho): **no te enrolles** stop jabbering on (colloq); **se ~on hablando** they got deep into conversation **(b)** (tener relaciones amorosas): **se ~on en la discoteca** they made out (AmE colloq) o (BrE colloq) they got off together in a disco; ~se **CON algn** to make out WITH sb (AmE colloq), to get off WITH sb (BrE colloq)

enroque m (en ajedrez) castling

enroscar [A2] vt ‹tornillo› to screw in; ‹cable/cuerda› to coil; ~ **algo EN algo** to wind sth AROUND o ONTO sth
■ **enroscarse** v pron **(a)** ‹‹víbora›› to coil up **(b)** ‹‹gato/persona›› to curl up

enrular [A1] vt (Col, CS) to curl

ensalada f (Coc) salad; ~ **de fruta** fruit salad

ensaladera f salad bowl

ensalzar [A4] vt ‹virtudes› to extol; ‹persona› to praise, sing the praises of

ensamblar [A1] vt to assemble

ensanchar [A1] vt **(a)** ‹calle› to widen; ‹vestido› to let out **(b)** ‹horizontes/posibilidades› to expand
■ **ensancharse** v pron **(a)** ‹‹calle/acera›› to widen, get wider; ‹‹jersey›› to stretch **(b)** ‹‹horizontes›› to expand

ensangrentado -da adj bloodstained

ensangrentar [A5] vt to stain ... with blood

ensañarse [A1] v pron: **se ensañaron con los prisioneros** they showed the prisoners no mercy o pity; **no te ensañes con él** don't take it out on him (colloq)

ensartar [A1] vt **(a)** ‹perlas/cuentas› to string **(b)** (con pincho) to skewer **(c)** (enhebrar) to thread **(d)** (clavar) ~ **algo EN algo** to stick sth IN(TO) sth

ensayar [A1] vt **(a)** ‹obra/baile› to rehearse **(b)** ‹método› to test, try out
■ ~ vi to rehearse

ensayo m ① **(a)** (Espec) rehearsal; ~ **general** (de obra teatral) dress rehearsal; (de concierto) final rehearsal **(b)** (prueba) trial, test; (intento) attempt ② (Lit) essay ③ (en rugby) try

enseguida adv at once, immediately, right away; **¡~ voy!** I'll be right with you; ~ **de almorzar** (esp AmL) right o straight after lunch

enseñado -da adj: **bien/mal ~** ‹niño› well/badly brought up; ‹animal› well/badly trained

enseñanza f **(a)** (docencia) teaching **(b)** (educación) education; ~ **a distancia** distance

learning; ~ **media** *or* **secundaria** high school
(AmE) *o* (BrE) secondary education; ~ **primaria**
elementary (AmE) *o* (BrE) primary education; ~
universitaria college (AmE) *o* (BrE) university
education

enseñar [A1] *vt* ⟨**1**⟩ **(a)** ⟨*asignatura/niño*⟩ to
teach; ⟨*animal*⟩ to train; ~**le a algn A hacer algo**
to teach sb to do sth **(b)** (dar escarmiento) to teach
⟨**2**⟩ (mostrar) ⟨*camino/procedimiento*⟩ to show
■ **enseñarse** *v pron* (Méx fam) ~**se A hacer algo**
(aprender) to learn to do sth; (acostumbrarse) to get
used TO doing sth

ensillar [A1] *vt* to saddle (up)

ensimismado -da *adj* [ESTAR] lost in
thought; ~ **EN algo** engrossed IN sth, absorbed IN
sth

ensordecedor -dora *adj* deafening

ensuciar [A1] *vt* **(a)** ⟨*ropa/mantel*⟩ to get ...
dirty; **lo vas a ~ todo de barro** you'll get
mud everywhere **(b)** (liter) ⟨*honor/nombre*⟩ to
sully, tarnish
■ **ensuciarse** *v pron* **(a)** (*refl*) «*persona*» to get
dirty; **no te ensucies los dedos** don't get your
fingers dirty **(b)** «*falda/suelo*» to get dirty; **que
no se te ensucie** don't get it dirty; **se me ensució
el vestido de grasa** I got grease on my dress

entablar [A1] *vt* **(a)** (iniciar) ⟨*conversación/
amistad*⟩ to strike up; ⟨*negociaciones*⟩ to enter
into **(b)** ⟨*partida*⟩ to set up

entablillar [A1] *vt* to splint, put ... in a splint

entallado -da *adj* ⟨*chaqueta/vestido*⟩ waisted;
⟨*camisa*⟩ tailored, fitted

ente *m* **(a)** (ser) being, entity **(b)** (organismo,
institución) body

entender [E8] *vt* to understand; ⟨*chiste*⟩ to
understand, get (colloq); **no te entiendo la letra** I
can't read your writing; **no entendí su nombre** I
didn't get his name; **lo entendió todo al revés** he
got it all completely wrong; **tú ya me entiendes**
you know what I mean; **me has entendido mal**
you've misunderstood me; **se hace ~** *or* (AmL) **se
da a ~** he makes himself understood; **me dio a ~
que ...** she gave me to understand that ...; **dar
algo a ~** to imply sth
■ ~ *vi* **(a)** (comprender) to understand **(b)** (saber) ~
DE algo to know ABOUT sth
■ **entenderse** *v pron* **(a)** (comunicarse) to
communicate; **se entienden por señas** they
communicate using sign language; ~**se CON algn**
to communicate WITH sb; **a ver si nos
entendemos ¿quién te pegó?** let's get this
straight, who hit you? **(b)** (llevarse bien); **lo que
pasa es que no nos entendemos** the thing is we
just don't get on very well; ~**se CON algn** to get
along *o* on WITH sb
⟨**2**⟩ (*refl*): **déjame, yo me entiendo** leave me alone,
I know what I'm doing

entendido -da *adj* ⟨**1**⟩ [ESTAR] (comprendido)
understood; **según tengo ~** as I understand it;
tenía ~ que ... I was under the impression that
...; **eso se da por ~** that goes without saying
⟨**2**⟩ [SER] (experto): **no soy muy ~ en estos temas**
I'm not very well up on these subjects; **es muy ~
en política** he's very knowledgeable about politics
■ *m,f* expert

entendimiento *m* **(a)** (acuerdo)

understanding **(b)** (capacidad para entender) mind;
todavía no tiene suficiente ~ he's not old enough
to understand

enterado -da *adj* ⟨**1**⟩ (de hecho, suceso): **¿estás
~ de lo ocurrido?** have you heard what's
happened?; **no estoy enterada de nada** I have no
idea what's going on; **darse por ~** to get the
message, take the hint ⟨**2**⟩ (Esp) (que sabe mucho)
knowledgeable, well-informed

enterarse *v pron* ⟨**1**⟩ (de suceso, noticia):
ahora me entero this is the first I've heard of it;
me enteré por tus padres I found out from your
parents; **le robaron el reloj y ni se enteró** they
stole her watch and she didn't even notice *o*
realize; **me enteré de la noticia por la radio** I
heard the news on the radio; **si papá se entera de
esto ...** if Dad finds out about this ...
⟨**2**⟩ (averiguar) to find out; ~ **DE algo** to find out
ABOUT sth
⟨**3**⟩ (esp Esp fam) (entender): **te voy a castigar ¿te
enteras?** I'll punish you, have I made myself
clear?; **¡para que te enteres!** (fam) so there! (colloq)

entereza *f* (serenidad, fortaleza) fortitude; (rectitud)
integrity; (firmeza) determination, strength of
mind

enternecedor -dora *adj* moving, touching

enternecer [E3] *vt* to move, touch
■ **enternecerse** *v pron* to be moved *o* touched

entero¹ -ra *adj* **(a)** (en su totalidad) whole; **una
caja entera de bombones** a whole *o* an entire box
of chocolates; **en el mundo ~** all over the world;
por ~ completely, entirely **(b)** (intacto) intact **(c)**
⟨*número*⟩ whole

entero² *m* **(a)** (Fin) point **(b)** (Mat) whole
number, integer **(c)** (de lotería) (whole) lottery
ticket

enterrador -dora *m,f* gravedigger

enterrar [A5] *vt* to bury; **lo entierran mañana**
the funeral is tomorrow

entibiar [A1] *vt* ⟨*líquido*⟩ (enfriar) to cool;
(calentar) to warm (up)

entidad *f* (frml) (organización, institución) entity,
body; ~ **deportiva** sporting body

entienda, entiendas, etc ▶ ENTENDER

entierro *m* (acto) burial; (ceremonia) funeral;
(procesión) funeral procession; **ir a un ~** to attend
a funeral

entoldado *m* (marquesina) awning; (carpa)
marquee

entonación *f* intonation

entonado -da *adj* ⟨**1**⟩ (Mús) in tune ⟨**2**⟩ [ESTAR]
(fam) (por el alcohol) tipsy (colloq), merry (BrE colloq)

entonar [A1] *vt* ⟨**1**⟩ ⟨*canción*⟩ to intone, sing;
⟨*voz*⟩ to modulate; ⟨*nota*⟩ to sing, give ⟨**2**⟩ (animar)
«*café/sopa*» ⟨*persona*⟩ to perk ... up
■ ~ *vi* (Mús) to sing in tune

entonces *adv* ⟨**1**⟩ (en aquel momento) then; **por**
or **en aquel ~** in those days ⟨**2**⟩ **(a)** (introduciendo
conclusiones) so; **¿~ vienes o te quedas?** so are
you coming with us or staying here? **(b)** (uso
expletivo) well, anyway; ~**, como te iba diciendo ...**
well *o* anyway, as I was saying ...

entornado -da *adj* ⟨*puerta*⟩ ajar, half-open;
⟨*ventana*⟩ slightly open; ⟨*ojos*⟩ half-closed

entorno *m* **(a)** (situación) environment **(b)** (Lit)
setting **(c)** (Inf) environment

entorpecer [E3] vt (a) (dificultar) ‹tráfico› to hold up, slow down; ‹planes/movimiento› to hinder; **estas cajas entorpecen el paso** these boxes are (getting) in the way **(b)** ‹entendimiento/reacciones› to dull
■ **entorpecerse** v pron ‹‹entendimiento/reacciones›› to become dulled

entrada f **1** (acción) entrance; **la ~ es gratuita** admission o entrance is free; **vigilaban sus ~s y salidas** they watched his comings and goings; **🅢 prohibida la entrada** no entry; **🅢 entrada libre** admission free; **la ~ de divisas** the inflow of foreign currency; **~ EN** or (esp AmL) **A algo** entry INTO sth; **forzaron su ~ en el** or **al edificio** they forced an entry into the building; **de ~** right from the start
2 (a) (en etapa, estado): **la ~ en vigor del nuevo impuesto** the coming into effect of the new tax **(b)** (ingreso, incorporación) entry; **la ~ de Prusia en la alianza** Prussia's entry into the alliance; **esto le facilitó la ~ a la universidad** that made it easier for him to get into university **(c)** (lugar de acceso) entrance; **espérame en** or **a la ~** wait for me at the entrance; **repartían folletos a la ~** they were handing out leaflets at the door **(d)** (vestíbulo) hall
3 (Espec) ticket; **los niños pagan media ~** it's half-price for children
4 (Com, Fin) **(a)** (Esp) (depósito) deposit **(b)** (ingreso) income; **~s y salidas** income and expenditure, receipts and outgoings
5 (de comida) starter
6 (Dep) **(a)** (en fútbol) tackle; **hacerle una ~ a algn** to tackle sb **(b)** (en béisbol) inning
7 (en el pelo): **tiene ~s** he has a receding hairline

entrado -da adj: **era entrada la noche** it was dark o night-time; **duró hasta bien entrada la tarde** it went on well into the evening

entrador -dora adj (AmL fam) (lanzado) daring, forward

entrante adj **(a)** (próximo): **el año ~** next year, the coming year **(b)** (nuevo) ‹gobierno/presidente› new, incoming (before n)

entrañable adj **(a)** ‹amistad› close, intimate; ‹amigo› very close, bosom (before n); ‹recuerdo› fond (before n) **(b)** ‹persona› pleasant, likable*

entrañar [A1] vt to entail, involve

entrañas fpl (vísceras) entrails (pl)

entrar [A1] vi **1** (acercándose) to come in; (alejándose) to go in; **déjame ~** let me in; **hazla ~** tell her to come in, show her in; **entró corriendo** he ran in, he came running in; **¿se puede ~ con el coche?** can you drive in?; **había gente entrando y saliendo** there were people coming and going; **¿cómo entró?** how did he get in?; **~ EN** or (esp AmL) **A algo** ‹a edificio/habitación› to go INTO sth; **entró en el** or **al banco** she went into the bank
2 (en etapa, estado) **~ EN algo** ‹en periodo/guerra/negociaciones› to enter sth; **~ en calor** to get warm; **entró en coma** he went into a coma
3 (a) (introducirse, meterse): **cierra la puerta, que entra frío** close the door, you're letting the cold in; **me entró arena en los zapatos** I've got sand in my shoes **(b)** (poderse meter): **¿entrará por la puerta?** will it get through the door?; (+ me/te/le etc): **estos vaqueros no me entran** I can't get into

these jeans; **el zapato no le entra** he can't get his shoe on; **no me entra la segunda** (Auto) I can't get it into second (gear)
4 ‹‹hambre›› (+ me/te/le etc): **le entró hambre** she felt o got hungry; **me ha entrado la duda** I'm beginning to have my doubts; **me entró sueño** I got o began to feel sleepy
5 (empezar) to start, begin; **entró de aprendiz** he started o began as an apprentice
6 (incorporarse) **~ EN** or (esp AmL) **A algo** ‹en empresa/ejército/club› to join sth; ‹en convento› to enter sth; **el año que entré en** or **a la universidad** the year I started college I've just joined the association
7 (estar incluido): **el postre no entra en el precio** dessert is not included in the price; **¿cuántas entran en un kilo?** how many do you get in a kilo?
■ **~** vt (traer) to bring in; (llevar) to take in; **¿cómo van a ~ el sofá?** how are they going to get the sofa in?

entre prep **1 (a)** (dos personas, cosas) between; **lo decidieron ~ ellos dos** they decided it between the two of them; **está ~ las dos casas** it's between the two houses; **~ paréntesis** in brackets; **cuando hablan ~ los dos** when they talk to each other **(b)** (más de dos personas, cosas) among; **los alumnos hablaban ~ ellos** the pupils were talking among themselves; **~ otras cosas** among other things; **se perdió ~ la muchedumbre** he disappeared into the crowd; **~ estas cuatro paredes** within these walls **(c)** (indicando cooperación, distribución): **~ los tres logramos levantarlo** we managed to lift it between the three of us; **le hicimos con regalo ~ todos** we all got together and brought him a present; **repártelos ~ los niños/~ todos** share them out among the children/between everybody
2 (en expresiones de tiempo): **abierto ~ semana** open during the week; **llegaré ~ las tres y las cuatro** I'll be arriving between three and four; **cualquier semana ~ julio y agosto** any week in July or August
3 **entre tanto** meanwhile, in the meantime
■ adv (esp AmL): **~ más come más/menos engorda** the more he eats the more/less he puts on weight

entreabierto -ta adj ‹puerta› ajar, half-open; ‹ventana/ojos/boca› half-open

entreabrir [I33] vt to half-open

entrecejo m space between the eyebrows; **fruncir el ~** to frown

entrecortado -da adj ‹respiración› difficult, labored*; **con la voz entrecortada por la emoción** in a voice choked with emotion

entrecruzar [A4] vt to intertwine, interweave

entredicho m **1** (duda): **estar en ~** to be in doubt o question; **poner algo en ~** ‹‹persona›› to question sth **2** (CS, Per) (entre dos personas) argument; (entre dos países) dispute

entrega f **1** (de pedido, paquete, carta) delivery; (de premio) presentation; **~ de premios** prize-giving; **la ~ de los documentos** the handing over of the documents; **el plazo para la ~ de solicitudes** the deadline for handing in o (frml) submitting applications; **servicio de ~ a domicilio** delivery service **2 (a)** (partida) delivery, shipment **(b)** (plazo, cuota) installment*

(c) (de enciclopedia) installment*, fascicle; (de revista) issue ③ (dedicación) dedication, devotion; (abandono) surrender

entregar [A3] *vt* ① (llevar) ⟨*pedido/paquete/ carta*⟩ to deliver
② **(a)** (dar) to give; **me entregó un cuestionario** she gave me *o* handed me a questionnaire; **no quiso entregármelo** he refused to hand it over to me **(b)** ⟨*premio/trofeo*⟩ to present; **~le algo a algn** to present sb WITH sth **(c)** ⟨*trabajo/deberes/ informe*⟩ to hand in, give in; ⟨*solicitud/impreso*⟩ to hand in, submit (frml)
③ **(a)** ⟨*ciudad/armas*⟩ to surrender; ⟨*poder/ control*⟩ to hand over **(b)** ⟨*delincuente/prófugo*⟩ to turn in, hand over; ⟨*rehén*⟩ to hand over **(c)** ⟨*novia*⟩ to give away **(d)** (dedicar) to devote
■ **entregarse** *v pron* ① (dedicarse) **~se a algo/ algn** to devote oneself TO sth/sb
② **(a)** (rendirse) to surrender, give oneself up; **~se a algo/algn** ⟨*al enemigo/a la policía*⟩ to give oneself up *o* surrender TO sth/sb **(b)** (abandonarse): **se entregó a la bebida** he gave himself over to drink

entrelazar [A4] *vt* ⟨*cintas/hilos*⟩ to interweave, intertwine; **con las manos entrelazadas** hand in hand
■ **entrelazarse** *v pron* to intertwine, interweave

entremedias, entremedio *adv* **(a)** (entre dos cosas) in between; **son muy caros o muy baratos, no hay nada ~** they're very expensive *o* very cheap, there's nothing in between; **lo metí ~** I put it in between **(b)** (mezclado con) **~ de algo** among; **~ de mis papeles/de la gente** among my papers/the people **(c)** (en el tiempo) in between

entremés *m* (Coc) hors d'oeuvre, starter

entremezclar [A1] *vt* to intermingle
■ **entremezclarse** *v pron* «*recuerdos*» to intermingle, become intermingled; «*culturas*» to mix, intermingle

entrenador -dora *m,f* (manager) coach, manager; (preparador físico) trainer

entrenamiento *m* **(a)** (por el entrenador) coaching, training **(b)** (ejercicios) training **(c)** (sesión) training session

entrenar [A1] *vt/vi* to train
■ **entrenarse** *v pron* to train

entrepierna *f* (Anat) crotch; (medida) inside leg measurement

entrepiso *m* (AmL) mezzanine

entreplanta *f* mezzanine

entretanto *adv* meanwhile, in the meantime

entretejer [E1] *vt* ⟨*hilos*⟩ (en tela) to weave; (entrelazar) to interweave

entretelones *mpl* (CS, Per) (de un caso) ins and outs (*pl*)

entretención *f* (AmL) ▶ ENTRETENIMIENTO

entretener [E27] *vt* ① «*crucigrama/libro*» to keep ... amused; «*obra/payaso*» to entertain; **pintar me entretiene** I enjoy painting ② **(a)** (distraer, apartar de una tarea) to distract **(b)** (retener) to keep, detain; **no te entretengo más** I won't keep *o* detain you any longer
■ **entretenerse** *v pron* ① **(a)** (divertirse) to amuse oneself; **se entretiene con cualquier cosa** «*adulto*» she's easily amused; «*niño*» she's

happy playing with anything **(b)** (pasar el tiempo) to keep (oneself) busy *o* occupied ② (demorarse) to hang around, dally about

entretenido -da *adj* ① [SER] ⟨*película/ conversación*⟩ entertaining, enjoyable; ⟨*persona*⟩ entertaining ② [ESTAR] ⟨*persona*⟩ (ocupado) busy

entretenimiento *m* entertainment; **lo hace por ~** he does it for pleasure *o* for fun

entretiempo *m* **(a)** (período entre estaciones): **de ~** ⟨*abrigo*⟩ lightweight; ⟨*ropa*⟩ spring/autumn (*before n*) **(b)** (Chi) (Dep) halftime

entrever [E29] *vt* **(a)** (ver confusamente) to make out **(b)** ⟨*solución/acuerdo*⟩ to begin to see; **ha dejado ~ que ...** she has hinted *o* suggested that ...

entreverado -da *adj* **(a)** (intercalado) interspersed **(b)** (fam) (desordenado, mezclado) muddled up, mixed up

entrevista *f* **(a)** (para trabajo, en periódico) interview **(b)** (period) (reunión) meeting

entrevistador -dora *m,f* interviewer

entrevistar [A1] *vt* to interview

entristecer [E3] *vt* to sadden
■ **entristecerse** *v pron* to grow sad

entrometerse [E1] *v pron* to meddle

entrometido -da *adj* meddling (*before n*), interfering (*before n*)
■ *m,f* meddler, busybody (colloq)

entronque *m* (AmL) (Ferr) junction

entumecerse [E3] *v pron* (perder la sensibilidad) to go numb; (perder la flexibilidad) to get stiff; **estar entumecido de frío** to be numb with cold

entusiasmado -da *adj* excited, enthusiastic; **está ~ con la idea** he's excited *o* enthusiastic about the idea

entusiasmar [A1] *vt* (apasionar): **lo entusiasma el fútbol** he's crazy about football; **no me entusiasma mucho la idea** I'm not very enthusiastic about the idea
■ **entusiasmarse** *v pron* **~se CON algo** to get excited *o* enthusiastic ABOUT sth

entusiasmo *m* enthusiasm

entusiasta *adj* enthusiastic
■ *mf* enthusiast

enumerar [A1] *vt* to list, enumerate (frml)

enunciar [A1] *vt* ⟨*idea/teoría*⟩ to state, enunciate (frml); ⟨*problema/teorema*⟩ to formulate

envainar [A1] *vt* ⟨*espada*⟩ to sheathe

envalentonar [A1] *vt* to make ... bolder, encourage
■ **envalentonarse** *v pron* (ponerse valiente) to become bolder *o* more daring; (insolentarse) to become defiant

envasar [A1] *vt* (en botellas) to bottle; (en latas) to can; (en paquetes, cajas) to pack

envase *m* (en general) container; (botella) bottle; (lata) can, tin (BrE)

envejecer [E3] *vi* **(a)** «*persona*» (hacerse más viejo) to age, grow old; (parecer más viejo) to age **(b)** «*vino/queso*» to mature, age
■ *vt* **(a)** ⟨*persona*⟩ «*tragedia/experiencia*» to age; «*ropa/peinado*» to make ... look older **(b)** ⟨*madera*⟩ to make ... look old; ⟨*vaqueros*⟩ to give ... a worn look

envejecido -da adj **(a)** ⟨persona⟩: **está tan ~**
he's aged so much, he looks so old **(b)** ⟨cuero/
madera⟩ distressed

envenenamiento m poisoning

envenenar [A1] vt to poison

■ **envenenarse** v pron (involuntariamente) to be
poisoned; (voluntariamente) to poison oneself

envergadura f (importancia) magnitude (frml),
importance; **de cierta ~** of some importance

enviado -da m,f (Pol) envoy; (Period) reporter,
correspondent

enviar [A17] vt **(a)** ⟨carta/paquete⟩ to send;
⟨pedido/mercancías⟩ to send, dispatch **(b)**
⟨persona⟩ to send; **me envió por pan** she sent me
out for bread

enviciarse [A1] v pron to become addicted,
get hooked (colloq); **~ CON algo** to become
addicted TO sth (colloq) hooked ON sth

envidia f envy, jealousy; **le da ~ que yo vaya**
he's envious o jealous because I'm going; **le
tienes ~** you are jealous of him; **me muero de ~**
I'm green with envy; **¡qué ~!** I'm so jealous!

envidiable adj enviable

envidiar [A1] vt to envy; **~le algo A algn** to
envy sb sth

envidioso -sa adj envious

envío m ⟨1⟩ (acción): **el ~ de los fondos** the
remittance o sending of the money; **fecha de ~**
date of dispatch, date sent; **~ contra reembolso**
COD, cash on delivery ⟨2⟩ (partida — de mercancías)
consignment, shipment; (— de dinero) remittance

enviudar [A1] vi to be widowed

envoltorio m **(a)** (de paquete, regalo) wrapping;
(de caramelo) wrapper **(b)** (bulto) bundle

envolver [E11] vt ⟨1⟩ ⟨paquete/regalo⟩ to wrap
(up); **¿me lo puede ~ para regalo?** could you gift
wrap it?; **~ algo/a algn EN algo** to wrap sth/sb
(up) IN sth ⟨2⟩ (rodear) «membrana/capa» to
surround; «humo/tristeza» to envelop
⟨3⟩ (involucrar) to involve

■ **envolverse** v pron **(a)** (refl) (en manta) to wrap
oneself (up) **(b)** (en delito, asunto) to become
involved

envuelto -ta adj ⟨1⟩ ⟨paquete/regalo⟩ wrapped;
~ para regalo gift-wrapped ⟨2⟩ (rodeado) **~ EN
algo** ⟨en humo/niebla⟩ enveloped IN sth; ⟨en
misterio⟩ cloaked o shrouded IN sth; ⟨en una
manta⟩ wrapped (up) IN sth ⟨3⟩ (involucrado) **~ EN
algo** involved IN sth

enyesar [A1] vt **(a)** (Const) to plaster **(b)**
⟨brazo/pierna⟩ to put ... in a plaster cast, put ...
in plaster (BrE)

enzarzarse [A4] v pron **~ EN algo** to get
involved IN sth

eñe f: name of the letter ñ

épica f **(a)** (género) epic poetry **(b)** (poema) epic

epicentro m epicenter*

épico -ca adj epic

epidemia f epidemic

epilepsia f epilepsy

epiléptico -ca adj/m,f epileptic

epílogo m (Lit) epilogue; (de suceso) conclusion

episodio m (Cin, Rad, TV) episode; (suceso)
episode, incident

epístola f (frml o hum) epistle (frml or hum)

epitafio m epitaph

época f **(a)** (período de tiempo) time, period; **en la
~ de Franco** in Franco's time; **la ~ de los Tudor**
the Tudor period; **muebles de ~** period furniture;
en aquella ~ in those days o at that time; **esa ~
de mi vida** that period of my life; **es música de mi
~** it's music from my time **(b)** (parte del año) time
of year; **la ~ de lluvias** the rainy season

epopeya f **(a)** (Lit) (poema) epic, epic poem **(b)**
(empresa difícil): **el viaje fue toda una ~** the journey
turned out to be a real ordeal

equilátero -ra adj equilateral

equilibrado -da adj ⟨persona/dieta⟩
well-balanced, balanced; ⟨lucha/partido⟩ close

equilibrar [A1] vt ⟨peso/carga/ruedas⟩ to
balance; **~ las diferencias económicas** to redress
economic imbalances

■ **equilibrarse** v pron «fuerzas» to even up;
«balanza de pagos» to be restored; «platillos de
la balanza» to balance out

equilibrio m (de fuerzas, estabilidad) balance;
perdió el ~ he lost his balance; **en estado de ~**
in equilibrium

equilibrista mf (Espec) tightrope walker

equinoccio m equinox; **~ de primavera/de
otoño** vernal/autumnal equinox

equipaje m baggage (esp AmE), luggage (BrE);
facturar el ~ to check in one's baggage o luggage;
~ de mano hand baggage o luggage; **viaja con
poco ~** he travels light

equipar [A1] vt **(a)** ⟨persona⟩ to equip, fit ...
out; **~ a algn CON or DE algo** to equip sb WITH sth
(b) ⟨casa⟩ to furnish; ⟨local/barco⟩ to fit out; (de
víveres) to provision; **una cocina bien equipada** a
well-equipped kitchen

equiparable adj comparable

equiparar [A1] vt **(a)** (poner al mismo nivel) **~
algo/a algn A or CON algo/algn** to put sth/sb on a
level with sth/sb **(b)** (comparar) **~ algo CON algo**
to compare sth TO o WITH sth

equipo m ⟨1⟩ (de trabajadores, jugadores) team; **el ~
local/visitante** the home/visiting team; **trabajo de
~** team work; **trabajar en ~** to work as a team;
~ de filmación film crew ⟨2⟩ (de materiales,
utensilios) equipment; **~ de pesca** fishing tackle;
~ de gimnasia gym kit; **~ de alta fidelidad** hi-fi
system

equis f: name of the letter x

equitación f riding, horseback riding (AmE),
horse riding (BrE); **practica (la) ~** he rides

equitativo -va adj ⟨persona⟩ fair; ⟨reparto⟩
equitable

equivalente adj equivalent; **~ A algo**
equivalent TO sth

■ m equivalent; **~ A or DE algo** equivalent OF sth

equivaler [E28] vi **~ A algo** to be equivalent

TO sth; **¿a cuánto equivalen mil euros en libras?** how much is a thousand euros equivalent to *o* worth in pounds?

equivocación *f* mistake; **por ~** by mistake, in error (fml)

equivocado -da *adj* **(a)** ⟨*dato/número/ respuesta*⟩ wrong **(b)** [ESTAR] ⟨*persona*⟩ mistaken, wrong

equivocar [A2] *vt* ⟨*persona*⟩ to make ... make a mistake, to make ... go wrong

■ **equivocarse** *v pron* (cometer un error) to make a mistake, (estar en un error) to be wrong *o* mistaken; **me equivoqué con él** I was wrong about him; **me equivoqué de autobús** I took the wrong bus; **no te equivoques de fecha** don't get the date wrong; **se equivocó de camino** he went the wrong way

era *f* (período, época) era, age

era, éramos, etc ▶ SER

eras ▶ SER

erección *f* erection

erecto -ta *adj* erect

eres ▶ SER

erguido -da *adj* upright

erguir [I26] *vt* (liter) ⟨*cabeza*⟩ to raise, lift; ⟨*cuello*⟩ to straighten

■ **erguirse** *v pron* (liter) «*persona*» to stand up; «*edificio/torre*» to rise

erigir [I7] *vt* **(a)** (fml) ⟨*edificio*⟩ to build, erect (fml); ⟨*monumento*⟩ to erect (fml), to raise (fml) **(b)** (fml) (convertir, elevar) **~ algo/a algn EN algo** to set sth/sb up AS sth

■ **erigirse** *v pron* (llegar a ser) **~se EN algo** to become sth; (atribuirse funciones de) to set oneself up AS sth

erizado -da *adj* (de punta): **tenía el pelo ~** her hair was standing on end

erizar [A4] *vt* ⟨*pelo/vello*⟩ to make ... stand on end

■ **erizarse** *v pron* ⟨*pelo*⟩ to stand on end

erizo *m* hedgehog; **~ de mar** sea urchin

ermita *f* chapel

ermitaño -ña *m,f* (asceta) hermit

erosión *f* erosion

erosionar [A1] *vt* to erode

■ **erosionarse** *v pron* to be/become eroded

erótico -ca *adj* erotic

erotismo *m* eroticism

erradicar [A2] *vt* (fml) to eradicate

errado -da *adj* ⨮1⨯ (desacertado): **cinco tiros ~s** five misses ⨮2⨯ (esp AmL) **(a)** [ESTAR] ⟨*persona*⟩ mistaken, wrong; **están muy ~s en estos cálculos** they're way off the mark with these calculations **(b)** [SER] ⟨*decisión*⟩ wrong; ⟨*política*⟩ misguided

errante *adj* **(a)** ⟨*persona*⟩ wandering (*before n*), roaming (*before n*); ⟨*pueblo*⟩ wandering (*before n*) **(b)** ⟨*mirada*⟩ faraway, distant; **una vida ~** a nomadic existence

errar [A26] *vt* ⟨*tiro/golpe*⟩ to miss; **erró su vocación** she chose the wrong vocation/career

■ **~** *vi* «*tirador*» to miss; **erró en su decisión** he made the wrong decision

errata *f* (error de imprenta) misprint, printer's error; (error de mecanografía) typing error

erre *f*: name of the letter r

erróneo -nea *adj* (fml) ⟨*decisión/afirmación*⟩ wrong, erroneous (fml)

error *m* mistake; **cometer un ~** to make a mistake *o* an error; **~ de ortografía** spelling mistake; **~ de cálculo** miscalculation; **~ de imprenta** misprint, printer's error; **por ~** by mistake, in error (fml)

eructar [A1] *vi* to belch, burp (colloq)

eructo *m* belch, burp (colloq)

erudición *f* erudition (fml), learning

erudito -ta *adj* ⟨*lenguaje/obra*⟩ erudite; ⟨*persona*⟩ learned, knowledgeable; **~ EN algo** learned IN sth, knowledgeable ABOUT sth

■ *m,f* scholar

erupción *f* **(a)** (de volcán) eruption; **el volcán entró en ~** the volcano erupted **(b)** (en la piel) rash, eruption (fml)

es ▶ SER

esbelto -ta *adj* slender

esbozar [A4] *vt* **(a)** ⟨*figura*⟩ to sketch **(b)** ⟨*idea/tema*⟩ to outline

esbozo *m* **(a)** (Art) sketch **(b)** (de proyecto) outline, rough draft

escabeche *m* pickling brine (*made with oil, vinegar, peppercorns and bay leaves*)

escabroso -sa *adj* **(a)** ⟨*terreno*⟩ rugged, rough **(b)** ⟨*asunto/problema/tema*⟩ thorny, tricky; ⟨*escena/relato*⟩ shocking

escabullirse [I9] *v pron* (escaparse) to slip away; **logró ~ entre la multitud** he managed to slip away into the crowd; **no puedes escabullirte de tus responsabilidades** you can't get away from your responsibilities

escafandra *f* diving suit

escala *f* ⨮1⨯ (en general) scale; **~ centígrada/ Fahrenheit** centigrade *o* Celsius/Fahrenheit scale; **~ de valores** set of values; **~ musical** (musical) scale; **la ~ social** the social scale; **hecho a ~** done to scale; **a gran ~** on a large scale ⨮2⨯ (Aviac, Náut) stopover; **hicimos ~ en Roma** we stopped over in Rome

escalada *f* ⨮1⨯ (Dep) (de montaña) climb, ascent ⨮2⨯ (aumento, subida): **una ~ de la violencia** an escalation of violence; **la ~ de los precios** the increase *o* escalation in prices

escalador -dora *m,f* (de montañas) mountaineer, climber; (de rocas) rock-climber; (en ciclismo) climber, mountain rider

escalafón *m* scale; **subir un puesto en el ~** to go up one step on the promotion ladder

escalar [A1] *vt* ⟨*montaña/pared*⟩ to climb, scale; (en jerarquía, clasificación) to climb (up)

■ **~** *vi* (Dep) to climb, go climbing

escaldar [A1] *vt* **(a)** ⟨*acelgas/tomates*⟩ to blanch, scald **(b)** ⟨*manos/persona*⟩ to scald

■ **escaldarse** *v pron* **(a)** (con agua, vapor) to scald oneself **(b)** «*bebé*» to get diaper (AmE) *o* (BrE) nappy rash

escalera *f* ⨮1⨯ (de edificio) stairs (*pl*), staircase; **bajó las ~s** he came downstairs *o* down the stairs; **el hueco de la ~** the stairwell; **~ (de) caracol** spiral staircase; **~ mecánica** escalator ⨮2⨯ (portátil) *tb* **~ de mano** ladder; (de tijera) stepladder ⨮3⨯ (en naipes) run; (juego de tablero) snakes and ladders

escalfar [A1] *vt* to poach

escalinata *f* staircase, steps (*pl*)

escalofriante *adj* ⟨crimen/escena⟩ horrifying; ⟨cifra⟩ staggering, incredible

escalofrío *m* shiver; **me da ～s** it makes me shiver *o* shudder; **tiene ～s** she's shivering

escalón *m* (peldaño) step; (travesaño) rung

escalonar [A1] *vt* ⟨pagos/vacaciones⟩ to stagger; ⟨terreno⟩ to terrace

escalope *m* escalope

escama *f* (a) (Zool) scale (b) (en la piel) flake

escamotear [A1] *vt* (a) (ocultar) ⟨naipe⟩ to palm; ⟨informe⟩ to keep ... secret; **nos escamoteaban la información** they were keeping the information (secret) from us (b) (robar) to swipe

escampar [A1] *v impers* to stop raining, to clear up
■ ～ *vi* (Col) to shelter

escanciar [A1] *vt* (frml) ⟨vino⟩ to serve; ⟨sidra⟩ to pour (*from a height*)

escandalizar [A4] *vt/vi* to shock
■ **escandalizarse** *v pron* to be shocked

escándalo *m* **1** (hecho, asunto chocante) scandal; **¡qué ～! ¡qué manera de vestir!** what a shocking *o* an outrageous way to dress!
2 (alboroto, jaleo) fuss; **tanto ～ para nada** all this fuss over nothing; **cuando lo sepa va a armar un ～** when she finds out she'll kick up a fuss; **no armen tanto ～** don't make such a racket *o* row (colloq); **nada de ～s dentro del local** we don't want any trouble in here

escandaloso -sa *adj* (a) ⟨conducta⟩ shocking, scandalous; ⟨ropa⟩ outrageous; ⟨película⟩ shocking; ⟨vida⟩ scandalous (b) (ruidoso) ⟨persona/griterío⟩ noisy; ⟨risa⟩ loud, uproarious

Escandinavia *f* Scandinavia

escandinavo -va *adj/m,f* Scandinavian

escaño *m* (Esp) (Pol) (cargo, asiento) seat; (banco) bench

escapada *f* (a) (huida) breakout, escape (b) (de un peligro) escape (c) (en ciclismo) breakaway

escapar [A1] *vi* **1** to escape; **～ DE algo** ⟨de cárcel/rutina/peligro⟩ to escape FROM sth; ⟨de castigo/muerte⟩ to escape sth
2 **dejar escapar** ⟨carcajada/suspiro⟩ to let out, give; ⟨oportunidad⟩ to pass up; ⟨persona/animal⟩ to let ... get away
■ **escaparse** *v pron* **1** «prisionero» to escape; «animal/niño» to run away; **～se DE algo** ⟨de cárcel/jaula⟩ to escape FROM sth; ⟨de situación/castigo⟩ to escape sth; **～se DE algn** ⟨de policía/perseguidor⟩ to escape (FROM) sth; **～se de casa** to run away from home; **se me escapó el perro** the dog got away from me
2 (+ *me/te/le etc*) (a) (involuntariamente): **se le escapó un grito** he cried out, he let out a cry (b) (pasar inadvertido): **no se le escapa nada** he doesn't miss anything; **se me escapó ese detalle** that detail escaped my notice
3 «gas/aire/agua» to leak

escaparate *m* (a) (esp Esp) (de tienda) shop window; (b) (Col) (vitrina) display cabinet; (aparador) sideboard (c) (Ven) (armario) wardrobe

escapatoria *f* (salida, solución) way out

escape *m* (a) (fuga) escape (b) (de gas, fluido) leak (c) (Auto) exhaust

escapismo *m* escapism

escarabajo *m* beetle

escaramuza *f* (Mil) skirmish; (Dep) scrimmage

escarbadientes *m* (*pl* ～) toothpick

escarbar [A1] *vi* (a) (en la tierra — haciendo un hoyo) to dig; (— superficialmente) to scrabble *o* scratch around (b) (buscando algo) **～ EN algo** ⟨en cajón/armario⟩ to rummage (about *o* around) IN sth; **perros escarbando en la basura** dogs rummaging through the garbage
■ ～ *vt*: **～ la tierra** (hacer un hoyo) to dig a hole; (superficialmente) to scratch around in the soil
■ **escarbarse** *v pron* (refl) ⟨nariz/dientes⟩ to pick

escarcha *f* frost

escarchar [A1] *vt* to crystallize

escarlata *adj inv/m* scarlet

escarlatina *f* scarlet fever, scarlatina

escarmentar [A5] *vi* to learn one's lesson; **¡para que escarmientes!** that'll teach you!; **no escarmienta** she never learns
■ ～ *vt* to teach ... a lesson

escarmiento *m* lesson; **habrá que darle un buen ～** he needs to be taught a good lesson

escarola *f* escarole, endive (BrE)

escarpado -da *adj* ⟨montaña/terreno⟩ precipitous; ⟨pared/acantilado⟩ sheer, steep

escarpín *m* (AmL) (calcetín — de bebé) bootee; (— de adulto) bed sock

escasear [A1] *vi*: **empiezan a ～ los alimentos** food is running short; **va a ～ el café** there's going to be a coffee shortage

escasez *f* shortage; **hubo ～ de agua** there was a water shortage; **por ～ de medios** owing to a lack of resources

escaso -sa *adj* (a) ⟨recursos económicos⟩ limited, scant; ⟨posibilidades⟩ slim, slender; ⟨visibilidad⟩ poor; ⟨conocimientos/experiencia⟩ limited (b) [ESTAR] (falto): **～ DE algo** ⟨de dinero/tiempo⟩ short OF sth

escatimar [A1] *vt* ⟨comida/tela⟩ to skimp on, be sparing with; **no ～on esfuerzos** they spared no effort

escayola *f* (Esp) (material) plaster; (Med) plaster cast

escayolar [A1] *vt* (Esp) to put ... in a (plaster) cast, to put ... in plaster (BrE)

escena *f* **1** (a) (de obra) scene; **la ～ del duelo** the duel scene (b) (sin art) (escenario): **poner en ～** to stage; **entrar en ～** to come/go on stage **2** **la ～ del accidente** (period) the scene of the accident; **no me hagas una ～** there's no need to make a scene

escenario *m* (Teatr) stage

escenografía *f* (decorado) scenery; (arte) scenography, set design

escenógrafo -fa *m,f* scenographer, set designer

escepticismo *m* skepticism*

escéptico -ca *adj* skeptical*
■ *m,f* skeptic*

esclarecer [E3] *vt* ⟨situación/hechos⟩ to clarify, elucidate (frml); ⟨crimen/misterio⟩ to clear up

esclavitud *f* slavery

esclavizar [A4] *vt* to enslave; **está esclavizado por el trabajo** he's a slave to his work

esclavo -va *m,f* slave; **es un ~ del trabajo** he is a slave to his work

esclerosis *f* sclerosis; **~ múltiple** multiple sclerosis

esclusa *f* (de canal) lock; (de presa) floodgate

escoba *f* (para barrer) broom; (de bruja) broomstick

escobilla *f* **(a)** (de motor) brush **(b)** (del limpiaparabrisas) wiper-blade, blade **(c)** (del inodoro) toilet brush

escocedura *f* irritation; (de bebé) diaper rash (AmE), nappy rash (BrE)

escocer [E10] *vi* «*herida/ojos*» to sting, smart

escocés -cesa *adj* **(a)** (*ciudad/persona*) Scottish; (*dialecto*) Scots **(b)** (*whisky*) Scotch; (*tela/manta*) tartan
■ *m,f* *(m)* Scotsman, Scot; *(f)* Scotswoman, Scot

Escocia *f* Scotland

escocido -da *adj* (*cuello/axila*) sore, chafed; **tiene las nalgas escocidas** he has diaper rash (AmE) *o* (BrE) nappy rash

escoger [E6] *vt* to choose; **escoge que quieras** pick *o* choose whichever (one) you want; **no hay mucho (de) donde ~** there isn't a great deal of choice, there isn't much to choose from

escogido -da *adj* **(a)** (selecto) (*mercancía*) choice; (*clientela*) select **(b)** (Méx fam) (manoseado) picked over

escolar *adj* school (*before n*)
■ *m,f* *(m)* schoolboy, schoolchild; *(f)* schoolgirl, schoolchild

escolaridad *f* education, schooling

escolarizar [A4] *vt* to educate, provide schooling for; **niños sin ~** children without any (formal) education *o* schooling

escoleta *f* (Méx) **(a)** (banda) band (*of amateur musicians*) **(b)** (ensayo) rehearsal

escollo *m* (Náut) reef; (dificultad) obstacle, hurdle

escolta *mf* (persona) escort; (en baloncesto) guard
■ *f* (grupo) escort

escoltar [A1] *vt* to escort

escombros *mpl* rubble

esconder [E1] *vt* to hide, conceal (frml)
■ **esconderse** *v pron* **1** (*refl*) «*persona*» to hide; **~se DE algn** to hide FROM sb **2** (estar oculto) to hide, lie hidden

escondidas *fpl* **1** (AmE) (Juego): **jugar a las ~** to play hide-and-seek **2** **a escondidas** in secret, secretly; **hacer algo a ~ de algn** to do sth behind sb's back

escondido -da *adj* **(a)** (oculto) hidden **(b)** (lejano) remote

escondite *m* **(a)** (para personas) hideout; (para cosas) hiding place **(b)** (Juego): **jugar al ~** to play hide-and-seek

escondrijo *m* hidden place, recess (liter)

escopeta *f* shotgun

escoria *f* (de fundición) slag; **la ~ de la sociedad** the dregs of society

Escorpio *m* (signo) Scorpio; **es (de) ~** he's a Scorpio
■ *mf* (*pl* **~** *or* **-pios**) (persona) *tb* **escorpio** Scorpio

escorpión *m* scorpion

escotado -da *adj* **(a)** (*blusa/vestido*) low-cut; **~ por detrás** cut low at the back **(b)** (RPl) (*zapato*) strapless

escote *m* (Indum) neck, neckline; (profundo) low-cut neck *o* neckline; **~ redondo** round neck; (en suéters) crew neck; **~ en pico** V neck; *pagar a ~* (Esp fam) to go Dutch

escotilla *f* hatch, hatchway

escozor *m* **(a)** (Med) stinging, burning sensation **(b)** (resentimiento, amargura) bitterness

escribanía *f* (RPl) (Der) (oficina) notary's office; (profesión): **ejerce la ~** he is a practicing notary (public)

escribano -na *m,f* **(a)** (Hist) (amanuense) scribe **(b)** (RPl) (notario) notary (public)

escribiente *mf* clerk

escribir [I34] *vt* **1** **(a)** (anotar) to write; **escríbelo aquí** write it down here **(b)** (ser autor de) (*libro/canción/carta*) to write
2 (ortográficamente) to write; **la escribió sin acento** she wrote it without an accent; **no sé cómo se escribe** I don't know how you spell it; **se escribe sin acento** it's written without an accent
■ **~** *vi* to write; **nunca le escribe** she never writes him (AmE) *o* (BrE) writes to him; **~ a máquina** to type
■ **escribirse** *v pron* (*recípr*): **me escribo con ella** we write to each other; **se escribe con un peruano** she has a Peruvian penfriend *o* penpal

escrito[1] -ta *adj* (*examen*) written; **por ~** in writing

escrito[2] *m* (documento) document

escritor -tora *m,f* writer, author

escritorio *m* **(a)** (mueble) desk **(b)** (AmL) (oficina, despacho) office; (en casa particular) study; **~ público** (en Méx) *office or stall offering letter writing, form-filling or typing services*

escritura *f* **1** (sistema de signos) writing; (letra) writing, handwriting **2** (Der) (documento) deed; **la ~ de la casa** the deeds *o* of the house

escrúpulo *m* scruple

escrupuloso -sa *adj* **(a)** (honrado) honest, scrupulous **(b)** (meticuloso) meticulous **(c)** (Esp) (aprensivo) fastidious

escrutinio *m* **(a)** (Pol) count; **los resultados del ~** the results of the ballot **(b)** (inspección) scrutiny

escuadra *f* **1** (instrumento — triangular) set square; (— de carpintero) square **2** (en el ejército) squad; (en la marina) squadron

escuadrón *m* **(a)** (Aviac) squadron **(b)** (de caballería) squadron; (más pequeño) troop

escuálido -da *adj* (*persona/animal*) skinny, scrawny

escuchar [A1] *vt* **(a)** (prestar atención) (*música/persona*) to listen to **(b)** (esp AmL) (oír) to hear
■ **~** *vi* to listen

escudarse [A1] *v pron*: **quiso ~ en su inmunidad diplomática** he tried to hide behind his diplomatic immunity

escudero *m* (Hist, Mil) squire

escudilla *f* bowl

escudo *m* **(a)** (Hist, Mil) shield **(b)** (emblema) *tb* **~ de armas** coat of arms **(c)** (en la solapa, etc) badge

escudriñar [A1] *vt* **(a)** (liter) (mirar intensamente) ··· ·❖

⟨*horizonte*⟩ to scan **(b)** (examinar) ⟨*persona*⟩ to scrutinize, examine; ⟨*casa/habitación*⟩ to search ... thoroughly

escuela *f* school; ~ **de conductores** *or* **choferes** (AmL) driving school; ~ **primaria** primary school; ~ **militar/naval** military/naval academy; ~ **pública** public (AmE) *o* (BrE) state school; E~ **de Medicina** Medical Faculty *o* School

escueto -ta *adj* ⟨*explicación*⟩ succinct; ⟨*lenguaje/estilo*⟩ concise, plain; **fue muy** ~ he was very succinct

escuincle -cla *m,f* (Méx fam) kid (colloq)

esculcar [A2] *vt* (AmC, Col, Méx, Ven) ⟨*cajones/papeles*⟩ to go through; ⟨*persona/casa*⟩ to search

esculpir [I1] *vt* ⟨*estatua/busto*⟩ to sculpt, sculpture; ⟨*inscripción*⟩ to engrave, carve
■ ~ *vi* to sculpt, sculpture

escultor -tora *m,f* sculptor

escultura *f* sculpture; ~ **en madera** wood carving

escupida *f* (RPl) gob (of spit) (colloq)

escupir [I1] *vi* to spit; ~**le A algn** to spit AT sb; **le escupió en la cara** he spat in her face
■ ~ *vt* **(a)** ⟨*comida*⟩ to spit out; ⟨*sangre*⟩ to spit, cough up **(b)** ⟨*llamas/lava*⟩ to belch out

escupitajo *m* gob (of spit) (colloq)

escupo *m* (Chi, Ven) gob (of spit) (colloq)

escurreplatos *m* (*pl* ~) (mueble) *cupboard with built-in plate rack*; (rejilla) plate rack

escurridizo -za *adj* ⟨*piel/jabón*⟩ slippery; ⟨*persona/respuesta*⟩ evasive; ⟨*idea/concepto*⟩ elusive

escurrir [I1] *vt* ⟨*ropa*⟩ to wring out, wring; ⟨*verduras/pasta*⟩ to strain, drain; ⟨*líquido*⟩ to drain (off)
■ ~ *vi* to drain; **dejar** ~ ⟨*platos*⟩ to leave ... to drain; ⟨*camisa*⟩ to leave ... to drip-dry
■ **escurrirse** *v pron* **1** **(a)** «*líquido*»: **cuelga la camisa para que se escurra el agua** hang the shirt out to drip-dry **(b)** ⟨*verduras/vajilla*⟩ to drain **2** **(a)** (fam) (escaparse, escabullirse) to slip away; ~**se DE algo** to wriggle *o* get out OF sth **(b)** (resbalarse, deslizarse) to slip

escúter *m* scooter

esdrújula *f* word with the stress on the antepenultimate syllable

ese¹ *f*: name of the letter s

ese², esa *adj dem* (*pl* **esos, esas**) that; (*pl*) those; **en** ~ **país/esos países** in that country/those countries

ése, ésa *pron dem* (*pl* **ésos, ésas**) [*The written accent may be omitted when there is no confusion with the adjective*] **(a)** that one; (*pl*) those; ~ *or* **ese es el tuyo** that (one) is yours; **prefiero ésos** *or* **esos** I prefer those (ones); [*usually indicates disapproval when used to refer to a person*] **ésa** *or* **esa no sabe lo que dice** (fam) she doesn't know what she's talking about **(b)** **ésas** (fam) (esas cosas, esos asuntos): **¡conque ésas** *or* **esas tenemos!** so that's it!; **¡no me vengas con ésas** *or* **esas!** don't give me that! (colloq)

esencia *f* essence

esencial *adj* (fundamental) essential; **coincidimos en lo** ~ we agree on the essentials *o* on the main points; **lo** ~ **es** ... the main *o* the most important thing is ...

esfera *f* **(a)** (Astron, Mat) sphere **(b)** (de reloj) face **(c)** (ámbito) sphere; **en las altas** ~**s de la política** in the highest political circles

esférico -ca *adj* spherical

esfero *m* (Col fam) ballpoint pen, biro® (BrE)

esfinge *f* sphinx

esforzar [A11] *vt* ⟨*voz/vista*⟩ to strain
■ **esforzarse** *v pron*: **se esforzó mucho** he tried very hard, he put in a lot of effort; **tienes que** ~**te más** you'll have to work harder; ~**se POR** *o* **EN hacer algo** to strive to do sth

esfuerzo *m* effort; **hizo el** ~ **de ser amable** he made an effort *o* tried to be friendly

esfumarse [A1] *v pron* **(a)** «*ilusiones/sueños*» to evaporate; «*temores*» to melt away, be dispelled **(b)** (fam) «*persona/dinero*» to vanish, disappear

esgrima *f* fencing

esgrimista *mf* fencer

esguince *m* sprain; **sufrió un** ~ **en el tobillo** he sprained his ankle

eslabón *m* link

eslálom (*pl* **-loms**), **eslalon** *m* slalom

eslavo -va *adj* Slavic, Slavonic
■ *m,f* Slav

eslogan *m* (*pl* **-lóganes**) slogan

eslovaco¹ -ca *adj* Slovakian
■ *m,f* Slovak

eslovaco² *m* (idioma) Slovak

Eslovaquia *f* Slovakia

esmaltar [A1] *vt* ⟨*metal*⟩ to enamel; ⟨*cerámica*⟩ to glaze

esmalte *m* **(a)** (capa — sobre metales) enamel; (— sobre cerámica) glaze; ~ **de** *or* **para uñas** nail polish *o* (BrE) varnish **(b)** (Odont) enamel **(c)** (Art) enamel

esmerado -da *adj* ⟨*persona*⟩ conscientious, painstaking; ⟨*presentación*⟩ careful, painstaking; ⟨*trabajo*⟩ carefully done

esmeralda *f* emerald

esmerarse [A1] *v pron* to go to a lot of trouble; **se esmera en hacerlo bien** she goes to great pains to do it properly

esmero *m* care

esmirriado -da *adj* (fam) ⟨*persona*⟩ skinny (colloq), scrawny (colloq); ⟨*animal*⟩ scrawny

esmog *m* smog

esmoquin *m* (*pl* **-móquines**) tuxedo (AmE), dinner jacket (BrE)

esnifar [A1] *vt* ⟨*cocaína*⟩ (arg) to snort (sl); ⟨*pegamento*⟩ to sniff (colloq)

esnob *adj* (*pl* **-nobs**) snobbish
■ *mf* (*pl* **-nobs**) snob

esnobismo *m* snobbery, snobbishness

eso *pron dem* **(a)** (*neutro*) that; **no digas ~** don't say that; **~ que te contaron** what they told you **(b)** (*en locs*) **a eso de** (at) around *o* about; **en eso: en ~ llegó su madre** (just) at that moment her mother arrived; **¡eso es!** that's it!; **y eso que ...** even though ...; **por ~** that's why **(c)** **¡eso!** (*interj*) exactly!

esófago *m* esophagus*

esos, esas *pron dem*: ▶ ESE²

ésos, ésas *adj dem*: ▶ ÉSE

espabilado -da *adj* **(a)** (*despierto*) awake **(b)** (*vivo, listo*) bright, smart; **tienes que ser más ~** you have to keep more on the ball
■ *m,f*: **los ~s de la clase** the smart ones of the class

espabilar [A1] *vt* **(a)** (*quitar el sueño*) to wake ... up **(b)** (*avivar*) to wise ... up (*colloq*)
■ *~ vi* **(a)** (*sacudirse el sueño*) to wake up **(b)** (*darse prisa*) to get a move on (*colloq*) **(c)** (*avivarse*) to wise up (*colloq*)
■ **espabilarse** *v pron* **(a)** (*sacudirse el sueño*) to wake (oneself) up **(b)** (*darse prisa*) to get a move on (*colloq*) **(c)** (*avivarse*) to wise up (*colloq*)

espaciado -da *adj* **(a)** (*en el espacio*): **los árboles están muy ~s** the trees are too far apart **(b)** (*en el tiempo*): **sus visitas se hicieron más espaciadas** her visits became more infrequent

espacial *adj* **(a)** (*cohete/vuelo*) space (*before n*) **(b)** (*Fís, Mat*) spatial

espacio *m* **1** **(a)** (*amplitud*) space, room; **ocupan demasiado ~** they take up too much space *o* room **(b)** (*entre líneas, palabras*) space; (*entre objetos*) space, gap; **rellenar los ~s en blanco** fill in the blank spaces *o* the blanks **(c)** (*recinto, área*) area **2** (Espac): **el ~** space; **~ aéreo** airspace **3** (*de tiempo*): **un corto ~ de tiempo** a short space of time; **por ~ de 24 horas** for 24 hours *o* for a period of 24 hours **4** **(a)** (Rad, TV) (*programa*) program*; **~ publicitario** advertising slot **(b)** (*en periódico, revista*) space

espacioso -sa *adj* spacious

espada *f* **1** (*arma*) sword **2** **(a)** (*carta*) *any card of the* ESPADAS *suit* **(b)** **espadas** *fpl* (*palo*) *one of the suits in a Spanish pack of cards*

espagetis, espaguettis *mpl* spaghetti

espalda *f* back; **ancho de ~s** broad-shouldered; **perdona, te estoy dando la ~** sorry, I've got my back to you; **de ~s a nosotros** with his/her back to us; **vuélvete de ~s** turn around *o* (BrE) round; **los 100 metros ~** the 100 meters backstroke; **tenderse de ~s** to lie on one's back; **lo atacaron por la ~** he was attacked from behind; **hacer algo a ~s de algn** to do sth behind sb's back

espantado -da *adj* **(a)** (*asustado*) frightened, scared; **salieron ~s** they ran off in fright **(b)** (*horrorizado*) horrified, appalled

espantapájaros *m* (*pl ~*) scarecrow

espantar [A1] *vt* **1** **(a)** (*ahuyentar*) (*peces/pájaros*) to frighten away **(b)** (*asustar*) (*caballo*) to frighten, scare **2** (*fam*) (*horrorizar*) to horrify, appall*
■ *~ vi* **(a)** (*fam*) (*asustar*): **es tan feo que espanta** he's absolutely hideous (*colloq*) **(b)** (Bol, Col, Ven fam) (*fantasma*): **en esa casa espantan** that house is haunted

espantarse *v pron* «*pájaro/peces*» to get frightened away; «*caballo*» to take fright, be startled

espanto *m* **1** **(a)** (*miedo*) fright, horror **(b)** (*uso hiperbólico*): **la noticia nos llenó de ~** we were horrified *o* appalled at the news; **hace un frío de ~** (*fam*) it's freezing *o* terribly cold (*colloq*); **ya está curada de ~** (*fam*) she's seen/heard it all before **2** (Bol, Col, Ven fam) (*espíritu*) ghost, spook (*colloq*)

espantoso -sa *adj* **(a)** (*escena/crimen*) horrific, appalling **(b)** (*fam*) (*uso hiperbólico*) (*comida/letra/tiempo*) atrocious; (*vestido/color*) hideous; (*ruido/voz*) terrible, awful; **pasé un frío ~** I was absolutely freezing (*colloq*)

España *f* Spain

español¹ -ñola *adj* Spanish
■ *m,f* (*persona*) (*m*) Spaniard, Spanish man; (*f*) Spaniard, Spanish woman; **los ~es** the Spanish, Spaniards, Spanish people

español² *m* (*idioma*) Spanish

esparadrapo *m* surgical tape

esparcir [I4] *vt* **(a)** (*libros/juguetes*) to scatter **(b)** (*rumor*) to spread **(c)** (Chi) (*mantequilla*) to spread
■ **esparcirse** *v pron* **(a)** «*líquido*» to spread; «*papeles/semillas*» to be scattered **(b)** «*noticia/rumor*» to spread

espárrago *m* asparagus; **mandar a algn a freír ~s** (*fam*) to tell sb to get lost (*colloq*)

espasmo *m* spasm

espátula *f* **(a)** (*paleta*) spatula; (Art) palette knife **(b)** (*para quitar pintura, papel*) scraper

especia *f* (*condimento*) spice

especial *adj* **(a)** (*en general*) special; **en ~** especially, particularly; **nadie en ~** nobody in particular; **un día muy ~ para mí** a very special day for me **(b)** (*difícil*) (*persona/carácter*) fussy

especialidad *f* **(a)** (*actividad, estudio*) specialty (AmE), speciality (BrE); **hizo dos años de ~** she did two years' specialization **(b)** (*de restaurante*) specialty (AmE), speciality (BrE)

especialista *adj* specialist (*before n*)
■ *mf* **(a)** (*experto*) specialist, expert **(b)** (Med) specialist; **un ~ de(l) corazón** a heart specialist **(c)** (Cin, TV) (*m*) stuntman; (*f*) stuntwoman

especialización *f* specialization

especializado -da *adj* **(a)** (*librería/restaurante*) specialty (*before n*) (AmE), specialist (*before n*) (BrE); **~ EN algo** specializing IN sth **(b)** (*lenguaje*) technical, specialized **(c)** (*obrero*) skilled, specialized (*before n*)

especializarse [A4] *v pron* to specialize

especie *f* **(a)** (Biol, Bot, Zool) species **(b)** (*clase*) kind, sort

especificar [A2] *vt* to specify

específico -ca *adj* specific

espécimen *m* (*pl* **-pecímenes**) (*ejemplar*) specimen; (*muestra*) sample, specimen

espectacular *adj* spectacular

espectáculo *m* **1** (*representación*) show; **un ~ de variedades** a variety show; **⑤ espectáculos** (*en periódicos*) entertainment guide; **el mundo del ~** showbusiness **2** (*visión, panorama*) sight; **un triste ~** a sad sight *o* spectacle

espectador -dora *m,f* (Dep) spectator; (Espec) ⋯⋗

member of the audience; **asistieron al estreno dos mil ~es** two thousand people attended the premiere

espectro m ⓵ (gama) spectrum ⓶ (fantasma) specter*, ghost; (amenaza) specter*

especulación f speculation

especulador -dora m,f speculator

especular [A1] vi to speculate

espejismo m (fenómeno óptico) mirage; (ilusión) illusion

espejo m mirror; **~ de cuerpo entero** full-length mirror; **~ lateral/retrovisor** wing/rear-view mirror; **mirarse al ~** to look (at oneself) in the mirror; **la obra es ~ de esa sociedad** the play mirrors that society

espeleología f spelunking, potholing (BrE)

espeluznante adj ⟨tragedia/estado/experiencia⟩ horrific, horrifying; ⟨grito⟩ terrifying, blood-curdling

espera f ⓵ (acción, período) wait; **una larga ~ a** long wait; **estoy a la ~ de una oferta concreta** I am waiting for a concrete offer; **en ~ de su respuesta saluda a Vd. atte.** (frml) I look forward to hearing from you, yours faithfully ⓶ (Der) respite

esperado -da adj (a) (aguardado) ⟨acontecimiento/carta⟩ eagerly awaited (b) (que es de esperar): **no obtuvo los resultados ~s** he didn't get the results he expected

esperanza f hope; **mi única ~** my only hope; **puso todas sus ~s en su hijo** he pinned all his hopes on his son; **hay ~s de éxito** there are hopes that he/it/they will succeed; **perdimos toda ~ de encontrarlos vivos** we gave up o lost hope of finding them alive; **fue con la ~ de que ...** he went in the hope that ...; **me dio ~s de que el niño mejoraría** he gave me hope that the child would recover; **~ de vida** life expectancy

esperanzado -da adj hopeful

esperanzador -dora adj encouraging

esperar [A1] vt ⓵ (a) ⟨autobús/persona/acontecimiento⟩ to wait for; **¿qué estás esperando para decírselo?** tell him! what are you waiting for? (b) (recibir) to meet; **la fuimos a ~ al aeropuerto** we went to meet her at the airport (c) ⟨sorpresa⟩ to await; **le espera un futuro difícil** he has a difficult future ahead of him ⓶ (a) (contar con, prever) to expect; **tal como esperábamos** just as we expected; **cuando uno menos lo espera** when you least expect it; **te espero alrededor de las nueve** I'll expect you around nine; **¿esperabas que te felicitara?** did you expect me to congratulate you?; **era de ~ que el proyecto fracasara** the project was bound to fail (b) ⟨niño/bebé⟩ to be expecting ⓷ (con esperanza) to hope; **eso espero** or **espero que sí** I hope so; **espero que no** I hope not; **~ hacer algo** to hope to do sth; **espero que no llueva** I hope it doesn't rain; **esperemos que no sea nada grave** let's hope it's nothing serious

■ **~** vi (a) (aguardar) to wait; **no podemos ~ más** we can't wait any longer; **espera a estar seguro** wait until you're sure; **~on** (a) **que él se fuera para entrar** they waited for him to go before they went in (b) «embarazada»: **estar esperando** to be expecting

■ **esperarse** v pron ⓵ (fam) (aguardar) to hang on (colloq), to hold on (colloq) ⓶ (fam) (prever) to expect; **¡quién se lo iba a ~!** who would have thought it!

esperma m or f (Biol) sperm
■ f (a) (sustancia) spermaceti (b) (Col) (vela) candle

espesar [A1] vt/vi to thicken
■ **espesarse** v pron «salsa» to thicken; «vegetación» to become thick, become dense

espeso -sa adj (a) ⟨salsa⟩ thick; ⟨vegetación/niebla⟩ dense, thick; ⟨nieve⟩ thick, deep; ⟨cabello/barba⟩ bushy, thick (b) (Per fam) (cargoso) annoying

espesor m thickness

espesura f vegetation; **se abrieron paso por entre la ~** they hacked a path through the vegetation

espía adj inv ⟨avión/satélite⟩ spy (before n); ⟨cámara⟩ hidden (before n), secret (before n)
■ mf (persona) spy

espiar [A17] vt ⟨enemigo/movimientos⟩ to spy on, keep watch on
■ **~** vi to spy

espiga f (Agr, Bot) (de trigo) ear, spike; (de flores) spike

espigón m (a) (rompeolas) breakwater (b) (Per, RPl) (en aeropuerto) terminal (building)

espina f (a) (de rosal, zarza) thorn; (de cactus) prickle (b) (de pez) bone (c) (Anat) spine; **~ dorsal** spine, backbone; **darle a algn mala ~** to make sb feel uneasy; **esto me da mala ~** I don't like the look of this

espinaca f spinach

espinazo m spine, backbone

espinilla f ⓵ (Anat) shin ⓶ (en la piel) (a) (de cabeza negra) blackhead (b) (AmL) (barrito) pimple, spot

espino m hawthorn

espinoso -sa adj ⓵ (a) ⟨rosal/zarza⟩ thorny; ⟨cactus⟩ prickly (b) ⟨pescado⟩ bony ⓶ ⟨problema/asunto⟩ thorny, knotty

espionaje m spying, espionage; **novela de ~** spy novel

espiral f (a) (forma, movimiento) spiral; **un cuaderno de ~(es)** a spiral-bound notebook; **escalera de ~** spiral staircase (b) (muelle) hairspring (c) (dispositivo intrauterino) coil

espirar [A1] vi to breathe out, exhale

espiritismo m spiritualism; **sesión de ~** séance

espiritista adj/mf spiritualist

espíritu m (a) (en general) spirit; **un ~ maligno** an evil spirit; **E~ Santo** Holy Ghost o Spirit; **con ~ de sacrificio** in a spirit of self-sacrifice; **el ~ de la ley** the spirit of the law (b) (naturaleza, carácter) nature; **tiene un ~ rebelde** she has a rebellious nature

espiritual adj spiritual
■ m: **tb ~ negro** (Negro) spiritual

espita f spigot (AmE), tap (BrE)

espléndido -da adj (a) ⟨fiesta/comida⟩ splendid, magnificent; ⟨día/tiempo⟩ splendid, marvelous*; ⟨regalo/joya/abrigo⟩ magnificent (b) (generoso) ⟨persona⟩ generous; ⟨regalo⟩ lavish, generous

esplendor *m* (a) (magnificencia) splendor*, magnificence (b) (apogeo) splendor*

espolear [A1] *vt* ‹caballo› to spur (on)

espoleta *f* (Arm) fuse

espolvorear [A1] *vt* to sprinkle

esponja *f* sponge

esponjoso -sa *adj* ‹masa/bizcocho› spongy, fluffy; ‹tejido› soft; ‹lana› fluffy

espontaneidad *f* spontaneity

espontáneo -nea *adj* ‹persona/gesto/ayuda› spontaneous; ‹actuación› impromptu
■ *m,f*: spectator who jumps into the ring to join in the bullfight

esporádico -ca *adj* ‹sucesos/visitas› sporadic, intermittent

esposado -da *adj* handcuffed, in handcuffs

esposas *fpl* handcuffs (*pl*)

esposo -sa *m,f* (*m*) husband; (*f*) wife

espray *m* (*pl* **-prays**) (a) (atomizador) spray (b) (pintura) spray paint

esprint *m* (*pl* **-prints**) sprint

espuela *f* spur

espuelear [A1] *vt* (AmL) to spur (on)

espuma *f* [1] (a) (del mar) foam; (al romper las olas) surf; (en agua revuelta) foam, froth (b) (del jabón) lather; **este jabón no hace ~** this soap doesn't lather; **un baño de ~** a foam *o* bubble bath; **~ de afeitar** shaving foam; **~ seca** carpet shampoo (c) (de la cerveza) head, froth (d) (Coc) (capa) scum [2] (a) (caucho celular) foam rubber (b) (tejido elástico) stretch nylon

espumadera *f* skimmer, slotted spoon

espumante *m* sparkling wine

espumillón *m* tinsel

espumoso¹ -sa *adj* ‹ola› foaming; ‹cerveza› frothy; ‹vino› sparkling

espumoso² *m* sparkling wine

esqueje *m* (para plantar) cutting; (para injertar) scion

esquela *f* (a) (AmL) (carta) note (b) (Andes) (papel) stationery set (c) (Esp) (aviso fúnebre) *tb* ~ **mortuoria** death notice

esqueleto *m* (a) (Anat) skeleton (b) (de edificio, novela) framework

esquema *m* [1] (croquis) sketch, diagram; (sinopsis) outline [2] (de ideas): **el ~ liberal** liberal philosophy *o* thinking; **no se sale de sus ~s** she doesn't change her way of thinking

esquemático -ca *adj* schematic; **el libro es algo ~** the book is a little oversimplified

esquematizar [A4] *vt/vi* to schematize

esquí *m* (*pl* **-quís** *or* **-quíes**) (tabla) ski; (deporte) skiing; **pista de ~** ski run, piste; **~ acuático** *or* **náutico** waterskiing; **hacer ~ acuático** to water-ski

esquiador -dora *m,f* skier

esquiar [A17] *vi* to ski

esquilar [A1] *vt* to shear, clip

esquimal *adj/mf* Eskimo

esquina *f* (a) (en calle) corner; **en la calle Vidal, ~ a (a)** Cádiz on the corner of Vidal (Street) and Cadiz (Street); **doblar la ~** to go round *o* turn the corner; **hace ~ con la plaza** it's on the corner of the square (b) (Dep): **sacar de ~** to take a corner (kick)

esquinazo *m* [1] (Esp): **darle (el) ~ a algn** (dejar plantado) to stand sb up; (esquivar) to give sb the slip [2] (Chi) (serenata) *serenade of traditional singing and dancing*

esquirol *mf* (pey) strikebreaker, scab (pej)

esquivar [A1] *vt* ‹persona/problema/dificultad› to avoid; ‹golpe/pregunta› to dodge, evade; ‹responsabilidad› to avoid, evade

esquivo -va *adj* ‹persona› (difícil de encontrar) elusive; (huraño) aloof, unsociable; (tímido) shy (b) ‹respuesta› elusive, evasive

esquizofrenia *f* schizophrenia

esquizofrénico -ca *adj/m,f* schizophrenic

estabilidad *f* stability

estabilizar [A4] *vt* to stabilize
■ **estabilizarse** *v pron* to stabilize

estable *adj* stable; ‹trabajo› steady

establecer [E3] *vt* [1] (a) ‹colonia/dictadura› to establish; ‹campamento› to set up; **estableció su residencia en Mónaco** he took up residence in Monaco (b) ‹relaciones/contacto› to establish [2] (dejar sentado) (a) ‹criterios/bases› to establish, lay down; ‹precio› to fix, set; ‹precedente› to establish, set (b) (frml) ‹ley/reglamento» (disponer) to state, establish (c) ‹récord/marca/moda› to set; ‹uso› to establish [3] (determinar) to establish
■ **establecerse** *v pron* ‹colono/emigrante» to settle; «comerciante/empresa» to set up

establecimiento *m* establishment

establo *m* stable

estaca *f* (a) (poste) stake, post (b) (para carpa) tent peg (c) (garrote) club, stick (d) (clavo de madera) peg

estación *f* [1] (de tren, metro, autobús) station; **~ de bomberos** (Col, Méx, Ven) fire station; **~ de policía** (Col, Ven) police station; **~ de esquí** ski resort; **~ de servicio** service station, gas (AmE) *o* (BrE) petrol station; **~ terminal** *or* **término** terminal, terminus (BrE) [2] (del año) season [3] (AmL) (emisora) radio station

estacionamiento *m* (a) (acción de estacionar) parking (b) (espacio para estacionar) parking space; (en recinto cerrado) (AmL) parking lot (AmE), car park (BrE)

estacionar [A1] *vt* to park
■ ~ *vi* to park; 🚫 **prohibido estacionar** no parking; **~ en doble fila** to double-park
■ **estacionarse** *v pron* (a) «crecimiento» to stop; «peso» to stabilize; «proceso/enfermedad» to halt (b) (Chi, Méx) «conductor» to park

estadía *f* (AmL) (en un lugar) stay

estadio *m* stadium

estadista *mf* (*m*) statesman; (*f*) stateswoman

estadística *f* (a) (estudio) statistical study (b) (cifra) statistic, figure (c) (disciplina) statistics

estadístico -ca *adj* statistical

estado *m* [1] (a) (en general) state; **~ de ánimo** state of mind; **~ de cuenta** bank statement; **~ de emergencia** *or* **excepción** state of emergency; **la casa está en buen ~** the house is in good condition (b) (Med) condition; **estar en ~** (euf) to be expecting (colloq); **quedarse en ~** (euf) to get pregnant (c) **estado civil** marital status [2] (nación, gobierno) state; **la seguridad del E~** national *o* state security; **~ de bienestar** welfare state

Estados Unidos m: tb los ~ ~ mpl the United States (+ sing or pl vb)

Estados Unidos Mexicanos mpl (frml) United States of Mexico (frml)

estadounidense adj American, US (before n)
■ mf American

estafa f (a) (Der) fraud, criminal deception (b) (fam) (timo) rip-off (colloq), con (colloq)

estafador -dora m.f (a) (Der) fraudster (b) (fam) (timador) swindler (colloq)

estafar [A1] vt (a) (Der) to swindle, defraud; ~le algo A algn to defraud sb OF sth, swindle sb OUT OF sth (b) (fam) (timar) to rip ... off (colloq), to con (colloq)

estafeta f: tb ~ de correos mail office (AmE), sub-post office (BrE)

estallar [A1] vi (a) «bomba» to explode; «neumático» to blow out, burst; «globo» to burst; «vidrio» to shatter; **hizo ~ el dispositivo** he detonated the device (b) «guerra/revuelta» to break out; «tormenta/escándalo/crisis» to break (c) «persona» (ponerse furioso) to blow one's top (colloq); ~ **EN algo** ‹en llanto/carcajadas› to burst INTO sth

estallido m (a) (de bomba) explosion; (de neumático) bursting; (de cristal) shattering (b) (de guerra) outbreak

estamento m (de sociedad) stratum, class

estampado¹ -da adj patterned, printed

estampado² m pattern; **los ~s están de moda** patterned o printed fabrics are in fashion

estampar [A1] vt (imprimir) ‹tela/diseño› to print; ‹metal› to stamp; (formando relieve) to emboss

estampida f stampede; **salir en** or **de ~** to stampede out

estampido m (de pistola) bang, report; (de bomba) bang

estampilla f (a) (AmL) (sello — postal) postage (stamp); (— fiscal) tax stamp (b) (sello de goma) rubber stamp

estampillar [A1] vt (AmL) (con sello fiscal o de correos) to stamp

estancado -da adj ‹agua› stagnant (b) (detenido): **las negociaciones están estancadas** negotiations are at a standstill (c) (con un problema) stuck, bogged down

estancamiento m stagnation

estancarse [A2] v pron (a) «agua» to become stagnant, to stagnate (b) «negociación/proceso» to come to a halt o standstill (c) (con un problema) to get bogged down o stuck

estancia f [1] (frml) (habitación) large room [2] (Esp, Méx) (permanencia) stay [3] (en el CS) (Agr) farm; (de ganado) ranch

estanciero -ra m,f (en el CS) (Agr) farmer; (de ganado) rancher

estanco m (tienda) tobacconist's

estándar adj/m standard

estandarte m standard, banner

estanque m pond

estanquillo m (Méx) general store (AmE), grocer's shop (BrE)

estante m shelf

estantería f shelves (pl); (para libros) bookcase, bookshelves (pl)

estaño m (elemento) tin; (para soldar) solder; (peltre) pewter

estar¹ [A27] cópula [1] (a) (seguido de adjetivos) [ESTAR denotes a changed condition or state as opposed to identity or nature, which is normally expressed by SER. ESTAR is also used when the emphasis is on the speaker's perception of things, of their appearance, taste, etc. The examples given below should be contrasted with those to be found in SER¹ cópula 1] to be; **estás más gordo** you've put on weight; **estoy cansada** I'm tired; **está muy simpático conmigo** he's being o he's been so nice to me (recently); **¡todo está tan caro!** things are o have become so expensive! (b) (con BIEN, MAL, MEJOR, PEOR): **están todos bien, gracias** they're all fine, thanks; **¡qué bien estás en esta foto!** you look great in this photo!; **está mal que no se lo perdones** it's wrong of you not to forgive him; ver tb BIEN, MAL, MEJOR, PEOR

[2] (hablando de estado civil) to be; **está casada con un primo mío** she's married to a cousin of mine

[3] (seguido de participios) ~ **sentado** to be sitting; **estaban abrazados** they had their arms around each other; ver tb v aux 2

[4] (seguido de preposición) to be; (para más ejemplos ver la preposición o el nombre correspondiente); **estoy a régimen** I'm on a diet; **¿a cómo está la uva?** how much are the grapes?; **está con el sarampión** she has (the) measles; **estoy de cocinera** I'm doing the cooking; **estamos sin electricidad** the electricity is off at the moment; **está sin pintar** it hasn't been painted yet
■ ~ vi [1] (en un lugar) to be; **¿dónde está Chiapas?** where's Chiapas?; **está a 20 kilómetros de aquí** it's 20 kilometers from here; **¿sabes dónde está Pedro?** do you know where Pedro is?; **¿está Rodrigo?** is Rodrigo in?; **solo ~é unos días** I'll only be staying a few days; **¿cuánto tiempo ~ás en Londres?** how long are you going to be in London (for)?

[2] (en el tiempo): **¿a qué (día) estamos?** what day is it today?; **¿a cuánto estamos hoy?** what's the date today?; **estamos a 28 de mayo** it's May 28th (AmE) o (BrE) the 28th of May; **estamos en primavera** it's spring

[3] (a) (tener como función, cometido): **para eso están los amigos** that's what friends are for; **estamos para ayudarlos** we're here to help them (b) (radicar) to lie; **en eso está el problema** that's where the problem lies

[4] (estar listo, terminado): **la carne todavía no está** the meat's not ready yet; **lo atas con un nudo y ya está** you tie a knot in it and that's it o there you are; **enseguida estoy** I'll be right with you

---

AmC	América Central		Arg	Argentina		Cu	Cuba		Per	Perú
AmL	América Latina		Bol	Bolivia		Ec	Ecuador		RPI	Río de la Plata
AmS	América del Sur		Chi	Chile		Esp	España		Ur	Uruguay
Andes	Región andina		CS	Cono Sur		Méx	México		Ven	Venezuela

5 (Esp) (quedar) (+ *me/te/le etc*) (+ *compl*): **te está pequeña** it's too small for you; **la 46 te está mejor** the 46 fits you better

■ ~ *v aux* **1** (con gerundio): **está lloviendo** it's raining; **estoy viendo que va a ser imposible** I'm beginning to see that it's going to be impossible **2** (con participio): **ese asiento está ocupado** that seat is taken; **ya está hecho un hombrecito** he's a proper young man now; *ver tb* ESTAR *cópula 3*

■ **estarse** *v pron* (*enf*) (permanecer) to stay; **¿no te puedes ~ quieto?** can't you stay *o* keep still?; **estese tranquilo** don't worry

estar² *m* (esp AmL) living room

estárter *m* choke

estatal *adj* state (*before n*)

estático -ca *adj* static

estatua *f* statue

estatura *f* height; **mide dos metros de ~** he's two meters (tall); **¿qué ~ tenía?** how tall was she?; **de mediana ~** of medium height

estatus *m* status

estatuto *m* (a) (Der, Pol) statute; (regla) rule (b) **estatutos** *mpl* (de empresa) articles of association (*pl*)

este¹ *adj inv* ⟨*región*⟩ eastern; **iban en dirección ~** they were heading east *o* eastward(s); **el ala/la costa ~** the east wing/coast ■ *m* (a) (parte, sector): **el ~** the east; **al ~ de Lima** to the east of Lima (b) (punto cardinal) east, East; **vientos del E~** easterly winds; **las ventanas dan al ~** the windows face east (c) **el Este** (Hist, Pol) the East; **los países del E~** the Eastern Bloc countries

este², esta *adj dem* (*pl* **estos, estas**) (a) this; (*pl*) these; **este chico** this boy; **estos dólares** these dollars; [*usually indicates a pejorative or emphatic tone when placed after the noun*] **la estúpida esta no me avisó** (fam) this idiot here didn't tell me (b) (como muletilla) well, er

éste, ésta *pron dem* (*pl* **éstos, éstas**) [*The written accent may be omitted when there is no confusion with the adjective*] this one; (*pl*) these; **~** *or* **este es el mío** this (one) is mine; **un día de éstos** *or* **estos** one of these days; **~** *or* **este es el que yo quería** this is the one I wanted; **prefiero éstos** *or* **estos** I prefer these (ones); [*sometimes indicates irritation, emphasis or disapproval*] **¡qué niña ésta!** (fam) honestly, this child!; **residente en ésta** *or* **esta** resident in Seville (*o* Lima *etc*)

estela *f* (de barco) wake; (de avión, cohete) trail

estelar *adj* (a) (Espec) star (b) (Astron) stellar

estelarizar [A4] *vt* (Méx) to star in

estepa *f* steppe

estera *f* mat

estercolero *m* dunghill, dung heap

estéreo *adj inv/m* stereo

estereofónico -ca *adj* stereophonic

estereotipado -da *adj* ⟨*frase*⟩ clichéd; ⟨*idea/personaje*⟩ stereotyped

estereotipo *m* stereotype

estéril *adj* (a) ⟨*animal/persona*⟩ sterile; ⟨*terreno*⟩ infertile, barren (b) ⟨*esfuerzo/discusión*⟩ futile (c) ⟨*gasa/jeringa*⟩ sterile

esterilidad *f* infertility; (de un hombre) sterility

esterilizar [A4] *vt* to sterilize

esterilla *f* (a) (alfombrilla) mat (b) (AmS) (mimbre) wicker

esternón *m* sternum, breastbone

estero *m* (a) (AmS) (laguna, pantano) marsh (b) (Chi) (arroyo) stream

esteroide *m* steroid

estética *f* (a) (Art) aesthetics (b) (Med) cosmetic surgery

esteticien, esteticista *mf* aesthetician, beautician

estético -ca *adj* aesthetic

estetoscopio *m* stethoscope

estiércol *m* (excremento) dung; (abono) manure

estigma *m* stigma

estilar [A1] *vi* (Chi) (gotear) to drip; (escurrir) to drain

■ **estilarse** *v pron* «*moda/peinado*» to be fashionable

estilista *mf* (a) (Lit) stylist (b) (diseñador de modas) designer (c) (AmL) (peluquero) hairstylist

estilístico -ca *adj* stylistic

estilizado -da *adj* (a) (Art) stylized (b) ⟨*cuerpo/figura*⟩ slender, slim

estilo *m* (a) (en general) style; **~ barroco** baroque style; **~ de vida** way of life, lifestyle; **ropa ~ deportivo** casual wear; **vestir con ~** to dress stylishly; **al ~ de mi tierra** the way they do it back home; **por el ~: son todos por el ~** they are all the same; **algo por el ~** something like that (b) (en natación) stroke, style; **~ libre** freestyle; **~ mariposa** butterfly; **~ pecho** *or* (Esp) **braza** breaststroke

estilográfica *f* fountain pen

estima *f* esteem; **ganarse la ~ de algn** to raise oneself in sb's esteem; **tener(le) ~ a algn** to think highly of sb; **tiene en gran ~ tu amistad** he values your friendship very highly

estimación *f* **1** (cálculo) estimate **2** (aprecio) esteem

estimado -da *adj* dear

estimar [A1] *vt* **1** (a) ⟨*persona*⟩ (respetar) to respect, hold ... in high esteem (frml); (tener cariño) to be fond of (b) ⟨*objeto*⟩ to value; **su piel es muy estimada** its skin is highly prized **2** (frml) (considerar) (+ *compl*) to consider, deem (frml)

estimulante *adj* stimulating

estimular [A1] *vt* (a) (en general) to stimulate (b) (alentar) ⟨*persona*⟩ to encourage

estímulo *m* (a) (incentivo) incentive (b) (Biol, Fisiol) stimulus

estirado -da *adj* (fam) stuck-up (colloq)

estirar [A1] *vt* **1** (a) ⟨*goma/elástico/suéter*⟩ to stretch; ⟨*cable/soga*⟩ to pull out, stretch (b) ⟨*sábanas/mantel*⟩ (con las manos) to smooth out; (con la plancha) to run the iron over **2** ⟨*brazos/piernas/músculo*⟩ to stretch; **estiró el cuello para poder ver** she craned her neck to be able to see **3** ⟨*dinero/comida/recursos*⟩ to make ... go further

■ **estirarse** *v pron* to stretch

estirón *m*: **dar** *or* **pegar un ~** (fam) to shoot up (colloq)

estirpe *f* stock, lineage

estítico -ca *adj* (Chi) constipated

estitiquez *f* (Chi) constipation

esto *pron dem (neutro)* this; ¿qué es ~? what's this?; ~ **es lo que quiero** this is what I want

estofado¹ -da *adj* stewed; (con menos líquido) braised

estofado² *m* stew

estoico -ca *adj* stoic, stoical

estomacal *adj* stomach (*before n*)

estómago *m* (Anat) stomach; **tengo dolor de** ~ I have a stomachache, my stomach hurts; **beber con el** ~ **vacío** to drink on an empty stomach; *revolverle el* ~ *a algn* to turn sb's stomach

estoperol *m* ⒈ (Andes) (en carretera) cat's eye ⒉ (Chi) (Dep) stud

estoque *m* sword (*used for killing bull*)

estorbar [A1] *vi* to be/get in the way
■ ~ *vt* to obstruct; **el piano estorbaba el paso** the piano was in the way

estorbo *m* (obstáculo) hindrance; (molestia) nuisance

estornudar [A1] *vi* to sneeze

estornudo *m* sneeze

estos -tas *adj dem*: ▶ ESTE²

éstos -tas *pron dem*: ▶ ÉSTE

estoy ▶ ESTAR¹

estrabismo *m* squint, strabismus (tech)

estrado *m* (tarima) platform, dais

estrafalario -ria *adj* ⟨persona/ideas/conducta⟩ eccentric; ⟨vestimenta⟩ outlandish, bizarre
■ *m,f* eccentric

estragón *m* tarragon

estragos *mpl*: **los** ~ **de la guerra** the ravages of war; **causar/hacer** ~**s** «⟨terremoto/inundación⟩» to wreak havoc; **la epidemia causó** ~ **entre la población** the epidemic devastated the population

estrambótico -ca *adj* ⟨persona/idea/conducta⟩ eccentric; ⟨vestimenta⟩ outlandish, bizarre

estrangulador -dora *m,f* strangler

estrangular [A1] *vt* **(a)** ⟨persona/animal⟩ to strangle, throttle **(b)** ⟨vena/conducto⟩ to strangulate

estraperlo *m* black market

estratagema *f* stratagem

estrategia *f* strategy

estratégico -ca *adj* strategic

estratosfera *f* stratosphere

estrechar [A1] *vt* ⒈ **(a)** ⟨falda/pantalones⟩ to take ... in; ⟨carretera⟩ to make ... narrower **(b)** ⟨relaciones/lazos⟩ to strengthen ⒉ (abrazar, apretar): **la estrechó entre sus brazos** he held her tightly in his arms; **me estrechó la mano** he shook my hand
■ **estrecharse** *v pron* ⒈ **(a)** «⟨carretera/acera⟩» to narrow, get narrower **(b)** «⟨relaciones/lazos⟩» to strengthen ⒉ (*recípr*) (apretarse): **se** ~**on en un abrazo** they embraced; **se** ~**on la mano** they shook hands

estrecho¹ -cha *adj* ⒈ ⟨calle/pasillo⟩ narrow; ⟨falda⟩ tight; **íbamos muy** ~**s** it was very cramped ⒉ ⟨amistad/colaboración/vigilancia⟩ close ⒊ (limitado) ⟨criterio⟩ narrow; **es muy** ~ **de miras** he's very narrow-minded

estrecho² *m* (Geog) strait, straits (*pl*); **el E**~ **de Gibraltar** the Strait(s) of Gibraltar

estrella *f* **(a)** (en general) star; ~ **de mar** starfish; ~ **fugaz** shooting star; ~ **polar** Pole Star; **un hotel de tres** ~**s** a three-star hotel; **una** ~ **de cine** a movie star **(b)** (asterisco) asterisk

estrellado -da *adj* (lleno de estrellas) starry; (en forma de estrella) star-shaped

estrellar [A1] *vt*: **estrelló un plato contra la pared** he smashed a plate against the wall; **estrelló el coche contra un árbol** he smashed his car into a tree
■ **estrellarse** *v pron* (chocar) to crash; **se estrelló con la moto** he had a motorcycle accident; ~**se CONTRA algo** «⟨coche⟩» to crash INTO sth; «⟨olas⟩» to crash AGAINST sth; **se estrelló contra el vidrio** he walked smack into the glass door

estremecedor -dora *adj* ⟨escena/noticia⟩ horrifying; ⟨grito/relato⟩ spine-chilling, hair-raising

estremecer [E3] *vt* to make ... shudder
■ ~ *vi* to shudder; **hacer** ~ **a algn** to make sb shudder
■ **estremecerse** *v pron* **(a)** «⟨persona⟩» ~**se DE algo** ⟨de miedo/horror⟩ to shudder WITH sth; ⟨de frío⟩ to shiver *o* tremble WITH sth; **se estremeció solo de pensarlo** he shuddered at the mere thought of it **(b)** «⟨edificio/ventana⟩» to shake

estremecimiento *m* (de miedo) shudder; **tenía** ~**s de frío** he was shivering with cold

estrenar [A1] *vt* ⒈ (Cin, Teatr): **la película se estrenó en marzo** the movie opened *o* (journ) had its premiere in March; **acaban de** ~ **la obra en Madrid** the play's just started showing *o* just opened in Madrid ⒉ (usar por primera vez): **voy a** ~ **corbata** I'm going to wear a new tie; **todavía no he estrenado la blusa** I still haven't worn the blouse; **todavía no estrenamos el gimnasio** we still haven't tried out the gymnasium

estreno *m* ⒈ (de película, nueva obra) premiere; (de nueva puesta en escena) opening night ⒉ (primer uso): **ir de** ~ to be wearing new clothes; **el** ~ **del local** the opening of the new premises

estreñido -da *adj* constipated

estreñimiento *m* constipation

estreñir [I15] *vi* to cause constipation
■ ~ *vt* to make ... constipated, bind (colloq)

estrés *m* stress

estresado -da *adj* under stress

estresante *adj* stressful

estría *f* **(a)** (de la piel) stretch mark **(b)** (de columna) groove, stria (tech)

estriado -da *adj* **(a)** ⟨piel⟩ stretch-marked **(b)** ⟨columna⟩ fluted

estribillo *m* (Lit) refrain; (Mús) chorus

estribo *m* **(a)** (Equ) stirrup; **perder los** ~**s** to fly off the handle, lose one's cool; **tomarse la del** ~ to have one for the road (colloq) **(b)** (de vehículo) running board; (de moto) footrest

estribor *m* starboard

estricto -ta *adj* strict

estridente *adj* **(a)** ⟨pitido/chirrido⟩ shrill **(b)** ⟨voz⟩ (agudo) shrill; (fuerte) strident **(c)** ⟨color⟩ garish, loud

estrofa *f* stanza, verse

estropajo *m* scourer

estropeado -da adj: **estar** ~ «zapato/sillón» to be falling apart; «motor/coche» to be broken down; ver tb ESTROPEAR

estropear [A1] vt ① (a) ‹aparato/mecanismo› to damage, break; ‹coche› to damage (b) (malograr) ‹plan/vacaciones› to spoil, ruin ② (deteriorar, dañar) ‹piel› to damage, ruin; ‹juguete› to break; ‹ropa› to ruin; **el calor estropeó la fruta** the heat made the fruit go bad
■ **estropearse** v pron ① (a) (averiarse) «motor/coche» to break down; **la lavadora está estropeada** the washing machine is broken (b) «plan/vacaciones» to go wrong ② (deteriorarse) «fruta» to go bad; «leche/pescado» to go off; «zapatos/chaqueta» to get ruined

estructura f structure

estructurar [A1] vt to structure, to organize

estruendo m (de las olas) roar; (de cascada, tráfico) thunder, roar; (de maquinaria) din

estrujar [A1] vt ① (a) (apretar arrugando) ‹papel› to crumple up, scrunch up; ‹tela› to crumple (up) (b) (para escurrir) to wring (out) (c) ‹uvas› to press ② ‹persona› to squeeze, hold ... tightly

estuche m (de gafas, lápices, violín) case; (de cubiertos) canteen; (de collar, reloj) box, case

estudiante mf (de universidad) student; (de secundaria) (high-school) student (AmE), (secondary school) pupil (BrE)

estudiantil adj student (before n)

estudiar [A1] vt ① (a) ‹asignatura› to study; (en la universidad) to study, read (frml); **¿qué carrera estudió?** what subject did he do at college/university? (b) ‹instrumento› to learn (c) ‹lección/tablas› to learn
② (observar) ‹rostro/comportamiento› to study
③ (considerar, analizar) ‹mercado/situación/proyecto› to study; ‹propuesta› to study, consider; ‹causas› to look into, investigate
■ ~ vi to study; **estudia en un colegio privado** he goes to a private school; **debes** ~ **más** you must work harder; **dejó de** ~ **a los 15 años** she left school at 15; ~ **PARA** algo to study to be sth
■ **estudiarse** v pron (enf) ‹lección› to study; ‹papel› to learn

estudio m ① (a) (Educ) (actividad): **primero está el** ~ studying o your studies o work must come first (b) (investigación, análisis) study; ~ **de mercado** market research (c) (de asunto, caso) consideration; **está en** ~ it is being considered ② (lugar) (a) (de artista) studio; (de arquitecto) office, studio (b) (Cin, Rad, TV) studio (c) (en casa) study; (apartamento) studio apartment ③ **estudios** mpl (Educ) education; ~**s superiores** higher education; **quiso darle** ~**s a su hijo** she wanted to give her son an education; **tener** ~**s superiores** to have a degree; **dejar los** ~**s** to give up one's studies

estudioso -sa adj studious
■ m,f scholar

estufa f (a) (de calefacción) stove; ~ **eléctrica** electric heater (b) (Col, Méx) (cocina) stove; ~ **de gas** gas stove o (BrE) cooker

estupefaciente m narcotic (drug); **tráfico de** ~**s** drug trafficking

estupefacto -ta adj astonished, amazed

estupendo¹ -da adj (a) (excelente) marvelous*, fantastic (colloq), great (colloq); **¡**~**!** great! (b) (guapo) gorgeous

estupendo² adv ‹cantar› marvelously*; **lo pasé** ~ I had a great o wonderful time

estupidez f (a) (cualidad) stupidity, foolishness (b) (dicho): **no digas estupideces** don't talk nonsense (c) (acto): **eso sería una** ~ that would be stupid o foolish

estúpido -da adj ‹persona› stupid; ‹argumento› stupid, silly; **¡ay, qué estúpida soy!** oh, how stupid of me!
■ m,f idiot, fool

estupor m astonishment

estuve, estuviste, etc ▶ ESTAR¹

ETA /'eta/ f (= **Euzkadi ta Azkatasuna**) ETA

etapa f stage; **por** ~**s** in stages; **la** ~ **más feliz de mi vida** the best o happiest time of my life

etarra mf: member of ETA

etcétera etcetera, and so on (and so forth)

etéreo -rea adj ethereal

eternidad f eternity

eterno -na adj eternal; ‹amor› everlasting

ética f ethics

ético -ca adj ethical

etimología f etymology

etíope, etiope adj/mf Ethiopian

Etiopía f Ethiopia

etiqueta f ① (a) (adherida) label (b) (atada) tag; (en prenda) label ② (protocolo) etiquette; **baile/traje de** ~ formal ball/dress

etiquetar [A1] vt ‹producto› to label; ‹persona› ~ **a** algn DE algo to label sb (AS) sth

étnico -ca adj ethnic

eucalipto m eucalyptus

Eucaristía f Eucharist

eufemismo m euphemism

euforia f elation, euphoria

eufórico -ca adj ecstatic, euphoric

euro m euro

eurocheque m eurocheque

eurodiputado -da m,f Euro MP, MEP, Member of the European Parliament

Europa f Europe

europeísta adj pro-European

europeo -pea adj/m,f European

Eurotunnel®, eurotúnel m Channel Tunnel

Eurozona f Eurozone

Euskadi f the Basque Country

euskera, eusquera adj/m Basque

eutanasia f euthanasia

evacuación f (desalojo) evacuation

evacuar [A18] or [A1] vt ‹local/zona/población› to evacuate

evadir [I1] vt (a) ‹pregunta/peligro/responsabilidad› to avoid; ‹tema› to dodge, evade (b) ‹impuestos› to evade
■ **evadirse** v pron (a) «preso» to escape (b) ~**se** DE algo ‹de responsabilidad/problema› to run away FROM sth; ‹de la realidad› to escape FROM sth

evaluación f (a) (de daños, situación)　····⋮›

assessment; (de datos, informes) evaluation, assessment **(b)** (Educ) (acción) assessment; (prueba, examen) test

evaluar [A18] *vt* ⟨pérdidas/situación⟩ to assess; ⟨datos⟩ to evaluate; ⟨alumno⟩ to assess

evangélico -ca *adj* **(a)** (del evangelio) evangelical **(b)** (protestante) protestant (*before n*)
■ *m,f* Protestant

evangelio *m* gospel

evaporación *f* evaporation

evaporarse [A1] *v pron* «líquido» to evaporate; «ayuda/dinero» to evaporate; «persona» (fam) to vanish *o* disappear into thin air

evasión *f* escape, breakout; ∼ **de impuestos** tax evasion

evasiva *f*: **me contestó con** ∼**s** she avoided *o* dodged the issue

evasivo -va *adj* evasive, noncommital

evento *m* **(a)** (period) (suceso) event **(b)** (caso) case; **en este** ∼ in such a case

eventual *adj* 1 (posible) ⟨problema/conflicto⟩ possible; ⟨gastos⟩ incidental; ⟨riesgos/pasivos⟩ contingent 2 ⟨trabajo/trabajador⟩ casual, temporary; ⟨cargo⟩ temporary

evidencia *f* **(a)** (pruebas) evidence, proof; **negar la** ∼ to deny the obvious *o* the facts **(b)** (cualidad) obviousness; **dejar** *or* **poner a algn en** ∼ to show sb up

evidente *adj* obvious, clear

evidentemente *adv* (indep) obviously, clearly

evitar [A1] *vt* **(a)** (eludir, huir de) to avoid; ∼ **hacer algo** to avoid doing sth **(b)** (impedir) to avoid, prevent; **para** ∼ **que sufran** to avoid *o* prevent them suffering **(c)** (remediar): **me puse a llorar, no lo puede** ∼ I started to cry, I couldn't help it **(d)** (ahorrar) ∼**le algo A algn** ⟨molestia/preocupación⟩ to save *o* spare sb sth
■ **evitarse** *v pron* ⟨problemas⟩ to save oneself; **evítese la molestia de ir a la tienda** avoid the inconvenience of going to the store

evolución *f* **(a)** (Biol) evolution **(b)** (de ideas, sociedad, enfermedad) development; (de enfermo) progress

evolucionado -da *adj* ⟨especie⟩ highly developed *o* evolved; ⟨sociedad/ideas⟩ advanced, highly developed

evolucionar [A1] *vi* **(a)** (Biol) to evolve **(b)** «ideas/sociedad/ciencia» to develop, evolve **(c)** «enfermo» to progress

exactamente *adv* exactly

exactitud *f* **(a)** (precisión) accuracy, precision; **las órdenes se cumplieron con** ∼ the orders were carried out to the letter **(b)** (veracidad, rigor) accuracy

exacto -ta *adj* **(a)** ⟨medida/cantidad⟩ exact; **40 kilos** ∼**s** exactly 40 kilos; **hay que ser muy** ∼ **en los cálculos** you have to be very accurate *o*

precise in your calculations **(b)** ⟨informe/mapa/descripción⟩ accurate **(c)** ⟨copia⟩ exact; ⟨reproducción⟩ accurate

exageración *f* exaggeration

exagerado -da *adj* **(a)** ⟨persona⟩: **¡qué** ∼ **eres!** you do exaggerate! **(b)** ⟨historia/relato⟩ exaggerated **(c)** (excesivo) ⟨precio⟩ exorbitant; ⟨cariño/castigo⟩ excessive; ⟨moda⟩ extravagant, way-out (colloq)

exagerar [A1] *vt* ⟨suceso/noticia⟩ to exaggerate
■ ∼ *vi* (al hablar) to exaggerate; (al hacer algo) to overdo it, go over the top (colloq)

exaltado -da *adj* **(a)** (vehemente) ⟨discurso⟩ impassioned **(b)** (excitado): **los ánimos estaban** ∼**s** feelings were running high; **estaba muy** ∼ he was really worked up **(c)** [SER] ⟨persona⟩ hotheaded
■ *m,f* hothead

exaltar [A1] *vt* 1 **(a)** (excitar) ⟨personas⟩ to excite; ⟨pasiones⟩ to arouse **(b)** (hacer enojar) to anger 2 (frml) (alabar) to extol (frml)
■ **exaltarse** *v pron* to get worked up

exalumno -na *m,f* (de colegio) ex-pupil; (de universidad) ex-student

examen *m* **(a)** (Educ) exam, examination (frml); ∼ **de admisión** entrance examination *o* test; ∼ **parcial** modular exam *o* test; **hacer** *or* (CS) **dar un** ∼ to take an exam; **presentarse a un** ∼ to take *o* (BrE) sit an exam; ∼ **de ingreso** entrance examination *o* test **(b)** (estudio, investigación) examination; **someter algo a** ∼ to examine sth; ∼ **médico** medical examination, medical

examinador -dora *adj* examining (*before n*)
■ *m,f* examiner

examinar [A1] *vt* to examine; ⟨situación/caso⟩ to study, consider
■ **examinarse** *v pron* (Esp) to take an exam

exangüe *adj* (liter) spent (liter), exhausted

exasperante *adj* exasperating

exasperar [A1] *vt* to exasperate
■ **exasperarse** *v pron* to get worked up *o* exasperated

excavación *f* excavation

excavadora *f* excavator

excavar [A1] *vt* **(a)** ⟨túnel/fosa⟩ to dig **(b)** (Arqueol) to excavate
■ ∼ *vi* to dig, excavate

excedencia *f* (Esp) extended leave of absence

excedente *adj* **(a)** ⟨producción⟩ excess (*before n*), surplus (*before n*) **(b)** (con permiso) (Esp) on extended leave of absence
■ *m* surplus

exceder [E1] *vt* **(a)** ⟨límite/peso⟩ to exceed **(b)** (superar, aventajar) ∼ **A algo** to be superior TO sth
■ **excederse** *v pron* (al beber, trabajar) to overdo it; **se excedió en sus críticas** she went too far in her criticism

excelencia *f* 1 (cualidad) excellence 2 (frml) (tratamiento): **Su E**∼ (*m*) His Excellency; (*f*) Her Excellency

excelente *adj* excellent

· ·

excéntrico -ca *adj/m,f* eccentric

excepción *f* exception; **esta norma tiene una** ~ there is an exception to this rule; **hacer una** ~ **(con algn)** to make an exception (for sb); **a excepción de** with the exception of, except for

excepcional *adj* ‹caso/circunstancia/talento› exceptional; ‹contribución/labor› outstanding

excepto *prep* except, apart from; **todos** ~ **yo** everyone but me

exceptuar [A18] *vt* to except (frml); **exceptuando un pequeño incidente** except for o with the exception of a minor incident

excesivo *adj* excessive

exceso *m* **(a)** (excedente) excess; ~ **de equipaje** excess baggage **(b)** (demasía): **un** ~ **de ejercicio** too much exercise; **me multaron por** ~ **de velocidad** I was fined for speeding; **en** ~ ‹beber/fumar/trabajar› too much **(c) excesos** *mpl* (abusos) excesses (*pl*)

excitabilidad *f* excitability

excitación *f* **(a)** (entusiasmo) excitement **(b)** (sexual) arousal, excitement

excitante *adj* ‹espectáculo/libro› exciting

excitar [A1] *vt* **(a)** (hacer enojar): **la discusión lo excitó mucho** he got very excited o worked up during the argument **(b)** (sobreexcitar) to get ... overexcited; **el café me excita** coffee makes me jumpy **(c)** (en sentido sexual) to arouse, excite **(d)** ‹deseo/odio/curiosidad› to arouse
■ **excitarse** *v pron* **(a)** (enojarse) to get agitated, get worked up **(b)** (sobreexcitarse) to get overexcited **(c)** (sexualmente) to get aroused, get excited

exclamación *f* exclamation

exclamar [A1] *vt* to exclaim

excluir [I20] *vt* to exclude; ‹posibilidad› to rule out

exclusión *f* exclusion

exclusiva *f* **(a)** (Period) (derechos) exclusive rights (*pl*); (reportaje) exclusive **(b)** (Esp) (Com) exclusive rights (*pl*); **tendrán la** ~ **de nuestros productos** they will be sole distributors of our products

exclusive *adj inv* (detrás del *n*): **del tres al quince, ambos** ~ from the third to the fifteenth not inclusive

exclusividad *f* **(a)** (de club, colegio, diseño) exclusiveness, exclusivity **(b)** (AmL) (Com) exclusive rights (*pl*), sole rights (*pl*)

exclusivo -va *adj* ‹club/diseño› exclusive; ‹distribuidor› sole; ‹derechos› exclusive, sole

excombatiente *mf* (*m*) veteran (AmE), ex-serviceman (esp BrE); (*f*) veteran (AmE), ex-servicewoman (esp BrE)

excomulgar [A3] *vt* to excommunicate

excomunión *f* excommunication

excremento *m* excrement

excursión *f* (viaje organizado) excursion, day trip; (paseo, salida) trip, excursion; **ir de** ~ **al campo** to go on a trip to the countryside

excursionismo *m* hiking

excursionista *mf* (que hace una excursión) tripper; (que hace excursionismo) hiker

excusa *f* **(a)** (pretexto) excuse **(b) excusas** *fpl* (disculpas) apologies (*pl*)

excusar [A1] *vt* **(a)** (disculpar) ‹comportamiento› to excuse **(b)** (eximir) ~ **a algn de algo/hacer algo** to excuse sb (FROM) sth/doing sth
■ **excusarse** *v pron* (frml) **(a)** (pedir perdón) to apologize **(b)** (ofrecer excusas) to excuse oneself

exento -ta *adj* (frml) [ESTAR] exempt; ~ **DE algo** exempt FROM sth; ~ **de impuestos** tax-exempt, tax-free (BrE)

exfoliador *m* (Col) notepad

exhaustivo -va *adj* exhaustive

exhausto -ta *adj* exhausted

exhibición *f* **(a)** (demostración) display **(b)** (de cuadros, artefactos) exhibition, display; **estar en** ~ to be on show o display

exhibicionista *mf* **(a)** (pervertido) exhibitionist, flasher (colloq) **(b)** (ostentoso) exhibitionist, show-off (colloq)

exhibir [I1] *vt* **(a)** ‹colección/modelos› to show, display **(b)** ‹película› to show, screen; ‹cuadro/obras de arte› to exhibit **(c)** (con orgullo) ‹regalos/trofeos› to show off
■ ~ *vi* (period) (Art) to exhibit
■ **exhibirse** *v pron* (mostrarse en público) to show oneself; (hacerse notar) to draw attention to oneself

exhumar [A1] *vt* to exhume, disinter

exigencia *f* **(a)** (pretensión) demand; **¡no me vengas con** ~**s!** don't start making demands **(b)** (requisito) requirement

exigente *adj* ‹persona/prueba› demanding; ‹clientela/paladar› discerning

exigir [I7] *vt* **(a)** ‹pago/respuesta/disciplina› to demand; **exigió que se retiraran** he demanded that they leave **(b)** (requerir) ‹concentración/paciencia› to call for, demand **(c)** (esperar de algn) (+ me/te/le etc): **le exigen demasiado en ese colegio** they ask too much of him at that school

exiliado -da *adj* exiled, in exile
■ *m,f* exile

exiliarse [A1] *v pron* to go into exile

exilio *m* exile

eximir [I1] *vt* (frml) to exempt; ~ **a algn DE algo/hacer algo** to exempt sb FROM sth/doing sth; **esto me exime de toda culpa** this relieves o absolves me of all responsibility

existencia *f* 1 **(a)** (hecho de existir) existence **(b)** (vida) life; **amargarle la** ~ **a algn** to make sb's life a misery 2 (Com) stock

existir [I1] *vi* **(a)** (en 3ª pers) (haber): **siempre ha existido rivalidad entre ellos** there has always been rivalry between them; **no existen pruebas** there is no evidence **(b)** (ser) to exist; **ya no existe** it doesn't exist anymore

éxito *m* success; **con** ~ successfully; **tener** ~ to be successful; ~ **de ventas** best-seller; ~ **de taquilla** a box-office hit

exitoso -sa *adj* (AmL) ‹campaña/gira› successful

éxodo *m* exodus; **el** ~ **rural** the drift from the land

exorbitante *adj* exorbitant

exorcismo *m* exorcism

exorcizar [A4] *vt* to exorcize

exótico -ca *adj* exotic

expandirse [I1] *v pron* to expand

expansión *f* expansion; **en** ~ expanding

expatriado -da *m,f* expatriate

expatriarse [A1] *or* [A17] *v pron* (emigrar) to leave one's country; (exiliarse) to go into exile

expectación *f* sense of expectancy *o* anticipation

expectante *adj* expectant; **esperaba** ∼ she waited expectantly

expectativa *f* **(a)** (espera): **estar a la** ∼ **(de algo)** to be waiting (for sth) **(b)** (esperanza) expectation; **defraudó las** ∼**s de su padre** he failed to live up to his father's expectations **(c) expectativas** *fpl* (perspectivas) prospects (*pl*); **tienen pocas** ∼**s de ganar** they have little hope of winning; ∼**s de vida** life expectancy

expedición *f* expedition; ∼ **de salvamento** (misión) rescue mission; (equipo) rescue party

expediente *m* **(a)** (documentos) file, dossier; ∼ **académico** student record **(b)** (investigación) investigation, inquiry **(c)** (medidas disciplinarias) disciplinary action; **le abrieron** ∼ disciplinary action was taken against him

expedir [I14] *vt* ⟨pasaporte/visa⟩ to issue

expendio *m* (AmL) (tienda) store (AmE), shop (BrE); (venta) sale; **un** ∼ **de licores** a package store (AmE), an off-licence (BrE)

expensas: **a expensas de algo** ⟨de ideales/salud⟩ at the expense of; **vive a** ∼ **de su familia** he lives off his family

experiencia *f* **(a)** (conocimiento, suceso) experience; **saber algo por** ∼ to know sth by *o* from experience; ∼ **piloto** pilot scheme **(b)** (experimento) experiment

experimentado -da *adj* experienced

experimental *adj* experimental

experimentar [A1] *vi* ∼ **con algo** to experiment ON *o* WITH sth
■ ∼ *vt* **(a)** ⟨sensación⟩ to experience, feel; ⟨tristeza/alegría⟩ to feel **(b)** (sufrir) ⟨cambio⟩ to undergo; **ha experimentado una leve mejoría** there's been a slight improvement in his condition

experimento *m* experiment

experto -ta *adj*: **es** ∼ **en casos de divorcio** he's an expert on divorce cases; ∼ **EN hacer algo** very good AT doing sth
■ *m,f* expert

expiar [A17] *vt* to expiate, atone for

explanada *f* (plataforma) raised area, terrace; (delante de un edificio) leveled* area; (al lado del mar) esplanade

explayarse [A1] *v pron* **(a)** (sobre un tema) to speak at length **(b)** (desahogarse) to unburden oneself **(c)** (esparcirse) to relax

explicación *f* explanation

explicar [A2] *vt* to explain; **no sé** ∼**lo** I don't know how to explain it
■ **explicarse** *v pron* **(a)** (comprender, concebir) to understand; **no me lo explico** I can't understand it *o* (colloq) I just don't get it **(b)** (hacerse comprender) to express oneself; **explícate** explain what you mean; **¿me explico?** do you understand what I mean?

explícito -ta *adj* explicit

exploración *f* **(a)** (de territorio) exploration; (de yacimientos) prospecting **(b)** (Mil) reconnaisance **(c)** (Med) examination, exploration

explorador -dora *m,f* **1** (expedicionario) explorer; (Mil) scout **2 exploradora** *f* (Col) (Auto) fog lamp

explorar [A1] *vt* ⟨región⟩ to explore; ⟨yacimientos⟩ to prospect for; (Inf) ∼ **la web** *or* **Red** to surf the Web **(b)** ⟨posibilidades⟩ to explore, investigate; ⟨situación⟩ to investigate, examine **(c)** (Mil) to reconnoiter*, scout; «⟨radar/sonar⟩» to scan

explosión *f* **(a)** (de bomba) explosion; **la bomba hizo** ∼ (period) the bomb exploded *o* went off **(b)** (de cólera, júbilo) outburst **(c)** (crecimiento brusco) explosion

explosivo¹ -va *adj* explosive; **materiales** ∼**s** explosives

explosivo² *m* explosive

explotación *f* **(a)** (de tierra, mina) exploitation, working; (de negocio) running, operation **(b)** (de trabajador) exploitation

explotador -dora *adj* exploitative
■ *m,f* exploiter

explotar [A1] *vt* **(a)** ⟨tierra⟩ to exploit, work; ⟨mina⟩ to operate, work; ⟨negocio⟩ to run, operate **(b)** ⟨idea/debilidad⟩ to exploit **(c)** ⟨trabajador⟩ to exploit
■ ∼ *vi* **(a)** «⟨bomba⟩» to explode, go off; «⟨caldera/máquina⟩» to explode, blow up **(b)** (fam) «⟨persona⟩» to explode, to blow a fuse (colloq)

exponer [E22] *vt* **1 (a)** (en museo) ⟨cuadro/escultura⟩ to exhibit, show **(b)** (en vitrina) to display **2** ⟨razones/hechos⟩ to set out, state; ⟨ideas/teoría⟩ to put forward; ⟨tema⟩ to present **3 (a)** (poner en peligro) to put ... at risk **(b)** (al aire, sol) ∼ **algo A algo** to expose sth TO sth
■ ∼ *vi* to exhibit, exhibit *o* show one's work
■ **exponerse** *v pron* ∼**se (A algo)** to expose oneself (TO sth); **te expones a que te multen** you're risking a fine

exportación *f* **(a)** (acción) exportation, export **(b) exportaciones** *fpl* (mercancías) exports (*pl*)

exportador -dora *adj*: **países** ∼**es de petróleo** oil-exporting countries; **una región** ∼**a de cítricos** a region that exports citrus fruit
■ *m,f* exporter

exportar [A1] *vt* to export

exposición *f* **1 (a)** (acción) exhibition, showing **(b)** (muestra — de cuadros, esculturas) exhibition; (— de productos, maquinaria) show **2** (de hechos, razones) statement; (de tema, teoría) presentation **3** (al aire, sol) exposure; (Fot) exposure

expositor -tora *m,f* **1** (de cuadros, maquinaria) exhibitor **2** (Col, Ven) (conferenciante) speaker

exprés *adj inv* (Esp) ⟨servicio/envío⟩ express (*before n*)
■ *m* (Esp) (Ferr) express train, fast train

expresar [A1] *vt* to express
■ **expresarse** *v pron* to express oneself

expresión *f* expression

expresividad *f* expressiveness

expresivo -va *adj* ⟨persona/rostro/lenguaje⟩ expressive

expreso¹ -sa *adj* **1** (explícito) express (*before n*) **2** ⟨tren⟩ express (*before n*), fast (*before n*); ⟨carta/envío⟩ express (*before n*); **por correo** ∼ express **3** ⟨café⟩ espresso

expreso² *m* 1 (Ferr) express train, fast train
2 (café) espresso

exprimidor *m* (manual) reamer (AmE), lemon
squeezer (BrE); (eléctrico) juicer

exprimir [I1] *vt* (a) ⟨naranja/limón⟩ to squeeze;
⟨ropa⟩ to wring (b) ⟨trabajadores⟩ to exploit

expropiación *f* (sin indemnización) expropriation; (con indemnización) compulsory purchase

expropiar [A1] *vt* (sin indemnización) to
expropriate; (con indemnización) to acquire ... by
compulsory purchase

expulsar [A1] *vt* 1 (a) (de institución) to expel;
(de local) to throw ... out, eject (frml) (b) (de
territorio) to expel, drive out (c) (Dep) to send off
2 ⟨aire/cálculo⟩ to expel

expulsión *f* expulsion; (Dep) sending-off

expurgar [A3] *vt* to expurgate

exquisito -ta *adj* ⟨comida⟩ delicious; ⟨tela/
poema/música⟩ exquisite; ⟨persona⟩ refined

éxtasis *m* ecstasy

extático -ca *adj* ecstatic

extender [E8] *vt* 1 ⟨periódico/mapa⟩ to open
... up *o* out; ⟨mantel/toalla⟩ to spread ... out
2 ⟨brazos⟩ to stretch out; ⟨alas⟩ to spread; **le
extendió la mano** he held out his hand to her
3 ⟨pintura/mantequilla⟩ to spread
4 (ampliar) ⟨poderes/plazo/permiso⟩ to extend
5 (frml) ⟨factura/cheque/escritura⟩ to issue;
⟨receta⟩ to make out, write
■ **extenderse** *v pron* 1 (en el espacio) (a)
«fuego/epidemia/noticia» to spread (b)
«territorio/propiedad» to stretch; **se extiende
hasta el río** it stretches down to the river (c)
«influencia/autoridad» to extend; **~se a algo** to
extend *to* sth
2 (en el tiempo) (a) «época/debate» to last (b)
«persona»: **se extendió demasiado en ese tema**
he spent too much time on that subject; **¿quisiera
~se sobre ese punto?** would you like to expand
on that point?

extendido -da *adj* (a) ⟨costumbre/error⟩
widespread (b) ⟨brazos/alas⟩ outstretched

extensión *f* 1 (a) (superficie): **una gran ~ de
terreno** a large expanse *o* stretch of land; **una ~
de 20 hectáreas** an area of 20 hectares (b)
(longitud) length; **la ~ de la novela** the length of
the novel; **por ~** by extension 2 (grado,
importancia) extent; **en toda la ~ de la palabra** in
every sense of the word 3 (a) (prolongación)
extension; **pidió una ~ del plazo** she asked for an
extension on the deadline (b) (de cable) extension
cord (AmE), extension lead (BrE); (línea telefónica)
extension

extenso -sa *adj* extensive

exterior *adj* 1 (a) ⟨aspecto⟩ external (before
n), outward (before n); ⟨bolsillo/temperatura/
mundo⟩ outside (before n); ⟨revestimiento/capa⟩
outer (before n) (b) ⟨habitación/apartamento⟩
outward-facing 2 ⟨comercio/política⟩ foreign
(before n)
■ *m* 1 (fachada) outside, exterior; (espacio
circundante) outside; **desde el ~ de la iglesia** from
outside the church 2 **el exterior** (países
extranjeros): **la influencia del ~** foreign influence;
las relaciones con el ~ relations with other
countries 3 **exteriores** *mpl* (Cin) location
shots (*pl*); **rodar en ~es** to film on location

exteriorizar [A4] *vt* to externalize, exteriorize

exterminar [A1] *vt* to exterminate

exterminio *m* extermination

externalizar [A4] *vt* ⟨servicios⟩ to outsource

externar [A1] *vt* (Méx) to display, show

externo -na *adj* (a) ⟨apariencia/signos⟩
outward (before n), external; ⟨influencia⟩ outside,
external; ⟨superficie⟩ external; ⟨ángulo⟩ exterior
(b) ⟨alumno⟩ day (before n)
■ *m,f* day pupil

extinción *f* (de especie, volcán) extinction; **una
especie en peligro de ~** an endangered species

extinguidor *m* (AmL) fire extinguisher

extinguir [I2] *vt* (a) ⟨especie⟩ to wipe out;
⟨violencia/injusticia⟩ to put an end to (b) ⟨fuego⟩
to extinguish, put out
■ **extinguirse** *v pron* (a) «especie» to become
extinct, die out (b) «fuego» to go out; «volcán»
to become extinct; «sonido» to die away (c)
«entusiasmo/amor» to die

extintor *m* (Esp): *tb* **~ de incendios** fire
extinguisher

extirpar [A1] *vt* (Med) to remove

extorsión *f* extortion

extorsionar [A1] *vt* to extort money from

extra *adj* (a) (Com) top quality, fancy grade
(AmE) (b) (adicional) ⟨gastos/ración⟩ additional,
extra; ⟨edición⟩ special
■ *adv* extra
■ *mf* (Cin) extra
■ *m* (gasto) extra expense; (paga) bonus

extracción *f* (a) (en general) extraction (b) *tb*
~ social background, origins (*pl*); **de ~ humilde**
of humble origins

extraconyugal *adj* extramarital

extracto *m* (a) (resumen) summary, abstract; **~
de cuenta** (bank) statement (b) (esencia) extract

extractor *m* extractor; **~ de aire** extractor fan

extradición *f* extradition

extraer [E23] *vt* (en general) to extract; ⟨bala⟩ to
remove; ⟨conclusión⟩ to draw

extraescolar *adj* extramural, out-of-school
(before n)

extralimitarse [A1] *v pron* to exceed one's
authority

extramatrimonial *adj* extramarital

extranjería *f* (Esp): **ley de ~** immigration laws

extranjero -ra *adj* foreign
■ *m,f* (a) (persona) foreigner (b) **extranjero** *m*:
al/en el ~ abroad; **noticias del ~** foreign news

extrañar [A1] *vt* (esp AmL) ⟨amigo/país⟩ to miss
■ **~** *vi* 1 (sorprender) (+ *me/te/le etc*) to surprise;
me extraña que no lo sepas I'm surprised you
didn't know that; **ya me extrañaba a mí que ...** I
thought it was strange that ... 2 (RPl) (tener
nostalgia) to be homesick
■ **extrañarse** *v pron* **~se DE algo** to be
surprised *at* sth

extrañeza *f* surprise; **me miró con ~** she
looked at me in surprise

extraño -ña *adj* (raro) strange, odd; **eso no
tiene nada de ~** there's nothing unusual about
that
■ *m,f* (desconocido) stranger

extraoficial *adj* unofficial

extraordinario -ria *adj* (en general) extraordinary; ‹*edición*› special; ‹*contribución*› extra, additional; **la película no fue nada ~** the movie was nothing special *o* nothing out of the ordinary

extraplano -na *adj* ‹*reloj/calculadora*› slimline; ‹*compresa*› extra-slim

extrarradio *m* outlying districts (*pl*), outskirts (*pl*)

extrasensorial *adj* extrasensory

extraterrestre *adj/mf* alien, extraterrestrial

extravagancia *f* (acto) outrageous thing (to do); (cualidad) extravagance

extravagante *adj* ‹*comportamiento/ideas*› outrageous, extravagant; ‹*persona/ropa*› flamboyant, outrageous

extraviado -da *adj* ‹*objeto/niño*› lost, missing; ‹*perro/gato*› stray

extraviar [A17] *vt* (frml) to mislay (frml), to lose
■ **extraviarse** *v pron* (frml) «*persona/animal*» to get lost; «*documento*» to go missing

extremado -da *adj* extreme

extremar [A1] *vt* (frml) to maximize (frml)
■ **extremarse** *v pron* ~ (**EN hacer algo**) to make a great effort (to do sth)

extremaunción *f* extreme unction

extremidad *f* **(a)** (extremo) end **(b)** **extremidades** *fpl* (Anat) extremities

extremista *adj* (extremo) extreme; (Pol) extremist
■ *mf* (Pol) extremist

extremo¹ -ma *adj* extreme; **un caso de extrema gravedad** an extremely serious case; **en caso ~** as a last resort; **~ derecha/izquierda** (Pol) extreme right/left; **~ derecho/izquierdo** (Dep) right/left wing; **E~ Oriente** Far East

extremo² *m* **(a)** (de palo, cable) end **(b)** (postura extrema) extreme; **va de un ~ a otro** she goes from one extreme to the other; **son ~s opuestos** they are complete opposites **(c)** (límite): **si se llega a ese ~ ...** if it gets that bad *o* to that point ...; **en último ~** as a last resort

extrovertido -da *adj/m,f* extrovert

exuberante *adj* exuberant; ‹*mujer*› voluptuous

exudar [A1] *vt* to exude

exultar [A1] *vi* to exult (frml), to rejoice

eyaculación *f* ejaculation

eyacular [A1] *vi* to ejaculate

Ff

F, f *f* (*read as* /'efe/) *the letter* F, f

fa *m* (nota) F; (en solfeo) fa, fah (BrE)

fábrica *f* factory; **una ~ de zapatos** a shoe factory; **~ de textiles/papel** textile/paper mill; **~ de cerveza** brewery; **~ de conservas** cannery

fabricación *f* manufacture; **la ~ de coches** car manufacture; **de ~ japonesa** made in Japan; **de ~ casera** home-made; **~ en serie** mass production

fabricante *mf* manufacturer

fabricar [A2] *vt* to manufacture; **~ en cadena/serie** to mass-produce; Ⓢ **fabricado en Perú** made in Peru

fábula *f* (Lit) fable; (mentira) fabrication

fabuloso -sa *adj* (maravilloso) (fam) fabulous (colloq)

facción *f* **(a)** (Pol) faction **(b)** **facciones** *fpl* (rasgos) features (*pl*)

faceta *f* facet

facha *f* (fam) (aspecto) look; **no me gustó su ~** I didn't like the look of him; **¿vas a salir con esa ~?** are you going out looking like that?; *estar hecho una ~* to be *o* look a sight (colloq)
■ *adj/mf* (Chi, Esp fam) fascist

fachada *f* **(a)** (de edificio) facade (tech), front **(b)** (apariencia) facade

fácil *adj* **1** **(a)** ‹*problema/lección/vida*› easy; **~ de entender** easy to understand **(b)** (pey) (en lo sexual) easy (pej), loose (pej) **2** (probable): **es ~ que se le olvide** he'll probably forget; **no es ~ que me lo den** they are unlikely to let me have it

facilidad *f* **1** **(a)** (cualidad de fácil) ease; **con ~** easily **(b)** (de una tarea) simplicity **2** (aptitud): **tener ~ para los idiomas/los números** to have a gift for languages/to be good at figures; **tiene ~ de palabra** he has a way with words **3** **facilidades** *fpl* **(a)** (posibilidades, oportunidades): **se le dieron todas las ~es** they gave her every chance **(b)** (Fin) *tb* **~es de pago** credit facilities (*pl*)

facilitar [A1] *vt* **(a)** (hacer más fácil) ‹*tarea*› to make ... easier, facilitate (frml) **(b)** (frml) (proporcionar) ‹*datos/información*› to provide

factible *adj* possible, feasible

factor *m* factor; **el ~ tiempo** the time factor

factoría *f* (fábrica) factory; (astillero) shipyard; (fundición) foundry

factura *f* **1** (Com) invoice (frml), bill; **pasarle ~ a algn** (Fin) to invoice sb **2** (RPl) (Coc) rolls, croissants, etc

facturación f [1] (Com) **(a)** (acción) invoicing **(b)** (volumen) turnover [2] (Ferr) registration; (Aviac) check-in

facturar [A1] vt [1] (Com) **(a)** ⟨mercancías/arreglo⟩ to invoice for, bill for **(b)** (refiriéndose al volumen de ventas) to turn over, have a turnover of [2] (Ferr) to register; (Aviac) to check in
■ ~ vi (Ferr) to register; (Aviac) to check in

facultad f [1] (capacidad) faculty; **está perdiendo ~es** he's losing his faculties; **~es mentales** (mental) faculties (pl) [2] (Educ) faculty; **F~ de Filosofía y Letras** Faculty of Arts

facultar [A1] vt (frml) **~ a algn PARA hacer algo** «jefe/presidente» to authorize sb to do sth; «carnet/documento» to entitle sb to do sth; «ley» to allow sb to do sth

faena f [1] (tarea) task, job; **es una ~ dura** it's hard work; **~s domésticas** housework; **~s agrícolas** farm work [2] (fam) **(a)** (mala pasada) dirty trick; **hacerle una ~ a algn** to play a dirty trick on sb (colloq) **(b)** (contratiempo) drag (colloq), pain (colloq)

fagot /fa'ɣo(t)/ m (instrumento) bassoon
■ mf (músico) bassoonist

faisán m pheasant

faja f **(a)** (prenda interior) girdle **(b)** (cinturón — de traje regional) wide belt; (— de sotana) sash; (— de smoking) cummerbund **(c)** (franja, zona) strip

fajo m (de billetes) wad, roll (AmE); (de papeles) bundle, sheaf

falange f [1] (Anat) phalanx, phalange [2] **(a)** (Mil) phalanx **(b)** (Hist, Pol) phalanx; **la F~** the Spanish Falangist Movement

falda f **(a)** (Indum) skirt; **~ escocesa** (de mujer) tartan skirt, kilt; (de hombre) kilt; **~ pantalón** split skirt, culottes (pl); **se enemistaron por un asunto de ~s** they fell out over a woman **(b)** (de montaña) side

faldón m, **faldones** mpl **(a)** (de camisa) shirttails; (de frac, chaqué) coattails **(b)** (de bebé) christening robe

falla f [1] **(a)** (de tela, cristal) flaw; **la pieza tenía una ~** the part was defective **(b)** (Geol) fault [2] **(a)** (de motor, máquina, sistema — en la composición) defect, fault; (— en el funcionamiento) failure; **~s en el sistema de seguridad** security failures **(b)** (de persona) mistake; **~ humana** (AmL) human error; **¡qué ~!** what a stupid mistake! **(c)** (Dep) miss [3] (AmL exc CS fam) (lástima) pity, shame [4] **(a)** (figura) model, figure (burned during the FALLAS) **(b)** **las Fallas** fpl (fiesta) the festival of San José in Valencia

fallado -da adj (CS) flawed, defective

fallar [A1] vi [1] «juez/jurado» **~ a** or **en favor/en contra de algn** to rule in favor* of/against sb [2] **(a)** «frenos/memoria» to fail; «planes» to go wrong; **le falló el corazón** his heart failed; **le falló la puntería** he missed; **a ti te falla** (AmL) (fam) you've a screw loose (colloq) **(b)** «persona» (+ me/te/le etc) to let ... down
■ ~ vt (errar) to miss; **fallé el tiro** I missed (the shot)

fallecer [E3] vi (frml o euf) to pass away (frml or euph), to die

fallecimiento m (frml) death, passing (frml or euph)

fallero -ra m,f: person who takes part in the preparation of the FALLAS

fallo m **(a)** (en concurso, certamen) decision; (Der) ruling, judgment **(b)** (Esp) ▶ FALLA 2

falluca f (Méx fam) (comercio ilegal) black market (gen in smuggled goods); (mercancía) smuggled goods (pl)

falsear [A1] vt ⟨hechos/datos⟩ to falsify; ⟨verdad/realidad⟩ to distort

falsedad f **(a)** (de afirmación) falseness; (de persona) insincerity, falseness **(b)** (mentira) lie

falsificador -dora m,f forger

falsificar [A2] vt **(a)** ⟨firma/billete/cheque⟩ to forge **(b)** ⟨documento⟩ (copiar) to forge, counterfeit; (alterar) to falsify

falso -sa adj **(a)** ⟨billete⟩ counterfeit, forged; ⟨cuadro⟩ forged; ⟨documento⟩ false, forged; ⟨diamante/joya⟩ fake; ⟨cajón/techo⟩ false **(b)** (insincero) ⟨persona⟩ insincere, false; ⟨sonrisa/promesa⟩ false **(c)** (no cierto) ⟨dato/nombre/declaración⟩ false; **eso es ~** that is not true o is untrue; **falsa alarma** false alarm; **~ testimonio** m (Der) false testimony, perjury

falta f [1] (carencia, ausencia) **~ DE algo** ⟨de interés/dinero⟩ lack OF sth; **~ de personal** staff shortage; **es la ~ de costumbre** it's because I'm/you're not used to it; **fue una ~ de respeto** it was very rude of you/him/her/them; **eso es una ~ de educación** that's bad manners; **a ~ de más información** in the absence of more information [2] (inasistencia) tb **~ de asistencia** absence; **le pusieron ~** they marked her down as absent [3] **(a)** **hacer falta: no hace ~ que se queden** there's no need for you to stay; **si hace ~ ...** if necessary ...; **hacen ~ dos vasos más** we need two more glasses; **le hace ~ descansar** he/she needs to rest **(b)** **sin falta** without fail [4] (defecto) fault; **a pesar de todas sus ~s** in spite of all his faults; **sacarle** or **encontrarle ~s a algo** to find fault with sth; **~ de ortografía** spelling mistake [5] (Dep) **(a)** (infracción — en fútbol, baloncesto) foul; (— en tenis) fault **(b)** (tiro libre — en fútbol) free kick; (— en balonmano) free throw

faltar [A1] vi [1] **(a)** (no estar) to be missing; **¿quién falta?** who's missing?; (en colegio, reunión) who's absent?; **te falta un botón** you have a button missing; **a esta taza le falta el asa** there's no handle on this cup **(b)** (no haber suficiente): **va a ~ vino** there won't be enough wine; **nos faltó tiempo** we didn't have enough time **(c)** (hacer falta): **le falta alguien que la aconseje** she needs someone to advise her; **les falta cariño** they need affection
[2] (quedar): **yo estoy lista ¿a ti te falta mucho?** I'm ready, will you be long?; **nos falta poco para terminar** we're almost finished; **me faltan tres páginas para terminar el libro** I have three pages to go to finish the book; **solo me falta pasarlo a máquina** all I have to do is type it out; **falta poco para Navidad** it's not long until Christmas; **faltan cinco minutos para que empiece** there are five minutes to go before it starts; **¡no faltaba más!** (respuesta — a un agradecimiento) don't mention it!; (— a una petición) of course, certainly!; (— a un ofrecimiento) I wouldn't hear of it!
[3] **(a)** (no asistir): **te esperamos, no faltes** we're expecting you, make sure you come; **~ A algo** ⟨al ⋯⟶

colegio⟩ to be absent FROM sth; ⟨*a una cita*⟩ to miss sth; ∼ **a clase** to skip lessons; **ha faltado dos veces al trabajo** she's been off work twice **(b)** (*no cumplir*): **faltó a su promesa** he didn't keep his promise; **¡no me faltes al respeto!** don't be rude to me

fama *f* **(a)** (renombre, celebridad) fame; **una marca de** ∼ **mundial** a world-famous brand; **dar** ∼ **a algo/algn** to make sth/sb famous **(b)** (reputación) reputation; **tener mala** ∼ to have a bad reputation; **tiene** ∼ **de ser severo** he has a reputation for being strict; **tiene** ∼ **de bromista** he's well known as a joker

familia *f* **(a)** (parientes) family; **una** ∼ **numerosa** a large family; **mi** ∼ **política** my wife's/husband's family, my in-laws (colloq); **es de buena** ∼ *or* **de** ∼ **bien** he's from a good family; **somos como de la** ∼ we're just like family; **le viene de** ∼ it runs in the family **(b)** (hijos) children; **no tienen** ∼ they don't have any children

familiar *adj* **(a)** ⟨*vida/vínculo*⟩ family (*before n*); ⟨*envase/coche*⟩ family (*before n*) **(b)** ⟨*trato/tono*⟩ familiar, informal; ⟨*lenguaje/expresión*⟩ colloquial **(c)** (conocido) ⟨*cara/lugar*⟩ familiar; **su voz me resulta** ∼ her voice is familiar
■ *mf* relative, relation

familiaridad *f* familiarity

familiarizarse [A4] *v pron* ∼ CON **algo** to familiarize oneself WITH sth, become familiar WITH sth

famoso -sa *adj* famous; ∼ POR **algo** famous FOR sth
■ *m,f* celebrity, famous person

fan *mf* (*pl* **fans**) fan

fanático -ca *adj* fanatical
■ *m,f* (en general) fanatic; **es un** ∼ **de la gimnasia** he's a gym fanatic; (de fútbol) (AmS period) fan

fanatismo *m* fanaticism

fanfarrón -rrona *adj* (fam) (al hablar) loudmouthed (colloq); (al actuar): **no seas** ∼ stop showing off
■ *m,f* (fam) (al hablar) loudmouth (colloq); (al actuar) show-off (colloq)

fanfarronear [A1] *vi* (fam) **(a)** (al hablar) to boast, brag **(b)** (al actuar) to show off (colloq)

fango *m* mud

fantasear [A1] *vi* to fantasize

fantasía *f* **1** **(a)** (imaginación) imagination **(b)** (ficción) fantasy; **vive en un mundo de** ∼ he's living in a fantasy world **2** (bisutería): **joyas de** ∼ costume jewelry*; **una pulsera de** ∼ an imitation diamond (*o* ruby *etc*) bracelet

fantasma *m* **(a)** (aparición) ghost **(b)** (amenaza) specter*

fantástico -ca *adj* fantastic

fantochear [A1] *vi* (AmL fam) ▶ FANFARRONEAR

faquir *m* fakir

faraón *m* Pharaoh

fardar [A1] *vi* (Esp fam) «*persona*» ▶ FANFARRONEAR

fardo *m* (de algodón, paja) bale; (de ropa) bundle

faringe *f* pharynx

faringitis *f* pharyngitis

farmacéutico -ca *adj* pharmaceutical
■ *m,f* druggist (AmE), chemist (BrE)

farmacia *f* **(a)** (tienda) drugstore (AmE), chemist's (BrE); ∼ **de guardia** *or* **de turno** duty chemist **(b)** (disciplina) pharmacy

faro *m* **(a)** (Náut) lighthouse **(b)** (Auto) headlight, headlamp; ∼ **antiniebla** fog light *o* (BrE) lamp

farol *m* (de alumbrado público) streetlight, streetlamp; (en jardín, portal) lantern, lamp; ∼ **de papel** paper lantern

farola *f* (luz) streetlight, streetlamp; (poste) lamppost

farolillo *m* (de papel) Chinese lantern

farra *f* (fam) ▶ JUERGA

farrear [A1] *vi* (AmL fam) to go out partying (colloq), go out on the town (colloq)
■ **farrearse** *v pron* (AmL fam) ⟨*fortuna/dinero*⟩ to blow (colloq); ⟨*oportunidad*⟩ to throw away

farrero -ra *adj/m,f* (AmL fam) ▶ FARRISTA

farrista *adj* (AmL fam): **estudiantes** ∼**s** students who are always out living it up
■ *mf* (AmL fam): **es un** ∼ he's always out living it up

farsa *f* (Teatr) farce; (engaño) sham, farce

farsante *mf* fraud, fake

fascículo *m* part (*of a serialized publication*), fascicle (tech)

fascinación *f* fascination

fascinante *adj* fascinating

fascinar [A1] *vi* (fam): **me fascinó ese programa** I found that program fascinating; **me fascina viajar** I love travelling
■ ∼ *vt* to fascinate, captivate

fascismo *m* fascism

fascista *adj/mf* fascist

fase *f* **(a)** (etapa) stage, phase; **la** ∼ **de clasificación** the preliminary round; **está todavía en** ∼ **de negociación** it is still being negotiated **(b)** (Astron, Elec, Fis, Quím) phase

fastidiado -da *adj* (esp Esp fam): **estoy un poco** ∼ I'm not too good *o* too well; **anda** ∼ **de los riñones** he's having trouble with his kidneys

fastidiar [A1] *vt* **(a)** (molestar, irritar) ⟨*persona*⟩ to bother, pester **(b)** (esp Esp fam) (estropear) ⟨*mecanismo/plan*⟩ to mess up; ⟨*fiesta/excursión*⟩ to spoil; ⟨*estómago*⟩ to upset
■ ∼ *vi*: **me fastidia tener que repetir las cosas** it annoys me to have to repeat things; **¡no fastidies! ¿de veras?** go on! you're kidding! (colloq)
■ **fastidiarse** *v pron* **(a)** (AmL fam) (molestarse) to get annoyed **(b)** (fam) (jorobarse): **tendré que** ∼**me** I'll have to put up with it (colloq); **¡te fastidias!** (Esp) tough! (colloq) **(c)** (Esp fam) (estropearse) «*velada/plan*» to be ruined

fastidio *m* (molestia) annoyance; **¡qué** ∼**!** what a nuisance!

fastidioso -sa *adj* **(a)** (molesto) ⟨*persona*⟩ tiresome, annoying; ⟨*trabajo*⟩ tiresome, irksome **(b)** (Méx, Per fam) (quisquilloso) fussy (colloq)

fastuoso -sa *adj* ⟨*salón*⟩ magnificent; ⟨*banquete*⟩ lavish

fatal *adj* **1** ⟨*accidente/enfermedad/consecuencias*⟩ fatal **2** (fam) (muy malo) terrible, awful; **fue un fin de semana** ∼ it was a terrible weekend; **me encuentro** ∼ I feel awful; **su padre está** ∼ his father's in a really bad way (colloq)
■ *adv* (esp Esp fam): **viste** ∼ he dresses really badly; **me caen** ∼ I can't stand them (colloq)

fatiga *f* (a) (cansancio) tiredness, fatigue (frml) (b) (ahogo) breathlessness

fatigado -da *adj* tired, weary

fatigar [A3] *vt* (físicamente) to tire ... out; (mentalmente) to tire

■ **fatigarse** *v pron* (a) (cansarse) to get tired, wear oneself out (colloq) (b) (ahogarse) to get breathless

fatigoso -sa *adj* ‹trabajo› tiring, exhausting

faul *m* (*pl* **fauls**) (AmL) foul

faulear [A1] *vt* (AmL) to foul

fauna *f* fauna

favor *m* (a) (ayuda, servicio) favor*; ¿me puedes hacer un ∼? can you do me a favor?; vengo a pedirte un ∼ I've come to ask you (for) a favor; ¿me harías el ∼ de copiarme esto? would you copy this for me, please?; hagan el ∼ de esperar would you mind waiting, please? (b) (*en locs*) a favor in favor*; dos votos a ∼ two votes in favor; en ∼ de in favour of; estar a ∼ de algo/algn/hacer algo to be in favor* of sth/sb/doing sth; por favor please

favorable *adj* favorable*

favorecedor -dora *adj* becoming

favorecer [E3] *vt* (a) (ayudar, beneficiar) to favor*; una política para ∼ la agricultura a policy to help agriculture (b) «peinado/color» (sentar bien) to suit

favoritismo *m* favoritism*

favorito -ta *adj/m,f* favorite*

fax *m* fax; mándaselo por ∼ fax it to him

faxear [A1] *vt* to fax, send ... by fax

Fdo (= firmado) (en correspondencia) signed

fe *f* (a) (Relig) faith; (creencia, confianza) faith; tener ∼ en algo/algn to have faith in sth/sb; puse toda mi ∼ en ti I put all my trust in you (b) (intención): no dudo de su buena ∼ I don't doubt his good intentions; actuar de buena/mala ∼ to act in good/bad faith

febrero *m* February; *para ejemplos ver* ENERO

fecha *f* date; ¿qué ∼ es hoy? what's the date today?, what date is it today?; con ∼ 7 de marzo (Corresp) dated March 7 *o* (BrE) 7th March; hasta la ∼ to date; el año pasado por estas ∼s this time last year; en ∼ próxima soon; ∼ de caducidad *or* (AmL) vencimiento (de medicamento) expiration date (AmE), expiry date (BrE); (de alimento) use-by date; ∼ de consumo preferente best-before date; ∼ límite *or* tope (para solicitud, suscripción) closing date; (para proyecto, trabajo) deadline

fechar [A1] *vt* to date

fechoría *f* misdeed

fecundación *f* fertilization; ∼ in vitro in vitro fertilization

fecundar [A1] *vt* ‹óvulo› to fertilize; ‹animal› to inseminate

fecundo -da *adj* (a) (Biol) ‹mujer› fertile (b) ‹región/tierra› fertile; ‹labor› fruitful

federación *f* federation

federal *adj* federal

felicidad *f* (a) (alegría) happiness (b) ¡felicidades! *interj* (por cumpleaños) Happy Birthday!; (en Navidad) Merry Christmas!; (por un logro) congratulations!

felicitación *f* (a) (escrito — por un logro) letter of congratulation; (— en Navidad) Christmas card

(*or* letter wishing sb Merry Christmas) (b) **felicitaciones** *fpl* (deseo — por un logro) congratulations (*pl*); (— en Navidad) greetings (*pl*) (c) ¡felicitaciones! *interj* (AmL) congratulations!

felicitar [A1] *vt* (a) (por un logro) to congratulate; ¡te felicito! congratulations!; me felicitó por el premio he congratulated me on winning the prize (b) (por Navidad) to wish ... (a) Merry Christmas; (por cumpleaños) to wish ... (a) Happy Birthday

feligrés -gresa *m,f* parishioner

feliz *adj* happy; les deseo que sean muy felices I wish you every happiness; ¡∼ cumpleaños! happy birthday!; ¡∼ Navidad! Merry Christmas!; ¡∼ Año Nuevo! Happy New Year!; ¡∼ viaje! have a good trip!

felpa *f* (Tex) (para toallas) toweling*; (en tapicería) plush

felpudo *m* doormat

femenil *adj* (Méx) ‹equipo/moda› ladies' (*before n*), women's (*before n*)

femenino -na *adj* (a) ‹equipo/moda› ladies' (*before n*), women's (*before n*); ‹hormona/sexo› female (b) ‹vestido/modales/chica› feminine (c) (Ling) feminine

femineidad, feminidad *f* femininity

feminismo *m* feminism

feminista *adj/mf* feminist

fenomenal *adj* (fam) great (colloq)

■ *adv* (fam): lo pasamos ∼ we had a great time (colloq); me vino ∼ it was exactly *o* just what I needed; ¡∼! great! (colloq)

fenómeno[1] -na *adj/adv* (AmL) ▶ FENOMENAL

fenómeno[2] *m* (suceso) phenomenon

feo[1], fea *adj* (a) ‹persona/edificio› ugly; ‹peinado› unflattering; es fea de cara she has a very plain face; es un barrio ∼ it's not a very nice neighborhood (b) ‹asunto/situación› unpleasant; ‹color/sabor› (esp AmL) unpleasant; ¡qué ∼ está el día! what an awful day!; la cosa se está poniendo fea things are getting nasty *o* ugly; es *or* (Esp) está muy ∼ hablar así it's not nice to talk like that

feo[2] *adv* (AmL) ‹oler/saber› bad; me miró ∼ she gave me a dirty look

féretro *m* coffin

feria *f* [1] (a) (exposición comercial) fair; (— en muestras) trade fair (b) (CS, Per) (mercado) (street) market [2] (a) (fiesta popular) festival (b) (parque de atracciones) fair [3] (Méx fam) (cambio, suelto) small change; (dinero) cash (colloq)

feriado *m* (AmL) (public) holiday

fermentar [A1] *vi/vt* to ferment

fermento *m* ferment

feroz *adj* (a) ‹animal› ferocious, fierce; ‹ataque/mirada/odio› fierce, vicious; ‹viento/tempestad› fierce, violent (b) (Col, Méx, Ven fam) (feo) horrendous (colloq)

ferretería *f* (tienda) hardware store, ironmonger's (BrE); (mercancías) hardware, ironmongery (BrE)

ferrocarril *m* railroad (AmE), railway (BrE)

ferrocarrilero -ra *adj* (Chi, Méx) rail (*before n*)

ferroviario -ria *adj* rail (*before n*)

ferry /'ferri/ m (pl **-rrys**) ferry

fértil adj fertile

fertilización f fertilization; ~ **in vitro** in vitro fertilization

fertilizante m fertilizer

fertilizar [A4] vt to fertilize, put fertilizer on

ferviente adj ⟨admiración/creyente⟩ fervent; ⟨deseo⟩ burning; ⟨fe/defensor⟩ passionate

fervor m fervor*; **con** ~ fervently

festejado -da m,f ⟨CS⟩ person celebrating his/ her birthday (o saint's day etc)

festejar [A1] vt (AmL) (celebrar) to celebrate

festejo m celebration, festivity

festín m feast, banquet

festival m festival; ~ **de cine** film festival

festividad f **(a)** (fiesta religiosa) feast, festivity **(b) festividades** fpl (festejos) festivities (pl)

festivo -va adj festive; ▶ DÍA 1B

fetidez f (cualidad) smelliness; (olor) stench

fétido -da adj fetid, foul-smelling

feto m fetus*

feúcho -cha adj (fam) ⟨mujer⟩ plain, homely (AmE colloq); **es** ~ he's not much to look at

feudalismo m feudalism

fiable adj reliable

fiaca adj inv (RPl fam) bone idle (colloq), lazy ■ f (Andes, CS fam) (pereza): **me da** ~ I can't be bothered

fiador -dora m,f (Com, Der, Fin) guarantor

fiambre m (Coc): **tb** ~**s** cold cuts (pl) (AmE), cold meats (pl) (BrE)

fiambrería f (AmL) delicatessen

fianza f **(a)** (Der) bail; **salió bajo** ~ she was released on bail **(b)** (Com) deposit

fiar [A17] vt ⟨mercancías⟩ to sell ... on credit ■ ~ vi **(a)** (dar crédito) to give credit **(b) ser de** ~ «persona» (digno de confianza) to be trustworthy; (responsable) to be reliable; «mecanismo/motor» to be reliable ■ **fiarse** v pron: **no me fío de lo que dice** I don't believe what he says; ~**se DE algn** to trust sb

fiasco m fiasco

fibra f fiber*; ~**s artificiales** man-made fibers; ~ **de vidrio** fiberglass*; ~ **óptica** optical fiber*

ficción f fiction

ficha f **1** (para datos) card; (de fichero) index card; ~ **médica** medical records (pl); ~ **policial** police record **2 (a)** (de teléfono, estacionamiento) token **(b)** (Jueg) (de dominó) domino; (de damas) checker(AmE), draught (BrE); (de otros juegos de mesa) counter; (de ruleta, póker) chip

fichaje m (Dep) (acción) signing (up); (jugador) signing, trade (AmE)

fichar [A1] vt **(a)** «policía» to open a file on **(b)** «equipo/club» to sign (up) ■ ~ vi (en fábrica, oficina — a la entrada) to clock in, punch in (AmE); (— a la salida) to clock out o (BrE) off, to punch out (AmE)

fichero m **(a)** (mueble para carpetas) filing cabinet **(b)** (cajón — de carpetas) filing draw; (— para tarjetas) card index draw **(c)** (caja) index card file (AmE), card index box (BrE) **(d)** (conjunto de fichas) file; (Inf) file

ficticio -cia adj ⟨personaje/suceso⟩ fictitious

fidelidad f **(a)** (de persona, animal) fidelity, faithfulness **(b)** (de reproducción) faithfulness, fidelity; (de instrumento) accuracy, precision

fideo m **(a)** (pasta fina) noodle; (muy finos) vermicelli **(b) fideos** mpl (RPl) (pasta en general) pasta

fiebre f **(a)** (Med) fever; **tener** ~ to be feverish, to have a fever (esp AmE), to have a temperature (esp BrE); **le bajó la** ~ his fever o temperature came down; ~ **del heno** hay fever; ~ **palúdica** malaria **(b)** (furor) obsession; **le dio la** ~ **de la limpieza** he went crazy and started cleaning the whole house (colloq); ~ **del oro** gold fever

fiel adj **(a)** ⟨persona/animal⟩ faithful; **serle** ~ **a algn** to be faithful to sb; ~ **al rey** loyal to the king **(b)** ⟨traducción/copia⟩ faithful, accurate ■ mf (Relig) **los** ~**es** the faithful

fieltro m felt

fiera f (animal) wild animal, beast (liter); **ponerse como** or **hecho una** ~ to go wild (colloq)

fiero -ra adj ⟨animal⟩ fierce, ferocious

fierro m **(a)** (AmL) (hierro) iron; (fam) (trozo de metal) piece of metal **(b) fierros** mpl (Méx fam) (en los dientes) braces (pl) (AmE), brace (esp BrE)

fiesta f **(a)** (celebración) party; ~ **de cumpleaños** birthday party; **dieron una gran** ~ they threw o had a big party; **estar de** ~ to be having a party; **aguar la** ~ to spoil the fun **(b)** (día festivo) (public) holiday; **el lunes es** ~ Monday is a holiday; ~ **nacional** (día festivo) public holiday; (Taur) bullfighting; ~ **patria** (AmL) independence day **(c) fiestas** fpl (festejos) fiesta, festival; (de fin de año, etc) festive season; **¡felices** ~**s!** Merry Christmas!; **¿dónde vas a pasar estas** ~**s?** where are you going to spend the vacation (AmE) o (BrE) holidays?

FIFA /'fifa/ f: **la** ~ FIFA

figura f figure; **tiene buena** ~ she has a good figure; **una** ~ **de las letras** an important literary figure; ~ **paterna** father figure

figuración f (imaginación) imagining; **son figuraciones tuyas** it's all in your imagination

figurado -da adj figurative; **en sentido** ~ in a figurative sense

figurar [A1] vi (en lista, documento) to appear ■ **figurarse** v pron to imagine; **me figuro que sí** I imagine so, I figure she (o he etc) will (AmE); **me figuro que tardaremos una hora** I reckon o (AmE) figure that it'll take us one hour; **¡figúrate, tardamos dos horas!** just imagine! it took us two hours; **ya me lo figuraba yo** I thought as much, so I thought

figurita f (de adorno) figurine; (lámina) (RPl) picture card

fijación *f* (Psic) fixation, obsession; ¡que ~ tienes con ese tema! you're obsessed with that subject!

fijar [A1] *vt* ☐1 **(a)** (poner, clavar) ⟨*poste/ estantería*⟩ to fix; **⑤ prohibido fijar carteles** stick no bills; **fijó la mirada en el horizonte** she fixed her gaze on the horizon **(b)** ⟨*atención/mente*⟩ to focus
☐2 **(a)** ⟨*residencia*⟩ to take up, establish (frml) **(b)** ⟨*fecha/cifra/precio*⟩ to set **(c)** «*reglamento/ley*» to state
■ **fijarse** *v pron* **(a)** (prestar atención): **fíjate bien en cómo lo hace** watch carefully how she does it; **fíjate en lo que haces** watch *o* pay attention to what you're doing **(b)** (darse cuenta) to notice; **¿te has fijado en que no discuten nunca?** have you noticed that they never quarrel?; **¡fíjate lo que ha crecido!** just look how she's grown!

fijo¹ -ja *adj* **(a)** (no movible) fixed; **una lámpara fija a la pared** a lamp fixed to the wall; **con los ojos ~s en ella** with his eyes fixed on her; **asegúrate de que la escalera está bien fija** make sure the ladder is steady **(b)** ⟨*sueldo/precios*⟩ fixed; ⟨*trabajo/empleado*⟩ permanent; ⟨*cliente*⟩ regular **(c)** (definitivo) ⟨*fecha*⟩ definite, firm

fijo² *adv* (fam): **¿crees que vendrá?** — **fijo** do you think she'll come? — definitely *o* (colloq) sure; ~ **que el domingo llueve** it's bound to rain on Sunday

fila *f* **(a)** (hilera) line; **formen ~ aquí** line up *o* form a line here; **en ~ india** in single file; **estacionado en doble ~** double-parked **(b)** (en teatro, aula) row **(c) filas** *fpl* (Mil) ranks (*pl*); **incorporarse a ~s** to join up; **lo llamaron a ~s** he was drafted

filamento *m* (Elec) filament; (hilo, fibra) thread

filatelia *f* stamp collecting, philately

filete *m* (de pescado) fillet; (de carne — bistec) steak; (— corte entre las costillas y el lomo) (Chi, Méx) fillet

filiación *f* (afiliación) affiliation; ~ **política** political affiliation

filial *adj* **(a)** ⟨*amor*⟩ filial **(b)** ⟨*compañía/ asociación*⟩ affiliate (*before n*), subsidiary
■ *f* subsidiary (company)

Filipinas *fpl*: *tb* **las ~** the Philippines

filipino -na *adj* Philippine, Filipino
■ *m,f* Filipino

film *m* (*pl* **films**) **(a)** (Cin, TV) movie, film (BrE) **(b)** (Coc) *tb* ~ **transparente** Saran wrap® (AmE), clingfilm (BrE)

filmadora *f* (AmL) movie camera (AmE), cinecamera (BrE)

filmar [A1] *vt* ⟨*película*⟩ to shoot; ⟨*persona/ suceso*⟩ to film

filmina *f* slide

filmoteca *f* film library

filo *m* **(a)** (de cuchillo, espada) cutting edge, blade; **no tiene mucho ~** it isn't very sharp; **le voy a dar ~** I'm going to sharpen it **(b)** (borde) edge; **el ~ de la mesa** the edge of the table; **al ~ de las siete** at seven o'clock sharp

filología *f* philology; **una licenciatura en ~ francesa** a degree in French

filólogo -ga *m,f* philologist; **soy ~** I have a degree in languages

filón *m* **(a)** (Min) seam, vein **(b)** (fam) (negocio) gold mine (colloq)

filoso -sa *adj* (AmL) ⟨*cuchillo/hoja*⟩ sharp

filosofía *f* philosophy

filosófico -ca *adj* philosophical

filósofo -fa *m,f* philosopher

filtración *f* (en general) leak ; (de información) leak; **la ~ de un informe** the leaking of a report

filtrar [A1] *vt* **(a)** ⟨*líquido/rayos*⟩ to filter **(b)** ⟨*informaciones/noticias*⟩ to leak
■ **filtrarse** *v pron* **(a)** «*agua*» to leak; «*humedad*» to seep; **la luz se filtraba por entre las persianas** light filtered through the shutters **(b)** «*noticia*» to leak

filtro *m* filter; ~ **solar** sunscreen

fin *m* ☐1 **(a)** (final) end; **a ~es de junio** at the end of June; **a ~ de mes** at the end of the month; ~ **de año** New Year's Eve; ~ **de semana** (sábado y domingo) weekend; **puso ~ a la discusión** she put an end to the discussion **(b)** (en locs) **por** *o* **al fin** at last; **en fin** (expresando resignación) ah well; **en ~ ¡sigamos!** anyway, let's carry on!; **a ~ de cuentas** in the end, at the end of the day; **al ~ y al cabo** after all
☐2 **(a)** (objetivo, finalidad) purpose; **el ~ de esta visita** the aim *o* purpose of this visit **(b)** (en locs) **a fin de que** (frml) in order to; **con este fin** (frml) with this aim (frml), to this end (frml); **con el fin** *or* **a fin de** (frml) with the aim *o* purpose of

final *adj* ⟨*decisión*⟩ final; ⟨*objetivo*⟩ ultimate
■ *m* end; **a ~es de junio** at the end of June; **un ~ feliz** a happy ending; **a ~ de la lista** at the bottom of the list; **al ~ tendrá que decidirse** he'll have to make his mind up in the end *o* eventually
■ *f* (Dep) **(a)** (en fútbol, tenis etc) final; **la ~ de copa** the cup final; **pasar a la ~** to go through to *o* make it to the final **(b) finales** *fpl* (en béisbol, baloncesto, fútbol americano) playoffs (*pl*)

finalidad *f* (propósito, utilidad) purpose, aim

finalista *adj*: **los dos equipos ~s** the two teams that reach (*o* reached *etc*) the final
■ *mf* finalist

finalizar [A4] *vt* to finish
■ *vi* to end; **una vez finalizada la reunión** once the meeting is/was over

financiación *f*, **financiamiento** *m* financing

financiar [A1] *vt* **(a)** ⟨*empresa/proyecto*⟩ to finance, fund **(b)** (AmL) (vender a plazos) to give credit facilities for

financiero -ra *adj* financial
■ *m,f* financier

financista *mf* (AmL) financier

finanzas *fpl* finances (*pl*)

finca *f* **(a)** (explotación agrícola) farm **(b)** (casa de campo) country estate **(c)** (Esp) (propiedad urbana) building

fincar [A2] *vt* (Méx) to build

fingido -da *adj* hypocritical, false

fingir [I7] *vt* **(a)** ⟨*alegría/desinterés*⟩ to feign, fake; **fingió no verme** she pretended not to see me **(b)** ⟨*voz*⟩ to imitate
■ ~ *vi* to pretend
■ **fingirse** *v pron*: **se fingió apenado** he pretended to be sorry

finlandés¹ -desa adj Finnish
■ m,f (persona) Finn
finlandés² m (idioma) Finnish
Finlandia f Finland
fino¹ -na adj ⓵ (en grosor) ⟨papel/capa/hilo⟩ fine, thin; ⟨loncha⟩ thin; ⟨arena/pelo/lluvia⟩ fine; ⟨labios⟩ thin; ⟨cintura/dedos⟩ slender; ⟨punta/lápiz⟩ fine ⓶ (en calidad) ⟨pastelería/bollería⟩ high quality; ⟨porcelana⟩ fine; ⟨lencería⟩ sheer ⓷ (en modales) refined ⓸ (a) ⟨oído/olfato⟩ acute (b) ⟨ironía/humor⟩ subtle
fino² m fino, dry sherry
firma f ⓵ (nombre) signature; (acción) signing ⓶ (empresa) company, firm (BrE)
firmamento m (liter) firmament (liter)
firmar [A1] vt/vi to sign
firme adj ⓵ ⟨escalera/silla/mesa⟩ steady; **terreno ~** solid ground; **con paso/pulso ~** with a firm step/steady hand; **una oferta en ~** a firm offer; **de ~** ⟨estudiar/trabajar⟩ hard ⓶ (Mil): **¡~s!** attention! ⓷ (a) ⟨persona⟩ firm; **mostrarse ~ con algn** to be firm with sb; **me mantuve ~ en mi idea** I stuck o kept to my idea (b) (delante del n) ⟨creencia/convicción⟩ firm
firmeza f (a) (de convicciones, carácter) strength; **con ~** firmly (b) (del terreno) firmness
fiscal adj fiscal, tax (before n)
■ mf ≈ district attorney (in US), ≈ public prosecutor (in UK)
fiscalizar [A4] vt to supervise, control
fisco m ≈ Treasury (in US), ≈ Exchequer (in UK)
fisgar [A3] vi (fam) to snoop (colloq); **andaba fisgando por las oficinas** he was snooping around the offices
fisgón -gona adj (fam) nosy (colloq)
■ m,f (fam) busybody (colloq)
fisgonear [A1] vi (fam) to nose around (colloq)
física f physics; **~ nuclear** nuclear physics
físico¹ -ca adj physical
■ m,f physicist
físico² m (cuerpo — de hombre, atleta) physique; (— de mujer) figure; (apariencia) appearance
fisionomía, fisonomía f (a) (de persona) features (pl) (b) (de objeto, lugar) appearance
fisioterapia f physiotherapy, physical therapy (AmE)
flaccidez f flaccidity
fláccido -da adj flaccid, flabby
flaco -ca adj thin, skinny (colloq)
flagelar [A1] vt to flagellate (frml); (Bib) to scourge
■ **flagelarse** v pron to flagellate oneself (frml), to whip oneself
flagrante adj ⟨mentira⟩ blatant; ⟨injusticia⟩ glaring, flagrant; **lo sorprendieron en ~ delito** they caught him red-handed
flama f (Méx) flame
flamable adj (Méx) inflammable, flammable
flamante adj (gen delante del n) (nuevo) brand-new; (vistoso) smart (colloq)
flamenco¹ -ca adj ⓵ ⟨cante/baile⟩ flamenco (before n) ⓶ (de Flandes) Flemish
■ m,f Fleming; **los ~s** the Flemish

flamenco² m ⓵ (Mús) flamenco ⓶ (idioma) Flemish ⓷ (Zool) flamingo
flan m (a) (dulce) crème caramel (b) (de arroz) mold*; (de pescado, verduras) terrine
flanco m (a) (Mil) flank (b) (de animal) flank, side; (de persona) side
Flandes m Flanders
flaquear [A1] vi «persona/fuerzas» to flag; **su voluntad empezó a ~** she began to lose heart
flaqueza f weakness
flash /'flas/ m (pl **flashes**) (Fot) flash
flato m (a) (Esp) (dolor en el costado): **tengo ~** I have a stitch (b) (Chi fam) (eructo) burp (colloq)
flauta f (Mús) flute; **~ dulce** recorder
■ mf flute player, flutist (AmE), flautist (BrE)
flautín m piccolo
■ mf piccolo (player)
flautista mf flute player, flutist (AmE), flautist (BrE)
flecha f arrow
flechazo m (a) (fam) (enamoramiento): **fue un ~** it was love at first sight (b) (herida) arrow wound
fleco m (Méx) (en el pelo) bangs (pl) (AmE), fringe (BrE)
flecos mpl (a) (adorno) fringe; **un chal con ~** a fringed shawl (b) (borde deshilachado) frayed edge
flema f phlegm
flemático -ca adj phlegmatic
flemón m boil, abscess; (en la encía) gumboil
flequillo m bangs (pl) (AmE), fringe (BrE)
fletar [A1] vt (Com, Transp) ⟨barco/avión⟩ to charter; ⟨autobús/camión⟩ to hire, rent (AmE)
flete m (a) (contratación — de barco, avión) charter; (— de autobús, camión) hire (b) (precio de contratación — de barco, avión) charter fee; (— de autobús, camión) hire charge, rental charge (AmE)
flexibilidad f flexibility
flexible adj flexible
flexión f (Dep) (de brazos) push-up, press-up (BrE); (de piernas) squat; **hacer flexiones** (de brazos) to do push-ups o press-ups; (de cintura) to touch one's toes
flexionar [A1] vt (Dep) ⟨pierna/rodillas⟩ to bend
flirt /'flirt/ m (pl **flirts**) (a) (relación) fling (b) (hombre) boyfriend; (mujer) girlfriend
flirtear [A1] vi to flirt
flojear [A1] vi (a) (debilitarse) to grow o get weak; **me flojean las piernas** my legs are getting weak (b) (fam) (holgazanear) to laze around
flojera f (a) (fam) (debilidad) lethargy (b) (fam) (pereza) laziness; **me da ~** I can't be bothered; **tengo ~** I feel lazy
flojo -ja adj ⓵ (a) ⟨nudo/tornillo/vendaje⟩ loose; ⟨cuerda/goma⟩ slack (b) ⟨débil⟩ weak (c) ⟨vientos⟩ light (d) ⟨café/té⟩ weak ⓶ (mediocre) ⟨trabajo/examen⟩ poor; ⟨película/vino⟩ second-rate; ⟨estudiante⟩ poor; **está ~ en física** he's weak in (AmE) o (BrE) at physics ⓷ ⟨persona⟩ (fam) (perezoso) lazy
■ m,f (fam) (perezoso) lazybones (colloq)
floppy /'flopi/ m (pl **floppys**) floppy disk, diskette
flor f (de planta) flower; (de árbol frutal) blossom; **~es secas** dried flowers; **un vestido de ~es** a

flowery dress; en ~ in flower o bloom/in blossom; ~ **de azahar** orange/lemon blossom; **la** ~ **y nata** the cream, the crème de la crème

flora f flora

florear [A1] vi **(a)** (Chi, Méx) (Bot) to flower, blossom **(b)** (Méx) (halagar): **le** ~**on mucho su vestido** her dress got a lot of compliments

florecer [E3] vi **(a)** «*tulipán/rosa*» to flower, bloom; «*árbol*» to flower, blossom **(b)** (prosperar) to flourish, thrive

floreciente adj flourishing, thriving

Florencia f Florence

florentino -na adj/m,f Florentine

florería f (AmL) florist's, flower shop

florero m vase

florido -da adj **(a)** ‹campo› full of flowers **(b)** ‹estilo/lenguaje› flowery

florín m (moneda holandesa) guilder

florista mf florist

floristería f florist's, flower shop

flota f **1** (de barcos, camiones, aviones) fleet **2** (Col) (autobús) bus (AmE), coach (BrE)

flotador m (en general) float; (para la cintura) rubber ring; (para los brazos) armband

flotante adj floating

flotar [A1] vi to float

flote: a ~ afloat; **mantenerse a** ~ to stay afloat; **logró mantener el negocio a** ~ he managed to keep the business afloat; **salir a** ~ «*cuerpo sumergido*» to float to the surface; «*país/persona en apuros*» to get back on its/one's feet

flotilla f (Náut) flotilla; (Aviac) fleet

fluctuar [A18] vi to fluctuate

fluidez f **(a)** (de expresión) fluency; **habla griego con** ~ she speaks Greek fluently **(b)** (de tráfico) smooth flow **(c)** (Fís, Quím) fluidity

fluido adj ‹estilo/language› fluent; ‹circulación› free-flowing; ‹movimientos› fluid, fluent ■ m fluid

fluir [I20] vi to flow

flujo m **1** (circulación, corriente) flow; ~ **sanguíneo** blood flow **2** (Med) (secreción) discharge; ~ **menstrual** menstrual flow **3** (Náut) tide; ~ **y reflujo** ebb and flow

fluminense adj of/from Rio de Janeiro

flúor, fluor m (gas) fluorine; (fluoruro) fluoride

fluorescente adj fluorescent

fluvial adj river (before n)

fobia f phobia; **tiene** ~ **a los aviones** he has a phobia about flying

foca f (animal) seal; (piel) sealskin

focal adj focal

foco m **1** **(a)** (Fís, Fot, Mat) focus **(b)** (centro, núcleo) focus; **fue el** ~ **de todas las miradas** everybody's eyes were focused on him **(c)** (de incendio) seat **2** **(a)** (reflector) (Cin, Teatr) spotlight; (en estadio, monumento) floodlight **(b)** (AmL) (Auto) light **(c)** (Ec, Méx, Per) (de lámpara) light bulb **(d)** (AmC) (linterna) flashlight (AmE), torch (BrE)

fogata f bonfire

fogón m (quemador) burner; (fogata) (AmL) bonfire, campfire; (de caldera) firebox

fogonazo m flash, explosion

fogueado -da adj (AmS fam) experienced

fogueo m (Mil): **un cartucho de** ~ a blank (cartridge)

folio m **(a)** (hoja) sheet (of paper); **papel tamaño** ~ A4 paper **(b)** (de un trabajo, una tesis) page

folk /'fo(l)k/ adj folk (before n) ■ m folk (music)

folklore m folklore

folklórico -ca adj **(a)** ‹danza/música/leyenda› folk (before n) **(b)** (fam) (pintoresco) quaint

follaje m foliage

folletín m (en periódicos, revistas) newspaper serial; (revista mala) rag (colloq); (película, novela mala) melodrama

folleto m (hoja) leaflet, flier (AmE); (librito) brochure, pamphlet; ~ **de viaje** travel brochure

follón m (Esp fam) **(a)** (trifulca) commotion, ruckus; (ruido) racket (colloq); din (AmE colloq); **armó un buen** ~ (montó una trifulca) he kicked up a hell of a fuss (colloq); (hizo ruido) he made such a racket o din (colloq) **(b)** (situación confusa, desorden) mess **(c)** (problema) trouble; **no te metas en follones** don't get into trouble

fomentar [A1] vt ‹industria/turismo› to promote; ‹ahorro/inversión› to encourage, boost; ‹disturbio/odio› to incite, foment (frml); ‹interés/afición› to encourage

fonda f **(a)** (esp AmL) (restaurant) cheap restaurant **(b)** (esp Esp) (pensión) boarding house **(c)** (Chi) (puesto) refreshment stand

fondista mf (Dep) long-distance runner

fondo m **1** **(a)** (parte más baja) bottom; **el** ~ **del mar** the bottom of the sea; **llegaré al** ~ **de esta cuestión** I'll get to the bottom of this matter **(b)** (parte de atrás — de pasillo, calle) end; (— de habitación) back; **al** ~ **de la sala** at the back of the room **(c)** (profundidad): **tiene poco** ~ it is not very deep **(d)** (de edificio) depth **(e)** (en cuadro, fotografía) background

2 (Lit) (contenido) content

3 (Fin) **(a)** (de dinero) fund; **hacer un** ~ **común** to start a joint fund o (colloq) a kitty **(b)** **fondos** mpl (dinero) money, funds (pl); **recaudar** ~**s** to raise money; **un cheque sin** ~**s** a dud o (AmE) rubber check (colloq)

4 (Dep) (en atletismo): **de** ~ ‹corredor/carrera/prueba› long-distance (before n)

5 (Méx) (Indum) slip, underskirt

6 (en locs) **a fondo** (loc adj) ‹estudio/investigación› in-depth (before n); ‹limpieza› thorough; (loc adv) ‹prepararse/entrenar› thoroughly; **conoce el tema a** ~ she knows the subject really well; **de fondo** ‹ruido/música› background (before n); **en el fondo: en el** ~ **nos llevamos bien** we get on all right, really; **en el** ~ **no es malo** deep down he's not a bad person

fonética f phonetics

fonógrafo m phonograph

fontanería f (esp Esp) plumbing

fontanero -ra m,f (esp Esp) plumber

footing /'futin/ m jogging; **hacer** ~ to jog

forajido -da m,f fugitive, outlaw

foráneo -nea adj foreign, strange

forastero -ra m,f stranger, outsider

forcejear [A1] vi to struggle

forcejeo m struggle

fórceps m (pl ~) forceps (pl)

forense adj forensic
■ mf forensic scientist

forestal adj forest (before n)

forjar [A1] vt **(a)** ⟨utensilio/pieza⟩ to forge; ⟨metal⟩ to work **(b)** ⟨porvenir⟩ to shape, forge; ⟨plan⟩ to make; ⟨ilusiones/esperanzas⟩ to build up **(c)** ⟨nación/bases⟩ to create; ⟨amistad/alianza⟩ to forge
■ **forjarse** v pron ⟨porvenir⟩ to shape, forge; ⟨ilusiones⟩ to build up

forma f **1** **(a)** (contorno, apariencia) shape; **en ~ de cruz** in the shape of a cross; **tiene la ~ de un platillo** it's the shape of a saucer; **dar ~ a algo** (al barro) to shape sth; (a proyecto) to give shape to sth **(b)** (tipo, modalidad) form; **distintas ~s de vida animal** different forms of animal life; **~ de pago** form o method of payment
2 (Dep, Med): **estar en ~** to be fit; **está en baja ~** he's not on form; **en plena ~** on top form; **en ~: nos divertimos en ~** we had a really good time
3 (manera, modo) way; **es su ~ de ser** it's just the way he is; **¡vaya ~ de conducir!** what a way to drive!; **~ de vida** way of life; **de ~ distinta** differently; **de cualquier ~** or **de todas ~s** anyway, in any case
4 formas fpl **(a)** (de mujer) figure **(b)** (apariencias) appearances (pl); **guardar las ~s** to keep up appearances
5 (Méx) (formulario) form

formación f **1** (en general) formation; **la ~ de un gobierno** the formation of a government
2 (educación recibida) education; (para trabajo) training; **~ profesional** or (CS) **vocacional** professional o vocational training

formal adj **1** (en general) formal; ⟨promesa/ oferta⟩ firm **2** ⟨persona⟩ (cumplidora) reliable, dependable; (responsable) responsible

formalidad f **1** (de persona) reliability; **no tiene ~** he's so unreliable **2** (requisito) formality

formalizar [A4] vt ⟨noviazgo/relación⟩ to make ... official; ⟨transacción/contrato⟩ to formalize

formar [A1] vt **1** **(a)** (crear) ⟨círculo/figura⟩ to make, form; ⟨asociación/gobierno⟩ to form, set up; ⟨barricada⟩ to set up; **¡formen parejas!** (en clase) get into pairs o twos!; (en baile) take your partners! **(b)** (Ling) to form **(c)** (Mil) ⟨tropas⟩ to have ... fall in
2 (componer) to make up; **un equipo formado por cinco personas** a team made up of five people; **~ parte de algo** to be part of sth, to belong to sth
3 ⟨carácter/espíritu⟩ to form, shape
4 (educar) to bring up; (para trabajo) to train
■ **~** vi (Mil) to fall in
■ **formarse** v pron **1** **(a)** (hacerse, crearse) «grupo/organismo» to form; **se formó una cola** a line (AmE) o (BrE) queue formed **(b)** (desarrollarse) «niño/huesos» to develop **(c)** ⟨idea/opinión⟩ to form
2 (educarse) to be educated; (para trabajo) to be trained

formatear [A1] vt (Inf) to format

formato m **1** **(a)** (tamaño, forma) format **(b)** (Inf) format; **sin ~** unformatted **2** (Méx) (formulario, solicitud) form

formidable adj/interj (fam) fantastic (colloq)

fórmula f **1** **(a)** (Mat, Quím) formula **(b)** (manera, sistema) way **(c)** (frase, expresión) standard expression, formula; **~s de cortesía** polite expressions **(d)** (Col) (receta médica) prescription
2 (Auto) formula; **un coche de F~ 1** a Formula 1 car

formular [A1] vt **1** ⟨queja⟩ to make, lodge; ⟨teoría/plan⟩ to formulate **2** (Col) «médico» to prescribe

formulario m form

forrado -da adj **1** ⟨prenda⟩ lined; ⟨sillón/ libro⟩ covered; **un abrigo ~ de seda** a coat lined with silk **2** [ESTAR] (fam) (de dinero) loaded (colloq)

forrar [A1] vt ⟨prenda⟩ to line; ⟨libro/sillón⟩ to cover
■ **forrarse** v pron (fam) tb **~se de dinero** to make a killing o mint (colloq)

forro m (de abrigo) lining; (de sillón) cover; (de libro) cover, jacket

fortalecer [E3] vt ⟨organismo/músculos/ amistad⟩ to strengthen
■ **fortalecerse** v pron «organismo/músculo» to get stronger

fortaleza f **1** (física) strength; (moral) fortitude, strength of spirit **2** (Mil) fortress

fortificar [A2] vt **(a)** (Mil) ⟨lugar/plaza⟩ to fortify **(b)** (dar fuerza) to strengthen, make ... stronger

fortín m (fuerte pequeño) (small) fort; (emplazamiento) pillbox, bunker

fortuito -ta adj ⟨encuentro/suceso⟩ chance (before n), fortuitous

fortuna f **(a)** (riqueza) fortune **(b)** (azar, suerte) fortune; **por ~** fortunately; **probar ~** to try one's luck

forzado -da adj forced, unnatural

forzar [A11] vt **1** (obligar) to force **2** **(a)** ⟨vista⟩ to strain; **estaba forzando la vista** I was straining my eyes **(b)** ⟨sonrisa⟩ to force **3** ⟨puerta/ cerradura⟩ to force

forzoso -sa adj ⟨aterrizaje/anexión/paro⟩ forced; ⟨jubilación/liquidación⟩ compulsory

fosa f (zanja) ditch; (hoyo) pit; (tumba) grave; **~ común** common o communal grave

fosfato m phosphate

fosforescente adj **(a)** (Fís) phosphorescent **(b)** ⟨color/pintura⟩ fluorescent

fósforo m **(a)** (Quím) phosphorus **(b)** (cerilla) match

fósil adj fossilized, fossil (before n)
■ m fossil

foso m **(a)** (zanja) ditch; (en fortificaciones) moat; (Equ) water jump **(b)** (Teatr) pit; **~ de la orquesta** orchestra pit **(c)** (Auto) (inspection) pit

foto f picture, photo (esp BrE); **me sacó** or **tomó una ~** he took a picture o photo of me; **~ de carné/pasaporte** passport photo

AmC	América Central	Arg	Argentina	Cu	Cuba	Per	Perú
AmL	América Latina	Bol	Bolivia	Ec	Ecuador	RPI	Río de la Plata
AmS	América del Sur	Chi	Chile	Esp	España	Ur	Uruguay
Andes	Región andina	CS	Cono Sur	Méx	México	Ven	Venezuela

fotocopia *f* photocopy, Xerox®; **hizo** *or* **sacó una ~ de la carta** he made *o* took a photocopy of the letter

fotocopiadora *f* photocopier, Xerox® machine

fotocopiar [A1] *vt* to photocopy, xerox

fotogénico -ca *adj* photogenic

fotografía *f* (técnica, arte) photography; (retrato, imagen) photograph

fotografiar [A17] *vt* to photograph, take a photograph of

fotográfico -ca *adj* photographic

fotógrafo -fa *m,f* photographer

fotomatón *m* photo booth

fotómetro *m* (Fot) exposure *o* light meter; (Fís) photometer

foul /'faul/ *m* (*pl* **fouls**) (AmL) foul

FP (en Esp) = **Formación Profesional**

frac *m* (*pl* **fracs** *or* **fraques**) (chaqueta) tail coat, tails (*pl*); (traje) morning suit

fracasado -da *adj* failed, unsuccessful
■ *m,f* failure

fracasar [A1] *vi* to fail

fracaso *m* failure

fracción *f* fraction

fractura *f* (a) (Med) fracture (b) (Geol) fault

fracturar [A1] *vt* to fracture
■ **fracturarse** *v pron* to fracture

fragancia *f* fragrance, perfume

fragata *f* frigate

frágil *adj* (a) (cristal/fuente) fragile (b) ⟨salud/constitución⟩ delicate; ⟨persona⟩ frail; ⟨economía⟩ fragile

fragmento *m* (a) (de jarrón) shard; (de hueso) fragment (b) (de conversación) snippet, snatch (c) (extracto de novela, carta) extract, passage

fragua *f* forge

fraguar [A16] *vt* (a) (Metal) to forge (b) ⟨complot⟩ to hatch; ⟨plan⟩ to conceive
■ ~ *vi* «cemento» to set

fraile *m* friar, monk

frailecillo *m* puffin

frambuesa *f* raspberry

francés¹ -cesa *adj* French
■ *m,f* (*m*) Frenchman; (*f*) Frenchwoman; **los franceses** the French, French people

francés² *m* (idioma) French

Francia *f* France

franco¹ -ca *adj* **1** (sincero) ⟨persona⟩ frank; ⟨sonrisa⟩ natural; **para serte ~ ...** to be frank *o* honest ...; **una mirada franca** an honest *o* open expression **2** (delante de *n*) (patente) ⟨mejoría/decadencia⟩ marked; **un clima de franca cordialidad** an atmosphere of genuine warmth **3** (Com) free; **~ de porte** carriage free; **paso ~** free passage; **~ de derechos** duty-free **4** [ESTAR] (a) (Mil) off duty (b) (RPl) (libre de trabajo): **el lunes estoy ~** I have Monday off

franco² *m* (unidad monetaria) franc

francotirador -dora *m,f* sniper

franela *f* (a) (Tex) flannel (b) (Ven) (camiseta) T-shirt (c) (Col) (camiseta de interior) undershirt (AmE), vest (BrE)

franja *f* (banda) stripe, band; (cinta, adorno) border, fringe

franquear [A1] *vt* **1** ⟨paso/entrada⟩ to clear; ⟨puerta⟩ to go through; ⟨umbral/río⟩ to cross **2** ⟨carta⟩ (pagar) to pay the postage on
■ **franquearse** *v pron* **~se CON algn** to confide IN sb

franqueo *m* postage

franqueza *f* frankness, openness; **hablar con (toda) ~** to be (perfectly) frank *o* honest

franquicia *f* **1** (exención) exemption; (en seguros) excess; **~ aduanera** (condición) duty-free status; (cantidad) duty-free allowance **2** (concesión) franchise

franquismo *m* Franco's regime

frasco *m* bottle; (de mermelada) jar

frase *f* (oración) sentence; (sintagma) phrase; **~ hecha** set phrase

fraternal *adj* brotherly, fraternal

fraude *m* fraud; **~ fiscal** tax evasion

fraudulento -ta *adj* ⟨negocio⟩ fraudulent; ⟨elecciones⟩ rigged

fray *m* (delante de *n* propio) Brother

frazada *f* (AmL) blanket; **~ eléctrica** electric blanket

frecuencia *f* frequency; **con ~** frequently; **~ modulada** frequency modulation, FM

frecuentar [A1] *vt* to frequent

frecuente *adj* ⟨llamada/visita⟩ frequent

freelance /'frilans/ *mf* freelancer; **trabaja de ~** he works freelance

freezer /'friser/ *m* (a) (AmL) (electrodoméstico) freezer, deep freeze (b) (Chi, Ven) (en el refrigerador) freezer (compartment)

fregadero *m* (de la cocina) kitchen sink; (para lavar ropa) (Méx) sink

fregado -da *adj* (AmL exc RPl fam) (a) (molesto) annoying; **¡no seas ~, hombre!** stop being such a pain (colloq) (b) (difícil) ⟨examen/tema⟩ tricky (colloq), tough (colloq); ⟨persona/carácter⟩ difficult (c) [ESTAR] (enfermo, delicado) in a bad way (colloq); (sin dinero) broke (colloq)
■ *m,f* (AmL exc RPl fam) (persona difícil) difficult person

fregar [A7] *vt* **1** (lavar, limpiar) to wash; **fregué el suelo** I washed the floor; (con cepillo) I scrubbed the floor; **~ los platos** to wash the dishes, to do the dishes (colloq) **2** (AmL exc RPl fam) (a) (molestar) to bug (colloq) (b) ⟨planes/vacaciones⟩ to ruin
■ ~ *vi* **1** (lavar los platos) to wash the dishes, to do the dishes (colloq); (limpiar) to clean; (restregar) to scrub **2** (AmL exc RPl fam) (molestar): **¡déjate de ~!** stop being such a pest!; **¡no friegues!** (no digas) you're kidding! (colloq)
■ **fregarse** *v pron* **1** (AmL fam) (embromarse): **¡te friegas!** tough! (colloq); **¡me fregué!** I've really done it now! (colloq) **2** (AmL exc RPl fam) (malograrse): **se ~on nuestros planes** that's ruined *o* messed up our plans (colloq)

fregona *f* (Esp) (utensilio) mop

freidora *f* deep fryer

freír [I35] *vt* to fry
■ **freírse** *v pron* to fry

frenada *f* (esp AmL) ▶ FRENAZO

frenar [A1] *vt* 1 (Transp) to brake 2 ⟨*proceso/ deterioro*⟩ to slow ... down; ⟨*alza/inflación*⟩ to curb, check; ⟨*progreso/desarrollo*⟩ to hold ... back ■ ∼ *vi* to brake, apply the brake(s) (frml)

frenazo *m* (fam): **oí el** ∼ I heard the screeching of brakes; **dio un** ∼ she slammed *o* jammed on her brakes

frenético -ca *adj* frenzied, frenetic; **ponerse** ∼ (fam) to go crazy *o* wild

frenillos *mpl* (AmL) (para los dientes) braces (*pl*) (AmE), brace (esp BrE)

freno *m* (a) (Mec, Transp) brake; ∼ **de mano** emergency brake (AmE), handbrake (BrE) (b) (Equ) bit (c) (contención): **poner** ∼ **a algo** (a gastos, importaciones) to curb sth; (a abusos) to put a stop to sth (d) **frenos** *mpl* (Méx) ▶ FRENILLOS

frente *f* forehead, brow (liter); **arrugar la** ∼ to frown
■ *m* 1 (a) (de edificio) front, facade (frml); **hacer** (le) ∼ **a algo** (a la realidad, una responsabilidad) to face up to sth; (a gastos, obligaciones) to meet sth; **hacerle** ∼ **a algn** (a enemigo, atacante) to face sb (b) (*en locs*) **al frente:** **dar un paso al** ∼ to take a step forward; **vive al** ∼ (Chi) she lives opposite; **estar al** ∼ **de algo** (de una clasificación) to be at the top of sth; (de una empresa) to be in charge of sth; **de frente** ⟨*chocar*⟩ head on; **una foto de** ∼ a full-face photo; **de frente a** (AmL) facing; **frente a** opposite; **estamos** ∼ **a un grave problema** we are faced with a serious problem
2 (Meteo, Mil, Pol) front

fresa *f* (planta) strawberry plant; (fruta) strawberry

fresco¹ -ca *adj* 1 (a) ⟨*viento*⟩ cool, fresh; ⟨*agua*⟩ cold; ⟨*bebida*⟩ cool, cold; **el tiempo está** ∼ the weather is a bit chilly (b) ⟨*ropa/tela*⟩ cool
2 (a) ⟨*pescado/fruta*⟩ fresh; **trae noticias frescas** she has the latest news; ⊕ **pintura fresca** wet paint (b) ⟨*cutis/belleza*⟩ fresh, young (c) (no viciado) ⟨*aire*⟩ fresh 3 ⟨*persona*⟩ (a) [SER] (fam) (descarado): **¡qué tipo más** ∼! that guy sure has some nerve! (colloq) (b) [ESTAR] (descansado) refreshed; (no cansado) fresh (c) (tranquilo): **él estaba tan** ∼ he was as cool as a cucumber
■ *m,f* (fam) (descarado): **¡eres un** ∼! you have a lot of nerve! (colloq)

fresco² *m* 1 (a) (aire) fresh air; **tomar el** ∼ to get some fresh air (b) (frío moderado): **hace un fresquito que da gusto** it's lovely and cool; **hace** ∼ it's chilly 2 (Art) fresco; **pintura al** ∼ fresco painting 3 (AmL) (gaseosa) soda (AmE), fizzy drink (BrE); (refresco de frutas) fruit drink

frescura *f* (descaro) nerve (colloq)

fresón *m* (long stem) strawberry

frialdad *f* (en general) coldness; **la** ∼ **de su mirada** the coldness in his eyes; **me trató con** ∼ he treated me coldly *o* frostily; **la** ∼ **del público** the audience's lack of enthusiasm

friega *f* (fricción) rub; **date una(s)** ∼**(s) en el pecho con esto** rub this on your chest

friega, friegas, etc ▶ FREGAR

frígido -da *adj* frigid

frigorífico *m* (a) (Esp) (nevera) refrigerator, fridge (b) (en tiendas) cold store (c) (AmS) (de carne) meat processing plant

frijol *m* (AmL exc CS) (Bot, Coc) bean; ∼ **colorado/ negro** kidney/black bean; **ganarse los** ∼**es** to earn a living

frío¹, fría *adj* 1 ⟨*comida/agua/motor/viento*⟩ cold; **tengo los pies** ∼**s** my feet are cold; **dejar** ∼ **a algn: la noticia lo dejó** ∼ (indiferente) he was quite unmoved by the news; (atónito) he was staggered by the news; **el jazz me deja fría** jazz does nothing for me 2 (a) ⟨*persona*⟩ cold; ⟨*público*⟩ unresponsive; ⟨*recibimineto*⟩ cool; **estuvo** ∼ **conmigo** he was cold towards me (b) ⟨*decoración/color*⟩ cold

frío² *m* cold; **no salgas con este** ∼ don't go out in this cold; **¡qué** ∼ **hace!** it's so cold!; **tener/ pasar** ∼ to be cold; **tengo** ∼ **en los pies** my feet are cold; **tomar** *or* (Esp) **coger** ∼ to catch cold

friolento -ta *adj* (AmL): **es muy** ∼ he really feels the cold

friolero -ra *adj* (Esp) ▶ FRIOLENTO

friso *m* frieze

fritanga *f* (a) (AmC, Andes, Méx) (alimento frito) fried snack (b) (pey) (comida frita) greasy fried food

frito -ta *adj* 1 (Coc) fried 2 (a) (fam) (harto) fed up (colloq); **me tienes** ∼ I'm fed up with you (b) (CS, Méx fam) (en apuros) done for (colloq)

frivolidad *f* (cualidad) frivolousness, frivolity; (cosa vana) triviality, frivolous thing

frívolo -la *adj* frivolous

frondoso -sa *adj* ⟨*árbol*⟩ leafy; ⟨*vegetación*⟩ lush; ⟨*bosque*⟩ thick

frontal *adj* ⟨*colisión*⟩ head-on; ⟨*ataque*⟩ direct, frontal (frml); ⟨*oposición*⟩ direct

frontenis *m* pelota (*played with tennis rackets*)

frontera *f* border, frontier (frml)

frontón *m* (juego) pelota; (cancha) pelota court; (pared) fronton

frotar [A1] *vt/vi* to rub
■ **frotarse** *v pron* (*refl*) ⟨*ojos/rodillas*⟩ to rub; ⟨*manos*⟩ to rub ... together

fructífero -ra *adj* fruitful, productive

fruncir [I4] *vt* (a) ⟨*tela*⟩ to gather (b) ∼ **el ceño** *or* **entrecejo** to frown

frustración *f* frustration

frustrado -da *adj* (a) ⟨*persona*⟩ frustrated; ⟨*actor/bailarina*⟩ frustrated (*before n*) (b) ⟨*atentado/intento*⟩ failed (*before n*)

frustrar [A1] *vt* ⟨*persona*⟩ to frustrate; ⟨*planes*⟩ to thwart; ⟨*esperanzas*⟩ to dash; **me frustra que no entiendan** I find it frustrating that they don't understand
■ **frustrarse** *v pron* «*planes*» to be thwarted, fail; «*esperanzas*» to come to nothing

fruta *f* fruit; **una** ∼ a piece of fruit; ∼ **confitada** *or* **escarchada** crystallized fruit, candied fruit; ∼ **del tiempo** *or* **de (la) estación** seasonal fruit

frutal *adj* fruit (*before n*)
■ *m* fruit tree

frutería *f* fruit store *o* shop, greengrocer's (BrE)

frutero¹ -ra *m,f* (vendedor) fruit seller, greengrocer (BrE)

frutero² *m* (recipiente) fruit bowl

frutilla *f* (Bol, CS) strawberry

fruto *m* 1 (Bot) fruit; ∼**s secos** nuts and dried fruit (*pl*) 2 (resultado, producto) fruit; **dar** *or* **rendir** ∼**s** to bear fruit; ∼ **DE algo** ⟨*de inversión*⟩ return

ON sth; ⟨de trabajo/investigación⟩ fruits OF sth; **todo fue ∼ de su imaginación** it was all a figment of his imagination

FTP m (= **protocolo de transferencia de archivo**) FTP

fucsia f fuchsia
■ m/adj inv fuchsia

fue ▶ IR, SER

fuego m **(a)** (en general) fire; ¡∼! fire!; **le prendieron ∼ a la casa** they set the house on fire; **abrieron ∼ sobre los manifestantes** they opened fire on the demonstrators; **∼s artificiales** fireworks (pl) **(b)** (para cigarrillo): **¿me da ∼, por favor?** have you got a light, please? **(c)** (Coc): **cocinar a ∼ lento** to cook over a low heat; (apenas hirviendo) to simmer; **poner la sartén al ∼** put the frying pan on to heat

fuel, fuel-oil m fuel oil

fuelle m bellows (pl)

fuente f **1** **(a)** (manantial) spring; **∼ termal** thermal spring **(b)** (origen) source; **la ∼ del río** the source of the river; **∼ de ingresos** source of income; **información de buena ∼** information from reliable sources **2** (construcción) fountain; **∼ de soda** (Chi, Méx) soda fountain (AmE), (place where drinks and ice creams are bought and consumed) **3** (plato) dish; **∼ de horno** ovenproof dish

fuera adv **1** **(a)** (lugar, parte) [Latin American Spanish also uses AFUERA in this sense] outside; **comeremos ∼** (en el jardín) we'll eat outside; (en un restaurante) we'll eat out; **por ∼ es rojo** it's red on the outside; **aquí ∼ se está muy bien** it's very nice out here; **se pasa el día ∼** she's out all day **(b)** (en el extranjero) abroad, out of the country; (del lugar de trabajo, de la ciudad, etc) away **2** **fuera de** (loc prep) **(a)** (en el exterior de, más allá de) out of; **está ∼ del país** he's out of the country; **ocurrió ∼ del edificio** it happened outside the building; **∼ de peligro/lugar** out of danger/place; **¡∼ (de aquí)!** get out (of here)! **(b)** (excepto) apart from; **∼ de eso, me encuentro bien** apart o (AmE) aside from that, I feel fine **3** (en otras locs): **fuera de combate: lo dejó ∼ de combate** (Dep) he knocked him out; **fuera de serie** ⟨jugador/cantante⟩ exceptional, outstanding; **fuera de sí: estaba ∼ de sí** he was beside himself; **fuera de temporada** out of season

fuera, fuéramos, etc ▶ IR, SER

fueraborda m outboard

fuereño -ña m,f (Méx fam): **un ∼** some guy from out of town (colloq)

fuero m **(a)** (jurisdicción) jurisdiction **(b)** (privilegio, derecho) privilege; **en mi/su ∼ interno** in my/his heart of hearts, deep down inside

fuerte adj **1** (en general) strong; **un equipo/una cuerda ∼** a strong team/rope **2** **(a)** ⟨viento⟩ strong; ⟨terremoto⟩ severe; ⟨lluvia/nevada⟩ heavy **(b)** ⟨dolor⟩ intense, bad; ⟨golpe⟩ heavy; ⟨resfriado⟩ bad; ⟨abrazo/beso⟩ big **(c)** ⟨ruido/música⟩ loud **(d)** ⟨olor/sabor/medicina⟩ strong; ⟨comida/dosis⟩ heavy **(e)** ⟨acento⟩ strong, thick **3** ⟨violento⟩ ⟨discusión⟩ violent, heated; ⟨película/escena⟩ shocking

■ adv **1** ⟨golpear/empujar⟩ hard; ⟨agarrar/apretar⟩ tightly; ⟨llover⟩ heavily **2** ⟨hablar⟩ loudly; **pon la radio más ∼** turn the radio up; **habla más ∼** speak up

■ m **(a)** (Mil) fort **(b)** (especialidad) strong point, forte

fuerza f **1** **(a)** (vigor, energía) strength; **tener ∼ to be strong; no me siento con ∼s** I don't have the strength; **tiene mucha ∼ en los brazos** she has very strong arms; **agárralo con ∼** hold on to it tightly; **empuja con ∼** push hard; **le fallaron las ∼s** his strength failed him; **recuperar ∼s** to get one's strength back; **gritó con todas sus ∼s** she shouted with all her might; **∼ de voluntad** willpower **(b)** (del viento, de olas) strength, force **(c)** (de estructura, material) strength **2** (violencia) force; **recurrir a la ∼** to resort to force; **∼ bruta** brute force **3** (Mil, Pol, Fís) force; **∼s políticas** political forces; **las ∼s armadas** the armed forces; **las ∼s de orden público** (period) the police; **∼ de gravedad** (force of) gravity **4** (en locs) **a la fuerza: a la ∼ tuvo que verme** he must have seen me; **lo llevaron a la ∼** they dragged me there; **comí a la ∼** I forced myself to eat; **entraron a la ∼** they forced their way in; **a fuerza de** by; **aprobó a ∼ de estudiar** he managed to pass by studying hard; **por fuerza: por ∼ tiene que saberlo** he must know about it; **por la fuerza** by force

fuerza, fuerzas, etc ▶ FORZAR

fuese, fuésemos, etc ▶ IR, SER

fuete m (AmL exc CS) riding crop; (más largo) whip

fuga f **1** (huida) escape; **un intento de ∼** an attempted escape; **se dieron a la ∼** they fled; **∼ de capitales** or **divisas** flight of capital; **∼ de cerebros** brain drain **2** (de líquido, gas) leak, escape (frml) **3** (Mús) fugue

fugarse [A3] v pron **(a)** (huir) to flee, run away; ⟨«preso»⟩ to escape; **∼ de algo** to escape FROM sth **(b)** ⟨«enamorados»⟩ to run away together

fugaz adj ⟨sonrisa/visión/amor⟩ fleeting; ⟨visita/tregua⟩ brief

fugitivo -va adj fugitive; **anda ∼** he is on the run

fui, fuimos, etc ▶ IR, SER

fuiste, etc ▶ IR, SER

fulano -na m,f (fam) (persona cualquiera) so-and-so; **don ∼ de tal** Mr so-and-so
■ m (fam) (tipo) guy (colloq)

fulminante adj ⟨enfermedad⟩ sudden and devastating; ⟨mirada⟩ withering; **tuvo un efecto ∼** it had an immediate and devastating effect

fulminantes mpl (AmL) (Jueg) caps (pl); **pistola de ∼** cap gun

fumador -dora m,f smoker; **∼ pasivo** passive smoker; **sección de ∼es/no ∼es** smoking/no-smoking section

fumar [A1] vt **1** ⟨cigarrillo/puro⟩ to smoke **2** (Méx fam) (hacer caso) to take notice of
■ ∼ vi to smoke; **∼ en pipa** to smoke a pipe

fumigar [A3] vt ⟨campo/cultivo⟩ to spray, dust; ⟨local⟩ to fumigate

función f **1** **(a)** (cometido, propósito) function; **tiene la ∼ de ...** it performs the function of ...; **salario en ∼ de la experiencia** salary according to experience **(b)** **funciones** mpl duties (pl); **en el ejercicio de sus funciones** in the performance of her duties; **el secretario en funciones** the acting secretary; **entrar en funciones** (AmL) ⟨«empleado»⟩ ⋯⋗

to take up one's post; «*presidente*» to assume office **2** (Fisiol, Mat, Ling) function **3** (de teatro, circo) performance; (de cine) showing, performance; ~ **de noche** late night performance

funcionamiento *m*: **me explicó su** ~ he explained (to me) how it works (*o* worked *etc*); **para el buen** ~ **de la escuela** for the smooth running of the school; **ponerse en** ~ «*hospital/estación/fábrica*» to become operational; «*central nuclear*» to come into operation; «*mecanismo/máquina*» to start up; «*servicio/sistema*» to start; **estar en** ~ to be running; **poner en** ~ «*central/fábrica*» to bring into operation; «*mecanismo/máquina*» to start ... up

funcionar [A1] *vi* «*aparato/máquina*» to work; «*servicio*» to operate; ❸ **no funciona** out of order; ~ **con pilas/gasolina** to run off batteries/on gasoline

funcionario -ria *m,f* **(a)** (empleado público) *tb* ~ **público** *o*r **del Estado** government employee; **un alto** ~ a senior *o* high-ranking official **(b)** (de organización internacional) member of staff, staff member **(c)** (RPI) (de empresa, banco) employee

funda *f* **(a)** (de libro) dustjacket; (de disco) sleeve **(b)** (de raqueta, cojín, sillón) cover **(c)** *tb* ~ **de almohada** pillowcase, pillowslip **(d)** (Odont) cap

fundación *f* **1** (institución) foundation; **una** ~ **benéfica** a charity **2** (de ciudad, escuela) founding; (de empresa, partido) establishment

fundado -da *adj* «*temor/sospecha*» justified, well founded

fundador -dora *m,f* founder

fundamental *adj* fundamental

fundamento *m* **(a)** (base, sustentación) foundation; **los rumores carecen de** ~ the rumors are totally without foundation **(b)** **fundamentos** *mpl* (nociones básicas) fundamentals (*pl*), basics (*pl*)

fundar [A1] *vt* **(a)** «*ciudad/hospital/escuela*» to found; «*partido/empresa*» to establish **(b)** (basar) «*sospecha/argumento*» ~ **algo EN algo** to base sth ON sth
■ **fundarse** *v pron* ~**se EN algo** «*afirmación/sospecha*» to be based ON sth; **¿en qué te fundas para decirlo?** what grounds do you have for saying that?

fundir [I1] *vt* **1** **(a)** «*metal/hierro*» to melt; «*mineral*» to smelt **(b)** «*estatua/campana*» to cast **2** (Elec) to blow **3** (fusionar) to merge
■ **fundirse** *v pron* **1** «*metal*» to melt; «*nieve/hielo*» to melt, thaw **2** (Elec): **se ha fundido la bombilla** the bulb has gone (colloq); **se fundieron los fusibles** the fuses blew **3** (fusionarse) «*empresas/partidos*» to merge; ~**se EN algo** to merge sth INTO sth

fundo *m* (Chi) country estate, large farm

fúnebre *adj* «*música/ambiente*» funereal; ▶ COCHE A, CORTEJO, ETC

funeral *m*, **funerales** *mpl* (exequias) funeral; (oficio religioso) funeral service

funeraria *f* undertaker's, funeral parlor*

funesto -ta *adj* disastrous, terrible

fungir [I7] *vi* (Méx, Per) ~ COMO *o*r DE **algo** to act AS sth

funicular *m* (tren) funicular (railway); (teleférico) cable car

furgón *m* (Auto) truck, van; (Ferr) boxcar (AmE), goods van (BrE)

furgoneta *f* (para carga) van; (para pasajeros) van, minibus

furia *f* fury; **estar/ponerse hecho una** ~ (fam) to be/to get furious

furioso -sa *adj* furious; **se puso** ~ he was furious, he flew into a rage

furor *m* **(a)** (rabia) fury, rage **(b)** (de las olas, del viento, de una tempestad) fury **(c)** (entusiasmo) enormous enthusiasm; **causar** *o*r **hacer** ~ to be all the rage (colloq)

furtivo -va *adj* **(a)** (ilegal): **la caza/pesca furtiva** poaching; **un cazador** ~ a poacher **(b)** «*mirada/caricia*» furtive

furúnculo *m* boil

fusible *m* (Elec) fuse; **saltaron los** ~**s** the fuses blew

fusil *m* **1** (Arm) rifle **2** (Méx fam) (plagio) plagiarism

fusilar [A1] *vt* **1** (Mil) to shoot; **fue fusilado** he was executed by firing squad **2** (fam) (plagiar) to plagiarize, lift (colloq)

fusión *f* **1** (de empresas, partidos) merger **2** **(a)** (de un metal) melting; (de metales, piezas) fusion, fusing together **(b)** (Fís) fusion

fusionar [A1] *vt* **(a)** «*piezas/metales*» to fuse, fuse together **(b)** «*empresas/partidos*» to merge **(c)** (Inf) to merge
■ **fusionarse** *v pron* **(a)** «*piezas/metales*» fuse (together) **(b)** «*empresas/partidos*» to merge; «*ideas*» to fuse

fusta *f* riding crop; (más larga) whip

fustigar [A3] *vt* «*caballo*» to whip

futbito *m* (Esp) five-a-side soccer *o* football, ≈ indoor soccer (AmE)

fútbol, (AmC, Méx) **futbol** *m* soccer, football (esp BrE); ~ **americano** American football; ~ **sala** five-a-side soccer *o* football, ≈ indoor soccer (AmE)

futbolín *m* **(a)** (juego) table football **(b)** **futbolines** *mpl* (local) amusement arcade

futbolista *mf* soccer *o* football player

futuro¹ -ra *adj* future (*before n*); **las futuras generaciones** future generations; **la futura mamá** the mother-to-be

futuro² *m* **1 (porvenir) future; **¿qué nos deparará el** ~? what will the future bring?; **en un** ~ **cercano** *o*r **próximo** in the near future; **en el** *o*r **en lo** ~ in future; **un empleo con/sin** ~ a job with good prospects/with no prospects; **su relación no tiene** ~ their relationship has no future **2** (Ling) future (tense)

Gg

G, g *f* (*read as* /xe/) *the letter* G, G

gabacho -cha *m,f* **(a)** (Chi, Esp fam & pey) (francés) frog (colloq & pej) **(b)** (Méx fam & pey) (extranjero) foreigner (*of North American or European origin*)

gabán *m* (abrigo — largo) overcoat; (— corto) jacket

gabardina *f* (prenda) raincoat; (tela) gabardine

gabinete *m* ⬚1 (despacho) office; (en una casa) study ⬚2 (conjunto de profesionales) department; (Pol) cabinet ⬚3 (armario —de la cocina) (Méx) kitchen cabinet *o* cupboard; (— del baño) (Col, Ven) bathroom cabinet

gacela *f* gazelle

gacho -cha *adj* **(a)** ⟨orejas⟩ drooping (*before n*); **con la cabeza gacha** with his head bowed **(b)** **a gachas** (agachado) crouching; (a gatas) on all fours

gachupín *m* (Méx pey) Spaniard

gaélico¹ -ca *adj* Gaelic

gaélico² *m* (idioma) Gaelic

gafar [A1] *vt* (Esp fam) to jinx

gafas *fpl* **(a)** (anteojos) glasses (*pl*), spectacles (*pl*) (frml); **unas ~s nuevas** a new pair of glasses; **~ de sol** sunglasses; **~ oscuras** dark glasses **(b)** (de protección) goggles (*pl*)

gafe *adj* (Esp fam): **es ~** she has a jinx on her; **no seas ~** don't say that, you'll bring us bad luck

gafo -fa *adj* (Ven fam) (estúpido) dumb (colloq)

gagá *adj inv* ⬚1 (fam) (senil) gaga (colloq) ⬚2 (Per fam) (elegante) smart (colloq)

gaita *f tb* **~ gallega/escocesa** (Galician/ Scottish) bagpipes (*pl*)

gaitero -ra *m,f* (Mús) (bag)piper

gajes *mpl*: **son (los) ~ del oficio** it's all part of the job

gajo *m* ⬚1 (de naranja, limón) segment ⬚2 (Col) (de pelo) lock

gala *f* **(a)** (cena) gala; **cena de ~** gala (dinner); (en el teatro) *tb* **función de ~** gala (evening *o* performance); **vestido de ~** formal *o* full dress; **hacer ~ de algo** to display sth **(b) galas** *fpl* (ropa) clothes (*pl*); **mis/tus mejores ~s** my/your best clothes *o* Sunday best

galán *m* **(a)** (actor) hero **(b)** (hum) (novio) young man (hum)

galante *adj* ⟨hombre⟩ gallant, attentive

galantería *f* **(a)** (caballerosidad) gallantry **(b)** (piropo) compliment; (gesto cortés) polite gesture, attention

galápago *m* (Zool) (tortuga — gigante) giant turtle; (— europea) terrapin

galaxia *f* galaxy

galera *f* ⬚1 (Hist, Náut) galley ⬚2 (RPl) (sombrero) top hat

galería *f* **(a)** (interior) corridor; (exterior) gallery

(c) (Teatr) gallery **(c) ~ comercial** shopping mall (AmE), shopping arcade (BrE); **~ de arte** art gallery

Gales *m*: *tb* **el país de ~** Wales

galés¹ -lesa *adj* Welsh
■ *m,f* (persona) (*m*) Welshman; (*f*) Welshwoman; **los galeses** the Welsh, Welsh people

galés² *m* (idioma) Welsh

galgo *mf* greyhound

galgódromo *m* (Méx) dog track

galicismo *m* gallicism

galimatías *m* (*pl* ~) (lenguaje incomprensible) gibberish; (de cosas, ideas) jumble

gallada *f* (Andes fam): **la ~** the crowd

gallego¹ -ga *adj* **(a)** (de Galicia) Galician **(b)** (AmL fam) (español) Spanish
■ *m,f* **(a)** (de Galicia) Galician **(b)** (AmL fam) (español) Spaniard

gallego² *m* (idioma) Galician

galleta *f* (Coc) (dulce) cookie (AmE), biscuit (BrE); (salada) cracker

gallina *f* ⬚1 (Zool) hen; (Coc) chicken; **~ clueca** (empollando) broody hen; (cuidando la pollada) mother hen; **gallinita ciega** blind man's buff ⬚2 **gallina** *mf* (fam) (cobarde) chicken (colloq)

gallinazo *m* (Zool) (de cabeza roja) turkey buzzard *o* vulture; (de cabeza negra) black vulture

gallinero *m* **(a)** (Zool) (corral) henhouse, coop **(b)** (fam) (sitio ruidoso) madhouse (colloq) **(c)** (fam) (en el cine, teatro): **el ~** the gods (colloq)

gallito *m* ⬚1 (fam) (persona) tough guy (colloq) ⬚2 (Col, Méx) (Dep) shuttlecock, birdie (AmE)

gallo¹ *m* ⬚1 (Zool) (ave) cockerel; **~ de pelea** *or* (AmS) **de riña** fighting *o* game cock; (más grande) rooster; **en menos (de lo) que canta un ~** in no time at all; **otro ~ cantaría** *or* **otro ~ me/te/nos cantara** (fam) things would be very different ⬚2 (Méx fam) (bravucón) macho, tough guy (colloq) ⬚3 (fam) **(a)** (de un cantante) false note **(b)** (de adolescente): **soltó un ~** his voice went squeaky ⬚4 (Méx) (serenata) serenade

gallo² -lla *adj* (AmL fam) tough (colloq)
■ *m,f* (Chi fam) (*m*) guy (colloq); (*f*) woman; **hola ~** hi, buddy (AmE) *o* (BrE) mate (colloq)

galón *m* ⬚1 (Mil) stripe ⬚2 (medida) gallon

galopante *adj* ⟨inflación/tuberculosis⟩ galloping (*before n*)

galopar [A1] *vi* (Equ) to gallop

galope *m* gallop; **a** *o* **al ~** at a gallop

galpón *m* (AmL) (cobertizo) shed; (almacén) storehouse

gama *f* **(a)** (de colores, productos) range **(b)** (de notas musicales) scale

gamba *f* (esp Esp) (Coc, Zool) shrimp (AmE), prawn (BrE)

gamberrada *f* (Esp) (grosería) loutish act; (acto violento) act of hooliganism

gamberrismo *m* (Esp) (comportamiento — escandaloso) loutishness; (— violento) hooliganism

gamberro -rra *m,f* (Esp) (grosero) lout; (vándalo) hooligan

gamín -mina *m,f* (Col) street urchin

gamo -ma *m,f* fallow deer

gamulán® *m* (CS) (prenda) sheepskin coat/jacket

gamuza *f* **(a)** (Zool) chamois **(b)** (piel) chamois (leather); (de otros animales) suede

gana *f* (deseo): ¡con qué ∼s me comería un helado! I'd love an ice cream!; lo hizo sin ∼s he did it very half-heartedly; siempre hace lo que le da la ∼ she always does just as she pleases; quería ir pero me quedé con las ∼s (fam) I wanted to go, but it wasn't to be; tener ∼s de hacer algo to feel like doing sth; (no) tengo ∼s de ir I (don't) feel like going; tengo ∼s de volver a verte I'm looking forward to seeing you again; le dieron ∼s de reírse she felt like bursting out laughing; se me quitaron las ∼s de ir I don't feel like going any more; tengo ∼s de que llegue el verano I'm looking forward to the summer; con ∼s: llover con ∼s to pour down; es feo/tonto con ∼s he is so ugly/stupid!; de buena/mala ∼ willingly/reluctantly

ganadería *f* (actividad) ranching, stockbreeding; (ganado) cattle (*pl*), livestock (+ *sing or pl vb*)

ganadero -ra *adj* ranching (*before n*), stockbreeding (*before n*)
■ *m,f* rancher, stockbreeder

ganado *m* cattle (*pl*), livestock (+ *sing or pl vb*); ∼ bovino *or* vacuno cattle (*pl*); ∼ caballar *or* equino horses (*pl*); ∼ en pie (AmL) cattle on the hoof (*pl*); ∼ ovino/porcino sheep (*pl*)/pigs (*pl*)

ganador -dora *adj* ⟨equipo/caballo⟩ winning (*before n*); la película ∼a del Oscar the Oscar-winning film
■ *m,f* winner

ganancia *f* (Com, Fin) profit; ∼ neta/bruta net/gross profit; ∼ del capital capital gain

ganar [A1] *vt* **1 (a)** ⟨sueldo⟩ to earn; lo único que quiere es ∼ dinero all he's interested in is making money **(b)** ⟨tiempo⟩ to gain; ¿qué ganas con eso? what do you gain by (doing) that? **(c)** (adquirir) ⟨experiencia⟩ to gain **2** ⟨partido/guerra/premio⟩ to win; le gané la apuesta I won my bet with him
■ ∼ *vi* **(a)** (vencer) to win; van ganando 2 a 1 they're winning 2-1; ∼le ∧ algn to beat sb; nos ∼on por cuatro puntos they beat us by four points **(b)** (aventajar): le ganas en estatura you're taller than him; me gana en todo he beats me on every count; salir ganando: salió ganando con el trato he did well out of the deal; al final salí ganando in the end I came out of it better off
■ **ganarse** *v pron* **1** (*enf*) (mediante el trabajo) to earn; ∼se la vida to earn a/one's living **2** (*enf*) ⟨premio/apuesta⟩ to win **3** ⟨afecto/confianza⟩ to win; se ganó el respeto de todos she won *o* earned everyone's respect **4** ⟨descanso⟩ to earn oneself; te lo has ganado you've earned it, you deserve it

ganchillo *m* (aguja) crochet hook; (labor) crochet; hacer ∼ to crochet

gancho *m* **1 (a)** (garfio) hook **(b)** (AmL) (para la ropa) hanger **(c)** (Andes, Ven) (imperdible) safety pin **2 (a)** (en boxeo) hook **(b)** (en baloncesto) hook shot

gandalla *mf* (Méx fam) (persona deshonesta) crook (colloq); (sinvergüenza) swine (colloq)

gandul -dula *m,f* (fam) lazybones (colloq)

ganga *f* (compra ventajosa) bargain; a precio de ∼ at a bargain *o* giveaway price

ganglio *m* (en los vasos linfáticos) gland; (de células nerviosas) ganglion

gangrena *f* gangrene

ganso -sa *m,f* **1** (Zool) (*m*) goose, gander; (*f*) goose **2** (fam) **(a)** (persona torpe) clumsy oaf (colloq) **(b)** (tonto) idiot, clown (colloq)

ganzúa *f* picklock

garabatear [A1] *vi/vt* (escribir) to scribble, scrawl; (dibujar) to doodle

garabato *m* **1 (a)** (dibujo) doodle **(b) garabatos** *mpl* (escritura) scrawl, scribble **2** (Chi) (palabrota) swearword

garaje /ga'raxe/ *m*, (esp AmL) **garage** /ga'raʒ/ *m* garage

garantía *f* **1** (Com) guarantee, warranty; estar bajo *or* en ∼ to be under guarantee *o* warranty **2 (a)** (Der) (fianza) surety, guarantee **(b)** (seguridad) guarantee **(c)** ∼s constitucionales constitutional rights (*pl*)

garantizar [A4] *vt* **1** (Com) ⟨producto⟩ to guarantee, warrant (AmE) **2** (asegurar) to guarantee

garapiña *f* (Méx) pineapple squash

garbanzo *m* chickpea

garbo *m* (elegancia) poise, grace; (gracia, desenvoltura) jauntiness

garfio *m* hook

gargajo *m* (fam) gob (sl)

garganta *f* **1 (a)** (Anat) throat; me dolía la ∼ I had a sore throat **(b)** (cuello) neck **2** (desfiladero) gorge, ravine; (entre montañas) narrow pass
■ *mf* (Per fam) scrounger (colloq)

gargantilla *f* choker, necklace

gárgara *f* gargle; hacer ∼s to gargle

garita *f* (de centinela) sentry box; (de portero) lodge

garito *m* gambling den

garra *f* **1 (a)** (de animal) claw; (de águila) talon **2** (arrojo, valor) fighting spirit; (personalidad) personality **3 garras** *fpl* (poder, dominio) clutches (*pl*)

garrafa *f* **(a)** (para vino) demijohn **(b)** (RPl) (para gas) cylinder

garrafal *adj* terrible; ⟨error⟩ monumental

garrapata *f* tick

garrapiñada *f* (esp AmL) caramel-coated peanuts/almonds (*pl*)

garrobo *m* (AmC) iguana

garrocha *f* **1** (Taur) lance, goad **2** (AmL) (Dep) pole

garrochista *mf* (AmL) pole-vaulter

garrotazo *m* (golpe) blow (*with a club*)

garrote *m* (palo) club, stick; (método de ejecución) garrotte

garúa *f* (AmL) drizzle

garuar [A18] *v impers* (AmL) to drizzle

garza *f* (Zool) heron

garzón ⋯⟶ género ⋯

garzón -zona *m,f* (Chi) *(m)* waiter; *(f)* waitress

gas *m* [1] (Fís, Quím) gas; ∼**es tóxicos** toxic fumes; ∼ **ciudad** town gas; ∼ **lacrimógeno/ licuado** tear/liquified gas [2] **gases** *mpl* (Fisiol) wind, gas (AmE)

gasa *f* (Med, Tex) gauze

gaseosa *f* **(a)** (bebida efervescente) soda (AmE), fizzy drink (BrE) **(b)** (CS) (cualquier refresco) soft drink

gaseoso -sa *adj* **(a)** ‹cuerpo/estado› gaseous **(b)** ‹bebida› carbonated, fizzy (BrE)

gásfiter *mf* (*pl* **-ters**) (Chi) plumber

gasfitería *f* (Chi, Per) plumbing

gasfitero -ra *m,f* (Per) plumber

gasoducto *m* gas pipeline

gas-oil, gasóleo *m* (para calefacción) (gas) oil; (para motores) diesel (fuel *o* oil)

gasolina *f* gasoline (AmE), gas (AmE), petrol (BrE); ∼ **normal** regular gasoline (AmE), two-star petrol (BrE); ∼ **sin plomo** unleaded gasoline (AmE) *o* (BrE) petrol; ∼ **super** premium gasoline (AmE), four-star petrol (BrE)

gasolinera *f* gas station (AmE), petrol station (BrE)

gastado -da *adj* ‹ropa/zapatos› worn-out; ‹político/cantante› washed-up (colloq)

gastador -dora *adj/m,f* spendthrift

gastar [A1] *vt* [1] (consumir) **(a)** ‹dinero› to spend; ∼ **algo EN algo** to spend sth ON sth **(b)** ‹gasolina/electricidad› to use [2] (desperdiciar, malgastar) ‹dinero/tiempo/energía› to waste [3] (desgastar) ‹ropa/zapatos› to wear out; ‹tacones› to wear down [4] (fam) (llevar, usar) ‹ropa/gafas› to wear; **gasto el 37** I'm a size 37 [5] ‹broma› to play; **le ∼on una broma** they played a joke *o* trick on him
■ **gastarse** *v pron* [1] (enf) ‹dinero› to spend [2] «pilas/batería» to run down; **se me gastó la tinta** I ran out of ink [3] «ropa/zapatos» (desgastarse) to wear out [4] (enf) (fam) (tener) to have; **se gasta un genio …** he has a terrible temper!

gasto *m* expense; **un ∼ innecesario** an unnecessary expense; **este mes he tenido muchos ∼s** this has been an expensive month for me; **el ∼ público** public expenditure; **∼s de correo** postage; **∼s de envío** postage and handling (AmE) *o* (BrE) packing

gastritis *f* gastritis

gastronomía *f* gastronomy

gata *f* [1] (Chi, Per) (Auto) jack; *ver tb* GATO¹ [2] **a gatas** (*loc adv*) (a cuatro patas): **ir** *or* **andar a ∼s** to crawl; **tuve que entrar a ∼s** I had to go in on all fours

gatear [A1] *vi* (andar a gatas) to crawl

gatera *f* cathole (AmE), cat flap (BrE)

gatillero *m* (Méx) gunman

gatillo *m* trigger; **apretar el ∼** to pull the trigger

gatito -ta *m,f* kitten

gato¹ -ta *m,f* (Zool) cat; ∼ **montés** wild cat; **aquí hay ∼ encerrado** there's something fishy going

on here; **le dieron ∼ por liebre** he was conned *o* had! (colloq); **llevarse el ∼ al agua** (fam) to pull it off (colloq)

gato² *m* [1] (Auto) jack [2] (Chi, Méx) (Jueg) ticktacktoe (AmE), noughts and crosses (BrE) [3] (Méx) (signo) hash sign

gauchada *f* (Bol, CS fam) favor*, good turn

gaucho *m* gaucho

gaveta *f* drawer

gavilán *m* sparrowhawk

gavilla *f* (de cereales) sheaf

gaviota *f* seagull, gull

gay /gai, gei/ *adj* (*pl* ∼ *or* **gays**) gay
■ *mf* *(m)* gay man, gay; *(f)* gay woman, lesbian

gazmoño -ña *adj* (pudoroso) prudish; (mojigato) sanctimonious

gaznate *m* (garganta) (fam) throat, gullet; **refrescar el ∼** (fam) to have a drink

gazpacho *m*: *tb* ∼ **andaluz** gazpacho (*cold soup made from tomatoes, peppers, etc*)

ge *f*: *name of the letter* G

gel *m* gel

gelatina *f* **(a)** (sustancia) gelatin* **(b)** (postre) Jell-O® (AmE), jelly (BrE)

gelatinoso -sa *adj* gelatinous

gema *f* gem

gemelo¹ -la *adj* twin (*before n*)
■ *m,f* twin

gemelo² *m* **(a)** (de camisa) cuff link **(b) gemelos** *mpl* (Ópt) binoculars (*pl*)

gemido *m* **(a)** (de dolor, pena) groan, moan **(b)** (de animal) whine

Géminis *m* (signo, constelación) Gemini; **es (de) ∼** she's (a) Gemini, she's a Geminian
■ *mf* (*pl* ∼) (persona) *tb* **géminis** Geminian, Gemini

gemir [I14] *vi* **(a)** «persona» to moan, groan **(b)** «animal» to whine

gen *m* gene

gendarme *mf* gendarme

gendarmería *f* gendarmerie

genealógico -ca *adj* genealogical

generación *f* generation

generacional *adj* generation (*before n*), generational

generador *m* generator

general *adj* **(a)** (no específico, global) general; **de interés ∼** of general interest; **hablando en líneas ∼es** broadly speaking; **un panorama ∼ de la situación** an overall view of the situation **(b)** (*en locs*) **en general** on the whole, in general; **el público en ∼** the general public; **por lo general** as a (general) rule
■ *mf* (Mil) general

generalidad *f* (vaguedad) general comment, generality; (mayoría) majority

generalizado -da *adj* widespread

generalizar [A4] *vi* to generalize, make generalizations
■ **generalizarse** *v pron* to spread

generalmente *adv* generally

generar [A1] *vt* to generate

género *m* [1] **(a)** (clase, tipo) kind, type; **el ∼** ⋯⟶

humano the human race, mankind **(b)** (Biol) genus **(c)** (Lit, Teatr) genre; **el ~ dramático** drama **(d)** (Ling) gender **2** (tela) cloth, material

generosidad *f* generosity

generoso -sa *adj* generous

genética *f* genetics

genéticamente *adv* genetically; **~ modificado** genetically modified, GM

genético -ca *adj* genetic

genial *adj* **(a)** ‹idea/escritor/pintor› brilliant **(b)** (fam) (estupendo) great (colloq), fantastic (colloq); (fam) (ocurrente, gracioso) witty, funny

genialidad *f* (cualidad) genius; (ocurrencia) brilliant idea, stroke of genius

geniecillo *m* elf

genio *m* **(a)** (carácter) temper; **tener buen/mal ~** to be even-tempered/bad-tempered **(b)** (lumbrera) genius **(d)** (ser fantástico) genie

genitales *mpl* genitals (*pl*), genital organs (*pl*)

genocidio *m* genocide

Génova *f* Genoa

gente *f*
─────────────────────────────────────
■ **Nota** Nótese que en español, cuando el nombre *gente* significa *personas*, se traduce al inglés por *people* con verbo en plural - *allí la gente es muy amable* = people are very nice there. Cuando tiene el sentido de *familia* se traduce al inglés por *family* con el verbo en singular o plural - *mi gente está de vacaciones* = my family is o are on holiday
─────────────────────────────────────
(a) (personas) people (*pl*); **la gente está asustada** people are frightened; **había muy poca/tanta ~** there were very few/so many people; **~ bien** (de respeto) respectable people; (adinerada) well-to-do people; **la ~ de a pie** the man in the street; **ser buena ~** to be nice (*o* kind *etc*); **ser ~** (AmS) to behave (properly) **(b)** (Méx) (persona) person
■ *adj* (AmL) (de buenas maneras) respectable; (amable) kind, good
■ *adv* (Chi, Méx): **se portó muy ~ conmigo** she was very good *o* kind to me

gentil *adj* (amable) kind

gentileza *f* (cualidad) kindness; (atención, gesto): **tuvo la ~ de cederme el asiento** she was kind enough to let me have her seat; **ni siquiera tuvo la ~ de avisarnos** he didn't even have the courtesy to inform us

gentilicio *m: name given to the people from a particular region or country*

gentío *m* crowd

gentuza *f* (pey) riffraff (pej), rabble (pej)

genuflexión *f* genuflection

genuino -na *adj* genuine

geografía *f* geography

geográfico -ca *adj* geographical

geología *f* geology

geólogo -ga *m,f* geologist

geometría *f* geometry

geométrico -ca *adj* geometric

geranio *m* geranium

gerencia *f* **(a)** (cargo) post *o* position of manager **(b)** (personas) management **(c)** (oficina) manager's office

gerenciar [A1] *vt* (AmL) to manage

gerente *mf* manager; **~ comercial** business manager

geriatría *f* geriatrics

geriátrico -ca *adj* geriatric

germen *m* **1** (microbio) germ **2** **(a)** (embrión) germ **(b)** (origen) seeds (*pl*)

germicida *m* germicide

germinar [A1] *vi* to germinate

gerundio *m* gerund

gestación *f* gestation

gesticular [A1] *vi* to gesticulate

gestión *f* **(a)** (trámite) step; **la única ~ que había hecho** the only step he had taken; **hizo gestiones para adoptar un niño** he went through the procedure for adopting a child; **su apoyo a las gestiones de paz** their support for the peace process **(b)** **gestiones** *fpl* (negociaciones) negotiations (*pl*)

gestionar [A1] *vt* ‹compra/préstamo› to negotiate; **le están gestionando el permiso de trabajo** they are getting his work permit sorted out *o* arranged

gesto *m* **1** (en general) gesture; **un ~ grosero** a rude gesture; **le hizo un ~ para que se callara** she gestured to him to be quiet **2** (expresión) expression; **hacer ~s** to make faces

gestoría *f* agency (*which obtains official documents on clients' behalf*)

ghetto /'geto/ *m* ghetto

Gibraltar *m* Gibraltar

gibraltareño -ña *adj/m,f* Gibraltarian

gigabyte /xɪvə'βaɪt/ *m* gigabyte

gigante[1] *adj* giant (*before n*)

gigante[2] **-ta** *m,f* (en cuentos) (*m*) giant; (*f*) giantess; (persona alta) giant

gigantesco -ca *adj* huge, gigantic

gil *mf* (RPl fam *o* vulg) jerk (sl)

gilipollas *adj inv* (Esp fam *o* vulg): **¡qué ~ es ese tío!** that guy's such a jerk! (sl & pej)
■ *mf* (*pl* **~**) (Esp fam *o* vulg) jerk (sl & pej)

gilipollez *f* (Esp fam *o* vulg): **decir gilipolleces** to talk garbage (AmE) *o* (BrE) rubbish; **no discutáis por esa ~** don't argue over a stupid *o* silly thing like that; **pagar tanto es una ~** it's stupid paying that much

gimnasia *f* gymnastics; (como asignatura) gym, PE (BrE); **hago ~ todos los días** I do exercises every day; **~ de mantenimiento** keep-fit

gimnasio *m* gymnasium, gym

gimnasta *mf* gymnast

gimotear [A1] *vi* to whine, whimper

ginebra *f* gin

Ginebra *f* Geneva

ginecólogo -ga *m,f* gynecologist*

gira *f* tour; **de ~** on tour

girar [A1] *vi* [1] **(a)** «*rueda*» to turn, go
around; «*disco*» to revolve, go around;
«*trompo*» to spin; ~ **ALREDEDOR DE algo/algn** to
revolve AROUND sth/sb **(b)** (darse la vuelta) to turn
[2] (torcer, desviarse) to turn; ~**on a la derecha** they
turned right
■ ~ *vt* [1] ‹*manivela/volante*› to turn [2] (Com, Fin)
‹*cheque/letra de cambio*› to draw

girasol *m* sunflower

giratorio -ria *adj* revolving (*before n*)

giro *m* [1] (en general) turn; **hizo un ~ a la
derecha** she made a right turn; **un ~ de 180
grados** a volte-face, an about-turn; **el ~ que
estaba tomando la conversación** the direction the
conversation was taking [2] (Fin): **enviar un ~** (a
través de un banco) to transfer money; (por correo) to
send a money order; ~ **bancario** (cheque) bank *o*
banker's draft; (transferencia) credit transfer; ~
postal money order

gis *m* (Méx) chalk

gitano -na *adj* gypsy (*before n*)
■ *m,f* gypsy

glacial *adj* **(a)** ‹*zona/período*› glacial **(b)**
‹*viento/temperatura*› icy

glaciar *m* glacier

gladiador *m* gladiator

gladiolo *m* gladiolus

glamoroso -sa *adj* glamorous

glándula *f* gland

glandular *adj* glandular

glicerina *f* glycerin

global *adj* global; ‹*informe*› full,
comprehensive; ‹*resultado*› overall; ‹*precio/
cantidad*› total

globo *m* [1] **(a)** (Aviac, Jueg, Meteo) balloon; ~
aerostático/sonda hot-air/observation balloon **(b)**
(de chicle) bubble **(c)** (de lámpara) globe **(d)** ~
ocular eyeball [2] (mundo) world; *tb* ~**terráqueo**
globe

glóbulo *m* (cuerpo esférico) globule; (corpúsculo)
corpuscle; ~ **blanco/rojo** white/red corpuscle

gloria *f* [1] **(a)** (Relig) glory; **estar/sentirse en la
~** to be in seventh heaven **(b)** (fama, honor) glory;
cubrirse de ~ to win glory [2] (personalidad)
figure; **es una de las ~s del deporte** he is one of
the great sporting figures *o* heroes

glorieta *f* **(a)** (plaza) square; (Auto) traffic circle
(AmE), roundabout (BrE) **(b)** (en el jardín) arbor*

glorioso -sa *adj* ‹*hecho*› glorious; ‹*personaje*›
great

glotón -tona *adj* gluttonous, greedy
■ *m,f* glutton

glotonería *f* gluttony

glúteo *m* gluteus

gnomo /'nomo/ *m* gnome

gobelino *m* Gobelin

gobernador -dora *m,f* governor

gobernante *adj* ‹*partido/organismo*› ruling
(*before n*), governing (*before n*)
■ *mf* leader, ruler

gobernar [A5] *vt* ‹*país*› to govern, rule; ‹*barco*›
to steer
■ ~ *vi* (Gob, Pol) to govern; (Náut) to steer

gobierna, gobiernas ▶ GOBERNAR

gobierno *m* government

goce *m* **(a)** (de derecho, título) enjoyment; **en
pleno ~ de sus facultades** in full possession of
her faculties **(b)** (placer) pleasure

gol *m* goal; **marcar** *or* **meter un ~** to score a goal

goleada *f* heavy defeat

goleador -dora *adj* high-scoring
■ *m,f* scorer, goal-scorer

golear [A1] *vt*: **el Madrid goleó al Osasuna** Real
Madrid thrashed Osasuna

golero -ra *m,f* (CS) goalkeeper

golf *m* golf

golfa *f* (fam) (prostituta) whore (colloq)

golfillo -lla *m,f* street urchin

golfista *mf* golfer

golfito *m* (AmL) mini-golf, miniature golf

golfo¹ -fa *m,f* **(a)** (holgazán) good-for-nothing,
layabout **(b)** (fam) (niño travieso) rascal (colloq),
little devil (colloq)

golfo² ** *m* (Geog, Náut) gulf; **G~ de México Gulf of
Mexico; **G~ de Vizcaya** Bay of Biscay

golilla *f* [1] (Indum) **(a)** (cuello fruncido) ruff **(b)**
(RPl) (pañuelo) neckerchief [2] (arandela) washer

gollete *m* neck (*of a bottle*); **estar hasta el ~**
(fam) to be fed up to the back teeth (colloq); **no
tiene ~** (RPl fam) it's the limit

golondrina *f* (Zool) swallow

golosa *f* (Col) hopscotch

golosina *f* (dulce) candy (AmE), sweet (BrE)

goloso -sa *adj* (amante de lo dulce): **es muy ~** he
has a really sweet tooth

golpe *m* [1] (choque, impacto) knock; **me di un ~
en la cabeza** I got a knock on the head, I hit *o*
banged my head; **darse un ~ contra algo** to bang
o knock into sth; **dio unos ~s en la mesa** he
tapped on the table; (más fuerte) he knocked on
the table; (aún más fuerte) he banged on the table;
a ~ de (Ven) around; **de ~ (y porrazo)** suddenly;
se abrió/cerró de ~ it flew open/slammed shut;
de un ~ (de una vez) all at once; (de un trago) in
one go *o* gulp
[2] **(a)** (al pegarle a algn) blow; **lo derribó de un ~**
he knocked him down with one blow; **casi lo
matan a ~s** they almost beat him to death;
siempre andan a ~s they're always fighting **(b)**
(marca) bruise, mark
[3] (Dep) stroke
[4] **(a)** (desgracia) blow **(b)** ~ **de suerte** stroke of
luck
[5] (fam) (atraco, timo) job (colloq); **dar el ~** to do the
job
[6] (Pol) *tb* ~ **de estado** coup (d'état)

golpear [A1] *vt* [1] ‹*objeto/superficie*› to bang;
(repetidamente) to beat; **no golpees la puerta al salir**
don't slam *o* bang the door as you go out; **la lluvia
golpeaba los cristales** the rain beat against the
window panes; **golpeó la mesa con el puño** he
banged his fist on the table
[2] (pegar) to hit; **algo me golpeó en la cara**
something hit me in the face; **su marido la golpea**
her husband hits her
■ ~ *vi* **(a)** (dar, pegar) ~ **CONTRA algo** to beat
AGAINST sth **(b)** (AmS) (llamar a la puerta) to knock
(c) (en fútbol americano) to scrimmage
■ **golpearse** *v pron* **(a)** (refl) ‹*cabeza/codo*› to
bang, hit **(b)** (AmL) «*puerta*» to bang

golpetazo *m* (fam) hard blow

golpeteo *m* (tamborileo) drumming, tapping; (de la lluvia) patter, pitter-patter; (de una puerta) banging

golpismo *m* pro-coup tendency

golpista *adj* ⟨minoría/tendencia⟩ in favor of a coup; **los militares** ~**s** the soldiers who took part in the coup

golpiza *f* (AmL) beating

goma *f* 1 (a) (caucho) rubber; **suelas de** ~ rubber soles (b) (pegamento) glue, gum; ~ **de mascar** chewing gum 2 (a) (para sujetar) rubber band, elastic band (BrE) (b) (de borrar) eraser (c) (RPl) (neumático) tire* 3 (AmC fam) (resaca) hangover; **ando de** ~ I've got a hangover

gomina *f* hair gel

gomita *f* 1 (RPl) (para sujetar) rubber band, elastic band (BrE) 2 (Chi, Méx, Ven) (dulce) gumdrop, gum (BrE)

góndola *f* gondola

googlear® *vt/i* (colloq) to google

gordo¹ -da *adj* 1 ⟨persona/piernas⟩ fat; **siempre ha sido** ~ he's always been overweight *o* fat; **estás** ~ you've put on weight; **es más bien gordita** she's quite plump 2 (grueso) ⟨libro/lana/ suéter⟩ thick 3 ⟨carne/tocino⟩ fatty
■ *m,f* (a) (persona) (*m*) fat man; (*f*) fat woman (b) (fam) (como apelativo ofensivo) fatso (colloq), fatty (colloq)

gordo² *m* (Jueg) (premio mayor) jackpot (*in the state lottery*)

gordura *f* (a) (grasa) fat (b) (exceso de peso) fatness; **me preocupa su** ~ I'm worried about how fat he is

gorgorito *m* trill

gorgotear [A1] *vi* (en cañería) to gurgle; (al hervir) to bubble

gorila *m* 1 (Zool) gorilla 2 (fam) (a) (matón) thug (b) (guardaespaldas) heavy (colloq) (c) (reaccionario) fascist (d) (Esp) (en un club) bouncer

gorjear [A1] *vi* «pájaro» to trill, warble; «niño» to gurgle

gorra *f* cap; (con visera) peaked cap; (de bebé) bonnet

gorrear [A1] *vt* 1 (fam) (pedir) to scrounge (colloq); **me gorreó $20** he scrounged $20 off me 2 (Chi fam) ⟨cónyuge⟩ to cheat on (colloq)

gorrero -ra *m,f* (AmL fam) (aprovechado) scrounger (colloq)

gorrión *m* sparrow

gorro *m* cap; ~ **de baño** (para nadar) bathing cap; (para la ducha) shower cap; **estar hasta el** ~ (fam) to be fed up to the back teeth (colloq)

gorrón -rrona *m,f* (Esp, Méx fam) scrounger (colloq)

gorronear [A1] *vt/vi* (Esp, Méx fam) to scrounge (colloq)

gota *f* 1 (de líquido) drop; ~**s de sudor** beads of sweat; **la** ~ **que colma** *or* **rebasa el vaso** the last straw; **parecerse/ser como dos** ~**s de agua** to be as like as two peas in a pod 2 (enfermedad) gout

gotear [A1] *vi* «líquido/grifo/vela» to drip; «cañería» to leak
■ ~ *v impers* (llovizna) to spit, drizzle

goteo *m* dripping

gotera *f* (a) (filtración) leak (b) (mancha) damp stain

gótico -ca *adj* Gothic

gourde *m* gourde (*Haitian unit of currency*)

gozador -dora *adj* (AmL) fun-loving

gozar [A4] *vi*: ~ **DE** algo to enjoy sth; ~ **de la vida** to enjoy life; **goza viéndolos jugar** she enjoys watching them play; ~ **CON** algo to enjoy sth; **goza de perfecta salud** he enjoys perfect health; **goza de una buena posición** he has a good position

gozne *m* hinge

gozo *m* 1 (a) (alegría) joy; **no caber en sí de** ~ to be beside oneself with joy (b) (placer) pleasure, enjoyment 2 **gozos** *mpl* (Relig) verses (*pl*)

GPS *m* GPS

grabación *f* recording; ~ **en video** video recording

grabado *m* engraving

grabador -dora *m,f* 1 (Art) engraver 2 **grabadora** *f* (a) (casa discográfica) record company (b) (magnetófono) tape recorder

grabar [A1] *vt/vi* (a) (Audio, TV) to record, tape (b) (Art) to engrave
■ **grabarse** *v pron*: **sus palabras se me** ~**on en la memoria** her words are etched on my memory; **su cara se me quedó grabada** I'll never forget her face

gracia *f*
I 1 (comicidad): **yo no le veo la** ~ I don't think it's funny; **tener** ~ «chiste/broma» to be funny; **me hace** ~ **que digas eso** it's funny you should say that; **no me hace ninguna** ~ **tener que ir** I don't relish the idea of having to go 2 (a) (chiste) joke; (broma) joke, trick (b) (de niño) party piece 3 (encanto, elegancia) grace; **con** ~ ⟨moverse/ bailar⟩ gracefully; **un vestido sin** ~ a very plain dress; **tiene mucha** ~ **para arreglar flores** she has a real flair for flower arranging
II **gracias** *fpl* (a) (expresión de agradecimiento): **darle las** ~**s a algn** to thank sb; **no dieron ni las** ~**s** they didn't even say thank you (b) (como interj) thank you, thanks (colloq); **muchas** ~**s** thank you very much, thanks a lot (colloq); **un millón de** ~**s por ayudarme/tu ayuda** thank you very much for helping me/your help (c) **gracias a thanks to**; ~**s a Dios** thank God

gracioso -sa *adj* 1 (divertido) ⟨chiste/persona⟩ funny; **¡qué** ~**!** how funny!; **hacerse el** ~ to play the fool 2 (atractivo) ⟨cara/figura⟩ attractive; **las pecas le dan un aspecto muy** ~ those freckles make her look really cute *o* sweet

grada *f* (a) (peldaño) step (b) **gradas** *fpl* (Dep) stand, grandstand

gradería *f*, (Esp) **graderío** *m* stands (*pl*)

gradiente *f* (AmL) (pendiente) slope, gradient

grado *m* 1 (en general) degree; **estamos a tres** ~**s bajo cero** it's three degrees below zero; ~ **centígrado** *or* **Celsius/Fahrenheit** degree centigrade *o* Celsius/Fahrenheit; **el** ~ **de confusión reinante** the degree of confusion that prevails; **en** ~ **sumo** extremely 2 (de escalafón) grade; (Mil) rank 3 (disposición): **de buen/mal** ~ willingly/unwillingly 4 (a) (esp AmL) (Educ) (curso, año) year (b) (título): **tiene el** ~ **de licenciado** he has a college (AmE) *o* (BrE) university degree

graduable *adj* adjustable

graduación *f* (a) (acción de regular) adjustment (b) (de bebida alcohólica) alcohol content (c) (Mil) rank (d) (Educ) graduation

graduado -da *adj* (a) ⟨gafas/lentes⟩ prescription (before n) (b) ⟨termómetro⟩ graduated
■ *m,f* (Educ) graduate

gradual *adj* gradual

graduar [A18] *vt* (a) (regular) to adjust (b) (marcar) ⟨instrumento/termómetro⟩ to calibrate
■ **graduarse** *v pron* (a) (Educ) to graduate (b) (Mil) to take a commission

graffiti /graˈfiti/ *mpl* graffiti

gráfico¹ -ca *adj* graphic; ⟨gesto⟩ expressive

gráfico² *m* (a) (Mat) graph (b) (Inf) graphic

grafología *f* graphology

gragea *f* (a) (Farm) tablet (b) (Coc) small candy (AmE) o (BrE) sweet

Gral. *m* (= **General**) Gen.

grama *f* (AmC, Ven) (césped) lawn

gramática *f* (disciplina) grammar; (libro) grammar (book)

gramatical *adj* grammatical

gramo *m* gram

gran *adj*: ▶ GRANDE

granada *f* [1] (Bot) pomegranate [2] (Arm, Mil) grenade; ~ **de mano** hand grenade

Granada *f* (en España) Granada; (en el Caribe) Grenada

granadilla *f* (fruta — redonda, oscura) passion fruit; (— más grande, amarilla) granadilla

granate *adj inv* maroon (before n)
■ *m* (color) maroon

Gran Bretaña *f* Great Britain

grande *adj* [GRAN is used before singular nouns]
[1] (a) (en dimensiones) ⟨casa/área/nariz⟩ big, large; **un tipo** ~ a big guy; **unos** ~ **almacenes** a department store (b) (en demasía) too big; **me queda** ~ it's too big for me (c) (en número) ⟨familia⟩ large; ⟨clase⟩big; **la gran parte** *or* **mayoría** the great majority
[2] (a) (alto) tall; **¡qué** ~ **está Andrés!** isn't Andrés tall! (b) (en edad): **cuando sea** ~ when I grow up; **ya son** ~s they are all grown up now
[3] (Geog): **el G**~ **Santiago** Greater Santiago
[4] ⟨delante del n⟩ (a) (notable, excelente) great; **un gran hombre** a great man (b) (poderoso) big; **los** ~s **bancos** the big banks; **a lo** ~ in style
[5] (a) (en intensidad, grado) ⟨pena/honor/ventaja⟩ great; ⟨explosión⟩ powerful; **¡me llevé un susto más** ~ ... ! I got such a fright!; **una temporada de gran éxito** a very o a highly successful season; **son** ~s **amigos** they're great friends; **eso es una gran verdad** that is absolutely true; **¡qué mentira más** ~! that's a complete lie! (b) (elevado): **a gran velocidad** at high o great speed; **volar a gran altura** to fly at a great height; **un gran número de personas** a large number of people; **objetos de gran valor** objects of great value; **en** ~: **lo pasamos en** ~ we had a great time (colloq)
■ *m,f* (a) (mayor): **la grande ya está casada** their eldest (daughter) is already married (b) (adulto): **los** ~s the grown-ups

grandeza *f* [1] (excelencia, nobleza) nobility; ~ **de alma** (liter) magnanimity; ~ **de ánimo** (liter)

valor* (liter) [2] (a) (dignidad de Grande) rank of grandee (b) (conjunto de Grandes): **la** ~ the (Spanish) nobility o grandees

grandilocuencia *f* grandiloquence

grandiosidad *f* grandeur

grandioso -sa *adj* ⟨espectáculo/obra⟩ impressive, magnificent (b) (rimbombante) ⟨gesto/palabras⟩ grandiose

granel: **a** ~ (a) (loc adj) (en abundancia) ⟨comida/bebida⟩ stacks of (b) (loc adv) **comprar/vender a** ~ ⟨vino/aceite⟩ to buy/sell ... by the liter (o pint etc); ⟨galletas/nueces⟩ to buy/sell ... loose; (en grandes cantidades) to buy/sell ... in bulk

granero *m* granary, barn

granito *m* (roca) granite

granizado *m* (bebida) *drink served on crushed ice*

granizar [A4] *v impers* to hail

granizo *m* (grano, bola) hailstone; (conjunto) hail

granja *f* (Agr) farm; ~ **avícola** poultry farm

granjearse [A1] *v pron* to earn, win

granjero -ra *m,f* farmer

grano *m* [1] (de arena, azúcar, trigo, arroz) grain; (de café) bean; (de mostaza) seed; ~s **de pimienta** peppercorns; **ir al** ~ (fam) to get (straight) to the point [2] (Med) spot, pimple (esp AmE) [3] (a) (de la piedra, la madera) grain (b) (Fot) grain

granuja *mf* rascal

grapa *f* [1] (a) (para papeles) staple; (para cables) cable clip (b) (Arquit) cramp iron [2] (CS) (aguardiente) grappa

grapadora *f* stapler

grapar [A1] *vt* to staple

grasa *f* [1] (a) (Biol, Coc) fat; **la comida tenía mucha** ~ the food was very greasy (b) (suciedad) grease; **está lleno de** ~ it's all greasy (c) (Mec) grease [2] (Méx) (betún) shoe polish

grasiento -ta *adj* greasy

grasitud *f* (AmL) greasiness

graso -sa *adj* (a) ⟨pelo/cutis⟩ greasy (b) (Coc) greasy, oily, fatty; **queso** ~ full fat cheese

grasoso -sa *adj* (AmL) greasy

gratificación *f* (a) (bonificación) bonus; (recompensa) reward (b) (satisfacción) gratification

gratificador -dora *adj* (AmL) rewarding, gratifying (frml)

gratificante *adj* rewarding, gratifying (frml)

gratificar [A2] *vt* (a) ⟨persona⟩ to give ... a bonus (b) (recompensar) to give ... a reward; **❸ se gratificará** reward offered

gratinado -da *adj* au gratin

gratinador *m* grill

gratis *adj/adv* free; **es** ~ it is free (of charge); **entramos** ~ we got in free o for nothing

gratitud *f* gratitude

grato -ta *adj* pleasant

gratuito -ta *adj* (a) (gratis) free (b) (infundado) ⟨afirmaciones⟩ unwarranted; ⟨insulto⟩ gratuitous

grava *f* gravel

gravamen *m* (impuesto) tax; (carga) burden; (sobre finca, casa) encumbrance

gravar [A1] *vt* (con impuesto) ⟨ingresos/productos⟩ to tax

grave *adj* [1] (a) [ESTAR] ⟨enfermo⟩ seriously ill ····>

g

(a) [SER] ⟨*herida/enfermedad*⟩ serious **2** ⟨*situación/asunto/error*⟩ serious **3** **(a)** ⟨*tono/ expresión/gesto*⟩ grave, solemn **(b)** ⟨*voz*⟩ deep **(c)** ⟨*sonido/nota*⟩ low **4** (Ling) ⟨*acento*⟩ grave; ⟨*palabra*⟩ paroxytone

gravedad *f* **1** (en general) seriousness; **está herido de** ~ he is seriously injured; **es un asunto de mucha** ~ it is a very serious matter **2** (Fís) gravity

gravilla *f* gravel

graznar [A1] *vi* «*cuervo*» to caw; «*ganso*» to honk; «*pato*» to quack

graznido *m* (del cuervo) caw; (del ganso) honk; (del pato) quack

Grecia *f* Greece

greda *f* (para cerámica) clay

grei *m* (Col) grapefruit

greifrú *mf* (*pl* **-frús**) (AmC, Ven fam) grapefruit

gremial *adj* **(a)** (profesional) ⟨*asociación*⟩ professional **(b)** (AmL) (sindical) union (*before n*)

gremialista *mf* (AmL) trade unionist

gremio *m* **(a)** (de oficio, profesión) trade **(b)** (CS, Per) (sindicato) union

greña *f* **(a)** (enredo) tangle **(b)** **en greña** (Méx) ⟨*trigo*⟩ unthreshed; ⟨*plata/azúcar*⟩ unrefined; ⟨*tabaco*⟩ leaf (*before n*) **(c)** **greñas** *fpl* untidy hair

gresca *f* (fam) (jaleo) rumpus (colloq); (riña) fight

griego¹ -ga *adj/m,f* Greek

griego² *m* (idioma) Greek

grieta *f* (en una pared) crack; (en la tierra) crack, crevice; (en la piel) crack

grifo¹ *m* **1** (Esp) (de lavabo, bañera) faucet (AmE), tap (BrE); **abrir/cerrar el** ~ to turn the faucet *o* tap on/off **2** (Per) (gasolinera) filling station **3** (Chi) (de incendios) fire hydrant, fireplug (AmE)

grifo² -fa *m,f* (Méx fam) pothead (sl), dopehead (sl)

grillo *m* **1** (Zool) cricket **2** **grillos** *mpl* (de los presos) fetters (*pl*), shackles (*pl*)

grima *f* (Esp fam): **darle** ~ **a algn** (repulsión) to make sb's flesh crawl; (dentera) to set sb's teeth on edge

gringo -ga *adj* **(a)** (AmL fam & pey) gringo, foreign (*of or relating to a person from a non-Spanish speaking country*) **(b)** (Andes fam) (rubio) fair-haired
■ *m,f* **(a)** (AmL fam & pey) (extranjero) gringo, foreigner (*from a non-Spanish speaking country*); (norteamericano) Yank (colloq & pej), Yankee (colloq & pej) **(b)** (Andes fam) (rubio) (*m*) fair-haired boy/ man; (*f*) fair-haired girl/woman

Gringolandia *f* (Andes fam & pey) Yankeeland (colloq & pej)

gripa *f* (Col, Méx) ▶ GRIPE

gripe *f* flu; **estar con/tener** ~ to have (the) flu

gris *adj/m* gray*

gritar [A1] *vi* to shout; **no hace falta que grites** there's no need to shout *o* yell; ~ **de dolor** to

scream with pain; ~ **de alegría** to shout for joy; ~ **pidiendo ayuda** to shout for help; ~**le A algn** to shout AT sb; (para llamarlo) to shout (out) TO sb
■ ~ *vt* to shout

griterío *m* shouting, clamor*

grito *m* **(a)** (de dolor, alegría) shout, cry; (de terror) scream; **un** ~ **de socorro** a cry for help; ~**s de protesta** shouts *o* cries of protest; **hablar a** ~**s** to talk at the top of one's voice; **ser el último** ~ to be the last word in fashion **(b)** (de pájaro, animal) call, cry

groenlandés -desa *adj* of/from Greenland

Groenlandia *f* Greenland

grosella *f* redcurrant

grosería *f* **(a)** (acción): **fue una** ~ **de su parte** it was very rude of him **(b)** (comentario) rude comment; **¡qué** ~**!** how rude!; **decir** ~**s** to swear

grosero -ra *adj* **(a)** (descortés) ⟨*persona/ lenguaje*⟩ rude **(b)** (vulgar) crude, vulgar
■ *m,f*: **es un** ~ (vulgar) he's so vulgar *o* crude!; (descortés) he's so rude!

grosor *m* thickness

grotesco -ca *adj* ⟨*personaje/mueca*⟩ grotesque; ⟨*espectáculo*⟩ hideous, grotesque

grúa *f* **(a)** (Const) crane **(b)** (Auto) (de taller) wrecker (AmE), breakdown van (BrE); (de la policía) tow truck; **se lo llevó la** ~ it was towed (away)

grueso -sa *adj* thick

grulla *f* crane

grumete *m* cabin boy

grumo *m* lump

grumoso -sa *adj* lumpy

gruñido *m* grunt; (del perro) growl

gruñir [I9] *vi* **(a)** «*cerdo*» to grunt; «*perro*» to growl **(b)** (fam) «*persona*» to grumble

gruñón -ñona *adj* (fam) grumpy (colloq)

grupa *f* rump, hindquarters (*pl*)

grupo *m* **(a)** (de personas, empresas, países) group; (de árboles) clump; ~ **sanguíneo** blood group; ~**s sociales** social groups; **de** ~ ⟨*terapia/trabajo*⟩ group (*before n*); **en** ~ ⟨*salir/trabajar*⟩ in a group/in groups **(b)** (Mús) *tb* ~ **musical** group, band

gruta *f* (natural) cave; (artificial) grotto

guaca *f* (Andes) pre-Columbian tomb

guacal *m* **(a)** (Col, Méx, Ven) (caja) wooden crate **(b)** (Ven) (medida) crate, crateload **(c)** (AmC) (calabaza) large gourd (*used for storing tortillas*)

guacamaya *f* (Méx) **1** (ave) macaw **2** (fam) (persona) loudmouth (colloq)

guacamayo *m* macaw

guacamole *m* guacamole

guachimán *m* (AmS fam) watchman

guachinango *m* (Méx) red snapper

guacho¹ -cha *adj* **1** (Andes, RPI) **(a)** (fam) ⟨*niño*⟩ orphaned; ⟨*perro*⟩ stray **(b)** (fam & pey) ⟨*hijo*⟩ bastard (*before n*) (pej) **2** (Chi, Per fam) ⟨*calcetín/guante*⟩ odd
■ *m,f* (Andes, RPI) **(a)** (fam) (niño abandonado) orphan,

waif; (perro) stray **(b)** (fam & pey) (hijo ilegítimo) bastard (vulg) **(c)** (insulto — a un hombre) bastard (pej); (— a una mujer) bitch (sl & pej)

guacho² *m* (Per) (de la lotería) *tenth share in a lottery ticket*

guaco *m* (Andes) pot (*found in pre-Columbian tomb*)

guadaña *f* scythe

guagua *f* (fam) **1** (Andes) (bebé) baby **2** (Cu) (autobús) bus

guaje -ja *m,f* **1** (Méx fam) sucker (colloq); *hacerle* ~ *a algn* (serle infiel) to cheat on sb (colloq); (engañarlo) to rip sb off (colloq); *hacerse* ~ to act dumb (colloq) **2** **guaje** *m* (Méx) **(a)** (planta, fruto) bottle gourd **(b)** (vasija) gourd **(c)** (instrumento) maraca (*made from a bottle gourd*)

guajiro -ra *m,f* **1** (en Cuba) peasant **(b)** (en Col, Ven) *native of the Guajira peninsula*

guajolote -ta *m,f* (Méx) turkey

guanábana *f* (fruto) soursop; (árbol) soursop tree

guanaco *m* **1** (Zool) guanaco **2** (Chi fam) (de la policía) water cannon

guanera *f* guano deposit

guanero -ra *adj* guano (*before n*)

guano *m* guano

guante *m* glove; ~s de lana/boxeo woollen/ boxing gloves; *echarle el* ~ *a algn* (fam) to nab sb (colloq)

guantera *f* glove compartment

guapetón -tona *adj* (fam) ⟨chico⟩ handsome; ⟨chica⟩ pretty

guapo -pa *adj* **1** ⟨hombre⟩ handsome, good-looking; ⟨mujer⟩ attractive, good-looking; ⟨bebé⟩ beautiful; *estás muy* ~ *con ese traje* you look very nice in that suit **2 (a)** (fam) (bravucón): *ponerse* ~ to get cocky (colloq) **(b)** (AmS fam) (valiente) gutsy (colloq)

guarangada *f* (RPI, Ven fam) ▶ GROSERÍA B

guarango -ga *adj* (CS, Ven fam) (grosero) rude, loutish

■ *m,f* (CS, Ven fam) (grosero) lout (colloq)

guaraní *adj/m,f* Guarani

■ *m* (idioma) Guarani

guarapear [A1] *vi* (Per fam) to get plastered (colloq)

guarda *mf* (de museo, parque) keeper; (de edificio público) *tb* ~ **jurado** security guard

guardabarros *m* (*pl* ~) **(a)** (Auto) fender (AmE), mudguard (BrE) **(b)** (de bicicleta) mudguard

guardabosque *mf* (en parque nacional) forest ranger

guardacostas *mf* (*pl* ~) **(a)** (persona) coastguard **(b) guardacostas** *m* (buque) coastguard vessel

guardaespaldas *mf* (*pl* ~) bodyguard

guardalíneas *mf* (*pl* ~) (Chi) (*m*) linesman; (*f*) lineswoman

guardameta *mf* goalkeeper

guardapelo *m* locket

guardapolvo *m* (bata — de niño) overall; (— de profesor, tendero) workcoat (AmE), overall (BrE)

guardar [A1] *vt* **1** (reservar) to save, keep; *guarda algo para después* save *o* keep sth for later

2 (a) (poner en un lugar) ⟨juguetes/libros⟩ to put ... away; *ya guardé toda la ropa de invierno* I've already put away all my winter clothes **(b)** (conservar, mantener) to keep; *lo guardó durante años* she kept it for years; ~ *las apariencias* to keep up appearances **(c)** ⟨secreto⟩ to keep; ⟨rencor⟩ to bear, harbor*; *guardo muy buenos recuerdos de él* I have very good memories of him

■ **guardarse** *v pron* **1 (a)** (quedarse con) to keep **(b)** (reservar) to save, keep **2** (poner en un lugar): *se guardó el cheque en el bolsillo* he put the check (away) in his pocket

guardarropa *m* **(a)** (en restaurantes, teatros) cloakroom **(b)** (ropa) wardrobe **(c)** (armario) dressing room

guardavallas *mf* (*pl* ~) (AmL) goalkeeper

guardería *f*: *tb* ~ **infantil** nursery

guardia *f* **1 (a)** (vigilancia): *estar de* ~ «soldado» to be on guard duty; «médico» to be on duty *o* call; «empleado» to be on duty; «marino» to be on watch; *montar* ~ to stand guard; *poner en* ~ *a algn* to warn sb **(b)** (en esgrima): *en* ~ on guard **2** (cuerpo militar) guard; *cambio de* ~ changing of the guard; *G~* Civil Civil Guard; ~ *municipal or urbana* police (*mainly involved in traffic duties*) **3 guardia** *mf* (*m*) policeman; (*f*) policewoman

guardiamarina *mf* midshipman

guardián -diana *m,f* **(a)** (de un edificio) security guard, guard **(b)** (protector, defensor) guardian

guarecer [E3] *vt* to shelter, protect

■ **guarecerse** *v pron* (refl) to shelter, take shelter

guarén *m* water rat

guargüero *m* (AmL fam) (garganta) throat

guarida *f* (de animales) den, lair; (de personas) hideout

guarnecer [E3] *vt* (Coc) to garnish

guarrada *f* (Esp fam) **(a)** (porquería, suciedad) mess (colloq) **(b)** (mala pasada) dirty trick (colloq) **(c)** (indecencia, vulgaridad): *no digas* ~s don't be filthy; *esa película es una* ~ that's a filthy movie

guarro -rra *m,f* (Esp fam) **(a)** (persona sucia) filthy pig (colloq) **(b)** (indecente, vulgar): *es un* ~ he's really disgusting

guarura *m* (Méx) bodyguard

guasa *f* (fam) (broma, burla) joke; *de* ~ as a joke; *no te lo tomes a* ~ it's no joke, it's no laughing matter

guasca *f* (Chi, Per) (ramal de cuero) strap

guasón -sona *m,f* (fam) (bromista) joker

guata *f* **1** (Esp) (algodón) wadding **2** (Andes fam) (barriga) paunch; *echar* ~ to get a paunch; *me duele la* ~ I've got a tummy ache (colloq)

Guatemala *f* Guatemala

guatemalteco -ca *adj/m,f* Guatemalan

guateque *m* (Esp, Méx fam) (fiesta) bash (colloq), party

guatitas *fpl* (Chi) tripe

guatón -tona *adj* (Chi, Per fam): *está muy* ~ he has a real paunch (colloq)

■ *m,f* (Chi, Per fam) fatty (colloq)

guau *interj* (del perro) woof!, bow-wow!

guayaba *f* (fruta) guava

guayabera *f*: loose lightweight shirt

guayabo *m* **1** (Bot) guava tree **2** (Col fam) (resaca) hangover

Guayana *f*: *tb* la ~ Francesa French Guiana

gubernatura *f* (Méx) government

güero -ra *adj* (Méx fam) (rubio) blond, fair-haired; (amarillo) yellow
■ *m,f* (Méx fam) (*m*) blond *o* fair-haired man; (*f*) blonde *o* fair-haired woman

guerra *f* **1** (Mil, Pol) war; **nos declararon la** ~ they declared war on us; **estar en** ~ to be at war; **hacerle la** ~ **a algn** to wage war on *o* against sb; ~ **bacteriológica** *or* **biológica** germ *o* biological warfare; ~ **civil** civil war; ~ **fría** cold war; ~ **mundial** world war; ~ **nuclear** nuclear war; ~ **química** chemical warfare **2** (fam) (problemas) trouble, hassle (colloq); **estos niños me dan mucha** ~ these kids give me a lot of hassle

guerrera *f* army jacket

guerrero -ra *adj* ⟨pueblo/espíritu⟩ warlike; **canto** ~ war cry
■ *m,f* warrior

guerrilla *f* **(a)** (grupo) guerrillas (*pl*) **(b)** (lucha) guerrilla warfare

guerrillero -ra *m,f* guerrilla

guía *f* **1** (libro, folleto) guide (book); (de calles) map; ~ **turística/de hoteles** tourist/hotel guide; ~ **telefónica** *or* **de teléfonos** telephone directory, phone book **2 guía** *mf* (persona) guide; ~ **de turismo** tourist guide

guiar [A17] *vt* to guide
■ **guiarse** *v pron* ~**se POR algo** ⟨por mapa/consejo⟩ to follow sth; ~**se por las apariencias** to be led by appearances; ~**se por el instinto** to follow one's instincts

guijarro *m* pebble

guillotina *f* guillotine

guillotinar [A1] *vt* to guillotine

guinda *f* morello cherry; (confitada) glacé cherry

guindar [A1] *vt* **1** (Esp arg) (robar) ⟨novia/trabajo⟩ to steal **2 (a)** (Col, Méx, Ven fam) ⟨ropa⟩ to hang up **(b)** (Col fam) ⟨hamaca⟩ to hang
■ **guindarse** *v pron* (Col, Méx, Ven) (colgarse) to hang

guindilla *f* chili

guindo *m* morello cherry tree

guiñar [A1] *vt* to wink; ~**le el ojo** *or* **un ojo a algn** to wink at sb

guiño *m* wink; **hacerle un** ~ **a algn** to give sb a wink

guion *m* **1 (a)** (Cin, TV) script; ~ **cinematográfico** screenplay **(b)** (esquema) outline, plan **2** (Impr) (en diálogo) dash; (en palabras compuestas) hyphen; **lleva** ~ it's hyphenated

guionista *mf* scriptwriter, screenwriter

güirila *f* (AmC) maize pancake

guirnalda *f* garland

guisante *m* (Esp) pea

guisar [A1] *vi* (Esp) to cook; **guisa muy bien** he's a very good cook
■ ~ *vt* (con bastante líquido) to stew; (con poco líquido) to braise

guiso *m* stew, casserole

guita *f* (arg) cash (colloq), dough (sl)

guitarra *f* guitar; ~ **eléctrica/española/clásica** electric/Spanish/classical guitar

guitarrear [A1] *vi* (Mús) to play the guitar

guitarrista *mf* guitarist

gula *f* greed, gluttony

gusano *m* **1 (a)** (como nombre genérico) worm; (lombriz de tierra) earthworm, worm **(b)** (larva — de mariposa) caterpillar; (— de mosca) maggot; ~ **de luz** glowworm; ~ **de seda** silkworm **2** (pey) (persona despreciable) worm (pej)

gustar [A1] *vi* **1** (+ *me/te/le etc*): **¿te gustó el libro?** did you like *o* enjoy the book?; **me gusta su compañía** I enjoy her company; **los helados no me/te/nos gustan** I/you/we don't like ice cream; **le gusta mucho la música** he likes music very much; **a Juan le gusta María** Juan likes María; **le gusta tocar la guitarra** she likes to play the guitar (AmE), she likes playing the guitar (BrE); **le gusta mucho viajar** she's very fond of traveling (colloq); **nos gusta dar un paseo después de comer** we like to have a walk after lunch; **¿te ~ía visitar el castillo?** would you like to visit the castle?; **me ~ía que vinieras temprano** I'd like you to come early
2 (en frases de cortesía) to wish (frml); **como guste** as you wish; **cuando usted guste** whenever it is convenient for you
■ ~ *vt* (AmL) (querer) to like; **¿gustan tomar algo?** would you like something to drink?

gusto *m* **1 (a)** (sentido, sabor) taste; **resulta amargo al** ~ it has a bitter taste; **tiene un** ~ **medio raro** it has a funny taste to it; **tiene** ~ **a fresa** it tastes of strawberry; **deja un** ~ **a menta** it has a minty aftertaste **(b)** (sentido estético) taste; **tiene muy buen** ~ **para vestirse** she has very good taste in clothes; **una broma de mal** ~ a tasteless joke; **para todos los** ~**s** to suit all tastes **2 (a)** (placer, agrado) pleasure; **tendré mucho** ~ **en acompañarlos** (frml) it will be a pleasure for me to accompany you (frml); **da** ~ **estar aquí** it's so nice (being) here; **me dio mucho** ~ **volverlo a ver** it was lovely to see him again; **por** ~ for fun, for pleasure; **un lugar donde se está a** ~ a place where you feel comfortable *o* at ease **(b)** (en fórmulas de cortesía): **mucho** ~ **(en conocerla)** pleased *o* nice to meet you; **el** ~ **es mío** the pleasure is mine

gustoso -sa *adj* willingly

gutural *adj* guttural

Hh

H, h *f* (*read as* /'atʃe/) *the letter* H, h (*ver tb* HACHE)

h. (= **hora**) hr

ha *interj* ah!, ha!

Ha. (= **hectárea**) ha., hectare

haba *f* (Bot) (broad) bean

Habana *f*: **La** ~ Havana

habanero -ra *adj/m,f* Havanan

habano *m* (cigarro) Havana cigar

haber¹ [E17] *v aux* (en tiempos compuestos) to have; **no habían llegado** they hadn't arrived; **de** ~**lo sabido** had I known, if I'd known; **¡deberías** ~**lo dicho!** you should have said so!

■ ~ *v impers*

I (existir, estar, darse): **hay una carta/varias cartas para ti** there's a letter/there are several letters for you; **¿hay un banco por aquí?** is there a bank near here?; **hubo dos accidentes** there were two accidents; **¿hay helado?** do you have any ice cream?; **no hay como un buen descanso** there's nothing like a good rest; **hubo varios heridos** several people were injured; **las hay rojas y verdes** there are red ones and green ones; **gracias — no hay de qué** thank you — don't mention it *o* not at all *o* you're welcome; **no hay de qué preocuparse** there's nothing to worry about; **¿qué hay de nuevo?** (fam) what's new?; **hola ¿qué hay?** (fam) hello, how are things?; **¿qué hubo?** (Andes, Méx, Ven fam) how are things?

II (ser necesario) *o* ~ **QUE + INF**: **hay que estudiar** you/we/they must study; **hubo que romperlo** we/they had to break it; **no hay que lavarlo** (no es necesario) you don't need *o* have to wash it; (no se debe) you mustn't wash it

haber² *m* (a) (bienes) assets (*pl*) (b) (en contabilidad) credit side (c) **haberes** *mpl* (frml) (ingresos) income, earnings (*pl*)

habichuela *f* (a) (semilla) bean (b) (Col) (con vaina) green bean, French bean (BrE)

hábil *adj* [1] (a) (diestro) ⟨*carpintero*⟩ skilled, adept; ⟨*conductor*⟩ good, skillful*; ⟨*juego/táctica*⟩ skillful* (b) (astuto, inteligente) clever, able [2] ⟨*horas/días*⟩ working (*before n*) [3] (Der) competent

habilidad *f* [1] (a) (para actividad manual, física) skill; **tiene** ~ **para la carpintería** he is good at carpentry (b) (astucia, inteligencia) skill, cleverness; **con** ~ cleverly, skillfully [2] (Der) competence

habilidoso -sa *adj* [SER] good with one's hands, handy

habilitación *f* [1] (de lugar) fitting out [2] (autorización) authorization [3] (Col) (Educ): **exámenes de** ~ retakes

habilitar [A1] *vt* [1] ⟨*lugar*⟩ to fit out [2] ⟨*persona/institución*⟩ to authorize; «*título*» to qualify, authorize; «*documento*» to authorize, empower [3] (Col) (Educ) to retake, to make up (AmE)

habiloso -sa *adj* (Chi fam) (inteligente) bright, smart (colloq)

habitable *adj* habitable

habitación *f* (cuarto) room; (dormitorio) bedroom; ~ **individual** single room

habitacional *adj* (CS) housing (*before n*)

habitante *mf* (Geog, Sociol) inhabitant; (de barrio) resident

habitar [A1] *vt* ⟨*vivienda*⟩ to live in; ⟨*isla/planeta*⟩ to inhabit

■ ~ *vi* (frml) to dwell (frml)

hábitat /'aβita(t)/ *m* (*pl* **-tats**) (Ecol, Zool) habitat; (Geog, Sociol) environment

hábito *m* [1] (costumbre) habit; **adquirir/tener el** ~ **DE hacer algo** to get into/have the habit OF doing sth [2] (de religioso) habit

habitual *adj* ⟨*sitio/hora*⟩ usual; ⟨*cliente/lector*⟩ regular

habituar [A18] *vt* ~ **a algn A algo** to get sb used to sth

■ **habituarse** *v pron* ~**se A algo** to get used TO sth, get *o* become accustomed TO sth

habla *f⁑* [1] (facultad) speech; **perder el** ~ to lose one's powers of speech; **al verla me quedé sin** ~ when I saw her I was speechless [2] (a) (idioma): **países de** ~ **hispana** Spanish-speaking countries (b) (manera de hablar): **de esta región** the local way of speaking [3] **al habla** (en el teléfono) speaking; **estamos al** ~ **con nuestro corresponsal** we have our correspondent on the line

hablado -da *adj* (a) ⟨*lenguaje*⟩ spoken (b) **bien/mal** ~ ⟨*persona*⟩ well-spoken/foul-mouthed

hablador -dora *adj* (a) (charlatán) talkative, chatty (colloq) (b) (chismoso) gossipy (c) (Méx fam) (mentiroso): **es tan** ~ he's such a fibber (colloq);

■ *m,f* (a) (charlatán) chatterbox (colloq) (b) (chismoso) gossip (colloq) (c) (Méx fam) (mentiroso) storyteller, fibber (colloq)

habladurías *fpl* idle gossip *o* talk

hablar [A1] *vi* [1] (a) (articular palabras) to speak; **habla más alto** speak up; **habla más bajo** keep your voice down (b) (expresarse) to speak; ~ **claro** (claramente) to speak clearly; (francamente) to speak frankly; ~ **por señas** to use sign language; **un político que habla muy bien** a politician who is a very good speaker; ~ **por** ~ to talk for the sake of it [2] (a) (conversar) to talk; **habla mucho** he talks a lot; **tenemos que** ~ we must (have a) talk; ~ **CON algn** to speak *o* talk TO sb; **tengo que** ~**te** *or* **que** ~ **contigo** I need to speak to you *o* have a word with you; **está hablando por teléfono** he's on the phone; **¡ni** ~! no way! (colloq), no chance! (colloq) (b) (bajo coacción) to talk (c) (murmurar) to talk, gossip; **dar que** ~ to start people talking (d) (rumorear): **se habla ya de miles de víctimas** there is already talk of thousands of casualties; **se habla de que va a renunciar** it is said *o* rumored that she's going to resign (e) (al teléfono): **¿con quién hablo?** who am I speaking with (AmE) *o* (BrE) speaking to? [3] (a) (tratar, referirse a) ~ **DE algo/algn** to talk   ⋯⋯

ABOUT sth/sb; ~ **de negocios** to talk (about) *o* discuss business; **siempre habla mal de ella** he never has a good word to say about her; **hablan muy bien de él** people speak very highly of him; **me ha hablado mucho de ti** she's told me a lot about you; **en tren sale caro, y no hablemos ya del avión** going by train is expensive, and as for flying …; **háblame de tus planes** tell me about your plans; ~ SOBRE *or* ACERCA DE algo to talk ABOUT sth **(b)** (dirigirse a) to speak; **no me hables así** don't speak to me like that; **háblale de tú** use the 'tú' form with him **(c)** (anunciar propósito) ~ DE **hacer algo** to talk OF doing sth; **habla de jubilarse** he's talking of retiring

4 (Méx) (por teléfono) to call, phone

■ ~ *vt* **1** ⟨*idioma*⟩ to speak

2 (tratar): **tenemos que** ~ **las cosas** we must talk things over; **ya lo** ~**emos más adelante** we'll talk about *o* discuss that later

■ **hablarse** *v pron*: **llevan meses sin** ~**se** they haven't spoken to each other for months; **no se habla con ella** he's not speaking *o* talking to her, he's not on speaking terms with her

habrá, habría, etc ▶ HABER¹

hacendado -da *adj* landowning (*before n*)
■ *m,f* landowner, owner of a ranch (*o* farm *etc*)

hacendoso -sa *adj* hardworking (*esp referring to housework*)

hacer [E18] *vt*

I **1** **(a)** (crear) ⟨*mueble/vestido*⟩ to make; ⟨*casa/carretera*⟩ to build; ⟨*nido*⟩ to build, make; ⟨*túnel*⟩ to make, dig; ⟨*dibujo/plano*⟩ to do, draw; ⟨*lista*⟩ to make, draw up; ⟨*resumen*⟩ to do, make; ⟨*película*⟩ to make; ⟨*nudo/lazo*⟩ to tie; ⟨*pan/pastel*⟩ to make, bake; ⟨*vino/café/tortilla*⟩ to make; ⟨*cerveza*⟩ to make, brew; **me hizo un lugar en la mesa** he made room for me at the table; **hacen buena pareja** they make a lovely couple **(b)** (producir, causar) ⟨*ruido*⟩ to make; **los chistes no me hacen gracia** I don't find jokes funny; **estos zapatos me hacen daño** these shoes hurt my feet

2 **(a)** (efectuar, llevar a cabo) ⟨*sacrificio*⟩ to make; ⟨*milagro*⟩ to work, perform; ⟨*deberes/ejercicios/limpieza*⟩ to do; ⟨*mandado*⟩ to run; ⟨*transacción/investigación*⟩ to carry out; ⟨*experimento*⟩ to do, perform; ⟨*entrevista*⟩ to conduct; ⟨*gira/viaje*⟩ to do; ⟨*regalo*⟩ to give; ⟨*favor*⟩ to do; ⟨*trato*⟩ to make; **me hicieron una visita** they paid me a visit; **aún queda mucho por** ~ there is still a lot (left) to do; **dar que** ~ to make a lot of work **(b)** ⟨*cheque/factura*⟩ to make out, write out **3** (formular, expresar) ⟨*declaración/promesa/oferta*⟩ to make; ⟨*proyecto/plan*⟩ to make, draw up; ⟨*crítica/comentario*⟩ to make, voice; ⟨*pregunta*⟩ to ask; **nadie hizo ninguna objeción** nobody raised any objections

4 **(a)** (refiriéndose a necesidades fisiológicas): ~ **caca** (fam) to do a poop (AmE) *o* (BrE) a pooh (colloq); ~ **pis** *or* **pipí** (fam) to have a pee (colloq); ~ **sus necesidades** (euf) to go to the bathroom *o* toilet (euph) **(b)** (refiriéndose a sonidos onomatopéyicos) to go; **las vacas hacen 'mu'** cows go 'moo'

5 (adquirir) ⟨*dinero/fortuna*⟩ to make; ⟨*amigo*⟩ to make

6 (preparar, arreglar) ⟨*cama*⟩ to make; ⟨*maleta*⟩ to pack; **hice el pescado al horno** I did *o* cooked the fish in the oven; **tengo que** ~ **la comida** I must make lunch; *ver tb* COMIDA B

7 (recorrer) ⟨*trayecto/distancia*⟩ to do, cover

8 (en cálculos, enumeraciones): **son 180 … y 320 hacen 500** that's 180 … and 320 is *o* makes 500

II **1** **(a)** (ocuparse en actividad) to do; ~ **la(s) compra(s)** to do the shopping; **¿hacemos algo esta noche?** what shall we do something tonight?; ~ **ejercicio** to do (some) exercise; **¿hace algún deporte?** do you play *o* do any sports?; ▶ AMOR 1B **(b)** (como profesión, ocupación) to do; **¿qué hace tu padre?** what does your father do? **(c)** (estudiar) to do

2 (realizar cierta acción, actuar de cierta manera) to do; **¡eso no se hace!** you shouldn't do that!; **¡qué le vamos a** ~**!** what can you *o* (frml) one do?; **toca bien el piano — antes lo hacía mejor** she plays the piano well — she used to play better; ~**la buena** (fam): **¡ahora sí que la hice!** now I've really done it!; ▶ TONTO *m,f*

III **1** (transformar en, volver) to make; **ella lo hizo posible** she made it possible; **hizo pedazos la carta** she tore the letter into tiny pieces; **ese vestido te hace más delgada** that dress makes you look thinner; ~ **algo** DE **algo** to turn sth INTO sth; **quiero** ~ **de ti un gran actor** I want to make a great actor of you

2 **(a)** (obligar a, ser causa de que) ~ **a algn hacer algo** to make sb do sth; **me hizo abrirla** he made me open it; **me hizo llorar** it made me cry; **hágalo pasar** tell him to come in; **me hizo esperar tres horas** she kept me waiting for three hours; ~ **que algo/algn haga algo** to make sth/sb do sth **(b)** (mandar hacer) ~ **hacer algo** to have *o* get sth done/made; **hice acortar las cortinas** I had *o* got the curtains shortened

■ ~ *vi*

I **1** (obrar, actuar): **déjame** ~ **a mí** just let me handle this *o* take care of this; **¿cómo se hace para que te den la beca?** what do you have to do to get the scholarship?; **hiciste bien en decírmelo** you did *o* were right to tell me; **haces mal en mentir** it's wrong of you to lie

2 (fingir, simular): **hice como que no oía** I pretended not to hear; **haz como si no lo conocieras** act as if *o* pretend you don't know him

3 (servir): **esta sábana hará de toldo** this sheet will do for *o* as an awning; **la escuela hizo de hospital** the school served as *o* was used as a hospital

4 (interpretar personaje) ~ DE **algo/algn** to play the part of) sth/sb

II (+ *compl*) (sentar): **tanto sol hace mal** (AmL) too much sun is not good for you; (+ *me/te/le etc*) **el descanso le hizo bien** the rest did him good; **la trucha me hizo mal** (AmL) the trout didn't agree with me

■ ~ *v impers* **1** (refiriéndose al tiempo atmosférico):

hace frío/sol it's cold/sunny; **hace tres grados** it's three degrees; **(nos) hizo un tiempo espantoso** the weather was terrible

2 (expresando tiempo transcurrido): **hace dos años que murió** he's been dead for two years; **hace mucho que lo conozco** I've known him for a long time; **hacía años que no lo veía** I hadn't seen him for *o* in years; **¿cuánto hace que se fue?** how long ago did she leave?; **hace poco/un año** a short time/a year ago; **hasta hace poco** until recently

■ **hacerse** *v pron*

I **1** (producirse) (+ *me/te/le etc*): **se me hizo un nudo en el hilo** I got a knot in the thread; **se le hizo una ampolla** she got a blister; *hacérsele algo a algn* (Méx): **por fin se le hizo ganar el premio** she finally got to win the award

2 (a) (*refl*) (hacer para sí) «*café/falda*» to make oneself; **se hicieron una casita** they built themselves a little house (b) (*caus*) (hacer que otro haga): **se hicieron una casita** they had a little house built; **se hizo la cirugía estética** she had plastic surgery

3 (causarse): **¿qué te hiciste en el brazo?** what did you do to your arm?; **¿te hiciste daño?** did you hurt yourself?

4 (refiriéndose a necesidades fisiológicas): **todavía se hace pis/caca** (fam) she still wets/messes herself

5 (*refl*) (adquirir) to make; **~se un nombre** to make a name for oneself

II **1** (a) (volverse, convertirse en) to become; **se hicieron amigos** they became friends; **se están haciendo viejos** they're getting *o* growing old (b) (resultar): **se hace muy pesado** it gets very boring; (+ *me/te/le etc*) **se me hizo interminable** it seemed interminable; **se me hace difícil creerlo** I find it very hard to believe (c) (*impers*): **se hace de noche muy pronto** it gets dark very early; **se está haciendo tarde** it's getting late (d) (cocinarse) «*pescado/guiso*» to cook (e) (AmL) (pasarle a): **¿qué se habrá hecho María?** what can have happened to María?

2 (acostumbrarse) **~se A algo** to get used TO sth

3 (fingirse): **no te hagas el inocente** don't act the innocent; **¿es bobo o se (lo) hace?** (fam) is he stupid or just a good actor? (colloq); **~se pasar por algn** (por periodista, doctor) to pass oneself off as sb

4 (moverse) (+ *compl*) to move; **~se a un lado** to move to one side

5 **hacerse de** (AmL) (de fortuna, dinero) to get; (de amigos) to make

hacha *f‡* (herramienta) ax (AmE), axe (BrE)

hache *f: the name of the letter* h

hachís *m* hashish, hash (colloq)

hacia *prep* (a) (dirección) toward (esp AmE) , towards (esp BrE); **~ el sur** southward(s), toward(s) the south; **~ adelante** forward(s); **~ adentro/arriba** inward(s)/upward(s); **el centro queda ~ allá** the center is (over) that way; **¿~ dónde tenemos que ir?** which way do we have to go? (b) (aproximación) toward(s); **llegaremos ~ las dos** we'll arrive toward(s) *o* at around two (c) (con respecto a) toward(s); **su actitud ~ mí** his attitude toward(s) *o* to me

hacienda *f* **1** (a) (esp AmL) (finca) estate; (dedicada a ganadería) ranch (b) (bienes) possessions (*pl*), property **2 Hacienda (a)** (ministerio) ≈ the Treasury Department (*in US*), ≈ the Treasury (*in*

UK) **(b)** (oficina) tax office; **el dinero que debo a H~** the money I owe the IRS (AmE) *o* (BrE) the Inland Revenue

hada *f‡* fairy; **el ~ madrina** the fairy godmother

haga, etc ▶ HACER

hago ▶ HACER

Haití *m* Haiti

haitiano -na *adj/m,f* Haitian

hala *interj* (Esp) (a) (para animar) come on! (b) (expresando sorpresa) wow!

halagador -dora *adj* flattering

halagar [A3] *vt* to flatter; **me halaga que me lo ofrezcas a mí** I am flattered that you're offering it to me; **le ~on el vestido** they complimented her on her dress

halago *m* praise; **~s** praise, flattery

halagüeño -ña *adj* «*palabras/frases*» flattering, complimentary; «*situación*» promising, encouraging; «*noticia*» encouraging; «*futuro*» promising

halcón *m* (Zool) falcon

hall /'xol/ *m* (*pl* **halls**) (de casa) hall, hallway; (de teatro, cine) foyer

hallaca *f* (Ven) cornmeal, meat and vegetables wrapped in banana leaves

hallar [A1] *vt* **1** (frml) (encontrar) to find; **halló la puerta abierta** she found the door open **2** (esp AmL) **(a)** (en frases negativas) (saber): **no halla cómo sentarse** she can't find a comfortable position to sit in; **no hallo cómo decírselo** I don't know how to tell her **(b)** (opinar, creer) to find

■ **hallarse** *v pron* **(a)** (frml) (estar, encontrarse) (+ *compl*) to be **(b)** (sentirse) (+ *compl*) to feel

hallazgo *m* find

hallulla *f* **1** (Chi) (pan) *slightly leavened white bread* **2** (Chi) (sombrero) straw boater

halo *m* (a) (aureola) halo **(b)** (de inocencia, santidad) aura

halógeno -na *adj* halogen (*before n*)

halterofilia *f* weightlifting

hamaca *f* **(a)** (para colgar) hammock **(b)** (RPl) (mecedora) rocking chair; (columpio) swing **(c)** (Esp) (asiento plegable) deckchair

hamacar [A2] *vt* (columpiar) (RPl) to swing; (mecer) (CS) to rock

■ **hamacarse** *v pron* (columpiarse) to swing; (mecerse) to rock (oneself)

hambre *f‡* **(a)** (sensación) hunger; **tengo ~** I'm hungry; **pasar ~** to go hungry; **morirse de ~** to starve to death; **me muero de ~** (fam) I'm starving (colloq) **(b)** (como problema) **el ~** hunger

hambreado -da *adj* (Andes, Méx, RPl) hungry, starving

hambriento -ta *adj* [ESTAR] hungry, starving (colloq); **~ DE algo** hungry FOR sth

■ *m,f*: **los ~s** hungry people

hamburguesa *f* (bistec) hamburger, beefburger (BrE); (sandwich) hamburger, burger

hampa *f‡*: **el ~** criminals (*pl*), the underworld

hámster /'xamster/ *m* (*pl* **-ters**) hamster

handicap /'xandikap/ *m* (*pl* **-caps**) handicap

hangar *m* hangar

haragán -gana *adj* lazy, idle

■ *m,f* shirker, layabout

harapiento -ta *adj* ragged

harapo *m* rag

haré, etc ▶ HACER

harén *m* harem

haría, etc ▶ HACER

harina *f* flour; ~ **de avena/maíz** oatmeal/ cornmeal

harinoso -sa *adj* floury

hartar [A1] *vt* ⟦1⟧ (cansar, fastidiar): **me hartó con sus quejas** I got tired of his complaints ⟦2⟧ (fam) (llenar): **nos hartaban a** *or* **de sopa** they fed us on nothing but soup; **lo ~on a palos** they gave him a real beating
■ **hartarse** *v pron* ⟦1⟧ (cansarse, aburrirse) to get fed up; ~**se DE algo/algn** to get tired *o* sick of sth/ sb, get fed up WITH sth/sb; ~**se DE hacer algo** to get tired *o* sick of doing sth, get fed up WITH doing sth ⟦2⟧ (llenarse): ~**se (DE algo)** to gorge oneself (ON sth), to stuff oneself (WITH sth) (colloq)

harto¹ -ta *adj* ⟦1⟧ (a) (cansado, aburrido) fed up; ~ **DE algo/algn** fed up WITH sth/sb, tired OF sth/ sb; ~ **DE hacer algo** tired OF doing sth, fed up WITH doing sth; **estaba harta de que le dijeran eso** she was tired of *o* fed up with them telling her that (b) (de comida) full ⟦2⟧ (*delante del n*) (mucho) (AmL exc RPl): **le llamé hartas veces** I phoned you lots of times; **tiene hartas ganas de verte** he really wants to see you
■ *pron* (AmL exc RPl): **tenía ~ que hacer** I had an awful lot to do; **¿tienes amigos allí? — ¡sí, ~s!** do you have friends there? — yes, lots

harto² *adv* (a) (AmL exc RPl) (modificando un adjetivo) very; **es ~ mejor que el hermano** he's much *o* a lot better than his brother (b) (modificando un verbo): **me gustó ~** I really liked it; **bailamos ~** we danced a lot

hasta *prep* ⟦1⟧ (en el tiempo) (a) until; **no descansó ~ terminar** she didn't rest until she'd finished; ~ **el momento** so far, up to now (b) **hasta que** until, till; **espera ~ que pare de llover** wait until *o* till it stops raining (c) **hasta tanto** until such time as (d) (AmC, Col, Méx) (con valor negativo): **cierran ~ las nueve** they don't close until *o* till nine (e) (en saludos): ~ **mañana** see you tomorrow; ~ **luego/pronto** see you (colloq), see you soon ⟦2⟧ (en el espacio) to; **el agua me llegaba ~ los hombros** the water came up to my shoulders; **el pelo le llega ~ la cintura** her hair goes down to her waist; **¿~ dónde llega?** how far does it go? ⟦3⟧ (en cantidades) up to; ~ **cierto punto** up to a point
■ *adv* even

hastiante *adj* boring, sickening

hastiarse [A17] *v pron* ~**se DE algo** to grow tired *o* weary OF sth; **hastiado de la vida** tired *o* weary of life

Hawai *m* Hawaii

hawaiano -na *adj/m,f* Hawaiian

hay ▶ HABER

haya *f* (árbol, madera) beech

haya, hayas, etc ▶ HABER

hayaca *f* (Ven) ▶ HALLACA

haz *m* (de leña, paja) bundle; (de trigo) sheaf; (de luz) beam

haz ▶ HACER

hazaña *f* (acción — heróica) great *o* heroic deed, exploit; (— de mucho esfuerzo) feat, achievement

hazmerreír *m* (fam) laughing stock

he ▶ HABER

hebilla *f* (de zapato) buckle; (de cinturón) clasp, buckle

hebra *f* (a) (Tex) thread, strand (b) (fibra vegetal, animal) fiber*; (c) (del gusano de seda) thread (d) (de la madera) grain

hebreo¹ -brea *adj/m,f* Hebrew

hebreo² *m* (idioma) Hebrew

heces *fpl*: ▶ HEZ

hechicero -ra *adj* ⟨persona⟩ enchanting, captivating; ⟨ojos/sonrisa⟩ captivating
■ *m,f* (a) (brujo) (*m*) sorcerer, wizard; (*f*) sorceress, witch (b) (de tribu) witch doctor

hechizar [A4] *vt* (a) «brujo» to cast a spell on, bewitch (b) (cautivar) to captivate

hechizo¹ -za *adj* (Chi, Méx) home-made

hechizo² *m* (a) (maleficio) spell (b) (atractivo, encanto) charm

hecho¹ -cha *pp* [*ver tb* HACER]
⟦1⟧ (manufacturado) made; ~ **a mano** handmade; **un traje ~ a (la) medida** a made-to-measure suit; **bien/mal ~** well/badly made ⟦2⟧ (refiriéndose a acción): **¡bien ~!** well done!; **no le avisé — pues mal ~** I didn't let him know — well you should have (done); **lo ~, ~ está** what's done is done ⟦3⟧ (convertido en): **estaba ~ una fiera** he was furious; **tú estás ~ un vago** you've become *o* turned into a lazy devil
■ *adj* (a) ⟨ropa⟩ ready-to-wear (b) (terminado) ⟨trabajo⟩ done (c) (esp Esp) ⟨carne⟩ done; **un filete muy/poco ~** a well-done/rare steak

hecho² *m* ⟦1⟧ (a) (acto, acción): **yo quiero ~s** I want action, I want something done; **demuéstramelo con ~s** prove it to me by doing something about it (b) (suceso, acontecimiento) event; **el lugar de los ~s** the scene of the crime ⟦2⟧ (realidad, verdad) fact; **de hecho** in fact

hechura *f* (a) (de traje, vestido): **no cobran por la ~** they don't charge for making it up (b) (modelo, estilo) style; **la falda tiene una ~ muy simple** the skirt is cut very simply (c) (forma) shape, form

hectárea *f* hectare

hedionder *f* stench, stink

hediondo -da *adj* (fétido) foul-smelling, stinking

hegemonía *f* hegemony, dominance

helada *f* frost

heladera *f* (para hacer helados) ice-cream maker; (nevera) (RPl) refrigerator, fridge; (para picnic) (Arg, Col) cool *o* cold box

heladería *f* ice-cream parlor*

heladero -ra *m,f* (esp AmL) ice-cream vendor *o* seller

helado¹ -da *adj* ⟦1⟧ (a) ⟨persona/manos⟩ freezing (colloq), frozen (colloq); ⟨casa/habitación⟩ freezing (colloq); **quedarse ~** (de asombro) to be stunned (b) ⟨comida⟩ stone-cold; ⟨líquido/bebida⟩ (muy frío) freezing; (que se ha enfriado) stone-cold; **servir el vino bien ~** (AmL) serve the wine well chilled ⟦2⟧ ⟨agua/estanque⟩ frozen

helado² *m* ice cream; ~ **de agua** (Andes) water ice, sherbet (AmE); (con palo) Popsicle® (AmE), ice lolly (BrE)

helar [A5] *vt/vi* to freeze
■ ~ *v impers*: **anoche heló** it went below freezing last night (AmE), there was a frost last night (BrE)
■ **helarse** *v pron* 1 «*río/charco*» to freeze (over); «*agua/plantas/cosecha*» to freeze 2 (fam) **(a)** «*persona*» to freeze **(b)** «*comida/café*» to get *o* go cold

helecho *m* (como nombre genérico) fern; (más específico) bracken

hélice *f* (de barco) propeller, screw; (de avión) propeller

helicóptero *m* helicopter

hematoma *m* (tumor) hematoma*; (moretón) bruise

hembra *adj inv* female
■ *f* **(a)** (Zool) female; **la ~ del faisán** the hen pheasant **(b)** (mujer) female, woman **(c)** (de enchufe, corchete) female (part)

hemisferio *m* **(a)** (Geog, Mat) hemisphere; **el ~ norte** the northern hemisphere **(b)** (Anat) cerebral hemisphere

hemofilia *f* hemophilia*

hemofílico -ca *adj/m,f* hemophiliac*

hemorragia *f* hemorrhage*

hemorroides *fpl* piles, hemorrhoids (tech)

hendidura *f* (en madera) crack; (en roca) fissure, crack

heno *m* hay

hepatitis *f* hepatitis

heráldica *f* heraldry

heraldo *m* herald

herbáceo -cea *adj* herbaceous

herbicida *m* herbicide, weedkiller

herbívoro -ra *adj* herbivorous
■ *m,f* herbivore

herboristería *f* herbalist's

heredar [A1] *vt* «*bienes/título/tradiciones*» to inherit; «*trono*» to succeed to; **heredó los ojos de su madre** he has his mother's eyes

heredero -ra *m,f* (*m*) heir; (*f*) heir, heiress; **príncipe ~** crown prince; **~ DE algo** heir TO sth

hereditario -ria *adj* hereditary

herejía *f* heresy

herencia *f* **(a)** (Der) inheritance; **le dejó en ~ la finca** he bequeathed *o* left her the farm **(b)** (patrimonio cultural, nacional) heritage **(c)** (Biol) heredity

herida *f* **(a)** (en el cuerpo): **sufrir ~s de carácter grave** to suffer serious injuries; **se hizo una ~ en la rodilla** he cut his knee; **curar una ~** to clean/dress a wound **(b)** (pena, sufrimiento) wound

herido -da *adj* **(a)** (físicamente) injured; **está gravemente ~** (por accidente) he is seriously injured; (por agresión) he has been seriously wounded; **~ de muerte** fatally wounded **(b)** (en sentimiento) «*persona*» hurt
■ *m,f*: **los ~s** the injured/wounded

herir [I11] *vt* **(a)** (físicamente) to wound **(b)** «*orgullo*» to hurt **(c)** «*vista*» to hurt

hermanar [A1] *vt* **(a)** (en sentimiento, propósito) to unite **(b)** «*ciudades*» to twin **(c)** «*calcetines*» to match up, put ... in pairs; «*fichas/naipes*» to match up

hermanastro -tra *m,f* **(a)** (con vínculo sanguíneo) (*m*) half brother; (*f*) half sister **(b)** (sin vínculo sanguíneo) (*m*) stepbrother; (*f*) stepsister

hermandad *f* **(a)** (de hombres) brotherhood, fraternity; (de mujeres) sisterhood **(b)** (asociación) association

hermano -na
■ *m,f* 1 (pariente) (*m*) brother; (*f*) sister; **mis ~s** (solo varones) my brothers; (varones y mujeres) my brothers and sisters; **~ gemelo/hermana gemela** twin brother/twin sister; **~ político/hermana política** brother-in-law/sister-in-law 2 (como apelativo) (Col, Per, Ven fam) buddy (AmE colloq), mate (BrE colloq) 3 **(a)** (religioso) (*m*) brother; (*f*) sister **(b)** (prójimo) (*m*) brother; (*f*) sister 4 (de guante, calcetín) pair
■ *adj* «*buque*» sister (*before n*); «*ciudades*» twin (*before n*)

hermético -ca *adj* **(a)** «*envase/cierre*» airtight, hermetic (tech) **(b)** «*persona/rostro*» inscrutable, secretive

hermoso -sa *adj* **(a)** (bello) beautiful, lovely **(b)** (magnífico) splendid **(c)** (lozano, corpulento) big and healthy, bonny (BrE) **(d)** (noble) noble

hermosura *f* **(a)** (cualidad) beauty, loveliness **(b)** (persona, cosa hermosa): **¡qué ~ de niño/paisaje!** what a beautiful child/landscape!

hernia *f* hernia, rupture; **~ discal** slipped disk*

herniarse [A1] *v pron* to get a hernia, rupture oneself

héroe *m* hero

heroico -ca *adj* heroic

heroína *f* 1 (persona) heroine 2 (droga) heroin

heroinómano -na *m,f* heroin addict

heroísmo *m* heroism

herpes *m* (*pl* ~) (en boca, genitales) herpes; (en cintura) shingles

herradura *f* horseshoe

herramienta *f* tool

herrería *f* blacksmith's, smithy

herrero -ra *m,f* blacksmith

herrumbre *f* rust

hervidero *m* (de moscas) swarm; (de chismes, delincuencia) hotbed; **un ~ de gente** a seething mass of people; **la casa era un ~** the house was buzzing

hervidor *m* (de agua) kettle; (de leche) milk pan

hervir [I11] *vi/vt* to boil; **el café está hirviendo** the coffee is boiling

heterosexual *adj/mf* heterosexual

hez *f* **(a)** (escoria) dregs (*pl*) **(b)** (Vin) *tb* **heces** sediment, lees (*pl*) **(c)** **heces** *fpl* (excrementos) feces* (*pl*)

hibernar [A1] *vi* to hibernate

híbrido¹ -da *adj* hybrid (*before n*)

híbrido² *m* hybrid

hice, hiciera, etc ▶ HACER

hidalgo *m* gentleman, nobleman (*from the lower ranks of the nobility*)

hidratante *adj* moisturizing (*before n*)

hidratar [A1] *vt* «*verduras*» to hydrate; «*piel*» to moisturize

hidrato *m* hydrate; ~**s de carbono** carbohydrates

hidráulico -ca *adj* hydraulic

hidroavión *m* seaplane

hidroeléctrico -ca *adj* hydroelectric

hidrofobia *f* hydrophobia (tech), rabies

hidrógeno *m* hydrogen

hiedra *f* ivy

hiel *f* bile

hiela, hielas, etc ▶ HELAR

hielo *m* ice; *romper el* ~ to break the ice

hiena *f* hyena

hierba *f* 1 (césped) grass; ~ *mala nunca muere* the Devil looks after his own 2 (a) (Bot, Coc, Med) herb; **malas** ~**s** weeds (b) (arg) (marihuana) grass (colloq)

hierbabuena *f* mint

hierbajo *m* (esp Esp) weed

hierro *m* (a) (Metal) iron; ~ **forjado** wrought iron; ~ **fundido** cast iron; *de* ~ iron (*before n*) (b) (de lanza, flecha) head, tip (c) (en golf) iron; **un** ~ **cuatro** a four iron

hígado *m* liver

higiene *f* hygiene

higiénico -ca *adj* hygienic

higo *m* (de la higuera) fig; ~ **chumbo** (Esp) prickly pear

higuera *f* fig tree

hijastro -tra *m,f* (*m*) stepson; (*f*) stepdaughter; **mis** ~**s** (varones y mujeres) my stepchildren

hijo -ja *m,f* 1 (pariente) (*m*) son; (*f*) daughter; **mis** ~**s** (solo varones) my sons; (varones y mujeres) my children; **espera un** ~ she's expecting a baby; **no tienen** ~**s** they don't have any children; ~ **adoptivo/hija adoptiva** adopted son/daughter; ~/ **hija de papá** rich kid (colloq); ~/**hija natural** illegitimate son/daughter; ~ **político/hija política** son-in-law/daughter-in-law; ~ **único/hija única** only child; **M. Pérez,** ~ M. Pérez Junior; ~ *de tigre sale pintado* (AmL fam) he's just like his father/mother 2 (apelativo): ¡~**, por Dios!** (hablándole a un niño) for heaven's sake, child!; (hablándole a un adulto) for heaven's sake, Pedro (o Luis *etc*)!

híjole *interj* (Méx) jeez! (AmE colloq), gosh (colloq)

hilacha *f* loose thread

hilar [A1] *vi* to spin; ~ **fino** to split hairs
■ ~ *vt* (a) ⟨algodón/lana⟩ to spin; «araña» to spin (b) ⟨ideas/hechos⟩ to string together

hilera *f* (a) (fila) row, line (b) (Mil) file (frml or liter) (c) (de ladrillos) course (d) (de semillas) row, drill

hilo *m* 1 (a) (en costura) thread; ~ **dental** dental floss (b) (lino) linen (c) (de araña) thread (d) (fam) (de las judías) string 2 (Elec) wire; ~ **musical** (Esp) piped music 3 (de relato, conversación) thread 4 (de sangre, agua) trickle

hilvanar [A1] *vt* 1 (coser) to baste (AmE), to tack (BrE) 2 ⟨frases/ideas⟩ to put together

himen *m* hymen

himno *m* (a) (religioso) hymn; (de colegio) school song *o* anthem; ~ **nacional** national anthem (b) (Lit) ode

hincada *f* (Col, Per) sharp pain

hincapié *m*: **hacer** ~ **en algo** to stress *o* emphasize sth

hincar [A2] *vt* (clavar) ~ **algo EN algo** ⟨estaca⟩ to drive *o* thrust sth INTO sth; **me hincó los dientes en la mano** it buried its teeth in *o* sunk its teeth into my hand
■ **hincarse** *v pron tb* ~**se de rodillas** to kneel

hincha *mf* (fam) (Dep) fan (colloq), supporter

hinchado -da *adj* ⟨vientre/pierna⟩ swollen; ⟨estilo/lenguaje⟩ overblown

hinchar [A1] *vt* (Esp) ⟨globo⟩ to inflate (frml), to blow up; ⟨rueda⟩ to inflate, pump up; ⟨suceso/ noticia⟩ (fam) to blow ... up (colloq)
■ ~ *vi* (CS fam) (fastidiar) «persona» to be a pain in the ass (AmE vulg) *o* (BrE vulg) arse; (+ *me/te/le etc*) **me hincha su actitud** his attitude really pisses me off (sl)
■ **hincharse** *v pron* (a) «vientre/pierna» (+ *me/ te/le etc*) to swell up (b) (fam) (enorgullecerse) to swell with pride (c) (Esp fam) (hartarse) ~**se DE algo** ⟨de pasteles/ostras⟩ to stuff oneself WITH sth

hinchazón *f* swelling

hindú *adj/mf* (a) (Relig) Hindu (b) (crit) (de la India) Indian

hinduismo *m* Hinduism

hinojo *m* (Bot, Coc) fennel

hiperactivo -va *adj* hyperactive

hipermercado *m* large supermarket, hypermarket (BrE)

hipertensión *f* high blood pressure, hypertension

hípica *f* equestrian sports (*pl*); (carreras) horse racing

hípico -ca *adj* ⟨deportes/centro⟩ equestrian (*before n*)

hipnosis *f* hypnosis

hipnotismo *m* hypnotism

hipnotizador -dora *adj* ⟨mirada⟩ hypnotic
■ *m,f* hypnotist

hipnotizar [A4] *vt* (Psic) to hypnotize; (fascinar) to mesmerize

hipo *m* hiccups (*pl*), hiccoughs (*pl*)

hipocondríaco -ca *m,f* hypochondriac

hipocresía *f* hypocrisy

hipócrita *adj* hypocritical
■ *mf* hypocrite

hipodérmico -ca *adj* hypodermic

hipódromo *m* (Equ, Ocio) racecourse, racetrack (AmE); (Hist) hippodrome

hipopótamo *m* hippopotamus

hipoteca *f* mortgage

hipotecar [A2] *vt* to mortgage

hipotecario -ria *adj* mortgage (*before n*)

hipótesis *f* hypothesis

hipotético -ca *adj* hypothetical

hippy, hippie /'xipi/ *adj* (*pl* **hippies**) hippy (*before n*), hippie (*before n*)
■ *mf* hippy, hippie

hiriente *adj* hurtful, wounding (*before n*)

hirviendo ▶ HERVIR

hisopo *m* (a) (bastoncillo) cotton swab (AmE), cotton bud (BrE) (Chi) (de afeitar) shaving brush

hispánico -ca *adj* (a) (de los países de habla hispana) Hispanic (b) (relativo a España) Spanish

hispanismo *m* (giro propio del español de España) word/expression peculiar to Spain; (palabra derivada del español) hispanicism; (estudio) Hispanic studies

hispano -na *adj* (a) (español) Spanish, Hispanic (frml); **países de habla hispana** Spanish-speaking countries (b) (hispanoamericano) Spanish American, Latin American; (en EE UU) Hispanic
■ *m,f* (a) (liter) (español) Spaniard (b) (hispanoamericano) Spanish American, Latin American; (en EE UU) Hispanic

Hispanoamérica *f* Spanish America

hispanoamericano -na *adj/m,f* Spanish American

hispanohablante, hispanoparlante *mf* Spanish speaker

histeria *f* hysteria; ~ **colectiva** mass hysteria

histérico -ca *adj* (Med, Psic) hysterical; (exaltado): **ponerse** ~ to have hysterics *o* a fit; **me pones** ~ you drive me mad
■ *m,f* (Med, Psic) hysteric; (exaltado): **es un** ~ he gets quite hysterical about things

historia *f* **1** (Hist) history; ~ **antigua** ancient history; ~ **clínica** medical history; **pasar a la** ~ (por ser importante) to go down in history; (perder actualidad) (fam): **aquello ya pasó a la** ~ that's ancient history now (colloq) **2** (relato) story; **la** ~ **de su vida** the story of his life **3** (fam) (cuento, asunto): **me vino con la** ~ **de que** ... he came up with this story *o* tale about ...; **déjate de** ~s stop making excuses; **se quejó de no sé qué** ~s he complained about something or other (colloq)

historiador -dora *m,f* historian

historial *m* record; ~ **clínico** *or* **médico** medical history; ~ **personal** resumé (AmE), curriculum vitae (BrE)

histórico -ca *adj* (real) historical; (importante) historic

historieta *f* comic strip, cartoon story

hit /'xit/ *m* (*pl* **hits**) hit

hito *m* (hecho trascendental) landmark, milestone

hizo ▶ HACER

Hnos. (= **hermanos**) Bros.

hobby /'xoβi/ *m* (*pl* **-bbies**) hobby

hocico *m* (de cerdo) snout; (de perro, lobo) snout, muzzle

hocicón -cona *m,f* (CS, Méx fam & pey) bigmouth (colloq & pej), blabbermouth (colloq & pej)

hockey /'x(o)oki/ *m* hockey; ~ **sobre hielo** ice hockey

hogar *m* home; **formar un** ~ to set up home; **artículos para el** ~ household goods; **las labores del** ~ housework; **quedarse sin** ~ to be left homeless; ~ **de ancianos** residential home for the elderly, old people's home (colloq)

hogareño -ña *adj* ⟨persona⟩ home-loving; ⟨vida/escena⟩ domestic (*before n*)

hoguera *f* bonfire; **murió en la** ~ he was burned at the stake

hoja *f* **1** (Bot) leaf **2** (a) (folio) sheet; ~ **de vida** (Col, Ven) resumé (AmE), curriculum vitae (BrE) (b) (de libro) page, leaf; **pasar las** ~s to turn the pages (c) (formulario) form, sheet; ~ **electrónica** spreadsheet program **3** (a) (de puerta, mesa) leaf (b) (de madera, metal) sheet (c) (de cuchillo) blade; ~ **de afeitar** razor blade

hojalata *f* tinplate

hojalatería *f* (Méx) body work (AmE), panel-beating (BrE)

hojalatero -ra *m,f* (Auto) (Méx) body shop worker (AmE), panel beater (BrE)

hojaldre *m* puff pastry, puff paste (AmE)

hojear [A1] *vt* to leaf *o* glance through

hojilla *f* (Ven) razor blade

hojuela *f* (AmL exc CS) flake

hola *interj* (saludo) hello, hi! (colloq)

holá *interj* (RPI) (por teléfono) hello?

holán *m* (Méx) flounce, frill

Holanda *f* Holland

holandés¹ -desa *adj* Dutch
■ *m,f* (*m*) Dutchman; (*f*) Dutchwoman; **los holandeses** the Dutch, Dutch people

holandés² *m* (idioma) Dutch

holgado -da *adj* (a) ⟨prenda⟩ loose-fitting, baggy (b) ⟨posición⟩ comfortable; **viven** ~s they're comfortably off (c) ⟨victoria/mayoría⟩ comfortable (d) (de espacio): **así iremos más** ~s we'll be more comfortable like that

holgar [A8] *vi* (en *3ª pers*) (frml) (estar de más): **huelga decir que** ... it goes without saying that ...; **huelgan los comentarios** what can one say?

holgazán -zana *adj* lazy
■ *m,f* idler, lazybones (colloq)

holgazanear [A1] *vi* to idle, laze *o* loaf around

holgura *f* (a) (bienestar económico, comodidad): **vivir con** ~ to live comfortably (b) (de prenda) fullness, looseness

hollejo *m* skin

hollín *m* soot

hombre *m* (a) (varón) man; ~s, **mujeres y niños** men, women and children; **no es lo bastante** ~ **para** ... he's not man enough to ...; **¡**~ **al agua!** man overboard!; **este** ~ **no sabe lo que dice** this guy doesn't know what he's talking about; ~ **de confianza** right-hand man; ~ **del tiempo** weatherman; ~ **de negocios** businessman; ~ **lobo** werewolf; ~ **medio** man in the street; ~ **rana** frogman, diver; ~ **precavido vale por dos** forewarned is forearmed (b) (especie humana): **el** ~ **man**
■ *interj*: **¡**~**!** **¡qué sorpresa!** well! what a nice surprise!; **¿te gustaría venir?** — **¡**~**!** I would you like to come? — you bet! what do you think?; ~, **no es lo mismo** come off it, it's not the same thing at all (colloq)

hombrera *f* (almohadilla) shoulder pad; (Mil) (de uniformes) epaulet

hombría *f* manliness

hombrillo *m* (Ven) shoulder (AmE), hard shoulder (BrE)

hombro *m* shoulder; **encogerse de** ~s to shrug (one's shoulders); **lo llevaron a** ~s they carried him on their shoulders *o* shoulder high; *arrimar el* ~ to pull one's weight, put one's shoulder to the wheel; *mirar a algn por encima del* ~ to look down on sb

hombruno -na *adj* (pey) ⟨*mujer*⟩ mannish, butch (colloq & pej); ⟨*gestos/modales*⟩ masculine, mannish

homenaje *m* (a) (tributo) tribute; **rendir(le)** ~ **a** algn to pay tribute *o* homage to sb; **en** ~ **a** in honor of (b) (acto): **le ofrecieron un** ~ they held a party (*o* reception, *etc*) in his honor

homeópata *mf* homeopath

homeopatía *f* homeopathy

homeopático -ca *adj* (Med) homeopathic

homicida *adj* (frml) ⟨*instinto*⟩ homicidal; ⟨*arma*⟩ murder (*before n*)
■ *mf* (frml) murderer, homicide (frml)

homicidio *m* (frml) homicide

homogéneo -nea *adj* ⟨*grupo*⟩ homogeneous; ⟨*masa/mezcla*⟩ smooth

homologación *f* 1 (a) (de un producto — recomendación) endorsement; (— autorización) authorization (b) (Dep) (de un récord) ratification 2 (equiparación) ~ **con** algo: **han pedido su** ~ **con los técnicos** they have asked for parity with the technicians; **la** ~ **de los títulos australianos con los europeos** the recognition of Australian qualifications as equivalent to European ones

homologar [A3] *vt* (a) ⟨*producto*⟩ (recomendar) to approve, endorse; (autorizar) to authorize, approve (b) (Dep) ⟨*récord*⟩ to ratify, recognize (c) ⟨*convenio*⟩ to recognize

homólogo -ga *adj* equivalent
■ *m,f* (period) counterpart

homosexual *adj/mf* homosexual

honda *f* (de cuero) sling; (con elástico) slingshot (AmE), catapult (BrE)

hondo¹ -da *adj* (a) ⟨*piscina/río*⟩ deep; **en lo más** ~ **de mi corazón** in my heart of hearts, deep down; **en lo** ~ **del valle** at the bottom of the valley (b) (*gen delante del n*) (frml) ⟨*pena/pesar*⟩ profound (frml), deep

hondo² *adv*: **respirar** ~ to breathe deeply

hondonada *f* hollow

Honduras *f* Honduras

hondureño -ña *adj/m,f* Honduran

honestidad *f* integrity, honesty

honesto -ta *adj* (íntegro) honest, honorable*

hongo *m* (a) (Bot, Med) fungus (b) (AmL) (Coc) mushroom (c) *tb* **sombrero de** ~ derby (AmE), bowler hat (BrE) (d) ~ **atómico** mushroom cloud

honor *m* (a) honor*; **tengo el** ~ **de ... it is my honor** *o* **I have the honor to ...; me hizo el** ~ **de recibirme** he did me the honor of receiving me; **en** ~ **a la verdad** to be truthful; **hacer** ~ **a su nombre** to live up to one's reputation (b) **honores** *mpl* (homenaje) honors* (*pl*); **le rindieron los** ~**es correspondientes a su rango** he was accorded the honors befitting his rank (frml)

honorable *adj* honorable*

honorario -ria *adj* honorary

honorarios *mpl* fees (*pl*)

honorífico -ca *adj* honorary

honra *f* (a) (en general) honor*; **¡y a mucha** ~**!** and proud of it! (b) ~**s fúnebres** *fpl* funeral rites (*pl*)

honradez *f* (honestidad) honesty; (decencia) decency

honrado -da *adj* (a) (honesto) honest, honorable* (b) ⟨*mujer*⟩ respectable

honrar [A1] *vt* 1 «*comportamiento/actitud*» to do ... credit *o* honor*; **nos honra hoy con su presencia** she is honoring us with her presence here today 2 (respetar) to honor*
■ **honrarse** *v pron* to be honored*

hora *f* 1 (período de tiempo) hour; **media** ~ half an hour, a half hour (AmE); **las** ~**s de mayor afluencia** the busiest time; **cobrar por** ~**s** to be paid by the hour; **45 euros por** ~ 45 euros an hour; ~ **libre** free period; ~ **pico** (AmL) *or* (Esp) **punta** rush hour; ~**s extra(s)** *o* **extraordinaria(s)** overtime 2 (a) (momento puntual) time; **¿tiene** ~**, por favor?** have you got the time, please?; **¿qué** ~ **es?** what's the time?, what time is it?; **pon el reloj en** ~ put the clock right; **todavía no es la** ~ it's not time yet; **nunca llegan a la** ~ they never arrive on time; **el avión llegó antes de (su)** ~ the plane arrived early (b) (momento sin especificar) time; **es** ~ **de irse a la cama** it's bedtime *o* time for bed; **a la** ~ **de almorzar** at lunchtime; **ya es** ~ **de irnos** it's time for us to go; **¡ya era** ~ **de que llamases!** it's about time you called; **a primera** ~ **de la mañana** first thing in the morning; **a última** ~ at the last moment; **a la** ~ **de**: **a la** ~ **de traducirlo** when it comes to translating it; **a la** ~ **de la verdad** when it comes down to it; **entre** ~**s** between meals; **hacer** ~ (Chi) to kill time 3 (cita) appointment; **pedir** ~ to make an appointment

horadar [A1] *vt* ⟨*roca*⟩ to bore through; ⟨*pared*⟩ to drill a hole in

horario *m* 1 (de trenes, aviones) schedule (AmE), timetable (BrE); (de clases) timetable; **tiene un** ~ **muy flexible** his hours are very flexible; **la empresa ofrece** ~ **flexible** the company offers flextime *or* (BrE) flexitime; ~ **continuo** *or* (AmL) **corrido** *or* (Esp) **intensivo** *continuous working day (usually from eight to three) with no break for lunch*; ~ **de visitas** visiting hours (*pl*); ~ **partido** *working day with a long break for lunch* 2 (de reloj) hour hand

horca *f* 1 (patíbulo) gallows (*pl*); (juego): **la** ~ hangman 2 (Agr) pitchfork, hayfork

horcajadas: **a** ~ (*loc adv*) astride

horchata *f* (de chufas) horchata (*cold drink made from tiger nuts*); (en Méx) *drink made from ground melon seeds*

horda *f* horde

horizontal *adj/f* horizontal

horizonte *m* (a) (línea) horizon (b) **horizontes** *mpl* (perspectivas) horizons (*pl*)

horma *f* (para hacer zapatos) last; (para conservar su forma) shoetree

hormiga *f* ant

hormigón *m* concrete

hormigueo *m* pins and needles (*pl*), tingling

hormiguero *m* (a) (Zool) (nido) ant's nest; (montículo) anthill (b) (de personas): **era un** ~ **de gente** it was swarming with people

hormona *f* hormone

hornada *f* (de pan, pasteles) batch

hornalla *f* (RPl) ▶ HORNILLO 1

hornilla *f* **(a)** (AmL exc CS) ▶ HORNILLO 1 **(b)** (Chi) ▶ HORNILLO 2

hornillo *m* 1 **(a)** (Esp) **(a)** (de gas) burner **(b)** (de una cocina eléctrica — espiral) ring; (— placa) hotplate 2 (cocinilla portátil) portable electric stove

horno *m* **(a)** (de cocina) oven; **resistente al** ∼ ovenproof; **pollo al** ∼ roast chicken; **pescado al** ∼ baked fish; **(b)** (Metal, Tec) furnace **(c)** (para cerámica) kiln

horóscopo *m* horoscope

horqueta *f* (Chi) (de jardinero) fork; (de campesino) pitchfork

horquilla *f* **(a)** (para pelo) hairpin **(b)** (Agr) pitchfork **(c)** (en bicicleta) fork

horrendo -da *adj* ▶ HORROROSO

horrible *adj* **(a)** ⟨accidente/muerte⟩ horrible, horrific **(b)** (feo) ⟨persona⟩ hideous, ugly; ⟨camisa/adorno⟩ horrible, hideous **(c)** ⟨tiempo⟩ terrible, awful **(d)** (inaguantable) unbearable

horripilante *adj* terrifying, horrifying

horror *m* 1 **(a)** (miedo, angustia) horror; **me causa** ∼ **verlo** it horrifies me to see it; **les tengo** ∼ **a los hospitales** I'm terrified of hospitals **(b)** (fam) (uso hiperbólico): **¡qué** ∼**!** how awful o terrible! 2 **horrores** *mpl* (cosas terribles) horrors (*pl*); **los** ∼**s de la guerra** the horrors of the war

horrorizar [A4] *vt* to horrify, appall
■ **horrorizarse** *v pron* to be horrified, be appalled; ∼**se DE algo** to be horrified BY o AT sth

horroroso -sa *adj* ⟨crimen⟩ horrific, horrifying; ⟨película/novela⟩ terrible, awful; ⟨persona/vestido⟩ awful, horrific (colloq); **tengo un hambre horrorosa** I'm absolutely starving (colloq)

hortaliza *f* vegetable

hortelano -na *m,f* truck farmer (AmE), market gardener (BrE)

hortensia *f* hydrangea

hortera *adj* (Esp fam) ⟨vestido/canción⟩ tacky (colloq); **es muy** ∼ he has very tacky taste

horticultor -ra *m,f* horticulturalist, gardener

horticultura *f* horticulture, gardening

hosco -ca *adj* ⟨persona/semblante⟩ surly, sullen

hospedaje *m* accommodations (AmE), accommodation (BrE)

hospedar [A1] *vt* to provide ... with accommodations (AmE) o (BrE) accommodation
■ **hospedarse** *v pron* to stay, put up (AmE colloq)

hospedería *f* (posada) inn; (Rel) hospice

hospicio *m* (para niños huérfanos) orphanage

hospital *m* hospital; ∼ **clínico** teaching hospital

hospitalario -ria *adj* **(a)** ⟨pueblo/persona⟩ hospitable, welcoming **(b)** (Med) hospital (*before n*)

hospitalidad *f* hospitality

hospitalizar [A4] *vt* to hospitalize
■ **hospitalizarse** *v pron* (AmL) to go into the hospital (AmE) o (BrE) into hospital

hostal *m* cheap hotel; ∼ **residencia** guesthouse, boarding house

hostelería *f* (Esp) ▶ HOTELERÍA

hostia *f* 1 (Relig) host 2 (Esp vulg o fam) (golpe) slap, smack in the face (o mouth *etc*); **se pegó una** ∼ **con el coche** he smashed his car up badly (colloq) 3 (uso expletivo) (Esp vulg o fam) **¡**∼**(s)!** jeez!

(AmE colloq), bloody hell! (BrE sl); **hace un frío de la** ∼ it's goddamn (AmE) o (BrE) bloody freezing! (sl); **¡qué** ∼**s ...!** what the hell ...! (sl)

hostigar [A3] *vt* 1 **(a)** (acosar) to bother, pester **(b)** (Mil) to harass **(c)** ⟨caballo⟩ to whip 2 (Andes fam) ⟨comida/bebida⟩ to pall on

hostigoso -sa *adj* (Andes) ⟨comida/bebida⟩ sickly, sickly-sweet; ⟨persona⟩ annoying, irritating

hostil *adj* [SER] ⟨medio/clima⟩ hostile; ⟨gente/actitud⟩ hostile, unfriendly

hostilidad *f* **(a)** (del clima) hostility; (de actitud) hostility, unfriendliness **(b)** **hostilidades** *fpl* hostilities (*pl*)

hotel *m* hotel; ∼ **residencia** guesthouse, boarding house

hotelería *f* (AmL) (negocio, industria) hotel and catering trade o business; (profesión) hotel management

hotelero -ra *adj* hotel (*before n*)
■ *m,f* hotel manager, hotelier

hoy *adv* 1 (este día) today; ∼ **hace un año** a year ago today; **¿a cuánto estamos** ∼**?** what's the date today? 2 **(a)** (actualmente) today, nowadays **(b)** (en locs) **hoy (en) día** nowadays, these days; **hoy por hoy** at this precise moment, at this moment in time

hoyo *m* (agujero) hole; (depresión) hollow; (fosa) pit; (en golf) hole; (sepultura) (fam) grave

hoyuelo *m* dimple

hoz *f* sickle

huacal *m* (Col, Méx, Ven) (caja) wooden crate

huachafo -fa *adj* (Per fam) **(a)** ⟨persona⟩ pretentious, affected **(b)** ⟨vestido/adorno⟩ tacky (colloq)

huachinango *m* (Méx) red snapper

huacho -cha *adj/m,f* ▶ GUACHO

huarache *m* (Méx) (Indum) sandal

huasca *f* (Chi, Per) ▶ GUASCA

huaso -sa *m,f* (Chi) **(a)** (campesino) peasant **(b)** (fam) (persona — rústica) hick (AmE colloq), country bumpkin (colloq); (—sin modales) uncouth yob (colloq)

hube, hubo, etc ▶ HABER

hucha *f* (Esp) moneybox, piggybank

hueco¹ -ca *adj* **(a)** [ESTAR] ⟨árbol/bola⟩ hollow; ⟨nuez⟩ empty, hollow; **tienes la cabeza hueca** (fam & hum) you've got a head full of sawdust (colloq & hum) **(b)** [SER] (vacío) ⟨palabras⟩ empty; ⟨estilo⟩ superficial; ⟨persona⟩ shallow, superficial **(c)** (esponjoso) ⟨lana⟩ soft; ⟨colchón⟩ soft, spongy **(d)** ⟨sonido/tos⟩ hollow; ⟨voz⟩ resonant

hueco² -n *m* **(a)** (cavidad en árbol, roca) hollow; (de ascensor) shaft; **suena a** ∼ it sounds hollow; **el** ∼ **de la escalera** the stairwell **(b)** (espacio) space; (entre dos dientes) gap; **un** ∼ **para aparcar** a parking space; **hazme un** ∼ make room for me; **llenar un** ∼ **en el mercado** to fill a gap in the market **(c)** (concavidad) hollow

huela, huele, etc ▶ OLER

huelga *f* strike; **hacer** ∼ to (go on) strike; **estar en** ∼ to be on strike

huelga, huelgan, etc ▶ HOLGAR

huelguista *mf* striker

huella *f* **(a)** (pisada — de persona) footprint, ⋯⋰

footstep; (— de rueda) track; **las ~s del animal** the
animal's tracks o pawprints (o hoofmarks etc);
~s dactilares fingerprints **(b)** (vestigio) mark; **sin
dejar ~** without (a) trace

huelo ▶ OLER

huemul m deer (native to the Southern Andes)

huérfano -na adj: **un niño ~** an orphan;
quedó ~ he was orphaned; **es ~ de padre** he
doesn't have a father
■ m,f orphan

huerta f **(a)** (huerto grande) (vegetable) garden;
(con frutales) orchard **(b)** (explotación agrícola) truck
farm (AmE), market garden (BrE)

huerto m (para verduras) vegetable garden; (con
frutales) orchard

hueso m ⌜1⌝ **(a)** (Anat) bone; **en los ~s** (fam)
nothing but skin and bone(s) (colloq) **(b)** (de)
color ~ off-white, bone-colored ⌜2⌝ (de fruta) pit
(AmE), stone (BrE)

huésped mf (en casa, hotel) guest

huesudo -da adj bony

hueva f ⌜1⌝ tb **~s** (Coc) roe; (Zool) spawn
⌜2⌝ (Andes vulg) (testículo): **~s** balls (vulg), bollocks
(BrE vulg)

huevada f (Andes vulg) (estupidez): **¿dónde
compraste esa ~?** where did you buy that crap
(sl) o (vulg) that shit?; **¡no digas ~s!** don't talk
crap! (sl); **déjate de ~s y ponte a trabajar** stop
screwing around (AmE) o (BrE) pissing about and
get on with some work (vulg)

huevear [A1] vi (Chi, Per vulg) (perder el tiempo) to
goof off (AmE colloq), to piss around (BrE sl)
■ **~** vt (Chi vulg) ⟨persona⟩ (molestar) to bug (colloq),
to hassle (colloq); (tomar el pelo a) to kid

hueveo m (Chi vulg) (tomadura de pelo) pisstake
(vulg); **agarrar a algn para el ~** to make fun of sb,
to take the piss out of sb (BrE sl)

huevera f ⌜1⌝ (para guardar huevos) egg box; (para
servir huevos) eggcup ⌜2⌝ (Per) (huevas) roe

huevo m ⌜1⌝ (Biol, Coc, Zool) egg; **~ a la copa** (Chi)
boiled egg; **~ de Pascua** Easter egg; **~ duro** or
(Ven) **sancochado** hard-boiled egg; **~ escalfado** or
(Méx, RPl) **poché** poached egg; **~ estrellado** (frito)
fried egg; **~ pasado por agua** or (Col, Méx) **tibio**
soft boiled egg; **~ revueltos** or (Col) **pericos**
scrambled eggs (pl); **a ~: tuve que leer el libro a
~** (Méx vulg) I had no damn o (BrE) bloody choice
but to read the book (sl); **comprar/vender a ~**
(Andes fam) to buy/sell for peanuts (colloq); **mirar a
~** (Chi fam) to look down on
⌜2⌝ (vulg) (testículo) ball (vulg); para modismos ver
COJONES 1

huevón -vona adj **(a)** (Andes, Ven fam o vulg)
(tonto, estúpido) (fam) dumb (colloq); **es tan ~** he's so
fucking stupid (vulg) **(b)** (Méx vulg) (holgazán) lazy
(colloq)
■ m,f **(a)** (Andes, Ven vulg) (imbécil) dickhead (vulg),
asshole (AmE vulg) **(b)** (Méx vulg) (holgazán) lazy
bum (colloq)

huida f (fuga) flight; **emprender la ~** to take
flight (frml)

huidizo -za adj ⟨mirada⟩ evasive, shy;
⟨carácter/persona⟩ elusive; ⟨animal⟩ timid

huila f (Chi) rag

huincha f **(a)** (Andes) (cinta) ribbon; (en carrera)
tape **(b)** (Andes) (para pelo) hair-band **(c)** (Bol, Chi,
Per) (para medir) tape measure

huipil m (en AmC, Méx) huipil (traditional
embroidered dress worn by Indian women)

huir [I20] vi **(a)** (escapar) to flee (liter or journ),
escape; **huyó de la cárcel** he escaped from prison;
~ del país to flee the country **(b)** (tratar de evitar)
~ DE algo to avoid sth; **~le A algn** to avoid sb

huira f (Per) rope

huiro m (Chi, Per) seaweed

hule m ⌜1⌝ (para mantel) oilcloth; (para ropa
impermeable) oilskin ⌜2⌝ (Méx) (goma) rubber

hule-espuma m (Méx) foam rubber

hulera f (AmC) slingshot (AmE), catapult (BrE)

hulla f coal

humanidad f **(a)** (los humanos): **la ~** the
human race, humanity, mankind **(b)** (piedad,
benevolencia) humanity **(c) humanidades** fpl
(estudios de letras) humanities (pl); (enseñanza
secundaria) (Chi) secondary education

humanista mf humanist

humanitario -ria adj humanitarian

humano¹ -na adj **(a)** ⟨naturaleza⟩ human
(before n) **(b)** (benevolente) humane

humano² m human being; **los ~s** humans

humareda f cloud of smoke

humeante adj ⟨leño/lava⟩ smoking; ⟨sopa/
café⟩ steaming (hot), piping hot

humear [A1] vi «chimenea/hoguera» to smoke;
«sopa/café» to steam

humectante m moisturizer

humedad f **(a)** (Meteo) dampness; (con calor)
humidity **(b)** (en paredes, suelo) damp

humedecer [E3] vt to moisten, dampen
■ **humedecerse** v pron «paredes/ropa» to get
damp

húmedo -da adj **(a)** (Meteo) damp; (con calor)
humid **(b)** ⟨suelo/casa/ropa⟩ damp **(c)** ⟨labios⟩
moist

humildad f **(a)** (sumisión) humility; **con ~**
humbly **(b)** (pobreza) humbleness, lowliness

humilde adj ⟨carácter/tono⟩ meek; ⟨vivienda/
ropa⟩ humble, lowly

humillación f humiliation

humillante adj humiliating

humillar [A1] vt to humiliate
■ **humillarse** v pron: **no se humilla ante nadie**
she doesn't kowtow to anyone; **no me voy a ~ a
pedirle que vuelva** I'm not going to demean
myself by begging him to come back

humita f ⌜1⌝ (CS) (Coc) flavored corn paste
wrapped in corn leaves ⌜2⌝ (Chi) (Indum) bow tie

humo m ⌜1⌝ (de tabaco, incendio) smoke; (gases)
fumes (pl); **echaba ~** smoke was pouring out of
it; **hacerse ~** (AmL fam) to make oneself scarce

(colloq) **2** **humos** *mpl* (aires) airs (*pl*); **¡qué ~s se da!** she really gives herself airs (colloq); **bajarle los ~s a algn** to take sb down a peg or two

humor *m* **(a)** (estado de ánimo) mood; **estar de buen ~** to be in a good mood; **no estoy de ~ para salir** I'm not in the mood to go out **(b)** (gracia) humor*

humorada *f* **(a)** (extravagancia): **hacer una ~** to do something crazy **(b)** (broma) little joke, witticism

humorista *mf* (autor) humorist, comic writer; (dibujante) cartoonist; (cómico) comic, comedian

humorístico -ca *adj* humorous

hundido -da *adj* **(a)** ‹barco› sunken **(b)** ‹ojos› deep-set; (por enfermedad) sunken

hundimiento *m* **(a)** (de barco) sinking **(b)** (de negocio) collapse **(c)** (de edificio — bajada de nivel) subsidence; (— derrumbe) collapse

hundir [I1] *vt* ‹barco› to sink; ‹persona› to destroy; ‹negocio/empresa› to drive ... under
■ **hundirse** *v pron* **(a)** «barco» to sink **(b)** (en barro, nieve) to sink **(c)** «empresa/negocio» to fold **(d)** «edificio» (bajar de nivel) to sink, subside; (derrumbarse) to collapse

húngaro¹ -ra *adj/m,f* Hungarian

húngaro² *m* (idioma) Hungarian

Hungría *f* Hungary

huracán *m* hurricane

huraño -ña *adj* ‹persona› unsociable; ‹animal› timid

hurgar [A3] *vi* ~ **EN algo** ‹en basura› to rummage *o* rake THROUGH sth; ~ **en el pasado** to delve into the past
■ **hurgarse** *v pron* (refl): **~se la nariz** to pick one's nose

hurguetear [A1] *vi* (CS) ~ **EN algo** ‹en papeles› to nose THROUGH sth; ‹en cartera› to rummage *o* ferret around IN sth
■ ~ *vt* ‹cajón/cartera› to rummage around in, rummage through
■ **hurguetearse** *v pron* (refl) (esp AmL) ▶ HURGARSE

hurra, hurrah *interj* hurrah!, hooray!

hurtadillas *fpl*: **entrar/salir a ~** to sneak in/out

hurtar [A1] *vt* (frml) to purloin (frml), to steal

hurto *m* (frml) (robo) robbery, theft; (en las tiendas) shoplifting

husmear [A1] *vt* to sniff
■ ~ *vi* **(a)** «perro» to sniff around **(b)** (fam) (fisgonear) to snoop, sniff (around) (colloq)

huso *m* spindle

huy *interj* (fam) (para expresar— dolor) ouch!, ow!; (— asombro) wow!; (— alivio) phew!

huya, huyas, etc ▶ HUIR

- -

I i

- -

I, i *f* (*pl* **íes**) (*read as* /i/) *tb* **i latina** the letter I, i; **i griega** *the letter* Y

iba, íbamos, etc ▶ IR

Iberia *f* Iberia

ibérico -ca *adj* Iberian

Iberoamérica *f* Latin America

iberoamericano -na *adj/m,f* Latin American

icaco *m* (Col, Méx, Ven) coco plum

iceberg /'aιsβer, 'iθe'βer/ *m* (*pl* **-bergs**) iceberg

icono, ícono *m* icon

ictericia *f* jaundice

ida *f* **(a)** (viaje) outward journey; **a la ~** on the way out; **¿cuánto cuesta la ~?** how much does it cost one way?; **¿saco de ~ y vuelta?** shall I buy a round-trip ticket (AmE) *o* (BrE) return ticket? **(b)** (partida) departure

idea *f* idea; **la ~ de libertad** the idea *o* concept of freedom; **es de ~s fijas** he has very set ideas about things; **no tiene ~ de cómo funciona** he has no idea how it works; **no tengo ~** I don't have a clue; **hacerse una ~ de la situación** to get an idea of the situation; **se me ocurre una ~** I've got an idea; **cambió de ~** she changed her mind; **hacerse (a) la ~ de algo** to get used to the idea of sth

ideal *adj* ideal

■ *m* **(a)** (prototipo) ideal **(b)** (aspiración) dream **(c) ideales** *mpl* (valores, principios) ideals (*pl*)

idealismo *m* idealism

idealista *adj* idealistic
■ *mf* idealist

idealizar [A4] *vt* to idealize

ídem *adv* ditto, idem (frml)

idéntico -ca *adj* identical; **es ~ al padre** (físicamente) he looks just like his father, he's the spitting image of his father (colloq); (en el carácter) he's exactly like his father; **~ A algo** identical TO sth

identidad *f* identity

identificar [A2] *vt* to identify
■ **identificarse** *v pron* **(a)** (compenetrarse, solidarizarse) **~se CON algo/algn** to identify WITH sth/sb **(b)** (demostrar la identidad) to identify oneself

ideología *f* ideology

ideológico -ca *adj* ideological

idílico -ca *adj* idyllic

idilio *m* **(a)** (Lit) idyll **(b)** (romance) romance

idioma *m* language

idiota *adj* (fam) (tonto) stupid, idiotic; **¡no seas ~!** don't be such an idiot!
■ *mf* (tonto) (fam) idiot, stupid fool (colloq)

idiotez *f* (fam) (cosa estúpida): **decir idioteces** to talk nonsense; **fue una ~ hacer eso** that was a stupid thing to do

ido, ida *adj* (distraído) ⟨mirada⟩ faraway (*before n*); **estás como** ~ you seem miles away

ídolo *m* idol

idóneo -nea *adj* suitable; **es la persona idónea para el cargo** he's suitable for the job, he's the right person for the job

iglesia *f* church; **no van a la** ~ they don't go to church; **casarse por la** ~ *or* (Bol, Per, RPl) **por** ~ to have a church wedding

iglú *m* igloo

ignorancia *f* ignorance; **por** ~ out of *o* through ignorance

ignorante *adj* (a) (sin instrucción) ignorant (b) (sin información): **estar** ~ **de algo** to be unaware of sth
■ *mf* ignoramus, ignorant fool (colloq)

ignorar [A1] *vt* (a) (desconocer): **lo ignoro** I've no idea; **ignoran las causas del accidente** they do not know what caused the accident; **ignora los peligros que le acechan** he's unaware of the dangers which await him (b) (no hacer caso de) to ignore

igual *adj* ⒈ (a) (idéntico): **de** ~ **peso** of equal *o* the same weight; **son** ~**es** they are the same *o* alike; **de forma son** ~**es** they're the same shape; ~ **A** *or* **QUE algo/algn** the same **AS** sth/sb; **es** ~**ita a** *or* **que su madre** (físicamente) she looks just like her mother; (en personalidad) she's exactly the same *o* just like her mother; **es** ~ **a x** (Mat) it equals x; **me/nos es** *or* **da** ~ I/we don't mind, it makes no difference to me/to us (b) (en una jerarquía) equal; ~**es ante la ley** equal in the eyes of the law
⒉ (en tenis): **quince** ~**es** fifteen all; **van** ~**es** they're even
■ *adv* ⒈ (a) (de la misma manera): **los trato a todos** ~ I treat them all the same (b) (*en locs*) **al igual que** (frml) as, like; **igual que: tiene pecas,** ~ **que su hermano** she has freckles, (just) like her brother; **se llama** ~ **que su padre** he's named after his father; **me aburrí** — ~ **que yo** I got bored — so did I *o* me too; **opino** ~ **que tú** I agree with you; **por igual** equally
⒉ (de todos modos) anyway
⒊ (expresando posibilidad): ~ **llueve y no podemos salir** it might rain and then we won't be able to go out; ~ **llamaron y no estábamos** they may have called and we weren't in
■ *mf* (par) equal; **le habló de** ~ **a** ~ he spoke to him on equal terms; **me trató de** ~ **a** ~ she treated me as an equal; **sin** ~ ⟨belleza/talento⟩ unequaled*, matchless (frml); **es un compositor sin** ~ he's unrivaled as a composer
■ *m* (signo) equals sign

igualado -da *adj* ⒈ (a) (Dep): **van muy** ~**s** they're very close, they're neck and neck; **quedaron** ~**s** they drew; **iban** ~**s a tres** they were level at three-three (b) ⟨superficie⟩ even, level ⒉ (Méx fam) (irrespetuoso) sassy (AmE colloq), cheeky (BrE colloq)

igualar [A1] *vt* ⒈ (a) ⟨superficie/terreno⟩ to level, level off; ⟨flequillo/dobladillo⟩ to even up, make ... straight (b) ⟨salarios⟩ to make ... equal *o* the same; ~ **algo CON** *or* **A algo** to make sth the same **AS** sth ⒉ ⟨éxito/récord⟩ to equal, match
■ **igualarse** *v pron*: **nada se le iguala** it has no equal, there's nothing like it; ~**se A** *or* **CON algo** to match *o* equal sth

igualdad *f* equality; ~ **de oportunidades** equal opportunities; **en** ~ **de condiciones** on equal terms

igualmente *adv* (a) (en fórmulas de cortesía): **que lo pases muy bien — igualmente** have a great time — you too *o* and you (b) ⟨bueno/malo⟩ equally (c) (frml) (también) likewise

iguana *f* (Zool) iguana

ilegal *adj* illegal; **de manera** ~ illegally

ilegible *adj* illegible, unreadable

ilegítimo -ma *adj* ⟨hijo⟩ illegitimate

ileso -sa *adj* unhurt, unharmed

ilícito -ta *adj* illicit

ilimitado -da *adj* unlimited

ilógico -ca *adj* illogical

iluminación *f* (de habitación) lighting; (de monumento) illumination; (Teatr) lighting

iluminar [A1] *vt* (a) ⟨calles⟩ to light, illuminate; ⟨monumento⟩ to illuminate; ⟨escenario⟩ to light (b) (con focos muy potentes) ⟨estadio⟩ to floodlight (c) ⟨rostro/ojos⟩ (liter) to light up

ilusión *f* ⒈ (a) (esperanza) hope; **no te hagas ilusiones** don't build your hopes up; **no me hago muchas ilusiones** I'm not very hopeful; **su mayor** ~ **es ...** her dearest *o* fondest wish is ... (b) (esp Esp) (alegría, satisfacción): **me hizo mucha** ~ I was thrilled; **le hace** ~ **el viaje** he's looking forward to the trip; **¡qué** ~**!** isn't it wonderful! ⒉ (noción falsa) illusion

ilusionar [A1] *vt*: **me ilusiona mucho** I'm very excited about it; **no la ilusiones** don't raise her hopes
■ **ilusionarse** *v pron* (a) (hacerse ilusiones) to build one's hopes up (b) (entusiasmarse) ~**se CON algo** to get excited **ABOUT** sth

iluso -sa *adj* naive
■ *m,f* dreamer

ilustración *f* illustration

ilustrado -da *adj* (a) ⟨revista/libro⟩ illustrated (b) (frml) ⟨persona⟩ erudite, learned

ilustrar [A1] *vt* to illustrate

ilustre *adj* illustrious, distinguished

imagen *f* ⒈ (a) (Fís, Ópt) image; (TV) picture, image (b) (foto) picture (c) (en espejo) reflection; **ser la viva** ~ **de algn** to be the image of sb (d) (en la mente) picture ⒉ (de político, cantante, país) image

imaginación *f* imagination; **¡ni (se) me pasó por la** ~**!** it never even crossed my mind!; **son imaginaciones tuyas** you're imagining things

imaginar [A1] *vt* (a) (suponer, figurarse) ▸ **IMAGINARSE** (b) (idear) ⟨plan/método⟩ to think up, come up with
■ **imaginarse** *v pron* to imagine; **me imagino que no querrá ir** I don't imagine *o* suppose he feels like going; **no te puedes** ~ **lo mal que nos trató** you've no idea how badly she treated us; **¿quedó contento? — ¡imagínate!** was he pleased? — what do you think!; **me imagino que sí** I suppose so; **me lo imaginaba más alto** I imagined he'd be taller

imaginario -ria *adj* imaginary

imaginativo -va *adj* imaginative

imán *m* magnet

imbécil *adj* (a) (fam) (tonto) stupid (b) (Med) imbecilic

■ *mf* **(a)** (fam) (tonto) stupid idiot, moron (colloq & pej) **(b)** (Med) imbecile

imberbe *adj*: un joven ∼ (sin barba) a beardless youth; (sin experiencia) a callow youth, a fresh-faced youth

imborrable *adj* lasting (*before n*), indelible

imitación *f* **(a)** (acción) imitation **(b)** (parodia) impression **(c)** (copia) imitation; bolso ∼ cuero imitation-leather bag

imitador -dora *m,f* (Teatr) impressionist, impersonator; (plagiario) imitator

imitar [A1] *vt* **(a)** ⟨persona⟩ (copiar) to copy, imitate; (para hacer reír) to do an impression of, mimic; se sentó y todos lo ∼on he sat down and everyone followed suit **(b)** ⟨voz/gesto/estilo⟩ to imitate; (para hacer reír) to imitate, mimic **(c)** (tener el aspecto de) to simulate

impaciencia *f* impatience

impacientarse [A1] *v pron* (por retraso) to get impatient; (exasperarse) to lose (one's) patience, get exasperated

impaciente *adj* **(a)** [SER] impatient **(b)** [ESTAR]: estaba ∼ he was (getting) impatient; ∼ POR hacer algo impatient to do sth

impactante *adj* ⟨noticia⟩ shocking; ⟨libro/imagen⟩ powerful; ⟨espectáculo/efecto⟩ stunning, impressive

impactar [A1] *vt* **(a)** (golpear) to hit **(b)** (impresionar) to have a profound impact on
■ ∼ *vi* **(a)** (impresionar) to shock **(b)** (chocar) to hit, strike

impacto *m* **(a)** (choque) impact; recibió un ∼ de bala she was shot **(b)** (huella, señal) hole, mark; el cadáver tiene varios ∼s de bala there are several bullet wounds in the body **(c)** (en el ánimo, público) impact **(d)** (Inf) hit

impago -ga *adj* (AmL) ⟨persona⟩ unpaid; ⟨deuda/impuesto⟩ unpaid, outstanding

impalpable *adj* impalpable

impar *adj* ⟨número⟩ odd
■ *m* odd number

imparcial *adj* impartial, unbiased

imparcialidad *f* impartiality

impasible *adj* impassive

impecable *adj* impeccable; va siempre ∼ she is always impeccably dressed

impedido -da *adj* disabled
■ *m,f* disabled person

impedimento *m* obstacle, impediment; si no surge ningún ∼ if there are no hitches; ∼ físico physical handicap

impedir [I14] *vt* **(a)** (imposibilitar) to prevent; nadie te lo impide nobody's stopping you; ∼le a algn hacer algo to prevent sb FROM doing sth; quiso ∼ que nos viéramos she tried to stop us seeing each other **(b)** ⟨paso/entrada⟩ to block **(c)** (dificultar) to hamper, hinder

impenetrable *adj* **(a)** ⟨bosque⟩ impenetrable; ⟨fortaleza⟩ impregnable **(b)** ⟨persona/expresión⟩ inscrutable; ⟨misterio/secreto⟩ unfathomable

impensable *adj* unthinkable, inconceivable

imperante *adj* ⟨moda/tendencia/condiciones⟩ prevailing (*before n*); ⟨dinastía/régimen⟩ ruling (*before n*)

imperativo¹ -va *adj* **(a)** (Ling) imperative **(b)** ⟨voz/tono⟩ commanding, authoritative

imperativo² *m* imperative

imperdible *m* safety pin

imperdonable *adj* ⟨error/comportamiento⟩ unforgivable, inexcusable

imperfección *f* **(a)** (en tela) flaw; (en mecanismo) defect **(b)** (cualidad) imperfection

imperfecto¹ -ta *adj* **1** ⟨trabajo/tela/facciones⟩ flawed **2** (Ling) imperfect

imperfecto² *m* imperfect (tense)

imperial *adj* ⟨dinastía/corona⟩ imperial

imperialismo *m* imperialism

imperialista *adj/mf* imperialist

imperio *m* empire

impermeable *adj* ⟨material/tela⟩ waterproof, impermeable (tech)
■ *m* (Indum) raincoat

impersonal *adj* impersonal

impersonar [A1] *vt* (Méx) to impersonate

impertinencia *f* **(a)** (cualidad) impertinence **(b)** (hecho, dicho): me dijo que me callara — ¡qué ∼! he told me to shut up — how impertinent!; me contestó con una ∼ she gave me a very cheeky reply

impertinente *adj* ⟨persona/pregunta/tono⟩ impertinent; ⟨comentario⟩ uncalled-for
■ *mf* (persona): eres una ∼ you're extremely impertinent

imperturbable *adj* **(a)** [SER] (sereno) imperturbable **(b)** [ESTAR] (ante un peligro) unperturbed **(c)** ⟨rostro/sonrisa⟩ impassive

ímpetu *m* **(a)** (Fís, Mec) impetus, momentum **(b)** (energía, ardor) vigor*, energy **(c)** (violencia) force

impetuoso -sa *adj* impetuous, impulsive

impida, impidas, etc ▶ IMPEDIR

implacable *adj* **(a)** ⟨odio/furia⟩ implacable; ⟨avance/lucha⟩ relentless; ⟨sol⟩ relentless **(b)** ⟨juez/crítico⟩ implacable **(c)** ⟨enemigo/contrincante⟩ ruthless

implantar [A1] *vt* **1** ⟨método/norma/moda⟩ to introduce; ⟨régimen político⟩ to establish; ⟨estado de excepción⟩ to impose **2** ⟨embrión/cabello⟩ to implant

implante *m* implant

implementar [A1] *vt* **1** ⟨medidas/plan⟩ to implement **2** (Ven) (instalar) to install*, set up

implicación *f* **1** (participación) involvement **2** implicaciones *fpl* (consecuencias) implications (*pl*)

implicancia *f* (AmL) (consecuencia) implication

implicar [A2] *vt* **1** (significar, conllevar) to entail, involve **2** (envolver, enredar) to involve; estuvo implicado en un delito (participó) he was involved in a crime; (estuvo bajo sospecha) he was implicated in a crime
■ **implicarse** *v pron* to get involved

implícito -ta *adj* implicit

implorar [A1] *vt* ⟨perdón/ayuda⟩ to beg for; ∼le algo A algn to beg sth OF sb; ∼le a algn QUE haga algo to implore o beg sb TO do sth

imponente *adj* ⟨belleza⟩ impressive; ⟨edificio/paisaje⟩ imposing, impressive

imponer [E22] *vt* (frml) **(a)** (imponer) to impose (frml); le impusieron una pena de un año de cárcel he was ···⟡

sentenced to one year in prison **(b)** ⟨*respeto*⟩ to command; ⟨*temor*⟩ to inspire, instill* **(c)** ⟨*moda*⟩ to set
■ **imponerse** *v pron* ① **(a)** (*refl*) ⟨*horario/meta*⟩ to set oneself **(b)** «*idea*» to become established **(c)** «*color/estilo*» to come into fashion ② (hacerse respetar) to assert oneself *o* one's authority ③ (frml) (vencer) to win; **se impondrá el sentido común** common sense will prevail

importación *f* **(a)** (acción) importation; **de ~** ⟨*artículos/mercancías*⟩ imported; ⟨*permiso*⟩ import (*before n*) **(b) importaciones** *fpl* (mercancías) imports (*pl*)

importado -da *adj* imported

importador -dora *adj*: **países ~es de petróleo** oil-importing countries
■ *m,f* importer

importancia *f* importance; **darle ~ a algo** to attach importance to sth; **quitarle ~ a algo** to play down the importance of sth; **detalles sin ~** minor *o* insignificant details; **no tiene ~** it doesn't matter; **darse ~** to give oneself airs

importante *adj* **(a)** ⟨*noticia/persona*⟩ important; ⟨*acontecimiento/cambio*⟩ important, significant; **dárselas de** *or* **hacerse el ~** to give oneself airs **(b)** ⟨*pérdidas*⟩ serious, considerable; ⟨*daños*⟩ severe, considerable; ⟨*cantidad*⟩ considerable, significant

importar [A1] *vi* **(a)** (tener importancia, interés) to matter; **no importa quién lo haga** it doesn't matter *o* it makes no difference who does it; **lo que importa es que te recuperes** the important thing is for you to get better; **no me importa lo que piense** I don't care what he thinks; **¿a mí qué me importa?** what do I care?; **¿a ti qué te importa?** what business is it of yours?; **yo no le importo** I don't mean a thing to him; **me importa un bledo** *or* **un comino** *or* **un pepino** *or* **un rábano** (fam) I couldn't care less, I don't give a damn (colloq); **meterse en lo que no le importa** (fam) to poke one's nose into other people's business (colloq); **no te metas en lo que no te importa** mind your own business! **(b)** (molestar): **no me ~ía venir el sábado** I wouldn't mind coming on Saturday; **no me importa que me llame a casa** I don't mind him calling me at home
■ **~** *vt* (Com, Fin) ⟨*productos*⟩ to import

importe *m* **(a)** (de factura, letra) amount; **el ~ total** the full *o* total amount; **el ~ de la compra** the purchase price **(b)** (costo) cost

importunar [A1] *vt* (frml) to inconvenience, disturb
■ **~** *vi*: **espero no ~** I hope it's not inconvenient, I hope I'm not disturbing you

importuno -na *adj* inopportune

imposibilitado -da *adj* [ESTAR] (Med) disabled

imposibilitar [A1] *vt* **(a)** (hacer imposible) to make ... impossible **(b)** (impedir) to prevent

imposible *adj* ① [SER] ⟨*sueño/amor*⟩ impossible; **me es ~ acompañarte** I won't be able to go with you; **es ~ que lo sepan** they can't

possibly know; **hicieron lo ~** they did everything they could ② (inaguantable) ⟨*persona*⟩ impossible; **está ~ hoy** he's (being) impossible today

impositivo -va *adj* ⟨*sistema/reforma*⟩ tax (*before n*)

impostor -tora *m,f* impostor

impotencia *f* (falta de poder) powerlessness, helplessness; (Med) impotence

impotente *adj* (incapaz, sin poder) powerless, helpless; (Med) impotent

impreciso -sa *adj* vague, imprecise; **un número ~ de personas** an indeterminate number of people

impredecible *adj* unpredictable

imprenta *f* (taller) printer's; (aparato) (printing) press

imprescindible *adj* ⟨*requisito/herramienta/ factor*⟩ essential, indispensable; **lleva lo ~** take the bare essentials; **es ~ hacerlo** it is essential to do it; **es ~ que nos acompañe** it is essential that you come with us

impresión *f* **(a)** (idea, sensación) impression; **nos causó** *or* **nos hizo muy buena ~** he made a very good impression on us; **da la ~ de ser demasiado ancho** it looks too wide; **me da/tengo la ~ de que me está mintiendo** I have a feeling he's lying to me; **cambiar impresiones** to exchange ideas **(b)** (sensación desagradable): **el accidente me produjo mucha ~** the accident really shocked me

impresionable *adj* squeamish, easily affected

impresionante *adj* ⟨*éxito/cantidad/paisaje*⟩ amazing, incredible; ⟨*accidente*⟩ horrific

impresionar [A1] *vt* ① **(a)** (causar buena impresión): **París me impresionó** I was really taken with Paris **(b)** (afectar) to affect; **verlo llorar me impresionó mucho** seeing him cry really affected *o* moved me **(c)** (alarmar) to shock; **me impresionó verla tan delgada** it shocked me to see her looking so thin **(d)** (sorprender) to strike ② (Fot) ⟨*película*⟩ to expose
■ **~** *vi* to impress

impresionismo *m* impressionism

impresionista *adj* ⟨*movimiento/pintor*⟩ Impressionist; ⟨*estilo/descripción*⟩ impressionistic

impreso¹ -sa *pp*: ▶ IMPRIMIR

impreso² *m* (formulario) form; **~ de solicitud** application form

impresora *f* (Inf) printer; **~ láser** *or* **de láser** laser printer

imprevisible *adj* ⟨*hecho/factor*⟩ unforeseeable; ⟨*persona*⟩ unpredictable

imprevisión *f* lack of foresight

imprevisto¹ -ta *adj* unforeseen, unexpected; **de modo ~** unexpectedly

imprevisto² *m* unforeseen event (*o* factor *etc*); **si no surge ningún ~** if nothing unexpected happens

imprimir [I36] *vt* (Impr) to print; **impreso en Perú** printed in Peru

improbable *adj* unlikely, improbable

impropio -pia *adj* **(a)** ⟨*actitud/respuesta*⟩ inappropriate; **un comportamiento ~ de una persona educada** behavior unbecoming to an educated person (frml) **(b)** (incorrecto) incorrect

improvisación *f* (acción) improvisation; (actuación) impromptu performance

improvisar [A1] *vt* to improvise; **~ una comida** to rustle up a meal
■ **~** *vi* «*actor/músico*» to improvise

improviso: **de ~** (*loc adv*) ⟨*llegar/aparecer*⟩ unexpectedly, out of the blue

imprudencia *f* imprudence; **no cometas esa ~** don't be so rash *o* reckless; **su ~ al conducir** his reckless driving

imprudente *adj* (que actúa sin cuidado) imprudent, careless; (temerario) reckless; **fuiste muy ~ al decírselo** it was very rash *o* imprudent of you to tell him

impúdico -ca *adj* (frml *o* hum) **(a)** (obsceno) indecent **(b)** (desvergonzado) shameless

impuesto *m* tax; **libre de ~s** tax-free, duty-free; **~ a** *or* **sobre la renta** income tax; **~ de circulación** road tax

impugnar [A1] *vt* ⟨*decisión/fallo*⟩ to contest, challenge

impulsar [A1] *vt* **(a)** ⟨*motor/vehículo*⟩ to propel, drive **(b)** ⟨*persona*⟩ to drive **(c)** ⟨*comercio, producción*⟩ to boost, give a boost to; ⟨*cultura/ relaciones*⟩ to promote

impulsivo -va *adj* impulsive

impulso *m* **(a)** (empuje) **un fuerte ~ para el comercio** a major boost for trade; **dar ~ a algo** (a comercio) to give a boost to sth; (a iniciativa) to give impetus to sth; **tomar** *or* **darse ~** to gather momentum, to get up speed (fig); ⟨*reacción, deseo*⟩ impulse; **mi primer ~ fue ...** my first instinct was ... **(c)** (Fís) impulse

impuntualidad *f* unpunctuality

impureza *f* impurity

impuro -ra *adj* impure

impuse, impuso, etc ▶ IMPONER

in *adj inv* ⟨*discoteca*⟩ trendy (colloq); **lo que está muy ~** the in thing (colloq), the trendy thing (colloq)

inaccesible *adj* **(a)** ⟨*montaña/persona/ concepto*⟩ inaccessible **(b)** (crit) ⟨*precios*⟩ prohibitive; ⟨*objetivo*⟩ unattainable

inaceptable *adj* unacceptable

inactividad *f* inactivity

inactivo -va *adj* inactive

inadaptación *f* failure to adapt

inadaptado -da *adj* maladjusted

inadecuado -da *adj* ⟨*color/traje*⟩ inappropriate, unsuitable; ⟨*norma/sistema*⟩ inadequate

inadmisible *adj* **(a)** ⟨*comportamiento/ pretensiones*⟩ unacceptable, inadmissible **(b)** (Der) inadmissible

inadvertido -da *adj* (no notado): **pasar ~** to go unnoticed

inagotable *adj* ⟨*fuente/reservas*⟩ inexhaustible, endless

inaguantable *adj* unbearable

inalámbrico -ca *adj* ⟨*teléfono*⟩ cordless; ⟨*comunicaciones*⟩ wireless

inalcanzable *adj* unattainable, unachievable

inanimado -da *adj* inanimate

inapetente *adj* lacking in appetite

inapreciable *adj* **1** (muy valioso) ⟨*ayuda/ amistad*⟩ invaluable; **un cuadro de un valor ~** a priceless painting **2** (insignificante) negligible

inapropiado -da *adj* inappropriate

inaudible *adj* inaudible

inaudito -ta *adj* ⟨*decisión/suceso*⟩ unprecedented

inauguración *f* opening, inauguration (frml)

inaugurar [A1] *vt* ⟨*teatro/hospital*⟩ to open, inaugurate (frml); ⟨*monumento*⟩ to unveil; ⟨*exposición/sesión*⟩ to open

inca *mf* Inca

incaico -ca *adj* Inca, Incaic

incalculable *adj* inestimable, incalculable

incandescente *adj* incandescent

incansable *adj* tireless

incapacidad *f* **1** (física) disability, physical handicap; (mental) mental handicap; (Der) incapacity; **~ laboral** invalidity **2** (ineptitud) incompetence; (falta de capacidad) inability **3** (Col) (baja) sick leave

incapacitado -da *adj* (físicamente) disabled, physically handicapped; (mentalmente) mentally handicapped

incapacitar [A1] *vt* «*enfermedad*» to incapacitate; **la lesión lo incapacita para su trabajo** the injury has made him unfit for work

incapaz *adj* [SER] (de un logro, una hazaña): **no lo conseguirá nunca, es ~** he'll never do it, he simply isn't capable; **es ~ de una cosa así** he's incapable of doing something like that; **es ~ de llamarme** he can't even be bothered to phone me
■ *mf* (inútil, inepto) incompetent (fool)

incendiar [A1] *vt* **(a)** (prender fuego a) to set fire to **(b)** (quemar) ⟨*edificio*⟩ to burn down; ⟨*coche*⟩ to burn; ⟨*pueblo/bosque*⟩ to burn ... to the ground
■ **incendiarse** *v pron* **(a)** (empezar a arder) to catch fire **(b)** (destruirse) «*edificio*» to be burned down; **los bosques que se ~on** the forests that were destroyed by fire

incendiario -ria *m,f* arsonist

incendio *m* fire; **~ provocado** arson attack

incentivo *m* incentive

incertidumbre *f* uncertainty

incesante *adj* incessant

incesto *m* incest

incestuoso -sa *adj* incestuous

incidente *m* incident

incienso *m* incense; (Bib) frankincense

incierto -ta *adj* (dudoso, inseguro) uncertain

incineración *f* **(a)** (de basura) incineration **(b)** (de cadáveres) cremation

incinerador *m* incinerator

incinerar [A1] *vt* ⟨*basura*⟩ to incinerate, burn; ⟨*cadáver*⟩ to cremate

incitar [A1] *vt* **~ a algn A algo** to incite sb TO sth; **~ a algn CONTRA algn** to incite sb AGAINST sb

incivilizado -da *adj* uncivilized

inclinación *f* **1 (a)** (pendiente) slope **(b)** (ángulo) inclination **2** (movimiento del cuerpo) bow; ⋯⋮

asintió con una ~ de la cabeza he nodded (his head) in agreement **3** (interés, tendencia): **tener ~ por** or **hacia la música** to have a musical bent o musical inclinations; **inclinaciones políticas/sexuales** political/sexual leanings

inclinado -da adj **1** ‹tejado/terreno› sloping; ‹torre› leaning (before n); ‹cuadro› crooked; **una pendiente muy inclinada** a very steep slope o incline **2** (predispuesto): **sentirse ~ a hacer algo** to feel inclined to do sth

inclinar [A1] vt **1** ‹botella/sombrilla/plato› to tilt; **inclinó la cabeza a un lado** she tilted her head to one side; **inclinó la cabeza en señal de asentimiento** he nodded (his head) in agreement; **~ el cuerpo** to bend over; (en señal de respeto) to bow; **el viento inclinaba los árboles** the wind bent the trees **2** (inducir, predisponer) ‹persona›: **ello me inclina a pensar que …** this inclines me to think that … (frml)

■ **inclinarse** v pron **1** (tender) ~**se A hacer algo** to be inclined to do sth; **me inclino por su candidato** I'm inclined to go for your candidate; **me ~ía por esta opción** I would tend to favor this option **2** (doblarse) to bend; (en señal de respeto) to bow; ~**se ante algn** to bow to sb; **se inclinó sobre la cuna** she leaned over the cradle; ~**se hacia adelante/atrás** to lean forward/back

incluir [I20] vt **1** (comprender) **(a)** ‹impuestos/gastos› to include; **$500 todo incluido** $500 all inclusive o all in **(b)** ‹tema/sección› to include, contain **2** (poner, agregar) **(a)** (en un grupo) to include **(b)** (en una carta) to enclose

inclusive adj inv inclusive; **del 10 al 18, ambos ~** from 10 to 18 inclusive; **domingos ~** including Sundays

incluso adv even

incógnita f **(a)** (Mat) unknown (factor o quantity) **(b)** (misterio) mystery

incógnito: **de ~** (loc adv) incognito

incoherente adj incoherent, illogical

incoloro -ra adj colorless*

incomible adj inedible, uneatable

incómodo -da adj **(a)** (en general) uncomfortable; **¿no estás ~ en esa silla?** aren't you uncomfortable in that chair?; **se siente muy ~ en las fiestas** he feels ill at ease o uncomfortable at parties **(b)** (inconveniente) inconvenient; **es muy ~ vivir tan lejos** it's very inconvenient living so far away

incompatibilidad f mutual incompatibility; **~ de caracteres** incompatibility

incompatible adj ‹personas/caracteres› incompatible; **el horario de clases es ~ con el de mi trabajo** the times of the classes clash with my work hours

incompetente adj/mf incompetent

incompleto -ta adj incomplete

incomprensible adj incomprehensible

incomprensión f lack of understanding

incomunicado -da adj ‹preso/prisionero› in solitary confinement; **hay varios pueblos ~s** several villages have been cut off

inconcebible adj inconceivable

inconcluso -sa adj unfinished

incondicional adj **(a)** ‹apoyo› unconditional, wholehearted; ‹obediencia› absolute; ‹aliado/admirador› staunch; ‹amigo› true, loyal **(b)** ‹rendición› unconditional

inconexo -xa adj unconnected

inconfesable adj unmentionable

inconformista adj/mf nonconformist

inconfundible adj unmistakable

incongruente adj ‹imágenes› unconnected; **decía palabras ~s** his words didn't make sense

inconsciencia f **(a)** (Med) unconsciousness **(b)** (insensatez) irresponsibility

inconsciente adj **1** [ESTAR] (Med) unconscious **2** [SER] (insensato) irresponsible **3** [SER] (no voluntario) ‹movimiento/gesto› unwitting, unconscious; **de una manera ~** unconsciously
■ mf irresponsible person; **son unos ~s** they are very irresponsible

inconsecuente adj: **ser ~ con uno mismo** to be inconsistent with one's principles

inconsistente adj **(a)** ‹material› flimsy, weak **(b)** ‹argumento› (falto de solidez) weak, flimsy; (falto de coherencia) inconsistent, flawed

inconsolable adj inconsolable

inconstante adj **(a)** (falto de perseverancia) lacking in perseverance **(b)** (voluble) fickle

inconstitucional adj unconstitutional

incontable adj countless, innumerable

incontrolado -da adj **(a)** ‹furia/pasión/ira› uncontrolled, unbridled (liter) **(b)** ‹llanto/risa› uncontrollable

inconveniencia f **(a)** (cualidad) inconvenience **(b)** (comentario inoportuno) tactless remark

inconveniente adj (incómodo) ‹hora/fecha› inconvenient
■ m **(a)** (problema) problem; **si no surge ningún ~** if everything goes according to plan, if there are no problems; **¿habría algún ~ en que nos quedemos?** would it be alright if we stayed? **(b)** (desventaja) drawback; **tiene sus ~s** it has its disadvantages o drawbacks **(c)** (objeción) objection; **no tengo ~** I have no objection; **no tengo ~ en decírselo** I don't mind telling him; **no veo ningún ~ en que venga** I see no reason why he shouldn't come

incordiar [A1] vt (Esp fam) to annoy, to pester (colloq)
■ ~ vi (Esp): **¡no incordies!** don't be such a nuisance!

incordio m (Esp fam) nuisance, pain in the neck (colloq)

incorporación f incorporation

incorporado -da adj integral, built-in

incorporar [A1] vt (frml) **1 (a)** (agregar) to add; **~ algo A algo** to add sth TO sth **(b)** (integrar) to incorporate **2** ‹enfermo/niño› to sit … up
■ **incorporarse** v pron (frml) **1** (a equipo, puesto) to join; ~**se A algo** to join sth **2** (levantarse) to sit up

incorrecto -ta adj **(a)** ‹respuesta/interpretación› incorrect, wrong **(b)** ‹comportamiento› impolite, discourteous (frml)

incorregible adj ‹mentiroso/idealista› incorrigible; ‹defecto› irremediable, irreparable

incredulidad *f* skepticism*

incrédulo -la *adj* skeptical*
■ *m,f* skeptic*

increíble *adj* incredible, unbelievable

incrementar [A1] *vt* (frml) to increase

incremento *m* (frml) increase

incriminar [A1] *vt* (frml) **(a)** «*pruebas*» to incriminate **(b)** (acusar, inculpar) to charge

incrustación *f* **(a)** (de madera, metal) inlay **(b)** (Col) (Odont) filling

incrustar [A1] *vt* ⟨*piedra preciosa*⟩ ~ algo EN algo to set sth IN sth
■ **incrustarse** *v pron* ~se EN algo «*bala*» to embed itself IN sth; «*suciedad*» to get embedded IN sth

incubadora *f* incubator

incubar [A1] *vt* to incubate

inculcar [A2] *vt* to instill*, inculcate (frml); **las ideas que les inculcan** the ideas they fill their heads with

inculto -ta *adj* (sin cultura) uncultured, uneducated; (ignorante) ignorant
■ *m,f* **(a)** (persona sin cultura): **es un** ~ he's uneducated **(b)** (persona ignorante) ignorant person

incumplido -da *adj* (AmL exc CS) unreliable

incumplidor -dora *adj* (CS) unreliable

incumplir [I1] *vt* ⟨*ley/promesa*⟩ to break; ⟨*contrato*⟩ to breach
■ ~ *vi* (AmL exc CS): **no me vayas a** ~ don't let me down; **incumplió a la cita** she didn't show *o* turn up

incurable *adj* incurable

indagación *f* (frml) investigation; **hacer indagaciones** to make inquiries, to investigate

indagar [A3] (frml) *vi* to investigate; ~ SOBRE algo to investigate sth

indecencia *f* **(a)** (cualidad) indecency **(b)** (cosa, hecho): **presentarse así en público es una** ~ it's indecent to appear in public like that

indecente *adj* ⟨*persona/vestido*⟩ indecent; ⟨*película/lenguaje*⟩ obscene
■ *mf* rude *o* shameless person

indecisión *f* indecision

indeciso -sa *adj* ⟨*persona*⟩ **(a)** [SER] indecisive **(b)** [ESTAR] undecided
■ *m,f* **(a)** (en general) indecisive person **(b)** (sobre un tema): **hay un gran número de** ~s there are a lot of people who are as yet undecided

indecoroso -sa *adj* unseemly, indecorous (frml)

indefenso -sa *adj* ⟨*niño/animal*⟩ defenseless*; ⟨*fortaleza*⟩ undefended

indefinido -da *adj* **(a)** ⟨*forma*⟩ undefined, vague; **un color** ~ a difficult color to describe **(b)** (ilimitado) indefinite, unlimited; **por tiempo** ~ for an indefinite *o* unlimited period

indemnización *f* **(a)** (por pérdidas sufridas) compensation, indemnity (frml); (por posibles pérdidas) indemnity (frml); ~ **por daños y perjuicios** damages (*pl*) **(b)** (por despido) severance pay

indemnizar [A4] *vt* **(a)** (por pérdidas sufridas) to compensate, indemnify (frml); (por posibles pérdidas) to indemnify (frml); **fue indemnizado con diez mil**

euros he was given ten thousand euros (in) compensation **(b)** (por despido) to pay severance pay to

independencia *f* independence

independentista *adj* ⟨*político/ideas*⟩ pro-independence (*before n*)
■ *mf* supporter of the independence movement

independiente *adj/mf* independent

independizarse [A4] *v pron* to become independent, gain independence; ~ DE algn to become independent of sb

indescriptible *adj* indescribable

indestructible *adj* indestructible

indeterminado -da *adj* **(a)** (indefinido) indefinite; **por tiempo** ~ indefinitely **(b)** (no establecido) undetermined **(c)** (vago, impreciso) ⟨*contorno/forma*⟩ indeterminate **(d)** (Ling) indefinite

India *f*: **la** ~ India

indicación *f* **(a)** (instrucción) instruction; **me dio indicaciones de cómo llegar** he gave me directions as to how to get there **(b)** (muestra) indication; **no dio ninguna** ~ **de sus intenciones** she gave no indication of her intentions

indicado -da *adj* **(a)** (adecuado) suitable; **es el menos** ~ **para hacerlo** he's the last person who should do it; **lo más** ~ **sería** ... the best thing to do would be ... **(b)** (señalado) ⟨*hora/fecha*⟩ specified

indicador *m* (Auto) **(a)** *tb* ~ **de dirección** indicator **(b)** (señal de tráfico) sign **(c)** (del aceite, la gasolina) gauge; ~ **de velocidad** speedometer

indicar [A2] *vt* to indicate, show; **hay una flecha que indica el camino** there's an arrow indicating the way; **¿me podría** ~ **cómo llegar allí?** could you tell me how to get there? **me indicó el lugar en el mapa** he showed me *o* pointed out the place on the map; **todo parece** ~ **que** ... there is every indication that ...; **el asterisco indica que** ... the asterisk indicates *o* shows that ...

indicativo *m* (Ling) indicative; **presente de** ~ present indicative

índice *m* **1** (de una publicación) index; (catálogo) catalog* **2** (Anat) index finger, forefinger **3** (tasa, coeficiente) rate; ~ **de natalidad** birth rate

indicio *m* **(a)** (señal, huella) sign, indication **(b)** (vestigio) trace, sign; ~s **de potasio** traces of potassium

Índico *adj*: **el** (Océano) ~ the Indian Ocean

indiferencia *f* indifference

indiferente *adj* **(a)** (poco importante, de poco interés): **es** ~ **que venga hoy o mañana** it doesn't matter *o* it makes no difference whether he comes today or tomorrow; **me es** ~ **su amistad** I'm not concerned *o* (colloq) bothered about his friendship **(b)** (poco interesado) indifferent; ~ A **algo** indifferent TO sth

indígena *adj* indigenous, native (*before n*)
■ *mf* native

indigestión *f* indigestion

indignación *f* indignation, anger; (más fuerte) outrage; **sentí una gran** ~ I was outraged

indignado -da *adj* indignant, angry; (más fuerte) outraged, incensed

indignante *adj* outrageous

indignar [A1] *vt* to make ... angry *o* indignant; (más fuerte) to outrage

■ **indignarse** *v pron* to get angry, become indignant; (más fuerte) to be outraged *o* incensed

indigno -na *adj* (a) (impropio) unworthy; ~ **DE algn** unworthy OF sb (b) (no merecedor) unworthy (c) (humillante) degrading, humiliating (d) (vergonzoso) shameful, disgraceful

indio -dia *adj* (a) (de América) (American) Indian, Amerindian (b) (de la India) Indian, of/ from India

■ *m,f* (a) (de América) (American) Indian, Amerindian (b) (de la India) Indian

indirecta *f* hint; **lanzar** *or* **soltar una** ~ to drop a hint

indirecto -ta *adj* indirect

indisciplinado -da *adj* ⟨alumno⟩ undisciplined, unruly; ⟨soldado⟩ insubordinate

indiscreción *f* (a) (dicho, declaración — que molesta) indiscreet *o* tactless remark; (— que revela un secreto) indiscreet *o* unguarded remark; ¿su edad, si no es ~? how old are you, if you don't mind my asking?; **cometió la** ~ **de preguntárselo** he was indiscreet *o* tactless enough to ask her (b) (cualidad) lack of discretion

indiscreto -ta *adj* (a) (falto de tacto) indiscreet, tactless (b) (que revela un secreto) indiscreet

indiscutible *adj* (a) ⟨pruebas/hecho/verdad⟩ indisputable (b) ⟨líder/campeón⟩ undisputed

indispensable *adj* ⟨persona⟩ indispensable; ⟨objeto⟩ indispensable, essential; **lleva lo** ~ take the bare essentials

indispuesto -ta *adj* (a) (enfermo) unwell, indisposed (frml) (b) (CS euf) ⟨mujer⟩: **está indispuesta** it's the time of the month (euph)

individual *adj* (a) ⟨características/libertades⟩ individual (b) ⟨cama/habitación⟩ single (before n); **mantel** ~ place mat (c) ⟨caso⟩ one-off (before n), isolated (d) (Dep) ⟨prueba/final⟩ singles (before n)

■ *m* (Dep) singles (*pl*); ~ **femenino** women's singles

individualismo *m* individualism

individualista *adj* individualistic

■ *mf* individualist

individuo *m* (a) (persona indeterminada): **un** ~ **alto** a tall man (b) (pey) (tipo) character (colloq), individual (colloq); **ese** ~ **que iba contigo** (fam) that guy you were with (colloq)

indivisible *adj* indivisible

Indochina *f* Indo-China

índole *f* (a) (tipo, clase) kind, nature; **un problema de** ~ **afectiva** a problem of an emotional nature (b) (manera de ser) nature; **ser de buena/mala** ~ to be good-natured/ill-natured

indolente *adj* lazy, slack, indolent

indoloro -ra *adj* painless

indomable *adj* (a) ⟨animal salvaje⟩ untamable*; ⟨caballo⟩ unbreakable (b) ⟨pueblo/

tribu⟩ indomitable, unconquerable; ⟨persona⟩ indomitable (c) (fam) ⟨pelo/remolino⟩ unruly, unmanageable

Indonesia *f* Indonesia

indonesio -sia *adj/m,f* Indonesian

indudable *adj* unquestionable; **es** ~ **que** ... there is no doubt that ...

indulgente *adj* (tolerante) indulgent; (para perdonar castigos) lenient; ~ **CON algn** indulgent WITH/lenient TOWARD(s) sb

indultar [A1] *vt* (Der) to pardon; (la pena de muerte) to reprieve

indulto *m* (Der) pardon; (de la pena de muerte) reprieve

indumentaria *f* clothing, clothes (*pl*), attire (frml)

industria *f* (Com, Econ) industry; ~ **del turismo** tourist industry; ~ **pesquera** fishing industry

industrial *adj* industrial

■ *mf* industrialist

industrialización *f* industrialization

industrializarse [A4] *v pron* to become industrialized

inédito -ta *adj* (a) ⟨obra/autor⟩ unpublished (b) (nuevo, sin precedente) unprecedented; **una técnica inédita en nuestro país** a technique unknown in our country

ineficacia *f* (de medida) ineffectiveness; (de método, persona) inefficiency

ineficaz *adj* (a) ⟨remedio/medida⟩ ineffectual, ineffective (b) ⟨método/sistema/persona⟩ inefficient

ineficiencia *f* inefficiency

ineficiente *adj* inefficient

inepto -ta *adj* inept, incompetent

■ *m,f* incompetent

inercia *f* (a) (Fís) inertia (b) **por** ~ (por rutina) out of habit; (por apatía) out of inertia *o* apathy

inescrutable *adj* inscrutable

inesperado -da *adj* unexpected; **de manera inesperada** unexpectedly

inestabilidad *f* instability

inestable *adj* (a) (en general) unstable (b) ⟨tiempo⟩ changeable, unsettled

inestimable *adj* ⟨ayuda⟩ invaluable

inevitable *adj* (ineludible) inevitable; ⟨cambio/ conflicto/controversia⟩ unavoidable; **era** ~ **que empeorase la situación** the situation was bound to get worse

inexcusable *adj* ⟨comportamiento/error⟩ inexcusable, unforgivable; ⟨deber⟩ inescapable, unavoidable

inexistente *adj* nonexistent

inexperiencia *f* inexperience

inexperto -ta *adj* (falto de experiencia) inexperienced; (falto de habilidad) inexpert, unskilled

inexplicable *adj* inexplicable

inexpresivo -va *adj* expressionless, inexpressive

infalibilidad *f* infallibility

infalible *adj* ⟨persona/método⟩ infallible; ⟨puntería⟩ unerring

infancia *f* (período) childhood

infante -ta *m,f* (hijo del Rey) (*m*) prince, infante; (*f*) princess, infanta

infantería *f* infantry; ∼ **de marina** marines (*pl*), Marine Corps

infantil *adj* (a) ⟨enfermedad⟩ children's (*before n*), childhood (*before n*); ⟨literatura/programa/moda⟩ children's (*before n*); ⟨rasgos/sonrisa⟩ childlike; ⟨población⟩ child (*before n*) (b) (pey) ⟨persona/actitud/reacción⟩ childish (pej), infantile (pej)

infarto *m* heart attack

infección *f* infection

infeccioso -sa *adj* infectious

infectar [A1] *vt* to infect
■ **infectarse** *v pron* to become infected

infelicidad *f* unhappiness

infeliz *adj* (a) ⟨persona/vida⟩ unhappy (b) ⟨intervención/tentativa⟩ unfortunate
■ *mf* poor wretch, poor devil

inferior *adj* [1] (en el espacio) ⟨piso/planta⟩ lower [2] (en jerarquía) ⟨especie/rango⟩ inferior [3] (en comparaciones) lower; **temperaturas** ∼**es a los 10°** temperatures lower than *o* below 10°; **un número** ∼ **al 20** a number below twenty

inferioridad *f* inferiority

infernal *adj* ⟨ruido⟩ infernal, hideous; ⟨música⟩ diabolical; **hacía un calor** ∼ it was baking hot (colloq)

infértil *adj* infertile

infertilidad *f* infertility

infestado -da *adj* ∼ **DE algo** ⟨de insectos, parásitos⟩ infested WITH sth; ∼ **de turistas** crawling with tourists

infestar [A1] *vt* to infest

infidelidad *f* infidelity, unfaithfulness

infiel *adj* (a) (desleal) unfaithful; **ser** ∼ **A algn/algo** to be unfaithful TO sb/sth (b) (Relig) unbelieving (*before n*), infidel (*before n*) (dated)

infiernillo *m* (Esp) kerosene stove, primus® stove (BrE)

infierno *m* (a) (en general) hell; ¡**vete al** ∼! (fam) go to hell! (sl); **su vida es un** ∼ her life is hell (b) (fam) (lugar — ruidoso) madhouse (colloq), bedlam (colloq); (— horrendo) hellhole (colloq)

infílder *mf* (Col, Ven) infielder

infiltración *f* infiltration

infiltrado -da *m,f* infiltrator

infiltrar [A1] *vt* to infiltrate; ∼ **a algn EN algo** to infiltrate sb INTO sth
■ **infiltrarse** *v pron* to infiltrate; ∼**se EN algo** ⟨en partido/organización⟩ to infiltrate sth

infinidad *f* (gran cantidad): **en** ∼ **de ocasiones** on countless occasions; ∼ **de veces** innumerable *o* countless times

infinitivo *m* infinitive

infinito¹ -ta *adj* (a) (Fil, Mat) infinite (b) ⟨bondad/sabiduría⟩ infinite; ⟨amor⟩ boundless (c) (delante del n, en pl) (innumerables) innumerable, countless

infinito² ** *m* (a) **el ∼ (Fil) the infinite; **mirar al** ∼ to look into the distance (b) (Mat) infinity

inflación *f* inflation

inflador *m* (Bol, Per, RPl) bicycle pump

inflamable *adj* flammable, inflammable

inflamación *f* (Med) inflammation; (Quím) ignition

inflamar [A1] *vt* (a) (Med) to inflame (b) (Quím) to ignite, set ... on fire
■ **inflamarse** *v pron* (a) (Med) to become inflamed (b) (Quím) to ignite

inflar [A1] *vt* (a) ⟨balón/rueda⟩ to inflate; ⟨globo⟩ to blow up (b) ⟨noticia/acontecimiento⟩ to exaggerate
■ **inflarse** *v pron* «velas» to swell, fill

inflexible *adj* inflexible; **se mostró** ∼ he refused to give in

inflexión *f* inflection

influencia *f* [1] (influjo) influence; **bajo la** ∼ **del alcohol** under the influence of alcohol; ∼ **EN** *or* **SOBRE algo** influence ON *o* UPON sth; ∼ **SOBRE algn** influence ON sb [2] **influencias** *fpl* (contactos) contacts (*pl*)

influenciable *adj* easily influenced

influenciar [A1] *vt* to influence

influir [I20] *vi* ∼ **EN algo/algn** to influence sth/sb, have an influence ON sth/sb
■ ∼ *vt* to influence

influyente *adj* influential

infografía *f* computer graphics

información *f* [1] (a) (datos, detalles) information; **el mostrador de** ∼ the information desk (b) (Telec) information (AmE), directory enquiries (BrE) [2] (Period, Rad, TV) news; **la** ∼ **internacional** the foreign news [3] (Inf) data (*pl*)

informado -da *adj* (sobre tema, noticia) informed; **está usted muy mal informada** you have been misinformed *o* wrongly informed; **fuentes bien informadas** reliable sources

informal *adj* [1] (a) ⟨persona⟩ unreliable (b) ⟨ropa/estilo⟩ informal, casual; ⟨cena/ambiente⟩ informal (c) (no oficial) ⟨reunión⟩ informal [2] (AmL) ⟨economía/sector⟩ black (*before n*), informal (*before n*)

informar [A1] *vt* ⟨persona/prensa⟩ to inform; **te han informado mal** you've been misinformed; **¿podría** ∼**me sobre los cursos de idiomas?** could you give me some information about language courses?
■ ∼ *vi* (dar noticias, información) to report; ∼ **SOBRE algo** to report ON sth, give a report ON sth; ∼ **DE algo** to announce sth
■ **informarse** *v pron* to get information; ∼**se SOBRE algo** to find out *o* inquire ABOUT sth

informática *f* computer science, computing

informático -ca *adj* computer (*before n*)

informativo -va *adj* (a) ⟨servicios/campaña⟩ information (*before n*); **programa** ∼ news program* (b) (instructivo) informative

informatizar [A4] *vt* to computerize

informe *m* [1] (exposición, dictamen) report; ∼ **médico** medical report [2] **informes** *mpl* (a) (datos) information, particulars (*pl*) (b) (de empleado) reference, references (*pl*); **pedir** ∼**s to** ask for a reference/for references

infovía *f* information highway

infracción *f* offense*, infraction (frml); ~ **de tráfico** traffic violation (AmE), driving offence (BrE)

infractor -tora *m,f* offender

infraestructura *f* infrastructure

in fraganti *loc adv* red-handed

infrarrojo -ja *adj* infrared

infringir [I7] *vt* to infringe, break

ínfulas *fpl*: **darse** *or* **tener muchas** ~ to put on *o* give oneself airs

infundado -da *adj* unfounded, groundless

infundir [I1] *vt* ⟨confianza/respeto⟩ to inspire; ⟨sospechas⟩ to arouse; **les infundía miedo** it filled them with fear; **para ~les ánimo** to give them encouragement

infusión *f* infusion; ~ **de manzanilla** chamomile tea

ingeniar [A1] *vt* ⟨método/sistema⟩ to devise, think up; **ingeniárselas** (fam): **se las ingenió para arreglarlo** he managed to fix it

ingeniería *f* engineering; ~ **civil** civil engineering

ingeniero -ra *m,f* engineer; ~ **agrónomo** agriculturist; ~ **civil/industrial** civil/industrial engineer; ~ **técnico** engineer (*qualified after a three-year university course*)

ingenio *m* ① (a) (talento) ingenuity, inventiveness; **aguzar el** ~ to rack one's brains (b) (chispa, agudeza) wit ② (aparato) device ③ (AmL) (refinería) *tb* ~ **azucarero** sugar refinery

ingenioso -sa *adj* (a) (lúcido) ⟨persona/idea⟩ clever, ingenious (b) (con chispa, agudeza) ⟨persona/dicho/chiste⟩ witty (c) ⟨aparato/invención⟩ ingenious

ingenuidad *f* naivety, ingenuousness

ingenuo -nua *adj* (a) naive, ingenuous
■ *m,f*: **es un** ~ he's so naive

Inglaterra *f* England

ingle *f* groin

inglés¹ -glesa *adj* (a) (de Inglaterra) English (b) (crit) (británico) British, English (crit)
■ *m,f* (a) (de Inglaterra) (m) Englishman; (f) Englishwoman; **los ingleses** the English, English people (b) (crit) ▶ BRITÁNICO

inglés² *m* (idioma) English

ingratitud *f* ingratitude

ingrato -ta *adj* (a) (desagradecido) ⟨persona⟩ ungrateful; ~ **con ella** ungrateful to her (b) (desagradable, difícil) ⟨vida⟩ hard; ⟨trabajo/tarea⟩ unrewarding
■ *m,f* ungrateful wretch (*o* swine *etc*) (colloq), ingrate (liter)

ingrediente *m* ingredient

ingresar [A1] *vi* ① «persona» (en organización, club) to join; (en colegio) to enter; (en el ejército) to join; **después de** ~ **en el hospital** after being admitted to (the) hospital; **ingresó cadáver** (Esp) he was dead on arrival
② «dinero» to come in
■ ~ *vt* ① ⟨persona⟩ (en hospital): **el médico decidió** ~**lo** the doctor decided to send him to hospital; **hubo que** ~**lo de urgencia** he had to be admitted as a matter of urgency; **fueron ingresados en esta prisión** they were taken to this prison
② (Esp) (Fin) ⟨dinero/cheque⟩ to pay in; ~ **una**

cantidad en una cuenta «persona» to pay a sum into an account; «banco» to credit an account with a sum

ingreso *m* ① (a) (en organización): **el año de mi** ~ **a** *or* **en la universidad/el ejército/la compañía** the year I started *o* entered university/joined the army/joined the company; **examen de** ~ entrance examination (b) (en hospital) admission ② (Fin) (a) (Esp) (depósito) deposit (b) **ingresos** *mpl* (ganancias) income; ~**s brutos/netos** gross/net income

íngrimo -ma *adj* (Col, Méx, Ven fam) (a) (sin compañía) all alone, all by oneself (b) ⟨lugar⟩ lonely, deserted

inhábil *adj* (a) (torpe) unskillful*, clumsy (b) (no apto) ~ **PARA algo** unsuited TO sth

inhabitado -da *adj* uninhabited

inhalación *f* inhalation; **hacer inhalaciones** to inhale; ~ **de pegamento** *or* (Méx) **cemento** glue sniffing

inhalador *m* inhaler

inhalar [A1] *vt* to inhale; ⟨pegamento⟩ to sniff

inhibición *f* inhibition

inhibir [I1] *vt* to inhibit
■ **inhibirse** *v pron* to become inhibited

inhóspito -ta *adj* inhospitable

inhumano -na *adj* (a) (falto de compasión) inhumane (b) (cruel) inhuman

iniciación *f* (a) (frml) (comienzo) beginning, start (b) (introducción) introduction; **curso de** ~ introductory course (c) (a una secta) initiation

inicial *adj* initial
■ ~ *f* (a) (letra) initial (b) (en béisbol) first base

iniciar [A1] *vt* (a) (frml) ⟨curso/viaje⟩ to begin, commence (frml); ⟨negociaciones/diligencias⟩ to initiate, commence (frml) (b) ~ **a algn EN algo** ⟨en secta⟩ to initiate sb INTO sth; ⟨en un arte⟩ to introduce sb TO sth
■ **iniciarse** *v pron* (a) «ceremonia/negociaciones» to begin, commence (frml) (b) «persona» ~**se EN algo** ⟨en secta⟩ to be initiated INTO sth; ⟨en un arte⟩ to take one's first steps IN sth

iniciativa *f* initiative; **tomó la** ~ he took the initiative

inicio *m* beginning, start

inigualable *adj* ⟨belleza⟩ matchless, incomparable; ⟨precios/oferta⟩ unbeatable

ininteligible *adj* unintelligible, incomprehensible

ininterrumpido -da *adj* ⟨lluvias/trabajo⟩ continuous, uninterrupted; ⟨sueño⟩ uninterrupted; ⟨línea⟩ continuous

injertar [A1] *vt* to graft

injerto *m* (a) (Agr) (acción) grafting; (tallo) graft, scion (b) (Med) graft

injusticia *f* (a) (acto injusto) injustice, act of injustice; **es una** ~ **que te hayan dicho eso** it's unfair of them to have said that to you (b) (cualidad) unfairness, injustice

injustificable *adj* unjustifiable

injustificado -da *adj* unwarranted, unjustified; **despido** ~ unfair dismissal

injusto -ta *adj* unfair; **ser** ~ **CON algn** to be unfair TO *o* ON sb

inmaculado -da *adj* (a) ⟨presentación/vestido/ superficie⟩ immaculate (b) ⟨fama⟩ impeccable

inmadurez *f* immaturity, lack of maturity

inmaduro -ra *adj* ⟨persona/animal⟩ immature; ⟨fruta⟩ unripe

inmediaciones *fpl* vicinity, surrounding area; **el hotel está en las ~ del aeropuerto** the hotel is in the vicinity of the airport; **en las ~ de la capital** in the area around the capital

inmediatamente *adv* immediately

inmediato -ta *adj* (a) ⟨efecto/respuesta⟩ immediate; **de ~** immediately, right away, straightaway (BrE) ⟨zona⟩ immediate; ⟨lugar/ pueblo⟩ **~ A algo** close TO sth

inmejorable *adj* ⟨resultados/posición⟩ excellent, unbeatable; **está en una situación ~** it is superbly located

inmenso -sa *adj* ⟨fortuna/cantidad⟩ immense, vast, huge; ⟨casa/camión⟩ huge, enormous; ⟨alegría/pena⟩ great, immense; **¡es ~!** it's absolutely huge!

inmerecido -da *adj* undeserved, unmerited

inmerso -sa *adj* ⟨submarino/buzo⟩ submerged; ⟨objeto⟩ immersed

inmigración *f* immigration

inmigrante *mf* immigrant

inmigrar [A1] *vi* to immigrate

inmiscuirse [I20] *v pron* **~ EN algo** to interfere IN sth, meddle IN sth

inmobiliaria *f* (a) (agencia) real estate agency (AmE), estate agent's (BrE) (b) (empresa propietaria) real estate company (AmE), property company (BrE) (c) (empresa constructora) property developer

inmoral *adj* immoral

■ *mf*: **eres un ~** you have no morals

inmoralidad *f* immorality

inmortal *adj/mf* immortal

inmortalidad *f* immortality

inmortalizar [A4] *vt* to immortalize

■ **inmortalizarse** *v pron* to achieve immortality, be immortalized

inmovible *adj* immovable

inmóvil *adj* still

inmovilismo *m* resistance to change, immobilism (frml)

inmovilizar [A4] *vt* [1] ⟨persona/país/vehículo⟩ to immobilize [2] (Com, Fin) ⟨capital⟩ to tie up

inmundo -da *adj* (a) ⟨lugar⟩ filthy (b) ⟨sabor/ comida⟩ foul, disgusting (c) (repulsivo) ⟨escena/ película⟩ filthy, disgusting

inmune *adj* immune; **~ A algo** immune TO sth

inmunidad *f* immunity

inmunizar [A4] *vt* to immunize; **~ a algn CONTRA algo** to immunize sb against sth

inmunodeficiencia *f* immunodeficiency

inmunológico -ca *adj* ⟨tolerancia⟩ immunological; ⟨sistema/reacción⟩ immune (before n)

inmutarse [A1] *v pron* «persona»: **cuando se lo dije ni se inmutó** she didn't bat an eyelash *o* (BrE) eyelid when I told her (colloq); **lo escuchó sin ~se** she listened to him unperturbed

innato -ta *adj* innate, inborn

innavegable *adj* ⟨río⟩ unnavigable; ⟨embarcación⟩ unseaworthy

innecesario -ria *adj* unnecessary

innegable *adj* undeniable

innovación *f* innovation

innovador -dora *adj* innovative

■ *m,f* innovator

innovar [A1] *vi* to innovate

innumerable *adj* innumerable

inocencia *f* innocence

inocentada *f* ≈ April Fools' joke (*played on 28 December*); **gastarle** *or* **hacerle ~s a algn** to play practical jokes on sb

inocente *adj* (a) (sin culpa) innocent; (Der) innocent, not guilty; **lo declararon ~** he was found not guilty (b) ⟨broma⟩ harmless (c) (ingenuo) naive, gullible

■ *mf* innocent; **no te hagas el ~** don't play the innocent

inodoro *m* (a) (wáter) toilet, lavatory (b) (taza) bowl, pan

inofensivo -va *adj* harmless, inoffensive

inolvidable *adj* unforgettable

inoportuno -na *adj* (a) ⟨visita/llamada⟩ untimely, inopportune; **llamó en un momento ~** he phoned at a bad moment (b) ⟨comentario/ crítica⟩ ill-timed, inopportune

inquebrantable *adj* ⟨fe⟩ unshakable, unyielding; ⟨lealtad⟩ unswerving; ⟨voluntad/ salud⟩ iron (before n)

inquietante *adj* ⟨noticia/cifras⟩ disturbing, worrying; ⟨síntoma⟩ worrying

inquietarse [A1] *v pron* to worry; **~ POR algo/algn** to worry ABOUT sth/sb

inquieto -ta *adj* (a) [ESTAR] (preocupado) worried (b) [SER] (emprendedor) enterprising; (vivo) lively, inquiring (before n) (c) (que se mueve mucho) restless

inquietud *f* (a) (preocupación) worry; **~ POR algo** concern ABOUT sth (b) (interés): **es una persona sin ~es** she has no interest in anything; **su ~ filosófica** his philosophical preoccupations

inquilino -na *m,f* (arrendatario) tenant

Inquisición *f* (Hist): **la ~** the Inquisition

inquisidor *m* inquisitor

insaciable *adj* insatiable; ⟨sed⟩ unquenchable

insalubre *adj* unhealthy

insalvable *adj* insurmountable, insuperable

insatisfacción *f* dissatisfaction

insatisfactorio -ria *adj* unsatisfactory

insatisfecho -cha *adj* (a) (descontento) dissatisfied; **~ CON algo/algn** dissatisfied WITH sth/sb (b) ⟨hambre/deseo⟩ unsatisfied

inscribir [I34] *vt* (en registro) to register; (en curso, escuela) to register, enroll*

■ **inscribirse** *v pron* «persona» (en curso, colegio) to enroll*, register; (en concurso) to enter; (en congreso) to register

inscripción *f* (a) (para curso) enrollment*, registration; (para concurso) entry; (en congreso) registration; **la ~ se cierra el ...** the last day for enrollment is ... (b) (de un nacimiento) registration (c) (leyenda, lema) inscription

inscrito -ta, (RPI) **inscripto -ta** *pp*: ▸ INSCRIBIR

insecticida *m* insecticide

insecto *m* insect

inseguridad *f* **(a)** (falta de confianza) insecurity;
~ **laboral** job insecurity **(b)** (falta de firmeza,
estabilidad) unsteadiness **(c)** (falta de garantías)
insecurity, lack of security **(d)** (en ciudad, barrio):
la ~ ciudadana the lack of safety on our streets

inseguro -ra *adj* **(a)** (falto de confianza) insecure
(b) (falto de firmeza, estabilidad) unsteady **(c)**
⟨situación/futuro⟩ insecure **(d)** ⟨ciudad/barrio⟩
unsafe, dangerous

inseminación *f* insemination; ~ **artificial**
artificial insemination

insensatez *f* **(a)** (cualidad) foolishness,
senselessness **(b)** (dicho, hecho): **lo que has dicho/
hecho es una ~** that was a stupid thing to say/do

insensato -ta *adj* foolish
■ *m,f* fool

insensible *adj* insensitive; ~ **al frío**
insensitive to the cold

inseparable *adj* inseparable

insertar [A1] *vt* to insert

inservible *adj* (inútil) useless; (inutilizable)
unusable

insignia *f* **(a)** (distintivo, emblema) insignia,
emblem; (prendedor) badge, button (AmE) **(b)**
(bandera) flag; (estandarte) standard, banner

insignificante *adj* ⟨asunto/detalle/suma⟩
insignificant, trivial; ⟨objeto/regalo⟩ small;
⟨persona⟩ insignificant

insinuación *f* hint; (que ofende) insinuation;
hacerle insinuaciones (amorosas) a algn ▶
INSINUARSE

insinuante *adj* ⟨mirada/voz⟩ suggestive;
⟨escote⟩ provocative

insinuar [A18] *vt* to imply, hint at; (algo ofensivo)
to insinuate
■ **insinuarse** *v pron*: **insinuársele a algn** to make
advances to sb, to make a pass at sb

insípido -da *adj* insipid, bland

insistencia *f* insistence; **con ~** insistently

insistente *adj* ⟨persona⟩ insistent;
⟨recomendaciones/pedidos⟩ repeated (*before n*),
persistent; ⟨timbrazos⟩ insistent, repeated (*before
n*)

insistir [I1] *vi* to insist; **ya que insistes** if you
insist; **es inútil que insistas** there's no point
going on about it; ~ **EN hacer algo** to insist ON
doing sth; **insiste en que lo hagamos** he insists
(that) we do it; **insiste en que es suyo** she is
adamant that it's hers; ~ **SOBRE** *or* **EN algo** to
stress sth

insociable *adj* unsociable

insolación *f* (Med) sunstroke; **agarrar una ~** to
get sunstroke

insolencia *f* **(a)** (cualidad) insolence **(b)** (dicho):
no pienso tolerar sus ~s I don't intend putting
up with his insolence *o* his insolent behavior;
contestarle así fue una ~ it was very rude of you
to answer him like that

insolente *adj* rude, insolent
■ *mf*: **es una ~** she's so rude *o* insolent

insólito -ta *adj* unusual

insolvencia *f* insolvency

insolvente *adj* insolvent

insomnio *m* insomnia

insonorizado -da *adj* soundproof

insoportable *adj* unbearable, intolerable

insostenible *adj* **(a)** ⟨situación/gasto⟩
unsustainable **(b)** ⟨posición/tesis⟩ untenable

inspección *f* inspection

inspeccionar [A1] *vt* to inspect

inspector -tora *m,f* inspector; ~ **de Hacienda**
revenue agent (AmE), tax inspector (BrE); ~ **de
policía** (police) inspector

inspiración *f* (Art, Lit, Mús) inspiration

inspirado -da *adj* inspired

inspirar [A1] *vt* **1** ⟨confianza⟩ to inspire;
⟨compasión⟩ to arouse, inspire; **sabe ~les
confianza** she knows how to inspire confidence in
them **2** «obra/canción/persona» to inspire
■ **inspirarse** *v pron*: **~se EN algo** «persona/obra/
ley» to be inspired BY sth

instalación *f* **(a)** (colocación) installation **(b)**
(equipo, dispositivo) system; **la ~ sanitaria** the
plumbing **(c) instalaciones** *fpl* (dependencias)
installations (*pl*); **instalaciones deportivas** sports
facilities

instalar [A1] *vt* **(a)** (colocar y conectar) ⟨teléfono/
lavaplatos⟩ to install; ⟨antena⟩ to erect, put up;
(Inf) ⟨programa⟩ to install **(b)** (colocar)
⟨archivador/piano⟩ to put **(c)** ⟨oficina/consultorio⟩
to open, set up
■ **instalarse** *v pron* to settle, install oneself

instantánea *f* snapshot

instantáneo -nea *adj* **(a)** ⟨resultado/crédito⟩
instant (*before n*); ⟨reacción⟩ instantaneous,
immediate **(b)** ⟨café⟩ instant (*before n*)

instante *m* moment; **un ~, por favor** just a
second *o* moment, please; **me llama a cada ~** he
calls me all the time; **al ~** right away,
straightaway (BrE)

instigar [A3] *vt* ~ **a algn A algo/hacer algo** to
incite sb TO sth/do sth

instintivo -va *adj* instinctive

instinto *m* instinct; **por ~** instinctively; ~ **de
conservación** survival instinct

institución *f* institution

instituto *m* institute; ~ **nacional de
bachillerato** (Esp) high school (AmE), secondary
school (BrE)

institutriz *f* governess

instrucción *f* **1** (educación) education;
(práctica) training; ~ **militar** military training
2 instrucciones *fpl* **(a)** (de aparato, juego)
instructions (*pl*); (para llegar a un lugar) directions
(*pl*) **(b)** (órdenes) instructions

instructor -tora *m,f* instructor

instruir [I20] *vt* (adiestrar, educar) ~ **a algn EN
algo** to instruct *o* train sb IN sth
■ **instruirse** *v pron* (refl) to broaden one's mind,
improve oneself

instrumental *adj* (Mús) instrumental

■ *m* (Med) equipment, set of instruments

instrumentar *vt* [A1] (Mús) to orchestrate

instrumento *m* **1** (en general) instrument; ~ de cuerda string instrument; ~s de precisión precision instruments **2** (medio) means

insubordinación *f* insubordination

insubordinarse [A1] *v pron* ~ (CONTRA algn) (desobedecer) to be insubordinate (TO sb); (sublevarse) to rebel (AGAINST sb)

insuficiencia *f* (escasez): ~ de medios lack of resources; ~ de personal staff shortage

insuficiente *adj* (a) ⟨medios/cantidad⟩ insufficient (b) (Educ) ⟨trabajo⟩ unsatisfactory ■ *m* (Esp) fail

insular *adj* insular

insulina *f* insulin

insulso -sa *adj* (a) ⟨comida⟩ insipid (b) ⟨persona⟩ insipid; ⟨conversación/libro⟩ dull

insultante *adj* insulting

insultar [A1] *vt* (a) (proferir insultos) to insult (b) (ofender) to insult, offend

insulto *m* insult

insumiso -sa *m,f: person refusing to do military service*

insumos *mpl* (esp AmL) consumables (*pl*)

insuperable *adj* (a) (insalvable) ⟨problema/dificultad⟩ insurmountable, insuperable (b) (inmejorable) ⟨calidad/precio⟩ unbeatable

insurgente *mf* (frml) rebel, insurgent (frml)

insurrección *f* (frml) insurrection (frml)

intachable *adj* impeccable, irreproachable

intacto -ta *adj* (íntegro, no dañado) intact

integración *f* integration

integrado -da *adj* integrated

integral *adj* (a) (completo, total) comprehensive (b) (incorporado) built-in

integrante *mf* member

integrar [A1] *vt* **1** (formar) ⟨grupo/organización⟩ to make up **2** (incorporar) ⟨idea/plan⟩ to incorporate **3** (Mat, Sociol) to integrate **4** (CS) ⟨suma/cantidad⟩ to pay
■ **integrarse** *v pron* (a) (asimilarse) to integrate, fit in; ~se A or EN algo to integrate INTO sth, fit INTO sth (b) (unirse) ~se A or EN algo to join sth

integridad *f* integrity

integrismo *m* fundamentalism

integrista *adj* fundamentalist ■ *mf* fundamentalist

íntegro -gra *adj* **1** ⟨texto⟩ unabridged; se proyectó en versión íntegra they screened the full-length version **2** ⟨persona⟩ upright

intelecto *m* intellect

intelectual *adj/mf* intellectual

inteligencia *f* **1** (a) (facultad, ser inteligente) intelligence (b) (comprensión) understanding **2** (Mil, Pol) intelligence

inteligente *adj* intelligent; ⟨persona⟩ intelligent, clever

inteligible *adj* intelligible

intemperie *f: pasar la noche a la ~* to spend the night out in the open; gente sin hogar que duerme a la ~ people who sleep rough

intención *f* intention; no fue mi ~ ofenderte I didn't mean to offend you; tiene buenas/malas intenciones she's well-intentioned/up to no good;

lo dijo con segunda *or* doble ~ she had an ulterior motive for saying it; con la mejor ~ with the best of intentions; lo que cuenta es la ~ it's the thought that counts; vine con (la) ~ de ayudarte I came to help you; tiene (la) ~ de abrir un bar she plans *o* intends to open a bar; no tengo la menor ~ de venderlo I have no intention whatsoever of selling it

intencionado -da *adj* (hecho a propósito) deliberate, intentional; mal ~ malicious, hostile; bien ~ well-intentioned

intendencia *f* (a) (Andes) (división territorial) administrative division (b) (RPl) (gobierno municipal) town/city council; (edificio) town/city hall

intendente *mf* (a) (Andes) governor (b) (RPl) mayor

intensidad *f* (a) (de terremoto) intensity, strength; (del viento) strength; (de dolor, sentimiento) intensity (b) (Elec, Fís) intensity

intensivo -va *adj* intensive

intenso -sa *adj* (a) ⟨frío/luz/color⟩ intense (b) ⟨emoción/mirada⟩ intense; ⟨dolor/sentimiento⟩ intense, acute (c) ⟨esfuerzo⟩ strenuous; ⟨negociaciones⟩ intensive

intentar [A1] *vt* to try; ¡inténtalo otra vez! try again!; ~ un aterrizaje de emergencia to attempt an emergency landing; ~ hacer algo to try to do sth; ¿has intentado que te lo arreglen? have you tried getting *o* to get it fixed?

intento *m* (a) (tentativa) attempt (b) (Méx) (propósito) intention, aim

intercalar [A1] *vt* ~ algo EN algo ⟨en texto⟩ to insert sth INTO sth; intercaló algunas citas en su discurso she interspersed her speech with some quotations; intercala uno rojo cada dos azules put a red one between every two blue ones

intercambiable *adj* interchangeable

intercambiar [A1] *vt* ⟨impresiones/ideas⟩ to exchange; ⟨sellos/revistas⟩ to swap

intercambio *m* (a) (de ideas, información, bienes) exchange (b) (de sellos, revistas) swap; (de estudiantes, prisioneros) exchange

interceder [E1] *vi* (frml) to intercede; intercedió por ellos ante el rey he interceded for them with the king

interceptar [A1] *vt* (a) ⟨correspondencia/mensaje⟩ to intercept (b) ⟨teléfono⟩ to tap (c) (Dep) ⟨balón/pase⟩ to intercept; ⟨golpe⟩ to block (d) ⟨calzada/carretera⟩ to block; ~ el paso to block the way

intercomunicar [A2] *vt* to link (up)

interés *m* **1** (en general) interest; de ~ turístico of interest to tourists; pon más ~ en tus estudios take more interest in your schoolwork; tengo especial ~ en que ... I am particularly concerned *o* keen that ...; tienen gran ~ en verlo they are very interested in seeing it; por tu propio ~ in your own interest, for your own good; actúa solo por ~ he acts purely in his own interest *o* out of self-interest; conflicto de intereses conflict of interests **2** (Fin) interest; a *or* con un ~ del 12% at 12% interest *o* at an interest rate of 12%; ganar intereses to earn interest; tipo de ~ rate of interest

interesado -da *adj* (a) [ESTAR] (que muestra ···⟶

interés) interested; ～ **EN algo** interested IN sth **(b)**
[SER] (egoísta) selfish; **actuó de manera interesada**
he acted selfishly **(c)** (parcial) biased, biassed
■ *m,f* **(a)** (que tiene interés) interested party (frml);
los ～s deberán ... all those interested *o* (frml) all
interested parties should ... **(b)** (que busca su
provecho): **es un ～** he always acts in his own
interest *o* out of self-interest

interesante *adj* interesting; **hacerse el ～**
(fam) to try to draw attention to oneself

interesar [A1] *vi* **(a)** (suscitar interés): (+ *me/te/le*
etc) **no me interesa la política** I'm not interested
in politics; **esto a ti no te interesa** this doesn't
concern you, this is no concern of yours **(b)**
(convenir): **～ía comprobar los datos** it would be
useful/advisable to check the data; **me interesa
este tipo de préstamo** this sort of loan would suit
me
■ ～ *vt* ～ **a algn EN algo** to interest sb IN sth, get
sb interested IN sth
■ **interesarse** *v pron* **(a)** (tener interés) to take
interest; **～se EN** *or* **POR algo** to take an interest
IN sth **(b)** (preguntar) **～se POR algo/algn** to ask *o*
inquire ABOUT sth/sb

interferencia *f* interference

interferir [I11] *vt* **(a)** (obstaculizar) to interfere in
(b) ⟨emisión⟩ to jam
■ ～ *vi* to interfere, meddle; ～ **EN algo** ⟨en asunto⟩
to interfere *o* meddle IN sth
■ **interferirse** *v pron* **～se EN algo** to interfere *o*
meddle IN sth

interfono *m* **(a)** (portero automático) intercom
(AmE), entryphone (BrE); (intercomunicador) intercom
(b) (para bebés) baby alarm

interinato *m* (esp AmL) (cargo) temporary post *o*
position

interino -na *adj* ⟨secretario/director⟩ acting
(before n); ⟨profesor⟩ substitute (AmE) (before n),
supply (BrE) (before n); ⟨gobierno⟩ interim (before
n); **médico ～** locum
■ *m,f* (funcionario) temporary clerk (*o* accountant
etc); (profesor) substitute teacher (AmE), supply
teacher (BrE); (médico) locum

interior *adj* **(a)** ⟨patio/escalera⟩ interior,
internal, inside (before n); ⟨habitación/piso⟩ *with
windows facing onto a central staircase or patio*
(b) ⟨bolsillo/revestimiento⟩ inside (before n); **en la
parte ～** inside *o* on the inside **(c)** ⟨vida/mundo⟩
inner **(d)** ⟨política/comercio⟩ domestic, internal
■ *m* **1** **(a)** (de cajón, maleta, coche) inside; (de
edificio) interior, inside; (de un país) interior; **en el
～ de la habitación** inside the room **(b)** (Méx, RPl,
Ven) (provincias) provinces (*pl*) **(c)** (de una persona):
en su ～ estaba muy intranquilo inside he was
very worried; **allá en su ～ la amaba** deep down
he really loved her
2 Interior *m* (period) (Ministerio del Interior)
Ministry of the Interior, ≈ Department of the
Interior (in US), ≈ Home Office (in UK)
3 interiores *mpl* (Col, Ven) (Indum) underwear

interjección *f* interjection

intermediario -ria *adj* intermediary
■ *m,f* **(a)** (Com) middleman, intermediary **(b)**
(mediador) intermediary, mediator, go-between

intermedio¹ -dia *adj* **(a)** ⟨punto/etapa⟩
intermediate; **alumnos de nivel ～** students at

intermediate level **(b)** ⟨calidad/tamaño⟩ medium
(before n); **un color ～ entre el gris y el verde** a
color halfway between gray and green

intermedio² *m* (Espec) intermission, interval

interminable *adj* ⟨serie/discusión/espera⟩
interminable, never-ending; ⟨cola/fila⟩ endless,
never-ending

intermitente *adj* **(a)** ⟨lluvia⟩ intermittent,
sporadic **(b)** ⟨luz⟩ flashing; ⟨señal⟩ intermittent
(c) ⟨fiebre⟩ intermittent
■ *m* turn signal (AmE), indicator (BrE)

internacional *adj* international; ⟨noticia⟩
foreign (before n), international (before n);
⟨política⟩ foreign (before n); **de fama ～**
internationally famous; Ⓢ **salidas internacionales**
international departures

internado¹ -da *adj* (AmL): **está ～** he's been
admitted to (the) hospital, he's been hospitalized

internado² *m* **(a)** (Educ) boarding school **(b)**
(Med) position or term as an intern or a houseman
at a hospital, internship (AmE)

internar [A1] *vt*: **la ～on en un manicomio** she
was put in an asylum; **lo ～on en el hospital** he
was admitted to (the) hospital; **tuvimos que ～lo**
we had to take him to (the) hospital
■ **internarse** *v pron* **(a)** (adentrarse) **～se EN algo**
⟨en bosque/espesura⟩ to penetrate INTO sth, to go
deep INTO sth **(b)** (AmL) (en hospital) to go into the
hospital

internauta *mf* Internet user

Internet /inter'ne/ *m* (a veces *f*): **(el) ～** the
Internet

interno¹ -na *adj* **1** (en general) internal **2** **(a)**
(Educ): **está ～ en un colegio inglés** he is a
boarder at an English school **(b)** (Med): **médico ～**
≈ intern (in US), ≈ houseman (in UK)
■ *m,f* **(a)** (Educ) boarder **(b)** (en cárcel) inmate **(c)**
(médico) ≈ intern (in US), ≈ houseman (in UK)

interno² *m* (RPl) (Telec) (extensión) extension

interponerse [E22] *v pron*: **se interpuso y
paró la pelea** he stepped in and stopped the fight;
nada se interpone en su camino nothing stands
in her way

interpretación *f* **(a)** (de un texto)
interpretation **(b)** (Cin, Mús, Teat) interpretation
(c) (traducción oral) interpreting; **～ simultánea**
simultaneous interpreting

interpretar [A1] *vt* **1** ⟨texto/comentario/
sueño⟩ to interpret; **interpretó mal tus palabras**
she misinterpreted what you said **2** **(a)** ⟨papel/
personaje⟩ to play **(b)** ⟨pieza/sinfonía⟩ to play,
perform; ⟨canción⟩ to sing

intérprete *mf* **1** (traductor oral) interpreter; ～
jurado sworn interpreter **2** (Mús) performer;
(cantante) singer

interpuesto -ta *pp*: ▶ INTERPONERSE

interrogación *f* **(a)** (de un sospechoso)
interrogation **(b)** (Chi) (Educ) test

interrogar [A3] *vt* ⟨testigo/acusado⟩ to
question, examine; ⟨detenido/sospechoso⟩ to
interrogate, question; ⟨examinando⟩ to examine

interrogatorio *m* (de acusado, testigo)
questioning, examination; (de detenido)
interrogation, questioning

interrumpir [I1] *vt* **1** (temporalmente) **(a)**
⟨persona/reunión⟩ to interrupt **(b)** ⟨suministro⟩ to
cut off; ⟨servicio⟩ to suspend; ⟨tráfico⟩ to hold up;

las obras no ~**án el paso** the work will not block the road **2** **(a)** (acortar) ⟨viaje/vacaciones/reunión⟩ to cut short **(b)** ⟨embarazo⟩ to terminate
■ ~ *vi* to interrupt
interrupción *f* interruption; ~ **(voluntaria) del embarazo** termination of pregnancy
interruptor *m* switch
intersección *f* **(a)** (en geometría) intersection **(b)** (frml) (Transp) intersection, junction
intertanto *m*: **en el** ~ (AmL) in the meantime
interurbano -na *adj* ⟨transporte/autobús/llamada⟩ long-distance; ⟨tren⟩ intercity
intervalo *m* **(a)** (de tiempo) interval; (entre clases) recess (AmE), break (BrE) **(b)** (Mús) interval **(c)** (Teatr) (intermedio) intermission (AmE), interval (BrE) **(d)** (en el espacio) gap
intervención *f* **(a)** (en general) intervention; **se probó su** ~ **en el atraco** his involvement in the robbery was proved; **una política de no** ~ a policy of nonintervention; ~ **quirúrgica** operation **(b)** (de droga, armas) seizure, confiscation
intervenir [I31] *vi* **(a)** (en debate, operación) to take part; (en espectáculo) to appear, perform **(b)** (mediar) to intervene, intercede (frml); **en mi decisión intervinieron muchos factores** there were many factors involved in my decision; ~ **en una pelea** o step in to stop a fight; (involucrarse) to get involved in a fight
■ ~ *vt* **1** **(a)** ⟨teléfono⟩ to tap **(b)** (tomar control de) ⟨empresa⟩ to place ... in administration **(c)** (inspeccionar) ⟨cuentas⟩ to audit, inspect **(d)** ⟨armas/droga⟩ to seize, confiscate **2** (operar) to operate on; **fue intervenido en una clínica privada** he underwent surgery in a private clinic
interviú *f* interview
intestinal *adj* intestinal
intestino *m* intestine, gut
inti *m* inti (former Peruvian unit of currency)
intimar [A1] *vi* ~ **CON algn** to get close TO sb
intimidación *f* intimidation
intimidad *f* **1** **(a)** (ambiente privado) privacy; **en la** ~ **del hogar** in the privacy of one's home **(b)** (relación estrecha) intimacy **2** **intimidades** *fpl* **(a)** (cosas íntimas) private life, personal o private affairs (pl) **(b)** (euf) (partes pudendas) private parts (pl) (euph), privates (pl) (colloq)
intimidante *adj* intimidating
intimidar [A1] *vt* **(a)** (atemorizar) to intimidate **(b)** (amenazar) to threaten
íntimo -ma *adj* **(a)** ⟨vida/diario/ceremonia⟩ private; ⟨secreto⟩ intimate; ⟨ambiente⟩ intimate; **una cena íntima** a small dinner (with a few friends/members of the family); (en pareja) a candlelit o romantic dinner **(b)** ⟨amistad⟩ close; ⟨amigo⟩ close, intimate (before n)
intocable *adj* **(a)** (sagrado) sacred, sacrosanct **(b)** ⟨tema⟩ taboo **(c)** ⟨casta⟩ untouchable
intolerable *adj* intolerable
intolerancia *f* intolerance
intolerante *adj* intolerant
intoxicación *f* (Med) intoxication, poisoning; ~ **alimenticia** food poisoning; ~ **etílica** (Med) alcohol poisoning
intoxicar [A2] *vt* to poison
■ **intoxicarse** *v pron* to get food poisoning

intranquilizar [A4] *vt* to worry
intranquilo -la *adj* **(a)** [ESTAR] (preocupado) worried, anxious **(b)** (agitado) restless
intranscendente *adj* ▶ INTRASCENDENTE
intransferible *adj* not transferable, untransferable
intransigente *adj* intransigent
intransitivo -va *adj* intransitive
intrascendente *adj* ⟨episodio/detalle⟩ insignificant, unimportant; ⟨comentario⟩ trivial
intravenoso -sa *adj* intravenous
intriga *f* intrigue; **novela/película de** ~ thriller
intrigante *mf* schemer, intriguer (AmE)
intrigar [A3] *vt* to intrigue
■ ~ *vi* to scheme
intrincado -da *adj* **(a)** ⟨problema/asunto⟩ intricate, complex; ⟨laberinto/sistema⟩ complicated **(b)** ⟨nudo⟩ tangled
introducción *f* introduction; ~ **A algo** introduction TO sth
introducir [I6] *vt* **1** (en general) to put ... in; ⟨moneda⟩ to insert; ~ **algo EN algo** to put sth INTO sth; ⟨moneda⟩ to insert sth IN sth **2** **(a)** ⟨cambios/medidas/ley⟩ to introduce, bring in; ⟨producto⟩ to introduce **(b)** ⟨contrabando/drogas⟩ to bring in, smuggle in **3** (presentar) ⟨acto/cantante⟩ to introduce
■ **introducirse** *v pron* **(a)** (meterse) «ladrón» to gain access; **la moneda se introdujo por una grieta** the coin fell down a crack **(b)** (entrar en uso) «moda» to come in; «costumbre» to be introduced **(c)** (hacerse conocido) «escritor/actor» to become known
introductorio -ria *adj* introductory
introvertido -da *adj* introverted
■ *m,f* introvert
intruso -sa *m,f* intruder; (Inf) cracker (colloq)
intuición *f* intuition; **hacer algo por** ~ to do sth intuitively; **tuve la** ~ **de que** ... I had a feeling that ...
intuir [I20] *vt* to sense; **intuía que me iba a llamar** I had a feeling he was going to ring me
intuitivo -va *adj* intuitive
inundación *f* (en área limitada, casa) flood; (en zona más amplia) floods (pl), flooding
inundar [A1] *vt* **(a)** «riada/aguas» to flood, inundate (frml); «turistas/manifestantes» to inundate, crowd **(b)** «persona» (con agua) to flood; (con productos) to flood, swamp; ~ **algo DE** or **CON algo** to flood sth WITH sth
■ **inundarse** *v pron* (de agua) to be flooded
inusitado -da *adj* unusual, rare
inusual *adj* unusual
inútil *adj* useless; **es** ~ **que insistas** there's no point (in) insisting
■ *mf*: **es un** ~ he's useless
invadir [I1] *vt* **(a)** «ejército/fuerzas» to invade **(b)** «espacio aéreo/aguas» to enter, encroach upon **(c)** «tristeza/alegría» to overcome, overwhelm
invalidez *f* (Med) disability, disablement
inválido -da *adj* (Med) ⟨persona⟩ disabled, handicapped
■ *m,f* invalid, disabled person
invariable *adj* **(a)** ⟨precio/estado⟩ constant, stable **(b)** (Ling) invariable

invasión f **1** (de zona, país) invasion **2** (Col) (chabolas) shantytown

invasor -sora m,f invader

invencible adj (a) ⟨luchador/equipo⟩ unbeatable, invincible (b) ⟨miedo/timidez⟩ insuperable, insurmountable

invención f (a) (en general) invention (b) (mentira) fabrication

inventar [A1] vt (a) ⟨aparato/sistema⟩ to invent (b) ⟨juego/palabra⟩ to make up, invent; ⟨cuento/ excusa/mentira⟩ to make up

inventario m (de negocio) inventory, stock list; (de casa) inventory

inventiva f inventiveness; tiene mucha ~ she's very inventive

invento m invention

inventor -tora m,f inventor

invernadero m greenhouse

invernal adj ⟨lluvias⟩ winter (before n); ⟨frío⟩ wintry

inverosímil adj implausible

inversión f **1** (de dinero, tiempo, esfuerzos) investment **2** (de posiciones, términos) reversal; (de una imagen) inversion; ~ térmica thermal inversion

inversionista mf investor

inverso -sa adj ⟨sentido/orden⟩ reverse; puedes ordenarlo así o a la inversa you can arrange it like this or the other way around

inversor -sora m,f investor

invertido -da adj ⟨posición/orden⟩ reversed; ⟨imagen/figura⟩ inverted, reversed

invertir [I11] vt **1** ⟨dinero/capital⟩ to invest; ⟨tiempo⟩ to invest, devote **2** ⟨orden/papeles/ términos⟩ to reverse; ⟨imagen/figura⟩ to invert, reverse
■ ~ vi to invest; ~ EN algo to invest IN sth
■ **invertirse** v pron «papeles/funciones» to be reversed

investigación f (a) (de caso, delito) investigation; (por comisión especial) inquiry (b) (Educ, Med, Tec) research; ~ científica scientific research; ~ de mercados market research

investigador -dora m,f (a) (que indaga) investigator (b) (Educ, Med, Tec) researcher

investigar [A3] vt (a) ⟨delito/caso⟩ to investigate (b) (Educ, Med, Tec) «persona» to research, do research into
■ ~ vi (a) «policía» to investigate (b) (Educ, Med, Tec) ~ SOBRE algo to research o do research INTO sth

invierno m winter; (en la zona tropical) rainy season; en ~ in winter, in wintertime; ropa de ~ winter clothes

invierta, inviertas, etc ▶ INVERTIR

invirtiera, invirtió, etc ▶ INVERTIR

invisible adj invisible

invitación f invitation

invitado -da m,f guest; tenemos ~s a cenar we have people coming to dinner; los ~s a la boda the wedding guests

invitar [A1] vt to invite; ~ a algn A algo to invite sb TO sth; te invito a una copa I'll buy o get you a drink; ~ a algn A hacer algo or A QUE haga algo to invite sb to do sth; me invitó a cenar (en casa) she invited me (round) to dinner; (en restaurante) she invited me out to dinner
■ ~ vi «persona»: invito yo it's on me, I'm buying; invita la casa it's on the house

invocar [A2] f (a) ⟨divinidad/santos⟩ to invoke (frml), to call on (b) ⟨auxilio/protección⟩ to appeal for

involucrar [A1] vt (a) (implicar) to involve; ~ a algn EN algo ⟨en asunto/crimen⟩ to involve sb IN sth (b) (AmL) (conllevar) to involve
■ **involucrarse** v pron «persona» to get involved

involuntario -ria adj ⟨error/movimiento/ gesto⟩ involuntary; ⟨testigo/cómplice⟩ unwitting

inyección f (Med) injection; (dosis) injection, shot (colloq); le puso una ~ she gave him an injection

inyectado -da adj: ojos ~s en sangre bloodshot eyes

inyectar [A1] vt to inject; le ~on morfina they gave him morphine injections/a shot of morphine
■ **inyectarse** v pron (refl) «persona» to give oneself an injection, inject oneself; se inyectó heroína he injected himself with heroin

ion m ion

ir [I27] vi
I 1 (a) (trasladarse, desplazarse) to go; ~ en taxi to go by taxi; iban a caballo/a pie they were on horseback/on foot; ~ por mar to go by sea; ¡Fernando! — ¡voy! Fernando! — (just) coming! o I'll be right there!; el ~ y venir de los invitados the coming and going of the guests; vamos a casa let's go home; ¿adónde va este tren? where's this train going (to)?; ~ de compras/de caza to go shopping/hunting; ya vamos para allá we're on our way; ¿por dónde se va a ...? how do you get to ...?; ~ por or (Esp) a por algo/algn to go to get sth/sb; voy (a) por pan I'm going to get some bread (b) (asistir) to go to; voy a clases nocturnas I go to evening classes; ya va al colegio she's already at school
2 (expresando propósito) ~ A + INF: ¿has ido a verla? have you been to see her?; ve a ayudarla go and help her; ver tb ~ V AUX 1
3 (al arrojar algo, arrojarse): tírame la llave — ¡allá va! throw me the key — here you are o there you go!; tírate del trampolín — ¡allá voy! jump off the board! — here I go/come!
4 «comentario»: no iba con mala intención it wasn't meant unkindly; eso va por ti también that goes for you too, and the same goes for you
II 1 (+ compl) (sin énfasis en el movimiento): iban cantando por el camino they sang as they went along; ¿van cómodos? are you comfortable?;

íbamos sentados we were sitting down; **vas muy cargada** you have a lot to carry; **yo iba a la cabeza** I was in the lead

2 (refiriéndose al atuendo): **iban de largo** they wore long dresses; **voy a ~ de Drácula** I'm going to go as Dracula; **iba de verde** she was dressed in green

3 (en calidad de) **~ DE algo** to go (along) AS sth; **yo fui de intérprete** I went along as interpreter

III 1 «*camino/sendero*» (llevar) **~ A algo** to lead TO sth, to go TO sth

2 (extenderse, abarcar): **la autopista va desde Madrid hasta Valencia** the highway goes from Madrid to Valencia; **el período que va desde ... hasta ...** the period from ... to ...

IV 1 (marchar, desarrollarse): **¿cómo va el nuevo trabajo?** how's the new job going?; **va de mal en peor** it's going from bad to worse; **¿cómo te va?** how's it going?, how are things? (colloq), what's up? (AmE colloq); **¿cómo les fue en Italia?** how was Italy?, how did you get on in Italy?; **me fue mal/ bien en el examen** I did badly/well in the exam; **¡que te vaya bien!** all the best!, take care!; **¡que te vaya bien (en) el examen!** good luck in the exam

2 (en competiciones): **¿cómo van? — 3-1** what's the score? — 3-1; **voy ganando yo** I'm ahead, I'm winning

3 (en el desarrollo de algo): **¿por dónde van en historia?** where have you got (up) to in history?; **¿todavía vas por la página 20?** are you still on page 20?

4 (estar en camino): **¡vamos para viejos!** we're getting on o old!; **va para los cincuenta** she's going on fifty; **ya va para dos años que ...** it's getting on for two years since ...

5 (sumar, hacer): **ya van tres veces que te lo digo** this is the third time I've told you; **con este van seis** six, counting this one

6 (haber transcurrido): **en lo que va del** or (Esp) **de año/mes** so far this year/month

V 1 (deber colocarse) to go; **¿dónde van las toallas?** where do the towels go?; **¡qué va!** (fam): **¿has terminado? — ¡qué va!** have you finished? — you must be joking!; **¿se disgustó? — ¡qué va!** did she get upset? — not at all!; **vamos a perder el avión — ¡qué va!** we're going to miss the plane — no way!

2 (a) (combinar) **~ CON algo** to go WITH sth (b) (sentar bien, convenir) (+ *me/te/le etc*): **el negro no te va bien** black doesn't suit you; **te ~á bien un descanso** a rest will do you good

3 (Méx) (tomar partido por, apoyar) **~le A algo/algn** to support sth/sb; **le va al equipo peruano** he supports the Peruvian team

VI 1 **vamos (a)** (expresando incredulidad, fastidio): **¡vamos! ¿eso quién se lo va a creer?** come off it o come on! who do you think's going to believe that? **(b)** (intentando tranquilizar, animar, dar prisa): **vamos, mujer, dile algo** go on, say something to him; **¡vamos, date prisa!** come on, hurry up! **(c)** (al aclarar, resumir): **eso sería un disparate, vamos, digo yo** that would be a stupid thing to do, well, that's what I think anyway; **vamos, que no es una persona de fiar** basically, he's not very trustworthy; **es mejor que el otro, vamos** it's better than the other one, anyway

2 **vaya (a)** (expresando sorpresa, contrariedad): **¡vaya! ¡tú por aquí!** what a surprise! what are you

doing here?; **¡vaya! ¡se ha vuelto a caer!** oh no o (colloq) damn! it's fallen over again! **(b)** (Esp) (para enfatizar): **¡vaya cochazo!** what a car!

■ **~** *v aux* **~ A + INF:** 1 (a) (para expresar tiempo futuro, propósito) to be going to + INF; **voy a estudiar medicina** I'm going to study medicine; **va a hacer dos años que ...** it's getting on for two years since ... **(b)** (en propuestas, sugerencias): **vamos a ver ¿cómo dices que te llamas?** now then, what did you say your name was?; **bueno, vamos a trabajar** all right, let's get to work

2 (al prevenir, hacer recomendaciones): **que no se te vaya a caer** make sure you don't drop it; **cuidado, no te vayas a caer** mind you don't fall (colloq); **lleva el paraguas, no vaya a ser que llueva** take the umbrella, in case it rains

3 (expresando un proceso paulatino): **poco a poco irá aprendiendo** she'll learn little by little; **ya puedes ~ haciéndote a la idea** you'd better get used to the idea; **la situación ha ido empeorando** the situation has been getting worse and worse

■ **irse** *v pron* 1 (marcharse) to leave; **¿por qué te vas tan temprano?** why are you leaving o going so soon?; **vámonos** let's go; **bueno, me voy** right then, I'm taking off (AmE) o (BrE) I'm off; **no te vayas** don't go; **vete a la cama** go to bed; **se fue de casa/de la empresa** she left home/the company; **vete de aquí** get out of here; **se han ido de viaje** they're away, they've gone away

2 (consumirse, gastarse): **¡cómo se va el dinero!** I don't know where the money goes!; **se me va medio sueldo en el alquiler** half my salary goes on the rent

3 (desaparecer) «*mancha/dolor*» to go; **se ha ido la luz** the electricity's gone off; (+ *me/te/le etc*) **¿se te ha ido el dolor de cabeza?** has your headache gone?

4 (salirse, escaparse) «*líquido/gas*» to escape; **se le está yendo el aire al globo** the balloon's losing air o going down

5 (caerse, perder el equilibrio) (+ *compl*): **~se de boca/espaldas** to fall flat on one's face/back; **me iba para atrás** I was falling backwards; **frenó y nos fuimos todos para adelante** he braked and we all went flying forwards

ira *f* rage, anger

Irak, Iraq *m* Iraq

Irán *m* Iran

iraní *adj/mf* Iranian

iraquí *adj/mf* Iraqi

irguieron, irguió, etc ▶ ERGUIR

iris *m* (*pl* **~**) iris

Irlanda *f* Ireland; **~ del Norte** Northern Ireland

irlandés¹ -desa *adj* Irish
■ *m,f* (persona) (*m*) Irishman; (*f*) Irishwoman; **los irlandeses** the Irish, Irish people

irlandés² *m* (idioma) Irish (Gaelic)

IRM *fpl* (= **Imágenes por resonancia magnética**) MRI

ironía *f* irony

irónico -ca *adj* (a) ‹*situación*› ironic (b) ‹*persona/comentario/tono*› sarcastic

irracional *adj* irrational

irradiar [A1] *vt* (a) ‹*calor/luz*› to radiate (b) ‹*simpatía/felicidad*› to radiate, irradiate

irrazonable *adj* unreasonable

irreal *adj* unreal

irrealizable *adj* ⟨*proyecto*⟩ unfeasible; ⟨*deseo*⟩ unattainable, unrealizable

irreconocible *adj* unrecognizable

irrecuperable *adj* unrecoverable, irretrievable

irreemplazable *adj* irreplaceable

irregular *adj* (en general) irregular; ⟨*letra/ superficie*⟩ irregular, uneven

irregularidad *f* irregularity

irrelevante *adj* irrelevant

irremediable *adj* irreparable

irrepetible *adj* unrepeatable; **una actuación** ∼ a once-in-a-lifetime performance

irreprochable *adj* irreproachable

irresistible *adj* (a) ⟨*sonrisa/mujer/hombre*⟩ irresistible; ⟨*deseo/tentación*⟩ irresistible (b) ⟨*dolor*⟩ unbearable

irrespetar [A1] *vt* (Col, Ven) ⟨*persona*⟩ to be rude to; ⟨*lugar sagrado*⟩ to desecrate

irrespetuoso -sa *adj* disrespectful

irrespirable *adj* unbreathable

irresponsabilidad *f* irresponsibility

irresponsable *adj* irresponsible
■ *mf*: **es un** ∼ he's irresponsible, he's an irresponsible person

irreversible *adj* irreversible

irritable *adj* irritable

irritación *f* (a) (Med) irritation, inflammation (b) (enfado) irritation, annoyance

irritante *adj* ⟨*situación/actitud*⟩ irritating, annoying

irritar [A1] *vt* (a) ⟨*piel/garganta*⟩ to irritate; **tiene la garganta irritada** his throat is sore *o* inflamed (b) ⟨*persona*⟩ to annoy, irritate
■ **irritarse** *v pron* (a) «*piel/ojos*» to become irritated (b) «*persona*» to get irritated

irrompible *adj* unbreakable

isla *f* (a) (Geog) island, isle (liter) (b) (Ven) (en autopistas) median strip (AmE), central reservation (BrE); ∼ **peatonal** safety island (AmE), traffic island (BrE)

Isla de Pascua *f*: **la** ∼ **de** ∼ Easter Island

Islam *m*: **el** ∼ Islam

islámico -ca *adj* Islamic

islamista *adj* Islamist
■ *mf* Islamist

islandés¹ -desa *adj* Icelandic
■ *m,f* (persona) Icelander

islandés² *m* (idioma) Icelandic

Islandia *f* Iceland

Islas Británicas *fpl* British Isles (*pl*)

Islas Canarias *fpl* Canary Islands (*pl*), Canaries (*pl*)

Islas Malvinas *fpl* Falkland Islands (*pl*)

isleño -ña *adj* ⟨*población/productos*⟩ island (*before n*)
■ *m,f* (habitante de una isla) islander

islote *m* small island, islet

ISP *m* (= **proveedor de servicios Internet**) ISP

Israel *m* Israel

israelí *adj/mf* Israeli

itacate *m* (Méx) pack, bundle

Italia *f* Italy

italiano¹ -na *adj/m,f* Italian

italiano² *m* (idioma) Italian

ítem *m* (*pl* **ítems**) item

itinerario *m* itinerary, route

IVA /'iβa/ *m* (= **Impuesto al Valor Agregado** *or* **sobre el Valor Añadido**) VAT

izar [A4] *vt* ⟨*vela/bandera*⟩ to hoist, raise, run up

izquierda *f* 1 (a) (mano izquierda): **la** ∼ the left hand (b) (lado) left; **la puerta de la** ∼ the door on the left, the left-hand door; **torció a la** ∼ he turned left; **ahí enfrente a la** ∼ over there on the left; **conducen por la** ∼ they drive on the left 2 (Pol) left; **de** ∼ *or* (Esp) **de** ∼**s** left-wing

izquierdo -da *adj* left (*before n*)

Jj

J, j *f* (*read as* /'xota/) *the letter* J, j

ja *interj* ha!

jabalí *m* (*pl* **-íes**) wild boar

jabalina *f* (a) (Arm, Dep) javelin (b) (Zool) wild sow

jabón *m* (producto) soap; **una barra** *or* **pastilla de** ∼ a bar *o* cake of soap; ∼ **de afeitar** shaving soap

jabonada *f* (con jabón): **dale una buena** ∼ wash it well in soapy water

jabonar [A1] *vt* ▶ ENJABONAR

jabonera *f* soap dish

jabonoso -sa *adj* soapy

jacal *m* (Méx) hut, small house (*made of adobe or reeds*)

jacarandá *m or f* jacaranda

jacinto *m* (Bot) hyacinth

jactarse [A1] *v pron* to boast, brag; ∼ **DE algo** to boast *o* brag ABOUT sth

Jacuzzi® /dʒəˈkuzi/ *m* Jacuzzi®

jade *m* jade

jadeante *adj*: **venía** ∼ **por la cuesta** he came up the hill (puffing and) panting; **con voz** ∼ in a breathless voice

jadear [A1] *vi* to pant

jadeo *m* panting

jaguar *m* jaguar

jagüey, jagüel *m* (AmL) pool

jai *f* (AmS fam) (alta sociedad) high society

jai alai *m* jai alai, pelota

jaiba *f* (AmL) crab; (de río) freshwater crab

jaibol *m* (Méx) highball (AmE), whisky and soda (BrE)

jalada *f* (Méx fam) **1** (tirón) pull, tug **2** (tontería, exageración): **esas son puras ~s** that's a load of garbage (AmE) *o* (BrE) rubbish (colloq)

jalado¹ -da *adj* **1** (AmC, Col, Méx fam) (borracho) tight (colloq) **2** (Méx fam) (descabellado) crazy (colloq) **3** (Per fam) ⟨*ojos*⟩ slanting
■ *m,f* (Per fam) oriental-looking person

jalado² *m* (Per arg) (Educ) fail

jalador -dora *adj* **1** (Méx fam) (a) (trabajador) hard-working (b) (animoso) willing (c) (que atrae) ⟨*oferta*⟩ attractive; ⟨*cantante/actor*⟩ popular **2** (Per arg) ⟨*profesor*⟩ tough (colloq)

jalapeño *m* (Méx) jalapeño pepper

jalar [A1] *vt* **1** (a) (AmL exc CS) (tirar de) to pull; **me jaló la manga** he pulled *o* tugged at my sleeve (b) (Méx) (agarrar y acercar) ⟨*periódico/libro*⟩ to pick up, take; ⟨*silla*⟩ to draw up **2** (Per arg) ⟨*alumno*⟩ to fail, flunk (esp AmE colloq) **3** (Per fam) (en automóvil, moto) to give … a lift *o* ride
■ ~ *vi* **1** (AmL exc CS) (tirar) to pull; **~ DE algo** to pull sth; **~ con algn** (Méx fam) (llevarse bien) to get on *o* along well with sb **2** (a) (Méx fam) (apresurarse) to hurry up, get a move on (colloq); **¡jálale!** hurry up! (b) (Col, Méx fam) (ir) to go; **jálale por el pan** go and get the bread **3** (Méx fam) «*motor/aparato*» to work; **mi coche no jalaba en la mañana** my car wouldn't start this morning; **¿cómo van los negocios? — jalando, jalando** how's business? — oh, not so bad (colloq) **4** (AmC fam) «*pareja*» to date, go out; «*persona*» **~ con algn** to date sb, go out WITH sb
■ **jalarse** *v pron* **1** (Méx) (*enf*) ▶ JALAR *vt* 1B **2** (Méx) (*enf*) (a) (irse) to go (b) (venir) to come **3** (Col, Méx fam) (emborracharse) to get tight (colloq)

jalea *f* jelly; **~ real** royal jelly

jaleo *m* (fam) (a) (alboroto, ruido) racket (colloq), row (colloq) (b) (confusión) muddle, mess; (desorden) mess; (problemas) hassle (colloq) (c) (actividad intensa): **hemos tenido mucho ~ en casa** everything's been very hectic at home; **con todo el ~ de la mudanza** with all the upheaval of the move (d) (riña) brawl

jallán *m* (AmC, Col) lout

jalón *m* (a) (AmL exc CS fam) (tirón) pull, yank; **de un ~** in one go (b) (Méx) (tramo) stretch

jalonazo *m* (AmL exc CS fam) tug, yank; **el carro iba a ~s** the car jerked *o* lurched along

jalonear [A1] *vt* (Méx, Per fam) to tug (at)
■ ~ *vi* (a) (AmL exc CS fam) (dar tirones) to pull, tug (b) (AmC fam) (regatear) to haggle

jamaica *f* (Bot) hibiscus

Jamaica *f* Jamaica

jamaicano -na *adj/m,f* Jamaican

jamás *adv* never; **~ volverá a suceder** it will never happen again; **nunca ~** never ever; **por** *or* **para siempre ~** for ever and ever

jamón *m* (Coc) ham; **~ serrano** ≈ Parma ham

jaña *f* (AmC fam) (compañera) girlfriend; (chica) girl

Japón *m*: *tb* **el ~** Japan

japonés¹ -nesa *adj/m,f* Japanese

japonés² *m* (idioma) Japanese

jaque *m* check; **~ mate** checkmate

jaqueca *f* migraine, severe headache

jarabe *m* **1** (Coc, Farm, Med) syrup; **~ para la tos** cough mixture *o* syrup **2** (Mús) *Mexican folk dance and music*

jarana *f* **1** (fam) (a) (bromas): **basta de ~** that's enough fun and games *o* fooling around (colloq) (b) (juerga): **salir de ~** to go out on the town *o* out partying (colloq) **2** (a) (baile) *folk dance from south-east Mexico* (b) (Per) (fiesta) party (*with folk music*)

jaranero -ra *adj* (fam): **es muy ~** he's always out on the town *o* out partying (colloq)

jardín *m* **1** (con plantas) garden; **~ botánico** botanical garden; **~ zoológico** zoological garden, zoo; **~ de infancia** *or* **de niños** nursery school, kindergarten **2** **los jardines** *mpl* (en béisbol) the outfield; **~ central** center* field

jardinear [A1] *vi* **1** (en béisbol) to field **2** (Chi) (en el jardín) to do the gardening

jardinera *f* (para la ventana) window box; (con pedestal) jardinière

jardinería *f* gardening

jardinero -ra *m,f* **1** (persona) gardener **2** (Dep) outfielder

jareta *f* (a) (para pasar una cinta) casing; (de adorno) tuck (b) (AmC) (bragueta) fly

jaripeo *m*: *Mexican rodeo*

jarra *f* **1** (a) (para servir) pitcher (AmE), jug (BrE) (b) (para beber) stein (AmE), tankard (BrE); **en ~s: con los brazos en ~s** (with) arms akimbo, hands on hips **2** (Méx fam) bender (colloq); **irse de ~** to go on a bender

jarro *m* (a) (para servir) pitcher (AmE), jug (BrE) (b) (AmS) (tazón) mug; (para cerveza) beer mug

jarrón *m* vase

jaspe *m* (piedra) jasper; (mármol) veined marble

jaspeado -da *adj* ⟨*mármol*⟩ veined; ⟨*tela/lana*⟩ flecked; ⟨*plumaje/huevos*⟩ speckled

jauja *f* (fam): **piensan que la universidad es ~** they think that university is a bed of roses; **¡esto es ~!** this is the life!

jaula *f* cage

jauría *f* (de perros) pack (of hounds)

jayán -yana *adj* (AmC fam) foul (colloq); **no seas ~** don't be a jerk *o* creep (colloq)

jazmín *m* jasmine

jazz /(d)ʒas/ *m* jazz

jebo -ba *m,f* (Ven arg) (a) (novio) (*m*) boyfriend; (*f*) girlfriend (b) **jeba** *f* (muchacha) chick (AmE colloq), bird (BrE colloq)

Jeep® /(d)ʒip/ *m* (*pl* **Jeeps**) Jeep®

jefatura *f* **1** (sede) headquarters (*sing o pl*) **2** (de partido) leadership

jefe -fa *m,f*, **jefe** *mf* (a) (superior) boss; **~ de estudios** director of studies; **~ de personal/ ventas** personnel/sales manager; **~ de redacción** editor-in-chief (b) (de empresa) manager; (de sección) head; (de tribu) chief **2** (Pol) leader; **~ de Estado/gobierno** head of state/government

jején *m*: *small mosquito*

jengibre *m* ginger

jeque *m* sheik, sheikh

jerarca *mf* leader

jerarquía *f* (a) (organización) hierarchy (b) (categoría, rango) rank

jerez *m* sherry

jerga *f* **1** (a) (de gremio, profesión) jargon; (de los adolescentes) slang (b) (galimatías) mumbo jumbo (colloq) **2** (Méx) (trapo) floorcloth

jergón *m* straw mattress

jeringa *f* (Med) syringe

jeringuilla *f* syringe

jeroglífico *m* (escritura) hieroglyphic, hieroglyph; (acertijo) rebus

jersey *m* (*pl* **-seys**) (a) /'ʒersi/ (AmL) (tela) jersey (b) /xer'sei/ (Esp) (prenda) sweater

Jerusalén *m* Jerusalem

Jesucristo Jesus Christ

jesuita *adj/m* Jesuit

Jesús (a) (Relig) Jesus (b) (*como interj*) ¡∼! (expresando — dolor, fatiga) heavens!; (— susto, sorpresa) good heavens!, good grief!; (cuando alguien estornuda) (Esp) bless you!

jet /'(d)ʒet/ *m* (*pl* **jets**) (Aviac) jet

jeta *f* (fam) (a) (cara) face, mug (colloq) (b) (AmL fam) (boca) trap (sl)

jet lag /'(d)ʒetlav/ *m* jet lag

jet set /'(d)ʒetset/ *m or* (Esp) *f* jet set

jíbaro -ra *adj/m,f* Jivaro

jibia *f* cuttlefish

jícama *f* yam bean

jícara *f* **1** (Méx) (Bot) calabash **2** (a) (Méx) (taza) (drinking) bowl (b) (Col, Méx) (vasija — de calabaza) gourd, calabash; (— de otro material) pot

jicote *m* (Méx) wasp

jicotera *f* (a) (Méx) (nido) wasp's nest (b) (ruido) row (colloq)

jilguero *m* goldfinch

jinete *mf* (Equ) (*m*) horseman, rider; (*f*) horsewoman, rider

jinetear [A1] *vt* **1** (Equ) (Chi) (montar) to ride **2** (Méx fam) ⟨dinero⟩ to speculate with

jirafa *f* (Zool) giraffe

jirón *m* **1** (de tela) shred; **hecho jirones** in tatters *o* shreds **2** (Per) (avenida) avenue, street

jitomate *m* (Méx) tomato

jo *interj* (Esp fam) (expresando — sorpresa) wow! (colloq); (— enfado, disgusto) damn it! (colloq)

jockey /'(d)ʒoki/ *mf* (*pl* **-ckeys**) jockey

jocoso -sa *adj* humorous, jocular

joda *f* (AmL fam)(a) (molestia) pain (colloq), drag (colloq) (b) (broma): **en** ∼ as a joke

joder¹ [E1] *vi* **1** (vulg) (copular) to screw (vulg), fuck (vulg)
2 (fam: en algunas regiones vulg) (molestar) to annoy (sl); **lo hace solo por** ∼ he only does it to annoy
■ ∼ *vt* **1** (vulg) (copular con) to screw (vulg), fuck (vulg)
2 (fam: en algunas regiones vulg) (a) (molestar) to bug (colloq) (b) (engañar) to rip ... off (colloq)
3 (fam: en algunas regiones vulg) ⟨televisor/reloj⟩ to

bust (colloq), to fuck up (vulg); ⟨planes⟩ to mess up (colloq), to screw up (vulg); ∼**la** (fam) to screw up (vulg)
■ **joderse** *v pron* (fam: en algunas regiones vulg) (a) (jorobarse): **y si no te gusta, te jodes** and if you don't like it, that's tough! (colloq) (b) ⟨espalda⟩ to do ... in (colloq); ⟨hígado/estómago⟩ to mess up (colloq) (c) «planes» to get screwed up (vulg), fucked up (vulg); **se ha jodido el motor** the engine's had it (colloq)

joder² *interj* (esp Esp fam: en algunas regiones vulg) (expresando — fastidio) for heaven's sake! (colloq), for fuck's sake! (vulg); (— asombro) good grief!, holy shit! (vulg)

jodido -da *adj* **1** (fam: en algunas regiones vulg) (a) [SER] (difícil) ⟨trabajo⟩ tricky, tough (colloq); ⟨persona⟩ difficult, pain in the neck (colloq) (b) ⟨delante del n⟩ (maldito) damn (colloq), fucking (vulg) (c) [SER] (AmL) (exigente) demanding, tough (colloq) **2** [ESTAR] (fam: en algunas regiones vulg) (a) (estropeado) ⟨ascensor/radio⟩ bust (colloq), fucked (vulg) (b) (enfermo) in a bad way (colloq) (c) (deprimido) down (colloq) **3** [SER] (Col fam) (astuto) sharp

jogging /'(d)ʒovin/ *m* (a) (Dep, Ocio) jogging; **hacer** ∼ to jog, go jogging (b) (RPI) (Indum) jogging suit

jojoto *m* (Ven) corn (AmE), maize (BrE)

jolgorio *m* revelry, merrymaking; **irse de** ∼ (fam) to go out on the town *o* out partying (colloq)

jonrón *m* (AmL) home run

Jordania *f* Jordan

jordano -na *adj/m,f* Jordanian

jornada *f* **1** (a) (period) (día) day (b) (Rels Labs) *tb* ∼ **laboral** working day; **trabajar** ∼ **completa/ media** ∼ to work full-time/part-time; ∼ **continuada** *or* **intensiva** or (Chi) **única** *working day with no break for lunch so as to finish earlier*; ∼ **partida** split shift (*working day with long break for lunch*) **2** (esp Col) (viaje) journey

jornal *m* day's wages (*pl*), day's pay; **trabajar a** ∼ to be paid on a daily basis

jornalero -ra *m,f* day laborer*

joroba *f* (a) (de persona, camello) hump (b) (fam) (molestia) drag (colloq), pain in the neck (colloq)

jorobado -da *adj* **1** (giboso) hunchbacked **2** (fam) (a) (enfermo, delicado): **todavía anda algo jorobada** she's still a bit low (colloq); **está** ∼ **del estómago** his stomach's been playing (him) up (colloq) (b) (sin dinero) broke (colloq) (c) ⟨asunto⟩ tricky
■ *m,f* hunchback

jorobar [A1] *vt* (fam) (a) (molestar) to bug (colloq) (b) (malograr) to ruin, spoil
■ ∼ *vi* (fam) (molestar) to annoy; **lo que más me joroba es** ... what really bugs *o* gets me is ... (colloq)
■ **jorobarse** *v pron* (fam) (a) (aguantarse): **y si no te gusta, te jorobas** and if you don't like it, that's tough (colloq) (b) (dañarse) ⟨hígado/estómago⟩ to

AmC	Central America	Arg	Argentina	Cu	Cuba
AmL	Latin America	Bol	Bolivia	Ec	Ecuador
AmS	South America	Chi	Chile	Esp	Spain
Andes	Andean Region	CS	Southern Cone	Méx	Mexico

Per	Peru
RPI	River Plate Area
Ur	Uruguay
Ven	Venezuela

mess up (colloq); ‹*espalda*› to do ... in (colloq) **(c)** «*plan*» to be scuppered (colloq); «*fiesta*» to be ruined

jorongo *m* (Méx) poncho

joropo *m*: *Colombian/Venezuelan folk dance*

jota *f* **(a)** (letra) *name of the letter* j; **ni** ~ (fam): **no entiendo/no veo ni** ~ I don't understand/I can't see a thing; **no sabe ni** ~ he doesn't have a clue (colloq) **(b)** (Mús) jota (*Aragonese folk song/dance*) **(c)** (en naipes) jack

joven *adj* young
■ *mf* (*m*) young person, young man; (*f*) young person, young woman; **de aspecto** ~ youthful looking; **los jóvenes de hoy** ... young people today ...

jovencito -ta (*m*) young man; (*f*) young lady, young woman; **moda para jovencitas** teenage fashions (*for girls*)

jovial *adj* jovial, cheerful

joya *f* **1** (alhaja) piece of jewelry*; ~**s** jewelry *o* jewels; ~ **de fantasía** piece *o* item of costume jewelry **2** (persona) gem, treasure; (cosa): **este coche es una** ~ this is a real gem of a car

joyería *f* (tienda) jeweler's*

joyero -ra *m,f* **(a)** (persona) jeweler* **(b) joyero** *m* (estuche) jewelry* box, jewel case

joystick /'(d)ʒojstik/ *m* joystick

jr (en Perú) (= **jirón**) street

Jr. (= **Júnior**) Jr

juanete *m* (Med) bunion

jubilación *f* (retiro) retirement; (pensión) pension; ~ **anticipada/forzosa** early/compulsory retirement

jubilado -da *adj* retired
■ *m,f* pensioner, retired person (*o* worker *etc*)

jubilar [A1] *vi* (Andes) to retire
■ **jubilarse** *v pron* (del trabajo) to retire

júbilo *m* jubilation

jubiloso -sa *adj* (liter) jubilant

judaísmo *m* Judaism

judía *f* (Esp) bean; ~ **verde** green bean

judicial *adj* judicial
■ *m* (Méx) policeman

judío -día *adj* **1** (Relig, Sociol) Jewish **2** (fam & pey) (tacaño) miserly, tightfisted (colloq)
■ *m,f* Jewish person, Jew

judo /'(d)ʒuðo/ *m* judo

juega, juegas, etc ▶ JUGAR

juego *m* **1** **(a)** (en general) play; **entrar en** ~ «*jugador*» to come on; «*factores/elementos*» to come into play; **estar en** ~ to be at stake; ~ **limpio/sucio** fair/foul play; **seguirle el** ~ **a algn** to go *o* play along with sb **(b)** (por dinero): **el** ~ gambling **(c)** (fam) (maniobras, estratagemas) game (colloq) **(d)** (en naipes) hand, cards (*pl*) **2** **(a)** (de mesa, de niños, etc) game; ~ **de azar** game of chance; ~ **de manos** conjuring trick; ~ **de palabras** pun, play on words; ~**s malabares** juggling; **J**~**s Olímpicos** Olympic Games (*pl*), Olympics (*pl*) **(b)** (AmL) (en la feria) fairground attraction, ride **(c)** (en tenis) game **(d)** **juegos** *mpl* (columpios, etc) swings, slide, etc (*in a children's playground*) **3** (conjunto) set; **un** ~ **de cuchillos/llaves** a set of knives/keys; **un** ~ **de platos** a dinner service; ~

de café/té coffee/tea set; ~ **de escritorio** desk set; **hacer** ~ «*colores/cortinas*» to go together; **te hace** ~ **con los zapatos** it goes with your shoes

juerga *f* (fam): **ir de** ~ to go out on the town *o* out partying (colloq); **organizar una** ~ to have *o* throw a party

juerguista *mf* (fam) reveller

jueves *m* (*pl* ~) Thursday; *para ejemplos ver* LUNES; **J**~ **Santo** Maundy Thursday

juez *mf*, **juez -za** *m,f* **(a)** (Der) judge **(b)** (Dep) referee; ~ **de banda** *or* **línea** (en fútbol, tenis) (*m*) linesman; (*f*) lineswoman; (en fútbol americano, rugby) line judge; ~ **de silla** umpire

jugada *f* **(a)** (con pelota — individual) move; (— entre varios) play **(b)** (en ajedrez, damas, etc) move; **hacerle una (mala)** ~ **a algn** to play a (dirty) trick on sb

jugado -da *adj* (Col, Méx) experienced

jugador -dora *m,f* (Dep) player; (en naipes, juegos de mesa) player; (que juega habitualmente por dinero) gambler

jugar [A15] *vi* **1** **(a)** (en general) to play; ~ **A algo** to play sth; ~ **a la pelota** to play ball; ~ **al fútbol** (Esp, RPl) to play football; ~ **a las muñecas** to play with dolls; ~ **limpio/sucio** to play fair/ dirty **(b)** (en ajedrez, damas) to move; (en naipes) to play; (en otros juegos) to play; **me tocaba** ~ **a mí** it was my turn/move/go **(c)** (apostar fuerte) to gamble **2 jugar con** (a) ‹*persona/sentimientos*› to play with, toy with **(b)** (manejar) ‹*colores/luz/palabras*› to play with
■ ~ *vt* **1** ‹*partido/carta*› to play **(b)** (AmL exc RPl) ‹*tenis/fútbol/ajedrez*› to play **2** (apostar) ~ **algo A algo** to bet sth ON sth **3** ‹*rol/papel*› to play
■ **jugarse** *v pron* **(a)** (gastarse en el juego) ‹*sueldo*› to gamble (away) **(b)** (arriesgar) ‹*reputación/vida*› to risk, put ... at risk; ~**se el pellejo** (fam) to risk one's neck (colloq) **(c)** (apostarse) ‹*recípr*›: **nos jugamos una comida** we bet a meal on it

jugarreta *f* (fam) dirty trick (colloq); **hacerle una** ~ **a algn** to play a dirty trick on sb

juglar *m* minstrel, jongleur

jugo *m* (líquido) juice; ~ **de tomate** tomato juice

jugoso -sa *adj* **(a)** ‹*fruta/carne*› juicy **(b)** ‹*historia/anécdota*› colorful*; ‹*chisme*› juicy **(c)** ‹*artículo/guion*› meaty **(d)** ‹*negocio*› lucrative, profitable

juguera *f* (CS) (para hacer jugos) juicer

juguete *m* toy; **un tren de** ~ a toy train

juguetear [A1] *vi* to play

juguetería *f* (tienda) toy store; (ramo) toy trade *o* business

juguetón -tona *adj* playful

juicio *m* **1** (facultad) judgment; **no está en su sano** ~ he's not in his right mind; **perder el** ~ to go out of one's mind **2** (prudencia, sensatez) sense **3** (opinión) opinion; **a mi** ~ in my opinion, to my mind; **lo dejo a tu** ~ I'll leave it up to you; ~ **de valor** value judgment **4** (Der) trial; **llevar a** ~ **a algn** to take sb to court; **ir a** ~ to go to court; ~ **civil/criminal** civil/criminal proceedings (*pl*); **el J**~ **Final** (Relig) the Final Judgment

juicioso -sa *adj* sensible

jul. (= **julio**) Jul

julepe *m* ⟦1⟧ (Jueg) *card game similar to whist*
⟦2⟧ (AmS fam) (susto) fright; **le da ~ la oscuridad**
she's terrified of the dark

julia *f* (Méx fam) Black Maria (colloq)

julio *m* (mes) July; *para ejemplos ver* ENERO

jumbo /'(d)ʒumbo/ *m* jumbo jet

jun. (= **junio**) Jun

junco *m* ⟦1⟧ (planta) rush, reed ⟦2⟧ (Náut) *tb* ~
chino junk

jungla *f* jungle

junio *m* June; *para ejemplos ver* ENERO

júnior /'(d)ʒunjo(r)/ *adj inv* ⟨equipo/categoría⟩
junior (*before n*), youth (*before n*) (BrE)
■ *mf* (*pl* ~**s**) (a) (Dep): **los ~s** the juniors (b) (el
más joven, el hijo) Junior
■ *m* (a) (Chi) (en oficina) office junior (b) (Méx) (hijo
de papá) rich kid (colloq)

junta *f* ⟦1⟧ (a) (comité, comisión) board, committee;
(de empresa) board; (reunión) meeting; ~ **directiva**
board of directors (b) (de militares) junta (c)
(gobierno regional) *autonomous government in some
regions of Spain* ⟦2⟧ (Mec) (acoplamiento) joint; (para
cerrar herméticamente) gasket

juntar [A1] *vt* (a) (unir) ⟨pies/manos/camas⟩ to
put ... together (b) (reunir) ⟨fichas/piezas⟩ to
collect up, gather together; ⟨dinero⟩ to save (up);
~ **sellos** (esp AmL) to collect stamps (c) (cerrar)
⟨puerta⟩ to push ... to
■ **juntarse** *v pron* ⟦1⟧ «*personas*» (a) (acercarse)
to move *o* get closer together (b) (reunirse) to get
together; ~**se con algn** to join sb, meet up with
sb (c) (como pareja) to live together; **se volvieron
a ~** they got back together again ⟦2⟧ (a)
«*desgracias/sucesos*» to come together (b)
«*carreteras/conductos*» to meet, join

junto -ta *adj* ⟦1⟧ (a) (unido, reunido) together;
**nunca había visto tanto dinero ~/tanta gente
junta** I'd never seen so much money/so many
people in one place (b) (*pl*) (cercanos, contiguos)
together; **están demasiado ~s** they're too close
together; **bailaban muy ~s** they were dancing
very close ⟦2⟧ (*como adv*) (a) ⟨estudiar/trabajar/
vivir⟩ together (b) ⟨llegar/saltar⟩ at the same
time; **¡ahora todos ~s!** all together now! ⟦3⟧ (*en
locs*) **junto a** next to; **junto con** (together) with

juntura *f* join, joint

Júpiter *m* Jupiter

jurado *m* (cuerpo) (Der) jury; (de concurso) panel
of judges, jury
■ *mf* (persona) (Der) juror, member of a jury; (de
concurso) judge, member of the jury

juramento *m* oath; **prestar ~** to take an oath;
tomarle ~ a algn (Der) to swear sb in; **bajo ~**
under *o* on oath

jurar [A1] *vt* to swear; **juró su cargo el 22 de
julio** he was sworn in on July 22; **~on (la)
bandera** *or* (AmL) **a la bandera** they swore
allegiance to the flag; **juró vengarse** he swore to
get his revenge; **no lo entiendo, te lo juro** I
honestly don't understand

■ ~ *vi* (a) (maldecir) to curse, swear (b) (prometer):
~ **en falso** *or* **vano** to commit perjury

jurídico -ca *adj* legal (*before n*)

jurisdicción *f* jurisdiction

justicia *f* (a) (equidad) justice; **pedir ~** to call
for justice; **en ~** in all fairness, to be fair; **la ~
de su decisión** the fairness of her decision; **nunca
se le ha hecho ~ como escritor** he has never
received due recognition as a writer (b) (sistema,
leyes): **la ~** the law; **huir de la ~** to flee from
justice *o* the law; **tomarse la ~ por su mano** to
take the law into one's own hands

justificable *adj* justifiable

justificación *f* (disculpa, razón) justification;
(Der) (prueba) proof

justificante *m* receipt; ~ **de pago** receipt,
proof of payment; ~ **de asistencia** certificate of
attendance; ~ **de ausencia** note explaining
reasons for one's absence

justificar [A2] *vt* (a) (en general) to justify; **eso
no justifica su actitud** that does not justify her
attitude; **sus sospechas no estaban justificadas**
his suspicions were not justified; **trabajar por tan
poco no se justifica** it isn't worth working for so
little (b) (disculpar) ⟨persona⟩ to find *o* make
excuses for
■ **justificarse** *v pron* to justify oneself, excuse
oneself

justo¹ -ta *adj* ⟦1⟧ ⟨persona/castigo/sociedad⟩
just, fair; ⟨causa⟩ just ⟦2⟧ (a) (exacto) ⟨medida/
peso/cantidad⟩ exact; **me dio el dinero ~** he gave
me the right money; **son 40 euros justas** that's 40
euros exactly; **buscaba la palabra justa** he was
searching for exactly *o* just the right word (b)
(apenas suficiente): **tener lo ~ para vivir** to have just
enough to live on; **andan muy ~s de dinero**
they're very short of money; **teníamos las sillas
justas** we had just enough chairs for everybody
(c) (ajustado): **estos zapatos me quedan demasiado
~s** these shoes are too tight (for me)

justo² *adv* (a) (exactamente) just; ~ **a tiempo** just
in time; **es ~ lo que quería** it's just *o* exactly
what I wanted; **vive ~ al lado** he lives just *o*
right next door; **y ~ hoy que pensaba salir** and
today of all days, when I was planning to go out
(b) (ajustado): **con el sueldo que gana vive muy ~**
he only just manages to scrape by on what he
earns; **me cupo todo, pero muy ~** I managed to
get everything in, but only just

juvenil *adj* ⟨moda⟩ young; ⟨aspecto⟩ youthful;
⟨categoría/competición⟩ junior (*before n*), youth
(*before n*) (BrE)
■ *mf* junior; **los ~es** the juniors

juventud *f* (edad) youth; (gente joven) youth;
¡esta ~ de hoy! young people today!

juzgado *m* court

juzgar [A3] *vt* (a) (Der) ⟨acusado⟩ to try; ⟨caso⟩
to try, judge (b) ⟨conducta/persona⟩ to judge; ~
mal a algn to misjudge sb (c) (considerar) to
consider; **a ~ por las apariencias** judging by
appearances

K k

K, k *f (read as* /ka/) *the letter* K, k

ka *f. name of the letter* k

kaleidoscopio *m* kaleidoscope

karate, kárate *m* karate

kárdex *m* (archivo) file; (mueble) filing cabinet

kart *m* (*pl* **karts**) kart

Kenia, Kenya *f* Kenya

kermesse /ker'mes/*f* (CS, Méx) charity fair, kermess (AmE), fête (BrE)

ketchup /'katʃup 'katsup/ *m* ketchup, catsup (AmE)

Kg. (= **kilogramo**) kg

kilo *m* kilogram, kilo

kilogramo *m* kilogram

kilometraje *m* ≈mileage

kilométrico -ca *adj* (fam) ⟨pasillo⟩ endless; **una cola kilométrica** a line (AmE) *o* (BrE) queue a mile long

kilómetro *m* kilometer*

kilovatio *m* kilowatt

kimono *m* kimono

kindergarten *m* (*pl* ~ *or* **-tens**) kindergarten

kiosco, kiosko *m* **(a)** (de periódicos) newsstand, newspaper kiosk; (de refrescos) drinks stand; (de helados) ice-cream stand; (de caramelos, tabaco) kiosk **(b)** (para orquesta) bandstand

kiwi /'kiwi/ *m* **(a)** (Bot) kiwifruit, Chinese gooseberry **(b)** (Zool) kiwi

klaxon *m* ▶ CLAXON

Kleenex®, kleenex /'klineks/ *m* (*pl* ~) tissue

Km. (= **kilómetro**) km

K.O. /'nokau(t)/ *or* (Esp) /'kao/ *m* KO; **lo dejó** ~ he knocked him out

koala *m* koala (bear)

kuchen /'kuxen/ *m* (Chi) (Coc) tart

Kurdistán *m* Kurdistan

kurdo -da *adj* Kurdish
■ *m,f* Kurd

Kuwait *m* Kuwait

Kuwaití *adj/mf* Kuwaiti

L l

L, l *f (read as* /'ele/) *the letter* L, l

l. (= **litro**) l, liter*

la *art: ver* **el**
■ *pron pers* **(a)** (referido — a ella) her; (— a usted) you; (— a cosa) it; **no** ~ **conozco** I don't know her; **¿**~ **atienden?** can I help you?; **yo se** ~ **llevo** I'll take it to him **(b)** (impers) you, one (frml)
■ *m* (nota) A; (en solfeo) la

laberinto *m* (de caminos, pasillos) maze, labyrinth; (en jardín, parque) maze

labia *f* (fam) gift of the gab (colloq)

labio *m* lip; **leer los** ~**s** to lip-read; **sin dispegar los** ~**s** without uttering a single word

labor *f* **(a)** (trabajo) work; **una** ~ **de equipo** teamwork; ~**es domésticas** housework; ~**es agrícolas** *or* **del campo** farm work **(b)** (de coser, bordar) needlework; (de punto) knitting

laborable *adj* **(a)** ⟨día⟩ working (before n) **(b)** ⟨tierra⟩ arable

laboral *adj* ⟨problemas/conflictos⟩ labor* (before n), work (before n); ▶ ACCIDENTE

laboratorio *m* laboratory

laborioso -sa *adj* ⟨persona⟩ hardworking, industrious; ⟨abejas⟩ industrious; ⟨tarea⟩ laborious

laborista *adj* Labour (before n)
■ *mf* member of the Labour Party

labrador -dora *m,f* (Agr) (propietario) farmer; (trabajador) farmworker

labrar [A1] *vt* ① (Agr) ⟨tierra⟩ to work ② ⟨madera⟩ to carve; ⟨piedra⟩ to cut; ⟨cuero⟩ to tool, work; ⟨metales⟩ to work
■ **labrarse** *v pron* (forjarse): ~**se un porvenir** to carve out a future for oneself

labriego -ga *m,f* farmworker

laburar [A1] *vi* (CS fam) to work

laca *f* (resina) lac, shellac; (barniz) lacquer; (para el pelo) hairspray

lacear [A1] *vt* (CS) ⟨ganado⟩ to lasso

lacio -cia *adj* ⟨pelo⟩ straight; ⟨cuerpo⟩ limp, weak

lacónico -ca *adj* laconic

lacrar [A1] *vt* (con cera) to seal

lacre *adj* (AmL) bright-red; (Chi) red
■ *m* sealing wax

lacrimógeno -na *adj* (fam) ⟨película⟩ weepy (colloq), tear-jerking (before n) (colloq); ▶ GAS

lactancia *f* (secreción de leche) lactation; **durante el período de** ~ while breastfeeding

lácteo -tea *adj* dairy (before n), milk (before n)

ladeado -da *adj*: **el cuadro está** ~ the picture ···⫶

is on a slant *o* is askew; **llevaba el sombrero** ∼ he wore his hat at an angle; **con la cabeza ladeada** with his head tilted to one side

ladear [A1] *vt* ‹*cabeza*› to tilt ... to one side; ‹*objeto*› to tilt

■ **ladearse** *v pron* (inclinarse) to lean to one side

ladera *f* hillside, mountainside; **la** ∼ **norte** the northern slope *o* side

ladino -na *adj* [1] (taimado) sly, cunning [2] (AmC, Méx) **(a)** (mestizo) mestizo, of mixed race **(b)** (hispanohablante) Spanish-speaking (*often used to refer to Indians who adopt Spanish ways*) [3] (Méx fam) (agudo) high-pitched, piercing
■ *m,f* (AmC, Méx) **(a)** (mestizo) mestizo, person of mixed race **(b)** (hispanohablante) Spanish-speaking Indian

lado *m* [1] **(a)** (en general) side; **está en el** ∼ **derecho** it is on the right-hand side; **a este/al otro** ∼ **del río** on this/on the other side of the river; **hacerse a un** ∼ to move to one side; **echarse a un** ∼ «*coche*» to swerve; «*persona*» to move over; **ponlas a un** ∼ set them aside; **¿de qué** ∼ **estás?** whose side are you on?; **cambiar de** ∼ (Dep) to change sides (AmE) *o* (BrE) ends; **ver el** ∼ **positivo de las cosas** to look on the bright side of things; **por el** ∼ **de mi padre** on my father's side (of the family) **(b)** (de papel, moneda, tela) side [2] (sitio, lugar): **a/en/por todos** ∼**s** everywhere; **en algún** ∼ somewhere; **en cualquier** ∼ anywhere; **ir de un** ∼ **para otro** to run around [3] (*en locs*) **al lado: viven en la casa de al** ∼ they live next door; **los vecinos de al** ∼ the next-door neighbors; **al lado de algn/algo** (contiguo a) next to sb/sth, beside sb/sth; (en comparación con) compared to sb/sth; **de lado** ‹*meter/colocar*› sideways; ‹*tumbarse/dormir*› on one's side; **de a** ∼ ‹*extenderse/cruzar*› from one side to the other; **por otro lado** (en cambio) on the other hand; (además) apart from anything else; **por un** ∼ ..., **pero por otro** ∼ ... on the one hand ..., but on the other hand ...; *dejar algo de* ∼ to leave sth aside *o* to one side; *ir cada uno por su* ∼: **cada uno se fue por su** ∼ they went their separate ways

ladrar [A1] *vi* **(a)** «*perro*» to bark **(b)** (fam) «*persona*» to yell (at) (colloq), to bark (colloq)

ladrido *m* bark; ∼**s** barking

ladrillo *m* brick; **(de) color** ∼ brick-red

ladrón -drona *m,f* [1] (de bolsos, coches) thief; (de bancos) bank robber; (de casas) burglar [2] **ladrón** *m* (Elec) adaptor

ladronzuelo -la *m,f* petty thief

lagartija *f* wall lizard

lagarto *m* [1] (Zool) lizard [2] (Col fam) (persona) crawler (colloq)

lago *m* lake

lágrima *f* (Fisiol) tear; **le caían las** ∼**s** tears were running down her face; **se le saltaron las** ∼**s** it brought tears to his eyes; ∼**s de cocodrilo** crocodile tears (*pl*); **llorar a** ∼ **viva** to cry one's eyes *o* heart out

lagrimal *m* **(a)** (extremo del ojo) corner of the eye **(b)** *tb* **conducto** ∼ tear duct

laguna *f* [1] (de agua dulce) lake, pool; (de agua salada) lagoon [2] **(a)** (en estudio, artículo) gap **(b)** (en la memoria) memory lapse

laico -ca *adj* secular, lay (*before n*)
■ *m,f* (*m*) layman, layperson; (*f*) laywoman, layperson

laísmo *m*: *use of* LA/LAS *instead of* LE/LES (*as in* LA/LAS DIJE QUE NO), *common in certain regions of Spain but not acceptable to most speakers*

laja *f* (AmS) slab

lama *m* lama
■ *f* (AmL) (musgo) moss; (verdín) green slime; (moho) mold*

lambetear [A1] *vt* (Col, Méx, Ven) to lick

lambiscón -cona *m,f* (Méx fam) bootlicker (colloq)

lambisquear [A1] *vt* **(a)** (Col) (lamer) to lick **(b)** (Méx fam) (lisonjear) to suck up to (colloq)

lamentable *adj* **(a)** ‹*conducta/error/suceso*› deplorable, terrible **(b)** ‹*pérdida*› sad; ‹*estado/aspecto*› pitiful; ‹*error*› regrettable

lamentación *f* lamentation (liter); **estoy harta de oír tus lamentaciones** (fam) I'm fed up with your complaining *o* grumbling

lamentar [A1] *vt* to regret; **lamento molestarlo** I'm sorry to disturb you; **lamentamos tener que comunicarle que ...** (frml) we regret to have to inform you that ...; **lo lamento mucho** I am very sorry
■ **lamentarse** *v pron* to complain, to grumble (colloq)

lamento *m* **(a)** (quejido — por un dolor físico) groan; (— por tristeza) wail **(b)** (elegía) lament

lamer [E1] *vt* «*persona/animal*» to lick

lámina *f* [1] (hoja, plancha) sheet [2] (Impr) **(a)** (plancha, ilustración) plate; (estampa) picture card **(b)** (Educ) wall chart

laminar [A1] *vt* to laminate

lámpara *f* lamp; ∼ **de pie/mesa** standard/table lamp

lamparín *m* (Per) kerosene lamp

lamparita *f* (RPl) (light) bulb

lampiño -ña *adj* (sin barba) smooth-faced; (con poco vello) with little body hair

lana *f* [1] (material) wool; (vellón, pelambre) fleece; ∼ **virgen** new wool; **una bufanda de** ∼ a wool *o* woolen scarf [2] (AmL fam) (dinero) dough (sl); **tienen mucha** ∼ they're loaded (colloq)

lanceta *f* **(a)** (Med) lancet **(b)** (Andes, Méx) (aguijón) sting

lancha *f* (barca grande) launch, cutter; (bote) motorboat; ∼ **fuera borda** (outboard) launch; ∼ **neumática** inflatable (dinghy); ∼ **salvavidas** lifeboat

langosta *f* (crustáceo) lobster; (insecto) locust

langostino *m* (grande) king prawn; (pequeño) prawn; ∼ **de río** crayfish, crawfish (esp AmE)

langüetear [A1] *vt* (Chi) to lick

languidecer [E3] *vi* «*persona*» to languish (liter); «*entusiasmo/conversación*» to flag

lánguido -da adj (a) (débil) listless, weak (b) ⟨mirada/aspecto⟩ languid

lanolina f lanolin

lanudo -da adj long-haired, shaggy

lanza f (arma — en las lides) lance; (— arrojadiza) spear
- m (Chi) (delincuente) pickpocket, thief

lanzacohetes m (pl ~) rocket launcher

lanzado -da adj [1] [SER] (fam) (precipitado) impulsive, impetuous; (decidido, atrevido) forward [2] (fam) (rápido): ir ~ to shoot along (colloq); pasar ~ to shoot past

lanzador -dora m,f (Dep) (de disco, jabalina) thrower; (en béisbol) pitcher; ~ de bala or (Esp) de peso shot-putter

lanzamiento m [1] (a) (de objetos, pelota) throwing; (de misil, torpedo) launch; (de bomba) dropping (b) (de cohete, satélite) launch (c) (Dep) (de disco, jabalina) throw; (de bala) put; (en béisbol) pitch; ~ de bala or (Esp) de peso shot put; ~ de disco/jabalina discus/javelin throwing [2] (de producto, libro) launch, launching [3] (CS) (Der) tb orden de ~ eviction order

lanzamisiles adj inv missile-launching (before n)
- m (pl ~) missile launcher

lanzar [A4] vt [1] (a) ⟨pelota/objetos/jabalina⟩ to throw; (en béisbol) to pitch (b) ⟨misil/satélite⟩ to launch; ⟨bomba⟩ to drop [2] ⟨producto/libro⟩ to launch [3] (a) ⟨ofensiva/ataque/crítica⟩ to launch (b) ⟨mirada⟩ to shoot, give; ⟨indirecta⟩ to drop; ⟨grito⟩ to give; **lanzó un grito de dolor** he cried out in pain
- ~ vi (en béisbol) to pitch
- **lanzarse** v pron (a) (refl) (arrojarse) to throw oneself; ~se al agua/al vacío to leap into the water/the void; ~se en paracaídas to parachute; (en una emergencia) to bale out (b) (abalanzarse, precipitarse): ~se sobre algo/algn to pounce on sth/sb; ~se al ataque to attack

lapa f (a) (molusco) limpet (b) (Ven) (mamífero) paca (c) (AmC) (ave) macaw

lapicera f (CS) pen; ~ fuente or estilográfica fountain pen

lapicero m (a) (portaminas) automatic pencil (AmE), propelling pencil (BrE) (b) (Esp) (lápiz) pencil (c) (AmC, Per) (bolígrafo) ballpoint pen

lápida f (en tumba) tombstone, gravestone; (losa conmemorativa) stone plaque

lapislázuli m lapis lazuli

lápiz m (de madera) pencil; (portaminas) automatic pencil (AmE), propelling pencil (BrE); con or a ~ in pencil; **lápices de colores** crayons (pl); ~ de labios lipstick; ~ de ojos eye pencil; ~ de pasta (Chi) ballpoint pen

lapso m (a) (de tiempo) space (b) (error, olvido) ▶ LAPSUS

lapsus m (pl ~) (error) slip, blunder; (olvido): tuve un pequeño ~ it slipped my mind

laptop m laptop (computer)

larga f (a) (largo plazo): a la ~ in the long run; darle ~s a algn/algo to put sb/sth off (b) (Auto) high beam (AmE), full o main beam (BrE)

largar [A3] vt [1] (a) (Náut) ⟨amarras/cabo⟩ to let out, pay out (b) (RPl) (soltar, dejar caer) to let ... go [2] ⟨discurso/sermón⟩ to give; ⟨palabrota/

insulto⟩ to let fly [3] (fam) (despedir) to fire, to give ... the boot (colloq); ⟨novio⟩ to ditch [4] (CS, Méx) (Dep) ⟨pelota⟩ to throw; ⟨carrera⟩ to start
- **largarse** v pron (a) (fam) (irse) to beat it (colloq); **¡yo me largo!** I'm taking off! (AmE), I'm off! (BrE) (colloq) (b) (CS fam) (empezar) to start, get going (colloq); ~se A hacer algo to start to do sth, to start doing sth

largavistas m (pl ~) (CS) binoculars (pl)

largo¹ -ga adj (a) (en general) long; **me queda largo** it's too long (for me); **es muy ~ de contar** it's a long story; **un tren de ~ recorrido** a long-distance train (b) (en locs) a lo largo ⟨cortar/partir⟩ lengthways; **a lo largo de** (de camino, río) along; (de jornada, novela) throughout; (de una semana, vida) in the course of; **de largo** ⟨vestirse⟩ to wear a long skirt/dress; ver tb PASAR I 1A; **va para ~** (fam) it's going to be a while

largo² m (a) (longitud) length; **¿cuánto mide de ~?** how long is it? (b) (en natación) lap (AmE), length (BrE)
- interj (fam) tb **¡~ de aquí!** get out of here!

largometraje m feature film, full-length film

larguero m (a) (Arquit, Const) (viga) crossbeam; (de puerta) jamb (b) (de cama) side (c) (Dep) crossbar

larguirucho -cha adj (fam) gangling (before n)

laringe f larynx

laringitis f laryngitis

larva f larva, grub

lasaña f lasagna, lasagne

lascivo -va adj lascivious, lustful

láser m laser

lástima f (a) (pena) shame, pity; **¡qué ~!** a shame o pity!; **me da ~ tirarlo** it seems a pity o shame to throw it out (b) (compasión): **sentir ~ por algn** to feel sorry for sb; **digno de ~** worthy of compassion

lastimadura f (AmL) graze

lastimar [A1] vt to hurt
- **lastimarse** v pron (refl) (esp AmL) to hurt oneself; ⟨dedo/rodillas⟩ to hurt

lastimero -ra adj pitiful

lastre m (a) (de buque, globo) ballast (b) (carga, estorbo) burden

lata f [1] (a) (hojalata) tin (b) (envase) can, tin (BrE); **sardinas en ~** canned o tinned sardines (c) (para galletas, etc) tin [2] (fam) (pesadez) nuisance, pain (colloq); **¡qué ~!** what a nuisance!; **dar (la) ~** (fam) to be a nuisance; **¡deja ya de darme ~!** stop bugging o pestering me! (colloq)

latente adj latent

lateral adj ⟨puerta/salida/calle⟩ side (before n); ⟨línea/sucesión⟩ indirect, lateral
- m (Dep) (poste) goalpost
- m or f (Auto) (calle perpendicular) side street; (calle paralela) service road, frontage road (AmE)
- mf (Dep) (alero) wing, winger; (defensa) left/right back

latido m (del corazón) heartbeat; (en la sien, una herida) throbbing

latifundio m large estate

latigazo m (a) (golpe) lash (b) (chasquido) crack of the whip

látigo m whip

latín *m* Latin

latino -na *adj* **(a)** ⟨*literatura/gramática/pueblo*⟩ Latin **(b)** (fam) (latinoamericano) Latin American
■ *m,f* **(a)** (español, italiano, etc) Latin **(b)** (fam) (latinoamericano) Latin American

Latinoamérica *f* Latin America

latinoamericano -na *adj/m,f* Latin American

latir [I1] *vi* **1** ⟨*corazón*⟩ to beat; ⟨*vena*⟩ to pulsate; ⟨*herida/sien*⟩ to throb **2 (a)** (Chi, Méx fam) (parecer) (+ *me/te/le etc*): **me late que no vendrá** I have a feeling *o* something tells me he isn't going to come **(b)** (Méx fam) (parecer bien, gustar) (+ *me/te/le etc*): **¿te late ir al cine?** do you feel like going to the movies?

latitud *f* (Astron, Geog) latitude; **la flora de otras ~es** the flora of other parts of the world

latón *m* **(a)** (Metal) brass **(b)** (RPl) (palangana) metal bowl

latonería *f* (Col) body shop

latoso -sa *adj* **(a)** (fam) (molesto) annoying, tiresome; **no seas ~** don't be such a pain (colloq) **(b)** (Andes fam) (aburrido) dull, boring
■ *m,f* **(a)** (fam) (pesado) pain (in the neck) (colloq) **(b)** (Andes fam) (aburrido) bore

laucha *f* (CS) mouse

laúd *m* lute

laurel *m* (árbol) laurel; (Coc) bay leaf

lava *f* lava

lavable *adj* washable

lavabo *m* **(a)** (pila) sink (AmE), washbasin (BrE) **(b)** (retrete) toilet, bathroom; ❾ **lavabos** rest rooms (*in US*), toilets (*in UK*)

lavadero *m* **(a)** (habitación) utility room, laundry room; (pila) sink; (al aire libre) washing place **(b)** (RPl) (lavandería) laundry **(c)** (Col) (tina de lavar) washtub

lavado¹ -da *adj* **(a)** ⟨*ropa/manos*⟩ washed **(b)** (RPl fam) ⟨*color*⟩ (descolorido) washed-out; (muy claro) light; ⟨*persona*⟩ pale

lavado² *m* **1 (a)** (de ropa) wash, washing; (de coche) wash; **~ en seco** dry cleaning; **hacerle un ~ de cerebro a algn** to brainwash sb; **le hicieron un ~ de estómago** they pumped his stomach out **(b)** (ropa, tanda) wash **2** (AmL) (de dinero) laundering

lavadora *f* washing machine

lavamanos *m* sink (AmE), washbasin (BrE)

lavanda *f* lavender
■ *m* lavander

lavandería *f* laundry; **~ automática** Laundromat® (AmE), launderette (BrE)

lavaplatos *mf* (*pl* ~) (persona) dishwasher
■ *m* (*pl*) **(a)** (máquina) dishwasher **(b)** (Andes) (fregadero) sink

lavar [A1] *vt* **1** ⟨*ropa/coche*⟩ to wash; ⟨*suelo*⟩ to mop; ⟨*fruta/verdura*⟩ to wash; **hay que ~lo en seco/a mano** it has to be dry-cleaned/hand-washed **2** (AmL) ⟨*dinero*⟩ to launder
■ *vi* **(a)** (lavar ropa) to do the laundry *o* (BrE) washing **(b)** (en peluquería): **~ y marcar** to shampoo and set
■ **lavarse** *v pron* **(a)** (refl) to have a wash; ⟨*cara/manos*⟩ to wash; ⟨*dientes*⟩ to clean, brush; **~se el pelo** *or* **la cabeza** to wash one's hair **(b)** (Col fam) (empaparse) to get soaked

lavarropas *m* (*pl* ~) (RPl) washing machine

lavatorio *m* **(a)** (CS) (lavamanos) sink (AmE), washbasin (BrE) **(b)** (Chi, Per) (palangana) washbowl (AmE), washbasin (BrE)

lavavajillas *m* (*pl* ~) (detergente) dishwashing liquid (AmE), washing-up liquid (BrE); (máquina) dishwasher

laxante *adj* laxative (*before n*)
■ *m* laxative

lazar [A4] *vt* (Méx) to rope, lasso

lazo *m* **1 (a)** (cinta) ribbon; (nudo decorativo) bow; **¿te hago un ~?** shall I tie it in a bow? **(b)** (Méx) (del matrimonio) cord with which the couple are symbolically united during the wedding ceremony **2 (a)** (Agr) lasso **(b)** (cuerda) (Col, Méx) rope; (para saltar) (Col) ▶ **CUERDA** 1B **(c)** (para cazar) snare, trap **3** (vínculo) bond, tie

le *pron pers* **1** (como objeto indirecto): **~ dije la verdad** (a él) I told him the truth; (a ella) I told her the truth; (a usted) I told you the truth; **~ di otra mano de barniz** I gave it another coat of varnish; **~ robaron el dinero** they stole the money from him; **a este libro ~ faltan páginas** there are some pages missing from this book **2** (como objeto directo) (esp Esp) (referido — a él) him; (— a usted) you; **¿le conoces?** do you know him?; **hoy no ~ puedo recibir** I can't see him/you today

leal *adj* loyal, trusty; ⟨*tropas*⟩ loyal

lealtad *f* loyalty

leasing /'lisin/ *m* (contrato) lease; (sistema) leasing

lección *f* lesson; **no me supe la ~** I hadn't learned the lesson; **eso te servirá de ~** let that be a lesson to you

lechal *adj* suckling

leche *f* **1** (de madre, de vaca) milk; **~ descremada** *or* (Esp) **desnatada** skim milk (AmE), skimmed milk (BrE); **~ en polvo** powdered milk; **~ entera** whole milk, full-cream milk **2** (en cosmética) milk, lotion **3** (Esp vulg) (mal humor): **tiene una ~ ...** he's got a foul temper; **hacer algo con mala ~** to do sth deliberately *o* to be nasty; **tener mala ~** to be bad-tempered **4** (Andes fam) (suerte) luck; **estar con** *o* **de ~** to be lucky

lechera *f* (para transportar) churn; (para servir) milk jug

lechería *f* dairy, creamery

lechero -ra *adj* **1 (a)** ⟨*industria/vaca*⟩ dairy (*before n*) **(b)** ⟨*producción*⟩ milk (*before n*) **2** (Col, Per fam) (afortunado) lucky
■ *m,f* (vendedor) (*m*) milkman; (*f*) milkwoman

lecho *m* **1** (liter) (cama) bed; **en su ~ de muerte** on her deathbed **2** (de río) bed; (capa, estrato) layer

lechón *m* (Coc) (cochinillo) suckling *o* sucking pig

lechosa *f* (AmC, Col, Ven) papaya

lechoso -sa *adj* ⟨*líquido*⟩ milky; ⟨*piel*⟩ pale

lechuga *f* lettuce

lechuza *f* owl

lectivo -va *adj* ⟨*día*⟩ school (*before n*); ⟨*año*⟩ academic (*before n*)

lector -tora *m,f* **(a)** (de libros, revistas) reader **(b)** (Esp) (Educ) foreign language assistant

lectura *f* **(a)** (acción) reading; **la ~ es su**

pasatiempo preferido reading is her favorite pastime **(b)** (texto) reading matter; ∼**s para niños** reading material for children

leer [E13] *vt* **(a)** ⟨*libro/texto*⟩ to read; ∼ **los labios** to lip-read; ∼**le el pensamiento a algn** to read sb's mind **(b)** (Educ) ⟨*tesis doctoral*⟩ to defend **(c)** (Inf) to scan
■ ∼ *vi* to read

legado *m* (Der) bequest, legacy

legal *adj* ⓵ (Der) **(a)** ⟨*trámite/documentos*⟩ legal **(b)** (lícito, permitido) lawful; **lo haré si es** ∼ I'll do it as long as it's within the law ⓶ (Col, Per arg) (estupendo) great (colloq)

legalización *f* (Der) (de droga, aborto) legalization; (de documento) authentication

legalizar [A4] *vt* (Der) ⟨*droga/aborto*⟩ to legalize; ⟨*documento*⟩ to authenticate

legaña *f* sleep; **tienes** ∼**s en los ojos** you have (some) sleep in your eyes

legar [A3] *vt* (en testamento) to bequeath, leave

legendario -ria *adj* legendary

legible *adj* legible

legión *f* (Hist, Mil) legion; (multitud) crowd

legionario¹ -ria *adj* legionary

legionario² -ria *m* (romano) legionary; (de otras asociaciones) legionnaire

legionela *f* legionnaire's disease

legislación *f* legislation

legislar [A1] *vi* to legislate

legislatura *f* **(a)** (mandato) term (of office); (año parlamentario) session **(b)** (AmL) (cuerpo) legislature

legítimo -ma *adj* ⓵ ⟨*hijo*⟩ legitimate; ⟨*esposa*⟩ lawful (*before n*); ⟨*heredero*⟩ rightful (*before n*); ⟨*derechos/reclamación/representante*⟩ legitimate; **en legítima defensa** in self-defense ⓶ ⟨*cuero*⟩ genuine, real; ⟨*oro*⟩ real

lego -ga *adj* ⓵ (seglar) lay (*before n*) ⓶ (ignorante): **soy** ∼ **en la materia** I know nothing at all about the subject
■ *m,f* **(a)** (fiel laico) layperson **(b)** (religioso) (*m*) lay brother; (*f*) lay sister **(c)** (Col) (curandero) quack

legua *f* league

legumbre *f* (garbanzo, lenteja, etc) pulse, legume; (hortaliza) vegetable

leído -da *adj*: **ser muy** ∼ to be well-read

leísmo *m*: *use of* LE/LES *instead of* LO/LOS/LA/LAS (*as in* ESTE LIBRO NO TE LE PRESTO), *common in certain regions of Spain but not acceptable to most speakers*

lejanía *f* remoteness; **en la** ∼ in the distance

lejano -na *adj* **(a)** ⟨*época/futuro*⟩ distant; ⟨*lugar*⟩ remote, far-off; **el L**∼ **Oriente** the Far East **(b)** ⟨*pariente*⟩ distant

lejía *f* bleach

lejísimos *adv* ⟨*quedar/estar*⟩ very far (away); **vive** ∼ she lives miles away

lejos *adv* ⓵ **(a)** (en el espacio) far; **no está muy** ∼ it isn't very far; **queda** ∼ **del centro** it's a long way from the center; **estaba** ∼ **de imaginarme la verdad** I was far from guessing the truth **(b)** (*en locs*) **a lo lejos** in the distance; **de lejos** from a distance; **ir demasiado** ∼ to go too far; **sin ir más** ∼ for example, for instance **(c)** (fam) (con mucho): **es** ∼ (CS) *o* (Col, Méx) **de** ∼ by far ⓶ (en el futuro) a long way off; **las vacaciones aún están** ∼**s** the holidays are still a long way off

lelo -la *adj* (fam) (tonto) slow on the uptake; (pasmado) speechless

lema *m* (de insignia, de persona) motto; (de partido, anuncio publicitario) slogan

lempira *m* lempira (*Honduran unit of currency*)

lencería *f* lingerie

lengua *f* ⓵ **(a)** (Anat) tongue; **se me traba la** ∼ I get tongue-tied; **irse de la** ∼ *or* **írsele la** ∼ **a algn** (fam): **no debía haberlo dicho pero se me fue la** ∼ I shouldn't have said it but it just slipped out; **no te vayas a ir de la** ∼ make sure you don't tell anybody; ▶ MALO 2 **(b)** (Coc) tongue **(c)** (de tierra) spit, tongue; (de fuego) tongue ⓶ (Ling) language; ∼ **materna** mother tongue

lenguado *m* sole

lenguaje *m* language

lengüeta *f* (de zapato) tongue; (Mús) reed

lente *m* [*en algunas regiones f*] lens; ∼ **de contacto** contact lens; *ver tb* LENTES

lenteja *f* lentil

lentejuela *f* sequin

lentes *mpl* (esp AmL) ▶ GAFAS A

lentilla *f* (Esp) contact lens

lentitud *f* slowness; **con** ∼ slowly

lento¹ -ta *adj* slow

lento² *adv* slowly

leña *f* wood, firewood

leñador -dora *m,f* woodcutter

leño *m* log

Leo *m* (signo) Leo; **es (de)** ∼ he's a (a) Leo;
■ *mf* (*pl* ∼) (persona) *tb* **leo** Leo

león -ona *m,f* (de África) (*m*) lion; (*f*) lioness

leonera *f* **(a)** (de león) lion's den **(b)** (Esp fam) (lugar desordenado) tip (colloq)

leopardo *m* leopard; ∼ **hembra** leopardess

leotardo *m*: *tb* ∼**s** (woolen) tights (*pl*)

lépero -ra *adj* (Méx) coarse

lepra *f* leprosy

leproso -sa *adj* leprous
■ *m,f* leper

lerdo -da *adj* (fam) (torpe) clumsy; (tonto) slow

les *pron pers* ⓵ (como objeto indirecto): ∼ **quiero mostrar algo** (a ellos, ellas) I want to show them something; (a ustedes) I want to show you something; ∼ **puse fundas a los muebles** I put covers on the furniture ⓶ (como objeto directo) (esp Esp) (referido — a ellos) them; (— a ustedes) you; **no** ∼ **reconocí** I didn't recognize them/you; **¿**∼ **atienden?** can I help you?

lesbiana *f* lesbian

lesear [A1] *vi* (Chi fam) (tontear) to clown *o* fool around (colloq); (bromear) to joke (colloq); (flirtear) to flirt; (perder el tiempo) to laze around

lesera *f* (Chi fam) nonsense, tripe (colloq)

lesión *f* injury; **sufrió una** ∼ **cerebral** he suffered brain damage

lesionado -da *adj* injured

lesionar [A1] *vt* ⟨*persona*⟩ to injure; **le** ∼**on la pierna en el partido** his leg was hurt *o* injured in the game
■ **lesionarse** *v pron* «*persona*» to injure oneself; ⟨*pierna/rodilla*⟩ to injure

leso -sa *adj* (Chi fam) dumb (colloq); **hacer** ∼ **a algn** (fam) to make a monkey out of sb (colloq)

letárgico -ca adj lethargic

letargo m lethargy

letra f **1** (a) (Impr, Ling) letter; ~ **bastardilla** or **cursiva** italic script, italics (pl); ~ **de imprenta** print; ~ **negrita** boldface, bold type; ~ **pequeña** or (AmS) **chica** small print (b) (caligrafía) writing, handwriting; **no entiendo tu** ~ I can't read your writing (c) **letras** fpl (carta breve): **solo unas ~s para decirte que ...** just a few lines to let you know that ... **2** (Mús) (de canción) words (pl), lyrics (pl) **3** (Fin) tb ~ **de cambio** bill of exchange, draft; **me quedan tres ~s por pagar** I still have three payments to make **4** **letras** fpl (Educ) arts (pl), liberal arts (pl) (AmE)

letrado -da adj learned
■ m,f (frml) lawyer

letrero m sign, notice; ~ **luminoso** neon sign

letrina f latrine

leucemia f leukemia

levadura f yeast; **pan sin** ~ unleavened bread; ~ **de cerveza** brewer's yeast; ~ **en polvo** (Esp) baking powder

levantado -da adj: **estar** ~ to be up

levantador -dora m,f (Dep) tb ~ **de pesas** weightlifter

levantamiento m (a) (sublevación) uprising (b) (de embargo, sanción) lifting; ~ **de pesas** weightlifting

levantar [A1] vt **1** (a) (del suelo) ⟨bulto/peso⟩ to lift, pick up (b) ⟨tapadera/mantel⟩ to lift (up); ⟨cabeza/mano/copa⟩ to raise; ⟨alfombra⟩ to lift up (c) ⟨persiana⟩ to pull up, raise (d) (elevar) ⟨voz⟩ to raise; **sin** ~ **la vista del libro** without looking up from her book (e) ⟨polvo⟩ to raise (f) (Jueg) ⟨carta⟩ to pick up
2 (a) ⟨ánimo⟩ to boost; ⟨moral⟩ to raise, boost (b) ⟨industria/economía⟩ to help ... to pick up
3 ⟨estatua/muro/edificio⟩ to erect, put up
4 ⟨embargo/sanción⟩ to lift; **le levantó el castigo** he let him off; **se levanta la sesión** the meeting is adjourned
5 ⟨rumor/protestas⟩ to spark (off); ⟨polémica⟩ to cause; ~ **sospechas** to arouse suspicion
6 ⟨campamento⟩ to strike; ~ **la mesa** (AmL) to clear the table
7 (en brazos) ⟨persona⟩ to pick up; (de la cama) to get ... out of bed; (poner de pie) to get ... up
8 (AmS) ⟨mujer⟩ to pick up (colloq)
■ **levantarse** v pron **1** (a) (de la cama) to get up (b) (ponerse en pie) to stand up, to rise (frml); **¿me puedo ~ de la mesa?** may I leave the table?
2 «polvareda» to rise; «temporal» to brew; «viento» to begin to blow, rise
3 (sublevarse) to rise (up)
4 (refl) ⟨solapas/cuello⟩ to turn up
5 (AmS fam) ⟨mujer⟩ to pick up (colloq)

levante m **1** (a) (Geog) (este) east (b) (viento) east wind **2** (AmS fam) (conquista) pick up

levar [A1] vt: ~ **anclas** to weigh anchor

leve adj (a) ⟨perfume/gasa⟩ delicate (b) ⟨sospecha/duda⟩ slight; ⟨sonrisa⟩ slight; ⟨brisa⟩ gentle, slight; ⟨golpe⟩ gentle, light; ⟨enfermedad⟩ mild; ⟨herida/lesión⟩ slight; ⟨pecado⟩ venial; ⟨castigo/sanción⟩ light; ⟨infracción⟩ minor

levita f (Indum) frock coat

léxico¹ -ca adj lexical

léxico² m (vocabulario) vocabulary, lexis (tech); (diccionario) lexicon; (glosario) glossary, lexicon

ley f **1** (en general) law; **violar la** ~ to break the law; **iguales ante la** ~ equal in the eyes of the law; ~ **de la oferta y la demanda** law of supply and demand; **la** ~ **del más fuerte** the survival of the fittest; ~ **pareja no es dura** (CS) a rule isn't unfair if it applies to everyone **2** (de oro, plata) assay value

leyenda f (a) (Lit) (narración) legend (b) (de moneda, escudo) legend; (de ilustración) caption, legend

leyeron, leyó, etc ▶ LEER

liado -da adj (fam) (a) (ocupado) tied up (b) (relacionado) ~ **CON algn** involved WITH sb

liana f liana

liar [A17] vt **1** (a) ⟨cigarrillo⟩ to roll (b) (atar) to tie (up); (envolver) to wrap (up); (en un fardo, manojo) to bundle (up) **2** (fam) (a) ⟨situación/asunto⟩ to complicate (b) (confundir) ⟨persona⟩ to confuse, get ... in a muddle (c) (en un asunto) ⟨persona⟩ to involve
■ **liarse** v pron **1** (fam) (a) «asunto» to get complicated (b) «persona» to get confused **2** (Esp fam) (a) (entretenerse): **nos liamos a hablar y ...** we got talking and ... (b) (emprenderla): **se ~on a golpes** they started throwing punches at each other

libanés -nesa adj/m,f Lebanese

Líbano m: tb el ~ Lebanon

libélula f dragonfly

liberación f (de preso, rehén) release, freeing; (de pueblo, país) liberation; **la** ~ **de la mujer** Women's Liberation, Women's Lib

liberado -da adj ⟨mujer⟩ liberated

liberal adj liberal
■ mf Liberal

liberalismo m liberalism

liberalizar [A4] vt ⟨comercio/importaciones⟩ to relax the restrictions on

liberar [A1] vt (a) ⟨prisionero/rehén⟩ to release, free; ⟨pueblo/país⟩ to liberate (b) (de una obligación) ~ **a algn DE algo** to free sb FROM sth
■ **liberarse** v pron ~**se DE algo** ⟨de ataduras/deudas⟩ to free oneself FROM sth

libertad f **1** (para actuar) freedom; **queda usted en** ~ you are free to go; **poner a algn en** ~ to release sb; ~ **bajo fianza** bail; ~ **condicional** parole; ~ **de expresión/de prensa** freedom of speech/of the press **2** (confianza): **pídelo con toda** ~ feel free to ask; **habla con toda** ~ speak freely; **tomarse la** ~ **de hacer algo** to take the liberty of doing sth

libertador -dora m,f liberator

libertinaje m licentiousness

libertino -na *adj* dissolute, licentious
■ *m,f* libertine

Libia *f* Libya

libidinoso -sa *adj* lustful

libido, líbido *f* libido

libio -bia *adj/m,f* Libyan

libra *f* pound; ~ **esterlina** pound sterling

Libra *m* (signo) Libra; **es (de)** ~ she's (a) Libra, she's a Libran
■ *mf* (*pl* ~ *or* **-bras**) (persona) *tb* **libra** Libran, Libra

libramiento *m* (Méx) (Transp) beltway (AmE), relief road (BrE)

librar [A1] *vt* ⟦1⟧ (liberar) ~ **a algn** DE **algo** ⟨*de peligro*⟩ to save sb FROM sth; ⟨*de obligación/ responsabilidad*⟩ to free sb FROM sth; **¡Dios nos libre!** God forbid! ⟦2⟧ ⟨*batalla/combate*⟩ to fight
■ **librarse** *v pron*: **se libró por poco** he had a lucky escape; ~**se** DE **algo** ⟨*de tarea/obligación*⟩ to get out of sth; ~**se de un castigo** to escape punishment; **se libró de tener que ayudarlo** she got out of having to help him; **se** ~**on de morir asfixiados** they escaped being suffocated; ~**se** DE **algn** to get rid OF sb

libre *adj* ⟦1⟧ ⟨*país/pueblo*⟩ free; **lo dejaron** ~ they set him free; **eres** ~ **de ir donde quieras** you're free to go wherever you want; ~ **albedrío** free will; ~ **cambio** *or* **comercio** free trade; ~ **mercado** free market ⟦2⟧ ⟨*traducción/adaptación*⟩ free; **los 200 metros** ~**s** the 200 meters freestyle ⟦3⟧ (no ocupado) ⟨*persona/tiempo/asiento*⟩ free; **¿tienes un rato** ~**?** do you have a (spare) moment?; **en sus ratos** ~**s** in her spare *o* free time; **tengo el día** ~ I have the day off ⟦4⟧ (exento): **artículos** ~**s de impuestos** duty-free goods

librecambista *adj* free-trade (*before n*)

librería *f* ⟦1⟧ (tienda) bookstore (AmE), bookshop (BrE); ~ **de ocasión** second-hand bookstore ⟦2⟧ (Esp) (mueble) bookcase

librero -ra *m,f* (a) (Com) bookseller (b) **librero** *m* (Chi, Méx) (mueble) bookcase

libreta *f* notebook; ~ **de ahorro** passbook, bankbook; ~ **de calificaciones** (AmL) school report

libretearse [A1] *v pron* (AmC fam) to play hooky (esp AmE colloq), to skive off (school) (BrE colloq)

libreto *m* ⟦1⟧ (a) (de ópera) libretto (b) (AmL) (guion) script ⟦2⟧ (Chi) *tb* ~ **de cheques** checkbook*

libro *m* (Impr) book; **un** ~ **de cocina** a cookbook; **llevar los** ~**s** (Fin) to do the bookkeeping; ~ **de bolsillo** paperback; ~ **de consulta** reference book; ~ **de escolaridad** school record; ~ **de familia** booklet recording details of one's marriage, children's birthdates, etc; ~ **de texto** textbook

liceal *mf* (Ur) high school student (AmE), secondary school pupil (BrE)

liceano -na *m,f* (Chi) ▶ LICEAL

liceísta *mf* (Ven) ▶ LICEAL

licencia *f* ⟦1⟧ (documento) license*; ~ **de caza** hunting permit; ~ **de conducir** *or* (AmC, Méx, Ven) **de manejar** driver's license (AmE), driving licence (BrE) ⟦2⟧ (a) (Mil) leave; **con** ~ on leave (b) (AmL) (de un trabajo) leave; **estar de** ~ to be on leave

licenciado -da *m,f* (a) (Educ) graduate; ~ **en Filosofía y Letras** ≈ arts *o* (AmE) liberal arts graduate (b) (AmC, Méx) (abogado) lawyer

licenciar [A1] *vt* ⟨*soldado*⟩ to discharge
■ **licenciarse** *v pron* «*estudiante*» to graduate

licenciatura *f* degree

licencioso -sa *adj* dissolute

liceo *m* (CS, Ven) high school (AmE), secondary school (BrE)

licitación *f* (esp AmL) tender; **se llamará a** ~ **para la construcción del puente** the construction of the bridge will be put out to tender

licitar [A1] *vt* (esp AmL) (llamar a concurso para) to invite tenders for; (presentar una propuesta para) to put in a tender for

lícito -ta *adj* (a) (dentro de la ley) ⟨*acto/conducta*⟩ legal, lawful; ⟨*jugada*⟩ legal (b) (admisible) justifiable, reasonable

licor *m* (bebida dulce) liqueur; (alcohol) liquor, spirits (*pl*)

licuado *m* (AmL) (con leche) (milk) shake; (de frutas) fruit drink

licuadora *f* blender, liquidizer (BrE)

licuar [A18] *vt* (a) (Coc) ⟨*frutas/verduras*⟩ to blend, liquidize (b) (Fís, Quím) to liquefy

líder¹ *mf* (a) (Com, Dep, Pol) leader (b) (*como adj*) ⟨*equipo/marca/empresa*⟩ leading (*before n*)

líder² **lideresa** *m,f* (Méx) (Dep, Pol) leader

liderazgo, liderato *m* leadership

lidiar [A1] *vt* ⟨*toro*⟩ to fight
■ ~ *vi*: ~ CON **algn/algo** to battle WITH sb/sth

liebre *f* ⟦1⟧ (Zool) hare ⟦2⟧ (Chi) (Transp) small bus

liendre *f* nit

lienzo *m* ⟦1⟧ (a) (Art) canvas (b) (Tex) cloth ⟦2⟧ (Arquit) (pared) wall

lifting /'liftin/ *m* facelift

liga *f* ⟦1⟧ (asociación) league; (Dep) league, conference (esp AmE) ⟦2⟧ (a) (Indum) garter (b) (AmL) (gomita) rubber *o* (BrE) elastic band

ligado *adj* [ESTAR] (conectado) connected, linked; (apegado) ~ A **algn** attached TO sb; **se siente muy** ~ **a su país** he feels a strong bond with his country

ligadura *f* (a) (Med) ligature (b) **ligaduras** *fpl* (ataduras) bonds (*pl*), ties (*pl*)

ligamento *m* ligament

ligar [A3] *vt* (a) (unir) to bind; **los ligaba una gran amistad** they were bound together by a strong friendship (b) (atar): **le** ~**on las manos** they tied his hands together; **un fajo de billetes ligados con una goma elástica** a bundle of bills held together with a rubber band (c) ⟨*metales*⟩ to alloy; ⟨*salsa*⟩ to bind
■ ~ *vi* (fam) (con el sexo opuesto): **salieron a** ~ they went out on the make *o* (BrE) pull (colloq); ~ CON **algn** to make out WITH sb (AmE), to get off WITH sb (BrE)
■ **ligarse** *v pron* (fam) (conquistar) to make out with (AmE colloq), to get off with (colloq BrE)

ligazón *f* connection, link

ligereza *f* ⟦1⟧ (de objeto) lightness ⟦2⟧ (a) (de carácter) flippancy; **con** ~ ⟨*actuar/hablar*⟩ flippantly (b) (acto, dicho irreflexivo): **cometió la** ~ **de mencionarlo** he thoughtlessly mentioned it ⟦3⟧ (agilidad) agility, nimbleness; (rapidez) speed

ligero¹ -ra *adj* ⟦1⟧ (liviano) (a) ⟨*paquete/gas/* ⋯⟶

‹metal› light; ‹tela› light, thin; ~ **de ropa** lightly dressed; **viajar ~ de equipaje** to travel light **(b)** ‹comida/masa› light **2** (leve) **(a)** ‹dolor/sabor/olor› slight; ‹inconveniente› slight, minor; ‹golpe› gentle, slight; **tener el sueño ~** to be a light sleeper **(b)** ‹sensación/sospecha› slight **3** (no serio) ‹conversación› lighthearted; ‹película/lectura› lightweight; **a la ligera** ‹actuar› without thinking, hastily; **todo se lo toma a la ligera** he doesn't take anything seriously **4** (ágil) ‹movimiento› agile, nimble; (rápido) ‹persona/animal/vehículo› fast

ligero² adv quickly, fast

light /lajt/ adj inv ‹cigarrillos› low-tar; ‹alimentos› low-calorie; ‹refresco› diet (before n)

ligue m (Esp, Méx fam) **(a)** (persona): **el nuevo ~ de Ana** Ana's new man (colloq) **(b)** (acción): **ir de ~** to go out on the make o (BrE) pull

liguero m garter belt (AmE), suspender belt (BrE)

lija f **(a)** (para madera, metales) tb **papel de ~** sandpaper **(b)** (Ven) ▶ LIMA 1B

lijar [A1] vt to sand (down)

lila f (Bot) lilac
■ adj (gen inv) ‹color› lilac
■ m (color) lilac

lima f **1** **(a)** (herramienta) file **(b)** (para uñas — de metal) nail file; (—de papel) emery board **2** (Bot) (fruto) lime; (árbol) lime (tree)

Lima f Lima

limar [A1] vt ‹uñas/metal› to file
■ **limarse** v pron ‹uñas› to file

limeño -ña adj of/from Lima
■ m,f person from Lima

limitación f **(a)** (restricción) restriction, limitation **(b)** (carencia) limitation; (defecto) shortcoming

limitado -da adj ‹poder/número/edición› limited; **estar ~ A/POR algo** to be restricted TO/BY sth

limitar [A1] vt ‹funciones/derechos› to limit, restrict
■ ~ vi ~ **CON algo** «país/finca» to border ON sth
■ **limitarse** v pron: **el problema no se limita a las ciudades** the problem is not confined o limited to cities; **me limité a repetir lo dicho** I just repeated what was said

límite m **1** (Geog, Pol) boundary **2** (tope) limit; **el ~ de velocidad** the speed limit; **su ambición no tiene ~s** his ambition knows no limits; **sin ~s** unlimited; **¡todo tiene un ~!** enough is enough! **3** (como adj inv): **tiempo ~** time limit; **situación ~** extreme situation; **fecha ~** deadline

limítrofe adj ‹país/provincia› neighboring* (before n); ‹conflicto› border (before n)

limo m **1** (barro) mud, slime **2** (Col) (Bot) lime (tree)

limón m **(a)** (fruto amarillo) lemon **(b)** (AmL) (árbol) lemon tree **(c)** (Méx, Ven) (fruto verde) lime

limonada f lemonade

limonero m lemon tree

limosna f alms (pl) (arch); **pedir ~** to beg; **dar ~** to give money to beggars

limosnear [A1] vi (AmL) to beg

limosnero -ra m,f (AmL) beggar

limpiabotas mf (pl ~) bootblack; (niño) shoeshine boy

limpiacristales m (pl ~) (Esp) (líquido) window cleaner
■ mf (persona) window cleaner

limpiador¹ -dora m,f (persona) cleaner

limpiador² m (Méx) (Auto) ▶ LIMPIAPARABRISAS

limpiamuebles m (pl ~) furniture polish

limpiaparabrisas m (pl ~) windshield wipers (pl) (AmE), windscreen wipers (pl) (BrE)

limpiar [A1] vt **1** **(a)** ‹casa/mueble/zapatos› to clean; ‹arroz/lentejas› to wash; ‹pescado› to clean; ‹aire/atmósfera› to clear; **lo limpió con un trapo** he wiped it with a cloth; ~ **algo en seco** to dry-clean sth **(b)** ‹nombre› to clear; ‹honor› to restore **2** (dejar libre) ~ **algo DE algo** to clear sth OF sth **3** (fam) **(a)** (en el juego) ‹persona› to clean … out (colloq) **(b)** «ladrones» ‹casa› to clean … out (colloq)
■ ~ vi to clean
■ **limpiarse** v pron (refl) ‹boca/nariz› to wipe; **se ~on los zapatos al entrar** they wiped their shoes as they came in

limpiavidrios mf (pl ~) (esp AmL) (persona) window cleaner
■ m (líquido) window cleaner

limpieza f **1** (estado, cualidad) cleanliness **2** (acción) cleaning; **la señora de la ~** the cleaning lady; ~ **de cutis** skin cleansing; ~ **en seco** drycleaning; ~ **general** spring-cleaning (AmE), spring-clean (BrE); ~ **étnica** ethnic cleansing **3** (por la policía) clean-up operation; (Pol) purge

limpio¹ -pia adj **1** **(a)** [ESTAR] ‹casa/vestido/vaso› clean **(b)** ‹aire› clean; ‹cielo› clear **(c)** **pasar algo en** or (Esp) **a ~** to make a clean (AmE) o (BrE) fair copy of sth **2** [SER] **(a)** ‹persona› clean **(b)** ‹dinero/campaña› clean; ‹elecciones/juego› fair, clean; **un asunto poco ~** an underhand business **(c)** (libre) ~ **DE algo** ‹de impurezas/polvo› free OF sth **3** (neto): **saca unos $70 ~s por mes** she makes $70 a month after deductions; **sacar en ~**: **no sacó nada en ~ de todo lo que dijo** he didn't make sense of anything he said; **lo único que saqué en ~ es que …** the only thing that I got clear was that …

limpio² adv ‹jugar/pelear› fairly, clean

linaje m descent, lineage (frml)

linaza f linseed

lince m (Zool) lynx; (persona): **es un ~ para los negocios** he's a very shrewd businessman

linchar [A1] vt to lynch

lindar [A1] vi ~ **CON algo** (limitar) to adjoin sth; (aproximarse a) to border ON sth, verge ON sth

lindo¹ -da adj **1** (bonito) ‹bebé› cute, sweet; ‹casa/canción› lovely; ‹cara› pretty **2** (esp AmL) (agradable) ‹gesto/detalle› nice; ‹fiesta/viaje› wonderful; ‹ceremonia› beautiful; **¡es una persona tan linda!** she's such a lovely person; **de lo ~** (fam): **nos divertimos de lo ~** we had a great time

lindo² adv (AmL) ‹cantar/bailar› beautifully; **se siente ~** (Méx) it feels wonderful

lindura f (AmL) delight; **me pareció una ~** I thought it was lovely

línea f **1** (en general) line; **la ~ de puntos** the

dotted line; **escribirle unas ~s a algn** to drop sb a line; **seguir la ~ del partido** to follow the party line; **en ~s generales** broadly speaking; **por ~ materna** on his (*o* her *etc*) mother's side; **~ de montaje** assembly line; **~ de gol** goal line; **~ de llegada** finishing line, wire (AmE); **~ de salida** starting line; **de primera ~** ⟨*tecnología*⟩ state-of-the-art; ⟨*producto*⟩ top-quality, high-class; ⟨*actor/jugador*⟩ first-rate; **leer entre ~s** to read between the lines
2 (Transp, Tele) line; **~ aérea** airline; **final de la ~** end of the line; **no hay ~ directa a Córdoba** there is no direct service to Cordoba; **intenté llamarte pero no había ~** I tried to ring you but the phone *o* the line was dead; **la ~ está ocupada** the line is busy
3 **(a)** (gama, colección) line, range; **nuestra nueva ~ de cosméticos** our new line *o* range of cosmetics **(b)** (estilo): **una ~ más clásica** a more classic look
4 (figura): **cuidar la ~** to watch one's figure

lineal *adj* linear

lingo *m* (Per) leapfrog

lingote *m* ingot

lingüística *f* linguistics

lingüístico -ca *adj* ⟨*fenómeno/aptitud*⟩ linguistic; ⟨*barrera*⟩ language (*before n*)

lino *m* (planta) flax; (tela) linen

linóleo *m* lino, linoleum

linterna *f* (fanal) lantern; (de pilas) flashlight (AmE), torch (BrE)

lío *m* **1** **(a)** (fam) (embrollo, confusión) mess; **armarse/hacerse un ~ (con algo)** to get into a mess (with sth) (colloq) **(b)** (fam) (problema, complicación) trouble; **meterse en un ~** to get oneself into trouble; **tiene ~s con la policía** he's in trouble with the police (colloq); **¡qué ~ se va a armar!** there's going to be hell to pay! (colloq) **(c)** (fam) (amorío) affair **2** (fardo) bundle

lioso -sa *adj* (fam) confusing, muddling

liquidación *f* **1** (en tienda) sale; **~ total** clearance sale **2** (de negocio, activo) liquidation **3** **(a)** (de cuenta, deuda) settlement **(b)** (Méx) (compensación por despido) severance pay

liquidar [A1] *vt* **1** ⟨*existencias*⟩ to sell off **2** ⟨*negocio*⟩ to wind up; ⟨*activo*⟩ to liquidate **3** **(a)** ⟨*deuda/cuenta*⟩ to settle; ⟨*sueldo/pago*⟩ to pay **(b)** (Méx) ⟨*trabajador*⟩ to pay … off **4** (fam) ⟨*persona*⟩ (matar) to do away with (colloq); (destruir) (AmL) to destroy (colloq)

liquidez *f* liquidity

líquido¹ -da *adj* **1** ⟨*sustancia*⟩ liquid **2** ⟨*sueldo/renta*⟩ net

líquido² *m* **1** (sustancia) liquid; **~ de frenos** brake fluid **2** (dinero) cash

lira *f* **(a)** (Mús) lyre **(b)** (Fin) lira

lírica *f* poetry

lírico -ca *adj* **(a)** (Lit, Mús) lyric **(b)** (Per, RPI fam) ⟨*persona*⟩ dreamy, starry-eyed (colloq)

lirio *m* iris

lirón *m* dormouse; ▶ DORMIR *vi*

lis *f* lily

lisiado -da *adj* crippled
■ *m,f* cripple; **un ~ de guerra** a disabled veteran

lisiarse [A1] *v pron* (refl): **se lisió la columna vertebral** he damaged his spine

liso -sa *adj* **1** ⟨*piel/superficie*⟩ smooth; ⟨*pelo*⟩ straight; ⟨*terreno*⟩ flat **2** (sin dibujos) plain **3** (Per fam) (insolente) fresh (AmE colloq), cheeky (BrE colloq)

lisonjero -ra *adj* ⟨*palabras*⟩ flattering; **es un hombre muy ~** he's a terrible flatterer

lista *f* **(a)** (de nombres, números) list; **pasar ~** (Educ) to take roll call, to take the register (BrE); **~ de boda** wedding list; **~ de espera** waiting list; **~ de éxitos** (Mús) charts (*pl*); (Lit) best-seller list **(b)** (raya) stripe; **a ~s** striped

listado *m* (Inf) printout; (lista) list; **~ electoral** (RPl) electoral roll *o* register

listar [A1] *vt* to list

listín *m* (Esp) *tb* **~ de teléfonos** telephone directory

listo -ta *adj* **1** [SER] ⟨*persona*⟩ clever, bright, smart (colloq); **se pasó de ~** he tried to be too clever; **estar ~** (fam): **ahora sí que estamos ~s** we're in real trouble now (colloq); **está lista si cree eso** if that's what she thinks, she's got another think coming (colloq) **2** **(a)** [ESTAR] (preparado) ready; **~ PARA algo/ hacer algo** ready FOR sth/to do sth **(b)** [ESTAR] (terminado) finished; **lo doblas así y ~** you fold it like this and that's it (finished) **(c)** (Andes fam) (manifestando acuerdo) okay (colloq)
■ *m,f* (esp Esp) **(a)** (inteligente) clever one; **el ~ de la clase** (pey) the class know-it-all (colloq & pej) **(b)** (vivo, astuto) tricky customer (colloq)

listón *m* **(a)** (de madera) strip; (en salto de altura) bar **(b)** (Méx) (cinta) ribbon

lisura *f* (Per) **(a)** (fam) (grosería) four-letter word (colloq) **(b)** (gracia) gracefulness

litera *f* (en dormitorio) bunk; (en barco) bunk, berth; (en tren) berth, couchette (BrE)

literal *adj* literal

literalmente *adv* ⟨*traducir*⟩ literally; ⟨*repetir*⟩ word for word

literario -ria *adj* literary

literato -ta *m,f* (*m*) man of letters; (*f*) woman of letters

literatura *f* literature; **~ infantil** juvenile books (AmE), children's books (BrE)

litigar [A3] *vi* to be at law *o* in litigation (frml), to be in dispute

litigio *m* **(a)** (Der) lawsuit **(b)** (disputa) dispute

litografía *f* (sistema) lithography; (grabado) lithograph

litoral *adj* coastal
■ *m* coast; **un largo ~** a long coastline

litro *m* liter*

Lituania *f* Lithuania

lituano¹ -na *adj/m,f* Lithuanian

lituano² *m* (idioma) Lithuanian

liturgia *f* liturgy

liviano -na *adj* (esp AmL) **(a)** ⟨*paquete/tela*⟩ light **(b)** ⟨*comida*⟩ light; **tiene un sueño muy ~** she's a very light sleeper **(c)** ⟨*obra/película*⟩ lightweight

lívido -da *adj* (pálido) pallid; (morado) livid

living /'liβin/ *m* (*pl* **-vings**) (esp AmS) living room

Ll, ll *f* (*read as* /'eʎe/) *combination traditionally considered as a separate letter in the Spanish alphabet*

llaga *f* (Med) sore, ulcer; (Bib) wound

llama f **1** (de fuego) flame; **la casa ardía en ~s** the house was in flames; **~ piloto** pilot light **2** (Zool) llama

llamada f call; **hacer una ~** to make a phone call; **~ a cobro revertido** or (Chi, Méx) **por cobrar** collect call (AmE), reverse-charge call (BrE); **~ de larga distancia** long-distance call; **~ local** or **urbana** local call; **~ al orden** call to order

llamado¹ -da adj **1** (por un nombre) called; **un lugar ~ La Dehesa** a place called La Dehesa; **el 747, también ~ 'jumbo'** the 747, also known as the jumbo jet; **el ~ 'boom' de los sesenta** the so-called 'boom' of the sixties **2** (a la fama, éxito) ▶ DESTINADO 1A

llamado² m (a) (AmL) (al público) ▶ LLAMAMIENTO (b) (Arg) (Telec) ▶ LLAMADA

llamamiento m call; **hacer un ~ a la calma** to appeal for calm

llamar [A1] vt **1** ‹bomberos/policía› to call; ‹médico› to call (out); ‹camarero/criada/ascensor› to call; ‹súbditos/servidores› to summon; ‹taxi› (por teléfono) to call; (en la calle) to hail; **lo llamó por señas** she beckoned to him; **el sindicato los llamó a la huelga** the union called them out on strike **2** (por teléfono) to phone, to call; **llamar a algn AL** (AmL) **celular** or (Esp) **al móvil** to call sb ON their cell phone (AmE) o mobile (BrE) **3** (a) (dar el nombre de) to call, name; (dar el título, apodo de) to call (b) (considerar) to call; **eso es lo que yo llamo un amigo** that's what I call a friend ■ ~ vi **1** (con los nudillos) to knock; (tocar el timbre) to ring (the doorbell); **llaman a la puerta** there's someone at the door **2** (Telec) «persona» to telephone, phone, call; «teléfono» to ring; **¿quién llama?** who's calling?; ver tb COBRO B ■ **llamarse** v pron to be called; **su padre se llama Pedro** his father is called Pedro; **¿cómo te llamas?** what's your name?

llamarada f (de fuego) sudden blaze, flare-up

llamativo -va adj ‹color› bright; ‹mujer/vestido› striking

llanamente adv: **lisa** or **simple y ~** ‹explicar/hablar› in straightforward terms; **lisa y ~, hay que despedirlos** they should be fired, it's as simple as that

llanero -ra m,f (a) (habitante del llano) (m) plainsman; (f) plainswoman (b) (vaquero) cattle herder, cowboy (of the Colombian/Venezuelan LLANOS)

llaneza f simplicity

llano¹ -na adj (a) ‹terreno/superficie› (horizontal) flat; (sin desniveles) even; **los 100 metros ~s** (RPl) the 100 meters dash o sprint (b) ‹persona› straightforward; ‹trato› natural; ‹lenguaje› plain

llano² m (a) (Geog) (llanura) plain (b) (extensión de terreno) area of flat ground

llanta f (a) (de metal) rim (b) (AmL) (neumático) tire*; **~ de repuesto** or (Méx) **de refacción** spare tire*

llanto m (de niño) crying; (de adulto) crying, weeping (liter)

llanura f (Geog) plain, prairie

llapa f ▶ YAPA

llave f **1** (en general) key; **cierra la puerta con ~** lock the door; **bajo ~** under lock and key; **la ~ del éxito** the key to success; **~ de contacto** ignition key; **~ maestra** master key, passkey **2** (Mec) (herramienta) wrench (AmE), spanner (BrE); **~ inglesa** monkey wrench **3** (a) (interruptor) switch; (en tubería) valve; **la ~ del gas** the gas jet (AmE) o (BrE) tap; **cerrar la ~ de paso** to turn the water/gas off at the main valve (AmE) o (BrE) at the mains (b) (AmL) (de lavabo, bañera) faucet (AmE), tap (BrE) **4** (en un texto) brace **5** (en lucha, judo) hold; **lo inmovilizó con una ~ (de brazo)** she got him in an armlock

llavero m key ring

llegada f (a) (de un viaje) arrival; (b) (Dep) (meta) finishing line, wire (AmE); (Equ) winning post

llegar [A3] vi **1** «persona/tren/carta» to arrive; **tienen que estar por** or **al ~** they'll be arriving any minute now; **~on cansadísimos** they were exhausted when they arrived; **¿falta mucho para ~?** is it much further (to go)?; **siempre llega tarde** he's always late; **no me llegó el telegrama** I didn't get the telegram; **~ A algo** ‹a país/ciudad› to arrive in sth; ‹a edificio› to arrive AT sth; **~ a casa** to arrive o get home; **el rumor llegó a oídos del alcalde** the rumor reached the mayor **2** ‹camino/ruta/tren» (ir) **~ A** or **HASTA** to go all the way to, go as far as; **solo llega al tercer piso** it only goes (up) to the third floor **3** «día/invierno» to come, arrive; **ha llegado el momento de …** the time has come to … **4** (a) (alcanzar) to reach; **~ A algo** ‹a acuerdo/conclusión› to reach sth, come to sth; ‹a estante/techo› to reach; **llegué a la conclusión de que…** I reached o came to the conclusion that …; **los pies no le llegan al suelo** her feet don't touch the floor; **la falda le llegaba a los tobillos** her skirt came down to her ankles; **el agua le llegaba al cuello** the water came up to her neck; **las cosas ~on a tal punto que …** things reached such a point that … (b) (expresando logro): **~á lejos** she'll go far o a long way; **así no vas a ~ a ningún lado** you'll never get anywhere like that; **llegó a (ser) director** he became director; **~ a viejo** to live to old age; **llegué a conocerlo mejor** I got to know him better **5** **~ A + INF** (a) (al extremo de): **llegó a amenazarme** she even threatened me; **no llegó a pegarme** he didn't actually hit me (b) (en oraciones condicionales): **si lo llego a saber, no vengo** if I'd known, I wouldn't have come; **si llego a enterarme de algo, te aviso** if I happen to hear anything, I'll let you know

llenado m filling, filling up

llenador -dora adj (CS) ‹comida› filling

llenar [A1] *vt* [1] **(a)** ⟨*vaso/plato/cajón*⟩ to fill; ⟨*tanque*⟩ to fill (up); ⟨*maleta*⟩ to fill, pack; **no me llenes el vaso** don't fill my glass right up; ∼ **algo DE/CON algo** to fill sth WITH sth **(b)** ⟨*formulario*⟩ to fill out, to fill in (esp BrE) [2] **(a)** (cubrir) ∼ **algo DE algo** to cover sth WITH sth **(b)** ⟨*vacante*⟩ to fill [3] (colmar) ⟨*persona*⟩: **la noticia nos llenó de alegría** we were overjoyed by the news; **nos llenó de atenciones** he made a real fuss of us [4] (hacer sentirse realizado) ⟨*persona*⟩: **su carrera no la llena** she doesn't find her career fulfilling
■ ∼ *vi* ⟨*comida*⟩ to be filling

■ **llenarse** *v pron* [1] **(a)** ⟨⟨*recipiente/estadio*⟩⟩ to fill (up); **el teatro solo se llenó a la mitad** the theater only filled to half capacity *o* was only half full; ∼**se DE algo** to fill WITH sth **(b)** (cubrirse) ∼**se DE algo** ⟨*de polvo/pelos*⟩ to be covered IN sth [2] ⟨*bolsillo/boca*⟩ to fill; ∼**se algo DE algo** to fill sth WITH sth [3] (colmarse): **su corazón se llenó de alegría** she filled with joy; **se** ∼**on de deudas** they got heavily into debt [4] ⟨⟨*persona*⟩⟩ (de comida): **con un plato de ensalada ya se llena** one plate of salad and she's full; **me llené** (colloq) I'm full (up) (colloq)

lleno¹ -na *adj* [1] **(a)** ⟨*estadio/autobús/copa*⟩ full; ∼ **DE algo** full OF sth **(b)** (cubierto) ∼ **DE algo** ⟨*de granos/manchas/polvo*⟩ covered IN sth **(c)** (después de comer) full (up) (colloq) [2] de **lleno** ⟨*consagrarse/dedicarse*⟩ fully; **el sol nos daba de** ∼ the sun was shining down on us

lleno² *m* sellout

llevadero -ra *adj* bearable

llevar [A1] *vt*
I [1] **(a)** (de un lugar a otro) to take; **le llevé unas flores** I took her some flowers; **te lo** ∼**é cuando vaya** I'll bring it when I come; **¿qué llevas en la bolsa?** what have you got in your bag?; **comida para** ∼ take out (AmE) *o* (BrE) takeaway meals **(b)** (transportar) ⟨*carga*⟩ to carry; **la ayudé a ∼ las bolsas** I helped her carry her bags **(c)** ⟨*persona*⟩ to take; **nos llevó a cenar** he took us out to dinner; **me llevó (en su coche) hasta la estación** she gave me a lift to the station; **lo llevaba en brazos/de la mano** she was carrying him in her arms/holding her hand **(d)** (tener consigo) ⟨*llaves/dinero/documentación*⟩ to have
[2] **(a)** (guiar, conducir) to take; **la llevaba de la mano** I/he was holding her hand; **esto no nos** ∼**á a ninguna parte** this won't get us anywhere **(b)** (impulsar, inducir) to lead; **esto me lleva a pensar que ...** this leads me to believe that ...
[3] **(a)** ⟨*ropa/perfume/reloj*⟩ to wear **(b)** (tener) ⟨*barba/bigote*⟩ to have; **llevaba el pelo corto** she had short hair
II [1] (tener a su cargo) ⟨*negocio/tienda*⟩ to run; ⟨*caso*⟩ to handle; ⟨*contabilidad*⟩ to do
[2] (esp Esp) (conducir) ⟨*vehículo*⟩ to drive; ⟨*moto*⟩ to ride
[3] ⟨*vida*⟩ to lead; ∼ **una vida tranquila** to lead a quiet; **¿cómo llevas el informe?** how are you getting on with the report?
[4] (seguir, mantener): ∼ **el ritmo** *or* **el compás** to keep time; **¿llevas la cuenta de lo que te debo?** are you keeping track of what I owe you?; **¿qué dirección llevaban?** which direction were they going in?
III [1] **(a)** (requerir) ⟨*tiempo*⟩ to take; **le llevó**

horas aprendérselo it took her hours to learn it **(b)** (aventajar) (+ *me/te/le etc*): **me lleva un año** he's a year older than me; **nos llevan un día de ventaja** they have a one-day lead over us
[2] (Esp) (cobrar) to charge
■ ∼ *v aux*: **llevo una hora esperando** I've been waiting for an hour; **lleva tres días sin comer** he hasn't eaten for three days; **el tren lleva una hora de retraso** the train's an hour late; **llevo revisada la mitad** I've already checked half of it
■ ∼ *vi* ⟨⟨*camino/carretera*⟩⟩ to go, lead

■ **llevarse** *v pron* [1] **(a)** (a otro lugar) to take; **la policía se llevó al sospechoso** the police took the suspect away; **¿quién se llevó mi paraguas?** who took my umbrella?; **el agua se llevó las casas** the water swept away the houses **(b)** ⟨*premio/dinero*⟩ to win **(c)** (quedarse con, comprar) to take; **me llevo este** I'll take this one **(d)** (Mat) to carry; **9 y 9 son 18, me llevo una** 9 plus 9 is 18, carry one **(e)** (Arg) ⟨*asignatura*⟩ to carry over
[2] ⟨*susto/regañina*⟩ to get; **me llevé una decepción** I was disappointed; **se llevó un buen recuerdo** he left here with pleasant memories
[3] ∼**se bien con algn** to get along with sb
[4] (hablando de modas) to be in fashion; **vuelven** ∼**se las faldas cortas** short skirts are back in fashion

llorar [A1] *vi* (derramar lágrimas) **(a)** ⟨⟨*persona*⟩⟩ to cry; **estaba a punto de** ∼ she was on the verge of tears; ∼ **DE algo** ⟨*de risa/rabia*⟩ to cry WITH sb; ⟨*de emoción*⟩ to weep with sth; ∼ **POR algo/algn** to cry over sth/sb **(b)** ⟨⟨*ojos*⟩⟩ (+ *me/te/le etc*) to water

lloriquear [A1] *vi* (fam) to whine (colloq)

lloro *m* crying, weeping (liter)

llorón -rona *adj* (fam): **es muy** ∼ he cries a lot; **no seas tan** ∼ don't be such a crybaby (colloq)
■ *m,f* **(a)** (fam) (que llora mucho) crybaby (colloq) **(b)** (Col, RPl, Ven fam) (quejón) whiner (colloq)

llover [E9] *v impers* to rain; **aquí llueve mucho** it rains a lot here; **llueve a cántaros** *or* **a mares** *or* **a chuzos** it's pouring (with rain)

llovizna *f* drizzle

lloviznar [A1] *v impers* to drizzle

llueva, llueve ▶ LLOVER

lluvia *f* **(a)** (Meteo) rain; **un día de** ∼ a rainy day; **zonas de mucha** ∼ areas of heavy rainfall; ∼ **radiactiva** nuclear fallout **(b)** (de balas) hail; (de críticas) hail, barrage

lluvioso -sa *adj* ⟨*tiempo/día/época*⟩ rainy; ⟨*región*⟩ wet

lo *art* [1]: **prefiero** ∼ **dulce** I prefer sweet things; ∼ **interesante del caso es ...** the interesting thing about the case is ...; **¿estoy en** ∼ **cierto?** am I right?; **en** ∼ **alto de la sierra** high up in the mountains; **ser** ∼ **más objetivo posible** to be as objective as possible; **me dijo** ∼ **de siempre** he came out with the same old story; **se ha enterado de** ∼ **nuestro/de** ∼ **de Pablo** she's found out about us/about Pablo; **voy a** ∼ **de Eva** (RPl) I'm going to Eva's (place)
[2] **(a)** lo cual which; ∼ **cual fue desmentido por el gobierno** which was denied by the Government **(b)** lo que what; **no entiendo** ∼ **que dices** I don't understand what you're saying; **pide** ∼ **que quieras** ask for whatever you want; **límpialo con un trapo o** ∼ **que sea** clean it with a cloth or whatever; **¡**∼ **que debe haber sufrido!** how she   ⸱⸱⸱⸡⸱

must have suffered!; ¡no te imaginas ~ que fue
aquello! you can't imagine what it was like!; ¡~
que es saber idiomas! it sure is something (AmE)
o (BrE) what it is to be able speak languages
■ *pron pers* **1** (a) (referido — a él) him; (— a usted)
you; (— a cosa, etc) it; **¿~ conozco?** do I know
you?; **~ compré hoy I** bought it today; **ya ~ sé I**
know (b) (*impers*): **duele que a uno ~ traten así**
it hurts when people treat you like that
2 (*con estar, ser*): **¿que si estoy harta? pues sí,
~ estoy** am I fed up? well, yes, I am; **si ella es
capaz, yo también ~ soy** if she can, so can I

loable *adj* commendable, praiseworthy

lobezno -na *m,f* wolf cub

lobo -ba *m,f* (Zool) wolf; **~ marino** seal

lóbrego -ga *adj* gloomy

lóbulo *m* lobe

locación *f* (Méx) (lugar): **visite el museo Rivera,
~: Calle Altavista** visit the Rivera Museum on
Altavista Street; **¿en qué ~?** whereabouts?

local *adj* local; **el equipo ~** the home team
■ *m* premises (*pl*)

localidad *f* **1** (población) town, locality (frml)
2 (Espec) seat, ticket

localización *f* **1** (a) (acción): **la ~ del barco**
the finding of the ship (b) (lugar) location **2** (de
productos) localization

localizar [A4] *vt* (a) ⟨persona/lugar/tumor⟩ to
locate; **estoy intentando ~la I** am trying to get
hold of her (b) ⟨incendio/epidemia⟩ to localize

loción *f* lotion

loco¹ -ca *adj* (a) (Med, Psic) mad, insane (b)
(chiflado) crazy (colloq), nuts (colloq); **este tipo está
medio ~** (fam) the guy's not all there (colloq); **eso
no lo hago (pero) ni ~** there's no way I'd do that;
hacer algo a lo ~ to do sth any which way (AmE)
o (BrE) any old how (colloq); **estar ~ de remate**
(fam) to be completely nuts (colloq); **tener ~** (Esp)
traer ~ a algn to be driving sb crazy (colloq);
volver ~ a algn to drive sb crazy (colloq); **volverse
~** to go mad (c) (entusiasmado): **está loca por él**
she's crazy about him (colloq); **está ~ por volver**
he's dying to come back (colloq) (d) (fam)
(ajetreado): **anda (como) ~ con los preparativos**
the preparations are driving him mad (colloq) (e)
(indicando gran cantidad): **tengo unas ganas locas de
verla** I'm dying to see her (colloq); **tuvo una suerte
loca** she was incredibly lucky (f) **estar ~ DE
algo:** ⟨de entusiasmo/furia/celos⟩ to be wild WITH
sth; ⟨de dolor/remordimiento⟩ to be racked WITH
sth; **estaba loca de alegría** she was blissfully
happy
■ *m,f* (enfermo mental) (*m*) madman; (*f*) madwoman;
se puso como un ~ he went crazy o mad;
corrimos como ~s (fam) we ran like crazy o mad
(colloq); **hacerse el ~** to act dumb (colloq)

loco² *m* (Chi) (Zool) abalone

locomoción *f* (a) (acción) locomotion (b) (Chi)
(Transp) *tb* **~ colectiva** public transport

locomotora *f* (Ferr) locomotive, engine

locuaz *adj* talkative, loquacious (frml)

locución *f* phrase

locura *f* (a) (demencia) madness, insanity; **lo que
hizo/dijo fue una ~** what he did/said was sheer
madness (b) (inclinación exagerada): **siente ~ por la
pequeña** she's absolutely besotted with the little
one; **la quiero con ~** I'm crazy about her (colloq)

locutor -tora *m,f* (en general) broadcaster
(informativo) newscaster (AmE), newsreader (BrE);
(deportivo) sports commentator; (de continuidad)
commentator, announcer (BrE)

lodo *m* mud; *para modismos ver* BARRO

logia *f* (a) (de los masones) lodge (b) (Arquit)
loggia

lógica *f* logic

lógico¹ -ca *adj* (a) (normal, natural) natural,
logical; **como es ~** naturally, obviously; **es ~
que así sea** it's (only) natural that it should be
so; **lo ~ seria ...** the logical thing would be ... (b)
⟨conclusión/consecuencia⟩ logical

lógico² *adv* (indep) (fam) of course

logotipo *m* logo, logotype

logrado -da *adj* (satisfactorio) successful;
(verosímil) ⟨retrato/personaje⟩ lifelike

lograr [A1] *vt* ⟨objetivo⟩ to attain, achieve;
⟨éxito⟩ to achieve; **logró el quinto puesto** she
managed fifth place; **~ hacer algo** to manage to
do sth

logro *m* (de un objetivo) achievement; (éxito)
success

loísmo *m*: *use of* LO/LOS *instead of* LE/LES *(as in
LO/LOS DIJE QUE NO), used in parts of Spain but
unacceptable to most speakers*

lolo -la *m,f* (Chi fam) teenager

loma *f* hill; (más pequeño) hillock

lombriz *f* (de tierra) worm, earthworm; (en el
intestino) (fam) worm (colloq)

lomo *m* (a) (de animal) back; **~ de burro** (RPl) *or*
(Chi) **de toro** (Auto) speed bump (b) (Coc) (de cerdo)
loin; (de vaca) (AmL) fillet steak (c) (de libro) spine;
(de cuchillo) back

lona *f* canvas

loncha *f* slice

lonche *m* (Per) (merienda) tea

lonchera *f* (AmL) lunch box

londinense *adj* ⟨público/teatro/periódico⟩
London (before *n*); **es ~** she's a Londoner
■ *mf* Londoner

Londres *m* London

longaniza *f*: spicy pork sausage

longitud *f* (a) (largo) length; **de 30 metros de ~**
30 meters long (b) (Astron, Geog) longitude; **~ de
onda** (Fís, Rad) wavelength

lonja *f* **1** (a) (loncha) slice (b) (RPl) (de cuero)
strip **2** (a) (Esp) (mercado de pescado) fish market
(b) (institución mercantil) guild; **~ de propiedad raíz**
(Col) association of realtors (AmE) o (BrE) estate
agents

loro¹ -ra *m,f* (Zool) parrot

loro² *m* (fam) (charlatán) chatterbox (colloq)

los, las *art; ver* el
■ *pron pers* **1** (referido — a ellos, ellas, cosas, etc)
them; (— a ustedes) you; **¿las atienden?** can I help
you? **2** (con el verbo haber): **las hay de muchos
tamaños** they come in many different sizes;
también ~ hay de chocolate we have chocolate
ones too

losa *f* (de sepulcro) tombstone; (de suelo) flagstone

lote *m* (a) (de un producto) batch; (en subastas) lot
(b) (terreno) plot (of land)

lotería *f* lottery; **me tocó** *or* **me gané la ~** I won the lottery

loto *m* lotus

loza *f* **(a)** (material) china **(b)** (vajilla) crockery; (de mejor calidad) china

lozano -na *adj* ⟨persona⟩ healthy-looking; ⟨cutis⟩ fresh; ⟨verduras⟩ fresh

Ltda (= **Limitada**) Ltd, Limited

lubina *f* sea bass

lubricante *adj* lubricating
■ *m* lubricant

lubricar [A2] *vt* to lubricate

lucero *m* bright star; **~ del alba** morning star

luces *fpl* ▶ LUZ

lucha *f* **(a)** (combate, pelea) fight; (para conseguir algo) struggle; **~ de clases** class struggle; **la ~ contra el cáncer** the fight against cancer **(b)** (Dep) wrestling; **~ libre** all-in wrestling

luchador -dora *m,f* **(a)** (persona esforzada) fighter **(b)** (Dep) wrestler

luchar [A1] *vi* **(a)** (combatir, pelear) to fight **(b)** (para conseguir algo) to struggle, fight; **~ para salir adelante** struggle hard to get on in life; **~ por la paz** to fight for peace **(c)** (batallar) **~ CON algo** ⟨con problema⟩ to wrestle WITH sth **(d)** (Dep) to wrestle

luche *m* (Chi) (Jueg) hopscotch

lucidez *f* lucidity

lucido -da *adj* ⟨fiesta⟩ magnificent, splendid; **su actuación no fue muy lucida** her performance wasn't particularly brilliant

lúcido -da *adj* **(a)** [SER] ⟨mente/análisis⟩ lucid, clear; ⟨persona⟩ clear-thinking **(b)** [ESTAR] ⟨enfermo⟩ lucid

luciente *adj* bright, shining

luciérnaga *f* glowworm; (insecto volador) firefly

lucir [I5] *vi* (aparentar) to look good, look special; **gasta mucho en ropa pero no le luce** she spends a fortune on clothes but it doesn't do much for her
■ **~** *vt* **(a)** (period) ⟨vestido/modelo⟩ to wear, sport (journ); ⟨peinado/collar⟩ to sport (journ) **(b)** ⟨figura/piernas⟩ to show off, flaunt
■ **lucirse** *v pron* **(a)** (destacarse) to excel oneself **(b)** (presumir) to show off

lucrativo -va *adj* lucrative, profitable; **una entidad sin fines ~s** a nonprofit (AmE) *o* (BrE) non-profit-making organization

lucro *m* profit, gain; **sin ánimo de ~** with no profit motive in mind

lúcuma *f* eggfruit

lúdico -ca *adj* ⟨fantasías/diversiones⟩ playful, ludic (before n) (liter)

luego *adv* ⓵ **(a)** (más tarde) later (on); (después de otro suceso — en el futuro) afterwards; (— en el pasado) then, next; **¡hasta ~!** goodbye!, see you!; **~ DE hacer algo** after doing sth **(b)** (Chi, Méx) (pronto) soon, quickly; **~ ~** (Méx) immediately ⓶ **(a)** (en el espacio): **hay una tienda y ~ está el banco** you come to a shop and the bank is next **(b)** (Méx) (cerca) nearby; **aquí ~** just here **(c)** (indicando orden, prioridad) then; **primero está él y ~ nosotros** he's first and then we're next ⓷ **desde luego** of course; **desde ~ que no** of course not
■ *conj* (frml) therefore

lugar *m* ⓵ (en general) place; **este es el ~** this is the place; **en cualquier otro ~** anywhere else; **en algún ~** somewhere; **cambiar los muebles de ~** to move the furniture around; **el ~ del suceso** the scene of the incident; **yo en tu ~ ...** if I were you ...; **ponte en mi ~** put yourself in my place; **se clasificó en primer ~** she finished in first place ⓶ (localidad, región): **los habitantes del ~** the local people; **~ y fecha de nacimiento** place and date of birth ⓷ **(a)** (espacio libre) room; **hacer ~ para algn/algo** to make room *o* space for sb/sth; **me hizo un ~** he made me some room **(b)** (asiento) seat ⓸ **dar lugar a** (a disputa, comentarios) to provoke, give rise to ⓹ (en locs) **en lugar de** instead of; **ella firmó en mi ~** she signed on my behalf; **en primer lugar** (antes que nada) first of all, firstly; **en último lugar** (finalmente) finally, lastly; **sin ~ a dudas** without doubt, undoubtedly; **tener ~** to take place

lugareño -ña *adj/mf* local

lugarteniente *mf* deputy

lúgubre *adj* gloomy

lujo *m* luxury; **no puedo permitirme el ~ de llegar tarde** I can't afford to be late; **nos dimos el ~ de viajar en primera** we treated ourselves and traveled first class; **a todo ~** in style; **de ~** luxury (before n); **con ~ de detalles** with a wealth of detail

lujoso -sa *adj* luxurious

lujuria *f* (liter) lust, lechery

lumbago *m* lumbago

lumbre *f* (de hoguera, chimenea) fire; (de la cocina): **puso el cazo en la ~** she put the saucepan on the stove

lumbrera *f* (fam) (persona brillante) genius, whiz* (colloq)

luminoso -sa *adj* **(a)** ⟨habitación⟩ bright, light; ⟨fuente⟩ luminous; ⟨letrero⟩ illuminated **(b)** ⟨idea⟩ bright, brilliant

luna *f* ⓵ (Astron) moon; **a la luz de la ~** in the moonlight; **hay ~** the moon's out; **~ creciente/menguante/llena/nueva** waxing/waning/full/new moon; **~ de miel** honeymoon; **estar en la ~** (fam) to have one's head in the clouds ⓶ (espejo) mirror; (de puerta, ventana) glass; (escaparate) window; (parabrisas) windshield (AmE), windscreen (BrE) ⓷ (de la uña) half-moon, lunule (tech)

lunar *adj* lunar
■ *m* **(a)** (en la piel) mole; (pintado) beauty spot **(b)** (en el pelo) gray* patch **(c)** (en un diseño) polka-dot

lunático -ca *adj* lunatic (before n)
■ *m,f* lunatic

lunes *m* (pl **~**) Monday; **el ~ por la mañana/noche** on Monday morning/night; **todos los ~** every Monday; **el próximo ~** next Monday; **el ~ pasado** last Monday; **el ~ es fiesta** Monday is a holiday; **nos vemos el ~** I'll see you on Monday; **los ~ voy a nadar** on Mondays I go swimming

luneta *f* ⓵ (Auto) window ⓶ (Col, Méx) (Teatr) orchestra seats (pl) (AmE), front stalls (pl) (BrE)

lunfardo *m* Buenos Aires slang

lupa *f* magnifying glass

lustrabotas *mf* (pl **~**) ▶ LUSTRADOR

lustrada *f* (AmS) polish, shine

lustrador -dora *m,f* (AmS) bootblack; (niño) shoeshine boy

lustrar [A1] *vt* (esp AmL) ⟨zapatos/muebles⟩ to polish
■ **lustrarse** *v pron* [1] (esp AmL) ⟨zapatos⟩ to polish [2] (AmC) (en una actividad) to excel

lustre *m* (a) (brillo) shine, luster*; **darle** *or* **sacarle** ∼ **a algo** to polish sth (b) (distinción) glory, distinction

lustrín *m* (AmS) (cajón) bootblack's box; (puesto) shoeshine stand

lustro *m* period of five years

luterano -na *adj/m,f* Lutheran

luto *m* mourning; **estar de** ∼ to be in mourning; ∼ **riguroso** deep mourning; **ir de** ∼ to wear mourning (clothes); **ponerse de** ∼ to go into mourning

Luxemburgo *m* Luxembourg

luxemburgués -guesa *adj* of/from Luxembourg

luz *f* [1] (en general) light; **la** ∼ **del sol** the sunlight; **me da la** ∼ **en los ojos** the light's in my eyes; **a plena** ∼ **del día** in broad daylight; **este reflector da mucha** ∼ this spotlight is very bright; **leer con poca** ∼ to read in poor light; **a la** ∼ **de los últimos acontecimientos** in the light of recent events; *a todas luces*: whichever way you look at it; **dar a** ∼ to give birth; **sacar algo a la** ∼ ⟨secreto/escándalo⟩ to bring sth to light; ⟨publicación⟩ to bring out; **salir a la** ∼ «⟨secreto/escándalo⟩» to come to light; «⟨publicación⟩» to come out

[2] (a) (fam) (electricidad) electricity; **les cortaron la** ∼ their electricity was cut off; **se fue la** ∼ (en una casa) the electricity went off; (en una zona) there was a power cut (b) (dispositivo) light; **encender** *or* (AmL) **prender** *or* (Esp) **dar la** ∼ to turn on *o* switch on the light; **apagar la** ∼ to turn off *o* switch off the light; **cruzar con la luz roja** to cross when the lights are red; **luces de estacionamiento** *or* (Esp) **de situación** parking lights (*pl*) (AmE), sidelights (*pl*) (BrE); **luces de cruce** *or* **cortas** *or* (AmL) **bajas** dipped headlights (*pl*); **poner las luces largas** *or* **altas** to put the headlights on high (AmE) *o* (BrE) full beam; ∼ **de frenado** stoplight, brake light (BrE); ∼ **de giro** (Arg) indicator

luzca, luzcan, etc ▶ LUCIR

M m

M, m *f* (read as /'eme/) the letter M, m

m (= **metro**) m, meter*

macabro -bra *adj* macabre

macaco -ca *m,f* (Zool) macaque

macana *f* [1] (AmL) (de policía) billy club (AmE), truncheon (BrE) [2] (a) (CS fam) (tontería, disparate): **decir** ∼**s** to talk nonsense; **no hagas la** ∼ **de renunciar** don't be so stupid as to resign (colloq) (b) (CS fam) (problema) trouble, snag; **¡qué** ∼ **que no puedas venir!** what a shame *o* (colloq) drag you can't come! (c) (RPl fam) (mentira) lie

macanear [A1] *vt* (Méx) (golpear) to beat
■ ∼ *vi* (RPl fam) (mentir) to lie; (decir tonterías) to talk garbage (AmE) *o* (BrE) rubbish (colloq)

macanudo -da *adj* (CS, Per fam) great (colloq)

macarrón *m* (a) (pasta) piece of macaroni; **macarrones** macaroni (b) (galleta) macaroon

macedonia *f* (de frutas) fruit salad, macedoine; (de verduras) mixed vegetables (*pl*), macedoine

macerar [A1] *vt* ⟨fruta⟩ to soak, macerate; ⟨carne⟩ to marinate, marinade

maceta *f* flowerpot

macetero *m* (a) (para tiestos) flowerpot holder (b) (AmS) (tiesto) large flowerpot; (jardinera) window box

machacar [A2] *vt* (a) ⟨ajo⟩ to crush; ⟨almendras⟩ to grind, crush; ⟨piedra⟩ to crush, pound (b) (fam) ⟨contrincante⟩ to thrash (colloq)
■ ∼ *vi* (a) (fam) (insistir): ∼ **con** *or* **sobre algo** to go on *o* harp on about sth (colloq) (b) (fam) (para un examen) to cram (colloq)

machacón -cona *adj* (insistente) insistent; (pesado) tiresome

machamartillo: **a** ∼ (loc adj) ⟨monárquico/feminista⟩ ardent, staunch; (loc adv) firmly

machete *m* (cuchillo) machete
■ *adj inv* (Ven fam) great (colloq)

machetero -ra *m,f* (cañero) cane cutter
■ *adj* (Méx fam) persevering

machismo *m* (actitud, ideología) sexism, male chauvinism

machista *adj* sexist, chauvinist
■ *mf* sexist, male chauvinist

macho *m* [1] (Biol, Zool) male; ∼ **cabrío** billy goat [2] (fam) (hombre fuerte) tough guy (colloq); (pey) macho man (colloq & pej) [3] (Mec, Tec) pin; (Elec) male (plug); (de un corchete) hook; (en carpintería) peg, pin
■ *adj* [1] ⟨animal/planta⟩ male; **ballena/elefante** ∼ bull whale/elephant; **gato** ∼ tomcat [2] (fam) (valiente, fuerte) tough, brave; (pey) macho (pej) [3] ⟨pieza⟩ male

machote -ta *m,f* **(a)** (fam) (hombre) tough guy (colloq); (pey) macho man (colloq & pej) **(b)** (fam & pey) (mujer) butch woman (colloq & pej)

machucar [A2] *vt* **(a)** ⟨*fruta*⟩ to bruise **(b)** (fam) ⟨*dedo*⟩ to crush **(c)** (Méx) ⟨*ajo*⟩ to crush

machucón *m* (AmL fam) (moretón) bruise

macilento -ta *adj* **(a)** ⟨*persona/cara*⟩ gaunt, haggard **(b)** ⟨*luz*⟩ wan (liter)

macillo *m* hammer

macizo¹ -za *adj* **(a)** [SER] (sólido) solid **(b)** [ESTAR] (fam) ⟨*persona*⟩ (robusto) strapping (colloq)

macizo² *m* (de montañas) massif; (de flores, arbustos) clump

maco *m* (Col) monkey

macramé *m* macramé

macrobiótico -ca *adj* macrobiotic

macroeconomía *f* macroeconomics

macuco -ca *adj* (Chi, Per fam) cute (AmE colloq), sharp (BrE colloq)

macuto *m* back pack, rucksack (BrE)

madalena *f* ≈cupcake (AmE), ≈fairycake (BrE)

madeja *f* (de lana, hilo) hank, skein

madera *f* (material) wood; (para construcción, carpintería) lumber (esp AmE), timber (BrE); ∼ **blanda/dura** softwood/hardwood; **es de** ∼ it's made of wood, it's wooden; **mesa de** ∼ wooden table; ∼ **de pino** pine (wood); **tener** ∼ **de algo** to have the makings of sth; **tocar** ∼ to knock (on) wood (AmE), touch wood (BrE)

maderero -ra *adj* timber (*before n*); lumber (*before n*) (esp AmE)
■ *m,f* timber merchant

madero *m* (piece of) timber

madrastra *f* stepmother

madrazo *m* (Méx fam) blow; **darle un** ∼ **a algn** to give sb a beating; **películas de** ∼ violent movies

madre *f* mother; **ser** ∼ to be a mother; ∼ **de familia** mother; ∼ **política** mother-in-law; ∼ **soltera** single *o* unmarried mother; ∼ **superiora** Mother Superior; **¡**∼ **mía!** *or* **¡mi** ∼**!** (my) goodness!, (good) heavens!; **me vale** ∼**s** (Méx vulg) I don't give a damn (colloq) *o* (vulg) shit; **salirse de** ∼ «*río*» to burst its banks; «*situación*» to get out of hand

madreperla *f* mother-of-pearl

madreselva *f* honeysuckle

Madrid *m* Madrid

madriguera *f* **(a)** (de conejos) warren, burrow; (de zorros) earth; (de tejones) set **(b)** (de maleantes) den, lair

madrileño -ña *adj* of/from Madrid
■ *m,f* person from Madrid

madrina

■ **Nota** En inglés *godmother* no se usa como apelativo

f [1] **(a)** (en bautizo) godmother; (en boda) ≈matron of honor* **(b)** (de barco) *woman who launches a ship* [2] (Méx fam) paddy wagon (AmE sl), police van (BrE)

madroño *m* (Bot) tree strawberry

madrugada *f* **(a)** (amanecer, alba) dawn, daybreak; **se levantó de** ∼ (muy temprano) she got up very early (in the morning); (al amanecer) she got up at dawn *o* daybreak **(b)** (después de

medianoche) (early) morning; **las tres de la** ∼ three o'clock in the morning; **llegó de** ∼ he arrived in the early hours of the morning *o* in the small hours

madrugador -dora *adj*: **ser** ∼ to be an early riser

madrugar [A3] *vi* to get up early

maduración *f* **(a)** (de fruta) ripening (process) **(b)** (de persona) maturing (process) **(c)** (de idea) development, maturing

madurar [A1] *vi* **(a)** «*fruta*» to ripen **(b)** «*persona*» to mature **(c)** «*ideas*» to mature, come to fruition
■ ∼ *vt* **(a)** ⟨*fruta*⟩ to ripen **(b)** ⟨*plan*⟩ to develop, bring to fruition

madurez *f* **(a)** (de fruta) ripeness **(b)** (de persona) maturity

maduro -ra *adj* [1] [ESTAR] ⟨*fruta*⟩ ripe [2] **(a)** [SER] (entrado en años) mature, of mature years **(b)** [SER] (sensato) mature; **es joven pero muy** ∼ he's young but very mature for his age

maestría *f* [1] (liter) (habilidad) skill, mastery [2] (esp AmL) (Educ) (postgrado) master's degree, master's

maestro -tra *m,f* [1] **(a)** (Educ) teacher, schoolteacher; **maestra jardinera** (Arg, Col) kindergarten teacher, nursery school teacher (BrE) **(b)** (en un arte): **es un** ∼ **de la danza española** he is a master of Spanish dance; **un** ∼ **de las letras españolas** a leading authority *o* an expert on Spanish literature **(c)** (en un oficio) master (*before n*); ∼ **carpintero** master carpenter **(d)** (Chi) (obrero) builder [2] (Mús) maestro [3] (en ajedrez) master

mafia *f* mafia

mafioso -sa *adj* mafia (*before n*)
■ *m,f* (criminal) gangster, racketeer; (de la Mafia siciliana) mafioso

magdalena *f* (Esp) ≈cupcake (AmE), ≈fairycake (BrE)

magia *f* magic; **hacer** ∼ to do magic (tricks)

mágico -ca *adj* **(a)** ⟨*poderes/número*⟩ magic (*before n*) **(b)** ⟨*belleza/ambiente*⟩ magical

magisterio *m* (enseñanza) teaching; (carrera) teacher training; **estudia** ∼ he's training to be a teacher

magistrado -da *m,f* judge

magistral *adj* ⟨*actuación/libro*⟩ masterly; ⟨*tono/actitud*⟩ magisterial (fml)

magnánimo -ma *adj* magnanimous

magnate *mf* magnate, tycoon; **los** ∼**s de la prensa** the press barons

magnesia *f* magnesia

magnesio *m* magnesium

magnético -ca *adj* magnetic

magnetismo *m* magnetism

magnetófono, magnetofón *m* (reel-to-reel) tape recorder

magnífico -ca *adj* **(a)** (estupendo) ⟨*edificio/panorama*⟩ magnificent, superb; ⟨*espectáculo/escritor/oportunidad*⟩ marvelous*, wonderful; **¡**∼**!** excellent! **(b)** (suntuoso) magnificent, splendid

magnitud *f* magnitude; **la** ∼ **de la tragedia** the extent *o* magnitude of the tragedy

magnolia *f* magnolia

mago -ga *m,f* (a) (prestidigitador) conjurer, magician (b) (en cuentos) wizard, magician (c) (persona habilidosa) wizard

magro -gra *adj* lean

magulladura *f* bruise

magullar [A1] *vt* to bruise
■ **magullarse** *v pron* to bruise

mahometano -na *adj* Islamic
■ *m,f* follower of Islam

mahonesa *f* mayonnaise

maicena® *f* cornstarch (AmE), cornflour (BrE)

maillot /maˈʝo(t)/ *m* (a) (traje de baño) swimsuit (b) (de ciclista) jersey

maíz *m* (planta) maize, corn (AmE); (Coc) corn (AmE), sweet corn (esp BrE); **~ tostado** *or* **pira** *or* **tote** (Col) popcorn

maizal *m* cornfield (AmE), maize field (BrE)

maizena® *f* cornstarch (AmE), cornflour (BrE)

majadería *f* (fam) (a) (cualidad) stupidity (b) (dicho, acto): **no dice más que ~s** he talks a lot of rubbish *o* nonsense (colloq); **fue una ~** it was a stupid thing to do

majadero -ra *adj* (fam) (insensato) stupid
■ *m,f* clown (colloq)

majar [A1] *vt* to crush

maje *mf* [1] (AmC arg) (individuo) (*m*) guy (colloq), bloke (BrE colloq); (*f*) girl [2] (Méx fam) (persona crédula) sucker (colloq)

majestad *f* [1] (aspecto grandioso) majesty [2] **su Majestad** (al referirse — al rey) His Majesty; (— a la reina) Her Majesty; (al dirigirse al rey, a la reina) Your Majesty; **sus M~es los Reyes** Their Majesties the King and Queen

majestuosidad *f* majesty

majestuoso -sa *adj* majestic

majo -ja *adj* (Esp fam) (a) (simpático) nice (b) (guapo) ⟨hombre⟩ handsome, good-looking; ⟨mujer⟩ good-looking, pretty (c) ⟨casa/vestido⟩ lovely, nice

mal *adj*: ▶ MALO
■ *adj inv* [1] [ESTAR] (enfermo) ill; (anímicamente) in a bad way (colloq); (incómodo) uncomfortable; **andar ~ del estómago** to have trouble with one's stomach; **¡este está ~ de la cabeza!** he's not right in the head; **esas cosas me ponen ~** things like that really upset me
[2] (fam) (en frases negativas) (refiriéndose al aspecto): **no está nada ~** she's/he's/it's not at all bad (colloq)
[3] (insatisfactorio): **estoy** *or* **salí muy ~ en esta foto** I look awful in this photograph; **le queda ~ ese color** that color doesn't suit her
[4] [ESTAR] (incorrecto) wrong
[5] (indicando escasez) **estar** *or* **ir ~ DE algo** ⟨de dinero/tiempo⟩ to be short OF sth
■ *adv* [1] (de manera no satisfactoria) ⟨vestir/cantar/jugar⟩ badly; **le fue ~ en los exámenes** his exams went badly; **te oigo muy ~** I can hardly hear you; **el negocio marcha ~** the business isn't doing well; **de ~ en peor** from bad to worse
[2] (desfavorablemente) badly, ill; **hablar ~ de algn** to speak badly *o* ill of sb
[3] (a) (de manera errónea) wrong, wrongly; **te han informado ~** you've been badly *o* wrongly informed; **te entendí ~** I misunderstood you (b) (de manera reprensible) ⟨obrar/partarse⟩ badly;

haces ~ en no ir a verla it's wrong of you not to go and see her; **me contestó muy ~** she answered me very rudely
[4] (desagradable) ⟨oler/saber⟩ bad; **aquí huele ~** there's a horrible smell *o* it smells in here
[5] (en locs) **hacer mal** (AmL) (a la salud): **esto hace ~ al hígado** this is bad for the liver; **el pescado me hizo ~** the fish didn't agree with me; **menos mal: ¡menos ~!** thank goodness!; **¡menos ~ que le avisaron a tiempo!** it's just as well they told him in time!; **tomarse algo a ~** to take sth to heart
■ *m* [1] (Fil) evil; **el bien y el ~** good and evil, right and wrong
[2] (daño, perjuicio): **el divorcio de sus padres le hizo mucho ~** her parents' divorce did her a lot of harm
[3] (cosa dañina) ill, evil; **los ~es sociales** the social ills; **no hay ~ que por bien no venga** every cloud has a silver lining
[4] (Med) (liter) (enfermedad) illness; **tiene ~ de amores** (fam) he's lovesick; **~ de (las) altura(s)** altitude sickness, mountain sickness
[5] (pena) trouble

malabarismo *m* juggling; **hacer ~s** «malabarista» to juggle; (en situación difícil) to do a juggling *o* balancing act

malabarista *mf* juggler

malacostumbrado -da *adj* spoiled*, pampered

malacostumbrar [A1] *vt* to spoil
■ **malacostumbrarse** *v pron* to become spoilt

malacrianza *f* (AmL) rudeness

malaria *f* malaria

Malasia *f* Malaysia

malasio -sia *adj/m,f* Malaysian

malayo¹ -ya *adj/m,f* Malay

malayo² *m* (idioma) Malay

malcriado -da *adj* (mimado) spoiled*; (travieso) bad-mannered, badly brought up

malcriar [A17] *vt* to spoil, bring ... up badly

maldad *f* (a) (cualidad) evilness, wickedness (b) (acto) evil deed, wicked thing

maldecir [I25] *vt* to curse
■ **~** *vi* (a) (renegar) to curse; **~ DE algo/algn** to speak ill OF sth/sb (b) (blasfemar) to swear, curse (AmE)

maldición *f* (a) (imprecación) curse; **nos echó una ~** she put a curse on us (b) (palabrota) swearword; **soltó una ~** he swore

maldiga, maldijo, etc ▶ MALDECIR

maldito -ta *adj* (fam) (expresando irritación) damn (before n) (colloq), wretched (before n) (colloq); **¡este ~ ruido!** this damn *o* wretched noise!; **¡maldita/~ sea!** damn (it)! (colloq)

maldoso -sa *adj* (Méx) mischievous

malecón *m* (a) (rompeolas) breakwater; (embarcadero) jetty (b) (AmL) (paseo marítimo) seafront

maleducado -da *adj* rude, bad-mannered

maléfico -ca *adj* ⟨poderes/espíritus⟩ evil; ⟨influencia⟩ harmful

malenseñado -da *adj* (CS) (maleducado) rude, bad-mannered; (mimado) spoiled

malenseñar [A1] *vt* (CS) to spoil

malentender [E8] *vt* to misunderstand

malentendido *m* misunderstanding

malestar *m* **(a)** (Med) discomfort **(b)** (desazón, inquietud) unease

maleta *f* ⚊1⚊ (valija) suitcase, case; **hacer la** ~ to pack (one's case) ⚊2⚊ (Chi, Per) ▶ MALETERA

maletera *f* (Chi, Per) trunk (AmE), boot (BrE)

maletero *m* **(a)** (Auto) trunk (AmE), boot (BrE) **(b)** (mozo de estación) porter

maletín *m* (para documentos) briefcase; (maleta pequeña) overnight bag, small case; (de médico) bag

malévolo -la *adj* malevolent, malicious

maleza *f* ⚊1⚊ (espesura) undergrowth; (malas hierbas) weeds (*pl*) ⚊2⚊ (AmL) (mala hierba) weed

malformación *f* malformation

malgastador -dora *adj* wasteful, spendthrift ■ *m,f* squanderer, spendthrift

malgastar [A1] *vt* ⟨tiempo/esfuerzo⟩ to waste; ⟨dinero/herencia⟩ to squander

malhablado -da *adj* foul-mouthed

malhechor -chora *m,f* criminal, delinquent

malhumorado -da *adj* **(a)** [SER] ⟨persona/gesto⟩ bad-tempered **(b)** [ESTAR] ⟨persona⟩ in a bad mood

malicia *f* **(a)** (intención malévola) malice, malevolence **(b)** (picardía) mischief

malicioso -sa *adj* **(a)** (malintencionado) malicious, spiteful **(b)** (pícaro) mischievous

maligno -na *adj* **(a)** ⟨tumor⟩ malignant **(b)** ⟨persona/intención⟩ evil; ⟨influencia⟩ harmful, evil

malinchista *adj* (Méx) *preferring foreign things*

malinformar [A1] *vt* (CS frml) to misinform (frml)

malintencionado -da *adj* ⟨persona/palabras⟩ malicious, spiteful; ⟨golpe⟩ malicious

malinterpretar [A1] *vt* to misinterpret

malla *f* ⚊1⚊ (red) mesh; **una** ~ **para los insectos** a screen *o* mesh to stop insects ⚊2⚊ **(a)** (para gimnasia) leotard; ~ **de baño** (RPl) bathing suit, swimsuit **(b) mallas** *fpl* (medias) tights (*pl*); (sin pie) leggings (*pl*)

Mallorca *f* Majorca

mallorquín¹ -quina *adj/m,f* Majorcan

mallorquín² *m* (idioma) Majorcan

mallugar [A3] *vt* (Méx, Ven) to bruise

malnutrición *f* malnutrition

malnutrido -da *adj* malnourished

malo -la *adj* [*The form* MAL *is used before masculine singular nouns*] ⚊1⚊ **(a)** [SER] (en general) bad; **una novela mala** a bad novel; **un mal amigo** a bad friend; **una mala caída** a bad fall; **soy muy** ~ **para los números** I'm very bad with figures; **¡qué mala suerte** *or* (fam) **pata!** what bad luck!, how unlucky!; **lo** ~ **es que** ... the thing *o* trouble is that ...; **las malas compañías** bad company; **mala hierba** weed; ~**s tratos** ill-treatment; **es** ~ **tomar tanto sol** it's not good to sunbathe so much; **tienes mala cara** *or* **mal aspecto** you don't look well **(b)** ⟨calidad/visibilidad⟩ poor; **tiene mala ortografía** her spelling is poor; **estar de malas** (de mal humor) (fam) to be in a bad mood; (con mala suerte) (esp AmL) to be unlucky; **más vale** ~ **conocido que bueno por conocer** better the devil you know (than the devil you don't)

⚊2⚊ [SER] ⟨persona⟩ (en sentido ético) nasty; (travieso) naughty; **¡qué** ~ **eres con tu hermano!** you're really horrible *o* nasty to your brother; **no seas mala, préstamelo** don't be mean *o* rotten, lend it to me (colloq); **una mala mujer** a loose woman; **una mujer mala** a wicked *o* an evil woman; **lo hizo a** *or* **con mala idea** he did it deliberately *o* to be nasty; **mala palabra** (esp AmL) rude *o* dirty word; **dicen las malas lenguas que ...** (fam) there's a rumor going around that ..., people are saying that ...; **hacerse mala sangre** to get upset *ver tb* LECHE 3

⚊3⚊ [ESTAR] **(a)** (en mal estado) ⟨alimento⟩: **el pescado/queso está** ~ the fish/cheese has gone bad, that fish/cheese is off (BrE) **(b)** (Esp, Méx fam) (enfermo) sick (AmE), ill (BrE); **el pobre está malito** the poor thing's not very well (colloq) ■ *m,f* (leng infantil *o* hum) baddy (colloq)

malograr [A1] *vt* ⟨oportunidad⟩ to waste; ⟨trabajo⟩ to ruin, spoil ■ **malograrse** *v pron* ⚊1⚊ «proyecto/cosecha» to fail ⚊2⚊ **(a)** «persona» (morir joven) to die young *o* before one's time **(b)** (Per) «reloj» to stop working; «lavadora» to break down

maloliente *adj* stinking, smelly

malparado -da *adj*: **salir** ~ to come off badly

malpensado -da *adj*: **no seas** ~ why do you always think the worst of people?

malsano -na *adj* ⟨clima/lugar⟩ unhealthy; ⟨influencia⟩ bad, unhealthy

malsonante *adj* rude

malta *f* **(a)** (cereal) malt **(b)** (Chi) (cerveza) stout

malteada *f* (AmL) milk shake

maltratar [A1] *vt* **(a)** ⟨persona/animal⟩ to maltreat, ill-treat, mistreat; (pegar) ⟨niño/mujer⟩ to batter **(b)** ⟨juguete/coche⟩ to mistreat, treat ... very roughly

maltrecho -cha *adj*: **lo dejaron muy** ~ they left him in a bad way

malucho -cha *adj* (fam) (algo enfermo): **estar** ~ to be *o* feel under the weather (colloq)

malva *adj inv/m* mauve ■ *f* mallow; ~ **real** hollyhock, rose mallow (AmE)

malvado -da *adj* wicked, evil

malvavisco *m* marshmallow

malvender [E1] *vt* to sell ... off cheap, sell ... at a loss

malversación *f*: *tb* ~ **de fondos** embezzlement (of funds)

malversar [A1] *vt* to embezzle, misappropriate

Malvinas *fpl*: **las** ~ the Falkland Islands, the Falklands

malvón *m* (RPl, Méx) geranium

mama *f* (Anat) breast; (Zool) mammary gland

mamá *f* (*pl* **-más**) (fam) mom (AmE colloq), mum (BrE colloq); (usado por niños) mommy (AmE colloq), mummy (BrE colloq)

mamadera *f* (CS, Per) (biberón) (feeding) bottle, baby bottle

mamado -da *adj* **(a)** (fam) (borracho) tight(colloq), sloshed (colloq) **(b)** (Col, Ven fam) (cansado) dead beat (colloq), shattered (colloq); (aburrido) bored

mamar [A1] *vi* ⚊1⚊ **(a)** «bebé» to feed; **dar de** ~ to breastfeed **(b)** «gato/cordero» to suckle ⚊2⚊ (fam) (beber alcohol) to booze (colloq)

mameluco m (AmL) **(a)** (de niño, bebé) rompers (pl), romper suit (BrE) **(b)** (pantalón con peto) overalls (pl) (AmE), dungarees (pl) (BrE); (de trabajo) coveralls (pl) (AmE), overalls (pl) (BrE)

mamífero adj mammalian
■ m mammal

mamila f (Méx) (biberón) (feeding) bottle; (tetilla) nipple (AmE), teat (BrE)

mampara f **(a)** (biombo, tabique) screen, partition **(b)** (Chi, Per) (puerta) inner door

mampostería f masonry

manada f **(a)** (Zool) (de elefantes) herd; (de leones) pride; (de lobos) pack **(b)** (fam) (de gente) herd

Managua f Managua

managüense adj of/from Managua

manantial m (de agua) spring

manar [A1] vi to pour

manatí m manatee

mancha f **1** **(a)** (de suciedad) spot, mark; (difícil de quitar) stain; **una ~ de grasa** a grease stain; **~s de humedad** damp patches; **~ de petróleo** oil slick **(b)** (borrón) blot **2** **(a)** (en la piel) mark **(b)** (en el pelaje, las plumas) patch; (del leopardo) spot **3** (liter) (imperfección, mácula) stain; **sin ~** ⟨alma⟩ pure; ⟨reputación⟩ spotless **4** (Per fam) (pandilla) gang

manchado -da adj ⟨mantel/vestido⟩ stained; **está ~ de vino** it has wine stains on it; **~ de sangre** blood-stained

manchar [A1] vt **1** (ensuciar) to mark, get ... dirty; (de algo difícil de quitar) to stain **2** ⟨reputación/honra/memoria⟩ to tarnish
■ ~ vi to stain
■ **mancharse** v pron **(a)** «ropa/mantel» to get dirty; (de algo difícil de quitar) to get stained; **~se DE** or **CON algo** to get stained WITH sth **(b)** (refl) «persona» to get dirty; **me manché la blusa de aceite** I got oil stains on my blouse

manchego -ga adj of/from La Mancha

manco -ca adj: **es ~ de un brazo/una mano** he only has one arm/hand

mancomunidad f community, association; **M~ Británica de Naciones** British Commonwealth

mancorna f (Col) cufflink

mancuernilla f (Méx) cufflink

manda f (Chi, Méx) offering, promise

mandadero -ra m,f (esp AmL) (m) office boy; (f) office girl

mandado¹ -da adj (Méx fam): **es muy ~** he's a real opportunist; **no seas mandada, solo te ofrecí uno** don't be so greedy, I only offered you one (colloq)
■ m,f (esp Esp) (subordinado) minion (hum or pej); **no soy más que un ~** I'm just following orders

mandado² m **(a)** (esp AmL) (compra): **hacer los ~s** or (Méx) **ir al ~** to do the shopping **(b)** (Méx) (cosa comprada): **¿me trajiste el ~?** did you get the shopping o the things I asked you for? **(c)** (diligencia) errand

mandamiento m **1** (Relig) commandment **2** (orden) order; (Der) warrant, order

mandar [A1] vt **1** **(a)** (ordenar): **a mí nadie me manda** nobody tells me what to do, nobody orders me about; **haz lo que te mandan** do as you're told; **la mandó callar** he told o ordered her to be quiet; **mandó que sirvieran la comida** she ordered lunch to be served **(b)** (recetar) to prescribe; **el médico le mandó descansar** the doctor advised him to rest **2** (enviar) to send; **la mandé por el pan** I sent her out to buy the bread **3** (AmL) (tratándose de encargos): **mis padres me ~on llamar** my parents sent for me; **mandó decir que ...** she sent a message to say that ...; **~ algo a arreglar** to get o have sth mended **4** (AmL fam) (arrojar, lanzar): **mandó la pelota fuera de la cancha** he kicked/sent/hit the ball out of play
■ **~** vi (ser el jefe) to be in charge, be the boss (colloq); **¿mande?** (Méx) (I'm) sorry?, pardon?; **¡María! — ¿mande?** (Méx) María! — yes?

mandarina f (Bot, Coc) mandarin (orange), tangerine

mandatario -ria m,f (Pol) tb **primer ~/primera mandataria** head of state

mandato m **1** **(a)** (período) term of office **(b)** (orden) mandate **2** (Der) mandate

mandíbula f jaw

mandil m (delantal) leather apron

mandioca f (planta) cassava; (fécula) tapioca

mando m **1** (en general) command; **entregarle el ~ a algn** to hand over command to sb; **dotes de ~** leadership qualities; **estar al ~ (de algo)** to be in charge (of sth) **2** (Auto, Elec) control; **~ a distancia** remote control

mandolina f mandolin

mandón -dona adj bossy

mandonear [A1] vt (fam) to boss ... around (colloq)

mandril m (Zool) mandrill

manearse [A1] v pron (Chi fam) to get in a tangle (colloq), to be all fingers and thumbs (colloq)

manecilla f hand; **la ~ grande/pequeña** the minute/hour hand

manejable adj **1** ⟨coche⟩ maneuverable*; ⟨máquina⟩ easy-to-use; ⟨pelo⟩ manageable **2** ⟨persona⟩ easily led, easily manipulated

manejar [A1] vt **1** (usar) ⟨herramienta/arma/diccionario⟩ to use; ⟨máquina⟩ to use, operate **2** (dirigir, llevar) ⟨negocio/empresa⟩ to manage; ⟨asuntos⟩ to manage, handle **3** (manipular) to manipulate **4** (AmL) ⟨auto⟩ to drive
■ ~ vi (AmL) to drive
■ **manejarse** v pron **1** (desenvolverse) to get by, manage **2** (Col) (comportarse) to behave

manejo m **1** (uso): **el ~ de la máquina es muy sencillo** the machine is easy to use o operate; **su ~ de la lengua** his use of the language **2** (de asunto, negocio) management **3** (AmL) (Auto) driving

manera f **1** (modo, forma) way; **yo lo hago a mi ~** I do it my way; **a ~ de** by way of; **de todas ~s**

AmC	América Central	Arg	Argentina	Cu	Cuba	Per	Perú
AmL	América Latina	Bol	Bolivia	Ec	Ecuador	RPI	Río de la Plata
AmS	América del Sur	Chi	Chile	Esp	España	Ur	Uruguay
Andes	Región andina	CS	Cono Sur	Méx	México	Ven	Venezuela

anyway; **su** ~ **de ser** the way she is; **se puede ir vestido de cualquier** ~ you can dress however you want; **no lo pongas así, de cualquier** ~ don't just put it in any which way (AmE) o (BrE) any old how; **de ninguna** ~ **lo voy a permitir** there's no way I'm going to allow it; **de alguna** ~ **tendré que conseguirlo** I'll have to get it somehow (or other); **no hay/hubo** ~ it is/it was impossible; **de** ~ **que** so; **de mala** ~ ⟨contestar⟩ rudely; ⟨tratar⟩ badly

[2] **maneras** *fpl* (modales) manners (*pl*)

manga *f* [1] (a) (de abrigo, blusa) sleeve; **sin** ~**s** sleeveless; **de** ~ **corta/larga** short-sleeved/ long-sleeved; **en** ~**s de camisa** in shirtsleeves; *tener (la)* ~ *ancha* to be tolerant o lenient (b) (capa de jerga) (AmC) poncho [2] (Coc) (filtro) strainer; (para repostería) *tb* ~ **pastelera** pastry bag [3] (Dep) round [4] (manguera) hose; ~ **de incendio** fire hose; ~ **de riego** hosepipe [5] (AmL) (de langostas) swarm

manglar *m* mangrove swamp

mangle *m* mangrove

mango *m* [1] (de cuchillo, paraguas) handle [2] (Bot) (árbol) mango (tree); (fruta) mango [3] (Méx fam & hum) (persona atractiva): **es un** ~ *«mujer»* she's a real stunner (colloq); *«hombre»* he's a real hunk (colloq)

mangonear [A1] *vi* (fam) (a) (mandonear) to order o (colloq) boss people around (b) (entrometerse) to meddle
■ ~ *vt* (fam) to boss ... around (colloq)

mangosta *f* mongoose

manguera *f* (para regar) hose, hosepipe; (de bombero) hose

maní *m* (*pl* **-níes** or (crit) **-níses**) (AmC, AmS) peanut

manía *f* [1] (obsesión, capricho): **tiene sus** ~**s** he has his funny little ways; **tiene la** ~ **de la limpieza** she has a mania for cleanliness o (colloq) a thing about cleaning; **le ha dado la** ~ **de vestirse de negro** she has this fad o craze of dressing in black; ~ **persecutoria** or **de persecución** persecution complex o mania [2] (antipatía): **tenerle** ~ **a algn** to have it in for sb (colloq)

maniaco -ca, maníaco -ca *m,f* (a) (Psic) manic (b) (fam) (loco) maniac; ~ **sexual** sex maniac

maniatar [A1] *vt* (a) ⟨persona⟩: **los ladrones lo** ~**on** the burglars tied his hands (b) ⟨animal⟩ to hobble

maniático -ca *adj* (a) (delicado, difícil) finicky, fussy (b) (obsesionado) obsessive

manicero -ra *m,f* (AmC, AmS) peanut seller

manicomio *m* mental hospital, lunatic asylum

manicura *f* manicure; **hacerse la** ~ (*refl*) to do one's nails; (*caus*) to have a manicure

manido -da *adj* ⟨frase⟩ hackneyed; ⟨tema⟩ stale

manifestación *f* [1] (Pol) demonstration [2] (expresión, indicio) sign; **las manifestaciones artísticas culturales de la época** the artistic cultural expression of the era

manifestante *mf* demonstrator

manifestar [A5] *vt* (a) (expresar) ⟨desaprobación/agradecimiento⟩ to express; ~**on**

su apoyo a esta propuesta they expressed their support for the proposal (b) (demostrar) ⟨emociones⟩ to show
■ **manifestarse** *v pron* [1] (hacerse evidente) to become apparent o evident; (ser evidente) to be apparent o evident [2] (Pol) to demonstrate, take part in a demonstration [3] (dar opinión): ~**se en contra/a favor de algo** to express one's opposition to/support for sth

manifiesta, manifiestas, etc ▶
MANIFESTAR

manifiesto¹ -ta *adj* (frml) manifest (frml), evident (frml); **poner algo de** ~ to highlight sth; **quedar de** ~ to become plain o obvious o evident

manifiesto² *m* (Pol) manifesto

manija *f* (esp AmL) handle

manilla *f* (a) (de reloj) hand (b) (de cajón) handle (c) (Col) (guante) baseball glove

manillar *m* (esp Esp) handlebars (*pl*)

maniobra *f* maneuver*; **estar de** ~**s** (Mil) to be on maneuvers

maniobrar [A1] *vi/vt* to maneuver*

manipulador -dora *adj* manipulative
■ *m,f* (aprovechado) manipulator

manipular [A1] *vt* [1] (a) ⟨mercancías⟩ to handle (b) ⟨aparato/máquina⟩ to operate, use [2] ⟨persona/información/datos⟩ to manipulate; ~ **los resultados** to fix o rig the results

maniquí *mf* (a) (persona) model (b) **maniquí** *m* (de sastre, escaparate) mannequin, dummy

manirroto -ta *adj* (a) (fam) extravagant (b) (generoso) generous, open-handed
■ *m,f* (fam) spendthrift

manitas *mf* (Esp, Méx fam) handyman (colloq)

manito -ta *m,f*: ▶ MANO²

manivela *f* crank, handle

manjar *m* delicacy; ~ **blanco** (Andes) ▶ DULCE DE LECHE

mano¹ *f* [1] (a) (Anat) hand; **tengo las** ~**s sucias** my hands are dirty; **levantar la** ~ to raise one's hands, put one's hand up; **¡** ~**s arriba!** or **¡arriba las** ~**s!** hands up!; **con la** ~ **en el corazón** hand on heart; **le hizo adiós con la** ~ he waved goodbye to her; **su carta pasó de** ~ **en** ~ her letter was passed around; **darle la** ~ **a algn** (para saludar) to shake hands with sb, to shake sb's hand; (para ayudar, ser ayudado) to give sb one's hand; **dame la** ~ hold my hand; **me tendió la** ~ he held out his hand to me; **me tomó de la** ~ she took me by the hand; **ir (tomados) de la** ~ to walk hand in hand; ~ **de obra** labor (b) (Zool) (de oso, perro) paw; (de mono) hand; (Equ) forefoot, front foot
[2] (control, posesión) *gen* ~**s** hands (*pl*); **ha cambiado de** ~**s** it has changed hands; **cayó en** ~**s del enemigo** it fell into the hands of the enemy; **haré todo lo que esté en mis** ~**s** I will do everything in my power; **la oportunidad se nos fue de las** ~**s** we let the opportunity slip through our fingers; **se tomó la justicia por su propia** ~ he took the law into his own hands
[3] (en fútbol) handball
[4] (del mortero) pestle
[5] (de pintura, barniz) coat
[6] (Jueg) (vuelta, juego) hand; (conjunto de cartas) hand; (jugador): **soy/eres** ~ it's my/your lead
[7] (*en locs*) **a mano** (no a máquina) by hand; **hecho** ⋯⃟

a ~ handmade; **escrito a** ~ handwritten; **tejido a ~** handwoven; **las tiendas me quedan muy a ~** the shops are very close by o near; **siempre tengo un diccionario a ~** I always keep a dictionary by me; **a la mano** (AmL) close at hand; **de mano** hand (*before n*); **en mano** ⟨*lápiz/copa*⟩ in hand; **agarrar** or (esp Esp) **coger a algn con las ~s en la masa** to catch sb red-handed; **agarrarle** or **tomarle la ~ a algo** (CS fam) to get the hang of sth (colloq); **bajo ~** on the quiet, on the sly (colloq); **con las ~s vacías** empty-handed; **darse la ~** (*para saludar*) to shake hands; (*para cruzar, jugar, etc*) to hold hands; **de segunda ~** secondhand; **echar** or **dar una ~** to give o lend a hand; **echar ~ a algo** (fam) to grab sth; **estar/quedar a ~** (AmL fam) to be even o quits (colloq); **lavarse las ~s** to wash one's hands; **levantarle la ~ a algn** to raise one's hand to sb; **llegar** or **pasar a las ~s** to come to blows; **pedir la ~ de algn** to ask for sb's hand in marriage; **ser la ~ derecha de algn** to be sb's right-hand man/woman; **tenderle una ~ a algn** to offer sb a (helping) hand; **tener ~ dura** to have a firm hand; **tener ~ para algo** to be good at sth; **traerse algo entre ~s** to be up to sth (colloq)

8 **(a)** (*lado*) side; **queda de esta ~** it's on this side of the street; **a ~ derecha** on the right **(b)** (Auto) side of the road

mano² **-na** *m,f* (AmL fam) (*apelativo*) buddy (AmE colloq), mate (BrE colloq)

manojo *m* bunch; **ser un ~ de nervios** to be a bundle of nerves

manoseado **-da** *adj* **(a)** ⟨*libro*⟩ well-thumbed; **fruta manoseada** fruit that has been handled by lots of people **(b)** ⟨*tema*⟩ hackneyed, well-worn

manosear [A1] *vt* **(a)** ⟨*objeto*⟩ to handle **(b)** (fam) ⟨*persona*⟩ to grope (colloq)

manotada *f* (Col) handful

manotazo *m* swipe

mansalva: **a ~** (*loc adv*) ⟨*disparar*⟩ at close range

mansión *f* mansion; **~ señorial** stately home

manso **-sa** *adj* **(a)** ⟨*caballo*⟩ tame; ⟨*toro*⟩ docile; ⟨*perro*⟩ friendly **(b)** (liter) ⟨*río*⟩ gently-flowing (liter)

manta *f* **1** (de cama) blanket **2** (Chi) (poncho) poncho **3** (Méx) (tela) *a coarse muslin-like cloth*, calico (BrE)

manteca *f* **(a)** (grasa) fat; (de cerdo) lard **(b)** (mantequilla) (RPl) butter; **~ de cacao** cocoa butter; **~ de maní** (RPl) peanut butter

mantecoso **-sa** *adj* greasy

mantel *m* (de mesa) tablecloth; (del altar) altar cloth; **~ individual** place mat

mantelería *f* table linen

mantención *f* (CS) maintenance

mantener [E27] *vt* **1** (económicamente) ⟨*familia/persona*⟩ to support, maintain; ⟨*amante*⟩ to keep **2** (conservar, preservar) to keep; **~ la calma** to keep calm; **~ el equilibrio** to keep one's balance; **~ algo en equilibrio** to balance sth; **para ~ su peso actual** to maintain his present weight **3** **(a)** ⟨*conversaciones*⟩ to have; ⟨*contactos*⟩ to maintain, keep up; ⟨*correspondencia*⟩ to keep up; ⟨*relaciones*⟩ to maintain **(b)** (cumplir) ⟨*promesa/palabra*⟩ to keep **4** (afirmar, sostener) to maintain

■ **mantenerse** *v pron* **1** (sustentarse económicamente) to support oneself

2 (en cierto estado, cierta situación) to keep; **~se en forma** to keep fit; **la torre aún se mantiene en pie** the tower is still standing; **~se en contacto** (**con algn**) to keep in touch (with sb) **3** (alimentarse): **~se a base de latas** to live off tinned food

mantenimiento *m* maintenance; **ejercicios de ~** keep-fit exercises

mantequilla *f* butter; **~ de cacao** (Chi, Per) cocoa butter

mantequillera *f* butter dish

mantiene, mantienes, etc ▶ MANTENER

mantilla *f* **(a)** (de mujer) mantilla **(b)** (de bebé) terry diaper (AmE), terry nappy (BrE)

manto *m* (Indum) cloak

mantón *m* shawl

mantuve, mantuvo, etc ▶ MANTENER

manual *adj* ⟨*trabajo/destreza*⟩ manual; **tener habilidad ~** to be good with one's hands
■ *m* manual, handbook

manualidades *fpl* handicrafts (*pl*)

manubrio *m* **(a)** (manivela) crank, handle **(b)** (AmL) (de bicicleta) handlebars (*pl*) **(c)** (Chi, Par) (de auto) steering wheel

manufacturar [A1] *vt* to manufacture

manuscrito¹ **-ta** *adj* hand-written, manuscript (frml)

manuscrito² *m* manuscript

manutención *f* maintenance

manzana *f* **1** (Bot) apple **2** (de edificios) block; **dar una vuelta a la ~** to go round the block **3** (AmL) (Anat) *tb* **~ de Adán** Adam's apple

manzanar *m* apple orchard

manzanilla *f* (planta) camomile; (infusión) camomile tea
■ *m* manzanilla (*dry sherry*)

manzano *m* apple tree

maña *f* **1** (habilidad) skill, knack (colloq); **tener** or **darse ~ para algo** to be good at sth; **más vale ~ que fuerza** brain is better than brawn **2** **mañas** *fpl* (artimañas) wiles (*pl*), guile **3** (capricho) bad habit; (manía) (AmL fam): **tiene ~s de viejo** he's like an old man with all his funny little ways (colloq); **tiene la ~ de morderse las uñas** he has the annoying habit of biting his nails

mañana *adv* tomorrow; **pasado ~** the day after tomorrow; **~ por la ~** tomorrow morning; **adiós, hasta ~** goodbye, see you tomorrow; **el día de ~** tomorrow
■ *m* future
■ *f* morning; **a la ~ siguiente** (the) next o the following morning; **a media ~ nos reunimos** we met mid-morning; **a las nueve de la ~** at nine (o'clock) in the morning; **en** or (esp Esp) **por** or (RPl) **a la(s) ~(s)** in the morning; **muy de ~** very early in the morning; **el tren de la ~** the morning train

mañanero **-ra** *adj* (fam): **soy muy ~** I'm a very early riser

mañanitas *fpl* (en Méx) *song often sung on birthdays*

mañosear [A1] *vi* (Chi fam) to play o act up (colloq)

mañoso **-sa** *adj* **1** (habilidoso) good with one's hands **2** (AmL) (caprichoso) difficult

mapa *m* map; ~ **de carreteras** road map; **cambios en el** ~ **político** changes in the political scene *o* landscape; *desaparecer del* ~ to disappear off the face of the earth

mapache *m* racoon

mapamundi *m* map of the world, world map

mapurite *m* (AmC, Ven) skunk

maqueta *f* (de edificio) model, mock-up

maquiladora *f* (Méx) (cross-border) assembly plant

maquillador -dora *m,f* makeup artist

maquillaje *m* makeup; ~ **de fondo** foundation

maquillar [A1] *vt* to make up
▪ **maquillarse** *v pron* to put one's makeup on, to make up

máquina *f* [1] **(a)** (aparato) machine; **¿se puede lavar a** ~? can it be machine-washed?; **escribir a** ~ to type; ~ **de afeitar** safety razor; (eléctrica) electric razor, shaver; ~ **de coser/lavar** sewing/washing machine; ~ **de escribir** typewriter; ~ **expendedora** vending machine; ~ **tragamonedas** *or* (Esp) **tragaperras** slot machine, fruit machine **(b)** (Jueg) fruit machine; (Fot) camera [2] **(a)** (Ferr, Náut) engine **(b)** (Ven fam) (auto) car

maquinación *f* plot, scheme

maquinar [A1] *vt* to plot, scheme

maquinaria *f* **(a)** (conjunto) machinery **(b)** (mecanismo) mechanism; **la** ~ **del estado** the state machinery

maquinilla *f* [1] *tb* ~ **de afeitar** safety razor; (eléctrica) electric razor, shaver [2] (AmC) (máquina de escribir) typewriter

maquinista *mf* [1] (operador de una máquina) machine operator [2] (Ferr) engine driver, engineer (AmE); (Náut) engineer

mar *m* (*sometimes f in literary language and in set idiomatic expressions*) [1] (Geog) sea; **a orillas del** ~ by the sea; **el fondo del** ~ the seabed, the bottom of the sea; ~ **abierto** open sea; **la corriente llevó la barca** ~ **adentro** the boat was swept out to sea by the current; **hacerse a la** ~ (liter) to set sail; **por** ~ by sea; ~ **Cantábrico** Bay of Biscay; ~ **de las Antillas** Caribbean Sea; ~ **Mediterráneo** Mediterranean Sea; ~ **gruesa** rough *o* heavy sea [2] (costa): **prefiero el** ~ **a la montaña** I prefer the seaside to the mountains

maraca *f* maraca

maracuyá *m* passion fruit

maraña *f* tangle; **la** ~ **burocrática** the tangle of bureaucracy

maratón *m or f* marathon

maravilla *f* [1] (portento, prodigio) wonder; **las** ~s **de la tecnología moderna** the wonders of modern technology; **mi secretaria es una verdadera** ~ my secretary is absolutely wonderful; **a las mil** ~s marvelously; **de** ~ wonderfully; **hacer** ~s to work wonders [2] (Bot) marigold

maravillar [A1] *vt* to amaze, astonish
▪ **maravillarse** *v pron* to be amazed *o* astonished; ~**se DE algo/algn** to marvel AT sth/sb

maravilloso -sa *adj* marvelous*, wonderful

marca *f* [1] **(a)** (señal, huella) mark **(b)** (en el ganado) brand [2] (Com) (de coches, cámaras) make; (de productos alimenticios, cosméticos, etc) brand; **comprar artículos de** ~ to buy brand products *o* brand names; **ropa de** ~ designer clothes; ~ **patentada** *or* **registrada** registered trademark [3] (Dep) record; **superar** *or* **batir una** ~ to break a record

marcado¹ -da *adj* marked; **un** ~ **acento escocés** a marked *o* pronounced Scottish accent

marcado² *m* **(a)** (del pelo) set **(b)** (de reses) branding

marcador *m* [1] (Dep) scoreboard; **¿cómo va el** ~? what's the score? [2] **(a)** (para libros) bookmark **(b)** (AmL) (rotulador) felt-tip pen, fiber-tip* pen

marcaje *m* (Dep) coverage, cover

marcapasos *m* (*pl* ~) pacemaker

marcar [A2] *vt* [1] **(a)** (con señal) ⟨ropa/página/baraja⟩ to mark; ⟨ganado⟩ to brand **(b)** «experiencia/suceso» (dejar huella) to mark [2] **(a)** (indicar, señalar) to mark; **el precio va marcado en la tapa** the price is marked on the lid; **el reloj marca las doce en punto** the time is exactly twelve o'clock **(b)** (hacer resaltar) ⟨cintura/busto⟩ to accentuate **(c)** (Mús): ~ **el compás/el ritmo** to beat time/the rhythm [3] ⟨pelo⟩ to set [4] (Telec) to dial [5] (Dep) **(a)** ⟨gol/tanto⟩ to score **(b)** ⟨jugador⟩ to mark
▪ ~ *vi* [1] (Dep) to score [2] (Telec) to dial
▪ **marcarse** *v pron*: ~**se el pelo** (*refl*) to set one's hair; (*caus*) to have one's hair set

marcha *f* [1] **(a)** (Mil) march; (manifestación) march; (caminata) hike, walk; **ir de** ~ to go walking *o* hiking; **recojan todo y ¡en** ~! pick up your things and off you/we go!; *ponerse en* ~ to set off **(b)** (en atletismo) *tb* ~ **atlética** walk [2] (paso, velocidad) speed; **el vehículo disminuyó la** ~ the car reduced speed *o* slowed down; **acelerar la** ~ to speed up; **a toda** ~ at full *o* top speed, flat out [3] (Auto) gear; **cambiar de** ~ to change gear; **meter la** ~ **atrás** to put the car into reverse; **dar** *or* **hacer** ~ **atrás** (Auto) to go into reverse; (arrepentirse, retroceder) to pull out, back out [4] (funcionamiento) running; **estar en** ~ «motor» to be running; «proyecto» to be up and running, to be under way; «gestiones» to be under way; **poner en** ~ ⟨coche/motor⟩ to start; ⟨plan/sistema⟩ to set … in motion; **ponerse en** ~ «tren» to move off [5] (curso, desarrollo) course; **la** ~ **de los acontecimientos** the course of events; **sobre la** ~: **hago correciones sobre la** ~ I make corrections as I go along; **lo decidiremos sobre la** ~ we'll play it by ear [6] (partida) departure [7] (Mús) march; ~ **nupcial** wedding march [8] (Esp fam) (animación, ambiente): **una ciudad con mucha** ~ a very lively city; **¡qué** ~ **tiene!** he's so full of energy

marchante -ta *m,f* [1] (de obras de arte) art dealer [2] (Méx) (en mercado — vendedor) stallholder; (— comprador) customer

marchar [A1] *vi* [1] «coche» to go, run; «reloj/máquina» to work; «negocio/relación/empresa» to work; **su matrimonio no marcha muy bien** his marriage isn't going *o* working very well [2] **(a)** (Mil) to march **(b)** (caminar) to walk

⋯⋄

marchitarse ⋯⟩ mármol

■ **marcharse** v pron (esp Esp) to leave; **se marcha a Roma** he's leaving for o going off to Rome

marchitarse [A1] v pron (a) «flores» to wither (b) (liter) «belleza/juventud» to fade

marchito -ta adj (a) ‹flores› withered (b) (liter) ‹belleza/juventud› faded

marchoso -sa adj (Esp fam) ‹ambiente/ciudad› lively; **es un tío ~** he's really into the night life (colloq), he's really into having a good time (colloq)

marcial adj martial

marciano -na adj/m,f Martian

marco m ① (a) (de cuadro) frame; (de puerta) doorframe (b) (Dep) goalposts (pl), goal (c) (Andes) (de bicicleta) frame ② (contexto) framework; **dentro del ~ de la ley** within the framework of the law ③ (Fin) mark

marea f tide; **cuando baja/sube la ~** when the tide goes out/comes in; **~ creciente** rising tide, flood tide; **~ menguante** falling tide, ebb tide; **~ negra** oil slick

mareado -da adj (a) (Med): **está ~** (con náuseas) he's feeling sick o queasy; (con pérdida del equilibrio, etc) he's feeling dizzy o giddy; (a punto de desmayarse) he's feeling faint (b) (confundido): **me tienes ~ con tanta cháchara** all your chatter is making my head spin

marear [A1] vt (a) (Med) (con náuseas) to make … feel sick o queasy; (con pérdida de equilibrio) to make … dizzy (b) (confundir) to confuse, get … confused o muddled; **me mareas con tantas preguntas** you're confusing me with all these questions

■ **marearse** v pron (a) (al viajar — en coche) to get carsick; (— en barco) to get seasick; (— en avión) to get airsick; (perder el equilibrio) to feel dizzy; (con alcohol) to get tipsy (b) (confundirse) to get muddled o confused

marejada f heavy sea, swell

maremoto m (a) (sismo) seaquake (b) (ola) tidal wave

mareo m (a) (del estómago) sickness, nausea; (producido por movimiento) motion sickness; (en coche) carsickness; (en avión) airsickness; (en barco) seasickness; (pérdida de equilibrio, etc) dizziness, giddiness; **me dio un ~** I felt dizzy (b) (confusión) muddle, mess

marfil m ivory

margarina f margarine

margarita f (Bot) (pequeña) daisy; (grande) marguerite

margen f (a veces m) (de río) bank; (de carretera) side

■ m ① (en general) margin; **~ de beneficio** or **ganancias** profit margin; **~ de error** margin of error; **ver nota al ~** see margin note; **al margen de** apart from: **al ~ de la ley** on the fringes of the law; **mantenerse al ~ de algo** to keep out of sth; **dejar a algn al ~** to leave sb out; **~ de acción/tiempo** leeway ② **márgenes** mpl (límites, parámetros) limits (pl); **dentro de ciertos márgenes** within certain limits

marginación f (Sociol) marginalization

marginado -da adj (a) (Sociol) marginalized (b) (excluido) excluded

■ m,f social outcast

marginal adj ① (Sociol): **en los barrios ~es** in the poor, outlying areas of the city ② (secundario) ‹posición› peripheral; ‹asunto› marginal, peripheral ③ (Impr): **una nota ~** a note in the margin, a marginal note

marginar [A1] vt (en la sociedad) to marginalize; (en un grupo) to ostracize

mariachi m mariachi musician

marialuisa f (Méx) mount, passe-partout

maricón¹ -cona adj (fam & pey) (a) (homosexual) queer (colloq & pej), bent (sl & pej) (b) (como insulto): **el muy ~** the bastard o (AmE) son of a bitch (vulg); **la muy maricona** the bitch (vulg) (c) (AmL) (cobarde) wimpy (colloq), wimpish (colloq)

maricón² m (fam & pey) fag (AmE colloq & pej), poof (BrE colloq & pej)

mariconera f (fam & hum) (men's) handbag

marido m husband

marihuana f marijuana

marihuanero -ra m,f (fam) dope fiend (colloq)

marimacho m or f (fam & pey) (a) (niña) tomboy (colloq) (b) (mujer hombruna) butch woman (colloq)

marimba f marimba (type of xylophone)

marina f ① (organización) navy; (barcos) fleet; **~ de guerra** navy ② (Art) seascape

marinar [A1] vt to marinate, marinade

marinera f ① (blusa) sailor top; (chaqueta) (Col) sailor jacket ② (baile) Andean folk dance

marinero m sailor

marino¹ -na adj ‹brisa/corriente› sea (before n); ‹fauna/biología› marine (before n)

marino² m (marinero) sailor; (oficial) naval officer; **~ mercante** merchant seaman

marioneta f puppet, marionette

mariposa f butterfly; **~ nocturna** moth; **estilo ~** butterfly; **nadar ~** or (Esp) **a** or (Méx) **de ~** to swim butterfly

mariquita f (Zool) ladybug (AmE), ladybird (BrE)

■ m (fam & pey) fag (AmE colloq & pej), poof (BrE colloq & pej)

mariscal m (Hist, Mil) marshal; **~ de campo** (Mil) field marshal; (en fútbol americano) quarterback

marisco m shellfish (pl), seafood

marisma f marsh

marisquería f seafood o shellfish restaurant/ bar/shop

marital adj ‹relaciones› marital (before n); ‹vida› married (before n)

marítimo -ma adj ‹comercio› maritime; ‹ruta/ agente› shipping (before n); ‹transporte› sea (before n); ‹ciudad› coastal, maritime; **un puerto ~** a seaport

marketing /'marketin/ m marketing

mármol m marble

AmC Central America	Arg Argentina	Cu Cuba	Per Peru
AmL Latin America	Bol Bolivia	Ec Ecuador	RPI River Plate Area
AmS South America	Chi Chile	Esp Spain	Ur Uruguay
Andes Andean Region	CS Southern Cone	Méx Mexico	Ven Venezuela

marmota *f* (a) (Zool) marmot (b) (fam) (persona dormilona) sleepyhead (colloq)

maroma *f* [1] rope [2] (a) (Andes) (acrobacia, malabarismo) trick, stunt; **las ~s del payaso** the clown's antics (b) (Méx) (voltereta) somersault, tumble; **dar una ~** to do a somersault

marqués -quesa *m,f* [1] (persona) (*m*) marquis, marquess (BrE); (*f*) marquise, marchioness (BrE) [2] **marquesa** *f* (Chi) (catre) bed

marquesina *f* (en parada, andén) shelter; (de teatro, hotel) marquee (AmE), canopy (BrE); (en estadio) roof

marquetería *f* marquetry

marranada *f* (fam) (faena) dirty trick

marrano -na *adj* filthy
■ *m,f* (fam) (a) (animal) (*m*) pig, hog; (*f*) pig, sow (b) (Col) (carne) pork (c) (persona grosera) dirty swine (colloq)

marraqueta *f* (Chi) bread roll

marrón *adj/m* brown; **zapatos ~ oscuro** dark brown shoes

marroquí *adj/mf* Moroccan

marroquinería *f* (a) (artículos de cuero) leather goods (*pl*) (b) (tienda) leather goods shop

marrueco *m* (Chi) fly, flies (*pl*)

Marruecos *m* Morocco

marsupial *adj/m* marsupial

marta *f* (pine) marten; **~ cibelina** sable

Marte *m* Mars

martes *m* (*pl* **~**) Tuesday; **~ (y) trece** ≈ Friday the thirteenth; **~ de carnaval** Shrove Tuesday, Mardi Gras; *para ejemplos ver* LUNES

martillar, martillear [A1] *vt/vi* to hammer

martilleo *m* hammering; **un ~ terrible en las sienes** a terrible pounding in the temples

martillero -ra *m,f* (CS, Per) auctioneer

martillo *m* hammer; **~ neumático** jackhammer, pneumatic drill

martín pescador *m* kingfisher

mártir *mf* martyr

martirio *m* (a) (muerte) martyrdom (b) (sufrimiento) torment, ordeal

martirizar [A4] *vt* (a) (matar) to martyr (b) (atormentar) to torment

marxismo *m* Marxism

marxista *adj/mf* Marxist

marzo *m* March; *para ejemplos ver* ENERO

mas *conj* (liter) but

más *adv* [1] (a) (comparativo): **¿tiene algo ~ barato/moderno?** do you have anything cheaper/more modern; **duran ~** they last longer; **me gusta ~ sin azúcar** I prefer it without sugar; **ahora la vemos ~** we see more of her now; **tendrás que estudiar ~** you'll have to study harder; **~ lejos/atrás** further away/back; **el ~ allá** the other world; **~ que nunca** more than ever; **me gusta ~ el vino seco que el dulce** I prefer dry wine to sweet, I like dry wine better than sweet; **pesa ~ de lo que parece** it's heavier than it looks; **es ~ complicado de lo que tú crees** it's more complicated than you think; **eran ~ de las cinco** it was after five o'clock; **~ de 30** more than 30, over 30 (b) (especialmente) particularly, especially

[2] (superlativo): **la ~ bonita/la ~ inteligente** the prettiest/the most intelligent; **el que ~ sabe** the one who knows most; **el que ~ me gusta** the one I like best; **estuvo de lo ~ divertido** it was great fun

[3] (*en frases negativas*): **no tiene ~ que tres meses** she's only three months old; **nadie ~ que ella** nobody but her; **no tengo ~ que esto** this is all I have; **no tuve ~ remedio** I had no alternative; **no juego ~** I'm not playing any more; **nunca ~** never again

[4] (con valor ponderativo): **¡cantó ~ bien...!** she sang so well!; **¡qué cosa ~ rara!** how strange!

■ *adj inv* [1] (comparativo): more; **~ dinero** more money; **una vez ~** once more; **ni un minuto ~** not a minute longer; **hoy hace ~ calor** it's warmer today; **son ~ que nosotros** there are more of them than us

[2] (superlativo): most; **el equipo que ganó ~ partidos** the team that won most games; **las ~ de las veces** more often than not

[3] (con valor ponderativo): **¡me da ~ rabia ...!** it makes me so mad!; **¡tiene ~ amigos ...!** he has so many friends!

[4] **¿qué ~?** what else?; **nada/nadie ~** nothing/nobody else; **algo/alguien ~** something/somebody else; **¿quién ~ vino?** who else came?; **¿algo ~? — nada ~ gracias** anything else? — no, that's all, thank you

■ *pron* [1] more; **¿te sirvo ~?** would you like some more?

[2] (*en locs*) **a lo más** at the most; **a más no poder: corrimos a ~ no poder** we ran as fast *o* hard as we could; **a más tardar** at the latest; **cuanto más** at the most; **de más: ¿tienes un lápiz de ~?** do you have a spare pencil?; **me dio cinco dólares de ~** he gave me five dollars too much; **no está de ~ repetirlo** there's no harm in repeating it; **es más** in fact; **más bien** (un poco) rather; **más o menos** (aproximadamente) more or less; (no muy bien) so-so; **ni más ni menos** no less; **no más** ▸ NOMÁS; **por más: por ~ que llores** however much you cry; **por ~ que trataba** however hard he tried; **¿qué más da?** what does it matter?; **sin más (ni más)** just like that

■ *prep* (a) (Mat) (en sumas) plus; **8+7 =15** (*read as: ocho más siete (es) igual (a) quince*) eight plus seven equals fifteen (b) (además de) plus; **mil pesos, ~ los gastos** a thousand pesos, plus expenses

■ *m* plus sign

masa *f* [1] (Coc) (a) (para pan, pasta) dough; (para empanadas, tartas) pastry; (para bizcocho) mixture; (para crepes) batter; **~ de hojaldre** puff pastry (b) (RPl) (pastelito) pastry, cake [2] (Pol, Sociol, Fís) mass; **educar a las ~s** to educate the masses [3] **en masa** (a) (*loc adj*) ⟨fabricación/despidos⟩ mass (*before n*) (b) (*loc adv*) ⟨acudir⟩ en masse

masacrar [A1] *vt* to massacre

masacre *f* massacre

masaje *m* massage; **darle ~s** *or* **un ~ a algn** to give sb a massage

masajear [A1] *vt* to massage

masajista *mf* [1] (que da masajes) (*m*) masseur; (*f*) masseuse [2] (en fútbol) coach, trainer

mascada *f* (a) (Chi) (mordisco) bite (b) (Méx) (pañuelo grande) scarf

mascar [A2] *vt* to chew

máscara f mask; ~ **antigás** gas mask; ~ **de oxígeno** oxygen mask; ~ **facial** face pack

mascarilla f mask; (en cosmética) face pack

mascota f (talismán) mascot; (animal doméstico) pet

masculino¹ -na adj (a) ⟨actitud/hormona⟩ male; ⟨mujer/aspecto⟩ masculine, manly (b) (Ling) masculine

masculino² m masculine

mascullar [A1] vt to mumble, mutter

masía f (granja) farm; (casa) country house

masificación f overcrowding

masificado -da adj ⟨universidad⟩ overcrowded

masilla f (para cristales) putty; (para rellenar grietas) mastic, filler

masivo -va adj (a) ⟨ejecución/migración⟩ mass (before n); ⟨protesta⟩ large-scale (before n), mass (before n); ⟨concurrencia⟩ massive (b) ⟨dosis⟩ massive, huge

masón adj Masonic
■ m Freemason, Mason

masonería f Freemasonry

masoquismo m masochism

masoquista adj masochistic
■ mf masochist

máster /'master/ m (pl **-ters**) [1] (Audio, Vídeo) master [2] (Educ) master's degree

masticar [A2] vt/vi to chew

mástil m (a) (Náut) mast; (para una bandera) flagpole, flagstaff (b) (de guitarra, violín) neck (c) (de carpa) centerpole*

mastín m mastiff

mastodonte m (a) (animal prehistórico) mastodon (b) (fam) (persona grande) giant

mastuerzo m (planta) (garden) cress

masturbación f masturbation

masturbarse [A1] v pron to masturbate

mata f [1] (arbusto) bush, shrub; (planta) (AmL) plant [2] (ramita) sprig; (de hierba) tuft [3] (fam) (de pelo) mane (colloq), mop (colloq)

matadero m slaughterhouse, abattoir

matado -da m,f (Méx fam & pey) grind (AmE colloq), swot (BrE colloq)

matador m matador

matamoscas m (pl ~) (a) (paleta) flyswatter (b) (spray) fly spray, fly killer

matanza f (acción de matar) killing, slaughter; (de res, cerdo) slaughter; **la ~ de gente inocente** the mass killing of innocent people

matapolillas m (pl ~) moth killer

matar [A1] vt [1] (a) ⟨persona⟩ to kill (b) (sacrificar) ⟨perro/caballo⟩ to put down, destroy; ⟨reses⟩ to slaughter; **lo mató un coche** he was run over and killed by a car (c) (en sentido hiperbólico): **la vas a ~ a disgustos** you'll be the death of her; **es para ~los** I could murder o kill them (colloq); **nos mataban de hambre** they used to starve us; **estos zapatos me están matando** these shoes are killing me!
[2] (fam) ⟨sed⟩ to quench; ⟨tiempo⟩ to kill; **compraron fruta para ~ el hambre** they bought some fruit to keep them going
■ ~ vi to kill
■ **matarse** v pron [1] (a) (morir violentamente) to be

killed; **casi me mato** I almost got killed (b) (refl) (suicidarse) to kill oneself; **se mató de un tiro** she shot herself
[2] (fam) (a) (esforzarse): **me maté estudiando** or (Esp) **a estudiar** I studied like crazy o mad (colloq) (b) (Méx fam) (para un examen) to cram (colloq), to swot (BrE colloq)

matarife m (en matadero) slaughterman

matarratas m (pl ~) (veneno) rat poison

matasellos m (pl ~) (a) (marca) postmark (b) (instrumento) datestamp, stamp

matazón f (Col, Méx, Ven fam) massacre, slaughter

mate adj or adj inv ⟨pintura/maquillaje⟩ matt; **fotos ~** photos with a matt finish
■ m [1] (en ajedrez) tb **jaque ~** checkmate, mate [2] (a) (infusión) maté; **cebar ~** to brew maté (b) (AmL) (calabaza) gourd

matear [A1] vi (CS fam) to drink maté
■ **matearse** v pron (Chi fam) to cram (colloq), to swot (Br colloq)

matemáticas fpl mathematics, math (AmE), maths (BrE)

matemático -ca adj mathematical
■ m,f mathematician

mateo -tea m,f (Chi fam) grind (AmE colloq), swot (BrE colloq)

materia f [1] (sustancia) matter; ~ **gris** gray* matter; ~ **prima** (Econ, Tec) raw material; (Fin) commodity [2] (a) (tema, asunto) subject; **en ~ de** as regards, with regard to (b) (asignatura) subject

material adj (a) ⟨necesidades/ayuda/valor⟩ material; **daños ~es** damage to property, material damage (b) ⟨autor/causante⟩ actual
■ m [1] (en general) material; ~**es para la construcción** building materials [2] (útiles) materials (pl); ~ **de oficina** office stationery; ~ **didáctico/escolar** teaching/school materials (pl)

materialismo m materialism

materialista adj materialistic
■ mf [1] (persona) materialist [2] (Méx) (constructor) building contractor; (camionero) truck driver, lorry driver (BrE)

maternal adj ⟨instinto⟩ maternal; ⟨amor⟩ motherly, maternal

maternidad f (a) (estado) motherhood, maternity (b) (hospital) maternity hospital; (sala) maternity ward

materno -na adj ⟨amor⟩ motherly; ⟨pariente⟩ maternal; ⟨lengua⟩ mother

matinal adj morning (before n)

matinée, matiné f (a) (AmS) (de tarde) matinée (b) (Méx) (de mañana) morning performance

matiz m (a) (de color) shade, hue (b) (de palabra, frase) nuance, shade of meaning; **tiene cierto ~ peyorativo** it has a slightly pejorative nuance (c) (de ironía) touch, hint

matizar [A4] vt [1] ⟨colores⟩ to blend [2] (concretar, puntualizar) to qualify, clarify

matón m (del barrio) thug; (en la escuela) bully; (criminal) thug, heavy (colloq)

matorral m (a) (conjunto de matas) thicket, bushes (pl) (b) (terreno) scrubland

matraca f [1] (juguete) rattle [2] (Méx fam) (coche) rattletrap (colloq)

matrero -ra adj [1] (Col fam) (basto) shoddy [2] (RPI) (fugitivo): **un gaucho ∼ a** gaucho on the run from the law [3] (Col) (traicionero) sly, crafty

matriarcado m matriarchy

matriarcal adj matriarchal

matrícula f [1] (Educ) (inscripción) registration, enrollment*; **derechos** or **tasas de ∼** registration fees; **∼ de honor** (Esp) ≈distinction, ≈magna cum laude [2] (Transp) (número) registration number; (placa) license* plate, number plate (BrE)

matricular [A1] vt (a) ⟨persona⟩ to register, enroll* (b) ⟨coche/barco⟩ to register
■ **matricularse** v pron (refl) to register, enroll*; **∼se EN algo** to enroll ON sth

matrimonial adj marital

matrimonio m (a) (institución) marriage, matrimony (frml); **contraer ∼** (frml) to marry (b) (pareja) (married) couple; **el ∼ Garrido** Mr and Mrs Garrido, the Garridos (c) (AmS exc RPI) (boda) wedding; **∼ civil/religioso** civil/church wedding

matriz f (a) (útero) womb, uterus (b) (molde) mold* (c) (de talonario) stub

matrona f (comadrona) midwife

matutino¹ -na adj morning (before n)

matutino² m morning paper

maullar [A23] vi to miaow

maullido m miaow

mausoleo m mausoleum

maxilar m jawbone, maxilla (tech)

máxima f maxim

máxime adv especially

máximo¹ -ma adj ⟨temperatura/velocidad⟩ top (before n), maximum (before n); ⟨carga/altura⟩ maximum (before n); ⟨punto⟩ highest; ⟨esfuerzo/ ambición⟩ greatest (before n); **el ∼ dirigente francés** the French leader

máximo² m maximum; **como ∼** at the most; **aprovechar algo al ∼** to make the most of sth; **se esforzó al ∼** she did her utmost; **rendir al ∼** «persona» to give a hundred percent; «máquina» to work to its full capacity

maya adj Mayan
■ mf Maya, Mayan; **los ∼s** the Maya o Mayas

mayo m May; **el primero de ∼** May Day; *para ejemplos ver* ENERO

mayonesa f mayonnaise, mayo (AmE) (colloq)

mayor adj [1] (a) (comparativo de GRANDE) ⟨número/porcentaje⟩ greater, higher; ⟨beneficio⟩ greater; **vuelan a ∼ altura** they fly at a greater height; **a ∼ escala** on a larger scale; **un número ∼ que 40** a number greater than 40 (b) (superlativo de GRANDE): **el ∼ número de accidentes** the greatest o highest number of accidents; **su ∼ preocupación** her greatest o biggest worry; **a la ∼ brevedad posible** as soon as possible; **la ∼ parte de los estudiantes** most students, the majority of students

[2] (en edad) (a) (comparativo) older; **∼ QUE algn** older THAN sb (b) (superlativo): **es la ∼ de las dos** she is the older o elder of the two; **mi hijo ∼** my eldest o oldest son (c) (anciano) elderly (d) (adulto): **las personas ∼es** adults, grown-ups (colloq); **cuando sea ∼** when I grow up; **ser ∼ de edad** (Der) to be of age; **soy ∼ de edad y haré lo que quiera** I'm over 18 (o 21 etc) and I'll do as I please

[3] (en nombres) (principal) main; **Calle M∼** Main Street (in US), High Street (in UK) [4] (Mús) major [5] (Com): **(al) por ∼** wholesale
■ mf (adulto) adult, grown-up (colloq); **solo para ∼es** adults only; **mis/tus ∼es** my/your elders; **∼ de edad** person who is legally of age

mayoral m (capataz) foreman; (de finca) farm manager, steward

mayordomo m (criado principal) butler, majordomo; (capataz) (CS) foreman; (portero) (Chi) superintendent (AmE), caretaker (BrE)

mayoría f majority; **la gran ∼ de ...** the great majority of ...; **ser ∼** or **estar en ∼** to be in the majority; **gobierno de la ∼** majority rule; **∼ absoluta/relativa** absolute/simple majority; **llegar a la ∼ de edad** to come of age

mayorista adj wholesale
■ mf wholesaler

mayoritario -ria adj (a) ⟨apoyo/decisión/ partido⟩ majority (before n) (b) (Fin) ⟨socio/ accionista⟩ principal

mayúscula f capital (letter), uppercase letter (tech); **se escribe con ∼** it is written with a capital letter; **rellenar en** or **con ∼s** write in block capitals o in capital letters

mayúsculo -la adj (a) ⟨letra⟩ capital (before n), upper-case (tech) (b) ⟨susto/error⟩ terrible

maza f (a) (Const) drop hammer (b) (de bombo) drumstick (c) (arma) mace

mazacote m (a) (fam) (Coc): **un ∼** a lumpy mess (b) (fam) (obra tosca) eyesore

mazamorra f (a) (AmS) milky pudding made with maize (b) (Per) pudding made with corn starch, sugar and honey (c) (Col) maize soup

mazapán m marzipan

mazmorra f dungeon

mazo m [1] (a) (herramienta) mallet; (del mortero) pestle; (para la carne) meat tenderizer; (porra) club (b) (en croquet, polo) mallet [2] (esp AmL) (manojo) bunch; (de naipes) deck (of cards) (AmE), pack (of cards) (BrE)

mazorca f (Bot, Coc) cob; **∼ de maíz** corncob

mazurca f mazurka

me pron pers me; **¿∼ lo prestas?** will you lend it to me o lend me it?; **∼ arregló el televisor** he fixed the television for me; **∼ lo quitó** he took it off me o away from me; **∼ robaron el reloj** my watch was stolen; **∼ miré en el espejo** (refl) I looked at myself in the mirror; **∼ corté el pelo** (refl) I cut my hair; (caus) I had my hair cut; **∼ equivoqué** I made a mistake; **∼ alegro mucho** I'm very pleased; **se ∼ murió el gato** my cat died

mear [A1] vi (vulg) to (have a) piss (vulg)
■ **mearse** v pron (fam) to wet oneself; **me estoy meando** I'm dying for a pee (colloq)

mecánica f mechanics

mecánico -ca adj mechanical
■ m,f (de vehículos) mechanic; (de maquinaria industrial) fitter; (de fotocopiadoras, lavadoras) engineer

mecanismo m mechanism; **∼ de defensa** defense* mechanism

mecanizado -da adj mechanized

mecanizar [A4] vt to mechanize

mecanografía f typing

mecanografiar [A17] vt to type

mecanógrafo -fa *m,f* typist

mecate *m* (AmC, Méx, Ven) string, cord; (más grueso) rope

mecedora *f* rocking chair

mecenas *mf* (*pl* ~) patron, sponsor

mecer [E2] *vt* ‹*bebé/cuna*› to rock; ‹*niño*› (en columpio) to push

■ **mecerse** *v pron* **(a)** (en mecedora) to rock; (en columpio) to swing **(b)** (bambolearse) to sway

mecha *f* **1** (de vela) wick; (de armas, explosivos) fuse **2 mechas** *fpl* (en peluquería) highlights (*pl*)

mechero *m* **(a)** (Esp) (encendedor) lighter **(b)** (Col) (candil) oil lamp

mechón¹ *m* **(a)** (de pelo) lock **(b)** (de lana) tuft **(c) mechones** *mpl* (Col) (en peluquería) highlights (*pl*)

mechón² -chona *m,f* (Chi) (estudiante) freshman, fresher (BrE)

medalla *f* (Dep, Mil) medal; (Relig) medallion (*with religious engraving on it*)

medallón *m* medallion

media *f* **1** (Indum) **(a)** (hasta el muslo) stocking; ~s con/sin costura seamed/seamless stockings **(b) medias** *fpl* (hasta la cintura) panty hose (*pl*) (AmE), tights (*pl*) (BrE); ~s bombacha(s) (RPI) *or* (Col, Ven) **pantalón** panty hose (*pl*) (AmE), tights (BrE) (*pl*) **(c)** (AmL) (calcetín) sock **2** (Mat) average; **la ~ de velocidad** the average speed **3 a medias** (*loc adv*) **(a)** (incompleto): **dejó el trabajo a ~s** he left the work half-finished; **me dijo la verdad a ~s** she didn't tell me the whole truth *o* story **(b)** (entre dos): **pagar a ~s** to pay half each, go halves; **lo hicimos a ~s** we did half (of it) each

mediación *f* mediation; **por ~ de** through

mediador -dora *m,f* mediator

mediados: **a ~ de mes** halfway through the month, in the middle of the month; **a ~ de los años 30** in the mid thirties

mediagua *f* (Andes) hut, shack

medialuna *f* **(a)** (esp RPI) (Coc) croissant (*often with ham and cheese*) **(b)** (Chi) (corral) ring

mediana *f* (Auto) median strip (AmE), central reservation (BrE)

medianero -ra *adj* dividing (*before n*)

mediano -na *adj* **(a)** ‹*tamaño/porción*› medium; ‹*coche*› medium-sized; **de mediana estatura/inteligencia** of average height/intelligence; **de mediana edad** middle-aged **(b)** (mediocre) average, mediocre

medianoche *f* midnight; **a ~** at midnight

mediante *prep* through, by means of

mediar [A1] *vi* **(a)** (intervenir) to mediate; ~ **EN algo** ‹*en conflicto/negociaciones*› to mediate IN sth, to act as mediator IN sth **(b)** (interceder) ~ **POR algn** to intercede FOR sb; ~ **ANTE algn** to intercede *o* intervene WITH sb

mediasnueves *fpl* (Col) mid-morning snack, elevenses (BrE colloq)

medicamento *m* (frml) medicine, medicament (frml)

medicatura *f* (Ven) first aid post, clinic

medicina *f* medicine

medicinal *adj* ‹*aguas/planta*› medicinal; ‹*champú/jabón*› medicated

medición *f* **(a)** (acción) measuring **(b)** (frml) (medida) measurement

médico¹ -ca *adj* medical; **un reconocimiento ~** a medical (examination)

médico² ** *mf* doctor; ~ **de cabecera family doctor *o* (AmE) physician, general practitioner, GP; ~ **de medicina general** general practitioner, GP

medida *f* **1** (Mat) (dimensión) measurement; **tomarle las ~s a algn** to take sb's measurements; **tomar las ~s de algo** to measure something **2** (*en locs*) **a** (**la**) **medida** ‹*traje/zapato*› custom-made (AmE), made-to-measure (BrE); **a medida que** as; **a ~ que fue creciendo** as he grew up **3** (utensilio) measure; (contenido) measure **4** (grado, proporción): **en gran/cierta ~** to a large/certain extent; **en la ~ de lo posible** as far as possible **5** (disposición) measure; **tomar ~s** to take steps *o* measures

medido -da *adj* (CS) ‹*persona/comportamiento*› restrained; **es muy ~ con la bebida** he's a very moderate drinker

medidor *m* (AmL) meter

medieval *adj* medieval

medio¹ -dia *adj* **1** (*delante del n*) (la mitad de): ~ **kilo** half a kilo; **media manzana** half an apple; **pagar ~ pasaje** to pay half fare *o* half price; **media hora** half an hour, a half hour (AmE); **dos horas y media** two and a half hours; **a las cinco y media** at half past five; **a media mañana/tarde** in the middle of the morning/afternoon; **a ~ camino** halfway; **media pensión** (en hoteles) half board; **(se) dio ~ vuelta y se fue** she turned on her heel and left; **un jugador de ~ campo** a midfield player; ~ **tiempo** (AmL) half-time; *mi media naranja* (fam & hum) my better half (colloq & hum) **2** (mediano, promedio) average; **el ciudadano ~** the average citizen; **a ~ y largo plazo** in the medium and long term

medio² ** *adv* half; **está ~ loca she's half crazy; **todo lo deja a ~ terminar** he leaves everything half finished

■ *m* **1** (Mat) (mitad) half **2** (centro) middle; **en (el) ~ de la habitación** in the middle *o* center of the room; **quitarse de en ~** *or* **del ~** to get out of the way **3 (a)** (recurso, manera) means (*pl*); **como ~ de coacción** as a means of coercion; **los ~s de comunicación** the media; ~ **de transporte** means of transport **(b) medios** *mpl* (recursos económicos) *tb* ~s **económicos** means (*pl*), resources (*pl*) **4** (*en locs*) **en medio de**: **en ~ de tanta gente** (in) among so many people; **en ~ de la confusión** in *o* amid all the confusion; **por medio** (CS, Per): **día/semana por ~** every other day/week; **dos casas** por ∼ every two houses; **por medio de** ⟨de proceso/técnica⟩ by means of; **por ∼ de tu primo** from o through your cousin

5 (a) ⟨círculo, ámbito⟩: **en ∼s literarios/políticos** in literary/political circles; **no está en su ∼** he's out of his element (b) (Biol) environment; **la adaptación al ∼** adaptation to one's environment; **∼ ambiente** environment; **que no da daña el ∼ ambiente** eco-friendly, environmentally friendly

mediocampista *mf* midfield player

mediocre *adj* mediocre

mediocridad *f* mediocrity

mediodía *m* (a) (las doce de la mañana) midday, noon; **a ∼** *or* **al ∼** at midday (b) (hora de comer) lunch time

Medio Oriente *m* Middle East, Mid-East (AmE)

medir [I14] *vt* **1** ⟨habitación/distancia/ velocidad⟩ to measure **2** (tener ciertas dimensiones) to be, measure; **mido 60 cm de cintura** I measure o I'm 60 cm round the waist; **¿cuánto mide de alto/largo?** how tall/long is it?; **mide casi 1,90 m** he's almost 1.90 m (tall) **3** (calcular, considerar) to consider, weigh up; **∼ los pros y contras de algo** to weigh up the pros and cons of sth.

■ **medirse** *v pron* **1** (*refl*) to measure oneself; ⟨caderas/pecho⟩ to measure **2** (Col, Méx, Ven) (probarse) to try on

meditación *f* meditation

meditar [A1] *vi* to meditate; **∼ sobre algo** to reflect o meditate on sth

■ **∼** *vt* (considerar) to think about; (durante más tiempo) to ponder, meditate on; **una decisión muy meditada** a very carefully thought-out decision

mediterráneo -nea *adj* Mediterranean

Mediterráneo *m*: *tb* **el (mar) ∼** the Mediterranean (sea)

médula *f* (Anat) marrow, medulla (tech); **∼ ósea** bone marrow; **británico hasta la ∼** British through and through

medusa *f* jellyfish, medusa

megafonía *f* PA system

megáfono *m* megaphone

mejicano -na *adj/m,f* Mexican

Méjico *m* ▶ MEXICO

mejilla *f* cheek; **poner la otra ∼** to turn the other cheek

mejillón *m* mussel

mejor *adj* **1** (a) (comparativo de BUENO) ⟨producto/profesor⟩ better; ⟨calidad⟩ better, higher, superior; **tanto ∼** so much the better; **cuanto más grande ∼** the bigger the better (b) (comparativo de BIEN) better; **está ∼ así** it's better like this

2 (a) (superlativo de BUENO) (entre dos) better; (entre varios) best; **mi ∼ amiga** my best friend; **productos de la ∼ calidad** products of the highest quality; **lo ∼ es que se lo digas** the best thing (to do) is to tell her; **le deseo lo ∼** I wish you the very best o all the best (b) (superlativo de BIEN): **la que está ∼ de dinero** the one who has the most money

■ *adv* **1** (comparativo) better; **luego lo pensé ∼** then I thought better of it; **pintas cada vez ∼** your painting is getting better and better; **me lleva dos años, ∼ dicho, dos y medio** she's two years older than me, or rather, two and a half

2 (superlativo) best; **este es el lugar desde donde se ve ∼** this is where you can see best (from); **la versión ∼ ambientada de la obra** the best-staged production of the play; **lo hice lo ∼ que pude** I did it as best I could o (frml) to the best of my ability; **a lo ∼** maybe, perhaps; **a lo ∼ vamos a Italia** we may o might go to Italy

3 (esp AmL) (en sugerencias): **∼ lo dejamos para otro día** why don't we leave it for another day?; **∼ me callo** I think I'd better shut up

■ *mf*: **el/la ∼** (de dos) the better; (de varios) the best; **es la ∼ de la clase** she's the best in the class

mejora *f* improvement

mejorana *f* marjoram

mejorar [A1] *vt* ⟨condiciones/situación/oferta⟩ to improve; ⟨marca⟩ to improve on, beat; **el tratamiento la mejoró** the treatment made her a lot better

■ **∼** *vi* «tiempo/calidad/situación» to improve, get better; «persona» (Med) to get better; **ha mejorado de aspecto** he looks a lot better

■ **mejorarse** *v pron* «enfermo» to get better; **que te mejores** get well soon, I hope you get better soon

mejoría *f* improvement; **le deseamos una pronta ∼** we wish you a speedy recovery

melancolía *f* melancholy, sadness

melancólico -ca *adj* melancholy

■ *m,f* melancholic

melaza *f* molasses

melé *f* (Dep) (libre) ruck, maul; (organizada) scrum

melena *f* (a) (pelo suelto) long hair (b) (estilo de corte) bob (c) (del león) mane

melenudo -da *adj* (fam) long-haired

melindroso -sa *adj* (a) (remilgado) affected (b) (Méx) (delicado) choosy, finicky (c) (mojigato) prudish

mellado -da *adj* ⟨diente/taza⟩ chipped; ⟨cuchillo/borde⟩ jagged

mellar [A1] *vt* (a) ⟨cuchillo/hoja⟩ to notch, nick; ⟨diente/porcelana⟩ to chip (b) (esp AmL) ⟨honor/ fama⟩ to damage

mellizo -za *adj* twin (*before n*)

■ *m,f* (*m*) twin (brother); (*f*) twin (sister); **tuvo ∼s** she had twins

melocotón *m* (a) (esp Esp) (fruta redonda) peach (b) (AmC) (fruta en forma de estrella) star fruit

melodía *f* melody, tune

melódico -ca *adj* melodic

melodioso -sa *adj* melodious, tuneful

melodrama *m* melodrama

melodramático -ca *adj* melodramatic

melómano -na *m,f* music lover

melón *m* (Bot) melon

meloso -sa *adj* ⟨persona/voz⟩ sickly-sweet; ⟨música/canción⟩ schmaltzy, slushy

membrana *f* membrane

membresía *f* (AmL frml) membership

membrete *m* letterhead; **papel con ∼** headed paper

membrillo *m* (árbol) quince (tree); (fruta) quince; **dulce de ∼** quince jelly

memorable *adj* memorable

memorándum *m* (*pl* **-dums**),

memorando *m* (nota) memorandum, memo

memoria *f* ① (en general) memory; **tener buena/mala** ∼ to have a good/poor memory; **si la** ∼ **no me falla** *or* **engaña** if my memory serves me right; **desde que tengo** ∼ for as long as I can remember; **aprender/saber algo de** ∼ to learn/ know sth by heart; **respetar la** ∼ **de algn** to respect the memory of sb; **a la** *or* **en** ∼ **de algn** in memory of sb ② **memorias** *fpl* (Lit) memoirs (*pl*) ③ **(a)** (Adm, Com) report; ∼ **anual** annual report **(b)** (Educ) written paper

memorial *m* memorial

memorizar [A4] *vt* to memorize

menaje *m*: **artículos de** ∼ household items; **sección de** ∼ **del hogar** household department

mención *f* mention; **hacer** ∼ **de algo** to mention sth

mencionar [A1] *vt* to mention; **no quiero oír** ∼ **ese nombre** I don't want to hear that name mentioned

mendicidad *f* begging

mendigar [A3] *vi* to beg
■ ∼ *vt* «*mendigo*» to beg for

mendigo -ga *m,f* beggar

mendrugo *m*: *tb* ∼ **de pan** piece of stale bread

menear [A1] *vt* ⟨*rabo*⟩ to wag; ⟨*cabeza*⟩ to shake; ⟨*caderas*⟩ to wiggle
■ **menearse** *v pron* **(a)** (con inquietud) to fidget **(b)** (provocativamente) to wiggle one's hips

menester *m* ① **ser** ∼ (fml) (ser necesario) to be necessary; **es** ∼ **que lo hagamos sin demora** we must do it without delay ② (fml) (tarea) occupation; **se ganaba la vida en los** ∼**es más diversos** he earned his living from some very diverse activities

menestra *f* vegetable stew

menguar [A16] *vi* ① (fml) «*temperatura/ nivel*» to fall, drop; «*cantidad/número/reservas*» to diminish ② (al tejer) to decrease
■ ∼ *vt* ① (fml) ⟨*responsabilidad/influencia*⟩ to diminish; ⟨*reputación*⟩ to damage ② ⟨*puntos*⟩ (en tejido) to decrease

meningitis *f* meningitis

menisco *m* cartilage, meniscus (tech)

menopausia *f* menopause

menopáusico -ca *adj* menopausal

menor *adj* ① **(a)** (comparativo de PEQUEÑO) ⟨*número/porcentaje*⟩ lower, smaller; **en** ∼ **medida/grado** to a lesser extent *o* degree; ∼ **QUE algo** lower THAN sth; **un ingreso** ∼ **que el mío** an income lower than mine **(b)** (superlativo de PEQUEÑO): **el país con el** ∼ **número de parados** the country with the lowest unemployment figures; **haciendo el** ∼ **ruido posible** making as little noise as possible; **el de** ∼ **tamaño** the smallest one ② (en edad) **(a)** (comparativo) younger; ∼ **QUE algn** younger THAN sb **(b)** (superlativo): **¿cuál es el** ∼ **de los hermanos?** who's the youngest of the brothers?; **el** ∼ **de los dos niños** the younger of the two boys ③ (secundario) ⟨*escritor/obra*⟩ minor; **lesiones de** ∼ **importancia** minor injuries ④ (Mús) minor ⑤ (Com): **(al) por** ∼ retail
■ *mf*: *tb* ∼ **de edad** minor; **ser** ∼ **de edad** to be a minor, to be under age; **película no apta para menores** film not suitable for under-18s

menorista *mf* (Col, Méx, Ven) retailer

menos *adv* ① (comparativo) less; **cada vez estudia** ∼ she's studying less and less; **ya me duele** ∼ it hurts less now; **ahora lo vemos** ∼ we don't see him so often now, we don't see so much of him now; **pesa** ∼ **de 50 kilos** it weighs less than *o* under 50 kilos; **éramos** ∼ **de diez** there were fewer than ten of us; **los niños de** ∼ **de 7 años** children under seven ② (superlativo) least; **es la** ∼ **complicada** it is the least complicated one; **el que** ∼ **me gusta** the one I like (the) least; **se esfuerza lo** ∼ **posible** he makes as little effort as possible; **cuando** ∼ **lo esperaba** when I was least expecting it
■ *adj inv* ① (comparativo) (en cantidad) less; (en número) fewer; **alimentos con** ∼ **fibra/calorías** food with less fiber/fewer calories; **hay** ∼ **errores** there are fewer mistakes; **mide medio metro** ∼ it's half a meter shorter; ∼ **estudiantes que el año pasado** fewer students than last year; **tengo** ∼ **tiempo que tú** I haven't as *o* so much time as you ② (superlativo) (en cantidad) least; (en número) fewest; **donde hay** ∼ **luz** where there's least light; **el que obtuvo** ∼ **votos** the one who got (the) fewest votes
■ *pron* ① (en cantidad) less; (en número) fewer; **sírveme** ∼ give me less; **ya falta** ∼ it won't be long now ② (*en locs*) **al menos** at least; **a menos que** unless; **cuando menos** at least; **de menos: me dió 100 pesos de** ∼ he gave me 100 pesos too little; **me cobró de** ∼ he undercharged me; **lo menos** the least; **menos mal** just as well, thank goodness; **por lo menos** at least; **eso es lo de** ∼ that's the least of my (*o* our *etc*) problems
■ *prep* ① (excepto): **todos** ∼ **Alonso** everybody except *o* but Alonso; ∼ **estos dos, ...** apart from *o* with the exception of these two, ...; **tres latas de pintura,** ∼ **la que usé para la puerta** three cans of paint, less what I used on the door ② **(a)** (Mat) (en restas, números negativos) minus **(b)** (Esp, RPl) (en la hora): **son las cinco** ∼ **diez/cuarto** it's ten to five/(a) quarter to five; **son** ∼ **veinte** it's twenty to

menoscabar [A1] *vt* ⟨*autoridad/fortuna*⟩ to diminish, reduce; ⟨*derechos*⟩ to impinge upon, infringe; ⟨*honor/fama/salud*⟩ to damage, harm

menospreciar [A1] *vt* **(a)** (despreciar) ⟨*persona/obra*⟩ to despise, look down on **(b)** (subestimar) to underestimate

menosprecio *m* contempt, scorn

mensaje *m* (en general) message; (nota) note; ∼ **de texto** text message

mensajero -ra *adj* messenger (*before n*)
■ *m,f* (en general) messenger; (Com) messenger, courier (BrE)

menso -sa *adj* (AmL fam) stupid

menstruación *f* menstruation; **estar con la** ∼ to have one's period

menstruar [A3] *vi* to menstruate

mensual *adj* ⟨*publicación/sueldo*⟩ monthly; **9.000 pesos** ∼**es** 9,000 pesos a month

mensualidad (a) *f* (sueldo) monthly salary **(b)** (cuota) monthly payment *o* installment*

menta *f* mint; **licor de** ∼ crème de menthe; **caramelos de** ∼ mints, peppermints

mentada *f* (Col, Méx, Ven euf) *tb* ~ **de madre** insult (*usually about a person's mother*)

mental *adj* mental

mentalidad *f* mentality; **tener una** ~ **muy cerrada** a very closed mind

mentalizar [A4] *vt* ~ **a algn DE algo** to make sb aware OF sth

■ **mentalizarse** *v pron* **(a)** (*prepararse mentalmente*) to prepare oneself (mentally), get into the right frame of mind **(b)** (*tomar conciencia*): **tuve que** ~**me de que mi carrera se había acabado** I had to come to terms with the fact that my career was over

mentar [A5] *vt* to mention

mente *f* mind; **tenía la** ~ **en blanco** my mind was a blank; **de repente me vino a la** ~ it suddenly came to me; **tener algo en** ~ to have sth in mind

mentecato -ta *m,f* fool

mentir [I11] *vi* to lie; **me mintió** he lied to me

mentira *f* lie; **eso es** ~ that's a lie; **¡**~**! yo no le pegué** that's a lie, I didn't hit him!; **¡parece** ~**! ¡cómo pasa el tiempo!** isn't it incredible! doesn't time fly!; ~ **piadosa** white lie; **una araña de** ~ *or* (Méx) **de** ~**s** (leng infantil) a toy spider; *una* ~ *como una casa or un templo* (fam) a whopping great lie (colloq), a whopper (colloq)

mentiroso -sa *adj*: **es muy** ~ he's an awful *o* terrible liar; (dicho sin ánimo de ofender) he's a real fibber (colloq)

■ *m,f* liar; (dicho sin ánimo de ofender) fibber (colloq)

mentolado -da *adj* menthol (*before n*)

mentón *m* chin

menú *m* (*pl* **-nús**) menu; ~ **del día** set menu

menudencia *f* ⓵ (cosa insignificante): **eso es una** ~ that's not important ⓶ **menudencias** *fpl* (AmL) (Coc) giblets (*pl*)

menudeo *m* (Col, Méx) retail trade; **ventas al** ~ retail sales

menudillos *mpl* giblets (*pl*)

menudo¹ -da *adj* ⓵ **(a)** 〈*persona*〉 slight **(b)** 〈*letra/pie*〉 small ⓶ (Esp) (en exclamaciones) (*delante del n*): **¡**~ **lío!** what a mess!; **¡**~ **cochazo!** that's some car! ⓷ **a menudo** often

menudo² -da *adj* (Col, Ven) (dinero suelto) loose change

meñique *m* little finger

meollo *m* **(a)** (Anat) marrow **(b)** (de un tema) heart

mercadería *f* (esp AmS) merchandise

mercadillo *m* street market

mercado *m* market; **ir al** ~ *or* (Col, Méx) **hacer el** ~ to go to market; ~ **de abastos** market (*selling fresh food*); ~ **de (las) pulgas** flea market; ~ **persa** (CS) bazaar, street market; **el** ~ **del petróleo** the oil market; **salir al** ~ to come onto the market; **el M**~ **Común** the Common Market; ~ **de divisas** foreign exchange market; ~ **de trabajo** job market; ~ **negro** black market; ~ **paralelo** parallel market

mercancía *f*, **mercancías** *fpl* (Com) goods (*pl*), merchandise

mercante *adj* merchant (*before n*)

mercantil *adj* 〈*ley/operación*〉 commercial, mercantile

merced *f* (arc) (favor) favor*; **conceder una** ~ to grant a favor; **a (la)** ~ **de** at the mercy of

mercenario -ria *adj/m,f* (Mil) mercenary

mercería *f* (tienda de hilos, botones) notions store (AmE), haberdashery (BrE); (ferretería) (Chi) hardware store

Mercosur *m*: *economic community comprising Argentina, Brazil, Paraguay and Uruguay*

mercurio *m* mercury

Mercurio *m* Mercury

merecedor -dora *adj* ~ **DE algo** worthy OF sth, deserving OF sth (frml)

merecer [E3] *vt* 〈*premio/castigo*〉 to deserve; **merece que le den el puesto** she deserves to get the job

■ **merecerse** *v pron* (enf) 〈*premio/castigo*〉 to deserve; **te lo tienes bien merecido** it serves you right; **se merece que la asciendan** she deserves to be promoted

merecido *m*: **recibió** *or* **se llevó su** ~ he got what he deserved

merendar [A5] *vi* to have a snack in the afternoon, have tea; **merendamos en el campo** we had a picnic (tea) in the country

■ ~ *vt* to have ... as an afternoon snack

merendero *m* (bar) outdoor bar; (instalaciones para picnics) picnic area

merengada *f* (Ven) milkshake

merengue *m* ⓵ (pastel) meringue ⓶ (baile) merengue

meridiano *m* meridian; ~ **cero** *or* **de Greenwich** /'grintʃ/ Greenwich Meridian

meridional *adj* southern

■ *mf* southerner

merienda *f* afternoon snack, tea; (para la escuela) (RPl) snack; **ir de** ~ **al campo** to go for a picnic (tea) in the country

mérito *m* merit, worth; **no le veo ningún** ~ **a eso** I can't see any merit in that; **una persona de** ~ a worthy person; **tener** ~ to be praiseworthy; **quitarle** ~**s a algn** to take the credit away from sb; **atribuirse el** ~ **de algo** to take the credit for sth

meritorio -ria *adj* [SER] (frml) commendable, praiseworthy (frml); ~ **DE algo** worthy OF sth

■ *m,f* unpaid trainee

merluza *f* (Coc, Zool) hake

mermar [A1] *vi* (frml) «*viento/frío*» to abate (frml); «*luz*» to fade

■ ~ *vt* (frml) to reduce

mermelada *f* (de cítricos) marmalade; (de otras frutas) jam

mero¹ -ra *adj* (*delante del n*) ⓵ (solo, simple) mere; **el** ~ **hecho de ...** the mere *o* simple fact of ...; **es un** ~ **juego** it's only *o* just a game ⓶ (AmC, Méx fam) (uso enfático): **¿cuántas quedaron?** — **una mera** how many were left? — just one; **el** ~ **día de su boda** the very day of her wedding; **el** ~ **patrón** the boss himself; **en la mera esquina** right on the corner

mero² *m* grouper; **el** ~ ~ (Méx fam) the boss

■ *adv* (Méx fam) **(a)** (casi) nearly, almost **(b)** (uso enfático): **así** ~ **me gustan los tacos** this is just how I like tacos; **ya** ~ right now; **aquí merito** right here

merodear [A1] *vi* to prowl

mersa *adj* (RPl fam & pey) 〈*ropa/lugar*〉 tacky (colloq); 〈*persona*〉 common (pej)   ⤳

■ *mf* (RPI fam & pey) **(a)** (persona): **es un** ~ he's so common (pej) **(b) la mersa** *f* the plebs (*pl*) (colloq & pej), the riffraff (hum *or* pej)

mes *m* month; **el** ~ **pasado/que viene** last/next month; **una vez al** ~ once a month; **tiene siete** ~**es** he's seven months old; **nos deben dos** ~**es** they owe us two months' rent (*o* pay *etc*)

mesa *f* **1** (mueble) table; **poner/recoger la** ~ to lay/clear the table; **bendecir la** ~ to say grace; **sentarse a la** ~ to sit at the table; **se levantó de la** ~ he got up from *o* left the table; **reservar** ~ to reserve a table; ~ **de centro** coffee table; ~ **de noche** *or* (RPI) **de luz** bedside table **2** (conjunto de personas) committee; ~ **redonda/de negociaciones** round/negotiating table

mesada *f* (AmL) (dinero) monthly allowance; (para niños) pocket money

mesero -ra *m,f* (AmL) (*m*) waiter; (*f*) waitress

meseta *f* (Geog) plateau

Mesías *m* Messiah

Mesoamérica *f* Middle America (*most of Mexico and Central America*)

mesón *m* **1** (bar) old-style bar/restaurant **2** (Chi) (en tienda) counter; (de bar) bar, counter; ~ **de información** information desk

mesonero -ra *m,f* **(a)** (de bar) (*m*) landlord; (*f*) landlady **(b)** (Ven) (camarero) (*m*) waiter; (*f*) waitress

mestizo -za *adj* **(a)** (*persona*) of mixed race (*particularly of Indian and white parentage*); **de sangre mestiza** of mixed blood **(b)** (*animal*) crossbred
■ *m,f* mestizo, person of mixed race

meta *f* **1** **(a)** (en atletismo) finishing line; (en ciclismo, automovilismo) finish; (en carreras de caballos) winning post **(b)** (en fútbol) goal **2** **(a)** (propósito) aim; **su única** ~ **es ganar dinero** his only aim *o* ambition is to earn money **(b)** (objetivo) goal; **trazarse** ~**s** to set oneself targets *o* goals

metabolismo *m* metabolism

metafísico -ca *adj* metaphysical

metáfora *f* metaphor

metal *m* **(a)** (material, elemento) metal; ~ **noble** *or* **precioso** precious metal **(b)** *tb* **metales** (Mús) brass (section)

metálico¹ -ca *adj* **(a)** (de metal) metallic, metal (*before n*) **(b)** (*sonido/brillo/color*) metallic

metálico² ** *m*: **pagar en ~ to pay (in) cash; **un premio en** ~ a cash prize

metalurgia *f* metallurgy

metalúrgico -ca *adj* metallurgical
■ *m,f* metalworker

metamorfosis, metamórfosis *f* (*pl* ~) metamorphosis

metate *m* (AmC, Méx) flat stone used for grinding corn

metedura de pata *f* (esp Esp fam) blunder, gaffe

metegol *m* (Arg) table football

meteorito *m* meteorite

meteoro *m* meteor

meteorología *f* meteorology

meteorológico -ca *adj* meteorological, weather (*before n*)

meteorólogo -ga *m,f* meteorologist

meter [E1] *vt* **1** **(a)** (introducir, poner) to put; ~ **algo EN algo** to put sth IN(TO) sth; ~ **la llave en la cerradura** to put the key into the lock; **logró** ~ **todo en la maleta** he managed to fit everything into the suitcase **(b)** (hacer entrar): ~ **a algn en la cárcel** to put sb in prison; **consiguió** ~**lo en la empresa** she managed to get him a job in the company **(c)** (involucrar) ~ **a algn EN algo** to involve sb IN sth, get sb involved IN sth **2** **(a)** (invertir) (*ahorros/dinero*) to put **(b)** (*tanto/gol*) to score **(c)** (en costura) (*dobladillo*) to turn up **(d)** (Auto): **mete** (**la**) **tercera** put it into third (gear); ~ **la marcha atrás** to get into reverse **3** (provocar, crear): ~**le prisa a algn** to rush sb; ~**le miedo a algn** to frighten *o* scare sb; **no metas ruido** keep the noise down

■ **meterse** *v pron* **1** **(a)** (entrar): **me metí en el agua** (en la playa) I went into the water; (en la piscina) I got into the water; **nos metimos en un museo** we went into a museum; ~**se en la cama/la ducha** to get into bed/the shower; **¿dónde se habrá metido el perro?** where can the dog have got to?; **se me metió algo en el ojo** I got something in my eye **(b)** (introducirse): **me metí el dedo en el ojo** I stuck my finger in my eye; **se metió el dinero en el bolsillo** he put the money in(to) his pocket **2** **(a)** (en trabajo): **se metió de secretaria** she got a job as a secretary; ~**se de** *or* **a cura/monja** to become a priest/nun **(b)** (involucrarse) ~**se EN algo** to get involved IN sth; **te has metido en un buen lío** you've got yourself into a fine mess; **no te metas en lo que no te importa** mind your own business; ~**se con algn** (fam) to pick on sb; ~**se por medio** to interfere

metiche *adj* (AmL fam) nosy (colloq)
■ *mf* busybody (colloq)

meticuloso -sa *adj* (*trabajo/investigación*) meticulous, thorough; (*persona*) meticulous

metida de pata *f* (AmL fam) blunder, gaffe

metódico -ca *adj* methodical

metodista *adj/mf* Methodist

método *m* method; **con** ~ methodically

metodología *f* methodology

metomentodo *mf* (*pl* ~) (fam) busybody (colloq)

metralla *f* (trozos) shrapnel; (munición) grapeshot

metralleta *f* submachine gun

métrico -ca *adj* metric, metrical

metro *m* **1** **(a)** (medida) meter*; ~ **cuadrado/cúbico** square/cubic meter; **vender algo por** ~(**s**) to sell sth by the meter; **los 100** ~**s valla** the 100-meter hurdles **(b)** (cinta métrica) tape measure **2** (Transp) subway (AmE), tube (BrE) **3** (en poesía) meter*

metrónomo *m* metronome

---

metrópolis (*pl* ~), **metrópoli** *f* metropolis

metropolitano¹ -na *adj* metropolitan

metropolitano² *m* subway (AmE), underground (BrE)

mexicanismo *m* Mexicanism

mexicano -na *adj/m,f* Mexican

México *m* Mexico; (capital) Mexico City

mexiquense *adj* (Méx) of/from Mexico City

mezcal *m* mescal

mezcla *f* **1** (proceso) **(a)** (en general) mixing **(b)** (de vinos, tabacos, cafés) blending **2** (combinación) **(a)** (de cosas diversas) mixture; (de vinos, tabacos, cafés) blend; (de tejidos) mix; **una ~ de harina y azúcar** a mixture of flour and sugar **(b)** (de razas, culturas) mix **(c)** (Audio) mix

mezclador -dora *m,f* (persona) *tb* ~ **de sonido** *or* **audio** sound mixer

mezcladora *f* (Const) mixer

mezclar [A1] *vt* **1** **(a)** (combinar) to mix; ~ **algo CON algo** to mix sth WITH sth **2** ‹*café/vino/tabaco*› to blend **2** ‹*documentos/ropa*› to mix up, get ... mixed up; ~ **algo CON algo** to get sth mixed up WITH sth **3** (involucrar) ~ **a algn EN algo** to get sb mixed up *o* involved IN sth

■ **mezclarse** *v pron* **1 (a)** (involucrarse) ~**se EN algo** to get mixed up *o* involved IN sth **(b)** (tener trato con) ~**se CON algn** to mix WITH sb **2** «*razas/culturas*» to mix

mezclilla *f* **(a)** (tela de mezcla) cloth of mixed fibers **(b)** (Chi, Méx) (tela de jeans) denim

mezcolanza *f* (pey) hodgepodge (esp AmE), hotchpotch (BrE)

mezquindad *f* **(a)** (cualidad — de tacaño) meanness, stinginess (colloq); (— de vil): smallmindedness, pettiness **(b)** (acción egoísta) mean thing to do

mezquino¹ -na *adj* **(a)** (tacaño) mean, stingy (colloq); (vil) mean, small-minded **(b)** (escaso) ‹*sueldo/ración*› paltry, miserable

mezquino² *m* (Col, Méx) wart

mezquita *f* mosque

mezzo-soprano *f* mezzo soprano

mg. (= **miligramo**) mg

mi *adj* (delante del n) my; ~**s libros** my books; **sí, ~ vida** yes, darling; **sí, ~ capitán** yes, sir
■ *m* (nota) E; (en solfeo) mi

mí *pron pers* me; **¿es para ~?** is it for me?; **por ~ no hay problema** as far as I'm concerned that's fine, that's fine by me; **¿y a ~ qué?** so what?, what do I care?; **a ~ no me importa** I couldn't care less; ~ **mismo/misma** (*refl*) myself

miau *m* miaow; **hacer ~** to miaow

mica *f* **1 (a)** (Min) mica **(b)** (AmL) (de un reloj) crystal **2** (Col) (de niño) potty (colloq)

mico -ca *m,f* (Zool) long-tailed monkey; (como término genérico) monkey

micrero -ra *m,f* (Chi) bus driver

micro *m* **1** (fam) (microbús) small bus; (autobús) (Arg) bus, coach (BrE) **2** (fam) (micrófono) mike (colloq)
■ *f* (Chi) bus

microbio *m* microbe

microbiología *f* microbiology

microbús *m* small bus

microchip /mikro'tʃip/ *m* (*pl* **-chips**) microchip

microcomputadora *f* (esp AmL) microcomputer, micro

microcosmos (*pl* ~), **microcosmo** *m* microcosm

microfilm (*pl* **-films**), **microfilme** *m* microfilm

micrófono *m* microphone; **hablar por el ~** to speak over the microphone

microondas *m* (*pl* ~) microwave (oven)

microordenador *m* (Esp) microcomputer, micro

microorganismo *m* microorganism

microscópico -ca *adj* microscopic

microscopio *m* microscope; **mirar algo al** *or* **por el ~** to look at sth under the microscope

mida, midas, etc ▶ MEDIR

miedo *m* fear; **¡qué ~ pasamos!** we were so frightened *o* scared!; **temblaba de ~** he was trembling with fear; **me da ~ salir de noche** I'm afraid to go *o* of going out at night; ~ **A algo/algn** fear OF sth/sb; **el ~ a lo desconocido** fear of the unknown; **le tiene ~ a su padre** he's scared *o* afraid of his father; ~ **a salir a escena** stage fright; **agarrarle** *or* (esp Esp) **cogerle ~ a algo/algn** to become frightened *o* scared of sth/sb; **por ~ a** for fear of; **tener ~** to be afraid *o* frightened *o* scared; **tiene ~ de caerse** he's afraid he might fall; **tengo ~ de que se ofenda** I'm afraid he will take offense

miedoso -sa *adj*: **¡no seas ~!** not te va a hacer daño don't be frightened *o* scared! it won't hurt you; **¡qué ~ es!** he's such a coward!
■ *m,f* coward, scaredy cat (colloq)

miel *f* honey; ~ **de palma** palm syrup

miembro *m* **1 (a)** (de organización, asociación) member **(b)** (como adj) ‹*estado/países*› member (before n) **2** (Anat) limb; ~**s anteriores/posteriores** fore/back limbs

mienta, mientas, etc ▶ MENTIR

mientras *adv* **1** (al mismo tiempo) *tb* ~ **tanto** in the meantime, meanwhile **2** (esp AmL) (cuanto): ~ **más se le da, más pide** the more you give him, the more he wants; ~ **menos coma, mejor** the less I eat the better
■ *conj* **1** (indicando simultaneidad) while; ~ **dormíamos** while we were asleep **2** (con idea de futuro, condición, etc) as long as; ~ **viva/él no se entere** as long as I live/he doesn't find out **3** **mientras que** (con valor adversativo) whereas, while

miércoles *m* (*pl* ~) Wednesday; ~ **de ceniza** Ash Wednesday; *para ejemplos ver* LUNES

mierda *f* **1** (vulg) (excremento) shit (vulg) **2** (vulg) **(a)** (cosa despreciable): **una ~ de empleo** a crappy *o* lousy job (colloq); **la película es una ~** the movie is (a load of) crap (sl) **(b)** (mugre) filth, crap (sl); **¡a la ~ con ... !** (vulg) to hell with ... ! (colloq); **irse a la ~** (vulg) ‹*proyecto/empresa*› to go to the dogs, go to pot (colloq); **mandar a algn a la ~** (vulg) to tell sb to go to hell (colloq) *o* (vulg) to screw himself/herself; **¡vete a la ~!** (vulg) go to hell! (colloq), fuck off! (vulg)

mies *f* ripe grain; ~**es** cornfields

miga *f* **1** (de pan) crumb; **hacer buenas/malas ~s (con algn)** to get on well/badly (with sb)

 ⋯

2 migas *fpl* (Coc) *breadcrumbs fried with garlic, etc* **3** (contenido, sustancia) substance; (dificultad) difficulties (*pl*); **el asunto tiene su ~** it has its difficulties *o* it's quite tricky

migajas *fpl* (de pan) breadcrumbs (*pl*); (sobras) leftovers (*pl*), scraps (*pl*)

migración *f* migration

migraña *f* migraine

mijo¹ *m* millet

mijo² -ja *pron* (apelativo) (AmL fam) dear; **¿qué le pasa, mijita?** what's the matter, darling? (colloq)

mil *adj inv/pron* thousand; **~ quinientos pesos** fifteen hundred pesos, one thousand five hundred pesos; **20 ~ millones** 20 billion (AmE), 20 thousand million (BrE); **tengo ~ cosas que hacer** I have a thousand and one things to do
■ *m* (number) one thousand

milagro *m* miracle; **alcancé el tren de ~** by a miracle I caught the train; **escaparon de ~** they had a miraculous escape; **hacer ~s** to work wonders

milagroso -sa *adj* miraculous

milanesa *f*: *thin breaded cutlet of meat/chicken*

milano *m* kite

milenio *m* millennium

milésima *f* thousandth

milésimo -ma *adj/pron* thousandth; **la milésima parte** a thousandth

milhojas *f* (*pl* **~**) (Coc) millefeuille

mili *f* (Esp fam) military service; **hacer la ~** to do one's military service

milicia *f* militia

miliciano -na *m,f* militiaman

milico *m* (AmL fam & pey) soldier; **los ~s** the military

miligramo *m* milligram

mililitro *m* milliliter*

milímetro *m* millimeter*

militancia *f* (filiación) political affiliation; (militantes) members (*pl*)

militante *adj* politically active
■ *mf* activist

militar¹ *adj* military
■ *mf* soldier, military man; **los ~es** the military

militar² [A1] *vi* to be politically active; **~ en un partido político** to be an active member of a political party

milla *f* mile

millar *m* thousand; **un ~ de seguidores** about a thousand supporters

millón *m* million; **15 mil millones** 15 billion (AmE), 15 thousand million (BrE); **un ~ de gracias** thank you very much

millonario -ria *adj*: **es ~** he's a millionaire
■ *m,f* millionaire

milonga *f* **1** (Mús) *a type of dance and music from the River Plate region* **2** (RPl arg) (a) (fiesta) party, bash (colloq) (b) (mujer fácil) slut (colloq & pej)

milonguero -ra *m,f* (RPl arg) reveler, raver (BrE colloq)

milpa *f* (AmC, Méx) (campo) field (*used mainly for the cultivation of maize*); (cultivo) crop

mimado -da *adj* spoiled, pampered
■ *m,f* spoiled child; **este niño es un ~** this child is spoiled *o* (pej) is a spoiled brat

mimar [A1] *vt* to spoil, pamper

mimbre *m* (material) wicker; **silla de ~** wicker *o* basket chair

mimbrera *f* (arbusto) osier; (sauce) willow

mímica *f* (Teatr) mime; (gestos, señas) sign language, mime

mimo *m* (a) (caricia) cuddle; **hacerle ~s a algn** to cuddle sb (b) (trato indulgente) pampering; **lo criaron con mucho ~** he had a very pampered upbringing
■ *mf* mime

mimosa *f* mimosa

min (= **minuto**) min

mina *f* **1** (yacimiento, excavación) mine; **~ de carbón** coalmine; **~ a cielo abierto** *or* (Andes) **a tajo abierto** strip mine (AmE), opencast mine (BrE); **es una ~ de información** he's a mine of information **2** (Mil, Náut) mine; **un campo de ~s** a minefield **3** (de lápiz) lead **4** (CS arg) (mujer) broad (AmE sl), bird (BrE sl)

minar [A1] *vt* (a) ‹campo/mar› to mine (b) (debilitar) ‹salud› to damage; ‹autoridad/moral› to undermine

minarete *m* minaret

mineral *adj* mineral
■ *m* (a) (sustancia) mineral (b) (de un metal) ore

minería *f* mining industry

minero -ra *adj* mining (*before n*)
■ *m,f* miner

mini *f* (fam) miniskirt, mini (colloq)

miniatura *f* (Art) miniature; **¡qué ~ de pie!** (fam) what a tiny little foot!

minicomputadora *f* (esp AmL) minicomputer

minifalda *f* miniskirt

minifundio *m* (propiedad) smallholding

mini-golf *m* miniature golf

mínima *f* minimum temperature

minimizar [A4] *vt* (reducir al mínimo) to minimize; (quitar importancia) to make light of, play down

mínimo¹ -ma *adj* (a) ‹temperatura/peso› minimum (*before n*); **no le importa lo más ~** he couldn't care less; **el trabajo no le interesa en lo más ~** he is not in the slightest (bit) interested in his work; **no tengo la más mínima idea** I haven't the faintest idea (b) (insignificante) ‹detalle› minor; ‹diferencia/beneficios› minimal

mínimo² *m* minimum; **reducir los gastos al ~** to keep costs to a minimum; **como ~** at least

miniordenador *m* (Esp) minicomputer

ministerial *adj* ‹reunión› cabinet (*before n*); ‹orden› ministerial

ministerio *m* **1** (Pol) ministry, department (AmE); **M~ de Hacienda** ≈ Treasury Department (*in US*), ≈ Treasury (*in UK*); **M~ del Interior** ≈ Department of the Interior (*in US*), ≈ Home Office (*in UK*); **M~ de Relaciones** *or* **Asuntos Exteriores** ≈ State Department (*in US*), ≈ Foreign Office (*in UK*) **2** (Relig) ministry

ministro -tra *m,f* minister, government minister; **M~ de Hacienda** ≈ Secretary of the Treasury (*in US*), ≈ Chancellor of the Exchequer (*in UK*); **M~ del Interior** ≈ Secretary of the

Interior (*in US*), ≈ Home Secretary (*in UK*); **M~ de Relaciones** *or* **Asuntos Exteriores** ≈ Secretary of State (*in US*), ≈ Foreign Secretary (*in UK*)

minoría *f* minority; **estar en ~** to be in a/the minority; **~ de edad** minority

minorista *adj* retail (*before n*)

■ *mf* retailer

minoritario -ria *adj* minority (*before n*)

mintiera, mintió, etc ▶ MENTIR

minucia *f* **(a)** (detalle pequeño) minor detail **(b)** (cualidad) detail; **explicar algo con ~** to explain sth in detail *o* thoroughly

minuciosidad *f* attention to detail

minucioso -sa *adj* ⟨*búsqueda/investigación/persona*⟩ meticulous, thorough; ⟨*informe*⟩ detailed

minúscula *f* lower case letter, minuscule (tech)

minúsculo -la *adj* **(a)** (diminuto) minute, tiny **(b)** ⟨*letra*⟩ lower case

minusvalía *f* [1] (física) physical handicap *o* disability; (psíquica) mental handicap [2] (Econ) drop *o* fall in value

minusválido -da *adj* (físico) physically handicapped, disabled; (psíquico) mentally handicapped

■ *m,f* (físico) disabled person, physically handicapped person; (psíquico) mentally handicapped person; **coches para ~s** cars for the disabled

minuta *f* [1] (de abogado, notario) bill [2] (plato rápido) (RPl) quick meal

minutero *m* minute hand

minuto *m* minute; **a tres ~s de su casa** three minutes (away) from his house

mío, mía *adj* (*detrás del n*) mine; **un primo ~** a cousin of mine; **eso es asunto ~** that's my business; **Muy señor ~** (Corresp) (frml) Dear Sir

■ *pron*: **el ~/la mía,** *etc* mine; **sus hijos y los ~s** their children and mine; **los idiomas no son lo ~** languages are not my thing; **los ~s** my family and friends

miope *adj* **(a)** (Med, Ópt) myopic (tech), nearsighted (AmE), short-sighted (BrE) **(b)** (falto de perspicacia) short-sighted

■ *mf* myopic person (tech), nearsighted person (AmE), short-sighted person (BrE)

miopía *f* **(a)** (Med, Ópt) myopia (tech), nearsightedness (AmE), short-sightedness (BrE) **(b)** (falta de perspicacia) shortsightedness

mira *f* **(a)** (Arm, Ópt) sight; **(b)** (intención, objetivo): **con ~s a reducir los gastos** with a view to reducing costs; **con la ~ puesta en el porvenir** with one's sight set on the future; **es muy estrecho de ~s** he's very narrow-minded

mirada *f* **(a)** (modo de mirar) look; **una ~ reprobatoria** a disapproving look; **su ~ era triste** he had a sad look in his eyes; **lo fulminó con la ~** she looked daggers at him **(b)** (vistazo, ojeada) glance; **echarle una ~ a algo** to take a quick glance at sth; **échales una ~ a los niños** have a look at the children **(c)** (vista): **tenía la ~ fija en el suelo** she had her eyes fixed on the ground; **recorrió la habitación con la ~** she cast her eyes over the room; **bajar/levantar la ~** to look down/up

miradero *m* (Col) viewpoint

mirado -da *adj* (considerado): **eso no está bien ~**

that's not approved of, that's looked down on; **está muy mal ~ en el barrio** he is not at all well thought of *o* well regarded in the neighborhood; *ver tb* MIRAR *vt*

mirador *m* viewpoint

miramiento *m*: **tratar a algn sin ningún ~** to treat sb with a total lack of consideration

mirar [A1] *vt* [1] **(a)** (observar, contemplar) to look at; **~ un cuadro** to look at a picture; **no me mires así** don't look at me like that; **~ a algn a los ojos** to look sb in the eye; **se me quedó mirando** he just stared at me; **miraba distraída por la ventana** he was gazing absent-mindedly out of the window; **miraba cómo lo hacía** he was watching how she did it; **ir a ~ escaparates** *or* (AmL) **vidrieras** to go window shopping **(b)** ⟨*programa/partido/televisión*⟩ to watch

[2] (fijarse) to look; **¡mira lo que has hecho!** look what you've done!; **mira bien que esté apagado** make sure *o* check it's off; **miré a ver si estaba listo** I had a look to see if he was ready

[3] (considerar): **míralo desde otro punto de vista** look at it from another point of view; **lo mires por donde lo mires** whatever *o* whichever way you look at it; **mirándolo bien** (pensándolo detenidamente) all things considered; (pensándolo mejor) on second thoughts; **~ a algn en menos** to look down on sb; **~ mal a algn** to disapprove of sb

[4] (expresando incredulidad, irritación, etc): **¡mira que poner un plato de plástico en el horno ...!** honestly *o* really! imagine putting a plastic dish in the oven ...! (colloq); **¡mira que eres tacaño!** boy, you're mean! (colloq); **¡mira las veces que te lo habré dicho ...!** the times I've told you!

■ **~** *vi* [1] (en general) to look; **he mirado por todas partes** I've looked everywhere; **~ por la ventana** to look out of the window; **¿miraste bien?** did you have a good look?, did you look properly?; **~ atrás** to look back

[2] (estar orientado) **~ A/HACIA algo** «*fachada*» to face sth; «*terraza/habitación*» to look out over sth, overlook sth; **ponte mirando hacia la ventana** stand (*o* sit *etc*) facing the window

[3] **mirar por (a)** (preocuparse por) to think of **(b)** (Col) (cuidar) to look after

■ **mirarse** *v pron* **(a)** (*refl*) to look at oneself; **~se en el espejo** to look at oneself in the mirror **(b)** (*recípr*) to look at each other

mirilla *f* peephole, spyhole

mirlo *m* blackbird

mirto *m* myrtle

misa *f* mass; **están en ~** they're at mass; **ir a ~** to go to mass; **decir ~** «*sacerdote*» to say *o* celebrate mass; **~ de cuerpo presente** funeral mass; **~ de difuntos** Requiem (mass); **~ de** *or* **del gallo** midnight mass (*on Christmas Eve*)

miscelánea *f* **(a)** (variedad) miscellany **(b)** (Méx) (tienda) small general store, corner shop (BrE)

misceláneo -nea *adj* miscellaneous

miserable *adj* **(a)** (pobre) ⟨*vivienda*⟩ miserable, wretched; ⟨*sueldo*⟩ paltry, miserable **(b)** (avaro) mean, stingy (colloq) **(c)** (malvado) malicious, nasty

■ *mf* wretch, scoundrel

miseria *f* [1] (pobreza) poverty, destitution [2] (cantidad insignificante) miserable amount, paltry ⋯⋗

amount; **gana una** ~ she earns a pittance

3 (desgracia) misfortune; **las ~s de la guerra** the miseries of war

misericordia *f* mercy, compassion

misericordioso -sa *adj* merciful

mísero -ra *adj* miserable

misil *m* missile; ~ **antiaéreo/balístico** antiaircraft/ballistic missile

misión *f* **1** (tarea) mission **2** (delegación): **una ~ científica** a team of scientists; **una ~ diplomática** a diplomatic delegation

misionero -ra *adj* missionary (*before n*)
■ *m,f* missionary

Misisipí *m* (río): **el (río)** ~ the Mississippi (River); (estado) Mississippi

mismo¹ -ma *adj* **1** **(a)** (*delante del n*) (expresando identidad) same; **hacer dos cosas al ~ tiempo** to do two things at once *o* at the same time **(b)** (*como pron*) same; **Roma ya no es la misma** Rome isn't the same any more; **el ~ que vimos ayer** the same one we saw yesterday

2 (uso enfático) **(a)** (refiriéndose a lugares, momentos, cosas): **en el ~ centro de Lima** right in the center of Lima; **en este ~ instante** this very minute; **eso ~ pienso yo** that's exactly what I think **(b)** (refiriéndose a personas): **el mismísimo presidente** the president himself; **te perjudicas a ti ~** you're only hurting yourself; **ella misma lo trajo** she brought it herself

3 lo mismo: **siempre dice lo ~** he always says the same thing; **lo ~ para mí** the same for me, please; **nuestra empresa, lo ~ que tantas otras** our company, like so many others; **los niños pueden ir lo ~ que los adultos** children can go as well as adults; **o lo que es lo ~** in other words; *da lo* ~ it doesn't matter; *me/le da lo* ~ I don't care/he/she doesn't care

mismo² adv (uso enfático): **aquí/ahora ~** right here/now; **hoy ~ te mando el cheque** I'll send you the check today; **ayer ~ hablé con él** I spoke to him only yesterday

miss /mis/ *f* beauty queen; **M~ Universo** Miss Universe

misterio *m* mystery

misterioso -sa *adj* mysterious

misticismo *m* mysticism

místico -ca *adj* ⟨experiencia⟩ mystic, mystical; ⟨escritor⟩ mystic (*before n*)
■ *m,f* mystic

mitad *f* **1** (parte) half; **la ~ de la población** half (of) the population; **solo quiero la ~** I only want half; **a ~ de precio** half price; **lo hizo en la ~ del tiempo** she did it in half the time; **~ y ~** half and half

2 (medio, centro): **cortar algo por la ~** to cut sth in half; **dividir algo por la ~** to halve sth; **a** *or* **en (la) ~ de la reunión** in the middle of the meeting; **a ~ de camino** halfway; **en la ~ de la película/del libro** halfway through the movie/the book

mítico -ca *adj* mythical

mitigar [A3] *vt* ⟨dolor⟩ to relieve, ease; ⟨pena/sufrimiento⟩ to alleviate; ⟨sed⟩ to quench

mitin, mitín *m* (Pol) political meeting, rally

mito *m* **(a)** (leyenda) legend **(b)** (invención, mentira) myth

mitología *f* mythology

mitológico -ca *adj* mythological

mixto¹ -ta *adj* mixed; **educación mixta** coeducation

mixto² *m* toasted sandwich (*with two different fillings*)

ml. (= mililitro) ml

mm. (= milímetro) mm

moaré *m* moiré

mobbing *m* (Esp) harrassment

mobiliario *m* furniture, furnishings (*pl*); **renovar el ~ del comedor** to refurnish the dining room; **~ de baño** bathroom furnishings (*pl*); **~ de cocina** kitchen fittings *o* units (*pl*)

moca *m*: *tb* **café ~** mocha; **tarta de ~** coffee cake

mocasín *m* moccasin

mochila *f* (de excursionista, soldado) backpack; (de escolar) satchel

mochilear [A1] *vi* (CS) to backpack

mochilero -ra *m,f* (CS) backpacker

moción *f* motion; **presentar una ~** to propose *o* (BrE) table a motion; **~ de censura** vote of censure *o* no confidence

moco *m* **(a)** (líquido) snot (colloq); **límpiate los ~s** wipe *o* blow your nose; **le colgaban los ~s** he had a runny nose (colloq) *o* (sl) snotty nose **(b)** (seco) booger (AmE colloq), bogey (BrE colloq)

mocoso -sa *m,f* (fam) squirt (colloq), pipsqueak (colloq)

moda *f* fashion; **la ~ joven** *or* **juvenil** young fashion; **la ~ de los 30** 30's fashion; **ir a la ~** to be trendy; **estar de ~** to be in fashion, be in (colloq); **ponerse/pasar de ~** to come into/go out of fashion; **seguir la ~** to follow fashion

modal *adj* modal

modales *mpl* manners (*pl*); **tener buenos/malos ~** to be well-mannered/bad-mannered

modalidad *f*: **varias ~es de pago** several methods *o* modes of payment; **la medalla de oro en la ~ de esquí alpino** the gold medal for downhill skiing

modelaje *m* (Andes, Ven) modeling*; **hacer ~** to model

modelar [A1] *vt* (Art) ⟨arcilla⟩ to model; ⟨estatua/figura⟩ to model, sculpt; ⟨carácter⟩ to mold*
■ ~ *vi* **1** (Art) to model **2** (Andes) (para fotos, desfiles) to model

modelo *adj inv* **(a)** ⟨niño/estudiante⟩ model (*before n*); ⟨comportamiento/carácter⟩ exemplary **(b)** (de muestra): **visité la casa ~** I visited the model home (AmE) *o* (BrE) the showhouse
■ *m* **1** (en general) model; **tomar/utilizar algo como ~** to take/use sth as a model; **tomó a su padre**

como ∼ he followed his father's example; ∼ **en** *or* **a escala** scale model ⟦2⟧ (Indum) design; **un** ∼ **de Franelli** a Franelli (design); **llegó con un nuevo modelito** (fam) she arrived wearing a new little number

■ *mf* model; **desfile de** ∼**s** fashion show

módem *m* (*pl* **-dems**) modem

moderación *f* moderation; **beber con** ∼ to drink in moderation

moderado -da *adj* **(a)** ⟨*persona/ comportamiento*⟩ restrained **(b)** ⟨*temperatura*⟩ moderate; ⟨*precio*⟩ reasonable; ⟨*ideología/facción*⟩ moderate

■ *m,f* moderate

moderador -dora *m,f* (en debate) moderator, chair; (Rad, TV) presenter

moderar [A1] *vt* ⟦1⟧ **(a)** ⟨*impulsos/aspiraciones*⟩ to curb, moderate; **por favor modera tu vocabulario** please mind your language **(b)** ⟨*gasto/consumo*⟩ to curb; ⟨*velocidad*⟩ to reduce ⟦2⟧ ⟨*debate/coloquio*⟩ to moderate, chair

■ **moderarse** *v pron*: **modérate, estás comiendo mucho** restrain yourself *o* (colloq) go easy, you're eating too much; ∼**se en los gastos** to cut down on spending

modernismo *m* (Arquit, Art, Lit) modernism; (cualidad) modernness, modernity

modernista *adj/mf* modernist

modernizar [A4] *vt* ⟨*fábrica/técnica/sociedad*⟩ to modernize; ⟨*costumbres*⟩ to update; ⟨*vestido/ abrigo*⟩ to do up

■ **modernizarse** *v pron*: **debes** ∼**te** you have to keep up with the times

moderno -na *adj* **(a)** (actual) modern; **el hombre** ∼ modern man; **una edición más** ∼ **a** a more up-to-date edition **(b)** (a la moda) ⟨*vestido/ peinado*⟩ fashionable, trendy **(c)** ⟨*edad/historia*⟩ modern

modestia *f* modesty

modesto -ta *adj* **(a)** (falto de pretensión) modest **(b)** (humilde) ⟨*familia*⟩ humble; ⟨*posición social*⟩ modest, humble **(c)** ⟨*sueldo/ingresos*⟩ modest

módico -ca *adj* reasonable

modificar [A2] *vt* **(a)** ⟨*aparato*⟩ to modify; ⟨*plan*⟩ to change; ⟨*horario/ley*⟩ to change, alter **(b)** (Ling) to modify; **modifica al verbo** it modifies the verb

■ **modificarse** *v pron* to change, alter

modismo *m* idiom

modista *mf* (que diseña) couturier, designer; (que confecciona) dressmaker

modistería *f* (Col) (actividad) dressmaking; (establecimiento) dressmaker's shop/workshop

modisto *m* couturier, designer

modo *m* ⟦1⟧ **(a)** (manera, forma) way, manner (frml); **el** ∼ **de hacerlo** the way of doing it; **del siguiente** ∼ in the following manner; **a mi** ∼ **de ver** to my way of thinking, in my opinion; **lo digas de ese** ∼ don't say it like that; **de un** ∼ **u otro** one way or another; **su** ∼ **de ser** the way he is; **◉ modo de empleo** instructions for use, directions; **me lo pidió de muy mal** ∼ (AmL) she asked me (for it) very rudely **(b)** (en locs) **a mi/ tu/su modo** (in) my/your/his (own) way; **de cualquier modo** (de todas formas) (*indep*) in any case, anyway; (sin cuidado) anyhow; **del mismo** *or* **de igual modo que** just as, in the same way

(that); **de modo que** (así que) so; (para que) so that; **de ningún modo** no way; **de ningún** ∼ **puedo aceptar** there's no way I can accept; **de todos modos** anyway, anyhow; **en cierto modo** in a way; **ni modo** (AmL exc CS fam) no way; **traté de persuadirlo pero ni** ∼ I tried to persuade him but it was no good; **ni** ∼ **que te quedes aquí** there's no way you're staying here (colloq)

⟦2⟧ **modos** *mpl* (modales) manners (*pl*); **con buenos/malos** ∼**s** politely/rudely *o* impolitely

modulación *f* modulation; ∼ **de amplitud/ frecuencia** amplitude/frequency modulation

modular [A1] *vt/vi* to modulate

módulo *m* **(a)** (de mueble) unit, module **(b)** (de prisión) unit **(c)** (Espac, Educ) module

mofarse [A1] *v pron* ∼ **DE algo/algn** to make fun of sth/sb

mofle *m* (AmC, Méx) muffler (AmE), silencer (BrE)

moflete *m* (fam) chubby cheek

mofletudo -da *adj* (fam) chubby-cheeked

mogolla *f* (Col) bread roll

mohair /mo'er/ *m* mohair

mohín *m* face; **hacer un** ∼ to make *o* (BrE) pull an angry face

mohíno -na *adj* **(a)** (enfurruñado): **está** ∼ **porque lo regañaron** he's sulking because he's been told off **(b)** (alicaído) depressed

moho *m* **(a)** (en fruta, pan) mold*, mildew; **criar** ∼ «*fruta/queso*» to go moldy* **(b)** (en cobre) patina, verdigris; (en hierro) rust

moisés *m* (cuna) cradle, Moses basket; (portátil) portacrib (AmE), carrycot (BrE)

mojado -da *adj* wet

■ *m,f* (Méx fam) wetback (colloq & pej)

mojar [A1] *vt* **(a)** ⟨*suelo/papel/pelo*⟩ (accidentalmente) to get *o* make ... wet; (a propósito) to wet; **pasó un coche y me mojó** a car went by and splashed me; ∼ **la cama** (euf) to wet the bed **(b)** (sumergiendo) ⟨*galleta/bizcocho*⟩ to dip, dunk (colloq)

■ **mojarse** *v pron* **(a)** «*persona/ropa/suelo*» to get wet; **se me** ∼**on los zapatos** my shoes got wet; **me mojé toda** I got soaked **(b)** ⟨*pelo/pies*⟩ (a propósito) to wet; (accidentalmente) to get ... wet

mojigatería *f* prudishness

mojigato -ta *adj* prudish

■ *m,f* prude

mojón *m* (señal) marker, boundary stone; (hito) landmark; (Auto) *tb* ∼ **kilométrico** ≈ milestone

molar *m* molar, back tooth

molcajete *m* (Méx) mortar

molde *m* **(a)** (para hornear) baking pan (AmE), baking tin (BrE); (para flanes, gelatina) mold*; ∼ **de pan** loaf pan (AmE) *o* (BrE) tin **(b)** (Tec) cast; **un** ∼ **de yeso** (Art) a plaster cast **(c)** (AmL) (para coser) pattern

moldeable *adj* **(a)** ⟨*barro*⟩ moldable*, malleable **(b)** ⟨*persona/carácter*⟩ malleable

moldear [A1] *vt* **(a)** (en bronce) to cast; (en barro) to mold*, model **(b)** ⟨*persona/carácter*⟩ to mold*, shape; ⟨*pelo*⟩ to style

moldura *f* molding*

mole *f* mass; **una** ∼ **de hormigón** a huge mass of concrete ⋯⟫

■ *m* (Méx) (salsa) chili sauce (*with chocolate and peanuts*); (plato) *turkey, chicken or pork with* MOLE *sauce*

molécula *f* molecule

moler [E9] *vt* ‹especias/café› to grind; ‹trigo› to grind, mill; ‹aceitunas› to crush; ‹carne› to grind (AmE), to mince (BrE); ‹plátano› (Chi, Méx) to mash; **café molido** ground coffee

molestar [A1] *vt* **1** **(a)** (importunar) to bother; **perdone que lo moleste** sorry to trouble *o* bother you **(b)** (interrumpir) to disturb **2** (ofender, disgustar) to upset

■ ~ *vi* **1** (importunar): **¿le molesta si fumo?** do you mind if I smoke?; **me molesta su arrogancia** her arrogance irritates *o* annoys me; **no me duele, pero me molesta** it doesn't hurt but it's uncomfortable **2** (fastidiar) to be a nuisance; **no quiero** ~ I don't want to be a nuisance *o* to cause any trouble

■ **molestarse** *v pron* **1** (disgustarse) to get upset; ~**se POR algo** to get upset ABOUT sth; ~**se CON algn** to get annoyed WITH sb **2** (tomarse el trabajo) to bother, trouble oneself (frml); **ni se molestó en llamarme** he didn't even bother to call me; **se molestó en venir hasta aquí a avisarnos** she took the trouble to come all this way to tell us

molestia *f* **1** **(a)** (incomodidad, trastorno): **ser una** ~ to be a nuisance; **siento causarte tantas** ~**s** I'm sorry to cause you so much trouble; **perdona la** ~**, pero ...** sorry to bother you, but ... **(b)** (trabajo) trouble; **se tomó la** ~ **de escribirnos** she took the trouble to write to us; **¿para qué te tomaste la** ~? why did you bother to do that?; **no es ninguna** ~ it's no trouble *o* bother **2** (malestar): ~**s estomacales** stomach problems *o* upsets; **no es un dolor, solo una** ~ it's not a pain, just a feeling of discomfort

molesto -ta *adj* **1** [SER] **(a)** (fastidioso) ‹ruido/tos› annoying, irritating; ‹sensación/síntoma› unpleasant **(b)** (violento, embarazoso) awkward, embarrassing **2** [ESTAR] (ofendido) upset; (irritado) annoyed; **está muy** ~ **por lo que hiciste** he's very upset/annoyed about what you did

molestoso -sa *adj* (AmL fam) annoying

molido -da *adj* **(a)** (fam) (agotado) bushed (AmE colloq), shattered (BrE colloq) **(b)** (Andes fam) (dolorido) stiff

molinero -ra *m,f* miller

molinillo *m* **(a)** (de café, especias) grinder, mill; ~ **de carne** grinder (AmE), mincer (BrE) **(b)** (juguete) pinwheel (AmE), windmill (BrE) **(c)** (Col, Méx) (para batir) whisk

molino *m* **(a)** (máquina — para el trigo) mill; (— para la carne) grinder (AmE), mincer (BrE) **(b)** (fábrica) mill; ~ **de agua** waterwheel; ~ **de viento** windmill; ~ **de papel** paper mill

molleja *f* (de res) sweetbread; (de ave) gizzard

mollera *f* (fam) head; **está mal de la** ~ he's off his head *o* rocker (colloq); **cerrado** *or* **duro de** ~ pigheaded (colloq)

molo *m* (Chi) *tb* ~ **de abrigo** breakwater, mole

molusco *m* mollusk*

momentáneo -nea *adj* **(a)** (breve) momentary **(b)** (pasajero) temporary

momento *m* **1** **(a)** (instante puntual) moment; **justo en ese** ~ just at that moment; **a partir de**

ese ~ from that moment on; **en todo** ~ at all times **(b)** (lapso breve) minute, moment; **dentro de un** ~ in a minute *o* moment; **¡un momentito!** (por teléfono) just a moment, just a minute; **eso te lo arreglo en un** ~ I'll fix that for you in no time at all **(c)** (época, período) time, period; **atravesamos** ~**s difíciles** we're going through a difficult time *o* period; **está en su mejor** ~ he is at his peak **(d)** (ocasión) time; **llegas en buen/mal** ~ you've arrived at the right time/at a bad time; **en ningún** ~ at no time **2** (*en locs*) **al momento** at once; **de momento** (ahora mismo) right now; (mientras tanto) for the time being; (por ahora) for the moment; **de un momento al otro** (dentro de muy poco) any minute now; **en cualquier momento** at any time; **en el momento** immediately; **en el momento menos pensado** when they (*o you etc*) least expect it; **por el momento** for the time being **3** (Fís, Mec) momentum

momia *f* mummy

mona *f* **1** (fam) (borrachera): **agarrar una** ~ to get plastered (colloq); **dormir la** ~ to sleep it off **2** **(a)** (en naipes) old maid **(b)** (Col) (para un álbum) picture card; **como la** ~ (CS fam) terrible

monada *f* (fam) **(a)** (cosa bonita): **¡qué** ~ **de vestido!** what a lovely dress! **(b)** (persona bonita): **su novia es una** ~ his girlfriend's really pretty; **¡qué** ~ **de niño!** what a lovely *o* (colloq) cute kid **(c)** (RPl) (persona encantadora) angel (colloq)

monaguillo *m* altar boy, acolyte, server

monarca *mf* monarch

monarquía *f* monarchy

monárquico -ca *adj* ‹régimen› monarchical; ‹persona/ideas› monarchist (*before n*)

■ *m,f* monarchist, royalist

monasterio *m* monastery

monástico -ca *adj* monastic

mondadientes *m* (*pl* ~) toothpick

mondar [A1] *vt* (Esp) ‹fruta/patatas› to peel

■ **mondarse** *v pron* (*refl*): **se mondaba los dientes** she was picking her teeth; ~**se de risa** (Esp fam) to die laughing

moneda *f* **1** **(a)** (pieza) coin; **una** ~ **de cinco pesos** a five-peso coin *o* piece **(b)** (de país) currency; **acuñar** ~ to mint money **2** **la Moneda** (en Chi) Presidential Palace

monedero *m* change purse (AmE), purse (BrE)

monerías *fpl* (fam): **hacer** ~ (tontear) to mess around (colloq); (hacer payasadas) to monkey *o* clown around (colloq)

mongólico -ca *adj* **(a)** (ant *o* crit) (Med) ‹rasgos› mongoloid (dated *or* crit); **niños** ~**s** Down's syndrome children **(b)** (fam & pey) (tonto) moronic (colloq & pej)

mongolismo *m* (ant *o* crit) Down's syndrome

monigote *m* (muñeco) rag doll; (de papel) paper doll; (dibujo) doodle

monitor -tora *m,f* **1** **(a)** (CS) (Dep): ~ **de esquí/natación** ski/swimming instructor; ~ **de tenis** tennis coach **(b)** (Educ) (en la escuela) (RPl) monitor; (en la universidad) (Col) *student who acts as an assistant teacher* **2** **monitor** *m* (Inf, Med, Tec) monitor

monja *f* nun; **meterse a** *or* **de** ~ to become a nun

monje *m* monk

mono¹ -na *adj* [1] (fam) ⟨*mujer*⟩ pretty, lovely-looking (colloq); ⟨*niño*⟩ lovely, cute (colloq); ⟨*vestido/piso*⟩ gorgeous, lovely [2] (Col) (rubio) ⟨*hombre/niño*⟩ blond; ⟨*mujer/niña*⟩ blonde [3] (Audio) mono
■ *m,f* [1] (Zool) monkey; **ser el último** ~ (fam) to be the lowest of the low [2] *m* **(a)** (de mecánico) coveralls (*pl*) (AmE), overalls (*pl*) (BrE) **(b)** (de moda — de cuerpo entero) jumpsuit; (— con peto) overalls (*pl*) (AmE), dungarees (*pl*) (BrE) **(c)** (Méx) (malla de bailarina) leotard

mono² *m* (monigote) [1] doodle; **una revista de monitos** (Andes, Méx) a comic; ~ **animado** (Chi) cartoon; ~ **de nieve** (Chi) snowman [2] **(a)** (de mecánico) coveralls (*pl*) (AmE), overalls (*pl*) (BrE), boiler suit (BrE) **(b)** (de moda — de cuerpo entero) jumpsuit; (— con peto) overalls (*pl*) (AmE), dungarees (*pl*) (BrE) **(c)** (Méx) (malla de bailarina) leotard [3] (arg) (síndrome de abstinencia) cold turkey (sl); **está con el** ~ he's gone cold turkey (sl)

monocarril *m* monorail

monocolor *adj* one-color* (*before n*)

monóculo *m* monocle

monogamia *f* monogamy

monógamo -ma *adj* monogamous
■ *m,f* monogamist

monografía *f* monograph

monográfico -ca *adj* monographic

monolingüe *adj* monolingual

monolítico -ca *adj* monolithic

monolito *m* monolith

monólogo *m* monologue

monoparental *adj*: **las familias** ~**es** one-parent families

monopatín *m* (con manillar) (CS) scooter; (sin manillar) (Esp) skateboard

monopolio *m* monopoly

monopolizar [A4] *vt* to monopolize

monorriel *m* (AmL) monorail

monosílabo *m* monosyllable

monoteísmo *m* monotheism

monotonía *f* (de tarea) monotony; (de sonido) monotone

monótono -na *adj* monotonous

monóxido *m* monoxide; ~ **de carbono** carbon monoxide

monseñor *m* Monsignor

monstruo *m* **(a)** (en general) monster **(b)** (fenómeno) phenomenon; **un** ~ **de la música pop** a pop phenomenon

monstruosidad *f* **(a)** (cosa fea, grande) monstrosity **(b)** (atrocidad) atrocity **(c)** (cualidad) monstrous nature, monstrousness

monstruoso -sa *adj* **(a)** ⟨*crimen/ comportamiento*⟩ monstrous, atrocious **(b)** ⟨*ser/ facciones*⟩ hideous, grotesque

monta *f* (monto) total (value); **de poca** ~ ⟨*asunto*⟩ of little importance *o* note; ⟨*escritor*⟩ third-rate; ⟨*daños*⟩ slight, minor

montacargas *m* (*pl* ~) freight *o* service elevator (AmE), service *o* goods lift (BrE)

montado -da *adj* ⟨*policía*⟩ mounted; **iba** ~ **a caballo** he was riding a horse; **estaba montada en su bicicleta** she was sitting on her bicycle; *ver tb* MONTAR

montador -dora *m,f* (Mec, Tec) fitter; (Cin, TV) film editor

montaje *m* **(a)** (de máquina, mueble) assembly **(b)** (de obra) staging; (de película) editing; **seguro que todo es un** ~ I bet it's all a big con *o* a set-up (colloq)

montallantas *m* (*pl* ~) (Col) (taller) *workshop where tires* are retreaded*; (mecánico) *person who retreads tires**

montaña *f* [1] (Geog) mountain; **tienen un chalet en la** ~ they have a chalet in the mountains; ~ **rusa** roller coaster [2] (montón) pile

montañero -ra *m,f* mountaineer, mountain climber

montañés -ñesa *adj* mountain (*before n*), highland (*before n*)
■ *m,f* highlander

montañismo *m* mountaineering, mountain climbing

montañoso -sa *adj* ⟨*cadena*⟩ mountain (*before n*); ⟨*terreno/país*⟩ mountainous

montar [A1] *vt* [1] **(a)** ⟨*caballo*⟩ (subirse a) to mount, get on; (ir sobre) to ride **(b)** (subir, colocar): **montó al niño en el poni** he lifted the boy up onto the pony [2] ⟨*vaca/yegua*⟩ to mount [3] **(a)** (poner, establecer) ⟨*feria/exposición*⟩ to set up; ⟨*negocio*⟩ to start up, set up **(b)** ⟨*máquina/ mueble*⟩ to assemble; ⟨*estantería*⟩ to put up; ⟨*tienda de campaña*⟩ to put up, pitch **(c)** ⟨*piedra preciosa*⟩ to set; ⟨*diapositiva*⟩ to mount **(d)** (organizar) ⟨*obra/producción*⟩ to stage [4] (Esp) ⟨*nata*⟩ to whip; ⟨*claras*⟩ to whisk
■ ~ *vi* [1] **(a)** (ir): ~ **a caballo/en bicicleta** to ride a horse/bicycle **(b)** (Equ) to mount [2] (cubrir parcialmente) ~ **SOBRE algo** to overlap sth
■ **montarse** *v pron* (en coche) to get in; (en tren, autobús, bicicleta) to get on; (en caballo) to mount, get on; **¿me dejas** ~**me en tu bicicleta?** can I have a ride on your bicycle?

monte *m* (Geog) **(a)** (montaña) mountain **(b)** (terreno — cubierto de maleza) scrubland, scrub; (— cubierto de árboles) woodland

montera *f* (gorra) cap; (de torero) bullfighter's hat

montés *adj* ⟨*animal/planta*⟩ wild

montevideano -na *adj* of/from Montevideo

Montevideo *m* Montevideo

montgomery *m* (CS) duffle coat

montículo *m* mound

montón *m* **(a)** (pila) pile; **del** ~ (fam) ordinary, average **(b)** (fam) (gran cantidad): **un** ~ **de gente** loads of people (colloq); **me gusta un** ~ I like her/ him/it a lot

montonero -ra *m,f* (guerrillero) guerrilla

montura *f* [1] (Equ) (silla) saddle; (animal) mount [2] **(a)** (de anteojos) frame **(b)** (engarce) setting, mount

monumental *adj* (fam) **(a)** ⟨*cocina/jardín*⟩ huge, massive **(b)** ⟨*error/esfuerzo*⟩ monumental

monumento *m* [1] (obra conmemorativa) monument; ~ **histórico/nacional** historical/ national monument; ~ **a los caídos** war memorial; ~ **funerario** commemorative stone [2] (obra excepcional) masterpiece, classic [3] (fam) (mujer atractiva) stunner (colloq)

monzón *m* monsoon

moña *f* (Taur) ribbon; (lazo) (RPI) bow

moño *m* **(a)** (peinado) bun; **se hizo un ~** she put her hair up in a bun; **estar hasta el ~** to be fed up (to the back teeth) (colloq) **(b)** (AmL) (lazo) bow

moñona *f* (Col fam) strike; **hacer ~** to get a strike

moqueta *f* (Esp) wall-to-wall carpet, fitted carpet (BrE)

moquillento -ta *adj* (Andes fam) **(a)** (resfriado) coldy (colloq) **(b)** (con mocos) ‹nariz› runny, snotty (colloq); ‹niño› runny-nosed, snotty-nosed (colloq)

moquillo *m* distemper

mora *f* (de zarzamora) blackberry; (de moral) mulberry; (de morera) white mulberry

morada *f* (frml o liter) dwelling (frml), abode (frml or liter)

morado¹ -da *adj* ‹color› purple; **~ del frío** blue with cold; **ponerle a algn un ojo ~** to give sb a black eye

morado² *m* (Esp, Ven) bruise

moral *adj* moral
■ *f* **1** (Fil, Relig) **(a)** (doctrina) moral doctrine **(b)** (moralidad) morality, morals (*pl*) **2** (estado de ánimo) morale; **levantarle la ~ a algn** to raise sb's morale, lift sb's spirits; **estar bajo de ~** to be feeling low; **tener la ~ alta** to be in good spirits
■ *m* mulberry (tree)

moraleja *f* moral

moralidad *f* morality, ethics (*pl*)

morar [A1] *vi* (liter) to dwell (liter)

moratón *m* bruise

morboso -sa *adj* ‹escena/película› gruesome; ‹persona/mente› ghoulish; (truculento, retorcido) morbid
■ *m,f* (fam) ghoul

morcilla *f* blood sausage (AmE), black pudding (BrE)

mordaz *adj* ‹estilo/lenguaje› scathing, caustic; ‹crítica› sharp, scathing

mordaza *f* **(a)** (en la boca) gag **(b)** (Tec) clamp

mordedura *f* bite

morder [E9] *vt* **1** (con los dientes) to bite; **el perro le mordió la mano** the dog bit her hand **2** (Méx fam) ‹policía/funcionario› to extract a bribe from
■ **~ vi** to bite
■ **morderse** *v pron* (refl) to bite oneself; **~se las uñas** to bite one's nails

mordida *f* **1** (CS) (en general) bite; (huella) toothmarks (*pl*) **2** (Méx fam) (soborno) bribe, backhander (BrE colloq)

mordisco *m* bite; **le dio un ~ en el brazo** it bit her (on the) arm

mordisquear [A1] *vt* to nibble

moreno -na *adj* **(a)** [SER] ‹persona› (de pelo oscuro) dark, dark-haired; (de tez oscura) dark; (de raza negra) (euf) dark-skinned (euph) **(b)** [ESTAR] (bronceado) brown, tanned **(c)** ‹piel› brown, dark
■ *m,f* **(a)** (de pelo oscuro) (*m*) dark-haired man (o

boy *etc*); (*f*) dark-haired woman (o girl *etc*), brunet* **(b)** (de tez oscura) dark person (o man *etc*); (de raza negra) (euf) dark-skinned person (o man *etc*) (euph), coloured man (o woman *etc*) (BrE euph)

morera *f* white mulberry tree

moretón *m* bruise

morfar [A1] *vi* (RPI arg) to eat

morfina *f* morphine

morgue *f* (AmL) morgue, mortuary

moribundo -da *adj* dying, moribund (frml)
■ *m,f* dying man (o woman *etc*)

morir [I37] *vi* **(a)** ‹‹persona/animal›› to die; **~ ahogado** to drown; **murió asesinada** she was murdered; **~ DE algo** ‹de vejez/cáncer› to die OF sth; **murió de hambre** she starved to death; **¡y allí muere!** (AmC fam) and that's all there is to it! **(b)** (liter) ‹‹civilización/costumbre›› to die out
■ **morirse** *v pron* ‹‹persona/animal/planta›› to die; **se les murió la madre** their mother died; **se me murió la perra** my dog died; **no te vas a ~ por ayudarlo** (fam) it won't kill you to help him (colloq); **como se entere me muero** (fam) I'll die if she finds out (colloq); **~se DE algo** ‹de un infarto/ de cáncer› to die OF sth; **se moría de miedo/ aburrimiento** he was scared stiff/bored stiff; **me muero de frío** I'm freezing; **me estoy muriendo de hambre** I'm starving (colloq); **me muero por una cerveza** I'm dying for a beer (colloq); **se muere por verla** he's dying to see her (colloq)

morisco -ca *adj* Moorish, Morisco

morisqueta *f* (CS): **hacer ~s** to make o (BrE) pull faces

mormado -da *adj* (Méx) ‹nariz› blocked; **estoy ~** I'm all stuffed up (colloq)

mormón -mona *adj/m,f* Mormon

moro -ra *adj* **1** (Hist) Moorish **2** (Esp) (de África del Norte) (fam & pey) North African; (referido a un hombre machista) (fam) chauvinistic, sexist
■ *m,f* **1** **(a)** (Hist) Moor **(b)** (mahometano) Muslim **2** (Esp) (de África del Norte) (fam & pey) North African; (hombre machista)
■ *m* (fam) sexist, male chauvinist pig

morocho -cha *adj* (AmS fam) (de pelo oscuro) dark, dark-haired; (de piel oscura) dark
■ *m,f* (de pelo oscuro) dark-haired person (o man *etc*); (de piel oscura) dark person (o man *etc*)

morral *m* **(a)** (al hombro) rucksack, haversack; (a la espalda) backpack, rucksack **(b)** (para el pienso) nosebag

morralla *f* **1** (cosas sin valor) junk **2** (chusma) riffraff, rabble **3** (Méx) (dinero suelto) loose change

morriña *f* (fam) homesickness; **tener ~** to feel o be homesick

morro *m* **1** **(a)** (hocico) snout **(b)** (Esp fam) (boca) *tb* **~s** mouth, chops (*pl*) (BrE colloq); **estar de ~s (con algn)** (Esp fam) to be in a bad mood (with sb) **(c)** (Esp fam) (descaro) nerve (colloq) **(d)** (Esp fam) (de coche, avión) nose **2** (cerro) hill

morrón *m* (CS) (pimiento) red pepper

morsa *f* walrus

mortadela f mortadella

mortaja f [1] (sábana) shroud [2] (Tec) mortise

mortal adj [1] (a) ‹ser› mortal (b) ‹herida› fatal, mortal; ‹dosis› fatal, lethal; ‹enfermedad/ veneno› deadly; **un golpe ~** a death blow [2] ‹odio/enemigo› mortal
■ mf mortal

mortalidad f mortality; **la ~ infantil** infant mortality

mortecino -na adj ‹luz› weak; ‹color› pale

mortero m mortar

mortífero -ra adj deadly, lethal

mortificar [A2] vt (a) (atormentar) to torment; **los celos lo mortifican** he's tortured o tormented by jealousy (b) (Relig) to mortify
■ **mortificarse** v pron (refl) (atormentarse) to fret, distress oneself; (Relig) to mortify the flesh

mortuorio -ria adj funeral (before n)

mosaico m (a) (Art) mosaic (b) (Méx, RPI) (baldosa) floor tile; **piso de ~** tiled floor (c) (Col) (foto) school/college photograph

mosca f fly; **no se oía ni una ~** you could have heard a pin drop (colloq); **por si las ~s** (fam) just in case (colloq)

moscardón m botfly

moscatel adj muscat (before n)
■ m muscatel

moscovita adj/mf Muscovite

Moscú m Moscow

mosqueado -da adj (esp Esp fam) (a) (molesto, disgustado) annoyed, sore (AmE colloq), cross (BrE colloq) (b) (desconfiado, suspicaz) suspicious, wary

mosquearse [A1] v pron (esp Esp fam) (a) (sospechar, desconfiar) to get suspicious, smell a rat (colloq) (b) (disgustarse) to get annoyed, get sore (AmE colloq), to get cross (BrE colloq)

mosquetero m musketeer

mosquitero m, **mosquitera** f (de ventana) mosquito netting; (de tela) mosquito net

mosquito m mosquito

mostaza f mustard; (color) : **(de) color ~** mustard, mustard-colored*

mosto m grape juice, must

mostrador m (en tienda) counter; (en bar) bar; (en aeropuerto) check-in desk

mostrar [A10] vt to show; **muéstrame cómo funciona** show me how it works
■ **mostrarse** v pron (+ compl): **se mostró muy atento con nosotros** he was very obliging (to us); **se ~on partidarios de la propuesta** they expressed support for the proposal

mota f [1] (partícula) tiny bit, dot; **una ~ de polvo** a speck of dust [2] (Tex): **una tela a ~s** a spotted fabric; **una lana azul con ~s de colores** blue wool with flecks of colors [3] (AmC, Méx arg) (marihuana) grass (colloq), weed (sl) [4] (a) (para empolvarse) powder puff (b) (Méx) (borla) pom-pom

mote m [1] (apodo) nickname; **le pusieron como ~ 'el Oso'** they nicknamed him 'the Bear' [2] (Andes) (trigo) boiled wheat; (maíz) boiled corn (AmE) o (BrE) maize

moteado -da adj ‹tela› ‹jaspeado› flecked; (a lunares) dotted, spotted; ‹piel› mottled

motel m motel

motín m (de tropas, tripulación) mutiny; (de prisioneros) riot, rebellion

motivación f (incentivo) motivation; (motivo) motive

motivar [A1] vt [1] (en general) to motivate; **motivado por la venganza** motivated by revenge; **¿qué te motivó a hacerlo?** what made you do it? [2] (causar) to bring about, cause

motivo m [1] (a) (razón, causa) reason, cause; **el ~ de su viaje** the reason for her trip; **por este ~ nos hallamos aquí** that's (the reason) why we're here; **con ~ de algo** on the occasion of sth; **no des ~s para que te critiquen** don't give them cause to criticize you; **hay ~s para preocuparse** there is cause for concern; **el adulterio es ~ suficiente de divorcio** adultery is sufficient grounds for divorce; **sin ningún ~** for no reason at all; **¡que sea un ~!** (Col fam) let's drink to that! (colloq) (b) (propósito, finalidad) purpose; **el ~ de esta carta es …** the purpose of this letter is … [2] (Art, Lit, Mús) motif; **~s decorativos** decorative motifs

moto f (motocicleta) motorcycle, motorbike (BrE); (motoneta, escúter) (motor) scooter; **fue en ~** he went on his motorcycle

motocicleta f motorcycle

motociclismo m motorcycling

motociclista mf motorcyclist

motocross, moto-cross m motocross

motoneta f (AmL) (motor) scooter

motor¹ -triz, motor -tora adj motor (before n)

motor² m [1] (Tec) engine; **~ fuera (de) borda** outboard motor [2] (impulsor) driving force

motora f small motorboat, powerboat

motorismo m motorcycling

motorista mf (a) (que va en moto) motorcyclist (b) (Col) (automovilista) motorist (frml), driver

motorizado -da adj ‹ejército› motorized
■ m,f (Ven) motorcycle messenger o (BrE) courier

motudo -da adj (CS fam) frizzy

mousse /mus/ f or m mousse

mouton /mu'ton/ m sheepskin

movedizo -za adj ‹niño› restless, fidgety

mover [E9] vt [1] (a) (trasladar, desplazar) to move (b) (Jueg) ‹ficha/pieza› to move (c) (agitar): **no muevas la cámara** keep the camera still; **el viento movía los árboles** the wind shook the trees; **movió la cabeza** (asintiendo) he nodded (his head); (negando) she shook her head; **mueve la cola** it wags its tail (d) (accionar) to drive [2] (inducir): **~ a algn a hacer algo** to move sb to do sth
■ ~ vi (Jueg) to move
■ **moverse** v pron (a) (en general) to move; **no te muevas de ahí** don't move; **la lámpara se movía con el viento** the lamp was moving o swaying in the wind (b) (apresurarse) to hurry up, get a move on (colloq)

movida f [1] (Jueg) move [2] (Esp) (fam) (a) (asunto, rollo): **no me interesa la ~ ecológica** I'm not into this ecology thing (colloq); **anda en ~s chuecas** (Méx) he's into some shady deals (colloq) (b) (actividad cultural): **la ~ madrileña** the Madrid scene; **donde está la ~** where it's all going on

movido -da adj (a) (Fot) blurred (agitado) ‹mar› rough, choppy; ‹día/año› hectic, busy; ‹fiesta› lively

móvil *adj* mobile
■ *m* 1 (frml) (impulso) motive 2 (adorno) mobile 3 (Esp) (teléfono) cell phone (AmE), mobile (BrE)
movilidad *f* mobility
movilización *f* 1 (a) (Mil) mobilization (b) (Rels Labs) (manifestación) demonstration; **un calendario de movilizaciones** a program of industrial action 2 (Chi) (Transp) public transportation (AmE), public transport (BrE)
movilizar [A4] *vt* ⟨tropas/población⟩ to mobilize
■ **movilizarse** *v pron* 1 (Mil, Rels Labs) to mobilize 2 (CS) (desplazarse) to move around
movimiento *m* 1 (a) (en general) movement; **el menor ~ de la mano** the slightest movement of the hand; **el ~ surrealista** the surrealist movement; **~ pictórico** school of painting; **~ sísmico** earth tremor (b) (Fis, Tec) motion, movement; **poner algo en ~** to set sth in motion; **se puso en ~** it started moving (c) (agitación, actividad) activity; **una calle de mucho ~** a very busy street 2 (Mús) (parte de obra) movement; (compás) tempo 3 (Jueg) move
mozárabe *adj* Mozarabic
■ *mf* Mozarab
mozo -za *adj*: **en mis años ~s** in my youth; **sus hijos ya son ~s** her children are quite grown-up now
■ *m,f* (a) (ant) (joven) (*m*) young boy; (*f*) young girl; **los ~s del pueblo** the young people in the village (b) (AmS) (camarero) (*m*) waiter; (*f*) waitress (c) (Ferr) *tb* **~ de equipajes** *or* **de estación** porter
muaré *m* moiré
mucamo -ma (AmL) (*m*) servant; (*f*) maid, servant; **mucama de hotel** chambermaid
muchacha *f*: *tb* **~ de servicio** maid; *ver tb* MUCHACHO
muchacho -cha *m,f* (*m*) kid (colloq), boy, guy (colloq); (*f*) girl
muchedumbre *f* crowd
mucho¹ *adv* (a) ⟨salir/ayudar⟩ a lot; ⟨trabajar⟩ hard; **no salen ~** they don't go out much *o* a lot; **me gusta muchísimo** I like it very much *o* a lot; **~ mejor** a lot better; **por ~ que insistas** no matter how much you insist; **después de ~ discutir** after much discussion (b) (en respuestas): **¿estás preocupado? — mucho** are you worried? **— (yes, I am,) very; ¿te gusta? — sí, ~** do you like it? — yes, very much
mucho² -cha *adj* (a) (sing) a lot of; (en oraciones negativas, interrogativas) much, a lot of; **~ vino** a lot of wine; **no gano ~ dinero** I don't earn much *o* a lot of money; **¿ves mucha televisión?** do you watch much *o* a lot of television; **tiene mucha hambre** he's very hungry (b) (*pl*) many, a lot of; **había ~s extranjeros/muchas personas allí** there were many *o* a lot of foreigners/people there; **hace ~s años** many years ago
■ *pron* 1 (referido a cantidad) (a) (sing) a lot; (en oraciones negativas) much; **~ de lo dicho** a lot of what was said; **tengo ~ que hacer** I have a lot to do; **eso no es ~** that's not much; **no queda mucha** there isn't much left (b) (*pl*) many; **~s creen que ...** many (people) believe that ...; **~s de nosotros** many of us
2 **mucho** (a) (referido a tiempo): **hace ~ que no la veo** I haven't seen her for a long time; **¿te falta**

~ para terminar? will it take you long to finish?; **~ antes** long before; **¿tuviste que esperar ~?** did you have to wait long? (b) (en locs) **como mucho** at (the) most; **con mucho** by far, easily; **ni mucho menos** far from it; **por mucho que ...** however much ...
mucosidad *f* mucus, mucosity
muda *f* (de ropa) change of clothes; (de la piel) shedding, sloughing off
mudanza *f* move, removal (BrE); **camión de ~s** moving (AmE) *o* (BrE) removal van; **estoy de ~** I'm in the process of moving (house)
mudar [A1] *vi* 1 (cambiar): **las serpientes mudan de piel** snakes slough off *o* shed their skin; **cuando mudó de voz** when his voice broke 2 (Méx) (cambiar los dientes) to lose one's milk teeth
■ **~** *vt* 1 ⟨bebé/sábanas⟩ to change 2 (Zool) ⟨piel/plumas⟩ to molt, shed
■ **mudarse** *v pron* (a) (de casa) to move (house); **se ~on a una casa más grande** they moved to a bigger house (b) (de ropa) to get changed, change (one's) clothes
mudéjar *adj/mf* Mudejar
mudo -da *adj* (a) (Med) dumb, mute; **es ~ de nacimiento** he was born mute; **se quedó ~ de asombro** he was dumbfounded (b) ⟨letra⟩ silent, mute
■ *m,f* mute
mueble *m* piece of furniture; **los ~s del dormitorio** the bedroom furniture; **~ bar** drinks cabinet, cocktail cabinet; **~ cama** foldaway bed
mueca *f*: **hacerle ~s a algn** to make *o* (BrE) pull faces at sb; **sus graciosísimas ~s** her funny faces; **una ~ burlona** a sneer
muela *f* 1 (Odont) molar, back tooth; (como término genérico) tooth; **me sacaron una ~** I had a tooth taken out; **tengo dolor de ~s** I have (a) toothache; **~ del juicio** wisdom tooth 2 (de molino) millstone; (para afilar) whetstone 3 (Col) (en calle) parking bay; (en carretera) rest stop (AmE), lay-by (BrE)
muelle *m* 1 (Náut) (saliente) pier, mole; (rústico, más pequeño) jetty; (sobre la costa) quay, wharf 2 (resorte) spring
muera, mueras, etc ▶ MORIR
muérdago *m* mistletoe
muerte *f* death; **condenado a ~** sentenced to death; **a la ~ de su padre** on her father's death; **~ de cuna** crib death (AmE), cot death (BrE); **me dio un susto de ~** (fam) she scared me to death (colloq); **dar ~ a algn** (frml) to kill sb; **de mala ~** (fam) ⟨pueblo/hotel⟩ grotty (colloq); **ser la ~** (fam) (ser atroz) to be hell *o* murder (colloq); (ser estupendo) to be fantastic (colloq)
muerto -ta *adj* 1 [ESTAR] (a) ⟨persona/animal/planta⟩ dead; **lo dieron por ~** he was given up for dead; **resultaron ~s 30 mineros** 30 miners died *o* were killed; **caer ~** to drop dead (b) (fam) (cansado) dead beat (colloq) (c) (fam) (pasando, padeciendo): **estar ~ de hambre/frío/sueño** to be starving/freezing/dead-tired (colloq); **estaba ~ de miedo** he was scared stiff (colloq); **~ de (la) risa** (fam): **estaba ~ de risa** he was laughing his head off
2 (a) ⟨pueblo/zona⟩ dead, lifeless (b) (inerte) limp

■ *m,f* [1] (persona muerta): **hubo dos ~s** two people died *o* were killed; **hacerse el ~** to pretend to be dead; *cargar con el ~* (fam) (con un trabajo pesado) to do the dirty work; *cargarle el ~ a algn* (fam) (responsabilizar) to pin the blame on sb; (endilgarle la tarea) to give sb the dirty work (colloq); *hacer el ~* to float on one's back
[2] **muerto** *m* (en naipes) dummy

muesca *f* (a) (hendidura) nick, notch (b) (para encajar) slot, groove

muesli /'musli/ *m* muesli

muestra *f* [1] (a) (de mercancía) sample (b) (de sangre, orina) specimen, sample (c) (en estadísticas) sample [2] (prueba, señal) sign; **una ~ de cansancio/falta de madurez** a sign of tiredness/ immaturity; **como *o* en ~ de mi gratitud** as a token of my gratitude [3] (exposición) exhibition, exhibit (AmE); (de teatro, cine) festival

mueva, muevas, etc ▶ MOVER

mufa *f* (RPl fam) (a) (mal humor) bad mood (b) (moho) mold*

mugido *m* moo; **los ~s de las vacas** the mooing of the cows

mugir [I7] *vi* «*vaca*» to moo; «*toro*» to bellow

mugre *f* (suciedad) dirt, filth; (grasa) grime

mugriento -ta *adj* filthy

mugroso -sa *adj* (Chi, Méx fam) filthy

mujer *f* (a) woman; **ser ~** to be a woman; **~ de la limpieza** cleaning lady, cleaner; **~ de mala vida** *or* **de mal vivir** prostitute; **~ de negocios** businesswoman; **hacerse ~** (euf) to reach puberty, become a woman (euph) (b) (esposa) wife

mujeriego *m* womanizer

mújol *m* gray* mullet

mula *f* mule; **~ de carga** pack mule; *terco/ tozudo como una ~* as stubborn as a mule (colloq)
■ *adj* (Méx fam) stubborn

mulato -ta *adj* of mixed race (*black and white*), mulatto (dated *or* pej)
■ *m,f* person of mixed race (*of a black and a white parent*), mulatto (dated *or* pej)

muleta *f* [1] (bastón) crutch; (apoyo) crutch, prop [2] (Taur) red cape (*attached to a stick*)

muletilla *f* tag, filler (tech)

mulita *f* (Per) (de pisco) glass, shot

mullido -da *adj* ‹colchón/sofá› soft; ‹hierba› springy

mulo *m* (male) mule

multa *f* fine; **le pusieron una ~** she was fined

multar [A1] *vt* to fine

multicine *m* multiscreen movie complex (AmE), multiscreen cinema (BrE)

multicolor *adj* multicolored*

multicultural *adj* multicultural

multimillonario -ria *adj*: **es ~** he is a multimillionaire; **un contrato ~** a multi-million dollar (*o* pound *etc*) contract
■ *m,f* multimillionaire

multinacional *adj/f* multinational

múltiple *adj* [1] ‹aplicaciones/causas› many, numerous [2] ‹flor/imagen/fractura› multiple

multiplicación *f* [1] (Biol, Mat) multiplication [2] (incremento) increase

multiplicar [A2] *vt* to multiply; **~ algo POR algo** to multiply sth BY sth
■ ~ *vi* to multiply
■ **multiplicarse** *v pron* [1] «*especie*» to multiply, reproduce [2] (aumentar) to increase several times over

múltiplo *m* multiple

multitud *f* [1] (muchedumbre) crowd [2] ~ DE **algo** (muchos): **tengo (una) ~ de cosas que hacer** I have dozens of things to do (colloq); **una ~ de usos** an enormous variety of uses

multitudinario -ria *adj* ‹manifestación/ movilizaciones› mass (*before n*); ‹concierto› with mass audiences

multiuso *adj inv* multipurpose (*before n*)

mundano -na *adj* (a) ‹problemas/placeres› worldly (b) ‹fiesta› society (*before n*)

mundial *adj* ‹historia/mercado› world (*before n*); **la marca ~** the world record; **de fama ~** world-famous; **es un problema ~** it's a global *o* worldwide problem
■ *m*: *tb* **~es** *mpl* World Championship(s); **el ~ de fútbol** the World Cup

mundialmente *adv*: **es ~ famoso** he is world famous; **un producto conocido ~** a product well-known throughout the world

mundo *m* [1] (en general) world; **artistas venidos de todo el ~** artists from all over the world; **el mejor del ~** the best in the world; **me parece lo más normal del ~** it seems perfectly normal to me; **es conocido en todo el ~** he is known worldwide; **el ~ árabe** the Arab world; **el ~ de la droga** the drugs world; **el ~ del espectáculo** showbusiness; **todo el ~ lo sabe** everybody knows it; **el ~ es un pañuelo** it's a small world; **por nada del *or* en el ~: yo no me lo pierdo por nada del ~** I wouldn't miss it for the world; **no lo vendería por nada en el ~** I wouldn't sell it for anything in the world *o* (colloq) for all the tea in China; *traer a algn/venir al ~* to bring sb/come into the world; *ver ~* to see the world [2] (planeta, universo) planet, world; **él vive en otro ~** he's on another planet *o* in another world

munición *f* (carga) *tb* **municiones** ammunition, munitions (*pl*)

municipal *adj* ‹impuesto› local; ‹elecciones/ piscina/mercado› municipal

municipalidad *f* ▶ MUNICIPIO

municipio *m* (territorio) municipality; (entidad) town council; (edificio) town hall

muñeca *f* [1] (a) (Jueg) doll; **~ de trapo** rag doll; **jugar a las ~s** to play with dolls; **ser** *or* *parecer una ~* to be a little doll (b) (fam) (como apelativo) darling, honey (colloq) [2] (Anat) wrist

muñeco *m* [1] (a) (con forma humana) doll; (con forma de animal) toy animal; **~ de peluche** stuffed animal (AmE), soft toy (BrE); **~ de nieve** snowman (b) (de ventrílocuo, sastre, etc) dummy (c) (dibujo) figure [2] **muñecos** *mpl* (Per fam): **estar con los ~s** to be very nervous

muñequera *f* (Dep) wristband; (Med) wrist bandage

muñón *m* (de un miembro) stump

mural *adj* wall (*before n*), mural (*before n*)
■ *m* mural

muralista *adj/mf* muralist

m

muralla *f* **(a)** (de ciudad) walls (*pl*), city wall; (de convento) wall; **la M∼ China** the Great Wall of China **(b)** (Chi) (pared) wall

murciélago *m* bat

muriera, murió, etc ▶ MORIR

murmullo *m* (de voces) murmur

murmuraciones *fpl* gossip

murmurador -dora *adj* gossipy
■ *m,f* gossip

murmurar [A1] *vt* **(a)** (hablar bajo) to murmur; **le murmuró algo al oído** he whispered something in her ear **(b)** (con enojo) to mutter; **— no pienso hacerlo — murmuró** I won't do it, she muttered **(c)** (en son de crítica): **cosas que se murmuran en la oficina** rumors that go around the office
■ ∼ *vi* (criticar) to gossip (*maliciously*); ∼ DE algn to gossip ABOUT sb

muro *m* wall; **M∼ de las Lamentaciones** *or* **los Lamentos** Wailing Wall

mus *m*: *a Spanish card game*

musa *f* (Mit) Muse; (inspiración) muse

muscular *adj* muscular

musculatura *f* muscles (*pl*), musculature (tech)

músculo *m* muscle; **sacar ∼** to flex one's muscles

musculoso -sa *adj* muscular

muselina *f* muslin

museo *m* museum; **∼ de cera** wax museum, waxworks (*pl*); **∼ de ciencias naturales** natural science museum

musgo *m* moss

música *f* music; **pon algo de ∼** put some music on; **∼ ambiental** background music; (en tienda, fábrica) piped *o* canned music

musical *adj/m* musical

músico -ca *m,f* (compositor) composer; (instrumentista) musician; **∼ callejero** street musician, busker (BrE)

musitar [A1] *vt* to whisper, murmur

muslera *f* thighband

muslo *m* (Anat) thigh (Coc); **∼s de pollo** chicken legs

mustio -tia *adj* ⟦1⟧ ⟨flor/planta⟩ withered ⟦2⟧ (Méx fam) (hipócrita) two-faced (colloq)

musulmán -mana *adj/m,f* Muslim, Moslem

mutable *adj* changeable, mutable (frml)

mutación *f* mutation

mutilado -da *m,f* disabled person; **un ∼ de guerra** a disabled serviceman

mutilar [A1] *vt* **(a)** ⟨persona/pierna⟩ to mutilate; **quedó mutilado en el accidente** he was maimed as a result of the accident **(b)** ⟨árbol/estatua⟩ to vandalize

mutua *f* benefit society (AmE), friendly society (BrE)

mutual *f* (CS) (de asistencia económica) benefit society (AmE), friendly society (BrE)

mutuo -tua *adj* mutual; **de ∼ acuerdo** by mutual *o* joint agreement; **redundará en beneficio ∼** it will be to our mutual benefit

muy *adv* **(a)** very; **∼ poca gente** very few people; **son ∼ amigos** they're great friends; **∼ admirado** much admired; **∼ respetado** highly respected; **∼ bien, sigamos adelante** OK *o* fine, let's go on; **por ∼ cansado que estés** however *o* no matter how tired you are **(b)** (demasiado) too; **quedó ∼ dulce** it's rather *o* too sweet

Nn

N, n *f* (*read as* /'ene/) *the letter* N, n

N. (= **norte**) North, N

nabo *m* turnip

nácar *m* mother-of-pearl, nacre

nacer [E3] *vi* ⟦1⟧ **(a)** «niño/animal» to be born; **¿dónde naciste?** where were you born?; **al ∼** at birth; **nació para (ser) músico** he was born to be a musician **(b)** «pollito/insecto» to hatch **(c)** «hoja/rama» to sprout **(d)** «río» to have its source; «carretera» to start **(e)** «pelo/plumas» to grow ⟦2⟧ (surgir) «amistad/relación» to spring up; **∼ DE algo** «problema/situación» to arise *o* spring FROM sth; **nació de ella invitarlo** it was her idea to invite him

nacido -da *adj* born; **un niño recién ∼** a newborn baby

naciente *adj* ⟨sol⟩ rising (*before n*); **el ∼ interés por la ecología** the new interest in ecology

nacimiento *m* ⟦1⟧ (de niño, animal) birth; **es argentino de ∼** he's Argentinian by birth; **es sorda de ∼** she was born deaf ⟦2⟧ (de idea, movimiento) birth; **el ∼ de una amistad duradera** the start *o* beginning of a lasting friendship ⟦3⟧ (belén) crib

nación *f* nation; **las Naciones Unidas** the United Nations (*pl*)

nacional *adj* **(a)** (de la nación) ⟨deuda/reservas/industria⟩ national; **en todo el territorio ∼**

283

nacionalidad ·····:· naturaleza ···

throughout the country; **un programa de difusión ~** a program broadcast nationwide **(b)** ⟨*vuelo*⟩ domestic
■ *mf* (frml) (ciudadano) national

nacionalidad *f* (ciudadanía) nationality

nacionalismo *m* nationalism

nacionalista *adj* nationalist (*before n*)
■ *mf* nationalist

nacionalización *f* (de industria) nationalization; (naturalización) naturalization

nacionalizar [A4] *vt* ⟨*industria*⟩ to nationalize; ⟨*persona*⟩ to naturalize
■ **nacionalizarse** *v pron* «*persona*» to become naturalized

naco -ca *adj* (Méx fam & pey) plebby (colloq & pej)
■ *m, f* pleb (colloq & pej)

nada *pron* ① **(a)** nothing; **es mejor que ~** it's better than nothing; **de ~ sirve que le compres libros** there's no point in buying him books; **antes que** *or* **de ~** first of all; **no quiere ~** he doesn't want anything; **¡no sirves para ~!** you're useless; **sin decir ~** without a word **(b)** (*en locs*) **de nada** you're welcome; **nada de nada** (fam) not a thing; **nada más: no hay ~ más** there's nothing else; **¿algo más? — ~ más** anything else? — no, that's it *o* that's all; **~ más fui yo** (Méx) I was the only one who went; **salí ~ más comer** I went out right *o* straight after lunch; **sacó (~ más ni) ~ menos que el primer puesto** she came first no less; **para nada: no me gustó para ~** I didn't like it at all; **por nada: la compraron por ~** they bought it for next to nothing; **discuten por ~** they argue over nothing; **llora por ~** she cries at the slightest little thing
② (Esp) (en tenis) love; **quince-~** fifteen-love
■ *adv* : **no está ~ preocupado** he isn't at all *o* the least bit worried; **esto no me gusta ~** I don't like this at all *o* (colloq) one bit

nadador -dora *m,f* swimmer

nadar [A1] *vi* **(a)** «*persona/pez*» to swim; **¿sabes ~?** can you swim?; **~ (estilo) mariposa/pecho** to do (the) butterfly/breaststroke; **~ de espalda** *or* (Méx) **de dorso** to do (the) back stroke **(b)** «*ramas/hojas*» (flotar) to float **(c) nadar en** (tener mucho): **~ en dinero** to be rolling in money (colloq); **el pollo nadaba en grasa** the chicken was swimming in grease
■ **~** *vt* to swim

nadie *pron* nobody, no one; **no me ayudó ~** nobody helped me; **no vi a ~** I didn't see anybody; **sin que ~ se diera cuenta** without anyone noticing

nado *m* **(a) a nado: cruzó el río a ~** he swam across the river **(b)** (Méx, Ven) (natación) swimming

nafta *f* **(a)** (Quím) naphtha **(b)** (RPl) (gasolina) gas (AmE), petrol (BrE)

naftalina *f* (Quím) naphthalene; (para ropa) mothballs (*pl*)

naguas *fpl* (Méx fam) petticoat

náhuatl¹ *adj/mf* (*pl* **nahuas**) Nahuatl

náhuatl² *m* (idioma) Nahuatl

nailon *m* nylon

naipe *m* (playing) card; **juegos de ~s** card games

nalga *f* (Anat) buttock; **una inyección en la ~** an injection in the buttock *o* bottom

nalgada *f* (Méx) smack on the bottom

nana *f* **(a)** (canción de cuna) lullaby **(b)** (fam) (abuela) grandma (colloq), granny (colloq) **(c)** (Andes, Ven) (niñera) nanny

naranja *f* (fruta) orange; **~ amarga** Seville orange
■ *m* (color) orange
■ *adj* (*gen inv*) orange

naranjada *f* orangeade

naranjal *m* orange grove

naranjo *m* orange tree

narciso *m* **(a)** (Bot) daffodil; (género) narcissus **(b)** (persona) narcissist

narcótico *m* narcotic

narcotraficante *mf* drug-trafficker

narcotráfico *m* drug trafficking

nardo *m* spikenard, nard

nariz *f* **(a)** (Anat) nose; **sonarse la ~** to blow one's nose; **no te metas los dedos en la ~** don't pick your nose; **en mis/sus propias narices** right under my/his nose; **estar hasta las narices de algo/algn** (fam) to be fed up (to the back teeth) with sth/sb (colloq); **meter las narices en** *or* **la ~ en algo** (fam) to poke one's nose into sth (colloq) **(b)** (de avión) nose

narizota *f* (fam) schnozzle (AmE colloq), conk (BrE colloq)

narración *f* (relato) story; (acción de contar) account

narrador -dora *m,f* narrator

narrar [A1] *vt* (frml) **(a)** «*película/libro*» ⟨*hazañas/experiencias*⟩ to tell of (frml), to relate; ⟨*historia*⟩ to tell, relate **(b)** «*persona*» ⟨*historia*⟩ to tell, narrate (frml)

narrativa *f* (género) fiction; (narración) narrative

narrativo -va *adj* narrative

nasal *adj* nasal

nata *f* **(a)** (sobre leche hervida) skin **(b)** (Esp) ▶ CREMA B

natación *f* swimming

natal *adj* **(a)** ⟨*país*⟩ native (*before n*); ⟨*ciudad*⟩ home (*before n*) **(b)** (Méx) (originario): **es ~ de Chiapas** she was born in Chiapas

natalidad *f* birthrate

natillas *fpl* custard

natividad *f* **(a) la ~** (nacimiento de Cristo) the Nativity **(b) la N~** (navidad) Christmas

nativo -va *adj* **(a)** ⟨*tierra/país/lengua*⟩ native **(b)** ⟨*flora/fauna*⟩ native; **~ DE algo** native TO sth
■ *m,f* (aborigen) native; (hablante) native speaker

nato -ta *adj* ⟨*artista/deportista*⟩ born (*before n*)

natural *adj* ① **(a)** ⟨*fenómeno/ingrediente*⟩ natural; ⟨*fruta*⟩ fresh; **al ~** ⟨*mejillones*⟩ in brine **(b)** (a temperatura ambiente) ⟨*cerveza/gaseosa*⟩ unchilled **(c)** (Mús) natural ② **(a)** (espontáneo) ⟨*gesto/persona*⟩ natural **(b)** (inherente) natural, innate **(c)** (normal) natural; **me parece lo más ~ del mundo** it seems perfectly natural to me ③ (frml) (nativo) **ser ~ DE** to be a native OF, to come FROM
■ *m* **(a)** (carácter) nature **(b)** (nativo) native; **los ~es del lugar** people from the area

naturaleza *f* **(a)** (Ecol): **la ~** nature; **~ muerta** still life **(b)** (índole) nature

naturalidad *f*: su ~ her natural manner; **con la mayor** ~ **del mundo** as if it were the most natural thing in the world

naturalización *f* naturalization

naturalizarse [A4] *v pron* to become naturalized

naturismo *m* (estilo de vida) natural lifestyle

naturista *adj* ‹médico/tratamiento› natural

naufragar [A3] *vi* (a) «barco» to be wrecked; «persona» to be shipwrecked (b) «plan/negocio» to go under

naufragio *m* (a) (Náut) shipwreck (b) (fracaso) failure

náufrago -ga *adj* shipwrecked
■ *m,f* (Náut) shipwrecked person

náuseas *fpl* nausea, sickness; **sentir** *or* **tener** ~ to feel sick *o* nauseous; **me da** ~ it makes me sick

náutico -ca *adj* nautical

navaja *f* (de bolsillo) penknife; (para afeitar) razor

navajazo *m* (herida) knife wound

naval *adj* naval

nave *f* ⟦1⟧ (Náut) (arc *o* liter) ship; ~ **espacial** spacecraft, spaceship ⟦2⟧ (de iglesia) nave

navegabilidad *f* (de río) navigability; (de embarcación) seaworthiness

navegable *adj* ‹río› navigable; ‹barco› seaworthy

navegación *f* (acción de navegar) navigation; (tráfico) shipping; ~ **aérea** aerial navigation; ~ **fluvial** river navigation

navegador *m* (Inf) browser

navegante *mf* (a) (arc) (marino) mariner (arch) (b) (que determina el rumbo) navigator

navegar [A3] *vi* (a) «nave» to sail (b) «persona» (a vela) to sail (c) (determinar el rumbo) to navigate (d) (Inf): ~ **en la web** *or* **Red** to surf the Web
■ ~ *vt* (liter) to sail

Navidad *f* Christmas; **el día de** ~ Christmas Day; **¡feliz** ~**!** happy Christmas!; **en** ~ at Christmas (time)

navideño -ña *adj* Christmas (before n)

navío *m* ship

nazi *adj/mf* Nazi

nazismo *m* Nazism

NE (= nordeste) NE

neblina *f* mist

nebuloso -sa *adj* (a) (Meteo) misty (b) ‹idea/imagen› hazy, nebulous

necedad *f* (a) (cualidad) crassness (b) (dicho, acto): **decir** ~**es** to talk nonsense; **es una** ~ it's sheer stupidity

necesario -ria *adj* (imprescindible) necessary; **haré lo que sea** ~ I'll do whatever's necessary; **si es** ~ if necessary, if need be; **no es** ~ there's no need, it isn't necessary; **me sentía** ~ I felt needed

neceser *m* (estuche) toilet kit (AmE), toilet bag (BrE); (maleta pequeña) overnight bag

necesidad *f* ⟦1⟧ (a) (urgencia, falta) need; **no hay** ~ **de que se entere** there's no need for her to know; **en caso de** ~ if necessary, if need be (b) (cosa necesaria) necessity, essential (c) (pobreza) poverty, need ⟦2⟧ **necesidades** *fpl* (a) (requerimientos) needs (pl), requirements (pl) (b)

(privaciones) hardship; **pasar** ~**es** to suffer hardship (c) **hacer sus** ~**es** (euf) to relieve oneself (euph)

necesitado -da *adj* (a) (falto) ~ **DE algo** ‹de dinero› short OF sth; ‹de afecto› in need OF sth (b) (pobre) in need, needy
■ *m,f* needy person; **los** ~**s** the needy

necesitar [A1] *vt* to need; ⊕ **se necesita vendedora** saleswoman required; **necesito verte hoy** I need to see you today
■ ~ *vi* (frml) ~ **DE algo** to need sth

necio -cia *adj* (a) (tonto) stupid (b) (AmC, Col, Ven fam) (travieso) naughty

néctar *m* nectar

nectarina *f* nectarine

nefasto -ta *adj* ‹consecuencias› disastrous; ‹influencia› harmful; ‹tiempo/fiesta› (fam) awful (colloq)

negación *f* (acción) denial, negation; (antítesis) antithesis; (Ling) negative

negado -da *adj*: **ser** ~ **para algo** to be useless *o* hopeless at sth

negar [A7] *vt* (a) ‹acusación/rumor› to deny; **no puedo** ~**lo** I can't deny it; **niega habértelo dicho** she denies having told you (b) (no conceder) ‹permiso/favor› to refuse; **les** ~**on la entrada** they were refused entry
■ ~ *vi*: ~ **con la cabeza** to shake one's head
■ **negarse** *v pron* (rehusar) to refuse; ~**se A hacer algo** to refuse to do sth; **se negó a que llamáramos a un médico** he refused to let us call a doctor

negativa *f* (ante acusación) denial; (a propuesta) refusal

negativo¹ -va *adj* negative

negativo² *m* (Fot) negative

negligé /neʋli'ʒe/ *m* negligee

negligencia *f* negligence

negociable *adj* negotiable

negociación *f* ⟦1⟧ (Pol, Rels Labs) negotiation ⟦2⟧ (Méx) (empresa) business

negociado *m* ⟦1⟧ (departamento) department ⟦2⟧ (AmS fam) (negocio sucio) shady deal (colloq)

negociador -dora *adj* negotiating (before n)
■ *m,f* negotiator

negociante *mf* (a) (Com, Fin) (m) businessman; (f) businesswoman (b) (pey) (mercenario) money-grubber (colloq & pej)

negociar [A1] *vt/vi* to negotiate

negocio *m* (a) (Com) business; **montar** *or* **poner un** ~ to set up a business; **dedicarse a los** ~**s** to be in business; **hablar de** ~**s** to talk business; **en el mundo de los** ~**s** in the business world (b) (transacción) deal; **un buen** ~ a good deal (c) (CS) (tienda) store (AmE), shop (BrE) (d) (fam) (asunto) business (colloq)

negra *f* (a) (Mús) crotchet (b) (en ajedrez): **las** ~**s** the black pieces

negrita *f* boldface, bold type; **en** ~**(s)** in boldface, in bold (type)

negro¹ -gra *adj* (a) ‹pelo/hombre/raza› black; ‹ojos› dark (b) (fam) (por el sol) tanned (c) (sombrío) black, gloomy; **lo ve todo tan** ~ she's always so pessimistic; **pasarlas negras** (fam) to have a rough time of it (colloq)
■ *m,f* (persona de raza negra) black person

negro² *m* (color) black

negrura *f* blackness

nene -na *m,f* (Esp, RPl fam) **(a)** (niño pequeño) (*m*) little boy; (*f*) little girl; **los ~s** the kids (colloq) **(b)** (apelativo cariñoso) darling, honey **(c) nena** *f* (arg) (mujer) chick (AmE colloq), bird (BrE colloq)

nené *mf* (Ven fam) (*m*) little boy; (*f*) little girl

neocelandés -desa *adj* of/from New Zealand
■ *m,f* New Zealander

neologismo *m* neologism

neonazi *adj/mf* neonazi

neoyorquino -na *adj* of/from New York
■ *m,f* New Yorker

nepotismo *m* nepotism

Neptuno *m* Neptune

nervio *m* ① **(a)** (Anat) nerve **(b)** (en la carne) sinew; **carne con ~s** gristly meat ② **nervios** *mpl* nerves (*pl*); **tiene los ~s destrozados** his nerves are in shreds; **está enfermo de los ~s** he suffers with his nerves; **tengo unos ~s ...** I'm *o* I feel so nervous; **me muero de ~s** I'm a nervous wreck (colloq); **ponerle a algn los ~s de punta** to get on sb's nerves

nerviosismo *m* nervousness; **el ~ que producen los exámenes** the feeling of nervousness *o* nerves that exams produce

nervioso -sa *adj* ① ⟨persona/animal⟩ **(a)** [SER] (excitable) nervous **(b)** [ESTAR] (preocupado, tenso) nervous; **estoy muy ~ por lo de los exámenes** I'm very nervous about the exams **(c)** [ESTAR] (agitado) agitated; **últimamente se le nota ~** he's been on edge *o* (colloq) uptight lately; **ese ruido me pone muy nerviosa** that noise is getting on my nerves; **me pongo ~ cada vez que la veo** I get flustered every time I see her ② ⟨trastorno⟩ nervous; ⟨célula⟩ nerve (*before n*)

nervudo -da *adj* sinewy

neto -ta *adj* **(a)** ⟨sueldo/precio⟩ net **(b)** (claro) ⟨silueta/perfil⟩ distinct, clear

neumático *m* tire (AmE), tyre (BrE)

neumonía *f* pneumonia

neura *adj* (fam): **eso me pone ~** that drives me crazy *o* (BrE) mad (colloq); **es tan ~** he's so neurotic
■ *mf* (fam) ① (persona): **es un ~** he's a complete neurotic (colloq) ② **neura** *f*: **está con la ~** she's in a real state (colloq)

neurasténico -ca *adj/m,f* **(a)** (Med) neurasthenic **(b)** (fam) ▸ NEURA

neurólogo -ga *m,f* neurologist

neurosis *f* neurosis

neurótico -ca *adj/m,f* neurotic

neutral *adj* neutral

neutralizar [A4] *vt* to neutralize

neutro¹ -tra *adj* **(a)** (Elec, Fís) neutral **(b)** (Biol, Ling) neuter

neutro² *m* **(a)** (Ling) neuter **(b)** (AmL) (Auto) neutral

nevada *f* snowfall

nevado -da *adj* ⟨cumbres/picos⟩ snowcapped, snow-covered; ⟨campos/techos⟩ covered with snow

nevar [A5] *v impers* to snow

nevasca *f*, (CS) **nevazón** *f* blizzard, snowstorm

nevera *f* **(a)** (refrigerador) refrigerator, fridge, icebox (AmE); **~ congelador** fridge-freezer **(b)** (para picnic) cooler (AmE), cool bag/box (BrE)

nevoso -sa *adj* snowy

nexo *m* (enlace, vínculo) link

ni *conj* **(a)** (con otro negativo): **no vino él ~ su mujer** neither he nor his wife came; **yo no pienso ir — ~ yo** (tampoco) I don't intend going — neither do I; **~ fumo ~ bebo** I don't smoke or drink, I neither smoke nor drink; **no nos avisó ~ a él ~ a mí** he didn't tell him or me (either); **~ siquiera** not even; **¿ ~ siquiera piensas llamarlo?** aren't you even going to call him?; **no vendieron ~ un libro** they didn't sell a single book **(b)** (expresando rechazo, enfado): **¡~ hablar!** out of the question!; **~ aunque me lo ruegue** not even if he gets down on his knees

Nicaragua *f* Nicaragua

nicaragüense *adj/mf* Nicaraguan

nicho *m* (Arquit) niche; (en cementerio) *deep recess in a wall used as a tomb*

nicotina *f* nicotine

nidada *f* (de huevos) clutch; (de crías) clutch, brood

nido *m* nest; **un ~ de ladrones** a den of thieves; **un ~ de amor** a love nest

niebla *f* fog; **había ~** it was foggy

niega, niegas, etc ▸ NEGAR

nieto -ta *m,f* (*m*) grandson, grandchild; (*f*) granddaughter, grandchild; **mis ~s** my grandchildren

nieva ▸ NEVAR

nieve *f* **(a)** (Meteo) snow **(b)** (Coc): **batir las claras a ⟨punto de⟩ ~** whisk the egg whites until stiff **(c)** (Méx) (helado) sorbet, water ice

nimiedad *f* triviality

nimio -mia *adj* trivial, petty

ningún *adj*: *apocopated form of* NINGUNO *used before masculine singular nouns*

ningunear [A1] *vt* (Méx fam) to treat ... like dirt (colloq)

ninguno -na *adj* (*see note under* NINGÚN) **(a)** (delante del n): **no prestó ninguna atención** he didn't pay any attention; **en ningún momento** never; **no lo encuentro por ningún lado** I can't find it anywhere **(b)** (detrás del n): **no hay problema ~** there's absolutely no problem
■ *pron* **(a)** (refiriéndose — a dos personas o cosas) neither; (— a más de dos) none; **~ de los dos vino** neither of them came; **no trajo ~ de los dos** she didn't bring either of them; **~ de nosotros la conoce** none of us know her **(b)** (nadie) nobody, no-one

niña *f* pupil; *ver tb* NIÑO *m,f*

niñera *f* nanny, nursemaid (AmE)

niñería *f* (pey): **déjate de ~s** stop being so childish

niñez *f* childhood

niño -ña *adj* (joven) young; (infantil, inmaduro) immature, childish
■ *m,f* **(a)** (*m*) boy, child; (*f*) girl, child; (bebé) baby; **¿te gustan los ~s?** do you like children?; **de ~** as a child; **~ bien** rich kid (colloq); **~ de pecho** small *o* young baby; **el ~ mimado de la maestra** the teacher's favorite* *o* pet; **~ prodigio** ···⊹

child prodigy **(b)** (con respecto a los padres) *(m)* son, child; *(f)* daughter, child; **tengo que llevar al ∼ al dentista** I have to take my son to the dentist

nipón -pona *adj/m,f* Japanese

níquel *m* nickel

níspero *m* loquat

nitidez *f* (de imagen, del día) clarity; (de recuerdo) vividness

nítido -da *adj* ⟨foto/imagen⟩ clear

nitrógeno *m* nitrogen

nivel *m* **(a)** (altura) level **(b)** (en escala, jerarquía) level; **conversaciones de alto ∼** high-level talks; **∼ de vida** standard of living; **no está al ∼ de los demás** he's not up to the same standard as the others; **el ∼ de las universidades mexicanas** the standard of Mexican universities

nivelar [A1] *vt* **(a)** (Const) ⟨suelo/terreno⟩ to level; ⟨estante⟩ to get ... level **(b)** ⟨presupuesto⟩ to balance

no *adv* **(a)** (como respuesta) no; (modificando adverbios, oraciones, verbos) not [*la negación de la mayoría de los verbos ingleses requiere el uso del auxiliar 'do'*] **¿te gustó? — no** did you like it? — no, I didn't; **¿vienes o ∼?** are you coming or not?; **∼ te preocupes** don't worry; **¿por qué ∼ quieres ir? — porque ∼** why don't you want to go? — I just don't **(b)** (con otro negativo): **∼ veo nada** I can't see a thing *o* anything; **∼ viene nunca** she never comes **(c)** (en coletillas interrogativas): **está mejor ¿∼?** she's better, isn't she?; **ha dimitido ¿∼?** he has resigned, hasn't he? **(d)** (expresando incredulidad): **se ganó la lotería — ¡no!** he won the lottery — he didn't! *o* no! **(e)** (sustituyendo a una cláusula): **creo que ∼** I don't think so; **¿te gustó? a mí ∼** did you like it? I didn't **(f)** (*delante de n, adj, pp*): **los ∼ fumadores** nonsmokers; **la ∼ violencia** non-violence; **un hijo ∼ deseado** an unwanted child

■ *m (pl* **noes**) no

NO (= **noroeste**) NW

Nobel *m* **(a)** *tb* **Premio ∼** Nobel Prize **(b)** (ganador) Nobel prizewinner

noble *adj* **(a)** (en general) noble; **un caballero de ∼ linaje** (liter) a knight of noble lineage (liter) **(b)** ⟨madera⟩ fine

■ *mf (m)* nobleman; *(f)* noblewoman; **los ∼** the nobles, the nobility

nobleza *f* nobility

nocaut *adj* (AmL): **lo dejó ∼** he/it knocked him out; **está ∼** he's out for the count

■ *m (pl* **-cauts**) (AmL) knockout

noche *f* **(a)** night; **la ∼ anterior** the night before, the previous evening; **esta ∼** tonight, this evening; **¡buenas ∼s!** (al saludar) good evening!; (al despedirse) goodnight **(b)** (*en locs*) **de noche** ⟨trabajar/conducir⟩ at night; ⟨vestido/función⟩ evening (*before n*); **hacerse de ∼** to get dark; **en la** *or* (esp Esp) **por la** *or* (RPI) **a la noche: en la ∼ fuimos al teatro** in the evening we went to the theater; **el lunes en la ∼** on Monday evening/ night; **de la ∼ a la mañana** overnight

Nochebuena *f* Christmas Eve

Nochevieja *f* New Year's Eve (*in the evening*)

noción *f* **(a)** (idea, concepto) notion, idea; **no tiene la menor ∼ del tema** he doesn't know the first thing about the subject **(b)** **nociones** *fpl* (conocimientos): **tengo nociones de ruso** I have a smattering of Russian; **las nociones de electrónica** the basics *o* rudiments of electronics

nocivo -va *adj* ⟨sustancia⟩ harmful; ⟨influencia⟩ damaging

noctámbulo -la *adj*: **siempre ha sido ∼** he's always been a night bird *o* (AmE) nighthawk (colloq)

nocturno -na *adj* **(a)** ⟨vuelo/tren/vida⟩ night (*before n*); ⟨clases⟩ evening (*before n*) **(b)** ⟨animal/planta⟩ nocturnal

nodriza *f* (ama de cría) wet nurse; (niñera) (ant) nursemaid

nogal *m* (árbol) walnut tree; (madera) walnut

nómada *adj* nomadic

■ *mf* nomad

nomás *adv* **(a)** (AmL): **pase ∼** come on in; **no lo vas a convencer así ∼** you're not going to convince him as easily as that; **déjelo aquí ∼** just leave it here; **lo dijo por molestar ∼** she only said it to be difficult **(b)** **nomás (que)** (Col, Méx fam) as soon as; **∼ (que) tenga dinero** as soon as I have some money

nombramiento *m* (designación) appointment; (documento) letter of appointment

nombrar [A1] *vt* **(a)** (citar, mencionar) to mention; **no lo volvió a ∼** she never mentioned his name *o* him again **(b)** (designar) to appoint

nombre *m* **(a)** (de cosa, persona, animal) name; **∼ y apellidos** full name, name in full; **∼ artístico** stage name; **∼ de pila** first name, christian name; **∼ de soltera** maiden name; **¿qué ∼ le pusieron?** what did they call him?; **lo conozco de ∼** I know him by name; **en ∼ de** (en representación de) on behalf of; (apelando a) in the name of; **a ∼ de** ⟨paquete/carta⟩ made payable to, made out to; **lo que ha hecho no tiene ∼** what she has done is unspeakable **(b)** (Ling) noun; **∼ compuesto** compound noun **(c)** (fama): **un científico de ∼** a renowned scientist; **hacerse un ∼ en la vida** to make a name for oneself

nómina *f* (lista de empleados) payroll; (hoja de pago) payslip; (suma de dinero) salary, wages (*pl*)

nominación *f* nomination

nominar [A1] *vt* to nominate

nominativo *adj* (Fin): **un cheque ∼ a favor de** ... a check made out to *o* payable to ...

nomo *m* gnome

non *adj* odd

■ *m* odd number; **pares y ∼es** odds and evens

noqueada *f* knockout

noquear [A1] *vt* to knock out

noratlántico -ca *adj* north-Atlantic (*before n*)

nordeste, noreste *adj inv* ⟨región⟩ northeastern; **iban en dirección ∼** they were heading northeast

■ *m* (punto cardinal) northeast, Northeast; **vientos del ~** northeasterly winds

nórdico -ca *adj* ‹país/pueblo› Nordic (*esp Scandinavian*)

noria *f* **(a)** (para sacar agua) waterwheel **(b)** (Ocio) Ferris wheel (AmE), big wheel (BrE)

norma *f* **(a)** (regla) rule, regulation; **~s de conducta** rules of conduct; **~s de seguridad** safety regulations; **tengo por ~ ...** I make it a rule ... **(b)** (manera común de hacer algo): **la ~ es que acudan los directivos** it is standard practice for the directors to attend

normal *adj* normal; **es ~ que reaccionen así** it's normal for them to react like that; **hoy en día es muy ~** it's very common nowadays; **no es ~ que haga tanto frío** it's unusual *o* it isn't normal for it to be so cold; **superior a lo ~** above-average; **~ y corriente** ordinary
■ *f* **(a)** (escuela): **la N ~** teacher training college **(b)** (gasolina) regular gas (AmE), two-star petrol (BrE)

normalidad *f* **(a)** (cualidad): **con ~** normally **(b)** (situación) normality, normalcy (AmE); **el país volvió a la ~** the country returned to normal

normalización *f* **(a)** (de situación) normalization **(b)** (estandarización) standardization

normalizar [A4] *vt* **(a)** ‹situación/relaciones› to normalize **(b)** (estandarizar) to standardize
■ **normalizarse** *v pron* **(a)** «situación/relaciones» to return to normal **(b)** (estandarizarse) to become standardized

normalmente *adv* normally, usually

noroeste *adj inv* ‹región› northwestern; **iban en dirección ~** they were heading northwest
■ *m* (punto cardinal) northwest, Northwest; **vientos del ~** northwesterly winds

norte *adj inv* ‹región› northern; ‹costa/ala› north (*before n*); **iban en dirección ~** they were heading north *o* northward(s)
■ *m* north, North; **al ~ de Matagalpa** to the north of Matagalpa; **vientos del N~** northerly winds; **caminaron hacia el N~** they walked north *o* northward(s); **la casa da al ~** the house faces north

Norteamérica *f* (América del Norte) North America; (EEUU) America, the States (colloq)

norteamericano -na *adj/m,f* (de América del Norte) North American; (estadounidense) American

norteño -ña, (Chi, Per) **nortino -na** *adj* northern
■ *m,f* northerner

Noruega *f* Norway

noruego¹ -ga *adj/m,f* Norwegian

noruego² *m* (idioma) Norwegian

nos *pron pers* **(a)** (como complemento directo, indirecto) us; **~ ayudaron mucho** they helped us a lot; **escúchanos** listen to us; **~ han robado el coche** our car's been stolen **(b)** (*refl*) ourselves; **~ hicimos daño** we hurt ourselves; **sentémonos** let's sit down **(c)** (*recípr*): **~ conocemos desde hace años** we have known each other for years

nosotros -tras *pron pers pl* **(a)** we; **¿quién lo trajo? — nosotros** who brought it? — we did; **ábrenos, somos nosotras** open the door, it's us; **~ mismos lo arreglamos** we fixed it ourselves **(b)** (en comparaciones, con preposiciones) us; **antes/después que ~** before/after us; **ven con ~** come with us

nostalgia *f* nostalgia; **siente ~ por su país** he feels homesick

nostálgico -ca *adj* nostalgic

nota *f* ⬚**1** (apunte, mensaje) note; **tomar ~ de algo** (apuntar) to make a note of sth; (fijarse) to take note of sth; **tomar ~s** to take notes; **~ a pie de página** footnote ⬚**2** **(a)** (Educ) (calificación) grade (AmE), mark (BrE) (Mús) note ⬚**3** (detalle) touch; **una ~ de humor** a touch of humor
■ *m* **(a)** (Educ) *grade between 7 and 8.5 on a scale from 1 to 10* **(b)** (persona importante) dignitary

notable *adj* ‹diferencia/mejoría› notable; **una actuación ~** an outstanding performance; **posee una ~ inteligencia** she is remarkably *o* extremely intelligent
■ *m* **(a)** (Educ) *grade between 7 and 8.5 on a scale from 1 to 10* **(b)** (persona importante) dignitary

notar [A1] *vt* **(a)** (advertir) to notice; **no noté nada extraño** I didn't notice anything strange; **hacer(le) ~ algo** (a algn) to point sth out (to sb); **te noto muy triste** you look very sad; **se le notaba indeciso** he seemed hesitant **(b)** (*impers*): **se nota que es novato** you can tell *o* see he's a beginner; **se te nota en la cara** it's written all over your face
■ **notarse** *v pron* (+ *compl*) to feel; **me noto rara con este vestido** I feel funny in this dress

notaría *f* **(a)** (profesión) *profession of notary*; (oficina) notary's office **(b)** (Col) (registro civil) registry office

notarial *adj* notarial

notario -ria *m,f* notary, notary public

noticia *f* ⬚**1** (información): **una ~** a piece *o* an item of news; **buenas/malas ~s** good/bad news; **la última ~ del programa** the final item on the news; **una ~ de última hora** a late *o* last-minute news item ⬚**2** **noticias** *fpl* **(a)** (referencias) news; **no hemos tenido ~s suyas** (provenientes de él) we haven't heard from him; (provenientes de otra persona) we haven't had (any) news of him **(b)** (Rad, TV) news

noticiario *m*, (AmL) **noticiero** *m* (Rad, TV) news; (Cin) newsreel

notificación *f* (frml) notification (frml)

notificar [A2] *vt* (frml) to notify

notorio -ria *adj* **(a)** (evidente) evident, obvious **(b)** (conocido) well-known **(c)** (notable) ‹descenso/mejora› marked

nov. (= **noviembre**) Nov

novato -ta *adj* inexperienced, new
■ *m,f* novice, beginner

novecientos -tas *adj/pron* nine hundred; *para ejemplos ver* QUINIENTOS

novedad *f* ⬚**1** **(a)** (innovación) innovation; **la última ~ en el campo de la informática** the latest innovation in the field of computing **(b)** (cualidad, cosa nueva) novelty; **eran una ~ en aquel entonces** they were a novelty then ⬚**2** (noticia): **¿alguna ~?** any news?; **eso no es ninguna ~** everybody knows that; **sin ~** ‹llegar› safely; **¿cómo sigue? — sin ~** how is he? — much the same

novedoso -sa *adj* ‹idea/enfoque› novel, original

novela *f* (Lit) novel; (TV) soap opera; **~ policíaca** detective novel *o* story; **~ rosa** (pey) novelette (pej), romantic novel

novelesco -ca *adj* ⟨*vida/historia*⟩ like something out of a novel; ⟨*viajes/andanzas*⟩ fabulous

novelista *mf* novelist

noveno¹ -na *adj/pron* ninth; **la novena parte** a ninth; *para ejemplos ver* QUINTO

noveno² *m* ninth

noventa *adj inv/pron/m* ninety; *para ejemplos ver* CINCUENTA

noviar [A1] *vi* (AmL fam) to go out together, to date (AmE); ~ **CON algn** to go out WITH sb, to date sb (AmE)

noviazgo *m*: **el ~ duró un año** they went out (together) for one year; **~s a larga distancia** long-distance relationships

novicio -cia *m,f* novice

noviembre *m* November; *para ejemplos ver* ENERO

novillo -lla *m,f* (*m*) young bull; (*f*) heifer; **hacer ~s** (fam) to play hooky (esp AmE colloq), to skive off (school) (BrE colloq)

novio -via *m,f* **(a)** (no formal) (*m*) boyfriend; (*f*) girlfriend; (después del compromiso) (*m*) fiancé; (*f*) fiancée **(b)** (el día de la boda) (*m*) groom; (*f*) bride; **los ~s** the bride and groom

nubarrón *m* storm cloud

nube *f* (Meteo) cloud; (de polvo, humo) cloud; (de insectos) cloud, swarm; **un cielo cubierto de ~s** an overcast *o* a cloudy sky; **~ atómica** mushroom cloud; **estar** or **andar en las ~s** (fam) to have one's head in the clouds

nublado -da *adj* ⟨*cielo/día*⟩ cloudy, overcast

nublar [A1] *vt* **(a)** ⟨*vista*⟩ to cloud **(b)** (liter) ⟨*felicidad*⟩ to cloud (liter)

■ **nublarse** *v pron* **(a)** «*cielo*» to cloud over **(b)** «*vista*» to cloud over

nubosidad *f*: **la ~ irá en aumento** it will become increasingly cloudy; **un día con mucha ~** a day with a lot of cloud about

nuboso -sa *adj* cloudy

nuca *f* back *o* nape of the neck

nuclear *adj* nuclear

núcleo *m* **(a)** (Biol, Fís) nucleus **(b)** (Elec) core

nudillo *m* knuckle

nudismo *m* nudism

nudista *adj/mf* nudist

nudo *m* **(a)** (en general) knot; **se hizo un ~ en el hilo** the thread got into a knot; **¿me haces el ~ de la corbata?** can you do my tie for me?; **tenía un ~ en la garganta** I had a lump in my throat **(b)** (de carreteras, vías férreas) junction

nuera *f* daughter-in-law

nuestro -tra *adj* our; **~ coche** our car; **un amigo ~** a friend of ours

■ *pron*: **el ~, la nuestra** *etc* ours; **es de los ~s** he's one of us; **nosotros a lo ~** let's just get on with our own business; **sabe lo ~** he knows about us

Nueva York *f* New York

Nueva Zelandia, Nueva Zelanda *f* New Zealand

nueve *adj inv/pron/m* nine; *para ejemplos ver* CINCO

nuevo -va *adj* **(a)** [SER] ⟨*estilo/coche/novio*⟩ new; **soy ~ en la oficina** I'm new in the office; **de ~** again; **¿qué hay de ~?** what's new? (colloq); **~ rico** nouveau riche **(b)** (delante del *n*) ⟨*intento/cambio*⟩ further; **ha surgido un ~ problema** another *o* a further problem has arisen; **N~ Testamento** New Testament **(c)** [ESTAR] (no desgastado) as good as new

Nuevo México *m* New Mexico

nuez *f* ⃞1 **(a)** (del nogal) walnut **(b)** (Méx) (pacana) pecan (nut) **(c)** **~ moscada** nutmeg ⃞2 (Anat) Adam's apple

nulidad *f* ⃞1 (Der) nullity ⃞2 (fam) (calamidad) dead loss (colloq); **soy una ~ para los idiomas** I'm useless at languages

nulo -la *adj* **(a)** (Der) ⟨*testamento/votación*⟩ null and void; ⟨*voto*⟩ void **(b)** ⟨*persona*⟩ useless (colloq), hopeless (colloq) **(c)** (inexistente): **mis conocimientos del tema son ~s** my knowledge of the subject is virtually nil

Núm., núm. (= **número**) no.

numerable *adj* countable

numeración *f* (acción) numbering; (números) numbers (*pl*); (sistema) numerals (*pl*)

numeral *adj/m* numeral

numerar [A1] *vt* to number

número *m* ⃞1 **(a)** (Mat) number; **~ de identificación personal** PIN number, Personal Identification Number; **~ de matrícula** license number (AmE), registration number (BrE); **~ de serie** serial number; **~ de teléfono/fax** phone/fax number; **una suma de seis ~s** a six figure sum; **problemas sin ~** innumerable *o* countless problems **(b)** (de zapatos) size; **¿qué ~ calzas?** what size shoe do you take? **(c)** (billete de lotería) lottery ticket ⃞2 **(a)** (Espec) act **(b)** (de publicación) issue

numeroso -sa *adj* ⟨*clase/grupo*⟩ large; ⟨*ocasiones/ejemplos*⟩ numerous, many

nunca *adv* never; **como ~** like never before; **casi ~** hardly ever; **más que ~** more than ever (before); **~ más** never again

nuncio *m* (Relig) *tb* **~ apostólico** papal nuncio

nupcial *adj* ⟨*festejos*⟩ (liter) nuptial (liter); ⟨*ceremonia*⟩ wedding (*before n*)

nupcias *fpl* (liter) nuptials (*pl*) (liter), wedding; **en 1970 se casó en segundas ~ con doña Inés Díaz** in 1970 he married his second wife, Inés Díaz

nutria *f* otter

nutrición *f* nutrition

nutrido -da *adj*: **mal ~** undernourished, malnourished; **bien ~** well-nourished

nutrir [I1] *vt* ⟨*organismo*⟩ to nourish; ⟨*niño/planta*⟩ to nourish, feed

nutritivo -va *adj* ⟨*alimento*⟩ nutritious; ⟨*valor*⟩ nutritional

nylon /ˈnajlon, niˈlon/ *m* nylon

Ññ

Ñ, ñ *f* (*read as* /'eɲe/) *the letter* Ñ, ñ
ñandú *m* rhea
ñandutí *m* nanduti (*fine Paraguayan lace*)
ñango -ga *adj* (Méx fam) wimpish (colloq)
ñapa *f* (AmL fam) *small amount of extra goods
given free*, lagniappe (AmE); **dar algo de ~** to
throw sth in (for free) (colloq); **me dio dos de ~**
she threw in a couple extra

ñato -ta *adj* (AmS fam) ⟨*persona*⟩ snub-nosed;
⟨*animal*⟩ pug-nosed
ñauca (Chi), (RPl) **ñaupa** *f* (fam): **es del año de
~** it's really ancient (colloq); **ropa del año de ~**
clothes that went out with the ark (colloq)
ñoquis *mpl* (Coc) gnocchi (*pl*)
ñorbo *m* (Ec, Per) passionflower
ñu *m* gnu, wildebeest

Oo

O, o *f* (*read as* /o/) *the letter* O, o
o *conj* or; **¿vienes o no?** are you coming or not?;
o ... o ... either ... or ...; **o mañana o el jueves**
either tomorrow or Thursday; [*between two digits*
o *is written with an accent*: **unas 100 ó 120** about
100 or 120]; **o sea** ▶ SER *vi* II

O. (= **oeste**) W, West
oasis *m* (*pl* ~) oasis
obcecarse [A2] *v pron* to become obsessed; **está
obcecado con la idea** he's obsessed with the idea
obedecer [E3] *vt* **(a)** ⟨*orden/norma*⟩ to obey,
comply with **(b)** ⟨*persona*⟩ to obey; **obedece a tu
madre** do as your mother tells you
■ ~ *vi* **(a)** «*persona*» to obey; **para que aprendas
a ~** to teach you to do as you're told **(b)**
«*mecanismo*» to respond **(c)** (frml) (a motivo, causa)
~ A algo to be due TO sth
obediente *adj* obedient
obelisco *m* obelisk
obertura *f* overture
obesidad *f* obesity
obeso -sa *adj* obese
obispo *m* bishop
objeción *f* objection; **nadie puso objeciones**
nobody objected *o* made any objection; **~ de
conciencia** conscientious objection
objetar [A1] *vt* to object; **¿tienes algo que ~?**
do you have any objection?
■ ~ *vi* (Esp fam) to declare oneself a conscientious
objector
objetividad *f* objectivity; **con ~** objectively
objetivo¹ -va *adj* objective
objetivo² *m* **[1]** (finalidad) objective, aim; (Mil)
objective **[2]** (Fot, Ópt) lens
objeto *m* **[1]** (cosa) object; **~s de valor**
valuables; **~s de uso personal** items *o* articles
for personal use; **~s perdidos** lost and found
(AmE), lost property (BrE); **~ volador no
identificado** unidentified flying object, UFO
[2] (a) (finalidad) aim, object; **con el ~ de hacer**

algo in order to do sth, with the aim of doing
sth; **con el ~ de que se conozcan** so that they
can get to know each other; **ser ~ de algo** (de
admiración/críticas) to be the object of sth; (de
investigación/estudio) to be the subject of sth; **ser ~
de malos tratos** to be ill-treated **(b)** (Ling) object
objetor -tora *m,f* objector; **~ de conciencia**
conscientious objector
oblicuo -cua *adj* ⟨*línea*⟩ oblique
obligación *f* **(a)** (deber) obligation; **cumplió con
sus obligaciones** he fulfilled his obligations; **tiene
(la) ~ de ...** it is his duty to ..., he has an
obligation to ...; **es mi ~ decírtelo** it is my duty
to tell you; **lo hace por ~** she does it out of
obligation; **si sus obligaciones se lo permiten** if
her commitments permit
obligado -da *adj* [ESTAR] ⟨*persona*⟩ obliged; **~
A hacer algo** obliged to do sth; **se vio ~ a
acompañarla** he felt obliged to accompany her
obligar [A3] *vt* **(a)** **~ a algn A hacer algo** to
force sb to do sth, to make sb do sth; **no lo
obligues a comer** don't force him to eat; **nos
obligan a llevar uniforme** we are required to wear
uniform; **~ a algn A QUE haga algo** to make sb
do sth **(b)** «*ley/disposición*» to bind
obligatorio -ria *adj* compulsory, obligatory;
no es ~ firmarlo it doesn't have to be signed
oboe *m* (instrumento) oboe
■ *mf* (músico) oboist
obra *f* **[1]** (creación artística) work; **sus primeras
~s** her earliest works; **una ~ de artesanía** a
piece of craftsmanship; **sus ~s de teatro** her
plays; **~ de arte** work of art; **~ maestra**
masterpiece **[2]** (acción): **mi buena ~ del día** my
good deed for the day; **~ benéfica** (acto) act of
charity; (organización) charity, charitable
organization **[3]** (Arquit, Const) **(a)** (construcción)
building work; **estamos de ~s** we're having
some building work done **(b)** (sitio) building *o*
construction site
obrar [A1] *vi* (actuar) to act; **~ de buena fe** to act
in good faith   ⋯⋯>

■ ~ vt ⟨milagros⟩ to work

obrera f (hormiga) worker (ant); (abeja) worker (bee); ver tb OBRERO m, f

obrero -ra adj ⟨barrio⟩ working-class; **el movimiento** ~ the workers' movement; **la clase obrera** the working class
■ m,f (de fábrica, industria) worker; **los ~s dejaron la arena en el jardín** the workmen left the sand in the garden

obsceno -na adj obscene

obscuro, etc ▶ OSCURO, ETC

obsequio m (frml) gift

observación f ① (examen, vigilancia) observation; **tener a algn en** ~ (Med) to keep sb under observation; **tener mucha capacidad de** ~ to be very observant ② (comentario) observation, remark; (en texto) note

observador -dora m,f observer

observar [A1] vt (a) (en general) to observe; **alguien la observaba** someone was watching o (frml) observing her (b) (notar) to observe (frml); **¿has observado algún cambio?** have you noticed o observed any changes?

observatorio m observatory

obsesión f obsession

obsesionar [A1] vt to obsess; **estaba obsesionado con la idea** he was obsessed with the idea
■ **obsesionarse** v pron to become obsessed

obsesivo -va adj obsessive

obsidiana f obsidian

obsoleto -ta adj obsolete

obstaculizar [A4] vt ⟨progreso/trabajo⟩ to hinder, hamper; ⟨tráfico⟩ to hold up; **no obstaculice el paso** don't stand in the way

obstáculo m obstacle

obstante: **no obstante** (sin embargo) nevertheless, nonetheless; (a pesar de) despite, in spite of

obstinado -da adj (a) (tozudo) obstinate, stubborn (b) (tenaz) tenacious, dogged

obstinarse [A1] v pron ~ **EN hacer algo** to (obstinately) insist ON doing sth; **se obstinó en no ir** he obstinately refused to go; **se ha obstinado en que hay que terminarlo hoy** he is bent on finishing it today

obstrucción f obstruction

obstruir [I20] vt ① (bloquear) ⟨conducto⟩ to block; ⟨salida⟩ to block, obstruct ② (entorpecer) ⟨plan/proceso⟩ to obstruct; ⟨tráfico⟩ to obstruct, hold up; ⟨progreso⟩ to impede ③ (Dep) to obstruct
■ **obstruirse** v pron to get blocked (up)

obtener [E27] vt ⟨premio⟩ to win, receive; ⟨resultado/autorización⟩ to obtain; ⟨calificación⟩ to obtain, set

obturador m (Fot) shutter

obtuve, obtuvo, etc ▶ OBTENER

obvio -via adj obvious

oca f (Zool) goose

ocasión f ① (a) (vez, circunstancia) occasion; con ~ de on the occasion of; **en alguna** ~ occasionally (b) (momento oportuno) opportunity; **no tuve** ~ **de hablarle** I didn't have an opportunity o a chance to talk to him ② (ganga) bargain; **de** ~ ⟨precios⟩ bargain (before n); ⟨muebles⟩ (usados) secondhand; (baratos) cut-rate o (BrE) cut-price; ⟨coches⟩ secondhand

ocasional adj ⟨encuentro⟩ chance (before n); ⟨trabajo⟩ temporary

ocasionar [A1] vt to cause

occidental adj ⟨zona⟩ western; ⟨cultura/países⟩ Western; **África O**~ West Africa
■ mf westerner

occidentalizarse [A4] v pron to become westernized

occidente m west

Oceanía f Oceania

océano m ocean

ochenta adj inv/pron/m eighty; para ejemplos ver CINCUENTA

ocho adj inv/pron/m eight; para ejemplos ver CINCO

ochocientos -tas adj/pron eight hundred; para ejemplos ver QUINIENTOS

ocio m (a) (tiempo libre) spare time, leisure time (b) (inactividad, holgazanería) inactivity, idleness

ociosidad f inactivity, idleness

ocioso -sa adj (inactivo) idle

ocre m : (de) color ~ ocher-colored*

oct. (= **octubre**) Oct

octavilla f pamphlet

octavo¹ -va adj/pron eighth; **la octava parte** an eighth; para ejemplos ver QUINTO

octavo² m eighth; ~**s de final** round before the quarter-finals

octubre m October; para ejemplos ver ENERO

oculista mf ophthalmologist

ocultar [A1] vt (en general) to conceal, hide; ⟨persona⟩ to hide; ~**le algo A algn** to conceal o hide sth FROM sb
■ **ocultarse** v pron (a) «persona» to hide (b) (estar oculto) to hide, lie hidden (c) «sol» to disappear

ocultismo m occult, occultism

oculto -ta adj (a) [ESTAR] (escondido) hidden (b) [SER] (misterioso) ⟨razón/designio⟩ mysterious, secret

ocupación f (empleo) occupation; (actividad) activity

ocupado -da adj (a) (atareado) busy (b) ⟨línea telefónica⟩ busy, engaged (BrE); **¿este asiento está** ~? is this seat taken? (c) ⟨territorio⟩ occupied

ocupante mf occupant; ~ **ilegal** squatter

ocupar [A1] vt ① ⟨espacio/tiempo⟩ to take up; **me ocupó toda la mañana** it took up my whole morning; **¿en qué ocupas tu tiempo libre?** how do you spend your spare time? ② «persona» (a) (situarse en) ⟨asiento⟩ to take; **volvió a** ~ **su asiento** she returned to her seat, she took her seat again; **ocupaban (todo) un lado**

de la sala they took up one (whole) side of the
room **(b)** (estar en) ⟨*vivienda*⟩ to live in, occupy;
⟨*habitación*⟩ to be in; ⟨*asiento*⟩ to be (sitting) in
(c) (en clasificación): **¿qué lugar ocupan en la liga?**
what position are they in the division? **(d)**
⟨*cargo*⟩ to hold, occupy (fml); ⟨*vacante*⟩ to fill
3 ⟨*fábrica/territorio*⟩ to occupy
4 (AmC, Chi, Méx) (usar) to use
■ **ocuparse** *v pron* **1** ⟨*de tarea/
trabajo*⟩ to take care OF sth; ⟨*de problema/asunto*⟩
to deal WITH sth; **yo me ∼é de eso** I'll see to that;
∼se DE algn ⟨*de niño/enfermo*⟩ to take care OF sb,
to look after sb
ocurrencia *f* (comentario gracioso) witty *o* funny
remark, witticism; (idea disparatada) crazy idea
ocurrente *adj* (gracioso) witty; (ingenioso) clever
ocurrir [I1] *vi* (en *3ª pers*) to happen; **ocurra lo
que ocurra** whatever happens; **lo que ocurre es
que ...** the trouble is (that) ...; **lamento lo
ocurrido** I'm sorry about what happened
■ **ocurrirse** *v pron* (en *3ª pers*): **se me ha
ocurrido una idea** I've had an idea; **no se les
ocurría nada** they couldn't think of anything; **di
lo primero que se te ocurra** say the first thing
that comes into your head; **¿cómo se te ocurrió
comprarlo?** whatever made you buy it?
odiar [A1] *vt* to hate; **odio planchar** I hate
ironing
odio *m* hate, hatred; **tenerle ∼ a algn** to hate sb
odioso -sa *adj* ⟨*trabajo/tema*⟩ horrible, hateful;
⟨*persona*⟩ horrible, odious
oeste *adj inv* ⟨*región*⟩ western; **conducían en
dirección ∼** they were driving west *o*
westward(s); **la costa ∼** the west coast
■ *m* **1 (a)** (parte, sector): **el ∼** the west; **en el ∼
de la provincia** in the west of the province; **al ∼
de Oaxaca** to the west of Oaxaca **(b)** (punto
cardinal) west, West; **vientos del O∼** westerly
winds; **caminaron hacia el O∼** they walked west
o westward(s) **2 el Oeste** (de los Estados Unidos)
the West; **una película del O∼** a Western
ofender [E1] *vt* to offend
■ **ofenderse** *v pron* to take offense*
ofensa *f* (agravio) insult
ofensiva *f* offensive
ofensivo -va *adj* offensive
oferta *f* **1 (a)** (proposición) offer **(b)** (Econ, Fin)
supply **2** (Com) offer; **están de** *or* **en ∼** they are
on special offer
oficial *adj* official
■ *mf* (de policía) police officer (*above the rank of
sergeant*); (Mil) officer
oficialismo *m* (AmL): **representantes del ∼**
representatives of the ruling *o* governing party
oficialista *adj* (AmL) ⟨*periódico*⟩
pro-government; ⟨*candidato*⟩ fielded by the party
in power
oficina *f* (despacho) office; **en horas de ∼** during
office hours; **∼ de empleo/turismo**
unemployment/tourist office
oficinista *mf* office worker
oficio *m* **1** (trabajo) trade; **carpintero de ∼**
carpenter by trade **2** (Der) **de ∼** court-appointed
(*before n*) **3** (Relig) service, office
ofimática *f* office automation
ofrecer [E3] *vt* **1 (a)** ⟨*ayuda/cigarrillo/empleo*⟩

to offer **(b)** ⟨*dinero*⟩ to offer; (en una subasta) to
bid **(c)** ⟨*fiesta*⟩ to give; ⟨*recepción*⟩ to lay on **(d)**
⟨*sacrificio/víctima*⟩ to offer (up)
2 (a) ⟨*oportunidad/posibilidad*⟩ to give, provide;
⟨*dificultad*⟩ to present **(b)** «*persona*»
⟨*resistencia*⟩ to put up, offer
■ **ofrecerse** *v pron* **1** «*persona*» to offer,
volunteer; **∼se A** *or* **PARA hacer algo** to offer *o*
volunteer TO do sth
2 (fml) (querer, necesitar) (*gen neg o interrog*):
¿qué se le ofrece, señora? what would you like,
madam? **si no se le ofrece nada más** if
there's nothing else I can do for you
ofrecimiento *m* offer
ofrenda *f* offering
ofuscarse [A2] *v pron* to get worked up
OGM *m* (= **organismo genéticamente
modificado**) GMO
ogro *m* ogre
oídas: de ∼ (*loc adv*) **lo conozco de ∼** I've
heard of him, I know of him
oído *m* **(a)** (Anat) ear; **me lo susurró al ∼** she
whispered it in my ear **(b)** (sentido) hearing; (para
la música, los idiomas) ear; **es duro de ∼** he's hard
of hearing; **aguzar el ∼** to prick up one's ears; **no
tiene ∼** she's tone-deaf, she has no ear for music;
tocar de ∼ (Mús) to play by ear
oiga, oigas, etc ▶ OÍR
oír [I28] *vt* **1** (percibir sonidos) to hear; **no oigo
nada** I can't hear anything *o* a thing; **se oyeron
pasos** I (*or* you *etc*) heard footsteps; **he oído
hablar de él** I've heard of him **2** (escuchar)
⟨*música/radio*⟩ to listen to **3** **oír misa** to go to
mass **4** **oiga/oye** (para llamar la atención) excuse
me; **¡oiga!** **se le cayó la cartera** excuse me, you've
dropped your wallet; **oye, si ves a Gustavo dile
que me llame** listen, if you see Gustavo tell him
to call me
■ *vi* to hear
ojal *m* buttonhole
ojalá *interj*: **seguro que apruebas — ¡∼!** I'm
sure you'll pass — I hope so!; **¡∼ que todo salga
bien!** let's hope everything turns out all right!; **∼
fuera rico!** if only I were rich!, I wish I was rich!
ojeada *f* glance; **echar una ∼ a algo** to have a
quick glance *o* look at sth
ojear [A1] *vt* to (have a) look at
ojeras *fpl* rings under the eyes (*pl*)
ojeriza *f* grudge; **tenerle ∼ a algn** to have a
grudge against sb
ojeroso -sa *adj*: **estar ∼** to have rings under
one's eyes
ojo *m* **1 (a)** (en general) eye; **un niño de ∼s
negros** a boy with dark eyes; **mirar fijamente a
los ∼** to stare straight into sb's eyes; **no me
quita los ∼s de encima** he won't take his eyes off
me; **a los ∼s de la sociedad** in the eyes of
society; **∼ de la cerradura** keyhole; **∼ de buey**
porthole; **∼ de vidrio** *or* (Esp) **cristal** glass eye; **∼
mágico** (AmL) spyhole, peephole; **∼ morado** *or*
(Méx) **moro** *or* (CS fam) **en tinta** black eye; **costar
un ∼ de la cara** (fam) to cost an arm and a leg
(colloq); **cuatro ∼s ven más que dos** two heads are
better than one; **en un abrir y cerrar de ∼s** in the
twinkling of an eye; **∼ por ∼** an eye for an eye
(b) (vista): **bajó los ∼s avergonzada** she lowered
her eyes in shame; **sin levantar los ∼s del libro** ⋯∴

without looking up from her book; *a* ~ (*de buen cubero*) *or* (AmS) *al* ~ at a guess; **echar un** ~ **a algo/algn** (fam) to have *o* take a (quick) look at sth/sb; **tener** ~ **de lince** *or* **de águila** to have eyes like a hawk

2 (perspicacia): ¡**vaya** ~ **que tiene!** he's pretty sharp *o* on the ball!; **tener** ~ **para los negocios** to have a good eye for business

3 (fam) (cuidado, atención): **hay que andar** *or* **ir con mucho** ~ you have to keep your eyes open; **¡**~**! que viene un coche** watch out! *o* be careful! there's a car coming

ojota *f* (CS) (para playa, piscina) thong (AmE), flip-flop (BrE); (calzado rústico) sandal

okey *interj* (esp AmL) OK!, okay!

okupa *mf* (Esp fam) squatter

ola *f* wave; ~ **de calor** heat wave; ~ **de frío** cold spell

olán *m* (Méx) flounce, frill

olé, ole *interj* olé!, bravo!

oleada *f* wave

oleaje *m* swell

óleo *m* (sustancia) oil; (cuadro) oil painting; **pintura al** ~ oil painting

oleoducto *m* (oil) pipeline

oler [E12] *vi* **1** (percibir olores) ~ **A algo** to smell sth; ¿**no hueles a humo?** can't you smell smoke? **2** (despedir olores) «*comida/perfume*» to smell; **¡qué bien/mal huele!** it smells good/awful!; **le huelen los pies** his feet smell; ~ **A algo** ⟨*a rosas/ajo*⟩ to smell *or* of sth **3** (fam) (expresando sospecha) (+ *me/te/le etc*): **esto me huele mal** it sounds fishy to me; **me huele que fue ella** I have a feeling it was her

■ ~ *vt* «*persona*» to smell; «*animal*» to sniff, smell

■ **olerse** *v pron* (fam) to suspect; **ya me lo olía** I thought so

olfatear [A1] *vt* **(a)** (oler con insistencia) to sniff **(b)** ⟨*rastro/presa*⟩ to scent, follow

olfato *m* (sentido) smell; (perspicacia, intuición) nose

oligarquía *f* oligarchy

olimpiada, olimpíada *f*: *tb* ~**s** Olympic Games (*pl*), Olympics (*pl*)

olímpico -ca *adj* **(a)** ⟨*campeón/récord*⟩ Olympic (*before n*) **(b)** (AmL fam) ⟨*pase/gol*⟩ fantastic (colloq), sensational (colloq)

olisquear [A1] *vt* to sniff

oliva *f* olive

olivar *m* olive grove

olivo *m* olive (tree)

olla *f* pot; ~ **a presión** pressure cooker

olmo *m* elm (tree)

olor *m* smell; **tiene un** ~ **raro** it has a funny smell; **tomarle el** ~ **a algo** (AmL) to smell sth; ~ **A algo** smell *or* of sth

oloroso -sa *adj* **(a)** ⟨*jabón/flor*⟩ scented, fragrant **(b)** ⟨*queso/pies*⟩ smelly

olote *m* (AmC, Méx) cob, corncob

olvidadizo -za *adj* forgetful

olvidar [A1] *vt* **1** ⟨*pasado/nombre*⟩ to forget; **había olvidado que ...** I had forgotten that ...; ~ **hacer algo** to forget to do sth **2** (dejar en un lugar) to forget, leave ... behind; **olvidó el pasaporte en casa** she left her passport at home

■ **olvidarse** *v pron* **1** (en general) to forget; ~**se**

DE algo to forget sth; ~**se DE hacer algo** to forget to do sth; (+ *me/te/le etc*) **¡ah! se me olvidaba** ah! I almost forgot; **se me olvidó decírtelo** I forgot to tell you **2** (dejar en un lugar) to forget, leave ... behind

olvido *m* **(a)** (abandono, indiferencia) obscurity; **caer en el** ~ to fall *o* sink into obscurity *o* oblivion **(b)** (descuido) oversight; **fue un** ~ it was an oversight, I forgot

ombligo *m* navel, belly button (colloq)

omisión *f* omission

omitir [I1] *vt* ⟨*frase/nombre*⟩ to omit; **omitió mencionar que ...** he failed to mention that ...

ómnibus *m* (*pl* ~ *or* **-buses**) (autobús — urbano) (Per, Ur) bus; (— de larga distancia) (Arg) bus, coach (BrE)

omnipotente *adj* omnipotent

omoplato, omóplato *m* shoulder blade, scapula (tech)

once *adj inv/pron/m* eleven; *para ejemplos ver* CINCO

ONCE /'onee/ *f* = **Organización Nacional de Ciegos Españoles**

onces *fpl* (Andes) tea

onda *f* (en general) wave; ~ **corta/larga** short/long wave; ~ **expansiva** blast, shock wave; **longitud de** ~ wavelength); **agarrarle la** ~ **a algo** (AmL fam) to get the hang of sth (colloq); **estar en la** ~ (fam) (a la moda) to be trendy (colloq); (al tanto) to be bang up to date (colloq); **¡qué buena/mala** ~**!** (AmL fam) that's great/terrible! (colloq); ¿**qué** ~**?** (AmL fam) what's up? (colloq)

ondear [A1] *vi* «*bandera*» to fly

ondulado *adj* ⟨*pelo*⟩ wavy; ⟨*terreno*⟩ undulating, rolling

ondulante *adj* ⟨*movimiento*⟩ undulatory; ⟨*terreno*⟩ undulating, rolling

ondularse [A1] *v pron* to go wavy

ONG *f* (= **Organización no Gubernamental**) NGO

onix *m* onyx

onomatopeya *f* onomatopoeia

onomatopéyico -ca *adj* onomatopoeic

ONU /'onu/ *f* (= **Organización de las Naciones Unidas**): **la** ~ the UN

onza *f* **1** (peso) ounce **2** (de chocolate) square

opaco -ca *adj* (no transparente) opaque; (sin brillo) dull

ópalo *m* opal

opción *f* option; **no tenía** ~ I had no option *o* choice; **con** ~ **a compra** with option to buy

opcional *adj* optional

open *m* open championship *o* tournament

ópera *f* (obra musical) opera; (edificio) opera house

operación *f* **(a)** (Mat) operation **(b)** (Med) operation; **una** ~ **a corazón abierto** open-heart surgery **(c)** (Fin) transaction **(d)** (misión) operation; ~ **de rescate** rescue operation

operador -dora *m,f* **(a)** (Inf, Tec, Telec) operator **(b)** (Cin, TV) (de cámara) (*m*) cameraman; (*f*) camerawoman; (de proyección) projectionist **(c)** (Chi, Méx) (obrero) ▶ OPERARIO **(d)** ~ **turístico** tour operator

operar [A1] *vt* **1** (Med) to operate on; **me van a** ~ **de la vesícula** I'm having a gallbladder operation; **lo** ~**on de apendicitis** he had his

appendix taken out **2** (frml) ⟨*cambio/ transformación*⟩ to produce, bring about **3** (Chi, Méx) ⟨*máquina*⟩ to operate
■ ~ *vi* (a) (Med) to operate (b) (frml) «*servicio/ vuelo*» to operate
■ **operarse** *v pron* **1** (Med) (*caus*) to have an operation; ~**se del corazón** to have a heart operation **2** (frml) «*cambio/transformación*» to take place

operario -ria *m,f* (frml) operator; **el ~ de la máquina** the machine operator

opinar [A1] *vi* to express an opinion; **prefiero no ~** I would prefer not to comment
■ ~ *vt* (a) (pensar) to think; **¿qué opinas del aborto?** what do you think about abortion?; **¿qué opinas de ella?** what do you think of her?; **no opino lo mismo** I do not share that view *o* opinion; **opino que debería renunciar** in my opinion he should resign (b) (expresar un juicio): **opinó que deberían aplazarlo** he expressed the view that it should be postponed

opinión *f* opinion; **en mi ~** in my opinion; **cambió de ~** he changed his mind; **la ~ pública** public opinion

opio *m* (Bot, Farm) opium

oponente *mf* opponent

oponer [E22] *vt* ⟨*resistencia*⟩ to offer, put up; ⟨*objeción*⟩ to raise
■ **oponerse** *v pron* (ser contrario) to object; ~**se A algo** to oppose sth; **nuestros caracteres se oponen** (*recípr*) we are opposites

oporto *m* (vino) port

oportunidad *f* **1** (momento oportuno, posibilidad) chance, opportunity; **a la primera ~** at the earliest opportunity; **tuve ~ (la) de conocerla** I got to meet her; **igualdad de ~es** equal opportunities **2** (AmL) (vez, circunstancia) occasion; **en aquella ~** that time *o* on that occasion

oportunismo *m* opportunism

oportunista *mf* opportunist

oportuno -na *adj* (a) ⟨*visita/lluvia*⟩ timely, opportune; **llegó en el momento ~** he arrived at just the right moment (b) ⟨*medida/respuesta*⟩ appropriate; **sería ~ avisarle** we ought to inform her; **estuvo muy ~** what he said was very much to the point

oposición *f* **1** (en general) opposition **2** (Esp, Ven) (concurso) (public) competitive examination; **hacer oposiciones** to take *o* (BrE) sit a competitive examination

opresión *f* (de un pueblo) oppression; (en el pecho) tightness

opresivo -va *adj* oppressive

oprimido -da *adj* ⟨*pueblo*⟩ oppressed

oprimir [I1] *vt* (a) (frml) (apretar, presionar) to press (b) (tiranizar) to oppress

optar [A1] *vi* **1** (decidirse) ~ **POR algo** to choose sth, opt **FOR** sth; ~ **POR hacer algo** to choose *o* opt to do sth **2** ~ **A algo** ⟨*a plaza/puesto*⟩ to apply **FOR** sth

optativo -va *adj* optional

óptica *f* (Fís, Ópt) optics; (tienda) optician's

óptico -ca *adj* optical
■ *m,f* optician

optimismo *m* optimism

optimista *adj* optimistic

■ *mf* optimist

óptimo -ma *adj* ⟨*posición*⟩ ideal, optimum; **en condiciones óptimas** ⟨*persona*⟩ in peak condition; ⟨*coche*⟩ in perfect condition; ⟨*alimento*⟩ fresh

opuesto -ta *adj* ⟨*versiones/opiniones*⟩ conflicting; ⟨*extremo/polo/lado*⟩ opposite; **tienen caracteres ~s** they have very different personalities; **venía en dirección opuesta** he was coming from the opposite direction

opulento -ta *adj* opulent, affluent

oración *f* (a) (Relig) prayer (b) (Ling) sentence

orador -dora *m,f* speaker

oral *adj* oral

órale *interj* (Méx fam) (expresando acuerdo) right!, OK!; (para animar) come on!

orangután *m* orangutan

orar [A1] *vi* (frml) (Relig) to pray

oratorio *m* (Relig) oratory, chapel; (Mús) oratorio

órbita *f* **1** (Astron) orbit; **poner en ~** to put into orbit **2** (Anat) (eye) socket, orbit (tech)

orca *f* killer whale

orden¹ *f* **1** (mandato) order; **deja de darme órdenes** stop ordering me about; **hasta nueva ~** until further notice; **estamos a la ~ para lo que necesite** (AmL) just let us know if there's anything we can do for you; **¡a la ~!** (Mil) yes, sir!; (fórmula de cortesía) (Andes, Méx, Ven) you're welcome, not at all; **~ de arresto** *or* **de busca y captura** arrest warrant; **~ de registro** *or* (Chi, Méx) **de cateo** search warrant; **~ judicial** court order **2** (Fin) order; **~ bancaria** banker's order **3** (Hist, Mil, Relig) order **4** (AmL) (pedido) order

orden² *m* **1** (en general) order; **en** *or* **por ~ alfabético** in alphabetical order; **por ~ de estatura** according to height; **vayamos por ~** let's begin at the beginning; **poner algo en ~** ⟨*habitación/armario/juguetes*⟩ to straight sth (up) (esp AmE), to tidy sth up (esp BrE); ⟨*asuntos/papeles*⟩ to sort sth up; ⟨*fichas*⟩ to put sth in order; **mantener el ~ en la clase** to keep order in the classroom; **~ del día** agenda; **~ público** public order; **alterar el ~ público** to cause a breach of the peace **2** (a) (frml) (carácter, índole) nature; **problemas de ~ económico** problems of an economic nature (b) (cantidad): **del ~ de** (frml) on the order of (AmE), in *o* of the order of (BrE)

ordenado -da *adj* (a) [ESTAR] (en orden) tidy (b) [SER] ⟨*persona*⟩ (metódico) organized, orderly; (para la limpieza) tidy

ordenador *m* (Esp) ▶ COMPUTADORA

ordenanza *m* (en oficinas) porter; (Mil) orderly, batman (BrE)

ordenar [A1] *vt* **1** ⟨*habitación/armario/juguetes*⟩ to straighten (up) (esp AmE), to tidy (up) (BrE); ⟨*fichas*⟩ to put in order; **ordené los libros por materias** I arranged the books according to subject **2** (a) (dar una orden) to order; **le ordenó salir de la oficina** she ordered him to leave the office (b) (AmL) (pedir) ⟨*taxi/bebida/postre*⟩ to order **3** ⟨*sacerdote*⟩ to ordain
■ **ordenarse** *v pron* to be ordained

ordeñar [A1] *vt* to milk

ordinal *m* ordinal (number)

ordinariez *f* (a) (falta de refinamiento) vulgarity; ⋯⟶

(grosería) rudeness, bad manners (*pl*); (en la manera de hablar) vulgarity, coarseness **(b)** (comentario — poco refinado) vulgar comment; (— grosero) rude comment

ordinario -ria *adj* ① (poco refinado) vulgar, common (pej); (grosero) rude, bad-mannered; (en el hablar) vulgar, coarse ② (de mala calidad) poor *o* bad quality ③ (no especial) ordinary; **correo ~** regular (AmE) *o* (BrE) normal delivery ④ **de ordinario** usually, normally; **hay menos gente que de ~** there are fewer people than usual *o* normal
■ *m,f* (persona — poco refinada) vulgar *o* (pej) common person; (— grosera) rude *o* bad-mannered person

orégano *m* oregano

oreja *f* (Anat) ear; **el perro puso las ~s tiesas** the dog pricked up its ears; **tirarle a algn de las ~s** *or* (AmL) **tirarle las ~s a algn** to pull sb's ears
■ *mf* (Méx fam) (soplón — de la policía) stool pigeon (colloq), grass (BrE colloq); (que escucha a escondidas) eavesdropper

orfanato, (Méx) **orfanatorio** *m* orphanage

orfelinato *m* orphanage

orgánico -ca *adj* organic

organismo *m* (Biol) organism; (Adm, Pol) organization

organización *f* organization

organizado -da *adj* organized

organizador -dora *m,f* organizer

organizar [A4] *vt* to organize, arrange
■ **organizarse** *v pron* to organize oneself

órgano *m* organ

orgasmo *m* orgasm

orgía *f* orgy

orgullo *m* pride; **con ~** proudly

orgulloso -sa *adj* **(a)** [ESTAR] (satisfecho) proud; **~ DE algn/algo** proud OF sb/sth **(b)** [SER] (soberbio) proud

orientación *f* **(a)** (de habitación, edificio) aspect (frml); **¿cuál es la ~ de la casa?** which way does the house face?; **la ~ de la antena** the way the antenna (AmE) *o* (BrE) aerial is pointing **(b)** (enfoque, dirección) orientation **(c)** (guía) guidance, direction; (acción de guiar) orientation; **~ profesional** (para estudiantes) vocational guidance, careers advice; (para desempleados) career guidance *o* advice **(d)** (en un lugar) bearings (*pl*)

oriental *adj* (del este) eastern; (del Lejano Oriente) oriental; (uruguayo) (AmL) Uruguayan
■ *mf* (del Lejano Oriente) oriental; (uruguayo) (AmL) Uruguayan

orientar [A1] *vt* ① **(a)** ⟨*reflector/antena*⟩ to position; **la casa está orientada al sur** the house faces south (frml) **(b)** (Náut) ⟨*velas*⟩ to trim ② (encaminar) ⟨*esfuerzos/política*⟩ to direct ③ ⟨*persona*⟩ **(a)** ⟨*faro/estrellas*⟩ to guide **(b)** (aconsejar) to advise; (mostrar el camino): **una mujer nos orientó** a woman told us the way
■ **orientarse** *v pron* (ubicarse) to get one's bearings, orient oneself; **~se por las estrellas** (Náut) to steer by the stars

oriente *m* (punto cardinal) east; (viento) east wind; **O~ Medio/Próximo** Middle/Near East

orificio *m* (frml) (de bala) hole; **los ~s de la nariz** the nostrils

origen *m* origin; **en su ~** originally, in the beginning; **dar ~ a algo** to give rise to sth; **país de ~** country of origin; **de ~ humilde** of humble origin(s)

original *adj/m* original

originalidad *f* (cualidad) originality; (comentario) clever remark

originar [A1] *vt* to start, give rise to
■ **originarse** *v pron* «*idea/costumbre*» to originate; «*movimiento*» to start, come into being, originate; «*incendio/disputa*» to start

originario -ria *adj* (de un lugar) native; **ser ~ de algo** «*persona*» to come from sth; «*especie*» to be native to sth

orilla *f* **(a)** (del mar, de lago) shore; (de río) bank; **viven a la ~ del mar** they live by the sea; **un paseo a la ~ del mar** a walk along the seashore **(b)** (de mesa, plato) edge **(c)** (dobladillo) hem

orillar [A1] *vt* ① ⟨*muro/costa/zona*⟩ to skirt (around) **(b)** (Col, Méx, Ven) (hacer a un lado): **orilló el coche** he pulled over ② (Méx) (obligar): **~ a algn A algo** to drive sb TO sth
■ **orillarse** *v pron* (Col, Méx, Ven) to move over

orina *f* urine

orinal *m* (de dormitorio) chamber pot; (para niños) pot, potty (colloq); (para enfermos) bedpan

orinar [A1] *vi* to urinate
■ **~** *vt*: **~ sangre** to pass blood
■ **orinarse** *v pron* to wet oneself; **se orina en la cama** he wets the bed

Orinoco *m*: **el (río) ~** the Orinoco (River)

oriundo -da *adj* ▶ ORIGINARIO

ornamentación *f* ornamentation

oro *adj inv* gold
■ *m* ① (metal) gold; **~ (de) 18 quilates** 18-carat gold; **bañado en ~** gold-plated; **~ negro** black gold; **ni por todo el ~ del mundo** not for all the tea in China (colloq) ② (en naipes) **(a)** (carta) *any card of the* OROS *suit* **(b)** **oros** *mpl* (palo) one of the suits in a Spanish pack of cards

orquesta *f* orchestra; **~ de jazz** jazz band

orquídea *f* orchid

ortiga *f* (stinging) nettle

ortodoxo -xa *adj* orthodox

ortografía *f* spelling, orthography (frml)

ortopédico -ca *adj* orthopedic*; ⟨*pierna*⟩ artificial

oruga *f* (Zool) caterpillar; (Auto) caterpillar *o* crawler track

orzuela *f* (Méx): **tengo ~** I've got split ends

orzuelo *m* sty*

os *pron pers* (Esp) **(a)** (complemento directo, indirecto) you; **~ veo mañana** I'll see you tomorrow; **~ lo prometió** she promised it to you **(b)** (*refl*)

AmC	Central America	Arg	Argentina	Cu	Cuba
AmL	Latin America	Bol	Bolivia	Ec	Ecuador
AmS	South America	Chi	Chile	Esp	Spain
Andes	Andean Region	CS	Southern Cone	Méx	Mexico

Per	Peru
RPI	River Plate Area
Ur	Uruguay
Ven	Venezuela

yourselves; **no ～ engañéis** don't kid yourselves **(c)** (*recípr*): **creía que ～ conocíais** I thought you knew each other

osar [A1] *vi* (liter) **～ + INF** to dare to + INF; **no osó decirles la verdad** he dared not tell them the truth (liter)

oscar /'oskar/ *m* (*pl* ～ *or* **-cars**) Oscar

oscilación *f* (movimiento) oscillation; (fluctuación) fluctuation

oscilar [A1] *vi* ⌐1⌐ «*péndulo*» to swing, oscillate (tech); «*aguja*» to oscillate; «*torre/ columna*» to sway ⌐2⌐ (fluctuar) «*cotización/ valores*» to fluctuate; **sus edades oscilaban entre** ... their ages ranged between ...

oscuras: **a ～** (*loc adv*) in darkness

oscurecer [E3] *v impers* to get dark
■ **～** *vt* ⟨*habitación/color*⟩ to darken, make ... darker

■ **oscurecerse** *v pron* to get darker

oscuridad *f* (de la noche, de lugar) darkness, dark; **¡qué ～!** it's so dark in here!

oscuro -ra *adj* ⌐1⌐ **(a)** ⟨*calle/habitación*⟩ dark; **a las seis ya está ～** at six it's already dark **(b)** ⟨*color/ojos/pelo*⟩ dark; **vestía de ～** she was wearing dark clothes ⌐2⌐ **(a)** (dudoso) ⟨*intenciones*⟩ dark; ⟨*asunto*⟩ dubious **(b)** (poco claro) ⟨*significado/asunto*⟩ obscure **(c)** (poco conocido) ⟨*escritor/orígenes*⟩ obscure

oso, osa *m,f* bear; **～ de felpa** *or* **peluche** teddy bear; **～ hormiguero** anteater, ant bear (AmE); **～ panda** panda; **～ polar** polar bear

ostensible *adj* obvious, evident

ostentación *f* ostentation

ostentar [A1] *vt* ⌐1⌐ (fml) (tener) ⟨*cargo/título*⟩ to hold ⌐2⌐ (exhibir) ⟨*alhajas/dinero*⟩ to flaunt
■ **～** *vi* to show off

ostentoso -sa *adj* ostentatious

ostión *m* **(a)** (CS) scallop **(b)** (Méx) oyster

ostra *f* oyster; **aburrirse como una ～** (fam) to get bored stiff *o* to death (colloq)

ostracismo *m* ostracism

OTAN /'otan/ *f* (= **Organización del Tratado del Atlántico Norte**) NATO

otitis *f* inflammation of the ear, otitis (tech)

otoñal *adj* ⟨*colores/paisaje*⟩ autumnal, fall (*before n*) (AmE), autumn (*before n*) (BrE)

otoño *m* fall (AmE), autumn (BrE); **en ～** in the fall, in (the) autumn

otorgar [A3] *vt* (fml) ⟨*premio*⟩ to award; ⟨*favor/ préstamo*⟩ to grant; ⟨*poderes*⟩ to bestow (fml), to give

otro, otra *adj* ⌐1⌐ (con carácter adicional) (*sing*) another; (*pl*) other; (con numerales) another;

¿puedo comer ～ trozo? can I have another piece?; **prueba otra vez** try again; **una y otra vez** time and time again; ▶ TANTO² *pron* 2
⌐2⌐ (diferente) (*sing*) another; (*pl*) other; **otra manera de hacerlo** another way of doing it; **¿no sabes ninguna otra canción?** don't you know any other songs?; **en ～ sitio** somewhere else; **en ～ momento** some other time
⌐3⌐ (estableciendo un contraste) other; **queda del ～ lado de la calle** it's on the other side of the street
⌐4⌐ (siguiente, contiguo) next; *ver tb* DÍA

■ *pron* ⌐1⌐ (con carácter adicional) (*sing*) another (one); **¿quieres ～?** would you like another (one)?
⌐2⌐ (diferente): **parece otra** she looks like a different person; **no voy a aceptar ningún ～** I won't accept any other; **lo cambié por ～** I changed it for another one; **¿no tiene ～s?** have you any other ones?; **～s piensan que no es así** others feel that this is not so
⌐3⌐ (estableciendo un contraste): **los ～s no están listos** (hablando — de personas) the others aren't ready; (— de cosas) the others *o* the other ones aren't ready
⌐4⌐ (siguiente, contiguo): **la semana que viene no, la otra** not next week, the week after; **uno detrás del ～** one after the other

ovación *f* (frml) ovation

ovalado -da *adj* oval

óvalo *m* oval

ovario *m* ovary

oveja *f* (nombre genérico) sheep; (hembra) ewe; **un rebaño de ～s** a flock of sheep; **la ～ negra** the black sheep; **la ～ descarriada** (Bib) the lost sheep

overol *m* (AmL) (pantalón con peto) overalls (*pl*) (AmE), dungarees (*pl*) (BrE); (con mangas) coveralls (*pl*) (AmE), overalls (*pl*) (BrE)

ovillo *m* ball (*of yarn*); **hacerse un ～** to curl up (in a ball)

ovni, OVNI /'oβni/ *m* (= **objeto volador** *or* **volante no identificado**) UFO

ovulación *f* ovulation

ovular [A1] *vi* to ovulate

óvulo *m* (Biol) ovule; (Farm) pessary

oxidado -da *adj* rusty

oxidarse [A1] *v pron* «*hierro*» to rust, go rusty, oxidize (tech); «*cobre*» to oxidize, form a patina

óxido *m* (herrumbre) rust; (Quím) oxide

oxígeno *m* oxygen

oye, etc ▶ OÍR

oyente *mf* **(a)** (Educ) occasional student, auditor (AmE) **(b)** (Rad) listener

oyera, oyese, etc ▶ OÍR

ozono *m* ozone; **la capa de ～** the ozone layer

Pp

P, p *f* (*read as* /pe/) *the letter* P, p

pabellón *m* ⌐1⌐ **(a)** (en hospital, cuartel) block,

building; (en feria, exposición) pavilion; (de palacio) pavilion; (en jardín) summerhouse **(b)** (de instrumento de viento) bell ⌐2⌐ (frml) (bandera) flag

paceño -ña adj of/from La Paz
■ m,f person from La Paz

pacer [E3] vi to graze

pacha f (AmC) baby's bottle

pachanga f (esp AmL fam) ▶ JARANA

pachanguero -ra adj (esp AmL fam) ▶
JARANERO

pachón -chona adj (Méx) ⟨suéter⟩ chunky;
⟨perro⟩ wooly*

pachucho -cha adj [ESTAR] (Esp fam)
⟨persona⟩ poorly (colloq); ⟨fruta⟩ overripe

pachuco -ca m,f (Méx) young Mexican
influenced by US culture

paciencia f patience; perder la ∼ to lose
patience; ten ∼ be patient, have a little patience

paciente adj (tolerante) patient
■ mf patient

pacificador -dora adj peace (before n)
■ m,f peacemaker

pacificar [A2] vt (Mil) to pacify (frml); (calmar) to
pacify, appease; ∼ los ánimos to calm people
down

pacífico -ca adj (a) ⟨manifestación/medios⟩
peaceful, pacific (frml) (b) ⟨carácter/persona⟩
peace-loving, peaceable; ⟨animal⟩ peaceful

Pacífico m: el (océano) ∼ the Pacific (Ocean)

pacifista adj/mf pacifist

paco -ca m,f (Andes fam) cop (colloq)

pacotilla f trash; de ∼ ⟨escritor/novela⟩
second-rate; ⟨reloj⟩ cheap, shoddy

pactar [A1] vt ⟨paz/tregua⟩ to negotiate, agree
terms for; ⟨plazo/indemnización⟩ to agree on
■ ∼ vi to make a pact, negotiate an agreement

pacto m pact, agreement; cumplir/romper un ∼
to abide by the terms of/to break an agreement;
P∼ de Varsovia Warsaw Pact

padecer [E3] vt ⟨enfermedad/hambre⟩ to suffer
from; ⟨desgracias/injusticias/privaciones⟩ to
suffer, undergo
■ ∼ vi to suffer; ∼ DE algo to suffer FROM sth;
padece del corazón he has heart trouble

padrastro m [1] (pariente) stepfather [2] (Anat)
hangnail

padre m [1] (pariente) father; mis ∼s my
parents; ∼ de familia father, family man
[2] (Relig) (sacerdote) father
■ adj (a) (fam) (grande) terrible (colloq) (b) [ESTAR]
(Méx fam) ⟨coche/persona⟩ great (colloq), fantastic

padrenuestro m Lord's Prayer

padrino m
━━━━━━━━━━━━━━━━━━━━━━━━
■ Nota En inglés godfather no se usa como
apelativo.Nótese también que cuando el plural
padrinos se refiere al padrino y a la madrina se
traduce por godparents.
━━━━━━━━━━━━━━━━━━━━━━━━
(a) (en bautizo) godfather; (de boda) man who gives
away the bride, usually her father (b) (en duelo)
second (c) (protector) sponsor, patron

padrón m (a) (Gob, Pol) register; ∼ electoral
(AmL) electoral roll o register (b) (Chi) (Auto)
registration documents (pl)

paella f paella

pág. f (= **página**) p.; 760 págs. 760 pp.

paga f (a) (acción de pagar) payment (b) (sueldo)

pay; ∼ de Navidad extra month's salary paid at
Christmas; ∼ extra or extraordinaria extra
month's salary gen paid twice a year

paganismo m paganism

pagano -na adj/m,f pagan; (pey) heathen

pagar [A3] vt (a) (abonar) ⟨cuenta/alquiler⟩ to
pay; ⟨deuda⟩ to pay (off), repay; ⟨comida/
entradas/mercancías⟩ to pay for; ¿cuánto pagas
de alquiler? how much rent do you pay?; le
pagan los estudios they are paying for his
education; no puedo ∼ tanto I can't afford (to
pay) that much; ∼ algo POR algo to pay sth FOR
sth (b) ⟨favor/desvelos⟩ to repay (c) (expiar)
⟨delito/atrevimiento⟩ to pay for; ∼ algo CON algo
to pay FOR sth WITH sth; ¡me las vas a ∼! you'll
pay for this!
■ ∼ vi (Com, Fin) to pay; ∼le a algn to pay sb

pagaré m promissory note, IOU

página f page; ∼s amarillas yellow pages; ∼
web (Inf) Web page; ∼ inicial or frontal or
principal (Inf) home page

pago m (a) (Com, Fin) payment; ∼ adelantado or
anticipado payment in advance; ∼ inicial down
payment; ∼ al contado/a plazos/en especie
payment in cash/by installments/in kind (b)
(recompensa) reward; en ∼ a algo as a reward for
sth

pagoda f pagoda

pai m (AmC, Méx) pie

país m (a) (unidad política) country; ∼ de origen
(de persona) home country, native land; (de
producto) country of origin; los P∼es Bajos the
Netherlands; el P∼ de Gales Wales; el P∼ Vasco
the Basque Country (b) (ciudadanos) nation (c) (en
ficción) land

paisaje m (a) (panorama) landscape, scenery (b)
(Art) landscape

paisanaje m civilians (pl); civil population

paisano -na m,f [1] (a) (compatriota) (m) fellow
countryman, compatriot; (f) fellow
countrywoman, compatriot (b) (de la misma zona,
ciudad): es un ∼ mío he's from the same area/
place as I am [2] (Indum): vestir de ∼ «soldado»
to wear civilian clothes o (colloq) civvies;
«policía» to be in/to wear plain clothes;
«sacerdote» to be in/to wear secular dress
[3] (a) (Per) mountain-dweller of Indian origin (b)
(RPl) peasant

paja f [1] (a) (Agr, Bot) straw; sombrero de ∼
straw hat; techo de ∼ thatched roof (b) (para
beber) (drinking) straw [2] (a) (fam) (en texto,
discurso) padding, waffle (BrE colloq) (b) (Col fam):
hablar or echar ∼ (decir mentiras) to tell lies;
(charlar) to chat, gab (colloq) [3] (AmC) (grifo) faucet
(AmE), tap (BrE)

pajar m (granero) barn; (desván) hayloft

pajarita f (a) tb ∼ de papel origami bird (b)
(Esp) (Indum) bow tie

pajarito m (cría) baby bird; (pájaro) (fam) little
bird, birdie (colloq)

pájaro m [1] (Zool) bird; ∼ carpintero
woodpecker; más vale ∼ en mano que cien or
ciento volando a bird in the hand is worth two in
the bush [2] (fam) (granuja) nasty piece of work
(colloq)

pajarraco m (fam) (a) (Zool) big, ugly bird (b)
(granuja) rogue

paje *m* **(a)** (Hist) page **(b)** (en boda) page (boy)

pajita, pajilla *f* (drinking) straw

pajizo -za *adj* straw-colored*

pajuerano -na *m,f* (RPl fam) country bumpkin, hick (AmE colloq)

Pakistán *m* Pakistan

pakistaní *adj/mf* Pakistani

pala *f* 1 (para cavar, de niño) spade; (para mover arena, carbón) shovel; (para recoger la basura) dustpan 2 (Coc) (para servir — pescado) slotted spatula (AmE), fish slice (BrE); (— tarta) cake slice 3 (de remo, hélice) blade; (de frontenis) racket; (de ping-pong) paddle, bat (BrE); (en piragüismo) paddle

palabra *f* 1 (vocablo) word; **una ~ de seis letras** a six-letter word; **no son más que ~s** it's all talk; **en pocas ~s, es un cobarde** in a word, he's a coward; **~ por ~** word for word; **yo no sabía ni una ~ del asunto** I didn't know a thing *o* anything about it; **no entendí (ni) una ~** I didn't understand a (single) word; **sin decir (una) ~** without a word; **~ compuesta** compound word; **tener la última ~** to have the final say 2 (promesa) word; **~ de honor** word of honor*; **una mujer de ~** a woman of her word; **cumplió con su ~** she kept her word; **nunca falta a su ~** he never breaks *o* goes back on his word 3 **(a)** (habla) speech; **el don de la ~** the gift of speech; **un acuerdo de ~** a verbal agreement; **no me dirigió la ~** she didn't speak to me; **dejar a algn con la ~ en la boca** to cut sb off in mid-sentence **(b)** (frml) (en ceremonia, asamblea): **pedir la ~** to ask for permission to speak; **tener/ tomar la ~** to have/to take the floor (frml)

palabrería *f*, **palabrerío** *m* talk; **no dice más que ~s** he's full of hot air (colloq)

palabrota *f* (fam) swearword; **decir ~s** to swear

palacio *m* **(a)** (residencia) palace; **el personal de ~** the Royal Household; **P~ Episcopal** Bishop's Palace; **P~ Real** Royal Palace **(b)** (edificio público) *large public building*; **P~ de Justicia** lawcourts (*pl*)

paladar *m* palate

paladear [A1] *vt* to savor*

palanca *f* 1 (en general) lever; (para forzar, abrir algo) crowbar; **lo levanté haciendo ~** I lifted it using a lever; **~ de cambios** gearshift (AmE), gear lever *o* stick (BrE); **~ de mando** joystick 2 (AmE fam) (influencia) influence; (persona influyente) contact

palangana *f* **(a)** (para fregar) bowl **(b)** (jofaina) washbowl (AmE), washbasin (BrE)

palanquear [A1] *vt* 1 (AmL) ▶ APALANCAR 2 (AmL fam) (usando influencias): **le ~on un puesto** they pulled some strings to get him a job (colloq) ■ ~ *vi* (AmL fam) to pull strings (colloq)

palapa *f* (Méx) palm shelter

palco *m* box

palenque *m* 1 (RPl) (poste) tethering post 2 (Méx) **(a)** (fiesta popular) festival (*with cockfights, music, etc*) **(b)** (para gallos) cockpit

Palestina *f* Palestine

palestino -na *adj/m,f* Palestinian

paleta *f* 1 **(a)** (de pintor) palette; (de cocina) spatula; (de ventilador) blade; (de albañil) trowel **(b)** (Dep) (de ping-pong) paddle, bat (BrE); (Jueg) (AmL) beach tennis 2 (fam) (diente) front tooth 3 (Coc)

shoulder; (Anat, Zool) (Andes) shoulder blade 4 **(a)** (Andes, Méx) (helado) Popsicle® (AmE), ice lolly (BrE) **(b)** (Méx) (dulce) lollipop

paletilla *f* **(a)** (Anat, Zool) shoulder blade **(b)** (Coc) shoulder

paleto -ta *m,f* (Esp fam & pey) country bumpkin, hick (AmE colloq & pej)

paliacate *m* (Méx) brightly colored* scarf

palidecer [E3] *vi* «*persona*» to turn *o* go pale

palidez *f* paleness

pálido -da *adj* ⟨*persona/luz/color*⟩ pale; **estás ~** you're very pale; **se puso ~** he went pale

paliducho -cha *adj* (fam) pale, peaky (colloq)

palillo *m* **(a)** (mondadientes) *tb* **~ de dientes** toothpick; (para comida oriental) chopstick; (de tambor) drumstick; (para tejer) (Chi) knitting needle **(c)** (fam) (persona flaca): **es un ~** he's as thin as a rake

palio *m* **(a)** (dosel) canopy **(b)** (prenda) pallium

paliza *f* 1 **(a)** (zurra) hiding, beating; **su padre le dio una buena ~** his father gave him a good hiding; **los matones le pegaron una ~** the thugs beat him up **(b)** (fam) (derrota) thrashing (colloq) 2 (fam) **(a)** (esfuerzo): **fue una ~ de viaje** the journey was a real killer; **darse la ~** (fam) (trabajando, estudiando) to work one's butt off (AmE colloq), to slog one's guts out (BrE colloq) **(b)** (aburrimiento) drag (colloq)

palizada *f* (valla) palisade; (terreno) fenced enclosure

pallar *m* (Per) (Bot, Coc) butter bean

palma *f* 1 **(a)** (de la mano) palm; **conocer algo como la ~ de la mano** to know sth like the back of one's hand 2 **(a)** (Bot) (planta) palm; (hoja) palm leaf; **~ de coco** (Col) coconut palm **(b)** (gloria, triunfo) distinction 3 **palmas** *fpl*: **dar** *or* **batir ~s** (aplaudir) to clap (one's hands), applaud; **tocar las ~s** (marcando el ritmo) to clap in time

palmada *f* **(a)** (golpecito amistoso) pat; **le dio una ~ en la espalda** he gave him a pat on the back; **me dio unas palmaditas en la mejilla** he patted me on the cheek **(b)** (para llamar la atención) clap; **dio unas ~s para pedir silencio** he clapped his hands for silence **(c)** (AmL) (golpe, azote) smack, slap

palmado *adj* **(a)** (AmC fam) (sin dinero) broke (colloq) **(b)** (Arg fam) (cansado) worn out (colloq)

palmatoria *f* candlestick

palmera *f* **(a)** (Bot) palm tree **(b)** (Coc) palmier

palmito *m* (planta) European fan palm; (tallo) palm heart

palmo *m* span, handspan; **casi un ~** several inches; **conocer algo ~ a ~** to know sth like the back of one's hand

palo *m* 1 **(a)** (trozo de madera) stick; (de valla, portería) post; (de herramienta) handle; (de tienda, carpa) tent pole; **~ de escoba** broomstick, broomhandle; **de tal ~, tal astilla** a chip off the old block, like father like son (*o* like mother like daughter etc) **(b)** (AmC, Col fam) (árbol) tree **(c)** (Dep) (de golf) (golf) club; (de hockey) hockey stick **(d)** (Náut) mast; **~ mayor** mainmast 2 (madera) wood; **cuchara de ~** wooden spoon 3 (fam) (golpe) blow (with a stick); **lo molieron a ~s** they beat him till he was black and blue 4 (en naipes) suit

paloma *f* (Zool) pigeon; (blanca) dove; (como ···⫶

símbolo) dove; ~ **de la paz** dove of peace; ~ **mensajera** carrier pigeon; ~ **torcaz** *or* **torcaza** ringdove, wood pigeon (BrE)

palomar *m* dovecot, pigeon loft

palomilla *f* ⟦1⟧ (mariposa nocturna) moth; (crisálida) chrysalis ⟦2⟧ (tuerca) wing nut, butterfly nut; (soporte) wall bracket ⟦3⟧ (Méx fam) (pandilla, grupo) gang
■ *mf* (Andes fam) (muchacho — callejero) street kid (colloq); (— travieso) little monkey (colloq), little devil (colloq)

palomita *f* ⟦1⟧ (Méx fam) (marca) check (AmE), tick (BrE) ⟦2⟧ **palomitas** *fpl: tb* ~**s de maíz** popcorn

palomo *m* (ave) cock pigeon

palote *m* ⟦1⟧ (en caligrafía) line, stroke ⟦2⟧ (RPl) (de amasar) rolling pin

palpable *adj* (claro, evidente) palpable (frml), obvious; (al tacto) palpable, tangible

palpar [A1] *vt* (Med) to palpate; (tantear) to touch, feel
■ **palparse** *v pron* ⟨bolsillo⟩ to feel

palpitación *f* palpitation

palpitar [A1] *vi* (a) «corazón» to beat (b) «vena/sien» to throb

pálpito *m* (AmS fam) feeling (colloq); **me dio el** *or* **tuve un** ~ I had a feeling *o* a hunch

palta *f* (Bol, CS, Per) (Bot, Coc) avocado (pear)

palto *m* (Bol, CS, Per) avocado tree

paludismo *m* malaria

palurdo -da *m,f* (fam) yokel (pej & hum), hick (AmE colloq & pej)

pamela *f* picture hat

pampa *f* pampa, pampas (*pl*); **la** ~ **argentina** the Argentinian Pampas; **la** ~ **salitrera** *region of nitrate deposits in northern Chile*

pampeano -na *adj* pampas (*before n*)

pamplinas *fpl* (fam) (a) (zalamerías) sweet talk (colloq); **no me vengas con** ~ don't try to sweet-talk me (colloq) (b) (tonterías) nonsense

pan *m* (Coc) bread; (pieza) loaf; (panecillo) roll; **¿quieres** ~? would you like some bread?; **una rebanada de** ~ a slice of bread; ~ **blanco/de centeno/integral** white/rye/whole wheat bread; ~ **de molde** *bread/loaf baked gen in a rectangular tin*, tin *o* pan loaf (BrE); ~ **de Pascua** (Chi) panettone; ~ **dulce** (con pasas) (RPl) panettone; (bollo) (AmC, Méx) bun, pastry; ~ **rallado** breadcrumbs (*pl*); ~ **tostado** toast; **un** ~ **tostado** (Chi, Méx) a piece of toast; **ganarse el** ~ to earn one's daily bread; **ser** ~ **comido** (fam) to be a piece of cake (colloq)

pana¹ *f* ⟦1⟧ (tela) corduroy; **pantalones de** ~ corduroy trousers ⟦2⟧ (Chi) (avería) breakdown

pana² *mf* (Ven fam) pal (Colloq), buddy (AmE colloq), mate (BrE colloq)

panacea *f* panacea

panadería *f* (tienda) bakery, baker's (shop); (fábrica) bakery

panadero -ra *m,f* baker

panal *m* honeycomb

panamá *m* panama hat

Panamá *m* (a) (país) Panama; **el Canal de** ~ the Panama Canal (b) (capital) *tb* **ciudad de** ~ Panama (City)

panameño -ña *adj/m,f* Panamanian

Panamericana *f*: **la** ~ the Pan-American Highway

pancarta *f* banner, placard

panceta *f* (a) (Esp) (sin curar) belly pork (b) (RPl) (curada) streaky bacon

pancho¹ -cha *adj* (tranquilo) calm; *quedarse tan* ~ (fam): **se lo dije y se quedó tan** ~ he didn't bat an eyelash *o* (BrE) eyelid when I told him

pancho² *m* (RPl) hot dog

pancito *m* (AmL) (bread) roll

páncreas *m* (*pl* ~) pancreas

panda *mf* panda
■ *f* (Esp fam) gang

pandemónium *m* pandemonium

pandereta *f* (Mús) tambourine

pandero *m* ⟦1⟧ (Mús) tambourine ⟦2⟧ (Per) (Fin) *cooperative savings scheme*

pandilla *f* (fam) gang

panecillo *m* (Esp) bread roll

panecito *m* (AmL) bread roll

panel *m* ⟦1⟧ (a) (de puerta, pared) panel (b) (tablero — de anuncios) noticeboard; (— en exposición) exhibition panel; (— en estación) arrivals/departures board (c) (de auto) dashboard (d) ~ **de instrumentos** instrument panel *o* console ⟦2⟧ (de personas) panel

panela *f* (Col, Ven) *brown sugarloaf*

panera *f* (para servir pan) bread basket; (para guardar pan) bread box (AmE), bread bin (BrE)

pánfilo -la *adj* (fam) dimwitted (colloq)
■ *m,f* (fam) dimwit (colloq)

panfleto *m* pamphlet

pánico *m* panic; **tenerle** ~ **a algo** to be terrified of sth; **sembrar el** ~ to spread panic

panocha *f* ⟦1⟧ (de maíz, trigo) ear ⟦2⟧ (Méx) (melaza) *candy made from molasses*

panorama *m* (a) (vista, paisaje) view, panorama (b) (perspectiva) outlook, prospect

panorámica *f* (Cin, TV) pan; (perspectiva) outlook

panorámico -ca *adj* panoramic

panque *m* (Méx) sponge cake

panqueque *m* (AmL) pancake, crepe

pantaletas *fpl* (AmC, Ven) panties (*pl*), knickers (*pl*) (BrE)

pantalla *f* ⟦1⟧ (Cin, Inf, TV) screen; ~ **de radar** radar screen; **la** ~ **chica** (AmL) the small screen ⟦2⟧ (a) (de lámpara) shade (b) (de chimenea) fireguard (c) (cobertura) front

pantalones *mpl*, **pantalón** *m* pants (*pl*) (AmE), trousers (*pl*) (BrE); **unos** ~ a pair of pants

o trousers; ~ **cortos** shorts (*pl*); ~ **de peto**
overalls (*pl*) (AmE), dungarees (*pl*) (BrE); ~
tejanos *or* **vaqueros** jeans (*pl*)

pantano *m* ⓵ (natural) marsh, swamp; (artificial)
reservoir ⓶ (dificultad) mess, predicament

pantanoso -sa *adj* ⓵ ⟨terreno⟩ marshy,
swampy ⓶ ⟨asunto/negocio⟩ difficult, tricky
(colloq)

panteón *m* (a) (monumento) pantheon,
mausoleum; ~ **familiar** *or* **de familia** family vault
(b) (AmL) (cementerio) cemetery

pantera *f* panther

panti *m* (*pl* **-tis**), (Méx) **pantimedia** *f* ▶ PANTY

pantomima *f* pantomime

pantorrilla *f* calf

pants *mpl* (Méx) tracksuit, sweat suit (AmE)

pantufla *f* slipper

panty *m* (*pl* **-tys**) panty hose (*pl*) (AmE), tights
(*pl*) (BrE)

panza *f* (a) (fam) (barriga) belly, paunch (colloq);
tener ~ to have a belly *o* paunch (b) (de cántaro)
belly (c) (de rumiante) rumen

panzada *f* (fam) ⓵ (en el agua) belly flop (colloq);
se dio una ~ he did a belly flop ⓶ (comilona):
darse una ~ **de algo** to pig out on sth (colloq)

panzón -zona *adj* (fam) potbellied (colloq)

pañal *m* diaper (AmE), nappy (BrE)

pañito *m* doily

paño *m* (a) (Tex) woollen cloth; **abrigo de** ~
wool coat; **en ~s menores** (fam & hum) in my/his
undies (colloq & hum) (b) (para limpiar) cloth; ~ **de**
cocina (para limpiar) dishcloth; (para secar)
teatowel; ~ **higiénico** sanitary napkin (AmE),
sanitary towel (BrE) (c) (de adorno) antimacassar

pañolenci *m* (CS) baize, felt

pañoleta *f* (de mujer) shawl; (de torero)
neckerchief

pañuelo *m* (para la nariz) handkerchief; (para la
cabeza) headscarf, scarf; (para el cuello) scarf,
neckerchief

papa¹ *m* pope; **el P**~ the Pope

papa² *f* (esp AmL) (Bot) potato; ~ **caliente** hot
potato; ~ **dulce** (AmL) sweet potato; ~**s fritas** (esp
AmL) (de paquete) potato chips (AmE) *o* (BrE) crisps
(*pl*); (de cocina) French fries (*pl*) (AmE), chips (*pl*)
(BrE); **ni** ~ (fam) not a thing; **no sé ni** ~ **de**
coches I haven't a clue about cars (colloq)

papá *m* (*pl* **-pás**) (fam) daddy (colloq), pop (AmE
colloq); **mis** ~**s** (AmL) my parents, my mom and
dad (AmE), my mum and dad (BrE colloq); **P**~ **Noel**
Santa Claus, Father Christmas

papada *f* (de persona) double chin, jowl

papagayo *m* ⓵ (ave) parrot; **recitar algo como**
un ~ to recite sth parrot-fashion ⓶ (Ven)
(juguete) kite

papalote *m* (AmC, Méx) (juguete) kite; (ala delta)
hang glider

Papanicolau *m* (AmL) smear test

papaya *f* papaya, pawpaw

papel *m* ⓵ (material) paper; **un** ~ a piece of
paper; **toalla de** ~ paper towel; ~ **carbón** carbon
paper; ~ **cuadriculado/rayado** squared/lined
paper; ~ **de aluminio** tinfoil, aluminum* foil; ~
de embalar/de envolver/de regalo wrapping
paper; ~ **higiénico** *or* **de water** toilet paper; ~
picado (RPI) confetti

⓶ (documento) document, paper; **no tenía los** ~**es**
en regla her papers were not in order
⓷ (a) (Cin, Teatr) role, part; **hace el** ~ **de monja**
she plays the part of a nun (b) (actuación)
performance; **hizo un lamentable** ~ **en el**
congreso his performance at the conference was
abysmal (c) (función) role; **juega un** ~ **importante**
en ... it plays an important role in ...

papeleo *m* (fam) red tape, paperwork

papelera *f* (a) (de oficina) wastepaper basket;
(en la calle) litter basket (AmE), litter bin (BrE) (b)
(fábrica) paper mill

papelería *f* (tienda) stationery store (AmE),
stationer's (BrE); **artículos de** ~ stationery

papelero -ra *adj* paper (*before n*)
■ *m,f* ⓵ (fabricante) paper manufacturer; (vendedor)
stationer ⓶ **papelero** *m* (CS) ▶ PAPELERA A

papeleta *f* (a) (de votación) ballot (paper); ~ **en**
blanco blank ballot (paper) (b) (de rifa) raffle
ticket (c) (de calificación) grade slip (d) (de empeño)
pawn ticket

papelillo *m* cigarette paper

papelitos *mpl* (Ur) confetti

papelón *m* (fam) (cosa vergonzosa): **hacer un** ~ to
make a fool of oneself; **¡qué** ~**!** how
embarrassing!

paperas *fpl* mumps

papi *m* (fam) ▶ PAPÁ

papilla *f* (para bebés) baby food, formula (AmE);
(para enfermos) puree, pap; **estar hecho** ~
⟨persona⟩ to be absolutely shattered (colloq)

papiro *m* papyrus

paprika *f* paprika

paquete¹ -ta *adj* (RPI fam) smart, chic

paquete² *m* ⓵ (a) (bulto envuelto) package,
parcel; **hacer un** ~ to wrap up a parcel; ~ **bomba**
parcel bomb; ~ **postal** parcel (*sent by mail*) (b)
(de galletas, cigarrillos) pack, packet (BrE); **un**
~ **de papas fritas** (AmL) a bag of chips (AmE), a
packet of crisps (BrE) ⓶ (conjunto) package; (Inf)
package ⓷ (Méx fam) (problema) headache

Paquistán *m* Pakistan

paquistaní *adj/mf* Pakistani

par *adj* ⟨número⟩ even; **jugarse algo a** ~**es o**
nones *to decide sth by guessing whether the*
number of objects held is odd or even
■ *m* ⓵ (a) (de guantes, zapatos) pair; **un** ~ **de**
preguntas/de veces a couple of questions/of
times; *a* ~**es** two at a time (b) (comparación)
equal; **sin** ~ (liter) incomparable, matchless (liter)
⓶ (Arquit) rafter; (abierto) **de** ~ **en** ~ wide open
⓷ (en golf) par; **sobre/bajo** ~ over/under par
■ *f* par; **a la** ~ (Fin) at par (for value); **sabroso a la** ~
que sano both tasty and healthy; **baila a la** ~ **que**
canta he dances and sings at the same time

para *prep*
ⓛ ⓵ (destino, finalidad, intención) for; **una carta para él**
a letter for him; **¿** ~ **qué sirve esto?** what's this
(used) for?; **champú** ~ **bebés** baby shampoo; ~
eso no voy I might as well not go; ~ **+ INF**:
ahorra ~ **comprarse un coche** he's saving up to
buy a car; **tomé un taxi** ~ **no llegar tarde** I took a
taxi so I wouldn't be late; **está listo** ~ **pintar** it's
ready to be painted *o* for painting; ~ **aprobar** (in
order) to pass; **entró en puntillas para no**
despertarla he went in on tiptoe so as not to

wake her; **lo dice ∼ que yo me preocupe** he (only) says it to worry me; **cierra ∼ que no nos oigan** close the door so (that) they don't hear us **2 (a)** (suficiencia) for; **no hay ∼ todos** there isn't enough for everybody; **no es ∼ tanto** it's not that bad; **soy lo bastante viejo (como) ∼ recordarlo** I'm old enough to remember it **(b)** (en comparaciones, contrastes): **hace demasiado frío ∼ salir** it's too cold to go out; **son altos ∼ su edad** they're tall for their age; **∼ lo que come, no está gordo** considering how much he eats, he's not fat; **¿quién es él ∼ hablarte así?** who does he think he is, speaking to you like that?; **es mucho ∼ que lo haga sola** it's too much for you to do it on your own

II 1 (dirección): **salieron ∼ el aeropuerto** they left for the airport; **empuja ∼ arriba** push up *o* upward(s); **¿vas ∼ el centro?** are you going to *o* toward(s) the center?

2 (tiempo) **(a)** (señalando una fecha, un plazo): **estará listo ∼ el día 15** it'll be ready by *o* for the 15th; **deberes ∼ el lunes** homework for Monday; **faltan cinco minutos ∼ que termine** there are five minutes to go before the end; **me lo prometió ∼ después de Pascua** he promised me it for after Easter; **¿cuánto te falta ∼ terminar?** how much have you got left to do?; **∼ entonces estaré en Madrid** I'll be in Madrid (by) then; **tengo hora ∼ mañana** I have an appointment (for) tomorrow **(b)** (AmL exc RPl) (al decir la hora) to; **son cinco ∼ las diez** it's five to ten **(c)** (duración): **∼ siempre** forever; **tengo ∼ rato** (fam) I'll be a while yet

parábola *f* **(a)** (Relig) parable **(b)** (Mat) parabola

parabrisas *m* (*pl* ∼) windshield (AmE), windscreen (BrE)

paracaídas *m* (*pl* ∼) (Aviac) parachute; **tirarse** *or* **lanzarse en ∼** to parachute

paracaidismo *m* parachuting

paracaidista *adj* parachute (*before n*)
■ *mf* **(a)** (Mil) paratrooper; (Dep) parachutist **(b)** (AmL fam) (en fiesta) gatecrasher; **llegar de ∼ to** come/go uninvited (*to a party*)

parachoques *m* (*pl* ∼) (Auto) bumper

parada *f* **1** (Transp) **(a)** (acción) stop **(b)** (lugar) *tb* **∼ de autobús** (*or* **de ómnibus** *etc*) bus stop; **me bajo en la próxima ∼** I'm getting off at the next stop; **∼ de taxi** taxi stand, taxi rank (BrE) **2** (Dep) (en fútbol) save, stop **3** (desfile) parade **4** (Per) (mercado) street market

paradero *m* **(a)** (frml) (de persona) whereabouts (*pl*) **(b)** (AmL exc RPl) ▶ PARADA 1B

parado -da *adj* **1** (detenido): **un coche ∼ en medio de la calle** a car sitting *o* stopped in the middle of the street; **no te quedes ahí ∼, ven a ayudarme** don't just stand there, help me **2** (AmL) **(a)** (de pie): **estar ∼** to stand, be standing **(b)** (erguido): **tengo el pelo todo ∼** my hair's standing on end; *ver tb* ▶ PARAR *vt* 2B **3** (Esp) (desempleado) unemployed **4** **salir (de algo) bien/mal parado** (de pelea, discusión) to come off well/badly (in sth); **es el que mejor ∼ ha salido** he's the one who's come off best
■ *m,f* (Esp) unemployed person; **los ∼s** the unemployed

paradoja *f* paradox

paradójico -ca *adj* paradoxical

parador *m* **(a)** (mesón) roadside bar/hotel **(b)** (en Esp) parador, state-owned hotel

parafina *f* **(a)** (sólida) paraffin (wax); **∼ líquida** mineral oil (AmE), liquid paraffin (BrE) **(b)** (AmL) (combustible) kerosene

paragolpes *m* (*pl* ∼) (RPl) bumper

paraguas *m* (*pl* ∼) umbrella

Paraguay *m*: *tb* **el ∼** Paraguay

paraguayo -ya *adj/m,f* Paraguayan

paragüero *m* umbrella stand

paraíso *m* (Relig) **el ∼** paradise, heaven; **∼ fiscal** tax haven

paraje *m* spot, place

paralela *f* **1** (línea) parallel (line) **2** **paralelas** *fpl* (Dep) parallel bars (*pl*)

paralelismo *m* parallelism, parallel

paralelo¹ -la *adj* **(a)** ⟨líneas/planos⟩ parallel; **∼ a algo** parallel ʀo sth **(b)** (*como adv*) ⟨marchar/crecer⟩ parallel

paralelo² *m* parallel

paralelogramo *m* parallelogram

paralímpico -ca *adj* paralympic; **los Juegos P∼s** the Paralympic Games

parálisis *f* paralysis; **∼ cerebral** cerebral palsy; **∼ infantil** poliomyelitis, infantile paralysis

paralítico -ca *adj* paralytic (*before n*); **se quedó ∼** he was paralyzed
■ *m,f* paralytic

paralizar [A4] *vt* **(a)** (Med) to paralyze; **se quedó paralizada de un lado** she was paralyzed down one side **(b)** ⟨industria/economía⟩ to paralyze; ⟨circulación/producción⟩ to bring ... to a halt *o* standstill

parámetro *m* parameter

paramilitar *adj* paramilitary

páramo *m* high plateau, bleak upland *o* moor

paramuno -na *m,f* (Col) *person from the high plateau*

paraninfo *m* main hall *o* auditorium

paranoia *f* paranoia

paranoico -ca *adj/m,f* paranoid

paranormal *adj* paranormal

parapente *m* paragliding

parapetarse [A1] *v pron* to take cover

parapeto *m* (Arquit) parapet; (barricada) barricade

paraplejía, paraplejia *f* paraplegia

parapléjico -ca *adj/m,f* paraplegic

parapsicología *f* parapsychology

parar [A1] *vi* **1** (detenerse) to stop; **paró en seco** she stopped dead; **ir/venir a ∼** to end up; **fue a ∼ a la cárcel** he ended up in prison; **¿a dónde habrá ido a ∼ aquella foto?** what can have happened to that photo?; **¡a dónde iremos a ∼!** I don't know what the world's coming to **2** (cesar) to stop; **para un momento** hang on a minute; **ha estado lloviendo sin ∼** it hasn't stopped raining; **no para quieto ni un momento** he can't keep still for a minute; **no para en casa** she's never at home; **∼ DE + INF** to stop -ING; **paró de llover** it stopped raining **3** (AmL) «obreros/empleados» to go on strike
■ ∼ *vt* **1 (a)** ⟨coche/tráfico/persona⟩ to stop; ⟨motor/máquina⟩ to stop, switch off **(b)** ⟨hemorragia⟩ to stanch (AmE), to staunch (BrE) **(c)** ⟨balón/tiro⟩ to save, stop; ⟨golpe⟩ to block

2 (AmL) **(a)** (poner de pie) to stand **(b)** (poner vertical) ‹vaso/libro› to stand ... up; **el perro paró las orejas** the dog pricked up its ears
■ **pararse** v pron **1** (detenerse) **(a)** «persona» to stop **(b)** «reloj/máquina» to stop; «coche/motor» to stall; **se me paró el reloj** my watch stopped **2** **(a)** (AmL) (ponerse de pie) to stand up; **párate derecho** stand up straight; **se paró en una silla** she stood on a chair; **¿te puedes ~ de cabeza/de manos?** can you do headstands/handstands? **(b)** (AmL) «pelo» (hacia arriba) to stick up; (en los lados) to stick out **(c)** (Méx, Ven) (levantarse de la cama) to get up

pararrayos m (pl ~) (en edificio) lightning rod (AmE), lightning conductor (BrE)
parasailing /'paraseɪlɪŋ/ m parasailing
parásito m parasite
parasol m (sombrilla) parasol, sunshade
parcela f plot (of land), lot (AmE)
parchar [A1] vt (AmL) (arreglar) to repair; (con parche) to patch (up)
parche m patch; **~ de nicotina** nicotine patch
parchís m (Esp, Méx) Parcheesi® (AmE), ludo (BrE)
parcial adj **1** ‹solución/victoria› partial **2** (no equitativo) biased, partial
■ m (examen) assessment examination (taken during the year and counting towards the final grade)
parcialidad f **(a)** (cualidad) partiality, bias **(b)** (seguidores) supporters (pl)
parco -ca adj **(a)** (lacónico) laconic **(b)** (sobrio, moderado) frugal; **ser ~ en palabras** to be sparing with words
pardo -da adj ‹color› dun, brownish-gray*
parecer¹ [E3] vi **1** (aparentar ser): **parece fácil** it looks easy; **no pareces tú en esta foto** this picture doesn't look like you (at all); **parecía de cuero** it looked like leather; **parece ser muy inteligente** she seems to be very clever **2** (expresando opinión) (+ me/te/le etc): **todo le parece mal** he's never happy with anything; **¿qué te pareciero n?** what did you think of them?; **vamos a la playa ¿te parece?** what do you think, shall we go to the beach?; **si te parece bien** if that's alright with you; **me parece que sí** I think so; **¿a ti qué te parece?** what do you think?; **me parece importante** I think it's important; **me pareció que no era necesario** I didn't think it necessary; **hazlo como mejor te parezca** do it however o as you think best; **me parece mal que vaya sola** I don't think it's right that she should go on her own **3** (dar la impresión) (en 3ª pers): **así parece** or **parece que sí** it looks like it; **aunque no lo parezca, está limpio** it might not look like it, but it's clean; **parece que va a llover** it looks like (it's going to) rain; **parece que fue ayer** it seems like only yesterday; **parece mentira que tenga 20 años** it's hard to believe o I can't believe that he's 20; **parece que fuera más joven** you'd think he was much younger
■ **parecerse** v pron **(a)** (asemejarse) **~se A algn/algo** (en lo físico) to look o to be like sb/sth; (en el carácter) to be like sb/sth **(b)** (recípr) to be alike; **no se parecen en nada** they're not/they don't look in the least bit alike; **se parecen mucho** they are very similar

parecer² m (opinión) opinion; **a mi ~** in my opinion; **son del mismo ~** they're of the same opinion
parecido¹ -da adj [SER] ‹personas› alike; ‹cosas› similar; **son muy parecidas de cara** they have very similar features; **una especie de capa o algo ~** a cape or something like that; **~ A algo** similar TO sth; **eres muy ~ a tu padre** you're a lot like your father
parecido² m resemblance, similarity; **tiene cierto ~ con su hermano** he bears some o a certain resemblance to his brother; **hay un ~ en sus estilos** there is a resemblance o similarity in their styles
pared f **1** **(a)** (Arquit, Const) wall; **viven ~ por medio** they live next door; **las ~es oyen** walls have ears **(b)** (de recipiente) side **(c)** (de montaña) face **2** (en fútbol) one-two
paredón m **(a)** (de roca) rock face, wall of rock **(b)** (pared gruesa) thick wall **(c)** (de fusilamiento) wall
pareja f **1** **(a)** (equipo, conjunto) pair; **salieron por ~s** they came out in pairs; **formar ~s** to get into pairs **(b)** (en una relación) couple; **hacen buena ~** they make a good couple **(c)** (en naipes) pair **2** **(a)** (compañero) partner **(b)** (de guante, zapato) pair; **no encuentro la ~ de este guante** I can't find the pair for this glove; **un calcetín sin ~** an odd sock
parejo -ja adj **1** **(a)** (esp AmL) (sin desniveles) even; **los dos ciclistas van muy ~s** the two cyclists are neck and neck; **el nivel en la clase es muy ~** the class are all at the same level **(b)** (afín, semejante) similar **(c)** (CS, Méx) (equitativo) ‹trato› equal; ‹ley› fair, impartial **2** (Méx fam) **al ~ (a la par)**: **trabajan al ~** they all do the same amount of work; **al ~ de los mejores del mundo** on a par with the world's best
parentela f (fam) clan (colloq), tribe (colloq)
parentesco m relationship; **tener ~ con algn** to be related to sb
paréntesis m (pl ~) **(a)** (signo) parenthesis, bracket (BrE); **cerrar el ~** close parentheses o brackets; **entre ~** (literal) in parentheses, in brackets; (a propósito) by the way **(b)** (digresión) digression, parenthesis
parezca, parezcas, etc ▶ PARECER¹
paria mf pariah
pariente mf, **pariente -ta** m,f (familiar) relative, relation; **~ lejano** distant relative o relation; **~ político** in-law
parir [I1] vi «mujer» to give birth; «vaca» to calve; «yegua/burra» to foal; «oveja» to lamb
■ vt **(a)** «mujer» to give birth to, have **(b)** «mamíferos» to have, bear (fml)
París m Paris
parisiense adj/mf Parisian
parisino -na adj/m,f Parisian
parking /'parkin/ m (esp Esp) parking lot (AmE), car park (BrE)
parlamentar [A1] vi **~ (con algn)** to talk (TO sb)
parlamentario -ria m,f member of parliament, parliamentarian
parlamento m (asamblea) parliament; (Lit, Teatr) speech

parlanchín -china adj (fam) chatty (colloq)
■ m,f (fam) chatterbox (colloq)

parlante m (AmL) (en lugar público) loudspeaker;
(de equipo de música) speaker

paro m ⓵ (esp AmL) (huelga) strike; **hacer un ~
de 24 horas** to go on a 24-hour strike; **están en** or
de ~ (AmL) they're on strike; **~ cívico** (Col)
community protest; **~ general** (esp AmL) general
strike ⓶ (Esp) **(a)** (desempleo) unemployment;
está en ~ he's unemployed **(b)** (subsidio)
unemployment benefit; **cobrar el ~** to claim
unemployment benefit ⓷ **~ cardíaco** or **cardiaco**
cardiac arrest

parodia f parody, send-up (colloq)

parpadear [A1] vi **(a)** «persona/ojo» to blink
(b) «luz» to flicker; «estrellas» to twinkle

párpado m eyelid

parque m ⓵ (terreno) park; **~ de atracciones** or
(Col, RPI) **de diversiones** or (Chi) **de entretenciones**
amusement park, funfair; **~ de bomberos** (Esp)
fire station; **~ natural** nature reserve; **~
zoológico** zoo ⓶ (para niños) playpen

parqué m (suelo) parquet (flooring)

parqueadero m (Col) parking lot (AmE), car
park (BrE)

parquear [A1] vt (Col) to park
■ **parquearse** v pron (Col) to park

parquet m (pl **-quets**) ▶ PARQUÉ

parquímetro m parking meter

parra f vine

párrafo m paragraph; **~ aparte** new paragraph

parral m (en un jardín) vine arbor*; (viñedo)
vineyard

parranda f (fam): **estar/irse de ~** to be/go out
on the town o out partying (colloq)

parrilla f ⓵ **(a)** (Coc) grill, broiler (AmE);
pescado a la ~ grilled o (AmE) broiled fish **(b)**
(restaurante) grillroom, grill bar **(c)** (de la chimenea)
grate ⓶ (AmL) (para el equipaje) luggage rack, roof
rack

parrillada f **(a)** (comida) grill, barbecue **(b)**
(RPI) (restaurante) grillroom, grill bar

párroco m parish priest

parroquia f (iglesia) parish church; (área)
parish; (feligreses) parishioners (pl)

parroquiano -na m,f **(a)** (Relig) parishioner
(b) (cliente) regular customer o (frml) patron

parsimonia f **(a)** (calma) calm **(b)** (frugalidad)
parsimony

parsimonioso -sa adj **(a)** (tranquilo)
phlegmatic, unhurried **(b)** (frugal) parsimonious

parte m ⓵ (informe, comunicación) report; **dar ~
de un incidente** «particular» to report an
incident; «autoridad» to file a report about an
incident; **dar ~ de enfermo** to call in sick; **~
meteorológico** weather report
⓶ (Andes) (multa) ticket (colloq), fine
■ f ⓵ **(a)** (porción, fracción) part; **tres ~s iguales**
three equal parts; **pasa la mayor ~ del tiempo al
teléfono** she spends most of her o the time on the
phone; **la mayor ~ de los participantes** the

majority of o most of the participants **(b)** (en una
distribución) share; **su ~ de la herencia** his share of
the inheritance **(c)** (de lugar) part; **¿de qué ~ de
México eres?** what part of Mexico are you from?;
en la ~ de atrás at the back
⓶ (en locs) **en parte** partly; **en gran ~** to a large
extent, largely; **en su mayor ~** for the most part;
de un tiempo a esta parte for some time now; **de
parte de algn** on behalf of sb; **llamo de ~ de
María** I'm ringing on behalf of María; **dale
recuerdos de mi ~** give him my regards; **vengo
de ~ del señor Díaz** Mr Díaz sent me; **¿de ~ de
quién?** (por teléfono) who's calling?, who shall I
say is calling? (frml); **formar parte de algo** «pieza/
sección» to be part of sth; «persona/país» to
belong to sth; **entrar a formar ~ de algo** to join
sth; **por mi/tu/su parte** as far as I'm/you're/he's
concerned; **por partes:** revisémoslo por ~s let's
go over it section by section; **vayamos por ~s**
let's take it step by step; **por otra parte** (además)
anyway, in any case; (por otro lado) however, on
the other hand; **por una parte ..., por la otra ...** on
the one hand ..., on the other ...
⓷ (participación) part; **tomar ~** to take part
⓸ (lugar): **vámonos a otra ~** let's go somewhere
else o (AmE) someplace else; **esto no nos lleva a
ninguna ~** this isn't getting o leading us
anywhere; **¿adónde vas? — a ninguna ~** where
are you going? — nowhere; **en cualquier ~**
anywhere; **a/en/por todas ~s** everywhere; **en
alguna ~** somewhere
⓹ (en negociación, contrato, juicio) party
⓺ (Teatr) part, role
⓻ (Méx) (repuesto) part, spare (part)

participación f ⓵ (intervención) participation;
la ~ del público audience participation; **~ EN
algo** «en debate/clase/huelga» participation in
sth; «en robo/fraude» involvement IN sth; «en
obra/película» role IN sth ⓶ **(a)** (en ganancias)
share **(b)** (en empresa) stockholding, interest **(c)**
(de lotería) share (in a lottery ticket)

participante adj participating (before n)
■ mf (en debate) participant; (en concurso)
contestant; (en carrera) competitor

participar [A1] vi **(a)** (tomar parte) **~ (EN algo)**
to take part (IN sth), participate (IN sth) (frml) **(b)**
~ EN algo (en ganancias) to have a share IN sth;
(en empresas) to have a stockholding IN sth

participio m participle; **~ pasado** or **pasivo**
past participle

partícula f particle

particular adj **(a)** (privado) «clases/profesor»
private; «teléfono» home (before n) **(b)** (específico)
«caso/aspecto» particular; **en ~** in particular,
particularly **(c)** (especial) «estilo/gusto» individual,
personal; **es un tipo muy ~** (fam) he's a very
peculiar guy; **no tiene nada de ~ que vaya**
there's nothing unusual o strange in her going; **la
casa no tiene nada de ~** there's nothing special
about the house
■ m **(a)** (frml) (asunto) matter, point; **sin otro ~
saluda a usted atentamente** sincerely yours

AmC	Central America	Arg	Argentina	Cu	Cuba
AmL	Latin America	Bol	Bolivia	Ec	Ecuador
AmS	South America	Chi	Chile	Esp	Spain
Andes	Andean Region	CS	Southern Cone	Méx	Mexico

Per	Peru
RPI	River Plate Area
Ur	Uruguay
Ven	Venezuela

(AmE), yours faithfully (BrE) **(b)** (persona)
(private) individual; **viajar como ~ to travel on
private o personal business

partida f ⬛1⬛ (Jueg) game; **una ~ de ajedrez/
cartas** a game of chess/cards; **echar una ~ to
have a game** ⬛2⬛ (en registro, contabilidad) entry; (en
presupuesto) item ⬛3⬛ (certificado) certificate; **~ de
defunción/nacimiento** death/birth certificate
⬛4⬛ (frml) (salida) departure, leaving

partidario -ria adj (a favor) **~ DE algo/hacer
algo** in favor* OF sth/doing sth
■ m,f supporter; **los ~s de Gaztelu** Gaztelu's
supporters; **los ~s de la violencia** those who
favor o advocate the use of violence

partido¹ -da adj ⬛1⬛ ⟨labios⟩ chapped;
⟨barbilla⟩ cleft ⬛2⬛ (Mat): **siete ~ por diez** seven
over ten; **nueve ~ por tres da ...** nine divided by
three gives ...

partido² m ⬛1⬛ **(a)** (de fútbol) game, match (BrE);
(de tenis) match; **echar un ~ to have a game; un
~ de béisbol** a baseball game; **~ amistoso**
friendly game o match; **~ de desempate** deciding
game, decider; **~ en casa/fuera de casa** home/
away match **(b)** (AmL) (partida) game; **un ~ de
ajedrez** a game of chess ⬛2⬛ (Pol) party; **~ de la
oposición** opposition party; **tomar ~ to take sides
⬛3⬛ (provecho): **sacar ~ de algo** to benefit from sth;
sacarle ~ a algo to make the most of sth ⬛4⬛ (para
casarse): **un buen ~** a good catch

partir [I1] vt **(a)** (con cuchillo) ⟨tarta/melón⟩ to
cut; **lo partió por la mitad** he cut it in half **(b)**
(romper) ⟨piedra/coco⟩ to break, smash; ⟨nuez/
avellana⟩ to crack; ⟨rama/palo⟩ to break **(c)** (con
golpe) ⟨labio⟩ to split (open); ⟨cabeza⟩ to split open
(d) «frío» ⟨labios⟩ to chap
■ ~ vi ⬛1⬛ **(a)** (marcharse) to leave, depart
(frml) **(b)** ⟨auto⟩ (Chi) to start
⬛2⬛ **(a)** **~ DE algo** ⟨de una premisa/un supuesto⟩
to start FROM sth **(b)** **a partir de** from; **a ~ de
ahora/ese momento** from now on/that moment
on; **a ~ de hoy** (as o starting) from today
■ **partirse** v pron **(a)** ⟨mármol/roca⟩ to split,
smash **(b)** (refl) ⟨labio⟩ to split; ⟨diente⟩ to break,
chip

partitura f (de obra orquestada) score

parto m (Med) labor*; **estar de ~** to be in labor;
fue un ~ difícil it was a difficult birth; **provocar
el ~** to induce labor; **~ sin dolor** pain-free labor*

parvulario m kindergarten, nursery school
(BrE)

pasa f raisin

pasable adj (tolerable) passable

pasabordo m (Col) boarding pass

pasada f **(a)** (con un trapo) wipe; (de barniz, cera)
coat **(b)** (paso): **trató el tema de ~** he dealt with
the subject in passing; **hacerle** or **jugarle una
mala ~ a algn** to play a dirty trick on sb

pasadizo m passageway, passage

pasado¹ -da adj ⬛1⬛ (en expresiones de tiempo): **el
año/sábado ~** last year/Saturday; **~s dos días**
after two days; **son las cinco pasadas** it's after o
past five o'clock; **~ mañana** the day after
tomorrow ⬛2⬛ (anticuado) tb **~ de moda**
old-fashioned ⬛3⬛ ⟨fruta⟩ overripe; ⟨arroz/pastas⟩
overcooked; ⟨leche⟩ sour; **el pescado está ~** the
fish is bad; **el filete muy ~, por favor** I'd like my
steak well done

pasado² m **(a)** (época pasada) past **(b)** (Ling)
past (tense)

pasador m **(a)** (de pelo — decorativo) barrette
(AmE), hair slide (BrE); (— en forma de horquilla)
(Méx) bobby pin (AmE), hair clip (BrE) **(b)** (de
corbata) tiepin **(c)** (Per) (cordón) shoelace

pasaje m ⬛1⬛ (esp AmL) (Transp) ticket; **un ~ de
ida/de ida y vuelta** a one-way/round-trip ticket
(AmE), a single/return ticket (BrE) ⬛2⬛ (callejón)
passage, narrow street; (galería comercial) arcade,
mall ⬛3⬛ (Lit, Mús) passage

pasajero -ra adj ⟨capricho/moda⟩ passing
(before n); ⟨amor⟩ fleeting (before n); ⟨molestia/
dolor⟩ temporary
■ m,f passenger

pasamanos m (pl ~) banister

pasamontañas m (pl ~) balaclava

pasapalo m (Ven fam) nibble (colloq)

pasaporte m passport; **sacar el ~** to get a
passport

pasapurés m (pl ~) (con manivela) food mill;
(para aplastar) potato masher

pasar [A1] vi
I ⬛1⬛ **(a)** (ir por un lugar) to come/go past; **no ha
pasado ni un taxi** not one taxi has come/gone
past; **los otros coches no podían ~** the other
cars weren't able to get past; **no dejan ~ a nadie**
they're not letting anyone through; **~ de largo** to
go right o straight past; **~ por la aduana** to go
through customs; **es un vuelo directo, no pasa
por Miami** it's a direct flight, it doesn't go via
Miami; **¿este autobús pasa por el museo?** does
this bus go past the museum?; **pasamos por
delante de su casa** we went past her house;
pasaba por aquí y ... I was just passing by o I
was in the area and ... **(b)** (deteniéndose en un
lugar): **¿podríamos ~ por el banco?** can we stop
off at the bank?; **pasa un día por casa** why don't
you drop o come by the house sometime?; **puede
~ a recogerlo mañana** you can come and pick it
up tomorrow **(c)** (atravesar) to cross; **~ de un lado
a otro** «persona/barco» to go o cross from one
side to the other; «humedad» to go through
from one side to the other **(d)** (caber): **no ~á por
la puerta** it won't go through the door
⬛2⬛ (entrar — acercándose al hablante) to come in; (—
alejándose del hablante) to go in; **pase, por favor**
please, do come in; **¡que pase el siguiente!** next,
please!; **haga ~ al Sr Díaz** show Mr Díaz in please
⬛3⬛ **(a)** (transmitirse, transferirse) «corona/título» to
pass; **pasó de mano en mano** it was passed
around (to everyone) **(b)** (comunicar): **te paso con
Javier** (en el mismo teléfono) I'll hand o pass you
over to Javier; (en otro teléfono) I'll put you
through to Javier
⬛4⬛ **(a)** (Educ) to pass; **~ de curso** to get through
o pass one's end-of-year exams **(b)** (ser aceptable):
no está perfecto, pero puede ~ it's not perfect,
but it'll do; **por esta vez, (que) pase** I'll let it pass
o go this time
⬛5⬛ **pasar por (a)** (ser tenido por): **podrían ~ por
hermanas** they could pass for sisters; ver tb
HACERSE II 3 **(b)** (experimentar) to go through; **~
por una crisis** to go through a crisis
II (suceder) to happen; **cuéntame lo que pasó** tell
me what happened; **lo que pasó es ...** the
thing o the problem is ...; **pase lo que pase**
whatever happens, come what may; **siempre pasa** ⋯⋗

igual *or* lo mismo it's always the same; ¿qué
pasa? what's the matter?, what's up? (colloq);
¿**qué te pasa?** what's the matter with you?; ¿**qué
te pasó en el ojo?** what happened to your eye?;
¿**qué le pasa a la tele?** what's wrong with the
TV?; **eso le pasa a cualquiera** that can happen to
anybody; **no le pasó nada** nothing happened to
him

III ⓵ (transcurrir) «*tiempo/años*» to pass, go by;
~**on muchos años** many years went by *o* passed;
ya han pasado dos horas it's been two hours
now; **un año pasa muy rápido** a year goes very
quickly; ¡**cómo pasa el tiempo!** doesn't time fly!

⓶ (cesar) «*crisis/mal momento*» to be over;
«*efecto*» to wear off; «*dolor*» to go away

⓷ (arreglárselas) ~ SIN **algo** to manage WITHOUT
sth

■ ~ *vt*

I ⓵ (a) (cruzar, atravesar) «*frontera*» to cross;
«*pueblo/ciudad*» to go through (b) (dejar atrás)
«*edificio/calle*» to go past (c) (adelantar, sobrepasar)
to overtake

⓶ (a) (hacer atravesar) ~ **algo** POR **algo** to put sth
THROUGH sth; ~ **la salsa por un tamiz** to put the
sauce through a sieve (b) (por la aduana —
legalmente) to take through; (— ilegalmente) to
smuggle

⓷ (hacer recorrer): ~ **la aspiradora** to vacuum, to
hoover (BrE); **pásale un trapo al piso** give the
floor a quick wipe; **hay que ~le una plancha** it
needs a quick iron

⓸ (exhibir, mostrar) «*película/anuncio*» to show

⓹ «*examen/prueba*» to pass

⓺ «*página/hoja*» to turn; ~ **por alto** «*falta/error*»
to overlook; «*tema/punto*» to leave out, omit

II ⓵ (entregar, hacer llegar): **pásaselo a Miguel** pass
it on to Miguel; ¿**me pasas el martillo?** can you
pass me the hammer?

⓶ (contagiar) to give, to pass on

III ⓵ (a) «*tiempo*» to spend; **pasamos las
Navidades en casa** we spent Christmas at home;
fuimos a Toledo a ~ el día we went to Toledo for
the day (b) (con idea de continuidad): **pasé toda la
noche en vela** I was awake all night; **pasa todo el
día al teléfono** she spends all day on the phone
(c) **pasarlo** *or* **pasarla bien** to have a good time;
¿**qué tal lo pasaste en la fiesta?** did you have a
good time at the party?, did you enjoy the party?;
lo pasé mal I didn't enjoy myself

⓶ (sufrir, padecer) «*penalidades/desgracias*» to go
through, to suffer; **pasé mucho miedo/frío** I was
very frightened/cold

■ **pasarse** *v pron*

I ⓵ (cambiarse) ~**se al enemigo** to go over to the
enemy

⓶ (a) (ir demasiado lejos) to go too far; **nos
pasamos de estación** we went past our station;
esta vez te has pasado (fam) you've gone too far
this time (b) (*enf*) (fam) (ir): **pásate por casa** come
round; ¿**podrías ~te por el mercado?** could you
go down to the market?

⓷ (a) «*peras/tomates*» to go bad, get overripe;
«*carne/pescado*» to go off, go bad; «*leche*» to go
off, go sour (b) (recocerse) «*arroz/pasta*» to get
overcooked

II ⓵ (a) (desaparecer) «*efecto*» to wear off;
«*dolor*» to go away; (+ *me/te/le etc*) **ya se me
pasó el dolor** the pain's gone *o* eased now; **espera**

a que se le pase el enojo wait until he's calmed *o*
cooled down (b) (transcurrir): **el año se ha pasado
muy rápido** this year has gone very quickly; *ver
tb* PASAR *vt* III 1A, B

⓶ (+ *me/te/le etc*) (a) (olvidarse): **se me pasó su
cumpleaños** I forgot his birthday (b) (dejar
escapar): **se me pasó la oportunidad** I missed the
opportunity

pasarela *f* (a) (en desfiles de modelos) runway
(AmE), catwalk (BrE) (b) (Náut) gangway

pasatiempo *m* (a) (entretenimiento) hobby,
pastime (b) **pasatiempos** *mpl* (en periódico)
puzzles (*pl*)

Pascua *f* (a) (fiesta de Resurrección) Easter (b)
(Navidad) Christmas (c) (fiesta judía) Passover

pase *m* ⓵ (a) (permiso) pass; ~ **de abordar**
(Méx) boarding pass; ~ **de periodista** press pass
(b) (para espectáculo) *tb* ~ **de favor** complimentary
ticket (c) (Col) (licencia de conducción) license*
⓶ (a) (Dep) (en fútbol, baloncesto, rugby) pass; (en
esgrima) feint (b) (Taur) pass (c) (en magia) sleight
of hand

pasear [A1] *vi* (a) (a pie) to go for a walk *o*
stroll; **salir a ~** to go out for a walk *o* stroll (b)
(en bicicleta) to go for a (bike) ride; (en coche) to go
for a drive
■ ~ *vt* «*perro*» to walk

paseo *m* ⓵ (a) (caminata) walk; **dar un ~** to go
for a walk *o* (colloq) stroll; **mandar a algn a ~**
(fam) to tell sb to get lost (colloq) (b) (en bicicleta)
ride; (en coche) drive; **fuimos a dar un ~ en coche**
we went for a drive (c) (AmL) (excursión) trip,
outing; **no vivo aquí, estoy de ~** I don't live here,
I'm just visiting ⓶ (en nombres de calles) walk,
avenue; ~ **marítimo** esplanade, seafront

pasillo *m* (corredor) corridor; (en avión) aisle

pasión *f* passion; **tiene ~ por el fútbol** he has a
passion for football

pasional *adj*: **un crimen ~** a crime of passion

pasito *adv* (Col, Ven) «*hablar*» quietly, softly;
poner ~ la música to turn the music down

pasivo¹ -va *adj* passive

pasivo² *m* (en negocio) liabilities (*pl*); (en cuenta)
debit side

pasmado -da *adj* (fam) «*persona*»: **la noticia me
dejó pasmada** I was stunned by the news (colloq)

pasmar [A1] *vt* (fam) to amaze, stun

paso *m* ⓵ (a) (acción): **el ~ del tren** the passing
of the train; **el ~ del tiempo** the passage of time;
el ~ de la dictadura a la democracia the
transition from dictatorship to democracy; **de ~:
están de ~** they're just visiting *o* just passing
through; **me pilla de ~** it's on my way; **y dicho
sea de ~ ...** and incidentally ... (b) (camino,
posibilidad de pasar) way; **abrir/dejar ~ a algn/algo**
to make way (for sth/sb); **me cerró el ~** she
blocked my way; **dejen el ~ libre** leave the way
clear; ⓢ **ceda el paso** yield (*in US*), give way (*in
UK*); ⓢ **prohibido el paso** no entry; ~ **de cebra**
zebra crossing; ~ **de peatones** crosswalk (AmE),
pedestrian crossing (BrE); ~**a nivel** grade *o*
(BrE) level crossing; ~ **elevado** *or* (Méx) **a desnivel**
overpass (AmE), flyover (BrE); ~ **subterráneo** (para
peatones) underpass, subway (BrE); (para vehículos)
underpass; **abrirse ~** to make one's way; (a
codazos) to elbow one's way; **salir al ~ de algn**
(abordar) to waylay sb; (detener) to stop sb

2 (Geog) (en montaña) pass; *salir del* ~ to get out of a (tight) spot *o* (AmE) crack (colloq)
3 **(a)** (al andar, bailar) step; **dio un ~ para atrás** he took a step backward(s); **oyó ~s** she heard footsteps; **entró con ~ firme** he came in purposefully; ~ **a** ~ step by step; *seguirle los ~s a algn* to tail sb; *seguir los ~s de algn* to follow in sb's footsteps **(b)** (distancia corta): **vive a dos ~s de mi casa** he lives a stone's throw (away) from my house; **está a un ~ de aquí** it's just around the corner/down the road from here **(c)** (avance) step forward; **eso ya es un ~ (adelante)** that's a step forward in itself **(d)** (de gestión) step
4 (ritmo, velocidad): **apretó/aminoró el ~ he** quickened his pace/he slowed down; **a este ~ ...** at this rate ...; *a ~ de hormiga or tortuga* at a snail's pace; *marcar el ~* to mark time
5 (en contador) unit

pasodoble *m* paso doble

pasota *mf* (Esp fam): **ese tío es un ~** that guy couldn't give a damn about anything (colloq)

pasparse [A1] *v pron* (RPl) «*cara/labios*» to get chapped

pasta *f* **1** (Coc) **(a)** (fideos, macarrones, etc) pasta **(b)** (Esp) (masa de harina) pastry; (galleta) *tb* ~ **de té** cookie **(c)** (de tomates, anchoas, etc) paste **2** **(a)** (materia moldeable) paste; ~ **dentífrica** *or* **de dientes** toothpaste; **un libro en ~** a book in boards; **libros de ~ blanda** (Méx) paperback books **(b)** (Chi) (betún) polish **3** (Esp fam) (dinero) money, dough (sl)

pastar [A1] *vi* to graze

pastel *m* **1** **(a)** (dulce) cake; ~ **de boda/ cumpleaños** wedding/birthday cake **(b)** (cubierto de masa) pie; ~ **de papas** (CS) shepherd's pie, cottage pie **2** (Art) pastel; **al ~ pastel** (*before n*)
■ *adj inv* pastel

pastelería *f* (tienda) cake shop, patisserie (BrE); (actividad) (cake) baking

pastelero -ra *m,f* (fabricante) patissier, pastry cook; (vendedor) cake seller

pasteurizado -da, pasterizado -da *adj* pasteurized

pastilla *f* **1** **(a)** (Farm, Med) (para tragar) pill, tablet; (para chupar) pastille, lozenge; ~**s para dormir** sleeping tablets *o* pills; ~**s para los nervios** tranquilizers **(b)** (caramelo) candy (AmE), sweet (BrE); ~ **de menta** mint **2** (de jabón) bar; (de chocolate) bar; (de caldo) cube **3** (Electrón) chip, microchip

pasto *m* **(a)** (Agr) pasture **(b)** (AmL) (hierba) grass; (extensión) lawn, grass

pastor -tora *m,f* **1** (Agr) (*m*) shepherd; (*f*) shepherdess; ~ **alemán** German shepherd, Alsatian **2** (Relig) minister

pastoso -sa *adj* **(a)** ‹*sustancia/masa*› doughy **(b)** ‹*boca/lengua*› furry **(c)** ‹*voz/tono*› rich, mellow

pata *f* **1** (Zool) **(a)** (pierna — de animal, ave) leg; **las ~s delanteras/traseras** the front/hind legs **(b)** (pie — de perro, gato) paw; (— de ave) foot **2** (de persona) (fam & hum) (pierna) leg; (pie) (AmL) foot; ~ **de palo** wooden leg; *a* ~ (fam & hum) on foot; *estirar la* ~ (fam) to kick the bucket (colloq); *meter la* ~ (fam) to put one's foot in it (colloq); ~**s**

(*para*) *arriba* (fam) upside down; *saltar a* (*la*) ~ *coja* to hop; *tener* ~ (AmL fam) to have contacts; ▶ MALO 1A
3 (de mueble) leg
■ *m* (Per fam) **(a)** (tipo) guy (colloq), bloke (BrE colloq) **(b)** (amigo) buddy (AmE colloq), mate (BrE colloq)

patada *f* **1** (puntapié) kick; **le dio una ~ al balón** he kicked the ball, he gave the ball a kick; **tiró la puerta abajo de una ~** he kicked the door down; **dio una ~ en el suelo** he stamped his foot; **los echaron a ~s** they were kicked out **2** (AmL) **(a)** (de arma) kick **(b)** (fam) (producida por la electricidad) shock (colloq); **me dio tremenda ~** I got a real shock

Patagonia *f*: **la ~** Patagonia

patagónico -ca *adj* Patagonian

patalear [A1] *vi* **(a)** (con enfado) to stamp (one's feet) **(b)** (en el aire, agua) to kick (one's legs in the air/water) **(c)** (fam) (protestar) to kick up a fuss (colloq)

pataleta *f* (fam) (de niño pequeño) tantrum; **le dio una ~** «*niño*» he threw a tantrum; «*adulto*» he had a fit (colloq)

patán *adj* (fam) loutish, uncouth; **no seas ~** don't be such a lout *o* so uncouth
■ *m* **1** (fam) (grosero) lout, yob (BrE colloq) **2** (Chi) (holgazán) good-for-nothing

patata *f* (Esp) potato; ~ **frita** (Esp) (de sartén) French fry, chip (BrE); (de bolsita) (potato) chip (AmE), (potato) crisp (BrE)

patatús *m* (fam) fit (colloq)

paté, pâté *m* pâté; ~ **de hígado** liver pâté

patear [A1] *vt* **(a)** «*persona*» to kick, boot (colloq) **(b)** (AmL) «*animal*» to kick
■ ~ *vi* **(a)** (dar patadas en el suelo) to stamp (one's feet) **(b)** (AmL) «*animal*» to kick

patentado -da *adj* ‹*invento*› patented; ‹*marca*› registered

patentar [A1] *vt* **1** ‹*marca*› to register; ‹*invento*› to patent **2** (CS) ‹*coche*› to register

patente *adj* clear, evident; **dejó ~ cuál era su objetivo** he made his aim quite clear
■ *f* **1** (de invento) patent **2** (Auto) **(a)** (CS) (impuesto) road tax; (placa) license* plate, numberplate (BrE); **el número de la ~** the registration number, the license number (AmE) **(b)** (Col) (carnet de conducir) driving license*

paternal *adj* paternal

paternalismo *m* paternalism

paternalista *adj* paternalistic

paternidad *f* **1** (del padre) **(a)** (Der) paternity (frml) **(b)** (circunstancia) fatherhood; **la ~ lo ha cambiado** fatherhood *o* being a father has changed him **2** (de los padres) parenthood

paterno -na *adj* **(a)** ‹*abuelo*› paternal (*before n*) **(b)** ‹*autoridad/herencia*› paternal; ‹*cariño*› paternal, fatherly; **su domicilio ~** her parents' home

patético -ca *adj* pathetic, moving

patetismo *m* pathos (liter); **imágenes de (un) gran ~** very moving images

patíbulo *m* **(a)** (tablado) scaffold **(b)** (horca) gallows

patilla *f* **1** **(a)** (barba) sideburn, sideboard (BrE) **(b)** (de las gafas) sidepiece, arm **2** (fruta) (Col, Ven) watermelon; (esqueje) (Chi) cutting

p

patín m (a) (con ruedas) (roller) skate; (para el hielo) (ice) skate; **le regalé unos patines** I gave him a pair of skates; ~ **en línea** Rollerblade® **(b)** (tabla) skateboard **(c)** (Esp) (bote) pedalo, pedal boat

pátina f patina

patinador -dora m,f (Dep) (sobre ruedas) (roller) skater; (sobre hielo) (ice) skater

patinaje m (sobre ruedas) roller skating; (sobre hielo) ice skating; ~ **artístico/de velocidad** figure/speed skating

patinar [A1] vi **1** **(a)** (Dep) (con ruedas) to skate, roller-skate; (sobre hielo) to skate, ice-skate **(b)** (resbalar) «*persona*» to slip, slide; «*vehículo*» to skid; «*embrague*» to slip **2** (fam) (equivocarse) to slip up

patinazo m **1** (de vehículo) skid; **el coche pegó un** ~ the car skidded **2** (fam) (equivocación) blunder, slip-up (colloq)

patineta f **(a)** (con manillar) scooter **(b)** (CS, Méx, Ven) (sin manillar) skateboard

patinete m scooter

patio m **1** (en una casa) courtyard, patio; (de escuela) playground, schoolyard **2** (Esp) (Cin, Teatr) tb ~ **de butacas** (Esp) orchestra (AmE), stalls (pl) (BrE)

patizambo -ba adj (con las piernas arqueadas — hacia adentro) knock-kneed; (— hacia afuera) bowlegged

pato¹ -ta m,f (Zool) duck

pato² m **1** (Esp fam) (persona) clodhopper (colloq) **2** (Andes, Méx) (Med) bedpan

patochada f (fam) piece of nonsense; **decir** ~**s** talk nonsense

patología f pathology

patológico -ca adj pathological

patón -tona adj (AmL fam) ▶ PATUDO 1

patoso -sa adj (Esp fam) clumsy
■ m,f (Esp fam) clumsy idiot (colloq)

patota f (AmL fam) mob, gang

patraña f tall story

patria f homeland, motherland, fatherland; **luchar por la** ~ to fight for one's country

patriarca m patriarch

patrimonio m patrimony; ~ **personal** personal assets (pl); **el** ~ **nacional** national wealth; ~ **histórico** heritage; ~ **artístico/cultural** artistic/cultural heritage

patriota adj patriotic
■ mf patriot

patriotero -ra adj jingoistic, chauvinistic
■ m,f jingoist, chauvinist

patriótico -ca adj patriotic

patriotismo m patriotism

patrocinador -dora m,f (de acto, proyecto) sponsor; (Art) patron

patrocinar [A1] vt **1** ⟨*acto/proyecto*⟩ to sponsor **2** (Chi, Méx) ⟨*abogado*⟩ to represent

patrón -trona m,f **1** **(a)** (Rels Labs) employer (frml), boss **(b)** (Esp) (de casa de huéspedes) (m)

landlord; (f) landlady **2** (Relig) patron saint **3** (CS fam) (como apelativo) (m) sir; (f) madam **4** **patrón** m **(a)** (en costura) pattern **(b)** (para mediciones) standard

patrono -na m,f **(a)** (esp AmL) (Relig) patron saint **(b)** (Rels Labs) employer

patrulla f patrol; **están de** ~ they are on patrol; **la** ~ **costera** the coastguard (patrol)
■ m or f (coche) patrol o squad car

patrullar [A1] vi/vt to patrol

patrullera f (lancha) patrol boat

patrullero m (barco) patrol boat; (avión) patrol plane; (coche — militar) patrol car; (— policial) (CS, Per) patrol o squad car

patudo -da adj **1** (AmL fam) (de pies grandes) with big feet;¡**qué niño tan** ~! what big feet he has! **2** (Chi fam) (descarado) nervy (AmE colloq), cheeky (BrE colloq)

paulatino -na adj gradual

paulista adj of/from São Paulo

pausa f **(a)** (interrupción) pause; (Rad, TV) break; **hacer una** ~ to pause/have a break **(b)** (Mús) rest

pauta f **1** (guía) guideline; ~**s de comportamiento** rules o norms of behavior **2** (de un papel) lines (pl)

pava f **1** (para calentar agua) kettle **2** (Col fam) (de cigarrillo) butt; ver tb PAVO

pavada f (RPI fam) **(a)** (dicho, acción) silly thing to say/do **(b)** (cosa insignificante) little thing

pavimentar [A1] vt (con asfalto) to surface, asphalt; (con cemento, adoquines) to pave

pavimento m (de asfalto) road surface; (de cemento, adoquines) paving

pavo -va m,f (Coc, Zool) turkey; ~ **real** peacock; **de** ~ (Chi, Per fam) ⟨*viajar/entrar*⟩ without paying
■ adj **(a)** (fam) (tonto, bobo) silly, dumb (AmE colloq) **(b)** (Chi fam) (ingenuo) naive (colloq)

pavonearse [A1] v pron (fam) to show off; ~ **DE algo** to brag o crow ABOUT sth (colloq)

pavor m terror; **me da** ~ it terrifies me; **les tiene** ~ **a los perros** (fam) she's terrified of dogs

pavoroso -sa adj terrifying, horrific

paya f (Chi), **payada** (RPI) f: improvised musical dialogue

payador m (CS) singer (who performs PAYADAS)

payasada f **1** (bufonada): **deja de hacer** ~**s** stop clowning around o acting the clown (colloq) **2** (fam) **(a)** (ridiculez) ridiculous thing to say/do **(b)** (Chi) (tontería) stupid thing to say/do; **son puras** ~**s** that's utter nonsense **(c)** (Chi) (cosa) thingamajig (colloq)

payasear [A1] vi (AmL fam) to clown around (colloq)

payaso -sa m,f **(a)** (Espec) clown; **hacer (se) el** ~ to clown around (colloq) **(b)** (persona — cómica) clown, comedian; (— poco seria) joker (colloq & pej)

payo -ya m,f (Esp) word used by gypsies to refer to a non-gypsy

paz f **(a)** (Mil, Pol) peace; **firmar la** ~ to sign a peace agreement o treaty; **en época de** ~ in

AmC	América Central	Arg	Argentina	Cu	Cuba
AmL	América Latina	Bol	Bolivia	Ec	Ecuador
AmS	América del Sur	Chi	Chile	Esp	España
Andes	Región andina	CS	Cono Sur	Méx	México

Per	Perú
RPI	Río de la Plata
Ur	Uruguay
Ven	Venezuela

peacetime; *hacer las paces* to make (it) up **(b)** (calma) peace; **no me dejan vivir en** ∼ they don't give me a moment's peace; **dejar algo/a algn en** ∼ to leave sth/sb alone; **descanse en** ∼ (frml) rest in peace (frml)

PC *m or f* personal computer, PC

P.D. (= *post data*) PS

pe *f*: name of the letter P

peaje *m* (dinero) toll; (lugar) toll barrier; **carretera de** ∼ toll road

pearse [A1] *v pron* (AmL fam) to fart (sl)

peatón *m* pedestrian

peatonal *adj* pedestrian (*before n*)

pebete -ta *m,f* (RPI fam) kid (colloq)

pebre *m*: sauce made with onion, chili, coriander, parsley and tomato

peca *f* freckle

pecado *m* **(a)** (Relig) sin; ∼ **capital** deadly sin; ∼ **mortal** mortal sin **(b)** (lástima) crime, sin

pecador -dora *m,f* sinner

pecaminoso -sa *adj* sinful

pecar [A2] *vi* (Relig) to sin

pecera *f* (redonda) goldfish bowl; (rectangular) fish tank

pechera *f* (de camisa, vestido) front

pecho *m* (tórax) chest; (mama) breast; **dar (el)** ∼ **a un niño** to breast-feed o suckle a child; *tomarse algo a* ∼ ⟨crítica⟩ to take sth to heart; ⟨responsabilidad⟩ to take sth seriously

pechuga *f* (de pollo) breast

pechugona *f* (fam & hum) big-breasted woman

pecoso -sa *adj* freckly

pectoral *adj* **1** ⟨músculos⟩ pectoral (*before n*) **2** (Med): **jarabe** ∼ cough mixture o syrup

peculiar *adj* **1** (característico) particular; **un rasgo** ∼ a particular trait; **con su** ∼ **buen humor** with his characteristic good humor **2** (poco común, raro) ⟨sensación⟩ peculiar, unusual

peculiaridad *f* peculiarity

pedagogía *f* pedagogy, teaching

pedagógico -ca *adj* pedagogical, teaching (*before n*)

pedagogo -ga *m,f* (estudioso) educationalist; (educador) educator, teacher, pedagogue (frml)

pedal *m* pedal; ∼ **de embrague/de freno** clutch/brake pedal; ∼ **de arranque** kickstart

pedalear [A1] *vi* to pedal

pedante *adj* pedantic
■ *mf* pedant

pedantería *f* pedantry

pedazo *m* **1** (trozo) piece; **un** ∼ **de pan** a piece of bread; **se hizo** ∼**s** it smashed (to pieces); **el coche saltó** o **voló en** ∼**s** the car was blown to pieces; **lo hice** ∼**s** I smashed it; *caerse a* ∼**s** to fall to pieces **2** (fam) (en insultos): **¡**∼ **de idiota!** you idiot! (colloq)

pederasta *m* (homosexual) homosexual; (pedófilo) pederast

pedernal *m* flint

pedestal *m* pedestal

pedestre *adj* prosaic

pediatra *mf* pediatrician*

pediatría *f* pediatrics*

pediátrico -ca *adj* pediatric*

pedicuro -ra *m,f* chiropodist

pedido *m* **1** (Com) order; **hacer un** ∼ to place an order **2** (AmL) (solicitud) request; **a** ∼ **de** at the request of

pedigree /peðiˈɣri/, **pedigrí** *m* pedigree; **un perro de** o **con** ∼ a pedigree dog

pedinche *mf* (Méx fam) scrounger (colloq)

pedir [I14] *vt* **1** **(a)** ⟨dinero/ayuda⟩ to ask for; **pidieron un préstamo al banco** they asked the bank for a loan; **pidió permiso para salir** she asked permission to leave; **pide limosna** he begs (for money); ∼**le algo a algn** to ask sb for sth; **le pidió ayuda** he asked her for help; **me pidió disculpas** o **perdón** he apologized (to me); ∼ **hora** to make an appointment; ∼ **la palabra** to ask for permission to speak; **me pidió que le enseñara** he asked me to teach him; ▶ PRESTADO **(b)** (en bar, restaurante) ⟨plato/bebida⟩ to order; ⟨cuenta⟩ to ask for
2 (Com) **(a)** (como precio) ∼ **algo** POR **algo** to ask sth FOR sth; **¿cuánto pide por la casa?** how much is she asking for the house? **(b)** ⟨mercancías⟩ to order
■ ∼ *vi* **(a)** (en bar, restaurante) to order **(b)** (mendigar) to beg

pedo *m* **1** (fam) (ventosidad) fart (sl); **tirarse un** ∼ to fart (sl), to let off (BrE colloq); *al* ∼ (RPI fam) for nothing **2** (arg) (borrachera): **agarró un buen** ∼ he got really plastered (colloq); **tenía un** ∼ **que no veía** he was blind drunk (colloq) **3** (Méx fam) (problema, lío) hassle (colloq); *hacérsela de* ∼ *a algn* (Méx vulg) to give sb hell (colloq)

pedofilia *f* pedophilia*

pedófilo *m* pedophile*

pedorreta *f* (fam) raspberry (colloq)

pedrada *f* **1** (golpe): **me dio una** ∼ **en la cabeza** she hit me on the head with a stone **2** (Méx fam) (indirecta) hint

pedrisco *m* hail

pega *f* **1** (Col fam) (broma) trick; **de** ∼ (Esp fam) ⟨araña/culebra⟩ joke (*before n*), trick (*before n*); ⟨revólver⟩ dummy (*before n*) **2** (Esp fam) (dificultad, inconveniente) problem, snag (colloq); **te ponen muchas** ∼**s** they make it really difficult for you **3** (Andes fam) **(a)** (trabajo) work; (empleo) work; **está sin** ∼ he's out of work **(b)** (lugar) work

pegadizo -za *adj* catchy

pegado -da *adj* [ESTAR] **(a)** (junto) ∼ A **algo**: **su casa está pegada a la mía** her house is right next to mine; **iba muy** ∼ **al coche de delante** he was too close to the car in front; **pon la cama pegada a la pared** put the bed right up against the wall **(b)** (adherido) stuck; (con cola, goma) glued; **está** ∼ **al suelo** it's stuck to the floor; **las piezas están pegadas** the pieces are glued together

pegajoso -sa *adj* **(a)** ⟨superficie/sustancia⟩ sticky **(b)** ⟨calor⟩ sticky **(c)** (fam) ⟨persona⟩ clinging (colloq) **(d)** (AmL fam) ⟨canción/música⟩ catchy

pegamento *m* glue, adhesive

pegar [A3] *vt* **1** **(a)** ⟨bofetada/patada⟩ to give; **le pegó una paliza terrible** she gave him a terrible beating; **le** ∼**on un tiro** they shot her **(b)** ⟨grito/chillido⟩ to let out; ∼ **un salto de alegría** to jump for joy; ∼**le un susto a algn** to give sb a fright

2 (a) (adherir) to stick; (con cola) to glue, stick **(b)** (coser) ⟨*mangas/botones*⟩ to sew on **(c)** (arrimar) to move ... closer

3 (fam) (contagiar) ⟨*enfermedad*⟩ to give; **me pegó la gripe** he gave me the flu

■ ~ *vi* **1 (a)** (golpear): ~**le a algn** to hit sb; (a un niño, como castigo) to smack sb; **le pega a su mujer** he beats his wife; **la pelota pegó en el poste** the ball hit the goalpost **(b)** (fam) (hacerse popular) ⟨*producto/moda*⟩ to take off; ⟨*artista*⟩ to be very popular

2 (a) (adherir) to stick **(b)** (armonizar) to go together; ~ **con algo** to go with sth; **no pega con el vestido** it doesn't go (very well) with the dress

■ **pegarse** *v pron* **1 (a)** (golpearse): **me pegué con la mesa** I knocked o hit myself on the table; **me pegué en la cabeza** I banged o knocked my head **(b)** (recípr) (darse golpes) to hit each other **2** ⟨*susto*⟩ to get; ~**se un tiro** to shoot oneself **3** (contagiarse) ⟨*enfermedad*⟩ to be infectious; **eso se pega** you can easily catch it; **se te va a ~ mi catarro** you'll catch my cold; **se le ha pegado el acento mexicano** he's picked up a Mexican accent

pegatina *f* (Esp) sticker

pegoste *mf* (Méx fam) hanger-on (colloq)

peinado¹ -da *adj*: **no estaba peinada** she hadn't combed her hair; **siempre va muy bien peinada** her hair always looks very nice

peinado² *m* (arreglo del pelo) hairstyle; **lavado y ~** shampoo and set

peinador -dora *m,f* (Méx, RPl) (persona) hairdresser, stylist

peinar [A1] *vt* **1 (a)** ⟨*melena/flequillo*⟩ (con peine) to comb; (con cepillo) to brush **(b)** ⟨*peluquero*⟩: **¿quién te peina?** who does your hair? **2** ⟨*lana*⟩ to card **3** (period) ⟨*área/zona*⟩ to comb

■ **peinarse** *v pron* **(a)** (refl) (con peine) to comb one's hair; (con cepillo) to brush one's hair **(b)** (caus) to have one's hair done; **me peino en esta peluquería** I have my hair done at this salon

peine *m* comb

peineta *f* **(a)** (para sujetar, adornar) ornamental comb **(b)** (Chi) (peine) comb

p. ej. (= **por ejemplo**) eg, for example

Pekín *m* Peking, Beijing

pekinés -nesa *m,f* Pekinese

pela *f* (Esp fam) (peseta) peseta

peladez *f* (Méx) rude word

pelado -da *adj* **1 (a)** (con el pelo corto): **lo dejaron ~ o con la cabeza pelada al rape)** they cropped his hair very short **(b)** (CS) (calvo) bald **2 (a)** ⟨*manzana*⟩ peeled; ⟨*hueso*⟩ clean; ⟨*almendras*⟩ blanched **(b)** ⟨*nariz/espalda*⟩: **tengo la nariz/espalda pelada** my nose/back is peeling **3** (Chi fam) ⟨*pies/trasero*⟩ bare; **ir a pie ~** to go barefoot **4** (Méx fam) (grosero) foulmouthed

■ *m,f* (CS fam) (calvo) baldy (colloq)

peladura *f* **(a)** (de fruta) peel; ~**s de papa** potato peelings **(b)** (Andes) (en la piel) graze

pelaje *m* (de animal) coat, fur

pelar [A1] *vt* **1 (a)** ⟨*fruta/zanahoria*⟩ to peel; ⟨*habas/marisco*⟩ to shell; ⟨*caramelo*⟩ to unwrap **(b)** ⟨*ave*⟩ to pluck **2** (rapar): **lo ~on al cero o al rape** they cropped his hair very short **3** (fam) (en

el juego) to clean ... out (colloq) **4** (Chi fam) ⟨*persona*⟩ to badmouth (AmE colloq), to slag off (BrE colloq)

■ **pelarse** *v pron* (a causa del sol) ⟨*persona*⟩ to peel; ⟨*cara/hombros*⟩ (+ *me/te/le etc*) to peel; **se te está pelando la nariz** your nose is peeling

peldaño *m* (escalón) step, stair; (travesaño) rung

pelea *f* **(a)** (discusión) quarrel, fight (colloq), argument; **buscar ~** to try to pick a quarrel o fight; **tuvimos una ~** we quarreled o had an argument **(b)** (en sentido físico) fight; ~ **de gallos** cockfight

peleado -da *adj* **(a)** (enfadado): **están ~s** they've fallen out; **estar ~ con algn** to have fallen out with sb **(b)** ⟨*partido/carrera/elecciones*⟩ keenly-contested

peleador -dora *adj* (fam) (que discute) argumentative; (que pelea): **es muy ~** he's always fighting

pelear [A1] *vi* **(a)** (discutir) to quarrel; ~**on por una tontería** they quarreled o (colloq) had a fight over a silly little thing **(b)** ⟨*novios*⟩ (discutir) to quarrel, argue; (terminar) to break up, split up **(c)** (en sentido físico) to fight; ~ **POR algo** to fight OVER sth

■ **pelearse** *v pron* **(a)** (discutir) to quarrel; (pegarse) to fight; ~**se POR algo** to quarrel/fight OVER sth **(b)** ⟨*novios*⟩ (discutir) to quarrel; (terminar) to break up, split up

pelele *m* **(a)** (de trapo) rag doll; (de paja) straw doll **(b)** (persona — manipulada) puppet; (— débil) (fam) wimp (colloq)

peletería *f* (oficio) fur trade; (tienda) furrier's, fur shop; (género) furs (*pl*)

peliagudo -da *adj* ⟨*problema*⟩ difficult, tricky; ⟨*asunto*⟩ thorny

pelícano *m* pelican

película *f* **1 (a)** (Cin, TV) movie, film (BrE); **hoy dan o** (Esp) **echan o ponen una ~** there's a movie o film on today, they're showing a movie o film today; ~ **de dibujos animados** cartoon; ~ **del Oeste o de vaqueros** Western; ~ **de miedo o de terror** horror movie o film; ~ **de suspenso o** (Esp) **suspense** thriller; ~ **muda** silent movie o film **(b)** (Fot) film **2** (capa fina — de aceite) film; (— de polvo) thin layer

peligrar [A1] *vi* to be at risk; **hacer ~ algo** to put sth at risk

peligro *m* danger; **estar en o correr ~** ⟨*persona*⟩ to be in danger; ⟨*vida*⟩ to be in danger o at risk; **un ~ para la salud** a health risk; **poner algo/a algn en ~** to put sth/sb at risk; **corren el ~ de perder la final** they're in danger of losing the final; **corres el ~ de que te despidan** you run the risk of being fired; **estar fuera de ~** to be out of danger; **Ⓢ peligro de incendio** fire hazard

peligrosidad *f* dangerousness

peligroso -sa *adj* dangerous

pelillo *m* small hair

pelirrojo -ja *adj* red-haired, ginger-haired

■ *m,f* redhead

pellejerías *fpl* (Andes fam) hard times (*pl*)

pellejo *m* **(a)** (piel — de animal) skin, hide; (— de persona) (fam) skin (colloq); **ponerse en el ~ de**

algn (fam) to put oneself in sb's shoes **(b)** (fam) (vida) neck (colloq); **jugarse** or **arriesgar el** ∼ to risk one's neck (colloq) **(c)** (odre) wineskin

pellizcar [A2] vt ⟨persona/brazo⟩ to pinch

pellizco m **(a)** (en la piel) pinch; **me dio un** ∼ **en la pierna** she pinched my leg **(b)** (fam) (cantidad pequeña) little bit; **un** ∼ **de sal** a pinch of salt

pelmazo -a adj (fam) boring
■ m,f (fam) bore

pelo m **1** (de personas) hair; ∼ **rizado/liso** or **lacio** curly/straight hair; **tiene mucho/poco** ∼ he has really thick/thin hair; **llevar el** ∼ **suelto** to wear one's hair down o loose; **se le está cayendo el** ∼ he's losing his hair; **con** ∼**s y señales** (fam) down to the last detail; **no tiene** ∼**s en la lengua** (fam) he doesn't mince his words; **se me/le ponen los** ∼**s de punta** (fam) it sends shivers down my/ his spine, it makes my/his hair stand on end; **tomarle el** ∼ **a algn** (fam) (bromeando) to pull sb's leg (colloq); (burlándose) to mess around with sb (AmE), to mess sb around (BrE) **2** (Zool) (filamento) hair; (pelaje — de perro, gato) hair, fur; (— de conejo, oso) fur; ∼ **de camello** camelhair **3** (de alfombra) pile

pelón -lona adj (fam) (sin pelo) bald
■ m,f **1** (fam) (sin pelo) baldy (colloq) **2** **pelón** m (RPl) (duranzo) nectarine

pelota f **1** (Dep, Jueg) ball; **una** ∼ **de fútbol** (esp AmL) a football; **jugar a la** ∼ to play ball; ∼ **vasca** jai alai, pelota; **darle** ∼ **a algn** (CS fam) to take notice of sb; **hacerle la** ∼ **a algn** (Esp fam) to suck up to sb (colloq) **2** **pelotas** fpl (vulg) (testículos) balls (pl) (colloq or vulg); **en** ∼**s** (vulg) (sin ropa) stark naked; (sin dinero) flat broke (colloq)
■ mf **1** (AmS vulg) (imbécil) jerk (sl) **2** (Esp fam) (adulador) creep (colloq)

pelotari mf jai alai o pelota player

pelotazo m (golpe): **me dio un** ∼ he hit me with the ball

pelotera f (fam) **(a)** (lío, jaleo) ruckus (AmE colloq), rumpus (BrE colloq) **(b)** (riña) argument, row (colloq)

pelotero -ra m,f **(a)** (AmL) (jugador — de béisbol) baseball player; (— de fútbol) soccer o football player, footballer **(b)** (Chi) (recogepelotas) (m) ballboy; (f) ballgirl

pelotón m **(a)** (Mil) squad; ∼ **de ejecución** or **fusilamiento** firing squad **(b)** (en ciclismo) bunch, pack; (en atletismo) pack **(c)** (fam) (de gente) gang (colloq)

pelotudo -da adj (AmS vulg): **¡qué** ∼**!** what a jerk! (sl)
■ m,f (AmS vulg) jerk (sl)

peluca f wig

peluche m felt, plush; **un juguete de** ∼ a cuddly toy; ▶ **oso**

pelucón -cona adj (Chi, Per fam) (con mucho pelo) hairy; (de pelo largo) long-haired

peludo -da adj ⟨hombre/brazo⟩ hairy; ⟨barba⟩ bushy; ⟨animal⟩ hairy, furry; ⟨cola⟩ bushy; ⟨lana/ jersey⟩ hairy

peluquería f **(a)** (establecimiento) hairdresser's, hairdressing salon **(b)** (oficio) hairdressing, hairstyling

peluquero -ra m,f hairdresser, hairstylist

peluquín m toupee, hairpiece

pelusa¹, pelusilla f **1** (en la cara) down, fuzz; (de fruta) down; (en jersey) ball of fluff o fuzz; (de suciedad) ball of fluff **2** (Esp fam) (celos) jealousy; **tener** ∼ to be jealous

pelusa² mf (Chi fam) (niño — callejero) street kid (colloq); (— travieso) little rascal (colloq)

pelvis f (pl ∼) pelvis

pena f **1** **(a)** (tristeza): **tenía/sentía mucha** ∼ he was o felt very sad; **me da** ∼ **verlo** it upsets me o it makes me sad to see it; **a mí la que me da** ∼ **es su mujer** it's his wife I feel sorry for; **está que da** ∼ she's in a terrible state **(b)** (lástima) pity, shame; **¡qué** ∼**!** what a pity o shame!; **es una** ∼ **que ...** it's a pity (that) ...; **vale** o **merece la** ∼ it's worth it; **vale la** ∼ **leerlo/visitarlo** it's worth reading/a visit **2** **penas** fpl **(a)** (problemas) sorrows (pl); **ahogar las** ∼**s** to drown one's sorrows; **me contó sus** ∼**s** he told me his troubles; **a duras** ∼**s** (apenas) hardly; (con dificultad) with difficulty **(b)** (penalidades) hardship **3** (Der) sentence; **la** ∼ **máxima** the maximum sentence; ∼ **capital** or **de muerte** death penalty **4** (AmL exc CS) (vergüenza) embarrassment; **¡qué** ∼**!** how embarrassing!; **me da mucha** ∼ **pedírselo** I'm too embarrassed to ask him

penal adj criminal (before n)
■ m **1** (cárcel) prison, penitentiary (AmE) **2** (AmL period) (Dep) penalty

pénal m (Andes) penalty

penalidades fpl hardship, suffering

penalizar [A4] vt (Der) to penalize

penalty /'penalti, pe'nalti/ m (pl **-tys**) penalty; **pitar** or **señalar** ∼ to award o give a penalty

penca f **(a)** (de hoja) main rib **(b)** (del nopal) stalk **(c)** (Méx) (de bananas) bunch

pendejada f **(a)** (AmL exc CS fam) (estupidez) stupid thing to say/do **(b)** (Per vulg) (mala jugada) dirty trick

pendejear [A1] vi (Méx fam) to clown around (colloq)

pendejez f (Méx vulg) stupidity

pendejo -ja adj **(a)** (AmL exc CS fam) (estúpido) dumb (AmE colloq), thick (BrE colloq) **(b)** (Per fam) (listo) sly, sharp (colloq)
■ m,f **(a)** (AmL exc CS fam) (estúpido) dummy (colloq), nerd (colloq); **hacerse el** ∼ (fam) (hacerse el tonto) to act dumb (colloq); (no hacer nada) to loaf around (colloq) **(b)** (Per fam) (persona lista) sly devil

pendenciero -ra adj quarrelsome
■ m,f troublemaker

pendiente adj **1** ⟨asunto/problema⟩ unresolved; ⟨cuenta⟩ outstanding **2** (atento): **está** ∼ **del niño a todas horas** she devotes every minute of the day to the child; **estoy** ∼ **de que me llamen** I'm waiting for them to call me
■ m (Esp) earring
■ f (de terreno) slope, incline; (de tejado) slope; **una** ∼ **muy pronunciada** a very steep slope o incline; **tiene mucha** ∼ it slopes steeply

péndulo m pendulum

pene m penis

penetración f penetration

penetrante adj **1** ⟨mirada/voz⟩ penetrating, piercing; ⟨olor⟩ pungent, penetrating; ⟨sonido⟩ piercing **(b)** ⟨viento/frío⟩ bitter, biting **2** ⟨inteligencia/mente/ironía⟩ sharp

p

penetrar [A1] *vi* (entrar) ~ POR algo «*agua/
humedad*» to seep THROUGH sth; «*luz*» to shine
THROUGH sth; «*ladrón*» to enter THROUGH sth; ~
EN algo to penetrate sth
■ ~ *vt* to penetrate; **la bala le penetró el pulmón**
the bullet penetrated *o* entered his lung
penicilina *f* penicillin
península *f* peninsula
peninsular *adj* peninsular
■ *mf*: **los ~es** people from mainland Spain
penique *m* penny
penitencia *f* [1] (Relig) penance; **en ~** as (a)
penance [2] (a) (Andes) (en juegos) forfeit; (b) (RPI
fam) (castigo) punishment; **el maestro me puso en
~** the teacher punished me
penitenciaría *f* penitentiary
penitente *mf* penitent
penoso -sa *adj* [1] (lamentable) terrible, awful
[2] (a) (triste) sad (b) ⟨*viaje*⟩ grueling*; ⟨*trabajo*⟩
laborious, difficult [3] (AmL exc CS fam) (a)
⟨*persona*⟩ shy (b) (embarazoso) embarrassing
pensamiento *m* [1] (a) (facultad) thought (b)
(cosa pensada) thought (c) (doctrina) thinking (d)
(máxima) thought [2] (Bot) pansy
pensar [A5] *vi* to think; **después de mucho ~**
... after much thought ...; **actuó sin ~** he did it
without thinking; **pensé para mí** *or* **para mis
adentros** I thought to myself; **~ EN algo/algn** to
think ABOUT sth/sb; **cuando menos se piensa** ...
just when you least expect it ...; **~ mal/bien de
algn** to think ill *o* badly/well of sb; **dar que** *or*
hacer ~ a algn to make sb think
■ ~ *vt* [1] (a) (creer, opinar) to think; **pienso que no**
I don't think so; **¿qué piensas del divorcio/del
jefe?** what do you think about divorce/the boss?
(b) (considerar) to think about; **lo ~é** I'll think
about it; **piénsalo bien antes de decidir** think it
over before you decide; **pensándolo bien,** ... on
second thought(s) *o* thinking about it, ...; **¡y ~
que ...!** (and) to think that ...!; **¡ni ~lo!** no way!
(colloq), not on your life! (colloq) (c) (Col) ⟨*persona*⟩
to think about
[2] (tener la intención de): **~ hacer algo** to think of
doing sth; **pensamos ir al teatro** we're thinking of
going to the theater; **no pienso ir** I'm not going
■ **pensarse** *v pron* (enf) (fam) ⟨*decisión/
respuesta*⟩ to think about; *ver tb* PENSAR *vt* 1B
pensativo -va *adj* pensive, thoughtful
pensión *f* [1] (Servs Socs) pension; **cobrar la ~**
to draw one's pension; **~ alimenticia**
maintenance; **~ de invalidez** disability
(allowance) (AmE), invalidity benefit (BrE) [2] (a)
(casa — de huéspedes) guesthouse, rooming house
(AmE), boarding house (BrE); (— para estudiantes)
student hostel; **~ completa** full board ▶ MEDIO¹ 1
(b) (alojamiento) accommodations (*pl*) (AmE),
lodging, accommodation (BrE) [3] (Col)
(mensualidad) tuition (AmE), school fees (*pl*) (BrE)
pensionado -da *m,f* [1] (Servs Socs) pensioner
[2] **pensionado** *m* (a) (Esp) (internado) boarding
school (b) (CS) (pensión para estudiantes) student
hostel

pensionarse [A1] *v pron* (Col) to retire
pensionista *mf* [1] (Servs Socs) pensioner
[2] (en casa de huéspedes) resident, lodger
pentágono *m* (a) (Mat) pentagon (b) **el
Pentágono** the Pentagon
pentagrama *m* (Mús) stave, staff
pentatlón *m* pentathlon
penúltimo -ma *adj* penultimate
■ *m,f*: **ser el ~** to be second to last
penumbra *f* (media luz) half-light, semidarkness
penuria *f* (a) (escasez) shortage, dearth; **pasar
~s** to suffer hardship (b) (pobreza) poverty
peña *f* [1] (roca) crag, rock [2] (a) (grupo) circle,
group; **~ taurina** bullfighting club (b) (AmL) *tb* **~
folklórica** folk club
peñasco *m* crag, rocky outcrop
peón *m* [1] (Const) laborer*; (Agr) (esp AmL)
agricultural laborer*, farm worker; **~ albañil**
(building) laborer*; **~ caminero** road worker
[2] (en ajedrez) pawn; (en damas) piece, checker
(AmE), draughtsman (BrE)
peonza *f* spinning top
peor *adj/adv* [1] (uso comparativo) worse; **va a ser
~ para él como no estudie** if he doesn't study so
much the worse for him; **y si vienen los dos,
tanto ~** and it'll be even worse if the two of them
come; **cada vez ~** worse and worse; **su situación
es ~ que la mía** his situation is worse than mine;
está ~ que nunca it's worse than ever
[2] (uso superlativo) worst; **el ~ alumno de la clase**
the worst pupil in the class; **lo ~ que puede
pasar** the worst (thing) that can happen; **en el ~
de los casos** if the worst comes to the worst; **el
lugar donde ~ se come** the worst place to eat in
■ *mf*: **el/la ~** (de dos) the worse; (de varios) the
worst
pepa *f* (AmS) (semilla — de uva, naranja) pip; (— de
durazno, aguacate) stone, pit
Pepe *diminutive of José*
pepenador -dora *m,f* (Méx) scavenger (*on
garbage dumps*)
pepenar [A1] *vt* (Méx fam) (en la basura) to
scavenge
pepinillo *m* gherkin
pepino *m* cucumber
pepita *f* (a) (de uva) pip; (de tomate) seed; (de
calabaza) (Méx) dried pumpkin seed (b) (de oro)
nugget
pepona *f* large doll
pequeño -ña *adj* (a) (de tamaño) small; **me
queda ~** it's too small for me; **en ~** in miniature
(b) (de edad) young, small; **mi hermano ~** my
younger *o* little brother; **cuando era ~** when I
was small *o* little (c) (de poca importancia)
⟨*distancia*⟩ short; ⟨*retraso*⟩ short, slight;
⟨*cantidad*⟩ small; ⟨*esfuerzo*⟩ slight; ⟨*problema/
diferencia*⟩ slight, small
■ *m,f*: **el ~/la pequeña** the little one (colloq); (edad
— de dos) the younger; (— de muchos) the youngest
pera *f* [1] (Bot) pear; **~ de agua** dessert pear;
pedirle ~s al olmo to ask the impossible [2] (de

goma) bulb **3** (en boxeo) punching ball (AmE), punchball (BrE) **4** (CS fam) (mentón) chin; (barba) goatee

peral *m* pear tree

percal *m* percale

percance *m* (contratiempo) mishap; (accidente) minor accidente

percatarse [A1] *v pron* to notice; ~ DE algo to notice sth

percebe *m* (molusco) goose barnacle

percepción *f* (por los sentidos) perception; ~ **extrasensorial** extrasensory perception, ESP

perceptible *adj* (por los sentidos) perceptible, noticeable

percha *f* (a) (para el armario) (coat) hanger (b) (gancho) coat hook; (perchero) coat stand

perchero *m* (de pared) coat rack; (de pie) coat stand

percibir [I1] *vt* **1** ⟨sonido/olor⟩ to perceive; ⟨peligro⟩ to sense **2** (fml) ⟨sueldo/cantidad⟩ to receive

percusión *f* percussion

perdedor -dora *adj* losing (before n)
■ *m,f* loser; **es un mal** ~ he's a bad loser

perder [E8] *vt* **1** (en general) to lose; **perdí el pasaporte** I lost my passport; **quiere** ~ **peso** he wants to lose weight; **con preguntar no se pierde nada** we've/you've nothing to lose by asking; ~ **la vida** to lose one's life, to perish; ▶ CABEZA 1E, VISTA 3; **yo no pierdo las esperanzas** I'm not giving up hope; ~ **la práctica** to get out of practice; ~ **el equilibrio** to lose one's balance; ~ **el conocimiento** to lose consciousness, to pass out; ~ **el ritmo** (Mús) to lose the beat; (en trabajo) to get out of the rhythm
2 (a) ⟨autobús/tren/avión⟩ to miss (b) ⟨ocasión/oportunidad⟩ to miss; **sin** ~ **detalle** without missing any detail (c) ⟨tiempo⟩ to waste; **¡no me hagas** ~ (el) **tiempo!** don't waste my time!; **no hay tiempo que** ~ there's no time to lose
3 (a) ⟨guerra/pleito/partido⟩ to lose (b) ⟨curso/año⟩ to fail; ⟨examen⟩ (Ur) to fail
4 ⟨agua/aceite/aire⟩ to lose
■ ~ *vi* **1** (ser derrotado) to lose; **perdieron 3 a 1** they lost 3-1; **no sabes** ~ you're a bad loser; **llevar las de** ~ to be onto a loser; **la que sale perdiendo soy yo** I'm the one who loses out *o* comes off worst
2 «cafetera/tanque» to leak
3 echar(se) a perder ▶ ECHAR I 1A, ECHARSE 1A
■ **perderse** *v pron* **1** ⟨persona/objeto⟩ to get lost; **siempre me pierdo en esta ciudad** I always get lost in this town; **se le perdió el dinero** he's lost the money; **cuando se ponen a hablar rápido me pierdo** when they start talking quickly I get lost
2 ⟨fiesta/película/espectáculo⟩ to miss

perdición *f* ruin

pérdida *f* (a) (en general) loss; ~ **de calor/energía** heat/energy loss; **tuvo una** ~ **de conocimiento** he lost consciousness, he passed out; *no tiene* ~ (Esp) you can't miss it (b) (Fin) loss; **la compañía sufrió grandes** ~s the company made a huge loss; ~ **materiales** damage; ~s **y ganancias** profit and loss (c) (desperdicio) waste; **fue una** ~ **de tiempo** it was a waste of time (d) (escape de gas, agua) leak

perdido -da *adj* **1** [ESTAR] (a) ⟨objeto/persona⟩ lost; **dar algo por** ~ to give sth up for lost; **de** ~ (Méx fam) at least (b) (confundido, desorientado) lost, confused (c) ⟨bala/perro⟩ stray (before n) **2** [ESTAR] (en un apuro): **si se enteran, estás** ~ if they find out, you've had it *o* you're done for (colloq) **3** (aislado) ⟨lugar⟩ remote, isolated; ⟨momento⟩ idle, spare **4** ⟨idiota⟩ complete and utter (before n), total (before n); ⟨loco⟩ raving (before n); ⟨borracho⟩ out and out (before n)
■ *m,f* degenerate

perdidoso -sa *m, f* (Méx) loser

perdigón *m* (Arm) pellet

perdiz *f* partridge

perdón *m* (Der) pardon; (Relig) forgiveness; **me pidió** ~ **por su comportamiento** he apologized to me for his behavior, he said he was sorry about his behavior; **con** ~ if you'll pardon the expression
■ *interj* (expresando disculpas) I beg your pardon (fml), excuse me (AmE), sorry; (para atraer la atención) excuse me, pardon me (AmE); (al pedir que se repita algo) sorry?, pardon me? (AmE)

perdonar [A1] *vt* (a) ⟨persona/falta/pecado⟩ to forgive; **te perdono** I forgive you; **perdona mi curiosidad, pero ...** forgive my asking but ...; **perdone que lo moleste, pero ...** sorry to bother you *o* (AmE) pardon me for bothering you, but ... (b) (Der) to pardon (c) ⟨deuda⟩ to write off; **le perdonó el castigo** she let him off the punishment
■ ~ *vi*: **perdone ¿me puede decir la hora?** excuse me *o* (AmE) pardon me, can you tell me the time?; **perdone ¿cómo ha dicho?** sorry? what did you say?, excuse *o* pardon me? what did you say? (AmE); **perdona, pero yo no dije eso** I'm sorry but that's not what I said

perdurar [A1] *vi* «duda/sentimiento/recuerdo» to remain, last; «crisis/situación/relación» to last

perecear [A1] *vi* (Col) to laze around

perecedero -ra *adj* ⟨producto⟩ perishable

perecer [E3] *vi* (fml) to die, perish (journ *or* liter)

peregrinación *f*, **peregrinaje** *m* pilgrimage

peregrino -na *adj* **1** ⟨idea/respuesta⟩ outlandish, peculiar **2** (a) ⟨ave⟩ migratory (b) ⟨monje⟩ wandering (before n)
■ *m,f* pilgrim

perejil *m* (Bot, Coc) parsley

perenne *adj* perennial; **árbol de hoja** ~ evergreen tree

pereza *f* laziness; **me da** ~ **ir** I can't be bothered to go; **tengo una** ~ **horrible** I feel terribly lazy; **¡qué** ~ **tener que ir!** what a bind *o* drag having to go! (colloq)

perezosa *f* (Col, Per) deck chair

perezoso -sa *adj* lazy, idle
■ *m,f* **1** (holgazán) lazybones (colloq) **2** **perezoso** *m* (Zool) sloth

perfección *f* perfection; **habla francés a la** ~ she speaks perfect French

perfeccionar [A1] *vt* (mejorar) to improve; (hacer perfecto) to perfect

perfeccionista *mf* perfectionist

perfecto¹ -ta *adj* (a) (ideal, excelente) perfect ···⊹

(b) (*delante del n*) (absoluto): **un ∼ caballero** a perfect gentleman; **es un ∼ desconocido** he is completely unknown

perfecto² *interj* fine!

perfil *m* **(a)** (del cuerpo, la cara) profile; **una foto de ∼** a profile photograph; **visto de ∼** seen from the side **(b)** (contorno, silueta) profile, silhouette

perfilar [A1] *vt* ⟨*plan/estrategia*⟩ to shape
■ **perfilarse** *v pron* **(a)** «*silueta/contorno*» to be outlined **(b)** (tomar forma) «*posición/actitud*» to become clear

perforación *f* **(a)** (en general) drilling, boring; (pozo) borehole **(b)** (Med) perforation **(c)** (en papeles, sellos) perforation

perforadora *f* **1** (Min, Tec) drill **2** (de papeles) hole puncher; (de sellos) perforator

perforar [A1] *vt* **1** **(a)** ⟨*pozo*⟩ to sink, drill, bore **(b)** ⟨*madera*⟩ to drill *o* bore holes/a hole in **(c)** «*ácido*» to perforate; «*bala*» to pierce **2** ⟨*papel/tarjeta*⟩ to perforate
■ **perforarse** *v pron* «*úlcera/intestino*» to become perforated

perfumar [A1] *vt* to perfume
■ **perfumarse** *v pron* (*refl*) to put perfume *o* scent on

perfume *m* perfume, scent

perfumería *f* perfumery

pergamino *m* (material) parchment; (documento) scroll

pérgola *f* pergola

pericia *f* (destreza) skill

periferia *f* **(a)** (de círculo) periphery, circumference **(b)** (de ciudad) outskirts (*pl*) **(c)** (Inf) peripherals (*pl*)

periférico¹ -ca *adj* ⟨*barrio/zona*⟩ outlying (*before n*)

periférico² *m* **1** (Inf) peripheral **2** (AmC, Méx) (carretera) beltway (AmE), ring road (BrE)

perilla *f* (barba) goatee; **venir de ∼(s)** (fam) to come in very handy (colloq)

perímetro *m* perimeter

periódico¹ -ca *adj* periodic

periódico² *m* newspaper, paper

periodiquero -ra *m,f* (Méx) news *o* newspaper vendor

periodismo *m* journalism

periodista *mf* journalist, reporter; **∼ gráfico** press photographer

período, periodo *m* period

peripecia *f* **(a)** (incidente): **un viaje lleno de ∼s** an eventful journey; **sus ∼s en el extranjero** her adventures abroad **(b)** (problema) vicissitude

periquito *m* (americano) parakeet; (australiano) budgerigar, budgie (colloq)

periscopio *m* periscope

peritaje *m* **(a)** (informe) expert's report; (de casa) survey (report) **(b)** (Educ) technical studies (*pl*)

perito -ta *m,f* (experto) expert; **∼ agrónomo** agricultural technician; **∼ industrial** engineer; **∼ mercantil** qualified accountant

peritonitis *f* (*pl* **∼**) peritonitis

perjudicado -da *adj*: **el que resultó ∼** the one who lost out *o* who was worst hit; **los más ∼s** the worst hit, the worst affected
■ *m,f*: **el ∼ fui yo** I was the one who lost out

perjudicar [A2] *vt* (dañar) to be detrimental to (frml), damage; **el tabaco perjudica la salud** smoking is detrimental to *o* damages your health; **estas medidas perjudican a los jóvenes** these measures are detrimental to *o* harm young people

perjudicial *adj* [SER] damaging, harmful, detrimental (frml); **∼ PARA algo/algn** damaging *o* harmful *o* detrimental TO sth/sb

perjuicio *m* (daño) damage; **no sufrió ningún ∼** it did him no harm *o* damage; **le causó un gran ∼** it was very damaging to him; **redunda *o* va en ∼ de todos** it works against *o* (frml) is detrimental to everyone; **sin ∼ para su salud** without detriment to his health (frml); **sin ∼ de que cambiemos de opinión** even though we may change our minds later

perjurio *m* perjury

perla *f* (joya) pearl; **∼ cultivada** *or* **de cultivo** cultured pearl

permanecer [E3] *vi* (frml) **(a)** (en lugar) to stay, remain (frml) **(b)** (en actitud, estado) to remain; **permaneció en silencio** he was *o* remained silent

permanencia *f* (en lugar) stay; (en organización, cargo) continuance (frml)

permanente *adj* permanent
■ *f* **1** (en el pelo) perm; **hacerse la ∼** to have one's hair permed, to have a perm **2** (Col) (juzgado) emergency court (*for cases of violent crime*)

permisible *adj* permissible

permisionario -ria *m,f* (Méx) concessionaire, official agent

permisivo -va *adj* permissive

permiso *m* **1** (autorización) permission; (documento) permit, license*; **me dio ∼** she gave me permission; **(con) permiso** (al abrirse paso) excuse me; (al entrar) may I come in?; **∼ de conducir** driver's license (AmE), driving licence (BrE); **∼ de residencia** residence permit, green card (AmE); **∼ de trabajo** work permit **2** (días libres) leave; **de ∼** on leave

permitir [I1] *vt* **(a)** (autorizar) to allow, permit (frml); **no le permitieron verla** he was not allowed to see her; **no van a ∼les la entrada** they're not going to let them in; **¿me permite?** (frml) may I? **(b)** (tolerar, consentir): **no te permito que me hables así** I won't have you speak *o* I won't tolerate you speaking to me like that; **si se me permite la expresión** if you'll pardon the expression **(c)** (hacer posible) to enable, to make ... possible; **esto ∼á mejores comunicaciones** this will enable better communications; **si el tiempo lo permite** weather permitting
■ **permitirse** *v pron* (*refl*) to allow oneself; (económicamente): **puedo/no puedo ∼me ese lujo** I can/can't afford that luxury

permutación *f* permutation

pernera *f* (del pantalón) leg

pero *conj* but; **ella fue, ∼ yo no** she went, but I didn't; **¡∼ si queda lejísimos!** but it's miles (away)!; **¿∼ tú estás loca?** are you crazy?
■ *m* **(a)** (defecto) defect, bad point; (dificultad, problema) drawback; **ponerle ∼s a algo/algn** to find fault with sth/sb **(b)** (excusa) objection; **¡no hay ∼ que valga!** I don't want any excuses (*o* arguments *etc*)

perogrullada *f* (fam) platitude, truism

Perogrullo *m*: **ser de** ~ to be patently obvious

perol *m* (pequeño) saucepan; (grande) pot

peroné *m* fibula

perorata *f* (fam) lecture (colloq)

perpendicular *adj/f* perpendicular

perpetrar [A1] *vt* to perpetrate (frml), to carry out

perpetuar [A18] *vt* to perpetuate

perpetuo -tua *adj* perpetual

perplejidad *f* perplexity, puzzlement

perplejo -ja *adj* perplexed, puzzled; **estar** ~ **con algo** to be puzzled *o* perplexed by sth

perra *f* [1] (Zool) dog, bitch [BITCH *solo se emplea cuando se quiere hacer referencia al sexo del animal*] *ver tb* PERRO [2] (Esp fam) **(a)** (rabieta) tantrum; **coger una** ~ to have *o* throw a tantrum **(b)** (manía) obsession; **le ha cogido la** ~ **de tener uno** he's obsessed with having one

perrada *f* (AmL fam) dirty trick

perrera *f* **(a)** (lugar) dog pound, dog's home **(b)** (vehículo) dog catcher's van

perrería *f* (fam) terrible thing (colloq)

perrero -ra *m,f* dog catcher, dog warden (BrE)

perrito *m* [1] (Zool) little dog; *ver tb* PERRO [2] (AmL) (Bot) snapdragon

perro -rra *m,f* (Zool) dog; ~ **callejero** stray (dog); ~ **de compañía** pet dog; ~ **guardián** guard dog; ~ **guía** *or* **lazarillo** guide dog; ~ **pastor** sheepdog; **perrito caliente** (Coc) hot dog; **perrito faldero** lapdog; ~ **policía** German shepherd, Alsatian (BrE); ~ **rastreador** (para seguir una huella) tracker dog; (para buscar drogas) sniffer dog; ~ **salchicha** dachshund, sausage dog (colloq); **de** ~**s** (fam) foul; **hace un tiempo de** ~**s** the weather's foul *o* horrible; **está de un humor de** ~**s** he's in a foul mood; **llevarse como** (el) ~ **y** (el) **gato** to fight like cats and dogs (AmE) *o* (BrE) cat and dog ■ *adj* (fam) **(a)** ⟨*vida/suerte*⟩ rotten (colloq), lousy (colloq) **(b)** ⟨*persona*⟩ nasty

persa *adj/mf* Persian ■ *m* (idioma) Persian

persecución *f* **(a)** (en sentido físico) pursuit; **salir en** ~ **de algn** to set off in pursuit of sb **(b)** (por la ideología) persecution; **sufrir persecuciones** to be subjected to persecution, to be persecuted

perseguir [I30] *vt* [1] **(a)** ⟨*fugitivo/delincuente/presa*⟩ to pursue, chase **(b)** (por la ideología) to persecute [2] ⟨*objetivo/fin*⟩ to pursue; ~ **la fama** to be in pursuit of fame; **me persigue la mala suerte** I'm dogged by bad luck

perseverante *adj* persevering, persistent

perseverar [A1] *vi* to persevere

Persia *f* Persia

persiana *f* **(a)** (que se enrolla *o* levanta) blind; ~ **veneciana** *or* **de lamas** Venetian blind **(b)** (AmL) (contraventana, postigo) shutter

persignarse [A1] *v pron* to cross oneself

persistencia *f* persistence

persistente *adj* persistent

persistir [I1] *vi*: **persiste el temporal** there is still a storm blowing; ~ **EN algo** to persist IN sth

persona *f* **(a)** (ser humano) person; **una** ~ **muy educada** a very polite person; **dos o más** ~**s** two or more people; **las** ~**s interesadas** ... all those interested ... **(b)** (en locs) **en persona** ⟨*ir/presentarse*⟩ in person; **no lo conozco en** ~ I

don't know him personally; **por persona** per person; **solo se venden dos entradas por** ~ you can only get two tickets per person; **la comida costó 20 dólares por** ~ the meal cost 20 dollars per *o* a head **(c)** (Ling) person

personaje *m* **(a)** (Cin, Lit) character **(b)** (persona importante) important figure, personage (frml); **un** ~ **de la política** an important political figure; **es todo un** ~ **en el pueblo** he's something of a local celebrity

personal *adj* personal; **objetos de uso** ~ personal effects ■ *m* (de fábrica, empresa) personnel (*pl*), staff (*sing or pl*); **estamos escasos de** ~ we're short-staffed

personalidad *f* **(a)** (Psic) personality **(b)** (persona importante) ▶ PERSONAJE B

personalizar [A4] *vi*: **no quiero** ~ I don't want to name names *o* mention any names ■ ~ *vt* to personalize

personería *f* (Col, RPI) legal capacity

personero -ra *m,f* (AmL) (representante) representative; (portavoz) (*m*) spokesman, spokesperson; (*f*) spokeswoman, spokesperson

personificar [A2] *vt* to personify; **es la bondad personificada** she is kindness itself

perspectiva *f* **(a)** (Arquit, Art) perspective; **en** ~ in perspective **(b)** (vista, paisaje) view, perspective (frml) **(c)** (punto de vista) perspective **(d)** (posibilidad) prospect; **las** ~**s son buenas** the prospects are good; **no tengo ningún plan en** ~ I've no plans for the immediate future

perspicacia *f* shrewdness, insight

perspicaz *adj* shrewd, perceptive

persuadir [I1] *vt* to persuade; ~ **a algn DE QUE** *or* **PARA QUE haga algo** to persuade sb to do sth

persuasión *f* persuasion

persuasivo -va *adj* persuasive

pertenecer [E3] *vi* **(a)** (ser propiedad) ~ **A algn/algo** to belong TO sb/sth **(b)** (formar parte) ~ **A algo** to belong to sth, be a member OF sth

perteneciente *adj*: **los países** ~**s al grupo** the countries belonging to *o* which are members of the group

pertenencia *f* **(a)** (a grupo, organización) membership **(b)** (frml) (propiedad): **los objetos de su** ~ his belongings **(c)** **pertenencias** *fpl* belongings (*pl*), possessions (*pl*)

pértiga *f* **(a)** (vara) pole **(b)** (Esp) (Dep) pole; **salto con** ~ pole vault

pertinente *adj* **(a)** (oportuno, adecuado) ⟨*medida*⟩ appropriate **(b)** (relevante) ⟨*observación/comentario*⟩ relevant, pertinent

perturbación *f* (alteración) disruption; (Psic) disturbance

perturbado -da *adj* disturbed ■ *m,f*: *tb* ~ **mental** mentally disturbed person

perturbar [A1] *vt* to disturb

Perú *m*: *tb* **el** ~ Peru

peruanismo *m* Peruvianism, Peruvian word/expression

peruano -na *adj/m,f* Peruvian

perversión *f* **(a)** (maldad) evil, wickedness **(b)** (corrupción) perversion

perverso -sa *adj* evil ■ *m,f* evil *o* wicked person

pervertido -da *m,f* pervert

pervertir [I11] *vt* to corrupt, pervert
■ **pervertirse** *v pron* to become corrupted

pesa *f* **(a)** (de balanza, reloj) weight **(b)** (Dep)
(grande) weight; (pequeña) dumbbell; **levantamiento
de ~s** weightlifting; *hacer* **~s** to do weight
training **(c)** (balanza) scales (*pl*)

pesadez *f* [1] (sensación de cansancio) heaviness
[2] (fam) **(a)** (aburrimiento, molestia) drag (colloq); **¡qué
~ de conversación!** what a boring conversation!
(b) (Andes) (broma) tiresome joke; (comentario)
nasty remark

pesadilla *f* **(a)** (sueño) nightmare, bad dream
(b) (situación) nightmare; **de ~** ‹viaje/visión›
nightmare (*before n*)

pesado -da *adj* [1] (en general) heavy;
‹estómago› bloated; ‹sueño› deep [2] **(a)** (fam)
(fastidioso, aburrido) ‹libro/película› tedious;
‹persona›: **¡qué ~ es!** he's such a pain in the
neck! (colloq); **no te pongas ~** don't be so
annoying *o* (colloq) such a pest! **(b)** (AmL) (difícil,
duro) ‹trabajo/tarea› heavy, hard [3] (Andes fam)
(antipático) unpleasant; **¡qué tipo tan ~!** what a
jerk! (colloq)
■ *m,f* **(a)** (fam) (latoso) pain (colloq), pest (colloq) **(b)**
(Andes fam) (antipático) jerk (colloq)

pesadumbre *f* grief, sorrow

pésame *m* condolences (*pl*); **darle el ~ a algn**
to offer sb one's condolences; **mi más sentido ~**
(fr hecha) my deepest sympathies

pesar¹ *m* [1] **(a)** (pena, tristeza) sorrow; **a ~ mío**
or **muy a mi ~** much to my regret
(b) (remordimiento) regret, remorse [2] **a pesar de**
despite, in spite of; **a ~ de todo** in spite of *o*
despite everything; **a ~ de que** even though

pesar² [A1] *vi* **(a)** «paquete/maleta» to be
heavy; **estas gafas no pesan** these glasses don't
weigh much; **no me pesa** it's not heavy
[2] (causar arrepentimiento) (+ *me/te/le* etc): **ahora me
pesa mucho** now I deeply regret it; **me pesa
haberlo ofendido** I'm very sorry I offended him
[3] **pese a** despite, in spite of; **pese a que** even
though; **mal que me/le pese** whether I like/he
likes it or not
■ **~** *vt* **(a)** ‹niño/maleta› to weigh; ‹manzanas› to
weigh (out) **(b)** (tener cierto peso) to weigh; **pesa 80
kilos** he weighs 80 kilos
■ **pesarse** *v pron* (*refl*) to weigh oneself

pesca *f* **(a)** (en general) fishing; **ir** *or* **salir de ~**
to go fishing; **~ con caña** angling; **~ con red** net
fishing; **~ submarina** underwater fishing **(b)**
(peces) fish (*pl*); **aquí hay mucha ~** there are a
lot of fish here **(c)** (lo pescado) catch

pescada *f* hake

pescadería *f* fish shop, fishmonger's (BrE)

pescadero -ra *m,f* fish dealer (AmE),
fishmonger (BrE)

pescadilla *f* whiting, young hake

pescado *m* (Coc) fish; (pez) (AmL) fish; **~ azul/
blanco** blue/white fish

pescador -dora (*m*) fisherman;
(*f*) fisherwoman

pescar [A2] *vt* ‹trucha/corvina› to catch;

fuimos a ~ trucha(s) we went trout-fishing, we
went fishing for trout [2] (fam) **(a)** ‹catarro/gripe›
to catch **(b)** ‹novio/marido› to get, hook (colloq &
hum) **(c)** ‹chiste/broma› to get (colloq) **(d)** (pillar) to
catch; **lo ~on robando** they caught him
red-handed (as he was stealing something)
■ **~** *vi* to fish; **~ a mosca** to fly-fish

pescuezo *m* (fam) neck

pese a *loc prep* ▶ PESAR² 3

pesebre *m* (en establo) manger, trough; (de
Navidad) crib

pesebrera *f* (Col) stable

pesero *m* (Méx) minibus

peseta *f* peseta (*former Spanish unit of
currency*)

pesimismo *m* pessimism

pesimista *adj* pessimistic
■ *mf* pessimist

pésimo -ma *adj* dreadful, terrible, abysmal

peso *m* [1] **(a)** (Fis, Tec) weight; **ganar/perder ~**
to gain *o* put on/lose weight; **~ bruto/neto** gross/
net weight **(b) al peso** by weight
[2] **(a)** (carga, responsabilidad) weight, burden;
quitarle un ~ de encima a algn to take a load *o* a
weight off sb's mind **(b)** (influencia) weight; **todo el
~ de la ley** the full weight of the law **(c) de peso**
‹argumento› strong, weighty; ‹razón› forceful
[3] (Dep) **(a)** (Esp) (en atletismo) shot; **lanzamiento
de ~** shot-put, shot-putting **(b)** (Esp) (en halterofilia)
weight; **levantamiento de ~s** weightlifting **(c)** (en
boxeo) weight; **~ ligero/mosca/pesado/pluma**
lightweight/flyweight/heavyweight/featherweight
[4] (báscula) scales (*pl*)
[5] (Fin) peso (*unit of currency in many Latin
American countries*)

pespunte *m* backstitch

pesquero -ra *adj* fishing (*before n*)

pesquisa *f* investigation, inquiry

pestaña *f* (Anat) eyelash

pestañear [A1] *vi* to blink; **sin ~** (literal)
without blinking; (sin inmutarse) without batting
an eyelash (AmE) *o* (BrE) eyelid

peste *f* **(a)** (Med, Vet) plague, epidemic; **~ cristal**
(Chi) chickenpox; **~ negra** Black Death **(b)** (AmL)
fam) (enfermedad contagiosa) bug (colloq); (resfriado)
cold **(c)** (fam) (mal olor) stink

pesticida *m* pesticide

pestilente *adj* ‹olor› foul

pestillo *m* (cerrojo) bolt; (de cerradura) latch,
catch; **echó** *or* **corrió el ~** she put the bolt across

petaca *f* **(a)** (cigarrera) cigarette case; (para
tabaco — de cuero) tobacco pouch; (— de metal)
tobacco tin **(b)** (para bebidas alcohólicas) hipflask

pétalo *m* petal

petanca *f* petanque

petardo *m* firecracker, banger (BrE)

petate *m* [1] (para dormir) bedroll; (bolsa)
knapsack [2] (Col, Méx) (estera) matting
[3] **petates** *mpl* (CS fam) (pertenencias) gear
(colloq)

petición *f* **(a)** (acción) request; **a ~ del público** by popular request *o* demand; **a ~ fiscal** at the prosecutor's request **(b)** (escrito) petition; **~ de divorcio** petition for divorce; **~ de extradición** application for extradition

petirrojo *m* robin

petiso -sa *m,f* **1** (AmS fam) (de baja estatura) shorty (colloq) **2** **petiso** *m* (CS) (Equ) small horse, pony

peto *m* **(a)** (de pantalón, delantal) bib; **pantalones de ~** (Esp) overalls (*pl*) (AmE), dungarees (*pl*) (BrE) **(b)** (de armadura) breastplate **(c)** (Taur) protective covering (*for picador's horse*) **(d)** (en béisbol) chest protector

petrificado -da *adj* ‹madera› petrified; ‹animal› fossilized; **al oírlo se quedó ~** he was thunderstruck when he heard

petrificar [A2] *vt* to petrify

■ **petrificarse** *v pron* to become petrified, turn to stone

petrodólar *m* petrodollar

petróleo *m* **(a)** (Min) oil, petroleum; **~ crudo** crude oil **(b)** (combustible) kerosene, paraffin (BrE)

petrolero¹ -ra *adj* oil (*before n*)

petrolero² *m* oil tanker

petrolífero -ra *adj* oil (*before n*);
▶ YACIMIENTO

petulante *adj* smug, self-satisfied

■ *mf* smug *o* self-satisfied fool

petunia *f* petunia

peyorativo -va *adj* pejorative

pez *m* fish; **~ de río** freshwater fish; **~ de colores** goldfish; **~ espada** swordfish; **~ gordo** (fam) (persona importante) bigwig (colloq); (en delito) big shot (colloq); **~ volador** flying fish; **estar** *or* **sentirse como ~ en el agua** to be in one's element

■ *f* (sustancia) pitch, tar

pezón *m* (Anat) nipple; (Zool) teat

pezuña *f* (Zool) hoof

piadoso -sa *adj* ‹personas› devout, pious; ‹obra› kind

pianista *mf* pianist

piano *m* piano; **~ de cola/de media cola** grand piano/baby grand; **~ vertical** upright piano

pianola *f* Pianola®, player piano

piar [A17] *vi* to chirp, tweet

PIB *m* (Esp) (= **Producto Interior Bruto**) GDP

pibe -ba *m,f* (RPl fam) kid (colloq)

pica *f* **1** (Arm) pike; (Taur) lance, goad; (para cavar) pick, pickax* **2** (Jueg) **(a)** (carta) spade **(b) picas** *fpl* (palo) spades

picada *f* **1** (AmL) (descenso pronunciado): **caer en ~** «avión» to nose-dive; «pájaro» to plunge, to dive; «acciones/valores» to plummet **2** (AmL) (aperitivo) nibbles (*pl*)

picadero *m* (para caballos) exercise ring; (escuela) riding school

picado¹ -da *adj* **(a)** ‹diente/muela› decayed, bad; ‹manguera/llanta› perished **(b)** ‹ajo/perejil› chopped; ‹carne› (Esp, RPl) ground (AmE), minced (BrE) **(c)** ‹manzana› rotten; ‹vino› sour **(d)** (fam) (enfadado, ofendido) put out (colloq), miffed (colloq) **(e)** ‹mar› choppy

picado² *m* (Esp) ▶ PICADA 1

picador *m* **(a)** (Taur) picador **(b)** (en mina) face worker

picadura *f* **1** (de mosquito, serpiente) bite; (de abeja) sting; (de polilla) hole **2** (en diente, muela) cavity

picaflor *m* (AmL) (Zool) hummingbird; (donjuán) (fam) womanizer

picana *f* (AmL) **(a)** (para bueyes) prod, goad **(b)** *tb* **~ eléctrica** cattle prod

picante *adj* **(a)** (Coc) ‹comida› hot **(b)** ‹chiste/libro› risqué; ‹comedia› racy

picaporte *m* (manivela) door handle; (mecanismo) latch

picar [A2] *vt* **1** **(a)** «mosquito/víbora» to bite; «abeja/avispa» to sting; **me ~on los mosquitos** I got bitten by mosquitoes; **una manta picada por las polillas** a moth-eaten blanket **(b)** «ave» ‹comida› to peck at; ‹enemigo› to peck **(c)** ‹anzuelo› to bite **(d)** (fam) (comer) to eat; **solo quiero ~ algo** I just want a snack *o* a bite to eat **(e)** ‹billete/boleto› to punch **(f)** (Taur) to jab **2** **(a)** (Coc) ‹carne› (Esp, RPl) to grind (AmE), to mince (BrE); ‹cebolla/perejil› to chop (up) **(b)** ‹hielo› to crush; ‹pared› to chip; ‹piedra› to break up, smash **3** ‹dientes/muelas› to rot, decay

■ **~** *vi* **1** **(a)** (morder el anzuelo) to bite, take the bait **(b)** (comer) to nibble **2** **(a)** (ser picante) to be hot **(b)** (producir comezón) «lana/suéter» to itch, be itchy; **me pica la espalda** my back itches *o* is itchy; **me pican los ojos** my eyes sting **3** (AmL) «pelota» to bounce **4** (RPl arg) (irse, largarse) to split (sl); **~le** (Méx fam) to get a move on (colloq)

■ **picarse** *v pron* **1** **(a)** «muelas» to decay, rot; «manguera/llanta» to perish; «cacerola/pava» to rust; «ropa» to get moth-eaten **(b)** «manzana» to go rotten; «vino» to go sour **2** «mar» to get choppy **3** (fam) (enfadarse) to get annoyed; (ofenderse) to take offense

picardía *f* **(a)** (astucia) craftiness, cunning **(b)** (malicia) mischief **(c)** (travesura) prank

picaresco -ca *adj* picaresque

pícaro -ra *adj* **(a)** (ladino) crafty, cunning **(b)** (malicioso) ‹persona› naughty, wicked (colloq); ‹chiste/comentario› naughty, racy; ‹mirada/sonrisa› mischievous, cheeky (BrE)

■ *m,f* **(a)** (Lit) rogue, villain **(b)** (astuto) cunning *o* crafty devil (colloq)

picatoste *m* (para sopa) crouton

picazón *f* irritation, itch

pichanga *f* (Chi) (partido — improvisado) kickabout, friendly game; (— malo) bad game

pichi *m* (Esp) jumper (AmE), pinafore (BrE)

pichí *m* (CS fam) wee-wee (used to or by children)

pichicatearse [A1] *v pron* (CS, Per fam) to take drugs

pichincha *f* (RPl fam) (ganga) bargain, steal (colloq)

pichirre *mf* (Ven fam) skinflint (colloq)

pichón -chona *m,f* (de paloma) young pigeon; (de otros pájaros) chick

picnic *m* (*pl* **-nics**) picnic

pico *m* **1** **(a)** (de pájaro) beak **(b)** (fam) (boca) mouth; **¡cierra el ~!** shut up (colloq), keep your ⋯⟶

trap shut! (colloq) **2** (a) ⟨cima, montaña⟩ peak (b) (en gráfico) peak (c) (en diseños, costura) point; **cuello de** ∼ V neck (de jarra, tetera) spout **3** (fam) (algo): **tiene 50 y** ∼ **de años** she's fifty odd o fifty something (colloq); **son las dos y** ∼ it's past o gone two; **tres metros y** ∼ (just) over three meters **4 picos** *mpl* (Méx) (zapatillas) spikes (*pl*) **5** (arg) shot

picor *m* irritation, itch

picoso *adj* (Méx) hot, spicy

picotazo *m* peck

picotear [A1] *vt* to peck
■ ∼ *vi* (fam) (entre comidas) to nibble, snack

picudo -da *adj* (a) ⟨nariz⟩ pointed, sharp (b) ⟨ave⟩ long-beaked

pida, pidas, etc ▶ PEDIR

pie¹ *m* **1** (a) (Anat) foot; **un dedo del** ∼ a toe; **tiene (los)** ∼**s planos** she has flat feet; ∼ **de atleta** athlete's foot (b) (*en locs*) **a pie** on foot; **ir a** ∼ to go on foot, walk; **hoy ando a** ∼ (AmL) I'm without wheels today; **de pie** standing; **ponte de** ∼ stand up; **en pie: estoy en** ∼ **desde las siete** I've been up since seven o'clock; **no puedo tenerme en** ∼ I can hardly walk/stand; **solo la iglesia quedó en** ∼ only the church remained standing; **mi oferta sigue en** ∼ my offer still stands; **a** ∼ **pelado** (Chi) barefoot, in one's bare feet; **de a** ∼ common, ordinary; **de la cabeza a los** ∼**s** *or* **de** ∼**s a cabeza** from head to foot o toe, from top to toe (colloq); **en** ∼ **de guerra** on a war footing; **en (un)** ∼ **de igualdad** on an equal footing; **hacer** ∼ to be able to touch the bottom; **levantarse con el** ∼ **derecho** to get off to a good start; **no tener ni** ∼**s ni cabeza** to make no sense whatsoever; **por mi/ tu/su** (*propio*) ∼ unaided, without any help **2** (a) (de calcetín, media) foot (b) (de lámpara, columna) base; (de copa — base) base; (— parte vertical) stem; (de montaña) foot (c) (de página, escrito) foot, bottom; **una nota a** *or* **al** ∼ **de página a** footnote; ∼ **de fotografía** caption; **al** ∼ **de la letra** ⟨copiar/repetir⟩ word by word, exactly (d) (de cama) *tb* ∼**s** foot
3 (a) (medida) foot (b) (Lit) foot

pie² /pai/ *m* (AmL) pie

piedad *f* (a) (compasión) mercy; **ten** ∼ **de nosotros** have mercy on us; **es un hombre sin** ∼ he's merciless; **¡por** ∼**!** for pity's sake! (b) (devoción) devotion

piedra *f* **1** (material) stone; (trozo) stone, rock (esp AmE); **casas de** ∼ stone houses; **me tiró una** ∼ he threw a stone o rock at me; ∼ **caliza** *or* **de cal** limestone; ∼ **de molino** millstone; ∼ **pómez** pumice stone; ∼ **preciosa** precious stone; **dejar a algn de** ∼ (fam) to stun sb; ⟨duro⟩ **como una** ∼ ⟨pan/asado⟩ rock hard; **tiene el corazón duro como una** ∼ he has a heart of stone **2** (de mechero) flint (b) (cálculo) stone; **tiene** ∼**s en el riñón/la vesícula** she has kidney stones/gallstones

piel *f* **1** (Anat, Zool) skin; ∼ **grasa/seca** oily o greasy/dry skin; ∼ **roja** *mf* (fam & pey) redskin (colloq & pej), Red Indian; **se me/te pone la** ∼ **de gallina** I/you get gooseflesh o goose pimples **2** (Indum) (a) (Esp, Méx) (cuero) leather; **guantes de** ∼ leather gloves; ∼ **de cocodrilo** crocodile skin; ∼ **de serpiente** snakeskin; ∼ **sintética** (cuero sintético) (Esp, Méx) synthetic leather; (imitación

nutria, visón, etc) synthetic fur (b) (de visón, zorro, astracán) fur; **abrigo de** ∼**(es)** fur coat (c) (sin tratar) pelt
3 (Bot) (de cítricos, papa) peel; (de manzana) peel, skin; (de otras frutas) skin

pienso *m* (comida) fodder, feed

pierda, pierdas, etc ▶ PERDER

pierna *f* (a) (Anat) leg; **con las** ∼**s cruzadas** cross-legged; **abrirse de** ∼**s** (en gimnasia) to do the splits (b) (Coc) leg; ∼ **de cordero** leg of lamb

pieza *f* **1** (a) (elemento, parte) piece (b) (de motor, reloj) part; ∼ **de recambio** *or* **de repuesto** spare part; **quedarse de una** ∼ to be dumbfounded; **ser de una sola** ∼ (AmL) to be as straight as a die (c) (en ajedrez) piece; (unidad, objeto) piece; **ser una** ∼ **de museo** (fam) to be a museum piece (d) (en caza) piece, specimen **2** (Mús, Teatr) piece **3** (esp AmL) (dormitorio) bedroom; (en hotel) room

pifia *f* **1** (a) (fam) (error) boob (colloq) (b) (en billar) miscue (c) (Chi) (defecto) fault **2** (Chi, Per) (del público) booing and hissing

pifiar [A1] *vt* **1** (fam) (fallar) to fluff (colloq); ∼**la** (fam) to blow it (colloq) **2** (Chi, Per) «*público*» to boo

pigmentación *f* pigmentation

pigmento *m* pigment

pigmeo -mea *adj/m,f* pygmy

pijama *m* pajamas (*pl*) (AmE), pyjamas (*pl*) (BrE)

pije *adj/mf* (Chi) ▶ PIJO

pijo -ja *adj* (Esp fam & pey) ⟨persona/moda/lugar⟩ posh (colloq & pej)
■ *m,f* (Esp fam & pey) rich kid (colloq & pej)

pila *f* **1** (Elec, Fís) battery; **funciona a** ∼**(s)** *or* **con** ∼**s** it runs on batteries, it's battery-operated **2** (fregadero) sink; (de una fuente) basin, bowl; ∼ **bautismal** baptismal font **3** (fam) (de libros, platos) pile, stack

pilar *f* (Arquit) pillar, column; (de puente) pier
■ *mf* (en rugby) prop (forward)

pilchas *fpl* (CS fam) clothes (*pl*), gear (colloq)

píldora *f* (a) (pastilla) pill, tablet (b) *tb* ∼ **anticonceptiva** (contraceptive) pill; **tomar la** ∼ to be on the pill; ∼ **del día siguiente** morning-after pill

pileta *f* (a) (RPl) (fregadero) kitchen sink; (del baño) washbowl (AmE), washbasin (BrE) (b) (RPl) (piscina) swimming pool (c) (Chi) (estanque) pond; (bebedero) drinking fountain

pillaje *m* pillage

pillar [A1] *vt* **1** (fam) (a) (atrapar) to catch; **le pilló un dedo** it caught o trapped her finger; **¡te pillé!** caught o got you! (b) ⟨catarro/resfriado⟩ to catch **2** (Esp fam) «*coche*» to hit
■ **pillarse** *v pron* ⟨dedos/manga⟩ to catch

pillo -lla *adj* (fam) (travieso) naughty, wicked (colloq); (astuto) crafty, cunning
■ *m,f* (fam) (travieso) rascal (colloq); (astuto) crafty o cunning devil (colloq)

pilón *m* **1** (a) (de fuente) basin (b) (Arquit) pillar; (de puente) pylon **2** (Méx fam) (en la compra) *small amount of extra goods given free*; **me dio tres manzanas de** ∼ he threw in three extra apples (for free)

pilotar [A1] *vt* **(a)** ⟨*avión*⟩ to pilot, fly; ⟨*barco*⟩ to pilot, steer; ⟨*coche*⟩ to drive; ⟨*moto*⟩ to ride **(b)** ⟨*empresa/país*⟩ to guide, steer

pilotear [A1] *vt* (AmL) ▶ PILOTAR

piloto *mf* 1 (Aviac, Náut) pilot; (de coche) driver; (de moto) rider; ~ **de carreras** racing driver; ~ **de pruebas** (de avión) test pilot; (de coche) test driver; (de moto) test rider 2 **piloto** *m* **(a)** (de aparato eléctrico, a gas) pilot light **(b)** (CS) (impermeable) raincoat 3 (*como adj inv*) ⟨*programa/producto*⟩ pilot (*before n*)

piltrafa *f* **(a)** (de comida) scrap **(b)** (cosa inservible) useless thing

pimentón *m* **(a)** (dulce) paprika; (picante) cayenne pepper **(b)** (AmS exc RPl) (fruto) pepper, capsicum

pimienta *f* pepper

pimiento *m* pepper, capsicum; ~ **rojo/verde** red/green pepper

pimpón *m* Ping-Pong®, table tennis

pin *m* (broche) pin

PIN *m* PIN

pináculo *m* (Arquit) pinnacle; (apogeo) peak

pinar *m* pine forest

pincel *m* (Art) paintbrush; (para maquillarse) brush

pincelada *f* brushstroke

pinchadiscos *mf* (*pl* ~) (Esp fam) disc jockey, DJ (colloq)

pinchar [A1] *vt* **(a)** ⟨*globo/balón*⟩ to burst; ⟨*rueda*⟩ to puncture **(b)** (con alfiler, espina) to prick **(c)** (para recoger) to spear 2 (fam) (poner una inyección) to give ... a shot (colloq) 3 ⟨*teléfono*⟩ to tap, bug 4 (Inf) to click on 5 (Esp fam) ⟨*discos*⟩ to play ■ ~ *vi* 1 **(a)** «*planta*» to be prickly 2 (Auto) to get a flat (tire*), get a puncture 3 (Chi fam) (con el sexo opuesto) ▶ LIGAR *vi* ■ **pincharse** *v pron* 1 (*refl*) «*persona*» (accidentalmente) to prick oneself; (inyectarse) (fam) to shoot up (sl), to jack up (sl) 2 «*rueda*» to puncture; «*globo/balón*» to burst; **se me pinchó un neumático** I got a flat (tire*) *o* a puncture

pinchazo *m* **(a)** (herida) prick; (inyección) shot (colloq) **(b)** (en una rueda) flat, puncture **(c)** (dolor agudo) sharp pain **(d)** (fam) (de droga) fix (colloq)

pinche *adj* **(a)** (AmL exc CS fam) (*delante del n*) (maldito): ¡~ **vida!** what a (lousy *o* rotten) life!; **por unos ~s pesos** for a few measly pesos (colloq); **vámonos de este ~ lugar** let's get out of this damn place! **(b)** (Méx fam) (de poca calidad) lousy (colloq); (despreciable) horrible **(c)** (AmC fam) (tacaño) tightfisted (colloq) ■ *mf* (Coc) kitchen assistant

pincho *m* 1 (de rosa, zarza) thorn, prickle (colloq) (de cactus) spine, prickle (colloq) 2 (Esp) (de aperitivo) bar snack

pingo -ga *m,f* (Méx fam) little scamp *o* rascal (colloq)

Ping-Pong® *m* Ping-Pong®, table tennis

pingüino *m* penguin

pino *m* 1 (Bot) (árbol) pine (tree); (madera) pine 2 (Esp) (en gimnasia): **hacer el** ~ to do a handstand 3 (Méx) (en bolos) pin

pinolillo *m* (AmC) (maíz) cornstarch (AmE), maize flour (BrE); (bebida) *drink made with cornstarch and water*

pinta *f* 1 (fam) (aspecto) look; **eso le da** ~ **de intelectual** it gives him an intellectual look; **tiene** ~ **de extranjero** he looks foreign; **¿dónde vas con esa(s) ~(s)?** where are you going looking like that?; *echar o tirar* (Andes) *or* (RPl) *hacer* ~ (fam) to impress 2 (en tela, animal) spot 3 (medida) pint 4 (Méx fam) (de la escuela): **irse de** ~ to play hooky* (esp AmE colloq), to skive off (school) (BrE colloq)

pintada *f* piece of graffiti; (Pol) slogan

pintado -da *adj* ⟨*vaca*⟩ spotted; ⟨*caballo*⟩ dappled, pied

pintalabios *m* (*pl* ~) (fam) lipstick

pintar [A1] *vt* **(a)** (en general) to paint; **pintó la puerta de rojo** she painted the door red; ~ **algo al óleo** to paint sth in oils **(b)** (fam) (dibujar) to draw ■ ~ *vi* 1 **(a)** (con pintura) to paint **(b)** (fam) (dibujar) to draw 2 (en naipes) to be trumps ■ **pintarse** *v pron* (*refl*) (maquillarse) to put on one's makeup; ~**se los labios** to put on some lipstick; ~**se los ojos** to put on eye makeup; ~**se las uñas** to paint one's nails

pintarrajear [A1] *vt* to daub

pintor -tora *m,f* (de cuadros) painter, artist; (de paredes) (house) painter; ~ **de brocha gorda** (de casas, barcos) painter

pintoresco -ca *adj* picturesque

pintura *f* **(a)** (arte, cuadro) painting; ~ **a la acuarela/al óleo** watercolor*/oil painting **(b)** (material) paint; (en cosmética) makeup

pinza *f* 1 **(a)** (para la ropa) clothespin (AmE), clothes peg (BrE) **(b)** (para el pelo) bobby pin (AmE), hairgrip (BrE) **(c)** (de un cangrejo) pincer **(d)** (en costura) dart; **un pantalón con ~s** pleated pants (AmE) *o* (BrE) trousers 2 *tb* ~**s (a)** (para depilar) tweezers (*pl*); (de cirujano) forceps (*pl*); (de cocina, chimenea) tongs (*pl*) **(b)** (alicates) pliers (*pl*)

piña *f* (Bot) (fruta) pineapple; (del pino) pine cone

piñata *f*: *container hung up during festivities and hit with a stick to release candy inside*

piñón *m* 1 (Bot) pine kernel *o* nut 2 (Mec) pinion; (de bicicleta) sprocket wheel

pío¹, pía *adj* devout, pious

pío² *m* peep, tweet; **no decir ni** ~ (fam) not to say a word

piojo *m* louse; ~**s** lice

piojoso -sa *adj* **(a)** (con piojos) lousy, lice-ridden **(b)** (fam) (sucio) filthy

piola *adj inv* (RPl fam) **(a)** (divertido) fun (*before n*) (colloq) **(b)** (astuto) crafty (colloq) **(c)** ⟨*ropa*⟩ trendy (colloq) ■ *f* (AmL) cord

piolet /pjo'le(t)/ *m* (*pl* **-lets**) ice ax*

pionero -ra *adj* pioneering (*before n*) ■ *m,f* pioneer

pipa *f* 1 (para fumar) pipe; **fumar (en)** ~ to smoke a pipe 2 (tonel) cask, barrel 3 (Esp) (de sandía, mandarina) pip; (de girasol, calabaza) seed; **pasarlo** ~ (fam) to have a great time 4 (Méx) (camión) tanker

pipí *m* (fam) pee (colloq), wee (BrE colloq); **hacer** ~ to have a pee *o* (BrE) wee

pique *m* 1 **a pique: una caída** *a or* (Méx) **en** ~ ⸰⸰⸰⟩

hasta el mar a vertical *o* sheer drop to the sea
below; **a pique de** on the point of, about to; *irse a*
~ «*barco*» to sink; «*negocio*» to go under
2 (fam) **(a)** (enfado, resentimiento): **tener un ~ con
algn** to be at odds with sb **(b)** (rivalidad) rivalry,
needle **3** **(a)** (carta) spade **(b) piques** *fpl* (palo)
spades (*pl*)

piqueta *f* pick, pickax*

piquete *m* **1** (de huelguistas) picket; (de soldados)
squad, picket (arch) **2** (Méx fam) **(a)** (herida) prick;
(inyección) shot (colloq), jab (colloq) **(b)** (de insecto)
sting, bite

pira *f* pyre

piragua *f* (Dep) canoe

piragüismo *m* canoeing

pirámide *f* pyramid

piraña *f* (Zool) piranha

pirarse [A1] *v pron* (Esp fam) to make oneself
scarce (colloq)

pirata *adj* **(a)** ⟨*barco*⟩ pirate (*before n*) **(b)**
(clandestino) ⟨*casete/copia*⟩ pirate (*before n*), bootleg
(*before n*) (colloq)
■ *mf* **(a)** (Náut) pirate; ~ **aéreo** hijacker **(b)** (de
casetes, vídeos) pirate

piratear [A1] *vt* ⟨*vídeos/casetes*⟩ to pirate;
⟨*sistema*⟩ to hack into

piratería *f* piracy; ~ **informática** hacking
(colloq)

Pirineos *mpl*, **Pirineo** *m*: **los ~** *or* **el Pirineo**
the Pyrenees (*pl*)

pirinola *mf* (Andes, Méx) (peonza) spinning top

pirómano -na *m,f* pyromaniac

piropear [A1] *vt* to make flirtatious/flattering
comments to

piropo *m* flirtatious/flattering comment

pirueta *f* (en danza) pirouette; (de un caballo)
pesade

pis *m* ▶ PIPÍ

pisada *f* (acción) footstep; (huella) footprint

pisapapeles *m* (*pl* ~) paperweight

pisar [A1] *vt* **1** **(a)** (con el pie) ⟨*mina/clavo*⟩ to
step on; ⟨*charco*⟩ to step in, tread in (esp BrE); **la
pisó sin querer** he accidentally stepped *o* (esp BrE)
trod on her foot; **❺ prohibido pisar el césped**
keep off the grass **(b)** (humillar) to trample on,
walk all over **2** (RPl, Ven) **(a)** (Coc) to mash **(b)**
(fam) (atropellar) to run over
■ ~ *vi* to tread; **pisó mal y se cayó** she lost her
footing and fell

pisca *f* (Méx) harvest

piscina *f* swimming pool; ~ **cubierta/
climatizada** covered/heated swimming pool

Piscis *m* (signo, constelación) Pisces; **es (de) ~**
he's *a* Pisces, he's a Piscean
■ *mf* (*pl* ~) (persona) *tb* **piscis** Piscean, Pisces

pisco *m* (aguardiente) ≈ grappa

piso *m* **1** **(a)** (de edificio) floor, story*; (de
autobús) deck; **una casa de seis ~s** a six-story
building; **un autobús de dos ~s** a double-decker
bus **(b)** (de pastel) layer **2** (AmL) **(a)** (suelo) floor

(b) (de carretera) road surface **3** (Esp) (apartamento)
apartment (esp AmE), flat (BrE); ~ **piloto** (Esp)
show apartment *o* (BrE) flat **4** (Chi) (taburete)
stool; (alfombrita) rug; (felpudo) doormat

pisotear [A1] *vt* **(a)** (con los pies) to trample,
stamp on **(b)** ⟨*persona/derecho*⟩ to ride roughshod
over

pisotón *m* stamp; **darle un ~ a algn** (intencional)
to stamp on sb's foot *o* toes; (sin querer) to tread *o*
step on sb's foot *o* toes

pista *f* **1** **(a)** (rastro) trail, track; **seguirle la ~ a
algn** to be/get on sb's trail **(b)** (indicio) clue **2** **(a)**
(carretera) road, track **(b)** (Chi) (carril) lane **(c)**
(Audio) track **3** **(a)** (en el circo) ring; (en el
picadero) ring; (en el hipódromo) track (AmE), course
(BrE); ~ **de aterrizaje** runway, landing strip; ~ **de
baile** dance floor; ~ **de esquí** ski slope, piste; ~
de hielo/de patinaje ice/skating rink **(b)** (Esp) (de
tenis) court

pistacho *m* pistachio (nut)

pistola *f* **(a)** (Arm) pistol; **a punta de ~** at
gunpoint **(b)** (para pintar) spray gun

pistolero *m* gunman

pistón *m* **(a)** (émbolo) piston **(b)** (de arma)
percussion cap **(c)** (de instrumento) key

pitada *f* **1** **(a)** (pitido) beep **(b)** (en espectáculo)
≈ booing and hissing, whistling (*as sign of
disapproval*) **2** (AmL) (de cigarrillo) puff, drag
(colloq)

pitar [A1] *vi* **(a)** «*guardia/árbitro*» to blow
one's whistle **(b)** «*vehículo*» to blow the horn, to
hoot **(c)** «*público*» (como protesta) to boo and hiss
■ ~ *vt* ⟨*falta*⟩ to blow for, award, call (AmE)

pitcher *mf* pitcher

pitido *m* (sonido agudo) whistle, whistling; (de
claxon) beep, hoot, honk

pitillera *f* cigarette case

pitillo *m* **1** (fam) (cigarrillo) smoke (colloq), fag
(BrE colloq) **2** (Col) (para beber) straw

pito *m* **1** **(a)** (silbato) whistle; **tocar el ~** to blow
the whistle; **tener voz de ~** (fam) to have a
squeaky voice **(b)** (fam) (de coche) horn, hooter;
(de tren) whistle; **tocar el ~** to hoot, honk **2** (Chi
fam) (de marihuana) joint (colloq), spliff (sl) **3** (fam)
(pene) weenie (AmE colloq), willy (BrE colloq)

pitón *f or m* python

pitonisa *f* fortuneteller

pitorrearse [A1] *v pron* (Esp fam) ~ **DE algn** to
make fun of sb

pituco -ca *adj* (CS, Per fam) **(a)** (elegante) posh
(colloq) **(b)** (engreído) stuck-up (colloq)
■ *m,f* (CS, Per fam) **es un ~** he's stuck-up (colloq)

pituto *m* (Chi fam) (para conseguir algo) contact

pívot *mf* (*pl* **-vots**) (Dep) center*, pivot

piyama *m or f* (AmL) pajamas (*pl*) (AmE),
pyjamas (*pl*) (BrE)

pizarra *f* (Min) slate **(b)** (en el aula)
blackboard, chalkboard; (del alumno) slate **(c)** (Cin)
clapperboard **(d)** (en béisbol) scoreboard

pizarrón *m* (AmL) blackboard, chalkboard

pizca f [1] (cantidad pequeña): **una** ∼ **de algo** (de sal, azúcar) a pinch of sth; (de vino, agua) a drop of sth; **no tiene ni** ∼ **de gracia** it's not the slightest bit funny [2] (Méx) (cosecha) harvest

pizcar [A2] vt (Méx) ‹maíz› to harvest; ‹algodón› to pick
■ ∼ vi (Méx) to take in the harvest

pizza /'pitsa, 'pisa/ f pizza

pizzería /pitse'ria, pise'ria/ f pizzeria

Pl. (= **Plaza**) Sq, Square

placa f [1] (lámina, plancha) sheet [2] **(a)** (con inscripción) plaque; **una** ∼ **con el nombre** a nameplate; ∼ **de matrícula** license (AmE) o (BrE) number plate **(b)** (de policía) badge [3] (Chi) (dentadura) dentures (pl), dental plate

placaje m (en fútbol americano) block; (en rugby) tackle

placar [A2] vt (en fútbol americano) to block; (en rugby) to tackle

placard /pla'kar/ m (RPl) built-in closet (AmE), fitted wardrobe (BrE)

placenta f placenta, afterbirth

placentero -ra adj pleasant, agreeable

placer [E4] vi (en 3ª pers) (+ me/te/le etc): **haz lo que te plazca** do as you please; **me place informarle que ...** (frml) it is my pleasure to inform you that ... (frml)
■ m (gusto, satisfacción) pleasure; **ha sido un** ∼ **conocerla** (frml) it has been a pleasure to meet you; **un viaje de** ∼ a pleasure trip

placero m (Per) street vendor

placidez f placidity, placidness, calmness

plácido -da adj placid, calm

plaga f **(a)** (de insectos, ratas) plague; **las ardillas son consideradas una** ∼ squirrels are considered to be a pest **(b)** (calamidad, azote) plague

plagado -da adj: **[ESTAR]** ∼ **DE algo** ‹de faltas/errores› riddled WITH sth; ‹de turistas/insectos› swarming WITH sth

plagiar [A1] vt ‹idea/libro› to plagiarize

plagio m (copia) plagiarism

plan m [1] (proyecto, programa) plan; **hacer** ∼**es to make plans;** ∼ **de estudios** syllabus [2] (fam) (cita, compromiso): **si no tienes otros** ∼**es** if you're not doing anything else; **¿tienes algún** ∼ **para esta noche?** do you have any plans for tonight?
[3] (fam) (actitud): **vienen en** ∼ **de diversión** they're here to have fun; **lo dijo en** ∼ **de broma** he was only kidding (colloq); **en** ∼ **económico** cheaply, on the cheap (colloq)

plana f [1] (de periódico) page; **aparece en primera** ∼ it's on the front page [2] (Educ) (ejercicio) handwriting exercise [3] **la** ∼ **mayor** (Mil) the staff officers (pl); (jefes) (fam) the top brass (colloq)

plancha f [1] **(a)** (electrodoméstico) iron **(b)** (acto) ironing; (ropa para planchar) ironing [2] **(a)** (Const, Tec) sheet **(b)** (Impr) plate [3] (utensilio de cocina) griddle; **filete a la** ∼ grilled steak [4] **(a)** (fam) (metedura de pata) boo-boo (colloq), boob (colloq) **(b)** (Chi fam) (vergüenza) embarrassment

planchar [A1] vt ‹sábana/mantel› to iron; ‹pantalones› to press, iron; ‹traje› to press
■ ∼ vi (con la plancha) to do the ironing

plancton m plankton

planeación f (Méx) planning

planeador m glider

planear [A1] vt to plan
■ ∼ vi (Aviac) to glide; «‹águila›» to soar; (Náut) to plane

planeta m planet

planetario m planetarium

planificación f planning; ∼ **familiar** family planning

planificar [A2] vt to plan, draw up a plan for

planilla f [1] **(a)** (tabla) table, chart; (lista) list **(b)** (AmL) (nómina) payroll; **estar en** ∼ to be on the payroll **(c)** (AmL) (personal) staff [2] **(a)** (Méx) (en elección) list of candidates **(b)** (Col) (censo electoral) electoral register

plano¹ -na adj [1] ‹superficie/terreno/zapato› flat; **los 100 metros** ∼**s** (AmL) the hundred meters dash o sprint [2] ‹figura/ángulo› plane

plano² m [1] (de edificio) plan; (de ciudad) street plan, map [2] (Mat) plane [3] **(a)** (nivel) level; **en el** ∼ **afectivo** on an emotional level **(b)** (Cin, Fot) shot [4] **de plano** ‹rechazar/rehusar› flatly

planta f [1] (Bot) plant; ∼ **de interior** houseplant, indoor plant [2] (Arquit) **(a)** (plano) plan **(b)** (piso) floor; **una casa de dos** ∼**s** a two-story house; ∼ **baja** first floor (AmE), ground floor (BrE) [3] (Tec) (instalación) plant [4] (del pie) sole

plantación f **(a)** (terreno plantado) field; (de árboles) plantation **(b)** (explotación agrícola) plantation **(c)** (acción) planting

plantado -da adj ∼ **DE algo** planted WITH sth; **dejar** ∼ **a algn** ▶ PLANTAR 2B

plantar [A1] vt [1] **(a)** ‹árboles/cebollas› to plant **(b)** ‹postes› to put in; ‹tienda› to pitch, put up [2] (fam) **(a)** (abandonar) ‹novio› to ditch (colloq), to dump (colloq); ‹estudios› to give up, to quit (AmE) **(b)** (dejar plantado) ‹persona› (en cita) to stand ... up; (el día de la boda) to jilt
■ **plantarse** v pron [1] (fam) (quedarse, pararse) to plant oneself (colloq) [2] (Jueg) (en cartas, apuesta) to stick

planteamiento m **(a)** (enfoque) approach **(b)** (exposición): **no les sabe dar el** ∼ **adecuado a sus ideas** he doesn't know how to set his ideas out; **ese no es el** ∼ **que me hicieron** that's not the way they explained the situation to me

plantear [A1] vt [1] **(a)** ‹teoría/razones› to set out **(b)** (exponer) ‹tema/pregunta› to raise; **me lo planteó de la siguiente manera** he explained it to me in the following way; ∼**le algo a algn** to raise sth with sb; **le** ∼**é la cuestión a mi jefe** I'll raise the matter with my boss; **nos** ∼**on dos opciones** they presented us with o gave us two options; **le planteé la posibilidad de ir a Grecia** I suggested going to Greece [2] ‹problemas/dificultades› to pose
■ **plantearse** v pron [1] (considerar) ‹problema/posibilidad› to think about, consider [2] (presentarse) «‹problema/posibilidad›» to arise

plantel m [1] (cuerpo) staff [2] (Agr) nursery [3] (AmL frml) (escuela) educational establishment (frml)

plantilla f [1] (de zapato) insole [2] (Esp) (personal) staff; (nómina) payroll; **estar en** ∼ to be on the staff o payroll [3] (para marcar, cortar) template; (para corregir exámenes) mask

plantón m **(a)** (fam) (espera) long wait; *darle el ~ a algn* ▶ PLANTAR 2B **(b)** (Méx) (para protestar) sit-in

plasma m (Biol, Fís) plasma

plasta f (fam) (masa — blanda) soft lump; (— aplastada) flat o shapeless lump

plasticina® f (CS) Plasticine®

plástico¹ -ca adj plastic

plástico² m **(a)** (material) plastic **(b)** (explosivo) plastic explosive, plastique **(c)** (fam) (tarjetas de crédito) credit cards (pl), plastic (colloq)

plastificar [A2] vt ‹tela› to plasticize; ‹carné/documento› to laminate

plata f ⏍1⏎ **(a)** (metal) silver; *~ de ley* hallmarked silver **(b)** (vajilla) silver, silverware ⏍2⏎ (AmS fam) (dinero) money; *tiene mucha ~* she has a lot of money

plataforma f platform; *~ de lanzamiento* launchpad

platal m (AmS fam) fortune (colloq)

platanal, platanar m banana plantation

platanera f (empresa) banana company

platanero m (árbol) banana tree

plátano m ⏍1⏎ (árbol) tb *~ oriental* plane tree ⏍2⏎ **(a)** (fruto que se come crudo) banana; (árbol) banana tree **(b)** (fruto para cocinar) plantain; (árbol) plantain

platea f **(a)** (patio de butacas) orchestra (AmE), stalls (pl) (BrE) **(b)** (localidad) seat (*in the orchestra/stalls*)

plateado -da adj **(a)** (del color de la plata) silver **(b)** (con baño de plata) silver-plated

platería f **(a)** (arte) silverwork **(b)** (objetos) silver(ware) **(c)** (tienda) silversmith's

plática f **(a)** (conferencia) talk **(b)** (esp AmL) (conversación) *[this noun is widely used in Mexico and Central America but is formal in other areas]* talk; *estar de ~* to talk, to chat (colloq)

platicar [A2] vi (esp AmL) *[this verb is widely used in Mexico and Central America but is literary in other areas]* to talk, chat (colloq) ■ *~ vt* (Méx) (contar) to tell

platillo m ⏍1⏎ **(a)** (plato pequeño) saucer; (de balanza) pan; (para limosnas) collection plate o bowl; *~ volador or* (Esp) *volante* flying saucer **(b)** (Mús) cymbal **(c)** (Dep) clay pigeon ⏍2⏎ (Méx) (en una comida) course

platino m ⏍1⏎ (metal) platinum ⏍2⏎ **platinos** mpl (Auto, Mec) (contact breaker) points (pl)

plato m ⏍1⏎ **(a)** (utensilio) plate; *lavar o fregar los ~s* to wash o do the dishes; *~ de postre* dessert plate; *~ hondo or sopero* soup dish; *~ llano or* (RPl) *playo or* (Chi) *bajo or* (Méx) *extendido* (dinner) plate **(b)** (para taza) tb *platito* saucer ⏍2⏎ (contenido) plate, plateful ⏍3⏎ **(a)** (receta) dish; *~ típico* typical dish **(b)** (en una comida) course; *~ central* (Ven) main course; *~ combinado* (Esp) *meal served on one plate, eg burger, eggs and fries*; *~ del día* dish of the day; *~ fuerte or principal* (Coc) main course ⏍4⏎ **(a)** (de balanza) (scale) pan **(b)** (de tocadiscos) turntable **(c)** (Dep) clay pigeon **(d)** (en béisbol) home plate

plató m set

platónico -ca adj platonic

platudo -da adj (AmS fam) well-heeled (colloq)

playa f **(a)** (extensión de arena) beach; (lugar de veraneo) seaside **(b)** *~ de estacionamiento* (CS, Per) parking lot (AmE), car park (BrE)

playera f (zapatilla) canvas shoe, beach shoe; (camiseta) (Méx) T-shirt

plaza f ⏍1⏎ (espacio abierto) square; *~ de armas* (Mil) parade ground; (lugar público) (Andes) main square; *~ de toros* bullring; *~ mayor* main square ⏍2⏎ **(a)** (esp AmL) (bolsa) market **(b)** (Esp) (mercado) market (place) **(c)** (puesto de trabajo) post, position; (en una clase, universidad) place; *hay varias ~s vacantes* there are several vacancies **(b)** (asiento) seat

plazo m ⏍1⏎ (de tiempo) period; *dentro de un ~ de dos meses* within a two-month period; *el ~ vence el próximo lunes* (para proyecto, trabajo) the deadline is next Monday; (para entrega de solicitudes) next Monday is the closing date; *tenemos un mes de ~ para pagar* we have one month to pay; *un objetivo a corto/largo ~* a short-term/long-term objective ⏍2⏎ (mensualidad, cuota) installment*; *pagar a ~s* to pay in installments; *comprar a ~s* to buy on installments

plazoleta, plazuela f small square

plebe f **(a)** (Hist) *la ~* the masses (pl), the populace **(b)** (pey) (chusma) rabble (pej), plebs (pl) (colloq & pej)

plebeyo -ya adj/m,f plebeian

plebiscito m plebiscite

plegable adj folding (before n)

plegar [A7] vt ‹papel› to fold; ‹silla› to fold up ■ **plegarse** v pron ⏍1⏎ (ceder) to yield, submit; *~se A algo* to yield TO sth, submit TO sth ⏍2⏎ (AmS) (unirse) to join in; *~se A algo* to join sth

plegaria f prayer

pleitear [A1] vi (AmL fam) (discutir) to argue

pleito m ⏍1⏎ (Der) action, lawsuit ⏍2⏎ (AmL) **(a)** (disputa, discusión) argument, fight (colloq) **(b)** (de boxeo) fight, boxing match

plenario -ria adj plenary, full

plenitud f: *en la ~ de algo* (de la vida) in the prime of sth; (de la carrera) at the height o peak of sth; *vivir la vida con ~* to live life to the full

pleno¹ -na adj **(a)** (completo, total) full; *en ~ uso de sus facultades* in full possession of his faculties **(b)** (uso enfático): *en ~ verano* in the middle of summer; *le dio una bofetada en plena cara* he slapped her right across the face; *a plena luz del día* in broad daylight; *a ~ sol* in the full sun

pleno² m ⏍1⏎ (reunión) plenary o full meeting/session ⏍2⏎ (Jueg) (en bolos) strike; (en lotería, bingo) full house; (en las quinielas) correct forecast o prediction

pliego m **(a)** (hoja de papel) sheet of paper **(b)** (Impr) section, signature **(c)** (documento) document

pliegue m **(a)** (en papel) fold, crease; (en la piel) fold; (en tela) pleat **(b)** (Geol) fold

plinto m (en gimnasia) box

plomería f (AmL) plumbing

plomero -ra m,f (AmL) plumber

plomizo -za adj ‹cielo› gray*, leaden (liter)

plomo m ⏍1⏎ **(a)** (metal) lead; *soldado de ~* tin

soldier **(b)** (arg) (balas) lead (sl) **2** (fam) (persona aburrida): **este profesor es un ~** this teacher is deadly boring (colloq) **3** (Esp) (fusible) fuse

pluma f **1** (de aves) feather; (antigua para escribir) quill; (como adorno) plume, feather; **mudar la ~** to molt* **2** (para escribir) pen; **~ atómica** (Méx) ballpoint pen; **~ estilográfica** or (AmL) **fuente** fountain pen

plumaje m (de ave) plumage; (en un casco) plume, crest

plumero m **(a)** (para limpiar) feather duster **(b)** (estuche) pencil case; (recipiente) pen holder

plumilla f **1** (para escribir) nib **2 (a)** (del limpiaparabrisas) blade **(b)** (Mús) brush **(c)** (Dep) shuttlecock

plumón m **1 (a)** (pluma suave) down **(b)** (edredón) down-filled quilt o (BrE) duvet **2** (Chi) (rotulador) felt-tip pen

plural adj/m plural; **tercera persona del ~** third person plural; **en ~** in the plural

pluralizar [A4] vi to generalize

pluscuamperfecto m pluperfect, past perfect

Plutón m Pluto

plutonio m plutonium

pluviosidad f rainfall

población f **1** (habitantes) population; (Zool) population, colony; **~ activa/pasiva** working/non-working population **2** (ciudad) town, city; (aldea) town, village; **~ callampa** (Chi) shantytown **3** (acción) settlement

poblado¹ -da adj **1** (habitado) populated; **poco ~** sparsely populated **2** ⟨barba/cejas⟩ bushy, thick; ⟨pestañas⟩ thick

poblado² m village

poblador -dora m,f **(a)** settler **(b)** (Chi) inhabitant of a shantytown

poblar [A10] vt **1** ⟨territorio/región⟩ **(a)** «colonos/inmigrantes» (ir a ocupar) to settle, populate **(b)** (habitar) to inhabit **2 ~ algo DE algo** ⟨bosque⟩ to plant sth WITH sth; ⟨río/colmena⟩ to stock sth WITH sth
■ **poblarse** v pron «tierra/colonia» to be settled

pobre adj **1 (a)** ⟨persona/barrio/nación⟩ poor; ⟨vestimenta⟩ poor, shabby **(b)** (escaso) ⟨vocabulario⟩ poor, limited; **aguas ~s en minerales** water with a low mineral content **(c)** (mediocre) ⟨examen/trabajo/actuación⟩ poor; ⟨salud⟩ poor, bad; ⟨argumento⟩ weak **(d)** ⟨tierra⟩ poor **2** (delante del n) (digno de compasión) poor; **~ animal** poor animal; **~, tiene hambre** poor thing, he's hungry; **¡~ de mí!** poor (old) me!
■ mf (necesitado) poor person, pauper (arch); **los ~s** the poor

pobreza f **(a)** (económica) poverty; **extrema ~** abject poverty **(b)** (mediocridad) poverty, poorness **(c)** (de la tierra) poorness, poor quality

poceta f (Ven) toilet bowl o pan

pocho -cha adj **1 (a)** (Esp fam) [ESTAR] ⟨persona⟩ off-color, peaked (AmE colloq) **(b)** ⟨fruta⟩ overripe; ⟨flor⟩ withered

pocilga f pigsty

pócima f (Farm) potion; (bebida) (fam) concoction (colloq)

poción f potion

poco¹ adv: **habla ~** he doesn't say much o a lot;

es muy ~ agradecido he is very ungrateful; **un autor muy ~ conocido** a very little-known author; **viene muy ~ por aquí** he hardly ever comes around; para locs ver POCO² 4

poco² -ca adj (con sustantivos no numerables) little; (en plural) few; **muy ~ vino** very little wine; **muy ~s niños** very few children; **había poquísimos coches** there were hardly any cars
■ pron **1** (poca cantidad, poca cosa): **había ~ que hacer** there was little to do; **por ~ que gane ...** no matter how little o however little she earns ...; **se conforma con ~** he's easily satisfied; **todo le parece ~** she is never satisfied; **~s quisieron ayudar** few were willing to help; **~s pueden permitirse ese lujo** not many people can afford to do that
2 poco (refiriéndose a tiempo): **lo vi hace ~** I saw him recently o not long ago; **hace muy ~ que lo conoce** she hasn't known him for very long; **tardó ~ en hacerlo** it didn't take him long to do it; **falta ~ para las navidades** it's not long till Christmas; **a ~ de venir él** soon o shortly after he came; **dentro de ~** soon; **~ antes de que ... a** short while o shortly before ...
3 un poco (a) (refiriéndose a cantidades) a little; (refiriéndose a tiempo) a while; **dame un ~** I'll have some o a little; **espera un ~** wait a while **(b)** un poco de (negativo) a bit of **(c)** un poco + ADJ/ADV: **un ~ caro/tarde** a bit o a little expensive/late
4 (en locs) a poco (Méx): **¡a ~ no está fabuloso Acapulco!** isn't Acapulco just fantastic!; **¡a ~ ganaron!** don't tell me they won!; de a poco (AmL) gradually, little by little; **poco a poco** gradually; **poco más o menos** approximately, roughly; **por poco** nearly

poda f (acción) pruning; (temporada) pruning season

podar [A1] vt ⟨árbol⟩ to prune

poder¹ [E21] v aux
I 1 (tener la capacidad o posibilidad de): **puedo ir ahora o mañana** I can go now or tomorrow; **no puedo pagar tanto** I can't pay that much; **no podía dormir** I couldn't sleep; **no va a ~ venir** he won't be able to come; **no pudo asistir** he was unable to o he couldn't attend; **¿pudiste hacerlo sola?** were you able to do it on your own?
2 (a) (expresando idea de permiso): **¿puedo servirme otro?** can o may I have another one?; **¿podría irme más temprano hoy?** could I leave earlier today?; **puedes hacer lo que quieras** you can do whatever you like; **no puede comer sal** he isn't allowed to eat salt; **¿se puede? — ¡adelante!** may I? — come in; **aquí no se puede fumar** smoking is not allowed here **(b)** (solicitando un favor): **¿puedes bajar un momento?** can you come down for a moment?; **¿podrías hacerme un favor?** could you do me a favor?
3 (expresando derecho moral): **no podemos hacerle eso** we can't do that to her
4 (en quejas, reproches): **podías** or **podrías haberme avisado** you could o might have warned me!
II 1 (con idea de esfuerzo) **1 ~ CON algo/algn**: **¿puedes con todo eso?** can you manage all that?; **no puedo con este niño** I can't cope with this child; **estoy que no puedo más** (cansado) I'm exhausted; (lleno) I can't eat anything else; **ya no puedo más** I can't go on like this
2 (con idea de eventualidad, posibilidad): **te podrías** or ⋯⋗

podías haber matado you could have killed yourself!; **no podía haber estado más amable** she couldn't have been kinder; **podría volver a ocurrir** it could happen again; **no pudo ser** it wasn't possible; **puede (ser) que tengas razón** you may *o* could be right; **puede que sí, puede que no** maybe, maybe not

3 (Méx) (doler): **nos pudo mucho la muerte de Julio** we were terribly upset by Julio's death

poder² *m* 1 (a) (control, influencia) power; **tiene mucho ~** he has a great deal of power; **estamos en su ~** we are in her power (b) (Pol) **el ~** power; **estar en el ~** to be in power; **tomar el ~** to take *o* seize power

2 (posesión): **la carta está en ~ de ...** the letter is in the hands of ...

3 (a) (derecho, atribución) power; **tener amplios ~es para hacer algo** to have wide-ranging powers to do sth (b) (Der) (documento) letter of authorization; (hecho ante notario) power of attorney; **casarse por ~** (AmL) *or* (Esp) **por ~es** to get married by proxy

4 (a) (capacidad, facultad) power; **su ~ de convicción** her power of persuasion; **~ adquisitivo** purchasing power (b) (de motor, aparato) power

poderío *m* power

poderoso -sa *adj* powerful

poderosos *mpl*: **los ~s** (los ricos) the wealthy; (los que tienen poder) the powerful

podio *m*, **pódium** *m* (*pl* **-diums**) (Dep) podium; (Mús) podium, rostrum

podólogo -ga *m,f* chiropodist, podiatrist (AmE)

podré, etc ▶ PODER¹

podría, etc ▶ PODER¹

podrido -da *adj* 1 (a) (descompuesto) rotten; **huele a** *or* (AmL) **hay olor a ~** there's a smell of something rotting *o* rotten (b) (corrompido) rotten, corrupt; **estar ~ de dinero** *or* (AmS) **estar ~ en plata/oro** (fam) to be stinking *o* filthy rich (colloq) 2 (RPI fam) (harto, aburrido) fed up (colloq)

podrir [I38] *vt* ▶ PUDRIR

poema *m* poem

poesía *f* (género) poetry; (poema) poem

poeta -tisa *m,f*, **poeta** *mf* poet

poético -ca *adj* poetic

póker *m* ▶ PÓQUER

polaco -ca *adj* Polish
■ *m,f* 1 (persona) Pole 2 **polaco** *m* (idioma) Polish

polar *adj* polar

polarizar [A4] *vt* (a) (Fot, Ópt) to polarize (b) ⟨atención⟩ to focus (c) ⟨nación/opiniones⟩ to polarize

polea *f* (Tec) pulley; (Náut) tackle

polémica *f* controversy, polemic (frml)

polémico -ca *adj* controversial, polemic (frml)

polemizar [A4] *vi* to argue

polen *m* pollen

poleo *m* pennyroyal

polera *f* (suéter) (RPI) polo neck; (Chi) (camiseta) T-shirt

polichinela *m* (títere) string puppet

policía *f* 1 (cuerpo) police; **la ~ está investigando el caso** the police are investigating the case; **~ antidisturbios** riot police; **~ de tráfico** *or* (AmL) **de tránsito** traffic police, highway patrol (AmE); **~ municipal** local *o* city police; **~ nacional** (state) police 2 **policía** (agente) (*m*) policeman, police officer; (*f*) policewoman, police officer

policíaco -ca, policiaco -ca *adj* ⟨novela/serie⟩ crime (*before n*), detective (*before n*)

policial *adj* police (*before n*)

polideportivo *m* sports center*

poliéster *m* polyester

poliestireno *m*: *tb* **~ expandible** polystyrene

polietileno *m* polyethylene (AmE), polythene (BrE)

polifacético -ca *adj* versatile, multifaceted

poligamia *f* polygamy

polígamo -ma *m,f* polygamist

políglota *mf* polyglot

polígono *m* 1 (Mat) polygon 2 (Esp) (zona) area, zone; (urbanización) development, housing estate; **~ industrial** (Esp) industrial area *o* zone

polilla *f* (Zool) moth; **~ de la madera** woodworm

Polinesia *f* Polynesia

polinesio¹ -sia *adj/m,f* Polynesian

polinesio² *m* (idioma) Polynesian

polinización *f* pollination

polio *f* polio

poliomielitis *f* poliomyelitis

politécnico -ca *adj* ⟨universidad⟩ specializing in technical or practical subjects; **escuela politécnica** technical college

politeísmo *m* polytheism

política *f* 1 (Pol) politics 2 (postura) policy; **~ interior/exterior** domestic/foreign policy

político -ca *adj* 1 (Pol) political 2 (diplomático) diplomatic, tactful 3 (en relaciones de parentesco): **la familia política** the in-laws
■ *m,f* politician

politizarse [A4] *v pron* to become politicized

póliza *f* 1 (de seguros) policy 2 (esp Esp) (sello) fiscal stamp

polizón *mf* stowaway; **viajar de ~** to stow away

polla *f* 1 (Esp vulg) (pene) cock (vulg), prick (vulg) 2 (a) (AmL) (apuesta) bet (b) (Per) (quiniela) ≈ sports lottery (*in US*), ≈ pools (*in UK*) (c) (Chi) (lotería) lottery; *ver tb* POLLO

pollera *f* (CS) (Indum) skirt

pollería *f* poultry store, poulterer's store

pollito -ta *m,f* chick

pollo -lla *m,f* (Zool) (a) (cría) chick (b) (adulto) chicken (c) (Coc) chicken; **~ asado** roast chicken

polluelo *m* chick

polo *m* 1 (a) (Geog) pole; **P~ Norte/Sur** North/South Pole (b) (Elec, Fís) pole; **~ negativo**

AmC	América Central	Arg	Argentina	Cu	Cuba
AmL	América Latina	Bol	Bolivia	Ec	Ecuador
AmS	América del Sur	Chi	Chile	Esp	España
Andes	Región andina	CS	Cono Sur	Méx	México

Per	Perú
RPI	Río de la Plata
Ur	Uruguay
Ven	Venezuela

negative pole; **ser** ∼**s opuestos** (fam) to be poles apart **2** (centro) center*, focus **3** (a) (Dep) polo **(b)** (Indum) polo shirt **4** (Esp) (helado) Popsicle® (AmE), ice lolly (BrE)

pololear [A1] *vi* (Chi) to have a boyfriend/ girlfriend; ∼ **CON algn** to go out WITH sb

pololo -la *m,f* (Chi fam) *(m)* boyfriend; *(f)* girlfriend

Polonia *f* Poland

poltrona *f* armchair, easy chair

polución *f* pollution; **la** ∼ **atmosférica** atmospheric pollution

polvareda *f* dust cloud

polvera *f* powder compact

polvo *m* **(a)** (suciedad) dust; **limpiar** *or* **quitar el** ∼ to do the dusting, to dust; **estar hecho** ∼ (agotado) to be all in (fam); (deprimido) to be devastated; (destruido) to be a wreck **(b)** (Coc, Quím) powder **(c)** **polvos** *mpl* (en cosmética) face powder; ∼**s de talco** talcum powder, talc (colloq)

pólvora *f* **(a)** (explosivo) gunpowder **(b)** (fuegos artificiales) fireworks *(pl)*

polvoriento -ta *adj* dusty

polvorín *m* **(a)** (almacén de explosivos) magazine **(b)** (lugar, país peligroso) powder keg

pomada *f* (Farm) ointment, cream; ∼ **de zapatos** (RPl) shoe polish

pomelo *m* (fruto) grapefruit; (árbol) grapefruit tree

pomo *m* (de puerta, mueble) handle, knob; (de espada) pommel

pompa *f* **1** *tb* ∼ **de jabón** bubble **2** (esplendor) pomp, splendor*; ∼**s fúnebres** *fpl* (ceremonia) funeral ceremony; (funeraria) funeral parlor*, funeral director's

pomposo -sa *adj* **(a)** ⟨boda/fiesta⟩ magnificent, splendid; ⟨lenguaje/estilo⟩ pompous, high-sounding **(b)** (ostentoso) pompous, ostentatious

pómulo *m* (hueso) cheekbone; (mejilla) cheek

pon ▶ PONER

ponchadura *f* (Méx) flat, puncture

ponchar [A1] *vt* (Méx) ⟨llanta/balón⟩ to puncture

■ **poncharse** *v pron* **1** (Méx) «balón» to puncture; **se nos ponchó una llanta** we had a flat tire *o* a puncture **2** (Col, Ven) (en béisbol) to fan (colloq), to strike out

ponche *m* (bebida) punch

poncho *m* poncho

ponderar [A1] *vt* **(a)** ⟨cálculo/índice⟩ to weight, adjust **(b)** (considerar) to weigh up, consider, ponder **(c)** (alabar) to praise, speak highly of

pondré, pondría, etc ▶ PONER

ponedora *f* layer, laying hen

poner [E22] *vt*

I **1** **(a)** (colocar) to put; **ponlo en el suelo** put it on the floor; **ponle el collar al perro** put the dog's collar on; ∼ **una bomba** to plant a bomb **(b)** ⟨anuncio/aviso⟩ to place, put **(c)** ⟨ropa⟩ (+ *me/te/ le etc*): **le puse el sombrero** I put his hat on (for him)

2 (agregar) to put

3 ⟨inyección/supositorio⟩ to give

4 **poner la mesa** to lay *o* set the table

5 (instalar, montar) **(a)** ⟨oficina/restaurante⟩ to open **(b)** ⟨cocina/teléfono/calefacción⟩ to install **(c)** ⟨cerradura/armario⟩ to fit

6 «ave» ⟨huevo⟩ to lay

7 (Esp) (servir, dar): **póngame un café, por favor** I'll have a coffee, please; **¿cuántos le pongo?** how many would you like?

II **1** ⟨dinero⟩ (contribuir) to put in; **pusimos 500 pesos cada uno** we put in 500 pesos each

2 ⟨atención⟩ to pay; ⟨cuidado/interés⟩ to take; **pon más cuidado en la presentación** take more care over the presentation

3 **(a)** (imponer) ⟨deberes⟩ to give, set; ⟨examen/ problema⟩ to set; **le pusieron una multa** he was fined **(b)** (oponer) ⟨inconvenientes⟩ to raise; **me pusieron problemas para entrar** they made it difficult for me to get in **(c)** (adjudicar) ⟨nota⟩ to give

4 (dar) ⟨nombre/apodo⟩ to give; ⟨ejemplo⟩ to give; **le pusieron Eva** they called her Eva

5 (enviar) ⟨telegrama⟩ to send

6 (escribir) ⟨dedicatoria/líneas⟩ to write

7 (Esp) (exhibir, dar) ⟨película⟩ to show; **¿ponen algo interesante en la tele?** is there anything interesting on TV?; **¿qué ponen en el Royal?** what's on *o* what's showing at the Royal?

III **1** **(a)** (conectar, encender) ⟨televisión/ calefacción⟩ to turn on, switch on, put on; ⟨programa/canal⟩ to put on; ⟨cinta/disco/música⟩ to put on; **puso el motor en marcha** she switched on *o* started the engine **(b)** (ajustar, graduar) ⟨despertador⟩ to set; **pon la música más alta** turn the music up; **puso el reloj en hora** she put the clock right

2 (Esp) (al teléfono): ∼ **a algn CON algo/algn** to put sb THROUGH TO sth/sb

IV (en estado, situación) (+ *compl*): ∼ **a algn nervioso** to make sb nervous; ∼ **a algn en un aprieto** to put sb in an awkward position

■ *vi* «ave» to lay

■ **ponerse** *v pron*

I **1** (refl) (colocarse): **pongámonos ahí** let's stand (*o* sit *etc*) there; ∼**se de pie** to stand (up); ∼**se de rodillas** to kneel (down), get down on one's knees

2 «sol» to set

3 (refl) ⟨calzado/maquillaje/alhaja⟩ to put on; **no tengo nada que** ∼**me** I don't have a thing to wear

II **1** (en estado, situación) (+ *compl*): ∼**se enfermo** to get sick; **se puso triste** she became sad; **cuando lo vio se puso muy contenta** she was so happy when she saw it; **se puso como loco** he went mad; ∼**se cómodo** to make oneself comfortable

2 (empezar) ∼**se A + INF** to start -ING, to start + INF; **se puso a llover** it started raining, it started to rain

III (Esp): ∼**se al teléfono** to come to the phone

ponga, pongas, etc ▶ PONER

poni *m* ▶ PONY

poniente *m* (occidente) west; (viento) west wind

pontífice *m* pontiff, pope

pony /'poni/ *m* (*pl* **-nies** *or* **-nys**) pony

pop *m* **1** (Mús) pop (music) **2** (Ur) (Coc) popcorn

popa *f* stern

popis, popoff *adj inv* (Méx fam) posh

popote *m* (Méx) straw

popular *adj* **1** **(a)** ⟨cultura/tradiciones⟩ ···⋮⋗

popular (*before n*); ⟨canción/baile/costumbres⟩ traditional **(b)** (Pol) ⟨movimiento/rebelión⟩ popular (*before n*) **2** (que gusta) ⟨actor/programa/deporte⟩ popular

popularidad *f* popularity

popularizar [A4] *vt* to popularize, make ... popular

■ **popularizarse** *v pron* to become popular

popurrí *m* (de cosas, colores) potpourri

póquer *m* (juego — de naipes) poker; (— de dados) poker dice; **un ~ de ases** four aces

poquísimo *adj* ▶ POCO

por *prep*

I **1** (causa) because of; **~ falta de dinero** because o owing to lack of money; **~ naturaleza** by nature; **~ necesidad** out of necessity; **~ eso no dije nada** that's why I didn't say anything; **fue ~ eso que no te llamé** that was why I didn't call you; **si no fuera ~ mi hijo** ... if it wasn't for my son ...; **me pidió perdón ~ haberme mentido** he apologized for lying o for having lied to me **2** (*en locs*) **por qué** why; **no dijo ~ qué** he didn't say why; **¿por qué no vienes conmigo?** why don't you come with me?; **por si** in case; **~ si no entiende** in case he doesn't understand; ▶ ACASO 2, MOSCA **3** (en expresiones concesivas): **~ más que me esfuerzo** however hard o no matter how hard I try; **~ (muy) fácil que sea** however easy o no matter how easy it is **4** **(a)** (modo): **colócalos ~ orden de tamaño** put them in order of size; **~ adelantado** in advance; **~ escrito** in writing **(b)** (medio): **se lo comunicaron ~ teléfono** they told him over the phone; **lo dijeron ~ la radio** they said it on the radio; **~ avión** by air; **la conocí ~ la voz** I recognized her by her voice; **me enteré ~ un amigo** I heard from o through a friend **5** **(a)** (proporción): **cobra $30 ~ clase** he charges $30 a o per class; **120 kilómetros ~ hora** 120 kilometers an o per hour; **~ metro/docena** by the meter/dozen; **tú comes ~ tres** you eat enough for three people; **tiene tres metros de largo ~ uno de ancho** it's three meters long by one meter wide; **uno ~ uno** one by one; ▶ CIENTO *m* B **(b)** (en multiplicaciones): **tres ~ cuatro (son) doce** three times four is twelve, three fours are twelve **6** **(a)** (sustitución) for; **su secretaria firmó ~ él** his secretary signed for him o on his behalf; **pasa ~ inglesa** she passes for an Englishwoman **(b)** (como): **~ ejemplo** for example **7** (introduciendo el agente) by; **compuesto ~ Mozart** composed by Mozart

II **1** (finalidad, objetivo): **pelearse ~ algo** to fight over sth; **lo hace ~ el dinero** he does it for the money; **no entré ~ no molestarlo** I didn't go in because I didn't want to disturb him; **~ QUE + SUBJ** (*here* POR QUE *can also be written* PORQUE): **estaba ansioso ~ que lo escucharan** he was eager for them to listen to him **2** (indicando inclinación, elección): **su amor ~ la música** her love of music; **no siento nada ~ él** I don't feel anything for him; **votó ~ ella** he voted for her **3** (en busca de): **salió/fue ~** or (Esp) **a ~ pan** he went (out) for some bread, he went (out) to get some bread **4** (en lo que respecta a): **~ mí que haga lo que quiera** as far as I'm concerned, he can do what he likes

5 (esp AmL) **estar ~ + INF** (estar a punto de) to be about to + INF; **está ~ terminar** he's about to finish; **deben (de) estar ~ llegar** they should be arriving any minute

III **1** **(a)** (lugar): **entró ~ la ventana** he came in through the window; **sal ~ aquí** go out this way; **se cayó ~ la escalera** he fell down the stairs; **¿el 121 va ~ (la) Avenida Rosas?** does the 121 go along Rosas Avenue?; **¿~ dónde has venido?** which way did you come?; **está ~ ahí** he's over there somewhere; **¿~ dónde está el hotel?** whereabouts is the hotel?; **viven ~ mi barrio** they live around my area; **voy ~ la página 15** I'm up to o I'm on page 15; **empieza ~ el principio** start at the beginning; **agárralo ~ el mango** hold it by the handle **(b)** (indicando extensión): **~ todos lados** or **~ todas partes** everywhere; **viajamos ~ el norte de Francia** we traveled around o in the North of France; *ver tb* DENTRO, FUERA, ENCIMA, ETC **2** (tiempo) for; **~ un mes** for a month; **~ el momento** or **~ ahora** for the time being, for now; *ver tb* MAÑANA, TARDE, NOCHE **3** (Esp) (ocasión) for; **me lo regaló ~ mi cumpleaños** she gave it to me for my birthday

porcelana *f* **(a)** (material) china; (de mejor calidad) porcelain **(b)** (objeto) piece of china/porcelain

porcentaje *m* percentage

porche *m* (de casa) porch; (soportal) arcade

porción *f* (de un todo) portion; (en reparto) share; (de comida) portion, helping, serving

pordiosero -ra *m,f* beggar

porfiado -da *adj* stubborn, pig-headed (colloq) ■ *m,f* (persona) stubborn creature (colloq)

porfiar [A17] *vi* (insistir) to insist; **no me porfíes, ya te dije que no** don't keep on o go on about it, I said no

pormenor *m* detail; **los ~es del incidente** the details of the incident; **entrar en ~es** to go into detail

pornografía *f* pornography

pornográfico -ca *adj* pornographic

poro *m* **1** (Anat, Biol) pore **2** (Méx) (puerro) leek

pororó *m* (RPI) popcorn

poroso -sa *adj* porous

poroto *m* (CS) bean; **~ verde** (Chi) green bean

porque *conj* **(a)** (indicando causa) because; **¿por qué no vas a ir? — ~ no** why don't you go? — because I don't want to **(b)** (indicando finalidad) ▶ POR II 1

porqué *m* reason; **quiero saber el ~** I want to know the reason

porquería *f* **1** **(a)** (suciedad) dirt **(b)** (cochinada): **no hagas ~s** don't do disgusting o filthy things like that; **la casa está hecha una ~** (fam) the house is in such a state (colloq) **2** (cosa de mala calidad): **el libro es una ~** the book's a piece of junk; **la comida es una ~** the food is dreadful o terrible

porra *f* **1** (de guardia, policía) nightstick (AmE), truncheon (BrE) **2** (fam) (expresando disgusto, enojo): **mandar a algn a la ~** (colloq) to tell sb to get lost (colloq); **¡vete** or **ándate a la ~!** go to hell! (colloq), get lost! (colloq); **mandar algo a la ~** (colloq) ⟨trabajo⟩ to chuck sth in (colloq) **3** (Jueg) draw, lottery **4** (Col, Méx fam) **(a)** (seguidores, hinchas) fans (*pl*) **(b)** (canto, grito): **¡una ~ para Villalva!**

three cheers for Villalva!; **la** ∿ **de la universidad** the college chant; **echarle** ∿**s a algn** (Méx fam) ⟨*a equipo/corredor*⟩ to cheer sb (on)

porrista *mf* **(a)** (Col, Méx) (seguidor) fan **(b) porrista** *f* (Col, Méx) (animadora) cheerleader

porro *m* (Esp arg) (de hachís) joint (colloq)

porrón *m* 1 **(a)** (de vino) wine bottle (*with a long spout for drinking from*) **(b)** (Arg) (de cerveza) bottle of beer 2 (CS) (pimiento) green pepper; (puerro) leek

portabebés *m* (*pl* ∿) portacrib® (AmE), carrycot (BrE)

portada *f* 1 (de libro) title page; (de periódico) front page; (de revista) cover 2 (de iglesia) front, facade

portadocumentos *m* (*pl* ∿) (AmL) (grande) briefcase, attaché case; (pequeño) document wallet

portador -dora *m,f* 1 (Med) (de virus, germen) carrier 2 (Com, Fin) bearer; **páguese al** ∿ pay the bearer

portaequipajes *m* (*pl* ∿) **(a)** (Auto) (para el techo) roofrack; (maletero) trunk (AmE), boot (BrE) **(b)** (en tren, autobús) luggage rack

portafolios *m* (*pl* ∿) (maletín) briefcase

portal *m* **(a)** (de casa — entrada) doorway; (— vestíbulo) hall **(b)** (de iglesia, palacio) portal **(c)** (en muralla) gate

portar [A1] *vt* (frml) ⟨*arma/bandera*⟩ to carry, bear (frml)
■ **portarse** *v pron* **(a)** (comportarse): ∿**se bien** to behave (oneself); ∿**se mal** to behave badly; ∿**se bien/mal CON algn** to treat sb well/badly**(b)** (cumplir): **el Zaragoza se portó en la final** Zaragoza delivered the goods in the final; **hoy te portaste** you've really excelled today

portátil *adj* portable
■ *m* laptop, portable computer

portaviones *m* (*pl* ∿) aircraft carrier

portavoz *mf* (*m*) spokesperson, spokesman; (*f*) spokesperson, spokeswoman

portazo *m* slam, bang; **dar un** ∿ to slam the door

porte *m* 1 (tamaño) size; **es de este** ∿ (AmL) it's about this big 2 (acción de portar) carrying; (costo) carriage; ∿**s pagados** freight/postage paid

porteño -ña *adj* of/from the city of Buenos Aires

portería *f* 1 **(a)** (de edificio) *desk/area from where the super/caretaker supervises the building* **(b)** (vivienda) super's *o* superintendent's apartment (AmE), caretaker's flat (*o* house *etc*) (BrE) 2 (Dep) goal

portero -ra *m,f* 1 (que abre la puerta) doorman, porter; (que cuida el edificio) super (AmE), superintendent (AmE), caretaker (BrE); ∿ **eléctrico** *or* (Esp) **automático** *m* entryphone 2 (Dep) goalkeeper

portezuela *f* door

pórtico *m* (entrada) portico, porch; (galería) arcade

portón *m* (puerta grande) large door; (puerta principal) front door; (en cerca) gate

portorriqueño -ña *adj/m,f* Puerto Rican

Portugal *m* Portugal

portugués¹ -guesa *adj/m,f* Portuguese

portugués² *m* (idioma) Portuguese

porvenir *m* future; **un joven sin** ∿ a young man with no future *o* no prospects

posada *f* **(a)** (arc) (taberna) inn (arch) **(b)** (cobijo) hospitality

posaderas *fpl* (fam) backside (colloq), butt (AmE colloq), bum (BrE colloq)

posar [A1] *vi* to pose
■ **posarse** *v pron* «*pájaro/insecto*» to alight, land; «*avión/helicóptero*» to land

posavasos *m* (*pl* ∿) coaster; (de cartón) beermat

pose *f* **(a)** (para foto) pose **(b)** (pey) (afectación) pose

poseedor -dora *m,f* (frml) (de título, récord, billete) holder

poseer [E13] *vt* **(a)** ⟨*tierras/fortuna*⟩ to own **(b)** ⟨*conocimientos*⟩ to have **(c)** ⟨*récord/título*⟩ to hold

posesión *f* possession; **tomar** ∿ **de algo** (de casa) to take possession of sth; (de cargo) to take up sth; **está en** ∿ **de todas sus facultades** he is in full possession of his faculties

posesivo -va *adj* possessive

posguerra *f* postwar period

posibilidad *f* 1 (circunstancia) possibility; **tener la** ∿ **de hacer algo** to have the chance of doing sth; **tiene muchas** ∿**es de salir elegido** he has a good chance of being elected; **existe la** ∿ **de que estés equivocado** you might just be wrong 2 **posibilidades** *fpl* **(a)** (medios económicos) means (*pl*); **vivo de acuerdo a mis** ∿**es** I live within my means; **la casa está por encima de mis** ∿**es** I can't afford the house **(b)** (potencial) potential; **un cantante con muchas** ∿**es** a singer of great potential

posibilitar [A1] *vt* to make ... possible

posible *adj* possible; **es** ∿ it's possible; **a ser** ∿ *or* **si es** ∿ if possible; **hicieron todo lo** ∿ they did everything possible *o* everything they could; **prometió ayudarlo dentro de lo** ∿ *or* **en lo** ∿ she promised to do what she could to help (him); **¡no es** ∿**!** that can't be true! (colloq); **en cuanto te sea** ∿ as soon as you can; **no creo que me sea** ∿ I don't think I'll be able to; **es** ∿ **hacerlo más rápido** it's possible to do it more quickly; **no me fue** ∿ **terminarlo** I wasn't able to finish it; **es** ∿ **que sea cierto** it might *o* may *o* could be true
■ *adv*: **lo más pronto** ∿ as soon as possible; **lo mejor** ∿ the best you can

posición *f* **(a)** (en general) position; **en** ∿ **vertical** in an upright position **(b)** (en la sociedad) social standing; **gente de buena** ∿ people of high social standing **(c)** (actitud) position, stance; **adoptar una** ∿ **intransigente** to take a tough stand *o* stance

positivo -va *adj* positive

poso *m* (del vino) sediment, lees (*pl*), dregs (*pl*); (del café) dregs (*pl*), grounds (*pl*)

posponer [E22] *vt* (aplazar) to postpone, put off

posta *f* 1 (AmL) (Dep) relay (race) 2 (AmC) (Mil) sentry post 3 (Esp) **a posta** on purpose, deliberately 4 (Chi) (centro médico) accident and emergency center*

postal *adj* ⟨*distrito/servicio*⟩ postal
■ *f* postcard

postdata *f* postscript

poste m (a) (de alambrado) (fence) post; (de teléfono, telégrafo) pole (b) (Dep) post, upright

postemilla f (AmL) gumboil, abscess

póster m (pl **-ters**) poster

postergar [A3] vt ① (esp AmL) (aplazar) ⟨juicio/ reunión⟩ to postpone, put back ② (relegar) ⟨empleado⟩ to pass over

posteridad f posterity

posterior adj ① (a) (en el tiempo) later, subsequent; **en años ~es** in later o subsequent years; **ese incidente fue ~ a su llegada** that incident happened after his arrival (b) (en orden) subsequent ② (trasero) ⟨patas⟩ back (before n), rear (before n); **la parte ~** the back o rear

posterioridad f: **con ~** subsequently, later

postgrado m postgraduate course

postgraduado -da adj/m,f postgraduate

postguerra f postwar period

postigo m shutter

postizo¹ -za adj (a) ⟨pestañas⟩ false; **dentadura postiza** dentures, false teeth (b) ⟨manga/cuello⟩ detachable

postizo² m hairpiece

postor m bidder

postrarse [A1] v pron (frml) (arrodillarse) to kneel

postre m dessert, pudding (BrE)
■ f: **a la ~** (loc adv) (frml) in the end

postulante -ta m,f (a) (AmL) (Pol) (candidato) candidate (b) (CS) (para puesto) applicant

postular [A1] vt (AmL) (Pol) ⟨candidato⟩ to nominate, propose
■ vi **~ PARA algo** (CS) ⟨para puesto⟩ to apply FOR sth
■ **postularse** v pron (AmL) to stand, run

póstumo -ma adj posthumous

postura f ① (del cuerpo) position ② (actitud) stance, stand; **adoptar una ~ firme con respecto a algo** to take a tough stance o stand on sth (b) (opinión) opinion; **tomar ~** to take a stand ③ (AmL) (de ropa, zapatos): **se le rompieron a la primera ~** they broke the first time she wore them; **~ de argollas** (Chi) (acción) exchange of rings (to seal one's engagement); (fiesta) engagement party

potable adj ⟨agua⟩ drinkable, potable (frml); ⊗ **agua no potable** not drinking water

potaje m (Coc) vegetable stew/soup (gen with pulses)

potasio m potassium

pote m (olla) pot; (de crema, maquillaje) (CS) pot, jar

potencia f power; **~ militar/nuclear** military/ nuclear power; **este niño es un artista en ~** this child has the makings of an artist

potencial adj (posible) potential; (Ling) conditional
■ m (capacidad, posibilidades) potential

potenciar [A1] vt (period) (a) ⟨desarrollo/ investigación/exportaciones⟩ to boost; ⟨relaciones/ unidad/talento⟩ to foster; ⟨cultura⟩ to promote (b) (mejorar) ⟨seguridad⟩ to improve

potentado -da m,f tycoon

potente adj (a) (en general) powerful (b) ⟨hombre⟩ virile

potestad f legal authority

potingue m (fam) cream, lotion

poto m (Andes fam) (de persona) butt (AmE colloq), bum (BrE colloq); (de botella) bottom

potpourrí /popu'rri/ m medley

potrero m (AmL) (terreno cercado) field; (para pastar) pasture

potrillo -lla m,f (Zool) foal

potro -tra m,f ① (caballo joven) (m) colt; (f) filly ② **potro** m (instrumento de tortura) rack; (cepo) stocks (pl); (en gimnasia) vaulting horse, buck

pozo m (a) (de agua) well; **~ ciego** or **negro** or **séptico** septic tank, cesspool, cesspit; **~ de petróleo** oil well (b) (en mina) shaft (c) (en río) deep pool

práctica f ① (a) (en actividad) practice; (en trabajo) experience; **perder la ~** to be out of practice (b) (de profesión) practicing* ② (aplicación) practice; **en la ~** in practice; **poner algo en ~** or **llevar algo a la ~** to put sth into practice ③ **prácticas** fpl (de Anatomía, Química) practicals (pl); (de maestro) teaching practice; **~s de tiro** target practice ④ (costumbre) practice

practicante adj (Rel) practicing* (before n)
■ mf (Med) nurse (specializing in giving injections, dressing wounds, etc)

practicar [A2] vt ① (a) ⟨idioma/pieza musical⟩ to practice*; ⟨tenis⟩ to play; **~ la natación** to swim; **no practica ningún deporte** he doesn't play o do any sport(s) (b) ⟨profesión⟩ to practice* ② (frml) (llevar a cabo, realizar) ⟨corte/ incisión⟩ to make; ⟨autopsia/operación⟩ to perform, do; ⟨redada/actividad⟩ to carry out; ⟨detenciones⟩ to make
■ **~** vi (repetir) to practice*; (ejercer) to practice*

práctico -ca adj ① ⟨envase/cuchillo⟩ useful, handy; ⟨falda/diseño⟩ practical; **es muy ~ tener el coche para hacer la compra** it's very handy o convenient having the car to do the shopping ② (no teórico) practical ③ ⟨persona⟩ [SER] (desenvuelto) practical

pradera f meadow; **las ~s de los Estados Unidos** the prairies of the United States

prado m (a) (Agr) meadow, field (b) (lugar de paseo) park (with lawns) (c) (Col) (jardín) garden, yard (AmE)

Praga f Prague

pragmático -ca adj pragmatic
■ m,f pragmatist

pragmatismo m pragmatism

preámbulo m (a) (de obra) introduction; (de constitución) preamble (b) (rodeo): **sin más ~s** without further ado; **dímelo sin tanto ~** stop beating about the bush and tell me (c) (de curso, negociaciones) preliminary

preaviso m notice

precalentamiento m (a) (Dep) warm-up (b) (del horno) preheating (c) (de motor) warming up

AmC	Central America	Arg	Argentina	Cu	Cuba

AmC Central America · Arg Argentina · Cu Cuba · Per Peru
AmL Latin America · Bol Bolivia · Ec Ecuador · RPI River Plate Area
AmS South America · Chi Chile · Esp Spain · Ur Uruguay
Andes Andean Region · CS Southern Cone · Méx Mexico · Ven Venezuela

precalentar [A5] *vt* ⟨*horno*⟩ to preheat; ⟨*motor*⟩ to warm up

precario -ria *adj* ⟨*vivienda*⟩ poor; ⟨*medios*⟩ scarce, meager*; ⟨*salud/situación*⟩ precarious, unstable; ⟨*gobierno/puesto*⟩ unstable

precaución *f* **1** (medida) precaution **2** (prudencia): **medida de** ∼ precautionary measure; **actuar con** ∼ to act with caution

precaverse [E1] *v pron* to take precautions

precavido -da *adj* cautious, prudent

precedencia *f* precedence, priority

precedente *adj* previous
■ *m* precedent; **sentar (un)** ∼ to set a precedent

preceder [E1] *vt* to precede

precepto *m* rule, precept (fml)

preciado -da *adj* ⟨*bien/objeto*⟩ prized, valued; ⟨*don*⟩ valuable

preciarse [A1] *v pron* **(a)** (estimarse): **un abogado que se precie no haría eso** no self-respecting lawyer would do that **(b)** (jactarse) ∼ **DE algo** to pride oneself ON sth

precintar [A1] *vt* **(a)** ⟨*paquete/botella*⟩ to seal **(b)** ⟨*local*⟩ (tras crimen) to seal; (clausurar) to close down (*often on health or safety grounds*)

precinto *m* seal

precio *m* **1** (de producto) price; ∼ **al contado/a plazos** cash/credit price; **¿qué** ∼ **tiene este vestido?** how much is this dress?; ∼ **de costo** *or* (Esp) **coste** cost price; ∼ **de venta al público** (de alimento, medicamento) recommended retail price; (de libro) published price; **no tener** ∼ to be priceless **2** (sacrificio, costo) price, cost; **a cualquier** ∼ at any price, whatever the cost

preciosidad *f*: **ser una** ∼ to be absolutely beautiful

precioso -sa *adj* (hermoso) beautiful, gorgeous, lovely; (de gran valor) precious, valuable

preciosura *f* (AmL) ▶ PRECIOSIDAD

precipicio *m* (despeñadero) precipice

precipitación *f* **1** (prisa) rush, hurry; **lo hizo con mucha** ∼ she did it in a rush *o* hurry **2** (Meteo) rainfall; **la** ∼ **mensual** the monthly rainfall; **habrá precipitaciones débiles** there will be some light rain

precipitado -da *adj* ⟨*decisión/actuación*⟩ hasty; ⟨*juicio*⟩ snap (*before n*)

precipitarse [A1] *v pron* **1** (en decisión, juicio) to be hasty; **te precipitaste juzgándolo así** you were rash to judge him like that **2** (apresurarse) to rush; ∼**se A hacer algo** to rush to do sth **3** **(a)** (caer) to plunge **(b)** (*refl*) (arrojarse) to throw oneself

precisado -da *adj* (AmL fml): **verse** ∼ **a hacer algo** to be forced *o* obliged to do sth

precisar [A1] *vt* **1** (determinar con exactitud) to specify **2** (necesitar) to need

precisión *f* **(a)** (exactitud) precision; **no puedo decírtelo con** ∼ I can't tell you exactly; **de** ∼ ⟨*instrumento/máquina*⟩ precision (*before n*) **(b)** (claridad, concisión) precision

preciso -sa *adj* **1** **(a)** (exacto, claro) precise **(b)** (*delante del n*) (como intensificador) very; **en este** ∼ **momento** this very minute, right now; **en el** ∼ **momento en que salía** just as he was going out; **en este** ∼ **lugar** in this very spot **2** (necesario) necessary; **si es** ∼ if necessary, if need be; **ser** ∼

hacer algo to be necessary to do sth; **es** ∼ **que la veas** you must see her; **no es** ∼ **que vayamos todos** there's no need for all of us to go

preconcebido -da *adj* preconceived

precoz *adj* ⟨*niño/desarrollo*⟩ precocious; ⟨*diagnóstico/fruto/helada*⟩ early

precursor -sora *m,f* precursor, forerunner

predecesor -sora *m,f* predecessor

predecir [I25] *vt* to predict, foretell (fml)

predestinación *f* predestination

predestinar [A1] *vt* to predestine; **estar** ∼ **a algo/hacer algo** to be predestined to sth/to do sth

predeterminar [A1] *vt* to predetermine

predicado *m* predicate

predicador -dora *m,f* preacher

predicamento *m* (AmL) (situación difícil) predicament

predicar [A2] *vt/vi* to preach

predicativo -va *adj* predicative

predicción *f* prediction, forecast

predicible *adj* (Andes) predictable

predilección *f* predilection; **tiene/siente** ∼ **por su hijo** she's especially fond of her son

predilecto -ta *adj/m,f* favorite*

predisponer [E22] *vt* **1** (Med) to predispose **2** (influir en) to prejudice; **lo predispusieron en contra mía** they prejudiced him against me

predisposición *f* **1** (Med) predisposition **2** (inclinación): **tener** ∼ **contra algn** to be prejudiced against sb

predispuesto -ta *adj* **(a)** [SER] (propenso) ∼ **A algo** prone TO sth **(b)** [ESTAR] (prejuiciado) ∼ **A FAVOR/EN CONTRA DE algo/algn** biased TOWARDS/ AGAINST sth/sb

predominante *adj* predominant

predominar [A1] *vi* «*actitud/opinión*» to prevail; ∼ **EN algo** to dominate sth; **el tema predominó en el congreso** the subject dominated the conference; ∼ **SOBRE algo** to be predominant OVER sth

predominio *m* predominance

preescolar *adj* ⟨*edad/educación*⟩ preschool (*before n*); **centro de educación** ∼ kindergarten, nursery school (BrE)

preestreno *m* preview

prefabricado -da *adj* prefabricated

prefacio *m* preface

prefecto *m* **(a)** (Relig) prefect **(b)** (Gob) (en Francia) prefect **(c)** (Per) (gobernador) civil governor **(d)** (Col) (Educ) *teacher responsible for discipline*

preferencia *f* **(a)** (prioridad) priority, precedence; (Auto) right of way, priority (BrE) **(b)** (predilección) preference; **tiene** ∼ **por el más pequeño** the youngest one is her favorite **(c)** (Espec) (localidad) grandstand

preferente *adj* (especial) special

preferible *adj* preferable, better; **es** ∼ **quedarse callado** it's better to stay quiet; **es** ∼ **a uno de plástico** it's better than *o* preferable to a plastic one; **es** ∼ **que no vayas** you'd better not go

preferido -da *adj/m,f* favorite*

preferir [I11] *vt* to prefer; **prefiero esperar aquí** ⋯❖

p

I'd rather wait here, I'd prefer to wait here; ∼ **algo A algo** to prefer sth TO sth; **prefiero que te quedes** I'd rather you stayed, I prefer you to stay
prefiera, prefieras, etc ▶ PREFERIR
prefijo *m* (Ling) prefix; (de teléfono) (dialing*) code
prefiriera, prefirió, etc ▶ PREFERIR
pregonar [A1] *vt* **(a)** ⟨noticia/secreto⟩ to make ... public **(b)** ⟨virtudes/méritos⟩ to extol **(c)** ⟨mercancía⟩ to hawk, cry
pregunta *f* question; **hacer/contestar una** ∼ to ask/answer a question
preguntar [A1] *vt* to ask; **eso no se pregunta** you shouldn't ask things like that; **la maestra me preguntó la lección** the teacher tested me on the lesson
■ ∼ *vi* to ask; **le preguntó sobre** *or* **acerca de lo ocurrido** he asked her (about) what had happened; ∼ **POR algo/algn** to ask ABOUT sth/sb; **preguntaban por un tal Mario** they were looking for *o* asking for someone called Mario
■ **preguntarse** *v pron* (*refl*) to wonder
prehistoria *f* prehistory
prehistórico -ca *adj* prehistoric
prejuiciado -da *adj* (AmL) prejudiced
prejuicio *m* prejudice; **tener** ∼**s raciales** to be racially prejudiced
prejuzgar [A3] *vt/vi* to prejudge
prelavado *m* prewash
preliminar *adj* preliminary
preludio *m* prelude
premamá *adj inv* (Esp fam) maternity (*before n*)
prematrimonial *adj* ⟨relaciones⟩ premarital
prematuro -ra *adj* premature
premeditación *f* premeditation
premeditado -da *adj* premeditated
premeditar [A1] *vt* to premeditate
premenstrual *adj* premenstrual
premiación *f* (AmL) (acción) awarding of prizes; (ceremonia) awards ceremony, prize-giving (BrE)
premiado -da *adj* ⟨número/boleto⟩ winning; ⟨novela/película/escritor⟩ prizewinning (*before n*); *ver tb* PREMIAR
premiar [A1] *vt* **(a)** ⟨actor/escritor⟩ to award a/the prize to, award ... a/the prize **(b)** ⟨generosidad/sacrificio⟩ to reward
premio *m* **(a)** (en general) prize; **conceder** *or* **dar un** ∼ to award *o* give a prize; **ganar** *or* **llevarse un** ∼ to win a prize; **el** ∼ **a la mejor película** the award *o* prize for the best movie; ∼ **de consolación** *or* (CS) **(de) consuelo** consolation prize; ∼ **gordo** jackpot; **P**∼ **Nobel** (galardón) Nobel Prize; (galardonado) Nobel Prize winner **(b)** (a esfuerzos, sacrificios) reward; **como** ∼ **a su dedicación** as a reward for your dedication
premisa *f* premise
premonición *f* premonition
prenatal *adj* prenatal (AmE), antenatal (BrE)
prenda *f* **1** (de vestir) garment; ∼ **íntima** undergarment, item of underwear **2** (señal, garantía) security, surety **3** (Jueg) forfeit
prendarse [A1] *v pron* (liter) ∼ **DE algn** to fall in love WITH sb
prender [E1] *vt* **1** ⟨persona⟩ to catch, seize **2** (sujetar) to pin; ⟨bajo/dobladillo⟩ to pin up

3 (a) ⟨cigarrillo/cerilla⟩ to light; ∼**(le) fuego a algo** to set fire to sth **(b)** (AmL) ⟨gas⟩ to light; ⟨estufa/horno⟩ to turn on; ⟨radio/luz/televisión⟩ to turn on, switch on
■ ∼ *vi* **1** «rama/planta» to take **2 (a)** «fósforo/piloto» to light; «leña» to catch (light) **(b)** (AmL) «luz/radio/televisión» to come on; **la televisión no prende** the TV won't come on **3** «idea/moda» to catch on
■ **prenderse** *v pron* **(a)** (con fuego) to catch fire **(b)** (AmL) «luz/radio/televisión» to come on
prensa *f* **(a)** (Impr, Period, Tec) press; **la** ∼ **oral** radio and television; **estar en** ∼ to be in *o* at the press **(b)** (periodistas) **la** ∼ the press; ∼ **amarilla** gutter press, yellow press; ∼ **del corazón** gossip magazines (*pl*); ∼ **roja** (CS) sensationalist press (*specializing in crime stories*)
preñado -da *adj* ⟨animal⟩ pregnant
preocupación *f* **(a)** (problema) worry; **les causa muchas preocupaciones** she causes them a lot of worry *o* problems **(b)** (inquietud) concern
preocupado -da *adj* worried; ∼ **POR algo** worried ABOUT sth
preocupante *adj* worrying
preocupar [A1] *vt* to worry; **no quiero** ∼**lo** I don't want to worry him; **le preocupa el futuro** she's worried *o* concerned about her future; **me preocupa que no haya llamado** it worries me that she hasn't phoned; **no me preocupa** it doesn't bother *o* worry me
■ **preocuparse** *v pron* **1** (inquietarse) to worry; ∼**se POR algo/algn** to worry ABOUT sth/sb **2** (ocuparse) ∼**se DE algo: me preocupé de que no faltara nada** I made sure *o* I saw to it that we had everything; **no se preocupó más del asunto** he gave the matter no further thought
preparación *f* **1** (de examen, discurso) preparation **2 (a)** (conocimientos, educación) education; (para trabajo) training **(b)** (de deportista) training; **su** ∼ **física es muy buena** he's in peak condition **3** (Farm, Med) preparation
preparado -da *adj* **1** (ESTAR) (listo, dispuesto) ready; ∼ **PARA algo** ready FOR sth; ¡∼**s, listos, ya!** get ready, get set, go! (AmE), on your marks, get set, go! (BrE) **2** (SER) (instruido, culto) educated; **un profesional muy bien** ∼ a highly-trained professional
preparar [A1] *vt* **1** ⟨plato⟩ to make, prepare; ⟨comida⟩ to prepare, get ... ready; ⟨medicamento⟩ to prepare, make up; ⟨habitación⟩ to prepare, get ... ready; ⟨cuenta⟩ to draw up (AmE), make up (BrE) **2** ⟨examen/prueba⟩ to prepare **3** ⟨persona⟩ (para examen) to tutor, coach (BrE); (para partido) to train, coach, prepare; (para tarea, reto) to prepare
■ **prepararse** *v pron* **1** (*refl*) (disponerse) ∼**se PARA algo** to get ready FOR sth **2** (*refl*) (formarse) to prepare; ∼**se PARA algo** ⟨para examen/competición⟩ to prepare for sth
preparativos *mpl* preparations (*pl*)
preparatoria *f* (Méx) three-year pre-university course and college where this is taught
preparatorio -ria *adj* ⟨curso⟩ preparatory; ⟨ejercicios⟩ warm-up (*before n*)
preponderante *adj* predominant, preponderant (fml)
preposición *f* preposition
prepotencia *f* arrogance

prepotente *adj* ⟨*persona*⟩ arrogant, overbearing; ⟨*actitud*⟩ high-handed

prepucio *m* foreskin, prepuce (tech)

presa *f* **1** (en caza) prey; **ser ~ de algo** (de terror, pánico) to be seized with sth **2** (dique) dam; (embalse) reservoir, lake **3** (AmS) (de pollo) piece

presagio *m* **(a)** (señal) omen **(b)** (premonición) premonition

prescindir [I1] *vi* **1** (arreglárselas sin) **~ DE algo/algn** to do WITHOUT sth/sb **2** (omitir) **~ DE algo** ⟨*de detalles/formalidades*⟩ to dispense WITH sth

prescribir [I34] *vt* to prescribe

prescripción *f* prescription; **por ~ facultativa** *or* **médica** on doctor's orders

prescrito -ta, prescripto -ta *pp* ▶ PRESCRIBIR

preselección *f*: **hacer una ~ de los candidatos** to draw up a shortlist of candidates; **una vez terminada la ~** once the initial selection process is/was complete

preseleccionar [A1] *vt* ⟨*candidatos/ solicitantes*⟩ to shortlist

presencia *f* **(a)** (en lugar, acto) presence; **su ~ me cohíbe** I feel awkward in his presence; **en ~ de algn** in the presence of sb **(b)** (euf) (aspecto físico) appearance; **se requiere buena ~** good *o* (BrE) smart appearance required **(c)** **~ de ánimo** (serenidad) presence of mind; (valor) courage, strength

presenciar [A1] *vt* ⟨*suceso/asesinato*⟩ to witness; ⟨*acto/espectáculo*⟩ to be present at, to attend

presentable *adj* presentable

presentación *f* (en general) presentation; (de personas) introduction

presentador -dora *m,f* presenter

presentar [A1] *vt* **1** **(a)** (mostrar) to present **(b)** (exponer por primera vez) ⟨*libro/disco*⟩ to launch; ⟨*obra de arte*⟩ to present; ⟨*colección de moda*⟩ to present, exhibit **(c)** (entregar) ⟨*informe/solicitud*⟩ to submit; ⟨*trabajo*⟩ to hand in; ⟨*renuncia*⟩ to hand in, submit **(d)** (enseñar) ⟨*carnet/pasaporte*⟩ to show **(e)** ⟨*disculpas/excusas*⟩ to make; ⟨*queja*⟩ to file, make; ⟨*cargos*⟩ to bring; **~on una denuncia** they reported the matter (to the police), they made an official complaint; **~ pruebas** to present evidence **(f)** (Mil): **~ armas** to present arms

2 (TV) ⟨*programa*⟩ to present, introduce
3 ⟨*persona*⟩ to introduce; **te presento a mi hermana** I'd like you to meet my sister, this is my sister
4 ⟨*novedad/ventaja*⟩ to offer; ⟨*síntoma*⟩ to show
■ **presentarse** *v pron* **1** **(a)** (en lugar) to turn up, appear; **~se (como) voluntario** to volunteer **(b)** **~se A algo** ⟨*a examen*⟩ to take sth; ⟨*a concurso*⟩ to enter sth; ⟨*a elecciones*⟩ to take part IN sth; **se presenta como candidato independiente** he's running (AmE) *o* (BrE) he's standing as an independent; **~se para un cargo** to apply for a post
2 «*dificultad/problema*» to arise, come up; «*oportunidad*» to arise
3 (darse a conocer) to introduce oneself

presente *adj* **1** (en un lugar) [ESTAR] present; **S Presente** (CS) (Corresp) ≈ by hand; **tener algo**

~ to bear sth in mind **2 (actual) present; **hasta el momento ~** up to the present time; **el día 15 del ~ mes** the 15th of this month; **en su atenta carta del 3 ~** (Méx frml) (Corresp) in your letter of the 3rd of this month *o* (frml) of the 3rd inst.
■ *m* **1** **(a)** (en el tiempo) **el ~** the present **(b)** (Ling) present (tense) **2** **los presentes** *mpl* (asistentes) those present

presentimiento *m* premonition; **tengo el ~ de que ...** I have a feeling that ...

presentir [I11] *vt* ⟨*desgracia*⟩ to have a premonition of; **presiento que ...** I have a feeling that ...

preservar [A1] *vt* **(a)** (proteger) to preserve **(b)** (AmL) (conservar, mantener) to maintain

preservativo *m* **1** (condón) condom **2** (Andes) (conservante) preservative

presidencia *f* **(a)** (Gob, Pol) (cargo) presidency; **~ municipal** (Méx) town hall **(b)** (de compañía, banco) presidency (esp AmE), chairmanship (BrE); (de reunión, comité) chairmanship, chair

presidente -ta *m,f* **(a)** (Gob, Pol) president; **el ~ del gobierno** the premier, the prime minister **(b)** (de compañía, banco) president (AmE), chairman (BrE) **(c)** (de reunión, comité, acto) chairperson, chair **(d)** (Der) (de tribunal) presiding judge/magistrate **(e)** (de jurado) chairman/chairwoman

presidiario -ria *m,f* convict, inmate, prisoner

presidio *m* (lugar) prison; (pena) prison sentence; **condenado a cinco años de ~** sentenced to five years imprisonment

presidir [I1] *vt* ⟨*país*⟩ to be president of; ⟨*reunión*⟩ to chair, preside at *o* over; ⟨*comité*⟩ to chair; ⟨*tribunal/cortes/jurado*⟩ to preside over; ⟨*compañía*⟩ to be president of (AmE), to be chairman of (BrE)

presilla *f* (para abrochar) eye; (lazo) loop

presión *f* **(a)** (Fís, Med, Meteo) pressure; **~ arterial** *or* **sanguínea** blood pressure **(b)** (coacción) pressure; **bajo ~** under pressure

presionar [A1] *vt* **(a)** (coaccionar) to put pressure on, to pressure (esp AmE), to pressurize (esp BrE) **(b)** ⟨*botón/timbre*⟩ to press
■ **~** *vi* (Dep) to put on the pressure

preso -sa *adj*: **estuvo ~ diez años** he was in prison for ten years; **llevarse a algn ~** to take sb prisoner
■ *m,f* prisoner

prestaciones *fpl* (Servs Socs) benefits (*pl*), assistance

prestado -da *adj*: **el libro está ~** the book is on loan *o* (colloq) is already out; **esta chaqueta es prestada** this jacket is borrowed; **pedir algo ~** to borrow sth; **me pidió el coche ~** she asked if she could borrow my car; **pídeselo ~** ask (him) if you can borrow it

prestamista *mf* moneylender

préstamo *m* (Econ, Fin) (acción — de prestar) lending; (— de tomar prestado) borrowing; (cosa prestada) loan

prestar [A1] *vt* **1** ⟨*dinero/libro*⟩ to lend; **¿me prestas el coche?** will you lend me your car?, can I borrow your car? **2** **(a)** ⟨*ayuda*⟩ to give; ⟨*servicio*⟩ to render; ⟨*servicio militar*⟩ to do **(b)** ⟨*atención*⟩ to pay **3** ⟨*juramento*⟩ to swear
■ **prestarse** *v pron* **1** (dar ocasión) **~se A algo** ⟨*críticas/malentendidos/abusos*⟩ to be open TO sth ····⁕

p

2 (ser apto, idóneo) ~**se** PARA algo to be suitable FOR sth **3** (*refl*) **(a)** (ofrecerse) ~**se a hacer algo** to offer to do dth **(b)** (en frases negativas): **no me presto a negocios sucios** I won't take part in anything underhand

prestidigitador -dora *m,f* conjurer

prestigio *m* prestige; **de** ~ prestigious

prestigioso -sa *adj* famous, prestigious

presumido -da *adj* **(a)** (engreído) conceited, full of oneself; (arrogante) arrogant **(b)** (coqueto) vain

presumir [I1] *vi* to show off; ~ DE algo ⟨*de dinero*⟩ (hablando) to boast *o* brag ABOUT sth; (enseñándolo) to flash sth around; **presume de guapo** he thinks he's good-looking
■ ~ *vt*: **se presume una reacción violenta** there is likely to be a violent reaction; **era de** ~ **lo que ocurriría** it was quite predictable what would happen

presunto -ta *adj* (*delante del n*) (frml) ⟨*asesino/ terrorista*⟩ alleged (*before n*)

presuntuoso -sa *adj* conceited, vain

presuponer [E22] *vt* to presuppose (frml), assume

presupuesto *m* **1** **(a)** (Fin) budget **(b)** (precio estimado) estimate; **hacer un** ~ to give an estimate **2** (supuesto) assumption, supposition

pretencioso -sa *adj* ⟨*casa/película*⟩ pretentious

pretender [E1] *vt*: **¿qué pretendes con esa actitud?** what do you hope to gain with that attitude?; **pretendía entrar sin pagar** he was trying to get in without paying; **no pretendo saberlo todo** I don't claim to know everything; **lo único que pretendía era ayudar** I was only trying to help; **¿pretendes que te crea?** do you expect me to believe you?

pretendido -da *adj* (*delante del n*) ⟨*interés/ amabilidad*⟩ feigned; **el** ~ **duque** the so-called duke; **con** ~ **interés** with false interest

pretendiente *mf* **1** (al trono) pretender; (a un puesto) applicant **2 pretendiente** *m* (de una mujer) suitor

pretensión *f* **1** (a trono, herencia) claim **2 pretensiones** *fpl* (ínfulas): **tener pretensiones** to be pretentious; **una película sin pretensiones** an unpretentious film

pretensioso -sa *adj* (AmL) vain

pretérito *m* preterit*; ~ **indefinido** simple past, preterit*; ~ **perfecto/pluscuamperfecto** present/past perfect

pretexto *m* pretext; **volvió con el** ~ **de recoger el paraguas** he went back on the pretext of getting his umbrella; **siempre sale con algún** ~ she always comes out with some excuse; **bajo ningún** ~ under no circumstances

prevalecer [E3] *vi* to prevail

prevención *f* **(a)** (de un mal, problema) prevention **(b)** (medida) precaution; **tomar prevenciones** to take precautionary measures

prevenido -da *adj* **(a)** (SER) (precavido)

well-prepared, well-organized; **es muy prevenida** she likes to be prepared *o* ready for all eventualities **(b)** (ESTAR) (advertido) forewarned; **ahora ya estás** ~ you've been warned

prevenir [I31] *vt* **(a)** ⟨*enfermedad/accidente*⟩ to prevent **(b)** (advertir, alertar) to warn
■ **prevenirse** *v pron* ~**se** CONTRA algo to take preventive *o* preventative measures AGAINST sth, take precautions AGAINST sth

preventiva *f* (Méx) yellow (AmE) *o* (BrE) amber light

preventivo -va *adj* preventive, preventative

prever [E29] *vt* **(a)** (anticipar) ⟨*acontecimiento/ consecuencias*⟩ to foresee, anticipate; ⟨*tiempo*⟩ to forecast; **se prevé un aumento de precios** a rise in prices has been predicted **(b)** (proyectar, planear): **medidas previstas por el gobierno** measures planned by the government; **tiene prevista su llegada a las 11 horas** it is due *o* scheduled to arrive at 11 o'clock; **todo salió tal como estaba previsto** everything turned out just as planned **(c)** ⟨*ley*⟩ to envisage
■ ~ *vi*: **como era de** ~ as was to be expected

previo -via *adj* **(a)** (anterior) ⟨*experiencia/ conocimientos*⟩ previous; **sin** ~ **aviso** without (prior) warning **(b)** ⟨*reunión/asunto*⟩ preliminary

previsible *adj* foreseeable

previsión *f* **(a)** (precaución) precaution; **en** ~ **de ...** as a precaution against ...; **por falta de** ~ owing to a lack of foresight **(b)** (predicción) forecast

previsor -sora *adj* (con visión de futuro) farsighted; (precavido) well-prepared

prieta *f* (Chi) blood sausage, black pudding (BrE)

prieto -ta *adj* (Méx fam) (oscuro) dark; (de piel oscura) dark-skinned

prima *f* **(a)** (de seguro) premium **(b)** (pago extra) bonus; ~ **de** *o* **por peligrosidad** danger money

primar [A1] *vi*: **debería** ~ **el interés público** the public interest should be (a) top priority; ~ **SOBRE algo** to take precedence *o* priority OVER sth

primaria *f* **1** (Educ) elementary *o* (BrE) primary education **2** (Pol) (en EEUU) primary

primario -ria *adj* **(a)** (básico) ⟨*necesidades/ objetivo*⟩ primary, basic **(b)** (primitivo) ⟨*instintos*⟩ primitive

primavera *f* **1** (estación) spring; **en** ~ in spring, in springtime **2** (Bot) primrose

primaveral *adj* ⟨*tiempo/moda*⟩ spring (*before n*); ⟨*ambiente*⟩ spring-like

primer ▶ PRIMERO

primera *f* **(a)** (Auto) first (gear) **(b)** (Transp) (clase) first class; **viajar en** ~ to travel first class; *ver tb* PRIMERO

primerizo -za *m,f* **(a)** (novice, beginner **(b) primeriza** *f* first-time mother

primero -ra *adj/pron* [PRIMER *is used before masculine singular nouns*] **1** (en el espacio, el tiempo) first; **el primer piso** the second (AmE) *o* (BrE) first floor; **en primer lugar ...** first (of all), ..., firstly, ...; **1°de julio** (*read as: primero de julio*)

1st July, July 1st (*léase: July the first*); Olaf I (*read as: Olaf primero*) Olaf I (*léase: Olaf the First*); **a primeras horas de la madrugada** in the early hours of the morning; **primera plana** front page; **∼s auxilios** *mpl* first aid; **primer plano** (Fot) close-up (shot)

2 (en calidad, jerarquía): **un artículo de primera calidad** a top-quality product; **de primera (categoría)** first-class, first-rate; **es el ∼ de la clase** he is top of the class; **primer ministro** Prime Minister

3 (básico, fundamental): **nuestro primer objetivo** our primary objective; **artículos de primera necesidad** basic necessities; **lo ∼ es ...** the most important thing is ...

■ *adv* 1 (en el tiempo) first

2 (en importancia): **estar ∼** to come first

primicia *f* (Period): **conseguimos la ∼ del reportaje** we were the first to carry the report; **una ∼ informativa** a scoop

primitivo -va *adj* primitive

primo -ma *adj* ⟨*número*⟩ prime; ⟨*materia*⟩ raw;
■ *m,f* (a) (*pariente*) cousin; **∼ hermano** first cousin (b) (Esp fam) (bobo) sucker (AmE colloq), mug (BrE colloq); **hacer el ∼** (Esp fam) to be taken for a ride

primogénito -ta *m,f* first *o* firstborn child

primordial *adj* ⟨*objetivo*⟩ fundamental, prime (*before n*); ⟨*interés/importancia*⟩ paramount

prímula *f* primula; (amarilla) primrose

princesa *f* princess

principal *adj* main; ⟨*papel*⟩ leading (*before n*); **lo ∼ es que...** the main thing is that...

príncipe *m* prince; **∼ heredero** crown prince

principiante *mf* beginner; **un error de ∼** a basic mistake

principio *m* 1 (comienzo) beginning; **a ∼s de temporada** at the beginning of the season; **empieza por el ∼** start at the beginning; **eso es un buen ∼** that's a good start; **en un** *or* **al ∼** at first, in the beginning 2 (a) (*postulado, norma moral*) principle; **es una mujer de ∼s** she's a woman of principle; **por ∼** on principle

pringar [A3] *vt* (fam) (ensuciar) to get ... dirty (with grease, oil etc)
■ **pringarse** *v pron* (fam) (ensuciarse) **∼se DE algo** ⟨*de grasa/mermelada*⟩ to get covered IN sth

pringoso -sa *adj* greasy

prioridad *f* priority

prisa *f* 1 (rapidez, urgencia) rush, hurry; **¿a qué viene tanta ∼?** what's the rush *o* hurry?; **con las ∼s olvidé decírselo** in the rush I forgot to tell her; **tenía ∼ por llegar a casa** he was in a rush to get home; **no me metas ∼** don't rush *o* hurry me; **tengo ∼** (Esp, Méx) I'm in a rush *o* a hurry; **darse ∼** to hurry (up) 2 (*en locs*) **a** *or* **de prisa** ▶ DEPRISA; **a toda prisa** as fast as possible; **correr prisa: estos no (me) corren ∼** there's no rush for these

prisco *m* (CS) *type of peach*

prisión *f* 1 (edificio) prison, jail, penitentiary (AmE) 2 (pena) prison sentence; **seis años de ∼** six years' imprisonment

prisionero -ra *m,f* prisoner; **lo hicieron ∼** he was taken prisoner *o* captured

prisma *m* (Fís, Ópt) prism; (perspectiva) perspective

prismáticos *mpl* binoculars (*pl*), field-glasses (*pl*); **unos ∼** a pair of binoculars

privacidad *f* privacy

privación *f* (a) (acción) deprivation; **la ∼ de libertad** deprivation of liberty (b) (falta, carencia) privation, deprivation; **pasar privaciones** to suffer privations *o* deprivations

privada *f* (Méx) private road (*with security control*)

privado -da *adj* (a) ⟨*reunión/vida*⟩ private; **en ∼** in private (b) (Col, Méx) (desmayado) unconscious (c) (Méx) ⟨*teléfono/número*⟩ unlisted (AmE), ex-directory (BrE)

privar [A1] *vt* 1 **∼ a algn DE algo** ⟨*de derecho/ libertad*⟩ to deprive sb OF sth 2 (Col, Méx) (dejar inconsciente) to knock ... unconscious
■ **privarse** *v pron* 1 **∼se DE algo** ⟨*de lujos/ placeres*⟩ to deprive oneself OF sth 2 (Col, Méx) (desmayarse) to lose consciousness, pass out

privatización *f* privatization

privatizar [A4] *vt* to privatize

privilegiado -da *adj* (a) ⟨*persona/clase*⟩ privileged (b) (excelente) ⟨*posición*⟩ privileged; ⟨*clima/inteligencia/memoria*⟩ exceptional
■ *m,f*: **unos pocos ∼s** a privileged few

privilegio *m* privilege

pro *m* (ventaja) advantage; **sopesar los ∼s y los contras de algo** to weigh up the pros and cons of sth
■ *prep*: **los sectores ∼ amnistía** the sectors in favor of an amnesty

proa *f* bow, prow

probabilidad *f* (Mat) probability; **con toda ∼** in all probability *o* likelihood; **¿qué ∼es tiene de ganar?** what are her chances of winning?

probable *adj* (posible) probable; **es ∼** probably; **es ∼ que llegue hoy** he will probably arrive today

probado -da *adj* (delante del *n*) proven

probador *m* fitting room, changing room (BrE)

probar [A10] *vt* 1 (demostrar) ⟨*teoría/inocencia*⟩ to prove 2 (a) ⟨*vino/sopa*⟩ to taste; (*por primera vez*) to try (b) ⟨*método*⟩ to try; ⟨*coche/mecanismo*⟩ to try out (c) ⟨*ropa*⟩ to try on; **∼le algo A algn** to try sth ON sb (d) (poner a prueba) ⟨*empleado/ honradez*⟩ to test; ⟨*arma/vehículo*⟩ to test (out)
■ **∼** *vi* (intentar) to try; **∼ A hacer algo** to try doing sth
■ **probarse** *v pron* ⟨*ropa/zapatos*⟩ to try on

probeta *f* test tube
■ *adj inv* ⟨*gemelos/hijos*⟩ test-tube (*before n*)

problema *m* problem; **resolver/solucionar un ∼** to solve a problem; **los coches viejos dan muchos ∼s** old cars give a lot of trouble; **no te hagas ∼** (AmL) don't worry about it

problemático -ca *adj* problematic, difficult

procaz *adj* ⟨*comentario/chiste*⟩ indecent, lewd; ⟨*lenguaje*⟩ obscene

procedencia *f* (a) (origen) origin (b) (de barco) port of origin

procedente *adj*: **el vuelo/tren ∼ de París** the flight/train from Paris

proceder [E1] *vi* 1 (provenir) **∼ DE algo** to come FROM sth 2 (actuar) to act, to proceed (frml); **procedió con mucha corrección** he behaved very correctly; **∼ contra algn** (Der) to iniciate ⋯✧

proceedings against sb **3** (frml) (iniciar) ~ **A algo**
to proceed TO sth **4** (ser conveniente): **procede
actuar rápidamente** it would be wise to act
swiftly; **rellenar lo que proceda** complete as
appropriate

procedimiento *m* **1** (método) procedure;
(Tec) process **2** (Der) proceedings (*pl*)

prócer *m* national hero (*esp of a struggle for
independence*)

procesado -da *m,f* (Der) accused, defendant

procesador *m* processor; ~ **de textos** word
processor

procesamiento *m* **1** (Der) prosecution, trial
2 (Tec, Inf) processing; ~ **de textos** word
processing

procesar [A1] *vt* **1** (Der) to try, prosecute
2 ⟨*materia prima/datos/solicitud*⟩ to process

procesión *f* procession

proceso *m* **1** (serie de acciones, sucesos) process
2 (Der) trial **3** (Inf) processing; ~ **de datos/
textos** data/word processing **4** (transcurso) course

proclamación *f* proclamation, declaration

proclamar [A1] *vt* to proclaim
■ **proclamarse** *v pron* to proclaim oneself

procrear [A1] *vi* to procreate, breed

procurador -dora *m,f* (Der) (abogado)
attorney, lawyer; (asistente) ≈ paralegal (*in US*),
≈ clerk (*in UK*)

procurar [A1] *vt* (intentar) ~ **hacer algo** to try to
do sth; **procura que no te vea** try not to let him
see you

prodigio *m* (a) (maravilla) wonder (b) (milagro)
miracle

prodigioso -sa *adj* prodigious, phenomenal;
⟨*éxito/jugador/músico*⟩ phenomenal

producción *f* **1** (Com, Econ) (proceso, acción)
production; (cantidad) output, production; ~ **en
cadena** *or* **serie** mass production **2** (Cin, Teatr, TV)
production

producir [I6] *vt* **1** (a) (en general) to produce
(b) ⟨*sonido*⟩ to cause, generate **2** (causar)
⟨*conmoción/reacción/explosión*⟩ to cause; **le
produjo una gran alegría** it made her very happy
■ **producirse** *v pron* **1** (frml) (tener lugar)
«*accidente/explosión*» to occur (frml), to take
place; «*cambio*» to occur (frml), to happen; **se
produjeron 85 muertes** there were 85 deaths, 85
people died *o* were killed **2** (*refl*) (frml) ⟨*heridas*⟩
to inflict ... on oneself (frml)

productividad *f* (cualidad) productivity;
(rendimiento) productivity, output

productivo -va *adj* productive; ⟨*empresa/
negocio*⟩ lucrative

producto *m* (a) (artículo producido) product; ~**s
agrícolas/de granja** agricultural/farm produce; ~
alimenticio foodstuff; ~ **lácteo** dairy product (b)
(resultado) result, product

productor -tora *adj* producing (*before n*)
■ *m,f* (a) (en general) producer (b) **productora** *f*
(empresa) production company

produje, produzca, etc ▶ PRODUCIR

proeza *f* (logro) feat, exploit; (Mil) heroic deed *o*
exploit

profanar [A1] *vt* ⟨*templo/sepultura*⟩ to
desecrate, defile

profano -na *adj* **1** (a) (no sagrado) ⟨*escritor/*

música⟩ secular, profane (frml); ⟨*fiesta*⟩ secular (b)
(antirreligioso) profane (frml), irreverent **2** (no
especializado): **soy ~ en la materia** I'm not an
expert on the subject
■ *m,f* **1** (Relig) (*m*) layman; (*f*) laywoman **2** (no
especialista) non-specialist

profecía *f* prophecy

proferir [I11] *vt* ⟨*palabras/amenazas*⟩ to utter;
⟨*insultos*⟩ to hurl

profesar [A1] *vt* (a) (declarar) ⟨*religión/doctrina*⟩
to profess (b) (sentir) ⟨*cariño*⟩ to feel; ⟨*respeto*⟩ to
have

profesión *f* (ocupación) profession; (en formularios)
occupation; ~ **liberal** profession

profesional *adj* ⟨*fotógrafo/deportista*⟩
professional (*before n*)
■ *mf* professional

profesionalidad *f* professionalism

profesionista *mf* (Méx) professional

profesor -sora *m,f* (de escuela secundaria)
teacher, schoolteacher; (de universidad) professor
(AmE), lecturer (BrE); **tiene un ~ particular** he has
a private tutor

profesorado *m* (cuerpo) faculty (AmE),
teaching staff (BrE); (actividad) teaching profession

profeta *m* prophet

profetizar [A4] *vt* to prophesy

prófugo -ga *m,f* (Der) fugitive; (Mil) deserter

profundidad *f* (a) (de pozo, río, mar) depth;
tiene 20 metros de ~ it's 20 meters deep (b) (de
conocimientos, ideas) depth; **en ~** ⟨*analizar*⟩ in
depth; ⟨*reformar*⟩ radically

profundizar [A4] *vi* ~ **EN algo** ⟨*en tema*⟩ to go
into sth in depth

profundo -da *adj* (a) ⟨*herida/pozo/raíz*⟩ deep;
un río poco ~ a shallow river (b) ⟨*pensamiento*⟩
profound, deep; ⟨*respeto/desprecio*⟩ profound;
⟨*lazos*⟩ strong; ⟨*desengaño*⟩ grave, terrible (c)
⟨*misterio*⟩ profound; ⟨*silencio*⟩ deep, profound (d)
⟨*voz/suspiro*⟩ deep (e) ⟨*sueño*⟩ deep, sound

progenitor -tora *m,f* (a) (antepasado) ancestor
(b) (frml) (*m*) (padre) father; (*f*) (madre) mother

programa *m* **1** (a) (Rad, TV) program*; ~
concurso quiz show; ~ **de entrevistas** chat show
(b) (folleto) program* **2** (programación, plan)
program* **3** (a) (político) program*; **su ~
electoral** their election manifesto (b) (Educ) (de
asignatura) syllabus; (de curso) curriculum, syllabus
4 (Inf, Elec) program*

programación *f* **1** (a) (Rad, TV) programs*
(*pl*) (b) (de festejos, visitas — lista) program*; (—
organización) organization, planning **2** (Inf)
programming

programador -dora *m,f* programmer

programar [A1] *vt* **1** (a) (Rad, TV) to schedule
(b) ⟨*actividades/eventos*⟩ to plan, draw up a
program* for; ⟨*horario/fecha*⟩ to schedule,
program*; ⟨*viaje*⟩ to organize (c) (Transp)
⟨*llegadas/salidas*⟩ to schedule, timetable (BrE)
2 (Inf) to program

progresar [A1] *vi* ⟨*persona*⟩ to make
progress, to progress; «*negociaciones/proyecto*»
to progress

progresión *f* (Mat, Mús) progression

progresista *adj/mf* progressive

progresivo -va *adj* progressive

progreso *m* **(a)** (adelanto): **supuso un gran ~** it was a great step forward; **hacer ~s** to make progress, **(b)** (evolución, desarrollo) progress

prohibición *f* (acción) prohibition, banning; (orden) ban

prohibir [I22] *vt* **(a)** ⟨acto/venta⟩ to ban, prohibit (frml); **iba en dirección prohibida** I was going the wrong way up a one-way street; **⊗ prohibido el paso** *or* **prohibida la entrada** no entry; **⊗ prohibido fumar** no smoking; **⊗ se prohíbe la entrada a menores de 16 años** over 16s only, no admission to persons under 16 years of age **(b)** **~le algo A** algn to ban sb FROM sth; **~le A** algn hacer algo to forbid sb to do sth, prohibit sb FROM doing sth (frml); **~ A** algn QUE haga algo to forbid sb to do sth

prohibitivo -va *adj* prohibitive

prójimo *m* (semejante) fellow man; **amar al ~** to love one's neighbor

prole *f* kids (*pl*) (colloq), offspring (hum)

proletario -ria *adj/m,f* proletarian

proliferar [A1] *vi* to proliferate, spread

prolífico -ca *adj* prolific

prolijo -ja *adj* **1** (extenso) protracted, long-winded; (minucioso) detailed **2** (RPl) (ordenado, aseado) ⟨persona/casa⟩ tidy; ⟨cuaderno⟩ neat

prólogo *m* (de libro) preface, foreword; (de acto) prelude

prolongación *f* extension

prolongado -da *adj* prolonged, lengthy

prolongar [A3] *vt* **(a)** ⟨contrato/plazo⟩ to extend; ⟨vacaciones/visita⟩ to prolong, extend; **~le la vida a** algn to prolong sb's life **(b)** ⟨línea/calle⟩ to extend

■ **prolongarse** *v pron* **(a)** (en el tiempo) «⟨debate/fiesta⟩» to go on, carry on **(b)** (en el espacio) «⟨carretera/línea⟩» to extend

promedio *m* **(a)** (Mat) average; **el ~ de mis ingresos** my average earnings; **como ~** on average **(b)** (nota media) average grade *o* (BrE) mark **(c)** (punto medio) mid-point

promesa *f* **(a)** (palabra) promise; **cumplí (con) mi ~** I kept my promise *o* word; **romper una ~** to break a promise **(b)** (persona) hope

prometedor -dora *adj* promising

prometer [E1] *vt* **(a)** (dar su palabra) to promise; **te lo prometo** I promise **(b)** (augurar) to promise

■ **~** *vi* «⟨persona/negocio⟩» to show *o* have promise

■ **prometerse** *v pron* **(a)** (en matrimonio) to get engaged **(b)** (refl) ⟨viaje/descanso⟩ to promise oneself

prometido -da *adj* **(a)** (para casarse) engaged **(b)** ⟨aumento/regalo⟩ promised; **cumplir con lo ~** to keep one's promise *o* word

■ *m, f* (*m*) fiancé; (*f*) fiancée

prominente *adj* prominent

promiscuidad *f* promiscuity

promiscuo -cua *adj* promiscuous

promoción *f* **1** **(a)** (de actividad, producto) promotion; **hacer la ~ de un producto** to promote a product **(b)** (ascenso) promotion **2** (Educ): **somos de la misma ~** we graduated at the same time

promocionar [A1] *vt* to promote

promontorio *m* (en tierra) hill, rise; (en el mar) promontory, headland

promotor -tora *m,f* (persona) **(a)** (Const) developer **(b)** (Espec) promoter **(c)** (de rebelión, huelga) instigator

promover [E9] *vt* ⟨ahorro/turismo⟩ to promote; ⟨conflicto/enfrentamientos⟩ to provoke; ⟨querella/pleito⟩ to bring

promulgar [A3] *vt* to enact, to promulgate (frml)

pronombre *m* pronoun

pronosticar [A2] *vt* ⟨tiempo/resultado⟩ to forecast; ⟨victoria/muerte⟩ to predict

pronóstico *m* **(a)** (predicción) forecast, prediction; **el ~ del tiempo** the weather forecast **(b)** (Med) prognosis **(c)** (en carreras de caballos) tip

prontitud *f* promptness

pronto¹ -ta *adj* **(a)** (rápido) ⟨entrega/respuesta⟩ prompt **(b)** (RPl) (preparado) ready

pronto² *adv* **1** **(a)** (en poco tiempo) soon; **¡hasta ~!** see you soon!; **lo más ~ posible** as soon as possible **(b)** (Esp) (temprano) early **2** (*en locs*) **de pronto** (repentinamente) suddenly; **por lo pronto** *or* **por de pronto** for the moment, for now; **tan pronto como** as soon as

pronunciación *f* pronunciation

pronunciado -da *adj* ⟨curva⟩ sharp, pronounced; ⟨pendiente⟩ steep, pronounced **(b)** ⟨facciones/rasgos⟩ pronounced, marked **(c)** ⟨tendencia⟩ marked, noticeable

pronunciamiento *m* rebellion, military uprising

pronunciar [A1] *vt* **1** **(a)** (Ling) to pronounce **(b)** ⟨discurso⟩ to deliver, give **2** (resaltar) to accentuate

■ **pronunciarse** *v pron* **1** (dar una opinión) **~se A FAVOR/EN CONTRA DE algo** to declare oneself to be in FAVOR OF/AGAINST sth **2** (acentuarse) to become more marked, become more pronounced

propaganda *f* **(a)** (Pol) propaganda **(b)** (Com, Marketing) advertising; **hacer ~ de un producto** to advertise a product **(c)** (material publicitario) advertisements (*pl*); **no trae más que ~** it has nothing but advertisements in it; **repartir ~** to hand out advertising leaflets

propagar [A3] *vt* **(a)** ⟨doctrina/rumores/enfermedad⟩ to spread, propagate **(b)** ⟨especie⟩ to propagate

■ **propagarse** *v pron* to spread; «⟨especie/sonido/luz⟩» to propagate

propasarse [A1] *v pron* **(a)** (excederse) to go too far, overstep the mark **(b)** (en sentido sexual) **~ CON** algn to make a pass AT sb

propenso -sa *adj* **~ A** algo prone TO sth

propiamente *adv* exactly; **no vive en Londres ~ dicho** he doesn't live in London proper

propiciar [A1] *vt* (favorecer) to favor*; (causar) to bring about

propicio -cia *adj* ⟨momento⟩ opportune, propitious (frml); ⟨condiciones⟩ favorable*, propitious (frml)

propiedad *f* **1** **(a)** (pertenencia) property; **son ~ del museo** they are the property of the museum; **la casa es ~ de mi hijo** the house belongs to my son **(b)** (lo poseído) property; **~ intelectual** copyright; **~ privada/pública** private/public property **2** (cualidad) property; (corrección): **con ~** ⟨hablar⟩ correctly; ⟨comportarse⟩ with decorum

P

propietario -ria *m,f* **(a)** (de comercio) owner, proprietor **(b)** (de casa) owner **(c)** (de tierras) landowner

propina *f* **(a)** (a camarero, empleado) tip, gratuity (frml); **dejó 25 pesos de** ∼ she left a 25 peso tip; **darle** ∼ **a algn** to tip sb **(b)** (Per) (de niño) pocket money

propio -pia *adj* ⊡ **(a)** (indicando posesión) own; ¿es ∼ o alquilado? is it your own or is it rented?; **tienen piscina propia** they have their own swimming pool **(b)** (de uno mismo) own; **por tu** ∼ **bien** for your own good; **todo lo hace en beneficio** ∼ everything he does is for his own gain; **lo vi con mis** ∼s **ojos** I saw it with my own two eyes o with my (very) own eyes ⊡ (característico, típico): **esa actitud es muy propia de él** that kind of attitude is very typical of him; **una enfermedad propia de la vejez** an illness common among old people; **no es un comportamiento** ∼ **de una señorita** it's not ladylike behaviour ⊡ (delante del n) (mismo): **fue el** ∼ **presidente** it was the president himself; **debe ser el** ∼ **interesado quien lo pida** it must be the person concerned who makes the request

proponer [E22] *vt* **(a)** ⟨idea⟩ to propose, suggest; ⟨brindis⟩ to propose; **nos propuso ir al campo** she suggested we go to the countryside; **te voy a** ∼ **un trato** I'm going to make you a proposition **(b)** ⟨persona⟩ (para cargo) to put forward, nominate; (para premio) to nominate **(c)** ⟨moción⟩ to propose **(d)** ⟨teoría⟩ to propound
■ **proponerse** *v pron*: ∼**se hacer algo** to set out to do sth; **me lo propuse como meta** I set myself that goal; **me propuse decírselo** I made up my mind o I decided to tell her

proporción *f* ⊡ (relación) proportion; **en** ∼ **a los ingresos** in proportion to income ⊡ **proporciones** *fpl* (dimensiones) proportions (pl)

proporcionado -da *adj*: ∼ **a la figura humana** in proportion to the human body; **mal** ∼ ⟨dibujo⟩ poorly proportioned; **es bajo pero bien** ∼ he's short but he's well-proportioned

proporcional *adj* proportional, proportionate

proporcionar [A1] *vt* ⟨materiales/información/comida⟩ to provide; ∼ **algo** A **algn** to provide sb WITH sth

proposición *f* proposal, proposition; ∼ **de matrimonio** proposal of marriage

propósito *m* **(a)** (intención) intention, purpose; **con el** ∼ **de verla** with the intention o purpose of seeing her; **tiene el firme** ∼ **de dejar de fumar** she's determined to give up smoking; **buenos** ∼s good intentions **(b) a propósito** (adrede) deliberately, on purpose; (por cierto) by the way

propuesta *f* **(a)** (sugerencia) proposal **(b)** (oferta) offer

propulsar [A1] *vt* ⟨desarrollo/actividad⟩ to promote, stimulate; ⟨avión/cohete⟩ to propel; ⟨vehículo⟩ to drive, propel

propulsión *f* propulsion; ∼ **a chorro** jet propulsion

propulsor -sora *adj* ⟨mecanismo⟩ driving (before n), propulsion (before n); ⟨cohete⟩ propulsion (before n)
■ *m,f* **(a)** (de actividad, idea) promoter **(b) propulsor** *m* (Tec) propellant

propuse, propuso, etc ▶ PROPONER

prórroga *f* **(a)** (extensión) extension; (Dep) overtime (AmE), extra time (BrE) **(b)** (aplazamiento) deferral, deferment

prorrogar [A3] *vt* **(a)** (alargar) to extend **(b)** (aplazar) ⟨fecha⟩ to postpone, put back

prosa *f* prose

prosaico -ca *adj* ⟨existencia/vida⟩ mundane, prosaic

proseguir [I30] *vi/vt* (frml) to continue

prospecto *m* **(a)** (de fármaco) directions for use (pl), patient information leaflet **(b)** (de propaganda) pamphlet, leaflet

prosperar [A1] *vi* **(a)** «negocio/país» to prosper, thrive; «persona» to do well, make good **(b)** «iniciativa/proyecto» (aceptarse) to be accepted, prosper

prosperidad *f* prosperity

próspero -ra *adj* prosperous

próstata *f* prostate (gland)

prostíbulo *m* brothel

prostitución *f* prostitution

prostituir [I20] *vt* to prostitute
■ **prostituirse** *v pron* to prostitute oneself

prostituto -ta *m,f* *(m)* male prostitute; *(f)* prostitute

protagonista *mf* **(a)** (personaje principal) main character **(b)** (actor) **el** ∼ **de la nueva serie** the actor who is playing the leading role in the new series; **los principales** ∼s **de nuestra historia** the major figures of our history

protagonizar [A4] *vt* **(a)** (Cin, Teatr) to star in, play the lead o leading role in **(b)** ⟨tiroteo⟩ to be involved in; ⟨debate⟩ to take part in; ⟨disturbios⟩ to be responsible for

protección *f* protection

proteccionismo *m* protectionism

proteccionista *adj/mf* protectionist

protector -tora *adj* protective; **sociedad** ∼**a de animales** society for the prevention of cruelty to animals
■ *m,f* (defensor) protector; (benefactor) patron

protectorado *m* protectorate

proteger [E6] *vt* **(a)** (en general) to protect; ∼ **algo/a algn** DE *or* CONTRA **algo/algn** to protect sth/sb FROM o AGAINST sth/sb **(b)** ⟨artes⟩ to champion, patronize; ⟨pintor/poeta⟩ to act as patron to
■ **protegerse** *v pron* (refl) ∼**se** DE *or* CONTRA **algo** to protect oneself FROM o AGAINST sth; ∼**se de la lluvia** to shelter from the rain

protegido -da *adj* **(a)** ⟨especie⟩ protected **(b)** ⟨vivienda⟩ subsidized **(c)** (Inf) write-protected

AmC	Central America	Arg	Argentina	Cu	Cuba	Per	Peru
AmL	Latin America	Bol	Bolivia	Ec	Ecuador	RPI	River Plate Area
AmS	South America	Chi	Chile	Esp	Spain	Ur	Uruguay
Andes	Andean Region	CS	Southern Cone	Méx	Mexico	Ven	Venezuela

■ *m,f* (*m*) protégé; (*f*) protégée

proteína *f* protein

prótesis *f* prosthesis

protesta *f* **1** (a) (queja) protest; **en señal de ~** in protest (b) (manifestación) demonstration, protest march (*o* rally *etc*) **2** (Méx) (a) (promesa) promise; **cumplieron con su ~** they kept their promise *o* word (b) ▶ JURAMENTO

protestante *adj/mf* Protestant

protestantismo *m* Protestantism

protestar [A1] *vi* (a) (mostrar desacuerdo) to protest; **~ CONTRA** algo to protest AGAINST *o* ABOUT sth (b) (quejarse) to complain; **~ POR** *or* **DE** algo to complain ABOUT sth

protocolo *m* (a) (ceremomial, etiqueta) protocol; (b) (Inf) protocol

prototipo *m* (a) (de especie) archetype, prototype (b) (Tec) prototype

protuberancia *f* bulge, protuberance (frml)

provecho *m* (a) (beneficio, utilidad) benefit; **no sacó mucho ~ de la experiencia** she didn't benefit much from the experience; **le sacó mucho ~ a su estancia** she got a lot out of her stay; **solo piensa en su propio ~** he's only out for himself (colloq); **de ~** ‹*estudiante*› hardworking; ‹*experiencia/visita*› worthwhile (b) (en la mesa): **¡buen ~!** (dicho por uno mismo) bon appetit!; (dicho por camarero) enjoy your meal!

provechoso -sa *adj* profitable, fruitful

proveedor -dora *m,f* supplier, purveyor (frml); **~ de servicios Internet** Internet service provider

proveer [E14] *vt* (suministrar) to provide; **~ a algn DE algo** to provide sb WITH sth; **iban provistos de botes salvavidas** they were equipped with *o* they carried lifeboats

■ **proveerse** *v pron* (*refl*): **~se DE algo** ‹*de herramientas/armas*› to equip oneself WITH sth; ‹*de comida*› to get sth

provenir [I31] *vi* **~ DE algo/algn** to come FROM sth/sb

proverbio *m* proverb

providencia *f* (Relig): **la (divina) P~** (divine) Providence

providencial *adj* (a) (oportuno) fortunate, lucky, providential (frml); **fue ~ que ...** it was fortunate that ... (b) (Relig) providential

provincia *f* **1** (Gob, Relig) province **2** **provincias** *fpl* (por oposición a la capital) provinces (*pl*); **la vida de ~s** provincial life

provinciano -na *adj* (a) (de provincias) provincial (b) (pey) (estrecho de miras) provincial, parochial

■ *m,f* (a) (de provincias): **los ~s** people from the provinces (b) (pey) (de mentalidad estrecha) provincial (c) (paleto) country bumpkin, hick (AmE colloq)

provisional *adj* provisional

provisiones *fpl* (víveres) provisions (*pl*)

provisto -ta *pp* ▶ PROVEER

provocación *f* provocation

provocador -dora *adj* provocative

■ *m,f* agitator

provocar [A2] *vt* **1** (a) ‹*explosión*› to cause; ‹*incendio*› to start; ‹*polémica*› to spark off,

prompt; ‹*reacción*› to cause (b) (Med) ‹*parto*› to induce **2** ‹*persona*› (al enfado) to provoke; (sexualmente) to lead ... on

■ **~** *vi* (Andes) (apetecer): **¿le provoca un traguito?** do you want a drink?, do you fancy a drink? (BrE colloq)

provocativo -va *adj* **1** (insinuante) provocative **2** (Col, Ven) (apetecible) tempting, mouthwatering

proxeneta *mf* (*m*) procurer (frml), pimp (colloq); (*f*) procuress (frml), pimp (colloq)

proximidad *f* (a) (en el tiempo, espacio) closeness, proximity (frml) (b) **proximidades** *fpl* (cercanías) vicinity

próximo -ma *adj* **1** (a) (siguiente) next; **el ~ jueves** next Thursday (b) (*como pron*): **esto lo dejamos para la próxima** we'll leave this for next time; **tome la próxima a la derecha** take the next (on the) right **2** [ESTAR] (cercano) (a) (en el tiempo) close; **la fecha ya está próxima** the day is close; **en fecha próxima** in the near future (b) (en el espacio) near, close; **~ A algo** close *o* near TO sth

proyección *f* (a) (Cin) showing (b) (de sombra) casting; (de luz) throwing

proyectar [A1] *vt* **1** (planear) to plan; **~ hacer algo** to plan to do sth **2** (a) ‹*película*› to show, screen; ‹*diapositivas*› to project, show (b) ‹*sombra*› to cast; ‹*luz*› to throw, project

proyectil *m* projectile, missile

proyecto *m* (a) (plan) plan; **¿qué ~s tienes para el próximo año?** what are your plans for next year?; **tiene un viaje en ~** she's planning a trip; **~ de ley** bill (b) (trabajo) project (c) (Arquit, Ing) plans and costing

proyector *m* **1** (Cin, Fot) projector **2** (Teatr) spotlight; (para monumentos) floodlight; (Mil) searchlight

prudencia *f* (cuidado) caution; (sabiduría) wisdom, prudence; **conduce con ~** drive carefully

prudente *adj* (sensato. responsable) prudent, sensible; (cauto, precavido) cautious, prudent

prueba *f* **1** (a) (demostración, testimonio) proof; **no hay ~s de que eso sea verdad** there's no proof that that's true; **eso es ~ de que le caes bien** that proves he likes you; **en** *or* **como ~ de mi agradecimiento** as a token of my gratitude (b) (Der) piece of evidence **2** (Educ) test; (Cin) screen test, audition; (Teatr) audition **3** (a) (ensayo, experimento) test; **vamos a hacer la ~** let's try; **~ de la alcoholemia** Breathalyzer® test, sobriety test (AmE), drunkometer test (AmE); **~ del embarazo** pregnancy test (b) (en locs) **a prueba: tomar a algn a ~** to take sb on for a trial period; **tener algo a ~** to have sth on trial; **poner algo a ~** to put sth to the test; **a ~ de golpes/de balas** shockproof/bulletproof (c) (en costura) fitting **4** (Fot, Impr) proof; **corregir ~s** to proofread **5** (Dep): **en las ~s de clasificación** in the qualifying heats; **la ~ de los 1.500 metros** the 1,500 meters (event *o* race)

prueba, pruebas, etc ▶ PROBAR

PSI *m* (= **provedor de sevicios Internet**) ISP

psicoanálisis *m* psychoanalysis

psicoanalista *mf* psychoanalyst
psicodélico -ca *adj* psychedelic
psicología *f* psychology
psicológico -ca *adj* psychological
psicólogo -ga *m,f* psychologist
psicópata *mf* psychopath
psicosis *f* (*pl* ~) psychosis
psicosomático -ca *adj* psychosomatic
psicoterapia *f* psychotherapy
psiquiatra *mf* psychiatrist
psiquiatría *f* psychiatry
psiquiátrico¹ -ca *adj* psychiatric (*before n*)
psiquiátrico² *m* psychiatric hospital, mental
hospital
psíquico -ca *adj* psychic
ptas, pts = pesetas
púa *f* ⎯1⎯ (a) (de erizo) spine, quill; (de alambre)
barb; (de peine) tooth (b) (Chi, Ven) (en zapatos de
atletismo) spike ⎯2⎯ (para guitarra) plectrum, pick; (de
tocadiscos) (RPl) needle
pub /puβ, pʌβ/ *m* (*pl* **pubs** *or* **pubes**) bar (*gen
with music, open late at night*)
pubertad *f* puberty
pubis *m* (*pl* ~) pubis
publicación *f* publication
publicar [A2] *vt* (a) ⟨artículo/noticia⟩ to
publish (b) (divulgar) to divulge, disclose
publicidad *f* (a) (de tema, suceso) publicity (b)
(Com, Marketing) advertising; **hacer** ~ **de algo** to
advertise sth
publicista *mf* (a) (AmL) (Com) advertising
executive *o* agent, publicist (b) (Period) publicist
publicitario -ria *adj* ⟨campaña/espacio⟩
advertising (*before n*); ⟨truco/montaje⟩ publicity
(*before n*)
público¹ -ca *adj* public; **hacer** ~ **algo** to
announce sth; **es un peligro** ~ he's a danger to
the public
público² *m* (en teatro) audience, public; (Dep)
spectators (*pl*); ⦿ **horario de atención al público**
(en oficinas públicas) opening hours; (en bancos)
hours of business; **película apta para todo(s) (los)**
~**(s)** 'G' movie (AmE), 'U' film (BrE); **el** ~ **en
general** the general public; **en** ~ ⟨hablar⟩ in
public; ⟨cantar/bailar⟩ in front of an audience;
salir al ~ (Andes) ⟨periódico/revista⟩ to come
out, appear; ⟨noticia/información⟩ to be
published
pucherazo *m* (fam) electoral rigging; **hubo** ~
the election was fixed *o* rigged
puchero *m* ⎯1⎯ (Coc) (recipiente) pot, stewpot;
(cocido) stew ⎯2⎯ (mueca) pout; **hacer** ~**s** to pout
pucho *m* (AmS fam) (a) (cigarrillo — de tabaco)
smoke (colloq), fag (BrE colloq); (— de marihuana)
joint (colloq) (b) (resto — de cigarrillo) butt, fag end
(BrE colloq); (— de comida) scrap; (— de bebida) drop
pude ▶ PODER
púdico -ca *adj* ⟨ropa⟩ modest;
⟨comportamiento/beso⟩ chaste
pudiera, pudiese, etc ▶ PODER
pudín *m* ▶ BUDÍN
pudiste, etc ▶ PODER
pudor *m* (a) (recato sexual) modesty; **no se
desnudó por** ~ she was too embarrassed *o* shy to

take her clothes off; **es una falta de** ~ it shows a
lack of (a sense of) decency (b) (reserva) reserve;
nos habló sin ~ he talked to us very openly
pudoroso -sa *adj* ▶ PÚDICO
pudrir [I38] *vt* (descomponer) ⟨carne/fruta/madera⟩
to rot, decay
■ **pudrirse** *v pron* ⎯1⎯ (descomponerse) «fruta/
carne» to rot, decay; «madera/tela» to rot;
«cadáver» to decompose, rot ⎯2⎯ (fam) (por el
abandono): ~**se en la cárcel** to rot in jail
pueblerino -na *adj* ⟨aire⟩ provincial; **¡qué** ~
eres! you're such a country bumpkin *o* (AmE
colloq) hick!
pueblo *m* ⎯1⎯ (poblado) village; (más grande) small
town; ~ **joven** (Per) shantytown ⎯2⎯ (a)
(comunidad) people; **un** ~ **nómada** a nomadic
people (b) (ciudadanos, nación) people; **el** ~ **vasco**
the Basque people
pueda, puedas, etc ▶ PODER
puente *m* ⎯1⎯ (Ing) bridge; ~ **colgante/giratorio**
suspension/swing bridge; ~ **levadizo** (en castillo)
drawbridge; (en carretera) lifting bridge; ~ **aéreo**
(servicio frecuente) shuttle (service); (Mil) airlift
⎯2⎯ (Mús, Odont) bridge; (de anteojos) bridge ⎯3⎯
(Elec) bridge (circuit) ⎯4⎯ (vacación) ≈ long
weekend (*linked to a public holiday by an extra
day's holiday in between*) ⎯5⎯ (Náut) *tb* ~ **de
mando** bridge
puerco -ca *adj* (fam & pey) (sucio) dirty;
(despreciable) low-down (colloq)
■ *m,f* ⎯1⎯ (a) (animal) (*m*) pig, hog, boar; (*f*) pig,
hog, sow; ~ **espín** porcupine (b) (Méx) (carne)
pork ⎯2⎯ (fam) (persona — sucia) pig (colloq); (—
despreciable) swine (colloq)
puericultor -tora *m,f*: nurse or doctor who
specializes in babycare/childcare
puericultura *f* babycare, childcare
pueril *adj* (a) (infantil) childish, puerile (frml) (b)
(ingenuo) naïve
puerro *m* leek
puerta *f* (de casa, coche, horno) door; (en jardín,
valla) gate; **llamar a la** ~ to ring the doorbell/
knock on the door; **te espero en la** ~ **del teatro**
I'll meet you at the entrance of the theater; **te
acompaño a la** ~ I'll see *o* show you out; **servicio**
~ **a** ~ door-to-door service; **un coche de dos** ~**s**
a two-door car; ~ **de embarque** gate; ~ **principal**
or **de la calle** (de casa) front door; (de edificio
público) main door *or* entrance; ~ **trasera** back
door
puerto *m* ⎯1⎯ (Náut) port, harbor*; **entrar a** ~ to
enter port *o* harbor; ~ **deportivo** marina; ~
franco *or* **libre** free port; ~ **pesquero** fishing port
⎯2⎯ (Geog) *tb* ~ **de montaña** (mountain) pass
Puerto Príncipe *m* Port-au-Prince
Puerto Rico *m* Puerto Rico
pues *conj* (a) (en general) well (b) (indicando
consecuencia) then; ~ **si te gusta tanto, cómpralo** if
you like it that much, then buy it
puesta *f* ⎯1⎯ (acción de poner): **hasta la** ~ **en
servicio de los autobuses** until the buses come
into service; **la** ~ **en libertad de los prisioneros**
the freeing *o* release of the prisoners; ~ **a punto**
(de vehículo) tune-up; (de máquina) adjustment; ~
de sol sunset; ~ **en escena** production; ~ **en
marcha** (de vehículo, motor) starting (up); ~ **al día**
updating ⎯2⎯ (de huevos) lay

puestero -ra *m,f* (AmL) **(a)** (vendedor) stallholder, market vendor **(b)** (en una estancia) farmer (*responsible for the running of part of a large ranch*)

puesto¹ -ta *adj*: ¿qué haces con el abrigo ∼? what are you doing with your coat on?; **tenía las botas puestas** she was wearing her boots; **la mesa estaba puesta** the table was laid; *ver tb* PONER

puesto² *m* **1** **(a)** (lugar, sitio) place; **se sentó en mi** ∼ he sat in my place **(b)** (en una clasificación) place, position; **sacó el primer** ∼ **de la clase** she came top *o* (AmE) came out top of the class **2** (empleo) position, job; ∼ **de trabajo** (empleo) job; (Inf) workstation **3** **(a)** (Com) (en mercado) stall; (quiosco) kiosk; (tienda) stand, stall **(b)** (de la policía, del ejército) post; ∼ **de socorro** first-aid post/ station **4** **puesto que** (*conj*) (frml) since

puf *m* (*pl* **pufs**) hassock (AmE), pouffe (BrE)
■ *interj* (expresando — repugnancia) ugh! (colloq), pee-yoo! (AmE); (— cansancio, sofoco) whew!, oof!

púgil *m* (period) boxer, pugilist (frml)

pugna *f* **(a)** (lucha) struggle **(b)** (conflicto): **tendencias/intereses en** ∼ conflicting trends/ interests; **entrar en** ∼ **con algo/algn** to clash *o* come into conflict with sth/sb

pugnar [A1] *vi* (liter) (luchar) ∼ POR + INF to strive to + INF (frml)

pujante *adj* booming (*before n*)

pujanza *f* vigor*, strength

pujar [A1] *vi* (luchar) ∼ POR algo/hacer algo to struggle POR sth/to do sth **2** (Esp) (en subasta) to bid **3** (Méx fam) (gemir) to moan, whimper

pulcro -cra *adj* (*persona/aspecto*) immaculate, neat and tidy; (*informe/trabajo*) meticulous

pulga *f* (Zool) flea; **tener malas** ∼**s** (fam) to be bad-tempered

pulgada *f* inch

pulgar *m* (de la mano) thumb; (del pie) big toe

pulgón *m* aphid, plant louse

pulido -da *adj* (*estilo/trabajo/lenguaje*) polished; (*modales*) refined

pulir [I1] *vt* **1** **(a)** (*metal/piedra/vidrio*) to polish **(b)** (*madera*) to sand **(c)** (lustrar) to polish **2** (refinar) (*estilo/trabajo*) to polish up; (*persona*) to make … more refined; (*idioma*) to brush up

pulla *f* gibe

pulmón *m* lung; ∼ **de acero** iron lung

pulmonía *f* pneumonia; ∼ **doble** double pneumonia

pulóver *m* (*pl* **-vers**) (suéter) pullover, sweater, jumper (BrE)

pulpa *f* (de fruta, vegetal) pulp; (de madera) (wood) pulp

pulpería *f* (AmL) local store

pulpero -ra *m,f* (AmL) local storekeeper

púlpito *m* pulpit

pulpo *m* (Zool) octopus

pulque *m* pulque (*drink made from fermented cactus sap*)

pulquería *f* (Méx) bar, restaurant (*serving pulque*)

pulquero -ra *m,f* (Méx) *owner of a* PULQUERÍA

pulsación *f* **1** (latido) beat **2** (en mecanografía) keystroke; ¿**cuántas pulsaciones piden por minuto?** ≈how many words a minute do they want?

pulsar [A1] *vt* **1** **(a)** (Mús) (*cuerda*) to pluck; (*tecla*) to press **(b)** (*botón*) to push, press; (*timbre*) press, ring **2** (*opinión/situación*) to gauge, assess

pulsera *f* bracelet; ∼ **de tobillo** ankle bracelet, anklet

pulso *m* **(a)** (Med) pulse; **tomarle el** ∼ **a algn** to take sb's pulse; **tomarle el** ∼ **a algo** to gauge sth **(b)** (firmeza en la mano): **tengo muy mal** ∼ I have a very unsteady hand; **me temblaba el** ∼ my hand was shaking; **a** ∼ (*levantar*) with one's bare hands; (*dibujar*) freehand

pulular [A1] *vi* **(a)** (bullir) «*muchedumbre*» to mill around **(b)** (abundar): **aquí pululan los mosquitos** there are swarms of mosquitos here

pulverizador *m* (de perfume) atomizer, spray; (de pintura) spray gun; (del carburador) jet

pulverizar [A4] *vt* (*líquido*) to atomize, spray; (*sólido*) to pulverize, crush

puma *m* (animal) cougar, mountain lion, puma

puna *f* **(a)** (páramo) high Andean plateau **(b)** (Andes) (soroche) mountain *o* altitude sickness

punki /'puŋki, 'pʌŋki/ *adj/mf* (fam) punk

punta *f* **1** **(a)** (de lengua, dedos) tip; (de nariz) end, tip; (de pan) end; (de pincel) tip; **vivo en la otra** ∼ **de la ciudad** I live on the other side *o* at the other end of town; **con la** ∼ **del pie** with the print of one's foot; **la** ∼ **del iceberg** the tip of the iceberg; **tener algo en la** ∼ **de la lengua** to have sth on the tip of one's tongue **(b)** **puntas** *fpl* (del pelo) ends (*pl*)
2 **(a)** (de aguja, clavo, cuchillo, lápiz) point; (de flecha, lanza) tip; ∼ **de lanza** spearhead; **sácale** ∼ **al lápiz** sharpen the pencil; **de** ∼ point first; **en** ∼ pointed; **por un extremo acaba en** ∼ it's pointed at one end **(b) a punta de** (AmL fam): **a** ∼ **de repetírselo mil veces** by telling him it a thousand times; **a** ∼ **de palos lo hicieron obedecer** they beat him until he did as he was told **3** (de pañuelo) corner
■ *adj inv*: **la hora** ∼ the rush hour

puntabola *f* (Bol) ballpoint pen, Biro® (BrE)

puntada *f* **1** (en costura) stitch **2** (CS) (de dolor) stab of pain, sharp pain **3** (Méx fam) (comentario ingenioso) quip, witticism

puntaje *m* (AmL) (en competencia, prueba) score; (Educ) grades (*pl*) (AmE), marks (BrE)

puntal *m* **(a)** (Const) prop **(b)** (sostén, apoyo) mainstay

puntapié *m* kick; **darle** *or* **pegarle un** ∼ **a algo/ algn** to kick sth/sb, to give sth/sb a kick; *para modismos ver* PATADA

puntear [A1] *vt* **1** (Mús) to pluck **2** (AmL) (Dep) to lead

punteo *m* plucking

puntería *f* aim; **tener buena/mala** ∼ to have a good/poor aim; **afinar la** ∼ to take careful aim; **¡qué** ∼**!** what a shot!

puntero *m* **1** (para señalar) pointer; (Inf) cursor; (de reloj) (Andes) hand **2** (Dep) **(a)** (equipo) leader, leaders (*pl*) **(b)** (Andes, RPI) (en fútbol) winger

puntiagudo -da *adj* (acabado en punta) pointed; (afilado) sharp

puntilla f **1** (Taur) dagger (*used to administer the coup de grâce in a bullfight*); **dar la ~** (Taur) to administer the coup de grâce **2** (punta del pie): **de ~s** *or* (AmL) **en ~s** on tiptoe; **entró de ~s** she tiptoed into the room **3** (encaje) lace edging

puntilloso -sa *adj* particular, punctilious

punto m **1** (a) (señal, marca) dot (b) (Ling) (sobre la 'i', la 'j') dot; (signo de puntuación) period (AmE), full stop (BrE); **~ decimal** decimal point ; **~ final** period (AmE), full stop (BrE); **~s suspensivos** ellipsis (tech), suspension points (*pl*) (AmE), dot, dot, dot; **~ y aparte** period (AmE) *o* (BrE) full stop, new paragraph; **~ y coma** semicolon; **~ com** (Com, Inf) dot com; **a ~ fijo** exactly, for certain; **... y punto** ... and that's that, ... period (AmE); ▶ **DOS**

2 (a) (momento, lugar) point; **en ese ~ de la conversación** at that point in the conversation; **el ~ donde ocurrió el accidente** the spot *o* place where the accident happened; **~ cardinal** cardinal point ; **~ ciego** blind spot; **~ de apoyo** (de palanca) fulcrum; **no hay ningún ~ de apoyo para la escalera** there is nowhere to lean the ladder; **~ de vista** (perspectiva) viewpoint, point of view; (opinión) views; **~ flaco/fuerte** weak/strong point; **~ muerto** (Auto) neutral; (en negociaciones) deadlock (b) (en geometría) point

3 (grado) point, extent; **hasta cierto ~ tiene razón** she's right, up to a point; **hasta tal ~ que ...** so much so that ...

4 (asunto, aspecto) point; **analizar algo ~ por ~** to analyze sth point by point; **los ~s a tratar en la reunión** the matters *o* items on the agenda for the meeting

5 (en locs) **a punto** (a tiempo) just in time; **estábamos a ~ de cenar** we were about to have dinner; **estuvo a ~ de caerse** he almost fell over; **batir las claras a ~ de nieve** beat the egg whites until they form stiff peaks; **en su punto** just right; **en punto: a las 12 en ~** at 12 o'clock sharp; **son las tres en ~** it's exactly three o'clock; **llegaron en ~** they arrived exactly on time

6 (a) (en costura, labores) stitch; **artículos de ~** knitwear; **hacer ~** (Esp) to knit; **~ (de) cruz** cross-stitch (b) (en cirugía) *tb* **~ de sutura** stitch

7 (unidad) (a) (Dep, Jueg) point; **~ para partido/set** (Méx) match/set point (b) (Educ) point, mark; (Fin) point

puntuación f **1** (Impr, Ling) punctuation **2** (a) (acción) (Educ) grading (AmE), marking (BrE); (Dep) scoring (b) (esp Esp) (Educ) grade (AmE), mark (BrE); (Dep) score

puntual *adj* **1** (a) ⟨*persona*⟩ punctual (b) (*como adv*) ⟨*llegar*⟩ punctually, on time **2** (detallado) detailed; (exacto) precise

puntualidad f punctuality

puntualizar [A4] *vt* (a) (especificar) to state (b) (señalar) to point out

puntuar [A18] *vt* **1** ⟨*examen/prueba*⟩ to grade (AmE), to mark (BrE) **2** ⟨*texto*⟩ to punctuate
■ ~ *vi* (a) «*partido/prueba*» **~ PARA algo** to count TOWARD(s) sth (b) «*deportista*» to score (points)

puntudo -da *adj* (Andes, RPI) ▶ **PUNTIAGUDO**

punzada f sharp pain, stab of pain; **me dio una ~ en el costado** I felt a sharp pain *o* a stab of pain in my side

punzante *adj* ⟨*objeto*⟩ sharp; ⟨*dolor*⟩ sharp, stabbing (*before n*); ⟨*palabras/comentario*⟩ biting, incisive; ⟨*estilo*⟩ caustic

punzón m (para hacer agujeros) bradawl, awl; (para hacer ojetes) hole punch; (de grabador, escultor) burin

puñado m handful

puñal m dagger

puñalada f (a) (navajazo) stab; **lo mató a ~s** she stabbed him to death (b) (herida) stab wound

puñeta f (Esp fam): **hacerle la ~ a algn** to mess things up for sb; **mandar a algn a hacer ~s** to tell sb to go to hell; **¡vete a hacer ~s!** go to hell! (colloq)

puñetazo m punch; **darle** *or* **pegarle un ~ a algn** to punch sb; **pegó un ~ en la mesa** he thumped the table with his fist; **le rompió la cara de un ~** he smashed his face in (colloq)

puñetero -ra *adj* (Esp fam) (a) (*delante del n*) (uso enfático) damn, blasted (b) [SER] ⟨*persona*⟩: **no seas ~** don't be a swine (colloq), don't be a jerk (colloq)

puño m **1** (Anat) fist; **apretar los ~s** to clench one's fists **2** (de camisa) cuff **3** (de espada) hilt; (de bastón) handle, haft; (de moto) grip

pupa f (a) (fam) (en los labios) cold sore (b) (Esp leng infantil) (dolor, daño): **mamá, (tengo) ~** mummy, it hurts; **¿te has hecho ~?** have you hurt yourself?

pupila f pupil

pupilo -la m,f (a) (de maestro) pupil; (de tutor) ward, charge (b) (RPI) (alumno interno) boarder

pupitre m desk

purasangre mf thoroughbred

puré m: **~ de verduras** puréed vegetables; **~ de tomates** tomato purée *o* paste; **~ de papas** *or* (Esp) **patatas** mashed *o* creamed potatoes

pureza f purity

purgante *adj/m* purgative, laxative

purgatorio m purgatory

purificador m purifier; **~ de ambientes** (Col) air freshener

purificadora f *tb* **~ de agua** water treatment plant, waterworks (*sing or pl*)

purificar [A2] *vt* to purify

puritanismo m puritanism

puritano -na *adj* (Relig) Puritanical, Puritan (*before n*); (mojigato) puritanical
■ m,f (Relig) Puritan; (mojigato) puritan

puro¹ -ra *adj* **1** (a) (sin mezcla) pure; (limpio) ⟨*aire*⟩ fresh, clean (b) (casto, inocente) ⟨*mujer*⟩ chaste, pure; ⟨*niño*⟩ innocent; ⟨*mirada/amor*⟩ innocent, pure **2** (*delante del n*) (a) (mero, simple) ⟨*verdad*⟩ plain, honest (colloq); ⟨*casualidad/coincidencia*⟩ pure, sheer; **lo hizo por ~ capricho** she did it purely on a whim; **de ~ cansancio**

from sheer exhaustion **(b)** (AmL fam) (sólo): **a ese bar van ~s viejos** only old men go to that bar; **son puras mentiras** it's just a pack of lies (colloq)
puro² *adv* (fam) (muy, tan): **se murió de ~ vieja** she just died of old age; **lo hizo de ~ egoísta** he did it out of sheer selfishness
■ *m* cigar
púrpura *f*: **(de) color ~** purple
purpurina *f* (en pinturas) metallic powder; (para adornar) glitter
pus *m* pus
puse, pusiera, etc ▶ PONER
pusilánime *adj* fainthearted, pusillanimous (frml)
pusiste, etc ▶ PONER

puso ▶ PONER
puta *f* (vulg & pey) (prostituta) whore (colloq & pej), hooker (colloq); **hijo (de) ~** son of a bitch (vulg), bastard (vulg)
putada *f* (vulg): **hacerle una ~ a algn** to play a dirty trick on sb (colloq)
putrefacción *f* putrefaction
putrefacto -ta, pútrido -da *adj* putrid
puya *f* **(a)** (Taur) point (*of the picador's lance*) **(b)** (comentario irónico) gibe; **lanzar** *or* **echar una ~** to make a gibe
puzzle /'pusle, 'puəle/ *m* (rompecabezas) (jigsaw) puzzle
Pza. *f* (= **Plaza**) Sq

Qq

Q, q *f* (*read as* /ku/) *the letter* Q, q

que *conj* **1** (oraciones subordinadas) **(a)** that; **creemos ~ esta es la solución** we believe that this is the solution; **estoy seguro de ~ vendrá** I'm sure (that) she'll come; **¿cuántos años crees ~ tiene?** how old do you think she is?; **eso de ~ estaba enfermo es mentira** (fam) this business about him being ill is a lie; **quiero ~ vengas** I want you to come; **dice ~ no vayas** she says you're not to go; **es importante ~ quede claro** it's important that it should be clear; **sería una lástima ~ no vinieras** it would be a shame if you didn't come **(b) es que: es ~ hoy no voy a poder** I'm afraid (that) I won't be able to today; **es ~ no tengo dinero** the trouble is I don't have any money **2 (a)** (en expresiones de deseo): **¡~ te mejores!** I hope you feel better soon; **¡~ se diviertan!** have a good time!; *ver tb* IR *v aux* 2 **(b)** (en expresiones de mandato): **¡~ te calles!** shut up! (colloq); **¡~ no!** I said no! **(c)** (en expresiones de sorpresa): **¿~ se casa?** she's getting married?; **¿cómo ~ no vas a ir?** what do you mean, you're not going? **(d)** (indicando persistencia): **se pasa dale ~ dale con lo mismo** he goes on and on about the same old thing; **y aquí llueve ~ llueve** and over here it just rains and rains **3** (introduciendo una consecuencia) that; **se parecen tanto ~ apenas los distingo** they're so alike (that) I can hardly tell them apart **4** (en comparaciones): **su casa es más grande ~ la mía** his house is bigger than mine; **tengo la misma edad ~ tú** I'm the same age as you **5** (fam) (en oraciones condicionales) if; **yo ~ tú** if I were you
■ *pron* **1** (refiriéndose a personas) **(a)** (*sujeto*) who; **los ~ estén cansados** those who are tired; **es la ~ manda aquí** she's the one who gives the orders here **(b)** (*complemento*): **la mujer ~ amo** the woman (that) I love; **las chicas ~ entrevistamos** the girls (that *o* who) we interviewed; **el único al ~ no le han pagado** the only one who hasn't been paid; **la persona de la ~ te hablé** the person (that *o* who) I spoke to you about **2** (refiriéndose a cosas, asuntos, etc) **(a)** (*sujeto*) that, which; **la pieza**

~ se rompió the part that *o* which broke; **eso es lo ~ me preocupa** that's what worries me **(b)** (*complemento*): **el disco ~ le regalé** the record (which *o* that) I gave her; **la casa en ~ vivo** the house (that) I live in; **¿sabes lo difícil ~ fue?** do you know how hard it was?; *ver tb* LO *art* 2B
qué *pron* **1** (interrogativo) **(a)** what; **¿~ es eso?** what's that?; **¿y ~?** so what?; **¿de ~ habló?** what did she talk about?; **¿sabes ~?** you know what *o* something?; **no sé ~ hacer** I don't know what to do **(b)** (al pedir que se nos repita algo) what; **¿qué?** what? **(c)** (en saludos): **¿~ tal?** how are you?; **¿~ es de tu vida?** how's life?
2 (en exclamaciones): **¡~ va a ser abogado ese!** him, a lawyer?; *ver tb* IR V1
■ *adj* **1** (interrogativo) what, which; **¿~ color quieres?** what *o* which color do you want? **2** (en exclamaciones) what; **¡~ noche!** what a night!
■ *adv*: **¡~ lindo!** how lovely!; **¡~ inteligente eres!** aren't you clever!; **¡~ bien (que) se está aquí!** it's so nice here!; **¡~ bien!** great!, good!
quebrada *f* **(a)** (despeñadero) gully; (más profunda) ravine **(b)** (AmS) (arroyo) stream
quebradero de cabeza *m* problem, headache (colloq)
quebradizo -za *adj* **(a)** (frágil) fragile; ‹uña/hueso› brittle **(b)** (que se desmenuza con facilidad) crumbly
quebrado¹ -da *adj* **1 (a)** ‹hueso› broken; ‹vaso/huevo› (roto) broken; (rajado) cracked **(b)** ‹voz› faltering **2** ‹empresa/comerciante› bankrupt **3 (a)** ‹línea› crooked, zigzag (*before n*) **(b)** (Mat): **número ~** fraction
quebrado² *m* fraction
quebradura *f* (esp AmL) crack
quebrar [A5] *vt* **1** (esp AmL) ‹lápiz/rama› to snap; ‹vaso/plato› (romper) to break; (rajar) to crack **2** (Méx fam) (matar) to kill
■ *vi* **1** (Com) ‹empresa/persona› to go bankrupt **2** (AmC) (romper una relación) to break up
■ **quebrarse** *v pron* **1** (esp AmL) **(a)** «lápiz/   ⋯⟶

rama» to snap; «*vaso/plato*» (romperse) to break;
(rajarse) to crack **(b)** ‹*pierna/brazo*› to break;
‹*diente*› to chip **2** (Col) (arruinarse) to go bankrupt

quechua *adj* Quechua
■ *mf* (persona) Quechuan
■ *m* (idioma) Quechua

quedar [A1] *vi*
I 1 (en un estado, una situación): ～ **viudo/huérfano**
to be widowed/orphaned; **quedó paralítico** he was
left paralyzed; **el coche quedó como nuevo** the
car is as good as new (now); **y que esto quede
bien claro** and I want to make this quite clear;
¿quién quedó en primer lugar? who was *o* came
first?
2 (en la opinión de los demás): **si no voy ～é mal
con ellos** it won't go down very well *o* it'll look
bad if I don't turn up; **lo hice para ～ bien con el
jefe** I did it to get in the boss's good books; **quedé
muy bien con el regalo** I made a very good
impression with my present; **me hiciste ～ muy
mal diciendo eso** you really showed me up
saying that; **nos hizo ～ mal a todos** he
embarrassed us all; **quedó en ridículo** (*por culpa
propia*) he made a fool of himself; (*por culpa ajena*)
he was made to look a fool
3 (permanecer): **¿queda alguien adentro?** is there
anyone left inside?; **le quedó la cicatriz** she was
left with a scar; **esto no puede ～ así** we can't
leave things like this; **nuestros planes ～on en
nada** our plans came to nothing; **～ atrás**
«*persona*» to fall behind; «*rencillas/problemas*»
to be in the past
4 (+ *me/te/le etc*) **(a)** «*tamaño/talla*»: **me queda
largo** it's too long for me; **la talla 12 le queda bien**
the size 12 fits (you/him) fine **(b)** (sentar): **el azul
le queda bien/mal** blue suits her/doesn't suit her
II (a) (acordar, convenir): **¿en qué ～on?** what did
you decide?; **¿entonces en qué quedamos?** so,
what's happening, then?; **～on en** *or* (AmL) **de no
decirle nada** they agreed *o* decided not to tell him
anything; **quedó en** *or* (AmL) **de venir a las nueve**
she said she would come at nine **(b)** (citarse): **¿a
qué hora quedamos?** what time shall we meet?;
quedé con unos amigos para cenar I arranged to
meet some friends for dinner
III (estar situado) to be; **queda justo enfrente de la
estación** it's right opposite the station; **me queda
muy lejos** it's very far from where I live (*o* work
etc)
IV (*en 3ª pers*) **1 (a)** (haber todavía) to be left;
¿te queda algo de dinero? do you have any
money left?; **¿queda café?** is there any coffee
left?; **solo quedan las ruinas** only the ruins
remain; **no nos queda más remedio que ir** we
have no choice but to go **(b)** (sobrar) «*comida/
vino*» to be left (over)
2 (faltar): **queda poco para que acabe la clase**
it's not long till the end of the class; **¿cuántos
kilómetros quedan?** how many kilometers are
there to go?; **todavía le quedan dos años** he
still has two years to go *o* do; **queda mucho por
ver** there is still a lot to see; **aún me queda
todo esto por hacer** I still have all this to do;
no me/le queda otra (fam) I have/he has no
choice
■ **quedarse** *v pron*
I 1 (a) (en un lugar, país) to stay; **～se en la cama**
to stay in bed **(b)** (en un estado, una situación)

(+ *compl*): **te estás quedando calvo** you're going
bald; **～se dormido** to fall asleep; **～se sin trabajo**
to lose one's job
2 (+ *me/te/le etc*) **(a)** (permanecer): **～se soltera** to
stay single; **no me gusta ～me sola en casa** I
don't like being alone in the house; **¡no te quedes
ahí parado!** don't just stand there!; **nos quedamos
charlando hasta tarde** we went on chatting until
late in the evening; **se me quedó mirando** he sat/
stood there staring at me; **de repente se me
quedó** (AmL) the engine suddenly died on me **(b)**
(Andes) (olvidarse): **se me quedó el paraguas** I left
my umbrella behind **(c)** (Esp) (llegar a ser): **la casa
se les está quedando pequeña** the house is
getting (to be) too small for them
II ‹*cambio/lápiz*› to keep; **se quedó con mi libro**
she kept my book; **me quedo con este** I'll take
this one

quehacer *m* (actividad, tarea) work; **～es
domésticos** housework, household chores; **el ～
diario** the daily routine

queja *f* (protesta) complaint; **presentar una ～** to
make a complaint

quejarse [A1] *v pron* **(a)** (protestar) to complain;
(refunfuñar) to grumble; **～ DE algo/algn** to
complain ABOUT sth/sb **(b)** (de una afección, un
dolor) **～ DE algo** to complain OF sth **(c)** (gemir) to
moan, groan

quejica *adj/mf* (Esp fam) ▶ QUEJÓN

quejido *m* groan, moan; (más agudo) whine; **un
～ de dolor** a cry of pain

quejón -jona *adj* (fam) whining (*before n*)
(colloq)
■ *m,f* (fam) crybaby (colloq)

quemada *f* **(a)** (Andes, Ven fam) (del sol): **pegarse
una ～** to get sunburned **(b)** (Méx) ▶ QUEMADURA

quemado -da *adj* **1** [ESTAR] **(a)** ‹*comida/
tostada*› burnt; **esto sabe a ～** this tastes burnt;
huele a ～ I can smell burning **(b)** (rojo) ‹*cara/
espalda*› burnt **(c)** (AmL) (bronceado) tanned,
brown **2** [ESTAR] (desgastado, agotado) burned-out

quemador *m* burner

quemadura *f* **(a)** (herida causada — por fuego,
ácido) burn; (— por líquido caliente) scald; **～ de sol**
sunburn **(b)** (en prenda — de cigarrillo) cigarette
burn; (— al planchar) scorch mark; (en mueble) burn
mark

quemar [A1] *vt* **1 (a)** ‹*basura/documentos/
leña/CDs*› to burn **(b)** ‹*herejes/brujas*› to burn …
at the stake
2 ‹*calorías*› to burn up; ‹*grasa*› to burn off
3 (a) ‹*comida/mesa/mantel*› to burn; (con la
plancha) to scorch **(b)** ‹*líquido/vapor*› to scald
(c) ‹*ácido*› ‹*ropa/piel*› to burn **(d)** ‹*motor*› to
burn … out; ‹*fusible*› to blow **(e)** ‹*sol*› ‹*plantas*›
to scorch; ‹*piel*› to burn; (broncear) (AmL) to tan
■ ～ *vi* **(a)** ‹*plato/sartén*› to be very hot; ‹*café/
sopa*› to be boiling (hot) (colloq) **(b)** ‹*sol*› to
burn
■ **quemarse** *v pron* **1 (a)** (refl) (con fuego, calor)
to burn oneself; (con líquido, vapor) to scald oneself;
‹*mano/lengua*› to burn; ‹*pelo/cejas*› to singe **(b)**
(al sol — ponerse rojo) to get burned; (— broncearse)
(AmL) to tan
2 (a) (destruirse) «*papeles*» to get burned;
«*edificio*» to burn down **(b)** (sufrir daños)
«*alfombra/vestido*» to get burned; «*comida*» to
burn; **se me ～on las tostadas** I burned the toast

3 «*persona*» (desgastarse) to burn oneself out

quemarropa: a ~ (*loc adv*) ⟨*disparar*⟩ at point-blank range; ⟨*preguntar*⟩ point-blank

quemazón *f* (sensación de ardor) burning

quena *f* reed flute (*used in Andean music*)

quepa, etc ▶ CABER

quepo ▶ CABER

querella *f* (a) (Der) private prosecution; **presentar ~ contra** algn to bring a private prosecution against sb (b) (disputa) dispute

querendón -dona *adj* (AmL fam) (cariñoso) affectionate; (enamoradizo) flighty

querer [E24] *vt*
I (amar) to love; **te querré siempre** I'll love you; **sus alumnos lo quieren mucho** his pupils are very fond of him; **¡por lo que más quieras!** for pity's sake!, for God's sake!
II **1** (a) (expresando deseo, intención, voluntad): **no sabe lo que quiere** she doesn't know what she wants; **quisiera una habitación doble** I'd like a double room; **¿qué más quieres?** what more do you want?; **hazlo cuando/como quieras** do it whenever/however you like; **iba a hacerlo pero él no quiso** I was going to do it but he didn't want me to; **tráemelo mañana ¿quieres?** bring it tomorrow, will you?; **no quiero** I don't want to; **quiero ir** I want to go; **quisiera reservar una mesa** I'd like to book a table; **quisiera poder ayudarte** I wish I could help you; **no quiso comer nada** she wouldn't eat anything; **quiero que estudies más** I want you to study harder; **¡qué quieres que te diga ...!** quite honestly *o* frankly ...; **el destino así lo quiso** it was destined to be; **~ es poder** where there's a will there's a way (b) (al ofrecer algo): **¿quieres un café?** would you like a coffee?; (menos formal) do you want a coffee? (c) (introduciendo un pedido): **¿querrías hacerme un favor?** could you do me a favor?; **¿te quieres callar?** be quiet, will you?
2 (*en locs*) **cuando quiera que** whenever; **donde quiera que** wherever; **queriendo** (adrede) on purpose, deliberately; **sin querer** accidentally; **fue sin ~** it was an accident; **querer decir** to mean; **¿qué quieres decir con eso?** what do you mean by that?
3 (como precio): **¿cuánto quieres por el coche?** how much do you want *o* are you asking for the car?
▪ **quererse** *v pron* (recípr): **se quieren mucho** they love each other very much

querido -da *adj* (a) (amado) ⟨*patria*⟩ beloved; **mis recuerdos más ~s** my fondest memories; **seres ~s** loved ones; **un profesor muy ~ por todos** a well-liked teacher (b) (Corresp) Dear (c) (Col fam) (simpático) nice
▪ *m,f* (a) (como apelativo) darling, dear, sweetheart (b) (amante) (*m*) fancy man; (*f*) fancy woman

querré, querría, etc ▶ QUERER

querubín *m* cherub

quesadilla *f* (a) (Méx) (tortilla): *tortilla filled with a savory mixture and topped with melted cheese* (b) (Ven) (panecillo) small roll (*flavored with cheese*)

quesera *f* cheese dish

queso *m* (Coc) cheese; **~ crema** (AmL) cream cheese; **~ fundido** processed cheese; **~ para untar** cheese spread

quetzal *m* (Fin) quetzal (*Guatemalan unit of currency*)

quicio *m* doorjamb; **sacar de ~ a** algn to drive sb crazy (colloq)

quid *m*: **el ~ de la cuestión** the crux of the matter

quiebra *f* (Com, Fin) (de empresa, individuo) bankruptcy; **declarse en ~** to go into liquidation

quiebra, quiebras, etc ▶ QUEBRAR

quien *pron* **1** (a) (sujeto) who, that; (complemento) who, that, whom (fml); **tienes que ser tú misma ~ lo decida** you are the one who *o* that has to decide; **es a él a ~ debemos agradecérselo** he's the one (who) we must thank; **la chica con ~ salía** the girl (who) I was going out with (b) (fml *o* liter) (en frases explicativas) who, whom (fml); **su hermano, a ~ no había visto, ...** her brother, who *o* whom she had not seen, ...
2 (la persona que): **~es hayan terminado** those who have finished; **~ lo haya encontrado** the person who found it; **~ se lo haya dicho** whoever told him

quién *pron* who; **¿~es eran?** who were they?; **¿~ de ustedes se atrevería?** which of you would dare?; **¿con ~es fuiste?** who did you go with?; **¿de ~ es esto?** whose is this?; **llegó una postal — ¿de ~?** there's a postcard — who's it from?

quienquiera *pron* (*pl* **quienesquiera**) whoever

quiera, quieras, etc ▶ QUERER

quieto -ta *adj* still; **¡estte ~!** keep still!

quietud *f* (ausencia de movimiento) stillness; (tranquilidad, sosiego) calm, peace

quihubo *interj* (Chi, Méx fam) hi! (colloq), how's it going? (colloq)

quihúbole *interj* (Méx fam) ▶ QUIHUBO

quijada *f* jaw (bone)

Quijote *m*: **Don ~** Don Quixote

quilate *m* karat (AmE), carat (BrE); **oro de 18 ~s** 18-karat gold

quilla *f* keel

quilombo *m* (Bol, RPl arg) (lío, jaleo) mess

quiltro -tra *m,f* (Chi fam) mongrel

quimera *f* (ilusión) illusion, chimera (liter)

química *f* chemistry

químico -ca *adj* chemical
▪ *m,f* chemist

quimioterapia *f* chemotherapy

quince *adj inv/pron/m* fifteen; **dentro de ~ días** in two weeks' time, in a fortnight's time (BrE); *para ejemplos ver tb* CINCO

quinceañero -ra *m,f* (de quince años) fifteen-year-old; (menos específico) teenager

quincena *f* (dos semanas) two weeks (*pl*), fortnight (BrE); **la primera ~ de marzo** the first two weeks in March

quincenal *adj* bimonthly (AmE), fortnightly (BrE)

quiniela *f* (Esp) (boleto) sports lottery ticket (AmE), pools coupon (BrE); (juego): **las ~s** the sports lottery (AmE), the football pools (BrE)

quinientos -tas *adj/pron* five hundred; **~ cinco** five hundred and five; **~ y pico** five hundred odd; **el ~ aniversario** the five hundredth anniversary

q

quinqué *m* oil lamp

quinquenal *adj* ⟨revisión/censo⟩ five-yearly, quinquennial (frml); **un plan** ∼ a five-year plan

quinta *f* **1** **(a)** (casa) *house in its own grounds, usually in the country* **(b)** (Agr) estate, farm **2** (Esp) (Mil) draft, call up

quintaesencia *f* quintessence (frml)

quinteto *m* quintet

quintillizo -za *m,f* quintuplet

quinto¹ -ta *adj/pron* fifth; **llegó en** ∼ **lugar** he came fifth; **Carlos V** (*read as: Carlos quinto*) Charles V (*read as: Charles the fifth*); **vive en el** ∼ **(piso)** she lives on the sixth (AmE) *o* (BrE) fifth floor; **la quinta parte** a fifth

quinto² *m* **1** **(a)** (partitivo) fifth; **tres** ∼**s** three-fifths **(b)** (en Méx) (moneda) five centavo coin; ***estar sin un*** ∼ (Méx fam) to be broke (colloq) **2** (Esp) (Mil) conscript

quíntuple *m* quintuple
■ *mf* (Chi, Ven) quintuplet

quíntuplo¹ -pla *adj* quintuple, fivefold

quíntuplo² *m* quintuple

quiosco *m* ▶ KIOSCO

quirófano *m* operating room (AmE), operating theatre (BrE)

quiromancia *f* palmistry, chiromancy (frml)

quirúrgico -ca *adj* surgical; **fue sometido a una intervención quirúrgica** (frml) he underwent surgery (frml)

quise, quisiera, etc ▶ QUERER

quisquilloso -sa *adj* (meticuloso, exigente) fussy, picky (colloq); (susceptible) touchy

quiste *m* cyst

quitaesmalte *m* nail polish remover

quitamanchas *m* (*pl* ∼) stain remover

quitar [A1] *vt* **1** (apartar, retirar): **¡quítalo de aquí!** get it out of here!; **quité la silla de en medio** I got the chair out of the way; **quita tus cosas de mi escritorio** take your things off my desk; ∼ **la mesa** (Esp) to clear the table; **¡quítame las manos de encima!** take your hands off me!; **no le puedo** ∼ **la tapa** I can't get the top off; **le quitó los zapatos** she took his shoes off
2 (+ *me/te/le etc*) **(a)** (de las manos): **le quitó la pistola al ladrón** he got *o* took the gun off the thief; **le quité el cuchillo** I took the knife (away) from her **(b)** (privar de) ⟨pasaporte/carnet de conducir⟩ to take away **(c)** ⟨cartera/dinero⟩ to take, steal; ⟨asiento/lugar⟩ to take
3 (restar) (+ *me/te/le etc*): **me quita mucho tiempo** it takes up a lot of my time; ∼**le años a algn** to take years off sb; ∼**le importancia a algo** to play sth down; **le quita valor** it detracts from its value
4 (hacer desaparecer) ⟨mancha⟩ to remove, get ... out; ⟨dolor⟩ to relieve, get rid of; ⟨sed⟩ to quench; ⟨apetito⟩ to take away; (+ *me/te/le etc*) **eso te** ∼**á el hambre** that will stop you feeling hungry; **hay que** ∼**le esa idea de la cabeza** we must get that idea out of his head
5 **quitando** (ger) (fam) except for
■ ∼ *vi* **1** (Esp fam): **¡quita (de ahí)!** get out of the way!
2 (en locs) **de quita y pon** ⟨funda/etiqueta⟩ removable; **eso no quita que ...** that doesn't mean that ...
■ **quitarse** *v pron* **1** (desaparecer) «mancha» to come out; «dolor» to go (away); **ya se me** ∼**on las ganas** I don't feel like it any more
2 (apartarse, retirarse) to get out of the way; **¡quítate de mi vista!** get out of my sight!
3 (refl) **(a)** ⟨prenda/alhaja/maquillaje⟩ to take off **(b)** ⟨dolor/resfriado⟩ to get rid of; ⟨miedo⟩ to overcome, get over; **se quita la edad** she lies about her age; ∼**se algo/a algn de encima** to get rid of sth/sb

quitasol *m* sunshade

quiteño -ña *adj* of/from Quito

Quito *m* Quito

quiubo *interj* (Chi, Méx fam) ▶ QUIHUBO

quizá, quizás *adv* maybe, perhaps

quórum /'kworum/ *m* (*pl* **-rums**) quorum

Rr

R, r *f* (*read as* /'ere/) *the letter* R

rábano *m* radish; ▶ IMPORTAR

rabia *f* **1** (enfermedad) rabies **2** **(a)** (expresando fastidio): **no sabes la** ∼ **que me da** you've no idea how much it annoys *o* irritates me; **¡qué** ∼**!** how annoying! **(b)** (furor, ira) anger, fury; **tener** ∼ to be angry; **con** ∼ angrily, in a rage **(c)** (antipatía, manía): **tenerle** ∼ **a algn** to have it in for sb (colloq)

rabiar [A1] *vi* (de furor, envidia): **el jefe está que rabia contigo** the boss is furious with you; **no lo hagas** ∼ don't annoy him

rabieta *f* tantrum; **le dio una** ∼ he threw a tantrum

rabino -na *m,f* rabbi

rabioso -sa *adj* **1** (Med, Vet) rabid **2** (furioso) furious

rabo *m* **(a)** (Zool) tail **(b)** (de letra) tail **(c)** (Bot) stem, stalk

AmC	Central America	Arg	Argentina	Cu	Cuba	Per	Peru
AmL	Latin America	Bol	Bolivia	Ec	Ecuador	RPI	River Plate Area
AmS	South America	Chi	Chile	Esp	Spain	Ur	Uruguay
Andes	Andean Region	CS	Southern Cone	Méx	Mexico	Ven	Venezuela

racha *f* **(a)** (secuencia) **una ∼ DE algo** ‹*de buena/ mala suerte*› a run *o* spell OF sth; ‹*de enfermedades/éxitos*› a string OF sth; **pasar una mala ∼** to go through bad times *o* (BrE) a bad patch; **tengo una buena ∼ , voy a seguir jugando** I'm on a winning streak so I'm going to carry on playing; **va/viene por ∼s** it goes/comes in phases **(b)** (Meteo) gust of wind

racial *adj* racial; ‹*disturbio*› race (*before n*)

racimo *m* bunch

raciocinio *m* (facultad) reason; (argumento) reasoning

ración *f* **(a)** (parte) share **(b)** (porción de comida) portion, helping; **una ∼ de calamares** a portion *o* plate of squid **(c)** (Mil) ration

racional *adj* rational

racionalizar [A4] *vt* to rationalize

racionamiento *m* rationing

racionar [A1] *vt* to ration

racismo *m* racism

racista *adj/mf* racist

radar *m* radar

radiación *f* radiation

radiactividad *f* radioactivity

radiactivo -va *adj* radioactive

radiador *m* radiator

radiante *adj* **(a)** (brillante) brilliant; **hace un sol ∼** it's brilliantly *o* beautifully sunny; **un día ∼** a bright, sunny day **(b)** [ESTAR] ‹*persona*› radiant; **∼ de alegría** radiant with happiness

radical *adj/mf* radical

radicar [A2] *vi* «*problema/dificultad*» to lie ■ **radicarse** *v pron* to settle

radio *m* **(a)** (Mat) radius **(b)** (distancia) range, radius; **en un ∼ de diez kilómetros** within a ten kilometer radius **(c)** (de rueda) spoke; **∼ de acción** (de avión, barco) operational range; (de organización) area of operations
■ *f or* (AmL exc CS) *m* **(a)** (medio de comunicación) radio; **por (la) ∼** on the radio; **escuchar la ∼** to listen to the radio **(b)** (aparato) radio **(c)** (emisora) radio station

radioactividad *f* radioactivity

radioactivo -va *adj* radioactive

radioaficionado -da *m,f* radio ham

radiocassette /rraðioka'set/, **radiocasete** *m* radio cassette player

radiodifusión *f* broadcasting

radiodifusora *f* (AmL fml) radio station

radiofónico -ca *adj* radio (*before n*)

radiografía *f* X-ray; **hacerse una ∼** to have an X-ray taken

radiólogo -ga *m,f* radiologist

radionovela *f* radio serial

radiooperador -dora *m,f* (AmL) radio operator

radiopatrulla *m* radio patrol car

radioterapia *f* radiotherapy

radioyente *mf* listener

raer [E16] *vt* ‹*superficie*› to scrape; ‹*barniz/ pintura*› to scrape off

ráfaga *f* (de viento) gust; (de ametralladora) burst

raid *m* (AmC) (en carro) ride; **pedir ∼** to hitch a ride *o* lift

raído -da *adj* worn-out, threadbare

raíz *f* (en general) root; **arrancar de ∼** ‹*planta*› to uproot; ‹*vello*› to remove … at the roots; **∼ cuadrada** (Mat) square root; **a ∼ de** as a result of; **echar raíces** «*planta/costumbre/ideología*» to take root; ‹*persona*› to put down roots

raja *f* **(a)** (en pared, cerámica) crack **(b)** (rotura — en costura) split; (— en tela) tear, rip **(c)** (abertura — en falda) slit; (— en chaqueta) vent **(d)** (de melón, salami) slice

rajar [A1] *vt* **1** **(a)** (agrietar) to crack, cause … to crack **(b)** (con cuchillo, navaja) ‹*neumático/lienzo*› to slash **2** **(a)** (CS fam) (criticar) to run … down **(b)** (Andes) (en examen) (fam) to fail, flunk (AmE colloq)
■ **rajarse** *v pron* **1** «*pared/cerámica*» to crack; «*tela*» to split, tear, rip **2** (fam) (acobardarse) to back off

rajatabla: a ∼ (*loc adv*) to the letter

rallador *m* grater

ralladura *f*: **∼ de limón** grated lemon rind

rallar [A1] *vt* to grate

ralo -la *adj* ‹*bosque*› sparse; ‹*monte*› bare; ‹*pelo/ barba*› thin, sparse

rama *f* branch; **una ramita de perejil** a sprig of parsley; **andarse/irse por las ∼s** to beat about the bush

ramada *f* **(a)** (AmS) (cobertizo) shelter (*made from branches*) **(b)** (Chi) (pérgola) arbor, arbour (BrE)

ramal *m* (Ferr) branch line; (Geog) branch; (cuerda) strap

rambla *f* **(a)** (RPl) (paseo marítimo) esplanade, promenade **(b)** (avenida) boulevard

ramera *f* prostitute

ramificación *f* ramification

ramificarse [A2] *v pron* **(a)** «*árbol/plantas/ nervios*» to branch **(b)** «*carretera/ciencia*» to branch **(c)** «*problema*» to ramify (frml), to become complex

ramillete *m* **(a)** (de flores) posy **(b)** (iró) (grupo selecto) bunch (colloq)

ramo *m* **1** (de flores) bunch; (para novia, dignatario) bouquet **2** **(a)** (en industria) industry **(b)** (Chi) (Educ) subject

rampa *f* (pendiente) ramp; **∼ de lanzamiento** launch pad

rana *f* (Zool) frog

ranchera *f* (Mús) *Mexican folk song*

ranchería *f* **(a)** (Col) ▶ RANCHERÍO **(b)** (Méx) dairy

rancherío *m* (CS) (poblado) settlement; (en suburbios) shantytown

ranchero -ra *adj* (Méx fam) shy
■ *m,f* (Méx) rancher

rancho *m* **1** (comida) food (*for a group of soldiers, workers, etc*) **2** **(a)** (AmL) (choza) hut; (casucha) hovel; (chabola) shack, shanty **(b)** (Méx) (hacienda) ranch

rancio -cia *adj* **1** ‹*mantequilla/tocino*› rancid **2** **(a)** ‹*vino*› mellow **(b)** (*delante del n*) ‹*abolengo/tradición*› ancient, long-established

rango *m* **1** **(a)** (Mil) rank **(b)** (categoría, nivel) level **2** (Chi) (lujo, pompa) luxury; (de persona) high social status

rangoso -sa *adj* (Chi) ‹*fiesta/casa*› lavish; ‹*persona*› of high social status

ranura *f* **(a)** (para monedas, tarjetas, cartas) slot; **por la ∼ de la puerta** through the chink *o* gap in the door **(b)** (en ensambladura, tornillo) groove

rapapolvo *m* (Esp) telling-off (colloq), talking-to (colloq)

rapar [A1] *vt* ‹*cabeza*› to shave; ‹*pelo*› to crop

rapaz *adj* (Zool) predatory; **ave ∼** bird of prey

rape *m* **(a)** (Coc, Zool) monkfish, goosefish (AmE) **(b) al rape: tiene el pelo cortado al ∼** he has closely-cropped hair

rápidamente *adv* quickly

rapidez *f* speed; **con ∼** quickly; **¡qué ∼!** that was quick!

rápido¹ *adv* ‹*hablar/trabajar*› quickly, fast; ‹*conducir/ir*› fast; **tráemelo ¡∼!** bring it to me, quick!

rápido² -da *adj* ‹*aumento*› rapid; ‹*cambio*› quick, rapid, swift; ‹*desarrollo*› rapid, swift; **a paso ∼** quickly, swiftly; **comida rápida** fast food
■ *m* (Ferr) express train, fast train
■ *m* **1** (Ferr) fast train **2 rápidos** *mpl* (Geog) rapids (*pl*)

rapiña *f* robbery, pillage

raptar [A1] *vt* (secuestrar) to kidnap, abduct (frml)

rapto *m* (secuestro) kidnapping, abduction (frml)

raptor -tora *m,f* kidnapper

raqueta *f* (de tenis, squash) racket; (para nieve) snowshoe

raquítico -ca *adj* ‹*niño/animal*› rickety, rachitic (tech); ‹*árbol*› stunted

rareza *f* **(a)** (de persona) peculiarity, quirk **(b)** (cosa poco común) rarity **(c)** (cualidad) rareness

raro -ra *adj* **(a)** (extraño) strange, odd, funny (colloq); **es ∼ que …** it's strange *o* odd *o* funny that …; **¡qué ∼!** how odd *o* strange!; **te noto muy ∼ hoy** you're acting very strangely today **(b)** (poco frecuente) rare; **salvo raras excepciones** with a few rare exceptions; **aquí es ∼ que nieve** it's very unusual *o* rare for it to snow here

ras: a ras de (*loc prep*): **llega a ∼ del suelo** it reaches down to the floor; **volar a ∼ de tierra** to fly very low

rasca *adj* (CS fam) **(a)** ‹*persona*› vulgar, common (pej); ‹*lugar/canción*› tacky (colloq) **(b)** (de mala calidad) trashy (colloq)

rascacielos *m* (*pl* ∼) skyscraper

rascar [A2] *vt* (con las uñas) to scratch **(b)** (con cuchillo) ‹*superficie*› to scrape; ‹*pintura*› to scrape off
■ **rascarse** *v pron* (*refl*) to scratch (oneself)

rasgado -da *adj* ‹*ojos*› almond (*before n*), almond-shaped

rasgar [A3] *vt* to tear, rip
■ **rasgarse** *v pron* to tear, rip

rasgo *m* **1 (a)** (característica) characteristic, feature **(b)** (gesto) gesture **(c)** (de la pluma) stroke; (en pintura) brushstroke; **a grandes ∼s** in outline, broadly speaking **2 rasgos** *mpl* (facciones) features (*pl*)

rasguear [A1] *vt* to strum

rasguñar [A1] *vt* to scratch
■ **rasguñarse** *v pron* (*refl*) (con uña, púa) to scratch oneself; (con algo áspero) to graze oneself; **me rasguñé la rodilla** I grazed my knee

rasguño *m* scratch

rasmillarse [A1] *v pron* (Chi fam) to graze oneself

raso¹ -sa *adj* **1** ‹*taza/cucharada*› level (*before n*) **2** (exterior) open country; **dormir al ∼** to sleep out in the open

raso² *m* satin

raspado *m* (Col, Méx) ▶ GRANIZADO

raspadura *f* (arañazo) scratch; (ralladura de metal, chocolate) shavings (*pl*)

raspar [A1] *vt* (con espátula) ‹*superficie*› to scrape; ‹*pintura*› to scrape off **(b)** (limar) to file, rasp **(c)** ‹*piel*› to scrape, graze
■ *vi* **(a)** ‹*toalla/manos*› to be rough; ‹*barba*› to scratch, be scratchy **(b)** ‹*garganta*› (+ *me/te/le etc*) to feel rough
■ **rasparse** *v pron* ‹*rodillas/codos*› (con algo puntiagudo) to scratch; (con algo áspero) to scrape, graze

raspón *m* (AmL) (por algo puntiagudo) scratch; (por algo áspero) graze, scrape; **hay un ∼ en la puerta** the door is scratched

rastra: a rastras (*loc adv*): **llevar algo/a algn a ∼s** to drag sth/sb; **fue a ∼s hasta la puerta** she dragged herself to the door

rastreador -dora *m,f* tracker

rastrear [A1] *vt* ‹*zona*› to comb **(b)** ‹*persona/satélite*› to track **(c)** ‹*río/lago*› ‹*pescadores*› to trawl; ‹*policías*› to drag, dredge

rastrero -ra *adj* **(a)** (despreciable) despicable, contemptible **(b)** ‹*tallo*› creeping (*before n*); ‹*animal*› crawling (*before n*)

rastrillo *m* **1** (Agr) rake **2** (Méx) (para afeitarse) safety razor

rastro *m* **1** (pista, huella) trail; (señal, vestigio) trace, sign; **sin dejar ∼** without (a) trace **2** (mercado) flea market

rasurador *m*, **rasuradora** *f* (AmC, Méx) electric razor *o* shaver

rasurar [A1] *vt* (AmL) to shave
■ **rasurarse** *v pron* (AmL) to shave

rata *f* **1** (Zool) rat; **hacerse la ∼** (RPl fam) to play hooky (esp AmE colloq), to skive off (school) (BrE colloq) **2** (Col) (Econ, Mat) (tasa) rate; (razón) ratio; (porcentaje) percentage
■ *mf* (fam) (tacaño) miser, stingy devil (colloq), tightwad (AmE colloq)

ratán *m* rattan

ratero -ra *m,f* (fam) (carterista) pickpocket; (ladrón) petty thief

ratificar [A2] *vt* ‹*tratado/contrato*› to ratify; ‹*persona*› (en un puesto) to confirm; ‹*noticia*› to confirm

rato *m* **(a)** (tiempo breve) while; **hace un ∼** a while ago; **espera un ratito** wait a minute (colloq); **en mis ∼s libres** in my spare time; **pasé un mal ∼** it was terrible; **iré dentro de un ∼** I'll go shortly **(b)** (en locs) **a cada rato** (AmL): **me interrumpe a cada ∼** he keeps interrupting me; **al (poco) rato** shortly afterwards; **al poco ∼ de irte tú** shortly *o* just after you left; **a ratos** from time to time; **para ∼** (fam): **tengo para ∼** I'll be a while, I'll be some time; **todavía hay para ∼** there's still a long way to go; **pasar el ∼** to while away the time

ratón¹ -tona *m,f* (Zool) mouse; **∼ de biblioteca** (fam) bookworm

ratón² *m* ⓵ (Inf) mouse; ~ **de bola** trackball ⓶ (AmC) **(a)** (Coc) *sinewy cut of meat* **(b)** (fam) (bíceps) biceps ⓷ (Ven fam) (resaca) hangover

ratonera *f* (trampa) mousetrap; (madriguera) mousehole

raudal *m* (de agua) torrent; **el agua entraba a ~es** the water poured out in torrents

ravioles, raviolis *mpl* ravioli

raya *f* ⓵ **(a)** (línea) line; (lista) stripe; **a** *or* **de ~s** ⟨tela/vestido⟩ striped; **pasarse de la ~** to overstep the mark, to go too far; **tener a algn a ~** to keep a tight rein on sb **(b)** (del pantalón) crease **(c)** (del pelo) part (AmE), parting (BrE); **hacerse la ~** to part one's hair **(d)** (Impr) dash ⓶ (Zool) ray, skate

rayado -da *adj* ⓵ ⟨papel⟩ lined, ruled (frml); ⟨tela/vestido⟩ striped, stripy (colloq) ⓶ [ESTAR] (AmS fam) (loco) screwy (colloq), nutty (colloq)

rayar [A1] *vt* **(a)** ⟨pintura/mesa⟩ to scratch **(b)** (garabatear) to scrawl
■ ~ *vi* ⓵ (dejar marca) to scratch ⓶ (aproximarse) ~ **EN** algo to border ON sth, verge ON sth ⓷ (Méx) «obreros» to get one's wages, to get paid
■ **rayarse** *v pron* ⓵ «superficie» to get scratched ⓶ (AmS fam) (volverse loco) to crack up (colloq)

rayo *m* ⓵ (en general) ray; **un ~ de luz** a ray *o* beam (of light); **un ~ de luna** a moonbeam; ~ **láser** laser beam; ~**s ultravioleta** ultraviolet rays (*pl*); ~**s X** X-rays (*pl*) ⓶ (Meteo) bolt (of lightning); **como un ~** (fam) ⟨salir⟩ like greased lightning (colloq) ⓷ (AmL) (de rueda) spoke

rayuela *f* **(a)** (juego de adultos) *game similar to pitch-and-toss* **(b)** (RPl) (juego de niños) hopscotch

raza *f* (etnia) race; (Agr, Zool) breed; **un perro de ~** a pedigree dog

razón *f* ⓵ (motivo, causa) reason; **la ~ por la que te lo digo** the reason (that) I'm telling you; **se enojó y con ~** she got angry and rightly so; **con ~ o sin ella** rightly or wrongly; **se quejan sin ~/con ~** they're complaining for no good reason/ they have good reason to complain; **¡con ~ no contestaban!** no wonder they didn't answer!; ~ **de más para ...** all the more reason to ...
⓶ (verdad, acierto): **tener** *or* **llevar ~** to be right; **tuve que darle la ~** I had to admit she was right; **tienes toda la ~** (fam) you're absolutely right ⓷ (habilidad para razonar) reason; **actuó guiado por la ~** he was guided by reason; **desde que tengo uso de ~** for as long as I can remember; **entrar en ~** to see reason *o* sense; **perder la ~** to go out of one's mind; (en sentido hiperbólico) to take leave of one's senses

razonable *adj* reasonable

razonamiento *m* reasoning

razonar [A1] *vi* to reason

re *m* (nota) D; (en solfeo) re, ray

reacción *f* ⓵ (en general) reaction ⓶ (Pol) (AmL) right wing

reaccionar [A1] *vi* to react; ~ **A** *or* **FRENTE A** *or* **ANTE** algo to react TO sth

reaccionario -ria *adj/m,f* reactionary

reacio -cia *adj* reluctant

reactor *m* **(a)** (Fís) reactor; ~ **nuclear** nuclear reactor **(b)** (Aviac) (motor) jet engine; (avión) jet (plane)

readmitir [I1] *vt* ⟨trabajador⟩ to reemploy; ⟨alumno⟩ to readmit

reafirmar [A1] *vt* to reaffirm, reassert

reajuste *m* adjustment; ~ **ministerial** cabinet reshuffle; ~ **salarial** wage settlement

real *adj* **(a)** (verdadero, no ficticio): **un hecho ~** a true story; **en la vida ~** in real life; **historias de la vida ~** real-life *o* true-life stories **(b)** (de la realeza) royal; **porque me da la ~ gana** (fam) because I damn well want to (colloq)
■ *m* **(a)** (Hist) real ⟨old Spanish coin⟩; **no valer un ~** (fam) to be worth nothing **(b)** (Fin) real (*Brazilian unit of currency*) **(c)** **reales** *mpl* (AmC fam) (dinero) cash (colloq)

realce *m*: **dar ~ A** algo ⟨a belleza/figura⟩ to enhance sth; ⟨a ocasión⟩ to add luster TO sth

realeza *f* royalty; **la ~** (personas) the royal family

realidad *f* reality; **la ~ paraguaya** the reality of life *o* of the situation in Paraguay; **esa es la dura ~** those are the harsh facts; **en ~** in reality, actually

realismo *m* realism

realista *adj* (pragmático) realistic; (Art, Lit, Fil) realist
■ *mf* realist

realizable *adj* feasible, practicable

realización *f* ⓵ (de tarea) carrying out, execution (frml); (de sueños, deseos) fulfillment*, realization ⓶ (Cin, TV) production

realizado -da *adj* fulfilled*

realizador -dora *m,f* producer

realizar [A4] *vt* **(a)** ⟨tarea⟩ to carry out, execute (frml); ⟨viaje/visita⟩ to make; ⟨entrevista/pruebas⟩ to conduct; ⟨encuesta/investigación⟩ to carry out; ⟨experimento⟩ to perform, do; ⟨compra/inversión⟩ to make; **realizó una magnífica labor** she did a magnificent job **(b)** ⟨ambiciones/ilusiones⟩ to fulfill*, realize
■ **realizarse** *v pron* «sueños/ilusiones» to come true, be realized; «persona» to fulfill* oneself

realmente *adv* really, in fact

realzar [A4] *vt* ⟨belleza/figura⟩ to enhance, set off; ⟨color⟩ to highlight, bring out

reanimar [A1] *vt* to revive
■ **reanimarse** *v pron* (recobrar fuerzas) to revive; (recobrar el conocimiento) to come to *o* around

reanudar [A1] *vt* (frml) ⟨conversaciones/negociaciones/viaje⟩ to resume; ⟨hostilidades⟩ to renew, resume; ⟨amistad/relación⟩ to renew, revive
■ **reanudarse** *v pron* to resume

reaparición *f* (de publicación, persona) reappearance; (de artista) comeback

reapertura *f* reopening

rearme *m* rearmament

reata *f* **(a)** (Méx) (cuerda) rope; (Agr) lasso **(b)** (Col) (correa) cartridge belt

reavivar [A1] *vt* to revive
■ **reavivarse** *v pron* to be revived

rebaja *f* **(a)** (descuento) discount, reduction; **nos hicieron una ~ del 10%** they gave us a 10% discount *o* reduction; **de ~** reduced **(b) rebajas** *fpl* (saldos) sale, sales (*pl*); **están de ~s** there's a sale on, they're having a sale

rebajar [A1] *vt* ⓵ ⟨precio⟩ to lower, bring ... down; ⟨artículo⟩ to reduce; **me rebajó $200** he took $200 off ⓶ ⟨peso/kilos⟩ to lose ···⫸

■ ~ *vi* (humillar) to degrade, be degrading

■ **rebajarse** *v pron* ~se A hacer algo to lower oneself TO doing sth; ~se ANTE algn to humble oneself BEFORE sb

rebalsarse [A1] *v pron* (CS) «*agua/cauce/ vaso*» to overflow; **se rebalsó el río** the river burst its banks

rebanada *f* slice

rebanar [A1] *vt* to slice, cut

rebaño *m* (de ovejas) flock; (de cabras) herd

rebasar [A1] *vt* **(a)** (sobrepasar) «*límite de velocidad*» to exceed, go over; «*cifras previstas*» to exceed; «*punto*» to go beyond; **el agua ha rebasado el límite** the water has risen above the limit **(b)** (Méx) (Auto) to pass, overtake

■ ~ *vi* (Méx) to pass, overtake (BrE)

rebatir [I1] *vt* to refute

rebeca *f* (Esp) cardigan

rebelarse [A1] *v pron* to rebel

rebelde *adj* **(a)** «*tropas/ejército*» rebel (*before n*) **(b)** «*niño/carácter*» unruly, rebellious **(c)** «*tos*» persistent; «*mancha*» stubborn

■ *mf* (Mil, Pol) rebel

rebeldía *f* (cualidad) rebelliousness

rebelión *f* rebellion, uprising

reblandecer [E3] *vt* to soften

■ **reblandecerse** *v pron* to become *o* go soft

rebobinar [A1] *vt* to rewind

rebosante *adj* ~ DE algo «*de alegría/ optimismo*» brimming WITH sth; «*de vino/agua*» filled to the brim WITH sth

rebosar [A1] *vi* **(a)** ~ DE algo «*de felicidad/ entusiasmo*» to be brimming *o* bubbling over WITH sth; «*de salud*» to be bursting *o* brimming WITH sth **(b)** «*agua/embalse*» to overflow

■ ~ *vt* «*alegría/felicidad*»: **rebosaba felicidad** she was radiant with happiness

rebotar [A1] *vi* «*pelota/piedra*» to bounce; «*bala*» to ricochet

rebote *m* **(a)** (al golpear algo): **la pelota dio un ~ en el poste** the ball bounced off the post; **de ~** «*pelota*» «*pegar/entrar*» on the rebound; **la bala le dio de ~** he was hit by a ricochet **(b)** (en baloncesto) rebound

rebozar [A4] *vt* to coat ... in batter (*o* in egg and breadcrumbs *etc*)

rebozo *m* (AmL) (Indum) shawl, wrap

rebuscado -da *adj* «*explicación*» over-elaborate, overcomplicated; «*ejemplo/ argumento*» far-fetched; «*estilo*» affected

rebuscar [A2] *vi*: **rebuscó entre los papeles** he searched through the papers; **rebuscaba en la basura** he was rummaging about in the garbage

rebuznar [A1] *vi* to bray

recadero -ra *m, f* messenger, runner

recado *m* **(a)** (mensaje) message; **le mandó ~ de que volviera** she sent word that he should return **(b)** (Esp) (encargo, diligencia) errand; **hacer un ~** to run an errand

recaer [E16] *vi* **1** «*enfermo*» to have *o* suffer a relapse **2** **(a)** «*sospechas/responsabilidad*» ~ SOBRE algn to fall ON sb **(b)** «*premio/ nombramiento*» ~ EN algn to go TO sb

recaída *f* relapse

recalcar [A2] *vt* to stress, emphasize

recalentamiento *m* overheating; ~ **global** global warming

recalentar [A5] *vt* **(a)** «*motor*» to cause ... to overheat **(b)** «*comida*» to heat up, warm up; **me dio un guiso recalentado** he gave me some reheated stew

■ **recalentarse** *v pron* to overheat, become overheated

recámara *f* (Méx) (dormitorio) bedroom; (muebles) bedroom furniture

recamarera *f* (Méx) chambermaid

recambio *m* **(a)** (Auto, Mec) spare (part); **rueda de ~** spare wheel **(b)** (de bolígrafo) refill

recapacitar [A1] *vi* to reconsider, think again; ~ SOBRE algo to reconsider sth

recargable *adj* «*batería/pila*» rechargeable; «*encendedor/pluma*» refillable

recargado -da *adj* «*decoración*» overelaborate; «*texto*» overwritten

recargar [A3] *vt* «*batería*» to recharge; «*encendedor/estilográfica*» to refill; «*arma/ programa*» to reload

■ **recargarse** *v pron* (Col, Méx, Ven) (apoyarse) ~se CONTRA algo to lean AGAINST sth

recargo *m* surcharge; **sin ~** at no extra charge

recatado -da *adj* (pudoroso) demure, modest

recato *m* (pudor) modesty

recauchar, (Esp) **recauchutar** [A1] *vt* to retread, remold*

recaudación *f* **(a)** (acción) collection **(b)** (ganancia — en tienda) takings (*pl*); (— en cine) box office receipts (*pl*); (— en estadio) gate

recaudador -dora *m,f: tb* ~ **de impuestos** tax collector

recaudar [A1] *vt* to collect

recelo *m* suspicion, distrust; **con ~** distrustfully

recepción *f* (en general) reception; (de mercancías) receipt (frml)

recepcionista *mf* receptionist

receptivo -va *adj* receptive

receptor -tora *m,f* **1** (Med, Ling) recipient **2** (Dep) (en fútbol americano) receiver; (en béisbol) catcher **3 receptor** *m* (Rad) radio, receiver; (TV) television (receiver *o* set)

recesión *f* recession

receso *m* (AmL) recess

receta *f* (Coc) recipe; (Med) prescription

recetar [A1] *vt* to prescribe

rechazar [A4] *vt* **(a)** «*invitación/propuesta/ individuo*» to reject; «*moción/enmienda*» to defeat; «*oferta/trabajo*» to turn down **(b)** «*ataque/ enemigo*» to repel, repulse **(c)** (Med) «*órgano*» to reject

rechazo *m* (de invitación, individuo, órgano) rejection; (de moción, enmienda) defeat

rechifla *f* whistling (*as a sign of disapproval*), ≈booing

rechinar [A1] *vi* «*polea/bisagra*» to creak, squeak; **le rechinan los dientes** he grinds his teeth

rechinón *m* (Méx) screech

rechistar [A1] *vi* ▶ CHISTAR

rechoncho -cha *adj* (fam) dumpy (colloq), short and fat

rechupete (fam): **de rechupete** (*loc adj*) ⟨*comida*⟩ delicious, scrumptious (colloq)

recibidor *m* entrance hall

recibimiento *m* reception

recibir [I1] *vt* (en general) to receive; **recibió muchos regalos** she got lots of gifts; **reciba un atento saludo de ...** (Corresp) sincerely yours (AmE), yours faithfully/sincerely (BrE); **~ a algn con los brazos abiertos** to welcome sb with open arms; **van a ir a ~lo** they are going to meet him; **el encargado la ~á enseguida** the manager will see you right away

■ **recibirse** *v pron* (AmL) (Educ) to graduate; **~se DE algo** to qualify AS sth

recibo *m* (en general) receipt; (de luz, teléfono) bill

reciclado, reciclaje *m* (a) (de papel, vidrio) recycling (b) (de persona) retraining

reciclar [A1] *vt* ⟨*papel/vidrio*⟩ to recycle

recién *adv* [1] (con participio): **pan ~ hecho** freshly baked bread; **está ~ pintado** it's just been painted; **tiene un año ~ cumplido** he's just one; **los ~ casados** the newlyweds; **un ~ nacido** a newborn baby [2] (AmL) (a) (hace poco tiempo) just; **~ llegaron** they have just arrived (b) (solo ahora) only just; **~ me entero** I've only just found out (c) (sólo) only; **~ voy por la página 20** I'm only on page 20; **~ el lunes iré** the first day I'll be able to go is Monday

reciente *adj* ⟨*acontecimiento/foto*⟩ recent; ⟨*huella*⟩ fresh; **en fecha ~** recently

recinto *m* enclosure; **el público abandonó el ~** the public left the premises/building; **~ ferial** (de muestras) showground, exhibition site; (de atracciones) fairground

recio -cia *adj* ⟨*hombre/aspecto*⟩ robust, sturdy

recipiente *m* (utensilio) container, receptacle (frml)

recíproco -ca *adj* reciprocal

recital *m* recital

recitar [A1] *vt* to recite

reclamación *f* (a) (petición, demanda) claim (b) (queja) complaint

reclamar [A1] *vt* (a) «*persona*» ⟨*derecho/indemnización*⟩ to claim; (con insistencia) to demand (b) «*situación/problema*» to require, demand

■ **~** *vi* to complain; **reclamó ante los tribunales** she took the matter to court

réclame *m or f* (AmL) commercial, advertisement; **~ publicitario** advertising

reclamo *m* (a) (de pájaro) call (b) (esp AmL) (para atraer la atención, provocar interés) lure (c) (AmL) (queja) complaint

reclinable *adj* reclining (*before n*)

reclinar [A1] *vt* to rest, lean

■ **reclinarse** *v pron* to lean back; **reclinado contra la pared** leaning against the wall

recluir [I20] *vt* (en prisión) to imprison; (en hospital psiquiátrico), to intern (frml)

reclusión *f* imprisonment; **~ perpetua** life imprisonment

recluso -sa *m,f* prisoner, inmate

recluta *mf* (Mil) recruit; (en servicio militar) conscript, recruit

reclutar [A1] *vt* to recruit

recobrar [A1] *vt* (a) ⟨*confianza/conocimiento*⟩ to regain; ⟨*salud/vista*⟩ to recover; **~ las fuerzas** to recover one's strength (b) ⟨*dinero/botín/joyas*⟩ to recover, retrieve (c) ⟨*ciudad/plaza fuerte*⟩ to recapture

■ **recobrarse** *v pron* **~se DE algo** ⟨*de enfermedad/susto*⟩ to recover FROM sth, get over sth; ⟨*de pérdidas económicas*⟩ to recoup sth

recogedor *m* dustpan

recogepelotas *mf* (*pl* **~**) (*m*) ball boy; (*f*) ball girl

recoger [E6] *vt* [1] (a) (levantar) ⟨*objeto/papeles*⟩ to pick up; **recogí el agua con un trapo** I mopped the water up (b) ⟨*casa/habitación*⟩ to straighten (up) (AmE), to tidy (up) (BrE); ⟨*platos*⟩ to clear away; **~ la mesa** to clear the table [2] (a) ⟨*dinero/firmas*⟩ to collect (b) ⟨*deberes/cuadernos*⟩ to collect, take in (c) ⟨*trigo/maíz*⟩ to harvest, gather in; ⟨*flores/hongos*⟩ to pick; ⟨*flores/hongos*⟩ to pick, gather (d) ⟨*tienda de campaña/vela*⟩ to take down (e) ⟨*pelo*⟩ to tie ... back; **le recogió el pelo en una cola** he tied her hair back in a ponytail [3] (ir a buscar) ⟨*persona*⟩ to pick up, fetch, collect; ⟨*paquete*⟩ to collect, pick up; ⟨*basura*⟩ to collect; ⟨*equipaje*⟩ to reclaim

■ **~** *vi* (guardar) to clear up, to straighten up (AmE), to tidy up (BrE)

■ **recogerse** *v pron* ⟨*pelo*⟩ to tie up; ⟨*falda*⟩ to gather up

recogida *f* (a) (de basura, correo) collection (b) (Agr) harvest

recolección *f* (a) (Agr) harvest (b) (de fondos, dinero) collection

recolectar [A1] *vt* (a) ⟨*trigo*⟩ to harvest, gather in; ⟨*fruta*⟩ to pick, harvest (b) ⟨*dinero*⟩ to collect

recomendación *f* (a) (consejo) advice (b) (para empleo) reference, recommendation

recomendado -da *adj* [1] (a) ⟨*método/producto*⟩ recommended (b) (apropiado) suitable; **no recomendada para menores de 15 años** not suitable for under-15s [2] (Col, Ur) ⟨*carta*⟩ registered

recomendar [A5] *vt* (a) ⟨*libro/restaurante/persona*⟩ to recommend (b) (aconsejar) to advise; **no te lo recomiendo** I wouldn't advise it

recomienda, recomiendas, etc ▶ RECOMENDAR

recompensa *f* reward

recompensar [A1] *vt* to reward

reconciliación *f* reconciliation

reconciliar [A1] *vt* to reconcile

■ **reconciliarse** *v pron* (a) **~se (CON algn)** to make (it) up (WITH sb) (b) **~se CON algo** ⟨*con idea/postura*⟩ to reconcile oneself TO sth

reconfortante adj ⟨palabras/pensamientos⟩ comforting; ⟨baño⟩ relaxing

reconfortar [A1] vt to comfort

reconocer [E3] vt 1 (a) ⟨hecho/error⟩ to admit; ⟨verdad/autoridad⟩ to acknowledge (b) ⟨hijo/gobierno/derecho⟩ to recognize 2 (identificar) ⟨persona/letra/voz⟩ to recognize 3 ⟨terreno⟩ to reconnoiter*

reconocimiento m (a) (en general) recognition (b) (Med) tb ~ médico medical (examination) (c) (de territorio) reconnaissance

reconquista f reconquest; **la R~** the Reconquest

reconquistar [A1] vt ⟨territorio⟩ to reconquer, regain; ⟨cariño/afecto⟩ to win back

reconstituyente m tonic, restorative

reconstruir [I20] vt to reconstruct

reconversión f (a) (reestructuración) restructuring, rationalization (b) (de un trabajador) tb ~ profesional retraining

reconvertir [I11] vt (a) ⟨industria⟩ to rationalize, restructure (b) ⟨profesional⟩ to retrain
■ **reconvertirse** v pron (a) «industria» to be rationalized o restructured (b) «profesional» to retrain

recopilación f compilation, collection

recopilar [A1] vt to compile, gather together

récord, record adj inv record (before n)
■ m (pl **-cords**) record; **batir un** ~ to break a record; **posee el** ~ **mundial** she is the world record holder

recordar [A10] vt 1 (a) ⟨nombre/fecha⟩ to remember, recall; **recuerdo que lo puse ahí** I remember o recall putting it there (b) (rememorar) ⟨niñez/pasado⟩ to remember 2 (a) (traer a la memoria) ~**le** A **algo/**QUE to remind sb ABOUT sth/to do sth; **les recuerdo que ...** I would like to remind you that ... (b) (por asociación, parecido) to remind; **me recuerdas a tu hermano** you remind me of your brother
■ ~ vi (acordarse) to remember; **si mal no recuerdo** if I remember right

recorrer [E1] vt (a) (viajar por): **recorrí toda España** I traveled o went all over Spain; (como turista) I toured all over Spain; ~ **mundo** to travel all around the world; **recorrimos toda la costa** we traveled the whole length of the coast (b) ⟨distancia/trayecto⟩ to cover, do (c) (con la mirada): **recorrió la sala con la mirada** he looked around the hall

recorrido m (a) (viaje): **un** ~ **por Perú** a trip around Peru; (turístico) a tour around Peru (b) (trayecto) route; **cubrir el** ~ to cover the route (c) (de proyectil) trajectory; (de balón) path (d) (en golf) round; (en esquí) run

recortable adj cutout (before n)

recortar [A1] vt 1 (a) ⟨figura/artículo/anuncio⟩ to cut out (b) ⟨pelo/puntas⟩ to trim 2 ⟨gastos/plantilla⟩ to reduce

recorte m 1 (de periódico, revista) cutting, clipping 2 (Fin) (acción) cutting; (efecto) cut, reduction

recostar [A10] vt (apoyar) to lean
■ **recostarse** v pron (a) (acostarse) to lie down; **recuéstate en el almohadón** lie back on the pillow

(b) (apoyarse) to lean; **recostados en el escritorio** leaning on the desk; **estaba recostado en un sillón** he was sitting back in an armchair

recoveco m: **un camino lleno de** ~**s** a road full of twists and turns; **en todos los** ~**s de la casa** in every nook and cranny of the house

recreativo -va adj recreational

recreo m (a) (diversión): **nos servía de** ~ it served as entertainment; **viaje de** ~ pleasure trip (b) (en el colegio) recess (AmE), break (BrE)

recriminar [A1] vt to reproach

recta f (Mat) straight line; (Dep) straight; ~ **final** (Dep) home stretch

rectángulo m rectangle

rectificar [A2] vt to correct
■ ~ vi (corregirse) to correct oneself

rectitud f rectitude (frml), honesty

recto¹ -ta adj (a) ⟨línea/nariz/falda⟩ straight (b) (honrado) honest, upright

recto² m (Anat) rectum
■ adv straight; **todo** ~ straight on

rector -tora m,f (de universidad) rector (AmE), vice-chancellor (BrE)

recuadro m box

recubrir [I33] vt ~ **algo** DE or CON **algo** to cover sth WITH sth

recuento m (de votos) recount

recuerdo m 1 (a) (reminiscencia) memory (b) (souvenir) souvenir; (regalo) memento, keepsake; **un** ~ **de familia** a family heirloom 2 **recuerdos** mpl regards (pl), best wishes (pl); **dale** ~**s** give him my regards

recuperación f (a) (en general) recovery (b) (Esp) (Educ) tb examen de ~ retake, makeup (exam) (AmE)

recuperar [A1] vt (a) ⟨dinero/joyas/botín⟩ to recover, get back; ⟨pérdidas⟩ to recoup (b) ⟨vista/salud⟩ to recover; ⟨confianza⟩ to regain; ~ **fuerzas** to get one's strength back (c) (compensar) ⟨tiempo perdido⟩ to make up for; **tienes que** ~ **esas tres horas** you have to make up those three hours (d) ⟨examen/asignatura⟩ to retake, make up (AmE)
■ **recuperarse** v pron ~**se** DE **algo** ⟨de enfermedad⟩ to recover FROM sth, recuperate FROM sth (frml); ⟨de sorpresa/desgracia⟩ to get over sth, recover FROM sth

recurrir [I1] vi (frente a problema) ~ A **algn** to turn TO sb; ~ A **algo** to resort TO sth

recursivo adj (Col) resourceful

recurso m 1 (medio): **agoté todos los** ~**s** I exhausted all the options; **como último** ~ as a last resort; **un hombre de** ~**s** a resourceful man 2 **recursos** mpl (medios económicos — de país) resources (pl); (— de persona) means (pl); ~**s energéticos** energy resources (pl); ~**s humanos** human resources (pl); ~**s naturales** natural resources (pl)

red f 1 (a) (para pescar) net (b) (Dep) net (c) (para pelo) hairnet (d) (en tren) (luggage) rack 2 (de comunicaciones, emisoras, transportes) network; (de comercios, empresas) chain, network; (de espionaje, contrabando) ring 3 (de electricidad) power supply, mains; (de gas) mains 4 **la Red** (Inf) the Net

redacción f 1 (a) (de carta) writing; (de

borrador) drafting; (de tratado) drawing-up, drafting **(b)** (lenguaje, estilo) wording, phrasing **2** (Educ) composition, essay **3** (Period) **(a)** (acción) writing **(b)** (equipo) editorial staff *o* team **(c)** (oficina) editorial department *o* office

redactar [A1] *vt* ‹*informe/artículo/composición*› to write; ‹*acuerdo/tratado*› to draw up
■ ~ *vi*: **redacta muy bien** she writes very well

redactor -tora *m,f* editor; ~ **jefe** editor in chief

redada *f* raid

redentor -tora *adj* redeeming
■ *m,f* redeemer

redimir [I1] *vt* to redeem

redoblar [A1] *vt* (aumentar) ‹*esfuerzos/críticas*› to redouble; ‹*vigilancia*› to step up, tighten
■ ~ *vi* «*tambor*» to roll

redoble *m* drumroll

redoma *f* (Ven) (Auto) traffic circle (AmE), roundabout (BrE)

redomado -da *adj* utter, out-and-out

redonda *f* **1** (Mús) semibreve **2** **a la redonda**: **en diez metros a la** ~ within a ten meter radius; **se oyó a varios kilómetros a la** ~ it could be heard for miles around

redondear [A1] *vt* **(a)** (dar forma curva) to round (off) **(b)** ‹*cifra/número*› to round off; (por lo alto) to round up; (por lo bajo) to round down
■ ~ *vi*: **digamos 200, para** ~ let's make it a round 200

redondel *m* (figura circular) ring

redondela *f* (Andes) ▶ REDONDEL

redondo -da *adj* **1** ‹*cara/espejo*› round; *caer (se)* ~ (desplomarse) to collapse; *en* ~ ‹*girar*› (right) around **2** ‹*cifra/número*› round **3** (perfecto): **un negocio** ~ a great *o* excellent deal; **nos salió todo** ~ everything turned out perfectly for us **4** (Méx) ‹*boleto/pasaje*› return (*before n*), round-trip (*before n*) (AmE)

reducción *f* reduction; ~ **de impuestos** tax cuts, reduction in taxes; **una** ~ **de personal** a reduction *o* cutback in the workforce

reducido -da *adj* **(a)** (pequeño) ‹*espacio/ presupuesto*› limited; ‹*tamaño*› small **(b)** (rebajado, achicado) ‹*precio/fotografía*› reduced; **un número** ~ **de personas** a small number of people; **trabaja jornada reducida** she is on short-time (working)

reducidor -dora *m,f* (AmS) (de objetos robados) receiver, fence (colloq)

reducir [I6] *vt* **1** **(a)** ‹*gastos/costos*› to cut, reduce; ‹*velocidad/producción/consumo*› to reduce; **debería** ~ **el consumo de sal** you should cut down on salt; ~ **algo A algo** to reduce sth TO sth; ~ **algo EN algo** to reduce sth BY sth **(b)** ‹*fotocopia/fotografía*› to reduce **2** **(a)** (transformar): ~ **los gramos a miligramos** to convert the grams to milligrams; **quedaron reducidos a cenizas** they were reduced to ashes **(b)** (AmS) ‹*objeto robado*› to receive, fence (colloq) **3** (dominar) ‹*enemigo/rebeldes*› to subdue; ‹*ladrón*› to overpower
■ **reducirse** *v pron*: **todo se reduce a tener tacto** it all comes down to being tactful

redundancia *f* (Ling) tautology, redundancy; **valga la** ~ if you'll forgive the repetition

redundante *adj* redundant

reedición *f* reissue, reprint

reeditar [A1] *vt* to reprint, reissue

reelegir [I8] *vt* to reelect

reembolsar [A1] *vt* ‹*gastos*› to refund, reimburse (fml); ‹*depósito*› to refund; ‹*préstamo*› to repay

reembolso *m* (de gastos) refund, reimbursement (fml); (de depósito) refund; (de préstamo) repayment; **contra** ~ cash on delivery, COD

reemplazar [A4] *vt* ‹*persona*› (durante período limitado) to substitute for, stand in for; (durante más tiempo) to replace; ‹*aparato/pieza*› to replace; ~ **algo/a algn POR** *o* **CON algo/algn** to replace sth/sb WITH *o* BY sth/sb

reemplazo *m* (durante período limitado) substitution; (durante más tiempo) replacement; **entró en** ~ **del jugador lesionado** he came on as a substitute for the injured player

reencarnación *f* reincarnation

reencarnarse [A1] *v pron* to be reincarnated; ~ **EN algn/algo** to be reincarnated AS sb/sth

reencuentro *m* reunion

reestreno *m* (de película) rerelease; (de obra teatral) revival

reestructurar [A1] *vt* to restructure

refacción *f* **1** (AmS) (para ampliar, mejorar) refurbishment **2** (Méx) (pieza de repuesto) spare part; **llanta de** ~ spare tire

refaccionar [A1] *vt* (AmS) to refurbish

refaccionaria *f* (Méx) (tienda) auto spares store; (taller) garage

referencia *f* reference; **hacer** ~ **a algo** to refer to *o* mention sth; **con** ~ **a ...** with reference to ...; **número de** ~ reference number; **tener buenas** ~**s** to have good references

referéndum *m* (*pl* **-dums**) referendum; **someter algo a** ~ to hold a referendum on sth

referente *adj*: **las noticias** ~**s al accidente** the news about the accident; **en lo** ~ **a ...** regarding ...

réferi, referí *mf* (AmL) referee

referirse [I11] *v pron* **(a)** (aludir) ~**se A algo/ algn** to refer TO sth/sb **(b)** (estar relacionado con): **por lo que se refiere a este asunto ...** with regard to this matter ..., as far as this matter is concerned ...

refilón: **de refilón** (*loc adv*): **lo miré de** ~ I gave him a sidelong glance; **la vi solo de** ~ I just caught a glimpse of her

refinado -da *adj* ‹*persona/modales*› refined; ‹*ironía*› subtle

refinar [A1] *vt* to refine; ‹*estilo*› to polish

refinería *f* refinery

reflector *m* **(a)** (pantalla reflectante) reflector **(b)** (foco) (Teatr) spotlight; (Dep) floodlight; (Mil) searchlight; (en monumento) floodlight

reflejar [A1] *vt* to reflect
■ **reflejarse** *v pron* **(a)** «*imagen*» to be reflected **(b)** «*emoción/cansancio/duda*» to show

reflejo¹ -ja *adj* reflex (*before n*)

reflejo² *m* **1** **(a)** (en general) reflection; (luz reflejada) reflected light **(b)** **reflejos** *mpl* (en peluquería) highlights (*pl*) **2** (Fisiol) reflex

reflexionar [A1] *vi* to reflect (fml); **¿has** ⋯⋗

reflexionado bien? have you thought it over *o* through carefully?; ~ **SOBRE** algo to think ABOUT sth, reflect on sth (frml)
reflexivo -va *adj* **(a)** (Ling, Mat) reflexive **(b)** ⟨*persona*⟩ thoughtful, reflective
reflujo *m* (de marea) ebb (tide)
reforestación *f* reforestation
reforestar [A1] *vt* to reforest
reforma *f* **(a)** (en general) reform; **la R~** (Relig) the Reformation **(b)** (en edificio, traje) alteration
reformar [A1] *vt* **(a)** (en general) to reform **(b)** ⟨*casa/edificio*⟩ to make alterations to
■ **reformarse** *v pron* to mend one's ways
reformatorio *m* reformatory
reforzar [A11] *vt* ⟨*puerta/costura*⟩ to reinforce; ⟨*guardia*⟩ to increase, strengthen; ⟨*relaciones*⟩ to reinforce; ⟨*medidas de seguridad*⟩ to step up, tighten
refrán *m* saying, proverb; **como dice el ~** as the saying goes
refregar [A7] *vt* ⟨*puños/cuello*⟩ to scrub
refrendar [A1] *vt* (Col, Méx) ⟨*pasaporte*⟩ to renew
refrescante *adj* refreshing
refrescar [A2] *vt* **(a)** ⟨*bebida*⟩ to cool; ⟨*ambiente*⟩ to make ... fresher *o* cooler **(b)** ⟨*conocimientos*⟩ to brush up (on)
■ ~ *v impers* to turn cooler
refresco *m* soft drink, soda (AmE)
refrigerador *m* **(a)** (nevera) refrigerator, fridge **(b)** (del aire acondicionado) cooling unit
refrigeradora *f* (Col, Per) refrigerator, fridge
refrigerar [A1] *vt* **(a)** ⟨*alimentos/bebidas*⟩ to refrigerate **(b)** ⟨*motor*⟩ to cool; ⟨*cine/bar*⟩ to air-condition; **❺** local refrigerado air-conditioned premises
refrito *m* (Coc): **un ~ de tomate y cebolla** fried onions and tomato
refuerzo *m* **(a)** (para puerta, pared, costura) reinforcement **(b)** (de vacuna) booster **(c)** **refuerzos** *mpl* (Mil) reinforcements (*pl*)
refugiado -da *adj* refugee (*before n*)
■ *m,f* refugee; **~ económico** economic refugee
refugiar [A1] *vt* to give ... refuge
■ **refugiarse** *v pron* to take refuge; **~se DE algo** ⟨*de bombardeo/ataque*⟩ to take refuge FROM sth; ⟨*de lluvia/tormenta*⟩ to take shelter FROM sth
refugio *m* **(a)** (de la lluvia, bombardeo) shelter; (en montaña) refuge, shelter **(b)** (de un ataque, perseguidores) refuge; **buscar ~** to seek refuge **(c)** (en calzada) traffic island
refunfuñar [A1] *vi* (fam) to grumble, grouch (colloq)
refunfuñón -ñona *adj* (fam) grouchy (colloq), grumpy (colloq)
regadera *f* **(a)** (para jardín) watering can **(b)** (Col, Méx, Ven) (de ducha) rose, shower head (AmE); (ducha) shower
regadío *m* (sistema) irrigation; **tierras de ~** irrigated land

regalado -da *adj* **(a)** (fam) (muy barato): **precios ~s** giveaway prices (colloq); **esos zapatos están ~s** those shoes are dirt cheap *o* are a steal (colloq) **(b)** (Chi, Méx, Ven fam) (muy fácil) easy
regalar [A1] *vt* **(a)** (obsequiar): **¿qué te ~on para tu cumpleaños?** what did you get for your birthday?; **le ~on un reloj de oro** he was given a gold watch **(b)** (vender muy barato) to sell ... at bargain prices
regaliz *m* licorice (AmE), liquorice (BrE)
regalo *m* **(a)** (obsequio) gift, present **(b)** (cosa barata) steal (colloq) **(c)** (deleite, festín) treat
regalón -lona *adj* (CS fam) spoiled
■ *m,f* (CS fam) spoilt brat (colloq)
regalonear [A1] *vt* (CS fam) to spoil
■ ~ *vi* (CS fam): **le encanta ~ con su abuela** she loves being made a fuss of by her grandmother
regañadientes: **a regañadientes** (*loc adv*) reluctantly, unwillingly
regañar [A1] *vt* (esp AmL) to scold, to tell ... off (colloq)
■ ~ *vi* (Esp) (pelearse) to quarrel
regañina, (Méx) **regañiza** *f* (fam) scolding, talking-to (colloq), telling-off (colloq)
regaño *m* (AmL fam) scolding, telling-off (colloq)
regar [A7] *vt* **(a)** ⟨*planta/jardín*⟩ to water; ⟨*tierra/campo*⟩ to irrigate; ⟨*calle*⟩ to hose down **(b)** «*río*» to water (AmC, Ven) ⟨*noticia/versión*⟩ to spread
regata *f* (carrera) yacht race; (serie de carreras) regatta
regate *m* (Esp) (en fútbol) feint
regatear [A1] *vi* (Com) to bargain, haggle
■ ~ *vt* **1** (escatimar): **no han regateado esfuerzos para ...** no efforts have been spared to ...; **sin ~ medios** whatever it takes **2** (Esp) (Dep) to get past, swerve past
regencia *f* (en lugar del soberano) regency
regenerar [A1] *vt* to regenerate
■ **regenerarse** *v pron* **(a)** (Biol, Tec) to be regenerated **(b)** «*persona*» to be reformed
regente *mf* regent
régimen *m* **1** (dieta) diet; **hacer ~** to be on a diet; **ponerse a ~** to go on a diet **2** (Pol) regime
regimiento *m* (Mil) regiment
regio -gia *adj* **(a)** (majestuoso) regal **(b)** (Col, CS fam) (estupendo) great (colloq); **te queda ~** it looks fantastic on you (colloq); **me viene ~** it suits me fine
región *f* region
regional *adj* regional
regir [I8] *vt* to govern
■ ~ *vi* «*ley/disposición*» to be in force, be valid; **ese horario ya no rige** that timetable is no longer valid
■ **regirse** *v pron* **~se POR algo** «*sociedad*» to be governed BY sth; «*economía/mercado*» to be controlled BY sth *o* subject to sth
registrar [A1] *vt* **1** **(a)** ⟨*nacimiento/defunción/patente*⟩ to register **(b)** ⟨*sonido/temperatura*⟩ to record; ⟨*temblor*⟩ to register **2** ⟨*equipaje/lugar/*

---

persona⟩ to search; **estaba registrando mis cajones** (fam) he was going through my drawers **3** (Méx) ⟨*carta*⟩ to register
■ **registrarse** *v pron* (inscribirse) to register; (en hotel) to register, check in

registro *m* **1** (libro) register; (acción de anotar) registration; (cosa anotada) record, entry; ∼ **civil** (oficina) registry, registry office (BrE) **2** (por la policía) search; **orden de** ∼ search warrant

regla *f* (a) (utensilio) ruler (b) (norma) rule; **todo está en** ∼ everything is in order; **por** ∼ **general** as a (general) rule (c) (menstruación) period; **tengo la** ∼ I have my period

reglamentario -ria *adj* ⟨*horario*⟩ set (*before n*); ⟨*uniforme/arma*⟩ regulation (*before n*)

reglamento *m* rules (*pl*), regulations (*pl*)

regocijarse [A1] *v pron* to rejoice; ∼ **DE** *or* **POR algo** (por buena noticia) to rejoice **AT** sth; (por mal ajeno) to take delight **IN** sth, delight **IN** sth

regocijo *m* (a) (júbilo, alborozo) rejoicing; (alegría) joy, delight; **sintió gran** ∼ **al verla** he was delighted to see her (b) (ante el mal ajeno) pleasure

regodearse [A1] *v pron* (a) (complacerse) to delight in, take great delight in; **se regodea haciéndome sufrir** he delights in making me suffer; ∼ **EN** *or* **CON algo** to delight **IN** sth, gloat **OVER** sth (b) (Chi) (al elegir) to hesitate

regordete -ta *adj* (fam) chubby

regresar [A1] *vi* to return, come/go back; **no sé cuándo va a** ∼ I don't know when he'll be back
■ ∼ *vt* (AmL exc CS) (a) ⟨*libro/llaves*⟩ to return, give back (b) ⟨*persona*⟩ to send ... back
■ **regresarse** *v pron* (AmL exc RPl) to return, go/come back; **ya se regresó** she's back now

regreso *m* (a) (vuelta) return; **emprendió el** ∼ she set off on the return journey *o* trip; **de** ∼ **paramos en León** on the way back we stopped in León (b) (AmL) (devolución) return

reguero *m* (rastro) trail

regulable *adj* adjustable

regulador *m* regulator

regular¹ *adj* **1** (en general) regular **2** (a) (no muy bien): **¿qué tal te va?** — **regular** how's it going? — so-so; **¿qué tal la película?** — **regular** how was the movie? — nothing special (b) (de tamaño) medium-sized, middling
■ *m* (calificación) fair

regular² [A1] *vt* **1** (a) ⟨*espejo/asiento*⟩ to adjust (b) ⟨*caudal/temperatura/velocidad*⟩ to regulate, control **2** ⟨*ley/norma*⟩ to regulate

regularidad *f* regularity; **con** ∼ regularly

regusto *m* aftertaste

rehabilitación *f* (a) (de enfermo, delincuente) rehabilitation (b) (en cargo) reinstatement (c) (de vivienda) renovation, restoration

rehabilitar [A1] *vt* (a) ⟨*paciente/delincuente*⟩ to rehabilitate (b) (en cargo) to reinstate (c) ⟨*vivienda/local*⟩ to renovate, restore

rehacer [E18] *vt* (volver a hacer) to redo; **trató de** ∼ **su vida** she tried to rebuild her life
■ **rehacerse** *v pron* ∼**se DE algo** to get over sth

rehén *m* hostage

rehogar [A3] *vt* to fry ... lightly

rehuir [I21] *vt* to shy away from

rehusar [A23] *vt/vi* to refuse

■ **rehusarse** *v pron* (esp AmL) to refuse

reilón -lona *adj* (Per, Ven fam) smiley (colloq)

reimpresión *f* (a) (acción) reprinting (b) (obra) reprint

reimprimir [I36] *vt* to reprint

reina *f* queen; ∼ **de belleza** beauty queen

reinado *m* reign

reinante *adj* (a) ⟨*casa/dinastía*⟩ reigning (b) ⟨*frío/lluvias*⟩ prevailing; **el malestar** ∼ **en el partido** the unease prevailing in the party

reinar [A1] *vi* (a) ⟨*monarca/dinastía*⟩ to reign (b) «*silencio/paz*» to reign; «*terror/buen tiempo*» to prevail

reincidente *mf* reoffender

reincidir [I1] *vi* (Der) to reoffend

reincorporarse [A1] *v pron* to return; ∼ **a filas** to rejoin the army

reiniciar [A1] *vt* to resume; (Inf) to reboot

reino *m* kingdom; ∼ **animal** animal kingdom; **el** ∼ **de la fantasía** the realm of fantasy

Reino Unido *m*: **el** ∼∼ the United Kingdom

reinserción *f*: *tb* ∼ **social** social rehabilitation, reintegration into society

reintegrar [A1] *vt* **1** ⟨*persona*⟩ (a cargo) to reinstate; (a la comunidad) to reintegrate; ∼ **a algn A** *or* **EN algo** ⟨*a cargo*⟩ to reinstate sb **IN** sth; ⟨*a la comunidad*⟩ to reintegrate sb **INTO** sth **2** (frml) ⟨*depósito*⟩ to refund, return; ⟨*gastos*⟩ to reimburse; ⟨*préstamo*⟩ to repay
■ **reintegrarse** *v pron* to return; ∼**se A algo** ⟨*a trabajo/equipo*⟩ to return **TO** sth; ∼**se en la comunidad** to reintegrate into the community

reintegro *m* (a) (en banco) withdrawal; (de depósito) refund; (de gastos) reimbursement; (de préstamo) repayment (b) (en lotería) refund (*of the ticket price*)

reír [I18] *vi* to laugh; **se echaron a** ∼ they burst out laughing
■ ∼ *vt* ⟨*gracia/chiste*⟩ to laugh at
■ **reírse** *v pron* to laugh; ∼**se a carcajadas** to guffaw; ∼**se DE algo/algn** to laugh **AT** sth/sb

reivindicación *f* (a) (demanda) demand, claim (b) (reconocimiento) recognition (c) (rehabilitación): **luchó por la** ∼ **de su buen nombre** she fought to vindicate her good name (d) (de atentado): **la** ∼ **del atentado** the claiming of responsibility for the attack

reivindicar [A2] *vt* (a) ⟨*derecho*⟩ to demand; ⟨*tierras*⟩ to claim (b) (rehabilitar) ⟨*imagen/reputación*⟩ to restore (c) ⟨*atentado*⟩ to claim responsibility for

reja *f* (a) (de ventana) grille (b) (para cercar) railing

rejego *adj* (Méx fam) ⟨*persona*⟩ mouthy (AmE), cheeky (BrE)

rejilla *f* (a) (de ventilación) grille; (Auto) grille; (del confesionario) screen; (del desagüe) grating (b) (para equipajes) luggage rack; (de horno) rack; (base de chimenea) grate

rejuntar [A1] *vt* (Méx fam) ⟨*reses*⟩ to round up; ⟨*borregos*⟩ to gather

rejuvenecer [E3] *vt* to rejuvenate
■ **rejuvenecerse** *v pron* to be rejuvenated

relación *f* **1** (a) (conexión) connection; **con** ∼ **a** *or* **en** ∼ **con** (con respecto a) in connection with; (en comparación con) relative to; **en** ∼ **con su carta** ⋯⊹

r

... with regard to *o* regarding your letter ... **(b)**
(correspondencia): **en una ~ de diez a uno** (Mat) in a
ratio of ten to one; **una ~ causa-efecto** a
relationship of cause and effect

2 **(a)** (entre personas) relationship; **las relaciones
entre padres e hijos** the relationship between
parents and their children; **estoy en buenas
relaciones con él** I'm on good terms with him **(b)**
relaciones *fpl* (influencias) contacts (*pl*),
connections (*pl*); (trato comercial, diplomático)
relations (*pl*); (trato carnal) sex; **relaciones
exteriores** foreign affairs; **relaciones
prematrimoniales** premarital sex; **relaciones
públicas** (actividad) public relations (*pl*); (persona)
public relations officer; (de cantante, artista) PR;
relaciones sexuales sexual relations

3 **(a)** (exposición) account **(b)** (lista) list

relacionado -da *adj* **(a)** [ESTAR] ⟨*temas/
ideas/hechos*⟩ related, connected **(b)** ⟨*persona*⟩:
está muy bien ~ he is very well connected; **estar
~ CON algn/algo** to be connected WITH sb/sth

relacionar [A1] *vt* (conectar) to relate, connect;
~ algo A *o* **CON algo** to relate *o* connect sth TO
sth

■ **relacionarse** *v pron* **(a)** **~se CON algo** ⟨*con
tema/asunto*⟩ to be related TO sth **(b)** «*persona*»
~se CON algn to mix WITH sb

relajación *f* (de músculos, mente) relaxation

relajado -da *adj* **(a)** (tranquilo) relaxed **(b)**
⟨*costumbres*⟩ dissolute, lax

relajante *adj* **1** ⟨*música/baño*⟩ relaxing
2 (CS fam) (empalagoso) sickly-sweet (pej)

relajar [A1] *vt* ⟨*músculo/persona/mente*⟩ to relax
■ ~ *vi* «*ejercicio/música*» to be relaxing
■ **relajarse** *v pron* **1** **(a)** (físicamente, mentalmente)
to relax; (tras período de tensión, mucho trabajo) to
relax, unwind **(b)** «*tensión*» to ease;
«*ambiente*» to become more relaxed
2 (degenerar) «*costumbres/moral*» to decline

relajo *m* **1** (de la moral) decline **2** (esp Esp fam)
(relax): **¡qué ~!** how relaxing! **3** **(a)** (Méx fam)
(persona divertida) laugh (colloq) **(b)** (persona
problemática) troublemaker

relamerse [E1] *v pron* (por algo sabroso) to lick
one's lips; (de satisfacción) to smack one's lips

relámpago *m* (Meteo) bolt *o* flash of lightning;
como un ~ ⟨*salir/pasar*⟩ like greased lightning

relatar [A1] *vt* ⟨*historia/aventura*⟩ to recount,
relate

relativo -va *adj* **1** (no absoluto) relative; **eso es
muy ~** that depends; **una enfermedad de relativa
gravedad** a relatively serious illness
2 (concerniente) **~ A algo** relating TO sth; **todo lo
~ a la política** anything to do with *o* related to
politics; **en lo ~ a este problema** with regard to
this problem

relato *m* **(a)** (historia, cuento) story, tale **(b)**
(relación) account

relax *m* relaxation

relegar [A3] *vt*: **se siente relegado** he feels left
out; **el problema quedó relegado a un segundo
plano** the matter was pushed into the
background; **relegado al olvido** consigned to
oblivion

relevante *adj* notable, outstanding

relevar [A1] *vt* **(a)** (sustituir) ⟨*guarda/enfermera*⟩

to relieve; ⟨*jugador*⟩ to replace, take over from;
~ la guardia (Mil) to change the guard **(b)**
(destituir) to remove
■ **relevarse** *v pron* to take turns, take it in
turn(s)

relevo *m* **(a)** **de ~** ⟨*conductor/equipo*⟩ relief
(*before n*) **(b)** (Dep) *tb* **~s** relay (race)

relieve *m* **1** **(a)** (Art, Geog) relief; **la costa tiene
un ~ muy accidentado** the coast is very rugged;
letras en ~ embossed letters **(b)** (parte que
sobresale): **el marco tiene un centímetro de ~** the
frame protrudes by a centimeter **2** (importancia)
prominence; **personas de ~** prominent people;
dar ~ a algo to lend (special) importance to sth;
poner de ~ to highlight

religión *f* religion

religiosidad *f* religiousness, religiosity

religioso -sa *adj* religious
■ *m,f* member of a religious order

relinchar [A1] *vi* to neigh, whinny

reliquia *f* relic; **una ~ de familia** a family
heirloom

rellano *m* (de escalera) landing; (de ladera,
montaña) shelf

rellenar [A1] *vt* **1** **(a)** ⟨*pavo/pimientos/cojín*⟩
to stuff; ⟨*pastel*⟩ to fill; **~ algo DE** *or* **CON algo** to
stuff/fill sth WITH sth **(b)** ⟨*agujero/grieta*⟩ to fill
2 (volver a llenar) to refill **3** ⟨*impreso/formulario*⟩
to fill out *o* in; ⟨*examen/discurso*⟩ to pad out

relleno¹ -na *adj* ⟨*pavo/pimientos*⟩ stuffed;
caramelos ~s de chocolate candies with a
chocolate filling

relleno² *m* (para pasteles, tortas) filling; (para
pavo, pimientos, cojín) stuffing; (de ropa interior)
padding; (para agujeros, grietas) filler

reloj *m* (de pared, mesa) clock; (de pulsera, bolsillo)
watch; **funciona como un ~** it's going like
clockwork; **contra ~** against the clock; **~ de
arena** hourglass; **~ de pie** grandfather clock;
~ de sol sundial; **~ despertador** alarm clock

relojería *f* (tienda, taller) clockmaker's,
watchmaker's; (actividad) watchmaking

relojero -ra *m,f* (de relojes — de pulsera)
watchmaker; (— de pared, mesa) clockmaker

reluciente *adj* ⟨*dientes/coche*⟩ gleaming;
⟨*metal/suelo*⟩ shiny, shining; **una mañana ~** a
bright, sunny morning

relucir [I5] *vi* «*sol*» to shine; «*estrellas*» to
twinkle, glitter; «*plata/zapatos*» to shine, gleam;
salir/sacar a ~ to come to the surface/to bring up

relumbrante *adj* brilliant, dazzling

relumbrar [A1] *vi* to shine brightly

remachar [A1] *vt* **(a)** ⟨*clavo*⟩ to clinch; ⟨*perno/
chapas*⟩ to rivet **(b)** (recalcar) to repeat, reiterate;
(finalizar) to round off, finish off
■ ~ *vi* (en tenis) to smash; (en vóleibol) to spike

remache *m* **1** (perno) rivet **2** (en tenis) smash;
(en vóleibol) spike

remangarse [A3] *v pron* (*refl*) ⟨*pantalones/
manga*⟩ to roll up; **se remangó para lavar los
platos** he rolled up his sleeves to wash the dishes

remanso *m* pool; **un ~ de paz** a haven of
peace (liter)

remar [A1] *vi* (en bote) to row; (en canoa) to
paddle

353

remarcar [A2] *vt* (hacer notar) to stress, emphasize

rematado -da *adj* complete, absolute; **es un loco ∼** he's a raving lunatic

rematar [A1] *vt* **1 (a)** ⟨actuación/intervención⟩ to round off, finish off; ⟨negocio⟩ to conclude, close; ⟨torre/bastón⟩ to top, crown; **y para ∼la** (fam) and to crown *o* cap it all (colloq) **(b)** ⟨costura⟩ to finish off **(c)** ⟨animal/persona⟩ to finish off
2 (en tenis) to smash; (en vóleibol) to spike; (en fútbol): **remató el centro a la portería** he hit the cross straight into the goal
3 (AmL) **(a)** (en subasta — vender) to auction; (— comprar) to buy ... at an auction **(b)** (liquidar) to sell ... off cheaply
■ ∼ *vi* **1** (terminar) ∼ **EN algo** to end **IN** sth
2 (en tenis) to smash; (en vóleibol) to spike; (en fútbol) to shoot; ∼ **de cabeza** to head the ball

remate *m* **1 (a)** (de activades, esfuerzos) culmination; **y como ∼** (fam) and to crown *o* cap it all (colloq) **(b)** (en costura) double stitch (*to finish off*) **2** (en tenis) smash; (en vóleibol) spike; (en fútbol) shot; ∼ **de cabeza** header **3** (AmL) (subasta) auction

remedar [A1] *vt* to mimic, ape

remediar [A1] *vt* **1** ⟨situación/problema⟩ to remedy; ⟨daño⟩ to repair; **¿qué piensas hacer para ∼lo?** what are you going to do to put things right?; **con llorar no remedias nada** crying won't solve anything **2** (evitar): **no lo puedo/pude ∼** I can't/couldn't help it

remedio *m* **1 (a)** (Med) (cura) remedy, cure **(b)** (esp AmL) (Farm) medicine **2** (solución) solution; **ya no tiene ∼** there's nothing we (*or* you *etc*) can do now; **su matrimonio no tiene ∼** her marriage is beyond hope; **un caso sin ∼** a hopeless case **3** (alternativa, recurso) option; **no queda más ∼ que ...** we have no alternative *o* choice but ...; **iré si no hay otro ∼** I'll go if I really have to *o* if I must

remendar [A5] *vt* to mend

remera *f* (RPl) (camiseta) T-shirt

remero -ra *m,f* (*m*) rower, oarsman; (*f*) rower, oarswoman

remesa *f* (de mercancías) consignment, shipment; (de dinero) remittance

remezón *m* (Andes) (temblor) earth tremor; (sacudida brusca) shake; (suceso inesperado) shake-up

remiendo *m* (pedazo de tela, cuero) patch; **le hizo un ∼** she mended *o* patched it

remilgado -da *adj* fussy

remilgón -gona, remilgoso -sa *adj* (delicado) (Andes, Méx) fussy; (difícil) (Méx) difficult

remisión *f* **1** (en texto) reference; ∼ **A algo** reference **TO** sth **2** (de enfermedad) remission **3** (Relig, Der) remission

remite *m* (persona) sender; (dirección) return address

remitente *mf* sender

remitir [I1] *vt* **(a)** (frml) (mandar) to send **(b)** ⟨lector/estudiante⟩ ∼ **A algn A algo** to refer sb **TO** sth
■ ∼ *vi* «fiebre» to drop, go down; «tormenta» to abate, subside
■ **remitirse** *v pron* ∼**se A algo** ⟨a obra⟩ to refer **TO** sth

remo *m* (con soporte) oar; (sin soporte) paddle

remodelación *f* (Arquit) remodeling*, redesigning; (de organización) reorganization, restructuring; (del gabinete) (Pol) reshuffle

remodelar [A1] *vt* ⟨plaza/barrio⟩ to remodel, redesign; ⟨organización⟩ to reorganize; ⟨gabinete⟩ to reshuffle

remojar [A1] *vt* ⟨ropa/lentejas⟩ to soak

remojo *m* (en agua): **poner algo a** *or* **en ∼** to put sth to soak; **dejar algo en ∼** to leave sth to soak

remojón *m* **1** (fam) (en agua) soaking, drenching; **¿quién quiere darse un ∼?** who's for a dip? (colloq) **2** (Méx fam) (de algo nuevo): **nos dio el ∼** (en el coche) he took us for a spin in his new car; (en la casa) he had us over for a housewarming party

remolacha *f* beet (AmE), beetroot (BrE); ∼ **azucarera** sugar beet

remolcador *m* (Náut) tug; (Auto) tow truck (AmE), breakdown van (BrE)

remolcar [A2] *vt* ⟨barco⟩ to tug; ⟨coche⟩ to tow

remolino *m* **(a)** (de viento) eddy, whirl **(b)** (de agua) eddy; (más violento) whirlpool **(c)** (en el pelo) cowlick

remolón -lona *adj* (fam) idle, lazy
■ *m,f* (fam) slacker (colloq)

remolque *m* **(a)** (vehículo) trailer **(b)** (acción) towing; **ir a ∼** (Auto) to be in tow **(c)** (AmS) (grúa) tow truck (AmE), breakdown van (BrE)

remontar [A1] *vt* **1** ⟨dificultad/problema⟩ to overcome, surmount (frml) **2 (a)** ∼ **el vuelo** «avión» to gain height; «pájaro» to fly *o* soar up **(b)** ∼ **el río** to go upriver **(c)** (RPl) ⟨barrilete⟩ to fly
■ **remontarse** *v pron* **1** «avión» to gain height; «pájaro» to soar up **2** (en el tiempo) to go back

remorder [E9] *vi* (+ me/te/le *etc*): **me remuerde haberlo dicho** I feel guilty for having said it; **¿no te remuerde la conciencia?** don't you feel guilty?

remordimiento *m* remorse; **sentir** *or* **tener ∼s de conciencia** to suffer pangs of conscience

remoto -ta *adj* **(a)** ⟨tiempo/época⟩ distant, far-off (*before n*) **(b)** ⟨lugar/mares/tierras⟩ remote, far-off **(c)** ⟨posibilidad⟩ remote, slim; ⟨esperanza⟩ faint; **no tengo (ni) la más remota idea** I haven't the remotest *o* faintest idea

remover [E9] *vt* **1 (a)** ⟨líquido/salsa⟩ to stir; ⟨ensalada⟩ to toss; ⟨tierra/piedras⟩ to turn over; ⟨escombros⟩ to dig about in; ⟨brasas⟩ to poke, stir **(b)** ⟨asunto⟩ to bring ... up again; ⟨pasado⟩ to revive, stir up **2** (frml) **(a)** ⟨impedimento/obstáculo⟩ to remove **(b)** (esp AmL) (destituir) ∼ **A algn DE algo** to remove sb **FROM** sth

remunerar [A1] *vt* to pay, remunerate (frml)

renacentista *adj* Renaissance (*before n*)

renacer [E3] *vi* to be reborn; **sentí ∼ la esperanza** I felt renewed hope

renacimiento *m* **(a)** (acción) revival, rebirth **(b)** (Art, Hist) **el R∼** the Renaissance

renacuajo *m* (Zool) tadpole; (niño, persona baja) (fam) shrimp (colloq)

rencilla *f* quarrel, row

rencor *m* resentment; **con el corazón lleno de** ····⟶

~ with his heart full of resentment; **no te guardo** ~ **I don't bear you any grudge; siento** ~ **por lo que me hizo** I feel bitter about what he did to me

rencoroso -sa *adj* [SER] resentful

rendición *f* surrender

rendido -da *adj* [ESTAR] (exhausto) exhausted; **cayó** ~ **(de cansancio)** he collapsed from exhaustion; *ver tb* RENDIR

rendidor -dora *adj* (AmL) ⟨*tierra*⟩ productive; **un detergente** ~ a detergent that goes a long way

rendija *f* (grieta) crack, crevice; (hueco) gap

rendimiento *m* **(a)** (de persona, coche) performance **(b)** (de máquina, factoría) output; **funciona a pleno** ~ it is working at full capacity **(c)** (de terreno) yield **(d)** (Fin) yield, return

rendir [I14] *vt* **1** ⟨*homenaje/tributo*⟩ to pay; ~**le culto a algn** to worship sb **2** (Fin) to yield; (producir) to produce **3** ⟨*persona*⟩: **me rindió el sueño** I was overcome by sleep; **tanto trabajo rinde a cualquiera** working that hard is enough to exhaust anyone **4** (CS) (Educ) ⟨*examen*⟩ to take, sit (BrE)

■ ~ *vi* **(a)** (cundir) (+ *me/te/le etc*): **me rindió mucho la mañana** I had a lot done this morning; **trabaja mucho pero no le rinde** he works hard but he doesn't make much headway **(b)** «*alumno/obrero/empleado*» to perform well **(c)** «*tela/arroz/jabón*» to go a long way

■ **rendirse** *v pron* (en pelea, guerra) to surrender; (en tarea, adivinanza) to give up

renegado -da *m,f* renegade

renegar [A7] *vi* **(a)** (Relig) to apostatize; ~ **DE algo** ⟨*de creencias/principios*⟩ to renounce sth **(b)** (maldecir) to swear, curse; (blasfemar) to blaspheme **(c)** (refunfuñar) to grumble; ~ **DE algo** to grumble ABOUT sth **(d)** (AmL) (enojarse) to get annoyed

RENFE /'rrenfe/ *f* = **Red Nacional de los Ferrocarriles Españoles**

renglón *m* (línea) line

rengo -ga *adj* (AmL) lame
■ *m,f* (AmL) lame person, cripple (pej)

renguear [A1] *vi* (AmL) to limp

renguera *f* (AmL) limp

reno *m* reindeer

renombrado -da *adj* well-known, renowned

renombre *m* renown; **de** ~ renowned

renovación *f* **(a)** (de pasaporte, contrato) renewal **(b)** (del mobiliario) complete change; (de edificio, barrio) renovation **(c)** (de organización, sistema) updating **(d)** (reanudación) renewal

renovar [A10] *vt* **(a)** ⟨*pasaporte/contrato*⟩ to renew **(b)** ⟨*mobiliario*⟩ to change; ⟨*edificio/barrio*⟩ to renovate **(c)** ⟨*organización/sistema*⟩ to update, bring up to date **(d)** ⟨*ataque/esperanza/promesa*⟩ to renew

■ **renovarse** *v pron* **(a)** «*sospechas/dolor/interés*» to be renewed **(b)** «*persona*» to be revitalized

renta *f* **(a)** (beneficio) income; **inversiones de** ~

fija fixed interest investments; **vivir de las** ~**s** (de dinero) to live off the interest; (de propiedades) to live off the rent **(b)** (esp Méx) (alquiler) rent

rentabilidad *f* profitability

rentable *adj* ⟨*inversión/negocio*⟩ profitable

rentar [A1] *vt* (Méx) **(a)** ⟨*departamento*⟩ «*propietario*» to rent out, let (BrE); «*usuario*» to rent **(b)** ⟨*coche*⟩ to rent, hire (BrE)

renuncia *f* **1** (dimisión) resignation; **presentar la** ~ to resign, tender one's resignation (fml) **2** (abandono) ~ **A** algo renunciation OF sth **3** (abnegación) self-sacrifice

renunciar [A1] *vi* (dimitir) to resign; ~ **A algo** ⟨*a puesto*⟩ to resign sth; ⟨*a derecho*⟩ to relinquish sth, renounce sth (fml); ⟨*a título*⟩ to give up sth, relinquish sth; ⟨*a trono*⟩ to renounce sth

reñido -da *adj* **1** ⟨*partido/batalla*⟩ hard-fought, tough **2** [ESTAR] **(a)** (peleado): **está** ~ **con su novia** he has fallen out with his girlfriend (colloq) **(b)** (en contradicción) ~ **CON algo** ⟨*con principios*⟩ against sth

reñir [I15] *vi* (esp Esp) **(a)** (discutir) to argue, quarrel **(b)** ~ **CON algn** (pelearse) to quarrel *o* have a row WITH sb; (enemistarse) to fall out WITH sb

■ ~ *vt* (Esp) (regañar) to scold, tell ... off (colloq)

reo *mf* (en lo penal — acusado) accused, defendant; (— condenado) convicted offender; (en lo civil) (Méx) defendant

reojo: **de reojo** (*loc adv*): **mirar a algn de** ~ to look at sb out of the corner of one's eye

reorganizar [A4] *vt* to reorganize

reparación *f* **(a)** (arreglo) repair; **taller de reparaciones** repair shop **(b)** (de daño, ofensa) redress, reparation

reparador -dora *adj* ⟨*sueño/descanso*⟩ refreshing

reparar [A1] *vt* **(a)** ⟨*coche*⟩ to repair, fix; ⟨*gotera/avería*⟩ to mend, fix **(b)** ⟨*error*⟩ to correct, put right; ⟨*ofensa/agravio*⟩ to make amends for, make up for; ⟨*daño/perjuicio*⟩ to make good, compensate for

■ ~ *vi* **1** ~ **EN algo** (darse cuenta) to notice sth; (considerar): **no repara en gastos** she spares no expense **2** (Méx) «*caballo/toro*» to rear, shy

reparo *m* **(a)** (inconveniente, objeción): **pone** ~**s a todo** she finds fault with everything; **no tengo ningún** ~ **en decírselo** I have no qualms about telling him **(b)** (duda) reservation

repartición *f* **(a)** (división) distribution, share-out **(b)** (CS) (departamento, sección) department; (del ejército) division

repartidor -dora *m,f* (*m*) delivery man; (*f*) delivery woman; (de periódicos) newspaper man (*o* boy *etc*)

repartir [I1] *vt* **(a)** ⟨*ganancias/trabajo*⟩ to distribute, share out **(b)** ⟨*panfletos/propaganda*⟩ to hand out, give out; ⟨*periódicos/correo*⟩ to deliver; ⟨*naipes/fichas*⟩ to deal **(c)** (esparcir) to spread, distribute

■ ~ *vi* (Jueg) to deal

reparto *m* ① (a) (distribución) distribution; (entre socios, herederos) share-out; **~ de premios** prize-giving (b) (servicio de entrega) delivery; **~ a domicilio** delivery service ② (Cin, Teatr) cast

repasador *m* (RPI) dish towel (AmE), tea towel (BrE)

repasar [A1] *vt* ‹lección/tema› to review (AmE), to revise (BrE); ‹lista/cuenta/carta› to go over, check
■ **~** *vi* to review (AmE), to revise (BrE)

repaso *m* (revisión — para aprender algo) review (AmE), revision (BrE); (— para detectar errores) check; **dio un ~ a sus apuntes** she went *o* looked over her notes

repatriado -da *m,f* repatriate

repatriar [A1 *or* A17] *vt* to repatriate

repelar [A1] *vi* (Méx fam) to grumble, to moan (BrE colloq)

repelente *adj* ‹persona› repulsive, repellent; ‹niño› obnoxious
■ *m* insect repellent

repeler [E1] *vt* ‹ataque/agresión› to repel, repulse (frml)
■ **~** *vi* (+ *me/te/le etc*): **las serpientes me repelen** I find snakes repellent *o* repulsive

repente: **de repente** (*loc adv*) (a) (de pronto) suddenly (b) (RPI, Per) (quizás) maybe, perhaps

repentino -na *adj* sudden

repentizar [A4] *vt/vi* to sight-read

repercusión *f* (consecuencia) repercussion

repercutir [I1] *vi* (a) «sonido» to reverberate (b) (afectar) **~ EN algo** to have an effect *o* an impact ON sth

repertorio *m* repertoire

repetición *f* (a) (de experimento, palabra) repetition; (de un sueño, fenómeno) recurrence (b) (de programa) repeat, rerun

repetido *adj* (a) ‹sello/disco›: **este lo tengo ~** I have two of these (b) (delante del n) ‹casos/avisos/intentos› repeated (before n)

repetir [I14] *vt* (a) ‹pregunta/explicación› to repeat; **¿me lo puedes ~?** could you repeat it, please?; **¡que no te lo tenga que volver a ~!** I don't let me have to tell you again! (b) ‹tarea› to do ... again; ‹programa› to repeat, rerun; ‹experimento/curso/asignatura› to repeat (c) ‹plato› to have a second helping of, to have seconds of (colloq)
■ **~** *vi* ① (volver a comer) to have a second helping, to have seconds (colloq)
② «pimientos/pepinos» to repeat; **el ajo me repite** garlic repeats on me
③ (Educ) to repeat a year/course
■ **repetirse** *v pron* (a) «fenómeno/incidente/sueño» to recur, happen again; «persona» to repeat oneself (b) (Chi) (volver a comer) to have a second helping, have seconds (colloq)

repetitivo -va *adj* repetitive

repicar [A2] *vi* to ring out, peal

repiquetear [A1] *vi* (a) «campanas» to peal, ring out (b) (golpear) «lluvia» to patter; **~ con los dedos en la mesa** to drum *o* tap one's fingers on the table

repiqueteo *m* (a) (de campanas) ringing, pealing (b) (de lluvia) pattering, pitter-patter (colloq); (con los dedos) drumming, tapping

repisa *f* (estante) shelf; (de chimenea) mantelpiece

repita, repitas, etc ▶ REPETIR

repleto -ta *adj* (a) ‹calle/vehículo/sala› **~ DE algo** full OF sth, packed WITH sth; **el tren iba ~** the train was packed *o* (colloq) jam-packed (b) ‹persona› replete (frml *o* hum), full

réplica *f* (a) (copia) replica (b) (Chi, Méx) (de terremoto) aftershock

replicar [A2] *vt* (frml) to retort, reply
■ **~** *vi* ① (argumentar) to argue ② (Der) to reply

repoblar [A10] *vt* (a) ‹río/lago› to restock (b) (de árboles) to reforest (c) (de personas) to repopulate, resettle

repollo *m* cabbage

reponer [E22] *vt* (a) (reemplazar) ‹existencias› to replace; ‹dinero› to put back, repay; **~ fuerzas** to get one's strength back (b) ‹funcionario/trabajador› to reinstate (c) ‹obra› to put ... on again, revive; ‹serie› to repeat, rerun; ‹película› to show ... again
■ **reponerse** *v pron* to recover

reportaje *m* (en periódico, revista) article, feature; (en televisión) report, item; (entrevista) (AmL) interview

reportar [A1] *vt* ① ‹beneficios/pérdidas› to produce, yield; **solo me reportó disgustos** it brought *o* caused me nothing but trouble ② (AmL) (denunciar, dar cuenta de) to report ③ (Méx) ▶ REPORTEAR
■ **reportarse** *v pron* (AmL) (presentarse) to report

reporte *m* (Méx) (informe) report; (queja) complaint

reportear [A1] *vt* (Andes) to cover, report on
■ **~** *vi* (Andes) to report

reportero -ra *m,f* reporter; **~ gráfico** press photographer

reposacabezas *m* (*pl* **~**) headrest

reposado -da *adj* [SER] ‹persona/temperamento› calm; ‹ademanes/habla› unhurried

reposar [A1] *vi* (a) (descansar) «persona» to rest; «restos mortales» to lie (b) «líquido/solución» to settle; **dejar ~ la masa** let the dough stand

reposición *f* (a) (reemplazo) replacement (b) (de serie) repeat, rerun; (de obra) revival; (de película) reshowing

reposo *m* (a) (descanso) rest (b) (Coc): **dejar en ~** leave to stand

repostar [A1] *vt* ‹gasolina› to fill up with; ‹provisiones› to stock up with
■ **~** *vi* (Auto) to fill up, to get some gas (AmE) *o* (BrE) petrol; (Aviac, Náut) to refuel

repostería *f* confectionery, baking (*of pastries, desserts*)

repostero -ra *m,f* (persona) confectioner, pastrycook

reprender [E1] *vt* to scold, tell ... off (colloq)

represa *f* (a) (en río — dique) dam; (— embalse) reservoir (b) (de molino) millpond

represalia *f* reprisal; **como ~ por ...** in retaliation for ...

representación *f* ① (acción) representation; **~ legal** legal representation; **asistió en ~ del Rey** she attended as the King's representative; **en ~** ···🢒

de mis **compañeros** on behalf of my companions
② (delegación) delegation ③ (Teatr) performance,
production ④ (símbolo) representation

representante *mf* representative; (de artista,
cantante) agent; **es** ~ **de una editorial** she
represents a publishing house

representar [A1] *vt* ① ⟨*persona/
organización/país*⟩ to represent ② ⟨*obra*⟩ to
perform, put on; ⟨*papel*⟩ to play ③ (aparentar) to
look; **no representa su edad** he doesn't look his
age ④ (simbolizar) to represent, symbolize
⑤ (reproducir) ⟨*dibujo/fotografía/escena*⟩⟩ to show,
depict; ⟨⟨*obra/novela*⟩⟩ to portray, depict
⑥ (equivaler a, significar) to represent; **esto
representa un aumento del 5%** this represents a
5% increase; **eso** ~**ía tres días de trabajo** that
would mean *o* involve three days' work

representativo -va *adj* representative

represión *f* repression

reprimenda *f* reprimand

reprimido -da *adj* repressed
■ *m,f*: **es un** ~ he's repressed

reprimir [I1] *vt* (a) ⟨*rebelión*⟩ to suppress,
crush (b) ⟨*risa/llanto/bostezo*⟩ to suppress, stifle
(c) (Psic) to repress
■ **reprimirse** *v pron* (refl) to control oneself

reprobar [A10] *vt* (a) ⟨*actitud/conducta*⟩ to
condemn (b) (AmL) ⟨*estudiante/materia/curso*⟩ to
fail; **me** ~**on en física** I failed physics

reprochar [A1] *vt* to reproach; ~**le algo a algn**
to reproach sb for sth

reproche *m* reproach; **hacerle** ~**s a algn** to
reproach sb

reproducción *f* reproduction

reproducir [I6] *vt* to reproduce
■ **reproducirse** *v pron* (a) (Biol, Bot) to
reproduce, breed (b) ⟨⟨*fenómeno*⟩⟩ to recur,
happen again

reproductor -tora *adj* ⟨*animal*⟩ breeding
(*before n*); ⟨*órgano*⟩ reproductive

reptar [A1] *vi* ⟨⟨*serpiente*⟩⟩ to slither;
⟨⟨*cocodrilo*⟩⟩ to crawl, slide

reptil *m* reptile

república *f* republic

República Dominicana *f* Dominican
Republic

republicano -na *adj/m,f* republican

República Oriental del Uruguay *f*
(frml) *official name of Uruguay*

repudiar [A1] *vt* ① ⟨*atentado/violencia*⟩ to
condemn ② (Der) ⟨*mujer*⟩ to disown, repudiate
(frml); ⟨*herencia*⟩ to repudiate

repuesto *m* (pieza) (spare) part; **de** ~ spare
(*before n*)

repugnancia *f*: **me causa** ~ I find him
repulsive *o* repugnant; **siento** ~ **hacia las
culebras** I find snakes repulsive

repugnante *adj* ⟨*olor*⟩ disgusting, revolting;
⟨*crimen*⟩ abhorrent, repugnant; ⟨*persona*⟩
(físicamente) repulsive, revolting; (moralmente)
repugnant

repugnar [A1] *vi*: **me repugna beber de un
vaso sucio** I find having to drink out of a dirty
glass disgusting; **me repugna su comportamiento**
I find his behavior disgusting *o* repulsive

repulsa *f* (condena) condemnation; (rechazo)
rejection

repulsivo -va *adj* ⟨*persona*⟩ (físicamente)
repulsive, revolting; (moralmente) repugnant; ⟨*olor*⟩
disgusting, revolting

reputación *f* reputation; ~ **de algo** reputation
as sth

requerir [I11] *vt* (a) (necesitar) to require (b)
⟨*documento*⟩ to require; ⟨*persona*⟩ to summon

requesón *m* curd (cheese)

requisar [A1] *vt* (a) (expropiar) ⟨*vehículo/
suministros*⟩ to requisition; (confiscar) ⟨*drogas/
objetos robados*⟩ to seize (b) (Col, Ven) (registrar) to
search

requisito *m* requirement; **reunir los** ~**s** to
fulfill *o* meet the requirements; ~ **previo**
prerequisite

res *f* (a) (animal) animal (b) (Col, Méx, Ven) (Coc) *tb*
carne de ~ beef

resaca *f* ① (de las olas) undertow ② (después de
beber) hangover

resaltador *m* (Col) highlighter

resaltante *adj* (AmL) outstanding

resaltar [A1] *vi* (sobresalir, destacarse) to stand
out; **hacer** ~ ⟨*color*⟩ to bring out; ⟨*importancia/
necesidad*⟩ to highlight, stress
■ ~ *vt* ⟨*cualidad/importancia/necesidad*⟩ to
highlight

resarcir [I4] *vt* ~ **a algn DE algo** ⟨*de daños/
inconvenientes*⟩ to compensate sb FOR sth; ⟨*de
gastos*⟩ to reimburse sb for sth
■ **resarcirse** *v pron* ~**se DE algo** (desquitarse) to
get one's own back FOR sth; (compensar) to make
up FOR sth

resbalada *f* (AmL) slip

resbaladilla *f* (Méx) slide, chute

resbaladizo -za *adj* (a) ⟨*superficie/carretera*⟩
slippery (b) ⟨*asunto/tema*⟩ delicate, tricky (colloq)

resbalar [A1] *vi* ① (caerse) to slip; **las lágrimas
le resbalaban por las mejillas** the tears ran *o*
trickled down his cheeks ② (fam) (ser indiferente):
todo lo que le digas le resbala anything you say
to him is just like water off a duck's back (colloq);
todo le resbala he couldn't care less about
anything (colloq)
■ **resbalarse** *v pron* (caerse) to slip

resbalín *m* (Chi) slide, chute

resbalón *m* slip

resbaloso -sa *adj* (AmL) ⟨*superficie*⟩ slippery

rescatar [A1] *vt* (a) (salvar) to rescue (b)
⟨*dinero/pulsera*⟩ to recover, get back

rescate *m* (a) (salvamento) rescue; **equipo de** ~
rescue team (b) (precio) ransom (c) (de dinero, joya)
recovery

rescoldo *m* embers (*pl*)

resecar [A2] *vt* ⟨*piel/ambiente*⟩ to make ... very
dry
■ **resecarse** *v pron* to dry up, get very dry

reseco -ca *adj* ⟨*planta*⟩ dried-up; ⟨*pan*⟩ dry;
⟨*tierra/garganta*⟩ parched

resentido -da *adj* (a) (dolorido) painful (b)
(disgustado) upset, hurt; (con rencor) resentful
■ *m,f*: **es un** ~ he has a chip on his shoulder

resentimiento *m* resentment, bitterness

resentirse [I11] *v pron* (a) (sentir dolor): **aún se
resiente de la lesión** he is still suffering the

effects of the injury; **aún se resienten de la derrota** they're still smarting from the defeat **(b)** (sufrir las consecuencias) «*salud/trabajo*» to suffer **(c)** (ofenderse, molestarse) to get upset

reseña *f* **(a)** (de congreso, reunión) summary, report; (de libro) review; **una ~ biográfica** a biographical outline **(b)** (descripción) description; (sobre escritor, deportista) profile

reserva *f* **1** (de habitación, pasaje) reservation; (de mesa) booking, reservation; **¿tiene ~?** do you have a reservation?, have you booked? **2** (cantidad guardada) reserve; **tengo otro par de ~** I have a spare pair **3** **(a)** (Dep) (equipo) reserves (*pl*); reserve team; (conjunto de suplentes) substitutes (*pl*) **(b)** (de indígenas) reservation; (de animales) reserve; **~ natural** nature reserve **4** (secreto, discreción): **en la más absoluta ~** in the strictest confidence **5** **reservas** *fpl* **(a)** (dudas) reservations (*pl*) **(b)** (reparos): **habló sin ~s** he talked openly *o* freely **6** (Méx): **a ~ de que (no) llueva** as long as *o* provided (that) it doesn't rain
■ *mf* (Dep) reserve

reservación *f* (AmL) ▶ RESERVA 1

reservado -da *adj* «*persona/actitud*» reserved; «*asunto/tema*» confidential; *ver tb* RESERVAR

reservar [A1] *vt* **1** «*asiento/habitación/mesa*» to reserve, book; «*pasaje/billete*» to book **2** (guardar) «*porción de comida/dinero*» to set aside; **nos reservaba una sorpresa** he had a surprise in store for us; **reservó lo mejor para el final** she kept the best till last
■ **reservarse** *v pron* **(a)** (para sí mismo) «*porción/ porcentaje*» to keep ... for oneself; **~se la opinión** to reserve judgment **(b)** (*refl*) (para otra tarea) to save oneself

resfriado¹ -da *adj*: **estoy (algo) ~** I have a (slight) cold

resfriado² *m* cold

resfriarse [A17] *v pron* to catch a cold

resfrío *m* (esp AmS) cold

resguardar [A1] *vt* **~ algo/a algn DE algo** «*de peligro/frío*» to protect sth/sb FROM sth
■ **resguardarse** *v pron* (de peligro) to protect oneself; (de la lluvia, el frío) to shelter, take shelter

resguardo *m* **1** (Esp) (de depósito) deposit slip; (en tintorería, zapatería) slip, ticket **2** (Col) (reserva) reservation, reserve **3** (Méx) (control, vigilancia) control

residencia *f* **1** **(a)** (en país, ciudad) residence; **fijar ~** to take up residence **(b)** (documento) *tb* **permiso de ~** residence permit **2** **(a)** (casa) residence **(b)** (de estudiantes) dormitory (AmE), hall of residence (BrE); (de enfermeras) hostel, home; **~ de ancianos** old people's home **(c)** (hostal, fonda) boarding house, guest house (*not providing meals*) **3** (AmL) (Med) residency (AmE), time spent as a houseman (BrE)

residencial *adj* residential
■ *f* (CS) guest house, boarding house

residente *adj* resident
■ *m,f* **(a)** (en país) resident **(b)** (médico) resident (AmE), houseman (BrE)

residir [I1] *vi* **(a)** «*persona*» to live, reside (frml) **(b)** «*encanto/interés*» (radicar) **~ EN algo** to lie IN sth

residuo *m* **(a)** (Mat) remainder; (Quím) residue **(b)** **residuos** *mpl* (desperdicios) waste, waste materials *o* products (*pl*); **~s radiactivos** radioactive waste

resignación *f* resignation

resignado -da *adj* resigned; **~ A algo** resigned TO sth

resignarse [A1] *v pron* to resign oneself; **~ a hacer algo** to resign oneself to doing sth

resina *f* resin

resistencia *f* **1** **(a)** (en general) resistance **(b)** (aguante físico) stamina; **prueba de ~** endurance test **2** (componente de circuito) resistor; (de secador, calentador) element

resistente *adj* «*material/metal*» resistant, tough; «*tela*» tough, hard-wearing; «*persona/ animal/planta*» tough, hardy; **~ al calor** heat-resistant

resistir [I1] *vt* **(a)** (aguantar) «*dolor/calor/ presión*» to withstand, take; **no la resisto** (Col, Per fam) I can't stand her **(b)** «*tentación/impulso*» to resist **(c)** «*ataque/enemigo*» to resist
■ **~** *vi* **(a)** (aguantar) «*cuerda/puerta*» to hold; **ya no resisto más** I can't stand (it) any more **(b)** «*ejército*» to hold out, resist
■ **resistirse** *v pron* **(a)** (oponer resistencia) to resist **(b)** (tener reticencia): **se resiste a aceptarlo** she's unwilling *o* reluctant to agree to it; **me resisto a creerlo** I find it hard to believe

resolución *f* **1** (de problema) solution; (de conflicto) settlement, resolution **2** (decisión) decision; **tomar una ~** to make a decision; **tomaron la ~ de emigrar** they decided to emigrate **3** (determinación) determination, resolve

resolver [E11] *vt* **(a)** «*crimen/problema/ misterio*» to solve, clear up; «*asunto/conflicto*» to resolve, settle; «*duda*» to clear up; **tiene resuelto su futuro** his future is sorted out **(b)** (decidir) to decide

resonancia *f* (Mús, Fís) resonance; (eco) echo; (de noticia, suceso) impact

resonante *adj* «*sonido*» resonant; «*éxito*» resounding, tremendous

resonar [A10] *vi* **(a)** (hacer eco) to echo, resound **(b)** «*gritos/risas*» to ring (out)

resoplar [A1] *vi* (por cansancio) to puff; (por enfado) to snort

resoplido *m* **(a)** (de enfado) snort **(b)** (de cansancio): **dando ~s** puffing and panting **(c)** (de caballo) snort

resorte *m* **(a)** (muelle) spring **(b)** (AmC, Col, Méx) (elástico) elastic

resortera *f* (Méx) slingshot (AmE), catapult (BrE)

respaldar [A1] *vt* «*persona*» (apoyar) to support, back; (en discusión) to back up; «*propuesta/plan*» to support, back; «*versión/teoría*» to support, back up

respaldo *m* **(a)** (de asiento) back **(b)** (apoyo) support, backing; **en ~ de** in support of **(c)** (Fin) backing

respectar [A1] *vi* (en 3ª pers): **en** or **por lo que a mí respecta** as far as I'm concerned

respectivo -va *adj* (correspondiente) respective

respecto *m*: **a este ~** on this respect, in this regard (frml); (con) **~ a algo** regarding sth, with regard to sth

r

respetable adj (digno de respeto) respectable; (considerable) considerable

respetar [A1] vt (a) ⟨persona⟩ to respect; **se hizo ∼ por todos** he won o gained everyone's respect (b) ⟨opinión/tradiciones⟩ to respect; ⟨señal/luz roja⟩ to obey; ⟨ley/norma⟩ to observe

respeto m (a) (consideración, deferencia) respect; **con ∼** respectfully, with respect; **por ∼ a algn/algo** out of consideration o respect for sb/sth; **faltarle al** or **CS el ∼ a algn** to be rude o disrespectful to sb; **presentaron sus ∼s a …** they paid their repects to … (frml) (b) (temor): **su presencia impone ∼** her presence commands (a feeling of) respect; **les tengo mucho ∼ a los perros** I have a healthy respect for dogs

respetuoso -sa adj ⟨persona/silencio⟩ respectful

respingado -da adj (AmL) ⟨nariz⟩ turned-up

respingo m start; **dio un ∼** he gave a start

respingón -gona adj (a) ⟨nariz⟩ turned-up (b) (Méx fam) ⟨persona⟩ touchy

respiración f (Fisiol) breathing, respiration (frml); **me quedé sin ∼** I was out of breath; **contener la ∼** to hold one's breath; **∼ boca a boca** mouth-to-mouth resuscitation, kiss of life

respirar [A1] vi to breathe; **respire hondo** take a deep breath
■ ∼ vt (a) ⟨aire⟩ to breathe; ⟨humo/gases⟩ to breathe in (b) ⟨tranquilidad⟩: **la paz que se respira aquí** the feeling of peace that you get here

respiratorio -ria adj respiratory

respiro m (descanso) break; **tomarse un ∼** to take a break o (colloq) have a breather

resplandecer [E3] vi «sol» to shine; «luna/metal/cristal» to gleam; «hoguera» to blaze

resplandeciente adj (a) ⟨luna/metal/cristal⟩ gleaming; ⟨sol⟩ dazzling (b) (limpio) ⟨cocina/coche⟩ sparkling clean

resplandor m (del sol) glare, brightness; (de luna, metal, cristal) gleam; (de relámpago, explosión) flash

responder [E1] vi ① (a) (contestar) to reply, answer, respond (frml); **respondió con una evasiva** he gave an evasive reply (b) (replicar) to answer back
② (reaccionar) to respond; **∼ A algo** ⟨a amenaza/estímulo⟩ to respond TO sth
③ (corresponder): **no responden a la descripción** they do not answer the description; **las cifras no responden a la realidad** the figures do not reflect the true situation
④ (responsabilizarse): **si ocurre algo, yo no respondo** if anything happens I will not be held responsible; **∼ ante la justicia** to answer for one's acts in a court of law; **yo respondo de su integridad** I will vouch for his integrity; **no respondo de lo que hizo** I am not responsible for what he did; **∼ POR algn** to vouch FOR sb
■ ∼ vt (a) (contestar) to reply, answer (b) ⟨pregunta⟩ to answer (c) ⟨llamada/carta⟩ to answer, reply to

respondón -dona adj (fam) ⟨niño⟩ mouthy (AmE colloq), cheeky (BrE colloq)
■ m,f (fam): **es un ∼** he's always answering back

responsabilidad f responsibility; **un puesto de mucha ∼** a post which involves a great deal of responsibility; **tener sentido de la ∼** to have a sense of responsibility; **cargó con toda la ∼** she took full responsibility

responsabilizar [A4] vt **∼ a algn DE algo** to hold sb responsible o accountable FOR sth
■ **responsabilizarse** v pron to take responsibility; **∼se DE algo** ⟨de tarea/error/accidente⟩ to take responsibility FOR sth; ⟨de atentado⟩ to claim responsibility FOR sth; ⟨de delito⟩ to admit responsibility FOR sth

responsable adj [SER] (concienzudo) responsible; **∼ DE algo** ⟨de tarea/error⟩ responsible FOR sth; (culpable) responsible FOR sth; ⟨de accidente/delito⟩ liable FOR sth; **nadie se ha hecho ∼ del atentado** no one has claimed responsibility for the attack
■ mf: **el ∼ de ventas** the person responsible for sales; **los ∼s serán castigados** those responsible will be punished

respuesta f (a) (a carta, mensaje) reply, answer, response (frml) (b) (reacción) response (c) (solución) answer, solution

resquebrajar [A1] vt ⟨loza/roca⟩ to crack; ⟨madera⟩ to split
■ **resquebrajarse** v pron «loza/roca» to crack; «madera» to split

resquicio m ① (grieta) crack; (abertura) gap ② (huella, resto) trace

resta f subtraction

restablecer [E3] vt ⟨relaciones/comunicaciones⟩ to re-establish; ⟨orden/democracia/normalidad⟩ to restore
■ **restablecerse** v pron to recover

restablecimiento m (de relaciones, comunicaciones) re-establishment; (de orden, paz) restoration; (de enfermo) recovery

restante adj remaining

restantes mpl/fpl: **los ∼s** the rest, the remainder

restar [A1] vt (a) (Mat) ⟨número⟩ to subtract, take away; **∼ algo DE algo** to take (away) o subtract sth FROM sth (b) ⟨gastos/cantidad⟩ to deduct, take away (c) (quitar): **∼le importancia a algo** to minimize o play down the importance of sth
■ ∼ vi ① (Mat) to subtract, take away ② (Esp) (Dep) to return (service)

restauración f restoration

restaurante m restaurant

restaurar [A1] vt to restore

resto m ① (a) (lo demás, lo que queda) **el ∼** the rest (b) (Mat) remainder ② **restos** mpl (humanos, arqueológicos) remains (pl); (de avión, barco siniestrado) wreckage; (de comida) leftovers (pl) ③ (Esp) (Dep) return (of service)

restregar [A7] vt ‹suelo› to scrub; ‹ropa› to rub, scrub
■ **restregarse** v pron (refl) ‹ojos/mejilla› to rub
restricción f restriction
restringido -da adj ‹libertad› restricted, limited; ‹posibilidades/cantidad› limited
restringir [I7] vt to restrict
resucitar [A1] vt (a) (Relig) to raise ... from the dead, to bring ... back to life (b) (Med) to resuscitate, revive (c) ‹costumbres/rencores› to revive, resurrect
■ ~ vi «persona» to rise (from the dead); «costumbre/grupo» to take on a new lease of life
resuelto -ta adj (a) [SER] ‹persona› decisive; **en tono** ~ decisively (b) [ESTAR] (decidido) determined, resolved (frml); ver tb RESOLVER
resultado m result; **como** ~ **de** as a result of; **mi idea dio** ~ my idea worked; **intentó convencerlo, pero sin** ~ she tried to persuade him, but without success o to no avail; ~ **final** (Dep) final score
resultar [A1] vi **1** (dar resultado) to work; **su idea no resultó** his idea didn't work (out) **2** (+ compl): **resulta más barato así** it works out cheaper this way; **me resulta simpático** I think he's very nice; **resultó ser un malentendido** it turned out to be o proved to be a misunderstanding; **resultó tal como lo planeamos** it turned out o worked out just as we planned **3** (en 3ª pers): **ahora resulta que era periodista** now it turns out that he was a journalist **4** (derivar) ~ EN algo to result IN sth, lead TO sth
resumen m summary; **hacer un** ~ **de un texto** to summarize a text; **en** ~ in short
resumidero m (AmL) drain
resumir [I1] vt (a) (condensar) ‹texto/libro› to summarize (b) (recapitular) ‹discurso/argumento› to sum up
■ ~ vi: **resumiendo ... in short ..., to sum up ...**
resurgir [I7] vi to reemerge
resurrección f resurrection
retachar [A1] vt (Méx fam) (a) ‹carta/trabajo› to reject, refuse to accept (b) (no dejar entrar): **nos** ~**on** they turned us away
■ ~ vi (Méx) «bala» to ricochet
retador -dora m,f (AmL) challenger
retaguardia f (Mil) rearguard
retahíla f string
retaliación f (AmL) retaliation
retar [A1] vt (a) (desafiar) to challenge (b) (CS) (regañar) to tell ... off (colloq), to scold
retardado -da adj **1** (Tec) delayed; **de apertura retardada** with time-delay lock **2** ‹persona› mentally handicapped o retarded
retardar [A1] vt (frenar) to delay, hold up, retard (tech); (posponer) to postpone
retén m (a) (patrulla) patrol; (pelotón) squad; (puesto de policía) police post (b) (Ven) (correccional) reformatory (AmE), remand home (BrE)
retener [E27] vt **1** (a) ‹datos/información› to keep back, withhold (b) ‹pasaporte/tarjeta› to retain (c) (Fin, Fisco) ‹dinero/cuota› to deduct, withhold **2** (a) «policía» ‹persona› to detain, hold (b) (hacer permanecer): **no te retendré mucho I**

won't keep you long **3** ‹calor/carga/líquidos› to retain **4** ‹atención/interés› to keep, retain **5** (recordar) to retain, keep ... in one's head
reticencia f (a) (renuencia) reluctance; **con** ~ reluctantly (b) (reserva) reticence
reticente adj (a) (reacio) reluctant (b) (reservado) reticent
retina f retina
retintín m (fam) (tonillo sarcástico) sarcastic tone of voice; **con** ~ sarcastically
retirada f (a) (en general) withdrawal (b) (Mil) retreat; **batirse en** ~ to retreat (c) (de actividad profesional) retirement (d) (de competición — antes de iniciarse) withdrawal; (— una vez iniciada) retirement
retirado -da adj **1** (a) ‹lugar/casa› remote, out-of-the-way; **una casa retirada de la calle** a house set back from the road; **un barrio** ~ **del centro** an outlying district (b) ‹vida› secluded, quiet **2** (jubilado) retired
retirar [A1] vt **1** (a) (quitar) to remove, take away; (apartar) to move away; **retiró la cacerola del fuego** he removed the saucepan from the heat; ~ **de la circulación** to withdraw from circulation (b) ‹cabeza/mano› to pull ... back (c) ‹embajador/tropas› to withdraw, pull out (d) (+ me/te/le etc) ‹apoyo› to withdraw; ‹pasaporte/carnet› to withdraw, take away **2** ‹afirmaciones/propuesta› to withdraw; **retiro lo dicho** I take back what I said **3** (de cuenta) ‹dinero› to withdraw
■ **retirarse** v pron **1** (a) (apartarse) to move back o away; (irse) to leave, withdraw (b) «ejército/tropas» to withdraw, pull out (c) (irse a dormir) to go to bed, retire (frml) **2** (jubilarse) to retire; (de competición — antes de iniciarse) to withdraw, pull out; (— una vez iniciada) to pull out
retiro m (a) (jubilación) retirement; (pensión) (retirement) pension (b) (AmL) (de fuerzas, empleados) withdrawal; (de apoyo, fondos) withdrawal
reto m (a) (desafío) challenge (b) (CS) (regañina) telling-off (colloq), scolding
retobar [A1] vi (Méx fam) to answer back
retocar [A2] vt ‹fotografía/maquillaje› to touch up, retouch
retoño m (Bot) shoot
retoque m: **dar los últimos** ~**s a algo** to put the final o the finishing touches to sth
retorcer [E10] vt to twist
■ **retorcerse** v pron **1** (a) (enrollarse) to become tangled (up) (b) «serpiente» to writhe (c) «persona»: ~**se de dolor** to writhe in agony; ▶ RISA **2** (refl) ‹manos› to wring
retorcido -da adj ‹persona/mente› twisted, devious; ‹estilo/argumento› convoluted, involved
retorcijón m (AmL) sharp pain (in the stomach or gut); **retorcijones de tripas** stomach cramps
retórico -ca adj rhetorical
retornable adj returnable; **no** ~ non-returnable
retornar [A1] vi/vt (frml o liter) to return
retorno m (frml o liter) (regreso, devolución) return; (viaje de regreso) return journey
retortijón m (Esp, Méx) ▶ RETORCIJÓN
retraído -da adj withdrawn, retiring (before n)

retransmisión *f* **(a)** (transmisión) transmission; ∼ **en directo** live broadcast *o* transmission **(b)** (repetición) repeat

retransmitir [I1] *vt* **(a)** (repetir) to repeat, rebroadcast (frml) **(b)** (Esp period) (Rad, TV) to broadcast

retrasado -da *adj* **(a)** [SER] (Med, Psic) mentally handicapped **(b)** [ESTAR] (en tarea, actividad): **está muy** ∼ **con respecto a los demás** he lags a long way behind the others; **están** ∼**s en los pagos** they are behind in their payments; **tengo trabajo** ∼ I have work to catch up on **(c)** ⟨país/sociedad⟩ backward **(d)** ⟨reloj⟩ slow
■ *m,f: tb* ∼ **mental** mentally handicapped person, (mentally) retarded person

retrasar [A1] *vt* **(a)** ⟨persona⟩ to make ... late; **el tráfico nos retrasó** we got held up in the traffic **(b)** ⟨producción/proceso⟩ to delay, hold up; **la niebla retrasó la salida del avión** the departure (of the plane) was delayed by fog **(c)** ⟨partida/fecha⟩ to postpone **(d)** ⟨reloj⟩ to put back
■ **retrasarse** *v pron* **(a)** (llegar tarde) to be late **(b)** «producción/trámite» to be delayed, be held up **(c)** (en trabajo, estudios, pagos) to fall behind; **se retrasó en presentarlo** she was late (in) submitting it **(d)** «reloj» to run slow

retraso *m* **(a)** (demora) delay; **viene con media hora de** ∼ it's (running) half an hour late; **llevamos un** ∼ **de dos meses sobre lo previsto** we're two months behind schedule **(b)** (de país) backwardness

retratar [A1] *vt* **(a)** (pintar) to paint a portrait of; (fotografiar) to photograph **(b)** ⟨realidad/costumbres⟩ to portray, depict

retrato *m* **(a)** (Art, Fot) portrait; **ser el vivo** ∼ **de algn** to be the (spitting) image of sb (colloq) **(b)** (descripción) depiction, portrayal

retreta *f* **1** (Mil) (toque) retreat **2** (AmL) (concierto) open-air concert

retribuir [I20] *vt* **(a)** ⟨esfuerzos/trabajo⟩ to pay **(b)** (recompensar) to reward **(c)** (AmL) ⟨favor⟩ to return

retroactivo -va *adj* retrospective, retroactive; **un aumento con efecto** ∼ **desde enero** an increase backdated to January

retroceder [E1] *vi* **(a)** «persona/coche» to go back, move back; «ejército» to withdraw, retreat **(b)** (volverse atrás) to back down

retroceso *m* **(a)** (movimiento hacia atrás) backward movement; (en plan, desarrollo) backward step **(b)** (de ejército) withdrawal, retreat **(c)** (Arm) recoil **(d)** (Ven) (Auto) reverse

retrógrado -da *adj* ⟨persona/actitud⟩ reactionary; ⟨planteamiento/idea⟩ retrograde
■ *m,f* reactionary

retroproyector *m* overhead projector

retrospectiva *f* retrospective

retrospectivo -va *adj* retrospective

retrovisor *m* (interior) (rear-view) mirror; (lateral) (wing) mirror

retumbar [A1] *vi* «voz/explosión» to boom; «eco» to resound; «paso» to echo; «trueno» to roll, boom; «habitación» to resound

reubicar [A2] *vt* (AmL) **(a)** ⟨trabajadores⟩ to relocate, redeploy; ⟨empresas⟩ to relocate;

⟨pobladores/damnificados⟩ to resettle **(b)** (cambiar de lugar) to put ... in a different place, change the position of

reuma, reúma *m or f* rheumatism

reumático -ca *adj* rheumatic

reunido -da *adj*: **estuvieron** ∼**s tres horas** the meeting lasted three hours; **está reunida** (Esp) she's in a meeting; *ver tb* REUNIR

reunificar [A2] *vt* ⟨nación⟩ to reunify; ⟨familia⟩ to reunite, bring together

reunión *f* **(a)** (para discutir algo) meeting; (de carácter social) gathering; (reencuentro) reunion **(b)** (de datos, información) gathering, collecting

reunir [I23] *vt* **1** ⟨cualidades/características⟩ to have; ⟨requisitos⟩ to satisfy, meet; ⟨condiciones⟩ to fulfill, satisfy **2** ⟨datos⟩ to gather; ⟨dinero/fondos⟩ to raise; ⟨información⟩ to gather together, collect **3** ⟨amigos/familia⟩ to get ... together; **reunió a los jefes de sección** he called a meeting of the heads of department
■ **reunirse** *v pron* «consejo/junta» to meet; «amigos/parientes» to get together; ∼**se CON algn** (encontrarse) to meet up WITH sb; (tener una reunión) to have a meeting WITH sb, meet WITH sb (AmE)

reutilizable *adj* reusable

reutilización *f* reuse, recycling

reutilizar [A4] *vt* to reuse

reválida *f* (RPI) validation

revalidación *f* **(a)** (Chi, Méx) (convalidación) validation **(b)** (Col, Ven) (del pasaporte) renewal

revalidar [A1] *vt* **1** ⟨campeonato/título⟩ to defend, win ... again; ⟨victoria⟩ to repeat **2** **(a)** (Chi, Méx) (convalidar) to validate **(b)** (Col, Ven) ⟨pasaporte⟩ to renew

revalorización *f* **(a)** (de una divisa) revaluation; (de una pensión) increase, adjustment **(b)** (de un activo) appreciation (frml), increase in value

revalorizar [A4] *vt* **(a)** ⟨moneda⟩ to revalue; ⟨pensiones⟩ to increase, adjust **(b)** ⟨sistema/situación⟩ to reassess
■ **revalorizarse** *v pron* «acciones/propiedad» to appreciate; «moneda» to gain in value

revancha *f* **(a)** (Dep, Jueg) return game **(b)** (desquite): **¡me tomaré la** ∼**!** I'll get my own back! (colloq)

revelación *f* **1** (de secreto, noticia) revelation, disclosure **2** (éxito, figura) revelation

revelado *m* developing

revelador -dora *adj* revealing

revelar [A1] *vt* **(a)** ⟨secreto/verdad⟩ to reveal **(b)** (Cin, Fot) to develop

revendedor -dora *m,f* (de entradas) scalper (AmE), ticket tout (BrE)

revender [E1] *vt* ⟨alimentos/artículos⟩ to resell; ⟨entradas⟩ to scalp (AmE), to tout (BrE); ⟨acciones⟩ to sell off

reventa *f* (de alimentos, artículos) resale; (de entradas) scalping (AmE), touting (BrE)

reventar [A5] *vi* **1** «globo» to burst, pop; «neumático» to blow out, burst; «ampolla/tubería» to burst; «ola» to break **2** **(a)** «persona» (uso hiperbólico): **si sigue comiendo así,**

va a ∼ if he carries on eating like that, he'll burst! **(b)** (fam) (irritar) to rile (colloq), to make ... mad (colloq); **me revienta cocinar** I hate cooking ■ ∼ *vt* ⟨globo/neumático⟩ to burst

■ **reventarse** *v pron* **(a)** «globo/tubería» ▶ REVENTAR *vi* 1 **(b)** (refl) ⟨grano⟩ to squeeze; ⟨ampolla⟩ to burst

reventón *m* ⒈ (de neumático) blowout; (de tubería) burst ⒉ (Méx fam) (fiesta) party

reverencia *f* (de hombre, niño) bow; (de mujer, niña) curtsy; **hacer una** ∼ «⟨hombre⟩» to bow; «⟨mujer⟩» to curtsy

reverendo -da *adj* **(a)** (Relig) reverend (before n) **(b)** (esp AmL fam) (como intensificador) (delante del n) ▶ SOBERANO 2

reversa *f* (Col, Méx) reverse; **meter** ∼ to put the car into reverse

reversible *adj* reversible

reverso *m* **(a)** (de papel, cuadro) back **(b)** (de moneda, medalla) reverse

revés *m* ⒈ **(a)** **el** ∼ (de prenda) the inside; (de tela) the back, the wrong side; (de papel, documento) the back **(b)** **al revés** (loc adv) (con lo de adelante atrás) back to front; (con lo de arriba abajo) upside down; (con lo de dentro fuera) inside out; **así no, va al** ∼ not that way, it goes the other way around o (BrE) round; **se puso los zapatos al** ∼ he put his shoes on the wrong feet; **todo lo entiende al** ∼ she's always getting the wrong end of the stick; **todo me sale al** ∼ nothing goes right for me; **saberse algo al** ∼ **y al derecho** to know sth (off) by heart ⒉ (Dep) backhand ⒊ (contratiempo) setback

revestir [I14] *vt* (cubrir) ⟨pared/suelo⟩ to cover; ⟨cable⟩ to sheathe, cover; ⟨tubería⟩ (con material aislante) to lag; **paredes revestidas de madera** wood-paneled walls

revienta, revientas, etc ▶ REVENTAR

revisación *f* (RPl) (Med, Odont) examination; (periódica) checkup

revisar [A1] *vt* **(a)** ⟨documento⟩ to go through, look through; ⟨traducción/cuenta⟩ to check, go through **(b)** ⟨criterio/doctrina/edición⟩ to revise **(c)** ⟨máquina/instalación/frenos⟩ to check; ⟨coche⟩ (hacer revisión periódica) (Esp) to service **(d)** (AmL) ⟨equipaje/bolsillos⟩ to search, go through **(e)** (AmL) ⟨paciente⟩ to examine; ⟨dentadura⟩ to check; **se hizo** ∼ **la dentadura** he had a dental checkup

revisión *f* **(a)** (de trabajo, documento) checking, check **(b)** (de criterio, doctrina) revision **(c)** (de instalación) inspection; (de frenos) check; (de coche) (Esp) service **(d)** (AmL) (de equipaje) inspection **(e)** (Med, Odont) checkup; ∼ **médica** (Esp) (periódica) checkup; (para trabajo) medical examination

revisor -sora *m,f* (Esp) ticket inspector

revista *f* **(a)** (publicación ilustrada) magazine; (de profesión) journal; ∼ **del corazón** real-life o true-romance magazine **(b)** (Espec, Teatr) revue; **teatro de** ∼ variety theater **(c)** (inspección) review; **pasar** ∼ **a las tropas** to inspect o review the troops

revistero *m* magazine rack

revitalizar [A4] *vt* to revitalize

revivir [I1] *vi* to revive ■ ∼ *vt* to relive

revocar [A2] *vt* ⒈ (Der) ⟨consentimiento/ testamento⟩ to revoke; ⟨fallo⟩ to reverse, revoke ⒉ (Const) ⟨pared interior⟩ to plaster; ⟨pared exterior⟩ to render

revolcar [A9] *vt*: **lo** ∼**on por el suelo** they knocked him to the ground and pushed him around ■ **revolcarse** *v pron* to roll around; (en lodo) to wallow, roll around

revolcón *m* (caída) tumble; (vuelta) roll

revolotear [A1] *vi* «⟨mariposa⟩» to flutter; «⟨polilla⟩» to flit; «⟨pájaro⟩» to flutter around; «⟨papeles/hojas⟩» to fly o swirl around

revoltijo, revoltillo *m* (fam) **(a)** (desorden) mess, jumble **(b)** (comida, bebida) mixture, concoction

revoltoso -sa *adj* ⟨niño⟩ naughty; ⟨soldados/ estudiantes⟩ rebellious

revolución *f* revolution

revolucionar [A1] *vt* **(a)** ⟨costumbres/ industria⟩ to revolutionize **(b)** ⟨niños⟩ to get ... excited; ⟨estudiantes/obreros⟩ to stir up

revolucionario -ria *adj/m,f* revolutionary

revolver [E11] *vt* **(a)** ⟨salsa/guiso⟩ to stir; **me revuelve el estómago** it turns my stomach **(b)** (AmL) ⟨dados⟩ to shake **(c)** ⟨cajones/papeles⟩ to rummage through, go through; «⟨ladrones⟩» ⟨casa⟩ to turn ... upside down ■ ∼ *vi*: **revolvió en mis cosas** he rummaged through my things

revólver *m* revolver

revuelo *m* (conmoción) stir

revuelta *f* **(a)** (de civiles) uprising; (de tropas) uprising, revolt; (de estudiantes, presos) riot **(b)** (jaleo) commotion, row (colloq)

revuelto¹ -ta *adj* **(a)** (desordenado) in a mess; ⟨pelo⟩ disheveled*; **tener el estómago** ∼ to feel sick o nauseous **(b)** ⟨mar⟩ rough; ⟨tiempo⟩ unsettled

revuelto² *m* vegetables sautéed with egg

rey *m* ⒈ **(a)** (monarca) king; **los R**∼**es de Suecia** the King and Queen of Sweden; **los R**∼**es y sus hijos** the royal couple and their children **(b)** (en ajedrez, naipes) king **(c)** (como apelativo) pet (colloq), precious (colloq) ⒉ **Reyes** Epiphany, January 6th; **Los R**∼**es Magos** the Three Wise Men, The Three Kings

rezagado -da *adj*: **quedar(se)** ∼ to fall o drop behind; **iban** ∼**s** they were lagging behind; **los alumnos más** ∼**s** the slower students

rezar [A4] *vi* (Relig) to pray; ∼ **POR algn/algo** to pray FOR sb/sth; **reza por que todo salga bien** pray that everything turns out all right ■ ∼ *vt* ⟨oración/rosario⟩ to say

rezo *m* prayer

rezongar [A3] *vi* to grumble ■ ∼ *vt* (AmC, Ur fam) (regañar) to tell ... off (colloq)

rezumar [A1] *vt/vi* to ooze

RFA *f* (= **República Federal de Alemania**) FRG

ría *f* ria (long, narrow, tidal inlet)

ría, rías, etc ▶ REÍR

riachuelo *m* stream, brook

riada *f* flood; (en área más extensa) flooding

ribera *f* **(a)** (orilla — de río) bank; (— de lago, mar) shore **(b)** (vega) strand, riverside

ribete *m* (adorno) trimming, edging

rico -ca *adj* ⓵ (a) ⟨*persona/país*⟩ rich, wealthy
(b) ⟨*tierra*⟩ rich; ⟨*vegetación*⟩ lush; ⟨*lenguaje/
historia*⟩ rich; ~ **EN** algo rich IN sth ⓶ (a)
⟨*comida*⟩ good, nice; ¡**esto está riquísimo!** this is
delicious! (b) (esp CS) ⟨*perfume*⟩ nice, lovely; ¡**qué
~ olor tiene!** what a lovely smell! (c) (fam) (mono)
⟨*niño/chica*⟩ lovely, cute (d) (AmL exc RPI)
(agradable) lovely, wonderful
■ *m,f* (a) (*m*) rich *o* wealthy man; (*f*) rich *o*
wealthy woman; **los ~s** rich people, the rich (b)
(como apelativo) (fam & iró) sweetie (colloq & iro),
honey (colloq & iro)

ricura *f* (fam): **tiene un bebé que es una ~** she
has the cutest little baby (colloq); **ven, ~** come
here, darling (colloq)

ridiculez *f* (a) (tontería, insignificancia): **lo que dijo
fue una ~** what he said was ridiculous; ¡**qué ~!**
that's ridiculous!; **pagué una ~ por esto** I paid
next to nothing for this (b) (cualidad)
ridiculousness

ridiculizar [A4] *vt* to ridicule

ridículo¹ -la *adj* (a) ⟨*persona/comentario/
vestimenta*⟩ ridiculous; **lo ~ de la situación era
que ...** the ridiculous thing about the situation
was that ...; **eso es ~** it's absurd *o* ridiculous (b)
⟨*cantidad/precios*⟩ ridiculous, ludicrous; ⟨*sueldo*⟩
ridiculous, laughable

ridículo² *m*: **sentido del ~** sense of the
ridiculous *o* absurd; **dejar** *or* **poner a algn en ~**
to make a fool of sb; **hacer el ~** to make a fool of
oneself

ríe, etc ▶ REÍR

riega, riegas, etc ▶ REGAR

riego *m* (a) (Agr) irrigation (b) **falta de ~
sanguíneo** insufficient blood supply

riel *m* rail

rienda *f* rein; **aflojar las ~s** to slacken the
reins; **llevar las ~s** to be in charge *o* control;
tomar las ~s to take charge

riesgo *m* risk; **un ~ para la salud** a health
hazard; **a ~ de perder su amistad** at the risk of
losing his friendship; **~s que hay que correr**
risks you have to take; **corres el ~ de perderlo**
you run the risk of losing it; **un seguro a** *or*
contra todo ~ an all-risks *o* a comprehensive
insurance policy

riesgoso -sa *adj* (AmL) risky

rifa *f* (sorteo) raffle, draw

rifar [A1] *vt* to raffle

rifle *m* rifle

rigidez *f* (a) (de material) stiffness, rigidity; (de
un miembro) stiffness (b) (de ley, doctrina, horario)
inflexibility; (de educación, dieta) strictness

rígido -da *adj* (a) ⟨*material*⟩ rigid, stiff (b)
⟨*educación/dieta*⟩ strict; ⟨*regla/horario/carácter*⟩
inflexible; ⟨*actitud*⟩ rigid, inflexible; ⟨*moral/
principios*⟩ strict

rigor *m* (en general) rigor*; (de medidas, castigo)
harshness, severity; **con todo el ~ de la ley** with

the full rigor of the law; **el ~ del invierno** the
rigors of winter; **con ~** rigorously, strictly; **los
saludos de ~** the usual greetings

riguroso -sa *adj* ⟨*método*⟩ rigorous; ⟨*dieta/
control/orden*⟩ strict; ⟨*examen*⟩ thorough;
rigurosas medidas de seguridad tight security (b)
⟨*juez*⟩ harsh; ⟨*maestro*⟩ strict; ⟨*castigo*⟩ severe,
harsh (c) ⟨*invierno*⟩ hard; ⟨*clima*⟩ harsh

rima *f* (de sonidos) rhyme

rimar [A1] *vi* to rhyme

rimbombante *adj* ⟨*estilo*⟩ grandiose,
overblown; ⟨*palabras*⟩ high-flown; ⟨*boda/fiesta*⟩
ostentatious, showy

rímel *m* mascara

rin *m* ⓵ (Col, Méx) (rueda) wheel; (llanta) rim
⓶ (Per) (teléfono) public telephone; (ficha)
(telephone) token

rincón *m* ⓵ (de habitación, armario) corner
⓶ (lugar) spot, place; **bellos rincones de Perú**
beautiful places *o* spots in Peru; **registraron hasta
el último ~ de la casa** they searched every nook
and cranny of the house

ring /rrin/ *m* (*pl* **rings**) (Dep) ring

rinoceronte *m* rhinoceros

riña *f* (a) (pelea) fight; **~ de gallos** (AmS)
cockfight (b) (discusión) quarrel, argument, row
(colloq)

riñón *m* (a) (Anat) kidney (b) (Coc) kidney (c)
riñones *mpl* (fam) (espalda baja) lower part of the
back, kidneys (*pl*)

río *m* river; **~ abajo/arriba** downstream/
upstream; **el R~ de la Plata** the River Plate

río, rio, etc ▶ REÍR

Río de Janeiro *m* Rio de Janeiro

rioplatense *adj* of/from the River Plate

riqueza *f* (a) (bienes) wealth; **las ~s del museo**
the treasures of the museum (b) (recursos): **las ~s
del suelo** the earth's riches; **las ~s naturales de
un país** a country's natural resources (c)
(variedad, abundancia) richness

risa *f* laugh; **una risita nerviosa** a nervous giggle
o laugh; ¡**qué ~!** what a laugh!, how funny!; **entre
las ~s del público** amid laughter from the
audience; **me entró la ~** I got the giggles; **da ~
oírla hablar** it's very funny hearing her talk;
morirse de (la) ~ (fam) to die laughing (colloq);
estábamos muertos de (la) ~ we were killing
ourselves laughing (colloq); **retorcerse de la ~** to
double up with laughter; **tomarse algo a ~** (fam)
to treat sth as a joke

risotada *f* guffaw

risueño -ña *adj* ⟨*cara/expresión*⟩ smiling;
⟨*persona*⟩ cheerful; ⟨*porvenir/perspectivas*⟩ bright

rítmico -ca *adj* rhythmic, rhythmical

ritmo *m* (a) (compás) rhythm; **al ~ de la música**
to the rhythm of the music, in time to the music;
llevaba el ~ con los pies he kept time with his
feet; **seguir el ~** to keep in time, follow the beat
(b) (velocidad) pace, speed; **llevan un buen ~ de**

trabajo they work at a steady pace o speed; **a este ~ no terminaremos nunca** at this rate we'll never finish; **el ~ de crecimiento** the rate of growth

rito m (Relig) rite; (costumbre) ritual

ritual adj/m ritual

rival adj rival (before n)
■ mf rival; **sin ~** unrivaled

rivalidad f rivalry

rizado -da adj ⟨pelo⟩ curly; ⟨mar⟩ slightly choppy

rizar [A4] vt ⟨pelo/melena⟩ to curl, perm
■ **rizarse** v pron **(a)** «pelo» (con la humedad) to frizz, go frizzy **(b)** (refl) ⟨pelo⟩ to curl

rizo m **(a)** (de pelo) curl **(b)** (Tex) bouclé **(c)** (Aviac) loop

róbalo m sea bass

robar [A1] vt ① **(a)** ⟨dinero/bolso⟩ to steal; ⟨banco⟩ to rob; **~le algo A algn** to steal sth FROM sb; **le robó dinero a su jefe** he stole some money from his boss; **le robaron el bolso** she had her bag stolen **(b)** (raptar) ⟨niño⟩ to abduct, kidnap ② (estafar) to cheat, rip off (colloq) ③ (Jueg) (en naipes, dominó) to draw, pick up (colloq)
■ ~ vi to steal; **~on en la casa de al lado** the house next door was broken into; **¡me han robado!** I've been robbed!

roble m (árbol) oak (tree); (madera) oak

robo m **(a)** (en banco, museo) robbery; (hurto de dinero, objeto) theft; **~ a mano armada** armed robbery **(b)** (en vivienda) burglary; (forzando la entrada) break-in **(c)** (fam) (estafa) rip-off (colloq)

robot m (pl **-bots**) robot; **~ de cocina** food processor

robustecer [E3] vt to strengthen
■ **robustecerse** v pron to become o grow stronger

robustez f robustness, sturdiness

robusto -ta adj ⟨árbol⟩ robust, strong; ⟨persona⟩ robust, sturdy; ⟨construcción⟩ sturdy

roca f rock

roce m **(a)** (contacto) rubbing; (fricción) friction; **no soporta el ~ de la sábana** he can't bear the sheet rubbing against his skin; **el ~ de su mejilla** the brush of her cheek; **tiene los puños gastados por el ~** his cuffs are worn **(b)** (trato frecuente) regular contact **(c)** (desacuerdo): **~s dentro del partido** friction within the party; **tener un ~ con algn** to have a brush with sb

rociar [A17] vt (con pulverizador) to spray; **lo ~on de keroseno** they doused it with kerosene; **rocíelo con limón** sprinkle with lemon

rocío m dew; **una gota de ~** a dewdrop

rock adj inv rock (before n)
■ m rock music; **~ duro** or **pesado** hard rock

rockero -ra adj ⟨grupo/ambiente⟩ rock (before n)
■ m,f rock artist o musician, rocker (colloq)

rocola f (AmL) jukebox

rocoso -sa adj rocky

rocote, rocoto m (AmS) hot pepper

rodaballo m turbot

rodachina f (Col) caster, roller

rodaja f slice; **en ~s** sliced

rodaje m **(a)** (Cin) filming, shooting **(b)** (Auto) breaking-in (AmE), running-in (BrE); **estar en ~** to be breaking in (AmE) o (BrE) running in

rodapié m baseboard (AmE), skirting board (BrE)

rodar [A10] vi ① «moneda/pelota» to roll; «rueda» to go round, turn; **la moneda rodó por la mesa** the coin rolled across the table; **rodó escaleras abajo** she went tumbling down the stairs ② (Cin) to film, shoot; **¡se rueda!** action!
■ ~ vt (Cin) to shoot, film

rodeado -da adj **~ DE algo** surrounded BY sth

rodear [A1] vt **(a)** ⟨edificio/persona⟩ to surround; **~ algo DE algo** to surround sth WITH sth; **las circunstancias que ~on su muerte** the circumstances surrounding his death; **le rodeó la cintura con los brazos** he put his arms around her waist **(b)** (AmL) ⟨ganado⟩ to round up ② (estar alrededor de) to surround; **todos los que lo rodean** everyone who works with him/knows him
■ **rodearse** v pron **~se DE algo/algn** to surround oneself WITH sth/sb

rodeo m **(a)** (desvío) detour; **dar un ~** to make a detour; **andarse con ~s** to beat about the bush **(b)** (Espec) rodeo

rodilla f knee; **ponerse de ~s** to kneel down, to get down on one's knees

rodillera f **(a)** (Dep) kneepad; (Med) knee bandage **(b)** (parche) knee patch

rodillo m (de cocina) rolling pin; (para pintar) paint roller; (de máquina de escribir) roller, platen

roedor -dora m,f rodent

roer [E13] vt ⟨hueso/cable⟩ to gnaw (at)

rogar [A8] vt: **te lo ruego** I beg you; **se ruega no fumar** you are kindly requested not to smoke; **te ruego que me perdones** please forgive me; **le rogó que tuviera misericordia** she begged him to have mercy
■ ~ vi (Relig) to pray; **roguemos al Señor** let us pray; **hacerse (de)** or (Méx) (del) ~ to play hard to get; **aceptó sin hacerse (de) ~** he accepted immediately, without any persuading

rojizo -za adj reddish

rojo¹ -ja adj ① **(a)** ⟨color/vestido⟩ red; **ponerse ~** «persona» to blush, turn red; «semáforo» to turn red, go red (BrE); **ponerse ~ de ira** to turn o (BrE) go red with anger **(b)** ⟨piel⟩ (por el sol) sunburnt, red ② (pey o hum) (Pol) **(a)** (de izquierda) red (pej or hum), commie (pej or hum) **(b)** (en la Guerra Civil española) Republican
■ m,f (pey o hum) **(a)** (izquierdista) red (pej or hum), commie (pej or hum) **(b)** (en la Guerra Civil española) Republican

rojo² m red; **al ~ vivo** ⟨metal⟩ red-hot

rol m **(a)** (lista) roll, list **(b)** (papel) role

rolar [A1] vi (Méx fam) (dar vueltas) to wander around
■ ~ vt (Méx fam) ⟨persona⟩ to move

rolarse v pron (recípr) (Méx fam) (turnarse) to take turns; **tenemos que ~nos el libro** we have to take turns with the book o pass the book around

rollizo -za adj chubby

rollo m ① **(a)** (de papel, tela, película) roll **(b)** (de cable, cuerda) reel **(c)** (fam) (de gordura) roll of fat ② **(a)** (Esp fam) (cosa aburrida) bore; **¡qué ~ de conferencia!** what a boring lecture! **(b)** (Esp, Méx fam) (lata) nuisance, pain (colloq); **¡qué ~!** what a nuisance o pain! ③ (fam) **(a)** (perorata) speech (colloq), lecture

r

(colloq); **siempre nos suelta el mismo** ∼ he always gives us the same speech; **bueno, corta el** ∼ **ya** OK, can it, will you? (AmE colloq), OK, put a sock in it, will you? (BrE colloq) **(b)** (mentira) story **4** (Esp, Méx fam) (asunto) business

■ *adj inv* (Esp fam) boring; **¡qué tío más** ∼**!** that guy's such a pain *o* bore! (colloq)

Roma *f* Rome

romance *m* romance

románico -ca *adj* ⟨*arquitectura/columna*⟩ Romanesque; ⟨*lengua*⟩ Romance (*before n*)

romano -na *adj* (Hist) Roman; (de la ciudad) of/from Rome, Roman

■ *m,f* (Hist) Roman; (de la ciudad) person from Rome

romanticismo *m* (Art, Lit, Mús) Romanticism; (sentimentalismo) romanticism

romántico -ca *adj/m,f* (Art, Lit, Mús) Romantic; (sentimental) romantic

rombo *m* **(a)** (Mat) rhombus **(b)** (carta) diamond **(c) rombos** *mpl* (palo) diamonds (*pl*)

romería *f* **(a)** (Relig) procession (*to a local shrine, gen followed by festivities*) **(b)** (AmL fam) (multitud) mass, crowd

romero *m* (Bot, Coc) rosemary

rompecabezas *m* (*pl* ∼) puzzle

rompehielos *m* (*pl* ∼) icebreaker

rompeolas *m* (*pl* ∼) breakwater

romper [E30] *vt* **1 (a)** ⟨*loza/mueble*⟩ to break; ⟨*ventana*⟩ to break, smash; ⟨*lápiz/cuerda*⟩ to break, snap **(b)** ⟨*hoja/póster*⟩ to tear; (en varios pedazos) to tear up **(c)** ⟨*camisa*⟩ to tear, split **2 (a)** ⟨*silencio/monotonía*⟩ to break; ⟨*tranquilidad*⟩ to disturb **(b)** ⟨*promesa/pacto*⟩ to break; ⟨*relaciones/compromiso*⟩ to break off

■ ∼ *vi* **1 (a)** ⟨*olas*⟩ to break **(b)** (liter) ⟨*alba*⟩ to break; **al** ∼ **el día** at daybreak, at the crack of dawn **(c)** (empezar): **rompió a llorar/reír** she burst into tears/burst out laughing

2 ⟨*novios*⟩ to break up, split up; ∼ **CON algn** ⟨*con novio*⟩ to split *o* break up WITH sb; ∼ **CON algo** ⟨*con el pasado*⟩ to break WITH sth; ⟨*con tradición*⟩ to break away FROM sth

■ **romperse** *v pron* **(a)** ⟨*vaso/plato*⟩ to break, smash, get broken *o* smashed; ⟨*papel*⟩ to tear, rip, get torn *o* ripped; ⟨*televisor/ascensor*⟩ (RPI) to break down **(b)** ⟨*pantalones/zapatos*⟩ to wear out **(c)** (*refl*) ⟨*brazo/pierna*⟩ to break

rompevientos *m* (*pl* ∼) (Méx, RPI) (pulóver) sweater; (anorak) windbreaker (AmE), windcheater (BrE)

ron *m* **(a)** (bebida) rum **(b)** (Per) (combustible) methanol

roncar [A2] *vi* (al dormir) to snore; (dormir) (fam) to sleep

roncha *f* (Med) (por picadura de insecto) bump; **se llenó de** ∼**s** she came out in a rash

ronco -ca *adj* **(a)** ⟨*persona*⟩ hoarse; **se quedó** ∼ **de tanto gritar** he shouted himself hoarse **(b)** ⟨*voz*⟩ husky

ronda *f* **1** (de soldado, guarda) patrol; (de enfermera) round; (de policía) patrol, beat; **hacer la** ∼ «*policía*» to patrol one's beat; «*soldado/guarda*» to be on patrol; «*repartidor*» to do one's round **2** (vuelta, etapa) round; (de bebidas) round **3** (CS, Per) (de niños): **formaron una** ∼

tomándose de la mano they held hands in a circle; **danzaban en** ∼ they were dancing around in a circle **4** (Esp, Méx) (serenata) serenade

rondar [A1] *vt* **(a)** «*vigilante/patrulla*» to patrol **(b)** «*pensamiento*»: **hace días que me ronda esa idea** that idea has been going round and round in my head for days **(c)** ⟨*lugar*⟩ to hang around **(d)** (acercarse a): **debe estar rondando los 60** she must be getting on for 60

■ ∼ *vi* (merodear) to hang around

ronquido *m* snore

ronronear [A1] *vi* to purr

roña *f* **1 (a)** (mugre) dirt, grime; **lleno de** ∼ covered in dirt *o* grime **(b)** (en metal) rust **(c)** (Vet) mange **2** (Méx) (juego) tag; **jugar a la** ∼ to play tag

roñoso -sa *adj* **1** [ESTAR] **(a)** (mugriento) grubby **(b)** (oxidado) rusty **(c)** (Vet) mangy **2** [SER] (fam) (tacaño) tight-fisted (colloq), stingy (colloq)

■ *m,f* (fam) scrooge (colloq), skinflint (colloq)

ropa *f* clothes (*pl*); **cambiarse de** ∼ to get changed, to change (one's clothes); **la** ∼ **sucia** the dirty laundry; **tengo un montón de** ∼ **para planchar** I've got a stack of ironing to do; ∼ **interior** underwear, underclothes (*pl*)

ropero *m* wardrobe

roquero -ra *adj/m,f* ▶ ROCKERO

rosa *f* **(a)** (flor) rose **(b)** (rosal) rosebush **(c)** (Chi) (nudo) bow

■ *adj* (gen inv) pink; **un vestido (de color)** ∼ a pink dress; **verlo todo de color** ∼ to see things through rose-colored glasses *o* (BrE) rose-tinted spectacles

■ *m* pink

rosado -da *adj* **(a)** ⟨*color/vestido*⟩ pink **(b)** ⟨*mejillas*⟩ rosy; ⟨*vino*⟩ rosé

■ *m* **(a)** (color) pink **(b)** (vino) rosé

rosal *m* (árbol) rosetree; (arbusto) rosebush

rosario *m* **(a)** (Relig) (rezo) rosary; (cuentas) rosary (beads) **(b)** (serie, sarta) string

rosca *f* **(a)** (de tornillo, tuerca) thread; **tapón de** ∼ screw top; *pasarse de* ∼: **el tornillo se pasó de** ∼ the screw isn't biting; **te has pasado de** ∼ (fam) you've gone too far **(b)** (Bol, Col) (círculo, grupo) clique, set

rosedal *m* (CS, Méx) rose garden

roseta *f* (Arquit) rose, rosette; (de ducha) showerhead; (de regadera) spinkler (AmE), rose (BrE)

rosetón *m* (ventana) rose window, rosette; (en el techo) ceiling rose

rosquilla *f*: type of doughnut

rosticería *f* (Méx) ▶ ROTISERÍA

rostizar [A4] *vt* (Méx) to roast; **pollo rostizado** roast chicken

rostro *m* **(a)** (cara) face **(b)** (Esp fam) (desfachatez) nerve (colloq), cheek (BrE colloq)

rotación *f* rotation

rotar [A1] *vt/vi* to rotate

■ **rotarse** *v pron* (en trabajo) to work on a rota system; ∼**se para hacer algo** to take it in turns to do sth

rotativo *m* **(a)** (period) (diario) newspaper **(b)** (Chi) (Cin) movie theater (AmE), cinema (BrE) (*showing a continuous performance*)

rotería f (Chi) (fam) (hecho): **fue una ~ no invitarlo** it was incredibly rude not to invite him; **me hizo una ~** he was rude to me

rotisería f (CS) delicatessen selling spit-roast chickens

roto¹ -ta adj [1] (a) ‹camisa› torn, ripped; ‹zapato› worn-out (b) ‹vaso/plato/brazo› broken (c) ‹papel› torn; **me devolvió el libro ~** the book was falling apart when he gave it back to me (d) (RPl) ‹televisor/heladera› broken; ‹coche› broken down [2] (Chi fam & pey) (a) ‹barrio/gente› lower-class (pej), plebby (colloq & pej) (b) (mal educado) rude
■ m,f [1] (Chi) (a) (fam & pey) (de clase baja) pleb (colloq & pej) (b) (fam & pey) (mal educado): **es una rota, nunca saluda** she's so rude, she doesn't even say hello [2] (Per fam) (chileno) Chilean

roto² m (Esp) (agujero) hole

rotonda f (glorieta) traffic circle (AmE), roundabout (BrE)

rotoso -sa adj (CS, Per fam) ‹persona/ropa› scruffy (b) (Chi fam & pey) ‹barrio/gente› lower-class (pej)

rótula f (Anat) kneecap

rotulador m (Esp) felt-tip pen

rótulo m (a) (Impr) (título) title; (encabezamiento) heading (b) (etiqueta) label (c) (letrero) sign

rotundo -da adj (a) ‹respuesta› categorical, emphatic; ‹negativa› categorical, outright (before n); **me contestó con un 'no' ~** his answer was an emphatic 'no' (b) ‹éxito/fracaso› resounding

rotura f: **hay una ~ en la cañería** there's a burst in the pipe; **sufrió ~ de cadera** she fractured her hip; **tiene ~ de ligamentos** she has torn ligaments; **tiene una ~ en la manga** (CS) it has a rip in the sleeve

round /rraun/ m (Dep) round

rozado -da adj (gastado) worn; (sucio) grubby

rozadura f scratch; **le hizo una ~ al coche** he scratched the car; **los zapatos nuevos le hicieron una ~** her new shoes rubbed

rozagante adj (AmL) healthy

rozamiento m friction

rozar [A4] vt (tocar ligeramente): **el gato me rozó la pierna** the cat brushed against my leg; **sus labios ~on mi frente** her lips brushed my forehead; **las sillas rozan la pared** the chairs rub o scrape against the wall; **la bala le rozó el brazo** the bullet grazed his arm; **me roza el zapato** my shoe's rubbing
■ **rozarse** v pron (a) (recípr) «cables/piezas» to chafe; «manos/labios» to touch (b) (refl) ‹brazo/rodillas› to graze (c) «cuello/puños» to wear (d) (Méx) «bebé» to get diaper rash (AmE), get nappy rash (BrE); **el bebé está rozado** the baby has diaper rash (AmE) o (BrE) nappy rash

Rte. (= **remite** or **remitente**) sender

ruana f ruana (Colombian, Venezuelan poncho)

rubeola f German measles

rubí m (a) (Min) ruby (b) (de reloj) jewel (c) (color) : **de color ~** ruby red

rubio -bia adj ‹pelo› fair, blonde; ‹hombre› fair-haired, blond; ‹mujer› fair-haired, blonde
■ m,f (m) blond o fair-haired man; (f) blonde o fair-haired woman, blonde (colloq)

rublo m ruble*

rubor m (a) (liter) (sonrojo) flush; **el ~ de sus mejillas la delató** her flushed cheeks betrayed her (b) (Méx, RPl) (cosmética) rouge, blusher

ruborizarse [A4] v pron to blush, to turn red (in the face), to flush

rúbrica f (de firma) flourish; (firma) signing

rubro m (esp AmL) (a) (área) area; **nuestro ~ de peletería** our line in furs; **trabaja en el ~ de la computación** he works in computers (b) (en contabilidad — apartado) heading; (— renglón) item

rucio -cia adj (a) ‹caballo› gray* (b) (Chi fam) ‹pelo› fair, blonde; ‹hombre› fair-haired, blond; ‹mujer› fair-haired, blonde

ruco -ca adj (Méx fam) old

rudimentario -ria adj rudimentary

rudimento m rudiment

rudo -da adj (tosco) rough, rude (arch)

rueca f distaff

rueda f (a) (de vehículo, mecanismo) wheel; **~ de molino** millstone; **~ dentada** gear wheel, cogwheel; **~ de recambio** or **repuesto** or (RPl) **de auxilio** spare wheel; **patinar sobre ~s** to roller-skate; **ir sobre ~s** to go o run smoothly (b) (neumático) tire*; **se me pinchó una ~** I got a flat tire o a puncture (c) (de mueble) caster, roller (d) (corro) ring, circle; **~ de prensa** press conference (e) (en gimnasia) cartwheel

ruedo m (a) (Taur) bullring (b) (esp AmL) (de falda, pantalón) hem

ruego m (a) (súplica) plea; **de nada te servirán tus ~s** your pleading will get you nowhere (b) (petición) request; **en respuesta a un ~ de sus oyentes** in response to a request from his listeners

rufián m (granuja) rogue, scoundrel (dated); (chulo) pimp

rugby /'rruvbi/ m rugby

rugido m roar

rugir [I7] vi «león/mar/viento» to roar

rugoso -sa adj rough, bumpy

ruibarbo m rhubarb

ruido m noise; **sin hacer ~** quietly; **no hagas tanto ~** don't make so much noise

ruidoso -sa adj ‹calle/máquina/persona› noisy

ruin adj (mezquino, vil) despicable, contemptible; (avaro) miserly, mean (BrE)

ruina f (a) (bancarrota) ruin; **dejar a algn en la ~** to ruin sb; **estar en la ~** «empresario» to be ruined; «país» to be in financial ruin; **la compañía está en la ~** the company has collapsed (b) (perdición) downfall; **el juego fue su ~** gambling was his downfall (c) (hundimiento) collapse; **la casa amenaza ~** the house is on the point of collapse (d) **ruinas** fpl (de edificio, ciudad) ruins (pl); **en ~s** in ruins

ruiseñor m nightingale

rulero m (Per, RPl) curler

ruleta f roulette

ruletero -ra m,f (Méx fam) cab o taxi driver, cabbie (colloq)

rulo m (para el pelo) curler, roller; (rizo) (CS, Per) curl

rulot f (Esp) trailer (AmE), caravan (BrE)

ruma f (Chi) pile, heap

Rumania, Rumanía f Romania

rumano[1] **-na** *adj/m,f* Romanian, Rumanian
rumano[2] *m* (idioma) Romanian, Rumanian
rumba *f* rumba
rumbo *m* (dirección) direction, course; (Náut) course; **caminar sin ~ fijo** to wander aimlessly; **partió (con) ~ a Toluca** he set off for Toluca; **navegar con ~ norte** to sail a northerly course; **los acontecimientos tomaron un ~ trágico** events took a tragic turn
rumiante *m* ruminant
rumiar [A1] *vi* «*vaca*» to chew the cud, ruminate
rumor *m* (a) (murmuración) rumor*; **circulan ~es de que ...** rumors are circulating that ..., rumor has it that ... (b) (sonido) murmur
rumorear [A1] *vt*: **se rumorea que ...** rumor has it that ...
rupestre *adj* ⟨*pintura/dibujo*⟩ cave (*before n*); ⟨*planta*⟩ rock (*before n*)
rupia *f* rupee

ruptura *f* (a) (de relaciones, negaciones) breaking-off; (de contrato) breach, breaking; (de matrimonio) breakup; (con pasado, tradición) break; **esa fue la causa de la ~ de las negociaciones** that was what caused the negotiations to be broken off (b) (Dep) (en tenis) service break
rural *adj* rural
Rusia *f* Russia
ruso[1] **-sa** *adj/m,f* Russian
ruso[2] *m* (idioma) Russian
rústica (esp Esp): **en rústica** (*loc adj*) ⟨*edición*⟩ paperback (*before n*); **un libro en ~** a paperback
rústico -ca *adj* (del campo) rustic; (basto) coarse
ruta *f* (a) (itinerario) route (b) (RPI) (carretera) road
rutina *f* routine; **inspección de ~** routine inspection; **por pura ~** out of habit
rutinario -ria *adj* (a) ⟨*trabajo/vida*⟩ monotonous (b) ⟨*inspección/procedimiento*⟩ routine (*before n*)

Ss

S, s *f* (*read as* /'ese/) *the letter* S, s
s. *m* (= **siglo**) C; **s.XX** C20
S (= **sur**) S, South
S. (= **santo**) St
S.A. (= **Sociedad Anónima**) ≈ Inc (*in US*), ≈ Ltd (*in UK*), ≈ PLC (*in UK*)
sábado *m* Saturday; (Relig) Sabbath; **S~ de Gloria** *or* **Santo** Easter Saturday; **~ inglés** (CS) *non-working Saturday*
sabana *f* (Geog) savanna*, grassland
sábana *f* sheet; **~ ajustable** *or* (Méx) **de cajón** fitted sheet; **~ bajera/encimera** bottom/top sheet
sabandija *f* [1] (insecto) creepy-crawly (colloq), bug; (reptil) creepy-crawly (colloq) [2] **sabandija** *mf* (AmL fam) (pícaro) rascal (colloq)
sabañón *m* chilblain
sabático -ca *adj* sabbatical
sabelotodo *mf* (fam) know-it-all (AmE colloq), know-all (BrE colloq)
saber[1] *m* knowledge; **una persona de gran ~** a person of great learning
saber[2] [E25] *vt* [1] (a) ⟨*nombre/dirección/canción*⟩ to know; **ya lo sé** I know; **no lo sé** I don't know; **no sé cómo se llama** I don't know his name; **¡yo qué sé!** how (on earth) should I know! (colloq); **que yo sepa** as far as I know; **~ algo DE algo** to know sth ABOUT sth; **sé muy poco de ese tema** I know very little about the subject; **no sabe lo que dice** he doesn't know what he's talking about (b) (enterarse) to find out; **lo supe**

por mi hermana I found out about it through my sister; **sin que lo supiéramos** without our knowing; **¡si yo lo hubiera sabido antes!** if I had only known before!; **¡cómo iba yo a ~ que ...!** how was I to know that ...!
[2] (ser capaz de): **~ hacer algo** to know how to do sth; **¿sabes nadar?** can you swim?, do you know how to swim?; **sabe escuchar** she's a good listener; **sabe hablar varios idiomas** she can speak several languages
■ **~** *vi*
I (a) (tener conocimiento) to know; **¿quién sabe?** who knows?; **~ DE algo/algn** to know OF sth/sb; **yo sé de un lugar donde te lo pueden arreglar** I know of a place where you can get it fixed (b) (tener noticias, enterarse): **no sé nada de ella desde hace más de un mes** I haven't heard from her for over a month; **yo supe del accidente por la radio** I heard about the accident on the radio
II (a) (tener sabor) (+ *compl*) to taste; **sabe dulce/bien** it tastes sweet/nice; **~ A algo** to taste OF sth; **no sabe a nada** it doesn't taste of anything; **sabe a podrido** it tastes rotten (b) (causar cierta impresión): **me sabe mal** *or* **no me sabe bien tener que decírselo** I don't like having to tell him
■ **saberse** *v pron* (enf) ⟨*lección/poema*⟩ to know
sabido -da *adj* [SER] well-known; **como es ~** as everybody knows
sabiduría *f* wisdom
sabiendas: **a sabiendas** (*loc adv*): **lo hizo a ~ de que me molestaba** he did it knowing full well *o* perfectly well that I found it annoying

AmC Central America	Arg Argentina	Cu Cuba	Per Peru
AmL Latin America	Bol Bolivia	Ec Ecuador	RPI River Plate Area
AmS South America	Chi Chile	Esp Spain	Ur Uruguay
Andes Andean Region	CS Southern Cone	Méx Mexico	Ven Venezuela

sabihondo -da *m,f* (fam) know-it-all (AmE colloq), know-all (BrE colloq)

sabio -bia *adj* (con grandes conococimientos) learned, wise; (sensato) ⟨*persona/medida*⟩ wise; ⟨*consejo*⟩ sound, wise

■ *m,f* (*m*) wise man, sage (liter); (*f*) wise woman

sable *m* ⟦1⟧ (Arm) saber*; (Náut) batten ⟦2⟧ (en heráldica) sable

sabor *m* **(a)** (de comida, bebida, etc) taste, flavor*; **con ～ a menta** mint-flavoured; **viene en tres ～es** it comes in three flavors; **no tiene ～** it has no taste to it **(b)** (carácter) flavor*

saborear [A1] *vt* to savor*; ⟨*éxito/triunfo*⟩ to relish

sabotaje *m* sabotage

saboteador -dora *m,f* saboteur

sabotear [A1] *vt* to sabotage

sabré, sabría, etc ▶ SABER

sabroso -sa *adj* ⟦1⟧ ⟨*comida*⟩ tasty, delicious; ⟨*chisme/historia*⟩ spicy (colloq), juicy (colloq) ⟦2⟧ (AmL fam) (agradable) ⟨*música/ritmo*⟩ pleasant, nice; ⟨*clima/agua*⟩ beautiful

sabrosón -sona *adj* **(a)** (AmL fam) ⟨*guiso*⟩ tasty, delicious; ⟨*fruta*⟩ delicious **(b)** (AmL fam) ⟨*clima*⟩ mild **(c)** (Col, Méx, Ven fam) ⟨*música*⟩ pleasant

sabueso *m* (Zool) bloodhound

sacacorchos *m* (*pl* ～) corkscrew

sacapuntas *m* (*pl* ～) pencil sharpener

sacar [A2] *vt*

I ⟦1⟧ (extraer) **(a)** ⟨*billetera/lápiz*⟩ to take out, get out; ⟨*pistola/espada*⟩ to draw; **～ algo DE algo** to take *o* get sth OUT OF sth; **lo saqué del cajón** I took *o* got it out of the drawer **(b)** ⟨*muela*⟩ to pull out, take out; ⟨*riñón/cálculo*⟩ to remove; **me ～on sangre** they took some blood **(c)** ⟨*diamantes/cobre/petróleo*⟩ to extract **(d)** ⟨*carta/ficha*⟩ to draw

⟦2⟧ (poner, llevar fuera) **(a)** ⟨*maceta/mesa/basura*⟩ to take out; **sácalo aquí al sol** bring it out here into the sun; **tuvimos que ～lo por la ventana** we had to get it out through the window; **～ el perro a pasear** to take the dog out for a walk; **～ el coche del garaje** to get the car out of the garage **(b)** (invitar): **el marido no la saca nunca** her husband never takes her out; **～ a algn a bailar** to ask sb to dance **(c)** ⟨*parte del cuerpo*⟩ to put out; **me sacó la lengua** he stuck *o* put his tongue out at me

⟦3⟧ (retirar) to take out; **～ dinero del banco** to take out *o* withdraw money from the bank

⟦4⟧ (de una situación difícil) **～ a algn DE algo** ⟨*de apuro/atolladero*⟩ to get sb OUT OF sth

⟦5⟧ (Esp) ⟨*dobladillo*⟩ to let down; ⟨*pantalón/falda*⟩ (alargar) to let down; (ensanchar) to let out

II (obtener) ⟦1⟧ ⟨*pasaporte/permiso*⟩ to get; ⟨*entrada/billete*⟩ to get, buy

⟦2⟧ **(a)** ⟨*votos/puntos/calificación*⟩ to get **(b)** ⟨*premio*⟩ to get, win **(c)** ⟨*conclusión*⟩ to draw **(d)** ⟨*suma/cuenta*⟩ to do, work out

⟦3⟧ ⟨*beneficio*⟩ to get; ⟨*ganancia*⟩ to make; **¿qué sacas con eso?** what do you gain by doing that?; **no sacó ningún provecho del curso** she didn't get anything out of the course

⟦4⟧ **～ algo DE algo** ⟨*idea/información*⟩ to get sth FROM sth; ⟨*porciones/unidades*⟩ to get sth OUT OF sth; **～le algo A algn** ⟨*dinero/información*⟩ to get sth OUT OF sb

⟦5⟧ ⟨*brillo*⟩ to bring out; **～le brillo a algo** to polish sth to a shine

III ⟦1⟧ **(a)** ⟨*libro*⟩ to publish, bring out; ⟨*disco*⟩ to bring out, release; ⟨*modelo/producto*⟩ to bring out **(b)** ⟨*tema*⟩ to bring up **(c)** ⟨*foto*⟩ to take; ⟨*copia*⟩ to make, take; ⟨*apuntes*⟩ to make, take; **～le una foto a algn** to take a photo of sb **(d)** (Esp) ⟨*defecto/falta*⟩ (+ *me/te/le etc*) to find; **a todo le tiene que ～ faltas** he always has to find fault with everything

⟦2⟧ **sacar adelante** ⟨*proyecto*⟩ (poner en marcha) to get sth off the ground; (salvar de la crisis) to keep sth going; **luché tanto para ～ adelante a mis hijos** I fought so hard to give my children a good start in life

⟦3⟧ (Dep) ⟨*tiro libre/falta*⟩ to take

IV (quitar) ⟦1⟧ (esp AmL) **(a)** **～le algo A algn** ⟨*botas/gorro*⟩ to take sth OFF sb **(b)** **～le algo A algo** ⟨*tapa/cubierta*⟩ to take sth OFF sth **(c)** (retirar): **saca esto de aquí** take this away; **saquen los libros de la mesa** take the books off the table **(d)** (hacer desaparecer) ⟨*mancha*⟩ to remove, get ... out

■ **～** *vi* (Dep) (en tenis, vóleibol) to serve; (en fútbol) to kick off

■ **sacarse** *v pron* (refl) ⟦1⟧ (extraer) ⟨*astilla/púa*⟩ to take ... out; ⟨*ojo*⟩ to poke ... out; **me tengo que ～ una muela** (caus) I have to have a tooth out; **～se algo DE algo** to take sth OUT OF sth; **sácate las manos de los bolsillos** take your hands out of your pockets

⟦2⟧ (AmL) (quitarse) ⟨*ropa/zapatos*⟩ to take off; ⟨*maquillaje*⟩ to remove, take off

⟦3⟧ **(a)** (caus) ⟨*foto*⟩: **tengo que ～me una foto** I have to have my photo taken **(b)** (AmL) ⟨*calificación/nota*⟩ to get

sacarina *f* saccharin

sacerdote *m* priest

sacerdotisa *f* priestess

saciar [A1] *vt* ⟨*hambre*⟩ to satisfy; ⟨*sed*⟩ to quench; ⟨*deseo*⟩ (liter) to satiate (liter); ⟨*ambición*⟩ to fulfill*, realize

■ **saciarse** *v pron*: comer/beber **hasta ～se** to eat/drink one's fill

saco *m* ⟦1⟧ ⟨*continente*⟩ sack; ⟨*contenido*⟩ sack, sackful; **～ de dormir** sleeping bag ⟦2⟧ (AmL) (de tela) jacket; **～ sport** (AmL) sports coat (AmE), sports jacket (BrE)

sacramento *m* sacrament; **los últimos ～s** the last rites

sacrificado -da *adj* ⟨*persona*⟩ selfless, self-sacrificing

sacrificar [A2] *vt* **(a)** (Relig) ⟨*cordero/víctimas*⟩ to sacrifice **(b)** ⟨*res/ganado*⟩ to slaughter; ⟨*perro/gato*⟩ (euf) to put ... to sleep (euph) **(c)** ⟨*carrera/juventud*⟩ to sacrifice

■ **sacrificarse** *v pron* to make sacrifices

sacrificio *m* **(a)** (privación, renuncia) sacrifice **(b)** (inmolación) sacrifice **(c)** (de res) slaughter

sacrilegio *m* sacrilege

sacrílego -ga *adj* sacrilegious

sacristán *m* sacristan, verger

sacristía *f* vestry, sacristy

sacudida *f* **(a)** (agitando) shake, shaking; (golpeando) beating **(b)** (de terremoto) tremor; (de explosión) blast; (de tren, coche) jerk, jolt **(c)** (fam) (descarga) electric shock

S

sacudir [I1] *vt* **1** **(a)** (agitar) ⟨*toalla/alfombra*⟩ to shake; (golpear) ⟨*alfombra/colchón*⟩ to beat; **sacudió la arena de la toalla** he shook the sand out of the towel **(b)** (fam) ⟨*niño*⟩ to clobber (colloq); **~ la cabeza** (para negar) to shake one's head; (para afirmar) to nod (one's head) **(c)** (hacer temblar) to shake **(d)** (CS, Méx) (limpiar) to dust, do the dusting **2** (conmover, afectar) to shake
■ **~** *vi* (CS, Méx) to dust
■ **sacudirse** *v pron* (*refl*) (quitarse) ⟨*arena/polvo*⟩ to shake off

sádico -ca *adj* sadistic
■ *m,f* sadist

sadismo *m* sadism

sadomasoquismo *m* sadomasochism

sadomasoquista *mf* sadomasochist

safari *m* **(a)** (gira, viaje) safari; **ir de ~** to go on safari **(b)** (zoológico) safari park

sagaz *adj* shrewd, astute

Sagitario *m* (signo, constelación) Sagittarius; **es (de) ~** she's (a) Sagittarian
■ *mf* (*pl* **~** *or* **-rios**) (persona) *tb* **sagitario** Sagittarian, Sagittarius

sagrado -da *adj* **1** (Relig) ⟨*altar*⟩ holy; ⟨*lugar*⟩ holy, sacred **2** (fundamental, intocable) sacred

Sahara /sa'ara/ *m*: **el (desierto del) ~** the Sahara (Desert)

sajón -jona *adj/m,f* Saxon

sal *f* **1** (Coc) salt; **mantequilla sin ~** unsalted butter; *echarle la ~ a algn* (Méx fam) to put a jinx on sb **2** (Quím) salt; **~ de fruta** liver salts (*pl*); **~es de baño** bath salts (*pl*)

sal ▶ SALIR

sala *f* **(a)** (de casa) *tb* **~ de estar** living room, lounge (BrE) **(b)** (de hotel) lounge; (en hospital) ward; (para reuniones, conferencias) hall; (Teatr) theater*; (Cin) movie theater (AmE), cinema (BrE); **~ cuna** (Chi) day nursery, creche; **~ de clases** (CS frml) classroom; **~ de conciertos** concert hall; **~ de embarque** departure lounge; **~ de espera** waiting room; **~ de exposiciones** gallery, exhibition hall; **~ de fiestas** night club (*usually featuring dancing and cabaret*); **~ de profesores** staff room **(c)** (sede de tribunal) courtroom, court

salado -da *adj* **1** (Coc) **(a)** (con sal) ⟨*almendras/bacalao*⟩ salted; ⟨*gusto*⟩ salty; **está demasiado ~** it's too salty **(b)** [SER] (no dulce) ⟨*plato/comida*⟩ savory* **2** **(a)** (fam) ⟨*persona*⟩ (gracioso) funny, witty **(b)** (fam) ⟨*chiste*⟩ risqué; ⟨*anécdota*⟩ spicy **3** (Méx fam) (que trae mala suerte) jinxed (colloq)

salamandra *f* (Zool) salamander; (estufa) salamander stove

salame *m* **(a)** (CS) (Coc) salami **(b)** (RPl fam) (tonto) idiot

salar¹ [A1] *vt* **(a)** (para conservar) ⟨*carne/pescado*⟩ to salt (down); ⟨*pieles*⟩ to salt **(b)** (para condimentar) to salt, add salt to
■ **salarse** *v pron* (Méx fam) (echarse a perder) «*planes*» to fall through; «*negocio*» to go bust

salar² *m* (Chi) salt pan, salt flat

salario *m* (frml) wage, salary

salchicha *f* sausage

salchichón *m*: *spiced sausage similar to salami*

salchichonería *f* (Méx) delicatessen

saldar [A1] *vt* **(a)** ⟨*cuenta*⟩ to settle; ⟨*deuda*⟩ to settle, pay (off) **(b)** ⟨*mercancías/productos*⟩ to sell off

saldo *m* **1** (de cuenta) balance; **~ a su/nuestro favor** credit/debit balance **2** **(a)** (artículo): **los ~s no se cambian** sale goods cannot be exchanged; **precios de ~** sale prices; **❺ venta de saldos** clearance sale **(b)** **saldos** *mpl* (rebajas) sales (*pl*)

saldré, saldría, etc ▶ SALIR

salero *m* **1** (recipiente) salt shaker (AmE), saltcellar (BrE) **2** (fam) (gracia): **tener ~** (contando chistes) to be funny; (bailando) to be stylish

salga, salgas, etc ▶ SALIR

salida *f*
I 1 (hacia el exterior) **1** **(a)** (lugar, puerta) exit; **~ de emergencia/incendios** emergency/fire exit; **todas las ~s de Bilbao** all the roads out of Bilbao; **es una calle sin ~** it's a dead end **(b)** (de tubería) outlet, outflow; (de circuito) outlet
2 **(a)** (acción): **me lo encontré a la ~** I met him on my way out; **nos encontramos a la ~ del concierto** we met at the door after the concert; **una ~ al campo** an outing *o* a trip to the country **(b)** (de líquido, gas, electricidad) output **(c) la ~ del sol** sunrise
II (partida) **1** (de tren, avión) departure; **el tren efectuará su ~ por la vía cinco** the train will leave from track five; **❺ salidas nacionales/internacionales** domestic/international departures **2** (Dep) (en una carrera) start
III 1 (solución): **no le veo ninguna ~ a esta situación** I can see no way out of this situation; **no nos queda otra ~** we have no other option **2** (Com, Fin) (gasto) payment

salido -da *adj* ⟨*ojos/dientes*⟩ protruding; ⟨*frente/mentón*⟩ prominent

saliente *adj* ⟨*pómulo/hueso*⟩ prominent; ⟨*cornisa/balcón*⟩ projecting
■ *f or* (Esp) *m* (de edificio, muro) projection; (de precipicio) ledge

salir [I29] *vi*
I 1 (partir) to leave; **¿a qué hora sale el tren?** what time does the train leave?; **el jefe había salido de viaje** the boss was away; **salió corriendo** (fam) she was off like a shot (colloq); **~ DE algo** to leave FROM sth; **¿de qué andén sale el tren?** what platform does the train leave from?; **~ PARA algo** to leave FOR sth
2 (al exterior — acercándose al hablante) to come out; (— alejándose del hablante) to go out; **no salgas sin abrigo** don't go out without a coat; **no puedo ~, me he quedado encerrado** I can't get out, I'm trapped in here; **~ DE algo** to come out/get out OF sth; **¡sal de ahí/de aquí!** come out of there/get out of here!; **¿de dónde salió este dinero?** where did this money come from?; **nunca ha salido de España** he's never been out of Spain; **~ por la ventana/por la puerta** to get out through the window/leave by the door; **salieron al balcón/al jardín** they went out onto the balcony/into the garden; **¿por aquí se sale a la carretera?** can I get on to the road this way?; **salió a hacer las compras** she's gone out (to do the) shopping
3 (habiendo terminado algo) to leave; **¿a qué hora sales de clase?** what time do you get out of class *o* finish your class?; **¿cuándo sale del hospital?** when is he coming out of (the) hospital?

4 **(a)** (como entretenimiento) to go out; ~ a cenar to go out for dinner **(b)** (tener una relación) to go out; ~ con algn to go out with sb
5 «*clavo/tapón/mancha*» to come out; «*anillo*» to come off
II **1** (aparecer, manifestarse) **(a)** «*cana/sarpullido*» to appear; (+ *me/te/le etc*) me empiezan a ~ canas I'm starting to go gray; le están saliendo los dientes she's teething; me salió una ampolla I've got a blister; le salió un sarpullido he came out in a rash; me salieron granos I broke out *o* (BrE) came out in spots; me sale sangre de la nariz my nose is bleeding; a la planta le están saliendo hojas nuevas the plant's putting out new leaves **(b)** «*sol*» (por la mañana) to rise, come up; (de detrás de una nube) to come out **(c)** (surgir) «*tema/idea*» to come up **(d)** «*carta*» (en naipes) to come up
2 **(a)** «*revista/novela*» to come out; «*disco*» to come out, be released; ~ al mercado to come on to the market **(b)** (en televisión, en el periódico) to appear **(c)** (en una foto) to appear; (+ *compl*) saliste muy bien en la foto you came out very well in the photo
III **1** (expresando logro) (+ *me/te/le etc*): no me sale esta ecuación I can't do this equation; ahora mismo no me sale su nombre (fam) I can't think of her name right now; no le salían las palabras he couldn't get his words out
2 **(a)** (costar) to work out; sale más barato/caro it works out less/more expensive **(b)** (resultar): todo salió bien everything turned out *o* worked out well; salió tal como lo planeamos it turned out just as we planned; no salió ninguna de las fotos none of the photographs came out; ¿qué número salió premiado? what was the winning number?; ~ bien/mal en un examen (Chi fam) to pass/fail an exam; (+ *me/te/le etc*) el postre no me salió bien the dessert didn't come out right
3 (de situación, estado) ~ DE algo «*de apuro*» to get out of sth; «*de depresión*» to get over sth; salieron ilesos del accidente they were not hurt in the accident; ~ *adelante* «*negocio*» to stay afloat, survive; «*propuesta*» to prosper; lograron ~ adelante they managed to get through it
4 (con preposición) **(a)** salir a (parecerse a) to take after **(b)** salir con (Col) (combinar con) to go with
■ **salirse** *v pron* **1** **(a)** (de borde, límite) «*agua*» to overflow; «*leche*» to boil over; ~se DE algo «*de carretera*» to come/go off sth; «*de tema*» to get off sth; el río se salió de su cauce the river overflowed its banks; procura no ~te del presupuesto try to keep within the budget **(b)** (por orificio, grieta) «*agua/tinta*» to leak (out), come out; «*gas*» to escape, come out
2 (soltarse) «*pedazo/pieza*» to come off; (+ *me/te/le etc*) estos zapatos se me salen these shoes are too big for me
3 (irse) to leave; ~se DE algo «*de asociación*» to leave sth; ~se con la suya to get one's (own) way

saliva *f* saliva, spit (colloq)
salivar [A1] *vi* to salivate
salmo *m* psalm
salmón *m* salmon
■ *adj inv* salmon-pink, salmon, salmon-colored*
salmonete *m* red mullet, surmullet (AmE)
salmuera *f* brine
salón *m* **(a)** (en casa particular) living room,

sitting room (BrE), lounge (BrE) **(b)** (en hotel) reception room, function room **(c)** (en palacio) hall **(d)** (de clases) classroom; ~ de actos auditorium (AmE), assembly hall (BrE); ~ de baile ballroom; ~ de belleza beauty salon, beauty parlor; ~ de fiestas (AmL) function room, reception room; ~ náutico/del automóvil boat/motor show
salpicadera *f* (Méx) (de coche, bicicleta) fender (AmE), mudguard (BrE)
salpicadero *m* (Esp) dashboard
salpicadura *f* splash
salpicar [A2] *vt* (de agua) to splash; (de barro, aceite) to splash, spatter
salpicón *m* (de pescado, ave) *chopped seafood or meat with onion, tomato and peppers*
salsa *f* **1** (Coc) sauce; (de jugo de carne) gravy; ~ bechamel *or* blanca bechamel (sauce); ~ de tomate (sofrito) tomato sauce; (catsup) (Col) ketchup, catsup (AmE) **2** (Mús) salsa
saltamontes *m* (*pl* ~) grasshopper
saltar [A1] *vi* **1** **(a)** (brincar) to jump; (más alto, más lejos) to leap; ~ a la cuerda *or* (Esp) comba to jump rope (AmE), to skip (BrE); ~ de alegría to jump for joy; «*aceite*» to spit; «*corcho*» to pop out; «*fusibles*» to blow; la bomba hizo ~ el coche por los aires the bomb blew the car into the air
■ ~ *vt* «*obstáculo/valla/zanja*» to jump (over); (apoyándose) to vault (over)
■ **saltarse** *v pron* **1** **(a)** (omitir) «*línea/página/nombre*» to skip, miss out; «*comida*» to miss, skip **(b)** «*semáforo/stop*» to jump
2 «*botón*» to come off, pop off; «*pintura*» to chip; se le ~on las lágrimas her eyes filled with tears
3 (Chi) «*diente/loza*» to chip
salteado -da *adj*: ¿se pueden contestar las preguntas salteadas? can we answer the questions in any order?; leí unos capítulos ~s I read a few odd chapters
saltear [A1] *vt* (Coc) to sauté
saltimbanqui *m* (Espec, Hist) tumbler, acrobat
salto *m* **1** **(a)** (brinco) jump; se levantó de un ~ (de la cama) he leapt *o* sprang out of bed; (del suelo) he leapt *o* jumped up from the floor; se puso en pie de un ~ she leapt *o* sprang to her feet; los pájaros se acercaban dando saltitos the birds were hopping closer to me/us; dar *or* pegar un ~ (dar un brinco) to jump; (de susto) to start, jump; daban ~s de alegría they were jumping for joy **(b)** (Dep) (en atletismo, esquí, paracaidismo) jump; (en natación) dive; ~ con pértiga *or* (AmL) garrocha pole vault; ~ de altura/longitud high/long jump; ~ (en) alto/(en) largo (AmL) high/long jump; ~ mortal somersault
2 (Geog) *tb* ~ de agua waterfall
saltón -tona *adj* «*ojos*» bulging

(tercera acepción de II, continúa):

2 (pasar) ~ DE algo A algo to jump FROM sth TO sth; saltaba de una idea a otra she kept jumping from one idea to the next
3 «*botón*» to come off, pop off; «*chispas*» to fly;

salud f [1] (Med) health; **estar bien de** ~ to be in good health; **gozar de buena** ~ to enjoy good health [2] ¡~! (al brindar) cheers!; (cuando alguien estornuda) (AmL) bless you!

saludable adj ⟨clima/alimentación⟩ healthy; ⟨experiencia⟩ salutary

saludar [A1] vt (a) ⟨persona⟩ to greet, say hello to; **saluda a tu hermano de mi parte** give my regards to your brother; **lo saluda atentamente** (Corresp) Sincerely (yours) (AmE), Yours sincerely (BrE); **los saludó con la mano** she waved at them (b) (Mil) to salute
■ ~ vi (a) (de palabra) to say hello (o good morning etc) (b) (con la mano) to wave (c) (Mil) to salute
■ **saludarse** v pron (recípr) to say hello to o greet each other

saludo m (a) greeting; **te mandan ~s** they send (you) their regards o best wishes; **~s** (Corresp) best wishes; **le hice un** ~ **con la mano** I gave him a wave, I waved to him (b) (Mil) salute

salva f: **una** ~ **de 21 cañonazos** a 21-gun salute o salvo; **una** ~ **de aplausos** a burst o round of applause

salvación f salvation

salvado m bran

salvador -dora m,f savior*

Salvador ▶ EL SALVADOR

salvadoreño -ña adj/m,f Salvadoran, Salvadorean

salvaguardar [A1] vt to safeguard

salvaguardia f safeguard, defense*

salvaje adj [1] (a) ⟨animal⟩ wild (b) (primitivo) ⟨tribu⟩ savage (c) ⟨vegetación/terreno⟩ wild [2] (cruel) ⟨persona/tortura⟩ brutal; ⟨ataque/matanza⟩ savage
■ mf (primitivo) savage; (bruto) (pey) animal, savage

salvamanteles m (pl ~) (para platos, fuentes) tablemat; (para vasos) coaster

salvamento m rescue; **equipo de** ~ rescue team

salvar [A1] vt [1] (en general) to save; ~ **algo/a algn DE algo** to save sth/sb FROM sth [2] (a) ⟨dificultad/obstáculo⟩ to overcome (b) ⟨distancia⟩ to cover (c) (Per, Ur) ⟨examen⟩ to pass
■ **salvarse** v pron to survive; **¡sálvese quien pueda!** every man for himself!; ~**se DE algo** ⟨de accidente/incendio⟩ to survive sth; **se ~on de una muerte segura** they escaped certain death

salvavidas mf (pl ~) (a) (persona) lifeguard (b) **salvavidas** m (flotador) life jacket, life preserver (frml)

salvia f sage

salvo: **a salvo** (loc adv) **poner algo a** ~ to put sth in a safe place; **los niños están a** ~ the children are safe o unharmed; **ponerse a** ~ to reach safety; **a** ~ **de** safe from
■ prep (excepto) except, apart from; ~ **que** unless

salvoconducto m safe-conduct

samba m or f samba

San adj (apócope de SANTO usado delante de nombres de varón excepto Domingo, Tomás y Tomé) St, Saint

sanar [A1] vi ⟨enfermo⟩ to get well, recover; ⟨herida⟩ to heal; ~ **DE algo** to recover FROM sth

sanatorio m (a) (para convalecientes) nursing home, sanitarium (AmE), sanatorium (BrE) (b) (hospital) clinic, hospital (usually private) (c) (Col, Ven) (hospital psiquiátrico) psychiatric hospital

sanción f [1] (castigo a empleado, obrero) disciplinary measure; (Der) sanction, penalty; **una** ~ **de tres partidos** a three-game ban o suspension; ~ **económica** (multa) fine; **sanciones económicas** (a país) economic sanctions [2] (de ley) sanction; (de costumbre) sanction (frml), authorization

sancionar [A1] vt [1] (multar) to fine; (castigar) ⟨empleado/obrero⟩ to discipline; ⟨jugador⟩ to penalize [2] ⟨ley/disposición/acuerdo/huelga⟩ to sanction; ⟨costumbre⟩ to approve, sanction

sancochar [A1] vt (AmL) (cocer a medias) to parboil

sandalia f sandal

sándalo m sandalwood

sandez f (fam) silly o stupid thing to say; **¡no digas sandeces!** don't talk nonsense!

sandía f watermelon

sándwich /'saŋgwɪtʃ/ m, **sándwiche** /'saŋgwɪtʃe/ m (esp AmL) (de pan de molde) sandwich; (de pancito) (filled) roll

sanfermines mpl: festival in Pamplona in which bulls are run through the streets

sangrar [A1] vi ⟨persona/herida/nariz⟩ to bleed

sangre f [1] (Biol) blood; **una transfusión de** ~ a blood transfusion; **no me salió** ~ it didn't bleed; **te sale** ~ **de** o **por la nariz** your nose is bleeding; **los ojos inyectados en** ~ bloodshot eyes; **animales de** ~ **fría/caliente** cold-blooded/warm-blooded animals; ~ **fría** calmness and courage; **a** ~ **fría** ⟨matar⟩ in cold blood; ▶ MALO 2 [2] (linaje) blood; **era de** ~ **noble** he was of noble blood o birth; **es de** ~ **mestiza** he is of mixed race; **no son de la misma** ~ they are not from the same family; ~ **azul** blue blood

sangría f [1] (bebida) sangria (type of red wine punch) [2] (a) (Med) bleeding (b) (de capital, recursos) outflow, drain [3] (Impr) indentation

sangriento -ta adj bloody

sangrón -grona adj (Méx fam) annoying
■ m,f (Méx fam) nuisance

sanguijuela f (a) (Zool) leech (b) (fam) (persona) leech, bloodsucker

sanguinario -ria adj ⟨persona⟩ cruel, bloodthirsty; ⟨animal⟩ vicious, ferocious

sanidad f [1] (calidad de sano) health, healthiness [2] (a) (salud pública) public health (b) **Sanidad** (sin art) (departamento) Department of Health

sanitario¹ -ria adj ⟨medidas⟩ public health

(*before n*); ⟨*condiciones*⟩ sanitary (*before n*);
servicios ∼s sanitation; **asistencia sanitaria**
health-care
sanitario² *m* **(a)** (retrete) toilet, lavatory **(b)**
sanitarios *mpl* (para cuarto de baño) bathroom
fittings (*pl*)
sano -na *adj* ⌐1⌐ ⟨*persona/planta/cabello*⟩
healthy; ⟨*clima/vida*⟩ healthy; ⟨*alimentación*⟩
healthy, wholesome; **∼ y salvo** safe and sound
⌐2⌐ (en sentido moral) wholesome; ⟨*lecturas/ideas*⟩
⟨*ambiente*⟩ healthy; ⟨*persona*⟩ good
San Salvador *m* San Salvador
sánscrito *m* Sanskrit
Santa Sede *f*: **la ∼ ∼** the Vatican, the Holy
See (frml)
Santiago (de Chile) *m* Santiago
Santiago (de Compostela) *m* Santiago
(de Compostela)
santiaguino -na *adj* of/from Santiago (*Chile*)
santiamén *m*: **en un ∼** (fam) in no time at all
santiguarse [A16] *v pron* (*refl*) to cross
oneself, make the sign of the cross
santo -ta *adj* ⌐1⌐ (Relig) **(a)** ⟨*lugar/mujer/vida*⟩
holy **(b)** (con nombre propio) St, Saint; **Santa Teresa**
Saint Theresa; *ver tb* SAN ⌐2⌐ (fam) (uso enfático)
blessed; **llovió todo el ∼ día** it rained the whole
blessed day (colloq)
■ *m,f* ⌐1⌐ (persona) saint; **una paciencia de ∼** the
patience of a saint; **no te hagas el ∼** don't come
over all virtuous; **∼ y seña** password ⌐2⌐ **santo**
m (festividad) name day, saint's day; (cumpleaños)
(esp AmL) birthday
Santo Domingo *m* (Geog) Santo Domingo;
(Relig) Saint Dominic
santuario *m* (Relig) sanctuary, shrine; (refugio)
sanctuary
saña *f* viciousness, brutality; **con ∼** brutally,
viciously
São Paulo *m* São Paulo
sapo *m* (Zool) toad
saque *m* **(a)** (en tenis, vóleibol) serve, service **(b)**
(en fútbol) kickoff; **∼ de banda** (en fútbol) throw-in;
(en rugby) line-out; **∼ de esquina** corner (kick); **∼
de puerta** *or* (CS) **valla** goal kick; **∼ inicial** kickoff
saquear [A1] *vt* ⟨*ciudad/población*⟩ to sack,
plunder; ⟨*tienda/establecimiento*⟩ to loot
sarampión *m* measles
sarape *m* (Méx) ▶ ZARAPE
sarcasmo *m* **(a)** (cualidad) sarcasm; **con ∼**
sarcastically **(b)** (comentario) sarcastic remark
sarcástico -ca *adj* sarcastic
sarcófago *m* sarcophagus
sardina *f* sardine
sardinel *m* (Col) **(a)** (de la acera) curb (AmE),
kerb (BrE) **(b)** (de ventana) windowsill
sargento *mf* (Mil) (en el ejército) sergeant; (en las
fuerzas aéreas) ≈ staff sergeant (*in US*), ≈ sergeant
(*in UK*)
sari *m* sari
sarita *f* (Per) straw hat
sarna *f* (Med) scabies; (Vet) mange
sarpullido *m* rash, hives (*pl*)
sarro *m* (en los dientes) plaque, tartar; (en la
lengua) fur; (en tetera eléctrica, cañería) scale
sarta *f* string

sartén *f*, (AmL) *m or f* frying pan, fry pan (AmE),
skillet
sastre *mf* (persona) tailor
sastrería *f* tailor's shop
Satanás, Satán *m* Satan
satánico -ca *adj* (del diablo) satanic; (malvado)
evil, satanic
satélite *m* satellite; **∼ artificial** artificial
satellite
satén, (AmL) **satín** *m* satin
sátira *f* satire
satírico -ca *adj* satirical
satirizar [A4] *vt* to satirize
satisfacción *f* satisfaction; **la ∼ del deber
cumplido** the satisfaction of a job well done; **es
una ∼ para mí estar aquí** it is a pleasure to be
here
satisfacer [E20] *vt* to satisfy; **su respuesta no
me satisface** I am not satisfied *o* happy with your
reply
■ **satisfacerse** *v pron* **(a)** (contentarse) to be
satisfied **(b)** (de agravio) to obtain satisfaction
satisfactorio -ria *adj* satisfactory
satisfaga, satisfará, etc ▶ SATISFACER
satisfecho -cha *adj* ⌐1⌐ [ESTAR] (complacido,
contento) satisfied, pleased ⌐2⌐ [ESTAR] (saciado,
lleno): **estoy ∼** I've had plenty; **no queda nunca ∼**
he never seems to be full
saturado -da *adj* (en general) saturated; ⟨*líneas
telefónicas*⟩ busy, engaged (BrE)
saturar [A1] *vt* to saturate
Saturno *m* Saturn
sauce *m* willow; **∼ llorón** weeping willow
saudí, saudita *adj/mf* (Saudi) Arabian
sauna *f or* (AmL) *m* sauna
savia *f* (Bot) sap
sávila *f* (Méx) aloe vera
saxo *m* (fam) **(a)** (instrumento) sax (colloq)
(b) saxo *mf* (persona) sax player (colloq)
saxofón, saxófono *m* saxophone
saxofonista *mf* saxophonist
sazón *f* ⌐1⌐ **(a)** (condimento) seasoning; (sabor)
flavor* **(b)** (de la fruta) ripeness; **estar en ∼** to be
ripe ⌐2⌐ **a la sazón** (liter) at that time
sazonar [A1] *vt* to season
schop /ʃop/ *m* (Chi) (vaso) beer mug; (cerveza)
keg beer
Scotch® /(e)s'kotʃ/ *m* (Andes) Scotch® tape
(AmE), Sellotape® (BrE)
scout /(e)s'kau(t)/ *mf* scout
se *pron pers* ⌐1⌐ [*seguido de otro pronombre:
sustituyendo a* LE, LES]: **ya ∼ lo he dicho** (a él)
I've already told him; (a ella) I've already told
her; (a usted, ustedes) I've already told you; (a ellos)
I've already told them; **el vestido tenía cuello
pero ∼ lo quité** the dress had a collar but I took
it off
⌐2⌐ (*en verbos pronominales*): **¿no ∼ arrepienten?**
«*ellos/ellas*» aren't they sorry?; «*ustedes*» aren't
you sorry?; **el barco ∼ hundió** the ship sank; **∼
secó/secaron** (*refl*) he dried himself/they dried
themselves; **∼ secó el pelo** (*refl*) she dried her
hair; **∼ hizo un vestido** (*refl*) she made herself a
dress; (*caus*) she had a dress made; **no ∼ hablan** ···❖

(*recípr*) they're not on speaking terms, they're not speaking to each other; ∼ **lo comió todo** (*enf*) he ate it all

3 **(a)** (*voz pasiva*): ∼ **oyeron unos gritos** there were shouts, I (*o* we *etc*) heard some shouts; ∼ **publicó el año pasado** it was published last year **(b)** (*impersonal*): **aquí** ∼ **está muy bien** it's very nice here; ∼ **castigará a los culpables** those responsible will be punished **(c)** (en normas, instrucciones): **¿cómo** ∼ **escribe tu nombre?** how is your name spelled?, how do you spell your name?; ∼ **pica la cebolla bien menuda** chop the onion finely

sé ▶ SABER, SER

sea, seas, etc ▶ SER

sebo *m* (grasa) grease, fat; (para jabón, velas) tallow; (Coc) suet

secador *m* **1** *tb* ∼ **de pelo** hairdryer **2** (Per) (paño) dishtowel (AmE), tea towel (BrE); (toalla) towel

secadora *f* (de ropa, tabaco) dryer; (para el pelo) (Méx) hairdryer

secano *m*: **de secano** ⟨*campo/tierra*⟩ dry, unirrigated

secar [A2] *vt* **(a)** ⟨*ropa/pelo/platos*⟩ to dry; ⟨*pintura/arcilla*⟩ to dry **(b)** ⟨*tierra/plantas/hierba*⟩ to dry up; ⟨*piel*⟩ to make ... dry
■ ∼ *vi* to dry
■ **secarse** *v pron* **1** **(a)** «*ropa/pintura/pelo*» to dry; «*piel*» to get dry; **se me seca mucho la piel** my skin gets very dry **(b)** «*herida*» to heal (up) **(c)** «*tierra/planta/hierba*» to dry up **(d)** «*río/pozo/fuente*» to dry up **(e)** «*arroz/guiso*» to go dry **2** (*refl*) «*persona*» to dry oneself; ⟨*manos/pelo*⟩ to dry; ⟨*lágrimas*⟩ to dry, wipe away

sección *f* **1** (corte) section **2** **(a)** (división, área — en general) section; (— de empresa, en grandes almacenes) department **(b)** (de periódico, orquesta) section **3** (Mil) platoon

seccionar [A1] *vt* (cortar) to cut off; (dividir en secciones) to section

seco -ca *adj* **1** **(a)** [ESTAR] ⟨*ropa/platos/pintura*⟩ dry; ⟨*boca/garganta*⟩ dry **(b)** [ESTAR] ⟨*planta/río/comida*⟩ dry **(c)** [SER] ⟨*clima/región*⟩ dry **2** ⟨*higos/flores*⟩ dried; **bacalao** ∼ stockfish, dried salt cod **3** [SER] (no graso) ⟨*piel/pelo*⟩ dry **4** [SER] (no dulce) ⟨*vino/licor/vermut*⟩ dry **5** ⟨*golpe/sonido*⟩ sharp; ⟨*tos*⟩ dry **6** ⟨*respuesta/carácter*⟩ dry; **estuvo muy** ∼ **conmigo** he was very short with me **7** (*en locs*) **en seco** ⟨*frenar/parar*⟩ sharply, suddenly; **limpieza en** ∼ dry cleaning

secreción *f* (de glándula) secretion; (de herida) discharge

secretaría *f* **1** **(a)** (cargo) office of secretary **(b)** (oficina) secretary's office **(c)** (departamento administrativo) secretariat **2** (Méx) (ministerio) department, ministry (BrE)

secretariado *m* secretarial work; **estudia** ∼ she's doing a secretarial course

secretario -ria *m,f* **1** **(a)** (trabajador administrativo) secretary **(b)** (de asociación, sociedad) secretary; ∼ **de dirección** secretary to the director; ∼ **general** secretary general **2** (Méx) (Gob, Pol) secretary of state, minister; **S**∼ **de Gobernación** (en Méx) Minister of the Interior, ≈ Home Secretary (*in UK*)

secretear [A1] *vi* (AmL fam) to whisper
■ **secretearse** *v pron* (AmL fam) to whisper

secreter *m* writing desk

secreto¹ -ta *adj* secret

secreto² *m* **(a)** (información confidencial) secret; **los preparamos en** ∼ we prepared them secretly *o* in secret; ∼ **a voces** open secret **(b)** (truco) secret; **el** ∼ **está en ...** the secret is in ...

secta *f* sect

sectario -ria *adj* sectarian

sector *m* **(a)** (grupo) sector, group **(b)** (Mat) sector **(c)** (de ciudad) area **(d)** (Com, Econ) sector

secuela *f* consequence

secuencia *f* sequence, series

secuestrador -dora *m,f* (de persona) kidnapper; (de avión) hijacker

secuestrar [A1] *vt* ⟨*persona*⟩ to kidnap; ⟨*avión*⟩ to hijack

secuestro *m* (de persona) kidnapping; (de avión) hijack(ing)

secundaria *f* **(a)** (enseñanza media) secondary education, high school (AmE) **(b)** (Méx) (instituto) middle school

secundario -ria *adj* ⟨*factor/problema*⟩ secondary; ⟨*actor/actriz*⟩ supporting (*before n*)

sed *f* thirst; **el agua le quitó la** ∼ the water quenched his thirst; **tengo** ∼ I'm thirsty; **me da** ∼ it makes me (feel) thirsty; **su** ∼ **de venganza/riqueza** her thirst for vengeance/riches

seda *f* (Tex) silk; (Odont) ∼ **dental** dental floss

sedal *m* fishing line

sedante *adj/m* (Med) sedative

sede *f* **(a)** (del gobierno) seat **(b)** (Relig) see **(c)** (de organización internacional) headquarters (*sing or pl*); (de compañía) headquarters (*sing or pl*), head office **(d)** (de congreso, feria) venue; **la** ∼ **de los Juegos Olímpicos** the venue for the Olympic Games

sedentario -ria *adj* sedentary

sediento -ta *adj* thirsty

sedimento *m* sediment, deposit

sedoso -sa *adj* silky

seducción *f* seduction

seducir [I6] *vt* **(a)** (en sentido sexual) to seduce **(b)** (fascinar, cautivar) to captivate **(c)** «*idea/proposición*» (atraer) to attract, tempt; **no me seduce la idea** the idea doesn't appeal to me at all

seductor -tora *adj* **(a)** (en sentido sexual) seductive **(b)** (que cautiva, fascina) enchanting, charming **(c)** ⟨*idea/proposición*⟩ attractive, tempting
■ *m,f* (*m*) seducer; (*f*) seducer, seductress

seg. *m* (= **segundo/segundos**) sec.

segar [A7] *vt* ⟨*mies*⟩ to reap (liter), to cut

seglar *adj* lay (*before n*)
■ *mf* (*m*) layman; (*f*) laywoman

segmento *m* (Mat) segment; (Zool) segment; (Com) sector

segregación *f* segregation; ∼ **racial** racial segregation

segregar [A3] *vt* ⟨*personas/grupos*⟩ to segregate

seguida: **en seguida** (*loc adv*) immediately,

right *o* (BrE) straight away; **vinieron en** ∼ they came at once *o* right away; **en** ∼ **voy/vuelvo** I'll be right there/back

seguido¹ -da *adj* consecutive, in a row; **faltó tres días** ∼**s** she was absent three days running *o* in a row; **pasaron tres autobuses** ∼**s** three buses went by one after the other; ∼ **DE algo/algn** followed BY sth/sb

seguido² *adv* [1] (recto, sin desviarse) straight on; **vaya todo** ∼ go straight on [2] (AmL) (a menudo) often

seguidor -dora *m,f* (de teoría, filósofo) follower; (Dep) supporter, fan

seguir [I30] *vt* [1] ⟨persona/vehículo/presa⟩ to follow; **camina muy rápido, no la puedo** ∼ she walks very fast, I can't keep up with her [2] ⟨camino/ruta⟩ to follow, go along; **siga esta carretera hasta llegar al puente** go along *o* follow this road as far as the bridge; **la saludé y seguí mi camino** I said hello to her and went on (my way); **la enfermedad sigue su curso normal** the illness is running its normal course [3] (a) ⟨instrucciones/consejo/flecha⟩ to follow (b) ⟨autor/método/tradición/moda⟩ to follow; ∼ **los pasos de algn** to follow in sb's footsteps [4] (a) ⟨trámite/procedimiento⟩ to follow; ⟨tratamiento⟩ to undergo (b) (Educ) ⟨curso⟩ to do, take [5] ⟨explicaciones/profesor⟩ to follow; **dicta demasiado rápido, no la puedo** ∼ she dictates too quickly, I can't keep up

■ ∼ *vi* [1] (a) (por un camino) to go on; **siga derecho** *or* **todo recto** keep *o* go straight on; **sigue por esta calle** go on down this street; ∼ **de largo** (AmL) to go straight past (b) seguir adelante to carry on; **resolvieron** ∼ **adelante con los planes** they decided to go ahead with their plans (c) (Col, Ven) (entrar): **siga por favor** come in, please [2] (en lugar, estado): **¿tus padres siguen en Ginebra?** are your parents still in Geneva?; **espero que sigan todos bien** I hope you're all keeping well; **sigue soltera** she's still single; **si las cosas siguen así ...** if things carry on like this ... [3] «tareas/buen tiempo/lluvia» to continue; «rumores» to persist; **sigo pensando que deberíamos haber ido** I still think we ought to have gone; ∼**é haciéndolo a mi manera** I'll go on *o* carry on doing it my way [4] (a) (venir después): **lee lo que sigue** read what comes next; **el capítulo que sigue** the next chapter (b) «historia/poema» to continue, go on

según *prep* [1] (de acuerdo con) according to; ∼ **Elena** according to Elena; ∼ **parece** apparently [2] (dependiendo de): ∼ **cómo lo hagas** depending (on) how you do it; **¿me llevas a casa? —** ∼ **dónde vivas** will you take me home? — (it) depends where you live
■ *adv* it depends; **puede resultar o no,** ∼ it may or may not work, it depends
■ *conj* (a medida que) as; ∼ **van entrando** as they come in

segunda *f* [1] (a) (Auto) (marcha) second (gear); **mete (la)** ∼ put it in second (gear) (b) (Transp) (clase) second class; **viajar en** ∼ to travel second class [2] **segundas** *fpl*: **todo lo dice con** ∼**s** there's a hidden meaning to everything he says

segundero *m* second hand

segundo¹ -da *adj/pron* (a) (ordinal) second; **relegar a algn a un** ∼ **plano** to push sb into the background; *para ejemplos ver* QUINTO (b) ⟨categoría/clase⟩ second
■ *m,f* deputy, second-in-command

segundo² *m* second; **un** ∼, **ahora te atiendo** just a second, I'll be right with you

seguridad *f* [1] (ausencia de peligro) safety; (protección contra robos, atentados) security; **medidas de** ∼ (contra accidentes, incendios) safety measures; (contra robos, atentados) security measures; **una prisión de alta** ∼ a high security prison; ∼ **ciudadana** public safety [2] (estabilidad, garantía) security; ∼ **social** social security [3] (a) (certeza) certainty; **podemos decir con** ∼ **que ...** we can say for sure *o* with certainty that ... (b) (confianza, aplomo) confidence, self-confidence

seguro¹ -ra *adj* [1] (a) [SER] (exento de riesgo) safe; **en un lugar** ∼ in a safe place (b) (estable) secure; **un trabajo** ∼ a secure job; **esa escalera no está segura** that ladder isn't safe *o* steady (c) [SER] (fiable) ⟨test/método⟩ reliable; ⟨anticonceptivo⟩ safe; **el cierre de la pulsera es muy** ∼ the fastener on the bracelet is very secure (d) [ESTAR] (a salvo) safe [2] (a) [ESTAR] (convencido) sure; **no estoy** ∼ I'm not sure; ∼ **DE algo** sure *o* certain OF sth (b) [SER] (que no admite duda) ⟨muerte/victoria⟩ certain; ⟨fecha⟩ definite; **todavía no es** ∼ it's not definite yet; **no te preocupes,** ∼ **que no es nada** don't worry, I'm sure it's nothing; ∼ **que se le olvida** he's sure *o* bound to forget (c) (con confianza en sí mismo) self-assured, self-confident

seguro² *m* [1] (a) (mecanismo — de armas) safety catch; (— de pulsera, collar) clasp, fastener; **echó el** ∼ **antes de acostarse** he locked the door before going to bed (b) (Méx) (imperdible) safety pin [2] (a) (contrato) insurance; ∼ **contra** *or* **a todo riesgo** comprehensive insurance, all-risks insurance; ∼ **contra** *or* **de incendios** fire insurance; ∼ **de desempleo** unemployment benefit; ∼ **de viaje** travel insurance; ∼ **de vida** life assurance, life insurance (b) (Seguridad Social): **el** ∼ *or* **el S**∼ the state health care system, ≈ Medicaid (*in US*), ≈ the National Health Service (*in UK*)
■ *adv*: **dijo que llegaría mañana** ∼ she said she'd definitely be arriving tomorrow; **no lo sabe** ∼ she doesn't know for sure *o* certain; ∼ **que sospecha lo nuestro** I'm sure he suspects we're up to something

seis *adj inv/pron/m* six; *para ejemplos ver* CINCO

seiscientos -tas *adj/pron* six hundred

seísmo *m* (Esp) (temblor) tremor; (terremoto) earthquake

selección *f* selection; **hizo una** ∼ **de los mejores** she selected the best ones; **la** ∼ **mexicana** (Dep) the Mexican national team

seleccionador -dora *m,f* (Dep) (a) (entrenador) coach (AmE), manager (BrE) (b) (miembro de una junta) selector

seleccionar [A1] *vt* to select, choose

selectividad *f* (a) (cualidad) selectivity (b) (Educ) (en Esp) *university entrance examination*

selectivo -va *adj* selective

selecto -ta *adj* ⟨*fruta/vino*⟩ select, choice; ⟨*ambiente/club*⟩ select, exclusive

sellar [A1] *vt* **1** **(a)** ⟨*pasaporte*⟩ to stamp **(b)** ⟨*plata/oro*⟩ to hallmark **2** (*cerrar*) to seal

sello *m* **1** (de correos) (postage) stamp; (útil de oficina) rubber stamp; (marca) stamp **2** **(a)** (en el oro, la plata) hallmark **(b)** (AmL) (de una moneda) reverse; ¿**cara o ∼?** (Andes, Ven) heads or tails? **(c)** (anillo) signet ring, seal ring **(d)** (distintivo) hallmark **(e)** (Mús) *tb* **∼ discográfico** record label **3** (precinto) seal

selva *f* (bosque) forest; (de vegetación tropical) jungle; **S∼ Negra** Black Forest; **∼ tropical** tropical rainforest, selva

semáforo *m* **(a)** (Auto) traffic lights (*pl*); **se pasó un ∼ en rojo** she went through *o* (AmE) ran a red light **(b)** (Ferr) stop signal **(c)** (Náut) semaphore

semana *f* **1** (periodo) week; **∼ laboral** workweek (AmE), working week (BrE); **S∼ Santa** Easter **2** (Col) (dinero) allowance, pocket money

semanal *adj* weekly

semanario *m* (Period) weekly magazine (*o* newspaper *etc*), weekly

semántico -ca *adj* semantic

sembrado¹ *m* sown field

sembrado² -da *m,f* (Méx) (Dep) seed

sembrar [A5] *vt* ⟨*terreno/campo*⟩ to sow; ⟨*trigo/ hortalizas*⟩ to sow, plant; **∼ algo DE algo** to plant sth WITH sth

semejante *adj* **(a)** (similar) similar; **∼ A algo** similar TO sth **(b)** (*delante del n*) (para énfasis): **¡cómo puedes decir ∼ cosa!** how can you say such a thing!; **nunca había oído ∼ estupidez** I'd never heard such nonsense *o* anything so stupid ■ *m*: **nuestros ∼s** our fellow men

semejanza *f* similarity; **a ∼ de sus antepasados** like his ancestors

semen *m* semen

semental *m* (caballo) stud horse; (toro) stud bull

semestral *adj* **(a)** (en frecuencia) ⟨*exámenes/ reuniones*⟩ half-yearly, six-monthly **(b)** (en duración) ⟨*curso*⟩ six-month (*before n*)

semestre *m* **(a)** (seis meses): **cada curso dura un ∼** each course lasts six months **(b)** (Educ) (en algunos países latinoamericanos) *tb* **∼ lectivo** semester (AmE), term (BrE)

semicírculo *m* semicircle

semicorchea *f* sixteenth note (AmE), semiquaver (BrE)

semidesnatado -da *adj* (Esp) semi-skimmed, half-cream (*before n*)

semifinal *f* semifinal

semifinalista *mf* semifinalist

semilla *f* seed

semillero *m* **(a)** (Agr, Bot) seedbed **(b)** (de discordias) source; (de delincuencia) hotbed, breeding ground

seminario *m* **(a)** (Relig) seminary **(b)** (Educ) seminar

seminarista *m* seminarian

semita *adj* Semitic
■ *mf* Semite

sémola *f* semolina; **∼ de arroz** ground rice

Sena *m*: **el ∼** the Seine

senado *m* senate

senador -dora *m,f* senator

sencillez *f* simplicity; **con ∼** ⟨*vestir*⟩ simply; ⟨*comportarse*⟩ with modesty; **habla con ∼** she uses plain language

sencillo¹ -lla *adj* **1** **(a)** ⟨*ejercicio/problema*⟩ simple, straightforward; **no fue ∼ hacerlos entrar** it wasn't easy getting them in **(b)** ⟨*persona*⟩ modest, unassuming; ⟨*vestido/estilo*⟩ simple, plain; ⟨*casa/comida*⟩ simple, modest **2** (Esp, Méx) (Transp) one-way (AmE), single (BrE)

sencillo² *m* **1** (disco) single **2** (AmL) (dinero suelto) change **3** (Esp, Méx) (Transp) one-way ticket (AmE), single (ticket) (BrE)

senda *f* **(a)** (camino) path **(b)** (Ur) (de carretera) lane

sendero *m* path, track

sendos -das *adj pl* (cada uno): **llevaban sendas pistolas** each of them was carrying *o* they were each carrying a gun; **con sendas fiestas en Madrid y Barcelona** with parties in both Madrid and Barcelona

Senegal *m* Senegal

senilidad *f* senility

seno *m* **(a)** (mama) breast; (pecho) bosom; **los ∼s** the breasts; **dar el ∼** (Ven) to breastfeed **(b)** (de organización, empresa) heart

sensación *f* **1** (percepción, impresión) feeling; **una ∼ de tristeza/impotencia** a feeling of sadness/ impotence; **una vaga ∼ de placer** a vague sensation of pleasure; **una ∼ de pérdida/espacio** a sense of loss/space; **tengo** *or* **me da la ∼ de que no vamos a ganar** I have a feeling we're not going to win **2** (furor, éxito) sensation; **ser una ∼** to be a sensation

sensacional *adj* sensational

sensacionalismo *m* sensationalism

sensacionalista *adj* ⟨*prensa*⟩ sensationalist (*before n*); ⟨*artículo/foto*⟩ sensationalistic

sensatez *f* sense; **tuvo la ∼ de …** she had the (good) sense to …; **obró con ∼** she acted sensibly

sensato -ta *adj* sensible

sensibilidad *f* **(a)** (en general) sensitivity **(b)** (en brazo, pierna) feeling

sensibilizar [A4] *vt* to raise … awareness

sensible *adj* **1** (en general) sensitive; **∼ A algo** sensitive TO sth **2** (*gen delante del n*) (frml) (ostensible) ⟨*cambio/diferencia*⟩ appreciable; ⟨*mejoría*⟩ noticeable; ⟨*aumento/pérdida*⟩ considerable

sensiblero -ra *adj* (pey) mawkish

sensitivo -va *adj* sensory

sensorial *adj* sensory

sensual *adj* ⟨*boca/cuerpo*⟩ sensual, sensuous; ⟨*placeres/gesto*⟩ sensual; ⟨*descripción*⟩ sensuous

sensualidad *f* (de boca, gesto) sensuality; (de descripción) sensuousness

sentada *f* **(a)** (protesta) sit-in, sit-down protest **(b)** de *or* en una sentada in one go

sentado -da *adj* sitting, seated (frml); estaban ~s a la mesa they were (sitting) at the table; dar algo por ~ to assume sth

sentador -dora *adj* (AmL) flattering, fetching

sentar [A5] *vi* (+ *me/te/le etc*) **(a)** «*ropa/color*» (+ *compl*): ese vestido le sienta de maravilla that dress really suits her **(b)** «*comida/bebida/clima*» (+ *compl*): el café no le sienta bien coffee doesn't agree with her; me sentó bien el descanso the rest did me a lot of good **(c)** «*actitud/ comentario*» (+ *compl*): me sentó mal que no me invitaran I was rather put out that they didn't ask me (colloq)

■ ~ *vt* [1] «*niño/muñeca*» to sit; «*invitado*» to seat, sit
[2] (establecer) to establish

■ **sentarse** *v pron* to sit; ~se a la mesa to sit at (the) table; siéntese, por favor please (do) sit down

sentencia *f* (Der) judgment, ruling

sentenciar [A1] *vt* to sentence; la ~on a muerte (Der) she was sentenced to death

sentido¹ -da *adj* [1] «*palabras/carta*» heartfelt; «*anhelo/dolor*» deep; mi más ~ pésame my deepest sympathy [2] [ESTAR] (AmL) (ofendido) hurt, offended

sentido² *m* [1] **(a)** (Fisiol) sense **(b)** (noción, idea) ~ DE algo sense OF sth; su ~ del deber her sense of duty; ~ común common sense; ~ del humor sense of humor*
[2] (conocimiento) consciousness; perder el ~ to lose consciousness; el golpe lo dejó sin ~ he was knocked unconscious by the blow
[3] (significado) sense; en el buen ~ de la palabra in the nicest sense of the word; en ~ literal in a literal sense; lo dijo con doble ~ he was intentionally ambiguous; el ~ de la vida the meaning of life; en cierto ~ … in a sense …; no le encuentro ~ a lo que haces I can't see any sense *o* point in what you're doing; esa política ya no tiene ~ that policy doesn't make sense anymore *o* is meaningless now; palabras sin ~ meaningless words
[4] (dirección) direction; gírese en ~ contrario al de las agujas del reloj turn (round) in a counterclockwise (AmE) *o* (BrE) an anticlockwise direction; venían en ~ contrario al nuestro they were coming in the opposite direction to us; calle de ~ único *or* (Méx) de un solo ~ one-way street

sentimental *adj* **(a)** (relativo a los sentimientos) sentimental **(b)** «*persona/canción/novela*» sentimental; ponerse ~ to get sentimental **(c)** «*aventura/vida*» love (*before n*)

sentimentalismo *m* sentimentalism

sentimiento *m* [1] **(a)** (emoción) feeling; ser de buenos ~s to be a caring person; no se deja llevar por los ~s she doesn't let herself get carried away by her emotions **(b)** (pesar): les acompaño en el ~ my commiserations
[2] **sentimientos** *mpl* feelings (*pl*); herir los ~s de algn to hurt sb's feelings

sentir [I11] *vt* [1] **(a)** «*dolor/pinchazo*» to feel; ~

hambre/frío/sed to feel hungry/cold/thirsty **(b)** «*emoción*» to feel; sentimos una gran alegría we were overjoyed; ~ celos to feel jealous
[2] **(a)** (oír) «*ruido/disparo*» to hear **(b)** (esp AmL) (percibir): siento olor a gas I can smell gas; le siento gusto a vainilla I can taste vanilla
[3] (lamentar): lo siento mucho I'm really sorry; sentí mucho no poder ayudarla I was very sorry not to be able to help her; ha sentido mucho la pérdida de su madre she has been very affected by her mother's death

■ **sentirse** *v pron* [1] (+ *compl*) to feel; me siento mal I don't feel well, I'm not feeling well; no me siento con ánimos I don't feel up to it
[2] (Chi, Méx) (ofenderse) to be offended *o* hurt; ~se CON algn to be offended *o* upset WITH algn

seña *f* [1] (gesto) sign; hacer una ~ to make a sign, to signal; les hice ~s de que se callaran I gestured *o* motioned to them to keep quiet
[2] **señas** *fpl* (dirección) address [3] **señas** *fpl* (indicios): dar ~s DE algo to show signs OF sth
[4] (RPl) ▶ SEÑAL 5

señal *f* [1] **(a)** (aviso, letrero) sign; ~es de tráfico traffic signs; S~ de la Cruz sign of the cross **(b)** (signo) signal; nos hacía ~es para que nos acercáramos she was signaling *o* gesturing for us to come nearer; ~ de auxilio *or* socorro distress signal **(c)** (Ferr) signal
[2] (marca, huella): pon una ~ en la página mark the page; ~es de violencia signs of violence
[3] (Rad, TV) signal **(b)** (Telec): la ~ para marcar the dial (AmE) *o* (BrE) dialling tone; la ~ de ocupado *or* (Esp) comunicando the busy signal (AmE), the engaged tone (BrE)
[4] (indicio) sign; eso es mala ~ that's a bad sign; no daba ~es de vida he showed no signs of life; en ~ de respeto/amor as a token of respect/love
[5] (Esp) (Com) (depósito) deposit, down payment

señalar [A1] *vt* [1] (indicar) «*ruta/camino*» to show; el reloj señalaba las doce the clock showed twelve; me señaló con el dedo he pointed at me (with his finger); ~le algo A algn to show sb sth, point sth out TO sb; me señaló con el dedo qué pasteles quería he pointed out (to me) which cakes he wanted
[2] (marcar con lápiz, rotulador) to mark
[3] (afirmar) to point out; señaló que … she pointed out that …
[4] (fijar) «*fecha*» to fix, set; en el lugar señalado in the appointed *o* agreed place
[5] (anunciar) to mark

■ ~ *vi* to point

señalización *f* **(a)** (en carretera, calle) signposting; (en edificio, centro comercial) signs (*pl*) **(b)** (Ferr) signaling*

señalizar [A4] *vt* **(a)** «*carretera/calle/ciudad*» to signpost; «*edificio/centro comercial*» to put up directions on/in **(b)** (Ferr) «*tramo/vía*» to install signals on

señor -ñora *m,f* [1] **(a)** (persona adulta) (*m*) man, gentleman; (*f*) lady; peluquería de ~as ladies' hairdresser's **(b)** (persona distinguida) (*m*) gentleman; (*f*) lady; es todo un ~ he's a real gentleman
[2] (dueño, amo): el ~/la ~a de la casa the gentleman/the lady of the house (frml)
[3] (Relig) **(a)** **Señor** *m* Lord **(b)** **Señora** *f*: Nuestra S~a de Montserrat Our Lady of Montserrat

⸱⸱⸱⸭

S

4 señora f (esposa) wife

5 (tratamiento de cortesía) **(a)** (con apellidos) (m) Mr; (f) Mrs; **los ~es de Paz** Mr and Mrs Paz **(b)** (frml) (con otros sustantivos): **la ~a directora está ocupada** the director is busy; **S~ Director** (Coresp) Dear Sir, Sir (frml) **(c)** (frml) (sin mencionar el nombre): **perdón, ~ ¿tiene hora?** excuse me, could you tell me the time?; **muy ~ mío/~es míos** (Coresp) Dear Sir/Sirs; **Teresa Chaves — ¿~a o ~ita?** Teresa Chaves — Miss, Mrs or Ms?; **los ~es han salido** Mr and Mrs Paz (o López etc) are not at home

señorial adj ⟨casa⟩ stately; ⟨ciudad⟩ noble

señorita f **1 (a)** (mujer joven) young lady **(b)** (joven distinguida) young lady **(c)** (maestra) teacher **2** (tratamiento de cortesía) **(a)** (con apellidos) Miss **(b)** (con nombres de pila): **~ Teresa ¿puede atender a la señora?** Teresa/Miss Chaves (o López etc), could you serve this lady please? **(c)** (maestra) Miss **(d)** (sin mencionar el nombre) (frml) Miss

señorito m (pey) rich young man, rich kid (colloq)

señuelo m (persona) bait; (para aves) decoy

sepa, sepas, etc ▶ SABER

separación f **1 (a)** (división) separation; **la ~ de la Iglesia y del Estado** the separation of the Church and the State **(b)** (espacio) gap, separation **2** (del matrimonio) separation

separado -da adj **1** ⟨persona⟩ separated **2 (a)** ⟨camas⟩ separate **(b) por separado** separately
■ m,f: **es hijo de ~s** his parents are separated

separador m **1** (de carpeta) divider **2** (Col) (Auto) median strip (AmE), central reservation (BrE)

separar [A1] vt **1 (a)** (apartar, alejar) to separate; **~ los machos de las hembras** to separate the males from the females; **separa la cama de la pared** move the bed away from the wall **(b)** (dividir un todo) to divide **(c)** (guardar, reservar) to put o set aside **2 (a)** (actuar de división) «valla/línea» to separate; **los Andes separan a Chile de Argentina** the Andes separate Chile from Argentina **(b)** (despegar): **no puedo ~ estas dos fotos** I can't get these two photographs apart
■ **separarse** v pron **(a)** «matrimonio» to separate; **~se DE algn** to separate FROM sb **(b)** (seguir direcciones distintas) to split up; **a mitad de camino nos separamos** we split up half way **(c)** (apartarse, alejarse): **no se separen, que los pequeños se pueden perder** please stay together in case the children get lost; **no me he separado nunca de mis hijos** I've never been away o apart from my children

separatismo m separatism

separatista mf separatist

separo m (Méx) cell

sepia f **(a)** (Coc, Zool) cuttlefish, sepia (tech) **(b)** (en pintura) sepia
■ m (color) sepia

septentrional adj northern

septiembre m September; para ejemplos ver ENERO

séptimo¹ -ma adj/pron seventh; **la séptima parte** a seventh; **el ~ arte** the movies (pl) (AmE), the cinema (BrE); para ejemplos ver QUINTO

séptimo² m seventh

sepulcral adj (liter) ⟨silencio⟩ deathly

sepulcro m tomb, sepulcher* (liter)

sepultar [A1] vt **(a)** (frml) ⟨muerto⟩ to inter (frml), to bury **(b)** (period) (cubrir): **fue sepultado por un alud de nieve** he was buried by an avalanche

sepultura f **(a)** (acción) burial **(b)** (tumba) tomb, grave

sepulturero -ra m,f gravedigger

sequedad f **(a)** (de terreno, región, piel) dryness **(b)** (de respuesta, tono) curtness

sequía f drought

séquito m (de rey) retinue, entourage

ser [E26] cópula **1** (seguido de adjetivos) to be [SER expresses identity or nature as opposed to condition or state, which is normally conveyed by ESTAR. The examples given below should be contrasted with those to be found in ESTAR¹ cópula 1] **es bajo/muy callado** he's short/very quiet; **es sorda de nacimiento** she was born deaf; **es inglés/católico** he's English/(a) Catholic; **era cierto** it was true; **sé bueno, estate quieto** be a good boy and keep still; **que seas muy feliz** I hope you'll be very happy; (+ me/te/le etc) **siempre le he sido fiel** I've always been faithful to her; ver tb IMPOSIBLE, DIFÍCIL etc **2** (hablando de estado civil) to be; **el mayor es casado** the oldest is married; **es viuda** she's a widow; ver tb ESTAR¹ cópula 2 **3** (seguido de nombre, pronombre) to be; **soy abogada** I'm a lawyer; **ábreme, soy yo** open the door, it's me **4** (con predicado introducido por 'de'): **esos zapatos son de plástico** those shoes are (made of) plastic; **soy de Córdoba** I'm from Cordoba; **es de los vecinos** it belongs to the neighbors, it's the neighbors'; **no soy de aquí** I'm not from around here **5** (hipótesis, futuro): **será un error** it must be a mistake; **¿será cierto?** can it be true?

■ ~ vi
I 1 (a) (existir) to be **(b)** (liter) (en cuentos): **érase una vez ...** once upon a time there was ...
2 (a) (tener lugar, ocurrir): **la fiesta va a ~ en su casa** the party is going to be (held) at her house; **¿dónde fue el accidente?** where did the accident happen? **(b)** (en preguntas): **¿qué habrá sido de él?** I wonder what happened to o what became of him; **¿qué es de Marisa?** (fam) what's Marisa up to (these days)? (colloq); **¿qué va a ser de nosotros?** what will become of us?
3 (sumar): **¿cuánto es (todo)?** how much is that (altogether)?; **son 3.000 pesos** that'll be o that's 3,000 pesos; **somos diez en total** there are ten of us altogether
4 (indicando finalidad, adecuación) **~ PARA algo** to be FOR sth; **este agua es para beber** this water is for drinking
II (en locs) **a no ser que** (+ subj) unless; **¿cómo es eso?** why is that?, how come? (colloq); **como/ cuando/donde sea: tengo que conseguir ese trabajo como sea** I have to get that job no matter what; **hazlo como sea, pero hazlo** do it any way o however you want but get it done; **el lunes o cuando sea** next Monday or whenever; **puedo dormir en el sillón o donde sea** I can sleep in the armchair or wherever you like o anywhere you like; **de ser así** (frml) should this be so o the case (frml); **¡eso es!** that's it!, that's right!; **es que ...:**

¿es que no lo saben? do you mean to say they don't know?; **es que no sé nadar** the thing is I can't swim; **lo que sea: cómete una manzana, o lo que sea** have an apple or something; **estoy dispuesta a hacer lo que sea** I'm prepared to do whatever it takes; **o sea: en febrero, o sea hace un mes** in February, that is to say a month ago; **o sea que no te interesa** in other words, you're not interested; **o sea que nunca lo descubriste** so you never found out; **(ya) sea ..., (ya) sea ...** either ..., or ...; **sea como sea** at all costs; **sea cuando sea** whenever it is; **sea donde sea** no matter where; **sea quien sea** whoever it is; **si no fuera/hubiera sido por ...** if it wasn't o weren't/hadn't been for ...
III (en el tiempo) to be; **¿qué fecha es hoy?** what's the date today?, what's today's date; **serían las cuatro cuando llegó** it must have been (about) four (o'clock) when she arrived; *ver tb v impers*
■ ~ *v impers* to be; **era primavera** it was spring(time)
■ ~ *v aux* (en la voz pasiva) to be; **fue construido en 1900** it was built in 1900
■ *m* **1** (a) (ente) being; **~ humano/vivo** human/living being (b) (individuo, persona): **un ~ querido** a loved one
2 (naturaleza): **desde lo más profundo de mi ~** from the bottom of my heart

Serbia *f* Serbia

serbio¹ -bia *adj/m,f* Serbian

serbio² *m* (idioma) Serbian

serbocroata *adj/mf* Serbo-Croat, Serbo-Croatian
■ *m* (idioma) Serbo-Croat

seré, seremos, etc ▶ SER

serenarse [A1] *v pron* (calmarse) to calm down

serenata *f* serenade; **dar una** *or* (Méx) **llevar ~** to serenade

serenidad *f* calmness, serenity; **no pierdas la ~** keep calm

sereno¹ -na *adj* (a) ⟨rostro/expresión/belleza⟩ serene; ⟨persona⟩ serene, calm (b) ⟨cielo⟩ cloudless, clear; ⟨tarde⟩ still; ⟨mar⟩ calm, tranquil (liter)

sereno² *m* (vigilante nocturno) night watchman

sería, etc ▶ SER

serial *m*, (CS) *f* ▶ SERIE 2

serie *f* **1** (a) (sucesión) series; **una ~ de pueblos** a series of villages (b) (clase) series; **coches de ~** production cars; **fabricación en ~** mass production; **producir/fabricar en ~** to mass produce; **fuera de ~** (fam) out of this world (colloq) (c) (Dep) heat **2** (Rad, TV) series; (historia continua) serial

seriedad *f* (a) (en general) seriousness (b) (sensatez, responsabilidad): **se comportó con mucha ~** she behaved very sensibly o responsibly; **¡un poco de ~!** let's be serious now!

serio -ria *adj* **1** (poco sonriente) serious **2** ⟨empleado⟩ responsible, reliable; ⟨empresa⟩ reputable **3** (a) ⟨cine/tema⟩ serious (b) ⟨grave⟩ ⟨enfermedad/problema⟩ serious; **tengo serias dudas acerca de él** I have serious doubts about him (c) **en serio** ⟨hablar⟩ in earnest; **¿lo dices en ~?** are you (being) serious?, do you really mean it?; **tomarse algo en ~** to take sth seriously

sermón *m* sermon; **me echó un ~** (fam) he gave me a lecture

seropositivo -va *adj* (en general) seropositive; (con el VIH) HIV positive

serpentear [A1] *vi* ⟨río⟩ to meander, wind; ⟨camino⟩ to wind, twist

serpentina *f* streamer

serpiente *f* snake, serpent; **~ (de) cascabel** rattlesnake; **~ pitón** python

serrar [A5] *vt* to saw (up)

serrín *m* sawdust

serruchar [A1] *vt* (AmL) to saw

serrucho *m* handsaw

servicentro *m* (Andes) service station

servicial *adj* helpful, obliging

servicio *m* **1** (a) (acción de servir) service; **estamos a su ~** we are at your service; **estar de ~** ⟨policía/bombero⟩ to be on duty; **~ público** public service; **~s informativos** broadcasting services (*pl*) (b) (favor) favor*, service (c) **servicios** *mpl* (asistencia) services (*pl*); **me ofreció sus ~s** he offered me his services **2** (funcionamiento) service, use; **está fuera de ~** it's out of service; **han puesto en ~ el nuevo andén** the new platform is now in use o is now open **3** (en hospital) department; **~ de urgencias** casualty department **4** (en restaurante, hotel) (a) (atención al cliente) service (b) (propina) service (charge) **5** (servidumbre): **entrada de ~** tradesman's entrance; **cuarto de ~** servant's quarters (frml), maid's room; **~ doméstico** (actividad) domestic service; (personas) servants (*pl*), domestic staff **6** (Mil) service; **~ militar** military service **7** (retrete) restroom (AmE), bathroom (esp AmE), toilet (esp BrE) **8** (en tenis) service, serve **9** (Relig) service **10** (AmL) (Auto) service

servidor -dora *m,f* **1** (a) (sirviente) servant (b) (frml) (Corresp): **su ⟨atento y⟩ seguro ~** your humble servant (frml) **2 servidor** *m* (Inf) server

servidumbre *f* **1** (esclavitud) servitude **2** (conjunto de criados) domestic staff, servants (*pl*)

servil *adj* (a) ⟨persona/actitud⟩ servile, obsequious (frml) (b) ⟨trabajo⟩ menial

servilleta *f* napkin, serviette (esp BrE)

servilletero *m* napkin ring, serviette ring (BrE)

servir [I14] *vi* **1** (ser útil): **esta caja no sirve** this box won't do o is no good; **ya no me sirve** it's (of) no use to me anymore; **¿para qué sirve este aparato?** what's this device for?; **no lo tires, puede ~ para algo** don't throw it away, it might come in useful for something; **este cuchillo no sirve para cortar pan** this knife is no good for cutting bread; **no sirves para nada** you're useless; **no creo que sirva para este trabajo** I don't think he's right o suitable for this job; **~ DE algo: de nada sirve llorar** it's no use o good crying; **¿de qué sirve?** what's the point o the use?; **esto te puede ~ de mesa** you can use this as a table **2** (a) (en la mesa) to serve (b) (trabajar de criado) to be in (domestic) service (c) (Mil) to serve (frml) **3** (Dep) (en tenis) to serve

■ ~ *vt* **1** ⟨*comida*⟩ to serve; ⟨*bebida*⟩ to serve, pour
2 (estar al servicio de) ⟨*persona/a la patria*⟩ to serve; ¿en qué puedo ~la? (frml) how can I help you?

■ **servirse** *v pron* (*refl*) ⟨*comida*⟩ to help oneself to; ⟨*bebida*⟩ to pour oneself, help oneself to

sésamo *m* sesame

sesear [A1] *vi*: *to pronounce the Spanish* [θ] *as* [s], *eg* /ser'βesa/ *instead of* /θer'βeθa/ *for* CERVEZA

sesenta *adj inv/m/pron* sixty; *para ejemplos ver* CINCUENTA

seseo *m*: *pronunciation of the Spanish* /θ/ *as* /s/, *eg* /ser'βesa/ *instead of* /θer'βeθa/ *for* CERVEZA

sesión *f* (a) (reunión) session; ~ de clausura closing session (b) (de tratamiento, actividad) session; (de fotografía, pintura) sitting (c) (de cine) showing, performance; (de teatro) show, performance; ~ de noche late evening performance

sesionar [A1] *vi* (AmL) to be in session

seso *m* (a) (Anat, Zool) brain (b) **sesos** *mpl* (Coc) brains (*pl*)

set *m* (*pl* **sets**) set

seta *f* (comestible) mushroom; (venenosa) toadstool

setecientos -tas *adj/pron* seven hundred; *para ejemplos ver* QUINIENTOS

setenta *adj inv/m/pron* seventy; *para ejemplos ver* CINCUENTA

setiembre *m* ▶ SEPTIEMBRE

seto *m* hedge

seudónimo *m* pseudonym; (de escritor) pen name, pseudonym

severidad *f* (de castigo, pena) severity, harshness; (de padre, educador) strictness; (de clima) harshness

severo -ra *adj* ⟨*padre/profesor*⟩ strict; ⟨*castigo*⟩ severe, harsh; ⟨*invierno*⟩ hard, severe; ⟨*dieta/ régimen*⟩ strict

Sevilla *f* Seville

sexismo *m* sexism

sexista *adj/mf* sexist

sexo *m* sex; el ~ débil the weaker sex; ~ seguro safe sex

sexto¹ -ta *adj/pron* sixth; *para ejemplos ver* QUINTO; la sexta parte a sixth; ~ sentido sixth sense

sexto² *m* sixth

sexual *adj* ⟨*relaciones/órganos/comportamiento*⟩ sexual; ⟨*educación/vida*⟩ sex (*before n*)

sexualidad *f* sexuality

sexy /'seksi, 'sesi/ *adj* (fam) sexy

sh, shh *interj* shush!, ssh!, hush!

sha, shah *m* shah

sheriff /'ʃerif/ *mf* sheriff

shock /ʃok/ *m* (a) (Med) shock; en estado de ~ in (a state of) shock (b) (sorpresa desagradable) shock

show /ʃou, tʃou/ *m* (*pl* **shows**) show

si *conj* **1** (a) (en general) if; ~ pudiera if I could;

~ lo hubiera *or* hubiese sabido ... if I'd known ..., had I known ...; empezó a decir que ~ esto, que ~ lo otro he said this, that and the other (b) (en frases que expresan deseo) if only; ¡~ yo lo supiera! if only I knew! (c) (en frases que expresan protesta, indignación, sorpresa): ¡pero ~ te avisé ...! but I warned you ...! (d) (planteando eventualidades, sugerencias): y ~ no quiere hacerlo ¿qué? and if she doesn't want to do it, what then?; ¿y ~ lo probáramos? why don't we give it a try? (e) (*en locs*) si no otherwise
2 (en interrogativas indirectas) whether; no sé ~ marcharme o quedarme I don't know whether to go or to stay

■ *m* (nota) B; (en solfeo) ti, te (BrE); ~ bemol/ sostenido B flat/sharp

sí *adv* **1** (respuesta afirmativa) yes; ¿has terminado? — sí have you finished? — yes (I have); decir que ~ con la cabeza to nod
2 (uso enfático): ahora ~ que lo has hecho bien now you've really done it! (colloq); tú ~ que sabes vivir you certainly know how to live!; eso ~ que es caro that *is* expensive; no puedo — ¡~ que puedes! I can't — yes, you can! o of course, you can!; que ~ cabe it does fit; es de muy buena calidad — eso ~ it's very good quality — (yes,) that's true
3 (sustituyendo a una cláusula): creo que ~ I think so; me temo que ~ I'm afraid so; ¿lloverá? — puede que ~ do you think it will rain? — it might; un día ~ y otro no every other day; no puedo ir pero ella ~ I can't go but she can

■ *m* yes

■ *pron pers* **1** (a) (*refl*) (él) himself; (ella) herself; (ellos, ellas) themselves; solo piensa en ~ mismo he only thinks of himself; parece muy segura de ~ (misma) she seems very sure of herself; fueron para convencerse a ~ mismos/mismas they went to convince themselves (b) (*refl*) (usted) yourself; (ustedes) yourselves; descríbase a ~ mismo describe yourself; léanlo para ~ (mismos) read it (to) yourselves (c) (*impers*): hay cosas que uno tiene que ver por ~ mismo there are some things you have to see for yourself
2 (*en locs*) entre sí (entre dos) between themselves; (entre varios) among themselves; lo discutieron entre ~ they discussed it between/ among themselves; no se respetan entre ~ they don't respect each other; de por sí: es de por ~ nervioso he is nervous by nature; el sistema es de por ~ complicado the system is in itself complicated; en sí (mismo): el hecho en ~ (mismo) no tenía demasiada importancia this in itself was not so important

siamés -mesa *adj* Siamese

■ *m,f* (gemelo) Siamese twins

sibarita *mf* (amante de los lujos) lover of luxury, sybarite (frml); (en cuestiones de comida) gourmet, epicure (frml)

Siberia *f* Siberia

Sicilia *f* Sicily

siciliano -na *adj/m,f* Sicilian

AmC	América Central		Arg	Argentina		Cu	Cuba		Per	Perú
AmL	América Latina		Bol	Bolivia		Ec	Ecuador		RPI	Río de la Plata
AmS	América del Sur		Chi	Chile		Esp	España		Ur	Uruguay
Andes	Región andina		CS	Cono Sur		Méx	México		Ven	Venezuela

sida *m* (= **Síndrome de Inmunodeficiencia Adquirida**) AIDS

sidecar /siðe'kar, 'saikar/ *m* (*pl* **-cares** or **-cars**) sidecar

sideral *adj* (Astron) sidereal

siderurgia *f* iron and steel industry

sidra *f* hard cider (AmE), cider (BrE)

siempre *adv* **1** always; ~ **se sale con la suya** he always gets his own way; **como** ~ as usual; **lo de** ~ the usual thing; **a la hora de** ~ at the usual time; **los conozco desde** ~ I've known them for as long as I can remember; **para** ~ (definitivamente) ⟨*regresar/quedarse*⟩ for good; (eternamente) ⟨*durar/vivir*⟩ for ever **2** (en todo caso) always; ~ **podemos modificarlo después** we can always modify it later **3** (AmL) (todavía) still; *¿*~ **viven en Malvín?** do they still live in Malvín? **4** (*en locs*) **siempre que** (cada vez que) whenever; (a condición de que) (+ *subj*) provided (that), providing (that) **5** (Méx) (en definitiva) after all; ~ **no se va** he's not leaving after all

sien *f* temple

sienta, sientas, etc ▶ SENTAR, SENTIR

sierra *f* **1** (Tec) saw; ~ **de mano** handsaw; ~ **mecánica** power saw **2** (Geog) (cordillera) mountain range; (zona montañosa): **fuimos a la** ~ we went to the mountains

Sierra Leona *f* Sierra Leone

sierraleonés -nesa *adj* of/from Sierra Leone

siervo -va *m,f* serf, slave

siesta *f* siesta, nap; **dormir la** ~ *or* **echar una** ~ to have a siesta *o* nap

siete *adj inv/pron* seven; *para ejemplos ver* CINCO
■ *m* (a) (cardinal) (number) seven; *para ejemplos ver* CINCO (b) (rotura) tear (*L-shaped*)

sietemesino -na *m,f* premature baby (*esp when born two months early*)

sífilis *f* syphilis

sifilítico -ca *m,f* person with *o* suffering from syphilis, syphilitic

sifón *m* **1** (a) (botella) siphon* (b) (Esp fam) (soda) soda (water) (c) (Col) (cerveza) draft* beer **2** (para trasvasar líquidos) siphon; (en fontanería) U-bend, trap

siga, sigas, etc ▶ SEGUIR

sigilo *m* stealth; **con** ~ stealthily

sigiloso -sa *adj* stealthy

sigla *f* abbreviation; (pronunciado como una palabra) acronym

siglo *m* (período) century; **hace** ~**s** *or* **un** ~ **que no le escribo** (fam) I haven't written to her for ages (colloq)

significación *f* (importancia) significance, importance

significado *m* **1** (de palabra) meaning; (de símbolo) meaning, significance **2** (importancia) ▶ SIGNIFICACIÓN

significar [A2] *vt* (a) (querer decir) to mean (b) (suponer, representar) ⟨*mejora/ruina*⟩ to represent; ⟨*esfuerzo/riesgo*⟩ to involve (c) (valer, importar) to mean

significativo -va *adj* **1** ⟨*cambio/detalle*⟩ significant **2** ⟨*gesto/sonrisa*⟩ meaningful

signo *m* **1** (en general) sign; ~ **de admiración** exclamation point (AmE), exclamation mark (BrE); ~ **de interrogación** question mark; ~ **de la victoria** V-sign; ~ **de puntuación** punctuation mark **2** (Astrol) *tb* ~ **del zodiaco** sign; *¿*de qué ~ eres? what sign are you?

sigo, sigue, etc ▶ SEGUIR

siguiente *adj* **1** (a) (en el tiempo) following (*before n*); **al día** ~ the next *o* the following day (b) (en secuencia) next; **en el capítulo** ~ in the next *o* following chapter (c) (*como n*): **serán los** ~**s en entrar** they'll be the next to go; **¡**(que pase) el ~! next please! **2** (que se va a nombrar) following (*before n*); **la carta decía lo** ~ ... the letter said the following ...

sílaba *f* syllable

silbar [A1] *vt* (a) ⟨*melodía*⟩ to whistle (b) ⟨*cantante/obra*⟩ (en señal de desaprobación) to whistle at, catcall
■ ~ *vi* (a) (Mús) to whistle (b) «*viento*» to whistle (c) «*oídos*»: **me silban los oídos** I've got a ringing *o* whistling in my ears

silbato *m* (a) (pito) whistle; **tocar el** ~ to blow the whistle (b) (Col period) (árbitro) referee

silbido *m* (a) (con la boca, un silbato) whistle; **dio un** ~ he whistled (b) (del viento, balas) whistling; (de respiración) wheezing (c) (en los oídos) ringing, whistling (d) **silbidos** *mpl* (en señal de desaprobacion) catcalls (*pl*)

silenciador *m* (a) (Auto) muffler (AmE), silencer (BrE) (b) (de arma) silencer

silencio *m* **1** (en general) silence; **deben guardar** ~ you must remain silent; **en el** ~ **más absoluto** in dead *o* total silence **2** (Mús) rest

silenciosamente *adv* silently, quietly

silencioso -sa *adj* **1** ⟨*máquina/motor*⟩ quiet, silent, noiseless; ⟨*persona*⟩ silent, quiet **2** ⟨*calle/barrio*⟩ quiet

silicona *f* silicone

silicosis *f* silicosis

silla *f* (a) (mueble) chair; ~ **de ruedas** wheelchair; ~ **eléctrica** electric chair; ~ **plegable** *or* **de tijera** folding chair (b) (Equ) *tb* ~ **de montar** saddle

sillín *m* (de bicicleta) saddle

sillón *m* armchair, easy chair

silogismo *m* syllogism

silueta *f* (a) (cuerpo) figure (b) (contorno) silhouette

silvestre *adj* wild

simbólico -ca *adj* symbolic

simbolizar [A4] *vt* to symbolize, represent

símbolo *m* symbol

simetría *f* symmetry

simétrico -ca *adj* symmetric, symmetrical

símil *m* (a) (comparación) comparison (b) (Lit) simile

similar *adj* similar; ~ A **algo** similar TO sth

similitud *f* similarity, resemblance

simio *m* ape, simian (tech)

simpatía *f* (a) (de una persona) friendliness (b) ···⫶

(sentimiento): **se ganó la(s) ∽(s) de todos** everyone came to like him; **no le tengo mucha ∽** I don't really like him

simpático -ca *adj* **(a)** ⟨*persona*⟩ nice; **me cae** *or* **me resulta muy ∽** I really like him **(b)** ⟨*gesto/ detalle*⟩ nice, lovely **(c)** ⟨*ambiente*⟩ pleasant, congenial; ⟨*paseo*⟩ pleasant, nice

simpatizante *mf* (de partido) supporter

simpatizar [A4] *vi* **(a)** (caerse bien) **∽ (CON algn)** to get on well (WITH sb); **∽on desde el primer momento** they took to each other right from the start **(b)** (Pol) **∽ CON algo** to be sympathetic TO sth, to sympathize WITH sth

simple *adj* **1** (sencillo, fácil) simple; ▶ LLANAMENTE **2** (*delante del n*) (mero) simple; **el ∽ hecho de ...** the simple fact of ...; **es un ∽ resfriado** it's just a common cold; **un ∽ soldado** an ordinary soldier **3** (tonto) simple, simple-minded
■ *mf* simpleton

simpleza *f* **(a)** (falta de inteligencia) simpleness; (ingenuidad) gullibility **(b)** (tontería): **deja de hacer/ decir ∽s** stop being silly; **discutieron por una ∽** they argued over a trifling matter

simplicidad *f* simplicity

simplificar [A2] *vt* to simplify

simplista *adj* simplistic

simposio, simposium *m* symposium

simulacro *m* **(a)** (cosa fingida): **no era de verdad, fue un ∽** it wasn't for real, they (*o* he *etc*) were (*o* was *etc*) just pretending **(b)** (farsa) sham; **∽ de ataque** mock attack; **∽ de incendio** fire drill, fire practice

simular [A1] *vt* ⟨*sentimiento*⟩ to feign; ⟨*accidente*⟩ to fake; ⟨*efecto/sonido*⟩ to simulate

simultánea *f* (en ajedrez) simultaneous match

simultáneo -nea *adj* simultaneous

sin *prep* **1** without; **∽ azúcar** without sugar; **seguimos ∽ noticias** we still haven't had any news; **agua mineral ∽ gas** still mineral water; **cerveza ∽ alcohol** non-alcoholic beer, alcohol-free beer; **me quedé ∽ pan** I ran out of bread **2 (a)** (con significado activo) without; **se fue ∽ pagar** he left without paying; **estuvo una semana ∽ hablarme** she didn't speak to me for a week; **sigo ∽ entender** I still don't understand; **la pisé ∽ querer** I accidentally trod on her foot **(b)** (con significado pasivo): **preguntas ∽ contestar** unanswered questions; **esto está aún ∽ terminar** it still isn't finished **3 ∽ QUE + SUBJ: no voy a ir ∽ que me inviten** I'm not going if I haven't been invited; **quítaselo ∽ que se dé cuenta** get it off him without his *o* without her noticing; ▶ EMBARGO 2

sinagoga *f* synagogue

sinceridad *f* sincerity; **te voy a contestar con toda ∽** I'm going to be quite honest *o* frank with you

sincero -ra *adj* sincere

sincronía *f* synchrony

sincronizar [A4] *vt* **(a)** ⟨*frecuencias/relojes*⟩ to synchronize; **∽ algo CON algo** to synchronize sth WITH sth **(b)** (Col) ⟨*carro*⟩ to tune

sindical *adj* union (*before n*), labor union (*before n*) (AmE), trade union (*before n*) (BrE)

sindicalismo *m* **(a)** (movimiento) labor union movement (AmE), trade union movement (BrE) **(b)** (sistema, ideología) unionism, trade unionism (BrE)

sindicalista *mf* **(a)** (Rels Labs) member of the unions, trade unionist (BrE) **(b)** (Pol) syndicalist

sindicalizarse [A4] *v pron* (formar un sindicato) to unionize, form a union; (afiliarse a un sindicato) to join a union

sindicato *m* (Rels Labs) union, labor union (AmE), trade union (BrE)

síndrome *m* syndrome; **∽ de abstinencia** withdrawal symptoms (*pl*); **∽ de inmunodeficiencia adquirida** Acquired Immune Deficiency Syndrome, AIDS; **el ∽ premenstrual** premenstrual syndrome *o* (BrE) tension, (BrE); **∽ de Down** Down's syndrome; **∽ de la clase turista** economy class syndrome

sinfín *m*: **un ∽ de** a great many

sinfonía *f* symphony

sinfónico -ca *adj* ⟨*música*⟩ symphonic; ⟨*orquesta*⟩ symphony (*before n*)

Singapur *m* Singapore

single /'singel/ *m* **1** (Mús) single **2** (en tenis) **(a)** (CS) (partido) singles (match) **(b) singles** *mpl* (AmL) (partido) singles (match)

singular *adj* singular
■ *m* singular; **en ∽** (Ling) in the singular

siniestro¹ -tra *adj* ⟨*mirada/aspecto*⟩ sinister; ⟨*intenciones*⟩ sinister, evil

siniestro² *m* (frml) (accidente) accident; (causado por una fuerza natural) disaster, catastrophe

sinnúmero *m* ▶ SINFÍN

sino *conj* but; **se comió no uno, ∽ tres** he ate not one, but three; **no hace ∽ criticar a los demás** he does nothing but criticize everybody else; **no vino, ∽ que llamó** he didn't come, he telephoned; **no solo ... ∽ que ...** not only ... but ...
■ *m* (liter) fate

sínodo *m* synod

sinónimo¹ -ma *adj* synonymous; **∽ DE algo** synonymous WITH sth

sinónimo² *m* synonym; **∽ DE algo** synonym FOR sth

sinsabores *mpl* (problemas) troubles (*pl*); (experiencias tristes) heartaches (*pl*)

sintáctico -ca *adj* syntactic

sintagma *m* syntagm, syntagma

sintaxis *f* syntax

síntesis *f* (*pl* ∽) **(a)** (resumen) summary **(b)** (deducción) synthesis; (combinación) synthesis, combination

sintético -ca *adj* ⟨*fibra*⟩ synthetic, man-made; ⟨*suelas*⟩ man-made

sintetizador *m* synthesizer

sintetizar [A4] *vt* **(a)** (resumir) to summarize **(b)** (combinar) to synthesize, combine

sintiera, sintió, etc ▶ SENTIR

síntoma *m* (Med) symptom; (señal) sign, indication

sintonía *f* **(a)** (Rad, TV): **están ustedes en la ∽ de Radio Victoria** you are listening to Radio Victoria; **para una mejor ∽** for better reception **(b)** (armonía): **en ∽ con el pueblo** in tune with the people

sintonizador *m* tuner

sintonizar [A4] *vt* ‹*emisora*› to tune (in) to
■ ~ *vi* (Rad, TV) to tune in
sinvergüenza *adj* **(a)** (canalla): ¡qué tipo más
~! what a swine! (colloq) **(b)** (hum) (pícaro)
naughty
■ *mf* **(a)** (canalla) swine (colloq); (estafador, ladrón)
crook (colloq) **(b)** (hum) (pícaro) rascal (hum)
síper *m* (Méx) zipper (AmE), zip (BrE)
siquiera *adv* ① (por lo menos) at least; dile ~
adiós at least say goodbye to her; ¡si (tan) ~ me
hubiera avisado ...! if only you'd warned me ...!
② (en frases negativas) even; ni ~ nos saludó he
didn't even say hello to us
sirena *f* ① (Mit) mermaid; (en mitología clásica)
siren ② (de fábrica, ambulancia, alarma) siren ③ (Col)
(en pirotecnia) rocket
Siria *f* Syria
sirope *m* syrup
sirviente -ta *m,f* (*m*) servant; (*f*) maid,
servant
sísmico -ca *adj* seismic
sismo *m* (terremoto) earthquake; (temblor) earth
tremor
sismógrafo *m* seismograph
sistema *m* ① (método) system; trabajar con ~
to work systematically *o* methodically ② (conjunto
organizado) system; ~ nervioso nervous system; ~
solar solar system; S~ Monetario Europeo
European Monetary System ③ (Inf) system;
entrar en el/salir del ~ to log on/off
sistemático -ca *adj* ‹*persona*› systematic,
methodical; ‹*método*› systematic
sistematizar [A4] *vt* to systematize
sitiar [A1] *vt* **(a)** (Mil) to besiege; estamos
sitiados we are under siege **(b)** (acorralar) to
corner
sitio *m* ① **(a)** (lugar) place; pon ese libro en su
~ put that book back in its place; cambié la tele
de ~ I moved the TV; déjalo en cualquier ~
leave it anywhere; tiene que estar en algún ~ it
must be around somewhere **(b)** (espacio) room,
space; ¿hay ~ para todos? is there (enough)
room for everyone?; hacer ~ to make room **(c)**
(plaza, asiento): guárdame el ~ keep my seat *o*
place; le cambié el ~ I changed places with him
(d) (Inf); *tb* ~ web Web site **(e)** (Méx) (parada de
taxis) taxi stand *o* rank **(f)** (Chi) (terreno urbano)
vacant lot
② (Mil) siege
situación *f* ① **(a)** (coyuntura) situation **(b)** (en
la sociedad) position, standing ② (emplazamiento)
position, situation (frml), location (frml)
situado -da *adj* **(a)** (ubicado) situated **(b)**
‹*persona*›: estar bien ~ to have a good position in
society
situar [A18] *vt* **(a)** (colocar, ubicar) ‹*fábrica/*
aeropuerto› to site, to locate (frml) **(b)** (Lit) ‹*obra/*
acción› to set **(c)** ‹*soldados*› to post, station
■ **situarse** *v pron* **(a)** (colocarse, ubicarse): con esta
victoria se sitúan en primer lugar this victory
puts them in first place; se situó entre los cinco
mejores she's got a place among the top five **(b)**
(socialmente): se ha situado muy bien he has done
very well for himself
siútico -ca *adj/m,f* (Chi) ▶ CURSI
skai®, **skay**® /(e)s'kai/ *m* imitation leather

S.L. *f* = **Sociedad Limitada**
slalom /(e)s'lalom/ *m* (*pl* **-loms**) slalom
slip /(e)s'lip/ (*pl* **slips**) *m* ① (prenda interior) **(a)**
(de hombre) underpants (*pl*), pants (*pl*) (BrE) **(b)**
(de mujer) panties (*pl*), knickers (*pl*) (BrE)
② (bañador) swimming trunks (*pl*)
SME *m* (= **Sistema Monetario Europeo**)
EMS
smog /(e)s'mok/ *m* (AmL) smog
snowboard /es'nobor(d)/ *m* snowboard
sobaco *m* armpit
sobado -da *adj* ‹*tapizado/cortinas/prenda*›
worn, shabby; ‹*libro*› dog-eared, well-thumbed
sobajear [A1] *vt* (AmL fam) ▶ SOBAR 1A, B
sobar [A1] *vt* ① **(a)** (manosear) ‹*tela/ropa/*
tapizado› to handle, finger **(b)** (fam) ‹*chica*› to
feel up (colloq), to grope (*esp* BrE colloq) **(c)** (Méx,
Per fam) (adular) to suck up to (colloq) ② (Col, Ven)
(dar masajes) to massage
soberanía *f* sovereignty
soberano -na *adj* ① ‹*estado/pueblo/poder*›
sovereign ② (fam) (enorme) tremendous; eso es
una soberana estupidez that's an absolutely
ridiculous thing to say/do
■ *m,f* (Gob, Pol) sovereign
soberbia *f* (orgullo) pride; (altivez) arrogance,
haughtiness
soberbio -bia *adj* ① ‹*persona/carácter*›
(orgulloso) proud; (altivo) arrogant, haughty
② (magnífico) superb, magnificent
sobornar [A1] *vt* to bribe, suborn (frml)
soborno *m* (acción) bribery; (dinero, regalo) bribe
sobra *f* ① de sobra **(a)** (mucho): hay comida de
~ there's plenty of food **(b)** (de más): tengo una
entrada de ~ I have a spare *o* an extra ticket; tú
aquí estás de ~ you're not wanted/needed here
(c) (muy bien): saber de ~ que ... to know full
well *o* perfectly well that ... ② **sobras** *fpl* (de
comida) leftovers (*pl*)
sobrado -da *adj* ① **(a)** ‹*experiencia*› ample,
more than enough; tengo ~s motivos para
sospechar I have every reason to be suspicious
(b) ‹*persona*›: estar ~ de algo to have plenty of
sth; no ando muy ~ de tiempo I'm a bit short of
time ② (Andes fam) (engreído) full of oneself (colloq)
sobrar [A1] *vi* **(a)** (quedar, restar): sobró mucha
comida there was a lot of food left over; ¿te ha
sobrado dinero? do you have any money left? **(b)**
(estar de más): ya veo que sobro aquí I can see I'm
not wanted/needed here; a mí no me sobra el
dinero I don't have money to throw around
(colloq); sobra un cubierto there's an extra place
sobre *m* ① (Corresp) envelope
② (cartera) clutch bag
■ *prep* ① (indicando posición) **(a)** (encima de) on; lo
dejé ~ la mesa I left it on the table; los puso uno
~ otro she placed them one on top of the other;
estamos ~ su pista we're on their trail **(b)** (por
encima de) over; volamos ~ Lima we flew over
Lima; en el techo, justo ~ la mesa on the ceiling
right above *o* over the table; 4.000 metros ~ el
nivel del mar 4,000 meters above sea level **(c)**
(alrededor de) on; gira ~ su eje it spins on its axis
② (en relaciones de jerarquía): amar a Dios ~ todas
las cosas to love God above all else
③ (acerca de) on; hay muchos libros ~ el tema
there are many books on *o* about the subject ···❖

4 (Esp) (con cantidades, fechas, horas) around, about (BrE); ~ **unos 70 kilos** around o about 70 kilos **5** **sobre todo** above all

sobrecama f or m (AmL exc CS) bedspread, counterpane

sobrecarga f **(a)** (en vehículo) excess load o weight **(b)** (de circuito, motor) overload; (de batería) overcharging

sobrecargar [A3] vt **(a)** ⟨vehículo/animal⟩ to overload **(b)** ⟨circuito/motor⟩ to overload; ⟨batería⟩ to overcharge **(c)** ⟨persona⟩ ~ **a algn DE algo** ⟨de trabajo/responsabilidad⟩ to overburden sb WITH sth

sobrecargo mf **(a)** (Aviac) (supervisor) purser, chief flight attendant; (auxiliar de vuelo) flight attendant **(b)** (Náut) purser

sobrecogedor -dora adj shocking, horrific

sobrecoger [E6] vt **(a)** (conmover) to move **(b)** (asustar) to strike fear into

sobredosis f (pl ~) overdose

sobregirado -da adj (esp AmL) overdrawn

sobregirar [A1] vt (esp AmL) to overdraw (on) ∎ **sobregirarse** v pron to overdraw

sobregiro m (esp AmL) overdraft

sobrehumano -na adj superhuman

sobrellevar [A1] vt ⟨dolor/enfermedad⟩ to endure, bear; ⟨tragedia⟩ to bear; ⟨soledad⟩ to endure

sobremesa f (conversación) after-lunch/ after-dinner conversation; **estuvimos de** ~ we sat around the table chatting

sobrenatural adj supernatural

sobrenombre m nickname

sobrepasar [A1] vt **(a)** ⟨nivel/cantidad⟩ to exceed, go above; ~ **el límite de velocidad** to exceed o go over the speed limit **(b)** ⟨persona⟩ (en capacidad) to outstrip; (en altura) to overtake

sobrepeso m (AmL) (exceso — de equipaje) excess (baggage); (— de carga) excess load o weight

sobreponerse [E22] v pron (recuperarse) to pull oneself together; ~**se A algo** to get over sth, recover FROM sth

sobrepuesto pp ▶ SOBREPONER

sobresaliente adj ⟨actuación⟩ outstanding; ⟨noticia/hecho⟩ most significant o important ∎ m (Educ) grade between 8.5 and 10 on a scale of 10

sobresalir [I29] vi **(a)** ⟨alero/viga⟩ to project, overhang; ⟨borde⟩ to protrude **(b)** (destacarse, resaltar) to stand out; **sobresale entre los demás** it/ she stands out from the rest; ~ **EN algo** ⟨en deportes/idiomas⟩ to excel o shine AT sth

sobresaltar [A1] vt to startle, make … jump ∎ **sobresaltarse** v pron to jump, be startled

sobresalto m fright

sobretiempo m (Chi, Per) **(a)** (horas extra, pago) overtime **(b)** (Dep) overtime (AmE), extra time (BrE)

sobretodo m overcoat

sobrevenir [I31] vi ⟨desgracia/accidente⟩ to strike

sobrevivencia f survival

sobreviviente adj/mf ▶ SUPERVIVIENTE

sobrevivir [I1] vi to survive; ~ **A algo** to survive sth

sobrevolar [A10] vt to fly over

sobrino -na m,f (m) nephew; (f) niece; **mis** ~**s** (solo varones) my nephews; (varones y mujeres) my nephews and nieces

sobrio -bria adj **1** [SER] **(a)** ⟨persona⟩ sober, restrained; ⟨hábitos⟩ frugal **(b)** ⟨decoración/estilo/ color⟩ sober **2** [ESTAR] (no borracho) sober

sobros mpl (AmC) leftovers (pl)

socarrón -rrona adj (sarcástico) sarcastic, snide; (taimado) sly, crafty

socavón m (hoyo) hole; (excavación) shaft, tunnel; (cueva) cave

sociable adj sociable

social adj social

socialdemocracia f social democracy

socialdemócrata adj social democratic ∎ mf social democrat

socialismo m socialism

socialista adj/mf socialist

socializar [A4] vt to socialize

sociedad f **1** (Sociol) society; ~ **de consumo** consumer society **2** (asociación, club) society **3** (Der, Fin) company; ~ **anónima** ≈ public corporation (in US), ≈ public limited company (in UK); ~ **de responsabilidad limitada** limited corporation (in US), (private) limited company (in UK); ~ **inmobiliaria** (Esp) (que construye) construction company; (que administra) real estate (AmE) o (BrE) property management company; ~ **mercantil** trading company **4** (clase alta) (high) society

socio -cia m,f **1** (miembro) member; **hacerse** ~ **de un club** to join a club **2** (Der, Fin) partner; ~ **accionista** shareholder **3** (fam) (camarada) buddy (AmE colloq), mate (BrE colloq)

sociología f sociology

sociológico -ca adj sociological

sociólogo -ga m,f sociologist

socorrer [E1] vt to help, come to the aid of

socorrido -da adj ⟨excusa/recurso⟩ handy, useful

socorrismo m (en el agua) lifesaving; (en la montaña) mountain rescue; (primeros auxilios) first aid

socorrista mf (en el agua) lifeguard, lifesaver; (en la montaña) mountain rescue worker; (de primeros auxilios) first-aider

socorro m help; **pedir** ~ to ask for help; ¡~! help!; **un grito de** ~ a cry for help

soda f **(a)** (bebida) soda water, soda (AmE) **(b)** (AmC) (cafetería) coffee bar

sodio m sodium

sofá m sofa, settee, couch

sofá-cama m sofa bed

··

AmC	Central America	Arg	Argentina	Cu	Cuba	Per	Peru
AmL	Latin America	Bol	Bolivia	Ec	Ecuador	RPI	River Plate Area
AmS	South America	Chi	Chile	Esp	Spain	Ur	Uruguay
Andes	Andean Region	CS	Southern Cone	Méx	Mexico	Ven	Venezuela

sofisticado -da *adj* sophisticated

sofocante *adj* stifling

sofocar [A2] *vt* ‹*fuego*› to smother, put out; ‹*motín/revolución*› to stifle, put down
■ **sofocarse** *v pron* (acalorarse) to get upset *o* (colloq) worked up

sofoco *m* **(a)** (fam) (disgusto): **estaba con un ~ terrible** I was so upset **(b)** (por el calor) suffocation; (en la menopausia) hot flash (AmE), hot flush (BrE)

sofreír [I35] *vt* to sauté, fry lightly

sofrito *m*: *fried tomatoes, onion, garlic, etc*

software /'sofwer/ *m* software

soga *f* (cuerda) rope

sois ▸ SER

soja *f* (Esp) soy (AmE), soya (BrE)

sol *m* **1** (Astron, Meteo) sun; **brillaba el ~** the sun was shining; **al salir/ponerse el ~** at sunrise/ sunset; **ayer hizo** *or* **hubo ~** it was sunny yesterday; **un día de ~** a sunny day; **en esa habitación no da el ~** that room doesn't get any sunlight *o* sun; **ayer hubo siete horas de ~** we had seven hours of sunshine yesterday; *tomar el ~* *or* (CS) *tomar* **~** to sunbathe
2 (fam) (persona encantadora): **es un ~** she's an angel (colloq)
3 (Mús) (nota) G; (en solfeo) so*, sol; **~ bemol/ sostenido** G flat/sharp
4 (moneda) sol (*Peruvian unit of currency*)

solamente *adv* ▸ SÓLO

solapa *f* (de chaqueta) lapel; (de bolsillo, libro, sobre) flap

solapado -da *adj* ‹*persona*› sly, underhand (BrE); ‹*maniobra*› surreptitious, sly

solar *adj* ‹*energía/año/placa*› solar; **los rayos ~es** the sun's rays
■ *m* **1** (terreno) piece of land, site **2** **(a)** (casa solariega) ancestral home **(b)** (linaje) lineage **3** (Per) (casa de vecindad) tenement building

solario, solárium *m* solarium

soldado *mf* soldier; **~ de caballería** cavalryman; **~ de infantería** infantryman; ; **~ raso** private; **~** *or* **soldadito de plomo** tin soldier

soldar [A10] *vt* (con estaño) to solder; (sin estaño) to weld

soleado -da *adj* sunny

soledad *f*: **en la ~ de su cuarto** in the solitude of his room; **bebe para olvidar su ~** she drinks to forget her loneliness; **no soporta la ~** he can't stand being alone; **pasó sus últimos años en ~** she spent her last years alone

solemne *adj* **1** (en general) solemn **2** (*delante del n*) (fam) ‹*mentira*› complete, downright

solemnidad *f* solemnity

soler [E9] *vi*: **suele venir una vez a la semana** she usually comes once a week; **no suele retrasarse** he's not usually late; **solía correr todos los días** he used to go for a run every day

solera *f* **1** (tradición, calidad): **una familia con ~** a family with a long pedigree, a long-established family **2** (CS) (Indum) sundress

solfear [A1] *vt* to sol-fa

solfeo *m* (asignatura) music theory, sol-fa

solicitado -da *adj* ‹*persona*› in demand; ‹*canción*› popular

solicitante *mf* applicant; **~ de asilo** asylum seeker

solicitar [A1] *vt* ‹*empleo/plaza*› to apply for; ‹*permiso/entrevista/información, servicios/apoyo/ cooperación*› to request, ask for

solícito -ta *adj* (dispuesto a ayudar) attentive; (amable) thoughtful, kind

solicitud *f* **(a)** (para trabajo) application; (para licencia) application, request; (para información, ayuda) request **(b)** (formulario) application form

solidaridad *f* solidarity; **en** *or* **por ~ con algn** in solidarity with *o* in sympathy with sb

solidario -ria *adj* (fraterno) supportive; **un gesto ~** a gesture of solidarity

solidarizar [A4] *vi* **~ con algn** to support sb
■ **solidarizarse** *v pron* **~se CON algn** to support sb; **~se CON algo** to support sth, to back sth

solidez *f* (de muro, edificio) solidity; (de argumento, empresa) soundness; (de relación) strength

sólido¹ -da *adj* **1** (en sentido físico) solid **2** **(a)** ‹*argumento/razonamiento*› solid, sound; ‹*preparación/principios*› sound **(b)** ‹*empresa*› sound; ‹*relación*› steady, strong

sólido² *m* **(a)** (Fís, Mat) solid **(b)** **sólidos** *mpl* (Med) solids (*pl*)

solista *mf* soloist

solitaria *f* tapeworm

solitario -ria *adj* **(a)** ‹*persona/animal*› solitary; ‹*vejez/niñez*› lonely; **(b)** ‹*calles*› empty, deserted; ‹*paraje/lugar*› lonely, solitary
■ *m,f* **1** (persona) loner **2** **solitario** *m* solitaire (AmE), patience (BrE)

sollozar [A4] *vi* to sob

sollozo *m* sob

solo¹ -la *adj* **(a)** (sin compañía): **estar/sentirse ~** to be/feel lonely; **lo dejaron ~** (sin compañía) they left him on his own *o* by himself; (para no molestar) they left him alone; **el niño ya camina ~** the baby's walking on his own now; **hacen los deberes ~s** they do their homework by themselves; **hablar ~** to talk to oneself; **a solas** alone, by oneself **(b)** ‹*café/té*› black; ‹*whisky*› straight, neat; ‹*pan*› dry **(c)** (*delante del n*) (único): **lo haré con una sola condición** I'll do it on one condition; **hay un ~ problema** there's just one problem

solo² *m* (Mús) solo

sólo *adv* [*The written accent may be omitted if there is no confusion with the adjective*] only; **~** *or* **solo quería ayudarte** I only wanted to help, I was only *o* just trying to help; **~** *or* **solo de pensarlo me dan escalofríos** just *o* merely thinking about it makes me shudder; **canto ~ porque me gusta** I sing just for pleasure

solomillo *m* fillet/tenderloin/sirloin steak

solsticio *m* solstice

soltar [A10] *vt* **1** (dejar ir) ‹*persona*› to release, to let ... go; **soltó al perro** he let the dog off the leash
2 (dejar de tener agarrado) to let go of; **no lo sueltes** don't let go of it; **soltó el dinero y huyó** he dropped/let go of the money and ran; **¡suelta la pistola!** drop the gun!
3 **(a)** (desatar) ‹*cuerda/cable*› to undo, untie; **~ amarras** to cast off **(b)** (aflojar): **suelta la cuerda poco a poco** let *o* pay out the rope gradually **(c)** ⋯⋗

S

⟨*freno*⟩ to release; ⟨*embrague*⟩ to let out **(d)** (desatascar) ⟨*cable/cuerda*⟩ to free; ⟨*tuerca*⟩ to undo, get ... undone **4** (desprender) ⟨*calor/vapor*⟩ to give off; ⟨*pelo*⟩ to shed **5** ⟨*carcajada*⟩ to let out; ⟨*palabrotas/disparates*⟩ to come out with; ⟨*grito*⟩ to let out

■ **soltarse** *v pron* **1** ⟨*refl*⟩ «*perro*» to get loose; **no te sueltes de la mano** don't let go of my hand **2** (desatarse) «*nudo*» to come undone, come loose; (aflojarse) «*nudo*» to loosen, come loose; «*tornillo*» to come loose

soltería *f*: *the fact or state of being unmarried*; (en hombre) bachelorhood (fml); (en mujer) spinsterhood (fml)

soltero -ra *adj* single; **soy** *or* (esp Esp) **estoy soltera** I'm single, I'm not married
■ *m,f* (*m*) single man, bachelor; (*f*) single woman, spinster (dated *or* pej)

solterón -rona *m,f* (pey) (*m*) old *o* confirmed bachelor; (*f*) old maid (pej)

soltura *f*: **habla dos idiomas con** ∼ he speaks two languages fluently; **se desenvuelve con** ∼ **en cualquier situación** she is at ease in any situation

soluble *adj* **1** (Quím) soluble; ∼ **en agua** water-soluble **2** ⟨*problema*⟩ soluble, solvable

solución *f* solution; **encontrar una** ∼ **a algo** to find a solution to sth

solucionar [A1] *vt* ⟨*problema*⟩ to solve; ⟨*asunto/conflicto*⟩ to settle, resolve
■ **solucionarse** *v pron* «*problema*» to be resolved; **al final todo se solucionó** everything worked out in the end

somalí *adj/mf* Somali

Somalia *f* Somalia

sombra *f* (lugar sin sol) shade; (proyección) shadow; **las** ∼**s de los árboles** the shadows of the trees; **sentarse a** *or* **en la** ∼ to sit in the shade; **este árbol casi no da** ∼ this tree gives hardly any shade; ∼ **de** *or* **para ojos** eyeshadow

sombrero *m* hat; ∼ **de copa** top hat; ∼ **de jipijapa** Panama (hat); ∼ **hongo** derby (AmE), bowler (hat) (BrE); ∼ **jarano** Mexican sombrero

sombrilla *f* **(a)** (de mano) parasol; (de playa) sunshade **(b)** (Col, Ven) (paraguas) lady's umbrella

sombrío -bría *adj* (liter) ⟨*lugar*⟩ (umbrío) dark **(b)** (lúgubre) cheerless, dismal; ⟨*persona*⟩ gloomy

someter [E1] *vt* **1** (dominar) ⟨*país*⟩ to subjugate; **fue necesario usar la fuerza para** ∼**lo** they had to use force to subdue him **2** (a torturas, presiones, prueba) to subject; **lo sometieron a un interrogatorio** they subjected him to an interrogation; ∼ **algo a votación** to put sth to the vote
■ **someterse** *v pron* **(a)** (a autoridad) to submit to, yield to; (a capricho) to give in to; (a ley) to comply with **(b)** (a prueba, examen, operación) to undergo

somier /so'mje(r)/ *m* (*pl* **-miers** *or* **-mieres**) sprung bed base

somnífero *m* sleeping pill, soporific (fml)

somnolencia *f* drowsiness, sleepiness

somnoliento -ta *adj* sleepy, drowsy

somos ▶ SER

son *m* **1** **(a)** (sonido) sound; **al** ∼ **del violín** to the strains *o* to the sound of the violin **(b)** **en son de**: **lo dijo en** ∼ **de burla** she said it

mockingly; **venimos en** ∼ **de paz** we come in peace **2** (canción latinoamericana) *song with a lively, danceable beat*

son ▶ SER

sonado -da *adj* **1** ⟨*boda/suceso/noticia*⟩ much-talked-about **2** **(a)** ⟨*boxeador*⟩ punch-drunk **(b)** (fam) (torpe) stupid (colloq) **3** (AmL fam) (en dificultades) [ESTAR] in a mess (colloq), in trouble (colloq)

sonaja *f* (Méx) rattle

sonajero *m* rattle

sonámbulo -la *adj* somnambulistic (fml); **es** ∼ he sleepwalks, he walks in his sleep
■ *m,f* sleepwalker, somnambulist (fml)

sonar [A10] *vi* **1** ⟨*teléfono/timbre*⟩ to ring; «*disparo*» to ring out; **el despertador sonó a las cinco** the alarm went off at five o'clock; ∼**on las doce en el reloj** the clock struck twelve; **me suenan las tripas** (fam) my tummy's rumbling (colloq) **2** (+ compl) **(a)** «*motor/instrumento*» to sound; «*persona*» to sound; **suena raro** it sounds funny; **sonaba preocupada** she sounded worried; **suena a hueco** it sounds hollow **(b)** «*palabra/ expresión*» to sound **3** **(a)** (resultar conocido) (+ me/te/le etc): **me suena tu cara** your face is *o* looks familiar; **¿te suena este refrán?** does this proverb ring a bell (with you) *o* sound familiar to you? **(b)** (parecer) ∼ **A algo** to sound like sth **4** (AmL fam) (fracasar): **soné en el examen** I blew it in the exam (colloq); **sonamos** we've blown it now (colloq)
■ ∼ *vt* **1** **(a)** (+ me/te/le etc) ⟨*nariz*⟩ to wipe **(b)** ⟨*trompeta*⟩ to play **2** (Méx fam) **(a)** (pegar) ⟨*persona*⟩ to thump (colloq), to clobber (colloq) **(b)** (en competición) to beat, thrash (colloq)
■ **sonarse** *v pron*: *tb* ∼**se la nariz** to blow one's nose

sonata *f* sonata

sonda *f* **(a)** (Med) catheter **(b)** (para perforar) drill **(c)** (Náut) sounding line, lead line **(d)** (Espac, Meteo) probe

sondeo *m* **1** (encuesta) poll, survey **2** (perforación) test drilling; (Náut) sounding; (Espac, Meteo) exploration

soneto *m* sonnet

sonido *m* sound

sonoro -ra *adj* ⟨*golpe*⟩ resounding (before n), loud; ⟨*voz/lenguaje*⟩ sonorous, resonant; (Ling) voiced

sonreír [I18] *vi* **(a)** «*persona*» to smile; ∼**(le)** A **algn** to smile AT sb **(b)** «*vida/fortuna*» (+ me/te/ le etc) to smile on

sonriente *adj* ⟨*ojos/expresión*⟩ smiling (before n); ⟨*persona*⟩ cheerful

sonrisa *f* smile

sonrojarse [A1] *v pron* to blush

sonsacar [A2] *vt*: **me costó trabajo** ∼**le la verdad** I had a hard time getting the truth out of her

soñado -da *adj* (AmL fam) divine (colloq), heavenly (colloq); *ver tb* SOÑAR

soñador -dora *adj* ⟨*mirada*⟩ dreamy, faraway; **soy muy** ∼ I'm a real dreamer
■ *m,f* dreamer

soñar [A10] *vt* **(a)** (durmiendo) to dream **(b)** (fantasear) to dream; **la casa soñada** her/his/their dream house

■ ~ *vi* **(a)** (durmiendo) to dream; ~ CON algo/algn to dream ABOUT sth/sb; **que sueñes con los angelitos** (fr hecha) sweet dreams **(b)** (fantasear) to dream; ~ **despierto** to daydream; ~ CON algo to dream OF sth

sopa *f* (caldo) soup; ~ **de sobre** packaged soup (AmE), packet soup (BrE)

sopapo *m* (fam) (bofetón) slap, smack (colloq)

sope *m* (Méx) *fried tortilla topped with refried beans, onion and hot sauce*

sopera *f* soup tureen

sopesar [A1] *vt* ‹situación/ventajas› to weigh up; ‹palabras› to weigh

soplar [A1] *vi* **1** **(a)** (con la boca) to blow **(b)** «viento» to blow **2** (fam) (en examen) to whisper (answers in an exam)

■ ~ *vt* **1** **(a)** ‹vela› to blow out; ‹fuego/brasas› to blow on **(b)** ‹vidrio› to blow **2** (fam) ‹respuesta› (en examen) to whisper **3** (fam) (robar) to swipe (colloq), to pinch (BrE colloq); (cobrar) to sting (colloq)

■ **soplarse** *v pron* (Méx, Per fam) (aguantar) ‹persona› to put up with; ‹discurso/película› to sit through, suffer

soplete *m* (para soldar) gas welding torch; (para quitar pintura) blowtorch

soplido *m* puff

soplo *m* **1** **(a)** (soplido) puff; **de un** ~ with one puff, in one go **(b)** (de aire) puff; (más fuerte) blast **(c)** (de viento) puff; (más fuerte) gust **2** (fam) (chivatazo): **alguien dio el** ~ **a la policía** someone tipped off the police (colloq) **3** (Med) heart murmur

soplón -plona *m,f* **(a)** (fam) (en colegio) tattletale (AmE colloq), telltale (BrE colloq) **(b)** (fam) (a la policía) informer, stoolie (AmE colloq), grass (BrE colloq)

soponcio *m* (fam) **(a)** (desmayo): **le dio un** ~ she fainted **(b)** (ataque de nervios) fit (colloq)

sopor *m* **(a)** (somnolencia) drowsiness, sleepiness **(b)** (letargo) torpor

soporífero -ra *adj* ‹efecto/discurso/clase› soporific

soportable *adj* bearable

soportal *m* **(a)** (de casa) porch **(b)** **soportales** *mpl* (de calle) arcade, colonnade

soportar [A1] *vt* **1** **(a)** ‹situación/frío/dolor› to put up with, bear, endure (frml); ‹persona› to put up with; **no soporto este calor/la gente así** I can't stand this heat/people like that **2** ‹peso/carga› to support, withstand; ‹presión› to withstand

soporte *m* **(a)** (de estante) bracket; (de viga) support; (de maceta, portarretratos) stand **(b)** (Inf) medium

soprano *mf* soprano

soquete *m* **1** (CS) (Indum) ankle sock **2** (Chi) (Elec) lampholder, socket **3** (Col, Méx, RPl fam) (tonto) fool, idiot

sor *f* (Relig) sister

sorber [E1] *vt* **(a)** (beber) to suck in *o* up; (tomar poco a poco) to sip **(b)** «esponja» to absorb, soak up

sorbete *m* sherbet (AmE), sorbet (esp BrE)

sorbo *m* **(a)** (cantidad pequeña) sip; **bébetelo a sorbitos** sip it **(b)** (trago grande) gulp; **de un** ~ in one gulp

sordera *f* deafness

sórdido -da *adj* ‹lugar/ambiente› squalid; ‹asunto/libro› sordid

sordina *f* (de trompeta, violín) mute; (de piano) damper

sordo -da *adj* **1** (Med) deaf; **se quedó** ~ he went deaf; **es** ~ **de nacimiento** he was born deaf **2** ‹ruido/golpe› dull, muffled; ‹dolor› dull; (Ling) voiceless

■ *m,f* deaf person; **hacerse el** ~ to pretend not to hear

sordomudo -da *adj* deaf-mute (*before n*), deaf and dumb (BrE)

■ *m,f* deaf-mute

soroche *m* (Andes) (en la montaña) mountain sickness, altitude sickness

sorprendente *adj* surprising

sorprender [E1] *vi* to surprise; **me sorprende que no lo sepas** I'm surprised you don't know

■ ~ *vt* (coger desprevenido) to surprise, catch ... unawares; **nos sorprendió la lluvia** we got caught in the rain

■ **sorprenderse** *v pron* to be surprised

sorprendido -da *adj* surprised; **me miró** ~ he looked at me in surprise; *ver tb* SORPRENDER

sorpresa *f* **(a)** (emoción) surprise; **se va a llevar una** ~ she's going to be surprised, she's in for a surprise (colloq); **tomar** *or* (esp Esp) **coger a algn de** ~ to take sb by surprise **(b)** (regalo) surprise

■ *adj inv* ‹fiesta/ataque› surprise (*before n*)

sorpresivo -va *adj* (AmL) surprise (*before n*), unexpected

sortear [A1] *vt* **1** ‹premio/puesto› to draw lots for; **se** ~**á un coche** there will be a prize draw for a car **2** **(a)** ‹bache/obstáculo› to avoid, negotiate **(b)** ‹problema/dificultad› to get around

sorteo *m* draw; **por** ~ by drawing lots

sortija *f* **(a)** (anillo) ring **(b)** (en el pelo) ringlet

sortilegio *m* (embrujo) spell, charm; (brujería) sorcery; (adivinación) fortune-telling

sos: *equivalent of 'eres' in Central America and the River Plate area*

SOS *m* SOS, distress call

sosa *f* soda

soslayo: **de soslayo** ‹mirada› sidelong (*before n*), sideways; ‹mirar› sideways

soso -sa *adj* **(a)** ‹comida› (sin sabor) bland, tasteless; **está** ~ (sin sabor) it's bland *o* tasteless; (sin sal) it needs more salt **(b)** ‹persona/película› boring, dull; ‹estilo› flat, drab

sospecha *f* suspicion; **tengo la** ~ **de que ...** I suspect *o* I have a feeling that ...

sospechar [A1] *vt* to suspect

■ ~ *vi* ~ DE algn to suspect sb, have one's suspicions ABOUT sb

sospechoso -sa *adj* ‹movimiento/comportamiento› suspicious; ‹paquete› suspicious, suspect; **tres hombres de aspecto** ~ three suspicious-looking men

■ *m,f* suspect

sostén *m* **(a)** (físico) support; (económico) means of support **(b)** (Indum) bra, brassiere

S

sostener [E27] *vt* **1** (apoyar) **(a)** ⟨*estructura/techo*⟩ to hold up, support; ⟨*carga/peso*⟩ to bear **(b)** (sustentar) ⟨*familia*⟩ to support, maintain **2** (sujetar, tener cogido) ⟨*paquete*⟩ to hold; **no tengas miedo, yo te sostengo** don't be afraid, I've got you *o* I'm holding you **3** ⟨*conversación/relación/reunión*⟩ to have **4** **(a)** (opinar) to hold **(b)** ⟨*argumento/afirmación*⟩ to support, back up **5** **(a)** ⟨*lucha/ritmo/resistencia*⟩ to keep up, sustain; **ella sostuvo mi mirada** she held my gaze **(b)** (Mús) ⟨*nota*⟩ to hold, sustain
■ **sostenerse** *v pron* **(a)** (no caerse): **la estructura se sostiene sola** the structure stays up without support; **apenas se sostenía en pie** he could hardly stand **(b)** (en un estado) to remain; **se sostuvo en el poder** she managed to remain in power

sostenido -da *adj* sharp; **re ~ D** D sharp

sostuve, sostuvo, etc ▶ SOSTENER

sota *f* jack (*in Spanish pack of cards*)

sotana *f* cassock, soutane

sótano *m* (habitable) basement; (para almacenamiento) cellar, basement

souvenir /suβe'nir/ *m* (*pl* **-nirs**) souvenir

soviético -ca *adj/m,f* (Hist) Soviet

soy ▶ SER

soya *f* (AmL) soy (AmE), soya (BrE)

sport /(e)s'por/ *m*: **ropa (de) ~** leisure wear, casual clothes (*pl*); **vestido de ~** casually dressed

spot /(e)s'pot/ *m* (*pl* **spots**) *tb* **~ publicitario** (espacio) slot; (anuncio) commercial, advertisement (BrE)

spray /(e)s'prai/ *m* (*pl* **sprays**) spray

Sr. *m* (= **señor**) Mr

Sra. *f* (= **señora**) Mrs

Sres. *mpl* = **señores**

Srta. *f* (= **señorita**) Miss

SS.MM. = **Sus Majestades**

Sta. (= **Santa**) St

status /(e)s'tatus/ *m* (*pl* **~**) status

Sto. (= **Santo**) St

stop /(e)s'top/ *m* (disco) stop sign

su *adj* (delante del *n*) (de él) his; (de ella) her; (de usted, ustedes) your; (de ellos, ellas) their; (de animal, cosa) its

suave *adj* **1** ⟨*piel/cutis*⟩ smooth, soft; ⟨*pelo*⟩ soft; ⟨*superficie/pasta*⟩ smooth **2** **(a)** ⟨*tono*⟩ gentle; ⟨*acento/música*⟩ soft **(b)** ⟨*color*⟩ soft, pale **(c)** ⟨*sabor*⟩ (no fuerte) delicate, mild; (sin acidez) smooth **3** **(a)** ⟨*movimiento/gesto*⟩ gentle, slight **(b)** ⟨*temperaturas/clima*⟩ mild; ⟨*brisa*⟩ gentle **(c)** ⟨*modales/carácter/reprimenda*⟩ mild, gentle **(d)** ⟨*cuesta/curva*⟩ gentle, gradual **(e)** ⟨*jabón/champú*⟩ gentle, mild **(f)** ⟨*laxante/sedante*⟩ mild **4** (Méx fam) (fantástico): **¡qué ~!** great! (colloq), fantastic! (colloq)

suavidad *f* (de la piel) smoothness, softness; (de jabón, champú, clima) mildness; (de tono, acento)

gentleness, softness; (de color) softness, paleness; (de movimiento) gentleness; (de carácter) mildness, gentleness

suavizante *m* (para el pelo) (Esp) conditioner; (para la ropa) (fabric) softener *o* conditioner

suavizar [A4] *vt* ⟨*piel*⟩ to leave ... smooth/soft; ⟨*color*⟩ to soften, tone down; ⟨*sabor*⟩ to tone down; ⟨*carácter*⟩ to mellow, make ... gentler; ⟨*dureza/severidad*⟩ to soften, temper; ⟨*situación*⟩ to calm, ease
■ **suavizarse** *v pron* «*piel*» to become smoother/softer; «*carácter*» to mellow, become gentler; «*situación*» to calm down, ease

subalterno -na *m,f* **(a)** (en jerarquía) subordinate **(b)** (Taur) *member of a matador's support team*

subarrendar [A5] *vt* to sublease, sublet

subasta *f* **(a)** (venta) auction; **sacar algo a ~** to put sth up for auction **(b)** (de obras) invitation to tender

subastar [A1] *vt* ⟨*cuadro*⟩ to auction, sell ... at auction; ⟨*contrato/obra pública*⟩ to put ... out to tender

subcampeón -peona *m,f* (en liga) runner-up; (en torneo eliminatorio) losing finalist

subcomisión *f* subcommittee

subcomité *m* subcommittee

subconsciente *adj/m* subconscious

subcontratar [A1] *vt* to subcontract

subdesarrollado -da *adj* underdeveloped

subdesarrollo *m* underdevelopment

subdirector -ra *m,f* (de organización) deputy director; (de comercio) assistant manager, deputy manager

súbdito -ta *m,f* subject

subdividir [I1] *vt* to subdivide

subestimar [A1] *vt* to underestimate

subida *f* **(a)** (pendiente) rise, slope **(b)** (a montaña) ascent, climb; (al poder) rise **(c)** (de temperatura, precios, salarios) rise, increase

subido -da *adj* ⟨*color*⟩ intense, deep

subir [I1] *vi* **1** **(a)** «*ascensor/persona/coche*» (ir arriba) to go up; (venir arriba) to come up; **hay que ~ a pie** you have to walk up; **ahora subo** I'll be right up; **el camino sube hasta la cima** the path goes up to *o* leads to the top of the hill **(b)** **~ A algo** ⟨*a autobús/tren/avión*⟩ to get on *o* ONTO sth; ⟨*a coche*⟩ to get IN *o* INTO sth; ⟨*a caballo/bicicleta*⟩ to get ON *o* ONTO sth, to mount sth (frml); **~ a bordo** to go *o* get on board **(c)** (de categoría) to go up; (en el escalafón) to be promoted **2** **(a)** «*marea*» to come in; «*aguas/río*» to rise **(b)** «*fiebre/tensión*» to go up, rise; «*temperatura*» to rise **3** «*precio/valor/cotización/salario*» to rise, go up
■ **~** *vt* **1** ⟨*montaña*⟩ to climb; ⟨*escaleras/cuesta*⟩ to go up, climb **2** **(a)** ⟨*objeto/niño*⟩ (traer arriba) to bring up; (llevar arriba) to take up; **tengo que ~ unas cajas al desván** I have to put some boxes up in the attic

AmC América Central	Arg Argentina	Cu Cuba	Per Perú
AmL América Latina	Bol Bolivia	Ec Ecuador	RPl Río de la Plata
AmS América del Sur	Chi Chile	Esp España	Ur Uruguay
Andes Región andina	CS Cono Sur	Méx México	Ven Venezuela

(b) (poner más alto) ‹*objeto*› to put up ... (higher); ‹*cuello de prenda*› to turn up: **sube al niño al caballo** lift the child onto the horse **(c)** ‹*persiana/telón/ventanilla*› to raise; ‹*pantalones*› to pull up; **¿me subes la cremallera?** will you zip me up?, will you fasten my zipper (AmE) *o* (BrE) zip? **(d)** ‹*dobladillo*› to take up; ‹*falda*› to take *o* turn up **(e)** (Inf) to upload
   3 (a) ‹*precios/salarios*› to raise, put up **(b)** ‹*volumen/radio/calefacción*› to turn up
■ **subirse** *v pron* **1 (a)** (a coche, autobús, etc) ▶ ∼ *vi* 1B **(b)** (trepar) to climb; **se subió al árbol/al muro** she climbed up the tree/(up) onto the wall; **estaba subido a un árbol** he was up a tree **(c)** (a la cabeza) (+ *me/te/le etc*): **el éxito se le subió a la cabeza** the success went to his head
   2 (*refl*) ‹*calcetines/pantalones*› to pull up; ‹*cuello*› to turn up

súbitamente *adv* suddenly

súbito -ta *adj* **(a)** (repentino) sudden; **de** ∼ suddenly, all of a sudden **(b)** (precipitado) hasty

subjetivo -va *adj* subjective

subjuntivo *m* subjunctive

sublevarse [A1] *v pron* to revolt, rise up, rebel

sublime *adj* ‹*acción/sacrificio*› noble; ‹*cuadro/música*› sublime

submarinismo *m* scuba diving

submarinista *mf* (buzo) scuba diver; (tripulante de submarino) submariner

submarino¹ -na *adj* underwater (*before n*), submarine (*before n*)

submarino² *m* submarine

subnormal *adj* **(a)** (Psic) mentally handicapped, subnormal **(b)** (fam & pey) (como insulto) moronic (colloq & pej)
■ *mf* **(a)** (Psic) mentally handicapped person **(b)** (fam & pey) (cretino) moron (colloq & pej), cretin (colloq & pej)

subordinado -da *adj/mf* subordinate

subordinar [A1] *vt* to subordinate; ∼ **algo A algo** to subordinate sth TO sth

subrayar [A1] *vt* **(a)** ‹*texto*› to underline, underscore **(b)** (poner énfasis en) to underline, emphasize, stress

subsanar [A1] *vt* ‹*error*› to rectify, correct; ‹*carencia*› to make up for; ‹*obstáculo/dificultad*› to overcome

subscribirse *etc* ▶ SUSCRIBIRSE, ETC

subsidio *m* subsidy; ∼ **de enfermedad** sickness benefit; ∼ **de desempleo** unemployment compensation (AmE), unemployment benefit (BrE)

subsistencia *f* subsistence, survival

subsistir [I1] *vi* «*persona/planta*» to survive, subsist (fml); «*creencia/tradición*» to persist, survive

subte *m* (RPl fam) subway (AmE), tube (BrE colloq)

subterráneo¹ -nea *adj* underground, subterranean

subterráneo² *m* **(a)** (pasaje) subway, tunnel **(b)** (RPl) (Transp) subway (AmE), underground (BrE)

subtitular [A1] *vt* to subtitle; **versión original subtitulada** original version with subtitles

subtítulo *m* subtitle

suburbano -na *adj* suburban

suburbio *m* (extrarradio) suburb; (barrio pobre) depressed area (*on the outskirts of town*)

subvención *f* subsidy, subvention (fml)

subvencionar [A1] *vt* to subsidize

subversivo -va *adj* subversive

subyacer [E5] *vi* ∼ (EN algo) to underlie (sth)

succionar [A1] *vt* to suck (up)

sucedáneo *m* substitute

suceder [E1] *vi* **1** (ocurrir) to happen; **¿le ha sucedido algo?** has something happened to him?; **le expliqué lo sucedido** I explained to him what had happened; **por lo que pueda** ∼ just in case
   2 (en el tiempo) «*hecho/época*» ∼ A **algo** to follow sth
■ ∼ *vt* (en trono, cargo) to succeed

sucesión *f* **1 (a)** (al trono, en un cargo) succession **(b)** (herederos) heirs (*pl*), issue (fml) **(c)** (Der) (herencia) estate, inheritance **2** (serie) succession, series

sucesivo -va *adj* consecutive; ∼**s gobiernos lo han intentado** successive governments have tried it; **en lo** ∼ from now on, in future

suceso *m* **(a)** (acontecimiento) event **(b)** (accidente, crimen): **el lugar del** ∼ the scene of the incident/crime/accident; **sección de** ∼**s** accident and crime reports

sucesor -sora *m,f* (al trono, en un puesto) successor; (heredero) heir, successor (fml)

suciedad *f* **(a)** (mugre) dirt **(b)** (estado) dirtiness

sucio -cia *adj* **1 (a)** [ESTAR] ‹*ropa/casa/vaso*› dirty; **hacer algo en** ∼ to do a rough draft of sth (AmE), do sth in rough (BrE) **(b)** ‹*lengua*› furred, coated **2** [SER] **(a)** ‹*trabajo*› dirty; ‹*dinero/negocio/juego*› dirty **(b)** ‹*lenguaje*› filthy; ‹*mente*› dirty; **una jugada sucia** a dirty trick

sucre *m* sucre (*Ecuadorean unit of currency*)

sucursal *f* (de banco, comercio) branch; (de empresa) office

sudadera *f* (Dep, Indum) (suéter) sweatshirt; (conjunto) (Col, Ven) tracksuit

Sudáfrica *f* South Africa

sudafricano -na *adj/m,f* South African

Sudamérica *f* South America

sudamericano -na *adj/m,f* South American

Sudán *m*: *tb* **el** ∼ (the) Sudan

sudanés -nesa *adj/m,f* Sudanese

sudar [A1] *vi* to sweat, perspire (fml)

sudario *m* shroud

sudeste *adj inv* ‹*región*› southeastern; **iban en dirección** ∼ they were heading southeast
■ *m* **(a)** (parte, sector): **el** ∼ the southeast, the Southeast **(b)** (punto cardinal) southeast, Southeast

sudoeste *adj inv* ‹*región*› southwestern; **iban en dirección** ∼ they were heading southwest
■ *m* **(a)** (parte, sector): **el** ∼ the southwest, the Southwest **(b)** (punto cardinal) southwest, Southwest

sudor *m* sweat, perspiration (fml)

sudoroso -sa *adj* sweaty

Suecia *f* Sweden

sueco¹ -ca *adj* Swedish
■ *m,f* (persona) Swede

S

sueco² *m* (idioma) Swedish; **me hice/se hizo el
∼** (fam) I/he pretended not to have heard (*o* seen
etc)

suegro -gra *m,f* (*m*) father-in-law; (*f*)
mother-in-law; **mis ∼s** my in-laws, my
mother-and father-in-law

suela *f* sole

sueldo *m* (de funcionario, oficinista) salary; (de
obrero) wage; **∼ base** base salary (AmE), basic
salary (BrE)

suelo *m* (a) (tierra) ground; **se cayó al ∼** she fell
over (b) (en casa) floor (c) (en calle, carretera) road
(surface) (d) (Agr) land (e) (territorio) soil; **el ∼
patrio** one's native soil *o* land

suelta, sueltas, etc ▶ SOLTAR

suelto¹ -ta *adj* ① (a) ⟨tornillo/tabla/hoja⟩
loose; ⟨cordones⟩ loose, untied (b) (libre): **el perro
está ∼ en el jardín** the dog's loose in the garden;
el asesino anda ∼ the murderer is on the loose
(c) ⟨vestido/abrigo⟩ loose; **déjate el pelo ∼** leave
your hair loose *o* down (d) (separado): **ejemplares
∼s** individual *o* single issues; **no los vendemos
∼s** ⟨yogures/sobres⟩ we don't sell them
individually *o* separately; ⟨caramelos/tornillos⟩
we don't sell them loose ② (a) (fraccionado):
dinero ∼ loose change; **diez euros sueltas** ten
euros in change (b) ⟨lenguaje/estilo⟩ fluent;
⟨movimientos⟩ fluid (c) (euf) ⟨vientre⟩ loose

suelto² *m* (Esp, Méx) (monedas) (small) change

suena, suenan, etc ▶ SONAR

sueño *m* ① (a) (estado) sleep; **oyó un ruido
entre ∼s** she heard a noise in her sleep; **tener el
∼ ligero/pesado** to be a light/heavy sleeper;
perder el ∼ (por algo) to lose sleep (over sth) (b)
(ganas de dormir): **¿tienes ∼?** are you tired/sleepy?;
el vino me dio ∼ the wine made me sleepy; **me
empezó a entrar ∼** I started feeling sleepy; **se me
quitó el ∼** I don't feel sleepy any more
② (a) (cosa soñada) dream; **un mal ∼** a bad
dream (b) (ilusión) dream; **la mujer de sus ∼s** the
woman of his dreams; **su ∼ dorado es llegar a
ser actriz** her (greatest) dream is to become an
actress

suero *m* (a) (Med) (*para alimentar*) saline solution;
(*para inmunizar*) serum (b) (de la sangre) blood
serum (c) (de la leche) whey

suerte *f* (a) (fortuna) luck; **buena/mala ∼** good/
bad luck; **ha sido una ∼ que vinieras** it was
lucky you came; **¡qué mala ∼!** how unlucky!;
¡qué ∼ tienes! you're so lucky!; **no tengo ∼** I'm
not a lucky person; **hombre de ∼** lucky man; **por
∼ no estaba sola** luckily *o* fortunately I wasn't
alone; **¡(que tengas) buena ∼!** good luck!; **probar
∼** to try one's luck; **traer** *or* **dar mala ∼** to bring
bad luck (b) (azar) chance; **echar algo a ∼s** (con
monedas) to toss for sth; (con pajitas) to draw
straws for sth (c) (destino) fate

suertero -tera *m,f* (Per) lottery ticket seller

suéter *m* sweater, pullover, jersey (BrE),
jumper (BrE)

suficiencia *f* (a) (aptitud) aptitude (b)
(*presunción*) self-satisfaction, smugness; **aire de ∼**
air of self-satisfaction

suficiente *adj* (a) (bastante) enough; **con esto
hay más que ∼** there's more than enough here
(b) ⟨persona⟩ self-satisfied, smug

■ *m* pass (*equivalent to a grade of 5 on a scale
from 0-10*)

sufijo *m* suffix

suflé *m* soufflé

sufragio *m* (sistema) suffrage; (voto) (frml) vote

sufrido -da *adj* ⟨persona⟩ long-suffering,
uncomplaining; ⟨ropa/tejido⟩ hard-wearing; **un
color ∼** a color that doesn't show the dirt

sufrimiento *m* suffering; **pasar ∼s** to suffer

sufrir [I1] *vt* (a) ⟨dolores/molestias⟩ to suffer;
sufre lesiones de gravedad he has serious
injuries (b) ⟨derrota/persecución/consecuencias⟩
to suffer; ⟨cambio⟩ to undergo; ⟨accidente⟩ to
have; **sufrió un atentado** there was an attempt on
his life; **el coche sufrió una avería** the car broke
down

■ **∼** *vi* to suffer; **∼ DE algo** to suffer FROM sth

sugerencia *f* suggestion

sugerente *adj* ⟨mirada/pose⟩ suggestive;
⟨vestido/blusa⟩ sexy

sugerir [I11] *vt* to suggest; **me sugirió que lo
probara** he suggested that I (should) try it; **¿qué
te sugiere este cuadro?** what does this picture
make you think of?

sugestión *f* (convencimiento): **es pura ∼** it's all
in your (*o* his *etc*) mind; **tiene gran poder de ∼**
he is very persuasive

sugestionarse [A1] *v pron* to get ideas into
one's head

sugestivo -va *adj* ⟨mirada⟩ suggestive;
⟨escote⟩ sexy; ⟨libro/idea⟩ stimulating

suicida *adj* suicidal
■ *mf* suicide victim

suicidarse [A1] *v pron* to commit suicide

suicidio *m* suicide

suite /swit/ *f* (Mús) suite

Suiza *f* Switzerland

suizo -za *adj/m,f* Swiss

sujetador *m* (Esp) bra, brassiere

sujetar [A1] *vt* ① (a) (mantener sujeto) to hold;
sujétalo bien, que no se escape hold it tight,
don't let it go; **tuvimos que ∼los para que no se
pegaran** we had to hold them back to stop them
hitting each other (b) (sostener) to hold; **sujétame
los paquetes** hold on to the packages for me (c)
(fijar, trabar — con clip) to fasten ... together; (— con
alfileres) to pin ... together
② (dominar) to subdue, conquer

■ **sujetarse** *v pron* ① (a) (agarrarse) **∼se A algo**
to hold on TO sth (b) (trabar, sostener): **se sujetaba
los pantalones con la mano** he held his trousers
up with his hand; **se sujetó la falda con un
imperdible** she fastened her skirt with a safety
pin
② (someterse) **∼se A algo** ⟨a ley/reglas⟩ to abide
BY sth

sujeto¹ -ta *adj* ① (sometido) **∼ A algo** ⟨a
cambios/revisión⟩ subject TO sth ② (fijo) secure

sujeto² *m* ① (individuo) character, individual
② (Fil, Ling) subject

sultán *m* sultan

suma *f* ① (cantidad) sum ② (Mat) addition; **hacer
∼s** to do addition, to do sums (BrE)

sumamente *adv* extremely, exceedingly (frml)

sumar [A1] *vt* **(a)** ⟨*cantidades*⟩ to add (up) **(b)** (totalizar) to add up to; **8 y 5 suman 13** 8 and 5 add up to *o* make 13
■ ~ *vi* to add up
■ **sumarse** *v pron* **(a)** (agregarse) ~se a algo: **esto se suma a los problemas ya existentes** this comes on top of *o* is in addition to any already existing problems **(b)** (adherirse) ~se a algo ⟨*a protesta/celebración*⟩ to join sth
sumario *m* ⟨1⟩ (Der) **(a)** (en lo penal) indictment **(b)** (juicio administrativo) disciplinary action ⟨2⟩ (índice) (table of) contents
sumergible *adj* ⟨*reloj*⟩ waterproof; ⟨*nave*⟩ submersible
sumergido -da *adj* ⟨*submarino*⟩ submerged; ⟨*ciudad*⟩ submerged, sunken
sumergir [I7] *vt* (en líquido) to immerse, submerge
■ **sumergirse** *v pron* **(a)** «*submarino/buzo*» to dive **(b)** (en ambiente) to immerse oneself
sumidero *m* drain
suministrar [A1] *vt* (frml) to supply; ~ algo a algn to supply sb with sth
suministro *m* supply
sumir [I1] *vt* ⟨1⟩ (sumergir) ~ algo/a algn en algo ⟨*en tristeza/desesperación*⟩ to plunge sth/sb into sth ⟨2⟩ (Col, Méx) (abollar) to dent, make a dent in
■ **sumirse** *v pron* ⟨1⟩ (hundirse) ~se en algo ⟨*en tristeza*⟩ to plunge into sth; ⟨*en pensamientos*⟩ to become lost in sth ⟨2⟩ (Col, Méx) (abollarse) to get dented
sumisión *f* (acción) submission; (actitud dócil) submissiveness
sumiso -sa *adj* submissive
sumo -ma *adj* utmost (*before n*); **de suma importancia** of the utmost importance; **con ~ cuidado** with the utmost care; **a lo ~** at most
suní *adj* Sunni
■ *mf* Sunni
sunita *mf* Sunni
■ *mf* Sunni
suntuoso -sa *adj* sumptuous; ⟨*palacio*⟩ magnificent
supe ▶ SABER
súper *adv* (fam): **lo pasamos ~ bien** we had a great *o* fantastic time (colloq); **es ~ bueno** it's great *o* fantastic (colloq); **lo hizo ~ rápido** he did it incredibly quickly
■ *f* ≈ premium grade gasoline (*in US*), ≈ four-star petrol (*in UK*)
superación *f* (de problema) surmounting, overcoming; (de récord) breaking, beating; (de teoría) superseding
superar [A1] *vt* ⟨1⟩ **(a)** (ser superior a) to exceed; **superó todas las expectativas** she exceeded all expectations; **nadie lo supera en experiencia** no one has more experience than him; **supera en estatura a su hermano** he's taller than his brother **(b)** (mejorar) ⟨*marca*⟩ to beat ⟨2⟩ **(a)** (vencer, sobreponerse a) ⟨*timidez/dificultad/etapa*⟩ to overcome; ⟨*trauma*⟩ to get over **(b)** (frml) ⟨*examen/prueba*⟩ to pass
■ **superarse** *v pron* to better oneself
superbloque *m* (Ven) large apartment building
superdotado -da *adj* highly gifted
■ *m,f* highly-gifted person

superficial *adj* ⟨1⟩ (frívolo) ⟨*persona*⟩ superficial, shallow; ⟨*charla/comentario*⟩ superficial ⟨2⟩ ⟨*herida*⟩ superficial; ⟨*marca/grieta*⟩ surface (*before n*)
superficie *f* ⟨1⟩ (parte expuesta, aparente) surface; **salir a la ~** to surface, come to the surface ⟨2⟩ (Mat) (área) area
superfluo -flua *adj* superfluous, unnecessary; ⟨*gastos*⟩ unnecessary
superior¹ *adj* ⟨1⟩ (en posición) ⟨*parte/piso*⟩ top (*before n*), upper (*before n*); ⟨*nivel*⟩ higher; ⟨*labio/mandíbula*⟩ upper (*before n*) ⟨2⟩ **(a)** (en calidad) superior; ~ a algo/algn superior to sth/sb; **se siente ~ a los demás** he thinks he's better than everyone else; **una inteligencia ~ a la media** above-average intelligence **(b)** (en jerarquía) ⟨*oficial*⟩ superior; ⟨*clase social*⟩ higher **(c)** (en cantidad, número): **los atacantes eran ~es en número** the attackers were greater *o* more in number; ~ a algo above sth; **un número ~ a 9** a number greater than *o* higher than *o* above 9
superior² -riora *m,f* **(a)** (Relig) (*m*) Superior; (*f*) Mother Superior **(b)** **superior** *m* (en rango) superior
superioridad *f* superiority
superlativo *m* superlative
supermercado *m* supermarket
superpoblación *f* (de una región) overpopulation; (de una ciudad) overcrowding
superpoblado -da *adj* ⟨*mundo/país*⟩ overpopulated; ⟨*barrio/ciudad*⟩ overcrowded
superpotencia *f* superpower
superstición *f* superstition
supersticioso -sa *adj* superstitious
supervisar [A1] *vt* to supervise
supervisor -sora *m,f* supervisor
supervivencia *f* survival
superviviente *adj* surviving (*before n*)
■ *mf* survivor
supiera, supiste, etc ▶ SABER
suplantar [A1] *vt* ⟨*persona*⟩ to impersonate, pass oneself off as
suplementario -ria *adj* ⟨*información/ingresos*⟩ additional, supplementary; ⟨*trabajo*⟩ extra
suplemento *m* supplement
suplencia *f* **(a)** (sustitución): **hacer una ~** «*profesor*» to do substitute (AmE) *o* (BrE) supply teaching **(b)** (trabajo) temporary job
suplente *mf* **(a)** (de médico) covering doctor (AmE), locum (BrE) **(b)** (de actor) understudy **(c)** (Dep) substitute **(d)** (de profesor) substitute (teacher) (AmE), supply teacher (BrE)
supletorio -ria *adj* ⟨*cama*⟩ extra, additional; **teléfono ~** extension
súplica *f* (ruego) entreaty, plea; (Der) petition
suplicante *adj* imploring (*before n*)
suplicar [A2] *vt* (rogar) to beg; ~le a algn que haga algo to beg *o* implore sb to do sth
suplicio *m* **(a)** (tortura) torture **(b)** (castigo) punishment
suplir [I1] *vt* ⟨1⟩ (compensar) ⟨*falta/deficiencia*⟩ to make up for ⟨2⟩ (reemplazar) ⟨*profesor/médico*⟩ to stand in for, substitute for; ⟨*jugador*⟩ to substitute ⟨3⟩ (Chi, Col, Ven) (suministrar) to supply

suponer [E22] *vt* ⓵ **(a)** (tomar como hipótesis) to suppose, assume; **supongamos que lo que dice es cierto** let's suppose *o* assume what he says is true; **suponiendo que todo salga bien** assuming everything goes OK **(b)** (imaginar): **supongo que tienes razón** I suppose you're right; **¿va a venir hoy? — supongo que sí** is she coming today? — I should think so *o* I suppose so; **es de ~ que se lo habrán dicho** presumably *o* I should think he's been told; **se supone que empieza a las nueve** it's supposed to start at nine ⓶ (significar, implicar) to mean; **eso supondría tener que repetirlo** that would mean having to do it again

suposición *f* supposition

supositorio *m* suppository

supremacía *f* supremacy

supremo -ma *adj* supreme

suprimir [I1] *vt* **(a)** ⟨impuesto/ley/costumbre⟩ to abolish; ⟨restricción⟩ to lift; ⟨servicio⟩ to withdraw; ⟨gasto/ruido/alcohol⟩ to cut out **(b)** (Impr) ⟨párrafo/capítulo⟩ to delete **(c)** ⟨noticia/detalles⟩ to suppress

supuesto¹ -ta *adj* **(a)** (falso) false; **un nombre ~** a false name; **el ~ mendigo** the supposed beggar **(b)** (que se rumorea) ⟨milagro⟩ alleged (*before n*) **(c)** **por supuesto** of course; **dar algo por ~** to take sth for granted

supuesto² *m* supposition

supurar [A1] *vi* to weep, ooze, suppurate (tech)

supuse, supuso, etc ▶ SUPONER

sur *adj inv* ⟨región⟩ southern; **conducían en dirección ~** they were driving south *o* southward(s); **la costa ~** the south coast
■ *m* **(a)** (parte, sector): **el ~** the south; **al ~ de Cartagena** to the south of Cartagena **(b)** (punto cardinal) south, South; **vientos del ~** southerly winds; **viajábamos hacia el ~** we were travelling south *o* southward(s)

Suráfrica *f* South Africa

surafricano -na *adj/m,f* South African

Suramérica *f* South America

suramericano -na *adj/m,f* South American

surco *m* ⓵ **(a)** (en la tierra) furrow **(b)** (en el agua) wake, track **(c)** (en disco) groove; (en superficie) groove, line; (marca de rueda) ruts, track ⓶ (Col) (de flores) flowered

sureño -ña *adj* southern
■ *m,f* southerner

sureste *adj inv/m* ▶ SUDESTE

surf /'surf/, **surfing** /'surfin/ *m* surfing

surfista *mf* surfer

surgir [I7] *vi* ⟨manantial⟩ to rise; ⟨problema/dificultad⟩ to arise, come up, emerge; ⟨interés/sentimiento⟩ to develop, emerge; ⟨idea⟩ to emerge, come up; ⟨tema⟩ to come up, crop up; ⟨movimiento/partido⟩ to come into being, arise

suroeste *adj inv/m* ▶ SUDOESTE

surrealismo *m* surrealism

surrealista *adj* ⟨artista/exposición⟩ surrealist (*before n*); ⟨estilo/efecto⟩ surrealistic

surtido¹ -da *adj* **(a)** ⟨bombones/galletas⟩ assorted **(b)** (provisto) stocked; **una tienda bien/mal surtida** a well-stocked/poorly-stocked shop

surtido² *m* (de bombones, galletas) assortment; (de herramientas, ropa) range, selection, assortment

surtidor *m* (aparato) gas pump (AmE), petrol pump (BrE); (estación de servicio) gas station (AmE), petrol station (BrE)

surtir [I1] *vt* **(a)** (proveer) **~ a algn DE algo** to supply sb WITH sth **(b)** **surtir efecto** to take effect
■ **surtirse** *v pron* **~se DE algo** ⟨de provisiones⟩ to stock up WITH sth

susceptibilidad *f* sensitivity, touchiness

susceptible *adj* ⟨persona⟩ sensitive, touchy; **~ A algo** sensitive TO sth

suscribirse [I34] *v pron* (refl) **~ A algo** to take out a subscription TO sth

suscripción *f* (a publicación) subscription

suscriptor -tora *m,f* subscriber

suspender [E1] *vt* ⓵ **(a)** ⟨pagos⟩ to suspend; ⟨garantía/derecho⟩ to suspend, withdraw; ⟨sesión⟩ to adjourn; ⟨vuelo⟩ (cancelar) to cancel; (aplazar) to postpone; ⟨viaje/reunión⟩ (cancelar) to call off; (aplazar) to put off; ⟨tratamiento⟩ to stop, suspend; ⟨servicio⟩ to suspend, discontinue; ⟨programa⟩ to cancel **(b)** ⟨empleado/jugador⟩ to suspend; ⟨alumno⟩ (AmL) to suspend ⓶ (colgar) **~ algo DE algo** to hang sth FROM sth ⓷ (Esp) ⟨asignatura/examen/alumno⟩ to fail
■ **~** *vi* (Esp) to fail

suspense *m* (Esp) ▶ SUSPENSO 1

suspensión *f* suspension

suspenso *m* ⓵ (AmL) (Cin, Lit) suspense; **película/novela de ~** thriller ⓶ (Esp) (Educ) fail, failure; **no he tenido ningún ~** I haven't failed anything

suspensores *mpl* (Chi) (tirantes) suspenders (*pl*) (AmE), braces (*pl*) (BrE)

suspicacia *f* suspicion

suspicaz *adj* suspicious

suspirar [A1] *vi* **(a)** (de pena, alivio) to sigh **(b)** (anhelar) **~ POR algo** to yearn *o* long FOR sth

suspiro *m* sigh; **un ~ de alivio** a sigh of relief

sustancia *f* substance

sustantivo *m* noun, substantive (frml)

sustentar [A1] *vt* **(a)** ⟨peso⟩ to support **(b)** ⟨persona/familia⟩ to support, maintain

sustento *m* **(a)** (apoyo) means of support **(b)** (alimento) sustenance

sustitución *f* **(a)** (permanente) replacement **(b)** (transitoria) substitution

sustituir [I20] *vt* **(a)** (permanentemente) to replace; **~ A algo** to replace sth; **~ algo/a algn POR algo/algn** to replace sth/sb WITH sth/sb **(b)** (transitoriamente) ⟨trabajador/profesor⟩ to stand in for; ⟨deportista⟩ to come on as a substitute for

sustituto -ta *m,f* **(a)** (permanente) replacement **(b)** (transitorio) substitute; (de médico) covering doctor (AmE), locum (BrE); (de actor) understudy; **el ∼ de la profesora de alemán** the substitute (AmE) *o* (BrE) stand-in for the German teacher

susto *m* (impresión momentánea) fright; **darle un ∼ a algn** to give sb a fright; **darse** *or* **llevarse un ∼** to get a fright (colloq)

susurrar [A1] *vi* **(a)** «*persona*» to whisper **(b)** (liter) «*agua*» to murmur; «*viento*» to sigh; «*hojas*» to rustle
■ **∼** *vt* to whisper; **le susurró algo al oído** she whispered something in his ear

susurro *m* **(a)** (murmullo) whisper **(b)** (liter) (del agua) murmuring; (del viento) sighing; (de las hojas) rustling

sutil *adj* **(a)** ⟨*diferencia*⟩ subtle, fine; ⟨*ironía*⟩ subtle; ⟨*mente/inteligencia*⟩ keen, sharp **(b)** ⟨*gasa/velo*⟩ fine; ⟨*fragancia*⟩ subtle, delicate

sutileza *f* subtlety

suyo -ya *adj* (de él) his; (de ella) hers; (de usted, ustedes) yours; (de ellos, ellas) theirs; **Marta y un amigo ∼** Marta and a friend of hers
■ *pron* **el ∼, la suya,** *etc* (de él) his; (de ella) hers; (de usted, ustedes) yours; (de ellos, ellas) theirs; **él me prestó el ∼** he lent me his

svástica *f* swastika

switch /ˈ(e)switʃ/ *m* **(a)** (Col, Ven, Méx) (interruptor) light switch **(b)** (Méx) (Auto) ignition switch

Tt

T, t *f* (*read as* /te/) *the letter* T, t

tabaco *m* **(a)** (planta, producto) tobacco; **∼ de hebra/de pipa** loose/pipe tobacco; **∼ negro/rubio** dark/Virginia tobacco **(b)** (Esp) (cigarrillos) cigarettes (*pl*) **(c)** (Col) (puro) cigar

tábano *m* horsefly

tabaquismo *m* nicotine poisoning; **∼ pasivo** passive smoking

tabasco *m* Tabasco® (sauce)

taberna *f* bar, tavern (arch), pub (BrE)

tabernáculo *m* tabernacle

tabernero -ra *m,f* (propietario) (*m*) bar owner, landlord (BrE); (*f*) bar owner, landlady (BrE); (camarero) (*m*) bartender; (*f*) barmaid

tabique *m* **(a)** (pared) partition **(b)** (Méx) (ladrillo) brick

tabla *f* **1** (de madera) plank; **las ∼s del suelo** the floorboards; **∼ de picar/planchar** chopping/ironing board; **tener ∼s** «*actor/cantante*» (fam) to be an old hand *o* an expert **2** (de surfing) surfboard; (de windsurf) sailboard, windsurfer; (para natación) float **3** (gráfico, listado) table; (Mat) *tb* **∼ de multiplicar** multiplication table **4** (de falda) pleat; **una falda de ∼s** a pleated skirt **5 tablas** *fpl* (en ajedrez): **acabar** *or* **quedar en ∼s** to end in a draw; **estar ∼s** (Méx fam) to be even *o* quits (colloq)

tablado *m* (para discursos) platform; (para espectáculos) stage

tablao *m*: *tb* **∼ flamenco** *bar or club where flamenco is performed*

tablero *m* **(a)** (en estación, aeropuerto) board; (para anuncios) bulletin board (AmE), noticeboard (BrE); **∼ de dibujo** drawing board; **∼ de instrumentos** *or* **de mandos** instrument panel **(b)** (Jueg) board; **un ∼ de ajedrez** a chessboard; **un ∼ de damas** a checkerboard (AmE), a draughtboard (BrE) **(c)** (pizarra) blackboard **(d)** (de mesa) top

tableta *f* **(a)** (Farm) tablet, pill **(b)** (de chocolate) bar

tablilla *f* (Méx) (de chocolate) bar

tablón *m* **(a)** (de madera) plank **(b)** *tb* **∼ de anuncios** (Esp) bulletin board (AmE), noticeboard (BrE)

tabú *adj inv* taboo
■ *m* (*pl* **-búes** *or* **-bús**) taboo

tabulador *m* tabulator, tab

taburete *m* stool

tacañería *f* stinginess, meanness (colloq)

tacaño -ña *adj* stingy, mean
■ *m,f* miser, tightwad (AmE colloq)

tacha *f* stain, blemish; **sin ∼** ⟨*reputación*⟩ unblemished, spotless; ⟨*conducta*⟩ irreproachable

tachadura *f* crossing out, correction

tachar [A1] *vt* **1** (en escrito) to cross out
2 (tildar) **∼ a algn DE algo** to brand *o* label sb AS sth

tacho *m* **(a)** (CS) (recipiente) (metal) container **(b)** (CS, Per) (papelero) wastebasket (AmE), wastepaper basket (BrE); **∼ de la basura** (en la cocina) garbage can (AmE), rubbish bin (BrE); (en la calle) garbage *o* trash can (AmE), dustbin (BrE)

tachón *m* (en escrito) crossing out

tachuela *f* (clavo) tack; (en cinturón) stud

tácito -ta *adj* ⟨*acuerdo*⟩ tacit, unspoken

taciturno -na *adj* **(a)** [SER] (callado, silencioso) taciturn, uncommunicative **(b)** [ESTAR] (triste) glum, gloomy

taco *m* **1** **(a)** (de madera) plug; (para tornillo) Rawl® (AmE), Rawplug® (BrE) **(b)** (de billetes) book; (de folletos) wad; (de queso, jamón) (Esp) cube **2** **(a)** (en billar) cue **(b)** (Col) (de golf) tee **3** **(a)** (de botas de deporte) cleat (AmE), stud (BrE) **(b)** (CS, Per) (tacón) heel; **zapatos de ∼ alto/bajo** high-heeled/low-heeled *o* flat shoes **4** **(a)** (Coc) taco **(b)** (Méx) (comida ligera) snack, bite to eat (colloq) **5** (Esp fam) (palabrota) swearword; **soltar ∼s** to swear **6** (Chi) (embotellamiento) traffic jam

tacón *m* heel; **zapatos de ∼ alto/bajo** high-heeled/low-heeled *o* flat shoes; **∼ de aguja** spike heel

táctica *f* tactic, strategy

táctico -ca *adj* tactical

táctil *adj* tactile

tacto *m* ⓵ (a) (sentido) sense of touch (b) (acción) touch; **áspero al** ~ rough to the touch (c) (cualidad) feel ⓶ (delicadeza) tact; **¡qué falta de ~!** how tactless!; **tiene mucho** ~ he's very tactful

Tahití *m* Tahiti

tailandés¹ **-desa** *adj/m,f* Thai

tailandés² *m* (idioma) Thai

Tailandia *f* Thailand

taimado -da *adj* ⓵ (astuto) crafty, cunning ⓶ (Chi) (malhumorado) sulky, huffy

taimarse [A1] *v pron* (Chi fam) (a) «*persona*» to get into a huff (colloq) (b) «*mula*» to balk

tajada *f* (a) (de melón, queso) slice (b) (Ven) (de plátano frito) slice of fried plantain

tajante *adj* ⟨*respuesta*⟩ categorical, unequivocal; ⟨*tono*⟩ sharp; **un 'no'** ~ an emphatic *o* categorical 'no'

tajear [A1] *vt* (AmL) to slash

tajo *m* ⓵ (corte) cut ⓶ (a) (Geol) gorge, ravine (b) (Min) face

tal *adj* ⓵ (dicho) such; **en** ~**es casos** in such cases; **nunca dije** ~ **cosa** I never said anything of the kind *o* such a thing ⓶ (seguido de consecuencia): **se llevó** ~ **disgusto que** ... she was so upset (that) ...; **había** ~ **cantidad de gente que** ... there were so many people that ... ⓷ (con valor indeterminado) such-and-such; ~ **día, en** ~ **lugar** such-and-such a day, at such-and-such a place; **llamó un** ~ **Méndez** a Mr Méndez phoned ■ *pron*: **eres un adulto, compórtate como** ~ you're an adult, behave like one; **que si** ~ **y que si cual** and so on and so forth; **son** ~ **para cual** they're as bad as each other ■ *adv* ⓵ (fam) (en preguntas): **hola ¿qué** ~? hello, how are you?; **¿qué** ~ **es Marisa?** what's Marisa like?; **¿qué** ~ **lo pasaron?** how did it go? ⓶ (en locs) **con tal de: hace cualquier cosa con** ~ **de llamar la atención** he'll do anything to get attention; **con** ~ **de no tener que volver** as long as I don't have to come back; **tal (y) como:** ~ **(y) como están las cosas** the way things are; **hazlo** ~ **(y) como te indicó** do it exactly as she told you; **tal cual: lo dejé todo** ~ **cual** I left everything exactly as it was; **tal vez** maybe

talacha *f* (a) (Méx) (reparación de llantas) flat *o* puncture repair (b) (Méx fam) (trabajo manual) work

taladradora *f* pneumatic drill

taladrar [A1] *vt* ⟨*pared/madera*⟩ to drill (through)

taladro *m* (a) (mecánico) hand drill; (eléctrico) electric *o* power drill (b) (agujero) drill hole

talante *m* (humor) mood; **estar de buen** ~ to be in a good mood

talar [A1] *vt* ⟨*árbol*⟩ to fell, cut down

talco *m* talc; **polvos de** ~ talcum powder

talento *m* (a) (aptitud) talent; **tiene** ~ **para la música** he has a talent *o* gift for music; **un joven de** ~ a talented young man (b) (persona) talented person

talentoso -sa *adj* talented, gifted

TALGO /'talγo/ *m* (= **Tren Articulado Ligero Goicoechea Oriol**) air-conditioned express train

talismán *m* talisman, lucky charm

talla *f* (a) (Indum) size; **¿cuál es su** ~? what size are you?; **de** *o* **en todas las** ~**s** in all sizes (b) (estatura) size, height; **de** ~ **mediana** of medium height

tallado *m* (de madera) carving; (de piedras preciosas) cutting

tallar [A1] *vt* ⓵ ⟨*madera*⟩ to carve; ⟨*escultura/mármol*⟩ to sculpt; ⟨*piedras preciosas*⟩ to cut ⓶ (Méx) (a) (para limpiar) to scrub (b) (para aliviar) to rub ■ ~ *vi* (Col) «*zapatos*» to be too tight ■ **tallarse** *v pron* (Méx) (a) (para limpiarse) to scrub oneself (b) (para aliviar) to rub oneself; ⟨*ojos*⟩ to rub

tallarín *m* noodle

talle *m* (a) (cintura) waist (b) (figura) figure (c) (en costura) trunk measurement; **es corta de** ~ she's short-waisted

taller *m* ⓵ (a) (Auto) *tb* ~ **mecánico** garage, repair shop (AmE) (b) (de carpintero, técnico) workshop ⓶ (Educ) workshop

tallo *m* stem, stalk

talón *m* ⓵ (a) (del pie, zapato, calcetín) heel; ~ **de Aquiles** Achilles' heel (b) (de zapato, calcetín) heel ⓶ (a) (AmL) (matriz) stub, counterfoil (b) (Esp) (cheque) check (AmE), cheque (BrE); (vale) chit; ~ **de compra** receipt

talonario *m* (de cheques) checkbook (AmE), chequebook (BrE); (de recibos) receipt book; (de volantes) book of vouchers

talonear [A1] *vt* (AmL) ⟨*caballo*⟩ to spur (on)

tamal *m* tamale

tamaño *m* size; **pañuelos de todos los** ~**s** handkerchiefs in all sizes; **de** ~ **bolsillo** pocket-size; **un busto** ~ **natural** a life-size bust

tamarindo *m* (a) (Bot) tamarind (b) (Méx fam) (agente) traffic cop (colloq)

tambache *m* (Méx fam) (bulto) bundle; (montón) pile

tambalearse [A1] *v pron vi* «*silla/botella*» to wobble; «*persona*» to stagger; **caminaba tambaleándose** he was staggering; **todo empezó a** ~ everything began to shake

también *adv* too, as well; ~ **habla ruso** she speaks Russian too *o* as well; **que te diviertas — tú** ~ have fun! — you too *o* and you; **Pilar fuma — yo** ~ Pilar smokes — so do I *o* (colloq) me too

tambo *m* ⓵ (Méx) (a) (recipiente) can (AmE), bin (BrE) (b) (fam) (cárcel) slammer (sl), can (AmE sl) ⓶ (Per) (tienda) wayside stall

tambor *m* ⓵ (a) (instrumento) drum; **un redoble de** ~**es** a drum roll (b) (persona) drummer ⓶ (a) (del freno) drum (b) (AmL) (barril) drum

tamborilear [A1] *vi* to drum, tap

Támesis *m*: **el** ~ the (River) Thames

tamiz *m* sieve; **pasar algo por el** ~ ⟨*harina*⟩ to sift sth; ⟨*salsa*⟩ to sieve sth

tamizar [A4] *vt* ⟨*harina*⟩ to sift; ⟨*salsa*⟩ to sieve

tampoco *adv* not ... either; **yo** ~ **entendí** I didn't understand either; **él no va, ni yo** ~ he isn't going and neither am I; **no he estado en Roma ni** ~ **en París** I've never been to Rome or Paris

tampón *m* (a) (para entintar) ink pad (b) (Farm, Med) tampon

tan *adv*: *apocopated form of* TANTO *used before adjectives (except some comparatives), adverbs, and adjectival or adverbial phrases*

tanda *f* **1** (grupo) batch, lot; **cada dos minutos hay una ~ de avisos** (AmL) every couple of minutes there's another lot of commercials; **los horneamos en dos ~s** we baked them in two batches **2** (AmC, Méx fam) (función — de teatro) performance; (— de cine) showing, performance **3** (Col, Méx) (ronda) round (of drinks)

tándem *m* (bicicleta) tandem

tanga *f or m* tanga

tangente *f* tangent; **irse** *or* **salirse por la ~** to go off at a tangent

tangerina *f* tangerine

tango *m* tango; **bailar el ~** to tango

tano -na *adj/m,f* (RPl fam & pey) Italian

tanque *m* **1** (Arm) (carro) tank **2** (de agua, gasolina) tank; (de gas, oxígeno) cylinder, bottle

tantear [A1] *vt* **(a)** (con el tacto) to feel **(b)** ‹situación› to weigh up, size up; ‹persona› to sound out **(c)** (calcular aproximadamente) to estimate
■ **~** *vi* to feel one's way

tanteo *m* (Dep) score

tantito *adv* (Méx fam) a bit; **espérame ~, ya voy** just wait a bit, I'm coming

tanto¹ *adv* **1** [*see note under* TAN] (aplicado a adjetivo o adverbio) so; (aplicado a verbo) so much; **es tan bonito** it's so beautiful; **¡es una chica tan amable!** she's such a nice girl!; **~ mejor** so much the better; **tan solo** only; **~ es así que ...** so much so that ...; **ya no salimos ~** we don't go out so often *o* so much now; **llegó tan tarde que ...** he arrived so late (that) ...; **no es tan tímida como parece** she's not as shy as she looks; **sale ~ como tú** he goes out as much as you do; **tan pronto como puedas** as soon as you can; **~ Suárez como Vargas votaron en contra** both Suárez and Vargas voted against **2** (AmL exc RPl) **qué tanto/qué tan: ¿qué ~ te duele?** how much does it hurt?; **¿qué tan alto es?** how tall is he?
■ *m* **1** (cantidad): **un ~ por ciento** a percentage; **hay que dejar un ~ de depósito** you have to put down a certain amount as a deposit **2** (punto — en fútbol) goal; (— en fútbol americano, tenis, juegos) point **3** (en locs) **al tanto: me puso al ~** she put me in the picture; **mantenerse al ~ de algo** to keep up to date with sth; **estar al ~** (pendiente, alerta) to be on the ball (colloq); **está al ~ de lo ocurrido** he knows what's happened; **un tanto** somewhat, rather; **un ~ triste** somewhat sad

tanto² -ta *adj* **(a)** (sing) so much; (pl) so many; **había ~ espacio/~s niños** there was so much space/there were so many children; **¡~ tiempo sin verte!** it's been so long!; **~ dinero/~s turistas como ...** as much money/as many tourists as ... **(b)** (fam) (expresando cantidades indeterminadas): **tenía setenta y ~s años** he was seventy something, he was seventy-odd (colloq)
■ *pron* **1** **(a)** (sing) so much; (pl) so many; **¡tengo ~ que hacer!** I've so much to do!; **vinieron ~s que ...** so many people came (that) ...; **¿de verdad gana ~?** does he really earn that much?; **no ser para ~** (fam): **duele, pero no es para ~** it hurts, but it's not *that* bad **(b)** (fam) (expresando cantidades indeterminadas): **hasta las tantas de la**

madrugada until the early hours of the morning; **treinta y tantas** thirty or so **(c)** (refiriéndose a tiempo): **hace ~ que no me llama** it's been so long since she called me; **aún faltan dos horas — ¿tanto?** there's still two hours to go — what? that long?
2 (en locs) **en tanto** while; **entre tanto** meanwhile, in the meantime; **otro tanto** as much again; **me queda otro ~ por hacer** I have as much again still to do; **por (lo) tanto** therefore

tañer [E7] *vt* (liter) ‹arpa› to strum
■ **~** *vi* «campana» to peal, ring out

tapa *f* **1** **(a)** (de caja, cacerola) lid; (de botella, frasco) top; **~ de rosca** screw top **(b)** (de lente, bolígrafo) cap; **la ~ del tanque de gasolina** the gas (AmE) *o* (BrE) petrol cap **2** **(a)** (de libro, revista) cover; (de disco) sleeve **(b)** (de tacón) heelpiece **(c)** (de bolsillo) flap **(d)** (Auto) head **3** (Esp) (para acompañar la bebida) tapa, bar snack

tapabarros *m* (*pl* ~) (Chi, Per) (de coche) fender (AmE), wing (BrE); (de bicicleta) splashguard (AmE), mudguard (BrE)

tapadera *f* **(a)** (de cazo) lid **(b)** (de fraude, engaño) cover, front **(c)** (Méx) (de botella) cap, top

tapado *m* **1** (RPl, Ven) (abrigo) (winter) coat **2** (Méx) (Pol) potential candidate (*with official support*)

tapadura *f* (Andes, Méx) filling

tapar [A1] *vt* **1** (cubrir) ‹caja› to put the lid on; ‹botella/frasco› to put the top on; ‹olla› to cover, put the lid on; ‹bebé/enfermo/cara› to cover **2** **(a)** ‹agujero/hueco› to fill in; ‹puerta/ventana› to block up **(b)** (Andes, Méx) ‹muela› to fill; **me ~on dos muelas** I had two fillings **(c)** ‹defecto/error› to cover up **3** **(a)** ‹vista/luz› to block **(b)** ‹salida/entrada› to block; ‹excusado/cañería› (AmL) to block
■ **taparse** *v pron* **1** (refl) (cubrirse) to cover oneself up; ‹cara› to cover **2** **(a)** «oídos/nariz» to get *o* become blocked; **tengo la nariz tapada** my nose is blocked **(b)** (AmL) «cañería/excusado» to get blocked

taparrabos *m* (*pl* ~) loincloth

tapatío -tía *adj* of/from Guadalajara (*in Mexico*)

tapeo *m* (Esp fam): **ir de ~** to go for a drink and a few tapas *o* bar snacks; **bares de ~** tapas bars

tapete *m* **1** (para mesa) decorative table cloth; (para sofá) antimacassar **2** (Col, Méx, Ven) (alfombra) rug

tapia *f* (muro) wall; (cerca) fence; **ser/estar más sordo que una ~** (fam) to be as deaf as a post (colloq)

tapiar [A1] *vt* **(a)** ‹espacio› to wall in **(b)** ‹puerta/ventana› to brick up

tapicería *f* **(a)** (de coches, muebles) upholstery **(b)** (arte) tapestry making; (tapiz) tapestry

tapicero -ra *m,f* (de muebles) upholsterer

tapilla *f* (Chi) heelpiece

tapir *m* tapir

tapiz *m* (para pared) tapestry; (para suelo) carpet

tapizado *m* upholstery

tapizar [A4] *vt* ‹sillón› to upholster; ‹pared› to line

tapón *m* **1** **(a)** (de vidrio, goma) stopper; (de corcho) cork; (del lavabo) plug; (de botella) (Esp) top ···❯

(b) (para los oídos) earplug; (de cerumen) plug
2 (a) (fam) (atasco) traffic jam, tailback (BrE) **(b)**
(en baloncesto) block **3** (CS) (Elec) fuse

taponar [A1] *vt* ‹agujero› to block
■ **taponarse** *v pron* **(a)** «oídos/nariz» to get
blocked **(b)** «cañería» to get blocked **(c)** (Col,
RPl) «ciudad/zona» to block

taquigrafía *f* shorthand, stenography (AmE)

taquilla *f* **(a)** (de cine) box office; (en estación,
estadio) ticket office **(b)** (cantidad recaudada) takings
(*pl*) **(c)** (casillero) rack, pigeonholes (*pl*)

taquillero -ra *m,f* box-office clerk

tara *f* **1** (peso) tare **2** (defecto) defect

tarántula *f* tarantula

tararear [A1] *vt* to la-la-la

tardado -da *adj* (Méx) ‹proceso/tarea›
time-consuming; ‹persona› slow

tardanza *f* delay; **sin ~** without delay; **perdona
la ~ en contestar** forgive my delay in replying;
me preocupa su ~ I'm worried that he's so late;
su ~ se debió a … his lateness was due to …

tardar [A1] *vt* (emplear cierto tiempo): **está
tardando mucho** she's taking a long time; **tarda
una hora en hacerse** it takes about an hour to
cook; **tardó un mes en contestar** it took him a
month to reply; **no tardo ni un minuto** I won't be
a minute; **¿cuánto se tarda en coche?** how long
does it take by car?
■ **~** *vi* (retrasarse) to be late; (emplear demasiado
tiempo) to take a long time; **empieza a las seis, no
tardes** it starts at six, don't be late; **parece que
tarda** he seems to be taking a long time; **¡no
tardo!** I won't be long!; **aún ~á en llegar** it'll be a
while yet before he gets here; **no ~on en
detenerlo** it didn't take them long to arrest him
■ **tardarse** *v pron* (Méx, Ven) ▶ TARDAR *vt, vi*

tarde *adv* late; **llegar ~** to be late; **se está
haciendo ~** it's getting late; **~ o temprano**
sooner or later
■ *f* (temprano) afternoon; (hacia el anochecer)
evening; **a las seis de la ~** at six in the evening;
¡buenas ~s! (temprano) good afternoon!; (hacia el
anochecer) good evening!; **en la** *or* (esp Esp) **por la**
or (RPl) **a la ~** in the afternoon/evening

tardón -dona *adj* (fam) slow
■ *m,f* (fam) slowpoke (AmE colloq), slowcoach (BrE
colloq)

tarea *f* **(a)** (trabajo) task, job; **las ~s de la casa**
the housework **(b)** (deberes escolares) homework

tarifa *f* **(a)** (baremo, escala) rate; **~s postales**
postal rates **(b)** (Transp) fare **(c)** (lista de precios)
price list **(d)** (arancel) tariff

tarima *f* (plataforma) dais

tarjar [A1] *vt* (Andes) to cross out, delete (fml)

tarjeta *f* card; **marcar** (AmL) *or* (Méx) **checar ~**
to clock in/out, punch in/out (AmE); **~ amarilla/
roja** yellow/red card; **~ de crédito** credit card; **~
de embarque** boarding pass *o* card; **~ de Navidad**
Christmas card; **~ de prepago** top-up card; **~ de**

visita *or* (Méx) **de presentación** (personal) visiting
card; (de negocios) business card; **~ postal/
telefónica** postcard/phonecard

tarro *m* **1** (recipiente— de vidrio) jar; (— de
cerámica) pot; (— de metal) (Chi) can, tin (BrE)
2 (Méx, Ven) (taza) mug

tarta *f* (Esp) cake; (de hojaldre — descubierta) tart;
(— cubierta) pie

tartamudear [A1] *vi* to stutter, stammer

tartamudo -da *adj* stuttering (*before n*),
stammering (*before n*); **es ~** he has a stutter *o*
stammer
■ *m,f*: **hay un ~ en mi clase** one of the boys in my
class has a stutter *o* stammer

tartera *f* (para cocinar) cake tin

tarumba *adj* crazy (colloq); **me vuelve ~** he
drives me crazy (colloq)

tasa *f* **(a)** (valoración) valuation **(b)** (impuesto) tax
(c) (índice) rate; **~ de desempleo** rate of
unemployment; **~ de mortalidad/natalidad**
mortality rate/birthrate

tasación *f* valuation

tasajear [A1] *vt* (Méx, Per) to slash

tasar [A1] *vt* ‹objeto/coche› to value

tasca *f* (taberna) bar, tavern

tata *m* (AmL fam) **(a)** (padre) dad (colloq), pop (AmE
colloq) **(b)** (abuelo) grandpa (colloq)

tatarabuelo -la *m,f* (*m*)
great-great-grandfather; (*f*)
great-great-grandmother; **mis ~s** my
great-great-grandparents

tataranieto -ta *m,f* (*m*) great-great-grandson;
(*f*) great-great-granddaughter; **sus ~s** his
great-great-grandchildren

ta-te-ti *m* (RPl) tic-tac-toe (AmE), noughts and
crosses (BrE)

tatuaje *m* (acción) tattooing; (dibujo) tattoo

tatuar [A18] *vt* to tattoo

taurino -na *adj* ‹temporada/afición›
bullfighting (*before n*), taurine (fml)

Tauro *m* (signo, constelación) Taurus; **es (de) ~**
he's (a) Taurus, he's a Taurean
■ *mf* (*pl* **-ros**) (persona) *tb* **tauro** Taurean, Taurus

taxi *m* taxi, cab; **~ colectivo** (Col) minibus

taxímetro *m* taximeter

taxista *mf* taxi driver, cabdriver

taza *f* **(a)** (recipiente) cup; **~ de café/té** coffee
cup/teacup **(b)** (contenido) cupful; **una ~ de azúcar**
a cupful of sugar; **tomar una ~ de té** to have a
cup of tea **(c)** (del retrete) (toilet) bowl **(d)** (de
fuente) basin

tazón *m* bowl

te *pron pers* **(a)** you; **no ~ lo quiero prestar** I
don't want to lend it to you; **¿~ lo paso a
máquina?** shall I type it for you?; **voy a serte
sincera** I'll be frank with you; **cuídate** (*refl*) look
after yourself; **¿~ has cortado el pelo?** (*caus*)
have you had your hair cut?; **¿~ sientes bien?**

are you feeling all right?; **no** ∼ **muevas** don't move (b) (*impers*): **cuando** ∼ **pasa eso** ... when that happens ...

■ *f: name of the letter* t

té *m* (a) (infusión, planta) tea; **¿quieres un** ∼? do you want a cup of tea? (b) (AmL) (reunión) tea party

tea *f* torch

teatral *adj* (a) (Teatr) ⟨grupo/temporada⟩ theater* (*before n*); **una obra** ∼ **a** play; **un autor** ∼ **a** playwright (b) ⟨persona/gesto/tono⟩ theatrical

teatro *m* ⟨1⟩ (Teatr) (a) (arte, actividad) theater*; **una obra de** ∼ **a** play; **actor de** ∼ stage actor; ∼ **de guiñol** puppet theater*; ∼ **de variedades** vaudeville (AmE), music hall (BrE) (b) (local) theater*; **un** ∼ **al aire libre** an open-air theater ⟨2⟩ (fam) (exageración): **es puro** ∼ it's all an act

tebeo *m* (Esp) comic (*for children*)

techo *m* (a) (cielo raso) ceiling (b) (AmL) (tejado, cubierta) roof; ∼ **corredizo** sunroof (c) (hogar, casa) house; **sin** ∼ homeless; **bajo el mismo** ∼ under the same roof

techumbre *f* roof

tecla *f* key

teclado *m* keyboard; ∼ **numérico** numeric keypad

teclear [A1] *vt* ⟨palabra/texto⟩ to key in, type in

■ ∼ *vi* (en máquina de escribir) to type; (en ordenador) to key

técnica *f* ⟨1⟩ (a) (método) technique (b) (destreza) skill ⟨2⟩ (tecnología) technology ⟨3⟩ (en baloncesto) technical foul

tecnicismo *m* (cualidad) technical nature; (palabra) technical term

técnico -ca *adj* technical

■ *m,f* (a) (en fábrica) technician (b) (de lavadoras, etc) repairman (AmE), engineer (BrE) (c) (Dep) trainer, coach (AmE), manager (BrE)

tecnicolor *m* Technicolor®

tecnología *f* technology; ∼ **punta** state-of-the-art technology

tecnológico -ca *adj* technological

tecolote *m* (Méx) (Zool) owl

tedio *m* boredom, tedium

teja *f* tile; ∼s **de pizarra** slates

tejado *m* (esp Esp) roof

tejano -na *adj/m,f* Texan

Tejas *m* Texas

tejaván *m* (Méx) shed

tejedor -dora *m,f* (a) (con telar) weaver (b) (con agujas, máquina) knitter

tejer [E1] *vt* (a) (en telar) to weave; **tejido a mano** hand-woven (b) (con agujas, a máquina) to knit; (con ganchillo) to crochet; **máquina de** ∼ knitting machine (c) «araña» to spin

■ ∼ *vi* (en telar) to weave; (con agujas, a máquina) to knit; (con ganchillo) to crochet

tejido *m* ⟨1⟩ (a) (tela) fabric; ∼s **sintéticos** synthetic fabrics (b) (AmL) (con agujas, máquina) knitting; (con ganchillo) crochet ⟨2⟩ (Anat) tissue

tejo *m* (a) (disco) disc (b) (juego — de niños) hopscotch; (— de adultos) *game similar to pitch-and-toss*

tejolote *m* (Méx) pestle

tejón *m* badger

tela *f* ⟨1⟩ (Tex) (material) material, fabric; ∼ **de lana** wool (fabric); ∼ **de araña** ▶ TELARAÑA; ∼ **metálica** wire mesh ⟨2⟩ (Art) (cuadro) canvas, painting ⟨3⟩ (membrana) skin, film

telar *m* (a) (máquina) loom (b) **telares** *mpl* (fábrica) textile mill

telaraña *f* spiderweb (AmE), spider's web (BrE); (polvorienta) cobweb; ∼ **mundial** World Wide Web

tele *f* (fam) TV (colloq), telly (BrE colloq)

telebanca *f* telebanking

telebanco *m* cash dispenser

telecomunicación *f* telecommunication

teleculebra *f* (Ven fam) soap opera (colloq)

telediario *m* (Esp) (television) news

teledirigido -da *adj* ⟨coche⟩ radio-controlled, remote-controlled; **misiles** ∼s guided missiles

teleférico *m* cable railway

telefonazo *m* (fam) buzz (colloq); **darle** *or* (Méx) **echarle un** ∼ **a algn** to give sb a buzz (colloq)

telefonear [A1] *vt* to telephone, phone, call; **¿puedo** ∼ **a Londres?** can I make a (telephone) call to London?

■ ∼ *vi* to telephone, phone

telefónico -ca *adj* telephone (*before n*)

telefonista *mf* telephone operator

teléfono *m* ⟨1⟩ (Telec) telephone, phone; **número de** ∼ phone number; **contestar el** ∼ to answer *o* (colloq) get the phone; **me colgó el** ∼ she hung up on me; **hablé por** ∼ **con ella** I spoke to her on the phone; **está hablando por** ∼ he's on the phone; **llamar a algn por** ∼ to call sb (up), phone sb; ∼ **celular** *or* (Esp) **móvil** mobile telephone; ∼ **rojo** hotline; ∼ **satélite** satellite telephone, satphone ⟨2⟩ (de la ducha) shower head

telegrafiar [A17] *vi/vt* to telegraph

telégrafo *m* telegraph

telegrama *m* telegram

telemarketing /teleˈmarketin/ *m* telemarketing

telenovela *f* soap opera

telepatía *f* telepathy

telescopio *m* telescope

telespectador -dora *m,f* viewer

telesquí *m* ski lift

teletexto, teletex *m* teletext, videotex

televentas *fpl* telesales

televidente *mf* viewer

televisar [A1] *vt* to televise

televisión *f* (a) (sistema) television; **¿qué hay en (la)** ∼? what's on television?; **lo transmitieron por** ∼ it was broadcast on television; ∼ **a** *or* **en color(es)** color* television; ∼ **de alta definición** high definition television, HDTV; ∼ **en blanco y negro** black and white television; ∼ **en circuito cerrado** closed circuit television; ∼ **por cable/por satélite** cable/satellite television; ∼ **matinal** breakfast television (b) (programación) television; **ver (la)** ∼ to watch television (c) (televisor) television (set)

televisor *m* television (set)

télex *m* (*pl* ∼) telex

telón *m* curtain; ∼ **de fondo** (Teatr) backdrop

tema *m* (a) (asunto, cuestión) matter; (de conferencia, composición) topic; (de examen) subject;   ⋯⋮

(Art, Cin, Lit) subject; **es un ~ delicado** it's a delicate matter; **~ de conversación** topic of conversation; **cambiar de ~** to change the subject **(b)** (Mús) (motivo) theme

temario *m* **(a)** (para examen) syllabus, list of topics **(b)** (en congreso) agenda

temblar [A5] *vi* **(a)** «*persona*» (de frío) to shiver; (por nervios, miedo) to shake, tremble; (+ me/te/le etc) «*párpado*» to twitch; «*mano*» to shake; «*voz*» to tremble; **la voz le temblaba de emoción** her voice was trembling with emotion **(b)** «*edificio/tierra*» to shake

■ **~** *v impers*: **¡está temblando!** (AmL) it's an earthquake!; **tembló ayer** there was a(n earth) tremor yesterday

temblor *m* **(a)** (de frío, fiebre) shivering; (de miedo, nervios) trembling, shaking; **con un ligero ~ en la voz** in a tremulous voice **(b)** *tb* **~ de tierra** (earth) tremor

tembloroso -sa *adj* **(a)** «*manos*» trembling, shaking; «*voz*» trembling, tremulous; **~ de frío** shivering with cold **(b)** «*llama/luz*» flickering, quivering

temer [E1] *vt* «*castigo/reacción*» to fear, dread; «*persona*» to be afraid of; **sus hijos le temen** her children are afraid of her; **temo ofenderlo** I'm afraid of offending him

■ **~** *vi* to be afraid; **no temas** don't be afraid

■ **temerse** *v pron* **(a)** (sospechar) to fear; **ya me lo temía** I knew this would happen; **me temo que tenía razón** I fear that he was right **(b)** (en fórmulas de cortesía) to be afraid; **me temo que no ha llegado** I'm afraid he hasn't arrived

temeridad *f* **(a)** (acción): **eso fue una ~** that was a very rash *o* bold thing to do **(b)** (cualidad) temerity; **conduce con ~** she drives recklessly

temible *adj* fearsome, fearful

temor *m* fear; **no dije nada por ~ a ofenderlo** I didn't say anything for fear of offending him

témpano *m* ice floe

témpera *f* tempera

temperamental *adj* (irascible, cambiable) temperamental; (de mucho carácter) spirited

temperamento *m* **(a)** (manera de ser) temperament; **son de ~s muy diferentes** they have very different temperaments **(b)** (vigor de carácter): **un chico con mucho ~** a boy with a lot of spirit

temperatura *f* temperature; **tomarle la ~ a algn** to take sb's temperature; **tiene ~** (CS) she has a fever (AmE) *o* (BrE) a temperature; **~ ambiente** room temperature

tempestad *f* storm, tempest (liter); **~ de arena** sandstorm

tempestuoso -sa *adj* stormy, tempestuous

templado -da *adj* **(a)** «*clima*» mild, temperate; «*zona*» temperate; «*día*» warm **(b)** «*agua/comida*» lukewarm

templo *m* temple

temporada *f* **(a)** (época establecida) season; **verduras de ~** seasonal vegetables; **fuera de/en ~** out of/in season; **~ alta/baja** high/low season **(b)** (período de tiempo) spell; **una ~ de mucho trabajo** a very busy spell *o* period

temporal *adj* **1** (transitorio) temporary **2** (relativo al tiempo) temporal

■ *m* (Meteo) storm; **~ de nieve** snowstorm, blizzard

temporalero -ra *m,f* (Méx) seasonal worker

temporario -ria *adj* (AmL) temporary

temprano *adv* early; **levantarse ~** to get up early; **por la mañana ~** in the morning

ten ▶ TENER

tenacidad *f* (perseverancia) tenacity

tenacillas *fpl* hair crimper

tenaz *adj* **(a)** «*persona*» tenacious **(b)** «*dolor*» persistent; «*mancha*» stubborn

tenaza *f*, **tenazas** *fpl* **(a)** (Mec, Tec) pliers (*pl*) **(b)** (de chimenea, cocina) tongs (*pl*) **(c)** (del cangrejo) pincer **(d)** (Méx) (de pelo) curling iron (AmE), hair crimper (BrE)

tendajón *m* (Méx) shack (*serving as a store or stall*)

tendal *m* (AmL) (para el café) drying area

tendedero *m* (cuerda) clothes-line; (caballete) clotheshorse

tendencia *f* tendency; **~s homosexuales** homosexual tendencies *o* leanings; **~ a algo** trend TOWARD(s) sth; **tiene ~ a exagerar** she has a tendency to exaggerate; **existe una ~ a la centralización** there is a trend toward centralization

tender [E8] *vt* **1** «*ropa*» (afuera) to hang out; (dentro de la casa) to hang (up); **tengo ropa tendida** I have some washing on the line

2 (a) (extender) «*manta*» to spread out, lay out; «*mantel*» to spread; **le tendió la mano** he held out his hand to him **(b)** (AmL) «*cama*» to make; «*mesa*» to lay, set **(c)** «*persona*» to lay

3 (a) «*cable*» (sobre superficie) to lay; (suspendido) to hang **(b)** «*vía férrea*» to lay

4 «*emboscada*» to lay, set; «*trampa*» to lay

■ **~** *vi* (inclinarse) **~ A hacer algo** to tend to do sth; **tiende a encoger** it tends to shrink

■ **tenderse** *v pron* (tumbarse) to lie down

tendero -ra *m,f* storekeeper (esp AmE), shopkeeper (esp BrE)

tendido *m* **1** (Elec) (cables) cables (*pl*), wires (*pl*) **2** (Col, Ven) (ropa de cama) bedclothes (*pl*)

tendón *m* tendon

tendré, tendría, etc ▶ TENER

tenebroso -sa *adj* «*lugar*» dark, gloomy; «*asunto/maquinaciones*» sinister; «*porvenir*» dismal, gloomy

tenedor *m* (cubierto) fork

tenencia *f* (Méx) (Auto) road tax

tener [E27] *vt* [*El uso de 'got' en frases como 'I've got a new dress' está mucho más extendido en el inglés británico que en el americano. Este prefiere la forma 'I have a new dress'*] **1 (a)** (poseer, disponer de) «*dinero/trabajo/tiempo*» to have; **¿tienen hijos?** do they have any children?, have they got any children?; **no tenemos pan** we don't have any bread, we haven't got any bread; **tiene el pelo largo** she has *o* she's got long hair **(b)** (llevar encima) «*lápiz/cambio*» to have; **¿tiene hora?** have you got the time? **(c)** (hablando de actividades, obligaciones) to have; **tengo invitados a cenar** I have *o* I've got some people coming to dinner; **tengo cosas que hacer** I have *o* I've got things to do **(d)** (dar a luz) «*bebé/gemelos*» to have

2 (a) (señalando características, tamaño) to have; **la casa tiene mucha luz** the house is very light; **tiene un metro de largo** it is one meter long; **le lleva 15 años — ¿y eso qué tiene?** (AmL fam) she's

15 years older than he is — so what does that matter? **(b)** (señalando edad) to be; **¿cuántos años tienes?** how old are you?; **tengo veinte años** I'm twenty (years old)

3 **(a)** (sujetar, sostener) to hold; **tenlo derecho** hold it upright **(b)** (tomar): **ten la llave** take o here's the key

4 **(a)** (sentir): **tengo hambre/frío** I'm hungry/cold; **le tengo mucho cariño** I'm very fond of him; **tengo el placer de** ... it gives me great pleasure to ... **(b)** (refiriéndose a enfermedades) ‹gripe/cáncer› to have; **tengo dolor de cabeza** I have o I've got a headache **(c)** (refiriéndose a experiencias) ‹discusión/accidente› to have; **que tengas buen viaje** have a good trip

5 (refiriéndose a actitudes): **ten más respeto** have a little more respect; **ten paciencia/cuidado** be patient/careful; **tiene mucho tacto** he's very tactful

6 (indicando estado, situación): **la mesa tiene una pata rota** one of the table legs is broken; **tengo las manos sucias** my hands are dirty; **tienes el cinturón desabrochado** your belt's undone; **me tiene muy preocupada** I'm very worried about it

■ ∼ v aux 1 ∼ **QUE hacer algo** ... (expresando obligación, necesidad) to have (got) to do sth; **tengo que estudiar hoy** I have to o I must study today; **tienes que comer más** you ought to eat more **(b)** (expresando propósito, recomendación): **tenemos que ir a ver esa película** we must go and see that movie; **tendrías que llamarlo** you should ring him **(c)** (expresando certeza): **tiene que estar en este cajón** it must be in this drawer; **¡tú tenías que ser!** it had to be you!

2 (con participio pasado): **tengo entendido que sí viene** I understand he is coming; **te tengo dicho que** ... I've told you before (that) ...; **teníamos pensado irnos hoy** we intended leaving today

3 (AmL) (en expresiones de tiempo): **tienen tres años de casados** they've been married for three years; **tenía un año sin verlo** she hadn't seen him for a year

■ **tenerse** v pron (sostenerse): **no podía** ∼**se en pie** he couldn't stand; **no** ∼**se de sueño** to be dead on one's feet

tenga, tengas, etc ▶ TENER

tenia f (Med) tapeworm, taenia (tech)

tenida f (Chi) outfit

teniente mf **(a)** (en ejército) lieutenant **(b)** (en fuerzas aéreas) ≈ first lieutenant (in US), ≈ flying officer (in UK)

tenis m (pl ∼) tennis; ∼ **de mesa** table tennis

tenista mf tennis player

tenor m (Mús) tenor

tensar [A1] vt ‹músculo› to tense; ‹cuerda/cable› to tighten; ‹arco› to draw; ‹relaciones/lazos› to strain

tensión f 1 **(a)** (de cuerda, músculo) tension **(b)** tb ∼ **arterial** blood pressure; **tomarle la** ∼ **a algn** to take sb's blood pressure; ∼ **nerviosa** nervous tension 2 (estrés) strain, stress; (en relaciones, situación) tension 3 (Elec) voltage

tenso -sa adj 1 ‹cuerda/cable› taut, tight; ‹músculo› tense 2 ‹persona/situación› tense; ‹relación› strained, tense

tentación f **(a)** (impulso) temptation; **no resistió la** ∼ **de comérselo** he couldn't resist the

temptation to eat it **(b)** (cosa, persona): **los bombones son mi** ∼ I can't resist chocolates (colloq)

tentáculo m tentacle

tentador -dora adj tempting

tentar [A5] vt 1 (atraer, seducir) ‹plan/idea› to tempt; ‹persona› to tempt; **me tienta tu propuesta** I am very tempted by your proposal; **estuve tentado de decírselo** I was tempted to tell him; ∼ **a algn** A **hacer algo** to tempt sb to do sth 2 (probar) **(a)** ‹cuerda/tabla› to test **(b)** (palpar) to feel

tentativa f attempt

tentempié m (bocado) snack

tenue adj **(a)** ‹luz› faint, weak; ‹voz/sonido/sonrisa› faint; ‹neblina/llovizna› light; ‹línea› faint, fine **(b)** ‹color› subdued, pale

teñir [I15] vt **(a)** ‹ropa/zapatos/pelo› to dye **(b)** (manchar) to stain; **la tinta le tiñó los dedos de rojo** the ink stained his fingers red

■ **teñirse** v pron (refl) ‹pelo/zapatos› to dye

teología f theology

teoría f theory; **en** ∼ in theory

teórico -ca adj ‹existencia/valor/curso› theoretical; **examen** ∼ theory (exam)

tequila m tequila

terapeuta mf therapist

terapéutico -ca adj therapeutic

terapia f therapy; ∼ **de pareja** marriage counseling*; ∼ **intensiva** (Méx, RPI) intensive care

tercer ▶ TERCERO[1]

tercera f (Auto) third (gear); **mete (la)** ∼ put it into third (gear)

tercermundista adj third-world (before n)

tercero[1] -ra adj/pron [TERCER is used before masculine singular nouns] third; **en el tercer piso** on the third floor; **el Tercer Mundo** the Third World; **personas de la tercera edad** senior citizens; **la tercera parte** a third; para ejemplos ver QUINTO

tercero[2] m third party; **seguro contra** ∼**s** third party insurance

tercio m **(a)** (tercera parte) third **(b)** (Taur) each of the three main stages of a bullfight

terciopelo m velvet

terco -ca adj stubborn, obstinate

tergiversar [A1] vt to distort, twist

termas fpl (baños) hot o thermal baths (pl); (manantial) hot o thermal springs (pl)

térmico -ca adj thermal

terminación f **(a)** (finalización) termination (frml) **(b)** (acabado) finish **(c)** (Ling) ending

terminal adj ‹enfermedad/caso› terminal; **los enfermos** ∼**es** the terminally ill

■ m (Elec, Inf) terminal

■ f (de autobuses) terminus, bus station; (Aviac, Inf) terminal

terminante adj ‹respuesta› categorical; ‹orden› strict

terminar [A1] vt ‹trabajo/estudio› to finish; ‹casa/obras› to finish, complete; ‹discusión/conflicto› to put an end to; **termina esa sopa** finish up that soup; ∼ **la comida con un café** to end the meal with a cup of coffee

■ ∼ vi 1 ‹persona› **(a)** (de hacer algo) to finish; ···>

t

~ DE hacer algo to finish doing sth; **déjame ~ de hablar** let me finish (speaking) **(b)** (en estado, situación) to end up; **terminé muy cansada** I ended up feeling very tired; **va a ~ mal** he's going to come to a bad end; **terminó marchándose** or **por marcharse** he ended up leaving

2 (a) «*reunión/situación*» to end, come to an end; **al ~ la clase** when the class ended; **esto va a ~ mal** this is going to turn out o end badly **(b)** (rematar) ~ **EN algo** to end IN sth; **termina en consonante** it ends in a consonant **(c)** (llegar a): **no termina de convencerme** I'm not totally convinced; **no terminaba de gustarle** she wasn't totally happy about it

3 terminar con (a) (acabar) ~ **CON algo** «*con libro/tarea*» to finish WITH sth; «*con problema/abuso*» to put an end to sth **(b)** ~ **CON algn** (pelearse) to finish WITH sb; (matar) to kill sb

■ **terminarse** *v pron* **1** «*azúcar/pan*» to run out; **se me terminó la lana** I've run out of wool **2** «*curso/reunión*» to come to an end, be over **3** (enf) «*libro/comida*» to finish, polish off

término *m* **1** (posición, instancia): **en primer ~** first, first of all; ~ **medio** happy medium; **por ~ medio** on average **2** (Ling) term; **en ~s reales** in real terms **3 términos** *mpl* (condiciones, especificaciones) terms (*pl*) **4** (Col, Méx, Ven) (Coc): **¿qué ~ quiere la carne?** how would you like your meat (done)?

termita *f* termite

termo® *m* (recipiente) Thermos®, vacuum flask

termómetro *m* thermometer

termostato *m* thermostat

ternera *f* veal

ternero -ra *m,f* calf

terno *m* (AmS) suit (*in some countries specifically a three-piece suit*)

ternura *f* tenderness; **con ~** tenderly

terquedad *f* obstinacy, stubbornness

terracería *f* (Méx) (camino) rough dirt track

terracota *f* terra-cotta

terrateniente *mf* landowner

terraza *f* **(a)** (balcón) balcony **(b)** (azotea) terrace **(c)** (de bar) *area outside a bar or café where tables are placed*; **sentémonos en la ~** let's sit outside **(d)** (Agr) terrace

terregal *m* (Méx) loose topsoil

terremoto *m* earthquake

terrenal *adj* worldly, earthly

terreno¹ -na *adj* (Relig) earthly

terreno² ** *m* **1 (a) (lote, parcela) plot of land, lot (AmE); **heredó unos ~s en Sonora** she inherited some land in Sonora; **un ~ plantado de viñas** a field planted with vines; **~ de juego** field, pitch **(b)** (extensión de tierra) land; **una casa con mucho ~** a house with a lot of land **2** (Geog) (refiriéndose al relieve) terrain; (refiriéndose a la composición) land, soil; **un ~ fértil** fertile land **3** (esfera, campo de acción) sphere, field; **en el ~ político** within the field of politics

terrestre *adj* **(a)** «*transportes/comunicaciones*»

land (*before n*), terrestrial (frml); **por vía ~** overland, by land; **fuerzas ~s** ground o land forces; **la superficie ~** the earth's surface **(b)** (Relig) «*vida*» earthly

terrible *adj* **(a)** «*tortura/experiencia*» terrible, horrific **(b)** (uso hiperbólico) terrible; **tengo un sueño ~** I'm terribly tired

territorial *adj* territorial

territorio *m* territory

terrón *m* (de azúcar) lump; (de tierra) clod, lump

terror *m* **(a)** (miedo) terror; **le tengo ~** it terrifies me, I find it terrifying; **de ~** «*novela/relato*» horror (*before n*) **(b)** (persona) terror

terrorífico -ca *adj* horrific

terrorismo *m* terrorism

terrorista *adj/mf* terrorist

terso -sa *adj* smooth

tertulia *f* (reunión) gathering (*to discuss philosophy, politics, art, etc*)

tertuliano -na *m,f* participant in a TERTULIA

tesina *f* dissertation (*submitted as part of a first degree*)

tesis *f* (*pl ~*) **(a)** (Educ, Fil) thesis; ~ **doctoral** doctoral thesis **(b)** (opinión): **los dos sostienen la misma ~** they are both of the same opinion; **esto confirma la ~ inicial** this confirms the initial theory

tesón *m* tenacity, determination

tesorería *f* (oficina) treasury; (cargo) post of treasurer

tesorero -ra *m,f* treasurer

tesoro *m* **(a)** (cosa valiosa) treasure **(b)** (persona) treasure, gem (colloq); **¿qué te pasa, ~?** what's the matter, darling?

test *m* (*pl* **tests**) test; **un examen tipo ~** a multiple-choice exam

testamento *m* will, testament (frml); **hacer ~** to make one's will

testarudo -da *adj* stubborn, pigheaded

testículo *m* testicle

testificar [A2] *vt/vi* to testify, give evidence

testigo *mf* witness; **ser ~ de algo** to witness sth, be a witness to sth

testimonio *m* **(a)** (Der) (declaración) testimony, statement **(b)** (prueba) proof, testimony (frml); **dar ~ de algo** to bear witness to sth

tétanos, tétano *m* tetanus

tetera *f* **(a)** (para servir té) teapot **(b)** (Andes, Méx) (para hervir agua) kettle **(c)** (Méx) (biberón) baby's bottle

tetero *m* (Col, Ven) baby's bottle

tetilla *f* **(a)** (Anat) nipple; (Zool) teat **(b)** (del biberón) teat

tetina *f* teat

tétrico -ca *adj* dismal, gloomy

textil *adj* textile (*before n*)

texto *m* text

textual *adj* «*traducción*» literal; «*palabras*» exact; «*cita*» direct

---

textura *f* texture

tez *f* complexion

ti *pron pers* **(a)** you; **para ∼** for you; **delante de ∼** in front of you; **a mí me gusta ¿y a ∼?** I like it, do you? **(b)** (*refl*): **∼ mismo/misma** yourself; **piensa un poco en ∼ mismo** just think of yourself a little **(c)** (*impers*) you; **si a ∼ te cuentan que ...** if someone tells you that ...

tianguis *m* (Méx) street market

tibio -bia *adj* **(a)** ⟨*agua/baño*⟩ lukewarm, tepid **(b)** ⟨*atmósfera/ambiente*⟩ warm **(c)** ⟨*relación*⟩ lukewarm; ⟨*acogida*⟩ unenthusiastic, cool

tiburón *m* **(a)** (Zool) shark **(b)** (fam) (persona) shark **(c)** (Fin) raider

tic *m* ⏦1⏦ (movimiento) *tb* **∼ nervioso** nervous tic ⏦2⏦ (marca en escrito) tick

tico -ca *adj/m,f* (AmL fam) Costa Rican

tiempo *m* ⏦1⏦ **(a)** (en general) time; **¡cómo pasa el ∼!** how time flies!; **te acostumbrarás con el ∼** you'll get used to it in time; **perder el ∼** to waste time; **¡no hay ∼ que perder!** there's no time to lose!; **para ganar ∼** (in order) to gain time; **∼ libre** spare time, free time; **¿cuánto ∼ hace que no lo ves?** how long is it since you last saw him?; **hace ∼ que no sé de él** I haven't heard from him for a long time; **ya hace ∼ que se marchó** she left quite some time ago; **¡cuánto ∼ sin verte!** I haven't seen you for ages; **la mayor parte del ∼** most of the time; **me llevó mucho ∼** it took me a long time; **no pude quedarme más ∼** I couldn't stay any longer; **poco ∼ después** a short time after; **de un ∼ a esta parte** for some time (now); **a ∼ completo/parcial** full time/part time; **no vamos a llegar a ∼** we won't get there in time; **al mismo ∼** at the same time; **avísame con ∼** let me know in good time; **¡qué ∼ aquellos!** those were the days!; **en aquellos ∼s** at that time, in those days **(b)** (temporada) season; **fruta del ∼** fruits in season **(c)** (momento propio, oportuno): **a su (debido) ∼** in due course; **cada cosa a su ∼** everything in (its own) good time **(d)** (edad de bebé): **¿cuánto ∼ tiene?** how old is he? ⏦2⏦ (Dep) (en partido) half; **primer ∼** first half ⏦3⏦ (Mús) (compás) tempo, time; (de sinfonía) movement ⏦4⏦ (Ling) tense ⏦5⏦ (Meteo) weather; **hace buen/mal ∼** the weather's good/bad; **del** *or* (Méx) **al ∼** ⟨*bebida*⟩ at room temperature

tienda *f* ⏦1⏦ (Com) (en general) store (esp AmE), shop (esp BrE); **ir de ∼s** to go shopping; **∼ de comestibles** *or* (AmC, Andes, Méx) **abarrotes** grocery store (AmE), grocer's (shop) (BrE) ⏦2⏦ (Dep, Mil, Ocio) *tb* **∼ de campaña** tent; **poner** *or* **montar una ∼** to put up *o* pitch a tent; **desmontar una ∼** to take down a tent

tiene, tienes, etc ▶ TENER

tienta *f*: **a tientas** (*loc adv*): **andar** *or* **ir a ∼s** to feel one's way; **buscó el timbre a ∼s** he fumbled *o* felt around for the bell

tierno -na *adj* ⏦1⏦ ⟨*carne*⟩ tender; ⟨*pan*⟩ fresh; ⟨*brote/planta*⟩ young, tender ⏦2⏦ ⟨*persona*⟩ affectionate, loving; ⟨*mirada/corazón*⟩ tender

tierra *f* ⏦1⏦ (campo, terreno) land; **∼s fértiles** fertile land; **∼ de cultivo** arable land ⏦2⏦ (suelo, superficie) ground; (materia, arena) earth; **cavar la ∼** to dig the ground; **un camión de ∼** a

truckload of soil *o* earth; **no juegues con ∼** don't play in the dirt; **un camino de ∼** a dirt road *o* track; **echar algo por ∼** ⟨*planes*⟩ to wreck, ruin; ⟨*argumentos*⟩ to demolish, destroy; ⟨*esperanzas*⟩ to dash ⏦3⏦ (AmL) (polvo) dust ⏦4⏦ (Elec) ground (AmE), earth (BrE); **estar conectado a ∼** *or* (AmL) **hacer ∼** to be grounded *o* earthed ⏦5⏦ (por oposición al mar, al aire) land; **viajar por ∼** to travel overland *o* by land; **∼ firme** solid ground; **tomar ∼** to land, touch down ⏦6⏦ (país, lugar): **su ∼ (natal)** his homeland, his native land; **costumbres de aquellas ∼s** customs in those places *o* countries; **la T∼ Santa** the Holy Land ⏦7⏦ (planeta) **la T∼** (the) Earth

tieso -sa *adj* ⏦1⏦ **(a)** (rígido) stiff; **con las orejas tiesas** with ears pricked up **(b)** (Col, Ven) (duro) ⟨*pan*⟩ hard; ⟨*carne*⟩ tough ⏦2⏦ ⟨*persona*⟩ (erguido) upright, erect; (orgulloso) stiff; **quedarse ∼** (fam) (helarse) to get frozen stiff (colloq)

tiesto *m* **(a)** (para plantas) flowerpot **(b)** (Chi) (palangana) basin

tifón *m* typhoon

tifus *m* **(a)** (transmitido por parásitos) typhus (fever) **(b)** (fiebre tifoidea) typhoid

tigre -gresa *m,f* (animal asiático) (*m*) tiger; (*f*) tigress

tijeras *fpl*, **tijera** *f* (para cortar papel, tela) scissors (*pl*); (para uñas) nail scissors (*pl*); (para césped) shears (*pl*); **unas ∼s** a pair of scissors; **∼ de podar** pruning shears (*pl*); **de ∼** ⟨*silla/cama*⟩ folding (*before n*); **escalera de ∼** stepladder

tila *f* (infusión) lime (blossom) tea

tilde *f* (acento) accent; (sobre la ñ) tilde, swung dash

tiliches *mpl* (Méx fam) stuff (colloq)

tilo *m* **(a)** (árbol) lime (tree) **(b)** (Chi) ▶ TILA

timador -dora *m,f* swindler, cheat

timar [A1] *vt* to swindle, cheat

timbal *m* (Mús) kettledrum; **los ∼es** the timpani, the timps (colloq)

timbrar [A1] *vt* ⟨*documento*⟩ to stamp; ⟨*carta*⟩ to frank
  ■ **∼** *vi* (Col, Méx) to ring the bell

timbre *m* ⏦1⏦ (para llamar) (door)bell; **tocar el ∼** to ring the bell; **∼ de alarma** alarm bell ⏦2⏦ (de sonido, voz) tone, timbre ⏦3⏦ **(a)** (sello) fiscal stamp **(b)** (Méx) (sello postal) (postage) stamp

timidez *f* (retraimiento) shyness; (falta de decisión, coraje) timidity

tímido -da *adj* (retraído) shy; (falto de decisión, coraje) timid

timo *m* (fam) con (colloq), scam (colloq)

timón *m* **(a)** (Aviac, Náut) rudder **(b)** (Col, Per) (volante) steering wheel; **ir al ∼** to be at the wheel

timonel *mf* (*m*) helmsman; (*f*) helmswoman

tímpano *m* (Anat) eardrum

tinaco *m* (Méx) water tank

tinaja *f* large earthenware jar

tinca *f* (Andes) (fam) (empeño) effort

tincada *f* (Andes fam) feeling, hunch (colloq)

tincar [A2] *vi* (Andes fam) **(a)** (parecer): **me tinca que ya no viene** I get the feeling she's not coming ⋯

(b) (parecer bien, gustar): **ese pescado me tinca** I like the look of that fish; **¿te tinca ir al cine?** do you feel like going to the movies?

tinieblas *fpl* darkness

tino *m* **(a)** (sentido común) sound judgment, good sense **(b)** (tacto) tact, sensitivity

tinta *f* ink; ∼ **China** India ink; **escribir con** ∼ to write in ink (AmE), Indian ink (BrE); **saber algo de buena** ∼ to have sth on good authority

tinte *m* ⒈ (acción) dyeing; (sustancia) dye ⒉ (Esp) (establecimiento) dry cleaner's

tintero *m* inkwell

tintín *m* (de campanilla) tinkling, jingling; (de copa) clinking

tinto¹ -ta *adj* ⟨vino/uva⟩ red

tinto² *m* ⒈ (Vin) red wine ⒉ (Col) (café) black coffee

tintorería *f* dry cleaner's

tiña *f* (Med) ringworm

tiñoso -sa *adj* (Med) scabby, mangy

tío, tía *m,f* ⒈ (pariente) (*m*) uncle; (*f*) aunt; **mis** ∼**s** (varones) my uncles; (varones y mujeres) my aunts and uncles ⒉ (Esp) (individuo) (fam) ▶ TIPO¹

tiovivo *m* (Esp) merry-go-round, carousel (AmE)

tipear [A1] *vt* (AmS) to type

típico -ca *adj* typical; ⟨plato/traje⟩ typical, traditional; **¡eso es** ∼ **de él!** that's typical of him!

tipo¹ -pa *m,f* (fam) (*m*) guy (colloq), bloke (BrE colloq); (*f*) woman

tipo² *m* ⒈ (clase) kind, type, sort; **todo** ∼ **de plantas** all kinds of plants; **no es mi** ∼ he's not my type ⒉ (figura — de mujer) figure; (— de hombre) physique ⒊ (*como adv*) (CS fam) around, about; **vénganse** ∼ **cuatro** come around about four o'clock

tique, tíquet (*pl* ∼**ts**) *m* **(a)** (de tren, bus) ticket **(b)** (recibo) receipt, sales slip (AmE)

tiquete *m* (Col) ▶ TIQUE

tira *f* (de papel, tela) strip; (de zapato) strap; ∼ **cómica** comic strip, strip cartoon
■ *mf* **(a)** (Chi, Méx fam) (agente) cop (colloq) **(b)** (Per, RPl arg) (detective infiltrado) police plant (colloq), undercover cop (colloq) **(c) la tira** *f* (Méx fam) (cuerpo) the cops (colloq)

tirabuzón *m* ⒈ (sacacorchos) corkscrew ⒉ (rizo, bucle) ringlet ⒊ (en béisbol) screwball

tirada *f* ⒈ (Jueg) (en juegos de mesa) throw ⒉ (Impr) print run; **un periódico con una** ∼ **de 300.000 ejemplares diarios** a newspaper with a daily circulation of 300,000 copies

tiradero *m* (Méx) (basurero) garbage (AmE) *o* (BrE) rubbish dump; (casa, habitación) mess, pigsty

tirado -da *adj* ⒈ (en desorden): **lo dejan todo** ∼ they leave everything lying around ⒉ (fam) [ESTAR] **(a)** (muy fácil) dead easy (colloq) **(b)** (muy barato) dirt cheap (colloq)

tirador¹ *m* **(a)** (de cajón, puerta) knob, handle **(b)** (tirachinas) slingshot (AmE), catapult (BrE) **(c) tiradores** *mpl* (Arg, Bol) (de pantalón) suspenders (*pl*) (AmE), braces (*pl*) (BrE)

tirador² -dora *m,f* (*m*) marksman; (*f*) markswoman; **es un buen** ∼ he's a good shot

tiraje *m* **(a)** (AmL) (Impr) ▶ TIRADA 2 **(b)** (CS) (de la chimenea) damper

tiranía *f* tyranny

tirano -na *adj* tyrannical
■ *m,f* tyrant

tirantas *fpl* (Col) suspenders (*pl*) (AmE), braces (*pl*) (BrE)

tirante *adj* **(a)** ⟨piel/costura/cuerda⟩ taut **(b)** ⟨situación⟩ tense; ⟨relaciones⟩ tense, strained
■ *m* ⒈ (Const) strut, brace ⒉ (Indum) **(a)** (de prenda) strap, shoulder strap; **pantalones de** ∼**s** overalls (*pl*) (AmE), dungarees (*pl*) (BrE) **(b) tirantes** *mpl* (Esp, Méx, Ven) (de pantalón) suspenders (*pl*) (AmE), braces (*pl*) (BrE)

tirar [A1] *vt* ⒈ **(a)** (lanzar) to throw; **tiró la pelota al aire** he threw the ball up in the air; ∼**le algo A algn** (para que lo agarre) to throw sb sth; (con agresividad) to throw sth AT sb **(b)** (desechar) to throw out *o* away **(c)** (desperdiciar) to waste; **¡qué manera de** ∼ **el dinero!** what a waste of money! ⒉ **(a)** (hacer caer) ⟨jarrón/silla⟩ to knock over; **el perro me tiró al suelo** the dog knocked me over **(b)** (derribar) ⟨pared/puerta⟩ to knock down ⒊ **(a)** ⟨bomba⟩ to drop; ⟨cohete⟩ to fire, launch; ⟨flecha⟩ to shoot **(b)** ⟨foto⟩ to take ⒋ (AmL) (atrayendo hacia sí) to pull; **tiró la cadena** he pulled the chain
■ ∼ *vi* ⒈ (atrayendo hacia sí) to pull; ∼ **DE algo** to pull sth; **no le tires del pelo** don't pull her hair ⒉ **(a)** (disparar) to shoot; ∼ **a matar** to shoot to kill **(b)** (Dep) to shoot; ∼ **al arco** (AmL) *or* (Esp) **a puerta** to shoot at goal **(c)** (Jueg) (descartarse) to throw away; (en juegos de dados) to throw; (en dardos) to throw; (en bolos) to bowl ⒊ **(a)** ⟨⟨chimenea/cigarro⟩⟩ to draw **(b)** ⟨⟨coche/motor⟩⟩ to pull ⒋ **tirando** *ger* (fam): **gano poco pero vamos tirando** I don't earn much but we're managing; **¿qué tal andas? — tirando** how are things? — not too bad ⒌ **tirar a** (tender a): **tira más bien a azul** it's more of a bluish color; **ella tira más a la madre** she takes after her mother more
■ **tirarse** *v pron* ⒈ **(a)** (lanzarse, arrojarse) to throw oneself; **se tiró por la ventana** he threw himself out of the window; ∼**se en paracaídas** to parachute; (en emergencia) to bale out; ∼**se al agua** to jump into the water; ∼**se de cabeza** to dive in, to jump in headfirst **(b)** (AmL) (tumbarse) to lie down ⒉ (fam) ⟨horas/días⟩ to spend; **se tiró dos años escribiéndolo** he spent two years writing it ⒊ (fam) (expulsar): ∼**se un pedo** to fart (sl)

tirita *f* (Esp) Band-Aid® (AmE), sticking plaster (BrE)

tiritar [A1] *vi* to shiver, tremble; ∼ **de frío** to shiver with cold

tiro *m* ⒈ (disparo) shot; **le dispararon un** ∼ they shot him; **lo mató de un** ∼ she shot him dead; **al** ∼ (Chi fam) right away, straightaway (BrE); **errar el** ∼ (literal) to miss; (equivocarse) to get it wrong ⒉ (en fútbol, baloncesto) shot; (deporte) shooting; ∼ **al arco** (deporte) archery; (en fútbol) (AmL) shot at goal; ∼ **al blanco** (deporte) target shooting; (lugar) shooting gallery; ∼ **al plato** skeet shooting (AmE), clay-pigeon shooting (BrE); ∼ **de esquina** (AmL) corner (kick); ∼ **libre** (en fútbol) free kick; (en baloncesto) free shot *o* throw ⒊ (de chimenea) flue; **tiene muy buen** ∼ it draws well ⒋ **animal/caballo de** ∼ draught animal/horse

tirón *m* **(a)** (movimiento) tug, pull; **me dio un ~ de pelo** he pulled my hair; **dale un ~ de orejas** tweak his ears for him (colloq); **el autobús avanzaba a tirones** the bus jerked along; *de un ~*: **me arrancó la cadena de un ~** he ripped the chain from my neck; **lo leyó/bebió de un ~** (fam) she read/downed it in one go **(b)** (de músculo): **sufrió un ~ en la pierna** he pulled a muscle in his leg **(c)** (forma de robo): **le dieron un** *or* **el ~** they snatched her bag

tironear [A1] *vi* (AmL fam) to tug, pull
■ ~ *vt* (AmL fam) to tug (at)

tiroteo *m* (tiros) shooting; (intercambio de tiros) shoot-out

tirria *f* (fam) grudge; **tenerle ~ a algn** to have a grudge against sb

tisú *m* (*pl* **-sús** *or* **-súes**) (pañuelo) tissue; (tela) lamé

titánico -ca *adj* huge, colossal (*before n*)

títere *m* **(a)** (marioneta, persona) puppet **(b)** **títeres** *mpl* (función) puppet show

titiritar [A1] *vi* to shiver, tremble

titiritero -ra *m,f* (de marionetas) puppeteer; (acróbata) acrobat

titubeante *adj* ⟨voz/respuesta⟩ faltering, halting; ⟨actitud⟩ hesitant

titubear [A1] *vi* **(a)** (dudar, vacilar) to hesitate; **sin ~** without hesitation **(b)** (balbucear) to stutter

titubeo *m* (duda, vacilación) hesitancy, hesitation

titulación *f* qualifications (*pl*); **personas con ~ universitaria** university graduates, college graduates (AmE)

titulado -da *adj* qualified
■ *m,f* graduate; **~ medio** *graduate with a qualification obtained after a three-year degree course as opposed to a five-year course*; **~ superior** *or* **universitario** university graduate, college graduate (AmE)

titular¹ *adj* ⟨médico/profesor⟩ permanent
■ *mf* (de pasaporte, cuenta, cargo) holder
■ *m* **(a)** (en periódico) headline **(b)** (Rad, TV) main story; **los ~es** the main stories, the news headlines

titular² [A1] *vt* ⟨obra⟩: **su novela titulada 'Julia'** his novel called *o* (frml) entitled 'Julia'
■ **titularse** *v pron* **(a)** «obra/película» to be called, be entitled (frml) **(b)** (Educ) to graduate, get one's degree; **~se EN/DE algo** to graduate IN/AS sth

título *m* **1** (en general) title; **un poema que lleva por ~ ...** a poem called *o* (frml) entitled ...; **el ~ de campeón juvenil** the junior title; **~ nobiliario** title; **a ~ de:** **a ~ de introducción** by way of introduction; **asiste a ~ de observador** he's attending as an observer **2** (Educ) degree; (diploma) certificate; **~ académico** academic qualification; **~ universitario** university degree, college degree (AmE)

tiza *f* (material) chalk; (barra) (piece of) chalk; (en billar) chalk

tizón *m* (leño) charred stick/log

toalla *f* **(a)** (tejido) toweling* **(b)** (para secarse) towel; **~ higiénica** sanitary napkin (AmE), sanitary towel (BrE); *tirar* or *arrojar la* ~ to throw in the towel

toallero *m* (barra) towel rail; (aro) towel ring

tobillera *f* **(a)** (Med) ankle support **(b)** (de ciclista) cycle clip

tobillo *m* ankle

tobogán *m* **(a)** (en parque) slide; (en piscina) water chute **(b)** (Aviac) escape chute **(c)** (trineo) toboggan

toca *f* (de religiosa) wimple; (de tocado) circlet

tocadiscos *m* (*pl* ~) record player

tocador *m* (mueble) dressing table

tocar [A2] *vt* **1** **(a)** (en general) to touch; (palpar) to feel; (manosear) to handle; **¡no vayas a ~ ese cable!** don't touch that cable!; **mis ahorros no los quiero ~** I don't want to touch my savings; **la planta ya toca el techo** the plant is already touching the ceiling **(b)** (hacer sonar) ⟨timbre/campana⟩ to ring; ⟨claxon⟩ to blow, sound **(c)** (Mús) ⟨instrumento/pieza⟩ to play **2** ⟨tema⟩ (tratar) to touch on, refer to; (sacar) to bring up **3** (atañer, concernir) to affect; **un problema que nos toca de cerca** a problem which affects us directly
■ ~ *vi* **1** **(a)** (AmL) (llamar) «persona» to knock at the door; **alguien está tocando (a la puerta)** there's somebody at the door **(b)** «campana/timbre» to ring; **las campanas tocaban a misa** the bells were ringing for mass **(c)** (Mús) to play **2** **(a)** (corresponder en reparto, concurso, sorteo): **a ella le toca la mitad de la herencia** she gets half of the inheritance; **le tocó el primer premio** she won the first prize; **me tocó la maestra más antipática del colegio** I got the most horrible teacher in the school **(b)** (ser el turno): **te toca a ti** it's your turn; **¿a quién le toca cocinar?** whose turn is it to do the cooking?
■ **tocarse** *v pron* **(a)** (refl) ⟨herida/grano⟩ to touch; ⟨barba⟩ to play with **(b)** (recípr) «personas» to touch each other; «cables» to touch

tocayo -ya *m,f* namesake

tocino *m* (para guisar) pork fat; (con vetas de carne) fatty salt pork; (para freír) bacon

tocología *f* obstetrics

tocólogo -ga *m,f* obstetrician

todavía *adv* **1** **(a)** (aún) still; **¿~ estás aquí?** are you still here? **(b)** (en frases negativas) yet; **~ no está lista** she isn't ready yet **2** (en comparaciones) even, still; **sus primos son ~ más ricos** her cousins are even richer *o* richer still **3** (fam) (encima) still; **¡y ~ se queja!** and he still complains!

todo¹ -da *adj* **1** (la totalidad de) all; **nos comimos ~ el pan** we ate all the bread; **toda la mañana** all morning, the whole morning; **invitó a toda la clase** she invited the whole class; **por ~s lados** all over the place; **~s ustedes lo sabían** you all knew; ▶ MUNDO 1 **2** (cualquier, cada): **~ artículo importado** all imported items, any imported item; **~ aquel que quiera** anyone who wishes to; **~s los días** every day **3** (uso enfático): **a toda velocidad** at top speed; **con toda inocencia** in all innocence; **le dieron ~ tipo de facilidades** they gave him all kind of facilities; **a ~ esto** (mientras tanto) meanwhile, in the meantime; (a propósito) incidentally, by the way
■ *pron* **1** **(a)** (sin excluir nada) everything; **lo perdieron ~** they lost everything; **~ le parece** ⋯✦

poco he's never satisfied; **come ~ lo que quieras** eat as much as you like; **~ o nada** all or nothing **(b)** **~s/todas** (referido a — cosas) all; (— a personas) all, everybody; **los compró ~s** she bought all of them; **vinieron ~s** they all came, everybody came; **buena suerte a ~s** good luck to everybody; **es el más alto de ~s** he's the tallest of the lot *o* of them all; **¿están ~s?** is everyone *o* everybody here?; **~s y cada uno** each and every one **2** (*en locs*) **con todo (y eso)** (fam) (aun así) all the same, even so; **de todo: come de ~** she'll eat anything; **venden de ~** they sell everything *o* all sorts of things; **hace de ~ un poco** he does a bit of everything; **del todo** totally **3** (*como adv*) **(a)** (completamente) all; **está ~ mojado** it's all wet **(b)** (en frases ponderativas) quite; **fue ~ un espectáculo** it was quite a show!

todo² *m*: **el/un ~** the/a whole; **jugarse el ~ por el ~** to risk *o* gamble everything on one throw

todopoderoso -sa *adj* all-powerful

Todopoderoso *m*: **el ~** the Almighty

todoterreno *m* (Auto) four-wheel-drive vehicle, 4 x 4 (*léase: four by four*)

Tokio *m* Tokyo

toldo *m* **(a)** (de terraza) canopy; (de tienda) awning; (en la playa) awning; (en camión) tarpaulin **(b)** (para fiestas) tent (AmE), marquee (BrE) **(c)** (RPl) (de los indios) hut

tolerable *adj* tolerable

tolerancia *f* tolerance

tolerante *adj* tolerant

tolerar [A1] *vt* to tolerate; **¡eso no se puede ~!** that's intolerable!; ⑤ **tolerada (para menores de 14 años)** (Esp) ≈PG; **le toleras demasiado** you're too lenient with him

toma *f* **1** **(a)** (Mil) capture, taking **(b)** (de universidad, fábrica) occupation; (de tierras) seizure **2** (Cin, Fot — imagen) shot; (— acción de filmar) take **3** (de medicamento) dose **4** (de datos) gathering; (de muestras) taking; **la ~ de decisiones** the decision-making **5** (AmL) (acequia) irrigation channel **6** **(a)** **~ de tierra** (Elec) ground (wire) (AmE), earth (wire) (BrE) **(b)** (Aviac) landing, touchdown

tomado -da *adj* **1** (*voz*): **tengo la voz tomada** I'm hoarse **2** (AmL fam) (*persona*) drunk

tomadura de pelo *f* **(a)** (broma, chiste) joke **(b)** (burla): **esto es una ~ de ~** they're just messing around with us (AmE) *o* (BrE) messing us around

tomar [A1] *vt* **1** (en general) to take; **tomé un libro de la estantería** I took a book from the shelf; **la tomé de la mano** I took her by the hand; **toma lo que te debo** here's what I owe you; **¿lo puedo ~ prestado?** can I borrow it?; **tomó el asunto en sus manos** she took charge of the matter; **~ precauciones/el tren/una foto** to take precautions/the train/a picture; **~le la temperatura a algn** to take sb's temperature; **~ algo por escrito** to write sth down; **~ algo/a algn POR algo/algn** to take sth/sb FOR sth/sb; **¿por quién me has tomado?** who *o* what do you take

me for?; **lo tomó a mal/a broma** he took it the wrong way/as a joke; **eso toma demasiado tiempo** that takes up too much time **2** **(a)** (beber) to drink; **el niño toma (el) pecho** the baby's being breast-fed **(b)** (servirse, consumir) to have; **¿qué vas a ~?** what are you going to have? **3** (esp AmL) **(a)** (contratar) to take on **(b)** «*profesor*» ‹*alumnos/clases*› to take on **(c)** «*colegio*» ‹*niño*› to take **4** (apoderarse de) ‹*fortaleza/tierras*› to seize; ‹*universidad/fábrica*› to occupy **5** (adquirir) ‹*forma*› to take; ‹*aspecto*› to take on; ‹*velocidad/altura*› to gain; ‹*costumbre*› to get into **6** (cobrar): **le he tomado cariño a esta casa/a la niña** I've become quite attached to this house/ quite fond of the girl **7** (exponerse a): **~ el aire** to get some (fresh) air; **~ (el) sol** to sunbathe; **vas a ~ frío** (CS) you'll get *o* catch cold

■ **~** *vi* **1** (asir): **toma, aquí tienes tus tijeras** here are your scissors; **tome, yo no lo necesito** take it, I don't need it **2** (esp AmL) (beber alcohol) to drink **3** (AmL) (ir) to go; **~on para el norte** they went north; **~ a la derecha** to turn *o* go right **4** «*injerto*» to take

■ **tomarse** *v pron* **1** ‹*vacaciones/tiempo*› to take; **se tomó el día libre** he took the day off **2** ‹*molestia/libertad*› to take; **~se la molestia/ libertad de hacer algo** to take the trouble to do sth/the liberty of doing sth **3** (*enf*) **(a)** ‹*café/vino*› to drink **(b)** ‹*medicamento/vitaminas*› to take **(c)** ‹*desayuno/ merienda/sopa*› to eat, have; ‹*helado/yogur*› to have **4** ‹*autobús/tren/taxi*› to take **5** (Med) **(a)** (*refl*) to take; **se tomó la temperatura** she took her temperature **(b)** (*caus*): **~se la tensión** to have one's blood pressure taken **6** (*caus*) (esp AmL) ‹*foto*› to have ... taken **7** (*enf*) (reaccionar frente a) ‹*comentario/noticia*› to take; **no te lo tomes a mal** don't take it the wrong way **8** (Chi) ‹*universidad/fábrica*› to occupy

tomate *m* tomato; **estar/ponerse (colorado) como un ~** (de vergüenza) to be/turn as red as a beet (AmE), to be/go as red as a beetroot (BrE); (por el sol) to be/turn as red as a lobster

tomavistas *m* (*pl* **~**) movie camera

toma y daca *m* give-and-take

tómbola *f* tombola

tomillo *m* thyme

tomo *m* volume

ton *m*: **hacer algo sin ~ ni son** to do sth for no reason

tonada *f* **(a)** (melodía) tune; (canción) ballad, song **(b)** (AmL) (acento) accent

tonel *m* barrel

tonelada *f* ton

tongo *m* (fam) (en partido, pelea) fix (colloq); **hubo ~** it was fixed (colloq)

tónica *f* **1** (bebida) tonic (water) **2** (tendencia, tono) trend, tendency

tónico¹ -ca *adj* **1** (Med) tonic (*before n*) **2** (a) ⟨*sílaba/vocal*⟩ tonic (*before n*), stressed **(b)** (Mús) tonic

tónico² *m* (Med) tonic; (en cosmética) toner

tono *m* **1** (a) (en general) tone; **en ∼ cariñoso** in an affectionate tone of voice; **en ∼ de reproche** reproachfully; **el ∼ en que lo dijo** the way he said it; **el ∼ general de la conversación** the general tone of the conversation **(b)** (Rad, Telec, TV) tone; **este teléfono no da** *or* **tiene ∼** I can't get a dial tone (AmE) *o* (BrE) dialling tone on this phone; **∼ de marcar** *or* (AmL) **de discado** *or* (AmS) **de discar** dial tone (AmE), dialling tone (BrE); **∼ de ocupado** busy signal (AmE), engaged tone (BrE); **no venir a ∼** to be out of place **2** (de color) shade; **subido de ∼** risqué **3** (Mús) key

tontear [A1] *vi* **(a)** (hacer el tonto) to play the fool; (decir tonterías) to talk nonsense **(b)** (flirtear) to fool around (colloq)

tontería *f* **(a)** (cosa tonta) silly *o* stupid thing; (dicho tonto) silly remark; **¡déjate de ∼s!** stop fooling around; **¡∼s!** nonsense! **(b)** (cosa insignificante) silly thing, small thing; **se enoja por cualquier ∼** she gets angry over the slightest little thing **(c)** (cualidad) stupidity

tonto -ta *adj* **1** (a) [SER] (falto de inteligencia) stupid, dumb (colloq); (ingenuo) silly **(b)** [ESTAR] (intratable) difficult, silly; (disgustado) upset **2** ⟨*excusa/error/historia*⟩ silly

■ *m,f* (falto de inteligencia) idiot, dummy (colloq); (ingenuo) idiot, fool; **hacer el ∼** (hacer payasadas) to play *o* act the fool; (actuar con necedad) to make a fool of oneself; **hacerse el ∼** to act dumb

topacio *m* topaz

toparse [A1] *v pron* **∼se CON algn** (tropezarse) to bump INTO sb; (encontrarse) to bump *o* run INTO sb; **∼se CON algo** (tropezarse) to bump INTO sth; (encontrarse) to come across sth

tope *m* **1** (a) (límite) limit; **han establecido un ∼ máximo** an upper limit has been set **(b)** (*como adj inv*) ⟨*edad/precio*⟩ maximum (*before n*); **fecha ∼** deadline **2** (a) (para las puertas) doorstop; (Ferr) buffer **(b)** (Méx) (Auto) speed bump **3** (Andes) (cima) top **4** (a) (Andes) (golpe, choque) bump **(b)** (Méx fam) (cabezazo): **me di un ∼** I bumped my head

tópico¹ -ca *adj* **1** ⟨*comentario/afirmación*⟩ trite **2** (Farm): **⊕ uso tópico** for external use only

tópico² *m* **(a)** (tema, asunto) topic, subject **(b)** (tema trillado) hackneyed subject; (expresión) cliché

top-less, topless /'toples/ *m*: **el ∼ es habitual aquí** it is quite normal for people to go topless here

topo *m* **(a)** (Zool) mole **(b)** (Col) (pendiente) earring

topografía *f* topography, surveying

toque *m* **1** (a) (de timbre) ring; (de campana) stroke, chime; **al ∼ de las doce** on the stroke of twelve; **∼ de queda** curfew **(b)** (Esp fam) (llamada) call, ring (BrE colloq) **2** (en béisbol) bunt **3** (detalle) touch; **falta darle los últimos ∼s** we have to put the finishing touches to it **4** (Méx fam) (descarga) electric shock

toquetear [A1] *vt* (fam) to touch; (sexualmente) to touch up

toquilla *f* shawl

tórax *m* thorax

torbellino *m* **(a)** (de viento) whirlwind; (de polvo) dust storm **(b)** (de actividad) whirl **(c)** (persona inquieta) bundle of energy

torcedura *f* sprain

torcer [E10] *vt* **1** ⟨*cuerpo*⟩ to twist; ⟨*cabeza*⟩ to turn; **me torció el brazo** she twisted my arm **2** ⟨*esquina*⟩ to turn **3** ⟨*curso/rumbo*⟩ to change

■ *∼ vi* (girar) ⟨*persona/vehículo*⟩ to turn; ⟨*camino*⟩ to bend, curve

■ **torcerse** *v pron* **1** ⟨*tobillo/muñeca*⟩ to sprain **2** ⟨*madera/viga*⟩ to warp

torcido -da *adj* **1** [ESTAR] **(a)** (con respecto a otra cosa) crooked; **tiene la nariz torcida** he has a crooked nose; **llevas la falda torcida** your skirt's twisted **(b)** (curvo) bent; **una rama torcida** a bent branch; **tiene las piernas torcidas** (para adentro) he is knock-kneed; (para afuera) he is bowlegged **2** ⟨*intenciones*⟩ devious, crooked

torcijón *m* stomach cramp

tordo -da *m,f* **(a)** (caballo) dapple, dapple-gray* **(b)** (pájaro) thrush

torear [A1] *vi* to fight; **quiere ∼** he wants to be a bullfighter

■ *∼ vt* **1** ⟨*toro/novillo*⟩ to fight **2** (fam) ⟨*perseguidor/pregunta*⟩ to dodge **(b)** (AmL) (provocar) to torment, needle

toreo *m* bullfighting

torero -ra *m,f* bullfighter, matador

tormenta *f* **1** (Meteo) storm; **∼ de nieve** snowstorm; (con viento) blizzard; **hacer frente a la ∼** to weather the storm **2** (de pasiones) storm; (de celos) frenzy

tormentoso -sa *adj* stormy

tornado *m* tornado

tornamesa *f or m* (Col, Méx) (plato giratorio) turntable

tornar [A1] *vi* (liter) **(a)** (regresar) to return; **tornó a nevar** it snowed again **(b)** (volver, hacer) to make, render

■ **tornarse** *v pron* (liter) to become; **∼se EN algo** to turn INTO sth

torneo *m* tournament

tornero -ra *m,f* lathe operator

tornillo *m* (Tec) screw; **te/le falta un ∼** you have/he has a screw loose (colloq)

torniquete *m* (Med) tourniquet

torno *m* **1** (a) (de carpintero) lathe; **∼ de alfarero** potter's wheel **(b)** (Odont) drill **(c)** (para alzar pesos) winch **2** **en torno a** around

toro *m* (animal) bull; **∼ bravo** *or* **de lidia** fighting bull; **los ∼s** (el espectáculo) bullfighting; **ir a los ∼s** to go to a bullfight

toronja *f* (AmL) grapefruit

torpe *adj* **(a)** (en las acciones) clumsy **(b)** (de entendimiento) slow (colloq) **(c)** (sin tacto) ⟨*persona/comentario*⟩ clumsy; **de manera ∼** clumsily

torpedo *m* **1** (Arm) torpedo **2** (Chi fam) (de estudiante) crib (note) (colloq)

torpeza *f* **1** (cualidad) **(a)** (en las acciones) clumsiness **(b)** (falta de inteligencia) stupidity; **perdona mi ∼, pero no entiendo** I'm sorry to be ⋯❖

so stupid *o* dim, but I don't understand **(c)** (falta de tacto) clumsiness **2** (dicho desacertado) gaffe; (acción desacertada) blunder

torrar [A1] *vt* to roast

torre *f* **(a)** (de castillo, iglesia) tower; (en punta) steeple, spire **(b)** (de cables de alta tensión) pylon; (de pozo de petróleo) derrick **(c)** (en ajedrez) rook, castle **(d)** (edificio alto) apartment block (AmE), tower block (BrE)

torreja *f* **1** (AmL) (pan frito) ▶ TORRIJA **2** (Chi) (rodaja) slice

torrencial *adj* torrential

torrente *m* (Geog) torrent

torrentoso -sa *adj* (AmL) fast-flowing

torreón *m* tower

torrija *f* piece *o* slice of French toast; ~**s** French toast

torsión *f* torsion

torso *m* (Anat) torso, trunk; (Art) bust

torta *f* **1** (CS, Ven) (de cumpleaños, etc) cake; (decorada, con crema, etc) gateau **2** (Méx) (bocadillo) sandwich **3** (fam) (golpe): **darle una ~ a algn** to hit *o* wallop sb (colloq); **pegarse una ~** to bang one's head (*o* arm *etc*); **liarse a ~s** to come to blows

tortazo *m* (fam) ▶ TORTA 3

tortícolis *f* stiff neck, torticollis (tech)

tortilla *f* **1** (de huevos) omelet*; **~ de papas** *or* (Esp) **de patatas** Spanish omelet* (*made with potatoes and sometimes onion*) **2** (de maíz) tortilla

tortillero -ra *m,f* tortilla seller

tórtola *f* turtledove

tortuga *f* (Zool) (de tierra) tortoise, turtle (AmE); (de mar) turtle

tortuoso -sa *adj* **(a)** ⟨sendero⟩ tortuous, winding **(b)** ⟨maquinaciones/conducta⟩ devious; ⟨mente⟩ devious, twisted

tortura *f* torture

torturar [A1] *vt* (con violencia física) to torture; (angustiar) to torment, torture

tos *f* cough; **tener ~** to have a cough; **~ convulsa** *or* **convulsiva** whooping cough

tosco -ca *adj* **(a)** ⟨utensilio/mueble/ construcción⟩ crude, basic; ⟨tela⟩ coarse, rough **(b)** ⟨persona/manos⟩ crude; ⟨lenguaje⟩ unrefined; ⟨modales⟩ coarse; ⟨facciones⟩ coarse

toser [E1] *vi* to cough

tostada *f* **(a)** (de pan) piece *o* slice of toast; **desayuno café con ~s** I have coffee and toast for breakfast **(b)** (Méx) (de tortilla) tostada (*fried maize tortilla*)

tostado -da *adj* ⟨pan/almendras⟩ toasted; ⟨café⟩ roasted; ⟨piel⟩ tanned

tostadora *f*, **tostador** *m* (para pan) toaster; (para café) roaster

tostar [A10] *vt* **(a)** ⟨pan/almendras⟩ to toast; ⟨café⟩ to roast **(b)** ⟨piel/persona⟩ to tan
■ **tostarse** *v pron* (broncearse) to tan

tostón *m* **1** **(a)** (Esp) (pan frito) crouton **(b)** (Ven) (plátano frito) fried plantain **2** (Esp fam) (cosa fastidiosa) drag (colloq); **darle el ~ a algn** (Esp fam) to pester somebody **3** (Méx fam) (moneda) fifty-cent coin

total *adj* **(a)** (absoluto) ⟨desastre/destrucción⟩ total; ⟨éxito⟩ resounding (*before n*), total; ⟨cambio⟩ complete **(b)** (global) ⟨costo/importe⟩ total
■ *m* total; **en ~** altogether
■ *adv* (indep) (fam) (al resumir una narración) so, in the end; **~, que me di por vencida** so in the end I gave up

totalidad *f*: **la ~ de la población** the whole *o* entire population; **fue destruido en su ~** it was totally destroyed; **se pagó en su ~** it was paid in full

totalitario -ria *adj* totalitarian

totalitarismo *m* totalitarianism

totogol *m* (Col) sports lottery (AmE), football pools (*pl*) (BrE)

totopo *m* (Méx) tortilla chip

totora *f* reed mace, bulrush

tóxico¹ -ca *adj* toxic

tóxico² *m* poison, toxin

toxicómano -na *m,f* drug addict

tozudo -da *adj* obstinate, stubborn
■ *m,f*: **es un ~** he's extremely stubborn *o* obstinate

traba *f* **1** (en ventana) catch; (de cinturón) belt loop **2** (dificultad, impedimento) obstacle; **me puso muchas ~s** he made things really difficult for me

trabajado -da *adj* ⟨diseño/bordado/plan⟩ elaborate

trabajador -dora *adj* (que trabaja mucho) hard-working
■ *m,f* worker; **un ~ no calificado** (AmL) *or* (Esp) **cualificado** an unskilled worker *o* laborer; **~ autónomo** self-employed worker *o* person; **~ de medio tiempo** (AmL) *or* (Esp) **a tiempo parcial** part-time worker; **~a social** (Méx) social worker

trabajar [A1] *vi* **1** (en general) to work; **~ por cuenta propia** to be self-employed; **~ jornada completa** *or* **a tiempo completo** to work full-time; **~ media jornada** to work part-time; **~ mucho** to work hard; **¿en qué trabajas?** what do you do (for a living)?; **estoy trabajando en una novela** I'm working on a novel; **~ DE algo** *o* **COMO algo** to work AS sth **2** (actuar) to act, perform; **¿quién trabaja en la película** who's in the movie?
■ *vt* **1 (a)** ⟨campo/tierra/madera⟩ to work **(b)** ⟨masa⟩ (con las manos) to knead, work **2** (perfeccionar, pulir) to work on

trabajo *m* **1 (a)** (empleo) job; **buscar ~** to look for work *o* for a job; **quedarse sin ~** to lose one's job; **un ~ fijo** a steady job; **un ~ de media jornada** a part-time job; **un ~ de jornada completa** *or* **a tiempo completo** a full-time job **(b)** (lugar) work; **está en el ~** she's at work; **ir al ~** to go to work
2 (actividad, labor) work; **~ en equipo** teamwork; **el ~ de la casa** housework; **los niños dan mucho ~** children are hard work; **¡buen ~!** well done!; **~ de campo** fieldwork; **~s forzados** hard labor*; **~s manuales** handicrafts (*pl*); **~ voluntario** voluntary *o* (AmE) volunteer work
3 (a) (tarea) job; **limpiar el horno es un ~ que odio** cleaning the oven is a job I hate **(b)** (obra escrita) piece of work; (en universidad, escuela) essay
4 (esfuerzo): **con mucho ~ consiguió levantarse** with great effort she managed to get up; **me cuesta ~ creerlo** I find it hard to believe

trabajoso -sa *adj* ‹*subida*› arduous; ‹*tarea*› laborious

trabalenguas *m* (*pl* ~) tongue twister

trabar [A1] *vt* ⏽**1**⏽ (a) ‹*puerta/ventana*› (para que no se abra) to hold ... shut; (para que no se cierre) to hold ... back *o* open (b) ‹*caballo*› to hobble ⏽**2**⏽ (a) ‹*conversación/amistad/relación*› to strike up (b) ‹*historia*› to weave together ⏽**3**⏽ ‹*proceso/ negociaciones*› to hamper the progress of
■ **trabarse** *v pron* «*cajón/cierre*» to get jammed *o* stuck; **se le traba la lengua** he gets tongue-tied

trabilla *f* (de pantalón) stirrup; (para cinturón) belt loop

trácala *m* (Méx, Ven fam) cheat
■ *f* (Méx, Ven fam) trick, swindle; **se la pasa haciendo ~** he's always cheating people

tracalada *f* (Andes fam) bunch (colloq)

tracalear [A1] *vt* (Méx, Ven fam) to cheat, swindle

tracalero -ra *adj* (Méx, Ven fam) dishonest

tracción *f* (Auto, Mec) traction, drive; **un vehículo con** *or* **de ~ a cuatro ruedas** a four-wheel-drive vehicle

tractor *m* tractor

tradición *f* (costumbre) tradition

tradicional *adj* traditional

tradicionalista *adj/mf* traditionalist

traducción *f* translation; **~ del inglés al español** translation from English into Spanish

traducir [I6] *vt* ‹*texto/escritor*› to translate; **~ DE algo A algo** to translate FROM sth INTO sth

traductor -tora *m,f* translator

traer [E23] *vt* ⏽**1**⏽ (de un lugar a otro) to bring; **me trajo en la moto** he brought me on his motorbike; **¿qué te trae por aquí?** what brings you here? ⏽**2**⏽ (ocasionar, causar) ‹*problemas/dificultades*› to cause; **~ buena suerte** to bring good luck ⏽**3**⏽ «*libro/artículo*» ‹*artículo/capítulo*› to have; **este diccionario no lo trae** it's not in this dictionary ⏽**4**⏽ (a) ‹*ropa/sombrero*› to wear (b) (tener consigo) to bring; **traje poco dinero** I didn't bring much money (with me)
■ **traerse** *v pron* ⏽**1**⏽ (*enf*) (a un sitio) to bring (along); **lo invité a él y se trajo a toda la familia** I invited him and he brought the whole family along ⏽**2**⏽ (fam) (tramar) to be up to (colloq); **¿qué se ~án esas dos?** what are those two up to?

traficante *mf* dealer, trafficker; **~ de drogas** drug dealer *o* trafficker; **~ de esclavos** slave trader

traficar [A2] *vi* **~ EN** *or* **CON algo** to deal IN sth

tráfico *m* ⏽**1**⏽ (de vehículos) traffic; **accidente de ~** road accident ⏽**2**⏽ (de mercancías) trade; **~ de armas** arms trade; **~ de drogas** drug dealing *o* trafficking

tragaluz *m* (en el techo) skylight; (en una puerta, ventana) fanlight

traganíqueles *m* (*pl* ~) (AmC) slot machine

tragaperras *m or f* (*pl* ~) (Esp fam) slot machine

tragar [A3] *vt* ⏽**1**⏽ ‹*comida/agua/medicina*› to swallow ⏽**2**⏽ (fam) (aguantar): **no lo trago** I can't stand him

■ **~** *vi* ⏽**1**⏽ (Fisiol) to swallow ⏽**2**⏽ (RPl fam) (estudiar) to cram
■ **tragarse** *v pron* ⏽**1**⏽ (*enf*) (a) ‹*comida*› to swallow; **~se el humo** to inhale (b) ‹*lágrimas*› to choke back; ‹*orgullo*› to swallow (c) «*máquina*» ‹*dinero/tarjeta*› to swallow up ⏽**2**⏽ (fam) (a) (soportar) ‹*obra/recital*› to sit through (b) (creerse) ‹*excusa/cuento*› to swallow, fall for (colloq)

tragedia *f* tragedy

trágico -ca *adj* (a) ‹*actriz/obra*› tragic (*before n*) (b) ‹*vida/final/consecuencia*› tragic; **no te pongas ~** don't be so melodramatic

tragicomedia *f* tragicomedy

trago *m* ⏽**1**⏽ (a) (de líquido) drink, swig; **un ~ de agua** a drink of water; **de un ~** in one gulp (b) (esp AmL fam) (bebida alcohólica) drink; **¿vamos a tomar un ~?** shall we go for a drink? ⏽**2**⏽ (experiencia): **pasar un ~ amargo** to have a rough time

traición *f* (a) (delito) treason (b) (acto desleal) treachery, betrayal; **lo mataron a ~** they killed him by treachery

traicionar [A1] *vt* (a) ‹*patria/amigo*› to betray (b) (delatar) «*mirada/nerviosismo*» to give ... away

traicionero -ra *adj* (a) ‹*persona/acción*› treacherous (b) ‹*mar/carretera*› treacherous, dangerous

traidor -dora *adj* traitorous, treacherous
■ *m,f* traitor; **~ A algo** traitor TO sth

traiga, traigas, etc ▶ TRAER

trailer /'trailer/ *m* (*pl* ~s) ⏽**1**⏽ (a) (AmL) (casa rodante) trailer (AmE), caravan (BrE) (b) (para caballos) horsebox ⏽**2**⏽ (Méx) (camión) semitrailer (AmE), articulated lorry (BrE)

tráiler *m* (*pl* ~s) ⏽**1**⏽ (Esp) (Cin) trailer ⏽**2**⏽ ▶ TRAILER

trailero -ra *m,f* (Méx) truck driver

traje *m* (de dos, tres piezas) suit; (vestido de mujer) dress; (Teatr) costume; (de país, región) dress; **~ de baño** (de hombre) swimming trunks (*pl*); (de mujer) bathing suit, swimsuit; **~ de etiqueta/gala** formal/evening dress; **~ largo** evening dress

traje, etc ▶ TRAER

trajera, trajese, etc ▶ TRAER

trajimos, trajiste, etc ▶ TRAER

trajín *m*: **un día de mucho ~** a very hectic day; **con todo este ~ ...** with all this coming and going...; **el ~ de las grandes ciudades** the hustle and bustle of big cities

trajinar [A1] *vi* (fam) to rush about (colloq)

trajiste, etc ▶ TRAER

trama *f* ⏽**1**⏽ (de tejido) weave, weft ⏽**2**⏽ (de película, novela) plot

tramar [A1] *vt* ‹*engaño*› to devise; ‹*venganza*› to plot; ‹*complot*› to hatch, lay; **¿qué andan tramando?** what are they up to? (colloq)

tramitación *f* processing; **la ~ del divorcio tardó años** the divorce proceedings took years

tramitar [A1] *vt* ‹*préstamo*› «*funcionario*» to deal with; «*interesado*» to arrange; **están tramitando el divorcio** «*cónyuges*» they have started divorce proceedings; **~ un permiso de trabajo** «*organismo*» to deal with a work permit application; «*interesado*» to apply for one's work permit

t

trámite m (proceso) procedure; (etapa) step, stage; **simplificar los ~s aduaneros** to simplify customs procedures; **el préstamo está en ~** the loan application is being processed; **tengo que hacer unos ~s en el centro** I have some business to attend to in the centre

tramo m (de carretera, vía) stretch; (de escalera) flight

tramoyista mf (Teatr) sceneshifter, stagehand

trampa f (a) (para animales) trap; (de lazo) snare (b) (ardid) trap; **le tendieron una ~** they laid o set a trap for him (c) (en el juego): **hacer ~(s)** to cheat; **eso es ~** that's cheating

trampilla f trapdoor

trampolín m (en natación — flexible) springboard; (— rígido) diving board; (en gimnasia) trampoline; (en esquí) ski jump

tramposo -sa adj: **ser ~** to be a cheat
■ m,f cheat

tranca f ⓵ (a) (de puerta, ventana) bar (b) (palo) cudgel, club ⓶ (esp AmL fam) (borrachera) bender (colloq); **agarrarse una ~** to get plastered o smashed (colloq) ⓷ (Ven fam) (Auto) holdup, tailback

trancar [A1] vt ‹puerta/ventana› to bar

trance m (Psic, Relig) trance; **estar en ~** to be in a trance

tranque m (CS) reservoir

tranquilidad f (a) (calma) peace; **ni un minuto de ~** not a moment's peace; **con ~** (sin prisas) at my (o your etc) leisure; (sin nerviosismo) calmly (b) (falta de preocupación): **llámame a la hora que sea, con toda ~** feel free to call me at any time; **lo hice para mi propia ~** I did it for my own peace of mind

tranquilizante adj (a) ‹noticia› reassuring; ‹música› soothing (b) (Med) tranquilizing*
■ m tranquilizer*

tranquilizar [A4] vt (a) (apaciguar) to calm ... down; **intenté ~lo** I tried to calm him down; **sus palabras la ~on** his words reassured her (b) (atenuar la preocupación): **eso me tranquiliza mucho** that makes me feel a lot better
■ **tranquilizarse** v pron (calmarse) to calm down; (dejar de preocuparse): **al oír su voz me tranquilicé** when I heard his voice I felt reassured

tranquilo¹ -la adj ⓵ [SER] ‹persona› (pacífico) calm (b) ‹mar/ambiente› calm; ‹lugar› quiet, peaceful, tranquil
⓶ [ESTAR] (a) (libre de preocupacion) ‹conciencia› clear; ‹persona›: **ahora que trabaja estoy más ~** I feel better now that he's found a job; **¡tranquilo! relax!**; **tú, ~, de eso me encargo yo** there's no need for you to worry, I'll take care of that; **lo hice para quedarme ~** I did it for my own peace of mind; **déjalo ~** leave him alone (b) (sin inmutarse): **su hermano en el hospital y él tan ~** his brother's in hospital and he doesn't seem at all bothered; **...y se quedó tan tranquila** ...and she didn't bat an eyelash (AmE) o (BrE) eyelid

tranquilo² adv (Méx fam): **te cuesta ~ unas 2,000 libras** it costs 2,000 pounds easily (colloq)

tranquiza f (Méx fam) hiding (colloq)

transa adj/mf (Méx fam) ▶ TRANZA

transacción f (Com, Fin) transaction, deal

transandino¹ -na adj trans-Andean

transandino² m trans-Andean railroad o railway

transar [A1] vi (AmL) (a) (hacer concesiones) ▶ TRANSIGIR A (b) (llegar a un acuerdo) to reach an agreement o a compromise; **~ EN algo** to settle FOR sth

transatlántico¹ -ca adj transatlantic

transatlántico² m ocean liner

transbordador m ferry

transbordar [A1] vt ‹mercancías/equipajes› to transfer
■ **~** vi «pasajeros» to change

transbordo m (a) (de viajeros) change; **hacer ~** to change (b) (de equipaje, mercancías) transfer

transcribir [I34] vt to transcribe

transcurrir [I1] vi (a) «tiempo/años» to pass, go by (b) «acontecimiento/acto» to take place

transcurso m course; **en el ~ del año** during the course of the year; **con el ~ del tiempo** as time goes/went by

transeúnte mf (peatón) passer-by; (no residente) non-resident

transexual adj/mf transsexual

transferencia f transfer; **~ bancaria** credit o bank transfer

transferir [I11] vt to transfer

transformación f (a) (cambio) transformation, change (b) (en rugby) conversion (c) (Ling) transformation

transformador m transformer

transformar [A1] vt (a) (convertir) to convert; **~ algo EN algo** to convert sth INTO sth (b) (cambiar radicalmente) ‹persona/situación/país› to transform, change o alter ... radically (c) (en rugby) to convert
■ **transformarse** v pron (a) (convertirse) **~se EN algo** to turn INTO sth (b) (cambiar radicalmente) «persona/país» to change completely, be transformed

transfusión f transfusion; **le hicieron una ~ de sangre** they gave him a blood transfusion

transgénico¹ -ca adj genetically modified

transgénico² m genetically modified organism (o product etc)

transgredir [I1] vt (frml) to transgress (frml)

transgresión f (frml) transgression (frml)

transgresor -sora m,f transgressor

transición f transition; **~ DE algo A algo** transition FROM sth TO sth

transigente adj accommodating

transigir [I7] vi (a) (hacer concesiones) to compromise, give way; **~ EN algo** to compromise ON sth (b) (tolerar) **~ CON algo** to tolerate sth, put up WITH sth

transistor m transistor

· ·

AmC	Central America	Arg	Argentina	Cu	Cuba	Per	Peru
AmL	Latin America	Bol	Bolivia	Ec	Ecuador	RPI	River Plate Area
AmS	South America	Chi	Chile	Esp	Spain	Ur	Uruguay
Andes	Andean Region	CS	Southern Cone	Méx	Mexico	Ven	Venezuela

transitar [A1] *vi* «*vehículo*» to travel; «*peatón*» to walk

transitivo -va *adj* transitive

tránsito *m* [1] (tráfico) traffic; ~ **rodado** vehicular traffic; **una calle de mucho** ~ a very busy road; **un accidente de** ~ (AmL) a road accident; **infracción de** ~ (AmL) traffic violation (AmE), motoring offense (BrE) [2] (paso) movement; **el** ~ **de turistas en los meses de verano** the movement of tourists during the summer months; **pasajeros en** ~ passengers in transit

transitorio -ria *adj* (a) ⟨*medida*⟩ provisional; ⟨*situación*⟩ temporary; ⟨*período*⟩ transitional (b) (efímero) transitory, fleeting

transmisión *f* (a) (acción) transmission (b) (Rad, TV) (señal) transmission; (programa) broadcast; **una** ~ **en directo/en diferido** a live/ prerecorded broadcast; ~ **de pensamiento** thought transference

transmisor *m* transmitter

transmitir [I1] *vt* [1] (Rad, TV) ⟨*señal*⟩ to transmit; ⟨*programa*⟩ to broadcast [2] (a) ⟨*sonido/movimiento*⟩ to transmit (b) ⟨*enfermedad/ lengua/costumbres*⟩ to transmit, pass on; ⟨*conocimientos*⟩ to pass on (c) ⟨*saludos/ felicidades*⟩ to pass on
■ ~ *vi* (Rad, TV) to transmit

transparentarse [A1] *v pron* (a) «*blusa/ falda*»: **una blusa que se transparenta** a see-through blouse; **con ese vestido se le transparenta la enagua** her petticoat shows through that dress (b) «*intenciones*» to be evident, be apparent

transparente *adj* (a) ⟨*cristal/agua*⟩ transparent, clear; ⟨*aire*⟩ clear (b) ⟨*tela/papel*⟩ transparent; ⟨*blusa*⟩ see-through (c) ⟨*persona/ carácter*⟩ transparent; ⟨*intenciones*⟩ clear, plain

transpirar [A1] *vi* (Fisiol) to perspire, sweat; (Bot) to transpire

transportador *m* (Mec) conveyor

transportar [A1] *vt* (a) ⟨*personas/mercancías*⟩ to transport; ~ **algo por aire** to ship sth by air (b) ⟨*energía/sonido*⟩ to transmit

transporte *m* [1] (de pasajeros, mercancías) transportation (esp AmE), transport (esp BrE); ~ **aéreo** airfreight; ~ **público** public transportation (AmE), public transport (BrE) [2] (medio, vehículo) means of transport [3] (gastos de viaje) traveling expenses

transportista *mf* haulage contractor

transversal *adj* ⟨*eje/línea*⟩ transverse; **una calle** ~ **al Paseo de Recoletos** a street which crosses the Paseo de Recoletos; **un corte** ~ a cross section
■ *f* (Mat) transversal

tranvía *m* (a) (vehículo urbano) streetcar (AmE), tram (BrE) (b) (Esp) (Ferr) local train

tranza *adj* (Méx fam) crooked
■ *mf* (Méx fam) (persona) con artist (colloq), shark (colloq)
■ *f* (Méx fam) (engaño, fraude) scam (colloq)

tranzar [A4] *vt* (Méx fam) ⟨*persona*⟩ to con (colloq)

trapear [A1] *vt* (AmL) to mop

trapecio *m* (a) (Mat) trapezoid (AmE), trapezium (BrE) (b) (Espec) trapeze

trapecista *mf* trapeze artist

trapero -ra *m,f* (ropavejero) junkman (AmE), rag and bone man (BrE) [2] **trapero** *m* (AmL) (para el suelo) floorcloth

trapo *m* (para limpiar) cloth; **pásale un** ~ **a la mesa** wipe the table; ~ **de cocina** dishtowel (AmE), tea towel (BrE); ~ **de sacudir** dust cloth (AmE), duster (BrE)

tráquea *f* windpipe, trachea

traquetear [A1] *vi* «*tren/carreta*» (hacer ruido) to clatter; (moverse) to jolt

traqueteo *m* (de tren, carreta — movimiento) jolting; (— ruido) clatter, clattering

tras *prep* [1] (a) (frml) (después de) after; ~ **interrogarlo lo pusieron en libertad** after questioning him they released him (b) (indicando repetición) after; **día** ~ **día** day after day [2] (a) (detrás de) behind; **la puerta se cerró** ~ **él** the door closed behind him; **la policía anda** ~ **él** the police are after him (b) (más allá de) beyond

trascendental *adj* (a) (importante) ⟨*noticia/ ocasión*⟩ momentous; (de gran alcance) ⟨*decisión/ cambio/efecto*⟩ far-reaching (b) (Fil) transcendental

trascendente *adj* (a) (importante) ⟨*hecho/ suceso*⟩ significant, important (b) (Fil) transcendent

trascender [E8] *vi* (ir más allá) ~ **DE** algo to transcend sth (frml), to go beyond sth
■ ~ *vt* to go beyond, transcend (frml)

trasero¹ -ra *adj* ⟨*puerta/habitación/asiento*⟩ back (*before n*); ⟨*rueda/pata/asiento*⟩ rear (*before n*), back (*before n*); ⟨*motor*⟩ rear-mounted

trasero² *m* (fam) (de persona) bottom, backside (colloq); (de animal) hindquarters (*pl*)

trasladar [A1] *vt* [1] (cambiar de sitio) ⟨*objeto/ oficina/tienda*⟩ to move; ⟨*preso/enfermo*⟩ to move, transfer; ⟨*información*⟩ to transfer; **los heridos fueron trasladados al hospital** the injured were taken to hospital [2] (cambiar de destino) ⟨*empleado/ funcionario*⟩ to transfer
■ **trasladarse** *v pron* (mudarse) to move

traslado *m* (de prisioneros) transferal; (de oficina) removal; (de empleados) transfer; (de objeto): **el** ~ **del cuadro se llevó a cabo ayer** the picture was moved yesterday; **gastos de** ~ relocation expenses

traslúcido -da *adj* translucent

trasluz *m*: **al** ~ against the light

trasmano: **a trasmano** (*loc adv*) out of the way; **vive muy a** ~ she lives in a very out-of-the-way place

trasnochar [A1] *vi* (no acostarse) to be up all night; (acostarse de madrugada) to stay up late
■ **trasnocharse** *v pron* (Col, Per, Ven) ▶ TRASNOCHAR

traspasar [A1] *vt* [1] (a) «*bala/espada*» to pierce, go through; «*líquido*» to go through, soak through (b) (sobrepasar) to go beyond [2] ⟨*bar/farmacia*⟩ (vender) to sell; (arrendar) to let, lease [3] ⟨*poderes/fondos/negocio*⟩ to transfer [4] (Dep) ⟨*jugador*⟩ to transfer, trade (AmE)

traspaso *m* [1] (a) (de bar, farmacia — venta) sale; (— arrendamiento) leasing, letting (b) (suma) premium [2] (de poderes, fondos, negocio) transfer [3] (Dep) (a) (de jugador) transfer, trade (AmE) (b) (suma) transfer fee

traspié *m* (tropezón) stumble; **dar un ~** to stumble

trasplantar [A1] *vt* (Bot, Med) to transplant

trasplante *m* (Bot, Med) transplant

trasquilar [A1] *vt* (a) ⟨*ovejas*⟩ to shear, clip (b) (fam) ⟨*pelo*⟩ to hack ... about (colloq); ⟨*persona*⟩ to scalp (colloq)

trastada *f* (a) (fam) (mala pasada) dirty trick; **hacerle una ~ a algn** to play a dirty trick on sb (b) (travesura) prank

traste *m* ① (Mús) fret ② (fam) (trasero) backside (colloq) ③ (AmC, Méx) (utensilio) utensil; **lavar los ~s** to do the dishes *o* (BrE) the washing-up

trastero *m* junk room, lumber room (AmE)

trastienda *f* back room (*of a shop*)

trasto *m* (fam) (cosa inservible) piece of junk (colloq); **el cuarto de los ~s** the junk room

trastornado -da *adj* ⟨*persona/mente*⟩ disturbed; **su muerte lo dejó ~** he was deeply disturbed *o* traumatized by his death

trastornar [A1] *vt* ① (Psic) to disturb; **la muerte de su hijo la trastornó** her son's death left her deeply disturbed; **esa chica lo ha trastornado** (fam) he's lost his head over that girl (colloq) ② (alterar la normalidad) to upset, disrupt

■ **trastornarse** *v pron* (Psic) to become disturbed

trastorno *m* ① (Med, Psic) disorder ② (alteración de la normalidad) disruption; **los ~s provocados por la huelga** the disruption caused by the strike; **me ocasionó muchos ~s** it caused me a great deal of inconvenience

trastrocar [A9] *vt* to alter, change; **~ algo EN algo** to transform *o* change sth INTO sth

trasvasar [A1] *vt* (a) ⟨*vino/aceite*⟩ to decant (b) (Inf) to download

tratado *m* ① (Der, Pol) treaty; **~ de paz** peace treaty ② (libro) treatise

tratamiento *m* ① (a) (en general) treatment; **estoy en ~ médico** I am undergoing medical treatment; **no me quejo del ~ que recibí** I can't complain about the treatment I received (b) (Inf) (de información, datos) processing; **~ de textos** word processing ② (título de cortesía) form of address

tratar [A1] *vi* ① (intentar) to try; **traten de llegar temprano** try to arrive early; **~é de que no vuelva a suceder** I'll try to make sure it doesn't happen again ② «*obra/libro/película*» **~ DE algo** to be ABOUT sth; **~ SOBRE algo** to deal WITH sth; **la conferencia ~á sobre medicina alternativa** the lecture will deal with alternative medicine ③ (tener contacto, relaciones) **~ CON algn** to deal WITH sb; **en mi trabajo trato con gente de todo tipo** in my job I deal with all kinds of people

■ **~** *vt* ① ⟨*persona/animal/instrumento*⟩ to treat; **me tratan muy bien** they treat me very well ② (frecuentar): **lo trataba cuando era joven** I saw quite a lot of him when I was young ③ ⟨*tema/asunto*⟩ to discuss, to deal with ④ (a) (Med) to treat (b) ⟨*sustancia/metal*⟩ to treat

■ **tratarse** *v pron* ① **~se CON algn** (ser amigo de) to be friendly WITH sb; (alternar) to socialize *o* mix WITH sb; **no nos tratamos mucho** (*recíp*) we don't have much to do with each other

② (+ *compl*) (*recípr*): **se tratan sin ningún respeto** they show no respect for each other ③ (Med) to have *o* undergo treatment ④ **tratarse de** (*en 3ª pers*) (a) (ser acerca de) to be about; **¿de qué se trata?** what's it about? (b) (ser cuestión de) to be a question of; **se trata de participar, no de ganar** it's a question of taking part, not of winning; **solo porque se trata de ti** just because it's you

trato *m* ① (a) (acuerdo) deal; **cerrar un ~** to finalize a deal; **¡~ hecho!** it's a deal! (b) **tratos** *mpl* (negociaciones): **estamos en ~s con otra compañía** we are talking to *o* negotiating with another company ② (a) (relación): **no tiene ~ con los vecinos** he doesn't have much to do with his neighbors; **tengo poco ~ con ella** I don't really have much contact with her *o* much to do with her (b) (manera de tratar) treatment; **le dan un ~ preferente** they give him preferential treatment

trauma *m* trauma

traumatizado -da *adj* traumatized

traumatizar [A4] *vt* to traumatize

■ **traumatizarse** *v pron* (fam) to be traumatized

través (a) **a través de** (*loc prep*) (de lado a lado) across; (por medio de) through; **pusieron barricadas a ~ de la calle** they erected barricades across the street; **se enteró a ~ de un amigo** she heard about it through a friend (b) **al** *or* (Méx) **de través** (*loc adv*) diagonally

travesaño *m* (a) (Const) crossbeam (b) (Dep) crossbar

travesía *f* ① (viaje) crossing ② (Esp) (callejuela) alleyway, side street

travesti, travestí *m* transvestite

travesura *f* prank; **hacer ~s** to play pranks

travieso -sa *adj* naughty, mischievous

trayecto *m* (a) (viaje) journey; **charlamos todo el ~** we chatted the whole journey (b) (ruta) route; **¿qué ~ hace este autobús?** which route does this bus take? (c) (trayectoria) trajectory, path

trayectoria *f* (a) (de proyectil, pelota) trajectory, path (b) (de persona, institución): **una brillante ~ profesional** a brilliant career; **una larga ~ democrática** a long democratic tradition

trayendo ▶ TRAER

trazar [A4] *vt* ① (a) ⟨*línea*⟩ to trace, draw; ⟨*plano*⟩ to draw; **~on la ruta a seguir** they traced out the route to be followed; **~ el contorno de algo** to outline sth (b) (Arquit) ⟨*puente/edificio*⟩ to design ② ⟨*plan/proyecto/estrategia*⟩ to draw up, devise

trazo *m* stroke

trébol *m* ① (Bot) clover ② (Jueg) (a) (carta) club (b) **tréboles** *mpl* (palo) clubs (*pl*)

trece *adj inv/m/pron* thirteen; *para ejemplos ver* CINCO; **mantenerse** *or* **seguir en sus ~** to stand one's ground

trecho *m* (a) (tramo) stretch (b) (distancia) distance; **aún nos queda un buen ~** we still have a good distance *o* a fair way to go

tregua *f* (a) (Mil) truce; **acordar una ~** to agree to a truce (b) (interrupción): **sin ~** relentlessly

treinta *adj inv/m/pron* thirty; *para ejemplos ver* CINCO, CINCUENTA

tremendo -da *adj* ① (a) (muy grande, extraordinario) ⟨*diferencia/cambio*⟩ tremendous, enormous; ⟨velocidad/éxito⟩ tremendous; ⟨chichón⟩ huge; **hace un frío** ~ it's incredibly cold! (colloq); **me dio (una) tremenda patada** he kicked me really hard **(b)** (terrible) ⟨ruido/dolor/situación⟩ terrible; **la película tiene unas escenas tremendas** (AmL) the film has some horrific scenes [2] (fam) ⟨persona⟩ terrible

trémulo -la adj (liter) ⟨manos⟩ trembling; ⟨voz⟩ tremulous; ⟨llama/luz⟩ flickering; **trémula de gozo** (liter) trembling with pleasure

tren m [1] (Ferr) train; **tomar** or (esp Esp) **coger el** ~ to take o catch the train; **ir en** ~ to go by train; **cambiar de** ~ to change trains; ~ **correo** or **postal** mail train; ~ **de alta velocidad** high-speed train; ~ **de cercanías** local o suburban train; ~ **directo** through train; ~ **expreso** or **rápido** express train [2] (fam) (ritmo) rate; **a este** ~ at this rate (colloq); ~ **de vida** lifestyle

trenazo m (Méx) train crash

trenca f (Esp) duffle o duffel coat

trenza f (de cintas, fibras) plait; (de pelo) braid (AmE), plait (BrE)

trepador -dora m,f [1] (Col, CS, Ven) social climber [2] **trepadora** f (Bot) climber

trepar [A1] vi to climb; ~ **a un árbol** to climb (up) a tree

tres adj inv/m/pron three; ~ **en raya** tic-tac-toe (AmE), noughts and crosses (BrE); **para ejemplos ver** CINCO

trescientos -tas adj/pron three hundred; **para ejemplos ver** QUINIENTOS

tresillo m (Esp) (sofá) three-seater sofa; (juego de muebles) suite

treta f **(a)** (ardid) trick, ruse **(b)** (en esgrima) feint

trial m motocross

triangular adj triangular

triángulo m [1] (Mat) triangle; ~ **rectángulo** right-angled triangle [2] **(a)** (en relaciones amorosas) (love) triangle **(b)** (Mús) triangle **(c)** (Auto) tb ~ **reflectante** advance-warning triangle

tribu f tribe

tribuna f **(a)** (para orador) platform, rostrum **(b)** (para autoridades) platform; (para espectadores) grandstand, stand; **la** ~ **de la prensa** the press box **(c)** (de iglesia) gallery

tribunal m [1] (Der) **(a)** (lugar) court; (jueces) judges (pl); ~ **militar** court martial, military court; ~ **supremo** ≈ supreme court (in US), ≈ high court (in UK); ~ **(tutelar) de menores** juvenile court **(b)** **tribunales** mpl (justicia): **acudir a los** ~**es** to go to court [2] (en examen) examining board; (en concurso) panel of judges

tributar [A1] vt **(a)** (Fisco) to pay **(b)** (rendir, ofrecer): ~ **un homenaje a algn** to pay tribute to sb

tributo m **(a)** (Fisco) tax **(b)** (ofrenda, homenaje) tribute; **rendirle** ~ **a algn/algo** to pay tribute to sb/sth

triciclo m tricycle

tricotar [A1] vt (Esp) to knit

tridimensional adj three-dimensional

trifulca f (fam) rumpus, commotion

trigal m wheat field

trigo m wheat

trigueño -ña adj ⟨pelo⟩ light brown; ⟨persona⟩ dark; **una niña de tez trigueña** an olive-skinned girl

trillar [A1] vt to thresh

trillizo -za m,f triplet

trilogía f trilogy

trimestral adj ⟨publicación/pago⟩ quarterly; **examen** ~ end-of-semester examination (AmE), end-of-term examination (BrE)

trimestre m **(a)** quarter, three-month period; **pago por** ~**s** I pay quarterly **(b)** (Educ) term, ≈ semester (in US)

trinar [A1] vi ⟨«pájaro»⟩ to sing

trinchar [A1] vt to carve

trinchera f **(a)** (Mil) trench **(b)** (Indum) trench coat

trineo m **(a)** (Dep, Jueg) sled (AmE), sledge (BrE) **(b)** (tirado por perros, caballos) sleigh

trinidad f trinity; **La (Santísima) T**~ (Relig) the Trinity

trino m trill

trío m trio

tripa f [1] **(a)** tb **tripas** fpl (intestino) intestine, gut; (visceras) (fam) innards (pl) (colloq); **se me revuelven las** ~**s de solo verlo** just looking at it turns my stomach **(b)** (material) gut [2] (Esp fam) (barriga) belly (colloq)

triple adj triple
■ m [1] (Mat): **el precio aumentó al** ~ the price tripled o trebled; **tardó el** ~ it took three times as long; **el** ~ **de tres es nueve** three times three equals nine [2] (Elec) three-way adapter o adaptor

triplicado: **por triplicado** (loc adv) in triplicate

triplicar [A2] vt ⟨capacidad/precio/ventas⟩ to treble; ⟨longitud/cifra⟩ to triple
■ **triplicarse** v pron to treble, triple

trípode m tripod

tripulación f crew

tripulante mf crew member; **los** ~**s** the crew

tripular [A1] vt to crew, man

triquiñuela f (fam) trick, dodge (colloq)

trisílabo -ba adj trisyllabic

triste adj [1] **(a)** [ESTAR] ⟨persona⟩ sad; **esa música me pone** ~ that music makes me sad **(b)** ⟨expresión/mirada⟩ sad, sorrowful **(c)** [SER] (que causa tristeza) ⟨historia/película/noticia⟩ sad; ⟨paisaje/color⟩ dismal, gloomy; ⟨lugar/ambiente⟩ gloomy [2] ⟨delante del n⟩ (miserable, insignificante) miserable; **por cuatro** ~**s pesos** for a few miserable pesos; **es la** ~ **realidad** it's the sad truth

tristeza f (de mirada, persona) sadness, sorrow; (de lugar, ambiente) gloominess

triturador m: ~ **de basura** garbage disposal unit (AmE), waste disposal unit (BrE); ~ **de ajos** garlic press

trituradora f crushing machine, crusher

triturar [A1] vt ⟨almendras/ajo⟩ to crush; ⟨minerales⟩ to grind, crush

triunfador -dora adj ⟨ejército⟩ triumphant; ⟨equipo⟩ winning (before n), triumphant
■ m,f winner

triunfal adj ⟨marcha/arco⟩ triumphal; ⟨gesto/sonrisa/entrada⟩ triumphant

t

triunfalismo *m* triumphalism

triunfar [A1] *vi* **(a)** (ganar) ~ SOBRE algo/algn to triumph OVER sth/sb; **triunfó en el concurso** she won the competition **(b)** (tener éxito) to succeed, be successful **(c)** *‹justicia/verdad/razón›* (prevalecer) to prevail, win out (AmE) *o* (BrE) through

triunfo *m* [1] **(a)** (victoria) victory; **el ~ del equipo irlandés** the Irish team's victory **(b)** (logro) triumph; **uno de los ~s de la ciencia** one of the triumphs of science **(c)** (éxito) success [2] (en naipes) trump; **palo del ~** trumps (*pl*)

trivial *adj* trivial

trivialidad *f* **(a)** (cualidad) triviality **(b)** (dicho) trivial *o* trite remark; (cosa) triviality

trivializar [A4] *vt ‹asunto›* to trivialize; *‹éxito›* to play down

trizarse [A4] *v pron* (Chi) (rajarse) *«anteojos/vaso»* to crack; *«diente»* to chip

trizas *fpl*: **hacer ~ algo** *‹tela/carta›* to tear sth to shreds; **el jarrón se cayó y se hizo ~** the vase fell and smashed (to bits *o* smithereens); **tengo los nervios hechos ~** my nerves are in shreds *o* tatters

trofeo *m* (premio) trophy

troglodita *mf* **(a)** (cavernícola) troglodyte **(b)** (fam) (bruto) lout

trolebús *m* trolleybus

tromba *f* (terrestre) whirlwind, tornado; (marina) waterspout; **~ de agua** downpour

trombón *m* [1] (instrumento) trombone [2] **trombón** *mf* (músico) trombonist

trombonista *mf* trombonist

trombosis *f* thrombosis

trompa *f* [1] (de elefante) trunk; (de insecto) proboscis [2] (boca) (AmL fam) lips (*pl*), mouth [3] (instrumento) horn [4] (Esp fam) (borrachera): **coger una ~** to get plastered (colloq) [5] **trompa** *mf* (músico) horn-player

trompada *f* (AmS fam) (puñetazo) punch; **darle** *or* **pegarle una ~ a algn** to punch sb

trompazo *m* (fam): **me di un ~ con la puerta** I walked (*o* ran *etc*) smack into the door (colloq)

trompear [A1] *vt* (AmL fam) to thump (colloq), to punch

trompeta *f* [1] (instrumento) trumpet [2] **trompeta** *mf* (persona) trumpet player; (Mil) trumpeter

trompetista *mf* trumpet player

trompicón *m*: **iba dando trompicones** he was staggering; **a trompicones** in fits and starts

trompo *m* **(a)** (Jueg) (spinning) top **(b)** (Auto) spin

trona *f* (Esp) high chair

tronar [A10] *v impers* to thunder
■ **~** *vi* [1] *«cañones/voz»* to thunder [2] (Méx fam) **(a)** (en relación) to split up (colloq) **(b)** (fracasar) to flop (colloq); (en examen) to fail
■ **~** *vt* [1] (AmC, Méx fam) (fusilar) to shoot [2] (Méx fam) *‹examen/alumno›* to fail, flunk (AmE colloq)

tronchar [A1] *vt ‹tallo/rama›* to snap
■ **troncharse** *v pron* *«tallo/rama»* to break *o* snap off; **~se de (la) risa** (Esp fam) to die laughing (colloq)

tronco *m* [1] (Bot) trunk; (leño) log [2] (en genealogía) stock [3] (Anat) trunk, torso

tronera *f* (en billar) pocket

trono *m* throne; **subir al ~** to come to the throne

tropa *f* **(a)** (soldados rasos): **la ~** the troops (*pl*) **(b)** **tropas** *fpl* (ejército, soldados) troops

tropel *m* (de personas) mob; **entraron al estadio en ~** they poured into the stadium

tropezar [A6] *vi* **(a)** (al caminar, correr) to stumble, trip; **~ CON algo** *‹con piedra/escalón›* to trip OVER sth; *‹con árbol/muro›* to walk (*o* run *etc*) INTO sth **(b)** (encontrarse) **~ CON algo** *‹con dificultad/problema›* to come up AGAINST sth; **~ CON algn** to run *o* bump INTO sb (colloq)
■ **tropezarse** *v pron* (encontrarse) **~se CON algn** to run *o* bump INTO sb (colloq)

tropezón *m* **(a)** (acción de tropezar) stumble; **dio un ~ y cayó** he stumbled and fell; **a tropezones** (fam) in fits and starts **(b)** (equivocación) mistake, slip

tropical *adj* tropical

trópico *m* tropic

tropiece, tropieces, etc ▶ TROPEZAR

tropieza, tropiezas, etc ▶ TROPEZAR

tropiezo *m* (contratiempo) setback, hitch; (equivocación) mistake, slip

trotar [A1] *vi* **(a)** *«caballo/jinete»* to trot **(b)** (fam) (ir de un lado a otro) to rush around **(c)** (CS, Méx) (como ejercicio) to jog

trote *m* [1] (Equ) trot; **al ~** at a trot [2] (fam) (ajetreo): **¡qué ~ he tenido hoy!** it's been so hectic today (colloq); **ya no estoy para esos ~s** I'm not up to that sort of thing any more

trovador *m* troubadour, minstrel

trozar [A4] *vt* (AmL) to cut ... into pieces, cut up

trozo *m* **(a)** (de pan, pastel) piece, bit, slice; (de madera, papel, tela) piece, bit; (de vidrio, cerámica) piece, fragment; **cortar la zanahoria en trocitos** dice the carrot **(b)** (Lit, Mús) passage

trucar [A2] *vt* **(a)** *‹dados/juego/elecciones›* to fix, rig **(b)** *‹fotografía›* to touch up

trucha *f* (Coc, Zool) trout

truco *m* trick; **el ~ está en...** the trick *o* secret is...; **pillarle el ~ a algo** to get the hang of sth

trueno *m* **(a)** (Meteo) thunderclap, clap of thunder; **~s** thunder **(b)** (de cañones) thunder

trueque *m* (cambio) barter

trufa *f* truffle

truncar [A2] *vt* **(a)** *‹frase/discurso/texto›* to cut short **(b)** *‹vida›* to cut short; *‹planes›* to frustrate, thwart; *‹ilusiones›* to shatter

tu *adj* (delante del *n*) your; **~s amigos** your friends

tú *pron pers* [familiar form of address] [1] (como sujeto, en comparaciones, con preposición) you; **¿quién**

lo va a hacer? — tú who's going to do it? — you are; llegó después que ∼ he arrived after you (did); entre ∼ y yo between you and me; tratar de ∼ a algn *to address sb using the familiar* TÚ *form* ⟨2⟩ (uno) you; te dan varias opciones y ∼ eliges una you're given several options and you choose one

tuba *f* tuba

tubérculo *m* (Bot) tuber

tuberculosis *f* tuberculosis

tuberculoso -sa *m,f* tuberculosis sufferer (*o* patient *etc*)

tubería *f* (cañería) pipe; (conjunto de tubos) piping, pipes (*pl*)

tubo *m* ⟨1⟩ (a) (cilindro hueco) tube; ∼ de escape exhaust (pipe) (b) (del órgano) pipe (c) (Chi, Méx) (para el pelo) roller, curler ⟨2⟩ (RPl) (del teléfono) receiver

tuco *m* (Per, RPl) (Coc) tomato sauce

tuerca *f* nut

tuerce, tuerces, etc ▶ TORCER

tuerto -ta *adj* one-eyed; es ∼ (sin un ojo) he only has one eye; (ciego de un ojo) he's blind in one eye
■ *m,f*: *person blind in one eye or with only one eye*

tuerza, tuerzas, etc ▶ TORCER

tuétano *m* marrow

tufo *m* (fam) (olor — a sucio, podrido) stink (colloq); (— a cerrado): aquí dentro hay un ∼ horrible it smells really stuffy in here

tugurio *m* (vivienda) hovel; (bar) dive

tul *m* tulle

tulipa *f* lampshade

tulipán *m* tulip

tullido -da *adj* crippled
■ *m,f* cripple

tumba *f* (excavada) grave; (construida) tomb

tumbar [A1] *vt* (a) (hacer caer) to knock down: lo tumbó en el primer asalto he knocked him down in the first round; un olor que te tumbaba a smell that knocked you backward(s) (b) (AmL) ⟨árbol⟩ to fell, cut down; ⟨muro/casa⟩ to demolish, knock down
■ **tumbarse** *v pron* to lie down

tumbo *m* ⟨1⟩ (vaivén): salió del bar dando ∼s he staggered out of the bar; la carreta iba dando ∼s por el camino the cart jolted along the path ⟨2⟩ (Bol) (fruta) passion fruit

tumbona *f* (Esp) sun lounger, deck chair

tumor *m* tumor*

tumulto *m* (multitud) crowd; (alboroto) commotion, tumult

tumultuoso -sa *adj* tumultuous

tuna *f* ⟨1⟩ (Bot, Coc) (planta, fruto) prickly pear ⟨2⟩ (Mús) tuna (*musical group made up of university students*)

tundra *f* tundra

túnel *m* tunnel; ∼ de lavado car wash

túnica *f* (Hist) tunic; (Relig) robe

tuntún *m* (fam): al ∼ ⟨elegir⟩ at random; contestó al ∼ he just said the first thing that came into his head

tupé *m* ⟨1⟩ (fam) (descaro) nerve ⟨2⟩ (Esp) (peluquín) toupee; (mechón de pelo) forelock

tupido¹ -da *adj* ⟨follaje/vegetación⟩ dense; ⟨tela⟩ closely-woven; ⟨cejas⟩ bushy; ⟨niebla⟩ thick

tupido² *adv* (Méx) intensely

turbante *m* turban

turbar [A1] *vt* ⟨1⟩ (liter o period) ⟨orden/silencio⟩ to disturb ⟨2⟩ (liter o period) (a) (aturdir, confundir): sus insistentes miradas la ∼on the way he kept looking at her embarrassed and confused her; su presencia lo turbó her presence made him uncomfortable
■ **turbarse** *v pron* (liter o period) (a) (aturdirse, confundirse): la besó en la mejilla y se turbó he kissed her on the cheek and she was covered with confusion (liter); se turbó ante tantos elogios such praise confused and embarrassed him

turbina *f* turbine

turbio -bia *adj* (a) ⟨agua⟩ cloudy; ⟨río⟩ muddy (b) ⟨visión/ojos⟩ blurred, misty (c) ⟨asunto/ negocio⟩ shady, murky

turbo *adj inv* turbocharged
■ *m* (turbocompresor) turbocharger; (automóvil) turbo

turbulencia *f* turbulence

turbulento -ta *adj* turbulent

turco¹ -ca *adj* (Geog) Turkish
■ *m,f* (a) (Geog) (persona) Turk (b) (AmL) (árabe) *term used (often pejoratively) to refer to someone of Middle Eastern origin*

turco² *m* (idioma) Turkish

turismo *m* (Com, Ocio) tourism; los ingresos del ∼ income from tourism; ∼ cultural heritage tourism; dependen del ∼ alemán they rely on German tourists; oficina de ∼ tourist office; hacer ∼ to travel (around)

turista *adj* tourist (*before n*); clase ∼ tourist *o* economy class
■ *mf* tourist

turistear [A1] *vi* (Andes, Méx) (en país) to tour around; (en ciudad) to do some sightseeing

turístico -ca *adj* ⟨información/folleto⟩ tourist (*before n*); ⟨viaje⟩ sightseeing (*before n*); ⟨empresa⟩ travel (*before n*); ⟨atracción/actividad/ lugar⟩ tourist (*before n*)

turnarse [A1] *v pron* to take turns

turnio -nia *adj* (Chi fam) ⟨persona⟩ cross-eyed; ⟨ojos⟩ squint

turno *m* (a) (horario de trabajo): hacer el ∼ de noche to work the night shift; estar de ∼ to be on duty (b) (personas) shift (c) (en un orden): cuando te toque el ∼ when your turn comes; cuidémoslo por ∼s let's take turns looking after him; pedir ∼ (Esp) *to ask who is last in the line* (AmE) *o* (BrE) *queue*

turquesa *f* (Min) turquoise
■ *m/adj inv* turquoise

Turquía *f* Turkey

turrón *m*: *type of candy traditionally eaten at Christmas*

tute *m*: *card game in which the object is to win all the kings or queens*

tutear [A1] *vt*: *to address sb using the familiar* TÚ *form*
■ **tutearse** *v pron*: *to address each other using the familiar* TÚ *form*

tutela *f* (a) (Der) guardianship, tutelage (b) (protección) protection

tuteo *m*: *use of the familiar* TÚ *form*

tutor -tora *m,f* **1** (Educ) (encargado de curso) course tutor, class teacher; (en la universidad) tutor **2** (Der) guardian

tutoría *f* **1** (Educ) tutorship **2** (Der) guardianship, tutelage

tutú *m* (Indum) tutu

tuve, tuviera, etc ▶ TENER

tuyo -ya *adj* yours; **esto es ~** this is yours; **¿es amigo ~?** is he a friend of yours?; **fue idea tuya** it was your idea
■ *pron:* **el ~, la tuya etc** yours; **la música no es lo ~** music isn't your strong point *o* your forte; **los ~s** (tu familia) your family and friends

twist /twis(t)/ *m* twist

U u

U, u *f* (*pl* **úes**) (*read as* /u/) *the letter* U, u

u *conj* [*used instead of* o *before* o- *or* ho-] or; **siete u ocho** seven or eight

ubicación *f* **(a)** (esp AmL) (situación, posición) location **(b)** (AmL) (localización): **se hizo difícil la ~ del avión** locating the airplane was very difficult

ubicar [A2] *vt* (AmL) **(a)** (colocar, situar): **me ~on a su lado** they placed me next to him; **~on las sillas para la reunión** they arranged the chairs for the meeting **(b)** (localizar) ⟨*persona/lugar*⟩ to find, locate **(c)** (identificar): **la ubico solo de nombre** I only know her by name; **lo ubiqué por el color** I recognized her by the color; **me suena el nombre, pero no lo ubico** the name rings a bell, but I can't quite place him
■ **ubicarse** *v pron* **1** (AmL) **(a)** (colocarse, situarse): **se ubicó en la primera fila** he sat in the front row **(b)** (en empleo) to get oneself a good job **(c)** (orientarse) to find one's way around; **¿te ubicas?** have you got your bearings? **2** (esp AmL) (estar situado) to be, be situated *o* located

ud. = **usted**

uds. = **ustedes**

UE *f* (= **Unión Europea**) EU

uf *interj* (expresando — cansancio, sofocación) whew! (colloq); (— repugnancia) yuck (colloq)

ufano -na *adj* **(a)** (satisfecho, orgulloso) proud **(b)** (engreído) self-satisfied, smug

ujier *m* uniformed doorman; (en tribunales) usher

úlcera *f* ulcer

ulpo *m* (Chi) *cold drink made with roasted flour and sugar*

ultimar [A1] *vt* **1** ⟨*preparativos*⟩ to complete; ⟨*detalles*⟩ to finalize **2** (AmL frml) (matar) to kill, murder

ultimátum *m* (*pl* ~ *or* **-tums**) ultimatum

último -ma *adj* (*delante del n*) **1** (en el tiempo) last; **a última hora** at the last minute *o* moment; **su ~ libro** his latest book; **en los ~s tiempos** recently; **¿cuándo fue la última vez que lo usaste?** when did you last use it?
2 (a) (en una serie) last; **estar en ~ lugar** to be last; **por última vez** for the last time; **como ~ recurso** as a last resort; **última voluntad** last wishes (*pl*) **(b)** (*como adv*) (CS) ⟨*salir/terminar*⟩ last
3 (en el espacio): **el ~ piso** the top floor; **la última fila** the back row
4 (definitivo): **es mi última oferta** it's my final offer
■ *m,f* last one; **era el ~ que me quedaba** it was my last one; **es el ~ de la clase** he's bottom of the class; **a ~s de** (Esp) toward(s) the end of; **por ~** finally, lastly

ultra *mf* (Esp) right-wing extremist

ultraderecha *f*: **la ~** the far *o* extreme right

ultraderechista *adj* extreme right-wing
■ *mf* right-wing extremist

ultrafino -na *adj* ultrafine, superfine

ultrajar [A1] *vt* (frml) ⟨*persona*⟩ to outrage, offend ... deeply; ⟨*bandera*⟩ to insult; ⟨*honor*⟩ to offend against

ultraje *m* outrage, insult

ultramarinos *mpl* (comestibles) groceries; **tienda de ~** grocery store (AmE), grocer's shop (BrE)

ultrasónico -ca *adj* ultrasonic

ultravioleta *adj* (*pl* ~ *or* **-tas**) ultraviolet

umbilical *adj* umbilical

umbral *m* **(a)** (de puerta) threshold **(b)** (borde, frontera) *tb* **~es** threshold; **en los ~es de la muerte** at death's door; **en los ~es de la civilización** at the dawn of civilization

un (*pl* **unos**), **una** (*pl* **unas**) *art* [*the masculine article* un *is also used before feminine nouns which begin with stressed* a *or* ha *e.g.* un arma poderosa, un hambre feroz] **1** (*sing*) a; ⟨*delante de sonido vocálico*⟩ an; (*pl*) some; **una nueva droga** a new drug; **un asunto importante** an important matter; **hay unas cartas para ti** there are some letters for you; **tiene unos ojos preciosos** he has lovely eyes
2 (con valor ponderativo): **tú haces unas preguntas ...** you do ask some questions!
3 (con nombres propios) a; **es un Miró** it's a Miró
4 (*pl*) (expresando aproximación) about; **tiene unos 30 años** she's about 30

una *pron* (*ver tb* un, uno): **a la ~, a las dos, ¡a las tres!** ready, steady, go!

unánime *adj* unanimous

unanimidad *f* unanimity; **por ~** unanimously

undécimo -ma *adj/pron* eleventh; *para ejemplos ver* quinto

UNED /u'neð/ *f* (en Esp) = **Universidad Nacional de Educación a Distancia**

UNESCO /u'nesko/ *f*: **la ~** UNESCO

ungüento *m* ointment

únicamente *adv* only

UNICEF /uni'sef, uni'θef/ *f*: **la ~** UNICEF

único -ca *adj* ⌐1⌐ **(a)** (solo) only; **soy hijo** ~ I'm an only child; **¡es lo** ~ **que faltaba!** that's all we needed! **(b)** ⟨*mercado/moneda*⟩ single; **tarifa única** flat rate; **talla única** one size ⌐2⌐ (extraordinario) extraordinary
■ *m,f*: **el** ~**/las únicas que tengo** the only one/ones I have

unicornio *m* unicorn

unidad *f* ⌐1⌐ **(a)** (Com, Mat) unit; **costo por** ~ unit cost; ~ **de peso** unit of weight; ~ **de cuidados intensivos** *or* (Esp) **de vigilancia** *or* (Arg, Méx) **terapia intensiva** *or* (Chi) **de tratamiento intensivo** intensive care unit ⌐2⌐ (unión, armonía) unity ⌐3⌐ (Inf): ~ **de disco** (Inf) disk drive

unido -da *adj* **(a)** ⟨*familia/amigos*⟩ close **(b)** (sobre un tema) united

unificación *f* unification

unificar [A2] *vt* ⟨*país*⟩ to unify; ⟨*precios*⟩ to standardize

uniforme *adj* ⟨*velocidad/temperaturas*⟩ constant, uniform; ⟨*superficie*⟩ even, uniform; ⟨*terreno*⟩ even, level; ⟨*paisaje/estilo*⟩ uniform; ⟨*criterios/precios*⟩ standard, uniform
■ *m* uniform

unilateral *adj* ⟨*desarme/decisión*⟩ unilateral; ⟨*criterio/opinión*⟩ one-sided

unión *f* ⌐1⌐ **(a)** (acción): **la** ~ **de las dos empresas** the merger of the two companies; **la** ~ **de estos factores** the combination of these factors **(b)** (agrupación) association **(c) la U**~ **Americana** (Méx) (Period) the United States ⌐2⌐ (relación) union, relationship; (matrimonio) union, marriage ⌐3⌐ (juntura) joint

Unión Europea *f*: **la** ~ ~ the European Union

Unión Soviética *f* (Hist): **la** ~ ~ the Soviet Union

unir [I1] *vt* ⌐1⌐ **(a)** ⟨*cables*⟩ to join; (con cola, pegamento) to stick … together; ⟨*esfuerzos*⟩ to combine **(b)** «*sentimientos/intereses*» to unite **(c)** ⟨*características/cualidades/estilos*⟩ to combine; ~ **algo A algo** to combine sth WITH sth ⌐2⌐ (comunicar) ⟨*lugares*⟩ to link ⌐3⌐ (fusionar) ⟨*empresas/organizaciones*⟩ to merge
■ **unirse** *v pron* ⌐1⌐ (aliarse) «*personas/colectividades*» to join together; **se unió a nuestra causa** he joined our cause ⌐2⌐ (juntarse) «*caminos*» to converge, meet ⌐3⌐ (fusionarse) «*empresas/organizaciones*» to merge

universal *adj* universal

universalidad *f* universality

universidad *f* university; ~ **a distancia** *or* (Méx) **abierta** open university; ~ **laboral** ≈ technical college (*school with emphasis on vocational training*)

universitario -ria *adj* university (*before n*)
■ *m,f* (estudiante) undergraduate, (university) student; (licenciado) (university) graduate

universo *m* universe

uno¹, una *adj* [UNO *becomes* UN *before a masculine noun or noun phrase*] one; **no había ni un asiento libre** there wasn't one empty seat *o* a single empty seat; **treinta y un pasajeros** thirty-one passengers; **el capítulo uno** chapter one

■ *pron* ⌐1⌐ (numeral) one; **uno a** *or* **por uno** one by one; **es la una** it's one o'clock; **más de uno/una** (fam) quite a few
⌐2⌐ (personal) (*sing*) one; (*pl*) some; **uno es mío, el otro no** one's mine, the other isn't; **¿te gustaron?** — **unos sí, otros no** did you like them? — some I did, others I didn't; **se ayudan los unos a los otros** they help one another
⌐3⌐ (fam) (alguien) (*m*) some guy (colloq); (*f*) some woman (colloq); **les pregunté a unos que estaban allí** I asked some people who were there
⌐4⌐ (uso impersonal) you; **uno no sabe qué decir** you don't *o* (frml) one doesn't know what to say; **nunca le dicen nada a uno** they don't tell you anything

uno² *m* (number) one; *para ejemplos ver* CINCO

untar [A1] *vt* **(a)** (cubrir): ~ **las galletas con miel** spread honey on the cookies; **se unta el molde con mantequilla** grease the cake tin (with butter) **(b)** (empapar) ~ **algo EN algo** to dip sth IN sth
■ **untarse** *v pron* **(a)** (ensuciarse): **se untó las manos de pintura** he got paint all over his hands **(b)** (ponerse): **se untó los hombros con bronceador** she rubbed suntan lotion on her shoulders

uña *f* **(a)** (Anat) (de la mano) nail, fingernail; (del pie) nail, toenail; **arreglarse** *or* **hacerse las** ~**s** (*refl*) to do one's nails; (*caus*) to have one's nails done **(b)** (de oso, gato) claw; (de caballo, oveja) hoof

uralita® *f* asbestos

uranio *m* uranium

Urano *m* Uranus

urbanidad *f* courtesy, urbanity (frml)

urbanismo *m* city (AmE) *o* (BrE) town planning

urbanización *f* (acción) urbanization, development; (núcleo residencial) (Esp) (housing) development

urbanizado -da *adj* built-up; **esta zona está muy urbanizada** this area is heavily developed

urbanizar [A4] *vt* ⟨*zona/terreno*⟩ to develop, urbanize; **una zona sin** ~ an undeveloped area

urbano -na *adj* ⟨*núcleo/transporte*⟩ urban, city (*before n*); ⟨*población*⟩ urban

urdir [I1] *vt* **(a)** (en telar) to warp; ⟨*puntos*⟩ to cast on **(b)** ⟨*plan*⟩ to devise, hatch

urgencia *f* **(a)** (cualidad) urgency; **con** ~ urgently **(b)** (Med) emergency; ❾ **urgencias** accident and emergency; **lo operaron de** ~ he had an emergency operation

urgente *adj* ⟨*asunto*⟩ pressing, urgent; ⟨*mensaje*⟩ urgent; ⟨*caso/enfermo*⟩ emergency (*before n*); ⟨*carta*⟩ express (*before n*)

urgido -da *adj* (AmL): **estaban** ~**s de dinero** they were in urgent need of money; **estamos** ~**s de tiempo** we are pressed for time

urgir [I7] *vi* (*en 3ªpers*): **urge la finalización del proyecto** the project must be finished as soon as possible; **me urge estar allí el martes** I absolutely must be there on/by Tuesday; **le urge el préstamo** he needs the loan urgently

urinario *m* urinal

urna *f* ⌐1⌐ (vasija) urn; (de exposición) display case; (para votar) ballot box; ~ **cineraria** funerary urn ⌐2⌐ (Chi, Ven) (ataúd) coffin, wooden box (euph)

urólogo -ga *m,f* urologist

urraca *f* magpie

URSS /urs/ f (Hist) (= **Unión de Repúblicas Socialistas Soviéticas**) USSR

urubú m black vulture

Uruguay m (a) (país) tb el ~ Uruguay (b) (río): el (río) ~ the Uruguay River

uruguayismo m Uruguayan word (o phrase etc)

uruguayo -ya adj/m,f Uruguayan

USA /'usa/ (fam) USA

usado -da adj (a) [SER] (de segunda mano) secondhand (b) [ESTAR] (gastado, viejo) worn

usar [A1] vt (a) (utilizar) to use; ¿qué champú usas? what shampoo do you use?; ~ algo/a algn DE or COMO algo to use sth/sb AS sth (b) (llevar) ‹alhajas/ropa/perfume› to wear; estos zapatos están sin ~ these shoes are unworn, these shoes have never been worn

■ **usarse** v pron (en 3ª pers) (esp AmL) (estar de moda) «color/ropa» to be in fashion, to be popular; ya no se usa hacer fiestas de compromiso people don't tend to have engagement parties any more

usina f (AmS) (fábrica) large factory; (industria) industry

uso m (a) (de producto, medicamento, máquina) use; instrucciones para su ~ instructions for use; hacer ~ de algo to use sth (b) (de facultad, derecho): en pleno ~ de sus facultades mentales in full possession of his mental faculties; hacer ~ de un derecho to exercise a right; desde que tengo ~ de razón ever since I can remember; hacer ~ de la palabra (frml) to speak (c) (de prenda): ropa de ~ diario everyday clothes; los zapatos ceden con el ~ shoes give with wear

usted pron pers [Polite form of address but also used in some areas, eg Colombia and Chile, instead of the familiar TÚ form] **1** (como sujeto, en comparaciones, con preposición) you; ¿quién lo va a hacer? — usted who's going to do it? — you (are); tratar a algn de ~ to address sb using the USTED form; muchas gracias — a ~ thank you very much — thank you; son de ~ they're yours **2** (uso impersonal) you, one (frml); le dicen eso y ~ no sabe qué contestar when they say that you just don't know what to say in reply

ustedes pron pers pl [Polite plural form of address also used in Latin American countries as the familiar plural form] you; ¿quién lo va a hacer? — ustedes who's going to do it? — you (are); ~ mismos lo dijeron you said so yourselves; son de ~ they're yours

usual adj usual, normal

usuario -ria m,f user

usurero -ra m,f usurer

usurpador -dora m,f usurper

usurpar [A1] vt (frml) ‹propiedad/título› to misappropriate; ‹territorio› to seize; ‹poder› to usurp

utensilio m (instrumento) utensil; (herramienta) tool; ~s de cocina kitchen o cooking utensils; ~s de laboratorio laboratory apparatus; ~s de pesca fishing tackle

útero m womb, uterus (tech)

útil adj useful

utilería f (esp AmL) (Cin, Teatr) props (pl)

utilero -ra m,f (esp AmL) (Cin, Teatr) props manager

útiles mpl (a) (herramientas, instrumentos) tools (pl), implements (pl); ~ de pesca fishing tackle; ~ de jardinería gardening tools (b) (AmL) (artículos escolares) tb ~ escolares pencils, pens, rulers, etc for school

utilidad f (a) (de aparato) usefulness; un coche me sería de mucha ~ a car would be of great use to me (b) **utilidades** fpl (AmL) (ganancia, beneficio) profits (pl)

utilitario m small (economical) car

utilización f use, utilization (frml)

utilizar [A4] vt to use, utilize (frml)

utopía f Utopia

utópico -ca adj Utopian

uva f grape; ~ blanca/negra white/black grape

uve f (Esp) name of the letter v; ~ doble (Esp) name of the letter w

uy interj (expresando — asombro) ooh! (colloq); (— malestar, disgusto) oh!; (— emoción súbita) ah!, oh!; (— dolor) ow!, ouch!

· ·

Vv

· ·

V, v f (read as /be/, /be 'korta/, /be 'tʃika/, /be pe'keɲa/ or (Esp) /'uβe/) the letter V, v

va, vas, etc ▶ IR

vaca f (a) (Zool) cow; estar como una ~ (fam) to be very fat; hacer una ~ (AmL fam) to make a collection (b) (Coc): (carne de) ~ beef; filete de ~ fillet steak

vacacionar [A1] vi (Méx) to spend one's vacation(s) o holidays

vacaciones fpl vacation(s) (esp AmE), holiday(s) (esp BrE); ~ de verano summer vacation o holidays; irse de ~ to go away on vacation o on holiday; estamos de ~ we're on

· ·

vacation o holiday; **tomarse unas** ∼ to take a vacation o holiday

vacacionista *mf* (Méx) vacationer (AmE), holidaymaker (BrE)

vacante *adj* ⟨puesto/plaza⟩ vacant; ⟨piso/asiento⟩ empty, unoccupied
■ *f* vacancy; **cubrir una** ∼ to fill a vacancy

vaciar [A17] *vt* **1 (a)** ⟨vaso/botella⟩ to empty; ⟨radiador⟩ to drain; ⟨bolsillo/cajón⟩ to empty; ⟨armario/habitación⟩ to clean out **(b)** ⟨contenido⟩ to empty (out) **2** (ahuecar) to hollow out
■ **vaciarse** *v pron* to empty

vacilación *f* hesitation, vacillation (frml); **tras un momento de** ∼ after a moment's hesitation

vacilante *adj* **(a)** (oscilante) unsteady, shaky; **con paso** ∼ unsteadily **(b)** (dubitativo) ⟨expresión⟩ doubtful; ⟨voz⟩ hesitant **(c)** ⟨luz⟩ flickering

vacilar [A1] *vi* **1 (a)** (dudar) to hesitate; **sin** ∼ without hesitating; **no vaciló en aceptar** he did not hesitate to accept, he accepted without hesitation **(b)** «fe/determinación» to waver **(c)** «luz» to flicker **2** (oscilar) «persona» to stagger, totter **3** (AmL exc CS fam) (divertirse) to have fun

vacile *m* (fam) (tomadura de pelo) joke; **basta de** ∼ that's enough kidding (colloq)

vacilón *m* (AmL fam) **(a)** (diversión): **le encanta el** ∼ he loves having a good time; **la fiesta fue un** ∼ the party was great fun **(b)** (tomadura de pelo) joke; **es puro** ∼ it's just a joke

vacío¹ -cía *adj* **(a)** ⟨botella/caja⟩ empty; ⟨calle/ciudad⟩ empty, deserted; ⟨casa⟩ empty, unoccupied; ⟨palabras/retórica⟩ empty; **con el estómago** ∼ on an empty stomach **(b)** (frívolo) ⟨persona⟩ shallow; ⟨vida/frase⟩ empty, meaningless

vacío² *m* **(a)** (Fis) vacuum; **envasado al** ∼ vacuum-packed **(b)** (espacio vacío) space; **mirar al** ∼ to gaze into space **(c)** (falta, hueco) gap; **dejó un** ∼ **en su vida** she left a gap o a void in his life; **una sensación de** ∼ a feeling of emptiness

vacuna *f* vaccine; **me tengo que poner la** ∼ I have to have my vaccination

vacunación *f* vaccination

vacunar [A1] *vt* to vaccinate; ∼ **a algn** CONTRA **algo** to vaccinate sb AGAINST sth
■ **vacunarse** *v pron* to get vaccinated; ∼**se** CONTRA **algo** to get vaccinated AGAINST sth

vacuno -na *adj* bovine; **ganado** ∼ cattle (*pl*)

vado *m* (de río) ford; **❾ vado permanente** no parking

vagabundear [A1] *vi* to drift (around)

vagabundo -da *adj* ⟨perro⟩ stray; **niños** ∼**s** street urchins
■ *m,f* tramp, vagrant

vagar [A3] *vi* to wander, roam

vagina *f* vagina

vago -ga *adj* **1** (fam) ⟨persona⟩ lazy, idle **2** ⟨recuerdo/idea⟩ vague, hazy; ⟨contorno/forma⟩ vague, indistinct; ⟨explicación/parecido⟩ vague
■ *m,f* (fam) layabout, slacker (colloq); **deja ya de hacer el** ∼ stop lazing around (colloq)

vagón *m* (de pasajeros) coach, car (AmE), carriage (BrE); ∼ **restaurante** dining o (BrE) restaurant car

vagoneta *f* (Méx) (para pasajeros) van, minibus

vaguedad *f* **(a)** (de palabras, ideas) vagueness

(b) (expresión imprecisa) vague remark; **¡déjate de** ∼**es y ve al grano!** stop being so vague o stop beating about the bush and get to the point

vaho *m* **(a)** (aliento) breath **(b)** (vapor) steam, vapor*; **(c)** (inhalación): **hacer** ∼**s** to inhale

vaina *f* **1** (de espada) scabbard; (de navaja) sheath **2** (Bot) (de habas, etc) pod **3** (Col, Per, Ven fam) **(a)** (problema, contrariedad): **¡qué** ∼! what a drag o pain (colloq); **la** ∼ **es que no sé cómo** the thing o problem is that I don't know how; **estoy metida en una** ∼ I'm in a spot of trouble (colloq) **(b)** (cosa, asunto) thing, thingamajig (colloq) **(c)** (comportamiento sospechoso): **tenían una** ∼ they were up to something funny; **¿qué** ∼ **te traes tú?** what are you up to?

vainilla *f* (Bot, Coc) vanilla

vais ▶ IR

vaivén *m* (de columpio, péndulo) swinging; (de tren) rocking; (de barco) rolling; (de mecedora) rocking; (de gente) toing and froing

vajilla *f* (en general) dishes (*pl*); (juego) dinner service o set

valdré, valdría, etc ▶ VALER

vale *m* **(a)** (para adquirir algo) voucher; (por devolución) credit note o slip; **un** ∼ **de descuento** a money-off coupon **(b)** (pagaré) IOU
■ *interj* ▶ VALER *vi* 4

valenciana *f* (Méx) cuff (AmE), turn-up (BrE)

valenciano¹ -na *adj/m,f* Valencian

valenciano² *m* (Ling) Valencian

valentía *f* bravery, courage; **con** ∼ courageously

valer [E28] *vt* **1** (tener un valor de) to be worth; (costar) to cost; **¿cuánto valen?** how much are they?, what do they cost?
2 (+ *me/te/le etc*) (ganar): **esta obra le valió un premio** this play earned o won her a prize
■ ∼ *vi* **1** (+ *compl*) (tener cierto valor) to be worth; (costar) to cost; **vale más, pero es mejor** it costs more but it's better; **cada cupón vale por un regalo** each voucher is worth a gift
2 (tener valor no material): **ha demostrado que vale** he has shown his worth; **como profesor no vale (nada)** as a teacher he's useless; **vales tanto como él** you're as good as he is; **hacerse** ∼ to assert oneself; **hacer** ∼ **algo** ⟨derecho⟩ to assert o enforce sth
3 (servir): **esta no vale, es muy ancha** this one's no good, it's too wide; **no le valió de nada protestar** protesting got him nowhere; **no** ∼ PARA **algo** to be useless o no good AT sth
4 **vale** (Esp fam) **(a)** (expresando acuerdo) OK; **¿a las ocho? — ¡vale!** at eight o'clock? — sure o fine o OK?; **¿vale?** OK?, all right? **(b)** (basta): **¿** ∼ **así?** is that OK o enough?
5 **más vale**: **más vale así** it's better that way; **más te vale ir** you'd better go
6 (a) (ser válido) «entrada/pasaporte» to be valid; «jugada/partido» to count **(b)** (estar permitido): **eso no vale, estás haciendo trampa** that's not fair, you're cheating; **no vale mirar** you're not allowed to look
7 (Méx fam) **(a)** (no importar): **a mí eso me vale** I don't give a damn about that (colloq) **(b)** (no tener valor) to be useless o no good (colloq) **(c)** (estropearse): **mi coche ya valió** my car's had it (colloq)

■ **valerse** *v pron* **1** (servirse) ~se DE algo/algn to use sth/sb

2 «*anciano/enfermo*»: ~se por sí mismo to look after oneself

3 (estar permitido, ser correcto): **no se vale golpear por debajo del cinturón** hitting below the belt is not allowed; **¡no se vale!** that's not fair!

valeroso -sa *adj* brave, courageous, valiant (liter)

valga, valgas, etc ▶ VALER

validar [A1] *vt* to validate

validez *f* validity

válido -da *adj* valid

valiente *adj* ⟨*persona*⟩ brave, courageous

valija *f* (RPl) suitcase; ~ **diplomática** diplomatic bag

valioso -sa *adj* ⟨*joya/consejo/experiencia*⟩ valuable; **un hombre** ~ a man of great worth

valla *f* (a) (cerca) fence (b) (Dep) (en atletismo) hurdle; (en fútbol) goal; ~ **publicitaria** billboard (AmE), hoarding (BrE)

valle *m* valley

valor *m* **1** (a) (Com, Fin) value; **libros por** ~ **de $150** books to the value of $150; **objetos de** ~ valuables; ~ **adquisitivo** purchasing power (b) (importancia, mérito) value; ~ **sentimental** sentimental value (c) (validez) validity; **sin la firma no tiene ningún** ~ it's not valid without the signature **2** (a) (coraje, valentía) courage; **me faltó** ~ I didn't have the courage; **armarse de** ~ to pluck up courage (b) (fam) (descaro, desvergüenza) nerve (colloq); **¡encima tiene el** ~ **de protestar!** and then she has the nerve to complain! **3** **valores** *mpl* (a) (principios morales) values (b) (Fin) securities, stocks, shares

valoración *f* (a) (de bienes, joyas) valuation; (de pérdidas, daños) assessment (b) (frml) (de suceso, trabajo) assessment, appraisal (frml)

valorar [A1] *vt* (a) ⟨*joya/cuadro*⟩ to value; ⟨*pérdida/daño*⟩ to assess; ~ **algo** EN **algo** to value/assess sth AT sth; **eso no se puede** ~ **en dinero** you cannot put a value on it (b) (frml) ⟨*trabajo/actuación*⟩ to assess (c) ⟨*amistad/lealtad*⟩ to value

valorización *f* (a) (tasación) ▶ VALORACIÓN A (b) (AmL) (aumento de valor) appreciation

vals *m* waltz; **bailar un** ~ to waltz

valuar *vt* [A18] (AmL) to value

válvula *f* valve

vamos ▶ IR

vampiresa *f* femme fatale, vamp (dated)

vampiro *m* (a) (en historias de horror) vampire; (explotador) vampire, bloodsucker (b) (Zool) vampire (bat)

van ▶ IR

vanagloriarse [A1] *v pron* ~ DE algo to boast o brag ABOUT sth

vandalismo *m* vandalism, hooliganism

vándalo -la *m,f* (gamberro) vandal, hooligan

vanguardia *f* (Mil) vanguard; (Art, Lit) avant-garde; **teatro de** ~ avant-garde theater; **ir** *or* **estar a la** ~ **(de algo)** to be in the vanguard (of sth)

vanguardista *adj* avant-garde

vanidad *f* vanity

vanidoso -sa *adj* (presumido) vain, conceited; (en cuanto al aspecto físico) vain

■ *m,f*: **es un** ~ he's so vain o conceited

vano -na *adj* (a) (ineficaz) ⟨*discusión/intento*⟩ vain, futile; ⟨*esfuerzo*⟩ futile; **en** ~ in vain (b) (falto de realidad) vain; **ilusiones vanas** wishful thinking (c) ⟨*palabra/promesa*⟩ empty

vapor *m* (a) (Fis, Quím) vapor*, steam (b) (Coc): **al** ~ steamed (c) (Náut) steamer, steamship

vaquero¹ -ra *adj* ⟨*falda/cazadora*⟩ denim; **un pantalón** ~ a pair of jeans o denims (b) ⟨*estilo*⟩ cowboy (*before n*)

■ *m,f* (Agr) (*m*) cowboy, cowhand; (*f*) cowgirl, cowhand

vaquero² *m* (Indum) *tb* ~s: **unos** ~s a pair of jeans o denims

vaquilla *f* heifer

vara *f* **1** (palo) stick, pole **2** (Per fam) (influencia) connections (*pl*) (colloq)

varado -da *adj* **1** (a) (Náut) ⟨*barco*⟩ aground (b) (AmL) (detenido): **miles de turistas se quedaron** ~s thousands of tourists were left stranded; **me quedé** ~ **con el trabajo** I got stuck with my work **2** (a) (Col, Méx fam) (sin dinero) broke (colloq) (b) (Andes) (sin empleo) out of work

variable *adj* ⟨*carácter/humor*⟩ changeable; **tiempo** ~ unsettled o changeable weather

variación *f* variation

variado -da *adj* (a) ⟨*programa/vida/trabajo*⟩ varied (b) (diverso): **ropa de colores** ~s clothes in a variety of colors

variante *f* **1** (de palabra) variant **2** (carretera) turnoff

variar [A17] *vi* «*precio/temperatura*» to vary; **las temperaturas varían entre 20°C y 25°C** temperatures range o vary between 20°C and 25°C; **para** ~ (iró) (just) for a change (iro)

■ ~ *vt* **1** (hacer variado) ⟨*menú*⟩ to vary; ⟨*producción*⟩ to vary, diversify **2** (cambiar) ⟨*decoración/rumbo*⟩ to change, alter

varicela *f* chicken pox

várices, (Esp) **varices** *fpl* ▶ VARIZ

varicoso -sa *adj* varicose

variedad *f* (a) (en general) variety (b) **variedades** *fpl* (Espec) vaudeville (AmE), variety (BrE)

varilla *f* (en general) rod; (de abanico, paraguas) rib; (de jaula) bar; (de rueda de bicicleta) spoke; (para medir el aceite) dipstick

vario -ria *adj* **1** ~s/**varias** (más de dos) several; **hace** ~s años several years ago **2** (variado, diverso) various; **asuntos** ~s various matters

varios -rias *pron* several; **lo compraron entre** ~s several of them got together to buy it

varita *f* wand; ~ **mágica** magic wand

variz (*pl* **várices** *or* (Esp) **varices**) *f* varicose vein

varón *adj* ⟨*heredero/descendiente*⟩ male; **un hijo** ~ a son

■ *m* (niño) boy; (hombre) man, male

varonil *adj* (a) (viril) manly, masculine; **voz** ~ masculine voice (b) ⟨*mujer*⟩ (hombruna) mannish, masculine

vas ▶ IR

vasallo *m* vassal

vasco¹ -ca *adj/m,f* Basque

vasco² *m* (idioma) Basque

vasectomía *f* vasectomy

vaselina *f* Vaseline®, petroleum jelly

vasija *f* (Arqueol) vessel (frml)

vaso *m* **1** (recipiente, contenido) glass; **un ~ de vino** (con vino) a glass of wine; (para vino) a wine glass; **~ de papel** paper cup **2** (Anat) vessel; **~ sanguíneo** blood vessel

vasto -ta *adj* (gen delante del n) ‹mar/llanura› vast, immense; ‹conocimientos/experiencia› vast

váter *m* (Esp fam) (inodoro) toilet, lavatory; (cuarto) bathroom (esp AmE), toilet (BrE)

Vaticano *m*: **el ~** the Vatican

vatio *m* watt

vaya, vayas, etc ▶ IR

Vd. = **usted**

ve *f* (AmL) *tb* **~ corta** *or* **chica** *or* **pequeña** *name of the letter* v

ve ▶ IR, VER²

vea, veas, etc ▶ VER²

vecindad *f* **1** (lugar, barrio) neighborhood*, area; (vecinos) residents (*pl*) **2** (Méx) (edificio) tenement house

vecindario ▶ VECINDAD 1

vecino -na *adj* **(a)** (contiguo) neighboring*; **los países ~s** the neighboring countries; **~ A algo** bordering ON sth, adjoining sth **(b)** (cercano) neighboring*, nearby

■ *m,f* **(a)** (persona que vive cerca) neighbor*; **mi ~ de al lado** my next-door neighbor **(b)** (habitante — de población, municipio) inhabitant; (— de barrio, edificio) resident

veda *f* (en caza y pesca) closed (AmE) *o* (BrE) close season; **la perdiz está en ~** it is the closed *o* close season for partridge

vedar [A1] *vt* **1** ‹caza/pesca› to prohibit, ban (*during the closed season*) **(b)** (prohibir) to ban

vedette /be'ðet/ *f* cabaret star

vegetación *f* **(a)** (Bot) vegetation **(b)** (Med) **vegetaciones** *fpl* adenoids (*pl*)

vegetal *adj* ‹vida› plant (*before n*); ‹aceite/reino› vegetable (*before n*)

■ *m* plant, vegetable

vegetar [A1] *vi* **(a)** (Bot) to grow **(b)** (fam) «persona» to vegetate (colloq & pej)

vegetariano -na *adj/m,f* vegetarian

vehemente *adj* vehement

vehículo *m* vehicle

veía, veíamos, etc ▶ VER

veinte *adj inv/m/pron* twenty; *para ejemplos ver* CINCO, CINCUENTA

veintitantos -tas *adj/pron* twenty-odd

veintiuno¹ -na *adj/pron* [VEINTIÚN *is used before masculine nouns and before feminine nouns which begin with accented* A *or* HA] twenty-one; **veintiún años** twenty-one years; *para ejemplos ver tb* CINCO

veintiuno² *m* (number) twenty-one

vejación *f* humiliation; **las vejaciones perpetradas por los guardias** the acts of humiliation carried out by the guards

vejestorio *m* **(a)** (fam) (persona): **la profesora es un ~** the teacher is ancient (colloq) **(b)** (AmL fam) (cosa) old relic (colloq)

vejez *f* old age

vejiga *f* (Anat) bladder

vela *f* **1** (para alumbrar) candle **2** (vigilia): **pasé la noche en ~** (por preocupación, dolor) I couldn't get to sleep all night; (cuidando a un enfermo) I was up all night **3** **(a)** (de barco) sail **(b)** (deporte) sailing; **hacer ~** to go sailing

velado -da *adj* ‹película› fogged; ‹amenaza/referencia› veiled; ‹sonido› muffled

velador¹ *m* **(a)** (mesa) pedestal table **(b)** (AmS) (mesilla de noche) bedside table, night stand (AmE)

velador² -dora *m,f* **1** (Méx) (de fábrica) watchman, guard **2** **veladora** *f* (Méx) (vela) candle

velar [A1] *vt* **1** **(a)** ‹difunto› to hold a wake over **(b)** ‹enfermo› to watch over **2** ‹película› to fog, expose

■ **~** *vi* **1** (permanecer despierto) to stay up *o* awake **2** (cuidar) **~ POR algo/algn** to watch OVER sth/sb

■ **velarse** *v pron* «película» to get fogged *o* exposed

velatorio *m* **(a)** (reunión) wake, vigil (frml) **(b)** (establecimiento) funeral parlor*; (sala) chapel of rest

velero *m* **(a)** (Náut) (grande) sailing ship; (pequeño) sailboat (AmE), sailing boat (BrE) **(b)** (Aviac) glider

veleta *f* **1** (para el viento) weather vane, weathercock **2** **veleta** *mf* (fam) (persona inconstante) fickle person

vello *m* **1** (pelusa) down; (en las piernas, etc) hair **2** (Bot) bloom

velo *m* veil

velocidad *f* **1** (en general) speed; **cobrar ~** to pick up *o* gather speed; **¿a qué ~ iba?** how fast was he going?; **disminuir la ~** to slow down; **a toda ~** at top speed; **la ~ con que lo hizo** the speed with which he did it **2** (Auto, Mec) gear; **un modelo de cinco ~es** a five-gear model

velocímetro *m* speedometer

velódromo *m* cycle track, velodrome

veloz *adj* ‹corredor› fast; ‹movimiento› swift, quick

ven ▶ VENIR, VER²

vena *f* **1** (Anat) vein; **cortarse las ~s** to slash *o* cut one's wrists **2** (Geol, Min) vein, seam **3** (de madera) grain; (de piedra) vein, stripe

venado *m* **(a)** (Zool) deer; **pintar ~** (Méx fam) to play hooky (esp AmE colloq), skive off (school) (BrE colloq) **(b)** (Coc) venison

vencedor -dora *adj* ‹ejército/país› victorious; ‹equipo/jugador› winning (*before n*)

■ *m,f* (en guerra) victor; (en competición) winner

vencer [E2] *vt* **(a)** ‹enemigo› to defeat, vanquish (liter); ‹rival/competidor› to defeat, beat; **no te dejes ~** don't give in **(b)** ‹miedo/pesimismo/obstáculo› to overcome **(c)** (dominar): **me venció el sueño** I was overcome by sleep

■ **~** *vi* **1** ‹ejército/equipo› to win, be victorious; **¡~emos!** we shall overcome! **2** **(a)** «pasaporte/garantía» to expire; **el lunes vence el plazo** Monday is the deadline **(b)** «letra» to be due for payment

■ **vencerse** *v pron* (AmL) «pasaporte/garantía» to expire; **se me venció el carnet** my card expired *o* ran out

vencido -da *adj* **1** ‹ejército/país› defeated, vanquished (liter); ‹equipo/jugador› losing (*before n*), ⋯◈

V

beaten; **darse por** ~ to give up o in **2** **(a)** ⟨visa/
pasaporte⟩ expired, out-of-date (before n); **estos
antibióticos están** ~**s** (AmE) these antibiotics are
past their expiration (AmE) o (BrE) expiry date **(b)**
⟨boleto/cheque⟩ out-of-date (before n) **(c)** ⟨letra/
intereses⟩ due for payment
■ m,f: **los** ~**s** the defeated, the vanquished (liter)
vencimiento m (de letra, pago) due date; (de
carnet, licencia) expiration (AmE) o (BrE) expiry date
venda f bandage; ~ **elástica** elastic bandage
vendaje m dressing; **poner un** ~ to put on a
dressing
vendar [A1] vt to bandage
vendaval m gale, strong wind
vendedor -dora m,f **(a)** (en mercado)
stallholder, stallkeeper (AmE); (en tienda)
salesclerk (AmE), shop assistant (BrE); (viajante,
representante) sales representative; ~ **a domicilio**
door-to-door sales agent; ~ **ambulante** peddler,
hawker; ~ **de periódicos** newspaper vendor o
seller **(b)** (Der) (propietario que vende) vendor
vender [E1] vt ⟨mercancías/casa⟩ to sell; **le
vendí el reloj** I sold him the watch; **vendió la casa
muy bien** she got a very good price for her house;
🄢 **se vende** for sale; **lo venden a $500 el kilo** they
sell it at $500 a kilo; **vendí el cuadro en** or **por
$20.000** I sold the painting for $20,000; **se vende
por kilo(s)/unidades** it's sold by the kilo/unit
■ ~ vi «producto» to sell
■ **venderse** v pron (dejarse sobornar) to sell out
vendimia f grape harvest, wine harvest
vendimiar [A1] vt to pick, harvest
vendré, vendría, etc ▶ VENIR
venduta f (Col) public sale (of household goods)
Venecia f Venice
veneno m **(a)** (sustancia tóxica) poison; (de culebra)
venom **(b)** (malevolencia) venom
venenoso -sa adj ⟨sustancia/planta⟩
poisonous; ⟨araña/serpiente⟩ poisonous,
venomous; ⟨palabras/mirada⟩ venomous
venerable adj/m,f venerable
venerar [A1] vt (adorar) to revere, worship;
(Relig) to venerate
venéreo -rea adj venereal
venezolanismo m Venezuelan word (o
phrase etc), Venezuelanism
venezolano -na adj/m,f Venezuelan
Venezuela f Venezuela
venga interj (Esp fam) **(a)** (para animar) come on
(b) (expresando insistencia): **y** ~ **a protestar** and they
just kept o went on (and on) complaining
vengáis, vengamos, etc ▶ VENIR
venganza f revenge, vengeance (liter)
vengar [A3] vt ⟨insulto/derrota⟩ to take revenge
for, to avenge; ⟨persona⟩ to avenge
■ **vengarse** v pron to take revenge; ~**se DE** or
POR algo to take revenge FOR sth; ~**se DE/EN algn**
to take (one's) revenge ON sb
vengativo -va adj vindictive, vengeful (liter)
vengo ▶ VENIR

venia f (AmS) (inclinación de cabeza) bow
venial adj venial
venida f **(a)** (llegada) arrival **(b)** (AmL) (vuelta): **a
la** or **de** ~ on the way back
venidero -ra adj future (before n)
venir [I31] vi **1** **(a)** (a un lugar) to come; **vine en
tren** I came by train; **¿a qué vino?** what did he
come by o around for?; **vine dormida todo el
tiempo** I slept (for) the whole journey; ~ **POR** or
(Esp) **A POR algn/algo** to come FOR sb/sth, come to
pick sb/sth up; **la vino a buscar su madre** her
mother came to pick her up; **ven a ver esto** come
and see this **(b)** (volver) to come back; **ahora
vengo** I'll be back in a moment; **no vengas tarde**
don't be late home o back **(c)** (salir): **me vino con
un cuento** he came up with some excuse; **no me
vengas con exigencias** don't start making
demands
2 **(a)** (tener lugar): **ahora viene esa escena que te
conté** that scene I told you about is coming up
now; **¿qué viene después de las noticias?** what's
on after the news?; **ya vendrán tiempos mejores**
things will get better **(b)** (indicando procedencia) ~
DE algo to come FROM sth; **viene de la India** it
comes from India; **le viene de familia** it runs in
his family; **¿a qué viene eso?** why do you say
that? **(c)** (indicando presentación) to come; **viene en
tres tamaños** it comes in three sizes **(d)** (estar
incluido): **viene en primera página** it's on the front
page; **no viene nada sobre la huelga** there's
nothing about the strike
3 (convenir): **estas cajas me vendrían muy bien**
these boxes would come in handy; **el jueves no
me viene bien** Thursday's no good for me; **me
vendría bien un descanso** I could do with a rest
4 (como aux): **esto viene a confirmar mis
sospechas** this confirms my suspicions; **hace
mucho que lo venía diciendo** I'd been saying so
all along
■ **venirse** v pron (enf) **(a)** (a un lugar) to come; **se
vinieron a pie** they came on foot; ~**se abajo**
«persona» to go to pieces; «techo» to fall in,
collapse; «estante» to collapse; «ilusiones» to go
up in smoke; «proyectos» to fall through **(b)**
(volver) to come back
venta f (Com) sale; ~ **al contado** cash sale; ~ **al
por mayor/menor** wholesale/retail; ~ **a plazos**
installment plan (AmE), hire purchase (BrE); ~
por catálogo or **correo** mail order; **pronto saldrá a
la** ~ it will be on sale soon; **estar en** or **a la** ~
«coche/bicicleta» to be for sale; «casa» to be
(up) for sale
ventaja f **(a)** (beneficio) advantage; **tiene la** ~ **de
que está cerca** it has the advantage of being
near; **tienes** ~ **por tu experiencia** you have an
advantage because of your experience **(b)** (en
carrera): **lleva una** ~ **de diez segundos** she has a
ten-second lead; **jugar con** ~ to be at an
advantage
ventajero -ra m,f (RPl) opportunist
ventajoso -sa adj **(a)** ⟨negocio⟩ profitable;
⟨acuerdo/situación⟩ favorable*, advantageous **(b)**
(Col) ⟨persona⟩ opportunistic

ventana *f* [1] (Arquit, Const, Inf) window; ~ emergente pop-up [2] (de la nariz) nostril

ventanilla *f* **(a)** (de coche, tren) window **(b)** (en oficinas) window; (en cines, teatros) box office; **horario de** ~ opening hours **(c)** (Inf) window

ventilación *f* **(a)** (posibilidad de ventilarse) ventilation **(b)** (acción de ventilar) airing

ventilador *m* (aparato) fan; (abertura) ventilator, air vent

ventilar [A1] *vt* ⟨*habitación*⟩ to air, ventilate; ⟨*ropa/colchón*⟩ to air

■ **ventilarse** *v pron* [1] «*habitación/ropa*» to air [2] (fam) (tomar el aire) to get a breath of fresh air, get some air

ventisca *f* snowstorm; (con más viento) blizzard

ventolera *f* gust of wind

ventosa *f* **(a)** (de goma, plástico) suction pad **(b)** (Zool) sucker

ventosidad *f* wind, flatulence

ventoso -sa *adj* windy

ventrículo *m* ventricle

ventrílocuo -cua *m,f* ventriloquist

ventura *f* [1] (liter) (suerte) fortune; **tiene la** ~ **de** ... he has the good fortune to ...; **echarle la buena** ~ **a algn** to tell sb's fortune [2] (*en locs*) **a la ventura: viven a la** ~ they take each day as it comes; **salieron a la** ~ they set out with no fixed plan

Venus *m* (Astron) Venus
■ *f* (Art, Mit) Venus

veo ▶ VER 2

ver¹ *m* [1] (aspecto): **ser de buen** ~ to be good-looking *o* attractive [2] (opinión): **a mi/su** ~ in my/his view

ver² [E29] *vt* [1] **(a)** (percibir con la vista) to see; **¿ves algo?** can you see anything?; **no se ve nada aquí** you can't see a thing in here; **lo vi hablando con ella** I saw him talking to her **(b)** (mirar) ⟨*programa/partido*⟩ to watch; ~ **(la) televisión** to watch television; **esa película ya la he visto** I've seen that movie before; *no poder (ni)* ~ **a algn**: **no la puede** ~ he can't stand her [2] (entender, notar) to see; **¿no ves lo que está pasando?** don't *o* can't you see what's happening?; **se la ve preocupada** she looks worried; *hacerse* ~ (RPl) to show off [3] **(a)** (constatar, comprobar) to see; **ve a** ~ **quién es** go and see who it is; **¡ya ~ás lo que pasa!** you'll see what happens; **¡ya se ~á!** we'll see **(b)** (ser testigo de) to see; **¡nunca he visto cosa igual!** I've never seen anything like it!; **¡si vieras lo mal que lo pasé!** you can't imagine how awful it was!; **¡hubieras visto cómo se asustaron!** (AmL) you should have seen the fright they got! [4] **a ver:** (vamos) **a** ~ **¿de qué se trata?** OK *o* all right, now, what's the problem?; **está aquí, en el periódico — ¿a** ~**?** it's here in the newspaper — let's see; **apriétalo a** ~ **qué pasa** press it and see what happens; **a** ~ **si escribes pronto** make sure you write soon [5] **(a)** (estudiar): **esto mejor que lo veas tú** you'd better have a look at this; **tengo que** ~ **cómo lo arreglo** I have to work out how I can fix it; **ya ~é qué hago** I'll decide what to do later **(b)** «*médico*» (examinar) to see; **¿la ha visto un médico?** has she been seen by a doctor yet? [6] **(a)** (juzgar, considerar): **yo eso no lo veo bien** I

don't think that's right; **a mi modo** *or* **manera de** ~ the way I see it **(b)** (encontrar) to see; **no le veo salida a esto** I can't see any way out of this; **no le veo la gracia** I don't think it's funny

[7] (visitar, entrevistarse con) ⟨*amigo/pariente*⟩ to see, visit; ⟨*médico/jefe*⟩ to see; **¡cuánto tiempo sin ~te!** I haven't seen you for ages!

[8] **tener ... que ver: ¿y eso qué tiene que** ~**?** and what does that have to do with it?; **no tengo nada que** ~ **con él** I have nothing to do with him; **¿qué tiene que** ~ **que sea sábado?** what difference does it make that it's Saturday?

■ ~ *vi* [1] (percibir con la vista) to see; **así no veo** I can't see like this; **no veo bien de lejos/de cerca** I'm shortsighted/longsighted [2] (constatar): **¿hay cerveza? — no sé, voy a** ~ is there any beer? — I don't know, I'll have a look; **pues ~ás, todo empezó cuando ...** well you see, the whole thing began when ... [3] (pensar) to see; **ya ~é** I'll see; *estar/seguir en* ~*emos* (AmL fam): **todavía está en ~emos** it isn't certain yet; **seguimos en ~emos** we still don't know anything

■ **verse** *v pron* [1] (*refl*) (percibirse, imaginarse) to see oneself [2] (hallarse) (+ *compl*) to find oneself; **me vi en un aprieto** I found myself in a tight spot; **me vi obligado a despedirlo** I had no choice but to dismiss him [3] (esp AmL) (parecer): **se ve bien con esa falda** she looks good in that skirt; **no se ve bien con ese peinado** that hairdo doesn't suit her [4] (*recípr*) **(a)** (encontrarse) to meet; **nos vemos a las siete** I'll meet *o* see you at seven; **¡nos vemos!** (esp AmL) see you! **(b)** (visitarse, encontrarse) to see each other; **nos vemos a menudo** we see each other often; ~**se con algn** to see sb

veraneante *mf* vacationer (AmE), holidaymaker (BrE)

veranear [A1] *vi*: **solía** ~ **en un pueblo** she used to spend her summer vacation (AmE) *o* (BrE) holidays in a small town

veraneo *m*: **fuimos de** ~ **al campo** we spent our summer vacation (AmE) *o* (BrE) holidays in the country; **lugar de** ~ summer resort

veraniego -ga *adj* summer (*before n*)

verano *m* summer; (en la zona tropical) dry season; **ropa de** ~ summer clothes

veras: de veras (*loc adv*) really; **lo siento de** ~ I really am sorry; **¡no lo dirás de** ~**!** you can't be serious!

verbal *adj* verbal

verbena *f* [1] (Bot) verbena [2] (fiesta popular) festival; (baile) open-air dance

verbo *m* (Ling) verb

verdad *f* **(a)** (en general) truth; **dime la** ~ tell me the truth; **es la pura** ~ it's the gospel truth; **a decir** ~ ... to tell you the truth ...; **la** ~**, no lo sé** I don't honestly know; **¡no es** ~**!** that's not true!; **eso es una gran** ~ that is so true! **(b)** (de verdad) (*loc adv*) really; (*loc adj*) real; **¡de** ~ **que me gusta!** I really do like it!; **una pistola de** ~ a real gun **(c)** (buscando corroboración): **es guapa ¿**~**?** she's beautiful, isn't she?; **¿**~ **que tú me entiendes?** you understand me, don't you?

verdadero -ra *adj* [1] **(a)** ⟨*premisa/historia*⟩ true; ⟨*caso/nombre*⟩ real **(b)** ⟨*pieles/joyas*⟩ real

2 (*delante del n*) (uso enfático) real; **se portó como un ~ imbécil** he behaved like a real o (colloq) proper idiot

verde *adj* **1** ‹*color/ojos/vestido*› green; **zapatos ~ oliva** olive-green shoes; **ojos ~ azulado** bluish o (BrE) bluey green eyes **2** ‹*fruta*› green, unripe; ‹*leña*› green; **estar ~** (fam) (no tener experiencia) to be green (colloq); (en una asignatura): **está ~ en historia** he doesn't know much about history (colloq) **3** (Pol) Green **4** (fam) ‹*chiste*› dirty, blue (colloq)
■ *m* (color) green; (Bot) greenery
■ *mf* (Pol) Green; **los ~s** the Greens

verdín *m* **(a)** (musgo) moss **(b)** (moho) mold*; (en el agua) slime; (en metal) verdigris

verdor *m* greenness

verdoso -sa *adj* greenish

verdugo *m* **1** **(a)** (en ejecuciones) executioner; (en la horca) hangman **(b)** (persona cruel) tyrant **2** (Indum) balaclava; (para el esquí) ski mask

verdulería *f* fruit and vegetable store, greengrocer's (BrE)

verdulero -ra *m,f* (persona) greengrocer

verdura *f* (Bot, Coc) vegetable; **sopa de ~(s)** vegetable soup

vereda *f* **(a)** (senda) path **(b)** (CS, Per) (acera) sidewalk (AmE), pavement (BrE) **(c)** (Col) (distrito) district

veredicto *m* (Der) verdict; (dictamen) opinion, verdict

vergonzoso -sa *adj* **1** (tímido) shy, bashful **2** ‹*asunto/comportamiento*› disgraceful, shameful

vergüenza *f* **1** (turbación) embarrassment; **no lo hagas pasar ~** don't embarrass him; **me da ~ pedírselo otra vez** I'm embarrassed to ask him again; **sentí ~ ajena** I felt embarrassed for him (o her *etc*) **2** (sentido del decoro) (sense of) shame; **no tiene ~** he has no (sense of) shame **3** (escándalo, motivo de oprobio) disgrace; **ser una ~ para algo/algn** to be a disgrace to sth/sb; **estos precios son una ~** these prices are outrageous

verídico -ca *adj* true

verificar [A2] *vt* ‹*hechos*› to establish, verify; ‹*resultado*› to check; ‹*pagos/cuentas*› to check, audit; ‹*máquina/instrumento*› to check, test

verja *f* (cerca) railings (*pl*); (puerta) wrought-iron gate; (de ventana) (wrought-iron) grille

vermut /ber'mu(t)/ *m* (*pl* **-muts**) vermouth
■ *f* (CS) early evening performance

verosímil *adj* ‹*excusa/versión*› plausible; ‹*argumento/historia*› realistic

verruga *f* **(a)** (Med) (en la mano, cara) wart; (en los pies) verruca **(b)** (Bot) wart

versículo *m* verse

versión *f* **(a)** (de obra, suceso) version; **~ original** *movie in its original language* **(b)** (traducción) translation **(c)** (modelo) model

verso *m* (Lit) (línea) line, verse; (poema) poem; (género) verse; **en ~** in verse

vértebra *f* vertebra

vertebrado¹ -da *adj* vertebrate

vertebrado² *m* vertebrate; **los ~s** the vertebrates

vertedero *m* **1** (para basura) dump; **un ~ de residuos nucleares** a dumping site for nuclear waste **2** (desagüe) outlet

verter [E31] *or* [E8] *vt* **(a)** (en un recipiente) ‹*agua/vino/trigo*› to pour **(b)** (derramar) ‹*líquido*› to spill; ‹*lágrimas/sangre*› (liter) to shed (liter) **(c)** ‹*residuos radiactivos*› to dump

vertical *adj* **1** **(a)** ‹*línea/madero*› vertical; **en posición ~** in a vertical position **(b)** (en crucigramas): **el tres ~** three down **2** (Pol, Rels Labs) vertical
■ *f* **(a)** (Mat, Tec) vertical line, vertical (tech) **(b)** (Dep) handstand

vértice *m* (de ángulo, figura) vertex, apex; (coronilla) crown

vertiente *f* **(a)** (de montaña, tejado) slope **(b)** (faceta, aspecto) aspect **(c)** (CS) (manantial) spring

vertiginoso -sa *adj* ‹*velocidad*› dizzy, giddy, vertiginous (frml)

vértigo *m* vertigo; **tener ~** to have vertigo; **me produce ~** it makes me dizzy o giddy

ves ► VER²

vesícula *f* vesicle; **~ biliar** gallbladder

vespa® *f* Vespa®, scooter

vespertino -na *adj* evening (*before n*); **diario ~** evening newspaper

vespino® *m* moped

vestíbulo *m* (de casa particular) hall; (de edificio público) lobby; (de teatro, cine) foyer

vestido¹ -da *adj* dressed; **bien ~** well/badly dressed; **¿cómo iba ~?** what was he wearing?; **iba vestida de azul** she was wearing blue; **~ de uniforme** in uniform; **¿de qué vas a ir ~?** what are you going to go as?

vestido² *m* **(a)** (de mujer) dress; **~ de baño** (Col) swimsuit; **~ de noche** evening dress; **~ de novia** wedding dress o gown **(b)** (Col) (de hombre) suit

vestidor *m* (en casa) dressing room; (en club, gimnasio) (Chi, Méx) locker room (AmE), changing room (BrE)

vestier *m* (Col) (en tienda) fitting room; (en club, gimnasio) locker room (AmE), changing room (BrE)

vestigio *m* trace; **no quedan ~s de aquella civilización** no trace remains of that civilization; **~s históricos** historical remains

vestir [I14] *vt* **1** **(a)** ‹*niño/muñeca*› to dress **(b)** (proporcionar ropa a) to clothe (frml) **(c)** (confeccionar ropa a) «*modisto*» to dress **2** (liter o period) (llevar puesto) to wear
■ **~** *vi* **1** «*persona*» to dress; **~ bien** to dress well; **~ DE algo** ‹*de uniforme/azul*› to wear sth; **~ de etiqueta** to wear formal dress **2** (ser elegante): **no sabe ~** he has no dress sense; **de ~** ‹*traje/zapatos*› smart
■ **vestirse** *v pron* (*refl*) **(a)** (ponerse ropa) to dress, get dressed; **date prisa, vístete** hurry up, get dressed **(b)** (de cierta manera): **se viste mal** he dresses badly; **se viste a la última moda** she wears the latest styles; **siempre se viste de verde** she always wears green **(c)** (disfrazarse) **~se DE algo** to dress up as sth

vestón *m* (CS) jacket

vestuario *m* **1** (conjunto de ropa) wardrobe; (Cin, Teatr) wardrobe **2** (en club, gimnasio) locker room (AmE), changing room (BrE)

veta *f* [1] (a) (en madera) streak (b) (en la carne) streak (c) (en roca, mármol) vein [2] (inclinación) bent, leanings (*pl*)

vetar [A1] *vt* to veto

veteranía *f* (experiencia) experience; (antigüedad) seniority

veterano -na *adj/m,f* veteran

veterinaria *f* (ciencia) veterinary science *o* medicine; (clínica) veterinary surgery

veterinario -ria *adj* ‹clínica› veterinary (*before n*); **médico ~** vet, veterinarian (AmE), veterinary surgeon (BrE)
■ *m,f* vet, veterinarian (AmE), veterinary surgeon (BrE)

veto *m* veto; **poner el ~ a algo** to veto sth

vez *f* [1] (ocasión) time; **una ~/dos veces** once/twice; **una ~ por semana** once a week; **me acuerdo de una/aquella ~ cuando ...** I remember once/that time when ...; **la última ~ que lo vi** the last time I saw him; **mil veces** *or* **miles de veces** a thousand times, thousands of times; **algunas veces** sometimes; **¿te has arrepentido alguna ~?** have you ever regretted it?; **érase una ~** (liter) once upon a time (liter); **por primera ~** for the first time; **otra ~** again; **déjalo para otra ~** leave it for another time *o* day; **otra ~ será** maybe next time; **una ~ más** once again
[2] (*en locs*) **a la vez** at the same time; **a veces** sometimes; **cada vez** every *o* each time; **cada ~ más** more and more; **lo encuentro cada ~ más viejo** he looks older every time I see him; **cada ~ menos** less and less; **de una vez** (expresando impaciencia) once and for all; (simultáneamente) in one go; **de vez en cuando** from time to time, every now and then; **en vez de** instead of; **rara vez** seldom, hardly ever; **una vez** once; **una ~ que hayas terminado** once *o* when you have finished
[3] (Esp) (turno en una cola): **¿quién tiene** *or* **me da la ~?** who's last?; **pedir la ~** to ask who's last

vi ▶ VER²

vía *f* [1] (a) (ruta, camino): **la ~ rápida** the fast route; **una ~ al diálogo** a channel *o* an avenue for dialogue; **¡dejen ~ libre!** clear the way!; **~ de comunicación** road (*o* rail *etc*) link; **V~ Láctea** Milky Way; **~ marítima** sea route, seaway (b) (medio de transporte): **por ~ aérea/marítima/terrestre** by air/by sea/by land; **◉ vía aérea** airmail (c) (medio, procedimiento) channels (*pl*); **por la ~ diplomática/política** through diplomatic/political channels
[2] **en vías de: está en ~s de solucionarse** it's in the process of being resolved; **países en ~s de desarrollo** developing countries; **una especie en ~s de extinción** an endangered species
[3] (Ferr) track; **saldrá por la ~ dos** it will depart from track (AmE) *o* (BrE) platform two
[4] (Anat, Med): **por ~ oral/venosa** orally/intravenously; **~s respiratorias/urinarias** respiratory/urinary tract
■ *prep* via; **~ Miami** via Miami

viable *adj* ‹proyecto/plan› viable, feasible; ‹bebé› viable

viaducto *m* viaduct

viajante *mf* traveling* salesman/saleswoman

viajar [A1] *vi* to travel; **~ en avión** to travel by plane; **~ en primera clase** to travel *o* go first class

viaje *m* trip, journey; **hacer un ~** to go on a trip *o* journey; **un ~ en tren** a train journey; **hizo el ~ en coche** he drove; **estar de ~** to be away; **salir de ~** to go on a trip; **en el ~ de vuelta** on the way back; **¡buen ~!** have a good trip!; **hicimos un ~ por todo Chile** we traveled all around Chile; **~ de negocios** business trip; **~ de novios** honeymoon; **~ organizado** package tour; **hice varios ~s para llevarlas todas** I made several trips to take them all

viajero -ra *m,f* traveler*; (pasajero) passenger

vial *adj* road (*before n*)

viáticos *mpl* (esp AmL) travel allowance

víbora *f* (a) (Zool) viper; **~ de cascabel** (Méx) rattlesnake (b) (fam & pey) (persona): **es una ~** he has a vicious tongue

vibración *f* vibration

vibrante *adj* ‹voz› vibrant, resonant; ‹discurso› vibrant

vibrar [A1] *vi* «cuerdas/cristales» to vibrate

vicaría *f* vicariate

vicario -ria *m,f* (párroco) vicar

vicecampeón -peona *m,f* runner-up

vicepresidencia *f* (Gob, Pol) vice presidency; (de empresa) vice presidency (AmE), deputy chairmanship (BrE)

vicepresidente -ta *m,f*, **vicepresidente** *mf* (Gob, Pol) vice president; (de empresa) vice president (AmE), deputy chairman/chairwoman (BrE)

vice versa *adv* vice versa

vichar [A1] *vi* (RPl fam) to peep (colloq)
■ **~** *vt* to peep at

viciado -da *adj* [1] ‹atmósfera› stuffy; **aquí dentro el aire está ~** it's very stuffy in here
[2] ‹estilo/dicción› marred

viciar [A1] *vt* ‹persona› to get ... into a bad habit; ‹estilo/lenguaje› to mar
■ **viciarse** *v pron* (a) «persona»: **~se con algo** to become addicted to sth (b) «estilo/lenguaje» to deteriorate

vicio *m* [1] (corrupción) vice; **darse al ~** to give oneself over to vice [2] (hábito): **el único ~ que tengo** my only vice *o* bad habit; **el juego se convirtió en ~ para él** his gambling became an addiction; **se queja de ~** (fam) she complains for the sake of it

vicioso -sa *adj* ‹persona› depraved, debauched
■ *m,f* dissolute person

víctima *f* victim; **~ DE algo** victim OF sth; **fue ~ de una emboscada** he was the victim of an ambush; **~s del cáncer** cancer victims

victoria *f* victory; (Dep) win; **no cantes ~ antes de tiempo** don't count your chickens before they're hatched

victorioso -sa *adj* victorious

vicuña *f* vicuna

vid *f* vine

vida *f* [1] (a) (Biol) life; **la ~ marina** marine life; **una cuestión de ~ o muerte** a matter of life and death; **quitarse la ~** to take one's (own) life (frml); **salir con ~** to escape alive (b) (viveza, vitalidad) life; **lleno de ~** full of life; **le falta ~** it's/she's/he's not very lively
[2] (extensión de tiempo, existencia) life; **a lo largo de su ~** throughout his life; **toda una ~** a lifetime; ⋯

la ~ **de un coche** the life-span of a car; **un amigo
de toda la** ~ a lifelong friend; *amargarle la* ~ *a
algn* to make sb's life a misery; *complicarse la* ~
to make life difficult for oneself; *de por* ~ for
life; *hacerle la* ~ *imposible a algn* to make sb's
life impossible
3 (manera de vivir, actividades) life; **lleva una** ~ **muy
ajetreada** she leads a very busy life; **¿qué es de
tu** ~? what have you been up to?; **hace** *or* **vive
su** ~ he lives his own life; **¡esto sí que es** ~**!** this
is the life!; **¡(así) es la** ~**!** that's life, such is life;
~ **privada** private life; **su** ~ **sentimental** his love
life; **una mujer de** ~ **alegre** a woman of easy
virtue; **¡qué** ~ **de perros!** it's a dog's life; **hacer**
~ **social** to socialize; *estar encantado de la* ~ to
be thrilled, to be over the moon (colloq)
4 (necesidades materiales): **la** ~ **está carísima** the
cost of living is very high; **ganarse la** ~ to earn
one's *o* a living; **tiene la** ~ **resuelta** he's set up for
life
5 (como apelativo) darling; **¡mi** ~**!** (my) darling!

vidente *mf* (que ve) sighted person; (que adivina)
clairvoyant

video, (Esp) **vídeo** *m* **(a)** (medio, sistema) video;
en ~ on video **(b)** (cinta) videocassette, videotape,
video (colloq); (grabación) video **(c)** (aparato) video
(cassette recorder), VCR

videocámara *f* video camera, camcorder

videoclip *m* video

videoclub *m* (*pl* **-clubs** *or* **-clubes**)
videoclub

videodisco *m* video disk

videojuego *m* video game

videoteca *f* video library

videotex *m* videotex(t), teletext

vidriado -da *adj* glazed

vidriera *f* **(a)** (puerta) glazed door; (ventana)
window; (en iglesia) *tb* ~ **de colores** stained glass
window **(b)** (AmL) (escaparate) shop window; **mirar**
~**s** to window-shop

vidrierista *mf* (AmL) window dresser

vidriero *m* glazier

vidrio *m* **(a)** (material) glass; **una botella de** ~ a
glass bottle; **fábrica de** ~ glassworks **(b)** (esp
AmL) (objeto): **limpiar los** ~**s** to clean the windows;
cambié uno de los ~**s** I replaced one of the panes
o windowpanes; **me corté con un** ~ I cut myself
on a piece of glass; **hay** ~**s rotos en la calle** there
is broken glass in the street; *pagar los* ~*s rotos*
to take the responsibility *o* the blame **(c)** (de reloj)
crystal, glass

vieira *f* (molusco) scallop; (concha) scallop shell

vieja *f* (Col, Méx, Ven fam) (mujer) broad (AmE sl),
bird (BrE sl); *ver tb* VIEJO *m,f*

viejo -ja *adj* **1** [SER] ⟨persona/animal⟩ old;
⟨coche/ropa/casa⟩ old; **hacerse** ~ to get old
2 (a) [ESTAR] ⟨persona/animal⟩ (envejecido) old;
ya está ~ he's old (ten) old; **¡qué vieja estoy!** I
look so old! **(b)** [ESTAR] ⟨zapatos/pantalones⟩
(desgastado) old

3 ⟨delante del n⟩ (antiguo) ⟨costumbre/amigo⟩ old;
los ~**s tiempos** the old days; **V**~ **Testamento** Old
Testament
■ *m,f* **1** (*m*) old man; (*f*) old woman; **los** ~**s** old
people, the elderly; **llegar a** ~ to reach old age;
se casó de ~ he was an old man when he got
married; **se murió de** ~ he died of old age; **V**~
Pascuero (Chi) ▶ PAPÁ NOEL; ~ **verde** *or* (Méx) ~
rabo verde (fam) dirty old man
2 (fam) (refiriéndose a los padres): **mi** ~/**mi vieja** my
old man/lady (colloq); **tus** ~**s** your folks, your
Mom and Dad
3 (AmL) (hablándole a un niño, al cónyuge etc) darling
(colloq), love (colloq); (a un amigo) buddy (AmE),
mate (BrE)
4 (Méx fam) (esposo) (*m*) old man (colloq); (*f*) old
woman *o* lady (colloq)

Viena *f* Vienna

viendo ▶ VER²

viene, vienes, etc ▶ VENIR

vienés -nesa *adj/m,f* Viennese

viento *m* **1** (en general) wind; **correr** *or* **hacer** ~
to be windy; **un** ~ **helado** an icy wind; ~ **en
contra/a favor** *or* **de cola** head/tail wind;
instrumento de ~ wind instrument **2** (de tienda
de campaña) guy (rope)

vientre *m* **(a)** (cavidad) abdomen; **el bajo** ~ the
lower abdomen; **hacer de** ~ to have a bowel
movement **(b)** (región exterior) stomach, belly
(colloq) **(c)** (de mujer embarazada) womb, belly
(colloq)

viera, vieras, etc ▶ VER²

viernes *m* (*pl* ~) Friday; **V**~ **Santo** Good
Friday; *para ejemplos ver* LUNES

viese, vieses, etc ▶ VER²

viga *f* (de madera) joist, beam; (de metal) beam,
girder

vigencia *f* validity; **entrar en** ~ ⟨«ley»⟩ to come
into force *o* effect

vigente *adj* ⟨pasaporte/contrato⟩ valid;
⟨legislación/precio⟩ current (*before n*); **estar** ~
⟨«ley»⟩ to be in force

vigésimo -ma *adj/pron* twentieth; ~ **primero**
twenty-first; **el** ~ **aniversario** the twentieth
anniversary; **la vigésima parte** a twentieth

vigía *mf* (persona) lookout

vigilancia *f* (atención, cuidado) vigilance; (por
guardias, la policía) surveillance; **estar bajo** ~ to be
under surveillance; **servicio de** ~ security patrol

vigilante *adj* vigilant, on the alert; **en actitud**
~ on the alert
■ *mf* (en tienda) store detective; (en banco, edificio
público) security guard; ~ **jurado/nocturno**
security guard/night watchman

vigilar [A1] *vt* **(a)** (cuidar, atender) to watch, keep
an eye on **(b)** ⟨preso/local⟩ to guard, keep watch
on; ⟨frontera/zona⟩ to guard, patrol; ⟨examen⟩ to
proctor (AmE), to invigilate at (BrE) **(c)** (fam)
(espiar) to watch
■ ~ *vi* to keep watch

AmC	Central America	Arg	Argentina	Cu	Cuba	Per	Peru
AmL	Latin America	Bol	Bolivia	Ec	Ecuador	RPI	River Plate Area
AmS	South America	Chi	Chile	Esp	Spain	Ur	Uruguay
Andes	Andean Region	CS	Southern Cone	Méx	Mexico	Ven	Venezuela

vigilia f [1] (vela) wakefulness; **de** ~ awake [2] (Relig) (víspera) vigil; (abstinencia) abstinence; (tiempo de abstinencia) day/period of abstinence

vigor m (a) (fuerza, energía) vigor*, energy; **con** ~ vigorously (b) **en vigor** ⟨estar⟩ in force; **entrar en** ~ to come into effect o force

vigoroso -sa adj ⟨persona/movimiento⟩ vigorous, energetic; ⟨esfuerzo⟩ strenuous

VIH m (= **virus de inmunodeficiencia humana**) HIV

vil adj (liter) ⟨acto/persona⟩ vile, despicable

villa f [1] (Hist) (población) town; ~ **miseria** (Arg) shantytown [2] (casa) villa

villancico m (Christmas) carol

villano -na m,f (persona ruin) rogue, scoundrel

vilo: en vilo (loc adv): **la levantó en** ~ he lifted her up; **permanecen en** ~ **esperando el resultado** they're on tenterhooks awaiting the result

vinagre m vinegar

vinagrera f (a) (para vinagre) vinegar bottle (b) **vinagreras** fpl (para aceite y vinagre) cruet set o stand

vinagreta f vinaigrette

vinatero -ra adj wine (before n)
■ m,f vintner (AmE), wine merchant (BrE)

vincha f (AmS) (elástica, rígida) hair-band; (hebilla del pelo) barrette (AmE), hair slide (BrE)

vinculación f (relación) links (pl), connections (pl); ~ **con** or **a algo/algn** links o connections WITH sth/sb

vincular [A1] vt (a) (conectar, relacionar) ~ **algo/a algn a** or **con algo/algn** to link sth/sb TO o WITH sth/sb; **están vinculados por lazos de amistad** they are linked by bonds o ties of friendship; **grupos estrechamente vinculados** closely linked groups (b) (comprometer) to bind, be binding on

vínculo m (unión, relación) tie, bond; ~**s familiares** family ties

vine ▶ VENIR

vinería f (AmL) wineshop, liquor store (specializing in wines)

vinero -ra adj (Chi, Per) wine (before n)

vinícola adj ⟨industria/producción⟩ wine (before n); ⟨región⟩ wine-producing, wine-growing

vinicultor -tora m,f wine producer, winegrower

viniera, viniese, etc ▶ VENIR

viniste, etc ▶ VENIR

vino m (bebida) wine; ~ **dulce/seco** sweet/dry wine; ~ **blanco/rosado/tinto** white/rosé/red wine; ~ **de la casa** house wine

vino ▶ VENIR

viña f vineyard

viñatero -ra adj (AmL) wine (before n), wine-growing (before n)
■ m,f (AmL) (a) (propietario) winegrower (b) (trabajador) vineyard worker

viñedo m vineyard

viola f (a) (instrumento) viola (b) **viola** mf (persona) viola player, violist (AmE)

violáceo -cea adj purplish

violación f (a) (de persona) rape (b) (de ley, acuerdo, derecho) violation; (de templo) violation

violador -dora m,f (a) (de persona) rapist (b) (de ley, acuerdo) violator

violar [A1] vt (a) ⟨persona⟩ to rape (b) ⟨ley⟩ to violate, break; ⟨tratado/derecho⟩ to violate; ⟨templo⟩ to violate

violencia f violence; **recurrir a la** ~ to resort to violence

violentar [A1] vt (a) (forzar) ⟨cerradura/puerta⟩ to force; ⟨persona⟩ to rape (b) (poner en situación embarazosa) to make ... feel awkward
■ **violentarse** v pron to get embarrassed

violento -ta adj [1] (en general) violent; **utilizar medios** ~**s** to use violent means [2] (incómodo) ⟨situación⟩ embarrassing, awkward; **le resulta** ~ **hablar del tema** she finds it embarrassing to talk about it; **estaba muy** ~ I felt very awkward

violeta f violet
■ m/adj violet

violín (a) m (instrumento) violin (b) **violín** mf (persona) violinist

violinista mf violinist

violón (a) m (instrumento) double bass (b) **violón** mf (persona) double bass player

violonchelista mf cellist

violonchelo m cello, violoncello

viral adj viral

virar [A1] vi (a) (Náut) to tack, go about (b) «vehículo/conductor» to turn; **viró bruscamente** she swerved (c) «política/partido» to veer

virgen adj (a) ⟨persona⟩: **una mujer/un hombre** ~ a virgin; **ser** ~ to be a virgin (b) ⟨cinta⟩ blank; ⟨película⟩ unexposed (c) ⟨selva⟩ virgin
■ f virgin; **la V**~ (Relig) the Virgin

virginidad f virginity

Virgo m (signo) Virgo; **es (de)** ~ she's (a) Virgo, she's a Virgoan
■ mf (pl ~ or **-gos**) (persona) tb **virgo** Virgo, Virgoan

viril adj ⟨cualidades⟩ virile, manly

virilidad f virility

virreinato m viceroyalty

virtual adj (a) (potencial) virtual (b) (tácito) implicit

virtud f (a) (cualidad) virtue (b) (capacidad) power; **con** ~**es curativas** with healing powers

virtuoso -sa adj virtuous
■ m,f virtuoso

viruela f (enfermedad) smallpox; (marca) pockmark

virus m (pl ~) virus

viruta f shaving

visa f, (Esp) **visado** m visa

visar [A1] vt ⟨documento⟩ to endorse; ⟨pasaporte⟩ to visa

visceral adj (a) (Anat) visceral (b) ⟨odio/impresión⟩ visceral, deep; **un sentimiento** ~ a gut feeling

vísceras fpl entrails (pl), viscera (pl)

visconde -desa m,f (m) viscount; (f) viscountess

viscosa f viscose

viscoso -sa adj viscous

visera f (de casco) visor; (de gorra) peak; (de jugador) eyeshade

visibilidad f visibility

visible adj (a) [SER] visible (b) (fam) [ESTAR] (presentable) presentable, decent

V

visillo *m* net curtain, lace curtain

visión *f* **1** **(a)** (vista) vision, sight; **perdió la ~ de un ojo** she lost the sight of one eye **(b)** (aparición) vision; *ver visiones* to be seeing things **2** (enfoque, punto de vista) view; **una ~ romántica de la vida** a romantic view of life; **tener ~ de futuro** to be forward-looking

visionario -ria *adj/m,f* visionary

visir *m* vizier

visita *f* **(a)** (acción) visit; **hacer(le) una ~ (a algn)** to pay (sb) a visit; **ir de ~** to go visiting; **horario de ~** visiting hours *o* times; **~ a domicilio** house call; **~ de cortesía** courtesy call, duty visit; **~ guiada** (AmL) guided tour **(b)** (visitante) visitor; (invitado) guest; **espera una ~ importante** he's expecting an important visitor; **tener ~** to have visitors/guests

visitador social -dora social *m,f* (AmL) social worker

visitante *adj* visiting (*before n*)
■ *mf* visitor

visitar [A1] *vt* **(a)** ⟨persona⟩ to visit, visit with (AmE) **(b)** ⟨lugar⟩ to visit
■ **visitarse** *v pron* (*recípr*) to visit each other

vislumbrar [A1] *vt* (en la distancia) to make out, discern (frml); (entre los árboles, las nubes) to glimpse; **a lo lejos se vislumbraba una iglesia** a church could just be made out in the distance

viso *m* (Indum) petticoat, underskirt

visón *m* mink

visor *m* **(a)** (en cámara) viewfinder; (para diapositivas) slide viewer **(b)** (Arm) sight

víspera *f* **(a)** (día anterior): **la ~** the day before **(b)** (tiempo anterior): **~s de fiesta** days prior to public holidays; **en ~s de un viaje** just before a journey

vista *f* **1** **(a)** (sentido) sight, eyesight; **tener buena ~** to have good eyesight; **ser corto de ~** to be near-sighted; **perdió la ~** he lost his sight; **~ cansada** eyestrain **(b)** (ojos) eyes; **le hace daño a la ~** it hurts his eyes; **lo operaron de la ~** he had an eye operation **2** (mirada): **alzar/bajar la ~** to look up/down **3** (*en locs*) **a la vista**: **ponlo bien a la ~** put it where it can be seen easily; **estar/no estar a la ~** to be within/out of sight; **a la ~ de todos** in full view of everyone; **¿tienes algún proyecto a la ~?** do you have any projects in view?; **a primera** *or* **simple vista** at first sight *o* glance; **con vistas a** with a view to; **en vista de** in view of; **en ~ de que ...** in view of the fact that ...; **¡hasta la vista!** see you!, so long! (colloq); *perder algo/a algn de ~* to lose sight of sth/sb; *perderse de ~* to disappear from view **4** (panorama) view; **con ~ al mar** with a sea view; **~ aérea** aerial view **5** (Der) hearing

vistazo *m* look; **darle** *or* **echarle un ~ a algo** to have a look at sth

viste, visteis ▶ VER2

viste, vistieron, etc ▶ VESTIR

visto¹ -ta *adj* **1** **(a)** (claro, evidente) obvious, clear; **está/estaba ~ que ...** it is/was clear *o* obvious that ... **(b)** (por lo visto) (*loc adv*) apparently **2** [ESTAR] (común, trillado): **un truco que está muy ~** an old trick; **eso ya está muy ~** that's not very original **3** (considerado): **en ciertos**

círculos **eso no está bien ~** in some circles that is not considered correct; **estaba mal ~ que las mujeres fumaran** it was not the done thing *o* it was frowned upon for women to smoke

visto² *m* **(a)** (Esp) check (AmE), tick (BrE) **(b)** **visto bueno** approval; **tiene que dar el ~ bueno** she has to give her approval

visto ▶ VESTIR, VER2

vistoso -sa *adj* bright and colorful*

visual *adj* visual; **campo ~** field of vision

vital *adj* **1** (fundamental) vital; **de ~ importancia** of vital importance **2** **(a)** (Biol, Med) ⟨órgano⟩ vital (*before n*) **(b)** ⟨persona⟩ dynamic, full of life

vitalicio -cia *adj* ⟨miembro/presidente⟩ life (*before n*); **cargo ~** post held for life

vitalidad *f* vitality

vitamina *f* vitamin

viticultor -tora *m,f* vine-grower

viticultura *f* vine-growing

vitorear [A1] *vt* to cheer

vitral *m* stained-glass window

vitrina *f* **(a)** (mueble — en tienda) showcase; (— en casa) glass cabinet, display cabinet **(b)** (AmL) (escaparate) shop window

vitrinear [A1] *vi* (Andes fam) to window-shop

viudez *f* (de mujer) widowhood; (de hombre) widowerhood

viudo -da *adj*: **su madre es** *or* (Esp) **está viuda** her mother is a widow; **(se) quedó ~ a los 40 años** he lost his wife *o* he was widowed when he was 40
■ *m,f* (*m*) widower; (*f*) widow

viva *m*: **dar ~s** to cheer; **fuera se oían ~s** cheering could be heard outside

vivacidad *f* (de persona) liveliness, vivacity; (de ojos) brightness

vivaracho -cha *adj* **(a)** ⟨ojos⟩ sparkling; ⟨niño⟩ lively **(b)** (AmL) (espabilado) crafty

vivaz *adj* ⟨persona⟩ lively, vivacious; ⟨ojos⟩ bright; ⟨imaginación⟩ vivid, lively

vivencia *f* experience

víveres *mpl* provisions (*pl*), supplies (*pl*)

vivero *m* (de plantas) nursery; (de peces) hatchery; (de moluscos) bed

viveza *f* **(a)** (rapidez, agilidad) liveliness; **~ de ingenio** readiness *o* sharpness of wit **(b)** (de recuerdo) vividness; **lo describió con gran ~** she described it very vividly **(c)** (de color) brightness; (de ojos, mirada) liveliness, brightness; (de emoción, deseo) strength, intensity

vividor -dora *m,f* pleasure seeker

vivienda *f*: **el problema de la ~** the housing *o* accommodation problem; **un bloque de ~s** an apartment building, a block of flats (BrE); **la construcción de 50 ~s** the construction of 50 homes *o* (frml) dwellings

vivir [I1] *vi* **1** (en general) to live; **vive solo** he lives alone *o* on his own; **~ para algo/algn** to live for sth/sb; **~ en paz** to live in peace; **la pintura no da para ~** you can't make a living from painting; **el sueldo no le alcanza para ~** his salary isn't enough (for him) to live on; **~ DE algo** ⟨de la caridad⟩ to live ON sth; ⟨del arte/de la pesca⟩ to make a living FROM sth; ▶ *ver tb* RENTA **2** (estar vivo) to be alive

3 (*como interj*): ¡**viva el Rey!** long live the King!; ¡**vivan los novios!** three cheers for the bride and groom!; ¡**viva!** ¡**viva!** hurray!

■ ~ *vt* **(a)** (pasar por): ~ **momentos difíciles** to live in difficult times; **los que vivimos la guerra** those of us who lived through the war **(b)** ⟨*personaje/música*⟩ to live **(c)** ⟨*vida*⟩ to live

vivisección *f* vivisection

vivo -va *adj* **1** **(a)** (con vida) alive; **no quedó nadie** ~ no one was left alive; **en** ~ ⟨*actuación/transmisión*⟩ live **(b)** ⟨*lengua*⟩ living (*before n*) **2** **(a)** ⟨*persona*⟩ (despierto, animado) vivacious, bubbly; ⟨*descripción*⟩ vivid, graphic; ⟨*relato/imaginación*⟩ lively **(b)** ⟨*color*⟩ bright, vivid; ⟨*llama/fuego*⟩ bright; ⟨*ojos/mirada*⟩ lively, bright **(c)** ⟨*sentimiento/deseo*⟩ intense, strong **3** (avispado, astuto) sharp; **no seas tan** ~ don't try to be clever

■ *m,f* (oportunista) sharp *o* smooth operator (colloq); (aprovechado) freeloader

vizconde -desa *m,f* (*m*) viscount; (*f*) viscountess

vocablo *m* (frml) word

vocabulario *m* vocabulary; ¡**qué** ~! what language!

vocación *f* vocation; **tiene** ~ **de músico** he has a vocation for music

vocacional *adj* vocational

vocal *adj* vocal

■ *f* **1** (Ling) vowel **2** **vocal** *mf* (de consejo, tribunal) member

vocalista *mf* vocalist, singer

vocalizar [A4] *vi* to vocalize

voceador *m* (Col, Méx) (de periódicos) newspaper vendor

vocear [A1] *vt* **(a)** ⟨*mercancías*⟩ to cry (dated); ⟨*noticias*⟩ to shout out **(b)** (hacer público) to spread **(c)** (corear) to shout **(d)** (Méx) ⟨*persona*⟩ to shout

vocerío *m* clamor*, shouting

vocero -ra *m, f* (AmL) (*m*) spokesman, spokesperson; (*f*) spokeswoman, spokesperson

vociferar [A1] *vi* to shout, vociferate (frml)

vodevil *m* vaudeville (AmE), variety (BrE)

vodka *m or f* /ˈbo(ð)ka/ vodka

volado -da **(a)** (Méx fam) (con moneda): **te lo juego a un** ~ I'll toss you for it; **echar un** ~ to toss *o* flip a coin **(b)** (RPl, Ven) (en costura) flounce

volador¹ -dora *adj* flying (*before n*)

volador² *m* (en pirotecnia) rocket

volanta *f* (RPl) horse-drawn carriage

volantazo *m* (Esp, Méx) swerve; **dar un** ~ to swerve

volante *m* **1** (Auto) steering wheel; **ir/ponerse al** ~ to be at/to take the wheel **2** **(a)** (AmL) (de propaganda) leaflet, flier **(b)** (Esp) (para el médico) referral note *o* slip **3** (en costura) flounce **4** (Dep) shuttlecock

volantín *m* **1** (Chi) (cometa) kite; **encumbrar un** ~ to fly a kite **2** (Per) (en gimnasia) somersault

volar [A10] *vi* **1** ⟨*pájaro/avión*⟩ to fly **2** **(a)** «*tiempo*» to fly; ¡**cómo vuela el tiempo!** doesn't time fly!; **las malas noticias vuelan** bad news travels fast **(b)** **volando** *ger* ⟨*comer/cambiarse*⟩ in a rush, in a hurry; **se fue volando** he/she rushed off; **sus clases se me pasan volando** her classes seem to go so quickly

3 **(a)** (con el viento) «*sombrero*» to blow off; ~**on todos los papeles** my papers blew all over the place **(b)** (fam) (desaparecer) «*dinero/pasteles*» to vanish, disappear

■ ~ *vt* **1** ⟨*puente/edificio*⟩ to blow up; ⟨*caja fuerte*⟩ to blow **2** (Méx, Ven fam) (robar) to swipe (colloq), to nick (BrE colloq)

■ **volarse** *v pron* **1** **(a)** (Col fam) «*preso*» to escape **(b)** (Col, Méx fam) «*alumno*» to play hooky (esp AmE colloq), to skive off (school) (BrE colloq) **2** **(a)** (Méx fam) (coquetear) to flirt **(b)** (Méx, Ven fam) (robar) to swipe (colloq), nick (BrE colloq)

volcán *m* volcano

volcánico -ca *adj* volcanic

volcar [A9] *vt* **1** **(a)** (tumbar) to knock over **(b)** ⟨*carga*⟩ to tip, dump **(c)** (vaciar) to empty (out) **(d)** (Inf) to dump

■ ~ *vi* «*automóvil/camión*» to overturn, turn over; «*embarcación*» to capsize

■ **volcarse** *v pron* **1** **(a)** «*vaso/botella*» to get knocked *o* tipped over **(b)** ▶ VOLCAR *vi* **2** (entregarse, dedicarse) ~**se A algo** ⟨*a tarea*⟩ to throw oneself INTO sth **3** (desvivirse) ~**se PARA** *or* **POR hacer algo** to go out of one's way to do sth; ~**se CON algn: se** ~**on conmigo** they bent over backwards to make me feel welcome

volea *f* volley

volear [A1] *vt/vi* (Dep) to volley

vóleibol, voleibol *m* volleyball

voleo *m*: **a** *or* **al** ~ (al azar) at random; **contesté al** ~ I said the first thing that came into my head

volibol *m* (Col, Méx, Ven) volleyball

voltaje *m* voltage

volteado -da *adj* (Col, Méx fam & pey) bent (pej), queer (pej)

voltear [A1] *vt* **1** **(a)** ⟨*mies*⟩ to winnow; ⟨*tierra*⟩ to turn (over) **(b)** (por el aire) «*toro*» to toss; «*caballo*» to throw **2** (AmL exc CS) **(a)** ⟨*tortilla/disco*⟩ to turn over; ⟨*cuadro*⟩ to turn ... around; ⟨*copa/jarrón*⟩ (poner — boca arriba) to turn ... the right way up; (— boca abajo) to turn ... upside down **(b)** ⟨*calcetín/manga*⟩ (poner — del revés) to turn ... inside out; (— del derecho) to turn ... the right way round; ~ **la página** to turn the page **3** (AmL exc CS) (dar la vuelta): **me volteó la espalda** she turned her back on me; **al oír su voz volteó la cara** when she heard his voice she turned her head **4** (CS) (tumbar, echar abajo) ⟨*bolos/botella*⟩ to knock over; ⟨*puerta*⟩ to knock down

■ **voltearse** *v pron* (AmL exc CS) (volverse, darse la vuelta) to turn around; (cambiar de ideas) to change one's ideas **(b)** (Méx) «*vehículo*» to overturn, turn over

voltereta *f* somersault

voltio *m* volt

voluble *adj* (inconstante) changeable, fickle

volumen *m* **1** (en general) volume; ~ **de ventas** volume of sales, turnover; **bajar/subir el** ~ to turn the volume down/up; **a todo** ~ on full volume, at full blast **2** (tomo) volume

voluminoso -sa *adj* ⟨*paquete*⟩ sizeable, bulky

voluntad *f* **1** **(a)** (facultad) will **(b)** (deseo) wish; **por expresa** ~ **de los familiares** by express wish of the family; **lo hizo por (su) propia** ~ he ···⟶

did it of his own free will; **manifestó su ~ de renunciar** he expressed his wish to resign; **por causas ajenas a su ~** for reasons beyond his control **2** ‹firmeza de intención› *tb* **fuerza de ~** willpower **3** ‹disposición, intención›: **con la mejor ~** with the best of intentions; **agradezco tu buena ~ I** appreciate your willingness to help; **mostrar buena ~ hacia algn** to show goodwill to *o* toward(s) sb

voluntario -ria *adj* (a) ‹acto/donación› voluntary; **fue una elección voluntaria I**/he did it of my/his own free will (b) (*como adv*) voluntarily

■ *m,f* volunteer

voluptuoso -sa *adj* voluptuous

volver [E11] *vi* **1** (regresar — al lugar donde se está) to come back; (— a otro lugar) to go back; **no sé a qué hora ~é I** don't know what time I'll be back; **¿cómo vas a ~?** how are you getting back?; **ha vuelto con su familia** she's gone back to her family; **~ A algo** ‹a un lugar› to go back TO sth; ‹a una situación/actividad› to return TO sth; **mañana volvemos a clases** tomorrow we go back to school; **quiere ~ al mundo del espectáculo** he wants to return to show business; **volviendo a lo que decía** ... to get *o* go back to what I was saying ...; **¿cuándo volviste de las vacaciones?** when did you get back from your vacation?; **ha vuelto de París** she's back from Paris **2** «calma/paz» to return; **~ A algo** to return TO sth **3** volver en sí to come to *o* round

■ **~ v aux: ~ a empezar** to start again *o* (AmE) over; **no ~á a ocurrir** it won't happen again; **lo tuve que ~ a llevar al taller I** had to take it back to the workshop

■ **~** *vt* **1** (dar la vuelta) (a) ‹colchón/tortilla› to turn (over); ‹tierra› to turn *o* dig over; ‹calcetín/chaqueta› (poner — del revés) to turn ... inside out; (— del derecho) to turn ... the right way round; ‹cuello› to turn; **~ la página** to turn the page (b) ‹cabeza› to turn; **volvió la mirada hacia mí** he turned his gaze toward(s) me (c) ‹esquina› to turn **2** (convertir en, poner): **la ha vuelto muy egoísta** it has made her very selfish; **me está volviendo loca** it's/he's/she's driving me mad **3** (Méx) **~ el estómago** to be sick

■ **volverse** *v pron* **1** (girar) to turn (around); **se volvió hacia él** she turned to face him; **no te vuelvas, que nos están siguiendo** don't look back, we're being followed; **se volvió de espaldas** he turned his back on me (*o* her *etc*); **~se boca arriba/abajo** to turn over onto one's back/stomach **2** (convertirse en, ponerse): **se ha vuelto muy antipático** he's become very unpleasant; **se vuelve agrio** it turns *o* goes sour; **se volvió loca** she went mad

vomitar [A1] *vi* to vomit, be sick; **tengo ganas de ~ I** think I'm going to vomit *o* be sick, I feel sick

■ **~** *vt* ‹comida› to bring up; ‹sangre› to cough up

■ **vomitarse** *v pron* (Col, Méx, Ven) to vomit, be sick

vómito *m* (a) (acción) vomiting; **¿ha tenido ~s?** have you been vomiting *o* (BrE) sick? (b) (cosa vomitada) vomit

voraz *adj* ‹persona/animal/apetito› voracious; ‹incendio/fuego› fierce

vos *pron pers* [*Familiar form of address which is widely used instead of* TÚ *mainly in the River Plate area and parts of Central America*] **1** (como sujeto, en comparaciones, con preposición) you; **¿quién lo va a hacer? — vos** who's going to do it? — you (are); **che, ~** hey, you; **~ misma que ~** less than you; **para/sin ~** for/without you **2** (uso impersonal) you; **dan tres opciones y ~ elegís** you're given three options and you choose one

vosear [A1] *vt* to address sb using the vos form

voseo *m* use of the vos form instead of TÚ

vosotros -tras *pron pers pl* [*Familiar form of address which is widely used in Latin America or in certain parts of Spain, where* USTEDES *is used instead*] you; **¿quién lo va a hacer? — vosotros** who's going to do it? — you (are); **lo podéis hacer ~ mismos** you can do it yourselves; **más que ~** more than you; **para ~** for you

votación *f* (acción) voting; (método) vote; **decidir por ~** to decide by ballot; **fue elegida por ~** she was elected *o* voted in; **hagamos una ~** let's vote on it; **una ~ a mano alzada** a vote by a show of hands

votante *mf* voter

votar [A1] *vi* to vote; **~ POR algo/algn** to vote FOR sth/sb; **~ A FAVOR DE/EN CONTRA DE algo** to vote FOR/AGAINST sth

■ **~** *vt* ‹candidato› to vote for; ‹reforma/aumento› to approve, vote to approve

voto *m* **1** (en general) vote; **~ secreto** secret ballot *o* vote; **por ~ a mano alzada** by a show of hands; **~ de confianza/censura** vote of confidence/no confidence; **~ en blanco** blank ballot paper; **~ por correo** postal vote, absentee ballot (AmE) **2** (Relig) vow; **hacer los ~s solemnes** to take solemn vows

voy ▶ IR

voyeurista /bwaje'rista, bojer'ista/ *mf* voyeur

voz *f* **1** (en general) voice; **levantar la ~** to raise one's voice; **tener la ~ tomada** to be hoarse; **hablar en ~ baja** to speak quietly; **en ~ alta** ‹hablar› loudly; ‹leer› aloud, out loud; **quedarse sin ~** to lose one's voice; **una pieza a cuatro voces** (Mús) a piece for four voices, a four-part piece; **~ activa/pasiva** (Ling) active/passive voice **2** voces *fpl* (gritos) shouting, shouts (*pl*); **hablar a voces** to talk in loud voices

vozarrón *m* booming voice

vudú *m* voodoo

vuela, vuelan, etc ▶ VOLAR

vuelco *m* **1** (sobre sí mismo): **dar un ~** «coche» to overturn, turn over; «embarcación» to capsize **2** (cambio radical): **las cosas pueden dar un ~**

things could change *o* alter drastically; **el mercado dio un ∼ favorable** the market registered a favorable upturn ③ (Inf) dump

vuelo *m* ① (a) (acción): **el ∼ de las gaviotas** the seagulls' flight; **remontar el ∼** to soar up; *alzar or levantar el* ∼ «*pájaro*» to fly away *o* off; «*avión*» to take off; «*persona*» to fly *o* leave the nest; *a ∼ de pájaro* (AmL): **un cálculo a ∼ de pájaro** a rough estimate; **lo leí a ∼ de pájaro** I just skimmed through it (b) (Aviac) flight; **son dos horas de ∼** it is a two-hour flight; **∼ charter/ regular** charter/schedule flight; **∼ internacional/ nacional** international/domestic *o* internal flight; **∼ sin motor** gliding, soaring (AmE)
② (en costura) (amplitud): **la falda tiene mucho ∼** it is a very full skirt
vuelo ▶ VOLAR

vuelta *f*
I ① (a) (circunvolución): **dar ∼s alrededor de algo** to go around sth; **da ∼s alrededor de su eje** it spins *o* turns on its axis; **dar la ∼ al mundo** to go around the world; **todo/la cabeza me da ∼s** everything's/my head's spinning; **dar una ∼ a la manzana** to go around the block; **dar toda la ∼** to go all the way around (b) (Dep) (en golf) round; (en carreras) lap; **∼ al ruedo** (Taur) lap of honor; **∼ ciclista** cycle race, tour (c) (en carretera) bend; **el camino da muchas ∼s** the road winds about a lot; **el autobús da muchas ∼s** the bus takes a very roundabout route
② (giro): **darle ∼ a algo** «*a llave/manivela*» to turn sth; **dale otra ∼** give it another turn; **el coche dio una ∼ de campana** the car turned (right) over; **∼ (de) carnero** (CS) somersault; **∼ en redondo** (vuelta completa) 360 degree turn, complete turn; (cambio radical) U-turn
③ (a) **darle la ∼ a algo** «*a disco/colchón*» to turn ... (over); «*a calcetín*» (ponerlo — del derecho) to turn ... the right way out; (— del revés) to turn ... inside out; «*a copa*» (ponerla — boca arriba) to turn ... the right way up; (— boca abajo) to turn ... upside down; **dar la ∼ a la página** to turn the page, turn over (b) (para cambiar de dirección, posición): **dar la ∼** (Auto) to turn (around); **darse la ∼** to turn (around)

④ (CS) **dar vuelta algo** «*disco/colchón*» to turn sth over; «*calcetín*» (ponerlo — del derecho) to turn the right way out; (— del revés) to turn sth inside out; «*copa*» (ponerla — boca arriba) to turn sth the right way up; (— boca abajo) to turn sth upside down; **dar la ∼ a la página** to turn the page, turn over; **dio ∼ la cara** she looked away; **¿damos ∼ aquí?** (Auto) shall we turn (around) here?; **darse ∼** «*persona*» to turn (around); «*vehículo*» to overturn; «*embarcación*» to capsize
⑤ (paseo): **dar una ∼** (a pie) to go for a walk; (en coche) to go for a drive; (— del revés) to go for a ride
⑥ (a) **a la vuelta (de la esquina)** (just) around the corner (b) **vuelta y vuelta** (Coc) rare
⑦ (a) (regreso) return; (viaje de regreso) return journey; **a la ∼ paramos para almorzar** on the way back we stopped for lunch; **a la ∼ se encontró con una sorpresa** when he got back he found a surprise; **¡hasta la ∼!** see you when you get back! (b) (a un estado anterior) **∼ A algo** return TO sth
⑧ (a) (Esp) (cambio) change; **quédese con la ∼** keep the change (b) **vueltas** (Col) (cambio, dinero suelto) change
⑨ (a) (en elecciones) round (b) (de bebidas) round
⑩ (Per, RPl fam) (vez) time; **de ∼** (de nuevo) again
⑪ (de collar) strand; (en labores de punto) row; (de pantalones) cuff (AmE), turn-up (BrE)

vuelto -ta *pp* ▶ VOLVER

vuelto *m* (AmL) change; **quédese con el ∼** keep the change

vuelva, vuelvas, etc ▶ VOLVER

vuestro -tra *adj* (a) (Esp) (de vosotros) your; **∼s libros** your books; **un amigo ∼** a friend of yours (b) (frml) your; **Vuestra Majestad** Your Majesty ■ *pron* (Esp): **el ∼, la vuestra,** *etc* yours; **sabe lo ∼** he knows about the two of you

vulcanizadora *f* (Chi, Méx) tire* repairshop

vulgar *adj* (a) (corriente, común) common; **un ∼ resfriado** a common cold (b) (poco refinado) vulgar, coarse (c) (no técnico) common, popular

vulgaridad *f* (cualidad) vulgarity, coarseness

vulnerable *adj* vulnerable

Ww

W, w *f* (*read as* /'doβle βe/, /'doβle u/ *or* (Esp) /'doβle 'uβe, /'uβe 'ðoβle/) *the letter* W, w
w. (= **watio**) w, watt
walkie-talkie /'wo(l)ki 'to(l)ki/ *m* (*pl* -**kies**) walkie-talkie
walkman® /'wo(l)kman/ *m* (*pl* -**mans**) Walkman®
wáter /'(g)water *or* (Esp) 'bater/ *m* (a) (inodoro) toilet (b) (cuarto) bathroom (esp AmE), toilet (BrE)
waterpolo /'(g)waterpolo/ *m* water polo
WC /'be θe, 'uβe 'ðoβle θe/ *m* WC
web /(g)web/ *f or m*: **la** *or* **el web** the Web
weekend /'wiken/ *m* weekend

western *m* (*pl* ∼ *or* -**terns**) western

whisky /'(g)wiski/ *m* (*pl* -**kies** *or* -**kys**) whiskey*; **∼ americano** bourbon

windsurf /'winsurf/ *m* (deporte) windsurfing; (tabla) windsurfer, sailboard

windsurfing /'winsurfin/ *m* windsurfing

windsurfista /winsur'fista/ *mf* windsurfer

WWW *m* WWW

Xx

X, x *f (read as* /'ekis/) *the letter* X, x
xenofobia *f* xenophobia
xenófobo -ba *adj* xenophobic
■ *m,f* xenophobe

xilofón, xilófono *m* xylophone

Yy

Y, y *f (read as* /i 'ɣrjeɣa/, /je/ *or* (RPl) /ʒe/) *the letter* Y, y

y *conj* **1** (en general) and; **habla inglés y alemán** he speaks English and German; **¡yo gano el dinero y él lo gasta!** I earn the money and he spends it! **2 (a)** (en preguntas): **¿y tu padre? ¿qué tal está?** and how's your father?; **yo no oigo nada ¿y tú?** I can't hear anything, can you? **(b)** (fam) (expresando indiferencia) so (colloq); **¿y qué?** so what?; **¿y a mí qué?** so, what's it to me? **3** (esp RPl fam) (encabezando respuestas) well; **¿fuiste? — y sí, no tuve más remedio** did you go? — well yes, I had no choice; **y bueno** oh well **4** (en números, la hora): **cuarenta y cinco** forty-five; **doscientos treinta y tres** two hundred and thirty-three; **la una y diez** ten after (AmE) *o* (BrE) past one

ya *adv* [*Both the simple past* YA TERMINÉ *and the present perfect* YA HE TERMINADO *are used to refer to the recent indefinite past. The former is the preferred form in Latin America while in Spain there is a tendency to use the latter*] **1 (a)** (en frases afirmativas o interrogativas) already; **¿~ te has gastado todo el dinero?** have you spent all the money already?; **~ terminé** I've (already) finished; **¿~ ha llegado Ernesto?** has Ernesto arrived yet?, did Ernesto arrive yet? (AmE); **aprietas este botón ¡y ~ está!** you press this button, and that's it! **(b)** (expresando que se ha comprendido) yes, sure (colloq) **2 (a)** (en frases negativas) any more; **ese color ~ no se lleva** nobody wears that color any more **(b)** **no ya ... sino** not (just) ... but **3** (enseguida, ahora) right now; **desde ~ te digo que no puede ser** (esp AmL) I can tell you right now that it's not possible; **~ mismo** (esp AmL) right away, straightaway (BrE); **¡~ voy!** coming!; **preparados listos ¡~!** on your mark(s), get set, go! **4** (con verbo en futuro): **~ te contaré** I'll tell you all about it; **~ lo entenderás** you'll understand one day **5** (uso enfático): **¡~ quisiera yo!** I should be so lucky!; **~ era hora** about time (too)!; **¡~ me tienes harta!** I'm (just about) fed up with you! **6** **ya que** since, as; **~ que estás aquí** since *o* as you're here

■ *conj*: **se puede solicitar ~ sea en persona o por teléfono** it can be ordered either in person or by telephone

yacer [E5] *vi* (frml) to lie (frml)

yacimiento *m* **(a)** (de mineral) deposit; **~ petrolífero** oilfield **(b)** (Arqueol) site

yámper *m* (Per) jumper (AmE), pinafore dress (BrE)

yanqui *adj* (*pl* **-quis**) (fam) Yankee (colloq)
■ *mf* Yank (colloq), Yankee (colloq)

yapa *f* (CS, Per fam) *small amount of extra goods given free*, lagniappe (AmE); **dar algo de ~** to throw sth in (for free) (colloq)

yate *m* yacht

yayo -ya *m,f* (fam) (*m*) grandpa (colloq), granddad (colloq); (*f*) granny (colloq), grandma (colloq)

yedra *f* ivy

yegua *f* (Zool) mare

yelmo *m* helmet

yema *f* **(a)** (de huevo) yolk **(b)** (dulce) *sweet made with egg yolk and sugar* **(c)** (del dedo) fingertip **(d)** (Bot) leaf bud

yen *m* yen

yendo ▶ IR

yerba *f* **(a)** *tb* **~ mate** maté **(b)** (Andes, Méx, Ven fam) (marihuana) grass (sl) **(c)** (césped) grass

yerbatero -ra *adj* maté (*before n*)
■ *m,f* (Andes) (curandero) witch doctor; (que vende hierbas medicinales) herbalist

yerga, yergue ▶ ERGUIR

yerno *m* son-in-law

yerra, yerras, etc ▶ ERRAR

yeso *m* **(a)** (Art, Const) plaster **(b)** (AmL) (Med) (plaster) cast; **me quitaron el ~** I had my cast taken off

yesquero *m* (Col, RPl, Ven) cigarette lighter

yo *pron pers* **(a)** (como sujeto) I; **~ que tú** if I were you; **¿quién quiere más? — ¡yo!** who wants some more? — me! *o* I do!; **soy ~** it's me; **¿quién, ~?** who, me?; **~ misma** myself; **estoy cansada — ~ también** I'm tired — so am I *o* me too **(b)** (en

comparaciones, con ciertas preposiciones) me; **come más que** ∼ he eats more than me *o* more than I do; **llegó después que** ∼ she arrived after me
yodo *m* iodine
yoga *m* yoga
yogui *m* yogi
yogurt (*pl* **-gurts, yogur**) *m* yogurt, yoghurt
yonqui *mf* (*pl* **-quis**) (fam) junkie (colloq)
yo-yo *m* (*pl* **-yos**) yo-yo
yuca *f* (tubérculo comestible) cassava, manioc; (planta ornamental) yucca
yudo *m* judo
yudoca *mf* judoka, judoist

yugo *m* yoke
Yugoslavia, Yugoeslavia *f* (Hist) Yugoslavia
yugoslavo -va, yugoeslavo -va *adj/m,f* (Hist) Yugoslavian
yugular *adj/f* jugular
yunque *m* anvil
yunta *f* (de bueyes) yoke
yute *m* jute
yuyo *m* (a) (Per, RPl) (hierba) herb; **té de** ∼**s** herbal tea (b) (RPl) (mala hierba) weed (c) (Per) (alga) seaweed

Zz

Z, z *f* (read as /ˈseta/ *or* (Esp) /ˈθeta/) *the letter* Z, z
zacate *m* (AmC, Méx) (a) (hierba) grass; (heno) hay (b) (estropajo) scourer
zafar [A1] *vt* (a) (Chi, Méx) ⟨brazo/dedo⟩ to dislocate (b) (Col, Ven) ⟨nudo⟩ to untie; ⟨tuerca⟩ to unscrew; ⟨persona/animal⟩ to let ... loose
  ■ **zafarse** *v pron* (a) (de compromiso) ∼**se de** algo to get *o* wriggle **OUT OF** sth (b) (soltarse) «persona/animal» to get loose, get away (c) (*refl*) (Chi, Méx) (dislocarse): ∼**se la muñeca** to dislocate one's wrist
zafiro *m* sapphire
zaga *f* (a) (Dep) defense* (b) **a la zaga** ⟨ir/ quedarse⟩ in the rear, behind
zaguán *m* hallway
zalamería *f*: *tb* ∼**s** sweet talk, flattery; **hacerle** ∼**s a** algn to sweet-talk sb
zalamero -ra *adj* ⟨palabras⟩ flattering; **¡qué** ∼ **estás!** you're being very nice (to me)! (iro)
zamarra *f* (chaqueta) leather/sheepskin jacket; (chaleco) leather/sheepskin jerkin
zamba *f* zamba (South American folk dance)
zambo -ba *adj* bowlegged
  ■ *m,f* (AmL) person of mixed black and Amerindian origin
zambomba *f* (Mús) traditional drum-like instrument
zambullida *f* (salto) dive, plunge; (baño) dip
zambullirse [I9] *v pron* (lanzarse) to dive (in); (sumergirse) to duck *o* dive underwater
zamuro *m* (Ven) turkey vulture
zanahoria *adj* (a) (RPl fam) (tonto) stupid (b) (Ven fam) (anticuado) square (colloq)
  ■ *mf* (a) (RPl fam) (tonto) idiot, nerd (colloq) (b) (Ven fam) (mojigato) straitlaced person; (anticuado) old fogey (colloq)
  ■ *f* (Bot, Coc) carrot
zanca *f* leg
zancada *f* stride; **bajaba la cuesta a** ∼**s** he came striding down the hill
zancadilla *f* trip; **me hizo** *or* (Esp) **puso una** ∼ he tripped me (up)

zancos *mpl* stilts (*pl*)
zancuda *f* wader, wading bird
zancudo¹ -da *adj* (a) ⟨ave⟩ wading (before n) (b) (fam) ⟨persona⟩ long-legged
zancudo² *m* (típula) crane fly, daddy longlegs; (mosquito) (AmL) mosquito
zángano -na *m,f* **1** (fam) (persona) lazybones (colloq) **2 zángano** *m* (abeja) drone
zanja *f* (para desagüe) ditch; (para cimientos, tuberías) trench; (acequia) irrigation channel
zanjar [A1] *vt* ⟨polémica/diferencias⟩ to settle, resolve; ⟨deuda⟩ to settle, pay off
zapallito *m* (CS): *tb* ∼ **largo** *or* **italiano** zucchini (AmE), courgette (BrE)
zapallo *m* (CS, Per) pumpkin
zapata *f* (Auto, Mec) brake shoe
zapateado *m* (a) (en general) ▶ ZAPATEO (b) (baile) zapateado (type of Flamenco dance)
zapatear [A1] *vi* (a) (en danza) to tap one's feet; (más fuerte) to stamp (in time to the music) (b) (para protestar, vitorear) to stamp (one's feet)
zapateo *m* tapping; (más fuerte) stamping
zapatería *f* (a) (tienda) shoe store (AmE), shoe shop (BrE) (b) (taller — de fabricación) shoemaker's, cobbler's; (— de reparación) shoe repairer's, cobbler's
zapatero -ra *m,f* shoemaker, cobbler
zapatilla *f* (a) (de lona) canvas shoe; (para deportes) sneaker (AmE), trainer (BrE); (alpargata) espadrille; (para ballet) ballet shoe; (pantufla) slipper (b) (Méx) (zapato de mujer) lady's shoe; ∼ **de piso** flat shoe
zapato *m* shoe; ∼**s bajos/de tacón** low-heeled/ high-heeled shoes; ∼ **de cordón** lace-up shoe; ∼ **de goma** (Ven) sneaker (AmE), trainer (BrE)
zaperoco *m* (Ven fam) riot
zar *m* tsar, czar
Zaragoza *f* Saragossa
zarandear [A1] *vt* (de un lado a otro) to shake; (para arriba y para abajo) to shake *o* jog up and down
  ■ **zarandearse** *v pron* (esp AmL) «tren» to ····❖

shake around; «*barco*» to toss about; **nos zarandeamos mucho durante el vuelo** we got shaken around o buffeted a lot during the flight

zarape *m* (en AmC, Méx) serape (*colorful blanket-like shawl worn esp by men*)

zarcillo *m* ☐1 (arete) earring ☐2 (Bot) tendril

zarina *f* czarina

zarpa *f* (a) (Zool) paw (b) (fam) (mano) paw (colloq)

zarpar [A1] *vi* to set sail, weigh anchor

zarpazo *m* (de gato, león) swipe; **me dio un ∼** it took a swipe at me (with its paw)

zarza *f* bramble, blackberry bush

zarzamora *f* (fruto) blackberry; (arbusto) bramble, blackberry bush

zarzo *m* (Col) loft, attic

zarzuela *f* (Espec, Mús) *traditional Spanish operetta*

zenit *m* zenith

zeppelin /sepe'lin, θepe'lin/, **zepelín** *m* zeppelin, airship

zeta *f*: name of the letter z

zigzag *m* (*pl* **-zags** *or* **-zagues**) zigzag

zigzaguear [A1] *vi* to zigzag

zinc *m* zinc; **techo de chapa de ∼** corrugated iron roof

zíper *m* (AmC, Méx, Ven) zipper (AmE), zip (BrE)

zócalo *m* ☐1 (rodapié) baseboard (AmE), skirting board (BrE) ☐2 (Méx) (plaza) main square

zodíaco, zodiaco *m* zodiac

zombi *mf* zombie

zona *f* ☐1 (área, región) area; **fue declarada ∼ neutral** it was declared a neutral zone; ❸ **zona de carga y descarga** loading and unloading only; **∼ comercial** commercial district; **∼ de castigo** penalty area; **∼ industrial** industrial park; **∼ peatonal** pedestrian precinct; **∼ roja** (AmL) (zona de prostitución) red-light district; **∼ verde** park, green space; **∼ cero** (en Nueva York) ground zero ☐2 (en baloncesto) free-throw lane, three-second area

zonzo -za *m,f* (AmL fam) idiot, fool

zoo *m* zoo

zoología *f* zoology

zoológico *m* zoo, zoological garden (frml)

zoólogo -ga *m,f* zoologist

zoom /sum, θum/ *m* zoom (lens)

zopenco -ca *adj* (fam) stupid, idiotic
▪ *m,f* (fam) blockhead (colloq)

zopilote *m* (AmC, Méx) turkey vulture

zoquete *adj* (fam) dim, dense (colloq)
▪ *mf* (fam) (persona) dimwit (colloq), blockhead
▪ *m* (CS) (Indum) sock, ankle sock

zorra *f* (fam & pey) (prostituta) whore (colloq & pej), tart (colloq & pej); *ver tb* ZORRO 1A, 2

zorrillo *m* (AmL) (mofeta) skunk

zorro -rra *m,f* ☐1 (a) (Zool) (*m*) fox; (*f*) vixen (b) (AmC, Méx fam) (oposum) opossum ☐2 (fam) (persona astuta) sly o crafty person ☐3 **zorro** *m* (piel) fox (fur); *ver tb* ZORRA

zorzal *m* thrush

zozobrar [A1] *vi* ☐1 «*barco*» (hundirse) to founder; (volcar) to capsize ☐2 «*proyecto/negocio*» to founder

zueco *m* clog

zumbar [A1] *vi* «*insecto*» to buzz; «*motor*» to hum, whirr; **pasar zumbando** «*bala/coche*» to whizz by; **me zumbaban los oídos** my ears were buzzing o ringing
▪ **∼** *vt* ☐1 (fam) ⟨persona⟩ to give ... a good hiding (colloq) ☐2 (Ven fam) (tirar) to chuck (colloq), to throw

zumbido *m* (de insecto) buzzing, droning; (de motor) humming, whirring

zumo *m* (esp Esp) juice

zurcir [I4] *vt* to darn, mend

zurdo -da *adj* left-handed; ⟨futbolista⟩ left-footed; ⟨boxeador/lanzador⟩ southpaw (*before n*)
▪ *m,f* left-handed person; (tenista) left-hander; (boxeador) southpaw

zurra *f* (fam) (good) hiding (colloq)

zurrar [A1] *vt* (fam) to wallop (colloq), to give ... a (good) thrashing o hiding (colloq)

zurrón *m* (de pastor) leather bag; (de cazador) hunter's pouch

Z

431

1 January **Año Nuevo** (New Year's Day). Public holiday in all Spanish-speaking countries.

5 January (Spain) The *cabalgata de los Reyes Magos* is a parade of floats symbolizing the Three Wise Men's journey to Bethlehem.

6 January **Día de Reyes** (Epiphany/Twelfth Night). In many Spanish-speaking countries, this is when presents are given, rather than on Christmas Day.

20 January **San Sebastián** (Saint Sebastian's Day). Celebrated in Spain with parades, sporting events, and bullfights, it is also a day of celebration for the people of the Basque city that bears the name of the saint.

February (Chile) **Festival de Viña del Mar** This hugely popular international music festival is staged over six days in February, in front of a live audience in a 15,000-seater amphitheater. The event is broadcast to viewers in 56 countries.

2 February **La Candelaria** (Candlemas). An occasion for celebrations and parades in many Spanish-speaking countries.

3 February **Fiesta de San Blas** (patron saint of Paraguay). Public holiday.

(Mexico) **Día de la Constitución** (Constitution Day). Public holiday.

26 February **Aberri Eguna** Basque national day and public holiday in the Basque country of Spain.

12–19 March **Las Fallas** is a key festival held in Valencia, eastern Spain. The high point is on the last night, when the *fallas* (groups of huge painted cardboard and wood figures depicting current events and famous people) are paraded through the streets. The best *falla* is 'pardoned' and placed in the *falla* museum; the others are burned.

21 March (Mexico) A public holiday to celebrate the anniversary of the birth of Benito Juárez, a famous 19th-century statesman, who was twice president.

14 April (Paraguay) **Día de la Independencia**. Public holiday.

23 April **San Jordi** The feast day of Catalonia's patron saint. Women traditionally give men books and men give women roses on this Catalan version of St Valentine's Day.

1 May **Día del Trabajo** (Labor Day). Public holiday in all Spanish-speaking countries.

5 May (Mexico) The anniversary of the victory of the state of Puebla over the French in 1862. Public holiday.

25 May (Argentina) The anniversary of the May revolution of 1810.

20 June (Argentina) **Día de la Bandera** (Argentinian National Day). Public holiday.

(Colombia) **Día de la Independencia**. Public holiday.

24 June **San Juan** (Feast of St John). Traditionally fires are lit on the night of San Juan in order to keep away the cold of winter. In some places, people will jump over the fires or walk through them barefoot.

5 July (Venezuela) **Día de la Independencia**. Public holiday.

6–14 July **Sanfermines.** The festival of *el encierro* (the 'running of the bulls') in Pamplona, northern Spain. The animals are released into the barricaded streets and people run in front of them, in honor of the town's patron saint, San Fermín, who was put to death by being dragged by bulls.

9 July (Argentina) **Día de la Independencia**. A public holiday.

16 July (Chile) **La Tirana** is a spectacular annual festival. The high point is on 16 July, the day of **La Virgen del Carmen**, Chile's patron saint. Costumed dancers perform for three days non-stop in front of a richly adorned statue of the Virgin.

25 July **Fiesta de Santiago** (Feast of St James). The *Camino de Santiago* is the pilgrimage from all over Europe to the holy city of Santiago de Compostela. The city streets are full of performers for two weeks of celebrations culminating in the *Festival del Apóstol*.

28 July (Peru) **Día de la Independencia**. A public holiday.

6 August (Bolivia) **Día de la Independencia**. A public holiday.

10 August (Ecuador) **Primer Grito de Independencia**. A public holiday.

17 August (Argentina) A public holiday. Anniversary of the death of San Martín, who liberated Argentina from Spanish rule in 1816.

25 August (Uruguay) **Día de la Independencia**. A public holiday.

11 September **Día Nacional de Cataluña**. Catalonian National Day and a public holiday in Catalonia.

13 September (Mexico) Commemoration of the *Niños Héroes* (child heroes) who fell while defending the castle of Chapultepec against European invaders in 1847.

15 September (Mexico) **Conmemoración de la Proclamación de la Independencia**. At 11 o'clock at night, people join in shouting, '*El Grito*' (the Cry for Freedom), in memory of Padre Hidalgo, the priest who in 1810 initiated the quest for independence from the Spanish.

18 September (Chile) **Día de la Independencia**. A public holiday.

12 October **Día de la Raza (Columbus Day)**. In Latin America, the anniversary of Columbus's discovery of the Americas in 1492. In Spain it is known as *día de la Hispanidad*, and celebrates the cultural ties shared by Spanish-speaking countries.

31 October **Todos los Santos** (All Saints). In the Spanish-speaking world on this and the following day, *el día de los Difuntos/Muertos*, people put flowers on friends' and relatives' graves. In Mexico this is an important festival in which Catholic traditions are mixed with those of pre-Hispanic religions.

10 November (Argentina) **Fiesta de la Tradición**. This countrywide festival is especially important in the town of San Antonio de Areco, near Buenos Aires. The capital also holds a festival in November, the **Semana de Buenos Aires**, in honor of its patron saint, San Martín de Tours.

20 November (Mexico) **Día de la Revolución de 1910**. Public holiday to celebrate the revolution of 1910.

12 December (Mexico) **Virgen de Guadalupe**. Music and dancing in honor of the patron saint of the country. The *concheros* wear bells around their ankles and dance to stringed instruments and conches.

16 December **Posada** A popular celebration in Mexico and Central America between 16 December and Christmas Day to commemorate the journey of Mary and Joseph to Bethlehem. Religious figures are carried on people's shoulders. Nine houses, or *posadas*, are visited by groups carrying the figures, who ask for shelter at each one. At the last house, the figures are taken in and put on an altar. The celebrations continue with food and drink, singing and dancing, and end with a *piñata*.

24 December **Nochebuena** In Spanish-speaking countries, Christmas Eve is celebrated rather than Christmas Day. Dinner is eaten before Midnight Mass (*misa del gallo*).

In Latin America, where many countries do not celebrate the *día de Reyes* (*see* 6 JANUARY), Christmas gifts are given on 24 December. This custom is spreading in Spain, though the *día de Reyes* is celebrated there.

25 December **Navidad** (Christmas Day). A time of great religious celebration in all Spanish-speaking countries. In many places, re-enactments of the nativity are held, with a variety of traditions, parades, and costumes.

28 December **Día de los Inocentes**. The equivalent to April Fool's Day in Spanish-speaking countries, it is a day for playing tricks on people. And if you trick someone into lending you money for that day, you keep it and tell them *que te lo paguen los Santos Inocentes* (let the Holy Innocents pay you back).

31 December **Nochevieja y Año Nuevo**. In Spain and in many other Spanish-speaking countries, it is customary to see the New Year in by eating twelve grapes for good luck, one on each chime of the clock at midnight.

Movable feasts and holidays

Martes de Carnaval (Shrove Tuesday) The last Tuesday before the beginning of *Cuaresma* (Lent). *Carnaval* is celebrated in many Spanish-speaking countries just before this date. In many places, there are masked balls and parades. The biggest in Spain are those in Cádiz, on the south coast, and Madrid, where a strange ceremony called *el entierro de la sardina* (literally, the burial of the sardine) takes place. In Mexico, the best-known are in Veracruz and Mazatlán.

Pascua (Easter); **Semana Santa** (Holy Week) The most important time of religious celebration throughout the Spanish-speaking world. In many places there are processions, in which statues of Christ or the Virgin Mary, often covered in jewels and flowers, are paraded through the streets.

Seville's famous **Feria de abril** (April festival) takes place in the week following Easter. On the site of the *feria* stand hundreds of *casetas*, or small marquees, in which people entertain, eat, drink, play music, and dance *sevillanas*, the popular dances of Andalucía. Many people dress up in colorful traditional costumes and ride on horseback or in horse-drawn carriages.

Corpus Christi Nine weeks after Easter is celebrated in most Spanish-speaking countries with religious parades.

Calendario / Calendar

1 de enero
New Year's Day (día de Año Nuevo). El primero de enero es festivo y normalmente es un día tranquilo en el que la gente se recupera de los festejos de la noche anterior.

2 de enero
Día festivo en Escocia.

6 de enero
Epiphany o Twelfth night (Día de Reyes). No hay ninguna costumbre en especial relacionada con este día, pero tradicionalmente se guarda el árbol de Navidad junto con el resto de los adornos navideños.

25 de enero
Burns Night. Es el aniversario del nacimiento del poeta escocés Robert Burns en el siglo XVIII. Los escoceses preparan una cena llamada *Burns Supper*, cuyo plato principal se llama *haggis* (estómago de oveja relleno con una mezcla de avena, hígado y otras vísceras, cebollas y especias) y que es acompañado a la mesa por un gaitero (*piper*) que toca la gaita escocesa.

2 de febrero
Groundhog Day. Según la tradición estadounidense, la pequeña marmota (*groundhog*) sale de su madriguera en este día, luego de su hibernación. Si está soleado y ve su sombra, regresa a su madriguera, y habrá otras seis semanas de tiempo invernal. Si no ve su sombra, la primavera comenzará temprano.

14 de febrero
St Valentine's Day. En el día de San Valentín los enamorados se intercambian flores y regalos. También es tradicional mandarle una tarjeta anónima a alguien que le guste a uno.

1 de marzo
St David's Day. San David es el santo patrono de Gales.

17 de marzo
St Patrick's Day. San Patricio es el santo patrono de Irlanda, es día festivo y se celebra por todos los irlandeses con música y bebida en cantidad.

1 de abril
El 1 de abril se celebra esta popular tradición de gastarle bromas a la gente desprevenida, especialmente en el sentido de hacer creer algo insólito para luego revelar la broma diciendo 'April Fool!' Los periódicos y otros medios de comunicación se suman a la diversión incluyendo alguna broma entre las noticias importantes.

23 de abril
St George's Day. San Jorge es el santo patrono de Inglaterra.

4 de julio
Independence Day. Día festivo en los Estados Unidos para celebrar el Día de la Independencia con desfiles, fuegos artificiales y banderas. La gente se reúne haciendo comidas al aire libre y parrilladas o asados.

12 de octubre
Columbus Day. Día festivo en los Estados Unidos, en el que se conmemora el descubrimiento de América por Cristóbal Colón en 1492.

31 de octubre
Halloween (víspera de Todos Santos). Ocasión en la que se mezcla la religión con antiguas creencias paganas. Los niños se disfrazan de fantasmas y brujas y visitan casas de la vecindad jugando a la "broma o golosina" (*trick or treat*). Si los vecinos no les dan dinero o golosinas, los niños les gastan una broma. En los Estados Unidos, las familias suelen hacer una fiesta de disfraces.

5 de noviembre
Bonfire Night/Guy Fawkes' Night En Gran Bretaña se celebra para conmemorar la noche, en 1605, en que un miembro del grupo de conspiradores católicos fue sorprendido tratando de prender fuego a la pólvora que se guardaba en los sótanos bajo el Parlamento. El objetivo de la fallida Conspiración de la Pólvora ('*Gunpowder Plot*') era el asesinato del rey Jaime I y todos los miembros del Parlamento. Hoy en día la gente se junta alrededor de fogatas – algunas veces de enormes proporciones – en cuya parte superior se ha colocado un muñeco de tamaño natural conocido como el '*guy*'. Los fuegos artificiales constituyen una parte fundamental de las celebraciones y muchos se organizan a traves del país. La comida tradicional de la '*Bonfire Night*' son las salchichas y patatas, por lo general cocinadas en las brazas de la fogata.

11 de noviembre
Remembrance Day (Poppy Day), en Estados Unidos, **Veterans' Day**. El día en que se conmemora el armisticio de 1918, y se recuerdan los caídos en las dos guerras mundiales y otros conflictos más recientes. También se lo conoce en Gran Bretaña como el día de la amapola (*Poppy Day*), ya que la gente lleva prendida una amapola roja de papel como signo recordatorio.

30 de noviembre
St Andrew's Day. San Andrés es el santo patrono de Escocia.

25 de diciembre
Christmas Day (el día de Navidad). Es
día festivo. Se intercambian regalos alrededor
del árbol de Navidad, y en muchas casas los
niños, al despertar, encuentran en su cama
una media llena de regalitos y golosinas que,
según la tradición, deja *Father Christmas*,
también conocido como *Santa Claus*.

26 de diciembre
Boxing Day en Gran Bretaña, **St Stephen's
Day** en Irlanda. Día festivo en ambos países.

31 de diciembre
New Year's Eve (la noche de Fin de Año)
llamada **Hogmanay** en Escocia, país donde se
acostumbra ir a visitar a amigos y vecinos
a medianoche, para comer y beber hasta las
primeras horas de la mañana. Antiguamente
era tradicional llevar un pedazo de carbón
como símbolo de buena suerte.

Fiestas móviles

El tercer lunes de febrero, es el día de los
Presidentes (**Presidents' Day**) en Estados
Unidos. Es día festivo en el que se celebran
los nacimientos de George Washington
y Abraham Lincoln.

Shrove Tuesday (martes de Carnaval) es
el último día de carnaval antes del comienzo
de la Cuaresma el miércoles de Ceniza.
Tradicionalmente se comen creps
o panqueques.

El cuarto domingo de la Cuaresma en Gran
Bretaña y el segundo domingo de mayo en
Estados Unidos, es el día de la Madre
(**Mother's Day** o **Mothering Sunday**).
Las madres suelen recibir tarjetas y pequeños
regalos de sus hijos.

El tercer domingo de junio es el día del
Padre (**Father's Day**) en el que los padres
suelen recibir tarjetas y pequeños regalos
de sus hijos.

Good Friday el Viernes Santo. Se celebra
en la iglesia, es día festivo.

Easter Sunday (el Domingo de Pascua).
La gente religiosa va a la iglesia. A los niños
se les dan huevos de Pascua.

Easter Monday El lunes siguiente al
Domingo de Pascua es día festivo en Gran
Bretaña e Irlanda.

El primer lunes de mayo (**Early May Bank
Holiday**) es día festivo en Gran Bretaña e
Irlanda

Whitsun o **Pentecost** El domingo de
Pentecostés es el séptimo después de la Pascua
de Resurrección (**Easter Sunday**). Se celebra
solamente en la iglesia.

El lunes siguiente solía ser día festivo en
Gran Bretaña, pero ha sido reemplazado por el
último lunes del mes de mayo (**Spring Bank
Holiday**).

El último lunes de agosto (**Late Summer
Bank Holiday**) es día festivo en Inglaterra,
Gales e Irlanda del Norte.

El primer lunes de septiembre es el día del
Trabajo (**Labor Day**) en Estados Unidos.
Es día festivo y se celebra con desfiles.

Thanksgiving (el día de Acción de Gracias)
en Estados Unidos, es el cuarto jueves de
noviembre. Es un día de festejos tanto
religiosos como familiares, que culmina con
una gran comida consistente en un pavo
acompañado con batatas y salsa de arándano,
seguido de un pastel de calabaza.

Advent El período que incluye los cuatro
domingos previos a la Navidad. Por tradición,
los niños tienen calendarios de Adviento
(*Advent Calendars*), con pequeñas 'ventanitas'
de papel que contienen ilustraciones
navideñas y algunas veces golosinas.

Calendario / Calendar

A-Z of Hispanic Life and Culture

ABC One of Spain's bestselling newspapers (www.abc.es). Founded in 1905, it supported the Nationalists in the GUERRA CIVIL and, since Spain's return to democracy, has supported the centre-right PP.

Alcázar de Sevilla, El Dating from the 12th and 13th centuries, this complex of buildings is Seville's oldest and most important civil edifice. It is the Seville residence of the Spanish royal family.

alfajor Derived from the Arabic word, *al ha'soo*, meaning filling, this is a delicacy made from almonds, hazelnuts, honey, cinnamon, cloves, coriander, and other ingredients. In Latin America it is a kind of sandwich made of soft biscuit and a filling that may be made of coconut, chocolate, or DULCE DE LECHE.

Alhambra, La This exquisite fortified palace of the Moorish kings of Granada was begun in the 13th century and named after the color of its walls '*qa'lat al-Hamra*' (red castle).

almuerzo In Mexico and Spain, *almuerzo* is the midday meal, also known as *comida*, or a light mid-morning snack. In most of Latin America it means lunch, and *comida* refers to the evening meal (*cena* in Mexico and Spain).

amates guerrenses In Mexico, these are paintings on paper made from the bark of the *amate* tree.

Andean Food is very varied and many of its ingredients, such as *kiwicha* (a cereal with a high protein content), *quinua* (a cereal grown high in the Andes), and the *tarwi* or *chocho*, are part of the Inca heritage. *Chuño* (potato flour) is very commonly used, as well as maize, sweet potatoes, avocado pears, and guinea-pig and alpaca meat. Among the most popular dishes are *humitas* (corn paste wrapped in corn leaves) and *anticuchos* (skewered ox heart cooked over a slow heat).

Antena 3 Spain's first private television channel, which began broadcasting in 1989. Its proprietors include the conservative newspapers LA VANGUARDIA and ABC.

araucano ▶ MAPUCHE

arpilleras Pieces of appliquéd textile folk art, common in South America. *Arpilleras* became a symbol of protest for mothers, sisters, and daughters of Chilean DESAPARECIDOS during the dictatorship of General Pinochet.

asado In Latin America, an open-air event at which meat is grilled. It also means the meat itself. Guests eat the meat with sausages and salad. Wine, beer, or CHICHA is drunk and there is singing to a guitar.

Asturiano ▶ BABLE

Audiencia Nacional The Spanish high court for crimes affecting the national interest, e.g. drug trafficking and large-scale fraud. It has powers of extradition.

autonomía ▶ COMUNIDADES AUTÓNOMAS

AVE – Alta Velocidad Española A high-speed train service linking Madrid with Seville and Huelva via Cadiz, established in 1992. Other lines under construction include Madrid to Barcelona, with an extension to France.

Aztecas A NÁHUATL-speaking people of Central America who, in the 14th century, established a brilliant but tyrannical civilization in central and southern Mexico. The capital was Tenochtitlán, which became Mexico City. Renowned for their jewelry, the Aztecs were also skilled architects. They worshipped the plumed serpent Quetzalcóatl and the war-god Huitzilopochtli, appeasing him with human sacrifice. The Aztec empire collapsed in 1521 after defeat by the Spanish under Hernán Cortés and Pedro de Alvarado.

Bable or **Asturiano** A variety of Castilian spoken in Asturias. It went into decline when the kingdom of Castile achieved political dominance and imposed Castilian on what became Spain. By the 20th century it was confined to rural areas. With the revival of Spanish regional languages Bable has seen a resurgence in use. On-line newspaper at www.Asturies.es

Bachillerato A traditional term for secondary education. Today, under the LOGSE (1990), it specifically means the last two years of secondary education (16–18 years) following ESO, for students who wish to go to university. In parts of Latin America *bachillerato* is the examination taken at the end of secondary education. In Peru it is the first university degree.

balsero A name for Cubans who try to enter the US by sailing to Florida in small boats and rafts. *See also* PATERA.

bar Bars (*bares*) in Spain sell hot and cold drinks, snacks such as tapas and raciónes, sandwiches, and pastries. They often provide full meals at lunch and they open from early in the morning until late at night.

barbacoa In Mexico, this is meat or poultry that is cooked in a hole in the ground lined with heated stones. In Peru it is known as *pachamanca* and in Chile *curanto*, where its main ingredient is seafood.

barrio A city neighborhood, defined by its geographical location, a characteristic of its inhabitants, a particular feature, or its history. Most *barrios* have very strong identities. Buenos Aires is unique, with a total of

46 distinctive *barrios*, including the oldest, San Telmo, and La Boca, popular with tourists for its brightly painted wooden houses.

Batasuna The political wing of ETA.

bayetón ▶ PONCHO

belén A nativity scene. In Spain it is traditional to have a *belén* at home at Christmas. Towns and cities in Spain often have a *belén viviente*, with real people playing the biblical characters.

bonoloto A Spanish state lottery established in 1988. *See also* LOTERÍA NACIONAL and LOTERÍA PRIMITIVA.

butifarra A type of sausage, generally made of pork, and typical of Cataluña. In Peru it is a sandwich of French bread, filled with a slice of Peruvian ham, onion sauce, and lettuce.

Cadena SER Spanish commercial radio station, offering a high level of information and political debate. Politically it is considered to be left of centre. See also RADIO ESPAÑOLA.

cafetería In Spain, a place to have a coffee, pastries, etc. Cafeterías are usually smarter than BARES and serve a wider variety of dishes.

cajeta ▶ DULCE DE LECHE

Caló The Indo-European language spoken by Spanish gypsies. It is not recognized as an official language, but there are many words of Caló origin in colloquial Spanish, such as *calé* (gypsy) and *payo*, the gypsy word for non-gypsies. *See also* GITANO.

Cámara de los Diputados ▶ CONGRESO DE LOS DIPUTADOS

Canal + (Canal Plus) A private subscription television channel in Spain, concentrating on sports events, especially soccer, and recently released movies. Its news style is neutral, but it openly supports the PSOE.

cantegril ▶ CHABOLAS

Caribbean and Central American music has its roots in the cultures of the original Caribbeans, the European conquerors, and those brought from Africa as slaves. Cuba is the most prolific producer of Caribbean music. The salsa, rumba, and merengue are well-known forms. Instruments used are the *guiro*, the *maraca* (a type of rattle), and the base drum. Typical is the *clave*, a percussion instrument made of two wooden cylinders that are struck together.

Carlismo (Carlism) means support for Don Carlos. Spain had three civil wars known as the *guerras carlistas* (1833–9, 1860, 1872–6). When Fernando VII died in 1833, he was succeeded not by his brother Don Carlos de Borbón, but by his daughter Isabel, under the regency of her mother María Cristina. This provoked a mainly northern-Spanish revolt, with guerrillas pitted against the forces of the central government. The Carlist Wars were also a confrontation between conservative rural Catholic Spain, especially the Basque provinces and Aragón, led by the Carlistas, and the progressive liberal urban middle classes allied with the army. Carlos died in 1855, but the Carlistas, representing political and religious traditionalism, supported his descendants' claims until reconciliation in 1977 with King Juan Carlos.

Carnaval ▶ TRADITIONS, FESTIVALS, AND HOLIDAYS

carné de identidad Identity card that all residents over a certain age in Spain and Latin America must carry at all times. Holders must quote their identity card number on most official forms. In Latin America the card is also known as the *cédula de identidad*, and in Spain as the *DNI* (*Documento Nacional de Identidad*).

Cartel de Juárez A powerful drugs cartel operating in Juárez on the US border. It was pre-eminent in the 1990s and aimed to bring drugs into the US.

cartel de Medellín y cartel de Cali The two most important Colombian drug cartels. From 1975, Colombia's role in the narcotics trade has become increasingly important. It is now a major supplier of cocaine to the western world. This has led to great tension within Colombia, and has also affected the country's international relations.

Casa Amarilla The headquarters of the Venezuelan State Department in Caracas. Also the name of the Presidential Palace in San José, Costa Rica.

Casa Rosada The Argentinian president's official residence in the Plaza de Mayo, Buenos Aires. It was painted pink to symbolize the union of two opposing political factions, one of whose banners was red, the other white.

Castellano In Spain the term Castellano, rather than Español, refers to the Spanish language as opposed to Catalan, Basque, etc. The choice of word has political overtones: Castellano has separatist connotations and Español is considered centralist. In Latin America, Castellano is the usual term for Spanish.

Catalán The language of Catalonia. Like Castilian, Catalan is a Romance language. Variants of it include MALLORQUÍN and VALENCIANO. Banned under Franco, Catalan has enjoyed a revival since Spain's return to democracy and now has around 11 million speakers. It is the medium of instruction in schools and universities, and its use is widespread in business, the arts, and the media. Many books are published in Catalan. *See also* LENGUAS COOFICIALES.

Culture

cédula de identidad ▶ CARNÉ DE IDENTIDAD

CEIP ▶ COLEGIO ESTATAL

chabolas The word used in Spain to describe the miserable slum dwellings that are built around the edges of a city. In Argentina they are called *villa miseria*; in Chile *población callampa*, in Colombia *barrio invasión*, in Uruguay *cantegril*, and in Venezuela *ranchos*.

charro A Mexican cowboy or -girl skilled in horsemanship. The traditional *charro* costume for a man consists of a high-crowned, wide-brimmed hat, tight trousers, a white shirt, waistcoat, and short jacket. A woman's outfit is similar but with a long, wide skirt. *Charros* originated *charrerías*, the culture associated with horse-riding and rodeo skills. They also take part in festivals known as *charreadas*.

Chicanos Mexican Americans, the descendants of Mexican immigrants living in the US. For long looked down on by Americans of European descent, Chicanos have found a new pride in their origins and culture. There are numerous Chicano radio stations and cultural organizations in the US, and many universities and colleges now offer courses in Chicano Studies.

chicha A Latin American drink, typically alcoholic, made of fermented maize. In some South American countries, *chicha* is drunk out of a bull's horn during FIESTAS PATRIAS. In Peru, the term *lo chicha* is used to denote anything relating to ordinary life and the common people. It also refers to a mixture of CUMBIA and HUAINO, Andean music.

chinampas ▶ XOCHIMILCO

chiringuito de playa In Spain, a kiosk or stall on a beach selling drinks and simple meals. Some have become well-known restaurants.

churro A typical Spanish food, consisting of a cylinder of dough, deep-fried in olive oil. *Churros* are often eaten with hot chocolate for breakfast.

cinema ▶ LATIN AMERICAN CINEMA

ciudad perdida ▶ CHABOLAS

coca Andean peasants in Peru, Bolivia, and Ecuador chew *coca* leaves mixed with bicarbonate of soda to combat cold and tiredness. They also make *mate de coca*, an infusion effective against altitude sickness. Much of the *coca* grown in the region goes to Colombia and reaches Europe and the US as cocaine. Governments in the region are now under international pressure to stop its cultivation, but *coca* farmers defend their right to grow it, both for their own use and because it is so profitable.

colegio concertado In Spain, a school that is privately owned but receives a government grant. Parents pay monthly fees, but not as much as in a COLEGIO PRIVADO. *Colegios concertados* normally cover all stages of primary and secondary education and often have religious connections.

colegio estatal In Spain, a school offering compulsory primary education for children aged from six to twelve. Some also offer non-compulsory classes for three to six year olds. Part of the free state school system, their official name is *CEIP* (*Colegios de Educación Infantil y Primaria*).

colegio privado A privately owned school that receives no government funds. Parents pay monthly fees. *Colegios privados* cover all stages of primary and secondary education.

comarca In Spain, a geographical, social, and culturally homogeneous region, with a clear natural or administrative demarcation.

comunidades autónomas In 1978 power in Spain was decentralized and the country was divided into *comunidades autónomas* or *autonomías* (autonomous regions), replacing the old *regiones.* The new communities have far greater autonomy from central government than the old *regiones,* and were a response to nationalist aspirations, which had built up under Franco. Some regions have more autonomy than others. The Basque Country, Catalonia, and Galicia, for example, had political structures, a desire for independence, and their own languages, which underpinned their claims to distinctive identities. Andalusia gained almost complete autonomy without having had a nationalist tradition. Other regions, such as Madrid, are to some extent artificial, having been created largely to complete the process. The *comunidades autónomas* are: Andalusia, Aragon, Asturias, Balearic Islands, the Basque Country (EUSKADI), Canary Islands, Cantabria, Castilla y León, Castilla-La Mancha, Catalonia, Extremadura, Galicia, Madrid, Murcia, Navarre, La Rioja, Valencia, and the North African cities of Ceuta and Melilla.

La Concertación A pro-democracy coalition founded in Chile in 1988 to oppose the then-president Augusto Pinochet. Its specific aim was to present a united front at the plebiscite on whether Pinochet should continue as president. Pinochet lost the plebiscite and the party has since facilitated a peaceful transition to democracy after years of dictatorship.

Condorito A cartoon character with a huge following throughout Latin America, Condorito (Little Condor) is a condor who lives in Pelotillehue. Created by the Chilean René Ríos in 1949, Condorito was used by Microsoft as the Hispanic American logo for Windows 98.

Congreso de los Diputados Also known as the *Cámara de los Diputados*, this is the lower house of the Spanish CORTES GENERALES. The number of members (*diputados*) ranges from 300 to 400. Members are elected every four years by proportional representation. Each of Spain's 52 provinces is treated as an electoral district. The *Congreso* legislates, approves the budget, elects the prime minister, controls the actions of the executive, and debates current national and international political issues.

Cono Sur describes the Spanish-speaking countries of the southern cone of Latin America, i.e. Argentina, Chile, Paraguay, and Uruguay.

Conquistadores The collective term for the succession of explorers, soldiers, and adventurers who, from the 16th century onward, led the settlement and exploitation of Spain's Latin American colonies. Among the best known are Hernán Cortés (Mexico), Hernando de Soto (Florida, Nicaragua), and the Pizarro brothers (Panama, Peru, Ecuador).

Constitución Española The current Spanish Constitution was approved in the CORTES GENERALES in December 1978. Generally well received, except in the Basque Country, which wanted independence, it is thought to have facilitated the successful transition from dictatorship to democracy.

copetín In the River Plate region of Latin America, an aperitif or light snack, or the social occasion at which they are eaten.

Correos The name of Spain's state-run post office. Stamps can be bought in ESTANCOS, although certified or express mail must be sent from a post office (*estafeta* or *oficina de correos*). Postboxes in Spain are silver with red and yellow hoops. There are also red boxes for urgent mail. In Latin America *correo*, in the singular, means both a post office and the mail system.

corrida A bullfight. Bullfighting remains popular in many parts of Spain and some Latin American countries, and is regularly broadcast on television. During the *corrida,* three bullfighters (*matadores*) fight a total of six bulls, two each. *See also* TOROS (LA FIESTA DE LOS).

corrido In Mexico, a ballad sung to guitar and trumpet accompaniment on subjects such as heroic deeds, love, and the lives of historical and fictional characters. *Corridos* are straightforward songs of ordinary people.

Cortes Generales The Spanish parliament, consisting of two houses, the lower house or CONGRESO DE LOS DIPUTADOS, and the upper house or SENADO. It is a legislative body, approves state budgets, and exercises other powers, including appointments to posts in institutions such as the TRIBUNAL CONSTITUCIONAL.

cuatro A four-stringed musical instrument, typical of Venezuela, similar to a smaller version of the guitar.

Cuban Revolution The guerrilla campaign (1956–9) that started the Cuban

Revolution (*Revolución cubana*) aimed to topple the corrupt regime of Fulgencio Batista and free Cuba from US economic domination. The new government of January 1959 set in motion wide-ranging social and political reforms. When Fidel Castro Ruz announced the expropriation of foreign-owned companies, the US imposed a trade embargo that has lasted into the new century. After the unsuccessful invasion by CIA-trained Cuban exiles at the Bay of Pigs (Playa Girón), bilateral relations worsened and Cuba sought support from the communist block. When the USSR collapsed in 1991, the Cuban economy was left in ruins. It recovered somewhat in the 1990s thanks to the growth of international tourism and new industries such as pharmaceuticals. Cuba is criticized by the US for not adopting parliamentary democracy, and the presence of a politically influential Cuban community in the United States has blocked normal relations between the countries. In Latin America, revolutionary Cuba has inspired political movements seeking to improve the lot of workers and peasants.

Culture

cumbia One of the most typical varieties of Colombian music and dance, also very popular in the rest of Latin America. It combines elements of African, Spanish, and native Colombian music.

curanto ▶ BARBACOA

Defensor del pueblo An ombudsman nominated by the Spanish Parliament to defend the rights of citizens against government maladministration. This post, under the same name, also exists in some Latin American countries.

desaparecidos The name for people who, in the 1970s, during the military dictatorships in Argentina, Chile, and Uruguay, were detained by the police, secret police, and the armed forces in a campaign to restore 'law and order'. Thousands of detainees were murdered and never seen again.

despacho de lotería y apuestas del estado Or simply *despacho de lotería*, this is a store in Spain licenced to sell lottery tickets.

Día de la Hispanidad (Día de la Raza) ▶ TRADITIONS, FESTIVALS, AND HOLIDAYS

Día de los (Santos) Inocentes ▶ TRADITIONS, FESTIVALS, AND HOLIDAYS

Día de todos los Santos or (in Spain) **de los Difuntos** or (in Latin America) **de los Muertos** ▶ TRADITIONS, FESTIVALS, AND HOLIDAYS

Día del Trabajo ▶ TRADITIONS, FESTIVALS, AND HOLIDAYS

Día Nacional de Catalunya ▶ TRADITIONS, FESTIVALS, AND HOLIDAYS

Culture

diablada A dance originating in Andean mining communities in which participants dress up as devils. It combines pagan and religious elements and is especially associated with Oruro, Bolivia, during carnival, and with the festival of LA TIRANA.

DNI – Documento Nacional de Identidad ▶ CARNÉ DE IDENTIDAD

dulce de leche A sort of caramel spread made of milk and sugar. It is called *manjar (blanco)* in the Andean region and *cajeta* in Mexico.

educación infantil In Spain, a period of voluntary pre-school education. It provides care and teaching for children from birth to the age of six, when they begin formal education. *See also* GUARDERÍAS and COLEGIOS.

educación secundaria ▶ ESO

education systems In Spain, as in Latin America, schooling begins with pre-school education or *Parvularia* (EP), which is not compulsory.

Education is usually compulsory between the ages of 6 and 16 and covers *educación* PRIMARIA or *básica* and *educación secundaria* or *media* (EM), both of which are free. Secondary education usually ends with a leaving certificate called the BACHILLERATO or *licencia*, according to country. Education is delivered in state and private schools, some of which, like the COLEGIOS CONCERTADOS in Spain, are state-subsidized. Illiteracy is still a problem in some Latin American countries: Guatemala has the worst rate at 44 percent; in Peru the rate is 15 percent.

empanada In Spain, a typically Galician delicacy consisting of puff pastry with a variety of fillings. In Latin America it is normally smaller and made with bread dough stuffed with fish, meat etc., oven-cooked or fried.

enchufe y enchufismo In Spain, *enchufe* refers to the use of personal connections to obtain a job or favor. *Enchufismo* is the practice of giving out jobs and other benefits on the basis of *enchufes*. In Latin America the term *palanca* is used for *enchufe*, but there is no equivalent for *enchufismo*.

enseñanza primaria ▶ PRIMARIA

enseñanza secundaria ▶ ESO

equeco or **ekeco** In Peru and Bolivia a lucky charm made of plaster or clay in the form of a smiling, open-armed human figure holding desirable objects. An *equeco* is supposed to bring prosperity to the owner.

Ertzaintza The Basque autonomous police force. Its members, *ertzaintzas*, wear a uniform of red sweaters and berets, and white jackets. Despite the *Ertzaintza's* wide range of responsibilities, the GUARDIA CIVIL and POLICÍA NACIONAL still operate in the Basque Country.

Escorial, El (San Lorenzo de El Escorial) Founded by Philip II in 1563, this site includes a complex of buildings making up the monastery, Philip II's chambers, and the Spanish royal family's mausoleum.

ESO – Enseñanza Secundaria Obligatoria One of the stages of secondary education established in Spain by the LOGSE. It begins at 12 years of age and ends at 16, the age at which compulsory education ends. The old division between a technical and an academic education is not as marked in ESO, as all secondary pupils receive basic professional training.

espalda mojada The name in Mexico for people who try to enter the US illegally by crossing the Rio Grande. In Spain the term refers to illegal immigrants from Morocco who cross the Straits of Gibraltar to enter Spain. In both countries *espaldas mojadas* are a source of cheap unskilled labor. *See also* PATERA.

Esquerra Republicana (EPC) A democratic Catalan party, left-wing in orientation, whose support and influence have grown recently.

esquinazo In Chile, a serenade of songs and folk dancing, performed as a surprise in honor of people or institutions, to mark a notable event.

estanco *Estancos* sell tobacco, stamps, transport passes, and other products whose sale is restricted. (Cigarettes can be bought in bars/cafés but at higher prices.) They also sell stationery and sometimes newspapers.

Estudiantina ▶ TUNA

ETA – Euskadi ta Askatasuna Its title means 'Basque homeland and liberty'. ETA is a terrorist organization founded in 1959 to fight for Basque independence. Its political wing, established in 1978 as Herri Batasuna (Popular Unity) and now called BATASUNA (Unity), has a number of elected representatives on local councils and in the Basque parliament. Opinion polls show a majority of Basques are opposed to the political violence and murder campaigns espoused by ETA.

Euskadi The most widely accepted term in the Basque language for the Basque country. The present COMUNIDAD AUTÓNOMA includes the three Basque provinces of Vizcaya, Guipúzcoa, and Álava, but not neighboring Navarre, which also has many Basque-speakers and cultural traditions. For this reason the most uncompromising of Basque separatists prefer the term EUSKAL HERRIA, which includes Euskadi, Navarre, and also the Basque *département* of southwest France, Iparralde.

Euskal Herria A name in Basque meaning 'Basque nation', used by some Basque nationalists in preference to EUSKADI, to refer to the greater Basque homeland.

Euskera The language of the Basque Country and Navarre, spoken by around 750,000 people; in Spanish *vasco* or *vascuence*. It is also spelled Euskara. Basque is unrelated to the Indo-European languages and its origins are unclear. Like Spain's other regional languages, Basque was banned under Franco. With the return of democracy, it became an official language alongside Spanish, in the regions where it is spoken. It is a compulsory school subject and needed for many official and administrative posts in the Basque Country. There is Basque language television and radio and a considerable number of books are published in Basque. *See also* LENGUAS COOFICIALES.

EZLN, the initials of the *Ejército Zapatista de Liberación Nacional*, the revolutionary movement founded in Chiapas, Mexico, in 1994, and led by the *mestizo* known as Subcomandante Marcos. Over the years the rebel group has succeeded in drawing support from other native ethnic groups seeking recognition of their rights.

Fallas ▶ TRADITIONS, FESTIVALS, AND HOLIDAYS

FARC (Fuerzas Armadas Revolucionarias de Colombia) Established in 1964 as an armed, economic, and social response to the aggressively liberal-conservative regime in Marquetalia. It describes itself as a people's army, but it is widely regarded as a terrorist organization that finances its activities through extortion, kidnapping, and drug-trafficking.

Feria de San Telmo (St Telmo market) This is one of the most important attractions in Buenos Aires life. It is held every Sunday in the Plaza Dorrego in the San Telmo district, where stalls offer antiques and bric-à-brac amid buskers, tango dancers, and mime artists.

Feria de Sevilla ▶ TRADITIONS, FESTIVALS, AND HOLIDAYS

Festival de Viña del Mar ▶ TRADITIONS, FESTIVALS, AND HOLIDAYS

fiesta de 15 The celebration of a girl's 15th birthday is a common Latin American custom. The girl often wears a pastel-colored dress. It is customary to have a tiered cake with floral decorations and there is music and dancing. In Mexico it is called the *quinceañera*.

fiestas patrias In Latin America, a period of one or more days on which each country celebrates its independence. There are usually military parades, firework displays, and folk activities.

flamenco Flamenco is performed in three forms: guitar, singing, and dancing. Its origins lie with the gypsies, and many of the best *cantaores* (flamenco singers), *bailaores* (dancers), and guitarists are gypsies. There are also Arabic and North African influences. Modern flamenco blends traditional forms with rock, jazz, and salsa. Most flamenco songs are folk songs, modified by oral tradition. The music and lyrics are improvised and never written down. An integral part of traditional flamenco is the *duende*, the idea that the performer becomes inspired by the emotion of the music or dance. But as flamenco becomes commercialized, rehearsed performances are more likely than spontaneous ones.

football is the most popular sport in Spain and most of Latin America, though in some Caribbean countries baseball is favorite. The *Copa América* is the continent's top football trophy and the oldest international football competition in the world. It was first held in 1916. Uruguay (once), Argentina (twice) and Brazil (five times) have all won the World Cup. Pelé and Diego Maradona, considered among the best footballers of all time, both come from Latin America. It is a way out of poverty for many young players.

Formación Profesional – FP After the ESO stage in the Spanish education system, pupils go on to BACHILLERATO, with its more traditional academic approach, or to *Formación Profesional*, which has a vocational focus. *FP* comprises two cycles, one for students from 16 to 18 and another, running parallel to university education, for students of 18 and over. After both cycles students qualify for a specific occupation, or to go on to more specialized courses. *See also* LOGSE.

fueros Medieval charters setting out the privileges granted to an individual, a town, or a territory. 'Foral' rights were held, for example, by the cities of León and Burgos, by the former kingdom of Navarre, and by the Basque provinces. Each Spanish monarch traditionally went to GUERNICA to reaffirm the rights of the Basques.

Gallego The language of Galicia, spoken by around 3 million people. It is an official requirement for many official and academic positions, and a compulsory school subject. Galician, a Romance language similar to Portuguese, was banned under Franco, but with the return to democracy, it became an official language in Galicia beside Castilian. Nowadays there is Galician radio and television, and a considerable amount of publishing. Galician has less social prestige than Catalan and Basque in their homelands. The middle classes have largely opted to use Castilian. *See also* LENGUAS COOFICIALES.

gaucho A peasant of the pampas of Argentina, Uruguay, and Brazil. Modern *gauchos* work as foremen on farms and ranches and take part in rodeos. *Gauchos* fought for Argentine independence from Spain, but later became involved in political disputes and suffered persecution. A literary genre, *literatura gauchesca*, grew up in the 18th and 19th centuries. The most famous work is *Martín Fierro*, an epic poem by José Hernández, about an Argentine *gaucho* suffering when the huge pampas are divided into ranches.

Culture

Traditionally *gauchos* wore baggy trousers, leather chaps, a *chiripá* (which went over their trousers and came up around their waist), boots, a hat, a leather waistcoat, a belt with a large buckle. They carried a *facón* – a large knife with a curved blade, and used *boleadoras*, ropes weighted at each end and thrown like lassos, to catch cattle.

gazpacho A cold soup made from tomatoes, cucumbers, and peppers which is typical of Andalusia.

Generación del 98/27 These two important groups of Spanish writers were inspired by events that united them and that initially defined their writing. The *Generación del 98* came into being after the loss of the Philippines and Cuba in the war with the US (1898), an event which underlined Spain's decline. Its most important members were Miguel de Unamuno, Ramón del Valle-Inclán, Pío Baroja, Azorín, and Antonio Machado. The *Generación del 27* was a group of writers who rose to prominence in the late 1920s (the group's name marked the third centenary of the death of the poet Góngora in 1927). Its writing focuses on the themes of love, death, and man's destiny, often seen through popular art forms. Its most prominent members were Federico García Lorca, Rafael Alberti, Dámaso Alonso, Vicente Aleixandre, and Miguel Hernández.

Generalitat The name of the autonomous governments of Catalonia and Valencia. A great deal of power has now been transferred to them from central government. The medieval term *generalitat* was revived in 1932, when Catalonia voted for its own devolved government. Franco abolished it, but it was restored in 1978 with the establishment of COMUNIDADES AUTÓNOMAS. The Valencian Generalitat is keen to preserve the traditions of the region from Catalan influence.

gestoría In Spain, an office that deals with government agencies on behalf of its clients. It is common practice to use a *gestoría* to avoid the problems of dealing with Spanish bureaucracy, despite the cost involved.

Giralda, La Today a bell tower, this was the tower of the largest mosque in Islamic Seville, built in the 12th century. It is the city's symbol and one of the finest towers of its type in the world.

Gitano A member of Spain's gypsy community. Gypsies often live in camps and retain their nomadic habits. They have preserved many of their customs and do not usually integrate into the mainstream of Spanish society. Their language is CALÓ. Gypsies have been a great influence on FLAMENCO, and many of the best performers are Gypsies.

Gordo, El In Spain, the name of the big prizes in the LOTERÍA NACIONAL and LOTERÍA PRIMITIVA, in particular the prize for the Christmas draw of the *Lotería Nacional*. In Latin America it also means a big lottery prize.

gringo A pejorative term in Latin America meaning a white English speaker, particularly a North American. In the 18th century it referred to a foreigner who spoke little or no Spanish.

Guaraní The name of a people who lived between the rivers Amazon and Plate, and their language. Guaraní is also an official language in Paraguay and is spoken in parts of Argentina, Bolivia, and Brazil. The Jesuit missionaries in Paraguay wrote Guaraní dictionaries and grammars, hymns and catechisms. Guaraní acquired a symbolic status in Paraguay during the Chaco War with Bolivia, 1932–5. Today, many Paraguayans with hardly any indigenous blood speak Guaraní better than Spanish.

guardería In Spain, a center for small children. *Guarderías* normally look after children from a few months old until the age of four, or sometimes up to the compulsory school age of six. Some *guarderías* are private, while some are run and subsidized by the local authority or the government.

Guardia Civil A rural paramilitary police force founded in Spain in 1844. It has been used by different governments to fight against organized labor, republicanism, and regional autonomy, and came to be seen as an instrument of state repression. The Civil Guard has adapted to the new democratic Spain and is involved in anti-terrrorist operations, the coastguard service, and environmental protection. Civil guards are armed and traditionally wore the *tricornio*, a black, patent-leather, three-cornered hat. In an effort to change its image, the Civil Guard now only wears the *tricornio* on ceremonial occasions, or when on duty in front of official buildings.

guayabera Originally from Cuba, this is a light, loose shirt worn over the trousers. It has become a symbol of a relaxed outlook on life and is fashionable with young Americans and Mexicans.

Guernica A Basque town destroyed in April 1937 by German bombers fighting on the Nationalist side in the Spanish Civil War (GUERRA CIVIL). The death toll among civilians shocked the world; the horror was vividly evoked in Pablo Picasso's painting, *Guernica*. Guernica (Gernika) is the site of the ancient Basque parliament and of the oak tree, the *árbol de Guernica*, beneath which Spanish kings traditionally swore to uphold Basque privileges, or FUEROS. *See also* EUSKADI.

Guerra Civil The Spanish Civil War of 1936–9 began when right-wing army officers led by General Francisco Franco rebelled against the elected government of the Spanish Republic. South and northwest Spain soon fell to Franco's *nacionalistas*, but in cities such as Madrid, Bilbao, and Barcelona, resistance was fierce. Franco's revolt was aided by Nazi Germany and Fascist Italy, while Britain and France declared a policy of non-intervention, blockading Spanish ports. The Soviet Union aided the

Republican government, and volunteers from around the world joined the *Brigadas Internacionales* to fight against Fascism. Resistance collapsed in 1939, and Franco established a dictatorship that only ended with his death in 1975. A period of great economic hardship followed the Civil War. The persecution of Republicans continued for many years.

Guerras de Independencia Spain's War of Independence against Napoléon Bonaparte's French occupation was ignited by the popular revolt in Madrid on 2 May 1808 against the French army. The reprisal executions are commemorated in a famous painting by Francisco de Goya. With support from the Duke of Wellington, Spanish resistance continued for over five years in a *guerra de guerrillas* that gave the world the concept of and the term, 'guerrilla warfare'. The autocratic Fernando VII was restored to the throne in 1814, and his first act was to abolish the progressive Constitution of Cadiz (1812). The Wars of Independence of Spain's Latin American colonies resulted in Argentina achieving

independence in 1816. Simón Bolívar of Caracas led a freedom movement that was to sweep South America and earned him the title *El Libertador*. By 1840 all the mainland Spanish colonies were independent. Others who played crucial roles in the independence struggles of Spain's colonies during the 19th century include Hidalgo, Morelos and Guerrero (Mexico), Sucre and Miranda (Venezuela, Peru), San Martín, Brown and Belgrano (Argentina), O'Higgins, San Martín (Chile), Céspedes and Martí (Cuba).

hallaca or **hayaca** This is a traditional Venezuelan dish made with maize dough and a highly seasoned stuffing. Rectangular in shape, it is wrapped in banana leaves and boiled. It is associated with Christmas.

Herri Batasuna ▶ ETA

huaco or guaco In the Andean region, a pre-conquest pot taken from a *huaca*, or Incaic burial place.

huaino or huayno The traditional dance and music of the Peruvian Andes. Characterized by distinctive rhythms, and by pairs of dancers performing reels without personal contact, it is also found with some variations in Ecuador, Bolivia, and the north of Chile.

huipil A traditional shirt worn by Indian and *mestizo* women in Mexico and Central America. Generally made of richly embroidered cotton, *huipiles* are very wide and low-cut, and are either waist- or thigh-length.

ICV – Iniciativa per Catalunya Verds The Catalan ecology party. It aims to promote ecological socialism and Catalan autonomy.

Incas Founded in the 12th century in the region of Lake Titicaca, by the

15th century the Andean empire of the Quechua-speaking Incas extended from southern Colombia down to Argentina and central Chile. Their society was rigidly divided into classes: the nobility, their servants, and the common people. The Incas worshipped the sun and the moon, and believed that Manco Capac, their first emperor, or *inca*, was descended from the sun. An extensive network of roads was built to facilitate control over the empire from its capital in Cuzco. The Incas left an impressive heritage of monuments, including the palace complex of MACHU PICCHU. The empire collapsed in 1533 when the Spanish conquistador Francisco Pizarro had the emperor Atahualpa executed, and occupied Cuzco.

INEM – Instituto Nacional de Empleo The Spanish department of employment. It is responsible for all aspects of employment, from unemployment benefits to employee protection. It is also an employment agency for hard-to-place job seekers, and runs training courses.

instituto In Spain, a center of secondary education providing ESO and BACHILLERATO. *Institutos* are part of the state school system.

insumiso In Spain, a person who refused to do either compulsory military service (abolished in 2001), or the alternative community service.

jerez (sherry) Sherry is produced in an area of chalky soil known as *albariza* lying between the towns of Puerto de Santa María, Sanlúcar de Barrameda, and Jerez de la Frontera in Cádiz province. It is from Jerez that sherry takes its English name. Sherries, made from grape varieties including Palomino and Pedro Ximénez, are drunk worldwide as an aperitif, and in Spain as an accompaniment to TAPAS. The styles of jerez vary from the pale *fino* and *manzanilla* to the darker aromatic *oloroso* and *amontillado*.

jorongo ▶ PONCHO

joropo A Venezuelan dance, its music, and the event at which they take place. The dance, also popular in Colombia, is performed to the harp, the *cuatro,* and other instruments.

jota In Spain, a song or dance typical of several regions. The music, which is very lively, is played on string and percussion instruments.

Junta Autonómica The name given to the governments of Spain's autonomous regions, with the exception of Catalonia and Valencia's GENERALITAT and Galicia's Xunta.

Latin American cinema For a long time a fractured industry led by Argentina, Brazil, and especially Mexico. Between 1930 and 1996 these countries accounted for 89 percent of the region's output. In the 1940s Mexican movies became popular, starring actors such as Dolores del Río

Culture

and Pedro Armendáriz. In countries such as Cuba, Chile, Bolivia, Peru, and Colombia, the film industry has been hampered by lack of resources and, in general, by poor demand in home markets, but it has also shown great originality. From the 1980s foreign investment has increased through co-productions and interest from European television companies. Today foreign interest is increasing and the industry's appeal is reaching beyond specialist film festivals to general audiences.

Latin American literature has its origins in the chronicles of the *conquistadores* and the missionary catechisms. The 19th century, with an increasing sense of national identity, saw the first Latin American novel (in 1816), written by the Mexican José Joaquín Fernández de Lizardi. The Venezuelan poet and critic, Andrés Bello, based his work on Latin American themes and created a new poetic genre. The Latin American short story came to maturity in the early 20th century, the work of the Uruguayan, Horacio Quiroga, with his stories of the jungle being especially noteworthy.

From 1910 Latin American fiction took off and in 1945 the Chilean, Gabriela Mistral, was awarded the Nobel Prize for Literature. Other winners of the prize have been: M. Ángel Asturias (Guatemala, 1967), P. Neruda (Chile, 1971), G. García Márquez (Colombia, 1982) and O. Paz (Mexico, 1998). Today Latin American writers are prominent, with authors such as M. Vargas Llosa (Peru), and Isabel Allende (Chile) selling to audiences worldwide.

Latin American universities From the 16th century to 1812, Spain founded 32 universities in its American colonies. The University of San Marcos in Peru, where many of the prominent figures in Latin American arts, science, and politics were students, was founded in 1551, as was the University of Mexico. Other universities founded by the Spaniards are: University of San Carlos (Guatemala, 1676), University of Havana (Cuba, 1728). In post-independence Latin America many more were founded, and in the 20th century private universities gained in importance.

lehendakari The president of the Basque autonomous government. The *lehendakari* is responsible for the administration of the Basque Country, and liaises with the prime minister of the Spanish central government. *See also* EUSKADI.

lenguas cooficiales The regional languages of Spain – CATALÁN, EUSKERA, and GALLEGO – which now have equal status with Castilian in the regions where they are spoken. Banned under Franco, they continued to be spoken privately. They are now widely used in public life, education, and the media, cinema, and literature.

libertadores, los The name given to the most important leaders of the Latin American independence movement of the early 19th century. Among the most prominent are Simón Bolívar (Venezuela), José de San Martín (Argentina) and Bernardo O'Higgins (Chile). They dreamed of a united, Spanish-speaking republic.

licenciatura The name given to the first university degree. Degree courses in Spain used to last five years. Now, after the passing of the LRU, degrees – except for medicine and architecture – normally take four years.

Líneas de Nasca The Nasca Lines are located in a desert area near the coastal town of Nasca. Almost 50 km (31 miles) in length and 15km (9 miles) wide, they have been declared a cultural heritage site by UNESCO. They consist of vast geometrical and animal figures, which can only be seen from the air. Created between 300 BC and AD 900 by the ancient Nasca people, they are one of the most important and intriguing legacies of the pre-Incaic cultures of Peru.

linguistic differences There are significant linguistic differences between different parts of the Spanish-speaking world. The pronoun *tú* is replaced by *vos* in the River Plate area and Central America. This change affects verb forms, e.g. *vos sos* for *tú eres*, etc. In Latin America the pronoun, *vosotros*, so common in Spain, is never used. There are words that have different preferred translations according to the country concerned, e.g. English bus (*autobús* in Spain) is a *camión* in Mexico and Central America, *colectivo* in Argentina, *micro* in Chile, *ómnibus* in Peru and Uruguay, *guagua* in Cuba. A word may have a vulgar or offensive meaning in some countries and not in others, e.g. *coger*, which has no vulgar connotations in Spain, is a taboo word in Mexico, Argentina, Uruguay, and Venezuela. In almost all of Latin America, the simple past tense is preferred to the present perfect; compare *fui a comprar* (Latin America) and *he ido a comprar* (Spain).

literature ▶ LATIN AMERICAN LITERATURE

LOGSE – Ley Orgánica de Ordenación General del Sistema Educativo A Spanish educational reform passed in 1990. A priority was to tackle the high rate of failure and non-attendance among school pupils. It established four stages of pre-university education: non-compulsory EDUCACIÓN INFANTIL, from birth to six years old; compulsory primary education (PRIMARIA), from six to twelve years; compulsory secondary education, ESO, from twelve to sixteen; and either two years of BACHILLERATO, leading to university entrance, or two years of *Formación Profesional Específica de Grado Medio*, vocational training that can lead to *Formación Profesional Específica de Grado Superior*. The division between vocational and academic studies is less marked than it was before.

Lotería Nacional A Spanish state-run lottery founded in 1812. There is an 'ordinary' draw on Thursdays and 'special' and 'extraordinary' draws, offering bigger prizes. The biggest are EL GORDO, drawn before Christmas, and El Niño, drawn at Epiphany. Other lotteries are the BONOLOTO, LOTERÍA PRIMITIVA, and the ONCE.

Lotería Primitiva or Loto A Spanish state lottery founded in 1985. As in the BONOLOTO, players choose six out of 49 numbers on a ticket and win the main prize if all the numbers are drawn. There are 'ordinary' draws on Thursdays and Saturdays, and a draw for a larger prize on the last Sunday of each month, known as EL GORDO, or *El Gordo de la Primitiva*.

loto ▶ LOTERÍA PRIMITIVA

LRU – Ley de Reforma Universitaria A Spanish law of 1983 that divided responsibility for universities between the state, the autonomous regions, and the universities. It gave universities academic independence and responsibility for hiring and promoting staff, and shortened degree courses from five to four years. Subjects offered were changed to meet the needs of the labor market.

lunfardo A form of Buenos Aires slang that originated in the underworld. It draws on many languages, including Italian, Portuguese, Spanish, French, German, and several African languages. It has found its way into popular songs and theater. *Lunfardo* words in standard colloquial speech are *morfar* (to eat), *güita* (money), and *mina* (woman).

machismo A concept deeply rooted in the Spanish-speaking world. It has its origin in a sense of honor, felt to depend on a man's actions and those of his close family, particularly the women. *Machismo* is present in the home, where even working women usually do most of the housework, and extends to the workplace. It can affect the legal status of women. In Spain legal reforms since the 1970s have contributed to undermining *machismo*.

Machu Picchu An Inca fortress and sacred city in the southern Peruvian Andes. The site covers an area of around 5 square miles (13 square kilometers) at an altitude of 7,874 feet (2,400 meters). It includes a temple and citadel and is surrounded by terraces. It was rediscovered in 1911 by the American, Hiram Bingham.

Mafalda is a comic-strip character created by the Argentinian Joaquín Salvador Lavado, known as Quino. She is an inquisitive, ingenuous six year old, who also reflects on life. She first appeared in the 1960s; the strip has been translated into 26 languages.

Mallorquín The variety of CATALÁN spoken in the Balearic Islands. Some people regard it as a separate language from Catalan, which enjoys official status, but it is not officially recognized as such.

manjar (blanco) ▶ DULCE DE LECHE

mañanitas In Mexico, a short love song sung on someone's birthday, or SANTO, or in honor of an important person. It is also a song that MARIACHIS sing at dawn serenades.

Mapuche The largest group of Araucanian-speaking South American Indians, living in the central valley of Chile. The Mapuche struggled for 350 years against Spanish and Chilean domination. After Chilean independence, the Mapuche were put in reservations. In the 1980s, the Chilean government transferred ownership of the land to individual Mapuche, who risk losing their land if they incur debts that they cannot repay. Originally the Mapuche were one part of the Araucanian people, but nowadays the two terms are used synonymously, as most Araucanians are Mapuche. Araucano or Mapuche is spoken in Chile and Argentina.

Mariachi The traditional Mexican musical ensembles, the lively *mestizo* music that they play, and the dance performed to it. The instruments used by *Mariachis* are the guitar, harp, *vihuela* (an early form of guitar), violin, and trumpet. *Mariachis* wearing costumes based on those worn by CHARROS can be seen in the Plaza Garibaldi, in Mexico City, where they are hired for parties, or to sing MANAÑITAS or serenades.

mate is a somewhat bitter infusion of the leaves of *yerba mate*, a caffeine-rich South American shrub. It is very typical of the River Plate region and is drunk through a straw (*bombilla*) from a gourd, also called a *mate*. Once associated with the GAUCHOS, it is common throughout the CONO SUR and is drunk at any time of day.

Mayas The Mayas, possibly of North American origin, settled in the Yucatán Peninsula around 2600 BC, and established a civilization that spread through Southern Mexico, into Guatemala, Belize, parts of Honduras and El Salvador, flourishing until the arrival of the Spanish in the 16th century. Their society was organized on the basis of city states grouped into confederations. Though lacking metal tools, the Mayas built stepped pyramids and other stone monuments, such as those at Chichén Itzá, Uxmal, and Petén.

mediasnueves ▶ ONCES

Mexican food is varied and among the tastiest in the world. Its most common ingredients are maize and beans, both foods with Mayan and Aztec origins. Chillies and cactus are also used. Dishes based on the *tortilla* (thin unleavened maize cake) are the most common and some, such as *tacos*, *enchiladas*, *quesadillas*, and *sopes*, are now well known internationally. Other typical dishes are *guacamole*, *pozole* (a kind of stew), *frijoles refritos*, and *frijoles de olla* (bean dishes). Cooking ingredients that originated in Mexico include chocolate, vanilla, maize,

Culture

pumpkins, zucchini or courgettes, and bell peppers.

mezcal An alcoholic drink similar to TEQUILA, obtained in Mexico by distilling the juice or *aguamiel* extracted from roasted tips of the maguey plant. Bottles of *mezcal* are usually sold containing a *gusano*, the larva of an insect that lives on the maguey. This is said to enhance the flavor.

mili In Spain, the colloquial term for compulsory military service. Abolished in 2001, it was for years an important factor in Spanish life. It was once an opportunity for many people to leave their home town and learn to read and write. One could avoid *la mili* by declaring oneself an *objetor de conciencia*. Conscientious objectors did community service, *prestación social sustitutoria*. Those who refused to do this were called INSUMISOS.

mojito a long Cuban drink made with rum, soda water, macerated mint leaves, sugar, and lemon juice.

Moncloa, Palacio de la The Spanish prime minister's official residence in Madrid.

Moneda, Palacio de la The Chilean presidential palace in Santiago.

Mossos d'Esqua The police force of the Catalan autonomous region. It has a wide range of responsibilities, but the GUARDIA CIVIL and POLICÍA NACIONAL also operate in Catalonia.

murales y muralistas mexicanos Mexico's muralist movement flourished between the two world wars during a time of nationalist fervor. It was led by Diego Rivera, José Clemente Orozco, and David Alfaro Siqueiros. Their work reflected revolutionary themes and the working-class struggle. They decorated many public buildings.

murga A band of street musicians common in Argentina and in the Montevideo (Uruguay) carnival. Performances of music and song comment on topical subjects of public interest. Bass drums and cymbals are characteristic of *murga* music.

Náhuatl was the main language of the Aztecs and is still spoken today in Mexico. Spanish words that come from Náhuatl include *chocolate*, *tomate*, *chile*, and *coyote*. *See also* AZTECAS.

natillas A custard-like dish made of eggs, milk, and sugar, popular as a dessert especially in Spain and also in Mexico.

NIF – Número de identificación fiscal Tax identification code that is compulsory for all residents of Spain. People must give it when applying for a loan, opening a bank account, sending invoices, etc.

Nochebuena ▶ TRADITIONS, FESTIVALS, AND HOLIDAYS

Nochevieja y Año Nuevo ▶ TRADITIONS, FESTIVALS, AND HOLIDAYS

ONCE – Organización Nacional de Ciegos Españoles Founded in 1938 to create employment for the blind, in 1981 ONCE launched a national lottery that is drawn every day except Saturday. Money raised is invested in training and social centers for blind people.

onces In some Andean countries, particularly Chile, *onces* is a light meal eaten between five and six p.m., the equivalent of 'afternoon tea' in Britain. In Colombia, *onces* is a light snack eaten between breakfast and lunch, like the British 'elevenses'. It is also known as *mediasnueves*.

onomástica ▶ SANTO

oposiciones In Spain, competitive examinations for people wanting a public-sector job, to teach in an INSTITUTO, or to become a judge. The large number of candidates (*opositores*) – many more than the number of posts available – means that the exams are very difficult.

Opus Dei Latin for 'God's Work', Opus Dei is a Catholic organization founded in Spain in 1928. It became very influential in Spanish society, above all by founding schools and universities. The aim was to create an élite which would spread Christian ideals throughout society. The University of Navarre is one of its foremost institutions.

paella In Spain *paella* (pronounced pa'elya) is associated with Valencia and is often called *paella valenciana*. It is made with rice, seafood, meat, and vegetables. Bell peppers, olive oil, and saffron are also essential.

paga extra or **paga extraordinaria** In Spain, a bonus payment equivalent to a month's salary, paid twice a year (in July and at Christmas) on top of the normal monthly salary. The bonuses are guaranteed to most permanent employees.

País, El The Spanish daily newspaper with the largest circulation (over 436,000). Its website is www.elpais.es. First published in 1976, it became a symbol of transition, and of the new Spanish democracy. The paper generally supports the PSOE.

Palacio de Oriente or **Palacio Real** is the official residence of the Spanish Royal Family. The Royal Family now lives in the Palacio de la ZARZUELA, on the outskirts of Madrid.

palanca ▶ ENCHUFE Y ENCHUFISMO

PAN – Partido de Acción Nacional Founded in 1939 as a conservative alternative to the then-President, Lázaro Cárdenas, PAN won the Mexican general elections in 2000, breaking the PRI's record of 71 years in power.

paraditas In Peru, street markets selling food.

Parador (Nacional de Turismo) A national chain of hotels in Spain. *Paradores* were designed to give buildings such as former palaces, castles, and monasteries a new lease of life and to bring tourism to economically disadvantaged areas. They are often luxurious but relatively inexpensive.

paro The name in Spain for both unemployment and unemployment benefit. The period for which *paro* can be claimed ranges from three months to a year, depending on how long a person has been working. The amount paid decreases over the period of unemployment.

pasapalo In Venezuela, small portions of food that are usually served with drinks at bars and social gatherings.

patera A boat with a shallow draft, used by illegal immigrants to cross the Straits of Gibraltar from Morocco to southern Spain. *See also* ESPALDA MOJADA.

pelota vasca A ball game, also known as *jai alai*, that developed in the Basque Country. It is played in Spain, Mexico, Cuba, and Florida in a *frontón*, a court with three high walls. The players use a *cesta*, a long, concave basket attached to their hand with a strap, to throw the ball against the walls and catch it. Spectators watch from behind a metal fence. Pelota is played by two teams of two players.

periódicos de las principales capitales de Latinoamérica BOGOTÁ: Newspapers represent the major political parties, but all are government controlled. Dailies include *El Tiempo* (www.eltiempo.com), *El Espectador* (www.elespectador.com), and *La República*. BUENOS AIRES: Important morning papers are: *La Prensa*, *La Nación* (www.lanacion.com.ar), the country's oldest, *The Buenos Aires Herald* (www.buenosairesherald.com), *The Standard*, the oldest English-language newspaper, and *Clarín* (www.clarín.com), a morning daily. *La Razón* and *La Crónica* come out in the evening. CARACAS: has a wide press service. The most important dailies are *El Nacional* (www.el-nacional.terra.com.ve), *El Universal* (www.eud.com), *Últimas Noticias*, *La Religión*, and *La Verdad* (www.laverdad.com), all appearing in the afternoon, and the evening newspapers *El Meridiano*, *El Mundo*, *El Globo*, and *Extra*. There is also an English-language daily, *The Daily Journal*. HAVANA: Has three dailies. The best known is *Granma* (www.granma.cubaweb.cu), official newspaper of the Cuban Communist Party. *Trabajadores* is published by the Cuban trade union movement, and the more lively *Juventud Rebelde* is aimed at a younger readership. LIMA: Has 12 dailies. *El Comercio* (www.elcomercioperu.com), founded in 1939, is Peru's oldest newspaper. *Ojo*, a morning newspaper, has the largest circulation. *El Peruano* (www.editoraperu.com) is the official state gazette, and *Expreso* is the leading opposition daily. MEXICO CITY: Has 20 dailies. The morning daily *Excelsior* (www.excelsior.com.mx), established in 1917, is often considered the nation's best and one of the most important newspapers of the Spanish-speaking world. *La Jornada* is another important daily, and there is an English-language daily, *The News*. MONTEVIDEO: The British, who occupied the city in 1807, published the first newspaper in the capital, *The Southern Star*. The city has had newspapers ever since, representing the views of all political parties and factions. SANTIAGO DE CHILE: There are almost a dozen newspapers. The most important dailies are *El Mercurio* (www.elmercurio.cl), founded in 1900, *La Nación*, and *La Tercera* (www.tercera.cl).

peronismo A political movement, known officially as *justicialismo*, named for the populist politician Colonel Juan Domingo Perón, elected President of Argentina in 1946. An admirer of Italian fascism, Perón claimed always to be a champion of the workers and the poor, the *descamisados* (shirtless ones), to whom his first wife Eva Duarte (Evita) became a sort of icon, especially after her death in 1952. Although he instituted some social reforms, Perón's regime proved increasingly repressive and he was ousted in an army coup in 1955. He returned from exile to become president again in 1973, but died in office a year later. His *Partido Justicialista* governed Argentina again from 1989 to 1999 under President Carlos Saúl Menem.

picaresca y pícaro A picaresque outlook on life, known in Latin America as *viveza criolla*, involves resorting to guile and trickery in order to get ahead or simply survive. In Spanish-speaking countries, this is often regarded as amusing or unavoidably necessary.

pincho In Spain, *pinchos* are small portions of food, often on a cocktail stick, eaten in a bar or café. Often free, they are similar to TAPAS, but much smaller. *See also* RACIÓN.

piñata A hollow figure made of cardboard, or a clay pot lined with colored paper. Filled with fruit, toys, etc., they are hung up at parties. People, blindfolded, then take turns to try to break them with a stick. They feature in Mexican *posadas* and in children's parties there, in Cuba, and in Spain.

piqueteros Organized groups of unemployed people who demand work by cutting road communications. They first appeared in 1996 in Cutral-Có, south-east of Buenos Aires. They now operate throughout Argentina, blocking roads until work is provided by the authorities.

pisco An alcoholic drink, produced by distilling grape juice, originally from Peru but now also characteristic of Chile.

Plata, Río de la Region around the estuary of the River Plate (*plata* means silver), which includes Uruguay and Argentina.

PNV – Partido Nacionalista Vasco The main Basque nationalist party..

población callampa o callampas ▶ CHABOLAS

Policía Nacional The National Police was set up in Spain in 1976. Its members patrol provincial capitals and big cities, which are responsible for its finance, administration, and recruitment. Although armed, it has never been considered a repressive force, unlike the GUARDIA CIVIL.

polla In Chile and Peru a word for an official lottery, whose proceeds go to charity. In some Latin American countries, a *polla* is a private bet on soccer games, horse races, etc.

poncho South American garment consisting of a blanket with a slit for the wearer's head. It generally reaches below the wearer's waist. In Colombia and Venezuela it is called a *ruana*. In the Andean region a poncho covering the whole body is a *bayetón*. The Mexican equivalent is the *jorongo*.

portero A superintendent in an apartment building. *Porteros* often have an apartment in the building as part of their pay. In many buildings access is now regulated by a *portero automático* (intercom). The *portero* and the female *portera* have a reputation for being inquisitive and fond of gossip.

posada ▶ TRADITIONS, FESTIVALS, AND HOLIDAYS

PP – Partido Popular One of Spain's two main national political parties, the other being the PSOE. The PP defines itself as a party of the center right.

Premio Cervantes A prize given in Spain for literary achievement. It is Spain's most prestigious literary prize.

Premios Goya del cine español The Spanish equivalent of Oscars, awarded in January every year by the AACC (*Academia de las Artes y las Ciencias Cinematográficas de España*).

prensa del corazón A type of magazine, with a huge readership in Spain, whose content revolves around the private lives of the rich and famous. The best-known example of the genre is the magazine *¡Hola!*, whose English-language version, *Hello*, has also proved very successful.

Presidente del Gobierno The president of the Spanish central government and the equivalent of the prime minister in the UK. He is appointed for a four-year term.

PRI – Partido Revolucionario Institucional Mexico's leading political party. Founded in 1929, it took its present name in 1946. It supports state intervention in economic, political, and cultural life. The PRI was in power for most of the 20th century.

primaria The name given in Spain to the first of the two compulsory levels of education. It is for pupils aged six to twelve and leads to the ESO.

provincia Each of the 55 administrative areas into which Spain is divided. Every *provincia* includes a main city or town, sometimes more, depending on its social and economic power. The provincial capital usually has the same name as the province.

PSOE – Partido Socialista Obrero Español One of Spain's two main national political parties, the PSOE was transformed from a democratic Marxist party to a liberal-democratic party in 1978. *See also* PP.

pub The name comes from English, but Spanish pubs are very different from British pubs. Usually stylish and modern, they cater to young people and are open very late. They always have music, which tends to be loud.

puente (literally, 'bridge') *Hacer puente* means that when a working day falls between two public holidays, it too is taken as a holiday.

pulque A thick, white, Mexican alcoholic drink made from fermented maguey juice; the sacred drink of the Aztecs. It is drunk without being aged, sometimes with added fruit or vegetable juice. *Pulquerías* are bars where it is drunk.

Quechua The language of the Incas, Quechua is spoken today by some 13 million people in Peru, Bolivia, Chile, Colombia, Ecuador, and Argentina. Since 1975 it has been an official language in Peru. The Quechua people are one of South America's most important ethnic minorities. Words derived from Quechua include coca, condor, and puma.

quinceañera ▶ FIESTA DE 15

ración In Spain, a *ración* is a serving of food eaten in a bar or café, generally with a drink. *Raciones* tend to be larger and more elaborate than TAPAS, and may include Spanish omelet, squid, octopus, cheese, ham, or chorizo. See also PINCHO.

radio española, la Radio broadcasting in Spain began in the 1920s. The state-run Radio Nacional de España (RNE) was established during the Civil War. *See also* CADENA SER.

RAE – Real Academia de la Lengua Española A body established in the 18th century to record and preserve the Spanish language. It is made up of *académicos*, normally well-known literary figures and/or experts on the Spanish language. The RAE publishes the *Diccionario de la Real Academia Española*, regarded as an authority on correct Spanish.

Ramblas, Las Also known as La Rambla (de Cataluña), this is one of the most pleasant thoroughfares in Barcelona. Gracious buildings overlook its central tree-lined area, and it is famous for its varied stalls, florists, pavement cafés, street artists, and strollers.

ranchos ▶ CHABOLAS

rastro In some parts of Spain, the name given to a weekly open-air flea market. 'El Rastro' is a big market of this type held in Madrid.

RCN – Radio Cadena Nacional of Columbia. It has won many awards for its news broadcasts and the help it has given to the community. RCN Internacional, New York, retransmits its output locally; broadcasts are also made to other countries.

Reconquista The period in Spain's history during which the Christian kingdoms slowly recovered the territories occupied by the Moslem Moors

of North Africa. The Moorish invasion of the Iberian peninsula began in AD 711 and was halted in 718. The expulsion of the last Moorish ruler of the kingdom of Granada in 1492 completed the Reconquest. The intervening 781 years saw periods of alternate conflict and coexistence between Moors and Christians.

RENFE – Red Nacional de los Ferrocarriles Españoles Spain's generally cheap and efficient state-run railroad system.

Reyes Magos ▶ TRADITIONS, FESTIVALS, AND HOLIDAYS

Río de la Plata ▶ PLATA, RÍO DE LA

ruana ▶ PONCHO

rumba This Cuban music and dance form has roots in African and Spanish music. Rumba bands include three conga drums and two drumsticks, which are used to beat a wooden sound box.

Sagrada Familia, La The building of this church, begun in 1882, was taken over by the Catalan architect Antonio Gaudí in 1884. It was unfinished at his death in 1926. Gothic in design and inspiration, it is of varying quality due to the many changes of plans throughout Gaudí's lifetime. Its silhouette is now universally recognized as the symbol of Barcelona.

Sanfermines ▶ TRADITIONS, FESTIVALS, AND HOLIDAYS

sangría A light alcoholic drink made from red wine, fruit juice, carbonated soft drinks, diced fruit, and spices.

Santería A religious cult, fusing African beliefs and Catholicism, which developed among African Yoruba slaves in Cuba. Rituals involve music, dancing, sacrificial offerings, and going into trances.

santo Most first names in Spanish-speaking countries are those of saints. A person's *santo*, (also known as *onomástico* in Latin America and *onomástica* in Spain) is the day of the saint that they are named for.

sarape A Mexican blanket in vivid colors, which men wear folded up over one shoulder. It is typical of the CHARRO (Mexican cowboy) costume. If it has a slit for wearing over the head, it is known as a *jorongo*. *See also* PONCHO.

sardana Traditional Catalan music and the dance performed to it. It is played by a band called a *cobla*. The dancers stand in circles, holding hands, and perform the steps as a group.

selectividad The universal university entrance exam in Spain. It is the only means of access to state-run universities.

Semana Santa ▶ TRADITIONS, FESTIVALS, AND HOLIDAYS

Senado The upper chamber of the Spanish Cortes Generales, and the place where it meets. There are 250 senators, most of whom are elected every four years, at general elections. A small number of senators are also elected by the autonomous governments. The Senado's functions include discussing, approving, and suggesting amendments to legislation passed by the CONGRESO DE LOS DIPUTADOS.

sobremesa The time when people stay at the table after a meal, especially lunch, talking, drinking coffee, and smoking. In television schedules, *programación de sobremesa* refers to afternoon viewing.

Spanish cinema began when Luis Buñuel started Spain's first cinema club in 1928. During the dictatorship, Spanish cinema was forced to adopt an educational and moralizing tone. But the 1980s saw a rebirth of the industry, with directors such as Pedro Almodóvar and Carlos Saura producing films that appealed to a worldwide audience. Spanish cinema currently enjoys international prestige, and actors such as Antonio Banderas and Penélope Cruz have had a major impact in Hollywood.

Spanish universities In 1218 Alfonso X of León founded the University of Salamanca, the country's oldest. Now there are 70 public and 19 private institutions in the 17 COMUNIDADES AUTÓNOMAS. Spain has the second highest number of university students in Europe: about 13 percent of the population have had a university education.

Sudaca A pejorative term (from Sudamérica) to refer to South Americans in Spain. It first appeared in the 1970s, when Chilean and Argentinian political refugees were arriving in Spain in great numbers.

tango The dance and music that originated in the poor quarters of Buenos Aires. The dance has slow rhythms, and partners dance close together with abrupt movements and pauses. It has become emblematic of Argentina.

tapas In Spain, small portions of food served in bars and cafés with a drink. They can be very elaborate, and people often order several to make a meal. The social aspect of having *tapas* is very important. The practice of going out for a drink and *tapas* is known as *tapeo*.

Telefé The abbreviation for Televisión Federal S.A., the most popular television channel in Argentina. Established in 1980, it is controlled by the Spanish multinational, Telefónica.

Televisa This Mexican television and media group is one of the biggest in Latin America. The group's soap operas are romantic dramas of 60 to 100 episodes, broadcast in Spanish and other languages throughout the world.

Teotihuacán The ruins of Teotihuacán lie northeast of Mexico City. The NÁHUATL name means 'city of the gods' or 'where men became gods'. Little is known about the city's founders or inhabitants, but it reached its peak between 300 and 600 AD. It includes the Pyramids of the Sun and Moon, the temple of Quetzalcóatl, the Great Compound, and the central complex, the Ciudadela. By 650 AD Teotihuacán was in decline; it was in ruins when the Aztecs found it in the 15th century.

tequila An alcoholic drink obtained in Mexico by fermenting and then distilling the juice, called *aguamiel*, of the maguey plant. *See also* MEZCAL.

Tirana, La ▶ TRADITIONS, FESTIVALS, AND HOLIDAYS

Toros (La fiesta de los) Bullfighting is popular in Spain and in Mexico, Colombia, Peru, and Venezuela. For some Spaniards it is crucial to their identity. The season runs from March to October in Spain, November to March in Latin America. The art of bullfighting is *tauromaquia*. The principal bullfighter is known as the matador. His outfit, the *traje de luces*, consists of a tight silk jacket and trousers, decorated with embroidery and epaulettes, and a black, two-cornered hat known as a *montera*.

Tribunal Constitucional The Spanish constitutional court, made up of 12 members. It decides all matters relating to constitutional legislation, including common law, international treaties, and regional statutes. All other constitutional bodies are subject to its control.

tuna A *tuna*, also called an *estudiantina*, is a group of strolling student players. The groups date from the 17th or 18th centuries. *Tunas* wear black velvet costumes, with doublets and capes. The ribbons on their capes show the faculties that they belong to.

Valenciano The variety of CATALÁN spoken in the autonomous region of
Valencia. Some people regard it as a separate language from Catalan,
which has official status, but it is not officially recognized as such.

La Vanguardia Founded in Barcelona in 1881, this is one of Spain's most
prestigious daily newspapers (www.lavanguardia.es).

vasco or vascuence ▶ EUSKERA

villa miseria ▶ CHABOLAS

viveza criolla ▶ PICARESCA Y PÍCARO

voladores A Mexican pre-Columbian ritual dance. Four or six men are
attached by ropes to a platform on top of a 17–27 m (60–90 ft) high pole. They
dance on the platform. At the end of the dance, they circle down to the
ground, hanging by their feet, as the ropes attaching them unwind.

weddings In traditional weddings, the conventions are similar
throughout the Spanish-speaking world. Shortly before the
wedding the groom has his *despedida de soltero*, or stag night; the
bride has her *despedida de soltera*. In church weddings, usually
the Catholic service, the chief participants, apart from the
priest, bride and groom, are the groom's mother, *madrina de la
boda*, who accompanies him to the altar, and the bride's father, or
padrino de la boda, who gives her away. Bridesmaids, *damas de
honor*, are not usual, but are becoming more common, especially
in Spain. The bride usually wears a long dress and veil. During
the ceremony, rings (*alianzas* or *anillos de boda*) are exchanged,
as well as *las arras*, 13 coins symbolizing the sharing of assets.
The couple are considered married when they say '*sí quiero*' or
'*sí acepto*' (equivalent to 'I do'). Rice is thrown at the couple as they leave the
church. A wedding feast follows, at which it is not usual to make speeches.
The newlyweds then go on their honeymoon, or *luna de miel*.

Xochimilco A city in central Mexico, situated on Lake Xochimilco and
famous for its *chinampas* or floating gardens. These were originally Aztec
rafts for transporting vegetables, fruit, and flowers to Mexico City by canal.
The *chinampas* are still cultivated in Xochimilco and other towns in the area.

zarzuela A musical drama consisting of alternating passages of dialog,
songs, choruses, and dancing, which originated in Spain in the 17th
century. Its name comes from the ZARZUELA palace, Madrid. It is also
popular in Latin America. After a decline, Zarzuela revived in the early
19th century. The revived *zarzuela* dealt with more popular themes and
was called *género chico*. A more serious version developed, known as
género grande.

Zarzuela (Palacio de la) The Madrid palace where the Spanish Royal
Family now lives. *See also* PALACIO DE ORIENTE.

La vida y cultura anglosajonas

ABC 1. (*American Broadcasting Company*) Una de las principales cadenas de televisión norteamericanas, actualmente propiedad de la compañía Walt Disney. **2.** (*Australian Broadcasting Corporation*) En Australia, la cadena nacional pública de radio y televisión financiada por el gobierno.

Aborigine Un individuo perteneciente al grupo de personas que fueron los primeros habitantes del continente australiano. Su modo de vida tradicional es la del cazador-recolector y data de los tiempos prehistóricos.

ACT (*American College Test*) Una prueba que los estudiantes de la mayor parte de los estados que forman Estados Unidos deben aprobar para ser admitidos en la universidad. Normalmente tiene lugar al final de la HIGH SCHOOL y cubre un número de materias principales, p.ej. inglés y matemáticas.

Advance Australia Fair El himno nacional de Australia.

African-American Este es el término de más amplia aceptación en Estados Unidos para referirse a norteamericanos de origen africano.

Afro-Caribbean El término de más amplia aceptación en Gran Bretaña para referirse a gente con antepasados africanos que procede del Caribe o que vive allí.

A level ▶ EXAMINATIONS

Alliance Party ▶ NORTHERN IRELAND

American Dream, The El sueño americano es la creencia, en Estados Unidos, de que cualquier persona que trabaje duro puede alcanzar el éxito económico o social. Para los inmigrantes y las minorías, este sueño también incluye libertad e igualdad de derechos.

American Football El fútbol americano se juega con dos equipos de once jugadores cada uno y con una pelota de forma ovalada. Es un deporte violento por lo que los jugadores usan cascos y almohadillas de protección. Lo más destacado de la temporada es el campeonato de la *National Football League*, el SUPER BOWL.

American Indian ▶ NATIVE AMERICAN

Anglican Church ▶ CHURCH OF ENGLAND

Anzac Un soldado miembro del *Australian and New Zealand Army Corps* que luchó en la Segunda Guerra Mundial. El cuerpo es especialmente recordado por el heroísmo demostrado en la desastrosa campaña de Galípoli en contra de los turcos en 1915–16. La valentía de los *Anzacs* jugó un papel importante en el establecimiento de la conciencia nacional en Australia y Nueva Zelanda y se la conmemora anualmente en el *Anzac Day* (25 de abril).

April Fool's Day ▶ DÍAS FESTIVOS, FIESTAS, Y TRADICIONES

Armistice Day ▶ POPPY DAY

Ashes *The Ashes* es un trofeo en forma de una pequeña urna por el cual compiten los equipos nacionales de críquet de Australia e Inglaterra. El nombre surgió de un obituario simulado publicado en *The Times* en 1882, después de que el equipo inglés fuera abiertamente derrotado. En él se lamentaba la muerte del críquet inglés diciendo que su cuerpo había sido incinerado y que se llevarían sus cenizas a Australia.

Asian-American Este es el término de más amplia aceptación hoy en día para referirse a norteamericanos de origen asiático, especialmente del Extremo Oriente.

A/S Level ▶ EXAMINATIONS

Australia Day Día festivo de carácter oficial que se celebra el primer lunes después del 26 de enero. Conmemora la llegada de los primeros colonos británicos en 1788 al entonces Port Jackson y que ahora es el puerto de Sydney.

Australian Rules Tipo de fútbol que se juega en Australia entre equipos de 18 jugadores en un campo ovalado con un balón grande, también ovalado. Es el deporte de invierno más polular en gran parte de Australia.

Authorized Version Traducción al inglés de la Biblia, publicada por primera vez en 1611. Fue producto de un grupo de eruditos bajo las órdenes del rey de Inglaterra James I, por lo que también se la conoce por la Biblia del rey James. Desde el siglo XVII al XX fue la única versión de la Biblia autorizada para usarse en la Iglesia Anglicana (CHURCH OF ENGLAND). Ha ejercido una profunda influencia en la literatura inglesa y el idioma inglés.

B & B ▶ BED AND BREAKFAST

backbencher Es un diputado (MP) del Parlamento británico que no tiene un puesto de responsabilidad en el gobierno o en la oposición. Los *backbenchers* ocupan los escaños posteriores de la Cámara de los Comunes. Se espera que voten como se lo ordena el WHIP del partido.

bank holiday Día festivo de carácter oficial en el Reino Unido, en que cierran los bancos, correos, la mayoría de las oficinas y muchas tiendas. Siempre cae en un lunes.

barrister ▶ LAWYER

baseball Es el deporte nacional de Estados Unidos. Se juega entre dos equipos; uno fildea mientras el otro batea. El objetivo de cada bateador es correr alrededor de cuatro bases para obtener 'carreras'. El torneo anual de béisbol más importante es la Serie Mundial (*World Series*).

BBC (*British Broadcasting Corporation*) Una de las principales cadenas de televisión y radiodifusión británicas. No se financia a través de la publicidad, sino que con los ingresos provenientes del pago de una licencia anual que se debe obtener para poder utilizar un receptor de televisión. Tiene la obligación de informar de un modo imparcial.

bed and breakfast Los *bed & breakfast* o *B&B* son casas privadas o pequeños hoteles que ofrecen alojamiento más el desayuno a precios generalmente módicos.

beer En la mayoría de los países de habla inglesa, el tipo de cerveza más común es la cerveza rubia. En Gran Bretaña es conocida por *lager*. Las cervezas originarias de Gran Bretaña se fabrican del grano del cereal de malta, como la cebada aromatizada con lúpulos. Son de color más oscuro, con espuma blanca y se beben a temperatura ambiente. La más popular se conoce por *bitter* debido a su sabor ligeramente amargo. *Stout* es un tipo de cerveza muy fuerte, de color casi negro. La marca más famosa de este tipo de cerveza es Guinness, que se fabrica en Dublín, Irlanda. *Ver tb* PUB.

Big Apple Apodo de la ciudad de Nueva York.

Bill of Rights Son las primeras diez enmiendas a la Constitución de EEUU. Los derechos que confieren a los estadounidenses incluyen la libertad de cultos, de expresión, de prensa y diversos derechos para el que es acusado de un delito. La Quinta Enmienda (*Fifth Amendment*) establece, entre otras cosas, que nadie está obligado a testificar en su propia contra. La Segunda otorga el derecho a portar armas.

Bonfire Night ▶ DÍAS FESTIVOS, FIESTAS, Y TRADICIONES

Booker Prize En el Reino Unido, un premio que se otorga cada octubre al autor de la mejor novela de ficción que se haya publicado el año anterior. Desde 2002 su nombre oficial es *Man Booker Prize*.

Boxing Day ▶ DÍAS FESTIVOS, FIESTAS, Y TRADICIONES

British Isles Las Islas Británicas comprenden Gran Bretaña (GREAT BRITAIN), Irlanda (tanto Irlanda del Norte como la República de Irlanda) y las islas más pequeñas que están a su alrededor, como las Islas Shetlands (*the Shetlands*), la Isla de Man (*Isle of Man*), y las Islas Anglonormandas (the CHANNEL ISLANDS).

broadsheets ▶ NEWSPAPERS

Broadway Una calle famosa por sus teatros que atraviesa el barrio neoyorquino de Manhattan. El término a menudo se usa para referirse al teatro y al mundo del espectáculo de EEUU en general. Antes del surgimiento de la industria del cine, era el principal lugar donde los actores podían hacerse famosos.

Buckingham Palace La residencia oficial del monarca británico, se sitúa en Londres. La ceremonia de la Guardia Montada, comúnmente conocida como el cambio de guardia, tiene lugar la mayoría de las mañanas del año, frente al Palacio de Buckingham, bajo el acompañamiento de la banda del regimiento.

Burns Night ▶ DÍAS FESTIVOS, FIESTAS, Y TRADICIONES

By-election Una elección especial que se lleva a cabo entre una elección general o local cuando hay una vacante debido a que un miembro del parlamento o un concejal ha dimitido o ha fallecido.

Cabinet El gabinete (ministerial) del gobierno británico es un cuerpo formado por unos 20 ministros (*ministers*) nombrados por el primer ministro y que se reúne regularmente para discutir asuntos administrativos y de política gubernamental. Cada uno de los ministros es responsable de un área específica, mientras que a la totalidad del gabinete le atañe decidir acerca de la política a seguir por el gobierno. El líder del principal partido de la oposición también nombra un gabinete, llamado gabinete en la sombra (SHADOW CABINET), con el objeto de que pueda gobernar en caso de que el gobierno sea derrotado.

Capitol El Capitolio o sede del Congreso (CONGRESS) de Estados Unidos, en Washington DC. Situado en Capitol Hill, a menudo la prensa emplea este nombre para hacer referencia al Congreso de EEUU.

CBS (*Columbia Broadcasting System*) Una de las tres primeras compañías de radio y televisión nacionales norteamericanas.

Channel Islands Un grupo de islas en el Canal de la Mancha que están más cerca de la costa de Francia que de la de Inglaterra. No forman parte del Reino Unido. Desde el punto de vista oficial son dependencias autónomas de la corona británica. Jersey y Guernsey son las más grandes de las Islas Anglonormandas.

Christmas Day ▶ DÍAS FESTIVOS, FIESTAS, Y TRADICIONES

Church of England La Iglesia Anglicana, protestante, es la Iglesia oficial de Inglaterra. Fue creada en 1534, bajo el reinado de Enrique VIII, por una ley suprema (*Act of Supremacy*) mediante la cual el rey reemplazó al Papa como jefe de la Iglesia en Inglaterra. En la actualidad el monarca lo sigue siendo, pero sus obispos y arzobispos son designados a propuesta del primer ministro. El jefe espiritual de la Iglesia es el Arzobispo de Canterbury. Inglaterra está dividida en 44 diócesis y 13.000 parroquias (*parishes*) cada una de las cuales está a cargo de un párroco (*vicar*). En 1992, el *General Synod* u organismo rector de la Iglesia, permitió a las mujeres ser párrocos. También se la conoce por la *Anglican Church* y es parte del grupo mundial de iglesias que comparten fundamentalmente las mismas creencias y organización, conocido como la *Anglican Communion* (Comunión Anglicana). La Iglesia Anglicana es conocida como la *Episcopalian Church* (Iglesia Episcopal) en Escocia y EEUU. En Irlanda como la *Church of Ireland* (Iglesia de Irlanda) y en Gales como la *Church in Wales* (Iglesia en Gales).

City The City es el área que se encuentra dentro de los límites de la antigua ciudad de Londres. Hoy en día es el centro financiero y de negocios de la capital. Allí tienen sus sedes centrales muchos bancos e instituciones financieras. A menudo, cuando se habla de The City, se está refiriendo a estas instituciones y no a la zona propiamente dicha.

Civil War 1. (en Inglaterra) Muchas de las causas que provocaron la guerra civil (1642–1651) entre los *Royalists* (monárquicos) o *Cavaliers* (partidarios del rey Carlos I) y las fuerzas parlamentarias (apodadas *Roundheads*) encabezadas por Oliver Cromwell tenían que ver con los problemas religiosos y económicos de la época. El intento de Carlos I de arrestar a los miembros del cuerpo legislativo al negarle éste los fondos necesarios para seguir gobernando como autócrata fue lo que desencadenó el conflicto militar. Vencido en las batallas de Marston Moor (1644) y Naseby (1645), el rey se entregó al ejército escocés un año más tarde. Condenado a muerte por una comisión parlamentaria bajo Cromwell, fue ajusticiado en 1649. Durante los años que siguieron, Cromwell disolvió el Parlamento en varias ocasiones y gobernó durante varios años como dictador. La monarquía fue restaurada en 1660 bajo Carlos II, hijo de Carlos I. **2. (en Estados Unidos)** La Guerra de Secesión (1861–5), entre los estados del norte y los del sur de EEUU, se inició principalmente a raíz del problema de los esclavos. Once estados del sur, donde la economía agrícola dependía del trabajo de éstos, en 1861 formaron la Confederate States of America, para separarse de la Unión. La Guerra estalló el 12 de abril. Al rendirse la Confederación el 9 de abril de 1865 se abolió la esclavitud y en 1870, posteriores enmiendas a la Constitución otorgaron a los negros, al menos en teoría, los mismos derechos de los blancos.

Clubbing Un pasatiempo entre los jóvenes del Reino Unido. '*Going clubbing*' significa ir de discotecas donde se sirven bebidas y a veces algo de comer; se toca música muy alto y se tiene una pista de baile. Se puede entrar mediante el pago de una suma, por lo general más alta antes de las 11 p.m. Estos lugares están vigilados por *bouncers* (gorilas).

CNN (*Cable News Network*) Una compañía de televisión norteamericana que emite programas informativos y de noticias vía satélite, las veinticuatro horas del día.

Cockney Una persona de clase obrera que ha nacido y se ha criado en el tradicional EAST END (barrio del este) de Londres. Es también el nombre del dialecto que hablan, que incluye un argot rítmico en el que, por ejemplo '*apples and pears*' significa '*stairs*' y '*trouble and strife*' significa '*wife*'.

common law En el derecho inglés, el término se refiere a la ley basada en la costumbre y en el fallo de los tribunales (derecho consuetudinario y jurisprudencia respectivamente), es decir que no ha sido creada en el Parlamento. A menudo se contrapone a derecho escrito (*statute law*). El derecho consuetudinario (*common law*) sólo rige cuando el derecho escrito no se pronuncia en una materia.

Commonwealth La Commonwealth o Comunidad Británica de Naciones, creada en 1931, es una asociación de estados independientes, en su mayoría ex colonias británicas, más algunas dependencias británicas, tales como Las Bermudas, Las Islas Malvinas y Gibraltar. Los miembros trabajan juntos para lograr ciertos fines como la paz mundial, fomento del comercio y la defensa de la democracia. Cada dos años se celebra una reunión de todos los jefes de gobierno de la Comunidad (*the Commonwealth Conference*), para debatir asuntos de carácter político y económico. Cada cuatro años se celebran los *Commonwealth Games*, competencia deportiva en el que uno de los miembros es el anfitrión.

community college Un tipo de universidad norteamericana donde se imparten cursos de nivel universitario de dos años de duración. Son cursos prácticos orientados a la población local.

comprehensive school Colegio británico de educación secundaria con alumnos de todos los niveles, cuyas edades están comprendidas entre los 11 y los 18 años. Estos colegios fueron introducidos en los años 60, con el fin de crear un sistema educativo más igualitario, en sustitución del sistema selectivo que operaba en esa época. *Ver tb* GRAMMAR SCHOOL.

Congress El Congreso es el organismo nacional legislativo de Estados Unidos. Se reúne en el Capitolio (CAPITOL) y está compuesto por dos cámaras, el Senado (SENATE), y la Cámara de Representantes (HOUSE OF REPRESENTATIVES). Se renueva cada dos años y su función es elaborar leyes. Toda nueva ley debe ser aprobada primero por las dos cámaras y posteriormente por el presidente (PRESIDENT).

Conservative Party El Partido Conservador es uno de los principales partidos políticos británicos. Se sitúa a la derecha del espectro político que apoya el sistema capitalista, la libre empresa y la privatización de la industria y los servicios públicos. Surgió alrededor de 1830 como resultado de la evolución del *Tory Party* y a menudo se le denomina aún por este nombre.

Constituency Una de la áreas en que se dividen, para efectos electorales, el RU, Canadá, y Australia.

Constitution La Constitución de los EEUU, escrita después de que el país se independizara de Gran Bretaña, fue ratificada en 1789 por representantes de cada una de las trece ex colonias que conformaban los Estados Unidos, incluidos algunos de los padres de la nación (FOUNDING FATHERS). La Constitución estableció los tres poderes de gobierno, el legislativo (CONGRESS), el judicial (SUPREME COURT), y el ejecutivo (PRESIDENT). La separación de poderes fue ideada a fin de evitar que cualquiera adquiriera demasiada autoridad. El texto básico de la Constitución nunca ha cambiado, pero desde 1789 se le han hecho 27 enmiendas. Las primeras diez enmiendas se conocen como *the* BILL OF RIGHTS.

council Gran Bretaña está dividida, con fines administrativos, en áreas. Las más grandes son los condados (COUNTIES) y en Escocia, regiones (*regions*); ambos se dividen en *districts*. Los *parish councils* (*community councils* en Escocia y Gales) son las unidades más pequeñas de gobierno local. Todos son dirigidos por *councils* que cuentan con poderes otorgados por el gobierno central. Están formados por representantes o *councillors* que son elegidos por los habitantes de la localidad. Sus responsabilidades incluyen la educación, los servicios sociales, los servicios de la policía y de los bomberos, bibliotecas, y otros servicios locales.

Country and Western También conocida como música country, es música popular en el estilo tradicional de la música folklórica de los blancos en los estados del sur de los EEUU y de las canciones de los vaqueros del oeste. Las canciones, por lo general, tratan temas personales y emotivos. Entre los cantantes famosos de este género se incluyen Johnny Cash, Willie Nelson, Dolly Parton, y Loretta Lynn.

county Región administrativa de Gran Bretaña que agrupa un número de distritos (*districts*). Los condados son las principales unidades administrativas de Gran Bretaña y muchos tienen demarcaciones que se remontan a muchos años atrás. Sin embargo, en las últimas décadas, éstas y sus nombres han cambiado mucho, y el término *county* a menudo ya no se usa. La mayoría de los estados en EEUU también están divididos en condados. Hay alrededor de 3.000 condados en EEUU.

courts En los Estados Unidos muchos tribunales son operados por cada estado por separado pero también existen tribunales federales que conocen, entre otros, de los conflictos entre los estados o los ciudadanos de diferentes estados. La SUPREME COURT (Tribunal Supremo) es un tribunal federal. La mayoría de los estados tienen distintos tribunales para los casos civiles y criminales y un tribunal supremo que actúa como el tribunal de apelación final. Un caso criminal típico en EEUU será juzgado en un tribunal comarcal con un funcionario conocido como el fiscal del distrito, que lleva la acusación. El juez lleva una toga negra y los abogados (o '*counsels*') llevan ropa normal. En Inglaterra y Gales, los tribunales locales son conocidos como *magistrates' courts* (equivalente a un tribunal de primera instancia). Por lo general, los preside un *magistrate*, que es un lego que no recibe remuneración. Éstos remiten los casos más graves a los tribunales que conocen de lo criminal (*crown courts*), en los que los *barristers* (abogados habilitados para actuar ante un tribunal superior) comparecen por la acusación y la defensa. El último tribunal de apelación es la Cámara de los Lores (HOUSE OF LORDS). En Escocia, que tiene un sistema legal propio, los casos menores son conocidos por los *magistrates' courts* o por un tribunal de la policía. Los casos más graves se tratan ante un *sheriff* (juez principal de un distrito). Los tribunales más altos se conocen como el *High Court of Justiciary* y el *Court of Session* para los casos criminales y civiles respectivamente. En Inglaterra , Gales y Escocia, los jueces y abogados llevan togas y pelucas cuando comparecen en el tribunal.

cricket El críquet se juega principalmente en Gran Bretaña y los países de la COMMONWEALTH. Dos equipos de once jugadores se turnan para batear y fildear; cuando están bateando, corren entre los '*wickets*' (palos) a fin de acumular carreras. *Ver* ASHES.

cuisine La cocina tradicional británica tiende a los platos fuertes que hacen entrar en calor, tales como el pescado frito con patatas fritas, estofados o guisos y postres a base de sebo. Sin embargo, en los últimos años, la cocina en los hogares británicos y en los restaurantes se ha vuelto mucho más variada y sofisticada, gracias a las influencias culinarias de Europa y de países como la India, China, y Tailandia, y de los chefs de la TV que han ayudado a promocionar una cocina más innovadora y, cada vez más, el uso de ingredientes autóctonos de alta calidad. En los EEUU gran parte de la cocina tradicional norteamericana se basa en los cultivos de los primeros colonos, por ejemplo el maíz y la calabaza. La influencia mexicana es grande, especialmente en el suroeste. Los inmigrantes judíos trajeron los *bagels* y los *pretzels* y los alemanes las hamburguesas, la base de gran parte de la industria de la comida rápida. La mayoría de los platos servidos en los restaurantes chinos, fuera de la China, en realidad, fueron desarrollados en EEUU.

Cup final ▶ FOOTBALL

degree A las personas que terminan una carrera universitaria en los países de habla inglesa, se les otorga un título. La calificación del primer nivel, es la licenciatura (*bachelor's degree*), la del segundo, es la maestría (*master's degree*), y la más alta , el doctorado (*doctorate*). La licenciatura en filosofía y letras, o su titular, se conoce como BA (en EEUU también como AB), una maestría en ciencias es una MSc (también ScM en EEUU) y el título de un doctor en filosofía es conocido casi en todas partes como un PhD.

Democratic Party Creado en 1792, es uno de los dos principales partidos políticos de Estados Unidos. El otro es el Partido Republicano (REPUBLICAN PARTY). El Partido Demócrata está considerado como el propulsor de políticas más liberales, especialmente referidas a temas que afectan a la sociedad. Por esta razón, consigue el apoyo de sindicatos y grupos minoritarios.

devolution En el Reino Unido, el término *devolution* implica la transferencia de competencias del gobierno central tanto a las naciones históricas de Escocia y Gales y a la provincia de Irlanda del Norte, como a

otras regiones periféricas del estado británico. Después de la victoria Laborista en las urnas en 1997, fueron inaugurados el Parlamento escocés y las Asambleas de Irlanda del Norte y de Gales. *Ver tb* SCOTLAND, NORTHERN IRELAND, WALES.

District Attorney ▶ COURTS

DIY Una actividad popular en el Reino Unido. *DIY* o *Do It Yourself* (Hágalo usted mismo), abarca una variedad de actividades, desde la pintura de paredes hasta la plomería, que se llevan a cabo para mejorar los hogares. El objetivo de los que las efectúan es evitar pedir ayuda profesional, pero se los suele considerar graciosos porque sus aptitudes no siempre están a la altura de sus aspiraciones.

Dow Jones Average También *Dow Jones Index* (índice Dow Jones), expresa en puntos el precio relativo de las acciones en la Bolsa de Nueva York de cada día de transacciones. Se basa en el precio promedio de ciertas acciones seleccionadas. Se emplea para medir la fuerza del mercado bursátil de EEUU.

Downing Street Una calle del céntrico barrio londinense de Westminster. El número 10 es la residencia oficial del primer ministro y el número 11 la del *chancellor of the Exchequer* (equivalente al cargo del Ministro de Economía y Hacienda). Los periodistas utilizan a menudo las expresiones Downing Street o Number 10 para referirse al despacho del Primer Ministro.

Driving En el RU, Australia, Nueva Zelanda y África del Sur, los vehículos se conducen por el lado izquierdo de la calzada. En EEUU y Canadá se conduce por el lado derecho como se hace en el resto de Europa.

East End Área de Londres que está al este de la CITY, tradicionalmente el lugar donde vive la clase obrera y donde se encontraba el puerto de

Londres que, en la actualidad, está casi cerrado a los barcos y toda el área a su alrededor ha sido considerablemente reurbanizada. Se la conoce como Docklands y contiene muchas viviendas de categoría como también recintos comerciales, tales como la torre y complejo Canary Wharf, centro de muchos periódicos destacados. El área está conectada al resto de Londres por el nuevo Tren Ligero de los Docklands.

East Side En Nueva York, el área al este de Central Park, tradicionalmente más rica y moderna que el área oeste de la ciudad.

Edinburgh Festival Un festival internacional de tres semanas de música, teatro, danza etc., que se viene celebrando cada agosto en Edimburgo desde 1947. Muchos turistas vienen a ver las actuaciones y los conciertos, incluida la gran cantidad que no forma parte oficial del festival y que se conoce como *Edinburgh Fringe*. En la actualidad, éste se considera tan importante como el festival mismo por la originalidad y nivel de su contenido.

education En EEUU la educación primaria y secundaria es proporcionada gratis por el gobierno federal nacional. Los niños empiezan formalmente el colegio a los cinco años, en un kindergarten. Éste conjuntamente con los próximos cinco o seis años de educación se conoce como ELEMENTARY SCHOOL. Le siguen ya sea dos años en un *junior high school*, o tres años en un *middle school*, y luego los últimos años de educación en un HIGH SCHOOL, hasta que se cumple 18 años. Después de esta edad la educación no es gratuita, aunque los gobiernos de cada estado subsidian la educación de las personas que viven en ellos. Alrededor del 45% de los norteamericanos sigue alguna clase de educación después de la secundaria y más del 20% se gradúa de algún instituto o universidad. En el Reino Unido, el colegio es obligatorio para los niños entre las edades de cinco y dieciséis años. La educación primaria se obtiene en un *infant school* seguida de un *primary school*. Después de los 11 años se empieza la educación secundaria, normalmente en un COMPREHENSIVE SCHOOL. Un número más reducido asiste a los GRAMMAR SCHOOLS selectivos. Después de los 16 años, algunos estudiantes dejan el colegio, otros prosiguen hacia la *further education* y otros continúan en el colegio para preparar los *A levels*. Si desean acceder a la educación superior, necesitan costearse tanto los gastos de su propio mantenimiento como los de matrícula, para lo cual un gran número solicita préstamos. La mayoría de los alumnos asiste a un colegio estatal y unos pocos a los *independent schools*, que son de pago.

Eisteddfod En Gales son festivales tradicionales durante los cuales individuos y grupos en representación de aldeas, iglesias, colegios o condados rivales compiten entre sí en la composición e interpretación de poesía, prosa y piezas musicales. Desde 1880 el *National Eisteddfod of Wales* que dura más de una semana viene celebrándose cada agosto en una localidad distinta de Gales. Todos los eventos se celebran en galés (WELSH).

elections En EEUU se celebran elecciones para ocupar el cargo de presidente (PRESIDENT), para llenar ambas cámaras del Congreso (CONGRESS) y cargos a nivel local y estatal. Los candidatos se presentan ya sea con el apoyo del Partido Republicano (REPUBLICAN PARTY) o del Partido Demócrata (DEMOCRATIC PARTY). El que desee presentarse como independiente, puede hacerlo elevando una petición con firmas que la apoyen. Las elecciones presidenciales se celebran cada cuatro años. Los partidos preseleccionan a sus candidatos mediante una serie de primarias (PRIMARY) celebradas en cada estado. La selección final de los candidatos para presidente y vicepresidente se efectúa en la convención o congreso que cada partido (*party convention*) celebra en los meses de julio y agosto. El presidente es elegido en noviembre mediante el sistema de colegios electorales (ELECTORAL COLLEGES). En el Reino Unido, las elecciones generales deben celebrarse por ley, cada cinco años. Sin embargo el primer

ministro puede convocar a elecciones anticipadas si parece que tiene buenas posibilidades de triunfar. En el Reino Unido hay 659 circunscripciones electorales (*constituencies*), cada una de las cuales elige un parlamentario (MP). El sistema electoral que se aplica es el *first-past-the-post system*, es decir que se resulta elegido por mayoría relativa. El líder del partido que obtiene el mayor número de escaños, pasa a ser el primer ministro y forma el nuevo gobierno.

electoral college Es el sistema adoptado por los EEUU para elegir presidente y vicepresidente, mediante el cual los votantes de cada estado eligen a compromisarios (*electors*) que conforman los colegios electorales, los que a su vez se comprometen a votar por un determinado candidato. Todos los votos de un estado van a un candidato. Sólo 270 votos (*electoral college votes*) se necesitan para obtener la victoria, todo lo cual significa que el presidente puede ser elegido sin obtener la mayoría del voto popular.

elementary school También *grade school*. En EEUU, un colegio de enseñanza primaria dirigido a niños de edades comprendidas entre 6 y 12 ó 13 años.

England De los países que conforman el Reino Unido, Inglaterra es el más grande en cuanto a territorio y el que tiene, con mucho, la población más grande. A trevés de la historia, pudo unir a sí a los otros países que ahora forman el RU, al ser el poder militar, político, y económico dominante en las Islas Británicas (BRITISH ISLES). En la actualidad este proceso se ha ido invirtiendo (*ver* DEVOLUTION). Escocia, Gales, e Irlanda del Norte tienen ahora parlamentos o asambleas separados para tratar sus asuntos nacionales, pero Inglaterra sigue gobernándose exclusivamente por el Parlamento Británico en Westminster.

English Breakfast Un desayuno caliente tradicional de huevos, tocino, pan, salchichas, champiñones y tomates, por lo general, fritos.

Estuary English Un tipo de inglés, criticado como feo y descuidado, que habla sobre todo la gente joven de Inglaterra. Mezcla la RECEIVED PRONUNCIATION con el acento COCKNEY. Se originó en el área alrededor del estuario del Río Támesis, pero se ha extendido ya a otras regiones.

Examinations En Inglaterra, Gales e Irlanda del Norte muchos escolares hacen los exámenes *General Certificate of Secondary Education* (*GCSE*) en una variada gama de asignaturas, al final del quinto año de la secundaria. Los que continúan en la educación escolar hacen el *Advanced Supplementary* (*A/S*) *Level* en un número menor de asignaturas, en el sexto año y el *Advanced Level* (*A Level*) en el último año. El ingreso a la universidad depende de que el estudiante apruebe al menos dos *A Levels*. Los que deseen estudiar asignaturas vocacionales hacen los exámenes *General National Vocational Qualifications* (*GNVQ*s) en los colegios y las escuelas politécnicas. En Escocia los estudiantes hacen los *Standard Grade*, al final del cuarto año de la secundaria y los *Higher* y *Advanced Higher* para poder entrar a la universidad. En los Estados Unidos, los exámenes públicos no son una característica de la educación. Los estudiantes obtienen su *high school diploma* al final de la educación secundaria, principalmente, basándose en las calificaciones otorgadas por los profesores de cada curso. Algunas universidades y colegios también exigen, antes de solicitar su ingreso, que los estudiantes hagan un examen nacional, el *American College Test* (*ACT*), en inglés, matemáticas y razonamiento científico. *Ver tb* EDUCATION.

Fifth Amendment ▶ BILL OF RIGHTS

Fish and chips Un plato británico popular, de filete de pescado rebozado y frito, acompañado de patatas fritas. En el RU muchos restaurantes de comida para llevar, se especializan en este plato y se los denomina *fish-and-chip shops*, *chip shops*, o *chippies*.

Flower of Scotland El himno nacional de Escocia.

Football Es el deporte más popular del Reino Unido. Muchos de los conocidos clubes de fútbol profesionales están basados en Londres (Arsenal, Chelsea, Tottenham Hotspur) o en las grandes ciudades de la región central de Inglaterra y del Norte (Manchester United, Newcastle United, Aston Villa). Todos los clubes profesionales y algunos no profesionales toman parte anualmente en una competición eliminatoria, la *FA Cup*. Los dos equipos ganadores juegan en la *Cup Final*, tradicionalmente, el partido más importante de la temporada. Escocia tiene una liga de fútbol separada que está organizada de manera similar.

Sus dos clubes más famosos, Celtic y Rangers, tienen su base en Glasgow. En EEUU, normalmente el fútbol recibe el nombre de '*soccer*' y la palabra '*football*' se refiere la fútbol americano.

Founding Fathers Aquellos norteamericanos que sentaron las bases del gobierno de EEUU en la *Federal Constitution Convention* en 1787, ocasión en que se redactó y firmó la Constitución (CONSTITUTION). Los más conocidos son George Washington, Thomas Jefferson, y Benjamin Franklin.

fraternity Una hermandad de varones en muchos establecimientos de la enseñanza superior en EEUU. Por lo general, sus miembros viven juntos en una *fraternity house*. Cada *fraternity* lleva como nombre el de dos o tres letras griegas, como por ejemplo '*Lambda Delta Chi*'. Hacen obras de caridad y a algunas de ellas les interesa el éxito académico. Han recibido críticas de elitistas y discriminatorias, pero en la actualidad vuelven a tener aceptación ya que su sistema comunitario reduce el costo de la vida para los estudiantes, en una época en que la educación es cada vez más cara. *Ver tb* SORORITY.

FTSE-100 (pronunciado '*Footsie one hundred*') Un promedio del valor de las acciones de las 100 empresas más grandes que aparecen en las listas de la Bolsa de Londres y que se publican diariamente en el periódico *Financial Times*. Se usan como un indicador importante del rendimiento de la economía británica.

further education En Gran Bretaña, el término *further education* se utiliza normalmente para referirse a cualquier tipo de enseñanza dirigida a personas que tengan más de 16 años, edad mínima en que se puede dejar la escolaridad obligatoria, y que no estén en la universidad, en cuyo caso se habla de *higher education*. Sin embargo, en los Estados Unidos, el término *further education* también se utiliza para referirse a la educación universitaria.

Gaelic Así se denominan varias lenguas de origen celta habladas en distintas regiones de las Islas Británicas. El *Scots Gaelic* es hablado por unas 50.000 personas que viven en las Highlands y en las islas del oeste de Escocia. En cuanto al *Irish* o *Irish Gaelic*, aunque casi 1,5 millones de personas afirman dominarlo, se calcula que apenas la mitad lo habla diariamente. En la Isla autónoma de Man, varios centenares de personas hablan hoy el *Manx Gaelic*.

Gap Year Así se denomina en Gran Bretaña el período entre el final de los estudios preuniversitarios y el comienzo de la carrera universitaria que toman muchos estudiantes para conseguir experiencia laboral y acumular fondos o para viajar a otros países.

GCSE ▶ EXAMINATIONS

Geordie Una persona de Newcastle upon Tyne en el norte de Inglaterra. La palabra también se usa para designar el acento o dialecto de estas personas.

Gettysburg Address Un discurso pronunciado por Abraham Lincoln en 1863, en la inauguración de un monumento a los caídos en la Batalla de Gettysburg durante la Guerra de Secesión (CIVIL WAR). Contiene la memorable definición de democracia como 'un gobierno del pueblo, por el pueblo y para el pueblo'.

GNVQ ▶ EXAMINATIONS

God Save the Queen Es el himno nacional británico. No se sabe quién escribió la letra o compuso su música, pero en el siglo dieciocho ya era una canción tradicional.

GP (*general practitioner*) Un médico generalista (también llamado *family doctor*), que trata a todo tipo de pacientes dentro de una localidad de Gran Bretaña. Es el equivalente al médico de familia. En un consultorio (*surgery*) suelen atender varios médicos (*group practice*). Cada consultorio tiene financiación directa o indirecta del gobierno.

grade school ▶ ELEMENTARY SCHOOL

grammar school En algunas áreas de Inglaterra y Gales, un tipo de colegio de enseñanza secundaria (*secondary school*) que admite a alumnos que han aprobado una prueba de aptitud. Desde 1965, estos colegios han sido reemplazados en su mayor parte por los COMPREHENSIVE SCHOOLS.

Great Britain Gran Bretaña es la más grande de la Islas Británicas (BRITISH ISLES). Incluye a Inglaterra, Escocia y Gales. A menudo el término '*Britain*' se emplea erróneamente para hacer referencia al Reino Unido (UNITED KINGDOM) o a Inglaterra.

green card En EEUU es un documento oficial que cualquier persona que no sea ciudadana americana debe obtener para tener el derecho a residir y trabajar en Estados Unidos. En el Reino Unido es un documento que el conductor o dueño de un automóvil debe conseguir de la compañía de seguros al llevarlo al extranjero para que siga vigente la cobertura de la póliza.

Greyhound bus Vehículo que pertenece a la mayor compañía de autobuses de los Estados Unidos (*The Greyhound Lines Company*). Circulan entre ciudades y grandes poblaciones a través de toda la geografía estadounidense y son muy usados por la gente joven y los turistas, quienes a menudo recorren grandes distancias en ellos.

Groundhog Day ▶ DÍAS FESTIVOS, FIESTAS, Y TRADICIONES

Guardian Angels Una organización formada por jóvenes en Estados

Culture

Unidos y creada para proteger a la población de la delincuencia. Sus miembros llevan gorras rojas y camisas que tienen el eslogan '*Dare to Care*' (o sea 'Atrévete a preocuparte por los demás'). Trabajan en colaboración con la policía y no van armados.

gun control El control de armas es uno de los temas más polémicos de EEUU. Muchos son de la opinión que se debería prohibir su posesión por parte de ciudadanos comunes, debido al gran número de delitos violentos cometidos con ellas. Otros opinan que tal prohibición contravendría la Constitución, la que establece el derecho a portar armas '*right to bear arms*'. La NATIONAL RIFLE ASSOCIATION se ha opuesto a toda ley relacionada con el tema. Sin embargo en 1993, el congreso aprobó la '*Brady Bill*' que restringe la venta y uso de cierto tipo de armas.

Gunpowder Plot ▶ BONFIRE NIGHT

Guy Fawkes' Night ▶ BONFIRE NIGHT

haka Un canto de guerra tradicional de los maoríes de Nueva Zelanda, que se acompaña pateando el suelo y con enérgicos movimientos de brazos. El equipo nacional de rugby de Nueva Zelanda, tradicionalmente ejecuta un *haka* antes de empezar un partido.

Halloween ▶ DÍAS FESTIVOS, FIESTAS, Y TRADICIONES

Harlem Un barrio en Manhattan, Nueva York, tradicionalmente el lugar donde vive una gran comunidad de negros con una fuerte tradición jazzística.

high school En Estados Unidos, el último ciclo del colegio secundario, generalmente para alumnos cuyas edades están comprendidas entre los 14 y los 18 años. En Gran Bretaña, algunos colegios secundarios también se llaman *high schools*.

holidays ▶ DÍAS FESTIVOS, FIESTAS, Y TRADICIONES

homecoming Un acontecimiento que se celebra cada año en los establecimientos de enseñanza superior en EEUU. Por lo general tiene lugar en el otoño cuando los antiguos alumnos regresan para participar en toda clase de actividades, entre las que se incluyen un *homecoming game* de fútbol, un *homecoming parade* y el *homecoming dance*. También se elige a la *homecoming queen*.

Honours List Cada año, en junio, para el cumpleaños de la reina (*Queen's* OFFICIAL BIRTHDAY) y para el día de Año Nuevo, se publica una lista con el nombre de las personas que se han distinguido por su labor, tanto a nivel nacional como local. Estas reciben una gran variedad de títulos honoríficos que van desde el de *Lord* o *Lady* (*peerage*), el de *Sir* (*knighthood*) o *Dame* (el equivalente para una mujer), hasta otros de menor importancia. También al final de cada legislatura antes de elecciones generales, el primer ministro propone una lista con los nombres de políticos para los *Dissolution Honours*.

House of Commons La Cámara de los Comunes es la cámara baja del Parlamento británico o HOUSES OF PARLIAMENT. Los parlamentarios elegidos para reunirse aquí se denominan MPs (*members of Parliament*).

House of Lords La Cámara de los Lores es la cámara alta del Parlamento británico. Su función es discutir y posteriormente aprobar o sugerir cambios a la legislación que haya sido aprobada en la Cámara de los Comunes (HOUSE OF COMMONS). Es también el último tribunal de apelación. Sus miembros son nombrados en su mayoría, y hasta 1999 un número de los cargos eran hereditarios. Se han propuesto unas medidas de reforma según las cuales un porcentaje de los lores serían elegidos directamente por el pueblo.

House of Representatives La Cámara de Representantes es la cámara baja del Congreso (CONGRESS) de Estados Unidos. Está formada por 435 representantes (REPRESENTATIVES) que son elegidos cada dos años. Cada estado de EEUU tiene un número de representantes proporcional a su población. Esta cámara es la encargada de introducir nueva legislación, por lo que toda nueva ley debe ser aprobada por ella.

Houses of Parliament Son las dos cámaras del Parlamento británico, la Cámara de los Comunes (HOUSE OF COMMONS) y la Cámara de los Lores (HOUSE OF LORDS). El Palacio de Westminster (*Palace of* WESTMINSTER), que es el grupo de edificios situados en el centro de Londres donde se reúnen los miembros de las dos cámaras, también se conoce con este nombre.

Hunting En EEUU, es un deporte para individuos o pequeños grupos que salen con escopetas a acechar o a cazar animales. En el RU este deporte se conoce por '*shooting*' y el término '*hunting*' se refiere a la caza tradicional, en la que un grupo de personas, con chaquetas rojas o negras, montan a caballo a través del campo siguiendo a una jauría que caza y finalmente mata a un animal; por lo general un zorro. En noviembre de 2004, el Parlamento británico aprobó una ley para prohibir la caza con jauría en Inglaterra y Escocia. Partidarios de este tipo de caza sostienen que la prohibición no sólo pondrá fin a una tradición que se remonta a cientos de años, sino que también tendrá graves efectos económicos y sociales en la vida rural y se han propuesto trabajar para levantar la prohibición.

Inauguration Day En EEUU, el día en que el nuevo presidente asume oficialmente el poder. La ceremonia de investidura siempre tiene lugar el 20 de enero, en Washington DC.

Independence Day ▶ DÍAS FESTIVOS, FIESTAS, Y TRADICIONES

independent school Un colegio de Gran Bretaña que no recibe dinero alguno del estado y se autofinancia mediante el pago de cuotas por parte de los padres. Los PUBLIC SCHOOLS y los PREPARATORY SCHOOLS están dentro de esta categoría.

infant school ▶ EDUCATION

IRA (*Irish Republican Army*) El IRA (Ejército Republicano Irlandés) es una organización paramilitar ilegal cuyo objetivo es la unificación de la República de Irlanda e Irlanda del Norte. En 1970, como respuesta a lo que se percibía como represión contra la minoría católica en Irlanda del Norte, una facción del IRA (*Provisional IRA*) empezó a cometer actos de terrorismo en Irlanda del Norte e Inglaterra. El acuerdo de Viernes Santo (*Good Friday Agreement*) del 1998 ha llevado a un período de relativa paz entre las comunidades enfrentadas en Irlanda del Norte. *Ver tb* SINN FEIN.

ITV (*Independent Television*) Un grupo de compañías de televisión comercial que ofrecen programaciones diferentes para quince regiones distintas del Reino Unido.

Ivy League El grupo de universidades más antiguas y más respetadas de EEUU, situadas en el noreste del país. Son: Harvard, Yale, Columbia University, Cornell University, Dartmouth College, Brown University, Princeton University y la University of Pennsylvania. El término proviene de la hiedra que crece en los antiguos edificios de las universidades.

John Bull Una figura imaginaria que se supone representa a Inglaterra o la esencia de ser inglés y que por lo general es representada por un hombre gordo de pantalones ajustados, que lleva un frac y un sombrero de copa baja y ala ancha. Muy poca gente moderna se identificaría con John Bull y es mucho menos símbolo patriótico que el Tío Sam (UNCLE SAM) en EEUU.

junior high school ▶ EDUCATION

junior school Un colegio estatal de Gran Bretaña para niños de entre 7 y 11 años.

King James Bible ▶ AUTHORIZED VERSION

kirk Palabra escosesa que significa iglesia. '*The Kirk*' quiere decir la *Church of Scotland* (Iglesia de Escocia).

kiwi Un pájaro que no vuela, auctóctono de Nueva Zelanda. Los neocelandeses y sus equipos deportivos se conocen por el apodo '*Kiwis*'.

Ku Klux Klan Una organización secreta en EEUU, que se opone a la igualdad de derechos para los afroamericanos (AFRICAN-AMERICANS). Se estableció en 1866, después de la abolición de la esclavitud. Declarada ilegal en 1871, resurgió en 1915, ampliando sus ataques para incluir también a los judíos, católicos y extranjeros. Durante los años 60 se opuso violentamente a la campaña por la igualdad de los derechos civiles de los afroamericanos. En la actualidad tiene poca influencia. Los miembros del KKK se visten con túnicas largas de color blanco y capuchones altos terminados en punta que les ocultan la cara.

Labor Day El Día del Trabajo es un día festivo de carácter nacional en EEUU, celebrado el primer lunes de septiembre en honor a los trabajadores.

Labor Party En Australia, es uno de los dos principales partidos políticos. Por lo general, es de una política de centro izquierda moderada.

Labour Party El Partido Laborista es uno de los tres principales partidos políticos de Gran Bretaña. Accedió por primera vez al poder en 1924 con el objetivo de representar los intereses de los trabajadores y sindicatos. En las últimas décadas, ha abandonado su postura de izquierda en puntos tales como la propiedad pública de la industria y los servicios, y hoy en día sus líderes prefieren denominarlo *New Labour*.

lawyer En el RU un abogado que lleva los asuntos legales normales y corrientes de las personas se llama *solicitor*. Los *barristers* representan a los clientes ante los tribunales superiores. Cuando una persona es acreditada *barrister*, se dice que ésta ha ingresado a la abogacía ('*has been called to the Bar*'). Los términos *barrister* y *solicitor* no se usan en EEUU, donde no se hace esta distinción entre diferentes tipos de abogados. Tanto en el RU como en EEUU, el término *counsel* se puede emplear para designar a un abogado o a un equipo de abogados que presentan un caso ante un tribunal.

Liberal Democratic Party Al Partido Demócrata Liberal también se lo conoce informalmente como los *Lib Dems*. Es el tercer partido en importancia en Gran Bretaña. Se formó en 1988 mediante la unión del Partido Liberal (*Liberal Party*) y el Partido Socialdemócrata (*Social Democratic Party*).

Liberal Party Un importante partido político en Australia que fundamentalmente aboga por políticas conservadoras.

licensing laws Las leyes que controlan la venta y el consumo de alcohol en Gran Bretaña, en PUBS, tiendas, supermercados y *off-licences*. Establecen dónde se puede vender, cuándo y a quién. Generalmente, los pubs sólo pueden vender bebidas alcohólicas entre las 11 a.m. y las 11 p.m. En EEUU hay leyes locales acerca de la venta y consumo del alcohol. Existen algunas ciudades secas (*dry*), donde está prohibida la venta de bebidas alcohólicas.

L-plates En el RU, es un pequeño cuadrado blanco de plástico con una letra 'L' en rojo, que se debe llevar en la parte delantera y trasera del vehículo conducido por una persona que está aprendiendo a conducir y que todavía no ha aprobado el examen correspondiente.

mayor En EEUU el alcalde (*mayor*) de una ciudad es elegido por sus habitantes. En Inglaterra y Gales, es el jefe de un ayuntamiento (COUNCIL) de una ciudad o un municipio (*borough*), elegido tradicionalmente por otros concejales (*councillors*). En algunas ciudades grandes se le confiere el título de *Lord Mayor* y su equivalente en Escocia es *provost* o *Lord Provost*. Llevan a cabo tareas oficiales pero tienen poco poder político. En los últimos años varias ciudades grandes han empezado a someter el cargo de alcalde a la votación popular. El primero de ellos, Ken Livingstone, fue elegido Alcalde de Londres (*Mayor of London*) en 2000.

member of Parliament ▶ MP

Memorial Day Un día festivo en EEUU en honor a los americanos caídos en la guerra. Tiene lugar, por lo general, el último lunes de mayo.

middle school ▶ EDUCATION

midterms (*midterm elections*) En EEUU una serie de elecciones para la Cámara de Representantes (HOUSE OF REPRESENTATIVES), celebradas en la mitad del mandato del presidente.

Mormon La *Church of Jesus Christ of Latter-Day Saints* cuenta hoy con unos 10 millones de miembros, denominados *Mormons*. Fue fundada en 1830 por Joseph Smith. Posteriormente, guiados por Brigham Young, sus miembros se trasladaron hacia el oeste para fundar Salt Lake City en el estado de Utah, la mayoría de cuyos habitantes son hoy mormones. Tienen reglas morales muy estrictas y no beben alcohol ni café.

Morris dancing Un tipo de baile floklórico que se originó en el RU. Se baila en formación, normalmente por varones ('*Morris men*'), que llevan camisa blanca, pantalones llenos de campanitas, sombrero de paja y que agitan pañuelos o palos.

Mother's Day (Mothering Sunday) ▶ DÍAS FESTIVOS, FIESTAS, Y TRADICIONES

motorways Gran Bretaña tiene un amplio sistema de autopistas (*motorways*) que tienen dos o tres carriles por calzada. Están señalizadas con la letra 'M' seguida de un número y tienen un límite de velocidad de 112 km/h (70 mph). En la actualidad sólo existe una autopista de peaje.

MP (*member of Parliament*) Un diputado, miembro de la Cámara de los Comunes (HOUSE OF COMMONS) que representa a una de las 659 circunscripciones electorales de Inglaterra, Escocia, Gales, e Irlanda del Norte.

NAACP (*National Association for the Advancement of Colored People*) Asociación fundada en 1909 para defender los derechos civiles de los afroamericanos (AFRICAN-AMERICANS). Jugó un papel muy importante en la campaña que culminó con la *Civil Rights Act of 1964*.

National Guard Una milicia voluntaria reclutada por cada uno de los estados norteamericanos, cuya historia remonta a la época colonial. En tiempos de desastre natural o emergencia civil puede ser declarada bajo mando federal, y hoy día se le considera parte del ejército nacional.

National Health Service (*NHS*) En Gran Bretaña, es el servicio público de asistencia médica, financiado en gran parte por el gobierno. La asistencia, por lo general, es gratuita. Se deben pagar la atención dental y las medicinas recetadas. Sin embargo, las personas que pertenecen a ciertos grupos, tales como los niños y los jubilados, no pagan por estos servicios.

National Insurance En Gran Bretaña, sistema de cotizaciones o contribuciones a la Seguridad Social (*National Insurance contributions*), que los empleados y empleadores deben realizar a fin de que el gobierno pueda financiar los diferentes beneficios sociales que proporciona, tales como las jubilaciones, y el NATIONAL HEALTH SERVICE. Cada persona debe tener un número de la Seguridad Social (*National Insurance Number*).

National Lottery La lotería nacional británica, mediante la cual se recauda dinero tanto para una amplia variedad de proyectos culturales o deportivos como para obras benéficas y la conservación del patrimonio nacional.

National Party Importante partido político en Nueva Zelanda, que aboga principalmente por políticas conservadoras.

National Rifle Association (*NRA*) Una organización en EEUU, que apoya el uso de armas de fuego para la caza, el deporte y la legítima defensa. Sus 3, 4 millones de miembros sostienen que la Constitución (CONSTITUTION) otorga a los ciudadanos el derecho a poseerlas.

National Trust Una fundación británica que tiene como objetivo la conservación de lugares de interés histórico o de belleza natural. Es una organización de beneficencia que cuida cerca de 248.000 hectáreas (612,000 acres) de campo, casi 960 km (600 millas) de costa y más de 200 inmuebles y jardines. En Escocia la organización recibe el nombre de *National Trust for Scotland*, y es independiente.

Native American El término de más amplia aceptación para referirse a los pueblos indígenas de América y el Caribe. De acuerdo al Bureau of Indian Affairs, organización del gobierno de EEUU que trata todos los asuntos relacionados con los indios, existen en ese país cerca de 550 tribus que totalizan alrededor de 1,2 millones de personas. De éstas cerca de un millón vive en reservaciones y cerca del 37% de éstos están desempleados. Muchas reservaciones abren casinos basándose en el hecho de que pueden establecer sus propias normas.

NBC (*National Broadcasting Company*) La primera compañía de radiodifusión que se fundó en Estados Unidos (1926). El primer canal de televisión de la NBC empezó a transmitir en 1940.

Newspapers El 95% de los Americanos lee la prensa local. En EEUU existe sólo un periódico de carácter nacional, el *USA Today*, los demás son locales. Algunos periódicos de ciudades grandes, tales como el *New York Times*, *Los Angeles Times*, y *The Washington Post*, se leen a través de todo el país. Además el *International Herald Tribune*, publicado fuera de EEUU, es leído por muchos americanos en el extranjero. *The Wall Street Journal* es el periódico de negocios más importante de EEUU, también publica el DOW JONES AVERAGE. La prensa americana todavía es, en líneas generales, conservadora debido a la necesidad de alcanzar el mayor número de ventas posible. En el RU hay dos tipos de periódicos; los de formato grande (*broadsheets*) y los tabloides (*tabloids*), publicados en formato más compacto y más cuadrado. Hasta hace poco todos los periódicos nacionales serios eran *broadsheets*. El *Daily Telegraph*, el *Guardian*, y el *Financial Times* han conservado este formato, pero *The Times* y *el Independent* actualmente se publican como tabloides, al igual que los periódicos nacionales populares. Entre estos últimos, los más conocidos son el *Sun*, *Mirror*, *Express*, y *el Mail*. Tienden a enfatizar los aspectos de interés humano de las noticias y a veces son de un tono sensacionalista. Tanto en EEUU como en el RU los periódicos que se publican los sábados y domingos son más voluminosos que los de los días de semana y normalmente traen por separado las secciones de las noticias, los deportes, cultura, etc.

Northern Ireland La provincia al noreste de la isla de Irlanda que continuó siendo parte del Reino Unido, con autonomía limitada, después de que el resto de Irlanda se independizara en 1920. La vida en Irlanda del Norte ha sido dominada por conflictos, entre la mayoría protestante, que desea retener el vínculo con el RU y la gran minoría católica que desea unirse a la República Irlandesa. Desde 1969 hasta 1998, la violencia fue frecuente en Irlanda del Norte y en el territorio de Gran Bretaña, a medida que la minoría católica hacía campaña en favor de los derechos civiles y las organizaciones paramilitares llevaban a cabo atentados terroristas y asesinatos. Durante gran parte de este período la privincia fue regida por el gobierno británico y muchas tropas británicas fueron emplazadas allí. El acuerdo de Viernes Santo (*Good Friday Agreement*) en 1998 ha terminado con la violencia y se ha reestablecido una autonomía limitada, sobre la base de un poder compartido. Sin embargo, el Parlamento de Irlanda del Norte, ha sido suspendido en varias ocasiones debido a que a los partidos políticos les ha resultado difícil la cooperación. Dentro de éstos también existen divisiones sectarias. El Partido Democrático Unionista (*Democratic Unionist Party*) y el más moderado Partido Unionista del Ulster

(*Ulster Unionist Party*) representan a la comunidad protestante mientras que SINN FEIN y el más moderado Partido Social Demócrata y Laborista representan a los católicos. El pequeño Partido Alianza (*Alliance Party*) se ha comprometido a no ser sectario. *Ver tb* IRA.

Number Ten ▶ DOWNING STREET

NVQ ▶ EXAMINATIONS

Official Birthday Es el segundo sábado de junio, día en que se celebra el cumpleaños del monarca inglés, aunque no es el día de su nacimiento. Se conmemora con *Trooping the Colour*, un desfile militar ante el monarca, y con la publicación de una HONOURS LIST, los *Birthday Honours*.

Old Glory ▶ STARS AND STRIPES

Open University (*OU*) Universidad a distancia británica fundada en 1969.

Oscars En la *Oscar Ceremony*, celebrada en Los Ángeles cada año desde 1929 por la *Academy of Motion Picture Arts and Sciences*, se otorgan los *Academy Awards*, apodados los *Oscars*, a aquellos artistas, directores, productores y guionistas de cine considerados por votación de sus colegas los mejores del año.

Oxbridge Un término para referirse conjuntamente a las dos universidades más antiguas y con más prestigio del Reino Unido, Oxford y Cambridge. Las clases altas, tradicionalmente, siempre han enviado a sus hijos a una u otra universidad. Se han hecho muchos esfuerzos en los últimos años para atraer a más estudiantes de todos los medios sociales y de colegios estatales (STATE SCHOOLS), muchos todavía provienen de los colegios privados (PUBLIC SCHOOLS).

Pancake Day ▶ SHROVE TUESDAY

pantomime Un tipo de representación teatral, dirigida a los niños y comunmente conocida también como *panto*, que tradicionalmente presentan los teatros británicos durante la época navideña. El argumento suele ser una adaptación cómica de un cuento tradicional y cuenta con un número de personajes de características exageradas e increíbles. También requiere de un gran nivel de participación por parte del público.

Parliament El Parlamento británico es el más alto organismo legislativo de Gran Bretaña y está formado por la Cámara de los Lores (HOUSE OF LORDS) y la Cámara de los Comunes (HOUSE OF COMMONS).

PBS (*Public Broadcasting Service*) Un servicio de radiodifusión estadounidense, financiado por el gobierno, famoso por la calidad de sus programas. Consiste en una asociación de emisoras locales que transmiten sin fines de lucro y sin publicidad.

Culture

Culture

Peace Corps El Cuerpo de Paz , fundado en 1961, es una agencia federal de los EEUU, compuesta por voluntarios que trabajan principalmente en países en vías de desarrollo en esferas tales como la enseñanza, la salud, la agricultura o proyectos medioambientales.

peer Hay dos clases de pares (*peers*) británicos: aquellos que heredan este título de nobleza (*hereditary peers*) y los que lo poseen de por vida (*life peers*) sin poder traspasarlo a su descendencia. Los pares tenían derecho a ocupar un escaño en la Cámara de los Lores (HOUSE OF LORDS). Se han propuesto medidas según las cuales un porcentaje de los lores serían elegidos directamente por el pueblo.

Pentagon, The El edificio de forma pentagonal, situado en Washington, donde se encuentra la oficina central del ministerio de defensa y de las fuerzas armadas de EEUU. A menudo la prensa utiliza el término '*The Pentagon*' para referirse al Estado Mayor.

Pledge of Allegiance Promesa de lealtad que los norteamericanos hacen a su bandera y a su patria. En muchos colegios, los niños la repiten cada mañana frente a la bandera y con una mano en el pecho.

Poppy Day ▶ DÍAS FESTIVOS, FIESTAS, Y TRADICIONES

preparatory school En EEUU los *preparatory schools* son colegios secundarios donde se les proporciona a los alumnos un régimen especial de enseñanza preuniversitaria. En Gran Bretaña, es un colegio privado, también llamado *prep school*, para alumnos de edades comprendidas entre siete y trece años. Algunos tienen régimen de internado y otros no, pero la mayoría son una mezcla de ambos. Normalmente no es un colegio mixto. Gran parte de los alumnos pasa, a continuación, a un colegio privado (PUBLIC SCHOOL).

President En Estados Unidos el presidente puede gobernar un máximo de dos legislaturas (*terms*) de cuatro años cada una. Es el jefe del Estado, es responsable de la política exterior y es comandante en jefe de las fuerzas armadas.

President's Day ▶ DÍAS FESTIVOS, FIESTAS, Y TRADICIONES

primary (*primary election*) Las elecciones primarias (*primaries*) se celebran en EEUU para seleccionar candidatos para una elección principal, especialmente la presidencial. Los candidatos para presidente (PRESIDENT) se eligen después de una serie de primarias estatales. *Ver tb* ELECTIONS.

primary school ▶ EDUCATION

Proms (*promenade concerts*) Una serie de conciertos de música clásica que tienen lugar, en el Albert Hall de Londres, todos los años, en el verano.

Provost ▶ MAYOR

pub (*public house*) Una casa abierta al público que vende bebidas alcohólicas y no alcohólicas. El *pub* tradicional casi imposible de reproducir fuera del RU. Sus orígenes remontan al tiempo de los romanos. Para finales del siglo XIV todo el que fabricara cerveza (*ale*) para vender, tenía que poner un letrero con el dibujo del signo del pub, lo que hoy sigue siendo una característica de estos establecimientos. Más que un bar, el *pub* (o '*local*') continúa siendo el centro social y cultural de muchos pueblos y otras comunidades.

public access channel Un canal de televisión en EEUU reservado para programas de personas y organizaciones que no persiguen fines de lucro.

public house ▶ PUB

public school En Inglaterra y Gales, un colegio privado para alumnos de edades comprendidas entre 13 y 18 años. La mayoría de los *public schools* tiene régimen de internado y a menudo son mixtos. En Escocia y Estados Unidos el término *public school* se utiliza para referirse a un colegio estatal. *Ver tb* PREPARATORY SCHOOL.

Pulitzer Prize Un premio de gran prestigio establecido en 1917, por Joseph Pulitzer, director de periódico y editor, que se otorga anualmente por los éxitos más destacados en el mundo del periodismo, la literatura y la música norteamericanos. Cada año se entregan trece premios.

Queen's English El inglés que habla y escribe la gente educada de Gran Bretaña. *Ver tb* RECEIVED PRONUNCIATION.

Received Pronunciation (*RP*) La pronunciación estándar del inglés británico, que se basa en el habla educada del sur de Inglaterra. Sólo alrededor del 5% de los habitantes de las islas británicas hablan con una RP. Durante un largo tiempo los locutores de la BBC hablaron con una RP, también conocida como '*BBC English*'.

Remembrance Sunday ▶ POPPY DAY

Representative Un miembro de la Cámara de Representantes (*House of Representatives*) de Estados Unidos.

Republican Party Uno de los dos principales partidos políticos de EEUU. Aunque el Partido Republicano fue fundado en 1854, por los que deseaban abolir la esclavitud, se considera más conservador que el Partido Demócrata (DEMOCRATIC PARTY), el otro partido.

rugby Un deporte que tuvo su origen en Gran Bretaña y que se juega con un balón ovalado. Los dos sistemas, el de la *rugby league* y el de la *rugby union*, difieren ligeramente en cuanto a las normas y al tanteo. Los equipos de la primera, están compuestos por trece jugadores, los de la segunda por quince. Los jugadores de *rugby league* siempre han sido profesionales, mientras que en la *rugby union* el profesionalismo fue aceptado sólo en 1995.

Salvation Army Una organización religiosa fundada en Gran Bretaña a finales del siglo XIX, cuyos miembros visten uniforme de estilo militar y llevan a cabo trabajos de beneficencia, especialmente para personas sin techo.

SAT En EEUU, corresponde a las siglas de *Scholastic Aptitude Test*. Una prueba de aptitud, que se hace normalmente en el último año del *high school*. Hay que aprobarlo para entrar a la mayor parte de las universidades. En Inglaterra y Gales, significa *Standard Assessment Test* o *Task*, prueba que se hace a los alumnos de todos los colegios, a los 7, 11, y 14 años, a fin de evaluar su progreso.

Scotland La parte más al norte del Reino Unido, cuya población se concentra principalmente en un cinturón central alrededor de dos ciudades

principales; Glasgow y Edimburgo, su capital. Escocia es conocida, especialmente, por la belleza de sus montañas y lagos, (llamados '*lochs*') de las Tierras Altas (*Highlands*), al noroeste de Edimburgo. Hasta el siglo XVI las guerras entre Inglaterra y Escocia eran frecuentes. En 1603, el rey James IV de Escocia pasó a ser también rey de Inglaterra (reinando aquí como James I) y la unión de los dos países se finalizó en 1707 cuando se disolvió el Parlamento escocés. Escocia, sin embargo, retuvo muchas de sus propias instituciones. Por ejemplo, tiene un sistema de educación distinto del resto del RU. Siempre ha habido escoceses que piensan que su país debería ser completamente independiente. En estos momentos este punto de vista está representado por el Partido Nacional Escocés (*Scottish National Party*), fundado en 1943 y que en la actualidad es el principal partido de la oposición en el nuevo Parlamento escosés. El parlamento para Escocia, en Edimburgo, fue restablecido en 1999, (*ver* DEVOLUTION). Tiene plena autoridad en asuntos legislativos y ejecutivos relativos a Escocia y, a diferencia de la Asemblea galesa, tiene poderes, aunque limitados, para subir o cambiar los impuestos. *Ver tb* TARTAN.

SDLP ▶ NORTHERN IRELAND

Senate El Senado es la cámara alta del Congreso (CONGRESS) de Estados Unidos. Está formado por 100 senadores (*senators*), dos por cada estado y son elegidos por períodos de seis años. Toda nueva ley debe ser aprobada por el Senado y la Cámara de Representantes (HOUSE OF REPRESENTATIVES), pero el Senado tiene responsabilidad especial en asuntos relacionados con la política exterior (PRESIDENT).

Shadow Cabinet ▶ CABINET

Shrove Tuesday ▶ DÍAS FESTIVOS, FIESTAS, Y TRADICIONES

Silicon Valley Así se apoda el Valle de Santa Clara, en California, donde se concentra un gran número de compañías de electrónica e informática. El nombre deriva del uso del silicio (*silicon*) en la electrónica.

Sinn Fein Partido político fundado en 1905 cuyo objetivo es la reunificación de los 32 condados de Irlanda dentro de la República establecida en 1949. Se le considera como la rama política del IRA, aunque niega todo vínculo orgánico con dicho movimiento paramilitar.

Smithsonian Institution Una institución nacional en EEUU que está compuesta de varios museos y centros de investigación en Washington DC. Comúnmente se la suele llamar '*the nation's attic*' ('el desván de la nación').

soap opera Nombre humorístico del culebrón o telenovela. Su nombre se debe al hecho de que las primeras *soap operas* (óperas de jabón) emitidas por radio en EEUU eran financiadas por compañías de jabón.

social security number Un número de identificación que toda persona debe tener en EEUU. En un principio fue un requisito para poder trabajar y recibir prestaciones de la seguridad social. Sin embargo, en 1987 el gobierno decidió que también los niños debían tenerlo. En la actualidad el número tiene una gran variedad de usos: aparece en cheques de banco, licencias de conducir y es el número de cada estudiante en los establecimientos de enseñanza superior.

Soho Un barrio de Londres famoso, principalmente por su vida nocturna un tanto atrevida, que ofrece espectáculos de *striptease* y *sex-shops*, como también muchos clubes nocturnos y restaurantes.

sorority Una hermandad de mujeres en muchos establecimientos de la enseñanza superior en EEUU. *Ver tb* FRATERNITY.

South Bank La orilla sur del río Támesis, en Londres, donde están situados muchos emplazamientos culturales, tales como el National Theatre, el Royal Festival Hall, el National Film Theatre, la galería de arte Tate Modern y el Globe Theatre. En este lugar también se encuentra el London Eye.

Speaker La persona que preside los debates en la Cámara de los Comunes (HOUSE OF COMMONS). Es elegida por los parlamentarios (MPS) de todos los partidos políticos.

Speaker of the House En EEUU, es la persona encargada de presidir la mayoría de las actividades de la Cámara de Representantes (HOUSE OF REPRESENTATIVES). Es responsable de mantener el orden durante los debates, de nombrar a los miembros de los comités y de remitirles los proyectos de ley. Es elegida por el partido mayoritario dentro de la Cámara, partido del cual es uno de sus dirigentes. Es la persona que sigue al vicepresidente en la sucesión a la presidencia.

Speakers' Corner Situado en la esquina noreste del Hyde Park en Londres, es el lugar donde, desde el siglo diecinueve, la gente pronuncia discursos sobre cualquier tema de su elección. El contenido de éstos muchas veces da origen a discusiones con los miembros del público.

Stars and Stripes La bandera de EEUU. Sus cincuenta estrellas (*stars*) representan los cincuenta estados y las trece franjas horizontales representan las primeras colonias que constituyeron Estados Unidos en la época de la independencia. También recibe el nombre de *Old Glory* o STAR-SPANGLED BANNER.

Star-Spangled Banner Uno de los nombres que recibe la bandera de EEUU, y así también se llama el himno nacional. Escrito en 1814, fue adoptado como tal sólo en 1931.

state school En Gran Bretaña, un colegio que está financiado directa o indirectamente por el gobierno, y que ofrece educación gratuita. La gran mayoría de los niños británicos va a este tipo de colegios.

State of the Union Address Un discurso pronunciado por el presidente de EEUU (PRESIDENT) y dirigido al Congreso (CONGRESS). Emana de la obligación, establecida en la Constitución (CONSTITUTION), de proporcionar 'información acerca del estado de la Unión'. En el discurso también se mencionan los logros del gobierno y se habla acerca de sus planes y políticas a seguir. Se transmite, en directo, por televisión.

Statue of Liberty La famosa estatua situada en la Liberty Island en la bahía de Nueva York, representa a una mujer que lleva la antorcha de la libertad. Fue un obsequio de Francia al pueblo de EEUU.

summer camp En EEUU, una de las miles de colonias de vacaciones en el campo, adonde los padres envían a sus hijos durante las vacaciones de verano a participar en actividades recreativas y deportivas tales como la natación, el senderismo o técnicas de supervivencia a la intemperie.

Super Bowl ▶ AMERICAN FOOTBALL

Supreme Court El más alto tribunal de EEUU, compuesto de nueve jueces, los *justices*, que son nombrados por el presidente (PRESIDENT) con la aprobación del Congreso (CONGRESS). Este Tribunal Supremo decide sobre la constitucionalidad de las leyes y cuenta así con el poder para impedir la aprobación de leyes tanto gubernamentales como estatales y locales. Además, funciona como tribunal de alzada para casos vistos por los tribunales inferiores. Los fallos del Tribunal Supremo sientan jurisprudencia, es decir pueden usarse como precedente por los demás tribunales.

Culture

tabloid ▶ NEWSPAPERS

tartan Un diseño de cuadrados y líneas de diferentes colores asociado con un clan escocés determinado o una tela tejida con este diseño que especialmente se usa para hacer artículos de vestir tradicionales de las tierras altas, como la falda escocesa tableada (*kilt*) que llevan los varones.

tea La tradicional bebida caliente, favorita de los británicos. En Gran Bretaña '*tea*' es también una comida pero tiene distintos significados dependiendo de la clase o las variantes regionales: Para algunos, especialmente para la clase media, es una pequeña comida que se toma a media tarde, alrededor de las 4 p.m. y que consiste en beber té con *scones* (bollos ingleses), galletas o pasteles. Ésta es la clase de comida que se sirve en un '*tea shop*' (salón de té). Para otros, es la comida principal de la tarde que se toma cuando se vuelve a casa del trabajo.

Teamsters El Teamsters Union, sindicato más grande de EEUU, cuenta con unos 1,5 millones de afiliados. Aunque en un principio representaba a los conductores de camiones (*teamsters*), en la actualidad pueden formar parte de él muchas otras profesiones.

Thanksgiving ▶ DÍAS FESTIVOS, FIESTAS, Y TRADICIONES

TOEFL (*Test of English as a Foreign Language*) Un examen que, a la hora de solicitar el ingreso a una universidad americana, evalúa el dominio del inglés de aquellos estudiantes cuya lengua materna no es este idioma.

Tory ▶ CONSERVATIVE PARTY

trick or treat ▶ HALLOWEEN

Uncle Sam Personaje imaginario que representa a EEUU, a su gobierno y ciudadanos. Tiene barba blanca y su vestimenta es roja, blanca, y azul. Lleva un sombrero alto con estrellas. Se utiliza para apelar al patriotismo norteamericano.

Union Jack o Union Flag El nombre que recibe la bandera del Reino Unido. Está formada por las cruces de San Jorge (St George), patrono de Inglaterra, de San Andrés (St Andrew), patrono de Escocia, y de San Patricio (St Patrick), patrono de Irlanda. Gales y su patrono San David no están representados en ella.

United Kingdom El Reino Unido de Gran Bretaña e Irlanda del Norte (United Kingdom of Great Britain and Northern Ireland) comprende Inglaterra, Escocia, Gales, e Irlanda del Norte. Es miembro de la COMMONWEALTH y de la Unión Europea.

Veterans Day ▶ DÍAS FESTIVOS, FIESTAS, Y TRADICIONES

Wales Parte del Reino Unido que limita con el centro-oeste de Inglaterra.

Culture

Los principales centros poblados e industriales se encuentran a lo largo de la costa sur, especialmente alrededor de las importantes ciudades de Cardiff, la capital y Swansea. La mayoría de las ciudades galesas se sitúan en la costa. El interior del país es montañoso y de escasa población. El idioma y el nacionalismo galés tiene más fuerza en el norte. La colonización inglesa de Gales empezó poco después de la conquista normanda en 1066 y continuó a través de la Edad Media. Eduardo I de Gales impuso la tradición de hacer Príncipe de Gales al hijo mayor del rey o de la reina. En el siglo XVI, Gales se integró con Inglaterra para efectos legales, administrativos y parlamentarios. En 1999, la Asamblea Nacional de Gales, normalmente conocida como la Asamblea galesa, se estableció como parte del proceso de descentralización (*ver* DEVOLUTION). Tiene poderes limitados para tratar asuntos galeses determinados, pero no tiene los poderes económicos del parlamento escocés.

Wall Street Una calle en Manhattan, Nueva York, donde se encuentran la Bolsa neoyorquina y las sedes de muchas instituciones financieras. Cuando se habla de Wall Street, a menudo se está refiriendo a ésas instituciones.

Weddings En los países angloparlantes una boda tradicional tiene lugar en una iglesia. La novia lleva un vestido blanco largo y llega acompañada por una o más *bridesmaids* (damas de honor). El padre entrega a la novia, el *best man* (un pariente o amigo que acompaña al novio) atiende al *bridegroom* (el novio). Los novios intercambian anillos, (*wedding rings* o *bands*). Después de la ceremonia, se reciben a los invitados en el *wedding reception* (banquete de bodas), donde el padre de la novia, el *best man* y el novio pronuncian discursos. Terminado el banquete, la pareja nupcial sale para pasar la *honeymoon* (luna de miel). Ya sea una boda religiosa o civil, ha sido costumbre, que antes de la boda, el novio y sus amigos salgan una noche para celebrar lo que se conoce por *stag party*, o en EEUU también *bachelor party* (despedida de soltero). Hoy en día la novia y sus amigas salen para celebrar la *hen night* o en EEUU también, *bachelorette party* (despedida de soltera). Además en EEUU se dan regalos a la novia en una fiesta que se llama *shower* que es organizada por una parienta o amiga, especialmente la dama de honor principal. Si la boda es por lo civil, el protocolo es más o menos similar, excepto que la ceremonia tiene lugar en el ayuntamiento o en una dependencia del mismo.

Welfare En EEUU el término '*welfare*' y '*welfare programs*' se usa para referirse a las distintas formas de ayuda gubernamental a disposición de los pobres, los enfermos, los desempleados y otras personas desfavorecidas. Los programas incluyen MEDICARE y MEDICAID y *food stamps*.

Welsh El idioma galés (*Cymraeg*) hoy comparte con el inglés cierta oficialidad administrativa en Gales. De origen céltico como el bretón y el córnico, sigue siendo la lengua materna de más del 20% de la población galesa, y ha experimentado un resurgimiento durante los últimos cuarenta años. Se estudia como materia obligatoria en la mayor parte de los colegios de Gales. Los letreros y otras señales de las ciudades aparecen normalmente en inglés y galés, al menos en teoría y según el antojo de cada ayuntamiento.

Westminster Un barrio central de Londres en el que se encuentran muchos de los principales edificios del gobierno, como son el Parlamento (HOUSES OF PARLIAMENT) y la residencia del primer ministro en DOWNING STREET, al igual que la Abadía de Westminster (Westminster Abbey). A menudo la prensa utiliza el término 'Westminster' para referirse al Parlamento británico.

West Side ▶ EAST SIDE

Whip En la Cámara de los Comunes (HOUSE OF COMMONS) británica, los *Whips* son parlamentarios (MPS) que tienen la responsabilidad de mantener la disciplina entre sus colegas de partido, y de asegurarse de que asistan a las sesiones y de que emitan su voto. En el Congreso (CONGRESS) de EEUU los *whips* tienen las mismas responsabilidades, también existen *Whips* de cada partido.

Whitehall Una calle del centro de Londres donde están situadas una gran parte de las oficinas del gobierno. Los periodistas utilizan a menudo el término para referirse al gobierno y la administración.

White House, The La residencia y el despacho oficial del presidente de Estados Unidos, situada en Washington. Los periodistas utilizan a menudo el término '*the White House*' para referirse al presidente y a sus consejeros.

World Series ▶ BASEBALL

Yankee Término peyorativo usado por los sureños durante la Guerra de Secesión para referirse a la gente de los estados norteños. Se usa hoy en todo el mundo para referirse a los estadounidenses en general. En los estados del sur aún se emplea en su sentido original, mientras que en los estados del norte suele aplicarse a los oriundos de Nueva Inglaterra.

yearbook Un anuario publicado por los estudiantes de un HIGH SCHOOL en EEUU, al final de cada curso. Contiene información sobre las actividades académicas y sociales de cada uno, conjuntamente con fotografías y dedicatorias.

Culture

Letter-writing / Redacción de cartas

Invitation (informal)

Madrid, 22 de abril del 2005

Querido James:

Te escribo para preguntarte si te apetecería ① pasar las vacaciones de verano con nosostros. A Tito y a Pilar les haría mucha ilusión (y también a Juan y a mí, por supuesto). Pensamos ir al noreste del país a finales de julio o a principios de agosto. Es una región realmente hermosa y nos encantaría que tú también vinieras. Es muy probable que llevemos tiendas de campaña ¡espero que no te importe dormir en el suelo!

Te agradecería que me avisaras lo más pronto posible si puedes venir.

Un cariñoso saludo,

Ana de Salas

① Or (in Latin America and also in Spain): si te gustaría.

Invitation (formal)

Invitations to parties are usually by word of mouth, while for weddings announcements are usually sent out.

Carmen S. de Pérez y Ramón Pérez Arrate, Lucía N. de Salas y Mario Salas Moro Participan a Ud. de la boda de sus hijos

Consuelo y Hernán

Y le invitan a la ceremonia religiosa que se efectuará en la Capilla del Sagrado Corazón, de Mirasierra, Madrid, el sábado 23 de julio del 2005 a las 7 p.m.

Y luego a una recepción en la Sala de Banquetes del Restaurante Galán en C/Los Santos 10 de Majadahonda, Madrid.

S.R.C.②

- In Latin America invitations to the reception are sent to relatives and close friends in a separate smaller card enclosed with the announcement.

- In Spanish-speaking countries, the answer is not usually given in writing.

② In Latin America: R.S.V.P.

Invitación (informal)

- La fecha también se puede escribir de la siguiente manera: April 10, 10 April, 10th April.
- La dirección del remitente va en el ángulo superior derecho de la carta y la fecha va inmediatamente debajo.

> 35 Winchester Drive
> Stoke Gifford
> Bristol
> BS34 8PD
>
> April 22nd 2005

Dear Luis,

Is there any chance of your coming to stay with us in the summer holidays? Roy and Debbie would be delighted if you could (as well as David and me, of course). We hope to go to North Wales at the end of July/beginning of August, and you'd be very welcome to come too. It's really beautiful up there. We'll probably take tents - I hope that's OK by you.

Let me know as soon as possible if you can manage it.

All best wishes

Rachel Hemmings

Letters / Cartas

Invitación (formal)

Invitación a una boda con recepción:

> Mr and Mrs Peter Thompson
> request the pleasure of your company
> at the marriage of their daughter
> Hannah Louise
> to
> Steven David Warner
> at St Mary's Church, Little Bourton
> on Saturday 23rd July 2005 at 2 p.m.
> And afterwards at the Golden Cross Hotel, Billing
>
> 23 Santers Lane
> Little Bourton
> Northampton
> NN6 1AZ
>
> R.S.V.P

Accepting an invitation

Winchester, 2 de mayo del 2005

Estimada Sra. de Salas:

Muchísimas gracias por su amable carta y su invitación ①.

No tengo nada planeado para las vacaciones de verano, así es que me encantaría acompañarles ② *al norte. Desgraciadamente, no podré quedarme más de cinco o seis días debido a que mi madre no se encuentra muy bien y no me gustaría estar mucho tiempo fuera de casa.*

Por favor dígame lo que tengo que llevar. ¿Hace mucho calor en la región adonde vamos? ¿Hay mar o río donde se pueda nadar? En cuanto a hacer camping, no tengo ningún problema. Nosotros siempre llevamos nuestras tiendas de campaña a todas partes.

Esperando verles ③ *pronto otra vez,*

Un afectuoso saludo,

James

① Since this is a letter from a younger person writing to the mother of a friend, he uses the formal usted form and the possessive su, and writes to her as Sra. de Salas and Estimada, which is normally used to begin a letter when the relationship is not too close. Querida ... could also be used (Estimado Sr. ... or Querido Sr. ... if the addressee is a man). On the other hand it was quite natural for Sra. de Salas to use the informal tú form to him.

② In Latin America: acompañarlos.

③ In Latin America: verlos.

■ Ending: This is normally used when the relationship is not too close, generally when the person is known to you but the usted form would be used. Un saludo muy afectuoso is also possible.

Aceptación de una invitación (informal)

Luis Villegas
Las Acacias 30
28020 Madrid

2 May 2005

Dear Mrs Hemmings ①,

Many thanks for your letter and kind invitation. Since I don't have anything fixed yet for the summer holidays, I'd be delighted to come. However I mustn't be away for more than four or five days since my mother hasn't been very well.

You must let me know what I should bring. How warm is it in North Wales? Can you swim in the sea? Camping is fine as far as I'm concerned, we take our tents everywhere.

Looking forward to seeing you soon,

Yours ②,

Luis

① Este es un encabezamiento relativamente formal, puesto que esta es una carta de una persona joven dirigida a la madre de un amigo.

② Otras alternativas para este tipo de carta: With best wishes, Yours sincerely, Kind/Kindest regards.

Respuesta a una invitación (formal)

Aceptando: Richard Willis has great pleasure in accepting Mr and Mrs Peter Thompson's kind invitation to the marriage of their daughter Hannah Louise to Steven Warner at St Mary's Church, Little Bourton, on Saturday 22nd July.

No aceptando: Richard Willis regrets that he is unable to accept Mr and Mrs Peter Thompson's kind invitation to ..., owing to a prior engagement.

- Se repiten los datos de la invitación, pero no en forma detallada.

- Si no se acepta la invitación, es de mejor educación enviar una carta a los padres de la novia, si se conocen personalmente.

Letters / Cartas

Replying to a job advertisement

■ *In Spain when the full address is given it is usually written in the top left-hand corner and in Latin America in the bottom left-hand corner, beneath the signature.*

■ *This is the most commonly used opening for a formal or business letter, or when the addressee is not personally known to you. Alternatively* Estimado Sr. *and, in Latin America,* De mi mayor consideración, *can also be used.*

■ *When the full address is given, the name of the town or city is not repeated in the date.*

David Baker
67 Whiteley Avenue
St George
Bristol
BS5 6TW

26 de septiembre de 2005

Gerente del Personal
Renos Software S.A.
Alcalá 52
28014 Madrid

Muy señor mío:

Con referencia al puesto de programador anunciado recientemente en El País del 12 de septiembre del presente, les agradecería me enviaran información más detallada acerca de la plaza vacante ①.

Actualmente estoy trabajando para una empresa de Bristol, pero mi contrato termina a finales de este mes y querría aprovechar esta oportunidad para ② trabajar en Madrid. Como se desprende del currículum vitae que adjunto, viví durante algún tiempo en España, tengo perfecto dominio del idioma español y también las cualificaciones ③ y experiencia requeridas.

Estaré disponible para asistir a una entrevista, en cualquier momento desde el 6 de octubre, fecha a partir de la cual se me puede contactar en la siguiente dirección en Madrid:

C/ Sevilla 25
28020 Madrid
Teléf. 91 429-96-67

Sin otro particular, quedo a la espera de su respuesta, ④
Atentamente, ⑤

① *Or if you have enough details and want to apply for the job right away:* quisiera solicitar la plaza vacante.

② *Or if you are unemployed:* Actualmente estoy buscando trabajo y quisiera ...

③ *In Latin America:* calificaciones.

④ *Or:* Agradeciendo de antemano su atención *or* En espera de su respuesta.

⑤ *Or:* Le *(Lo in Latin America)* saluda atentamente. Me despido de usted atentamente, Muy atentamente, *or* Esperando su respuesta, se despide atentamente *are also possible.*

Respuesta a un anuncio de trabajo

C/Islas Baleares 18. 2º B
FUENCARRAL
28080 Madrid
Spain

13th February 2005

The Personnel Manager ①
Patterson Software plc
Milton State
Bath BA6 8YZ

Dear Sir o Madam ①,

I am interested in the post of programmer advertized in The Guardian of 12 February and would be very grateful if you could send me further particulars. ②

I am currently working for the Sempo Corporation, but my contract finishes at the end of the month, and I would like ③ to work in England. As you can see from my CV (enclosed), I have an excellent command of English and also the required qualifications and experience.

I will be available for interview any time after 6th March, from which date I can be contacted at the following address in the UK:

c/o Lewis
51 Dexter Road
London N7 6BW
Tel. 0207 607 5512

I look forward to hearing from you. ④

Yours sincerely

María Luisa Márquez Blanco

Encl.

① Otra alternativa puede ser Ms Angela Summers, ..., si en el anuncio aparece Reply to Angela Summers o Dear Ms Summers, Dear Mrs Wright, si en el anuncio sólo se indica el apellido.

② O and would like to apply for this position, si en el anuncio se incluye suficiente información acerca del puesto.

③ O si se encuentra desempleado: I am currently looking for work and I would like ...

④ También: Thanking you in anticipation/advance.

Curriculum Vitae (CV), (*AmE*) Resumé

CURRÍCULUM VITAE

Nombre y apellidos	David Baker
Fecha de nacimiento	30/6/78
Lugar	Londres
Estado civil	Soltero ①
Domicilio actual	67 Whiteley Avenue
	St George
	Bristol
	BS5 6TW
	Gran Bretaña
Teléfono	+44 (0)117 945 3421

DATOS ACADÉMICOS

1993-95   GCSE (equivalente a la ESO en España) en 9 asignaturas.

1995-97   A Levels (equivalente al Curso de Orientación Universitaria en España) en Matemáticas, Informática y Español, Croydon Sixth Form College.

1997-98   Trabajos temporales de oficina en España y estudios de Español para los negocios en clases nocturnas.

1999-2001 Universidad de Aston, Birmingham, BSc en Informática (equivalente a Licenciatura en Ciencias de la Información).

EXPERIENCIA PROFESIONAL

2001-02   Trabajo de práctica como programador de software para IBM, desarrollo de programas para la industria, con especialidad en infografía.

2002-al presente Programador para Wondersoft plc, Bristol.

IDIOMAS

Inglés   Lengua materna.

Español Dominio total, hablado y escrito.

Francés Bueno.

AFICIONES

Leer, viajar, esquí, tenis.

---

① Or: Casado (sin hijos *or* con un hijo/dos/tres *etc*, hijos), Divorciado (sin hijos *or* con un hijo/dos/tres *etc*, hijos).

Currículum Vitae

CURRICULUM VITAE ①

Name:	María Luisa Márquez Blanco
Address:	C/Islas Baleares 18. 2ºB
	FUENCARRAL
	28080 Madrid
	Spain
Telephone:	(+34) 91. 243 53 94
Nationality:	Spanish
Date of Birth:	11/3/78

EDUCATION:

1996-2000   Degree Course in Information Technology and English at Universidad Complutense of Madrid.

1992- 1996   BUP (secondary education)/COU (equivalent to A levels) at the Instituto de Enseñanza Media in Fuencarral.

EMPLOYMENT:

2002-present   Program development engineer with Sempo Informática, Madrid, specializing in computer graphics.

2001-02   Trainee programmer with Oregón-España, Madrid.

FURTHER SKILLS:

Languages: Spanish (mother tongue),

English (fluent, spoken and written),

French (good).

Interests: Travel, fashion, tennis.

① O: Resumé (AmE).

Letters / Cartas

Booking a hotel room

Luis Granados
C/Felipe V 32
Segovia

23 de abril del 2005

Sr. Director
Hotel Los Palomos
C/Piedrabuena 40
Cádiz

Apreciado señor: ①

Su hotel aparece en un folleto turístico sobre la zona para el año 2005 y me ha causado muy buena impresión. Por ello le escribo para reservar una habitación doble con baño y una habitación individual ② para nuestro hijo, desde el 6 hasta 14 de agosto (nueve noches). Preferiblemente ambas habitaciones con vista al mar.

Si tiene disponibilidad para esas fechas, le rogaría que me comunicara el precio y si se requiere depósito.

Sin otro particular le saluda ③ atentamente,

Luis Granados

① *Also:* Estimado Sr.

② *Or:* una habitación doble y una individual para nuestro hijo, ambas con baño.

③ *In Latin America:* lo saluda ...

Reserva de habitación en un hotel

The Manager
Torbay Hotel
Dawlish
Devon
EX37 2LR

35 Prince Edward Road
Milton ML7 3AA

Tel. 01865 322435

23rd April 2005

Dear Sir or Madam,

I saw your hotel listed in the Inns of Devon guide for last year, and wish to reserve a double (or twin-bedded) room with shower ① in a quiet position from August 2nd-11th (nine nights), also a single room for my son.

If you have anything suitable for this period please let me know the price and whether you require a deposit.

Yours faithfully,

Charles Fairhurst

. . . .

Sending an e-mail

The illustration shows a typical interface for sending e-mail.

Querida Cristina:

Solo un par de líneas para confirmar el recibo de tu e-mail de prueba.
Me alegro que desde ahora nos podamos comunicar por Internet.
Quedo a la espera del documento adjunto que me prometiste.

Un fuerte abrazo,

Carmen

Letters / Cartas

Para enviar correo electrónico

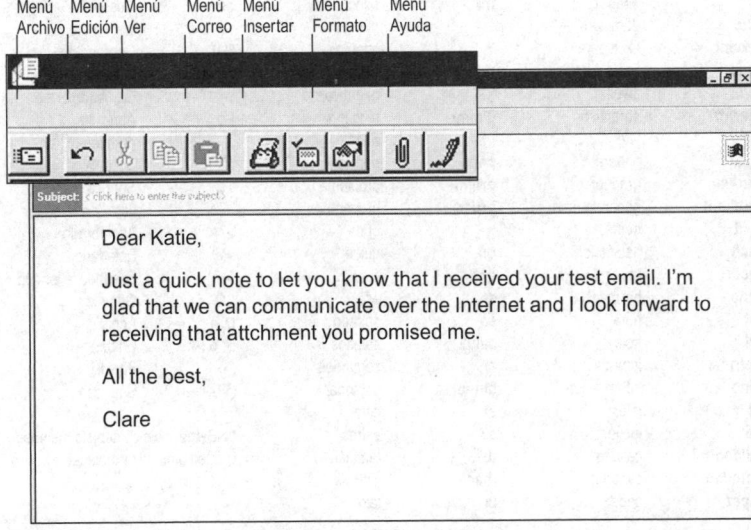

Dear Katie,

Just a quick note to let you know that I received your test email. I'm
glad that we can communicate over the Internet and I look forward to
receiving that attchment you promised me.

All the best,

Clare

SMS (electronic text messaging)

The basic principles governing Spanish SMS abbreviations are similar to English ones. Certain words or syllables can be represented by letters or numbers that sound the same but take up less space. Also, points, accents and other diacritics are generally omitted altogether. For example, the syllable -ca can be replaced by the letter k and the conjunction 'que' by 'ke'. Another way of shortening words is simply to omit certain letters, especially vowels. For example, 'bastante' becomes 'bstnt' and 'gente' becomes 'gnt'.

As in English, 'emoticons' are very popular, and some of the more established ones are included in the table below.

Glossary of Spanish SMS abbreviations

Abbreviation	Full word	Abbreviation	Full word	Abbreviation	Full word
a2	adiós	kro	caro	txt	texto
aa	años	lgr	lugar	t2	todos
archvo	archivo	lu	lunes	vi	viernes
artclo	artículo	mar	martes	xa	para
bstnt	bastante	mñna/mñn	mañana	x	por
b	beso	mktg	marketing	xfa	por favor
cia	compañía	+	más	xq	porque
compljo	complejo	+tikr	masticar	xtrangro	extranjero
complikdo	complicado	mjr	mejor		
comnikr	comunicar	msj/sms	mensaje/		
d	de		mens.móvil	*Emoticons**	
dcir	decir	msjr	mensajero	:-)	Cara feliz
dd	días	mm	meses	:-|	Ceñudo
dir	dirección	mi	miércoles	:-e	Desilusión
do	domingo	'	minuto	:-(	Cara triste
exclnt	excelente	's	minutos	%-)	Confundido
fsta	fiesta	nd	nada	:~(o :'-(	Llorando
fvor	favor	-	negativo, no	;-)	Guiñando el ojo
garntzr	garantizar	0/ning	ninguno	|-o	Aburrido,
gf	jefe	nka	nunca		durmiendo
gral	general	pers	personas	:-\	Escéptico
grduar	graduar	prblm	problema	:-D	Sonrisa grande,
gralmnt	generalmente	prpar2	preparados		cara sonriente
gnt	gente	q	que	:-<>	Asombrado
hab	habitación	qn	quien	:-@	Enfadado
hcer	hacer	qndo	cuando	:-p	Sacando la lengua
hno	hermano	s	ese	:-O	Gritando
hr	hora	sa	sábado	O:-)	Ángel
hl	hola	salu2	saludos	:-* o :-x	Un beso
infrmal	informal	"	segundos	:-o	Shock
info	información	stndar	estándar	@}-,-'—	Una rosa
jf	jefe	st	este		
ju	jueves	s3	estrés	* NB: the '-' which depicts the nose
klidad	calidad	tb	también	is often omitted or replaced by an 'o'
kntidad	cantidad	thanx	gracias	e.g., :) or :o)
kpaz	capaz	tx	taxi		

SMS (mensajería electrónica de texto)

SMS es la abreviatura inglesa de "Short Message (o Messaging) Service", que se traduce como "Servicio de Mensajes Cortos".

Los principios básicos que rigen el uso de las abreviaturas SMS en inglés son bastante simples. Se pueden utilizar todas las abreviaturas y signos convencionales ingleses establecidos, pero sin puntos. Algunas palabras o sílabas se pueden representar con una letra o un número que suene igual o parecido. Por ejemplo, la letra 'C' suena igual que la palabra 'see' (o tambien 'sea'), 'U' suena igual que 'you', el número '8' ('eight') se puede sustituir por el sonido /-ayt/. De este modo, 'see you later' se abrevia como CUL8R, a lo cual se podría contestar GR8 ('great'). También es común simplemente omitir ciertas letras, especialmente las vocales. Por ejemplo, 'message' se convierte en MSG, 'please' se sustituye por PLS y 'speak' se cambia por SPK. La mayoría de las abreviaturas SMS se derivan de las letras iniciales de frases comunes, como por ejemplo FYI 'for your information', TTYL 'talk to you later'. Estas abreviaturas pueden parecer un poco crípticas al principio, pero con la práctica es fácil aprender a identificar su significado. Igual que en español los 'emoticonos' son muy populares en los mensajes SMS. Algunos de los más comunes se incluyen más abajo.

Glosario de abreviaturas en inglés de SMS

Abreviatura	Palabra completa	Abreviatura	Palabra completa	Abreviatura	Palabra completa
@	at	LOL	lots of luck/	XLNT	excellent
ADN	any day now		laughing out loud	XOXOX	hugs and kisses
AFAIK	as far as I know	MOB	Mobile	YR	your
ATB	all the best	MSG	message	1	one
B	be	MYOB	mind your own	2	to, too
B4	before		business	2DAY	today
B4N	bye for now	NE	any	2MORO	tomorrow
BBL	be back late(r)	NE1	anyone	2NITE	tonight
BCNU	be seeing you	NO1	no one	3SUM	threesome
BFN	bye for now	OIC	oh, I see	4	for
BRB	be right back	OTOH	on the other hand		
BTW	by the way	PCM	please call me		
BWD	backward	PLS	please	*Emoticonos**	
C	see	PPL	people		
CU	see you	R	are	:-)	Smiling, happy face
CUL8R	see you later	ROFL	rolling on the	:-|	Frowning
F2F	face to face		floor, laughing	:-e	Disappointed
F2T	free to talk	RU	are you	:-(	Unhappy face
FWD	forward	RUOK	are you OK?	%-)	Confused
FWIW	for what it's worth	SIT	stay in touch	:-~(or :'-(	Crying
FYI	for your information	SOM1	someone	;-)	Winking happy face
GAL	get a life	SPK	speak	|-o	Tired, asleep
GR8	great	THKQ	thank you	:-\	Sceptical
H8	hate	TTYL	talk to you later	:-D	Big smile, laughing face
HAND	have a nice day	TX	thanks	:-<>	Amazed
HTH	hope this helps	U	you	X=	Fingers crossed
IC	I see	UR	you are	:-p	Tongue sticking out
ILUVU	I love you	W/	with	:-O	Shouting
IMHO	in my humble opinion	WAN2	want to	O:-)	Angel
IMO	in my opinion	WAN2TLK	want to talk?	:-* or :-x	Big kiss!
IOW	in other words	WERV U BIN	where have you	:-o	"Oooh!", shocked face
JIC	just in case		been?	@}-,-'—	A rose
JK	just kidding	WKND	weekend		
KIT	keep in touch	WOT	what	*NB: el '-' que representa la nariz se	
KWIM	know what I mean?	WU	what's up?	puede omitir o sustituir por una 'o',	
L8	late	X	kiss	por ej., :) o :o)	
L8R	later				

A, a /eɪ/ *n* (a) (letter) A, a *f* (b) (Mus) la *m*

a /ə, *stressed form* eɪ/ (*before vowel* **an**) *indef art* un, una; **a Mrs Smith called** llamó una tal señora Smith; **have you got a car?** ¿tienes coche?; **he didn't say a word** no dijo ni una palabra; **she's a dentist** es dentista; **what a shock!** ¡qué susto!; **it costs 2 dollars a pound** cuesta 2 dólares la libra

AA *n* ⟦1⟧ (*no art*) = **Alcoholics Anonymous** ⟦2⟧ (in US) = **Associate in Arts** ⟦3⟧ (in UK) = **Automobile Association**

AAA *n* = **American Automobile Association**

aback /ə'bæk/ *adv* ▶ TAKE ABACK

abacus /'æbəkəs/ *n* (*pl* **-cuses** *or* **-ci** /-saɪ/) ábaco *m*

abandon¹ /ə'bændən/ *vt* ⟨home/family⟩ abandonar; ⟨project/idea/search⟩ renunciar a; ⟨hope⟩ perder*; **to ~ ship** abandonar el barco

abandon² *n*: **they were dancing with gay ~** bailaban desenfrenadamente

abandoned /ə'bændənd/ *adj* ⟨vehicle/cottage/wife⟩ abandonado

abase /ə'beɪs/ *v refl* **to ~ oneself** humillarse

abashed /ə'bæʃt/ *adj* (*pred*) avergonzado

abate /ə'beɪt/ *vi* «storm/wind» amainar; «anger» aplacarse*; «noise/violence» disminuir*; «pain» calmarse

abattoir /'æbətwɑːr ‖'æbətwɑː(r)/ *n* matadero *m*

abbey /'æbi/ *n* (*pl* **abbeys**) abadía *f*

abbot /'æbət/ *n* abad *m*

abbreviate /ə'briːvieɪt/ *vt* abreviar

abbreviation /ə'briːvi'eɪʃən/ *n* abreviatura *f*

ABC *n* ⟦1⟧ (alphabet, rudiments) abecé *m* ⟦2⟧ (in US) (*no art*) (= **American Broadcasting Company**) la ABC

abdicate /'æbdɪkeɪt/ *vt/i* abdicar*

abdication /'æbdɪ'keɪʃən/ *n* abdicación *f*

abdomen /'æbdəmən/ *n* abdomen *m*

abduct /æb'dʌkt ‖əb'dʌkt/ *vt* (fml) raptar, secuestrar

abduction /æb'dʌkʃən ‖əb'dʌkʃən/ *n* (fml) rapto *m*, secuestro *m*

abet /ə'bet/ *vt* **-tt-** ▶ AID²

abeyance /ə'beɪəns/ *n*: **to be in ~** estar* suspendido

abhor /əb'hɔːr ‖əb'hɔː(r)/ *vt* **-rr-** (fml) detestar

abide /ə'baɪd/ *vt* tolerar, soportar

■ **abide by** [*v* + *prep* + *o*] ⟨verdict/rules⟩ acatar

ability /ə'bɪləti/ *n* (*pl* **-ties**) capacidad *f*; **to the best of one's ~** lo mejor que uno pueda

abject /'æbdʒekt/ *adj* (fml) (*before n*) ⟨slave/flattery⟩ abyecto; **in ~ poverty** en la mayor miseria

ablaze /ə'bleɪz/ *adj* (*pred*): **to be ~** arder

able /'eɪbl/ *adj* ⟦1⟧ (*pred*) **to be ~ to +** INF poder* + INF; (referring to particular skills) saber* +

INF; **to be ~ to see/hear** poder* ver/oír ⟦2⟧ **abler** /'eɪblər ‖'eɪblə(r)/, **ablest** /'eɪbləst ‖'eɪblɪst/ (proficient) hábil

able-bodied /'eɪbəl'bɑːdid ‖,eɪbəl'bɒdid/ *adj* sano, no discapacitado

abnormal /'æb'nɔːrməl ‖æb'nɔːməl/ *adj* anómalo, anormal

abnormality /'æbnər'mæləti ‖,æbnɔː'mæləti/ *n* (*pl* **-ties**) anomalía *f*, anormalidad *f*

aboard¹ /ə'bɔːrd ‖ə'bɔːd/ *adv* (on ship, plane) a bordo

aboard² *prep* a bordo de; **~ the bus/train** en el autobús/tren

abode /ə'bəʊd/ *n* (liter or hum) morada *f* (liter o hum); **of no fixed ~** (Law) sin domicilio fijo

abolish /ə'bɑːlɪʃ ‖ə'bɒlɪʃ/ *vt* abolir*

abolition /'æbə'lɪʃən/ *n* abolición *f*

abominable /ə'bɑːmənəbəl ‖ə'bɒmɪnəbəl/ *adj* (a) (horrible) ⟨deed⟩ abominable (b) (awful) (colloq) ⟨weather/food⟩ espantoso

abomination /ə'bɑːmə'neɪʃən ‖ə,bɒmɪ'neɪʃən/ *n* abominación *f*

aboriginal¹ /'æbə'rɪdʒənl/ *adj* aborigen

aboriginal² *n* (a) (indigenous inhabitant) aborigen *mf* (b) ▶ ABORIGINE

Aborigine /'æbə'rɪdʒəni/ *n* aborigen australiano, -na *m,f*

abortion /ə'bɔːrʃən ‖ə'bɔːʃən/ *n* aborto *m* (provocado); **to have an ~** hacerse* un aborto, abortar

abortive /ə'bɔːrtɪv ‖ə'bɔːtɪv/ *adj* frustrado

abound /ə'baʊnd/ *vi* abundar; **to ~ IN** *o* **WITH** sth abundar EN algo

about¹ /ə'baʊt/ *adv* ⟦1⟧ (approximately) más o menos, aproximadamente; **she must be ~ 60** debe (de) tener unos 60 años; **at ~ six o'clock** alrededor de *or* a eso de las seis; **~ a month ago** hace cosa de un mes

⟦2⟧ **to be about to +** INF estar* a punto de + INF ⟦3⟧ (movement): **she can't get ~ very easily** le cuesta desplazarse; **he was waving a knife ~** blandía un cuchillo

⟦4⟧ (in the vicinity, in circulation) (esp BrE): **is Teresa ~?** ¿Teresa anda por aquí?; **there's a lot of flu ~** hay mucha gente con gripe

about² *prep* ⟦1⟧ (a) (concerning) sobre, acerca de; **what's the play ~?** ¿de qué se trata la obra?; **he wants to see you about something** quiere verte acerca de *or* por algo; **she won — how ~ that!** ganó — ¡pues qué te parece! *or* ¡pues mira tú! (b) (pertaining to): **there's something ~ him that I don't like** tiene un no sé qué que no me gusta ⟦2⟧ (engaged in): **while you're ~ it, could you fetch my book?** ¿ya que estás me traes el libro?

aboutface /ə'baʊt'feɪs/, (BrE also) **about-turn** /-'tɜːrn ‖-'tɜːn/ *n* cambio *m* radical de postura

above¹ /ə'bʌv/ *prep* ⟦1⟧ (a) (on top of, over) encima de; **~ sea level** sobre el nivel del mar (b) (upstream of) más allá *or* más arriba de ⟦2⟧ (superior ⋯⟫

to) por encima de; *to get* ~ *oneself* (pej) subirse a la parra **3** (more than): ~ **average** por encima de la media; ~ **and beyond** más allá de

above² /adv/ **1** (on top, higher up) arriba **2** (in text): **as shown** ~ como se demostró anteriormente *or* más arriba; **see** ~, **page 43** véase página 43

above³ *adj* (fml) (*before n*): **for the** ~ **reasons** por dichas razones, por lo antedicho

above: ~**board** /əˈbʌvˈbɔːrd ‖əˌbʌvˈbɔːd/ *adj* (*pred*) legítimo; **open and** ~**board** sin tapujos; ~**mentioned** /əˈbʌvˈmentʃənd ‖əˌbʌvˈmenʃənd/ *adj* antedicho (fml)

abrasive /əˈbreɪsɪv/ *adj* ⟨*powder*⟩ abrasivo; ⟨*surface*⟩ áspero; ⟨*tone/manner*⟩ áspero

abreast /əˈbrest/ *adv* **(a)** (side by side): **to march four** ~ marchar en columna de cuatro en fondo **(b)** (up to date): **to keep** ~ **of sth** mantenerse* al día en *or* al corriente de algo

abridge /əˈbrɪdʒ/ *vt* ⟨*book*⟩ compendiar; ~**d edition** edición *f* condensada

abroad /əˈbrɔːd/ *adv* ⟨*live/work*⟩ en el extranjero *or* en el exterior; ⟨*go*⟩ al extranjero, al exterior; **I've never been** ~ nunca he salido del país

abrupt /əˈbrʌpt/ *adj* ⟨*departure/conclusion*⟩ repentino; ⟨*rise/decline*⟩ abrupto; ⟨*manner*⟩ brusco

abruptly /əˈbrʌptli/ *adv* ⟨*end/stop*⟩ repentinamente; ⟨*rise/fall*⟩ bruscamente; ⟨*speak/act*⟩ abruptamente

abscess /ˈæbses/ *n* absceso *m*

abscond /æbˈskɑːnd ‖əbˈskɒnd/ *vi* (fml) fugarse*

absence /ˈæbsəns/ *n* **(a)** (of person) ausencia *f* **(b)** (lack) ~ **of sth** falta *f* DE algo

absent /ˈæbsənt/ *adj* ausente; **to be** ~ **FROM sth** faltar A algo

absentee /ˌæbsənˈtiː/ *n* (*pl* **-tees**) ausente *mf*

absenteeism /ˌæbsənˈtiːɪzəm/ *n* ausentismo *m or* (Esp) absentismo *m*

absentminded /ˈæbsəntˈmaɪndəd ‖æbsəntˈmaɪndɪd/ *adj* (temporarily) distraído; (habitually) despistado

absolute /ˈæbsəluːt/ *adj* **1** (complete) ⟨*trust/confidence*⟩ absoluto; **it was an** ~ **disaster** fue un absoluto desastre *or* un desastre total **2** ⟨*right*⟩ incuestionable; ⟨*pardon/freedom*⟩ incondicional; ⟨*guarantee/monarchy/rule*⟩ absoluto

absolutely /ˈæbsəˈluːtli/ *adv* ⟨*deny/reject*⟩ rotundamente; ⟨*impossible*⟩ absolutamente; **I'm** ~ **certain** estoy segurísima *or* absolutamente segura; **you're** ~ **right!** ¡tienes toda la razón!

absolution /ˈæbsəˈluːʃən/ *n* absolución *f*

absolve /əbˈzɑːlv ‖əbˈzɒlv/ *vt* **to** ~ **sb OF sth** absolver* a algn DE algo; **to** ~ **sb FROM sth** eximir a algn DE algo

absorb /əbˈzɔːrb ‖əbˈzɔːb/ *vt* ⟨*light/energy*⟩ absorber; ⟨*impact/shock*⟩ amortiguar*; ⟨*information*⟩ asimilar; **to be** ~**ed IN sth** estar* absorto EN algo

absorbent /əbˈsɔːrbənt ‖əbˈzɔːbənt/ *adj* absorbente

absorbent cotton *n* (AmE) algodón *m* (hidrófilo)

absorption /əbˈsɔːrpʃən ‖əbˈzɔːpʃən/ *n* absorción *f*

abstain /əbˈsteɪn/ *vi* **1** (in vote) abstenerse* **2** (refrain) **to** ~ **FROM sth/-ING** abstenerse* DE algo/+ INF

abstract /ˈæbstrækt/ *adj* abstracto

absurd /əbˈsɜːrd ‖əbˈsɜːd/ *adj* absurdo

absurdity /əbˈsɜːrdəti ‖əbˈsɜːdəti/ *n* (*pl* **-ties**) lo absurdo

abundance /əˈbʌndəns/ *n* abundancia *f*

abundant /əˈbʌndənt/ *adj* ⟨*resources*⟩ abundante; ⟨*enthusiasm*⟩ desbordante

abuse¹ /əˈbjuːs/ *n* **1** (insulting language) insultos *mpl*; **a term of** ~ un insulto **2** (misuse) abuso *m*; **sexual** ~ abusos *mpl* deshonestos; **child** ~ malos tratos *mpl* a la infancia; (sexual) abusos *mpl* deshonestos (*a un niño*); **drug** ~ consumo *m* de drogas

abuse² /əˈbjuːz/ *vt* **1** **(a)** (use wrongly) ⟨*power/hospitality*⟩ abusar de **(b)** ⟨*child/woman*⟩ maltratar; (sexually) abusar de **2** (insult) insultar

abusive /əˈbjuːsɪv/ *adj* insultante

abysmal /əˈbɪzməl/ *adj* pésimo

abyss /əˈbɪs/ *n* (liter) abismo *m*

a/c (= **account**) cta.

AC /ˈeɪˈsiː/ **(a)** (= **alternating current**) CA **(b)** (esp AmE) = **air conditioning**

A/C = **air conditioning**

academic¹ /ˈækəˈdemɪk/ *adj* **1** **(a)** ⟨*career/record*⟩ académico **(b)** ⟨*child/student*⟩ intelectualmente capaz **2** (abstract) ⟨*question/debate*⟩ puramente teórico

academic² *n* académico, -ca *m,f*

academy /əˈkædəmi/ *n* (*pl* **-mies**) academia *f*; (*before n*) **A**~ **Award** Oscar *m*

accede /əkˈsiːd/ *vi* (fml) **to** ~ **TO sth** (grant) acceder A algo

accelerate /əkˈseləreɪt/ *vi* «*vehicle*» acelerar; «*person*» acelerar; (Auto) apretar* el acelerador; «*process/growth*» acelerarse ■ ~ *vt* acelerar

accelerator /əkˈseləreɪtər ‖əkˈseləreɪtə(r)/ *n* acelerador *m*

accent /ˈæksent ‖ˈæksənt, ˈæksənt/ *n* **(a)** (Ling, Mus) acento *m* **(b)** (emphasis) énfasis *m*

accentuate /əkˈsentʃueɪt/ *vt* **(a)** ⟨*difference*⟩ hacer* resaltar; ⟨*fact/necessity*⟩ subrayar; ⟨*eyes/features*⟩ realzar*, hacer* resaltar **(b)** ⟨*syllable/word*⟩ acentuar*

accept /əkˈsept/ *vt* aceptar; **do you** ~ **that you were wrong?** ¿reconoces que estabas equivocado?

acceptable /əkˈseptəbəl/ *adj* (satisfactory) aceptable; (tolerable) admisible

acceptance /əkˈseptəns/ *n* **1** (of offer, responsibility) aceptación *f* **2** (approval) aprobación *f*

access¹ /'ækses/ n acceso m; (before n) ~ road carretera f de acceso

access² vt (Comput) obtener* acceso a, entrar a

accessible /ək'sesəbəl/ adj accesible

accession /ək'seʃən, æk'seʃən/ n (frml) **(a)** (to throne, power) acceso m **(b)** (acquisition) adquisición f

accessory /æk'sesəri/ n (pl **-ries**) **1** **(a)** (extra) accesorio m **(b)** **accessories** pl (Clothing) accesorios mpl **2** (Law) ~ (**TO** sth) cómplice mf (**EN** algo)

accident /'æksədənt ‖'æksɪdənt/ n **(a)** (mishap) accidente m **(b)** (chance) casualidad f; **by** ~ **(b)** (by chance) por casualidad; (unintentionally) sin querer

accidental /ˌæksə'dentl̩ ‖ˌæksɪ'dentl̩/ adj ⟨discovery/meeting⟩ fortuito; ⟨blow⟩ accidental; ~ **death** muerte f por caso fortuito

accidentally /ˌæksə'dentli ‖ˌæksɪ'dentəli/ adv **(a)** (unintentionally) sin querer **(b)** (by chance) por casualidad, de manera fortuita

accident-prone /'æksədəntprəʊn ‖'æksɪdəntprəʊn/ adj propenso a los accidentes

acclaim¹ /ə'kleɪm/ vt aclamar

acclaim² n aclamación f

acclimate /'ækləmeɪt/ vt (AmE) ▶ ACCLIMATIZE

acclimatize /ə'klaɪmətaɪz/ vt aclimatar; **to become ~d TO** sth aclimatarse A algo

accolade /'ækəleɪd/ n (praise) elogio m; (honor) honor m; (award) galardón m

accommodate /ə'kɑːmədeɪt ‖ə'kɒmədeɪt/ vt **1** **(a)** (provide lodging for) ⟨guests⟩ alojar **(b)** (have room for) tener* cabida para **2** (cater to) ⟨wish/need⟩ tener* en cuenta

accommodating /ə'kɑːmədeɪtɪŋ ‖ə'kɒmədeɪtɪŋ/ adj complaciente

accommodation /əˌkɑːmə'deɪʃən ‖əˌkɒmə'deɪʃən/ n **1** **(a)** (AmE also) **accommodations** (lodgings) alojamiento m **(b)** (seat, berth) (AmE) plaza f **2** (agreement, compromise) acuerdo m

accompaniment /ə'kʌmpənimənt/ n acompañamiento m

accompanist /ə'kʌmpənəst ‖ə'kʌmpənɪst/ n acompañante mf

accompany /ə'kʌmpəni/ vt **-nies, -nying, -nied (a)** (go with) acompañar **(b)** (Mus) acompañar

accomplice /ə'kɑːmpləs ‖ə'kʌmplɪs/ n cómplice mf

accomplish /ə'kɑːmplɪʃ ‖ə'kʌmplɪʃ/ vt ⟨task⟩ llevar a cabo; ⟨goal⟩ lograr

accomplished /ə'kɑːmplɪʃt ‖ə'kʌmplɪʃt/ adj ⟨performer/liar/thief⟩ consumado; ⟨performance⟩ logrado

accomplishment /ə'kɑːmplɪʃmənt ‖ə'kʌmplɪʃmənt/ n **(a)** (of aim) logro m **(b)** (success) logro m **(c)** (skill) habilidad f

accord /ə'kɔːrd ‖ə'kɔːd/ n acuerdo m; **of one's own** ~ (de) motu proprio

accordance /ə'kɔːrdn̩s ‖ə'kɔːdn̩s/ n: **in** ~ **with** de acuerdo con or a, según

according /ə'kɔːrdɪŋ ‖ə'kɔːdɪŋ/ **according to** prep según

accordion /ə'kɔːrdiən ‖ə'kɔːdiən/ n acordeón m

accost /ə'kɔːst ‖ə'kɒst/ vt abordar

account /ə'kaʊnt/ n

I **1** (explanation) explicación f; (version) versión f; (report) informe m; **by all** ~**s** a decir de todos **2** (consideration): **to take sth into** ~ tener* algo en cuenta **3** (in phrases) **on account of** (as prep) debido a; **on no account** de ningún modo, de ninguna manera; **on sb's account** por algn

II **1** (with bank, at shop) cuenta f **2** **accounts** (Busn, Fin) (+ pl vb) contabilidad f

■ **account for** [v + prep + o] **1** **(a)** (provide record of, justify) ⟨expenditure/time⟩ dar* cuentas de **(b)** (explain) explicar*; **there's no** ~**ing for taste** sobre gustos no hay nada escrito **2** (add up to): **wages** ~ **for 70% of the total** los sueldos representan or al 70% del total

accountable /ə'kaʊntəbəl/ adj (pred) responsable; **to be** ~ **to sb** (**FOR** sth) ser* responsable ANTE algn (**DE** algo)

accountancy /ə'kaʊntn̩si/ n contabilidad f

accountant /ə'kaʊntn̩t/ n contador, -dora m,f (AmL), contable mf (Esp)

accredit /ə'kredət ‖ə'kredɪt/ vt (usu pass) acreditar

accrue /ə'kruː/ vi acumularse

■ ~ vt acumular

accumulate /ə'kjuːmjəleɪt ‖ə'kjuːmjʊleɪt/ vt ⟨wealth/interest⟩ acumular; ⟨information/evidence⟩ reunir*

■ ~ vi acumularse

accuracy /'ækjərəsi/ n (of measurement, instrument, description, translation) exactitud f; (of weapon) precisión f; (of aim, blow) lo certero

accurate /'ækjərət/ adj ⟨measurement/instrument/description/translation⟩ exacto; ⟨weapon/aim/blow⟩ certero

accusation /ˌækjə'zeɪʃən ‖ˌækjuː'zeɪʃən/ n acusación f

accuse /ə'kjuːz/ vt acusar

accused /ə'kjuːzd/ n (pl ~) (Law) **the** ~ el acusado, la acusada; (pl) los acusados, las acusadas

accusing /ə'kjuːzɪŋ/ adj acusador

accustom /ə'kʌstəm/ vt **to** ~ **sb TO** sth/-**ING** acostumbrar a algn A algo/+INF

accustomed /ə'kʌstəmd/ adj (pred) **to be** ~ **TO** sth/-**ING** estar* acostumbrado A algo/+ INF; **to become** ~ **TO** sth/-**ING** acostumbrarse A algo/+ INF

AC/DC /'eɪsiː'diːsiː/ adj (Elec) CA/CC

ace /eɪs/ n **(a)** (in cards, dice) as m **(b)** (expert, champion) as m

ache¹ /eɪk/ vi **(a)** «tooth/ear/leg» doler*; **my back** ~**s** me duele la espalda **(b)** **aching** pres p ⟨shoulders/muscles⟩ dolorido

ache² n dolor m (sordo y continuo); ~**s and pains** achaques mpl

achieve /ə'tʃiːv/ vt **(a)** (accomplish) lograr **(b)** (attain) ⟨success/victory⟩ conseguir*, obtener*; ⟨aim⟩ lograr, conseguir*; ⟨ambition⟩ hacer* realidad

achievement /ə'tʃiːvmənt/ n **(a)** (feat) logro m **(b)** (success) éxito m; **a sense of** ~ la satisfacción de haber logrado algo

Achilles heel /ə'kɪliːz/ n talón m de Aquiles

acid¹ /'æsəd ‖'æsɪd/ n ácido m

acid², acidic /ə'sɪdɪk/ *adj* ácido

acid rain *n* lluvia *f* ácida

acknowledge /ək'nɑ:lɪdʒ ‖ək'nɒlɪdʒ/ *vt* [1] (a) (admit) ⟨*mistake/failure*⟩ admitir (b) (recognize) ⟨*skill/authority/right*⟩ reconocer*; ⟨*quotations/sources*⟩ hacer* mención de (c) (express appreciation of) agradecer* [2] ⟨*letter/order*⟩ acusar recibo de; ⟨*greeting*⟩ responder a; ⟨*person*⟩ saludar

acknowledgment, acknowledgement /ək'nɑ:lɪdʒmənt ‖ək'nɒlɪdʒmənt/ *n* (a) (recognition) reconocimiento *m* (b) (confirmation, response): I've had no ~ of my letter no han acusado recibo de mi carta (c) **acknowledgments** *pl* (in book) lista *f* de menciones

acne /'ækni/ *n* acné *m or f*, acne *f*‡

acorn /'eɪkɔːn ‖'eɪkɔːn/ *n* bellota *f*

acoustic /ə'kuːstɪk/ *adj* acústico

acoustics /ə'kuːstɪks/ *n* (of room) (+ *pl vb*) acústica *f*

acquaintance /ə'kweɪntns/ *n* (a) (person) conocido, -da *m,f* (b) (with person) relación *f*; to make sb's ~ conocer* a algn (c) (knowledge) ~ WITH sth conocimiento *m* DE algo

acquainted /ə'kweɪntɪd ‖ə'kweɪntɪd/ *adj* (*pred*) (a) to be ~ WITH sb conocer* a algn (b) to be ~ WITH sth (be informed of) estar* al corriente DE algo; (be familiar with) estar* familiarizado CON algo

acquiesce /ˌækwi'es/ *vi* to ~ (IN sth/-ING) consentir* (algo/EN + INF)

acquire /ə'kwaɪr ‖ə'kwaɪə(r)/ *vt* ⟨*collection/skill*⟩ adquirir*; ⟨*reputation*⟩ hacerse*

acquired /ə'kwaɪrd ‖ə'kwaɪəd/ *adj* ⟨*characteristic*⟩ adquirido; it's an ~ taste es algo a lo que se le va tomando el gusto con el tiempo

acquisition /ˌækwə'zɪʃən ‖ˌækwɪ'zɪʃən/ *n* adquisición *f*

acquit /ə'kwɪt/ *vt* -tt- to ~ sb (OF sth) absolver* a algn (DE algo)

acre /'eɪkər ‖'eɪkə(r)/ *n* acre *m* (*0,405 hectáreas*)

acrid /'ækrəd ‖'ækrɪd/ *adj* acre

acrobat /'ækrəbæt/ *n* acróbata *mf*

acrobatic /ˌækrə'bætɪk/ *adj* acrobático

across¹ /ə'krɔːs ‖ə'krɒs/ *adv* (a) (indicating movement): the boatman ferried them ~ el barquero los cruzó (b) (indicating position) del otro lado; she sat ~ from me estaba sentada frente a mí (c) (in width, diameter): it is 20m ~ tiene or mide 20m de ancho

across² *prep* (a) (from one side to other): they ran ~ the road cruzaron la calle corriendo (b) (on the other side of): they live just ~ the road viven justo enfrente; it's ~ the river está al otro lado del río

acrylic /ə'krɪlɪk/ *n* acrílico *m*; (before n) acrílico

act¹ /ækt/ *vi* [1] (a) (take action, do sth) actuar* (b) ⟨*drug/chemical*⟩ hacer* efecto (c) (serve) to ~ AS sth servir* DE algo; she will ~ as interpreter hará de intérprete (d) **acting** *pres p* ⟨*chairman/director*⟩ interino [2] (behave) comportarse*; don't ~ dumb ¡no te hagas el tonto! [3] (perform) actuar*; (as profession) ser* actor/actriz

act for [*v* + *prep* + *o*] (represent) representar

act on [*v* + *prep* + *o*] (a) (follow) ⟨*advice*⟩ seguir*; ⟨*orders*⟩ cumplir (b) (affect) «*drug/chemical*» actuar* sobre

act out [*v* + *o* + *adv*, *v* + *adv* + *o*] representar

act² *n* [1] (deed) acto *m*; to catch sb in the ~ agarrar *or* (esp Esp) coger* a algn con las manos en la masa [2] (Govt) ley *f* [3] (a) (division of play) acto *m* (b) (routine) número *m*; to get one's ~ together organizarse* [4] (pretense): it was all a big ~ era puro cuento (fam)

acting /'æktɪŋ/ *n* (performance) interpretación *f*; have you done any ~ before? ¿has hecho teatro/cine alguna vez?

action /'ækʃən/ *n* [1] (a) (practical measures): prompt ~ by the police saved several lives la rápida actuación de la policía salvó varias vidas; to take ~ (against sb/sth) tomar medidas (contra algn/algo); ~! (Cin) ¡acción! (b) (in phrases) to put sth into ~ poner* algo en práctica; to be out of ~ «*car*» estar* averiado; «*person*» estar* fuera de circulación [2] (deed) acto *m* [3] (Mil) acción *f* (de guerra) [4] (a) (plot of play, movie) acción *f* (b) (exciting activity) animación *f* [5] (a) (movement) movimiento *m* (b) (operation) funcionamiento *m* (c) (of drug, chemical) acción *f*

action: ~-packed *adj* lleno de acción; ~ replay *n* (BrE) repetición *f* de la jugada

active /'æktɪv/ *adj* [1] ⟨*person/life*⟩ activo; ⟨*volcano*⟩ en actividad [2] (Ling) activo

activist /'æktəvəst ‖'æktɪvɪst/ *n* activista *mf*

activity /æk'tɪvəti/ *n* (*pl* -ties) actividad *f*

actor /'æktər ‖'æktə(r)/ *n* actor, actriz *m,f*

actress /'æktrəs/ *n* actriz *f*

actual /'æktʃuəl/ *adj* (before n) (a) (real) real; in ~ fact en realidad (b) (precise, very) mismo; on the ~ day of the election el mismo día de las elecciones

actually /'æktʃuəli/ *adv* en realidad; ~, I'd rather not go la verdad es que preferiría no ir

acumen /ə'kjuːmən ‖'ækjuːmən/ *n* sagacidad *f*, perspicacia *f*; business ~ visión *f* para los negocios

acupuncture /'ækjəˌpʌŋktʃər ‖'ækjʊˌpʌŋktʃə(r)/ *n* acupuntura *f*

acute /ə'kjuːt/ *adj* [1] ⟨*condition/pain*⟩ agudo; ⟨*crisis/shortage*⟩ grave; ⟨*anxiety*⟩ profundo; ⟨*sense of smell*⟩ fino; ⟨*sight/hearing*⟩ agudo [2] (Ling) ⟨*accent*⟩ agudo

ad /æd/ *n* (colloq) ▶ ADVERTISEMENT

AD (= **Anno Domini**) después de Cristo; (written form) d. de C., d. de J.C.

Adam /'ædəm/ *n* Adán; ~'s apple nuez *f* (de Adán)

adamant /'ædəmənt/ *adj* ⟨*refusal*⟩ firme; she was ~ that she wouldn't go se mantuvo firme en su decisión de no ir

adapt /ə'dæpt/ *vt* adaptar

~ *vi* to ~ (TO sth/-ING) adaptarse (A algo/+ INF)

adaptable /ə'dæptəbəl/ *adj* adaptable

adaptation /ˌædæp'teɪʃən/ *n* adaptación *f*

adapter, adaptor /əˈdæptər ‖əˈdæptə(r)/ *n*
(plug — with several sockets) enchufe *m* múltiple; (—
for different sockets) adaptador *m*

add /æd/ *vt* 1 (put in in addition) añadir; **at least I
think so, she** ~**ed** —al menos eso creo —añadió
2 (Math) sumar; ~ **the numbers together** suma
los números
3 **added** *past p* ⟨*bonus/incentive*⟩ adicional;
with ~**ed vitamins** con vitaminas
■ **add to** [*v + prep + o*] ⟨*building*⟩ ampliar*;
⟨*confusion/difficulties*⟩ aumentar
■ **add up** 1 [*v + adv*] (Math) cuadrar **(b)**
(make sense) (colloq) ⟨*story/facts*⟩ cuadrar; **it just
doesn't** ~ **up** no tiene sentido
2 [*v + o + adv, v + adv + o*] (Math) ⟨*figures*⟩
sumar; ⟨*bill*⟩ hacer*, preparar
■ **add up to** [*v + adv + prep + o*] «*figures*»
sumar en total; «*total*» ascender* a

adder /ˈædər ‖ˈædə(r)/ *n* víbora *f*

addict /ˈædɪkt/ *n* adicto, -ta *m,f*; **drug** ~
drogadicto, -ta *m,f*

addicted /əˈdɪktəd ‖əˈdɪktɪd/ *adj* **to be** ~ **(TO
sth)** ser* adicto (A algo)

addiction /əˈdɪkʃən/ *n* adicción *f*

addictive /əˈdɪktɪv/ *adj* ⟨*drug*⟩ que crea
adicción; ⟨*activity*⟩ que crea hábito

addition /əˈdɪʃən/ *n* 1 **(a)** (Math) suma *f*,
adición *f* (frml) **(b)** (adding) adición *f* **(c)** (*in
phrases*) **in addition** además; **in addition to**
además 2 (extra thing): **the latest** ~**s to our
library** las últimas adquisiciones de nuestra
biblioteca

additional /əˈdɪʃnəl ‖əˈdɪʃənl̩/ *adj* ⟨*cost/
weight*⟩ extra, adicional

additive /ˈædətɪv ‖ˈædɪtɪv/ *n* aditivo *m*

address[1] /ˈædres ‖əˈdres/ *n* 1 **(a)** (of house,
offices etc) dirección *f*, señas *fpl*; ⑤ **address** (on
form) domicilio; (*before n*) ~ **book** libreta *f* de
direcciones **(b)** (Comput) dirección *f* 2 (speech)
discurso *m* 3 **form of** ~ tratamiento *m*

address[2] /əˈdres/ *vt* 1 (AmE alsó) /ˈædres/
⟨*mail*⟩ ponerle* la dirección a 2 **(a)** (speak to)
⟨*person*⟩ dirigirse* a; ⟨*assembly*⟩ pronunciar un
discurso ante **(b)** (direct) (frml) ⟨*question/remark*⟩
dirigir* 3 (deal with, confront) ⟨*problem/issue*⟩
tratar
■ *v refl* **(a)** (speak to) **to** ~ **oneself TO sb** dirigirse*
A algn **(b)** (turn one's attention to) (frml) **to** ~ **oneself
TO sth** dedicarse* A algo

addressee /ˌædreˈsiː/ *n* destinatario, -ria *m,f*

adept /əˈdept/ *adj* experto

adequate /ˈædɪkwət/ *adj* ⟨*help/funding*⟩
suficiente; ⟨*standard/explanation*⟩ adecuado

adhere /ædˈhɪr ‖ədˈhɪə(r)/ *vi* (frml) **(a)** (stick) to
~ **(TO sth)** adherirse* A algo **(b) to** ~ **TO sth** ⟨*to
principles/cause*⟩ adherirse* A algo; ⟨*to
regulations*⟩ observar algo

adhesive[1] /ædˈhiːsɪv ‖ədˈhiːsɪv/ *adj* adhesivo

adhesive[2] *n* adhesivo *m*

ad hoc /ˈædˈhɑːk ‖ˌædˈhɒk/ *adj* ⟨*arrangement/
measure*⟩ ad hoc; ~ ~ **committee** comisión *f*
especial *or* ad hoc

adjacent /əˈdʒeɪsn̩t/ *adj* ⟨*fields*⟩ adyacente;
⟨*rooms*⟩ contiguo; ~ **TO sth** ⟨«*field*»⟩ adyacente A
algo; «*room*» contiguo A algo

adjective /ˈædʒɪktɪv/ *n* adjetivo *m*

adjoin /əˈdʒɔɪn/ *vt* (frml) **(a)** (be adjacent to) lindar
con **(b) adjoining** *pres p* ⟨*houses*⟩ contiguo; **the**
~**ing room** el cuarto de al lado

adjourn /əˈdʒɜːrn ‖əˈdʒɜːn/ *vt* ⟨*talks/trial*⟩
suspender; **the meeting was** ~**ed** se levantó la
sesión
■ ~ *vi*: **the court** ~**ed** el tribunal levantó la sesión

adjournment /əˈdʒɜːrnmənt ‖əˈdʒɜːnmənt/ *n*
suspensión *f*

adjudicate /əˈdʒuːdɪkeɪt/ *vi* (give judgment)
arbitrar
■ ~ *vt* (frml) ⟨*competition*⟩ juzgar*; ⟨*claim*⟩ decidir
sobre

adjust /əˈdʒʌst/ *vt* ⟨*instrument/prices/wages*⟩
ajustar; ⟨*volume/temperature/speed*⟩ regular; **he**
~**ed his tie** se arregló la corbata
■ ~ *vi* **to** ~ **(TO sth/-ING)** adaptarse (A algo/+ INF)

adjustable /əˈdʒʌstəbəl/ *adj* ⟨*focus/
temperature*⟩ regulable

adjustment /əˈdʒʌstmənt/ *n* 1 (to machine,
instrument, figures) ajuste *m*; (to clothes) arreglo *m*;
(to plan, system) cambio *m* 2 (act, process) **(a)** (of
machine, instrument) ajuste *m* **(b)** (of person)
adaptación *f*

ad-lib /ˈædˈlɪb/ *vt/i* -**bb**- improvisar

administer /ədˈmɪnəstər ‖ədˈmɪnɪstə(r)/ *vt* **(a)**
(manage) administrar **(b)** (frml) ⟨*punishment/drug*⟩
administrar

administration /ədˌmɪnəˈstreɪʃən
‖ədˌmɪnɪˈstreɪʃən/ *n* **(a)** (of institution, business,
estate) administración *f* **(b)** (managing body)
administración *f*; (Pol) gobierno *m*,
administración *f* **(c)** (of justice, medicine)
administración *f*

administrative /ədˈmɪnəstreɪtɪv
‖ədˈmɪnɪstrətɪv/ *adj* administrativo

administrator /ədˈmɪnəstreɪtər
‖ədˈmɪnɪstreɪtə(r)/ *n* administrador, -dora *m,f*

admirable /ˈædmərəbəl/ *adj* ⟨*honesty/work*⟩
digno de admiración; ⟨*plan*⟩ excelente

admiral /ˈædmərəl/ *n* almirante *mf*

admiration /ˌædməˈreɪʃən/ *n* admiración *f*

admire /ədˈmaɪr ‖ədˈmaɪə(r)/ *vt* admirar

admirer /ədˈmaɪrər ‖ədˈmaɪərə(r)/ *n*
admirador, -dora *m,f*

admission /ədˈmɪʃən/ *n* 1 **(a)** (to building,
exhibition) entrada *f*; (price) (precio *m* de) entrada *f*;
(into college, society) ingreso *m* **(b)** (into hospital)
ingreso *m* 2 (confession) admisión *f*; **he was, by
his own** ~**, a poor father** él mismo admitía que
no era un buen padre

admit /ədˈmɪt/ -**tt**- *vt* 1 **(a)** (allow entry) dejar
entrar; ⟨*light/air*⟩ permitir entrar; ⑤ **admit one**
entrada individual **(b)** ⟨*patient*⟩ ingresar,
internar (CS, Méx) 2 (confess) ⟨*crime/mistake*⟩
admitir; **to** ~ **sth TO sb** confesarle* algo A algn
■ **admit to** [*v + prep + o*] (confess) ⟨*error*⟩
admitir; ⟨*crime*⟩ declararse culpable de

admittance /ədˈmɪtns/ *n* (frml) ~ **(TO sth)**
acceso *m* (A algo); ⑤ **no admittance** prohibida la
entrada

admittedly /ədˈmɪtədli ‖ədˈmɪtɪdli/ *adv*
(indep): ~**, it wasn't an easy task, but ...** hay que
reconocer que no era una tarea fácil pero ...

admonish /ædˈmɑːnɪʃ ‖ədˈmɒnɪʃ/ *vt* (frml) **to**
~ **sb (FOR sth)** amonestar a algn (POR algo)

ado /əˈduː/ n: without further o more ~ sin más (preámbulos)

adolescence /ˈædəˈlesn̩s/ n adolescencia f

adolescent¹ /ˈædəˈlesn̩t/ n adolescente mf

adolescent² adj adolescente

adopt /əˈdɑːpt ‖əˈdɒpt/ vt (a) ⟨child⟩ adoptar (b) ⟨idea/custom/title⟩ adoptar (c) ⟨recommendation⟩ aprobar*

adopted /əˈdɑːptəd ‖əˈdɒptɪd/ adj ⟨son/country⟩ adoptivo; she's ~ es adoptada

adoption /əˈdɑːpʃən ‖əˈdɒpʃən/ n (a) (of child) adopción f (b) (of approach, custom, title) adopción f (c) (of report, motion) aprobación f

adoptive /əˈdɑːptɪv ‖əˈdɒptɪv/ adj ⟨before n⟩ adoptivo

adorable /əˈdɔːrəbəl/ adj ⟨house/hat⟩ divino; ⟨child⟩ adorable

adoration /ˈædəˈreɪʃən/ n adoración f

adore /əˈdɔːr ‖əˈdɔː(r)/ vt (a) (love, worship) adorar (b) **adoring** pres p ⟨gaze⟩ lleno de adoración; ⟨mother⟩ amantísimo (c) (like, enjoy): I ~ figs me encantan los higos

adorn /əˈdɔːrn ‖əˈdɔːn/ vt (frml or liter) adornar

adornment /əˈdɔːrnmənt ‖əˈdɔːnmənt/ n adorno m

adrenaline /əˈdrenl̩ən ‖əˈdrenəlɪn/ n adrenalina f

Adriatic /ˈeɪdriˈætɪk/ n the ~ (Sea) el (mar) Adriático

adrift /əˈdrɪft/ adj ⟨pred⟩ (Naut) a la deriva; to come o go ~ «plans» fallar

adroit /əˈdrɔɪt/ adj (a) ⟨answer/speaker⟩ hábil (b) ⟨movement⟩ ágil; ⟨player⟩ diestro

adulation /ˈædʒəˈleɪʃən ‖ˌædjʊˈleɪʃən/ n adulación f

adult¹ /əˈdʌlt, ˈædʌlt/ n adulto, -ta m,f

adult² adj (a) (physically mature) adulto (b) (mature) ⟨behavior/approach⟩ maduro, adulto (c) (suitable for adults) para mayores or adultos

adult education n educación f para adultos; ⟨before n⟩ ⟨class⟩ para adultos

adultery /əˈdʌltəri/ n adulterio m

adulthood /əˈdʌlthʊd, ˈædʌlthʊd/ n edad f adulta, adultez f

advance¹ /ədˈvæns ‖ədˈvɑːns/ vi «person/vehicle» avanzar*; «science/society» avanzar*, progresar
■ ~ vt **1** (a) (move forward) ⟨troops⟩ avanzar* (b) (further) ⟨knowledge⟩ fomentar; ⟨interests/cause⟩ promover* **2** (a) ⟨date/meeting⟩ adelantar (b) ⟨money/wages⟩ anticipar

advance² n **1** (of person, army, vehicle) avance m; (of civilization, science) avance m, progreso m **2** advances pl (overtures) insinuaciones fpl **3** (a) (early payment) anticipo m (b) (loan) préstamo m **4** in advance: to pay in ~ pagar* por adelantado; it was planned well in ~ se planeó con mucha antelación

advance³ adj ⟨before n⟩: ~ booking is essential es imprescindible hacer la reserva por anticipado

advanced /ədˈvænst ‖ədˈvɑːnst/ adj ⟨civilization/course/student⟩ avanzado

advantage /ədˈvæntɪdʒ ‖ədˈvɑːntɪdʒ/ n (a) (superior factor) ventaja f (b) (gain): to take ~ of sth aprovechar algo; (pej) aprovecharse de algo; to take ~ of sb (exploit) aprovecharse de algn; to turn sth to one's ~ sacar* provecho de algo (c) (in tennis) (no pl) ventaja f

advantageous /ˌædvænˈteɪdʒəs ‖ˌædvənˈteɪdʒəs/ adj ⟨arrangement⟩ ventajoso; ⟨position/situation⟩ de ventaja

advent /ˈædvent/ n (a) (arrival) llegada f (b) **Advent** (Relig) Adviento m

adventure /ədˈventʃər/ n aventura f; ⟨before n⟩ ⟨story/film⟩ de aventuras

adventurous /ədˈventʃərəs/ adj ⟨traveler⟩ intrépido; ⟨spirit/person⟩ aventurero

adverb /ˈædvɜːrb ‖ˈædvɜːb/ n adverbio m

adversary /ˈædvərseri ‖ˈædvəsəri/ n (pl -ries) (frml) adversario, -ria m,f

adverse /ˈædvɜːrs, ædˈvɜːrs ‖ˈædvɜːs/ adj adverso

adversity /ædˈvɜːrsəti ‖ədˈvɜːsəti/ n (pl -ties) adversidad f

advert /ˈædvɜːrt ‖ˈædvɜːt/ n (BrE colloq) ▶ ADVERTISEMENT

advertise /ˈædvərtaɪz ‖ˈædvətaɪz/ vt ⟨product⟩ hacerle* publicidad a, hacerle* réclame a (AmL); I saw it ~d on TV lo vi anunciado en la tele
■ ~ vi hacer* publicidad

advertisement /ˈædvərˈtaɪzmənt ‖ədˈvɜːtɪsmənt/ n anuncio m, aviso m (AmL)

advertiser /ˈædvərtaɪzər ‖ˈædvətaɪzə(r)/ n anunciante mf

advertising /ˈædvərtaɪzɪŋ ‖ˈædvətaɪzɪŋ/ n (a) (action, business) publicidad f; ⟨before n⟩ ⟨campaign/slot⟩ publicitario; ~ agency agencia f de publicidad (b) (advertisements) propaganda f

advice /ədˈvaɪs/ n (counsel) consejos mpl; (professional) asesoramiento m; a piece of ~ un consejo; to give sb ~ aconsejar a algn; to take sb's ~ seguir* los consejos de algn

advisable /ədˈvaɪzəbəl/ adj aconsejable

advise /ədˈvaɪz/ vt **1** (a) (recommend) aconsejar; to ~ sb to + INF aconsejar(le) A algn QUE (+ subj); they ~d him against marrying so young le aconsejaron que no se casara tan joven (b) (give advice to) aconsejar; (professionally) asesorar **2** (inform) (frml) informar; (in writing) notificar* (frml)
■ ~ vi aconsejar; (professionally) asesorar; to ~ AGAINST sth/-ING desaconsejar algo/+ INF

adviser, advisor /ədˈvaɪzər ‖ədˈvaɪzə(r)/ n consejero, -ra m,f; (professional) asesor, -sora m,f

advisory /ədˈvaɪzəri/ adj ⟨body/service⟩ consultivo; in an ~ capacity en calidad de asesor

advocate¹ /'ædvəkət/ n (a) (supporter, defender) ~ (OF sth) defensor, -sora *m,f* (DE algo) (b) (in a court of law) abogado, -da *m,f*

advocate² /'ædvəkeɪt/ vt recomendar*, abogar* por

Aegean /ɪ'dʒiːən/ n the ~ (Sea) el (mar) Egeo

aerial¹ /'eriəl Il'eəriəl/ adj (before n) aéreo; ~ photograph aerofoto *f*

aerial² n (esp BrE) antena *f*

aerobics /e'rəʊbɪks, ə- Ileə'rəʊbɪks/ n (+ sing or pl vb) aerobic(s) *m*, aerobismo *m* (CS)

aerodynamic /'erəʊdaɪ'næmɪk Il,eərəʊdaɪ'næmɪk/ adj aerodinámico

aeroplane /'erəpleɪn Il'eərəpleɪn/ n (BrE) avión *m*

aerosol /'erəsɑːl Il'eərəsɒl/ n aerosol *m*, spray *m*

aerospace /'erəʊspeɪs Il'eərəʊspeɪs/ adj (before n) ‹research/industry› aeroespacial

aesthetic, (AmE also) **esthetic** /es'θetɪk Ili:s'θetɪk/ adj estético

afar /ə'fɑːr Ilə'fɑː(r)/ adv (liter) lejos

affable /'æfəbəl/ adj afable

affair /ə'fer Ilə'feə(r)/ n **1** (a) (case) caso *m* (b) (event): the wedding was a small, family ~ la boda se celebró en la intimidad; it was a very formal ~ fue una ocasión muy ceremoniosa (c) (business, concern) asunto *m* (d) affairs pl (matters) asuntos *mpl* **2** (liaison) affaire *m*

affect /ə'fekt/ vt (have effect on) afectar a; ‹organ/nervous system› comprometer

affected /ə'fektəd Ilə'fektɪd/ adj afectado

affection /ə'fekʃən/ n cariño *m*

affectionate /ə'fekʃnət/ adj cariñoso

affiliate /ə'fɪlieɪt/ vt (often pass) afiliar

affiliation /ə'fɪli'eɪʃən/ n afiliación *f*; her political ~s su filiación política

affinity /ə'fɪnəti/ n (pl **-ties**) afinidad *f*

affirm /ə'fɜːrm Ilə'fɜːm/ vt declarar

affirmative /ə'fɜːrmətɪv Ilə'fɜːmətɪv/ adj afirmativo

affix /ə'fɪks/ vt (fml) ‹stamp/seal› poner*; ‹notice› fijar

afflict /ə'flɪkt/ vt «disease/problem» aquejar

affliction /ə'flɪkʃən/ n (a) (suffering) aflicción *f* (b) (cause of suffering) desgracia *f*; (ailment) mal *m*

affluence /'æfluəns/ n prosperidad *f*

affluent /'æfluənt/ adj ‹suburb/country› próspero; ‹person› acomodado

afford /ə'fɔːrd Ilə'fɔːd/ vt: I can't ~ a new car no me alcanza el dinero para comprarme un coche nuevo; you can't ~ to miss this opportunity no puedes perderte esta oportunidad

affordable /ə'fɔːrdəbəl Ilə'fɔːdəbəl/ adj asequible

affront /ə'frʌnt/ n (fml) afrenta *f*

Afghan¹ /'æfgæn/ adj afgano

Afghan² n afgano, -na *m,f*

Afghanistan /æf'gænəstæn Ilæf'gænɪstɑːn/ n Afganistán *m*

afield /ə'fiːld/ adv: she travels as far ~ as China viaja a lugares tan distantes como la China; we had to look further ~ for help tuvimos que buscar ayuda en otra parte

afloat /ə'fləʊt/ adj (pred) a flote; to stay ~ mantenerse* a flote

afoot /ə'fʊt/ adj (pred): plans are ~ to create ... hay planes de crear ...; what's ~? ¿qué se está tramando?

aforementioned /ə'fɔːr'mentʃənd Ilə,fɔː'menʃənd/ adj (fml) (before n) ‹clause/statement› anteriormente mencionado, antedicho (fml); the ~ person el susodicho, la susodicha (fml o hum)

afraid /ə'freɪd/ adj (pred) **1** (scared): to be ~ OF sb/sth tenerle* miedo A algn/A algo; there's nothing to be ~ of no tienes nada que temer **2** (sorry): she's not in, I'm ~ lo siento pero no está; I'm ~ not me temo que no

afresh /ə'freʃ/ adv: to start ~ empezar* de nuevo, volver* a empezar

Africa /'æfrɪkə/ n África *f*‡

African¹ /'æfrɪkən/ adj africano

African² n africano, -na *m,f*

African-American¹ /'æfrɪkənə'merɪkən/adj norteamericano de origen africano

African-American² n norteamericano, -na *m,f* de origen africano

Afro-American¹ /'æfrəʊə'merɪkən/ adj afroamericano

Afro-American² n afroamericano, -na *m,f*

Afro-Caribbean /,æfrəʊ,kærɪ'biːən/ adj (BrE) afroantillano, afrocaribeño

after¹ /'æftər Il'ɑːftə(r)/ prep **1** (following in time) después de; I'll be at home ~ eight o'clock estaré en casa después de *or* a partir de las ocho; it's just ~ midnight son las doce pasadas; it's a quarter ~ two (AmE) son las dos y cuarto; the day ~ the party al día siguiente de la fiesta **2** (in sequence, rank) tras; day ~ day día tras día; do go in ~ you! pase — ¡primero usted! **3** (a) (behind): shut the door ~ you cierra la puerta al salir (b) (in pursuit of) tras; he ran ~ them corrió tras ellos; he's ~ her money anda a la caza de su dinero (fam); see also ASK AFTER **4** after all después de todo

after² conj: it happened ~ you left ocurrió después de que tú te fuiste; ~ examining it después de examinarlo

after³ adv (a) (afterward, following) después; the day ~ al día siguiente (b) (behind) detrás

aftereffect /'æftərɪ,fekt Il'ɑːftərɪ,fekt/ n (of drug) efecto *m* secundario; (of problem) secuela *f*

aftermath /'æftərmæθ Il'ɑːftəmæθ, 'ɑːftəmɑː θ/ n (a) (subsequent period): in the ~ of the riots tras los disturbios (b) (consequences) repercusiones *fpl*

afternoon /'æftər'nuːn Il,ɑːftə'nuːn/ n **1** (time of day) tarde *f*; on Friday ~ el viernes por *or* (AmL) en la tarde; he came in the ~ vino por la tarde, vino en la tarde (AmL); good ~! ¡ buenas tardes! **2** afternoons (as adv) por las tardes, en las tardes (AmL)

after: ~shave (lotion) n loción *f* para después de afeitarse, aftershave *m*; ~thought n: it occurred to me as an ~thought that ... después se me ocurrió qué ...; it was added on as an ~thought fue una idea de último momento

afterward /'æftərwərd Il'ɑːftəwəd/, (BrE also) **afterwards** /-z/ adv después

again /ə'gen, ə'geɪn/ adv otra vez, de nuevo; **to do sth** ~ volver* a hacer algo, hacer* algo otra vez or de nuevo; **never** ~! ¡nunca más!

against /ə'genst, ə'geɪnst/ prep contra; **I've nothing** ~ **her** no tengo nada contra ella or en contra suya or en contra de ella; **I'm** ~ **capital punishment** estoy en contra de la pena de muerte; **he put a cross** ~ **my name** puso una cruz al lado de mi nombre

age¹ /eɪdʒ/ n **1** (of person, animal, thing) edad f; **he is six years of** ~ tiene seis años; **to be under** ~ ser* menor de edad; (before n) ~ **group** grupo m etario (frml) **2 (a)** (epoch, period) era f; **through the** ~**s** a través de los tiempos **(b)** (long time) (colloq): **I haven't seen her for** ~**s** hace siglos que no la veo (fam)

age² (pres p **aging** or **ageing**; past p **aged** /eɪdʒd/) vi «person» envejecer*; «cheese» madurar
■ ~ vt «person» hacer* envejecer; «wine» añejar

aged adj **1** /'eɪdʒəd ‖'eɪdʒɪd/ (elderly) anciano **2** /eɪdʒd/ (pred): **he was** ~ **20** tenía 20 años de edad

ageing adj/n ▶ AGING

ageism /'eɪdʒɪzəm/ n discriminación f por razones de edad

ageist /'eɪdʒəst ‖'eɪdʒɪst/ adj que discrimina a las personas en razón de su edad

agency /'eɪdʒənsi/ n (pl **-cies) (a)** (office) agencia f **(b)** (branch) sucursal f **(c)** (department) organismo m

agenda /ə'dʒendə/ n orden m del día, agenda f

agent /'eɪdʒənt/ n **1** (person) agente mf **2** (substance) agente m

aggravate /'ægrəveɪt/ vt **(a)** (make worse) agravar **(b)** (annoy) (colloq) exasperar

aggression /ə'greʃən/ n **(a)** (feeling, attitude) agresividad f **(b)** (unprovoked attack) agresión f

aggressive /ə'gresɪv/ adj «person/country» agresivo; «tactics/strategy» de agresión

aghast /ə'gæst ‖ə'gɑːst/ adj (pred) aterrado

agile /'ædʒaɪl ‖'ædʒaɪl/ adj ágil

agility /ə'dʒɪləti/ n agilidad f

aging¹ /'eɪdʒɪŋ/ adj (before n) «person» envejecido

aging² n envejecimiento m

agitate /'ædʒəteɪt ‖'ædʒɪteɪt/ vt **(a)** (disturb) «surface/liquid» agitar **(b)** (upset) inquietar
■ ~ vi **to** ~ **FOR/AGAINST sth** hacer* campaña A FAVOR DE/EN CONTRA DE algo

agitated /'ædʒəteɪtəd ‖'ædʒɪteɪtɪd/ adj «movements/gestures» nervioso; **to become/get** ~ ponerse* nervioso

agitation /ˌædʒə'teɪʃən ‖ˌædʒɪ'teɪʃən/ n agitación f

AGM n (BrE) = **annual general meeting**

agnostic /æg'nɑːstɪk ‖æg'nɒstɪk/ n agnóstico, -ca m,f

ago /ə'gəʊ/ adv: **five days** ~ hace cinco días; **a long time** ~ hace mucho (tiempo)

agog /ə'gɑːg ‖ə'gɒg/ adj (pred): **I was all** ~ estaba que me moría de curiosidad

agonize /'ægənaɪz/ vi: **stop agonizing, just do it** no le des más vueltas al asunto y hazlo; **he** ~**d over the decision** le costó muchísimo decidirse

agonizing /'ægənaɪzɪŋ/ adj «experience» angustioso; «pain» atroz; «decision» muy difícil

agony /'ægəni/ n (pl **-nies**): **he was in** ~ estaba desesperado de dolor; **she's going through agonies of doubt** las dudas la están atormentando; **to prolong the** ~ alargar* el martirio

agoraphobia /ˌægərə'fəʊbiə/ n agorafobia f

agree /ə'griː/ vt **1 (a)** (be in agreement over) **to** ~ (THAT) estar* de acuerdo (EN QUE); **yes, it must feel odd, he** ~**d** —sí, debe resultar extraño — asintió **(b)** (reach agreement over) decidir; **it was** ~**d that he should go on his own** se decidió que fuera él solo; **to** ~ **WHEN/WHAT/HOW** etc ponerse* de acuerdo EN CUÁNDO/EN QUÉ/EN CÓMO etc; **to** ~ **to + INF** quedar EN + INF; **(c)** (decide on) «price» acordar*
2 (a) (consent) **to** ~ **to + INF** aceptar + INF **(b)** (admit) **to** ~ (THAT) reconocer* (QUE)
■ ~ vi **1** (be of same opinion) estar* de acuerdo; **to** ~ **ABOUT sth** estar* de acuerdo EN algo **2 (a)** (get on well) congeniar (fam) **(b)** (tally) «statements/figures» concordar*
■ **agree on** [v + prep + o] «date/details» acordar*; **we** ~ **on the colour** estamos de acuerdo en el color
■ **agree to** [v + prep + o] «terms/conditions» aceptar
■ **agree with** [v + prep + o] **(a)** (approve of) estar* de acuerdo con **(b) to** ~ **with sb** «food/heat/climate» sentarle* bien a algn

agreeable /ə'griːəbəl/ adj **1** (pleasant) agradable **2** (willing) (pred): **bring her along, if she's** ~ **to coming** tráela, si quiere venir; **he seemed quite** ~ **to coming** parecía dispuesto a venir

agreed /ə'griːd/ adj **1** (in agreement) (pred) de acuerdo **(b)** (prearranged): **we met at ten, as** ~ nos encontramos a las diez como habíamos quedado; (before n) «price/terms» acordado

agreement /ə'griːmənt/ n **1 (a)** (shared opinion) acuerdo m; **to be in** ~ **(with sb)** estar* de acuerdo (con algn) **(b)** (written arrangement) acuerdo m; (Busn) contrato m **2** (consent) consentimiento m

agricultural /ˌægrɪ'kʌltʃərəl/ adj agrícola

agriculture /'ægrɪkʌltʃər ‖'ægrɪkʌltʃə(r)/ n agricultura f

aground /ə'graʊnd/ adv: **to go** o **run** ~ (ON sth) encallar (EN algo)

ahead /ə'hed/ adv **1 (a)** (indicating movement): **go straight** ~ siga todo recto; **I'll go on** ~ yo iré delante **(b)** (indicating position): **the post office is straight** ~ la oficina de correos está siguiendo recto **(c)** (in race, competition): **our team was** ~ nuestro equipo llevaba la delantera **(d)** (in time): **the months** ~ los meses venideros, los próximos meses
2 ahead of **(a)** (in front of) delante de **(b)** (in race, competition) por delante de; **the Japanese are way** ~ **of us in this field** los japoneses nos llevan mucha ventaja en este campo **(c)** (before): **she got there an hour** ~ **of him** llegó una hora antes que él

aid¹ /eɪd/ n **(a)** (assistance, support) ayuda f; **to come/go to sb's** ~ venir*/ir* en ayuda de algn **(b)** (monetary) ayuda f, asistencia f; **a concert in** ~ **of ...** un concierto a beneficio de ...

aid² vt ayudar; **to** ~ **and abet sb** (Law) instigar* or secundar a algn (en la comisión de un delito)

aide /eɪd/ *n* asesor, -sora *m,f*

AIDS /eɪdz/ *n* (= **acquired immune deficiency syndrome**) sida *m*, SIDA *m*

ailing /'eɪlɪŋ/ *adj* ⟨person⟩ enfermo; ⟨economy⟩ renqueante

ailment /'eɪlmənt/ *n* enfermedad *f*, dolencia *f* (frml)

aim¹ /eɪm/ *vt*: he ~ed the gun at her le apuntó con la pistola; she ~ed a blow at his head intentó darle en la cabeza; the movie is ~ed at a young audience la película está dirigida a un público joven

■ ~ *vi* (a) ⟨point weapon⟩ apuntar; to ~ AT sth/sb apuntar(le) A algo/algn (b) ⟨intend⟩ to ~ to + INF querer* + INF

aim² *n* (a) ⟨goal, object⟩ objetivo *m* (b) ⟨with weapon⟩ puntería *f*; to take ~ hacer* puntería, apuntar

aimless /'eɪmləs ‖'eɪmlɪs/ *adj* ⟨wandering⟩ sin rumbo (fijo); ⟨existence⟩ sin norte

ain't /eɪnt/ ⟨colloq & dial⟩ (a) = **am not** (b) = **is not** (c) = **are not** (d) = **has not** (e) = **have not**

air¹ /er ‖eə(r)/ *n* 1 aire *m*; to go by ~ ir* en avión; to be up in the ~ «plans» estar* en el aire; to vanish into thin ~ esfumarse; ⟨before n⟩ ⟨route/attack⟩ aéreo; ⟨pollution⟩ de la atmósfera; ~ **pressure** presión *f* atmosférica 2 (Rad, TV): to be on the ~ estar* en el aire; to come *o* go on the ~ salir* al aire 3 (a) ⟨manner, look, atmosphere⟩ aire *m* (b) **airs** *pl* ⟨affectations⟩ aires *mpl*

air² *vt* 1 (a) ⟨clothes/linen⟩ airear, orear; ⟨bed/room⟩ ventilar, airear (b) ⟨opinion/grievance⟩ manifestar*; ⟨knowledge⟩ hacer* alarde de 2 ⟨broadcast⟩ (AmE) ⟨program⟩ transmitir, emitir

air: ~ **bag** *n* (Auto) bolsa *f* de aire; ~ **base** *n* base *f* aérea; ~ **bed** *n* (BrE) colchón *m* inflable; ~**borne** *adj* (a) ⟨seeds/dust⟩ transportado por el aire; ⟨troops/units⟩ aerotransportado (b) ⟨off the ground⟩: the plane is now ~borne el avión ha despegado; ~**conditioned** /'erkən'dɪʃənd ‖'eəkəndɪʃənd/ *adj* con aire acondicionado, climatizado; ~ **conditioning** *n* aire *m* acondicionado

aircraft /'erkræft ‖'eəkrɑːft/ *n* (*pl* ~) avión *m*

aircraft carrier *n* portaaviones *m*

air: ~**fare** *n* precio *m* del pasaje *or* (Esp tb) del billete de avión; ~**fares are set to rise** van a subir las tarifas aéreas; ~**field** *n* aeródromo *m*; ~ **force** *n* ⟨of nation⟩ fuerza *f* aérea; ~ **freshener** /'freʃnər ‖'freʃnə(r)/ *n* ambientador *m*, desodorante *m* ambiental *or* de ambientes (CS); ~ **gun** *n* ⟨revolver⟩ pistola *f* de aire comprimido; ⟨rifle⟩ escopeta *f* *or* rifle *m* de aire comprimido; ~ **hostess** *n* azafata *f*, aeromoza *f* (AmL); ~ **letter** *n* aerograma *m*; ~**lift** *n* puente *m* aéreo; ~**line** *n* línea *f* aérea, aerolínea *f*; ~**mail** *n* correo *m* aéreo; to send sth (by) ~**mail** mandar algo por avión *or* por vía aérea; ⟨before n⟩ ⟨paper/envelope⟩ de avión; ~**plane** *n* (AmE) avión *m*; ~**port** *n* aeropuerto *m*; ~ **raid** *n* ataque *m* aéreo; ⟨before n⟩ ~**raid shelter** refugio *m* antiaéreo; ~**ship** *n* dirigible *m*, zepelín *m*; ~**sick** *adj*: to be ~sick estar* mareado (en un avión); to get ~sick marearse (al viajar en avión); ~**sickness** *n* mareo *m* (al viajar en avión); ~ **strike** *n* ataque *m* aéreo; ~**strip** *n*

pista *f* de aterrizaje; ~**tight** *adj* ⟨room/box⟩ hermético; ⟨alibi/argument⟩ a toda prueba; ~ **traffic control** *n* control *m* del tráfico aéreo; ~ **traffic controller** *n* controlador aéreo, controladora aérea *m,f*; ~**worthy** *adj*: to be ~worthy estar* en condiciones de vuelo

airy /'eri ‖'eəri/ *adj* **airier, airiest** (a) ⟨room/house⟩ espacioso y aireado (b) ⟨manner/reply⟩ displicente

aisle /aɪl/ *n* ⟨gangway⟩ pasillo *m*; (Archit) nave *f* lateral

ajar /ə'dʒɑːr ‖ə'dʒɑː(r)/ *adj* ⟨pred⟩ entreabierto

AK = **Alaska**

akin /ə'kɪn/ *adj* ⟨pred⟩ to be ~ (TO sth) ser* similar (A algo)

AL = **Alabama**

Ala = **Alabama**

à la carte /'ɑːlə'kɑːrt ‖,ɑːlɑː'kɑːt/ *adj/adv* a la carta

alarm¹ /ə'lɑːrm ‖ə'lɑːm/ *n* 1 ⟨apprehension⟩ gran preocupación *f* 2 ⟨warning, device⟩ alarma *f*

alarm² *vt* ⟨worry⟩ alarmar; ⟨scare⟩ asustar

alarm clock *n* ⟨reloj *m*⟩ despertador *m*

alarmed /ə'lɑːrmd ‖ə'lɑːmd/ *adj* ⟨apprehensive⟩: don't be ~ no te asustes; I began to be ~ empecé a alarmarme

alarming /ə'lɑːrmɪŋ ‖ə'lɑːmɪŋ/ *adj* alarmante

alas /ə'læs/ *interj* ⟨liter *or* frml⟩ ¡ay! (liter)

Albania /æl'beɪniə/ *n* Albania *f*

Albanian¹ /æl'beɪniən/ *adj* albanés

Albanian² *n* (a) ⟨person⟩ albanés, -nesa *m,f* (b) ⟨language⟩ albanés *m*

albeit /ɔːl'biːɪt/ *conj* ⟨frml⟩ aunque

albino /æl'baɪnəʊ ‖æl'biːnəʊ/ *n* (*pl* **-nos**) albino, -na *m,f*; ⟨before n⟩ albino

album /'ælbəm/ *n* (a) ⟨book⟩ álbum *m*; **photograph ~** álbum de fotos (b) ⟨Audio⟩ álbum *m*

alchemist /'ælkəmɪst ‖'ælkəmɪst/ *n* alquimista *mf*

alcohol /'ælkəhɔːl ‖'ælkəhɒl/ *n* alcohol *m*

alcoholic¹ /'ælkə'hɔːlɪk ‖,ælkə'hɒlɪk/ *adj* alcohólico

alcoholic² *n* alcohólico, -ca *m,f*

alcoholism /'ælkəhɔːlɪzəm ‖'ælkəhɒlɪzəm/ *n* alcoholismo *m*

alcove /'ælkəʊv/ *n* ⟨recess⟩ hueco *m*; ⟨niche⟩ hornacina *f*

alderman /'ɔːldərmən ‖'ɔːldəmən/ *n* (*pl* **-men** /-mən/) (a) ⟨in UK⟩ regidor, -dora *m,f* (b) ⟨in US⟩ concejal *m*

alderwoman /'ɔːldər,wʊmən ‖'ɔːldə,wʊmən/ *n* (*pl* **-women**) ⟨in US⟩ concejala *f*

ale /eɪl/ *n* cerveza *f*

alert¹ /ə'lɜːrt ‖ə'lɜːt/ *adj* alerta *adj inv*; to be ~ ⟨vigilant⟩ estar* alerta; ⟨lively-minded⟩ estar* despierto

alert² *n* alerta *f*; to be on the ~ estar* alerta

alert³ *vt* to ~ sb (TO sth) alertar a algn (DE algo)

A level *n* ⟨in UK⟩ *estudios de una asignatura a nivel de bachillerato superior*

alga /'ælgə/ *n* (*pl* **algae** /'ældʒiː, 'ælgiː/) alga *f*‡

algebra /'ældʒɪbrə ‖'ældʒɪbrə/ *n* álgebra *f*‡

Algeria /æl'dʒɪriə ‖æl'dʒɪəriə/ *n* Argelia *f*

Algerian /ælˈdʒɪriən ‖ælˈdʒɪriən/ *adj* argelino

alias /ˈeɪliəs/ *adv* alias

alibi /ˈæləbaɪ ‖ˈælɪbaɪ/ *n* coartada *f*

alien¹ /ˈeɪliən/ *n* **(a)** (foreigner) extranjero, -ra *m,f* **(b)** (in science fiction) extraterrestre *mf*

alien² *adj* **(a)** (strange, foreign) extraño; **to be ~ TO sb/sth** serle* ajeno A algn/algo **(b)** (in science fiction) (*before n*) extraterrestre

alienate /ˈeɪliəneɪt/ *vt* (Pol, Psych) alienar; (estrange): **he has ~d all his friends** ha hecho que todos sus amigos se alejen *or* se distancien de él

alight¹ /əˈlaɪt/ *adj* (*pred*) **to be ~** estar* ardiendo; **to set sth ~** prender(le) fuego a algo

alight² *vi* (fml) «*passenger*» apearse (fml); (land) «*bird/insect*» posarse

align /əˈlaɪn/ *vt* alinear

alignment /əˈlaɪnmənt/ *n* **(a)** (Tech) alineación *f* **(b)** (Pol) alineamiento *m*

alike¹ /əˈlaɪk/ *adj* (*pred*) parecido

alike² *adv* «*think/act*» igual; **popular with young and old ~** popular tanto entre los jóvenes como entre los mayores

alimony /ˈæləməʊni ‖ˈælɪməni/ *n* pensión *f* alimenticia

alive /əˈlaɪv/ *adj* (*pred*) vivo; **is he still ~?** ¿todavía vive?; **to stay ~** sobrevivir; **she's ~ and well** está sana y salva; **the place was ~ with insects** el lugar estaba plagado de insectos

alkaline /ˈælkəlaɪn/ *adj* alcalino

all¹ /ɔːl/ *adj* (*before n*) todo, -da; (*pl*) todos, -das; **~ four of us went** fuimos los cuatro; **~ morning** toda la mañana; *or* **~ the stupid things to do!** ¡qué estupidez!; *see also* ALL³ 3D

all² *pron* ☐1 (everything) (+ *sing vb*) todo; **will that be ~, madam?** ¿algo más señora?; **when ~ is said and done** a fin de cuentas; **for ~ I care** por lo que a mí me importa

☐2 **all of: ~ of the children go to school** todos los niños van al colegio; **~ of the cheese** todo el queso

☐3 (*after n, pron*) todo, -da; (*pl*) todos, -das; **it was ~ gone** no quedaba nada

☐4 (*in phrases*) **(a)** all in all en general **(b)** all told en total **(c)** all and ~ y todo; **he ate it, skin and ~** se lo comió con la cáscara y todo **(d)** at all: **they don't like him at ~** no les gusta nada; **thank you — not at ~** gracias — de nada *or* no hay de qué; **it's not at ~ bad** no está nada mal **(e)** in all en total

all³ *adv* ☐1 (completely): **you've gone ~ red** te has puesto todo colorado/toda colorada; **she was ~ alone** estaba completamente sola

☐2 (each, apiece) (Sport): **the score was one ~** iban (empatados) uno a uno; **30 ~ 30** iguales

☐3 (*in phrases*) **(a)** all along desde el primer momento **(b)** all but casi; **the game had ~ but finished** ya casi había terminado el partido **(c)** all that (particularly) (*usu neg*): **I don't know her ~ that well** no la conozco tan bien; **I don't care ~ that much** no me importa demasiado **(d)** all the

(+ *comp*): **~ the more reason to fire them!** ¡más razón para echarlos!; **~ the more so because ...** tanto más cuanto que ...

Allah /ˈælə/ *n* Alá

all: ~-American /ˈɔːləˈmerəkən ‖ˌɔːləˈmerɪkən/ *adj* «*boy/girl*» típicamente americano; **~-around** /ˈɔːləˈraʊnd/ *adj* (AmE) (*before n*) **(a)** (versatile) «*athlete/scholar*» completo **(b)** «*experience/visibility*» amplio

allay /əˈleɪ/ *vt* «*doubt/fear*» disipar

all-clear /ˈɔːlˈklɪr ‖ˈɔːlˈklɪə(r)/ *n*: **to give sb/sth the ~** dar* luz verde a algn/algo

allegation /ˌælɪˈɡeɪʃən/ *n* acusación *f*

allege /əˈledʒ/ *vt* afirmar; **she is ~d to have accepted bribes** se dice que aceptó sobornos

alleged /əˈledʒd/ *adj* (*before n*) «*thief/violation*» presunto

allegedly /əˈledʒədli ‖əˈledʒɪdli/ *adv* (*indep*) supuestamente

allegiance /əˈliːdʒəns/ *n* lealtad *f*; (political) filiación *f*

allergic /əˈlɜːrdʒɪk ‖əˈlɜːdʒɪk/ *adj* alérgico; **to be ~ TO sth** ser alérgico A algo

allergy /ˈælərdʒi ‖ˈælədʒi/ *n* (*pl* **-gies**) alergia *f*

alleviate /əˈliːvieɪt/ *vt* «*pain*» aliviar; «*problem*» paliar

alley /ˈæli/ *n* (*pl* **alleys**) callejón *m*

alleyway /ˈæliweɪ/ *n* callejón *m*

alliance /əˈlaɪəns/ *n* alianza *f*

allied /ˈælaɪd/ *adj* **(a)** (combined) (*pred*) **~ WITH** *o* **TO sth** unido A algo **(b)** «*nations/groups*» aliado **(c)** (related) «*subjects/industries*» relacionado

alligator /ˈæləɡeɪtər ‖ˈælɪɡeɪtə(r)/ *n* aligátor *m*

all: ~-important /ˈɔːlɪmˈpɔːrtnt ‖ˌɔːlɪmˈpɔːtnt/ *adj* de suma importancia; **~-night** /ˈɔːlˈnaɪt/ *adj* «*party/show*» que dura toda la noche; «*café/store*» que está abierto toda la noche

allocate /ˈæləkeɪt/ *vt* asignar; (distribute) repartir; **$3 million has been ~d for research** se han destinado tres millones de dólares a la investigación

allot /əˈlɑːt ‖əˈlɒt/ *vt* **-tt-** (distribute) repartir; (assign) asignar

all: ~out /ˈɔːlˈaʊt/ *adj* «*attack*» con todo; «*opposition*» acérrimo; «*strike*» general; «*war*» total; **~ over** *adv* «*search*» por todas partes; **people came from ~ over** vino gente de todas partes

allow /əˈlaʊ/ *vt* ☐1 **(a)** (permit) permitir; 🚫 **no dogs allowed** no se admiten perros **(b)** (give, grant) dar*; **they are ~ed an hour for lunch** les dan una hora para comer; **within the time ~ed** dentro del plazo concedido ☐2 (plan for): **~ a good two hours to reach the coast** calculen que les va a llevar por lo menos dos horas llegar a la costa; **I normally ~ about £50 for spending money** normalmente calculo unas 50 libras para gastos ☐3 (Sport) «*referee*» «*goal*» dar* por bueno

■ **allow for** [*v + prep + o*] «*contingency*» tener* en cuenta

allowance /əˈlaʊəns/ n [1] (from employer) complemento m; (from state) prestación f; (private) asignación f; (from parents) mensualidad f, mesada f (AmL) [2] **to make ~(s) for sb** ser* indulgente con algn; **we've made ~(s) for delays** hemos tenido en cuenta posibles retrasos

alloy /ˈælɔɪ/ n aleación f

all-powerful /ˈɔːlˈpaʊərfəl ‖ˌɔːlˈpaʊəfəl/ adj todopoderoso

all right¹ adj (pred): **are you ~ ~?** ¿estás bien?; **the hotel looks ~** el hotel no parece estar mal; **do I look ~ in this dress?** ¿estoy bien con este vestido?; **I'll pay you back tomorrow: is that ~ ~?** mañana te devuelvo el dinero ¿okey? or (Esp) ¿vale?; **I'm sorry — that's ~ ~** lo siento — no tiene importancia; **it's ~ ~: I'm not going to hurt you** tranquilo, que no te voy a hacer daño

all right² adv bien

all right³ interj (colloq): **I won't be home till late, ~ ~?** volveré tarde ¿okey? or (Esp) ¿vale? (fam); **can I come too? — all right** ¿puedo ir yo también? — bueno

all: ~-round /ˈɔːlˈraʊnd/ adj (esp BrE) ▶ ALL-AROUND; **A~ Saints' Day** n día m de Todos los Santos; **~-time** adj ⟨record⟩ sin precedentes; ⟨favorite⟩ de todos los tiempos

allude /əˈluːd/ vi **to ~ TO sth/sb** aludir A algo/ algn

alluring /əˈlʊrɪŋ ‖əˈlʊərɪŋ/ adj seductor

allusion /əˈluːʒən/ n alusión f

ally¹ /ˈælaɪ/ n (pl **allies**) aliado, -da m,f

ally² v refl **allies, allying, allied: to ~ oneself WITH sb** aliarse CON algn; see also ALLIED

almanac /ˈɔːlmənæk/ n (yearbook) anuario m; (calendar) almanaque m

almighty /ɔːlˈmaɪti/ adj todopoderoso

almond /ˈɑːmənd/ n almendra f

almost /ˈɔːlmoʊst/ adv casi

■ **Note** Where almost is used with a verb in the past tense, it is translated by casi or por poco, and the verb is usually in the present tense: I almost fell casi me caigo; we almost missed the train casi or por poco perdemos el tren.In some Latin American countries the preterite tense is often used: we almost missed the train casi or por poco perdimos el tren.

---

alms /ɑːmz/ pl n limosnas fpl

aloft /əˈlɔːft ‖əˈlɒft/ adv en el aire; **he held the cup ~** levantó la copa en alto

alone¹ /əˈləʊn/ adj **(a)** (without others) solo; **I want to be ~ with you** quiero estar a solas contigo; **leave me ~** ¡déjame en paz! **(b) let alone: I can't afford beer, let ~ champagne** no puedo comprar ni cerveza, para qué hablar de champán; **she can't sew a button on, let ~ make a dress** no sabe ni pegar un botón menos aún hacer un vestido

alone² adv solo

along¹ /əˈlɔːŋ ‖əˈlɒŋ/ adv **(a)** (forward): **a bit further ~ on the right** un poco más adelante, a mano derecha; **I was walking ~** iba caminando; see also COME, GET, MOVE etc ALONG **(b)** (with one): **why don't you come ~?** ¿por qué no vienes conmigo/con nosotros?; **she brought her brother ~** trajo a su hermano; see also SING ALONG **(c) along with** (junto) con

along² prep: **we walked ~ the shore** caminamos por la playa; **a bit further ~ the road** un poco más adelante

alongside¹ /əˈlɔːŋsaɪd ‖əˈlɒŋsaɪd/ prep al lado de

alongside² adv al costado

aloof /əˈluːf/ adj distante

aloud /əˈlaʊd/ adv en alto, en voz alta

alphabet /ˈælfəbet/ n alfabeto m

alphabetical /ˌælfəˈbetɪkəl/ adj alfabético; **in ~ order** en or por orden alfabético

alpine /ˈælpaɪn/ adj **(a)** (of high mountains) alpino **(b) Alpine** ⟨scenery/people⟩ de los Alpes, alpino

Alps /ælps/ pl n **the ~** los Alpes

already /ɔːlˈredi/ adv ya; **I've ~ been there** ya he estado allí, ya estuve allí (AmL)

alright /ɔːlˈraɪt/ adj/adv/interj ▶ ALL RIGHT

Alsatian /ælˈseɪʃən/ n (esp BrE) ▶ GERMAN SHEPHERD (DOG)

also /ˈɔːlsəʊ/ adv **(a)** (as well) también **(b)** (moreover) (as linker) además

altar /ˈɔːltər ‖ˈɔːltə(r)/ n altar m

alter /ˈɔːltər ‖ˈɔːltə(r)/ vt ⟨text/situation⟩ cambiar; ⟨garment⟩ arreglar
■ ~ vi cambiar

alteration /ˌɔːltəˈreɪʃən/ n (to text) cambio m; (to building) reforma f; (to garment) arreglo m

alternate¹ /ˈɔːltərnət ‖ɔːlˈtɜːnət/ adj (before n) **(a)** (every second): **she works ~ Tuesdays** trabaja un martes sí y otro no; **write on ~ lines** escriba dejando un renglón por medio **(b)** (happening by turns) alterno **(c)** (AmE) ▶ ALTERNATIVE¹ A

alternate² /ˈɔːltərneɪt ‖ˈɔːltəneɪt/ vt/i alternar

alternately /ˈɔːltərnətli ‖ɔːlˈtɜːnətli/ adv: **he and she take the class ~** se turnan para dar la clase

alternating /ˈɔːltərneɪtɪŋ ‖ˈɔːltəneɪtɪŋ/ adj alterno

alternating current n corriente f alterna

alternative¹ /ɔːlˈtɜːrnətɪv ‖ɔːlˈtɜːnətɪv/ adj (before n) **(a)** (other) ⟨plan/method⟩ diferente **(b)** (progressive) ⟨lifestyle/medicine⟩ alternativo

alternative² n alternativa f

alternatively /ɔːlˈtɜːrnətɪvli ‖ɔːlˈtɜːnətɪvli/ adv (indep): **~, you could stay with us** si no, te podrías quedar con nosotros

although /ɔːlˈðəʊ/ conj aunque

altitude /ˈæltətuːd ‖ˈæltɪtjuːd/ n altitud f

alto¹ /ˈæltəʊ/ n (pl **altos**) contralto f

alto² adj alto

altogether /ˌɔːltəˈgeðər ‖ˌɔːltəˈgeðə(r)/ adv **(a)** (completely) totalmente; **the decision wasn't ~ wise** la decisión no fue del todo acertada **(b)** (in total) en total **(c)** (on the whole) (indep) en general

aluminum /əˈluːmɪnəm/, (BrE) **aluminium** /ˌæljəˈmɪniəm/ n aluminio m

always /ˈɔːlweɪz/ adv siempre

am¹ /æm, weak form əm/ 1st pers sing of BE

am² /ˈeɪem/ (before midday) a.m.; **at 7 ~** a las 7 de la mañana or 7 a.m.

amalgamate /əˈmælgəmeɪt/ vt ⟨collections/ indexes⟩ unir, amalgamar; ⟨companies/ departments⟩ fusionar
■ ~ vi «companies» fusionarse

amass /ə'mæs/ *vt* ⟨*fortune*⟩ amasar; ⟨*arms/ information/debts*⟩ acumular

amateur¹ /'æmətər ‖'æmətə(r)/ *n* amateur *mf*

amateur² *adj* ⟨*athlete/musician*⟩ amateur; ⟨*sport/competition*⟩ para amateurs; **an ~ photographer** un aficionado a la fotografía

amaze /ə'meɪz/ *vt* asombrar

amazed /ə'meɪzd/ *adj* ⟨*expression*⟩ de asombro; **to be ~** estar* asombrado

amazement /ə'meɪzmənt/ *n* asombro *m*

amazing /ə'meɪzɪŋ/ *adj* increíble

Amazon /'æməzɑːn ‖'æməzən/ *n* **(a)** (Myth) amazona *f* **(b)** (Geog) **the ~** el Amazonas; ⟨*before n*⟩ ⟨*rain forest*⟩ amazónico

ambassador /æm'bæsədər ‖æm'bæsədə(r)/ *n* embajador, -dora *m,f*

amber /'æmbər ‖'æmbə(r)/ *n* **(a)** (substance, color) ámbar *m* **(b)** (BrE Aut) amarillo

ambidextrous /'æmbɪ'dekstrəs/ *adj* ambidiestro, ambidextro

ambiguity /'æmbə'gjuːəti ‖,æmbɪ'gjuːəti/ *n* (*pl* **-ties**) ambigüedad *f*

ambiguous /æm'bɪgjuəs/ *adj* ambiguo

ambition /æm'bɪʃən/ *n* ambición *f*

ambitious /æm'bɪʃəs/ *adj* **(a)** ⟨*person/plan*⟩ ambicioso **(b)** (overadventurous) ⟨*pred*⟩: **aren't you being a bit ~?** ¿no estás pretendiendo hacer demasiado?

ambivalent /æm'bɪvələnt/ *adj* ambivalente

amble /'æmbəl/ *vi*: **to ~ along** ir* tranquilamente

ambulance /'æmbjələns ‖'æmbjʊləns/ *n* ambulancia *f*

ambulanceman /'æmbjələnsmən ‖'æmbjʊlənsmən/ *n* (*pl* **-men** /-mən/) (BrE) ambulanciero *m*

ambush¹ /'æmbʊʃ/ *vt* tenderle* una emboscada a

ambush² *n* emboscada *f*

ameba /ə'miːbə/ (AmE) ▶ AMOEBA

amen /'ɑː'men, 'er'men/ *interj* amén

amenable /ə'miːnəbəl/ *adj* ⟨*temperament*⟩ dócil; **they proved quite ~ to the idea** se mostraron bien dispuestos frente a la idea

amend /ə'mend/ *vt* **(a)** ⟨*text*⟩ corregir* **(b)** (Law) enmendar*

amendment /ə'mendmənt/ *n* **(a)** (alteration) corrección *f* **(b)** (Law) enmienda *f*

amends /ə'mendz/ *pl n*: **to make ~ to sb** desagraviar a algn; **to make ~** reparar el daño

amenity /ə'miːnəti/ *n* (*pl* **-ties**) servicio *m*

America /ə'merəkə ‖ə'merɪkə/ *n* (USA) Norteamérica *f*, Estados *mpl* Unidos, América *f*; (continent) América *f*

American¹ /ə'merəkən ‖ə'merɪkən/ *adj* (of USA) estadounidense, norteamericano, americano

American² *n* (from USA) estadounidense *mf*, norteamericano, -na *m,f*, americano, -na *m,f*

amethyst /'æməθəst ‖'æməθɪst/ *n* amatista *f*

amiable /'ermiəbəl/ *adj* afable

amicable /'æmɪkəbəl/ *adj* ⟨*person*⟩ amigable; ⟨*relations*⟩ cordial

amid /ə'mɪd/, **amidst** /ə'mɪdst/ *prep* en medio de, entre

amiss /ə'mɪs/ *adj* ⟨*pred*⟩: **there was nothing ~** no había ningún problema; **there's something ~** pasa algo

ammunition /'æmjə'nɪʃən ‖,æmjʊ'nɪʃən/ *n* munición *f*

amnesia /æm'niːʒə ‖æm'niːziə/ *n* amnesia *f*

amnesty /'æmnəsti/ *n* (*pl* **-ties**) amnistía *f*

amoeba, (AmE also) **ameba** /ə'miːbə/ *n* ameba *f*, amiba *f*

amok /ə'mʌk ‖ə'mɒk/ *adv* **to run ~** ⟨*person*⟩ tener* un ataque de locura

among /ə'mʌŋ/, **amongst** /ə'mʌŋst/ *prep* entre

amount /ə'maʊnt/ *n* cantidad *f*
■ **amount to** [*v + prep + o*] **(a)** (add up to) ⟨*debt/ assets*⟩ ascender* a **(b)** (be equivalent to) equivaler* a; **it ~s to the same thing** viene a ser lo mismo

amp /æmp/ *n* **(a)** (Elec) amperio *m* **(b)** (amplifier) (colloq) amplificador *m*

amphetamine /æm'fetəmiːn/ *n* anfetamina *f*

amphibian /æm'fɪbiən/ *n* (Zool) anfibio *m*

amphibious /æm'fɪbiəs/ *adj* anfibio

amphitheater, (BrE) **amphitheatre** /'æmfɪ'θiːətər ‖'æmfɪ'θiːətə(r)/ *n* anfiteatro *m*

ample /'æmpəl/ *adj* **(a)** ⟨*space*⟩ amplio; ⟨*funds/ resources*⟩ abundante; ⟨*helping*⟩ generoso **(b)** (plenty) ⟨*pred*⟩ más que suficiente

amplifier /'æmpləfaɪər ‖'æmplɪfaɪə(r)/ *n* amplificador *m*

amplify /'æmpləfaɪ ‖'æmplɪfaɪ/ *vt* **-fies,** **-fying, -fied** amplificar*

amputate /'æmpjəteɪt ‖'æmpjʊteɪt/ *vt* amputar

Amtrak /'æmtræk/ *n* (in US) Ferrocarriles *mpl* de los EEUU

amuse /ə'mjuːz/ *vt* **(a)** (entertain) entretener* **(b)** (make laugh) divertir*
■ *v refl* **to ~ oneself** (entertain oneself) entretenerse*; (have fun) divertirse*

amused /ə'mjuːzd/ *adj* ⟨*expression*⟩ divertido; **she was ~ at the look on his face** le hizo gracia la cara que puso

amusement /ə'mjuːzmənt/ *n* **(a)** (entertainment) distracción *f*, entretención *f* (AmL) **(b)** (mirth) diversión *f*; **much to our ~** para nuestro gran regocijo; ⟨*before n*⟩ **~ arcade** sala *f* de juegos recreativos; **~ park** parque *m* de diversiones *or* (Esp) atracciones

amusing /ə'mjuːzɪŋ/ *adj* divertido

an /æn, *weak form* ən/ *indef art before vowel* ▶ A

anachronism /ə'nækrənɪzəm/ *n* anacronismo *m*

anaemia *etc* (BrE) ▶ ANEMIA *etc*

anaesthetic *n* (BrE) ▶ ANESTHETIC

anagram /'ænəgræm/ *n* anagrama *m*

analogy /ə'nælədʒi/ *n* (*pl* **-gies**) analogía *f*

analyse *vt* (BrE) ▶ ANALYZE

analysis /ə'næləsəs ‖ə'nælɪsɪs/ *n* (*pl* **-lyses** /-lɪsiːz/) **(a)** (examination) análisis *m* **(b)** (Psych) psicoanálisis *m*, análisis *m*

analyst /'ænələst ‖'ænəlɪst/ *n* **(a)** (of data) analista *mf* **(b)** (Psych) psicoanalista *mf*, analista *mf*

analytical /'ænə'lɪtɪkəl/ *adj* analítico

analyze, (BrE) **analyse** /'ænəlaız/ vt **(a)**
⟨data⟩ analizar* **(b)** (Psych) psicoanalizar*,
analizar*

anarchist /'ænərkəst ‖'ænəkıst/ n anarquista
mf

anarchy /'ænərki ‖'ænəki/ n anarquía f

anatomy /ə'nætəmi/ n anatomía f

ancestor /'ænsestər ‖'ænsestə(r)/ n
antepasado, -da m,f

ancestry /'ænsestri/ n ascendencia f

anchor¹ /'æŋkər ‖'æŋkə(r)/ n (Naut) ancla f‡

anchor² vt ⟨ship⟩ anclar; ⟨rope/tent⟩ sujetar

anchor: ~man /'æŋkərmæn ‖'æŋkəmæn/ n
(pl **-men** /-men/) (TV) presentador m;
~woman n (TV) presentadora f

anchovy /'æntʃəʊvi ‖'æntʃəvi/ n (pl **-vies** or
-vy) anchoa f

ancient /'eınʃənt/ adj **(a)** ⟨civilizations/ruin⟩
antiguo; A~ Greek griego m clásico **(b)** (colloq)
(old) ⟨car⟩ del año de la pera (fam)

and /ænd, weak form ənd/ conj

■ Note The usual translation of and, y, becomes e
when it precedes a word beginning with i, hi, or y.

(a) y; bread ~ butter pan con mantequilla **(b)** (in
numbers): one ~ a half uno y medio; two hundred
~ twenty doscientos veinte **(c)** (showing continuation,
repetition): faster ~ faster cada vez más rápido **(d)**
(with inf): try ~ finish this today trata de
terminar esto hoy

Andalusia /ændə'luːʒə ‖,ændə'luːsiə/ n
Andalucía f

Andalusian¹ /,ændə'luːʒən ‖,ændə'luːsiən/
adj andaluz

Andalusian² n andaluz, -luza m,f

Andes /'ændiːz/ pl n the ~ los Andes

Andorra /æn'dɔːrə/ n Andorra f

anecdote /'ænıkdəʊt/ n anécdota f

anemia, (BrE) **anaemia** /ə'niːmiə/ n anemia f

anemic, (BrE) **anaemic** /ə'niːmık/ adj
anémico

anemone /ə'neməni/ n (Bot) anémona f

anesthetic, (BrE) **anaesthetic** /'ænəs'θetık
‖,ænıs'θetık/ n anestésico m; to be under ~
estar* bajo los efectos de la anestesia

anesthetize, (BrE) **anaesthetize**
/ə'nesθetaız ‖ə'niːsθetaız/ vt anestesiar

anew /ə'nuː ‖ə'njuː/ adv (liter) de nuevo, otra
vez

angel /'eındʒəl/ n ángel m

angelic /æn'dʒelık/ adj angelical

anger /'æŋgər ‖'æŋgə(r)/ n ira f, enojo m (esp
AmL), enfado m (esp Esp)

angina /æn'dʒaınə/ n angina f (de pecho)

angle /'æŋgəl/ n ①① ángulo m; she wore her hat
at an ~ llevaba el sombrero ladeado ②② (point of
view) perspectiva f

angler /'æŋglər ‖'æŋglə(r)/ n pescador, -dora
m,f (de caña)

Anglican¹ /'æŋglıkən/ n anglicano, -na m,f

Anglican² adj anglicano

angling /'æŋglıŋ/ n pesca f (con caña)

Anglo-Saxon¹ /'æŋgləʊ'sæksən/ adj
anglosajón

Anglo-Saxon² n **(a)** (person) anglosajón, -jona
m,f **(b)** (language) anglosajón m

Angola /æŋ'gəʊlə/ n Angola f

Angolan /æŋ'gəʊlən/ adj angoleño

angrily /'æŋgrəli ‖'æŋgrıli/ adv con ira

angry /'æŋgri/ adj **angrier, angriest**
⟨person⟩ enojado (esp AmL), enfadado (esp Esp); to
get ~ enojarse (esp AmL), enfadarse (esp Esp)

anguish /'æŋgwıʃ/ n angustia f

angular /'æŋgjələr ‖'æŋgjʊlə(r)/ adj ⟨shape⟩
angular; ⟨features⟩ anguloso

animal /'ænəməl ‖'ænıməl/ n animal m

animate /'ænəmeıt ‖'ænımeıt/ vt animar

animated /'ænəmeıtəd ‖'ænımeıtıd/ adj
animado

animation /'ænə'meıʃən ‖,ænı'meıʃən/ n
animación f

animator /'ænəmeıtər ‖'ænımeıtə(r)/ n
animador, -dora m,f

animosity /'ænə'mɑːsəti ‖,ænı'mɒsəti/ n (pl
-ties) animosidad f

aniseed /'ænəsiːd ‖'ænısiːd/ n anís m

ankle /'æŋkəl/ n tobillo m; (before n) ~ boot
botín m; ~ sock calcetín m corto, soquete m (CS)

annex¹ /ə'neks/ vt ⟨territory⟩ anexar

annex², (BrE) **annexe** /'æneks/ n anexo m,
anejo m

annihilate /ə'naıəleıt/ vt ⟨army/city⟩ aniquilar

anniversary /'ænə'vɜːrsəri ‖,ænı'vɜːsəri/ n
(pl **-ries**) aniversario m; ⟨wedding⟩ ~
aniversario m de boda de casados

announce /ə'naʊns/ vt **(a)** ⟨flight/guest/
marriage⟩ anunciar **(b)** (declare) anunciar **(c)**
(AmE Rad, TV) ⟨game/race⟩ comentar

announcement /ə'naʊnsmənt/ n anuncio m

announcer /ə'naʊnsər ‖ə'naʊnsə(r)/ n (Rad,
TV) **(a)** (commentator) (AmE) comentarista mf **(b)**
(between programs) (BrE) locutor, -tora m,f de
continuidad

annoy /ə'nɔɪ/ vt molestar, irritar

annoyance /ə'nɔɪəns/ n **(a)** (irritation) irritación
f; (anger) enojo m (esp AmL), enfado m (esp Esp) **(b)**
(cause of irritation) molestia f

annoyed /ə'nɔɪd/ adj enojado (esp AmL),
enfadado (esp Esp)

annoying /ə'nɔɪŋ/ adj ⟨person⟩ pesado; ⟨noise/
habit⟩ molesto; how ~! ¡qué rabia!

annual¹ /'ænjuəl/ adj (before n) anual

annual² n ① (plant) planta f anual
② (publication) anuario m

annually /'ænjuəli/ adv anualmente

annul /ə'nʌl/ vt **-ll-** anular

annulment /ə'nʌlmənt/ n anulación f

anoint /ə'nɔɪnt/ vt ungir*

anonymity /,ænə'nıməti/ n anonimato m

anonymous /ə'nɑːnəməs/ adj
anónimo; to remain ~ permanecer* en el
anonimato; ~ letter anónimo m

anorak /'ænəræk/ n (BrE) anorak m

anorexia (nervosa) /'ænə'reksiə (nər'vəʊsə)
‖,ænə'reksiə (nɜː'vəʊsə)/ n anorexia f (nerviosa)

another¹ /ə'nʌðər ‖ə'nʌðə(r)/ adj otro, otra;
(pl) otros, otras

another² pron otro, otra

answer¹ /'ænsər ǁ'ɑ:nsə(r)/ n ⬛**1** **(a)** (reply) respuesta f, contestación f; in ~ to your question para contestar tu pregunta **(b)** (response): her ~ to his rudeness was to ignore it respondió a su grosería ignorándola; **Britain's ~ to Elvis Presley** el Elvis Presley británico ⬛**2** **(a)** (in exam, test, quiz) respuesta f **(b)** (solution) solución f; ~ TO sth solución DE algo

answer² vt ⬛**1** **(a)** (reply to) ⟨person/letter⟩ contestar **(b)** ⟨telephone⟩ contestar, atender* (AmL), coger* (Esp); **will you ~ the door?** ¿vas tú (a abrir)? **(c)** ⟨critic/criticism⟩ responder a ⬛**2** (fit): **to ~ (to) a description** responder a una descripción
■ ~ vi contestar, responder
■ **answer back** ⬛**1** [v + adv] (rudely) contestar ⬛**2** [v + o + adv] **to ~ sb back** contestarle mal or de mala manera a algn
■ **answer for** [v + prep + o] (accept responsibility for) ⟨conduct/consequences⟩ responder de; **his parents have a lot to ~ for** sus padres tienen mucha culpa

answerable /'ænsərəbəl ǁ'ɑ:nsərəbəl/ adj: **she said she was not ~ for his behavior** dijo que ella no era responsable de lo que él hiciera; **I'm ~ to no one** no tengo que rendirle cuentas a nadie

answering machine /'ænsərɪŋ ǁ'ɑ:nsərɪŋ/ n contestador m (automático)

answerphone /'ænsərfəʊn ǁ'ɑ:nsəfəʊn/ n contestador m (automático)

ant /ænt/ n hormiga f

antagonize /æn'tægənaɪz/ vt suscitar el antagonismo de

Antarctic¹ /ænt'ɑ:rktɪk ǁæn'tɑ:ktɪk/ adj antártico; **the ~ Ocean** el Océano Antártico; **the ~ Circle** el círculo polar antártico

Antarctic² n **the ~** la región antártica

Antarctica /ænt'ɑ:rktɪkə ǁæn'tɑ:ktɪkə/ n la Antártida

anteater /'ænt,i:tər ǁ'ænt,i:tə(r)/ n oso m hormiguero

antecedent /,æntə'si:dn̩t ǁ,æntɪ'si:dənt/ n antecedente m

antelope /'æntələʊp ǁ'æntɪləʊp/ n (pl ~s or ~) antílope m

antenatal /'ænti'neɪtl̩/ adj prenatal; ~ **clinic** consulta médica para mujeres embarazadas

antenna /æn'tenə/ n **(a)** (pl **-nae** /-ni:/) (Zool) antena f **(b)** (pl **-nas**) (Rad, TV) antena f

anthem /'ænθəm/ n himno m; **national ~** himno nacional

anthology /æn'θɑːlədʒi ǁæn'θɒlədʒi/ n (pl **-gies**) antología f

anthropologist /'ænθrə'pɑːlədʒəst ǁ,ænθrə'pɒlədʒɪst/ n antropólogo, -ga m,f

anthropology /'ænθrə'pɑːlədʒi ǁ,ænθrə'pɒlədʒi/ n antropología f

anti- /'æntaɪ, 'ænti ǁ'ænti/ pref anti-

antiaircraft /'æntar'erkræft ǁ,ænti'eəkrɑ:ft/ adj antiaéreo

antibiotic /'æntɪbar'ɑːtɪk ǁ,æntibar'ɒtɪk/ n antibiótico m

antibody /'ænti,bɑːdi ǁ'ænti,bɒdi/ n (pl **-dies**) anticuerpo m

anticipate /æn'tɪsəpeɪt ǁæn'tɪsɪpeɪt/ vt ⬛**1** **(a)** (expect) ⟨consequences⟩ prever*; **I don't ~ any problems** no creo que vaya a haber ningún problema **(b)** (look forward to) esperar ⬛**2** **(a)** (foresee and act accordingly) ⟨movements/objections/ needs⟩ prever* **(b)** (pre-empt) anticiparse a

anticipation /æn'tɪsə'peɪʃən ǁæn,tɪsɪ'peɪʃən/ n **(a)** (foresight) previsión f; **thanking you in ~** agradeciéndole de antemano su atención **(b)** (expectation) expectativa f

anticlimax /'æntar'klaɪmæks ǁ,ænti'klaɪmæks/ n suceso caracterizado por un descenso de la tensión; (disappointment) decepción f

anticlockwise /'æntɪ'klɑːkwaɪz ǁ,ænti'klɒkwaɪz/ adj/adv (BrE) en sentido contrario a las agujas del reloj

antics /'æntɪks/ pl n (clowning) payasadas fpl; (of naughty children) travesuras fpl

antidote /'æntɪdəʊt/ n ~ (TO sth) antídoto m (CONTRA algo)

antifreeze /'æntifri:z/ n anticongelante m

antihero /'ænti,hɪərəʊ ǁ'ænti,hɪərəʊ/ n (pl **-roes**) antihéroe m

antipathy /æn'tɪpəθi/ n (pl **-thies**) antipatía f

antiperspirant /'æntɪ'pɜ:rspərənt ǁ,ænti'pɜ:spɪrənt/ n antitranspirante m

antique¹ /æn'ti:k/ n antigüedad f; (before n) ~ **shop** tienda f de antigüedades

antique² adj antiguo

antiquity /æn'tɪkwəti/ n (pl **-ties**) ⬛**1** (ancient times, age) antigüedad f ⬛**2** **antiquities** pl antigüedades fpl

anti-Semitic /'æntɪsə'mɪtɪk ǁ,æntɪsɪ'mɪtɪk/ adj antisemita

anti-Semitism /,ænti'semətɪzəm ǁ,ænti'semɪtɪzəm/ n antisemitismo m

antiseptic¹ /'æntɪ'septɪk/ n antiséptico m

antiseptic² adj (Pharm) antiséptico

antisocial /'æntɪ'səʊʃəl/ adj **(a)** (offensive to society) antisocial **(b)** (unsociable) poco sociable

antithesis /æn'tɪθəsəs ǁæn'tɪθəsɪs/ n (pl **-eses** /-əsi:z/) antítesis f

antler /'æntlər ǁ'æntlə(r)/ n cuerno m, asta f; **the animal's ~s** la cornamenta del animal

anus /'eɪnəs/ n ano m

anvil /'ænvəl ǁ'ænvɪl/ n yunque m

anxiety /æŋ'zaɪəti/ n (pl **-ties**) **(a)** (distress, concern) preocupación f **(b)** (problem, worry) preocupación f **(c)** (Med, Psych) ansiedad f

anxious /'æŋkʃəs/ adj **(a)** (worried) preocupado **(b)** (worrying) ⟨time/moment⟩ (lleno) de preocupación **(c)** (eager) deseoso; **he's very ~ to please** tiene mucho afán de agradar

anxiously /'æŋkʃəsli/ adv **(a)** (worriedly) con preocupación **(b)** (eagerly) ansiosamente

any¹ /'eni/ adj

AmC	América Central	Arg	Argentina	Cu	Cuba
AmL	América Latina	Bol	Bolivia	Ec	Ecuador
AmS	América del Sur	Chi	Chile	Esp	España
Andes	Región andina	CS	Cono Sur	Méx	México

Per	Perú
RPI	Río de la Plata
Ur	Uruguay
Ven	Venezuela

I ⓵ (*in questions*) **(a)** (+ *pl n*): **are there ~
questions?** ¿alguien tiene alguna pregunta?; **does
she have ~ children?** ¿tiene hijos? **(b)** (+ *uncount
n*): **do you need ~ help?** ¿necesitas ayuda?; **do
you want ~ more café?** ¿quieres más café? **(c)**
(+ *sing count n: as indef art*) algún, -guna; **is
there ~ chance they'll come?** ¿existe alguna
posibilidad de que vengan?
⓶ (*in 'if' clauses and suppositions*) **(a)** (+ *pl n*):
call me if there are ~ changes llámame si hay
algún cambio; **if you see ~ flowers, buy some** si
ves flores, compra algunas **(b)** (+ *uncount n*): **let
me know if you have ~ pain** avíseme si siente
dolor; **take ~ money you need** toma el dinero
que necesites **(c)** (+ *sing count n*): **~ upset could
kill him** cualquier disgusto podría matarlo; **~ act
of disobedience will be punished** toda
desobediencia será castigada
⓷ (*with neg and implied neg*) **(a)** (+ *pl n*): **don't
buy ~ more eggs** no compres más huevos; **aren't
there ~ apples left?** ¿no queda ninguna
manzana? **(b)** (+ *uncount n*): **don't make ~ noise**
no hagas ruido; **it doesn't make ~ sense** no tiene
ningún sentido
II ⓵ **(a)** (no matter which): **take ~ book you want**
llévate cualquier libro; **~ day now** cualquier día
de estos **(b)** (every, all): **in ~ large school, you'll
find that ...** en cualquier *or* todo colegio grande,
verás que ...
⓶ (countless, a lot): **~ number/amount of sth**
cualquier cantidad de algo

any² *pron* ⓵ (*in questions*) **(a)** (*referring to pl n*)
alguno, -na; **those chocolates were nice, are there
~ left?** ¡qué ricos esos bombones! ¿queda alguno?
(b) (*referring to uncount n*): **we need sugar; did
you buy ~?** nos hace falta azúcar ¿compraste?; **is
there ~ of that cake left?** ¿queda algo de ese
pastel?
⓶ (*in 'if' clauses and suppositions*) **(a)** (*referring
to pl n*): **buy some red ones if you can find ~**
compra algunas rojas si encuentras; **if ~ of my
friends calls, take a message** si llama alguno de
mis amigos, toma el recado **(b)** (*referring to
uncount n*): **help yourself to cake if you want ~**
sírvete pastel si quieres
⓷ (*with neg and implied neg*) **(a)** (*referring to pl
n*): **some children were here — I didn't see ~**
aquí había algunos niños — yo no vi (a) ninguno
or no los vi; **you'll have to go without cigarettes; I
forgot to buy ~** te vas a tener que arreglar sin
cigarrillos porque me olvidé de comprar **(b)**
(*referring to uncount n*): **she offered me some
wine, but I didn't want ~** me ofreció vino, pero no
quise; **I didn't understand ~ of that lecture** no
entendí nada de esa conferencia

any³ *adv* ⓵ (*with comparative*): **do you feel ~
better now?** ¿te sientes (algo) mejor ahora?; **they
don't live here ~ more** ya no viven aquí ⓶ (at all)
(AmE): **have you thought about it ~ since then?**
¿has pensado en ello desde entonces?; **it doesn't
seem to have affected him ~** no parece haberlo
afectado en absoluto

anybody /'enɪˌbɑːdi ‖ 'enɪˌbɒdi/ *pron* ⓵ **(a)**
(somebody) (*in interrog, conditional sentences*)
alguien; **will ~ be seeing Emma today?** ¿alguno
de ustedes va a ver a Emma hoy? **(b)** (*with neg*)
nadie; **don't tell ~!** ¡no se lo digas a nadie! ⓶ **(a)**
(whoever, everybody): **give it to ~ you like** dáselo a
quien quieras; **~ who's been to Paris knows ...**

cualquier persona que haya estado en París sabe
...; **before ~ could stop her** antes de que nadie
pudiera detenerla **(b)** (no matter who) cualquiera;
~ could do it cualquiera podría hacerlo

anyhow /'enɪhaʊ/ *adv* ⓵ ▶ ANYWAY
⓶ (haphazardly) de cualquier manera

anyone /'enɪwʌn/ *pron* ▶ ANYBODY

anyplace /'enɪpleɪs/ *adv* (AmE) ▶ ANYWHERE¹ 1

anything /'enɪθɪŋ/ *pron* ⓵ **(a)** (something) (*in
interrog, conditional sentences*) algo; **have you
ever heard ~ so ridiculous?** ¡habráse oído
semejante ridiculez! **(b)** (a single thing) (*with neg*)
nada; **don't say ~!** ¡no digas nada!
⓶ **(a)** (whatever): **~ you say!** ¡lo que tú digas!;
we'll do ~ we can to help haremos todo lo que
podamos para ayudar **(b)** (no matter what): **~ is
possible** todo es posible; **~ could happen** podría
pasar cualquier cosa
⓷ (used for emphasis): **was it interesting? — ~
but!** ¿fue interesante? — ¡qué va!; **the portrait
doesn't look ~ like her** el retrato no se parece en
nada a ella

anyway /'enɪweɪ/ *adv* ⓵ (in any case) de todos
modos ⓶ (changing the subject, moving conversation on)
(*as linker*) bueno; **~, to cut a long story short, ...**
bueno, en resumidas cuentas ...

anywhere¹ /'enɪhwer ‖ 'enɪweə(r)/ *adv* ⓵ **(a)**
(no matter where) en cualquier sitio *or* lugar; **you
can sit ~ you like** te puedes sentar donde quieras
(b) (in, to any unspecified place): **have you seen my
book ~?** ¿has visto mi libro por alguna parte *or*
por algún lado?; **we never go ~ together** nunca
vamos juntos a ningún lado ⓶ **anywhere near: is
it ~ near Portland?** ¿queda cerca de Portland?; **we
aren't ~ near ready yet** todavía no estamos listos
ni mucho menos

anywhere² *pron*: **is there ~ that sells oysters?**
¿hay algún sitio donde vendan ostras?; **she hasn't
~ to stay** no tiene donde quedarse

apace /ə'peɪs/ *adv* (liter *or* journ) a paso *or* ritmo
acelerado

apart /ə'pɑːrt ‖ ə'pɑːt/ *adv* ⓵ **(a)** (separated):
they've lived ~ for some years ya hace algunos
años que viven separados; **keep them ~**
manténgalos separados **(b)** (into pieces): ▶ COME,
FALL, PULL, TAKE *etc* APART
⓶ (distant): **in places as far ~ as Tokyo and Paris**
en lugares tan alejados el uno del otro como
Tokio y París
⓷ (excluded) (*after n*): **these faults ~ ...** aparte de
estos defectos ...; **joking ~ ...** bromas aparte ...
⓸ **apart from** (*as prep*) **(a)** (except for) excepto,
aparte de **(b)** (separated from): **she always sits ~
from the rest of the group** siempre se sienta
apartada del resto del grupo

apartheid /ə'pɑːrteɪt ‖ ə'pɑːteɪt/ *n* apartheid *m*

apartment /ə'pɑːrtmənt ‖ ə'pɑːtmənt/ *n* (set of
rooms) apartamento *m*, departamento *m* (AmL),
piso *m* (Esp); (*before n*) **~ building** edificio *m* de
apartamentos *or* (AmL tb) de departamentos

apathetic /ˌæpə'θetɪk/ *adj* apático

apathy /'æpəθi/ *n* apatía *f*

ape¹ /eɪp/ *n* simio *m*, mono *m*

ape² *vt* remedar, imitar

aperitif /ə'perəˈtiːf ‖ ə'perətif/ *n* aperitivo *m*

aperture /'æpərt∫ər ‖'æpət∫ə(r)/ n (a) (Opt, Phot) apertura f (b) (hole, opening) (frml) orificio m; (long and narrow) rendija f

apex /'eɪpeks/ n (pl **apexes** or **apices**) (a) (Math) vértice m (b) (pinnacle) cúspide f (c) (pointed end, tip) ápice m

APEX /'eɪpeks/ adj (= **advance purchase excursion**) (before n) ⟨ticket/booking⟩ Apex adj inv

aphid /'eɪfəd ‖'eɪfɪd/ n afidido m, áfido m

aphrodisiac /ˌæfrə'dɪziæk/ n afrodisíaco m

apices /'eɪpəsiːz ‖'eɪpɪsiːz/ pl of APEX

apiece /ə'piːs/ adv cada uno

apocalypse /ə'pɑːkəlɪps ‖ə'pɒkəlɪps/ n apocalipsis m

apologetic /əˌpɑːlə'dʒetɪk ‖ə,pɒlə'dʒetɪk/ adj ⟨letter/look⟩ de disculpa; she was very ~ se deshizo en disculpas

apologize /ə'pɑːlədʒaɪz ‖ə'pɒlədʒaɪz/ vi pedir* perdón, disculparse; we ~ for the delay rogamos disculpen el retraso; you must ~ to her for being so rude tienes que pedirle perdón por haber sido tan grosero

apology /ə'pɑːlədʒi ‖ə'pɒlədʒi/ n (pl **-gies**) (often pl) disculpa f; please accept my apologies le ruego me disculpe

apostle /ə'pɑːsəl ‖ə'pɒsəl/ n apóstol m

apostrophe /ə'pɑːstrəfi ‖ə'pɒstrəfi/ n apóstrofo m

appall, (BrE) **appal** /ə'pɔːl/ vt (BrE) **-ll-** horrorizar*

appalling /ə'pɔːlɪŋ/ adj ⟨conditions⟩ atroz; the play is absolutely ~ la obra es pésima

apparatus /ˌæpə'rætəs ‖ˌæpə'reɪtəs/ n (pl ~) (a) (equipment) aparatos mpl; a piece of ~ un aparato (b) (Pol) aparato m

apparel /ə'pærəl/ n (a) (finery) (liter) atavío m (liter) (b) (AmE Busn) ropa f

apparent /ə'pærənt/ adj (a) (evident): for no ~ reason sin motivo aparente; it was ~ that ... estaba claro que ..., era evidente que ... (b) (seeming) ⟨interest/concern⟩ aparente

apparently /ə'pærəntli/ adv (a) (indep) al parecer, por lo visto, según parece (b) (seemingly) ⟨intelligent/happy⟩ aparentemente

apparition /ˌæpə'rɪʃən/ n aparición f

appeal¹ /ə'piːl/ n **1** (call) llamamiento m, llamado m (AmL); (request) solicitud f, pedido m (AmL); (plea) ruego m **2** (Law) apelación f **3** (fund, organization) campaña para recaudar fondos **4** (attraction) atractivo m

appeal² vi **1** (call) to ~ FOR sth ⟨for funds⟩ pedir* algo; the police ~ed to witnesses to come forward la policía hizo un llamamiento or (AmL tb) un llamado para que se presentaran testigos del hecho **2** (Law) apelar **3** (be attractive) to ~ TO sb atraerle* A algn
■ ~ vt (AmE) ⟨decision/verdict⟩ apelar contra or de

appealing /ə'piːlɪŋ/ adj atractivo

appear /ə'pɪr ‖ə'pɪə(r)/ vi **1** (a) (come into view) aparecer* (b) (be published): to ~ (in print) publicarse* (c) (Law) comparecer*; to ~ in court comparecer* **2** (seem) parecer*; so it ~s eso parece; to ~ to + INF parecer* + INF; we ~ to be lost parece que nos hemos perdido

appearance /ə'pɪrəns ‖ə'pɪərəns/ n **1** (a) (coming into view) aparición f (b) (Law) comparecencia f (c) (of book) publicación f **2** (a) (look) aspecto m (b) **appearances** pl apariencias fpl; to keep up ~s guardar las apariencias

appease /ə'piːz/ vt ⟨person⟩ apaciguar*; ⟨anger⟩ aplacar*

appendices /ə'pendəsiːz ‖ə'pendɪsiːz/ pl of APPENDIX

appendicitis /əˌpendə'saɪtəs ‖ə,pendɪ'saɪtɪs/ n apendicitis f

appendix /ə'pendɪks/ n (pl **-dixes** or **-dices**) apéndice m

appetite /'æpətaɪt ‖'æpɪtaɪt/ n apetito m

appetizer /'æpətaɪzər ‖'æpɪtaɪzə(r)/ n (a) (drink) aperitivo m (b) (snack) aperitivo m, tapa f (Esp), botana f (Méx)

appetizing /'æpətaɪzɪŋ ‖'æpɪtaɪzɪŋ/ adj apetitoso

applaud /ə'plɔːd/ vt/i aplaudir

applause /ə'plɔːz/ n aplausos mpl

apple /'æpəl/ n manzana f; (before n) ~ pie pastel m de manzana, pay m de manzana (Méx); ~ tree manzano m

appliance /ə'plaɪəns/ n aparato m; electrical ~s electrodomésticos mpl

applicable /'æplɪkəbəl, ə'plɪkəbəl/ adj (frml): these regulations are only ~ to foreigners estas normas se refieren únicamente a los extranjeros; delete as ~ tache lo que no corresponda

applicant /'æpləkənt ‖'æplɪkənt/ n (for job) candidato, -ta m,f, postulante mf (CS), aplicante mf (Ven)

application /ˌæplə'keɪʃən ‖ˌæplɪ'keɪʃən/ n **1** (request) solicitud f; ~ FOR sth ⟨for loan/grant/visa⟩ solicitud DE algo; (before n) ~ form (impreso m de) solicitud f **2** (a) (of method, skills, theory) aplicación f (b) (of paint, ointment) aplicación f

applied /ə'plaɪd/ adj aplicado

apply /ə'plaɪ/ **applies, applying, applied** vt (a) (put on) aplicar* (b) ⟨method/theory/rules⟩ aplicar*; to ~ the brakes frenar; she applied herself to her work se puso a trabajar con diligencia
■ ~ vi (a) (make application): please ~ in writing to ... diríjase por escrito a ...; to ~ FOR sth ⟨for loan/permission⟩ solicitar algo; to ~ for a job solicitar un trabajo, aplicar* a un trabajo (Ven), postular para un trabajo (CS) (b) (be applicable) «regulation/criterion» aplicarse*

appoint /ə'pɔɪnt/ vt **1** (name, choose) nombrar **2** (frml) ⟨date⟩ designar (frml)

appointment /ə'pɔɪntmənt/ n **1** (arrangement to meet) cita f; (with doctor, hairdresser) hora f, cita f; to make an ~ pedir* hora or una cita **2** (a) (act of appointing) nombramiento m (b) (post) (frml) puesto m

appraisal /ə'preɪzəl/ n (of situation, employee) evaluación f; (of work, novel) valoración f; (of property) tasación f

appraise /ə'preɪz/ vt ⟨situation/employee⟩ evaluar*; ⟨novel/painting⟩ valorar; ⟨property⟩ tasar, avaluar* (AmL)

appreciable /ə'priːʃəbəl/ adj ⟨change/difference⟩ apreciable; ⟨loss/sum⟩ importante

appreciate /əˈpriːʃieɪt/ vt (a) (value) ⟨food/ novel⟩ apreciar (b) (be grateful for) agradecer* (c) (understand) ⟨danger/difficulties⟩ darse* cuenta de; I ~ that, but … lo comprendo, pero …
■ ~ vi «shares/property» (re)valorizarse*

appreciation /əˌpriːʃiˈeɪʃən/ n (a) (gratitude) agradecimiento m (b) (discriminating enjoyment): he showed a genuine ~ of music demostró saber apreciar la música

appreciative /əˈpriːʃətɪv/ adj (a) (grateful) ⟨smile/gesture⟩ de agradecimiento (b) (of art, good food) apreciativo

apprehend /ˈæprɪˈhend/ vt (frml) apresar, detener*

apprehension /ˌæprɪˈhentʃən ‖ˌæprɪˈhenʃən/ n aprensión f

apprehensive /ˌæprɪˈhensɪv/ adj ⟨look⟩ aprensivo, de aprensión; I'm rather ~ about the consequences estoy algo inquieto por lo que pueda pasar

apprentice¹ /əˈprentəs ‖əˈprentɪs/ n aprendiz, -diza m,f

apprentice² vt: to be ~d TO sb estar* de aprendiz CON algn

apprenticeship /əˈprentəsʃɪp ‖əˈprentɪsʃɪp/ n aprendizaje m (de un oficio); to serve an ~ in sth hacer* el aprendizaje de algo

approach¹ /əˈprəʊtʃ/ vi acercarse*, aproximarse
■ ~ vt (a) (draw near to) aproximarse or acercarse* a (b) (talk to): have you ~ed her about it? ¿ya se lo ha planteado?, ¿ya ha hablado con ella del asunto?; he ~ed me for a loan se dirigió a mí para pedirme un préstamo (c) (tackle) ⟨problem/ question⟩ enfocar*

approach² n ① (method, outlook) enfoque m ② (overture — offering sth) propuesta f; (— requesting sth) solicitud f, petición f, pedido m (AmL) ③ (drawing near): at the ~ of winter al acercarse el invierno ④ (means of entering) acceso m

approachable /əˈprəʊtʃəbəl/ adj ⟨person/ place⟩ accesible

appropriate¹ /əˈprəʊpriət/ adj apropiado

appropriate² /əˈprəʊprieɪt/ vt ⟨possessions⟩ apropiarse de; ⟨money⟩ destinar

approval /əˈpruːvəl/ n aprobación f; on ~ a prueba

approve /əˈpruːv/ vi to ~ (OF sth/sb): they don't ~ of my smoking les parece mal que fume; mother seems to ~ of him a mamá parece gustarle; I don't ~ of his methods no estoy de acuerdo con sus métodos
■ ~ vt ⟨decision/plan⟩ aprobar*

approving /əˈpruːvɪŋ/ adj ⟨smile/look⟩ de aprobación

approximate /əˈprɑːksəmət ‖əˈprɒksɪmət/ adj aproximado

approximately /əˈprɑːksəmətli ‖əˈprɒksɪmətli/ adv aproximadamente

approximation /əˌprɑːksəˈmeɪʃən ‖əˌprɒksɪˈmeɪʃən/ n aproximación f

apricot /ˈæprɪkɑːt ‖ˈeɪprɪkɒt/ n albaricoque m or (Méx) chabacano m or (AmS) damasco m

April /ˈeɪprəl ‖ˈeɪprɪl/ n abril m; (before n) ~ Fools' Day ≈ el día de los (Santos) Inocentes (en EEUU y GB se celebra el 1° de abril)

apron /ˈeɪprən/ n delantal m, mandil m (Esp)

apt /æpt/ adj (a) (fitting, suitable) acertado (b) (likely) to be ~ to + INF ser* propenso a + INF

aptitude /ˈæptətuːd ‖ˈæptɪtjuːd/ n ~ (FOR sth) aptitud f (PARA algo)

aquarium /əˈkweriəm ‖əˈkweəriəm/ n (pl -riums or -ria /-riə/) acuario m

Aquarius /əˈkweriəs ‖əˈkweəriəs/ n (a) (sign) (no art) Acuario (b) (person) Acuario or acuario mf, acuariano, -na m,f

aquatic /əˈkwætɪk, əˈkwɑːtɪk ‖əˈkwætɪk/ adj acuático

AR = Arkansas

Arab¹ /ˈærəb/ adj árabe

Arab² n árabe mf

Arabian /əˈreɪbiən/ adj árabe; the ~ Sea el Mar de Omán

Arabic¹ /ˈærəbɪk/ adj árabe; a~ numerals números mpl arábigos

Arabic² n árabe m

arable /ˈærəbəl/ adj arable; ~ land tierras fpl de cultivo

arbiter /ˈɑːrbətər ‖ˈɑːbɪtə(r)/ n árbitro, -tra m,f

arbitrary /ˈɑːrbəˌtreri ‖ˈɑːbɪtrəri/ adj arbitrario

arbitrate /ˈɑːrbətreɪt ‖ˈɑːbɪtreɪt/ vt ⟨dispute⟩ arbitrar (en)
■ ~ vi arbitrar

arbitration /ˌɑːrbəˈtreɪʃən, ˌɑːbɪˈtreɪʃən/ n arbitraje m

arc /ɑːrk ‖ɑːk/ n arco m

arcade /ɑːrˈkeɪd ‖ɑːˈkeɪd/ n (a) (Archit) arcada f; (around square, along street) soportales mpl, recova f (Arg) (b) (of shops) galería f comercial

arch¹ /ɑːrtʃ ‖ɑːtʃ/ n arco m

arch² vt ⟨eyebrows/back⟩ arquear
■ ~ vi formar un arco

archaeologist etc (BrE) ▶ ARCHEOLOGIST etc

archaic /ɑːrˈkeɪɪk ‖ɑːˈkeɪɪk/ adj arcaico

archangel /ˈɑːrkˌeɪndʒəl ‖ˈɑːkˌeɪndʒəl/ n arcángel m

archbishop /ˈɑːrtʃˈbɪʃəp ‖ˌɑːtʃˈbɪʃəp/ n arzobispo m

archenemy /ˈɑːrtʃˈenəmi ‖ˌɑːtʃˈenəmi/ n (pl -mies) archienemigo, -ga m,f

archeologist, (BrE) **archaeologist** /ˈɑːrkiɑːlədʒəst ‖ˌɑːkiˈɒlədʒɪst/ n arqueólogo, -ga m,f

archeology, (BrE) **archaeology** /ˈɑːrkiɑːlədʒi ‖ˌɑːkiˈɒlədʒi/ n arqueología f

archer /ˈɑːrtʃər ‖ˈɑːtʃə(r)/ n arquero, -ra m,f

archery /ˈɑːrtʃəri ‖ˈɑːtʃəri/ n tiro m con or al arco

architect /ˈɑːrkətekt ‖ˈɑːkɪtekt/ n arquitecto, -ta m,f

architecture /ˈɑːrkətektʃər ‖ˈɑːkɪtektʃə(r)/ n arquitectura f

archive /ˈɑːrkaɪv ‖ˈɑːkaɪv/ n (often pl) archivo m

Arctic¹ /ˈɑːrktɪk ‖ˈɑːktɪk/ adj ártico; the ~ Ocean el Océano (Glacial) Ártico, el Ártico; the ~ Circle el círculo polar ártico

Arctic² n the ~ la región ártica, el Ártico

ardent /ˈɑːrdnt ‖ˈɑːdnt/ adj ⟨supporter⟩ apasionado; ⟨plea/desire⟩ ferviente

ardor, (BrE) **ardour** /'ɑːrdər ‖'ɑːdə(r)/ n (liter) (zeal) fervor m, ardor m; (love) pasión f

arduous /'ɑːrdʒuəs ‖'ɑːdjuːəs/ adj ⟨task⟩ arduo; ⟨training/conditions⟩ duro; ⟨march/climb⟩ difícil

are /ɑːr ‖ɑː(r), weak form ər/ 2nd pers sing, 1st, 2nd & 3rd pers pl pres of BE

area /'eriə ‖'eəriə/ n **1** (geographical) zona f, área f‡, región f; (neighborhood) barrio m; (urban) zona f **2** (part of room, building) zona f; **play ~** zona de recreo **3** (expanse, patch): **the shaded ~ represents ...** el área sombreada representa ...; **the wreckage was scattered over a wide ~** los restos del siniestro quedaron esparcidos sobre una extensa zona **4** (Math) superficie f, área f‡; (of room, land) superficie f **5** (field, sphere) terreno m; (of knowledge) campo m

area code n (AmE) código m de la zona (AmL), prefijo m (local) (Esp)

arena /ə'riːnə/ n **(a)** (of stadium) arena f **(b)** (scene of activity) ruedo m; **the political ~** el ruedo político

aren't /ɑːrnt ‖ɑːnt/ = **are not**

Argentina /'ɑːrdʒən'tiːnə ‖,ɑːdʒən'tiːnə/ n Argentina f

Argentine /'ɑːrdʒəntaɪn ‖'ɑːdʒəntaɪn/ adj argentino

Argentinian¹ /'ɑːrdʒən'tɪniən ‖,ɑːdʒən'tɪniən/ adj argentino

Argentinian² n argentino, -na m,f

arguably /'ɑːrgjuəbli ‖'ɑːgjuːəbli/ adv (indep): **this is ~ his best novel** podría decirse que esta es su mejor novela

argue /'ɑːrgjuː ‖'ɑːgjuː/ vi **1** (quarrel) discutir; (more heatedly) pelear(se), reñir* (esp Esp); **don't ~ with me!** ¡no me discutas! **2** (reason): **she ~s convincingly** sabe expresar su punto de vista de manera muy convincente; **he ~s against changing the law** da razones en contra de que se cambie la ley
■ **~** vt **(a)** (put forward) ⟨case⟩ exponer* **(b)** (present as argument) argüir*, sostener*; **supporters of the bill ~ that ...** los partidarios del proyecto arguyen or sostienen que ...

argument /'ɑːrgjəmənt ‖'ɑːgjʊmənt/ n **1** (quarrel) discusión f; (more heated) pelea f, riña f (esp Esp); **to have an ~ with sb** tener* una discusión con algn; (more heatedly) pelearse or (esp Esp) reñir* con algn **2** (debate) polémica f **3** **(a)** (case) ~ (FOR/AGAINST) sth razones fpl or argumentos mpl (A FAVOR/EN CONTRA DE) algo **(b)** (line of reasoning) razonamiento m

argumentative /'ɑːrgjə'mentətɪv ‖,ɑːgjʊ'mentətɪv/ adj discutidor

arid /'ærəd ‖'ærɪd/ adj árido

Aries /'eriːz ‖'eəriːz/ n **(a)** (sign) (no art) Aries **(b)** (person) Aries or aries m,f, ariano, -na m,f

arise /ə'raɪz/ vi (past **arose**; past p **arisen** /ə'rɪzən/) ⟨difficulty/opportunity⟩ surgir*; **if the need ~s** si fuera necesario

aristocracy /'ærə'stɑːkrəsi ‖,ærɪ'stɒkrəsi/ n (pl **-cies**) aristocracia f

aristocrat /ə'rɪstəkræt ‖'ærɪstəkræt/ n aristócrata m,f

aristocratic /ə'rɪstə'krætɪk ‖,ærɪstə'krætɪk/ adj aristocrático

arithmetic /ə'rɪθmətɪk/ n aritmética f

Ariz = **Arizona**

Ark¹ = **Arkansas**

Ark² /ɑːrk ‖ɑːk/ n arca f‡; **Noah's ~** el arca de Noé

arm¹ /ɑːrm ‖ɑːm/ n **1** (Anat) brazo m; **they walked along ~ in ~** iban del brazo **2** **(a)** (of chair, crane) brazo m **(b)** (of garment) manga f **3** **arms** pl (weapons) armas fpl

arm² vt armar; see also ARMED

armament /'ɑːrməmənt ‖'ɑːməmənt/ n armamento m

arm: ~band n (to denote rank, mourning etc) brazalete m; (for swimming) flotador m (que se coloca en el brazo), alita f (AmS); **~chair** n sillón m, butaca f

armed /ɑːrmd ‖ɑːmd/ adj ⟨resistance/struggle⟩ armado; **the ~ forces** las fuerzas armadas; **~ robbery** robo m a mano armada

Armenia /ɑːr'miːniə ‖ɑː'miːniə/ n Armenia f

Armenian /ɑːr'miːniən ‖ɑː'miːniən/ adj armenio

armistice /'ɑːrməstəs ‖'ɑːmɪstɪs/ n armisticio m

armor, (BrE) **armour** /'ɑːrmər ‖'ɑːmə(r)/ n armadura f; **suit of ~** armadura f

armored, (BrE) **armoured** /'ɑːrmərd ‖'ɑːməd/ adj blindado

armor-plated, (BrE) **armour-plated** /'ɑːrmər'pleɪtəd ‖,ɑːmə'pleɪtɪd/ adj blindado

armory, (BrE) **armoury** /'ɑːrməri ‖'ɑːməri/ n (pl **-ries**) **(a)** (storehouse) arsenal m **(b)** (factory) (AmE) fábrica f de armas

arm: ~pit n axila f, sobaco m; **~rest** n (of chair, sofa) brazo m; (of car, airplane seat) apoyabrazos m

arms race n carrera f armamentista

army /'ɑːrmi ‖'ɑːmi/ n (pl **armies**) ejército m

aroma /ə'rəumə/ n aroma m

aromatic /'ærə'mætɪk/ adj aromático

arose /ə'rəuz/ past of ARISE

around¹ /ə'raund/ adv **1** **(a)** (in a circle): **~ and ~ they drove** estuvieron dando vueltas y vueltas con el coche **(b)** (so as to face in different direction): **she glanced ~** echó un vistazo a su alrededor; see also TURN etc AROUND **(c)** (on all sides): **there's nothing for miles ~** no hay nada en millas a la redonda; **everyone crowded ~** todo el mundo se apiñó alrededor **2** (in the vicinity): **is John ~?** ¿anda or está John por ahí?; **there's no one ~** aquí no hay nadie **3** (from one place to another): **he keeps following me ~** me sigue a todas partes; **he knows his way ~** conoce la ciudad (or la zona etc)

AmC	Central America	Arg	Argentina	Cu	Cuba	Per	Peru
AmL	Latin America	Bol	Bolivia	Ec	Ecuador	RPI	River Plate Area
AmS	South America	Chi	Chile	Esp	Spain	Ur	Uruguay
Andes	Andean Region	CS	Southern Cone	Méx	Mexico	Ven	Venezuela

4 (approximately) más o menos; **he must be ∼ 35** debe (de) tener unos 35; **at ∼ five thirty** alrededor de *or* a eso de las cinco y media, sobre las cinco y media (Esp); **∼ 1660** alrededor de 1660

around² *prep* **1** (encircling) alrededor de; **he put his arm ∼ her** la rodeó con el brazo; **they sailed ∼ the world** dieron la vuelta al mundo en un velero **2** **(a)** (in the vicinity of) alrededor de; **do you live ∼ here?** ¿vives por aquí? **(b)** (within, through): **they traveled ∼ Europe** viajaron por Europa; **she took them ∼ the house** les mostró la casa

arouse /əˈraʊz/ *vt* ⟨*interest/suspicion*⟩ despertar*; (sexually) excitar

arrange /əˈreɪndʒ/ *vt* **1** **(a)** (put in certain order, position) ⟨*furniture/flowers*⟩ arreglar **(b)** (put in order) arreglar **2** (fix up in advance) ⟨*meeting/party*⟩ organizar*; ⟨*date/fee*⟩ fijar; ⟨*deal/appointment*⟩ concertar*; ⟨*loan*⟩ tramitar; **she had ∼d to meet them for lunch** había quedado en encontrarse con ellos para comer, había quedado con ellos para comer (Esp)

▪ ∼ *vi*: **could you ∼ for the carpets to be cleaned?** ¿podría encargarse de que alguien venga a limpiar las alfombras?; **we've ∼d for you to see the specialist** le hemos pedido hora *or* una cita con el especialista

arrangement /əˈreɪndʒmənt/ *n* **1** (of furniture) disposición *f*; **a flower ∼** un arreglo floral **2** (agreement): **we made an ∼ to meet the next day** quedamos en encontrarnos al día siguiente; **I have an ∼ with the bank** tengo un acuerdo con el banco **3** **arrangements** *pl* (plans) planes *mpl*; (for a funeral) preparativos *mpl*; **what are the sleeping ∼s?** ¿cómo vamos (*or* van *etc*) a dormir? **4** (Mus) arreglo *m*

array /əˈreɪ/ *n* selección *f*

arrears /əˈrɪrz ‖əˈrɪəz/ *pl n* atrasos *mpl*; **to be in ∼ with the rent** estar* atrasado en el pago del alquiler; **salaries are paid monthly in ∼** los sueldos se pagan mensualmente, una vez cumplido cada mes de trabajo

arrest¹ /əˈrest/ *n* detención *f*, arresto *m*; **to be under ∼** estar* detenido *or* arrestado

arrest² *vt* **1** (detain) detener*, arrestar **2** ⟨*progress/growth*⟩ (hinder) dificultar; (halt) detener*; ⟨*decline*⟩ atajar

arrival /əˈraɪvəl/ *n* llegada *f*, arribo *m* (esp AmL frml); **on ∼** al llegar

arrive /əˈraɪv/ *vi* llegar*; **to ∼ AT** llegar* A

arrogance /ˈærəgəns/ *n* arrogancia *f*

arrogant /ˈærəgənt/ *adj* arrogante

arrow /ˈærəʊ/ *n* flecha *f*

arse /ɑːrs ‖ɑːs/ *n* (BrE vulg) culo *m* (fam: en algunas regiones vulg)

arsenal /ˈɑːrsṇəl ‖ˈɑːsənḷ/ *n* arsenal *m*

arson /ˈɑːrsṇ ‖ˈɑːsṇ/ *n* incendiarismo *m*

arsonist /ˈɑːrsṇəst ‖ˈɑːsənɪst/ *n* incendiario, -ria *m,f*, pirómano, -na *m,f*

art /ɑːrt ‖ɑːt/ *n* **1** **(a)** arte *m*; **she's studying ∼** estudia Bellas Artes; (*before n*) ⟨*class*⟩ de arte; (in school) de dibujo; **∼ gallery** (museum) museo *m* de arte; (commercial) galería *f* de arte; **∼ school** *o* **college** escuela *f* de Bellas Artes **(b)** (artwork) trabajos *mpl* artísticos; **∼s and crafts** artesanía **2** **arts** *pl* **(a) the ∼s** la cultura y las artes **(b)** (BrE Educ) letras *fpl*

artefact /ˈɑːrtɪfækt ‖ˈɑːtɪfækt/ *n* (BrE) artefacto *m*

artery /ˈɑːrtəri ‖ˈɑːtəri/ *n* (*pl* **-ries**) arteria *f*

arthritis /ɑːrˈθraɪtɪs ‖ɑːˈθraɪtɪs/ *n* artritis *f*

artichoke /ˈɑːrtətʃəʊk ‖ˈɑːtɪtʃəʊk/ *n* **(a)** (globe ∼) alcachofa *f*, alcaucil *m* (RPl) **(b)** (Jerusalem ∼) aguaturma *f*, pataca *f*

article /ˈɑːrtɪkəl ‖ˈɑːtɪkəl/ *n* **1** (thing, item) artículo *m*; **an ∼ of clothing** una prenda (de vestir) **2** (in newspaper, encyclopedia) artículo *m* **3** (Ling) artículo *m*

articulate¹ /ɑːrˈtɪkjʊleɪt ‖ɑːˈtɪkjʊleɪt/ *vt* **(a)** ⟨*idea/feeling*⟩ expresar **(b)** ⟨*word/sound*⟩ articular

articulate² /ɑːrˈtɪkjʊlət ‖ɑːˈtɪkjʊlət/ *adj* ⟨*utterance*⟩ articulado; **he's very ∼** se expresa muy bien

articulated lorry /ɑːrˈtɪkjʊleɪtəd ‖ɑːˈtɪkjəleɪtɪd/ *n* (BrE) camión *m* articulado

artifact /ˈɑːrtɪfækt/, (BrE) **artefact** *n* artefacto *m*

artificial /ˌɑːrtəˈfɪʃəl ‖ˌɑːtɪˈfɪʃəl/ *adj* artificial; ⟨*leather*⟩ sintético; ⟨*arm/leg*⟩ ortopédico; **∼ respiration** respiración *f* artificial

artillery /ɑːrˈtɪləri ‖ɑːˈtɪləri/ *n* artillería *f*

artisan /ˈɑːrtəzən/ *n* artesano, -na *m,f*

artist /ˈɑːrtəst ‖ˈɑːtɪst/ *n* **(a)** (writer, musician, painter, sculptor) artista *mf* **(b)** (performer) (Mus) intérprete *mf*; (Theat) actor, -triz *m,f*, artista *mf*

artistic /ɑːrˈtɪstɪk ‖ɑːˈtɪstɪk/ *adj* artístico

as¹ /æz, *weak form* əz/ *conj* **1** **(a)** (when, while) cuando; **∼ she was eating breakfast ...** cuando *or* mientras tomaba el desayuno ... **(b)** (indicating progression) a medida que; **∼ the date drew closer, ...** a medida que se acercaba la fecha, ... **2** (because, since) como **3** (though): **try ∼ he might, he could not open it** por más que trató, no pudo abrirlo; **strange ∼ it may seem** por extraño que parezca **4** (in accordance with) como; **∼ I was saying** como iba diciendo **5** **(a)** (in the way that) como; **do ∼ I say** haz lo que te digo; **I'm only interested in the changes ∼ they affect me** solo me interesan los cambios en la medida en que me afectan a mí **(b)** (in phrases) **as it is: we've got too much work ∼ it is** ya tenemos demasiado trabajo; **as it were** por así decirlo **6** (in comparisons of equal degree) **as ... as** tan ... como; **there weren't ∼ many people ∼ last time** no había tanta gente como la última vez **7** **as if/as though** como si (+ *subj*)

as² *adv* **1** (equally): **it's not ∼ cold today** hoy no hace tanto frío; **I can't run ∼ quickly now** no puedo correr tan rápido ahora **2 as ... as: ∼ many ∼ 400 people** hasta 400 personas; **∼ long ago ∼ 1960** ya en 1960

as³ *prep* **1** (in the condition, role of): **∼ a child she adored dancing** de pequeña le encantaba bailar; **∼ a teacher ...** como maestro ...; **he works ∼ a clerk** trabaja de oficinista **2** (in phrases) **as for** en cuanto a; **as of** *o* **as from** desde, a partir de

asbestos /æsˈbestəs/ *n* asbesto *m*, amianto *m*

ASBO *n* /ˈæzbəʊ/ (BrE) = **Anti-Social Behaviour Order**

ascend /əˈsend/ *vi* (frml) **(a)** «*person/rocket*» ascender* (frml) **(b) ascending** *pres p* ⟨*slope/spiral/scale*⟩ ascendente   ···⫸

a

■ ~ *vt* (fml) ⟨*steps*⟩ subir; ⟨*mountain*⟩ escalar

ascension /ə'sentʃən ‖ə'senʃən/ *n* the A~ (Relig) la Ascensión

ascent /ə'sent/ *n* **(a)** (of mountain) escalada *f* **(b)** (rise) ascenso *m* **(c)** (slope) subida *f*

ascertain /'æsər'teɪn‖,æsə'teɪn/ *vt* establecer*

ASCII /'æski/ (*no art*) (= **American standard code for information interchange**) ASCII *m*

ascribe /ə'skraɪb/ *vt* to ~ sth TO sth/sb atribuirle* algo A algo/algn

aseptic /eɪ'septɪk/ *adj* aséptico

ash /æʃ/ *n* **1** **(a)** (*often pl*) ceniza *f* **(b)** **ashes** *pl* (cremated remains) cenizas *fpl* **2** ~ **(tree)** fresno *m*

ashamed /ə'ʃeɪmd/ *adj* (*pred*) avergonzado, apenado (AmL exc CS); **she was** ~ **of what she'd done** estaba avergonzada de *or* (AmL exc CS) apenada por lo que había hecho; **to be** ~ **OF sb** avergonzarse* DE algn; **he's** ~ **to ask** le da vergüenza *or* (AmL exc CS) pena preguntar

ashcan /'æʃkæn/ *n* (AmE) ▶ GARBAGE CAN

ashore /ə'ʃɔːr/ *adv* en tierra; **to go** ~ desembarcar*; **we swam** ~ nadamos hasta la orilla

ash: ~**tray** *n* cenicero *m*; **A**~ **Wednesday** *n* miércoles *m* de Ceniza

Asia /'eɪʒə, 'eɪʃə ‖'eɪʃə/ *n* Asia *f*‡

Asian¹ /'eɪʒən, 'eɪʃən ‖'eɪʃən/ *adj* **(a)** (of Asia) asiático **(b)** (from the Indian subcontinent) (BrE) *de India, Pakistán etc*

Asian² *n* **(a)** (from Asia) asiático, -ca *m,f* **(b)** (from the Indian subcontinent) (BrE) *persona proveniente de India, Pakistán etc*

aside¹ /ə'saɪd/ *adv* **1** a un lado; *see also* PUT ASIDE, SET ASIDE, STAND² 2A, STEP ASIDE, TAKE ASIDE **2** **aside from** (*as prep*) (esp AmE) **(a)** (except for) aparte de **(b)** (as well as) aparte de, además de

aside² *n* aparte *m*

ask /æsk ‖ɑːsk/ *vt* **1** (inquire) preguntar; (inquire of) preguntarle a; **to** ~ **sb sth** preguntarle algo A algn; **have you** ~**ed him about his trip?** ¿le has preguntado por el viaje?
2 (request) ⟨*approval/advice/favor*⟩ pedir*; **to** ~ **sb FOR sth** pedirle* algo A algn; **to** ~ **sb to + INF** pedirle* A algn QUE (+ *subj*); **I** ~**ed to see the manager** pedí hablar con el director
3 (invite) invitar; **to** ~ **sb** (TO sth) invitar A algn (A algo); **to** ~ **sb out** invitar a algn a salir
■ ~ *vi* **1** (inquire) preguntar
2 (request): **there's no harm in** ~**ing** con preguntar no se pierde nada; **to** ~ **FOR sth** pedir* algo; **to** ~ **FOR sb** preguntar POR algn
■ **ask after** [*v + prep + o*] preguntar por

askance /ə'skæns/ *adv*: **to look** ~ **at sb** mirar a algn con recelo

askew /ə'skjuː/ *adv* torcido

asleep /ə'sliːp/ *adj* (*pred*): **to be** ~ estar* dormido; **to fall** ~ dormirse*

asparagus /ə'spærəgəs/ *n* espárrago *m*

ASPCA *n* = **American Society for the Prevention of Cruelty to Animals**

aspect /'æspekt/ *n* **1** (feature, facet) aspecto *m* **2** (fml) (orientation) orientación *f*

aspersions /ə'spɜːrʒənz ‖ə'spɜːʃənz/ *pl n* (sometimes sing): **to cast** ~ **on sth/sb** poner* algo/a algn en entredicho

asphalt /'æsfɔːlt ‖'æsfælt/ *n* asfalto *m*

asphyxiate /æs'fɪksieɪt/ *vt* asfixiar

aspiration /'æspə'reɪʃən ‖,æspɪ'reɪʃən/ *n* aspiración *f*

aspire /ə'spaɪr ‖ə'spaɪə(r)/ *vi* **(a)** to ~ TO sth aspirar A algo **(b)** **aspiring** *pres p*: **aspiring writers** personas que aspiran a ser escritores

aspirin /'æsprən ‖'æsprɪn/ *n* (*pl* ~ *or* **-rins**) aspirina *f*

ass /æs/ *n* **1** **(a)** (donkey) (liter) asno *m*, jumento *m* (liter) **(b)** (idiot) (colloq) imbécil *mf* **2** (part of body) (AmE vulg) culo *m* (fam: en algunas regiones vulg)

assailant /ə'seɪlənt/ *n* (fml) agresor, -sora *m,f*

assassin /ə'sæsn ‖ə'sæsɪn/ *n* asesino, -na *m,f* (*de un personaje importante*)

assassinate /ə'sæsɪneɪt ‖ə'sæsɪneɪt/ *vt* asesinar (*a un personaje importante*)

assassination /ə'sæsə'neɪʃən ‖ə,sæsɪ'neɪʃən/ *n* asesinato *m* (*de un personaje importante*)

assault¹ /ə'sɔːlt/ *n* **1** (Law) (violence) agresión *f*, (molestation) agresión *f* sexual **2** **(a)** (Mil) asalto *m* **(b)** (onslaught) ~ (ON sth) ataque *m* (A algo)

assault² *vt* (use violence against) agredir*; (sexually) agredir* sexualmente

assemble /ə'sembəl/ *vt* **(a)** (construct) montar; ⟨*model*⟩ armar **(b)** (get together) reunir* **(c)** (gather) ⟨*facts*⟩ recopilar; ⟨*collection*⟩ reunir*
■ ~ *vi* (gather) reunirse*

assembly /ə'sembli/ *n* (*pl* **-blies**) **1** **(a)** (coming together) reunión *f* **(b)** (group) concurrencia *f* **(c)** (Govt) asamblea *f* **(d)** (Educ) (*no art*) reunión de profesores y alumnos, al iniciarse la jornada escolar **2** (Tech)(process) montaje *m*; (*before n*) ~ **line** cadena *f* de montaje

assent¹ /ə'sent/ *n* asentimiento *m*; **to give one's** ~ **to sth** dar* su (*or mi etc*) conformidad a algo

assent² *vi* asentir*; **to** ~ **TO sth** acceder A algo

assert /ə'sɜːrt ‖ə'sɜːt/ *vt* **(a)** (declare) afirmar **(b)** (demonstrate, enforce) ⟨*superiority*⟩ reafirmar; ⟨*rights/claims*⟩ hacer* valer
■ *v refl* to ~ **oneself** hacerse* valer

assertion /ə'sɜːrʃən ‖ə'sɜːʃən/ *n* **(a)** (declaration) afirmación *f* **(b)** (demonstration) reafirmación *f*

assertive /ə'sɜːrtɪv ‖ə'sɜːtɪv/ *adj* ⟨*tone*⟩ autoritario; **to be** ~ ser* firme y enérgico

assess /ə'ses/ *vt* ⟨*value/amount*⟩ calcular; ⟨*student/performance*⟩ evaluar*; ⟨*situation*⟩ aquilatar

assessment /ə'sesmənt/ *n* (of performance, results) evaluación *f*; (of amount) cálculo *m*

asset /'æset/ *n* **(a)** (valuable quality): **her intelligence is her greatest** ~ su inteligencia es su gran baza; **she's an** ~ **to the company** es una empleada muy valiosa para la compañía **(b)** **assets** *pl* (Fin) activo *m*

asset stripping /'strɪpɪŋ/ *n* vaciamiento *m*

assiduous /ə'sɪdʒuəs ‖ə'sɪdjʊəs/ *adj* (fml) ⟨*student*⟩ diligente

assign /ə'saɪn/ *vt* **(a)** (appoint) to ~ **sb** TO sth nombrar a algn PARA algo **(b)** (allocate) asignar

assignment /ə'saɪnmənt/ n ① (a) (mission) misión f (b) (task) función f (c) (schoolwork) tarea f ② (a) (posting) nombramiento m (b) (allocation) asignación f

assimilate /ə'sɪməleɪt ‖ə'sɪmɪleɪt/ vt asimilar

assimilation /ə'sɪmə'leɪʃən ‖ə,sɪmɪ'leɪʃən/ n asimilación f

assist /ə'sɪst/ vt ayudar

assistance /ə'sɪstəns/ n ayuda f

assistant¹ /ə'sɪstənt/ n (a) (in shop) dependiente, -ta m,f, empleado, -da m,f (AmL) (b) (subordinate, helper) ayudante mf; **clerical ~** auxiliar administrativo, -va m,f (c) (language ~) (BrE) (in university) ayudante mf or (Esp) lector, -tora m,f; (in school) auxiliar mf de lengua

assistant² adj (before n): **~ manager** subdirector, -tora m,f

associate¹ /ə'səʊʃieɪt, -sieɪt/ vt (a) (involve, connect) (usu pass) vincular (b) (link in mind) asociar
■ ~ vi **to ~ (with sb)** relacionarse (con algn)

associate² /ə'səʊʃiət, -siət/ n (a) (in business, profession) colega mf (b) (member of professional body) colegiado, -da m,f

associate³ /ə'səʊʃiət, -siət/ adj (before n) ⟨member⟩ no numerario; ⟨editor/professor⟩ (AmE) adjunto

association /ə'səʊʃi'eɪʃən, -si'eɪʃən/ n asociación f; **in ~ with** (as prep) en asociación con

assorted /ə'sɔːtəd ‖ə'sɔːtɪd/ adj (before n) surtido

assortment /ə'sɔːtmənt ‖ə'sɔːtmənt/ n surtido m

assuage /ə'sweɪdʒ/ vt (liter) (a) (satisfy) ⟨hunger/ desire⟩ saciar (liter) (b) (ease) ⟨pain/grief⟩ aliviar (c) (calm) ⟨anxiety⟩ calmar; ⟨fear⟩ disipar

assume /ə'suːm ‖ə'sjuːm/ vt ① (suppose) suponer* ② (frml) ⟨duties/command/responsibility⟩ asumir; **~d name** nombre m ficticio

assumption /ə'sʌmpʃən/ n ① (supposition): **the ~ was that ...** se suponía que ...; **his reasoning is based on the ~ that ...** su razonamiento se basa en el supuesto de que ... ② (frml) (of duties, leadership, responsibility) asunción f

assurance /ə'ʃʊərəns ‖ə'ʃʊərəns, ə'ʃɔːrəns/ n ① (guarantee): **she gave me her ~ that ...** me aseguró que ... ② (self-confidence) seguridad f en sí mismo ③ (insurance) (BrE) seguro m

assure /ə'ʃʊr ‖ə'ʃʊə(r), ə'ʃɔː(r)/ vt ① (a) (guarantee) asegurar (b) (convince) convencer* ② (make certain) **to ~ sb (of) sth: this work will ~ me (of) a regular income** este trabajo me asegurará una entrada fija ③ (insure) (BrE) ⟨life⟩ asegurar

asterisk /'æstərɪsk/ n asterisco m

asteroid /'æstərɔɪd/ n asteroide m

asthma /'æzmə ‖'æsmə/ n asma f‡

asthmatic /æz'mætɪk ‖æs'mætɪk/ adj asmático

astonish /ə'stɑːnɪʃ ‖ə'stɒnɪʃ/ vt asombrar; (more intensely) dejar pasmado

astonished /ə'stɑːnɪʃt ‖ə'stɒnɪʃt/ adj asombrado; **the ~ look on their faces** la cara de asombro que pusieron; **I'm ~ (that) he got so far** me asombra que haya llegado tan lejos

astonishing /ə'stɑːnɪʃɪŋ ‖ə'stɒnɪʃɪŋ/ adj asombroso; (more intensely) pasmoso

astonishment /ə'stɑːnɪʃmənt ‖ə'stɒnɪʃmənt/ n asombro m; (more intense) estupefacción f

astound /ə'staʊnd/ vt dejar estupefacto

astounded /ə'staʊndəd/ adj atónito

astounding /ə'staʊndɪŋ/ adj increíble

astray /ə'streɪ/ adv: **to go ~** (get lost) extraviarse*; (do wrong) (euph or hum) descarriarse*; **to lead sb ~** (euph or hum) llevar a algn por mal camino

astride /ə'straɪd/ prep: **he sat ~ the fence/ horse** estaba sentado en la valla/montado en el caballo a horcajadas

astringent /ə'strɪndʒənt/ adj astringente

astrologer /ə'strɑːlədʒər/ n astrólogo, -ga m,f

astrology /ə'strɑːlədʒi ‖ə'strɒlədʒi/ n astrología f

astronaut /'æstrənɔːt/ n astronauta mf

astronomer /ə'strɑːnəmər ‖ə'strɒnəmə(r)/ n astrónomo, -ma m,f

astronomical /'æstrə'nɑːmɪkəl ‖,æstrə'nɒmɪkəl/ adj astronómico

astronomy /ə'strɑːnəmi ‖ə'strɒnəmi/ n astronomía f

astute /ə'stuːt ‖ə'stjuːt/ adj ⟨person⟩ sagaz; ⟨decision⟩ inteligente

asylee /asaɪ'liː/ n (AmE) asilado -da m,f político -ca

asylum /ə'saɪləm/ n (a) (refuge) asilo m (b) (lunatic ~) manicomio m; **~ seeker** solicitante mf de asilo

at /æt, weak form ət/ prep ① (location) en; **she's ~ the office** está en la oficina; **he's ~ the bank** ha ido al banco ② (direction): **to point ~ sth/sb** señalar algo/a algn; **he smiled ~ me** me sonrió ③ (time): **~ 6 o'clock** a las seis; **~ Christmas** en Navidad, por Navidades (Esp); **~ night** por la noche, de noche ④ (indicating state): **~ a disadvantage** en desventaja; **~ war/peace** en guerra/paz (b) (occupied with): **people ~ work** gente trabajando; **children ~ play** niños jugando ⑤ (with measurements, numbers, rates etc): **they sell them ~ around $80** las venden a alrededor de $80 ⑥ (because of): **he was surprised ~ the decision** le sorprendió la decisión

ate /eɪt/ past of EAT

atheism /'eɪθiɪzəm/ n ateísmo m

atheist /'eɪθiəst ‖'eɪθiɪst/ n ateo, atea m,f

Athens /'æθənz/ n Atenas f

athlete /'æθliːt/ n atleta mf

athlete's foot n pie m de atleta

athletic /æθ'letɪk/ adj atlético

athletics /æθ'letɪks/ n (+ sing or pl vb) (a) (active sports) (AmE) deportes mpl (b) (track and field) (esp BrE) atletismo m

Atlantic¹ /ət'læntɪk/ adj atlántico

Atlantic² n **the ~ (Ocean)** el (océano) Atlántico

atlas /'ætləs/ n atlas m

ATM n (AmE) (= **automated** or **automatic teller machine**) cajero m automático

atmosphere /'ætməsfɪr ‖'ætməsfɪə(r)/ n (a) (of planet) atmósfera f (b) (feeling, mood) ambiente m

atmospheric /'ætməs'ferɪk/ adj atmosférico

atom /'ætəm/ n átomo m

atomic /ə'tɑːmɪk ‖ə'tɒmɪk/ adj ‹warfare/ energy› atómico; ~ **bomb** bomba f atómica

atone /ə'təʊn/ vi (fml) to ~ **FOR** sth ‹for sins› expiar* algo; ‹for crime/harm› reparar algo

atrocious /ə'trəʊʃəs/ adj (a) (very bad) (colloq) ‹spelling/manners› espantoso (fam) (b) (horrifying) ‹injuries/conditions› atroz

atrocity /ə'trɑːsəti ‖ə'trɒsəti/ n (pl **-ties**) atrocidad f

attach /ə'tætʃ/ vt (fasten) sujetar; (tie) atar, amarrar (AmL exc RPl); (stick) pegar*; (to letter, document) adjuntar; **it is ~ed to the wall with screws** está sujeto a la pared con tornillos; **the ~ed form** el formulario adjunto; **to ~ importance to sth** dar(le) importancia a algo

attaché /ˌætæ'ʃeɪ ‖ə'tæʃeɪ/ n agregado, -da m,f

attaché case n maletín m

attached /ə'tætʃt/ adj (pred) (fond) **to be ~ TO sb/sth** tenerle* mucho cariño A algn/algo

attachment /ə'tætʃmənt/ n 1 (a) (part) accesorio m (b) (Comput) documento m adjunto 2 (fondness) ~ **(TO sb/sth)** cariño m **(POR** algn/ algo)

attack¹ /ə'tæk/ n (a) (physical, verbal) ataque m; **terrorist ~s** atentados mpl terroristas (b) (Med) ataque m; **heart ~** infarto m

attack² vt 1 (physically, verbally) atacar* 2 ‹task› acometer; ‹problem› combatir ■ ~ vi (Mil, Sport) atacar*

attacker /ə'tækər ‖ə'tækə(r)/ n agresor, -sora m,f

attain /ə'teɪn/ vt (fml) ‹position/goal› alcanzar*, lograr; ‹ambition› realizar*

attempt¹ /ə'tempt/ vt (a) (try) **to ~ to + INF/-ING** tratar DE or intentar + INF (b) (have a try at) «student» «exam question» intentar responder a (fml) (c) **attempted** past p: **~ed suicide/ murder** intento m de suicidio/tentativa f de asesinato

attempt² n intento m; **I made an ~ at conversation** traté de or intenté entablar conversación; **to make an ~ on sb's life** atentar contra la vida de algn

attend /ə'tend/ vt 1 (fml) (a) (be present at) asistir a (fml) (b) (go to regularly) ‹church/school/ classes› ir* a 2 ‹patient› atender* ■ ~ vi 1 (be present) asistir 2 (pay attention) **to ~ (TO sth)** atender* (A algo), poner* atención (A algo) (AmL) ■ **attend to** [v + prep + o] ‹patient/customer› atender*; ‹correspondence/filing› ocuparse de

attendance /ə'tendəns/ n (a) (presence) asistencia f; **to be in ~** estar* presente (b) (people present): **what was the ~?** ¿cuántos asistentes hubo?; **to take ~** (AmE) pasar lista

attendant /ə'tendənt/ n (in museum, parking lot) guarda m; (in pool, toilets) encargado, -da m,f

attention /ə'tentʃən ‖ə'tenʃən/ n 1 (a) (concentration) atención f; **to pay ~ to sth/sb** prestarle atención a algo/algn (b) (notice) atención f; **to catch sb's ~** atraer* la atención de algn; **it has been brought to my ~** o **it has come to my ~ that …** me han informado que … (c) (care) atención f 2 (Mil): **to stand to ~** ponerse* en posición de firme(s)

attentive /ə'tentɪv/ adj atento

attenuate /ə'tenjueɪt/ vt atenuar*; **attenuating circumstances** circunstancias fpl atenuantes

attic /'ætɪk/ n desván m, ático m, altillo m (esp AmL)

attire /ə'taɪr ‖ə'taɪə(r)/ n (liter) atuendo m (frml), atavío m (liter)

attitude /'ætətuːd ‖'ætɪtjuːd/ n actitud f

attorney /ə'tɜːrni ‖ə'tɜːni/ n (pl **-neys**) (AmE) abogado, -da m,f; see also POWER OF ATTORNEY

Attorney General n (pl **~s** or **~s ~**) (in US — at national level) ≈Ministro, -tra m,f de Justicia; (— at state level) ≈Fiscal mf General

attract /ə'trækt/ vt atraer*

attraction /ə'trækʃən/ n (a) (Phys) atracción f (b) (interest): **I still feel a great ~ toward the place** todavía me atrae mucho el lugar; **what's the ~?** ¿qué atractivo tiene? (c) (attractive feature) atractivo m; **tourist ~** atracción f turística

attractive /ə'træktɪv/ adj atractivo

attribute¹ /ə'trɪbjət ‖ə'trɪbjuːt/ vt **to ~ sth TO sth/sb** atribuirle* algo A algo/algn

attribute² /'ætrəbjuːt ‖'ætrɪbjuːt/ n atributo m

attrition /ə'trɪʃən/ n 1 (destruction) desgaste m; **war of ~** guerra f de desgaste 2 (AmE Lab Rel) bajas fpl vegetativas

aubergine /'əʊbərʒiːn ‖'əʊbəʒiːn/ n (BrE) berenjena f

auburn /'ɔːbərn ‖'ɔːbən/ adj castaño rojizo adj inv

auction¹ /'ɔːkʃən/ n subasta f, remate m (AmL)

auction² vt subastar, rematar (AmL)

auctioneer /'ɔːkʃəˈnɪr ‖ˌɔːkʃəˈnɪə(r)/ n subastador, -dora m,f, rematador, -dora m,f (AmL)

audacious /ɔː'deɪʃəs/ adj (a) (daring) ‹act/plan› audaz (b) (impudent) ‹behavior/person› atrevido

audacity /ɔː'dæsəti/ n (daring) audacia f; (impudence) atrevimiento m

audible /'ɔːdəbəl/ adj audible

audience /'ɔːdiəns/ n 1 (at play, film) público m; (at concert, lecture) auditorio m; (TV) audiencia f 2 (interview) audiencia f

audio- /'ɔːdiəʊ/ pref audio-

audio: ~**book** n audiolibro m; ~**-visual** adj audiovisual

audit¹ /'ɔːdət ‖'ɔːdɪt/ vt (a) (Busn, Fin) ‹accounts› auditar (b) (AmE Educ) ‹classes/course› asistir como oyente a

···

AmC	América Central	Arg	Argentina	Cu	Cuba	Per	Perú
AmL	América Latina	Bol	Bolivia	Ec	Ecuador	RPl	Río de la Plata
AmS	América del Sur	Chi	Chile	Esp	España	Ur	Uruguay
Andes	Región andina	CS	Cono Sur	Méx	México	Ven	Venezuela

audit² *n* (Busn, Fin) **(a)** (inspection) auditoría *f* **(b)** (report) (AmE) informe *m* de auditoría

audition¹ /ɔː'dɪʃən/ *vi*: **to ~ (FOR sth)** dar* una audición (PARA algo)

audition² *n* audición *f*

auditor /'ɔːdətər ‖'ɔːdɪtə(r)/ *n* **(a)** (Busn, Fin) auditor, -tora *m,f* **(b)** (AmE Educ) oyente *mf*

auditorium /ˌɔːdə'tɔːriəm ‖ˌɔːdɪ'tɔːriəm/ *n* (*pl* **-riums** *or* **-ria** /-riə/) auditorio *m*

augment /ɔːg'ment/ *vt* (frml) aumentar, incrementar (frml)

augur /'ɔːgər ‖'ɔːgə(r)/ *vi*: **to ~ well/ill** ser* de buen/mal agüero

august /ɔː'gʌst/ *adj* augusto

August /'ɔːgəst/ *n* agosto *m*

aunt /ænt ‖ɑːnt/ *n* tía *f*

auntie, aunty /'ænti ‖'ɑːnti/ *n* (colloq) tía *f*, tiíta *f* (fam)

au pair /'əʊˈper ‖,əʊ'peə(r)/ *n* au pair *mf*

aura /'ɔːrə/ *n* halo *m*, aura *m*

aural /'ɔːrəl/ *adj* auditivo

auspices /'ɔːspəsəz ‖'ɔːspɪsɪz/ *pl n* (frml): **under the ~ of sb/sth** bajo los auspicios de algn/algo

auspicious /ɔː'spɪʃəs/ *adj* (frml) prometedor, auspicioso (CS)

austere /ɔː'stɪr ‖ɒ'stɪə(r), ɔː'stɪə(r)/ *adj* austero

austerity /ɔː'sterəti ‖ɒ'sterəti, ɔː'sterəti/ *n* austeridad *f*

Australasia /ˌɔːstrə'leɪʒə, -'leɪʃə ‖ˌɒstrə'leɪʒiə, -'leɪʃə/ *n* Australasia *f*

Australia /ɔː'streɪliə ‖ɒ'streɪliə/ *n* Australia *f*

Australian¹ /ɔː'streɪliən ‖ɒ'streɪliən/ *adj* australiano

Australian² *n* australiano, -na *m,f*

Austria /'ɔːstriə ‖'ɒstriə/ *n* Austria *f*

Austrian¹ /'ɔːstriən ‖'ɒstriən/ *adj* austriaco, austríaco

Austrian² *n* austriaco, -ca *m,f*, austríaco, -ca *m,f*

authentic /ə'θentɪk ‖ɔː'θentɪk/ *adj* **(a)** (genuine) auténtico **(b)** (realistic) ⟨*atmosphere*⟩ realista

authenticate /ə'θentɪkeɪt ‖ɔː'θentɪkeɪt/ *vt* **(a)** (declare genuine) autenticar* **(b)** (prove, confirm) probar*

authenticity /ˌɔːθen'tɪsəti/ *n* (of manuscript, painting) autenticidad *f*

author /'ɔːθər ‖'ɔːθə(r)/ *n* (writer) escritor, -ra *m,f*; (in relation to her/his works) autor, -tora *m,f*

authoritarian /ɔː'θɒːrə'teriən ‖ɔː,θɒrɪ'teəriən/ *adj* autoritario

authoritative /ə'θɒːrəteɪtɪv ‖ɔː'θɒrətətɪv/ *adj* **1** ⟨*manner/tone*⟩ de autoridad **2** (reliable, respected) ⟨*source*⟩ fidedigno; ⟨*work/study*⟩ autorizado

authority /ə'θɒːrəti ‖ɔː'θɒrəti/ *n* (*pl* **-ties**) **1** **(a)** (power) autoridad *f* **(b)** (authorization) **~ to + INF** autorización *f* PARA + INF **2** (person, body) autoridad *f*; **she was detained by the Belgian authorities** fue detenida por las autoridades belgas **3** **(a)** (expert) **~ (ON sth)** autoridad *f* (EN algo) **(b)** (source) autoridad *f*; **to have sth on good ~** saber* algo de buena fuente

authorize /'ɔːθəraɪz/ *vt* **(a)** ⟨*publication/*

transaction⟩ autorizar*; ⟨*funds*⟩ aprobar* **(b)** (empower) **to ~ sb to + INF** autorizar* a algn PARA + INF

autistic /ɔː'tɪstɪk/ *adj* autista

autobiographical /'ɔːtəˌbaɪə'græfɪkəl/ *adj* autobiográfico

autobiography /'ɔːtəbar'ɑːgrəfi ‖'ɔːtəbaɪɒgrəfi/ *n* (*pl* **-phies**) autobiografía *f*

autocratic /'ɔːtə'krætɪk/ *adj* autocrático

autograph¹ /'ɔːtəgræf ‖'ɔːtəgrɑːf/ *n* autógrafo *m*

autograph² *vt* autografiar*

automata /ɔː'tɑːmətə ‖ɔː'tɒmətə/ *pl of* AUTOMATON

automate /'ɔːtəmeɪt/ *vt* automatizar*

automatic¹ /'ɔːtə'mætɪk/ *adj* automático

automatic² *n* (car) coche *m* automático; (pistol) automática *f*

automatically /'ɔːtə'mætɪkli/ *adv* automáticamente

automation /'ɔːtə'meɪʃən/ *n* automatización *f*

automaton /ɔː'tɑːmətən ‖ɔː'tɒmətən/ *n* (*pl* **automata** *or* **-tons**) autómata *m*

automobile /'ɔːtəməbiːl/ *n* (esp AmE) coche *m*, carro *m* (AmL exc CS), auto *m* (esp CS), automóvil *m* (frml)

autonomous /ɔː'tɑːnəməs ‖ɔː'tɒnəməs/ *adj* autónomo

autonomy /ɔː'tɑːnəmi ‖ɔː'tɒnəmi/ *n* autonomía *f*

autopsy /'ɔːtɑːpsi ‖'ɔːtɒpsi/ *n* (*pl* **-sies**) autopsia *f*

autumn /'ɔːtəm/ *n* (esp BrE) otoño *m*; (*before n*) ⟨*day/weather*⟩ de otoño, otoñal

auxiliary¹ /ɔːg'zɪljəri/ *adj* auxiliar

auxiliary² *n* (*pl* **-ries**) auxiliar *mf*; **nursing ~** enfermero, -ra *m,f* auxiliar

avail¹ /ə'veɪl/ *v refl* (frml) **to ~ oneself OF sth** aprovechar algo

avail² *n* (liter): **to no ~** en vano

available /ə'veɪləbəl/ *adj* **(a)** (obtainable) (*pred*): **to be readily ~** ser* fácil de conseguir; **brochures are ~ on request** hay folletos a disposición de quien los solicite **(b)** (at sb's disposal) ⟨*resources/manpower*⟩ disponible; **to make sth ~ to sb** poner* algo a disposición de algn **(c)** (free, contactable) (*pred*) libre; (for work, job) disponible

avalanche /'ævəlæntʃ ‖'ævəlɑːnʃ/ *n* alud *m*, avalancha *f*

avant-garde /'ɑːvɑːn'gɑːrd ‖,ævɒn'gɑːd/ *adj* vanguardista, de vanguardia

avarice /'ævərəs ‖'ævərɪs/ *n* (liter) codicia *f* (liter)

avaricious /'ævə'rɪʃəs/ *adj* (liter) codicioso

Ave (= **Avenue**) Avda., Av.

avenge /ə'vendʒ/ *vt* vengar*

avenue /'ævənuː ‖'ævənjuː/ *n* **1** **(a)** (tree-lined walk) paseo *m* (arbolado) **(b)** (broad street) avenida *f* **2** (means, method) vía *f*

average¹ /'ævərɪdʒ, 'ævərɪdʒ/ *n* (Math) promedio *m*, media *f*

average² *adj* **(a)** (Math) ⟨*time/age*⟩ medio, promedio *adj inv*; **he is of ~ height** es de   ⋯⟶

estatura mediana **(b)** (typical): **the ~ family** la familia tipo **(c)** (ordinary): **how was the movie? — average** ¿qué tal la película? — normal
■ **average out** [*v + adv*]: **our speed ~d out at about 60mph** hicimos una media *or* un promedio de 60 millas por hora

averse /ə'vɜːrs ‖ə'vɜːs/ *adj* (*pred*) **to be ~ TO sth** ‹*to an idea*› ser* reacio A algo

aversion /ə'vɜːrʒən, -ʃən ‖ə'vɜːʃən/ *n* (*no pl*) aversión *f*

avert /ə'vɜːrt ‖ə'vɜːt/ *vt* **(a)** ‹*eyes/gaze*› apartar **(b)** ‹*danger/suspicion*› evitar; ‹*accident/strike*› impedir*

aviary /'eɪvieri ‖'eɪvɪəri/ *n* (*pl* **-ries**) pajarera *f*

aviation /'eɪvi'eɪʃən/ *n* aviación *f*

avid /'ævəd ‖'ævɪd/ *adj* ‹*reader/interest*› ávido; ‹*fan/follower*› ferviente

avocado /'ævə'kɑːdəʊ/ *n* (*pl* **-dos**) ~ (**pear**) aguacate *m or* (Bol, CS, Per) palta *f*

avoid /ə'vɔɪd/ *vt* ‹*obstacle/place/topic*› evitar; ‹*blow*› esquivar; **why are you ~ing me?** ¿por qué me rehúyes?

avoidable /ə'vɔɪdəbəl/ *adj* evitable

avowed /ə'vaʊd/ *adj* (*before n*) declarado

await /ə'weɪt/ *vt* esperar

awake[1] /ə'weɪk/ *adj* (*pred*) **to be ~** estar* despierto

awake[2] (*past* **awoke**; *past p* **awoken**), **awaken** /ə'weɪkən/ *vt/i* despertar*

awakening /ə'weɪkənɪŋ/ *n* despertar *m*

award[1] /ə'wɔːrd ‖ə'wɔːd/ *vt* **(a)** ‹*prize/medal/ pay increase*› conceder; ‹*honor*› conferir* **(b)** (Sport) ‹*penalty/free kick*› conceder

award[2] *n* **(a)** (prize) galardón *m*; (medal) condecoración *f* **(b)** (sum of money) asignación *f*

award-winning /ə'wɔːrd,wɪnɪŋ ‖ə'wɔːd,wɪnɪŋ/ *adj* (*before n*) galardonado

aware /ə'wer ‖ə'weə(r)/ *adj* (conscious) (*pred*) **to be ~ OF sth** ser* *or* (Chi, Méx) estar* consciente DE algo; **is your father ~ that you drink?** ¿sabe tu padre que bebes?

awareness /ə'wernəs ‖ə'weənɪs/ *n* conciencia *f*

awash /ə'wɔːʃ ‖ə'wɒʃ/ *adj* (*pred*) **to be ~ (WITH sth)** estar* inundado (DE algo)

away /ə'weɪ/ *adv* **1** (from place, person): **I looked ~** aparté la vista; **he limped ~** se alejó cojeando **2** **(a)** (in the distance): **it isn't far ~** no queda lejos; **it's 20 miles ~** queda a 20 millas; **Easter is a long way ~** falta mucho para Pascua **(b)** (absent): **she's**

~ in Canada está en Canadá; **I'll be ~ all next week** toda la semana que viene no voy a estar **(c)** (esp BrE Sport): **to play ~** jugar* fuera (de casa) **3** (continuously): **he's been painting ~ all morning** se ha pasado toda la mañana pintando; **I could hear him singing ~** lo oía cantar **4** **away from** (*as prep*) **(a)** (in opposite direction to): **she pulled him ~ from the cliff edge** lo apartó del borde del acantilado **(b)** (at a distance, separated from) lejos de; **to get ~ from it all** alejarse del mundanal ruido

awe /ɔː/ *n* sobrecogimiento *m*; **to be in ~ of sb** sentirse* intimidado por algn

awe-inspiring /'ɔːɪn'spaɪrɪŋ ‖'ɔːɪn,spaɪərɪŋ/ *adj* impresionante

awesome /'ɔːsəm/ *adj* imponente

awestruck /'ɔːstrʌk/ *adj* atemorizado

awful /'ɔːfəl/ *adj* (colloq) ‹*journey/weather/day*› horrible; ‹*clothes*› horroroso; ‹*joke/movie*› malísimo; **I felt ~** me sentía fatal

awkward /'ɔːkwərd ‖'ɔːkwəd/ *adj* **1** (clumsy) ‹*movement/person*› torpe; ‹*phrase*› poco elegante **2** **(a)** (difficult, inconvenient) ‹*shape/angle*› incómodo; **at a rather ~ moment** en mal momento; **she could make things very ~ for you** te podría hacer la vida imposible **(b)** (difficult to deal with) difícil **3** **(a)** (embarrassing) ‹*decision/ subject*› delicado; **you've put me in a very ~ position** me has puesto en una situación muy violenta **(b)** (embarrassed) ‹*silence*› incómodo; **I felt very ~** me sentí muy incómodo

awning /'ɔːnɪŋ/ *n* toldo *m*

awoke /ə'wəʊk/ *past of* AWAKE[2]

awoken /ə'wəʊkən/ *past p of* AWAKE[2]

awry /ə'raɪ/ *adj* (*pred*) torcido; **to go ~** salir* mal

ax[1], (BrE) **axe** /æks/ *n* hacha *f*‡; **to have an ~ to grind** tener* un interés personal

ax[2], (BrE) **axe** *vt* (journ) ‹*project/services/jobs*› suprimir; ‹*employee*› despedir*

axis /'æksəs ‖'æksɪs/ *n* (*pl* **axes** /'æksiːz/) eje *m*

axle /'æksəl/ *n* eje *m*

AZ = **Arizona**

Azerbaijan /'æzərbaɪ'dʒɑːn ‖,æzəbaɪ'dʒɑːn/ *n* Azerbaiyán *m*, Azerbaiján *m*

Azerbaijani /'æzərbaɪ'dʒɑːni ‖,æzəbaɪ'dʒɑːni/ *adj* azerbaiyaní

Aztec[1] /'æztek/ *adj* azteca

Aztec[2] *n* azteca *mf*

azure /'æʒər ‖'æʒə(r), 'æzjʊə(r)/ *adj* (liter) azur (liter)

Bb

B, b /biː/ n **(a)** (letter) B, b f **(b)** (Mus) si m
b (= **born**) n.

BA n = **Bachelor of Arts**

babble /'bæbəl/ vi (talk foolishly) parlotear (fam); (talk unintelligibly) farfullar; «*baby*» balbucear; **a babbling brook** (liter) un arroyo rumoroso (liter)

baby /'beɪbi/ n (pl **babies**) **(a)** (infant) bebé m, niño, -ña m,f, bebe, -ba m,f (Per, RPl), guagua f (Andes); **to have a ~** tener* un hijo or un niño **(b)** (animal) cría f **(c)** (youngest member) benjamín, -mina m,f

baby: **~ buggy, ~ carriage** n (AmE) cochecito m de bebé, carriola f (Méx); **~-sit** vi (pres p **-sitting**; past & past p **-sat**) cuidar niños, hacer* de canguro (Esp); **~-sitter** /'beɪbi,sɪtər ‖ 'beɪbi,sɪtə(r)/ n baby sitter mf, canguro mf (Esp)

bachelor /'bætʃələr ‖ 'bætʃələ(r)/ n [1] (single man) soltero m [2] (Educ) licenciado, -da m,f; **B~ of Arts/Science** (degree) licenciatura f en Filosofía y Letras/en Ciencias

back¹ /bæk/ n [1] (Anat) (of human) espalda f; (of animal) lomo m; **they laugh at him behind his ~** se ríen de él a sus espaldas; **to turn one's ~ on sb** volverle* la espalda a algn
[2] **(a)** (of chair) respaldo m; (of dress, jacket) espalda f; (of electrical appliance, watch) tapa f **(b)** (reverse side — of envelope, photo) dorso m; (— of head) parte f posterior; (— of hand) dorso m; **your sweater is on ~ to front** te has puesto el suéter al revés; ▶ HAND¹ 2
[3] (rear part): **the ~ of the house** la parte de atrás de la casa; **at the ~ of the drawer** en el fondo del cajón; **we sat at the ~** nos sentamos al fondo; **I'll sit in the ~** (of car) yo me siento detrás or (en el asiento de) atrás; **in the ~ of beyond** quién sabe dónde, donde el diablo perdió el poncho (AmS fam), en el quinto pino (Esp fam)
[4] (Sport) defensa mf, zaguero, -ra m,f

back² adj (before n, no comp) [1] ‹door› trasero; ‹garden› de atrás [2] (of an earlier date): **~ number** o **issue** número m atrasado; **~ pay** atrasos mpl

back³ adv [1] (indicating return, repetition): **the journey ~** el viaje de vuelta; **he's ~ from Paris** ha vuelto de París; **long hair is ~** (in fashion) vuelve (a estar de moda) el pelo largo; **to run/fly ~** volver* corriendo/en avión; **he asked for the ring ~** pidió que le devolviera el anillo; *see also* GO, TAKE *etc* BACK
[2] (in reply, reprisal): **he slapped her and she slapped him ~** él la abofeteó y ella le devolvió la bofetada
[3] (backward): **take two steps ~** da dos pasos atrás
[4] (in the past): **~ in 1972** (ya) en 1972
[5] **back and forth** = **backward(s) and forward(s)**: ▶ BACKWARD² A

back⁴ vt [1] **(a)** ‹person/decision› respaldar **(b)** (bet money on) ‹horse/winner› apostar* por

[2] (reverse): **he ~ed the car out of the garage** sacó el coche del garaje dando marcha atrás or (Col, Méx) en reversa
[3] (Mus) acompañar
■ **~** vi «*vehicle/driver*» dar* marcha atrás, meter reversa (Col, Méx); **he ~ed into a lamppost** se dio contra una farola al dar marcha atrás or al meter reversa
■ **back away** [v + adv] echarse atrás
■ **back down** [v + adv] volverse* atrás
■ **back out** [v + adv] volverse* atrás; **they ~ed out of the deal** no cumplieron el trato
■ **back up** [1] [v + o + adv, v + adv + o] **(a)** (support) respaldar, apoyar **(b)** (Comput) ‹file› hacer* una copia de seguridad de
[2] [v + adv] (reverse) dar* marcha atrás, meter reversa (Col, Méx)

back: **~ache** n dolor m de espalda; **~bencher** /'bæk'bentʃər ‖ ,bæk'bentʃə(r)/, **~ bench MP** n (in UK) diputado, -da m,f (sin cargo específico en el gobierno o la oposición); **~bone** n (Anat) columna f (vertebral); (main strength) columna f vertebral, eje m; **~date** /'bæk'deɪt/ vt ‹wage increase› pagar* con retroactividad; ‹check› ponerle* una fecha anterior a; **~drop** n telón m de fondo

backer /'bækər ‖ 'bækə(r)/ n patrocinador, -dora m,f

backfire /'bækfaɪr ‖ bæk'faɪə(r)/ vi **(a)** «*car*» producir* detonaciones en el escape **(b)** (fail) fracasar

background¹ /'bækgraʊnd/ n **(a)** (of picture, scene) fondo m; **she prefers to stay in the ~** prefiere permanecer en un segundo plano **(b)** (of events) ~ (**TO sth**) antecedentes mpl (DE algo) **(c)** (of person — origin) origen m; (— education) formación f; (— previous activities) experiencia f

background² adj (before n) ‹noise/music› de fondo; **~ reading** lecturas fpl preparatorias (acerca del momento histórico, antecedentes etc)

backhand /'bækhænd/ n revés m

backing /'bækɪŋ/ n **(a)** (support) respaldo m **(b)** (Mus) acompañamiento m

backlash /'bæklæʃ/ n reacción f violenta; (Mech Eng) contragolpe m

backless /'bækləs ‖ 'bæklɪs/ adj sin espalda

back: **~log** n atraso m; **a ~log of work** trabajo atrasado; **~pack** n mochila f; **~ seat** n asiento m trasero or de atrás; **~side** /'bæk'saɪd/ n (colloq) trasero m (fam); **~stage** /'bæk'steɪdʒ/ adj/adv entre bastidores; **~street** n callejuela f; (before n) ‹abortion› clandestino; **~stroke** n estilo m espalda; **~track** vi **(a)** (retrace one's steps) retroceder **(b)** (reverse opinion, plan) dar* marcha atrás; **~up** n **(a)** (support) respaldo m, apoyo m; (before n) ‹team/equipment› de refuerzo **(b)** (Comput) copia f de seguridad; (before n) ‹disk/file› de reserva, de seguridad

backward¹ /'bækwərd ‖ 'bækwəd/ adj   ⋯❖

1 (before n) ⟨movement⟩ hacia atrás; **a ~ glance** una mirada atrás **2** ⟨child⟩ retrasado; ⟨nation⟩ atrasado

backward², (esp BrE) **backwards** /'bækwərdz ‖'bækwədz/ adv **(a)** (toward rear) hacia atrás; **~ and forward(s)** para atrás y para adelante; ▶ KNOW¹ vt 1A **(b)** (back to front, in reverse order) al revés

back yard n (paved) patio m trasero; (grassed) (AmE) jardín m trasero, fondo m (RPI)

bacon /'beɪkən/ n tocino m or (Esp) bacon m or (RPI) panceta f

bacteria /bæk'tɪriə ‖bæk'tɪəriə/ pl n bacterias mpl

bad¹ /bæd/ adj

■ Note The usual translation of bad, malo, becomes mal when it is used before a masculine singular noun.

(comp **worse**; superl **worst**) **1** (not good) malo; **to be ~ AT sth/-ING** ser* malo PARA algo/+ INF; **to go from ~ to worse** ir* de mal en peor; **too much food is ~ for you** comer demasiado es malo; **she's got a ~ knee** tiene problemas con la rodilla; **I feel ~ about not having written to her** me da no sé qué no haberle escrito; **to be in a ~ way** (colloq) estar* fatal (fam) **2** (serious) ⟨mistake/injury⟩ grave; ⟨headache⟩ fuerte **3** (rotten) ⟨egg/fruit⟩ podrido; **to go ~** echarse a perder

bad² n: **all the ~ that he's done** todo el mal que ha hecho; **there's good and ~ in everybody** todos tenemos cosas buenas y malas

bad³ adv (esp AmE colloq): **to need sth real ~** necesitar algo desesperadamente

bade /bæd, beɪd/ past of BID¹ vt 2

badge /bædʒ/ n (pin-on) chapa f, botón m (AmL); (sew-on) insignia f

badger¹ /'bædʒər ‖'bædʒə(r)/ n tejón m

badger² vt fastidiar

badly /'bædli/ adv (comp **worse**; superl **worst**) **1** (poorly) ⟨play/sing⟩ mal **2** (improperly) ⟨behave/treat⟩ mal **3** (as intensifier) ⟨fail⟩ miserablemente; **~ injured** gravemente herido

badly off adj (comp **worse off**; superl **worst off**) (pred) mal de dinero

badminton /'bædmɪntn/ n bádminton m

bad-tempered /'bæd'tempərd ‖,bæd'tempəd/ adj ⟨reply/tone⟩ malhumorado; ⟨person⟩ (as permanent characteristic) de mal genio; (in a bad mood) de mal humor

baffle /'bæfəl/ vt **(a)** (perplex) desconcertar* **(b)** (frustrate) ⟨efforts⟩ frustrar

baffled /'bæfəld/ adj perplejo; ⟨expression⟩ de perplejidad

bag /bæg/ n **1** **(a)** (container, bagful) bolsa f; **a paper ~** una bolsa de papel; (hand~) (esp BrE) cartera f or (Esp) bolso m or (Méx) bolsa f **(b)** (piece of luggage) maleta f, valija f (RPI), petaca f (Méx); **to pack one's ~s** hacer* la maleta (or

valija etc) **2** (of skin) bolsa f; **to have ~s under one's eyes** (of skin) tener* bolsas en los ojos; (dark rings) tener* ojeras

baggage /'bægɪdʒ/ n equipaje m; (before n) **~ room** (AmE) consigna f

baggy /'bægi/ adj **-gier, -giest** ancho, guango (Méx)

bagpipes /'bægpaɪps/ pl n gaita f

Bahamas /bə'hɑːməz/ pl n the **~** las Bahamas

bail /beɪl/ n (Law) fianza f; **he was released on ~** fue puesto en libertad bajo fianza

■ **bail out** **1** [v + o + adv, v + adv + o] **(a)** (Law): **to ~ sb out** pagarle* la fianza a algn **(b)** (Naut) ⟨water⟩ achicar* **2** [v + o + adv, v + adv + o] (rescue) sacar* de apuros **3** [v + adv] (Aviat) tirarse en paracaídas

bailiff /'beɪləf ‖'beɪlɪf/ n (Law) **(a)** (in UK) alguacil mf **(b)** (in US) funcionario que custodia al acusado en el juzgado

bait¹ /beɪt/ n cebo m

bait² vt **1** ⟨hook/trap⟩ cebar **2** (persecute) acosar

bake /beɪk/ vt: **~ in a hot oven** hornear en horno caliente; **she ~s her own bread** hace el pan en casa; **~d potato** papa f or (Esp) patata f asada

■ ~ vi hacer* pasteles (or pan etc)

baked beans /beɪkt/ pl n **(a)** (in can) frijoles mpl or (Esp) judías fpl or (CS) porotos mpl en salsa de tomate **(b)** (dish) (AmE) el mismo plato preparado con cerdo

baker /'beɪkər ‖'beɪkə(r)/ n panadero, -ra m,f; **~'s** (shop) panadería f

bakery /'beɪkəri/ n (pl **-ries**) panadería f

baking /'beɪkɪŋ/ n: **we do a lot of ~** hacemos muchos pasteles (or pan etc); (before n) **~ dish** fuente f para el horno; **~ powder** polvo m de hornear, Royal® m, levadura f en polvo (Esp); **~ tin** molde m; **~ tray** bandeja f (de horno)

balance¹ /'bæləns/ n **1** (apparatus) balanza f **2** (equilibrium) equilibrio m; **to lose one's ~** perder* el equilibrio **3** **(a)** (in accounting) balance m **(b)** (bank ~) saldo m **(c)** (difference, remainder) resto m; (of sum of money) saldo m

balance² vt **1** ⟨load⟩ equilibrar; ⟨object⟩ mantener* en equilibrio **2** (Fin) ⟨account⟩ hacer* el balance de

balanced /'bælənst/ adj equilibrado

balance of payments n balanza f de pagos

balcony /'bælkəni/ n (pl **-nies**) **(a)** (Archit) balcón m; (large) terraza f **(b)** (Theat) (in US) platea f alta; (in UK) galería f

bald /bɔːld/ adj **-er, -est** **(a)** ⟨man⟩ calvo, pelón (AmC, Méx), pelado (CS); **to go ~** quedarse calvo (or pelón etc) **(b)** (worn) ⟨tire⟩ gastado

bale /beɪl/ n paca f

■ **bale out** (BrE) ▶ BAIL OUT

Balearic Islands /'bæli'ærɪk/ pl n the **~ ~** las (Islas) Baleares

baleful /'beɪlfəl/ adj torvo

Balkan /'bɔːlkən/ *adj* balcánico

Balkans /'bɔːlkənz/ *pl n* **the ~** los países balcánicos

ball /bɔːl/ *n* ⓵ (in baseball, golf) pelota *f*, bola *f*; (in basketball, football) pelota *f* (esp AmL), balón *m* (esp Esp); (in billiards) bola *f*; **to be on the ~** (colloq) ser* muy espabilado ⓶ **(a) to play ~ (with sb)** (lit: play game) jugar* a la pelota (con algn); (cooperate) (colloq) cooperar (con algn) **(b)** (base~) (AmE) béisbol *m* ⓷ **(a)** (round mass) bola *f*; (of string, wool) ovillo *m* **(b)** (Anat): **the ~ of the foot** la parte anterior de la planta del pie ⓸ (dance) baile *m*

ballad /'bæləd/ *n* (narrative poem, song) romance *m*; (sentimental song) balada *f*

ballast /'bæləst/ *n* (Aviat, Naut) lastre *m*

ballerina /,bælə'riːnə/ *n* bailarina *f* (de ballet)

ballet /'bæleɪ/ *n* ballet *m*; (*before n*) **~ dancer** bailarín, -rina *m,f* de ballet

ball game *n* juego *m* de pelota; (baseball game) (AmE) partido *m* de béisbol; (US football game) (AmE) partido *m* de fútbol *or* (AmC, Méx) futbol americano

ballistics /bə'lɪstɪks/ *n* (+ *sing vb*) balística *f*

balloon /bə'luːn/ *n* **(a)** (toy) globo *m*, bomba *f* (Col), chimbomba *f* (AmC) **(b)** (Aviat) globo *m*

ballot /'bælət/ *n* votación *f*; (*before n*) **~ box** urna *f*; **~ (paper)** papeleta *f*, boleta *f* electoral (Méx, RPl)

ball: **~park** *n* (AmE Sport) estadio *m or* (Méx) parque *m* de béisbol; (*before n*) **a ~park figure** una cifra aproximada; **~player** *n* (AmE) (in baseball) jugador, -dora *m,f* de béisbol, beisbolista *mf*; (in US football) jugador, -dora *m,f* de fútbol *or* (AmC, Méx) de futbol americano; (in basketball) jugador, -dora *m,f* de baloncesto, baloncestista *mf*, basquetbolista *mf* (AmL); **~point (pen)** *n* bolígrafo *m*, esfero(gráfico) *m* (Col), pluma *f* atómica (Méx), birome *f* (RPl), lápiz *m* de pasta (Chi); **~room** *n* sala *f or* salón *m* de baile; **~room dancing** *n* baile *m* de salón

balm /bɑːm/ *n* bálsamo *m*

Baltic /'bɔːltɪk/ *n* **the ~** (Sea) el (mar) Báltico

bamboo /'bæm'buː ‖ bæm'buː/ *n* (*pl* **-boos**) bambú *m*

ban¹ /bæn/ *vt* **-nn-** ⟨book/smoking⟩ prohibir*; ⟨organization⟩ proscribir*; **he was ~ned from the club** le prohibieron la entrada al club

ban² *n* prohibición *f*

banal /bə'næl, 'beɪnəl ‖ bə'nɑːl/ *adj* banal

banana /bə'nænə ‖ bə'nɑːnə/ *n* plátano *m*, banana *f* (Per, RPl), banano *m* (AmC, Col), cambur *m* (Ven)

band /bænd/ *n* ⓵ **(a)** (group) grupo *m*; (of thieves, youths) pandilla *f* **(b)** (Mus) (jazz ~) grupo *m or* conjunto *m* de jazz; (rock ~) grupo *m* de rock ⓶ **(a)** (ribbon) cinta *f*; (strip — of cloth) banda *f*; (— for hat) cinta *f* **(b)** (stripe) franja *f*

■ **band together** [*v + adv*] unirse

bandage¹ /'bændɪdʒ/ *n* venda *f*

bandage² *vt* vendar

Band-Aid® /'bændeɪd/ *n* (AmE) curita® *f*, tirita® *f* (Esp)

B & B /'biːən'biː/ *n* = **bed and breakfast**

bandit /'bændət ‖ 'bændɪt/ *n* bandido, -da *m,f*, bandolero, -ra *m,f*

band: **~stand** *n* quiosco *m* de música; **~wagon** *n*: *to jump on the ~wagon* subirse al carro

bandy¹ /'bændi/ *adj* **-dier, -diest** arqueado, torcido

bandy² **-dies, -dying, -died** *vt* ⟨remarks/ jokes⟩ intercambiar

bane /beɪn/ *n*: **to be the ~ of sb's life** ser* la cruz de algn

bang¹ /bæŋ/ *n* ⓵ (loud noise) estrépito *m*; (explosion) explosión *f* ⓶ (blow) golpe *m*, trancazo *m* ⓷ **bangs** *pl* (AmE) (fringe) flequillo *m*, cerquillo *m* (AmL), chasquilla *f* (Chi), capul *f* (Col), fleco *m* (Méx), pollina *f* (Ven)

bang² *vt* **(a)** (strike) golpear **(b)** (slam): **he ~ed the door** dio un portazo (fam)

■ **~** *vi* **(a)** (strike) **to ~ on sth** golpear algo; **to ~ INTO sth** darse* CONTRA algo **(b)** (slam) ⟨*door*⟩ cerrarse* de un golpe

bang³ *adv* ⓵: **to go ~** ⟨*gun*⟩ dispararse ⓶ (*as intensifier*) (esp BrE colloq): **~ on time** a la hora justa

banger /'bæŋər ‖ 'bæŋə(r)/ *n* (BrE colloq) **(a)** (sausage) salchicha *f* **(b)** (firework) petardo *m* **(c)** (car) (old ~) cacharro *m* (fam)

Bangkok /'bæŋkɑːk ‖ ,bæŋ'kɒk/ *n* Bangkok *m*

Bangladesh /'bɑːŋglə'deʃ ‖ ,bæŋglə'deʃ/ *n* Bangladesh *m*

Bangladeshi /'bɑːŋglə'deʃi ‖ ,bæŋglə'deʃi/ *adj* bangladesí

bangle /'bæŋgəl/ *n* pulsera *f*, brazalete *m*; (thin, of gold or silver) esclava *f*, aro *m*

banish /'bænɪʃ/ *vt* (exile) desterrar*; ⟨fear/ doubts⟩ hacer* olvidar **(b)** (prohibit) prohibir*

banister /'bænəstər ‖ 'bænɪstə(r)/ *n* pasamanos *m*

bank¹ /bæŋk/ *n* ⓵ **(a)** (Fin) banco *m*; (*before n*) **~ balance** saldo *m* **(b)** (store, supply) banco *m*; **blood ~** banco de sangre ⓶ (edge of river) orilla *f*, ribera *f* ⓷ **~ of earth/snow** montículo *m* de tierra/nieve

bank² *vt* depositar *or* (esp Esp) ingresar (en el banco)

■ **~** *vi* ⓵ (Fin): **I ~ with the National** tengo la cuenta en el National ⓶ (Aviat) ladearse

■ **bank on** [*v + prep + o*] ⟨victory/help⟩ contar* con; **I wouldn't ~ on it** yo no me confiaría demasiado

bank: **~ account** *n* cuenta *f* bancaria; **~book** *n* libreta *f* de ahorros; **~card** *n* (AmE) tarjeta *f* de crédito (*expedida por un banco*); (BrE) tarjeta *f* bancaria

banker /'bæŋkər ‖ 'bæŋkə(r)/ *n* **(a)** (Fin) banquero, -ra *m,f* **(b)** (in gambling) banca *f*

bank holiday *n* (BrE) día *m* festivo, feriado *m* (esp AmL)

banking /'bæŋkɪŋ/ *n* banca *f*

bank: **~ note** *n* **(a)** (promissory note) (AmE) pagaré *m* **(b)** (paper money) (BrE) billete *m* de banco; **~ rate** *n* tasa *f or* (esp Esp) tipo *m* de interés

bankrupt¹ /'bæŋkrʌpt/ *adj* en quiebra, en bancarrota; **to be ~** estar* en quiebra *or* en bancarrota; **to go ~** quebrar*, ir* a la bancarrota

bankrupt² *n* fallido, -da *m,f*

b

bankrupt³ *vt* llevar a la quiebra *or* a la bancarrota

bankruptcy /'bæŋkrʌptsi/ *n* (*pl* **-cies**) quiebra *f*, bancarrota *f*

banner /'bænər ‖'bænə(r)/ *n* (flag) estandarte *m*; (in demonstration) pancarta *f*

bannister *n* ▶ BANISTER

banns /bænz/ *pl n* amonestaciones *fpl*

banquet /'bæŋkwət ‖'bæŋkwɪt/ *n* banquete *m*

banter /'bæntər ‖'bæntə(r)/ *n* bromas *fpl*

baptism /'bæptɪzəm/ *n* bautismo *m*

Baptist /'bæptəst ‖'bæptɪst/ *n* baptista *mf*, bautista *mf*

baptize /bæp'taɪz/ *vt* bautizar*

bar¹ /baːr ‖baː(r)/ *n* **1** (rod, rail) barra *f*; (— on cage, window) barrote *m* **2** (Sport) (cross∼) (in soccer) larguero *m*; (in rugby) travesaño *m*; (in high jump) barra *f or* (Esp) listón *m*; (horizontal ∼) barra *f* (fija) **3** (block) barra *f*; ∼ **of chocolate** barra *f* de chocolate; **gold** ∼ lingote *m* de oro; ∼ **of soap** pastilla *f or* (CS) barra *f* de jabón **4** (establishment) bar *m*; (counter) barra *f*, mostrador *m* **5** (Law) **the Bar** (legal profession) (AmE) la abogacía; (barristers) (BrE) el conjunto de BARRISTERS **6** (Mus) compás *m*

bar² *vt* **-rr-** **1** (secure) ⟨door/window⟩ atrancar* **2** (block) ⟨path/entrance⟩ bloquear **3** (prohibit) ⟨smoking/jeans⟩ prohibir*; ⟨person/group⟩ excluir*

bar³ *prep* salvo, excepto, a *or* con excepción de

barb /baːrb ‖baːb/ *n* (of fishhook, arrow) lengüeta *f*

Barbados /baːr'beɪdəʊs ‖baː'beɪdɒs/ *n* Barbados *m*

barbarian /baːr'beriən ‖baː'beərɪən/ *n* bárbaro, -ra *m*,*f*

barbaric /baːr'bærɪk ‖baː'bærɪk/ *adj* (primitive) primitivo; (brutal) brutal

barbarity /baːr'bærəti ‖baː'bærəti/ *n* (*pl* **-ties**) brutalidad *f*

barbecue /'baːrbɪkjuː ‖'baːbɪkjuː/ *n* **1** (grid and fireplace) barbacoa *f*, parrilla *f*, asador *m* (AmL) **2** (social occasion) barbacoa *f*, parrillada *f*, asado *m* (AmL)

barbed wire /baːrbd ‖baːbd/ *n* alambre *m* de púas *or* (Esp tb) de espino

barber /'baːrbər ‖'baːbə(r)/ *n* peluquero *m*, barbero *m* (ant); **the** ∼**('s)** la peluquería

barbwire /'baːrb'waɪr ‖ˌbaː'b'waɪə(r)/ *n* (AmE)
▶ BARBED WIRE

bar code *n* código *m* de barras

bare¹ /ber ‖beə(r)/ *adj* **barer** /'berər ‖'beərə(r)/, **barest** /'berəst ‖'beərɪst/ (uncovered) ⟨blade/flesh/walls⟩ desnudo; ⟨head⟩ descubierto; ⟨foot⟩ descalzo; ⟨floorboards⟩ sin alfombrar; ⟨tree⟩ pelado; ⟨wire⟩ pelado *or* (Esp) desnudo; ⟨room⟩ con pocos muebles; **the** ∼ **essentials** lo estrictamente esencial; **he gave me the** ∼ **facts** se ciñó a los hechos; **to lay sth** ∼ poner* *or* dejar algo al descubierto

bare² *vt*: **to** ∼ **one's head** descubrirse* (la cabeza); **the dog** ∼**d its teeth** el perro enseñó *or* mostró los dientes

bareback /'berbæk ‖'beəbæk/ *adv* ⟨ride⟩ a pelo

barefoot¹ /'berfʊt ‖'beəfʊt/ *adj* descalzo

barefoot² *adv*: **she ran** ∼ corrió descalza

barely /'berli ‖'beəli/ *adv* (hardly) apenas

bargain¹ /'baːrgən ‖'baːgən/ *n* **1** (cheap purchase) ganga *f*; (*before n*) ⟨*price*⟩ de ganga *or* oferta **2** (deal, agreement) trato *m*, acuerdo *m*; **to strike a** ∼ llegar a un acuerdo; **into** *o* (AmE also) **in the** ∼ encima, por si fuera poco

bargain² *vi* (a) (haggle) regatear (b) (negotiate) negociar

■ **bargain for** [*v* + *prep* + *o*]: **we hadn't** ∼**ed for such an eventuality** no habíamos tenido en cuenta esa posibilidad; **I got more than I had** ∼**ed for** no me esperaba algo así

bargaining /'baːrgənɪŋ ‖'baːgənɪŋ/ *n* (a) (haggling) regateo *m* (b) (negotiating) negociaciones *fpl*; (*before n*) ⟨*strategy/position*⟩ negociador

barge¹ /baːrdʒ ‖baːdʒ/ *n* barcaza *f*

barge² *vi* (+ *adv compl*): **he** ∼**d past (me)** me dio un empujón para pasar; **he always** ∼**s in when we're trying to talk** siempre se entromete cuando queremos hablar

baritone /'bærətəʊn ‖'bærɪtəʊn/ *n* barítono *m*

bark¹ /baːrk ‖baːk/ *n* **1** (on tree) corteza *f* **2** (of dog) ladrido *m*

bark² *vi* ladrar;
■ ∼ *vt* (shout) espetar; **to** ∼ **(out) an order** gritar una orden

barkeep /'baːrkiːp ‖'baːkiːp/, **barkeeper** /-ˌkiːpər ‖-ˌkiːpə(r)/ *n* (AmE) (male) barman *m*, camarero *m* (Esp, Ven); (female) mesera *f or* (Esp, Ven) camarera *f or* (AmS) moza *f*

barley /'baːrli ‖'baːli/ *n* cebada *f*

bar: ∼**maid** *n* mesera *f or* (Esp, Ven) camarera *f or* (AmS) moza *f*; ∼**man** /'baːrmæn ‖'baːmən/ *n* (*pl* **-men** /-mən/) (BrE) barman *m*, camarero *m* (Esp, Ven)

barn /baːrn ‖baːn/ *n* (a) (for crops) granero *m*; (for livestock) establo *m* (b) (for vehicles) (AmE) cochera *f*

barometer /bə'raːmətər ‖bə'rɒmɪtə(r)/ *n* barómetro *m*

baron /'bærən/ *n* (a) (nobleman) barón *m* (b) (magnate) magnate *m*

baroness /'bærə'nes, 'bærənəs/ *n* baronesa *f*

barracks /'bærəks/ *n* (*pl* ∼) (+ *sing or pl vb*) cuartel *m*

barrage /bə'raːʒ ‖'bæraːʒ/ *n* (Mil) (action) descarga *f*; (fire) cortina *f* de fuego

barrel /'bærəl/ *n* **1** (container) barril *m*, tonel *m* **2** (of handgun) cañón *m*; (of cannon) tubo *m*

barren /'bærən/ *adj* **-er**, **-est** ⟨land/soil⟩ estéril; ⟨tree/plant/animal⟩ (no comp) estéril; ⟨woman⟩ (dated or liter) infecunda

barrette /baː'ret ‖ba'ret/ *n* (AmE) pasador *m*, broche *m* (Méx, Ur), hebilla *f* (Arg)

barricade¹ /'bærəkeɪd ‖ˌbærɪ'keɪd/ *n* barricada *f*

barricade² *vt* cerrar* con barricadas; **they** ∼**d themselves into the building** se atrincheraron en el edificio

barrier /'bæriər ‖'bæriə(r)/ *n* barrera *f*; **language** ∼ barrera idiomática

Barrier Reef *n* **the Great** ∼ ∼ el Gran Arrecife Coralino, la Gran Barrera Coral

barrister /'bærəstər ‖'bærɪstə(r)/ *n* (BrE) abogado, -da *m*,*f* (habilitado para alegar ante un tribunal superior)

barrow /'bærəʊ/ n (wheel~) carretilla f

bar: ~**stool** n taburete m; ~**tender** n (esp AmE) (male) barman m, camarero m (Esp, Ven); (female) mesera f or (Esp, Ven) camarera f or (AmS) moza f

barter /'bɑːrtər ‖'bɑːtə(r)/ vt cambiar, trocar* ■ ~ vi hacer* trueques

base¹ /beɪs/ n [1] (of column, wall) base f; (of mountain, tree) pie m; (of spine, skull) base f; (of lamp) pie m [2] (foundation, basis) base f [3] (of patrol, for excursion) base f; (of organization) sede f [4] (in baseball) base f

base² vt [1] (found) to ~ sth ON sth ⟨opinion/ conclusion⟩ basar algo EN algo; **the movie is ~d on a real event** la película se basa en una historia real [2] (locate) basar; **the company is ~d in Madrid** la compañía tiene su base en Madrid

base³ adj **baser, basest** ⟨conduct/motive⟩ abyecto

baseball /'beɪsbɔːl/ n **(a)** (game) béisbol m; (before n) ~ **bat** bate m de béisbol **(b)** (ball) pelota f de béisbol

basement /'beɪsmənt/ n sótano m

base pay n (AmE) sueldo m base or básico

bases¹ /'beɪsiːz/ pl of BASIS

bases² /'beɪsəz ‖'beɪsɪz/ pl of BASE¹

bash¹ /bæʃ/ n (colloq) [1] (blow) golpe m, madrazo m (Méx fam) [2] (party) juerga f (fam)

bash² vt (colloq) pegarle* a

bashful /'bæʃfəl/ adj tímido, penoso (AmL exc CS)

basic /'beɪsɪk/ adj [1] (fundamental) fundamental [2] (simple, rudimentary) ⟨knowledge/need⟩ básico; ⟨hotel/food⟩ sencillo [3] (Econ) ⟨pay⟩ básico

basically /'beɪsɪkli/ adv fundamentalmente

basics /'beɪsɪks/ pl n lo básico

basil /'beɪzəl ‖'bæzəl/ n albahaca f

basin /'beɪsn̩/ n **(a)** (for liquid, food) cuenco m, bol m, tazón m **(b)** (hand ~) (BrE) lavamanos m, lavabo m, pileta f (RPl) **(c)** (Geog, Geol) cuenca f

basis /'beɪsəs ‖'beɪsɪs/ n (pl **bases** /'beɪsiːz/) [1] (foundation, grounds) base f [2] (system, level) (no pl): **employed on a daily** ~ contratado por día; **on a regional** ~ a nivel regional

bask /bæsk ‖bɑːsk/ vi: **to** ~ **in the sun** disfrutar (del calor) del sol; **she** ~**ed in their adulation** se deleitaba or se regodeaba con su adulación

basket /'bæskət ‖'bɑːskɪt/ n [1] (for shopping) canasta f (esp AmL), cesta f (esp Esp) [2] (in basketball) **(a)** (goal) canasta f, cesto m **(b)** (score) canasta f, enceste m

basketball /'bæskətbɔːl ‖'bɑːskɪtbɔːl/ n **(a)** (game) baloncesto m, básquetbol m (AmL) **(b)** (ball) pelota f de básquetbol or (Esp) balón m de baloncesto

Basque¹ /bæsk ‖bæsk, bɑːsk/ adj vasco; **the** ~ **Country** el País Vasco, Euskadi m

Basque² n **(a)** (person) vasco, -ca m,f **(b)** (language) euskera m, vasco m, vascuence m

bass¹ n /beɪs/ (pl ~**es**) (Mus) **(a)** (voice, singer) bajo m **(b)** (double bass or bass guitar) (contra)bajo m **(c)** (Audio) graves mpl

bass² adj ⟨voice⟩ de bajo

bass clef clave f de fa

bassoon /bə'suːn/ n fagot m

bastard /'bæstərd ‖'bɑːstəd/ n [1] (illegitimate child) bastardo, -da m,f [2] (colloq or vulg) cabrón m (fam o vulg), hijo m de puta (vulg)

baste /beɪst/ vt **(a)** (Culin) rociar con su jugo o con mantequilla etc durante la cocción **(b)** (sew loosely) hilvanar

bastion /'bæstʃən ‖'bæstiən/ n **(a)** (Archit) bastión m **(b)** (stronghold) baluarte m, bastión m

bat¹ /bæt/ n [1] (in baseball, cricket) bate m; (in table tennis) (BrE) paleta f, raqueta f [2] (Zool) murciélago m

bat² vi -tt- (Sport) batear

batch /bætʃ/ n (of cakes) hornada f; (of goods) (Busn) lote m; (of trainees, candidates) grupo m; (of mail, paperwork) pila f; (Comput) lote m

bated /'beɪtəd ‖'beɪtɪd/ adj: **with** ~ **breath** con ansiedad

bath¹ /bæθ ‖bɑːθ/ n (pl **baths** /bæðz ‖bɑːðz/) [1] **(a)** (wash) baño m; **to have** o (AmE also) **take a** ~ bañarse, darse* un baño **(b)** (tub) bañera f, tina f (AmL) [2] **baths** pl (swimming ~s) (BrE) piscina f, alberca f (Méx), pileta f (RPl)

bath² (BrE) vt bañar

bathe /beɪð/ vt (wash) ⟨wound/eyes⟩ lavar; ⟨baby/dog⟩ (AmE) bañar ■ ~ vi **(a)** (take bath) (AmE) bañarse **(b)** (go swimming) (BrE) bañarse

bathing suit, (BrE also) **bathing costume** /'beɪðɪŋ/ n traje m de baño, bañador m (Esp), malla f (de baño) (RPl), vestido m de baño (Col)

bath: ~**mat** n alfombrilla f or tapete m or (Chi) piso m de baño; ~**robe** n bata f de baño, albornoz m (Esp); ~**room** n **(a)** (room with bath) (cuarto m de) baño m **(b)** (toilet) (esp AmE) baño m, servicio m; ~**tub** n bañera f, tina f (AmL), bañadera f (Arg)

baton /bə'tɑːn ‖'bætən/ n **(a)** (Mus) batuta f **(b)** (truncheon) (BrE) bastón m **(c)** (in relay race) testigo m

battalion /bə'tæljən/ n batallón m

batter¹ /'bætər ‖'bætə(r)/ vt [1] (beat) ⟨victim/ opponent⟩ apalear; ⟨child/wife⟩ maltratar [2] (cover with batter) rebozar*

batter² n [1] (for fried fish, etc) rebozado m; (for pancakes) masa f; (for cake) (AmE) masa f [2] (in baseball) bateador, -dora m,f

battered /'bætərd ‖'bætəd/ adj ⟨car⟩ abollado; ⟨hat/suitcase⟩ estropeado; ⟨reputation/image⟩ maltrecho; ⟨baby/wife⟩ maltratado

battering ram /'bætərɪŋ/ n ariete m

battery /'bætəri/ n (pl **-ries**) [1] (in radio, lamp) pila f; (in car, motorcycle) batería f [2] (artillery) batería f [3] (Agr) batería f (conjunto de jaulas instaladas para la explotación avícola intensiva); (before n) ⟨eggs/hens⟩ de criadero, de batería; ~ **farming** cría f intensiva

battle¹ /'bætl̩/ n batalla f; **to fight a losing** ~ luchar por una causa perdida

battle² vi luchar

battle: ~**field** n campo m de batalla; ~**ground** n campo m de batalla

battlements /'bætl̩mənts/ pl n almenas fpl

battleship /'bætl̩ʃɪp/ n acorazado m

baud /bɔːd/ n (Comput) baudio m

bawdy /'bɔːdi/ adj **-dier, -diest** subido de tono

bawl /bɔːl/ *vi* (a) (shout) vociferar (b) (cry noisily) berrear

bay[1] /beɪ/ *n* ①︎ (Geog) bahía *f* ②︎ (a) (loading ∼) muelle *m or* plataforma *f* de carga (b) (area, recess) espacio *m* ③︎: at ∼ acorralado; to keep *o* hold sth/sb at ∼ mantener* algo/a algn a raya ④︎ ∼ (tree) laurel *m*

bay[2] *vi* «*hounds*» aullar*

bayleaf /'beɪliːf/ *n* (*pl* **-leaves**) hoja *f* de laurel

bayonet /'beɪənət/ *n* bayoneta *f*

bay window *n* ventana *f* en saliente

bazaar /bə'zɑːr ‖ bə'zɑː(r)/ *n* (a) (oriental market) bazar *m* (b) (charity sale) venta *f* benéfica

BBC *n* (= **British Broadcasting Corporation**) the ∼ la BBC

BC (= **before Christ**) antes de Cristo; (written form) aC, a. de C., a. de J.C.

be /biː, *weak form* bi/ (*pres* **am, are, is**; *past* **was, were**; *past p* **been**) *vi* [*See notes at* SER *and* ESTAR]

I ①︎ (*followed by an adjective*): she's French es francesa; he's worried está preocupado; how are you? ¿cómo estás?; I'm much better estoy *or* me encuentro mucho mejor; she's pregnant/tired/ill está embarazada/cansada/enferma; I'm cold/hot/hungry/thirsty tengo frío/calor/hambre/sed; he's dead está muerto; he's blind es *or* (Esp tb) está ciego; he's short es bajo; Tony is married/divorced Tony está *or* (esp AmL) es casado/divorciado; these shoes are new estos zapatos son nuevos; she was very rude to me estuvo *or* fue muy grosera conmigo; she's very rude es muy grosera; ∼ good sé bueno

②︎ (*followed by a noun*): if I were you, I'd stay yo que tú me quedaría

③︎ (a) (talking about age) tener*; how old are you? ¿cuántos años tienes?; I'm 31 tengo 31 años; Paul was four last Monday Paul cumplió cuatro años el lunes pasado; our house is over 100 years old nuestra casa tiene más de 100 años (b) (giving cost, measurement, weight): they are $15 each cuestan *or* valen 15 dólares cada una; two plus two is four dos más dos son cuatro; how tall is he? ¿cuánto mide?; Jim's over six feet tall Jim mide más de seis pies

II ①︎ (a) (exist, live): to let sth/sb ∼ dejar tranquilo algo/a algn (b) (in expressions of time): I'm drying my hair, I won't ∼ long me estoy secando el pelo, enseguida estoy; the party is tomorrow la fiesta es mañana

②︎ (be situated, present) estar*; where is the library? ¿dónde está la biblioteca?

③︎ (*only in perfect tenses*) (visit) estar*; I've never been to India nunca he estado en la India

■ ∼ *v impers* ①︎ (a) (talking about physical conditions, circumstances): it's cold/hot hace frío/calor; it's so noisy in here! ¡qué ruido hay aquí! (b) (in expressions of time) ser*; it's three o'clock son las tres; it's Wednesday today hoy es miércoles (c) (talking about distance) estar*; it's 500 miles from here to Detroit Detroit queda a 500 millas de aquí

②︎ (introducing person, object) ser*; it's me/Daniel soy yo/es Daniel

■ ∼ *v aux* ①︎ **to** ∼ **-ING** estar* + GER; I'm working estoy trabajando; how long have you been waiting? ¿cuánto (tiempo) hace que esperas?; when are you seeing her? ¿cuándo la vas a ver?

②︎ (*in the passive voice*) ser* [*The passive voice, however, is less common in Spanish than it is in English*] it was built in 1903 fue construido en 1903, se construyó en 1903, lo construyeron en 1903; it is known that ... se sabe que ...

③︎ **to** ∼ **to** + INF (a) (with future reference): the dessert is (still) to come todavía falta el postre (b) (expressing possibility): what are we to do? ¿qué podemos hacer?; it was nowhere to ∼ found no se lo pudo encontrar por ninguna parte

④︎ (a) (*in tag questions*): she's right, isn't she? tiene razón, ¿no? *or* ¿verdad? (b) (*in elliptical uses*): are you disappointed? — yes, I am/no, I'm not ¿estás desilusionado? — sí (, lo estoy)/no (, no lo estoy); she was told the news, and so was he/but I wasn't a ella le dieron la noticia, y también a él/pero a mí no

beach /biːtʃ/ *n* playa *f*

beacon /'biːkən/ *n* (light) faro *m*; (fire) almenara *f*

bead /biːd/ *n* cuenta *f*, abalorio *m*; (drop) gota *f*; ∼s of sweat gotas *fpl* de sudor

beady /'biːdi/ *adj*: ∼ eyes ojos redondos y brillantes

beak /biːk/ *n* pico *m*

beaker /'biːkər ‖ 'biːkə(r)/ *n* (a) (Chem) vaso *m* de precipitados (b) (cup) (BrE) taza *f* (*gen alta y sin asa*)

be-all and end-all /'biːɔːlən'endɔːl/ *n*: it is the ∼ ∼ ∼ of his life es su razón de ser; work isn't the ∼ ∼ ∼ el trabajo no lo es todo

beam[1] /biːm/ *n* ①︎ (in building) viga *f*; (in ship) bao *m* ②︎ (ray) rayo *m*; (broad) haz *m* de luz; keep the headlights on high *o* (BrE) full ∼ main ∼ (Auto) deja las (luces) largas *or* (Chi) altas

beam[2] *vi* (a) (shine) brillar (b) (smile) sonreír* (*abiertamente*)

■ ∼ *vt* (broadcast) transmitir

bean /biːn/ *n* (a) (fresh, in pod) ▶ GREEN BEAN (b) (dried) frijol *m or* (Esp) alubia *f or* judía *f or* (CS) poroto *m or* (Ven) caraota *f*; to be full of ∼s (colloq) estar* lleno de vida

bean: ∼ curd *n* tofu *m*, queso *m* de soya (AmL) *or* (Esp) soja; ∼shoot, ∼ sprout *n* frijol *m* germinado *or* (Esp) judía *f* germinada *or* (CS) poroto *m* germinado; (of soy bean) brote *m or* germinado *m* de soya (AmL) *or* (Esp) soja

bear[1] /ber ‖ beə(r)/ (*past* **bore**; *past p* **borne**) *vt* ①︎ (a) (support) ⟨*weight*⟩ aguantar; ⟨*cost*⟩ correr con; ⟨*responsibility*⟩ cargar* con (b) (endure) ⟨*pain/uncertainty*⟩ soportar (c) (put up with, stand) (colloq) (*with can*) ⟨*person*⟩ aguantar (fam); ⟨*noise*⟩ aguantar (d) (stand up to): her argument doesn't ∼ close scrutiny su razonamiento no resiste un análisis cuidadoso; it doesn't ∼ thinking about da miedo solo de pensarlo

AmC	América Central	Arg	Argentina	Cu	Cuba	Per Perú
AmL	América Latina	Bol	Bolivia	Ec	Ecuador	RPI Río de la Plata
AmS	América del Sur	Chi	Chile	Esp	España	Ur Uruguay
Andes	Región andina	CS	Cono Sur	Méx	México	Ven Venezuela

2 **(a)** (carry) (liter) ⟨*banner/coffin*⟩ llevar, portar (liter) **(b)** (harbor): **she's not one to ~ a grudge** no es rencorosa; **to ~ sb malice** guardarle rencor a algn

3 (have, show) ⟨*title/signature*⟩ llevar; ⟨*scars*⟩ tener*; ⟨*resemblance*⟩ tener*

4 **(a)** (produce) ⟨*fruit/crop*⟩ dar*; ⟨*interest*⟩ devengar* **(b)** (give birth to) ⟨*child*⟩ dar* a luz; *see also* BORN¹

■ **~** *vi* (turn) torcer*; **~ left** tuerza a la izquierda
■ **bear out** [*v + o + adv, v + adv + o*] ⟨*theory*⟩ confirmar
■ **bear up** [*v + adv*]: **she bore up well under the strain** sobrellevó muy bien la situación
■ **bear with** [*v + prep + o*] ⟨*person/mood*⟩ tener* paciencia con; **if you'll just ~ with me for a moment, ...** (asking to wait) si tienen la bondad de esperar un momento, ...; (asking for patience) si puedo poner a prueba su paciencia, ...

bear² *n* oso, osa *m,f*

bearable /ˈberəbəl ‖ˈbeərəbəl/ *adj* soportable

beard /bɪrd ‖bɪəd/ *n* barba *f*

bearded /ˈbɪrdəd ‖ˈbɪədɪd/ *adj* con *or* de barba

bearer /ˈberər ‖ˈbeərə(r)/ *n* **(a)** (of news) portador, -dora *m,f* **(b)** (carrier, porter) portador, -dora *m,f*, porteador, -dora *m,f* **(c)** (holder — of check) portador, -dora *m,f*; (— of passport) titular *mf*

bearing /ˈberɪŋ ‖ˈbeərɪŋ/ *n* **1** **(a)** (Aviat, Naut) demora *f*; **to get/lose one's ~s** orientarse/ desorientarse **(b)** (relevance): **that has no ~ on the subject** eso no tiene ninguna relación con el tema **2** (way of standing) porte *m*

beast /biːst/ *n* bestia *f*

beat¹ /biːt/ (*past* **beat**; *past p* **beaten** /ˈbiːtṇ/) *vt* **1** **(a)** (hit) golpear; ⟨*carpet*⟩ sacudir; ⟨*wings*⟩ batir; ⟨*child/wife*⟩ maltratar **(b)** (hammer) ⟨*metal*⟩ batir **(c)** (Culin) batir
2 ⟨*opponent*⟩ ganarle a; ⟨*record*⟩ batir; **our prices can't be ~en** nuestros precios son imbatibles
3 (arrive before, anticipate): **I ~ him to the telephone** llegué antes que él al teléfono; **to ~ sb to it** adelantársele a algn
3 (Mus) ⟨*time*⟩ marcar*

■ **~** *vi* **(a)** (strike): **he could hear them ~ing on the door** los oía golpear la puerta; **the waves were ~ing against the cliff** las olas golpeaban contra el acantilado **(b)** (pulsate) «*heart*» latir, palpitar; «*drum*» redoblar; «*wings*» batir
■ **beat down** **1** [*v + o + adv, v + adv + o*] ⟨*door*⟩ tirar abajo; ⟨*crop*⟩ aplastar
2 [*v + adv*] «*sun*» caer* de lleno; «*rain*» llover* con fuerza
■ **beat up** [*v + o + adv, v + adv + o*] (colloq) darle* una paliza a (fam)
■ **beat up on** [*v + adv + prep + o*] (AmE colloq) darle* una paliza a

beat² *n* **1** (of heart) latido *m*; (of drum) golpe *m*
2 (Mus) (rhythmic accent) tiempo *m*; (rhythm) ritmo *m* **3** (of policeman) ronda *f*

beat³ *adj* (colloq) (*pred*): **to be** (dead) **~** estar* reventado (fam)

beaten /ˈbiːtṇ/ *past p of* BEAT¹

beating /ˈbiːtɪŋ/ *n* **(a)** (thrashing) paliza *f* **(b)** (defeat) paliza *f* (fam) **(c)** (surpassing): **her time will take some ~** va a ser difícil superar su marca

beautiful /ˈbjuːtəfəl ‖ˈbjuːtɪfəl/ *adj* **(a)** (in

appearance) precioso, hermoso, bello (liter) **(b)** (very good) (colloq) ⟨*meal/weather*⟩ estupendo **(c)** (kind) (esp AmE) ⟨*person*⟩ encantador

beautifully /ˈbjuːtəfli ‖ˈbjuːtɪfəli/ *adv* (excellently, very well) ⟨*sing/dance*⟩ maravillosamente (bien); **she was ~ dressed** iba elegantísima

beauty /ˈbjuːti/ *n* (*pl* **-ties**) **1** (quality) belleza *f*, hermosura *f*; (*before n*) **~ contest** *o* (esp AmE) **pageant** concurso *m* de belleza; **~ queen** reina *f* de la belleza **2** (woman) belleza *f*

beauty: **~ salon** *n* salón *m* de belleza; **~ shop** *n* (AmE) salón *m* de belleza; **~ spot** *n* **1** (place) lugar *m* pintoresco; **2** (on face) lunar *m*

beaver /ˈbiːvər ‖ˈbiːvə(r)/ *n* castor *m*

became /bɪˈkeɪm/ *past of* BECOME

because /bəˈkɔːz, bɪˈkʌz/ *conj* **1** porque **2** **because of** (*as prep*) por, a *or* por causa de (frml)

beck /bek/ *n*: **to be at sb's ~ and call** estar* siempre a entera disposición de algn

beckon /ˈbekṇ/ *vt*: **to ~ sb over** hacerle* señas a algn para que se acerque
■ **~** *vi* hacer* una seña; **she ~ed to him to follow** le hizo señas para que la siguiera

become /bɪˈkʌm/ (*past* **became**; *past p* **become**) *vi*: **to ~ famous** hacerse* famoso; **to ~ accustomed to sth** acostumbrarse a algo; **she soon became bored** pronto se aburrió; **the heat became unbearable** el calor se hizo insoportable; **they became friends** se hicieron amigos
■ **~** *vt* **(a)** (befit) (frml) (*often neg*) ser* apropiado para **(b)** (suit) favorecer*
■ **become of** (*usu interrog*) ser* de; **what's to ~ of me?** ¿qué va a ser de mí?

becoming /bɪˈkʌmɪŋ/ *adj* **(a)** (fitting) (frml) apropiado **(b)** ⟨*outfit/hat*⟩ favorecedor, sentador (AmL)

bed /bed/ *n* **1** (for sleeping) cama *f*; **to make the ~** hacer* *or* (AmL tb) tender* la cama; **to get into/ out of ~** acostarse*/levantarse; **to go to ~** acostarse*; **he's in ~ with measles** está en cama con sarampión; **we put the children to ~ early** acostamos a los niños temprano **2** (for plants) arriate *m*, cantero *m* (RPl) **3** (of river) lecho *m*, cauce *m*; (of sea) fondo *m* **4** (base, support) base *f*

bed: ~ and breakfast /ˈbedṇˈbrekfəst/ *n* **(a)** (service): **they do ~ and breakfast** dan alojamiento y desayuno **(b)** (establishment) ≈pensión *f*; **~clothes** *pl* ropa *f* de cama

bedding /ˈbedɪŋ/ *n* **(a)** ▶ BEDCLOTHES **(b)** (for animals) cama *f*

bedlam /ˈbedləm/ *n* (colloq): **there was ~ when he announced the news** se armó la de San Quintín cuando anunció la noticia (fam)

bedpan /ˈbedpæn/ *n* (Med) cuña *f*

bedraggled /bɪˈdrægəld/ *adj* desaliñado; ⟨*hair*⟩ despeinado

bed: ~ridden *adj* postrado en cama; **~room** *n* dormitorio *m*, cuarto *m*, pieza *f* (esp AmL), recámara *f* (esp Méx); **~side** *n*: **they sat at his ~side throughout the night** pasaron toda la noche junto a su cabecera; (*before n*) **~side table** mesita *f* de noche, velador *m* (AmS), mesa *f* de luz (RPl); **~sit, ~sitter** /ˈbed.sɪtər ‖/ˌbedˈsɪtə(r)/ *n* (BrE colloq) habitación *f* amueblada (*cuyo alquiler suele incluir el uso de baño y cocina comunes*); **~sore** ⋯

n escara *f*, úlcera *f* de decúbito (frml) (*llaga que se produce por estar mucho tiempo en cama*); **~spread** *n* cubrecama *m*, colcha *f*; **~time** *n* hora *f* de acostarse

bee /biː/ *n* **1** (Zool) abeja *f* **2** (social gathering) (esp AmE) círculo *m*

beech /biːtʃ/ *n* **~ (tree)** haya *f*

beef /biːf/ *n* carne *f* de vaca *or* (AmC, Méx) de res, ternera *f* (Esp)

beefburger /'biːfˌbɜːrgər ‖ 'biːfˌbɜːgə(r)/ *n* (esp BrE) hamburguesa *f*

bee: ~hive *n* colmena *f*; **~line** *n*: **to make a ~line for sb/sth** (colloq) irse* derechito a algn/algo (fam)

been /bɪn ‖ biːn/ **(a)** *past p of* BE **(b)** *past p of* GO[1] *vi* I 2

beep[1] /biːp/ *n* (colloq) pitido *m*

beep[2] *vt/i* (colloq) pitar

beer /bɪr ‖ bɪə(r)/ *n* cerveza *f*

beer: ~ garden *n*: *jardín o patio abierto de un bar*; **~ mat** *n* posavasos *m* (*de cartón*)

beeswax /'biːzwæks/ *n* cera *f* de abeja

beet /biːt/ *n* (*pl* **~s**) (AmE) remolacha *f or* (Méx) betabel *m or* (Chi) betarraga *f*

beetle /'biːtl/ *n* escarabajo *m*

beetroot /'biːtruːt/ *n* (BrE) ▶ BEET

befall /bɪ'fɔːl/ *vt* (*past* **befell** /bɪ'fel/ *past p* **befallen** /bɪ'fɔːlən/) (liter) sucederle *or* ocurrirle a

before[1] /bɪ'fɔːr ‖ bɪ'fɔː(r)/ *prep* **1** **(a)** (preceding in time) antes de; **~ long** dentro de poco; **~ going in** antes de entrar **2** **(a)** (in front of) delante de, ante (frml) **(b)** (in rank, priority): **she puts her work ~ her family** antepone el trabajo a su familia

before[2] *conj* **(a)** (earlier than) antes de que (+ *subj*), antes de (+ *inf*) **(b)** (rather than) antes que

before[3] *adv* (preceding) antes; **the day ~** el día anterior; **have you been to Canada ~?** ¿ya has estado en el Canadá?

beforehand /bɪ'fɔːrhænd ‖ bɪ'fɔːhænd/ *adv* (earlier) antes; (in advance) de antemano

befriend /bɪ'frend/ *vt* hacerse* amigo de

beg /beɡ/ **-gg-** *vt* **1** ⟨money/food⟩ pedir*, mendigar* **2** (frml) (entreat) ⟨person⟩ suplicarle* a, rogarle* a **(b)** (ask for) ⟨forgiveness⟩ suplicar*, rogar*

■ **~** *vi* «*beggar*» pedir*, mendigar*; **to ~ for mercy** pedir* *or* suplicar* clemencia

began /bɪ'ɡæn/ *past of* BEGIN

beget /bɪ'ɡet/ *vt* (*pres p* **begetting**; *past* **begot** *or* (arch) **begat** /bɪ'ɡæt/; *past p* **begotten**) (liter) engendrar

beggar /'beɡər ‖ 'beɡə(r)/ *n* mendigo, -ga *m,f*

begin /bɪ'ɡɪn/ (*pres p* **beginning**; *past* **began**; *past p* **begun**) *vt* empezar*, comenzar*; **to ~ -ING/to + INF** empezar* *or* comenzar* A + INF

■ **~** *vi* empezar*, comenzar*; «*custom*» originarse; **to ~ with** para empezar

beginner /bɪ'ɡɪnər ‖ bɪ'ɡɪnə(r)/ *n* principiante *mf*

beginning /bɪ'ɡɪnɪŋ/ *n* **(a)** (in time, place) principio *m*; **at the ~ of the year/of June** a principios del año/de junio; **I'll start again from the ~** volveré a empezar desde el principio; **from**

~ to end de principio a fin **(b)** (origin, early stage) (*often pl*) comienzo *m* **(c)** (start, debut) (*no pl*) comienzo *m*

begot /bɪ'ɡɑːt ‖ bɪ'ɡɒt/ *past of* BEGET

begotten /bɪ'ɡɑːtn̩ ‖ bɪ'ɡɒtn̩/ *past p of* BEGET

begrudge /bɪ'ɡrʌdʒ/ *vt*: **I ~ paying so much** me da rabia pagar tanto; **I don't ~ you your success** no te envidio el éxito que tienes

beguile /bɪ'ɡaɪl/ *vt* (charm) cautivar, seducir*

beguiling /bɪ'ɡaɪlɪŋ/ *adj* cautivador, seductor

begun /bɪ'ɡʌn/ *past p of* BEGIN

behalf /bɪ'hæf ‖ bɪ'hɑːf/ *n*: **on o** (AmE also) **in ~ of sb, on o** (AmE also) **in sb's ~** **1** (as representative of): **I'd like to thank you on ~ of the team** quisiera darle las gracias en nombre de *or* de parte de todo el equipo; **he accepted the award on her ~** aceptó el premio en su nombre **2** (in the interest of): **he argued on her ~ that ...** alegó en su defensa *or* en su favor que ...

behave /bɪ'heɪv/ *vi* **(a)** (act) comportarse; (esp of children) portarse **(b)** (be good) «*child/animal*» portarse bien, comportarse

■ *v refl* **to ~ oneself** portarse bien, comportarse

behavior, (BrE) **behaviour** /bɪ'heɪvjər ‖ bɪ'heɪvjə(r)/ *n* conducta *f*, comportamiento *m*

behead /bɪ'hed/ *vt* decapitar

beheld /bɪ'held/ *past and past p of* BEHOLD

behind[1] /bɪ'haɪnd/ *prep* **1** **(a)** (to the rear of) detrás de, atrás de (AmL); **we're ten years ~ the Japanese in microelectronics** llevamos un retraso de diez años respecto a los japoneses **(b)** (on the other side of) detrás de, atrás de (AmL) **2** (responsible for) detrás de; **the motives ~ his decision** los motivos que lo llevaron a esa decisión **3** (in time): **all that is ~ us now** todo eso ha quedado atrás; **I'm ~ schedule** voy retrasado (con el trabajo *or* los preparativos *etc*)

behind[2] *adv* **(a)** (to the rear, following): **he ran along ~** iba corriendo detrás *or* (AmL tb) atrás; **I was attacked from ~** me atacaron por la espalda; **keep an eye on the car ~** no pierdas de vista al coche de atrás **(b)** (in race, competition): **England were two goals ~** Inglaterra iba perdiendo por dos goles **(c)** (in arrears): **I'm ~ with my work/payments** estoy atrasada con el trabajo/en los pagos

behind[3] *n* (colloq & euph) trasero *m* (fam)

behold /bɪ'həʊld/ (*past and past p* **beheld**) *vt* (liter) contemplar (liter)

beige /beɪʒ/ *adj* beige *adj inv*, beis *adj inv* (Esp)

Beijing /'beɪ'dʒɪŋ/ *n* Beijing *m*

being /'biːɪŋ/ *n* ser *m*

Belarus /'belə'ruːs/ *n* Bielorrusia *f*

belated /bɪ'leɪtəd ‖ bɪ'leɪtɪd/ *adj* tardío

belch /beltʃ/ *vi* «*person*» eructar; **flames ~ed from the cannon** la boca del cañón escupía llamas

Belgian[1] /'beldʒən/ *adj* belga

Belgian[2] *n* belga *mf*

Belgium /'beldʒəm/ *n* Bélgica *f*

belie /bɪ'laɪ/ *vt* **belies, belying, belied (a)** (disguise) no dejar traslucir **(b)** (show to be false): **this ~s the notion that ...** esto demuestra que no es cierto que ...

belief /bə'li:f ‖br'li:f/ n **(a)** (conviction, opinion) creencia f **(b)** (confidence) ∼ **IN** sb/sth confianza f or fe f **EN** algn/algo **(c)** (Relig) fe f

believable /bə'li:vəbəl ‖br'li:vəbəl/ adj ⟨story/ account⟩ verosímil

believe /bə'li:v ‖br'li:v/ vt **(a)** ⟨statement/story⟩ creer*; ⟨person⟩ creerle* a; **I don't** ∼ **it!** ¡no puedo creerlo!; **to make** ∼ **(that)** hacer* de cuenta que **(b)** (think) creer*
■ ∼ vi creer*; **to** ∼ **IN** sth/sb creer* **EN** algo/algn

believer /bə'li:vər ‖br'li:və(r)/ n creyente mf

belittle /br'lɪtl/ vt ⟨achievements⟩ menospreciar; ⟨person⟩ denigrar

bell /bel/ n **(a)** (of church, clock) campana f; (on cat, toy) cascabel m; (on door, bicycle) timbre m; (of telephone, timer) timbre m; **to ring a** ∼**:** **the name rings a** ∼ me suena el nombre; (before n) ∼ **tower** campanario m

belligerent /bə'lɪdʒərənt/ adj agresivo

bellow /'beləʊ/ vi bramar; (shout) gritar

bellows /'beləʊz/ n (pl ∼) (for fire) fuelle m

bell pepper n (AmE) ▶ CAPSICUM

belly /'beli/ n (pl **-lies**) **(a)** (of person) vientre m, barriga f (fam); (of animal) panza f, vientre m; (before n) ∼ **button** (colloq) ombligo m; **to do a** ∼ **flop** darse* un planchazo or (Andes) un guatazo (fam)

belong /br'lɔ:ŋ ‖br'lɒŋ/ vi **1** **(a)** (be property) **to** ∼ **TO** sb ser* **DE** algn, pertenecerle* a algn **(b)** (be member) **to** ∼ **TO** sth ⟨to a club⟩ ser* socio **DE** algo; ⟨to a union/political party⟩ estar* afiliado a algo **2** (have as usual place) ir*; **put them back where they** ∼ vuélvelos a poner en su lugar

belongings /br'lɔ:ŋɪŋz ‖br'lɒŋɪŋz/ pl n pertenencias fpl

beloved /br'lʌvəd ‖br'lʌvɪd/ adj (before n) querido

below¹ /br'ləʊ/ prep **1** (under) debajo de, abajo de (AmL) **2** (inferior, junior to) por debajo de **3** (less than) por debajo de; ∼ **zero** bajo cero

below² adv **1** (underneath) abajo; **put it on the shelf** ∼ ponlo en el estante de abajo **2** (in text) más abajo **3** (of temperature): **20** (degrees) ∼ 20 (grados) bajo cero

belt¹ /belt/ n **1** (Clothing) cinturón m **2** (Mech Eng) correa f

belt² vt (colloq) darle* una paliza a

beltway /'beltweɪ/ n (AmE) carretera f de circunvalación

bemoan /br'məʊn/ vt lamentarse de

bemused /br'mju:zd/ adj de desconcierto

bench /bentʃ/ n **1** **(a)** (seat) banco m **(b)** (work∼) mesa f de trabajo **2** (Law) **the bench** or **the Bench** (judges collectively) la judicatura; (tribunal) el tribunal

bend¹ /bend/ n **(a)** (in road, river) curva f **(b)** **bends** pl **the** ∼**s** la enfermedad del buzo

bend² (past and past p **bent**) vt ⟨wire/branch⟩ torcer*, curvar; ⟨back/leg⟩ doblar; ❸ **do not bend** no doblar
■ ∼ vi **(a)** «pipe/wire» torcerse* **(b)** «person» ▶ BEND DOWN **(c)** ⟨road/river⟩ hacer* una curva
■ **bend down** [v + adv] agacharse
■ **bend over** [v + adv] inclinarse

beneath¹ /br'ni:θ/ prep **1** (under) bajo **2** **(a)** (inferior to): **she married** ∼ **her** no se casó bien **(b)** (unworthy of): **it's** ∼ **her** es indigno de ella; **you're** ∼ **contempt** no mereces ni desprecio

beneath² adv: **the floor** ∼ el piso de abajo; **I wondered what lay** ∼ me preguntaba qué habría debajo or abajo

benefactor /'benəfæktər ‖'benɪfæktə(r)/ n benefactor, -tora m,f

beneficial /'benə'fɪʃəl ‖,benɪ'fɪʃəl/ adj beneficioso

beneficiary /'benə'fɪʃieri ‖,benɪ'fɪʃəri/ n (pl **-ries**) beneficiario, -ria m,f

benefit¹ /'benəfɪt ‖'benɪfɪt/ n **1** (good) beneficio m, bien m; (advantage) provecho m; **to give sb the** ∼ **of the doubt** darle* a algn el beneficio de la duda **2** (Soc Adm) prestación f; see also UNEMPLOYMENT **3** (concert, performance) beneficio m; (before n) con fines benéficos

benefit² **-t-** or (AmE also) **-tt-** vt beneficiar
■ ∼ vi beneficiarse; **to** ∼ **FROM** sth beneficiarse **CON** algo

benevolent /bə'nevələnt/ adj ⟨person/smile⟩ benévolo; ⟨gesture⟩ de benevolencia

benign /br'naɪn/ adj **(a)** ⟨person/attitude⟩ benévolo **(b)** (Med) benigno

bent¹ /bent/ past and past p of BEND²

bent² adj **1** ⟨pipe⟩ curvado, torcido **2** (determined) **to be** ∼ **ON doing sth** estar* empeñado **EN** hacer algo

bequeath /br'kwi:ð, -'kwi:θ/ vt **to** ∼ sth **TO** sb legarle* algo **A** algn

bequest /br'kwest/ n legado m

berate /br'reɪt/ vt (frml) **to** ∼ sb (**FOR** sth) reprender a algn (**POR** algo)

bereaved /br'ri:vd/ adj desconsolado (por la muerte de un ser querido)

bereavement /br'ri:vmənt/ n dolor m (por la muerte de un ser querido)

beret /bə'reɪ ‖'bereɪ/ n boina f

Berlin /'bɜ:r'lɪn ‖bɜ:'lɪn/ n Berlín m

Bermuda /bər'mju:də ‖bə'mju:də/ n las (islas) Bermudas

berry /'beri/ n (pl **-ries**) (Bot) baya f; (Culin) fresas, frambuesas, moras etc

berserk /bər'sɜ:rk ‖bə'sɜ:k/ adj: **to go** ∼ ponerse* como una fiera

berth¹ /bɜ:rθ ‖bɜ:θ/ n **(a)** (bunk) litera f, cucheta f (RPl); (cabin) camarote m **(b)** (mooring) atracadero m; **to give sb a wide** ∼ eludir a algn

berth² vt/i atracar*

beseech /br'si:tʃ/ vt (past & past p **beseeched** or **besought**) (liter) suplicar*, rogar*

beset /br'set/ vt (pres p **besetting**; past & past p **beset**) «anxieties/fears» acuciar; **he was** ∼ **by doubts** lo acosaban las dudas

beside¹ /br'saɪd/ prep **(a)** (at the side of) al lado de; **to be** ∼ **oneself**: **he was** ∼ **himself with rage** estaba fuera de sí (de la rabia); **she's** ∼ **herself with happiness** está que no cabe en sí de la alegría **(b)** (compared with) comparado con **(c)** (extraneous to): **that's** ∼ **the point** eso no tiene nada que ver **(d)** ▶ BESIDES¹

beside² adv **(a)** (alongside) al lado **(b)** ▶ BESIDES²

besides¹ /bɪˈsaɪdz/ *prep* **(a)** (in addition to) además de **(b)** (apart from) excepto, aparte de
besides² *adv* además
besiege /bɪˈsiːdʒ/ *vt* sitiar, asediar; **the village was ~d by reporters** el pueblo se vio asediado por periodistas
besotted /bɪˈsɒtəd ‖bɪˈsɒtɪd/ *adj* (*usu pred*): **he's totally ~ with her** está perdidamente enamorado de ella
besought /bɪˈsɔːt/ *past & past p of* BESEECH
bespectacled /bɪˈspektɪkəld/ *adj* de anteojos *or* lentes (AmL), con gafas (esp Esp)
best¹ /best/ *adj* (*superl of* GOOD¹) mejor; **for the ~ part of an hour/a month** durante casi una hora/un mes; **she's not very tolerant at the ~ of times** la tolerancia no es precisamente una de sus características
best² *adv* (*superl of* WELL¹,²) mejor; **I did it as ~ I could** lo hice lo mejor que pude; **it's ~ forgotten** más vale olvidarlo
best³ *n* **1** **the ~ (a)** (+ *sing vb*) lo mejor; **to do one's ~** hacer* todo lo posible; **we'll just have to make the ~ of what we've got** tendremos que arreglarnos con lo que tenemos; **(b)** (+ *pl vb*): **they're (the) ~ of friends** son de lo más amigos; **she can ski with the ~ of them** (colloq) esquía tan bien como el mejor **2 (a) at best: at ~, we'll just manage to cover costs** como mucho, podremos cubrir los gastos **(b) at/past one's best: at his ~, his singing rivals that of Caruso** en sus mejores momentos puede compararse a Caruso; **the roses were past their ~** las rosas ya no estaban en su mejor momento **3 (a)** (in greetings): **all the ~!** ¡buena suerte! **(b)** (Sport) récord *m*; **a personal ~ for Flynn** un récord para Flynn
best man *n*: *amigo que acompaña al novio el día de la boda*, ≈padrino *m*, testigo *m*
bestow /bɪˈstəʊ/ *vt* (frml or liter) **to ~ sth ON** *o* **UPON sb** ⟨*title/award*⟩ conferirle* algo A algn (frml)
best-seller /ˈbestˈselər ‖ˌbestˈselə(r)/ *n* (book) bestseller *m*; (product) superventas *m*; (author) autor, -tora *m,f* de bestsellers
bet¹ /bet/ *n* apuesta *f*; **I had a ~ with Charlie that Brazil would win** le aposté a Charlie que ganaría Brasil; **your best ~ is to stay here** lo mejor que puedes hacer es quedarte aquí
bet² (*pres p* **betting**; *past & past p* **bet**) *vt* apostar*
■ ~ *vi* jugar*; **to ~ ON sth/sb** apostarle* A algo/ algn; **I wouldn't ~ on it if I were you** yo no estaría tan seguro, yo no me fiaría
betray /bɪˈtreɪ/ *vt* ⟨*ally*⟩ traicionar; **he ~ed us to the enemy** nos vendió al enemigo; **her voice ~ed her nervousness** su voz revelaba el miedo que sentía
betrayal /bɪˈtreɪəl/ *n* traición *f*
betrothal /bɪˈtrəʊðəl/ *n* (frml) esponsales *mpl* (frml)
better¹ /ˈbetər ‖ˈbetə(r)/ *adj* **1** (*comp of*

GOOD¹) mejor; **to get ~** mejorar; **if they can both come, so much the ~** si pueden venir los dos, mucho *or* tanto mejor **2** (*pred*) (recovered from illness): **to be ~** estar* mejor; **to get ~** recuperarse
better² *adv* **1** (*comp of* WELL¹,²) mejor **2 had better** (ought): **I'd ~ leave before it gets dark** va a ser mejor que me vaya antes de que oscurezca; **well, I'd ~ be off** bueno, me tengo que ir
better³ *n* **(a)** (superior of two): **the ~ of the two** el mejor de los/las dos; **for the ~** para bien; **to get the ~ of sb/sth** ganarle la batalla a algn/algo **(b) betters** *pl* (superiors) superiores *mpl*; **his elders and ~s** sus mayores
better⁴ *vt* mejorar; **to ~ oneself** superarse
better-off /ˌbetərˈɔːf ‖ˌbetərˈɒf/ *adj* (*pred* **better off**) **(a)** (financially) de mejor posición económica **(b)** (emotionally, physically) (*pred*) mejor
betting shop /ˈbetɪŋ/ *n* (BrE) agencia *f* de apuestas
between¹ /bɪˈtwiːn/ *prep* entre
between² *adv*: **the one ~** el/la de en medio
beverage /ˈbevərɪdʒ/ *n* bebida *f*
beware /bɪˈwer ‖bɪˈweə(r)/ *vi* (only in inf and imperative): **~!** ¡(ten) cuidado!; ⑤ **beware of the dog** cuidado con el perro
bewildered /bɪˈwɪldərd ‖bɪˈwɪldəd/ *adj* desconcertado; (overwhelmed) apabullado
bewildering /bɪˈwɪldərɪŋ/ *adj* desconcertante; (overwhelming) apabullante
bewitch /bɪˈwɪtʃ/ *vt* (cast spell on) embrujar; (entrance, delight) cautivar
beyond¹ /bɪˈɑːnd ‖bɪˈjɒnd/ *prep* **1** (on other side of): **I live just ~ the station** vivo justo pasando la estación; **~ this point** de aquí en adelante **2 (a)** (further than): **try to think ~ the immediate future** trata de pensar más allá del futuro inmediato **(b)** (more than, apart from): **I can't tell you anything ~ that** no te puedo decir nada más que eso **3** (past): **it's ~ repair** ya no tiene arreglo; **circumstances ~ our control** circunstancias ajenas a nuestra voluntad; **it's ~ me what she sees in him** (colloq) no puedo entender qué es lo que ve en él; **to live ~ one's means** vivir por encima de sus (*or* mis *etc*) posibilidades
beyond² *adv* **(a)** (in space) más allá **(b)** (in time): **we're planning for the year 2000 and ~** estamos haciendo planes para el 2000 y más allá del 2000
bias /ˈbaɪəs/ *n* parcialidad *f*; **the course has a scientific ~** el curso tiene un enfoque científico
biased, biassed /ˈbaɪəst/ *adj* ⟨*report/criticism*⟩ tendencioso; ⟨*judge*⟩ parcial; **to be ~ AGAINST/TOWARD(S) sth/sb** estar* predispuesto EN CONTRA DE/A FAVOR DE algo/algn
bib /bɪb/ *n* **(a)** (for baby) babero *m* **(b)** (on dungarees) peto *m*
Bible /ˈbaɪbəl/ *n* Biblia *f*
biblical /ˈbɪblɪkəl/ *adj* bíblico
bibliography /ˌbɪbliˈɑːgrəfi ‖ˌbɪbliˈɒgrəfi/ *n* (*pl* **-phies**) bibliografía *f*

AmC Central America	Arg Argentina	Cu Cuba	Per Peru
AmL Latin America	Bol Bolivia	Ec Ecuador	RPI River Plate Area
AmS South America	Chi Chile	Esp Spain	Ur Uruguay
Andes Andean Region	CS Southern Cone	Méx Mexico	Ven Venezuela

b

bicarbonate of soda /baɪˈkɑːrbəneɪt ‖baɪˈkɑːbəneɪt/ n bicarbonato m de sodio or de soda or (Esp) de sosa

biceps /ˈbaɪseps/ n (pl ~) bíceps m

bicker /ˈbɪkər ‖ˈbɪkə(r)/ vi pelear, discutir

bicycle /ˈbaɪsɪkəl/ n bicicleta f

bid[1] /bɪd/ vt **1** (pres p **bidding**; past & past p **bid**) (at auction) ofrecer* **2** (pres p **bidding**; past **bade** or **bid**; past p **bidden** or **bid**) (liter) **(a)** (wish, say): **to ~ sb farewell** despedirse* de algn **(b)** (request) **to ~ sb (to)** + INF pedirle* a algn QUE + SUBJ

■ ~ vi (pres p **bidding**; past & past p **bid**) (at auction) hacer* ofertas, pujar; **to ~ FOR sth** pujar POR algo

bid[2] n **1** (at auction) oferta f, puja f **2** (attempt) intento m, tentativa f; (unsuccessful) intentona f, intento m; **~ to** + INF intento m DE + INF

bidden /ˈbɪdn̩/ past p of BID[1] vt 2

bidder /ˈbɪdər ‖ˈbɪdə(r)/ n postor, -tora m,f

bidding /ˈbɪdɪŋ/ n **1** (at auction): **the ~ opened at $100** la subasta abrió con una oferta de $100 **2** (wishes): **they had servants to do their ~** tenían criados para lo que se les antojara; **at his father's ~** a petición de su padre

bide /baɪd/ vt: **to ~ one's time** esperar el momento oportuno

bidet /bɪˈdeɪ ‖ˈbiːdeɪ/ n bidet m, bidé m

biennial /baɪˈeniəl/ adj bienal

bier /bɪr ‖bɪə(r)/ n andas fpl

bifocals /ˈbaɪfəʊkəlz/ pl n anteojos mpl or (esp Esp) gafas fpl bifocales

big /bɪɡ/ adj

■ Note The usual translation of big, grande, becomes gran when it is used before a singular noun.

-gg- grande; **a ~ garden** un jardín grande, un gran jardín; **how ~ is the table?** ¿cómo es de grande la mesa?; **a ~ hug/kiss** un abrazote/ besote (fam); **a ~ decision** una gran decisión; **our ~gest customer** nuestro cliente más importante; **she's really ~ in Europe** es muy conocida en Europa; **my ~ brother** mi hermano mayor

bigamist /ˈbɪɡəmɪst ‖ˈbɪɡəmɪst/ n bígamo, -ma m,f

bigamy /ˈbɪɡəmi/ n bigamia f

big: **~ business** n el gran capital; **to be ~ business** ser* un gran negocio; **~-headed** /ˈbɪɡˈhedəd ‖ˌbɪɡˈhedɪd/ adj (colloq) creído (fam); **~ league** n (in US) (Sport) liga f mayor; (top rank) los grandes; **~mouth** n (colloq) (boaster) fanfarrón, -rrona m,f; (gossip) chismoso, -sa m,f, cotilla mf (Esp fam), hocicón, -cona m,f (Chi, Méx fam)

bigot /ˈbɪɡət/ n intolerante mf

bigotry /ˈbɪɡətri/ n intolerancia f

big: **~ shot** n (colloq) pez m gordo (fam); **~ top** n carpa f de circo

bike /baɪk/ n (colloq) (bicycle) bici f (fam); (motorcycle) moto f

bikini /bɪˈkiːni/ n bikini m or (RPl) f

bilateral /ˈbaɪˈlætərəl/ adj bilateral

bilberry /ˈbɪlˌberi ‖ˈbɪlbəri/ n (pl **-ries**) arándano m

bilingual /baɪˈlɪŋɡwəl/ adj bilingüe

bilious /ˈbɪliəs/ adj: **to feel ~** sentirse* descompuesto; **~ attack** ataque m al or de hígado

bill[1] /bɪl/ n **1** **(a)** (invoice) factura f, cuenta f; **the telephone ~** la cuenta or (Esp tb) el recibo del teléfono **(b)** (in restaurant) (esp BrE) cuenta f, adición f (RPl) **2** (AmE Fin) (banknote) billete m **3** (Govt) proyecto m de ley **4** (program) programa m; **to top the ~** encabezar* el reparto **5** (certificate): **~ of sale** contrato m de venta; **a clean ~ of health** (favorable report) el visto bueno **6** (beak) pico m

bill[2] vt **1** (invoice, charge) pasarle la cuenta or la factura a **2** (advertise) ⟨play/performer⟩ anunciar

billboard /ˈbɪlbɔːrd/ n cartelera f

billet /ˈbɪlət ‖ˈbɪlɪt/ vt alojar

billfold /ˈbɪlfəʊld/ n (AmE) billetera f, cartera f

billiards /ˈbɪljərdz ‖ˈbɪljədz/ n (+ sing vb) billar m

billion /ˈbɪljən/ n mil millones mpl, millar m de millones

billow /ˈbɪləʊ/ vi **(a)** **~ (out)** ⟨sail/parachute⟩ hincharse **(b)** ⟨smoke⟩: **smoke ~ed from the window** nubes de humo salían de or por la ventana

billy /ˈbɪli/ n (pl **-lies**) **~ (goat)** macho m cabrío

bin /bɪn/ n (for kitchen refuse etc) (BrE) cubo m or (CS) tacho m or (Méx) bote m or (Col) caneca f or (Ven) tobo m de la basura; (wastepaper basket) (BrE) papelera f, papelero m, caneca f (Col); (litter ~) papelera f, basurero m (Chi, Méx), caneca f (Col)

binary /ˈbaɪnəri/ adj binario

bind[1] /baɪnd/ vt (past & past p **bound**) **1** (tie, fasten) ⟨person⟩ atar, amarrar; ▶ BOUND[4] 1A **2** **(a)** (wrap) envolver* **(b)** **~ (up)** ⟨wound⟩ vendar **3** (Law) obligar* **4** ⟨book⟩ encuadernar **5** (Culin) ligar*

bind[2] n (colloq) (difficult situation) aprieto m, apuro m; (nuisance) (BrE) lata f (fam), rollo m (Esp fam)

binder /ˈbaɪndər ‖ˈbaɪndə(r)/ n (file, folder) carpeta f

binding[1] /ˈbaɪndɪŋ/ n **(a)** (book cover) tapa f, cubierta f **(b)** (tape) ribete m

binding[2] adj ⟨promise/commitment⟩ que hay que cumplir; (Law) vinculante

binge /bɪndʒ/ n (colloq): **to go on a ~** irse* de juerga (fam)

bingo /ˈbɪŋɡəʊ/ n bingo m

binliner /ˈbɪnˌlaɪnər ‖ˈbɪnˌlaɪnə(r)/ n (BrE) bolsa f de (la) basura

binoculars /bəˈnɑːkjələrz ‖bɪˈnɒkjʊləz/ pl n gemelos mpl, prismáticos mpl, anteojos fpl de larga vista (esp AmL)

biochemistry /ˈbaɪəʊˈkeməstri/ n bioquímica f

biodegradable /ˈbaɪəʊdɪˈɡreɪdəbəl/ adj biodegradable

biodiversity /ˌbaɪəʊdaɪˈvɜːsəti/ n biodiversidad f

biographer /baɪˈɑːɡrəfər ‖baɪˈɒɡrəfə(r)/ n biógrafo, -fa m,f

biographical /ˈbaɪəˈɡræfɪkəl/ adj biográfico

biography /baɪˈɑːɡrəfi ‖baɪˈɒɡrəfi/ n (pl **-phies**) biografía f

biological /ˈbaɪəˈlɑːdʒɪkəl ‖ˌbaɪəˈlɒdʒɪkəl/ adj biológico

biologist /baɪˈɑːlədʒəst ‖barˈɒlədʒɪst/ n
biólogo, -ga m,f

biology /baɪˈɑːlədʒi ‖barˈɒlədʒi/ n biología f

biopsy /ˈbaɪɑːpsi ‖ˈbaɪɒpsi/ n (pl **-sies**)
biopsia f

birch /bɜːrtʃ ‖bɜːtʃ/ n ~ (**tree**) abedul m

bird /bɜːrd ‖bɜːd/ n (small) pájaro m; (large) ave
f‡; **to kill two ~s with one stone** matar dos
pájaros de un tiro

bird: ~**cage** n jaula f de pájaros; (large)
pajarera f; ~ **of prey** n (pl ~**s of prey**) ave f‡
rapaz or de rapiña or de presa; ~'**s-eye view**
n vista f aérea; ~**watcher** /ˈbɜːrdwɑːtʃər
‖ˈbɜːd,wɒtʃə(r)/ n observador, -dora m,f de aves;
~**watching** /ˈbɜːrd,wɑːtʃɪŋ ‖ˈbɜːd,wɒtʃɪŋ/ n
observación f de las aves (como hobby)

Biro®, **biro** /ˈbaɪrəʊ ‖ˈbaɪərəʊ/ n (pl **biros**)
(BrE) bolígrafo m, birome f (RPl), esfero m (Col),
lápiz m de pasta (Chi), boli m (Esp fam)

birth /bɜːrθ ‖bɜːθ/ n nacimiento m; (childbirth)
parto m; **at** ~ al nacer; **date of** ~ fecha f de
nacimiento; **to give** ~ dar* a luz, parir

birth: ~ **certificate** n partida f or certificado
m or (Méx) acta f de nacimiento; ~ **control** n
control m de la natalidad

birthday /ˈbɜːrθdeɪ ‖ˈbɜːθdeɪ/ n cumpleaños m;
(of institution) aniversario m; **it'll be his fifth** ~
cumple cinco años; **happy** ~! ¡feliz cumpleaños!;
(before n) **cake/card/party**) de cumpleaños

birth: ~**mark** n mancha f or marca f de
nacimiento, antojo m; ~**place** n (of person) lugar
m de nacimiento; (of movement, fashion, idea) cuna f

biscuit /ˈbɪskɪt/ n (Culin) (**a**) (BrE) bollo m,
panecillo m, bísquet m (Méx) (**b**) (cookie, cracker)
(BrE) galleta f, galletita f (RPl)

bisect /baɪˈsekt/ vt bisecar*

bisexual /ˌbaɪˈsekʃuəl/ adj bisexual

bishop /ˈbɪʃəp/ (**a**) n (Relig) obispo m (**b**) (in
chess) alfil m

bison /ˈbaɪsn̩/ n (pl ~) bisonte m

bit¹ /bɪt/ past of BITE¹

bit² n [1] (fragment, scrap) pedazo m, trozo m; **to
smash sth to** ~s hacer* pedazos algo; ~**s and
pieces** (assorted items) cosas fpl; (belongings) cosas
fpl; (broken fragments) pedazos mpl
[2] (section, piece) parte f
[3] **a bit of** (+ uncount noun) un poco de; **they
have quite a** ~ **of work to do** tienen bastante
trabajo que hacer
[4] **a bit** (as adv) (**a**) (somewhat) un poco; **the
town's changed a** ~ la ciudad ha cambiado algo
or un poco; **they hasn't changed a** ~ no ha
cambiado (para) nada (**b**) (a while) un momento
or rato
[5] (in adv phrases) (**a**) **bit by bit** poco a poco, de
a poco (AmL) (**b**) **every bit: I'm every** ~ **as
disappointed as you** estoy absolutamente tan
decepcionado como tú
[6] (Comput) bit m
[7] (of bridle) freno m, bocado m

bitch /bɪtʃ/ n [1] (female dog) perra f [2] (spiteful
woman) (AmE vulg, BrE sl) bruja f (fam), arpía f
(fam), cabrona f (Esp, Méx vulg)

bite¹ /baɪt/ (past **bit**; past p **bitten**) vt
«person/dog» morder*; «bug» picar*; **to** ~ **off**

more than one can chew tratar de abarcar más
de lo que se puede; **once bitten, twice shy** el gato
escaldado del agua fría huye
∎ ~ vi [1] (**a**) «person/dog» morder*;
«mosquito» picar*; «wind/frost» cortar; **to** ~
INTO sth darle* un mordisco A algo (**b**) (take bait)
«fish» picar* [2] «law/recession» hacerse*
sentir

bite² n [1] (act) mordisco m; (fierce) tarascada f
[2] (wound — from insect) picadura f; (— from dog,
snake) mordedura f [3] (snack) (colloq) (no pl)
bocado m; **to have a** ~ (to eat) comer un bocado,
comer algo

biting /ˈbaɪtɪŋ/ adj «wind» cortante; «sarcasm/
criticism» mordaz

bit part n papel m pequeño

bitten /ˈbɪtn̩/ past p of BITE¹

bitter¹ /ˈbɪtər ‖ˈbɪtə(r)/ adj [1] (**a**) (in taste)
amargo (**b**) (very cold) «weather» glacial; «wind/
frost» cortante [2] (**a**) (painful, hard)
«disappointment» amargo; **they fought on to the** ~
end lucharon valientemente hasta el final (**b**)
«person» resentido, amargado (**c**) «enemies/
hatred» implacable; «struggle» enconado

bitter² n (BrE) tipo de cerveza ligeramente
amarga

bitterly /ˈbɪtərli ‖ˈbɪtəli/ adv [1] «cold»: **it was**
~ **cold** hacía un frío glacial [2] (**a**)
«disappointed» tremendamente; «weep/complain/
say» amargamente (**b**) (implacably)
implacablemente

bitterness /ˈbɪtərnəs ‖ˈbɪtənɪs/ n [1] (of taste)
amargor m [2] (of person, disappointment) amargura f

bittersweet /ˈbɪtərswiːt ‖ˌbɪtəˈswiːt/ adj
agridulce; «chocolate» (AmE) amargo

bizarre /bɪˈzɑːr ‖brˈzɑː(r)/ adj «story/
coincidence» extraño; «appearance/behavior»
estrambótico

black¹ /blæk/ adj **-er, -est** [1] «dress/hair/
ink» negro; «sky» oscuro; «coffee» negro (AmL),
solo (Esp), tinto (Col), puro (Chi); «tea» solo, sin
leche, puro (Chi);~ **cloud** nubarrón m [2] also
Black «person/community» negro [3] (sad,
hopeless) negro

black² n [1] (color) negro m [2] also **Black**
(person) negro, -gra m,f [3] (freedom from debt): **to
be in the** ~ no estar* en números rojos
∎ **black out** [1] [v + adv] (lose consciousness)
perder* el conocimiento [2] [v + o + adv, v + adv
+ o] (in wartime) «windows» tapar; «lights» apagar*;
(by accident) «town/district» dejar sin luz

black: ~ **and white** n (Cin, Phot, TV) blanco y
negro m; **she sees things in** ~ **and white** para
ella no hay términos medios; ~**-and-white**
/ˈblækənˈhwaɪt ‖ˈblækənˈwaɪt/ adj (pred ~ **and
white**) en blanco y negro; ~ **belt** n cinturón m
negro, cinta f negra (Méx); (person) cinturón mf
negro, cinta mf negra (Méx); ~**berry**
/blæk,beri‖ˈblækbəri/ n mora f; ~**bird** n
(European) mirlo m; (North American) totí m;
~**board** n pizarra f, pizarrón m (AmL), tablero
m (Col); ~ **box** n (Aviat) caja f negra; ~**currant**
/ˈblækˈkɜːrənt ‖ˌblækˈkʌrənt/ n grosella f negra

blacken /ˈblækən/ vt (**a**) (make black)
ennegrecer* (**b**) (defame) «person» deshonrar;
«reputation» manchar

black: ~ **eye** n ojo m morado, ojo m a la

funerala (Esp fam), ojo *m* en compota (CS fam), ojo *m* en tinta (Chi fam); **~head** *n* espinilla *f*; **~ hole** *n* agujero *m* negro; **~ ice** *n capa fina de hielo en las carreteras*

blacklist¹ /'blæklɪst/ *n* lista *f* negra

blacklist² *vt* poner* en la lista negra

blackmail¹ /'blækmeɪl/ *n* chantaje *m*

blackmail² *vt* chantajear, hacerle* chantaje a

black: ~ mark *n* punto *m* en contra; **~ market** *n* mercado *m* negro; **~out** /'blækaʊt/ *n* [1] (loss of consciousness) desvanecimiento *m*, desmayo *m*; [2] (in wartime) *oscurecimiento de la ciudad para que esta no sea visible desde los aviones enemigos*; **B~ Sea** *n* **the B~ Sea** el Mar Negro; **~ sheep** *n* oveja *f* negra; **~smith** *n* herrero *m*

bladder /'blædər ‖'blædə(r)/ *n* (Anat) vejiga *f*

blade /bleɪd/ *n* [1] (of knife, razor) hoja *f* [2] (of propeller) pala *f*, paleta *f* [3] (Bot) (of grass) brizna *f*

blame¹ /bleɪm/ *vt* echarle la culpa a, culpar; **to ~ sb FOR sth** culpar a algn DE algo, echarle la culpa DE algo A algn; **to be to ~ for sth** tener* la culpa de algo; **to ~ sth ON sb/sth** echarle la culpa DE algo A algn/algo

blame² *n* culpa *f*; **it's always me that gets the ~** siempre me echan la culpa a mí

bland /blænd/ *adj* **-er, -est (a)** ‹*colors/music*› soso; ‹*food/taste*› insípido; ‹*statement/reply*› anodino; ‹*smile/manner*› insulso **(b)** (mild) ‹*food*› suave

blank¹ /blæŋk/ *adj* **(a)** (empty) ‹*page/space*› en blanco; ‹*tape*› virgen; **my mind went ~** me quedé en blanco; **a ~ expression** un rostro carente de expresión **(b)** (uncompromising) ‹*refusal/rejection*› rotundo **(c)** (Mil) ‹*ammunition*› de fogueo

blank² *n* **(a)** (empty space) espacio *m* en blanco; ***to draw a ~*** no obtener* ningún resultado **(b)** (Mil) cartucho *m* de fogueo

blank check, (BrE) **cheque** *n* cheque *m* en blanco

blanket¹ /'blæŋkət ‖'blæŋkɪt/ *n* manta *f*, cobija *f* (AmL), frazada *f* (AmL)

blanket² *adj* (*before n, no comp*) ‹*measure*› global

blare /bler ‖bleə(r)/*vi* atronar*

■ **blare out** [*v + adv + o*]: **the radio was blaring out music** el radio emitía música retumbante

blasphemous /'blæsfəməs/ *adj* blasfemo

blasphemy /'blæsfəmi/ *n* (*pl* **-mies**) blasfemia *f*

blast¹ /blæst ‖blɑ:st/ *n* [1] (of air, wind) ráfaga *f*; (of water) chorro *m* [2] (explosion) (journ) explosión *f* [3] (of sound) toque *m*; **he had the TV on full ~** tenía la tele a todo lo que daba (fam)

blast² *vt* **(a)** (blow) ‹*rock*› volar*; **they used dynamite to ~ the safe open** usaron dinamita para volar la caja fuerte **(b)** (attack) (journ) atacar*

■ **blast off** [*v + adv*] despegar*

blast-off /'blæstɔ:f ‖'blɑ:stɒf/ *n* despegue *m*

blatant /'bleɪtn̩t/ *adj* ‹*prejudice/disrespect*› descarado; ‹*lie*› flagrante; ‹*incompetence*› patente

blatantly /'bleɪtn̩tli/ *adv* descaradamente; **it's ~ obvious that ...** está clarísimo que ...

blaze¹ /bleɪz/ *n* [1] (in grate) fuego *m*; (bonfire) fogata *f*; (flames) llamaradas *fpl*; (dangerous fire) (journ) incendio *m* [2] (dazzling display) (*no pl*): **a ~ of color** un derroche de color; **in a ~ of glory** cubierto de gloria

blaze² *vi* «*fire*» arder; «*lights*» brillar; «*eyes*» centellear

blazer /'bleɪzər ‖'bleɪzə(r)/ *n* blazer *m*

bleach¹ /bli:tʃ/ *n* lejía *f*, blanqueador *m* (Col, Méx), lavandina *f* (Arg), agua *f*‡ Jane® (Ur), cloro *m* (AmC, Chi)

bleach² *vt* ‹*cloth*› (in the sun) blanquear; (with bleach) poner* en lejía (*or* blanqueador *etc*)

bleachers /'bli:tʃərz ‖'bli:tʃəz/ *pl n* (AmE) tribuna *f* descubierta

bleak /bli:k/ *adj* **-er, -est (a)** ‹*landscape*› inhóspito; ‹*room*› lóbrego **(b)** ‹*winter*› crudo; ‹*day*› gris y deprimente **(c)** (miserable, cheerless) ‹*prospects/news*› sombrío

bleary-eyed /'blɪri'aɪd ‖'blɪəri'aɪd/ *adj* con cara de sueño

bleat /bli:t/ *vi* balar

bleed /bli:d/ (*past & past p* **bled** /bled/) *vi* sangrar; **he bled to death** murió desangrado

■ **~** *vt* **(a)** (Med) sangrar; ***to ~ sb dry*** chuparle la sangre a algn (fam) **(b)** ‹*brakes/radiator*› purgar*

bleeding /'bli:dɪŋ/ *n* hemorragia *f*

bleep¹ /bli:p/ *n* pitido *m*

bleep² *vi* (BrE) emitir un pitido

blemish /'blemɪʃ/ *n* (on skin) imperfección *f*; (on reputation) mancha *f*

blend¹ /blend/ *n* combinación *f*, mezcla *f*

blend² *vt* mezclar, combinar; (in blender) licuar*

■ **~** *vi* «*flavors/colors*» armonizar*

■ **blend in** [1] [*v + o + adv, v + adv + o*] ‹*ingredients*› añadir y mezclar [2] [*v + adv*] (merge, harmonize) armonizar*

blender /'blendər ‖'blendə(r)/ *n* licuadora *f*

bless /bles/ *vt* (*past* **blessed**; *past p* **blessed** *or* (arch) **blest**) **(a)** (Relig) bendecir* **(b)** (*in interj phrases*) **~ you!** (to sb who sneezes) ¡salud! *or* (Esp) ¡Jesús!; **~ my soul!** (colloq) ¡válgame Dios!

blessed /'blesəd ‖'blesɪd/ *adj* bienaventurado

blessing /'blesɪŋ/ *n* [1] **(a)** (Relig — benediction) bendición *f*; (— of bread, wine) consagración *f* **(b)** (approval) aprobación *f* [2] (fortunate thing) bendición *f* (del cielo); ***to be a mixed ~*** tener* sus pros y sus contras

blest /blest/ (arch) *past & past pt of* BLESS

blew /blu:/ *past of* BLOW²

blight¹ /blaɪt/ *n* (Agr, Hort) añublo *m*; (loosely) peste *f*; (curse) plaga *f*

blight² *vt* ‹*crop/career/health*› arruinar; ‹*region*› asolar*; ‹*hopes*› malograr

blind¹ /blaɪnd/ *adj* [1] **(a)** (Med) ciego; **to go ~** quedarse ciego; **to be ~ TO sth** no ver* algo **(b)** (Auto) ‹*corner*› de poca visibilidad [2] ‹*faith/fury*› ciego

blind² *vt* **(a)** (permanently) dejar ciego **(b)** «*ambition/passion*» cegar*, enceguecer* (AmL); «*light/wealth*» deslumbrar

blind³ *n* [1] (outside window) persiana *f*; (roller ~) persiana *f* (de enrollar), estor *m* (Esp); (venetian ~) persiana *f* veneciana [2] (blind people) (+ *pl vb*) **the ~** los ciegos

blind date *n* cita *f* con un desconocido/una desconocida

blinders /'blaɪndərz ‖'blaɪndəz/ n pl (AmE) (on horse) anteojeras fpl

blindfold¹ /'blaɪndfəʊld/ vt vendarle los ojos a

blindfold² n venda f (para tapar los ojos)

blindfold³ adv con los ojos vendados

blindly /'blaɪndli/ adv (a) (without seeing) ‹grope› a ciegas (b) (without reasoning) ‹follow› ciegamente

blindness /'blaɪndnəs ‖'blaɪndnɪs/ n ceguera f

blind spot n (a) (weak point) punto m flaco (b) (Auto) punto m ciego

blink¹ /blɪŋk/ n parpadeo m, pestañeo m; **to be on the ~** (colloq) no marchar, no andar* bien (AmL)

blink² vi «eye/person» pestañear, parpadear; «light» parpadear

blinker /'blɪŋkər ‖'blɪŋkə(r)/ n **1** (a) (Auto colloq) intermitente m, direccional f (Col, Méx), señalizador m (de viraje) (Chi) (b) (AmE Transp) señal f intermitente **2 blinkers** pl (on horse) anteojeras fpl

blinkered /'blɪŋkərd ‖'blɪŋkəd/ adj ‹attitude› de miras estrechas; ‹view/outlook› estrecho

blip /blɪp/ n (a) (sound) bip m, pitidito m (b) (irregularity) accidente m; (problem) problema m pasajero

bliss /blɪs/ n dicha f

blissful /'blɪsfəl/ adj ‹smile› de gozo

blissfully /'blɪsfəli/ adv ‹smile/sigh› con gran felicidad

blister¹ /'blɪstər ‖'blɪstə(r)/ n (a) (Med) ampolla f (b) (on paintwork) ampolla f, burbuja f

blister² vi ampollarse

blithely /'blaɪðli/ adv alegremente

blitz /blɪts/ n (a) (Aviat, Mil) bombardeo m aéreo (b) (intense attack): this weekend we're going to have a ~ on the garden (colloq) este fin de semana vamos a atacar el jardín

blizzard /'blɪzərd ‖'blɪzəd/ n ventisca f

bloated /'bləʊtəd ‖'bləʊtɪd/ adj hinchado

blob /blɑːb ‖blɒb/ n (a) (drip) gota f (b) (indistinct shape) mancha f

bloc /blɑːk ‖blɒk/ n (Pol) bloque m

block¹ /blɑːk ‖blɒk/ n **1** (of stone, wood) bloque m; (starting ~) (Sport) taco m de salida; (of paper) bloc m

2 (a) (space enclosed by streets) manzana f; (distance between two streets): **it's eight ~s from here** (AmE) está a ocho cuadras or (Esp) calles de aquí (b) (building): **a ~ of flats** (BrE) un edificio de apartamentos or de departamentos (AmL), una casa de pisos (Esp); **an office ~** un edificio de oficinas

3 (section of text) sección f, bloque m

4 (Comput) bloque m

5 (blockage) obstrucción f, bloqueo m; **I have a mental ~ about physics** tengo un bloqueo mental con la física

6 (Sport) bloqueo m

block² vt **1** (a) (obstruct) ‹road/entrance› bloquear; **you're ~ing my way** me estás

impidiendo el paso; **that fat man is ~ing my view** ese gordo no me deja ver (b) ‹drain/sink› atascar*, tapar (AmL); **my nose is ~ed** tengo la nariz tapada

2 (a) (prevent) ‹progress› obstaculizar*; ‹funds/sale› congelar (b) (Sport) bloquear

■ **~** vi (Sport) bloquear

■ **block in** [v + o + adv, v + adv + o] cerrarle* el paso a

■ **block off** [v + o + adv, v + adv + o] ‹street› cortar

■ **block out** [v + o + adv, v + adv + o] (a) (shut out) ‹thought› ahuyentar (b) (obstruct) ‹light› tapar

■ **block up** [v + o + adv, v + adv + o] (a) (seal) ‹entrance/window› tapar (b) (cause obstruction in) ‹drain/sink› atascar*, tapar (AmL); **my nose is ~ed up** tengo la nariz tapada

blockade¹ /blɑːˈkeɪd ‖blɒˈkeɪd/ n bloqueo m

blockade² vt bloquear

blockage /'blɑːkɪdʒ ‖'blɒkɪdʒ/ n (in pipe, road) obstrucción f; (Med) oclusión f

block capitals, block letters pl n (letras fpl) mayúsculas fpl de imprenta

bloke /bləʊk/ n (BrE colloq) tipo m (fam), tío m (Esp fam)

blond /blɑːnd ‖blɒnd/ adj (f **blonde**) rubio or (Méx) güero or (Col) mono or (Ven) catire

blood /blʌd/ n sangre f; **in cold ~** a sangre fría; (before n) **~ donor** donante mf de sangre; **~ group** grupo m sanguíneo; **~ test** análisis m de sangre; **~ transfusion** transfusión f de sangre

blood: ~ bath n masacre f; **~curdling** /'blʌd,kɜːrdlɪŋ ‖'blʌd,kɜːdlɪŋ/ adj espeluznante, aterrador

bloodless /'blʌdləs ‖'blʌdlɪs/ adj ‹coup› sin derramamiento de sangre

blood: ~ pressure n tensión f or presión f (arterial); **~shed** n derramamiento m de sangre; **~shot** adj rojo, inyectado de sangre; **~ sport** n deporte m sangriento; **~stain** n mancha f de sangre; **~-stained** /'blʌdsteɪnd/ adj manchado de sangre; **~stream** n the ~stream el torrente sanguíneo; **~thirsty** adj (a) (cruel) sanguinario (b) ‹story/description› sangriento; **~ vessel** n vaso m sanguíneo

bloody¹ /'blʌdi/ adj **-dier, -diest** **1** (a) ‹hands/clothes› ensangrentado; ‹wound› que sangra, sangrante (b) ‹battle› sangriento **2** (esp BrE vulg or colloq) (no comp) (expressing annoyance, surprise, shock etc): **where's that ~ dog?** ¿dónde está ese maldito or (Méx) pinche perro? (fam); **~ hell!** ¡coño! (vulg), ¡chingado! (Méx vulg), ¡hostias! (Esp vulg)

bloody² adv (BrE vulg or colloq) (as intensifier): **the weather was ~ awful!** ¡hizo un tiempo de mierda! (vulg)

bloom¹ /bluːm/ n **1** (a) (flower) flor f (b) **to be in ~** estar* en flor; **to be in full ~** estar* en plena floración **2** (on fruits, leaves) vello m

bloom² vi «plant/garden» florecer*; «flower» abrirse*

blossom¹ /'blɑːsəm ‖ 'blɒsəm/ n (a) (mass of flowers) flores fpl (b) (by single bloom) flor f

blossom² vi (a) (flower) «tree» florecer* (b) (flourish) «arts» florecer*; «person/relationship» alcanzar* su plenitud

blot¹ /blɑːt ‖ blɒt/ n (a) (of ink) borrón m (b) (blemish): **the factory is a ~ on the landscape** la fábrica afea el paisaje

blot² -tt- vt (a) (stain, smear) ⟨page/word⟩ emborronar (b) (dry) ⟨ink⟩ secar* (con papel secante)
■ **blot out** [v + o + adv, v + adv + o] ⟨word⟩ tachar; ⟨view⟩ tapar; ⟨memory⟩ borrar

blotchy /'blɑːtʃi ‖ 'blɒtʃi/ adj **blotchier, blotchiest** ⟨skin⟩ lleno de manchas

blotting paper /'blɑːtɪŋ ‖ 'blɒtɪŋ/ n papel m secante

blouse /blaʊs ‖ blaʊz/ n blusa f

blow¹ /bləʊ/ n golpe m; **to come to ~s** llegar* a las manos; **his death came as a ~ to us** su muerte fue un duro golpe para nosotros

blow² (past **blew**; past p **blown**) vt
⟦1⟧ (propel): **stop ~ing smoke in my face!** ¡no me eches el humo a la cara!; **a gust of wind blew the door shut** una ráfaga de viento cerró la puerta de golpe; **the plane was ~n off course** el viento sacó el avión de su curso
⟦2⟧ (a) (make by blowing): **to ~ bubbles** hacer* pompas de jabón (b) (clear): **to ~ one's nose** sonarse* la nariz (c) (play) ⟨note⟩ tocar*; ⟨signal⟩ dar*; **the referee blew the whistle** el árbitro tocó el silbato or pito
⟦3⟧ (a) (smash) ⟨bridge/safe⟩ volar* (b) (burn out) ⟨fuse⟩ hacer* saltar, quemar (c) (burst) ⟨gasket⟩ reventar*
⟦4⟧ (colloq) (a) (squander) ⟨money⟩ despilfarrar (b) (spoil): **I blew it** la pifié (fam); **I blew the oral test** la pifié en el oral (fam), la regué en el oral (Méx fam)
■ **~** vi ⟦1⟧ (a) «wind» soplar (b) «person» soplar; **she came up the stairs, puffing and ~ing** subió las escaleras bufando y resoplando
⟦2⟧ (be driven by wind): **litter was ~ing everywhere** volaba basura por todas partes; **his hat blew off** se le voló el sombrero; **the door blew open** la puerta se abrió con el viento
⟦3⟧ (produce sound) «whistle» sonar*
⟦4⟧ (burn out) «fuse» saltar, quemarse
■ **blow down** ⟦1⟧ [v + o + adv, v + adv + o] tirar (abajo)
⟦2⟧ [v + adv] caerse* (con el viento)
■ **blow out** ⟦1⟧ [v + o + adv, v + adv + o] ⟨match/flame⟩ apagar* (soplando); **to ~ sb's brains out** (colloq) saltarle la tapa de los sesos a algn (fam)
⟦2⟧ [v + adv] «candle» apagarse*
■ **blow over** [v + adv] «trouble» caer* en el olvido; «storm» pasar
■ **blow up** ⟦1⟧ [v + adv] (a) (explode) «bomb» estallar; «car» saltar por los aires (b) (begin) «wind/storm» levantarse; «conflict» estallar; **the affair blew up into a major scandal** el caso terminó en un gran escándalo
⟦2⟧ [v + o + adv, v + adv + o] (a) ⟨mine/car⟩ volar* (b) ⟨balloon⟩ inflar (c) (colloq) ⟨incident⟩ exagerar (d) ⟨photo⟩ ampliar*

blow: ~-by-~ /'bləʊbɑr'bləʊ/ adj (before n) ⟨account⟩ con pelos y señales (fam); **~-dry** vt

-dries, -drying, -dries: **to ~-dry one's hair** hacerse* un brushing (secarse el pelo con secador de mano y cepillo); **~gun** n (AmE) cerbatana f

blown /bləʊn/ past p of BLOW²

blow: ~out n (a) (feast) (colloq) comilona f (fam) (b) (burst tire) reventón m; **~pipe** n cerbatana f; **~torch** n soplete m

blubber¹ /'blʌbər ‖ 'blʌbə(r)/ n grasa f de ballena

blubber² vi (colloq & pej) lloriquear

bludgeon /'blʌdʒən/ vt aporrear

blue¹ /bluː/ adj **bluer, bluest** ⟦1⟧ ⟨dress/sea/sky⟩ azul ⟦2⟧ (pornographic) (colloq) verde, porno adj inv, colorado (Méx) ⟦3⟧ (unhappy) (esp AmE) triste, deprimido

blue² n azul m; **out of the ~** ⟨call/arrive⟩ cuando menos se (or me etc) lo esperaba

blue: ~bell n jacinto m silvestre; **~berry** /'bluːˌberi ‖ 'bluːbəri/ n arándano m; **~-blooded** /'bluːˈblʌdəd ‖ ˌbluːˈblʌdɪd/ adj de sangre azul; **~bottle** n mosca f azul; **~collar** /'bluːˈkɑːlər ‖ ˌbluːˈkɒlə(r)/ adj ⟨union⟩ obrero; ⟨job⟩ manual; **~-collar workers** los obreros; **~print** n (of technical drawing) plano m; (plan of action) programa m

blues /bluːz/ pl n ⟦1⟧ (depression) (colloq): **the ~** la depre (fam) ⟦2⟧ (Mus) blues m

bluff¹ /blʌf/ vi hacer* un bluff or (Col, Méx) blof
■ **~** vt: **he managed to ~ his way out of it** logró salir del apuro embaucándolos

bluff² n (pretense) bluff m, blof m (Col, Méx); **to call sb's ~** poner* a algn en evidencia

blunder¹ /'blʌndər ‖ 'blʌndə(r)/ vi ⟦1⟧ (move clumsily, stumble): **he ~ed into the table** se topó con el jefe en el pasillo; **he ~ed around in the dark** andaba dando tumbos en la oscuridad ⟦2⟧ (make mistake) cometer un error garrafal

blunder² n (mistake) error m garrafal; (faux pas) metedura f or (AmL tb) metida f de pata (fam)

blunt¹ /blʌnt/ adj **-er, -est** (a) (not sharp) ⟨pencil⟩ desafilado, mocho (esp AmL); ⟨tip/edge⟩ romo; **a ~ instrument** un objeto contundente (b) (straightforward) ⟨person/manner⟩ directo, franco; ⟨refusal⟩ rotundo

blunt² vt (a) ⟨pencil⟩ despuntar; ⟨knife/scissors⟩ desafilar (b) (make dull) ⟨senses/intellect⟩ embotar

bluntly /'blʌntli/ adv ⟨say⟩ sin rodeos; ⟨refuse⟩ rotundamente

blur /blɜːr ‖ blɜː(r)/ -rr- vt ⟨outline⟩ desdibujar; ⟨distinction⟩ hacer* menos claro; ⟨memory⟩ hacer* borroso
■ **~** vi «outline» desdibujarse

blurred /blɜːrd ‖ blɜːd/ adj ⟨outline/vision⟩ borroso

blurt out /blɜːrt ‖ blɜːt/ [v + o + adv, v + adv + o] espetar

blush /blʌʃ/ vi ruborizarse*, ponerse* colorado

blusher /'blʌʃər ‖ 'blʌʃə(r)/ n colorete m, rubor m (Méx, RPl)

bluster¹ /'blʌstər ‖ 'blʌstə(r)/ vi bravuconear

bluster² n bravatas fpl, bravuconería f

B-movie /'biːˌmuːvi/ n película f de serie B or de bajo presupuesto

boa /'bəʊə/ n (Zool) boa f; **a ~ constrictor** una boa constríctor

boar /bɔːr ‖bɔː(r)/ n (pl ∼s or ∼) **(a)** (male pig) cerdo m macho, verraco m **(b)** (wild ∼) jabalí m

board¹ /bɔːrd ‖bɔːd/ n **1** (plank) tabla f, tablón m

2 (a) (diving ∼) trampolín m **(b)** (for surfing, windsurfing) tabla f (de surf) **(c)** (Games) tablero m

3 (a) (notice∼) tablero m or (Esp) tablón m de anuncios, cartelera f (AmL), diario m mural (Chi) **(b)** (sign) letrero m, cartel m **(c)** (score∼) marcador m **(d)** (blackboard) pizarra f, pizarrón m (AmL), tablero m (Col)

4 (a) (committee) junta f, consejo m **(b)** (administrative body): the Water/Gas B∼ la compañía del agua/gas **(c)** ∼ **(of directors)** (Busn) junta f directiva, consejo m de administración **(d)** (of examiners) tribunal m

5 (provision of meals): ∼ **and lodging** comida y alojamiento m; **full/half** ∼ pensión f completa/media pensión f

6 (in phrases) **across the board:** they have promised to reduce taxation across the ∼ han prometido una reducción general de impuestos; **on board** a bordo; **on** ∼ **the ship/plane** a bordo del barco/avión

board² vt **1** (go aboard): **to** ∼ **a ship** embarcar(se)*, abordar (Méx) **2** (accommodate) hospedar

■ ∼ vi **1** (go aboard) embarcar(se)*, abordar (Col, Méx) **2** (be accommodated) **to** ∼ **WITH sb** alojarse or hospedarse en casa de algn

■ **board up** [v + o + adv, v + adv + o] cerrar* con tablas

boarder /'bɔːrdər ‖'bɔːdə(r)/ n **(a)** (lodger) huésped mf **(b)** (at boarding school) (esp BrE) interno, -na m,f

board game n juego m de mesa

boarding /'bɔːrdɪŋ ‖'bɔːdɪŋ/: ∼ **card** n ▶ ∼ PASS; ∼ **house** n pensión f; ∼ **pass** n tarjeta f de embarque, pase m de abordar (Chi, Méx); ∼ **school** n internado m

board: ∼**room** n sala f or salón m de juntas; ∼**walk** n (AmE) paseo marítimo entarimado

boast¹ /bəʊst/ vi presumir, fanfarronear (fam); **to** ∼ ABOUT sth alardear or jactarse or vanagloriarse DE algo

■ ∼ vt **(a)** (brag): **I won, he** ∼**ed** —gané yo —dijo vanagloriándose **(b)** (possess) contar* con

boast² n alarde f

boastful /'bəʊstfəl/ adj jactancioso

boat /bəʊt/ n barco m; (small, open) bote m, barca f; **by** ∼ en barco

boating /'bəʊtɪŋ/ n: **to go** ∼ ir* a dar un paseo en bote or barca

boat: ∼**man** n cobertizo m (para botes); ∼**man** /'bəʊtmən/ n (pl **-men** /-mən/) barquero m; ∼ **race** n regata f; ∼**swain** /'bəʊsn/ n contramaestre m

bob¹ /bɑːb ‖bɒb/ n **1 (a)** (movement of head) inclinación f **(b)** (curtsy) reverencia f **2** (haircut) melena f

bob² vi **-bb-** (move abruptly): **the cork** ∼**bed up and down on the water** el corcho cabeceaba en el agua

bobbin /'bɑːbən ‖'bɒbɪn/ n bobina f

bobby /'bɑːbi ‖'bɒbi/**:** ∼ **pin** n (AmE) horquilla

f, pasador m (Méx), pinche m (Chi); ∼ **socks,** (AmE also) ∼ **sox** /sɑːks ‖sɒks/ pl n calcetines mpl cortos

bode /bəʊd/ vi (liter): **to** ∼ **well/ill** ser* buena/ mala señal

bodice /'bɑːdəs ‖'bɒdɪs/ n (of dress) canesú m; (undergarment) corpiño m

bodily¹ /'bɑːdəli ‖'bɒdɪli/ adj (before n) corporal; ∼ **functions** funciones fpl fisiológicas

bodily² adv: **they dragged him** ∼ **into the car** lo agarraron y lo metieron en el coche a la fuerza

body /'bɑːdi ‖'bɒdi/ n (pl **bodies**) **1 (a)** (of human, animal) cuerpo m; (before n) ∼ **language** lenguaje m corporal **(b)** (trunk) cuerpo m **(c)** (dead) cadáver m; **over my dead** ∼! ¡tendrán (or tendrá etc) que pasar por encima de mi cadáver! **2** (main part — of plane) fuselaje m; (— of ship) casco m; (Auto) carrocería f

3 (a) (organization) organismo m **(b)** (unit) (no pl): **they walked out in a** ∼ salieron en masa **(c)** (collection): **a** ∼ **of evidence** un conjunto de pruebas; **a growing** ∼ **of opinion** una creciente corriente de opinión **(d)** (of water) masa f

4 (object) cuerpo m; **heavenly** ∼ (poet) cuerpo m celeste

5 (density — of wine) cuerpo m; (— of hair) volumen m, cuerpo m

body: ∼ **builder** n fisiculturista mf; ∼ **building** n fisiculturismo m; ∼**guard** n guardaespaldas mf; (group) escolta f; ∼ **stocking** n body m; ∼**work** n carrocería f

bog /bɔːg, bɑːg ‖bɒg/ n ciénaga f; (peat ∼) tremedal m

■ **bog down: -gg-** [v + o + adv] (usu pass): **to** ∼**ged down with work** estar* inundado de trabajo; **don't get** ∼**ged down in too much detail** no te enredes con demasiados detalles

boggle /'bɑːgəl ‖'bɒgəl/ vi: **the mind** ∼**s** (hum) uno se queda helado, uno alucina (Esp, Méx fam)

bogus /'bəʊgəs/ adj ⟨claim/name⟩ falso; ⟨argument⟩ falaz

Bohemian /bəʊ'hiːmiən/ adj also **bohemian** (unconventional) bohemio

boil¹ /bɔɪl/ n **1** (Med) furúnculo m **2** (boiling point): **the vegetables are on the** ∼ las verduras se están haciendo; **bring the water to the** ∼ dejar que el agua rompa el hervor

boil² vi ⟨water/vegetables⟩ hervir*; **the rice has** ∼**ed dry** el arroz se ha quedado sin agua

■ ∼ vt **1** (bring to boiling point) hervir*; (keep at boiling point) hervir*, dejar hervir; (cook in boiling water) cocer*, hervir* **2 boiled** past p ⟨potatoes/rice⟩ hervido; ⟨ham⟩ cocido; ⟨egg⟩ (soft) pasado por agua; (hard) duro

■ **boil down to** [v + adv + prep + o] reducirse* a

■ **boil over** [v + adv] ⟨milk⟩ irse* por el fuego; ⟨pan⟩ desbordarse; ⟨person⟩ perder* el control

boiler /'bɔɪlər ‖'bɔɪlə(r)/ n caldera f

boiler suit n (BrE) overol m (AmL), mono m (Esp, Méx)

boiling /'bɔɪlɪŋ/ adj (colloq): **this coffee is** ∼ este café está hirviendo; **I'm** ∼ estoy asado (fam); **it's** ∼ **hot today/in here** (as adv) hace un calor espantoso hoy/aquí

boiling point n punto m de ebullición

boisterous /'bɔɪstərəs/ adj bullicioso

bold /bəʊld/ adj **-er, -est** [1] (daring) audaz [2] (impudent) ‹smile/advances› descarado [3] ‹pattern› llamativo; ‹color› fuerte

boldly /'bəʊldli/ adv [1] (daringly) con audacia, audazmente [2] (impudently) descaradamente

Bolivia /bə'lɪvɪə/ n Bolivia f

Bolivian¹ /bə'lɪvɪən/ adj boliviano

Bolivian² n boliviano, -na m,f

bollard /'bɑːlərd ‖'bɒlɑːd/ n **(a)** (on quay) noray m, bolardo m **(b)** (by road) (BrE) baliza f

bolster¹ /'bəʊlstər ‖'bəʊlstə(r)/ vt to ~ (up) ‹popularity/economy› reforzar*; ‹argument› reafirmar; ‹morale› levantar

bolster² n cabezal m (almohada de forma cilíndrica)

bolt¹ /bəʊlt/ n [1] (Tech) tornillo m, perno m [2] **(a)** (on door) pestillo m, pasador m, cerrojo m **(b)** (on firearm) cerrojo m

bolt² vt [1] (fasten with bolt) atornillar, sujetar con un tornillo or perno [2] ‹door› echarle el pestillo or el pasador or el cerrojo a [3] ~ (down) ‹food/meal› engullir*
■ ~ vi ‹horse› desbocarse*; ‹person› salir* disparado

bolt³ adv: ~ upright muy erguido; he sat ~ upright in bed se irguió en la cama

bomb¹ /bɑːm ‖bɒm/ n bomba f; (before n) ~ disposal desactivación f de explosivas; ~ scare amenaza f de bomba; ~ squad (colloq) brigada f antiexplosivos

bomb² vt (from air) bombardear; (plant bomb in) colocar* una bomba en

bombard /bɑːm'bɑːrd ‖bɒm'bɑːd/ vt (Mil) bombardear; she was ~ed with questions la acribillaron a preguntas

bomber /'bɑːmər ‖'bɒmə(r)/ n **(a)** (aircraft) bombardero m **(b)** (terrorist) terrorista mf (que perpetra atentados colocando bombas)

bomber jacket n chaqueta f or (Esp) cazadora f or (Méx) chamarra f or (RPl) campera f de aviador

bombing /'bɑːmɪŋ ‖'bɒmɪŋ/ n **(a)** (from aircraft) bombardeo m **(b)** (by terrorists) atentado m (terrorista)

bombshell /'bɑːmʃel ‖'bɒmʃel/ n (shocking news) bomba f

bona fide /'bəʊnəfaɪd ‖,bəʊnə'faɪdi/ adj genuino, auténtico

bonanza /bə'nænzə/ n **(a)** (piece of luck) filón m **(b)** (plentiful supply) superabundancia f

bond¹ /bɑːnd ‖bɒnd/ n [1] **(a)** (link) vínculo m **(b)** bonds pl (fetters) cadenas fpl [2] (adhesion) adherencia f

bond² vi **(a)** (stick) adherirse* **(b)** (form relationship) establecer* vínculos afectivos
■ ~ vt (stick) to ~ sth TO sth adherir* or pegar* algo A algo

bondage /'bɑːndɪdʒ ‖'bɒndɪdʒ/ n (enslavement) (liter) cautiverio m (liter)

bone¹ /bəʊn/ n **(a)** (Anat) hueso m; to have a ~ to pick with sb tener* que ajustar cuentas con algn **(b)** (of fish) espina f

bone² vt ‹meat› deshuesar; ‹fish› quitarle las espinas a

bone: ~ china n porcelana f fina; ~-dry /'bəʊn'draɪ/ (pred ~ dry) adj completamente seco

bonfire /'bɑːnfaɪr ‖'bɒnfaɪə(r)/ n hoguera f

bonnet /'bɑːnət ‖'bɒnɪt/ n [1] (Clothing) sombrero m; (for baby) gorrito m [2] (BrE Auto) capó m, capote m (Méx)

bonus /'bəʊnəs/ n [1] (payment to employee) plus m, prima f [2] (added advantage): (added) ~ ventaja f

bony /'bəʊni/ adj **bonier, boniest (a)** ‹knee› huesudo **(b)** (made of bone) óseo

boo¹ /buː/ interj ¡bu!

boo² n ≈ silba f

boo³, boos, booing, booed vt/i abuchear

booby /buːbi/ n: ~ prize n premio m al peor; ~ trap n (Mil) trampa f; (bomb) bomba f trampa; ~-trap vt -pp- (Mil): his car was ~-trapped le pusieron una bomba en el coche

book¹ /bʊk/ n [1] (printed work) libro m; to go by the ~ ceñirse* (estrictamente) a las normas or reglas; to throw the ~ at sb castigar* duramente a algn [2] **(a)** (exercise ~) cuaderno m **(b)** (note~) libreta f or cuaderno m (de apuntes) [3] (set — of samples) muestrario m; (— of matches, stamps) librito m [4] **books** pl (Busn, Fin): the ~s los libros

book² vt (esp BrE) [1] **(a)** ‹room/seat/flight› reservar; ‹appointment› concertar*; the hotel/flight is fully ~ed el hotel/vuelo está completo; I'm ~ed (up) all this week tengo toda la semana ocupada **(b)** ‹performer› contratar [2] (record) ‹order› asentar* [3] **(a)** (record charge against) multar **(b)** (in soccer) (BrE) amonestar
■ ~ vi (esp BrE) hacer* una reserva
■ **book in** [v + o + adv, v + adv + o] (reserve room for): she'd ~ed us in at the Hilton nos había reservado habitación en el Hilton
■ **book up** [v + o + adv, v + adv + o] (reserve) (often pass): the hotels are all ~ed up los hoteles están todos completos; tonight's performance is ~ed up no quedan localidades para la función de esta noche

book: ~case n biblioteca f, librería f (Esp), librero m (Méx); ~end n sujetalibros m

booking /'bʊkɪŋ/ n (esp BrE) **(a)** (reservation) reserva f, reservación f (AmL) **(b)** (engagement) compromiso m

booking office n (BrE Theat) taquilla f, boletería f (AmL)

bookkeeping /'bʊk,kiːpɪŋ/ n contabilidad f, teneduría f de libros

booklet /'bʊklət ‖'bʊklɪt/ n folleto m

bookmaker n /'bʊk,meɪkər ‖'bʊk,meɪkə(r)/ corredor, -dora m,f de apuestas

bookmark¹ /'bʊkmɑːrk ‖'bʊkmɑːk/ n **(a)** (for book) señalador m, marcador m **(b)** (Comput) marcador m

bookmark² vt marcar

book: ~seller n librero, -ra m,f; ~shelf n **(a)** (shelf) estante m, balda f (Esp) (para libros) **(b)** ~shelves ▶ BOOKCASE; ~shop n librería f; ~store n (AmE) librería f; ~ token n (BrE) cheque m regalo, vale m (canjeable por libros)

boom¹ /buːm/ n [1] (Econ, Fin) boom m [2] (sound of guns, explosion) estruendo m

boom² *vi* 1 «*guns*» tronar*; «*voice/thunder*» retumbar 2 (*usu in -ing form*) «*market/industry*» vivir un boom

boomerang /'buːməræŋ/ *n* bumerang *m*

booming /'buːmɪŋ/ *adj* (a) ‹*sound*› retumbante (b) ‹*industry*› en auge

boon /buːn/ *n* gran ayuda *f*

boost¹ /buːst/ *n* (uplift): **to give a ~ to sth** dar* empuje a algo; **it was a tremendous ~ to her confidence** le dio mucha más confianza en sí misma

boost² *vt* ‹*economy/production*› estimular; ‹*sales*› aumentar; ‹*morale*› levantar

booster /'buːstər ‖'buːstə(r)/ *n* (a) (Rad, Telec, TV) repetidor *m* (b) (Med) ~ (**shot**) (vacuna *f* de) refuerzo *m*

booster cable *n* (AmE) cable *m* de arranque

boot¹ /buːt/ *n* 1 (Clothing) bota *f*; (short) botín *m* 2 (kick) (colloq) (*no pl*) patada *f*, puntapié *m* 3 (BrE Auto) maletero *m*, portamaletas *m*, cajuela *f* (Méx), baúl *m* (Col, CS, Ven), maleta *f* (Chi), maletera *f* (Per) 4 **to boot** (*as linker*) para rematarla

boot² *vt* (a) (kick) (colloq) darle* un puntapié a (b) (Comput) ~ (**up**) cargar*

booth /buːθ ‖buːð, buːθ/ *n* (a) (cabin) cabina *f*; **photo ~** fotomatón *m* (b) (polling ~) cabina *f* de votación (c) (telephone ~) cabina *f* (de teléfono) (d) (stall — at fair) barraca *f*, caseta *f*; (— at exhibition) stand *m*

bootleg /'buːtleg/ *adj* (*before n*) ‹*liquor*› de contrabando; ‹*tape*› pirata *adj inv*

booty /'buːti/ *n* botín *m*

booze¹ /buːz/ *n* (colloq) bebida *f*, trago *m* (esp AmL fam)

booze² *vi* (colloq) beber, tomar (esp AmL)

border¹ /'bɔːrdər ‖'bɔːdə(r)/ *n* 1 (Pol) frontera *f*; (*before n*) ‹*dispute/town*› fronterizo 2 (a) (edge) borde *m* (b) (edging — on fabric, plate) cenefa *f*

border² *vt* (a) ‹*country/state*› limitar con; ‹*fields/lands*› lindar con (b) (edge — with ribbon, binding) ribetear
■ **border on** [*v + prep + o*] (a) «*country*» limitar con (b) (verge on) rayar en, lindar con

borderline /'bɔːrdərlaɪn ‖'bɔːdəlaɪn/ *adj* ‹*case/score*› dudoso; ‹*candidate*› en el límite entre el aprobado y el reprobado *or* (Esp) el suspenso

bore¹ /bɔːr ‖bɔː(r)/ *past of* BEAR¹

bore² *vt* 1 ‹*shaft/tunnel*› hacer*, abrir* 2 (weary) aburrir

bore³ *n* 1 (person) pesado, -da *m,f* (fam); (thing) aburrimiento *m*, lata *f* (fam) 2 (of cylinder, gun barrel) calibre *m*

bored /bɔːrd ‖bɔːd/ *adj* aburrido; **to be ~ WITH sth** estar* aburrido DE algo; **to get ~** aburrirse

boredom /'bɔːrdəm ‖'bɔːdəm/ *n* aburrimiento *m*

boring /'bɔːrɪŋ/ *adj* aburrido, aburridor (AmL)

born¹ /bɔːrn ‖bɔːn/ (*past p of* BEAR¹): **to be ~** nacer*

born² *adj* (*before n*) ‹*teacher/leader*› nato; **he's a ~ loser** siempre ha sido *or* será un perdedor

born-again /'bɔːrnəgen ‖,bɔːnə'gen/ *adj* (*before n*): ~ **Christian** cristiano -na renacido -da

borne /bɔːrn ‖bɔːn/ *past p of* BEAR¹

borough /'bɜːrəʊ ‖'bʌrə/ *n* (a) (in US) distrito *m* municipal (b) (in UK) municipio *m*

borrow /'bɑːrəʊ ‖'bɒrəʊ/ *vt* 1 (a) (have on loan): **may I ~ your pencil?** ¿me prestas *or* (Esp tb) me dejas el lápiz?; **to ~ sth FROM sb** pedirle* prestado algo A algn; **I ~ed $5,000 from the bank** pedí un préstamo de 5.000 dólares al banco (b) (from library) sacar* 2 ‹*idea*› sacar*; ‹*word*› tomar

borrower /'bɑːrəʊər ‖'bɒrəʊə(r)/ *n* (a) (Fin) prestatario, -ria *m,f* (b) (from library) usuario, -ria *m,f*

borrowing /'bɑːrəʊɪŋ ‖'bɒrəʊɪŋ/ *n* (Fin) préstamos *mpl*

Bosnia Herzegovina /'bɑːzniə,hertsəgəʊ'viːnə ‖,bɒzniə,hɜːtsəgəʊ'viːnə/ *n* Bosnia Herzegovina *f*

Bosnian /'bɑːzniən ‖'bɒzniən/ *adj* bosnio

bosom /'bʊzəm/ *n* (a) (breast, chest) (liter) pecho *m*; (*before n*) ‹*friend*› del alma (b) (of woman — bust) pecho *m*, busto *m*; (— breast) pecho *m*, seno *m* (c) (heart, center) (liter) seno *m*

boss /bɑːs ‖bɒs/ *n* (colloq) (a) (superior) jefe, -fa *m,f*; (employer, factory owner) patrón, -trona *m,f* (b) (leader) dirigente *mf*
■ **boss around,** (BrE also) **boss about** [*v + o + adv*] (colloq) mandonear (fam)

bossy /'bɑːsi ‖'bɒsi/ *adj* **bossier, bossiest** (colloq) mandón (fam)

bosun /'bəʊsn/ *n* ▶ BOATSWAIN

botanic /bə'tænɪk/, **-ical** /-ɪkəl/ *adj* botánico

botanist /'bɑːtnɪst ‖'bɒtənɪst/ *n* botánico, -ca *m,f*

botany /'bɑːtni ‖'bɒtəni/ *n* botánica *f*

botch /bɑːtʃ ‖bɒtʃ/ *vt* (colloq) ~ (**up**) ‹*repair*› hacer* una chapuza de (fam); ‹*plan*› estropear

both¹ /bəʊθ/ *adj* ambos, -bas, los dos, las dos

both² *pron* ambos, -bas, los dos, las dos; **we ~ like chess** a los dos nos gusta el ajedrez; **the coats are ~ too big** los dos abrigos son demasiado grandes

both³ *conj* **both ... and ...:** ~ **Paul and John are in Italy** tanto Paul como John están en Italia, Paul y John están los dos en Italia; **she ~ wrote and played the music** compuso y tocó la música ella misma

bother¹ /'bɑːðər ‖'bɒðə(r)/ *vt* (a) (irritate, pester) molestar; **sorry to ~ you** perdone (que lo moleste) (b) (trouble) preocupar; **she's very quiet, but don't let it ~ you** es muy callada, no te inquietes por ello (c) (make effort) **not to + ~ -ING:** **don't ~ writing a long letter** no hace falta que escribas una carta larga; **to ~ to + INF** tomarse la molestia DE + INF

b

■ ~ *vi* **(a)** (make effort) molestarse **(b)** (worry) **to ~ ABOUT** sth/sb preocuparse POR algo/algn

bother² *n* molestia *f*; (work) trabajo *m*; (problems) problemas *mpl*

bothered /'bɑːðərd ‖'bɒðəd/ *adj* (*pred*): **I can't be ~ to go** me da pereza ir; **she yelled at him, but he wasn't a bit ~** le pegó un berrido, pero él ni se inmutó

bottle¹ /'bɑːtḷ ‖'bɒtḷ/ *n* (container, contents) botella *f*; (of perfume) frasco *m*; **baby's ~** biberón *m*, mamila *f* (Méx), mamadera *f* (CS, Per), tetero *m* (Col); (*before n*) **~ opener** abrebotellas *m*, destapador *m* (AmL)

bottle² *vt* **(a)** ⟨*wine/milk*⟩ embotellar; **~d milk** leche *f* en or de botella; **~d water** agua *f*‡ embotellada **(b)** (BrE) ⟨*fruit/vegetables*⟩ poner* en conserva

■ **bottle up** [*v + o + adv, v + adv + o*] (colloq) ⟨*emotion*⟩ reprimir

bottle: ~ bank *n* contenedor *m* de recogida de vidrio; **~feed** *vt* (*past & past p* **-fed**) alimentar con biberón or (Méx) con mamila or (CS, Per) con mamadera or (Col) con tetero; **~neck** *n* (narrow stretch of road) cuello *m* de botella; (hold-up) embotellamiento *m*

bottom¹ /'bɑːtəm ‖'bɒtəm/ *n* **1** **(a)** (of box, bottle, drawer) fondo *m*; (of hill, stairs) pie *m*; (of page) final *m*, pie *m*; (of pile) parte *f* de abajo; **to get to the ~ of sth** llegar* al fondo de algo **(b)** (underneath — of box) parte *f* de abajo; (— of ship) fondo *m* **(c)** (of bed) pies *mpl*; (of garden) fondo *m*; (of road) final *m* **(d)** (of sea, river, lake) fondo *m* **2** (of hierarchy): **he is at the ~ of the class** es el último de la clase; **she started out at the ~** empezó desde abajo **3** **(a)** (of person) trasero *m* (fam), traste *m* (CS fam) **(b)** (of pyjamas, tracksuit) (*often pl*) pantalón *m*, pantalones *mpl*; (of bikini) parte *f* de abajo

bottom² *adj* (*before n*) ⟨*shelf/layer*⟩ de más abajo; ⟨*grade*⟩ más bajo; ⟨*part/edge/lip*⟩ inferior

bottomless /'bɑːtəmləs ‖'bɒtəmlɪs/ *adj* ⟨*well/shaft*⟩ sin fondo

bough /baʊ/ *n* rama *f*

bought /bɔːt/ *past & past p of* BUY¹

boulder /'bəʊldər ‖'bəʊldə(r)/ *n* roca *f* (*grande, alisada por la erosión*)

boulevard /'bʊləvɑːrd ‖'buːləvɑːd/ *n* bulevar *m*

bounce¹ /baʊns/ *vi* **(a)** «*ball/object*» rebotar, picar* (AmL), botar (Esp, Méx); **the child was bouncing up and down on the sofa** el niño saltaba en el sofá **(b)** «*check*» (colloq) ser* devuelto, rebotar (fam)

■ ~ *vt* **(a)** ⟨*ball/object*⟩ hacer* rebotar, hacer* picar (AmL), (hacer*) botar (Esp, Méx) **(b)** ⟨*check*⟩ (colloq) devolver*

■ **bounce back** [*v + adv*] (colloq) levantarse

bounce² *n* **(a)** (action) rebote *m*, pique *m* (AmL) **(b)** (springiness, vitality): **this shampoo puts the ~ back into your hair** este champú les da nueva vida a sus cabellos; **she's full of ~** es una persona llena de vida

bouncer /'baʊnsər ‖'baʊnsə(r)/ *n* (colloq) gorila *m* (fam), sacabullas *m* (Méx fam)

bound¹ /baʊnd/ *n* **1** **bounds** *pl* (limits) límites *mpl*; **within the ~s of possibility** dentro de lo

posible; **the shop is out of ~s to schoolchildren** los niños tienen prohibido entrar en la tienda **2** (jump) salto *m*, brinco *m*

bound² *vi* saltar; **to ~ in/out** entrar/salir* dando saltos

bound³ *past & past p of* BIND¹

bound⁴ *adj* **1** **(a)** (tied up) atado, amarrado (AmL exc RPl) **(b)** (obliged): **they are ~ by law to supply the goods** están obligados por ley a suministrar los artículos; **I'm duty ~ to tell you the truth** es mi deber decirte la verdad **2** (*pred*) (certain): **it was ~ to happen sooner or later** tarde o temprano tenía que suceder; **it was ~ to go wrong** no cabía duda de que iba a salir mal **3** (headed) (*pred*): **the truck was ~ for Italy** el camión iba rumbo a Italia; **they are Moscow ~** van camino a Moscú

boundary /'baʊndri, -dəri/ *n* (*pl* **-ries**) límite *m*

bountiful /'baʊntɪfəl/ *adj* (liter) ⟨*king/nature*⟩ munificente (liter); ⟨*harvest/gifts*⟩ copioso

bounty /'baʊnti/ *n* (*pl* **-ties**) **1** (liter) (generosity) munificencia *f* (liter) **2** (reward) recompensa *f*; (*before n*) **~ hunter** cazador, -dora *m,f* de recompensas

bouquet /bəʊˈkeɪ, buːˈkeɪ ‖bəʊˈkeɪ, bəʊˈkeɪ/ *n* **1** (of flowers) ramo *m*; (small) ramillete *m* **2** (of wine) bouquet *m*

bourbon /'bɜːrbən ‖'bɜːbən/ *n* bourbon *m*

bourgeois /'bʊrʒwɑː ‖'bɔːʒwɑː, 'bʊəʒ-/ *adj* burgués

bout /baʊt/ *n* **1** (period, spell): **I had a ~ of flu** tuve una gripe or (Col, Méx) una gripa muy mala; **a drinking ~** una borrachera **2** (in boxing, wrestling) combate *m*, encuentro *m*

boutique /buːˈtiːk/ *n* boutique *f*

bow¹ /baʊ/ *n* **1** (movement) reverencia *f* **2** (of ship) (*often pl*) proa *f*

bow² /baʊ/ *vi* hacer* una reverencia; **they ~ed to government pressure** cedieron ante la presión del gobierno

■ ~ *vt* ⟨*head*⟩ inclinar

■ **bow out** [*v + adv*] retirarse

bow³ /bəʊ/ *n* **1** (knot) lazo *m*, moño *m* (esp AmL) **2** (weapon) arco *m* **3** (Mus) arco *m*

bow⁴ /bəʊ/ *vi* ⟨*branch/plank*⟩ arquearse, pandearse (esp AmL)

bowel /'baʊəl/ *n* (Anat) intestino *m* grueso; **in the ~s of the earth** (liter) en las entrañas de la tierra

bowl¹ /bəʊl/ *n* **1** **(a)** (container) (Culin) bol *m*, tazón *m*, cuenco *m*; (for washing etc) palangana *f*, barreño *m*; **fruit ~** frutero *m*, frutera *f* (CS); **soup ~** sopero *m* **(b)** (contents) bol *m*, tazón *m* **(c)** (of toilet) taza *f* **2** (in game of bowls) bola *f*, bocha *f*; *see also* BOWLS

bowl² *vt/i* lanzar*

■ **bowl over** [*v + o + adv, v + adv + o*] derribar; **we were ~ed over by the beauty of the island** la belleza de la isla nos dejó pasmados

bowlegged /'bəʊlegd/ *adj* patizambo

bowler /'bəʊlər ‖'bəʊlə(r)/ *n* **1** (in cricket) lanzador, -dora *m,f*; (in bowling, bowls) jugador, -dora *m,f* **2** **~ (hat)** bombín *m*, sombrero *m* de hongo

b

bowling /'bəʊlɪŋ/ n (a) (in bowling alley) bolos mpl (b) (on grass) ▶ BOWLS

bowling: ~ **alley** n bolera f, bowling m; ~ **green** n: pista donde se juega a los BOWLS

bowls /bəʊlz/ n (+ sing vb) juego semejante a la petanca que se juega sobre césped

bow tie /bəʊ/ n corbata f de moño (AmL), pajarita f (Esp)

box¹ /bɑːks ‖bɒks/ n **1** (container, contents) caja f; (large) cajón m; (for watch, pen) estuche m **2** (on form) casilla f **3** (a) (in theater) palco m (b) (booth) cabina f

box² vi boxear

■ ~ vt poner* en una caja, embalar

■ **box in** [v + o + adv, v + adv + o] (a) (restrict, surround) cerrarle* el paso a (b) (enclose) ⟨pipes⟩ esconder (tapando con una tabla etc)

boxer /'bɑːksər ‖'bɒksə(r)/ n (a) (person) boxeador, -dora m,f (b) (dog) bóxer mf

boxer shorts pl n calzoncillos mpl, calzones mpl (Méx), interiores mpl (Col, Ven)

boxing /'bɑːksɪŋ ‖'bɒksɪŋ/ n boxeo m; (before n) ~ **ring** ring m, cuadrilátero m

Boxing Day /'bɑːksɪŋ ‖'bɒksɪŋ/ n: el 26 de diciembre, día festivo en Gran Bretaña

box: ~ **number** n (at post office) apartado m (de correos), apartado m postal (Méx), casilla f postal or de correo (CS); ~ **office** n taquilla f, boletería f (AmL)

boy /bɔɪ/ n (a) (baby, child) niño m, chico m (b) (son) hijo m, chico m (c) (young man) (colloq) muchacho m, chico m

boy band /bɔɪ bænd/ n (colloq) grupo m de pop de chicos

boycott¹ /'bɔɪkɑːt ‖'bɔɪkɒt/ n boicot m

boycott² vt boicotear

boyfriend /'bɔɪfrend/ n novio m

boyish /'bɔɪɪʃ/ adj ⟨enthusiasm/smile⟩ de chico, de niño; (used of woman) de muchacho, de chico

boy scout n boy scout m, explorador m

bra /brɑː/ n sostén m, sujetador m (Esp), brasier m (Col, Méx), corpiño m (RPI), soutien m (Ur)

brace¹ /breɪs/ n **1** (support) abrazadera f **2** (Dent) ▶ 4B **3** (drill) berbiquí m **4 braces** pl n (a) (BrE Clothing) tirantes mpl, cargaderas fpl (Col), tiradores mpl (RPI), suspensores mpl (Chi) (b) (esp AmE Dent) aparato(s) m(pl), frenos mpl (Méx), fierros mpl (Méx, Per), frenillos mpl (Chi) **5** (pl ~) (pair) (BrE) par m

brace² vt (support) apuntalar

■ v refl **to** ~ **oneself for sth** prepararse para algo

bracelet /'breɪslət ‖'breɪslɪt/ n pulsera f, brazalete m

bracing /'breɪsɪŋ/ adj vigorizante

bracken /'brækən/ n helechos mpl

bracket¹ /'brækət ‖'brækɪt/ n **1** (a) (Print) (square bracket) corchete m (b) (parenthesis) (BrE) paréntesis m **2** (category): income ~ nivel m de ingresos; the 25-30 age ~ el grupo etario de entre 25 y 30 años **3** (support) soporte m; (for shelves) escuadra f

bracket² vt (a) ⟨word/phrase⟩ poner* entre corchetes; (in parentheses) (BrE) poner* entre paréntesis (b) (categorize) catalogar*

brag /bræg/ vi/t -**gg**- fanfarronear (fam)

braid¹ /breɪd/ n (a) (of hair) (esp AmE) trenza f (b) (Tex) galón m

braid² vt trenzar*

braille, Braille /breɪl/ n braille m, Braille m

brain /breɪn/ n cerebro m; (before n) ~ **damage** lesión f cerebral; ~ **tumor** tumor m cerebral

brain: ~**child** n creación m; ~**-dead** adj clínicamente muerto

brains /breɪnz/ n **1** (+ pl vb) (a) (substance) sesos mpl; (Culin) sesos mpl (b) (intelligence) inteligencia f **2** (+ sing vb) (mastermind) cerebro m, autor, -tora m,f intelectual (AmL); he's the ~ of the family es la lumbrera de la familia

brain: ~**wash** vt hacerle* un lavado de cerebro a; ~**wave** n (colloq) idea f genial, lamparazo m (Col fam)

braise /breɪz/ vt estofar

brake¹ /breɪk/ n (on vehicle) freno m; (before n) ~ **lights** luces fpl de freno

brake² vi/t frenar

bramble /'bræmbəl/ n zarza f

bran /bræn/ n salvado m, afrecho m

branch¹ /brɑːntʃ ‖brɑːntʃ/ n (of tree) rama f; (of river, road, railway) ramal m; (of family, field of study) rama f; (of company, bank) sucursal f

branch² vi «river/family» ramificarse*; «road» bifurcarse*; **a path** ~**es (off) to the right** un sendero sale a la derecha

■ **branch out** [v + adv] (a) (take on new activity) diversificar* sus (or nuestras etc) actividades; the company has ~ed out into publishing la compañía ha diversificado sus actividades lanzándose al campo editorial (b) (become independent): he has ~ed out on his own «business partner» se ha establecido por su cuenta

brand¹ /brænd/ n **1** (a) (Busn) marca f (b) (type) tipo m; (style) estilo m **2** (identification mark) marca f (hecha a fuego)

brand² vt (a) (mark) ⟨cattle⟩ marcar* (con hierro candente) (b) (label) **to** ~ **sb** AS **sth** tachar a algn DE algo

brandish /'brændɪʃ/ vt blandir

brand: ~ **name** n marca f; ~**-new** /'brænd'nuː ‖,brænd'njuː/ adj nuevo

brandy /'brændi/ n (pl -**dies**) coñac m

brash /bræʃ/ adj -**er**, -**est** excesivamente desenvuelto

brass /bræs ‖brɑːs/ n (a) (Metall) latón m; (before n) ⟨button⟩ dorado (b) (Mus) (+ sing or pl vb) bronces mpl, metales mpl

brass band n banda f de música, tambora f (Méx)

brassiere /brə'zɪr ‖'bræziə(r)/ n ▶ BRA

brass knuckles pl n (AmE) nudilleras fpl de metal, manoplas fpl (AmL)

brat /bræt/ n (pej) mocoso, -sa m,f (pey)

bravado /brə'vɑːdəʊ/ n bravuconadas fpl

brave¹ /breɪv/ adj -**ver**, -**vest** valiente

brave² vt ⟨peril⟩ afrontar; **to** ~ **the weather** hacerle frente al mal tiempo

brave³ n **1** (North American Indian) guerrero m, piel roja **2** (liter) (+ pl vb) the ~ los valientes

bravely /'breɪvli/ adv valientemente

bravery /'breɪvəri/ n valentía f, valor m

bravo /'brɑːvəʊ ‖brɑː'vəʊ/ interj ¡bravo!

brawl¹ /brɔːl/ *n* pelea *f*

brawl² *vi* pelearse

brawny /'brɔːni/ *adj* **-nier, -niest** musculoso

bray /breɪ/ *vi* «*donkey*» rebuznar; «*person*» cacarear

brazen /'breɪzn̩ ‖ 'breɪzən/ *adj* descarado

brazier /'breɪʒər, 'breɪziər ‖ 'breɪziə(r)/ *n* brasero *m*

Brazil /brə'zɪl/ *n* Brasil *m*

Brazilian /brə'zɪliən/ *adj* brasileño

brazil nut /brə'zɪl/ *n* coquito *m* del Brasil, castaña *f* de Pará (RPl)

breach¹ /briːtʃ/ *n* **1** (of law) infracción *f*; ~ of contract incumplimiento *m* de contrato; she was arrested for ~ of the peace la detuvieron por alterar el orden público **2** (gap, opening) (frml) brecha *f* **3** (break) (frml) ruptura *f*

breach² *vt* **(a)** (*rule*) infringir*, violar; (*security*) poner* en peligro **(b)** (frml) (*defenses*) abrir* una brecha en

bread /bred/ *n* pan *m*; ~ and butter pan con mantequilla *or* (RPl) manteca

bread: ~**bin** *n* (BrE) ▶ ~BOX; ~**board** *n* tabla *f* de cortar el pan; ~**box** *n* (AmE) panera *f* (*para guardar el pan*); ~**crumb** *n* miga *f* (de pan); ~**crumbs** (Culin) pan *m* rallado *or* (Méx) molido; ~**line** *n*: they're on the ~**line** (colloq) apenas tienen para vivir

breadth /bredθ/ *n* **(a)** (width) anchura *f*, ancho *m* **(b)** (extent) amplitud *f*; ~ of vision amplitud de miras

breadwinner /'bred,wɪnər ‖ 'bred,wɪnə(r)/ *n*: she's the ~ of the family es la que mantiene a la familia

break¹ /breɪk/ (*past* **broke**; *past p* **broken**) *vt* **1** (*window/plate*) romper*; (*stick*) partir, quebrar* (AmL); he broke his wrist se rompió la muñeca

2 (render useless) (*machine*) romper*, descomponer* (AmL)

3 (violate) (*rule*) infringir*; (*promise*) no cumplir; (*contract*) incumplir; (*strike*) romper*; ▶ LAW B

4 (end) (*strike*) poner* fin a; (*drug ring*) desarticular; (*impasse*) salir* de; (*habit*) dejar

5 **(a)** (ruin) (*person/company*) arruinar a **(b)** (crush) (*person*) destrozar*

6 (impart): Sue broke the news to him Sue le dio la noticia; they broke it to her gently se lo dijeron con mucho tacto

7 (exceed) (*record*) batir

8 (disrupt) (*pattern/monotony*) romper*

9 (decipher) (*code*) descifrar

■ ~ *vi* **1** «*window/plate*» romperse*; «*stick*» partirse, quebrarse* (AmL)

2 (give in) «*resistance*» desmoronarse; she broke under constant interrogation no resistió el constante interrogatorio

3 **(a)** (begin) «*storm*» estallar; «*day*» romper* **(b)** (change) «*weather*» cambiar; his voice is ~ing le está cambiando la voz; his voice broke (with emotion) se le entrecortó la voz

4 «*wave/surf*» romper*

■ **break away** [*v* + *adv*] to ~ away (FROM sth) «*piece*» desprenderse (DE algo); «*faction/region*» escindirse (DE algo)

■ **break down**

I [*v* + *adv*] **1** «*vehicle/machine*» estropearse,

averiarse*, descomponerse* (AmL), quedarse en pana (Chi), quedarse varado (Col); «*system*» fallar; «*talks*» fracasar

2 (lose composure) perder* el control

II [*v* + *o* + *adv*, *v* + *adv* + *o*] **1** (*door/barrier*) echar abajo

2 (divide up) (*expenditure*) desglosar; (*sentence*) descomponer*; the process can be broken down into three steps el proceso puede dividirse en tres pasos

■ **break in** **1** [*v* + *adv*] «*intruder*» entrar (*para robar etc*)

2 [*v* + *o* + *adv*, *v* + *adv* + *o*] (*horse*) domar

■ **break into** [*v* + *prep* + *o*] (*building*) entrar en (*para robar etc*)

■ **break off** **1** [*v* + *o* + *adv*, *v* + *adv* + *o*] **(a)** (detach) partir **(b)** (*engagement/diplomatic relations*) romper*

2 [*v* + *adv*] (snap off, come free) «*piece of ice*» desprenderse; the handle broke off se le rompió el asa

■ **break out** [*v* + *adv*] **1** (start) «*war/epidemic/rioting*» estallar

2 (escape) «*prisoner*» escaparse, fugarse*

■ **break through** **1** [*v* + *adv*] (penetrate) (Mil) penetrar en las defensas enemigas; «*sun*» salir*

2 [*v* + *prep* + *o*] (*barrier*) atravesar*, romper*; they broke through our defenses penetraron en nuestras defensas

■ **break up**

I [*v* + *o* + *adv*, *v* + *adv* + *o*] **1** (divide) (*land*) dividir; (*ship*) desaguazar*; (*sentence*) descomponer*

2 **(a)** (*demonstration*) disolver* **(b)** (wreck, ruin) (*home*) deshacer*

II [*v* + *adv*] **(a)** «*lovers/band*» separarse; their marriage broke up su matrimonio fracasó; to ~ up WITH sb romper* CON algn **(b)** «*meeting*» terminar; «*crowd*» dispersarse

break² *n* **1** **(a)** (Rad, TV) pausa *f* (comercial); (Theat) entreacto *m*, intermedio *m* **(b)** (rest period) descanso *m*; (at school) (BrE) recreo *m* **(c)** (short vacation) vacaciones *fpl* **(d)** (change, respite) cambio *m*; I need a ~ from all this necesito descansar de todo esto; (a holiday) necesito un cambio de aires

2 (gap) interrupción *f* **3** (fracture) fractura *f*, rotura *f*; to make a clean ~ cortar por lo sano

breakable /'breɪkəbəl/ *adj* frágil

breakage /'breɪkɪdʒ/ *n* **(a)** (action) rotura *f* **(b)** **breakages** *pl* (objects broken) roturas *fpl*

break: ~**away** *n* (separation) ruptura *f*, escisión *f*; (before *n*) (*faction*) disidente, escindido; ~**down** *n* **1** **(a)** (failure — of car, machine) avería *f*, descompostura *f* (Méx), varada *f* (Col), pana *f* (Chi); (— of service, communications) interrupción *f*; (— of negotiations) fracaso *m*; (before *n*) ~**down truck** grúa *f* **(b)** (nervous ~**down**) crisis *f* nerviosa; **2** (analysis): a ~**down of expenditure** un desglose de los gastos

breaker /'breɪkər ‖ 'breɪkə(r)/ *n* gran ola *f*

breakfast /'brekfəst/ *n* desayuno *m*; to have ~ desayunar, tomar el desayuno; (before *n*) ~ **television** televisión *f* matinal

break-in /'breɪkɪn/ *n* robo *m* (con escalamiento)

breaking /'breɪkɪŋ/**:** ~ **and entering** /'breɪkɪŋəndentərɪŋ/ *n* allanamiento *m* de morada; ~ **point** *n* límite *m*

break: ~**through** *n* gran avance *m*; ~**up** *n* ···❖

b

(of structure, family) desintegración *f*; (of empire, company) desmembramiento *m*; (of political party) disolución *f*; (of talks) fracaso *m*; **the ~up of their marriage** su separación; **~water** *n* rompeolas *m*

breast /brest/ *n* (a) (of woman) pecho *m*, seno *m*; (*before n*) ~ **cancer** cáncer *m* de mama *or* de pecho (b) (chest) (liter) pecho *m* (c) (Culin) (of chicken, turkey) pechuga *f*

breast: **~feed** (*past & past p* **-fed**) *vt* darle* el pecho a, darle* de mamar a ■ ~ *vi* dar* el pecho, dar* de mamar; **~stroke** *n* (estilo) pecho *m* (AmL), braza *f* (Esp)

breath /breθ/ *n* aliento *m*; **to have bad ~** tener* mal aliento; **to take a ~** aspirar, inspirar; **take a deep ~** respire hondo; **out of ~** sin aliento; **to hold one's ~** contener* la respiración; **to take sb's ~ away** dejar a algn sin habla

Breathalyzer®, Breathalyser® /'breθəlaɪzər ‖'breθəlaɪzə(r)/ *n* alcohómetro *m*, alcoholímetro *m*; (*before n*) ~ **test** prueba *f* del alcohol *or* de la alcoholemia

breathe /bri:ð/ *vi* respirar
■ ~ *vt* ‹air/fumes› aspirar, respirar
■ **breathe in** [1] [*v + adv*] aspirar [2] [*v + o + adv, v + adv + o*] ‹air/fumes› aspirar, respirar
■ **breathe out** [1] [*v + adv*] espirar [2] [*v + o + adv, v + adv + o*] ‹smoke› expeler; ‹air› exhalar

breathing /'bri:ðɪŋ/ *n* respiración *f*

breathing space *n* respiro *m*

breathless /'breθləs ‖'breθlɪs/ *adj*: **the blow left me ~** el golpe me dejó sin aliento; **he arrived ~** llegó jadeando

breathtaking /'breθ,teɪkɪŋ/ *adj* impresionante

bred /bred/ *past & past p of* BREED²

breeches /'brɪtʃəz ‖'brɪtʃɪz/ *pl n* (knee ~) (pantalones *mpl*) bombachos *mpl*; (riding ~) pantalones *mpl* de montar

breed¹ /bri:d/ *n* (of animals) raza *f*; (of plants) variedad *f*

breed² (*past & past p* **bred**) *vt* ‹animals› criar*; ‹violence› engendrar
■ ~ *vi* reproducirse*

breeder /'bri:dər ‖'bri:də(r)/ *n* (of animals) criador, -dora *m,f*; (of plants) cultivador, -dora *m,f*

breeding /'bri:dɪŋ/ *n* (a) (reproduction) reproducción *f* (b) (raising — of animals) cría *f*; (— of plants) cultivo *m* (c) (upbringing): **politeness is a sign of good ~** la cortesía es señal de buena educación

breeze¹ /bri:z/ *n* brisa *f*

breeze² *vi* (colloq): **to ~ in/out** entrar/salir* tan campante (fam)

breezy /'bri:zi/ *adj* **-zier, -ziest** [1] (windy) ‹spot› ventoso; **it's a bit ~ today** hace un poco de vientecito hoy [2] (lively) (colloq) ‹person› dinámico

brethren /'breðrən/ *pl n* (arch *or* liter) hermanos *mpl*

brevity /'brevəti/ *n* brevedad *f*

brew /bru:/ *vt* (a) ‹beer› fabricar* (b) ‹tea› preparar (c) ‹mischief› tramar

■ ~ *vi* (a) (make beer) fabricar* cerveza (b) ‹tea›: **the tea is ~ing** el té se está haciendo (c) ‹storm› avecinarse; ‹trouble› gestarse

brewer /'bru:ər ‖'bru:ə(r)/ *n* cervecero, -ra *m,f*

brewery /'bru:əri/ *n* (*pl* **-ries**) fábrica *f* de cerveza, cervecería *f*

bribe¹ /braɪb/ *n* soborno *m*

bribe² *vt* sobornar

bribery /'braɪbəri/ *n* soborno *m*

bric-a-brac /'brɪkəbræk/ *n* baratijas *fpl*

brick /brɪk/ *n* ladrillo *m*

bricklayer /'brɪk,leɪər ‖'brɪk,leɪə(r)/ *n* albañil *m*

bridal /'braɪdl/ *adj* ‹procession› nupcial; ‹shop› para novias

bride /braɪd/ *n* novia *f*; **the ~ and groom** los novios; (after ceremony) los recién casados

bride: **~groom** *n* novio *m*; **~smaid** *n* dama *f* de honor; (child) niña *que acompaña a la novia*

bridge¹ /brɪdʒ/ *n* [1] (a) puente *m* (b) (on ship) puente *m* (de mando) (c) (of nose) caballete *m* [2] (Dent) puente *m* [3] (card Game) bridge *m*

bridge² *vt* ‹river› tender* un puente sobre; ‹differences› salvar

bridle /'braɪdl/ *n* brida *f*

brief¹ /bri:f/ *adj* breve; **in ~** en resumen

brief² *n* (a) (Law) expediente *entregado por el abogado al* BARRISTER (b) (instructions) instrucciones *fpl* (c) (area of responsibility) competencia *f*

brief³ *vt* ‹lawyer› instruir*; ‹pilot/spy› darle* instrucciones a; ‹committee› informar

briefcase /'bri:fkeɪs/ *n* maletín *m*, portafolio(s) *m* (esp AmL)

briefing /'bri:fɪŋ/ *n* (a) (~ session) sesión *f* para dar instrucciones (b) (press ~) reunión *f* informativa (para la prensa)

briefly /'bri:fli/ *adv* (a) ‹visit/rule› por poco tiempo (b) ‹reply/speak› brevemente (c) (indep) en resumen

briefs /bri:fs/ *pl n* (man's) calzoncillos *mpl*, slip *m*; (woman's) calzones *mpl* (esp AmL), bragas *fpl* (Esp), bombachas *fpl* (RPI), pantaletas *fpl* (AmC, Ven)

brigade /brɪ'geɪd/ *n* brigada *f*

bright /braɪt/ *adj* **-er, -est** [1] (a) ‹star/light› brillante; ‹room› con mucha luz (b) ‹color› fuerte [2] (a) (cheerful) ‹eyes› lleno de vida (b) (hopeful) ‹future› prometedor; **to look on the ~ side of sth** mirar el lado bueno de algo [3] (intelligent) ‹person› inteligente; **whose ~ idea was it to ...?** (iro) ¿quién tuvo la brillante idea de ...? (iró)

brighten /'braɪtn/ *vi* (a) (become brighter) ‹light› hacerse* más brillante (b) ~ (**up**) (become cheerful, hopeful) ‹person› animarse; ‹situation/prospects› mejorar
■ ~ *vt* (a) (make brighter) iluminar (b) ~ (**up**) ‹room› alegrar; ‹occasion/party› animar

brightly /'braɪtli/ *adv* (a) ‹shine› intensamente (b) ‹say/smile› alegremente

brights /braɪts/ *pl n* (Auto) (AmE colloq) (luces *fpl*) largas *or* (Andes, Méx) altas *fpl*

brilliance /'brɪljəns/ *n* **(a)** (brightness) resplandor *m* **(b)** (skill, intelligence) brillantez *f*

brilliant /'brɪljənt/ *adj* **(a)** ⟨*light*⟩ brillante; ⟨*sunshine*⟩ radiante; ⟨*red/green*⟩ brillante **(b)** ⟨*student/performance*⟩ brillante

brilliantly /'brɪljəntli/ *adv* **(a)** ⟨*shine*⟩ intensamente **(b)** ⟨*write*⟩ con brillantez

brim¹ /brɪm/ *n* 1 (of hat) ala *f*; 2 (of vessel) borde *m*

brim² *vi* **-mm-**: her eyes were ∼ming with tears tenía los ojos llenos de lágrimas; **to ∼ with confidence** rebosar seguridad

brine /braɪn/ *n* **(a)** (saltwater) salmuera *f* **(b)** (seawater) agua *f* salada *or* de mar

bring /brɪŋ/ (*past & past p* **brought**) *vt* traer*; **I couldn't ∼ myself to do it** no pude hacerlo; **it brought tears to my eyes** hizo que se me llenaran los ojos de lágrimas; **to ∼ sth to bear: to ∼ pressure to bear on sb** ejercer* presión sobre algn
▪ **bring about** [*v + o + adv, v + adv + o*] dar* lugar a
▪ **bring along** [*v + o + adv, v + adv + o*] traer*
▪ **bring back** [*v + o + adv, v + adv + o*] **(a)** (return): **I'll ∼ your book back tomorrow** te devolveré *or* (AmL exc CS) te regresaré el libro mañana; **to ∼ sb back to life** devolverle* la vida a algn **(b)** ⟨*gift/souvenir*⟩ traer* **(c)** (reintroduce) ⟨*custom*⟩ volver* a introducir **(d)** (recall) recordar*; **it brought back memories** me (*or* le *etc*) trajo recuerdos
▪ **bring down** [*v + o + adv, v + adv + o*] **(a)** (lower) ⟨*price*⟩ reducir*; ⟨*temperature*⟩ hacer* bajar **(b)** (cause to fall) ⟨*tree/wall*⟩ tirar; ⟨*player/opponent/plane*⟩ derribar; ⟨*government*⟩ derrocar*
▪ **bring forward** [*v + o + adv, v + adv + o*] **(a)** (present) ⟨*witness*⟩ hacer* comparecer; ⟨*evidence/idea*⟩ presentar **(b)** (to earlier time) ⟨*meeting/appointment*⟩ adelantar
▪ **bring home** [*v + o + adv, v + adv + o*]: **her letter brought home to me the seriousness of the situation** su carta me hizo dar cuenta cabal de la gravedad de la situación
▪ **bring off** [*v + o + adv, v + adv + o*] ⟨*feat/victory*⟩ conseguir*, lograr; ⟨*plan*⟩ llevar a cabo; ⟨*deal*⟩ conseguir*
▪ **bring on** [*v + o + adv, v + adv + o*] ⟨*attack/breakdown*⟩ provocar*; **what brought this on?** ¿esto a qué se debe?
  2 [*v + o + prep + o*] (cause to befall): **he brought it all on himself** él (mismo) se lo buscó
▪ **bring out** [*v + o + adv, v + adv + o*] **(a)** ⟨*product/model*⟩ sacar* (al mercado); ⟨*edition/book*⟩ publicar* **(b)** (accentuate): **children ∼ out the best in her** el trato con niños hace resaltar sus mejores cualidades
▪ **bring together** [*v + o + adv, v + adv + o*]: **the conference will ∼ together scientists from all over the world** el congreso reunirá a científicos de todo el mundo; **a tragedy like this can ∼ a family together** una tragedia así puede unir a una familia
▪ **bring up** [*v + o + adv, v + adv + o*] **(a)** (rear) ⟨*child*⟩ criar* **(b)** (mention) ⟨*subject*⟩ sacar* **(c)** (vomit) vomitar, devolver*

brink /brɪŋk/ *n* borde *m*; **to be on the ∼ of -ING** estar* a punto de +INF

brisk /brɪsk/ *adj* **(a)** (lively, quick) ⟨*pace*⟩ rápido y enérgico; ⟨*walk*⟩ a paso ligero; **ice-cream sellers did a ∼ trade** los vendedores de helados vendieron muchísimo **(b)** (efficient) ⟨*person/manner*⟩ enérgico *or* dinámico y eficiente

bristle¹ /'brɪsəl/ *n* (on animal) cerda *f*; (on person): **his face was covered in ∼(s)** tenía la barba crecida

bristle² *vi* **(a)** (stand up) «*hair*» erizarse*, ponerse* de punta **(b)** (show annoyance) erizarse*

Britain /'brɪtn̩ ‖ 'brɪtən/ *n* Gran Bretaña *f*

British¹ /'brɪtɪʃ/ *adj* británico

British² *pl n* **the ∼** los británicos

Britisher /'brɪtɪʃər ‖ 'brɪtɪʃə(r)/ *n* (AmE) británico, -ca *m,f*

British: ∼ Isles *pl n* **the ∼ Isles** las Islas Británicas; **∼ Summer Time** *n hora de verano en Gran Bretaña, adelantada en una hora con respecto a la hora de Greenwich*

Briton /'brɪtn̩ ‖ 'brɪtən/ *n* ciudadano británico, ciudadana británica *m,f*; **the ancient ∼s** los antiguos britanos

Brittany /'brɪtni ‖ 'brɪtəni/ *n* Bretaña *f*

brittle /'brɪtl̩/ *adj* quebradizo

broach /brəʊtʃ/ *vt* ⟨*subject*⟩ mencionar

broad¹ /brɔːd/ *adj* 1 ⟨*avenue*⟩ ancho; ⟨*valley*⟩ grande; ⟨*forehead*⟩ despejado; ⟨*grin*⟩ de oreja a oreja 2 **(a)** (extensive) ⟨*syllabus*⟩ amplio; ⟨*interests*⟩ numeroso; **in its ∼est sense** en su sentido más amplio **(b)** (general) ⟨*guidelines/conclusions*⟩ general 3 **(a) a ∼ hint** una indirecta muy clara **(b)** ⟨*accent*⟩ cerrado

broad² *n* (woman) (AmE sl) tipa *f* (fam), vieja *f* (Col, Méx, Ven fam)

broadband¹ /'brɔːdbænd/ *nu* (Electron) banda *f* ancha

broadband² *adj* de banda ancha

broad bean *n* haba *f*

broadcast¹ /'brɔːdkæst ‖ 'brɔːdkɑːst/ *vt/i* (*past & past p* **broadcast**) transmitir, emitir

broadcast² *n* programa *m*, emisión *f* (frml)

broadcaster /'brɔːdkæstər ‖ 'brɔːdkɑːstə(r)/ *n*: presentador, locutor etc de radio o televisión

broadcasting /'brɔːdkæstɪŋ ‖ 'brɔːdkɑːstɪŋ/ *n* (Rad) radiodifusión *f*; (TV) televisión *f*

broaden /'brɔːdn̩/ *vt* ⟨*scope/horizons/interests*⟩ ampliar*

broadly /'brɔːdli/ *adv*: **the two systems are ∼ similar** en líneas generales, los dos sistemas son similares; **∼ speaking** en líneas generales

broad: ∼-minded /'brɔːd'maɪndəd ‖ ,brɔːd'maɪndɪd/ *adj* de criterio amplio; **∼sheet** *n*: periódico de formato grande

brocade /brəʊ'keɪd ‖ brə'keɪd/ *n* brocado *m*

broccoli /'brɑːkəli/ *n* brócoli *m*, brécol *m*

brochure /brəʊ'ʃʊr ‖ 'brəʊʃə(r)/ *n* folleto *m*

brogue /brəʊg/ *n* 1 (shoe) *zapato bajo de cuero* 2 (Irish accent) (*no pl*) acento *m* irlandés

broil /brɔɪl/ *vt* asar a la parrilla *or* al grill

broiler /'brɔɪlər/ *n* (AmE) parrilla *f*, grill *m*

broke¹ /brəʊk/ *past of* BREAK¹

broke² *adj* (colloq) (*pred*): **to be ~** estar* pelado; **to be flat ~** estar* pelado *or* (Esp) sin un duro *or* (Col) en la olla

broken¹ /'brəʊkən/ *past p of* BREAK¹

broken² *adj* 1 (a) ⟨*window/vase/chair/glass*⟩ roto; ⟨*bone*⟩ roto, quebrado (AmL) (b) (not working) roto 2 ⟨*voice*⟩ quebrado; **to die of a ~ heart** morirse* de pena; **he's a ~ man** está destrozado 3 ⟨*home/marriage*⟩ deshecho 4 (imperfect): **in ~ English** en inglés chapurreado

broken-down /'brəʊkən'daʊn/ *adj* ⟨*car/ machine*⟩ averiado, descompuesto (AmL), en pana (Chi), varado (Col); ⟨*shed/gate*⟩ destartalado

broker /'brəʊkər ‖'brəʊkə(r)/ *n* (a) (agent) agente *mf*; **insurance ~** agente *mf* de seguros (b) (stock~) corredor, -dora *m,f* de bolsa

bronchitis /brɑ:ŋ'kaɪtəs ‖brɒŋ'kaɪtɪs/ *n* bronquitis *f*

bronze /brɑ:nz ‖brɒnz/ *n* (Metall) bronce *m*

brooch /brəʊtʃ/ *n* prendedor *m*, broche *m*

brood¹ /bru:d/ *n* (of birds) nidada *f*; (of mammals) camada *f*; (of children) (hum) prole *f* (fam & hum)

brood² *vi* (reflect): **she sat ~ing on the unfairness of life** rumiaba lo injusta que era la vida; **stop ~ing over it** deja de darle vueltas al asunto

brook /brʊk/ *n* arroyo *m*

broom /bru:m/ *n* 1 (brush) escoba *f* 2 (plant) retama *f*, hiniesta *f*

broomstick /'bru:mstɪk/ *n* palo *m* de escoba; (of a witch) escoba *f*

broth /brɔ:θ ‖brɒθ/ *n* caldo *m*

brothel /'brɑ:θəl ‖'brɒθəl/ *n* burdel *m*

brother /'brʌðər ‖'brʌðə(r)/ *n* hermano *m*; **do you have any ~s and sisters?** ¿tienes hermanos?

brotherhood /'brʌðərhʊd ‖'brʌðəhʊd/ *n* (a) (fellowship) fraternidad *f* (b) (association) hermandad *f*; (Relig) cofradía *f*

brother-in-law /'brʌðərɪn,lɔ:/ *n* (*pl* **brothers-in-law**) cuñado *m*

brotherly /'brʌðərli ‖'brʌðəli/ *adj* fraternal

brought /brɔ:t/ *past & past p of* BRING

brow /braʊ/ *n* (a) (forehead) (liter) frente *f* (b) (eye~) ceja *f* (c) (of hill) cima *f*

browbeat /'braʊbi:t/ *vt* (*past* **browbeat**; *past p* **browbeaten** /'braʊ,bi:tn̩/) intimidar

brown¹ /braʊn/ *adj* **-er, -est** ⟨*shoe/dress/eyes*⟩ marrón, café *adj inv* (AmC, Chi, Méx), carmelito (Col); ⟨*hair*⟩ castaño; ⟨*skin/person*⟩ (naturally) moreno; (suntanned) bronceado; **to get ~** broncearse

brown² *n* marrón *m*, café *m* (AmC, Chi, Méx), carmelito *m* (Col)

brown³ *vt* (a) (Culin) dorar (b) (tan) broncear

brown bread *n* pan *m* negro *or* (Esp) moreno

brownie /'braʊni/ *n* 1 (cake) bizcocho de chocolate y nueces 2 **Brownie**, (BrE) **Brownie** (Guide) alita *f*

brown: ~ paper *n* papel *m* de estraza; **~ rice** *n* arroz *m* integral; **~ sugar** *n* azúcar *m* moreno, azúcar *f* morena

browse /braʊz/ *vi* (look) mirar (*en una tienda, catálogo etc*); **she was browsing through a magazine** estaba hojeando una revista

browser /'braʊzər ‖'braʊzə(r)/ *n* (Comput) navegador *m*

bruise¹ /bru:z/ *n* moretón *m*, cardenal *m*, morado *m* (Esp, Ven)

bruise² *vt* ⟨*body/arm*⟩ contusionar (fml); ⟨*fruit*⟩ magullar, mallugar* (Méx, Ven)

brunch /brʌntʃ/ *n* (colloq) brunch *m* (*combinación de desayuno y almuerzo*)

brunette /bru:'net/ *n* morena *f*, morocha *f* (CS)

brunt /brʌnt/ *n*: **to bear** *o* **take the ~ of sth** sufrir algo

brush¹ /brʌʃ/ *n* 1 (for cleaning) cepillo *m*; (for hair) cepillo *m*; (paint~) pincel *m*; (large) brocha *f* 2 (of fox) cola *f* 3 (a) (act): **I gave my hair a ~** me cepillé el pelo (b) (faint touch) roce *m* (c) (encounter) **~ WITH sth/sb** ⟨*with the law/the police*⟩ roce *m* CON algo/algn 4 (scrub) maleza *f*

brush² *vt* (a) (clean, groom) ⟨*jacket/hair*⟩ cepillar; **to ~ one's teeth** lavarse los dientes (b) (sweep): **he ~ed the crumbs off the table** quitó las migas de la mesa (c) (touch lightly) rozar*
■ **~** *vi* **to ~** AGAINST **sth/sb** rozar* algo/a algn
■ **brush off** [*v* + *o* + *adv*, *v* + *adv* + *o*] (a) ⟨*mud/ hair*⟩ quitar (cepillando) (b) ⟨*advances/ suggestions*⟩ no hacer* caso de
■ **brush up** (a) [*v* + *o* + *adv*, *v* + *adv* + *o*] (colloq) darle* un repaso a (b) [*v* + *adv*] **to ~ up ON sth** darle* un repaso A algo

brusque /brʌsk ‖brʊsk/ *adj* brusco

Brussels /'brʌsəlz/ *n* Bruselas *f*

brussels sprout, Brussels Sprout *n* col *f or* (AmS) repollito *m* de Bruselas

brutal /'bru:tl̩/ *adj* brutal

brutality /bru:'tæləti/ *n* (*pl* **-ties**) brutalidad *f*

brutally /'bru:tl̩i/ *adv* (a) (cruelly) ⟨*attack/treat*⟩ brutalmente (b) (mercilessly) ⟨*frank*⟩ crudamente

brute¹ /bru:t/ *n* (colloq) (a) (person) animal *mf* (fam) (b) (animal) bestia *f* (fam)

brute² *adj* (before *n*) **~ force** fuerza *f* bruta

BS *n* (AmE), **BSc** *n* (BrE) = **Bachelor of Science**

BST = **British Summer Time**

bubble¹ /'bʌbəl/ *n* (of air, gas) burbuja *f*; (of soap) pompa *f*

bubble² *vi* 1 (form bubbles) «*lava*» bullir*; «*champagne*» burbujear 2 «*person*»: **she ~s with enthusiasm** rebosa (de) entusiasmo

bubble: ~ bath *n* baño *m* de burbujas *or* espuma *f*; **~ gum** *n* chicle *m* (de globos), chicle *m* de bomba (Col, Ven), chicle *m* globero (Ur); **~-wrapped** *adj* envuelto en plástico con burbujas

bubbly /'bʌbli/ *adj* **-lier, -liest** (a) ⟨*person*⟩ lleno de vida; ⟨*personality*⟩ efervescente (b) (full of bubbles) burbujeante

Bucharest /'bu:kərest ‖bu:kə'rest/ *n* Bucarest *m*

buck¹ /bʌk/ *n* 1 (male deer) ciervo *m* (macho); (male rabbit) conejo *m* (macho) 2 (dollar) (esp AmE colloq) dólar *m*, verde *m* (AmL fam) 3 (responsibility): **to pass the ~** (colloq) pasar la pelota (fam); **the ~ stops here** la responsabilidad es mía (*or* nuestra *etc*)

buck² *vi* «*horse*» corcovear
■ **~** *vt* ⟨*trend*⟩ resistirse a

■ **buck up** (colloq) ⟦1⟧ [*v* + *adv*] (become cheerful) levantar el ánimo ⟦2⟧ [*v* + *o* + *adv*, *v* + *adv* + *o*] (cheer up) ⟨*person*⟩ levantarle el ánimo a

bucket /'bʌkət ‖'bʌkɪt/ *n* balde *m* or (Esp) cubo *m* or (Méx) cubeta *f* or (Ven) tobo *m*; **to kick the ∼** (colloq & hum) estirar la pata (fam & hum)

buckle¹ /'bʌkəl/ *n* hebilla *f*

buckle² *vt* abrochar

■ ∼ *vi* (bend, crumple) «*wheel/metal*» torcerse*; **his knees ∼d beneath him** se le doblaron las rodillas

bud /bʌd/ *n* brote *m*, yema *f*; (of flower) capullo *m*

Budapest /'buːdəpest ‖,buːdə'pest/ *n* Budapest *m*

Buddha /'buːdə ‖'bʊdə/ *n* Buda *m*

Buddhism /'buːdɪzəm ‖'bʊdɪzəm/ *n* budismo *m*

Buddhist¹ /'buːdəst ‖'bʊdɪst/ *n* budista *mf*

Buddhist² *adj* budista

budding /'bʌdɪŋ/ *adj* (before *n*) ⟨*artist/genius*⟩ en ciernes

buddy /'bʌdi/ *n* (*pl* **-dies**) (AmE colloq) amigo *m*, compinche *m* (fam), cuate *m* (Méx fam)

budge /bʌdʒ/ *vi* (*usu with neg*) **(a)** (move) moverse* **(b)** (change opinion) cambiar de opinión

■ ∼ *vt* **(a)** (move) correr **(b)** (persuade) convencer*

budgerigar /'bʌdʒəriɡɑːr ‖'bʌdʒəriɡɑː(r)/ *n* periquito *m*

budget¹ /'bʌdʒət ‖'bʌdʒɪt/ *n* presupuesto *m*

budget² *vi* administrarse; **to learn to ∼** aprender a administrar el dinero; **I hadn't ∼ed for staying in a hotel** no había contado con gastos de hotel

budgie /'bʌdʒi/ *n* (BrE colloq) periquito *m*

buff¹ /bʌf/ *n* (colloq) aficionado, -da *m,f*; **film ∼** cinéfilo, -la *m,f*

buff² *vt* ⟨*metal*⟩ pulir; ⟨*shoes*⟩ sacar* brillo a

buffalo /'bʌfələʊ/ *n* (*pl* **-loes** or **-los**) **(a)** (wild ox) búfalo *m*; (water ∼) búfalo *m* de agua, carabao *m* **(b)** (bison) (AmE) bisonte *m*

buffer /'bʌfər ‖'bʌfə(r)/ *n* ⟦1⟧ **(a)** (AmE Auto) parachoques *m*, paragolpes *m* (RPl) **(b)** (BrE Rail) (on train) tope *m*; (in station) parachoques *m*; (before *n*) ∼ **state** estado *m* tapón ⟦2⟧ (Comput) memoria *f* intermedia

buffet¹ /bə'feɪ ‖'bʊfeɪ, 'bʌfeɪ/ *n* ⟦1⟧ (meal) buffet *m* ⟦2⟧ (BrE) **(a)** (in train) bar *m*; (before *n*) ∼ **car** (also AmE) coche *m* restaurante, coche *m* comedor **(b)** (cafetería) bar *m* (en una estación)

buffet² /'bʌfət ‖'bʌfɪt/ *vt* zarandear, sacudir

bug¹ /bʌɡ/ *n* ⟦1⟧ (biting insect) chinche *f* or *m*; (any insect) (esp AmE) bicho *m* ⟦2⟧ (germ, disease) (colloq): **he picked up a stomach ∼** se agarró algo al estómago; **she got the travel ∼** le entró la fiebre de los viajes ⟦3⟧ (listening device) (colloq) micrófono *m* oculto

bug² *vt* **-gg-** (colloq) ⟦1⟧ ⟨*room/telephone*⟩ colocar* micrófonos ocultos en ⟦2⟧ (bother, irritate) fastidiar

bugger /'bʌɡər ‖'bʌɡə(r)/ *n* (BrE vulg) hijo, -ja *m,f* de puta (vulg)

buggy /'bʌɡi/ *n* (*pl* **-gies**) ⟦1⟧ (horse-drawn vehicle) calesa *f* ⟦2⟧ (baby ∼) (baby carriage) (AmE) cochecito *m*; (pushchair) (BrE) sillita *f* de paseo (*plegable*)

bugle /'bjuːɡəl/ *n* clarín *m*

build¹ /bɪld/ (*past & past p* **built**) *vt* ⟨*house/road/ship/wall*⟩ construir*; ⟨*fire/nest*⟩ hacer*

■ **build up** ⟦1⟧ [*v* + *o* + *adv*, *v* + *adv* + *o*] **(a)** (make

bigger, stronger) fortalecer* **(b)** (accumulate) ⟨*supplies/experience*⟩ acumular; ⟨*reserves*⟩ acrecentar* **(c)** (develop) ⟨*reputation*⟩ forjarse; **to ∼ up one's hopes** hacerse* ilusiones; **he built the firm up from nothing** levantó la empresa de la nada ⟦2⟧ [*v* + *adv*] (increase) «*pressure/noise*» ir* en aumento; **the tension ∼s up to a climax** la tensión va en aumento hasta llegar a un punto culminante

build² *n* complexión *f*

builder /'bɪldər ‖'bɪldə(r)/ *n* albañil *mf*; (contractor) contratista *mf*

building /'bɪldɪŋ/ *n* **(a)** (edifice) edificio *m* **(b)** (construction) construcción *f*; (before *n*) ∼ **contractor** contratista *mf* (de obras); ∼ **site** obra *f*

building society *n* (in UK) sociedad *f* de crédito hipotecario

buildup /'bɪldʌp/ *n* **(a)** (accumulation) acumulación *f*; (of tension, pressure) aumento *m* **(b)** (of troops) concentración *f* **(c)** (publicity) propaganda *f*

built /bɪlt/ *past & past p of* BUILD¹

built: ∼**-in** /'bɪlt'ɪn/ *adj* (before *n*) ⟨*bookcase/desk*⟩ empotrado; ⟨*equipment*⟩ fijo; ⟨*mechanism/feature*⟩ incorporado; ∼**-up** /'bɪlt'ʌp/ *adj* (before *n*) ⟨*area*⟩ urbanizado

bulb /bʌlb/ *n* ⟦1⟧ (Bot, Hort) (of flower) bulbo *m*, papa *f* (Chi); (of garlic) cabeza *f* ⟦2⟧ (light ∼) bombilla *f* or (Méx) foco *m* or (Col, Ven) bombillo *m* or (RPl) bombita *f* or lamparita *f* or (Chi) ampolleta *f* or (AmC) bujía *f*

bulbous /'bʌlbəs/ *adj* ⟨*growth*⟩ bulboso; ⟨*nose*⟩ protuberante

Bulgaria /bʌl'ɡeriə ‖bʌl'ɡeəriə/ *n* Bulgaria *f*

Bulgarian¹ /bʌl'ɡeriən ‖bʌl'ɡeəriən/ *adj* búlgaro

Bulgarian² *n* **(a)** (person) búlgaro, -ra *m,f* **(b)** (language) búlgaro *m*

bulge¹ /bʌldʒ/ *n* bulto *m*

bulge² *vi* **(a)** (protrude) sobresalir*; **the bag was bulging with books** la bolsa estaba repleta de libros **(b) bulging** *pres p* ⟨*pocket/bag*⟩ repleto; ⟨*eyes*⟩ saltón

bulimia (nervosa) /bjuː'liːmiə(nɜːr'vəʊsə) ‖bjuː'lɪmiə(nɜː'vəʊsə)/ *n* bulimia *f* (nerviosa)

bulk /bʌlk/ *n* ⟦1⟧ **(a)** (Busn) (large quantity): **in ∼** en grandes cantidades **(b)** (large mass) mole *f* ⟦2⟧ (largest part): **the ∼ of sth** la mayor parte de algo

bulky /'bʌlki/ *adj* **-kier, -kiest** ⟨*package*⟩ voluminoso; ⟨*person*⟩ corpulento; ⟨*sweater*⟩ (AmE) grueso

bull /bʊl/ *n* toro *m*

bull: ∼**dog** *n* bul(l)dog *m*; ∼**doze** *vt* demoler*; ∼**dozer** /'bʊldəʊzər ‖'bʊldəʊzə(r)/ *n* bulldozer *m*, topadora *f* (Arg)

bullet /'bʊlət ‖'bʊlɪt/ *n* bala *f*

bulletin /'bʊlətn ‖'bʊlətɪn/ *n* (notice) anuncio *m*; (newsletter) boletín *m*; (report) (Journ) boletín *m* (informativo)

bulletin board *n* (AmE) tablero *m* or (Esp) tablón *m* de anuncios, cartelera *f* (AmL), diario *m* mural (Chi)

bulletproof /'bʊlətpruːf ‖'bʊlɪtpruːf/ *adj* ⟨*vest*⟩ antibalas *adj inv*; ⟨*vehicle*⟩ blindado

bull: ~**fight** n corrida f de toros; ~**fighter** n torero, -ra m,f; ~**fighting** n (deporte m de) los toros; (art) tauromaquia f; ~**frog** n rana f toro

bullion /'bʊljən ‖'bʊliən/ n: **gold/silver** ~ oro/plata en lingotes

bullock /'bʊlək/ n (a) (castrated bull) buey m (b) (young bull) (esp AmE) novillo m

bull: ~**ring** n plaza f de toros; ~**seye** n diana f; ~**shit** /'bʊlʃɪt/ n (vulg) sandeces fpl (fam), pendejadas (AmL exc CS vulg), gilipolleces fpl (Esp arg), huevadas fpl (Andes, Ven vulg), boludeces fpl (Col, RPl vulg), mamadas fpl (Méx vulg)

bully[1] /'bʊli/ n (pl **-lies**) matón, -tona m,f

bully[2] vt **-lies, -lying, -lied** intimidar

bum /bʌm/ n (colloq) [1] (a) (worthless person) vago, -ga m,f (fam) (b) (vagrant) (AmE) vagabundo, -da m,f [2] (buttocks) (BrE) trasero m (fam), culo m (fam o vulg), traste m (CS fam), poto m (Chi, Per fam)

bumblebee /'bʌmbəlˌbiː/ n abejorro m

bumbling /'bʌmblɪŋ/ adj torpe

bump[1] /bʌmp/ n [1] (blow) golpe m; (jolt) sacudida f; (collision) topetazo m [2] (lump — on surface) bulto m; (— on head) chichón m; (— on road) bache m

bump[2] vt: I ~ed my elbow on o against the door me di en el codo con or contra la puerta; I ~ed the post as I was reversing choqué con or contra el poste al dar marcha atrás

■ ~ vi (hit, knock) **to** ~ (**AGAINST** sth) darse* or chocar* (**CONTRA** or **CON** sth algo)

■ **bump into** [v + prep + o] (a) (collide with) darse* or chocar* contra (b) (meet by chance) (colloq) toparse or tropezarse* con

bumper[1] /'bʌmpər ‖'bʌmpə(r)/ n (Auto) parachoques m, paragolpes m (AmL)

bumper[2] adj (before n) ⟨crop/year⟩ récord adj inv; ⟨edition⟩ extra; ⟨pack⟩ gigante

bumper car n coche m de choque, autito m chocador (RPl), carro m loco (Andes), carrito m chocón (Méx, Ven)

bumpkin /'bʌmpkɪn/ n: (country) ~ pueblerino, -na m,f, paleto, -ta m,f (Esp fam), pajuerano, -na m,f (RPl fam)

bumpy /'bʌmpi/ adj **-pier, -piest** ⟨surface⟩ desigual; ⟨road⟩ lleno de baches; **we had a** ~ **flight** el avión se movió mucho

bun /bʌn/ n [1] (a) (sweetened) bollo m (b) (bread roll) panecillo m, pancito m (CS), bolillo m (Méx) [2] (hairstyle) moño m, rodete m (RPl), chongo m (Méx) [3] **buns** pl (AmE colloq) trasero m (fam), culo m (fam o vulg), traste m (CS fam), poto m (Chi, Per fam)

bunch /bʌntʃ/ n (a) (of flowers) ramo m, bonche m (Méx); (small) ramillete m; (of bananas) racimo m, penca f (Méx), cacho m (RPl); (of grapes) racimo m; (of keys) manojo m (b) (group) grupo m; **they're an odd** ~ son gente de lo más rara

bundle[1] /'bʌndl/ n (of clothes) lío m, fardo m, atado m (AmL); (of newspapers, letters) paquete m; (of money) fajo m; (of sticks) haz m, atado m (AmL)

bundle[2] vt (a) (make into a bundle) liar*, atar (b)

(push) (+ adv compl): **she** ~**d them off to school** los despachó al colegio; **they** ~**d him into the car** lo metieron a empujones en el coche

bung /bʌŋ/ n tapón m

bungalow /'bʌŋgələʊ/ n casa f de una planta

bungle /'bʌŋgəl/ vt echar a perder; **a** ~**d attempt** un intento fallido

bungling /'bʌŋglɪŋ/ adj (before n, no comp) torpe

bunion /'bʌnjən/ n juanete m

bunk /bʌŋk/ n litera f

■ **bunk off** ▶ SKIVE OFF

bunk bed n litera f

bunny (pl **-nies**), **bunny rabbit** /'bʌni/ n (used to or by children) conejito m (fam)

bunting /'bʌntɪŋ/ n (esp AmE) tela usada para la confección de banderas

buoy /bɔɪ, 'buːi ‖bɔɪ/ n boya f

■ **buoy up** [v + o + adv, v + adv + o] (a) ⟨boat/person⟩ mantener* a flote (b) (keep cheerful) animar

buoyant /'bɔɪənt/ adj (a) (able to float) flotante (b) ⟨mood/spirits⟩ optimista (c) (Fin) ⟨currency⟩ fuerte; ⟨market⟩ alcista

burble /'bɜːrbəl ‖'bɜːbəl/ vi (a) ⟨stream/spring⟩ borbotar, borbotear (b) (talk meaninglessly) parlotear (fam), cotorrear (fam); (talk excitedly) hablar atropelladamente

burden[1] /'bɜːrdn ‖'bɜːdn/ n carga f

burden[2] vt cargar*; **I don't want to** ~ **you with my problems** no te quiero preocupar con mis problemas

bureau /'bjʊrəʊ ‖'bjʊərəʊ/ n (pl **bureaus** or **bureaux** /-z/) [1] (a) (agency) agencia f (b) (government department) (AmE) departamento m [2] (a) (chest of drawers) (AmE) cómoda f (b) (desk) (BrE) buró m, escritorio m

bureaucracy /bjʊ'rɑːkrəsi ‖bjʊə'rɒkrəsi/ n (pl **-cies**) burocracia f

bureaucrat /'bjʊrəkræt ‖'bjʊərəkræt/ n burócrata mf

bureaucratic /ˌbjʊrə'krætɪk ‖ˌbjʊərə'krætɪk/ adj burocrático

bureau de change /ˌbjʊrəʊdə'ʃɑːnʒ ‖ˌbjʊərəʊdə'ʃɑʒ/ n (pl **bureaux de change**) (casa f de) cambio m

burgeon /'bɜːrdʒən ‖'bɜːdʒən/ vi (liter) florecer*

burglar /'bɜːrglər ‖'bɜːglə(r)/ n ladrón, -drona m,f; (before n) ~ **alarm** alarma f antirrobo

burglarize /'bɜːrgləraɪz ‖'bɜːgləraɪz/ vt (AmE) robar

burglary /'bɜːrgləri ‖'bɜːgləri/ n (pl **-ries**) robo m (con allanamiento de morada o escalamiento)

burgle /'bɜːrgəl ‖'bɜːgəl/ vt robar

burial /'beriəl/ n entierro m

Burkina Faso /bɜːr'kiːnə'fæsəʊ ‖ˌbɜːkiːnə'fæsəʊ/ n Burkina Faso m

burlesque /bɜːr'lesk ‖bɜː'lesk/ n obra f burlesca

AmC	Central America
AmL	Latin America
AmS	South America
Andes	Andean Region

Arg	Argentina
Bol	Bolivia
Chi	Chile
CS	Southern Cone

Cu	Cuba
Ec	Ecuador
Esp	Spain
Méx	Mexico

Per	Peru
RPl	River Plate Area
Ur	Uruguay
Ven	Venezuela

burly /'bɜːrli ‖'bɜːli/ adj **-lier, -liest** fornido

Burma /'bɜːrmə ‖'bɜːmə/ n Birmania f

Burmese[1] /'bɜːr'miːz ‖bɜːˈmiːz/ adj birmano

Burmese[2] n (pl ~) **(a)** (person) birmano, -na m,f; **(b)** (language) birmano m

burn[1] /bɜːrn ‖bɜːn/ (past & past p **burned** or **burnt**) vi [1] **(a)** «fire/building/wood/coal» arder; «food» quemarse **(b)** (in sun) «skin» quemarse [2] (sting) «eyes/wound» escocer*, arder (esp AmL); **a ~ing sensation** un escozor, un ardor (esp AmL)
■ ~ vt [1] **(a)** «letter/rubbish/food» quemar; «building/town» incendiar; **I ~ed a hole in my sleeve** me quemé la manga (con un cigarrillo etc) **(b)** (injure) quemar [2] (Comput) «CD» quemar
■ **burn down** [1] [v + o + adv, v + adv + o] incendiar [2] [v + adv] incendiarse

burn[2] n quemadura f

burner /'bɜːrnər ‖'bɜːnə(r)/ n quemador m

burning /'bɜːrnɪŋ ‖'bɜːnɪŋ/ adj (before n) **(a)** (hot) «sand» ardiente; «sun» abrasador **(b)** (intense) «desire» ardiente; «hatred» violento

burnt /bɜːrnt ‖bɜːnt/ past & past p of BURN[1]

burp v eructar

burrow[1] /'bərəʊ ‖'bʌrəʊ/ n madriguera f; (of rabbits) conejera f

burrow[2] vi cavar

bursar /'bɜːrsər ‖'bɜːsə(r)/ n administrador, -dora m,f

burst[1] /bɜːrst ‖bɜːst/ (past & past p **burst**) vi [1] «balloon/tire» reventarse*; «pipe» reventar*, romperse*; «dam» romperse*; **to ~ open** abrirse* de golpe [2] (move suddenly) (+ adv compl): **he ~ into the room** entró de sopetón en la habitación; **they ~ through the police cordon** rompieron el cordón policial
■ ~ vt «balloon/bubble» reventar*; **the river ~ its banks** el río se desbordó
■ **burst into** [v + prep + o]: **to ~ into tears** echarse a llorar; **to ~ into song** ponerse* a cantar; **to ~ into flames** estallar en llamas

burst[2] n [1] (of applause) salva f; (of activity) arrebato m; (of gunfire) ráfaga f [2] (of pipe) rotura f

bursting /'bɜːrstɪŋ ‖'bɜːstɪŋ/ adj (pred, no comp) **to be ~** (WITH sth) estar* repleto (DE algo); **he was ~ with energy** rebosaba (de) energía

bury /'beri/ **buries, burying, buried** vt (inter) enterrar*; **the village was buried by the avalanche** el pueblo fue sepultado por la avalancha; **he buried his head in his hands** ocultó la cabeza entre las manos
■ v refl **to ~ oneself IN sth** (in one's work/one's books) enfrascarse* EN algo

bus /bʌs/ n (pl **buses** or (AmE also) **busses**) (Transp) **(a)** (local) autobús m, bus m (AmL), camión m (AmC, Méx), colectivo m (Arg), ómnibus m (Per, Ur), micro f (Chi), guagua f (Cu); (before n) **~ conductor** cobrador, -dora m,f, guarda mf (RPl) de autobuses; **~ driver** conductor, -tora m,f or chofer mf or (Esp) chófer mf de autobús, camionero, -ra m,f (AmC, Méx), colectivero, -ra m,f (Arg), microbusero, -ra m,f (Chi); **~ stop** parada f or (AmL exc RPl) paradero m de autobús (or bus etc) **(b)** (long-distance) autobús m, autocar m (Esp), pullman m (CS)

bush /bʊʃ/ n [1] (shrub) arbusto m; **to beat about the ~** andarse* con rodeos [2] (wild country) **the ~** el monte

bushy /'bʊʃi/ adj **bushier, bushiest** «beard» poblado; «eyebrows» tupido; «undergrowth» espeso

busily /'bɪzəli ‖'bɪzɪli/ adv «work» afanosamente

business /'bɪznəs/ n [1] (Busn) **(a)** (world of commerce, finance) negocios mpl; (before n) **~ studies** (ciencias fpl) empresariales fpl **(b)** (commercial activity, trading) comercio m; **the firm has been in ~ for 50 years** la empresa tiene 50 años de actividad comercial; **they went into ~ together** montaron un negocio juntos; **she's away on ~** está de viaje por negocios; **to go out of ~** cerrar*; **to get down to ~** ir* al grano; **to mean ~** decir* algo muy en serio; (before n) «appointment/lunch» de trabajo, de negocios; **~ hours** horas fpl de oficina; **~ letter** carta f comercial; **~ trip** viaje m de negocios **(c)** (custom, clients): **to lose ~** perder* clientes or clientela [2] **(a)** (firm) negocio m, empresa f **(b)** (branch of commerce): **I'm in the antiques ~** trabajo en la compra y venta de antigüedades; **the music ~** la industria de la música [3] (rightful occupation, concern) asunto m; **mind your own ~!** ¡no te metas en lo que no te importa!; **that's none of your ~** eso no es asunto tuyo [4] (affair, situation, activity) (colloq) (no pl) asunto m; **what's all this ~ about you leaving?** ¿qué es eso de que te vas?

business: **~like** adj «person/manner» (serious) formal; (efficient) eficiente; «discussion» serio; **~man** /'bɪznəsmæn ‖'bɪznɪsmən/ n (pl **-men** /-men ‖-mən/) empresario m, hombre m de negocios; **~woman** n empresaria f, mujer f de negocios

busker /'bʌskər ‖'bʌskə(r)/ n (BrE) músico m callejero

bust[1] /bʌst/ vt **(a)** (past & past p **busted** or (BrE also) **bust**) (break) (colloq) romper* **(b)** (past & past p **busted**) (raid) (sl) «person» agarrar (fam), trincar* (Esp fam); «premises» hacer* una redada en

bust[2] n **(a)** (sculpture) busto m **(b)** (bosom) busto m, pecho m

bust[3] adj (bankrupt) (colloq): **to go ~** quebrar*, ir(se)* a la bancarrota, fundirse (Per, RPl fam)

bustle[1] /'bʌsəl/ vi **(a)** (move busily): **to ~ around** ir* de aquí para allá **(b)** (be crowded, lively) «street/store» **to ~** (WITH sth) bullir* (DE algo)

bustle[2] n ajetreo m

bustling /'bʌslɪŋ/ adj «street/shop» animado

bust-up /'bʌstʌp/ n **(a)** (breakup) ruptura f **(b)** (quarrel) (BrE colloq) pelea f, bronca f (fam)

busy[1] /'bɪzi/ adj **busier, busiest** [1] «person» ocupado; **the children keep me very ~** los niños me tienen muy atareada [2] «street/market» concurrido; **I've had a ~ day** he tenido un día de mucho trabajo; **a ~ road** una carretera con mucho tráfico [3] (AmE Telec) ocupado (AmL), comunicando (Esp); **the ~ signal** la señal de ocupado or (Esp) de comunicando

busy[2] v refl **busies, busying, busied**: **to ~ oneself WITH sth** entretenerse* CON algo

busybody /'bɪziˌbɑːdi ‖'bɪziˌbɒdi/ n (pl **-dies**) (colloq) entrometido, -da m,f, metomentodo mf (fam)

··· but ···> byroad

b

but¹ /bʌt, *weak form* bət/ *conj* pero; **not ... ~ ...
no ... sino ...;** ~ **then you never were very
ambitious, were you?** pero la verdad es que tú
nunca fuiste muy ambicioso ¿no?; **not only did
she hit him, ~ she also ...** no solo le pegó, sino
que también ...

but² *prep:* **everyone ~ me** todos menos *or*
excepto yo; **the last street ~ one** la penúltima
calle; ~ **for them, we'd have lost everything** de no
haber sido por ellos, habríamos perdido todo

but³ *adv* (frml): **we can ~ try** con intentarlo no se
pierde nada

butane /'bjuːteɪn/ *n* butano *m*

butcher¹ /'bʊtʃər ‖'bʊtʃə(r)/ *n* **(a)** (meat dealer)
carnicero, -ra *m,f*; ~**'s (shop)** carnicería *f* **(b)**
(murderer) asesino, -na *m,f*

butcher² *vt* **(a)** ‹cattle/pig› matar, carnear (CS)
(b) ‹people› masacrar

butler /'bʌtlər ‖'bʌtlə(r)/ *n* mayordomo *m*

butt¹ /bʌt/ **1 (a)** (of rifle) culata *f* **(b)** ~
(end) (blunt end) extremo *m* **(c)** (of cigarette) colilla
f, bacha *f* (Méx fam) **2** (target of jokes or criticism)
blanco *m* **3 (a)** (from goat) topetazo *m* **(b)** (head
~) cabezazo *m* **4** (buttocks) (AmE colloq) trasero *m*
(fam), culo *m* (fam o vulg), traste *m* (CS fam), poto
m (Chi, Per fam)

butt² *vt* ‹goat› topetar
■ **butt in** [*v + adv*] interrumpir

butter¹ /'bʌtər ‖'bʌtə(r)/ *n* mantequilla *f*,
manteca *f* (RPl)

butter² *vt* ‹bread› untar con mantequilla *or*
(RPl) manteca

butter: ~ **bean** *n* **(a)** (dried bean) *tipo de frijol
blanco*, poroto *m* de manteca (RPl) **(b)** (wax bean)
(AmE) *tipo de frijol fresco con vaina amarilla*;
~**cup** *n* ranúnculo *m*; ~**fly** *n* **(a)** (Zool)
mariposa *f*; **to have ~flies (in one's stomach)**
ponerse*/estar* nervioso **(b)** (swimming stroke)
estilo *m* mariposa

buttock /'bʌtək/ *n* nalga *f*

button¹ /'bʌtn̩/ *n* botón *m*

button² *vt* abotonar
■ ~ *vi* abotonarse
■ **button up** [*v + o + adv, v + adv + o*] abotonar

buttonhole /'bʌtn̩həʊl/ *n* **(a)** (Clothing) ojal *m*
(b) (flower) (BrE) *flor que se lleva en el ojal*

buttress /'bʌtrəs ‖'bʌtrɪs/ *n* (Archit)
contrafuerte *m*; **flying ~** arbotante *m*

buxom /'bʌksəm/ *adj* con mucho busto *or*
pecho

buy¹ /baɪ/ (*past & past p* **bought**) *vt* comprar;
to ~ sb sth comprarle algo a algn; **to ~ sth** FROM
sb comprarle algo a algn; **to ~ sth** FOR **sb**
comprar algo PARA algn
■ ~ *vi* comprar; **to ~** FROM **sb** comprarle A algn
■ **buy off** [*v + o + adv, v + adv + o*] sobornar
■ **buy out** [*v + o + adv, v + adv + o*] ‹partner/
shareholder› comprarle su parte a
■ **buy up** [*v + adv + o*] comprarse todas las
existencias de

buy² *n* compra *f*

buyer /'baɪər ‖'baɪə(r)/ *n* **(a)** (customer)
comprador, -dora *m,f* **(b)** (buying agent) encargado,
-da *m,f* de compras

buzz¹ /bʌz/ *n* (of insect) zumbido *m*; (of voices)
rumor *m*; (as signal) zumbido *m*

buzz² *vi* «insect» zumbar; «telephone/alarm
clock» sonar*; **my ears were** ~**ing** me zumbaban
los oídos

buzzard /'bʌzərd ‖'bʌzəd/ *n* **(a)** (hawk) (esp BrE)
águila *f‡* ratonera **(b)** (vulture) (AmE) aura *f‡*,
gallinazo *m*, zopilote *m* (AmC, Méx)

buzzer /'bʌzər ‖'bʌzə(r)/ *n* timbre *m*

by¹ /baɪ/ *prep* **1** (indicating agent, cause) (*with
passive verbs*) por [*The passive voice is, however,
less common in Spanish than it is in English*] **she
was brought up ~ her grandmother** la crio su
abuela; **a play ~ Shakespeare** una obra de
Shakespeare
2 (a) (indicating means, method): **made ~ hand**
hecho a mano; **to travel ~ car/train/plane** viajar
en coche/tren/avión; **to pay ~ credit card** pagar*
con tarjeta de crédito; **I'll begin ~ introducing
myself** empezaré por presentarme **(b)** (owing to,
from): ~ **chance** por casualidad; **they have lost
public support ~ being too extreme** han perdido
apoyo popular por ser demasiado extremistas
3 (a) (at the side of, near to) al lado de; **it's right ~
the door** está justo al lado de la puerta **(b)** (to
hand) (AmE): **I always keep some money ~ me**
siempre llevo algo de dinero encima
4 (a) (past): **I said hello, but he walked right ~
me** lo saludé pero él pasó de largo **(b)** (via,
through) por; ~ **land/sea/air** por tierra/mar/avión
5 (a) (indicating rate) por; **we are paid ~ the
hour** nos pagan por hora(s) **(b)** (indicating extent of
difference): **she broke the record ~ several seconds**
batió el récord en *or* por varios segundos **(c)**
(indicating gradual progression): **one ~ one** uno por
uno
6 (a) (not later than): **he told her to be home ~ 11**
le dijo que volviera antes de las 11; **they should
be there ~ now** ya deberían estar allí; ~ **the time
he arrived, Ann had left** cuando llegó, Ann se
había ido **(b)** (during, at) ~ **day/night** de día/noche
7 (according to): ~ **that clock it's almost half past**
según ese reloj son casi y media; **that's fine ~ me**
por mí no hay problema
8 (Math) por; **multiply two ~ three** multiplica dos
por tres; **a room 20ft ~ 12ft** una habitación de 20
pies por 12
9 (by oneself (alone, without assistance) solo

by² *adv* **(a)** (past): **she rushed ~ without seeing
me** pasó corriendo y no me vio; **they watched the
parade march ~** vieron pasar el desfile **(b)** (to sb's
residence): **call** *o* **stop ~ on your way to work** pasa
por casa de camino al trabajo **(c)** (*in phrases*): **by
and by:** ~ **and ~ they came to the clearing** al
poco rato llegaron al claro; **by and large** por lo
general, en general

bye, (AmE) **'bye** /baɪ/ *interj* (colloq) ¡adiós!, ¡chao
or chau! (esp AmL fam)

bye-bye /'baɪ'baɪ/ *interj* (colloq) ¡adiós!,
¡chaucito! (AmL fam), ¡chaíto! (Chi fam)

by: ~**gone** *adj* (liter) (*before n*) ‹age/days› de
antaño (liter); **to let ~gones be ~gones** olvidar el
pasado; ~**law** *n* (BrE) ordenanza *f* municipal

bypass¹ /'baɪpæs ‖'baɪpɑːs/ *n* **(a)** (road) (BrE)
carretera *f* de circunvalación **(b)** (Med) bypass *m*

bypass² *vt* **(a)** (circumvent) ‹person/difficulty›
eludir **(b)** (Transp) «road» circunvalar; «driver»
evitar entrar en

by: ~**-product** *n* (in manufacture) subproducto *m*;
(consequence) consecuencia *f*; ~**road** *n* carretera

f secundaria; **~stander** /ˈbaɪˌstændər
‖ˈbaɪˌstændə(r)/ *n*: **they opened fire, killing
innocent ~standers** abrieron fuego y mataron a
varias personas inocentes *or* a varios transeúntes
byte /baɪt/ *n* byte *m*, octeto *m*

by: ~way *n* camino *m* (*apartado*); **~word** *n*:
to be a ~word FOR sth ser* sinónimo DE algo;
~-your-leave /ˈbaɪʤərˈliːv ‖ˌbaɪjɔːˈliːv/ *n*:
without so much as a ~-your-leave sin (ni)
siquiera pedir permiso

Cc

C, c /siː/ *n* **(a)** (letter) C, c *f* **(b)** (Mus) re *m*
c (a) (Corresp) = **copy to (b)** (in US) (= **cent(s)**)
centavo(s) *m*(*pl*) **(c)** = **circa**

C (= **Celsius** *or* **centigrade**) C

ca = **circa**

CA, Ca = **California**

cab /kæb/ *n* **1** (taxi) taxi *m*; (*before n*) **~ driver**
taxista *mf* **2** (driver's compartment) cabina *f*

cabaret /ˌkæbəˈreɪ ‖ˈkæbəreɪ/ *n* cabaret *m*

cabbage /ˈkæbɪʤ/ *n* repollo *m*, col *f*

cabin /ˈkæbən ‖ˈkæbɪn/ *n* **(a)** (hut) cabaña *f* **(b)**
(Naut) camarote *m* **(c)** (Aerosp, Auto, Aviat) cabina *f*

cabinet /ˈkæbənət ‖ˈkæbɪnɪt/ *n* **1** (cupboard)
armario *m*; (with glass front) vitrina *f* **2** *also*
Cabinet (Govt) gabinete *m* (ministerial)

cable /ˈkeɪbəl/ *n* **(a)** (Elec, Naut) cable *m* **(b)**
(Telec) cable *m* **(c)** ▶ CABLE TELEVISION

cable: ~ car *n* (suspended) teleférico *m*;
(funicular) funicular *m*; (streetcar) (AmE) tranvía *m*;
~ television *n* televisión *f* por cable,
cablevisión *f* (esp AmL)

caboose /kəˈbuːs/ *n* (AmE Rail) furgón *m* de
cola

cache /kæʃ/ *n* alijo *m*

cackle /ˈkækəl/ *vi* «*hen*» cacarear; «*person*»
reírse* socarronamente

cactus /ˈkæktəs/ *n* (*pl* **-ti** /-taɪ/ *or* **-tuses**)
cactus *m*

caddie, caddy (*pl* **-dies**) /ˈkædi/ *n* caddie *mf*

cadet /kəˈdet/ *n* cadete *mf*

cadge /kæʤ/ (colloq) *vt* **to ~ sth FROM *o* OFF sb**
gorronearle *or* gorrearle *or* (RPl) garronearle *or*
(Chi) bolsearle algo A algn (fam)

Caesarean (section) /sɪˈzæriən
‖sɪˈzeəriən/ *n* ▶ CESAREAN (SECTION)

café, cafe /kæˈfeɪ ‖ˈkæfeɪ/ *n* (coffee bar) café *m*,
cafetería *f*; (restaurant) *restaurante económico*

cafeteria /ˌkæfəˈtɪriə ‖ˌkæfəˈtɪəriə/ *n* (in
hospital, college) cantina *f*, cafetería *f*; (restaurant)
restaurante *m* autoservicio, self-service *m*

caffeine /kæˈfiːn ‖ˈkæfiːn/ *n* cafeína *f*

cage¹ /keɪʤ/ *n* jaula *f*; (in basketball) canasta *f*,
cesta *f*; (in ice hockey) portería *f*, meta *f*, arco *m*
(Col, CS)

cage² *vt* (*usu pass*) enjaular

Cairo /ˈkaɪrəʊ ‖ˈkaɪərəʊ/ *n* El Cairo

cajole /kəˈʤəʊl/ *vt* convencer* con zalamerías

cake¹ /keɪk/ *n* (Culin) (large) pastel *m*, tarta *f*

(Esp), torta *f* (esp CS); (small, individual) pastel *m*,
masa *f* (RPl); **to be a piece of ~** (colloq) ser* pan
comido (fam)

cake² *vt* (*usu pass*): **our shoes were ~d with
mud** teníamos los zapatos cubiertos de barro
endurecido

cake tin *n* (BrE) (for baking) molde *m* (para
pastel); (for storage) lata *f* (*para guardar pasteles*)

Cal = **California**

calamity /kəˈlæməti/ *n* (*pl* **-ties**) calamidad *f*

calcium /ˈkælsiəm/ *n* calcio *m*

calculate /ˈkælkjəleɪt ‖ˈkælkjʊleɪt/ *vt* calcular

calculating /ˈkælkjəleɪtɪŋ/ *adj* calculador

calculation /ˌkælkjəˈleɪʃən/ *n* cálculo *m*

calculator /ˈkælkjəleɪtər/ *n* calculadora *f*

calendar /ˈkæləndər ‖ˈkælɪndə(r)/ *n*
calendario *m*, almanaque *m*; (*before n*) **~ month**
mes *m* (del calendario)

calf /kæf ‖kɑːf/ *n* (*pl* **calves**) **1** (Zool) **(a)**
(animal) ternero, -ra *m*,*f*, becerro, -rra *m*,*f* **(b)**
(leather) (piel *f* or cuero *m* de) becerro *m* **2** (Anat)
pantorrilla *f*

caliber, (BrE) **calibre** /ˈkæləbər ‖ˈkælɪbə(r)/ *n*
calibre *m*

Calif = **California**

calipers, (BrE) **callipers** /ˈkæləpərz
‖ˈkælɪpəz/ *pl n* **(a)** (for measuring) calibrador *m*
(b) (Med) aparato *m* ortopédico (*para la pierna*)

call¹ /kɔːl/ *n* **1** (by telephone) llamada *f*; **to give
sb a ~** llamar a algn (por teléfono); **~ sb ON
their cell phone** (AmE) *o* (BrE) **mobile** llamar a
alguien AL celular (AmL) *or* móvil (AmL Esp)
2 (a) (of person — cry) llamada *f*, llamado *m*
(AmL); (— shout) grito *m* **(b)** (of animal) grito *m*; (of
bird) reclamo *m*
3 (summons): **to be on ~** estar* de guardia;
beyond the ~ of duty más de lo que el deber
exigía (*or* exige *etc*) (frml)
4 (demand) llamamiento *m*, llamado *m* (AmL);
there were ~s for his resignation pidieron su
dimisión
5 (*usu with neg*) **(a)** (reason) motivo *m* **(b)**
(demand) demanda *f*; **there's not much ~ for this
product** no hay mucha demanda para este
producto
6 (visit) visita *f*
7 (Sport) decisión *f*, cobro *m* (Chi)

call² *vt* **(a)** (shout) llamar; **to ~ the roll** *o* **register**
(Educ) pasar lista **(b)** ⟨*police/taxi/doctor*⟩ llamar;
⟨*strike*⟩ llamar a, convocar* **(c)** (by telephone)
llamar **(d)** (name, describe as) llamar; **we ~ her
Betty** la llamamos *or* (esp AmL) le decimos Betty; ⋯▸

what are you going to ∼ the baby? ¿qué nombre le van a poner al bebé?; **what's this** ∼ed **in Italian?** ¿cómo se llama esto en italiano?
■ ∼ *vi* **(a)** «*person*» llamar **(b)** (by telephone) llamar; **who's** ∼ing, **please?** ¿de parte de quién, por favor? **(c)** (visit) pasar
■ **call around** [*v + adv*] **(a)** (Telec) llamar (*a varias personas*) **(b)** (visit) pasar (por casa)
■ **call at** [*v + prep + o*]: «*train*» parar en; **I** ∼ed **at your place yesterday** ayer pasé por tu casa
■ **call back** 1 (Telec) [*v + o + adv*] llamar más tarde
2 [*v + adv*] (Telec) volver* a llamar
■ **call for** [*v + prep + o*] **(a)** (require) ‹*skill/courage*› requerir*, exigir* **(b)** (demand) pedir* **(c)** (collect) pasar a buscar *or* a recoger
■ **call in** 1 [*v + o + adv, v + adv + o*] **(a)** ‹*expert/doctor*› llamar **(b)** ‹*coin/note*› retirar de circulación
2 [*v + adv*] **to** ∼ **in** (on sb) pasar a ver a algn
■ **call off** [*v + o + adv, v + adv + o*] **(a)** (cancel) suspender **(b)** ‹*dog*› llamar
■ **call on** [*v + prep + o*] **(a)** (visit) pasar a ver a **(b)** ▶ CALL UPON
■ **call out** [*v + o + adv, v + adv + o*] **(a)** ‹*fire brigade/doctor*› llamar **(b)** (utter): **he** ∼ed **out her name** la llamó
■ **call round** [*v + adv*] (BrE) ▶ CALL AROUND
■ **call up** [*v + o + adv, v + adv + o*] **(a)** ‹*spirits*› invocar* **(b)** (telephone) (esp AmE) llamar **(c)** (Mil) (*often pass*) llamar (a filas)
■ **call upon** [*v + prep + o*] **(a)** (invite): **to** ∼ **upon sb to speak** dar* la palabra a algn **(b)** (appeal to) apelar a

call: ∼ **box** *n* (BrE) cabina *f* telefónica; ∼ **center,** (BrE) ∼ **centre** *n* (Telec) centro *m* de llamadas

caller /'kɔːlər ‖ 'kɔːlə(r)/ *n*: **we didn't have many** ∼s no vino mucha gente; (Telec) no tuvimos *or* no hubo muchas llamadas; **the** ∼ **didn't leave her name** la persona que llamó no dejó su nombre

callipers *n* (BrE) ▶ CALIPERS

callous /'kæləs/ *adj* insensible, cruel

callus /'kæləs/ *n* (*pl* **-luses**) (Med) callo *m*

calm¹ /kɑːm/ *adj* **-er, -est** ‹*sea*› en calma, calmo (esp AmL); ‹*person/voice*› tranquilo, calmo (esp AmL)

calm² *vt* tranquilizar*, calmar
■ **calm down (a)** [*v + o + adv, v + adv + o*] tranquilizar*, calmar **(b)** [*v + adv*] tranquilizarse*; ∼ **down!** ¡tranquilízate!, ¡tranquilo!

calm³ *n* calma *f*

calmly /'kɑːmli/ *adv* con calma

Calor Gas® /'kælər ‖ 'kælə(r)/ *n* (BrE) (gas *m*) butano *m*, supergás® *m* (RPl)

calorie /'kæləri/ *n* (Culin) (kilo)caloría *f*

calves /kævz ‖ kɑːvz/ *pl of* CALF

camcorder /'kæm,kɔːrdər ‖ 'kæm,kɔːdə(r)/ *n* videocámara *f*, camcórder *m*

came /keɪm/ *past of* COME

camel /'kæməl/ *n* camello *m*

cameo /'kæmiəʊ/ *n* 1 (jewelry) camafeo *m* 2 (Cin, TV) actuación *f* especial

camera /'kæmərə/ *n* cámara *f* (fotográfica), máquina *f* fotográfica *or* de fotos

camera: ∼**man** /'kæmərəmæn/ *n* (*pl* **-men** /-men/) camarógrafo, -fa *m,f*, cameraman *mf* (esp AmL), cámara *mf* (Esp); ∼**work** *n* fotografía *f*

Cameroon /'kæməˈruːn/ *n* Camerún *m*

camomile /'kæməmaɪl/ *n* ▶ CHAMOMILE

camouflage¹ /'kæməflɑːʒ/ *n* camuflaje *m*

camouflage² *vt* camuflar, camuflajear (AmL)

camp¹ /kæmp/ *n* (collection of tents, huts) campamento *m*; (summer) ∼ (in US) campamento *m* de verano, colonia *f* de vacaciones *or* verano

camp² *vi* acampar; **to go** ∼ing ir* de camping

camp³ *adj* **(a)** (effeminate) amanerado, afeminado **(b)** ‹*performance*› afectado, exagerado

campaign¹ /kæmˈpeɪn/ *n* campaña *f*

campaign² *vi* (Pol, Sociol) **to** ∼ **FOR/AGAINST sth** hacer* una campaña A FAVOR DE/EN CONTRA DE algo

campaigner /kæmˈpeɪnər ‖ kæmˈpeɪnə(r)/ *n* (Pol, Sociol) defensor, -sora *m,f*

camper /'kæmpər ‖ 'kæmpə(r)/ *n* **(a)** (person) campista *mf* **(b)** (Transp) cámper *f*

campground /'kæmpɡraʊnd/ (AmE), **campsite** /'kæmpsaɪt/ *n* camping *m*

camping /'kæmpɪŋ/ *n*: **I like** ∼ me gusta ir de camping

campus /'kæmpəs/ *n* (*pl* **-puses**) campus *m*

can¹ /kæn/ *n* **(a)** (container) lata *f*, bote *m* (Esp), tarro *m* (Chi); (*before n*) ∼ **opener** abrelatas *m* **(b)** (for petrol, water) bidón *m*; (for garbage) (AmE) cubo *m or* (CS) tacho *m or* (Col) caneca *f*, bote *m* (Méx), tobo *m* de la basura (Ven)

can² *vt* **-nn-** (put in cans) enlatar; (bottle) (AmE) ‹*fruit*› preparar conservas de

can³ /kæn, *weak form* kən/ *v mod*

■ **Note** When *can* means *to be capable of* or *to be allowed to*, it is translated by *poder*: *he can't eat* no puede comer; *can you come out tonight?* ¿puedes salir esta noche? When *can* means *to know how to*, it is translated by *saber*: *can you swim?* ¿sabes nadar?; *she can already read and write* ya sabe leer y escribir.When *can* is used with a verb of perception such as *see, hear,* or *feel*, it is often not translated: *can you see her from here?* ¿la ves desde aquí?; *she couldn't feel anything* no sentía nada.

(*past* **could**) 1 (indicating ability) poder*; (referring to particular skills) saber*; **she couldn't answer the question** no pudo contestar la pregunta; ∼ **you swim?** ¿sabes nadar?
2 **(a)** (with verbs of perception): **I** ∼'t **see very well** no veo muy bien; ∼ **you hear me?** ¿me oyes? **(b)** (with verbs of mental activity): **I** ∼'t **understand it** no lo entiendo; ∼'t **you tell he's lying?** ¿no te das cuenta de que está mintiendo?
3 **(a)** (indicating, asking etc permission) poder*; ∼ **I come with you?** ¿puedo ir contigo? **(b)** (in requests)

AmC	América Central	Arg	Argentina	Cu	Cuba	Per	Perú
AmL	América Latina	Bol	Bolivia	Ec	Ecuador	RPl	Río de la Plata
AmS	América del Sur	Chi	Chile	Esp	España	Ur	Uruguay
Andes	Región andina	CS	Cono Sur	Méx	México	Ven	Venezuela

poder*; ~ **you turn that music down, please?** ¿puedes bajar esa música, por favor? **(c)** (in offers): ~ **I help you?** ¿me permite?; (in shop) ¿lo/la atienden?, ¿qué desea?; ~ **I carry that for you?** ¿quieres que (te) lleve eso? **(d)** (in suggestions, advice): ~**'t you give it another try?** ¿por qué no lo vuelves a intentar?

    4 (indicating possibility) poder*; **it** ~**'t be true!** ¡no puede ser!, ¡no es posible!

Canada /'kænədə/ n (el) Canadá m

Canadian¹ /kə'neɪdɪən/ adj canadiense

Canadian² n canadiense mf

canal /kə'næl/ n canal m

Canaries /kə'neriz ‖kə'neəriz/ pl n the ~ (las) Canarias

canary /kə'neri ‖kə'neəri/ n (pl **-ries**) canario m

Canary Islands pl n the ~ ~ las Islas Canarias

cancel /'kænsəl/, (BrE) **-ll-** vt cancelar; ‹check› anular

    ■ **cancel out** [v + o + adv, v + adv + o] ‹deficit/ loss› compensar; ‹debt› cancelar

cancellation /ˌkænsə'leɪʃən/ n cancelación f; (Theat) devolución f

cancer /'kænsər ‖'kænsə(r)/ n 1 (disease) cáncer m 2 **Cancer** (Astrol) **(a)** (sign) (no art) Cáncer **(b)** (person) Cáncer or cáncer mf, canceriano, -na m,f

candid /'kændəd ‖'kændɪd/ adj franco

candidate /'kændədeɪt ‖'kændɪdət/ n candidato, -ta m,f

candle /'kændḷ/ n (for domestic use) vela f; (for altar) cirio m

candle: ~**light** n: **by** ~**light** a la luz de una vela/de las velas; ~**stick** n candelero m; (flat) palmatoria f

candy /'kændi/ n (pl **-dies**) (AmE) **(a)** (confectionery) golosinas fpl, dulces mpl (AmL exc RPl) **(b)** (individual piece) caramelo m, dulce m (AmL exc RPl)

cane¹ /keɪn/ n 1 (for wickerwork) mimbre m 2 (walking stick) bastón m; (for punishment) palmeta f; (for supporting plants) rodrigón m

cane² vt castigar* con la palmeta

canine¹ /'keɪnaɪn/ n 1 (Zool) canino m, cánido m 2 ~ (**tooth**) (diente m) canino m, colmillo m

canine² adj canino

canister /'kænəstər ‖'kænɪstə(r)/ n **(a)** (for tea, coffee) lata f, bote m (Esp) **(b)** (Mil) bote m (de humo, metralla etc)

cannabis /'kænəbəs ‖'kænəbɪs/ n hachís m, cannabis m

canned /kænd/ adj **(a)** ‹food› enlatado, en or de lata, en conserva **(b)** (pre-recorded) (colloq) ‹music› enlatado (fam); ‹laughter› grabado

cannibal /'kænəbəl ‖'kænɪbəl/ n caníbal mf, antropófago, -ga m,f

cannon /'kænən/ n (pl also ~) cañón m

cannonball /'kænənbɔːl/ n (Mil) bala f de cañón

cannot /'kænɑːt ‖'kænɒt/ = **can not**

canoe¹ /kə'nuː/ n canoa f, piragua f

canoe² vi **-noes, -noeing, -noed** ir* en canoa or piragua

canoeing /kə'nuːɪŋ/ n piragüismo m, canotaje m

canopy /'kænəpi/ n (pl **-pies**) (over bed, throne) dosel m, baldaquín m, baldaquino m; (over person) palio m, dosel m

can't /kænt ‖kɑːnt/ = **can not**

canteen /kæn'tiːn/ n 1 (dining hall) (BrE) cantina f, comedor m, casino m (Chi) (en un lugar de trabajo, colegio etc) 2 (water bottle) cantimplora f

canter /'kæntər ‖'kæntə(r)/ vi ir* a medio galope

canvas /'kænvəs/ n 1 (cloth) lona f 2 (Art) (for painting) lienzo m, tela f

canvass /'kænvəs/ vt 1 (Pol): **to** ~ **voters in an area** hacer* campaña entre los votantes de una zona 2 (scrutinize) (AmE): **to** ~ **the votes** hacer* el escrutinio de los votos

    ■ ~ vi (Pol) **to** ~ (**FOR sb**) hacer* campaña (A or EN FAVOR DE algn)

canyon /'kænjən/ n cañón m

cap¹ /kæp/ n 1 (hat) gorra f; **swimming** ~ gorro m or (esp AmL) gorra f de baño; **baseball/ golf** ~ gorra de béisbol/golf 2 (of bottle) tapa f, tapón m; (metal) chapa f, tapa f, (of pen) capuchón m, tapa f 3 (upper limit) tope m

cap² vt **-pp-** 1 ‹bottle/tube› tapar 2 (crown): **to** ~ **it all off** o (BrE) **to** ~ **it all** ... para colmo (de desgracias or de males) ..., para rematarla ... (fam) 3 ‹expenditure› poner* un tope a 4 (Dentistry): **to have a tooth** ~**ped** ponerse* una funda or una corona

CAP n (= **Common Agricultural Policy**) PAC f

capability /ˌkeɪpə'bɪləti/ n (pl **-ties**) **(a)** (ability) capacidad f **(b) capabilities** pl aptitudes fpl

capable /'keɪpəbəl/ adj **(a)** (competent) capaz **(b)** (pred) (able) **to be** ~ **OF** -**ING** ser* capaz DE + INF

capacity /kə'pæsəti/ n (pl **-ties**) 1 **(a)** (maximum content) capacidad f; (before n) **a** ~ **crowd** un lleno completo **(b)** (output) capacidad f 2 (ability) capacidad f; ~ **FOR sth** capacidad DE algo; ~ **to** + INF capacidad PARA + INF; **the job was beyond her** ~ el trabajo estaba por encima de su capacidad 3 (role) calidad f; **in his** ~ **as union delegate** en su calidad de delegado del sindicato

cape /keɪp/ n 1 (Clothing) capa f 2 (Geog) cabo m

caper¹ /'keɪpər ‖'keɪpə(r)/ n 1 (jump) salto m 2 (prank) travesura f 3 (Bot, Culin) alcaparra f

caper² vi correr y brincar*, dar* saltos or brincos

capital¹ /'kæpətḷ ‖'kæpɪtḷ/ n **(a)** (city) capital f **(b)** (letter) mayúscula f **(c)** (Fin) capital m

capital² adj **(a)** (Law): ~ **punishment** pena f capital **(b)** (Geog, Pol): ~ (**city**) capital f **(c)** (Print) ‹letter› mayúscula

capitalism /'kæpətḷɪzəm ‖'kæpɪtəlɪzəm/ n capitalismo m

capitalist¹ /'kæpətḷəst ‖'kæpɪtəlɪst/ n capitalista mf

capitalist² adj capitalista

capitulate /kəˈpɪtʃəleɪt ‖kəˈpɪtjʊleɪt/ vi capitular

Capricorn /ˈkæprɪkɔːrn ‖ˈkæprɪkɔːn/ n **(a)** (sign) (no art) Capricornio **(b)** (person) Capricornio or capricornio mf, capricorniano, -na m,f

caps = **capital letters**

capsicum /ˈkæpsɪkəm/ n pimiento m, pimentón m (AmS exc RPl), ají m (RPl)

capsize /ˈkæpsaɪz ‖kæpˈsaɪz/ vi volcarse*

capsule /ˈkæpsəl ‖ˈkæpsjuːl/ n cápsula f

captain[1] /ˈkæptən ‖ˈkæptɪn/ n **(a)** (rank) capitán m **(b)** (person in command) capitán, -tana m,f; (of airline plane) comandante mf

captain[2] vt (Naut, Sport) capitanear

caption /ˈkæpʃən/ n (under picture) leyenda f, pie m de foto (or ilustración etc); (headline) título m

captivate /ˈkæptəveɪt ‖ˈkæptɪveɪt/ vt cautivar

captive[1] /ˈkæptɪv/ n (liter) cautivo, -va m,f

captive[2] adj: **to take/hold sb** ∼ tomar prisionero/mantener* cautivo a algn; **to have a** ∼ **audience** tener* un público que no tiene más remedio que escuchar

captivity /kæpˈtɪvəti/ n cautiverio m, cautividad f

captor /ˈkæptər ‖ˈkæptə(r)/ n captor, -tora m,f

capture[1] /ˈkæptʃər ‖ˈkæptʃə(r)/ vt [1] ⟨person/animal⟩ capturar; ⟨city⟩ tomar [2] **(a)** ⟨attention/interest⟩ captar, atraer* **(b)** ⟨mood/atmosphere⟩ captar, reproducir*

capture[2] n (of person, animal) captura f; (of city) conquista f, toma f

car /kɑːr ‖kɑː(r)/ n **(a)** (Auto) coche m, automóvil m (frml), carro m (AmL exc CS), auto m (esp CS) **(b)** (Rail, Transp) vagón m, coche m

caramel /ˈkɑːrml ‖ˈkærəmel, -məl/ n caramelo m

carat /ˈkærət/ n **(a)** (for gold) (AmE also **karat**) quilate m; (before n) **18-**∼ **gold** oro m de 18 quilates **(b)** (for precious stones) quilate m

caravan /ˈkærəvæn/ n **(a)** (group) caravana f **(b)** (vehicle) (BrE) caravana f, rulot f (Esp), casa f rodante (CS), tráiler m (Andes, Méx); (before n) ∼ **park** o **site** camping m para caravanas

carbohydrate /ˌkɑːrbəʊˈhaɪdreɪt ‖ˌkɑːbəˈhaɪdreɪt/ n hidrato m de carbono

car bomb n coche m bomba

carbon /ˈkɑːrbən ‖ˈkɑːbən/ n carbono m

carbon: ∼ **copy** n copia f (hecha con papel carbón); ∼ **dioxide** /daɪˈɒksaɪd ‖daɪˈɒksaɪd/ n anhídrido m carbónico; ∼ **monoxide** /məˈnɒksaɪd ‖məˈnɒksaɪd/ n monóxido m de carbono

carburetor, (BrE) **carburettor** /ˌkɑːrbəˈreɪtər ‖ˌkɑːbəˈretə(r)/ n carburador m

carcass, (BrE also) **carcase** /ˈkɑːrkəs ‖ˈkɑːkəs/ n (dead animal) cuerpo de animal muerto; (for meat) res f (muerta)

card /kɑːrd ‖kɑːd/ n [1] **(a)** (for identification, access) tarjeta f; (business ∼) tarjeta (de visita); (credit ∼) tarjeta (de crédito) **(b)** (greeting ∼) tarjeta f (de felicitación) **(c)** (index ∼) ficha f; (before n) ∼ **index** fichero m **(d)** (post∼) (tarjeta f) postal f [2] (thin cardboard) cartulina f [3] (playing

card) carta f, naipe m, baraja f (AmC, Col, Méx, RPl); **to play** ∼**s** jugar* a las cartas or (Col) jugar* cartas

cardamom /ˈkɑːrdəməm ‖ˈkɑːdəməm/ n cardamomo m

cardboard /ˈkɑːrdbɔːrd ‖ˈkɑːdbɔːd/ n (stiff) cartón m; (thin) cartulina f; (before n) ∼ **box** caja f de cartón

cardiac /ˈkɑːrdiæk ‖ˈkɑːdiæk/ adj cardíaco; ∼ **arrest** paro m cardíaco

cardigan /ˈkɑːrdɪɡən ‖ˈkɑːdɪɡən/ n cárdigan m, chaqueta f de punto, rebeca f (esp Esp), saco m (tejido) (AmL)

cardinal /ˈkɑːrdnəl ‖ˈkɑːdɪnl/ n [1] (Relig) cardenal m [2] ∼ **(number)** número m cardinal

care[1] /ker ‖keə(r)/ n [1] (attention, carefulness) cuidado m, atención f; **to take** ∼ tener* cuidado; **take** ∼! (saying goodbye) ¡cuídate!; (as a warning) ¡ten cuidado!
[2] (of people): **medical** ∼ asistencia f médica; (of animals, things) cuidado m; **in** ∼ **of** (AmE), ∼ **of** (BrE) (on letters) en casa de
[3] **to take** ∼ **of sb/sth (a)** (look after) ⟨of patient⟩ atender* a algn, cuidar de algn; ⟨of children⟩ cuidar a or de algn, ocuparse de algn; ⟨of pet/plant/machine⟩ cuidar algo; **I can take** ∼ **of myself** yo sé cuidarme **(b)** (deal with) ocuparse or encargarse* de algn/algo
[4] (worry) preocupación f

care[2] vi **to** ∼ (ABOUT sth/sb) preocuparse (POR algo/algn); **I don't** ∼ no me importa
■ ∼ vt **(a)** (feel concern) (usu neg, interrog): **I couldn't** ∼ **less what he does** me tiene sin cuidado lo que haga **(b)** (wish) (frml) **to** ∼ **to + INF**: **would you** ∼ **to join us for dinner?** ¿le gustaría cenar con nosotros?
■ **care for** [v + prep + o] **(a)** (look after) ⟨patient⟩ cuidar (de), atender* **(b)** (be fond of) querer*, sentir* afecto or cariño por

career[1] /kəˈrɪr ‖kəˈrɪə(r)/ n carrera f

career[2] vi ir* a toda velocidad

carefree /ˈkerfriː ‖ˈkeəfriː/ adj despreocupado

careful /ˈkerfəl ‖ˈkeəfəl/ adj [1] (cautious) cuidadoso, prudente; **(be)** ∼ **(ten)** cuidado; **to be** ∼ **OF/WITH sth** tener* cuidado CON algo [2] (painstaking) ⟨planning⟩ cuidadoso; ⟨work⟩ cuidado, esmerado; ⟨worker⟩ meticuloso

carefully /ˈkerfli ‖ˈkeəfəli/ adv ⟨handle/drive⟩ con cuidado; ⟨plan/examine⟩ cuidadosamente; ⟨designed/chosen⟩ con esmero

careless /ˈkerləs ‖ˈkeəlɪs/ adj ⟨person⟩ descuidado; ⟨work⟩ poco cuidado; ⟨driving⟩ negligente; **you made some** ∼ **mistakes** cometiste errores por descuido

carelessly /ˈkerləsli ‖ˈkeəlɪsli/ adv sin cuidado, sin la debida atención

carelessness /ˈkerləsnəs ‖ˈkeəlɪsnɪs/ n falta f de atención or de cuidado

carer /ˈkerər ‖ˈkeərə(r)/ n: persona que tiene a su cuidado a un incapacitado, cuidador, -dora m, f (Esp)

caress[1] /kəˈres/ n caricia f

caress[2] vt acariciar

caretaker /ˈkerˌteɪkər ‖ˈkeəˌteɪkə(r)/ n conserje mf

cargo /ˈkɑːrɡəʊ ‖ˈkɑːɡəʊ/ n (pl **-goes** or **-gos**) **(a)** (load) cargamento m **(b)** (goods) carga f

Caribbean¹ /ˌkærəˈbiːən, kəˈrɪbiən ‖ˌkærɪˈbiːən/ adj caribeño, del Caribe

Caribbean² n the ~ (Sea) el (mar) Caribe; the ~ (region) el Caribe, las Antillas

caricature /ˈkærɪkətʃʊr ‖ˈkærɪkətʃʊə(r)/ n caricatura f

caring /ˈkerɪŋ ‖ˈkeərɪŋ/ adj ⟨society/approach⟩ humanitario; ⟨person⟩ (kindly) bondadoso; (sympathetic) comprensivo

carnage /ˈkɑːrnɪdʒ ‖ˈkɑːnɪdʒ/ n carnicería f

carnation /kɑːrˈneɪʃən ‖kɑːˈneɪʃən/ n clavel m

carnival /ˈkɑːrnəvəl ‖ˈkɑːnɪvəl/ n carnaval m

carnivorous /kɑːrˈnɪvərəs ‖kɑːˈnɪvərəs/ adj carnívoro

carol /ˈkærəl/ n villancico m

carousel /ˌkærəˈsel/ n (a) (esp AmE) ▶ MERRY-GO-ROUND (b) (for baggage) cinta f or correa f transportadora (c) (in shops) (AmE) expositor m giratorio

car park n (BrE) (open space) ▶ PARKING LOT; (building) ▶ PARKING GARAGE

carpenter /ˈkɑːrpəntər ‖ˈkɑːpəntə(r)/ n carpintero, -ra m,f

carpentry /ˈkɑːrpəntri ‖ˈkɑːpəntri/ n carpintería f

carpet /ˈkɑːrpət ‖ˈkɑːpɪt/ n (a) (rug) alfombra f, tapete m (Col, Méx, Ven); ▶ SWEEP² vt 1B (b) (wall-to-wall) alfombra f, moqueta f (Esp), moquette f (RPl) (c) (of flowers, leaves, moss) (liter) alfombra f (liter)

carphone /ˈkɑːrfəʊn ‖ˈkɑːfəʊn/ n teléfono m de automóvil

carriage /ˈkærɪdʒ/ n 1 (a) (horse-drawn) carruaje m, coche m (b) (BrE Rail) vagón m (c) (baby ~) (AmE) cochecito m, carriola f (Méx) 2 (transport) transporte m 3 (bearing) (frml) porte m

carrier /ˈkæriər ‖ˈkæriə(r)/ n 1 (company) compañía f or empresa f de transportes; (Aviat) línea f aérea 2 (of disease, gene) portador, -dora m,f

carrier bag n (BrE) bolsa f (de plástico or papel)

carrion /ˈkæriən/ n carroña f

carrot /ˈkærət/ n zanahoria f

carry /ˈkæri/ -ries, -rying, -ried vt 1 (a) (bear, take) llevar; **I can't ~ this, it's too heavy** no puedo cargar con esto, pesa demasiado (b) (have with one) llevar encima (c) (be provided with) ⟨guarantee⟩ tener* (d) (be pregnant with) estar* embarazada or encinta de 2 (a) (convey) ⟨goods/passengers⟩ llevar, transportar; **she was carried along by the crowd** fue arrastrada por la multitud (b) (channel, transmit) ⟨oil/water/sewage⟩ llevar (c) ⟨disease⟩ ser* portador de 3 (support) ⟨weight⟩ soportar 4 (involve, entail) ⟨responsibility⟩ conllevar 5 (gain support for) ⟨bill/motion⟩ aprobar* 6 (stock) ⟨model⟩ tener*, vender

■ ~ vi: **sound carries further in the mountains** en la montaña los sonidos llegan más lejos; **her voice carries well** su voz tiene mucha proyección

■ **carry away** [v + o + adv, v + adv + o] (usu pass): **I got carried away and painted the window as well** me entusiasmé y pinté la ventana también; **there's no need to get carried away** no te pases

■ **carry off** [v + o + adv, v + adv + o] 1 (abduct) ⟨victim/hostage⟩ llevarse 2 (a) (win) ⟨trophy/cup⟩ llevarse (b) (succeed with): **she tried to appear disinterested but failed to ~ it off** intentó aparentar desinterés pero no lo logró

■ **carry on** 1 (a) [v + o + adv, v + adv + o] ⟨practice⟩ seguir* or continuar* con (b) [v + adv + o] ⟨conversation/correspondence⟩ mantener* 2 [v + adv] (a) (continue) seguir*, continuar* (b) (make a fuss) (colloq): **what a way to ~ on!** ¡qué manera de hacer escándalo, por favor!

■ **carry out** [v + o + adv, v + adv + o] ⟨work/repairs/investigation⟩ llevar a cabo; ⟨order⟩ cumplir; ⟨duty⟩ cumplir con

carry: ~**all** n (AmE) bolso m de viaje, bolsón m (RPl); ~**cot** n (BrE) cuna f portátil; ~**-on** adj (AmE) (before n) ⟨bag/baggage⟩ de mano; ~**out** n (esp AmE) comida preparada o bebida que se vende para consumir fuera del lugar de venta

car: ~ **seat** n asiento m del coche; (for infant) asiento m de bebé (para el coche); ~**sick** adj mareado (por viajar en coche)

cart¹ /kɑːrt ‖kɑːt/ n (a) (waggon) carro m, carreta f (b) (in supermarket, airport) (AmE) carrito m

cart² vt (colloq): **I had to ~ the books around all day** tuve que cargar con los libros todo el día

cartel /kɑːrˈtel ‖kɑːˈtel/ n cártel m

carthorse /ˈkɑːrthɔːrs ‖ˈkɑːthɔːs/ n caballo m de tiro

cartilage /ˈkɑːrtl̩ɪdʒ ‖ˈkɑːtɪlɪdʒ/ n cartílago m

carton /ˈkɑːrtn̩ ‖ˈkɑːtn̩/ n (of cigarettes) cartón m; **a ~ of milk** una leche en cartón

cartoon /kɑːrˈtuːn ‖kɑːˈtuːn/ n (a) (humorous drawing) chiste m (gráfico), viñeta f (Esp), mono m (Chi) (b) (Cin) dibujos mpl animados

cartridge /ˈkɑːrtrɪdʒ ‖ˈkɑːtrɪdʒ/ n (for gun, pen) cartucho m

cartwheel /ˈkɑːrthwiːl ‖ˈkɑːtwiːl/ n voltereta f lateral, rueda f, rueda f de carro (Méx, RPl)

carve /kɑːrv ‖kɑːv/ vt 1 (Art) ⟨wood/stone⟩ tallar; ⟨figure/bust⟩ esculpir, tallar; ⟨initials⟩ grabar 2 (Culin) ⟨meat⟩ cortar, trinchar

■ **carve out** [v + o + adv, v + adv + o] ⟨reputation⟩ forjarse; ⟨name⟩ hacerse*

carving /ˈkɑːrvɪŋ ‖ˈkɑːvɪŋ/ n talla f, escultura f

carving knife n trinchante m, cuchillo m de trinchar

car wash n túnel m or tren m de lavado

cascade¹ /kæsˈkeɪd/ n cascada f

cascade² vi caer* en cascada

case /keɪs/ n 1 (matter) caso m; **to lose/win a ~** (Law) perder*/ganar un pleito or juicio 2 (a) (Med, Soc Adm) caso m (b) (eccentric) (colloq) caso m (fam) 3 (instance, situation) caso m; **if that's the ~** si es así; **in that ~, I'm not interested** en ese caso, no me interesa 4 (in phrases) **in any case** de todas maneras or formas; **in case** (as conj): **make a note in ~ you forget** apúntalo por si te olvidas; **just in case** por si acaso ⋯⟩

5 (argument): **she has a good** ~ sus argumentos son buenos; **there is a** ~ **for doing nothing** hay razones para no hacer nada
6 (a) (suit~) maleta *f*, valija *f* (RPI) **(b)** (attaché ~) maletín *m* **(c)** (crate) caja *f*, cajón *m*, jaba *f* (Chi, Per); (of wine, liquor) *caja de 12 botellas* **(d)** (hard container — for small objects) estuche *f*; (— for large objects) caja *f*; (soft container) funda *f*

case: ~ **history** *n* (Med) historial *m* clínico, historia *f* clínica (AmL); ~ **study** *n* estudio *m*

cash¹ /kæʃ/ *n* **(a)** (notes and coins) dinero *m* (en) efectivo; **(in)** ~ en efectivo; ~ **on delivery** entrega *f* contra reembolso; (*before n*) ⟨*payment*⟩ en efectivo; ⟨*refund*⟩ al contado **(b)** (funds) (colloq) dinero *m*, lana *f* (AmL fam), plata *f* (AmS fam), tela *f* (Esp fam)
cash² *vt* ⟨*check*⟩ cobrar
■ **cash in** **1** [*v + o + adv, v + adv + o*] (exchange for money) canjear **2** [*v + adv*] (profit) **to** ~ **in** (**ON** sth) aprovecharse (DE algo)
cash: ~ **and carry** *n*: tienda de venta al por mayor; ~ **crop** *n* cultivo *m* industrial *or* comercial; ~ **desk** *n* (BrE) caja *f*; ~ **dispenser** *n* (BrE) cajero *m* automático *or* permanente
cashew (nut) /'kæʃuː/ *n* anacardo *m*, castaña *f* de cajú (CS, Ven), nuez *f* de la India (Méx)
cash flow *n* flujo *m* de caja, cash-flow *m*
cashier /kæ'ʃɪr ‖ kæ'ʃɪə(r)/ *n* cajero, -ra *m,f*
cashier's check *n* (AmE) cheque *m* bancario *or* de caja *or* de gerencia
cashmere /'kæʒmɪr ‖ kæ,ʃ'mɪə(r)/ *n* cachemir *m*, cachemira *f*
cash: ~**point** *n* (BrE) cajero *m* automático *or* permanente; ~ **register** *n* caja *f* registradora
casing /'keɪsɪŋ/ *n* (cover) cubierta *f*; (case) caja *f*
casino /kə'siːnəʊ/ *n* (*pl* **-nos**) casino *m*
cask /kæsk ‖ kɑːsk/ *n* barril *m*, tonel *m*
casket /'kæskət ‖ 'kɑːskɪt/ *n* **(a)** (for jewels) cofre *m* **(b)** (coffin) (AmE) ataúd *m*, féretro, cajón (AmL)
casserole /'kæsərəʊl/ *n* **(a)** (dish) cazuela *f* **(b)** (food) guiso *m*, guisado *m* (Méx)
cassette /kə'set/ *n* (Audio) cassette *f or m*; (*before n*) ~ **player** pasacintas *m*, cassette *m* (Esp), pasacassettes *m* (RPI), tocacassettes *m* (Chi)
cast¹ /kæst ‖ kɑːst/ *n* **1 (a)** (molded object) (Art) vaciado *m*; (Metall) pieza *f* fundida **(b)** (mold) molde *m* **2** (Cin, Theat) (+ *sing or pl vb*) reparto *m*, elenco *m* (esp AmL)
cast² (*past & past p* **cast**) *vt* **1 (a)** ⟨*stone*⟩ arrojar, lanzar*, tirar*; ⟨*line*⟩ lanzar*; ⟨*net*⟩ echar **(b)** ⟨*shadow/light*⟩ proyectar; **to** ~ **doubt on sth** poner* algo en duda **(c)** ⟨*vote*⟩ emitir **2** «*snake*» ⟨*skin*⟩ mudar de, mudar **3** (Cin, Theat) ⟨*role*⟩ asignar; **she was** ~ **as the princess** le dieron el papel de la princesa
■ ~ *vi* (in angling) lanzar*
■ ~ **away** [*v + o + adv*]: **they were** ~ **away on a desert island** llegaron a una isla desierta tras naufragar

■ **cast off** [*v + adv*] **1 (a)** (in knitting) cerrar* **(b)** (Naut) soltar* amarras
2 [*v + o + adv, v + adv + o*] **(a)** (in knitting) ⟨*stitch*⟩ cerrar* **(b)** (abandon) ⟨*friend/lover*⟩ dejar
■ **cast on** **1** [*v + adv*] (in knitting) poner* *or* montar los puntos
2 [*v + o + adv, v + adv + o*] ⟨*stitch*⟩ montar, poner*
■ **cast out** [*v + o + adv, v + adv + o*] (liter) expulsar
castanets /'kæstə'nets/ *pl n* castañuelas *fpl*
castaway /'kæstəweɪ ‖ 'kɑːstəweɪ/ *n* náufrago, -ga *m,f*
caste /kæst ‖ kɑːst/ *n* casta *f*
caster /'kæstər ‖ 'kɑːstə(r)/ *n* ruedecita *f*, ruedita *f* (esp AmL)
caster sugar *n* (BrE) azúcar blanca de granulado muy fino
Castile /kæs'tiːl ‖ kæ'stiːl/ *n* Castilla *f*
Castilian¹ /kæs'tɪljən ‖ kə'stɪliən/ *adj* castellano
Castilian² *n* **(a)** (person) castellano, -na *m,f* **(b)** (language) castellano *m*
cast: ~ **iron** *n* hierro *m* fundido *or* colado; ~**-iron** *adj* (*before n*) ⟨*guarantee*⟩ sólido; ⟨*alibi*⟩ a toda prueba
castle /'kæsəl ‖ 'kɑːsəl/ *n* **(a)** (Archit) castillo *m* **(b)** (in chess) torre *f*
castoff /'kæstɔːf ‖ 'kɑːstɒf/ *n*: **she gave me her** ~**s** me dio la ropa que ya no quería
castrate /'kæstreɪt ‖ kæs'treɪt/ *vt* castrar
casual /'kæʒuəl/ *adj* **1 (a)** (superficial) (*before n*) ⟨*inspection*⟩ superficial; **a** ~ **acquaintance** un conocido, una conocida; ~ **sex** relaciones *fpl* sexuales promiscuas **(b)** (chance) (*before n*) ⟨*visit/reader*⟩ ocasional **(c)** (informal) ⟨*chat*⟩ informal; ⟨*clothes*⟩ de sport, informal **2** (unconcerned) ⟨*attitude/tone*⟩ despreocupado; ⟨*remark*⟩ hecho al pasar **3** (not regular) ⟨*employment/labor*⟩ eventual, ocasional
casually /'kæʒuəli/ *adv* **(a)** (informally) ⟨*dressed*⟩ de manera informal; ⟨*chat*⟩ informalmente **(b)** (with indifference) con indiferencia
casualty /'kæʒuəlti/ *n* (*pl* **-ties**) **1** (injured person) herido, -da *m,f*; (dead person) víctima *f*; (Mil) baja *f* **2** (hospital department) (BrE) (*no art*) urgencias *fpl*
cat /kæt/ *n* gato, -ta *m,f*; **to let the** ~ **out of the bag** descubrir* el pastel, levantar la liebre *or* (RPI) la perdiz; **to rain** ~**s and dogs** llover* a cántaros
Catalan¹ /'kætl̩æn ‖ 'kætəlæn/ *adj* catalán
Catalan² *n* **(a)** (person) catalán, -lana *m,f* **(b)** (language) catalán *m*
catalog¹, catalogue /'kætɔːg ‖ 'kætəlɒg/ *n* catálogo *m*
catalog², catalogue *vt* catalogar*
Catalonia /'kætl̩'əʊniə ‖ ,kætə'ləʊniə/ *n* Cataluña *f*
catalyst /'kætl̩əst ‖ 'kætəlɪst/ *n* catalizador *m*

AmC	Central America	Cu	Cuba	Per	Peru
AmL	Latin America	Arg	Argentina	Ec	Ecuador	RPI	River Plate Area
AmS	South America	Bol	Bolivia	Esp	Spain	Ur	Uruguay
Andes	Andean Region	Chi	Chile	Méx	Mexico	Ven	Venezuela
		CS	Southern Cone		

catalytic converter /,kætl'ıtık kən'vɜːrtər ‖,kætə'lıtık kən'vɜːtə(r)/ n catalizador m

catapult¹ /'kætəpʊlt ‖'kætəpʌlt/ n (Aviat, Mil) catapulta f

catapult² vt catapultar

cataract /'kætərækt/ n **1** (over a precipice) catarata f; (in a river) rápido m **2** (Med) catarata f

catarrh /kə'tɑːr ‖kə'tɑː(r)/ n catarro m

catastrophe /kə'tæstrəfi/ n catástrofe f

catch¹ /kætʃ/ (past & past p **caught**) vt
1 ⟨ball/object⟩ agarrar, coger* (esp Esp)
2 (capture) ⟨mouse/lion⟩ atrapar, coger* (esp Esp); ⟨fish⟩ pescar*, coger* (esp Esp); ⟨thief⟩ atrapar
3 (a) (take by surprise) agarrar, pillar (fam), pescar* (fam); **we got caught in the rain** nos sorprendió la lluvia (b) (intercept) ⟨person⟩ alcanzar*; ~ **you later** (colloq) nos vemos
4 (a) ⟨train/plane⟩ (take) tomar, coger* (esp Esp); (be in time for) alcanzar* (b) (manage to see, hear): **we'll just ~ the end of the game** todavía podemos pescar el final del partido (fam); **we could ~ a movie before dinner** (AmE) podríamos ir al cine antes de cenar
5 (entangle, trap): **I caught my skirt on a nail** se me enganchó or (Méx tb) se me atoró or (Chi) se me pescó la falda en un clavo; **I caught my finger in the drawer** me pillé or (AmL tb) me agarré el dedo en el cajón
6 (hear or understand clearly): **did you ~ what she said?** ¿oíste lo que dijo?
7 ⟨disease⟩ contagiarse de; **to ~ a cold** resfriarse*, agarrar or (esp Esp) coger* un resfriado
8 (hit): **he caught his head on the beam** se dio en la cabeza con la viga

■ ~ vi **1** (a) (grasp) agarrar, coger* (esp Esp), cachar (Méx) (b) (become hooked) engancharse **2** (ignite) ⟨fire⟩ prender, agarrar (AmL)

■ **catch on** [v + adv] (colloq) (a) (become popular) ⟨fashion/idea⟩ imponerse*; ⟨game/style⟩ ponerse* de moda (b) (understand) caer* (fam)

■ **catch out** [v + o + adv, v + adv + o] **to ~ sb out** pillar or agarrar a algn desprevenido (b) (trick) pillar (fam), agarrar (CS fam)

■ **catch up** **1** [v + adv] (with work, studies) ponerse* al día; **to ~ up WITH sb/sth** (physically) alcanzar* a algn/algo; **she had to ~ up with the rest of the class** tuvo que ponerse al nivel del resto de la clase
2 [v + o + adv] (draw level with) (BrE) alcanzar*
3 (trap, involve) **to be/get caught up in sth** ⟨in barbed wire/thorns⟩ estar*/quedar enganchado/atrapado en algo; ⟨in scandal/dispute⟩ verse* envuelto en algo; ⟨in excitement/enthusiasm⟩ contagiarse de algo; **I got caught up in the traffic** me agarró or (esp Esp) me cogió el tráfico

catch² n **1** (a) (Sport) atrapada f, atajada f (CS) (b) (of fish) pesca f **2** (on door) pestillo m, pasador m (AmL); (on window, box, necklace) cierre m **3** (hidden drawback) trampa f; **I knew there'd be a ~ in it somewhere** ya sabía yo que tenía que haber gato encerrado; **it's a C~-22 situation** es una situación sin salida

catcher /'kætʃər ‖'kætʃə(r)/ n (in baseball) receptor, -tora m,f, catcher mf

catching /'kætʃıŋ/ adj (pred) contagioso

catchment area /'kætʃmənt/ n zona f de captación (distrito que corresponde a un hospital, colegio etc)

catch: ~**phrase** n (of person) latiguillo m; (of political party) eslogan m; ~**word** n (a) (slogan) eslogan m (b) ▶ ~PHRASE

catchy /'kætʃi/ adj **catchier, catchiest** pegadizo, pegajoso (AmL exc RPl)

categorical /'kætə'gɔːrıkəl ‖,kætə'gɒrıkəl/ adj categórico; ⟨refusal⟩ rotundo

categorize /'kætəgəraız/ vt ⟨things⟩ clasificar*; ⟨people⟩ catalogar*

category /'kætəgəːri ‖'kætəgəri/ n (pl **-ries**) categoría f

cater /'keıtər ‖'keıtə(r)/ vt (AmE) encargarse* del buffet de

■ **cater to,** (BrE) **cater for** [v + prep + o]: **to ~ to o for people of all ages** ofrecer* servicios para gente de todas las edades; **we try to ~ to o for all needs** tratamos de satisfacer todas las necesidades

caterer /'keıtərər ‖'keıtərə(r)/ n: persona o firma que se encarga del servicio de comida y bebida para fiestas, cafeterías etc

catering /'keıtərıŋ/ n (a) (provision of food): **to do the ~** encargarse* del servicio de comida y bebida (or del buffet etc) (b) (trade, department) restauración f

caterpillar /'kætərpılər ‖'kætəpılə(r)/ n oruga f, azotador m (Méx), cuncuna f (Chi)

cathedral /kə'θiːdrəl/ n catedral f

Catholic¹ /'kæθəlık/ n católico, -ca m,f

Catholic² adj **1** (Relig) católico; **the Roman ~ Church** la iglesia católica (apostólica romana) **2 catholic** ⟨tastes/interests⟩ variado

Catholicism /kə'θɑːləsızəm ‖kə'θɒlısızəm/ n catolicismo m

cat: ~**nap** n siestecita f; **C~'s-eye**® n (Transp) catafaros m, ojo m de gato (CS), estoperol m (Col)

catsup /'kætsəp/ n (AmE) ▶ KETCHUP

cattle /'kætl/ pl n ganado m, reses fpl; (before n) ~ **breeder** ganadero, -ra m,f

catwalk /'kætwɔːk/ n pasarela f

Caucasian /kɔː'keızən/ n (Anthrop) caucásico, -ca m,f; **the suspect is a male ~** el sospechoso es un hombre de raza blanca

caught /kɔːt/ past & past p of CATCH¹

cauliflower /'kɑːlıflauər ‖'kɒlıflauə(r)/ n coliflor f

cause¹ /kɔːz/ n **1** (a) (of accident, event, death) causa f (b) (reason, grounds) motivo m, razón f; **there's no ~ for concern** no hay por qué preocuparse **2** (ideal, movement) causa f

cause² vt causar; **to ~ sb problems** causarle problemas a algn; **to ~ sb/sth TO + INF** hacer* que algn/algo (+ subj)

causeway /'kɔːzweı/ n (path) paso m elevado; (road) carretera f elevada

caustic /'kɔːstık/ adj cáustico

caution¹ /'kɔːʃən/ n (a) (care, prudence) cautela f, prudencia f (b) (warning) advertencia f, aviso m; (Law, Sport) amonestación f

caution² vt (a) (warn) advertir* (b) (inform of rights) informar de sus derechos

cautious /'kɔːʃəs/ adj cauteloso, cauto

cautiously /'kɔːʃəsli/ adv cautelosamente

cavalry /'kævəlri/ n caballería f

cave /keɪv/ n cueva f; (before n) ~ **painting** pintura f rupestre
■ **cave in** [v + adv] derrumbarse

caveman /'keɪvmæn/ n (pl **-men** /-men/) hombre m de las cavernas

cavern /'kævərn II'kævən/ n caverna f

caviar, caviare /'kæviɑːr II'kæviɑː(r)/ n caviar m

cavity /'kævəti/ n (pl **-ties**) cavidad f; (Dent) caries f

caw /kɔː/ vi graznar

CBS n (in US) (no art) (= **Columbia Broadcasting System**) la CBS

cc (= **cubic centimeter** o (BrE) **centimetre**) c.c.

CCTV n = **closed-circuit television**

CD n (= **compact disc** or (AmE also) **disk**) CD m

CD-ROM n (= **compact disc read-only memory**) CD-ROM m

cease /siːs/ vt (a) to ~ to + INF/ to ~ -ING dejar DE + INF (b) ⟨production/publication⟩ interrumpir, suspender
■ ~ vi ⟨noise⟩ cesar; ⟨production⟩ interrumpirse; ⟨work⟩ detenerse*

cease-fire /'siːsfaɪr II'siːsfaɪə(r)/ n alto m el fuego, cese m del fuego (AmL)

ceaseless /'siːsləs II'siːslɪs/ adj incesante

cedar /'siːdər II'siːdə(r)/ n cedro m

cede /siːd/ vt to ~ sth (TO sb) ceder(le) algo (A algn)

ceiling /'siːlɪŋ/ n (Const) techo m, cielo m raso; (upper limit) límite m, tope m

celebrate /'seləbreɪt II'selɪbreɪt/ vt celebrar
■ ~ vi: we won: let's ~! ¡ganamos, vamos a celebrarlo!

celebration /'seləbreɪʃən/ n (event) fiesta f; he attended the ~s asistió a los festejos

celebrity /sə'lebrəti II sɪ'lebrəti/ n (pl **-ties**) famoso, -sa m,f; celebridad mf

celery /'seləri/ n apio m, celeri m (Ven)

celibate /'seləbət II'selɪbət/ adj célibe

cell /sel/ n 1 (in prison) celda f 2 (Biol, Elec) célula f

cellar /'selər II'selə(r)/ n sótano m; (for coal) carbonera f; (for wine) bodega f

cello /'tʃeləʊ/ n (pl **-los**) violoncelo m, violonchelo m, chelo m

cellophane, (BrE) **Cellophane**® /'seləfeɪn/ n celofán m

cellphone /'selfəʊn/ n teléfono m celular (AmL), teléfono m móvil (Esp)

cellulite /'seljəlaɪt II'seljʊlaɪt/ n celulitis f

celluloid /'seljəlɔɪd II'seljʊlɔɪd/ n celuloide m

cellulose /'seljələʊs II'seljʊləʊs/ n celulosa f

Celsius /'selsiəs/ adj: **20 degrees ~** 20 grados centígrados or Celsio(s)

Celt /kelt/ n celta mf

Celtic /'keltɪk/ adj celta

cement¹ /sɪ'ment/ n cemento m

cement² vt (a) (Const) unir con cemento (b) ⟨friendship/alliance⟩ consolidar, fortalecer*

cement mixer n hormigonera f

cemetery /'semətri II'semətri/ n (pl **-ries**) cementerio m

censor¹ /'sensər II'sensə(r)/ n censor, -sora m,f

censor² vt censurar

censorship /'sensərʃɪp II'sensəʃɪp/ n censura f

censure /'sentʃər II'sensjə(r)/ vt censurar

census /'sensəs/ n (pl **-suses**) censo m

cent /sent/ n (of dollar) centavo m; (of euro) céntimo m

centenary /sen'tenəri II sen'tiːnəri/ n (pl **-ries**) centenario m

centennial /sen'teniəl/ n (esp AmE) centenario m

center¹, (BrE) **centre** /'sentər II'sentə(r)/ n 1 (middle point, area) centro m 2 (site of activity) centro m 3 (Sport) (in US football, rugby) centro mf; (in basketball) pivot mf, pivote mf (AmL)

center², (BrE) **centre** vt centrar
■ ~ vi (a) (focus on) to ~ ON o UPON sth/sb centrarse EN algo/algn (b) (revolve around) to ~ ON o AROUND sth/sb girar ALREDEDOR DE algo/algn

center: ~ **forward** n delantero mf centro; ~ **half** (pl **halfs** or **halves**) n medio mf centro; ~**piece** n (decoration) centro m (de mesa); (main feature) eje m

centigrade /'sentɪɡreɪd/ adj centígrado

centimeter, (BrE) **centimetre** /'sentə,miːtər II'sentɪ,miːtə(r)/ n centímetro m

centipede /'sentəpiːd II'sentɪpiːd/ n ciempiés m

central /'sentrəl/ adj (a) (main) central; ⟨problem⟩ fundamental (b) (in the center) ⟨area/street⟩ céntrico; in ~ **Chicago** en el centro de Chicago

central: C~ America n Centroamérica f, América f Central; **C~ American** adj centroamericano, de (la) América Central; **C~ Europe** n Europa f Central; ~ **heating** n calefacción f central

centralize /'sentrəlaɪz/ vt centralizar*

central reservation n (BrE) mediana f, bandejón m (central) (Chi), camellón m (Méx)

centre etc (BrE) ▶ CENTER etc

century /'sentʃəri/ n (pl **-ries**) siglo m; **in the 19th ~** en el siglo XIX

ceramic /sə'ræmɪk II sɪ'ræmɪk/ adj ⟨pot⟩ de cerámica; ~ **tile** (for walls) azulejo m; (for floors) baldosa f (de cerámica)

ceramics /sə'ræmɪks II sɪ'ræmɪks/ n (+ pl vb) objetos mpl de cerámica, cerámicas fpl

cereal /'sɪriəl II'sɪəriəl/ n (a) (plant, grain) cereal m (b) (breakfast ~) cereales mpl

cerebral palsy /sə'riːbrəl 'pɔːlzi II'serɪbrəl 'pɔːlzi/ n parálisis f

ceremonial /ˌserə'məʊniəl II ˌserɪ'məʊniəl/ adj ⟨robes⟩ ceremonial; ⟨occasion⟩ solemne

ceremony /'serəməʊni II'serɪməni/ n (pl **-nies**) ceremonia f

certain /'sɜːrtn̩ II'sɜːtn̩/ adj 1 (a) (definite) seguro; **to make ~ OF sth** asegurarse or cerciorarse DE algo; **for ~** con certeza (b) (convinced) ⟨pred⟩ **to be ~ (OF sth)** estar* seguro (DE algo); **I checked the list to make ~ (that) ...** revisé la lista para asegurarme de que ...

2 (*particular*) (*before n*) cierto; **he has a ~ something** tiene un no sé qué *or* (un) algo especial

certainly /'sɜːrtn̩li ‖'sɜːtn̩li/ *adv* (a) (definitely): **we're almost ~ going to win** es casi seguro que vamos a ganar; **do you see what I mean? — certainly** ¿te das cuenta de lo que quiero decir? — desde luego (b) (emphatic): **I ~ won't be buying anything there again!** por cierto que no voy a volver a comprar nada allí; **may I use your phone? — certainly!** ¿puedo llamar por teléfono? — pues claro ¡(no) faltaría más!; **~ not!** ¡de ninguna manera!

certainty /'sɜːrtn̩ti ‖'sɜːtn̩ti/ *n* (*pl* **-ties**) certeza *f*, seguridad *f*; **defeat is now a ~** la derrota es algo seguro

certificate /sər'tɪfɪkət ‖sə'tɪfɪkət/ *n* certificado *m*

certify /'sɜːrtəfaɪ ‖'sɜːtɪfaɪ/ *vt* **-fies, -fying, -fied** (a) 〈*facts/claim/death*〉 certificar*; **this is to ~ that ...** por la presente certifico que ... (b) (*declare insane*) (*usu pass*) declarar demente (c) (*license*) (AmE): **he isn't certified to teach in this state** no está habilitado para ejercer la docencia en este estado (d) **certified** *past p* (AmE) certificado; **certified public accountant** contador público, contadora pública *m,f* (AmL), censor jurado, censora jurada *m,f* de cuentas (Esp)

cervical /'sɜːrvɪkəl ‖'sɜːvɪkəl, sɜː'vaɪkəl/ *adj* del cuello del útero; **~ smear** (BrE) citología *f*, Papanicolau *m* (AmL)

cervix /'sɜːrvɪks ‖'sɜːvɪks/ *n* (*pl* **-vixes** *or* **-vices** /-vəsiːz/) cuello *m* del útero

Cesarean (section), Cesarian (section) /sɪ'zæriən ‖sɪ'zeəriən/ *n* (AmE) cesárea *f*

cesspit /'sespɪt/ *n* pozo *m* negro *or* séptico *or* ciego

cf (compare) cf.

CFC *n* = **chlorofluorocarbon**

ch *n* (*pl* **chs**) (= **chapter**) c.

chafe /tʃeɪf/ *vt/i* rozar*

chaff /tʃæf ‖tʃɑːf/ *n* barcia *f*

chagrin /ʃə'grɪn ‖'ʃægrɪn/ *n* (liter) disgusto *m*; **to his ~** para su disgusto

chain¹ /tʃeɪn/ *n* cadena *f*; **a ~ of events** una cadena de acontecimientos

chain² *vt* **to ~ sth/sb TO sth** encadenar algo/a algn A algo

chain: **~ reaction** *n* reacción *f* en cadena; **~smoke** *vi* fumar un cigarrillo tras otro; **~ store** *n* tienda *f* de una cadena

chair¹ /tʃer ‖tʃeə(r)/ *n* **1** (seat) silla *f*; (arm~) sillón *m*, butaca *f* (esp Esp) **2** (a) (at university) cátedra *f* (b) (in meeting) presidencia *f*; **to take the ~** presidir

chair² *vt* 〈*meeting*〉 presidir

chair: **~lift** *n* telesilla *f or* (Esp) telesquí *m*; **~man** /'tʃermən ‖'tʃeəmən/ *n* (*pl* **-men** /-mən/) presidente, -ta *m,f*; **~woman** *n* presidenta *f*

chalet /'ʃæleɪ/ *n* (a) (cabin) chalet *m* (*de montaña*) (b) (in motel) bungalow *m*

chalk /tʃɔːk/ *n* **1** (Geol) creta *f*, caliza *f* **2** (for writing) tiza *f*, gis *m* (Méx)

challenge¹ /'tʃæləndʒ ‖'tʃælɪndʒ/ *vt* **1** (a) (summon) desafiar*, retar; **to ~ sb to + INF** desafiar* a algn A QUE (+ *subj*) (b) (question) 〈*authority/findings*〉 cuestionar **2** (stop) (Mil) darle* el alto a

challenge² *n* desafío *m*, reto *m*

challenger /'tʃæləndʒər ‖'tʃælɪndʒə(r)/ *n* contendiente *mf*, rival *mf*

chamber /'tʃeɪmbər ‖'tʃeɪmbə(r)/ *n* **1** (room) (arch) cámara *f* (arc) **2** (of gun) recámara *f*

chamber: **~maid** *n* camarera *f* (*en un hotel*); **~ music** *n* música *f* de cámara; **~ of commerce** *n* cámara *f* de comercio; **~ pot** *n* orinal *m or* (AmL exc RPl) bacinilla *f or* (CS) escupidera *f*

chameleon /kə'miːliən/ *n* camaleón *m*

chamois (leather) /'ʃæmi/ *n* gamuza *f*

chamomile /'kæməmaɪl/ *n* manzanilla *f*, camomila *f*; **~ tea** manzanilla *f*

champagne /ʃæm'peɪn/ *n* champán *m*, champaña *f or m*

champion¹ /'tʃæmpiən/ *n* (a) (Sport) campeón, -peona *m,f* (b) (of cause) defensor, -sora *m,f*

champion² *vt* abogar* por, defender*

championship /'tʃæmpiənʃɪp/ *n* (Sport) (*often pl*) campeonato *m*

chance¹ /tʃæns ‖tʃɑːns/ *n* **1** (fate) casualidad *f*, azar *m*; **by ~** por *or* de casualidad; (*before n*) 〈*meeting*〉 fortuito **2** (risk) riesgo *m*; **don't take any ~s** no te arriesgues **3** (opportunity) oportunidad *f* **4** (likelihood) posibilidad *f*, chance *f or m* (esp AmL); **(the) ~s are (that) ...** (colloq) lo más probable es que ...

chance² *vt*: **to ~ it** arriesgarse*

chancellor /'tʃænslər ‖'tʃɑːnsələ(r)/ *n* (a) **Chancellor (of the Exchequer)** (in UK) ≈ministro, -tra *m,f* de Economía/Hacienda (b) (premier) canciller *mf* (c) (of university) rector, -tora *m,f*

chandelier /ˌʃændə'lɪr ‖ˌʃændə'lɪə(r)/ *n* araña *f* (*de luces*)

change¹ /tʃeɪndʒ/ *n* **1** (a) cambio *m*; **a ~ in temperature** un cambio de temperatura; **for a ~** para variar (b) (of clothes) muda *f* **2** (a) (coins) cambio *m*, monedas *fpl*, sencillo *m* (AmL), menudo *m* (Col), dinero *m* suelto, plata *f* suelta (AmS) (b) (money returned) cambio *m*, vuelto *m* (AmL), vuelta *f* (Esp), vueltas *fpl* (Col)

change² *vt* cambiar; **the witch ~d her into a stone** la bruja la convirtió en una piedra; **to ~ one's clothes** cambiarse de ropa; **to ~ color** cambiar de color; **let's ~ the subject** cambiemos de tema; **I wouldn't want to ~ places with her** no quisiera estar en su lugar; **to change train(s)** hacer* transbordo, cambiar (de tren); **to ~ dollars into pesos** cambiar dólares a *or* (Esp tb) en pesos

■ ~ *vi* **1** (a) (become different) cambiar; **to ~ INTO sth** convertirse* EN algo (b) **changing** *pres p* 〈*needs/role/moods*〉 cambiante **2** (a) (put on different clothes) cambiarse; **she ~d into a black dress** se cambió y se puso un vestido negro; **to get ~d** cambiarse (b) (Transp) cambiar, hacer* transbordo

■ **change over** [*v + adv*] cambiar

changeable /'tʃeɪndʒəbəl/ *adj* cambiante

change: **~over** *n* (transition) **~over (FROM sth) (TO sth)** cambio *m* (DE algo) (A algo); **~ purse** *n* (AmE) monedero *m*, portamonedas *m*

changing room /'tʃeɪndʒɪŋ/ n (BrE) **(a)** (Sport) vestuario m, vestidor m (Chi, Méx) **(b)** (in shop) probador m

channel¹ /'tʃænl/ n **1** (strait) canal m; (course of river) cauce m; (navigable course) canal m; **the (English) C~** el Canal de la Mancha **2** (for irrigation) canal m, acequia f **3** (system, method) vía f; **you must go through the official ~s** tiene que hacer el trámite por los conductos oficiales **4** (Comput, TV) canal m

channel² vt, (BrE) **-ll-** ⟨water/proposals/complaints⟩ canalizar*; ⟨efforts/energies⟩ encauzar*

channel: C~ Islands pl n the C~ Islands las Islas Anglonormandas, las islas del Canal de la Mancha; **C~ Tunnel** n the C~ Tunnel el Eurotúnel, el túnel del Canal de la Mancha

chant¹ /tʃænt ‖tʃɑ:nt/ n (of demonstrators) consigna f; (of sports fans) alirón m, canción f

chant² vt/i (Mus, Relig) salmodiar; «crowd» gritar

chaos /'keɪɑ:s ‖'keɪɒs/ n caos m

chaotic /ker'ɑ:tɪk ‖ker'ɒtɪk/ adj caótico

chap /tʃæp/ n (colloq) tipo m (fam)

chap. n (pl **chaps**) (= **chapter**) c., cap.

chapel /'tʃæpəl/ n capilla f

chaperon, chaperone /'ʃæpərəʊn/ n (of young lady) acompañanta f, chaperona f; (for young people) (AmE) acompañante mf

chaplain /'tʃæplən ‖'tʃæplɪn/ n capellán m

chapped /tʃæpt/ adj ⟨lips⟩ agrietado

chapter /'tʃæptər ‖'tʃæptə(r)/ n capítulo m

char /tʃɑ:r ‖tʃɑ:(r)/ vt **-rr-** carbonizar*

character /'kærəktər ‖'kærəktə(r)/ n **1** (of person, thing) carácter m; **to be in/out of ~** ser*/no ser* típico; **her face is full of ~** tiene una cara con mucha personalidad **2 (a)** (in novel, play, movie) personaje m **(b)** (person) tipo m (fam) **(c)** (eccentric person) caso m **3** (symbol) carácter m

characteristic¹ /'kærəktə'rɪstɪk/ n característica f

characteristic² adj característico

characterize /'kærəktəraɪz/ vt caracterizar*

charade /ʃə'reɪd ‖ʃə'rɑ:d/ n farsa f; **~s** (+ sing vb) (game) charada f

charcoal /'tʃɑ:rkəʊl ‖'tʃɑ:kəʊl/ n carbón m (vegetal); (Art) carboncillo m, carbonilla f (RPl)

charge¹ /tʃɑ:rdʒ ‖tʃɑ:dʒ/ n **1** (Law) cargo m, acusación f; **to bring o press ~s against sb** formular cargos contra algn **2** (price) precio m; (fee) honorario m; **free of ~** gratuitamente, gratis **3** (responsibility): **the person in ~** la persona responsable; **to be in ~ of sth/sb** tener* algo/a algn a su (or mi etc) cargo; **to take ~ of** (of situation) hacerse* cargo de; (of class, guests) hacerse* cargo de, encargarse* de; (of task) encargarse* de, ocuparse de **4** (Elec, Phys) carga f **5** (of explosive) carga f **6** (attack) carga f

charge² vt **1** (accuse) **to ~ sb WITH sth/-ING** acusar a algn DE algo/+ INF **2** (ask payment) cobrar **3** (obtain on credit): **to ~ sth TO sb** cargar*

algo a la cuenta de algn **4 (a)** (entrust) (frml) **to ~ sb WITH sth/-ING** encomendar* A algn algo/QUE (+ subj) **(b)** (allege) (AmE) aducir* **5** (attack) (Mil) cargar* contra; «animal» embestir* or arremeter contra **6** (Elec) ⟨battery⟩ cargar*
■ ~ vi **to ~** (AT sth/sb) (Mil) cargar* (CONTRA algo/algn); «animal» arremeter or embestir* (CONTRA algo/algn)

charge: ~ account n cuenta f de crédito; **~ card** n tarjeta f de pago

charger /'tʃɑ:rdʒər ‖'tʃɑ:dʒə(r)/ n (battery ~) cargador m de pilas; (Auto) cargador m de baterías

chariot /'tʃæriət/ n carro m (de guerra)

charisma /kə'rɪzmə/ n carisma m

charismatic /'kærəz'mætɪk ‖,kærɪz'mætɪk/ adj carismático

charitable /'tʃærətəbəl ‖'tʃærɪtəbəl/ adj **(a)** (generous, giving) caritativo **(b)** (kind) ⟨person⟩ bueno; ⟨interpretation⟩ benévolo, generoso

charity /'tʃærəti/ n (pl **-ties**) **1 (a)** (organization) organización f benéfica or de beneficencia **(b)** (relief) obras fpl de beneficencia; **to raise money for ~** recaudar dinero para un fin benéfico; (before n) ⟨work⟩ de beneficencia, benéfico **2** (generosity, kindness) caridad f

charm¹ /tʃɑ:rm ‖tʃɑ:m/ n **1 (a)** (attractiveness) encanto m **(b)** (attractive quality, feature) encanto m **2** (spell) hechizo m **3** (amulet) amuleto m, fetiche m; (on bracelet) dije m

charm² vt cautivar

charming /'tʃɑ:rmɪŋ ‖'tʃɑ:mɪŋ/ adj ⟨person⟩ encantador; ⟨room/house⟩ precioso

chart¹ /tʃɑ:rt ‖tʃɑ:t/ n **1** (Aviat, Naut) carta f de navegación; (diagram, graph) gráfico m; (table) tabla f **2 charts** pl (best-selling records) **the ~s** la lista de éxitos

chart² vt ⟨course⟩ trazar*; ⟨progress/changes⟩ (follow closely) seguir* atentamente; (record) registrar gráficamente

charter¹ /'tʃɑ:rtər ‖'tʃɑ:tə(r)/ n **1 (a)** (constitution) carta f **(b)** (guarantee of rights) fuero m, privilegio m **2** (Transp) (before n) ⟨flight/plane⟩ chárter adj inv

charter² vt **1** ⟨plane/ship/bus⟩ fletar, alquilar **2** (BrE) **chartered** past p ⟨engineer/surveyor⟩ colegiado; **~ed accountant** contador público, contadora pública m,f (AmL), censor jurado, censora jurada m,f de cuentas (Esp)

chase¹ /tʃeɪs/ n persecución f

chase² vt perseguir*
■ ~ vi: **we ~d after the thief** fuimos tras el ladrón; **to ~ after girls** ir* detrás de las chicas
■ **chase up** [v + o + adv, v + adv + o] (colloq): **~ up this order for me, please** averíguame qué pasó con este pedido, por favor; **I'll have to ~ him up about the report** voy a tener que recordarle lo del informe

chasm /'kæzəm/ n sima f, abismo m

chassis /'tʃæsi ‖'ʃæsi/ n (pl **chassis** /'tʃæsiz ‖'ʃæ-/) (Auto) chasis m, bastidor m (Esp)

chastise /tʃæs'taɪz/ vt (fml) (verbally) reprender; (physically) castigar*

chastity /'tʃæstəti/ n castidad f

chat¹ /tʃæt/ n charla f, conversación f (esp AmL), plática f (AmC, Méx)

chat² vi -tt- to ~ (TO o WITH sb) charlar or (esp AmL) conversar or (AmC, Méx) platicar* (CON algn)

chat: ~ **line** n chat m; ~ **room** n chat m; ~ **show** n (BrE) programa m de entrevistas

chatter /'tʃætər ‖'tʃætə(r)/ vi «person» charlar; «monkeys» parlotear; «birds» cotorrear; his teeth are ~ing le castañetean los dientes

chatterbox /'tʃætərbɑːks ‖'tʃætəbɒks/ n charlatán, -tana m,f

chatty /'tʃæti/ adj -tier, -tiest ‹person› conversador; ‹letter› simpático y lleno de noticias

chauffeur /'ʃəʊfər ‖'ʃəʊfə(r)/ n chofer mf or (Esp) chófer mf

chauvinism /'ʃəʊvənɪzəm ‖'ʃəʊvɪnɪzəm/ n chovinismo m; **male** ~ machismo m

chauvinist /'ʃəʊvənəst ‖'ʃəʊvɪnɪst/ n chovinista mf; **(male)** ~ machista m

cheap /tʃiːp/ adj -er, -est 1 (a) (inexpensive) barato; ‹restaurant/hotel› económico 1 (b) (shoddy) ‹merchandise/jewelry› ordinario, de baratillo; ‹mechanic/electrician› (AmE) chapucero 2 (a) (vulgar, contemptible) ‹joke/gimmick› de mal gusto; ‹trick/tactics› bajo; ‹liar/crook› vil (b) (worthless) ‹flattery/promises› fácil

cheapen /'tʃiːpən/ vt quitarle valor a, degradar

cheaply /'tʃiːpli/ adv ‹buy/sell/get› barato; ‹dress/eat/live› con poco dinero

cheat¹ /tʃiːt/ vt estafar, engañar
■ ~ vi (a) (act deceitfully) hacer* trampas (b) (be unfaithful) to ~ ON sb engañar a algn

cheat² n (swindler) estafador, -dora m,f; (at cards, in exam) tramposo, -sa m,f

check¹ /tʃek/ n 1 (stop, restraint) control m 2 (inspection — of passport, documents) control m; (— of work) examen m, revisión f; (— of machine, product) inspección f; to keep a ~ on sth controlar algo 3 (before n) ‹jacket/shirt› a or de cuadros 4 (in chess) jaque m 5 (Fin), (BrE) **cheque** cheque m, talón m (Esp); to pay by ~ pagar* con cheque or (Esp) con talón 6 (restaurant bill) (AmE) cuenta f, adición f (RPl) 7 (tick) (AmE) signo m, tic m, visto m (Esp), palomita f (Méx fam)

check² vt 1 (restrain) ‹anger/impulse› contener* 2 (a) (inspect) ‹passport/ticket› revisar, checar* (Méx); ‹machine/product› inspeccionar; ‹quality› controlar; ‹temperature/pressure/volume› comprobar*, checar* (Méx) (b) (verify) ‹facts/information› comprobar*, verificar*, checar* (Méx); ‹accounts/bill› revisar 3 (AmE) (a) (in cloakroom) dejar en el guardarropa; (in baggage office) dejar or (frml) depositar en consigna (b) (Aviat) ‹baggage› facturar, chequear (AmL) 4 (tick) (AmE) marcar*, hacer* un tic or (Méx fam) una palomita en, poner* un visto en (Esp)
■ ~ vi comprobar*, verificar*, checar* (Méx)
■ **check in** 1 [v + adv] (at airport) facturar or (AmL tb) chequear el equipaje; (at hotel) registrarse 2 [v + o + adv, v + adv + o] (Aviat) ‹luggage› facturar, chequear (AmL)

■ **check out** 1 [v + adv] dejar el hotel (or pensión etc) (habiendo pagado la factura etc) 2 [v + adv] (tally) (AmE) ‹story› cuadrar 3 [v + o + adv, v + adv + o] (a) ‹facts/story› verificar*, comprobar*, checar* (Méx) (b) (esp AmE) ‹shopping› «customer» pagar*; «cashier» cobrar
■ **check up** [v + adv]: we ~ed up and found out he was lying hicimos averiguaciones y comprobamos que mentía; can you ~ up on that? ¿puedes comprobarlo?

checkbook, (BrE) **chequebook** /'tʃekbʊk/ n chequera f, talonario m de cheques (esp Esp)

checked /tʃekt/ adj (no comp) a or de cuadros

checker /'tʃekər ‖'tʃekə(r)/ n (AmE) (cashier) cajero, -ra m,f

checkered, (BrE) **chequered** /'tʃekərd ‖'tʃekəd/ adj ‹career/history› accidentado

checkers /'tʃekərz ‖'tʃekəz/ n (AmE) (+ sing vb) damas fpl

check-in /'tʃekɪn/ n facturación f de equipajes

checking account /'tʃekɪŋ/ n (AmE) cuenta f corriente

check: ~**list** n lista f de control; ~**mate** n (jaque m) mate m; ~**out** n caja f; ~**point** n control m; ~**room** n (AmE) guardarropa m; ~**up** n (Med) chequeo m, revisión f

cheek /tʃiːk/ n 1 (of the face) mejilla f, cachete m (AmL fam) 2 (colloq) (impudence) descaro m, cara f (fam)

cheekbone /'tʃiːkbəʊn/ n pómulo m

cheeky /'tʃiːki/ adj -kier, -kiest (esp BrE) ‹boy/girl› fresco, descarado; ‹grin› pícaro

cheep /tʃiːp/ vi piar*

cheer¹ /tʃɪr ‖tʃɪə(r)/ n 1 (of encouragement, approval) ovación f, aclamación f; three ~s for Fred! ¡viva Fred! 2 **cheers** pl (as interj) (drinking toast) ¡salud!

cheer² vt (a) (shout in approval) aclamar, vitorear (b) ~ (on) (shout encouragement at) animar
■ ~ vi aplaudir
■ **cheer up** 1 [v + adv] animarse 2 [v + o + adv, v + adv + o] ‹person› animar

cheerful /'tʃɪrfəl ‖'tʃɪəfəl/ adj alegre; ‹news/prospect› alentador

cheerleader /'tʃɪr,liːdər ‖'tʃɪə,liːdə(r)/ n animador, -dora m,f (en encuentros deportivos, mítines políticos), porrista mf (Col, Méx)

cheese /tʃiːz/ n queso m

cheese: ~**board** n tabla f de quesos; ~**cake** n tarta f de queso; ~**burger** n hamburguesa f con queso; ~**cloth** n estopilla f, bambula f

cheetah /'tʃiːtə/ n guepardo m, chita f

chef /ʃef/ n chef m, jefe -fa m,f de cocina

chemical¹ /'kemɪkəl/ n sustancia f química, producto m químico

chemical² adj químico

chemist /'kemɪst ‖'kemɪst/ n (a) (scientist) químico, -ca m,f (b) (pharmacist) (BrE) farmacéutico, -ca m,f; the ~'s la farmacia

chemistry /'kemɪstri ‖'kemɪstri/ n química f

chemotherapy /'kiːməʊ'θerəpi/ n quimioterapia f

cheque /tʃek/ n (BrE) ▶ CHECK¹ 5

chequebook /'tʃekbʊk/ n (BrE) ▶ CHECKBOOK

chequered /'tʃekərd ‖ 'tʃekəd/ adj (BrE) ▶ CHECKERED

cherish /'tʃerɪʃ/ vt (a) (care for, value) apreciar (b) (cling to) ⟨memory/hope⟩ conservar

cherry /'tʃeri/ n (pl **-ries**) cereza f; (before n) ∼ **tree** cerezo m

chess /tʃes/ n ajedrez m

chessboard /'tʃesbɔːrd ‖ 'tʃesbɔːd/ n tablero m de ajedrez

chest /tʃest/ n **1** (Anat) pecho m; **to get sth off one's** ∼ desahogarse* contando/confesando algo **2** (box) arcón m **3** (AmE) (treasury) tesorería f; (funds) fondos mpl

chestnut¹ /'tʃesnʌt/ n castaña f; (before n) ∼ **tree** castaño m

chestnut² adj castaño

chest of drawers n (pl ∼s ∼ ∼) cómoda f

chew /tʃuː/ vt ⟨food⟩ mascar*, masticar*; ⟨gum⟩ mascar*

chewing gum /'tʃuːɪŋ/ n chicle m

chick /tʃɪk/ n (young bird) polluelo, -la m,f; (young chicken) pollito, -ta m,f

chicken /'tʃɪkən ‖ 'tʃɪkɪn/ n (a) (hen) gallina f; (as generic term) pollo m (b) (Culin) pollo m
■ **chicken out** [v + adv] (colloq) acobardarse, achicarse* (fam), rajarse (fam)

chickenpox /'tʃɪkənpɑːks ‖ 'tʃɪkɪnpɒks/ n varicela f, peste f cristal (Chi)

chickpea /'tʃɪkpiː/ n garbanzo m

chicory /'tʃɪkəri/ n (Bot) endivia f; (in coffee) achicoria f

chief¹ /tʃiːf/ n jefe, -fa m,f, líder mf; ∼ **of police** jefe de policía

chief² adj (before n, no comp) principal

chief: ∼ **constable** n jefe, -fa m,f de policía; ∼ **justice** n (in US) presidente, -ta m,f del tribunal

chilblain /'tʃɪlbleɪn/ n sabañón m

child /tʃaɪld/ n (pl **children** /'tʃɪldrən/) (a) (boy) niño m; (girl) niña f (b) (son) hijo m; (daughter) hija f

childbirth /'tʃaɪldbɜːrθ ‖ 'tʃaɪldbɜːθ/ n parto m

childhood /'tʃaɪldhʊd/ n niñez f, infancia f

childish /'tʃaɪldɪʃ/ adj infantil

childlike /'tʃaɪldlaɪk/ adj ingenuo, de niño

children /'tʃɪldrən/ pl of CHILD

Chile /'tʃɪli/ n Chile m

Chilean¹ /'tʃɪliən/ adj chileno

Chilean² n chileno, -na m,f

chili, chilli /'tʃɪli/ n (pl **-lies**) ají m, chile m

chill¹ /tʃɪl/ n (a) (coldness — of weather) frío m, fresco m (b) (Med) enfriamiento m, resfriado m

chill² vt enfriar*; ⟨wine/food⟩ poner* a enfriar

chilli n (pl **-lies**) ▶ CHILI

chilly /'tʃɪli/ adj **-lier, -liest** frío

chime¹ /tʃaɪm/ n (of bells, clock) campanada f; (of doorbell) campanilla f

chime² vi «bell» sonar*; «clock» dar* la hora

chimney /'tʃɪmni/ n chimenea f

chimney sweep n deshollinador, -dora m,f

chimpanzee /'tʃɪmpænˈziː ‖ ˌtʃɪmpənˈziː/ n chimpancé m

chin /tʃɪn/ n barbilla f, mentón m

china /'tʃaɪnə/ n loza f; (fine) porcelana f

China /'tʃaɪnə/ n China f

Chinese¹ /tʃaɪˈniːz/ adj chino

Chinese² n (pl ∼) (a) (person) chino, -na m,f (b) (language) chino m

chink /tʃɪŋk/ n grieta f, abertura f

chip¹ /tʃɪp/ n **1** (a) (of wood) astilla f; (of stone) esquirla f; **to have a** ∼ **on one's shoulder** ser* un resentido (b) (in cup) desportilladura f **2** (Culin) (a) (in packet) (AmE) papa f or (Esp) patata f frita, papa f chip (Ur) (b) (French fry) (BrE) papa f or (Esp) patata f frita **3** (Games) ficha f **4** (Comput, Electron) chip m

chip² **-pp-** ⟨crockery⟩ desportillar, cascar* (RPl), saltar (Chi); ⟨tooth⟩ romper* un trocito de
■ ∼ vi «china/cup» desportillarse, cascarse* (RPl), saltarse (Chi); «paint/varnish» saltarse, desconcharse

chipboard /'tʃɪpbɔːrd ‖ 'tʃɪpbɔːd/ n (a) (of wood) madera f prensada or aglomerada, aglomerado m (b) (of paper) (AmE) cartón m prensado

chipmunk /'tʃɪpmʌŋk/ n ardilla f listada

chiropodist /kəˈrɑːpədɪst ‖ kɪˈrɒpədɪst/ n pedicuro, -ra m,f, podólogo, -ga m,f, callista mf

chirp /tʃɜːrp ‖ tʃɜːp/ vi piar*

chisel¹ /'tʃɪzəl/ n (for stone) cincel m; (for wood) formón m, escoplo m

chisel² vt, (BrE) **-ll-** ⟨stone⟩ cincelar; ⟨wood⟩ labrar

chivalry /'ʃɪvəlri/ n caballerosidad f, cortesía f

chives /tʃaɪvz/ pl n cebollinos mpl, cebolletas fpl

chlorine /'klɔːriːn/ n cloro m

chlorofluorocarbon /'klɔːrəʊˈflʊərəʊˈkɑːrbən ‖ ˌklɔːrəʊˌflʊərəʊˈkɑːbən, -flɔːrə-/ n clorofluorocarbono m

chloroform /'klɔːrəfɔːrm ‖ 'klɒrəfɔːm/ n cloroformo m

chocolate /'tʃɑːklət ‖ 'tʃɒklət/ n (a) chocolate m; (candy, sweet) bombón m (b) (drinking ∼) chocolate m en polvo; **a cup of hot** ∼ una taza de chocolate

choice¹ /tʃɔɪs/ n (a) (act, option) elección f; **I don't work here out of** ∼ no es por (mi) gusto que trabajo aquí (b) (person, thing chosen): **she's a possible** ∼ **for the job** es una de las candidatas posibles para el puesto; **it was an unfortunate** ∼ **of words** no fue la mejor manera de decirlo (c) (variety) (no pl) surtido m, selección f

choice² adj **choicer, choicest** ⟨fruit/wine⟩ selecto; ⟨beef/veal⟩ (in US) de primera

choir /kwaɪr ‖ 'kwaɪə(r)/ n coro m

choke¹ /tʃəʊk/ vt estrangular, ahogar*, asfixiar
■ ∼ vi ahogarse*, asfixiarse; **to** ∼ **ON sth** atragantarse or (AmL tb) atorarse CON algo

choke² n (Auto) choke m, estárter m, cebador m (RPl), ahogador m (Chi, Méx)

cholera /'kɑːlərə ‖ 'kɒlərə/ n cólera m

cholesterol /kəˈlestərəʊl ‖ kəˈlestərɒl/ n colesterol m

choose /tʃuːz/ (past **chose**; past p **chosen**) vt (a) (select) elegir*, escoger*; ⟨candidate⟩ elegir* (b) (decide) **to** ∼ **to** + INF decidir + INF, optar POR + INF
■ ∼ vi elegir*, escoger*

choosy /'tʃuːzi/ adj **-sier, -siest** (colloq) exigente

chop¹ /tʃɑːp ‖tʃɒp/ n **1** (with ax, cleaver) hachazo m; (with hand) manotazo m; (in karate) golpe m **2** (Culin) chuleta f, costilla f (AmS)

chop² -**pp**- vt (a) (cut) ⟨wood⟩ cortar; ⟨meat/apple⟩ cortar (en trozos pequeños); ⟨parsley/onion⟩ picar* (b) **chopped** past p ⟨onions/herbs⟩ picado; ⟨meat⟩ (AmE) molido or (Esp, RPl) picado
■ **chop down** [v + o + adv, v + adv + o] cortar
■ **chop off** [v + o + adv, v + adv + o] ⟨branch⟩ cortar
■ **chop up** [v + o + adv, v + adv + o] ▶ CHOP² A

chopper /'tʃɑːpər ‖'tʃɒpə(r)/ n (a) (hatchet) hacha f; pequeña (b) (helicopter) (colloq) helicóptero m

chopping board /'tʃɑːpɪŋ ‖'tʃɒpɪŋ/ n tabla f de picar

choppy /'tʃɑːpi ‖'tʃɒpi/ adj **-pier, -piest** ⟨sea⟩ picado

chopstick /'tʃɑːpstɪk ‖'tʃɒpstɪk/ n palillo m (para comer comida oriental)

chord /kɔːrd ‖kɔːd/ n (Mus) acorde m

chore /tʃɔːr ‖tʃɔː(r)/ n (routine task) tarea f; (tedious task) lata f (fam)

choreographer /ˌkɔːri'ɑːgrəfər ‖ˌkʊri'ɒgrəfə(r)/ n coreógrafo, -fa m,f

choreography /ˌkɔːri'ɑːgrəfi ‖ˌkʊri'ɒgrəfi/ n coreografía f

chortle /'tʃɔːrtl ‖'tʃɔːtl/ vi reírse* (con satisfacción)

chorus /'kɔːrəs/ n **1** (+ sing o pl vb) (in musical, opera) coro m **2** (refrain) estribillo m; (choral piece) coral m

chose /tʃəʊz/ past of CHOOSE

chosen /'tʃəʊzən/ past p of CHOOSE

Christ /kraɪst/ n (a) (Relig) Cristo (b) (as interj) (colloq) ¡Jesús! (fam); **for ~'s sake!** ¡por amor de Dios!

christen /'krɪsn/ vt bautizar*

christening /'krɪsnɪŋ/ n bautismo m, bautizo m

Christian¹ /'krɪstʃən/ n cristiano, -na m,f

Christian² adj cristiano

Christianity /ˌkrɪsti'ænəti, ˌkrɪstʃi- ‖ˌkrɪsti'ænəti/ n (faith) cristianismo m; (believers) los cristianos

Christian name n nombre m de pila

Christmas /'krɪsməs/ n Navidad f, Pascua f (Chi, Per); (~time) las Navidades, la Navidad, la Pascua (Chi, Per); **merry o** (BrE also) **happy ~!** ¡Feliz Navidad!, ¡Felices Pascuas!; (before n) ~ **cake** pastel m de Navidad (pastel de frutas cubierto de mazapán y azúcar glaseado); ~ **card** tarjeta f de Navidad, tarjeta f de Pascua (Chi, Per), crismas m (Esp); ~ **Day** día m de Navidad or (Chi, Per tb) de Pascua; ~ **Eve** (day) la víspera de Navidad; (evening) Nochebuena f; ~ **tree** árbol m de Navidad or (Chi, Per tb) de Pascua

chrome /krəʊm/ n cromo m

chromium /'krəʊmiəm/ n cromo m

chromosome /'krəʊməsəʊm/ n cromosoma m

chronic /'krɑːnɪk ‖'krɒnɪk/ adj (Med) crónico; ⟨unemployment/shortages⟩ crónico; ⟨smoker/liar⟩ empedernido

chronicle /'krɑːnɪkəl ‖'krɒnɪkəl/ n crónica f

chronological /ˌkrɑːnə'lɑːdʒɪkəl ‖ˌkrɒnə'lɒdʒɪkəl/ adj cronológico

chrysalis /'krɪsələs ‖'krɪsəlɪs/ n crisálida f

chubby /'tʃʌbi/ adj **-bier, -biest** (colloq) ⟨legs/cheeks/face⟩ regordete (fam); ⟨person⟩ gordinflón (fam)

chuck /tʃʌk/ vt (colloq) (a) (throw) tirar, aventar* (Méx) (b) (throw away) tirar, botar (AmL exc RPl) (c) (give up) (colloq) ⟨job⟩ dejar, plantar (fam); ⟨boyfriend/girlfriend⟩ plantar (fam), botar (AmC, Chi fam), largar* (RPl fam)

chuckle /'tʃʌkəl/ vi reírse*

chum /tʃʌm/ n (colloq) amigo, -ga m,f, compinche mf (fam), cuate m (Méx fam), pata m (Per fam), pana mf (Ven fam)

chunk /tʃʌŋk/ n pedazo m, trozo m

chunky /'tʃʌŋki/ adj **-kier, -kiest** ⟨person⟩ fornido; ⟨sweater⟩ grueso

church /tʃɜːrtʃ ‖tʃɜːtʃ/ n iglesia f

churchgoer /'tʃɜːrtʃˌgəʊər ‖'tʃɜːtʃˌgəʊə(r)/ n practicante mf

churn¹ /tʃɜːrn ‖tʃɜːn/ n mantequera f

churn² vt ⟨milk⟩ batir; ⟨butter⟩ hacer*
■ **churn out** [v + o + adv, v + adv + o] (colloq) producir* como salchichas (fam)
■ **churn up** [v + o + adv, v + adv + o] revolver*

chute /ʃuːt/ n tolva f, vertedor m; (in swimming pool, amusement park) tobogán m, rodadero m (Col)

CIA n (= **Central Intelligence Agency**) CIA f

cider /'saɪdər ‖'saɪdə(r)/ n (a) (alcoholic) sidra f; **hard ~** (AmE) sidra f fermentada (b) (non-alcoholic) (AmE): (sweet) ~ jugo m or (Esp) zumo m de manzana

cigar /sɪ'gɑːr ‖sɪ'gɑː(r)/ n cigarro m, puro m, tabaco m (Col)

cigarette /ˌsɪgə'ret/ n cigarrillo m; (before n) ~ **end** colilla f; ~ **holder** boquilla f; ~ **lighter** encendedor m, mechero m (Esp)

cinch /sɪntʃ/ n (colloq) (no pl) (easy task): **it's a ~** es pan comido (fam), es tirado (Esp fam), es una papa or un bollo (RPl fam), es botado (Chi fam)

cinder /'sɪndər ‖'sɪndə(r)/ n (a) (ember) carbonilla f, carboncillo m; **the dinner was burnt to a ~** la cena estaba carbonizada (b) **cinders** pl (ashes) ceniza f, rescoldo m

cinecamera /'sɪniˌkæmərə/ n (BrE) filmadora f (AmL), tomavistas m (Esp); (large, professional) cámara f cinematográfica

cinema /'sɪnəmə ‖'sɪnəmɑː/ n cine m

cinnamon /'sɪnəmən/ n canela f

cipher /'saɪfər ‖'saɪfə(r)/ n clave f, cifra f

circa /'sɜːrkə ‖'sɜːkə/ prep alrededor de, hacia

circle¹ /'sɜːrkəl ‖'sɜːkəl/ n círculo m; **their ~ of friends** su círculo de amigos; **to come/go full ~** volver* al punto de partida

circle² vt **1** (move around) dar* vueltas alrededor de; (be around) rodear, cercar* **2** (draw circle around) trazar* un círculo alrededor de
■ ~ vi dar* vueltas; «aircraft/bird» volar* en círculos

circuit /'sɜːrkət ‖'sɜːkɪt/ n **1** (passage around) recorrido m, vuelta f **2** (Elec) circuito m

circular¹ /'sɜːrkjələr ‖'sɜːkjʊlə(r)/ adj circular

circular² n circular f

circulate /'sɜːrkjələɪt ‖'sɜːkjʊleɪt/ vi circular
■ ~ vt ⟨report/news⟩ hacer* circular, divulgar*

circulation /'sɜːrkjə'leɪʃən ‖,sɜːkjʊ'leɪʃən/ n
circulación f

circumcise /'sɜːrkəmsaɪz ‖'sɜːkəmsaɪz/ vt
circuncidar

circumference /sər'kʌmfərəns
‖səˈkʌmfərəns/ n circunferencia f

circumflex (accent) /'sɜːrkəmfleks
‖'sɜːkəmfleks/ n (acento m) circunflejo m

circumstance /'sɜːrkəmstæns
‖'sɜːkəmstəns/ n ⓵ (condition, fact) circunstancia
f; in o under the ~s dadas las circunstancias;
under no ~s bajo ningún concepto, bajo ninguna
circunstancia ⓶ **circumstances** pl (financial
position): a person in my ~s una persona en mi
situación económica

circumstantial /'sɜːrkəm'stæntʃəl
‖,sɜːkəm'stænʃəl/ adj ⟨evidence⟩ circunstancial

circus /'sɜːrkəs ‖'sɜːkəs/ n circo m

cirrhosis /sə'rəʊsəs ‖sɪ'rəʊsɪs/ n cirrosis f

CIS n (= **Commonwealth of Independent
States**) CEI f

cistern /'sɪstərn ‖'sɪstən/ n cisterna f

cite /saɪt/ vt citar

citizen /'sɪtəzən ‖'sɪtɪzən/ n ciudadano, -na m,f

citizenship /'sɪtəzənʃɪp ‖'sɪtɪzənʃɪp/ n
ciudadanía f

citrus /'sɪtrəs/ adj (before n) cítrico

city /'sɪti/ n (pl **cities**) ciudad f; (before n) ~
center centro m de la ciudad

city: ~ **hall** n (AmE) ayuntamiento m,
municipio m; ~ **planner** n (AmE) urbanista mf;
~ **planning** n (AmE) urbanismo m

civic /'sɪvɪk/ adj ⟨authorities⟩ civil; ⟨leader⟩ de
la ciudad; ⟨duty/virtues⟩ cívico; ~ **center** edificios
mpl municipales

civil /'sɪvəl ‖'sɪvl/ adj (a) (of society, citizens) civil
(b) (polite) cortés

civilian /sə'vɪljən ‖sɪ'vɪljən/ n civil mf

civilization /'sɪvələ'zeɪʃən ‖,sɪvəlaɪ'zeɪʃən/ n
civilización f

civilized /'sɪvəlaɪzd/ adj ⟨society⟩ civilizado;
⟨person⟩ educado

civil: ~ **liberties** pl n derechos mpl civiles; ~
rights pl n derechos mpl civiles; ~ **servant** n
funcionario, -ria m,f (del Estado); ~ **service** n
the ~ service la administración pública;
(employees) el funcionariado (del Estado); ~ **war**
n guerra f civil; the C~ War (in US) la guerra de
Secesión

claim¹ /kleɪm/ n ⓵ (demand): wage o pay ~
reivindicación f salarial; insurance ~
reclamación f al seguro; a ~ for expenses una
solicitud de reembolso de gastos ⓶ (to right, title)
~ (to sth) derecho m (a algo) ⓷ (allegation)
afirmación f

claim² vt ⓵ (a) ⟨throne/inheritance/land⟩
reclamar; ⟨right⟩ reivindicar*; ⟨diplomatic

immunity⟩ alegar* **(b)** ⟨lost property⟩ reclamar
(c) ⟨social security/benefits⟩ (apply for) solicitar;
(receive) cobrar; you can ~ your expenses back
puedes pedir que te reembolsen los gastos
⓶ (allege, profess): no one has ~ed responsibility
for the attack nadie ha reivindicado el atentado;
he ~ed (that) he knew nothing about it aseguraba
or afirmaba no saber nada de ello

claimant /'kleɪmənt/ n (a) (Soc Adm)
solicitante mf (b) (to throne) pretendiente, -ta m,f

clairvoyant /kler'vɔɪənt ‖kleə'vɔɪənt/ n
clarividente mf

clam /klæm/ n almeja f
■ **clam up**: -mm- [v + adv] (colloq) ponerse* muy
poco comunicativo

clamber /'klæmbər ‖'klæmbə(r)/ vi trepar;
they ~ed over the wall treparon al muro y
saltaron

clammy /'klæmi/ adj -**mier**, -**miest**
⟨handshake⟩ húmedo; ⟨weather⟩ bochornoso

clamor, (BrE) **clamour** /'klæmər ‖'klæmə(r)/
vi gritar; to ~ FOR sth ⟨for war/resignation⟩
pedir* algo a gritos

clamp¹ /klæmp/ n (a) (Const) abrazadera f; (in
carpentry) tornillo m de banco **(b)** (wheel ~) (BrE)
cepo m

clamp² vt (a) (join, fasten) sujetar con
abrazaderas **(b)** (BrE Auto) (colloq) ⟨car⟩ ponerle* el
cepo a
■ **clamp down** [v + adv] to ~ down ON sth/sb
tomar medidas drásticas CONTRA algo/algn

clampdown /'klæmpdaʊn/ n (colloq): a ~ on
illegal immigrants medidas fpl drásticas contra
los inmigrantes ilegales; there's been a ~ on
loans se ha restringido severamente la concesión
de créditos

clan /klæn/ n clan m

clandestine /klæn'destən ‖klæn'destɪn/ adj
clandestino

clang /klæŋ/ vi «bells» sonar*

clank /klæŋk/ vi hacer* ruido

clap¹ /klæp/ n (a) (applause): to give sb a ~
aplaudir a algn (b) a ~ of thunder un trueno

clap² -pp- vt (applaud) aplaudir; to ~ one's
hands to the music dar* palmadas al compás de
la música
■ ~ vi (applaud) aplaudir; (to music etc) dar* una
palmada

clapping /'klæpɪŋ/ n aplausos mpl

clarify /'klærəfaɪ ‖'klærɪfaɪ/ -**fies**, -**fying**,
-**fied** vt (a) (explain, make clear) aclarar (b) (purify)
⟨butter/wine⟩ clarificar*

clarinet /'klærə'net/ n clarinete m

clarity /'klærəti/ n claridad f

clash¹ /klæʃ/ n ⓵ (of interests) conflicto m; (of
cultures, personalities) choque m; (of opinions, views)
disparidad f ⓶ (between armies, factions)
enfrentamiento m, choque m ⓷ (noise): the ~ of
the cymbals el sonido de los platillos

clash² vi (a) «personalities» chocar*; «colors/

---

patterns» desentonar **(b)** «armies/factions/
leaders» chocar* **(c)** «dates» coincidir **(d)**
«cymbals/swords» sonar* (al entrechocarse)
clasp¹ /klæsp ‖klɑːsp/ n broche m, cierre m
clasp² vt: **she ~ed her bag firmly** sujetó
firmemente el bolso; **he ~ed her in his arms** la
estrechó entre sus brazos
class¹ /klæs ‖klɑːs/ n **1** (social stratum) clase f
2 (group of students) clase f; (lesson) clase f; **the ~
of '86** la promoción del 86 **3** (group, type) clase f
4 **(a)** (Transp) clase f **(b)** (in UK) (Post): **send the
letter first/second ~** manda la carta por correo
preferente/normal **5** (style) (colloq) clase f
class² vt catalogar*
classic¹ /'klæsɪk/ adj clásico; ‹scene/line›
memorable
classic² n clásico m; see also CLASSICS
classical /'klæsɪkəl/ adj (of Greece, Rome)
clásico; **~ music** música f clásica
classics /'klæsɪks/ n (+ sing vb) clásicas fpl
classification /'klæsəfə'keɪʃən
‖,klæsɪfɪ'keɪʃən/ n clasificación f
classified /'klæsəfaɪd ‖'klæsɪfaɪd/ adj **(a)**
(categorized) clasificado; **~ advertising** anuncios
mpl por palabras, avisos mpl clasificados (AmL)
(b) (secret) ‹information› secreto
classify /'klæsəfaɪ ‖'klæsɪfaɪ/ vt **-fies,
-fying, -fied** ‹books/data› clasificar*
class: ~mate n compañero, -ra m,f de clase;
~room n aula f‡, clase f
clatter¹ /'klætər ‖'klætə(r)/ vi «pans» hacer*
ruido; «typewriter» repiquetear
clatter² n (of trains) traqueteo m; (of typewriters)
repiqueteo m; (of hooves) chacoloteo m
clause /klɔːz/ n **(a)** (in contract) cláusula f **(b)**
(Ling) oración f, cláusula f
claustrophobia /'klɔːstrə'fəʊbiə
‖,klɒstrə'fəʊbiə/ n claustrofobia f
claustrophobic /'klɔːstrə'fəʊbɪk
‖,klɒstrə'fəʊbɪk/ adj claustrofóbico
claw /klɔː/ n (of tiger, lion) zarpa f, garra f; (of
eagle) garra f; (of crab, lobster) pinza f
clay /kleɪ/ n arcilla f; (for children) (AmE)
plastilina® f, plasticina® f (CS)
clean¹ /kliːn/ adj **-er, -est** limpio; ‹joke›
inocente; ‹game/player› limpio; ‹driver's license›
donde no constan infracciones; ‹stroke/features›
bien definido, nítido; **she made a ~ break with
the past** cortó radicalmente con el pasado
clean² adv (colloq) **(a)** (completely): **I ~ forgot
about it** se me olvidó por completo **(b)** (fairly)
‹fight/play› limpio, limpiamente
clean³ vt **(a)** limpiar; ‹blackboard› borrar; **to
~ one's teeth** lavarse los dientes; **you can ~ it
off with a sponge** lo puedes quitar con una
esponja **(b)** (dry-clean) limpiar en seco
■ **clean out** [v + o + adv, v + adv + o] (clean
thoroughly) vaciar* y limpiar (a fondo)
■ **clean up** **1** [v + o + adv, v + adv + o]
(physically, morally) limpiar **2** [v + adv] (do cleaning)
limpiar
clean-cut /'kliːn'kʌt/ adj ‹outline› bien
definido; ‹appearance› muy cuidado
cleaner /'kliːnər ‖'kliːnə(r)/ n **(a)** (person)
limpiador, -dora m,f **(b)** (substance) producto m de
limpieza

cleaning /'kliːnɪŋ/ n limpieza f; (before n) **~
fluid** líquido m limpiador; **the ~ lady** la señora
de la limpieza
cleanliness /'klenlɪnəs ‖'klenlɪnɪs/ n
limpieza f; **personal ~** el aseo personal
cleanse /klenz/ vt limpiar
cleanser /'klenzər ‖'klenzə(r)/ n (for household
use) producto m de limpieza; (for skin) leche f (or
crema f etc) limpiadora or de limpieza
clean-shaven /'kliːn'ʃeɪvən/ adj ‹face› bien
afeitado or (esp Méx) rasurado
cleansing /'klenzɪŋ/ adj limpiador; **~ lotion**
loción f limpiadora or de limpieza
clear¹ /klɪr ‖klɪə(r)/ adj **-er, -est** **1** ‹sky›
despejado; **she has very ~ skin** tiene muy buen
cutis; **to keep a ~ head** mantener* la mente
despejada **2** (distinct) ‹outline/picture› nítido,
claro; ‹voice› claro **3** **(a)** (plain, evident): **it's a ~
case of suicide** es un caso evidente de suicidio; **it
became ~ that ...** se hizo evidente que ... **(b)**
‹explanation/instructions› claro **4** (free,
unobstructed) ‹space/road› despejado
clear² adv: **stand ~ of the doors** manténganse
alejados de las puertas; **the curtains should hang
~ of the radiators** las cortinas no deben tocar los
radiadores; **to keep/stay ~ (of sth)** mantenerse*
alejado (de algo), no acercarse* (a algo)
clear³ vt **1** (make free, unobstructed) ‹room›
vaciar*; ‹surface› despejar; ‹drain/pipe›
desatascar*, destapar (AmL); ‹building› desalojar;
‹land› despoblar de árboles, desmontar; **to ~ the
table** levantar or (Esp tb) quitar la mesa; **to ~
one's throat** carraspear
2 (free from suspicion) ‹name› limpiar; **he was ~ed
of all charges** lo absolvieron de todos los cargos
4 (authorize) autorizar*
5 ‹debt/account› liquidar, saldar
■ ~ vi **1** ‹sky/weather/traffic› despejarse;
«water» aclararse; «fog/smoke» levantarse
2 (Fin) «check» ser* compensado
■ **clear off** [v + adv] (colloq) largarse* (fam)
■ **clear out** [v + o + adv, v + adv + o] ‹cupboard/
drawer› vaciar* y ordenar
■ **clear up** **1** [v + o + adv, v + adv + o] **(a)**
‹crime› esclarecer*; ‹misunderstanding/doubts›
aclarar **(b)** ‹rubbish/toys› recoger*
2 [v + adv] **(a)** (tidy) ordenar **(b)** ‹weather»
despejar **(c)** (get better) ‹cough/cold› mejorarse;
the rash has ~ed up se le (or me etc) ha ido el
sarpullido
clearance /'klɪrəns ‖'klɪərəns/ n
1 (authorization) autorización f; (from customs)
despacho m de aduana **2** (of building land)
desmonte m, despeje m **3** (of stock) liquidación f
clear-cut /'klɪr'kʌt ‖,klɪə'kʌt/ adj claro, bien
definido
clearing /'klɪrɪŋ ‖'klɪərɪŋ/ n (in forest) claro m
clearly /'klɪrli ‖'klɪəli/ adv ‹visible/marked›
claramente; ‹speak/write/think› con claridad,
claramente; **it's ~ impossible** es a todas luces
imposible, está claro que es imposible
cleavage /'kliːvɪdʒ/ n escote m
cleaver /'kliːvər ‖'kliːvə(r)/ n cuchilla f de
carnicero
clef /klef/ n clave f

cleft¹ /kleft/ adj ‹chin› partido; ~ **palate** paladar m hendido, fisura f del paladar

cleft² n hendidura f, grieta f

clench /klentʃ/ vt (a) ‹fist/jaw› apretar* (b) (grip) apretar*, agarrar

clergy /'klɜːrdʒi ‖ 'klɜːdʒi/ n (+ sing or pl vb) clero m

clerical /'klerɪkəl/ adj ⃞1 (Relig) clerical ⃞2 ‹job/work› de oficina; ~ **assistant** oficinista mf

clerk /klɜːrk ‖ klɑːk/ n (in office) empleado (administrativo), empleada (administrativa) m,f, oficinista mf; (in bank) empleado, -da m,f, bancario, -ria m,f (CS); (sales ~) (AmE) vendedor, -dora m,f, dependiente, -ta m,f; (desk ~) (AmE) recepcionista mf

clever /'klevər ‖ 'klevə(r)/ adj **-verer, -verest** (a) (intelligent) inteligente, listo (b) (artful) (pej) listo (c) (skillful, adept) ‹player/politician› hábil; ‹invention/solution› ingenioso

cliché /kliːˈʃeɪ/ n lugar m común, cliché m

click¹ /klɪk/ vt ⃞1 ‹fingers› chasquear, tronar* (Méx); ‹tongue› chasquear ⃞2 (Comput) hacer* clic en, pinchar

click² n (of fingers, tongue) chasquido m; (of camera, switch, mouse) clic m

client /'klaɪənt/ n cliente, -ta m,f

clientele /ˌklaɪənˈtel ‖ ˌkliːɒnˈtel, ˌkliːənˈtel/ n (+ sing or pl vb) clientela f

cliff /klɪf/ n acantilado m; (not by sea) precipicio m

cliffhanger /'klɪfˌhæŋər ‖ 'klɪfˌhæŋə(r)/ n situación f de suspenso or (Esp) de suspense

climate /'klaɪmət ‖ 'klaɪmɪt/ n clima m

climax /'klaɪmæks/ n (pl **-maxes**) clímax m; (orgasm) orgasmo m

climb¹ /klaɪm/ vt ‹mountain› escalar, subir a; ‹tree› trepar a, subirse a, treparse a (esp AmL); ‹stairs› subir

■ ~ vi (a) (clamber) trepar, treparse; **she ~ed onto the table** se subió a la mesa, trepó or se trepó a la mesa (b) (rise) subir

■ **climb down** ⃞1 [v + prep + o] ‹rope› bajarse por; ‹tree› bajarse de ⃞2 [v + adv] (concede) (colloq) ceder

climb² n (a) (ascent) subida f (b) (Aviat) ascenso m

climber /'klaɪmər ‖ 'klaɪmə(r)/ n (a) (rock ~) escalador, -dora m,f; (mountaineer) alpinista mf, andinista mf (AmL) (b) (Hort) enredadera f, trepadora f

climbing /'klaɪmɪŋ/ n (Sport) alpinismo m, andinismo m (AmL)

clinch /klɪntʃ/ vt ‹deal› cerrar*; ‹title› ganar; ‹argument› resolver* de forma contundente

cling /klɪŋ/ vi (past & past p **clung**) ⃞1 (a) (hold fast) **to ~ TO sth/sb** estar* aferrado A algo/ algn (b) (be dependent) (pej) **to ~ (TO sb)** pegársele* A algn ⃞2 (stick) **to ~ (TO sth)** pegarse* (A algo)

clingfilm /'klɪŋfɪlm/ n (BrE) film m transparente (para envolver alimentos)

clinic /'klɪnɪk/ n (treatment center) centro m médico; (in state hospital) consultorio m; (private hospital) clínica f

clinical /'klɪnɪkəl/ adj (a) (Med) (before n) clínico (b) (unemotional) ‹manner/detachment› frío

clink /klɪŋk/ vt hacer* tintinear

■ vi tintinear

clip¹ /klɪp/ n ⃞1 (device) clip m, gancho m ⃞2 (from film) fragmento m, clip m

clip² vt **-pp-** ⃞1 (a) (cut) ‹hair/nails/grass/ hedge› cortar; ‹sheep› trasquilar; ‹dog› recortarle el pelo a (b) (punch) ‹ticket› picar*, perforar ⃞2 (cut out) (AmE) recortar ⃞3 (attach) sujetar (con un clip)

clip-on /'klɪpɑːn ‖ 'klɪpɒn/ adj (before n) ‹sunglasses› que se engancha; ‹earrings› de clip

clippers /'klɪpərz ‖ 'klɪpəz/ pl n (for nails) cortaúñas m; (for hair) maquinilla f (para cortar el pelo); (for hedge, lawn) podadera f, tijeras fpl de podar

clipping /'klɪpɪŋ/ n (from newspaper) recorte m

clique /kliːk/ n camarilla f

cloak¹ /kləʊk/ n capa f; (disguise) tapadera f

cloak² vt ‹purpose/activities› encubrir*; ~**ed in secrecy** rodeado de un velo de misterio

cloakroom /'kləʊkruːm, -rʊm/ n guardarropa m

clock /klɑːk ‖ klɒk/ (a) n (timepiece) reloj m; **to work around o round the ~** trabajar las veinticuatro horas del día (b) (Auto) (mileometer) cuentakilómetros m; (speedometer) velocímetro m

■ **clock in,** (BrE) **clock on** [v + adv] fichar, marcar* or (Méx) checar* tarjeta (al entrar al trabajo)

■ **clock out,** (BrE) **clock off** [v + adv] fichar, marcar* or (Méx) checar* tarjeta (al salir del trabajo)

clockwise¹ /'klɑːkwaɪz ‖ 'klɒkwaɪz/ adj ‹direction› de las agujas del reloj

clockwise² adv en el sentido de las agujas del reloj

clockwork /'klɑːkwɜːrk ‖ 'klɒkwɜːk/ n mecanismo m de relojería; **like/regular as ~** como un reloj; (before n) ~ **toy** (esp BrE) juguete m de cuerda

clog¹ /klɑːg ‖ klɒg/ n zueco m

clog² **-gg-** ~ **(up)** vt ‹pipe/filter› obstruir*, atascar*

■ ~ vi «pipe/filter» obstruirse*, atascarse*

cloister /'klɔɪstər ‖ 'klɔɪstə(r)/ n claustro m

clone /kləʊn/ vt clonar

close¹ /kləʊs/ adj **closer, closest** ⃞1 (a) (near) próximo, cercano (b) ‹shave› al ras, apurado; **that was a ~ shave** (colloq) se salvó (or me salvé etc) por un pelo or por los pelos (fam) ⃞2 ‹link/connection› estrecho; ‹contact› directo; ‹relative› cercano; **they are ~ friends** son muy amigos ⃞3 (in similarity): **he bears a ~ resemblance to his brother** tiene un gran parecido a or con su hermano ⃞4 ‹fit› ajustado ⃞5 (careful) ‹examination› detenido; **to keep a ~ watch on sth/sb** vigilar algo/a algn de cerca ⃞6 ‹contest/ finish› reñido ⃞7 ‹weather/atmosphere› pesado, bochornoso

close² /kləʊs/ adv **closer, closest** ⃞1 (in position) cerca; **to draw/get/come ~** acercarse*; ~ **TO sth/sb** cerca DE algo/algn ⃞2 (in intimacy): **the tragedy brought them ~r together** la tragedia los acercó más ⃞3 (in approximation): **the temperature is ~ to ...** la temperatura es de casi ...; **he was ~ to**

tears estaba a punto de llorar **4** (*in phrases*) **close by** cerca; **close together** (physically) juntos; **close up** de cerca

close³ /kləʊz/ *n* fin *m*; **to come/draw to a ~** llegar*/acercarse* a su fin

close⁴ /kləʊz/ *vt* cerrar*
■ ~ *vi* **1** «*door/window*» cerrar(se)*; «*gap/ wound*» cerrarse*
2 «*shop/library/museum*» cerrar*
3 (a) (finish, end) «*lecture/book*» terminar, concluir* (b) **closing** *pres p* «*minutes*» último; «*speech*» de clausura
■ **close down** **1** [*v* + *o* + *adv*, *v* + *adv* + *o*] «*shop/factory*» cerrar*
2 [*v* + *adv*] «*shop/factory*» cerrar*
■ **close in** [*v* + *adv*] «*pursuers/enemy*» acercarse*; **to ~ in on** sth/sb cercar* algo a algn (b) «*winter*» acercarse* (c) (get shorter) «*day*» acortarse
■ **close off** [*v* + *o* + *adv*, *v* + *adv* + *o*] clausurar
■ **close out** [*v* + *o* + *adv*, *v* + *adv* + *o*] (AmE) liquidar
■ **close up** **1** [*v* + *adv*] «*shop/museum*» cerrar*; «*wound/gash*» cerrarse*
2 [*v* + *o* + *adv*, *v* + *adv* + *o*] «*shop/museum*» cerrar*

closed /kləʊzd/ *adj* cerrado

closed circuit *n* circuito *m* cerrado; (*before n*) **closed-circuit television** televisión *f* en circuito cerrado

close /kləʊs/**:** **~-fitting** *adj* ajustado, ceñido; **~-knit** *adj* unido

closely /ˈkləʊsli/ *adv* **1** «*connected/associated*» estrechamente; **they worked ~ with the French** trabajaron en estrecha colaboración con los franceses **2** (a) (at a short distance) «*follow/mark*» de cerca (b) (carefully) «*study/examine*» detenidamente; «*watch*» de cerca; «*question*» a fondo; **a ~ guarded secret** un secreto muy bien guardado **3** (in approximation): **somebody who resembled her ~** alguien que se le parecía mucho

closet /ˈklɑːzət ‖ ˈklɒzɪt/ *n* (AmE) (cupboard) armario *m*, placard *m* (RPl); (for clothes) armario *m*, closet (AmL exc RPl), placard *m* (RPl)

close-up /ˈkləʊsʌp/ *n* primer plano *m*

closing /ˈkləʊzɪŋ/: **~ date** *n* fecha *f* límite, fecha *f* tope; **~ time** *n* hora *f* de cierre

closure /ˈkləʊʒər ‖ ˈkləʊʒə(r)/ *n* cierre *m*

clot¹ /klɑːt ‖ klɒt/ *n* (blood ~) coágulo *m*

clot² *vi* **-tt-** «*blood*» coagularse

cloth /klɔːθ ‖ klɒθ/ *n* (a) (fabric) tela *f*, género *m*; (thick, woolen) paño *m* (b) (for cleaning) trapo *m*

clothe /kləʊð/ *vt* vestir*

clothes /kləʊðz/ *pl n* ropa *f*; **he had no ~ on** estaba desnudo; (*before n*) **~ brush** cepillo *m* para *or* de la ropa, escobilla *f* de ropa (Chi); **~ horse** tendedero *m* (plegable); **~ line** cuerda *f* de tender; **~ shop** tienda *f or* casa *f* de modas

clothespin /ˈkləʊðzpɪn/ (AmE), **clothes-peg** /ˈkləʊðzpeg/ (BrE) *n* pinza *f or* (Arg) broche *m or* (Chi) perrito *m or* (Ur) palillo *m* (de tender la ropa)

clothing /ˈkləʊðɪŋ/ *n* ropa *f*

cloud¹ /klaʊd/ *n* (a) (Meteo) (single) nube *f*; (mass) nubes *fpl*, nubosidad *f* (b) (of smoke, dust) nube *f*; (of suspicion) halo *m*, nube *f*

cloud² *vt* «*view/vision*» nublar

■ **cloud over** [*v* + *adv*] nublarse

cloudiness /ˈklaʊdinəs ‖ ˈklaʊdɪnɪs/ *n* (of sky) lo nublado; (of liquid) lo turbio

cloudless /ˈklaʊdləs ‖ ˈklaʊdlɪs/ *adj* totalmente despejado, sin una nube

cloudy /ˈklaʊdi/ *adj* **-dier, -diest** «*day/sky*» nublado; «*liquid*» turbio; **it's ~** está nublado

clout¹ /klaʊt/ *n* (a) (colloq) **1** (blow) tortazo *m* (fam) **2** (power, influence) peso *m*, influencia *f*

clout² *vt* (colloq) darle* un tortazo a (fam)

clove /kləʊv/ *n* (a) (spice) clavo *m* (de olor) (b) (of garlic) diente *m*

clover /ˈkləʊvər ‖ ˈkləʊvə(r)/ *n* trébol *m*

clown¹ /klaʊn/ *n* payaso, -sa *m,f*

clown² *vi* **~ (around** *o* **about)** hacer* payasadas, payasear (AmL fam), hacer* el payaso (Esp)

cloying /ˈklɔɪɪŋ/ *adj* empalagoso

club¹ /klʌb/ *n* **1** (a) (cudgel) garrote *m*, cachiporra *f* (b) (golf ~) palo *m* de golf **2** (society, association) club *m* **3** (Games) **clubs** *pl* (suit) (+ *sing or pl vb*) tréboles *mpl*; (in Spanish pack) bastos *mpl*

club² **-bb-** *vt* aporrear

■ ~ *vi* (visit nightclubs): **to go ~bing** ir* de nightclubs

cluck /klʌk/ *vi* «*hen*» cloquear

clue /kluː/ *n* pista *f*; (in crosswords) clave *f*; **not to have a ~** (colloq) no tener* ni (la más mínima *or* la menor) idea (fam)

clump /klʌmp/ *n* (a) (of trees) grupo *m*; (of flowers) macizo *m* (b) (of earth) terrón *m*

clumsily /ˈklʌmzəli ‖ ˈklʌmzɪli/ *adv* «*handle/ apologize*» torpemente

clumsy /ˈklʌmzi/ *adj* **-sier, -siest** «*person/ movement*» torpe; «*tool/shape*» tosco; «*translation*» burdo

clung /klʌŋ/ *past & past p of* CLING

cluster¹ /ˈklʌstər ‖ ˈklʌstə(r)/ *n* (of people, buildings, stars) grupo *m*; (of berries, bananas) racimo *m*

cluster² *vi* apiñarse, agruparse

clutch¹ /klʌtʃ/ *n* **1** **clutches** *pl* garras *fpl*; **to be in/fall into sb's ~es** estar*/caer* en las garras de algn **2** (Auto) embrague *m*, clutch *m* (AmC, Col, Méx) **3** (of eggs) nidada *f*

clutch² *vt* tener* firmemente agarrado

■ ~ *vi* **to ~ at** sth tratar de agarrarse DE algo

clutter /ˈklʌtər ‖ ˈklʌtə(r)/ *vt* **~ (up)** abarrotar

cluttered /ˈklʌtərd ‖ ˈklʌtəd/ *adj* abarrotado de cosas

cm (= **centimeter(s)** *or* (BrE) **centimetre(s))** cm.

c/o (= **in care of** *or* (BrE) **care of**): **John Smith, c/o Ana Mas** John Smith, en casa de Ana Mas

Co (a) /kəʊ/ (= **company**) Cía. (b) (Geog) = **County**

CO **1** (Geog) = **Colorado** **2** (Mil) = **Commanding Officer**

coach¹ /kəʊtʃ/ *n* **1** (a) (horse-drawn carriage) coche *m* (de caballos), carruaje *m* (b) (long-distance bus) (BrE) autobús *m*, autocar *m* (Esp), pullman *m* (CS) **2** (Rail) (a) (AmE) vagón *m* de tercera (clase) (b) (BrE) vagón *m* **3** (a) (tutor) profesor, -sora ⋯⃗

coach ⋯⟶ coin

coin² *vt* ⟨*word/expression*⟩ acuñar; **to ~ a phrase** (set phrase) como se suele decir

coin box *n* depósito *m* de monedas

coincide /'kəʊən'saɪd ǁ,kəʊm'saɪd/ *vi* **to ~ (with sth)** coincidir (CON algo)

coincidence /kəʊ'ɪnsədəns ǁkəʊ'ɪnsɪdəns/ *n* casualidad *f*, coincidencia *f*

coincidental /kəʊˌɪnsə'dentḷ ǁkəʊ'ɪnsɪdentḷ/ *adj* casual, fortuito

coin-operated /'kɔɪn'ɑːpəreɪtəd ǁ'kɔɪnˌɒpəreɪtɪd/ *adj* que funciona con monedas

coke /kəʊk/ *n* **1** (fuel) (carbón *m* de) coque *m* **2** (cocaine) (colloq) coca *f* (fam) **3 Coke®** (colloq) Coca-Cola® *f*

colander /'kʌləndər ǁ'kʌləndə(r)/ *n* colador *m*, escurridor *m* (de pasta, verduras)

cold¹ /kəʊld/ *adj* frío; **I'm ~** tengo frío; **my feet are ~** tengo los pies fríos, tengo frío en los pies; **it's ~ today** hoy hace frío; **your dinner's getting ~** se te está enfriando la comida; **I got a very ~ reception** me recibieron con mucha frialdad; **I came to the job ~** empecé el trabajo sin ninguna preparación

cold² *n* **1** (low temperature) frío *m*; **come in out of the ~** entra, que hace frío; **to feel the ~** ser* friolento *or* (Esp) friolero, sentir* el frío **2** (Med) resfriado *m*, constipado *m* (Esp), resfrío *m* (CS); **to have a ~** estar* resfriado

cold: ~-blooded /'kəʊld'blʌdəd ǁ,kəʊld'blʌdɪd/ *adj* **(a)** ⟨*murder*⟩ a sangre fría; ⟨*killer*⟩ despiadado, cruel **(b)** (Zool) de sangre fría; **~ cream** *n* crema *f* limpiadora *or* de limpieza, cold cream *f*; **~ cuts** *pl n* (AmE) fiambres *mpl*; **~-hearted** /'kəʊld'hɑːrtəd ǁ,kəʊld'hɑːtɪd/ *adj* frío, insensible

coldly /'kəʊldli/ *adv* con frialdad, fríamente

cold: ~ sore *n* herpes *m* (labial), fuego *m* (AmL), pupa *f* (Esp fam); **~ storage** *n* almacenamiento *m* en cámaras frigoríficas; **~ war** *n* guerra *f* fría

coleslaw /'kəʊlslɔː/ *n* ensalada de repollo, zanahoria y cebolla con mayonesa

collaborate /kə'læbəreɪt/ *vi* colaborar

collaboration /kəˌlæbə'reɪʃən/ *n* (cooperation) colaboración *f*; (with enemy) colaboracionismo *m*

collaborator /kə'læbəreɪtər ǁkə'læbəreɪtə(r)/ *n* (partner) colaborador, -dora *m,f*; (with enemy) colaboracionista *mf*

collapse¹ /kə'læps/ *vi* **1** «*building*» derrumbarse, desmoronarse **2** «*person*» desplomarse; (Med) sufrir un colapso **3** (fail) fracasar **4** (fold up) «*table/chair*» plegarse*

collapse² *n* **(a)** (of building) derrumbe *m*, desmoronamiento *m* **(b)** (Med) colapso *m* **(c)** (of company) quiebra *f*

collapsible /kə'læpsəbəl/ *adj* plegable

collar /'kɑːlər ǁ'kɒlə(r)/ *n* **(a)** (Clothing) cuello *m* **(b)** (for animal) collar *m*

collarbone /'kɑːlərbəʊn ǁ'kɒləbəʊn/ *n* clavícula *f*

colleague /'kɑːliːɡ ǁ'kɒliːɡ/ *n* colega *mf*

collect¹ /kə'lekt/ *vt* **1** ⟨*information/evidence/data*⟩ reunir*; ⟨*dust*⟩ acumular **2** (as hobby) coleccionar, juntar (esp AmL) **3** (fetch, pick up)

recoger* **4** (obtain payment) ⟨*rent*⟩ cobrar; ⟨*taxes*⟩ recaudar **5** (put in order): **give me some time to ~ my thoughts** déjame pensar un momento
■ **~** *vi* **1** **(a)** (gather, assemble) «*people*» reunirse* **(b)** (accumulate) «*dust/water*» acumularse **2** (for charity etc) recaudar dinero

collect² *adj* (AmE) ⟨*call*⟩ a cobro revertido, por cobrar (Chi, Méx)

collect³ *adv* (AmE) ⟨*call*⟩ a cobro revertido, por cobrar (Chi, Méx)

collection /kə'lekʃən/ *n* **1** **(a)** (of evidence) recopilación *f*; (of rent, debts) cobro *m*; (of taxes) recaudación *f* **(b)** (act of fetching): **the goods are ready for ~** puede recoger *or* pasar a buscar las mercancías **(c)** (of mail, refuse) recogida *f* **2** (of money) colecta *f* **3** (group of objects) colección *f*

collective /kə'lektɪv/ *adj* (usu before n) colectivo

collector /kə'lektər ǁkə'lektə(r)/ *n* **(a)** coleccionista *mf*; **a ~'s item** una pieza de colección **(b)** (official) cobrador, -dora *m,f*

college /'kɑːlɪdʒ ǁ'kɒlɪdʒ/ *n* **(a)** (university) (esp AmE) universidad *f* **(b)** (for vocational training) escuela *f*, instituto *m*; *see also* TEACHERS COLLEGE **(c)** (department of university) facultad *f*, departamento *m*; (in Britain) colegio *m* universitario

collegiate /kə'liːdʒət, -dʒiət/ *adj* (esp AmE) universitario

collide /kə'laɪd/ *vi* «*vehicle*» chocar*, colisionar (frml); **to ~ with sth/sb** chocar* CON algo/algn; **we ~ed in the corridor** nos chocamos en el pasillo

collie /'kɑːli ǁ'kɒli/ *n* collie *mf*, pastor escocés, pastora escocesa *m,f*

collision /kə'lɪʒən/ *n* (of cars, trains) choque *m*, colisión *f* (frml); (of boats) abordaje *m*, colisión *f* (frml)

colloquial /kə'ləʊkwiəl/ *adj* coloquial

collusion /kə'luːʒən/ *n* colusión *f*

Colo = **Colorado**

cologne /kə'ləʊn/ *n* (eau de ~) colonia *f*

Colombia /kə'lʌmbiə/ *n* Colombia *f*

Colombian /kə'lʌmbiən/ *adj* colombiano

colon /'kəʊlən/ *n* **(a)** (Anat) colon *m* **(b)** (in punctuation) dos puntos *mpl*

colonel /'kɜːrnḷ ǁ'kɜːnḷ/ *n* coronel, -nela *m,f*

colonial /kə'ləʊniəl/ *adj* colonial

colonize /'kɑːlənaɪz ǁ'kɒlənaɪz/ *vt* colonizar*

colony /'kɑːləni ǁ'kɒləni/ *n* (*pl* **-nies**) colonia *f*

color¹, (BrE) **colour** /'kʌlər ǁ'kʌlə(r)/ *n* **1** color *m*; **what ~ is the ball?** ¿de qué color es la pelota?; (before n) ⟨*photograph*⟩ en colores *or* (Esp) en color; ⟨*television*⟩ a color(es) *or* en colores *or* (Esp) en color **2 colors** *pl* **(a)** (flag) bandera *f*; **with flying ~s**: **he passed his exams with flying ~s** le fue estupendamente en los exámenes **(b)** (BrE Sport): **the team ~s** los colores del equipo

color², (BrE) **colour** *vt* **(a)** (Art) pintar, colorear; **to ~ sth blue** colorear algo de azul **(b)** (dye) teñir* **(c)** (influence, bias) ⟨*atmosphere*⟩ empañar; **you shouldn't let that ~ your judgment** no deberías dejar que eso influya en tu opinión ⋯⋰

■ ~ vi (flush) ruborizarse*, sonrojarse, ponerse* colorado

color: ~-**blind** adj daltónico, daltoniano; ~-**coded** /'kʌlər'kəʊdəd ‖ˌkʌlə'kəʊdɪd/ adj codificado con colores

colored, (BrE) **coloured** /'kʌlərd ‖'kʌləd/ adj ⟨walls/blouse⟩ de color

-**colored,** (BrE) -**coloured** /ˌkʌlərd ‖'kʌləd/ suff: slate~/coral~ de color pizarra/coral

colorful, (BrE) **colourful** /'kʌlərfəl ‖'kʌləfəl/ adj ⟨clothes/plumage⟩ de colores muy vivos; ⟨parade/description⟩ lleno de color

coloring, (BrE) **colouring** /'kʌlərɪŋ/ n **1** (of skin) color m, tono m; (of fur, plumage) colorido m **2** (food ~) colorante m

colorless, (BrE) **colourless** /'kʌlərləs ‖'kʌləlɪs/ adj incoloro, sin color; ⟨person/life⟩ anodino, gris

color: ~ **scheme** n (combinación f de) colores mpl; ~ **supplement** n suplemento m a todo color or en color

colossal /kə'lɑːsəl ‖kə'lɒsəl/ adj (colloq) colosal

colour etc (BrE) ► COLOR etc

colt /kəʊlt/ n potro m

column /'kɑːləm ‖'kɒləm/ n columna f

columnist /'kɑːləmnəst, 'kɑːləməst ‖'kɒləmnɪst, 'kɒləmɪst/ n columnista mf

coma /'kəʊmə/ n (pl ~s) (Med) coma m

comb¹ /kəʊm/ n (for hair) peine m, peinilla f (AmL), peineta f (Chi)

comb² vt (a) (pass a comb through): to ~ one's hair peinarse (b) (search) ⟨area/field⟩ peinar

combat¹ /kəm'bæt ‖'kɒmbæt/ vt, (BrE) -tt- combatir

combat² /'kɑːmbæt ‖'kɒmbæt/ n combate m

combination /ˌkɑːmbə'neɪʃən ‖ˌkɒmbɪ'neɪʃən/ n combinación f

combine /kəm'baɪn/ vt ⟨elements⟩ combinar; ⟨ingredients⟩ (Culin) mezclar; ⟨efforts⟩ aunar*
■ ~ vi ⟨elements⟩ combinarse; ⟨ingredients⟩ mezclarse; ⟨teams/forces⟩ unirse

combined /kəm'baɪnd/ adj conjunto; our ~ efforts led to success la suma de nuestros esfuerzos nos condujo al éxito

combine harvester /'kɑːmbaɪn 'hɑːrvəstər ‖'kɒmbaɪn 'hɑːvɪstə(r)/ n cosechadora f

combustion /kəm'bʌstʃən/ n combustión f; (before n) ~ **engine** motor m de combustión

come /kʌm/ (past **came**; past p **come**) vi
1 (a) (advance, approach, travel) venir*; ~ **here** ven (aquí); we've ~ **a long way since ...** (made much progress) hemos avanzado mucho desde que ...; can I ~ **with you?** ¿puedo ir contigo?, ¿te puedo acompañar?; **after a while, you'll ~ to a crossroads** al cabo de un rato, llegarás a un cruce; **I'm coming, I won't be a moment** enseguida voy (b) (originate): **where do you ~ from?** ¿de dónde eres?; **it ~s from Italy** viene de Italia (c) (to come and go ir* y venir*; **three o'clock came and went and he still hadn't arrived** pasaron las tres y no llegaba
2 (a) (occur in time, context): **Christmas is coming** ya llega la Navidad; **it came as a complete surprise** fue una sorpresa total; **to take life as it ~s** aceptar la vida tal (y) como se presenta; ~ **what may** pase lo que pase (b) (as prep) para; **I'll**

be tired out ~ Friday estaré agotado para el viernes (c) **coming** pres p: **this coming Friday** este viernes que viene (d) **to come** (in the future) (as adv): **in years to** ~ en años venideros; **a taste of things to** ~ una muestra de lo que nos espera
3 (reach) (+ adv compl) llegar*; **the water came up to our knees** el agua nos llegaba a las rodillas
4 (be gained): **it'll** ~, **just keep practicing** ya te va a salir; sigue practicando; **driving didn't** ~ **easily to me** aprender a manejar or (Esp) conducir no me fue fácil
5 (be available, obtainable) (+ adv compl) venir*; **sugar ~s in half-pound bags** el azúcar viene en paquetes de media libra; **the car ~s with the job** el coche te lo dan con el trabajo
6 (+ adv compl) (a) (in sequence, list, structure): **Cancer ~s between Gemini and Leo** Cáncer está entre Géminis y Leo (b) (in race, competition) llegar*; **to** ~ **first** (in a race) llegar* el primero; (in an exam) quedar or salir* el primero (c) (be ranked) estar*; **my children** ~ **first** primero están mis hijos
7 (a) (become) (+ adj compl): **my dream has** ~ **true** mi sueño se ha hecho realidad (b) (reach certain state) **to** ~ **to + INF** llegar* a + INF; ~ **to think of it ...** ahora que lo pienso ...
8 (in phrases) **come, come!** ¡vamos, vamos!, ¡dale! (CS fam); **how come?** (colloq) ¿cómo?

■ **come across 1** [v + prep + o] (find) encontrar(se)*; (meet) ⟨person⟩ encontrarse* con **2** [v + adv] (communicate, be communicated) ⟨meaning⟩ ser* comprendido; ⟨feelings⟩ transmitirse; **he came across very well in the interview** hizo muy buena impresión en la entrevista

■ **come along** [v + adv] **1** (in imperative) (a) (hurry up): ~ **along, children** ¡vamos, niños!, ¡apúrense, niños! (AmL), ¡órale, niños! (Méx fam) (b) (as encouragement, rebuke) ~ **along!** ¡vamos! **2** (accompany): **can I** ~ **along?** ¿puedo ir (yo) también?; ~ **along with me** ven conmigo, acompáñame **3** (progress) ir*, marchar

■ **come apart** [v + adv] (a) (fall apart) deshacerse* (b) (have detachable parts) desmontarse

■ **come around,** (BrE also) **come round 1** [v + prep + o] (turn) ⟨bend⟩ tomar; ⟨corner⟩ doblar **2** [v + adv] (a) (visit) (esp BrE) venir* (a casa) (b) (recover consciousness) volver* en sí (c) (change mind): **he'll** ~ **around eventually** ya se va a convencer

■ **come away** [v + adv] **1** (leave, depart) **to** ~ **away** (FROM sth) ⟨from meeting/stadium⟩ salir* (DE algo) **2** (become detached) ⟨handle⟩ salirse*

■ **come back** [v + adv] (a) (return) volver* (b) (be remembered): **it's all coming back (to me)** estoy volviendo a recordarlo todo

■ **come down** [v + adv] **1** (a) (descend) bajar (b) (reach) llegar* (c) (collapse) ⟨ceiling/wall⟩ caerse* (d) ⟨plane⟩ aterrizar*; (in accident) caer* **2** (decrease) ⟨price⟩ bajar

■ **come down to** [v + adv + prep + o] (impers) ser* cuestión de

■ **come forward** [v + adv] ⟨witness⟩ presentarse; ⟨volunteer⟩ ofrecerse*; ⟨culprit⟩ darse* a conocer

■ **come in** [v + adv] **1** (enter) entrar; ~ **in!** ¡adelante!

2 (a) «*boat*» llegar* (b) «*tide*» subir
3 (be received) «*applications/reports/donations*» llegar*
4 (play useful role): **where do I ~ in?** ¿cuál es mi papel?; **that's where these boxes ~ in** para eso están las cajas
■ **come in for** [*v + adv + prep + o*] ‹*criticism*› ser* objeto de
■ **come into** [*v + prep + o*] (a) (enter into) entrar en, entrar a (AmL) (b) (inherit) heredar (c) (be, become relevant): **principles don't ~ into it** no es cuestión de principios
■ **come off** **1** (a) (detach itself) «*handle*» soltarse*; «*button*» desprenderse; «*wallpaper*» despegarse*; «*dirt/grease*» quitarse (b) [*v + prep + o*] (fall off) ‹*horse/ motorcycle*› caerse* de
2 [*v + adv*] (fare, acquit oneself): **he always ~s off worst** siempre sale perdiendo
3 [*v + prep + o*] (a) (stop taking) ‹*drug*› dejar de tomar (b) (be serious): **~ off it!** (colloq) ¡anda! ¡no digas tonterías! (fam)
■ **come on** [*v + adv*] **1** (urging sb) (*only in imperative*): **~ on!** ¡vamos! ¡date prisa! *or* (AmL tb) ¡apúrate!, ¡órale! (Méx fam)
2 (a) (begin) «*night/winter*» entrar (b) (begin to operate) «*heating/appliance*» encenderse*, ponerse* en funcionamiento; «*light*» encenderse*
■ **come out**
I [*v + adv* (*+ prep + o*)] **1** (from inside) salir*
2 «*tooth/hair*» caerse*; «*stain*» salir*
II [*v + adv*] **1** (appear) «*sun/stars*» salir*; «*flowers*» florecer*, salir*
2 (be said, spoken) salir*; (be revealed, emphasized) ‹*secret/truth*› revelarse, salir* a la luz
3 (a) (declare oneself) declararse; **to ~ out on strike** declararse en huelga (b) (as being gay) destaparse (fam), declararse abiertamente homosexual
4 «*newspaper/record/product*» salir*
■ **come over** **1** [*v + adv*] (to sb's home) venir* (a casa)
2 [*v + prep + o*] (affect, afflict): **I don't know what came over me** no sé qué me pasó
■ **come round** (BrE) ▶ COME AROUND
■ **come through** **1** «*message/news/supplies*» llegar*; **you're coming through loud and clear** te recibimos muy bien
2 [*v + prep + o*] ‹*ordeal/illness*› salir* de; ‹*war*› sobrevivir a
■ **come to**
I [*v + prep + o*] **1** (a) (reach) llegar* a; **what's the world coming to!** ¡hasta dónde vamos a llegar! (b) (occur) «*idea/answer/name*» ocurrirse; **it came to me in a flash** se me ocurrió de repente (c) (be a question of): **when it ~s to ...** cuando se trata de ...
2 (amount to) «*total*» ascender* a (fml); **it ~s to $15 exactly** son 15 dólares justos; **the plan never came to anything** el plan nunca llegó a nada
II [*v + adv*] (recover consciousness) volver* en sí
■ **come up** [*v + adv*] **1** (a) (ascend, rise) «*person*» subir; «*sun/moon*» salir* (b) (approach) acercarse*; **to ~ up TO sb** acercársele* A algn
2 (a) (occur, arise) «*problem*» surgir*; **something important has just ~ up** acaba de surgir algo importante (b) (be raised, mentioned) «*subject/point*» surgir*; «*name*» ser* mencionado

■ **come up against** [*v + adv + prep + o*] ‹*opposition/prejudice*› enfrentarse a
■ **come up for** [*v + adv + prep + o*]: **the car is coming up for its annual service** dentro de poco hay que hacerle la revisión anual al coche; **I should ~ up for promotion next year** me deberían considerar para un ascenso el año que viene
■ **come up to** [*v + adv + prep + o*] (a) (reach as far as) llegar* a *or* hasta (b) (attain) ‹*standard*› alcanzar*, llegar* a
■ **come up with** [*v + adv + prep + o*] ‹*plan/ scheme*› idear; ‹*proposal*› presentar; ‹*money*› conseguir*; **if you can ~ up with a better idea** si a ti se te ocurre algo mejor

comeback /'kʌmbæk/ *n* **1** (return, revival) vuelta *f*, retorno *m*; **to make a ~** volver* a la escena (*or* a la política *etc*) **2** (redress) (*no pl*): **the trouble is that you have no ~ at all** el problema es que no puedes hacer ninguna reclamación

comedian /kə'miːdiən/ *n* humorista *mf*, cómico, -ca *m,f*

comedy /'kɒmədi ǁ'kɒmədi/ *n* (*pl* **-dies**) (a) (play, film) comedia *f* (b) (comic entertainment) humorismo *m*; (*before n*) ‹*show/program*› humorístico

comet /'kɒmət ǁ'kɒmɪt/ *n* cometa *m*

comfort¹ /'kʌmfərt ǁ'kʌmfət/ *n* **1** (a) (physical, material) comodidad *f*, confort *m* (b) (sth pleasant, luxury) comodidad *f* **2** (mental) consuelo *m*; **to take ~ from sth** consolarse* con algo

comfort² *vt* ‹*child/bereaved person*› consolar*

comfortable /'kʌmftərbəl ǁ'kʌmftəbəl/ *adj* **1** ‹*chair/clothes*› cómodo; ‹*house/room*› confortable; **a ~ lifestyle** una vida desahogada **2** ‹*margin/majority*› amplio, holgado

comfortably /'kʌmftərbli ǁ'kʌmftəbli/ *adv* ‹*lie/sit*› cómodamente; ‹*live/win*› holgadamente

comforter /'kʌmfərtər ǁ'kʌmfətə(r)/ *n* (a) (bedcover) (AmE) edredón *m* (b) (for baby) (BrE) ▶ PACIFIER

comforting /'kʌmfərtɪŋ ǁ'kʌmfətɪŋ/ *adj* ‹*words*› de consuelo; **it's a ~ thought** es reconfortante pensarlo

comic¹ /'kɒmɪk ǁ'kɒmɪk/ *adj* ‹*actor/scene*› cómico; ‹*writer*› humorístico

comic² *n* **1** (comedian) cómico, -ca *m,f*, humorista *mf* **2** (a) (BrE) (book) comic *m*, libro *m* de historietas; (magazine) ▶ COMIC BOOK (b) **comics** *pl* (comic strips) (AmE) tiras *fpl* cómicas, historietas *fpl*, monitos *mpl* (Andes, Méx)

comical /'kɒmɪkəl ǁ'kɒmɪkəl/ *adj* cómico

comic: ~ book *n* (AmE) revista *f* de historietas, tebeo *m* (Esp), revista *f* de chistes (RPl); (for adults) comic *m*; **~ strip** *n* tira *f* cómica, historieta *f*

coming /'kʌmɪŋ/ *adj* (*before n*) ‹*week/year*› próximo; **this ~ Monday** este lunes, el lunes que viene

comma /'kɒmə ǁ'kɒmə/ *n* coma *f*

command¹ /kə'mænd ǁkə'mɑːnd/ *vt* **1** (a) (order) **to ~ sb to + INF** ordenarle A algn QUE (+ *subj*) (b) ‹*army/ship*› estar* al mando de **2** ‹*wealth/resources*› contar* con **3** ‹*respect*› imponer*; ‹*fee*› exigir*; ‹*price*› alcanzar*

command² *n* **1** (a) (order) orden *f* (b) ···⟩

(authority) mando *m*; **under sb's** ~ bajo las órdenes *or* el mando de algn **2** (mastery) dominio *m* **3** (Comput) orden *f*, comando *m*

commandant /'kɑːməndænt ‖'kɒməndænt/ *n* comandante *mf*

commandeer /ˌkɑːmənˈdɪr ‖ˌkɒmənˈdɪə(r)/ *vt* (Mil) requisar

commander /kəˈmændər ‖kəˈmɑːndə(r)/ *n* **(a)** (officer in command) comandante *mf* **(b)** (navy rank) ≈ capitán *m* de fragata

commanding /kəˈmændɪŋ ‖kəˈmɑːndɪŋ/ *adj* **(a)** ‹position› de superioridad; ‹lead› considerable **(b)** ‹presence› que impone; ‹tone› autoritario

commanding officer *n* oficial *mf* al mando

commandment /kəˈmændmənt ‖kəˈmɑːndmənt/ *n* precepto *m*; **the Ten C~s** los diez mandamientos

commando /kəˈmændəʊ ‖kəˈmɑːndəʊ/ *n* (*pl* **-dos** *or* **-does**) comando *m*

commemorate /kəˈmeməreɪt/ *vt* conmemorar

commence /kəˈmens/ *vi* (frml) «session/ celebration» dar* comienzo (frml); «person» comenzar*

■ ~ *vt* (frml) ‹work/discussion› dar* comienzo a (frml)

commend /kəˈmend/ *vt* **1 (a)** (praise) elogiar **(b)** (recommend) recomendar* **2** (frml) (entrust) to ~ **sb/sth TO sb** encomendar(le)* algn/algo A algn

commendable /kəˈmendəbəl/ *adj* loable, encomiable

commendation /ˌkɑːmənˈdeɪʃən ‖ˌkɒmenˈdeɪʃən/ *n* **(a)** (praise) (frml) encomio *m* (frml), elogios *mpl* **(b)** (award) mención *f* de honor, accésit *m*

comment¹ /'kɑːment ‖'kɒment/ *n* **(a)** (remark) comentario *m* **(b)** (reaction) comentarios *mpl*; **no ~** sin comentarios

comment² *vi* to ~ (ON sth) hacer* comentarios (SOBRE algo)

■ ~ *vt* comentar

commentary /'kɑːmənteri ‖'kɒməntəri, -tri/ *n* (*pl* **-ries**) (Rad, Sport, TV) comentarios *mpl*, crónica *f*, (analysis) comentario *m*

commentator /'kɑːmənteɪtər ‖'kɒmənteɪtə(r)/ *n* comentarista *mf*

commerce /'kɑːmərs ‖'kɒmɜːs/ *n* comercio *m*

commercial¹ /kəˈmɜːrʃəl ‖kəˈmɜːʃəl/ *adj* comercial

commercial² *n* spot *m* publicitario, anuncio *m*, aviso *m* (AmL), comercial *m* (AmL)

commercialize /kəˈmɜːrʃəlaɪz ‖kəˈmɜːʃəlaɪz/ *vt* comercializar*

commiserate /kəˈmɪzəreɪt/ *vi*: **I ~d with him about losing his job** le dije cuánto sentía que se hubiera quedado sin trabajo

commiseration /kəˌmɪzəˈreɪʃən/ *n* (often *pl*) conmiseración *f*

commission¹ /kəˈmɪʃən/ *n* **1** (group)

comisión *f* **2** (for sales) comisión *f* **3 (a)** (for music, painting, building) encargo *m*, comisión *f* (esp AmL) **(b)** (office) (Govt) cargo *m*

commission² *vt* **1 (a)** to ~ **sb to + INF** ‹artist/writer/researcher› encargarle* a algn que (+ *subj*) **(b)** ‹painting/novel/study› encargar*, comisionar (esp AmL) **2 (a)** (Mil) nombrar oficial; ~**ed officer** oficial *mf* (del ejército) (*con grado de teniente o superior a teniente*) **(b)** (Naut) ‹ship› poner* en servicio

commissioner /kəˈmɪʃənər ‖kəˈmɪʃənə(r)/ *n* **(a)** (commission member) comisionado, -da *m,f*, miembro *mf* de la comisión **(b)** (of police) (BrE) inspector, -tora *m,f* jefe

commit /kəˈmɪt/ **-tt-** *vt* **1** (perpetrate) ‹crime/ error/sin› cometer **2** (assign) ‹funds/time/ resources› asignar **3** (send): to ~ **sb to an asylum** internar a algn en un manicomio

■ *v refl* to ~ (oneself) TO -ING/+ INF comprometerse (A + INF)

commitment /kəˈmɪtmənt/ *n* **1 (a)** (responsibility) responsabilidad *f*; (obligation) obligación *f* **(b)** (engagement) compromiso *m* **2** (dedication) dedicación *f*

committed /kəˈmɪtəd ‖kəˈmɪtɪd/ *adj* ‹Christian/feminist› comprometido; ‹teacher/ worker› entregado a su trabajo

committee /kəˈmɪti/ *n* (of club, society) comité *m*, comisión *f*; (of parliament) comisión *f*

commodity /kəˈmɑːdəti ‖kəˈmɒdəti/ *n* (*pl* **-ties**) **(a)** (product) artículo *m*, producto *m*, mercadería *f* (AmS) **(b)** (Fin) materia *f* prima

common¹ /'kɑːmən ‖'kɒmən/ *adj* **1 (a)** (widespread, prevalent) común; **the ~ cold** el resfriado común **(b)** (average, normal) ‹soldier› raso; **the ~ people** la gente común y corriente **(c)** (low-class, vulgar) ordinario **2 (a)** (shared, mutual) común **(b)** (public): **it's ~ knowledge** todo el mundo lo sabe

common² *n* **1** (in phrases) **in common** en común; **to have sth in ~ (with sb)** tener* algo en común (con algn); *see also* COMMONS **2** (in UK) terreno perteneciente al municipio

common: ~ **law** *n* derecho *m* consuetudinario; (before *n*) **common-law wife** concubina *f*, conviviente *f* (Chi); **C~ Market** *n* **the C~ Market** el Mercado Común; ~**-or-garden** /'kɑːmənɔːrˈgɑːrdn ‖'kɒmənɔːˈgɑːdn/ *adj* (BrE colloq) vulgar *or* común y corriente

commonplace /'kɑːmənpleɪs ‖'kɒmənpleɪs/ *adj* (ordinary) común; (trite) banal

Commons /'kɑːmənz ‖'kɒmənz/ *n* (in UK) (+ *sing or pl vb*) **the ~** la Cámara de los Comunes

common sense *n* sentido *m* común

Commonwealth /'kɑːmənwelθ ‖'kɒmənwelθ/ *n* **the ~** la *or* el Commonwealth

commotion /kəˈməʊʃən/ *n* (no-*pl*) **(a)** (outrage) conmoción *f*; **to cause (a)** ~ producir* una conmoción **(b)** (noise) alboroto *m*

communal /kəˈmjuːnḷ ‖'kɒmjʊnḷ, kəˈmjuːnḷ/

adj **(a)** ⟨*land/ownership*⟩ comunal; ⟨*kitchen/ bathroom*⟩ común; ⟨*life*⟩ comunitario **(b)** (between groups) ⟨*violence*⟩ interno

commune /'kɑːmjuːn ‖'kɒmjuːn/ *n* comuna *f*

communicate /kə'mjuːnɪkeɪt/ *vi* comunicarse*
■ ~ *vt* comunicar*

communication /kə,mjuːnə'keɪʃən ‖kə,mjuːnɪ'keɪʃən/ *n* **1** (act) comunicación *f* **2** **communications** *pl* comunicaciones *fpl*

communicative /kə'mjuːnəkeɪtɪv ‖kə'mjuːnɪkətɪv/ *adj* comunicativo

communion /kə'mjuːnjən/ *n* **1** (Holy C~) la Santa *or* Sagrada Comunión **2** (exchange of ideas, fellowship) (frml) comunión *f*

communism, Communism /'kɑːmjənɪzəm ‖'kɒmjʊnɪzəm/ *n* comunismo *m*

communist¹, Communist /'kɑːmjənəst ‖'kɒmjʊnɪst/ *adj* comunista

communist², Communist *n* comunista *mf*

community /kə'mjuːnəti/ *n* (*pl* **-ties**) comunidad *f*; **the city's black ~** la población *or* comunidad negra de la ciudad

community: ~ **center**, (BrE) ~ **centre** *n* centro *m* social; ~ **chest** *n* (in US) *fondos reunidos voluntariamente por la comunidad, destinados a beneficencia y bienestar social*; ~ **service** trabajo *m* comunitario ⟨*prestado en lugar de cumplir una pena de prisión*⟩

commute /kə'mjuːt/ *vi* viajar todos los días ⟨*entre el lugar de residencia y el de trabajo*⟩
■ ~ *vt* ⟨*sentence/punishment*⟩ conmutar

commuter /kə'mjuːtər ‖kə'mjuːtə(r)/ *n*: *persona que viaja diariamente una distancia considerable entre su lugar de residencia y el de trabajo*

compact¹ /kəm'pækt/ *adj* compacto

compact² /'kɑːmpækt ‖'kɒmpækt/ *n* **1** (**powder**) ~ polvera *f* **2** (agreement) (frml) pacto *m*

compact disc, compact disk /'kɑːmpækt ‖'kɒmpækt/ *n* disco *m* compacto, compact-disc *m*; (*before n*) ~ ~ **player** (reproductor *m* de) compact-disc *m*

companion /kəm'pænjən/ *n* compañero, -ra *m,f*

companionship /kəm'pænjənʃɪp/ *n* compañía *f*

company /'kʌmpəni/ *n* (*pl* **-nies**) *n* **1** (companionship, companions) compañía *f*; **to keep sb ~** hacerle* compañía a algn; **to part ~** separarse; **she's excellent ~** es muy agradable (*or* divertido *etc*) estar con ella; **we've got ~** tenemos visita **2** (Busn) compañía *f*, empresa *f*; (*before n*) ⟨*car*⟩ de la compañía *or* empresa **3** **(a)** (Theat) compañía *f* **(b)** (Mil) compañía *f* **(c)** (Naut) ship's ~ tripulación *f*, dotación *f*

comparable /'kɑːmpərəbəl ‖'kɒmpərəbəl/ *adj* comparable

comparative¹ /kəm'pærətɪv/ *adj* relativo; ⟨*literature/linguistics*⟩ comparado; ⟨*analysis/ study*⟩ comparativo

comparative² *n* (Ling) comparativo *m*

compare /kəm'per ‖kəm'peə(r)/ *vt* **(a)** (make comparison between) comparar; **to ~ sth/sb TO** *o*

WITH sth/sb comparar algo/a algn CON algo/algn **(b)** (liken) **to ~ sth/sb TO sth/sb** comparar algo/a algn CON *or* A algo/algn
■ ~ *vi*: **how do the two models ~ for speed?** en cuanto a velocidad ¿qué diferencia hay entre los dos modelos?; **this novel ~s favorably with the previous one** esta novela no desmerece de la anterior

comparison /kəm'pærəsən ‖kəm'pærɪsən/ *n* comparación *f*

compartment /kəm'pɑːtmənt ‖kəm'pɑːtmənt/ *n* **(a)** (of bag, desk, refrigerator) compartimento *m*, compartimiento *m* **(b)** (in train) (BrE Rail) compartimento *m*, compartimiento *m*

compass /'kʌmpəs/ *n* **(a)** (magnetic ~) brújula *f* **(b)** (Math) (*often pl*) compás *m*

compassion /kəm'pæʃən/ *n* compasión *f*

compassionate /kəm'pæʃənət/ *adj* compasivo

compatible /kəm'pætəbəl/ *adj* **(a)** ⟨*people/ ideas/principles*⟩ compatible **(b)** (Comput) compatible; **an IBM ~ computer** una computadora *or* (Esp tb) un ordenador compatible con IBM

compel /kəm'pel/ *vt* **-ll-** **to ~ sb to + INF** obligar* a algn A + INF

compelling /kəm'pelɪŋ/ *adj* ⟨*argument*⟩ convincente; ⟨*book*⟩ absorbente

compendium /kəm'pendiəm/ *n* (*pl* **-diums** *or* **-dia** /-dɪə/) (BrE) **(a)** (book) compendio *m* **(b)** (of games) juegos *mpl* reunidos

compensate /'kɑːmpənseɪt ‖'kɒmpenseɪt/ *vt* indemnizar*, compensar; **to ~ sb FOR sth** indemnizar* *or* compensar a algn POR algo
■ ~ *vi* **to ~ FOR sth** compensar algo

compensation /'kɑːmpən'seɪʃən ‖,kɒmpen'seɪʃən/ *n* **(a)** (recompense) indemnización *f*, compensación *f*; **I received $20,000 as** *o* **in ~ for the damage** me dieron 20.000 dólares de indemnización *or* en compensación por los daños **(b)** (remuneration) (AmE) remuneración *f*

compete /kəm'piːt/ *vi* competir*; **to ~ FOR sth** competir* POR algo

competence /'kɑːmpətəns ‖'kɒmpɪtəns/ *n* competencia *f*

competent /'kɑːmpətənt ‖'kɒmpɪtənt/ *adj* competente

competition /'kɑːmpə'tɪʃən ‖,kɒmpə'tɪʃən/ *n* **1** **(a)** (competing) competencia *f*; **to be in ~ with sb/sth** competir* con algn/algo **(b)** (opposition) competencia *f* **2** (contest) concurso *m*; (Sport) competencia *f* (AmL), competición *f* (Esp)

competitive /kəm'petətɪv ‖kəm'petɪtɪv/ *adj* competitivo

competitiveness /kəm'petətɪvnəs ‖kəm'petɪtɪvnɪs/ *n* **(a)** (of business, economy) competitividad *f* **(b)** (of person) espíritu *m* competitivo

competitor /kəm'petətər ‖kəm'petɪtə(r)/ *n* **(a)** (contestant) participante *mf*, concursante *mf* **(b)** (rival) (Busn) competidor, -dora *m,f*, rival *mf*; (Sport) contrincante *mf*

compile /kəm'paɪl/ *vt* **(a)** ⟨*dictionary/index*⟩ compilar **(b)** ⟨*information*⟩ recopilar, reunir*

complacent /kəm'pleɪsnt/ *adj* ⟨*person*⟩ satisfecho de sí mismo; ⟨*attitude*⟩ displicente

complain /kəm'pleɪn/ *vi/t* quejarse

complaint /kəm'pleɪnt/ *n* **(a)** (grievance) queja *f*, reclamo *m* (AmL); **to make a ~** quejarse **(b)** (ailment) dolencia *f* (frml)

complement¹ /'kɑːmpləmənt ‖'kɒmplɪmənt/ *n* [1] **~** (TO sth) complemento *m* (DE algo) [2] (full number): **the orchestra had the full ~ of strings** la orquesta contaba con una sección de cuerdas completa

complement² *vt* complementar

complementary /'kɑːmplə'mentri ‖,kɒmplɪ'mentri/ *adj* complementario

complete¹ /kəm'pliːt/ *adj* [1] **(a)** (entire) completo **(b)** (finished) terminado, concluido [2] (thorough, absolute) (*as intensifier*) total, completo; **it came as a ~ surprise** fue una auténtica sorpresa

complete² *vt* **(a)** (finish) ⟨building/education⟩ acabar, terminar; ⟨sentence⟩ cumplir; ⟨investigations⟩ completar, concluir* **(b)** (make whole) ⟨set/collection⟩ completar **(c)** (fill in) (frml) ⟨form⟩ llenar, rellenar

completely /kəm'pliːtli/ *adv* completamente, totalmente

completion /kəm'pliːʃən/ *n* finalización *f*, terminación *f*

complex¹ /'kɑːmpleks ‖'kɒmpleks/ *adj* complejo

complex² *n* [1] (buildings) complejo *m* [2] (Psych) complejo *m*

complexion /kəm'plekʃən/ *n* cutis *m*; (in terms of color) tez *f*

complexity /kəm'pleksəti/ *n* (*pl* **-ties**) complejidad *f*

complicate /'kɑːmpləkeɪt ‖'kɒmplɪkeɪt/ *vt* complicar*

complicated /'kɑːmpləkeɪtəd ‖'kɒmplɪkeɪtɪd/ *adj* complicado

complication /'kɑːmplə'keɪʃən ‖,kɒmplɪ'keɪʃən/ *n* complicación *f*; **~s set in** (Med) surgieron complicaciones

compliment¹ /'kɑːmpləmənt ‖'kɒmplɪmənt/ *n* **(a)** (expression of praise) cumplido *m*, halago *m*; **to pay sb a ~** hacerle* un cumplido a algn, halagar* a algn **(b) compliments** *pl* (best wishes) saludos *mpl*; **with the ~s of the management** gentileza de la casa

compliment² *vt* **to ~ sb** (ON sth) felicitar a algn (POR algo)

complimentary /'kɑːmplə'mentəri ‖,kɒmplɪ'mentri/ *adj* **(a)** (flattering) elogioso, halagüeño **(b)** (free) ⟨copy⟩ de obsequio *or* regalo; **~ ticket** invitación *f*

comply /kəm'plaɪ/ *vi* **-plies, -plying, -plied**: **to ~ with a request/an order** acceder a una solicitud/cumplir una orden

component¹ /kəm'pəʊnənt/ *n* componente *m*; (Auto) pieza *f*; (Electron) componente *m*

component² *adj* componente; ⟨element⟩ constituyente; **~ part** componente *m*

compose /kəm'pəʊz/ *vt* [1] (constitute) (*usu pass*) **to be ~d of OR sth** estar* compuesto DE algo [2] ⟨music⟩ componer*; ⟨letter⟩ redactar [3] (calm, control) (liter): **to ~ oneself** serenarse, recobrar la compostura

composed /kəm'pəʊzd/ *adj* sereno

composer /kəm'pəʊzər ‖kəm'pəʊzə(r)/ *n* compositor, -tora *m,f*

composition /'kɑːmpə'zɪʃən ‖,kɒmpə'zɪʃən/ *n* composición *f*

compost /'kɑːmpəʊst ‖'kɒmpɒst/ *n* abono *m* orgánico

composure /kəm'pəʊʒər ‖kəm'pəʊʒə(r)/ *n* compostura *f*

compound¹ /'kɑːmpaʊnd ‖'kɒmpaʊnd/ *adj* ⟨number/interest⟩ compuesto

compound² /'kɑːmpaʊnd ‖'kɒmpaʊnd/ *n* [1] **(a)** (Chem) compuesto *m* **(b)** (word) palabra *f* compuesta [2] (residence) complejo *m* habitacional; (for prisoners etc) barracones *mpl*

compound³ /kəm'paʊnd ‖kəm'paʊnd/ *vt* ⟨problem⟩ agravar; ⟨risk/difficulties⟩ acrecentar*

comprehend /'kɑːmprɪ'hend ‖,kɒmprɪ'hend/ *vt* comprender

comprehension /'kɑːmprɪ'hentʃən ‖,kɒmprɪ'henʃən/ *n* **(a)** (understanding) comprensión *f* **(b)** (school exercise) (BrE) ejercicio *m* de comprensión

comprehensive /'kɑːmprɪ'hensɪv ‖,kɒmprɪ'hensɪv/ *adj* **(a)** ⟨survey/report⟩ exhaustivo, global; ⟨view⟩ integral, de conjunto; ⟨list/range⟩ completo; ⟨insurance/cover⟩ contra todo riesgo **(b)** (Educ) (in UK) relativo al sistema educativo en el cual no se separa a los alumnos según su nivel de aptitud

comprehensive (school) *n* (in UK) instituto de segunda enseñanza para alumnos de cualquier nivel de aptitud

compress¹ /kəm'pres/ *vt* comprimir

compress² /'kɑːmpres ‖'kɒmpres/ *n* compresa *f*

comprise /kəm'praɪz/ *vt* **(a)** (consist of) comprender **(b)** (constitute, make up) componer*

compromise¹ /'kɑːmprəmaɪz ‖'kɒmprəmaɪz/ *n* acuerdo *m* mutuo, arreglo *m*, compromiso *m*

compromise² *vi* transigir*, transar (AmL) ■ **~** *vt* **(a)** (discredit) comprometer; **to ~ oneself** ponerse* en una situación comprometida **(b)** (endanger) comprometer

compromising /'kɑːmprəmaɪzɪŋ ‖'kɒmprəmaɪzɪŋ/ *adj* ⟨evidence⟩ comprometedor; ⟨situation⟩ comprometido

compulsion /kəm'pʌlʃən/ *n* **(a)** (force, duress) coacción *f* **(b)** (obsession) compulsión *f*

compulsive /kəm'pʌlsɪv/ *adj* **(a)** (compelling): **the book is ~ reading** es uno de esos libros que se empiezan y no se pueden dejar **(b)** (obsessive) ⟨behavior⟩ compulsivo; **he's a ~ eater/liar** come/miente por compulsión

compulsory /kəm'pʌlsəri/ *adj* ⟨attendance⟩ obligatorio; ⟨retirement⟩ forzoso; **~ education** enseñanza *f* obligatoria

computer /kəm'pjuːtər ‖kəm'pjuːtə(r)/ *n* computadora *f* (esp AmL), computador *m* (esp AmL), ordenador *m* (Esp); (before *n*) ⟨society/age/revolution⟩ de la informática; ⟨program/game⟩ de computadora (*or* ordenador *etc*)

computer: ~ crime *n* delito *m* informático; **~ dating** *n* citas *fpl* por computadora *or* (Esp tb) ordenador

computerize /kəm'pju:təraɪz/ *vt* computarizar*, computerizar*; ⟨company/ department⟩ informatizar*

computer: ～-literate *adj* capacitado para operar un ordenador; **～ programmer** *n* programador, -dora *m,f*; **～ programming** *n* programación *f*; **～ science** *n* informática *f*; **～ studies** *n* informática *f*, computación *f*

computing /kəm'pju:tɪŋ/ *n* informática *f*, computación *f*

comrade /'kɒmræd ‖'kɒmreɪd/ *n* compañero, -ra *m,f*, camarada *mf*

con¹ /kɑːn ‖kɒn/ *n* **1** (fraud) (colloq) timo *m* (fam), estafa *f* **2** (convict) (sl) preso, -sa *m,f* **3** (colloq) (objection) contra *m; see also* PRO 2

con² *vt* **-nn-** (colloq) timar (fam), estafar

concave /'kɑːnkeɪv ‖'kɒŋkeɪv/ *adj* cóncavo

conceal /kən'si:l/ *vt* ⟨object/facts⟩ ocultar; ⟨emotions⟩ disimular; **to ～ sth FROM sb** ocultar(le) algo A algn

concede /kən'si:d/ *vt* **(a)** (admit) reconocer* **(b)** (allow) ⟨right/privilege⟩ conceder **(c)** (give away) ⟨game/penalty⟩ conceder

conceit /kən'si:t/ *n* engreimiento *m*, presunción *f*

conceited /kən'si:təd ‖kən'si:tɪd/ *adj* engreído, presuntuoso

conceivable /kən'si:vəbəl/ *adj* imaginable

conceive /kən'si:v/ *vt* **1** (a) (devise) ⟨plan⟩ concebir* **(b)** (imagine) imaginar; (consider) considerar **2** ⟨child⟩ concebir*
■ **～** *vi* concebir*

concentrate¹ /'kɑːnsəntreɪt ‖'kɒnsəntreɪt/ *vt* **to ～ sth (ON sth)** concentrar algo (EN algo)
■ **～** *vi* ⟨person⟩ concentrarse; ⟨talks⟩ centrarse; **～ on getting this finished** concéntrate en terminar esto

concentrate² *n* concentrado *m*

concentrated /'kɑːnsəntreɪtəd ‖'kɒnsəntreɪtɪd/ *adj* **(a)** ⟨effort⟩ intenso y continuado **(b)** ⟨solution/juice⟩ concentrado

concentration /'kɑːnsən'treɪʃən ‖,kɒnsən'treɪʃən/ *n* concentración *f*

concentration camp *n* campo *m* de concentración

concept /'kɑːnsept ‖'kɒnsept/ *n* concepto *m*

conception /kən'sepʃən/ *n* **1** (idea) noción *f* **2** (of baby, plan) concepción *f*

concern¹ /kən'sɜːrn ‖kən'sɜːn/ *n* **1** (business, affair) asunto *m*; **that's no ～ of yours** eso no es asunto tuyo **2** (a) (anxiety) preocupación *f*, inquietud *f* **(b)** (interest) **～ FOR sb/sth** interés *m* POR algn/algo; **to be of ～ to sb** importarle a algn **3** (firm) empresa *f*; ▶ GOING²

concern² *vt* **1** (affect, involve) concernir*, incumbir; **to be ～ed WITH sth** ocuparse DE algo; **as far as I'm ～ed** en lo que a mí respecta, por mi parte; **to whom it may ～** (frml) a quien corresponda (frml) **2** (a) (interest) interesar **(b)** (worry, bother) preocupar, inquietar **3** (relate to): **item one ～s the new office** el primer punto trata de la nueva oficina

concerned /kən'sɜːrnd ‖kən'sɜːnd/ *adj* ⟨person⟩ preocupado; ⟨look⟩ de preocupación; **to be ～ ABOUT/FOR sb/sth** estar* preocupado POR algn/algo

concerning /kən'sɜːrnɪŋ ‖kən'sɜːnɪŋ/ *prep* sobre, acerca de, con respecto a

concert¹ /'kɑːnsərt ‖'kɒnsət/ *n* concierto *m*; **in ～** en vivo, en concierto; ⟨before n⟩ **～ hall** sala *f* de conciertos, auditorio *m*

concert² /kən'sɜːrt ‖kən'sɜːt/ *vt* (frml) concertar*, coordinar; **we made a ～ed effort to …** coordinamos *or* concertamos nuestros esfuerzos para …

concerto /kən'tʃertəʊ ‖kən'tʃɜːtəʊ, kən'tʃeətəʊ/ *n* (*pl* **-tos** *or* **-ti** /-ti/) concierto *m*

concession /kən'seʃən/ *n* concesión *f*

conciliation /kən'sɪli'eɪʃən/ *n* conciliación *f*

conciliatory /kən'sɪliətɔːri ‖kən'sɪliətəri/ *adj* conciliador, conciliatorio

concise /kən'saɪs/ *adj* conciso

conclude /kən'klu:d/ *vt* **1** (a) (end) concluir*, finalizar* **(b)** (settle) ⟨deal⟩ cerrar*; ⟨agreement⟩ llegar* a; ⟨treaty⟩ firmar; ⟨alliance⟩ pactar **2** (infer) concluir* (frml)
■ **～** *vi* concluir* (frml), terminar

conclusion /kən'klu:ʒən/ *n* **1** (end) conclusión *f*; **in ～** (as linker) para concluir **2** (decision, judgment) conclusión *f*; **to come to o reach a ～** llegar* a una conclusión; **to jump to ～s** precipitarse (a sacar conclusiones)

conclusive /kən'klu:sɪv/ *adj* ⟨evidence/argument⟩ concluyente; ⟨victory⟩ decisivo

concoct /kən'kɑːkt ‖kən'kɒkt/ *vt* ⟨meal/drink⟩ preparar; ⟨excuse/story⟩ inventarse; ⟨plan⟩ tramar

concrete¹ /kɑːn'kri:t, 'kɑːnkri:t ‖'kɒnkri:t/ *adj* concreto

concrete² /'kɑːnkri:t ‖'kɒnkri:t/ *n* hormigón *m*, concreto *m* (AmL)

concur /kən'kɜːr ‖kən'kɜː(r)/ *vi* **-rr-** (frml) **to ～ (WITH sb/sth)** coincidir (CON algn/algo)

concuss /kən'kʌs/ *vt* (*usu pass*): **to be ～ed** sufrir una conmoción (cerebral) *or* una concusión

concussion /kən'kʌʃən/ *n* conmoción *f* cerebral, concusión *f*

condemn /kən'dem/ *vt* **1** (a) (sentence) condenar **(b)** (censure) condenar **2** (a) (declare unusable) ⟨building⟩ declarar ruinoso **(b)** (in US: convert to public use) ⟨building⟩ expropiar (*por causa de utilidad pública*)

condemnation /'kɑːndem'neɪʃən ‖,kɒndem'neɪʃən/ *n* condena *f*

condensation /'kɑːnden'seɪʃən ‖,kɒnden'seɪʃən/ *n* **(a)** (process) condensación *f* **(b)** (on windows etc) vapor *m*, vaho *m*

condense /kən'dens/ *vt* **1** (abridge) ⟨book/article⟩ condensar **2** (Chem) condensar

condensed /kən'denst/ *adj* condensado; **～ milk** leche *f* condensada

condescend /'kɑːndɪr'send ‖,kɒndɪ'send/ *vi* **to ～ to + INF** dignarse *or* condescender* A + INF

condescending /'kɑːndɪr'sendɪŋ ‖,kɒndɪ'sendɪŋ/ *adj* ⟨tone/smile⟩ condescendiente

condiment /'kɑːndəmənt ‖'kɒndɪmənt/ *n* (seasoning) condimento *m*, aliño *m*; (relish) salsa *f* (*para condimentar*)

condition¹ /kən'dɪʃən/ *n* **1** (stipulation, requirement) condición *f*; **on ～ that** con la condición de que **2** (a) (state) (*no pl*) estado *m*, ···❖

condiciones *fpl*; **in good ~ en buen estado (b)** (state of fitness): **to be in/out of ~ estar*/no estar*** en forma **(c)** (Med) afección *f* (frml), enfermedad *f* **3 conditions** *pl* **(a)** (circumstances) condiciones *fpl*; **working/housing ~s** condiciones de trabajo/vivienda **(b)** (Meteo): **weather ~s are good** el estado del tiempo es bueno

condition² *vt* **(a)** (influence, determine) condicionar **(b)** ⟨hair⟩ acondicionar

conditional /kən'dɪʃnəl ‖ kən'dɪʃənl/ *adj* **(a)** (provisional) condicional **(b)** (Ling) condicional

conditioner /kən'dɪʃnər ‖ kən'dɪʃnə(r)/ *n* (hair ~) acondicionador *m*, enjuague *m* (AmL), suavizante *m* (Esp), bálsamo *m* (Chi); (fabric ~) suavizante *m*

conditioning /kən'dɪʃnɪŋ/ *n* (Psych) condicionamiento *m*

condo /'kɑːndəʊ ‖ 'kɒndəʊ/ *n* (AmE colloq) ▶ CONDOMINIUM

condolences /kən'dəʊlənsɪz/ *pl n* (frml) condolencias *fpl* (frml)

condom /'kɑːndəm ‖ 'kɒndɒm/ *n* preservativo *m*, condón *m*

condominium /ˌkɑːndə'mɪniəm ‖ ˌkɒndə'mɪniəm/ *n* (pl ~s) (AmE) apartamento *m*, piso *m* (Esp) (*en régimen de propiedad horizontal*)

condone /kən'dəʊn/ *vt* aprobar*

conduct¹ /'kɑːndʌkt ‖ 'kɒndʌkt/ *n* conducta *f*

conduct² /kən'dʌkt/ *vt* **(a)** ⟨inquiry/experiment/business⟩ llevar a cabo, realizar*; ⟨conversation⟩ mantener* **(b)** (Mus) dirigir* **(c)** ⟨visitor/tour/party⟩ guiar* **(d)** ⟨heat/electricity⟩ conducir*

conductor /kən'dʌktər ‖ kən'dʌktə(r)/ *n* **1** (Mus) director, -tora *m,f* (de orquesta) **2** (on bus) cobrador, -dora *m,f*, guarda *mf* (RPl); (on train) (AmE) cobrador, -dora *m,f* **3** (Elec, Phys) conductor *m*

cone /kəʊn/ *n* **(a)** (Auto, Math) cono *m* **(b)** (ice-cream ~) cucurucho *m or* barquillo *m or* (Ven) barquilla *f or* (Col) cono *m*

confectionery /kən'fekʃəneri ‖ kən'fekʃənəri/ *n* productos *mpl* de confitería

confer /kən'fɜːr ‖ kən'fɜː(r)/ **-rr-** *vt* (bestow) conceder, conferir* (frml); **to ~ sth ON** *o* **UPON sb/sth** concederle *or* (frml) conferirle* algo A algn/algo
■ ~ *vi* (discuss) consultar

conference /'kɑːnfrəns ‖ 'kɒnfərəns/ *n* **(a)** (large assembly, convention) congreso *m*, conferencia *f*; (*before n*) **~ center** *o* (BrE) **centre** centro *m* de conferencias **(b)** (meeting, discussion) conferencia *f*; (*before n*) **~ room** sala *f* de juntas

confess /kən'fes/ *vt* confesar*
■ ~ *vi* **(a)** (admit) confesar* **(b)** (Relig) confesarse*

confession /kən'feʃən/ *n* **(a)** (statement) confesión *f* **(b)** (Relig) confesión *f*

confetti /kən'feti/ *n* confeti *m or* (Chi) chaya *f or* (RPl) papel *m* picado *or* (Ven) papelillos *mpl*

confide /kən'faɪd/ *vi* (tell secrets) **to ~ IN sb** confiarse* A algn
■ ~ *vt* **to ~ sth TO sb** confiarle* algo A algn

confidence /'kɑːnfədəns ‖ 'kɒnfɪdəns/ *n* **1** **(a)** (trust, faith) confianza *f* **(b)** (self-confidence) confianza *f* en sí mismo **2** (confidentiality): **he took her into his ~** se confió a ella; **in ~** en confianza

confidence game *n* (AmE), **confidence trick** *n* estafa *f*, timo *m* (fam)

confident /'kɑːnfədənt ‖ 'kɒnfɪdənt/ *adj* **(a)** (sure) ⟨statement/forecast⟩ hecho con confianza; **to be ~ OF sth** confiar* EN algo **(b)** (self-confident) ⟨person⟩ seguro de sí mismo

confidential /ˌkɑːnfə'dentʃəl ‖ ˌkɒnfɪ'denʃəl/ *adj* confidencial

confidentiality /ˌkɑːnfə'dentʃi'æləti ‖ ˌkɒnfɪdenʃɪ'æləti/ *n* confidencialidad *f*

configure /kən'fɪgjər/ *vt* configurar

confine /kən'faɪn/ *vt* **(a)** (limit, restrict) **to ~ sth TO sth** limitar algo A algo **(b)** (shut in, imprison) ⟨person⟩ confinar, recluir*; ⟨animal⟩ encerrar*

confined /kən'faɪnd/ *adj* ⟨space⟩ limitado

confinement /kən'faɪnmənt/ *n* **(a)** (act, state) reclusión *f*, confinamiento *m* **(b)** (in childbirth) parto *m*

confines /'kɑːnfaɪnz/ *pl n* confines *mpl*

confirm /kən'fɜːrm ‖ kən'fɜːm/ *vt* **1** **(a)** (substantiate) ⟨report/reservation⟩ confirmar **(b)** **confirmed** *past p* ⟨bachelor/liar⟩ empedernido **2** (Relig) confirmar

confirmation /ˌkɑːnfər'meɪʃən ‖ ˌkɒnfə'meɪʃən/ *n* **1** **(a)** (substantiation) confirmación *f* **(b)** (ratification) (frml) ratificación *f* **2** (Relig) confirmación *f*

confiscate /'kɑːnfəskeɪt ‖ 'kɒnfɪskeɪt/ *vt* confiscar*

conflict¹ /'kɑːnflɪkt ‖ 'kɒnflɪkt/ *n* conflicto *m*

conflict² /kən'flɪkt/ *vi* discrepar

conflicting /kən'flɪktɪŋ/ *adj* ⟨interests⟩ opuesto; ⟨views/accounts/emotions⟩ contradictorio

conform /kən'fɔːrm ‖ kən'fɔːm/ *vi* **(a)** (be in accordance) **to ~ TO** *o* **WITH sth** ajustarse A *or* cumplir CON algo **(b)** (act in a conformist way) ser* conformista; **he usually ~s to their wishes** por lo general se aviene a sus deseos

confound /kən'faʊnd/ *vt* **(a)** (perplex) ⟨person⟩ confundir **(b)** (thwart) ⟨atttempt⟩ frustrar

confront /kən'frʌnt/ *vt* **(a)** (come face to face with) ⟨danger/problem⟩ afrontar, enfrentar; **police were ~ed by a group of demonstrators** la policía se vio enfrentada a un grupo de manifestantes **(b)** (face up to) ⟨enemy/fear/crisis⟩ hacer* frente a

confrontation /ˌkɑːnfrʌn'teɪʃən ‖ ˌkɒnfrʌn'teɪʃən/ *n* **(a)** (conflict) enfrentamiento *m*, confrontación *f* **(b)** (encounter) confrontación *f*

confuse /kən'fjuːz/ *vt* **1** **(a)** (bewilder) confundir **(b)** (blur) ⟨situation⟩ complicar* **2** (mix up, be unable to distinguish) ⟨ideas/sounds⟩ confundir

confused /kən'fjuːzd/ *adj* **(a)** (perplexed) confundido; **to get ~** confundirse **(b)** (unclear) ⟨argument⟩ confuso

confusing /kənˈfjuːzɪŋ/ adj confuso

confusion /kənˈfjuːʒən/ n (a) (turmoil) confusión f (b) (disorder) desorden m

congeal /kənˈdʒiːl/ vi «fat» solidificarse*; ∼ed blood sangre f coagulada

congested /kənˈdʒestəd ‖kənˈdʒestɪd/ adj (a) (with traffic) congestionado; (with people) abarrotado de gente (b) (Med) congestionado

congestion /kənˈdʒestʃən/ n (a) (with traffic) congestión f; (with people) abarrotamiento m (b) (Med) congestión f

Congo /ˈkɒŋɡəʊ ‖ˈkɒŋɡəʊ/ n el Congo

congratulate /kənˈɡrætʃəleɪt ‖kənˈɡrætjʊleɪt/ vt felicitar; to ∼ sb ON sth/-ING felicitar or darle* la enhorabuena a algn POR algo/+ INF

congratulation /kənˌɡrætʃəˈleɪʃən ‖kənˌɡrætjʊˈleɪʃən/ n (a) (praise) felicitación f (b) **congratulations** pl enhorabuena f, felicitaciones fpl; (as interj) ∼s! ¡enhorabuena!, ¡felicitaciones! (AmL)

congregate /ˈkɒŋɡrɪɡeɪt ‖ˈkɒŋɡrɪɡeɪt/ vi congregarse*

congregation /ˈkɒŋɡrɪˈɡeɪʃən ‖ˌkɒŋɡrɪˈɡeɪʃən/ n (Relig) (attending service) fieles mpl; (parishioners) feligreses mpl

congress /ˈkɒŋɡrəs ‖ˈkɒŋɡres/ n (a) (conference) congreso m (b) **Congress** (in US) el Congreso (de los Estados Unidos)

congress: ∼man /ˈkɒŋɡrəsmən ‖ˈkɒŋɡresmən/ n (pl -men /-mən/) (in US) miembro m del Congreso; **∼woman** n (in US) miembro f del Congreso

conifer /ˈkɒnəfər ‖ˈkɒnɪfə(r)/ n conífera f

conjecture¹ /kənˈdʒektʃər ‖kənˈdʒektʃə(r)/ n: it's pure ∼ no son más que conjeturas

conjecture² vt/i (frml) conjeturar

conjugal /ˈkɒndʒəɡəl ‖ˈkɒndʒʊɡəl/ adj (frml) conyugal

conjunctivitis /kənˈdʒʌŋktɪˈvaɪtəs ‖kənˌdʒʌŋktɪˈvaɪtɪs/ n conjuntivitis f

conjurer /ˈkɒndʒərər ‖ˈkʌndʒərə(r)/ n prestidigitador, -dora m,f, mago, -ga m,f

conjure up /ˈkɒndʒər ‖ˈkʌndʒə(r)/ [v + o + adv, v + adv + o] (evoke) evocar*; it ∼s ∼ images of ... hace pensar en ...

conjuror n ▶ CONJURER

con man n estafador m, timador m

Conn = Connecticut

connect /kəˈnekt/ vt ⊡ (a) (attach) to ∼ sth (TO sth) conectar algo (A algo) (b) (link together) «rooms/buildings» comunicar*; «towns» conectar (c) (Telec): I'm trying to ∼ you un momento que lo comunico or (Esp) le pongo con el número (d) «phone/gas» conectar
⊡ (associate) «people/ideas/events» relacionar
■ ∼ vi ⊡ (a) (be joined together) «rooms» comunicarse*; «pipes» empalmar (b) (be fitted) to ∼ (TO sth) estar* conectado (a algo)
⊡ (Transp) to ∼ WITH sth «train/flight» enlazar* CON algo, conectar CON algo (AmL)
■ **connect up** ⊡ [v + o + adv, v + adv + o] «wires/apparatus» conectar
⊡ [v + adv] «wires» conectarse; it all ∼s up todo está relacionado

connected /kəˈnektəd ‖kəˈnektɪd/ adj «ideas/events» relacionado; to be ∼ed WITH sth estar* relacionado CON algo

connection /kəˈnekʃən/ n ⊡ (a) (link) ∼ (WITH sth) enlace m or conexión f (CON algo) (b) (Elec) conexión f ⊡ (Transp) ∼ (WITH sth) conexión f or enlace m (CON algo) ⊡ (relation) relación f or conexión f ⊡ **connections** pl (links, ties) lazos mpl; (influential people) contactos mpl, conexiones fpl (AmL)

connive /kəˈnaɪv/ vi (a) (plot) to ∼ (WITH sb) actuar* en complicidad (CON algn) (b) (cooperate) to ∼ AT sth ser* cómplice EN algo

connoisseur /ˈkɒnəˈsɜːr ‖ˌkɒnəˈsɜː(r)/ n entendido, -da m,f

connotation /ˈkɒnəˈteɪʃən ‖ˌkɒnəˈteɪʃən/ n connotación f

conquer /ˈkɒŋkər ‖ˈkɒŋkə(r)/ vt «country/mountain» conquistar; «enemy/fear» vencer

conqueror /ˈkɒŋkərər ‖ˈkɒŋkərə(r)/ n conquistador, -dora m,f

conquest /ˈkɒŋkwest ‖ˈkɒŋkwest/ n conquista f

conscience /ˈkɒntʃəns ‖ˈkɒnʃəns/ n conciencia f; to have a clear ∼ tener* la conciencia tranquila

conscientious /ˈkɒntʃiˈentʃəs ‖ˌkɒnʃiˈenʃəs/ adj «work» concienzudo; «student» aplicado

conscientious objector n /əbˈdʒektər ‖əbˈdʒektə(r)/ objetor, -tora m,f de conciencia

conscious /ˈkɒntʃəs ‖ˈkɒnʃəs/ adj ⊡ (a) (awake, alert) (no comp) consciente (b) (aware) (pred) to be ∼ OF sth ser* or (Chi, Méx tb) estar* consciente DE algo ⊡ (deliberate) «decision» deliberado; she made a ∼ effort to be nice se esforzó por ser amable

consciousness /ˈkɒntʃəsnəs ‖ˈkɒnʃəsnɪs/ n (a) (state of being awake, alert) conocimiento m (b) (awareness) conciencia f

conscript¹ /ˈkɒnskrɪpt ‖ˈkɒnskrɪpt/ n recluta mf, conscripto, -ta m,f (AmL)

conscript² /kənˈskrɪpt/ vt reclutar

conscription /kənˈskrɪpʃən/ n conscripción f (esp AmL), reclutamiento m (para el servicio militar obligatorio en casos de guerra)

consecrate /ˈkɒnsəkreɪt ‖ˈkɒnsɪkreɪt/ vt consagrar

consecutive /kənˈsekjətɪv ‖kənˈsekjʊtɪv/ adj «numbers» consecutivo; he was absent on three ∼ days faltó tres días seguidos

consensus /kənˈsensəs/ n consenso m

consent¹ /kənˈsent/ vi acceder; to ∼ TO sth acceder A or consentir* EN algo

consent² n consentimiento m de común acuerdo; age of ∼ (Law) edad a partir de la cual es válido el consentimiento que se da para tener relaciones sexuales

consequence /ˈkɒnsəkwens ‖ˈkɒnsɪkwəns/ n ⊡ (result) consecuencia f ⊡ (importance) trascendencia f

consequently /ˈkɒnsəkwentli ‖ˈkɒnsɪkwəntli/ adv consiguientemente, por consiguiente

conservation /ˈkɑːnsərˈveɪʃən ‖ˌkɒnsəˈveɪʃən/ n protección f or conservación f del medio ambiente

conservationist /ˈkɑːnsərˈveɪʃənəst ‖ˌkɒnsəˈveɪʃənɪst/ n conservacionista mf

conservative /kənˈsɜːrvətɪv ‖kənˈsɜːvətɪv/ adj **(a)** (traditional) conservador **(b) Conservative** (in UK) (before n) conservador **(c)** (cautious) cauteloso; **a ~ estimate** un cálculo por lo bajo

Conservative n (in UK) conservador, -dora m,f

conservatory /kənˈsɜːrvətɔːri ‖kənˈsɜːvətri/ n (pl **-ries) (a)** (greenhouse) jardín m de invierno **(b)** (school of music) conservatorio m

conserve /kənˈsɜːrv ‖kənˈsɜːv/ vt **(a)** (preserve) ⟨wildlife/rivers⟩ proteger*, conservar **(b)** (save) ⟨energy/resources⟩ conservar

consider /kənˈsɪdər ‖kənˈsɪdə(r)/ vt **(a)** (think about, of) considerar; **we're ~ing moving house** estamos pensando en mudarnos; **~ yourself lucky** puedes darle por afortunado **(b)** (take into account) tener* en cuenta, considerar; **all things ~ed, I think that ...** bien considerado, creo que ...

considerable /kənˈsɪdərəbəl/ adj ⟨achievement/risk⟩ considerable; ⟨sum⟩ importante; **with ~ difficulty** con bastante dificultad

considerably /kənˈsɪdərəbli/ adv bastante, considerablemente

considerate /kənˈsɪdərət/ adj atento, considerado

consideration /kənˈsɪdəˈreɪʃən/ n ① **(a)** (attention, thought): **their case has been given careful ~** su caso ha sido estudiado or considerado detenidamente; **to take sth into ~** tener* algo en cuenta **(b)** (factor): **a major ~ is the cost** un factor muy a tener en cuenta es el costo ② (thoughtfulness) consideración f ③ (importance): **of little/no ~** de poca/ninguna importancia

considering¹ /kənˈsɪdərɪŋ/ prep teniendo en cuenta

considering² conj: **~ (that) she's only two years old** teniendo en cuenta que tiene solo dos años

consignment /kənˈsaɪmmənt/ n **(a)** (goods sent) envío m, remesa f **(b)** (sending) envío m

consist /kənˈsɪst/ vi **to ~ OF sth** constar DE algo

consistency /kənˈsɪstənsi/ n (pl **-cies) (a)** (regularity) regularidad f **(b)** (of mixture) consistencia f

consistent /kənˈsɪstənt/ adj **(a)** (compatible) **to be ~ (WITH sth)** «statements/beliefs» concordar* (CON algo) **(b)** (constant) ⟨excellence/failure⟩ constante; ⟨denial⟩ sistemático

consistently /kənˈsɪstəntli/ adv **(a)** (without change) ⟨argue⟩ coherentemente; ⟨behave⟩ consecuentemente **(b)** (constantly) ⟨claim/refuse⟩ sistemáticamente

consolation /ˈkɑːnsəˈleɪʃən ‖ˌkɒnsəˈleɪʃən/ n consuelo m; (before n) **~ prize** premio m de consolación, premio m (de) consuelo (CS)

console¹ /ˈkɑːnsəʊl ‖ˈkɒnsəʊl/ n consola f

console² /kənˈsəʊl/ vt consolar*

consolidate /kənˈsɑːlədeɪt ‖kənˈsɒlɪdeɪt/ vt **(a)** (reinforce) ⟨support/position⟩ consolidar **(b)** (combine) ⟨companies⟩ fusionar; ⟨debts⟩ consolidar

consonant /ˈkɑːnsənənt ‖ˈkɒnsənənt/ n consonante f

consort /ˈkɑːnsɔːrt ‖ˈkɒnsɔːt/ n (frml) consorte mf (frml)

consortium /kənˈsɔːrʃjəm ‖kənˈsɔːtiəm/ n (pl **-tia** /-tiə/ or **-tiums**) consorcio m

conspicuous /kənˈspɪkjuəs/ adj ⟨hat/badge⟩ llamativo; ⟨differences/omissions⟩ manifiesto, evidente; **to make oneself ~** llamar la atención; **to be ~ by one's absence** brillar por su (or mi etc) ausencia

conspiracy /kənˈspɪrəsi/ n (pl **-cies**) conspiración f

conspirator /kənˈspɪrətər ‖kənˈspɪrətə(r)/ n conspirador, -dora m,f

conspire /kənˈspaɪr ‖kənˈspaɪə(r)/ vi conspirar; **to ~ to + INF** conspirar PARA + INF

constable /ˈkɑːnstəbəl ‖ˈkʌnstəbəl/ n (BrE) agente mf de policía

constant /ˈkɑːnstənt ‖ˈkɒnstənt/ adj **(a)** (continual) ⟨pain/complaints⟩ constante **(b)** (unchanging) ⟨temperature/speed⟩ constante **(c)** (loyal) (liter) fiel, leal

constantly /ˈkɑːnstəntli ‖ˈkɒnstəntli/ adv constantemente

constellation /ˈkɑːnstəˈleɪʃən ‖ˌkɒnstəˈleɪʃən/ n constelación f

constipated /ˈkɑːnstəpeɪtəd ‖ˈkɒnstɪpeɪtɪd/ adj estreñido

constipation /ˈkɑːnstəˈpeɪʃən ‖ˌkɒnstɪˈpeɪʃən/ n estreñimiento m

constituency /kənˈstɪtʃuənsi ‖kənˈstɪtjuənsi/ n (pl **-cies**) (area) circunscripción f or distrito m electoral; (supporters) electores mpl potenciales (de una circunscripción electoral)

constituent¹ /kənˈstɪtʃuənt ‖kənˈstɪtjuənt/ n ① (Pol) elector, -tora m,f ② (component) (frml) componente m, elemento m constitutivo or constituyente

constituent² adj (before n) ⟨part/element⟩ constitutivo, constituyente

constitute /ˈkɑːnstətuːt ‖ˈkɒnstɪtjuːt/ vt (frml) constituir* (frml)

constitution /ˈkɑːnstəˈtuːʃən ‖ˌkɒnstɪˈtjuːʃən/ n ① (of country) constitución f; (of association, party) estatutos mpl ② (of person) constitución f

constitutional /ˈkɑːnstəˈtuːʃnəl ‖ˌkɒnstɪˈtjuːʃənl/ adj constitucional

constrain /kənˈstreɪn/ vt (often pass) obligar*

constraint /kənˈstreɪnt/ n **(a)** (compulsion) coacción f **(b)** (restriction) (often pl) restricción f, limitación f

constrict /kənˈstrɪkt/ vt ⟨opening/channel⟩ estrechar; ⟨flow/breathing⟩ dificultar; ⟨freedom⟩ coartar

construct /kənˈstrʌkt/ vt **(a)** (build) (frml) construir* **(b)** (put together) ⟨model⟩ armar, montar

construction /kənˈstrʌkʃən/ n ① **(a)** (of building) construcción f; (before n) ⟨industry/worker⟩ de la construcción **(b)** (Ling, Math) construcción f ② (structure) estructura f

constructive /kən'strʌktɪv/ *adj* constructivo

consul /'kɑːnsəl ‖'kɒnsəl/ *n* cónsul *mf*

consulate /'kɑːnsələt ‖'kɒnsjʊlət/ *n* consulado *m*

consult /kən'sʌlt/ *vt* consultar
■ ~ *vi*: I ought to ~ with my wife first primero debería consultárselo a mi mujer

consultancy /kən'sʌltənsi/ *n* (*pl* **-cies**) (Busn) asesoría *f*, consultoría *f*

consultant /kən'sʌltənt/ *n* (adviser) asesor, -sora *m,f*, consultor, -tora *m,f*; (BrE Med) especialista *mf*

consultation /'kɑːnsəl'teɪʃən ‖,kɒnsəl'teɪʃən/ *n* (a) (with doctor, lawyer) consulta *f* (b) (of dictionary, notes) consulta *f* (c) (discussion): there was no ~ with the tenants no se consultó a los inquilinos; in ~ with sb en conferencia con algn

consulting /kən'sʌltɪŋ/ *adj* (before *n*) (Med): ~ room consultorio *m*, consulta *f*

consume /kən'suːm ‖kən'sjuːm/ *vt* consumir; he was ~d by *o* with jealousy lo consumían los celos

consumer /kən'suːmər ‖kən'sjuːmə(r)/ *n* consumidor, -dora *m,f*; (before *n*) ~ goods artículos *mpl* *or* bienes *mpl* de consumo; the ~ society la sociedad de consumo

consummate¹ /'kɑːn,səmət ‖'kɒnsəmət/ *adj* (frml) (before *n*) ⟨actor/liar⟩ consumado

consummate² /'kɑːnsəmeɪt ‖'kɒnsəmeɪt/ *vt* consumar

consumption /kən'sʌmpʃən/ *n* consumo *m*

contact¹ /'kɑːntækt ‖'kɒntækt/ *n* (a) (physical) contacto *m*; to come into ~ with sth hacer* contacto con algo (b) (communication) contacto *m*; to come in/into ~ with sb tratar a algn; to be/get in ~ with sb estar*/ponerse* en contacto con algn

contact² *vt* ponerse* en contacto con

contact lens *n* lente *f or* (AmL) lente *m* de contacto, lentilla *f* (Esp)

contagious /kən'teɪdʒəs/ *adj* contagioso

contain /kən'teɪn/ *vt* [1] (hold) contener* [2] ⟨enemy/fire/epidemic⟩ contener*; ⟨anger/laughter⟩ contener*; to ~ oneself contenerse*

container /kən'teɪnər ‖kən'teɪnə(r)/ *n* (receptacle) recipiente *m*; (as packaging) envase *m*; (Transp) contenedor *m*, contáiner *m*; (before *n*) ~ ship buque *m* portacontenedores

contaminate /kən'tæmɪneɪt ‖kən'tæmɪneɪt/ *vt* contaminar

contamination /kən'tæmə'neɪʃən ‖kən,tæmɪ'neɪʃən/ *n* contaminación *f*

contd (= **continued**) sigue

contemplate /'kɑːntəmpleɪt ‖'kɒntəmpleɪt/ *vt* contemplar; I ~d phoning her pensé (en) llamarla

contemporary¹ /kən'tempərəri ‖kən'tempərəri/ *adj* (a) (of the same period) ⟨person⟩ contemporáneo, coetáneo; ⟨object⟩ de la época (b) (present-day) contemporáneo, actual

contemporary² *n* (*pl* **-ries**) (a) (sb living at same time) contemporáneo, -nea *m,f*, coetáneo, -na *m,f* (b) (sb of same age): he looks older than his contemporaries parece mayor que la gente de su edad

contempt /kən'tempt/ *n* desprecio *m*; to be beneath ~ ser* despreciable; ~ (**of court**) (Law) desacato *m* al tribunal

contemptible /kən'temptəbəl/ *adj* despreciable

contemptuous /kən'temptʃuəs ‖kən'temptʃʊəs/ *adj* despectivo

contend /kən'tend/ *vi* (a) (compete) to ~ (WITH sb) (FOR sth) competir* (CON algn) (POR algo) (b) (face) to ~ WITH sth lidiar CON algo
■ ~ *vt* argüir*

contender /kən'tendər ‖kən'tendə(r)/ *n* ~ (FOR sth) aspirante *mf* (A algo)

content¹ /'kɑːntent ‖'kɒntent/ *n* [1] **contents** *pl* (of box, bottle) contenido *m*; ~s (of book) índice *m* de materias; (in magazine) sumario *m* [2] (amount contained) contenido *m*

content² /kən'tent/ *adj* (pred) contento

content³ /kən'tent/ *v refl* to ~ oneself WITH sth/-ING contentarse CON algo/+ INF

contented /kən'tentəd/ *adj* ⟨sigh/purr⟩ de satisfacción; ⟨person/workforce⟩ satisfecho; to be ~ WITH sth contentarse CON algo

contention /kən'tentʃən ‖kən'tenʃən/ *n* [1] (dispute): there is considerable ~ over ... existe un gran desacuerdo sobre ... [2] (assertion) opinión *f*; it is her ~ that ... ella sostiene que ...

contentious /kən'tentʃəs ‖kən'tenʃəs/ *adj* ⟨issue⟩ polémico

contentment /kən'tentmənt/ *n* satisfacción *f*

contest¹ /'kɑːntest ‖'kɒntest/ *n* (a) (competition) (Games) concurso *m*; (Sport) competencia *f* (AmL), competición *f* (Esp); (in boxing) combate *m* (b) (struggle) lucha *f*

contest² /kən'test/ *vt* (a) ⟨allegation⟩ refutar; ⟨will⟩ impugnar; ⟨decision⟩ protestar contra (b) ⟨election⟩ presentarse como candidato a

contestant /kən'testənt/ *n* concursante *mf*

context /'kɑːntekst ‖'kɒntekst/ *n* contexto *m*

continent /'kɑːntɪnənt ‖'kɒntɪnənt/ *n* continente *m*; the C~ Europa *f* (continental)

continental /'kɑːntɪŋ'entl̩ ‖,kɒntɪ'nentl̩/ *adj* continental; C~ (European) de Europa (continental)

continental: ~ **breakfast** *n* desayuno *m* continental (desayuno de café o té y bollos con mantequilla y mermelada); ~ **quilt** *n* (BrE) ▶ DUVET

contingency /kən'tɪndʒənsi/ *n* (*pl* **-cies**) (eventuality) contingencia *f*; (before *n*) ⟨fund⟩ (para casos) de emergencia; a ~ plan un plan para prever

continual /kən'tɪnjuəl/ *adj* continuo, constante

continually /kən'tɪnjuəli/ *adv* continuamente, constantemente

continuation /kən'tɪnju'eɪʃən/ *n* continuación *f*

continue /kən'tɪnjuː/ *vi* continuar*, seguir*; we ~d on our way reanudamos el camino
■ ~ *vt* (a) (keep on) continuar*, seguir* con; to ~ -ING to + INF continuar* *or* seguir* + GER (b) (resume) continuar*, seguir* con, proseguir* (frml); to be ~d continuará (c) (extend, prolong) prolongar*

continuity /ˌkɑːntn̩'uːəti ‖ˌkɒntrɪ'njuːɪti/ n
continuidad f

continuous /kən'tɪnjuəs/ adj continuo; ~
assessment (Educ) evaluación f continua

continuously /kən'tɪnjuəsli/ adv
continuamente, sin interrupción

contort /kən'tɔːrt ‖kən'tɔːt/ vt ‹face› contraer*;
to ~ oneself contorsionarse
■ ~ vi crisparse

contortion /kən'tɔːrʃən ‖kən'tɔːʃən/ n
contorsión f

contour /'kɑːntʊr ‖'kɒntʊə(r)/ n contorno m;
(before n) ~ line curva f de nivel, cota f

contraband /'kɑːntrəbænd ‖'kɒntrəbænd/ n
contrabando m

contraception /'kɑːntrə'sepʃən
‖ˌkɒntrə'sepʃən/ n anticoncepción f,
contracepción f

contraceptive /'kɑːntrə'septɪv
‖ˌkɒntrə'septɪv/ n anticonceptivo m,
contraconceptivo m

contract¹ /'kɑːntrækt ‖'kɒntrækt/ n
(agreement, document) contrato m; (for public works)
contrata f; ~ killer asesino, -na m,f a sueldo,
sicario, -ria m,f

contract² /kən'trækt/ vt also /'kɑːntrækt/ (a)
(place under contract) ‹person› contratar (b) ‹debt/
disease› contraer* (fml) (c) ‹muscle› contraer*
■ ~ vi (become smaller/tighter) contraerse*

■ **contract out** /'kɑːntrækt ‖'kɒntrækt/ [v + o
+ adv, v + adv + o] ‹job/work› subcontratar

contraction /kən'trækʃən/ n contracción f

contractor /kən'træktər ‖kən'træktə(r)/ n
contratista mf

contradict /'kɑːntrə'dɪkt ‖ˌkɒntrə'dɪkt/ vt
contradecir*

contradiction /'kɑːntrə'dɪkʃən
‖ˌkɒntrə'dɪkʃən/ n contradicción f; a ~ in terms
un contrasentido

contradictory /'kɑːntrə'dɪktəri
‖ˌkɒntrə'dɪktəri/ adj contradictorio

contralto /kən'træltəʊ/ n (pl ~s) contralto f

contraption /kən'træpʃən/ n (colloq) artilugio
m

contrary¹ adj [1] /'kɑːntreri ‖'kɒntrəri/ (a)
(opposed, opposite) contrario (b) ~ to (as prep)
contrariamente a, al contrario de [2] /'kɑːntreri,
kən'treri ‖kən'treəri/ (obstinate): he's so ~
siempre tiene que llevar la contraria

contrary² /'kɑːntreri ‖'kɒntrəri/ n (pl -ries):
the ~ lo contrario; on the ~ (as linker) al
contrario

contrast¹ /'kɑːntræst ‖'kɒntrɑːst/ n contraste
m; by ~ (as linker) por contraste; in ~ to o with
(as prep) en contraste con

contrast² /kən'træst ‖kən'trɑːst/ vt contrastar
■ ~ vi (a) (differ) contrastar (b) **contrasting**
pres p ‹opinions/approaches› contrastante

contribute /kən'trɪbjət, -bjuːt/ vt (a) ‹money/
time› contribuir* con, aportar, hacer* una

aportación or (esp AmL) un aporte de;
‹suggestions/ideas› aportar (b) ‹article/poem/
paper› escribir*
■ ~ vi (a) (play significant part) to ~ (TO sth)
contribuir* (A algo) (b) (give money) contribuir*
(c) (participate) to ~ TO sth participar EN algo (d)
(Journ) to ~ TO sth escribir* PARA algo

contribution /'kɑːntrə'bjuːʃən
‖ˌkɒntrɪ'bjuːʃən/ n (a) (participation, part played)
contribución f (b) (payment, donation) contribución
f; (to a fund) aportación f, aporte m (esp AmL)

contributor /kən'trɪbjətər ‖kən'trɪbjʊtə(r)/ n
(a) (writer) colaborador, -dora m,f (b) (donor)
donante mf

contrive /kən'traɪv/ vt (a) (manage) to ~ to +
INF lograr + INF/QUE (+ subj), ingeniárselas or
arreglárselas PARA + INF/PARA QUE (+ subj) (b)
(create) ‹method/device› idear

contrived /kən'traɪvd/ adj artificioso

control¹ /kən'trəʊl/ vt **-ll-** controlar; ‹traffic›
dirigir*; to ~ oneself controlarse

control² n [1] control m; to be in ~ of sth
dominar algo; to gain ~ of sth hacerse* con;
circumstances beyond our ~ circunstancias
ajenas a nuestra voluntad; to be out of ~ estar*
fuera de control; to get out of ~ descontrolarse
[2] price ~(s) control m de precios [3] **controls**
pl (of vehicle) mandos mpl [4] (mastery) dominio m

controlled /kən'trəʊld/ adj ‹voice/emotion›
contenido; ‹response› mesurado; ‹conditions/
experiment› controlado

controller /kən'trəʊlər ‖kən'trəʊlə(r)/ n
director, -tora m,f

control: ~ room n (Mil, Naut) centro m de
operaciones; (Audio, Rad, TV) sala f de control; ~
tower n torre f de control

controversial /'kɑːntrə'vɜːrʃəl
‖ˌkɒntrə'vɜːʃəl/ adj controvertido

controversy /'kɑːntrəvɜːrsi ‖'kɒntrəvɜːsi,
kən'trɒvəsi/ n (pl -sies) controversia f

conundrum /kə'nʌndrəm/ n adivinanza f

conurbation /'kɑːnɜːr'beɪʃən ‖ˌkɒnɜː'beɪʃən/
n conurbación f

convalesce /'kɑːnvə'les ‖ˌkɒnvə'les/ vi
recuperarse, convalecer*

convene /kən'viːn/ vi reunirse*

convenience /kən'viːniəns/ n (a) (comfort,
practicality) conveniencia f; at your ~ cuando le
resulte conveniente (b) (amenity, appliance): with
every modern ~ con todas las comodidades
modernas

convenience food n comida f de
preparación rápida

convenient /kən'viːniənt/ adj (a) (opportune,
suitable) conveniente (b) (practical) práctico; a very
~ way of storing things una manera muy
práctica de guardar las cosas (c) (handy, close): it's
very ~ having the school so near resulta muy
práctico tener la escuela tan cerca

conveniently /kən'viːniəntli/ adv (a) (handily)
convenientemente (b) (expediently): the

AmC	Central America	Arg	Argentina	Cu	Cuba	Per	Peru
AmL	Latin America	Bol	Bolivia	Ec	Ecuador	RPI	River Plate Area
AmS	South America	Chi	Chile	Esp	Spain	Ur	Uruguay
Andes	Andean Region	CS	Southern Cone	Méx	Mexico	Ven	Venezuela

government ~ forgets its election promises le
resulta muy cómodo al gobierno olvidarse de sus
promesas electorales

convent /'kɑːnvənt ‖'kɒnvənt/ n convento m

convention /kən'ventʃən ‖kən'venʃən/ n
1 (a) (social code) convenciónes fpl,
convencionalismos mpl (b) (established practice)
convención f **2** (agreement) convención f
3 (conference) convención f, congreso m

conventional /kən'ventʃṇəl ‖kən'venʃənl/
adj convencional

converge /kən'vɜːrdʒ ‖kən'vɜːdʒ/ vi «lines/
roads» converger*, convergir*; «crowd/armies»
reunirse*

conversation /'kɑːnvərseɪʃən
‖ˌkɒnvə'seɪʃən/ n conversación f

conversational /'kɑːnvərseɪʃṇəl
‖ˌkɒnvə'seɪʃənl/ adj familiar, coloquial

converse /kən'vɜːrs ‖kən'vɜːs/ vi conversar

conversion /kən'vɜːrʒən ‖kən'vɜːʃən/ n **1**
(a) (change) conversión f (b) (of house): to do a ~
transformar una casa (c) (Relig) conversión f
2 (in rugby) conversión f, transformación f

convert¹ /'kɑːnvɜːrt ‖'kɒnvɜːt/ n converso, -sa
m,f

convert² /kən'vɜːrt ‖kən'vɜːt/ vt **1** ‹building›
remodelar; ‹vehicle› transformar; to ~ sth INTO
sth convertir* algo EN algo **2** (cause to change
view, religion) convertir* **3** (in rugby) transformar,
convertir*
■ ~ vi (Pol, Relig) convertirse*

convertible¹ /kən'vɜːrtəbəl ‖kən'vɜːtəbəl/
adj convertible

convertible² n (Auto) descapotable m,
convertible m (AmL)

convex /'kɑːnveks ‖'kɒnveks/ adj convexo

convey /kən'veɪ/ vt ‹goods/people› transportar;
‹feeling› expresar; ‹thanks› hacer* llegar

conveyor (belt) /kən'veɪər ‖kən'veɪə(r)/ n
cinta f or correa f transportadora, banda f
transportadora (Méx)

convict¹ /'kɑːnvɪkt ‖'kɒnvɪkt/ n recluso, -sa
m,f, presidiario, -ria m,f

convict² /kən'vɪkt/ vt (often pass) declarar
culpable, condenar; to be ~ed OF sth ser*
condenado POR algo

conviction /kən'vɪkʃən/ n **1** (Law) condena f
2 (certainty) convicción f

convince /kən'vɪns/ vt convencer*; to ~ sb
THAT convencer* a algn DE QUE

convinced /kən'vɪnst/ adj (persuaded) (pred):
to be ~ OF sth/THAT estar* convencido DE algo/
DE QUE

convincing /kən'vɪnsɪŋ/ adj convincente

convivial /kən'vɪviəl/ adj ‹atmosphere› cordial;
‹person› simpático

convoy /'kɑːnvɔɪ ‖'kɒnvɔɪ/ n convoy m

convulsion /kən'vʌlʃən/ n convulsión f

coo /kuː/ vi ‹dove/pigeon» arrullar

cook¹ /kʊk/ n cocinero, -ra m,f; he's a good ~
cocina muy bien, es muy buen cocinero

cook² vt ‹food/meal› hacer*, preparar
■ ~ vi (a) (prepare food) cocinar, guisar (b) (become
ready) ‹food» hacerse*

cookbook /'kʊkbʊk/ n libro m de cocina or de
recetas

cooker /'kʊkər ‖'kʊkə(r)/ n (BrE) (stove) cocina
f or (Col, Méx) estufa f

cookery /'kʊkəri/ n cocina f; (before n) ~ book
(BrE) ▶ COOKBOOK

cookie /'kʊki/ n (AmE Culin) galleta f, galletita f
(RPl)

cooking /'kʊkɪŋ/ n: to do the ~ cocinar; it is
used in ~ se usa para cocinar; home ~ la
comida casera; Spanish ~ la cocina española

cooky n ▶ COOKIE

cool¹ /kuːl/ adj -er, -est **1** (cold) fresco; it's ~
today hace or está fresco hoy **2** (reserved, hostile)
‹reception/behavior› frío **3** (calm) sereno,
tranquilo; keep ~! ¡tranquilo!, no te pongas
nervioso; he's a very ~ customer tiene una
sangre fría impresionante **4** (sl) (trendy, laid-back):
he's really ~ es muy en la onda (fam)

cool² n **1** (low temperature): let's stay here in the
~ quedémonos aquí al fresco **2** (composure)
calma f; to keep/lose one's ~ mantener*/perder*
la calma

cool³ vt ‹air/room› refrigerar; ‹engine/food/
enthusiasm› enfriar*
■ ~ vi ‹air/room› refrigerarse; «engine/food/
enthusiasm» enfriarse*
■ **cool down** [v + adv] (a) (become cooler) «food/
iron» enfriarse*; «person» refrescarse* (b)
(become calmer) calmarse
■ **cool off** [v + adv] (a) (become cooler) «person»
refrescarse* (b) (become calmer) calmarse

coolly /'kuːlli/ adv (a) (calmly) con serenidad or
calma (b) (boldly) descaradamente, con la mayor
frescura (c) (with reserve, hostility) fríamente, con
frialdad

coop /kuːp/ n: chicken/hen ~ gallinero m
■ **coop up** [v + o + adv, v + adv + o] (usu
passive) encerrar*

co-op /'kəʊɑːp ‖'kəʊɒp/ n cooperativa f

cooperate /kəʊ'ɑːpəreɪt ‖kəʊ'ɒpəreɪt/ vi
cooperar, colaborar

cooperation /kəʊˌɑːpə'reɪʃən
‖kəʊˌɒpə'reɪʃən/ n cooperación f, colaboración f

cooperative¹ /kəʊ'ɑːpərətɪv ‖kəʊ'ɒpərətɪv/
adj (a) ‹attitude› de colaboración, cooperativo
(b) ‹effort/venture› conjunto

cooperative² n cooperativa f

co-opt /kəʊ'ɑːpt ‖kəʊ'ɒpt/ vt: to ~ sb onto a
committee invitar a algn a formar parte de una
comisión

coordinate¹ /kəʊ'ɔːrdṇeɪt ‖ˌkəʊ'ɔːdɪneɪt/ vt
coordinar

coordinate² /kəʊ'ɔːrdṇət ‖kəʊ'ɔːdɪnət/ n
1 (Math) coordenada f **2** **coordinates** pl
prendas fpl para combinar, coordinados mpl

coordination /kəʊˌɔːrdṇ'eɪʃən
‖kəʊˌɔːdɪ'neɪʃən/ n coordinación f

coordinator /kəʊ'ɔːrdṇeɪtər ‖kəʊ'ɔːdɪneɪtə(r)/
n coordinador, -dora m,f

coowner /'kəʊ'əʊnər ‖kəʊ'əʊnə(r)/ n
copropietario, -ria m,f

cop /kɑːp ‖kɒp/ n (colloq) poli mf (fam), tira mf
(Méx fam), cana mf (RPl arg), cachaco, -ca m,f (Per
fam), paco, -ca m,f (Chi fam)

cope /kəʊp/ vi: I can't ~ with all this work no
doy abasto or no puedo con tanto trabajo; how do
you ~ without a washing machine? ¿cómo te las ⠂⠂⠆

arreglas sin lavadora?; **how is he coping on his own?** ¿qué tal se las arregla solo?; **these are some of the problems they have to** ~ **with** estos son algunos de los problemas a los que tienen que enfrentarse

Copenhagen /'kəʊpən'heɪgən/ n Copenhague m

copious /'kəʊpiəs/ adj copioso

copper /'kɑːpər ǁ 'kɒpə(r)/ n ① (a) (metal) cobre m (b) **coppers** pl (coins) (colloq) peniques mpl, perras fpl (Esp fam), quintos mpl (Méx fam), chauchas fpl (Chi fam), vintenes mpl (Ur fam) (c) (color) color m cobre; (before n) cobrizo ② (police officer) (colloq) ▶ COP

co-production /'kəʊprə,dʌkʃən/ n coproducción f

copy¹ /'kɑːpi ǁ 'kɒpi/ n (pl **copies**) ① (of painting, document) copia f ② (of newspaper, book) ejemplar m ③ (text): **he/she must be able to produce clear** ~ debe saber redactar con claridad

copy² copies, copying, copied vt ① (a) (reproduce, transcribe) copiar (b) (photocopy) fotocopiar ② (imitate) (painter/singer) copiarle a; (style/behavior) copiar

copy: ~**cat** n (colloq) copión, -piona m,f (fam), imitamonos mf (Méx fam); ~**right** n copyright m, derechos mpl de reproducción

coral /'kɒrəl ǁ 'kɒrəl/ n coral m

cord /kɔːrd ǁ kɔːd/ n ① (a) (string, rope) cuerda f; (of pajamas, curtains) cordón m (b) (AmE Elec) cordón m, cable m (c) (Anat) ▶ SPINAL CORD, UMBILICAL CORD, VOCAL CORDS ② (Tex) pana f, corderoy m (AmS), cotelé m (Chi)

cordial¹ /'kɔːrdʒəl ǁ 'kɔːdiəl/ adj cordial

cordial² n refresco m (concentrado)

cordless /'kɔːrdləs ǁ 'kɔːdlɪs/ adj inalámbrico

cordon /'kɔːrdn̩ ǁ 'kɔːdn̩/ n cordón m
■ **cordon off** [v + o + adv, v + adv + o] acordonar

corduroy /'kɔːrdərɔɪ ǁ 'kɔːdərɔɪ/ n pana f, corderoy m (AmS), cotelé m (Chi)

core¹ /kɔːr ǁ kɔː(r)/ n (of apple, pear) corazón m; (of Earth) centro m; (of nuclear reactor) núcleo; (of problem) meollo m

core² vt (apple) quitarle el corazón a

coriander /'kɔːriændər ǁ ,kɒri'ændə(r)/ n cilantro m, culantro m

cork /kɔːrk ǁ kɔːk/ n corcho m

corkscrew /'kɔːrkskruː ǁ 'kɔːkskruː/ n sacacorchos m, tirabuzón m

corn /kɔːrn ǁ kɔːn/ n ① (a) (cereal crop — in general) grano m; (maize) (AmE) maíz m; (wheat) (BrE) trigo m; (oats) (BrE) avena f (b) (foodstuff) maíz m, choclo m (AmS); ~ **on the cob** mazorca f de maíz or (AmS) de choclo, elote f (Méx) ② (on toe) callo m

corner¹ /'kɔːrnər ǁ 'kɔːnə(r)/ n ① (a) (inside angle — of room, cupboard) rincón m; (— of field) esquina f; (— of mouth) comisura f; (— of page) ángulo m (b) (outside angle — of street, page) esquina f; (— of table) esquina f, punta f; (bend in road) curva f; **I'll meet you on** o **at the** ~ te veo en la esquina; **to cut** ~**s** (financially) hacer* economías; (in a process) simplificar*; (before n) ~ **shop** (BrE) tienda f de la esquina; (local shop) tienda f de barrio

② (in soccer) (~ kick) córner m, tiro m or saque m de esquina
③ (in boxing) esquina f

corner² vt ① (trap) acorralar ② (monopolize) acaparar
■ ~ vi tomar una curva; **this car** ~**s well** este coche tiene buen agarre en las curvas

cornerstone /'kɔːrnərstəʊn ǁ 'kɔːnəstəʊn/ n piedra f angular

corn: ~**flakes** pl n copos mpl or hojuelas fpl de maíz; ~**flour** n (BrE) maizena® f

Cornish /'kɔːrnɪʃ ǁ 'kɔːnɪʃ/ adj de Cornualles

cornstarch /'kɔːrnstɑːrtʃ ǁ 'kɔːnstɑːtʃ/ n (AmE) maizena® f

Cornwall /'kɔːrnwɔːl ǁ 'kɔːnwɔːl/ n Cornualles m

corny /'kɔːrni ǁ 'kɔːni/ adj -**nier**, -**niest** (colloq) (a) (song/movie) cursi, sensiblero (b) (BrE) (joke) malo

coronary¹ /'kɔːrəneri ǁ 'kɒrənri/ adj coronario

coronary² n (pl -**ries**) infarto m (de miocardio)

coronation /'kɔːrə'neɪʃən ǁ ,kɒrə'neɪʃən/ n coronación f

coroner /'kɔːrənər ǁ 'kɒrənə(r)/ n: funcionario encargado de investigar las causas de muertes violentas, repentinas o sospechosas, ≈ juez mf de instrucción

corporal /'kɔːrprəl ǁ 'kɔːpərəl/ n cabo m

corporal punishment n castigos mpl corporales

corporate /'kɔːrpərət ǁ 'kɔːpərət/ adj ① (a) (of a company) (headquarters/lawyer) de la empresa or compañía (b) (mentality/jargon) empresarial ② (joint, collective) (action/decision) colectivo

corporation /'kɔːrpə'reɪʃən ǁ ,kɔːpə'reɪʃən/ n (company — in US) sociedad f anónima; (— in UK) compañía f, empresa f, corporación f

corpse /kɔːrps ǁ kɔːps/ n cadáver m

corpuscle /'kɔːrpʌsəl ǁ 'kɔːpʌsəl/ n corpúsculo m

corral /kə'ræl ǁ kɒ'rɑːl/ n corral m

correct¹ /kə'rekt/ vt corregir*

correct² adj correcto

correction /kə'rekʃən/ n corrección f

correctly /kə'rektli/ adv correctamente

correlate /'kɔːrəleɪt ǁ 'kɒr-/ vi to ~ (**with** sth) estar* correlacionado (con algo)

correlation /,kɔːrə'leɪʃən ǁ ,kɒrə'leɪʃən/ n correlación f (fml)

correspond /'kɔːrə'spɑːnd ǁ ,kɒrə'spɒnd/ vi ① (a) (tally) to ~ (**with** sth) corresponderse or concordar* (con algo) (b) (be equivalent) to ~ (**to** sth) equivaler* or corresponder (a algo) ② (communicate by letter) to ~ (**with** sb) mantener* correspondencia (con algn)

correspondence /'kɔːrə'spɑːndəns ǁ ,kɒrə'spɒndəns/ n ① (agreement) correspondencia f ② (letters, letter writing) correspondencia f

correspondence course n curso m por correspondencia

correspondent /ˈkɔːrəˈspɑːndənt ‖ˌkɒrəˈspɒndənt/ n (a) (letter writer) corresponsal mf (b) (Journ) corresponsal mf

corridor /ˈkɔːrədər ‖ˈkɒrɪdɔː(r)/ n pasillo m, corredor m

corroborate /kəˈrɑːbəreɪt ‖kəˈrɒbəreɪt/ vt corroborar

corrode /kəˈrəʊd/ vt corroer*
■ ~ vi corroerse*

corrosion /kəˈrəʊʒən/ n (a) (action) corrosión f (b) (substance) herrumbre f, orín m

corrosive /kəˈrəʊsɪv/ adj corrosivo

corrugated /ˈkɔːrəgeɪtəd ‖ˈkɒrəgeɪtɪd/ adj ondulado; ~ cardboard cartón m corrugado; ~ iron chapa f de zinc, calamina f (Chi, Per)

corrupt[1] /kəˈrʌpt/ vt (deprave) corromper; (bribe) sobornar; (Comput) corromper

corrupt[2] adj ‹person/government› corrompido, corrupto

corruption /kəˈrʌpʃən/ n corrupción f

corset /ˈkɔːrsət ‖ˈkɔːsɪt/ n (often pl) corsé m

cosmetic /kɑːzˈmetɪk ‖kɒzˈmetɪk/ adj (a) (beautifying) ‹before n› ‹powder/cream› cosmético; ~ surgery cirugía f estética (b) (superficial) ‹reforms/changes› superficial

cosmetics /kɑːzˈmetɪks ‖kɒzˈmetɪks/ pl n cosméticos mpl

cosmic /ˈkɑːzmɪk ‖ˈkɒzmɪk/ adj cósmico

cosmonaut /ˈkɑːzmənɔːt ‖ˈkɒzmənɔːt/ n cosmonauta mf

cosmopolitan /ˌkɑːzməˈpɑːlətn̩ ‖ˌkɒzməˈpɒlɪtn̩/ adj cosmopolita

cosmos /ˈkɑːzməʊs ‖ˈkɒzmɒs/ n the ~ el cosmos

cost[1] /kɔːst ‖kɒst/ n [1] (a) (expense) (often pl) costo m (esp AmL), coste m (Esp); to cut ~s reducir* los gastos (b) **costs** pl (Law) costas fpl [2] (loss, sacrifice): she helped me out, at great ~ to herself sacrificó mucho al ayudarme; at all ~s a toda costa

cost[2] vt [1] (past & past p cost) (a) «article/ service» costar* (b) (cause to lose) costar*; one slip ~ him the title un error le costó el título [2] (past & past p costed) (calculate cost of) calcular el costo or (Esp) coste de

co-star /ˈkəʊstɑːr ‖ˈkəʊstɑː(r)/ n coprotagonista mf

Costa Rica /ˈkɔːstəˈriːkə ‖ˌkɒstəˈriːkə/ n Costa Rica f

Costa Rican[1] /ˈkɔːstəˈriːkən ‖ˌkɒstəˈriːkən/ adj costarricense

Costa Rican[2] n costarricense mf

cost-effective /ˈkɔːstɪˈfektɪv ‖ˌkɒstɪˈfektɪv/ adj rentable

costly /ˈkɔːstli ‖ˈkɒstli/ adj -lier, -liest costoso

cost of living n costo m or (Esp) coste m de (la) vida; ~ price n precio m de costo or (Esp) de coste

costume /ˈkɑːstuːm ‖ˈkɒstjuːm/ n (a) (style of dress) traje m; (for parties, disguise) disfraz m (b) (wardrobe) (Theat) vestuario m; (individual outfit) traje m (c) (swimming ~) traje m de baño

costume jewelry, (BrE) **costume jewellery** n bisutería f, alhajas fpl de fantasía

cosy[1] /ˈkəʊzi/ adj cosier, cosiest (BrE) ▸ COZY[1]

cosy[2] n (pl cosies) (BrE) ▸ COZY[2]

cot /kɑːt ‖kɒt/ n (a) (campbed) (AmE) catre m (b) (for child) (BrE) cuna f, cama f ‹con barandas›

cottage /ˈkɑːtɪdʒ ‖ˈkɒtɪdʒ/ n casita f

cottage cheese n requesón m

cotton /ˈkɑːtn̩ ‖ˈkɒtn̩/ n (a) (cloth) algodón m; ‹before n› ‹dress/sheet/print› de algodón (b) (thread) (BrE) hilo m (de coser) (c) (absorbent ~) (AmE) algodón m (hidrófilo)

cotton wool n (BrE) algodón m (hidrófilo)

couch /kaʊtʃ/ n (sofa) sofá m; (doctor's, psychoanalyst's) diván m

couch potato /kaʊtʃ/ n (colloq) teleadicto, -ta m,f (fam)

cough[1] /kɔːf ‖kɒf/ n tos f; ‹before n› ~ mixture jarabe m para la tos

cough[2] vi toser
■ ~ vt ~ (up) expectorar
■ **cough up** [1] [v + adv + o] (pay) (colloq) ‹money› soltar* (fam), aflojar (fam) [2] [v + adv] (pay) soltar* la plata or (Esp) la pasta or (AmL tb) la lana (fam)

could /kʊd/ v mod [1] past of CAN[3]
[2] (indicating possibility) poder*; I would help you if I ~ te ayudaría si pudiera; you ~ have killed us all! ¡podrías or podías habernos matado a todos!; you ~ be right puede (ser) que tengas razón [3] (a) (asking permission): ~ I use your bathroom? ¿podría or me permitiría pasar al baño? (b) (in requests): ~ you sign here please? ¿quiere firmar aquí, por favor? [4] (a) (in suggestions) poder*; you ~ try doing it this way podrías tratar de hacerlo de esta manera (b) (indicating strong desire) poder*; I ~ have killed her la hubiera matado, la podría or podía haber matado

couldn't /ˈkʊdn̩t/ = **could not**

council /ˈkaʊnsəl/ n (a) (advisory group) consejo m (b) (Govt) ayuntamiento m, municipio m; ~ housing (BrE) viviendas de alquiler subvencionadas por el ayuntamiento

councillor n (BrE) ▸ COUNCILOR

Council of Europe n the ~ ~ ~ el Consejo de Europa

councilor, (BrE) **councillor** /ˈkaʊnsələr ‖ˈkaʊnsələ(r)/ n concejal, -jala m,f

council tax n (in UK) ≈ contribución f (municipal or inmobiliaria)

counsel[1] /ˈkaʊnsəl/ n (pl ~) (no art) (Law) abogado, -da m,f; ~ for the defense abogado defensor, abogada defensora m,f; ~ for the prosecution fiscal mf

counsel[2] vt, (BrE) **-ll-** (frml) aconsejar

counseling, (BrE) **counselling** /ˈkaʊnsəlɪŋ/ n (Educ, Psych) orientación f psicopedagógica

counselor, (BrE) **counsellor** /ˈkaʊnsələr ‖ˈkaʊnsələ(r)/ n (a) (Educ, Psych) consejero, -ra m,f, orientador, -dora m,f (b) (AmE Law) abogado, -da m,f

count[1] /kaʊnt/ n [1] (a) (act of counting) recuento m, cómputo m; (of votes) escrutinio m, recuento m, cómputo m, conteo m (Andes, Ven); to keep/ lose ~ of sth llevar/perder* la cuenta de algo (b) (total) total m; the final ~ (of votes) el recuento or ⋯▸

cómputo final **2** (point): **it has been criticized on several ~s** ha sido criticado por varios motivos **3** (rank) conde *m*

count² *vt* **1** (enumerate, add up) contar*
2 (include) contar*; **not ~ing the driver** sin contar al conductor
3 (consider) considerar; **to ~ oneself lucky** darse* por afortunado
■ **~** *vi* **1** (enumerate) contar*
2 (be valid, matter) contar*; **that doesn't ~** eso no cuenta *or* no vale; **every minute ~s** cada minuto cuenta
■ **count for** [*v* + *prep* + *o*] contar*; **your opinion ~s for a great deal/won't ~ for much** tu opinión importa mucho/no va a contar mucho
■ **count on** [*v* + *prep* + *o*] **(a)** (rely on) ⟨*friend/ help*⟩ contar* con **(b)** (expect) esperar; **we hadn't ~ed on that happening** no esperábamos que fuera a pasar eso
■ **count out 1** [*v* + *o* + *adv*]: **you can ~ me out** a mí no me incluyan, no cuenten conmigo
2 [*v* + *o* + *adv*, *v* + *adv* + *o*] ⟨*money/objects*⟩ contar* (*uno por uno*)

countdown /'kaʊntdaʊn/ *n* cuenta *f* atrás *or* regresiva, conteo *m* regresivo (Andes, Ven)

counter¹ /'kaʊntər ‖'kaʊntə(r)/ *n* **1** (in shop) mostrador *m*; (in café) barra *f*; (in bank, post office) ventanilla *f*; (in kitchen) (AmE) encimera *f*
2 (Games) ficha *f*

counter² *vt* **(a)** (oppose) ⟨*deficiency/trend*⟩ contrarrestar **(b)** (in debate) ⟨*idea/statement*⟩ rebatir, refutar; **to ~ THAT** responder *or* replicar* QUE

counter³ *adv*: **to run** *o* **go ~ to sth** ser* contrario a *or* oponerse* a algo

counteract /'kaʊntər'ækt/ *vt* contrarrestar

counterattack¹ /'kaʊntərə'tæk/ *n* contraataque *m*

counterattack² *vi* contraatacar*

counterbalance /'kaʊntər'bæləns ‖'kaʊntə,bæləns/ *n* contrapeso *m*

counterclockwise /'kaʊntər'klɑːkwaɪz ‖,kaʊntə'klɒkwaɪz/ (AmE) *adj/adv* en sentido contrario a las agujas del reloj

counterfeit¹ /'kaʊntərfɪt ‖'kaʊntəfɪt/ *n* falsificación *f*

counterfeit² *adj* ⟨*money*⟩ falso

counter: ~foil *n* talón *m* (AmL), matriz *f* (Esp); **~part** *n* (person) homólogo, -ga *m,f*; (thing) equivalente *m* (Mus) contrapunto *m*; **~point** *n* (Mus) contrapunto *m*; **~productive** /'kaʊntərprə'dʌktɪv ‖,kaʊntəprə'dʌktɪv/ *adj* contraproducente

countess /'kaʊntəs ‖'kaʊntes/ *n* condesa *f*

countless /'kaʊntləs ‖'kaʊntlɪs/ *adj* ⟨*stars/ hours*⟩ incontables, innumerables

country /'kʌntri/ *n* (*pl* **-tries**) **1** (nation) país *m*; (people) pueblo *m*; (native land) patria *f* **2** (rural area) **the ~** el campo; *(before n)* ⟨*people*⟩ del campo; ⟨*cottage*⟩ de campo **3** (region) terreno *m* **4** (Mus) (música *f*) country *m*

country: ~-and-western /'kʌntriən'westərn

country /'kʌntriən'westən/ *n* (música *f*) country *m*; **~ dancing** *n* (esp BrE) danzas *fpl* folklóricas; **~ house** *n* casa *f* solariega; **~man** /'kʌntrimən/ *n* (*pl* -**men** /-mən/) (fellow ~man) (liter) compatriota *m*; **~side** *n* campiña *f*, campo *m*; **~wide** /'kʌntri'waɪd/ *adj/adv* a escala nacional

county /'kaʊnti/ *n* (*pl* -**ties**) condado *m*

county: ~ council *n* (in UK) corporación de gobierno a nivel de condado; **~ court** *n* (in US) juzgado *m* comarcal; (in UK) juzgado *m* comarcal (*que conoce de causas de derecho civil*)

coup /kuː/ *n* (*pl* **~s** /kuːz/) **1** (successful action) golpe *m* maestro **2** **~ (d'état)** /deɪta:/ (Pol) golpe *m* (de estado)

couple¹ /'kʌpəl/ *n* **1** (two people) (+ *sing* o *pl* *vb*) pareja *f*; **a married ~** un matrimonio **2** (two or small number): **a ~ (of sth)** (+ *pl* *vb*) un par (de algo)

couple² *vt* **(a)** (connect) (Rail) enganchar; ⟨*theories/events*⟩ asociar; **to ~ sth/sb WITH sth/sb** asociar algo/a algn CON algo/algn **(b)** (combine) (*often pass*): **the fall in demand, ~d with competition from abroad** el descenso de la demanda, unido a la competencia extranjera

coupon /'kuːpɑːn ‖'kuːpɒn/ *n* **(a)** (voucher — for discount) vale *m*; (— in rationing) cupón *m* de racionamiento **(b)** (form — in advertisement) cupón *m*; (— for competition) boleto *m*

courage /'kərɪdʒ ‖'kʌrɪdʒ/ *n* valor *m*, coraje *m*

courageous /kə'reɪdʒəs/ *adj* ⟨*person*⟩ valiente, corajudo; ⟨*words*⟩ valiente; ⟨*act*⟩ valeroso

courgette /kʊr'ʒet ‖kɔː'ʒet/ *n* (BrE) ▶ ZUCCHINI

courier /'kʊriər ‖'kʊriə(r)/ *n* **(a)** (guide) guía *mf* **(b)** (messenger) (BrE) mensajero, -ra *m,f*, correo *mf*, rutero, -ra *m,f*

course /kɔːrs ‖kɔːs/ *n* **1** **(a)** (of river) curso *m*; (of road) recorrido *m* **(b)** (way of proceeding): **the best ~ of action** las mejores medidas que se pueden tomar **(c)** (progress, direction) (*no pl*): **in the normal ~ of events** normalmente; **in due ~** a su debido tiempo; **it changed the ~ of history** cambió el curso de la historia
2 of course claro, desde luego, por supuesto; **of ~ not** claro *or* por supuesto que no
3 (Aviat, Naut) rumbo *m*; **to go off ~** desviarse* de rumbo; **to change ~** cambiar de rumbo
4 **(a)** (Educ) curso *m*; **~ IN/ON sth** curso DE/ SOBRE algo; **to take a ~** hacer* un curso **(b)** (Med): **a ~ of treatment** un tratamiento
5 (part of a meal) plato *m*; **main ~** plato principal *or* fuerte; **a three-~ meal** una comida de dos platos y postre
6 (Sport) (race~) hipódromo *m*, pista *f* (de carreras); (golf ~) campo *m* *or* (CS tb) cancha *f* (de golf)

court¹ /kɔːrt ‖kɔːt/ *n* **1** (Law) **(a)** (tribunal) tribunal *m*; **to take sb to ~** demandar a algn, llevar a algn a juicio; *(before n)* **~ case** causa *f*, juicio *m* **(b)** (building) juzgado *m* **2** (of sovereign) corte *f* **3** (Sport) cancha *f* (AmL), pista *f* (Esp) **4** (courtyard) patio *m*

AmC	América Central	Arg	Argentina	Cu	Cuba	Per	Perú
AmL	América Latina	Bol	Bolivia	Ec	Ecuador	RPI	Río de la Plata
AmS	América del Sur	Chi	Chile	Esp	España	Ur	Uruguay
Andes	Región andina	CS	Cono Sur	Méx	México	Ven	Venezuela

court² *vt* **(a)** ⟨*girl*⟩ (dated) cortejar (ant), hacerle* la corte a (ant) **(b)** (seek) ⟨*danger/favor*⟩ buscar*; ⟨*danger*⟩ exponerse* a

courteous /'kɜːrtiəs ‖ 'kɜːtiəs/ *adj* cortés

courtesy /'kɜːrtəsi ‖ 'kɜːtəsi/ *n* cortesía *f*; ∼ **of** por atención de

courthouse /'kɔːrthaʊs ‖ 'kɔːthaʊs/ *n* juzgado *m*

courtier /'kɔːrtiər ‖ 'kɔːtiə(r)/ *n* cortesano, -na *m,f*

court-martial¹ /'kɔːrt'mɑːrʃəl ‖ ˌkɔːt'mɑːʃəl/ *n* (*pl* **courts-martial** /'kɔːrts-/) consejo *m* de guerra

court-martial² *vt*, (BrE) **-ll-** formarle consejo de guerra a

court: ∼**room** *n* sala *f* (*de un tribunal*); ∼ **shoe** *n* (BrE) zapato *m* (de) salón; ∼**yard** *n* patio *m*

cousin /'kʌzn̩/ *n* primo, -ma *m,f*; **first** ∼ primo hermano *or* carnal, prima hermana *or* carnal; **second** ∼ primo segundo, prima segunda

cove /kəʊv/ *n* cala *f*, caleta *f*

covenant /'kʌvənənt/ *n* pacto *m*

cover¹ /'kʌvər ‖ 'kʌvə(r)/ *n* ⊡ **(a)** (lid, casing) tapa *f*, cubierta *f*; (for cushion, sofa, typewriter) funda *f*; (for book) forro *m* **(b)** **covers** *pl* (bedclothes) **the** ∼**s** las mantas, las cobijas (AmL), las frazadas (AmL)

⊡ (of book) tapa *f*, cubierta *f*; (of magazine) portada *f*, carátula *f* (Andes); (front ∼) portada *f*; **to read sth from** ∼ **to** ∼ leer* algo de cabo a rabo

⊡ **(a)** (shelter, protection): **to take** ∼ guarecerse*, ponerse* a cubierto; **to run for** ∼ correr a guarecerse *or* a ponerse a cubierto; **under** ∼ **of darkness** al abrigo de la oscuridad **(b)** (front, pretense) tapadera *f*, pantalla *f*; **to blow sb's** ∼ desenmascarar a algn

⊡ (insurance) (BrE) cobertura *f*

cover² *vt* ⊡ **(a)** (overlay) cubrir*; **to be** ∼**ed IN sth** estar* cubierto DE algo **(b)** ⟨*hole/saucepan*⟩ tapar **(c)** ⟨*cushion*⟩ ponerle* una funda a; ⟨*book*⟩ forrar; ⟨*sofa*⟩ tapizar*, recubrir* **(d)** ⟨*passage/ terrace*⟩ techar, cubrir*

⊡ **(a)** (extend over) ⟨*area/floor*⟩ cubrir*; ⟨*page*⟩ llenar **(b)** (travel) ⟨*distance*⟩ recorrer

⊡ **(a)** (deal with) ⟨*syllabus*⟩ cubrir*; ⟨*topic*⟩ tratar **(b)** (report on) (Journ) cubrir*

⊡ **(a)** (hide) tapar; **to** ∼ **one's head** cubrirse* (la cabeza) **(b)** (mask) ⟨*surprise/ignorance*⟩ disimular; ⟨*mistake*⟩ ocultar

⊡ **(a)** (guard, protect) cubrir* **(b)** (point gun at) apuntarle a **(c)** (Sport) ⟨*opponent*⟩ marcar*; ⟨*shot/ base*⟩ cubrir*

⊡ (Fin) **(a)** ⟨*costs/expenses*⟩ cubrir*; ⟨*liabilities*⟩ hacer* frente a; **will $100** ∼ **it?** ¿alcanzará con 100 dólares? **(b)** (insurance) cubrir*

■ ∼ *vi* **(a)** (deputize) **to** ∼ **FOR sb** sustituir* a algn **(b)** (conceal truth) **to** ∼ **FOR sb** encubrir* a algn

■ **cover up** ⊡ [*v* + *o* + *adv*, *v* + *adv* + *o*] **(a)** (cover completely) cubrir*, tapar **(b)** (conceal) ⟨*facts/ truth*⟩ ocultar; ⟨*mistake*⟩ disimular

⊡ [*v* + *adv*] (conceal error) disimular; (conceal truth) **to** ∼ **up FOR sb** encubrir* a algn

coverage /'kʌvərɪdʒ/ *n* (Journ) cobertura *f*

cover-alls /'kʌvərɔːlz/ *pl n* (AmE) overol *m* (AmL), mono *m* (Esp, Méx)

covering letter /'kʌvərɪŋ/ *n* carta *f* adjunta

covert /'kəʊvərt ‖ 'kʌvət, 'kəʊ-/ *adj* encubierto

cover-up /'kʌvərʌp/ *n* (of crime) encubrimiento *m*

covet /'kʌvət/ *vt* codiciar

cow /kaʊ/ *n* **(a)** (Agr) vaca *f* **(b)** (female whale, elephant, seal) hembra *f*

coward /'kaʊərd ‖ 'kaʊəd/ *n* cobarde *mf*

cowardice /'kaʊərdəs ‖ 'kaʊədɪs/ *n* cobardía *f*

cowardly /'kaʊərdli ‖ 'kaʊədli/ *adj* cobarde

cowboy /'kaʊbɔɪ/ *n* (in Western US) vaquero *m*; (in Wild West) vaquero *m*, cowboy *m*

cower /'kaʊər ‖ 'kaʊə(r)/ *vi* encogerse* (de miedo)

coworker /'kəʊ'wɜːrkər ‖ kəʊ'wɜːkə(r)/ *n* (esp AmE) (workmate) colega *mf*, compañero, -ra *m,f* de trabajo; (collaborator) colaborador, -dora *m,f*

coy /kɔɪ/ *adj* **coyer, coyest** (shy) tímido; (evasive) evasivo

coyote /kaɪ'əʊti ‖ kɔɪ'əʊti/ *n* (*pl* **-otes** *or* **-ote**) coyote *m*

cozy¹, (BrE) **cosy** /'kəʊzi/ *adj* **cozier, coziest (a)** ⟨*room*⟩ acogedor **(b)** ⟨*chat*⟩ íntimo y agradable

cozy², (BrE) **cosy** *n* (*pl* **-ies**) (tea ∼) cubreteteras *m*

CPA *n* (in US) = **Certified Public Accountant**

crab /kræb/ *n* (animal, meat) cangrejo *m*, jaiba *f* (AmL)

crack¹ /kræk/ *n* ⊡ **(a)** (in ice, wall, pavement) grieta *f*; (in glass, china) rajadura *f* **(b)** (chink, slit) rendija *f* ⊡ **(a)** (sound — of whip, twig) chasquido *m*; (— of rifle shot) estallido *m*; (— of thunder) estruendo *m* ⊡ (blow) golpe *m* ⊡ (instant): **at the** ∼ **of dawn** al amanecer ⊡ (attempt) (colloq) intento *m*; **to have a** ∼ **at sth** intentar algo ⊡ (colloq) (wisecrack) comentario *m* socarrón ⊡ (drug) crack *m*

crack² *adj* (*before n*) ⟨*shot/troops*⟩ de primera

crack³ *vt* ⊡ ⟨*cup/glass*⟩ rajar; ⟨*ground/earth/ skin*⟩ agrietar; **he** ∼**ed a rib** se fracturó una costilla

⊡ **(a)** (break open) ⟨*egg/nut*⟩ cascar*; ⟨*safe*⟩ forzar*; ⟨*drugs ring/spy ring*⟩ desmantelar **(b)** (decipher, solve) ⟨*code*⟩ descifrar; ⟨*problem*⟩ resolver*

⊡ (make cracking sound with) ⟨*whip*⟩ (hacer*) chasquear; ⟨*finger/knuckle*⟩ hacer* crujir

⊡ (hit sharply) pegar*

⊡ ⟨*joke*⟩ (colloq) contar*

■ ∼ *vi* ⊡ **(a)** «*cup/glass*» rajarse*; «*rock/paint/ skin*» agrietarse **(b)** (make cracking sound) «*whip*» chasquear; «*bones/twigs*» crujir **(c)** «*voice*» quebrarse* **(d)** (break down): **she** ∼**ed under the strain** sufrió una crisis nerviosa a causa de la tensión

⊡ (be active, busy): **to get** ∼**ing** (colloq) poner(se)* manos a la obra

■ **crack down** [*v* + *adv*] **to** ∼ **down ON sb/sth** tomar medidas enérgicas CONTRA algn/algo

■ **crack up** [*v* + *adv*] **(a)** (break down) (colloq) «*person*» sufrir un ataque de nervios, sucumbir a la presión **(b)** (burst out laughing) (colloq) soltar* una carcajada

cracked /krækt/ *adj* **(a)** ⟨*cup/glass*⟩ rajado; ⟨*rib*⟩ fracturado; ⟨*wall/ceiling*⟩ con grietas; ⟨*lips*⟩ partido; ⟨*skin*⟩ agrietado **(b)** (crazy) (colloq) ⟨*person*⟩ loco, chiflado (fam) **(c)** ⟨*voice*⟩ cascado

cracker /'krækər ‖'krækə(r)/ n **1** (biscuit) cracker f, galleta f (salada) **2** (a) (fire~) petardo m (b) (BrE) sorpresa f (que estalla al abrirla) **3** (Comput colloq) intruso, -sa m,f

crackle¹ /'krækəl/ vi «fire» crepitar; «twigs/paper» crujir

crackle² n (of twigs, paper) crujido m; (of fire) chisporroteo m

cradle¹ /'kreɪdl/ n cuna f

cradle² vt «baby» acunar, mecer*

craft /krɑːft ‖krɑːft/ n **1** (a) (trade) oficio m; (skill) arte m (b) **crafts** pl artesanía f; see also ART 1B **2** (guile, deceit) (liter) artimañas fpl **3** (pl ~) (Naut) embarcación f; (Aerosp, Aviat) nave f

craftsman /'krɑːftsmən ‖'krɑːftsmən/ n (pl -men /mən/) artesano m, artífice m

crafty /'krɑːfti ‖'krɑːfti/ adj -tier, -tiest «person» astuto; «methods/tactics» hábil

craggy /'krægi/ adj -gier, -giest escarpado; he had a ~, weather-beaten face tenía un rostro curtido y de facciones bien marcadas

cram /kræm/ -mm- vt (stuff) meter; the room was ~med with books la habitación estaba abarrotada de libros; I ~med three meetings into one morning logré asistir a tres reuniones en una mañana
■ ~ vi (for exam) empollar (Esp fam), zambutir (Méx), tragar* (RPI fam), matearse (Chi fam), empacarse* (Col fam)

cramp¹ /kræmp/ n (in leg) calambre m, rampa f (Esp); **stomach ~s** retorcijones mpl or (Esp) retortijones mpl en el estómago

cramp² vt (limit) «work/progress» entorpecer*; to ~ sb's style cortarle los vuelos a algn

cramped /kræmpt/ adj «handwriting» apretado; they work in ~ conditions están muy estrechos en el trabajo; they live in ~ conditions viven hacinados

cranberry /'krænˌberi ‖'krænbəri/ n (pl -ries) arándano m (rojo y agrio)

crane¹ /kreɪn/ n **1** (for lifting) grúa f **2** (Zool) grulla f

crane² vt: to ~ one's neck estirar el cuello

crank /kræŋk/ n **1** (a) (Mech Eng) cigüeñal m (b) ~ (handle) (Auto) manivela f (de arranque) **2** (colloq) (a) (eccentric) maniático, -ca m,f (b) (bad-tempered person) (AmE) cascarrabias mf

cranny /'kræni/ n (pl -nies) ranura f; ▶ NOOK

crap /kræp/ n (a) (excrement) (vulg) mierda f (vulg) (b) (nonsense) (sl) estupideces fpl, pendejadas fpl (Esp fam o vulg), pendejadas fpl (AmL exc CS fam), huevadas fpl (Andes, Ven vulg), boludeces fpl (Col, RPI vulg)

crash¹ /kræʃ/ n (a) (loud noise) estrépito m (b) (collision, accident) accidente m, choque m (c) (financial failure) crac m, crack m

crash² vt **1** (smash): he ~ed the car tuvo un accidente con el coche, chocó **2** (colloq) to ~ a party colarse* en una fiesta (fam)
■ ~ vi (a) (collide) to ~ (INTO sth) estrellarse or chocar* (CONTRA algo) (b) (make loud noise) «thunder» retumbar; the dishes ~ed to the floor los platos se cayeron al suelo estrepitosamente (c) (Fin) «shares» caer* a pique

crash³ adj (before n) «program/course» intensivo; ~ diet régimen m muy estricto

crash: ~ barrier n barrera f de protección; ~ helmet n casco m (protector); ~-landing /'kræʃˌlændɪŋ/ n aterrizaje m forzoso

crate /kreɪt/ n cajón m (de embalaje), jaba f (Chi)

crater /'kreɪtər ‖'kreɪtə(r)/ n cráter m

cravat /krə'væt/ n pañuelo m de cuello (de caballero)

crave /kreɪv/ vt «admiration» ansiar*; «affection» tener* ansias de; «food/drink» morirse* por (fam)

craving /'kreɪvɪŋ/ n (a) (strong desire) ansias fpl (b) (in pregnancy) antojo m

crawfish /'krɔːfɪʃ/ n (pl -fish or -fishes) ▶ CRAYFISH

crawl¹ /krɔːl/ vi **1** (a) (creep) arrastrarse; «baby» gatear, ir* a gatas; «insect» andar* (b) (go slowly) «traffic/train» avanzar* muy lentamente **2** (teem): the beach was ~ing with tourists la playa estaba plagada de turistas **3** (demean oneself) (colloq) arrastrarse

crawl² n **1** (slow pace) (no pl): to go at a ~ avanzar* muy lentamente **2** (swimming stroke) crol m

crayfish /'kreɪfɪʃ/ n (pl -fish or -fishes) (freshwater) ástaco m, cangrejo m de río; (marine) langosta f (pequeña), cigala f

crayon /'kreɪɑːn ‖'kreɪən/ n (pencil) lápiz m de color; (wax ~) crayola® f, crayón m (Méx, RPI), lápiz m de cera (Chi)

craze /kreɪz/ n (fashion) moda f; (fad) manía f

crazy /'kreɪzi/ adj -zier, -ziest loco; to go ~ volverse* loco; to be ~ ABOUT o (AmE) FOR o (AmE) OVER sb estar* loco POR algn (fam)

creak /kriːk/ vi «door» chirriar*; «bedsprings/floorboards/joints» crujir

cream¹ /kriːm/ n **1** (Culin) crema f (de leche) (esp AmL), nata f (Esp) **2** (lotion) crema f **3** (elite) the ~ of society la flor y nata de la sociedad **4** (color) color m crema

cream² adj color crema adj inv

cream³ vt «butter/sugar» batir (hasta obtener una consistencia cremosa); ~ed potatoes puré m de papas or (Esp) patatas

cream cheese n queso m crema (AmL), queso m para untar (Esp)

creamer /'kriːmər ‖'kriːmə(r)/ n **1** (jug) (AmE) jarrita f para crema **2** (powder) leche f en polvo

creamy /'kriːmi/ adj -mier, -miest (containing cream) con crema; (smooth) cremoso

crease¹ /kriːs/ n (in paper, clothes) arruga f; (in trousers) raya f, pliegue m (Méx, Ven)

crease² vi arrugarse*
■ ~ vt «clothes» arrugar*; «paper» doblar, plegar*

create /kri'eɪt/ vt crear; «impression» producir*

creation /kri'eɪʃən/ n creación f

creative /kri'eɪtɪv/ adj creativo

creativity /ˌkriːeɪ'tɪvəti/ n creatividad f

creator /kri'eɪtər ‖kri'eɪtə(r)/ n creador, -dora m,f

creature /'kriːtʃər ‖'kriːtʃə(r)/ n (a) (animate being) criatura f; **sea ~** animal m marino (b) (person) ser m, criatura f

creche, crèche /kreʃ/ n (a) (hospital for foundlings) (AmE) orfanato m, orfelinato m, orfanatorio *m* **(b)** (day nursery) (BrE) guardería *f* (infantil) (*puede ser en el lugar de trabajo para los empleados etc.*)

credentials /krɪˈdentʃəlz ‖krɪˈdenʃəlz/ *pl n* (of ambassador) cartas *fpl* credenciales; (references) referencias *fpl*; (identifying papers) documentos *mpl* (de identidad)

credibility /ˌkredəˈbɪləti/ *n* credibilidad *f*

credible /ˈkredəbəl/ *adj* creíble

credit¹ /ˈkredət ‖ˈkredɪt/ *n* ☐ (Fin) **(a)** (in store) crédito *m*; **on ~** a crédito **(b)** (in banking): **to keep one's account in ~** mantener* un saldo positivo; (*before n*) **~ balance** saldo *m* positivo; **~ limit** límite *m* de crédito **(c)** (on balance sheet) saldo *m* acreedor *or* a favor

☒ (honor, recognition) mérito *m*; **Jim must take the ~ for the excellent organization** la excelente organización es obra de Jim; **your children are a ~ to you** puedes estar orgulloso de tus hijos

☒ (Educ) **(a)** (for study) crédito *m* (*unidad de valor de una asignatura dentro de un programa de estudios*) **(b)** (grade) ≈ notable *m*

☒ **credits** *pl* (Cin, TV, Video) créditos *mpl*

credit² *vt* ☐ **to ~ money to an account** abonar *or* ingresar dinero en una cuenta ☒ **(a)** (ascribe to) **please, ~ me with some intelligence** reconóceme algo de inteligencia, por favor; **they are ~ed with having invented the game** se les atribuye la invención del juego **(b)** (believe) creer*

credit card *n* tarjeta *f* de crédito

creditor /ˈkredətər ‖ˈkredɪtə(r)/ *n* acreedor, -dora *m,f*

creed /kriːd/ *n* credo *m*

creek /kriːk/ *n* **(a)** (stream) (AmE) arroyo *m*, riachuelo *m* **(b)** (inlet) (BrE) cala *f*

creep¹ /kriːp/ (*past & past p* **crept**) *vi* (+ *adv compl*) **(a)** (crawl) arrastrarse **(b)** (move stealthily): **to ~ into a room** entrar en un cuarto sigilosamente; **a note of suspicion crept into his voice** se empezó a notar un elemento de sospecha en su voz

creep² *n* (colloq) **(a)** (unpleasant person) asqueroso, -sa *m,f* **(b)** (favor-seeking person) adulador, -dora *m,f*, pelota *mf* (Esp fam), chupamedias *mf* (CS, Ven fam), lambiscón, -cona *m,f* (Méx fam), lambón, -bona *m,f* (Col fam)

creeper /ˈkriːpər ‖ˈkriːpə(r)/ *n* planta *f* trepadora

cremate /ˈkriːmeɪt ‖krɪˈmeɪt/ *vt* incinerar, cremar

cremation /krɪˈmeɪʃən/ *n* incineración *f*, cremación *f*

crematorium /ˈkriːməˈtɔːriəm ‖ˌkreməˈtɔːriəm/ *n* (*pl* **-riums** *or* **-ria** /-riə/) crematorio *m*

crepe, crêpe /kreɪp/ *n* ☐ (fabric) crep *m*, crepé *m* ☒ (pancake) (Culin) crep *m*, crêpe *f*, panqueque *m* (AmC, CS), crepa *f* (Méx)

crepe paper *n* papel *m* crepé *or* crep

crept /krept/ *past & past p of* CREEP¹

crescendo /krəˈʃendəʊ ‖krɪˈʃendəʊ/ *n* (*pl* **-dos**) (Mus) crescendo *m*; (climax) punto *m* culminante

crescent /ˈkresn̩t/ *n* ☐ (moon) creciente *m* ☒ **(a)** (shape) media luna *f* **(b)** (street) *calle en forma de media luna*

cress /kres/ *n* mastuerzo *m*

crest /krest/ *n* ☐ (Zool) (of skin) cresta *f*; (of feathers) penacho *m* ☒ (in heraldry) emblema *m*, divisa *f* ☒ (of wave) cresta *f*; (of mountain) cima *f*

crestfallen /ˈkrestˌfɔːlən/ *adj* alicaído

crevice /ˈkrevəs ‖ˈkrevɪs/ *n* grieta *f*

crew /kruː/ *n* **(a)** (Aviat, Naut) tripulación *f* **(b)** (team) equipo *m*; **film ~** (Cin) equipo *m* de rodaje **(c)** (gang, band) banda *f*, pandilla *f*

crew: ~ cut *n* pelo *m* cortado al rape; **~ neck** *n* cuello *m* redondo

crib /krɪb/ *n* ☐ **(a)** (child's bed) (AmE) cuna *f* **(b)** (Nativity scene) nacimiento *m*, pesebre *m*, belén *m* (Esp) ☒ (Agr) **(a)** (manger) pesebre *m* **(b)** (for storing grain) (AmE) granero *m*

crick /krɪk/ *vt*: **to ~ one's neck** hacer* un mal movimiento con el cuello

cricket /ˈkrɪkət ‖ˈkrɪkɪt/ *n* ☐ (Zool) grillo *m* ☒ (Sport) críquet *m*

cricketer /ˈkrɪkətər ‖ˈkrɪkɪtə(r)/ *n* jugador, -dora *m,f* de críquet

crime /kraɪm/ *n* **(a)** (wrongful act) delito *m*; (murder) crimen *m* **(b)** (criminal activity) delincuencia *f*; **~ wave** ola *f* delictiva

criminal¹ /ˈkrɪmənl ‖ˈkrɪmɪnl/ *n* delincuente *mf*; (serious offender) criminal *mf*

criminal² *adj* ⟨*act*⟩ delictivo; ⟨*organization/mind*⟩ criminal; **~ court** juzgado *m* en lo penal; **~ law** derecho *m* penal; **~ offense** delito *m*

criminal record *n* antecedentes *mpl* penales, prontuario *m* (CS)

crimson¹ /ˈkrɪmzən/ *n* carmesí *m*

crimson² *adj* carmesí *adj inv*

cringe /krɪndʒ/ *vi* **(a)** (shrink, cower) encogerse* **(b)** (grovel) arrastrarse

crinkle /ˈkrɪŋkəl/ **~ (up)** *vt* arrugar* ■ ~ *vi* arrugarse*

cripple¹ /ˈkrɪpəl/ *n* lisiado, -da *m,f*

cripple² *vt* **(a)** (lame, disable): **he was ~d for life** quedó lisiado de por vida; **he's ~d with arthritis** la artritis lo tiene casi inmovilizado **(b)** (make inactive, ineffective) ⟨*ship/plane*⟩ inutilizar*; ⟨*industry*⟩ paralizar*

crippling /ˈkrɪplɪŋ/ *adj* ⟨*costs/debts*⟩ agobiante; ⟨*losses/strike*⟩ de consecuencias catastróficas; ⟨*pain*⟩ atroz

crisis /ˈkraɪsəs ‖ˈkraɪsɪs/ *n* (*pl* **-ses** /-siːz/) crisis *f*; (*before n*) **to reach ~ point** hacer* crisis

crisp¹ /krɪsp/ *adj* **-er, -est** ☐ **(a)** (crunchy) ⟨*toast/bacon*⟩ crujiente, crocante (RPl); ⟨*lettuce*⟩ fresco; ⟨*apple/snow*⟩ crujiente **(b)** ⟨*sheets*⟩ limpio y almidonado **(c)** (cold) ⟨*air*⟩ frío y vigorizante ☒ (brisk, concise) ⟨*manner*⟩ seco; ⟨*style*⟩ escueto

crisp² *n* (potato ~) (BrE) papa *f or* (Esp) patata *f* frita (*de bolsa*), papa *f* chip (Ur)

crisscross¹ /ˈkrɪskrɔːs ‖ˈkrɪskrɒs/ *adj* entrecruzado

crisscross² *vt* entrecruzar*

criterion /kraɪˈtɪriən ‖kraɪˈtɪəriən/ *n* (*pl* **-ria** /-riə/) criterio *m*

critic /ˈkrɪtɪk/ *n* (Art, Theat, Lit) crítico, -ca *m,f*; (detractor) detractor, -tora *m,f*

critical /ˈkrɪtɪkəl/ *adj* ☐ ⟨*remark/report*⟩ crítico ☒ **(a)** (very serious) ⟨*condition/shortage*⟩ crítico **(b)** (crucial) ⟨*period*⟩ crítico

critically /'krɪtɪkli/ adv ① ⟨ill⟩ gravemente ② (a) (as a critic): she looked ∼ at her reflection miró con ojo crítico la imagen que le devolvía el espejo (b) (censoriously): she spoke rather ∼ of him habló de él en tono de crítica

criticism /'krɪtəsɪzəm ‖'krɪtɪsɪzəm/ n crítica f

criticize /'krɪtəsaɪz ‖'krɪtɪsaɪz/ vt criticar*

croak¹ /krəʊk/ n (of frog) croar m; (of raven) graznido m; (of person) voz f ronca

croak² vi ⟨frog⟩ croar; ⟨raven⟩ graznar; «person» hablar con voz ronca
■ ∼ vt decir* con voz ronca

Croat /'krəʊæt/ n croata mf

Croatia /krəʊ'eɪʃə/ n Croacia f

Croatian /krəʊ'eɪʃən/ adj croata

crochet¹ /krəʊ'ʃeɪ ‖'krəʊʃeɪ/ vt tejer a crochet or a ganchillo; (before n) ∼ hook aguja f de crochet, ganchillo f, crochet m (Chi)

crochet² n crochet m, ganchillo m

crockery /'krɑːkəri ‖'krɒkəri/ n vajilla f, loza f

crocodile /'krɑːkədaɪl ‖'krɒkədaɪl/ n cocodrilo m

crocus /'krəʊkəs/ n (pl **-cuses**) azafrán m de primavera

crook /krʊk/ n sinvergüenza mf

crooked /'krʊkəd ‖'krʊkɪd/ adj (a) ⟨line/legs⟩ torcido, chueco (AmL); ⟨back⟩ encorvado; ⟨path⟩ sinuoso (b) (dishonest) (colloq) ⟨person/deal⟩ deshonesto, chueco (Chi, Méx fam)

crop¹ /krɑːp ‖krɒp/ n ① (a) (quantity of produce) cosecha f (b) (type of produce) cultivo m ② (haircut) corte m de pelo muy corto ③ (riding ∼) fusta f, fuete m (AmL exc CS)

crop² **-pp-** vt ⟨hair⟩ cortar muy corto
■ **crop up** [v + adv] (colloq) surgir*

croquet /krəʊ'keɪ ‖'krəʊkeɪ/ n croquet m

croquette /krəʊ'ket/ n (potato ∼) rollito de puré de papa envuelto en pan rallado y frito

cross¹ /krɔːs ‖krɒs/ n ① (a) (Relig) cruz f (b) (mark, sign) cruz f ② (hybrid) cruce m, cruza f (AmL) ③ (Sport) (in soccer) pase m cruzado (b) (in boxing) cruzado m, cross m

cross² vt ① (go across) ⟨road/river/desert⟩ cruzar*; it ∼ed my mind that ... se me ocurrió que ... ② ⟨arms/legs⟩ cruzar* ③ ⟨plants/breeds⟩ cruzar* ④ (go against) ⟨person⟩ contrariar*; ⟨plans⟩ frustrar
■ ∼ vi (a) (walk across road) cruzar* (b) «paths/letters» cruzarse*
■ v refl to ∼ oneself persignarse, santiguarse*
■ **cross out** [v + o + adv, v + adv + o] tachar

cross³ adj **-er, -est** (esp BrE) enojado (esp AmL), enfadado (esp Esp); **to get** ∼ enojarse (esp AmL), enfadarse (esp Esp)

cross: ∼**bar** n (on bicycle) barra f; (of goal) larguero m; ∼**bow** /'krɔːsbəʊ ‖'krɒsbəʊ/ n ballesta f; ∼**breed** vt (past & past p **-bred**) cruzar*; ∼**-Channel** /'krɔːs'tʃæn‖,krɒs'tʃæn/ adj (before n) ⟨ferry/traffic⟩ que cruza el Canal de la Mancha; ∼**-check** /'krɔːs'tʃek ‖,krɒs'tʃek/ vt

⟨facts/references⟩ verificar* (consultando otras fuentes); **to** ∼**-check** sth AGAINST sth cotejar algo CON algo; ∼**-country** /'krɔːs'kʌntri ‖,krɒs'kʌntri/ adj ⟨route/drive⟩ campo a través; ∼**-examination** /'krɔːs,ɪgˌzæmə'neɪʃən ‖,krɒs,ɪgˌzæmɪ'neɪʃən/ n repregunta fpl, contrainterrogación f (Chi); ∼**-examine** /'krɔːs,ɪg'zæmən ‖'krɒsɪg'zæmɪn/ vt ⟨witness⟩ repreguntar; ∼**-eyed** /'krɔːs'aɪd ‖'krɒsaɪd/ adj bizco; ∼**fire** n fuego m cruzado

crossing /'krɔːsɪŋ ‖'krɒsɪŋ/ n ① (across sea) travesía f, cruce m (AmS) ② (for pedestrians) cruce m peatonal or de peatones

cross: ∼**-legged** /'krɔːs'legd‖,krɒs'legd/ adv con las piernas cruzadas (en el suelo); ∼**-purposes** /'krɔːs'pɜːrpəsəz ‖,krɒs'pɜːpəsɪz/ pl n: we're (talking) at ∼**-purposes** estamos hablando de cosas distintas; ∼**question** /'krɔːs'kwestʃən ‖,krɒs'kwestʃən/ vt interrogar*; ∼**-reference** /'krɔːs'refrəns ‖,krɒs'refrəns/ n remisión f; ∼**roads** n (pl ∼**roads**) cruce m, encrucijada f (liter); ∼ **section,** (BrE) ∼**-section** /'krɔːs'sekʃən ‖,krɒs'sekʃən/ n (Biol, Eng) sección f, corte m transversal; ∼**walk** n (AmE) cruce m peatonal or de peatones; ∼**word** (puzzle) n crucigrama m, palabras fpl cruzadas (CS)

crotch /krɑːtʃ ‖krɒtʃ/ n entrepierna f

crotchet /'krɑːtʃət ‖'krɒtʃɪt/ n (BrE Mus) negra f

crouch /kraʊtʃ/ vi agacharse, ponerse* en cuclillas

croupier /'kruːpiər ‖'kruːpiə(r)/ n crupier mf, croupier mf

crow¹ /krəʊ/ n cuervo m; **as the** ∼ **flies** en línea recta

crow² vi (a) «cock» cacarear (b) (exult) alardear

crowbar /'krəʊbɑːr ‖'krəʊbɑː(r)/ n palanca f

crowd¹ /kraʊd/ n (a) (gathering of people) muchedumbre f, multitud f; **the game attracted a good** ∼ el partido atrajo mucho público (b) (masses, average folk) (pej): **to follow the** ∼ seguir* (a) la manada; **to stand out from the** ∼ destacar(se)* (c) (group, set) (colloq): **they are a nice** ∼ son gente simpática

crowd² vi aglomerarse
■ ∼ vt ⟨hall/entrance⟩ llenar, abarrotar

crowded /'kraʊdəd ‖'kraʊdɪd/ adj ⟨street/room/bus⟩ abarrotado, atestado; **the beach gets very** ∼ la playa se llena de gente

crown¹ /kraʊn/ n ① (of monarch) corona f ② (top — of hill) cima f; (— of tree) copa f; (— of tooth) corona f; (— of head) coronilla f; (— of hat) copa f ③ (Fin) corona f

crown² vt ① (make monarch) coronar ② (be culmination of) coronar; **to** ∼ **it all, I lost my wallet** y para rematarla, perdí la billetera

crown court n (in UK) juzgado m (que conoce de causas de derecho penal)

crowning /'kraʊnɪŋ/ adj (before n) ⟨success/achievement⟩ supremo, mayor

crown: ~ **jewels** pl n joyas fpl de la corona;
~ **prince** n príncipe m heredero

crow's feet pl n patas fpl de gallo

crucial /'kru:ʃəl/ adj crucial, decisivo

crucifixion /'kru:sə'fɪkʃən ‖ˌkru:sɪ'fɪkʃən/ n
crucifixión f

crucify /'kru:səfaɪ ‖'kru:sɪfaɪ/ vt (past & past p
-**fied**) crucificar*

crude /kru:d/ adj -**der**, -**dest** (a) (vulgar)
ordinario, grosero (b) (unsophisticated)
rudimentario, burdo (c) (containing impurities)
(before n) ‹oil› crudo

cruel /'kru:əl/ adj **crueller**, **cruellest** cruel

cruelty /'kru:əlti/ n (pl -**ties**) crueldad f

cruet /'kru:ət ‖'kru:ɪt/ n (Culin) vinagrera f,
aceitera f, alcuza f (Chi)

cruise¹ /kru:z/ vi ① (a) (Naut) hacer* un
crucero (b) ‹police car› patrullar ② (travel at
steady speed) ‹plane› volar*; ‹car› ir* (a una
velocidad constante)

cruise² n crucero m

cruiser /'kru:zər ‖'kru:zə(r)/ n (warship) crucero
m; (cabin ~) lancha f

crumb /krʌm/ n miga f

crumble /'krʌmbəl/ vi ‹cake/soil›
desmenuzarse*; ‹wall› desmoronarse;
‹democracy/resolve› desmoronarse
∎ ~ vt ‹earth/cake› desmenuzar*; ‹bread›
desmigajar

crummy /'krʌmi/ adj -**mier**, -**miest** (colloq)
malo, horrible

crumpet /'krʌmpət ‖'krʌmpɪt/ n (Culin)
panecillo de levadura que se come tostado

crumple /'krʌmpəl/ vt ‹paper/clothes› arrugar*;
‹metal› abollar; **she ~d the sheet of paper into a
ball** hizo una bola estrujando la hoja de papel

crunch¹ /krʌntʃ/ vt (a) (eat noisily) mascar*,
ronchar (b) (crush) aplastar (haciendo crujir)

crunch² n ① (noise) crujido m ② (crisis): **when
it comes to the ~** a la hora de la verdad

crunchy /'krʌntʃi/ adj -**chier**, -**chiest**
crujiente

crusade /kru:'seɪd/ n (a) (Hist) also **Crusade**
cruzada f (b) (campaign) cruzada f

crush¹ /krʌʃ/ vt ① (squash) ‹box/car/person/
fingers› aplastar; ‹grapes› prensar; ‹dress/suit›
arrugar* ② (subdue) ‹resistance/enemy› aplastar

crush² n ① (crowd) (no pl) aglomeración f
② (infatuation) (colloq) enamoramiento m; **to have a
~ on sb** estar* chiflado por algn (fam)

crush barrier n valla f de protección

crushing /'krʌʃɪŋ/ adj ‹defeat› aplastante;
‹reply/contempt› apabullante

crust /krʌst/ n (a) (on bread) corteza f (b) (thin
outer layer) costra f, corteza f; **the earth's ~** la
corteza terrestre

crustacean /krʌ'steɪʃən/ n crustáceo m

crusty /'krʌsti/ adj -**tier**, -**tiest** (a) (crispy)
‹bread› crujiente (b) (irascible) malhumorado

crutch /krʌtʃ/ n ① (walking aid) muleta f
② (BrE) ▶ CROTCH

crux /krʌks/ n (no pl) **the ~** (of the matter) el
quid (de la cuestión)

cry¹ /kraɪ/ n (pl **cries**) ① (a) (exclamation)
grito m; **to be a far ~ from sth** ser* muy distinto

de or a algo (b) (of street vendor) pregón m (c) (no
pl) (call of seagull) chillido m ② (weep) (colloq) (no
pl) llanto m; **to have a ~** llorar

cry² **cries**, **crying**, **cried** vi ① (weep) llorar
② (call) ‹bird› chillar; ‹person› gritar
∎ **cry out** [v + adv] (call out) gritar (b) (need)
to ~ out FOR sth pedir* algo a gritos

crypt /krɪpt/ n cripta f

cryptic /'krɪptɪk/ adj enigmático

crystal /'krɪstl/ n (a) (Chem) cristal m (b) ~
(glass) cristal m

crystal: ~ **ball** n bola f de cristal; ~-**clear**
/'krɪstl'klɪr ‖'krɪstl'klɪə(r)/ adj ‹water› (liter)
cristalino; ‹sound/image› nítido, claro

crystallize /'krɪstəlaɪz/ vt (a) (Chem, Geol)
cristalizar*; ‹idea/plan› materializar* (b) (Culin)
‹fruit› confitar, escarchar, abrillantar (RPl),
cristalizar* (Méx)

CS gas /'si:'es/ n gas m lacrimógeno

CST (in US) = **Central Standard Time**

CT = **Connecticut**

cub /kʌb/ n (a) (young animal) cachorro m (b)
Cub (Scout) lobato m

Cuba /'kju:bə/ n Cuba f

Cuban¹ /'kju:bən/ adj cubano

Cuban² n cubano, -na m,f

cubbyhole /'kʌbihəʊl/ n cuchitril m

cube¹ /kju:b/ n (solid, shape) cubo m; (of meat,
cheese) dado m, cubito m; (of sugar) terrón m

cube² vt (Math) elevar al cubo, cubicar*

cubic /'kju:bɪk/ adj (of measure, shape) cúbico; ~
capacity volumen m; (of engine) cilindrada f,
cubicaje m

cubicle /'kju:bɪkəl/ n (in dormitory, toilets)
cubículo m; (booth) cabina f; (in store) probador m

cuckoo /'ku:ku: ‖'kʊku:/ n (pl **cuckoos**)
cuco m, cucú m, cuclillo m

cuckoo clock n reloj m de cuco or cucú

cucumber /'kju:kʌmbər ‖'kju:kʌmbə(r)/ n
pepino m

cud /kʌd/ n: **to chew the ~** (lit) ‹cow› rumiar;
‹person› rumiar el asunto

cuddle¹ /'kʌdl/ vt abrazar*

cuddle² n abrazo m

cuddly /'kʌdli/ adj -**dlier**, -**dliest** adorable; ~
toy muñeco m de peluche

cudgel /'kʌdʒəl/ n garrote m, porra f

cue /kju:/ n ① (Mus) entrada f; (Theat) pie m;
right on ~ en el momento justo ② (in snooker)
taco m

cuff¹ /kʌf/ n ① (a) (of sleeve) puño m; (of pants)
(AmE) vuelta f or (Chi) bastilla f or (Méx)
valenciana f or (RPl) botamanga f (b) (in phrases)
off the cuff (as adv): **he spoke off the ~** habló
improvisando; (as adj): **an off-the-~ speech** un
discurso improvisado ② (blow — on side of head)
cachete m, bofetón m, cachetada f (AmL); (— on
head) coscorrón m

cuff² vt darle* un cachete (or coscorrón etc) a

cuff link n gemelo m or (Col) mancorna f or
(Chi) collera f or (Méx) mancuernilla or
mancuerna f

cuisine /kwɪ'zi:n/ n cocina f

cul-de-sac /'kʌldɪsæk/ n calle f sin salida or
(Col) ciega or (RPl) cortada f

cull /kʌl/ vt sacrificar de forma selectiva

culminate /'kʌlmɪneɪt ‖'kʌlmɪneɪt/ vi (reach peak) **to ~ IN sth** culminar **EN** algo

culprit /'kʌlprət ‖'kʌlprɪt/ n culpable mf

cult /kʌlt/ n (belief, worship) culto m; (sect) secta f; (before n) **~ figure** ídolo m

cultivate /'kʌltəveɪt ‖'kʌltɪveɪt/ vt cultivar

cultural /'kʌltʃərəl/ adj cultural

culture¹ /'kʌltʃər ‖'kʌltʃə(r)/ n **1** (civilization) cultura f; (before n) **~ shock** choque m cultural or de culturas **2** (Agr, Biol) cultivo m

culture² vt cultivar

cultured /'kʌltʃərd ‖'kʌltʃəd/ adj ‹person/mind› culto; ‹tastes› refinado

cumbersome /'kʌmbərsəm ‖'kʌmbəsəm/ adj ‹movements/gait› pesado y torpe

cumin /'kʌmən ‖'kʌmɪn/ n comino m

cumulative /'kjuːmjələtɪv ‖'kjuːmjʊlətɪv/ adj acumulativo

cunning /'kʌnɪŋ/ adj (a) (clever, sly) astuto; ‹smile› malicioso (b) (ingenious) ‹device› ingenioso

cup¹ /kʌp/ n **1** (a) (container, contents, cupful) taza f; **paper ~** vaso m de papel (b) (goblet) copa f **2** (trophy) copa f

cup² vt **-pp-: to ~ one's hands** (to drink) ahuecar* las manos; (to shout) hacer* bocina (con las manos)

cupboard /'kʌbərd ‖'kʌbəd/ n (a) (cabinet) armario m; (in dining-room) aparador m (b) (full-length, built-in) (BrE) armario m or (AmL exc RPl) clóset m or (RPl) placard m

curable /'kjʊrəbəl ‖'kjʊərəbəl/ adj curable

curate /'kjʊrət ‖'kjʊərət/ n coadjutor m

curator /kjʊ'reɪtər ‖kjʊə'reɪtə(r)/ n (of museum, art gallery) conservador, -dora m,f; (of exhibition) comisario, -ria m,f

curb¹ /kɜːrb ‖kɜːb/ n **1** (restraint) freno m **2 curb**, (BrE) **kerb** (in street) bordillo m (de la acera), borde m de la banqueta (Méx), cuneta f (Chi), sardinel m (Col), cordón m de la vereda (RPl)

curb² vt (control) ‹anger› dominar, refrenar; ‹spending/prices› poner* freno a, frenar

curd /kɜːrd ‖kɜːd/ n (often pl) cuajada f

curdle /'kɜːrdl̩ ‖'kɜːdl̩/ vi (a) (go bad, separate) «milk/sauce» cortarse (b) (form curds) «milk» cuajarse

cure¹ /kjʊr ‖kjʊə(r)/ vt **1** (Med) curar **2** ‹meat› curar

cure² n cura f

curfew /'kɜːrfjuː ‖'kɜːfjuː/ n toque m de queda

curiosity /ˌkjʊriˈɑːsəti ‖ˌkjʊəriˈɒsəti/ n (pl **-ties**) curiosidad f

curious /'kjʊriəs ‖'kjʊəriəs/ adj (a) (inquisitive) curioso (b) (strange) curioso, extraño

curiously /'kjʊriəsli ‖'kjʊəriəsli/ adv (with curiosity) con curiosidad; (strangely) curiosamente; **~ enough**, ... (indep) curiosamente, ...

curl¹ /kɜːrl ‖kɜːl/ n rizo m, rulo m (CS), chino m (Méx); (ringlet) bucle m, tirabuzón m

curl² vt ‹hair› rizar*, encrespar (CS), enchinar (Méx), enrular (RPl)

■ **~** vi «hair» rizarse*, encresparse (CS), enchinarse (Méx), enrularse (RPl); «paper/leaf/edge» ondularse

■ **curl up** [v + adv] (twist) «leaf/pages» ondularse; «cat» hacerse* un ovillo; **to ~ up in a chair** acurrucarse* en un sillón

curler /'kɜːrlər ‖'kɜːlə(r)/ n (for hair) rulo m, rulero m (RPl), marrón m (Col), tubo m (Chi, Méx)

curling irons, curling tongs /'kɜːrlɪŋ ‖'kɜːlɪŋ/ pl n tenacillas fpl (para rizar el pelo)

curly /'kɜːrli ‖'kɜːli/ adj **-lier, -liest** ‹hair› rizado, crespo (CS), chino (Méx); ‹tail› enroscado

currant /'kɜːrənt ‖'kʌrənt/ n pasa f de Corinto

currency /'kɜːrənsi ‖'kʌrənsi/ n (pl **-cies**) moneda f; **foreign ~** moneda f extranjera, divisas fpl

current¹ /'kɜːrənt ‖'kʌrənt/ adj **1** (before n) (a) (existing) ‹situation/prices› actual; ‹year› en curso (b) (most recent) ‹issue› último **2** (a) (valid) ‹license/membership› vigente (b) (prevailing) ‹opinion/practice› corriente

current² n (Elec) corriente f

current: ~ account n (BrE) cuenta f corriente; **~ affairs** pl n sucesos mpl de actualidad

currently /'kɜːrəntli ‖'kʌrəntli/ adv (a) (at present) actualmente (b) (commonly) comúnmente

curriculum /kə'rɪkjələm ‖kə'rɪkjʊləm/ n (pl **-lums** or **-la** /-lə/) (a) (range of courses) plan m de estudios (b) (for single course) programa m (de estudio), currículo m, currículum m (AmL)

curriculum vitae /'viːtaɪ/ n (pl **curricula vitae**) (BrE) currículum m (vitae), historial m personal

curry¹ /'kɜːri ‖'kʌri/ n (pl **curries**) curry m

curry² vt **-ries, -rying, -ried 1** (Culin) preparar al curry; **curried chicken** pollo m al curry **2** ▶ FAVOR¹ 1A

curse¹ /kɜːrs ‖kɜːs/ n (a) (evil spell) maldición f (b) (oath) maldición f, palabrota f

curse² vt/i maldecir*

cursor /'kɜːrsər ‖'kɜːsə(r)/ n cursor m

cursory /'kɜːrsəri ‖'kɜːsəri/ adj ‹glance› rápido; ‹description› somero; ‹interest› superficial

curt /kɜːrt ‖kɜːt/ adj cortante, seco

curtail /kɜːr'teɪl ‖kɜː'teɪl/ vt (cut short) abreviar; (restrict) restringir*; (reduce) reducir*

curtain /'kɜːrtn̩ ‖'kɜːtn̩/ n (at window) cortina f; (Theat) telón m

curtain call n salida f a escena (para saludar), telón m (Méx)

curtsey /'kɜːrtsi/ n (pl **-seys**) (esp BrE) ▶ CURTSY¹

curtsey vi **-seys, -seying, -seyed** (BrE) ▶ CURTSY²

curtsy¹ /'kɜːrtsi ‖'kɜːtsi/ n (pl **-sies**) reverencia f (que hacen las mujeres agachándose)

curtsy² vi **-sies, -sying, -sied** hacer* una reverencia

curve¹ /kɜːrv ‖kɜːv/ n curva f

curve² vi «surface» estar* curvado; «river/ball» describir* una curva

curved /kɜːrvd ‖kɜːvd/ adj curvo

cushion¹ /'kʊʃən/ n almohadón m; (before n) **~ cover** funda f de almohadón

cushion² vt ‹blow› amortiguar*; (protect) **to ~ sb AGAINST sth** proteger* a algn CONTRA algo

cuss /kʌs/ (esp AmE colloq) vi (a) (complain) despotricar* (b) (swear) maldecir*

custard /'kʌstərd ‖'kʌstəd/ n (a) (sauce) (BrE) crema f; (cold, set) ≈ natillas fpl (b) (egg ∼) especie de flan

custodian /kʌ'stəʊdiən/ n (a) (of morals, tradition) guardián, -diana m,f, custodio, -dia m,f (b) (of museum, library) conservador, -dora m,f

custody /'kʌstədi/ n [1] (detention): **to be in** (police) ∼ estar* detenido [2] (of child) custodia f

custom /'kʌstəm/ n [1] (convention, tradition, habit) costumbre f [2] (patronage) (esp BrE): **I'll take my ∼ elsewhere** dejaré de ser su cliente [3] **customs** pl aduana f

customary /'kʌstəməri/ adj (a) (traditional) tradicional; **it is ∼ to + INF** es la costumbre + INF (b) (habitual) habitual, acostumbrado

custom-built /'kʌstəm'bɪlt/ adj ⟨car⟩ hecho de encargo; ⟨house⟩ construido según las especificaciones del cliente

customer /'kʌstəmər ‖'kʌstəmə(r)/ n cliente, -ta m,f; (before n) ❸ **customer services** información y reclamaciones

customize /'kʌstəmaɪz/ vt ⟨car/program⟩ hacer* (or adaptar etc) según los requisitos del cliente

custom-made /'kʌstəm'meɪd/ adj hecho de encargo; ⟨suit/shoes⟩ a la medida

cut¹ /kʌt/ n [1] (a) (wound) tajo m, corte m (b) (incision) corte m [2] (a) (reduction): **to make ∼s in essential services** hacer* recortes en los servicios esenciales (b) (in text, film) corte m (c) (power ∼) apagón m [3] (a) (⟨hair∼⟩) corte m de pelo (b) (of suit) corte m [4] (of meat — type) corte m; (— piece) trozo m [5] (share) (colloq) tajada f (fam), parte f [6] (blow — with knife) cuchillada f

cut² (pres p **cutting**; past & past p **cut**) vt [1] ⟨wood/paper/wire/rope⟩ cortar; **to ∼ sth in half** cortar algo por la mitad; **I ∼ my finger** me corté el dedo; **to cut sb's throat** degollar* a algn; see also SHORT² 1

[2] (a) (trim) ⟨hair/nails⟩ cortar; ⟨grass/corn⟩ cortar, segar*; **to get one's hair ∼** cortarse el pelo (b) (shape) ⟨glass/stone⟩ tallar; ⟨key⟩ hacer* [3] (reduce) ⟨level/number⟩ reducir*; ⟨budget⟩ recortar; ⟨price/rate⟩ rebajar; ⟨service/workforce⟩ hacer* recortes en [4] (a) (shorten) ⟨text⟩ acortar (b) (remove) ⟨scene⟩ cortar (c) ⟨film⟩ (edit) editar; ⟨⟨censors⟩⟩ hacer* cortes en [5] (in cards) ⟨deck⟩ cortar [6] (colloq) (cease): **∼ the jokes!** ¡basta ya de bromas!

■ ∼ vi [1] ⟨⟨knife/scissors⟩⟩ cortar; **the rope ∼ into her wrists** la cuerda le estaba cortando las muñecas [2] (Cin, Rad): **∼!** ¡corte(n)! [3] (in cards) cortar

■ **cut across** [v + prep + o] (a) (take shortcut across) cortar por (b) (cross boundaries of) trascender*

■ **cut back** [1] [v + o + adv, v + adv + o] (a) (prune) ⟨hedge⟩ podar (b) (reduce) ⟨spending⟩ recortar
[2] [v + adv] (make reductions) hacer* economías; **to ∼ back ON sth** reducir* algo

■ **cut down** [1] [v + o + adv, v + adv + o] (a) (fell) ⟨tree⟩ cortar, talar (b) (kill) matar
[2] [v + adv] (make reductions): **cigarette? — no, thanks, I'm trying to ∼ down** ¿un cigarrillo? —

no, gracias, estoy tratando de fumar menos; **you should ∼ down on carbohydrates** debería reducir el consumo de hidratos de carbono

■ **cut in** [v + adv] (a) (interrupt) interrumpir (b) (Auto) atravesarse*

■ **cut off** [1] [v + o + adv, v + adv + o] (sever) ⟨branch/limb⟩ cortar
[2] [v + o + adv, v + adv + o] (interrupt, block) ⟨supply/route⟩ cortar
[3] [v + o + adv] (a) (isolate) aislar*; **to feel ∼ off** sentirse* aislado; **the town was ∼ off** la ciudad quedó sin comunicaciones (b) (on telephone): **we were ∼ off** se cortó la comunicación

■ **cut out** [1] [v + o + adv, v + adv + o] ⟨article/ photograph⟩ recortar
[2] [v + o + adv, v + adv + o] (a) ⟨dress/cookies⟩ cortar (b) (exclude) ⟨noise/carbohydrates⟩ eliminar; **he ∼ me out of his will** me excluyó de su testamento; **∼ it out!** (colloq) ¡basta ya!
[3] (suit): **to be ∼ out FOR sth** estar* hecho para algo
[4] [v + adv] ⟨⟨engine⟩⟩ pararse

■ **cut up** [v + o + adv, v + adv + o] ⟨vegetables/ wood⟩ cortar en pedazos

cut³ adj (before n) ⟨flowers⟩ cortado; ⟨glass⟩ tallado

cutback /'kʌtbæk/ n recorte m

cute /kjuːt/ adj **cuter, cutest** (a) (sweet) ⟨baby/face⟩ mono (fam), cuco (fam), rico (CS fam) (b) (attractive) (AmE) guapo

cut-glass /'kʌt'glæs ‖kʌt'glɑːs/ adj de cristal tallado

cuticle /'kjuːtɪkəl/ n cutícula f

cutlery /'kʌtləri/ n cubiertos mpl, cubertería f, cuchillería f (Chi)

cutlet /'kʌtlət ‖'kʌtlɪt/ n chuleta f (pequeña)

cut: ∼**off** (point) n límite m; ∼**-price** /'kʌt'praɪs/ adj (BrE) ▶ -RATE; ∼**-rate** /'kʌt'reɪt/ adj (AmE) a precio rebajado; ∼**throat** adj ⟨competition⟩ feroz, salvaje

cutting¹ /'kʌtɪŋ/ n [1] (a) (from newspaper) (BrE) recorte m (b) (from plant) esqueje m [2] (for road, railway) (BrE) zanja f

cutting² adj (a) (before n) ⟨tool/blade⟩ cortante (b) (cold) ⟨wind⟩ cortante (c) (hurtful) ⟨remark⟩ hiriente

CV n = **curriculum vitae**

cwt n = **hundredweight**

cyanide /'saɪənaɪd/ n cianuro m

cybercafé /'saɪbər₁kæfeɪ ‖'saɪbə₁kæfeɪ/ n cibercafé m

cyberspace /'saɪbərspeɪs ‖'saɪbəspeɪs/ n ciberespacio m

cycle¹ /'saɪkəl/ n [1] (process) ciclo m [2] (Elec, Comput) ciclo m [3] (bicycle) bicicleta f

cycle² vi ir* en bicicleta

cycling /'saɪklɪŋ/ n ciclismo m

cyclist /'saɪkləst ‖'saɪklɪst/ n ciclista mf

cyclone /'saɪkləʊn/ n ciclón m

cylinder /'sɪləndər ‖'sɪlɪndə(r)/ n [1] (Math) cilindro m [2] (a) (of engine) cilindro m (b) (container — for liquid gas) tanque m or (Esp) bombona f or (RPl) garrafa f or (Chi) balón m

cymbal /'sɪmbəl/ n platillo m, címbalo m

cynic /'sɪnɪk/ n cínico, -ca m,f

cynical /'sɪnɪkəl/ adj cínico

cynicism /'sɪnəsɪzəm/ n cinismo m
cypher n (esp BrE) ▶ CIPHER
cypress /'saɪprəs/ n ciprés m
Cyprus /'saɪprəs/ n Chipre f
cyst /sɪst/ n quiste m
cystic fibrosis /'sɪstɪkfaɪ'brəʊsəs ‖'sɪstɪkfaɪ'brəʊsɪs/ n fibrosis f cística or pancreática
cystitis /sɪ'staɪtəs ‖sɪ'staɪtɪs/ n cistitis f
czar /zɑːr ‖zɑː(r)/ n (esp AmE) ▶ TSAR

Czech¹ /tʃek/ adj checo
Czech² n (a) (person) checo, -ca m,f (b) (language) checo m
Czechoslovakia /'tʃekəslə'vɑːkɪə ‖,tʃekəslə'vækiə/ n (Hist) Checoslovaquia f
Czechoslovakian /'tʃekəslə'vɑːkiən ‖,tʃekəslə'vækiən/ adj (Hist) checoslovaco
Czech Republic n the ~ ~ la Républica Checa

Dd

D, d /diː/ n (a) (letter) D, d f (b) (Mus) re m
d' = **do**; d'you go there often? ¿vas ahí a menudo?
'd /d/ (a) = **had** (b) = **would** (c) = **did**
DA n (in US) = **district attorney**
dab /dæb/ vt: ~ the stain with a damp cloth frote suavemente la mancha con un trapo húmedo; ~ antiseptic on the cut dese unos toques de antiséptico en la herida
dabble /'dæbəl/ vi: to ~ in politics/journalism tener* escarceos con la política/el periodismo
dad /dæd/ n (colloq) papá m (fam)
daddy /'dædi/ n papi m (fam)
daddy longlegs /'lɔːŋlegz ‖'lɒŋlegz/ n (pl ~ ~) (colloq) (a) (harvestman) (AmE) segador m, falangio m (b) (cranefly) (BrE) típula f
daffodil /'dæfədɪl/ n narciso m
daft /dæft ‖dɑːft/ adj -er, -est (esp BrE colloq) tonto, bobo (fam)
dagger /'dægər ‖'dægə(r)/ n daga f, puñal m
dahlia /'dæljə ‖'deɪlɪə/ n dalia f
daily¹ /'deɪli/ adj (before n) ⟨newspaper/prayers⟩ diario; ⟨walk/visit⟩ diario, cotidiano
daily² adv a diario, diariamente
daily³ n (pl -lies) diario m, periódico m
dainty /'deɪnti/ adj -tier, -tiest ⟨flowers/vase⟩ delicado; ⟨appearance⟩ delicado, refinado
dairy /'deri ‖'deəri/ n (pl -ries) (a) (on farm) lechería f; (before n) ⟨produce⟩ lácteo; ⟨butter/cream⟩ de granja; ⟨cow/industry⟩ lechero (b) (shop) lechería f; (company) central f lechera
daisy /'deɪzi/ n (pl -sies) (cultivated) margarita f; (wild) margarita f de los prados, maya f
dally /'dæli/ vi -lies, -lying, -lied perder* el tiempo
dam¹ /dæm/ n dique m, presa f, represa f (AmS)
dam² vt -mm- construir* una presa or (AmS) una represa en

damage¹ /'dæmɪdʒ/ n **1** (to object) daño m; (to reputation, cause) daño m, perjuicio m
2 damages pl (Law) daños y perjuicios mpl
damage² vt ⟨building/vehicle⟩ dañar; ⟨health⟩ perjudicar*, ser* perjudicial para; ⟨reputation/cause⟩ perjudicar*, dañar
damaging /'dæmɪdʒɪŋ/ adj perjudicial
dame /deɪm/ n **1 Dame** (title in UK) Dame (título honorífico) **2** (woman) (AmE sl) tipa f (fam), tía f (Esp fam)
damn¹ /dæm/ vt (a) (Relig) condenar (b) (condemn) condenar
damn² n (colloq) (no pl): not to give a ~: I don't give a ~ what they think me importa un bledo lo que piensen (fam), me vale madres lo que piensen (Méx vulg)
damn³ interj (colloq) ¡caray! (fam & euf)
damn⁴ adj (colloq) (before n) (as intensifier) condenado (fam), maldito (fam), pinche (Méx fam)
damnation /dæm'neɪʃən/ n condenación f
damned /dæmd/ ▶ DAMN⁴
damning /'dæmɪŋ/ adj (a) (condemnatory) ⟨evidence⟩ condenatorio (b) (critical) ⟨appraisal⟩ crítico
damp¹ /dæmp/ adj -er, -est húmedo; to smell ~ oler* a humedad
damp² n humedad f
damp³ vt ~ (down) ⟨fire⟩ sofocar*; ⟨enthusiasm/excitement⟩ apagar*, enfriar*
damp course n membrana f aislante
dampen /'dæmpən/ vt **1** (moisten) humedecer*, mojar **2** (discourage) ⟨hopes⟩ hacer* perder; ⟨enthusiasm⟩ hacer* perder, apagar*
damper /'dæmpər ‖'dæmpə(r)/ n (of piano) sordina f; to put a ~ on sth (colloq): the bad news put a ~ on the celebrations la mala noticia estropeó las fiestas
damp: ~-proof vt proteger* contra la humedad; **~-proof course** n ▶ DAMP COURSE
damson /'dæmzən/ n ciruela f damascena

dance¹ /dæns ‖dɑːns/ n (a) (act, occasion) baile m; (before n) ⟨music⟩ de baile, bailable (b) (set of steps) baile m, danza f (c) (art form) danza f, baile m

dance² vi ⟦1⟧ (a) (to music) bailar (b) (skip) dar* saltos ⟦2⟧ «⟨eyes/flames⟩» (liter) bailar, danzar* (liter)
■ ~ vt ⟨waltz/tango⟩ bailar

dancer /'dænsər ‖'dɑːnsə(r)/ n bailarín, -rina m,f

dancing /'dænsɪŋ ‖'dɑːnsɪŋ/ n baile m; (before n) ⟨lesson/shoes⟩ de baile

dandelion /'dændəlaɪən ‖'dændɪlaɪən/ n diente m de león

dandruff /'dændrʌf/ n caspa f; (before n) ~ shampoo champú m anti-caspa

Dane /deɪn/ n danés, -nesa m,f, dinamarqués, -quesa m,f

danger /'deɪndʒər ‖'deɪndʒə(r)/ n peligro m; in ~ en peligro or en riesgo; to be in ~ of -ING correr peligro or riesgo de + INF; (before n) to be on the ~ list encontrarse* en estado grave; ~ signal señal f

dangerous /'deɪndʒərəs/ adj peligroso

dangerously /'deɪndʒərəsli/ adv peligrosamente

dangle /'dæŋɡəl/ vi colgar*, pender
■ ~ vt hacer* oscilar

Danish¹ /'deɪnɪʃ/ adj danés, dinamarqués

Danish² n danés m

Danish (pastry) n: bollo cubierto de azúcar glaseado

dank /dæŋk/ adj frío y húmedo

dapper /'dæpər ‖'dæpə(r)/ adj atildado, pulcro

dare¹ /der ‖deə(r)/ n reto m, desafío m

dare² v mod atreverse a, osar (liter); how ~ you! ¡cómo te atreves!; I ~ say you've had enough estarás harto(, me imagino)
■ ~ vt ⟦1⟧ (be so bold) to ~ to + INF atreverse a + INF, osar + INF (liter) ⟦2⟧ (challenge) to ~ sb to + INF retar or desafiar* a algn a + INF or A QUE (+ subj)

daredevil /'der‚devl ‖'deə‚devl/ n corajudo, -da m,f (fam); (before n) ⟨feat/exploit⟩ temerario

daring¹ /'derɪŋ ‖'deərɪŋ/ adj (a) ⟨explorer/pilot⟩ osado; ⟨plan⟩ audaz (b) ⟨dress/film⟩ atrevido

daring² n (a) (courage) arrojo m, coraje m (b) (audacity) audacia f

dark¹ /dɑːrk ‖dɑːk/ adj -er, -est ⟦1⟧ (unlit) ⟨room/night⟩ oscuro; it's getting ~ está oscureciendo, se está haciendo de noche ⟦2⟧ (a) (in color) oscuro; ~ chocolate chocolate m sin leche; ~ glasses anteojos mpl oscuros (esp AmL), gafas fpl negras (Esp) (b) (in complexion) moreno

dark² n (absence of light) the ~ la oscuridad; to wait until ~ esperar hasta que anochezca; to keep sb in the ~ about sth ocultarle algo a algn

Dark Ages pl n the ~ ~ la Alta Edad Media, la Edad de las tinieblas

darken /'dɑːrkən ‖'dɑːkən/ vt (a) (make dark) oscurecer* (b) (make somber) ensombrecer*
■ ~ vi (a) (grow dark) ⟨room/color/sky⟩» oscurecerse* (b) (grow somber) ensombrecerse*

darkness /'dɑːrknəs ‖'dɑːknɪs/ n oscuridad f

darkroom /'dɑːrkruːm, -rʊm ‖'dɑːkruːm, -rʊm/ n cuarto m oscuro

darling¹ /'dɑːrlɪŋ ‖'dɑːlɪŋ/ n (as form of address) cariño

darling² adj (before n) querido

darn¹ /dɑːrn ‖dɑːn/ vt zurcir*

dart¹ /dɑːrt ‖dɑːt/ n (a) (weapon) dardo m (b) (Games) dardo m (c) (Clothing) pinza f

dart² vi: to ~ into/out of a room entrar como una flecha en/salir* como una flecha de una habitación
■ ~ ⟨look⟩ lanzar*

dartboard /'dɑːrtbɔːrd ‖'dɑːtbɔːd/ n diana f

darts /dɑːrts ‖dɑːts/ n (+ sing vb) dardos mpl

dash¹ /dæʃ/ n ⟦1⟧ (small amount) poquito m; a ~ of milk un chorrito de leche ⟦2⟧ (punctuation mark) guion m

dash² vt ⟦1⟧ (hurl) tirar; she ~ed the plate to pieces hizo añicos or trizas el plato; the ship was ~ed against the rocks el barco se estrelló contra las rocas ⟦2⟧ (disappoint) ⟨hopes⟩ (usu pass) defraudar
■ ~ vi: I ~ed to the rescue me lancé al rescate; she ~ed out salió disparada
■ **dash off** ⟦1⟧ [v + o + adv, v + adv + o] (write hurriedly) escribir* corriendo ⟦2⟧ [v + adv] (leave hastily) irse* corriendo

dashboard /'dæʃbɔːrd ‖'dæʃbɔːd/ n tablero m de mandos, salpicadero m (Esp)

data /'deɪtə/ n ⟦1⟧ (facts, information) (+ pl vb) datos mpl, información f ⟦2⟧ (Comput) (+ sing vb) datos mpl

data: ~base n base f de datos; ~ highway n (Comput) autopista f de datos

date¹ /deɪt/ n ⟦1⟧ (of appointment, battle) fecha f; what's the ~ today? ¿a qué fecha estamos?; to ~ hasta la fecha, hasta el momento ⟦2⟧ (colloq) (appointment) cita f; Greg has a ~ with Ana on Sunday Greg sale con Ana el domingo ⟦3⟧ (fruit) dátil m

date² vt ⟦1⟧ (a) (mark with date) fechar (b) (give date to) ⟨remains/pottery/fossil⟩ datar, determinar la antigüedad de ⟦2⟧ (betray age) (colloq): that really ~s you eso te delata tu edad, eso demuestra lo viejo que eres
■ ~ vi ⟦1⟧ (originate in) datar; it ~s from the 14th century data del siglo XIV; his title ~s back to the 14th century los orígenes de su título se remontan al siglo XIV ⟦2⟧ (become old-fashioned) pasar de moda

dated /'deɪtəd ‖'deɪtɪd/ adj ⟨fashion/word⟩ anticuado; his plays are ~ sus obras han perdido actualidad

date: ~ rape n violación f (cometida durante una cita); ~ stamp n (instrument) fechador m; (date) fecha f; ~-stamp vt fechar

daub /dɔːb/ vt (smear) to ~ sth WITH sth embadurnar algo DE algo

daughter /'dɔːtər ‖'dɔːtə(r)/ n hija f

daughter-in-law /'dɔːtərɪnlɔː/ n (pl daughters-in-law) nuera f

daunt /dɔːnt/ vt (usu pass) amilanar, intimidar

daunting /'dɔːntɪŋ/ adj ⟨prospect⟩ desalentador, sobrecogedor; ⟨task⟩ de enormes proporciones

dawdle /'dɔːdl/ vi entretenerse*

dawn¹ /dɔːn/ n amanecer m; at ~ al amanecer, al alba (liter)

dawn² *vi* (liter) «*day*» amanecer*, clarear, alborear (liter); «*new age*» alborear (liter), nacer*
■ **dawn on** [*v* + *prep* + *o*]: **it gradually ~ed on me that ...** fui cayendo en la cuenta de que ...

dawn chorus *n* the ~ ~ el trino de los pájaros al amanecer

day /deɪ/ *n* **1** día *m*; (working day) jornada *f*, día *m*; **twice a** ~ dos veces al día; **all** ~ todo el día; **every** ~ todos los días; **one of these** ~**s** un día de estos; ~ **by** ~ día a día, de día en día; **it's not my/his** ~ no es mi/su día; **to take a** ~ **off (from work)** tomarse un día libre; **in this** ~ **and age** hoy (en) día, el día de hoy; **these** ~**s** hoy (en) día; **that'll be the** ~ (colloq & iro) cuando las ranas críen cola; **have a good** *o* **nice** ~! (AmE) ¡que le vaya bien!; **to call it a** ~ (temporarily) dejarlo para otro día; (permanently) dejar de trabajar (*or* estudiar *etc*); **to make someone's** ~ (colloq) alegrarle la vida a algn
2 days (*as adv*): **to work** ~**s** trabajar durante el día

day: ~**break** *n* alba *f*‡ (liter), amanecer *m*; ~-**care center** *n* (AmE) guardería *f* infantil

daydream¹ /'deɪdriːm/ *n* ensueño *m*, ensoñación *f*

daydream² *vi* soñar* despierto, fantasear

day: ~**light** *n* luz *f* (del día); ~**light (saving) time** *n* (AmE) hora *f* de verano; ~ **release** *n* (in UK) *sistema que permite a un empleado ausentarse regularmente de su trabajo para seguir estudios relacionados con el mismo*; ~**room** *n*: *sala de estar comunal en hospitales, prisiones etc*; ~**time** *n*: **in** *o* **during the** ~**time** de día *or* durante el día; ~-**to**-~ /'deɪtə'deɪ/ *adj* (before n) «*occurrence*» cotidiano, diario; «*chores/difficulties*» de cada día; «*existence*» diario; ~ **trip** *n* excursión *f* de un día; ~-**tripper** /,trɪpər ‖ ,trɪpə(r)/ *n* excursionista *mf*

daze /deɪz/ *n* (*no pl*) aturdimiento *m*; **to go about in a** ~ estar* en las nubes

dazed /deɪzd/ *adj* aturdido

dazzle /'dæzəl/ *vt* «*light*» deslumbrar, encandilar; «*beauty/wit*» deslumbrar

dazzling /'dæzlɪŋ/ *adj* (bright) «*light/glare*» deslumbrante, resplandeciente, que encandila; (impressive) «*wit/looks*» deslumbrante, deslumbrador

DC (a) (= **direct current**) CC (b) = **District of Columbia**

D-day /'diːdeɪ/ *n* (a) (in World War II) día *m* D (*día del desembarco aliado en Normandía*) (b) (important day) el día señalado

DE = **Delaware**

DEA *n* (= **Drug Enforcement Administration**) DEA *f*

deacon /'diːkən/ *n* diácono *m*

deaconess /'diːkənəs ‖ ,diːkə'nes, 'diːkənɪs/ *n* diaconisa *f*

dead¹ /ded/ *adj* **1** (no longer alive) muerto; **he's** ~ está muerto; **to drop** ~ caerse* muerto; **I wouldn't be seen** ~ **in that dress** (colloq) yo no me pondría ese vestido ni muerta *or* ni loca; ▶ BODY 1c **2** (numb) (*usu pred*) dormido; **to go** ~ «*limb*» dormirse* **3** (very tired, ill) (colloq) muerto (fam) **4** (obsolete) «*language*» muerto; «*custom*» en desuso **5** (a) (not functioning) «*wire/circuit*»

desconectado; «*telephone*» desconectado, cortado; «*battery*» descargado (b) (not alight) «*fire/match*» apagado (c) (not busy) «*town/hotel/party*» muerto

dead² *adv* **1** (a) (exactly) «*right*» (b) (directly) justo, directamente; ~ **ahead** justo delante (c) (suddenly): **to stop** ~ parar en seco **2** (colloq) «*straight/level*» completamente; ~ **slow** lentísimo; **to be** ~ **certain** estar* totalmente seguro; **it was** ~ **easy** estuvo regalado *or* tirado (fam)

dead³ *pl n*: **the** ~ los muertos

deaden /'dedn̩/ *vt* «*impact*» amortiguar; «*noise/vibration*» reducir*; «*pain*» atenuar*, aliviar; «*nerve*» insensibilizar*; «*faculties*» entorpecer*

dead: ~ **end** *n* callejón *m* sin salida; ~-**end** /'ded'end/ *adj* «*street*» sin salida, ciego (Andes, Ven); **a** ~-**end job** (colloq) un trabajo sin porvenir *or* futuro; ~**line** *n* fecha *f* tope *or* límite, plazo *m* de entrega; ~**lock** *n* (*no pl*) punto *m* muerto

deadly¹ /'dedli/ *adj* -**lier**, -**liest 1** (fatal) «*disease/poison*» mortal; «*weapon*» mortífero **2** (dull) (colloq) aburridísimo, terriblemente aburridor (AmL)

deadly² *adv* (as intensifier) «*dull*» terriblemente

dead: ~**pan** *adj* «*expression*» de póquer *or* (fam) de palo; «*voice/delivery*» deliberadamente inexpresivo; **D**~ **Sea** *n* the **D**~ **Sea** el Mar Muerto; ~ **weight** *n* peso *m* muerto

deaf /def/ *adj* sordo; **to go** ~ quedarse sordo; ~ **and dumb** sordomudo

deaf-aid /'defeɪd/ *n* (BrE) audífono *m*

deafen /'defən/ *vt* ensordecer*

deafening /'defənɪŋ/ *adj* ensordecedor

deaf-mute /'def'mjuːt/ *n* sordomudo, -da *m,f*

deafness /'defnəs ‖ 'defnɪs/ *n* sordera *f*

deal¹ /diːl/ *n* **1** (indicating amount): **it makes a great/good** ~ **of difference** cambia mucho/bastante las cosas; **we've seen a great** ~ **of her lately** la hemos visto mucho *or* muy a menudo últimamente
2 (a) (agreement) trato *m*, acuerdo *m*; **to do a** ~ **with sb** llegar* a un acuerdo con algn, hacer* un trato *or* un pacto con algn; **it's no big** ~ no es nada del otro mundo (b) (financial arrangement) acuerdo *m* (c) (bargain): **you'll get a better** ~ **if you shop around** lo conseguirás más barato si vas a otras tiendas
3 (treatment) trato *m*; **she's had a raw** ~ **in life** la vida la ha tratado muy mal

deal² (*past & past p* **dealt**) *vt/i* (Games) dar*, repartir
■ **deal in** [*v* + *prep* + *o*] (Busn) dedicarse* a la compra y venta de, comerciar en
■ **deal out** [*v* + *o* + *adv*, *v* + *adv* + *o*] «*gifts/money*» repartir, distribuir*
■ **deal with** [*v* + *prep* + *o*] **1** (do business with) «*company*» tener* relaciones comerciales con; **I prefer to** ~ **with her** yo prefiero tratar con ella **2** (a) (tackle, handle) «*complaint*» ocuparse de, atender*; «*situation*» manejar (b) (be responsible for) ocuparse *or* encargarse* de **3** «*issue*» (discuss, treat) tratar; (have as subject) tratar de

dealer /'diːlər ‖ 'diːlə(r)/ *n* **1** (a) (trader): **she's a car** ~ se dedica a la compra-venta de coches; **visit your local Hoover** ~ visite a su representante Hoover más próximo; **drug** ~

traficante *mf* de drogas **(b)** (Fin) corredor, -dora *m,f* de bolsa *or* de valores [2] (Games): **the** ∼ el que da *or* reparte las cartas

dealing /'diːlɪŋ/ *n* [1] **(a)** (business methods): **the company has a reputation for honest/shady** ∼ la empresa tiene fama de honradez en los negocios/ de hacer negocios turbios **(b) dealings** *pl* (contacts, relations) relaciones *fpl*, trato *m* [2] (trafficking) tráfico *m*

dealt /delt/ *past & past p of* DEAL[2]

dean /diːn/ *n* [1] (Relig) deán *m* [2] **(a)** (in university) decano, -na *m,f* **(b)** (in college, secondary school) (AmE) *docente a cargo del asesoramiento y de la disciplina de los estudiantes*

dear¹ /dɪr ‖dɪə(r)/ *adj* **dearer, dearest** [1] (loved) querido [2] (in direct address) **(a)** (in speech): **my** ∼ **Mrs Harper, I can assure you that ...** mi buena señora (Harper), le aseguro que ... **(b)** (in letter writing): **D**∼ **Mr Jones** Estimado Sr. Jones; **D**∼ **Sir or Madam** Estimado/a Señor(a), Muy señor mío/señora mía; **D**∼ **Jimmy** Querido Jimmy [3] (lovable) adorable [4] (expensive) caro

dear² *interj*: **oh** ∼**!** ¡ay!, ¡qué cosa!

dear³ *n* (*as form of address*) querido, -da, cariño; **(you) poor** ∼**!** ¡pobre ángel!, ¡pobrecito!

dearly /'dɪrli ‖'dɪəli/ *adv* [1] (*as intensifier*): **I love him** ∼ lo quiero mucho *or* de verdad; ∼ **beloved** (fml) (Relig) (amados) hermanos [2] (at great cost) caro *adj*

death /deθ/ *n* muerte *f*, fallecimiento *m* (fml); **to put sb to** ∼ ejecutar a algn; **to be worried to** ∼ (colloq) estar* preocupadísimo

death: ∼**bed** *n* lecho *m* de muerte; ∼ **certificate** *n* certificado *m* de defunción; ∼ **penalty** *n* the ∼ **penalty** la pena de muerte; ∼ **row** /rəʊ/ *n* (*no art*) pabellón *m* de los condenados a muerte, corredor *m* de la muerte; ∼ **sentence** *n*: **the** ∼ **sentence** la pena de muerte; ∼ **squad** *n* escuadrón *m* de la muerte; ∼ **toll** *n* número *m* de víctimas (mortales) *or* de muertos; ∼ **trap** *n*: *edificio, vehículo etc muy poco seguro*; ∼ **warrant** *n* sentencia *f* de muerte; ∼ **wish** *n* (*no pl*) (Psych) pulsión *f* de muerte

debar /dɪ'bɑːr ‖dɪ'bɑː(r)/ *vt* **-rr-** (fml) **the fact that she didn't have a degree** ∼**red her from promotion** el hecho de no tener un título universitario le impedía ascender; **he was** ∼**red from taking his final exam** se le prohibió rendir el examen final

debase /dɪ'beɪs/ *vt* **(a)** (devalue) ⟨*ideal/principle*⟩ degradar, envilecer*; ⟨*language*⟩ corromper, viciar **(b)** (demean) ⟨*person*⟩ degradar, rebajar

debate¹ /dɪ'beɪt/ *n* **(a)** (public, parliamentary) debate *m* **(b)** (discussion) debate *m*, discusión *f*

debate² *vt* **(a)** ⟨*question/topic/motion*⟩ debatir, discutir **(b)** (weigh up) ⟨*idea/possibility*⟩ darle* vueltas a, considerar

debauchery /dɪ'bɔːtʃəri/ *n* disipación *f*, libertinaje *m*

debenture /dɪ'bentʃər ‖dɪ'bentʃə(r)/ *n* ∼ **(bond)** (Fin) obligación *f*, bono *m*

debilitating /dɪ'bɪlɪteɪtɪŋ ‖dɪ'bɪlɪteɪtɪŋ/ *adj* ⟨*disease*⟩ debilitante; ⟨*climate*⟩ extenuante

debit¹ /'debət ‖'debɪt/ *n* débito *m*, cargo *m*; (*before n*) ∼ **card** tarjeta *f* de cobro automático

debit² *vt* (Fin) debitar, cargar*

debonair /ˌdebə'ner ‖ˌdebə'neə(r)/ *adj* (suave) elegante y desenvuelto; (courteous) cortés, afable

debriefing /'diː'briːfɪŋ/ *n*: **they were sent for** ∼ los llamaron para que rindiesen informe *or* diesen parte de su misión

debris /də'briː ‖'debriː, 'deɪbriː/ *n* **(a)** (rubble) escombros *mpl*; (of plane, ship) restos *mpl*; (rubbish) desechos *mpl* **(b)** (Geol) detritos *mpl*

debt /det/ *n* **(a)** (indebtedness) endeudamiento *m*; **I'm $200 in** ∼ debo 200 dólares, tengo deudas por 200 dólares; **to be in** ∼ **to sb** (fml) estarle* en deuda a algn, estar* en deuda con algn; **to get into** ∼ endeudarse, llenarse *or* cargarse* de deudas **(b)** (money owing) deuda *f*; **bad** ∼**s** deudas incobrables

debtor /'detər ‖'detə(r)/ *n* deudor, -dora *m,f*

debunk /'diː'bʌŋk/ *vt* (colloq) desacreditar

debut, début /'deɪbjuː, 'de-/ (*pl* **-buts** /-bjuːz/) *n* debut *m*

decade /'dekeɪd/ *n* década *f*

decadence /'dekədəns/ *n* decadencia *f*

decadent /'dekədənt/ *adj* decadente

decaffeinated /'diː'kæfəneɪtəd ‖ˌdiː'kæfneɪtɪd/ *adj* descafeinado

decanter /dɪ'kæntər ‖dɪ'kæntə(r)/ *n* licorera *f*

decapitate /dɪ'kæpɪteɪt/ *vt* decapitar

decathlon /dɪ'kæθlən/ *n* decatlón *m*

decay¹ /dɪ'keɪ/ *vi* ⟨*foodstuffs/corpse*⟩ descomponerse*, pudrirse*; ⟨*wood*⟩ pudrirse*; ⟨*tooth*⟩ cariarse, picarse*; ⟨*building/machine*⟩ deteriorarse; ⟨*empire/culture/civilization*⟩ decaer*, declinar

decay² *n* (of organic matter) descomposición *f*; (tooth ∼) caries *f*; (of building) deterioro *m*; (of culture) decadencia *f*

deceased¹ /dɪ'siːst/ *n* (*pl* ∼) (fml) **the** ∼ el difunto, la difunta; (*pl*) los difuntos, las difuntas (fml)

deceased² *adj* (fml) difunto

deceit /dɪ'siːt/ *n* engaño *m*

deceitful /dɪ'siːtfəl/ *adj* ⟨*person*⟩ falso, embustero; ⟨*action*⟩ engañoso

deceive /dɪ'siːv/ *vt* engañar

deceiver /dɪ'siːvər ‖dɪ'siːvə(r)/ *n* impostor, -tora *m,f*

decelerate /'diː'seləreɪt/ *vi* (fml) ⟨*vehicle/ driver*⟩ reducir* *or* aminorar la velocidad

December /dɪ'sembər ‖dɪ'sembə(r)/ *n* diciembre *m*

decency /'diːsṇsi/ *n* **(a)** (of dress, conduct) decencia *f*, decoro *m* **(b)** (propriety) buena educación *f*, consideración *f*; **she didn't even have the** ∼ **to ask me** ni siquiera tuvo la consideración de preguntarme

decent /'diːsṇt/ *adj* [1] (appropriate, respectable) decente, decoroso [2] (acceptable) ⟨*person*⟩ pasable, aceptable; ⟨*meal/housing*⟩ decente, como es debido

decently /'diːsṇtli/ *adv* [1] (respectably) ⟨*dress/ behave*⟩ decentemente, con decencia [2] (acceptably) ⟨*perform/cook*⟩ bastante bien

decentralize /diː'sentrəlaɪz/ *vt* descentralizar*

deception /dɪ'sepʃən/ *n* engaño *m*

decibel /'desəbəl ‖'desɪbel/ n decibelio m, decibel m

decide /dɪ'saɪd/ vt **1** (make up one's mind) decidir; **to ~ to + INF** decidir or resolver + INF **2** (settle) ⟨question/issue⟩ decidir; ⟨outcome⟩ determinar
■ ~ vi decidirse

decided /dɪ'saɪdəd ‖dɪ'saɪdɪd/ adj **(a)** (definite) (before n) ⟨improvement/advantage⟩ claro, marcado **(b)** (determined) ⟨character/tone⟩ decidido

deciduous /dɪ'sɪdʒuəs ‖dɪ'sɪdjʊəs/ adj de hoja caduca, caducifolio (téc)

decimal¹ /'desəməl ‖'desɪməl/ adj decimal

decimal² n decimal m

decimalization /desəmələ'zeɪʃən ‖,desɪməlar'zeɪʃən/ n decimalización f, conversión f al sistema decimal

decimal point n ≈ coma f (decimal o de los decimales), punto m decimal

decimate /'desəmeɪt ‖'desɪmeɪt/ vt diezmar

decipher /dɪ'saɪfər ‖dɪ'saɪfə(r)/ vt descifrar

decision /dɪ'sɪʒən/ n decisión f; **to make** o (BrE also) **take a ~** tomar una decisión

decision-making /dɪ'sɪʒən,meɪkɪŋ/ n toma f de decisiones; (before n) ⟨body/process⟩ decisorio

decisive /dɪ'saɪsɪv/ adj **1** (conclusive) ⟨battle/factor⟩ decisivo; ⟨victory⟩ contundente **2** (purposeful) ⟨person⟩ decidido, resuelto; ⟨leadership/answer⟩ firme

deck¹ /dek/ n **1** **(a)** (Naut) cubierta f **(b)** (of stadium) (AmE) nivel m **(c)** (sun ~) terraza f **(d)** (of bus) (BrE) piso m **2** (Audio) deck m (AmL), pletina f (Esp) **3** (AmE Games) **~ (of cards)** baraja f, mazo m (de naipes or cartas) (esp AmL)

deck² vt **1** (adorn) **to ~ sth (out) WITH sth** engalanar or adornar algo CON algo; **he was all ~ed out in his Sunday best** iba muy endomingado (fam) **2** (knock down) (AmE colloq) tumbar (fam)

deckchair /'dektʃer ‖'dektʃeə(r)/ n silla f de playa, perezosa f (Col, Per), reposera f (RPl)

declaim /dɪ'kleɪm/ vt/i declamar

declaration /deklə'reɪʃən/ n **1** (statement) declaración f **2** (Law) (finding) pronunciamiento m (oficial); (statement) declaración f

declare /dɪ'kler ‖dɪ'kleə(r)/ vt **(a)** (state, announce) ⟨intention⟩ declarar; ⟨opinion⟩ manifestar*; **to ~ war** declarar la guerra; **to ~ war on sb/sth** declararle la guerra a algn/algo **(b)** (Tax) ⟨goods/income⟩ declarar

decline¹ /dɪ'klaɪn/ n (no pl) **(a)** (decrease) descenso m, disminución f **(b)** (downward trend) declive m, decadencia f, deterioro m; **to be in ~** estar* en declive or en decadencia

decline² vi **1** **(a)** (decrease) «production/strength» disminuir*, decrecer*; «interest» disminuir*, decaer* **(b)** (deteriorate) «health» deteriorarse; «industry/region/standards» decaer* **(c) declining** pres p ⟨industry/region/

standards⟩ en declive, en decadencia **2** (refuse): **I invited him, but he ~d** lo invité, pero rehusó or declinó mi invitación
■ ~ vt ⟨offer/invitation⟩ rehusar, declinar

decode /'diː'kəʊd/ vt ⟨signal⟩ descodificar*; ⟨message⟩ descifrar

decompose /'diːkəm'pəʊz/ vi descomponerse*, pudrirse*

decor, décor /deɪ'kɔːr ‖'deɪkɔː(r)/ n (furnishings) decoración f

decorate /'dekəreɪt/ vt **(a)** ⟨room/house⟩ (with paint) pintar; (with wallpaper) empapelar **(b)** ⟨Christmas tree⟩ adornar, decorar (AmL); ⟨cake⟩ decorar

decoration /dekə'reɪʃən/ n **1** **(a)** (act) decoración f **(b)** (ornamentation) decoración f **(c)** (ornament) adorno m **2** (Mil) condecoración f

decorative /'dekərətɪv/ adj ⟨object⟩ ornamental, de adorno

decorator /'dekəreɪtər ‖'dekəreɪtə(r)/ n **(a)** (painter) pintor, -tora m,f; (paperhanger) empapelador, -dora m,f **(b)** (designer) decorador, -dora m,f, interiorista mf

decorous /'dekərəs/ adj (frml) decoroso

decorum /dɪ'kɔːrəm/ n decoro m

decoy /'diːkɔɪ/ n (lure) señuelo m; (in hunting) señuelo m, reclamo m

decrease¹ /dɪ'kriːs, 'diːkriːs/ vi **(a)** (in quantity) «amount/numbers» disminuir*, decrecer*; «prices» bajar; «speed» disminuir* **(b)** (in intensity) «quality» disminuir*, bajar; «power/effectiveness» disminuir*, decrecer*; «interest» disminuir*, decaer*
■ ~ vt disminuir*, reducir*

decrease² /'diːkriːs, dɪ'kriːs/ n disminución f, descenso m

decree¹ /dɪ'kriː/ n decreto m

decree² vt decretar

decrepit /dɪ'krepət ‖dɪ'krepɪt/ adj **(a)** (dilapidated) ⟨bus/furniture⟩ destartalado; ⟨house⟩ deteriorado, viejo y en mal estado **(b)** (infirm) ⟨person/animal⟩ decrépito

decriminalize /diː'krɪmɪnəlaɪz/ vt despenalizar*

dedicate /'dedɪkeɪt/ vt **(a)** (devote) **to ~ sth TO sth/-ING** dedicar* algo A algo/+ INF **(b)** ⟨poem/book⟩ dedicar*

dedicated /'dedɪkeɪtəd ‖'dedɪkeɪtɪd/ adj **1** ⟨musician/nurse/teacher⟩ de gran dedicación, dedicado or entregado a su (or mi etc) trabajo; **to be ~ TO sth** estar* dedicado or entregado A algo **2** (Comput) (before n) dedicado

dedication /dedɪ'keɪʃən/ n **1** (devotion) dedicación f, entrega f **2** (written message) dedicatoria f

deduce /dɪ'duːs ‖dɪ'djuːs/ vt deducir*, inferir*

deduct /dɪ'dʌkt/ vt deducir*, descontar*

deduction /dɪ'dʌkʃən/ n **1** (subtraction) deducción f, descuento m **2** (reasoning, conclusion) deducción f

---

deed /diːd/ n **1** (action) hecho m **2** (Law) escritura f

deed poll n (BrE): **to change one's name by** ∼ ∼ ≈ cambiarse el apellido oficialmente

deem /diːm/ vt (fml) considerar, juzgar*

deep¹ /diːp/ adj **-er, -est 1 (a)** ⟨water⟩ profundo; ⟨hole/pit⟩ profundo, hondo; ⟨gash⟩ profundo; ⟨dish⟩ hondo; ⟨pan⟩ alto; **the ditch is 6 ft** ∼ la zanja tiene 6 pies de profundidad **(b)** (horizontally) ⟨shelf⟩ profundo; **the soldiers were standing 12** ∼ los soldados formaban columnas de 12 en fondo **2** ⟨sigh/groan⟩ profundo, hondo; **take a** ∼ **breath** respire hondo **3 (a)** ⟨voice⟩ profundo, grave; ⟨note⟩ grave **(b)** ⟨color⟩ intenso, subido **4 (a)** (intense) ⟨sleep/love/impression⟩ profundo; **it is with** ∼ **regret that ...** es con gran or profundo pesar que ... **(b)** ⟨thoughts⟩ profundo **(c)** ⟨mystery/secret⟩ profundo

deep² adv **-er, -est 1** (of penetration): **to dig** ∼ cavar hondo; **feelings run very** ∼ **among the population** hay un sentir muy fuerte entre la población; **he looked** ∼ **into her eyes** la miró fijamente a los ojos; **to go** ∼**er (into sth)** ahondar or profundizar* más (en algo) **2** (situated far from edge): ∼ **in the forest** en lo profundo del bosque; ∼ **down you know I'm right** en el fondo sabes que tengo razón

deepen /ˈdiːpən/ vt **1** ⟨canal/well⟩ hacer* más profundo or hondo **2** ⟨knowledge⟩ profundizar* or ahondar en; ⟨concern⟩ aumentar; ⟨friendship⟩ estrechar
■ ∼ vi **1** «gorge/river» hacerse* or volverse* más hondo or profundo **2** «concern/love» hacerse* más profundo; «friendship» estrecharse; «mystery» crecer*, aumentar; «crisis» acentuarse*

deep: ∼ **end** n the ∼ **end** (of swimming pool) la parte honda, lo hondo (fam); **to throw sb in** (**at**) **the** ∼ **end** meter a algn de lleno en lo más difícil; ∼ **freeze** n congelador m, freezer f (AmL); ∼**-fry** /ˈdiːpˈfraɪ/ vt **-fries, -frying, -fried** freír* (en abundante aceite)

deeply /ˈdiːpli/ adv **1** ⟨sigh⟩ profundamente; **to breathe** ∼ respirar hondo **2** ⟨think⟩ a fondo; ⟨concerned⟩ profundamente; ⟨interested⟩ sumamente

deep: ∼**-sea** /ˈdiːpˈsiː/ adj (before n) ∼**-sea diving** buceo m de altura or en alta mar; ∼**-sea fishing** pesca f de altura; ∼**-seated** /ˈdiːpˈsiːtəd ‖ ˌdiːpˈsiːtɪd/ adj ⟨prejudice/conviction⟩ profundamente arraigado; ⟨problem⟩ de raíces profundas; ∼**-set** /ˈdiːpˈset/ adj ⟨eyes⟩ hundido

deer /dɪr ‖ dɪə(r)/ n (pl ∼) ciervo m, venado m

deface /dɪˈfeɪs/ vt ⟨wall/notice⟩ pintarrajear

defamation /ˌdefəˈmeɪʃən/ n (fml) difamación f

default¹ /dɪˈfɔːlt/ n **1** (omission) omisión f; (on payments) mora f; (failure to appear) incomparecencia f; (Law) rebeldía f **2** (lack) falta f; **he was elected by** ∼ fue elegido por ausencia de otros candidatos; (before n) ∼ **option** (Comput) opción f por defecto

default² vi **(a)** (Fin) **to** ∼ (**ON sth**) no pagar* (algo) **(b)** (Law) estar* en rebeldía **(c)** (Sport) no presentarse

defeat¹ /dɪˈfiːt/ n **1** (by opponent) derrota f **2** (of motion, bill) (Adm, Govt) rechazo m

defeat² vt **1** ⟨opponent⟩ derrotar, vencer* **2** ⟨hopes/plans⟩ frustrar; **that would** ∼ **the object of the exercise** eso iría en contra de lo que se pretende lograr **3** (Adm, Govt) ⟨opposition⟩ derrotar; ⟨bill/motion⟩ rechazar* **4** (baffle) (colloq): **it** ∼**s me** no alcanzo a comprenderlo

defeatist /dɪˈfiːtəst ‖ dɪˈfiːtɪst/ adj derrotista

defect¹ /ˈdiːfekt/ n defecto m; **a speech** ∼ un defecto en el habla

defect² /dɪˈfekt/ vi (Pol) desertar*, defeccionar (period)

defective /dɪˈfektɪv/ adj defectuoso

defector /dɪˈfektər ‖ dɪˈfektə(r)/ n desertor, -tora m,f

defence etc (BrE) ▶ DEFENSE etc

defend /dɪˈfend/ vt defender*
■ ∼ vi **1** (Law) actuar* por la defensa **2** (Sport): **he's better at** ∼**ing** juega mejor como defensa

defendant /dɪˈfendənt/ n (Law) (in civil case) demandado, -da m,f; (in criminal case) acusado, -da m,f

defender /dɪˈfendər ‖ dɪˈfendə(r)/ n **(a)** (of cause, course of action, opinion) defensor, -sora m,f **(b)** (Sport) defensa mf

defending /dɪˈfendɪŋ/ adj: **the** ∼ **champion** el actual campeón (que defiende su título)

defense, (BrE) **defence** /dɪˈfens, ˈdiːfens ‖ dɪˈfens/ n **1 (a)** (Mil) defensa f **(b)** (on personal level) defensa f **2 (a)** (protection) defensa f, protección f **(b)** (apologia) defensa f **3 defenses** pl (Mil, Med, Psych) defensas fpl **4** (Law) defensa f **5 (a)** (Sport) defensa f **(b)** (in chess) defensa f

defenseless, (BrE) **defenceless** /dɪˈfensləs ‖ dɪˈfenslɪs/ adj indefenso

defensive /dɪˈfensɪv/ adj defensivo

defer /dɪˈfɜːr ‖ dɪˈfɜː(r)/ **-rr-** vt (fml) diferir* (fml), aplazar*, postergar* (esp AmL)
■ **defer to** [v + prep + o] (fml) deferir* a (fml)

deference /ˈdefərəns/ n (fml) deferencia f

deferential /ˌdefəˈrentʃəl ‖ ˌdefəˈrenʃəl/ adj deferente

deferment /dɪˈfɜːrmənt ‖ dɪˈfɜːmənt/ n (fml) aplazamiento m

defiance /dɪˈfaɪəns/ n **an act of** ∼ un desafío, un acto de rebeldía; **in** ∼ **of her orders** haciendo caso omiso de sus órdenes

defiant /dɪˈfaɪənt/ adj ⟨attitude/tone⟩ desafiante; ⟨person⟩ rebelde

deficiency /dɪˈfɪʃənsi/ n (pl **-cies**) deficiencia f

deficient /dɪˈfɪʃənt/ adj (fml) deficiente, insuficiente

deficit /ˈdefəsɪt ‖ ˈdefɪsɪt/ n déficit m

define /dɪˈfaɪn/ vt **(a)** (state meaning of, describe) ⟨word/position⟩ definir **(b)** ⟨powers/duties⟩ delimitar **(c)** (characterize) distinguir*

definite /ˈdefənət, ˈdefnət ‖ ˈdefɪnɪt/ adj **1 (a)** (final) ⟨date/price/offer⟩ definitivo, en firme **(b)** (certain) seguro, confirmado **(c)** (firm, categorical) ⟨tone⟩ firme, terminante **(d)** (distinct): **it's a** ∼ **advantage/possibility** es, sin duda, una ventaja/posibilidad **2** (Ling): ∼ **article** artículo m determinado or definido

definitely /ˈdefənətli, ˈdefnətli ‖ ˈdefɪnɪtli/ adv **(a)** (without doubt): **it's** ∼ **true** es indudablemente ⋯⋗

cierto; **he ~ said we should meet here** seguro que dijo que nos encontráramos aquí **(b)** (definitively) ⟨*arrange/agree*⟩ definitivamente

definition /ˌdefəˈnɪʃən ‖ ˌdefɪˈnɪʃən/ *n* ①︎ **(a)** (statement of meaning) definición *f*; **by ~** por definición **(b)** (categorization) definición *f*, delimitación *f*

definitive /dɪˈfɪnətɪv/ *adj* (*no comp*) **(a)** (final) ⟨*verdict/victory*⟩ definitivo **(b)** (authoritative) ⟨*biography/study*⟩ de mayor autoridad

deflate /dɪˈfleɪt/ *vt* **(a)** ⟨*balloon/tire*⟩ desinflar **(b)** (humble): **to ~ sb** bajarle los humos a algn **(c)** (depress) deprimir; **I felt ~d** me sentí por los suelos

deflation /dɪˈfleɪʃən/ *n* deflación *f*

deflect /dɪˈflekt/ *vt* **to ~ sth** (FROM sth) desviar* algo (DE algo)
■ **~** *vi* desviarse*

defogger /ˈdiːˌfɔːɡər ‖ ˌdiːˈfɒɡə(r)/ *n* (AmE) desempañador *m*

deforestation /diːˌfɔːrəˈsteɪʃən ‖ diːˌfɒrɪˈsteɪʃən/ *n* deforestación *f*, despoblación *f* forestal (Esp)

deformed /dɪˈfɔːrmd ‖ dɪˈfɔːmd/ *adj* deforme

deformity /dɪˈfɔːrməti ‖ dɪˈfɔːməti/ *n* (*pl* **-ties**) deformidad *f*

defraud /dɪˈfrɔːd/ *vt* ⟨*person*⟩ estafar

defray /dɪˈfreɪ/ *vt* (fml) ⟨*cost*⟩ sufragar* (fml)

defrost /diːˈfrɔːst ‖ diːˈfrɒst/ *vt* ⟨*food*⟩ descongelar; ⟨*refrigerator*⟩ deshelar*, descongelar
■ **~** *vi* «*meat*» descongelarse; «*refrigerator*» deshelarse*, descongelarse

deft /deft/ *adj* **-er, -est** ⟨*movement*⟩ hábil, diestro

deftly /ˈdeftli/ *adv* hábilmente, con destreza

defunct /dɪˈfʌŋkt/ *adj* ⟨*idea/theory*⟩ caduco; ⟨*institution*⟩ desaparecido, extinto, fenecido (fml)

defuse /diːˈfjuːz/ *vt* ⟨*bomb*⟩ desactivar; ⟨*situation*⟩ distender*; ⟨*crisis*⟩ calmar

defy /dɪˈfaɪ/ *vt* **defies, defying, defied (a)** (disobey) ⟨*order/authority*⟩ desacatar, desobedecer* **(b)** (resist): **to ~ understanding/description** ser* incomprensible/indescriptible **(c)** (ignore) ⟨*danger/death*⟩ desafiar*

degenerate¹ /dɪˈdʒenəreɪt/ *vi* degenerar; «*health*» deteriorarse

degenerate² /dɪˈdʒenərət/ *adj* degenerado

degeneration /dɪˌdʒenəˈreɪʃən/ *n* **(a)** (deterioration) degeneración *f*, deterioro *m* **(b)** (Med) (of tissue, organs) degeneración *f*

degrade /dɪˈɡreɪd/ *vt* degradar

degrading /dɪˈɡreɪdɪŋ/ *adj* degradante

degree /dɪˈɡriː/ *n* ①︎ (level, amount) grado *m*, nivel *m*; **there's a ~ of truth in what she says** hay cierta verdad en lo que dice; **to a ~** (extremely) en grado sumo; (to some extent) hasta cierto punto ②︎ (grade, step) grado *m*; **first/third ~ burns** quemaduras *fpl* de primer/tercer grado; **first/ second ~ murder** (in US) homicidio *m* en primer/ segundo grado; **by ~s** gradualmente, paulatinamente
③︎ (Math, Geog, Meteo, Phys) grado *m*; **12 ~s below zero** 12 grados bajo cero; **this wine is 12 ~s proof** este vino es de *or* tiene 12 grados

④︎ (Educ) título *m*; **first ~** licenciatura *f*; **he has o** (fml) **holds a ~ in chemistry** es licenciado en química

dehydrated /ˈdiːhaɪdreɪtəd ‖ ˌdiːhaɪˈdreɪtɪd/ *adj* deshidratado; **to become ~** deshidratarse

dehydration /ˌdiːhaɪˈdreɪʃən/ *n* deshidratación *f*

deign /deɪn/ *vi* **to ~ to + INF** dignarse (A) + INF

deity /ˈdiːəti/ *n* (*pl* **-ties**) deidad *f*

dejected /dɪˈdʒektəd ‖ dɪˈdʒektɪd/ *adj* abatido, desalentado

Del = Delaware

delay¹ /dɪˈleɪ/ *vt* ①︎ (make late, hold up) retrasar, demorar (esp AmL) ②︎ (defer) ⟨*decision/payment*⟩ retrasar, demorar (esp AmL)
■ **~** *vi* tardar, demorar (esp AmL)

delay² *n* **(a)** (waiting) tardanza *f*, dilación *f*, demora *f* (esp AmL) **(b)** (holdup) retraso *m*, demora *f* (esp AmL); **~s can be expected on major roads** se puede esperar embotellamientos en las principales carreteras

delayed action /dɪˈleɪd/ *n* acción *f* retardada

delectable /dɪˈlektəbəl/ *adj* **(a)** (delicious) delicioso, exquisito **(b)** (delightful) delicioso, encantador

delegate¹ /ˈdelɪɡeɪt/ *vt/i* delegar*

delegate² /ˈdelɪɡət/ *n* delegado, -da *m,f*

delegation /ˌdelɪˈɡeɪʃən/ *n* delegación *f*

delete /dɪˈliːt/ *vt* suprimir, eliminar; (by crossing out) tachar; (Comput) borrar, suprimir

delete key *n* (Comput) tecla *f* de borrar, tecla *f* de borrado

deliberate¹ /dɪˈlɪbərət, -brət/ *adj* ①︎ (intentional) ⟨*act/attempt*⟩ deliberado, intencionado ②︎ **(a)** (considered) reflexivo **(b)** (unhurried) pausado, lento

deliberate² /dɪˈlɪbəreɪt/ *vi* (fml) **to ~** (ABOUT/ ON sth) deliberar (SOBRE algo)
■ **~** *vt* (fml) deliberar sobre

deliberately /dɪˈlɪbərətli, -brətli/ *adv* ①︎ (intentionally) adrede, a propósito ②︎ (unhurriedly) pausadamente, con parsimonia

deliberation /dɪˌlɪbəˈreɪʃən/ *n* (fml) **(a)** (consideration) deliberación *f* **(b) deliberations** *pl* (decision-making) deliberaciones *fpl*

delicacy /ˈdelɪkəsi/ *n* (*pl* **-cies**) ①︎ **(a)** (fineness, intricacy) delicadeza *f*, lo delicado; (fragility) fragilidad *f*, lo delicado **(b)** (tact) delicadeza *f* **(c)** (subtleness) lo delicado ②︎ (choice food) manjar *m*, exquisitez *f*

delicate /ˈdelɪkət/ *adj* ①︎ **(a)** (fine, intricate) ⟨*lace/features*⟩ delicado; ⟨*workmanship*⟩ fino, esmerado **(b)** (fragile, needing care) delicado ②︎ **(a)** (needing skill, tact) delicado **(c)** (tactful) delicado, discreto ③︎ (subtle) ⟨*shade/taste*⟩ delicado

delicately /ˈdelɪkətli/ *adv* ①︎ ⟨*carve/paint*⟩ con delicadeza, delicadamente ②︎ ⟨*treat*⟩ con delicadeza ③︎ ⟨*patterned/perfumed*⟩ delicadamente

delicatessen /ˌdelɪkəˈtesən/ *n* charcutería *f*, rotisería *f* (CS), salsamentaria *f* (Col), salchichonería *f* (Méx)

delicious /dɪˈlɪʃəs/ *adj* delicioso

delight¹ /dɪˈlaɪt/ *n* **(a)** (joy) placer *m*, deleite *m*; **to take ~ in sth** disfrutar *or* gozar* con algo **(b)** (source of joy) placer *m*

delight² *vt* **(a)** (make very happy) llenar de

alegría; **his success** ⁓**ed them** su éxito los llenó de alegría **(b)** (give pleasure to) deleitar; **the clown** ⁓**ed the children** el payaso hizo las delicias de *or* deleitó a los niños

■ ⁓ *vi* **to** ⁓ **IN** -ING deleitarse + GER

delighted /dɪˈlaɪtəd ‖dɪˈlaɪtɪd/ *adj* ⟨*grin/look*⟩ de alegría; **I'm** ⁓ **(that) you can come** me alegra mucho que puedas venir; **to be** ⁓ **WITH sth/sb** estar* encantado CON algo/algn

delightful /dɪˈlaɪtfəl/ *adj* ⟨*weather/evening*⟩ muy agradable, delicioso; ⟨*person*⟩ encantador; ⟨*dress*⟩ precioso

delineate /dɪˈlɪnieɪt/ *vt* (fml) **(a)** (draw) trazar*, delinear **(b)** (describe) ⟨*problem*⟩ definir

delinquency /dɪˈlɪŋkwənsi/ *n* (Law, Sociol) delincuencia *f*

delinquent /dɪˈlɪŋkwənt/ *n* delincuente *mf*

delirious /dɪˈlɪriəs/ *adj* **(a)** (Med) delirante; **to be** ⁓ delirar, desvariar* **(b)** (wildly excited, happy) (colloq) loco de alegría (fam)

deliver /dɪˈlɪvər ‖dɪˈlɪvə(r)/ *vt* **1** **(a)** (hand over) entregar* **(b)** (distribute) repartir ⟨*a domicilio*⟩ **2** **(a)** (administer) ⟨*blow/punch*⟩ propinar, asestar **(b)** (issue) ⟨*ultimatum/lecture/sermon*⟩ dar*; ⟨*warning*⟩ hacer*; ⟨*speech*⟩ pronunciar; ⟨*judgment*⟩ dictar, pronunciar, emitir **(c)** (produce, provide): **he promised much, but** ⁓**ed little** cumplió muy poco de lo mucho que había prometido **(d)** (Sport) ⟨*ball*⟩ lanzar* **(e)** (in elections) (AmE) ⟨*state*⟩ ganar **3** (Med): **her husband** ⁓**ed the baby** su marido la asistió en el parto

■ ⁓ *vi* **1** (Busn): **we** ⁓ **free of charge** hacemos reparto(s) a domicilio gratuitamente **2** (produce the necessary) (colloq) cumplir

delivery /dɪˈlɪvəri/ *n* (*pl* **-ries**) **1** **(a)** (act) entrega *f*; (before n) ⁓ **charges** gastos *mpl* de envío *or* transporte; ⁓ **man** repartidor *m*; ⁓ **truck** *o* (BrE) **van** camioneta *f or* furgoneta *f* de los repartos **(b)** (occasion) reparto *m*; **is there a** ⁓ **on Saturdays?** ¿hay reparto los sábados? **(c)** (consignment) partida *f*, remesa *f* **2** (of baby) parto *m*, alumbramiento *m* (fml) **3** (manner of speaking) expresión *f* oral

delta /ˈdeltə/ *n* delta *m*

delude /dɪˈluːd/ *vt* engañar

deluge /ˈdeljuːdʒ/ *n* **1** **(a)** (flood) inundación *f* **(b)** (downpour) diluvio *m* **2** (of protests, questions, letters) aluvión *m*, avalancha *f*

delusion /dɪˈluːʒən/ *n* (mistaken idea) error *m*; (vain hope) falsa ilusión *f*

deluxe /dəˈlʊks/ *adj* de lujo

delve /delv/ *vi* (liter) **to** ⁓ **INTO sth** ahondar EN algo; **to** ⁓ **into the past** hurgar* en el pasado

demand[1] /dɪˈmænd ‖dɪˈmɑːnd/ *vt* **1** «*person*» (call for, insist on) exigir*; **the unions are** ⁓**ing better conditions** los sindicatos reclaman mejores condiciones **2** (require) ⟨*determination/perseverance*⟩ exigir*, requerir*

demand[2] *n* **1** (claim) exigencia *f*, (Lab Rel, Pol) reivindicación *f*, reclamo *m*; (request) petición *f*, pedido *m* (AmL); **the** ⁓**s of the job** las exigencias del trabajo; **abortion on** ⁓ libre aborto *m* **2** (requirement) demanda *f*; **he's in great** ⁓ está muy solicitado, es popular

demanding /dɪˈmændɪŋ ‖dɪˈmɑːndɪŋ/ *adj* ⟨*job*⟩ que exige mucho; ⟨*book/music*⟩ difícil; ⟨*teacher*⟩ exigente

demarcation /ˈdiːmɑːrˈkeɪʃən ‖ˌdiːmɑːˈkeɪʃən/ *n* demarcación *f*; (before n) ⁓ **line** línea *f* de demarcación

demean /dɪˈmiːn/ *vt* (fml) degradar

demeaning /dɪˈmiːnɪŋ/ *adj* degradante

demeanor, (BrE) **demeanour** /dɪˈmiːnər ‖dɪˈmiːnə(r)/ *n* (fml) **(a)** (behavior) comportamiento *m*, conducta *f* **(b)** (bearing) porte *m*

demented /dɪˈmentəd ‖dɪˈmentɪd/ *adj* ⟨*person*⟩ demente; ⟨*screams/mutterings*⟩ enloquecido

dementia /dɪˈmentʃə ‖dɪˈmenʃə/ *n* demencia *f*

demerara (sugar) /ˌdeməˈrɑːrə ‖ˌdeməˈreərə/ *n* (BrE) azúcar *f* morena, azúcar *m* moreno

demerit /diːˈmerət ‖diːˈmerɪt/ *n* (fml) demérito *m* (fml)

demise /dɪˈmaɪz/ *n* (no pl) (fml) **(a)** (death) fallecimiento *m* (fml), deceso *m* (AmL fml) **(b)** (end) desaparición *f*

demister /ˈdiːˈmɪstər ‖ˌdiːˈmɪstə(r)/ *n* (BrE) desempañador *m*

demo /ˈdeməʊ/ *n* (*pl* **demos**) **1** (Mus) demostración *f*; (before n) ⁓ **tape** cinta *f* de demostración **2** (protest) (BrE colloq) manifestación *f*

demobilize /ˈdiːˈməʊbəlaɪz ‖diːˈməʊbɪlaɪz/ *vt* desmovilizar*

democracy /dɪˈmɑːkrəsi ‖dɪˈmɒkrəsi/ *n* (*pl* **-cies**) democracia *f*

democrat /ˈdeməkræt/ *n* **(a)** (believer in democracy) demócrata *mf* **(b)** **Democrat** (in US) demócrata *mf*

democratic /ˌdeməˈkrætɪk/ *adj* **(a)** ⟨*country/election*⟩ democrático **(b)** **Democratic** (in US) demócrata

demographic /ˌdeməˈgræfɪk/ *adj* demográfico

demography /dɪˈmɑːgrəfi ‖dɪˈmɒgrəfi/ *n* demografía *f*

demolish /dɪˈmɑːlɪʃ ‖dɪˈmɒlɪʃ/ *vt* ⟨*structure/building*⟩ demoler*, derribar, echar abajo; ⟨*argument/theory*⟩ demoler*, echar por tierra

demolition /ˌdeməˈlɪʃən/ *n* (of building) demolición *f*, derribo *m*; (of theory) demolición *f*, destrucción *f*

demon /ˈdiːmən/ *n* demonio *m*

demonstrate /ˈdemənstreɪt/ *vt* **(a)** (show) ⟨*need/ability*⟩ demostrar* **(b)** (Marketing) hacer* una demostración de

■ ⁓ *vi* (Pol) manifestarse*

demonstration /ˌdemənˈstreɪʃən/ *n* **1** **(a)** (expression) muestra *f*, demostración *f* **(b)** (display) demostración *f* **2** (Pol) manifestación *f*

demonstrative /dɪˈmɑːnstrətɪv ‖dɪˈmɒnstrətɪv/ *adj* efusivo, expresivo, demostrativo (AmL)

demonstrator /ˈdemənstreɪtər ‖ˈdemənstreɪtə(r)/ *n* manifestante *mf*

demoralize /dɪˈmɔːrəlaɪz ‖dɪˈmɒrəlaɪz/ *vt* desmoralizar*

demoralizing /dɪˈmɔːrəlaɪzɪŋ ‖dɪˈmɒrəlaɪzɪŋ/ *adj* desalentador, desmoralizante

demote /dɪˈməʊt, ˈdiː-/ vt (in organization) bajar de categoría; (Mil) degradar

demotion /dɪˈməʊʃən, diː-/ n (in organization) descenso m de categoría; (Mil) degradación f

demur /dɪˈmɜːr ‖dɪˈmɜː(r)/ vi -rr- (fml) objetar

demure /dɪˈmjʊr ‖dɪˈmjʊə(r)/ adj recatado

den /den/ n 1 (of animals, thieves) guarida f 2 (room) (colloq) cuarto m de estar; (for study, work) estudio m

denial /dɪˈnaɪəl/ n 1 (of accusation, fact): **to issue a ~ of** sth desmentir* algo; **to be in ~** no querer reconocer algo 2 (of request, rights) denegación f 3 (repudiation) negación f, rechazo m 4 (abstinence) renuncia f

denier /ˈdenjər ‖ˈdenɪə(r)/ n denier m

denigrate /ˈdenɪɡreɪt/ vt (fml) ‹character/person› denigrar; ‹effort› menospreciar

denim /ˈdenəm ‖ˈdenɪm/ n(Tex) tela f vaquera or de jeans, mezclilla f (Chi, Méx); (before n) ‹jacket/skirt› vaquero, tejano (Esp), de mezclilla (Chi, Méx)

Denmark /ˈdenmɑːrk ‖ˈdenmɑːk/ n Dinamarca f

denomination /dɪˌnɑːməˈneɪʃən ‖dɪˌnɒmɪˈneɪʃən/ n 1 (Relig) confesión f 2 (of currency) valor m, denominación f (AmL)

denominator /dɪˈnɑːməneɪtər ‖dɪˈnɒmɪneɪtə(r)/ n (Math) denominador m

denote /dɪˈnəʊt/ vt denotar

denouement /ˌdeɪnuːˈmɑːn ‖deɪˈnuːmɔːn/ n desenlace m

denounce /dɪˈnaʊns/ vt denunciar

dense /dens/ adj **denser, densest** 1 (a) (closely spaced) ‹forest/jungle› espeso; ‹population/traffic› denso; ‹crowd› compacto, apretado (b) (thick) ‹fog/mist/smoke› denso, espeso (c) (Phys) denso (d) (complicated) ‹prose/article› denso 2 (stupid) (colloq) burro (fam), duro de entendederas (fam)

densely /ˈdensli/ adv ‹populated/forested› densamente; ‹packed› apretadamente

density /ˈdensəti/ n (pl **-ties**) densidad f; (of fog) lo espeso, densidad f

dent¹ /dent/ n (in metal) abolladura f, abollón m; (in wood) marca f

dent² vt ‹metal› abollar; ‹wood› hacer* una marca en; ‹popularity› afectar; ‹pride› hacer* mella en

dental /ˈdentl̩/ adj dental; ‹school› de odontología

dental floss /flɑːs ‖flɒs/ n hilo m or seda f dental

dentist /ˈdentəst ‖ˈdentɪst/ n dentista mf, odontólogo, -ga m,f (fml)

dentistry /ˈdentəstri ‖ˈdentɪstri/ n odontología f

dentures /ˈdentʃərz ‖ˈdentʃəz/ pl n dentadura f postiza

deny /dɪˈnaɪ/ vt **denies, denying, denied** 1 ‹accusation/fact› negar*; ‹rumors› desmentir* 2 (refuse) ‹request› denegar*

deodorant /diːˈəʊdərənt/ n desodorante m

depart /dɪˈpɑːrt ‖dɪˈpɑːt/ vi (Transp) salir*, partir (frml); «person» (frml) partir (frml), salir*

department /dɪˈpɑːrtmənt ‖dɪˈpɑːtmənt/ n 1 (of store) sección f; (of company) departamento m, sección f 2 (a) (Govt) ministerio m, secretaría f (Méx) (b) (AmE Adm): **the police/fire ~** el cuerpo de policía/bomberos 3 (Educ) departamento m

department store n (grandes) almacenes mpl, tienda f de departamentos (Méx)

departure /dɪˈpɑːrtʃər ‖dɪˈpɑːtʃə(r)/ n(Transp) salida f, partida f (frml); (of person) (frml) partida f (frml), ida f; **point of ~** punto m de partida; **a ~ from the norm** una desviación de la norma; (before n) ~ **lounge** sala f de embarque

depend /dɪˈpend/ vi **to ~ on** sb/sth depender DE algn/algo

dependable /dɪˈpendəbəl/ adj ‹person› formal, digno de confianza; ‹ally/workman› digno de confianza

dependant, (AmE also) **dependent** /dɪˈpendənt/ n carga f familiar, familiar mf a su (or mi etc) cargo

dependence /dɪˈpendəns/ n dependencia f

dependent¹ /dɪˈpendənt/ adj (a) (reliant) (pred) **to be ~ on** sth/sb depender DE algo/algn (b) (conditional) (pred) **to be ~ on** sth depender DE algo

dependent² n (AmE) ▶ DEPENDANT

depict /dɪˈpɪkt/ vt (fml) (a) (portray) representar (b) (describe) describir*, pintar

depiction /dɪˈpɪkʃən/ n (fml) (a) (representation) representación f (b) (description) descripción f

depilatory /dɪˈpɪlətɔːri ‖dɪˈpɪlətri/ n (pl **-ries**) depilatorio m

deplete /dɪˈpliːt/ vt (reduce) ‹supply/stock› reducir*; (exhaust) ‹energy source› agotar

deplorable /dɪˈplɔːrəbəl/ adj (a) (disgraceful) deplorable, vergonzoso (b) (regrettable) lamentable

deplore /dɪˈplɔːr ‖dɪˈplɔː(r)/ vt (fml) (a) (condemn) deplorar, condenar (b) (regret) deplorar, lamentar

deploy /dɪˈplɔɪ/ vt 1 (position) (Mil) desplegar* 2 (distribute, use) (frml) utilizar*, hacer* uso de

deport /dɪˈpɔːrt ‖dɪˈpɔːt/ vt deportar

deportation /ˈdiːpɔːrˈteɪʃən ‖ˌdiːpɔːˈteɪʃən/ n deportación f

deportment /dɪˈpɔːrtmənt ‖dɪˈpɔːtmənt/ n (frml) (a) (carriage) porte m (b) (conduct) conducta f

depose /dɪˈpəʊz/ vt ‹dictator/ruler› deponer*, derrocar*; ‹champion/king› destronar

deposit¹ /dɪˈpɑːzət ‖dɪˈpɒzɪt/ vt 1 (a) (set down) depositar, poner* (b) (Geol) ‹silt› depositar 2 (a) (leave) depositar (b) ‹money› depositar, ingresar (Esp)

deposit² n 1 (a) (payment into account) depósito m, ingreso m (Esp); (before n) ~ **account** cuenta f de ahorros (b) (down payment — on large amounts) depósito m, entrega f inicial; (— on small amounts) depósito m, señal f, seña f (RPl) (c) (security) depósito *m*, fianza *f* **2** (accumulation — of silt, mud) depósito *m*; (— of dust) capa *f* **3** (Min) (of gas) depósito *m*; (of gold, copper) yacimiento *m*

depot /'diːpəʊ ‖'depəʊ/ *n* **1** (a) (storehouse) depósito *m*, almacén *m* (b) (Mil) depósito *m* **2** (esp AmE) (bus station) terminal *f or* (Chi) *m*, estación *f* de autobuses; (train station) estación *f* **3** (esp BrE) (storage area) (a) (for buses) garage *m* (esp AmL), cochera *f* (Esp), depósito *m* (Chi) (b) (for trains) depósito *m* de locomotoras

depraved /dɪ'preɪvd/ *adj* depravado

depravity /dɪ'prævəti/ *n* depravación *f*

deprecating /'deprɪkeɪtɪŋ/ *adj* (fml) (a) (disapproving) (remark) de desaprobación, reprobatorio (b) (belittling) (smile/laugh) de desprecio

depreciate /dɪ'priːʃieɪt/ *vt* (Fin) depreciar ■ ~ *vi* (Fin) depreciarse

depress /dɪ'pres/ *vt* **1** (sadden) deprimir, abatir **2** (press down) (lever) bajar; (button) pulsar (fml) **3** (Econ) (market) deprimir; (prices/ wages) reducir*, hacer* bajar

depressed /dɪ'prest/ *adj* **1** (dejected) deprimido, abatido; **to get** ~ deprimirse, dejarse abatir **2** (Econ) (economy/market/area) deprimido

depressing /dɪ'presɪŋ/ *adj* deprimente

depression /dɪ'preʃən/ *n* **1** (despondency) depresión *f*, abatimiento *m* **2** (in flat surface) depresión *f* **3** (Econ) depresión *f*, crisis *f*

deprivation /'deprə'veɪʃən ‖,deprɪ'veɪʃən/ *n* (lack, loss) privación *f*; (hardship) privaciones *fpl*, penurias *fpl*

deprive /dɪ'praɪv/ *vt*: **to** ~ **sb** OF **sth** privar a algn DE algo

deprived /dɪ'praɪvd/ *adj* (child) carenciado, desventajado; (region) carenciado

dept (= **department**) Dpto.

depth /depθ/ *n* **1** (a) (of hole, water) profundidad *f*; **out of one's** ~: **when it comes to computers I'm out of my** ~ estoy muy flojo en informática; **don't go out of your** ~ (in water) no vayas donde no haces pie *or* no tocas fondo (b) (of shelf, cupboard) profundidad *f*, fondo *m*; (of hem) ancho *m* **2** (of emotion, knowledge) profundidad *f*; **to study sth in** ~ estudiar algo a fondo *or* en profundidad **3** (of voice) profundidad *f*; (of sound) intensidad *f* **4** **depths** *pl n*: **in the** ~**s of the ocean** en las profundidades del océano; **in the** ~**s of despair** en lo más hondo de la desesperación

deputation /'depjə'teɪʃən ‖,depjʊ'teɪʃən/ *n* delegación *f*

deputy /'depjəti/ *n* (*pl* **-ties**) **1** (a) (second-in-command) segundo, -da *m,f*; (substitute) suplente *mf*, reemplazo *mf* (b) ~ (**sheriff**) (AmE Law) ayudante *mf* del sheriff **2** (Govt) diputado, -da *m,f*

derail /dɪ'reɪl/ *vt* (a) (train) hacer* descarrilar (b) (upset) (plan) desbaratar

deranged /dɪ'reɪndʒd/ *adj* trastornado

derby /'dɜːrbi ‖'dɑːbi/ *n* (*pl* **derbies**) **1** (Sport): **the D**~ (in UK) el Derby, el clásico de Epsom; **the Kentucky D**~ el Derby de Kentucky **2** (hat) (AmE) bombín *m*, sombrero *m* de hongo

deregulate /'diː'regjəleɪt ‖,diː'regjʊleɪt/ *vt* desregular, liberalizar*

deregulation /'diː'regjə'leɪʃən ‖diː,regjʊ'leɪʃən/ *n* desregulación *f*, liberalización *f*

derelict /'derəlɪkt/ *adj* abandonado y en ruinas

deride /dɪ'raɪd/ *vt* ridiculizar*, burlarse de

derision /dɪ'rɪʒən/ *n* escarnio *m* (fml), irrisión *f* (fml)

derisive /dɪ'raɪsɪv/ *adj* (smile/laughter) burlón; (attitude/remark) desdeñoso y burlón

derisory /dɪ'raɪzəri/ *adj* (sum/offer) irrisorio

derivative¹ /dɪ'rɪvətɪv/ *adj* (unoriginal) (novel) carente de originalidad; (plot/theme) manido, trillado; (artist/writer) adocenado

derivative² *n* (in industry) derivado *m*

derive /dɪ'raɪv/ *vt* **children can** ~ **great enjoyment from the simplest things** las cosas más simples pueden dar enorme placer a un niño; **the name is** ~**d from the Greek** el nombre viene *or* deriva del griego ■ ~ *vi* **to** ~ **FROM sth** «(attitude/problem)» provenir* DE algo; «idea» tener* su origen EN algo; (Ling) derivar(se) DE algo

dermatitis /'dɜːrmə'taɪtəs ‖,dɜːmə'taɪtɪs/ *n* dermatitis *f*

derogatory /dɪ'rɑːgətɔːri ‖dɪ'rɒgətri/ *adj* despectivo, peyorativo

descant /'deskænt/ *n* contrapunto *m*

descend /dɪ'send/ *vi* (move downwards) descender* (fml), bajar; **in** ~**ing order of importance** en orden decreciente *or* descendente de importancia; **don't** ~ **to his level** no te pongas a su nivel ■ ~ *vt* descender* (fml), bajar

descendant /dɪ'sendənt/ *n* descendiente *mf*

descended /dɪ'sendəd ‖dɪ'sendɪd/ *adj* (pred) **to be** ~ **FROM sb** ser* descendiente DE algn, descender* DE algn

descendent *n* (AmE) ▶ DESCENDANT

descent /dɪ'sent/ *n* **1** (a) (by climbers, plane) descenso *m*, bajada *f* (b) (in terrain) pendiente *f*, bajada *f* **2** (decline) caída *f* **3** (lineage) ascendencia *f*

describe /dɪ'skraɪb/ *vt* describir*; **he** ~**s himself as a socialist** se define como socialista

description /dɪ'skrɪpʃən/ *n* descripción *f*; **of every** ~ de todo tipo, de toda clase

descriptive /dɪ'skrɪptɪv/ *adj* descriptivo

desecrate /'desɪkreɪt/ *vt* profanar

desert¹ /'dezərt ‖'dezət/ *n* (Geog) desierto *m*; (before n) (region/climate) desértico; (tribe/sand) del desierto

desert² /dɪ'zɜːrt ‖dɪ'zɜːt/ *vt* (a) (fml) (place) abandonar, huir* de (b) (family) abandonar; (cause) desertar de ■ ~ *vi* (Mil) desertar

deserted /dɪ'zɜːrtəd ‖dɪ'zɜːtɪd/ *adj* (a) (streets/ village) desierto (b) (husband/wife) abandonado

deserter /dɪ'zɜːrtər ‖dɪ'zɜːtə(r)/ *n* desertor, -tora *m,f*

desertion /dɪ'zɜːrʃən ‖dɪ'zɜːʃən/ *n* (a) (Mil) deserción *f* (b) (of family, place) abandono *m*

desert island /'dezərt ‖'dezət/ *n* isla *f* desierta

deserts /dɪ'zɜːrts ‖dɪ'zɜːts/ *pl n*: **to get one's just** ~ recibir su (*or* tu *etc*) merecido

deserve /dɪˈzɜːrv ‖dɪˈzɜːv/ vt merecer(se)*;
they got what they ~d se llevaron su merecido

deserving /dɪˈzɜːrvɪŋ ‖dɪˈzɜːvɪŋ/ adj ⟨cause/
case⟩ meritorio; the ~ poor los pobres dignos de
ayuda

desiccated /ˈdesɪkeɪtəd ‖ˈdesɪkeɪtɪd/ adj
seco; ~ coconut coco m rallado

design¹ /dɪˈzam/ n [1] (a) (of product, car,
machine) diseño m; (drawing) diseño m, boceto m
(b) (pattern, decoration) diseño m, motivo m, dibujo
m (c) (product, model) modelo m [2] (a) (Art)
diseño m (b) (style) estilo m, líneas fpl [3] (a)
(plan) (liter) plan m; by ~ deliberadamente (b)
designs pl n (intentions) propósitos mpl,
designios mpl (liter)

design² vt ⟨house/garden⟩ diseñar, proyectar;
⟨dress/product⟩ diseñar; ⟨course/program⟩
planear, estructurar; a statement ~ed to reassure
the public una declaración destinada a
tranquilizar al público

designate¹ /ˈdezɪgneɪt/ vt [1] (name officially)
nombrar, designar [2] (call) (fml) designar

designate² /ˈdezɪgneɪt, -nət ‖ˈdezɪgnət/ adj
(after n): the governor ~ quien ha sido nombrado
gobernador

designer /dɪˈzamər ‖dɪˈzamə(r)/ n diseñador,
-dora m,f; (before n) ⟨clothes/jeans⟩ de diseño
exclusivo; ⟨furniture/pen/baby⟩ de diseño

desirable /dɪˈzaɪrəbəl ‖dɪˈzaɪrəbəl/ adj (a)
⟨property/location⟩ atractivo (b) (sexually) ⟨man/
woman⟩ atractivo, deseable, apetecible (c)
⟨outcome⟩ deseable, conveniente; ⟨option⟩
conveniente, aconsejable

desire¹ /dɪˈzaɪr ‖dɪˈzaɪə(r)/ n [1] (wish) deseo m,
anhelo m (liter) [2] (lust) deseo m

desire² vt (a) (want) ⟨happiness/success⟩ desear;
to leave a lot to be ~d dejar bastante que desear
(b) (lust after) ⟨person⟩ desear

desirous /dɪˈzaɪrəs ‖dɪˈzaɪərəs/ adj (fml)
(pred): we are ~ of your success le deseamos
éxito

desist /dɪˈzɪst/ vi (fml) to ~ (FROM sth/-ING)
(cease) desistir (DE algo/+ INF); (abstain)
abstenerse* (DE algo/+ INF)

desk /desk/ n (a) (table) escritorio m, mesa f de
trabajo; (in school) pupitre m; (before n) ⟨lamp⟩ de
escritorio, de (sobre)mesa; a ~ job un trabajo de
oficina (b) (service counter) mostrador m (c) (Journ)
sección f

desktop /ˈdesktɑːp ‖ˈdesktɒp/ adj (before n)
⟨calculator/computer⟩ de escritorio, de
(sobre)mesa; ~ publishing autoedición f, edición
f electrónica

desolate /ˈdesələt/ adj [1] (deserted) ⟨place/
landscape⟩ desierto, desolado [2] ⟨person⟩
desconsolado, desolado; ⟨outlook/existence⟩
sombrío, lúgubre

despair¹ /dɪˈsper ‖dɪˈspeə(r)/ n desesperación
f; to be in ~ estar* desesperado

despair² vi perder* las esperanzas,
desesperar(se); honestly, I ~ of you!
¡francamente, eres un caso perdido!

despairing /dɪˈsperɪŋ ‖dɪˈspeərɪŋ/ adj ⟨look/
cry⟩ de desesperación

despatch /dɪˈspætʃ/ vt/n ▶ DISPATCH¹,²

desperate /ˈdespərət/ adj [1] (frantic) ⟨person/

attempt⟩ desesperado; to be ~ estar desesperado
[2] (critical) ⟨state/situation⟩ grave, desesperado;
⟨need⟩ apremiante

desperately /ˈdespərətli/ adv ⟨struggle⟩
desesperadamente; ⟨need⟩ urgentemente, con
urgencia

desperation /ˌdespəˈreɪʃən/ n desesperación f

despicable /dɪˈspɪkəbəl/ adj vil, despreciable

despise /dɪˈspaɪz/ vt despreciar
(profundamente)

despite /dɪˈspaɪt/ prep a pesar de

despondent /dɪˈspɑːndənt ‖dɪˈspɒndənt/ adj
abatido, descorazonado

despot /ˈdespɑːt ‖ˈdespɒt/ n déspota mf

dessert /dɪˈzɜːrt ‖dɪˈzɜːt/ n postre m

dessertspoon /dɪˈzɜːrtspuːn ‖dɪˈzɜːtspuːn/ n
cuchara f de postre

destabilize /diːˈsteɪbəlaɪz/ vt desestabilizar*

destination /ˌdestəˈneɪʃən ‖ˌdestɪˈneɪʃən/ n
(a) (end of journey) destino m (b) (purpose) meta f

destined /ˈdestənd ‖ˈdestɪnd/ adj (pred)
[1] (fated) to be ~ to + INF estar* (pre)destinado A
+ INF [2] (a) (intended) ~ FOR sth destinado A algo
(b) (bound, on way): ~ for the West Indies con
destino al Caribe

destiny /ˈdestəni ‖ˈdestɪni/ n (pl -nies)
destino m, sino m (liter)

destitute /ˈdestətuːt ‖ˈdestɪtjuːt/ adj indigente

destroy /dɪˈstrɔɪ/ vt (a) (ruin, wreck) ⟨building/
forest⟩ destruir*; ⟨reputation/confidence⟩ acabar
con; ⟨life⟩ arruinar (b) ⟨animal⟩ sacrificar* (euf)

destroyer /dɪˈstrɔɪər ‖dɪˈstrɔɪə(r)/ n
destructor m

destruction /dɪˈstrʌkʃən/ n [1] (of city, books,
forest) destrucción f; (of reputation, civilization) ruina f,
destrucción f; (slaughter) exterminación f [2] (cause
of downfall) (fml) ruina f, perdición f [3] (damage)
destrucción f, estragos mpl, destrozos mpl

destructive /dɪˈstrʌktɪv/ adj ⟨storm/weapon⟩
destructor; ⟨tendency⟩ destructivo; ⟨child⟩
destrozón; ⟨criticism⟩ destructivo, negativo

desultory /ˈdesəltɔːri ‖ˈdezəltəri/ adj ⟨effort/
attempt⟩ desganado

detach /dɪˈtætʃ/ vt (separate) separar, quitar;
(unstick) despegar*; the headrest can be ~ed el
apoyacabezas se puede desmontar or quitar

detachable /dɪˈtætʃəbəl/ adj ⟨cover⟩ de quita
y pon, de quitar y poner; ⟨lining⟩ desmontable

detached /dɪˈtætʃt/ adj [1] ⟨person/manner⟩
(aloof) distante, indiferente; (objective) objetivo,
imparcial [2] (BrE) ⟨house⟩ no adosado

detachment /dɪˈtætʃmənt/ n [1] (aloofness)
distancia f, indiferencia f; (objectivity) objetividad
f, imparcialidad f [2] (act of detaching) (fml)
desprendimiento m [3] (Mil) destacamento m

detail¹ /dɪˈteɪl, ˈdiːteɪl ‖ˈdiːteɪl/ n [1] (a)
(particular) detalle m, pormenor m; he asked for
further ~s pidió más información or información
más detallada (b) (embellishment) detalle m (c)
(insignificant matter) minucia f, detalle m (sin
importancia) [2] (minutiae) detalles mpl; to go into
~ entrar en detalles or pormenores; to explain
sth in ~ explicar* algo detalladamente or
minuciosamente

detail² vt [1] (describe) exponer* en detalle,
detallar [2] (Mil) destacar*

detailed /'di:teɪld/ adj ‹description› detallado, minucioso, pormenorizado; ‹examination› minucioso, detenido

detain /dɪ'teɪn/ vt (a) (delay) (frml): **don't let me ~ you** no quiero entretenerlo or demorarlo (b) (in custody) detener*

detect /dɪ'tekt/ vt ‹object/substance› detectar

detection /dɪ'tekʃən/ n [1] (of error) descubrimiento m; (of act, crime, criminal): **to escape ~** pasar desapercibido or inadvertido [2] (of substance) detección f

detective /dɪ'tektɪv/ n (private) detective mf; (in police force) agente mf, oficial mf; (before n) ~ **story** novela f policíaca or policial

detector /dɪ'tektər ‖dɪ'tektə(r)/ n detector m

detente /deɪ'tɑ:nt/ n (Pol) distensión f

detention /dɪ'tentʃən ‖dɪ'tenʃən/ n [1] (in custody) detención f [2] (Educ): **to be in ~** estar* castigado

deter /dɪ'tɜ:r ‖dɪ'tɜ:(r)/ vt -rr- ‹person› disuadir, hacer* disuadir; ‹crime/war› impedir*; **to ~ sb FROM sth/-ING** disuadir a algn DE algo/ + INF

detergent /dɪ'tɜ:rdʒənt ‖dɪ'tɜ:dʒənt/ n (Chem) detergente m; (for clothes) detergente m; (for dishes) lavavajillas m

deteriorate /dɪ'trɪəreɪt ‖dɪ'tɪərɪəreɪt/ vi «health/relationship/material» deteriorarse; «weather/work» empeorar

deterioration /dɪ'tɪrɪə'reɪʃən ‖dɪ,tɪərɪə'reɪʃən/ n deterioro m

determination /dɪ'tɜ:rmə'neɪʃən ‖dɪ,tɜ:mɪ'neɪʃən/ n determinación f, resolución f

determine /dɪ'tɜ:rmən ‖dɪ'tɜ:mɪn/ vt [1] (ascertain) establecer*, determinar [2] (a) (influence) determinar, condicionar (b) (mark) ‹boundary/limit› definir, demarcar* [3] (liter) (resolve) decidir; **to ~ to + INF** decidir + INF, tomar la determinación DE + INF

determined /dɪ'tɜ:rmənd ‖dɪ'tɜ:mɪnd/ adj ‹mood/person› decidido, resuelto; **to be ~ to + INF** estar* decidido A + INF, estar* empeñado EN + INF; **to be ~ THAT** estar* resuelto or decidido A QUE (+ subj)

deterrent /dɪ'terənt/ n: **it may act as a ~ to thieves** puede servir para disuadir a los ladrones; **the nuclear ~** las armas nucleares como fuerza disuasoria

detest /dɪ'test/ vt detestar, odiar

dethrone /dɪ'θrəʊn/ vt destronar

detonate /'detəneɪt/ vt hacer* detonar

detour[1] /'di:tər ‖'di:tʊə(r)/ n (a) (deviation) rodeo m, vuelta f; **to make a ~** dar* un rodeo, desviarse* (b) (AmE Transp) desvío m, desviación f

detour[2] vt (AmE) ‹traffic› desviar*

detract /dɪ'trækt/ vi: **I didn't wish to ~ from her achievement** no quise quitarle méritos or restarle valor a su logro; **it ~s from the beauty of the painting** desmerece la belleza del cuadro

detractor /dɪ'træktər ‖dɪ'træktə(r)/ n detractor, -tora m,f

detriment /'detrəmənt ‖'detrɪmənt/ n (frml) detrimento m, perjuicio m; **to the ~ of sb/sth** en detrimento or perjuicio de algn/algo

devalue /'di:'vælju:/ vt (Fin) devaluar*

devastate /'devəsteɪt/ vt (a) (lay waste) devastar, asolar* (b) (overwhelm) ‹opposition/

argument› aplastar, demoler*; **I was ~d when I heard** quedé deshecho or anonadado cuando me enteré

devastating /'devəsteɪtɪŋ/ adj (a) ‹punch/ shock› devastador (b) ‹accuracy/logic› abrumador, apabullante; ‹reply/defeat› demoledor, aplastante; ‹beauty› irresistible

devastation /'devə'steɪʃən/ n devastación f

develop /dɪ'veləp/ vt [1] (a) (elaborate, devise) desarrollar (b) (improve) ‹skill/ability/quality› desarrollar (c) (exploit) ‹land/area› urbanizar* (d) (expand) ‹business/range› ampliar* (e) (create) ‹drug/engine› crear [2] (acquire) ‹immunity/ resistance› desarrollar; ‹disease› contraer* (frml); **the machine ~ed a fault** la máquina empezó a funcionar mal [3] (Phot) revelar
■ ~ vi [1] (a) (grow) «person/industry» desarrollarse; «interest» crecer*, aumentar (b) (evolve) **to ~ INTO sth** convertirse* or transformarse EN algo [2] (appear) «problem/ complication» surgir*, aparecer*; «crisis» producirse*

developer /dɪ'veləpər ‖dɪ'veləpə(r)/ n [1] (of land, property) promotor inmobiliario, promotora inmobiliaria m,f [2] (Phot) revelador m

developing /dɪ'veləpɪŋ/ adj ‹country› en vías de desarrollo

development /dɪ'veləpmənt/ n [1] (of person, idea, situation) desarrollo m [2] (of drug, engine) creación f [3] (of land, area) urbanización f [4] (housing ~) complejo m habitacional, fraccionamiento m (Méx), urbanización f (Esp) [5] (Econ) desarrollo m [6] (happening, event) acontecimiento m, suceso m

deviant /'di:viənt/ adj ‹practices/conduct› desviado, que se aparta de la norma; ‹person/ personality› anormal

deviate /'di:vieɪt/ vi **to ~ FROM sth** ‹from course› desviarse* DE algo; ‹from truth/norm› apartarse DE algo

deviation /'di:vi'eɪʃən/ n desviación f

device /dɪ'vaɪs/ n [1] (gadget, tool) artefacto m, dispositivo m, aparato m; (mechanism) dispositivo m, mecanismo m [2] (stratagem) recurso m, estratagema f; **to leave sb to her/his own ~s** dejar que algn se las arregle solo

devil /'devl/ n [1] (a) (Relig) diablo m, demonio m (b) (evil spirit) demonio m [2] (colloq) (person): **he's a little ~!** ¡es un diablillo!; **poor ~!** ¡pobre diablo!

devious /'di:viəs/ adj (a) (underhand) ‹person› taimado, artero (b) (roundabout) ‹route/path› tortuoso, sinuoso

devise /dɪ'vaɪz/ vt ‹plan/system› idear, crear, concebir*; ‹machine/tool› inventar

devoid /dɪ'vɔɪd/ adj (pred) (frml) **to be ~ OF sth** carecer* DE algo

devolution /'devə'lu:ʃən ‖,di:və'lu:ʃən/ n (a) (delegation) delegación f, transferencia f (b) (BrE Govt) transferencia de competencias del gobierno central a un gobierno regional

devolve /dɪ'vɑ:lv ‖dɪ'vɒlv/ vt (frml) ‹power› delegar*, transferir*; ‹privilege/right› conceder

devote /dɪ'vəʊt/ vt **to ~ sth TO sth/-ING** dedicar* algo A algo/ + INF
■ v refl **to ~ oneself TO sth/-ING** dedicarse* A algo/ + INF

devoted ⋯▷ differentiate

614

devoted /dɪˈvəʊtəd ‖dɪˈvəʊtɪd/ adj (a) (loving) ⟨couple/family⟩ unido; **to be ~ TO sb** sentir* devoción POR algn (b) (dedicated) ⟨before n⟩ ⟨follower/admirer⟩ ferviente, devoto; ⟨service/ friendship⟩ leal

devotion /dɪˈvəʊʃən/ n (love) devoción f; (loyalty) lealtad f

devour /dɪˈvaʊr ‖dɪˈvaʊə(r)/ vt devorar

devout /dɪˈvaʊt/ adj (a) (Relig) devoto, piadoso (b) (earnest) (frml) ⟨before n⟩ ⟨supporter⟩ ferviente

dew /du: ‖dju:/ n rocío m

dexterity /dekˈsterəti/ n (manual) destreza f, habilidad f; (skill) habilidad f

diabetes /ˌdaɪəˈbi:ti:z/ n diabetes f

diabetic¹ /ˌdaɪəˈbetɪk/ adj diabético; ⟨jam/ chocolate⟩ para diabéticos

diabetic² n diabético, -ca m,f

diabolical /ˌdaɪəˈbɑːlɪkəl ‖ˌdaɪəˈbɒlɪkəl/ adj ⟨machinations⟩ diabólico, satánico; ⟨cruelty⟩ perverso, satánico

diagnose /ˈdaɪəɡnəʊs, -əʊz ‖ˈdaɪəɡnəʊz/ vt ⟨illness⟩ diagnosticar*; ⟨cause/fault⟩ determinar

diagnosis /ˌdaɪəɡˈnəʊsəs ‖ˌdaɪəɡˈnəʊsɪs/ n (pl **-ses** /-si:z/) diagnóstico m

diagonal /daɪˈæɡənl/ adj ⟨line⟩ diagonal; ⟨path⟩ en diagonal

diagram /ˈdaɪəɡræm/ n diagrama m, esquema m, gráfico m

dial¹ /ˈdaɪl ‖ˈdaɪəl/ n (on clock, watch) esfera f; (on measuring instrument) cuadrante m; (of telephone) disco m; (on radio) dial m

dial², (BrE) **-ll-** vt/i (Telec) marcar*, discar* (AmL)

dialect /ˈdaɪəlekt/ n dialecto m

dialling tone /ˈdaɪlɪŋ ‖ˈdaɪəlɪŋ/ n (BrE) ▶ DIAL TONE

dialogue, (AmE also) **dialog** /ˈdaɪəlɔ:ɡ ‖ˈdaɪəlɒɡ/ n diálogo m

dial tone n tono m de marcar or (AmL) de discado

diameter /daɪˈæmətər ‖daɪˈæmɪtə(r)/ n diámetro m

diamond /ˈdaɪəmənd/ n 1 (Min) diamante m; (cut) brillante m, diamante m 2 (shape) rombo m 3 (Games) **diamonds** (suit) (+ sing or pl vb) diamantes mpl

diaper /ˈdaɪpər ‖ˈdaɪəpə(r)/ n (AmE) pañal m

diaphragm /ˈdaɪəfræm/ n 1 (Anat) diafragma m 2 (contraceptive) diafragma m

diarrhea, (BrE) **diarrhoea** /ˌdaɪəˈri:ə ‖ˌdaɪəˈriə/ n diarrea f

diary /ˈdaɪəri/ n (pl **-ries**) 1 (personal record) diario m 2 (book for appointments) agenda f

dice¹ /daɪs/ n (pl ~) dado m

dice² pl of DIE² and of DICE¹

dice³ vt (Culin) cortar en dados or cubitos

dictate /ˈdɪkteɪt ‖dɪkˈteɪt/ vt 1 (read out) dictar 2 (prescribe, lay down) ⟨law⟩ establecer*, dictar; ⟨common sense⟩ dictar

dictation /dɪkˈteɪʃən/ n (Corresp, Educ) dictado m

dictator /ˈdɪkteɪtər ‖dɪkˈteɪtə(r)/ n dictador, -dora m,f

dictatorial /ˌdɪktəˈtɔ:riəl/ adj dictatorial

dictatorship /dɪkˈteɪtərʃɪp ‖dɪkˈteɪtəʃɪp/ n dictadura f

diction /ˈdɪkʃən/ n dicción f

dictionary /ˈdɪkʃəneri ‖ˈdɪkʃənri, ˈdɪkʃənəri/ n (pl **-ries**) diccionario m

did /dɪd/ past of DO¹

didactic /daɪˈdæktɪk/ adj didáctico

diddle /ˈdɪdl/ vt (colloq) estafar, timar (fam)

didn't /ˈdɪdnt/ = **did not**

die¹ /daɪ/ **dies, dying, died** vi (a) (stop living) morir*; (violently) matarse, morir*; **to be dying FOR sth** (colloq) morirse* POR algo; **to be dying to + INF** (colloq) morirse* POR + INF, morirse* de ganas de + INF (b) (stop functioning) «engine/motor» apagarse*, dejar de funcionar
  ■ ~ vt: **to ~ a natural death** morir* de muerte natural; **to ~ a violent death** tener* or sufrir una muerte violenta
  ■ **die away** [v + adv] «storm/wind» amainar; «anger» pasar
  ■ **die down** [v + adv] «fire/noise» irse* apagando; «storm/wind» amainar; «anger/ excitement» calmarse
  ■ **die out** [v + adv] «race/species» extinguirse*; «custom» morir*, caer* en desuso

die² n (pl **dice**) (Games) dado m

diehard /ˈdaɪhɑ:rd ‖ˈdaɪhɑ:d/ n intransigente mf; ⟨before n⟩ intransigente, acérrimo

diesel¹ /ˈdi:zəl/ n (a) (vehicle) coche m (or camión m etc) diesel, diesel m (b) (fuel) diesel m, gasóleo m, gas-oil m

diesel² adj ⟨before n⟩ diesel adj inv

diet¹ /ˈdaɪət/ n (a) (special food) régimen m, dieta f; **to be/go on a ~** estar*/ponerse* a régimen or a dieta; ⟨before n⟩ ⟨cola⟩ light adj inv (b) (nourishment) alimentación f, dieta f (alimenticia); **they live on a ~ of rice and fish** se alimentan de arroz y pescado

diet² vi hacer* régimen or dieta

differ /ˈdɪfər ‖ˈdɪfə(r)/ vi 1 (a) (be at variance) diferir*; **how do they ~?** ¿en qué difieren? (b) (be unlike) ser* distinto or diferente; **to ~ FROM sb/sth** diferenciarse or diferir* DE algn/algo 2 (disagree) discrepar, diferir* (frml)

difference /ˈdɪfrəns/ n diferencia f; **to tell the ~** notar or ver* la diferencia; **it could make a ~ in** o (BrE) **to the outcome** podría influir en el resultado; **it will make no ~ to you** a ti no te va a afectar

different /ˈdɪfrənt/ adj (a) (not the same) distinto, diferente; **~ FROM** o **TO** o (AmE also) **THAN sth/sb** distinto or diferente DE or A algo/ algn (b) (unusual) distinto, original

differential /ˌdɪfəˈrentʃəl ‖ˌdɪfəˈrenʃəl/ n diferencial m

differentiate /ˌdɪfəˈrentʃieɪt ‖ˌdɪfəˈrenʃieɪt/ vi distinguir*

AmC Central America	Arg Argentina	Cu Cuba	Per Peru
AmL Latin America	Bol Bolivia	Ec Ecuador	RPl River Plate Area
AmS South America	Chi Chile	Esp Spain	Ur Uruguay
Andes Andean Region	CS Southern Cone	Méx Mexico	Ven Venezuela

■ ~ *vt* (frml): **to ~ sth** (FROM sth) diferenciar *or* distinguir* algo (DE algo)

differently /'dɪfrəntli/ *adv*: they think ~ no piensan igual *or* del mismo modo; **I view things** ~ yo veo las cosas de otra forma *or* otro modo

difficult /'dɪfɪkəlt/ *adj* difícil; the ~ **part is** ... lo difícil es ..., la dificultad está en ...; **he's finding it** ~ **to give up smoking** le está resultando difícil dejar de fumar, le está costando dejar de fumar

difficulty /'dɪfɪkəlti/ *n* (*pl* **-ties**) **(a)** (of situation, task) dificultad *f*; **she had great** ~ **walking** caminaba con mucha dificultad **(b)** (problem) dificultad *f*, problema *m*; **to get into difficulties** meterse en líos

diffident /'dɪfədənt ‖'dɪfɪdənt/ *adj* (person) poco seguro de sí mismo; (smile) tímido

diffuse¹ /dɪ'fjuːz/ *vt* (heat) difundir, esparcir*; (light) tamizar*, difuminar; (knowledge) (frml) difundir

diffuse² /dɪ'fjuːs/ *adj* difuso

dig¹ /dɪg/ (*pres p* **digging**; *past & past p* **dug**) *vt* ⏍1⏍ (ground) cavar; (hole/trench) (by hand) cavar; (by machine) excavar ⏍2⏍ (jab, thrust) **to ~ sth** INTO sth clavar algo EN algo

■ ~ *vi* ⏍1⏍ (excavate — by hand) cavar; (— by machine) excavar; «dog» escarbar; **to ~ for oil** hacer* prospecciones petrolíferas ⏍2⏍ (search) buscar*; **she dug in her pockets for the key** buscó la llave en los bolsillos

■ **dig up** [v + o + adv, v + adv + o] **(a)** (lawn) levantar; (weeds/tree) arrancar* **(b)** (body/ treasure) desenterrar* **(c)** (facts) (colloq) sacar* a la luz

dig² *n* ⏍1⏍ (Archeol) excavación *f* ⏍2⏍ (jab — with elbow) codazo *m*; (— with pin) pinchazo *m* ⏍3⏍ (critical remark) (colloq) pulla *f*; (hint) indirecta *f*; **to have a** ~ **at sb/sth** meterse con algn/algo

digest¹ /daɪ'dʒest, də- ‖daɪ'dʒest, dɪ-/ *vt* (food) digerir*; (assimilate mentally) asimilar, digerir* (fam)

digest² /'daɪdʒest/ *n* (summary) compendio *m*; (journal) boletín *m*, revista *f*

digestible /daɪ'dʒestəbəl, də- ‖daɪ'dʒestəbəl, dɪ-/ *adj* (Physiol) digerible; (comprehensible) fácil de asimilar *or* (fam) digerir

digestion /daɪ'dʒestʃən, də- ‖daɪ'dʒestʃən, dɪ-/ *n* digestión *f*

digestive /daɪ'dʒestɪv, də- ‖daɪ'dʒestɪv, dɪ-/ *adj* digestivo

digger /'dɪgər ‖'dɪgə(r)/ *n* (machine) excavadora *f*; (person) excavador, -dora *m,f*

digit /'dɪdʒət ‖'dɪdʒɪt/ *n* ⏍1⏍ (Math) dígito *m* (frml) ⏍2⏍ (Anat) dedo *m*

digital /'dɪdʒətəl ‖'dɪdʒɪtl/ *adj* digital

digital: ~ **camera** *n* cámara *f* (fotográfica) digital; ~ **video disc** *n* videodisco *m* digital

dignified /'dɪgnəfaɪd ‖'dɪgnɪfaɪd/ *adj* **(a)** (person/reply) digno, circunspecto; (silence/ attitude) digno **(b)** (stately) majestuoso

dignity /'dɪgnəti/ *n* (of person) dignidad *f*; (of occasion) solemnidad *f*

digress /daɪ'gres/ *vi*: but I ~ pero estoy divagando; **to ~** FROM sth apartarse DE algo

digression /daɪ'greʃən/ *n* digresión *f*

dike /daɪk/ *n* ⏍1⏍ **(a)** (to keep out water) dique *m* **(b)** (causeway) terraplén *m* **(c)** (ditch) acequia *f* ⏍2⏍ ▸ DYKE 2

dilapidated /də'læpədeɪtəd ‖dɪ'læpɪdeɪtɪd/ *adj* (building) ruinoso; (car) destartalado

dilate /daɪ'leɪt/ *vi* dilatarse

dilemma /də'lemə, daɪ- ‖dɪ'lemə, daɪ-/ *n* dilema *m*

diligence /'dɪlədʒəns ‖'dɪlɪdʒəns/ *n* diligencia *f*

diligent /'dɪlədʒənt ‖'dɪlɪdʒənt/ *adj* (worker) diligente, cumplidor; (student) aplicado, diligente; (work/study) esmerado, concienzudo

dilute /daɪ'luːt ‖daɪ'ljuːt/ *vt* diluir*

dim¹ /dɪm/ *adj* **-mm-** ⏍1⏍ **(a)** (dark) (room) oscuro, poco iluminado; (light) débil, tenue **(b)** (indistinct) (memory/shape) borroso; (idea) vago **(c)** (gloomy) (prospects) nada halagüeño, nada prometedor ⏍2⏍ (stupid) (colloq) corto (de luces) (fam), tonto (fam)

dim² *vt* **-mm-** (lights) atenuar*; **to ~ one's headlights** (AmE) poner* las (luces) cortas *or* de cruce *or* (AmL tb) las (luces) bajas

dime /daɪm/ *n* (AmE colloq) moneda de diez centavos

dimension /de'mentʃən, daɪ- ‖dɪ'menʃən, daɪ-/ *n* dimensión *f*

dime store *n* (AmE) tienda que vende artículos de bajo precio, ≈ baratillo *m*

diminish /də'mɪnɪʃ ‖dɪ'mɪnɪʃ/ *vi* «cost/ number» disminuir*, reducirse*; «enthusiasm» disminuir*, apagarse*

■ ~ *vt* (size/cost) reducir*, disminuir*; (enthusiasm) disminuir*

diminutive /də'mɪnjətɪv ‖dɪ'mɪnjʊtɪv/ *adj* diminuto, minúsculo

dimly /'dɪmli/ *adv* (shine) débilmente; **a ~ lit room** una habitación poco iluminada *or* iluminada por una luz tenue

dimmer /'dɪmər ‖'dɪmə(r)/ *n* potenciómetro *m*, dimmer *m*

dimple /'dɪmpəl/ *n* (in cheeks, chin) hoyuelo *m*

dimwit /'dɪmwɪt/ *n* (colloq) tarado, -da (mental) *m,f* (fam)

din /dɪn/ *n* (colloq) (no *pl*) (of conversation, voices) barullo *m* (fam), bulla *f* (fam); (of drill, traffic) estruendo *m*, ruido *m*

dine /daɪn/ *vi* (frml) cenar

diner /'daɪnər ‖'daɪnə(r)/ *n* ⏍1⏍ (person) comensal *mf* ⏍2⏍ **(a)** (restaurant) (AmE) cafetería *f* **(b)** ▸ DINING CAR

dinghy /'dɪŋgi, 'dɪŋi/ *n* (*pl* **-ghies**) (sailing boat) bote *m*; (inflatable o rubber ~) bote *m* neumático

dingy /'dɪndʒi/ *adj* **-gier, -giest** (building/ room) lúgubre; (furnishings) deslucido; (dirty) sucio

dining /'daɪnɪŋ/**:** ~ **car** *n* coche *m* restaurante, coche *m* comedor; ~ **room** *n* comedor *m*; ~ **table** *n* mesa *f* (de comedor)

dinner /'dɪnər ‖'dɪnə(r)/ *n* **(a)** (in evening) cena *f*, comida *f* (AmL); **to eat** *o* **have ~** cenar, comer (AmL) **(b)** (formal) cena *f* (de gala) **(c)** (at midday) almuerzo *m*, comida *f* (esp Esp, Méx); **to eat** *o* (BrE) **have ~** almorzar*, comer (esp Esp, Méx)

dinner: ~ **dance** *n* cena *f* con baile, comida *f* bailable (esp AmL), cena-baile *f* (Méx); ~ **jacket** *n* (esp BrE) esmoquin *m*, smoking *m*; ~ **party** *n* cena *f*, comida *f* (AmL); ~ **plate** *n* plato *m* llano *or* (Méx) plano *or* (RPl tb) playo *or* (Chi) bajo; ~ ⋯⋮

service *n* vajilla *f*; ~ **table** *n* mesa *f*; ~**time** *n* (in evening) hora *f* de cenar *or* (esp AmL) de comer; (at midday) hora *f* de almorzar *or* (esp Esp, Méx) de comer

dinosaur /'daɪnəsɔːr ‖'daɪnəsɔː(r)/ *n* dinosaurio *m*

dint /dɪnt/ *n*: **by ~ of sth** a fuerza de algo

diocese /'daɪəsəs ‖'daɪəsɪs/ *n* diócesis *f*

dip[1] /dɪp/ **-pp-** *vt* [1] **to ~ sth IN(TO) sth** meter algo EN algo; (into liquid) mojar algo EN algo [2] (Agr) ⟨*sheep*⟩ desinfectar ⟨*haciendo pasar por un baño*⟩ [3] (a) (lower) ⟨*head*⟩ agachar, bajar (b) (BrE Auto): **to ~ one's headlights** poner* las (luces) cortas *or* de cruce *or* (AmL tb) las (luces) bajas
■ ~ *vi* (a) (decrease) «*sales/prices*» bajar (b) (move downward) «*aircraft/bird*» bajar en picada *or* (Esp) en picado

dip[2] *n* [1] (swim) (colloq) (*no pl*) chapuzón *m* (fam) [2] (Agr) baño *m* desinfectante [3] (depression, hollow) hondonada *f* [4] (in sales, production) caída *f*, descenso *m* [5] (Culin) *salsa en la que se mojan diferentes bocaditos (en una fiesta etc)*

diphthong /'dɪfθɔːŋ ‖'dɪfθɒŋ/ *n* diptongo *m*

diploma /də'pləʊmə ‖dɪ'pləʊmə/ *n* diploma *m*

diplomacy /də'pləʊməsi ‖dɪ'pləʊməsi/ *n* diplomacia *f*

diplomat /'dɪpləmæt/ *n* diplomático, -ca *m,f*

diplomatic /ˌdɪplə'mætɪk/ *adj* (a) (Govt) (*before n*) diplomático; ~ **immunity** inmunidad *f* diplomática (b) (tactful) diplomático

dipstick /'dɪpstɪk/ *n* varilla *f* (medidora) del aceite

dire /daɪr ‖'daɪə(r)/ *adj* **direr, direst** [1] (a) ⟨*news/consequences*⟩ funesto, nefasto; **to be in ~ straits** estar* en una situación desesperada (b) (very bad) (BrE colloq) espantoso (fam), atroz [2] (ominous) ⟨*warning*⟩ serio, grave [3] (desperate) ⟨*need/misery*⟩ extremo

direct[1] /də'rekt, daɪ- ‖daɪ'rekt, dɪ-/ *adj* [1] (a) ⟨*route/flight*⟩ directo; ⟨*contact*⟩ directo; ⟨*cause/consequence*⟩ directo (b) (Ling) (*before n*) ⟨*question/command*⟩ en estilo directo; ~ **discourse** *o* (BrE) **speech** estilo *m* directo [2] (frank, straightforward) ⟨*person/manner*⟩ franco, directo; ⟨*question*⟩ directo

direct[2] *adv* [1] ⟨*write/phone*⟩ directamente; ⟨*go/travel*⟩ (BrE) directo, directamente [2] (straight) directamente; ~ **from Paris** (Rad, TV) en directo desde París

direct[3] *vt* [1] (a) (give directions to) indicarle* el camino a (b) (address) ⟨*letter/parcel*⟩ mandar, dirigir* [2] (aim) dirigir*; **it was ~ed at us** iba dirigido a nosotros [3] ⟨*play/orchestra/traffic*⟩ dirigir* [4] (order) (fml) ordenar; **to ~ sb to + INF** ordenarle A algn QUE (+ *subj*)
■ ~ *vi* (Cin, Theat) dirigir*

direct: ~ **billing** /'bɪlɪŋ/ *n* (AmE) débito *m* bancario *or* (Esp) domiciliación *f* de pagos; ~ **current** *n* corriente *f* continua; ~ **debit** *n* ▶ BILLING; ~ **dialing,** (BrE) ~ **dialling** *n* discado *m* directo *or* automático

direction /də'rekʃən, daɪ- ‖daɪ'rekʃən, dɪ-/ *n* [1] (course, compass point) dirección *f*; **sense of ~** sentido *m* de (la) orientación; **in the ~ of** en dirección a [2] (purpose): **he lacks ~** no tiene un

norte [3] (supervision) dirección *f* [4] **directions** *pl* (for route) indicaciones *fpl*; (for task, use, assembly) instrucciones *fpl*, indicaciones *fpl*

directive /də'rektɪv, daɪ- ‖daɪ'rektɪv, dɪ-/ *n* directriz *f*, directiva *f* (esp AmL)

directly /də'rektli, daɪ- ‖daɪ'rektli, dɪ-/ *adv* [1] (a) (without stopping) ⟨*go/drive/fly*⟩ directamente, directo (b) (without intermediaries) ⟨*report/deal*⟩ directamente; **he's ~ responsible** es el responsable directo (c) (exactly) ⟨*opposite/above*⟩ justo (d) (in genealogy) ⟨*related/descended*⟩ por línea directa [2] (frankly, straightforwardly) ⟨*ask*⟩ directamente; ⟨*speak*⟩ con franqueza [3] (now, at once) inmediatamente, ahora mismo

director /də'rektər, daɪ- ‖daɪ'rektə(r), dɪ-/ *n* [1] (of company) directivo, -tiva *m,f*; (of department, project) director, -tora *m,f*; *see also* MANAGING DIRECTOR [2] (Cin, Theat) director, -tora *m,f*; (esp AmE Mus) director, -tora *m,f*

directory /də'rektəri, daɪ- ‖daɪ'rektəri, dɪ-/ *n* (*pl* **-ries**) (a) (telephone ~) guía *f* telefónica *or* de teléfonos, directorio *m* telefónico (Col, Méx) (b) (index, yearbook) directorio *m*, guía *f*

dirt /dɜːrt ‖dɜːt/ *n* suciedad *f*, mugre *f*

dirty[1] /'dɜːrti ‖'dɜːti/ *adj* **-tier, -tiest** [1] (soiled) sucio; **to get ~** ensuciarse [2] (a) (obscene) ⟨*story/book*⟩ cochino (fam), guarro (Esp fam); ⟨*leer/grin*⟩ lascivo; ⟨*joke*⟩ verde *or* (Méx) colorado; ⟨*magazine*⟩ porno *adj inv* (b) (shameful) ⟨*job/work*⟩ sucio; **to do sb's ~ work** hacerle* el trabajo sucio a algn

dirty[2] *vt* **dirties, dirtying, dirtied** ensuciar

dirty old man *n* (colloq) viejo *m* verde (fam)

disability /ˌdɪsə'bɪləti/ *n* (*pl* **-ties**) (a) (state) invalidez *f*, discapacidad *f*; (*before n*) ⟨*pension/allowance*⟩ por invalidez (b) (particular handicap) problema *m*

disable /dɪs'eɪbl/ *vt* (a) «*illness/accident/injury*» dejar inválido (*or* lisiado *or* ciego *etc*) (b) ⟨*machine/weapon*⟩ (Mil) inutilizar*

disabled /dɪs'eɪbld/ *adj* discapacitado, minusválido

disabuse /ˌdɪsə'bjuːz/ *vt* (fml) desengañar; **I tried to ~ him of the notion that ...** intenté sacarlo del error de que ...

disadvantage /ˌdɪsəd'væntɪdʒ ‖ˌdɪsəd'vɑːntɪdʒ/ *n* desventaja *f*, inconveniente *m*; **to be at a ~** estar* en desventaja

disadvantageous /ˌdɪsædvæn'teɪdʒəs ‖ˌdɪsædvən'teɪdʒəs/ *adj* desventajoso, desfavorable

disaffected /ˌdɪsə'fektəd ‖ˌdɪsə'fektɪd/ *adj* desafecto

disagree /ˌdɪsə'griː/ *vi* [1] (a) (differ in opinion) **to ~ (WITH sb/sth)** no estar* de acuerdo (CON algn/algo), discrepar (DE algn/algo) (fml) (b) (conflict) «*figures/accounts*» no coincidir, discrepar [2] (cause discomfort) «*food*» **to ~ WITH sb** sentarle* *or* caerle* mal A algn

disagreeable /ˌdɪsə'griːəbl/ *adj* ⟨*smell/experience/person*⟩ desagradable; ⟨*task/job*⟩ ingrato, desagradable

disagreement /ˌdɪsə'griːmənt/ *n* (a) (difference of opinion) desacuerdo *m*, disconformidad *f* (b) (quarrel) discusión *f* (c) (disparity) discrepancia *f*

disallow /ˌdɪsə'laʊ/ *vt* (fml) ⟨*claim/evidence*⟩ (Law) rechazar*, desestimar; ⟨*goal*⟩ anular

disappear /ˌdɪsəˈpɪr ‖ˌdɪsəˈpɪə(r)/ *vi* **(a)**
(become invisible) desaparecer* **(b)** (go away) «*pain/
problems*» desaparecer*, irse*; «*worries/fears*»
desvanecerse*

disappearance /ˌdɪsəˈpɪrəns ‖ˌdɪsəˈpɪərəns/
n desaparición *f*

disappoint /ˌdɪsəˈpɔɪnt/ *vt* ‹*person*›
decepcionar; ‹*hopes/desires*› defraudar

disappointed /ˌdɪsəˈpɔɪntəd ‖ˌdɪsəˈpɔɪntɪd/
adj (*pred*) **to be** ~ estar* desilusionado *or*
decepcionado; **I'm ~ with the results** los
resultados me han decepcionado

disappointing /ˌdɪsəˈpɔɪntɪŋ/ *adj*
decepcionante

disappointment /ˌdɪsəˈpɔɪntmənt/ *n* **(a)**
(emotion) desilusión *f*, decepción *f* **(b)** (letdown)
decepción *f*, chasco *m*

disapproval /ˌdɪsəˈpruːvəl/ *n* desaprobación *f*

disapprove /ˌdɪsəˈpruːv/ *vi*: **he ~s of smoking**
está en contra del tabaco *or* del cigarrillo; **she
~s of her son's fiancée** no tiene buen concepto
de la novia de su hijo

disapproving /ˌdɪsəˈpruːvɪŋ/ *adj* ‹*tone/look*›
de reproche

disarm /dɪsˈɑːrm ‖dɪsˈɑːm/ *vt* ①‹*troops/
opposition*› desarmar; ‹*bomb/mine*› desactivar;
‹*criticism*› desbaratar ② (win confidence of)
desarmar
■ ~ *vi* desarmarse

disarmament /dɪsˈɑːrməmənt
‖dɪsˈɑːməmənt/ *n* desarme *m*

disarming /dɪsˈɑːrmɪŋ ‖dɪsˈɑːmɪŋ/ *adj* que
desarma

disarray /ˌdɪsəˈreɪ/ *n* (of political party)
desorganización *f*; (of appearance) desaliño *m*; **her
papers were in total ~** sus papeles estaban
completamente desordenados

disassociate /ˌdɪsəˈsəʊʃɪeɪt, -sɪeɪt/ *vt* ▶
DISSOCIATE

disaster /dɪˈzæstər ‖dɪˈzɑːstə(r)/ *n* ① (flood,
earthquake) catástrofe *f*, desastre *m*; (crash, sinking)
siniestro *m*, desastre *m*; (*before n*) ~ **fund** fondo
m para los damnificados ② **(a)** (fiasco) desastre
m **(b)** (hopeless person) (colloq) desastre *m* (fam)
③ (misfortune): ~ **struck** ocurrió *or* se produjo una
catástrofe

disaster area *n* zona *f* siniestrada, zona *f* de
desastre; **my room is a real ~ ~** (colloq & hum) mi
habitación es una desastre (fam)

disastrous /dɪˈzæstrəs ‖dɪˈzɑːstrəs/ *adj*
desastroso, catastrófico

disband /dɪsˈbænd/ *vt* ‹*organization*› disolver*;
‹*army*› licenciar
■ ~ *vi* «*organization*» disolverse*; «*group*»
desbandarse

disbelief /ˌdɪsbəˈliːf/ *n* incredulidad *f*

disbelieve /ˌdɪsbəˈliːv/ *vt* (fml) ‹*statement*› no
creer*; ‹*person*› no creerle* a

disc /dɪsk/ *n* (esp BrE) ▶ DISK

discard /dɪˈskɑːrd ‖dɪˈskɑːd/ *vt* **(a)** (dispose of)
desechar, deshacerse* de **(b)** ‹*idea/belief*›
desechar **(c)** (shed) ‹*skin/leaves*› mudar **(d)** (take
off) ‹*clothing*› desembarazarse* de

discern /dɪˈsɜːrn ‖dɪˈsɜːn/ *vt* (fml) distinguir*,
percibir

discerning /dɪˈsɜːrnɪŋ ‖dɪˈsɜːnɪŋ/ *adj* ‹*reader/
customer*› exigente, con criterio; ‹*palate/taste*›
exigente, fino; ‹*ear/eye*› educado

discharge¹ /dɪsˈtʃɑːrdʒ ‖dɪsˈtʃɑːdʒ/ *vt* ① **(a)**
(release) ‹*prisoner*› liberar, poner* en libertad;
‹*patient*› dar* de alta; ‹*juror*› dispensar;
‹*bankrupt*› rehabilitar **(b)** (dismiss) (fml)
despedir* ② **(a)** (send out) ‹*fumes*› despedir*;
‹*electricity*› descargar*; ‹*sewage/waste*› verter*
(b) (unload) ‹*cargo*› descargar* **(c)** (shoot) ‹*volley/
broadside*› descargar* ③ **(a)** ‹*duty*› cumplir con
(b) ‹*debt*› saldar, liquidar

discharge² /ˈdɪstʃɑːrdʒ ‖ˈdɪstʃɑːdʒ/ *n*
① (release — from army) baja *f*; (— from hospital) alta
f; (— from prison) puesta *f* en libertad ② **(a)** (Med)
secreción *f*; (vaginal ~) flujo *m* (vaginal) **(b)** (of
toxic fumes, gases) emisión *f*; (of sewage, waste)
vertido *m* **(c)** (Elec) descarga *f* ③ (of debt, liabilities)
liquidación *f*, pago *m*; (of duty) (fml) cumplimiento
m

disciple /dɪˈsaɪpəl/ *n* (Relig) discípulo, -la *m,f*;
(adherent) seguidor, -dora *m,f*

disciplinary /ˈdɪsəpləneri ‖ˌdɪsɪˈplɪnəri/ *adj*
disciplinario

discipline¹ /ˈdɪsəplən ‖ˈdɪsɪplɪn/ *n* disciplina
f

discipline² *vt* **(a)** (control) ‹*child/pupils*›
disciplinar; ‹*emotions*› controlar **(b)** (punish)
‹*employee*› sancionar **(c)** (train) ‹*body/mind*›
disciplinar

disc jockey *n* disc(-)jockey *mf*, pinchadiscos
mf (Esp fam)

disclaim /dɪsˈkleɪm/ *vt* (deny): **she ~ed all
knowledge of his whereabouts** negó conocer su
paradero; **he ~ed any connection with him** negó
tener ninguna relación con él

disclaimer /dɪsˈkleɪmər ‖dɪsˈkleɪmə(r)/ *n*
(Law) descargo *m* de responsabilidad

disclose /dɪsˈkləʊz/ *vt* revelar

disclosure /dɪsˈkləʊʒər ‖dɪsˈkləʊʒə(r)/ *n*
revelación *f*

disco /ˈdɪskəʊ/ *n* (*pl* **-cos**) discoteca *f*, disco *f*
(fam)

discolor, (BrE) **discolour** /dɪsˈkʌlər
‖dɪsˈkʌlə(r)/ *vt* (fade) decolorar; (stain) dejar
amarillento, manchar

discomfort /dɪsˈkʌmfərt ‖dɪsˈkʌmfət/ *n* **(a)**
(lack of comfort) incomodidad *f*; (pain) molestia(s)
f(pl), malestar *m* **(b)** (emotional, mental) inquietud
f, desasosiego *m*

disconcert /ˌdɪskənˈsɜːrt ‖ˌdɪskənˈsɜːt/ *vt*
desconcertar*

disconcerting /ˌdɪskənˈsɜːrtɪŋ
‖ˌdɪskənˈsɜːtɪŋ/ *adj* desconcertante

disconnect /ˌdɪskəˈnekt/ *vt* desconectar; **I
didn't pay my bills, so I was ~ed** me cortaron el
teléfono (*or* el gas *etc*) por no pagar

discontent /ˌdɪskənˈtent/ *n* descontento *m*

discontented /ˌdɪskənˈtentəd
‖ˌdɪskənˈtentɪd/ *adj* descontento

discontinue /ˌdɪskənˈtɪnjuː/ *vt* ‹*production*›
suspender; ‹*model*› discontinuar*, descontinuar*;
‹*action/suit*› (Law) desistir de

discord /ˈdɪskɔːrd ‖ˈdɪskɔːd/ *n* ① (conflict)   ⋯⊹

discordia f ② (Mus) **(a)** (lack of harmony) discordancia f, disonancia f **(b)** (chord) acorde m disonante

discotheque /'dɪskətek/ n ▶ DISCO

discount¹ /'dɪskaʊnt/ n descuento m; **at a ∼** ⟨sell⟩ con descuento, a precio reducido; (before n) ⟨store⟩ de saldos; ⟨goods⟩ de saldo

discount² /'dɪskaʊnt, dɪs'kaʊnt ‖ dɪs'kaʊnt/ vt ① (Busn) **(a)** ⟨amount⟩ descontar* **(b)** ⟨goods⟩ rebajar **(c)** ⟨price⟩ reducir* ② (disregard) ⟨possibility⟩ descartar; ⟨claim/criticism⟩ pasar por alto

discourage /dɪs'kʌrɪdʒ ‖ dɪs'kʌrɪdʒ/ vt **(a)** (depress) desalentar*, desanimar **(b)** (deter) ⟨crime/speculation⟩ poner* freno a; ⟨burglar⟩ ahuyentar, disuadir **(c)** (dissuade) **to ∼ sb FROM -ING: she ∼d me from taking the exam** trató de convencerme de que no me presentara al examen

discouraging /dɪs'kʌrɪdʒɪŋ ‖ dɪs'kʌrɪdʒɪŋ/ adj ⟨news/result⟩ desalentador

discourse /'dɪskɔːrs ‖ 'dɪskɔːs/ n (frml) **(a)** (dissertation) disertación f **(b)** (talk) conversación f

discourteous /dɪs'kɜːrtɪəs ‖ dɪs'kɜːtɪəs/ adj descortés

discover /dɪs'kʌvər ‖ dɪs'kʌvə(r)/ vt descubrir*

discoverer /dɪs'kʌvərər ‖ dɪs'kʌvərə(r)/ n descubridor, -dora m,f

discovery /dɪs'kʌvəri/ n (pl **-ries**) descubrimiento m

discredit¹ /dɪs'kredət ‖ dɪs'kredɪt/ vt desacreditar

discredit² n descrédito m

discreet /dɪs'kriːt/ adj **(a)** (tactful) ⟨person/inquiries⟩ discreto **(b)** (restrained) ⟨elegance/colors⟩ discreto, sobrio

discreetly /dɪs'kriːtli/ adv discretamente, con discreción

discrepancy /dɪs'krepənsi/ n (pl **-cies**) discrepancia f

discretion /dɪs'kreʃən/ n ① (tact) discreción f ② (judgment) criterio m; **at the committee's ∼** a criterio or a discreción de la comisión

discretionary /dɪs'kreʃəneri ‖ dɪs'kreʃənəri, -ənri/ adj discrecional

discriminate /dɪs'krɪmɪneɪt ‖ dɪr'skrɪmɪneɪt/ vi ① (act with prejudice) hacer* discriminaciones, discriminar; **to ∼ AGAINST sb** discriminar a algn ② **(a)** (distinguish) distinguir*, discriminar **(b)** (be discerning) discernir*, utilizar* el sentido crítico

discriminating /dɪs'krɪmɪneɪtɪŋ ‖ dɪr'skrɪmɪneɪtɪŋ/ adj ⟨critic/customer⟩ exigente; ⟨judgment⟩ sagaz; ⟨taste⟩ refinado, educado

discrimination /dɪs'krɪmə'neɪʃən ‖ dɪr,skrɪmɪ'neɪʃən/ n ① (unfair treatment) discriminación f ② (discernment) criterio m, discernimiento m

discus /'dɪskəs/ n (pl **-cuses**) disco m

discuss /dɪs'kʌs/ vt (talk about) ⟨person⟩ hablar de; ⟨topic⟩ hablar de, tratar; (debate) debatir; ⟨plan/problem⟩ discutir

discussion /dɪs'kʌʃən/ n discusión f, debate m

disdain /dɪs'deɪn/ n desdén m

disdainful /dɪs'deɪnfəl/ adj ⟨manner/tone⟩ despectivo, desdeñoso

disease /dɪ'ziːz/ n enfermedad f, dolencia f (frml)

diseased /dɪ'ziːzd/ adj ⟨organ/tissue⟩ afectado; ⟨plant/animal⟩ enfermo

disembark /'dɪsəm'bɑːrk ‖ ,dɪsɪm'bɑːk/ vi desembarcar*

disembodied /'dɪsəm'bɑːdid ‖ ,dɪsɪm'bɒdid/ adj incorpóreo

disembowel /'dɪsəm'baʊəl ‖ ,dɪsɪm'baʊəl/ vt, (BrE) **-ll-** destripar

disenchanted /'dɪsɪn'tʃæntəd ‖ ,dɪsɪn'tʃɑːntɪd/ adj **to be ∼ WITH sb/sth** estar* desilusionado CON or DE algn/DE algo

disenfranchise /'dɪsɪn'fræntʃaɪz ‖ ,dɪsɪn'fræntʃaɪz/ vt ⟨person⟩ privar del derecho al voto; ⟨place⟩ privar del derecho de representación

disengage /'dɪsɪn'geɪdʒ ‖ ,dɪsɪn'geɪdʒ/ vt ① **(a)** (extricate) soltar* **(b)** (Mil) ⟨troops/forces⟩ retirar ② (Tech) ⟨gears/mechanism⟩ desconectar

disentangle /'dɪsɪn'tæŋgəl ‖ ,dɪsɪn'tæŋgəl/ vt ⟨rope/hair/wool⟩ desenredar, desenmarañar; ⟨mystery⟩ esclarecer*, desentrañar

disfavor, (BrE) **disfavour** /dɪs'feɪvər ‖ dɪs'feɪvə(r)/ n (frml) desaprobación f

disfigure /dɪs'fɪɡjər ‖ dɪs'fɪɡə(r)/ vt ⟨face/person⟩ desfigurar; ⟨landscape/building⟩ afear, estropear

disgrace¹ /dɪs'ɡreɪs/ n vergüenza f; **she was sent upstairs in ∼** la mandaron arriba castigada

disgrace² vt **(a)** (bring shame on) ⟨person/family/school⟩ deshonrar **(b)** (destroy reputation of) ⟨enemy/politician⟩ desacreditar

disgraceful /dɪs'ɡreɪsfəl/ adj vergonzoso

disgruntled /dɪs'ɡrʌntld/ adj ⟨child/look⟩ contrariado; ⟨employee⟩ descontento

disguise¹ /dɪs'ɡaɪz/ vt **(a)** ⟨person⟩ disfrazar*; ⟨voice⟩ cambiar **(b)** (conceal) ⟨mistake⟩ ocultar; ⟨disapproval/contempt⟩ disimular

disguise² n disfraz m; **in ∼** disfrazado

disgust¹ /dɪs'ɡʌst/ vt darle* asco a

disgust² n (revulsion) indignación f; (physical, stronger) asco m, repugnancia f; **she stormed out of the meeting in ∼** salió indignada or furiosa de la reunión

disgusted /dɪs'ɡʌstəd ‖ dɪs'ɡʌstɪd/ adj indignado; (stronger) asqueado

disgusting /dɪs'ɡʌstɪŋ/ adj **(a)** ⟨smell/taste/food⟩ asqueroso, repugnante **(b)** ⟨conduct/attitude⟩ vergonzoso

dish /dɪʃ/ n ① **(a)** (plate) plato m; (serving ∼) fuente f; **to wash the ∼es** lavar los platos **(b)** (amount) plato m ② (Culin) plato m ③ (Telec, TV) antena f parabólica

AmC	América Central	Arg	Argentina	Cu	Cuba	Per	Perú
AmL	América Latina	Bol	Bolivia	Ec	Ecuador	RPI	Río de la Plata
AmS	América del Sur	Chi	Chile	Esp	España	Ur	Uruguay
Andes	Región andina	CS	Cono Sur	Méx	México	Ven	Venezuela

dishcloth ⋯⟶ dispensation ⋯

dish up [*v + o + adv, v + adv + o*] [*v + adv*] (Culin) servir*

dishcloth /'dɪʃklɔːθ ‖ 'dɪʃklɒθ/ *n* **(a)** (for drying) paño *m* de cocina, repasador *m* (RPl), limpión *m* (Col) **(b)** (BrE) ▶ DISHRAG

disheartening /dɪs'hɑːrtnɪŋ ‖ dɪs'hɑːtnɪŋ/ *adj* descorazonador, desalentador

disheveled, (BrE) **dishevelled** /dɪ'ʃevəld/ *adj* despeinado

dishonest /dɪs'ɑːnəst ‖ dɪs'ɒnɪst/ *adj* ⟨person/ answer⟩ deshonesto; ⟨dealings/means⟩ fraudulento, deshonesto

dishonesty /dɪs'ɑːnəsti ‖ dɪs'ɒnɪsti/ *n* deshonestidad *f*, falta *f* de honradez; (of statement) falsedad *f*; (of dealings) fraudulencia *f*

dishonor, (BrE) **dishonour** /dɪs'ɑːnər ‖ dɪs'ɒnə(r)/ *n* deshonra *f*, deshonor *m*

dishonorable, (BrE) **dishonourable** /dɪs'ɑːnərəbəl ‖ dɪs'ɒnərəbəl/ *adj* deshonroso

dish: ~**rag** *n* (AmE) trapo *m*, bayeta *f*, fregón *m* (RPl); ~ **soap** *n* (AmE) lavavajillas *m*, detergente *m*; ~**towel** *n* ▶ DISHCLOTH A; ~**washer** /'dɪʃwɔːʃər ‖ 'dɪʃwɒʃə(r)/ *n* (machine) lavaplatos *m*, lavavajillas *m*; ~**washing liquid** /'dɪʃwɔːʃɪŋ ‖ 'dɪʃwɒʃɪŋ/ *n* (AmE) ▶ ~ SOAP; ~**water** *n* agua *f‡* de fregar *or* de lavar los platos

disillusion /dɪsə'luːʒən ‖ dɪsɪ'luːʒən/ *vt* desilusionar

disillusionment /dɪsə'luːʒənmənt ‖ dɪsɪ'luːʒənmənt/ *n* desilusión *f*

disinfect /dɪsɪn'fekt ‖ dɪsɪn'fekt/ *vt* desinfectar

disinfectant /dɪsɪn'fektənt ‖ dɪsɪn'fektənt/ *n* desinfectante *m*

disinformation /ˌdɪsɪnfər'meɪʃən ‖ dɪsɪnfə'meɪʃən/ *n* desinformación *f*

disinherit /dɪsɪn'herət ‖ dɪsɪn'herɪt/ *vt* desheredar

disintegrate /dɪs'ɪntəgreɪt ‖ dɪs'ɪntɪgreɪt/ *vi* desintegrarse

disintegration /dɪsˌɪntə'greɪʃən ‖ dɪsˌɪntɪ'greɪʃən/ *n* desintegración *f*

disinterested /dɪs'ɪntrəstəd ‖ dɪs'ɪntrəstɪd/ *adj* ⟨decision/advice⟩ imparcial; ⟨action⟩ desinteresado

disjointed /dɪs'dʒɔɪntəd ‖ dɪs'dʒɔɪntɪd/ *adj* inconexo, deshilvanado

disk /dɪsk/ *n* **(a)** (flat, circular object) disco *m* **(b)** (Comput, Audio, Anat) disco *m*

disk drive *n* unidad *f* de disco

diskette /dɪs'ket/ *n* disquete *m*

dislike¹ /dɪs'laɪk/ *vt*: I ~ dogs no me gustan los perros; **he** ~**s wearing a tie** le desagrada *or* no le gusta llevar corbata

dislike² *n* **(a)** (emotion): I **have a strong** ~ **of dogs** no me gustan nada los perros, (les) tengo aversión a los perros; **to take a** ~ **to sb** tomarle antipatía a algn **(b)** (sth disliked): **you'll have to tell us all your likes and** ~**s** tendrás que decirnos lo que te gusta y lo que no te gusta

dislocate /'dɪsləkeɪt/ *vt* (Med) dislocarse*

dislodge /dɪs'lɑːdʒ ‖ dɪs'lɒdʒ/ *vt* (shift, remove) sacar*; **the wind** ~**d some tiles** el viento causó que se soltaran varias tejas

disloyal /dɪs'lɔɪəl/ *adj* desleal

dismal /'dɪzməl/ *adj* **(a)** (gloomy) ⟨place/tone⟩

sombrío, deprimente, lúgubre **(b)** (very bad) ⟨news/prophecy⟩ funesto; ⟨future⟩ muy negro; ⟨weather⟩ malísimo; ⟨results/performance⟩ pésimo

dismantle /dɪs'mæntl/ *vt* ⟨machinery/ furniture⟩ desmontar; ⟨organization⟩ desmantelar

dismay¹ /dɪs'meɪ/ *n* consternación *f*; **they looked at him in** *o* **with** ~ lo miraron consternados; **much to my/his** ~ para mi/su desgracia

dismay² *vt* consternar

dismember /dɪs'membər ‖ dɪs'membə(r)/ *vt* ⟨animal⟩ descuartizar*; ⟨corpse⟩ desmembrar*

dismiss /dɪs'mɪs/ *vt* **1** **(a)** ⟨employee⟩ despedir*; ⟨executive, minister⟩ destituir* **(b)** (send away) ⟨class⟩ dejar salir **2** ⟨possibility/ suggestion⟩ descartar, desechar; ⟨request/petition/ claim⟩ desestimar, rechazar* **3** (Law) ⟨charge/ appeal⟩ desestimar; **to** ~ **a case** sobreseer* una causa

dismissal /dɪs'mɪsəl/ *n* **(a)** (of employee) despido *m*; (of executive, minister) destitución *f* **(b)** (sending away) autorización *f* para retirarse **(c)** (of theory, request) rechazo *m* **(d)** (Law) desestimación *f*

dismount /dɪs'maʊnt/ *vi* desmontar

disobedience /'dɪsə'biːdiəns/ *n* desobediencia *f*

disobedient /'dɪsə'biːdiənt/ *adj* desobediente

disobey /'dɪsə'beɪ/ *vt/i* desobedecer*

disorder /dɪs'ɔːrdər ‖ dɪs'ɔːdə(r)/ *n* **1** **(a)** (confusion) desorden *m* **(b)** (unrest) desórdenes *mpl*, disturbios *mpl* **2** (Med) afección *f* (frml), problema *m*

disorderly /dɪs'ɔːrdərli ‖ dɪs'ɔːdəli/ *adj* **(a)** (untidy) desordenado **(b)** (unruly) ⟨crowd⟩ alborotado; ⟨person⟩ revoltoso; ~ **conduct** alteración *f* del orden público

disorganized /dɪs'ɔːrgənaɪzd ‖ dɪs'ɔːgənaɪzd/ *adj* desorganizado

disorient /dɪs'ɔːrient/, **disorientate** /dɪs'ɔːrienteɪt/ *vt* desorientar

disown /dɪs'əʊn/ *vt* **(a)** (repudiate) renegar* de, repudiar **(b)** (deny responsibility for) no reconocer* como propio

disparaging /dɪs'pærədʒɪŋ/ *adj* desdeñoso, despreciativo

disparity /dɪs'pærəti/ *n* (inequality) disparidad *f*; (difference) discrepancia *f*

dispassionate /dɪs'pæʃənət/ *adj* ⟨account⟩ desapasionado, objetivo; ⟨adjudication/onlooker⟩ imparcial

dispatch¹ /dɪ'spætʃ/ *vt* **1** (send) despachar, enviar* **2** **(a)** (carry out) (frml) ⟨task/duty⟩ despachar **(b)** (kill) (euph) ⟨person/animal⟩ despachar (euf) **(c)** (consume) (hum) ⟨food/drink⟩ despacharse (hum)

dispatch² *n* **1** (message) despacho *m*; (Mil) parte *m* **2** (sending) despacho *m*, envío *m*, expedición *f*

dispel /dɪ'spel/ *vt* **-ll-** **(a)** ⟨doubts/fear⟩ disipar, hacer* desvanecer **(b)** ⟨fog⟩ disipar

dispensary /dɪ'spensəri/ *n* (*pl* **-ries**) (in hospital) dispensario *m*, farmacia *f*; (in school) enfermería *f*

dispensation /'dɪspən'seɪʃən/ *n* **1** **(a)** (exemption) exención *f* **(b)** (Relig) dispensa *f* **2** (of justice) administración *f*

dispense /dɪˈspens/ vt **1** (a) ⟨grants/alms⟩ dar*; ⟨advice⟩ ofrecer*, dar*; ⟨favors⟩ conceder* (b) «machine» ⟨coffee/soap⟩ expender **2** ⟨drugs/ prescription⟩ despachar, preparar **3** (administer) ⟨justice⟩ administrar
■ **dispense with** [v + prep + o] prescindir de

dispenser /dɪˈspensər ‖ dɪˈspensə(r)/ n (device): **a cash ~** un cajero automático; **a soap ~** un dispositivo que suministra jabón

disperse /dɪˈspɜːrs ‖ dɪˈspɜːs/ vt dispersar
■ ~ vi dispersarse

dispirited /dɪˈspɪrətəd ‖ dɪˈspɪrɪtɪd/ adj ⟨person⟩ desanimado, abatido

displace /dɪsˈpleɪs/ vt (a) (Phys) ⟨liquid/ volume⟩ desplazar* (b) (replace) reemplazar* (c) (force from home) ⟨refugees/workers⟩ desplazar*

display¹ /dɪˈspleɪ/ vt (a) (put on show) ⟨exhibit⟩ exponer*; ⟨data/figures⟩ (Comput) visualizar* (b) (flaunt) ⟨finery/erudition⟩ hacer* despliegue or gala de; ⟨muscles⟩ lucir*, hacer* alarde de (c) (reveal) ⟨anger/interest⟩ demostrar*, manifestar*; ⟨feelings⟩ exteriorizar*, demostrar*; ⟨tendencies/ symptoms⟩ presentar; ⟨skill/courage⟩ demostrar*

display² n **1** (a) (exhibition) exposición f, muestra f; (show) show m; **to be on ~** «painting/ wares» estar* expuesto; (before n) **~ cabinet** vitrina f (b) (of feeling) exteriorización f, demostración f; (of courage, strength, knowledge) despliegue m; (of ignorance) demostración f **2** (Comput, Electron) display m, visualizador m **3** (Journ, Print) (before n) **~ advertising** anuncios mpl destacados

displease /dɪsˈpliːz/ vt desagradar, contrariar*

displeasure /dɪsˈpleʒər ‖ dɪsˈpleʒə(r)/ n desagrado m

disposable /dɪˈspəʊzəbəl/ adj **1** ⟨cup/razor/ pen⟩ desechable, de usar y tirar **2** ⟨income⟩ disponible

disposal /dɪˈspəʊzəl/ n **1** (removal, riddance): **the problem of the ~ of waste** el problema de cómo deshacerse de residuos; **arrangements were made for the ~ of the body** se hicieron arreglos para que el cadáver fuera inhumado (or trasladado al crematorio etc) **2** (power to use) disposición f; **to have sth at one's ~** disponer* de algo, tener* algo a su (or mi etc) disposición

disposed /dɪˈspəʊzd/ adj (pred) (a) (inclined) **to be ~ to + INF** estar* dispuesto A + INF (b) (liable) (frml) **to be ~ TO sth** ser* propenso A algo, tener* propensión A algo

dispose of /dɪˈspəʊz/ [v + prep + o] **1** (a) (get rid of) ⟨refuse/evidence⟩ deshacerse* de; ⟨rival/ opponent⟩ deshacerse* de, liquidar (fam) (b) (sell) ⟨house/car/land⟩ vender, enajenar (frml) (c) (deal with) ⟨problem/question/objection⟩ despachar **2** (have use of) (frml) ⟨funds/resources⟩ disponer* de

disposition /ˌdɪspəˈzɪʃən/ n **1** (a) (personality) manera f or modo m de ser, temperamento m (b) (inclination) (no pl) (frml) **~ TO sth** predisposición f A algo **2** (arrangement) disposición f

dispossess /ˌdɪspəˈzes/ vt (frml) **to ~ sb OF sth** desposeer* or despojar a algn DE algo (frml)

disproportionate /ˌdɪsprəˈpɔːrʃnət ‖ ˌdɪsprəˈpɔːʃənət/ adj ⟨number/size⟩ desproporcionado

disprove /dɪsˈpruːv/ vt ⟨claim/assertion/charge⟩ desmentir*; ⟨doctrine/theory⟩ rebatir, refutar

dispute¹ /dɪˈspjuːt/ n (a) (controversy, clash) polémica f, controversia f (b) (debate) discusión f; (quarrel) disputa f (c) (Lab Rel) conflicto m (laboral)

dispute² vt **1** (a) (contest) discutir, cuestionar (b) ⟨will/decision⟩ impugnar (c) (argue) ⟨point/ question⟩ debatir, discutir (d) **disputed** past p ⟨decision⟩ discutido, polémico; ⟨territory⟩ en litigio **2** (fight for) ⟨possession/victory/territory⟩ disputarse

disqualify /dɪsˈkwɑːləfaɪ ‖ dɪsˈkwɒlɪfaɪ/ vt -fies, -fying, -fied (a) (make ineligible): **as a professional she was disqualified from entering the Olympics** el hecho de ser profesional le impedía participar en las Olimpíadas; **a criminal record disqualifies you from jury service** tener antecedentes penales inhabilita para ser miembro de un jurado (b) (debar) (Sport) descalificar*

disquiet /dɪsˈkwaɪət/ n (frml) inquietud f, intranquilidad f, desasosiego m

disregard¹ /ˌdɪsrɪˈɡɑːrd ‖ ˌdɪsrɪˈɡɑːd/ vt ⟨danger/difficulty⟩ ignorar, despreciar; ⟨advice⟩ hacer* caso omiso de, no prestar atención a; ⟨feelings/wishes⟩ no tener* en cuenta

disregard² n **~ FOR sth/sb** indiferencia f HACIA algo/algn

disrepair /ˌdɪsrɪˈper ‖ ˌdɪsrɪˈpeə(r)/ n mal estado m; **to be in (a state of) ~** estar* en mal estado

disreputable /dɪsˈrepjətəbəl ‖ dɪsˈrepjʊtəbəl/ adj ⟨person/firm⟩ de dudosa reputación, de mala fama; ⟨nightclub/district⟩ de mala fama; ⟨conduct/ action⟩ vergonzoso

disrepute /ˌdɪsrɪˈpjuːt/ n (frml): **to fall into ~** caer* en descrédito; **to bring sth into ~** desacreditar algo

disrespect /ˌdɪsrɪˈspekt/ n **~ (FOR sth)** falta f de respeto (HACIA algo); **I meant no ~** no fue mi intención ofenderlo, no quise faltarle al or (CS) respeto

disrespectful /ˌdɪsrɪˈspektfəl/ adj ⟨person⟩ irrespetuoso; ⟨attitude⟩ irreverente

disrupt /dɪsˈrʌpt/ vt ⟨meeting/class⟩ perturbar el desarrollo de; ⟨traffic/communications⟩ crear problemas de, afectar a; ⟨plans⟩ desbaratar, trastocar*

disruption /dɪsˈrʌpʃən/ n trastorno m

disruptive /dɪsˈrʌptɪv/ adj ⟨influence⟩ perjudicial, negativo; **a ~ pupil** un alumno problema

dissatisfaction /ˌdɪsˌsætəsˈfækʃən ‖ ˌdɪsˌsætɪsˈfækʃən/ n descontento m, insatisfacción f

dissatisfied /ˌdɪsˈsætəsfaɪd ‖ dɪˈsætɪsfaɪd/ adj descontento, insatisfecho

dissect /dɪˈsekt, daɪ-/ vt ⟨animal/body⟩ diseccionar, hacer* la disección de

disseminate /dɪˈsemənɪt ‖ dɪˈsemɪneɪt/ vt (frml) diseminar

dissent /dɪˈsent/ n (frml) desacuerdo m

dissertation /ˌdɪsərˈteɪʃən ‖ ˌdɪsəˈteɪʃən/ n (in US: for PhD) tesis f (doctoral); (in UK: for lower degree) tesis f, tesina f

disservice /ˌdɪs'sɜːrvəs ‖dɪs'sɜːvɪs/ n (frml): this report does him a ~ este informe no le hace justicia

dissident /'dɪsədənt ‖'dɪsɪdənt/ n disidente mf

dissimilar /dɪ'sɪmələr ‖dɪ'sɪmɪlə(r)/ adj distinto, diferente

dissipate /'dɪsəpeɪt ‖'dɪsɪpeɪt/ vt (frml) (a) (squander) ⟨inheritance⟩ disipar, dilapidar; ⟨energy/talents⟩ desperdiciar (b) (dispel) ⟨anxiety⟩ disipar, hacer* desvanecer
■ ~ vi (frml) «anger/doubts» disiparse, desvanecerse*

dissociate /dɪ'səʊʃieɪt, -sieɪt/ vt (a) (separate) disociar (b) (distance) **to ~ oneself FROM sb/sth** desvincularse DE algn/algo

dissolute /'dɪsəluːt/ adj disoluto

dissolve /dɪ'zɑːlv ‖dɪ'zɒlv/ vt disolver*
■ ~ vi disolverse*

dissuade /dɪ'sweɪd/ vt **to ~ sb (FROM sth)** disuadir a algn (DE algo); **I managed to ~ her from leaving** logré convencerla de que no se fuera

distance¹ /'dɪstəns/ n distancia f; **in the (far) ~** en la distancia or lejanía, a lo lejos; **to keep one's ~** (remain aloof) guardar las distancias; (lit: keep away) no acercarse*

distance² v refl **to ~ oneself (FROM sb/sth)** (emotionally) distanciarse (DE algn/algo); (deny involvement) desvincularse (DE algn/algo)

distance learning n enseñanza f a distancia

distant /'dɪstənt/ adj ⟨spot/country⟩ distante, lejano; ⟨relative⟩ lejano; **in the ~ past** en el pasado remoto

distantly /'dɪstəntli/ adv ⟨hear/see⟩ en la lejanía; **we are ~ related** somos parientes lejanos

distaste /dɪs'teɪst/ n desagrado m

distasteful /dɪs'teɪstfəl/ adj (a) (unpleasant) ⟨task/chore⟩ desagradable (b) (offensive) ⟨remark/picture⟩ de mal gusto

distend /dɪ'stend/ vt dilatar, hinchar
■ ~ vi dilatarse, hincharse

distill, (BrE) **distil** vt **-ll-** /dɪ'stɪl/ destilar

distillery /dɪ'stɪləri/ n (pl **-ries**) destilería f

distinct /dɪ'stɪŋkt/ adj [1] ⟨shape/outline⟩ definido, claro, nítido; ⟨likeness⟩ obvio, marcado; ⟨improvement⟩ decidido, marcado; ⟨possibility⟩ nada desdeñable [2] (different, separate) distinto, bien diferenciado **we are talking about English people as ~ from British people** nos referimos a los ingleses en particular y no a los británicos

distinction /dɪ'stɪŋkʃən/ n [1] (a) (difference) distinción f; **we must make o draw a ~ between ... debemos distinguir entre ...** (b) (act of differentiating) distinción f; **without ~ of race or creed** sin distinción de raza o credo [2] (a) (merit, excellence): **a writer of ~** un distinguido or destacado escritor; **a car of ~** un coche de categoría (b) (distinguished appearance) distinción f (c) (mark of recognition) honor m, distinción f (d) (BrE Educ) mención f especial

distinctive /dɪ'stɪŋktɪv/ adj ⟨marking/plumage⟩ distintivo, característico; ⟨gesture/laugh⟩ personal, inconfundible; ⟨decor/dress⟩ particular

distinctly /dɪ'stɪŋktli/ adv (a) ⟨speak/

enunciate⟩ con claridad (b) ⟨hear⟩ perfectamente, claramente; **I ~ remember telling you** me acuerdo perfectamente or muy bien de que te lo dije

distinguish /dɪ'stɪŋgwɪʃ/ vt [1] (a) (differentiate) distinguir*, diferenciar (b) **distinguishing** pres p ⟨feature/mark⟩ distintivo, característico [2] (make out) distinguir*
■ ~ vi distinguir*

distinguished /dɪ'stɪŋgwɪʃt/ adj distinguido

distort /dɪ'stɔːrt ‖dɪ'stɔːt/ vt (a) (deform) ⟨metal/object⟩ deformar (b) (Opt) ⟨image/reflection⟩ deformar, distorsionar (c) (Electron) ⟨signal/sound⟩ distorsionar (d) (misrepresent) ⟨facts/statement⟩ tergiversar, distorsionar

distortion /dɪ'stɔːrʃən ‖dɪ'stɔːʃən/ n (a) (of metal, object) deformación f; (of features) distorsión f (b) (Opt) deformación f, distorsión f (c) (of facts, news) tergiversación f, distorsión f

distract /dɪ'strækt/ vt (a) (divert) ⟨person⟩ distraer* (b) (amuse) entretener*, distraer*

distraction /dɪ'strækʃən/ n [1] (a) (interruption) distracción f (b) (entertainment) (frml) entretenimiento m, distracción f [2] (madness): **to drive sb to ~** sacar* a algn de quicio

distraught /dɪ'strɔːt/ adj ⟨voice/person⟩ consternado, angustiado

distress¹ /dɪ'stres/ n angustia f, aflicción f; **he was in great ~** sufría mucho

distress² vt (upset) afligir*; (grieve) consternar

distressed /dɪ'strest/ adj afligido

distressing /dɪ'stresɪŋ/ adj ⟨news/circumstance⟩ penoso, angustiante

distribute /dɪ'strɪbjət, -bjuːt ‖dɪ'strɪbjuːt/ vt distribuir*; ⟨profits⟩ repartir

distribution /ˌdɪstrɪ'bjuːʃən/ n distribución f, reparto m; (of dividends) reparto m

distributor /dɪ'strɪbjətər ‖dɪ'strɪbjʊtə(r)/ n [1] (Busn) distribuidor m; (Cin) distribuidora f [2] (Auto, Elec) distribuidor m (del encendido)

district /'dɪstrɪkt/ n [1] (a) (region) zona f, región f (b) (locality) barrio m [2] (Govt) (in US: of state, city) distrito m

district: **~ attorney** n (in US) fiscal mf del distrito; **~ court** n (in US) tribunal m de distrito; **~ nurse** n (in UK) enfermero que tiene a su cuidado a los pacientes de un distrito

distrust¹ /dɪs'trʌst/ vt desconfiar* de, no fiarse* de

distrust² n desconfianza f, recelo m

distrustful /dɪs'trʌstfəl/ adj desconfiado, receloso

disturb /dɪ'stɜːrb ‖dɪ'stɜːb/ vt [1] (a) (interrupt): **the noise ~ed my concentration** el ruido me hizo perder la concentración; **the calm was ~ed by the arrival of the tourists** la llegada de los turistas vino a perturbar la calma (b) (inconvenience) molestar (c) (burst in upon) ⟨thief⟩ sorprender [2] (disarrange): **she found that her papers had been ~ed** notó que alguien había tocado sus papeles [3] (trouble) perturbar, inquietar, llenar de inquietud

disturbance /dɪ'stɜːrbəns ‖dɪ'stɜːbəns/ n [1] (a) (noisy disruption): **to cause/create a ~** provocar*/armar un alboroto (b) (interruption) interrupción f [2] (of routine) alteración f [3] (riot) disturbio m

disturbed /dɪˈstɜːbd ‖dɪˈstɜːbd/ *adj* **1** (a) (Psych) ⟨*person/mind*⟩ trastornado (b) (perturbed) (*pred*): **I was greatly ~ to hear of his misfortune** la noticia de su desgracia me impresionó *or* afectó muchísimo **2** (restless) ⟨*sleep*⟩ agitado, inquieto

disturbing /dɪˈstɜːbɪŋ ‖dɪˈstɜːbɪŋ/ *adj* (worrying, upsetting) inquietante, perturbador; (alarming) alarmante

disuse /dɪsˈjuːs ‖dɪsˈjuːs/ *n* desuso *m*

disused /dɪʃˈjuːzd ‖dɪsˈjuːzd/ *adj* ⟨*factory/quarry*⟩ abandonado; ⟨*machinery*⟩ en desuso

ditch¹ /dɪtʃ/ *n* zanja *f*; (at roadside) cuneta *f*; (for irrigation) acequia *f*

ditch² *vt* **1** (abandon) (colloq) ⟨*girlfriend/boyfriend*⟩ plantar (fam), botar (AmC, Chi fam); ⟨*object*⟩ deshacerse* de, botar (AmL exc RPl), tirar (Esp, RPl); ⟨*plan*⟩ abandonar, desechar **2** (Aviat): **to ~ a plane** hacer* un amaraje *or* amarizaje *or* amerizaje (forzoso)

dither /ˈdɪðər ‖ˈdɪðə(r)/ *vi* (colloq) (a) (become agitated) (AmE) ponerse* muy nervioso (b) (be indecisive) titubear, vacilar

ditto /ˈdɪtəʊ/ *adv* (colloq): **I'm fed up — ditto!** estoy harto — ¡y yo ídem de ídem! (fam)

divan /dɪˈvæn/ *n* (a) (sofa) diván *m*, canapé *m* (b) **~ (bed)** cama *f* turca

dive¹ /daɪv/ *vi* (*past* **dived** *or* (AmE also) **dove**; *past p* **dived**) (a) (from height) zambullirse*, tirarse (al agua), tirarse *or* echarse un clavado (AmL) (b) (from surface) «*person/whale*» sumergirse*, zambullirse*; «*submarine*» sumergirse* (c) (swoop) «*plane/bird*» bajar en picada *or* (Esp) en picado

dive² *n* **1** (a) (into water) zambullida *f*, clavado *m* (AmL); (Sport) salto *m* (de trampolín), clavado *m* (AmL) (b) (of submarine, whale) inmersión *f* (c) (swoop) descenso *m* en picada *or* (Esp) en picado **2** (lunge, sudden movement) (colloq): **he made a ~ for the gun** se abalanzó sobre la pistola **3** (disreputable club, bar) (colloq) antro *m*

dive-bomb /ˈdaɪvbɑːm ‖ˈdaɪvbɒm/ *vt* bombardear en picada *or* (Esp) en picado

diver /ˈdaɪvər ‖ˈdaɪvə(r)/ *n* (a) (from diving board *etc*) saltador, -dora *m,f*, clavadista *mf* (b) (deep-sea) buzo *mf*, submarinista *mf*

diverge /daɪˈvɜːrdʒ ‖daɪˈvɜːdʒ/ *vi* (a) «*lines/paths*» separarse (b) «*opinions/explanations*» divergir*

diverse /daɪˈvɜːrs ‖daɪˈvɜːs/ *adj* (a) (varied) ⟨*interests/tastes*⟩ diversos, variados; **plant life in the area is extremely ~** la vegetación en la zona es muy variada (b) (unlike) diferentes, distintos

diversion /dəˈvɜːrʒən ‖daɪˈvɜːʃən/ *n* **1** (a) (of river) desviación *f* (b) (of funds) malversación *f* (c) (BrE Transp) desvío *m*, desviación *f* **2** (distraction) (Mil) diversión *f*, divertimiento *m* estratégico **3** (amusement) (fml) diversión *f*, entretenimiento *m*

diversity /dəˈvɜːrsəti ‖daɪˈvɜːsəti/ *n* diversidad *f*

divert /dəˈvɜːrt ‖daɪˈvɜːt/ *vt* **1** (a) (redirect) ⟨*stream/flow*⟩ desviar*; ⟨*traffic*⟩ (BrE) desviar* (b) (ward off) ⟨*blow/attack*⟩ eludir, esquivar **2** (distract) ⟨*attention/thoughts*⟩ distraer* **3** (amuse) (fml) divertir*, entretener*

divest /daɪˈvest/ *vt* (fml) **to ~ sb OF sth** despojar a algn DE algo (fml)

divide /dəˈvaɪd ‖dɪˈvaɪd/ *vt* **1** (a) (split up) dividir; **to ~ sth INTO sth** dividir algo EN algo (b) (separate) **to ~ sth FROM sth** separar algo DE algo (c) (share) ⟨*cake/money/work*⟩ repartir **2** (cause to disagree) dividir **3** (Math) dividir; ▶ FOUR¹
■ **~** *vi* **1** (a) (fork) «*road/river*» dividirse (b) (split) «*group/particles/cells*» dividirse **2** (Math) dividir
■ **divide up 1** [*v + o + adv, v + adv + o*] dividir **2** [*v + adv*] dividirse

divided /dəˈvaɪdəd ‖dɪˈvaɪdɪd/ *adj* ⟨*opinion*⟩ dividido

divided highway *n* (AmE) autovía *f*, carretera *f* de doble pista

dividend /ˈdɪvədend ‖ˈdɪvɪdend/ *n* dividendo *m*; **to pay ~s** dar* dividendos, reportar beneficios

divider /dəˈvaɪdər ‖dɪˈvaɪdə(r)/ *n* (a) (screen) mampara *f*; (in filing system) separador *m* (b) **dividers** *pl* (Math) compás *m* de puntas fijas

dividing line /dəˈvaɪdɪŋ ‖dɪˈvaɪdɪŋ/ *n* línea *f* divisoria

divine¹ /dəˈvaɪn ‖dɪˈvaɪn/ *adj* **1** (*before n*) ⟨*intervention/inspiration*⟩ divino **2** (wonderful) divino, precioso

divine² *vt* (a) (discover, guess) (liter) adivinar (b) ⟨*water/minerals*⟩ descubrir* (con una varita de zahorí)

diving /ˈdaɪvɪŋ/ *n* (a) (from height) saltos *mpl* de trampolín, clavados *mpl* (AmL) (b) (under water) submarinismo *m*, buceo *m*

diving: ~ board *n* trampolín *m*; **~ suit** *n* escafandra *f*, traje *m* de buzo

divinity /dəˈvɪnəti ‖dɪˈvɪnəti/ *n* (*pl* **-ties**) (fml) (a) (divine nature, being) divinidad *f* (b) (theology) teología *f*

division /dəˈvɪʒən ‖dɪˈvɪʒən/ *n* **1** (a) (distribution) reparto *m*, división *f* (b) (boundary) división *f*; **class ~s** divisiones de clase (c) (part) división *f* **2** (disagreement) desacuerdo *m* **3** (department) división *f*, sección *f* **4** (Mil) división *f* **5** (Sport) (a) (in boxing) categoría *f* (b) (in US: area) zona *f* (c) (in UK: by standard) división *f* **6** (Math) división *f*

divisive /dəˈvaɪsɪv ‖dɪˈvaɪsɪv/ *adj* divisivo

divorce¹ /dəˈvɔːrs ‖dɪˈvɔːs/ *n* divorcio *m*

divorce² *vt* (Law) divorciarse de; **to get ~d** divorciarse
■ **~** *vi* divorciarse

divorcee /dəˌvɔːrˈseɪ ‖dɪˌvɔːˈsiː/ *n* divorciado, -da *m,f*

divulge /daɪˈvʌldʒ/ *vt* divulgar*; **to ~ sth TO sb** revelarle algo A algn

DIY *n* (BrE) (= **do-it-yourself**) bricolaje *m*

AmC	Central America	Arg	Argentina	Cu	Cuba	Per	Peru
AmL	Latin America	Bol	Bolivia	Ec	Ecuador	RPl	River Plate Area
AmS	South America	Chi	Chile	Esp	Spain	Ur	Uruguay
Andes	Andean Region	CS	Southern Cone	Méx	Mexico	Ven	Venezuela

dizzy /'dɪzɪ/ adj **-zier, -ziest** (a) (giddy) ⟨sensation⟩ de mareo; **to feel ∼** estar* mareado (b) (causing dizziness) ⟨speed⟩ vertiginoso; ⟨height⟩ de vértigo

DJ n = **disc jockey**

DNA n (= **deoxyribonucleic acid**) ADN m

do[1] /duː, weak form dʊ, də/ (3rd pers sing pres **does**; pres **doing**; past **did**; past p **done**) vt
[1] hacer*; **to have something/nothing to ∼** tener* algo/no tener* nada que hacer; **it was a silly thing to ∼** fue una estupidez; **can I ∼ anything to help?** ¿puedo ayudar en algo?
[2] (carry out) ⟨job/task⟩ hacer*; **to ∼ the cooking** cocinar; **well done!** ¡muy bien!
[3] (achieve, bring about): **she's done it: it's a new world record** lo ha logrado: es una nueva marca mundial; **it was climbing those stairs that did it** fue por subir esa escalera; **that mustache really does something for him** la verdad es que le queda muy bien el bigote
[4] (a) (fix, arrange, repair): **I have to ∼ my nails** me tengo que arreglar las uñas; **she had her hair done** se hizo peinar (b) (clean) ⟨dishes⟩ lavar; ⟨brass/windows⟩ limpiar
[5] (make, produce) ⟨meal⟩ preparar, hacer*; ⟨drawing/translation⟩ hacer*
[6] (travel): **he was ∼ing 100 mph** iba a 100 millas por hora; **the car has only done 4,000 miles** el coche solo tiene 4.000 millas

∎ ∼ vi [1] (act, behave) hacer*; **∼ as you're told!** ¡haz lo que se te dice!; **his concern to ∼ well by his son** su preocupación por hacer todo lo posible por su hijo
[2] (get along, manage): **how are you ∼ing?** (colloq) ¿qué tal estás or andas or te va?; **how do you ∼?** (as greeting) mucho gusto, encantado; **how are we ∼ing for time?** ¿cómo or qué tal vamos or andamos de tiempo?; **she did well in her exams** le fue bien en los exámenes; **he's done well for himself** ha sabido abrirse camino
[3] (go on, happen) (colloq) (in -ing form): **there's nothing ∼ing in town** no pasa nada en el pueblo; **nothing ∼ing!** ¡ni hablar!, ¡ni lo sueñes!
[4] (be suitable, acceptable): **look, this won't ∼!** ¡mira, esto no puede ser!; **it's not ideal, but it'll ∼** no es lo ideal, pero sirve; **this box will ∼ for o as a table** esta caja nos servirá de mesa
[5] (be enough) ser* suficiente, alcanzar*, bastar*; **that'll ∼!** ¡shut up! ¡basta! ¡cállate la boca!

∎ ∼ v aux [El verbo auxiliar no se usa para formar el negativo (I 1) y el interrogativo (I 2), para agregar énfasis (I 3) o para sustituir a un verbo usado anteriormente (II)]
I [1] (used to form negative, interrogative, exclamations): **I ∼ not o don't know** no sé; **not only does it cost more, it also …** no solo cuesta más, sino que también …; **did I frighten you?** ¿te asusté?; **doesn't it make you sick!** ¡dime si no es asqueante!
[2] (emphasizing): **you ∼ exaggerate!** ¡cómo exageras!; **you must admit, she did look ill** tienes que reconocer que tenía mala cara
II [1] (in elliptical uses): **∼ you live here? — yes, I ∼/no, I don't** ¿vives aquí? — sí/no; **she says she understands, but she doesn't** dice que comprende, pero no es así
[2] (in tag questions): **you know Bob, don't you?** conoces a Bob, ¿no? or ¿verdad? or ¿no es cierto?; **I told you, didn't I?** te lo dije ¿no? or ¿no es cierto?

∎ **do away with** [v + adv + prep + o] (a) (abolish) ⟨privilege/tax⟩ abolir*, suprimir; ⟨need⟩ eliminar, acabar con (b) (kill) (colloq) eliminar, liquidar (fam)
∎ **do up** [v + o + adv, v + adv + o] (a) (fasten) ⟨coat/necklace/button⟩ abrochar; ⟨zipper⟩ subir; **to ∼ up one's shoes** atarse los cordones or (Méx) las agujetas or (Per) los pasadores (de los zapatos) (b) (wrap up) ⟨parcel⟩ envolver* (c) (dress up) (colloq): **she was all done up** estaba muy elegante (d) (colloq) ⟨house⟩ arreglar (pintando, empapelando etc)
∎ **do with** [v + prep + o] [1] (benefit from) (with can, could): **that door could ∼ with a coat of paint** no le vendría mal una mano de pintura a esa puerta; **you could ∼ with a change** te hace falta or te vendría bien un cambio
[2] (expressing connection) **I don't want to have anything to ∼ with him/this business** yo no quiero tener nada que ver con él/este asunto; **it's nothing to ∼ with you!** ¡no es nada que te concierna or que te importe a ti
∎ **do without** [1] [v + prep + o]: **to ∼ without sth/sb** prescindir de or arreglárselas sin algo/algn
[2] [v + adv] arreglárselas

do[2] /duː/ n (pl **dos**) [1] (party, gathering) (colloq) fiesta f, reunión f [2] **do's and don'ts** (rules) normas fpl

do[3] /dəʊ/ n (pl **dos**) (Mus) do m

docile /'dɑːsəl ‖ 'dəʊsaɪl/ adj dócil, sumiso

dock[1] /dɑːk ‖ dɒk/ n [1] (Naut) (a) (wharf, quay) muelle m; (for cargo ships) dársena f [2] (before n) ⟨worker/strike⟩ portuario **docks** pl puerto m [2] (Law) (no pl) **the ∼** el banquillo de los acusados [3] (Bot) acedera f

dock[2] vt [1] (a) ⟨tail⟩ cortar (b) ⟨wages⟩ descontar* dinero m [2] ⟨vessel/ship⟩ fondear, atracar*
∎ ∼ vi (a) (Naut) «ship/vessel» atracar*, fondear (b) (Aerosp) acoplarse

docker /'dɑːkər ‖ 'dɒkə(r)/ n (BrE) estibador, -dora m,f

dockyard /'dɑːkjɑːrd ‖ 'dɒkjɑːd/ n (often pl) astillero m

doctor[1] /'dɑːktər ‖ 'dɒktə(r)/ n [1] (Med) médico, -ca m,f, doctor, -tora m,f, facultativo, -va m,f (frml); **D∼ Jones** el doctor Jones [2] (Educ) doctor, -tora m,f

doctor[2] vt (pej) (a) ⟨food/drink⟩ adulterar (b) ⟨text⟩ arreglar (c) ⟨results/evidence⟩ falsificar*

doctoral /'dɑːktərəl ‖ 'dɒktərəl/ adj ⟨thesis/dissertation⟩ doctoral

doctorate /'dɑːktərət ‖ 'dɒktərət/ n doctorado m

doctrine /'dɑːktrɪn ‖ 'dɒktrɪn/ n doctrina f

document[1] /'dɑːkjəmənt ‖ 'dɒkjʊmənt/ n documento m

document[2] vt /'dɑːkjəmənt ‖ 'dɒkjʊment/ documentar

documentary[1] /'dɑːkjəˈmentəri ‖ ˌdɒkjʊˈmentrɪ/ adj documental

documentary[2] n (pl **-ries**) documental m

documentation /ˌdɑːkjəmənˈteɪʃən ‖ ˌdɒkjʊmenˈteɪʃən/ n documentación f

dodge /dɑːdʒ ‖ dɒdʒ/ vt (a) ⟨blow⟩ esquivar; ⟨pursuer⟩ eludir (b) ⟨question⟩ esquivar, soslayar; ⟨problem/issue⟩ soslayar; ⟨work/responsibility⟩ eludir; ⟨tax⟩ evadir

■ ~ *vi* echarse a un lado, apartarse; **she** ~d **behind the car** se escondió rápidamente detrás del coche

dodgem (car) /'dɑː.dʒəm ‖'dɒdʒəm/ *n* ▶ BUMPER CAR

dodger /'dɑː.dʒər ‖'dɒdʒə(r)/ *n*: **tax** ~ -sora *m,f* de impuestos; **fare** ~ *persona que intenta viajar sin pagar en un medio de transporte público*

doe /dəʊ/ *n* (of deer) hembra *f* de gamo, gama *f*; (of rabbit) coneja *f*

does /dʌz, *weak form* dəz/ *3rd pers sing pres of* DO[1]

doesn't /'dʌznt/ = **does not**

dog[1] /dɔːg ‖dɒg/ *n* (Zool) perro, -rra *m,f*; (male canine) macho *m*; **it's** ~ **eat** ~ hay una competencia brutal; **to go to the** ~**s** venirse* abajo; **let sleeping** ~**s lie** mejor no revolver el asunto; (*before n*) ~ **show** exposición *f* canina

dog[2] *vt* **-gg-** (*often pass*) perseguir*

dog-eared /'dɔːgɪrd ‖'dɒgɪəd/ *adj* sobado y con las esquinas dobladas

dogged /'dɔːgəd ‖'dɒgɪd/ *adj* obstinado

doggedly /'dɔːgədli ‖'dɒgɪdli/ *adv* obstinadamente

doggerel /'dɔːgərəl ‖'dɒgərəl/ *n* ripios *mpl*

doghouse /'dɔːghaʊs ‖'dɒghaʊs/ *n* (AmE) casa *f or* casilla *f or* (Esp) caseta *f or* (Chi) casucha *f* del perro, perrera *f* (Col); **to be in the** ~ (also BrE colloq) haber* caído en desgracia

dogma /'dɔːgmə ‖'dɒgmə/ *n* dogma *m*

dogmatic /dɔːg'mætɪk ‖dɒg'mætɪk/ *adj* dogmático

do-gooder /'duːˌgʊdər ‖duː'gʊdə(r)/ *n* (pej) hacedor, -dora *m,f* de buenas obras (hum)

dog: ~ **paddle** *n* estilo *m* perro *or* perrito; ~**sbody** *n* (esp BrE colloq): **I'm just the general** ~**sbody around here** yo aquí no soy más que el botones

doh /dəʊ/ *n* (Mus) do *m*

doily /'dɔɪli/ *n* (*pl* **-lies**) **(a)** (on plate) blonda *f* **(b)** (under plate, ornament) tapete *m*, pañito *m*, carpeta *f* (Col, CS)

doing /'duːɪŋ/ *n* **1** (action): **that takes some** ~ eso no es nada fácil; **it was none of our** ~ nosotros no tuvimos nada que ver **2 doings** *pl* (activities, events) actividades *fpl*

do-it-yourself /'duːətʃərˈself ‖ˌduːɪtjɔːˈself/ *n* bricolaje *m*

doldrums /'dəʊldrəmz, 'dɑː.l- ‖'dɒldrəmz/ *pl n*: **to be in the** ~ estar* de capa caída

dole /dəʊl/ *n* (BrE): **to be on the** ~ estar* cobrando subsidio de desempleo *or* (Chi tb) de cesantía, estar* en el paro (Esp)

■ **dole out** [*v + o + adv, v + adv + o*] ⟨*food/ money*⟩ dar*, repartir

doleful /'dəʊlfəl/ *adj* ⟨*face/look*⟩ compungido, triste; ⟨*sound/voice*⟩ plañidero, lúgubre

doll /dɑːl ‖dɒl/ *n* muñeca *f*

■ **doll up** [*v + o + adv*] (colloq): **to get (all)** ~ed up emperifollarse (fam)

dollar /'dɑːlər ‖'dɒlə(r)/ *n* dólar *m*; **you can bet your bottom** ~ (colloq) puedes estar seguro, te lo doy firmado (fam); (*before n*) ~ **bill** billete *m* de un dólar; ~ **sign** signo *m or* símbolo *m* del dólar

dollhouse /'dɑːlhaʊs ‖'dɒlhaʊs/ (AmE) *n* casa *f* de muñecas

dollop /'dɑːləp ‖'dɒləp/ *n* (colloq) (served with a spoon) cucharada *f*; (serving, measure) porción *f*

doll's house *n* (BrE) casa *f* de muñecas

dolly /'dɑːli ‖'dɒli/ *n* (*pl* **-lies**) (used to or by children) muñequita *f*

dolphin /'dɑːlfən ‖'dɒlfɪn/ *n* (*pl* ~**s** *or* ~) delfín *m*

domain /də'meɪn, dəʊ-/ *n* **(a)** (sphere of influence, activity) campo *m*, esfera *f*; **in the public** ~ de(l) dominio público **(b)** (Comput) dominio *m*

dome /dəʊm/ *n* (Archit) cúpula *f*

domestic /də'mestɪk/ *adj* **1 (a)** (of the home) ⟨*life/problems*⟩ doméstico; ~ **violence** violencia *f* en el hogar **(b)** (home-loving) casero, hogareño **2** ⟨*animal*⟩ doméstico **3** (Econ, Pol) ⟨*affairs/ policy/market*⟩ interno; ⟨*produce/flight*⟩ nacional

domesticated /də'mestɪkeɪtəd ‖də'mestɪkeɪtɪd/ *adj* ⟨*animal/species*⟩ domesticado

domesticity /ˌdəʊmes'tɪsəti ‖ˌdɒmes'tɪsəti, dəʊ-/ *n* (fml *or* hum) domesticidad *f*

domestic science *n* economía *f* doméstica, hogar *m* (Esp)

domicile /'dɑːməsaɪl ‖'dɒmɪsaɪl/ *n* (fml) domicilio *m* (fml)

dominance /'dɑːmənəns ‖'dɒmɪnəns/ *n* **(a)** (supremacy) dominio *m*, dominación *f* **(b)** (predominance) predominio *m*, preponderancia *f*

dominant /'dɑːmənənt ‖'dɒmɪnənt/ *adj* **(a)** (more powerful) ⟨*nation/influence*⟩ dominante **(b)** (predominant) ⟨*crop/industry*⟩ predominante, preponderante **(c)** (Biol, Ecol) dominante

dominate /'dɑːməneɪt ‖'dɒmɪneɪt/ *vt* dominar

domination /ˌdɑːmə'neɪʃən ‖ˌdɒmɪ'neɪʃən/ *n* dominación *f*

domineering /ˌdɑːmə'nɪrɪŋ ‖ˌdɒmɪ'nɪərɪŋ/ *adj* dominante

Dominican Republic /də'mɪnɪkən/ *n* **the** ~ ~ la República Dominicana

dominion /də'mɪnjən/ *n* (liter) dominio *m*

domino /'dɑːmənəʊ ‖'dɒmɪnəʊ/ *n* (*pl* **-noes**) **(a)** (counter) ficha *f* de dominó **(b) dominoes** (+ *sing vb*) dominó *m*

don /dɑːn ‖dɒn/ *vt* **-nn-** (put on) (liter) ponerse*

donate /'dəʊneɪt, dəʊ'neɪt/ *vt* donar

donation /dəʊ'neɪʃən/ *n* **(a)** (gift) donativo *m*, donación *f* **(b)** (act) donación *f*

done[1] /dʌn/ *past p of* DO[1]

done[2] *adj* (*no comp*) **1** (*pred*) **(a)** (finished) hecho **(b)** (cooked) cocido **2** (accepted): **it's not** ~ *o* **not the** ~ **thing** no está bien visto

donkey /'dɑːŋki ‖'dɒŋki/ *n* (*pl* **-keys**) burro *m*, asno *m*

donor /'dəʊnər ‖'dəʊnə(r)/ *n* donante *mf*

don't /dəʊnt/ = **do not**

doodle /'duːdl/ *vi/t* garabatear, garrapatear

doom[1] /duːm/ *vt* (*usu pass*) condenar

doom[2] *n* **(a)** (fate) sino *m* (liter); (death) muerte *f* **(b)** (ruin) fatalidad *f*

doomsday /'duːmzdeɪ/ *n* (arch) día *m* del Juicio Final

door /dɔːr ‖dɔː(r)/ *n* puerta *f*; **double** ~**s** puerta de dos hojas; **there's someone at the** ~ llaman a la puerta; **tickets are available at the ～** se pueden comprar las localidades en la puerta *or* a la entrada; **he's not allowed out of ～** no le permiten salir; *to show sb the ～* mostrarle* *or* enseñarle la puerta a algn, echar a algn

door: ～bell *n* timbre *m*; **～ knob** *n* pomo *m* (de la puerta); **～man** /'dɔːrmən ‖'dɔːmən/ *n* (*pl* **-men** /-mən/) portero *m*; **～mat** *n* felpudo *m*; **～step** *n* umbral *m*; **～stop** *n* cuña *f* (*para mantener la puerta abierta*); **～to-～** /'dɔːrtə'dɔːr ‖,dɔːtə'dɔː(r)/ *adj* ⟨*delivery/service*⟩ de puerta a puerta; **a ～-to-～ salesman** un vendedor ambulante (*que va de puerta a puerta*); **～way** *n* entrada *f*

dope¹ /dəʊp/ *n* ⏍**1** (a) (drugs) (sl) droga *f*, pichicata *f* (CS, Per fam); (cannabis) hachís *m*, chocolate *m* (Esp arg) (b) (Sport) estimulante *m*, droga *f*, doping *m*; (*before n*) ⟨*test*⟩ antidoping *adj inv* ⏍**2** (information) (sl) información *f* ⏍**3** (stupid person) (colloq) imbécil *mf*, tarugo *mf* (fam)

dope² *vt* (colloq) ⟨*person/racehorse*⟩ dopar (fam), drogar*; ⟨*food/drink*⟩ poner* droga en

dopey, dopy /'dəʊpi/ *adj* **dopier, dopiest** (colloq) **(a)** (stupid) lelo (fam), bobo (fam) **(b)** (befuddled) atontado, grogui (fam)

dormant /'dɔːrmənt ‖'dɔːmənt/ *adj* ⏍**1** **(a)** ⟨*animal/plant*⟩ aletargado **(b)** ⟨*volcano*⟩ inactivo ⏍**2** (frml) ⟨*idea/emotion*⟩ latente

dormice /'dɔːrmaɪs ‖'dɔːmaɪs/ *pl of* DORMOUSE

dormitory /'dɔːrmətɔːri ‖'dɔːmɪtri/ *n* (*pl* **-ries**) **(a)** (in school, hostel) dormitorio *m*; (*before n*) **～ town** (BrE) ciudad *f* dormitorio **(b)** (students' residence) (AmE) residencia *f* de estudiantes

dormouse /'dɔːrmaʊs ‖'dɔːmaʊs/ *n* (*pl* **-mice** /-maɪs/) lirón *m*

dorsal /'dɔːrsəl ‖'dɔːsəl/ *adj* dorsal

DOS /dɑːs ‖dɒs/ *n* (= **disk-operating system**) DOS *m*

dosage /'dəʊsɪdʒ/ *n* dosis *f*

dose¹ /dəʊs/ *n* (of medication) dosis *f*; **a bad ～ of flu** (colloq) una gripe *or* (Col, Méx) una gripa muy mala

dose² *vt*: **I'm all ～d up with painkillers** me he tomado no sé cuántos analgésicos

dossier /'dɒːsieɪ ‖'dɒsiə(r), -ieɪ/ *n* dossier *m*, expediente *m*

dot¹ /dɑːt ‖dɒt/ *n* punto *m*; **～ ～ ～** puntos suspensivos; **on the ～** en punto

dot² *vt* **-tt-** ⏍**1** (add dot) puntuar*; **to sign on the ～ted line** firmar la línea punteada *or* de puntos ⏍**2** (scatter) (*usu pass*) salpicar*; **her family is ～ted about all over Europe** su familia está desperdigada por toda Europa

dot.com /kɑːm ‖kɒm/ *n* (Comput) punto *m* com; (*before n*) ⟨*company*⟩ punto com

dote /dəʊt/ *vi* **to ～ ON sb** adorar a algn

doting /'dəʊtɪŋ/ *adj*: **his ～ mother** su madre, que lo adora

dotty /'dɑːti ‖'dɒti/ *adj* **-tier, -tiest** (colloq) ⟨*person*⟩ chiflado (fam); ⟨*idea*⟩ descabellada

double¹ /'dʌbəl/ *adj* doble; ⟨*bed*⟩ de matrimonio, de dos plazas (AmL); **it's ～ that** es el doble de eso; **my number is ～ three seven ～ four eight** (esp BrE) mi número es tres tres siete, cuatro cuatro ocho; **it's spelled with a ～ 't'** se

escribe con dos tes; **～ bend** curva *f* en S (*read as: curva en ese*); **inflation reached ～ figures** la inflación alcanzó/rebasó el 10%

double² *adv* ⟨*pay/earn/cost*⟩ el doble; **she spends ～ what she earns** gasta el doble de lo que gana; **to see ～** ver* doble

double³ *n* ⏍**1** **(a)** (hotel room) doble *f* **(b)** (of spirits): **I'll have a ～** (deme) uno doble ⏍**2** (lookalike) doble *mf* ⏍**3** (Sport) (double win) doblete *m* ⏍**4** (pace): **at** *o* **on the ～** (Mil) a paso ligero

double⁴ *vt* **(a)** (increase twofold) ⟨*earnings/profits*⟩ doblar, duplicar*; ⟨*efforts*⟩ redoblar **(b)** (Games) ⟨*stake/call/bid*⟩ doblar

■ **～** *vi* ⏍**1** (increase twofold) ⟨*price/amount*⟩ duplicarse*, doblarse ⏍**2** (have dual role): **the table ～s as a desk** la mesa también se usa como escritorio; **somebody ～d for him in the dangerous scenes** alguien lo doblaba en las escenas peligrosas

■ **double back** [*v + adv*] ⟨*person/animal*⟩ volver* sobre sus pasos; **the path ～d back on itself** el camino doblaba sobre sí mismo

■ **double up** [*v + adv* (+ *o*)] **(a)** (bend): **to ～ up with laughter** morirse* *or* desternillarse de risa; **he was ～d up with pain** se retorcía de dolor **(b)** (redouble) (AmE) doblar

double: **～ act** *n*: **they are a ～ act** actúan en pareja; **～-barreled**, (BrE) **～-barrelled** /'dʌbəl'bærəld/ *adj* **(a)** ⟨*shotgun*⟩ de dos cañones **(b)** ⟨*surname*⟩ compuesto; **～ bass** *n* contrabajo *m*; **～-book** /'dʌbəl'bʊk/ *vt* (BrE): **the room had been ～-booked** la habitación había sido reservada para dos personas distintas; **～-breasted** /'dʌbəl'brestəd ‖,dʌbəl'brestɪd/ *adj* cruzado; **～-check** /'dʌbəl'tʃek/ *vi* volver* a mirar, verificar* dos veces ■ **～** *vt* ⟨*facts/information*⟩ volver* a revisar; **～ chin** *n* papada *f*, **～-click** /'dʌbəl'klɪk/ *vi* (Comput) hacer* doble click; **～ cream** *n* (BrE) crema *f* doble, nata *f* para montar (Esp), doble crema *f* (Méx); **～-cross** /'dʌbəl'krɔːs ‖,dʌbəl'krɒs/ *vt* traicionar; **～-decker** /'dʌbəl'dekər ‖,dʌbəl'dekə(r)/ *n* **～-decker** (bus) (esp BrE) autobús *m* de dos pisos; **～ Dutch** *n* (colloq) chino *m* (fam); **～-edged** /'dʌbəl'edʒd/ *adj* ⟨*knife/blade/scheme*⟩ de doble filo; ⟨*remark/comment*⟩ de doble sentido; **～ glazing** /'dʌbəl'gleɪzɪŋ/ *n* (BrE) doble ventana *f*; **～-jointed** /'dʌbəl'dʒɔɪntəd ‖,dʌbəl'dʒɔɪntɪd/ *adj*: **he's ～-jointed** tiene articulaciones dobles

doubles /'dʌbəlz/ *pl n* dobles *mpl*

double standard *n*: **to have ～ ～s** aplicar* una ley para unos y otra para otros

doubly /'dʌbli/ *adv* ⟨*difficult/dangerous/ interesting*⟩ doblemente

doubt¹ /daʊt/ *n* (uncertainty) duda *f*; **no ～ she will phone** con seguridad que llama, seguro que llama; **if in ～, don't go** si estás en (la) duda, no vayas; **I have my ～s** tengo mis dudas

doubt² *vt* **(a)** ⟨*fact/truth*⟩ dudar de **(b)** (consider unlikely) dudar; **to ～** (THAT) *o* **if** *o* **whether** dudar QUE (+ *subj*)

doubtful /'daʊtfəl/ *adj* **(a)** (full of doubt) ⟨*expression/tone*⟩ de indecisión *or* duda, dubitativo; **I am ～ as to its value** tengo mis dudas acerca de su valor **(b)** (in doubt) dudoso; **the outcome remains ～** el resultado sigue siendo dudoso *or* incierto

doubtfully /'daʊtfəli/ adv ⟨say⟩ sin convicción; ⟨agree⟩ con reserva

doubtless /'daʊtləs ‖ 'daʊtlɪs/ adv sin duda, indudablemente

dough /dəʊ/ n ① (Culin) masa f ② (money) (sl) guita f (arg), lana f (AmL fam), plata f (AmS fam), pasta f (Esp fam)

doughnut /'dəʊnʌt/ n donut m, rosquilla f

dour /daʊr, dʊr ‖ dʊə(r)/ adj adusto

douse /daʊs/ vt ⟨flames⟩ sofocar*

dove¹ /dʌv/ n paloma f

dove² /dəʊv/ (AmE) past of DIVE¹

dovetail /'dʌvteɪl/ vi encajar

dowager /'daʊədʒər ‖ 'daʊədʒə(r)/ n: viuda de un noble

dowdy /'daʊdi/ adj -dier, -diest ⟨woman⟩ sin gracia, sin estilo

down¹ /daʊn/ adv ① (a) (in downward direction): to go ~ bajar; to look ~ mirar (hacia or para) abajo; from the waist ~ desde la cintura para abajo; ~ with tyranny! ¡abajo la tiranía! (b) (downstairs): can you come ~? ¿puedes bajar? ② (a) (of position) abajo; two floors ~ dos pisos más abajo; ~ here/there aquí/allí (abajo) (b) (downstairs): I'm ~ in the cellar estoy aquí abajo, en el sótano (c) (lowered, pointing downward) bajado; face ~ boca abajo (d) (prostrate): I was ~ with flu all last week estuve con gripe toda la semana pasada ③ (of numbers, intensity): my temperature is ~ to 38° C la fiebre me ha bajado a 38° C; they were two goals ~ iban perdiendo por dos goles ④ (a) (in, toward the south): to go/come ~ south ir*/venir* al sur (b) (at, to another place) (esp BrE): ~ on the farm en la granja; I'm going ~ to the library voy a la biblioteca ⑤ (a) (dismantled, removed): the room looks bare with the pictures ~ la habitación queda desnuda sin los cuadros; once this wall is ~ una vez que hayan derribado esta pared (b) (out of action): the telephone lines are ~ las líneas de teléfono están cortadas; the system is ~ (Comput) el sistema no funciona ⑥ down to (a) (as far as) hasta; ~ to the present day hasta nuestros días (b) (reduced to): we're ~ to our last can of tomatoes nos queda solo una lata de tomates

down² prep ① (in downward direction): we ran ~ the slope corrimos cuesta abajo; it fell ~ a hole se cayó por un agujero; halfway ~ the page hacia la mitad de la página ② (along): we drove on ~ the coast seguimos por la costa; the library is just ~ the street la biblioteca está un poco más allá

down³ adj ① (before n) (going downward): the ~ escalator la escalera mecánica de bajada or para bajar ② (depressed) (colloq) (pred) deprimido

down⁴ n (a) (on bird) plumón m (b) (on face, body) vello m, pelusilla f (c) (on plant, fruit) pelusa f

down⁵ vt (a) (drink) beberse or tomarse rápidamente (b) (knock down) ⟨person⟩ tumbar, derribar

down: ~ and out adj (colloq) (pred): to be ~

and out estar* en la miseria; ~cast adj (a) (dejected) alicaído, abatido (b) (directed downward): with ~cast eyes con la mirada baja; ~fall n (of person) perdición f, ruina f; (of king, dictator) caída f; ~grade ⟨employee/hotel⟩ bajar de categoría; ~hearted /'daʊn'hɑːrtəd ‖ daʊn'hɑːtɪd/ adj desanimado, desmoralizado; ~hill /'daʊn'hɪl/ adv ⟨walk/run⟩ cuesta abajo; to go ~hill ir* cuesta abajo, ir* de mal en peor

Downing Street /'daʊnɪŋ/ n Downing Street (calle de Londres donde se encuentra la residencia oficial del primer ministro británico)

download /'daʊn'ləʊd/ vt (Comput) bajar, descargar*

downmarket¹ /'daʊn'mɑːrkət ‖ daʊn'mɑːkɪt/ adv: the paper has gone ~ el diario ha perdido categoría; (deliberately) el diario se dirige ahora a un sector más popular del público

downmarket² adj ⟨newspaper⟩ popular; ⟨store⟩ barato

down: ~ payment n cuota f or entrega f inicial, entrada f (Esp), pie m (Chi); ~pour n aguacero m, chaparrón m

downright¹ /'daʊnraɪt/ adj ⟨lie/insolence⟩ descarado; ⟨crook/liar/rogue⟩ redomado, de tomo y lomo (fam); ⟨madness⟩ total y absoluto

downright² adv: it was ~ dangerous! ¡fue peligrosísimo!; he was ~ rude! ¡estuvo de lo más grosero!

downriver /'daʊn'rɪvər ‖ daʊn'rɪvə(r)/ adv río abajo

Down's syndrome /daʊnz/ n síndrome m de Down; (before n) ⟨child⟩ afectado por el síndrome de Down

downstairs¹ /'daʊn'sterz ‖ daʊn'steəz/ adv abajo; he went ~ to open the door bajó a abrir la puerta

downstairs² n planta f baja; (before n) ⟨neighbor/toilet⟩ (del piso) de abajo

down: ~stream /'daʊn'striːm/ adv río abajo; ~-to-earth /'daʊntʊ'ɜːrθ ‖ daʊntə'ɜːθ/ adj (pred ~ to earth) realista, práctico

downtown¹ /'daʊn'taʊn/ n (AmE) centro m (de la ciudad); (before n) ~ New York el centro de Nueva York

downtown² adv (AmE): to go/live ~ ir* al/ vivir en el centro

downtrodden /'daʊn'trɑːdn ‖ 'daʊn'trɒdn/ adj oprimido

downward¹ /'daʊnwərd ‖ 'daʊnwəd/ adj ⟨direction/pressure⟩ hacia abajo; ⟨movement/ spiral⟩ descendente; ⟨tendency⟩ (Fin) a la baja

downward² /'daʊnwərd ‖ 'daʊnwəd/, (esp BrE) **downwards** /-z/ adv hacia abajo

downwind /'daʊn'wɪnd/ adv en la dirección del viento

dowry /'daʊəri/ n (pl -ries) dote f

doze /dəʊz/ vi dormitar
■ **doze off** [v + adv] quedarse dormido, dormirse*

dozen¹ /'dʌzn̩/ n (pl ~ or ~s) docena f; **four dollars a** o **per** ~ cuatro dólares la docena; **I got** ~s **of cards** recibí montones de tarjetas (fam)

dozen² adj docena f de; **a** ~/two ~ **eggs** una docena/dos docenas de huevos

dozy /'dəʊzi/ adj **dozier, doziest** amodorrado, adormilado

Dr /'dɑːktər ‖ 'dɒktə(r)/ (title) (= **Doctor**) Dr., Dra.

drab /dræb/ adj ‹clothing/decor/appearance› soso, sin gracia; ‹life/occupation› gris, monótono

draft¹ /dræft ‖ drɑːft/ n [1] (BrE) **draught** (cold air) corriente f de aire [2] (formulation) versión f [3] (Fin) cheque m or efecto m bancario [4] (AmE) **the** ~ (Mil) el llamamiento or (AmL tb) llamado a filas

draft² vt [1] (formulate) ‹document/contract/letter› redactar el borrador de; ‹speech› preparar [2] (conscript) (AmE) reclutar, llamar a filas

draftproof /'dræftpruːf ‖ 'drɑːftpruːf/ adj hermético

draftsman, (BrE) **draughtsman** /'dræftsmən ‖ 'drɑːftsmən/ n (pl **-men** /-mən/) dibujante mf

drafty, (BrE) **draughty** /'dræfti ‖ 'drɑːfti/ adj **-tier, -tiest** con corrientes de aire

drag¹ /dræg/ **-gg-** vt [1] (haul) arrastrar, llevar a rastras; **I couldn't** ~ **myself away** (colloq) no tenía fuerzas para irme [2] (allow to trail) ‹tail/garment/anchor› arrastrar; **to** ~ **one's feet** o **heels** dar(le)* largas al asunto [3] (Comput) ~ **(and drop)** arrastrar (y soltar)

■ ~ vi [1] (a) (trail) «anchor» garrar; «coat» arrastrar (b) (lag) rezagarse* [2] (go on slowly) «work/conversation» hacerse* pesado; «film/play» hacerse* largo

■ **drag on** [v + adv] alargarse* (interminablemente)

drag² n (no pl) [1] (tiresome thing): **what a** ~! ¡qué lata! (fam) [2] (resistant force) resistencia f al avance [3] (women's clothes): **in** ~ vestido de mujer

dragon /'drægən/ n dragón m

dragonfly /'drægənflaɪ/ n (pl **-flies**) libélula f, caballito m del diablo, matapiojos m (Andes)

drain¹ /dreɪn/ n [1] (a) (pipe) sumidero m, resumidero m (AmL); **the** ~**s** (of town) el alcantarillado; (of building) las tuberías de desagüe (b) (grid) (BrE) sumidero m, resumidero m (AmL) [2] (plughole) desagüe m [3] (no pl) (cause of depletion) **a** ~ **on the country's resources** una sangría para el país; **the extra work is an enormous** ~ **on my energy** el trabajo extra me está agotando

drain² vt [1] (a) ‹container/tank› vaciar*; ‹land/swamp› drenar, avenar; ‹blood› drenar; ‹sap/water› extraer* (b) (Culin) ‹vegetables/pasta› escurrir, colar* (c) (Med) drenar [2] (drink up) ‹glass/cup› vaciar*, apurar [3] (consume, exhaust) ‹resources/strength› agotar, consumir

■ ~ vi (a) (dry) ‹dishes› escurrir(se) (b) (disappear): **all the strength seemed to** ~ **from my limbs** los brazos y las piernas se me quedaron como sin fuerzas (c) (discharge) «pipes/river» desaguar*

drainage /'dreɪnɪdʒ/ n (a) (of household waste) desagüe m (de aguas residuales); (of rainwater)

canalización f (de agua de lluvia); (before n) ~ **system** (red f de) alcantarillado m (b) (of fields, marshes) drenaje m, avenamiento m

drainboard /'dreɪnbɔːrd ‖ 'dreɪnbɔːd/ n (AmE) escurridero m

draining board /'dreɪnɪŋ/ n (BrE) escurridero m

drainpipe /'dreɪnpaɪp/ n tubo m or caño m del desagüe, bajante f

drake /dreɪk/ n pato m (macho)

drama /'drɑːmə/ n (pl **-mas**) [1] (Theat) (a) (play) obra f dramática, drama m (b) (plays collectively) teatro m, drama m; (dramatic art) arte m dramático [2] (excitement) dramatismo m

dramatic /drə'mætɪk/ adj [1] (Theat) (before n) dramático, teatral [2] (a) (striking) ‹change/improvement› espectacular, drástico; ‹increase› espectacular (b) (momentous) ‹events/development› dramático

dramatically /drə'mætɪkli/ adv (a) (exaggeratedly) ‹pause/announce› dramáticamente, de manera teatral or histriónica (b) (strikingly) ‹change/improve/increase› de manera espectacular

dramatics /drə'mætɪks/ n (Theat) (+ sing vb): **amateur** ~ teatro m amateur or de aficionados

dramatist /'dræmətɪst/ n dramaturgo, -ga m,f

dramatize /'dræmətaɪz/ vt [1] ‹story/novel› (Theat) dramatizar*, hacer* una adaptación teatral de; (Cin) llevar al cine [2] (exaggerate) ‹situation/event› dramatizar*, exagerar

drank /dræŋk/ past of DRINK²

drape /dreɪp/ vt (a) (arrange): **they** ~**d a flag over the tomb** colocaron una bandera formando pliegues sobre la tumba; **she** ~**d herself over the sofa** se tendió sobre el sofá (b) (cover) cubrir*

drapes /dreɪps/ pl n (AmE) cortinas fpl

drastic /'dræstɪk/ adj drástico, radical

drastically /'dræstɪkli/ adv drásticamente

draught /dræft ‖ drɑːft/ n [1] (storage under pressure): **beer on** ~ cerveza f de barril; (before n) ‹beer/cider› de barril [2] (liter) (of water, beer) trago m [3] (BrE) ▶ DRAFT¹ 1

draughtproof /'dræftpruːf ‖ 'drɑːftpruːf/ adj (BrE) ▶ DRAFTPROOF

draughts /dræfts ‖ drɑːfts/ n (BrE) (+ sing vb) damas fpl

draughtsman /'dræftsmən ‖ 'drɑːftsmən/ n (BrE) ▶ DRAFTSMAN

draughty /'dræfti ‖ 'drɑːfti/ adj (BrE) ▶ DRAFTY

draw¹ /drɔː/ (past **drew**; past p **drawn**) vt [1] (a) (move by pulling) ‹curtains/bolt› (open) descorrer; (shut) correr; **he drew her to one side** la llevó a un lado, la llevó aparte (b) (pull along) ‹cart/sled› tirar de, arrastrar [2] (a) (pull out) ‹tooth/cork› sacar*, extraer* (frml); ‹gun› desenfundar, sacar*; ‹sword› desenvainar, sacar* (b) (cause to flow) sacar*; **to** ~ **blood** sacar* sangre, hacer* sangrar; **to** ~ **breath** respirar [3] (a) (Fin) ‹salary/pension› cobrar, percibir (frml); ‹check› girar, librar (b) (derive) ‹strength/lesson› sacar* [4] (establish) ‹distinction/parallel› establecer* [5] (a) (attract) ‹customers/crowd› atraer*; **to be** ····⫶

d

~n to sb/sth sentirse* atraído por algn/algo **(b)**
(elicit) ⟨praise⟩ conseguir*; ⟨criticism/protest⟩
provocar*, suscitar
⑥ (sketch) ⟨flower/picture⟩ dibujar; ⟨line⟩ trazar*
⑦ (BrE Games, Sport) empatar
■ ~ vi ① (move): **to ~ close to sth/sb** acercarse* a
algo/algn; **to ~ to a close** terminar, finalizar*
(fml); **the train drew out of/into the station** el tren
salió de/entró en la estación; **to ~ ahead of sb/
sth** adelantarse a algn/algo
② (Art) dibujar
③ (BrE Games, Sport) empatar; (in chess game)
hacer* tablas
■ **draw back** [v + adv] **(a)** (retreat) retirarse **(b)**
(recoil) retroceder
■ **draw in** ① [v + o + adv, v + adv + o] **(a)**
(retract) ⟨claws⟩ esconder, retraer* **(b)** (into quarrel,
war) involucrar; (into conversation) darle*
participación a
② [v + adv] **(a)** (arrive) «train» llegar* **(b)**
«days/nights» hacerse* más corto
■ **draw on** [v + prep + o] (make use of) ⟨resources/
reserves⟩ recurrir a, hacer* uso de; **she drew on
her own experiences** se inspiró en sus propias
experiencias
■ **draw out** ① [v + adv] **(a)** (depart) «train»
salir* **(b)** (become longer) hacerse* más largo
② [v + o + adv, v + adv + o] **(a)** (prolong)
alargar*, estirar **(b)** (extract, remove) ⟨tooth/thorn⟩
sacar*, extraer* (fml); ⟨wallet/handkerchief⟩
sacar*; ⟨information⟩ sacar*, sonsacar*;
⟨confession⟩ arrancar* **(c)** (withdraw) ⟨money⟩
sacar*
■ **draw up** ① [v + adv] «car» detenerse*, parar
② [v + o + adv, v + adv + o] **(a)** (prepare, draft)
⟨contract/treaty⟩ redactar, preparar; ⟨list/plan⟩
hacer* **(b)** (arrange in formation) ⟨troops/competitors⟩
alinear, formar **(c)** (bring near) ⟨chair⟩ acercar*,
arrimar

draw² n ① (raffle) sorteo m ② (tie) (Games, Sport)
empate m

draw: ~**back** n inconveniente m, desventaja f;
~**bridge** n puente m levadizo

drawer n /drɔːr ‖'drɔ:(r)/ ① (in furniture) cajón
m, gaveta f (esp AmC, Méx) ② **drawers** pl
(Clothing) calzones mpl

drawing /'drɔːɪŋ/ n dibujo m

drawing: ~ **pin** n (BrE) ▶ THUMBTACK; ~
room n sala f, salón m

drawl /drɔːl/ n: acento caracterizado por la
longitud de las vocales

drawn¹ /drɔːn/ past p of DRAW¹

drawn² adj ⟨features/face⟩ demacrado

drawstring /'drɔːstrɪŋ/ n cordón m (del que se
tira para cerrar algo); (before n) ⟨bag/waist⟩
fruncido con un cordón o una cinta

dread¹ /dred/ vt tenerle* terror or pavor a

dread² n terror m

dreadful /'dredfəl/ adj ⟨news/experience/
weather⟩ espantoso, terrible; **I feel ~** me siento
pésimo

dreadfully /'dredfəli/ adv (as intensifier)
⟨upset/late⟩ terriblemente, enormemente

dream¹ /driːm/ n sueño m; **a ~ come true** un
sueño hecho realidad; (before n) **he lives in a ~
world** vive de ilusiones, vive en las nubes

dream² (past & past p **dreamed** or (BrE also)

dreamt /dremt/) vi soñar*; **to ~ ABOUT sth/sb**
soñar* CON algo/algn; **would you do that? — I
wouldn't ~ of it!** ¿harías eso? — ¡ni pensarlo!
■ ~ vt soñar*; **I never ~ed he'd be so rude** nunca
(me) imaginé que iba a ser tan grosero
■ **dream up** [v + o + adv, v + adv + o] ⟨plan⟩
idear

dreamer /'driːmər ‖'driːmə(r)/ n soñador,
-dora m,f

dreamt /dremt/ (BrE) past & past p of DREAM²

dreamy /'driːmi/ adj -**mier**, -**miest (a)**
(abstracted) ⟨person⟩ soñador, fantasioso; ⟨gaze⟩
distraído **(b)** ⟨music⟩ etéreo, sutil

dreary /'drɪri/ adj -**rier**, -**riest (a)**
⟨room/landscape⟩ deprimente, lóbrego, sombrío;
⟨weather⟩ gris, deprimente **(b)** ⟨work/routine⟩
monótono, aburrido, aburridor (AmL)

dredge /dredʒ/ vt dragar*
■ **dredge up** [v + o + adv, v + adv + o] ⟨mud/
sand⟩ dragar*; ⟨story/scandal⟩ desenterrar*

dredger /'dredʒər ‖'dredʒə(r)/ n (machine)
draga f; (vessel) dragador m, draga f

dregs /dregz/ pl n posos mpl, cunchos mpl (Col),
conchos mpl (Chi); **the ~ of society** la escoria de
la sociedad

drench /drentʃ/ vt (usu pass) empapar

dress¹ /dres/ n ① (for woman, girl) vestido m
② (style of dressing): **they adopted Western ~**
adoptaron el modo de vestir or la vestimenta
occidental; (before n) **she has no ~ sense** tiene
mal gusto para vestirse

dress² vt ① (put clothes on) vestir*; **to get ~ed**
vestirse*; **he was ~ed in white** iba (vestido) de
blanco ② (Culin) **(a)** (prepare) ⟨chicken/fish⟩
preparar **(b)** (season) ⟨salad⟩ aliñar ③ (Med)
⟨wound⟩ vendar
■ ~ vi vestirse*
■ **dress up** [v + adv] **(a)** (dress smartly) ponerse*
elegante **(b)** (in fancy dress) disfrazarse*; **to ~ up
AS sth** disfrazarse* DE algo

dresser /'dresər ‖'dresə(r)/ n ① (person): **he's
a stylish ~** (se) viste con mucho estilo ② **(a)** (in
bedroom) (AmE) tocador m **(b)** (in kitchen) (BrE)
aparador m

dressing /'dresɪŋ/ n ① (Med) apósito m, gasa f;
(bandage) vendaje m ② (Culin) (for salad) aliño m,
aderezo m; (stuffing) (AmE) relleno m

dressing: ~ **gown** n bata f, salto m de cama
(CS); ~ **room** n (Theat) camerino m; (in house)
vestidor m; ~ **table** n tocador m

dress: ~**maker** n modista mf; (designer)
modisto, -ta m,f; ~ **rehearsal** n ensayo m
general; ~ **suit** n traje m de etiqueta

dressy /'dresi/ adj -**sier**, -**siest** elegante

drew /druː/ past of DRAW¹

dribble /'drɪbəl/ vi ① (drool) babear ② (Sport)
driblar, driblear

dribs and drabs /ˌdrɪbzən'dræbz/ pl n: **in ~
~ ~** poquito a poco

dried /draɪd/ adj ⟨figs/flowers⟩ seco; ⟨fish⟩
salado, seco; ⟨milk/eggs⟩ en polvo

drier /'draɪər ‖'draɪə(r)/ n ▶ DRYER

drift¹ /drɪft/ vi ① **(a)** (on water) moverse*
empujado por la corriente **(b)** (be adrift) «boat/
person» ir* a la deriva **(c)** (in air) «balloon»
moverse* empujado por el viento ② (proceed

aimlessly): **the crowd began to ~ away** la muchedumbre comenzó a dispersarse; **to ~ apart** «*couple/friends*» distanciarse ③ (pile up) «*sand/snow*» amontonarse

drift² n ① (of sand) montón m; (of snow) ventisquero m ② (meaning) (no pl) sentido m; **I didn't quite catch your ~** no entendí or capté muy bien lo que querías decir ③ (movement): **the ~ from the land** el éxodo rural

driftwood /'drɪftwʊd/ n madera, tablas etc que flotan en el mar a la deriva o que arrastra el mar hasta la playa

drill¹ /drɪl/ n ① (electric o power ~) taladradora f, taladro m; (hand ~) taladro m (manual); (Dent) torno m, fresa f; (Eng, Min) perforadora f, barreno m; (drill head) broca f ② (a) (Mil) instrucción f (b) (Educ) ejercicio m

drill² vt ① «*hole*» hacer*, perforar; «*wood/metal*» taladrar, perforar, barrenar; «*tooth*» trabajar or limpiar con la fresa ② (Mil) «*soldiers*» instruir*
■ ~ vi perforar, hacer* perforaciones; **to ~ for oil** perforar en busca de petróleo

drily /'draɪli/ adv secamente, con sequedad

drink¹ /drɪŋk/ n ① (a) (any liquid) bebida f (b) (alcohol) bebida f ② (a) (amount drunk, served, sold): **have a ~ of** water/milk bebe or (esp AmL) toma un poco de agua/leche (b) (alcoholic) copa f, trago m (fam); **to have a ~** tomar una copa

drink² (past **drank**; past p **drunk**) vt/i beber, tomar (esp AmL)
■ **drink up** ① [v + adv] bebérselo or (esp AmL) tomárselo todo, terminar su (or mi etc) copa (or leche etc) ② [v + o + adv, v + adv + o] beberse, tomarse (esp AmL)

drinkable /'drɪŋkəbəl/ adj «*water*» potable

drink-driving /,drɪŋk'draɪvɪŋ/ n BrE ▶ DRUNK DRIVING

drinker /'drɪŋkər ‖ 'drɪŋkə(r)/ n: **he's a heavy ~** es un gran bebedor or un bebedor empedernido; **I'm a beer ~ myself** yo prefiero la cerveza

drinking /'drɪŋkɪŋ/ n (a) (of liquid) beber (b) (of alcohol): **his ~ is causing concern** lo mucho que bebe está causando preocupación

drinking: ~ **chocolate** n chocolate m en polvo; ~ **water** n agua f‡ potable

drip¹ /drɪp/ vi -pp- «*washing/hair*» chorrear, gotear; «*faucet/tap*» gotear; **water was ~ping from the ceiling** el techo goteaba, caían gotas del techo

drip² n ① (of rainwater, tap) (no pl) goteo m ② (Med) suero m, gota a gota m ③ (ineffectual person) (colloq) soso, -sa m,f (fam)

drip-dry /'drɪp'draɪ/ adj «*fabric/garment*» de lava y pon, de lavar y poner

dripping /'drɪpɪŋ/ adj (colloq) empapado; (as intensifier) **to be ~ wet** estar* chorreando or empapado

drive¹ /draɪv/ (past **drove**; past p **driven**) vt ① (Transp) (a) «*car/bus/train*» manejar or (Esp) conducir* (b) (convey in vehicle) llevar en coche ② (a) (cause to move) (+ adv compl): **the Indians were ~n off their land** los indios fueron expulsados de sus tierras; **we drove them away with sticks** los ahuyentamos con palos (b) (Sport) «*ball*» mandar, lanzar* (c) (provide power for, operate) hacer* funcionar, mover*

③ (make penetrate) «*nail*» clavar; «*stake*» hincar*
④ (a) (cause to become) volver*; **to ~ sb mad** volver* loco a algn; **he ~s me crazy with his incessant chatter** me saca de quicio con su constante cháchara (b) (compel to act) **to ~ sb to +** INF llevar or empujar a algn A + INF; **she is ~n by ambition** la impulsa or motiva la ambición (c) (overwork): **he drove them mercilessly** los hizo trabajar como esclavos; **she ~s herself too hard** se exige demasiado a sí misma
■ ~ vi manejar or (Esp) conducir*; **she ~s to work** va a trabajar en coche
■ **drive out** [v + o + adv, v + adv + o] expulsar

drive² n ① (in vehicle): **to go for a ~** ir* a dar un paseo or una vuelta en coche; **it's a three-hour ~** es un viaje de tres horas en coche
② (a) (leading to house) camino m, avenida f (que lleva hasta una casa) (b) (in front of house) entrada f (para coches)
③ (in golf, tennis) golpe m fuerte
④ (a) (energy) empuje m, dinamismo m (b) (compulsion) (Psych) impulso m, instinto m; **the sex ~** el apetito sexual
⑤ (a) (organized effort) campaña f (b) (attacking move) (Mil) ofensiva f, avanzada f (c) (in US football) ataque m
⑥ (a) (propulsion system) transmisión f, propulsión f (b) (Auto): **front-wheel/rear-wheel ~** tracción f delantera/trasera

drive-in /'draɪvɪn/ n (AmE) (cinema) autocine m; (restaurant) drive in m (restaurante que sirve a los clientes en el propio automóvil)

drivel /'drɪvəl/ n tonterías fpl, estupideces fpl

driven /'drɪvən/ past p of DRIVE¹

driver /'draɪvər ‖ 'draɪvə(r)/ n (of car, truck, bus) conductor, -ra m,f, chofer m or (Esp) chófer mf; (of racing car) piloto mf; **she's a good ~** maneja or (Esp) conduce bien

driver's license n (AmE) licencia f or (Esp) permiso m de conducción; (less formally) carné m or permiso m (de conducir) (Esp), carné m (Chi) or (Ur) libreta f or (AmC, Méx, Ven) licencia f or (Col) pase m (de manejar), registro m (Arg), brevete m (Per)

driving¹ /'draɪvɪŋ/ n (Auto) conducción f (frml)

driving² adj (a) «*rain*» torrencial; «*wind*» azotador (b) (dynamic): **she's the ~ force behind the project** es el alma-máter or la impulsora del proyecto

driving: ~ **instructor** n instructor, -tora m,f de autoescuela; ~ **licence** n (BrE) ▶ DRIVER'S LICENSE; ~ **test** n examen m de conducir or (AmL tb) de manejar

drizzle¹ /'drɪzəl/ n llovizna f, garúa f (AmL)

drizzle² v impers lloviznar, garuar* (AmL)

droll /drəʊl/ adj (a) (comic) gracioso, con chispa (b) (quaint, curious) curioso

drone¹ /drəʊn/ n ① (bee) zángano m ② (sound — of bees, traffic, aircraft) zumbido m; (— of voice) cantinela f (fam), sonsonete m

drone² vi «*bee/engine/plane*» zumbar; **she ~d (on) for hours** estuvo horas con la misma perorata (fam)

drool /druːl/ vi «*dog/baby*» babear; **we ~ed at the sight of the cakes** se nos hizo la boca agua or agua la boca al ver los pasteles

droop /druːp/ vi (a) (sag) «*flowers*» ponerse* ⋯⋗

mustio; **his shoulders ~ed** se encorvó **(b)** (flag)
«*spirits*» flaquear, decaer*; «*person*»
desfallecer*, decaer* **(c) drooping** *pres p* ⟨*head*⟩
gacho; ⟨*flowers*⟩ mustio

drop¹ /drɑːp ‖drɒp/ *n* **1 (a)** (of liquid) gota *f*;
she's had a ~ too much ha bebido más de la
cuenta **(b) drops** *pl* (Med) gotas *fpl*; **nose ~s**
gotas para la nariz **(d)** (candy): **acid ~s** caramelos
mpl ácidos; **chocolate ~s** pastillas *fpl* de
chocolate **2** (fall) (*no pl*) (in temperature) descenso
m; (in prices) caída *f*, baja *f*; **a sheer ~** una caída a
plomo; **at the ~ of a hat** en cualquier momento

drop² **-pp-** *vt* **1 (a)** (accidentally): **I/he ~ped the
cup** se me/le cayó la taza; **don't ~ it!** ¡que no se
te caiga! **(b)** (deliberately) ⟨*cup/vase*⟩ dejar caer,
tirar; ⟨*bomb/supplies*⟩ lanzar*; **~ that gun!** ¡suelta
ese revólver!
2 (lower) ⟨*hem*⟩ alargar*, bajar; ⟨*eyes/voice*⟩ bajar
3 (a) (set down) ⟨*passenger/cargo*⟩ dejar **(b)**
(deliver) pasar a dejar
4 (send) (colloq) ⟨*card/letter*⟩ mandar; **~ me a line**
a ver si me mandas *or* me escribes unas líneas
5 (utter) ⟨*hint/remark*⟩ soltar*, dejar caer; **to let it
~ that** ... (inadvertently) dejar escapar que ...;
(deliberately) dejar caer que ...
6 (a) (omit) ⟨*letter/syllable/word*⟩ omitir; **to ~ sb
from a team** sacar* a algn de un equipo **(b)** (give
up, abandon) ⟨*case*⟩ abandonar; ⟨*charges*⟩ retirar;
⟨*plan/idea*⟩ abandonar, renunciar a; ⟨*friend/
associate*⟩ dejar de ver a; **to ~ the subject** dejar
el tema
■ ~ *vi* **1 (a)** (fall) «*object*» caer(se)*; «*plane*»
bajar, descender*; **he ~ped to the ground**
(deliberately) se tiró al suelo; (fell) cayó de un golpe
(b) (collapse) desplomarse
2 (a) (decrease) «*wind*» amainar;
«*temperature*» bajar, descender*; «*prices*»
bajar, experimentar un descenso (frml); «*voice*»
bajar **(b)** (in height) «*terrain*» caer*
■ **drop in** [*v* + *adv*] (colloq) pasar; **to ~ in on sb**
pasar a ver a algn, caerle* a algn (fam)
■ **drop off** **1** [*v* + *adv*] **(a)** (fall off) caerse* **(b)**
(fall asleep) dormirse*, quedarse dormido **(c)**
(decrease) «*sales/numbers*» disminuir*
2 [*v* + *o* + *adv*] ⟨*person/goods*⟩ dejar
■ **drop out** [*v* + *adv*]: **to ~ out of school**
abandonar los estudios; **to ~ out (of a
competition/race)** (before event) no presentarse (a
un concurso/una carrera); (during event)
abandonar (un curso/una carrera); **to ~ out (of
society)** marginarse, convertirse* en un
marginado

drop-dead /ˈdrɑːpˈded ‖ˈdrɒpded/ *adv*: **~
gorgeous** que te caes de espaldas de guapo

droplet /ˈdrɑːplət ‖ˈdrɒplɪt/ *n* gotita *f*

dropper /ˈdrɑːpər ‖ˈdrɒpə(r)/ *n* cuentagotas *m*,
gotero *m*

droppings /ˈdrɑːpɪŋz ‖ˈdrɒpɪŋz/ *pl n* (of bird,
flies) excremento *m* (frml), cagadas *fpl* (fam); (of
rabbit, sheep) cagarrutas *fpl*

dross /drɑːs ‖drɒs/ *n* **(a)** (waste) basura *f* **(b)**
(Metall) escoria *f*

drought /draʊt/ *n* sequía *f*

drove¹ /drəʊv/ *past of* DRIVE¹

drove² *n* **(a)** (of animals) manada *f* **(b) droves**
pl (of people) hordas *fpl*, manadas *fpl*

drown /draʊn/ *vt* **1** ⟨*person/animal*⟩ ahogar*
2 ~ **(out)** (make inaudible) ⟨*noise/cries/screams*⟩
ahogar*
■ ~ *vi* ahogarse*, morir* ahogado

drowsy /ˈdraʊzi/ *adj* **-sier, -siest**
somnoliento, adormilado

drudge /drʌdʒ/ *n* esclavo, -va *m,f*

drudgery /ˈdrʌdʒəri/ *n*: **this job is sheer ~** este
trabajo es una pesadez

drug¹ /drʌg/ *n* **(a)** (narcotic) droga *f*,
estupefaciente *m* (frml); **to be on ~s** drogarse* **(b)**
(medication) medicamento *m*, medicina *f*, fármaco
m (frml)

drug² *vt* **-gg-** drogar*

drug addict *n* drogadicto, -ta *m,f*

druggist /ˈdrʌgɪst/ *n* (AmE) farmacéutico, -ca
m,f

drug: ~store *n* (AmE) *establecimiento que vende
medicamentos, periódicos y una gran
variedad de artículos*; **~taker** /ˌteɪkər
‖ˌteɪkə(r)/ *n* consumidor, -dora *m,f* de drogas;
~taking *n* consumo *m* de drogas

drum¹ /drʌm/ *n* **1** (Mus) **(a)** tambor *m* **(b)**
drums *pl* (in band) batería *f* **2 (a)** (container)
bidón *m* **(b)** (machine part) tambor *m* **(c)** (spool)
tambor *m*

drum² **-mm-** *vt* ⟨*table/floor*⟩ golpetear; **to ~
one's fingers** tamborilear con los dedos
■ ~ *vi* **(a)** (Mus) tocar* el tambor **(b)** (beat, tap)
«*person*» dar* golpecitos, tamborilear; «*rain/
hail/hooves*» repiquetear
■ **drum up** [*v* + *adv* + *o*] ⟨*support*⟩ conseguir*,
obtener*

drum: ~beat *n* son *m* del tambor; **~kit** *n*
batería *f*

drummer /ˈdrʌmər ‖ˈdrʌmə(r)/ *n* (pop, jazz)
batería *mf*, baterista *mf* (AmL); (military) tambor *m*

drumstick /ˈdrʌmstɪk/ *n* **1** palillo *m* (de
tambor), baqueta *f* **2** (Culin) muslo *m*, pata *f*

drunk¹ /drʌŋk/ *past p of* DRINK²

drunk² *adj* (pred) borracho; **to get ~**
emborracharse; **~ and disorderly** (Law) en estado
de embriaguez y alterando el orden público (frml)

drunk³ *n* borracho, -cha *m,f*

drunkard /ˈdrʌŋkərd ‖ˈdrʌŋkəd/ *n* (frml & pej)
borracho, -cha *m,f*, beodo, -da *m,f* (frml)

drunk driving *n* (AmE) conducción *f* de un
vehículo bajo los efectos del alcohol

drunken /ˈdrʌŋkən/ *adj* (before *n*) ⟨*person/mob*⟩
borracho; ⟨*orgy/brawl*⟩ de borrachos

drunkenness /ˈdrʌŋkənnəs ‖ˈdrʌŋkənnɪs/ *n*
borrachera *f*, embriaguez *f* (frml)

dry¹ /draɪ/ *adj* **drier, driest** **1 (a)** (not wet)
⟨*ground/washing*⟩ seco **(b)** (lacking natural moisture)
⟨*leaves/skin/hair*⟩ seco; ⟨*cough*⟩ seco **(c)** (dried-up)
⟨*well/river*⟩ seco; **to run ~** «*river/well*» secarse*
(d) (not rainy, not humid) ⟨*climate/weather/heat*⟩
seco; **tomorrow will be ~** mañana no lloverá

2 (not sweet) ⟨*wine/sherry*⟩ seco **3** (ironic) ⟨*humor/wit*⟩ mordaz **4** (dull, boring) ⟨*lecture/book*⟩ árido

dry² dries, drying, dried *vt* secar*; to ~ one's eyes secarse* *or* (liter) enjugarse* las lágrimas
■ ~ *vi* secarse*
■ **dry up** [*v + adv*] (a) «*stream/pond*» secarse* (*completamente*) (b) «*funds/resources/inspiration*» agotarse

dry: ~ **clean** *vt* limpiar en seco; ~ **cleaner('s)** *n* tintorería *f*; ~ **dock** *n* dique *m* seco

dryer /'draɪər ‖'draɪə(r)/ *n* (a) (for clothes — machine) secadora *f*; (— rack) tendedor *m*, tendedero *m*; (spin ~) secadora *f* (centrífuga); (tumble ~) secadora *f* (de aire caliente) (b) ▸ HAIRDRIER

dry: ~ **goods** *pl n* (a) (clothing) (AmE) artículos *mpl or* prendas *fpl* de confección; (*before n*) ~ **goods store** tienda *f* de confecciones (b) (groceries) (BrE) comestibles *mpl* no perecederos; ~ **ice** *n* hielo *m* seco

dryly *adv* ▸ DRILY

dryness /'draɪnəs ‖'draɪnɪs/ *n* **1** (of ground, hair, skin, climate) sequedad *f* **2** (of wine, sherry) lo seco **3** (of humor, wit) lo mordaz

dry: ~ **rot** *n* putrefacción *f de la madera producida por un hongo*; ~ **wall,** (BrE) ~**-stone wall** *n* muro *m* de mampostería sin mortero

dual /'dju:əl ‖'dju:əl/ *adj* (*before n*) ⟨*role/ function*⟩ doble; ⟨*nationality*⟩ doble

dual: ~ **carriageway** /'kærɪdʒweɪ/ *n* (BrE) autovía *f*, carretera *f* de doble pista; ~**-control** /'du:əlkən'trəʊl ‖,dju:əlkən'trəʊl/ *adj* ⟨*car/ brakes*⟩ de doble mando *or* control; ~**-purpose** /'du:əl'pɜ:rpəs ‖,dju:əl'pɜ:pəs/ *adj* ⟨*utensil*⟩ de doble uso; ⟨*cleaner*⟩ de doble acción; ⟨*furniture*⟩ de doble función *or* uso

dub /dʌb/ *vt* **-bb-** **1** (nickname) apodar **2** (a) (Cin) ⟨*film*⟩ doblar (b) (Audio) mezclar

dubious /'du:biəs ‖'dju:biəs/ *adj* (a) (questionable) ⟨*honor/achievement*⟩ dudoso, discutible; ⟨*past*⟩ turbio; ⟨*motives/person*⟩ sospechoso (b) (doubtful) to be ~ (ABOUT sth/sb) tener* reservas *or* dudas (SOBRE *or* ACERCA DE algo/algn)

duchess /'dʌtʃəs ‖'dʌtʃɪs/ *n* duquesa *f*

duchy /'dʌtʃi/ *n* (*pl* **duchies**) ducado *m*

duck¹ /dʌk/ *n* pato, -ta *m,f*

duck² *vi* (bow down) agacharse; (hide): **I ~ed behind a pillar** me escondí rápidamente detrás de una columna
■ ~ *vt* **1** (lower) ⟨*head*⟩ agachar, bajar **2** (submerge) hundir **3** (dodge) ⟨*question*⟩ eludir, esquivar; ⟨*responsibility*⟩ evadir, eludir

duckling /'dʌklɪŋ/ *n* patito *m*, anadón *m*

duct /dʌkt/ *n* (Tech, Anat) conducto *m*

dud¹ /dʌd/ *n* (colloq) (a) (useless thing) birria *f* (fam), porquería *f* (fam) (b) (useless person) calamidad *f*, inútil *mf*

dud² *adj* (colloq) (a) (useless, valueless) ⟨*note/coin*⟩ falso; ⟨*check*⟩ sin fondos (b) (Mil) ⟨*shell/bomb*⟩ que no estalla

dude /du:d ‖dju:d/ *n* (AmE sl) tipo *m* (fam), tío *m* (Esp fam)

dudgeon /'dʌdʒən/ *n:* in high ~ indignadísimo, lleno de indignación

due¹ /du: ‖dju:/ *adj* **1** (*pred*): the rent is ~ hay que pagar el alquiler; the respect ~ to one's elders el respeto que se les debe a los mayores; it's all ~ to you todo gracias a ti, te lo debemos todo a ti; when is the next train ~? ¿cuándo llega el próximo tren?; she's ~ back tomorrow vuelve mañana, su regreso está previsto para mañana **2** (*before n*) ⟨*consideration/regard*⟩ debido; with all ~ respect con el debido respeto **3** due to (*as prep*) (crit) debido a

due² *adv:* the fort is ~ west of the town el fuerte está justo *or* exactamente al oeste del pueblo; we headed ~ north nos dirigimos derecho hacia el norte

due³ *n* **1** to give him his ~, he is efficient tienes que reconocer que es eficiente **2** dues *pl n* (subscription) cuota *f*

duel /'dju:əl ‖'dju:əl/ *n* duelo *m*

duet /du:'et ‖dju:'et/ *n* dúo *m*

duffel bag, (BrE) **duffle bag** /'dʌfəl/ *n* talego *m*, tula *f* (Col), bolso *m* marinero (RPl)

duffel coat, (BrE) **duffle coat** /'dʌfəl/ *n* trenca *f*, montgomery *m* (CS)

dug /dʌg/ *past & past p of* DIG¹

dugout /'dʌgaʊt/ *n* **1** (Mil) refugio *m* subterráneo **2** ~ (**canoe**) piragua *f* **3** (in baseball) dogaut *m*, caseta *f*

duke /du:k ‖dju:k/ *n* duque *m*

dull¹ /dʌl/ *adj* **1** (a) (not bright) ⟨*color*⟩ apagado; ⟨*light/glow*⟩ pálido; ⟨*eyes/complexion*⟩ sin brillo (b) (not shiny) ⟨*finish*⟩ mate; ⟨*hair*⟩ sin brillo (c) (overcast) ⟨*day/morning*⟩ gris, feo **2** (boring) ⟨*speech/person*⟩ aburrido **3** (a) ⟨*faculties*⟩ torpe, lerdo; ⟨*pain/ache*⟩ sordo; ⟨*sound*⟩ sordo, amortiguado (b) ⟨*edge/blade*⟩ romo, embotado

dull² *vt* (a) (make less bright) ⟨*color/surface*⟩ quitar el brillo a, opacar* (b) (make less sharp) ⟨*pain*⟩ aliviar, calmar; ⟨*senses*⟩ entorpecer*, embotar

dully /'dʌlli/ *adv* (a) (dimly) ⟨*glow/shine*⟩ débilmente, pálidamente (b) (boringly) ⟨*talk/write*⟩ de manera aburrida

duly /'du:li ‖'dju:li/ *adv* debidamente; permission was ~ granted el permiso fue concedido, como era de esperar

dumb /dʌm/ *adj* **1** (unable to speak) mudo; to be struck ~ quedarse mudo *or* sin habla **2** (stupid) (colloq) bobo (fam)
■ **dumb down** [*v + adv + o, v + o + adv*] bajar el nivel intelectual de

dumb: ~**bell** *n* pesa *f*, mancuerna *f*; ~**found** /'dʌm'faʊnd/ *vt* (*usu pass*) anonadar; ~**struck** *adj* estupefacto; ~**waiter** /'dʌm'weɪtə ‖,dʌm'weɪtə(r)/ *n* (elevator) montaplatos *m*; (table) mesita *f* rodante

dummy¹ /'dʌmi/ *n* **1** (a) (in window display, for dressmaker) maniquí *m* (b) (in tests, stunts) muñeco *m* (c) (in US football) domi *m* **2** (for baby) (BrE) ▸ PACIFIER **3** (fool) (colloq) bobo, -ba *m,f* (fam)

dummy² *adj* ⟨*gun/telephone*⟩ de juguete

dump¹ /dʌmp/ *n* **1** (a) (place for waste) vertedero *m* (de basura), basural *m* (AmL), tiradero *m* (Méx) **2** (temporary store) (Mil) depósito *m* **3** (unpleasant place) (colloq) lugar *m* de mala muerte **4** to be (down) in the ~s (colloq) estar* *or* andar* con la depre (fam)

dump² *vt* **1** (get rid of) ‹*waste/refuse*› tirar, botar (AmL exc RPl); ‹*boyfriend/girlfriend*› (colloq) plantar (fam), botar (AmS exc RPl fam), largar* (RPl fam) **2** **(a)** (set on ground) ‹*load/sand*› descargar*, verter*; **where can I ~ my things?** (colloq) ¿dónde puedo dejar *or* poner mis cosas? **(b)** (Comput) ‹*data/disks*› volcar*

dumper (**truck**) /'dʌmpər ‖'dʌmpə(r)/ *n* ▶ DUMP TRUCK

dumpling /'dʌmplɪŋ/ *n*: bola de masa que se come en sopas o guisos

Dumpster® /'dʌmpstər ‖'dʌmpstə(r)/ *n* (AmE) contenedor *m* (*para escombros*)

dump truck *n* volquete *m*, camión *m* volteador (RPl) *or* (Méx) de volteo, volqueta *f* (Col)

dumpy /'dʌmpi/ *adj* **-pier, -piest** regordete

dunce /dʌns/ *n* (pej) burro, -rra *m,f*

dune /duːn ‖djuːn/ *n* duna *f*

dung /dʌŋ/ *n* **(a)** (feces) boñiga *f*, bosta *f* **(b)** (manure) (esp BrE) estiércol *m*

dungarees /ˌdʌŋɡə'riːz/ *pl n* (workman's) overol *m*; (fashion) pantalón *m* de peto *m*

dungeon /'dʌndʒən/ *n* mazmorra *f*, calabozo *m*

duo /'duːəʊ ‖'djuːəʊ/ *n* (*pl* **-os**) dúo *m*

dupe¹ /duːp ‖djuːp/ *vt* engañar, embaucar*

dupe² *n* inocentón, -tona *m,f*, primo, -ma *m,f* (Esp fam)

duplex /'duːpleks ‖'djuːpleks/ *n* (AmE) ~ (apartment) dúplex *m*; ~ (house) casa de dos viviendas adosadas

duplicate¹ /'duːplɪkət ‖'djuːplɪkət/ *adj* (before *n*): **a ~ copy** un duplicado; **a ~ key** un duplicado *or* una copia de una llave

duplicate² /'duːplɪkət ‖'djuːplɪkət/ *n* duplicado *m*, copia *f*

duplicate³ /'duːplɪkeɪt ‖'djuːplɪkeɪt/ *vt* **(a)** (copy) ‹*letter/document*› hacer* copias de **(b)** (repeat) ‹*work/efforts*› repetir* (*en forma innecesaria*)

durable /'dʊrəbəl ‖'djʊərəbəl/ *adj* durable

duration /dʊ'reɪʃən ‖djʊə'reɪʃən/ *n* duración *f*

duress /dʊ'res ‖djʊə'res/ *n*: **under ~** bajo coacción

during /'dʊrɪŋ ‖'djʊərɪŋ/ *prep* durante

dusk /dʌsk/ *n* anochecer *m*

dust¹ /dʌst/ *n* polvo *m*; **to bite the ~** «*person*» morder* el polvo

dust² *vt* **1** (remove dust from): **to ~ the furniture** quitarles el polvo a los muebles, sacudir los muebles (CS, Méx) **2** (sprinkle) **to ~ sth WITH sth** espolvorear algo CON algo

dust: ~**bin** /'dʌstbɪn, 'dʌsbɪn/ *n* (BrE) cubo *m* *or* (CS, Per) tacho *m or* (Méx) tambo *m or* (Col) caneca *f or* (Ven) tobo *m* de la basura; ~**cart** /'dʌstkɑːrt, 'dʌskɑːrt ‖'dʌstkɑːt, dʌskɑːt/ *n* (BrE) camión *m* de la basura; ~ **cloth** *n* (AmE) trapo *m* del polvo, trapo *m* de sacudir (CS, Méx), sacudidor *m* (Méx)

duster /'dʌstər ‖'dʌstə(r)/ *n* **1** (Clothing) (housecoat) (AmE) guardapolvo *m* **2** (BrE) **(a)** (for blackboard) borrador *m* **(b)** ▶ DUST CLOTH

dust: ~ **jacket** *n* sobrecubierta *f*; ~**man** /'dʌstmən, 'dʌsmən/ *n* (*pl* **-men** /-mən/) (BrE) basurero *m*; ~**pan** /'dʌstpæn, 'dʌspæn/ *n* pala *f*, recogedor *m*

dusty /'dʌsti/ *adj* **-tier, -tiest** ‹*furniture*› cubierto de polvo; ‹*road/plain*› polvoriento

Dutch¹ /dʌtʃ/ *adj* holandés; **to go ~** pagar* a escote (fam), pagar* *or* ir* a la americana (AmL), pagar* *or* ir* a la inglesa (Chi fam)

Dutch² *n* **(a)** (language) holandés *m* **(b)** (people) (+ *pl vb*) **the ~** los holandeses

Dutch: ~**man** /'dʌtʃmən/ *n* (*pl* **-men** /-mən/) holandés *m*; ~**woman** *n* holandesa *f*

dutiful /'duːtɪfəl ‖'djuːtɪfəl/ *adj* consciente de sus deberes

duty /'duːti ‖'djuːti/ *n* (*pl* **duties**) **1** (obligation) deber *m*, obligación *f* **2** **(a)** (service) servicio *m*; **to do ~ as sth** hacer* las veces de algo, servir* de algo **(b)** (in phrases) **to be on/off ~** «*nurse/doctor*» estar*/no estar* de turno *or* guardia; «*policeman/fireman*» estar*/no estar* de servicio **(c)** **duties** *pl n* (responsibilities) (frml) funciones *fpl*, responsabilidades *fpl* **3** (Tax) (*often pl*) impuesto *m*

duty: ~**-free** /'duːti'friː ‖ˌdjuːti'friː/ *adj* libre de impuestos; ~**-free shop** *n* duty free *m*, tienda *f* libre de impuestos

duvet /'duːveɪ ‖/ *n* (BrE) edredón *m* (nórdico)

DVD *n* = **digital video disc**

dwarf¹ /dwɔːrf ‖dwɔːf/ *n* (*pl* ~**s** *or* **dwarves** /dwɔːrvz/) enano, -na *m,f*; (before *n*) ‹*tree/species*› enano

dwarf² *vt* ‹*building*› hacer* parecer pequeño

dwell /dwel/ (*past & past p* **dwelt** *or* **dwelled**) *vi* (liter) morar (liter), vivir
■ **dwell on** [*v + prep + o*]: **try not to ~ on the past** trata de no pensar demasiado en el pasado; **the documentary ~s excessively on ...** el documental se detiene demasiado *or* hace demasiado hincapié en ...

dwelling /'dwelɪŋ/ *n* **(a)** (habitation) (liter) morada *f* (liter) **(b)** (house) (frml) vivienda *f*

dwelt /dwelt/ *past & past p of* DWELL

dwindle /'dwɪndl̩/ *vi* **(a)** «*numbers/population*» disminuir*, menguar*, reducirse* **(b)** **dwindling** *pres p*: **dwindling resources** recursos *mpl* cada vez más limitados

dye¹ /daɪ/ *n* tintura *f*, tinte *m*

dye² **dyes, dyeing, dyed** *vt* teñir*

dying /'daɪɪŋ/ *adj* (before *n*) **(a)** (near death, extinction) ‹*person/animal*› moribundo, agonizante; ‹*race/art*› en vías de extinción **(b)** (related to time of death) ‹*wish/words/breath*› último, postrero (liter)

dyke /daɪk/ *n* **1** ▶ DIKE 1 **2** (lesbian) (sl & often pej) tortillera *f* (arg)

dynamic /daɪ'næmɪk/ *adj* dinámico

dynamism /'daɪnəmɪzəm/ *n* dinamismo *m*

dynamite /'daɪnəmaɪt/ *n* dinamita *f*

dynamo /'daɪnəməʊ/ *n* (*pl* **-mos**) dínamo *m or* dinamo *m* (AmL), dinamo *f or* dínamo *f* (Esp)

dynasty /'daɪnəsti ‖'dɪnəsti/ *n* (*pl* **-ties**) dinastía *f*

dysentery /'dɪsn̩teri ‖'dɪsəntri/ *n* disentería *f*

dysfunction /dɪs'fʌŋkʃən/ *n* disfunción *f*

dysfunctional /dɪs'fʌŋkʃnəl ‖dɪs'fʌŋkʃənl̩/ *adj* disfuncional

dyslexia /dɪs'leksiə/ *n* dislexia *f*

dyslexic /dɪs'leksɪk/ *adj* disléxico

Ee

E, e /iː/ *n* **(a)** (letter) E, e *f* **(b)** (Mus) mi *m*

E (= **east**) E

each¹ /iːtʃ/ *adj* cada *adj inv*

each² *pron* **1** cada uno, cada una; **he questioned ~ of them in turn** les preguntó uno por uno **2** **each other: they are always criticizing ~ other** siempre se están criticando el uno al otro; (if more than two people) siempre se están criticando unos a otros; **their respect for ~ other** su mutuo respeto

each³ *adv*: **we were paid $10 ~** nos pagaron 10 dólares a cada uno; **the apples are 20 cents ~** las manzanas valen 20 centavos por pieza *or* cada una

eager /ˈiːɡər ‖ ˈiːɡə(r)/ *adj* (excited, impatient) impaciente, ansioso; (keen) entusiasta; **he's ~ to please** está deseoso de complacer; **she is ~ for change** tiene muchos deseos de cambio

eagerly /ˈiːɡərli ‖ ˈiːɡəli/ *adv* ⟨accept/agree⟩ con entusiasmo; ⟨await⟩ ansiosamente, con ansiedad e impaciencia; ⟨listen/read⟩ con avidez

eagle /ˈiːɡəl/ *n* águila *f‡*

ear /ɪr ‖ ɪə(r)/ *n* **1** **(a)** (Anat) oreja *f*, (organ) oído *m* **(b)** (sense of hearing) (*no pl*) oído *m*; **to play sth by ~** tocar* algo de oído **2** (of corn) espiga *f*

ear: ~ache *n* dolor *m* de oído; **~drum** *n* tímpano *m*

earl /ɜːrl ‖ ɜːl/ *n* conde *m*

early¹ /ˈɜːrli ‖ ˈɜːli/ *adj* **-lier, -liest** **1** (before expected time) ⟨arrival/elections⟩ anticipado; **to be ~** «*person*» llegar* temprano; **the bus was ~** el autobús pasó (*or* salió *etc*) antes de la hora **2** **(a)** (before normal time): **to have an ~ night** acostarse* temprano; **~ retirement** jubilación *f* anticipada **(b)** ⟨crop/variety⟩ temprano, tempranero **3** (far back in time): **~ man** el hombre primitivo; **his earliest memories** sus primeros recuerdos **4** (toward beginning of period): **it's too ~ to tell** es demasiado pronto para saber; **in ~ June** a principios de junio; **he was in his ~ twenties** tenía poco más de veinte años

early² *adv* **-lier, -liest** **1** (before expected time) temprano **2** (before usual time) temprano, pronto (Esp) **3** (toward beginning of period): **~ in the morning** por la mañana temprano; **~ in the year** a principios de año; **~ (on) in her career** en los comienzos de su carrera **4** (soon) pronto; **they won't be here till nine at the earliest** por temprano que lleguen no estarán aquí antes de las nueve

ear: ~mark *vt* ⟨money/funds⟩ destinar; **~muffs** *pl n* orejeras *fpl*

earn /ɜːrn ‖ ɜːn/ *vt* **1** ⟨money/wages⟩ ganar; ⟨interest⟩ dar* **2** ⟨respect/gratitude⟩ ganarse; ⟨promotion⟩ ganar

earnest¹ /ˈɜːrnəst ‖ ˈɜːnɪst/ *adj* **(a)** (sincere) (fml) ⟨effort/attempt⟩ serio; ⟨wish⟩ ferviente **(b)** (serious) serio

earnest² *n* in **~** en serio

earnings /ˈɜːrnɪŋz ‖ ˈɜːnɪŋz/ *pl n* ingresos *mpl*

ear: ~plug *n* tapón *m* para el oído; **~ring** *n* arete *m* (AmL), aro *m* (CS), pendiente *m* (Esp), caravana *f* (Ur); **~shot** *n*: **to be within/out of ~shot** estar*/no estar* lo suficientemente cerca como para oír

earth /ɜːrθ ‖ ɜːθ/ *n* **1** **(a)** (Astron, Relig) tierra *f*; **the ~** *o* **E~** la Tierra **(b)** (*as intensifier*): **why on ~ didn't you warn me?** ¿por qué diablos no me avisaste? **2** (land, soil) tierzra *f* **3** (BrE Elec) tierra *f*

earthenware /ˈɜːrθənwer ‖ ˈɜːθənweə(r)/ *n* (material) barro *m* (cocido); (dishes) vajilla *f* de barro (cocido)

earth: ~quake *n* terremoto *m*; **~worm** *n* lombriz *f* (de tierra)

earwig /ˈɪrwɪɡ ‖ ˈɪəwɪɡ/ *n* tijereta *f*, cortapicos *m*

ease¹ /iːz/ *n* **1** (facility) facilidad *f*; **~ of operation** facilidad de manejo; **for ~ of access** para facilitar el acceso; **with ~** fácilmente **2** **(a)** (freedom from constraint): **at ~** a gusto; **to put sb at his/her ~** hacer* que algn se sienta a gusto **(b)** (Mil): **(stand) at ~!** ¡descansen!

ease² *vt* **1** **(a)** (relieve) ⟨pain⟩ calmar, aliviar; ⟨tension⟩ hacer* disminuir, aliviar; ⟨burden⟩ aligerar; **to ~ sb's mind** tranquilizar* a algn **(b)** (make easier) ⟨situation⟩ paliar; ⟨transition⟩ facilitar; **to ~ the way for sth** preparar el terreno para algo **2** **(a)** ⟨rules/restrictions⟩ relajar **(b)** ⟨belt/rope⟩ aflojar **3** (move with care) (+ *adv compl*): **they ~d him into the wheelchair** lo sentaron con cuidado en la silla de ruedas; **he ~d the key into the lock** introdujo la llave en la cerradura con cuidado
■ **~** *vi* «*pain*» aliviarse, calmarse; «*tension*» disminuir*
■ **ease off** [*v* + *adv*] «*rain*» amainar; «*pain*» aliviarse, calmarse; «*pressure/traffic*» disminuir*
■ **ease up** [*v* + *adv*] (slacken pace — of life) tomarse las cosas con más calma; (— of work, activity) bajar el ritmo

easel /ˈiːzəl/ *n* caballete *m*

easily /ˈiːzəli ‖ ˈiːzɪli/ *adv* **1** **(a)** (without difficulty) fácilmente, con facilidad **(b)** (readily) ⟨break/stain/cry⟩ con facilidad **2** (by far) con mucho, (de) lejos (AmL fam); **there's ~ enough for everybody** hay de sobra para todos

east¹ /iːst/ *n* **1** (point of the compass, direction) este *m*; **the ~, the E~** (region) el este **2** **the East** (the Orient) (el) Oriente

east² *adj* (*before n*) este *adj inv*, oriental; ⟨wind⟩ del este

east³ *adv* al este

east: ~bound *adj* que va (*or* iba *etc*) en dirección este *or* hacia el este; **E~ End** *n* (in UK) **the E~ End of (London)** barrio del este de Londres de tradición obrera

Easter /'i:stər ‖'i:stə(r)/ n Pascua f (de Resurrección); (before n) ~ **Day** o **Sunday** (el) Domingo de Pascua or Resurrección; ~ **egg** huevo m de Pascua

easterly /'i:stərli ‖'i:stəli/ adj ⟨wind⟩ del este; **in an ~ direction** hacia el este, en dirección este

eastern /'i:stərn ‖'i:stən/ adj **(a)** (Geog) (before n) oriental, este adj inv; **heavy rain over ~ England** fuertes lluvias en or sobre el este de Inglaterra; **the ~ states** los estados del este; **E~ Europe** Europa Oriental or del Este **(b)** (oriental) ⟨appearance/custom⟩ oriental

eastward¹ /'i:stwərd ‖'i:stwəd/ adj (before n): **in an ~ direction** en dirección este, hacia el este

eastward², (BrE) **eastwards** /-z/ adv hacia el este

easy¹ /'i:zi/ adj **easier, easiest** [1] (not difficult) fácil; **it's ~ to see that ...** es fácil ver que ...; **she was an ~ winner** ganó sin problemas [2] (undemanding) ⟨life⟩ fácil; **to be ~ on the eye** ser* agradable a la vista

easy² adv [1] (without difficulty): **money doesn't come ~** el dinero no es fácil de conseguir; **~ come, ~ go** así como viene se va [2] (slowly, calmly) despacio, con calma; **~ does it** despacio; **to take it ~** tomárselo con calma

easy: ~ chair n sillón m, poltrona f, butaca f; **~going** /'i:zi'gəʊɪŋ/ adj: **she's very ~going** es una persona de trato fácil or sin complicaciones

eat /i:t/ (past **ate**; past p **eaten**) vt/i comer
■ **eat away** [v + o + adv, v + adv + o] ⟨rats/mice⟩ roer*; ⟨moths⟩ picar*, comerse; ⟨acid⟩ corroer*
■ **eat into** [v + prep + o] ⟨acid/rust⟩ corroer*; ⟨profits/savings⟩ comerse
■ **eat up** [1] [v + o + adv, v + adv + o] (finish) ⟨meal/food⟩ comerse [2] [v + adv] (finish meal) terminar (de comer) [3] [v + adv + o] (consume) ⟨fuel/electricity⟩ consumir, gastar [4] [v + o + adv] ⟨curiosity/ambition⟩ consumir

eaten /'i:tn̩/ past p of EAT

eater /'i:tər ‖'i:tə(r)/ n: **he's a big ~** come mucho, es muy comelón or (CS, Esp) comilón (fam); **we're big meat ~s** comemos mucha carne

eaves /i:vz/ pl n alero m

eavesdrop /'i:vzdrɒp ‖'i:vzdrɒp/ vi **-pp-** **to ~ (on sth/sb)** escuchar (algo/a algn) a escondidas

ebb¹ /eb/ n reflujo m; **the ~ and flow of the tide** el flujo y reflujo de la marea; **to be at a low ~** ⟨person⟩ estar* decaído; ⟨diplomatic relations⟩ estar* en un punto bajo

ebb² vi **(a)** ⟨tide⟩ bajar, retroceder; **to ~ and flow** fluir* y refluir* **(b)** (dwindle) decaer*
■ **ebb away** [v + adv]: **his life was ~ing away** se consumía poco a poco; **I felt my strength ~ing away** sentí que me abandonaban las fuerzas

ebb tide n reflujo m

ebony /'ebəni/ n **(a)** (wood) ébano m **(b)** (color) color m (de) ébano; (before n) ⟨hair/skin⟩ negro como el ébano

EC n **(a)** (= **European Commission**) CE f **(b)** (= **European Community**) CE f

eccentric¹ /ɪk'sentrɪk, ek-/ adj excéntrico

eccentric² n excéntrico, -ca m,f

eccentricity /'eksen'trɪsəti/ n (pl **-ties**) excentricidad f

ecclesiastical /ɪ'kli:zi'æstɪkəl/ adj eclesiástico

echo¹ /'ekəʊ/ n (pl **-oes**) eco m

echo² vi ⟨footsteps/voices⟩ hacer* eco

eclair /eɪ'kleə(r), ɪ'kleə(r)/ n: pastel individual relleno de crema

eclipse¹ /ɪ'klɪps/ n eclipse m

eclipse² vt eclipsar

eco-friendly /'i:kəʊˌfrendli/ adj ecológico, que no daña el medio ambiente

ecological /'i:kə'lɒ:dʒəkəl/ adj ecológico

ecologist /ɪ'kɑ:lədʒəst ‖ i:'kɒlədʒɪst/ n (student of ecology) ecólogo, -ga m,f; (conservationist) ecologista mf

ecology /ɪ'kɑ:lədʒi ‖ɪ'kɒlədʒi/ n ecología f

e-commerce /i:'kɑ:mərs ‖i:'kɒmɜ:s/ n. comercio m electrónico, e-comercio m

economic /ˌi:kə'nɒmɪk/ adj económico; **~ refugee** refugiado -da m, f económico -ca

economical /'ekə'nɑ:mɪkəl, 'i:k- ‖ˌi:kə'nɒmɪkəl, ˌek-/ adj económico

economics /'ekə'nɑ:mɪks, 'i:k- ‖ˌi:kə'nɒmɪks, ˌek-/ n **(a)** (+ sing vb) economía f **(b)** (financial aspect) (+ pl vb) aspecto m económico

economist /ɪ'kɑ:nəməst ‖ɪ'kɒnəmɪst/ n economista mf

economize /ɪ'kɑ:nəmaɪz ‖ɪ'kɒnəmaɪz/ vi economizar*; **to ~ on sth** economizar* algo

economy /ɪ'kɑ:nəmi, i:- ‖ɪ'kɒnəmi/ n (pl **-mies**) [1] (economic state or system of country) economía f [2] (a) (saving): **to make economies** economizar*, hacer* economía(s) **(b)** (thrift) economía f; (before n) ⟨pack/size⟩ familiar; **~ class** clase f turista; **~ class syndrome** síndrome m de la clase turista

ecosystem /'i:kəʊˌsɪstəm/ n ecosistema m

ecstasy /'ekstəsi/ n (pl **-sies**) **(a)** (state) éxtasis m **(b)** (drug) éxtasis m

ecstatic /ɪk'stætɪk/ adj ⟨look/expression⟩ extasiado, extático; ⟨applause⟩ clamoroso

Ecuador /'ekwədɔ:r ‖'ekwədɔ:(r)/ n Ecuador m

Ecuadorean¹ /'ekwə'dɔ:rɪən/ adj ecuatoriano

Ecuadorean² n ecuatoriano, -na m,f

eczema /ɪg'zi:mə, 'egzəmə ‖'eksɪmə/ n eczema m

eddy¹ /'edi/ n (pl **eddies**) remolino m, torbellino m

eddy² vi **eddies, eddying, eddied** ⟨water⟩ formar remolinos; ⟨smoke/dust⟩ arremolinarse

Eden /'i:dn̩/ n Edén m

edge¹ /edʒ/ n [1] **(a)** (no pl) (border, brink — of town) afueras fpl; (— of forest) lindero m, borde m; (— of river, lake) orilla f, margen m; (— of cliff) borde m **(b)** (of plate, table, chair) borde m; (of coin) canto *m*; (of page) margen *m* **2** (cutting part) filo *m*; **to be on** ~ estar* nervioso, tener* los nervios de punta (fam)

edge² *vt*: **the collar was** ~**d with fur** el cuello estaba ribeteado de piel; **the paper was** ~**d in black** el papel tenía un borde negro
■ ~ *vi* (+ *adv compl*): **to** ~ **forward/closer/away** ir* avanzando/acercándose/alejándose (poco a poco)

edging /'edʒɪŋ/ *n* borde *m*

edgy /'edʒi/ *adj* tenso, con los nervios de punta

edible /'edəbəl/ *adj* (safe to eat) comestible; (eatable) pasable, comible

edifying /'edəfaɪɪŋ ‖'edɪfaɪɪŋ/ *adj* edificante

Edinburgh /'edn,bɜːrə, -rəʊ ‖'edmbrə/ *n* Edimburgo *m*

edit /'edət ‖'edɪt/ *vt* **1** ⟨manuscript⟩ (correct) corregir*, editar; (cut) recortar, editar **2** ⟨movie/tape⟩ editar **3** (manage) ⟨newspaper/magazine⟩ dirigir*

edition /ɪ'dɪʃən/ *n* edición *f*

editor /'edətər ‖'edɪtə(r)/ *n* **1** (of text) redactor, -tora *m,f*, editor, -tora *m,f*, (of collected works, series) editor, -tora *m,f* **2** (of newspaper, magazine) director, -tora *m,f*, redactor, -tora *m,f* responsable **3** (of movie, radio show) editor, -tora *m,f*

editorial¹ /'edə'tɔːriəl ‖,edɪ'tɔːriəl/ *adj* **(a)** (Publ) ⟨assistant/director⟩ de redacción **(b)** (Journ) ⟨comment/decision/freedom⟩ editorial

editorial² *n* editorial *m*

EDT (in US) = **Eastern Daylight Time**

educate /'edʒəkeɪt ‖'edjʊkeɪt/ *vt* **(a)** (teach, school) educar* **(b)** (make aware) concientizar* *or* (Esp) concienciar

educated /'edʒəkeɪtəd ‖'edjʊkeɪtɪd/ *adj* ⟨person⟩ culto; **to make an** ~ **guess** hacer* una conjetura hecha con cierta base

education /'edʒə'keɪʃən ‖,edjʊ'keɪʃən/ *n* educación *f*; (before *n*) ⟨system/policy⟩ educativo

educational /'edʒə'keɪʃnəl ‖,edjʊ'keɪʃənl/ *adj* **(a)** ⟨establishment⟩ docente, de enseñanza; ⟨toy⟩ educativo **(b)** (instructive) instructivo

Edwardian /ed'wɔːrdiən ‖ed'wɔːdiən/ *adj* eduardiano

EEC *n* (= **European Economic Community**) CEE *f*

eel /iːl/ *n* anguila *f*

e'er /er ‖eə(r)/ *adv* (poet & arch) ▶ EVER

eerie /'ɪri ‖'ɪəri/ *adj* **eerier, eeriest** ⟨atmosphere/silence/cry⟩ inquietante, espeluznante; ⟨glow/place⟩ fantasmagórico

efface /ɪ'feɪs/ *vt* (frml) borrar

effect¹ /ɪ'fekt/ *n* **1** **(a)** (consequence) efecto *m*; **to take** ~ surtir efecto **(b) in effect** de hecho, realmente **(c)** (phenomenon) efecto *m*
2 (impression) impresión *f*; **he only did it for** ~ lo hizo sólo para llamar la atención
3 (applicability, operation): **to come into** ~, **to take** ~ entrar en vigor *or* en vigencia
4 (meaning): **a statement was issued to the** ~ **that ...** (frml) se hizo público un comunicado anunciando que ...; **he said it wasn't true, or words to that** ~ dijo que no era verdad o algo de ese tenor

5 effects *pl* **(a)** (special ~s) (Cin, TV) efectos *mpl* especiales **(b)** (belongings) (frml) efectos *mpl* (frml)

effect² *vt* (frml) ⟨reconciliation/cure⟩ lograr; ⟨escape⟩ llevar a cabo; ⟨repairs/payment⟩ efectuar* (frml)

effective /ɪ'fektɪv/ *adj* **(a)** (producing the desired result) ⟨method/treatment⟩ eficaz, efectivo **(b)** (striking) ⟨design/contrast⟩ de mucho efecto **(c)** (real) (before *n*) ⟨control/leader⟩ efectivo

effectively /ɪ'fektɪvli/ *adv* **(a)** ⟨manage/spend⟩ con eficacia, eficazmente **(b)** ⟨contrast/decorate⟩ con mucho gran efecto; ⟨speak⟩ convincentemente **(c)** (in effect) (indep) de hecho

effeminate /ə'femənət ‖ɪ'femɪnət/ *adj* afeminado

effervescent /'efər'vesənt ‖,efə'vesənt/ *adj* ⟨liquid/personality⟩ efervescente

efficiency /ɪ'fɪʃənsi/ *n* (*pl* **-cies**) (of person, system) eficiencia *f*; (Mech Eng, Phys) rendimiento *m*

efficient /ɪ'fɪʃənt/ *adj* ⟨person/system⟩ eficiente; ⟨machine/engine⟩ de buen rendimiento

efficiently /ɪ'fɪʃəntli/ *adv* eficientemente

effigy /'efədʒi ‖'efɪdʒi/ *n* (*pl* **-gies**) efigie *f*

effluent /'efluənt/ *n* (liquid waste) vertidos *mpl*; (sewage) aguas *fpl* residuales

effort /'efərt ‖'efət/ *n* esfuerzo *m*; **to make an** ~ hacer* un esfuerzo, esforzarse*; **it's not worth the** ~ no merece *or* vale la pena

effortless /'efərtləs ‖'efətlɪs/ *adj* ⟨grace⟩ natural; ⟨prose/style⟩ fluido

e.g. (for example) p. ej. *or* vg. *or* e.g.; (in speech) por ejemplo

egalitarian /ɪ'gælə'teriən ‖ɪ,gælɪ'teəriən/ *adj* igualitario

egg /eg/ *n* huevo *m*
■ **egg on** [*v* + *o* + *adv*, *v* + *adv* + *o*] incitar

egg: ~**cup** *n* huevera *f*; ~**plant** *n* (AmE) berenjena *f*; ~**shell** *n* cáscara *f* de huevo; ~ **timer** *n* (with sand) reloj *m* de arena (de tres minutos); (clockwork) avisador *m*; ~ **white** *n* clara *f* de huevo; ~ **yolk** *n* yema *f* de huevo

ego /'iːgəʊ, 'egəʊ/ *n* (*pl* **egos**) **(a)** (Psych) **the** ~ el yo, el ego **(b)** (self-regard) amor *m* propio, ego *m*

ego trip *n* (colloq): **his autobiography is simply an** ~ ~ su autobiografía es un regodeo ególatra

Egypt /'iːdʒəpt ‖'iːdʒɪpt/ *n* Egipto *m*

Egyptian¹ /ɪ'dʒɪpʃən/ *adj* egipcio

Egyptian² *n* egipcio, -cia *m,f*

eiderdown /'aɪdərdaʊn ‖'aɪdədaʊn/ *n* edredón *m*

eight /eɪt/ *adj/n* ocho *adj inv/m*; *see also* FOUR¹

eighteen /'eɪ'tiːn/ *adj/n* dieciocho *adj inv/m*; *see also* FOUR

eighteenth¹ /'eɪ'tiːnθ/ *adj* decimoctavo

eighteenth² *adv* en decimoctavo lugar

eighteenth³ *n* **(a)** (Math) dieciochoavo *m*; (part) dieciochoava parte *f* **(b)** (birthday): **it's her** ~ **today** hoy cumple dieciocho años

eighth¹ /eɪtθ/ *adj* octavo

eighth² *adv* en octavo lugar

eighth³ *n* (Math) octavo *m*; (part) octava parte *f*

eighth note *n* (AmE) corchea *f*

eightieth¹ /'eɪtiəθ/ *adj* octogésimo

eighttieth² *adv* en octogésimo lugar

eighttieth³ *n* (Math) octentavo *m*; (part) ochentava *or* octogésima parte *f*

eighty /'eɪti/ *adj/n* ochenta *adj inv/m*; *see also* FOUR¹

Eire /'erə ‖ 'eərə/ *n* Eire *m*, Irlanda *f*

either¹ /'iːðər, 'aɪðər ‖ 'iːðə(r), 'aɪðə(r)/ *conj* either ... or ... o ... o ...

■ Note In the usual translation of *either ... or*, *o ... o*, *o* becomes *u* when it precedes a word beginning with *o* or *ho*.

either² *adj*: you can take ~ route puedes tomar cualquiera de las dos rutas; on ~ side of the path a ambos lados del camino

either³ *pron* (*esp BrE*) cualquiera; (*with neg*) ninguno, -na; (*in questions*) alguno, -na

either⁴ *adv* (*with neg*) tampoco; she can't cook and he can't ~ ella no sabe cocinar y él tampoco

ejaculate /ɪ'dʒækjəleɪt ‖ ɪ'dʒækjʊleɪt/ *vi* (Physiol) eyacular

eject /ɪ'dʒekt/ *vt* ‹troublemaker/cassette› expulsar
■ ~ *vi* (Aviat) eyectarse

eke out /iːk/ [*v + adv + o, v + o + adv*] (a) (make last) ‹resources/funds› estirar, hacer* alcanzar (b) (barely obtain): to ~ out a living ganarse la vida a duras penas

elaborate¹ /ɪ'læbərət/ *adj* ‹decoration/design/ hairstyle› complicado; ‹meal› de mucho trabajo; ‹plan› minucioso

elaborate² /ɪ'læbəreɪt/ *vt* elaborar
■ ~ *vi* dar* (más) detalles

elapse /ɪ'læps/ *vi* transcurrir

elastic¹ /ɪ'læstɪk/ *n* (a) (Tex) elástico *m* (b) (garter) (AmE) liga *f* (c) (AmE) ▶ ELASTIC BAND

elastic² *adj* ‹waistband/garter› de elástico; ‹stocking› elastizado; ‹fiber/properties› elástico

elastic band *n* (*esp BrE*) goma *f* (elástica), gomita *f*, liga *f* (Méx), caucho *m* (Col), elástico *m* (Chi), banda *f* elástica (Ven)

elated /ɪ'leɪtəd ‖ ɪ'leɪtɪd/ *adj* eufórico

elbow¹ /'elbəʊ/ *n* codo *m*

elbow² *vt* darle* un codazo a; they ~ed us out of the way nos apartaron a empujones

elbow: ~ **grease** *n* (colloq): put some ~ grease into it! ¡dale con más fuerza! (fam); ~ **room** *n* espacio *m*

elder¹ /'eldər ‖ 'eldə(r)/ *adj* mayor

elder² *n* ① (a) (older person): she's my ~ by two years me lleva dos años, es dos años mayor que yo (b) (senior person): the village/tribal ~s los ancianos del pueblo/de la tribu (c) (Relig) miembro *m* del consejo ② (Bot) saúco *m*

elderberry /'eldər,beri ‖ 'eldəberi/ *n* (*pl* -ries) baya *f* del saúco

elderly¹ /'eldərli ‖ 'eldəli/ *adj* mayor, de edad

elderly² *pl n* the ~ los ancianos

eldest /'eldəst ‖ 'eldɪst/ *adj* (*before n*) ‹brother/ sister/child› mayor; the ~ (*as pron*) el/la mayor, el/la de más edad

elect¹ /ɪ'lekt/ *vt* ① (Adm, Govt) elegir*
② (choose) (frml) to ~ to + INF optar POR + INF

elect² *adj* (*after n*): the president ~ el presidente electo, la presidenta electa

election /ɪ'lekʃən/ *n* (a) (event) elecciones *fpl*; to call/hold an ~ convocar*/celebrar elecciones; (*before n*) ‹campaign/speech› electoral; ‹day/ results› de las elecciones (b) (act) elección *f*

elector /ɪ'lektər ‖ ɪ'lektə(r)/ *n* elector, -tora *m,f*

electoral /ɪ'lektərəl/ *adj* (*usu before n*) ‹system/reform› electoral; ~ **register** *o* **roll** padrón *m* (AmL) *or* (Esp) censo *m* *or* (Chi, Ven) registro *m* *or* (Col) planilla *f* electoral

electorate /ɪ'lektərət/ *n* (+ *sing or pl vb*) electorado *m*

electric /ɪ'lektrɪk/ *adj* eléctrico; ‹fence› electrificado; ‹performance/atmosphere› electrizante

electrical /ɪ'lektrɪkəl/ *adj* eléctrico

electric: ~ **blanket** *n* manta *f* or (AmL exc CS) cobija *f* or (CS) frazada *f* eléctrica; ~ **chair** *n* silla *f* eléctrica

electrician /ɪ,lek'trɪʃən/ *n* electricista *mf*

electricity /ɪ,lek'trɪsəti/ *n* electricidad *f*

electric shock *n* descarga *f* eléctrica

electrify /ɪ'lektrəfaɪ ‖ ɪ'lektrɪfaɪ/ *vt* -fies, -fying, -fied electrificar*; (excite, thrill) electrizar*

electrocute /ɪ'lektrəkjuːt/ *vt* electrocutar

electrode /ɪ'lektrəʊd/ *n* electrodo *m*

electrolysis /ɪ'lek'trɑːləsɪs ‖ ɪ,lek'trɒləsɪs/ *n* electrólisis *f*

electron /ɪ'lektrɑːn ‖ ɪ'lektrɒn/ *n* electrón *m*

electronic /ɪ'lek'trɑːnɪk ‖ ɪ,lek'trɒnɪk/ *adj* electrónico

electronic mail *n* correo *m* electrónico

electronics /ɪ'lek'trɑːnɪks ‖ ɪ,lek'trɒnɪks/ *n* (a) (subject) (+ *sing or pl vb*) electrónica *f*; (*before n*) ‹industry› electrónico (b) (circuitry) (+ *sing or pl vb*) sistema *m* electrónico

elegance /'eləgəns/ *n* elegancia *f*

elegant /'eləgənt/ *adj* elegante

element /'eləmənt ‖ 'elɪmənt/ *n* ① (a) (part, group) elemento *m*; an ~ of doubt algo de duda; extremist ~s in society elementos extremistas de la sociedad (b) **elements** *pl* (rudiments): the basic ~s of self-defense los principios elementales de la defensa personal ② (Chem) elemento *m* ③ **elements** *pl* (weather) (liter) the ~s los elementos ④ (preferred environment) elemento *m*; to be in one's ~ estar* en su (*or* mi *etc*) elemento ⑤ (of kettle, heater) resistencia *f*, elemento *m* (CS)

elementary /'elə'mentəri ‖ ,elɪ'mentri/ *adj* elemental

elementary: ~ **school** *n* (in US) escuela *f* (de enseñanza) primaria; ~ **teacher** *n* (in US) maestro, -tra *m,f* de enseñanza primaria

elephant /'eləfənt ‖ 'elɪfənt/ *n* elefante, -ta *m,f*

elevate /'eləveɪt ‖ 'elɪveɪt/ *vt* (a) (promote): to ~ sb to the peerage concederle a algn el título de lord/lady; he's been ~d to the position of manager (hum) lo han ascendido a director (b) (frml) ‹spirit› elevar (c) ‹load/platform› elevar (frml), subir

elevated railroad /'eləveɪtəd ‖ 'elɪveɪtɪd/ *n* (AmE) ferrocarril *m* elevado

elevation /'elə'veɪʃən ‖ ,elɪ'veɪʃən/ *n* ① (promotion) elevación *f* ② (angle) elevación *f* ③ (altitude) altura *f*

elevator /'eləveɪtər ‖'elɪveɪtə(r)/ n **(a)** (for passengers) (AmE) ascensor m, elevador m (Méx) **(b)** (for goods) elevador m, montacargas m

eleven¹ /ɪ'levən/ n **(a)** (number) once m; *see also* FOUR¹ **(b)** (in soccer, field hockey) equipo m, once m (period)

eleven² adj once adj inv

eleventh¹ /ɪ'levənθ/ adj undécimo

eleventh² adv en undécimo lugar

eleventh³ n (Math) onceavo m; (part) onceava parte f

elf /elf/ n (pl **elves**) geniecillo m, elfo m

elicit /ɪ'lɪsɪt ‖ɪ'lɪsɪt/ vt ⟨laughter/smile⟩ provocar*; **to ~ sth** (FROM sb) ⟨explanation/reply⟩ obtener* algo (DE algn)

eligible /'elɪdʒəbəl ‖'elɪdʒəbəl/ adj **(a)** (qualified, suitable) ⟨applicant/candidate⟩ que reúne los requisitos necesarios; **he's ~ for a grant** tiene derecho a solicitar una beca; **he is not ~ to compete** no reúne los requisitos necesarios para competir **(b)** (marriageable): **an ~ bachelor** un buen partido

eliminate /ɪ'lɪməneɪt ‖ɪ'lɪmɪneɪt/ vt eliminar; ⟨possibility/suspect⟩ descartar

elimination /ɪlɪmə'neɪʃən ‖ɪ,lɪmɪ'neɪʃən/ n (getting rid of) eliminación f; (ruling out) descarte m; **by a process of ~** por (un proceso de) eliminación or descarte

elite¹ /eɪ'liːt, i-/ n (+ sing or pl vb) elite f, élite f

elite² adj (before n) selecto, de elite or élite

elitism /eɪ'liːtɪzəm, i-/ n elitismo m

elitist /eɪ'liːtɪst, i-/ adj elitista

elixir /ɪ'lɪksər ‖ɪ'lɪksə(r)/ n elixir m

Elizabethan /ɪ'lɪzə'biːθən/ adj isabelino

elk /elk/ n (pl **~s** or **~**) (European animal) alce m; (American animal) uapití m

elm /elm/ n **~ (tree)** olmo m

elocution /'elə'kjuːʃən/ n dicción f, elocución f

elongated /ɪ'lɔːŋgeɪtəd ‖'iːlɒŋgeɪtɪd/ adj alargado

elope /ɪ'ləʊp/ vi fugarse* (con un amante, novio para casarse)

eloquent /'eləkwənt/ adj elocuente

El Salvador /el'sælvədɔːr ‖,el'sælvədɔː(r)/ n El Salvador

else /els/ adv **1** (after pron): **somebody** o **someone ~** otra persona; **everybody** o **everyone ~** todos los demás; **everything ~** todo lo demás; **there's not much ~ we can do** no podemos hacer mucho más; **nobody ~** nadie más; **they have nowhere ~ to go** no tienen ningún otro sitio or lugar adonde ir; **anything ~?** ¿algo más? **2** (with interrog): **what/who ~?** ¿qué/quién más?; **what ~ can you expect from her?** ¿qué otra cosa se puede esperar de ella? **3 or else** (as conj) si no

elsewhere /'elshwer ‖,els'weə(r)/ adv: **to go ~** ir* a otro sitio or lugar; **~ in Europe** en otras partes or otros lugares de Europa

elude /iː'luːd ‖ɪ'luːd/ vt (avoid) eludir; (escape from) escaparse de

elusive /iː'luːsɪv ‖ɪ'luːsɪv/ adj ⟨enemy/prey⟩ escurridizo, difícil de aprehender; ⟨goal/ agreement⟩ difícil de alcanzar

elves /elvz/ pl of ELF

emaciated /ɪ'meɪʃieɪtəd ‖ɪ'meɪsieɪtɪd/ adj ⟨person/animal⟩ escuálido; ⟨body/face⟩ consumido

E-mail, e-mail /'iː-meɪl/ n correo m electrónico

emanate /'eməneɪt/ vi **to ~ FROM sth** ⟨gas/ light/sound⟩ emanar DE algo; ⟨ideas/ suggestions⟩ provenir* DE algo

emancipate /ɪ'mænsəpeɪt ‖ɪ'mænsɪpeɪt/ vt (frml) emancipar

emancipated /ɪ'mænsəpeɪtəd ‖ɪ'mænsɪpeɪtɪd/ adj emancipado; ⟨viewpoint/ lifestyle⟩ independiente y progresista

emancipation /ɪ,mænsə'peɪʃən ‖ɪ,mænsɪ'peɪʃən/ n (frml) emancipación f

embankment /ɪm'bæŋkmənt/ n (for road, railroad) terraplén m; (as protection) muro m de contención

embargo /ɪm'bɑːrgəʊ ‖ɪm'bɑːgəʊ/ n (pl **-goes**) embargo m, prohibición f; **to put an ~ on sth** imponer* un embargo sobre algo

embark /ɪm'bɑːrk ‖ɪm'bɑːk/ vi **(a)** (on ship, plane) embarcar(se)* **(b)** (start) **to ~ ON** o **UPON sth** ⟨on career/new life⟩ emprender algo; ⟨on adventure/undertaking⟩ embarcarse* EN algo

embarrass /ɪm'bærəs/ vt hacerle* pasar vergüenza a, avergonzar*

embarrassed /ɪm'bærəst/ adj: **an ~ silence** un silencio violento; **I'm ~** me da vergüenza, me da pena (AmL exc CS)

embarrassing /ɪm'bærəsɪŋ/ adj ⟨situation/ question⟩ embarazoso; **how ~!** ¡qué vergüenza or (AmL exc CS) pena!

embarrassment /ɪm'bærəsmənt/ n **(a)** (shame) bochorno m, vergüenza f, pena f (AmL exc CS) **(b)** (cause of shame): **he's an ~ to his friends** les hace pasar vergüenza a sus amigos

embassy /'embəsi/ n (pl **-sies**) embajada f

embed /ɪm'bed/ vt **-dd-** (in rock, wood) enterrar*; **the bullet was ~ded in his arm** la bala quedó alojada en el brazo

ember /'embər ‖'embə(r)/ n brasa f, ascua f

embezzle /ɪm'bezəl/ vt desfalcar*, malversar

embittered /ɪm'bɪtəd ‖ɪm'bɪtəd/ adj ⟨person⟩ amargado; ⟨fighting/rivalry⟩ enconado

emblem /'embləm/ n emblema m

embody /ɪm'bɑːdi ‖ɪm'bɒdi/ vt **-dies, -dying, -died (a)** (personify) encarnar, personificar* **(b)** (express) ⟨thought/idea⟩ plasmar, expresar

emboss /ɪm'bɑːs, ɪm'bɔːs ‖ɪm'bɒs/ vt **(a)** ⟨leather/metal⟩ repujar **(b) embossed** past p ⟨stationery⟩ con membrete en relieve; ⟨wallpaper⟩ estampado en relieve

embrace¹ /ɪm'breɪs/ vt **(a)** (hug) abrazar* **(b)** ⟨idea/principle⟩ abrazar*; ⟨lifestyle/religion⟩ adoptar
■ **~** vi abrazarse*

embrace² n abrazo m

embrocation /'embrə'keɪʃən/ n linimento m, embrocación f (ant)

embroider /ɪm'brɔɪdər ‖ɪm'brɔɪdə(r)/ vt ⟨cloth/design⟩ bordar; ⟨story⟩ adornar

embroidery /ɪm'brɔɪdəri/ n (pl **-ries**) bordado m

embroil /ɪm'brɔɪl/ vt: **to be/become ~ed in sth** estar*/verse* envuelto en algo

embryo /'embriəʊ/ n (pl **-os**) embrión m

emend /iː'mend ‖ɪ'mend/ vt (frml) enmendar*

··· emerald ···> encounter

638

emerald /ˈemərəld/ n **(a)** (gem) esmeralda f;
(b) (color) verde m esmeralda

emerge /ɪˈmɜːrdʒ ǁɪˈmɜːdʒ/ vi **(a)** (come out)
salir*, aparecer* **(b)** (become evident, known)
«problem» surgir*; «pattern» dibujarse;
«truth» revelarse; «facts» salir* a la luz

emergency /ɪˈmɜːrdʒənsi ǁɪˈmɜːdʒənsi/ n (pl
-cies) **(a)** (serious situation) emergencia f; **in an ~**
o **in case of ~** en una emergencia or en caso de
emergencia **(b)** (Med) urgencia f; (before n) «case/
operation» de urgencia **(c)** (Govt): **a state of ~**
was declared se declaró el estado de excepción

emergency: ~ exit n salida f de
emergencia; **~ landing** n aterrizaje m forzoso;
~ stop n parada f de emergencia

emery /ˈeməri/: **~ board** n lima f de esmeril;
~ paper n papel m de lija

emigrant /ˈemɪɡrənt ǁˈemɪɡrənt/ n emigrante
mf

emigrate /ˈemɪɡreɪt ǁˈemɪɡreɪt/ vi emigrar

emigration /eməˈɡreɪʃən ǁemɪˈɡreɪʃən/ n
emigración f

eminent /ˈemənənt ǁˈemɪnənt/ adj eminente,
ilustre

emission /iːˈmɪʃən ǁɪˈmɪʃən/ n emisión f

emit /iːˈmɪt ǁiˈmɪt/ vt -tt- «gas/smell/vapor»
despedir*; «heat/light/radiation/sound» emitir

emotion /ɪˈməʊʃən/ n **(a)** (feeling) sentimiento
m **(b)** (strength of feeling) emoción f

emotional /ɪˈməʊʃənəl ǁɪˈməʊʃənəl/ adj **(a)**
«disorder» emocional **(b)** (sensitive) «person/nature»
emotivo **(c)** (upset) emocionado; **to get ~**
emocionarse **(d)** (moving) «speech/experience/scene»
emotivo

empathize /ˈempəθaɪz/ vi **to ~ with sb**
establecer* lazos de empatía con algn,
identificarse* con algn

empathy /ˈempəθi/ n empatía f

emperor /ˈempərər ǁˈempərə(r)/ n emperador
m

emphasis /ˈemfəsəs ǁˈemfəsɪs/ n (pl -ses
/-siːz/) énfasis m; **to lay** o **put ~ on sth** hacer*
hincapié or poner* énfasis en la importancia de
algo

emphasize /ˈemfəsaɪz/ vt «phrase/word»
enfatizar*; «fact/point/warning» recalcar*, hacer*
hincapié en; «fault/value» poner* de relieve;
«shape/feature» resaltar, hacer* resaltar

emphatic /ɪmˈfætɪk/ adj «gesture/tone»
enérgico, enfático; «assertion/refusal» categórico

empire /ˈempaɪr ǁˈempaɪə(r)/ n imperio m

employ /ɪmˈplɔɪ/ vt **(a)** «person» (take on)
contratar, emplear; (have working) emplear, dar*
empleo a **(b)** «method/tactics/tool» emplear

employee /ɪmˈplɔɪiː/ n empleado, -da m,f

employer /ɪmˈplɔɪər ǁɪmˈplɔɪə(r)/ n
empleador, -dora m,f, (of domestic worker etc)
patrón, -trona m,f

employment /ɪmˈplɔɪmənt/ n **(a)** (work)

trabajo m; **to be in ~** tener* trabajo; (before n) **~**
agency agencia f de trabajo **(b)** (availability of work)
empleo m; **full ~** pleno empleo m

empress /ˈemprəs ǁˈemprɪs/ n emperatriz f

empty¹ /ˈempti/ adj **-tier, -tiest** «container/
table» vacío; «words/gesture/life» vacío; «threat/
promise» vano

empty² -ties, -tying, -tied «container/
warehouse» vaciar*; **she emptied the contents all**
over the floor vació la caja (or el bolso etc) en el
suelo
■ ~ vi «room/street» vaciarse*; «river/stream»
to ~ into sth desaguar* en algo
■ **empty out** [v + o + adv, v + adv + o] «bag/
drawer/pockets» vaciar*; «garbage» tirar, botar
(AmL exc RPI)

empty³ n (pl -ties) (colloq) (bottle) envase m
(vacío), casco m (Esp, Méx)

empty-handed /ˈempti'hændəd
ǁempti'hændɪd/ adv con las manos vacías

emu /ˈiːmjuː/ n emú m

emulate /ˈemjəleɪt ǁˈemjʊleɪt/ vt emular

emulsion /ɪˈmʌlʃən/ n **~ (paint)** pintura f al
agua

enable /ɪˈneɪbəl/ vt **(a)** (provide means for) **to ~**
sb to + inf permitir(le) a algn + inf **(b)** (make
possible) posibilitar, permitir

enact /ɪnˈækt/ vt **1** (Govt, Law) «law»
promulgar* **2** «play/role» representar

enamel /ɪˈnæməl/ n esmalte m

enamored, (BrE) **enamoured** /ɪˈnæmərd
ǁɪˈnæməd/ adj (frml) **to be ~ of sb** estar*
enamorado or prendado de algn; **I'm not very ~**
of the idea no estoy muy entusiasmado con la
idea

enc (= **enclosed**) anexo

encampment /ɪnˈkæmpmənt/ n campamento
m

encase /ɪnˈkeɪs/ vt revestir*, recubrir*; **~d in**
sth revestido or recubierto de algo

enchant /ɪnˈtʃænt ǁɪnˈtʃɑːnt/ vt (delight, charm)
cautivar; (Occult) hechizar*

enchanting /ɪnˈtʃæntɪŋ ǁɪnˈtʃɑːntɪŋ/ adj
encantador

encircle /ɪnˈsɜːrkəl ǁɪnˈsɜːkəl/ vt «camp/house»
rodear; «waist/wrist» ceñir*

enclave /ˈenkleɪv/ n enclave m

enclose /ɪnˈkləʊz/ vt **1** **(a)** (surround)
encerrar*; (fence in) cercar* **(b)** **enclosed** past p
«area/space» cerrado **2** (in letter) adjuntar,
acompañar

enclosure /ɪnˈkləʊʒər ǁɪnˈkləʊʒə(r)/ n recinto
m; **a fenced ~** un cercado

encode /ɪnˈkəʊd, en-/ vt codificar*, cifrar

encompass /ɪnˈkʌmpəs/ vt (frml) abarcar*

encore /ˈɑːnkɔːr ǁˈɒŋkɔː(r)/ n bis m; (as interj)
¡otra!

encounter¹ /ɪnˈkaʊntər ǁɪnˈkaʊntə(r)/ vt **(a)**

AmC Central America	Arg Argentina	Cu Cuba	Per Peru
AmL Latin America	Bol Bolivia	Ec Ecuador	RPI River Plate Area
AmS South America	Chi Chile	Esp Spain	Ur Uruguay
Andes Andean Region	CS Southern Cone	Méx Mexico	Ven Venezuela

(be faced with) ⟨*danger/difficulty/opposition*⟩ encontrar*, encontrarse* con **(b)** (come across) tropezar* *or* toparse con

encounter² *n* encuentro *m*

encourage /ɪnˈkʌrɪdʒ ‖ɪnˈkɜːrɪdʒ/ *vt* **(a)** (give hope, courage to) animar, alentar*; **she/it ~d me to carry on** me animó a seguir adelante **(b)** ⟨*industry/competition/growth*⟩ fomentar

encouragement /ɪnˈkʌrɪdʒmənt ‖ɪnˈkɜːrɪdʒmənt/ *n* ánimo *m*

encouraging /ɪnˈkʌrɪdʒɪŋ ‖ɪnˈkɜːrɪdʒɪŋ/ *adj* alentador

encroach /ɪnˈkrəʊtʃ/ *vi* **to ~ on** *o* **upon sth** ⟨*on land*⟩ invadir algo; ⟨*on rights*⟩ cercenar algo

encrypt /enˈkrɪpt/ *vt* (Comput) cifrar

encumber /ɪnˈkʌmbər ‖ɪnˈkʌmbə(r)/ *vt* cargar*

encyclopedia, (BrE also) **encyclopaedia** /ɪnˌsaɪkləˈpiːdiə/ *n* enciclopedia *f*

end¹ /end/ *n* ⓵ **(a)** (extremity — of rope, stick) extremo *m*, punta *f*; (— of nose) punta *f*; (— of street) final *m*; **for weeks on ~** durante semanas y semanas, durante semanas enteras; **it measures five feet (from) ~ to ~** mide cinco pies de un lado al otro *or* de punta a punta; **to make ~s meet** llegar* a fin de mes **(b)** (remaining part) final *m*, resto *m* ⓶ **(a)** (finish, close) fin *m*, final *m*; **at the ~ of January** a fines *or* a finales de enero; **in the ~** al final; **to put an ~ to sth** poner* fin *or* poner* punto final a algo **(b)** (death, destruction) final *m*, fin *m* **(c)** (outcome) final *m* ⓷ (purpose) fin *m*; **to this ~** (frml) con este fin (frml)

end² *vt* **(a)** (stop) ⟨*argument/discussion/fight*⟩ terminar; ⟨*gossip/speculation*⟩ acabar *or* terminar con **(b)** (conclude) terminar
■ **~** *vi* acabar, terminar
■ **end up** [*v* + *adv*] terminar, acabar

endanger /ɪnˈdeɪndʒər ‖ɪnˈdeɪndʒə(r)/ *vt* ⟨*life*⟩ poner* en peligro; ⟨*chances/reputation*⟩ hacer* peligrar **(b) endangered** *past p* ⟨*species*⟩ en peligro

endear /ɪnˈdɪr ‖ɪnˈdɪə(r)/ *vt* **to ~ oneself to sb** granjearse el cariño de algn

endearing /ɪnˈdɪrɪŋ ‖ɪnˈdɪərɪŋ/ *adj* atractivo

endearment /ɪnˈdɪrmənt ‖ɪnˈdɪəmənt/ *n* expresión *f* de cariño

endeavor¹, (BrE) **endeavour** /ɪnˈdevər ‖ɪnˈdevə(r)/ *n* (frml) esfuerzo *m*, intento *m*

endeavor², (BrE) **endeavour** *vt* (frml) **to ~ to + INF** intentar por todos los medios + INF, esforzarse* POR + INF

ending /ˈendɪŋ/ *n* **(a)** (conclusion) final *m*, desenlace *m* **(b)** (Ling) desinencia *f*, terminación *f*

endless /ˈendləs ‖ˈendlɪs/ *adj* **(a)** ⟨*journey/meeting*⟩ interminable; ⟨*plain/patience*⟩ sin límites; ⟨*chatter/complaining*⟩ continuo **(b)** (innumerable) innumerable; **the possibilities are ~** las posibilidades son infinitas

endorse /ɪnˈdɔːrs ‖ɪnˈdɔːs/ *vt* ⓵ (approve) ⟨*statement/decision*⟩ aprobar* ⓶ (sign) ⟨*check/bill*⟩ endosar

endorsement /ɪnˈdɔːrsmənt ‖ɪnˈdɔːsmənt/ *n* ⓵ **(a)** (approval) aval *m*, aprobación *f* **(b)** (Pol) refrendo *m* ⓶ (on driving licence) (BrE) anotación *f* (*de una infracción de tráfico*)

endow /ɪnˈdaʊ/ *vt* **(a)** (provide) (*usu pass*) **~ed with sth** dotado DE algo **(b)** (provide income for) ⟨*college/school/hospital*⟩ dotar (de fondos) a

endowment /ɪnˈdaʊmənt/ *n* (Fin) donación *f*

end product *n* producto *m* final

endurance /ɪnˈdʊrəns ‖ɪnˈdjʊərəns/ *n* (physical) resistencia *f*; (mental) entereza *f*; (*before n*) **~ test** prueba *f* de resistencia

endure /ɪnˈdʊr ‖ɪnˈdjʊə(r)/ *vt* soportar
■ **~** *vi* «*fame/friendship/memories*» perdurar

enemy /ˈenəmi/ *n* (*pl* **-mies**) enemigo, -ga *m,f*

energetic /ˌenərˈdʒetɪk ‖ˌenəˈdʒetɪk/ *adj* ⟨*person*⟩ lleno de energía; ⟨*exercise*⟩ enérgico

energy /ˈenərdʒi ‖ˈenədʒi/ *n* energía *f*; (power, effort) energías *fpl*

enforce /ɪnˈfɔːrs ‖ɪnˈfɔːs/ *vt* ⟨*law/regulation*⟩ hacer* respetar *or* cumplir; ⟨*claim/right*⟩ hacer* valer

engage /ɪnˈgeɪdʒ/ *vt* ⓵ ⟨*attention/interest*⟩ captar ⓶ ⟨*cog/wheel*⟩ engranar con; ⟨*gear*⟩ engranar ⓷ (hire) ⟨*staff/performer*⟩ contratar
■ **~** *vi* (take part) **to ~ in sth** ⟨*in politics/voluntary work/study*⟩ dedicarse* A algo; **they ~d in a variety of activities** participaron en una variedad de actividades

engaged /ɪnˈgeɪdʒd/ *adj* ⓵ (betrothed) prometido, comprometido (AmL); **to be ~ TO sb** estar* prometido A algn, estar* comprometido CON algn (AmL); **to get ~** prometerse, comprometerse (AmL) ⓶ (*pred*) **(a)** (occupied) (frml) ocupado; **I'm otherwise ~** tengo otro compromiso; **they are ~ in a new business venture** tienen un nuevo negocio entre manos **(b)** (BrE) ⟨*toilet*⟩ ocupado **(c)** (BrE Telec) ocupado, comunicando (Esp); **the ~ tone** *o* **signal** la señal de ocupado *or* (Esp) de comunicando

engagement /ɪnˈgeɪdʒmənt/ *n* ⓵ (pledge to marry) compromiso *m*; (period) noviazgo *m*; (*before n*) **~ ring** anillo *m* de compromiso ⓶ (appointment) compromiso *m*

engine /ˈendʒən ‖ˈendʒɪn/ *n* **(a)** (motor) motor *m* **(b)** (locomotive) locomotora *f*, máquina *f*

engine driver *n* (BrE) maquinista *mf*

engineer¹ /ˌendʒəˈnɪr ‖ˌendʒɪˈnɪə(r)/ *n* ⓵ **(a)** (graduate) ingeniero, -ra *m,f* **(b)** (for maintenance) (BrE) técnico *mf*, ingeniero, -ra *m,f* (Méx) ⓶ (AmE Rail) maquinista *mf*

engineer² *vt* ⟨*plan*⟩ urdir, tramar; ⟨*defeat/downfall*⟩ fraguar*

engineering /ˌendʒəˈnɪrɪŋ ‖ˌendʒɪˈnɪərɪŋ/ *n* ingeniería *f*

England /ˈɪŋglənd/ *n* Inglaterra *f*

English¹ /ˈɪŋglɪʃ/ *adj* inglés

English² *n* **(a)** (language) inglés *m*; (*before n*) ⟨*lesson/teacher*⟩ de inglés **(b)** (people) (+ *pl vb*) **the ~** los ingleses

English: ~man /ˈɪŋglɪʃmən/ *n* (*pl* **-men** /-mən/) inglés *m*; **~woman** *n* inglesa *f*

engrave /ɪnˈgreɪv/ *vt* grabar

engraving /ɪnˈgreɪvɪŋ/ *n* grabado *m*

engross /ɪnˈgrəʊs/ *vt* absorber*; **to be ~ed IN sth** estar* absorto EN algo

engulf /ɪnˈgʌlf/ *vt* «*flames/fire/waves*» envolver*; «*lava*» sepultar; «*feeling*» asaltar

enhance /ɪn'hæns ‖m'hɑːns/ vt ⟨beauty/taste⟩ realzar*; ⟨value⟩ aumentar; ⟨reputation/ performance⟩ mejorar

enigma /ɪ'nɪgmə/ n (pl -mas) enigma m

enigmatic /'enɪg'mætɪk/ adj enigmático

enjoy /ɪn'dʒɔɪ/ vt **1** (like): I ~ traveling/music me gusta viajar/la música; I ~ed the party lo pasé bien en la fiesta **2** (have, experience) ⟨good health⟩ disfrutar de, gozar* de
- v refl to ~ oneself divertirse*, pasarlo or pasarla bien

enjoyable /ɪn'dʒɔɪəbəl/ adj agradable

enjoyment /ɪn'dʒɔɪmənt/ n placer m

enlarge /ɪn'lɑːrdʒ ‖m'lɑːdʒ/ vt ⟨hole/area⟩ agrandar; ⟨gland/heart⟩ dilatar; ⟨room/office⟩ ampliar*; ⟨print/photograph⟩ ampliar*

enlighten /ɪn'laɪtn̩/ vt ⟨people/population⟩ ilustrar (frml); would you care to ~ me? ¿te importaría explicarme?

enlightened /ɪn'laɪtn̩d/ adj ⟨person/view⟩ progresista; ⟨decision⟩ inteligente

Enlightenment /ɪn'laɪtn̩mənt/ n (Hist) the (Age of) ~ la Ilustración, el Siglo de las Luces

enlist /ɪn'lɪst/ vi alistarse
- ~ vt ⟨soldiers/helpers/members⟩ reclutar, alistar; ⟨sailors⟩ enrolar; ⟨support/aid⟩ conseguir*

enlisted man /ɪn'lɪstəd ‖m'lɪstɪd/ n (AmE) soldado m raso

en masse /ɑːn'mæs ‖ɒn'mæs/ adv en masa

enmity /'enməti/ n (pl -ties) (frml) enemistad f

enormous /ɪ'nɔːrməs ‖ɪ'nɔːməs/ adj enorme, inmenso

enormously /ɪ'nɔːrməsli ‖ɪ'nɔːməsli/ adv ⟨enjoy/benefit⟩ enormemente; he's ~ fat es gordísimo

enough¹ /ɪ'nʌf/ adj bastante, suficiente; (pl) bastantes, suficientes; they had more than ~ time tuvieron tiempo de sobra

enough² pron: they don't pay us ~ no nos pagan bastante or lo suficiente; I've had ~! ¡ya estoy harto!

enough³ adv you don't go out ~ no sales lo suficiente; make sure it's big ~ asegúrate de que sea lo suficientemente grande; curiously ~ curiosamente

■ **Note** Where the meaning ... enough to ... is being translated, the translation uses the structure lo bastante or lo suficiente ... como para ...: you aren't eating enough (to stay healthy) no estás comiendo lo suficiente or lo bastante (como para mantenerte saludable).

enquire etc (BrE) /ɪn'kwaɪr ‖m'kwaɪə(r)/ ▶ INQUIRE etc

enrage /ɪn'reɪdʒ/ vt enfurecer*

enrich /ɪn'rɪtʃ/ vt enriquecer*

enroll, (BrE) **enrol** /ɪn'rəʊl/ vi-ll- matricularse, inscribirse*
- ~ vt matricular, inscribir*

enrollment, (BrE) **enrolment** /ɪn'rəʊlmənt/ n inscripción f, matrícula f

en route /ɑːn'ruːt ‖ɒn'ruːt/ adv por el camino, de camino

ensemble /ɑːn'sɑːmbəl ‖ɒn'sɒmbəl/ n **1** (group of performers) conjunto m **2** (Clothing) conjunto m

enslave /ɪn'sleɪv/ vt esclavizar*

ensue /ɪn'suː ‖m'sjuː/ vi seguir*; in the ensuing fight en la pelea que tuvo lugar a continuación

en suite /,ɑːn'swiːt ‖,ɒn'swiːt/ adj adjunto, en suite

ensure /ɪn'ʃʊr ‖m'ʃʊə(r), m'ʃɔː(r)/ vt asegurar

entail /ɪn'teɪl/ vt ⟨risk⟩ implicar*, suponer*; ⟨expense⟩ acarrear, suponer*; ⟨responsibility⟩ conllevar

entangle /ɪn'tæŋgəl/ vt enredar

enter /'entər ‖'entə(r)/ vt **1** (a) ⟨room/house/ country⟩ entrar en, entrar a (esp AmL) (b) (penetrate) entrar en **2** (begin) ⟨period/phase⟩ entrar en **3** (a) (join) ⟨army⟩ alistarse en, entrar en; ⟨firm/organization⟩ entrar en, incorporarse a (b) (begin to take part in) ⟨war/negotiations⟩ entrar en; ⟨debate/dispute⟩ sumarse a (c) ⟨student/ candidate⟩ presentar (d) ⟨race⟩ inscribirse* (para tomar parte) en; to ~ a competition presentarse a un concurso **4** (a) (record — in register) inscribir*; (— in ledger, book) anotar (b) (Comput) dar* entrada a
- ~ vi **1** entrar **2** to ~ (FOR sth) ⟨for competition/race⟩ inscribirse* (EN algo); ⟨for examination⟩ presentarse (A algo)

enterprise /'entərpraɪz ‖'entəpraɪz/ n **1** (a) (project) empresa f (b) (initiative, daring) empuje m **2** (a) (company) empresa f (b) (business activity): free ~ la libre empresa; private ~ la iniciativa privada; (sector) el sector privado

entertain /'entər'teɪn ‖,entə'teɪn/ vt **1** (amuse) ⟨audience⟩ entretener* **2** (frml) ⟨idea/suggestion⟩ contemplar; ⟨doubt/suspicions⟩ abrigar* (frml)
- ~ vi **1** (provide entertainment) entretener* **2** (have guests) recibir

entertainer /'entər'teɪnər ‖,entə'teɪnə(r)/ n artista mf (del mundo del espectáculo); (presenter of program) (Rad, TV) animador, -dora m,f

entertaining /'entər'teɪnɪŋ ‖,entə'teɪnɪŋ/ adj ⟨book/movie/anecdote⟩ entretenido; ⟨person⟩ divertido

entertainment /'entər'teɪnmənt ‖,entə'teɪnmənt/ n (a) (amusement) entretenimiento m (b) (show) espectáculo m

enthrall, (BrE) **enthral** /ɪn'θrɔːl/ vt -ll- cautivar

enthusiasm /ɪn'θuːziæzəm ‖m'θjuːziæzəm/ n entusiasmo m

enthusiast /ɪn'θuːziæst ‖m'θjuːziæst/ n entusiasta mf

enthusiastic /ɪn'θuːzi'æstɪk ‖m,θjuːzi'æstɪk/ adj entusiasta

entice /ɪn'taɪs/ vt atraer*

entire /ɪn'taɪr ‖m'taɪə(r)/ adj (a) (whole) (before n) entero (b) (intact) (pred) intacto

entirely /ɪn'taɪrli ‖m'taɪəli/ adv totalmente, completamente

entirety /ɪn'taɪrəti ‖m'taɪərəti/ n: in its ~ íntegramente, en su totalidad

entitle /ɪn'taɪtl̩/ vt **1** (give right) to ~ sb TO sth darle* a algn derecho A algo; to be ~d TO sth tener* derecho A algo **2** (name) (frml) (often pass) titular

entity /'entəti/ n (pl -ties) entidad f

entourage /'ɑːntʊˈrɑːʒ ‖,ɒntʊˈrɑːʒ/ n séquito m

641

entrails ⋯⋗ equivalent ⋯

entrails /'entreɪlz/ pl n (of person) entrañas fpl; (of animal) vísceras fpl

entrance¹ /'entrəns/ n **1 (a)** (way in) entrada f **(b)** (foyer) hall m; (before n) ~ **hall** hall m, vestíbulo m **(c)** (access) (fml) entrada f **2** (admission — to club, museum) entrada f; (— to school, university) ingreso m; (before n) ~ **fee** (for entry) (precio m de) entrada f; (to join club) cuota f de ingreso or inscripción; (for exam, competition) cuota f or tasa f de inscripción **3** (act of entering) entrada f; (Theat) entrada f en escena

entrance² /ɪn'trɑːns ‖ ɪn'trɑːns/ vt embelesar, extasiar*

entrant /'entrənt/ n (in competition) participante mf; (for exam) candidato, -ta m,f

entreat /ɪn'triːt/ vt (liter) suplicar*, rogar*

entreaty /ɪn'triːti/ n (pl **-ties**) (liter) súplica f, ruego m

entrepreneur /ˌɑːntrəprə'nɜːr ‖ ˌɒntrəprə'nɜː(r)/ n empresario, -ria m,f

entrust /ɪn'trʌst/ vt **to ~ sth TO sb** encomendarle* or confiarle* algo A algn

entry /'entri/ n (pl **entries**) **1** (coming, going in) entrada f **2** (access) entrada f, acceso m; **⊘ no entry** (on door) prohibida la entrada; (on road sign) prohibido el paso **3 (a)** (in accounts) entrada f, asiento m **(b)** (in diary) anotación f, entrada f **(c)** (in dictionary — headword) entrada f; (in encyclopedia — article) artículo m **4** (in contest): **the winning ~ in the painting competition** el ejemplar ganador del concurso de pintura; **there were 20 entries** hubo 20 inscripciones **5** (door, gate) (AmE) entrada f

entryphone /'entrɪfəʊn/ n (BrE) portero m eléctrico or (Esp) automático, interfón m (Méx), intercomunicador m (Ven)

entwine /ɪn'twaɪn/ vt (liter) entrelazar*

envelop /ɪn'veləp/ vt envolver*

envelope /'envələʊp/ n sobre m

enviable /'enviəbəl/ adj envidiable

envious /'enviəs/ adj envidioso; (expression) (lleno) de envidia

environment /ɪn'vaɪrənmənt ‖ ɪn'vaɪərənmənt/ n **(a)** (Ecol) **the ~** el medio ambiente **(b)** (surroundings): **she's studying gorillas in their natural ~** estudia a las gorilas en su entorno or hábitat natural; **the home ~** el ambiente del hogar

environmental /ɪnˌvaɪrən'mentl ‖ ɪnˌvaɪərən'mentl/ adj **(a)** (Ecol) (factor) ambiental; (damage) al medio ambiente, medioambiental; ~ **groups** grupos mpl ecologistas **(b)** (of surroundings) (factor) ambiental; (influence) del ambiente or entorno

environment-friendly /ɪn'vaɪrənmənt,frendli ‖ ɪn'vaɪərənmənt,frendli/ adj: ~ **products** productos mpl ecológicos, productos mpl que no dañan al medio ambiente

environs /ɪn'vaɪrənz ‖ ɪn'vaɪərənz/ pl n alrededores mpl, entorno m

envisage /ɪn'vɪzɪdʒ/ vt **(a)** (foresee) prever* **(b)** (visualize) imaginarse

envision /ɪn'vɪʒən/ vt (AmE) prever*

envoy /'envɔɪ/ n enviado, -da m,f

envy¹ /'envi/ n envidia f

envy² vt **envies, envying, envied** envidiar

enzyme /'enzaɪm/ n enzima f

epic¹ /'epɪk/ adj (usu before n) (poem/poetry/film) épico; (achievement/struggle) colosal, de epopeya

epic² n (poem) poema m épico; (film) superproducción f; (novel) epopeya f

epidemic /'epə'demɪk ‖ ,epɪ'demɪk/ n epidemia f

epigram /'epəgræm ‖ 'epɪgræm/ n epigrama m

epilepsy /'epəlepsi ‖ 'epɪlepsi/ n epilepsia f

epileptic /'epə'leptɪk ‖ ,epɪ'leptɪk/ adj (fit/attack) epiléptico, de epilepsia; **she's ~** es epiléptica

epilogue, (AmE also) **epilog** /'epəlɔːg ‖ 'epɪlɒg/ n epílogo m

Epiphany /ɪ'pɪfəni/ n **the ~** la Epifanía (del Señor)

episode /'epəsəʊd ‖ 'epɪsəʊd/ n episodio m

epistle /ɪ'pɪsəl/ n epístola f

epitaph /'epətæf ‖ 'epɪtɑːf/ n epitafio m

epitome /ɪ'pɪtəmi/ n (embodiment) personificación f; (typical example) arquetipo m

epitomize /ɪ'pɪtəmaɪz/ vt tipificar*; «person» ser* la personificación de

epoch /'epək ‖ 'iːpɒk/ n era f, época f

equal¹ /'iːkwəl/ adj igual; ~ **opportunities** igualdad f de oportunidades; **he doesn't feel ~ to the task** no se siente capaz de hacerlo

equal² n igual mf

equal³ vt, (BrE) **-ll-** **1** (Math) ser* igual a; **three times three ~s nine** tres por tres son nueve or es igual a nueve **2** (record/time) igualar

equality /ɪ'kwɑːləti ‖ ɪ'kwɒləti/ n igualdad f

equalize /'iːkwəlaɪz/ vt (incomes) equiparar; (pressure/weight) igualar; ■ ~ vi (Sport) empatar

equalizer /'iːkwəlaɪzər ‖ 'iːkwəlaɪzə(r)/ n (Sport) gol m de la igualada or del empate

equally /'iːkwəli/ adv **1 (a)** (in equal amounts) (divide/share) por igual **(b)** (without bias) (treat) de la misma manera, (por) igual **2** (to an equal degree) igualmente; ~ **easily** con igual or con la misma facilidad **3** (indep) **(a)** (just as possibly) ~ (well) de igual modo **(b)** (at the same time) (as linker) al mismo tiempo

equate /ɪ'kweɪt/ vt (compare) equiparar; (identify) identificar*

equation /ɪ'kweɪʒən/ n ecuación f

equator /ɪ'kweɪtər ‖ ɪ'kweɪtə(r)/ n **the ~** o **E~** el ecuador

equilibrium /'iːkwə'lɪbriəm ‖ ,iːkwɪ'lɪbriəm/ n (pl **-riums** or **-ria** /-riə/) equilibrio m

equinox /'iːkwənɒks, 'ek- ‖ 'iːkwɪnɒks, 'ek-/ n equinoccio m

equip /ɪ'kwɪp/ vt **-pp- (a)** (furnish, supply) (troops/laboratory) equipar; **to ~ sth/sb WITH sth** proveer* algo/a algn DE algo **(b)** (prepare, make capable) preparar

equipment /ɪ'kwɪpmənt/ n equipo m; **office ~** mobiliario, máquinas y material de oficina; **sports ~** artículos mpl deportivos

equity /'ekwəti/ n **1** (fairness) (fml) equidad f (fml) **2** (Busn, Fin) **(a)** (shareholders' interest in company) patrimonio m neto **(b) equities** pl n (shares) valores mpl de renta variable

equivalent¹ /ɪ'kwɪvələnt/ adj **(a)** (equal) (size/ ⋯⋗

value› equivalente; **to be ~ TO sth/-ING**
equivaler* A algo/+ INF **(b)** (corresponding)
‹*position/term*› equivalente

equivalent² *n* equivalente *m*

era /'ɪrə, 'erə ‖ 'ɪərə/ *n* era *f*, época *f*

eradicate /ɪ'rædəkeɪt ‖ ɪ'rædɪkeɪt/ *vt*
erradicar*

erase /ɪ'reɪs ‖ ɪ'reɪz/ *vt* borrar

eraser /ɪ'reɪsər ‖ ɪ'reɪzə(r)/ *n* goma *f* (de borrar)

erect¹ /ɪ'rekt/ *adj* **1** ‹*bearing/posture*› erguido
2 (Physiol) erecto

erect² *vt* ‹*altar/monument*› erigir* (frml),
levantar; ‹*barricade/wall*› levantar; ‹*tent*› armar

erection /ɪ'rekʃən/ *n* **1** (frml) **(a)** (of building,
monument) construcción *f*; (of barricade)
levantamiento *m* **(b)** (building) construcción *f*
2 (Physiol) erección *f*

erode /ɪ'rəʊd/ *vt* ‹*water/wind/waves*›
erosionar; ‹‹*acid*›› corroer*; ‹*confidence/faith*›
minar

erosion /ɪ'rəʊʒən/ *n* (by water, wind, waves)
erosión *f*; (by acid) corrosión *f*; (of confidence, power,
rights) menoscabo *m*

erotic /ɪ'rɑːtɪk ‖ ɪ'rɒtɪk/ *adj* erótico

err /er ‖ ɜː(r)/ *vi* (frml): **to ~ IN sth** equivocarse*
EN algo; **to ~ on the side of caution** pecar* de
cauteloso

errand /'erənd/ *n* mandado *m* (esp AmL), recado
m (Esp); **to run an ~ for sb** hacerle* un mandado
or (Esp) recado a algn

erratic /ɪ'rætɪk/ *adj* ‹*performance/work*›
desigual; ‹*person/moods*› imprevisible; ‹*course*›
errático

erroneous /ɪ'rəʊnɪəs/ *adj* erróneo

error /'erər ‖ 'erə(r)/ *n* error *m*

error message *n* (Comput) mensaje *m* de
error

erstwhile /'ɜːrsthwaɪl ‖ 'ɜːstwaɪl/ *adj* (liter)
antiguo

erudite /'erjədaɪt ‖ 'eruːdaɪt/ *adj* (frml) erudito

erupt /ɪ'rʌpt/ *vi* **(a)** ‹‹*volcano/geyser*›› entrar en
erupción **(b)** (break out) ‹‹*violence/fighting*››
estallar

eruption /ɪ'rʌpʃən/ *n* **(a)** (of volcano) erupción *f*
(b) (of violence) brote *m*; (of anger) estallido *m*

escalate /'eskəleɪt/ *vi* **(a)** ‹‹*fighting/violence/
dispute*›› intensificarse*; ‹‹*prices/claims*››
aumentar **(b) escalating** *pres p* ‹*dispute/
tension*› creciente

escalator /'eskəleɪtər ‖ 'eskəleɪtə(r)/ *n*
escalera *f* mecánica

escapade /'eskəpeɪd/ *n* aventura *f*

escape¹ /ɪ'skeɪp/ *vi* **1 (a)** (flee) escaparse;
‹‹*prisoner*›› fugarse*; **to ~ FROM sth** ‹*from
prison*› fugarse* DE algo; ‹*from cage/zoo*›
escaparse DE algo; ‹*from danger/routine*› escapar
DE algo **(b)** ‹‹*air/gas/water*›› escaparse **2** (from
accident, danger) salvarse
■ **~** *vt* ‹*pursuer/police*› escaparse de; ‹*capture*›

salvarse de; ‹*responsibilities/consequences*›
librarse de; **that detail had ~d my notice** se me
había escapado ese detalle

escape² *n* **(a)** (from prison) fuga *f*, huida *f*; **to
make one's ~** escaparse **(b)** (from accident, danger): **to
have a miraculous ~** salvarse milagrosamente;
there's no ~ no hay escapatoria posible **(c)** (of
gas, air, water) escape *m* **(d)** (from reality) evasión *f*
(e) (Comput): **press ~** pulse la tecla de escape;
‹*before n*› **~ key** tecla *f* de escape

escapist /ɪ'skeɪpəst ‖ ɪ'skeɪpɪst/ *adj* escapista

escort¹ /'eskɔːrt ‖ 'eskɔːt/ *n* **1** (guard) escolta *f*;
under police ~ escoltado por la policía
2 (companion) acompañante *mf*; (male companion)
(frml) acompañante *m*

escort² /ɪ'skɔːrt ‖ ɪ'skɔːt/ *vt* **(a)** (accompany)
acompañar; ‹*prisoner/intruder*› llevar **(b)** (for
protection) ‹*politician/procession/ship*› escoltar

Eskimo *n* (*pl* **-mos**) esquimal *mf*

esoteric /'esə'terɪk ‖ ,iːsəʊ'terɪk, ,esəʊ-/ *adj*
esotérico

espadrille /,espə'drɪl/ *n* alpargata *f*

especially /ɪ'speʃli/ *adv* especialmente;
everyone was bored, ~ me estaba todo el mundo
aburrido, sobre todo *or* especialmente yo

espionage /'espɪənɑːʒ/ *n* espionaje *m*

Esquire /ɪ'skwaɪr ‖ ɪ'skwaɪə(r)/ *n* (as title):
Frederick Saunders, ~ Sr. Frederick Saunders,
Sr Don Frederick Saunders (esp Esp)

essay /'eseɪ/ *n* (literary composition) ensayo *m*;
(academic composition) trabajo *m*, ensayo *m*;
(language exercise) composición *f*, redacción *f*

essence /'esns/ *n* **1 (a)** (central feature, quality)
esencia *f*; **in ~** en esencia **(b)** (personification)
personificación *f* **2** (Culin): **vanilla ~** esencia *f* de
vainilla

essential¹ /ɪ'sentʃəl ‖ ɪ'senʃəl/ *adj* esencial

essential² *n* **(a)** (sth indispensable) imperativo
m, elemento *m* esencial **(b) essentials** *pl n*
(fundamental features) puntos *mpl* esenciales

essentially /ɪ'sentʃəli ‖ ɪ'senʃəli/ *adv*
esencialmente; (indep) en lo esencial

EST (in US) = **Eastern Standard Time**

establish /ɪ'stæblɪʃ/ *vt* **(a)** ‹*colony/company*›
establecer*, fundar; ‹*committee/fund*› instituir*,
crear **(b)** ‹*procedure/diplomatic relations*›
establecer* **(c)** (prove) ‹*guilt/innocence*›
establecer*; (ascertain) ‹*motive/fact/identity*›
establecer*

established /ɪ'stæblɪʃt/ *adj* **1** ‹*expert/
company*› de reconocido prestigio; ‹*star*› de
renombre; ‹*reputation*› sólido; ‹*practice*›
establecido; ‹*fact*› comprobado **2** ‹*church/
religion*› oficial

establishment /ɪ'stæblɪʃmənt/ *n* **1 (a)** (of
colony, business) fundación *f*; (of committee) creación
f **(b)** (of criteria, relations) establecimiento *m* **2**
‹*club, hotel, shop*› establecimiento *m* **3 the
Establishment** la clase dirigente, el establishment

estate /ɪ'steɪt/ *n* **1 (a)** (land, property) finca *f*,
propiedad *f* **(b)** (group of buildings): **a private ~** un

AmC	América Central	Arg	Argentina	Cu	Cuba
AmL	América Latina	Bol	Bolivia	Ec	Ecuador
AmS	América del Sur	Chi	Chile	Esp	España
Andes	Región andina	CS	Cono Sur	Méx	México

Per	Perú
RPI	Río de la Plata
Ur	Uruguay
Ven	Venezuela

complejo habitacional, una urbanización (Esp), un fraccionamiento (Méx) **2** (Law) patrimonio *m*; (of deceased person) sucesión *f* **3** ~ **(car)** (BrE) ▶ STATION WAGON

estate agent *n* (BrE) agente *mf* de la propiedad inmobiliaria

esteem /ɪ'stiːm/ *n* estima *f*; **I hold him in high ~** lo aprecio mucho

esthetic /es'θetɪk ‖ ɪs'θetɪk/ *adj* estético

estimate¹ /'estəmeɪt ‖ 'estɪmeɪt/ *vt* **(a)** (calculate approximately) ⟨*price/number/age*⟩ calcular **(b) estimated** *past p* ⟨*cost/speed*⟩ aproximado; **~d time of arrival** hora *f* de llegada previsto **(c)** (form judgment of) ⟨*outcome/ability*⟩ juzgar*, valorar

estimate² /'estəmət ‖ 'estɪmət/ *n* **(a)** (rough calculation) cálculo *m* aproximado **(b)** (of costs) (Busn) presupuesto *m*

estimation /estə'meɪʃən ‖ estɪ'meɪʃən/ *n* **(a)** (judgment, opinion) juicio *m*, valoración *f* **(b)** (esteem): **to go up/down in sb's ~** ganarse/perder* la estima de algn

Estonia /es'təʊniə/ *n* Estonia *f*

Estonian /es'təʊniən/ *adj* estonio

estrange /ɪ'streɪndʒ/ *vt*: **his ~d wife** su mujer, de quien está separado

estuary /'estʃʊeri ‖ 'estjʊəri/ *n* (*pl* **-ries**) estuario *m*

etc (= et cetera) etc.

et cetera /ɪt'setrə/ *adv* etcétera

etch /etʃ/ *vt* (Art, Print) grabar

etching /'etʃɪŋ/ *n* grabado *m*

eternal /ɪ'tɜːrnl ‖ ɪ'tɜːnl/ *adj* eterno; (colloq) ⟨*noise/complaints*⟩ constante

eternity /ɪ'tɜːrnəti ‖ ɪ'tɜːnəti/ *n* (*pl* **-ties**) eternidad *f*

ethereal /ɪ'θɪriəl ‖ ɪ'θɪəriəl/ *adj* (liter) etéreo (liter)

ethical /'eθɪkəl/ *adj* ⟨*dilemma*⟩ ético; ⟨*code*⟩ de conducta

ethics /'eθɪks/ *n* **1** (Phil) (+ *sing vb*) ética *f* **2** (+ *pl vb*) (morality) ética *f*

Ethiopia /iːθi'əʊpiə/ *n* Etiopía *f*

Ethiopian /iːθi'əʊpiən/ *adj* etíope

ethnic /'eθnɪk/ *adj* ⟨*origin/group*⟩ étnico; ⟨*culture/art/vote*⟩ de las minorías étnicas; **an ~ minority** una minoría étnica; **~ cleansing** limpieza *f* étnica

etiquette /'etɪket/ *n* etiqueta *f*

etymology /etə'mɒlədʒi ‖ etɪ'mɒlədʒi/ *n* (*pl* **-gies**) etimología *f*

EU *n* = **European Union**

eucalyptus /juːkə'lɪptəs/ *n* (*pl* **-tuses**) eucalipto *m*

Eucharist /'juːkərəst ‖ 'juːkərɪst/ *n* Eucaristía *f*

eulogy /'juːlədʒi/ *n* (*pl* **-gies**) (liter) elogio *m*, loa *f* (liter)

eunuch /'juːnək/ *n* eunuco *m*

euphemism /'juːfəmɪzəm/ *n* eufemismo *m*

euphemistic /juːfə'mɪstɪk/ *adj* eufemístico

euphoria /juː'fɔːriə/ *n* euforia *f*

euphoric /juː'fɔːrɪk ‖ juː'fɒrɪk/ *adj* eufórico

euro /'jʊərəʊ ‖ 'jʊərəʊ/ *n* (*pl* **euros**) euro *m*

eurocheque /'jʊərəʊtʃek ‖ 'jʊərəʊtʃek/ *n* (BrE) eurocheque *m*

Europe /'jʊərəp ‖ 'jʊərəp/ *n* **(a)** (Geog) Europa *f* **(b)** (the EC) (BrE) Europa *f*

European¹ /'jʊərə'piːən ‖ jʊərə'piən/ *adj* europeo

European² *n* europeo, -pea *m,f*

European: ~ Commission *n* Comisión *f* Europea, Comisión *f* de las Comunidades Europeas; **~ (Economic) Community** *n* Comunidad *f* (Económica) Europea; **~ Union** *n* Unión *f* Europea

Eurozone /'jʊərəʊzəʊn/ *n* Eurozona *f*

euthanasia /'juːθə'neɪʒə ‖ juːθə'neɪziə/ *n* eutanasia *f*

evacuate /ɪ'vækjueɪt/ *vt* evacuar*

evacuation /ɪ'vækju'eɪʃən/ *n* evacuación *f*

evade /ɪ'veɪd/ *vt* ⟨*arrest/enemy/responsibility*⟩ eludir, evadir; ⟨*question/issue*⟩ eludir; ⟨*regulations/military service*⟩ eludir; ⟨*taxes*⟩ evadir

evaluate /ɪ'væljueɪt/ *vt* ⟨*ability/data*⟩ evaluar* **(b)** (value) (AmE) valorar, tasar, avaluar* (AmL)

evangelical /'iːvæn'dʒelɪkəl/ *adj* evangélico

evaporate /ɪ'væpəreɪt/ *vi* «*liquid/support/opposition*» evaporarse; «*hope/fear*» desvanecerse*; «*confidence*» esfumarse

evaporated milk /ɪ'væpəreɪtɪd ‖ ɪ'væpəreɪtɪd/ *n* leche *f* evaporada, leche *f* condensada (*sin azúcar*)

evasion /ɪ'veɪʒən/ *n* evasión *f*

evasive /ɪ'veɪsɪv/ *adj* ⟨*reply*⟩ evasivo

eve /iːv/ *n* (day, night before) (liter or journ) víspera *f*

even¹ /'iːvən/ *adv* **1** **(a)** hasta, incluso **(b)** (*with neg*): **he can't ~ sew a button on** no sabe ni pegar un botón; **you're not ~ trying** ni siquiera lo estás intentando **(c)** (*with comparative*) aún, todavía **2** (*in phrases*) **even if** aunque (+ *subj*); **even so** aun así; **even though** aun cuando, a pesar de que

even² *adj* **1** **(a)** (flat, smooth) ⟨*ground/surface*⟩ plano; ⟨*coat of paint*⟩ uniforme **(b)** (regular, uniform) ⟨*color/lighting*⟩ uniforme, parejo (AmL); ⟨*breathing*⟩ acompasado; ⟨*temperature*⟩ constante **2** (equal) ⟨*distribution*⟩ equitativo; **to break ~** recuperar los gastos; **to get ~** desquitarse; **I'll get ~ with her** me las pagará **3** (divisible by two) ⟨*number*⟩ par

even³ *vt* **1** (level) ⟨*surface*⟩ allanar, nivelar **2** (make equal) ⟨*score*⟩ igualar; ⟨*contest/situation*⟩ equilibrar

■ **even out** **1** [*v + o + adv, v + adv + o*] compensar, nivelar **2** [*v + adv*] compensarse, nivelarse

■ **even up** [*v + o + adv, v + adv + o*] ⟨*numbers/amounts*⟩ equilibrar

evening /'iːvnɪŋ/ *n* **1** **(a)** (after dark) noche *f*; (before dark) tarde *f*; **good ~** (early on) buenas tardes; (later) buenas noches; (*before n*) **~ meal** cena *f* **(b)** (period of entertainment) velada *f* (frml), noche *f* **2** **evenings** (*as adv*) (before dark) por la tarde, en la tarde (AmL), a la tarde *or* de tarde (RPl); (after dark) por la noche, de noche, en la noche (AmL)

evening: ~ **class** n clase f nocturna; ~ **dress** n **(a)** (for woman) traje m de noche **(b)** (formal wear) traje m de etiqueta

evenly /'iːvənli/ adv **1** (equally) ⟨distribute/divide⟩ equitativamente; ⟨spread⟩ uniformemente **2 (a)** (calmly) ⟨say/speak⟩ sin alterar la voz **(b)** (steadily) ⟨breathe⟩ con regularidad

event /ɪ'vent/ n **1 (a)** (happening, incident) acontecimiento m **(b)** (Sport) prueba f **2** (in phrases) **in the event: in the ~ of the reactor becoming overheated** en caso de que el reactor se recalentara; **in any event** en todo caso; **at all events** de cualquier modo

eventful /ɪ'ventfəl/ adj ⟨week⟩ lleno de incidentes; ⟨life⟩ rico en experiencias

eventuality /ɪˌventʃu'æləti/ n (pl -ties) eventualidad f

eventually /ɪ'ventʃuəli/ adv finalmente, al final

ever /'evər ‖ 'evə(r)/ adv **1** (at any time): **have you ~ visited London?** ¿has estado en Londres (alguna vez)?; **nobody ~ comes to see me** nunca viene nadie a verme; **hardly ~** casi nunca **2** (after comp or superl): **these are our worst ~ results** estos son los peores resultados que hemos tenido hasta ahora; **the situation is worse than ~** la situación está peor que nunca **3** (always, constantly) **as ever** como siempre; **ever since: ~ since we first saw her** desde que la vimos por primera vez; **we've been friends ~ since** somos amigos desde entonces; **for ever** para siempre **4** (as intensifier): **when will you ~ learn?** ¿cuándo vas a aprender?; **thanks ~ so much** (esp BrE colloq) muchísimas gracias

ever-: ~**green** adj ⟨tree/shrub⟩ de hoja perenne; ~**lasting** /'evər'læstɪŋ ‖ˌevə'lɑːstɪŋ/ adj eterno

every /'evri/ adj **1** (each): **~ room was searched** se registraron todas las habitaciones; **~ minute is precious** cada minuto es precioso; **she comes ~ month** viene todos los meses **2** (indicating recurrence) cada; **~ three days, ~ third day** cada tres días; **~ other day** un día sí, otro no, día por medio (CS, Per); **~ so often** cada tanto, de vez en cuando **3** (very great, all possible): **they have ~ confidence in us** confían plenamente en nosotros; **she made ~ effort to satisfy him** hizo lo indecible por satisfacerlo

everybody /'evrɪˌbɑːdi ‖'evrɪˌbɒdi/ pron todos; **is that ~?** ¿están todos?, ¿está todo el mundo?

everyday /'evrɪdeɪ/ adj (before n) ⟨occurrence/problems/activities⟩ de todos los días, cotidiano; ⟨suit/clothes⟩ de diario; ⟨expression⟩ corriente, de todos los días; ⟨life⟩ diario, cotidiano

everyone /'evrɪwʌn/ pron ▶ EVERYBODY

everything /'evriθɪŋ/ pron todo

everywhere /'evrihwer ‖'evrɪweə(r)/ adv ⟨be⟩ en todas partes; **I've looked ~ for it** lo he buscado por todas partes or por todos lados; **they go ~ by car** van a todos lados or a todas partes en coche

evict /ɪ'vɪkt/ vt ⟨tenant/squatter⟩ desahuciar, desalojar; ⟨demonstrators⟩ desalojar

eviction /ɪ'vɪkʃən/ n (of tenant, squatter) desalojo m, desahucio m

evidence /'evədəns ‖'evɪdəns/ n **1** (Law) **(a)** (proof) pruebas fpl **(b)** (testimony) testimonio m; **to give ~** declarar, prestar declaración **2** (sign, indication) indicio m, señal f

evident /'evədənt ‖'evɪdənt/ adj evidente

evidently /'evədəntli ‖'evɪdəntli/ adv **(a)** ⟨embarrassed/unsuitable⟩ claramente, obviamente **(b)** (indep) aparentemente, según parece

evil[1] /'iːvəl/ adj ⟨demon/wizard⟩ malvado; ⟨deeds/thoughts/character⟩ de gran maldad; ⟨influence⟩ maléfico; ⟨plan/suggestion⟩ diabólico; ⟨spirit⟩ maligno

evil[2] n mal m

evildoer /'iːvəl'duːər ‖'iːvəlˌduːə(r)/ n malhechor, -chora m,f

evocative /ɪ'vɑːkətɪv ‖ɪ'vɒkətɪv/ adj evocador

evoke /ɪ'vəʊk/ vt ⟨response/admiration/sympathy⟩ provocar*; ⟨memories/associations⟩ evocar*

evolution /'evə'luːʃən ‖ˌiːvə'luːʃən/ n evolución f

evolve /ɪ'vɑːlv ‖ɪ'vɒlv/ vi evolucionar

ewe /juː/ n oveja f (hembra)

ex- /'eks/ pref ex⟨-⟩; ~**wife** ex⟨-⟩esposa

exact[1] /ɪg'zækt/ adj **(a)** (precise) ⟨number/size/time/date⟩ exacto **(b)** (accurate) ⟨description/definition⟩ preciso

exact[2] vt ⟨promise⟩ arrancar*; **he ~ed his revenge** se vengó

exacting /ɪg'zæktɪŋ/ adj ⟨work/job⟩ que exige mucho; ⟨supervisor/employer⟩ exigente; ⟨standards/conditions⟩ riguroso

exactly /ɪg'zæktli/ adv ⟨measure/calculate⟩ exactamente; **at ~ six-thirty** a las seis y media en punto

exaggerate /ɪg'zædʒəreɪt/ vi/t exagerar

exaggeration /ɪg'zædʒə'reɪʃən/ n exageración f

exalt /ɪg'zɔːlt/ vt (fml) **(a)** (elevate) exaltar (frml), elevar **(b)** (praise) ensalzar*, exaltar (frml)

exam /ɪg'zæm/ n ▶ EXAMINATION 1

examination /ɪg'zæmə'neɪʃən ‖ɪgˌzæmɪ'neɪʃən/ n **1** (Educ) (fml) examen m **2 (a)** (inspection — of accounts) revisión f, inspección f; (— of passports) control m; (— by doctor) reconocimiento m, examen m, revisación f (RPl) **(b)** (study, investigation) examen m; **on closer ~** al examinarlo más de cerca

examine /ɪg'zæmən ‖ɪg'zæmɪn/ vt **1 (a)** (inspect) examinar; ⟨accounts⟩ inspeccionar, revisar; ⟨baggage⟩ registrar, revisar (AmL) **(b)** (Med, Dent) examinar, revisar (AmL) **(c)** (study, investigate) examinar, estudiar **2 (a)** (Educ) examinar **(b)** (Law) ⟨witness/accused⟩ interrogar*

examiner /ɪg'zæmənər ‖ɪg'zæmɪnə(r)/ n examinador, -dora m,f

example /ɪg'zæmpəl ‖ɪg'zɑːmpəl/ n **1** (specimen, sample) ejemplo m; **for ~** por ejemplo **2 (a)** (model) ejemplo m **(b)** (warning): **to make an ~ of sb** darle* un castigo ejemplar a algn

exasperated /ɪg'zæspəreɪtəd ‖ɪg'zæspəreɪtɪd/ adj exasperado

exasperating /ɪg'zæspəreɪtɪŋ/ adj exasperante

exasperation /ɪg'zæspə'reɪʃən/ n exasperación f

excavate /'ekskəveɪt/ *vt/i* excavar

excavation /ˌekskə'veɪʃən/ *n* excavación *f*

exceed /ɪk'si:d/ *vt* **(a)** (be greater than) exceder de **(b)** (go beyond) ‹*limit/minimum*› rebasar; ‹*expectations/hopes*› superar; ‹*powers*› (frml) excederse en

excel /ɪk'sel/ **-ll-** *vi* **to** ~ **AT/IN** sth destacar* EN algo
■ *v refl* **to** ~ **oneself** lucirse*

excellence /'eksələns/ *n* excelencia *f*

excellent /'eksələnt/ *adj* excelente; (Educ) sobresaliente

except /ɪk'sept/ *prep* **(a)** (apart from): ~ **(for)** menos, excepto, salvo **(b)** ~ **for** (if it weren't for) si no fuera por

exception /ɪk'sepʃən/ *n* **1** excepción *f* **2** (offense): **to take** ~ **to** sth ofenderse por algo

exceptional /ɪk'sepʃnəl ‖ɪk'sepʃənl/ *adj* excepcional

excerpt /'eksɜ:rpt ‖'eksɜ:pt/ *n* pasaje *m*

excess¹ /ɪk'ses/ *n* **1** (*no pl*) exceso *m* **2** (surplus) excedente *m*; **in** ~ **of** superior a

excess² /ɪk'ses ‖'ekses/ *adj*: ~ **baggage/weight** exceso *m* de equipaje/de peso

excessive /ɪk'sesɪv/ *adj* ‹*price/charges*› excesivo; ‹*demands/pressure/interest*› exagerado

exchange¹ /ɪks'tʃeɪndʒ/ *n* **1** **(a)** (of information, greetings, insults) intercambio *m*; (of prisoners, hostages) canje *m*; **in** ~ **for** sth a cambio de algo **(b)** (of students) intercambio *m* **(c)** (dialogue) intercambio *m* de palabras **(d)** (of currency) cambio *m* **2** (Telec) (telephone ~) central *f* telefónica

exchange² *vt* **(a)** (give in place of) **to** ~ sth **FOR** sth cambiar algo POR algo **(b)** ‹*information/addresses*› intercambiar(se); ‹*blows*› darse*; ‹*insults*› intercambiar; ‹*prisoners/hostages*› canjear

exchange rate *n* tasa *f* or (esp Esp) tipo *m* de cambio

Exchequer /'ekstʃekər ‖ɪks'tʃekə(r)/ *n* (in UK) **the** ~ el tesoro público, el erario público; *see also* CHANCELLOR A

excise /'eksaɪz/ *n* impuestos *mpl* internos

excitable /ɪk'saɪtəbəl/ *adj* excitable

excite /ɪk'saɪt/ *vt* **1** **(a)** (make happy, enthusiastic) entusiasmar; (make impatient, boisterous) ‹*children*› alborotar **(b)** (sexually) excitar **2** ‹*interest/admiration*› despertar*; ‹*envy/curiosity*› provocar*

excited /ɪk'saɪtəd ‖ɪk'saɪtɪd/ *adj* **(a)** (happy, enthusiastic) ‹*person*› entusiasmado, excitado; ‹*shouts*› de excitación *or* entusiasmo; **to get** ~ entusiasmarse **(b)** (nervous, worried) ‹*person*› excitado, agitado; ‹*voice/gesture*› vehemente, ansioso **(c)** (impatient, boisterous) ‹*children*› excitado, alborotado **(d)** (sexually) excitado

excitement /ɪk'saɪtmənt/ *n* (enthusiasm, happiness) excitación *f*, entusiasmo *m*; (agitation) agitación *f*, alboroto *m*

exciting /ɪk'saɪtɪŋ/ *adj* ‹*events/experience*› emocionante; ‹*film/story*› apasionante

exclaim /ɪk'skleɪm/ *vi/t* exclamar

exclamation /ˌeksklə'meɪʃən/ *n* exclamación *f*

exclamation point, (BrE) **exclamation mark** *n* signo *m* de admiración

exclude /ɪk'sklu:d/ *vt* excluir*

excluding /ɪk'sklu:dɪŋ/ *prep* sin incluir, excluyendo

exclusion /ɪk'sklu:ʒən/ *n* exclusión *f*

exclusive /ɪk'sklu:sɪv/ *adj* **1** ‹*rights/ownership/privileges*› exclusivo; ‹*story/interview*› en exclusiva **2** ‹*club/gathering*› selecto, exclusivo

excommunicate /ˌekskə'mju:nəkeɪt ‖ˌekskə'mju:nɪkeɪt/ *vt* excomulgar*

excrement /'ekskrəmənt ‖'ekskrɪmənt/ *n* (frml) excremento *m* (frml)

excruciating /ɪk'skru:ʃieɪtɪŋ/ *adj* ‹*pain*› atroz; ‹*boredom/embarrassment*› espantoso

excursion /ɪk'skɜ:rʒən ‖ɪk'skɜ:ʃən/ *n* excursión *f*

excuse¹ /ɪk'skju:z/ *vt* **1** **(a)** (forgive) ‹*mistake/misconduct*› disculpar, perdonar; ~ **me!** ¡perdón!; ~ **me, please** (con) permiso **(b)** (justify) ‹*conduct/rudeness*› excusar, justificar* **2** (release from obligation) disculpar; **to** ~ **sb (FROM)** sth dispensar a algn DE algo

excuse² /ɪk'skju:s/ *n* excusa *f*; **to make** ~**s** poner* excusas

ex-directory /'eksdaɪr'rektəri, -də- ‖ˌeksdaɪr'rektəri, -dɪ-/ *adj* (BrE Telec) que no figura en la guía telefónica, privado (Méx)

execute /'eksɪkju:t/ *vt* **1** (carry out, perform) ejecutar; ‹*duties*› desempeñar **2** (put to death) ejecutar

execution /ˌeksɪ'kju:ʃən/ *n* **1** (of order, plan) ejecución *f*; (of duties) desempeño *m* **2** (putting to death) ejecución *f*

executioner /'eksɪr'kju:ʃnər ‖ˌeksɪr'kju:ʃənə(r)/ *n* verdugo *m*

executive¹ /ɪg'zekjətɪv ‖ɪg'zekjʊtɪv/ *adj* **1** (Adm, Busn) (managerial) ejecutivo; ‹*washroom/suite/jet*› para ejecutivos; ‹*car/briefcase*› de ejecutivo **2** (Govt) ‹*powers/branch*› ejecutivo

executive² *n* **1** (manager) ejecutivo, -va *m,f* **2** **(a)** (branch of government) **the** ~ el (poder) ejecutivo **(b)** (~ committee) (esp BrE) comisión *f* directiva

executor /ɪg'zekjətər ‖ɪg'zekjʊtə(r)/ *n* albacea *mf*, testamentario, -ria *m,f*

exemplify /ɪg'zempləfaɪ ‖ɪg'zemplɪfaɪ/ *vt* **-fies, -fying, -fied** **(a)** (give example of) ejemplificar* **(b)** (be example of) demostrar*

exempt /ɪg'zempt/ *adj*: **to be** ~ **FROM** sth estar* exento DE algo

exemption /ɪg'zempʃən/ *n* ~ **FROM** sth exención *f* or exoneración *f* DE algo

exercise¹ /'eksərsaɪz ‖'eksəsaɪz/ *n* **1** (physical) ejercicio *m*; **to take** ~ hacer* ejercicio **2** (Sport, Educ) ejercicio *m*; (Mil) ejercicios *mpl*, maniobras *fpl* **3** (undertaking): **a public relations** ~ una operación de relaciones públicas **4** (use — of rights, power) (frml) ejercicio *m*; (— of caution, patience) uso *m*

exercise² *vt* **1** ‹*body*› ejercitar; ‹*dog*› pasear; ‹*horse*› ejercitar **2** ‹*power/control/right*› ejercer*; ‹*patience/tact*› hacer* uso de
■ ~ *vi* hacer* ejercicio

exercise book *n* cuaderno *m*

exert /ɪg'zɜːrt ‖ɪg'zɜːt/ vt ejercer*; ⟨force⟩ emplear

∎ v refl to ~ oneself hacer* un (gran) esfuerzo

exertion /ɪg'zɜːrʃən ‖ɪg'zɜːʃən/ n (often pl) esfuerzo m

exhale /eks'heɪl/ vi espirar

exhaust¹ /ɪg'zɔːst/ n (a) (~ pipe) tubo m or (RPl) caño m de escape, mofle m (AmC, Méx), exhosto m (Col) (b) (system) escape m, exhosto m (Col) (c) (fumes) gases mpl del tubo de escape

exhaust² vt agotar

exhausted /ɪg'zɔːstəd ‖ɪg'zɔːstɪd/ adj agotado

exhausting /ɪg'zɔːstɪŋ/ adj agotador

exhaustion /ɪg'zɔːstʃən/ n agotamiento m

exhaustive /ɪg'zɔːstɪv/ adj (frml) exhaustivo

exhibit¹ /ɪg'zɪbət ‖ɪg'zɪbɪt/ vt [1] ⟨goods/ paintings⟩ exponer* [2] (frml) ⟨skill/dexterity⟩ demostrar*; ⟨fear/courage⟩ mostrar*; ⟨symptoms⟩ presentar

exhibit² n (a) (in gallery, museum) objeto en exposición (b) (Law) documento u objeto que se exhibe en un juicio como prueba (c) (exhibition) (AmE) exposición f

exhibition /ˌeksə'bɪʃən ‖ˌeksɪ'bɪʃən/ n (of paintings, goods) exposición f; **to make an ~ of oneself** dar* un espectáculo

exhilarate /ɪg'zɪləreɪt/ vt (a) (make happy) llenar de júbilo (b) (stimulate) tonificar*

exhilarating /ɪg'zɪləreɪtɪŋ/ adj ⟨experience⟩ excitante; ⟨climate⟩ tonificante

exile¹ /'eksaɪl/ n (a) (person — voluntary) exiliado, -da m,f, exilado, -da m,f; (— expelled) desterrado, -da m,f, exiliado, -da m,f, exilado, -da m,f (b) (state) exilio m, destierro m

exile² vt desterrar*, exiliar, exilar

exist /ɪg'zɪst/ vi [1] (be real) existir [2] (survive) subsistir

existence /ɪg'zɪstəns/ n [1] (being) existencia f; **this is the only copy in ~** este es el único ejemplar existente [2] (life) vida f, existencia f

existing /ɪg'zɪstɪŋ/ adj existente

exit /'egzət ‖'eksɪt/ n salida f

exodus /'eksədəs/ n (no pl) éxodo m

exorbitant /ɪg'zɔːrbətənt ‖ɪg'zɔːbɪtənt/ adj (frml) ⟨price/rent⟩ exorbitante

exorcize /'eksɔːrsaɪz ‖'eksɔːsaɪz/ vt exorcizar*

exotic /ɪg'zaːtɪk ‖ɪg'zɒtɪk/ adj exótico

expand /ɪk'spænd/ vt [1] (enlarge) expandir; ⟨lungs⟩ ensanchar; ⟨chest⟩ desarrollar; ⟨horizons⟩ ampliar*; ⟨influence/role⟩ extender* [2] ⟨story/ summary⟩ ampliar*

∎ ~ vi (a) «metal/gas» expandirse; «elastic/ rubber band» expandirse (b) **expanding** pres p ⟨industry/market⟩ en expansión

expanse /ɪk'spæns/ n extensión f

expansion /ɪk'spæntʃən ‖ɪk'spænʃən/ n expansión f

expatriate /eks'peɪtrɪət ‖eks'pætrɪət/ n expatriado, -da m,f

expect /ɪk'spekt/ vt [1] (anticipate) esperar; **is he**

coming tonight? — I ~ so ¿va a venir esta noche? — supongo que sí; **we're not ~ing any trouble** no creemos que vaya a haber problemas; **to ~ to + INF: she ~s to win the match** espera ganar el partido

[2] (imagine) suponer*, imaginarse

[3] (await) esperar; **I'll ~ you at eight** te espero a las ocho; **to be ~ing a baby** esperar un bebé

[4] (require): **he ~ed me to pay** esperaba que yo pagara; **that's the least you'd ~** es lo menos que se puede esperar

∎ ~ vi (colloq): **she's ~ing** está esperando (familia)

expectancy /ɪk'spektənsi/ n expectación f; **life ~** esperanza f or expectativas fpl de vida

expectant /ɪk'spektənt/ adj expectante

expectation /'ekspek'teɪʃən/ n [1] (anticipation): **in ~ of victory** previendo la victoria; **an atmosphere of great ~** un ambiente de gran expectación [2] **expectations** pl (of inheritance, promotion) expectativas fpl

expedient¹ /ɪk'spiːdɪənt/ adj (frml) (usu pred) conveniente

expedient² n (frml) recurso m, expediente m (frml)

expedition /'ekspə'dɪʃən ‖ˌekspɪ'dɪʃən/ n expedición f

expel /ɪk'spel/ vt -ll- expulsar

expendable /ɪk'spendəbəl/ adj prescindible

expenditure /ɪk'spendɪtʃər ‖ɪk'spendɪtʃə(r)/ n (amount) gastos mpl; (spending) gasto m

expense /ɪk'spens/ n [1] (cost, outlay) gasto m; **they had a good laugh at my ~** se partieron de risa a costa mía; **at the ~ of sth/sb** (with the loss of) a expensas de algo/algn [2] **expenses** pl (Busn) (incidental costs) gastos mpl

expense account n cuenta f de gastos de representación

expensive /ɪk'spensɪv/ adj caro

experience¹ /ɪk'spɪrɪəns ‖ɪk'spɪərɪəns/ n experiencia f

experience² vt ⟨loss/setback/delays⟩ sufrir; ⟨difficulty⟩ tener*; ⟨change/improvement/pleasure/ pain⟩ experimentar

experienced /ɪk'spɪrɪənst ‖ɪk'spɪərɪənst/ adj ⟨secretary/chef⟩ con experiencia; ⟨driver⟩ experimentado

experiment¹ /ɪk'sperəmənt ‖ɪk'sperɪmənt/ n experimento m

experiment² vi **to ~ ON sth/sb** experimentar CON algo/algn; **to ~ WITH sth** experimentar CON algo

experimental /ɪk'sperə'mentl̩ ‖ɪk̩sperɪ'mentl̩/ adj experimental

expert¹ /'ekspɜːrt ‖'ekspɜːt/ n experto, -ta m,f

expert² adj experto; **~ witness** perito, -ta m,f

expertise /'ekspɜːr'tiːz ‖ˌekspɜː'tiːz/ n pericia f

expire /ɪk'spaɪr ‖ɪk'spaɪə(r)/ vi (run out) «visa/ passport/ticket» caducar*; «lease/contract» vencer*

expiry /ɪk'spaɪrɪ ‖ɪk'spaɪərɪ/ *n* vencimiento *m*, caducidad *f*

explain /ɪk'spleɪn/ *vt* explicar*
■ *v refl* **to ~ oneself** explicarse*
■ **explain away** [*v + o + adv, v + adv + o*] 〈*fact/ result*〉 encontrar* una explicación convincente para

explanation /ˌeksplə'neɪʃən/ *n* explicación *f*

explanatory /ɪk'splænətɔːri ‖ɪk'splænətri/ *adj* explicativo

explicit /ɪk'splɪsət ‖ɪk'splɪsɪt/ *adj* explícito; 〈*denial/refutation*〉 categórico

explode /ɪk'spləʊd/ *vi* (a) 《*gunpowder/bomb*》 estallar, hacer* explosión, explotar; 〈*vehicle*》 hacer* explosión; (with emotion) explotar, estallar (b) 《*population/costs*》 dispararse
■ ~ *vt* [1] 〈*bomb/dynamite*〉 explosionar, hacer* explotar *or* estallar [2] (discredit) 〈*theory*〉 rebatir; 〈*myth*〉 destruir*

exploit¹ /ɪk'splɔɪt/ *vt* explotar; 〈*situation/ relationship*〉 aprovecharse de

exploit² /'eksplɔɪt/ *n* hazaña *f*

exploitation /ˌeksplɔɪ'teɪʃən/ *n* explotación *f*

exploration /ˌeksplə'reɪʃən/ *n* exploración *f*

exploratory /ɪk'splɔːrətɔːri ‖ɪk'splɒrətəri/ *adj* 〈*talks*〉 preliminar; 〈*surgery*〉 exploratorio

explore /ɪk'splɔːr ‖ɪk'splɔː(r)/ *vt* 〈*territory/ town*〉 explorar; 〈*topic/possibility*〉 investigar*

explorer /ɪk'splɔːrər ‖ɪk'splɔːrə(r)/ *n* (a) (traveler) explorador, -dora *m,f* (b) **Explorer** (in US) boy scout *m* (mayor de 14 años)

explosion /ɪk'spləʊʒən/ *n* (of bomb, gas) explosión *f*, estallido *m*; (of anger) estallido *m*, explosión *f*

explosive¹ /ɪk'spləʊsɪv/ *adj* explosivo

explosive² *n* explosivo *m*

exponent /ɪk'spəʊnənt/ *n* (of idea, theory) defensor, -sora *m,f*; (of art style) exponente *mf*

export¹ /ek'spɔːt ‖ɪk'spɔːt/ *vt* exportar

export² /'ekspɔːt ‖'ekspɔːt/ *n* (a) (item exported) artículo *m or* producto *m* de exportación (b) (act of exporting) exportación *f*

exporter /ek'spɔːrtər ‖ɪk'spɔːtə(r)/ *n* exportador, -dora *m,f*

expose /ɪk'spəʊz/ *vt* [1] (lay bare) 〈*nerve/wire/ wound*〉 exponer*; **to ~ oneself to criticism** exponerse* a las críticas [2] (uncover) 〈*secret/ scandal*〉 poner* al descubierto, sacar* a la luz; 〈*inefficiency/weaknesses*〉 poner* en evidencia; 〈*criminal*〉 desenmascarar [3] (Phot) exponer*

exposition /ˌekspə'zɪʃən/ *n* exposición *f*

exposure /ɪk'spəʊʒər ‖ɪk'spəʊʒə(r)/ *n* [1] (a) (contact) **~ TO** sth exposición *f* A algo (b) (Med) congelación *f*; **to die from ~** morir* de frío [2] (a) (unmasking): **she was threatened with public ~** amenazaron con ponerla al descubierto (b) (publicity) publicidad *f* [3] (Phot) exposición *f*

expound /ɪk'spaʊnd/ *vt* (fml) exponer*

express¹ /ɪk'spres/ *vt* expresar

express² *n* (train) expreso *m*, rápido *m*; (bus) directo *m*

express³ *adj* [1] (fast) 〈*train*〉 expreso, rápido; 〈*bus*〉 directo; 〈*delivery/letter*〉 exprés *adj inv* [2] (specific) (fml) 〈*intention/wish*〉 expreso

expression /ɪk'spreʃən/ *n* expresión *f*

expressive /ɪk'spresɪv/ *adj* expresivo

expressly /ɪk'spreslɪ/ *adv* (fml) expresamente

expressway /ɪk'spresweɪ/ *n* (AmE) autopista *f*; (urban) vía *f* rápida

expropriate /eks'prəʊprɪeɪt/ *vt* expropiar

expulsion /ɪk'spʌlʃən/ *n* expulsión *f*

exquisite /ek'skwɪzət ‖'ekskwɪzɪt/ *adj* (a) 〈*dress/meal/taste*〉 exquisito; 〈*carving/brooch*〉 de exquisita factura; 〈*work/workmanship*〉 intrincado (b) 〈*pleasure*〉 infinito

ex-serviceman /'eks'sɜːrvəsmən ‖ˌeks'sɜːvɪsmən/ *n* (*pl* **-men** /-mən/) soldado (*or* marinero *etc*) *m* retirado

extend /ɪk'stend/ *vt* [1] (a) (stretch out) 〈*limbs/ wings/telescope*〉 extender*; 〈*rope/wire*〉 tender* (b) (lengthen) 〈*road/line/visit*〉 prolongar*; 〈*lease/ contract/deadline*〉 prorrogar* (c) (enlarge) 〈*house/ room*〉 ampliar*; 〈*range/scope/influence*〉 extender* [2] (offer) (fml): **to ~ an invitation to sb** invitar a algn; (of written invitations) cursarle invitación a algn (fml)
■ ~ *vi* (a) (stretch) 《*fence/property/influence*》 extenderse* (b) (in time) 《*talks*》 prolongarse* (c) (become extended) 《*ladder/antenna*》 extenderse*

extension /ɪk'stentʃən ‖ɪk'stenʃən/ *n* [1] (a) (of power, meaning) extensión *f* (b) (lengthening) prolongación *f*; (of deadline) prórroga *f*, extensión *f* [2] (to building) ampliación *f* [3] (Telec) (a) (line) extensión *f*, interno *m* (RPl), anexo *m* (Chi) (b) (telephone) supletorio *m*

extension cord, (BrE) **extension lead** *n* extensión *f*, alargador *m*, alargue *m* (RPl)

extensive /ɪk'stensɪv/ *adj* 〈*area/field*〉 extenso; 〈*knowledge*〉 vasto; 〈*experience/coverage*〉 amplio; 〈*search/inquiries*〉 exhaustivo; 〈*damage/repairs*〉 de consideración

extensively /ɪk'stensɪvlɪ/ *adv* (a) (widely): **he's traveled ~** ha viajado por todas partes; **this technique is used ~** esta técnica es de uso extendido (b) (thoroughly, at length) 〈*research/ investigate*〉 exhaustivamente

extent /ɪk'stent/ *n* [1] (size, area) extensión *f* [2] (range, degree — of knowledge) amplitud *f*; (— of problem) alcance *m*; **to some ~** hasta cierto punto; **to a large ~** en gran parte

extenuate /ɪk'stenjueɪt/ *vt* (fml) atenuar*; **extenuating circumstances** circunstancias *fpl* atenuantes, atentuantes *mpl or fpl*

exterior¹ /ek'stɪrɪər ‖ɪk'stɪərɪə(r)/ *adj* 〈*wall/ surface*〉 exterior

exterior² *n* exterior *m*

exterminate /ɪk'stɜːrməneɪt ‖ɪk'stɜːmɪneɪt/ *vt* exterminar

external /ek'stɜːrnl̩ ‖ɪk'stɜːnl̩/ *adj* (a) (exterior) 〈*appearance/sign*〉 externo, exterior; 〈*wall*〉 exterior; 〈*wound/treatment*〉 externo (b) 〈*aid/ influence*〉 del exterior; 〈*pressure/evidence*〉 externo (c) (foreign) 〈*affairs/trade/policy*〉 exterior

extinct /ɪk'stɪŋkt/ *adj* 〈*animal/species*〉 extinto, desaparecido; 〈*volcano*〉 extinto, apagado

extinction /ɪk'stɪŋkʃən/ *n* extinción *f*

extinguish /ɪk'stɪŋgwɪʃ/ *vt* (a) 〈*fire*〉 extinguir*; 〈*candle/cigar*〉 apagar* (b) (liter) 〈*hope/ memory*〉 apagar* (liter); 〈*passion/life*〉 extinguir* (liter)

extinguisher /ɪk'stɪŋgwɪʃər ‖ɪk'stɪŋgwɪʃə(r)/ *n* (fire ~) extinguidor *m* (AmL), extintor *m* (Esp)

extortion /ɪk'stɔːrʃən ‖ɪk'stɔːʃən/ n extorsión f

extortionate /ɪk'stɔːrʃənət ‖ɪk'stɔːʃənət/ adj ⟨fee/price⟩ abusivo; ⟨demand⟩ excesivo

extra¹ /'ekstrə/ adj (a) (additional) ⟨before n⟩ de más; **we need ~ staff** necesitamos más personal; **at no ~ charge** sin cargo adicional; **they organized three ~ flights** organizaron tres vuelos adicionales; **~ time** (in soccer) prórroga f (b) (especial) ⟨before n⟩ ⟨care/caution⟩ especial

extra² adv (a) (as intensifier): **~ long** extralargo; **I worked ~ hard** trabajé más que nunca (b) (more): **to charge ~ for sth** cobrar algo aparte

extra³ n ① (additional payment or expense) extra m; **optional ~s** (Auto) equipamiento m opcional, extras mpl ② (Cin) extra mf

extract¹ /ɪk'strækt/ vt extraer*

extract² /'ekstrækt/ n ① (excerpt) fragmento m ② (concentrate) extracto m

extraction /ɪk'strækʃən/ n ① (a) (Dent) extracción f (b) (of mineral, juice) extracción f ② (ancestry) extracción f; **of Polish ~** de extracción polaca

extradite /'ekstrədaɪt/ vt extraditar

extradition /ˌekstrə'dɪʃən/ n extradición f; ⟨before n⟩ ⟨order/treaty⟩ de extradición

extraordinary /ɪk'strɔːrdneri ‖ɪk'strɔːdņri/ adj ① (exceptional) extraordinario; (very odd) ⟨sight/appearance⟩ insólito; (incredible) increíble ② (frml) (Adm, Govt) ⟨powers/meeting⟩ extraordinario

extrapolate /ɪk'stræpəleɪt/ vt (frml) extrapolar

extrasensory /'ekstrə'sensəri/ adj extrasensorial; **~ perception** percepción f extrasensorial

extravagance /ɪk'strævəgəns/ n ① (a) (lavishness, wastefulness) despilfarro m, derroche m (b) (luxury) lujo m ② (of gestures, dress) extravagancia f; (of claim, story) lo insólito

extravagant /ɪk'strævəgənt/ adj (a) (lavish, wasteful) ⟨person⟩ derrochador, despilfarrador; ⟨lifestyle⟩ de lujo (b) ⟨claim/notions⟩ insólito; ⟨praise/compliments⟩ exagerado; ⟨behavior/dress/gesture⟩ extravagante

extravaganza /ɪk'strævə'gænzə/ n gran espectáculo m (realizado con alarde de color, fantasía y dinero)

extreme¹ /ɪk'striːm/ adj (a) (very great) ⟨poverty/caution/urgency⟩ extremo; ⟨annoyance/relief⟩ enorme; ⟨heat⟩ extremado (b) (not moderate) ⟨action/measure⟩ extremo; ⟨opinion⟩ extremista (c) (outermost) ⟨before n⟩: **in the ~ north/south** en la zona más septentrional/meridional

extreme² n extremo m; **~s of temperature** temperaturas fpl extremas

extremely /ɪk'striːmli/ adv (as intensifier) sumamente; **it's ~ difficult** es dificilísimo

extremist /ɪk'striːməst ‖ɪk'striːmɪst/ n extremista mf

extremity /ɪk'streməti/ n (pl **-ties**) ① (a) (farthest point) extremo m (b) **extremities** pl (Anat) extremidades fpl ② (critical degree, situation) (frml) extremo m

extricate /'ekstrəkeɪt ‖'ekstrɪkeɪt/ vt sacar* (con dificultad)

extrovert¹ /'ekstrəvɜːrt ‖'ekstrəvɜːt/ adj extrovertido

extrovert² /'ekstrəvɜːrt ‖'ekstrəvɜːt/ n extrovertido, -da m,f

exude /ɪg'zuːd ‖ɪg'zjuːd/ vt ⟨resin/fluid⟩ exudar; ⟨charm/confidence⟩ emanar

exult /ɪg'zʌlt/ vi (frml) exultar (frml)

exultation /'egzʌl'teɪʃən/ n (frml) exultación f (frml)

eye¹ /aɪ/ n ① (a) (Anat) ojo m; **as far as the ~ can/could see** hasta donde alcanza/alcanzaba la vista; **I can't believe my ~s** si no lo veo, no lo creo; **to see ~ to ~ with sb** (usu with neg) estar* de acuerdo con algn; **to be up to one's ~s in sth** estar* hasta aquí de algo (fam) (b) (look, gaze) mirada f; **before my very ~s** ante mis propios ojos; **nothing caught my ~ in the store** no vi nada que me llamara la atención en la tienda; **to keep an ~ on sth/sb** vigilar or cuidar algo/a algn (c) (attention): **the company has been in the public ~ a lot recently** últimamente se ha hablado mucho de la compañía; **to have one's ~ on sth** echarle el ojo a algo (fam) (d) (ability to judge) ojo m; **to have an ~ for design** tener* ojo para el diseño ② (a) (of needle) ojo m (b) (of hurricane, storm) ojo m (c) (in potato) ojo m

eye² vt ⟨pres p **eying** or (BrE) **eyeing**⟩ mirar

eye: ~ball /'aɪbɔːl/ n globo m ocular; **~brow** n ceja f; **to raise one's ~brows** arquear las cejas; **to raise one's ~brows at sth** asombrarse ante algo; **~catching** adj llamativo; **~drops** pl n colirio m

eyeful /'aɪfʊl/ n: **I got an ~ of dust** se me llenó el ojo de polvo

eye: ~glasses pl n (AmE) gafas fpl, anteojos mpl (esp AmL), lentes mpl (esp AmL); **~lash** n pestaña f

eyelet /'aɪlət ‖'aɪlɪt/ n ojete m

eye: ~lid n párpado m; **~liner** n delineador m (de ojos); **~opener** n (colloq) (no pl) revelación f; **~ shadow** n sombra f de ojos; **~sight** n vista f; **~sore** n monstruosidad f, adefesio m; **~strain** n fatiga f visual; **~wash** n colirio m; **it's a lot of ~wash** (colloq) es un cuento chino (fam); **~witness** /'aɪ'wɪtnəs ‖'aɪwɪtnɪs/ n testigo mf ocular

Ff

F, f /ef/ *n* **(a)** (letter) F, f *f* **(b)** (Mus) fa *m*
F (= **Fahrenheit**) F
fa /fɑ:/ *n* (Mus) fa *m*
FA *n* (in UK) = **Football Association**
fable /'feɪbəl/ *n* fábula *f*
fabric /'fæbrɪk/ *n* **(a)** (Tex) tela *f* **(b)** (of building, society) estructura *f*
fabricate /'fæbrɪkeɪt/ *vt* **(a)** (invent) inventar(se) **(b)** (manufacture) fabricar*
fabulous /'fæbjələs ǁ'fæbjʊləs/ *adj* **(a)** (wonderful) (colloq) magnífico **(b)** (imaginary) fabuloso
facade, façade /fə'sɑ:d/ *n* fachada *f*
face¹ /feɪs/ *n* **1** (of person, animal) cara *f*, rostro *m*; **a new ∼** una cara nueva; **in the ∼ of stiff opposition** en medio de una fuerte oposición; **to fall flat on one's ∼** caerse* de bruces; **to keep a straight ∼: I could hardly keep a straight ∼** casi no podía aguantarme (de) la risa; **to make** *o* (BrE also) **pull a ∼** poner* mala cara; **to put a brave ∼ on it** poner(le)* al mal tiempo buena cara; **to sb's ∼** *a* or en la cara
2 (a) (appearance, nature) *(no pl)* fisonomía *f*; **on the ∼ of it** aparentemente **(b)** (dignity): **to lose ∼** desprestigiarse; **to save ∼** guardar las apariencias
3 (of coin, medal, solid) cara *f*; (of clock, watch) esfera *f*, carátula *f* (Méx)
4 (of cliff) pared *f*; **to disappear off the ∼ of the earth** desaparecer* de la faz de la tierra
face² *vt* **1** (be opposite): **she turned to ∼** him se volvió hacia él; **the hotel ∼s the sea** el hotel está frente al mar
2 (confront) enfrentarse a; **to be ∼d with sth** estar* *o* verse* frente a algo
3 (a) (be presented with) *(problem/increase)* enfrentarse a **(b)** (bear): **I can't ∼ going through all that again** no podría volver a pasar por todo eso; **I can't ∼ food first thing in the morning** no puedo ni oler la comida temprano por la mañana
■ **∼** *vi*: **the house ∼s north** la casa está orientada al norte; **I was facing the other way** miraba para el otro lado
■ **face up to** [*v* + *adv* + *prep* + *o*] afrontar
face: ∼cloth, (BrE also) **∼ flannel** *n* toallita *f* *(para lavarse)*; **∼ lift** *n* lifting *m*, estiramiento *m* (facial); **the building was given a ∼ lift** remozaron el edificio; **∼ pack** *n* mascarilla *f* *(de belleza)*
facet /'fæsət ǁ'fæsɪt/ *n* faceta *f*
facetious /fə'si:ʃəs/ *adj* burlón
face: ∼ to ∼ *adv* cara a cara; **∼ value** *n* valor *m* nominal; **to take sb/sth at ∼ value: I took her/what she said at ∼ value** me fie de ella/yo me creí lo que dijo
facial /'feɪʃəl/ *adj* facial
facile /'fæsaɪl ǁ'fæsaɪl/ *adj* superficial, simplista
facilitate /fə'sɪləteɪt ǁfə'sɪlɪteɪt/ *vt* (fml) facilitar
facility /fə'sɪləti/ *n* (*pl* **-ties**) **1 facilities** *pl*:

facilities for the disabled instalaciones *fpl* para minusválidos; **the hotel has conference facilities** el hotel dispone de sala(s) de conferencia **2** (building) (AmE) complejo *m*, centro *m*
-facing /'feɪsɪŋ/ *suff*: **north/south∼** que da al norte/sur
facsimile /fæk'sɪməli/ *n* facsímil(e) *m*
fact /fækt/ *n* **1** (sth true) hecho *m*; **hard ∼s** datos *mpl* concretos; **to face (the) ∼s** aceptar la realidad **2** (reality): **this novel is based on ∼** esta novela está basada en hechos reales; **in ∼** de hecho, en realidad; **the ∼ of the matter is (that)** … el hecho es que …
fact: ∼-finding /'fækt,faɪndɪŋ/ *adj* (*before n*) de investigación, investigador; **∼ sheet** *n* resumen *m* de datos esenciales
faction /'fækʃən/ *n* facción *f*
factor /'fæktər ǁ'fæktə(r)/ *n* factor *m*
factory /'fæktri, -təri/ *n* (*pl* **-ries**) fábrica *f*
factory: ∼ farming *n* (BrE) cría *f* intensiva; **∼ ship** *n* buque *m* factoría
factual /'fæktʃuəl/ *adj* *(account)* que se atiene a los hechos
faculty /'fækəlti/ *n* (*pl* **-ties**) **1** (sense) facultad *f* **2** (Educ) **(a)** (of university, college) facultad *f* **(b)** (academic personnel) (AmE) cuerpo *m* docente
fad /fæd/ *n* moda *f* pasajera
fade /feɪd/ *vi* **1** *(color)* apagarse*; *(fabric)* perder* color, desteñirse* **2 (a)** (disappear) *(hope/memories)* desvanecerse*; *(beauty)* marchitarse; *(interest)* decaer*; *(sound)* debilitarse **(b)** *(flower/plant)* ajarse
■ **∼** *vt* *(fabric)* desteñir*, hacer* perder el color a
■ **fade away** [*v* + *adv*] irse* apagando
faded /'feɪdəd ǁ'feɪdɪd/ *adj* *(color)* apagado; *(fabric)* desteñido
faeces /'fi:si:z/ *pl n* (fml) ► FECES
fag /fæg/ *n* **1** (male homosexual) (AmE sl & pej) maricón *m* (fam & pey) **2** (cigarette) (BrE colloq) cigarrillo *m*, pitillo *m* (fam)
fah /fɑ:/ *n* (BrE Mus) fa *m*
Fahrenheit /'færənhaɪt/ *adj* Fahrenheit *adj inv*
fail¹ /feɪl/ *vi* **1** (not succeed) *(marriage/business/plan)* fracasar; **if all else ∼s** como último recurso; **he ∼ed to live up to our expectations** no dio todo lo que se esperaba de él
2 (a) *(brakes/lights)* fallar **(b)** *(crop)* perderse*, malograrse **(c) failing** *pres p*: **he could no longer read because of his ∼ing eyesight** la vista se le había deteriorado tanto que ya no podía leer; **he retired because of ∼ing health** se retiró porque su salud se había deteriorado mucho
3 (in exam) ser* reprobado (AmL), suspender (Esp)
■ **∼** *vt* **1 (a)** *(exam)* no pasar, ser* reprobado en ⋯

(AmL), suspender (Esp), reprobar* (Méx), perder* (Col, Ur), salir* mal en (Chi) **(b)** ⟨*student*⟩ reprobar* *or* (Esp) suspender
2 (let down): **his courage ~ed him** le faltó valor; **words ~ me!** ¡es el colmo!

fail² *n* 1 (in exam, test) (BrE) reprobado *m or* (Esp) suspenso *m or* (RPl) aplazo *m* 2 **without ~** sin falta

failing¹ /'feɪlɪŋ/ *n* defecto *m*

failing² *prep:* ~ **that, try bleach** si eso no resulta, prueba con lejía

fail-safe /'feɪlseɪf/ *adj* ⟨*mechanism*⟩ de seguridad

failure /'feɪljər ‖ 'feɪljə(r)/ *n* (unsuccessful thing, act, person) fracaso *m*; **engine ~** falla *f* mecánica *or* (Esp) fallo *m* mecánico; **power ~** apagón *m*; **heart ~** insuficiencia *f* cardíaca; **~ to carry out orders** el incumplimiento de las órdenes

faint¹ /feɪnt/ *adj* **-er, -est** ⟨*line*⟩ apenas visible; ⟨*light*⟩ débil; ⟨*noise*⟩ apenas perceptible; ⟨*hope/ smile*⟩ ligero; **I feel ~** estoy mareado; **I haven't the ~est** (idea) (colloq) no tengo la más mínima idea

faint² *vi* desmayarse

faint³ *n* desmayo *m*

faintly /'feɪntli/ *adv* **(a)** (barely perceptibly) ⟨*see/ hear*⟩ apenas; ⟨*shine*⟩ débilmente **(b)** (slightly) ⟨*amused*⟩ ligeramente; ⟨*amusing/ridiculous*⟩ algo

fair¹ /fer ‖ feə(r)/ *adj* **-er, -est** 1 (just) ⟨*person/ decision*⟩ justo; ⟨*contest/election*⟩ limpio; **~ enough** bueno, está bien; **I've had my ~ share of problems recently** ya he tenido bastantes problemas últimamente; **~ and square:** he won **~ and square** ganó en buena ley 2 ⟨*hair*⟩ rubio, güero (Méx), mono (Col), catire (Ven); ⟨*skin*⟩ blanco 3 (beautiful) (liter) hermoso, bello 4 **(a)** (quite good) ⟨*work*⟩ pasable; **we have a ~ chance of winning** tenemos bastantes posibilidades de ganar **(b)** (considerable) (*before n*) ⟨*number/ amount*⟩ bueno 5 (Meteo): **the weather tomorrow will be ~** mañana va a hacer buen tiempo

fair² *adv* (impartially) ⟨*play*⟩ limpio, limpiamente

fair³ *n* 1 (market) feria *f*; (trade ~) feria *f* industrial/comercial 2 (funfair) (BrE) feria *f*

fair: ~ground *n* (funfair) (BrE) feria *f*; (permanent) parque *m* de diversiones *or* (Esp) atracciones; **~-haired** /'fer'herd ‖ ,feə'heəd/ *adj* (BrE) rubio, güero (Méx), mono (Col), catire (Ven)

fairly /'ferli ‖ 'feəli/ *adv* 1 (justly) ⟨*play*⟩ limpio; ⟨*judge*⟩ con imparcialidad; ⟨*divide*⟩ equitativamente 2 (moderately) bastante; **I'm ~ sure** estoy casi segura

fairness /'fernəs ‖ 'feənɪs/ *n* imparcialidad *f*; **in all ~** sinceramente

fair: ~ play *n* juego *m* limpio; **~-sized** /'fer'saɪzd ‖ ,feə'saɪzd/ *adj* (*before n*) bastante grande

fairy /'feri ‖ 'feəri/ *n* (*pl* **-ries**) hada *f*‡

fairy: ~ godmother *n* hada *f*‡ madrina; **~land** *n* el país de las hadas; **~ story, ~ tale** *n* cuento *m* de hadas

faith /feɪθ/ *n* 1 (trust) confianza *f*; **to have ~ IN sb/sth** tener* confianza *or* fe EN algn/algo 2 (Relig) fe *f*

faithful /'feɪθfəl/ *adj* fiel

faithfully /'feɪθfəli/ *adv* **(a)** (in letters): **yours ~** (esp BrE) (le saluda) atentamente **(b)** ⟨*serve/ record*⟩ fielmente

faith healer /'hiːlər ‖ 'hiːlə(r)/ *n* curandero, -ra *m,f*

fake¹ /feɪk/ *n* (object) falsificación *f*; (person) farsante *mf*

fake² *adj* ⟨*jewel/document*⟩ falso; ⟨*fur*⟩ sintético

fake³ *vt* ⟨*document/signature*⟩ falsificar*; ⟨*results/evidence*⟩ falsear
■ ~ *vi* fingir*

falcon /'fælkən ‖ 'fɔːlkən/ *n* halcón *m*

Falkland Islands /'fɔːlklənd/, **Falklands** /'fɔːlkləndz/ *pl n* **the ~ ~,the ~** las (Islas) Malvinas

fall¹ /fɔːl/ *n* 1 (tumble, collapse) caída *f* 2 (autumn) (AmE) otoño *m* 3 (decrease): **a ~ in temperature** un descenso de (las) temperaturas; **a ~ in prices** una bajada de precios 4 (of snow) nevada *f*; (of rocks) desprendimiento *m* 5 **falls** *pl* (waterfall) cascada *f*; (higher) catarata *f*

fall² (*past* **fell**; *past p* **fallen**) *vi* 1 **(a)** (tumble) caerse*; **I fell over a piece of wood** tropecé con un trozo de madera; **I fell down the stairs** me caí por la escalera **(b)** (descend) «*night/rain*» caer* 2 «*temperature/price*» bajar; **his face fell** puso cara larga 3 (be captured, defeated) **to ~** (TO **sb**) ⟨*city/ country*⟩ caer* (en manos de algn) 4 (pass into specified state): **to ~ ill** *o* (esp AmE) **sick** caer* *or* (Esp tb) ponerse* enfermo, enfermarse (AmL); **to ~ silent** callarse 5 (land): **Christmas ~s on a Thursday this year** este año Navidad cae en (un) jueves; **the burden will ~ on the poor** los pobres serán los que sufrirán la carga
■ **fall apart** [*v* + *adv*] «*clothing*» deshacerse*; «*system*» venirse* abajo; «*relationship*» irse* a pique
■ **fall back** [*v* + *adv*] «*troops*» replegarse*
■ **fall back on** [*v* + *adv* + *prep* + *o*] ⟨*one's parents*⟩ recurrir a; ⟨*resources*⟩ echar* mano de
■ **fall behind** [*v* + *adv*] [*v* + *prep* + *o*] (in class, race) rezagarse*, quedarse atrás; **to ~ behind WITH sth** ⟨*with payments*⟩ atrasarse EN algo
■ **fall down** [*v* + *adv*] «*person/tree*» caerse*; «*house/wall*» venirse* abajo
■ **fall for** [*v* + *prep* + *o*] **(a)** (be attracted to) ⟨*man/ woman*⟩ enamorarse de **(b)** (be deceived by) ⟨*trick/ story*⟩ tragarse* (fam)
■ **fall in** [*v* + *adv*] **(a)** (tumble in) caerse* (*a un pozo, al agua etc*) **(b)** (collapse) «*roof*» venirse* abajo **(c)** (form ranks) (Mil) formar filas
■ **fall off** [*v* + *adv*] **(a)** (tumble down) caerse* (*de una bicicleta, un caballo etc*) **(b)** (break off) «*button/handle*» caerse* **(c)** (decline) «*production/attendance*» decaer*

■ **fall out** [*v* + *adv*] **(a)** (drop out) caerse* **(b)** (break ranks) (Mil) romper* filas **(c)** (quarrel) «*friends*» pelearse

■ **fall over** [*v* + *adv*] «*person/object*» caerse*

■ **fall through** [*v* + *adv*] (fail) no salir* adelante

fallacy /'fæləsi/ *n* (*pl* **-cies**) falacia *f*

fallen /'fɔːlən/ *past p of* FALL²

fallible /'fæləbəl/ *adj* falible

falling /'fɔːlɪŋ/**: ~-off** /'fɔːlɪŋ'ɔːf ‖ˌfɔːlɪŋ'ɒf/ *n* ▶ FALLOFF; **~-out** /'fɔːlɪŋ'aʊt/ *n* (AmE) pelea *f*

falloff /'fɔːlɔːf ‖ 'fɔːlɒf/ *n* (*no pl*) (in speed) disminución *f*

Fallopian tube /fə'ləʊpiən/ *n* trompa *f* de Falopio

fallout /'fɔːlaʊt/ *n* lluvia *f* radiactiva; (*before n*) **~ shelter** refugio *m* antinuclear

fallow /'fæləʊ/ *adj* «*land*» en barbecho

false /fɔːls/ *adj* «*statement/pride/name*» falso; «*belief*» erróneo; «*eyelashes/fingernails*» postizo; **true or ~?** ¿verdadero o falso?

false alarm *n* falsa alarma *f*

falsehood /'fɔːlshʊd/ *n* (fml) falsedad *f*

falsely /'fɔːlsli/ *adv* «*accuse*» falsamente

false: ~ start *n* (Sport) salida *f* en falso; (to career, speech) intento *m* fallido; **~ teeth** *pl n* dentadura *f* postiza

falsify /'fɔːlsəfaɪ ‖ 'fɔːlsɪfaɪ/ *vt* **-fies, -fying, -fied** «*accounts/evidence*» falsificar*; «*truth*» falsear

falter /'fɔːltər ‖ 'fɔːltə(r)/ *vi* **(a)** (speak hesitantly) titubear, balbucear **(b)** «*enthusiasm/interest*» decaer*; «*courage/resolve*» flaquear

fame /feɪm/ *n* fama *f*

familiar /fə'mɪljər ‖ fə'mɪliə(r)/ *adj* **(a)** (well-known) «*sound/face*» familiar, conocido; **the name sounds ~** el nombre me suena **(b)** (having knowledge of) **to be ~ WITH sth/sb** estar* familiarizado CON algo/algn

familiarity /fəˌmɪli'ærəti/ *n* (*pl* **-ties**) **(a)** (knowledge): **she claimed extensive ~ with the method** dijo estar muy familiarizada con el método; **some ~ with computers would be an asset** se valorará la experiencia previa con computadoras **(b)** (of person, book, landscape) familiaridad *f*; **~ breeds contempt** lo que se tiene no se aprecia

familiarize /fə'mɪljəraɪz ‖ fə'mɪliəraɪz/ *vt* **to ~ oneself WITH sth** familiarizarse* CON algo

family /'fæmli, 'fæməli ‖ 'fæmɪli, 'fæmli/ *n* (*pl* **-lies**) (relatives) familia *f*; (*before n*) «*business*» familiar; «*fortune*» de la familia

family: ~ planning *n* planificación *f* familiar; **~ tree** *n* árbol *m* genealógico

famine /'fæmən ‖ 'fæmɪn/ *n* hambruna *f*

famished /'fæmɪʃt/ *adj* famélico; **I'm ~!** (colloq) ¡estoy muerto de hambre! (fam)

famous /'feɪməs/ *adj* famoso

fan¹ /fæn/ *n* **1** (hand-held) abanico *m*; (mechanical) ventilador *m* **2** (of group, actor) fan *mf*; (of football team) hincha *mf*

fan² -nn- *vt* «*person*» abanicar*; «*interest/curiosity*» avivar

■ **fan out** [*v* + *adv*] «*searchers*» abrirse* en abanico

fanatic /fə'nætɪk/ *n* fanático, -ca *m,f*

fanatical /fə'nætɪkəl/ *adj* «*believer*» fanático; «*belief*» ciego

fan belt *n* correa *f* or (Méx) banda *f* del ventilador

fanciful /'fænsɪfəl/ *adj* **(a)** (impractical) «*idea*» extravagante **(b)** (elaborate) «*design*» imaginativo

fan club *n* club *m* de fans

fancy¹ /'fænsi/ *vt* **fancies, fancying, fancied** (esp BrE) **1** (expressing surprise) (*in interj*): (just) **~ that!** ¡pues mira tú!; **~ meeting them here!** ¡qué casualidad encontrarnos con ellos aquí! **2** (feel desire for) (colloq): **I really ~ an ice-cream** ¡qué ganas de tomarme un helado!; **do you ~ going to see a movie?** ¿tienes ganas de ir al cine? **3** (be physically attracted to) (colloq): **I ~ her/him** me gusta mucho **4** (imagine) (fml) **to ~ (THAT): she fancied she saw his face in the crowd** creyó ver su cara entre la multitud

fancy² *adj* **-cier, -ciest (a)** (elaborate) elaborado **(b)** (superior) (pej) «*hotel*» de campanillas; «*car*» lujoso; «*ideas*» extravagante

fancy³ *n* (*pl* **-cies**) **1** (liking) (*no pl*): **to take a ~ to sb: she seems to have taken a ~ to you** parece que le has caído en gracia; **to tickle sb's ~: the idea rather tickled my ~** la idea me resultó atractiva **2** (imagination) imaginación *f*

fancy: ~ dress *n* (BrE) disfraz *m*; (*before n*) **~-dress party** fiesta *f* de disfraces; **~-free** /'fænsi'friː/ *adj* ▶ FOOTLOOSE; **~ goods** *pl n* (Busn) artículos *mpl* para regalo

fanfare /'fænfer ‖ 'fænfeə(r)/ *n* fanfarria *f*

fang /fæŋ/ *n* (of dog) colmillo *m*; (of snake) diente *m*

fan heater *n* electroconvector *m*

fanny /'fæni/ *n* (*pl* **-nies**) (buttocks) (AmE sl) culo *m* (fam: en algunas regiones vulg), traste *m* (CS fam), poto *m* (Chi, Per fam)

fantasize /'fæntəsaɪz/ *vi* fantasear

fantastic /fæn'tæstɪk/ *adj* **(a)** (wonderful) (colloq) fantástico **(b)** (incredible) «*story*» absurdo

fantasy /'fæntəsi/ *n* (*pl* **-sies**) **(a)** (unreality) fantasía *f* **(b)** (daydream) sueño *m*

FAQ *pl n* (Comput) = **frequently asked questions**

far¹ /fɑːr ‖ fɑː(r)/ *adv* **1** (*comp* **further** or **farther**; *superl* **furthest** or **farthest**) **(a)** (in distance) lejos; **how ~ is it?** ¿a qué distancia está?; **~ away in the distance** a lo lejos **(b)** (in progress): **the plans are now quite ~ advanced** los planes están ya muy avanzados; **that girl will go ~** esa chica va a llegar lejos **(c)** (in time): **Christmas isn't ~ away** o **off now** ya falta poco para Navidad; **I can't remember that ~ back** no recuerdo cosas tan lejanas **(d)** (in extent, degree): **the new legislation doesn't go ~ enough** la nueva legislación no tiene el alcance necesario; **his jokes went a bit too ~** se pasó un poco con esos chistes

2 (very much): **~ better** mucho mejor

3 (*in phrases*) **as** o **so far as: as** o **so ~ as I know** que yo sepa; **by far: their team was by ~ the worst** su equipo fue con mucho el peor; **so far: so ~, everything has gone according to plan** hasta ahora todo ha salido de acuerdo a lo planeado

far² *adj* (*comp* **farther**; *superl* **farthest**) **(a)** (distant) lejano **(b)** (most distant, extreme) (*before n*, ⋯⋗

no comp): **at the ~ end of the room** en el otro extremo de la habitación; **the ~ left/right** (Pol) la extrema izquierda/derecha

faraway /'fɑːrə'weɪ/ *adj* (*before n*) ‹*lands*› lejano; ‹*look*› ausente

farce /fɑːrs ‖fɑːs/ *n* farsa *f*

farcical /'fɑːrsɪkəl ‖'fɑːsɪkəl/ *adj* ridículo

fare /fer ‖feə(r)/ *n* **1** (cost of travel — by air) pasaje *m or* (Esp) billete *m*; (— by bus, train) boleto *m or* (esp Esp) billete *m*; **~s will rise again next year** las tarifas subirán de nuevo en el próximo año **2** (food and drink) comida *f*

Far East *n* **the ~ ~** el Lejano *or* Extremo Oriente

farewell¹ /'fer'wel ‖,feə'wel/ *n* despedida *f*

farewell² *interj* (liter) adiós

far-fetched /'fɑːr'fetʃt ‖,fɑː'fetʃt/ *adj* exagerado

farm¹ /fɑːrm ‖fɑːm/ *n* (small) granja *f*, chacra *f* (CS, Per); (large) hacienda *f*, cortijo *m* (Esp), rancho *m* (Méx), estancia *f* (RPl), fundo *m* (Chi); (*before n*) ‹*machinery/worker*› agrícola

farm² *vt* ‹*land*› cultivar

■ **farm out** [*v + o + adv, v + adv + o*] ‹*work*› encargar* (*a terceros*)

farmer /'fɑːrmər ‖'fɑːmə(r)/ *n* agricultor, -tora *m,f*, granjero, -ra *m,f*, chacarero, -ra *m,f* (CS, Per); (owner of large farm) hacendado, -da *m,f*, ranchero, -ra *m,f* (Méx), estanciero, -ra *m,f* (RPl), dueño, -ña *m,f* de fundo (Chi)

farm: ~hand *n* peón *m or* (Esp) mozo *m* de labranza; **~house** *n* casa *f* de labranza, alquería *f* (*en Esp*), ≈ casco *m* de la estancia (*en RPl*)

farming /'fɑːrmɪŋ ‖'fɑːmɪŋ/ *n* (of land) labranza *f*; (of animals) crianza *f*; (*before n*) ‹*community*› agrícola; ‹*methods*› de labranza

farm: ~land *n* tierras *fpl* de labranza; **~yard** *n* corral *m*

far: ~off /'fɑːr'ɔːf ‖'fɑːrɒf/ *adj* (*pred* ~ **off**) (in space) remoto; (in time) distante; **~reaching** /'fɑːr'riːtʃɪŋ ‖,fɑː'riːtʃɪŋ/ *adj* de gran alcance; **~sighted** /'fɑːr'saɪtəd ‖,fɑː'saɪtɪd/ *adj* (a) (showing foresight) con visión de futuro (b) (AmE Med) hipermétrope

fart¹ /fɑːrt ‖fɑːt/ *n* (vulg) pedo *m* (fam)

fart² *vi* (vulg) tirarse *or* echarse un pedo (fam)

farther¹ /'fɑːrðər ‖'fɑːðə(r)/ *adv comp of* FAR¹ 1

farther² *adj comp of* FAR²

farthest¹ /'fɑːrðəst ‖'fɑːðɪst/ *adv superl of* FAR¹ 1

farthest² *adj superl of* FAR²

fascinate /'fæsn̩eɪt ‖'fæsɪneɪt/ *vt* fascinar

fascinated /'fæsn̩eɪtəd ‖'fæsɪneɪtɪd/ *adj* fascinado

fascinating /'fæsn̩eɪtɪŋ ‖'fæsɪneɪtɪŋ/ *adj* fascinante

fascination /'fæsn̩'eɪʃən ‖,fæsɪ'neɪʃən/ *n* fascinación *f*

fascism /'fæʃɪzəm/ *n* fascismo *m*

fascist¹ /'fæʃəst ‖'fæʃɪst/ *n* fascista *mf*

fascist² *adj* fascista

fashion¹ /'fæʃən/ *n* **1** (vogue) moda *f*; **to be in/ out of ~** estar* de moda/estar* pasado de moda; (*before n*) **~ designer** diseñador, -dora *m,f* de

modas **2** (custom) costumbre *f* **3** (manner) manera *f*; **after a ~**: **can you swim? — well, after a ~** ¿sabes nadar? — bueno, a mi manera

fashion² *vt* crear

fashionable /'fæʃnəbəl/ *adj* ‹*clothes/designs*› a la moda; ‹*restaurant/people/idea*› de moda

fashionably /'fæʃnəbli/ *adv* a la moda

fashion show *n* desfile *m* de modas

fast¹ /fæst ‖fɑːst/ *adj* **-er, -est** **1** (a) (speedy) rápido (b) (of clock, watch) (*pred*): **my watch is five minutes ~** mi reloj (se) adelanta cinco minutos **2** (permanent) ‹*color*› inalterable

fast² *adv* **1** (quickly) rápidamente, rápido **2** (firmly): **the car was stuck ~ in the mud** el coche estaba atascado en el barro completamente; **to be ~ asleep** estar* profundamente dormido

fast³ *vi* ayunar

fast⁴ *n* ayuno *m*

fasten /'fæsn̩ ‖'fɑːsn̩/ *vt* (a) (attach) sujetar; (tie) atar (b) (do up, close) ‹*case*› cerrar*; ‹*coat/seat belt*› abrochar
■ **~** *vi* «*suitcase*» cerrar*; «*skirt/necklace*» abrocharse

fastener /'fæsnər ‖'fɑːsnə(r)/ *n* cierre *m*

fast: ~ food *n* comida *f* rápida; **~-forward** /'fæst'fɔːrwərd ‖,fɑːst'fɔːwəd/ *vt/i* avanzar*

fastidious /fæs'tɪdiəs/ *adj* (a) (demanding) muy exigente (b) (fussy) maniático, mañoso (AmL)

fast track *n* vía *f* rápida

fat¹ /fæt/ *adj* **-tt-** ‹*person/animal*› gordo; ‹*book/ cigar*› grueso; **to get ~** engordar; **a ~ lot of good that'll do!** (iro) ¡para lo que va a servir!

fat² *n* grasa *f*

fatal /'feɪtl/ *adj* (a) (causing death) mortal (b) (disastrous) ‹*decision/mistake*› fatídico

fatalistic /'feɪtl'ɪstɪk ‖,feɪtə'lɪstɪk/ *adj* fatalista

fatality /fer'tæləti ‖fə'tæləti/ *n* (*pl* **-ties**) muerto *m*

fatally /'feɪtli ‖'feɪtəli/ *adv* mortalmente

fate /feɪt/ *n* (a) (destiny) destino *m* (b) (*no pl*) (one's lot, end) suerte *f*

fated /'feɪtəd ‖'feɪtɪd/ *adj* (destined) **to be ~ to +** INF (liter) estar* predestinado A + INF

fateful /'feɪtfəl/ *adj* (a) (momentous) ‹*day/ decision*› fatídico (b) (prophetic) ‹*words*› profético

father¹ /'fɑːðər ‖'fɑːðə(r)/ *n* padre *m*

father² *vt* ‹*child*› engendrar, tener*

Father Christmas *n* (BrE) Papá *m* Noel, viejo *m* Pascuero (Chi)

fatherhood /'fɑːðərhʊd ‖'fɑːðəhʊd/ *n* paternidad *f*

father: ~-in-law *n* (*pl* **~s-in-law**) suegro *m*; **~land** *n* patria *f*

fatherly /'fɑːðərli ‖'fɑːðəli/ *adj* paternal

fathom¹ /'fæðəm/ *n* braza *f*

fathom² *vt* **~ (out)** entender*

fatigue /fə'tiːg/ *n* fatiga *f*

fatten /'fætn̩/ *vt* ~ (up): ‹*animal*› cebar

fattening /'fætn̩ɪŋ/ *adj*: **cakes are extremely ~** los pasteles engordan muchísimo

fatty /'fæti/ *adj* **-tier, -tiest** ‹*food/substance*› graso, grasoso (AmL)

faucet /'fɔ:sət/ n (AmE) llave f or (Esp) grifo m
or (RPl) canilla f or (Per) caño m or (AmC) paja f,
chorro m (AmC, Ven)

fault¹ /'fɔ:lt/ n **1** (responsibility, blame) culpa f;
they're always finding ~ with me todo lo que
hago les parece mal **2** **(a)** (failing) defecto m; **she
is generous to a ~** es generosa en extremo **(b)** (in
machine) avería f; (in goods) defecto m **3** (Geol)
falla f **4** (in tennis, show jumping) falta f

fault² vt encontrarle* defectos a

faultless /'fɔ:ltləs ‖'fɔ:ltlɪs/ adj impecable

faulty /'fɔ:lti/ adj **-tier, -tiest** ⟨goods/design⟩
defectuoso; ⟨workmanship⟩ imperfecto

faux pas /fəʊ'pɑ:/ n (pl ~ /-z/ or (AmL tb) /-z/) metedura f
or (AmL tb) metida f de pata (fam)

favor¹, (BrE) **favour** /'feɪvər ‖'feɪvə(r)/ n
1 (approval): **to find ~ with sb** (frml) tener* buena
acogida por parte de algn (frml); **to curry ~ with
sb** tratar de congraciarse con algn **2** **in ~** a
favor; **to be in ~ of sth** estar* a favor de algo
3 (act of kindness) favor m; **to do/ask sb a ~**
hacerle*/pedirle* un favor a algn

favor², (BrE) **favour** vt **(a)** (be in favor of) estar*
a favor de **(b)** (benefit) favorecer* **(c)** (treat
preferentially) favorecer*

favorable, (BrE) **favourable** /'feɪvrəbəl/ adj
favorable; **to be ~ to** sth favorecer* algo

favorite¹, (BrE) **favourite** /'feɪvrət ‖'feɪvərɪt/
adj preferido

favorite², (BrE) **favourite** n **(a)** (person, thing)
preferido, -da m,f; (Sport) favorito, -ta m,f **(b)** (of
teacher, ruler) favorito, -ta m,f

favoritism, (BrE) **favouritism** /'feɪvrətɪzəm
‖'feɪvərɪtɪzəm/ n favoritismo m

fawn¹ /fɔ:n/ n **1** (young deer) cervato m
2 (color) beige m, beis m (Esp); (before n)
⟨sweater/coat⟩ beige adj inv, beis adj inv (Esp)

fawn² vi (flatter) **to ~ on sb** «person» (pej)
adular a algn

fax¹ /fæks/ n fax m; (before n) ~ **machine** fax m

fax² vt faxear

faze /feɪz/ vt (colloq) perturbar

FBI n (in US) (= **Federal Bureau of
Investigation**) FBI m

FDA n (in US) = **Food and Drug
Administration**

fear¹ /fɪr ‖fɪə(r)/ n miedo m, temor m; ~ **of
heights** miedo a las alturas; **no ~!** (as interj)
(colloq) ¡ni loco! or ¡ni muerto!

fear² vt **(a)** (dread) temer **(b)** (suspect) **to ~
(THAT)** temerse QUE
■ ~ vi temer; **to ~ for sb/sth** temer POR algn/algo

fearful /'fɪrfəl ‖'fɪəfəl/ adj **1** (frightening)
aterrador **2** (timid) miedoso

fearless /'fɪrləs ‖'fɪəlɪs/ adj intrépido

fearsome /'fɪrsəm ‖'fɪəsəm/ adj ⟨enemy⟩
aterrador; ⟨task⟩ tremendo

feasibility /ˌfi:zə'bɪləti/ n viabilidad f; (before
n) ~ **study** estudio m de viabilidad

feasible /'fi:zəbəl/ adj (practicable) viable;
(possible) posible

feast¹ /fi:st/ n **1** (banquet) banquete m **2** (Relig)
fiesta f; (before n) ~ **day** día m festivo

feast² vi festejar
■ ~ vt **to ~ one's eyes ON sth** regalarse los ojos
CON algo

feat /fi:t/ n hazaña f

feather /'feðər ‖'feðə(r)/ n pluma f; **as light as
a ~** ligero or (esp AmL) liviano como una pluma;
(before n) ~ **bed** colchón m de plumas; ~ **duster**
plumero m

feature¹ /'fi:tʃər ‖'fi:tʃə(r)/ n **1** **(a)** (of face)
rasgo m **(b)** (of character, landscape, machine, style)
característica f **2** **(a)** ~ **(film)** película f **(b)**
(Journ) artículo m **(c)** (Rad, TV) documental m

feature² vt **1** (Journ, Cin): **he was ~d in 'The
Globe'** recently 'The Globe' publicó un artículo
sobre él hace poco; **featuring John Ball** con la
actuación de John Ball **2** **(a)** (have as feature)
«hotel/house» ofrecer* **(b)** (depict) mostrar*
■ ~ vi figurar; **rice ~s prominently in their diet** el
arroz ocupa un lugar importante en su
alimentación

February /'februeri ‖'februəri/ n febrero m

feces, (BrE) **faeces** /'fi:si:z/ pl n (frml) heces
fpl (frml)

fed /fed/ past & past p of FEED¹

federal /'fedərəl/ adj federal

federal: F~ Republic of Germany n the
F~ **Republic of Germany** la República Federal de
Alemania; **F~ Reserve Board** n (in US) la
Junta de Gobernadores de la Reserva Federal

federation /ˌfedə'reɪʃən/ n federación f

fed up adj (colloq) (usu pred) **to be ~** (WITH
sb/sth/-ING) estar* harto (DE algn/algo/+ INF)

fee /fi:/ n **(a)** (payment — to doctor, lawyer)
honorarios mpl; (— to actor, singer) caché m **(b)**
(charge) (often pl): **on payment of a small ~** por
una módica suma; **membership ~(s)** cuota f (de
socio)

feeble /'fi:bəl/ adj **-bler** /-blər ‖-blə(r)/, **-blest**
/-bləst ‖-blɪst/ **(a)** (weak) débil **(b)** (poor) ⟨joke⟩
flojo; ⟨excuse⟩ pobre

feed¹ /fi:d/ (past & past p fed) vt **1** **(a)** (give
food to) dar* de comer a; ⟨baby⟩ (breastfeed) darle*
el pecho a; (with a bottle) darle* el biberón or (CS,
Per) la mamadera or (Col, Ven) el tetero a **(b)**
(provide food for) alimentar **(c)** (give as food) **to ~
sth TO sb** dar* algo (de comer) A algn **2** (insert)
to ~ sth INTO sth ⟨into a machine⟩ introducir*
algo EN algo **3** (sustain) ⟨imagination/rumor⟩
avivar; ⟨hope/fire⟩ alimentar
■ ~ vi comer; **to ~ ON sth** alimentarse DE algo

feed² n **(a)** (act of feeding): **it's time for the baby's
~** es hora de darle de comer al niño **(b)** (food)
alimento m; (for cattle) pienso m

feedback /'fi:dbæk/ n (reaction) reacción f;
(Audio, Electron) retroalimentación f

feeding bottle /'fi:dɪŋ/ n (BrE) biberón m,
mamila f (Méx), mamadera f (CS, Per), tetero m
(Col)

feel¹ /fi:l/ (past & past p felt) vi **1** (physically,
emotionally) sentirse*; **to ~ hot/cold/hungry/thirsty**
tener* calor/frío/hambre/sed
2 (have opinion): **it's something I ~ strongly about**
es algo que me parece muy importante; **how do
you ~ about these changes?** ¿qué opinas de estos
cambios?
3 **to ~ like -ING** (be in the mood for) tener* ganas
DE + INF
4 (seem): **your hands ~ cold** tienes las manos
frías; **how does that ~? — it's still too tight**
¿cómo lo sientes? — todavía me queda apretado ⋯⸬

5 (grope) to ~ FOR sth buscar* algo a tientas
■ ~ vt **1** (touch) tocar*; to ~ one's way ir* a tientas
2 ⟨sensation/movement/shame⟩ sentir*; I couldn't ~ my fingers no sentía los dedos
3 (consider) considerar; I ~ that ... me parece que ...

feel² n (no pl) **1** (a) (sensation) sensación f (b) (sense of touch) tacto m **2** (a) (atmosphere — of house, room) ambiente m (b) (instinct): to have a ~ for sth tener* sensibilidad para algo; to get the ~ of sth acostumbrarse a algo

feeler /'fi:lər ‖ 'fi:lə(r)/ n (a) (Zool) (antenna) antena f; (tentacle) tentáculo m (b) (tentative approach): to put out ~s tantear el terreno

feeling /'fi:lɪŋ/ n **1** (a) (physical sensitivity) sensibilidad f (b) (physical, emotional sensation) sensación f **2** (a) (sincere emotion) sentimiento m (b) (sensitivity) sentimientos mpl **3** (opinion) opinión f **4** (no pl) (impression) impresión f; I've a ~ that he knows already tengo or me da la sensación de que ya lo sabe

feet /fi:t/ n pl of FOOT¹

feign /feɪn/ vt fingir*

feline /'fi:laɪn/ adj felino

fell¹ /fel/ past of FALL²

fell² vt ⟨tree⟩ talar; ⟨person⟩ derribar

fellow¹ /'feləʊ/ n **1** (man) tipo m (fam), hombre m **2** (member — of college) miembro del cuerpo docente y de la junta rectora de una universidad; (— of learned society) miembro mf de número

fellow² adj (before n): ~ worker/traveler compañero, -ra m,f de trabajo/viaje; ~ citizen conciudadano, -na m,f; he has no love for his ~ men no le tiene amor al prójimo

fellow feeling n camaradería f

fellowship /'feləʊʃɪp/ n **1** (Educ) (a) (at university) título m de FELLOW¹ 2 (b) (endowment) beca f de investigación **2** (a) (companionship) (liter) hermandad f (liter) (b) (fraternity) fraternidad f

felon /'felən/ n (in US law) delincuente mf (que ha cometido un delito grave)

felony /'feləni/ n (pl **-nies**) (in US Law) delito m grave

felt¹ /felt/ n fieltro m

felt² past & past p of FEEL¹

felt pen, felt-tip (pen) /'felttɪp/ n rotulador m, marcador m (AmL)

female¹ /'fi:meɪl/ adj ⟨sex⟩ femenino; ⟨animal/plant⟩ hembra; the victim was ~ la víctima era una mujer

female² n hembra f; (woman, girl) mujer f

feminine /'femənən ‖ 'femɪnɪn/ adj femenino

femininity /ˌfemə'nɪnəti ‖ ˌfemɪ'nɪnəti/ n femineidad f, feminidad f

feminism /'femənəzəm ‖ 'femɪnɪzəm/ n feminismo m

feminist¹ /'femənəst ‖ 'femɪnɪst/ n feminista mf

feminist² adj feminista

fence¹ /fens/ n **1** (a) (barrier) cerca f, cerco m (AmL); to sit on the ~ nadar entre dos aguas (b) (in showjumping) valla f **2** (receiver of stolen goods) (colloq) persona que comercia con objetos robados, reducidor, -dora m,f (AmS)

fence² vt cercar*
■ ~ vi (Sport) practicar* la esgrima
■ **fence in** [v + adv + o, v + o + adv] cercar*
■ **fence off** [v + adv + o, v + o + adv] separar con una cerca

fencer /'fensər ‖ 'fensə(r)/ n esgrimista mf

fencing /'fensɪŋ/ n **1** (Sport) esgrima f **2** (a) (material) materiales para cercos o vallas (b) (fence) cerca f

fend /fend/ vi: to ~ for oneself valerse* por sí mismo
■ **fend off** [v + o + adv, v + adv + o] ⟨attack/enemy⟩ rechazar*; ⟨blow⟩ esquivar; ⟨questions⟩ eludir

fender /'fendər ‖ 'fendə(r)/ n **1** (around fireplace) rejilla f **2** (on car) (AmE) guardabarros m or (Méx) salpicadera f or (Chi, Per) tapabarro(s) m; (on boat) defensa f

fennel /'fenl/ n hinojo m

ferment /fər'ment ‖ fə'ment/ vi fermentar

fern /fɜːrn ‖ fɜːn/ n helecho m

ferocious /fə'rəʊʃəs/ adj feroz

ferocity /fə'rɑːsəti ‖ fə'rɒsəti/ n ferocidad f

ferret /'ferət ‖ 'ferɪt/ n hurón m
■ **ferret around, ferret about** [v + adv] husmear
■ **ferret out** [v + o + adv, v + adv + o] (colloq) descubrir*

ferry¹ /'feri/ n (pl **-ries**) (boat) transbordador m, ferry m; (smaller) balsa f

ferry² vt **-ries, -rying, -ried** llevar; we ~ the children to and from school in the car llevamos a los niños al colegio y los vamos a buscar en coche

fertile /'fɜːrtl ‖ 'fɜːtaɪl/ adj ⟨woman/animal/plant/soil⟩ fértil; ⟨seed/egg⟩ fecundado; ⟨imagination⟩ fértil

fertility /fər'tɪləti ‖ fə'tɪləti/ n fertilidad f

fertilize /'fɜːrtlaɪz ‖ 'fɜːtɪlaɪz/ vt ⟨egg/plant/cell⟩ fecundar; ⟨soil/crop⟩ abonar

fertilizer /'fɜːrtlaɪzər ‖ 'fɜːtɪlaɪzə(r)/ n fertilizante m

fervent /'fɜːrvənt ‖ 'fɜːvənt/ adj ferviente

fervor, (BrE) fervour /'fɜːrvər ‖ 'fɜːvə(r)/ n fervor m

fester /'festər ‖ 'festə(r)/ vi enconarse

festival /'festəvəl ‖ 'festɪvəl/ n (a) (Relig) fiesta f (b) (Cin, Mus, Theat) festival m (c) (celebration) fiesta f

festive /'festɪv/ adj festivo; the ~ season (set phrase) las Navidades

festivity /fes'tɪvəti/ n (usu pl) celebración f

festoon /fe'stuːn/ vt to ~ sth/sb (WITH sth) adornar algo/a algn (CON algo)

AmC	Central America	Arg	Argentina	Cu	Cuba
AmL	Latin America	Bol	Bolivia	Ec	Ecuador
AmS	South America	Chi	Chile	Esp	Spain
Andes	Andean Region	CS	Southern Cone	Méx	Mexico

Per	Peru
RPI	River Plate Area
Ur	Uruguay
Ven	Venezuela

fetch /fetʃ/ vt [1] (bring) traer*, ir* a por (Esp) [2] (sell for) (colloq): **the car ~ed $4,000** el coche se vendió en 4.000 dólares
■ ~ vi: **to ~ and carry** ser* el recadero/la recadera
fetching /'fetʃɪŋ/ adj ‹smile› atractivo; ‹dress/ hat› sentador, que sienta bien (Esp)
fete, fête /feɪt/ n **(a)** (fund-raising event) (BrE) feria f (benéfica), kermesse f (CS, Méx), bazar m (Col) **(b)** (party) (AmE) fiesta f (en un jardín)
fetish /'fetɪʃ/ n fetiche m
fetter /'fetər ‖ 'fetə(r)/ vt (liter) encadenar; **he felt ~ed by convention** se sentía prisionero de los convencionalismos
fetters /'fetərz ‖ 'fetəz/ pl n (liter) grillos mpl
fettle /'fetl/ n: **to be in fine ~** estar* en (buena) forma
fetus, (BrE) **foetus** /'fi:təs/ n feto m
feud¹ /fju:d/ n contienda f (frml)
feud² vi contender* (frml)
feudal /'fju:dl/ adj feudal
fever /'fi:vər ‖ 'fi:və(r)/ n fiebre f
feverish /'fi:vərɪʃ/ adj (Med) con fiebre; (frantic) febril
fever pitch n: **to reach ~ ~** llegar* al paroxismo
few¹ /fju:/ adj **-er, -est** pocos, -cas; **the last ~ days have been difficult** estos últimos días han sido difíciles; **there were ~er people than usual** había menos gente que de costumbre; **I've been there a ~ times** he estado allí unas cuantas veces
few² pron **-er, -est** pocos, -cas; **the privileged ~** la minoría privilegiada; **a ~ of us complained** algunos (de nosotros) nos quejamos
fiancé /'fi:ɑ:n'seɪ, fi:'ɑ:nseɪ ‖ fi:'ɒnseɪ/ n prometido m
fiancée /'fi:ɑ:n'seɪ, fi:'ɑ:nseɪ ‖ fi:'ɒnseɪ/ n prometida f
fiasco /fi'æskəʊ/ n (pl **-cos** or **-coes**) fracaso m
fib¹ /fɪb/ n (colloq) mentirilla f, bola f (fam)
fib² vi **-bb-** (colloq) mentir*, decir* mentirillas or (fam) bolas
fiber, (BrE) **fibre** /'faɪbər ‖ 'faɪbə(r)/ n fibra f; (dietary) ~ fibra f
fiberglass /'faɪbərɡlæs ‖ 'faɪbəɡlɑ:s/ n fibra f de vidrio
fickle /'fɪkəl/ adj veleidoso
fiction /'fɪkʃən/ n ficción f
fictional /'fɪkʃnəl ‖ 'fɪkʃənl/ adj ficticio
fictitious /fɪk'tɪʃəs/ adj **(a)** (false) ‹name› ficticio **(b)** (imaginary) imaginario
fiddle¹ /'fɪdl/ n [1] (violin) violín m; **as fit as a ~** rebosante de salud [2] (cheat) (BrE colloq) chanchullo m (fam)
fiddle² vt (BrE colloq) ‹accounts› hacer* chanchullos con (fam); ‹results› amañar
■ ~ vi (fidget) **to ~ with sth** juguetear con algo
fiddler /'fɪdlər ‖ 'fɪdlə(r)/ n violinista mf
fidelity /fə'deləti ‖ fɪ'deləti/ n fidelidad f
fidget /'fɪdʒət ‖ 'fɪdʒɪt/ vi: **stop ~ing** ¡estate quieto!
field¹ /fi:ld/ n [1] (Agr) campo m [2] (Sport) **(a)** (area of play) campo m, cancha f (AmL) **(b)** (competitors) (+ sing o pl vb): **to lead the ~** llevar la delantera; **our products lead the ~** nuestros

productos son los líderes del mercado [3] (of study, work) campo m; (of activities) esfera f [4] (Opt, Phot, Phys) campo m; **~ of vision** campo visual
field² vt (Sport) fildear
field: ~ **day** n: **to have a ~ day** hacer* su agosto; ~ **glasses** pl n gemelos mpl, prismáticos mpl; ~ **hockey** n (AmE) hockey m (sobre hierba); ~ **marshal** n mariscal m de campo; ~ **trip** n viaje m de estudio; ~**work** n trabajo m de campo
fiend /fi:nd/ n **(a)** (demon) demonio m **(b)** (cruel person) (journ or hum) desalmado, -da m,f
fiendish /'fi:ndɪʃ/ adj **(a)** (wicked) diabólico **(b)** (very difficult) (colloq) endemoniado (fam)
fierce /fɪrs ‖ fɪəs/ adj **fiercer, fiercest (a)** ‹dog/lion› fiero; ‹temper› feroz **(b)** ‹hatred/love› intenso; ‹fighting› encarnizado; ‹criticism/ opposition› violento **(c)** ‹storm› violento; ‹wind› fortísimo; **the ~ tropical sun** el implacable sol del trópico
fiercely /'fɪrsli ‖ 'fɪəsli/ adv **(a)** ‹growl› con ferocidad **(b)** ‹fight› con fiereza; ‹criticize› duramente; ‹competitive/independent› extremadamente
fiery /'faɪri ‖ 'faɪəri/ adj **-rier, -riest** ‹glow› ardiente; ‹red› encendido; ‹heat/sun› abrasador; ‹liquor› muy fuerte; ‹temper› exaltado; ‹speech› fogoso
FIFA /'fi:fə/ n (no art) la FIFA
fifteen /fɪf'ti:n/ adj/n quince adj inv/m; see also FOUR¹
fifteenth¹ /fɪf'ti:nθ/ adj decimoquinto
fifteenth² adv en decimoquinto lugar
fifteenth³ n (Math) quinceavo m; (part) quinceava parte f
fifth¹ /fɪfθ/ adj quinto
fifth² adv en quinto lugar
fifth³ n [1] **(a)** (Math) quinto m; (part) quinta parte f, quinto m **(b)** (Mus) quinta f **(c)** (in competition): **he finished a disappointing ~** llegó en un deslucido quinto lugar [2] ~ **(gear)** (no art) quinta f
fiftieth¹ /'fɪftiəθ/ adj quincuagésimo
fiftieth² adv en quincuagésimo lugar
fiftieth³ n (Math) cincuentavo m; (part) cincuentava or quincuagésima parte f
fifty /'fɪfti/ adj/n cincuenta adj inv/m; see also FOUR¹
fifty-fifty¹ /'fɪfti'fɪfti/ adv (colloq) a medias
fifty-fifty² adj (colloq): **a ~ chance** un 50% de posibilidades; **on a ~ basis** a medias
fig /fɪɡ/ n higo m; (before n) ~ **tree** higuera f
fight¹ /faɪt/ (past & past p **fought**) vi ‹army/ country/animal» luchar; «person» pelear; **to ~ FOR/AGAINST sb/sth** luchar POR/CONTRA algn/algo; **to ~ OVER sth** pelearse POR algo
■ ~ vt [1] **(a)** ‹army/country› luchar contra **(b)** ‹fire/disease/measure› combatir [2] **(a)** (conduct): **they fought a long war against the rebels** lucharon contra los rebeldes durante largo tiempo **(b)** (contest) ‹election› presentarse a; **we intend to ~ the case** (Law) pensamos llevar el caso a los tribunales (or defendernos etc)
■ **fight back** [1] [v + adv] defenderse*; **to ~ back AGAINST sb/sth** luchar CONTRA algn/algo ⋯⋙

2 [v + o + adv, v + adv + o] ⟨tears⟩ contener*; ⟨anger⟩ reprimir
■ **fight off** [v + o + adv, v + adv + o] ⟨attack/ enemy⟩ rechazar*; ⟨cold⟩ combatir
■ **fight out** [v + o + adv]: you'll have to ∼ it out among yourselves tendrán que resolverlo entre ustedes
fight² n **1** (a) (between persons) pelea f; (between armies, companies) lucha f (b) (boxing match) pelea f **2** (a) (struggle) lucha f (b) (quarrel) pelea f
fighter /'faɪtər ‖ 'faɪtə(r)/ n **1** (a) (person) luchador, -dora m,f (b) (boxer) boxeador, -dora m,f **2** (plane) caza m; (before n) ∼ **pilot** piloto m de caza
fighting /'faɪtɪŋ/ n (Mil) enfrentamientos mpl; (brawling, arguing) peleas fpl
figment /'fɪgmənt/ n: **a ∼ of the imagination** (un) producto de la imaginación
figurative /'fɪgjərətɪv ‖ 'fɪgərətɪv/ adj figurado
figure¹ /'fɪgjər ‖ 'fɪgə(r)/ n **1** (digit) cifra f; **recent ∼s show that ...** estadísticas recientes muestran que ... **2** (a) (person) figura f; **a public ∼** un personaje público (b) (body shape) figura f **3** (Art, Math, Mus) figura f
figure² vi **1** (feature) figurar; **to ∼ prominently** destacarse* **2** (make sense) (colloq): **it just doesn't ∼** no me lo explico
■ ∼ vt (reckon) (AmE colloq) calcular
■ **figure on** [v + prep + o] (AmE colloq) contar* con
■ **figure out** [v + o + adv, v + adv + o] (a) (understand) entender* (b) (calculate) ⟨sum/result⟩ calcular; ⟨problem⟩ resolver*
figure: ∼**head** n (Naut) mascarón m de proa; **he's merely a ∼head** no es más que una figura decorativa; ∼ **of speech** n figura f retórica; ∼ **skating** n patinaje m artístico
Fiji /'fi:dʒi:/ n Fiji
filament /'fɪləmənt/ n filamento m
filch /fɪltʃ/ vt (colloq) birlar (fam)
file¹ /faɪl/ n **1** (a) (tool) lima f **2** (a) (folder) carpeta f; (box ∼) clasificador m; (for card index) fichero m (b) (collection of documents) archivo m; (of a particular case) expediente m (c) (Comput) archivo m
file² vt **1** (sort) ⟨papers⟩ archivar **2** ⟨application/suit⟩ presentar **3** ⟨metal⟩ limar; **to ∼ one's nails** limarse las uñas
■ ∼ vi **1** (walk in line) (+ adv compl): **they ∼d into the room** entraron en la habitación en fila; **the crowd ∼d past the tomb** la multitud desfiló ante la tumba **2** (Law): **to ∼ for divorce** presentar una demanda de divorcio
file: ∼ **card** n (AmE) ficha f; ∼ **clerk** n (AmE) administrativo, -va m,f (encargado de archivar)
filing /'faɪlɪŋ/ n: **there's a lot of ∼ to do** hay mucho que archivar
filing: ∼ **cabinet** n archivador m; ∼ **clerk** n (BrE) ▶ FILE CLERK
Filipino /'fɪlə'pi:nəʊ ‖ ˌfɪlɪ'pi:nəʊ/ adj filipino
fill¹ /fɪl/ vt **1** (a) (make full) **to ∼ sth** (WITH sth) llenar algo (DE algo); ⟨cake/sandwich⟩ rellenar algo (DE algo) (b) (plug) ⟨hole/crack⟩ rellenar; ⟨tooth⟩ empastar, tapar (Andes), emplomar (RPl), calzar* (Col)
2 ⟨vacancy⟩ cubrir*
■ ∼ vi «bath/auditorium» **to ∼** (WITH sth) llenarse (DE algo)

■ **fill in 1** [v + o + adv, v + adv + o] (a) ⟨hole/ outline⟩ rellenar (b) ⟨form⟩ rellenar
2 [v + o + adv] (inform) (colloq) **to ∼ sb in** (ON sth) poner* a algn al corriente (DE algo)
3 [v + adv] (deputize) **to ∼ in FOR sb** sustituir* a algn
■ **fill out** [v + o + adv, v + adv + o] ⟨form⟩ rellenar
■ **fill up 1** [v + o + adv, v + adv + o] (a) (make full) llenar (b) (Auto): ∼ **her up!** ¡llénelo!
2 [v + adv] (a) (become full) llenarse (b) (buy fuel) echar gasolina
fill² n: **to eat one's ∼ of sth** (liter) comer algo hasta saciarse; **to have had one's ∼ of sth** estar* harto de algo
filler /'fɪlər ‖ 'fɪlə(r)/ n (for cracks) masilla f
fillet¹ /'fɪlət ‖ 'fɪlɪt/ n (of beef) filete m, solomillo m (Esp), lomo m (AmS); (of pork) lomo m; (of fish) filete m; (before n) **a ∼ steak** un filete, un solomillo de ternera (Esp), un bife de lomo (RPl)
fillet² vt ⟨meat⟩ cortar en filetes; ⟨fish⟩ quitarle la espina a
filling¹ /'fɪlɪŋ/ n **1** (Dent) empaste m, tapadura f (Chi, Méx), emplomadura f (RPl), calza f (Col)
2 (Culin) relleno m
filling² adj: **pasta's very ∼** la pasta llena mucho
filling station n ▶ GAS STATION
filly /'fɪli/ n (pl **-lies**) potra f
film¹ /fɪlm/ n **1** (a) (Phot) película f (fotográfica) (b) (movie) película f, film(e) m (period); (before n) ∼ **star** estrella f de cine **2** (a) (thin covering) película f (b) (wrap) film m transparente
film² vt ⟨scene⟩ filmar; ⟨novel/play⟩ llevar al cine
■ ∼ vi rodar*; ∼**ing starts tomorrow** el rodaje empieza mañana
filmstrip /'fɪlmstrɪp/ n: película o serie de fílminas para proyección fija
Filofax® /'faɪləfæks/ n filofax® m
filter¹ /'fɪltər ‖ 'fɪltə(r)/ n **1** (device) filtro m; (before n) ∼ **coffee** café m americano (BrE Transp) flecha f (que autoriza el giro a derecha o izquierda en algunos semáforos); (before n) ∼ **lane** carril m de giro
filter² vt filtrar
■ ∼ vi «gas/light/sound» filtrarse
filter-tipped /'fɪltər'tɪpt ‖ ˌfɪltə'tɪpt/ adj con filtro
filth /fɪlθ/ n mugre f
filthy /'fɪlθi/ adj **-thier, -thiest** (a) (dirty) mugriento (b) (obscene) ⟨language⟩ obsceno (c) (unpleasant) (BrE colloq) ⟨weather/habit⟩ asqueroso (fam)
fin /fɪn/ n aleta f
final¹ /'faɪnl/ adj **1** (last) (before n) último; **a ∼ demand (for payment)** (Busn) un último aviso de pago **2** (definitive) final; **the judges' decision is ∼** (frml) la decisión del jurado es inapelable
final² n **1** (Games, Sport) (often pl) final f
2 finals pl (Educ) exámenes mpl finales
finale /fə'næli ‖ fɪ'nɑːli/ n (a) (Mus) final m (b) (Theat) apoteosis f
finalist /'faɪnləst ‖ 'faɪnlɪst/ n finalista mf
finalize /'faɪnlaɪz ‖ 'faɪnəlaɪz/ vt ultimar
finally /'faɪnli ‖ 'faɪnəli/ adv (a) (lastly) (indep) por último (b) (at last) por fin

finance¹ /fə'næns, faɪ- ‖'faɪmæns, far'næns/ *n*
(a) (banking, business) finanzas *fpl* (b) **finances**
pl recursos *mpl* financieros (c) (funding)
financiación *f*, financiamiento *m* (esp AmL)

finance² *vt* financiar

financial /fə'nænt∫əl ‖far'nænt∫əl/ *adj* ⟨*system/
risk*⟩ financiero; ⟨*difficulties/independence*⟩
económico; ⟨*news*⟩ de economía, de negocios; ~
advice asesoría *f* económica; ~ **management**
gestión *f* financiera

financial year *n* (BrE) (of company) ejercicio
m; (of government) año *m* fiscal

financier /'fman'sɪr ‖far'nænsɪə(r)/ *n*
financiero, -ra *m,f*

find¹ /faɪnd/ (*past & past p* **found**) *vt*
encontrar*; **I can't** ~ **it** no lo encuentro; **I found
(that) it was easier to do it this way** descubrí que
era más fácil hacerlo así; **I** ~ **that hard to believe!**
¡me cuesta creerlo!; **to** ~ **sb guilty/not guilty** (Law)
declarar a algn culpable/inocente
■ *v refl* **to** ~ **oneself** encontrarse* a sí (*or* mí *etc*)
mismo
■ **find out** ①[*v + o + adv, v + adv + o*] (discover)
⟨*truth*⟩ descubrir*; ⟨*information*⟩ (by making
enquiries) averiguar*
② [*v + adv*] (a) (learn) enterarse; **to** ~ **out ABOUT
sth** enterarse DE algo (b) (make inquiries)
averiguar*

find² *n* hallazgo *m*

findings /'faɪndɪŋz/ *pl n* conclusiones *fpl*

fine¹ /faɪn/ *adj* **finer, finest** ① (*usu before n*)
(a) (excellent) ⟨*house/speech/example*⟩ magnífico;
⟨*wine/ingredients*⟩ de primera calidad (b) (fair)
⟨*weather*⟩ bueno ② (colloq) (*pred*) (a) (in good
health) muy bien (b) (OK) bien; (perfect) perfecto
③ (thin, delicate) ⟨*hair/china/point*⟩ fino ④ (subtle)
⟨*distinction/nuance*⟩ sutil; ⟨*balance*⟩ delicado;
⟨*adjustment*⟩ preciso

fine² *adv* (adequately) bien; (very well) muy bien

fine³ *n* multa *f*

fine⁴ *vt* multar

fine art *n* arte *m*; **the** ~ ~**s** las bellas artes; **to
have (got) sth down to a** ~ ~ hacer* algo a la
perfección

finely /'faɪnli/ *adv* (a) (in small pieces): **to chop
sth** ~ picar* algo muy fino (b) (subtly) ⟨*adjust*⟩
con precisión

fine print *n* (AmE) **the** ~ ~ la letra pequeña *or*
menuda, la letra chica (AmL)

finery /'faɪnəri/ *n*: **in all their** ~ con sus mejores
galas

finesse /fə'nes ‖fɪ'nes/ *n* (a) (refinement) finura *f*
(b) (tact) diplomacia *f*

fine-tooth(ed) comb /faɪn'tu:θ(t)/ *n*: **to go
over sth with a** ~**-tooth(ed) comb** mirar algo con
lupa

finger¹ /'fɪŋgər ‖'fɪŋgə(r)/ *n* (of hand, glove) dedo
m; **index** ~ (dedo) índice *m*; **middle** ~ (dedo)
corazón *m or* medio *m*; **ring** ~ (dedo) anular *m*;
little ~ (dedo) meñique *m*; **to cross one's** ~**s: I'll
keep my** ~**s crossed for you** ojalá (que) tengas
suerte; **to snap one's** ~**s** chasquear *or* (Méx)
tronar* los dedos

finger² *vt* toquetear, tentalear (Méx)

finger: ~**nail** *n* uña *f*; ~**print** *n* huella *f*
digital; ~**tip** *n* yema *f* del dedo

finish¹ /'fɪnɪ∫/ *vt* ① (a) (complete) terminar,
acabar; **we** ~ **work at four o'clock today** hoy
salimos a las cuatro; **to** ~ **-ING** terminar *or*
acabar DE + INF (b) (consume) ⟨*drink/rations*⟩
terminar, acabar
② ⟨*cloth/porcelain*⟩ terminar; ⟨*wood*⟩ pulir
③ (destroy) (colloq) acabar con
■ ~ *vi* terminar, acabar
■ **finish off** ①[*v + o + adv, v + adv + o*] (a)
(complete) terminar, acabar (b) (exhaust) dejar
agotado (c) (consume) terminar (d) (kill) matar
② [*v + adv*] (conclude) terminar, acabar
■ **finish up** ①[*v + o + adv, v + adv + o*] ⟨*food/
paint*⟩ terminar
② [*v + adv*] (end up) acabar

finish² *n* ① (*no pl*) (end) fin *m*, final *m*; (of race)
llegada *f* ② (surface texture) acabado *m*

finished /'fɪnɪ∫t/ *adj* (*pred*) (a) (complete,
achieved): **to get sth** ~ terminar *or* acabar algo;
I'm ~ **with the scissors** no necesito más la tijera
(b) (ruined) acabado

finishing /'fɪnɪ∫ɪŋ/: ~ **line** *n* (BrE) ▶ FINISH
LINE; ~ **school** *n*: colegio privado para
señoritas donde se aprende a comportarse en
sociedad; ~ **touch** *n*: **to put the** ~ **touch(es) to
sth** darle* los últimos toques a algo

finish line, (BrE) **finishing line** *n* meta *f*,
línea *f* de llegada

finite /'faɪnaɪt/ *adj* finito

Finland /'fɪnlənd/ *n* Finlandia *f*

Finn /fɪn/ *n* finlandés, -desa *m,f*, finés, -nesa *m,f*

Finnish¹ /'fɪnɪ∫/ *adj* finlandés, finés

Finnish² *n* finlandés *m*

fiord /fi'ɔːrd ‖fi'ɔːd/ *n* fiordo *m*

fir /fɜːr ‖fɜː(r)/ *n* abeto *m*

fire¹ /faɪr ‖'faɪə(r)/ *n* ① (a) (flames) fuego *m*; **to
be on** ~ estar* en llamas; **to set sth on** ~ *o* **to set**
~ **to sth** prenderle fuego a algo; **to catch** ~
prender fuego (b) (outdoors) hoguera *f*; (in hearth)
fuego *m* ② (blaze which destroys a building) incendio
m; (*as interj*) ~! ¡fuego!; (*before n*) ~ **curtain**
telón *m* contra incendios; **this is a** ~ **hazard** esto
podría causar un incendio ③ (heater) (BrE) estufa
f ④ (of guns) fuego *m*; **to open** ~ **on sb/sth** abrir*
fuego sobre algn/algo

fire² *vt* ① ⟨*gun/shot*⟩ disparar; ⟨*rocket*⟩ lanzar*;
to ~ **questions at sb** hacerle* preguntas a algn
② (dismiss) (colloq) echar, despedir*
③ ⟨*imagination*⟩ avivar
■ ~ *vi* (shoot) disparar; **to** ~ **AT sb/sth** disparar
CONTRA algn/algo; **ready, aim,** ~! apunten ¡fuego!

fire: ~ **alarm** *n* (apparatus) alarma *f* contra
incendios; (signal) alarma *f*; ~**arm** *n* arma *f*‡ de
fuego; ~ **department,** (BrE) ~ **brigade** *n*
cuerpo *m* de bomberos; ~ **door** *n* puerta *f*
contra incendios; ~ **drill** *n* simulacro *m* de
incendio; ~ **engine** *n* (BrE) ▶ ~ TRUCK; ~
escape *n* escalera *f* de incendios; ~
extinguisher *n* extinguidor *m* (de incendios)
(AmL), extintor *m* (Esp); ~**fighter** *n* bombero *mf*;
~ **guard** *n* rejilla *f* (*de chimenea*); ~**lighter** *n*:
*líquido o pastilla utilizados para facilitar el
encendido del fuego de leña o carbón*; ~**man**
/'faɪrmən ‖'faɪəmən/ (*pl* **-men** /-mən/) *n*
bombero *m*; ~**place** *n* chimenea *f*; ~**proof** *adj*
ignífugo; ~**side** *n* hogar *m*; ~ **station** *n*
estación *f or* (Esp) parque *m or* (RPl) cuartel *m* de ····❥

bomberos, bomba *f* (Chi); **~ truck** *n* (AmE) carro *m or* (Esp) coche *m* de bomberos, autobomba *m* (RPI), bomba *f* (Chi); **~wood** *n* leña *f*; **~works** *pl n* fuegos *mpl* artificiales

firing /'faɪrɪŋ ‖ faɪrɪŋ/ **: ~ line** *n*: **to be on o** (BrE) **in the ~ line** (exposed to criticism) estar* expuesto a las críticas; (Mil) estar* en la línea de combate; **~ squad** *n* pelotón *m* de fusilamiento

firm¹ /fɜːrm ‖fɜːm/ *adj* **1** **(a)** (secure) ⟨grasp⟩ firme **(b)** (not yielding) ⟨surface/muscles⟩ firme; ⟨mattress⟩ duro; ⟨foundation⟩ sólido **2** **(a)** (steadfast) ⟨friendship⟩ sólido; ⟨support⟩ firme **(b)** (strict) estricto **3** (definite) ⟨offer/date⟩ en firme

firm² *n* empresa *f*, firma *f*

firmly /'fɜːrmli ‖'fɜːmli/ *adv* ⟨grasp/believe⟩ con firmeza; ⟨fixed/supported⟩ firmemente

first¹ /fɜːrst ‖fɜːst/ *adj*

■ **Note** The usual translation of *first*, *primero*, becomes *primer* when it precedes a masculine singular noun.

1 (initial) primero; **the ~ president of the USA** el primer presidente de los EE UU; **who's going to be ~?** ¿quién va a ser el primero?; **~ things first** primero lo más importante **2** (elliptical use): **he'll be arriving on the ~ (of the month)** llegará el primero *or* (Esp tb) el uno (del mes); **she was the ~ to arrive** fue la primera en llegar **3** (*in phrases*) **at first** al principio; **from first to last** de(l) principio a(l) fin

first² *adv* **1** **(a)** (ahead of others) primero; **he came ~ in the exam** sacó la mejor nota en el examen; **I always put my children ~** para mí antes que nada están mis hijos; **ladies ~** primero las damas **(b)** (before other actions, events) primero **(c)** (beforehand) antes **(d)** (for the first time) por primera vez **2** (*in phrases*) **first and foremost** ante todo; **first and last** por encima de todo; **first of all** en primer lugar

first³ **(a)** **~ (gear)** (Auto) (*no art*) primera *f* **(b)** (original idea, accomplishment) primicia *f*

first: ~ aid *n* primeros auxilios *mpl*; (before n) **~-aid kit** botiquín *m* (de primeros auxilios); **~-aid station** *o* (BrE) **post** puesto *m* de primeros auxilios; **~ class** *adv* ⟨travel⟩ en primera (clase); **~-class** /'fɜːrst'klæs ‖,fɜːst'klɑːs/ *adj* (*pred* **~ class**) **(a)** (of highest grade) ⟨hotel/ticket⟩ de primera clase; ⟨travel⟩ en primera (clase) **(b)** (excellent) de primera **(c)** (BrE Corresp) **~-class mail** correspondencia enviada a una tarifa superior, que garantiza una rápida entrega; **~-hand** /'fɜːrst'hænd ‖,fɜːst'hænd/ *adj* ⟨news⟩ de primera mano; **~ lady** *n* primera dama *f*

firstly /'fɜːrstli ‖'fɜːstli/ *adv* (as linker) en primer lugar

first: ~ name *n* nombre *m* de pila; **~-rate** /'fɜːrst'reɪt ‖,fɜːst'reɪt/ *adj* de primera; **~-time buyer** *n*: persona que compra algo, gen una vivienda, por primera vez

fiscal /'fɪskəl/ *adj* fiscal

fiscal year *n* (AmE) año *m* fiscal

fish¹ /fɪʃ/ *n* (*pl* **fish** *or* **fishes**) **(a)** (Zool) pez *m*; (before n) **~ pond** estanque *m*; **~ tank** pecera *f* **(b)** (Culin) pescado *m*; **~ and chips** (esp BrE) pescado *m* frito con papas *or* (Esp) patatas fritas

fish² *vi* pescar*; **to go ~ing** ir* de pesca; **to ~ FOR sth** ⟨for trout⟩ pescar* algo; ⟨for compliments⟩ andar* a la caza de algo; **to ~ (around) in one's pockets/bag** rebuscar* en los bolsillos/la bolsa ■ **fish out** [*v + o + adv, v + adv + o*] sacar*

fish: ~bone *n* espina *f* (de pez); **~cake** *n* ≈ croqueta *f* (de pescado y papas)

fisherman /'fɪʃərmən ‖'fɪʃəmən/ *n* (*pl* **-men** /-mən/) pescador *m*

fishery /'fɪʃəri/ *n* (*pl* **-eries**) **1** ▶ FISH FARM **2** **fisheries** *pl* (industry) industria *f* pesquera, pesca *f*

fish: ~ farm *n* piscifactoría *f*; **~ finger** *n* (BrE) ▶ FISH STICK; **~hook** *n* anzuelo *m*

fishing /'fɪʃɪŋ/ *n* pesca *f*; (before n) ⟨industry/port/vessel/fleet⟩ pesquero

fishing: ~ net *n* red *f* de pesca; **~ pole** (AmE), **~ rod** *n* caña *f* de pescar

fish: ~monger /'fɪʃ,mɑːŋgər ‖'fɪʃ,mʌŋgə(r)/ *n* (BrE) pesficadero, -ra *m,f*; **at the ~monger('s)** en la pescadería; **~net** *n* **(a)** (Tex) red *f* ▶ FISHING NET **(b)** (Tex) red *f*; (before n) ⟨stockings⟩ de malla gruesa *or* de red; **~ slice** *n* (BrE) espumadera *f*; **~ stick** *n* (AmE) palito *m* de bacalao (*or* merluza *etc*) (trozo de pescado rebozado y frito)

fishy /'fɪʃi/ *adj* **fishier, fishiest** **1** ⟨smell/taste⟩ a pescado **2** (suspicious) (colloq) sospechoso

fission /'fɪʃən/ *n* fisión *f*

fist /fɪst/ *n* puño *m*

fistfight /'fɪstfaɪt/ *n* pelea *f* (a puñetazos)

fit¹ /fɪt/ *adj* **-tt-** **1** (healthy) en forma; **to keep ~** mantenerse* en forma; **to be ~ to + INF** ⟨to play/travel⟩ estar* en condiciones DE + INF **2** (suitable) ⟨person/conduct⟩ adecuado; **this isn't ~ to eat** (harmful) esto no está en buenas condiciones; (unappetizing) esto está incomible; **he's not ~ to be a father** no es digno de ser padre; **he did not see ~ to reply to our letter** ni se dignó contestar a nuestra carta

fit² **-tt-** *vt* **1** **(a)** (Clothing): **the dress ~s you perfectly** el vestido te queda perfecto; **the jacket doesn't ~ me** la chaqueta no me queda bien **(b)** (be right size, shape for) ⟨socket⟩ encajar en **(c)** (correspond to) ⟨theory⟩ concordar* con; **to ~ a description** responder a una descripción **2** (install) (esp BrE) ⟨carpet/lock⟩ poner*; ⟨double glazing⟩ instalar **3** (accommodate) **to ~ sth INTO sth** meter algo EN algo

■ **~** *vi* **(a)** (Clothing): **these shoes don't ~** estos zapatos no me quedan bien; **to make sth ~** ajustar algo **(b)** (be right size, shape) ⟨lid⟩ ajustar; «key/peg» encajar **(c)** (correspond) «facts/description» encajar

■ **fit in 1** [*v + adv*] **(a)** (have enough room) caber* **(b)** (accord) «detail/event» **to ~ in (WITH sth)** concordar* (CON algo) **(c)** (belong): **she doesn't ~**

in here esto no es para ella **(d)** (conform to): **he'll have to ∼ in with our plans** tendrá que amoldarse a nuestros planes

2 [*v + o + adv, v + adv + o*] **(a)** (find space for) acomodar **(b)** (find time for): **I can ∼ you in at ten o'clock** puedo atenderla a las diez; **she hoped to ∼ in some sightseeing** esperaba tener un poco de tiempo para salir a conocer el lugar

■ **fit out** [*v + o + adv, v + adv + o*] equipar; **to ∼ sb out WITH sth** ⟨*with boots/equipment*⟩ equipar a algn CON algo; ⟨*with uniform*⟩ proveer* a algn DE algo

fit³ *n* **1** **(a)** (attack) ataque *m*; **epileptic ∼** ataque epiléptico; **to have a ∼** (colloq): **I nearly had a ∼** casi me da un ataque (fam) **(b)** (short burst): **a ∼ of coughing** un acceso de tos; **in ∼s and starts** a los tropezones **2** (of clothes) (*no pl*): **my new jacket is a good ∼** la chaqueta nueva me queda bien; **it's a tight ∼** es muy entallado

fitful /'fɪtfəl/ *adj* ⟨*progress/sunshine*⟩ intermitente; ⟨*sleep*⟩ irregular

fitfully /'fɪtfəli/ *adv* de manera irregular

fitness /'fɪtnəs ‖'fɪtnɪs/ *n* **1** (healthiness) salud *f*; (**physical**) **∼** (buena) forma *f* física **2** (suitability) aptitud *f*

fitted /'fɪtəd ‖'fɪtɪd/ *adj* **(a)** ⟨*cupboard*⟩ empotrado; ⟨*shelves*⟩ hecho a medida; ⟨*sheet*⟩ ajustable, de cajón (Méx); **∼ carpet** (esp BrE) alfombra *f* de pared a pared, moqueta *f* (Esp) **(b)** ⟨*kitchen*⟩ integral

fitter /'fɪtər ‖'fɪtə(r)/ *n* **1** (Clothing) probador, -dora *m,f* **2** (mechanic — in garage) mecánico, -ca *m,f*; (— in car industry, shipbuilding) operario, -ria *m,f*

fitting¹ /'fɪtɪŋ/ *adj* ⟨*conclusion*⟩ adecuado; ⟨*tribute*⟩ digno

fitting² *n* **1** (Clothing) **(a)** (trying on) prueba *f* **(b)** (BrE) (size — of clothes) medida *f*; (— of shoe) horma *f* **2** **(a)** (accessory) accesorio *m* **(b)** **fittings** *pl* (esp BrE Const) accesorios *mpl*; **electrical ∼s** instalaciones *fpl* eléctricas; **bathroom ∼s** grifería *f* y accesorios *mpl* de baño

fitting room *n* probador *m*

five /faɪv/ *adj/n* cinco *adj inv/m*; *see also* FOUR¹

fiver /'faɪvər ‖'faɪvə(r)/ *n* **(a)** ($5) (AmE sl) cinco dólares *mpl* **(b)** (£5) (BrE colloq) cinco libras *fpl*

fix¹ /fɪks/ *vt*

I **1** ⟨*plank/shelf*⟩ sujetar; **to ∼ a notice on a door** poner* un anuncio en una puerta; **to ∼ sth in one's memory** grabar algo en la memoria **2** (direct steadily): **his eyes were ∼ed on the road ahead** tenía la mirada fija en la carretera; **he ∼ed her with a stony gaze** clavó en ella una mirada glacial

II **1** ⟨*date/time/price*⟩ fijar **2** (repair) (colloq) arreglar **3** (prepare) (esp AmE colloq) preparar **4** (colloq) ⟨*election/contest*⟩ amañar (fam)

■ **∼ vi** (make plans) (AmE): **we're ∼ing to go fishing on Sunday** estamos planeando ir de pesca el domingo

■ **fix up** [*v + o + adv, v + adv + o*] **(a)** (provide for): **I need somewhere to stay: can you ∼ me up?** necesito alojamiento ¿me lo puedes arreglar?; **she ∼ed me up with a job** me encontró un trabajo **(b)** (repair) ⟨*house/room*⟩ (AmE) arreglar

fix² *n* (predicament) (colloq) aprieto *m*, apuro *m*

fixation /fɪk'seɪʃən/ *n* obsesión *f*

fixed /fɪkst/ *adj* **1** ⟨*price/rate/ideas*⟩ fijo; ⟨*principles/position*⟩ rígido; **a ∼-term contract** un contrato a plazo fijo **2** ⟨*gaze*⟩ fijo; ⟨*smile*⟩ petrificado

fixed: ∼ assets *pl n* activo *m* fijo; **∼-rate** /'fɪkst'reɪt/ *adj* a una tasa de interés fija *or* (esp Esp) a tipo de interés fijo

fixture /'fɪkstʃər ‖'fɪkstʃə(r)/ *n* **1** **(a)** (in building) *elemento de la instalación, como los artefactos del baño, cocina etc* **(b)** (permanent feature) parte *f* integrante **2** (BrE Sport) encuentro *m*

fizz /fɪz/ *vi* ⟨*champagne/cola*⟩ burbujear

fizzle out /'fɪzəl/ [*v + adv*] ⟨*fire/firework*⟩ apagarse*; ⟨*excitement*⟩ esfumarse

fizzy /'fɪzi/ *adj* **-zier, -ziest** gaseoso, efervescente; **∼ water** (colloq) agua *f* ⁑ mineral con gas

fjord /fi'ɔːrd ‖fɪ'ɔːd/ *n* fiordo *m*

FL, Fla = **Florida**

flabbergasted /'flæbər,gæstəd ‖'flæbə,ɡɑːstɪd/ *adj* estupefacto

flabby /'flæbi/ *adj* **-bier, -biest** ⟨*stomach*⟩ fofo; ⟨*muscle*⟩ flojo

flag¹ /flæg/ *n* bandera *f*

flag² **-gg-** *vi* ⟨*person/animal*⟩ desfallecer*; ⟨*interest/conversation/spirits*⟩ decaer*; ⟨*attendance*⟩ disminuir*

■ **∼ vt** **(a)** (mark with flags) marcar* con banderas **(b)** (mark for special attention) marcar*

■ **flag down** [*v + o + adv, v + adv + o*] parar (haciendo señas)

flagpole /'flæɡpəʊl/ *n* asta *f* ⁑ de (la) bandera

flagrant /'fleɪɡrənt/ *adj* flagrante

flag: ∼ship *n* (Naut) buque *m* insignia; (showpiece) producto *m* (*or* programa *m etc*) bandera; **∼stone** *n* losa *f*

flair /fler ‖fleə(r)/ *n* **(a)** (natural aptitude) (*no pl*): **a ∼ for languages/business** facilidad *f* para los idiomas/olfato *m* para los negocios **(b)** (stylishness) estilo *m*

flak /flæk/ *n* **(a)** (Aviat, Mil) fuego *m* antiaéreo **(b)** (criticism) críticas *fpl*

flake¹ /fleɪk/ *n* (of snow, cereals) copo *m*; (of paint, rust, skin) escama *f*

flake² *vi* ⟨*paint/plaster*⟩ descascararse

flaky, flakey /'fleɪki/ *adj* **-kier, -kiest** ⟨*piecrust*⟩ hojaldrado; ⟨*paint/plaster*⟩ que se desconcha; **∼ pastry** *masa tipo hojaldre*

flamboyant /flæm'bɔɪənt/ *adj* **(a)** (dashing) ⟨*style/person*⟩ exuberante; ⟨*gesture*⟩ ampuloso **(b)** (brilliant) ⟨*color*⟩ vistoso; ⟨*hat/dress*⟩ llamativo

flame /fleɪm/ *n* **(a)** llama *f*; **to be in ∼s** estar* (envuelto) en llamas; **to go up in ∼s** incendiarse **(b)** (lover): **he's an old ∼ of mine** es un antiguo enamorado mío

flame: ∼proof *adj* ⟨*fabric*⟩ ininflamable; ⟨*dish*⟩ resistente al fuego; **∼thrower** /'fleɪm'θrəʊər ‖'fleɪm,θrəʊə(r)/n lanzallamas *m*

flamingo /flə'mɪŋɡəʊ/ *n* (*pl* **-gos** *or* **-goes**) flamenco *m*

flammable /'flæməbəl/ *adj* inflamable, flamable (Méx)

flan /flæn/ *n* (sweet) tarta *f*, kuchen *m* (Chi); (individual) tartaleta *f*, tarteleta *f* (RPl)

flank¹ /flæŋk/ n **(a)** (of animal) ijada f, ijar m; (of person) costado m **(b)** (Mil, Sport) flanco m

flank² vt (often pass) flanquear

flannel /'flænl/ n 1 **(a)** (fabric) franela f; (before n) ⟨shirt/nightgown⟩ de franela **(b) flannels** pl (trousers) pantalón m de franela 2 (face ∼) (BrE) toallita f (para lavarse)

flap¹ /flæp/ n 1 **(a)** (cover) tapa f; (of pocket, envelope) solapa f; (of table) hoja f; (of jacket, coat) faldón m; (of tent) portezuela f; (ear ∼) orejera f; **a cat ∼** una gatera **(b)** (Aviat) alerón m 2 (motion) aletazo m 3 (commotion, agitation) (colloq): **to be in/get into a ∼** estar*/ponerse* como loco (fam)

flap² -**pp**- vi «sail/curtain» agitarse; «flag» ondear
■ ∼ vt ⟨wings⟩ batir; ⟨arms⟩ agitar

flapjack /'flæpdʒæk/ n 1 (pancake) (esp AmE) crepe o panqueque pequeño y grueso 2 (cookie) (BrE) tipo de galleta dulce de avena

flare /fler ‖fleə(r)/ n 1 **(a)** (marker light) bengala f; (on runway, road) baliza f **(b)** (sudden light) destello m; (flame) llamarada f 2 (Clothing) **(a)** (on jacket) vuelo m **(b) flares** (BrE) pantalones mpl acampanados
■ **flare up** [v + adv] **(a)** «fire» llamear; «fighting» estallar **(b)** «infection/disease» recrudecer* **(c)** (lose temper) explotar

flared /flerd ‖fleəd/ adj ⟨skirt⟩ con mucho vuelo, evasé (RPl); ⟨trousers⟩ acampanado

flare-up /'flerʌp ‖'fleərʌp/ n (of violence) brote m

flash¹ /flæʃ/ n 1 **(a)** (of light) destello m; (from explosion) fogonazo m; **a ∼ of inspiration** un ramalazo de inspiración; (as) **quick as a ∼** como un rayo; **in a ∼**: **it came to me in a ∼** de repente lo vi claro **(b)** (Phot) flash m 2 (news ∼) avance m informativo

flash² vt 1 (direct): **they ∼ed a light in my face** me enfocaron la cara con una luz; **to ∼ one's headlights at sb** hacerle* una señal con los faros a algn
2 (show) ⟨card⟩ mostrar*, enseñar (esp Esp); **she loves ∼ing her money around** le encanta ir por ahí haciendo ostentación de su dinero
■ ∼ vi 1 **(a)** (emit sudden light) destellar **(b)** (Auto) hacer* una señal con los faros **(c) flashing** pres p ⟨sign/light⟩ intermitente; ⟨eyes/smile⟩ brillante 2 (move fast) (+ adv compl): **a message ∼ed across the screen** un mensaje apareció fugazmente en la pantalla; **to ∼ by** o **past** «train/car/person» pasar como una bala

flash: ∼back n (Cin, Lit) flashback m; **∼bulb** n (Phot) lámpara f de flash; **∼cube** n (Phot) cubo m (de) flash; **∼ gun** n flash m electrónico; **∼light** n (AmE) linterna f

flashy /'flæʃi/ adj -**shier**, -**shiest** llamativo

flask /flæsk ‖flɑːsk/ n (bottle) frasco m; (in laboratory) matraz m; (hip ∼) petaca f, nalguera f (Méx); (vacuum ∼) (BrE) termo m

flat¹ /flæt/ adj -**tt**- 1 **(a)** ⟨surface⟩ plano; ⟨countryside⟩ llano; **∼ feet** pies mpl planos; **I was ∼ on my back for two months** estuve en cama durante dos semanas **(b)** ⟨dish⟩ llano, bajo (Chi), playo (RPl); **∼ shoes** zapatos mpl bajos, zapatillas fpl de piso (Méx) **(c)** (deflated) ⟨ball⟩ desinflado,

ponchado (Méx); **you have a ∼ tire** o (BrE) **tyre** tienes un neumático desinflado or (Méx) una llanta ponchada
2 **(a)** ⟨lemonade/beer⟩ sin efervescencia **(b)** ⟨battery⟩ descargado
3 (dull, uninteresting) ⟨conversation/party⟩ soso (fam); ⟨joke⟩ sin gracia; ⟨voice⟩ monótono; **to fall ∼** «play/project» fracasar*; **the joke fell very ∼** el chiste no hizo ni pizca de gracia
4 (total, firm) ⟨denial/refusal⟩ rotundo
5 (Mus) (referring to key) bemol; **A ∼** la m bemol
6 (fixed) (before n) ⟨rate⟩ fijo

flat² adv 1 **(a)** ⟨refuse/turn down⟩ de plano **(b)** (exactly): **it took him two hours ∼** tardó dos horas justas 2 (Mus) demasiado bajo

flat³ n 1 (apartment) (BrE) apartamento m, departamento m (AmL), piso m (Esp) 2 **(a)** (surface — of sword) cara f de la hoja; (— of hand) palma f **(b)** (level ground) llano m 3 (Mus) bemol m

flatly /'flætli/ adv de plano

flatmate /'flætmeɪt/ n (BrE) compañero, -ra m,f de apartamento or (Esp) de piso

flat out¹ adj (colloq) (pred) (prostrate) tirado

flat out² adv (at full speed) (colloq) a toda máquina

flat-rate /'flæt'reɪt/ adj (BrE) a una tasa de interés fija or (esp Esp) a tipo de interés fijo

flatten /'flætn/ vt ⟨surface⟩ aplanar; ⟨path/lawn⟩ allanar; ⟨city⟩ arrasar

flatter /'flætər ‖'flætə(r)/ vt **(a)** (gratify) halagar* **(b)** (show to advantage) favorecer*

flattering /'flætərɪŋ/ adj **(a)** ⟨words/speech⟩ halagador **(b)** ⟨clothes/hairstyle⟩ favorecedor

flattery /'flætəri/ n halagos mpl

flaunt /flɔːnt/ vt ⟨possessions⟩ hacer* ostentación de; ⟨knowledge⟩ alardear de

flavor¹, (BrE) **flavour** /'fleɪvər ‖'fleɪvə(r)/ n sabor m, gusto m

flavor², (BrE) **flavour** vt sazonar; **chocolate-∼ed** con sabor or gusto a chocolate

flavoring, (BrE) **flavouring** /'fleɪvərɪŋ/ n condimento m

flaw /flɔː/ n (in material, character) defecto m; (in argument) error m

flawless /'flɔːləs ‖'flɔːlɪs/ adj ⟨performance/logic⟩ impecable; ⟨conduct⟩ intachable; ⟨complexion/gem⟩ perfecto

flax /flæks/ n lino m

flay /fleɪ/ vt desollar*

flea /fliː/ n pulga f; (before n) ⟨collar/powder⟩ antipulgas adj inv

flea market n mercado m de las pulgas or (CS) de pulgas, rastro m (Esp)

fleck¹ /flek/ n (of dust) mota f; (of paint, mud) salpicadura f

fleck² vt (with mud) salpicar*; **beige ∼ed with brown** beige moteado de marrón

fled /fled/ past & past p of FLEE

fledgling, fledgeling /'fledʒlɪŋ/ n polluelo m; (before n) **a ∼ democracy** una democracia en ciernes

flee /fliː/ (past & past p **fled**) vi huir*
■ ∼ vt huir* de

fleece¹ /fliːs/ n (on sheep) lana f; (from sheep) vellón m

fleece² vt (colloq) desplumar (fam)

fleet /fliːt/ n **(a)** (naval unit, body of shipping) flota f **(b)** (navy) armada f **(c)** (of cars) parque m móvil, flota f

fleeting /ˈfliːtɪŋ/ adj (usu before n) fugaz

Flemish¹ /ˈflemɪʃ/ adj flamenco

Flemish² n flamenco m

flesh /fleʃ/ n carne f; **in the ∼** en persona; **∼ and blood: after all, I'm only ∼ and blood** después de todo, soy de carne y hueso

fleshy /ˈfleʃi/ adj **-shier, -shiest** adj ⟨arms/person⟩ rollizo; ⟨plant/leaf⟩ carnoso

flew /fluː/ past of FLY²

flex¹ /fleks/ vt ⟨arm/knees/body⟩ doblar; **to ∼ one's muscles** (to warm up) hacer* ejercicios de calentamiento; (in body building) mostrar* los músculos; «regime» mostrar* su poderío

flex² n (BrE) cable m (eléctrico)

flexible /ˈfleksəbəl/ adj flexible

flextime /ˈflekstaɪm/, (BrE) **flexitime** /ˈfleksɪtaɪm/ n horario m flexible

flick¹ /flɪk/ vt **(a)** (strike lightly): **she ∼ed a piece of bread at me** me tiró un pedazo de pan **(b)** (remove): **he ∼ed the ash off his lapel** se sacudió la ceniza de la solapa

■ **flick through** [v + prep + o] ⟨book⟩ hojear; ⟨pages⟩ pasar

flick² n (of tail) coletazo m; (of wrist) giro m

flicker¹ /ˈflɪkər ‖ ˈflɪkə(r)/ vi parpadear

flicker² n parpadeo m

flier /ˈflaɪər ‖ ˈflaɪə(r)/ n **1** **(a)** (pilot) aviador, -dora m,f **(b)** (passenger) usuario -ria m,f (regular) del avion **2** (handbill) (AmE) folleto m (publicitario), volante m (AmL)

flight /flaɪt/ n **1** **(a)** (of bird, aircraft) vuelo m; (of ball, projectile) trayectoria f; **in ∼** en vuelo **(b)** (air journey) vuelo m; (before n) **∼ path** ruta f; **∼ recorder** caja f negra **2** (group of birds) bandada f **3** (of stairs) tramo m **4** (act of fleeing) huida f; **to take ∼** darse* a la fuga

flight: ∼ attendant n auxiliar mf de vuelo; **∼ deck** n (on plane) cabina f de mando; (on aircraft carrier) cubierta f de vuelo

flimsy /ˈflɪmzi/ adj **-sier, -siest** **(a)** ⟨material/garment⟩ ligerísimo **(b)** ⟨construction/object⟩ endeble **(c)** ⟨excuse⟩ pobre; ⟨argument/evidence⟩ poco sólido

flinch /flɪntʃ/ vi estremecerse*

fling¹ /flɪŋ/ vt (past & past p flung) lanzar*, aventar* (Col, Méx, Per)

fling² n (colloq) **(a)** (love affair) aventura f; **to have a ∼** tener* una aventurilla **(b)** (wild time) juerga f (fam); **to have a ∼** irse* de juerga

flint /flɪnt/ n **(a)** (Geol) sílex m, pedernal m; (piece of stone) pedernal m **(b)** (for cigarette lighter) piedra f

flip /flɪp/ **-pp-** vt tirar, aventar* (Méx); **we'll ∼ a coin to decide** vamos a echarlo a cara o cruz or (Andes, Ven) a cara o sello or (Arg) a cara o ceca, vamos a echar un volado (Méx)

■ **∼** vi (sl) (lose self-control) perder* la chaveta (fam)

flip-flop /ˈflɪpflɑːp ‖ ˈflɪpflɒp/ n (BrE) ▶ THONG B

flippant /ˈflɪpənt/ adj ⟨remark⟩ frívolo; ⟨attitude⟩ displicente

flipper /ˈflɪpər ‖ ˈflɪpə(r)/ n aleta f

flip side n **the ∼** (Audio) la cara B; (of a situation) (colloq) la otra cara de la moneda (fam)

flirt¹ /flɜːrt ‖ flɜːt/ vi flirtear

flirt² n: **he is a terrible ∼** le encanta flirtear

flirtation /flɜːrˈteɪʃən ‖ flɜːˈteɪʃən/ n **(a)** (relationship) flirt m **(b)** (coquetry) flirteo m

flit /flɪt/ vi **-tt-** «bird/butterfly/bat» revolotear

float¹ /fləʊt/ vi **(a)** (on water) flotar; **to ∼ (up) to the surface** salir* a flote **(b)** «cloud/smoke» flotar en el aire

■ **∼** vt **1** ⟨ship/boat⟩ poner* a flote; ⟨raft/logs⟩ llevar **2** (Fin) **(a)** (establish): **to ∼ a company** introducir* una compañía en Bolsa **(b)** ⟨shares/stock⟩ emitir **(c)** ⟨currency⟩ dejar flotar **3** (circulate) ⟨idea⟩ presentar

float² n **1** **(a)** (for fishing, for buoyancy) flotador m **(b)** (in cistern, carburetor) flotador m **(c)** (raft, platform) plataforma f (flotante) **2** **(a)** (in parade) carroza f, carro m alegórico (CS, Méx) **(b)** (milk ∼) (BrE) furgoneta f (del reparto de leche) **3** (ready cash) caja f chica; (Busn, Fin) fondo m fijo

floating /ˈfləʊtɪŋ/ adj (before n) **1** ⟨harbor/restaurant⟩ flotante **2** (Fin) ⟨currency⟩ flotante; ⟨assets⟩ circulante **3** ⟨population⟩ flotante; ⟨voter⟩ (BrE) indeciso

flock¹ /flɑːk ‖ flɒk/ n (+ sing or pl vb) (of sheep) rebaño m; (of birds) bandada f; (of people) (often pl) tropel m, multitud f

flock² vi acudir (en gran número, en masa)

floe /fləʊ/ n témpano m de hielo

flog /flɑːg ‖ flɒg/ vt **-gg-** **1** (beat) azotar **2** (sell) (BrE sl) vender

flood¹ /flʌd/ n (of water) inundación f; (of complaints, calls) avalancha f; **she was in ∼s of tears** estaba hecha un mar de lágrimas

flood² vt inundar; ⟨engine⟩ ahogar*; **to ∼ the market with imports** (Busn) inundar el mercado de productos importados

■ **∼** vi «river/sewers» desbordarse; «mine/basement» inundarse; (Auto) ahogarse*; **to ∼ in** «sunshine» entrar a raudales; **donations came ∼ing in** llovieron los donativos

flooding /ˈflʌdɪŋ/ n inundación f

floodlight¹ /ˈflʌdlaɪt/ n reflector m, foco m

floodlight² vt (past & past p **floodlit** /ˈflʌdlɪt/) **(a)** iluminar (con reflectores o focos) **(b)** **floodlit** past p ⟨arena/building⟩ iluminado; ⟨game⟩ que se juega con luz artificial

flood: ∼ tide n pleamar f; **∼water** n (often pl) crecida f

floor¹ /flɔːr ‖ flɔː(r)/ n **1** **(a)** (of room, vehicle) suelo m, piso m (AmL) **(b)** (for dancing) pista f (de baile) **(c)** (of ocean, valley, forest) fondo m **2** (storey) piso m; **we live on the first/second ∼** (AmE) vivimos en la planta baja/el primer piso or (Chi) en el primer/segundo piso; (BrE) vivimos en el primer/segundo piso or (Chi) en el segundo/tercer piso

floor² vt **(a)** (knock down) derribar **(b)** (nonplus) (colloq) dejar helado (fam)

floorboard /ˈflɔːrbɔːrd ‖ ˈflɔːbɔːd/ n tabla f del suelo, duela f (Méx)

flooring /ˈflɔːrɪŋ/ n revestimiento m para suelos

floor show n espectáculo m (de cabaret)

flop¹ /flɑːp ‖ flɒp/ vi **-pp-** **1** (fall, move slackly) (+ ⋯⟶

adv compl): she ~ped down into a chair se dejó caer en un sillón; he ~ped down exhausted onto the bed se desplomó en la cama muerto de cansancio **2** (fail) (colloq) fracasar estrepitosamente

flop² n (colloq) fracaso m

floppy¹ /'flɑ:pi ‖'flɒpi/ adj ⟨hat/bag⟩ flexible; ⟨ears/tail⟩ caído

floppy² n (pl **-pies**) (colloq) ► FLOPPY DISK

floppy disk n disquete m, floppy (disk) m

floral /'flɔːrəl/ adj ⟨fabric/dress⟩ floreado; a ~ print un estampado de flores

florid /'flɔːrəd ‖'flɒrɪd/ adj (a) (red) ⟨complexion⟩ rubicundo (b) (ornate) ⟨decoration/ style⟩ recargado; ⟨language⟩ florido

florist /'flɔːrəst ‖'flɒrɪst/ n (person) florista mf; is there a ~'s near here? ¿hay una floristería or (AmL tb) florería cerca de aquí?

flotation /fləʊ'teɪʃən/ n (of company) salida f a Bolsa; (of shares) emisión f

flotsam /'flɑːtsəm ‖'flɒtsəm/ n restos mpl flotantes (de un naufragio); ~ and jetsam desechos mpl

flounce¹ /flaʊns/ vi (+ adv compl): to ~ in/out entrar/salir* indignado (or airado etc)

flounce² n (ruffle) volante m, elán m (Méx), volado m (RPI), vuelo m (Chi)

flounder /'flaʊndər ‖'flaʊndə(r)/ vi (a) (in water) luchar para mantenerse a flote (b) «speaker» quedarse sin saber qué decir

flour /flaʊər ‖'flaʊə(r)/ n harina f

flourish¹ /'flɜːrɪʃ ‖'flʌrɪʃ/ vi «arts/trade» florecer*; «business» prosperar; «plant» darse* or crecer* bien
■ ~ vt ⟨stick/letter⟩ blandir

flourish² n (a) (showy gesture) floreo m (b) (embellishment) floritura f, firulete m (AmL); (in signature) rúbrica f

flourishing /'flɜːrɪʃɪŋ ‖'flʌrɪʃɪŋ/ adj ⟨business⟩ próspero

flout /flaʊt/ vt desobedecer* abiertamente

flow¹ /fləʊ/ vi (a) «liquid/electric current» fluir*; «tide» subir; «blood» correr; (from wound) manar (b) (run smoothly, continuously) «traffic» circular con fluidez; «music/words» fluir*

flow² n **1** (a) (of liquid, current) flujo m (b) (of traffic, information) circulación f; (of capital, money) movimiento m **2** (stream — of water, lava) corriente f

flow chart, flow diagram n organigrama m

flower¹ /flaʊər ‖'flaʊə(r)/ n flor f

flower² vi florecer*, florear (Chi, Méx)

flower: ~bed n arriate m (Esp, Méx), parterre m (Esp), cantero m (Cu, RPI); ~pot n maceta f, tiesto m (Esp), macetero m (AmS)

flowery /'flaʊri ‖'flaʊəri/ adj ⟨pattern⟩ floreado; ⟨meadow⟩ florido; ⟨style/prose⟩ florido

flowing /'fləʊɪŋ/ adj (a) ⟨beard/robe⟩ largo y suelto (b) ⟨handwriting/movement⟩ fluido

flown /fləʊn/ past p of FLY²

flu /fluː/ n gripe f, gripa f (Col, Méx)

fluctuate /'flʌktʃueɪt ‖'flʌktjʊeɪt/ vi fluctuar*

fluctuation /ˌflʌktʃu'eɪʃən ‖ˌflʌktjʊ'eɪʃən/ n fluctuación f

flue /fluː/ n tiro m

fluency /'fluːənsi/ n fluidez f

fluent /'fluːənt/ adj: to speak ~ Italian hablar italiano con fluidez

fluently /'fluːəntli/ adv con fluidez

fluff /flʌf/ n pelusa f

fluffy /'flʌfi/ adj **-fier, -fiest** ⟨fabric/garment⟩ suave y esponjoso; ⟨fur/hair⟩ suave y sedoso

fluid¹ /'fluːəd ‖'fluːɪd/ n fluido m

fluid² adj fluido

fluke /fluːk/ n (colloq) chiripa f (fam)

flummox /'flʌməks/ vt (colloq) desconcertar*

flung /flʌŋ/ past & past p of FLING¹

fluorescent /flʊ'resənt ‖fluə'resənt, flɔː-/ adj fluorescente; ~ light tubo m fluorescente, tubolux® m (RPI)

fluoride /'flʊəraɪd ‖'flɔːraɪd/ n (Chem) fluoruro m; (Dent) flúor m; (before n) ~ toothpaste dentífrico m con flúor

flurry /'flɜːri ‖'flʌri/ n (pl **-ries**) **1** (of snow, wind) ráfaga f; (of rain) chaparrón m **2** (sudden burst): a ~ of excitement/activity una oleada de emoción/un frenesí de actividad

flush¹ /flʌʃ/ n **1** (a) (blush) rubor m (b) (of anger, passion) arrebato m; in the first ~ of success con la euforia del triunfo **2** (in cards) flor f

flush² vt **1** ⟨toilet⟩: to ~ the toilet tirar de la cadena, jalarle (a la cadena) (AmL exc CS) **2** (drive out) ~ (out) ⟨person/criminal⟩ hacer* salir
■ ~ vi **1** ⟨toilet⟩ funcionar **2** (blush) «person/ face» (with anger) enrojecer*; (with embarrassment) ruborizarse*

flush³ adj alineado

flushed /flʌʃt/ adj ⟨cheeks⟩ colorado; ~ with success exaltado por el éxito

fluster /'flʌstər ‖'flʌstə(r)/ vt poner* nervioso; to get ~ed ponerse* nervioso

flute /fluːt/ n flauta f

flutter¹ /'flʌtər ‖'flʌtə(r)/ vi «bird/butterfly» revolotear; «flag» ondear, agitarse; «heart» latir con fuerza
■ ~ vt ⟨wings⟩ batir, sacudir

flutter² n ~ (of wings) (no pl) aleteo m

flux /flʌks/ n: to be in (a state of) ~ estar* en un estado de cambio

fly¹ /flaɪ/ n (pl **flies**) **1** (insect) mosca f **2** (on trousers) (often pl in BrE) bragueta f, marrueco m (Chi)

fly² (3rd pers sing pres **flies**; pres p **flying**; past **flew**; past p **flown**) vi **1** (a) ⟨bird/bee⟩ volar*; «passenger» ir* en avión; to ~ away irse* volando; to ~ in/out ⟨bird/bee⟩ entrar/salir* volando; ⟨plane/pilot⟩ llegar*/salir* (en avión) (b) «flag» ondear **2** (a) (rush) «person» correr, ir* (or salir* etc) volando; **to ~ AT sb** lanzarse* SOBRE algn; **to ~ into a rage** ponerse* hecho una furia **(b)** (move, be thrown) volar*; **I tripped and went ~ing** tropecé y salí volando **(c)** (pass quickly) «*time*» pasar volando

■ ~ *vt* [1] **(a)** (control) ⟨*plane/glider/balloon*⟩ pilotar; ⟨*kite*⟩ hacer* volar *or* encumbrar (Andes), remontar (RPl) **(b)** (carry) ⟨*cargo*⟩ transportar (*en avión*); ⟨*person*⟩ llevar (*en avión*) **(c)** (travel over) ⟨*distance*⟩ recorrer (*en avión*) [2] ⟨*flag*⟩ izar*, enarbolar

flyer /'flaɪər ‖'flaɪə(r)/ *n* ► FLIER

flying¹ /'flaɪɪŋ/ *adj* (*before n*) **(a)** (hurried): **a ~ visit** una visita relámpago **(b)** ⟨*glass/debris*⟩ que vuela (por los aires)

flying² *n* **(a)** (as pilot) pilotaje *m*; (*before n*) ⟨*time/lesson*⟩ de vuelo; ⟨*helmet/jacket*⟩ de piloto **(b)** (as passenger): **I hate ~** odio viajar en avión

flying: ~ saucer *n* platillo *m* volador *or* (Esp) volante; **~ start** *n* salida *f* lanzada; **to get off to a ~ start** «*person/business*» empezar* con muy buen pie

fly: ~leaf *n* guarda *f*; **~-on-the-wall** *adj* ⟨*documentary*⟩ en el que las cámaras son meras espectadoras de la acción; **~over** *n* (BrE Transp) paso *m* elevado, paso *m* a desnivel (Méx); **~ spray** *n* insecticida *m* (*en aerosol*); **~swatter** /'flaɪˌswɑːtər ‖'flaɪˌswɒtə(r)/ *n* matamoscas *m*; **~wheel** *n* volante *m*

FM *n* (= **frequency modulation**) FM *f*

foal /fəʊl/ *n* (male) potro *m*, potrillo *m*; (female) potranca *f*, potra *f*

foam¹ /fəʊm/ *n* espuma *f*

foam² *vi* «*sea/waves*» hacer* espuma; **to ~ at the mouth** echar espuma por la boca

foam rubber *n* goma espuma *f*, hule *m* espuma (Méx)

fob /fɑːb ‖fɒb/ *n* (watchchain) leontina *f*; (*before n*) **~ watch** reloj *m* de bolsillo

■ **fob off: -bb-** [*v + o + adv*] (placate) **to ~ sb off** (WITH sth) engatusar a algn (CON algo)

focal /'fəʊkəl/ *adj* (*before n*) **(a)** (Opt) focal **(b)** ⟨*issue*⟩ central

focal point *n* **(a)** (Opt) foco *m* **(b)** (of attention, activity) centro *m*

focus¹ /'fəʊkəs/ *n* (*pl* **-cuses** *or* **foci** /'fəʊsaɪ/) [1] (Opt, Phot) foco *m*; **to be in/out of ~** estar* enfocado/desenfocado [2] (central point) centro *m*

focus² **-s-** *or* **-ss-** *vt* **(a)** (Opt, Phot) enfocar* **(b)** (concentrate) **to ~ sth** (ON sth) ⟨*attention*⟩ centrar algo (EN algo)

■ ~ *vi* **(a)** «*camera/eyes*» enfocar* **(b)** «*lecturer/chapter/attention*» **to ~ ON sth/sb** centrarse EN algo/algn

focus group *n* grupo *m* analizado

fodder /'fɑːdər ‖'fɒdə(r)/ *n* forraje *m*

foe /fəʊ/ *n* (liter) enemigo, -ga *m,f*

foetus /'fiːtəs/ *n* (BrE) ► FETUS

fog /fɔːg ‖fɒg/ *n* (Meteo) niebla *f*

fogbound /'fɔːgbaʊnd ‖'fɒgbaʊnd/ *adj* ⟨*airport/road*⟩ afectado por la niebla; ⟨*plane/ferry*⟩ retenido a causa de la niebla

foggy /'fɔːgi ‖'fɒgi/ *adj* **-gier, -giest (a)** ⟨*day*⟩ de niebla; ⟨*weather*⟩ nebuloso; **it's ~** hay niebla **(b)** (confused) confuso

fog: ~horn *n* sirena *f* (*de niebla*); **~ light, ~ lamp** *n* (BrE) faro *m* antiniebla

foible /'fɔɪbəl/ *n* debilidad *f*

foil¹ /fɔɪl/ *n* **(a)** (metal sheet) lámina *f* de metal **(b)** (Culin) (kitchen **~**) papel *m* de aluminio *or* de plata

foil² *vt* ⟨*plan/attempt*⟩ frustrar

foist /fɔɪst/ *vt* **to ~ sth** (OFF) ON *o* ONTO sb endilgarle* algo a algn

fold¹ /fəʊld/ *vt* [1] **(a)** (bend, bring together) ⟨*paper/sheet*⟩ doblar; **to ~ one's arms** cruzar* los brazos [2] (Culin) **to ~ sth INTO sth** incorporar algo A algo

■ ~ *vi* [1] **(a)** «*chair/table*» plegarse*; «*map/poster*» doblarse **(b)** folding *pres p* ⟨*chair/table*⟩ plegable [2] (fail) «*project*» venirse* abajo; «*play*» bajar de cartel; «*business*» cerrar* (sus puertas)

■ **fold up** [*v + o + adv, v + adv + o*] ⟨*sheet/newspaper*⟩ doblar; ⟨*chair/table*⟩ plegar*

fold² *n* [1] (crease) doblez *m* [2] (sheep pen) redil *m*

-fold /fəʊld/ *suff*: **his income increased five~** sus ingresos se multiplicaron por cinco *or* se quintuplicaron; **the problem is three~** el problema tiene tres aspectos

folder /'fəʊldər ‖'fəʊldə(r)/ *n* **(a)** (for papers) carpeta *f* **(b)** (Comput) carpeta *f*

foliage /'fəʊlɪdʒ/ *n* follaje *m*

folio /'fəʊliəʊ/ *n* (*pl* **folios**) (sheet) pliego *m*; (numbered leaf) folio *m*

folk /fəʊk/ *n* [1] **(a)** (*pl* **folks**) (people, colloq) gente *f* **(b)** **folks** *pl* (esp AmE colloq) (relatives) familia *f*; (parents) padres *mpl*, viejos *mpl* (fam) [2] (+ *pl vb*) (Anthrop) pueblo *m*; (*before n*) ⟨*art/medicine*⟩ popular; ⟨*dancing*⟩ folklórico

folk: ~lore *n* folklore *m*; **~ music** *n* (traditional) música *f* folklórica; (modern) música *f* folk; **~ song** *n* (traditional) canción *f* popular; (modern) canción *f* folk

follow /'fɑːləʊ ‖'fɒləʊ/ *vt* [1] (go, come after) seguir*; **the lecture was ~ed by a discussion** después de la conferencia hubo un debate [2] (keep to, conform to) ⟨*road*⟩ seguir* (por); ⟨*trail*⟩ seguir*; ⟨*instructions*⟩ seguir*; ⟨*order*⟩ cumplir; ⟨*fashion/example*⟩ seguir* [3] (pay close attention to) ⟨*movement/progress*⟩ seguir* de cerca; ⟨*news*⟩ mantenerse* al tanto de; ⟨*TV serial*⟩ seguir* [4] ⟨*argument/reasoning*⟩ entender*

■ ~ *vi* [1] (come after): **you go first, and I'll ~** tú ve delante que yo te sigo; **the winners were as ~s ...** los ganadores fueron ... [2] (be logical consequence) deducirse*; **that doesn't necessarily ~** una cosa no implica la otra [3] (understand) entender*

■ **follow up** [*v + o + adv, v + adv + o*] seguir*

follower /'fɑːləʊər ‖'fɒləʊə(r)/ *n* seguidor, -dora *m,f*

following¹ /'fɑːləʊɪŋ ‖'fɒləʊɪŋ/ *adj* (*before n*) (next) siguiente; (on) **the ~ day** al día siguiente

following² *n* [1] (followers) seguidores *mpl*; (admirers) admiradores *mpl* [2] (what, who comes next) **the ~: the ~ are to play in tomorrow's game** ... los siguientes jugarán en el partido de mañana ...; **the letter said the ~ ...** la carta decía lo siguiente ...

f

follow-up /ˈfɑːləʊʌp ‖ˈfɒləʊʌp/ n (sequel) continuación f; (before n): she sent a ~ letter mandó una segunda (or tercera etc) carta

folly /ˈfɑːli ‖ˈfɒli/ n (pl **-lies**) locura f

fond /fɑːnd ‖fɒnd/ adj **-er, -est** [1] (pred): she's very ~ of Sue le tiene mucho cariño a Sue; he was ~ of chocolate le gustaba el chocolate [2] (before n) (loving) ⟨gesture/look⟩ cariñoso

fondle /ˈfɑːndl ‖ˈfɒndl/ vt acariciar

fondly /ˈfɑːndli ‖ˈfɒndli/ adv (a) (lovingly) cariñosamente; ⟨remember⟩ con cariño (b) (foolishly) ingenuamente

fondness /ˈfɑːndnəs ‖ˈfɒndnɪs/ n (love) cariño m; (liking) afición f

font /fɑːnt ‖fɒnt/ n [1] (baptismal) pila f bautismal [2] (a) (Print) fuente f (b) (Comput) font m, fuente f, juego m de caracteres

food /fuːd/ n (a) (in general) comida f; (before n) ⟨shortage/exports⟩ de alimentos (b) (specific kind) alimento m

food: ~ **poisoning** n intoxicación f (por alimentos); ~ **processor** /ˈprɑːsesər, ˈprəʊ- ‖ˈprəʊsesə(r)/ n robot m de cocina; ~**stuffs** pl n productos mpl alimenticios

fool¹ /fuːl/ n idiota mf; to make a ~ of oneself hacer* el ridículo

fool² vt engañar
■ **fool around** (BrE also) **fool about** [v + adv] hacer* payasadas, hacer* el tonto (Esp)

foolhardy /ˈfuːlhɑːrdi ‖ˈfuːlhɑːdi/ adj imprudente

foolish /ˈfuːlɪʃ/ adj ⟨person/prank⟩ tonto; ⟨look/ grin⟩ de tonto; ⟨decision/plan⟩ insensato

fool: ~**proof** adj ⟨idea/plan⟩ infalible; ⟨machine⟩ sencillo de manejar; ~**scap** /ˈfuːlskæp/ n pliego de aprox 33 x 22 cm

foot¹ /fʊt/ n (pl **feet**) [1] (of person) pie m; (of animal) pata f; (on sewing machine) pie m; to be on one's feet estar* de pie, estar* parado (AmL); to go/come on ~ ir*/venir* a pie; to find one's feet: it didn't take him long to find his feet in his new school no tardó en habituarse a la nueva escuela; to put one's ~ down (be firm) imponerse*; (accelerate vehicle) (colloq) apretar* el acelerador, meterle (AmL fam); to put one's ~ in it (colloq) meter la pata (fam); under sb's feet: the cat keeps getting under my feet el gato siempre me anda alrededor
[2] (lower end) (no pl) pie m; the ~ of the bed los pies de la cama
[3] (measure) (pl **foot** or **feet**) pie m

foot² vt: to ~ the bill pagar*

footage /ˈfʊtɪdʒ/ n (Cin) secuencias fpl (filmadas)

foot-and-mouth (disease) /ˈfʊtn̩ˈmaʊθ/ n fiebre f aftosa, glosopeda f

football /ˈfʊtbɔːl/ n [1] (a) (American ~) fútbol m or (AmC, Méx) futbol m americano (b) (soccer) fútbol m or (AmC, Méx) futbol m; (before n) ~ match partido m de fútbol or (AmC, Méx) futbol; ~ player ▶ FOOTBALLER [2] (ball) balón m or (esp AmL) pelota f de fútbol or (AmC, Méx) futbol

footballer /ˈfʊtbɔːlər ‖ˈfʊtbɔːlə(r)/ n (BrE) futbolista mf, jugador, -dora m,f de fútbol or (AmC, Méx) futbol

football: ~ **pool** n (AmE) apuesta f colectiva, polla f (AmL); ~ **pools** pl n (BrE) the ~ pools

juego de apuestas en que se trata de acertar los resultados de los partidos de la liga de fútbol, ≈el pronóstico deportivo (en Méx), ≈las quinielas (en Esp), ≈el prode (en Arg), ≈el totogol (en Col), ≈la polla-gol (en Chi), ≈la polla (en Per)

-footed /ˈfʊtəd ‖ˈfʊtɪd/ suff: four~ de cuatro patas; light~ ligero de pies

foot: ~**hills** pl n estribaciones fpl; ~**hold** n punto m de apoyo (para el pie); to gain a ~hold «ideology» prender*

footing /ˈfʊtɪŋ/ n (no pl) [1] (balance) equilibrio m; to miss one's ~ resbalar [2] (basis): on an equal ~ en igualdad de condiciones

foot: ~**lights** pl n candilejas fpl; ~**loose** adj libre y sin compromiso; ~loose and fancy-free libre como el viento; ~**man** /ˈfʊtmən/ n (pl **-men** /-mən/) lacayo m; ~**note** n nota f a pie de página; ~**path** n (path) sendero m; (pavement) (BrE) acera f, banqueta f (Méx), vereda f (CS, Per); ~**print** n huella f; ~**step** n paso m; ~**wear** n calzado m

for¹ /fɔːr ‖fɔː(r), weak form fər ‖fə(r)/ prep
I [1] (intended for) para; is there a letter ~ me? ¿hay carta para mí?; my love ~ her mi amor por ella
[2] (a) (on behalf of, representing): I did it ~ you lo hice por ti; he plays ~ England forma parte de or juega en la selección inglesa; D ~ David D de David (b) (as): we're having chicken ~ dinner vamos a cenar pollo; I can see him now ~ what he is ahora me doy cuenta de cómo es en realidad (c) (in favor of) a favor de
[3] (indicating purpose): what's that ~? ¿para qué es eso?; it's ~ decoration es de adorno; it's ~ your own good! ¡es por tu (propio) bien!
[4] (giving reason) por; ~ that reason por esa razón; if it weren't ~ Joe ... si no fuera por Joe ...
[5] (in exchange for) por; I bought the book ~ $10 compré el libro por 10 dólares; she left him ~ somebody else lo dejó por otro
[6] (as concerns) para; it's too cold ~ me here aquí hace demasiado frío para mí
[7] (a) (in spite of): ~ all her faults, she's been very kind to us tendrá sus defectos, pero con nosotros ha sido muy buena (b) (with infinitive clause): it's unusual ~ me to forget a name es raro que se me olvide un nombre; it's not ~ me to decide no me corresponde a mí decidir
II [1] (in the direction of) para; the plane ~ New York el avión para or de Nueva York
[2] (a) (indicating duration): he spoke ~ half an hour habló (durante) media hora; I've only been here ~ a day solo llevo un día aquí; how long are you going ~? ¿por cuánto tiempo vas? (b) (on the occasion of) para; he gave it to me ~ my birthday me lo regaló para mi cumpleaños (c) (by, before) para; we have to be there ~ six o'clock tenemos que estar allí a las seis
[3] (indicating distance): we drove ~ 20 miles hicimos 20 millas; we could see ~ miles se podía ver hasta muy lejos

for² conj (liter) pues (liter), puesto que (frml)

forage /ˈfɔːrɪdʒ ‖ˈfɒrɪdʒ/ vi (a) «animal» forrajear (b) (for supplies) to ~ FOR sth buscar* algo

foray /ˈfɔːreɪ ‖ˈfɒreɪ/ n (Mil) incursión f

forbid /fərˈbɪd ‖fəˈbɪd/ vt (past **forbad(e)** /fərˈbæd, -ˈbeɪd ‖fəˈbæd, -ˈbeɪd/; past p

forbidden /fər'bɪdṇ ‖fəbɪdṇ/ (not allow)
prohibir*; **to ~ sb to + INF** prohibirle* A algn +
INF, prohibirle* A algn QUE (+ *subj*)

force¹ /fɔːs ‖fɔːrs/ n fuerza f; **the (armed) ~s**
las fuerzas armadas; **a ~ eight gale** vientos de
fuerza ocho; **to join ~s with sb** unirse a algn; **to
come into ~** entrar en vigor *or* vigencia; **to be in
~** estar* en vigor *or* vigencia

force² vt **1** (compel) **to ~ sb to + INF** obligar* a
algn A + INF **2** (push, drive) ⟨door/link⟩ forzar*;
they ~d their way in entraron por la fuerza
■ **force down** [v + o + adv, v + adv + o] **(a)**
⟨aircraft/pilot⟩ obligar* a aterrizar **(b)** ⟨food⟩
tragar* (*a duras penas*)

forced /fɔːrst ‖fɔːst/ adj (before n) ⟨labor/smile⟩
forzado; ⟨landing/stopover⟩ forzoso

force-feed /'fɔːrs'fiːd ‖'fɔːsfiːd/ vt (past & past
p **-fed**) alimentar por la fuerza

forceful /'fɔːrsfəl ‖'fɔːsfəl/ adj **(a)** (vigorous)
⟨person⟩ con carácter; ⟨personality⟩ fuerte **(b)**
(persuasive) ⟨words/argument⟩ convincente

forceps /'fɔːrsəps ‖'fɔːseps/ pl n fórceps m

forcible /'fɔːrsəbəl ‖'fɔːsəbəl/ adj forzoso

ford /fɔːrd ‖fɔːd/ n vado m

fore /fɔːr ‖fɔː(r)/ n: **to come to the ~** «issue»
saltar a primera plana

forearm /'fɔːr.ɑːrm ‖'fɔːr.ɑːm/ n antebrazo m

foreboding /fɔːr'bəʊdɪŋ ‖fɔː'bəʊdɪŋ/ n **(a)**
(apprehension) aprensión f **(b)** (presentiment)
premonición f

forecast¹ /'fɔːrkæst ‖'fɔːkɑːst/ n (weather ~)
pronóstico m del tiempo; (prediction) previsión f

forecast² vt (past & past p **forecast** *or*
forecasted) ⟨weather⟩ pronosticar*; ⟨result/
trend⟩ prever*

forecourt /'fɔːrkɔːrt ‖'fɔːkɔːt/ n patio m
delantero

forefathers /'fɔːr.fɑːðərz ‖'fɔːfɑːðəz/ pl n (liter)
antepasados mpl

forefinger /'fɔːr.fɪŋgər ‖'fɔː.fɪŋɡə(r)/ n índice
m

forefront /'fɔːrfrʌnt ‖'fɔːfrʌnt/ n: **in** o **at the ~
of** sth al frente de algo; (in the vanguard) a la
vanguardia de algo

forego /fɔːr'gəʊ ‖fɔː'gəʊ/ vt (3rd pers sing pres
-goes; pres p **-going**; past **-went**; past p
-gone) ▸ FORGO

foregone /'fɔːrgɑːn ‖'fɔːɡɒn/ adj: **the result
was a ~ conclusion** el resultado era de prever

foreground /'fɔːrɡraʊnd ‖'fɔːɡraʊnd/ n: **in the
~** en primer plano

forehand /'fɔːrhænd ‖'fɔːhænd/ n golpe m de
derecho

forehead /'fɑːrəd, 'fɔːrhed ‖'fɒrɪd, 'fɔːhed/ n
frente f

foreign /'fɔːrən, 'fɑː- ‖'fɒrən/ adj **1 (a)**
⟨custom/country/language⟩ extranjero **(b)** ⟨policy/
trade/relations⟩ exterior; **~ debt** deuda f externa
2 (Med) extraño; **a ~ body** un cuerpo extraño

foreigner /'fɔːrənər, 'fɑː- ‖'fɒrənə(r)/ n
extranjero, -ra m,f

foreign: ~ exchange n divisas fpl; **F~
Minister** n ministro, -tra *or* (Méx) secretario,
-ria m,f de relaciones *or* (Esp) asuntos exteriores,
canciller mf (AmS); **F~ Office** n (in UK) the **F~**

Office el Foreign Office, el ministerio de
relaciones exteriores de Gran Bretaña; **F~
Secretary** n (in UK) ▸ F~ MINISTER

foreleg /'fɔːrleg ‖'fɔːleg/ n pata f delantera

foreman /'fɔːrmən ‖'fɔːmən/ n (pl **-men**
/-mən/) **(a)** (supervisor) capataz m **(b)** (of jury)
presidente m

foremost¹ /'fɔːrməʊst ‖'fɔːməʊst/ adj más
importante

foremost² adv en primer lugar

forename /'fɔːrneɪm ‖'fɔːneɪm/ n nombre m
(de pila)

forensic /fə'rensɪk/ adj (before n) forense

forerunner /'fɔːr.rʌnər ‖'fɔː.rʌnə(r)/ n
precursor, -sora m,f

foresee /fɔːr'siː ‖fɔː'siː/ vt (past **foresaw**;
past p **foreseen**) prever*

foreshore /'fɔːrʃɔːr ‖'fɔːʃɔː(r)/ n: parte de la
playa entre la pleamar y la bajamar

foresight /'fɔːrsaɪt ‖'fɔːsaɪt/ n previsión f

foreskin /'fɔːrskɪn ‖'fɔːskɪn/ n prepucio m

forest /'fɔːrəst ‖'fɒrɪst/ n (wood) bosque m;
(tropical) selva f; (before n) forestal

forestall /fɔːr'stɔːl ‖fɔː'stɔːl/ vt **(a)** (prevent)
prevenir* **(b)** (preempt) adelantarse a

forestry /'fɔːrəstri ‖'fɒrɪstri/ n silvicultura f

foretaste /'fɔːrteɪst ‖'fɔːteɪst/ n anticipo m

foretell /fɔːr'tel ‖fɔː'tel/ vt (past & past p
foretold) predecir*

forever /fə'revər ‖fə'revə(r)/ adv: **those days
are gone ~** esos días no volverán; **nothing lasts
~** nada dura eternamente

forewarn /fɔːr'wɔːrn ‖fɔː'wɔːn/ vt **to ~ sb OF
sth** advertir* A algn DE algo

forewent /fɔːr'went ‖fɔː'went/ past of FOREGO

foreword /'fɔːrwɜːrd ‖'fɔːwɜːd/ n prólogo m

forfeit¹ /'fɔːrfət ‖'fɔːfɪt/ vt ⟨property⟩ perder* el
derecho a; ⟨rights/respect/game⟩ perder*

forfeit² n **(a)** (penalty) multa f **(b)** (Games)
prenda f

forgave /fər'ɡeɪv ‖fə'ɡeɪv/ past of FORGIVE

forge¹ /fɔːrdʒ ‖fɔːdʒ/ vt **1** ⟨metal/bond⟩ forjar
2 (counterfeit) falsificar*

forge² n **(a)** (smithy) forja f **(b)** (furnace) fragua f

forger /'fɔːrdʒər ‖'fɔːdʒə(r)/ n falsificador, -dora
m,f

forgery /'fɔːrdʒəri ‖'fɔːdʒəri/ n (pl **-ries**)
falsificación f

forget /fər'ɡet ‖fə'ɡet/ (pres p **forgetting**;
past **forgot**; past p **forgotten**) vt olvidarse de,
olvidar
■ ~ vi: **to ~** (ABOUT sth) olvidarse (DE algo)

forgetful /fər'ɡetfəl ‖fə'ɡetfəl/ adj olvidadizo

forget-me-not /fər'ɡetmiːnɑːt ‖fə'ɡetmɪnɒt/
n nomeolvides f

forgive /fər'ɡɪv ‖fə'ɡɪv/ vt (past **forgave**; past
p **forgiven**) perdonar; **to ~ sb FOR sth**
perdonarle algo a algn

forgiveness /fər'ɡɪvnəs ‖fə'ɡɪvnɪs/ n (quality)
clemencia f; **to ask sb's ~ for sth** pedirle* perdón
a algn por algo

forgo /fɔːr'ɡəʊ ‖fɔː'ɡəʊ/ vt (3rd pers sing pres
-goes; pres p **-going**; past **-went**; past p
-gone) (frml) privarse de

forgot /fər'ɡɑːt ‖fə'ɡɒt/ past of FORGET

forgotten /fəˈrˈgɑːtn̩ ‖fəˈgɒtn̩/ *past p of* FORGET

fork¹ /fɔːrk ‖fɔːk/ *n* (Culin) tenedor *m*; (for gardening) horca *f*

fork² *vi* (a) (split) «branch/road/river» bifurcarse* (b) (turn): **to ~ (to the) right** desviarse* a la derecha

forklift (truck) /ˈfɔːrkˈlɪft ‖ˈfɔːklɪft/ *n* carretilla *f* elevadora (de horquilla)

forlorn /fərˈlɔːrn ‖fəˈlɔːn/ *adj* (a) ⟨glance/smile⟩ triste; ⟨appearance⟩ de tristeza y desamparo (b) ⟨attempt⟩ desesperado

form¹ /fɔːrm ‖fɔːm/ *n* **1** (shape, manner) forma *f* **2** (type, kind) tipo; **other ~s of life** otras formas de vida **3** (fitness, ability) forma *f*; **to be on ~** estar* en forma **4** (document) formulario *m*, forma *f* (Méx) **5** (BrE Educ) (class) clase *f*; (year) curso *m*

form² *vt* ⟨character/shape/company/basis⟩ formar; ⟨opinion⟩ formarse; ⟨habit⟩ adquirir* ∎ ~ *vi* «idea/plan» tomar forma; «ice/fog» formarse

formal /ˈfɔːrməl ‖ˈfɔːməl/ *adj* ⟨reception/dinner/language⟩ formal; ⟨manner/person⟩ ceremonioso; **~ dress** traje *m* de etiqueta

formality /fɔːrˈmælət̬i ‖fɔːˈmæləti/ *n* (*pl* **-ties**) **1** (formal quality) ceremonia *f* **2** (convention) formalidad *f*

formalize /ˈfɔːrməlaɪz ‖ˈfɔːməlaɪz/ *vt* formalizar*

formally /ˈfɔːrməli ‖ˈfɔːməli/ *adv* ⟨invite/reprimand⟩ formalmente

format¹ /ˈfɔːrmæt ‖ˈfɔːmæt/ *n* formato *m*

format² *vt* **-tt-** formatear

formation /fɔːrˈmeɪʃən ‖fɔːˈmeɪʃən/ *n* formación *f*

former¹ /ˈfɔːrmər ‖ˈfɔːmə(r)/ *adj* **1** (previous) antiguo **2** (first-mentioned) primero

former² *n* **the ~** el primero, la primera; (*pl*) los primeros, las primeras

formerly /ˈfɔːrmərli ‖ˈfɔːməli/ *adv* antes

formidable /ˈfɔːrmədəbəl ‖ˈfɔːmɪdəbəl, fɔːˈmɪdəbəl/ *adj* ⟨task⟩ imponente; ⟨problem/obstacle⟩ tremendo; ⟨opponent⟩ temible

formula /ˈfɔːrmjələ ‖ˈfɔːmjʊlə/ *n* (*pl* **-las** *o* (frml) **-lae** /-liː/) fórmula *f*; **~ one** (motor racing) fórmula uno

formulate /ˈfɔːrmjəleɪt ‖ˈfɔːmjʊleɪt/ *vt* formular

fornication /ˌfɔːrnəˈkeɪʃən ‖ˌfɔːnɪˈkeɪʃən/ *n* (frml) fornicación *f* (frml)

for-profit /fərˈprɑːfət ‖fəˈprɒfɪt/ *adj* comercial, con fines de lucro

forsake /fərˈseɪk ‖fəˈseɪk/ *vt* (*past* **forsook** /fərˈsʊk ‖fəˈsʊk/; *past p* **forsaken** /fərˈseɪkən ‖fəˈseɪkən/) (liter) (a) (abandon) abandonar (b) (relinquish) ⟨pleasure/habits⟩ renunciar a

fort /fɔːrt ‖fɔːt/ *n* fuerte *m*; (small) fortín *m*

forte /ˈfɔːrteɪ ‖ˈfɔːteɪ/ *n* fuerte *m*

forth /fɔːrθ ‖fɔːθ/ *adv* (liter) (a) (out): **~ he went**

---

to battle with his enemy marchó a luchar con su enemigo (b) (in time): **from this day ~** de hoy en adelante

forthcoming /ˈfɔːrθˈkʌmɪŋ ‖ˌfɔːθˈkʌmɪŋ/ *adj* **1** (a) (approaching) (*usu before n*) ⟨event⟩ próximo (b) (about to appear) ⟨article/record⟩ de próxima aparición; ⟨film⟩ a estrenarse próximamente **2** (available) (*pred*): **no explanation was ~** no dieron (or dio *etc*) ninguna explicación **3** (open, helpful): **he was not very ~** no estuvo muy comunicativo

forthright /ˈfɔːrθraɪt ‖ˈfɔːθraɪt/ *adj* directo

forthwith /ˌfɔːrθˈwɪð ‖fɔːθˈwɪθ/ *adv* (frml or liter) inmediatamente

fortieth¹ /ˈfɔːrtiəθ ‖ˈfɔːtiəθ/ *adj* cuadragésimo

fortieth² *adv* en cuadragésimo lugar

fortieth³ *n* (Math) cuarentavo *m*; (part) cuarentava *or* cuadragésima parte *f*

fortification /ˈfɔːrtəfəˈkeɪʃən ‖ˌfɔːtɪfɪˈkeɪʃən/ *n* (Mil) fortificación *f*

fortify /ˈfɔːrtəfaɪ ‖ˈfɔːtɪfaɪ/ *vt* **-fies, -fying, -fied** ⟨town/building⟩ fortificar*; ⟨person/determination⟩ fortalecer*; ⟨argument⟩ reforzar*; **fortified wine** vino *m* fortificado

fortnight /ˈfɔːrtnaɪt ‖ˈfɔːtnaɪt/ *n* (esp BrE) quince días, dos semanas

fortnightly¹ /ˈfɔːrtnaɪtli ‖ˈfɔːtnaɪtli/ *adv* (esp BrE) cada dos semanas

fortnightly² *adj* (esp BrE) quincenal

fortress /ˈfɔːrtrəs ‖ˈfɔːtrɪs/ *n* fortaleza *f*

fortuitous /fɔːrˈtuːət̬əs ‖fɔːˈtjuːɪtəs/ *adj* fortuito

fortunate /ˈfɔːrtʃnət ‖ˈfɔːtʃənət/ *adj* afortunado; **it was ~ that he came** fue una suerte que viniera

fortunately /ˈfɔːrtʃnət̬li ‖ˈfɔːtʃənətli/ *adv* (*indep*) afortunadamente

fortune /ˈfɔːrtʃən ‖ˈfɔːtʃən, ˈfɔːtʃuːn/ *n* **1** (money, prosperity) fortuna *f*; (a lot of money) (colloq) (*no pl*) dineral *m*, platal *m* (AmL fam), pastón *m* (Esp fam) **2** (destiny) destino *m*; **to tell sb's ~** decirle* la buenaventura a algn **3** (luck) **good ~** suerte *f*

fortune-teller /ˈfɔːrtʃənˌtelər ‖ˈfɔːtʃənˌtelə(r), ˈfɔːtʃuːn-/ *n* adivino, -na *m,f*

forty /ˈfɔːrti ‖ˈfɔːti/ *adj/n* cuarenta *adj inv/m*; *see also* FOUR¹

forum /ˈfɔːrəm/ *n* foro *m*

forward¹ /ˈfɔːrwərd ‖ˈfɔːwəd/, (esp BrE) **forwards** /ˈfɔːrwərdz ‖ˈfɔːwədz/ *adv* (a) ⟨bend/slope/lean⟩ hacia adelante (b) (in time) (frml) en adelante; **from this day ~** desde hoy en adelante

forward² *adj* **1** (before n) ⟨movement⟩ hacia adelante **2** (advance): **~ planning** planificación *f* **3** (assertive) atrevido

forward³ *vt* (send) (Busn) enviar*; ⊛ **please forward** hacer* seguir

forward⁴ *n* (Sport) delantero *mf*

forwent /fɔːrˈwent ‖fɔːˈwent/ *past of* FORGO

fossil /ˈfɑːsəl ‖ˈfɒsəl/ *n* fósil *m*

---

fossil fuel *n* combustible *m* fósil

foster¹ /'fɒːstər ‖'fɒstə(r)/ *vt* [1] ⟨*child*⟩ (BrE) *acoger en el hogar sin adoptarlo legalmente* [2] ⟨*suspicion/talent*⟩ fomentar; ⟨*reconciliation*⟩ promover*

foster² *adj* ⟨*child*⟩ ≈adoptivo; ~ **home** casa *f* de acogida de menores

fought /fɒːt/ *past & past p of* FIGHT¹

foul¹ /faʊl/ *adj* **-er, -est** [1] (offensive) ⟨*smell*⟩ nauseabundo; ⟨*taste*⟩ repugnante [2] (horrible) (colloq) ⟨*person*⟩ asqueroso (fam); ⟨*weather*⟩ pésimo [3] (obscene) ⟨*language/gesture*⟩ ordinario

foul² *n* falta *f*, faul *m or* foul *m* (AmL)

foul³ *vt* [1] (pollute) contaminar [2] (a) (block) ⟨*drain/chimney*⟩ obstruir* (b) (entangle) ⟨*rope/ chain*⟩ enredar [3] (Sport) cometer una falta *or* (AmL tb) un foul *or* faul contra, faulear (AmL)

foul: ~-mouthed /faʊl'maʊðd/ *adj* malhablado; ~ **play** *n* (a) (Law): they suspect ~ play sospechan que se trata de un crimen (b) (Sport) juego *m* sucio

found¹ /faʊnd/ *past & past p of* FIND¹

found² *vt* [1] (a) (establish) fundar (b)
founding *pres p* fundador [2] (base) **to ~ sth on** sth fundar algo EN algo

foundation /faʊn'deɪʃən/ *n* [1] (a) (establishing) fundación *f* (b) (institution) fundación *f* [2] (*often pl*) (a) (Const) cimientos *mpl* (b) (groundwork, basis) fundamentos *mpl*; (*before n*) ~ **course** curso *m* preparatorio [3] (grounds) fundamento *m* [4] (cosmetic) base *f* de maquillaje

founder¹ /'faʊndər ‖'faʊndə(r)/ *n* fundador, -dora *m,f*

founder² *vi* «*ship*» hundirse; «*plan/project*» irse* a pique

foundry /'faʊndri/ *n* (*pl* **-ries**) fundición *f*

fountain /'faʊntn̩ ‖'faʊntn/ *n* (a) (ornamental) fuente *f* (b) (drinking ~) fuente *f*, bebedero *m* (CS, Méx)

fountain pen *n* pluma *f* (estilográfica), pluma *f* fuente (AmL), estilográfica *f*, lapicera *f* fuente (CS)

four¹ /fɒːr ‖fɒː(r)/ *n* cuatro *m*; **4 + 1 = 5** (*léase: four plus one equals o is five*) 4 + 1 = 5 (*read as: cuatro más uno es igual a cinco*); **4 - 1 = 3** (*léase: four minus one equals o is three*) 4 - 1 = 3 (*read as: cuatro menos uno es igual a tres*); **3 x 4 = 12** (*léase: three times four equals o is twelve, o three fours are twelve*) 3 x 4 = 12 (*read as: tres (multiplicado) por cuatro (son) doce*); **4 ÷ 2 = 2** (*léase: four divided by two equals o is two*) 4 ÷ 2 = 2 (*read as: cuatro dividido por dos es (igual a) dos*); **on all ~s** en *or* a cuatro patas, a gatas

four² *adj* cuatro *adj inv*

four: ~-by-~ *n* todoterreno *m*; **~-poster** **(bed)** /fɒːr'pəʊstər ‖fɒː'pəʊstə(r)/ *n*: cama con cuatro columnas, gen con dosel; **~-seater** /fɒːr'siːtər ‖fɒː.siːtə(r)/ *n* coche *m*/avión *m* de cuatro plazas

foursome /'fɒːrsəm ‖'fɒːsəm/ *n*: grupo de cuatro personas

fourteen /fɒːr'tiːn ‖fɔː'tiːn/ *adj/n* catorce *adj inv/m; see also* FOUR¹

fourteenth¹ /fɒːr'tiːnθ ‖fɔː'tiːnθ/ *adj* decimocuarto

fourteenth² *adv* en decimocuarto lugar

fourteenth³ *n* (Math) catorceavo *m*; (part) catorceava parte *f*

fourth¹ /fɒːrθ ‖fɔːθ/ *adj* cuarto

fourth² *adv* **(a)** (in position, time, order) en cuarto lugar **(b)** (fourthly) en cuarto lugar

fourth³ *n* [1] (part) cuarto *m* [2] ~ **(gear)** (Auto) (*no art*) cuarta *f*

fourthly /'fɔːrθli ‖'fɔːθli/ *adv* (*indep*) en cuarto lugar

four-wheel drive /ˌfɔːr'hwiːl ‖ˌfɔː'wiːl/ *n* tracción *f* integral

fowl /faʊl/ *n* (*pl* ~**s** *or* ~) ave *f*‡ (de corral)

fox¹ /fɑːks ‖fɒks/ *n* zorro *m*

fox² *vt* (colloq) confundir

fox: ~glove *n* dedalera *f*, digital *f*; **~-hunting** *n* caza *f* del zorro

foyer /'fɔɪeɪ/ *n* (of theatre) foyer *m*; (of hotel) vestíbulo *m*

fracas /'freɪkəs, 'frækəs ‖'frækɑː/ *n* (*pl* **fracases** *or* (BrE) **fracas** /-z/) (liter) altercado *m*

fraction /'frækʃən/ *n* fracción *f*

fracture¹ /'fræktʃər ‖'fræktʃə(r)/ *n* fractura *f*

fracture² *vt* fracturar

fragile /'frædʒəl ‖'frædʒaɪl/ *adj* **(a)** ⟨*object/ china/glass*⟩ frágil; ⟨*relationship/link/agreement*⟩ precario **(b)** ⟨*person*⟩ débil; ⟨*health*⟩ delicado

fragment /'frægmənt/ *n* fragmento *m*

fragrance /'freɪgrəns/ *n* (smell) fragancia *f*; (perfume) perfume *m*

fragrant /'freɪgrənt/ *adj* fragante

frail /freɪl/ *adj* **-er, -est** **(a)** (physically delicate) ⟨*person*⟩ débil; ⟨*health*⟩ delicado **(b)** (morally weak) débil **(c)** (fragile) precario

frame¹ /freɪm/ *n* **(a)** (structure — of building, ship, plane) armazón *m or f*; (— of car, motorcycle, bed, door) bastidor *m*; (— of bicycle) cuadro *m*, marco *m* (Chi, Col) **(b)** (edge — of picture, window, door) marco *m* **(c)** frames *pl* (for spectacles) montura *f*

frame² *vt* [1] ⟨*picture/photograph*⟩ enmarcar*; ⟨*plan/policy/question*⟩ formular, elaborar [2] (incriminate unjustly) (colloq): I was ~d me tendieron una trampa para incriminarme

frame: ~ of mind *n* (*pl* ~**s of mind**) estado *m* de ánimo; **~work** *n* (basis) marco *m*; (plan) esquema *m*; (Eng) armazón *m or f*

franc /fræŋk/ *n* franco *m*

France /fræns ‖frɑːns/ *n* Francia *f*

franchise /'fræntʃaɪz/ *n* [1] (Busn) **(a)** (right — to operate retail outlet) franquicia *f*; (— to market product, service) concesión *f* **(b)** (retail outlet) franquicia *f* [2] (Pol frml) **the** ~ el derecho de *or* al voto

frank¹ /fræŋk/ *adj* **-er, -est** **(a)** (candid) sincero **(b)** (outspoken) franco

frank² *vt* **(a)** ⟨*letter/parcel/envelope*⟩ franquear **(b)** (postmark) ⟨*stamp/letter*⟩ matasellar

frankfurter /'fræŋkfɜːrtər ‖'fræŋkfɜːtə(r)/ *n* salchicha *f* de Frankfurt *or* (Arg, Col) de Viena, frankfurter *m* (Ur), vienesa *f* (Chi), salchicha *f* alemana (Ven)

frankincense /'fræŋkənsens ‖'fræŋkɪnsens/ *n* incienso *m*

frankly /'fræŋkli/ *adv* francamente

frantic /ˈfræntɪk/ adj (a) (very worried) desesperado (b) (frenzied) ⟨activity⟩ frenético

fraternal /frəˈtɜːrnl ‖ frəˈtɜːnl/ adj ⟨love⟩ fraternal, fraterno; ⟨jealousy⟩ entre hermanos

fraternity /frəˈtɜːrnəti ‖ frəˈtɜːnəti/ n (pl **-ties**) ① (virtue of brotherhood) fraternidad f ② (a) (Relig) hermandad f (b) (university club) asociación f estudiantil

fraternize /ˈfrætərnaɪz ‖ ˈfrætənaɪz/ vi confraternizar*

fraud /frɔːd/ n ① (deception) fraude m ② (person) farsante mf

fraudulent /ˈfrɔːdʒələnt ‖ ˈfrɔːdjʊlənt/ adj fraudulento

fraught /frɔːt/ adj (a) (pred) to be ~ WITH sth ⟨with danger/problems⟩ estar* lleno DE algo (b) (tense) ⟨atmosphere/relationship⟩ tirante

fray¹ /freɪ/ vi ⟨cloth/collar/rope⟩ deshilacharse; ⟨wire⟩ pelarse

fray² n refriega f

frayed /freɪd/ adj (a) ⟨collar/cloth⟩ deshilachado; ⟨rope/wire⟩ desgastado (b) ⟨nerves⟩ crispado; **tempers were getting ~** se estaban exaltando los ánimos

freak¹ /friːk/ n (a) (abnormal specimen) fenómeno m; (monster) monstruo m (b) (unnatural event) fenómeno m

freak² adj (before n) ⟨weather⟩ inusitado; ⟨happening⟩ inesperado
▪ **freak out** (sl) ① [v + adv] flipar (arg), friquear(se) (Méx arg) ② [v + o + adv] alucinar (fam), friquear (Méx arg)

freckle /ˈfrekəl/ n peca f

free¹ /friː/ adj freer /ˈfriːər ‖ ˈfriːə(r)/, freest /ˈfriːəst ‖ ˈfriːɪst/ ① (a) (at liberty) libre; **to set sb ~** dejar or poner* a algn en libertad (b) ⟨country/people/press⟩ libre; **the right of ~ speech** la libertad de expresión (c) (loose) suelto; **to work ~** soltarse* ② (pred) (without, rid of) ~ **FROM** o **OF sth** libre DE algo; ~ **of o from** additives sin aditivos; ~ **of charge** gratis ③ (costing nothing) ⟨ticket/sample⟩ gratis adj inv; ⟨schooling/health care⟩ gratuito ④ (not occupied) ⟨table/time⟩ libre

free² adv (a) (without payment) gratuitamente; **I got in for ~** (colloq) entré gratis (b) (without restriction) ⟨roam/run⟩ a su (or mi etc) antojo

free³ vt ① (liberate) ⟨prisoner/hostage⟩ poner* or dejar en libertad; ⟨animal⟩ soltar*; ⟨nation/slave⟩ liberar ② (a) (release) ⟨bound person⟩ soltar*; ⟨trapped person⟩ rescatar (b) (loose, clear) ⟨sth stuck or caught⟩ desenganchar

-free /ˈfriː/ suff: **trouble~** sin problemas; **nuclear~ zone** zona f desnuclearizada

freedom /ˈfriːdəm/ n libertad f

freedom fighter n guerrillero, -ra m,f

free: ~**-for-all** /ˈfriːfərˈɔːl/ n gresca f; ~**hold** adj (esp BrE): ~hold property bien m raíz (que se compra o vende en plena propiedad junto con el suelo sobre el que está edificado); ~ **kick** n (in soccer) tiro m libre; (in rugby) patada f libre

freelance¹ /ˈfriːlæns ‖ ˈfriːlɑːns/ adj por cuenta propia, por libre (Esp)

freelance² adv por cuenta propia, por libre (Esp)

freely /ˈfriːli/ adv ① (a) (without restriction) libremente (b) (openly) ⟨speak/write⟩ con libertad (c) (willingly) ⟨offer⟩ de buen grado ② (a) (generously) ⟨spend/give⟩ a manos llenas (b) (copiously) ⟨flow/pour⟩ profusamente

free: F~mason /ˈfriːˈmeɪsən ‖ ˈfriːˈmeɪsən/ n masón, -sona m,f, francmasón, -sona m,f; ~**range** /ˈfriːˈreɪndʒ/ adj (BrE) ⟨chicken/eggs⟩ de granja; ~**style** n estilo m libre; ~ **trade** n libre comercio m; ~**ware** n (Comput) programas mpl de libre distribución; ~**way** n (AmE) autopista f (sin peaje); ~**wheel** /ˈfriːˈhwiːl ‖ ˌfriːˈwiːl/ vi: he ~wheeled down the hill (on bike) bajó la cuesta sin pedalear; (in car) bajó la cuesta en punto muerto; ~ **will** n: of one's own ~ will por su (or mi etc) propia voluntad

freeze¹ /friːz/ (past froze; past p frozen) vi ① «pipe/lock/ground/person» helarse*; **I'm freezing!** ¡estoy helado! ② (stand still) quedarse inmóvil
■ ~ vt ⟨water/stream/pipe⟩ helar*; ⟨food⟩ congelar ② (Fin) ⟨assets/account/prices⟩ congelar
■ ~ v impers helar*
▪ **freeze over** [v + adv] helarse*
▪ **freeze up** [v + adv] helarse*

freeze² n congelación f; **a wage/price ~** una congelación salarial/de precios

freezer /ˈfriːzər ‖ ˈfriːzə(r)/ n (deep freeze) freezer m; (freezing compartment) congelador m

freezing¹ /ˈfriːzɪŋ/ adj ⟨temperatures⟩ bajo cero; ⟨weather⟩ con temperaturas bajo cero; ⟨hands/feet⟩ helado; **it's ~ (cold) in here** aquí hace un frío que pela (fam)

freezing² n ① ~ **(point)** punto m de congelación; **three degrees below ~** tres grados sobre/bajo cero ② (process) congelación f

freight /freɪt/ n (a) (goods transported) carga f (b) (transportation) transporte m, flete m (AmL)

freighter /ˈfreɪtər ‖ ˈfreɪtə(r)/ n buque m de carga

freight train n tren m de carga

French¹ /frentʃ/ adj francés

French² n (a) (language) francés m (b) (people) + pl vb the ~ los franceses

French: ~ **bean** pl n (BrE) ▶ GREEN BEAN; ~ **doors** pl n (AmE) ▶ ~ WINDOWS; ~ **dressing** n aliño para ensaladas a base de aceite, vinagre y mostaza; (AmE) aderezo (para ensaladas) a base de aceite, vinagre y tomate; ~ **fries** pl n papas fpl or (Esp) patatas fpl fritas, papas fpl a la francesa (Col, Méx); ~**man** /ˈfrentʃmən/ n (pl -men) (man) francés m; ~ **windows** pl n puerta f ventana, cristalera f (Esp); ~**woman** n francesa f

frenetic /frəˈnetɪk/ adj ⟨activity⟩ frenético; ⟨attempt⟩ desesperado

frenzy /ˈfrenzi/ n (no pl) frenesí m

frequency /ˈfriːkwənsi/ n (pl -cies) frecuencia f

frequent¹ /ˈfriːkwənt/ adj ⟨attempts/journeys⟩ frecuente; ⟨visitor⟩ asiduo

frequent² /friːˈkwent/ vt frecuentar

frequently /ˈfriːkwəntli/ adv con frecuencia, a menudo

fresh /freʃ/ adj -er, -est ① (a) (not stale, frozen or canned) ⟨food⟩ fresco; **to get some ~ air** tomar el fresco (b) (not tired) ⟨complexion/appearance⟩

fresco ② (not salty): ~ **water** agua *f*‡ dulce ③ **(a)** (new, clean) ⟨*clothes/linen*⟩ limpio **(b)** (new, additional) ⟨*supplies/initiative*⟩ nuevo

freshen /'freʃən/ *vt* refrescar*

■ **freshen up** [*v* + *adv*] lavarse

fresher /'freʃər ‖'freʃə(r)/ *n* (BrE colloq) ▸ FRESHMAN

freshly /'freʃli/ *adv* recién

freshman /'freʃmən/ *n* (*pl* **-men** /-mən/) (Educ) estudiante *mf* de primer año, mechón, -chona *m,f* (Chi fam)

freshness /'freʃnəs ‖'freʃnɪs/ *n* frescura *f*

freshwater /'freʃˌwɔːtər ‖'freʃˌwɔːtə(r)/ *adj* (*before n*) de agua dulce

fret /fret/ *vi* **-tt-** preocuparse

fretful /'fretfəl/ *adj* **(a)** (querulous) quejoso **(b)** (anxious) inquieto

friar /'fraɪər ‖'fraɪə(r)/ *n* fraile *m*

friction /'frɪkʃən/ *n* ① (Phys, Tech) rozamiento *m*, fricción *f* ② (discord) tirantez *f*

Friday /'fraɪdeɪ, -di/ *n* viernes *m*; *see also* MONDAY

fridge /frɪdʒ/ *n* (colloq) nevera *f*, refrigerador *m*, frigorífico *m* (Esp), heladera *f* (RPl), refrigeradora *f* (Col, Per)

fried /fraɪd/ *adj* frito; **a ~ egg** un huevo frito *or* (Méx) estrellado

friend /frend/ *n* amigo, -ga *m,f*; **he soon made ~s with her** en poco tiempo se hizo amigo suyo

friendliness /'frendlməs ‖'frendlmɪs/ *n* simpatía *f*

friendly /'frendli/ *adj* **-lier, -liest** ⟨*person/ pet*⟩ simpático; ⟨*place/atmosphere*⟩ agradable; ⟨*welcome*⟩ cordial; **to be ~ WITH sb** ser* amigo, -ga DE algn **(b)** (good-natured) ⟨*rivalry/match*⟩ amistoso

friendship /'frendʃɪp/ *n* amistad *f*

frieze /friːz/ *n* (on building, wall) friso *m*; (on wallpaper) greca *f*

frigate /'frɪgət ‖'frɪgɪt/ *n* fragata *f*

fright /fraɪt/ *n* **(a)** (fear) miedo *m*; **to take ~ at sth** asustarse por algo **(b)** (shock) susto *m*

frighten /'fraɪtn/ *vt* asustar

■ **frighten away, frighten off** [*v* + *o* + *adv*, *v* + *adv* + *o*] espantar

frightened /'fraɪtnd/ *adj* ⟨*person/animal*⟩ asustado; **to be ~ OF sb/sth** tenerle* miedo A algn/algo

frightening /'fraɪtnɪŋ/ *adj* ⟨*experience*⟩ espantoso; (stronger) aterrador

frightful /'fraɪtfəl/ *adj* ① (horrific) aterrador ② (BrE colloq) (very unpleasant) horroroso

frigid /'frɪdʒəd ‖'frɪdʒɪd/ *adj* frígido

frill /frɪl/ *n* volante *m or* (RPl) volado *m or* (Méx) olán *m or* (Chi) vuelo *m*; **a ceremony with no ~s** una ceremonia sencilla

frilly /'frɪli/ *adj* **-lier, -liest** ⟨*dress/petticoat*⟩ de volantes *or* (RPl) de volados *or* (Méx) de olanes *or* (Chi) de vuelos

fringe /frɪndʒ/ *n* ① (on shawl, carpet, tablecloth) fleco *m* ② (of hair) (BrE) flequillo *m*, cerquillo *m* (AmL), fleco *m* (Méx), chasquilla *f* (Chi), capul *m* (Col), pollina *f* (Ven) ③ (periphery) (*often pl*): **to live on the ~(s) of society** vivir al margen de la sociedad; (*before n*) ⟨*area/group*⟩ marginal; ⟨*music/medicine*⟩ alternativo

fringe benefit *n* **(a)** (Lab Rel) incentivo *m* **(b)** (incidental advantage) ventaja *f* adicional

frisk /frɪsk/ *vt* cachear, catear (Méx)

frisky /'frɪski/ *adj* **-kier, -kiest** retozón

fritter /'frɪtər ‖'frɪtə(r)/ *n* buñuelo *m*, fruta *f* de sartén (Esp)

■ **fritter away** [*v* + *o* + *adv*, *v* + *adv* + *o*] ⟨*money*⟩ malgastar; ⟨*fortune*⟩ dilapidar; ⟨*time*⟩ desperdiciar

frivolous /'frɪvələs/ *adj* frívolo

frizzy /'frɪzi/ *adj* **-zier, -ziest** crespo, chino (Méx), como mota (CS)

frock /frɑːk ‖frɒk/ *n* vestido *m*

frog /frɔːg ‖frɒg/ *n* rana *f*; **to have a ~ in the o one's throat** tener* carraspera

frog: ~man /'frɔːgmən ‖'frɒgmən/ *n* (*pl* **-men** /-mən/) hombre *m* rana; **~spawn** *n* (BrE) huevos *mpl* de rana

frolic /'frɑːlɪk ‖'frɒlɪk/ *vi* **-ck-** retozar*

from /frɑːm ‖frɒm, *weak form* frəm/ *prep* ① (indicating starting point) desde; **~ the beginning** desde el principio ② (indicating distance): **2cm ~ the edge** a 2cm del borde; **we're still three hours ~ Tulsa** todavía faltan tres horas para llegar a Tulsa ③ (after): **~ today** a partir de hoy; **50 years ~ now** dentro de 50 años ④ (indicating origin) de; **I'm ~ Texas** soy de Texas; **the flight ~ Madrid** el vuelo procedente de Madrid; **a letter ~ my lawyer** una carta de mi abogado ⑤ **from ... to ...: they flew ~ New York to Lima** volaron de Nueva York a Lima; **they stretch ~ Derbyshire to the borders of Scotland** se extienden desde el condado de Derbyshire hasta el sur de Escocia; **we work ~ nine to five** trabajamos de nueve a cinco; **~ $50 to $100** entre 50 y 100 dólares ⑥ (as a result of) de; **his eyes were red ~ crying** tenía los ojos rojos de tanto llorar; **~ experience I would say that ...** según mi experiencia diría que ... ⑦ (out of, off) de; **~ the cupboard/shelf** del armario/estante; **if you take 5 ~ 10** si le restas 5 a 10 ⑧ (with preps & advs): **~ above/below** desde arriba/abajo; **he crawled out ~ under the table** salió gateando de debajo de la mesa

frond /frɑːnd ‖frɒnd/ *n* (of fern) fronda *f*; (of palm) hoja *f*

front¹ /frʌnt/ *n* ① (forward part) frente *m*; (of building) frente *m*, fachada *f*; (of dress) delantera *f*; **you sit in the ~** siéntate delante *or* (esp AmL) adelante ② (*in phrases*) **in front** (*as adv*) delante, adelante (esp AmL); **in front of sb/sth** delante *or* (esp AmL) adelante de algn/algo; (facing) enfrente de algn/algo ③ (Meteo, Mil, Pol) frente *m* ④ (outward show) fachada *f*; (— for illegal activity) pantalla *f* ⑤ (overlooking sea) paseo *m* marítimo, malecón *m* (AmL), rambla *f* (RPl)

front² *adj* (at front) ⟨*seat/wheel/leg*⟩ delantero, de delante *or* (esp AmL) de adelante; **the ~ door** la puerta de (la) calle; **the ~ yard** o (BrE) **garden** el jardín del frente; **a ~-row seat** un asiento en primera fila

frontbencher /frʌntˈbentʃər   ⋯⋗

‖ˌfrʌntˈbentʃə(r)/ *n* (BrE) *diputado con cargo ministerial en el gobierno o en el gabinete fantasma*

frontier /frʌnˈtɪr ‖ˈfrʌntɪə(r)/ *n* frontera *f*; (*before n*) ⟨*guard/zone*⟩ fronterizo

frontispiece /ˈfrʌntɪspiːs/ *n* frontispicio *m*

front room *n* salón *m*, living *m* (esp AmL)

frost¹ /frɔːst ‖frɒst/ *n* **(a)** (sub-zero temperature) helada *f* **(b)** (frozen dew) escarcha *f*

frost² *vt* **1** (Meteo) helar*; ⟨*plant*⟩ quemar **2** (AmE Culin) bañar

frostbite /ˈfrɔːstbaɪt ‖ˈfrɒstbaɪt/ *n* congelación *f*

frosting /ˈfrɔːstɪŋ ‖ˈfrɒstɪŋ/ *n* (AmE Culin) baño *m*

frosty /ˈfrɔːsti ‖ˈfrɒsti/ *adj* **-tier, -tiest** ⟨*weather/air*⟩ helado; ⟨*night*⟩ de helada; ⟨*manner/reception*⟩ glacial

froth /frɔːθ ‖frɒθ/ *n* espuma *f*

frothy /ˈfrɔːθi ‖ˈfrɒθi/ *adj* **frothier, frothiest** espumoso

frown¹ /fraʊn/ *vi* fruncir* el ceño; **to ~ AT sb** mirar a algn con el ceño fruncido
■ **frown on, frown upon** [*v + prep + o*]: that sort of thing is ~ed upon eso está muy mal visto

frown² *n* ceño *m* fruncido

froze /frəʊz/ *past of* FREEZE¹

frozen¹ /ˈfrəʊzn̩/ *past p of* FREEZE¹

frozen² *adj* **1 (a)** ⟨*water/lock/pipe/food*⟩ congelado; ⟨*region*⟩ helado; **my feet are ~** (colloq) tengo los pies helados **(b)** (Fin) ⟨*prices/incomes*⟩ congelado **2** (motionless): **I stood there ~ (to the spot)** me quedé allí clavado, paralizado por el terror

frugal /ˈfruːɡəl/ *adj* frugal

fruit /fruːt/ *n* **1 (a)** (collectively) fruta *f*; **dried ~** (BrE) fruta *f* seca; (*before noun*) **~ juice** jugo *m or* (Esp) zumo *m* de frutas; **~ tree** árbol *m* frutal **(b)** (type — as food) fruta *f*; (Bot) fruto *m* **2** (product) fruto *m*; **to bear ~** dar* (su) fruto

fruit: **~cake** *n* plum-cake *m*, ponqué *m* de frutas (Col), fruit cake *m* (Méx), budín *m* inglés (RPl); **~ cocktail** *n* (dish) ensalada *f or* macedonia *f or* cóctel *m* de frutas; **~ cup** *n* (AmE) ▶ ~ COCKTAIL

fruitful /ˈfruːtfəl/ *adj* provechoso, fructífero

fruition /fruːˈɪʃən/ *n* (frml): **their plan never came to ~** su plan nunca cristalizó

fruitless /ˈfruːtləs ‖ˈfruːtlɪs/ *adj* infructuoso

fruit: **~ machine** *n* (BrE) máquina *f* tragamonedas *or* (Esp tb) tragaperras; **~ salad** *n* **(a)** (AmE) ensalada *de frutas, gen en gelatina* **(b)** (BrE) ▶ FRUIT COCKTAIL

frustrate /ˈfrʌstreɪt ‖frʌsˈtreɪt/ *vt* frustrar

frustrated /ˈfrʌstreɪtəd ‖frʌsˈtreɪtɪd/ *adj* **(a)** (thwarted) frustrado **(b)** (dissatisfied) descontento; (sexually) ~ sexualmente frustrado

frustrating /ˈfrʌstreɪtɪŋ ‖frʌsˈtreɪtɪŋ/ *adj* frustrante

frustration /frʌsˈtreɪʃən/ *n* frustración *f*

fry¹ /fraɪ/ **fries, frying, fried** *vt* freír*
■ **~** *vi* freírse*

fry² *n* (*pl* **fries**) **1 fries** *pl* (French fries) papas *or* (Esp) patatas fritas, papas *fpl* a la francesa (Col, Méx) **2 (a)** (+ *pl vb*) (Zool) alevines *mpl*, majuga *f* (Ur) **(b)** (people): **small ~** gente *f* de poca monta

frying pan /ˈfraɪŋ/, (AmE also) **fry pan** *n* sartén *f*, sartén *m or f* (AmE)

ft = **foot/feet**

FTP *n* (Comput) (= **file transfer protocol**) FTP *m*

fuchsia /ˈfjuːʃə/ *n* (Bot) fucsia *f*, aljaba *f* (RPl)

fuck /fʌk/ *vt* (vulg) (copulate with) joder (vulg), tirarse (vulg), follarse (Esp vulg), coger* (Méx, RPl, Ven vulg)
■ **~** *vi* (vulg) joder (vulg), tirar (vulg), coger* (Méx, RPl, Ven vulg), follar (Esp vulg), cachar (Chi, Per vulg)
■ **fuck off** [*v + adv*] (vulg): **~ off!** ¡vete a la mierda! (vulg), ¡vete a tomar por (el) culo! (Esp vulg), ¡vete a la chingada! (Méx vulg), ¡andá a cagar! (RPl vulg)

fucking /ˈfʌkɪŋ/ *adj* (vulg) (*before n*): **~ hell!** ¡puta madre! (vulg)

fudge¹ /fʌdʒ/ *n* (Culin) *especie de caramelo de dulce de leche*

fudge² *vt* (colloq) **(a)** (falsify) ⟨*figures*⟩ amañar **(b)** (evade) ⟨*issue*⟩ esquivar

fuel¹ /ˈfjuːəl/ *n* combustible *m*

fuel² *vt* (BrE) **-ll- 1** ⟨*ship/plane*⟩ abastecer* de combustible; ⟨*stove/furnace*⟩ alimentar **2** ⟨*hope/passion*⟩ alimentar; ⟨*debate*⟩ avivar; ⟨*fear*⟩ exacerbar

fuel oil *n* fuel-oil *m*

fugitive /ˈfjuːdʒətɪv/ *n* fugitivo, -va *m,f*

fulfill, (BrE) **fulfil** /fʊlˈfɪl/ **-ll-** *vt* **1 (a)** (carry out) ⟨*duty*⟩ cumplir con; ⟨*task*⟩ llevar a cabo **(b)** (obey, keep) ⟨*order/promise/contract*⟩ cumplir **(c)** (serve) ⟨*need*⟩ satisfacer* **(d)** (meet) ⟨*requirements*⟩ satisfacer* **2** (realize) ⟨*ambition*⟩ hacer* realidad; ⟨*potential*⟩ alcanzar* **3** (make content) ⟨*person*⟩ satisfacer*
■ *v refl* **to ~ oneself** realizarse*

fulfilled /fʊlˈfɪld/ *adj* (usu pred) realizado

fulfillment, (BrE) **fulfilment** /fʊlˈfɪlmənt/ *n* **(a)** (of duty, promise) cumplimiento *m* **(b)** (satisfaction): **her family gave her a sense of ~** su familia la hacía sentirse realizada

full¹ /fʊl/ *adj* **-er, -est 1** (filled) lleno; **I'm ~ (up)** estoy lleno; **~ OF sth** lleno DE algo **2 (a)** (complete) ⟨*report/description*⟩ detallado; ⟨*name/answer*⟩ completo; **you have my ~ support** tienes todo mi apoyo; **to lead a very ~ life** llevar una vida muy activa **(b)** (maximum): **at ~ speed** a toda velocidad; **~ employment** (Econ) pleno empleo *m* **3** ⟨*figure*⟩ regordete

full² *adv* **1** (*as intensifier*) **~ well** muy bien **2** (directly): **the sun was shining ~ in my face** el sol me daba de lleno en la cara **3** **in full**: **write your name in ~** escriba su nombre completo; **it will be paid in ~** será pagado en su totalidad

full: **~-blown** /ˈfʊlˈbləʊn/ *adj* (*before n*)

verdadero; **~-fledged** /'fʊl'fledʒd/ *adj* (AmE) 🔟 ⟨*chick*⟩ capaz de volar; 🔁 ⟨*lawyer/nurse*⟩ hecho y derecho; **~-grown** /'fʊl'grəʊn/ *adj* (*before n*) totalmente desarrollado; **~ house** *n* (Cin, Theat) lleno *m*; **~-length** /'fʊl'leŋθ/ *adj* ⟨*portrait/mirror*⟩ de cuerpo entero; ⟨*dress/skirt*⟩ largo

fullness /'fʊlnəs ‖'fʊlnɪs/ *n* plenitud *f*; *in the ~ of time* con el tiempo

full: **~-scale** /fʊl'skeɪl/ *adj* 🔟 (actual size) a escala natural; 🔁 (major) ⟨*work*⟩ de envergadura; ⟨*investigation*⟩ a fondo; ⟨*test*⟩ a escala real; ⟨*war*⟩ declarado; **~-size** /fʊl'saɪz/, **~-sized** /-d/ *adj* **(a)** (life-size) de tamaño natural **(b)** (of adult size) ⟨*bicycle/bed*⟩ de adulto; **~ stop** *n* (BrE) punto *m*

full-time[1] /'fʊltaɪm/ *adj* ⟨*student/soldier*⟩ de tiempo completo; ⟨*employment/post*⟩ de jornada completa

full-time[2] /fʊl'taɪm/ *adv* a tiempo completo

fully /'fʊli/ *adv* 🔟 **(a)** (completely): **I ~ understand** comprendo muy bien; **she's a ~ trained nurse** es una enfermera diplomada **(b)** (in full) enteramente 🔁 (at least) por lo menos, como poco

fully-fledged /'fʊli'fledʒd/ *adj* (BrE) ▶ FULL-FLEDGED

fulsome /'fʊlsəm/ *adj* ⟨*praise*⟩ empalagoso; ⟨*manner*⟩ excesivamente efusivo

fumble /'fʌmbəl/ *vi*: **she ~d in her pockets** revolvió en sus bolsillos; **he ~d for the right words** tartamudeó, tratando de encontrar las palabras adecuadas; **she ~d with her buttons** intentó torpemente abrocharse/desabrocharse

fume /fjuːm/ *vi* 🔟 (smoke) (Chem) despedir* gases 🔁 (be angry) (colloq): **she was absolutely fuming** estaba que echaba humo

fumes /fjuːmz/ *pl n* gases *mpl*

fumigate /'fjuːməgeɪt ‖'fjuːmɪgeɪt/ *vt* fumigar*

fun /fʌn/ *n* diversión *f*; **to have ~** divertirse*; **he's good ~** es muy divertido; **to do sth for ~** hacer* algo por gusto; **to make ~ of sb/sth** reírse* de algn/algo

function[1] /'fʌŋkʃən/ *n* 🔟 (of tool, organ, person) función *f*; **to carry out/perform a ~** cumplir/ desempeñar una función 🔁 (reception, party) recepción *f* 🔢 (Comput, Math) función *f*; (*before n*) **~ key** tecla *f* de función

function[2] *vi* **(a)** (operate) «*machine/organ*» funcionar **(b)** (serve) **to ~ AS sth** «*object/ building*» hacer* (las veces) DE algo

functional /'fʌŋkʃənl ‖'fʌŋkʃənl/ *adj* **(a)** (functioning) ⟨*machine/part*⟩ en buen estado (de funcionamiento) **(b)** (practical) ⟨*furniture/design*⟩ funcional

fund[1] /fʌnd/ *n* **(a)** (money reserve) fondo *m* **(b)** **funds** *pl* (resources, money) fondos *mpl*

fund[2] *vt* **(a)** (finance) ⟨*research/organization*⟩ financiar **(b)** (Fin) ⟨*debt*⟩ consolidar

fundamental /ˌfʌndə'mentl/ *adj* **(a)** (basic) ⟨*principle/error/concept*⟩ fundamental **(b)** (essential) ⟨*skill/constituent*⟩ esencial **(c)** (intrinsic, innate) ⟨*absurdity/truth*⟩ intrínseco

fundamentalism /ˌfʌndə'mentəlɪzəm/ *n* integrismo *m*, fundamentalismo *m*

fundamentalist /ˌfʌndə'mentləst ‖ˌfʌndə'mentəlɪst/ *n* integrista *mf*, fundamentalista *mf*

fundamentally /ˌfʌndə'mentli ‖ˌfʌndə'mentəli/ *adv* **(a)** (radically) ⟨*different/ mistaken*⟩ fundamentalmente **(b)** (in essence) ⟨*correct/justified*⟩ esencialmente

fundamentals /ˌfʌndə'mentlz/ *pl n* fundamentos *mpl*

funding /'fʌndɪŋ/ *n* (act) financiación *f*; (resources) fondos *mpl*

fund-raising /'fʌnd'reɪzɪŋ ‖'fʌnd,reɪzɪŋ/ *n* recaudación *f* de fondos

funeral /'fjuːnərəl/ *n* funerales *mpl*

funeral: **~ director** *n* (fml) director, -tora *m,f* de una funeraria; **~ home** (AmE), **~ parlour** (BrE) *n* funeraria *f*

funfair /'fʌnfer ‖'fʌnfeə(r)/ *n* (BrE) (traveling) feria *f*; (permanent) parque *m* de diversiones *or* (Esp) de atracciones

fungus /'fʌŋgəs/ *n* (*pl* **fungi** /'fʌŋgaɪ/) hongo *m*

funnel /'fʌnl/ *n* **(a)** (for pouring) embudo *m* **(b)** (on steamship, steam engine) (BrE) chimenea *f*

funnily /'fʌnli ‖'fʌnɪli/ *adv* **(a)** (strangely) (esp BrE) de modo extraño **(b)** **~ enough** (*indep*) casualmente

funny /'fʌni/ *adj* **-nier, -niest** 🔟 (amusing) ⟨*joke*⟩ gracioso; ⟨*person*⟩ divertido 🔁 (strange) raro; **(it's) ~ (that) you should mention it** es curioso que lo menciones; **to taste/smell ~** saber*/oler* raro 🔢 (colloq) (unwell): **I feel a bit ~** me siento medio mal

fur /fɜːr ‖fɜː(r)/ *n* **(a)** (of animal) (Zool) pelo *m*, pelaje *m*; (Clothing) piel *f*; (*before n*) **~ coat** abrigo *m* de piel *or* (Esp tb) de pieles **(b)** (pelt) piel *f*

furious /'fjʊriəs ‖'fjʊəriəs/ *adj* **(a)** (angry) furioso **(b)** (violent, intense) ⟨*struggle*⟩ feroz; ⟨*speed*⟩ vertiginoso; ⟨*storm*⟩ violento; ⟨*activity*⟩ febril

furiously /'fjʊriəsli ‖'fjʊəriəsli/ *adv* **(a)** (angrily) con furia **(b)** (violently, intensely) frenéticamente

furlough /'fɜːrləʊ ‖'fɜːləʊ/ *n* (AmE) permiso *m*, licencia *f*; **on ~** de permiso, con licencia

furnace /'fɜːrnəs ‖'fɜːnɪs/ *n* (in industry) horno *m*; (for heating) caldera *f*

furnish /'fɜːrnɪʃ ‖'fɜːnɪʃ/ *vt* 🔟 **(a)** ⟨*house/ room*⟩ amueblar, amoblar* (AmL) **(b)** **furnished** *past p* ⟨*room/apartment*⟩ amueblado, amoblado (AmL) 🔁 (supply) (fml) proporcionar; **to ~ sb WITH sth** ⟨*with information*⟩ proporcionarle algo a algn

furnishings /'fɜːrnɪʃɪŋz ‖'fɜːnɪʃɪŋz/ *pl n*: *mobiliario, cortinas, alfombras, etc*

furniture /'fɜːrnɪtʃər ‖'fɜːnɪtʃə(r)/ *n* (in home, office) muebles *mpl*, mobiliario *m*; **a piece of ~** un mueble; (*before n*) **~ mover** *o* (BrE) **remover** empresa *f* de mudanzas; **~ polish** cera *f* para muebles

furor /'fjʊrɔːr ‖'fjʊərɔː(r)/, (BrE) **furore** /fjʊ'rɔːri ‖fjʊə'rɔːri/ *n* escándalo *m*

furrow /'fɜːrəʊ ‖'fʌrəʊ/ *n* surco *m*

furry /'fɜːri/ *adj* **-rier, -riest** ⟨*animal*⟩ peludo; ⟨*toy*⟩ de peluche; ⟨*covering/lining*⟩ afelpado

further[1] /'fɜːrðər ‖'fɜːðə(r)/ *adv* 🔟 *comp of* FAR[1] **(a)** (in distance): **they live even ~ away** ellos viven aún más lejos; **how much ~ is it?** ¿cuánto camino nos queda por hacer?; **~ on, there's another set of traffic lights** más adelante, hay otro semáforo **(b)** (in progress): **the legislation should have gone ~** la legislación debería haber ido ···⟩

más lejos; **have you got any ~ with that essay?** ¿has adelantado ese trabajo? **(c)** (in time): **we must look back even ~** tenemos que retroceder aún más en el tiempo; **this vase dates back even ~** este jarrón es aún más antiguo **(d)** (in extent, degree): **I'll look ~ into that possibility** voy a estudiar esa posibilidad más a fondo; **the situation is ~ complicated by her absence** el hecho de que ella no esté complica aún más la situación

2 **further to** (Corresp) (as prep): **~ to your letter of June 6, ...** con relación a su carta del 6 de junio, ...

3 (furthermore) (as linker) además

further² adj más; **have you any ~ questions?** ¿tienen más preguntas?; **until ~ notice** hasta nuevo aviso

further³ vt ‹cause/aims› promover*; ‹career/ interests› favorecer*

further education n (BrE) programa de cursos de extensión cultural para adultos

furthermore /'fɜːrðərmɔːr ‖ ˌfɜːðə'mɔː(r)/ adv además

furthest /'fɜːrðəst ‖ 'fɜːðɪst/ adv superl of FAR¹ 1

furtive /'fɜːrtɪv ‖ 'fɜːtɪv/ adj **(a)** (stealthy) ‹movement/look› furtivo; ‹person› solapado **(b)** (suspicious, shifty) ‹appearance› sospechoso; ‹manner› solapado

furtively /'fɜːrtɪvli ‖ 'fɜːtɪvli/ adv ‹creep› sigilosamente; ‹peep/listen› a hurtadillas

fury /'fjʊri ‖ 'fjʊəri/ n (pl **furies**) ira f

fuse¹ /fjuːz/ n **1** (Elec) fusible m, plomo m (Esp), tapón m (CS) **2** (for explosives) mecha f

fuse² vt **1** (Elec) **(a)** (short-circuit) (BrE): **to ~ the**

lights hacer* saltar los fusibles or (CS tb) los tapones, fundir los plomos (Esp) **(b) fused** past p con fusible **2 (a)** (melt together) alear **(b)** (merge) fusionar

fuse box n caja f de fusibles or (Esp tb) de plomos or (CS tb) de tapones

fuselage /'fjuːzəlɑːʒ/ n fuselaje m

fusion /'fjuːʒən/ n fusión f

fuss¹ /fʌs/ n alboroto m; **to kick up a ~** armar un lío, montar un número (Esp fam); **to make** o (AmE also) **raise a ~** hacer* un escándalo

fuss² vi preocuparse

fussbudget /'fʌs'bʌdʒɪt/, (BrE also) **fusspot** /'fʌspɑːt ‖ 'fʌspɒt/ n maniático, -ca m,f, mañoso, -sa m,f (AmL)

fussy /'fʌsi/ adj **-sier, -siest** exigente; **I'm a ~ eater** soy muy maniático or (AmL tb) mañoso para comer

futile /'fjuːtl ‖ 'fjuːtaɪl/ adj ‹attempt› inútil; ‹suggestion/question› trivial

futility /fjʊ'tɪləti/ n inutilidad f

future¹ /'fjuːtʃər ‖ 'fjuːtʃə(r)/ n **1** (time ahead) **the ~** el futuro; **in ~** de ahora en adelante **2** (prospects) futuro m; **a job with a ~** un trabajo con futuro **3** (Ling) futuro m **4 futures** pl (Fin) futuros mpl

future² adj (before n) **(a)** ‹husband/home› futuro **(b)** (Ling): **the ~ tense** el futuro

futuristic /'fjuːtʃə'rɪstɪk/ adj futurista

fuze /fjuːz/ n (AmE) ▶ FUSE¹ 2

fuzzy /'fʌzi/ adj **-zier, -ziest** **1** ‹hair› muy rizado; ‹beard› enmarañado **2** (blurred) ‹sound› confuso; ‹picture/outline› borroso

Gg

G, g /dʒiː/ n **(a)** (letter) G, g f **(b)** (Mus) sol m

g (= gram(s)) g., gr.

G (in US) (Cin) (= **general**) apta para todo público

GA, Ga = Georgia

gab /gæb/ vi **-bb-** (colloq) charlar (fam)

gabble /'gæbəl/ vi (speak incoherently) hablar atropelladamente, farfullar; (speak quickly) parlotear (fam)

gable /'geɪbəl/ n gablete m; **~ (end)** hastial m

gadget /'gædʒət ‖ 'gædʒɪt/ n (colloq) aparato m, chisme m (Esp fam)

Gaelic /'geɪlɪk/ n gaélico m

gaffe /gæf/ n metedura f or (AmL tb) metida f de pata (fam)

gag¹ /gæg/ n **1** (for mouth) mordaza f **2** (joke) (colloq) chiste m, gag m

gag² **-gg-** vt amordazar*
■ ~ vi hacer* arcadas

gage /geɪdʒ/ vt/n (AmE) ▶ GAUGE¹,²

gaggle /'gægəl/ n (of geese) bandada f

gain¹ /geɪn/ vt **1** (acquire) ‹control› conseguir*; ‹experience› adquirir*; ‹recognition› obtener* **2** (increase) ‹strength/speed› ganar **3** ‹time› ganar; **my watch is ~ing ten minutes a day** mi reloj se adelanta diez minutos por día
■ ~ vi **1 (a)** (improve) **to ~ in value** subir or aumentar de valor; **she's gradually ~ing in confidence** poco a poco va adquiriendo confianza en sí misma **(b)** (benefit) beneficiarse **2 (a)** (go fast) «clock/watch» adelantar(se) **(b)** (move nearer) **to ~ ON sb** acortar (las) distancias con respecto a algn

gain² n **1** (profit) ganancia f **2** (increase) aumento m

gainful /'geɪnfəl/ adj retribuido

gait /geɪt/ n (no pl) modo m de andar

gala /'gælə, 'geɪlə ‖ 'gɑːlə/ n fiesta f

Galapagos Islands /gə'lɑːpəgəs ‖ gə'læpəgəs/ pl n the **~ ~** las Islas Galápagos

galaxy /'gæləksi/ n (pl **-xies**) galaxia f

gale /geɪl/ n vendaval f; (before n) **~-force winds** vientos mpl (huracanados)

Galicia /gə'lɪʃiə, gə'lɪsiə/ n Galicia f

Galician¹ /gə'lɪʃiən, gə'lɪsiən/ n **(a)** (person) gallego, -ga m,f **(b)** (language) gallego m

Galician² adj gallego

gallant adj **(a)** /'gælənt/ (brave) (liter) aguerrido (liter) **(b)** /gə'lænt/ (chivalrous) galante

gall bladder /gɔ:l/ n vesícula f (biliar)

galleon /'gæliən/ n galeón m

gallery /'gæləri/ n (pl **-ries**) **1** (Art) museo m (de Bellas Artes); (commercial) galería f (de arte) **2** (Archit) galería f; (for press, spectators) tribuna f

galley /'gæli/ n **1** (ship) galera f **2** (kitchen on boat, plane) cocina f

gallon /'gælən/ n galón m (EEUU: 3,78 litros, RU: 4,55 litros)

gallop¹ /'gæləp/ n galope m

gallop² vi galopar

gallows /'gæləʊz/ n (pl ~) (+ sing o pl vb) horca f

gallstone /'gɔ:lstəʊn/ n cálculo m biliar

galore /gə'lɔ:r ‖gə'lɔ:(r)/ adj (after n) en abundancia

galvanize /'gælvənaɪz/ vt **1** (rouse) to ~ sb (INTO sth/-ING) impulsar a algn (A algo /+ INF) **2 galvanized** past p ‹iron/steel› galvanizado

Gambia /'gæmbiə/ n Gambia f

gambit /'gæmbət ‖'gæmbɪt/ n (stratagem) táctica f; (in chess) gambito m

gamble¹ /'gæmbəl/ vi jugar*; to ~ on a horse apostar* a un caballo
■ ~ vt jugarse*

gamble² n (no pl) **(a)** (bet) apuesta f **(b)** (risk): to take a ~ arriesgarse*

gambler /'gæmblər/ n jugador, -dora m,f

gambling /'gæmblɪŋ/ n juego m

gambol /'gæmbəl/ vi, (BrE) **-ll-** retozar*

game¹ /geɪm/ n **1** **(a)** (amusement) juego m **(b)** (type of sport) deporte m **2** **(a)** (complete match) (Sport) partido m; (in board games, cards) partida f **(b)** (part of tennis, squash match) juego m **3** (underhand scheme, ploy) juego m **4** (in hunting) caza f; **big** ~ caza mayor **5** (Culin) caza f

game² adj we're going swimming, are you ~? vamos a nadar ¿te apuntas?; **she's ~ for anything** se apunta a todo

game: ~**keeper** n guardabosque(s) mf; ~ **reserve** n coto m de caza; ~ **show** n programa m concurso

gammon /'gæmən/ n (esp BrE) jamón m fresco

gamut /'gæmət/ n gama f; **to run the (whole)** ~ **of sth** cubrir* toda la gama de algo

gander /'gændər ‖'gændə(r)/ n (Zool) ganso m (macho)

gang /gæŋ/ n (of criminals) banda f; (of youths, children) pandilla f
■ **gang up** [v + adv] (colloq) **to** ~ **up** AGAINST o ON **sb** ponerse*/estar* en contra de algn

gang: ~**land** n (journ) hampa f‡, mundo m del crimen organizado; ~**master** (BrE) contratista m de mano de obra indocumentada; ~**plank** n plancha f

gangrene /'gæŋgri:n/ n gangrena f

gangster /'gæŋstər ‖'gæŋstə(r)/ n gángster mf

gangway /'gæŋweɪ/ n **1** (walkway) pasarela f **2** (between rows of seats) (BrE) pasillo m

gantlet /'gɔ:ntlət/ n (AmE) ▶ GAUNTLET

gaol /dʒeɪl/ n/vt (esp BrE) ▶ JAIL¹, ²

gap /gæp/ n **1** (space) espacio m; (in fence, hedge) hueco m **2** **(a)** (in knowledge) laguna f **(b)** (in time) intervalo m, interrupción f **(c)** (disparity) distancia f, brecha f **(d)** (void) vacío m

gape /geɪp/ vi **1** (stare) mirar boquiabierto **2** (be open) estar* abierto

gaping /'geɪpɪŋ/ adj ‹wound› abierto; ‹hole› enorme

garage /gə'rɑ:ʒ ‖'gærɑ:dʒ, -ɪdʒ/ n **1** (for parking) garaje m, garage m (esp AmL) **2** **(a)** (for repairs) taller m (mecánico), garaje m, garage m (esp AmL) **(b)** (for fuel) (BrE) ▶ GAS STATION

garb /gɑ:rb ‖gɑ:b/ n (liter o hum) atuendo m (liter o hum)

garbage /'gɑ:rbɪdʒ ‖'gɑ:bɪdʒ/ n **(a)** (AmE) (refuse) basura f; (before n) ~ **dump** vertedero m (de basuras), basurero m, basural m (AmL) **(b)** (junk) (colloq) trastos mpl, cachivaches mpl (fam), porquerías fpl (fam); **this book is absolute** ~ este libro es una auténtica porquería

garbage: ~ **bag** n (AmE) bolsa f de la basura; ~ **can** n (AmE) cubo m or (CS) tacho m or (Col) caneca f or (Méx) bote m or (Ven) tobo m de la basura; ~**man** /'gɑ:rbɪdʒmæn/ n (pl **-men** /-men/) (AmE) basurero m; ~ **truck** n (AmE) camión m de la basura

garbled /'gɑ:rbəld ‖'gɑ:bəld/ adj ‹account› confuso; ‹message› incomprensible

garden¹ /'gɑ:rdn ‖'gɑ:dn/ n **(a)** (for ornamental plants) jardín m; (for vegetables) huerta f, huerto m **(b) gardens** pl (public, on private estate) jardines mpl, parque m

garden² vi trabajar en el jardín

garden center, (BrE) **garden centre** n vivero m, centro m de jardinería

gardener /'gɑ:rdnər ‖'gɑ:dnə(r)/ n jardinero, -ra m,f

gardening /'gɑ:rdnɪŋ ‖'gɑ:dnɪŋ/ n jardinería f; (vegetable growing) horticultura f; **he does the** ~ él se encarga del jardín

garden: ~ **party** n recepción f al aire libre; ~**-variety** adj (AmE colloq) (before n) vulgar or común y corriente

gargle /'gɑ:rgəl ‖'gɑ:gəl/ vi hacer* gárgaras

gargoyle /'gɑ:rgɔɪl ‖'gɑ:gɔɪl/ n gárgola f

garish /'gerɪʃ ‖'geərɪʃ/ adj ‹color› chillón, charro (AmL fam); ‹garment› estridente, charro (AmL fam)

garland /'gɑ:rlənd ‖'gɑ:lənd/ n guirnalda f

garlic /'gɑ:rlɪk ‖'gɑ:lɪk/ n ajo m

garment /'gɑ:rmənt ‖'gɑ:mənt/ n prenda f (de ropa)

garnet /'gɑ:rnət ‖'gɑ:nɪt/ n granate m

garnish¹ /'gɑ:rnɪʃ ‖'gɑ:nɪʃ/ vt adornar

garnish² n adorno m, aderezo m; (more substantial) guarnición f

garret /'gærət/ n buhardilla f

garrison /'gærəsən ‖'gærɪsən/ n **(a)** (place) plaza f fuerte or de armas **(b)** (troops) guarnición f

garrulous /'gærələs/ adj charlatán

garter /'gɑ:rtər ‖'gɑ:tə(r)/ n liga f

gas¹ /gæs/ n (pl **gases** or **gasses**) **1** (Phys) ⋯▸

gas m ② **(a)** (fuel) gas m; *(before n)* ⟨ring/heater⟩ de or a gas **(b)** (anesthetic) gas m ③ (gasoline) (AmE) ▶ GASOLINE ④ (flatulence) (AmE) gases mpl

gas² vt -ss- (Mil) gasear; (kill) asfixiar con gas; (in gas chamber) ejecutar en la cámara de gas

gas chamber n cámara f de gas

gaseous /'gæsiəs/ adj gaseoso

gash¹ /gæʃ/ n tajo m, corte m profundo

gash² vt hacer* un tajo en, cortar (profundamente)

gasket /'gæskət ‖'gæskɪt/ n junta f

gas: ∼light n (illumination) luz f de gas; ∼ **mask** n máscara f antigás

gasoline /'gæsəliːn/ n (AmE) gasolina f, nafta f (RPI), bencina f (Andes)

gasp¹ /gæsp ‖gɑːsp/ vi **(a)** (inhale sharply) dar* un grito ahogado **(b)** (pant) respirar entrecortadamente, jadear
■ ∼ vt decir* jadeando

gasp² n exclamación f, grito m (entrecortado o ahogado)

gas: ∼ pedal n (esp AmE) acelerador m; ∼ **pump** n (AmE) (in service station) surtidor m, bomba f bencinera (Andes); ∼ **station** n (AmE) estación f de servicio or (RPI tb) de nafta, gasolinera f, bomba f (Andes, Ven), grifo m (Per); ∼ **tank** n (AmE) depósito m or tanque m de gasolina or (RPI) de nafta or (Andes) de bencina

gastric /'gæstrɪk/ adj gástrico

gastroenteritis /'gæstrəʊ‚entə'raɪtəs ‖‚gæstrəʊ‚entə'raɪtɪs/ n gastroenteritis f

gasworks /'gæswɜːks ‖'gæswɜːks/ n (pl ∼) (+ sing o pl vb) fábrica f de gas

gate /geɪt/ n **(a)** (to garden — wooden) puerta f (del jardín); (— wrought-iron) verja f, cancela f (Esp); (to field) tranquera f (AmL), portillo m (Esp) **(b)** (to castle, city) (usu pl) puerta f **(c)** (controlling admission) entrada f **(d)** (at airport) puerta f (de embarque)

gate: ∼crash vi colarse*; ∼**way** n verja f, portalón m

gather¹ /'gæðər ‖'gæðə(r)/ vi congregarse*, reunirse*
■ ∼ vt ① **(a)** (collect) ⟨wood/berries⟩ recoger*, coger* (esp Esp); ⟨information⟩ reunir*, juntar; ⟨people⟩ reunir*; to ∼ **dust** juntar or acumular polvo **(b)** ⟨thoughts⟩ poner* en orden; ⟨strength⟩ juntar, hacer* acopio de **(c)** ⟨speed⟩ ir* adquiriendo ② (conclude) deducir*; **I** ∼ **you're moving** tengo entendido que te mudas (de casa) ③ (by sewing) fruncir*
■ **gather in** [v + o + adv, v + adv + o] recoger*

gather² n fruncido m, frunce m

gathering¹ /'gæðərɪŋ/ n (meeting) reunión f; (group of people) concurrencia f

gathering² adj *(before n)* creciente; **the ∼ storm** la tormenta que se avecinaba

gaudy /'gɔːdi/ adj chillón, charro (AmL fam)

gauge¹, (AmE also) **gage** /geɪdʒ/ vt **(a)** (estimate) ⟨size⟩ calcular **(b)** (judge) ⟨effects⟩ evaluar* **(c)** (measure) medir*

gauge², (AmE also) **gage** n ① (instrument) indicador m ② (measure, indication) indicio m ③ (Rail): **narrow ∼** vía f estrecha, trocha f angosta (CS)

gaunt /gɔːnt/ adj ⟨person⟩ descarnado, delgado y adusto; (from illness, tiredness) demacrado

gauntlet /'gɔːntlət ‖'gɔːntlɪt/ n guante m (con el puño largo); (of suit of armor) guantelete m, manopla f

gauze /gɔːz/ n (Tex, Med) gasa f; (fine mesh) malla f

gave /geɪv/ past of GIVE¹

gavel /'gævəl/ n mazo m or martillo m (usado por jueces, subastadores etc)

gay /geɪ/ adj ① (homosexual) gay adj inv ② (dated) (merry) alegre

gaze¹ /geɪz/ vi mirar (larga y fijamente); **to ∼ AT sth/sb** mirar algo/a algn

gaze² n mirada f (larga y fija)

gazelle /gə'zel/ n (pl ∼s or ∼) gacela f

gazette /gə'zet/ n gaceta f

gazetteer /‚gæzə'tɪr ‖‚gæzə'tɪə(r)/ n índice m geográfico

GB = **Great Britain**

GCSE n (in UK) = **General Certificate of Secondary Education** ≈ bachillerato m elemental (exámenes que se toman en diferentes asignaturas alrededor de los 16 años)

gear¹ /gɪr ‖'gɪə(r)/ n ① (Mech Eng) engranaje m; (Auto) marcha f, velocidad f, cambio m; **to shift** o (BrE) **change ∼** cambiar de marcha, cambiar de velocidad, hacer* un cambio ② **(a)** (equipment) equipo m; (tools) herramientas fpl; (fishing ∼) aparejo(s) m(pl) de pesca **(b)** (miscellaneous items) (colloq) cosas fpl

gear² vt orientar; **(to be) ∼ed TO/TOWARD sth/sb** (estar*) dirigido A algo/algn
■ **gear up** ① [v + adv] (prepare) prepararse ② [v + o + adv, v + adv + o] preparar

gearbox /'gɪrbɑːks ‖'gɪəbɒks/ n (Auto) caja f de cambios or velocidades

gee /dʒiː/ interj (AmE colloq): ∼, **I'm sorry to hear that** oye, lo siento; ∼, **thanks!** ¡pero … gracias!

geese /giːs/ pl of GOOSE

gel¹ /dʒel/ n gel m

gel² vi -ll- **(a)** ⟨liquid⟩ gelificarse* **(b)** (BrE) ⟨plans/ideas⟩ cuajar

gelatin /'dʒelətn ‖'dʒelətɪn/, **gelatine** /'dʒelətiːn/ n gelatina f

gem /dʒem/ n **(a)** (stone) gema f, piedra f preciosa/semipreciosa; (jewel) joya f, alhaja f **(b)** (wonderful example) joya f

Gemini /'dʒemɪnaɪ, -niː ‖'dʒemɪnaɪ, -niː/ n **(a)** (sign) (no art) Géminis **(b)** (person) Géminis or géminis mf, geminiano, -na m,f

gender /'dʒendər ‖'dʒendə(r)/ n **(a)** (Ling) género m **(b)** (sex) sexo m

gene /dʒiːn/ n gen m, gene m

genealogy /‚dʒiːni'ælədʒi/ n genealogía f

general¹ /'dʒenrəl/ adj ① (not detailed or specific)

general; **in** ~ en general **2** (widespread) ⟨tendency⟩ generalizado **3** (usual) general; **as a** ~ **rule** por lo general, por regla general **4** (chief) ⟨manager⟩ general **5** (Med) ⟨anesthetic⟩ general

general² n (Mil) general mf

general: ~ **delivery** n (AmE) lista f de correos, poste f restante (AmL); ~ **election** n elecciones fpl generales

generalization /ˌdʒenrələˈzeɪʃən ‖ˌdʒenrəlaɪˈzeɪʃən/ n generalización f

generalize /ˈdʒenrəlaɪz/ vi/t generalizar*

general knowledge n cultura f general

generally /ˈdʒenrəli/ adv (a) (usually, as a rule) generalmente, por lo general (b) (broadly) ⟨indep⟩ ~ (**speaking**) por lo general, en general (c) (as a whole) en general

general: ~ **practitioner** n médico, -ca m,f de medicina general; ~ **public** n the ~ **public** el público en general, el gran público; ~**-purpose** adj ⟨tool⟩ para todo uso; ⟨dictionary⟩ de uso general; ~ **store** n (AmE) tienda f (que vende todo tipo de artículos en una comunidad pequeña), almacén m (CS); ~ **strike** n huelga f general, paro m general (AmL)

generate /ˈdʒenəreɪt/ vt generar

generation /ˌdʒenəˈreɪʃən/ n **1** generación f; **the older** ~ la gente de más edad; **first-**~ **computers** computadoras fpl or (Esp tb) ordenadores mpl de primera generación **2** (act of generating) generación f

generation gap n brecha f generacional

generator /ˈdʒenəreɪtər ‖ˈdʒenəreɪtə(r)/ n generador m, grupo m electrógeno

generic /dʒəˈnerɪk/ adj ⟨term⟩ genérico

generosity /ˌdʒenəˈrɑːsəti ‖ˌdʒenəˈrɒsəti/ n generosidad f

generous /ˈdʒenrəs ‖ˈdʒenərəs/ adj (a) (open-handed) generoso (b) (ample, large) abundante, generoso

genetic /dʒəˈnetɪk ‖dʒɪˈnetɪk/ adj genético

genetically /dʒəˈnetɪkli/ adv genéticamente; ~ **modified** transgénico, genéticamente modificado

genetics /dʒəˈnetɪks ‖dʒɪˈnetɪks/ n (+ sing vb) genética f

genial /ˈdʒiːnjəl ‖ˈdʒiːniəl/ adj ⟨person⟩ simpático; ⟨welcome/smile⟩ cordial

genie /ˈdʒiːni/ n genio m

genitals /ˈdʒenətlz ‖ˈdʒenɪtlz/ pl n genitales mpl

genius /ˈdʒiːniəs/ n **1** (clever person) genio m **2** (brilliance) genialidad f

genre /ˈʒɑːnrə ‖ˈʒɒnrə/ n género m

gent /dʒent/ n (BrE colloq) caballero m; ⊖ **Gents** Caballeros

gentle /ˈdʒentl/ adj **gentler** /ˈdʒentlər ‖ˈdʒentlə(r)/, **gentlest** /ˈdʒentləst ‖ˈdʒentlɪst/ **1** (a) ⟨person⟩ dulce; ⟨character⟩ suave (b) (of voice): **in a** ~ **voice** en un tono suave or dulce **2** ⟨murmur/breeze⟩ suave; ⟨exercise⟩ moderado; ⟨slope⟩ poco empinado; ⟨reminder⟩ discreto

gentleman /ˈdʒentlmən/ n (pl **-men** /-mən/) (a) (man) caballero m, señor m (b) (well-bred man) caballero m

gently /ˈdʒentli/ adv (a) (not roughly or violently)

⟨handle⟩ con cuidado; ⟨tap⟩ ligeramente; ⟨hint⟩ con tacto (b) (tenderly) dulcemente; (tactfully) con delicadeza

gentry /ˈdʒentri/ n (+ sing o pl vb) alta burguesía f, pequeña nobleza f

genuine /ˈdʒenjuən ‖ˈdʒenjʊm/ adj (a) ⟨interest/person⟩ genuino, sincero; ⟨inquiry/buyer/mistake⟩ serio; **it was a** ~ **mistake** fue realmente un error (b) ⟨antique⟩ auténtico; ⟨leather⟩ legítimo

genuinely /ˈdʒenjuənli ‖ˈdʒenjʊmli/ adv (a) (sincerely) sinceramente (b) (really) realmente

geographical /ˌdʒiːəˈɡræfɪkəl ‖ˌdʒɪəˈɡræfɪkəl/ adj geográfico

geography /dʒiːˈɑːɡrəfi ‖dʒɪˈɒɡrəfi/ n geografía f

geological /ˌdʒiːəˈlɑːdʒɪkəl ‖ˌdʒɪəˈlɒdʒɪkəl/ adj geológico

geologist /dʒiːˈɑːlədʒəst ‖dʒiˈɒlədʒɪst/ n geólogo, -ga m,f

geology /dʒiːˈɑːlədʒi ‖dʒiˈɒlədʒi/ n geología f

geometrical /ˌdʒiːəˈmetrɪkəl ‖ˌdʒɪəˈmetrɪkəl/ adj geométrico

geometry /dʒiːˈɑːmətri ‖dʒiˈɒmətri/ n geometría f

Georgia /ˈdʒɔːrdʒə ‖ˈdʒɔːdʒə/ n (a) (republic in the Caucasus) Georgia f (b) (US state) Georgia f

Georgian¹ /ˈdʒɔːrdʒən ‖ˈdʒɔːdʒən/ adj (a) (of Georgia in the Caucasus) georgiano (b) (of Georgia in USA) georgiano (c) (in architecture, UK history) georgiano

Georgian² n (a) (from the Caucasus) georgiano, -na m,f (b) (language) georgiano m (c) (from USA) georgiano, -na m,f

geriatric /ˈdʒeriˈætrɪk/ adj (Med) ⟨patient⟩ anciano; ⟨ward⟩ de geriatría

geriatrician /ˌdʒerɪəˈtrɪʃən/ n geriatra mf

germ /dʒɜːrm ‖dʒɜːm/ n **1** (Med) microbio m, germen m **2** (Biol, Bot) germen m

German¹ /ˈdʒɜːrmən ‖ˈdʒɜːmən/ adj alemán

German² n (a) (language) alemán m (b) (person) alemán, -mana m,f

German: ~ **measles** n (+ sing vb) rubéola f, rubeola f; ~ **shepherd** (**dog**) n pastor m or (CS) ovejero m alemán

Germany /ˈdʒɜːrməni ‖ˈdʒɜːməni/ n Alemania f

germinate /ˈdʒɜːrməneɪt ‖ˈdʒɜːmɪneɪt/ vi germinar

gerund /ˈdʒerənd/ n gerundio m

gestation /dʒeˈsteɪʃən/ n gestación f

gesticulate /dʒeˈstɪkjəleɪt ‖dʒeˈstɪkjʊleɪt/ vi gesticular

gesture¹ /ˈdʒestʃər ‖ˈdʒestʃə(r)/ n (a) (of body) gesto m, ademán m (b) (token, expression) gesto m; **a** ~ **of good will** un gesto de buena voluntad; **it was a nice** ~ fue todo un detalle

gesture² vi hacer* gestos

get /ɡet/ (pres p **getting**; past **got**; past p **got** or (AmE also) **gotten**) vt

I **1** (a) (obtain) conseguir*, obtener*; ⟨job/staff⟩ conseguir*; ⟨idea⟩ sacar*; **where did you** ~ **that beautiful rug?** ¿dónde conseguiste esa alfombra tan preciosa? (b) (buy) comprar; **I got it from Harrods** lo compré en Harrods (c) (achieve, win) ⟨prize/grade⟩ sacar*, obtener* (frml) (d) (on the ⋯❯

telephone) ⟨*person*⟩ lograr comunicarse con; **you've got the wrong number** se ha equivocado de número

2 **(a)** (receive) ⟨*letter/reward/reprimand*⟩ recibir; **I got a stereo for my birthday** me regalaron un estéreo para mi cumpleaños **(b)** (be paid) ⟨*salary/pay*⟩ ganar; **I got £200 for the piano** me dieron 200 libras por el piano **(c)** (experience) ⟨*shock/surprise*⟩ llevarse; **I ~ the feeling that ...** tengo la sensación de que ... **(d)** (suffer): **how did you ~ that bump on your head?** ¿cómo te hiciste ese chichón en la cabeza?

3 (fetch) ⟨*hammer/scissors*⟩ traer*, ir* a buscar; ⟨*doctor/plumber*⟩ llamar; **~ your coat** anda *or* vete a buscar tu abrigo

4 **(a)** (take hold of) agarrar, coger* (*esp Esp*) **(b)** (catch, trap) pillar (*fam*), agarrar (*AmL*), coger* (*esp Esp*)

5 (contract) ⟨*cold/flu*⟩ agarrar, pescar* (*fam*), pillar (*fam*), coger* (*esp Esp*)

6 (catch) ⟨*bus/train*⟩ tomar, coger* (*Esp*)

7 (colloq) **(a)** (irritate) fastidiar **(b)** (puzzle): **what ~s me is how ...** lo que no entiendo es cómo ...

8 **(a)** (understand) (colloq) entender*; **don't ~ me wrong** no me malentiendas **(b)** (take note of): **did you ~ the number?** ¿tomaste nota del número?

9 (possess) **to have got** ▶ HAVE *vt*

II **1** (bring, move, put) (+ *adv compl*): **we'll ~ it there by two o'clock** lo tendremos allí antes de las dos; **they couldn't ~ it up the stairs** no lo pudieron subir por las escaleras

2 (cause to be) (+ *adj compl*): **he got the children ready** preparó a los niños; **I can't ~ the window open** no puedo abrir la ventana; **they got their feet wet** se mojaron los pies

3 **to ~ sb/sth** + *pp* **(a)** (with action carried out by subject): **we must ~ some work done** tenemos que trabajar un poco; **to ~ oneself organized** organizarse* **(b)** (with action carried out by somebody else): **he got the house painted** hizo pintar la casa; **I must ~ this watch fixed** tengo que llevar a *or* (*AmL tb*) mandar a arreglar este reloj

4 (arrange, persuade, force) **to ~ sb/sth to + INF: I'll ~ him to help you** (order) le diré que te ayude; (ask) le pediré que te ayude; (persuade) lo convenceré de que te ayude; **I can't ~ it to work** no puedo hacerlo funcionar

■ ~ *vi* **1** (reach) (+ *adv compl*) llegar*; **can you ~ there by train?** ¿se puede ir en tren?

2 (become): **to ~ tired** cansarse; **to ~ dressed** vestirse*; **he got very angry** se puso furioso; ▶ MARRIED, COLD *etc*

3 **to ~ to + INF (a)** (come to) llegar* a + INF; **I never really got to know him** nunca llegué a conocerlo de verdad **(b)** (have opportunity to): **in this job you ~ to meet many interesting people** en este trabajo uno tiene la oportunidad de conocer a mucha gente interesante; **when do we ~ to open the presents?** ¿cuándo podemos abrir los regalos?

4 (start) **to ~ -ING** empezar* a + INF, ponerse* a + INF

■ **get about** [*v* + *adv*] [*v* + *prep* + *o*] (BrE) ▶ GET AROUND I 1

■ **get above** [*v* + *prep* + *o*]: **to ~ above oneself** llenarse de ínfulas

■ **get across** **1** [*v* + *prep* + *o*] [*v* + *adv*] (cross) ⟨*river*⟩ atravesar*, cruzar*; ⟨*road*⟩ cruzar*

2 [*v* + *o* + *adv*, *v* + *adv* + *o*] ⟨*meaning/concept*⟩ hacer* entender

3 [*v* + *adv*] (be understood) «*teacher/speaker*» hacerse* entender

■ **get ahead** [*v* + *adv*] **(a)** (get in front) «*student/worker*» adelantar **(b)** (progress, succeed) progresar

■ **get along** [*v* + *adv*] **1** (manage, cope) arreglárselas

2 (progress) «*work/patient*» marchar, andar*; **he's ~ting along just fine at school** le va muy bien en el colegio

3 (be on good terms) **to ~ along (WITH sb)** llevarse bien (CON algn)

■ **get around**

I **1** [*v* + *adv*] **(a)** (walk, move about) caminar, andar* **(b)** (using transport, car) desplazarse* **(b)** (travel) viajar **(c)** (circulate): **it *o* word got around that ...** pronto corrió el rumor de que ...

2 [*v* + *prep* + *o*] (gather in circle): **we can't all ~ around this table** no cabemos todos alrededor de esta mesa

II [*v* + *prep* + *o*] **(a)** (avoid, circumvent) ⟨*difficulty/obstacle*⟩ sortear, evitar; ⟨*rule/law*⟩ eludir el cumplimiento de **(b)** (persuade) ⟨*person*⟩ engatusar

III [*v* + *adv*] (go) ir*; (come) venir*

■ **get around to** [*v* + *adv* + *prep* + *o*]: **I meant to write to you, I just never got around to it** tenía intenciones de escribirte pero nunca llegué a hacerlo; **I must ~ around to writing those letters** debo ponerme a escribir esas cartas

■ **get at** [*v* + *prep* + *o*] **1** **(a)** (reach) ⟨*pipe/wire*⟩ llegar* a **(b)** (ascertain) ⟨*facts/truth*⟩ establecer*

2 (nag, criticize) (colloq) criticar*, meterse con (fam)

3 (hint at, mean) (colloq): **what are you ~ting at?** ¿qué quieres decir?

■ **get away** [*v* + *adv*] **1** (escape) escaparse

2 **(a)** (leave) salir* **(b)** (go on vacation) irse* de vacaciones; **to ~ away from it all** alejarse del mundanal ruido

■ **get away with** [*v* + *adv* + *prep* + *o*] **1** (make off with) llevarse, escaparse con

2 **(a)** (go unpunished for): **you won't ~ away with this** esto no va a quedar así; **don't let them ~ away with it** no dejes que se salgan con la suya **(b)** (be let off with) ⟨*fine/warning*⟩ escaparse *or* librarse con

■ **get back** **1** [*v* + *adv*] **(a)** (return) volver*, regresar; (arrive home) llegar* (a casa) **(b)** (retreat): **~ back!** ¡atrás!

2 [*v* + *o* + *adv*, *v* + *adv* + *o*] (regain possession of) ⟨*property*⟩ recuperar; ⟨*health*⟩ recobrar; **we never got our money back** no nos devolvieron el dinero

■ **get behind** **1** [*v* + *adv*] (fall behind) **to ~ behind (WITH sth)** atrasarse (CON algo)

2 [*v* + *prep* + *o*] **(a)** (move to rear of) ponerse* detrás de; (fall behind) rezagarse*, quedarse atrás

■ **get by** [*v* + *adv*] (manage) arreglárselas; **I speak enough French to ~ by** me defiendo en francés; **to ~ by ON sth** arreglárselas CON algo

■ **get down** **1** [*v* + *adv*] **(a)** (descend) bajar **(b)** (crouch) agacharse

2 [*v* + *o* + *adv*, *v* + *adv* + *o*] **(a)** (take, lift, bring down) bajar **(b)** (write down) anotar, tomar nota de

3 [*v* + *o* + *adv*] **(a)** (reduce) ⟨*costs/inflation*⟩ reducir*; ⟨*blood pressure*⟩ bajar **(b)** (depress) deprimir

4 [v + prep + o] (descend) ⟨stairs⟩ bajar; ⟨ladder⟩ bajarse de; ⟨rope⟩ bajar por
■ **get down to** [v + adv + prep + o] (start work on) ponerse* a
■ **get in** **1** (a) [v + adv] (enter) entrar (b) [v + prep + o] ▶ GET INTO 1A
2 [v + adv] (a) (arrive) «person/train» llegar* (b) (gain admission to, be selected for) entrar, ser* admitido (c) (be elected) (Pol) ganar, resultar elegido
3 [v + o + adv, v + adv + o] (a) (bring in, collect up) ⟨washing/chairs⟩ entrar; ⟨harvest⟩ recoger* (b) (buy, obtain) (BrE) ⟨wood/coal/food⟩ aprovisionarse de (c) (call out) ⟨doctor/plumber⟩ llamar (d) (interpose) ⟨blow/kick⟩ dar*; ⟨remark⟩ hacer*
■ **get into** **1** [v + prep + o] (a) (enter) ⟨house⟩ entrar en or, (AmL tb) a; ⟨car⟩ subir a; ⟨hole⟩ meterse en (b) (arrive at) ⟨station/office⟩ llegar* a (c) (be selected for, elected to) ⟨college/club/Congress⟩ entrar en or (AmL tb) a (d) (put on) ⟨coat/robe⟩ ponerse*; (fit into) I can't ∼ into this dress any more este vestido ya no me entra (e) (into a given state): to ∼ into a rage/a mess ponerse* furioso/meterse en un lío; (f) (affect): I don't know what's got into him lately no sé qué le pasa últimamente
2 [v + o + prep + o] (a) (bring, take, put in) meter (b) (involve): you got me into this tú me metiste en esto
■ **get off** **1** [v + adv] [v + prep + o] (a) (alight, dismount) bajarse; to ∼ off a train/horse/bicycle bajarse de un tren/caballo/una bicicleta (b) (remove oneself from) ⟨flowerbed/lawn⟩ salir* de (c) (finish) ⟨work/school⟩ salir* de
2 [v + adv] (a) (leave) «person/letter» salir* (b) (escape unpunished) «person accused» salir* libre; he got off lightly o (AmE also) easy no recibió el castigo que se merecía; he got off with a fine se escapó con solo una multa
3 [v + prep + o] (a) (get up from) ⟨floor⟩ levantarse de (b) (deviate from) ⟨track/tourist routes⟩ salir* or alejarse de; ⟨point⟩ desviarse* or irse* de; I tried to ∼ him off the subject intenté hacerlo cambiar de tema (c) (evade) ⟨duty⟩ librarse or salvarse de
4 [v + o + adv] (remove) ⟨lid/top/stain⟩ quitar
5 [v + o + adv] (send, see off): we got the children off to school mandamos a los niños a la escuela
6 (save from punishment) salvar
■ **get on**
I [v + adv] **1** (move on) seguir* adelante; to ∼ on TO sth pasar A algo; ∼ on with what you're doing sigue con lo que estás haciendo
2 (a) (fare): how's Joe ∼ing on nowadays? ¿qué tal anda Joe?; how did he ∼ on at the interview? ¿cómo le fue en la entrevista? (b) (succeed) tener* éxito; to ∼ on in life tener éxito en la vida
3 (be friends, agree) to ∼ on (WITH sb) llevarse bien (CON algn)
4 (in -ing form) (a) (in time) it's ∼ting on se está haciendo tarde (b) (in age): she's ∼ting on (in years) está vieja, ya no es joven
II [v + adv] [v + prep + o] (climb on, board) subirse; to ∼ on the bus/a horse subirse al autobús/subirse a un caballo
III [v + o + adv] [v + o + prep + o] (place, fix on) poner; I can't ∼ the top on (it) no puedo ponerle la tapa

IV [v + o + adv] (put on) ⟨clothes⟩ ponerse*
■ **get on for** [v + adv + prep + o] (approach) (BrE) (usu in -ing form): it's ∼ting on for six o'clock van a ser las seis; he must be ∼ting on for 40 debe (de) andar rondando los 40
■ **get onto** [v + prep + o] **1** (a) (contact) ⟨person/department⟩ ponerse* en contacto con (b) (begin discussing) ⟨subject⟩ empezar* a hablar de
2 (mount, board) ⟨table/bus/train⟩ subirse a; ⟨horse/bicycle⟩ montarse en
■ **get out**
I [v + adv] **1** (a) (of car, bus, train) bajar(se); (of hole) salir*; (of bath) salir*; to ∼ out of bed levantarse (de la cama) (b) (of room, country) salir*; ∼ out! ¡fuera (de aquí)!
2 (a) (escape) ⟨animal/prisoner⟩ escaparse (b) (become known) «news/truth» saberse*
II [v + o + adv, v + adv + o] (a) (remove, extract) ⟨stopper/nail⟩ sacar*; ⟨stain⟩ quitar, sacar* (esp AmL) (b) (take out) ⟨knife/map⟩ sacar* (c) (withdraw) ⟨money⟩ sacar* (d) (borrow) ⟨library book⟩ sacar*
III [v + o + adv] **1** (remove) ⟨tenant⟩ echar; ∼ that dog out of here! ¡saquen (a) ese perro de aquí!; I can't ∼ you out of this mess no te puedo sacar de este lío
2 (send for) ⟨doctor/repairman⟩ llamar
■ **get out of** **1** [v + adv + prep + o] (a) (avoid) ⟨obligation⟩ librarse or salvarse de; to ∼ out of -ING librarse or salvarse de + INF (b) (give up): you must ∼ out of that bad habit tienes que sacarte esa mala costumbre; I'd got out of the habit of setting my alarm clock había perdido la costumbre de poner el despertador
2 [v + o + adv + prep + o] (a) (extract) ⟨information/truth⟩ sonsacar*, sacar* (b) (derive, gain) ⟨money/profit⟩ sacar*
■ **get over** **1** [v + prep + o] ⟨river/chasm⟩ cruzar*; ⟨wall/fence⟩ pasar por encima de; ⟨hill/ridge⟩ atravesar*; ⟨obstacle⟩ superar
2 [v + prep + o] ⟨loss/tragedy/difficulty⟩ superar; ⟨illness/shock⟩ reponerse* de; he's very disappointed — he'll ∼ over it ha quedado muy decepcionado — ya se le pasará
3 [v + o + adv] (cause to come, take): ∼ those documents over to Wall Street right away manda esos documentos a Wall Street enseguida; to ∼ sth over with: I'd like to ∼ it over with as quickly as possible quisiera salir de eso or quitarme eso de encima lo más pronto posible
4 [v + o + adv] (communicate) ⟨emotion⟩ comunicar*
■ **get past** **1** [v + adv] (move past) pasar
2 [v + prep + o] (a) (move past) ⟨vehicle⟩ pasar, adelantarse a; ⟨opponent/attacker⟩ eludir (b) (get beyond) ⟨obstacle⟩ superar; ⟨semifinals⟩ pasar
■ **get round** (esp BrE) ▶ GET AROUND
■ **get through**
I [v + prep + o] [v + adv] (a) (pass through) ⟨gap/hole⟩ pasar por (b) (ordeal) superar; ⟨winter/difficult time⟩ pasar (c) (Sport) ⟨heat⟩ pasar
II [v + adv] **1** (a) (reach destination) «supplies/messenger» llegar* a destino; «news/report» llegar* (b) (on the telephone) to ∼ through (TO sb/sth) comunicarse* (CON algn/algo) (c) (make understand): am I ∼ting through to you? ¿me entiendes?; I can't ∼ through to him no logro hacerme entender con él
2 (finish) (AmE) terminar, acabar   ⬦

III [v + prep + o] **(a)** (use up) (BrE) ‹money›
gastarse; ‹materials› usar; ‹shoes› destrozar* **(b)**
(deal with): **I've only got ten more pages to ~
through** me quedan solo diez páginas por leer (or
estudiar etc)

IV [v + o + adv] [v + o + prep + o] (bring through)
pasar; **to ~ sth through customs** pasar algo por
la aduana

V [v + o + adv] **(a)** (send) ‹supplies/message›
hacer* llegar **(b)** (make understood) hacer*
entender

■ **get together** ①[v + adv] **(a)** (meet up)
reunirse*, quedar (Esp); (have a family reunion)
juntarse, reunirse* **(b)** (join forces) «nations/
unions» unirse **(c)** (become couple, team) (colloq)
juntarse
②[v + o + adv, v + adv + o] (assemble) ‹people/
money› reunir*; **~ your things together** junta or
recoge tus cosas

■ **get up** ①[v + prep + o] [v + adv] (climb up)
subir; **to ~ up on sth** subir(se) a algo
②[v + adv] **(a)** (out of bed) levantarse **(b)** (stand
up) levantarse
③[v + o + adv] (raise, lift) ‹person› levantar
④[v + o + adv, v + adv + o] (develop, arouse)
‹appetite/enthusiasm› despertar*; ‹speed› agarrar,
coger* (esp Esp); **she didn't want to ~ their hopes
up** no quería esperanzarlos

■ **get up to** [v + adv + prep + o] ①(reach): **when
he got up to them ...** cuando los alcanzó ...; **we
got up to page 161** llegamos hasta la página 161
②(be involved in) (colloq) hacer*; **to ~ up to
mischief** hacer* travesuras or de las suyas

get: ~away n huida f, fuga f; **to make one's
~away** escaparse, huir*; **~-together** n (colloq)
reunión f

geyser /ˈgaɪzər ‖ˈgiːzə(r)/ n (Geog) géiser m

Ghana /ˈgɑːnə/ n Ghana f

Ghanaian /gɑːˈneɪən/ adj ghanés

ghastly /ˈgæstli ‖ˈgɑːstli/ adj **(a)** (very bad,
awful) (colloq) espantoso, horrendo (fam) **(b)**
(horrible, hideous) horrible, espantoso

gherkin /ˈgɜːrkən ‖ˈgɜːkɪn/ n pepinillo m

ghetto /ˈgetəʊ/ n (pl **-tos** or **-toes**) gueto m

ghost /gəʊst/ n fantasma m, espíritu m

ghostly /ˈgəʊstli/ adj **-lier, -liest** fantasmal,
fantasmagórico

ghoul /guːl/ n **(a)** (person) morboso, -sa m,f **(b)**
(evil spirit) demonio m necrófago

GI n (colloq) soldado m estadounidense

giant¹ /ˈdʒaɪənt/ n gigante, -ta m,f

giant² adj (before n) ‹organization› gigantesco;
‹insect› gigante; ‹stride› gigantesco

gibber /ˈdʒɪbər ‖ˈdʒɪbə(r)/ vi farfullar

gibberish /ˈdʒɪbərɪʃ/ n galimatías m; **to talk ~**
decir* sandeces (fam)

gibe /dʒaɪb/ n pulla f

giblets /ˈdʒɪbləts ‖ˈdʒɪblɪts/ pl n menudillos
mpl, menudos mpl

Gibraltar /dʒəˈbrɔːltər ‖dʒɪˈbrɔːltə(r)/ n
Gibraltar

giddy /ˈgɪdi/ adj **-dier, -diest** ‹sensation› de
mareo or aturdimiento; **to feel ~** sentirse*
mareado

gift /gɪft/ n ①(present) regalo m; **it was a ~** me
lo regalaron, es un regalo ②(talent) don m; **she
has a ~ for poetry** tiene talento para la poesía

gift certificate n (AmE) vale m ‹canjeable
por artículos en una tienda›, cheque regalo m

gifted /ˈgɪftəd ‖ˈgɪftɪd/ adj ‹person› de talento,
talentoso

gift: ~ token, ~ voucher n (BrE) ▶ GIFT
CERTIFICATE; **~-wrap** vt **-pp-** envolver* para
regalo or (frml) obsequio

gig /gɪg/ n (sl) actuación f

gigabyte /ˈgɪgəbaɪt/ n gigabyte m

gigantic /dʒaɪˈgæntɪk/ adj gigantesco; ‹success/
appetite› enorme; ‹effort› titánico

giggle¹ /ˈgɪgəl/ vi reírse* tontamente

giggle² n risita f

gild /gɪld/ vt dorar

gill n ①/dʒɪl/ medida para líquidos equivalente
a la cuarta parte de una pinta o 0,142 l ②/gɪl/
(Zool) agalla f, branquia f

gilt /gɪlt/ n dorado m

gimmick /ˈgɪmɪk/ n **(a)** (ingenious idea, device)
truco m **(b)** (catch, snag) (AmE) trampa f

gin /dʒɪn/ n ginebra f, gin m

ginger¹ /ˈdʒɪndʒər ‖ˈdʒɪndʒə(r)/ n jengibre m

ginger² adj ‹hair› color zanahoria; ‹cat› rojizo

ginger: ~ ale n ginger ale m, refresco m de
jengibre; **~ beer** n cerveza f de jengibre;
~bread n (cake) pan m de jengibre; (cookie)
galleta f de jengibre

gipsy, Gipsy /ˈdʒɪpsi/ n ▶ GYPSY

giraffe /dʒəˈræf ‖dʒɪˈrɑːf/ n jirafa f

girder /ˈgɜːrdər ‖ˈgɜːdə(r)/ n viga f (de metal)

girdle /ˈgɜːrdl ‖ˈgɜːdl̩/ n faja f

girl /gɜːrl ‖gɜːl/ n ①**(a)** (baby, child) niña f, nena
f (esp RPI) **(b)** (young woman) chica f, muchacha f
②(daughter) hija f, niña f

girl: ~friend n **(a)** (of man) novia f **(b)** (of
woman) (esp AmE) amiga f; (in lesbian couple)
compañera f; **~ guide** (BrE) ▶ GIRL SCOUT

girlish /ˈgɜːrlɪʃ ‖ˈgɜːlɪʃ/ adj de niña

girl scout n (AmE) guía f (de los scouts),
exploradora f

giro /ˈdʒaɪrəʊ/ n (pl **-ros**) (in UK) (system)
transferencia f, giro m

girth /gɜːrθ ‖gɜːθ/ n ①(of person, object)
circunferencia f ②(Equ) cincha f

gist /dʒɪst/ n lo esencial; **to get the ~ of sth**
captar lo esencial de algo

give¹ /gɪv/ (past gave; past p given) vt
I ①**(a)** (hand, pass) dar*; **~ her/me/them a glass
of water** dale/dame/dales un vaso de agua **(b)** (as
gift) regalar; **to ~ sb a present** hacerle* un regalo
a algn, regalarle algo a algn **(c)** (donate) dar*,
donar **(d)** (dedicate, devote) ‹love/affection› dar*;

⟨*attention*⟩ prestar; **I'll ~ it some thought** lo pensaré **(e)** (sacrifice) ⟨*life*⟩ dar*, entregar* **(f)** ⟨*injection/sedative*⟩ dar*, administrar (frml)

2 (a) (supply, grant) ⟨*help*⟩ dar*, brindar; ⟨*idea*⟩ dar* **(b)** (allow, concede) ⟨*opportunity/permission*⟩ dar*, conceder (frml)

3 (a) (cause) ⟨*pleasure/shock*⟩ dar*; ⟨*cough*⟩ dar* **(b)** (yield) ⟨*results/fruit*⟩ dar*

4 (a) (award, allot) ⟨*title/authority/right*⟩ dar*, otorgar* (frml); ⟨*contract*⟩ dar*, adjudicar*; ⟨*mark*⟩ dar*, poner* **(b)** (entrust) ⟨*task/responsibility*⟩ dar*, confiar*

5 (pay, exchange) dar*; **I'd ~ anything for a cigarette** no sé qué daría por un cigarrillo

6 (care) (colloq): **I don't ~ a damn** me importa un bledo (fam)

II 1 (convey, state) ⟨*apologies/information*⟩ dar*; **she gave a detailed description of the place** describió el lugar detalladamente

2 (make sound, movement) ⟨*cry/jump*⟩ dar*; ⟨*laugh*⟩ soltar*

3 (indicate) ⟨*speed/temperature*⟩ señalar

4 (hold) ⟨*party/dinner*⟩ dar*, ofrecer* (frml); ⟨*concert*⟩ dar*; ⟨*speech*⟩ decir*

■ ~ *vi* **1 (a)** (yield under pressure) ceder, dar* de sí **(b)** (break, give way) «*planks/branch*» romperse*

2 (make gift) dar*; **to ~ to charity** dar* dinero a organizaciones de caridad

■ **give away** [*v + o + adv, v + adv + o*] **1 (a)** (free of charge) regalar **(b)** ⟨*prizes*⟩ hacer* entrega de

2 (a) (disclose) revelar; **he didn't ~ anything away** no dejó entrever nada **(b)** (betray) delatar

3 ⟨*bride*⟩ entregar* en matrimonio

■ **give back** [*v + o + adv, v + adv + o*] devolver*

■ **give in** [*v + adv*] (surrender, succumb) ceder; (in guessing games) rendirse*; **we will not ~ in to terrorists** no vamos a ceder frente a los terroristas

■ **give off** [*v + adv + o*] ⟨*smell/fumes*⟩ despedir*, largar* (RPl fam); ⟨*heat*⟩ dar*; ⟨*radiation*⟩ emitir

■ **give out 1** [*v + o + adv, v + adv + o*] ⟨*leaflets*⟩ repartir, distribuir*

2 [*v + adv + o*] **(a)** (let out) ⟨*cry/yell*⟩ dar* **(b)** (emit) ⟨*heat*⟩ dar*; ⟨*signal*⟩ emitir

■ **give up**

I [*v + o + adv, v + adv + o*] **1 (a)** (renounce, cease from) ⟨*alcohol*⟩ dejar; ⟨*fight*⟩ abandonar; **to ~ up hope** perder* las esperanzas; **to ~ up -ING** dejar DE + INF **(b)** (relinquish, hand over) ⟨*territory/position*⟩ ceder; **to ~ up one's seat for sb** cederle el asiento a algn

2 (surrender): **to ~ oneself up** entregarse*

II [*v + adv*] **(a)** (cease fighting, trying) rendirse*; **I've ~n up on them** yo con ellos no insisto más, no pierdo más tiempo **(b)** (stop doing sth) dejar

III [*v + o + adv*] (abandon hope for): **to ~ sb up for lost** dar* a algn por desaparecido

give² *n* elasticidad *f*

give: ~-and-take /ˈgɪvənˈteɪk/ *n* concesiones *fpl* mutuas, toma y daca *m*; **~away** *n* **1** (evidence): **her accent is a real ~away** el acento la delata *or* (fam) la vende; **2 (a)** (free gift) regalo *m*; (*before n*) **at ~away prices** a precio de regalo **(b)** (sth easily done, obtained): **the last question was a ~away** la última pregunta estaba regalada *or* tirada (fam)

given¹ /ˈgɪvən/ *past p of* GIVE¹

given² *adj* ⟨*amount/time*⟩ determinado, dado

given³ *prep* **1** (in view of) dado **2** (*as conj*) ~ (THAT) dado que

give name *n* (AmE) nombre *m* de pila

glacé /ˈglæseɪ ‖ˈglæseɪ/ *adj* (*before n*) glaseado

glacier /ˈgleɪʃər ‖ˈglæsɪə(r), ˈgleɪsɪə(r)/ *n* glaciar *m*

glad /glæd/ *adj* **-dd-** (*pred*) **to be ~** (ABOUT sth) alegrarse DE algo; **to be ~** (THAT) alegrarse DE QUE (+ *subj*); **I'm only too ~ to help** es un placer poder ser útil

gladden /ˈglædn̩/ *vt* (liter) llenar de alegría *or* (liter) de gozo

gladly /ˈglædli/ *adv* con mucho gusto

glamor /ˈglæmər ‖ˈglæmə(r)/ *n* (AmE) ▶ GLAMOUR

glamorous /ˈglæmərəs/ *adj* ⟨*person/dress*⟩ glamoroso; ⟨*lifestyle*⟩ sofisticado; ⟨*job*⟩ rodeado de glamour

glamour, (AmE also) **glamor** /ˈglæmər ‖ˈglæmə(r)/ *n* glamour *m*

glance¹ /glæns ‖glɑːns/ *n* mirada *f*; **to take a ~ at sth** echarle un vistazo *or* una ojeada a algo; **at first ~** a primera vista

glance² *vi* mirar; **to ~ AT sth** echarle una ojeada *or* un vistazo A algo; **to ~ AT sb** echarle una mirada A algn

glancing /ˈglænsɪŋ ‖ˈglɑːnsɪŋ/ *adj* (*before n*): **to strike sb a ~ blow** pegarle* a algn de refilón

gland /glænd/ *n* **(a)** (organ) glándula *f* **(b)** (lymph node) ganglio *m*

glandular fever /ˈglændjələr ‖ˈglændjʊlə(r)/ *n* mononucleosis *f* (infecciosa)

glare¹ /gler ‖gleə(r)/ *n* **1** (stare) mirada *f* (*hostil, feroz, de odio etc*) **2** (light) resplandor *m*

glare² *vi* **1** (stare) **to ~ AT sb** fulminar a algn con la mirada **2** (shine) brillar

glaring /ˈglerɪŋ ‖ˈgleərɪŋ/ *adj* **(a)** ⟨*light*⟩ deslumbrante **(b)** (flagrant) (*before n*) ⟨*error*⟩ mayúsculo

glass /glæs ‖glɑːs/ *n* **1** (material) vidrio *m*, cristal *m* (Esp) **2** (vessel) vaso *m*; (with stem) copa *f*; **a ~ of wine** una copa de vino **3 glasses** *pl* (spectacles) gafas *fpl*, lentes *mpl* (esp AmL), anteojos *mpl* (esp AmL) **4** (magnifying ~) lupa *f*, lente *f* de aumento

glassblowing /ˈglæsˌbləʊɪŋ ‖ˈglɑːsˌbləʊɪŋ/ *n* soplado *m* del vidrio

glassy /ˈglæsi ‖ˈglɑːsi/ *adj* **(a)** (like glass) vítreo **(b)** (dull, lifeless) ⟨*stare*⟩ vidrioso

glaze¹ /gleɪz/ *n* **(a)** (on pottery) vidriado *m* **(b)** (Culin) glaseado *m*

glaze² *vt* **1** (fit with glass) ⟨*window/door*⟩ acristalar; **to ~ a window** ponerle* vidrio(s) *or* (Esp) cristal(es) a **2** (make shiny, glossy) **(a)** ⟨*pottery*⟩ vidriar **(b)** (Culin) glasear

■ ~ *vi* (over) «*eyes*» vidriarse

glazed /gleɪzd/ *adj* **1** (fitted with glass) ⟨*window/door*⟩ con vidrio *or* (Esp) cristal **2 (a)** (Culin) glaseado **(b)** ⟨*expression*⟩ vidrioso

glazier /ˈgleɪʒər ‖ˈgleɪzɪə(r)/ *n* vidriero, -ra *m,f*, cristalero, -ra *m,f* (Esp)

gleam¹ /gliːm/ *vi* «*metal*» relucir*

gleam² *n* (on metal, water) reflejo *m*; **he had a wicked ~ in his eyes** sus ojos despedían un destello maleficioso

gleaming /ˈgliːmɪŋ/ *adj* reluciente

glean /gliːn/ *vt* ‹*information*› recoger*

glee /gliː/ *n* regocijo *m*

gleeful /'gliːfəl/ *adj* lleno de alegría

glen /glen/ *n* cañada *f*

glib /glɪb/ *adj* **-bb-** ‹*remark/answer*› simplista; ‹*salesman/politician*› con mucha labia

glide /glaɪd/ *vi* **1** (move smoothly over a surface) deslizarse* **2** «*bird/plane*» planear

glider /'glaɪdər ‖'glaɪdə(r)/ *n* planeador *m*

glimmer¹ /'glɪmər ‖'glɪmə(r)/ *vi* brillar con luz trémula

glimmer² *n* luz *f* débil; **a ~ of hope** un rayo de esperanza

glimpse¹ /glɪmps/ *n*: **I caught a ~ of the room** pude ver brevemente la habitación; **a ~ of life in rural England** una visión de la vida en la Inglaterra rural

glimpse² *vt* alcanzar* a ver

glint¹ /glɪnt/ *vi* destellar

glint² *n* (of metal, light) destello *m*; (in eye) (*no pl*) chispa *f*, brillo *m*

glisten /'glɪsən/ *vi* brillar

glitter¹ /'glɪtər ‖'glɪtə(r)/ *vi* relumbrar

glitter² *n* (a) (sparkle) (*no pl*) destello *m* (b) (superficial attractiveness) oropel *m* (c) (decoration) purpurina *f*, brillantes *mpl* (Arg), brillantina *f* (Ur, Ven), brillo *m* (Chi)

gloat /gləʊt/ *vi* **to ~** (**OVER** sth) regodearse (CON algo)

global /'gləʊbəl/ *adj* (a) (worldwide) a escala mundial, global; **~ warming** calentamiento *m* global (b) (overall, comprehensive) global

globe /gləʊb/ *n* (a) (world) **the ~** el globo (b) (model) globo *m* terráqueo

globe: ~ artichoke *n* alcachofa *f*, alcaucil *m* (RPl); **~trotter** /'gləʊb,trɑːtər ‖'gləʊb,trɒtə(r)/ *n* trotamundos *mf*

globule /'glɑːbjuːl ‖'glɒbjuːl/ *n* glóbulo *m*

gloom /gluːm/ *n* (a) (darkness) penumbra *f*, oscuridad *f* (b) (melancholy) melancolía *f*

gloomily /'gluːməli ‖'gluːmɪli/ *adv* ‹*sigh/stare*› tristemente; ‹*predict*› con pesimismo

gloomy /'gluːmi/ *adj* **-mier, -miest** (a) (dark) ‹*day/place*› sombrío (b) (dismal) ‹*person*› lúgubre, fúnebre; ‹*prospect*› nada halagüeño; ‹*prediction*› pesimista

glorify /'glɔːrəfaɪ ‖'glɔːrɪfaɪ/ *vt* **-fies, -fying, -fied** ‹*person*› ensalzar*; ‹*violence/war*› exaltar

glorious /'glɔːriəs/ *adj* (a) (deserving glory) glorioso (b) (wonderful) ‹*view/weather*› maravilloso

glory¹ /'glɔːri/ *n* (*pl* **-ries**) (a) (fame) gloria *f* (b) (beauty, magnificence) esplendor *m*

glory² *vi* **-ries, -rying, -ried**: **to ~ IN sth** (take pleasure) disfrutar DE algo; (in unpleasant way) regodearse CON algo

gloss /glɑːs ‖glɒs/ *n* (a) (shine) brillo *m*; (*before n*) **~ finish** acabado *m* brillante (b) **~** (**paint**) (pintura *f* al or de) esmalte *m*

■ **gloss over** [*v* + *adv* + *o*] (make light of) quitarle importancia a; (ignore) pasar por alto

glossary /'glɑːsəri ‖'glɒsəri/ *n* (*pl* **-ries**) glosario *m*

glossy /'glɑːsi ‖'glɒsi/ *adj* **-sier, -siest** ‹*coat of animal*› brillante, lustroso; ‹*hair*› brillante,

brilloso (AmL); ‹*photograph*› brillante; **~ magazine** revista *f* ilustrada (*impresa en papel satinado*)

glove /glʌv/ *n* guante *m*

glove compartment *n* guantera *f*

glow¹ /gləʊ/ *vi* ‹*fire*› brillar; «*metal*» estar* al rojo vivo; **to ~ with health** rebosar (de) salud; **to be ~ing with happiness** estar* radiante de felicidad

glow² *n* (*no pl*) brillo *m*; **he felt a ~ of pride** sintió una oleada de orgullo

glower /'glaʊər ‖'glaʊə(r)/ *vi* tener* el ceño fruncido; **to ~ AT sb** lanzarle* miradas fulminantes/una mirada fulminante A algn

glowing /'gləʊɪŋ/ *adj* (a) (shining) ‹*before n*› ‹*cheeks*› encendido; **the ~ embers** las brasas (b) (expressing praise) ‹*report*› elogioso

glucose /'gluːkəʊs, -kəʊz/ *n* glucosa *f*

glue¹ /gluː/ *n* goma *f* de pegar, pegamento *m*

glue² *vt* **glues, glueing, glued** (a) (stick) pegar* (b) (fix): **he was ~d to the television** estaba pegado a la televisión

glum /glʌm/ *adj* **-mm-** apesadumbrado

glut /glʌt/ *n* superabundancia *f*

glutton /'glʌtn̩/ *n* glotón, -tona *m,f*

gluttony /'glʌtəni ‖'glʌtəni/ *n* glotonería *f*

glycerin /'glɪsərən ‖'glɪsərɪn/, **glycerine** /'glɪsərən ‖'glɪsəriːn/ *n* glicerina *f*

GM *adj* = **genetically modified**

GMO *n* (= **genetically modified organism**) OGM *m*

GMT (= **Greenwich Mean Time**) GMT

gnarled /nɑːrld ‖nɑːld/ *adj* ‹*wood/fingers*› nudoso; ‹*tree*› retorcido

gnash /næʃ/ *vt*: **to ~ one's teeth** hacer* rechinar los dientes

gnat /næt/ *n* jején *m*; (general usage) mosquito *m*

gnaw /nɔː/ *vt* roer*

■ **~** *vi* **to ~ AT sth** roer* algo

gnome /nəʊm/ *n* gnomo *m*

go¹ /gəʊ/ (*3rd pers sing pres* **goes**; *past* **went**; *past p* **gone**) *vi*

I **1** (a) (move, travel) ir*; **where do we ~ from here?** ¿y ahora qué hacemos? (b) (start moving, acting): **ready, (get) set, ~!** preparados *or* en sus marcas, listos ¡ya!; **let's ~!** ¡vamos!; **here ~es!** ¡allá vamos (*or* voy *etc*)!

2 (*past p* **gone/been**) (a) (travel to) ir*; **she's gone to France** se ha ido a Francia; **I have never been abroad** no he estado nunca en el extranjero; **to ~ by car/bus** ir* en coche/autobús; **to ~ on foot** ir* a pie; **to ~ for a walk** ir* a dar un paseo; **~ and see what she wants** anda *or* vete a ver qué quiere (b) (attend) ir*; **to ~ on a course** hacer* un curso; **to ~ -ING** ir* A + INF; **to ~ swimming** ir* a nadar

3 (attempt, make as if to) **to ~ to +** INF ir* A + INF

II **1** (leave, depart) «*visitor*» irse*; «*train*» salir*, marcharse (esp Esp); «*bus/train*» salir*; ▶ **LET²** 1c

2 (a) (pass) «*time*» pasar; **the time ~es quickly** el tiempo pasa volando (b) (disappear) «*headache/pain/fear*» pasarse *or* irse* (+ *me/te/le etc*) (c) «*money*» (be spent) irse*; (be used up) acabarse

3 (a) (be disposed of): **that sofa will have to ~**

nos vamos (or se van etc) a tener que deshacer de
ese sofá **(b)** (be sold) venderse; **the painting went
for £1,000** el cuadro se vendió en 1.000 libras
4 (a) (cease to function, wear out) «*bulb/fuse*»
fundirse; «*thermostat/fan/exhaust*» estropearse;
her memory/eyesight is ~ing está fallándole la
memoria/la vista; **my legs went (from under
me)** me fallaron las piernas **(b)** (die) (colloq)
morir*
5 to go (a) (remaining): **only two weeks to ~ till
he comes** solo faltan dos semanas para que
llegue; **I still have 50 pages to ~** todavía me
faltan or me quedan 50 páginas **(b)** (take away)
(AmE): **two burgers to ~** dos hamburguesas para
llevar
III 1 (a) (lead) «*path/road*» ir*, llevar **(b)**
(extend, range) «*road/railway line*» ir*; **it only
~es as far as Croydon** solo va hasta Croydon
2 (have place) ir*; (fit) caber*; *see also* GO IN, GO
INTO
IV 1 (a) (become): **to ~ blind** quedarse ciego; **to
~ crazy** volverse* loco; **her face went red** se puso
colorada **(b)** (be, remain): **to ~ barefoot** ir* or
andar* descalzo; **to ~ hungry** pasar hambre
2 (turn out, proceed, progress) ir*; **how are things
~ing?** ¿cómo van or andan las cosas?
3 (a) (be available) (only in -ing form): **I'll take
any job that's ~ing** estoy dispuesto a aceptar el
trabajo que sea **(b)** (be in general): **it's not
expensive as dishwashers ~** no es caro, para lo
que cuestan los lavavajillas
V 1 (a) (function, work) «*heater/engine/clock*»
funcionar **(b) to get going: the car's OK once it
gets ~ing** el coche marcha bien una vez que
arranca; **we'd better get ~ing** más vale que nos
vayamos; **we tried to get a fire ~ing** tratamos de
hacer fuego **(c)** (keep going) (continue to function)
aguantar; (not stop) seguir*; **to keep a project
~ing** mantener* a flote un proyecto
2 (continue, last out) seguir*; **the club's been ~ing
for 12 years now** el club lleva 12 años
funcionando
3 (a) (sound) «*bell/siren*» sonar* **(b)** (make
sound, movement) hacer*
4 (a) (contribute): **everything that ~es to make a
good school** todo lo que contribuye a que una
escuela sea buena; **it just ~es to show: we can't
leave them on their own** está visto que no los
podemos dejar solos **(b)** (be used) **all their savings
are ~ing toward the trip** van a gastar todos sus
ahorros en el viaje; **the money will ~ to pay the
workmen** el dinero se usará para pagar a los
obreros
5 (run, be worded) decir*; **how does the song ~?**
¿cómo es la (letra/música de la) canción?
6 (a) (be permitted): **anything ~es** todo vale **(b)**
(be necessarily obeyed, believed): **what the boss says
~es** lo que dice el jefe, va a misa **(c)** (match, suit)
pegar*, ir*
■ **~** v aux (only in -ing form) **to be ~ing to + INF**
(expressing intention, prediction) ir* A + INF
■ **go about** [v + prep + o] **(a)** (tackle) «*task*»
acometer; **how would you ~ about solving this
equation?** ¿cómo harías para resolver esta
ecuación? **(b)** (occupy oneself with): **to ~ about
one's business** ocuparse de sus (or mis etc) cosas
■ **go after** [v + prep + o] (pursue, chase)
perseguir*, dar* caza a
■ **go against** [v + prep + o] **(a)** (oppose, resist)

⟨*instructions/policy/person*⟩ oponerse* a, ir* en
contra de **(b)** (be unfavorable to): **the decision went
against them** la decisión les fue desfavorable
■ **go ahead** [v + adv] (proceed, begin) **to ~ ahead
(WITH sth)** seguir* adelante (CON algo); **may I ask
you a question? — ~ ahead!** ¿le puedo hacer una
pregunta? — por supuesto or (AmL tb) pregunte
nomás
■ **go along** [v + adv] **(a)** (accompany, be present) ir*
(b) (proceed, progress) ir*; **I usually make
corrections as I ~ along** normalmente hago
correcciones sobre la marcha **(c)** (acquiesce): **to ~
along with a proposal** secundar una propuesta
■ **go around**, (BrE also) **go round**
I [v + prep + o] **1 (a)** (turn) ⟨*corner*⟩ doblar, dar*
la vuelta a, dar* vuelta (CS); ⟨*bend*⟩ tomar **(b)**
(make detour) ⟨*obstacle*⟩ rodear
2 (visit, move through) ⟨*country/city*⟩ recorrer;
⟨*museum/castle*⟩ visitar; **to ~ around the world**
dar* la vuelta al mundo
II [v + adv] **1 (a)** (move, travel, be outdoors)
andar*; **to ~ around -ING** ir* por ahí + GER **(b)**
(circulate) ⟨*joke/rumor*⟩ correr **(c)** (be sufficient for
everybody): **there aren't enough to ~ around** no
alcanzan
2 (revolve) «*wheel/world*» dar* vueltas
3 (visit) ir*; **I'll ~ around and see him** iré a verlo
■ **go away** [v + adv] **(a)** (depart, leave) irse* **(b)**
(from home): **I'm ~ing away this weekend** voy a
salir este fin de semana; **to ~ away on vacation**
irse* de vacaciones **(c)** (disappear, fade away)
«*smell*» irse*; «*pain*» pasarse or irse* (+ me/te/
le etc)
■ **go back** [v + adv] **1** (return) volver*; **~ back!**
¡vuelve atrás!, ¡retrocede!
2 (a) (date, originate) «*tradition/dynasty*»
remontarse; **we ~ back a long way** (colloq) nos
conocemos desde hace mucho **(b)** «*clocks*»
atrasarse
■ **go back on** [v + adv + prep + o] ⟨*one's
promise*⟩ dejar de cumplir; ⟨*one's word*⟩ faltar a
■ **go before** [v + prep + o] ⟨*court/committee*⟩
presentarse ante
■ **go by 1** [v + adv] **(a)** (move past) pasar; **to let
an opportunity ~ by** dejar pasar una oportunidad
(b) (elapse) «*days/years*» pasar; **as time goes by**
con el tiempo
2 [v + prep + o] **(a)** (be guided by) ⟨*instinct*⟩
dejarse llevar por; ⟨*rules*⟩ seguir* **(b)** (base
judgment on) ⟨*appearances*⟩ guiarse* or dejarse
llevar por; **if previous experience is anything to ~
by** a juzgar por lo que ha sucedido en otras
ocasiones
■ **go down** [v + adv] **1 (a)** (descend) «*person*»
bajar; «*sun*» ponerse*; «*curtain*» (Theat) caer*
(b) (fall) «*boxer/horse*» caerse*; «*plane*» caer*,
estrellarse **(c)** (sink) «*ship*» hundirse **(d)**
«*computer*» dejar de funcionar, descomponerse*
(AmL) **(e)** (be defeated) (Sport) perder*; **to ~ down
fighting** caer* luchando
2 (a) (decrease) «*temperature/exchange rate*»
bajar; «*population/unemployment*» disminuir*;
to ~ down in value perder* valor **(b)** (decline)
«*standard/quality*» empeorar **(c)** (abate) «*wind/
storm*» amainar; «*floods/swelling*» bajar; **his
temperature's gone down** le ha bajado la fiebre
(d) (deflate) «*tire*» perder* aire
3 (extend): **this road ~es down to the beach**

 ⋯▸

este camino baja a *or* hasta la playa; **the skirt ~es down to her ankles** la falda le llega a los tobillos

4 (a) (be swallowed): **it just won't ~ down** no lo puedo tragar; **it went down the wrong way** se me fue por el otro camino **(b)** «*present/proposal/ remarks*»: **how did the announcement ~ down?** ¿qué tipo de acogida tuvo el anuncio?; **that won't ~ down too well with your father** eso no le va a caer muy bien a tu padre

5 (be recorded, written): **all these absences will ~ down on your record** va a quedar constancia de estas faltas en tu ficha; **to ~ down in history as sth** pasar a la historia como algo

▪ **go down with** [*v + adv + prep + o*] (BrE): **to ~ down with flu/hepatitis** caer* en cama con gripe/ caer* enfermo de hepatitis

▪ **go for** [*v + prep + o*] **1 (a)** (head toward, reach for): **he went for his gun** fue a echar mano de la pistola **(b)** (attack): **he went for Bill** se le echó encima a Bill

2 (choose) decidirse por

3 (aim at): **~ for it!** ¡haz la tentativa!, ¡a por ello! (Esp)

▪ **go in** [*v + adv*] **1 (a)** (enter) entrar **(b)** «*screw/ key*» entrar; **the big case won't ~ in** la maleta grande no cabe **(c)** (go to work) ir* a trabajar

2 (be obscured) «*sun/moon*» ocultarse

▪ **go in for** [*v + adv + prep + o*] **(a)** (enter) «*competition*» participar en; «*exam/test*» presentarse a **(b)** (take up, practice): **he'd thought of ~ing in for teaching** había pensado dedicarse a la enseñanza

▪ **go into** [*v + prep + o*] **1 (a)** (enter) «*room/ building*» entrar en, entrar a (AmL) **(b)** (crash into) «*car/wall*» chocar* contra **(c)** (fit into) entrar en

2 (a) (start, embark on) «*phase/era*» entrar en **(b)** (enter certain state) «*coma/trance*» entrar en **(c)** (enter profession) «*television/Parliament*» entrar en

3 (a) (discuss, explain) entrar en; **I don't want to ~ into that** no quiero entrar en ese tema **(b)** (investigate, analyze) «*problem/motives*» analizar*

4 (be devoted to): **after all the money/work that has gone into this!** ¡después de todo el dinero/ trabajo que se ha metido en esto!

▪ **go off**
I [*v + adv*] **1** (depart) irse*, marcharse (esp Esp); **to ~ off with sth** llevarse algo

2 «*milk/meat/fish*» echarse a perder

3 (a) «*bomb/firework*» estallar; «*gun*» dispararse **(b)** «*alarm*» sonar*

4 (stop operating) «*heating/lights*» apagarse*
II [*v + prep + o*] (lose liking for) (BrE): **to ~ off one's food** perder* el apetito; **I've gone off the idea** ya no me atrae la idea

▪ **go on** [*v + adv*] **1 (a)** (go further) seguir*; **I can't ~ on** no puedo más **(b)** (go ahead): **you ~ on, we'll follow** tú vete que nosotros ya iremos; **he went on ahead to look for a hotel** él fue antes para buscar hotel

2 (continue) «*fight/struggle*» continuar*; **we can't ~ on like this** no podemos seguir así; **the**

discussion went on for hours la discusión duró horas; **to ~ on -ING** seguir* + GER; **he went on to become President** llegó a ser presidente; **to ~ on WITH sth** seguir* CON algo; **~ on!** (encouraging, urging) ¡dale!, ¡vamos!, ¡ándale! (Méx), ¡ándele! (Col), ¡venga! (Esp)

3 (a) (continue speaking) seguir*, continuar* **(b)** (talk irritatingly) (pej): **he went on and on** siguió dale que dale; **to ~ on ABOUT sth** hablar insistentemente DE algo

4 (happen): **what's ~ing on?** ¿qué pasa?; **is there anything ~ing on between them?** ¿hay algo entre ellos?; **how long has this been ~ing on?** ¿desde cuándo viene sucediendo esto?

5 (a) (onto stage) salir* a escena; (onto field of play) salir* al campo **(b)** (fit, be placed): **the lid won't ~ on** no le puedo (*or* podemos *etc*) poner la tapa

▪ **go out** [*v + adv*] **1 (a)** (leave, exit) salir*; **to ~ out hunting/shopping** salir* de caza/de compras **(b)** (socially, for entertainment) salir*; **to ~ out for a meal** salir* a comer fuera **(c)** (as boyfriend, girlfriend) **to ~ out (WITH sb)** salir* (CON algn)

2 (a) (be broadcast) «*TV, radio program*» emitirse **(b)** (be issued, distributed): **a warrant has gone out for her arrest** se ha ordenado su detención; **the invitations have already gone out** ya se han mandado las invitaciones

3 (be extinguished) «*fire/cigarette/light*» apagarse*

4 «*tide*» bajar

5 (become outmoded) «*clothes/style*» pasar de moda

▪ **go over**
I [*v + prep + o*] **1** (check) «*text/figures/work*» revisar; «*car*» revisar; «*house/premises*» inspeccionar

2 (revise, review) «*notes/chapter*» repasar
II [*v + adv*] **1** (make one's way, travel) ir*; **she went over to Jack and took his hand** se acercó a Jack y le tomó la mano

2 (change sides) pasarse

▪ **go past** [*v + adv*] [*v + prep + o*] pasar

▪ **go round** (BrE) ▶ GO AROUND

▪ **go through**
I [*v + prep + o*] **1 (a)** (pass through) «*process/ stage*» pasar por **(b)** (perform): **let's ~ through the procedure once more** repitamos otra vez todos los pasos del procedimiento **(c)** (endure) «*ordeal/ hard times*» pasar por

2 (a) (search) «*attic/suitcase*» registrar, revisar (AmL); «*drawers/desk*» hurgar* en; **to ~ through sb's mail** abrirle* las cartas a algn **(b)** ▶ GO OVER I 2

3 (consume, use up) «*money/fortune*» gastarse; **he ~es through ten shirts a week** ensucia diez camisas por semana
II [*v + adv*] **(a)** (be carried out) «*changes/ legislation*» ser* aprobado; «*business deal*» llevarse a cabo; **when his divorce ~es through** cuando obtenga el divorcio **(b)** (Sport): **to ~ through to the next round** pasar a la siguiente etapa

▪ **go through with** [*v + adv + prep + o*] «*threat/ plans*» llevar a cabo

▪ **go together** [*v + adv*] «*colors/patterns*» combinar; **lamb and mint sauce ~ well together** el cordero queda muy bien con salsa de menta ▶

AmC	América Central	Arg	Argentina	Cu	Cuba	Per	Perú
AmL	América Latina	Bol	Bolivia	Ec	Ecuador	RPI	Río de la Plata
AmS	América del Sur	Chi	Chile	Esp	España	Ur	Uruguay
Andes	Región andina	CS	Cono Sur	Méx	México	Ven	Venezuela

■ **go under** [v + adv] **(a)** (sink) «*ship*» hundirse; «*submarine/diver*» sumergirse* **(b)** (fail, go bankrupt) hundirse

■ **go up** [v + adv] **1 (a)** (ascend) «*person*» subir; «*balloon/plane*» subir; «*curtain*» (Theat) levantarse **(b)** (approach) **to ~ up TO sb/sth** acercarse* A algn/algo **2 (a)** (increase) «*temperature/price/cost*» subir, aumentar; «*population/unemployment*» aumentar; **to ~ up in price** subir *or* aumentar de precio **(b)** (improve) «*standard*» mejorar **3** (burst into flames) prenderse fuego; (explode) estallar; **to ~ up in flames** incendiarse

■ **go with** [v + prep + o] **(a)** (be compatible with): **this sauce ~es well with hamburgers** esta salsa queda muy bien con hamburguesas; **choose a tie to ~ with your shirt** elija una corbata que quede bien con su camisa **(b)** (accompany, be associated with): **the house ~es with the job** la casa va con el puesto

■ **go without (a)** [v + prep + o] (do without) pasar sin; **she often went without food** a menudo pasaba sin comer; **they went without food/sleep for days** (not by choice) no comieron nada/no durmieron durante días **(b)** [v + adv]: **in order to feed her children she herself often went without** para darles de comer a los niños a menudo pasaba privaciones; **there's no coffee left, you'll just have to ~ without** no queda café, así que tendrás que pasar sin él

go² n (pl **goes**) **1 (a)** (attempt): **at one ~** (AmE), **in one ~** (BrE) «*empty/eat*» de un tirón (fam); ‹*drink*› de un trago; **she succeeded in lifting it at the third ~** consiguió levantarlo al tercer intento; **I want to have a ~ at learning Arabic** quiero intentar aprender árabe; **have a ~** prueba a ver, inténtalo; **to have a ~ at sb** (colloq): **she had a ~ at me for not having told her** se la agarró conmigo por no habérselo dicho (fam) **(b)** (turn): **whose ~ is it?** ¿a quién le toca?; **it's my ~** me toca a mí **2** (energy, drive) empuje m; (*to be*) **on the ~: I've been on the ~ all morning** no he parado en toda la mañana

goad /gəʊd/ vt ‹*person*› acosar; ‹*animal*› aguijonear

go-ahead /'gəʊəhed/ n: **to give sb/sth the ~** darle* luz verde a algn/algo

goal /gəʊl/ n **1** (Sport) **(a)** (structure) portería f, arco m (AmL) **(b)** (point) gol m **2** (aim) meta f

goal: ~keeper n portero, -ra m,f, guardameta m,f, arquero, -ra m,f (AmL); **~post** n poste m de la portería *or* (AmL tb) del arco; **~tender** n (AmE) ▶ **~KEEPER**

goat /gəʊt/ n (Zool) cabra f

gobble /'gɑːbəl ‖ 'gɒbəl/ vt engullirse*

■ **gobble up** [v + o + adv, v + adv + o] tragarse*

gobbledygook /'gɑːbəldiɡuːk ‖ 'gɒbəldiˌɡuːk/ n (colloq & pej) jerigonza f

go-between /'gəʊbɪtwiːn/ n (intermediary) intermediario, -ria m,f; (messenger) mensajero, -ra m,f

goblet /'gɑːblət ‖ 'gɒblɪt/ n copa f

goblin /'gɑːblən ‖ 'gɒblɪn/ n duende m travieso, trasgo m

god /gɑːd ‖ gɒd/ n **1 God** Dios m; **G~ bless (you)** que Dios te bendiga; **G~!** ¡Dios (santo)! **2** (deity, idol) dios m

god: ~child n ahijado, -da m,f; **~dam, ~damn** adj (AmE sl) (*before n*) condenado (fam); **~daughter** /'gɑːdˌdɔːtər ‖ 'gɒdˌdɔːtə(r)/ n ahijada f

goddess /'gɑːdəs ‖ 'gɒdɪs/ n diosa f

god: ~father /'gɑːdˌfɑːðər ‖ 'gɒdˌfɑːðə(r)/ n padrino m; **~mother** /'gɑːdˌmʌðər ‖ 'gɒdˌmʌðə(r)/ n madrina f; **~parent** /'gɑːdˌperənt ‖ 'gɒdˌpeərənt/ n (man) padrino m; (woman) madrina f; **my ~parents** mis padrinos; **~send** n bendición f (del cielo); **~son** n ahijado m

goggle /'gɑːɡəl ‖ 'gɒɡəl/ vi (pej) **to ~ AT sth/sb** mirar algo/a algn con los ojos desorbitados

goggles /'gɑːɡəlz ‖ 'gɒɡəlz/ pl n (Sport) gafas fpl or anteojos mpl (esp AmL) de esquí (or natación etc); (for welders) gafas fpl protectoras, anteojos mpl protectores (esp AmL)

going¹ /'gəʊɪŋ/ n (no pl) **1** (progress): **once at the top, the ~ was easier** una vez en la cima, la marcha fue más fácil; **I found that lecture hard ~** me resultó difícil seguir la conferencia; **the novel was heavy ~** la novela era pesada **2** (departure) partida f **3** (situation) situación f; **if I were you, I'd buy it while the ~ is good** yo que tú lo compraría ahora, aprovechando el buen momento; **when the ~ got tough** cuando las cosas se pusieron difíciles

going² adj (*before n*) **(a)** (in operation) en marcha; **a ~ concern** (Busn) un negocio *or* una empresa en marcha **(b)** (present, current): **that's the ~ rate** es lo que se suele cobrar/pagar

gold /gəʊld/ n **1** (metal) oro m; (money) (monedas fpl de) oro m; (*before n*) ‹*ring/medal*› de oro **2** (color) dorado m, color m (de) oro

gold dust n oro m en polvo

golden /'gəʊldən/ adj **1 (a)** (made of gold) de oro **(b)** (in color) dorado **2 (a)** (happy, prosperous) ‹*years*› dorado **(b)** (excellent): **a ~ opportunity** una excelente oportunidad

golden: ~ age n época f dorada, edad f de oro; **~ wedding (anniversary)** n bodas fpl de oro

gold: ~fish n (pl **-fish** or **-fishes**) pececito m (rojo); (plural) peces mpl de colores; **~ leaf** n oro m batido, pan m de oro; **~ mine** n mina f de oro; **~plated** /'gəʊldˈpleɪtəd ‖ ˌɡəʊldˈpleɪtɪd/ adj chapado en oro; **~ rush** n fiebre f del oro; **~smith** n orfebre mf

golf /gɑːlf ‖ ɡɒlf/ n golf m

golf: ~ ball n (Sport) pelota f de golf; **~ club (a)** (stick) palo m de golf **(b)** (place) club m de golf; **~ course** n campo m *or* (AmL tb) cancha f de golf

golfer /'gɑːlfər ‖ 'ɡɒlfə(r)/ n golfista mf

gone¹ /ɡɔːn ‖ ɡɒn/ past p of GO¹

gone² adj (pred) **(a)** (not here): **my briefcase is ~!** ¡se me ha desaparecido la cartera!; **how long has she been ~?** ¿cuánto hace que se fue? **(b)** (past): **those days are (long) ~** de eso hace ya mucho, ha llovido mucho desde entonces **(c)** (used up): **the money is all ~** se ha acabado el dinero, no queda nada de dinero

gone³ prep (BrE): **it's just ~ five** acaban de dar las cinco

gong /ɡɑːŋ ‖ ɡɒŋ/ n gong m

gonna /ɡənə ‖ 'ɡɒnə/ (colloq) (= **going to**) ▶ GO¹ v aux

gonorrhea ⋯⟶ gotten

684

gonorrhea, (BrE) **gonorrhoea** /ˌgɑːnəˈriːə ‖ˌɡɒnəˈriːə/ *n* gonorrea *f*

goo /guː/ *n* (colloq) mugre *f*

good¹ /ɡʊd/ *adj*

■ Note The usual translation of *good, bueno*, becomes *buen* when it precedes a masculine singular noun.

(*comp* **better;** *superl* **best**) **1** ⟨*food/quality/ book/work/reputation*⟩ bueno; **it smells ∼** huele bien; **her French is very ∼** habla muy bien (el) francés; **is this a ∼ time to phone?** ¿es buena hora para llamar?; **it's ∼ to be back home** ¡qué alegría estar otra vez en casa!; **I had a ∼ night's sleep** dormí bien

2 (advantageous, useful) ⟨*deal/offer/advice*⟩ bueno; **burn it; that's all it's ∼ for** quémalo, no sirve para otra cosa; **∼ idea!, ∼ thinking!** ¡buena idea!

3 (healthy) ⟨*diet/habit/exercise*⟩ bueno; **I'm not feeling too ∼** (colloq) no me siento bien; **spinach is ∼ for you** las espinacas son buenas para la salud

4 (attractive): **it looks ∼** tiene buen aspecto; **that dress looks really ∼ on her** ese vestido le queda *or* le sienta muy bien

5 (a) (in interj phrases): **∼!** now to the next question bien, pasemos ahora a la siguiente pregunta; **∼ for you!** ¡bien hecho! (b) (for emphasis) (colloq) **I'll do it when I'm ∼ and ready** lo haré cuando me parezca; **the water's ∼ and hot** el agua está bien caliente (c) **as good as: it's as ∼ as new** está como nuevo; **he as ∼ as admitted it** prácticamente lo admitió

6 (skilled, competent) bueno; **he's no ∼ in emergencies** en situaciones de emergencia no sabe qué hacer; **to be ∼ at languages** tener* facilidad para los idiomas; **he is ∼ with children** tiene buena mano con los niños; **she is ∼ with her hands** es muy habilidosa

7 (well-behaved, virtuous) bueno; **∼ boy!** ¡muy bien!

8 (kind) bueno; **she was very ∼ to me** fue muy amable conmigo

9 (valid) ⟨*argument/excuse*⟩ bueno; **this ticket is ∼ for another week** este billete vale para una semana más; **it's simply not ∼ enough!** ¡esto no puede ser!

10 (substantial, considerable) ⟨*meal/salary/distance*⟩ bueno; **there were a ∼ many people there** había bastante gente allí

11 (not less than): **it'll take a ∼ hour** va a llevar su buena hora *or* una hora larga; **a ∼ half of all the people interviewed** más de la mitad de los entrevistados

good² *n* **1** (moral right) bien *m*; **to do ∼** hacer* el bien; **there is some ∼ in everyone** todos tenemos algo bueno; **to be up to no ∼** (colloq) estar* tramando algo, traerse* algo entre manos

2 (a) (benefit) bien *m*; **no ∼ will come of it** nada bueno saldrá de ello; **to do sb ∼** hacerle* bien a algn (b) (use): **this knife is no ∼ (at all)** este cuchillo no sirve (para nada); **this book is no ∼** este libro no vale nada (c) **for good** para siempre

3 goods *pl* (a) (merchandise) artículos *mpl*, mercancías *fpl*, mercaderías *fpl* (AmS); **manufactured ∼s** productos *mpl* manufacturados, manufacturas *fpl* (b) (property) (frml) bienes *mpl*

goodbye¹ /ɡʊdˈbaɪ/ *interj* ¡adiós!, ¡chao! *or* ¡chau! (esp AmL)

goodbye² *n*: **to say ∼ to sb** decirle* adiós a algn

good: G∼ Friday *n* Viernes *m* Santo; **∼-humored,** (BrE) **∼-humoured** /ˈɡʊdˈhjuːmərd ‖ˌɡʊdˈhjuːməd/ *adj* ⟨*person*⟩ (permanent characteristic) alegre, jovial; (in good mood) de buen humor; ⟨*joke*⟩ sin mala intención; **∼-looking** /ˈɡʊdˈlʊkɪŋ/ *adj* ⟨*man*⟩ buen mozo (esp AmL), guapo (esp Esp); **a ∼-looking woman** una mujer bonita *or* (esp Esp) guapa; **∼-natured** /ˈɡʊdˈneɪtʃərd ‖ˌɡʊdˈneɪtʃəd/ *adj* (as permanent characteristic) bueno, de natural bondadoso

goodness /ˈɡʊdnəs ‖ˈɡʊdnɪs/ *n* **1** (a) (moral worth) bondad *f* (b) (of food) valor *m* nutritivo **2** (*in interj phrases, as intensifier*): (my) **∼!** ¡Dios (mío)!; **∼ me!** ¡Dios mío!, ¡válgame Dios!

goodwill /ˈɡʊdˈwɪl/ *n* (a) (benevolence) buena voluntad *f* (b) (Busn, Fin) fondo *m* de comercio, llave *f* (CS)

goofy /ˈɡuːfi/ *adj* **-fier, -fiest** (AmE sl) ⟨*person*⟩ memo (fam); ⟨*smile*⟩ bobalicón (fam)

google® /ˈɡuːɡəl/ *vt/i* colloq googlear

goose /guːs/ *n* (*pl* **geese**) (a) (Zool) oca *f*, ganso *m* (b) (Culin) ganso *m*

goose: ∼berry /ˈguːsˌberi ‖ˈɡʊzbəri/ *n* **1** (Bot) grosella *f* espinosa, uva *f* espina; **2** (unwanted third person) (BrE colloq) carabina *f* (fam), chaperón, -rona *m,f*, violinista *mf* (Chi fam); **to play ∼berry** hacer* de carabina (Esp fam), tocar* el violín (Chi fam); **∼ bumps** *pl n* (AmE colloq), **∼flesh** *n*, **∼ pimples** *pl n* carne *f* de gallina

gore /ɡɔːr ‖ɡɔː(r)/ *vt* cornear

gorge¹ /ɡɔːrdʒ/ *n* (Geog) desfiladero *m*, cañón *m*

gorge² *v refl* **to ∼ oneself** atiborrarse de comida

gorgeous /ˈɡɔːrdʒəs ‖ˈɡɔːdʒəs/ *adj* (a) (lovely) (colloq) ⟨*girl*⟩ precioso, guapísimo; ⟨*dress*⟩ precioso, divino; ⟨*day*⟩ maravilloso, espléndido (b) (splendid) ⟨*color*⟩ magnífico

gorilla /ɡəˈrɪlə/ *n* gorila *m*

gorse /ɡɔːrs ‖ɡɔːs/ *n* aulaga *f*, tojo *m*

gory /ˈɡɔːri/ *adj* **gorier, goriest** (colloq) sangriento

gosh /ɡɑːʃ/ *interj* (colloq) ¡(mi) Dios!, ¡Dios mío!

gospel /ˈɡɑːspəl ‖ˈɡɒspəl/ *n* (a) **Gospel** (in New Testament) evangelio *m* (b) (Christian teaching) (no *pl*) Evangelio *m*; (before *n*) **it's ∼** (truth) es la pura verdad (c) **∼ (music)** (Mus) gospel *m*

gossamer /ˈɡɑːsəmər ‖ˈɡɒsəmə(r)/ *n* (liter) telaraña *f*; (before *n*) ⟨*threads*⟩ tenue

gossip¹ /ˈɡɑːsəp ‖ˈɡɒsɪp/ *n* (a) (speculation, scandal) chismorreo *m* (fam), cotilleo *m* (Esp fam); **an interesting piece of ∼** un chisme interesante; (before *n*) **∼ column** crónica *f* de sociedad (b) (chat): **to have a ∼ with sb** chismorrear (fam) *or* (Esp fam) cotillear con algn (c) (person) chismoso, -sa *m,f* (fam), cotilla *mf* (Esp fam)

gossip² *vi* (a) (chatter) chismorrear (fam), cotillear (Esp fam) (b) (spread tales) contar* chismes

got /ɡɑːt ‖ɡɒt/ **1** *past & past p of* GET **2** (crit) *pres of* HAVE

Gothic /ˈɡɑːθɪk ‖ˈɡɒθɪk/ *adj* (Archit, Lit) gótico

gotta /ˈɡɑːtə ‖ˈɡɒtə/ (sl) = **have got to**

gotten /ˈɡɑːtn̩ ‖ˈɡɒtn̩/ (AmE) *past p of* GET

gouge /gaʊdʒ/ vt ‹hole› abrir*
■ **gouge out** [v + o + adv, v + adv + o] sacar*

gourd /gʊrd, gɔːrd ‖ gʊəd/ n (Bot) calabaza f, jícaro m (AmC, Col, Méx)

gourmet /'gʊrmeɪ ‖ 'gʊəmeɪ/ n gourmet mf, gastrónomo, -ma m,f

gout /gaʊt/ n gota f

govern /'gʌvərn ‖ 'gʌvən/ vt (a) ‹rule› gobernar* (b) ‹determine› determinar (c) **governing** pres p ‹party› de gobierno; ‹principle› rector; ~ing body organismo m rector
■ ~ vi gobernar*

governess /'gʌvərnəs/ n institutriz f

government /'gʌvərnmənt ‖ 'gʌvənmənt/ n gobierno m; (before n) ~ **policy** política f gubernamental

governor /'gʌvənər ‖ 'gʌvənə(r)/ n 1 (of state, province, colony) gobernador, -dora m,f 2 (of institution): **prison** ~ (BrE) director, -tora m,f de una cárcel; **school** ~ (BrE) miembro de un consejo escolar

gown /gaʊn/ n 1 (a) ‹dress› vestido m; **evening** ~ traje m de fiesta (b) ‹night~› (AmE) camisón m 2 (a) (Educ, Law) toga f (b) (Med) bata f

GP n (= **general practitioner**) médico, -ca m,f de medicina general; **my** ~ mi médico de cabecera

GPS n (= **Global Positioning System**) GPS m

gr (= **gram(s)**) gr., g.

grab /græb/ **-bb-** vt (a) ‹seize› ‹rope/hand› agarrar; ‹chance› aprovechar (b) ‹appropriate› ‹land› apropiarse de; ‹money› llevarse (c) ‹appeal to› (colloq) «idea» atraer*; **how does that** ~ **you?** ¿qué te parece?
■ ~ vi: **to** ~ **AT sth**: **she** ~**bed at the rope** trató de agarrar la cuerda

grace /greɪs/ n 1 (elegance — of movement) gracia f, garbo m; (— of expression, form) elegancia f
2 (a) (courtesy) cortesía f, gentileza f (b) (good nature): **to do sth with good/bad** ~ hacer* algo de buen talante/a regañadientes (c) (good quality): **her saving** ~ **is her sense of humor** lo que la salva es que tiene sentido del humor; **social** ~**s** modales mpl
3 (Relig) (a) (mercy) gracia f; **by the** ~ **of God** ... gracias a Dios ... (b) (prayer): **to say** ~ (before a meal) bendecir* la mesa
4 (respite) gracia f; **16 days'** ~ (BrE Law) 16 días de gracia

graceful /'greɪsfəl/ adj ‹dancer/movement› lleno de gracia, grácil (liter); ‹style› elegante

gracefully /'greɪsfəli/ adv con gracia or garbo

gracious¹ /'greɪʃəs/ adj (a) ‹smile/act› gentil, cortés (b) (merciful) misericordioso

gracious² interj: (good o goodness) ~! (expressing surprise) ¡Dios Santo!; (expressing exasperation) ¡por favor!

graciously /'greɪʃəsli/ adv ‹smile/apologize› gentilmente

grade¹ /greɪd/ n 1 (a) (quality) calidad f; ~ **A tomatoes** tomates mpl de la mejor calidad (b) (degree, level): **it divides hotels into four** ~**s** divide a los hoteles en cuatro categorías (c) (in seniority) grado m (del escalafón); (Mil) rango m 2 (Educ) (a) (class) (AmE) grado m, año m, curso m (b) (in exam) nota f

grade² vt 1 (a) (classify) clasificar* (b) (order in ascending scale) ‹exercise/questions› ordenar por grado de dificultad (c) (mark) (AmE) ‹test/exercise› corregir* y calificar* (d) **graded** past p ‹produce› clasificado 2 (make more level) ‹surface/ soil› (AmE) nivelar

grade: ~ **crossing** n (AmE) paso m a nivel, crucero m (Méx); ~ **school** n (AmE) escuela f primaria

gradient /'greɪdiənt/ n (slope) pendiente f, gradiente f (AmL)

gradual /'grædʒuəl/ adj ‹improvement› gradual; ‹slope› no muy empinado

gradually /'grædʒuəli/ adv ‹improve› gradualmente, poco a poco; ‹rise/slope› suavemente

graduate¹ /'grædʒueɪt/ vi 1 (Educ) (a) (from a college, university) terminar la carrera, recibirse (AmL), graduarse*; (obtain bachelor's degree) licenciarse (b) (from high school) (AmE) terminar el bachillerato, recibirse de bachiller (AmL) 2 (progress) **to** ~ (**FROM sth**) **TO sth** pasar (DE algo) A algo

graduate² /'grædʒuət/ n (a) (from higher education) persona con título universitario; (with a bachelor's degree) licenciado, -da m,f; (before n) ‹course/student› de posgrado or postgrado; **he went to** ~ **school** (AmE) hizo un curso de posgrado (b) (from high school) (AmE) bachiller mf

graduated /'grædʒueɪtəd ‖ 'grædʒueɪtɪd/ adj (a) (progressive) ‹scale› graduado; ‹payments› escalonado (b) (calibrated) ‹flask/test tube› graduado

graduation /ˌgrædʒu'eɪʃən/ n (Educ) graduación f

graffiti /grə'fiːti/ n (+ sing o pl vb) graffiti mpl

graft¹ /græft ‖ grɑːft/ vt (Hort) injertar

graft² n 1 (Hort, Med) injerto m 2 (bribery, corruption) (AmE colloq) chanchullos mpl (fam)

grain /greɪn/ n 1 (of cereal, salt, sugar, sand) grano m 2 (Agr) grano m, cereal m 3 (of wood — pattern) veta f, veteado m; (— texture) grano m; **to go against the** ~: **it goes against the** ~ **for me to support them** apoyarlos va en contra de mis principios

gram, (BrE also) **gramme** /græm/ n gramo m

grammar /'græmər ‖ 'græmə(r)/ n gramática f

grammar school n (a) (in US) ▶ ELEMENTARY SCHOOL (b) (in UK) colegio de enseñanza secundaria para ingresar al cual hay que aprobar un examen de aptitud

grammatical /grə'mætɪkəl/ adj (a) (of grammar) gramatical (b) (correct) gramaticalmente correcto

gramme /græm/ n (BrE) ▶ GRAM

granary /'greɪnəri, 'grænəri ‖ 'grænəri/ n (pl **-ries**) granero m

grand /grænd/ adj **-er, -est** 1 (a) (impressive) magnífico (b) (ostentatious) ‹gesture› grandilocuente; ‹entrance› triunfal (c) (ambitious, lofty) ‹vision› grandioso; ‹ideal› elevado (d) (overall) (before n, no comp) global; **the** ~ **total** el total 2 (formal, ceremonial) ‹opening/occasion› solemne 3 (very good) (colloq) ‹day/weather› espléndido

grandad /'grændæd/ n abuelo m

grand: G~ Canyon n the G~ Canyon el Cañón del Colorado; **~child** /ˈgræntʃaɪld/ n nieto, -ta m,f; **~dad** /ˈgrændæd/ n abuelo m; **~daughter** /ˈgræn,dɔːtər ‖ˈgræn,dɔːtə(r)/ n nieta f

grandeur /ˈgrændʒər ‖ˈgrændʒə(r)/ n grandiosidad f

grandfather /ˈgræn,fɑːðər ‖ˈgræn,fɑːðə(r)/ n abuelo m; (before n) ~ **clock** reloj m de pie

grandiose /ˈgrændɪəʊs/ adj ⟨claim/scheme/ notion⟩ fatuo; ⟨speech⟩ altisonante

grand: ~ jury n (in US) jurado m de acusación (jurado que decide si hay suficientes pruebas para procesar); **~ma** /ˈgrænmɑː/ n (colloq) abuela f; **~mother** /ˈgræn,mʌðər ‖ˈgræn,mʌðə(r)/ n abuela f; **~pa** /ˈgrænpɑː/ n abuelo m; **~parent** /ˈgræn,perənt ‖ˈgræn,peərənt/ n abuelo, -la m,f; my **~parents** mis abuelos; **~ piano** n piano m de cola; **~son** /ˈgrænsʌn/ n nieto m; **~stand** n tribuna f; (before n) ⟨ticket/seat⟩ de tribuna

granite /ˈgrænət ‖ˈgrænɪt/ n granito m

granny, grannie /ˈgræni/ n (pl **-nies**) abuelita f (fam)

grant¹ /grænt ‖grɑːnt/ vt **1** (a) ⟨desire/ request⟩ conceder (b) ⟨interview/asylum⟩ conceder (c) ⟨land/pension⟩ otorgar* **2** (admit) reconocer* **3 granted** past p (admittedly): **~ed,** it's very expensive, but ... de acuerdo, es muy caro, pero ...; **to take sth for ~ed** dar* algo por sentado

grant² n (subsidy — to body, individual) subvención f, subsidio m (AmL); (— to student) (esp BrE) beca f

granulated /ˈgrænjəleɪtəd ‖ˈgrænjʊleɪtɪd/ adj: ~ **sugar** azúcar f granulada, azúcar m granulado

granule /ˈgrænjuːl/ n gránulo m

grape /greɪp/ n (fruit) uva f; **it's sour ~s** (set phrase) las uvas están verdes (fr hecha)

grape: ~fruit n (pl **-fruit** or **-fruits**) toronja f (AmL exc CS), pomelo m (CS, Esp); **~vine** n (a) (Agr, Bot) parra f (b) (source of information) (colloq): **I heard it on o through the ~vine** me lo dijo un pajarito (fam), lo he escuchado en radio macuto (Esp fam)

graph /græf ‖grɑːf/ n gráfico m, gráfica f

graphic /ˈgræfɪk/ adj **1** (vivid) ⟨account/ description⟩ muy gráfico; **in ~ detail** con todo lujo de detalles **2** (Art) gráfico; **~ design** diseño m gráfico

graphics /ˈgræfɪks/ pl n **1** (graphic design) diseño m gráfico **2** (Comput) gráficos mpl

graph paper n papel m milimetrado or (Méx) cuadriculado

grapple /ˈgræpl/ vi **to ~** ⟨WITH sb/sth⟩ forcejear ⟨CON algn/algo⟩; **to ~ with one's conscience** tener* escrúpulos de conciencia

grasp¹ /græsp ‖grɑːsp/ vt **1** (a) (seize) ⟨object/ person⟩ agarrar; ⟨opportunity/offer⟩ aprovechar (b) (hold tightly) tener* agarrado **2** (understand) ⟨concept⟩ captar

■ ~ vi **to ~ AT sth** tratar de agarrar algo; ⟨opportunity⟩ aprovechar

grasp² n (no pl) **1** (a) (grip): **he tightened his ~ on my arm** me apretó más el brazo (b) (reach) alcance m **2** (understanding) comprensión f; (knowledge) conocimientos mpl

grasping /ˈgræspɪŋ ‖ˈgrɑːspɪŋ/ adj avaricioso

grass /græs ‖grɑːs/ n **1** (a) (as pasture) pasto m, zacate m (Méx); (lawn) césped m, hierba f, pasto m (AmL), grama (AmC, Ven); **the ~ is always greener on the other side** nadie está contento con su suerte (b) (Bot) hierba f **2** (marijuana) (sl) maría f (arg), hierba f (arg), monte m (AmC, Col, Ven arg), mota f (Méx arg)

grass: ~hopper /ˈgræs,hɑːpər ‖ˈgrɑːs,hɒpə(r)/ n saltamontes m; **~ roots** pl n (ordinary members) (before n) ⟨support/opinion⟩ de las bases

grassy /ˈgræsi ‖ˈgrɑːsi/ adj **-sier, -siest** cubierto de hierba

grate¹ /greɪt/ vt (Culin) rallar; **~d cheese** queso m rallado

■ ~ vi (a) (irritate) ser* crispante (b) (make harsh noise) chirriar*

grate² n (metal frame in fireplace) rejilla f; (fireplace) chimenea f

grateful /ˈgreɪtfəl/ adj agradecido; **I'm very ~ to you for your advice** le agradezco mucho sus consejos

grater /ˈgreɪtər ‖ˈgreɪtə(r)/ n rallador m

gratify /ˈgrætɪfaɪ ‖ˈgrætɪfaɪ/ vt **-fies, -fying, -fied** (a) (fulfill) satisfacer* (b) (give satisfaction) complacer*

grating¹ /ˈgreɪtɪŋ/ adj (a) (harsh) ⟨noise/sound⟩ chirriante (b) (irritating) crispante

grating² n rejilla f

gratitude /ˈgrætətuːd ‖ˈgrætɪtjuːd/ n gratitud f

gratuitous /grəˈtuːətəs ‖grəˈtjuːɪtəs/ adj (pej) gratuito

grave¹ /greɪv/ adj **graver, gravest 1** ⟨error/danger/voice⟩ grave **2** /grɑːv/ (Ling) ⟨accent⟩ grave

grave² n tumba f, sepultura f

gravedigger /ˈgreɪv,dɪgər ‖ˈgreɪv,dɪgə(r)/ n sepulturero, -ra m,f

gravel /ˈgrævəl/ n grava f; (finer) gravilla f

gravely /ˈgreɪvli/ adv (a) (seriously) gravemente (b) (solemnly) con gravedad

grave: ~stone n lápida f; **~yard** n cementerio m, panteón m (Méx)

gravitate /ˈgrævəteɪt ‖ˈgrævɪteɪt/ vi: **people of similar interests naturally ~ toward each other** uno tiende a acercarse a gente con intereses afines; **young people tend to ~ toward the big cities** las grandes ciudades son un polo de atracción para los jóvenes

gravity /ˈgrævəti/ n **1** (Phys) gravedad f **2** (seriousness) gravedad f

gravy /ˈgreɪvi/ n (Culin) salsa hecha con el jugo de la carne asada

gray¹, (BrE) **grey** /greɪ/ adj **-er, -est** gris; ⟨outlook/future⟩ poco prometedor; **a ~ hair** una cana; **she has ~ hair** es canosa

---

AmC Central America	Arg Argentina	Cu Cuba	Per Peru
AmL Latin America	Bol Bolivia	Ec Ecuador	RPI River Plate Area
AmS South America	Chi Chile	Esp Spain	Ur Uruguay
Andes Andean Region	CS Southern Cone	Méx Mexico	Ven Venezuela

g

gray², (BrE) **grey** *n* gris *m*

graze¹ /greɪz/ *vt* **(a)** (cut, injure) rasguñarse **(b)** (touch, brush) rozar*

■ ~ *vi* (Agr) pastar

graze² *n* rasguño *m*

grease¹ /griːs/ *n* grasa *f*

grease² *vt* **(a)** (lubricate) ⟨*machinery/hinge*⟩ engrasar **(b)** (Culin): **to ~ (with butter)** enmantequillar, enmantecar* (RPl); **to ~ (with oil)** aceitar

grease: ~paint *n* maquillaje *m* teatral; **~proof paper** *n* (BrE) papel *m* encerado *or* (Esp) parafinado, papel *m* manteca (RPl), papel *m* mantequilla (Chi)

greasy /ˈgriːsi/ *adj* **-sier, -siest (a)** (soiled) ⟨*hands*⟩ grasiento; ⟨*overalls*⟩ cubierto de grasa **(b)** (containing grease) ⟨*food*⟩ graso; (pej) grasiento **(c)** ⟨*hair/skin*⟩ graso, grasoso (esp AmL)

great¹ /greɪt/ *adj* [1] (*before n*) (large in size, number, quantity) (*sing*) gran (*delante del n*); (*pl*) grandes (*delante del n*); **a ~ many people** muchísima gente [2] (*before n*) **(a)** (important) ⟨*landowner/occasion*⟩ (*sing*) gran (*delante del n*); (*pl*) grandes (*delante del n*); **Catherine the G~** Catalina la Grande **(b)** (genuine, real) ⟨*friend/rival*⟩ (*sing*) gran (*delante del n*); (*pl*) grandes (*delante del n*) [3] (excellent) (colloq) ⟨*goal/movie/meal*⟩ sensacional; **he's a really ~ guy** es un tipo *or* (Esp tb) tío sensacional (fam); (*as interj*) **(that's) ~!** ¡fenomenal!, ¡estupendo! (fam)

great² *adv* (esp AmE colloq) fenomenal (fam)

great: ~-aunt /ˈgreɪt'ænt ‖ˌgreɪt'ɑːnt/ *n* tía *f* abuela; **G~ Britain** *n* Gran Bretaña *f*; **G~ Dane** *n* gran danés *m*; **~granddaughter** /ˈgreɪt'græn,dɔːtər ‖ˌgreɪt'græn,dɔːtə(r)/ *n* bisnieta *f*, biznieta *f*; **~grandfather** /ˈgreɪt'græn,fɑːðər ‖ˌgreɪt'græn,fɑːðə(r)/ *n* bisabuelo *m*; **~grandmother** /ˈgreɪt'græn,mʌðər ‖ˌgreɪt'græn,mʌðə(r)/ *n* bisabuela *f*; **~grandson** /ˈgreɪt'grænsʌn/ *n* bisnieto *m*, biznieto *m*

greatly /ˈgreɪtli/ *adv* (*as intensifier*) ⟨*admire/improve*⟩ enormemente

great-uncle /ˈgreɪt'ʌŋkəl/ *n* tío *m* abuelo

Greece /griːs/ *n* Grecia *f*

greed /griːd/ *n* **(a)** (for food) gula *f*, angurria *f* (CS) **(b)** (for power, money) codicia *f*

greedy /ˈgriːdi/ *adj* **-dier, -diest (a)** (for food, drink) glotón, angurriento (CS) **(b)** (for power, wealth) **to be ~ FOR sth** tener* ansias DE algo

Greek¹ /griːk/ *adj* griego

Greek² *n* **(a)** (language) griego *m* **(b)** (person) griego, -ga *m*,*f*

green¹ /griːn/ *adj* **-er, -est** [1] (in color) verde; **he was ~ with envy** se moría de envidia; **to have a ~ thumb** *o* (BrE) **~ fingers** tener* mano para las plantas [2] **(a)** (unripe) verde **(b)** (colloq) (*pred*) (inexperienced) verde (fam) [3] (Pol) verde, ecologista

green² *n* [1] (color) verde *m* [2] (in village, town) ≈ plaza *f* (*con césped*) [3] **greens** *pl* (vegetables) verdura *f* (*de hoja verde*)

green: ~back *n* (AmE colloq) dólar *m*, verde *m* (esp AmL fam); **~ bean** *n* habichuela *f or* (Esp) judía *f* verde *or* (Méx) ejote *m or* (RPl) chaucha *f or* (Chi) poroto *m* verde *or* (Ven) vainita *f*; **~ belt** *n* (esp BrE) zona *f* verde; **~ card** *n* (in US)

permiso *m* de residencia y trabajo; **~field site** *n*: terreno en zona rural; **~fly** *n* (*pl* **-flies** *or* **-fly**) (BrE) pulgón *m*; **~grocer** *n* (BrE) verdulero, -ra *m*,*f*; **the ~grocer('s)** la verdulería; **~house** *n* invernadero *m*; (*before n*) **the ~house effect** (Ecol) el efecto invernadero; **G~land** /ˈgriːnlənd/ *n* Groenlandia *f*; **~ onion** *n* (AmE) cebolleta *f*, cebollino *m*; **~ pepper** *n* ▶ PEPPER¹ 2

Greenwich Mean Time /ˈgrenɪdʒ, ˈgrenɪtʃ/ *n* hora *f* de Greenwich

greet /griːt/ *vt* [1] **(a)** (welcome, receive) ⟨*guest/client*⟩ recibir **(b)** (say hello to) saludar [2] (reactto) acoger* [3] (meet): **a strange sight ~ed our eyes** un extraño espectáculo se ofreció a nuestra vista

greeting /ˈgriːtɪŋ/ *n* **(a)** (spoken) saludo *m*; (*as interj*) **~s!** (arch *or* hum) ¡buenas! (fam) **(b)** (message) (*usu pl*): **❺ birthday/Christmas greetings** feliz cumpleaños/Navidad; (*before n*) **a ~ o** (BrE also) **~s card** una tarjeta de felicitación

gregarious /grɪˈgeriəs ‖grɪˈgeəriəs/ *adj* ⟨*person*⟩ sociable; (Zool) gregario

Grenada /grəˈneɪdə/ *n* Granada *f*

grenade /grəˈneɪd/ *n* granada *f*

grew /gruː/ *past of* GROW

grey *adj/n* (BrE) ▶ GRAY¹,²

greyhound /ˈgreɪhaʊnd/ *n* galgo *m*

grid /grɪd/ *n* [1] (grating over opening) rejilla *f* [2] (on map) (Geog) cuadriculado *m*; (*before n*) **~ reference** coordenadas *fpl* cartográficas

griddle /ˈgrɪdl/ *n* plancha *f*

grid: ~iron /ˈgrid'aɪərn ‖ˈgrɪdaɪən/ *n* [1] (Culin) parrilla *f*; [2] (in US football) campo *m*, cancha *f* (AmL), emparrillado *m* (Méx); **~lock** *n* (esp AmE) paralización *f* total del tráfico; **~locked** /ˈgrɪdlɑːkt ‖ˈgrɪdlɒkt/ *adj* colapsado, paralizado

grief /griːf/ *n* dolor *m*, profunda pena *f*; **to come to ~** ⟨*plans*⟩ fracasar, irse* al traste (fam); **he'll come to ~ one day** va a acabar mal

grievance /ˈgriːvəns/ *n* **(a)** (ground for complaint) motivo *m* de queja; **to air one's ~s** quejarse **(b)** (Lab Rel) queja *f* formal; (*before n*) **~ procedure** procedimiento *m* conciliatorio

grieve /griːv/ *vi* sufrir; **to ~ FOR sb** llorar a algn

■ ~ *vt* apenar

grievous /ˈgriːvəs/ *adj* (liter) ⟨*loss*⟩ doloroso; ⟨*wound/injury*⟩ de extrema gravedad; **~ bodily harm** (Law) lesiones *fpl* (corporales) graves

grill¹ /grɪl/ *vt* [1] (BrE Culin) (in electric, gas grill) hacer* al grill; (over hot fire) hacer* a la parrilla [2] (interrogate) (colloq) interrogar*

grill² *n* **(a)** (on stove) (esp BrE) grill *m*, gratinador *m* **(b)** (on barbecue) parrilla *f*

grille /grɪl/ *n* **(a)** (partition) reja *f* **(b)** (protective covering) (Tech) rejilla *f*; (Auto) calandra *f*

grim /grɪm/ *adj* **-mm-** ⟨*person/expression*⟩ adusto; (gloomy) ⟨*outlook/situation*⟩ nefasto; **she carried on with ~ determination** siguió adelante, resuelta a no dejarse vencer

grimace¹ /ˈgrɪməs, grɪˈmeɪs/ *n* mueca *f*

grimace² *vi* hacer* una mueca

grime /graɪm/ *n* mugre *f*

grimy /ˈgraɪmi/ *adj* **-mier, -miest** mugriento

grin¹ /grɪn/ *vi* **-nn-** sonreír* (*abiertamente o burlonamente*); **to ~ and bear it** aguantarse

grin² n sonrisa f

grind¹ /graɪnd/ (past & past p **ground**) vt ⟨coffee/wheat⟩ moler*; (in mortar) machacar*; ⟨meat⟩ (AmE) moler* or (Esp, RPI) picar*; ⟨crystals/ ore⟩ triturar; **he ~s his teeth in his sleep** le rechinan los dientes cuando duerme

■ **~** vi (move with friction) rechinar, chirriar*; **to ~ to a halt** o **standstill** ⟨vehicle⟩ pararse or detenerse* con un chirrido; «negotiations» llegar* a un punto muerto

grind² n (a) (drudgery) (colloq) (no pl): **the daily ~** el monótono trajín diario (b) (over-conscientious worker) (AmE colloq): **she's the office ~** es la niña aplicada de la oficina (iró)

grinder /'graɪndər ‖'graɪndə(r)/ n (machine) molinillo m; **a coffee ~** un molinillo de café

grindstone /'graɪnstəʊn, 'graɪndstəʊn ‖'graɪndstəʊn/ n muela f, piedra f de afilar; **back to the ~!** ¡de vuelta al yugo!

grip¹ /grɪp/ n 1 (a) (hold): **she held his arm in a strong ~** lo tenía agarrado or asido fuertemente del brazo; **he kept a firm ~ on expenses** llevaba un rígido control de los gastos; **get a ~ on yourself!** ¡contrólate!; **the region is in the ~ of an epidemic** una epidemia asola la región; **to come to ~s with sth** ⟨idea/situation⟩ aceptar or asumir algo; **to get to ~s with sth** ⟨subject⟩ entender* algo; ⟨new system⟩ aprender algo (b) (of tires) adherencia f
2 (on handle) empuñadura f
3 (hair ~) (BrE) horquilla f, pinche m (Chi), pasador m (Méx)

grip² vt **-pp-** 1 (take hold of) agarrar; (have hold of) tener* agarrado 2 (of feelings, attention): **the audience was ~ped by the play** la obra captó la atención del público

gripping /'grɪpɪŋ/ adj apasionante

grisly /'grɪzli/ adj **-lier, -liest** truculento

gristle /'grɪsəl/ n cartílago m

grit¹ /grɪt/ n 1 (a) (dirt) polvo m (b) (gravel) arenilla f 2 (courage) (colloq) agallas fpl (fam)
3 **grits** pl (hominy ~s) (AmE Culin) sémola f de maíz

grit² vt **-tt-** (a) (BrE) ⟨road⟩ echar arenilla en (b) ▶ TOOTH A

grizzly /'grɪzli/ n (pl **-lies**), **grizzly bear** oso m pardo

groan¹ /grəʊn/ vi 1 (a) (with pain, suffering) gemir* (b) (with dismay) gruñir* (c) (creak) «door/ timber» crujir 2 (grumble) (colloq) refunfuñar (fam)

groan² n (a) (of pain, suffering) quejido m (b) (of dismay) gruñido m (c) (creak) crujido m

grocer /'grəʊsər ‖'grəʊsə(r)/ n tendero, -ra m,f, almacenero, -ra m,f (esp CS); **the ~'s** (BrE) la tienda de comestibles or de ultramarinos, la bodega (Cu, Per, Ven), la tienda de abarrotes (AmC, Andes, Méx), el almacén (esp CS)

grocery /'grəʊsəri/ n (pl **-ries**) (a) (shop) tienda f de comestibles or de ultramarinos, bodega f (Cu, Per, Ven), tienda f de abarrotes (AmC, Andes, Méx), almacén m (esp CS) (b) **groceries** pl (provisions) comestibles mpl, provisiones fpl

groggy /'grɑːgi ‖'grɒgi/ adj **-gier, -giest** (colloq) grogui (fam)

groin /grɔɪn/ n (Anat) ingle f

groom¹ /gruːm/ vt (a) ⟨dog⟩ cepillar; ⟨horse⟩

cepillar, almohazar* (b) (make neat, attractive) (usu pass): **well ~ed** bien arreglado (c) (prepare) preparar; **to ~ sb for sth** preparar a algn para algo

groom² n 1 (Equ) mozo m de cuadra
2 (bride~) novio m

groove /gruːv/ n ranura f; (Audio) surco m

grope /grəʊp/ vi andar* a tientas; **to ~ FOR sth** buscar* algo a tientas
■ **~** vt ⟨person⟩ (colloq) manosear, meterle mano a (fam)

gross¹ /grəʊs/ adj 1 (extreme, flagrant) (before n) ⟨disregard/injustice⟩ flagrante; ⟨exaggeration⟩ burdo 2 (total) ⟨weight/profit/income⟩ bruto; **~ national product** (Econ) producto m nacional bruto 3 (a) (fat) obeso (b) (disgusting) ⟨person⟩ asqueroso; ⟨language/joke⟩ soez

gross² vt ⟨worker/earner⟩ tener* una entrada bruta de; **their profits ~ed 2 million** tuvieron beneficios brutos de 2 millones

gross³ n 1 (pl **~**) (144) gruesa f 2 (pl **grosses**) (gross profit) (AmE) ingresos mpl brutos

grossly /'grəʊsli/ adv ⟨exaggerated/unfair⟩ terriblemente

grotesque /grəʊ'tesk/ adj grotesco

grotto /'grɑːtəʊ ‖'grɒtəʊ/ n (pl **-toes** or **-tos**) gruta f

ground¹ /graʊnd/ n 1 (land, terrain) terreno m; **to gain/lose ~** ganar/perder* terreno; **to stand one's ~** (in argument) mantenerse* firme; (in battle) no ceder terreno
2 **grounds** pl (premises) terreno m; (gardens) jardines mpl
3 (surface of the earth) suelo m; (soil) tierra f; **to break new ~** abrir* nuevos caminos; **to get off the ~** ⟨plan/project⟩ llegar* a concretarse; «talks» empezar* a encaminarse; **to get sth off the ~** ⟨project⟩ poner* algo en marcha; **to suit sb down to the ~** (colloq) ⟨arrangement⟩ venirle* de perlas a algn (fam); «hat» quedarle que ni pintado a algn (fam)
4 (matter, subject): **we covered a lot of ~ in our discussions** tratamos muchos puntos en nuestras conversaciones
5 (outdoor site): **football ~** (BrE) campo m de fútbol, cancha f de fútbol (AmL); **recreation ~** parque m (donde se practican deportes)
6 (AmE Elec) tierra f
7 (justification) (usu pl) motivo m; **~s for divorce** causal f de divorcio; **on ~s of ill health** por motivos de salud; **they refused, on the ~s that ...** se negaron, alegando que ...
8 **grounds** pl (dregs): **coffee ~s** posos mpl de café

ground² vt 1 (usu pass) (a) (base) ⟨argument/ theory⟩ fundar (b) (instruct): **we were well ~ed in German** se nos dio una sólida base en alemán 2 ⟨plane⟩ retirar del servicio (b) ⟨child/ teenager⟩ (esp AmE colloq): **I can't go out tonight; I'm ~ed** no puedo salir esta noche, estoy castigado or no me dejan 3 (Naut) ⟨ship⟩ hacer* encallar

ground³ past & past p of GRIND¹

ground⁴ adj ⟨coffee/pepper⟩ molido; **~ beef** (AmE) carne f molida or (Esp, RPI) picada

ground: ~cloth, (BrE) **~sheet** n suelo m

impermeable (*de una tienda de campaña*); **~ control** *n* control *m* de tierra; **~ floor** *n* (BrE) the **~ floor** la planta baja, el primer piso (Chi)

grounding /'graʊndɪŋ/ *n* (*no pl*) base *f*

groundless /'graʊndləs/ *adj* infundado

ground: ~ level *n*: at **~ level** a ras del suelo; above **~ level** sobre el nivel del suelo; below **~ level** bajo tierra; **~ rule** *n* **1** (guiding principle) directriz *f*; **2** (AmE Sport) regla *f* de terreno *or* de campo, regla local (Ven); **~sheet** *n* (BrE) ▶ GROUNDCLOTH; **~work** *n* trabajo *m* preliminar *or* de base; **~ zero** *n* (in New York) zona *f* cero; (in atomic warfare) hipocentro *m*

group¹ /gruːp/ *n* **1** (+ *sing o pl vb*) **(a)** (of people) grupo *m*; **a women's/gay ~** una agrupación de mujeres/gay; (*before n*) ⟨*discussion/visit*⟩ de grupo; (*portrait*⟩ de conjunto **(b)** (Mus) grupo *m*, conjunto *m* **2** (Busn, Chem, Math) grupo *m*

group² *vt* agrupar
■ **~** *vi*: to **~ together** agruparse

grouse¹ /graʊs/ *n* (*pl* **~**) (bird) urogallo *m*

grouse² *vi* (colloq) gruñir* (fam); to **~ ABOUT sb/sth** quejarse DE algn/algo

grout /graʊt/ *vt* ⟨*tiles*⟩ enlechar

grove /grəʊv/ *n* (of trees) bosquecillo *m*; **an orange ~** un naranjal

grovel /'grɑːvəl ‖ 'grʊvəl/ *vi*, (BrE) **-ll-** (physically) postrarse; (abase oneself) arrastrarse

grow /grəʊ/ (*past* **grew**; *past p* **grown**) *vi* **1** (get bigger) crecer*; (develop emotionally) madurar; (expand, increase) ⟨*city/company/influence*⟩ crecer*; ⟨*quantity/population/membership*⟩ aumentar; **his hair has ~n** le creció el pelo; **the economy is ~ing again** la economía vuelve a experimentar un período de crecimiento *or* expansión
2 (a) (become): to **~ careless** volverse* descuidado; to **~ old** envejecer* **(b)** (get) to **~ to + INF**: **she grew to love him** llegó a quererlo
■ **~** *vt* ⟨*flowers/plants/crops*⟩ cultivar; to **~ a beard** dejarse (crecer) la barba; to **~ one's hair (long)** dejarse crecer el pelo
■ **grow into** [*v* + *prep* + *o*] **(a)** (become) convertirse* en **(b)** (grow to fit): **she will soon ~ into these dresses** pronto podrá usar estos vestidos
■ **grow on** [*v* + *prep* + *o*] (colloq): **it ~s on you** ⟨*music/place*⟩ llega a gustar con el tiempo
■ **grow out of** [*v* + *adv* + *prep* + *o*] **(a)** ⟨*habit*⟩ perder*, quitarse (con el tiempo o la edad); **it's just a phase, she'll ~ out of it** son cosas de la edad, ya se le pasará **(b)** ⟨*clothes*⟩: **she's ~n out of those shoes already** esos zapatos ya le quedan chicos *or* (Esp) le están pequeños
■ **grow up** [*v* + *adv*] **(a)** (spend childhood) criarse*, crecer* **(b)** (become adult) hacerse* mayor; **when I ~ up** cuando sea grande; **~ up!** ¡no seas infantil! **(c)** (arise) ⟨*friendship/custom/feeling*⟩ surgir*; ⟨*settlement/town*⟩ desarrollarse

grower /'grəʊə(r)/ *n* cultivador, -dora *m,f*

growing /'grəʊɪŋ/ *adj* (*before n*) **(a)** ⟨*quantity/ reputation*⟩ cada vez mayor; ⟨*influence*⟩ creciente **(b)** ⟨*child*⟩: **you need a lot to eat; you're a ~ boy** tienes que comer mucho, estás creciendo **(c)** ⟨*plant/stem/vegetable*⟩ que está creciendo

growl¹ /graʊl/ *vi* gruñir*

growl² *n* gruñido *m*

grown¹ /grəʊn/ *past p of* GROW

grown² *adj*: **he's a ~ man** es un hombre hecho y derecho; **when the young are fully ~** (Zool) cuando las crías han alcanzado su pleno desarrollo

grown-up¹ /'grəʊnʌp/ *n* persona *f* mayor

grown-up² *adj* **(a)** (adult) mayor **(b)** (mature) (colloq) maduro, adulto

growth /grəʊθ/ *n* **1** (of animals, humans) crecimiento *m* **2** (of population, city, business) crecimiento *m*; (of quantity, profits) aumento *m*; (in popularity) aumento *m* **3 (a)** (what grows): **new ~** brotes *mpl* nuevos; **several days' ~ of beard** una barba de varios días **(b)** (Med) bulto *m*, tumor *m*

growth industry *n* industria *f* en crecimiento *or* en expansión

grub /grʌb/ *n* **1** (Zool) larva *f* **2** (food) (colloq) comida *f*, papeo *m* (Esp arg), morfe *m* (CS arg)

grubby /'grʌbi/ *adj* **-bier, -biest** mugriento

grudge¹ /grʌdʒ/ *n* rencilla *f*; **to bear sb a ~** tenerle* *or* guardarle rencor a algn

grudge² *vt* ▶ BEGRUDGE

grueling, (BrE) **gruelling** /'gruːəlɪŋ/ *adj* ⟨*journey*⟩ extenuante; ⟨*experience/ordeal*⟩ penoso

gruesome /'gruːsəm/ *adj* truculento

gruff /grʌf/ *adj* **-er, -est** ⟨*voice*⟩ áspero; ⟨*manner/reply*⟩ brusco

grumble /'grʌmbəl/ *vi* refunfuñar (fam), rezongar*; to **~ ABOUT sth/sb** quejarse DE algo/ algn

grumpy /'grʌmpi/ *adj* **-pier, -piest** ⟨*person*⟩ gruñón; ⟨*remark/voice*⟩ malhumorado

grunt¹ /grʌnt/ *vi* gruñir*

grunt² *n* gruñido *m*

guarantee¹ /ˌgærən'tiː/ *n* garantía *f*

guarantee² *vt* garantizar*

guarantor /ˌgærən'tɔːr ‖ ˌgærən'tɔː(r)/ *n* garante *mf*

guard¹ /gɑːrd ‖ gɑːd/ *vt* **(a)** ⟨*building/prisoner*⟩ vigilar; ⟨*person/reputation*⟩ proteger*; ⟨*secret*⟩ guardar **(b)** (AmE Sport) marcar*
■ **guard against** [*v* + *prep* + *o*] ⟨*injury/ temptation*⟩ evitar; ⟨*risk*⟩ protegerse* contra

guard² *n* **1 (a)** (sentry, soldier) guardia *mf*; **security ~** guarda *mf* de seguridad; **prison ~** (AmE) carcelero, -ra *m,f*, oficial *mf* de prisiones **(b)** (squad) (*no pl*) guardia *f* **(c)** (Sport) (in US football) defensa *mf*; (in basketball) escolta *mf* **2** (surveillance) guardia *f*; **to be on ~** estar* de guardia; (*before n*) **~ duty** guardia *f*, posta *f* (AmC) **3** (in boxing, fencing) guardia *f*; **to be on/off (one's) ~** estar* alerta/desprevenido **4 (a)** (fire ~) guardallama(s) *m* **(b)** (on machinery) cubierta *f* (*or* dispositivo *m* etc) de seguridad **5** (BrE Rail) jefe, -fa *m,f* de tren

guard dog *n* perro *m* guardián

guarded /'gɑːrdəd ‖ 'gɑːdɪd/ *adj* ⟨*reply/ admission*⟩ cauteloso; ⟨*optimism*⟩ cauto

guardian /'gɑːrdiən ‖ 'gɑːdiən/ *n* **(a)** (of child) tutor, -tora *m,f* **(b)** (protector) defensor, -sora *m,f*, custodio, -dia *m,f*

guardian angel *n* ángel *m* de la guarda, ángel *m* custodio

guard: ~**rail** n (in staircase) barandilla f; (in roads etc) barrera f de seguridad; ~**'s van** n (BrE Rail) furgón m de cola

Guatemala /ˈɡwɑːtəˈmɑːlə/ n Guatemala f

Guatemalan¹ /ˈɡwɑːtəˈmɑːlən/ adj guatemalteco

Guatemalan² n guatemalteco, -ca m,f

Guernsey /ˈɡɜːrnzi ‖ˈɡɜːnzi/ n Guernesey

guerrilla /ɡəˈrɪlə/ n guerrillero, -ra m,f; (before n) ⟨tactics/leader⟩ guerrillero; ~ **warfare** guerrilla f

guess¹ /ɡes/ n: **have a** ~! ¡a ver si adivinas!; **your** ~ **is as good as mine** quién sabe, vete tú a saber

guess² vt (a) (conjecture, estimate) adivinar; ~ **what!** ¿sabes qué?; **you'll never** ~ **what he said** no te puedes imaginar lo que dijo (b) (suppose) (esp AmE colloq) suponer*; **I** ~ **so** supongo (que sí)
■ ~ vi: **how did you** ~? ¿cómo adivinaste? or (Esp) ¿cómo lo has adivinado?; **to** ~ **right** acertar*, adivinar, atinar(le) (Méx)

guesswork /ˈɡeswɜːrk ‖ˈɡeswɜːk/ n conjeturas fpl

guest /ɡest/ n (visitor) invitado, -da m,f; (in hotel) huésped mf, cliente, -ta m,f; (before n) ~ **list** lista f de invitados; ~ **speaker** conferenciante invitado, -da m,f; ~ **star** estrella f invitada

guest: ~**house** n (a) (in US, attached to mansion) pabellón m de huéspedes (b) (Tourism) (in UK) casa f de huéspedes, pensión f; ~**room** n cuarto m de huéspedes or (Chi) de alojados

guffaw¹ /ɡʌˈfɔː/ n risotada f

guffaw² vi reírse* a carcajadas

guidance /ˈɡaɪdns/ n orientación f; **he needs** ~ necesita que lo orienten; (before n) ~ **counselor** (AmE) orientador, -dora m,f vocacional

guide¹ /ɡaɪd/ n ①︎ (a) (Tourism) (person) guía mf; (publication) guía f (b) (adviser) consejero, -ra m,f ②︎ **Guide** (BrE) exploradora f, guía f ③︎ (indicator) guía f; **to use** o **take sth as a** ~ guiarse* por algo

guide² vt (a) ⟨tourist/stranger⟩ guiar*; **a priest** ~**d them round the cathedral** un sacerdote les hizo de guía en la catedral (b) (help, advise) guiar*, aconsejar (c) (steer, manipulate) (+ adv compl): **the captain** ~**d the ship between the rocks** el capitán condujo or guio el barco por entre las rocas

guide: ~**book** n guía f; ~ **dog** n perro m guía, perro m lazarillo

guided tour /ˈɡaɪdəd ‖ˈɡaɪdɪd/ n visita f guiada

guideline /ˈɡaɪdlaɪn/ n pauta f

guild /ɡɪld/ n (a) (of workers) gremio m (b) (club, society) asociación f

guile /ɡaɪl/ n astucia f

guillotine /ˈɡɪlətiːn/ n guillotina f

guilt /ɡɪlt/ n (a) (blame) culpa f; (Law) culpabilidad f (b) (Psych) culpa f

guilty /ˈɡɪlti/ adj **-tier, -tiest** (a) (Law) (no

comp) culpable; **to be** ~ **of sth** ser* culpable DE algo (b) (ashamed, remorseful) culpable (c) (shameful) (before n) ⟨secret⟩ vergonzoso

guinea /ˈɡɪni/ n guinea f

guinea pig n (a) (Zool) cobayo m, cobaya f, conejillo m de Indias, cuy m (AmS) (b) (person) conejillo m de Indias

guise /ɡaɪz/ n: **under the** ~ **of friendship** bajo una apariencia de amistad; **in many different** ~s de muchas formas distintas

guitar /ɡəˈtɑːr ‖ɡɪˈtɑː(r)/ n guitarra f

guitarist /ɡəˈtɑːrəst ‖ɡɪˈtɑːrɪst/ n guitarrista mf

gulf /ɡʌlf/ n (a) (Geog) golfo m (b) (gap) abismo m

gull /ɡʌl/ n (Zool) gaviota f

gullet /ˈɡʌlət ‖ˈɡʌlɪt/ n garganta f

gulley /ˈɡʌli/ n (pl **-leys**) ▶ GULLY

gullible /ˈɡʌləbəl/ adj crédulo

gully /ˈɡʌli/ n (pl **-lies**) (a) (small valley) barranco m (b) (channel) surco m, cauce m

gulp¹ /ɡʌlp/ vi tragar* saliva
■ ~ vt ~ (**down**) ⟨food⟩ engullir*; ⟨drink/medicine⟩ beberse de un trago

gulp² n (of liquid) trago m; (of air) bocanada f: **in one** ~ de un trago

gum /ɡʌm/ n ①︎ (Anat) encía f ②︎ (chewing ~) chicle m, goma f de mascar ③︎ (a) (glue) (BrE) goma f de pegar (b) (from plant) resina f

gun /ɡʌn/ n (pistol) pistola f, revólver m; (shotgun, rifle) escopeta f, fusil m, rifle m; (artillery piece) cañón m
■ **gun down** [v + o + adv, v + adv + o] abatir a tiros

gun: ~**dog** n perro m de caza; ~**fight** n tiroteo m, balacera f (AmL); ~**fire** n disparos mpl; (from heavy artillery) cañoneo m, cañonazos mpl; ~**man** /ˈɡʌnmən/ n (pl **-men** /-mən/) pistolero m, gatillero m (Méx); ~**point** n: **at** ~**point** a punta de pistola; ~**powder** n pólvora f; ~**running** n tráfico m de armas; ~**shot** n disparo m; (before n) ~**shot wound** herida f de bala; ~**smith** n armero, -ra m,f

gurgle¹ /ˈɡɜːrɡəl ‖ˈɡɜːɡəl/ vi «water/brook» borbotar; «baby» gorjear

gurgle² n (of water, liquid) borboteo m; (of delight) gorjeo m

gush /ɡʌʃ/ vi «liquid» salir* a borbotones

gushing /ˈɡʌʃɪŋ/ adj (pej) demasiado efusivo

gusset /ˈɡʌsət ‖ˈɡʌsɪt/ n entretela f

gust /ɡʌst/ n ráfaga f

gusto /ˈɡʌstəʊ/ n entusiasmo m; **with** ~ ⟨eat⟩ con ganas; ⟨sing/play⟩ con brío

gusty /ˈɡʌsti/ adj **-tier, -tiest** ⟨wind⟩ racheado; ⟨weather/day⟩ ventoso

gut¹ /ɡʌt/ n (a) (intestine) intestino m (b) (belly) (colloq) barriga f (fam); (before n) ⟨reaction⟩ instintivo

gut² vt **-tt-** (a) ⟨fish/chicken/rabbit⟩ limpiar (b) ⟨building⟩ destruir* el interior de

---

AmC	América Central	Arg	Argentina	Cu	Cuba
AmL	América Latina	Bol	Bolivia	Ec	Ecuador
AmS	América del Sur	Chi	Chile	Esp	España
Andes	Región andina	CS	Cono Sur	Méx	México

Per	Perú
RPI	Río de la Plata
Ur	Uruguay
Ven	Venezuela

guts /gʌts/ *n* 1 (+ *pl vb*) (colloq) (bowels) tripas *fpl* (fam) 2 (+ *sing o pl vb*) (courage) (colloq) agallas *fpl* (fam)

gutter /'gʌtər ‖'gʌtə(r)/ *n* **(a)** (on roof) canaleta *f*, canalón *m* (Esp) **(b)** (in street) alcantarilla *f* **(c)** (lowest section of society) **the ∼** el arroyo; (*before n*) **the ∼ press** la prensa sensacionalista

guttural /'gʌtərəl/ *adj* gutural

guy /gaɪ/ *n* (colloq) **(a)** (man) tipo *m* (fam), tío *m* (Esp fam), chavo *m* (Méx fam) **(b)** **guys** *pl* (people) (AmE) gente *f*

Guyana /gaɪˈænə/ *n* Guyana *f*, Guayana *f*

Guyanese /ˌgaɪəˈniːz/ *adj* guyanés, guayanés

guzzle /'gʌzəl/ *vt* **(a)** (drink greedily) chupar (fam) **(b)** (eat greedily) (BrE) engullirse*, tragarse*

gym /dʒɪm/ *n* **(a)** (gymnasium) gimnasio *m* **(b)** (gymnastics) gimnasia *f*

gymnasium /dʒɪmˈneɪziəm/ *n* (*pl* **-siums** *or* **-sia** /-ziə/) gimnasio *m*

gymnast /'dʒɪmnæst/ *n* gimnasta *mf*

gymnastics /dʒɪmˈnæstɪks/ *n* **(a)** (activity) (+ *sing vb*) gimnasia *f* **(b)** (exercises) (+ *pl vb*) gimnasia *f*

gynecologist, (BrE) **gynaecologist** /'gaɪnəˈkɑːlədʒəst ‖ˌgaɪnəˈkɒlədʒɪst/ *n* ginecólogo, -ga *m,f*

gynecology, (BrE) **gynaecology** /'gaɪnəˈkɑːlədʒi ‖ˌgaɪnəˈkɒlədʒi/ *n* ginecología *f*

gypsy, Gypsy /'dʒɪpsi/ *n* (*pl* **-sies**) gitano, -na *m,f*

gyrate /'dʒaɪreɪt ‖dʒaɪˈreɪt/ *vi* girar

H h

H, h /eɪtʃ/ *n* H, h *f*

haberdashery /'hæbərˌdæʃəri ‖'hæbəˌdæʃəri/ *n* **(a)** (clothes) (AmE) ropa *f* y accesorios *mpl* para caballeros **(b)** (sewing materials) (BrE) (artículos *mpl* de) mercería *f*

habit /'hæbət ‖'hæbɪt/ *n* 1 **(a)** (usual piece of behavior) costumbre *f*, hábito *m*; (bad) vicio *m*, mala costumbre *f*, mal hábito *m*; **to get out of/ into the ∼ of doing sth** perder*/tomar la costumbre de hacer algo **(b)** (customary behavior) costumbre *f*; **by** *or* **out of** *or* **from force of ∼** por fuerza de la costumbre 2 (Clothing) hábito *m*

habitat /'hæbətæt ‖'hæbɪtæt/ *n* hábitat *m*

habitation /ˌhæbəˈteɪʃən ‖ˌhæbɪˈteɪʃən/ *n* (frml): **unfit for human ∼** inhabitable

habitual /həˈbɪtʃuəl/ *adj* **(a)** (usual) habitual, acostumbrado **(b)** (compulsive) ⟨*liar/gambler*⟩ empedernido

hack¹ /hæk/ *vt* cortar a tajos, tajear (Andes)
■ ∼ *vi* 1 (to cut): **to ∼ at sth** darle* (golpes) a algo; **we ∼ed through the undergrowth** nos abrimos paso a machetazos (*or* hachazos *etc*) a través de la espesura 2 (Comput colloq) **to ∼ into** ⟨*system*⟩ piratear

hack² *n* 1 (pej *or* hum) (writer) escritorzuelo, -la *m,f* (pey); (journalist) gacetillero, -ra *m,f* (pey) 2 (horse — for hire) caballo *m* de alquiler; (— worn-out) jaco *m*, jamelgo *m* 3 (AmE colloq) **(a)** (taxi driver) taxista *mf*, tachero, -ra *m,f* (RPI fam), ruletero, -ra *m,f* (Méx fam) **(b)** (taxi) taxi *m*, tacho *m* (RPI fam)

hacker /'hækər ‖'hækə(r)/ *n* (Comput colloq) pirata informático, -ca *m,f*

hacking /'hækɪŋ/ *adj* ⟨*cough*⟩ áspero

hackles /'hækəlz/ *pl n* **to make sb's ∼ rise** poner* furioso a algn; **his ∼ rose** se enfureció

hackneyed /'hæknid/ *adj* manido, trillado

hacksaw /'hæksɔː/ *n* sierra *f* de arco (*para metales*)

had /hæd, *weak form* həd, əd/ *past & past p of* HAVE

haddock /'hædək/ *n* (*pl* **∼**) **(a)** (Zool) eglefino *m* **(b)** (Culin) abadejo *m*

hadn't /'hædn̩t/ = **had not**

haem- *etc* (BrE) ▶ HEM- *etc*

hag /hæg/ *n* bruja *f*, arpía *f*

haggard /'hægərd ‖'hægəd/ *adj* demacrado

haggis /'hægəs ‖'hægɪs/ *n* (*pl* **-gis** *or* **-gises**) *plato escocés hecho con vísceras de cordero y avena*

haggle /'hægəl/ *vi* regatear

Hague /heɪg/ *n* **The ∼** La Haya

hail¹ /heɪl/ *n* **(a)** (Meteo) granizo *m*, pedrisco *m* **(b)** (of bullets, insults) (*no pl*) lluvia *f*

hail² *v impers* (Meteo) granizar*
■ *vt* 1 (call to) ⟨*person*⟩ llamar; ⟨*ship*⟩ saludar; ⟨*taxi*⟩ hacerle* señas a 2 (acclaim, welcome) ⟨*king/ leader*⟩ aclamar; **it was ∼ed as a major breakthrough** fue acogido como un importantísimo avance
■ ∼ *vi* **to ∼ FROM** «*person*» ser* DE

hail: H∼ Mary /'meri ‖'meəri/ *n* Avemaría *m*; **∼stone** *n* granizo *m*, piedra *f* (de granizo)

hair /her ‖heə(r)/ *n* **(a)** (on human head) pelo *m*, cabello *m* (frml *o* liter); **to have one's ∼ done** peinarse (*en la peluquería*); (*before n*) ⟨*gel/ lacquer/oil*⟩ para el pelo; ⟨*transplant*⟩ capilar **(b)** (on human body) vello *m*; (on animal, plant) pelo *m* **(c)** (single strand) pelo *m*

hair: ∼band *n* (elastic) cinta *f*, huincha *f* (Bol, Chi, Per), balaca *f* (Col), banda *f* (Méx), vincha *f* (RPI, Ven); (rigid) diadema *f*, cintillo *m*, vincha *f* (RPI, Ven); **∼brush** *n* cepillo *m* (del pelo); **∼clip** *n* (BrE) horquilla *f*, pinche *m* (Chi), pasador *m* (Méx); **∼cut** *n* corte *m* de pelo; **∼do** *n* (colloq) peinado *m*; **∼dresser** *n* peluquero, -ra *m,f*; **the ∼dresser's** la peluquería; **∼drier, ∼dryer** *n* secador *m or* (Méx) secadora *f*; **∼grip** *n* (BrE) horquilla *f*, pinche *m* (Chi), pasador *m* (Méx); **∼line** *n* **(a)** (where hair begins) nacimiento *m* del ····❖

pelo **(b)** (fine line) línea *f* delgada; (*before n*) **a ~line fracture** una pequeña fisura; **~net** *n* redecilla *f*; **~piece** *n* postizo *m*; **~pin** *n* horquilla *f* (de moño); (*before n*) **~pin turn** *o* (BrE) **bend** curva *f* muy cerrada; **~raising** /'her,reɪzɪŋ ‖'heə,reɪzɪŋ/ *adj* espeluznante; **~'s breadth, ~sbreadth** *n* (*no pl*): **by a ~'s breadth** por un pelo (fam); **~slide** *n* (BrE) ▶ BARRETTE; **~spray** *n* laca *f*, fijador *m* (*para el pelo*); **~style** *n* peinado *m*, corte *m* de pelo

hairy /'heri ‖'heəri/ *adj* **-rier, -riest** ‹*legs/ chest*› peludo, velludo

Haiti /'heɪti/ *n* Haití *m*

Haitian /'heɪʃən/ *adj* haitiano

hake /heɪk/ *n* (*pl* ~) merluza *f*

halal /hɑːˈlɑːl/ *adj* (Culin) ‹*meat*› de animales faenados *or* (Esp) sacrificados según la ley musulmana

hale /heɪl/ *adj* (liter): **~ and hearty** (fuerte) como un roble

half¹ /hæf ‖hɑːf/ *n* (*pl* **halves**) ①**(a)** (part) mitad *f*; **to break sth in ~** romper* algo por la mitad *or* en dos; **to go halves** (colloq) pagar* a medias **(b)** (Math) medio *m* **(c)** (elliptical use): **an hour and a ~** una hora y media; **it's ~ past ten** son las diez y media ②(Sport) **(a)** (period) tiempo *m* **(b)** (of pitch) campo *m* **(c)** (interval) (AmE) descanso *m*, medio tiempo *m* (AmL)

half² *pron* la mitad

half³ *adj* medio, -dia; **~ a pint of milk** media pinta de leche; **one and a ~ hours** una hora y media

half⁴ *adv* medio; **she was ~ asleep** estaba medio dormida *or* semidormida; **the work is only ~ done** el trabajo está a medio hacer; **she is ~ Italian, ~ Greek** es hija de italianos y griegos; **they are paid ~ as much as we are** les pagan la mitad que a nosotros

half- /'hæf ‖hɑːf/ *pref*: **~closed/~open** entreabierto; **~starved** medio muerto de hambre

half: **~ a dozen** *n* (*no pl*) media docena *f*; **~ a dozen eggs** media docena de huevos; **~ an hour** *n* media hora *f*; **~ brother** *n* hermanastro *m*, medio hermano *m*; **~hearted** /'hɑːf'hɑːrtəd ‖,hɑːf'hɑːtɪd/ *adj* poco entusiasta; **~hour** /'hæfaʊr ‖,hɑːf'aʊə(r)/ *n* media hora *f*; **~light** *n* penumbra *f*; **~mast** /'hæf'mæst ‖,hɑːf'mɑːst/ *n*: **at ~mast** a media asta; **~ measures** *pl n* medias tintas *fpl*; **~moon** /'hæf'muːn ‖,hɑːf'muːn/ *n* media luna *f*; **~ note** *n* (AmE) blanca *f*; **~penny** /'heɪpni/ *n* (Hist) (*pl* **-pennies**) (coin) medio penique *m* **(b)** (*pl* **-pence** /'heɪpəns/) (value) medio penique *m*; **~ price** *n* mitad *f* de precio; **it's ~ price** está a mitad de precio; **~ sister** *n* hermanastra *f*, media hermana *f*; **~staff** *n* (AmE) ▶ ~MAST; **~ term** *n* (in UK) vacaciones *fpl* de mitad de trimestre; **~time** *n* **(a)** (Sport) descanso *m*, medio tiempo *m* (AmL); **(b)** (Busn, Lab Rel) media jornada *f*

half-way¹ /'hæfweɪ ‖,hɑːf'weɪ/ *adv* (at, to mid point) a mitad de camino; **I'm about ~ through** voy por la mitad; **to meet sb ~** (compromise) llegar* a una solución intermedia con algn; (lit: on journey) encontrarse* con algn a mitad de camino

half-way² *adj* (*before n*) ‹*point*› medio; ‹*stage*› intermedio; **the ~ mark** el punto medio, la mitad

half-yearly /'hæfjɪrli ‖,hɑːf'jɪəli/ *adj* semestral

hall /hɔːl/ *n* ①**(a)** (vestibule) vestíbulo *m*, entrada *f* **(b)** (corridor) (AmE) pasillo *m*, corredor *m* ②**(a)** (for gatherings) salón *m* **(b)** (in castle, mansion) sala *f* ③(student residence) (BrE) residencia *f* universitaria *or* de estudiantes, colegio *m* mayor (Esp) ④(large country house) (BrE) casa *f* solariega

halleluja /ˌhælɪˈluːjə ‖,hælɪˈljʉːjə/ *interj* ¡aleluya!

hallmark /'hɔːlmɑːrk ‖'hɔːlmɑːk/ *n* **(a)** (on gold, silver) contraste *m*, sello *m* (de contraste) **(b)** (distinguishing characteristic) distintivo *m*, sello *m*

hallo /həˈləʊ/ *interj* ▶ HELLO

hall of residence *n* (*pl* **~s of residence**) (BrE) ▶ HALL 3

Halloween, Hallowe'en /ˌhæləʊˈiːn/ *n* víspera *f* del día de Todos los Santos

hallucination /həˌluːsṇˈeɪʃən ‖həˈluːsɪˈneɪʃən/ *n* alucinación *f*

hallway /'hɔːlweɪ/ *n* ▶ HALL 1

halo /'heɪləʊ/ *n* (*pl* **-los** *or* **-loes**) **(a)** (Art, Relig) aureola *f*, halo *m* **(b)** (Astron, Opt) halo *m*

halt¹ /hɔːlt ‖hɒlt, hɔːlt/ *n*: **to come to a ~** pararse

halt² *vi* detenerse* (frml); **~!** (Mil) ¡alto!
■ ~ *vt* ‹*vehicle/troops*› detener* (frml); ‹*process*› atajar, detener* (frml); ‹*work/production*› interrumpir

halter /'hɔːltər ‖'hɒltə(r), 'hɔː-/ *n* cabestro *m*, ronzal *m*

halve /hæv ‖hɑːv/ *vt* **(a)** (reduce by half) ‹*expense/time/length*› reducir* a la mitad *or* en un 50%; ‹*number*› dividir por dos **(b)** (divide into halves) partir por la mitad
■ ~ *vi* reducirse* a la mitad *or* en un 50%

halves /hævz ‖hɑːvz/ *pl of* HALF¹

ham /hæm/ *n* ①(Culin) (cured) jamón *m* (crudo), jamón *m* serrano (Esp); (cooked) jamón *m* (cocido), jamón *m* (de) York (Esp) ②(Theat) *actor* extravagantemente histriónico

hamburger /'hæmbɜːrgər ‖'hæmbɜːgə(r)/ *n* hamburguesa *f*

hamlet /'hæmlət ‖'hæmlɪt/ *n* aldea *f*, caserío *m*

hammer¹ /'hæmər ‖'hæmə(r)/ *n* martillo *m*

hammer² *vt* ‹*nail*› clavar (con un martillo); ‹*metal*› martillar, batir
■ ~ *vi* (strike) dar* golpes; (with hammer) dar* martillazos; **to ~ at** *or* **on the door** golpear la puerta
■ **hammer home** [*v + o + adv, v + adv + o*] ‹*nail*› remachar; ‹*point*› recalcar*, machacar*
■ **hammer out** [*v + o + adv, v + adv + o*] ‹*metal/ dent*› alisar a martillazos; ‹*compromise/deal*› negociar (con mucho toma y daca)

hammock /'hæmək ‖*n* hamaca *f*, hamaca *f* paraguaya (RPl); (Naut) coy *m*

hamper¹ /'hæmpər ‖'hæmpə(r)/ *vt* dificultar

hamper² *n* cesta *f*, canasta *f*

hamster /'hæmstər ‖'hæmstə(r)/ *n* hámster *m*

hamstring /'hæmstrɪŋ/ *n* (of person) ligamento *m* de la corva; (of horse) tendón *m* del corvejón *or* jarrete

hand¹ /hænd/ *n* ①(Anat) mano *f*; **~s off!** ¡quita

las manos de ahí!; ~s up all those in favor que
levanten la mano los que estén a favor; ~s up!
¡manos arriba!

2 (in phrases) **at hand: help was at** ~ la ayuda
estaba en camino; **by hand** ‹make/write/wash› a
mano; ‹deliver› en mano; **hand in hand** (tomados
or agarrados or (esp Esp) cogidos) de la mano;
poverty and disease go ~ **in** ~ la pobreza y la
enfermedad van de la mano; **on hand: the police
were on** ~ la policía estaba cerca; **to have sth on**
~ tener* algo a mano; **out of hand: the situation
is getting out of** ~ la situación se nos (or les etc)
va de las manos; **to reject sth out of** ~ rechazar*
algo de plano; **to hand** (BrE) (within reach) al
alcance de la mano, a (la) mano; (available)
disponible; **to beat sb/win** ~s **down** ganarle a
algn/ganar sin problemas; **to get one's** ~s **on sb/
sth: just wait till I get my** ~s **on him!** ¡vas a ver
cuando lo agarre!; **she can't wait to get her** ~s **on
the new computer** se muere por usar la
computadora nueva; **to give sb/have a free** ~
darle* a algn/tener* carta blanca; **to know a place
like the back of one's** ~ conocer* un sitio al
dedillo; **to try one's** ~ (at sth) probar* (a hacer
algo)

3 **(a)** (agency) mano f; **to have a** ~ **in sth** tener*
parte en algo; **the town had suffered at the** ~s **of
invaders** la ciudad había sufrido a manos de los
invasores **(b)** (assistance) (colloq): **to give sb a** ~
echarle or darle* una mano a algn; **if you need a**
~ si necesitas ayuda **(c) hands** pl (possession,
control, care): **to change** ~s cambiar de dueño; **in
good/capable** ~s en buenas manos; **my life is in
your** ~s mi vida depende de ti; **we've got a
problem on our** ~s tenemos un problema; **the
matter is out of my** ~s el asunto no está en mis
manos

4 (side): **on sb's right/left** ~ a la derecha/
izquierda de algn; **on the one** ~ ... **on the other**
(~) ... por un lado ... por otro (lado) ...

5 (Games) **(a)** (set of cards) mano f, cartas fpl **(b)**
(round of card game) mano f

6 **(a)** (worker) obrero, -ra m,f; (farm ~) peón m
(b) (Naut) marinero m **(c)** (experienced person): **an
old** ~ un veterano, una veterana

7 (applause) (colloq) (no pl): **a big** ~ **for** ... un
gran aplauso para ...

8 (handwriting) (liter) letra f

9 (on clock) manecilla f, aguja f, puntero m
(Andes)

hand² vt **to** ~ **sb sth, to** ~ **sth TO sb** pasarle
algo A algn

■ **hand around,** (BrE also) **hand round** [v + o +
adv, v + adv + o] (distribute) repartir, distribuir*;
(offer round) ‹cakes› ofrecer*

■ **hand down** [v + o + adv, v + adv + o] (pass
down) ‹custom/heirloom/story› transmitir; ‹clothes›
pasar

■ **hand in** [v + o + adv, v + adv + o] ‹homework/
form/ticket› entregar*; ‹resignation› presentar

■ **hand on** [v + o + adv, v + adv + o] ‹skills/
knowledge› transmitir, pasar; ‹object/photograph›
pasar

■ **hand out** [v + o + adv, v + adv + o] repartir,
distribuir*; ‹advice› dar*

■ **hand over** [v + o + adv, v + adv + o] **(a)**
(relinquish) entregar* **(b)** (transfer) transferir*

■ **hand round** (BrE) ▶ HAND AROUND

hand: ~**bag** n (used by women) cartera f or (Esp)

bolso m or (Méx) bolsa f; (small suitcase) (AmE)
maletín m; ~ **baggage,** (BrE) ~ **luggage** n
equipaje m de mano; ~**ball** n **(a)** (game — in US)
frontón m, pelota f; (— in Europe) balonmano m,
handball m (AmL) **(b)** (in soccer) mano f; ~**book**
n manual m; ~**brake** n (on bicycle) (AmE) freno
m (de pastilla); (BrE Auto) freno m de mano;
~**craft** n ▶ HANDICRAFT; ~ **cream** n crema f
de manos or para las manos; ~**cuff** vt esposar,
ponerle* esposas a; ~**cuffs** pl n esposas fpl

handful /'hændfʊl/ n **(a)** (amount) puñado m **(b)**
(small number) (+ sing o pl vb) puñado m; **a** ~ **of
people** unas cuantas personas **(c)** (troublesome
person or people) (no pl): **that child is a real** ~ ese
niño da mucho trabajo

hand grenade n granada f (de mano)

handicap¹ /'hændɪkæp/ n **1** **(a)** (disability):
physical ~ impedimento m físico; **mental** ~
retraso m mental **(b)** (disadvantage) desventaja f
2 (Sport) (in golf, polo) hándicap m; (penalty)
desventaja f

handicap² vt **-pp-** ‹person/chances›
perjudicar*

handicapped /'hændɪkæpt/ adj disminuido,
discapacitado, minusválido; **mentally/physically**
~ disminuido or discapacitado or minusválido
psíquico/físico

handicraft /'hændɪkræft ‖'hændɪkrɑːft/,
handcraft n **(a)** (skill) artesanía f, trabajo m
artesanal **(b)** (product) producto m de artesanía

handiwork /'hændiwɜːrk ‖'hændiwɜːk/ n **(a)**
(craftsmanship) trabajo m **(b)** (product) artesanías
fpl, objetos mpl artesanales **(c)** (doing) (pej) obra
f; **it looks like Laura's** ~ **to me** a mí me parece
obra de Laura

handkerchief /'hæŋkərtʃəf, -tʃiːf
‖'hæŋkətʃɪf, -tʃiːf/ n (pl **-chieves** /-tʃiːvz/ or
-chiefs) pañuelo m

handle¹ /'hændl/ n (of cup, jug, bag) asa f‡; (of
door) picaporte m; (knob) pomo m; (of drawer)
tirador m, manija f; (of broom, knife, spade) mango
m; (of wheelbarrow) brazo m; (of pump) manivela f

handle² vt **1** **(a)** (touch) tocar*; ❾ **handle with
care** frágil **(b)** (manipulate, manage) ‹vehicle/
weapon› manejar; ‹chemicals› manipular **2** (deal
with) ‹people› tratar; ‹situation/affair› manejar; **he
can't** ~ **the job** (colloq) no puede con el trabajo
3 **(a)** (be responsible for) ‹business/financial
matters› encargarse* or ocuparse de, llevar **(b)**
(do business in) ‹goods/commodities› comerciar con
(c) ‹computer» ‹data› procesar

handlebar /'hændlbɑːr ‖'hændlbɑː(r)/ n (often
pl) ~**(s)** manillar m, manubrio m (AmL)

handling /'hændlɪŋ/ n **1** (treatment — of situation)
manejo m; (— of subject) tratamiento m **2** **(a)**
(Busn) porte m **(b)** (Aviat) handling m **(c)** (Auto)
manejo m

handling charge n cargo m por
tramitación

hand: ~ **luggage** n (BrE) equipaje m de mano;
~**-made** /'hænd'meɪd/ adj hecho a mano;
~**-me-down** n: prenda usada o heredada;
~**out** n **(a)** (of money, food) dádiva f **(b)** (advertising
leaflet) folleto m **(c)** (at lecture, in class) notas fpl
(que se distribuyen a los asistentes); ~**picked**
/'hænd'pɪkt/ adj cuidadosamente seleccionado;
~**rail** n (on stairs, slope) pasamanos m; (on bridge, ···⟩

ship) baranda *f*, barandilla *f*; ~**set** *n* auricular *m*, tubo *m* (RPl); ~**shake** *n* apretón *m* de manos; ~ **signal** *n* (Auto) seña *f* (*hecha con la mano*); (by referee, coach) (AmE) señal *f*

handsome /'hænsəm/ **handsomer, handsomest** *adj* **(a)** (attractive) ⟨*man*⟩ apuesto, buen mozo (AmL), guapo (esp Esp, Méx) **(b)** ⟨*gift/ offer*⟩ generoso

hand: ~**s-on** /'hændz'ɑ:n ‖'hændz,ɒn/ *adj* (*before n*) ⟨*instruction/experience*⟩ práctico **(b)** (Comput) manual; ~**stand** *n*: to do a ~**stand** hacer* la vertical *or* (Esp) el pino, pararse de manos (AmL); ~**-to-mouth** /'hændtə'mavθ/ *adj* pobre, precario; ~**-wash** /'hænd'wɔːʃ ‖'hænd,wɒʃ/ *vt* lavar a mano; ~**writing** *n* letra *f*, ~**written** /'hænd'rɪtn/ *adj* manuscrito, escrito a mano

handy /'hændi/ *adj* **-dier, -diest** (colloq) ☐1 (*pred*) **(a)** (readily accessible) a mano **(b)** (conveniently situated) cerca, a mano ☐2 (useful) práctico; **to come in** ~ venir* bien, resultar útil ☐3 ⟨*person*⟩ hábil, habilidoso

handyman /'hændimæn/ *n* (*pl* **-men** /-men/) *hombre habilidoso para trabajos de carpintería, albañilería etc*

hang[1] /hæŋ/ *vt* ☐1 (*past & past p* **hung**) **(a)** (suspend) ⟨*coat/picture*⟩ colgar* **(b)** (put in position) ⟨*door/gate*⟩ colocar* **(c)** to ~ one's head bajar la cabeza
☐2 (*past & past p* **hanged** *or* **hung**) (execute) ahorcar*
■ ~ *vi* ☐1 (*past p* **hung**) **(a)** (be suspended) colgar*, estar* colgado; **to** ~ **BY/FROM/ON sth** colgar* DE algo; **it's** ~**ing on the wall** está colgado en la pared **(b)** (hover) «*fog/smoke*» flotar; «*bird*» planear, cernerse*; **he still has the court case** ~**ing over him** todavía tiene el juicio pendiente **(c)** «*clothing/fabric*» caer*
☐2 (*past & past p* **hanged** *or* **hung**) (be executed): **he should** ~ **for his crime** debería ir a la horca por este crimen
■ **hang about** [*v* + *adv*] ▶ HANG AROUND
■ **hang around** (colloq) [*v* + *adv*] **(a)** (wait) esperar **(b)** (stay) quedarse **(c)** (spend time idly): **they just** ~ **on street corners** pasan el tiempo en la calle, holgazaneando; **to** ~ **around WITH sb** andar* *or* juntarse CON algn
■ **hang on** ☐1 [*v* + *adv*] **(a)** (wait) esperar **(b)** (keep hold) **to** ~ **on TO sth: you** ~ **on to this end of the rope** tú sostén esta punta de la cuerda **(c)** (keep) (colloq) **to** ~ **on TO sth** conservar *or* guardar algo **(d)** (in a crisis) aguantar, resistir
☐2 [*v* + *prep* + *o*] (depend on) «*outcome/decision*» depender de
■ **hang out** ☐1 [*v* + *o* + *adv*, *v* + *adv* + *o*] ⟨*washing*⟩ tender*, colgar*; ⟨*flag*⟩ poner*
☐2 [*v* + *adv*] (dangle) «*wires*» estar* suelto; **with his shirt/tongue** ~**ing out** con la camisa/la lengua afuera
■ **hang up** ☐1 [*v* + *adv*] (put down receiver) colgar*, cortar (CS)
☐2 [*v* + *o* + *adv*, *v* + *adv* + *o*] ⟨*coat*⟩ colgar*

hang[2] *n* (*no pl*) **to get the** ~ **of sth** (colloq)

agarrarle la onda a algo (AmL fam), cogerle* el tranquillo a algo (Esp fam), agarrarle la mano a algo (CS fam)

hangar /'hæŋər ‖'hæŋə(r)/ *n* hangar *m*

hanger /'hæŋər ‖'hæŋə(r)/ *n* (clothes or coat ~) percha *f*, gancho *m* (para la ropa) (AmL)

hang: ~ **glider** *n* ala *f*; delta, deslizador *m* (Méx); ~ **gliding** /'glaɪdɪŋ/ *n* vuelo *m* con ala delta *or* (Méx) en deslizador

hanging /'hæŋɪŋ/ *n* ☐1 (execution) ejecución *f* (*en la horca*) ☐2 (wall ~) tapiz *m*

hanging basket *n*: cesto colgante para plantas

hang: ~**man** *n* (*pl* **-men** /-mən/) verdugo *m*; ~**over** *n* **(a)** (from drinking) resaca *f*, cruda *f* (AmC, Méx fam), guayabo *m* (Col fam), ratón *m* (Ven fam) **(b)** (something surviving) vestigio *m*, reliquia *f*; ~**-up** *n* (colloq) complejo *m*, trauma *m*

hanker /'hæŋkər ‖'hæŋkə(r)/ *vi* **to** ~ AFTER *o* FOR sth anhelar *or* ansiar* algo

hanky, hankie /'hæŋki/ *n* (*pl* **-kies**) (colloq) pañuelo *m*

Hanukkah, Hanukah /'hɑːnəkə/ *n* Januká *m*, Hanukkah *m* (*fiesta judía de la dedicación del Templo*)

haphazard /'hæp'hæzərd ‖,hæp'hæzəd/ *adj* **(a)** (random): **they promote people in a very** ~ **way** ascienden a la gente caprichosamente *or* al azar **(b)** (without order): **his approach is very** ~ no es coherente en su enfoque

hapless /'hæpləs ‖'hæplɪs/ *adj* (*before n*) (liter *or* journ) desafortunado, desventurado (liter)

happen /'hæpən/ *vi* ☐1 **(a)** (occur) pasar, suceder, ocurrir **(b)** (befall, become of) **to** ~ **TO sb** pasarle A algn ☐2 **to** ~ **to + INF: she** ~**ed to be there** dio la casualidad de que estaba ahí; **if you** ~ **to see her ...** si por casualidad la ves ...
■ ~ *v impers*: **it (just) so** ~**s that ...** da la casualidad de que ...

happening /'hæpənɪŋ/ *n* suceso *m*

happily /'hæpəli ‖'hæpɪli/ *adv* ☐1 **(a)** ⟨*smile/ laugh*⟩ alegremente; **to be** ~ **married** ser* feliz en el matrimonio **(b)** (gladly) (*usu before vb*) ⟨*help*⟩ con mucho gusto ☐2 (fortunately) (*indep*) por suerte, afortunadamente

happiness /'hæpinəs ‖'hæpinɪs/ *n* felicidad *f*

happy /'hæpi/ *adj* **-pier, -piest** ☐1 **(a)** (joyful, content) ⟨*person/home*⟩ feliz; ⟨*smile*⟩ de felicidad, alegre **(b)** (pleased) (*pred*) **to be** ~ alegrarse **(c)** (satisfied) (*pred*) **to be** ~ (WITH sth) estar* contento (CON algo) ☐2 ⟨*days/occasion*⟩ feliz; ~ **birthday** feliz cumpleaños

happy-go-lucky /'hæpigəv'lʌki/ *adj* despreocupado

harangue /hə'ræŋ/ *vt* arengar*

harass /'hærəs, hə'ræs/ *vt* **(a)** (persistently annoy) acosar **(b)** (Mil) hostigar*

harassment /'hærəsmənt, hə'ræs-/ *n* acoso *m*; **racial** ~ hostilidad *f* racial; **sexual** ~ acoso *m* sexual

harbor¹, (BrE) **harbour** /'hɑːrbər ‖'hɑːbə(r)/ *n* puerto *m*

harbor², (BrE) **harbour** *vt* (a) (shelter) ⟨*fugitive*⟩ albergar*, dar* refugio a (b) ⟨*desire/ suspicion*⟩ albergar* (liter); **to ~ a grudge** guardar rencor

hard¹ /hɑːrd ‖hɑːd/ *adj* **-er, -est** ☐ (a) (firm, solid) ⟨*object/surface*⟩ duro (b) (forceful) ⟨*push/ knock*⟩ fuerte
☐ (a) (difficult) ⟨*question/subject*⟩ difícil; ⟨*task*⟩ arduo; **I find that ~ to believe** me cuesta creerlo; **to learn sth the ~ way** aprender algo a base de cometer errores (b) (severe) ⟨*winter/climate/ master*⟩ duro, severo; **to give sb a ~ time** hacérselas* pasar mal a algn; **don't be too ~ on him** no seas demasiado duro con él; **~ luck** mala suerte (c) (tough, cynical) ⟨*person/attitude*⟩ duro
☐ (concentrated, strenuous) ⟨*work*⟩ duro; **children are very ~ work** los niños dan mucho trabajo; **he's a ~ worker** es muy trabajador
☐ (definite) ⟨*evidence*⟩ concluyente
☐ (sharp, harsh) ⟨*light/voice*⟩ fuerte
☐ (a) (in strongest form): **~ drugs** drogas *fpl* duras; **~ liquor** bebidas *fpl* (alcohólicas) fuertes; **~ porn** porno *m* duro (b) ⟨*water*⟩ dura

hard² *adv* **-er, -est** ☐ (a) (with force) ⟨*pull/ push*⟩ con fuerza; ⟨*hit*⟩ fuerte (b) (strenuously) ⟨*work*⟩ mucho, duro (c) (intently) ⟨*listen*⟩ atentamente ☐ (heavily) ⟨*rain/snow*⟩ fuerte, mucho; ⟨*pant/breathe*⟩ pesadamente ☐ (severely): **to be ~ hit** ser* muy afectado; **to feel ~ done by:** **she feels ~ done by** piensa que la han tratado injustamente

hard: **~-and-fast** /'hɑːrdn̩'fæst ‖'hɑːdən'fɑːst/ *adj* (no comp, usu before n) absoluto; **~back** *n* (book) libro *m* de tapa dura *or* en cartoné; **~ball** *n* (AmE) béisbol *m*; **~board** *n* cartón *m* madera; **~-boiled** /'hɑːrd'bɔɪld ‖,hɑːd'bɔɪld/ *adj* (a) ⟨*egg*⟩ duro (b) (unsentimental) endurecido; **~ disk** *n* disco *m* duro; **~-earned** /'hɑːrd'ɜːrnd ‖'hɑːd,ɜːnd/ *adj* (usu before n) ⟨*cash*⟩ ganado con el sudor de la frente

harden /'hɑːrdn̩ ‖'hɑːdn̩/ *vt* (a) (make hard) ⟨*clay/cement/skin*⟩ endurecer*; ⟨*steel/glass*⟩ templar (b) (make tough, unfeeling) ⟨*person*⟩ endurecer*; **you must ~ your heart and tell him to go** tienes que hacerte fuerte y decirle que se vaya
■ **~** *vi* (a) (become hard, rigid) endurecerse* (b) (become inflexible) «*attitude*» volverse* inflexible

hardened /'hɑːrdn̩d ‖'hɑːdn̩d/ *adj* (before n) ⟨*sinner/drinker*⟩ empedernido; ⟨*criminal*⟩ habitual

hard: **~ hat** *n* (Clothing, Const) casco *m*; **~-headed** /'hɑːrd'hedəd ‖,hɑːd'hedɪd/ *adj* (a) (practical, realistic) práctico, realista (b) (stubborn) (AmE) testarudo, cabezota (fam); **~-hearted** /'hɑːrd'hɑːrtəd ‖,hɑːd'hɑːtɪd/ *adj* duro de corazón; **~-hitting** /'hɑːrd'hɪtɪŋ ‖,hɑːd'hɪtɪŋ/ *adj* implacable, feroz; **~ labor**, (BrE) **~ labour** *n* trabajos *mpl* forzados; **~-liner** /'hɑːrd'laɪnər ‖,hɑːd'laɪnə(r)/ *n* partidario, -ria *m,f* de la línea dura

hardly /'hɑːrdli ‖'hɑːdli/ *adv* (a) (scarcely): **~ anyone/anything** casi nadie/nada; **~ ever** casi nunca; **he ~ knew her** apenas la conocía (b) (surely not): **it's ~ what you'd call a masterpiece** no es precisamente una obra maestra

hardness /'hɑːrdnəs ‖'hɑːdnɪs/ *n* dureza *f*

hard: **~ of hearing** *adj* duro de oído; **~-pressed** /'hɑːrd'prest ‖,hɑːd'prest/ *adj* (pred) **~ pressed** ⟨*industry/nation/staff*⟩ en apuros; **~ sell** *n* (no pl) venta *f* agresiva

hardship /'hɑːrdʃɪp ‖'hɑːdʃɪp/ *n*: **to experience o suffer great ~** pasar muchos apuros; **the ~s of the journey** las penurias del viaje

hard: **~ shoulder** *n* (BrE) arcén *m*, berma *f* (Andes), acotamiento *m* (Méx), banquina *f* (RPl), hombrillo *m* (Ven); **~ up** *adj* (colloq) (pred) **to be ~ up** estar* mal de dinero; **~ware** /'hɑːrdwer ‖'hɑːdweə(r)/ *n* (a) (ironmongery) ferretería *f*; (before n) **~ware store** ferretería *f* (b) (Mil): **military ~ware** armamento *m* (c) (Comput) hardware *m*, soporte *m* físico, equipo *m*; **~-wearing** /'hɑːrd'werɪŋ ‖,hɑːd'weərɪŋ/ *adj* (BrE) resistente; **~-working** /'hɑːrd'wɜːrkɪŋ ‖,hɑːd'wɜːkɪŋ/ *adj* trabajador

hardy /'hɑːrdi ‖'hɑːdi/ *adj* **-dier, -diest** ⟨*person/animal*⟩ fuerte; ⟨*plant*⟩ resistente (a las heladas etc)

hare /her ‖heə(r)/ *n* liebre *f*

haricot (bean) /'hærɪkəʊ/ *n* frijol *m or* (Esp) alubia *f or* judía *f or* (CS) poroto *m* (de color blanco)

hark back /hɑːrk ‖hɑːk/ *vi* **to ~ ~ TO sth** «*person*» rememorar algo; «*book*» evocar* algo

harm¹ /hɑːrm ‖hɑːm/ *n* daño *m*; **to do ~ to sb/ sth** hacerle* daño a algn/algo; **there's no ~ in asking** con preguntar no se pierde nada; **he won't come to any ~** no le va a pasar nada; **to be out of ~'s way** estar* a salvo

harm² *vt* ⟨*person/object*⟩ hacerle* daño a; ⟨*reputation/career*⟩ perjudicar*

harmful /'hɑːrmfəl ‖'hɑːmfəl/ *adj* ⟨*substance*⟩ nocivo; ⟨*influence*⟩ pernicioso, dañino; ⟨*effect*⟩ perjudicial

harmless /'hɑːrmləs ‖'hɑːmlɪs/ *adj* ⟨*animal/ person*⟩ inofensivo; ⟨*substance*⟩ inocuo; ⟨*joke/ suggestion/fun*⟩ inocente

harmonica /hɑːr'mɑːnɪkə ‖hɑː'mɒnɪkə/ *n* armónica *f*

harmonious /hɑːr'məʊniəs ‖hɑː'məʊniəs/ *adj* armonioso

harmonize /'hɑːrmənaɪz ‖'hɑːmənaɪz/ *vi* (Mus) cantar en armonía; (be in accord) «*colors/ideas*» armonizar*
■ **~** *vt* ⟨*policies/plans*⟩ armonizar

harmony /'hɑːrməni ‖'hɑːməni/ *n* (pl **-nies**) (Mus) armonía *f*; **in ~** en armonía

harness¹ /'hɑːrnəs ‖'hɑːnɪs/ *n* (a) (for horse) arnés *m*, arreos *mpl* (b) (for baby, on parachute) arnés *m* (c) (safety ~) arnés *m* de seguridad

harness² *vt* (a) (put harness on) ⟨*horse*⟩ enjaezar*, ponerle* los arreos *or* el arnés a (b) (utilize) ⟨*energy/resources*⟩ aprovechar, utilizar*

harp /hɑːrp ‖hɑːp/ *n* arpa *f*♯
■ **harp on** [v + adv] (colloq) **to ~ on ABOUT sth** insistir SOBRE algo

harpoon¹ /hɑːr'puːn ‖hɑː'puːn/ *n* arpón *m*

harpoon² *vt* arponear

harrowing /'hærəʊɪŋ/ *adj* ⟨*experience*⟩ angustioso, terrible; ⟨*tale*⟩ desgarrador

harry /'hæri/ *vt* **-ries, -rying, -ried** (a) (raid) ⟨*enemy*⟩ hostilizar* (b) (pester) hostigar*, acosar

harsh /hɑːrʃ ‖hɑːʃ/ adj ⟨punishment⟩ duro, severo; ⟨words/conditions⟩ duro; ⟨light⟩ fuerte; ⟨climate⟩ riguroso; ⟨contrast⟩ violento; ⟨color⟩ chillón; ⟨sound⟩ discordante; ⟨tone/texture⟩ áspero

harshly /'hɑːrʃli ‖'hɑːʃli/ adv ⟨judge/punish/ speak⟩ severamente, con severidad

harvest¹ /'hɑːrvəst ‖'hɑːvɪst/ n **(a)** (of grain) cosecha f, siega f; (of fruit, vegetables) cosecha f, recolección f; (of grapes) vendimia f **(b)** (yield) cosecha f

harvest² vt ⟨crop/wheat⟩ cosechar; ⟨grapes⟩ vendimiar; ⟨field⟩ realizar* la cosecha en

harvester /'hɑːrvəstər ‖'hɑːvɪstə(r)/ n **(a)** (machine) cosechadora f **(b)** (person) segador, -dora m,f

has /hæz, weak form həz, əz/ 3rd pers sing pres of HAVE

has-been /'hæzbɪn ‖'hæzbiːn/ n (colloq & pej) nombre m del pasado

hash /hæʃ/ n **(a)** (Culin) plato de carne y verduras picadas y doradas **(b)** (muddle): to make a ~ of sth (colloq) hacer* algo muy mal

hash browns pl n (AmE colloq) papas y cebolla doradas en la sartén

hashish /'hæʃiːʃ/ n hachís m

hasn't /'hæznt/ = has not

hassle¹ /'hæsəl/ n (colloq) lío m (fam), rollo m (fam)

hassle² vt (colloq) fastidiar, jorobar (fam)

haste /heɪst/ n prisa f, apuro m (AmL)

hasten /'heɪsn̩/ vt ⟨process⟩ acelerar; ⟨defeat/ death⟩ adelantar
■ ~ vi apresurarse, apurarse (AmL)

hastily /'heɪstəli ‖'heɪstɪli/ adv **(a)** (quickly) ⟨built/thought up⟩ a toda prisa, apresuradamente **(b)** (rashly) ⟨speak/act⟩ con precipitación, precipitadamente

hasty /'heɪsti/ adj **-tier, -tiest (a)** (quick) ⟨glance/meal⟩ rápido **(b)** (rash) ⟨move/decision/ judgment⟩ precipitado; I think you're being rather ~ creo que te precipitas

hat /hæt/ n sombrero m

hatch¹ /hætʃ/ vt **(a)** ⟨egg⟩ incubar **(b)** ~ (out) ⟨chick⟩ empollar **(c)** (devise) (pej) ⟨plot/scheme⟩ tramar, urdir
■ ~ vi **(a)** ⟨egg⟩ romperse* **(b)** ~ (out) ⟨chick⟩ salir* del cascarón, nacer*

hatch² n **(a)** (opening, cover) trampilla f; (Aviat, Naut) escotilla f **(b)** (serving ~) ventanilla f (que comunica cocina y comedor)

hatchback /'hætʃbæk/ n (car) coche m con tres/cinco puertas; (door) puerta f trasera

hatchet /'hætʃət ‖'hætʃɪt/ n hacha f‡, hachuela f; to bury the ~ enterrar* el hacha de guerra

hate¹ /heɪt/ vt odiar, detestar

hate² n **(a)** (hatred) odio m **(b)** (object of hatred) ▶ PET² B

hatred /'heɪtrəd ‖'heɪtrɪd/ n odio m

hat trick n: to score a ~ marcar* tres goles (or tantos etc) en un partido

haughty /'hɔːti/ adj **-tier, -tiest** altivo, altanero

haul¹ /hɔːl/ vt **(a)** (drag) ⟨logs/load⟩ llevar arrastrando; the fishermen ~ed in their nets los pescadores cobraron las redes **(b)** (Transp) transportar

haul² n **1** (catch — of fish) redada f; (— of stolen goods) botín m **2** (distance) (Transp) recorrido m, trayecto m

haulage /'hɔːlɪdʒ/ n **(a)** (activity) transporte m; (before n) ~ **contractor** transportista mf **(b)** (charge) (gastos mpl de) transporte m

hauler /'hɔːlər ‖'hɔːlə(r)/, (BrE) **haulier** /'hɔːljə(r)/ n (person) transportista mf; (business) empresa f de transportes

haunch /hɔːntʃ/ n (usu pl) (of animal) anca f‡; (of horse) grupa f, anca f‡; (of person) cadera f

haunt¹ /hɔːnt/ vt «ghost» rondar; «memory/ idea» perseguir*

haunt² n: we went to all her old ~s fuimos a todos los sitios a los que solía ir

haunted /'hɔːntəd ‖'hɔːntɪd/ adj ⟨house⟩ embrujado; ⟨look⟩ angustiado

haunting /'hɔːntɪŋ/ adj evocador e inquietante

Havana /hə'vænə/ n La Habana

have /hæv, weak forms həv, əv/ (3rd pers sing pres **has**; past & past p **had**) vt
I **1** (possess) tener*; I ~ o (esp BrE) **I've got two cats** tengo dos gatos
2 (hold, have at one's disposal) tener*; **can I ~ a sheet of paper?** ¿me das una hoja de papel?; **I've (got) a lot to do** tengo mucho que hacer
3 **(a)** (receive) ⟨letter/news⟩ tener*, recibir; **to ~ had it** (colloq): **I've had it** (I'm in trouble) estoy frito (AmL), me la he cargado (Esp fam); (I've lost my chance) la he fastidiado (fam); **to ~ it in for sb** (colloq) tenerle* manía or tirria a algn (fam) **(b)** (obtain) conseguir*; **they were the only seats to be had** eran los únicos asientos que había
4 (consume) ⟨steak/spaghetti⟩ comer, tomar (Esp); ⟨champagne/beer⟩ tomar; ⟨cigarette⟩ fumar(se); **to ~ something to eat/drink** comer/beber algo; **to ~ breakfast** desayunar; **to ~ lunch** almorzar* or (esp Esp, Méx) comer; **to ~ dinner** cenar, comer (AmL)
5 **(a)** (experience, undergo) ⟨accident⟩ tener*; **~ a nice day!** ¡adiós!; ¡que le (or te etc) vaya bien!; **we had a very pleasant evening** pasamos una noche muy agradable; **she had a heart attack** le dio un ataque al corazón **(b)** (organize) ⟨party⟩ hacer*, dar*; ⟨meeting⟩ tener* **(c)** (suffer from) ⟨cancer/ diabetes/flu⟩ tener*; **to ~ a cold** estar* resfriado
6 (give birth to) ⟨baby⟩ tener*
7 (colloq) (swindle, dupe): **you've been had!** ¡te han timado or engañado!
II **1** (causative use): **we'll ~ it clean in no time** enseguida lo limpiamos or lo dejamos limpio; **he had them all in tears** los hizo llorar a todos; **you had me worried** me tenías preocupado; **to ~ sth +** PAST P: **we had it repaired** lo hicimos arreglar, lo mandamos (a) arreglar (AmL); **to ~ one's hair cut** cortarse el pelo
2 (indicating what happens to sb): **to have sth +** PAST P: **he had his bicycle stolen** le robaron la bicicleta
3 **(a)** (allow) (with neg) tolerar, consentir*; **I won't ~ it!** ¡no lo consentiré or toleraré! **(b)** (accept, believe) aceptar, creer*; **she wouldn't ~ it** no lo quiso aceptar or creer
4 (indicating state, position) tener*; **I had the radio on** tenía la radio puesta

■ ~ *v aux*
I [1] (*used to form perfect tenses*) haber*; **I ~/had seen her** la he/había visto; **~ you been waiting long?** ¿hace mucho que esperas?; **if I'd known that …** si hubiera sabido que …; **when he had finished, she …** cuando terminó *or* (liter) cuando hubo terminado, ella …
[2] **(a)** (in tags): **you've met Joe, ~n't you?** conoces a Joe ¿no? *or* ¿no es cierto? *or* ¿no es verdad?; **you ~n't lost the key, ~ you?** ¡no habrás perdido la llave …! **(b)** (elliptical use): **you may ~ forgiven him, but I ~n't** puede que tú lo hayas perdonado, pero yo no; **the clock has stopped — so it has!** el reloj se ha parado — ¡es verdad! *or* ¡es cierto!; **you've forgotten something — ~ I?** te has olvidado de algo — ¿sí?
II (expressing obligation): **to ~ to + INF** tener* QUE + INF; **you don't ~ to be an expert to realize that** no hay que *or* no se necesita ser un experto para darse cuenta de eso
■ **have back** [1] [*v + o + adv, v + adv + o*] (receive back): **can I ~ the ring back?** ¿me devuelves el anillo?
[2] [*v + o + adv*] ⟨*guests*⟩ **to ~ sb back** (invite again) volver* a invitar a algn; (reciprocate invitation) devolverle* a algn una invitación
■ **have on** [*v + o + adv*] (tease) (colloq) **to ~ sb on** tomarle el pelo a algn (fam)
■ **have out** [*v + o + adv*] **(a)** (have removed): **to ~ a tooth out** sacarse* una muela; **she had her tonsils out** la operaron de las amígdalas **(b)** (discuss forcefully) **to ~ it out WITH sb** ponerle* las cosas claras A algn

haven /'heɪvən/ *n* **(a)** (refuge) refugio *m* **(b)** (port) (liter) puerto *m*

haven't /'hævənt/ = **have not**

haversack /'hævərsæk ‖ 'hævəsæk/ *n* mochila *f*, morral *m*

haves /hævz/ *pl n* **the ~ and the have-nots** los ricos y los pobres *or* los desposeídos

havoc /'hævək/ *n*: **the accident caused ~** el accidente creó gran confusión; **the children created ~** los niños armaron un lío tremendo (fam); **to play ~ with sth** trastocar* *or* desbaratar algo

Hawaii /hə'waɪi:/ *n* Hawai *m*

Hawaiian /hə'waɪən/ *adj* hawaiano

hawk¹ /hɔ:k/ *n* halcón *m*

hawk² *vt* ⟨*goods/wares*⟩ vocear, pregonar

hawthorn /'hɔ:θɔ:rn ‖ 'hɔ:θɔ:n/ *n* espino *m*

hay /heɪ/ *n* heno *m*

hay: ~ fever *n* fiebre *f* del heno; **~rick** /'heɪrɪk/ *n* almiar *m*; **~seed** *n* (AmE sl) ► YOKEL; **~stack** *n* almiar *m*; **~wire** *adj* (colloq) (*pred*): **to go ~wire** «*person*» perder* la chaveta (fam); «*machine*» estropearse, descomponerse* (AmL)

hazard¹ /'hæzərd ‖ 'hæzəd/ *n* peligro *m*, riesgo *m*

hazard² *vt* (frml) ⟨*remark/question*⟩ aventurar; **to ~ a guess** aventurar una respuesta

hazard lights, (BrE also) **hazard warning lights** *pl n* (Auto) luces *fpl* de emergencia

hazardous /'hæzərdəs ‖ 'hæzədəs/ *adj* peligroso, arriesgado

haze /heɪz/ *n* (*no pl*) (due to humidity) neblina *f*, bruma *f*; (due to heat) calima *f*

hazel /'heɪzəl/ *n* **(a)** (plant) avellano *m* **(b)** (wood) (madera *f* de) avellano *m* **(c)** (color) color *m* avellana; (*before n*) ⟨*eyes*⟩ color avellana *adj inv*

hazelnut /'heɪzəlnʌt/ *n* avellana *f*

hazy /'heɪzi/ *adj* **hazier, haziest (a)** ⟨*day*⟩ (due to humidity) neblinoso, brumoso; (due to heat) de calima **(b)** ⟨*memory/idea/distinction*⟩ vago, confuso

he /hi:, *weak form* i/ *pron* él
■ Note Although *él* is given as the main translation of *he*, it is in practice used only for emphasis, or to avoid ambiguity: *he went to the theater* fue al teatro; *she went to the theater, he went to the cinema* ella fue al teatro y él fue al cine; *he did it* él lo hizo.

head¹ /hed/ *n* [1] (Anat) cabeza *f*; **a fine ~ of hair** una buena cabellera; **from ~ to foot** *o* **toe** de pies a cabeza, de arriba (a) abajo; **~ over heels: she tripped and went ~ over heels down the steps** tropezó y cayó rodando escaleras abajo; **to be ~ over heels in love** estar* locamente enamorado; **to go to sb's ~** subírsele a la cabeza a algn; **to make ~ or tail** *or* (AmE also) **~s or tails of sth** entender* algo
[2] (mind, brain) cabeza *f*; **I said the first thing that came into my ~** dije lo primero que se me ocurrió; **she added it up in her ~** hizo la suma mentalmente; **she has a good ~ for business** tiene cabeza para los negocios; **I've no ~ for heights** sufro de vértigo; **it never entered my ~ that …** ni se me pasó por la cabeza que …; **to keep/lose one's ~** mantener*/perder* la calma
[3] **(a)** (of nail, tack, pin) cabeza *f*; (of spear, arrow) punta *f*; (of hammer) cabeza *f*; (on beer) espuma *f* **(b)** (top end — of bed, table) cabecera *f*; (— of page, letter) encabezamiento *m*; (— of procession, line) cabeza *f*
[4] **(a)** (chief) director, -tora *m,f*; **~ of state** jefe, -fa *m,f* de Estado; **the ~ of the household** el/la cabeza de familia; (*before n*) ⟨*waiter*⟩ maître *m*, capitán *m* de meseros (Méx) **(b)** (~ teacher) (esp BrE) director, -tora *m,f* (de colegio)
[5] (person): **$15 per ~** 15 dólares por cabeza *or* persona
[6] (crisis): **to come to a ~** hacer* crisis
[7] (magnetic device) (Audio, Comput) cabeza *f*, cabezal *m* (of drill) cabezal *m*
[8] (Geog) cabo *m*

head² *vt* [1] **(a)** ⟨*march/procession*⟩ encabezar*, ir* a la cabeza de **(b)** ⟨*revolt*⟩ acaudillar; ⟨*team*⟩ capitanear; ⟨*expedition/department*⟩ dirigir*
[2] (direct) (+ *adv compl*) ⟨*vehicle/ship*⟩ dirigir*
[3] (in soccer) ⟨*ball*⟩ cabecear
[4] ⟨*page/chapter*⟩ encabezar*
■ ~ *vi*: **to ~ west/north** ir* en dirección oeste/norte
■ **head for** [*v + prep + o*] **(a)** (go toward) «*ship*» ir* con rumbo a; **to ~ for home** ponerse* en camino a casa; **the car was ~ing straight for me** el coche venía derecho hacia mí **(b)** (be in danger of): **to be ~ed** *o* **~ing for sth** ir* camino de algo
■ **head off** [1] [*v + adv*] (set out) salir*
[2] [*v + o + adv, v + adv + o*] **(a)** (get in front of) atajar, cortarle el paso a **(b)** (prevent, forestall) ⟨*criticism/threat*⟩ prevenir*

head: ~ache *n* dolor *m* de cabeza; **I've got a ~ache** tengo dolor de cabeza, me duele la cabeza; ⋯⁖

∼**band** n cinta f del pelo, vincha f (AmS), huincha f (Bol, Chi, Per); ∼**board** n cabecera f; ∼**dress** n tocado m

headed /'hedəd ‖'hedɪd/ adj ‹notepaper› con membrete, membretado, membreteado (Andes)

header /'hedər ‖'hedə(r)/ n (in soccer) cabezazo m

head: ∼**first** /'hed'fɜːrst ‖,hed'fɜːst/ adv (a) (with head foremost) de cabeza (b) (over-hastily) precipitadamente; ∼**hunt** vt ofrecerle* un puesto a; ∼**hunter** n (Busn) cazatalentos m

heading /'hedɪŋ/ n (title) encabezamiento m, título m, acápite m (AmL); (letterhead) membrete m

head: ∼**lamp** n faro m; ∼**land** /'hedlənd/ n cabo m; ∼**light** n faro m; ∼**line** n titular m; **the news** ∼**lines** el resumen informativo or de noticias; ∼**long** adv (a) (hastily) precipitadamente (b) (with head foremost) de cabeza; ∼**master** /'hed'mæstər ‖,hed'mɑːstə(r)/ n director m (de colegio); ∼**mistress** /'hed'mɪstrəs ‖,hed'mɪstrɪs/ n directora f (de colegio); ∼ **office** n (oficina f) central f; ∼**-on** /'hed'ɑːn ‖,hed'ɒn/ adj ‹crash/collision› frontal, de frente; ∼**phones** pl n auriculares mpl, cascos mpl; ∼**quarters** /'hed'kwɔːrtərz ‖,hed'kwɔːtəz/ n (pl ∼**quarters**) (+ sing or pl vb) oficina f central; (Mil) cuartel m general; ∼**rest** n reposacabezas m, apoyacabezas m; ∼**room** n altura f

heads /hedz/ adv (on coin) cara f, águilaʒ̞ (Méx); ∼ **or tails?** ¿cara o cruz, ¿águila o sol? (Méx), ¿cara o sello? (Andes, Ven), ¿cara o ceca? (Arg)

head: ∼**scarf** n pañuelo m (de cabeza); ∼**set** n auriculares mpl, cascos mpl; ∼**stand** n: to do a ∼**stand** pararse de cabeza (AmL), hacer* el pino (Esp); ∼ **start** n ventaja f; ∼**stone** n lápida f; ∼**strong** adj testarudo, obstinado; ∼**teacher** /'hed'tiːtʃər ‖,hed'tiːtʃə(r)/ n (BrE) director, -tora m,f (de colegio); ∼**way** n: to make ∼**way** hacer* progresos, avanzar*

heady /'hedi/ adj **-dier, -diest** ‹scent› embriagador; ‹wine› que se sube a la cabeza

heal /hiːl/ vt curar
■ ∼ vi cicatrizar*, cerrarse*

health /helθ/ n salud f; **to be in good/poor** ∼ estar* bien/mal de salud; **your (good)** ∼**!** (proposing a toast) ¡salud!; (before n) ‹policy/ services› sanitario, de salud pública; ‹inspector/ regulations› de sanidad; ∼ **hazard** riesgo m or peligro m para la salud

health: ∼ **care** n asistencia f sanitaria or médica; ∼ **centre** n (BrE) centro m médico or de salud; ∼ **food** n alimentos mpl naturales; ∼ **insurance** n seguro m de enfermedad; ∼ **service** n (in UK) ▶ NATIONAL HEALTH (SERVICE)

healthy /'helθi/ adj **-thier, -thiest** [1] (a) (in good health) ‹person/animal/complexion› sano; **she has a** ∼ **appetite** tiene buen apetito (b) (promoting good health) ‹diet/living/environment› sano, saludable (c) (sound) ‹respect› sano [2] ‹economy/ finances› próspero

heap¹ /hiːp/ n (a) (pile) montón m, pila f (b) (car) (colloq) cacharro m (fam)

heap² vt (a) (make pile) amontonar, apilar (b) (supply liberally): **she** ∼**ed his plate with food** le llenó el plato de comida; **a** ∼**ing** (AmE) o (BrE) ∼**ed spoonful** (Culin) una cucharada colmada

hear /hɪr ‖hɪə(r)/ ‹past & past p **heard** /hɜːrd ‖hɜːd/› vt [1] ‹sound› oír*
[2] (get to know) oír*; **I've** ∼**d so much about you** me han hablado tanto de ti, he oído hablar tanto de ti; **he's very ill, I** ∼ me han dicho que está muy enfermo
[3] (listen to) (a) ‹lecture/broadcast/views› escuchar, oír* (b) (Law) ‹case› ver*; ‹charge› oír*
■ ∼ vi [1] (perceive) oír*; ∼, ∼! ¡eso, eso!, ¡bien dicho!
[2] (get news): **have you** ∼**d?** ¿te has enterado?; **to** ∼ **ABOUT sth** enterarse DE algo; **I haven't** ∼**d from them for months** hace meses que no sé nada de ellos or que no tengo noticias suyas
■ **hear of** [v + prep + o] (a) (encounter, come to know of): **I've** ∼**d of him** he oído hablar de él; **if you** ∼ **of anything interesting, let me know** si te enteras de algo interesante, me lo dices (b) (have news of) tener* noticias or saber* de (c) (allow): **I won't** ∼ **of it!** ¡ni hablar!
■ **hear out** [v + o + adv, v + adv + o] escuchar (hasta el final)

hearing /'hɪrɪŋ ‖'hɪərɪŋ/ n [1] (sense) oído m [2] (a) (consideration) **to give sb a** ∼ escuchar a algn (b) (trial) vista f

hearing aid n audífono m

hearsay /'hɪrseɪ ‖'hɪəseɪ/ n habladurías fpl

hearse /hɜːrs ‖hɜːs/ n coche m fúnebre

heart /hɑːrt ‖hɑːt/ n [1] (Anat) corazón m; (before n) ‹disease› del corazón, cardíaco; ‹operation› de(l) corazón
[2] (seat of emotions): **to have a kind** ∼ tener* buen corazón, ser* de buen corazón; **to have sb's interests at** ∼ preocuparse por algn; **to learn/ know sth by** ∼ aprender/saber* algo de memoria; **my/her/his** ∼ **wasn't in it** lo hacía sin ganas; **to take sth to** ∼ tomarse algo a pecho
[3] (courage, morale) ánimos mpl; **to lose** ∼ descorazonarse, desanimarse; **to take** ∼ animarse; **not to have the** ∼ **to do sth: I didn't have the** ∼ **to tell him** no tuve valor para decírselo
[4] (a) (central part): **the** ∼ **of the city/country** el corazón or centro de la ciudad/del país; **the** ∼ **of the matter** el meollo del asunto (b) (of cabbage, lettuce) cogollo m
[5] (Games) **hearts** (suit) (+ sing or pl vb) corazones mpl

heart: ∼**ache** n pena f, dolor m; ∼ **attack** n ataque m al corazón, infarto m; ∼**beat** n latido m (del corazón); ∼**break** n (a) (grief) congoja f, sufrimiento m (b) (cause of grief) desengaño m; ∼**breaking** adj desgarrador; ∼**broken** adj ‹look/sobs› desconsolado; **she was** ∼**broken when he died** su muerte la dejó destrozada; ∼**burn** n ardor m de estómago; ∼**felt** adj sincero

hearth /hɑ:rθ ‖ hɑ:θ/ n chimenea f, hogar m

heartily /'hɑ:rtl̩i ‖ 'hɑ:tɪli/ adv (a) (warmly) ⟨congratulate/greet⟩ efusivamente (b) (with enthusiasm) ⟨laugh/eat⟩ con ganas

heartless /'hɑ:rtləs ‖ 'hɑ:tlɪs/ adj ⟨person⟩ sin corazón; ⟨refusal⟩ cruel

heart: ∼-shaped adj ⟨card/cake⟩ con forma de corazón; ⟨face⟩ en forma de corazón; **∼-to-∼** n (colloq) charla f íntima

hearty /'hɑ:rti ‖ 'hɑ:ti/ adj **-tier, -tiest** ⟨person⟩ campechano; ⟨welcome⟩ caluroso; ⟨appetite⟩ bueno

heat¹ /hi:t/ n ▣ (a) (warmth) calor m (b) (for cooking) fuego m ▣ in the ∼ of the moment en un momento de enojo (or exaltación etc) ▣ (estrus) celo m; **to be in** o (BrE) **on ∼** estar* en celo ▣ (Sport) (prueba) eliminatoria f

heat² vt calentar*; ⟨house⟩ calentar*, calefaccionar (CS)

■ **heat up** ▣ [v + adv] calentarse* ▣ [v + o + adv, v + adv + o] calentar*

heated /'hi:təd ‖ 'hi:tɪd/ adj (a) (warmed) ⟨pool⟩ climatizado; ⟨seat/rear window⟩ térmico (b) (impassioned) ⟨argument⟩ acalorado; **to get ∼** acalorarse

heater /'hi:tər ‖ 'hi:tə(r)/ n calentador m, estufa f; (water ∼) calentador m (de agua)

heath /hi:θ/ n brezal m, monte m

heathen /'hi:ðən/ n pagano, -na m,f

heather /'heðər ‖ 'heðə(r)/ n brezo m

heating /'hi:tɪŋ/ n calefacción f

heat wave n ola f de calor

heave¹ /hi:v/ vt ▣ (a) (move with effort): **we ∼d the box onto the shelf** con esfuerzo logramos subir la caja al estante; **they ∼d it into place** lo colocaron empujando/levantándolo (b) (throw) (colloq) tirar ▣ (utter): **to ∼ a sigh** suspirar

■ ∼ vi ▣ (pull) tirar, jalar (AmL exc CS) ▣ (rise and fall): **his chest ∼d** respiraba agitadamente

heave² n (pull) tirón m, jalón m (AmL exc CS); (push) empujón m

heaven /'hevən/ n cielo m; **(good) ∼s!** ¡Dios mío!; **thank ∼** gracias a Dios

heavenly /'hevənli/ adj (a) (Relig) celestial (b) (Astron) celeste (c) (superb) (colloq) divino (fam)

heavily /'hevəli ‖ 'hevɪli/ adv ▣ (a) ⟨tread/fall⟩ pesadamente; **to be ∼ built** ser* corpulento; **to breathe ∼** jadear (b) (thickly) ⟨underlined⟩ con trazo grueso; **she was ∼ made-up** iba muy maquillada ▣ (a) (copiously) ⟨rain/snow⟩ mucho (b) (immoderately) ⟨drink/smoke⟩ en exceso (c) (greatly): **to borrow ∼** contraer* considerables deudas; **∼ pregnant** en avanzado estado de gravidez (frml) or (period) de gestación

heavy¹ /'hevi/ adj **-vier, -viest** ▣ (a) (weighty) ⟨load/suitcase/weight⟩ pesado; ⟨fabric/garment⟩ grueso, pesado; ⟨saucepan⟩ de fondo grueso; ⟨boots⟩ fuerte; ⟨work⟩ pesado; **it's very ∼** es muy pesado, pesa mucho (b) (large-scale) (before n) ⟨artillery/machinery⟩ pesado ▣ (a) (ponderous) ⟨tread/footstep/fall⟩ pesado; ⟨thud⟩ sordo ⟨features⟩ tosco; ⟨irony⟩ poco sutil ▣ (a) (oppressive) ⟨clouds/sky⟩ pesado (b) (loud) ⟨sigh⟩ profundo ▣ (a) (bigger than usual) ⟨expenditure⟩ cuantioso (b) (intense) ⟨book⟩ pesado, denso; ⟨rain⟩ fuerte; ⟨traffic⟩ denso;

⟨schedule⟩ apretado; **to be a ∼ drinker/smoker** beber/fumar mucho (c) (severe) ⟨sentence⟩ severo; ⟨casualties⟩ numeroso; ⟨blow⟩ duro, fuerte

heavy² n (pl **-vies**) (colloq) matón m (fam)

heavy: ∼ cream n (AmE) crema f doble, nata f para montar (Esp), doble crema f (Méx); **∼-duty** /'hevi'du:ti ‖ ,hevi'dju:ti/ adj ⟨material/sacks⟩ muy resistente; ⟨machine⟩ para uso industrial; ⟨clothing/overalls⟩ de trabajo; **∼-handed** /'hevi'hænded ‖ ,hevi'hændɪd/ adj torpe; **∼ metal** n (Mus) heavy m (metal), rock m duro

heavyweight¹ /'heviweɪt/ n (Sport) peso mf pesado; **a political ∼** un peso pesado de la política

heavyweight² adj (a) (Sport) (before n) ⟨boxer/wrestler⟩ de la categoría de los pesos pesados; ⟨title⟩ de los pesos pesados (b) (Tex) ⟨cotton/denim⟩ grueso y resistente

Hebrew¹ /'hi:bru:/ adj hebreo

Hebrew² n hebreo m

Hebrides /'hebrədi:z ‖ 'hebrɪdi:z/ pl n **the ∼** las (islas) Hébridas

heck /hek/ n (colloq & euph): **∼!** ¡caray! (fam & euf); **what the ∼!** ¡qué diablos! (fam)

heckle /'hekl/ vt interrumpir (con preguntas o comentarios molestos)

heckler /'heklər ‖ 'heklə(r)/ n: persona que interrumpe a un orador para molestar

hectare /'hekter ‖ 'hekteə(r)/ n hectárea f

hectic /'hektɪk/ adj ⟨day/week⟩ ajetreado, agitado; ⟨journey/pace⟩ agotador; ⟨activity⟩ frenético, febril

he'd /hi:d/ (a) = **he had** (b) = **he would**

hedge¹ /hedʒ/ n seto m (verde or vivo)

hedge² vt ⟨field/garden⟩ cercar* (con seto)

■ ∼ vi (evade the issue) dar* rodeos

hedgehog /'hedʒhɔ:g ‖ 'hedʒhɒg/ n erizo m

hedgerow /'hedʒrəʊ/ n (usu pl) seto m (verde or vivo)

hedonism /'hi:dn̩ɪzəm ‖ 'hi:dənɪzəm/ n hedonismo m

hedonist /'hi:dn̩əst ‖ 'hi:dənɪst/ n hedonista mf

heed¹ /hi:d/ n: **to take ∼** tener* cuidado

heed² vt prestar atención a, hacer* caso de

heedless /'hi:dləs ‖ 'hi:dlɪs/ adj (frml) **∼ of** sth: **∼ of the danger ...** haciendo caso omiso del peligro ...

heel¹ /hi:l/ n (a) (Anat) talón m (b) (of shoe) tacón m, taco m (CS)

heel² vt ⟨shoes⟩ ponerles* tacones or (CS) tacos nuevos a; ⟨high-heeled shoes⟩ ponerles* tapas or (Chi) tapillas a

hefty /'hefti/ adj **-tier, -tiest** (colloq) (a) (large and heavy) ⟨person⟩ robusto, fornido, corpulento; ⟨load/case⟩ pesado (b) (strong) fuerte (c) (substantial) ⟨price/salary⟩ alto; ⟨fine⟩ considerable

heifer /'hefər ‖ 'hefə(r)/ n vaquilla f, novilla f

height /haɪt/ n ▣ (a) (tallness — of object) altura f; (— of person) estatura f, talla f; **what ∼ are you?** ¿cuánto mides? (b) (Aviat) altura f; **to gain/lose ∼** ganar/perder* altura ▣ (peak) (no pl): **to be at the ∼ of one's power** estar* en la cima o en la cumbre or en la cúspide de su (or mi etc) poder; **at the ∼ of the season** en plena temporada; **it's the ∼ of stupidity** es el colmo de la estupidez

····⫶

3 heights *pl* **(a)** (high ground) cerros *mpl*, cumbres *fpl* **(b) to be afraid of ~s** sufrir de vértigo

heighten /'haɪtn/ *vt* ⟨*effect/impression*⟩ destacar*, realzar*; ⟨*suspense/admiration/respect*⟩ aumentar

heinous /'heɪnəs/ *adj* (frml) atroz, abyecto

heir /er ‖eə(r)/ *n* heredero, -ra *m,f*; **~ to sth** (to fortune, title) heredero DE algo; (to throne) heredero A algo

heiress /'erəs ‖'eəres/ *n* heredera *f*

heirloom /'erluːm ‖'eəluːm/ *n* reliquia *f*

heist /haɪst/ *n* (AmE colloq) golpe *m* (fam), atraco *m*

held /held/ *past & past p of* HOLD¹

helicopter /'helɪkɑːptər ‖'helɪkɒptə(r)/ *n* helicóptero *m*

heliport /'heləpɔːrt ‖'helɪpɔːt/ *n* helipuerto *m*

helium /'hiːliəm/ *n* helio *m*

hell /hel/ *n* 1 (Relig) infierno *m*; **three months of sheer ~** tres meses infernales; **to make sb's life ~** (colloq) hacerle* la vida imposible a algn 2 (colloq) (*as intensifier*): **how/why the ~ ...?** ¿cómo/por qué demonios *or* diablos ...? (fam); **he's a o one ~ of a guy** es un tipo sensacional (fam); **to run like ~** correr como un loco (fam); **oh, well, what the ~!** bueno ¿qué importa? (fam)

he'll /hiːl/ **(a)** = **he will (b)** = **he shall**

hello /hə'ləʊ/ *interj* **(a)** (greeting) ¡hola! **(b)** (answering the telephone) sí, aló (AmS), diga *or* dígame (Esp), bueno (Méx), olá (RPl)

helm /helm/ *n* (Naut) timón *m*

helmet /'helmət ‖'helmɪt/ *n* (headgear) casco *m*; (armor) yelmo *m*

help¹ /help/ *vt* 1 (assist) ayudar; **to ~ sb (to) + INF** ayudar a algn A + INF 2 (avoid, prevent) (*usu neg or interrog*): **I can't ~ it** no lo puedo remediar; **they can't ~ being poor** no tienen la culpa de ser pobres ■ **~** *vi* ⟨*person/remark*⟩ ayudar; ⟨*tool*⟩ servir* ■ *v refl* **to ~ oneself** 1 (assist) ayudarse (a sí mismo) 2 (resist impulse) (*usu neg*) controlarse; **I can't ~ myself** no me puedo controlar 3 (take) **to ~ oneself (TO sth)** ⟨*to food/a drink*⟩ servirse* (algo) ■ **help out** 1 [*v + o + adv, v + adv + o*] ayudar 2 [*v + adv*] ayudar

help² *n* **(a)** (rescue) ayuda *f*; (*as interj*) **~!** ¡socorro!, ¡auxilio! **(b)** (assistance) ayuda *f*; **can I be of (any) ~ to you?** ¿la/lo puedo ayudar (en algo)?

help desk *n* servicio *m* de asistencia, ayuda *f* al usuario

helper /'helpər ‖'helpə(r)/ *n* ayudante, -ta *m,f*

helpful /'helpfəl/ *adj* **(a)** (obliging) ⟨*person/ attitude*⟩ servicial, amable **(b)** (useful) ⟨*advice*⟩ útil

helping /'helpɪŋ/ *n* porción *f* (esp AmL), ración *f* (esp Esp)

helpless /'helpləs ‖'helplɪs/ *adj* **(a)** (defenseless) ⟨*prey/victim*⟩ indefenso **(b)** (powerless) ⟨*look/expression*⟩ de impotencia; **to be ~ to + INF** ser* incapaz DE + INF **(c)** (incapacitated): **to leave sb ~** dejar a algn sin recursos

helplessly /'helpləsli ‖'helplɪsli/ *adv* ⟨*look on/ stand by*⟩ sin poder hacer nada; ⟨*struggle/try*⟩ en vano, inútilmente

helpline /'helplaɪn/ *n* servicio *m* telefónico de asistencia, línea *f* directa

helter-skelter /'heltər'skeltər ‖,heltə'skeltə(r)/ *adv* atropelladamente, a la desbanda

hem /hem/ *n* dobladillo *m*, basta *f* (Chi) ■ **hem in: -mm-** [*v + o + adv, v + adv + o*] encerrar*

hemisphere /'heməsfɪr ‖'hemɪsfɪə(r)/ *n* (Geog) hemisferio *m*

hemline /'hemlaɪn/ *n* bajo *m*, ruedo *m*

hemoglobin, (BrE) **haemoglobin** /'hiːmə,gləʊbən ‖,hiːmə'gləʊbɪn/ *n* hemoglobina *f*

hemophilia, (BrE) **haemophilia** /'hiːmə'fɪliə/ *n* hemofilia *f*

hemophiliac, (BrE) **haemophiliac** /,hiːmə'fɪliæk/ *n* hemofílico, -ca *m,f*

hemorrhage¹, (BrE) **haemorrhage** /'hemərɪdʒ/ *n* (Med) hemorragia *f*

hemorrhage², (BrE) **haemorrhage** *vi* «*patient*» tener* *or* (frml) sufrir una hemorragia; «*wound/blood vessel*» sangrar mucho

hemorrhoids, (BrE) **haemorrhoids** /'hemərɔɪdz/ *pl n* hemorroides *fpl*, almorranas *fpl*

hemp /hemp/ *n* (fiber) cáñamo *m*; (drug) marihuana *f*, cannabis *m*; (plant) cannabis *m*, cáñamo *m* índico *or* de la India

hen /hen/ *n* (chicken) gallina *f*; (female bird) hembra *f*

hence /hens/ *adv* 1 **(a)** (that is the reason for) de ahí **(b)** (therefore) por lo tanto, por consiguiente 2 (from now) (frml): **a few years ~** dentro de algunos años

henceforth /'hens'fɔːrθ ‖,hens'fɔːθ/ *adv* (liter) a partir de ahora, de ahora en adelante

henchman /'hentʃmən/ *n* (*pl* **-men** /-mən/) secuaz *m*

henna /'henə/ *n* henna *f*

hen: ~ night, hen party *n* **(a)** (all-female celebration) fiesta *f* de mujeres **(b)** (before wedding) despedida *f* de soltera; **~pecked** /'henpekt/ *adj* (colloq): **a ~pecked husband** un marido dominado por su mujer, un mandilón (Méx fam), un calzonazos (Esp fam)

hepatitis /'hepə'taɪtəs ‖,hepə'taɪtɪs/ *n* hepatitis *f*

her¹ /hɜːr ‖hɜː(r), *weak form* ər ‖ə(r)/ *pron* 1 **(a)** (as direct object) la; **I can't stand ~** no la soporto; **call ~** llámala **(b)** (as indirect object) le; (with direct object pronoun present) se; **I wrote ~ a letter** le escribí una carta **(c)** (after preposition) ella 2 (emphatic use) ella; **it's ~** es ella

her² *adj*

──────────

■ **Note** The translation *su* agrees in number with the noun which it modifies: *her* is translated by *su, sus,* according to what follows: *her father/mother* su padre/ madre; *her books/magazines* sus libros/revistas.

──────────

(*sing*) su; (*pl*) sus; **she took ~ hat off** se quitó el sombrero; **she broke ~ arm** se rompió el brazo

herald¹ /'herəld/ *n* (Hist) heraldo *m*

herald² *vt* anunciar

heraldry /'herəldri/ n heráldica f

herb /ɜːrb, hɜːrb ‖ hɜːb/ n hierba f, yuyo m (Per, RPl)

herbal /'ɜːrbəl, 'hɜːrbəl ‖ 'hɜːbəl/ adj ‹shampoo› de hierbas; ~ **tea** (esp BrE) ▶ HERB TEA

herb tea n infusión f, agua f‡ (AmC, Andes), té m de yuyos (Per, RPl)

herd¹ /hɜːrd ‖ hɜːd/ n **(a)** (of cattle) manada f, vacada f; (of goats) rebaño m; (of pigs) piara f, manada f; (of wild animals) manada f **(b)** (of people) (pej) tropel m

herd² vt ‹animals› arrear, arriar (RPl); **the refugees were ~ed into trucks** metieron a los refugiados en camiones como si fueran ganado

here /hɪr ‖ hɪə(r)/ adv **1 (a)** (at, to this place) aquí, acá (esp AmL); (less precise) acá **(b)** (in phrases) **here and there** aquí y allá; **here, there and everywhere** por todas partes **2** (calling attention to sth, sb): **~'s £20** toma 20 libras; **~ he is** aquí está **3 (a)** (present): **he isn't ~ today** hoy no está **(b)** (arrived): **they're ~!** ¡ya llegaron!, ¡ya están aquí! **4** (as interj): **~, let me do it** trae, deja que lo haga yo

hereabouts /'hɪrə'baʊts ‖ ˌhɪərə'baʊts/ adv por aquí, por acá

hereafter /ˌhɪr'æftər ‖ ˌhɪər'ɑːftə(r)/ adv (frml: used esp in legal texts) (from now on) de aquí en adelante; (in the future) en el futuro, en lo sucesivo

hereditary /hə'redəteri ‖ hɪ'redɪtri/ adj hereditario

heredity /hə'redəti ‖ hɪ'redəti/ n herencia f

heresy /'herəsi/ n (pl **-sies**) herejía f

heretic /'herətɪk/ n hereje mf

heritage /'herətɪdʒ/ n (no pl) patrimonio m; (before n) ‹tourism/tourist› cultural

hermetically /hɜːr'metɪkli ‖ hɜː'metɪkli/ adv: **~ sealed** herméticamente cerrado

hermit /'hɜːrmət ‖ 'hɜːmɪt/ n ermitaño, -ña m,f, eremita mf

hernia /'hɜːrniə ‖ 'hɜːniə/ n hernia f

hero /'hɪrəʊ ‖ 'hɪərəʊ/ n (pl **heroes**) héroe m; (of novel, film) protagonista mf

heroic /hɪ'rəʊɪk/ adj heroico

heroin /'herəʊɪn/ n heroína f; (before n) ~ **addict** heroinómano, -na m,f

heroine /'herəʊɪn/ n (brave, admirable woman) heroína f; (of novel, film) protagonista f

heroism /'herəʊɪzəm/ n heroísmo m

heron /'herən/ n garza f (real)

hero worship n adoración f (de alguien a quien se tiene como ídolo)

herpes /'hɜːrpiːz ‖ 'hɜːpiːz/ n herpes m, herpe f

herring /'herɪŋ/ n (pl **herrings** or **herring**) arenque m

hers /hɜːrz ‖ hɜːz/ pron

■ Note The translation suyo reflects the gender and number of the noun it is standing for; hers is translated by el suyo, la suya, los suyos, las suyas, depending on what is being referred to.

(sing) suyo, -ya; (pl) suyos, -yas, de ella; **they're ~** son suyos/suyas, son de ella; ~ **is blue** el suyo/la suya es azul; el/la de ella es azul; **a friend of ~** un amigo suyo or de ella

herself /hər'self ‖ hə'self/ pron **(a)** (reflexive): **she cut ~** se cortó; **she bought ~ a hat** se

compró un sombrero; **she only thinks of ~** solo piensa en sí misma; **by ~** sola; **she was talking to ~** estaba hablando sola **(b)** (emphatic use) ella misma; **she told me so ~** me lo dijo ella misma **(c)** (normal self): **she's not ~** no es la de siempre

he's /hiːz/ **(a)** = **he is** (b) = **he has**

hesitant /'hezətənt ‖ 'hezɪtənt/ adj ‹voice› vacilante; ‹manner› inseguro; ‹steps› vacilante; **he seemed a little ~** parecía un poco indeciso

hesitate /'hezəteɪt ‖ 'hezɪteɪt/ vi vacilar, titubear

hesitation /'hezə'teɪʃən ‖ ˌhezɪ'teɪʃən/ n vacilación f

heterosexual¹ /'hetərəʊ'sekʃuəl/ adj heterosexual

heterosexual² n heterosexual mf

heterosexuality /'hetərəʊˌsekʃu'æləti/ n heterosexualidad f

hew /hjuː/ vt (past **hewed**; past p **hewed** or **hewn** /hjuːn/) (extract) extraer*; (fashion) ‹stone› labrar

hexagon /'heksəgɑːn ‖ 'heksəgən/ n hexágono m

hey /heɪ/ interj **(a)** (calling attention) ¡eh! **(b)** (expressing dismay, protest, indignation) ¡oye!, ¡oiga(n)!

heyday /'heɪdeɪ/ n apogeo m, auge m; **in his ~** en sus buenos tiempos

HGV n (BrE) (= **heavy goods vehicle**) vehículo m pesado

hi /haɪ/ interj (colloq) ¡hola! (fam)

HI = Hawaii

hiatus /haɪ'eɪtəs/ n (pl **-tuses**) (frml) paréntesis m (frml)

hibernate /'haɪbərneɪt ‖ 'haɪbəneɪt/ vi hibernar

hibernation /'haɪbər'neɪʃən ‖ ˌhaɪbə'neɪʃən/ n hibernación f; **to go into ~** entrar en estado de hibernación

hiccough /'hɪkʌp/ n/vi ▶ HICCUP¹,²

hiccup¹ /'hɪkʌp/ n **(a)** hipo m; **to have (the) ~s** tener* hipo **(b)** (brief interruption) dificultad f

hiccup² vi, (BrE also) **-pp-** hipar

hick /hɪk/ n (AmE colloq & pej) pueblerino, -na m,f, paleto, -ta m,f (Esp fam & pey), pajuerano, -na m,f (RPl fam & pey)

hid /hɪd/ **(a)** past of HIDE¹ **(b)** (arch) past p of HIDE¹

hidden¹ /'hɪdn/ adj ‹entrance/camera/reserves› oculto; ‹cost› no aparente

hidden² past p of HIDE¹

hide¹ /haɪd/ (past **hid** /hɪd/; past p **hidden** or (arch) **hid**) vt **(a)** (conceal) esconder; **she hid the money from the police** escondió el dinero para que no lo encontrara la policía; **to ~ oneself** esconderse **(b)** (keep secret) ‹feelings/thoughts› ocultar; **to ~ sth FROM sb** ocultarle algo A algn **(c)** (mask, screen) tapar

■ ~ vi esconderse

■ **hide away 1** [v + adv] esconderse **2** [v + o + adv, v + adv + o] esconder

hide² n (raw) piel f; (tanned) cuero m

hide: hide-and-seek **~-and-seek** /'haɪdn'siːk/, (AmE & Scot also) **~-and-go-seek** /'haɪdngəʊ'siːk/ n: **to play ~-and-seek** jugar* al ⋯⋗

escondite, jugar* a las escondidas (AmL);
~away *n* **(a)** (hiding place) (AmE) escondite *m* **(b)**
(secluded spot) rincón *m*

hideous /'hɪdɪəs/ *adj* ⟨monster/sight⟩
horroroso, horrible; ⟨crime/fate⟩ espantoso;
⟨color/furniture⟩ (colloq) horrendo, espantoso

hideout /'haɪdaʊt/ *n* guarida *f*

hiding /'haɪdɪŋ/ *n* 1 (concealment): **to be in ~/go
into ~** estar* escondido/esconderse; ⟨before n⟩ ~
place escondite *m*, escondrijo *m* 2 (beating)
(colloq) paliza *f*, tunda *f*

hierarchy /'haɪərɑːrki ‖ 'haɪərɑːki/ *n* (pl
-chies) jerarquía *f*

hieroglyphics /haɪərə'glɪfɪks/ *pl n*
jeroglíficos *mpl*

hi-fi /'haɪfaɪ/ *n* **(a)** (equipment) alta fidelidad *f* **(b)**
(set) equipo *m* de alta fidelidad, hi-fi *m*

higgledy-piggledy /'hɪgəldi'pɪgəldi/ *adv*
(colloq) sin orden ni concierto, de cualquier
manera

high¹ /haɪ/ *adj* **-er, -est** 1 **(a)** (tall) ⟨wall/
mountain⟩ alto; **how ~ is it?** ¿qué altura tiene?;
the tower is 40 m ~ la torre tiene 40 m de alto *or*
de altura **(b)** (high up) ⟨window/balcony⟩ alto;
⟨plateau⟩ elevado; **at a ~ altitude** a gran altitud;
~ cheekbones pómulos *mpl* salientes **(c)** (in
status) ⟨office/rank⟩ alto; **he has friends in ~
places** tiene amigos muy bien situados; **~
society** la alta sociedad **(d)** (morally, ethically)
⟨ideals/principles⟩ elevado **(e)** (in pitch) ⟨voice⟩
agudo; ⟨note⟩ alto
2 (greater than usual) ⟨temperature/speed/pressure⟩
alto; ⟨wind⟩ fuerte; **unemployment is very ~** hay
mucho desempleo; **to be ~ in vitamins** ser* rico
en vitaminas
3 (climactic) culminante; **the ~ point** el punto
culminante
4 **(a)** (happy, excited): **she was in ~ spirits** estaba
muy animada **(b)** (intoxicated) (colloq) drogado,
colocado (Esp fam)
5 (of time): **~ noon** mediodía *m*; **in ~ summer** en
pleno verano
6 ⟨meat⟩ pasado; ⟨game⟩ que tiene un olor
fuerte

high² *adv* **-er, -est** 1 ⟨fly⟩ alto; **~ up** arriba,
en lo alto; **to search ~ and low (for sth)** remover*
cielo y tierra (para encontrar algo) 2 (in pitch)
⟨sing⟩ alto

high³ *n* 1 (level) récord *m* 2 (Meteo) (anticyclone)
zona *f* de altas presiones; (high temperature)
máxima *f* 3 (top gear) (AmE Auto) ⟨no art⟩ directa
f

high- /haɪ/ *pref*: **~quality** de alta calidad, de
gran calidad; **~speed** ⟨train⟩ de alta velocidad

high: **~brow** *adj* (colloq) ⟨tastes⟩ de intelectual;
⟨art/music⟩ para intelectuales; **~chair** *n* silla *f*
alta (para niño); **~class** /'haɪ'klæs ‖ haɪ'klɑːs/
adj ⟨restaurant/hotel⟩ de lujo; ⟨merchandise⟩ de
primera calidad; **H~ Court** *n* (in England and
Wales) una de las dos ramas del Tribunal
Supremo, con competencia para conocer de causas
civiles cuyo coste excede cierta cuantía

higher /'haɪər ‖ 'haɪə(r)/ *adj* **(a)** comp of HIGH¹
(b) ⟨before n⟩ ⟨mammals/organs⟩ superior

higher education *n* enseñanza *f* superior

high: **~ finance** *n* altas finanzas *fpl*; **~flier,
~flyer** /'haɪ'flaɪər ‖ haɪ'flaɪə(r)/ *n* persona *f*
muy prometedora; **~flown** *adj* altisonante;
~frequency /'haɪ'friːkwənsi/ *adj* de alta
frecuencia; **~grade** *adj* de calidad superior;
~handed /'haɪ'hændəd ‖ haɪ'hændɪd/ *adj*
arbitrario; **~heeled** /'haɪ'hiːld/ *adj* de tacón *or*
(CS) de taco alto; **~ jump** *n* salto *m* de altura,
salto *m* alto (AmL); **~lands** /'haɪləndz/ *pl n* **(a)**
(uplands) tierras *fpl* altas, altiplanicie *f* **(b)** (in
Scotland) **the H~lands** las *or* los Highlands, las
tierras altas; **~level** /'haɪ'levəl/ *adj* **(a)** ⟨talks/
delegation⟩ de alto nivel **(b)** ⟨bridge/road⟩
elevado **(c)** (Comput) de alto nivel

highlight¹ /'haɪlaɪt/ *vt* (past & past p
-lighted) 1 (call attention to) ⟨problem/question⟩
destacar*, poner* de relieve 2 (Art, Phot)
realzar*, dar* realce a

highlight² *n* 1 (most memorable part) lo más
destacado; **her performance was the ~ of the
evening** su actuación fue el plato fuerte de la
velada 2 **(a)** (Art, Phot) toque *m* de luz **(b)**
highlights *pl* (in hair) reflejos *mpl*, claritos *mpl*
(RPl), visos *mpl* (Chi), luces *fpl* (Méx), mechones
mpl (Col)

highlighter /'haɪlaɪtər ‖ 'haɪlaɪtə(r)/ *n* **(a)**
(makeup) sombra *f* clara de ojos **(b)** (pen)
rotulador *m*, marcador *m* (AmL)

highly /'haɪli/ *adv* **(a)** (to a high degree): **~
unlikely** muy poco probable; **~ intelligent**
inteligentísimo; **~ trained** altamente capacitado
(b) (favorably): **his boss speaks/thinks very ~ of
him** su jefe habla muy bien/tiene muy buena
opinión de él **(c)** (at a high rate): **a ~ paid job** un
trabajo muy bien pagado

highly-strung /'haɪli'strʌn/ *adj* (BrE) ▶
HIGH-STRUNG

Highness /'haɪnəs ‖ 'haɪnɪs/ *n*: **Her/His/Your
(Royal) ~** Su Alteza (Real)

high: **~-pitched** /'haɪ'pɪtʃt/ *adj* ⟨voice/sound⟩
agudo; ⟨instrument⟩ de tono agudo *or* alto;
~-powered /'haɪ'paʊərd ‖ haɪ'paʊəd/ *adj* ⟨car/
machine⟩ muy potente, de gran potencia;
⟨executive/campaign⟩ dinámico, enérgico; ⟨job⟩ de
alto(s) vuelo(s); **~-profile** /'haɪ'prəʊfaɪl/ *adj*
prominente; **~-ranking** /'haɪ'ræŋkɪŋ/ *adj*
⟨officer⟩ de alto rango; ⟨official⟩ alto, de alta
jerarquía; **~ rise** *n* (esp AmE) torre *f* (de
apartamentos *or* (Esp) pisos); **~-rise** /'haɪ'raɪz/
adj ⟨before n⟩ ⟨building/block⟩ alto, de muchas
plantas; ⟨apartment⟩ de una torre, de un edificio
alto; **~-risk** /'haɪ'rɪsk/ *adj* de alto riesgo;
~road *n* carretera *f*; **~ school** *n* colegio *m*
secundario, ≈ instituto *m* (en Esp), ≈ liceo *m* (en
CS, Ven); **~ season** *n* temporada *f* alta;
~-spirited /'haɪ'spɪrɪtəd ‖ haɪ'spɪrɪtɪd/ *adj*
lleno de vida, brioso; **~ street** *n* (BrE) calle *f*
principal, calle *f* mayor (Esp); **~-strung**
/'haɪ'strʌn/, (BrE) **highly-strung** *adj* ⟨person⟩

AmC Central America	Arg Argentina	Cu Cuba	Per Peru
AmL Latin America	Bol Bolivia	Ec Ecuador	RPl River Plate Area
AmS South America	Chi Chile	Esp Spain	Ur Uruguay
Andes Andean Region	CS Southern Cone	Méx Mexico	Ven Venezuela

nervioso; ⟨*dog/horse*⟩ muy excitable; **∼-tech**
/'haɪtek/ *adj* de alta tecnología; ⟨*era*⟩ high tech
adj inv; **∼-up** *n* (esp AmE colloq) gerifalte *mf*,
capo, -pa *m,f* (fam); **∼way** *n* (main road) carretera
f; (public way) vía *f* pública; (*before n*) ⟨*patrol/
patrolman*⟩ (AmE) de carretera; **H∼way Code**
n (in UK) Código *m* de la Circulación;
∼wayman /'haɪweɪmən/ *n* (*pl* **-men** /-mən/)
salteador *m* de caminos, bandolero *m*; **∼ wire** *n*
cuerda *f* floja

hijack¹ /'haɪdʒæk/ *vt* secuestrar

hijack² *n* secuestro *m*

hijacker /'haɪdʒækər ‖ 'haɪdʒækə(r)/ *n*
secuestrador, -dora *m,f*; (of planes) pirata áereo,
-rea *m,f*

hike¹ /haɪk/ *n* **1** (long walk) caminata *f*,
excursión *f* **2** (increase) subida *f*

hike² *vi* (walk) ir* de caminata *or* de excursión;
to go hiking hacer* excursionismo

hiker /'haɪkər ‖ 'haɪkə(r)/ *n* excursionista *mf*

hilarious /hɪ'leriəs ‖ hɪ'leəriəs/ *adj*
divertidísimo, comiquísimo

hill /hɪl/ *n* (low) colina *f*, cerro *m*, collado *m*;
(higher) montaña *f*; (slope, incline) cuesta *f*

hill: **∼billy** *n* (AmE colloq) rústico, -ca *m,f*,
paleto, -ta *m,f* (Esp fam & pey), pajuerano, -na *m,f*
(RPl fam & pey); **∼side** *n* ladera *f*; **∼top** *n* cima
f, cumbre *f*

hilly /'hɪli/ *adj* **-lier, -liest** accidentado

hilt /hɪlt/ *n* empuñadura *f*, puño *m*

him /hɪm/, *weak form* ɪm/ *pron* **1** **(a)** (as direct
object) lo, le (Esp); **I saw ∼** lo *or* (Esp tb) le vi; **call
∼** llámalo, llámale (Esp) **(b)** (as indirect object) le;
(with direct object pronoun present) se; **I sent ∼ a card**
le mandé una tarjeta **(c)** (after preposition) él
2 (emphatic use) él; **it's ∼** es él

Himalayas /'hɪmə'leɪəz/ *pl n* **the ∼** el
Himalaya

himself /hɪm'self/ *pron* **(a)** (reflexive): **he cut/
hurt ∼** se cortó/lastimó; **he bought ∼ a hat** se
compró un sombrero; **he only thinks of ∼** solo
piensa en sí mismo; **by ∼** solo; **he was talking to
∼** estaba hablando solo **(b)** (emphatic use) él
mismo; **he told me so ∼** me lo dijo él mismo **(c)**
(normal self): **he's not ∼** no es el de siempre

hind /haɪnd/ *adj* (*before n, no comp*) ⟨*legs*⟩
trasero

hinder /'hɪndər ‖ 'hɪndə(r)/ *vt* dificultar

Hindi /'hɪndi/ *n* indi *m*, hindi *m*

hindrance /'hɪndrəns/ *n* estorbo *m*

hindsight /'haɪndsaɪt/ *n*: **with (the benefit of)
∼** a posteriori, en retrospectiva

Hindu¹ /'hɪndu:/ *n* hindú *mf*

Hindu² *adj* hindú

Hinduism /'hɪndu:ɪzəm/ *n* hinduismo *m*

hinge¹ /hɪndʒ/ *n* (of door, window, gate) bisagra *f*,
gozne *m*; (of box, lid) bisagra *f*

hinge² **hinges, hinging, hinged** *vi* **to ∼ ON
sth** (turn) girar SOBRE algo; (be fixed) ir* asegurado
con bisagras A algo; (depend) depender DE algo

hint¹ /hɪnt/ *n* **1** **(a)** (oblique reference)
insinuación *f*, indirecta *f*; (clue) pista *f*; **to drop a
∼ to sb** lanzarle* una indirecta a algn; **to take
the ∼** captar *or* (Esp tb) coger* la indirecta **(b)**

(trace – of bitterness, sadness) dejo *m*; (– of color)
toque *m*, matiz *m*; (– of garlic, lemon) dejo *m*, gusto
m **2** (tip) consejo *m*

hint² *vt* insinuar*, dar* a entender
■ **∼** *vi* lanzar* indirectas; **to ∼ AT sth** insinuar*
or dar* a entender algo

hip¹ /hɪp/ *n* cadera *f*

hip² *interj*: **∼, ∼, hooray** *o* **hurrah!** ¡hurra!, ¡viva!

hippie /'hɪpi/ *n* ▶ HIPPY

hippo /'hɪpəʊ/ *n* (*pl* **-pos**) (colloq) hipopótamo *m*

hippopotamus /'hɪpə'pɑːtəməs
‖ ,hɪpə'pɒtəməs/ *n* (*pl* **-muses** *or* **-mi** /-maɪ/)
hipopótamo *m*

hippy, hippie /'hɪpi/ *n* (*pl* **-pies**) hippy *mf*

hire¹ /haɪr ‖ 'haɪə(r)/ *vt* **1** **(a)** ⟨*hall/boat/suit*⟩
alquilar, arrendar* **(b)** (Busn, Lab Rel) ⟨*staff/
person*⟩ contratar **(c)** **hired** *past p* ⟨*car*⟩
alquilado **2** ▶ HIRE OUT
■ **hire out** [*v + o + adv, v + adv + o*] (BrE)
alquilar, arrendar*

hire² *n* **1** (of hall/car/suit) alquiler *m*, arriendo *m*;
ⓢ **for hire** se alquila *or* se arrienda; (on taxis)
libre **2** (payment) alquiler *m*, arriendo *m*

hire purchase *n* (BrE) compra *f* a plazos; **to
buy sth on ∼ ∼** comprar algo a plazos, comprar
algo en cuotas (esp AmL)

his¹ /hɪz, *weak form* ɪz/ *adj*

■ **Note** The translation *su* agrees in number with the
noun which it modifies; *his* is translated by *su*, *sus*,
according to what follows: *his father/mother* su padre/
madre; *his books/magazines* sus libros/revistas.

(*sing*) su; (*pl*) sus; **he injured ∼ knee** se lesionó
la rodilla

his² *pron*

■ **Note** The translation *suyo* reflects the gender and
number of the noun it is standing for; *his* is translated
by *el suyo*, *la suya*, *los suyos*, *las suyas*, depending
on what is being referred to.

(*sing*) suyo, -ya; (*pl*) suyos, -yas, de él; **they're ∼**
son suyos/suyas, son de él; **∼ is blue** el suyo/la
suya es azul, el/la de él es azul; **a friend of ∼** un
amigo suyo *or* de él

Hispanic¹ /hɪ'spænɪk/ *adj* hispánico, hispano;
⟨*community/voter*⟩ (in US) hispano

Hispanic² *n* (esp AmE) hispano, -na *m,f*

hiss¹ /hɪs/ *vi* silbar; ⟨⟨*cat*⟩⟩ bufar
■ **∼** *vt* decir* entre dientes

hiss² *n* (of snake, audience) silbido *m*; (of cat)
bufido *m*

historian /hɪ'stɔːriən/ *n* historiador, -dora *m,f*

historic /hɪ'stɔːrɪk ‖ hɪ'stɒrɪk/ *adj* **(a)**
(momentous) ⟨*event/moment*⟩ memorable **(b)** (old)
⟨*house/building*⟩ histórico

historical /hɪ'stɔːrɪkəl ‖ hɪ'stɒrɪkəl/ *adj* **(a)**
(relating to history) histórico **(b)** (crit) ▶ HISTORIC

history /'hɪstəri/ *n* (*pl* **-ries**) **1** historia *f*; **the
worst earthquake in ∼** el peor terremoto de la
historia **2** (record, background) historial *m*

hit¹ /hɪt/ (*pres p* **hitting**; *past & past p* **hit**) *vt*
1 **(a)** (deal blow to) ⟨*door/table*⟩ dar* un golpe en,
golpear; ⟨*person*⟩ pegarle* a **(b)** (strike) golpear;
the truck ∼ a tree el camión chocó con *or* contra
un árbol; **the house was ∼ by a bomb** una bomba
cayó sobre la casa; **the bullet ∼ him in the leg** la ⋯⋗

bala le dio *or* lo alcanzó en la pierna; **to ~ one's head on sth** darse* un golpe en la cabeza contra algo; **to ~ it off with sb** congeniar con algn
2 (a) (strike accurately) ‹*target*› dar* en **(b)** (attack) ‹*opponent/enemy*› atacar* **(c)** (score) (Sport) anotarse, marcar*
3 (affect adversely) afectar (a)
4 (a) (meet with, run into) ‹*difficulty/problem*› toparse con **(b)** (reach) llegar* a, alcanzar*
5 (occur to): **suddenly it ~ me: why had he ... ?** de repente se me ocurrió: ¿por qué había ... ?
■ **hit back (a)** [*v + adv*] (strike in return) devolver* el golpe; **she ~ back at her critics** arremetió contra sus detractores **(b)** [*v + o + adv*] devolverle* el golpe a
■ **hit on** [*v + prep + o*] ‹*solution*› dar* con
■ **hit out** [*v + adv*] **(a)** (strike) **to ~ out (AT sb)** (once) lanzar*(le) un golpe (A algn); (repeatedly) tirar(le) golpes (A algn) **(b)** (attack verbally) **to ~ out AT o AGAINST sth/sb** atacar* algo/a algn
■ **hit upon** ▶ HIT ON

hit² *n* **1 (a)** (blow, stroke) (Sport) golpe *m* **(b)** (in shooting) blanco *m* **2** (success) (colloq) éxito *m*
3 (Comput) impacto *m*

hit: ~-and-miss /'hɪtən'mɪs/ *adj* (*pred* ~ **and miss**) ▶ HIT-OR-MISS; **~-and-run** /'hɪtən'rʌn/ *adj* (*before n*) ‹*driver*› que se da a la fuga tras atropellar a algn

hitch¹ /hɪtʃ/ *n* **1** (difficulty) complicación *f*, problema *m*, pega *f* (Esp fam); **a technical ~** un problema técnico **2** (limp) (AmE) cojera *f*, renguera *f* (AmL)

hitch² *vt* **1** (attach) **to ~ sth TO sth** enganchar algo A algo **2** (thumb) (colloq): **to ~ a ride** *o* (BrE also) **a lift** hacer* dedo (fam), hacer* autostop, ir* de aventón (Col, Méx fam), pedir* cola (Ven fam)
■ **~** *vi* ▶ HITCHHIKE

hitch: ~hike *vi* hacer* autostop, hacer* dedo (fam), ir* de aventón (Col, Méx fam), pedir* cola (Ven fam); **~hiker** *n* autoestopista *mf*

hi-tech /'haɪ'tek/ *adj* ▶ HIGH-TECH

hitherto /'hɪðər'tuː ‖ ,hɪðə'tuː/ *adv* (fml) hasta ahora, hasta la fecha

hit: ~ list *n* (colloq) (murder list) lista *f* de sentenciados; (blacklist) lista *f* negra; **~ man** *n* (colloq) (assassin) asesino *m* a sueldo, sicario *m*; **~-or-miss** /'hɪtər'mɪs ‖ ,hɪtɔː'mɪs/ *adj* (*pred* ~ **or miss**) ‹*method/approach*› poco científico

hitter /'hɪtər ‖ 'hɪtə(r)/ *n* (in baseball) bateador, -dora *m,f*; (in US football) liniero, -ra *m,f*

HIV *n* (= **Human Immunodeficiency Virus**) VIH *m*, virus *m* del sida; **he's ~ positive** es seropositivo

hive /haɪv/ *n* (home of bees) colmena *f*; (bee colony) enjambre *m*

hives /haɪvz/ *n* (Med) urticaria *f*

HM (= **Her/His Majesty**) S.M.

HMS (in UK) = **Her/His Majesty's Ship**

hoard¹ /hɔːrd ‖ hɔːd/ *n* (of food) reserva *f*; **a ~ of treasure** un tesoro escondido

hoard² *vt* acumular, juntar; (anticipating a shortage) acaparar

hoarding /'hɔːrdɪŋ ‖ 'hɔːdɪŋ/ *n* **1** (anticipating a shortage) acaparamiento *m* **2** (billboard) (BrE) valla *f* publicitaria, barda *f* de anuncios (Méx)

hoarse /hɔːrs ‖ hɔːs/ *adj* **hoarser, hoarsest** ronco

hoax /həʊks/ *n* (deception) engaño *m*; (joke) broma *f*; (tall story) patraña *f*

hob /hɑːb ‖ hɒb/ *n* **(a)** (beside open fire) placa *f* **(b)** (of cooker) (BrE) hornillas *fpl* (AmL exc CS), hornillos *mpl* (Esp), hornallas *fpl* (RPl), platos *mpl* (Chi)

hobble /'hɑːbəl ‖ 'hɒbəl/ *vi* cojear, renguear (AmL)

hobby /'hɑːbi ‖ 'hɒbi/ *n* (*pl* **-bies**) hobby *m*, pasatiempo *m*, afición *f*

hobnailed /'hɑːbneɪld ‖ 'hɒbneɪld/ *adj* con tachuelas

hobo /'həʊbəʊ/ *n* (*pl* **-boes** *or* **-bos**) (AmE colloq) vagabundo, -da *m,f*, linyera *mf* (CS fam)

hockey /'hɑːki ‖ 'hɒki/ *n* **(a)** (ice ~) (AmE) hockey *m* sobre hielo **(b)** (played on grass) (BrE) hockey *m* (sobre hierba)

hod /hɑːd ‖ hɒd/ *n* (for bricks) capacho *m* (*para acarrear ladrillos*)

hoe¹ /həʊ/ *n* azada *f*, azadón *m*

hoe² *vt* azadonar, pasar la azada por

hog¹ /hɔːg ‖ hɒg/ *n* **1** (AmE Agr, Zool) cerdo, -da *m,f*, puerco, -ca *m,f*, chancho, -cha *m,f* (AmL) **2** (person) (colloq) tragón, -gona *m,f* (fam), angurriento, -ta *m,f* (CS fam)

hog² *vt* **-gg-** (colloq) ‹*food/bathroom/limelight*› acaparar; ‹*discussion*› monopolizar*

Hogmanay /'hɑːgmənei ‖ 'hɒgmənei/ *n* (Scot) Nochevieja *f*, noche *f* de fin de año

hoist¹ /hɔɪst/ *vt* (lift) levantar, alzar*; ‹*sail/flag*› izar*

hoist² *n* (elevator) montacargas *m*; (crane, derrick) grúa *f*

hokum /'həʊkəm/ *n* (colloq) **(a)** (nonsense) paparruchas *fpl* (fam) **(b)** (corny material) (AmE) recursos efectistas de tipo melodramático o cómico

hold¹ /həʊld/ (*past & past p* **held**) *vt* **1 (a)** (have in one's hand(s)) tener* (en la mano); **will you ~ this for me?** ¿me puedes tener *or* (esp AmL) agarrar esto por favor? **(b)** (clasp): **~ it with both hands** sujétalo *or* (esp AmL) agárralo con las dos manos; **he was ~ing her hand** la tenía agarrada *or* (esp Esp) cogida de la mano **(c)** (grip) (Auto) agarrar, adherirse*
2 (have room for) ‹*cup/jug*› tener* una capacidad de; «*stadium*» tener* capacidad *or* cabida para; **this report ~s all the answers to ...** este informe contiene todas las respuestas a ...; **who knows what the future ~s** quién sabe qué nos deparará el futuro
3 (a) (keep in position) ‹*ladder*› sujetar, sostener* **(b)** (maintain) ‹*attention/interest*› mantener*; **she held the lead throughout the race** se mantuvo a la cabeza durante toda la carrera
4 (a) (keep) ‹*tickets/room*› reservar, guardar **(b)** (detain, imprison): **she is being held at the police station for questioning** está detenida en la comisaría para ser interrogada **(c)** (restrain) detener* **(d)** (control) «*troops/rebels*» ocupar
5 (a) (have) ‹*passport/permit*› tener*, estar* en posesión de (fml); ‹*degree/shares*› tener*; ‹*record*› ostentar, tener* **(b)** ‹*post/position*› tener*, ocupar; **he ~s the view that ...** sostiene *or* mantiene que ... **(b)** (consider) considerar; (assert) sostener*, mantener*; **to ~ sb responsible for sth** responsabilizar* a algn de algo **(c)** (conduct) ‹*meeting/elections*› celebrar; ‹*demonstration*› hacer*; ‹*party*› dar*; ‹*conversation*› mantener*

⑥ (stop): ~ **it!** ¡espera!

■ ~ *vi* ① (clasp, grip): ~ **tight!** ¡agárrate fuerte!
② **(a)** (stay firm) «*rope/door*» aguantar, resistir **(b)** (continue) «*weather*» seguir* *or* continuar* bueno; **if our luck ~s** si nos sigue acompañando la suerte

■ **hold against** [*v* + *o* + *prep* + *o*]: **I won't ~ that against him** no se lo voy a tomar en cuenta

■ **hold back** ① [*v* + *o* + *adv*, *v* + *adv* + *o*] **(a)** (restrain) ‹*crowds/water/tears*› contener* **(b)** (withhold, delay) ‹*information*› no revelar; ‹*payment*› retrasar
② [*v* + *adv*] (restrain oneself) contenerse*, frenarse

■ **hold down** [*v* + *o* + *adv*, *v* + *adv* + *o*] **(a)** (force, press down) ‹*lid/papers*› sujetar; ‹*person*› inmovilizar **(b)** ‹*job*›: **he can't ~ down a job** es incapaz de tener un trabajo y cumplir con él **(c)** (limit) ‹*price/increase*› moderar, contener*

■ **hold in** [*v* + *o* + *adv*, *v* + *adv* + *o*] ‹*stomach*› meter; ‹*feelings/laughter*› contener*

■ **hold off** ① [*v* + *o* + *adv*, *v* + *adv* + *o*] **(a)** (resist) ‹*attack/enemy*› resistir **(b)** (defeat) ‹*challenger/rival*› derrotar
② [*v* + *adv*] (be delayed): **if the rain ~s off** si no empieza a llover

■ **hold on** [*v* + *adv*] **(a)** (wait) esperar **(b)** (survive) resistir, aguantar **(c)** (clasp, grip) agarrarse; **to ~ on TO sth/sb** agarrarse A *or* DE algo/algn **(d)** (keep) **to ~ on TO sth** ‹*receipt/photo*› conservar *or* guardar algo

■ **hold out** ① [*v* + *o* + *adv*, *v* + *adv* + *o*] (extend) ‹*hands/arms*› tender*, alargar*
② [*v* + *adv* + *o*] **(a)** (offer) ‹*possibility*› ofrecer*; ‹*hope*› dar* **(b)** (have, retain) ‹*hope*› tener*; **I don't ~ out much hope of getting the job** no tengo muchas esperanzas de que me den el trabajo
③ [*v* + *adv*] **(a)** (survive, last) «*person*» aguantar **(b)** (resist, make a stand) ‹*army/town*› resistir

■ **hold over** [*v* + *o* + *adv*, *v* + *adv* + *o*] (postpone) ‹*meeting/decision*› aplazar*, postergar* (esp AmL)

■ **hold together** ① [*v* + *adv*] «*arguments*» tener* lógica *or* solidez; «*people*» mantenerse* unidos
② [*v* + *o* + *adv*] (keep united) ‹*family/group*› mantener* unido

■ **hold up** ① [*v* + *o* + *adv*, *v* + *adv* + *o*] **(a)** (raise) ‹*hand/banner*› levantar; ‹*head*› mantener* erguido **(b)** (support) ‹*roof/walls*› sostener* **(c)** (delay) ‹*person/arrival*› retrasar; ‹*progress*› entorpecer* **(d)** (rob) atracar*, asaltar
② [*v* + *adv*] «*theory/argument*» resultar válido

■ **hold with** [*v* + *prep* + *o*] (*usu neg*) estar* de acuerdo con

hold² *n* ① **(a)** (grip, grasp): **to catch** *o* **grab** *o* **take ~ of sth** agarrar *or* (esp Esp) coger* algo; (so as not to fall etc) agarrarse *or* asirse *or* a algo; **to get ~ of sb** (find) localizar* *or* (AmL tb) ubicar* a algn; **to get ~ of sth** (manage to get) conseguir* algo **(b)** (control): **the ~ they have over the members of the sect** el dominio que ejercen sobre los miembros de la secta
② **(a)** (in wrestling, judo) llave *f*; **with no ~s barred** sin ningún tipo de restricciones **(b)** (in mountaineering) asidero *m*
③ (delay, pause) demora *f*; **I've got Mr Brown on ~** (Telec) el Sr Brown está esperando para hablar con usted; **to put sth on ~** ‹*project*› dejar algo aparcado

④ (of ship, aircraft) bodega *f*

holdall /'həʊldɔːl/ *n* (BrE) bolso *m* de viaje, bolsón *m* (RPl)

holder /'həʊldər ‖'həʊldə(r)/ *n* ① (of permit, passport, job) titular *mf*; (of ticket) poseedor, -dora *m,f*; (of bonds etc) titular *mf*, tenedor, -dora *m,f*; (of title, cup) poseedor, -dora *m,f* ② (wallet) funda *f*

holdup /'həʊldʌp/ *n* **(a)** (delay) demora *f*, retraso *m*; (in traffic) atasco *m*, embotellamiento *m* **(b)** (armed robbery) atraco *m*

hole /həʊl/ *n* ① **(a)** (in belt, material, clothing) agujero *m*; (in ground) hoyo *m*, agujero *m*; (in road) bache *m*; (in wall) boquete *m*; **to make a ~ in sth** hacer* un agujero en algo, agujerear algo **(b)** (in argument, proposal) punto *m* débil; **to pick ~s in sth** encontrarle* defectos *or* faltas a algo **(c)** (of animal) madriguera *f* ② (in golf) hoyo *m*
③ (unpleasant place) (colloq): **this town is a real ~!** ¡qué pueblo de mala muerte! (fam)

holiday /'hɒlədeɪ ‖'hɒlədeɪ/ *n* **(a)** (day) fiesta *f*, día *m* festivo, (día *m*) feriado *m* (AmL) **(b)** (period away from work) (esp BrE) (*often pl*) vacaciones *fpl*, licencia *f* (Col, Méx, RPl); **to go/be on ~** irse*/estar* de vacaciones; ‹*before o*› ‹*mood/spirit*› festivo; ‹*cottage*› de vacaciones **(c)** (BrE Educ) (*often pl*) vacaciones *fpl*

holiday: ~ **camp** *n* (BrE) colonia *f* de vacaciones; ~**maker** *n* (BrE) turista *mf*; (on summer holidays) veraneante *mf*; ~ **resort** *n* centro *m* turístico

Holland /'hɒlənd ‖'hɒlənd/ *n* Holanda *f*

holler /'hɑːlər ‖'hɒlə(r)/ *vt/i* (AmE colloq) gritar

hollow¹ /'hɑːləʊ ‖'hɒləʊ/ *adj* ① ‹*tree/tooth/wall*› hueco; ‹*sound*› hueco; ‹*voice*› apagado; ‹*cheeks/eyes*› hundido ② ‹*success/triumph*› vacío; ‹*person*› vacío, vacuo; ‹*promises/threats*› vano, falso; ‹*words*› hueco, vacío

hollow² *n* **(a)** (empty space) hueco *m*; (depression) hoyo *m*, depresión *f* **(b)** (dell, valley) hondonada *f*

■ **hollow out** [*v* + *o* + *adv*, *v* + *adv* + *o*] vaciar*, ahuecar*

holly /'hɑːli ‖'hɒli/ *n* acebo *m*

holocaust /'həʊləkɔːst, 'hɑː- ‖'hɒləkɔːst/ *n* hecatombe *f*, desastre *m*; **nuclear ~** holocausto *m* nuclear; **the H~** el Holocausto

hologram /'həʊləgræm, 'hɑː- ‖'hɒləgræm/ *n* holograma *m*

holster /'həʊlstər ‖'həʊlstə(r)/ *n* pistolera *f*, funda *f* de pistola (*or* revólver *etc*)

holy /'həʊli/ *adj* **-lier, -liest** ‹*ground/place*› sagrado, santo; ‹*day*› de precepto, de guardar; ‹*water*› bendito; ‹*person/life/virtue*› santo; **the H~ Bible** la Sagrada *or* Santa Biblia; **H~ Week** Semana Santa

holy: **H~ Ghost** *n* **the H~ Ghost** el Espíritu Santo; **H~ Spirit** *n* **the H~ Spirit** el Espíritu Santo

homage /'hɑːmɪdʒ ‖'hɒmɪdʒ/ *n* (frml) homenaje *m*; **to pay ~ to sb/sth** rendir* homenaje a algn/algo

home¹ /həʊm/ *n* ① (of person) **(a)** (dwelling) casa *f* **(b)** (in wider sense): **New York is my ~ now** Nueva York es donde vivo ahora; **~ sweet ~** hogar dulce hogar; **to leave ~** irse* de casa **(c)** (family environment) hogar *m*
② (of animal, plant) (Bot, Zool) hábitat *m*
③ **at home (a)** (in house) en casa **(b)** (at ease): ⋯⋰

make yourself at ~ ponte cómodo, estás en tu casa **(c)** (not abroad): **at** ~ **and abroad** dentro y fuera del país **(d)** (Sport) en casa
4 (institution) (for children) asilo *m* (AmL), orfanatorio *m* (Méx), centro *m* de acogida de menores (Esp); (for old people) residencia *f* de ancianos; **dogs'** ~ (BrE) perrera *f*
■ **home in** [*v* + *adv*] **to** ~ **in** ON **sth** localizar* y dirigirse* HACIA algo

home² *adv* 1 (where one lives) ⟨come/arrive⟩ a casa; **I'll be** ~ **at five** estaré en casa a las cinco
2 (to desired place): **to hit** ~ dar* en el blanco; **to drive sth** ~ (**to sb**) hacer(le)* entender algo (a algn)

home³ *adj* (before *n*) **(a)** ⟨address/telephone number⟩ particular; ⟨background/environment⟩ familiar; ⟨cooking/perm⟩ casero; ~ **delivery** (of purchases) entrega *f* a domicilio;~ **visit** (by doctor) (BrE) visita *f* a domicilio **(b)** (of origin): ~ **state** (in US) estado *m* natal *or* de procedencia **(c)** (not foreign) ⟨affairs/market⟩ nacional **(d)** (Sport) ⟨team⟩ de casa, local; ⟨game⟩ en casa

home: ~ **base** *n* (AmE) **(a)** (Busn, Mil) base *f* de operaciones **(b)** (in baseball) ▶ HOME PLATE; **~boy** *n* (AmE sl) compinche *m* (fam), cuate *m* (Méx fam); ~ **brew** *n* cerveza hecha en casa; **~coming** *n* **(a)** (return home) regreso *m*, vuelta *f* (*a casa, a la patria etc*) **(b)** (at school, college) (AmE) *fiesta estudiantil al comienzo del año académico con asistencia de ex-alumnos*; **H~ Counties** *pl n* (in UK) **the H~ Counties** *los condados de los alrededores de Londres*; **~-grown** *adj* (from one's garden) de la huerta propia; (not foreign) del país, local, nacional; ~ **help** *n* (BrE) auxiliar *mf*

homeland /ˈhəʊmlənd/ *n* patria *f*, tierra *f* natal; (before *n*) ~ **security** seguridad *f* de las fronteras

homeless /ˈhəʊmləs/ *adj* sin hogar, sin techo

homely /ˈhəʊmli/ *adj* **-lier, -liest (a)** (characteristic of home) ⟨meal/food⟩ casero; ⟨atmosphere/room⟩ acogedor, hogareño **(b)** (plain) (AmE) feo

home: ~**-made** /ˈhəʊmˈmeɪd/ *adj* ⟨clothes⟩ hecho en casa; ⟨food⟩ casero; ~**-maker** *n* ama *f♯* de casa; ~ **movie** *n* película *f* casera; ~ **office** *n* (AmE) oficina *f* central; **H~ Office** (in UK) **the H~ Office** el Home Office, el Ministerio del Interior británico

homeopathic, (BrE) **homoeopathic** /ˈhəʊmiəˈpæθɪk/ *adj* homeopático

home: ~ **owner** *n* propietario, -ria *m,f* (*de una vivienda*); ~ **page** *n* (Comput) página *f* frontal, página *f* inicial; ~ **plate** *n* home *m*, pentágono *m* (Méx)

homer /ˈhəʊmər/ *n* (AmE colloq) ▶ HOME RUN

home: ~**room** *n* (AmE Educ) clase *f* or aula *f♯* del curso; ~ **rule** *n* autogobierno *m*; ~ **run** *n* cuadrangular *m*, jonrón *m* (AmL); **H~ Secretary** *n* (in UK) ministro, -tra *m,f* del Interior; ~**sick** *adj*: **I am** *o* **feel** ~**sick** echo de menos *or* (AmL tb) extraño a mi familia (*or mi país etc*)

homestead /ˈhəʊmsted/ *n* (AmE) casa *f* (*en una granja, hacienda etc*)

home: ~ **straight,** ~ **stretch** *n* (Sport) recta *f* final *or* de llegada; ~**town** /ˈhəʊmˈtaʊn/ *n* ciudad *f*/pueblo *m* natal; ~ **truth** *n* (*usu pl*) verdad *f* (*desagradable*)

homeward¹ /ˈhəʊmwərd ‖ ˈhəʊmwəd/ **(a)** (BrE also) **homewards** /-z/ *adv* ⟨travel/journey/sail⟩ de vuelta a casa **(b) to be** ~ **bound** ir* de camino *or* de vuelta a casa

homeward² *adj* (before *n*) ⟨journey⟩ de vuelta *or* de regreso

homework /ˈhəʊmwɜːrk ‖ ˈhəʊmwɜːk/ *n* deberes *mpl*, tarea *f*

homey /ˈhəʊmi/ *adj* **homier, homiest** (AmE colloq) ⟨atmosphere/place⟩ hogareño, acogedor; ⟨manner⟩ campechano

homicidal /ˈhɑːmɪˈsaɪdl ‖ ˌhɒmɪˈsaɪdl/ *adj* ⟨tendency⟩ homicida; ⟨rage⟩ asesino

homicide /ˈhɑːməsaɪd ‖ ˈhɒmɪsaɪd/ *n* **(a)** (crime, act) homicidio *m* **(b)** (murderer) (frml) homicida *mf*

homing /ˈhəʊmɪŋ/ *adj* (before *n*) ⟨instinct⟩ de volver al hogar; ⟨device/missile⟩ buscador; ~ **pigeon** paloma *f* mensajera

homoeopathic /ˈhəʊmiəˈpæθɪk/ *adj* (BrE) ▶ HOMEOPATHIC

homogeneous /ˈhəʊməˈdʒiːniəs ‖ ˌhɒməˈdʒiːniəs/ *adj* homogéneo

homosexual¹ /ˈhəʊməˈsekʃʊəl ‖ ˌhəʊməˈsekʃʊəl, ˌhɒmə-/ *adj* homosexual

homosexual² *n* homosexual *mf*

homosexuality /ˈhəʊməˈsekʃʊˈæləti ‖ ˌhəʊməsekʃʊˈæləti, ˌhɒmə-/ *n* homosexualidad *f*

Hon /ɑːn ‖ ɒn/ (in UK) **= Honourable**

Honduran¹ /hɑːnˈdʊrən ‖ hɒnˈdjʊərən/ *adj* hondureño

Honduran² *n* hondureño, -ña *m,f*

Honduras /hɑːnˈdʊrəs ‖ hɒnˈdjʊərəs/ *n* Honduras *f*

hone /həʊn/ *vt* ⟨blade/edge⟩ afilar; ⟨style/skill⟩ afinar

honest /ˈɑːnəst ‖ ˈɒnɪst/ *adj* **(a)** (trustworthy, upright) ⟨person/action⟩ honrado, honesto; ⟨face⟩ de persona honrada *o* honesta **(b)** (sincere) ⟨appraisal/opinion⟩ sincero; **to be** ~ **with you** ... si quieres que te diga la verdad ...

honestly /ˈɑːnəstli ‖ ˈɒnɪstli/ *adv* **(a)** (sincerely) ⟨answer/say/think⟩ sinceramente, francamente **(b)** (indep) en serio, de verdad **(c)** (as interj) (expressing exasperation) ¡por favor! **(d)** (legitimately) ⟨act/earn⟩ con honradez, honradamente

honesty /ˈɑːnəsti ‖ ˈɒnɪsti/ *n* **(a)** (probity) honradez *f*, honestidad *f*, rectitud *f* **(b)** (truthfulness) franqueza *f*, sinceridad *f*; **in all** ~ ... para ser sincero ...

honey /ˈhʌni/ *n* (*pl* **honeys**) 1 miel *f* 2 (*as form of address*) (colloq) cariño (fam)

honey: ~ **bee** *n* abeja *f*; ~**comb** *n* panal *m*; ~**moon** *n* luna *f* de miel; ~**suckle** *n* madreselva *f*

Hong Kong /'hɒːŋ'kɑːŋ ‖,hɒŋ'kɒŋ/ n
Hong-Kong m

honk vi (hoot) «goose» graznar; «driver» tocar*
el claxon, pitar

honor¹, (BrE) **honour** /'ɑːnər ‖'ɒnə(r)/ n
[1] (good name) honor m [2] (privilege, mark of
distinction) honor m; **to have the** ~ **to +** INF o of
-ING (frml) tener* el honor DE + INF (frml); **a
reception in** ~ **of the delegates** una recepción en
honor de los delegados [3] **Honor** (as title) Your/
His H~ Su Señoría [4] **honors** pl (a) (special
mention) (before n) ~s list (AmE) cuadro m de
honor (b) (Educ): **to graduate with** ~s licenciarse
con matrícula (de honor) or con honores; (before
n) **an honours degree** (BrE) ≈ una licenciatura

honor², (BrE) **honour** vt [1] (show respect)
honrar [2] (a) (keep to) «agreement/obligation»
cumplir (con) (b) (Fin) «bill/debt» satisfacer*
(frml), pagar*; «check/draft» pagar*, aceptar

honorable, (BrE) **honourable** /'ɑːnərəbəl
‖'ɒnərəbəl/ adj [1] (a) (honest, respectable)
«person/action» honorable (b) (creditable) «peace/
settlement» honroso [2] **Honourable** (in UK)
tratamiento dado a representantes parlamentarios
y a hijos de vizcondes, barones y condes

honorary /'ɑːnəreri ‖'ɒnərəri/ adj honorario;
«doctorate» honoris causa

honour etc (BrE) ▶ HONOR etc

hood /hʊd/ n [1] (on coat, jacket) capucha f;
(pointed) capirote m; (of monk) capucha f,
capuchón m [2] (a) (on chimney, cooker) campana f;
(on machine) cubierta f (b) (AmE Auto) capó m (c)
(folding cover) (BrE) capota f

hoodlum /'huːdləm/ n (a) (thug) (AmE) matón,
-tona m,f (fam), gorila mf (b) (rowdy youth)
vándalo, -la m,f, gamberro, -rra m,f (Esp)

hoodwink /'hʊdwɪŋk/ vt engañar; **to** ~ **sb
INTO** -ING engañar a algn PARA QUE (+ subj)

hoof /hʊf ‖huːf/ n (pl **hoofs** or **hooves**) (of
horse) casco m, vaso m (RPl), pezuña f (Méx); (of
cow) pezuña f

hoof-and-mouth disease /'hʊfən'maʊθ
‖,huːfən'maʊθ/ n (AmE) fiebre f aftosa, glosopeda
f (téc)

hook¹ /hʊk/ n [1] (a) gancho m; (for hanging
clothes) percha f, gancho m; (for fishing) anzuelo m;
to take the phone off the ~ descolgar* el teléfono;
to let sb off the ~ dejar salir a algn del
atolladero (b) (Clothing) corchete m, ganchito m;
~s and eyes corchetes (macho y hembra) [2] (in
boxing) gancho m

hook² vt (grasp, secure) enganchar
■ **hook up** [1] [v + o + adv, v + adv + o] (a)
(fasten) «dress/bra» abrochar (b) (connect, link)
enganchar [2] [v + adv] (a) (Rad, TV) conectarse,
transmitir en cadena (b) (fasten) «dress»
abrocharse

hooked /hʊkt/ adj [1] (hook-shaped) «tool» en
forma de gancho; «beak» ganchudo; «nose»
aguileño [2] (addicted) (colloq) **to be/get** ~ **ON sth**
estar* enviciado/enviciarse CON algo, estar
enganchado/engancharse A algo (fam)

hooker /'hʊkər ‖'hʊkə(r)/ n (esp AmE colloq)
prostituta f, puta f (vulg)

hooky, hookey /'hʊki/ n: **to play** ~ (esp AmE
colloq) faltar a clase, hacer* novillos or (Méx) irse*

de pinta or (RPl) hacerse* la rata or la rabona or
(Per) la vaca or (Chi) hacer* la cimarra or (Col)
capar clase or (Ven) jubilarse (fam)

hooligan /'huːlɪɡən/ n vándalo, -la m,f,
gamberro, -rra m,f (Esp)

hoop /huːp/ n aro m

hooray /hʊ'reɪ/ interj ¡hurra!

hoot¹ /huːt/ n (of owl) grito m, ululato m; ~s of
laughter risotadas fpl, carcajadas fpl

hoot² vi «owl» ulular; «car/driver» tocar* el
claxon, pitar

hooter /'huːtər ‖'huːtə(r)/ n (BrE) (a) (siren)
sirena f (b) (horn) claxon m, bocina f

hoover /'huːvər ‖'huːvə(r)/ (BrE) vt pasar la
aspiradora or el aspirador por, aspirar (AmL)

Hoover®, hoover /'huːvər ‖'huːvə(r)/ n (BrE)
aspiradora f, aspirador m

hooves /hʊvz ‖huːvz/ pl of HOOF

hop¹ /hɑːp ‖hɒp/ n [1] (jump – of person) salto m
a la pata coja, brinco m de cojito (Méx); (– of
rabbit) salto m, brinco m; (– of bird) saltito m
[2] (Bot, Culin) (usu pl) lúpulo m

hop² -pp- vi (a) «frog/rabbit» brincar*, saltar;
«bird» dar* saltitos (b) «person/child» saltar a
la pata coja, brincar* de cojito (Méx) (c) (move
quickly) (colloq): ~ **in,** I'll take you to the station
súbete, que te llevo a la estación; **to** ~ **on a bus**
tomarse un autobús
■ ~ vt (AmE colloq) «flight/train» tomar, pillar (fam)

hope¹ /həʊp/ n esperanza f; **she did it in the** ~
of a reward lo hizo con la esperanza de obtener
una recompensa

hope² vi esperar; **I** ~ **so/not** espero que sí/que
no; **we're hoping for good weather** esperamos
tener buen tiempo
■ ~ vt **to** ~ (THAT) esperar QUE (+ subj); **to** ~ **to +**
INF esperar + INF

hope chest n (AmE) baúl m or arcón m del
ajuar

hopeful¹ /'həʊpfəl/ adj (a) «person»
esperanzado, optimista (b) (promising)
esperanzador, prometedor

hopeful² n aspirante mf, candidato, -ta m,f

hopefully /'həʊpfəli/ adv (a) (in hopeful way):
can you pay me in dollars? she asked ~ —
¿puedes pagarme en dólares? —preguntó
esperanzada (b) (crit) (indep): **when do you leave?**
— ~, **on Friday** ¿cuándo te vas? — el viernes,
espero

hopeless /'həʊpləs ‖'həʊplɪs/ adj [1] (allowing
no hope) «situation» desesperado; «task» imposible;
he's a ~ **case** «patient» está desahuciado;
(colloq) «pupil» no tiene remedio [2] (incompetent,
inadequate) (colloq): **you're** ~! ¡eres un inútil!; **the
train service on this line is** ~ el servicio de
trenes en esta línea es desastroso or es un
desastre; **to be** ~ **AT sth** ser* negado PARA algo

hopelessly /'həʊpləsli ‖'həʊplɪsli/ adv (a)
(irredeemably) (as intensifier): **to be** ~ **lost/in love**
estar* completamente perdido/perdidamente
enamorado (b) (without hope) sin esperanzas

hopelessness /'həʊpləsnəs ‖'həʊplɪsnɪs/ n
(a) (of situation) lo desesperado (b) (despair)
desesperanza f

hopping /'hɑːpɪŋ ‖'hɒpɪŋ/ adj: **to be** ~ **mad**
(colloq) estar* furioso

hopscotch /ˈhɒpskɒːtʃ ‖ ˈhɒpskɒtʃ/ n: to play ∼ jugar* al tejo or (Méx) al avión or (RPl) a la rayuela or (Col) a la golosa or (Chi) al luche

horde /hɔːrd ‖ hɔːd/ n (colloq) multitud f, horda f

horizon /həˈraɪzən/ n (Geog) the ∼ el horizonte

horizontal /ˌhɒrəˈzɑːntl̩ ‖ ˌhɒrɪˈzɒntl̩/ adj horizontal

hormone /ˈhɔːrməʊn ‖ ˈhɔːməʊn/ n hormona f; (before n) ∼ **replacement therapy** terapia f hormonal sustitiva

horn /hɔːrn ‖ hɔːn/ n **1** (Zool) (of animal) cuerno m, asta f‡, cacho m (AmS), guampa f (CS) **2** (Mus) **(a)** (wind instrument) cuerno m **(b)** (French ∼) trompa f **3** (Auto) claxon m, bocina f; (Naut) sirena f

hornet /ˈhɔːrnət ‖ ˈhɔːnɪt/ n avispón m

horoscope /ˈhɔːrəskəʊp ‖ ˈhɒrəskəʊp/ n horóscopo m

horrendous /hɔːˈrendəs ‖ hɒˈrendəs/ adj **(a)** (horrifying) ⟨crime/account⟩ horrendo, horroroso **(b)** (dreadful) (colloq) ⟨price/mistake⟩ terrible

horrible /ˈhɔːrəbəl ‖ ˈhɒrɪbəl/ adj horrible, horroroso

horrid /ˈhɔːrəd ‖ ˈhɒrɪd/ adj (esp BrE colloq) ⟨weather/taste⟩ horroroso

horrific /hɔːˈrɪfɪk ‖ hɒˈrɪfɪk, hə-/ adj horroroso, espantoso

horrify /ˈhɔːrəfaɪ ‖ ˈhɒrɪfaɪ/ vt **-fies, -fying, -fied** horrorizar*

horrifying /ˈhɔːrəfaɪɪŋ ‖ ˈhɒrɪfaɪɪŋ/ adj horroroso, horrendo, horripilante

horror /ˈhɔːrər ‖ ˈhɒrə(r)/ n horror m; (before n) ⟨movie/story⟩ de terror

horror-struck /ˈhɔːrərstrʌk ‖ ˈhɒrəstrʌk/ adj horrorizado

hors d'oeuvre /ɔːrˈdɜːrv ‖ ɔːˈdɜːvrə/ n (pl **hors d'oeuvres** /-ˈdɜːrv ‖ -ˈdɜːvrə/) entremés m, botana f (Méx)

horse /hɔːrs ‖ hɔːs/ n **1** (Zool) caballo m; **I could eat a** ∼ tengo un hambre canina; (before n) ∼ **riding** (BrE) equitación f **2** (vaulting ∼) potro m, caballo m (Méx)

horse: ∼**back** n: on ∼back a caballo; (before n) ∼back **riding** (AmE) equitación f; ∼**box** n (BrE) ▶ ∼CAR; ∼**car** n (AmE) (for transporting horses) remolque m or trailer m (para transportar caballos); ∼ **chestnut** n **(a)** (tree) castaño m de Indias **(b)** (fruit) castaña f de Indias; ∼**-drawn** adj tirado por caballos; ∼**fly** n tábano m; ∼**man** /ˈhɔːrsmən ‖ ˈhɔːsmən/ n (pl **-men** /-mən/) jinete m; ∼**power** n caballo m (de fuerza); ∼ **racing** n carreras fpl de caballos, hípica f; ∼**radish** /ˈhɔːrsˌrædɪʃ ‖ ˈhɔːsrædɪʃ/ n rábano m picante; ∼**shoe** n herradura f; ∼ **show** n concurso m hípico

horticulture /ˈhɔːrtəˌkʌltʃər ‖ ˈhɔːtɪˌkʌltʃə(r)/ n horticultura f

hose /həʊz/ n **1** (∼pipe) manguera f, manga f; (Auto) manguito m **2** (Clothing) (+ pl vb) **(a)** (tights) (Hist, Theat) calzas fpl, malla f **(b)** (AmE) ▶ PANTYHOSE
- **hose down** [v + o + adv, v + adv + o] lavar (con manguera)

hosepipe /ˈhəʊzpaɪp/ n (esp BrE) ▶ HOSE 1

hosiery /ˈhəʊʒəri ‖ ˈhəʊʒɪəri/ n (fml) calcetería f

hospice /ˈhɑːspəs ‖ ˈhɒspɪs/ n: residencia para enfermos desahuciados

hospitable /hɑːˈspɪtəbəl ‖ hɒˈspɪtəbəl/ adj hospitalario

hospital /ˈhɑːspɪtl̩ ‖ ˈhɒspɪtl̩/ n hospital m

hospitality /ˌhɑːspəˈtæləti ‖ ˌhɒspɪˈtæləti/ n hospitalidad f

hospitalize /ˈhɑːspɪtl̩aɪz ‖ ˈhɒspɪtl̩aɪz/ vt hospitalizar*, internar (CS, Méx)

host¹ /həʊst/ n **1** **(a)** (person dispensing hospitality) anfitrión, -triona m,f; (before n) ⟨country/government⟩ anfitrión **(b)** (Rad, TV) presentador, -dora m,f **2** (of parasite) huésped m **3** (multitude) gran cantidad f **4** **the Host** (Relig) la Sagrada Hostia

host² vt **(a)** (be the venue for) ⟨conference/event⟩ ser* la sede de **(b)** (Rad, TV) ⟨program⟩ presentar

hostage /ˈhɑːstɪdʒ ‖ ˈhɒstɪdʒ/ n rehén m

hostel /ˈhɑːstl̩ ‖ ˈhɒstl̩/ n **(a)** (youth ∼) albergue m juvenil or de juventud **(b)** (for students) (BrE) residencia f; (for homeless people, battered wives etc) hogar m

hostess /ˈhəʊstəs ‖ ˈhəʊstes/ n **(a)** (in private capacity) anfitriona f (aire ∼) (esp BrE) ▶ STEWARDESS B **(c)** (on TV show) (presenter) presentadora f; (assistant) azafata f

hostile /ˈhɑːstl̩ ‖ ˈhɒstaɪl/ adj hostil

hostility /hɑːˈstɪləti ‖ hɒˈstɪləti/ n hostilidad f

hot /hɑːt ‖ hɒt/ adj **-tt-** **1** **(a)** ⟨food/water⟩ caliente; ⟨weather/day/country⟩ caluroso; ⟨climate⟩ cálido; **it's** ∼ **today** hoy hace calor; **I'm** ∼ tengo calor; **to be** ∼ «object» estar* caliente; **to get** ∼ «oven/iron/radiator» calentarse* **(b)** (spicy) picante, picoso **2** **(a)** (fresh) ⟨news/scent⟩ reciente, fresco **(b)** (current) ⟨story/issue⟩ de plena actualidad **(c)** (popular, in demand) ⟨product⟩ de gran aceptación; ⟨play/movie⟩ taquillero **3** (colloq) (knowledgeable, keen): **he's very** ∼ **on current affairs** está muy al tanto en temas de actualidad; **she's** ∼ **on punctuality** le da mucha importancia a la puntualidad

hot: ∼ **air** n palabrería f; ∼**-air balloon** /ˈhɑːt'er ‖ ˌhɒt'eə/ n globo m de aire caliente; ∼**bed** n (of crime, unrest) semillero m; ∼**-blooded** /ˈhɑːt'blʌdəd ‖ ˌhɒt'blʌdɪd/ adj apasionado; ∼ **dog** n perro m or perrito m caliente, pancho m (RPl)

hotel /həʊˈtel/ n hotel m

hotelier /həʊˈteljər ‖ həʊˈteliə(r)/ n hotelero, -ra m,f

hot: ∼ **flush,** (AmE) ∼ **flash** n sofoco m, bochorno m, calor m (RPl fam); ∼**headed** /ˈhɑːt'hedəd ‖ ˌhɒt'hedɪd/ adj exaltado; ∼**house** n invernadero m; (before n) ⟨plant/flowers⟩ de invernadero; ∼ **line** n (Pol) teléfono m rojo; (for public) línea f directa

hotly /ˈhɑːtli ‖ ˈhɒtli/ adv ⟨dispute/deny⟩ con vehemencia; ⟨debated⟩ acaloradamente

hot: ∼ **pepper** n (AmE) pimiento m picante, ají m picante (AmS), chile m (Méx); ∼**plate** n (for cooking) placa f, hornilla f (AmL exc CS), hornalla f (RPl), plato m (Chi); (for keeping food warm) calientaplatos m; ∼ **seat** n (colloq): **to be in the** ∼ **seat** estar* en la línea de fuego; ∼**shot** n personaje m; ∼ **spot** n (colloq) **(a)** (Pol) punto m conflictivo **(b)** (night club) club m nocturno; ∼ **spring** n fuente f termal; ∼**-tempered**

/ˈhɑːtˈtempərd ‖ˌhɒtˈtempəd/ *adj* irascible;
∼-water bottle /ˈhɑːtˈwɔːtər ‖ˌhɒtˈwɔːtə/ *n*
bolsa *f* de agua caliente

hound¹ /haʊnd/ *n* perro *m* de caza, sabueso *m*

hound² *vt* acosar

hour /aʊr ‖aʊə(r)/ *n* **(a)** (60 minutes) hora *f* **(b)**
(time of day) hora *f*; **on the ∼** a la hora en punto;
at 1600 ∼s a las 16:00 horas **(c)** (particular moment)
momento *m*; **her finest ∼** su mejor momento

hourly¹ /ˈaʊrli ‖ˈaʊəli/ *adj* ⟨*rate/wage*⟩ por
hora

hourly² *adv* **(a)** (every hour) ⟨*run/broadcast*⟩
cada hora **(b)** (by the hour) ⟨*pay/charge*⟩ por
hora(s)

house¹ /haʊs/ *n* (*pl* **houses** /ˈhaʊzəz
‖ˈhaʊzɪz/) [1] (dwelling, household) casa *f*; **to put
one's (own) ∼ in order** poner* sus (*or* mis *etc*)
asuntos en orden; **to set up ∼** poner* casa
[2] (Govt) Cámara *f*; **the H∼ of Representatives** (in
US) la Cámara de Representantes *or* de
Diputados; **the H∼ of Commons/of Lords** (in UK)
la Cámara de los Comunes/de los Lores; **the H∼s
of Parliament** (in UK) el Parlamento
[3] (Busn) casa *f*, empresa *f*; **publishing ∼**
editorial *f*; **drinks are on the ∼** invita la casa;
(*before n*) **∼ wine** vino *m* de la casa
[4] (Theat) **(a)** (auditorium) sala *f* **(b)** (audience)
público *m*

house² /haʊz/ *vt* **(a)** (accommodate) ⟨*person/
family*⟩ alojar **(b)** (contain) ⟨*office/museum*⟩
albergar*

house /haʊs/: **∼ arrest** *n* arresto *m*
domiciliario; **∼boat** *n* casa *f* flotante; **∼bound**
adj: **she's 85 and completely ∼bound** tiene 85
años y está completamente confinada a su casa;
∼broken *adj* (AmE) ⟨*pet*⟩ enseñado; **∼fly** *n*
mosca *f* común *or* doméstica

household /ˈhaʊshəʊld/ *n* casa *f*; **∼s with
more than one wage earner** las familias *or* (fml)
los hogares donde trabajan dos o más personas;
(*before n*) **a ∼ name** un nombre muy conocido

householder /ˈhaʊshəʊldər ‖ˈhaʊshəʊldə(r)/
n dueño, -ña *m,f* de casa

house /haʊs/: **∼-hunt** *vi* (*usu in* -ing *form*)
buscar* casa (*para comprar o alquilar*);
∼husband *n* (hum) hombre que se ocupa de la
casa mientras su mujer sale a trabajar, amo *m* de
casa (hum); **∼keeper** *n* (woman) ama *f* de llaves;
(in hotel) gobernanta *f*; (man) encargado *m* de la
casa; **∼keeping** *n* (running of home) gobierno
m de la casa **(b) ∼keeping** (money) dinero *m*
(para los gastos) de la casa; **∼maid** *n* criada *f*,
mucama *f* (AmL); **∼plant** *n* planta *f* de interior;
∼-proud *adj* (esp BrE) muy meticuloso (*en la
limpieza y el arreglo de la casa*); **∼-to-∼**
/ˈhaʊstəˈhaʊs/ *adj* ⟨*inquiries/search*⟩ puerta a
puerta; **∼-trained** *adj* (BrE) ⟨*pet*⟩ enseñado;
∼warming (party) /ˈhaʊsˌwɔːrmɪŋ
‖ˈhaʊsˌwɔːmɪŋ/ *n*: fiesta de inauguración de una
casa; **∼wife** *n* ama *f* de casa; **∼work** *n* tareas
fpl domésticas, trabajo *m* de la casa

housing /ˈhaʊzɪŋ/ *n* **(a)** (dwellings) viviendas *fpl*
(b) (provision of houses): **the government's policy
on ∼** la política del gobierno en cuanto al
problema de la vivienda

housing: ∼ association *n* (in UK) asociación
que construye o renueva viviendas para
alquilarlas a precios módicos; **∼ development**

n (AmE) complejo *m* habitacional, urbanización *f*
(Esp), fraccionamiento *m* (Méx); **∼ estate** *n*
(BrE) **(a)** (council estate) urbanización de viviendas
de alquiler subvencionadas por el ayuntamiento
(b) (privately owned) ▶ **∼** DEVELOPMENT; **∼
project** *n* (in US) complejo *m* de viviendas
subvencionadas

hovel /ˈhʌvəl ‖ˈhɒvəl/ *n* casucha *f*, rancho *m*
(RPl)

hover /ˈhʌvər ‖ˈhɒvə(r)/ *vi* «*helicopter*»
sostenerse* en el aire (*sin avanzar*); «*bird*»
cernerse*; **the temperature ∼ed around 20°** la
temperatura rondaba los 20°; **the waiter ∼ed
around, waiting for a tip** el mesero estuvo
rodando la mesa, esperando una propina

hovercraft /ˈhʌvərkræft ‖ˈhɒvəkrɑːft/ *n* (*pl*
-craft *or* **-crafts**) aerodeslizador *m*

how /haʊ/ *adv* [1] (in questions) cómo; **∼ are you?**
¿cómo estás?
[2] (*with adjs, advs*) **(a)** (in questions): **∼ wide is it?**
¿cuánto mide *or* tiene de ancho?, ¿qué tan ancho
es? (AmL exc CS); **∼ heavy is it?** ¿cuánto pesa?; **∼
often do you meet?** ¿con qué frecuencia se
reúnen?; **∼ old are you?** ¿cuántos años tienes?
(b) (in exclamations) qué; **∼ strange/rude!** ¡qué
raro/grosero!
[3] (*in phrases*) **how about** *o* (colloq) **how's about
sth: Thursday's no good; ∼ about Friday?** el
jueves no puede ser ¿qué te parece el viernes?; **I'd
love to go; ∼ about you?** me encantaría ir ¿y a
ti?; **how come** (colloq): **∼ come the door's locked?**
¿cómo es que la puerta está cerrada con llave?

however /haʊˈevər ‖haʊˈevə(r)/ *adv* [1] (*as
linker*) sin embargo, no obstante (fml) [2] (*used
before adj or adv*) (no matter how): **∼ hard she tried
... por más que trataba ...** [3] (interrog) cómo

howl¹ /haʊl/ *vi* **(a)** ⟨*dog/wolf*⟩ aullar*;
«*person*» dar* alaridos; «*wind/gale*» aullar*,
bramar **(b)** (weep noisily) (colloq) berrear (fam)

howl² *n* (of dog, wolf) aullido *m*; (of person)
alarido *m*, aullido *m*

hp (= **horsepower**) CV, HP

HP *n* (BrE) = **hire purchase**

HQ *n* = **headquarters**

hr (= **hour**) h.

HRH (in UK) (= **Her/His Royal Highness**)
S.A.R.

HRT *n* = **hormone replacement therapy**

HTML *n* (Comput) (= **hypertext markup
language**) HTML *m*

hub /ˈhʌb/ *n* **(a)** (of wheel) cubo *m* **(b)** (focal point)
centro *m*

hub cap *n* tapacubos *m*, taza *f* (RPl)

huddle¹ /ˈhʌdl/ *vi* **(a)** **∼ (together)** (crowd
together) apiñarse **(b)** **∼ (up)** (curl up) acurrucarse*

huddle² *n* (tight group) grupo *m*, corrillo *m*; (in
US football) timbac *m*, jol *m*

hue /hjuː/ *n* (liter) (color) color *m*; (shade) tono *m*

hue and cry *n* (*no pl*) revuelo *m*

huff /hʌf/ *n* (*no pl*): **to be in a ∼** estar*
enfurruñado, estar* con mufa (RPl fam)

hug¹ /hʌg/ *vt* -**gg**- **(a)** (embrace) abrazar* **(b)**
(keep close to) ir* pegado a

hug² *n* abrazo *m*

huge /ˈhjuːdʒ/ *adj* enorme

hull /hʌl/ *n* (of ship, plane, tank) casco *m*

hullo /hə'ləʊ ‖hʌ'ləʊ/ (esp BrE) ▶ HELLO

hum¹ /hʌm/ **-mm-** *vi* «*machinery/bee/wire*» zumbar; «*person*» tararear (*con la boca cerrada*)
■ ~ *vt* «*tune*» tararear (*con la boca cerrada*)

hum² *n* (*no pl*) (of bees, machinery) zumbido *m*; (of voices, traffic) murmullo *m*

human¹ /'hju:mən/ *adj* humano

human² *n* ser* *m* humano

human being *n* ser *m* humano

humane /hju:'meɪn/ *adj* humanitario, humano

humanism /'hju:mənɪzəm/ *n* humanismo *m*

humanist /'hju:mənəst ‖'hju:mənɪst/ *n* humanista *mf*

humanitarian /hju:'mænə'teriən ‖hju:,mænɪ'teəriən/ *adj* humanitario

humanities /hju:'mænətiz/ *n* (a) (+ *pl vb*) the ~ las humanidades, las artes y las letras (b) (discipline) (+ *sing vb*) humanidades *fpl*

humanity /hju:'mænəti/ *n* humanidad *f*

human: ~ nature *n* naturaleza *f* humana; **~ rights** *pl n* derechos *mpl* humanos

humble /'hʌmbəl/ *adj* humilde

humbly /'hʌmbli/ *adv* humildemente

humdrum /'hʌmdrʌm/ *adj* monótono, rutinario

humid /'hju:məd ‖'hju:mɪd/ *adj* húmedo

humidity /hju:'mɪdəti/ *n* humedad *f*

humiliate /hju:'mɪlieɪt/ *vt* humillar

humiliating /hju:'mɪlieɪtɪŋ/ *adj* humillante

humiliation /hju:'mɪli'eɪʃən/ *n* humillación *f*

humility /hju:'mɪləti/ *n* humildad *f*

humor¹, (BrE) **humour** /'hju:mər ‖'hju:mə(r)/ *n* humor *m*

humor², (BrE) **humour** *vt* seguirle* la corriente a

humorless, (BrE) **humourless** /'hju:mərləs ‖'hju:mələs/ *adj* «*person*» sin sentido del humor

humorous /'hju:mərəs/ *adj* «*novel/play/speech*» humorístico; «*situation*» cómico, gracioso

humour *n/vt* (BrE) ▶ HUMOR¹,²

hump /hʌmp/ *n* (a) (of camel) joroba *f*, giba *f*; (of person) joroba *f* (b) (in ground) montículo *m*

hunch¹ /hʌntʃ/ *vt* «*back/shoulders*» encorvar

hunch² *n* (intuitive feeling) (colloq) presentimiento *m*, pálpito *m*, corazonada *f*

hunch: ~back *n* (person) jorobado, -da *m,f*; (hump) joroba *f*; **~backed** /'hʌntʃbækt/ *adj* jorobado

hundred /'hʌndrəd/ *n* cien *m*; **a/one ~** cien; **a/one ~ and one** ciento uno; **two ~** doscientos; **five ~** quinientos; **five ~ pages** quinientas páginas; **in (the year) fifteen ~** en el (año) mil quinientos; **she lived in the seventeen ~s** vivió en el siglo XVIII; **ten ~s are a thousand** diez centenas son un millar; **they are sold by the ~** o in **~s** se venden de a cien *or* (Esp) de cien en cien; **a/one ~ thousand/million** cien mil/millones; **~s of times** cientos de veces

hundredfold /'hʌndrədfəʊld/ *adj/adv* ▶ -FOLD

hundredth¹ /'hʌndrədθ/ *adj* centésimo

hundredth² *adv* en centésimo lugar

hundredth³ *n* (Math) centésimo *m*; (part) centésima parte *f*

hundredweight /'hʌndrədweɪt/ *n* (*pl* ~) unidad de peso equivalente a 45,36kg. en EEUU y a 50,80kg. en RU

hung /hʌŋ/ *past & past p of* HANG¹

Hungarian¹ /hʌŋ'geriən ‖hʌŋ'geəriən/ *adj* húngaro

Hungarian² *n* (a) (language) húngaro *m* (b) (person) húngaro, -ra *m,f*

Hungary /'hʌŋgəri/ *n* Hungría *f*

hunger /'hʌŋgər ‖'hʌŋgə(r)/ *n* (a) (physical) hambre *f*; (b) (strong desire) (*no pl*): **a ~ for adventure** un ansia *f* or (liter) hambre de aventura

hunger strike *n* huelga *f* de hambre

hung: ~ jury *n*: jurado que se disuelve al no ponerse de acuerdo sus miembros; **~over** /hʌŋ'əʊvər‖hʌŋ'əʊvə(r)/ *adj* **to be ~over** tener* resaca *or* (Col fam) guayabo *or* (AmL, Méx fam) cruda *or* (Ven fam) ratón

hungrily /'hʌŋgrəli ‖'hʌŋgrɪli/ *adv* ávidamente

hungry /'hʌŋgri/ *adj* **-grier, -griest** hambriento; **to be ~** tener* hambre; **to be ~ FOR sth** estar* ávido DE algo

hunk /hʌŋk/ *n* (a) (chunk) trozo *m*, pedazo *m* (b) (man) (colloq): **he's a real ~** está buenísimo (fam)

hunt¹ /hʌnt/ *vt* **1** «*game/fox*» cazar* **2** (search for) buscar*
■ ~ *vi* (a) (pursue game) cazar*; **to go ~ing** ir* de caza *or* de cacería (b) (search) **to ~ (FOR sth)** buscar* (algo)
■ **hunt down** [*v + o + adv, v + adv + o*] «*animal/fugitive*» darle* caza a

hunt² *n* **1** (a) (chase) caza *f*, cacería *f* (b) (hunters) partida *f* de caza, cacería *f* **2** (search) búsqueda *f*

hunter /'hʌntər ‖'hʌntə(r)/ *n* (person) cazador, -dora *m,f*; (horse) caballo *m* de caza

hunting /'hʌntɪŋ/ *n* (Sport) caza *f*, cacería *f*

hurdle /'hɜ:rdl ‖'hɜ:dl̩/ *n* (a) (Sport) (obstacle) obstáculo *m*, valla *f*; *see also* HURDLES (b) (problem) obstáculo *m*

hurdles /'hɜ:rdlz ‖'hɜ:dl̩z/ *n* (+ *sing vb*) vallas *fpl*

hurl /hɜ:rl ‖hɜ:l/ *vt* tirar, arrojar, lanzar*

hurrah /hʊ'rɑ:/, **hurray** /hʊ'reɪ/ *interj* ▶ HOORAY

hurricane /'hɜ:rəkeɪn ‖'hʌrɪkən, -keɪn/ *n* huracán *m*

hurry¹ /'hɜ:ri ‖'hʌri/ *n* (*no pl*) prisa *f*, apuro *m* (AmL); **I'm in a ~** tengo prisa, estoy apurado (AmL); **he wrote it in a ~** lo escribió deprisa (fam)

hurry² **-ries, -rying, -ried** *vi* (a) (make haste) darse* prisa, apurarse (AmL) (b) (move hastily) (+ *adv compl*): **she hurried after him** corrió tras él; **he hurried back/in/out** volvió/entró/salió corriendo

---

AmC	Central America	Arg	Argentina	Cu	Cuba	Per Peru
AmL	Latin America	Bol	Bolivia	Ec	Ecuador	RPI River Plate Area
AmS	South America	Chi	Chile	Esp	Spain	Ur Uruguay
Andes	Andean Region	CS	Southern Cone	Méx	Mexico	Ven Venezuela

711

■ ~ *vt* **(a)** ⟨*person*⟩ meterle prisa a, apurar (AmL) **(b)** ⟨*work*⟩ hacer* apresuradamente

■ **hurry away, hurry off** [*v + adv*] alejarse rápidamente

■ **hurry up** **1** [*v + adv*] darse* prisa, apurarse (AmL) **2** [*v + o + adv*, *v + adv + o*] ⟨*person*⟩ meterle prisa a, apurar (AmL); ⟨*work*⟩ acelerar, apurar (AmL)

hurt¹ /hɜːrt ‖hɜːt/ (*past & past p* **hurt**) *vt* **1** **(a)** (cause pain): **you're ~ing her/me!** ¡le/me estás haciendo daño!, ¡la/me estás lastimando! (esp AmL) **(b)** (injure): **I ~ my ankle** me hice daño en el tobillo, me lastimé el tobillo (esp AmL); **to ~ oneself, to get ~** hacerse* daño, lastimarse (esp AmL)

2 (distress emotionally): **I've been ~ too often** me han hecho sufrir demasiadas veces; **to ~ sb's feelings** herir* los sentimientos de algn

■ ~ *vi* **1** (be source of pain) doler*; **my leg ~s** me duele la pierna

2 (have adverse effects): **it won't ~ to postpone it for a while** no pasa nada si lo dejamos por el momento

3 (suffer adverse effects) (AmE colloq): **to be ~ing** estar* pasándola *or* pasándolo mal (fam)

hurt² *n* (emotional) dolor *m*, pena *f*

hurt³ *adj* **(a)** (physically) ⟨*finger/foot*⟩ lastimado; **she was badly ~** estaba gravemente herida **(b)** (emotionally) ⟨*feelings/pride*⟩ herido; ⟨*tone/ expression*⟩ dolido; **to feel/be ~** sentirse*/estar* dolido

hurtful /'hɜːrtfəl ‖'hɜːtfəl/ *adj* hiriente

hurtle /'hɜːrtl̩ ‖'hɜːtl̩/ *vi* (+ *adv compl*): **to ~ along/past** ir*/pasar volando *or* a toda velocidad

husband /'hʌzbənd/ *n* marido *m*, esposo *m*

hush¹ /hʌʃ/ *n* (*no pl*) silencio *m*

hush² *vt* (quieten) hacer* callar; (calm down) calmar

■ **hush up** **1** [*v + o + adv*, *v + adv + o*] ⟨*scandal/ story*⟩ acallar **2** [*v + adv*] (be quiet) (AmE colloq) callarse

hush³ *interj*: ~! ¡shh!, ¡chitón!

hushed /hʌʃt/ *adj* (*before n*) silencioso; **in ~ tones** en voz muy baja, en murmullos

hush-hush *adj* (colloq) super secreto (fam)

husk /hʌsk/ *n* (of wheat, rice) cáscara *f*, cascarilla *f*; (of maize) chala *f or* (Esp) farfolla *f*

husky¹ /'hʌski/ *adj* **-kier, -kiest** ronco

husky² *n* (*pl* **-kies**) husky *mf*, perro, -rra *m,f* esquimal

hustings /'hʌstɪŋz/ *pl n* **the ~** la campaña electoral

hustle¹ /'hʌsəl/ *vt* **1** **(a)** (move hurriedly) (+ *adv compl*): **she was ~d into the car** la metieron en el coche a empujones; **he was ~d away by his bodyguards** sus guardaespaldas se lo llevaron precipitadamente **(b)** (pressure) apremiar, meterle prisa a, apurar (AmL) **2** (AmE colloq) **(a)** (obtain aggressively) hacerse* con **(b)** (hawk, sell) vender

hustle² *n* **1** (hurry) ajetreo *m*; **the ~ and bustle of the big city** el ajetreo y bullicio de la gran ciudad **2** (trick, swindle) (AmE colloq) chanchullo *m* (fam)

hustler /'hʌslər ‖'hʌslə(r)/ *n* (AmE) **(a)** (hard worker) (colloq) persona *f* trabajadora **(b)** (swindler) (sl) estafador, -dora *m,f* **(c)** (prostitute) (sl) puto, -ta *m,f* (vulg)

hut /hʌt/ *n* **(a)** (cabin) cabaña *f*; (of mud, straw) choza *f* **(b)** (hovel) casucha *f*

hutch /'hʌtʃ/ *n* (rabbit ~) conejera *f*

hyaena /haɪ'iːnə/ *n* ▶ HYENA

hybrid /'haɪbrəd ‖'haɪbrɪd/ *n* híbrido *m*

hydrant /'haɪdrənt/ *n* boca *f* de riego, toma *f* de agua, hidrante *m* (AmC, Col); (fire ~) boca *f* de incendios *or* (Esp) de riego, toma *f* de agua, hidrante *m* de incendios (AmC, Col), grifo *m* (Chi)

hydraulic /haɪ'drɔːlɪk ‖haɪ'drɔːlɪk, haɪ'drɒlɪk/ *adj* hidráulico

hydrocarbon /ˌhaɪdrəʊ'kɑːrbən ‖ˌhaɪdrə'kɑːbən/ *n* hidrocarburo *m*

hydroelectric /'haɪdrəʊɪ'lektrɪk/ *adj* hidroeléctrico

hydrofoil /'haɪdrəfɔɪl/ *n* (vessel) hidrodeslizador *m*, aliscafo *m*

hydrogen /'haɪdrədʒən/ *n* hidrógeno *m*

hyena /haɪ'iːnə/ *n* hiena *f*

hygiene /'haɪdʒiːn/ *n* higiene *f*

hygienic /haɪ'dʒiːnɪk/ *adj* higiénico

hymn /hɪm/ *n* (Relig) cántico *m*, himno *m*

hype¹ /haɪp/ *n* (colloq) despliegue *m or* bombo *m* publicitario

hype² *vt* (colloq) promocionar con bombos y platillos *or* (Esp) a bombo y platillo

■ **hype up** [*v + adv + o*, *v + o + adv*] (colloq) ⟨*movie*⟩ promocionar con bombos y platillos *or* (Esp) a bombo y platillo; ⟨*person*⟩ poner* nervioso

hyperactive /'haɪpər'æktɪv/ *adj* hiperactivo

hypermarket /'haɪpər,mɑːrkət ‖'haɪpəmɑːkɪt/ *n* (BrE) hipermercado *m*

hypertension /'haɪpər'tenʃən ‖ˌhaɪpə'tenʃən/ *n* hipertensión *f*

hypertext markup language /'haɪpərtekst ‖'haɪpətekst/ *n* (Comput) lenguaje *m* de marcado de hipertexto

hyperventilate /'haɪpər'ventleɪt ‖ˌhaɪpə'ventɪleɪt/ *vi* hiperventilarse

hyphen /'haɪfən/ *n* guion *m*

hypnosis /hɪp'nəʊsəs ‖hɪp'nəʊsɪs/ *n* hipnosis *f*

hypnotic /hɪp'nɑːtɪk ‖hɪp'nɒtɪk/ *adj* ⟨*suggestion/state*⟩ hipnótico; ⟨*voice/eyes/rhythm*⟩ hipnotizador, hipnotizante

hypnotism /'hɪpnətɪzəm/ *n* hipnotismo *m*

hypnotist /'hɪpnətəst ‖'hɪpnətɪst/ *n* hipnotizador, -dora *m,f*

hypnotize /'hɪpnətaɪz/ *vt* hipnotizar*

hypoallergenic /'haɪpəʊ,æler'dʒenɪk ‖ˌhaɪpəʊ,ælə'dʒenɪk/ *adj* hipoalérgeno

hypochondriac /'haɪpə'kɑːndriæk ‖ˌhaɪpə'kɒndriæk/ *n* hipocondríaco, -ca *m,f*

hypocrisy /hɪ'pɑːkrəsi ‖hɪ'pɒkrəsi/ *n* (*pl* **-sies**) hipocresía *f*

hypocrite /'hɪpəkrɪt/ *n* hipócrita *mf*

hypocritical /'hɪpə'krɪtɪkəl/ *adj* hipócrita

hypodermic¹ /'haɪpə'dɜːrmɪk ‖ˌhaɪpə'dɜːmɪk/ *adj* hipodérmico

hypodermic² *n* (aguja *f*) hipodérmica *f*

hypothermia /'haɪpə'θɜːrmiə ‖ˌhaɪpə'θɜːmiə/ *n* hipotermia *f*

hypothesis /haɪ'pɑːθəsəs ‖haɪ'pɒθəsɪs/ *n* (*pl* **-ses** /-siːz/) hipótesis *f*

hypothetical /'haɪpə'θetɪkəl/ *adj* hipotético

hysterectomy /ˌhɪstəˈrektəmi/ n (pl **-mies**) histerectomía f

hysteria /hɪˈstɪriə ‖ hɪˈstɪəriə/ n histerismo m, histeria f

hysterical /hɪˈsterɪkəl/ adj **(a)** (Psych) histérico **(b)** (very funny) (colloq) para morirse de (la) risa

hysterics /hɪˈsterɪks/ pl n **(a)** (nervous agitation) histeria f, histerismo m; **to go into** or **have ∼** ponerse* histérico **(b)** (laughter) (colloq) **to be in ∼** estar* como loco

I i

I, i /aɪ/ n I, i f

I /aɪ/pron yo

■ **Note** Although yo is given as the main translation of I, it is in practice used only for emphasis, or to avoid ambiguity: I went to the theater fui al teatro; I was singing, he was playing the piano yo cantaba y él tocaba el piano; I did it yo lo hice.

IA = **Iowa**

IBA n (in UK) = **Independent Broadcasting Authority**

Iberian /aɪˈbɪriən ‖ aɪˈbɪəriən/ adj ibérico

ice[1] /aɪs/ n [1] (frozen water) hielo m; **to break the ∼** (overcome reserve) romper* el hielo; (make a start) (AmE) dar* los primeros pasos [2] (sherbet) (AmE) sorbete m, helado m de agua (AmL), nieve f (Méx)

ice[2] vt ⟨cake⟩ bañar ⟨con fondant⟩

Ice Age n: **the ∼** la edad de hielo

iceberg /ˈaɪsbɜːrg ‖ ˈaɪsbɜːg/ n iceberg m

ice: **∼box** n **(a)** (refrigerator) (AmE colloq & dated) refrigerador m, nevera f, heladera f (RPl) **(b)** (freezing compartment) (BrE) congelador m; **∼ cream** n helado m; **∼ cube** n cubito m de hielo

iced /aɪst/ adj [1] (chilled) helado [2] (Culin) glaseado

ice hockey n hockey m sobre hielo

Iceland /ˈaɪslənd/ n Islandia f

Icelandic[1] /aɪsˈlændɪk/ adj islandés

Icelandic[2] n islandés m

ice: **∼ lolly** n (BrE) paleta f helada or (Esp) polo m or (RPl) palito m helado or (CS) chupete m helado; **∼ rink** n (BrE) pista f de (patinaje sobre) hielo; **∼ skating** n patinaje m sobre hielo

icicle /ˈaɪsɪkəl/ n carámbano m (de hielo)

icing /ˈaɪsɪŋ/ n (Culin) glaseado m

icing sugar n (BrE) azúcar m or f glas(é) or (RPl) impalpable or (Chi) flor or (Col) en polvo

icon /ˈaɪkɑːn ‖ ˈaɪkɒn/ n icono m, ícono m

icy /ˈaɪsi/ adj **icier, iciest** **(a)** ⟨wind/rain⟩ helado, glacial; ⟨feet/hands⟩ helado; (as adv) **∼ cold** helado **(b)** ⟨stare/reception⟩ glacial **(c)** ⟨roads/ground⟩ cubierto de hielo

ID **(a)** = **identification** **(b)** = **Idaho**

idea /aɪˈdiːə ‖ aɪˈdiə/ n idea f; **I had an ∼** se me ocurrió una idea; **that's the general ∼** de eso se trata; **that's not my ∼ of fun** eso no es lo que yo entiendo por diversión; **where is he? — (I've) no ∼!** ¿dónde está? — (no tengo) ni idea

ideal[1] /aɪˈdiːəl/ adj ideal

ideal[2] n ideal m

idealism /aɪˈdiːəlɪzəm/ n idealismo m

idealist /aɪˈdiːəlɪst ‖ aɪˈdiːəlɪst/ n idealista mf

idealistic /aɪˌdiːəˈlɪstɪk ‖ ˌaɪdɪəˈlɪstɪk/ adj idealista

idealize /aɪˈdiːəlaɪz ‖ aɪˈdɪəlaɪz/ vt idealizar*

ideally /aɪˈdiːəli ‖ aɪˈdɪəli/ adv ⟨located/placed/equipped⟩ inmejorablemente; **they are ∼ suited** están hechos el uno para el otro; **∼, no one would have to do it** (indep) lo ideal sería que nadie tuviera que hacerlo

identical /aɪˈdentɪkəl/ adj idéntico; **∼ twins** gemelos mpl univitelinos (téc), gemelos mpl (AmL), gemelos mpl idénticos (Esp); **to be ∼ TO** o **WITH sth** ser* idéntico A algo

identification /aɪˌdentəfəˈkeɪʃən ‖ aɪˌdentɪfɪˈkeɪʃən/ n **(a)** (act of identifying) identificación f **(b)** (evidence of identity): **have you got any ∼?** ¿tiene algún documento que acredite su identidad?

identification parade n (BrE) rueda f de identificación or de sospechosos

identify /aɪˈdentəfaɪ ‖ aɪˈdentɪfaɪ/ **-fies, -fying, -fied** vt identificar*
■ v refl (reveal identity) **to ∼ oneself** identificarse*
■ **∼** vi **to ∼ WITH sb/sth** identificarse* CON algn/ algo

Identikit® /aɪˈdentəkɪt ‖ aɪˈdentɪkɪt/ n: **∼ picture** Identikit® m, retrato m hablado (AmS) or (Méx) reconstruido or (Esp) robot

identity /aɪˈdentəti/ n (pl **-ties**) identidad f; (before n) **∼ card** carné m or (AmL tb) cédula f de identidad; **∼ theft** robo m de identidad

ideological /ˈaɪdiəˈlɑːdʒɪkəl ‖ ˌaɪdɪəˈlɒdʒɪkəl/ adj ideológico

ideology /ˈaɪdiˈɑːlədʒi ‖ ˌaɪdiˈɒlədʒi/ n (pl **-gies**) ideología f

idiom /ˈɪdiəm/ n modismo m

idiomatic /ˌɪdiəˈmætɪk/ adj idiomático

idiosyncrasy /ˌɪdiəˈsɪŋkrəsi/ n (pl **-sies**) idiosincrasia f

idiosyncratic /ˌɪdiəsɪŋˈkrætɪk ‖ ˌɪdiəsɪŋˈkrætɪk/ adj idiosincrásico

idiot /ˈɪdiət/ n idiota mf

idiotic /ˌɪdiˈɑːtɪk ‖ ˌɪdiˈɒtɪk/ adj idiota

idle[1] /ˈaɪdl/ adj **idler** /ˈaɪdlər ‖ ˈaɪdlə(r)/, **idlest** /ˈaɪdləst ‖ ˈaɪdlɪst/ [1] **(a)** (not in use or employment): **to be ∼** «worker» no tener* trabajo; «machine/

factory» estar* parado **(b)** (unoccupied) ‹*hours/ moment*› de ocio **2** (lazy) holgazán **3** (frivolous): **it was ~ curiosity** era pura curiosidad; **~ speculation** conjeturas *fpl* inútiles

idle² *vi* **(a)** (be lazy) holgazanear **(b)** (Auto) «*engine*» andar* al ralentí

idleness /'aɪdl̩nəs ‖'aɪdl̩nɪs/ *n* **(a)** (involuntary inactivity) inactividad *f* **(b)** (laziness) holgazanería *f*

idol /'aɪdl̩/ *n* ídolo *m*

idolize /'aɪdl̩aɪz/ *vt* idolatrar

idyll /'aɪdl̩ ‖'ɪdɪl/ *n* idilio *m*

idyllic /aɪ'dɪlɪk ‖ɪ'dɪlɪk/ *adj* idílico

i.e. /'aɪ'iː/ (that is) (in writing) i.e.; (in speech) esto es

if /ɪf/ *conj* **1** (on condition that) si; **~ I were you, I wouldn't do it** it yo en tu lugar *or* yo que tú, no lo haría; **she was very offhand, ~ not downright rude** estuvo muy brusca, por no decir verdaderamente grosera; **~ nothing else** aunque no sea más que eso; **~ so** (*as linker*) si es así **2** (whether) si **3** (though) aunque, si bien

igloo /'ɪgluː/ *n* iglú *m*

ignite /ɪg'naɪt/ *vt* prenderle fuego a ∎ *vi* «*fuel/paper*» prenderse fuego

ignition /ɪg'nɪʃən/ *n* **(a)** (act) encendido *m* **(b)** (mechanism) (Auto) encendido *m*; (before *n*) **~ key** llave *f* de contacto *or* (AmL tb) del arranque

ignorance /'ɪgnərəns/ *n* ignorancia *f*

ignorant /'ɪgnərənt/ *adj* (lacking knowledge) ignorante; **to be ~ of sth** ignorar algo

ignore /ɪg'nɔːr ‖ɪg'nɔː(r)/ *vt* ‹*person/remark*› ignorar; ‹*warning*› hacer* caso omiso de; **we can't ~ the fact that** ... no podemos dejar de tener en cuenta el hecho de que ...

IL = **Illinois**

ilk /ɪlk/ *n* tipo *m*

ill¹ /ɪl/ *adj* **1** **-er, -est** (unwell) enfermo; **to feel ~** sentirse* mal **2** (bad) (*before n*): **~ effects** efectos *mpl* negativos; **his ~ health** su mala salud

ill² *adv* (*no comp*) **(a)** (hardly): **I can ~ afford to buy a new car** mal puedo yo permitirme comprar un coche nuevo **(b)** (badly) (frml) mal; **to speak ~ of sb** hablar mal de algn

ill³ *n* mal *m*

Ill = **Illinois**

I'll /aɪl/ = **I will, I shall**

ill: ~-advised /'ɪləd'vaɪzd/ *adj* ‹*action*› desacertado; **you would be ~-advised to go** no sería aconsejable que fueras; **~ at ease** *adj* (*pred*) (uncomfortable) incómodo; (anxious) inquieto; **~-bred** /'ɪl'bred/ *adj* sin educación

illegal /ɪ'liːgəl/ *adj* **(a)** (unlawful) ilegal **(b)** (AmE Sport) antirreglamentario

illegible /ɪ'ledʒəbəl/ *adj* ilegible

illegitimate /'ɪlɪ'dʒɪtəmət ‖ˌɪlɪ'dʒɪtɪmət/ *adj* ilegítimo

ill: ~-fated /'ɪl'feɪtəd ‖ˌɪl'feɪtɪd/ *adj* infortunado; **~ feeling** *n* resentimiento *m*, rencor *m*; **~-gotten** /'ɪl'gɑːtn̩ ‖ˌɪl'gɒtn̩/*adj*: **~-gotten gains** dinero *m* mal habido

illicit /ɪ'lɪsət ‖ɪ'lɪsɪt/ *adj* ilícito

ill-informed /'ɪlɪn'fɔːrmd ‖ˌɪlɪn'fɔːmd/ *adj* mal informado

illiteracy /ɪ'lɪtərəsi/ *n* analfabetismo *m*

illiterate /ɪ'lɪtərət/ *adj* analfabeto

illness /'ɪlnəs ‖'ɪlnɪs/ *n* enfermedad *f*

illogical /ɪ'lɑːdʒɪkəl ‖ɪ'lɒdʒɪkəl/ *adj* ilógico

ill: ~-treat /'ɪl'triːt/ *vt* maltratar; **~-treatment** /'ɪl'triːtmənt/ *n* malos tratos *mpl*

illuminate /ɪ'luːmənɪt ‖ɪ'luːmɪneɪt/ *vt* iluminar

illumination /ɪˌluːmə'neɪʃən ‖ɪˌluːmɪ'neɪʃən/ *n* iluminación *f*

illusion /ɪ'luːʒən/ *n* **(a)** (false appearance): **to give *o* create an ~ of sth** dar* la impresión de algo; (Art) crear la ilusión de algo; **an optical ~** una ilusión óptica **(b)** (false idea) ilusión *f*

illustrate /'ɪləstreɪt/ *vt* **1** ‹*book/magazine*› ilustrar **2** **(a)** (explain by examples) ilustrar **(b)** (show) poner* de manifiesto

illustration /'ɪlə'streɪʃən/ *n* **1** (picture, technique) ilustración *f* **2** (example) ejemplo *m*

illustrator /'ɪləstreɪtər ‖'ɪləstreɪtə(r)/ *n* ilustrador, -dora *m,f*

illustrious /ɪ'lʌstriəs/ *adj* (liter) ilustre

ill will *n* **(a)** (hostility) animadversión *f* **(b)** (spite) rencor *m*

I'm /aɪm/ = **I am**

image /'ɪmɪdʒ/ *n* imagen *f*; **to be the (spitting) ~ *o* spit and ~ of sb** ser* la viva imagen de algn

imagery /'ɪmɪdʒəri/ *n* imaginería *f*, imágenes *fpl*

imaginable /ɪ'mædʒənəbəl ‖ɪ'mædʒɪnəbəl/ *adj* imaginable

imaginary /ɪ'mædʒəneri ‖ɪ'mædʒɪnəri/ *adj* imaginario

imagination /ɪˌmædʒə'neɪʃən ‖ɪˌmædʒɪ'neɪʃən/ *n* imaginación *f*

imaginative /ɪ'mædʒənətɪv ‖ɪ'mædʒɪnətɪv/ *adj* imaginativo

imagine /ɪ'mædʒən ‖ɪ'mædʒɪn/ *vt* **(a)** (picture to oneself) imaginarse; **I can just ~ her saying that** ya me la imagino diciendo eso **(b)** (fancy mistakenly): **you're imagining things** son imaginaciones *or* figuraciones tuyas **(c)** (assume) imaginarse; **I ~ she's very tired** me imagino que estará muy cansada

imbalance /ɪm'bæləns/ *n* desequilibrio *m*

imbecile /'ɪmbəsəl ‖'ɪmbəsiːl/ *n* imbécil *mf*

imbed /ɪm'bed/ *vt* **-dd-** (AmE) ▶ EMBED

IMF *n* (= **International Monetary Fund**) FMI *m*

imitate /'ɪməteɪt ‖'ɪmɪteɪt/ *vt* imitar

imitation¹ /'ɪmə'teɪʃən ‖ˌɪmɪ'teɪʃən/ *n* imitación *f*

imitation² *adj* ‹*gold/pearls*› de imitación

immaculate /ɪ'mækjələt ‖ɪ'mækjʊlət/ *adj* impecable

immaterial /'ɪmə'tɪriəl ‖ˌɪmə'tɪəriəl/ *adj* irrelevante

immature /'ɪmə'tʊr ‖ˌɪmə'tjʊə(r)/ *adj* **(a)** ‹*tree/ animal*› joven; ‹*fruit*› verde, inmaduro **(b)** (childish) ‹*person/attitude*› inmaduro

immaturity /'ɪmə'tʊrəti ‖ˌɪmə'tjʊərəti/ *n* inmadurez *f*

immediate /ɪ'miːdiət/ *adj* **1** **(a)** (instant, prompt) inmediato **(b)** ‹*problem/need*› urgente, apremiante **2** (*before n*) (close): **in the ~ future** en el futuro inmediato; **in the ~ vicinity** en las inmediaciones

immediately /ɪ'mi:diətli/ adv [1] (at once) inmediatamente [2] ⟨before/after/above/below⟩ justo

immemorial /ˌɪmə'mɔːriəl/ adj (liter) inmemorial (liter)

immense /ɪ'mens/ adj inmenso, enorme

immensely /ɪ'mensli/ adv ⟨enjoy/like⟩ enormemente; ⟨popular/powerful⟩ inmensamente

immerse /ɪ'mɜːrs ‖ɪ'mɜːs/ vt (a) (submerge) to ∼ sth/sb (IN sth) sumergir* algo/a algn (EN algo) (b) (absorb, involve) to be ∼d IN sth estar* absorto EN algo

immersion heater /ɪ'mɜːrʒən ‖ɪ'mɜːʃən/ n calentador m eléctrico (de agua), termo m (Chi), termofón m (RPI)

immigrant /'ɪməgrənt ‖'ɪmɪgrənt/ n inmigrante mf; ⟨before n⟩ ⟨worker/population⟩ inmigrante

immigration /ˌɪmə'greɪʃən ‖ˌɪmɪ'greɪʃən/ n inmigración f

imminent /'ɪmənənt ‖'ɪmɪnənt/ adj inminente

immobile /ɪ'məʊbəl ‖ɪ'məʊbaɪl/ adj inmóvil

immobilize /ɪ'məʊbəlaɪz ‖ɪ'məʊbɪlaɪz/ vt inmovilizar*

immoderate /ɪ'mɑːdərət ‖ɪ'mɒdərət/ adj ⟨demands/appetite⟩ desmedido

immodest /ɪ'mɑːdəst ‖ɪ'mɒdɪst/ adj (a) (conceited) presuntuoso, inmodesto (b) (indecent) ⟨behavior/suggestion⟩ impúdico, inmodesto

immoral /ɪ'mɔːrəl ‖ɪ'mɒrəl/ adj inmoral

immorality /ˌɪmɔː'ræləti ‖ˌɪmə'ræləti/ n inmoralidad f

immortal /ɪ'mɔːrtl̩ ‖ɪ'mɔːtl̩/ adj inmortal

immortality /ˌɪmɔːr'tæləti ‖ˌɪmɔː'tæləti/ n inmortalidad f

immortalize /ɪ'mɔːrtl̩aɪz ‖ɪ'mɔːtl̩aɪz/ vt inmortalizar*

immune /ɪ'mjuːn/ adj (a) (not susceptible) to be ∼ TO sth ser* inmune A algo (b) ⟨before n⟩ ⟨system/response⟩ inmunológico

immunity /ɪ'mjuːnəti/ n inmunidad f

immunization /'ɪmjənə'zeɪʃən ‖ˌɪmjʊnər'zeɪʃən/ n inmunización f

immunize /'ɪmjənaɪz ‖'ɪmjʊnaɪz/ vt inmunizar*

imp /ɪmp/ n diablillo m (fam)

impact /'ɪmpækt/ n impacto m

impair /ɪm'per ‖ɪm'peə(r)/ vt afectar; ∼ed vision/hearing problemas mpl de vista/audición

impale /ɪm'peɪl/ vt to ∼ sth/sb ON sth atravesar* algo/a algn CON algo

impart /ɪm'pɑːrt ‖ɪm'pɑːt/ vt (frml) ⟨news⟩ comunicar*; ⟨knowledge⟩ impartir; ⟨feeling/quality⟩ conferir* (frml)

impartial /ɪm'pɑːrʃəl ‖ɪm'pɑːʃəl/ adj imparcial

impassable /ɪm'pæsəbəl ‖ɪm'pɑːsəbəl/ adj ⟨river/barrier⟩ infranqueable; ⟨road⟩ intransitable

impasse /'ɪmpæs ‖'æmpæs/ n impasse m

impassioned /ɪm'pæʃənd/ adj apasionado

impassive /ɪm'pæsɪv/ adj impasible

impatience /ɪm'peɪʃəns/ n impaciencia f

impatient /ɪm'peɪʃənt/ adj ⟨person⟩ impaciente; ⟨gesture/voice⟩ de impaciencia

impatiently /ɪm'peɪʃəntli/ adv con impaciencia

impeach /ɪm'piːtʃ/ vt (Law) acusar a un alto cargo de delitos cometidos en el desempeño de sus funciones

impeccable /ɪm'pekəbəl/ adj impecable

impecunious /'ɪmpɪ'kjuːniəs/ adj (liter or hum) sin peculio (liter o hum)

impede /ɪm'piːd/ vt dificultar

impediment /ɪm'pedəmənt ‖ɪm'pedɪmənt/ n (a) (hindrance) impedimento m (b) (physical defect) defecto m; a speech ∼ un defecto del habla

impel /ɪm'pel/ vt -ll- impeler

impending /ɪm'pendɪŋ/ adj ⟨before n⟩ inminente

impenetrable /ɪm'penətrəbəl/ adj impenetrable

imperative¹ /ɪm'perətɪv/ adj [1] (a) (essential) imprescindible, fundamental (b) ⟨need⟩ imperioso, imperativo [2] (Ling) ⟨mood⟩ imperativo; ⟨sentence⟩ en imperativo

imperative² n imperativo m

imperceptible /'ɪmpər'septəbəl ‖ˌɪmpə'septəbəl/ adj imperceptible

imperfect¹ /ɪm'pɜːrfɪkt ‖ɪm'pɜːfɪkt/ adj imperfecto

imperfect² n imperfecto m

imperfection /'ɪmpər'fekʃən ‖ˌɪmpə'fekʃən/ n imperfección f

imperial /ɪm'pɪriəl ‖ɪm'pɪəriəl/ adj ⟨of empire⟩ ⟨before n⟩ imperial, del imperio

imperialism /ɪm'pɪriəlɪzəm ‖ɪm'pɪəriəlɪzəm/ n imperialismo m

imperialist /ɪm'pɪriələst ‖ɪm'pɪəriəlɪst/ n imperialista mf

imperil /ɪm'perəl ‖ɪm'perɪl, ɪm'perəl/ vt, (BrE) -ll- poner* en peligro

imperious /ɪm'pɪriəs ‖ɪm'pɪəriəs/ adj imperioso

impermeable /ɪm'pɜːrmiəbəl ‖ɪm'pɜːmiəbəl/ adj impermeable

impersonal /ɪm'pɜːrsn̩əl ‖ɪm'pɜːsn̩l̩/ adj impersonal

impersonate /ɪm'pɜːrsəneɪt ‖ɪm'pɜːsəneɪt/ vt (a) (pretend to be) hacerse* pasar por (b) (mimic) imitar, impersonar (Méx)

impersonator /ɪm'pɜːrsəneɪtər ‖ɪm'pɜːsəneɪtə(r)/ n imitador, -dora m,f, impersonador, -dora m,f (Méx)

impertinent /ɪm'pɜːrtn̩ənt ‖ɪm'pɜːtɪnənt/ adj impertinente

impervious /ɪm'pɜːrviəs ‖ɪm'pɜːviəs/ adj (a) ⟨rock/material⟩ impermeable (b) (unaffected) to be ∼ TO sth ⟨to criticism/doubt⟩ ser* impermeable A algo

impetuous /ɪmˈpetʃuəs/ adj ⟨person⟩ impetuoso; ⟨action/decision⟩ impulsivo

impetus /ˈɪmpətəs/ ‖ /ˈɪmpɪtəs/ n ímpetu m

impinge /ɪmˈpɪndʒ/ vi to ~ ON o UPON sth ⟨privacy/freedom⟩ vulnerar algo

implacable /ɪmˈplækəbəl/ adj implacable

implant /ɪmˈplænt/ ‖ /ɪmˈplɑːnt/ vt (a) ⟨idea/ideal⟩ inculcar* (b) ⟨embryo/hair⟩ implantar

implausible /ɪmˈplɔːzəbəl/ adj inverosímil

implement[1] /ˈɪmpləmənt/ vt implementar

implement[2] /ˈɪmpləmənt/ n instrumento m, implemento m (AmL)

implementation /ˌɪmpləmənˈteɪʃən/ nu implementación f, puesta f en marcha

implicate /ˈɪmpləkeɪt/ ‖ /ˈɪmplɪkeɪt/ vt implicar*

implication /ˌɪmpləˈkeɪʃən/ ‖ /ˌɪmplɪˈkeɪʃən/ n [1] (consequence, significance) repercusión f, implicación f [2] (involvement) implicación f

implicit /ɪmˈplɪsət/ adj (a) ⟨threat⟩ implícito (b) ⟨confidence/trust⟩ incondicional, total

implode /ɪmˈpləʊd/ vi implosionar

implore /ɪmˈplɔːr/ ‖ /ɪmˈplɔː(r)/ vt implorar

imply /ɪmˈplaɪ/ vt **implies, implying, implied** [1] (suggest, hint) dar* a entender, insinuar* [2] (involve) implicar*, suponer*

impolite /ˌɪmpəˈlaɪt/ adj maleducado, descortés

import[1] /ˈɪmpɔːrt/ ‖ /ˈɪmpɔːt/ n [1] (Busn) (a) (act) importación f (b) (article): **a foreign** ~ un artículo de importación [2] (significance) (frml) importancia f

import[2] /ɪmˈpɔːrt/ ‖ /ɪmˈpɔːt/ vt importar

importance /ɪmˈpɔːrtn̩s/ ‖ /ɪmˈpɔːtn̩s/ n importancia f

important /ɪmˈpɔːrtn̩t/ ‖ /ɪmˈpɔːtn̩t/ adj importante

importer /ɪmˈpɔːrtər/ ‖ /ɪmˈpɔːtə(r)/ n importador, -dora m,f

impose /ɪmˈpəʊz/ vt imponer*
■ ~ vi molestar; **to** ~ **on sb's goodwill** abusar de la buena voluntad de algn

imposing /ɪmˈpəʊzɪŋ/ adj imponente

imposition /ˌɪmpəˈzɪʃən/ n (a) (enforcement) imposición f (b) (taking unfair advantage) abuso m

impossibility /ɪmˌpɑːsəˈbɪləti/ ‖ /ɪmˌpɒsəˈbɪləti/ n imposibilidad f

impossible[1] /ɪmˈpɑːsəbəl/ ‖ /ɪmˈpɒsəbəl/ adj (a) ⟨job/request⟩ imposible; **it's** ~ **for me to arrive by twelve** me es imposible llegar para las doce (b) (intolerable) intolerable

impossible[2] n **to ask/attempt the** ~ pedir*/intentar lo imposible

impostor /ɪmˈpɑːstər/ ‖ /ɪmˈpɒstə(r)/ n impostor, -tora m,f

impotence /ˈɪmpətəns/ n impotencia f

impotent /ˈɪmpətənt/ adj impotente

impound /ɪmˈpaʊnd/ vt (a) ⟨possessions/assets⟩ incautar(se de) (b) ⟨vehicle⟩ llevar al depósito municipal

impoverished /ɪmˈpɑːvərɪʃt/ ‖ /ɪmˈpɒvərɪʃt/ adj (financially, spiritually) empobrecido; ⟨soil/diet⟩ pobre

impractical /ɪmˈpræktɪkəl/ adj poco práctico

impregnable /ɪmˈpregnəbəl/ adj ⟨fortress⟩ inexpugnable; ⟨organization⟩ impenetrable

impregnate /ɪmˈpregneɪt/ ‖ /ˈɪmpregneɪt/ vt [1] (saturate) **to** ~ **sth WITH sth** impregnar algo CON o DE algo [2] (make pregnant) (frml) fecundar

impresario /ˌɪmprəˈsɑːriəʊ/ ‖ /ˌɪmprɪˈsɑːriəʊ/ (pl **-os**) n empresario, -ria m,f teatral

impress /ɪmˈpres/ vt [1] (make impression on): **we were** ~**ed by your work** tu trabajo nos causó muy buena impresión; **he only did it to** ~ **her** lo hizo sólo para impactarla [2] (emphasize) **to** ~ **sth ON** o **UPON sb** recalcarle* algo a algn
■ ~ vi impresionar

impression /ɪmˈpreʃən/ n [1] (a) (idea, image) impresión f; **to be under the** ~ **(that) ...** creer* o pensar* que ... (b) (effect) impresión f; **to make** o **create a good/bad** ~ **on sb** causarle a algn una buena/mala impresión [2] (imprint) impresión f, huella f [3] (impersonation) imitación f

impressionable /ɪmˈpreʃn̩əbəl/ adj (a) (easily influenced) influenciable (b) (easily frightened, upset) impresionable

impressionism /ɪmˈpreʃn̩ɪzəm/ n impresionismo m

impressionist /ɪmˈpreʃn̩əst/ ‖ /ɪmˈpreʃn̩ɪst/ n (a) (Art) impresionista mf (b) (impersonator) imitador, -dora m,f

impressive /ɪmˈpresɪv/ adj ⟨record/work⟩ admirable; ⟨building/ceremony⟩ imponente

imprint[1] /ˈɪmprɪnt/ n marca f, huella f

imprint[2] /ɪmˈprɪnt/ vt (physically) imprimir*; (on mind) grabar

imprison /ɪmˈprɪzən/ vt (Law) encarcelar

imprisonment /ɪmˈprɪzənmənt/ n (act) encarcelamiento m; (state) prisión f; **life** ~ cadena f perpetua

improbable /ɪmˈprɑːbəbəl/ ‖ /ɪmˈprɒbəbəl/ adj (a) (unlikely) improbable (b) (implausible) inverosímil

impromptu /ɪmˈprɑːmptu/ ‖ /ɪmˈprɒmptjuː/ adj improvisado

improper /ɪmˈprɑːpər/ ‖ /ɪmˈprɒpə(r)/ adj [1] ⟨behavior/language⟩ indecoroso; ⟨suggestion⟩ deshonesto [2] (incorrect) (frml) ⟨use⟩ indebido; ⟨term⟩ incorrecto

improve /ɪmˈpruːv/ vt (a) ⟨design/results⟩ mejorar; ⟨chances⟩ aumentar; **to** ~ **one's mind** cultivarse (b) ⟨property⟩ hacer* mejoras en
■ ~ vi «situation/weather/health» mejorar; «chances» aumentar

improvement /ɪmˈpruːvmənt/ n (in design, situation) mejora f; (in health) mejoría f

improvise /ˈɪmprəvaɪz/ vi/t improvisar

imprudent /ɪmˈpruːdn̩t/ adj (frml) imprudente

impudence /ˈɪmpjədəns/ ‖ /ˈɪmpjʊdəns/ n insolencia f

impudent /ˈɪmpjədənt/ ‖ /ˈɪmpjʊdənt/ adj insolente

impulse /ˈɪmpʌls/ n impulso m; **I did it on** ~ lo hice sin pensarlo

impulsive /ɪmˈpʌlsɪv/ adj impulsivo

impunity /ɪmˈpjuːnəti/ n (frml) impunidad f

impure /ˈɪmˈpjʊr/ ‖ /ɪmˈpjʊə(r)/ adj impuro

impurity /ɪmˈpjʊrəti/ ‖ /ɪmˈpjʊərəti/ n (pl **-ties**) impureza f

in[1] /ɪn/ prep [1] (a) (indicating place, location) en; ~ **Japan** en (el) Japón; **he went** ~ **the shop** entró en la tienda; **who's that** ~ **the photo?** ¿quién es ese ···⊹

de la foto?; ~ **here/there** aquí/allí dentro *or* (esp AmL) adentro; ~ **the rain** bajo la lluvia **(b)** *(with superl)* de; **the highest mountain** ~ **Italy** la montaña más alta de Italia; **the worst storm** ~ **living memory** la peor tormenta que se recuerda ② (indicating time) en; ~ **spring/January/1924** en primavera/enero/1924; **at four o'clock** ~ **the morning** a las cuatro de la mañana; **she did it** ~ **three hours** lo hizo en tres horas; ~ **two months' time** dentro de dos meses

③ **(a)** (indicating manner) en; ~ **dollars** en dólares; ~ **French** en francés; ~ **twos** de dos en dos, de a dos (AmL); **cut it** ~ **half** córtalo por la mitad; **they came** ~ **their thousands** vinieron miles y miles **(b)** (wearing): **he turned up** ~ **a suit** apareció de traje; **are you going** ~ **that dress?** ¿vas a ir con ese vestido?

④ (indicating circumstances, state): **the company is** ~ **difficulties** la empresa está pasando dificultades; **to be** ~ **a good mood** estar* de buen humor; **he's** ~ **pain** está dolorido; **low** ~ **calories** bajo en calorías

⑤ (indicating ratio): **one** ~ **four** uno de cada cuatro; **she's one** ~ **a million** es única

⑥ **(a)** (+ *gerund*): ~ **so doing, they set a precedent** al hacerlo, sentaron precedente **(b) in that** (*as conj*): **the case is unusual** ~ **that ...** el caso es poco común en el sentido de que ...

in² *adv* ① **(a)** (inside): **is the cat** ~? ¿el gato está dentro *or* (esp AmL) adentro?; ~ **you go!** ¡entra! **(b)** (at home, work): **is Lisa** ~? ¿está Lisa?; **there was nobody** ~ no había nadie

② **(a)** (in position): **she had her curlers** ~ llevaba *or* tenía los rulos puestos **(b)** (at destination): **the train isn't** ~ **yet** el tren no ha llegado todavía; **application forms must be** ~ **by October 5** las solicitudes deben entregarse antes del 5 de octubre

③ (involved): **we were** ~ **on the planning stage** participamos en la planificación; *to be* ~ *for sth*: **it looks like we're** ~ **for some rain** parece que va a llover; **you're** ~ **for a big surprise** te vas a llevar una buena sorpresa

in³ *adj* ① **(a)** (fashionable) (colloq) (*no comp*): **black is** ~ **this season** el negro está de moda esta temporada; **the** ~ **place** el lugar in (fam) **(b)** (exclusive, private) (*before n*): **an** ~ **joke** un chiste para iniciados ② (*pred*) (in tennis, badminton, etc): **the ball was** ~ la pelota fue buena *or* cayó dentro *or* (esp AmL) adentro

in⁴ *n*: **the** ~**s and outs (of sth)** los pormenores (de algo)

in⁵ (*pl* **in** *or* **ins**) = **inch(es)**

IN = **Indiana**

inability /ˌɪnəˈbɪlɪti/ *n* incapacidad *f*, ~ **to +** INF incapacidad PARA + INF

inaccessible /ˌɪnəkˈsesəbəl ‖ ˌɪnæksˈsesəbəl/ *adj* inaccesible

inaccurate /ɪnˈækjərət/ *adj* **(a)** ⟨*translation/estimate*⟩ inexacto **(b)** ⟨*aim/shot*⟩ impreciso

inactive /ɪnˈæktɪv/ *adj* inactivo

inactivity /ˌɪnækˈtɪvəti/ *n* inactividad *f*

inadequate /ɪnˈædɪkwət/ *adj* **(a)** ⟨*resources/measures*⟩ insuficiente **(b)** ⟨*person*⟩ inepto

inadvertently /ˌɪnədˈvɜːrtn̩tli ‖ ˌɪnədˈvɜːtn̩tli/ *adv* sin querer

inadvisable /ˌɪnədˈvaɪzəbəl/ *adj* desaconsejable

inane /ɪˈneɪm/ *adj* estúpido, idiota

inanimate /ɪnˈænəmət ‖ ɪnˈænɪmət/ *adj* inanimado

inapplicable /ɪnˈæplɪkəbəl, ˌɪnəˈplɪkəbəl/ *adj* inaplicable, no aplicable

inappropriate /ˌɪnəˈprəʊprɪət/ *adj* ⟨*measure/dress*⟩ inadecuado; ⟨*moment*⟩ inoportuno

inarticulate /ˌɪnɑːrˈtɪkjələt ‖ ˌɪnɑːˈtɪkjʊlət/ *adj* ⟨*babbling/grunt*⟩ inarticulado; ⟨*person*⟩ con dificultad para expresarse

inasmuch as /ˌɪnəzˈmʌtʃ/ *conj* (fml) **(a)** (since, seeing that) ya que, puesto que **(b)** ▶ INSOFAR AS

inattentive /ˌɪnəˈtentɪv/ *adj* ⟨*pupil/listener*⟩ distraído, poco atento

inaudible /ɪnˈɔːdəbəl/ *adj* inaudible

inaugural /ɪnˈɔːgjərəl ‖ ɪˈnɔːgjʊrəl/ *adj* **(a)** ⟨*speech/lecture*⟩ inaugural **(b)** (of official) ⟨*speech*⟩ de toma de posesión; ⟨*ceremony*⟩ de investidura

inaugurate /ɪnˈɔːgjəreɪt ‖ ɪˈnɔːgjʊreɪt/ *vt* **(a)** (begin, open) inaugurar **(b)** (fml) ⟨*president*⟩ investir*

inauguration /ɪˈnɔːgjəˈreɪʃən ‖ ɪˌnɔːgjʊˈreɪʃən/ *n* **(a)** (investiture) investidura *f*; (*before n*) I~ **Day** (in US) día de la toma de posesión del presidente de los EEUU **(b)** (opening) inauguración *f*

inbreeding /ˈɪnˌbriːdɪŋ/ *n* endogamia *f*

Inc /ɪŋk/ (AmE) = **Incorporated**

Inca¹ /ˈɪŋkə/ *adj* incaico, inca

Inca² *n* inca *mf*

incapable /ɪnˈkeɪpəbəl/ *adj* (*pred*) **(a)** (not able) **to be** ~ OF -ING ser* incapaz DE + INF **(b)** (helpless) inútil, incapaz

incapacitate /ˌɪnkəˈpæsəteɪt ‖ ˌɪnkəˈpæsɪteɪt/ *vt* **(a)** (disable) incapacitar **(b)** (Law) inhabilitar

incarcerate /ɪnˈkɑːrsərəɪt ‖ ɪnˈkɑːsəreɪt/ *vt* encarcelar

incarnate /ɪnˈkɑːrnət ‖ ɪnˈkɑːnət/ *adj* (liter) (*usu pred*) encarnado

incarnation /ˌɪnkɑːrˈneɪʃən ‖ ˌɪnkɑːˈneɪʃən/ *n* encarnación *f*

incendiary /ɪnˈsendieri ‖ ɪnˈsendiəri/ *adj* incendiario

incense¹ /ˈɪnsens/ *n* incienso *m*

incense² /ɪnˈsens/ *vt* indignar

incentive /ɪnˈsentɪv/ *n* incentivo *m*

inception /ɪnˈsepʃən/ *n* (fml) inicio *m*

incessant /ɪnˈsesn̩t/ *adj* incesante

incessantly /ɪnˈsesn̩tli/ *adv* sin cesar

incest /ˈɪnsest/ *n* incesto *m*

incestuous /ɪnˈsestʃuəs ‖ ɪnˈsestjʊəs/ *adj* incestuoso

inch¹ /ɪntʃ/ *n* pulgada *f* (*2,54 centímetros*); **I've searched every** ~ **of the house** he buscado hasta en el último rincón de la casa; **she wouldn't budge** *o* **give an** ~ no cedió ni un ápice

inch² *vi*: **to** ~ **forward** avanzar* lentamente

incidence /ˈɪnsədəns ‖ ˈɪnsɪdəns/ *n* ① (frequency) índice *m* ② (Opt, Phys) incidencia *f*

incident /ˈɪnsədənt ‖ ˈɪnsɪdənt/ *n* incidente *m*

incidental /ˌɪnsəˈdentl ‖ ˌɪnsɪˈdentl/ *adj* **(a)** (accompanying) ⟨*effect*⟩ secundario; ⟨*advantage/benefit*⟩ adicional; ⟨*expenses*⟩ imprevisto **(b)** (minor) incidental

incidentally /ˌɪnsəˈdentl̩i ‖ ˌɪnsɪˈdentl̩i/ *adv* (*indep*) a propósito

incinerate /ɪnˈsɪnəreɪt/ *vt* incinerar
incinerator /ɪnˈsɪnəreɪtər ‖ɪnˈsɪnəreɪtə(r)/ *n* incinerador *m*
incision /ɪnˈsɪʒən/ *n* incisión *f*
incisor /ɪnˈsaɪzər ‖ɪnˈsaɪzə(r)/ *n* incisivo *m*
incite /ɪnˈsaɪt/ *vt* ⟨hatred/violence⟩ instigar* a, incitar a; ⟨person⟩ **to ~ sb TO sth/+ INF** instigar* *or* incitar a algn A algo/+ INF
inclination /ˈɪnkləˈneɪʃən ‖ˌɪnklɪˈneɪʃən/ *n* **(a)** (leaning) tendencia *f*, inclinación *f*; **to have an/no ~ to + INF** tener*/no tener* deseos de + INF
incline¹ /ɪnˈklaɪn/ *vt* (fml) ⟨head⟩ inclinar
■ **~** *vi* (fml) **to ~ TO sth: she ~s to the opposite view** se inclina a pensar lo contrario
incline² /ˈɪnklaɪn/ *n* (fml) pendiente *f*
inclined /ɪnˈklaɪnd/ *adj* (disposed) **~ to + INF: I'm ~ to agree** yo me inclino a pensar lo mismo; **she's ~ to be irritable in the morning** tiende a estar de mal humor por la mañana
include /ɪnˈkluːd/ *vt* incluir*; (with letter) adjuntar; **service isn't ~d** el servicio no está incluido
including /ɪnˈkluːdɪŋ/ *prep*: **up to and ~ page 25** hasta la página 25 inclusive; **not ~ insurance** sin incluir el seguro
inclusion /ɪnˈkluːʒən/ *n* inclusión *f*
inclusive /ɪnˈkluːsɪv/ *adj* ⟨price/charge⟩ global; **to be ~ OF sth** incluir* algo
incognito /ˌɪnkɑːgˈniːtəʊ ‖ˌɪnkɒgˈniːtəʊ/ *adv* de incógnito
incoherent /ˈɪnkəʊˈhɪrənt ‖ˌɪnkəʊˈhɪərənt/ *adj* incoherente
income /ˈɪnkʌm/ *n* ingresos *mpl*
income: ~ support *n* (in UK) *subsidio otorgado a personas de bajos ingresos*; **~ tax** *n* impuesto *m* sobre *or* a la renta, impuesto *m* a los réditos (Arg)
incoming /ˈɪnkʌmɪŋ/ *adj* (before n) **(a)** (inbound): **the area has been closed to ~ traffic** no se permite la entrada de vehículos a la zona; **the secretary takes all ~ calls** la secretaria atiende todas las llamadas **(b)** (about to take office) ⟨president⟩ entrante
incommunicado /ˈɪnkəˈmjuːnəˈkɑːdəʊ ‖ˌɪnkəˌmjuːnɪˈkɑːdəʊ/ *adj* (pred) **to be ~** estar* incomunicado
incomparable /ɪnˈkɑːmpərəbəl ‖ɪnˈkɒmpərəbəl/ *adj* (liter) incomparable
incompatibility /ˌɪnkəmpætəˈbɪləti/ *n* incompatibilidad *f*
incompatible /ˈɪnkəmˈpætəbəl/ *adj* incompatible
incompetence /ɪnˈkɑːmpətəns ‖ɪnˈkɒmpɪtəns/ *n* incompetencia *f*
incompetent /ɪnˈkɑːmpətənt ‖ɪnˈkɒmpɪtənt/ *adj* ⟨person⟩ incompetente; ⟨work⟩ deficiente
incomplete /ˈɪnkəmˈpliːt/ *adj* **(a)** (with sth or sb missing) incompleto **(b)** (unfinished) inacabado
incomprehensible /ɪnˈkɑːmprəˈhensəbəl ‖ɪnˌkɒmprɪˈhensəbəl/ *adj* incomprensible
incomprehension /ɪnˈkɑːmprɪˈhentʃən ‖ɪnˌkɒmprɪˈhenʃən/ *n* incomprensión *f*
inconceivable /ˈɪnkənˈsiːvəbəl/ *adj* inconcebible
inconclusive /ˈɪnkənˈkluːsɪv/ *adj* ⟨evidence/findings⟩ no concluyente

incongruous /ɪnˈkɑːŋgruəs ‖ɪnˈkɒŋgruəs/ *adj* ⟨behavior/remark⟩ fuera de lugar, inapropiado; ⟨appearance⟩ extraño, raro
inconsequential /ɪnˈkɑːnsəˈkwentʃəl ‖ɪnˌkɒnsɪˈkwenʃəl/ *adj* intrascendente
inconsiderate /ˈɪnkənˈsɪdərət/ *adj* desconsiderado
inconsistent /ˈɪnkənˈsɪstənt/ *adj* **(a)** (contradictory) contradictorio; **to be ~ WITH sth** no concordar* CON algo; ⟨with principles/ideas⟩ no compadecerse* CON algo **(b)** (changeable) ⟨person/attitude⟩ inconsecuente
inconspicuous /ˈɪnkənˈspɪkjuəs/ *adj* que no llama la atención
incontinent /ɪnˈkɑːntɪnənt ‖ɪnˈkɒntɪnənt/ *adj* (Med) incontinente
inconvenience¹ /ˈɪnkənˈviːniəns/ *n* **(a)** (unsuitability, troublesomeness) inconveniencia *f* **(b)** (trouble) molestias *fpl* **(c)** (drawback, nuisance) inconveniente *m*
inconvenience² *vt* causarle molestias a
inconvenient /ˈɪnkənˈviːniənt/ *adj* ⟨moment⟩ poco conveniente; ⟨position⟩ poco práctico
incorporate /ɪnˈkɔːrpəreɪt ‖ɪnˈkɔːpəreɪt/ *vt* ⒈ **(a)** (take in) ⟨idea/plan⟩ incorporar; **to ~ sth INTO sth** incorporar algo A algo **(b)** (include, contain) incluir* ⒉ (Busn, Law) ⟨business/enterprise⟩ constituir* (en sociedad)
incorrect /ˈɪnkəˈrekt/ *adj* ⟨answer/spelling⟩ incorrecto; ⟨statement/belief⟩ equivocado
incorrigible /ɪnˈkɔːrədʒəbəl ‖ɪnˈkɒrɪdʒəbəl/ *adj* incorregible
increase¹ /ɪnˈkriːs/ *vi* «number/size/prices/output» aumentar; «influence/popularity» crecer*; **to ~ in size** aumentar de tamaño; **to ~ in number** crecer* en número; **to ~ in value** aumentar de valor
■ **~** *vt* aumentar
increase² /ˈɪnkriːs/ *n* aumento *m*; **to be on the ~** estar* *or* ir* en aumento
increasing /ɪnˈkriːsɪŋ/ *adj* (before n) creciente
increasingly /ɪnˈkriːsɪŋli/ *adv*: **~ difficult** cada vez más difícil; **it is becoming ~ clear that** ... resulta cada vez más claro que ...
incredible /ɪnˈkredəbəl/ *adj* increíble
incredibly /ɪnˈkredəbli/ *adv* (colloq) (as intensifier) increíblemente
incredulous /ɪnˈkredʒələs ‖ɪnˈkredjʊləs/ *adj* de incredulidad
increment /ˈɪŋkrəmənt/ *n* (in salary) incremento *m* (salarial) (fml)
incriminate /ɪnˈkrɪmineɪt ‖ɪnˈkrɪmɪneɪt/ *vt* incriminar (fml)
incriminating /ɪnˈkrɪmineɪtɪŋ ‖ɪnˈkrɪmɪneɪtɪŋ/ *adj* ⟨evidence/document⟩ comprometedor
incubate /ˈɪŋkjəbeɪt ‖ˈɪŋkjʊbeɪt/ *vt* incubar
■ **~** *vi* «bird» empollar; «egg/bacteria» incubarse
incubation /ˈɪŋkjəˈbeɪʃən ‖ˌɪŋkjʊˈbeɪʃən/ *n* incubación *f*
incubator /ˈɪŋkjəbeɪtər ‖ˈɪŋkjʊbeɪtə(r)/ *n* incubadora *f*
inculcate /ˈɪnkʌlkeɪt/ *vt* (fml) **to ~ sth IN(TO) sb**, **to ~ sb WITH sth** inculcarle* algo A algn, inculcar* algo EN algn

incumbent¹ /ɪnˈkʌmbənt/ *adj* (frml) **to be ~ ON** *o* **UPON sb** incumbirle A algn

incumbent² *n* titular *mf* del cargo

incur /ɪnˈkɜːr ‖ ɪnˈkɜː(r)/ *vt* **-rr-** (frml) ⟨anger⟩ provocar*, incurrir en (frml); ⟨penalty⟩ acarrear; ⟨damage/loss⟩ sufrir; ⟨debt/liability⟩ contraer*; ⟨expense⟩ incurrir en (frml)

incurable /ɪnˈkjʊrəbəl ‖ ɪnˈkjʊərəbəl/ *adj* ⟨illness⟩ incurable; ⟨optimist/romantic⟩ empedernido

incursion /ɪnˈkɜːrʒən ‖ ɪnˈkɜːʃən/ *n* incursión *f*

Ind = Indiana

indebted /ɪnˈdetəd ‖ ɪnˈdetɪd/ *adj* **to be ~ TO sb (FOR sth)** estar* en deuda con algn (POR algo)

indecency /ɪnˈdiːsnsɪ/ *n* indecencia *f*

indecent /ɪnˈdiːsnt/ *adj* indecente

indecent assault *n* abusos *mpl* deshonestos

indecipherable /ˈɪndɪˈsaɪfərəbəl/ *adj* indescifrable

indecision /ˈɪndɪˈsɪʒən/ *n* indecisión *f*

indecisive /ˈɪndɪˈsaɪsɪv/ *adj* **(a)** (hesitant) indeciso **(b)** (inconclusive) no decisivo

indeed /ɪnˈdiːd/ *adv* ⟨1⟩ (as intensifier): thank you very much ~ muchísimas gracias; this is ~ a great privilege este es un auténtico or verdadero privilegio ⟨2⟩ (in fact): the wheel was ~ loose en efecto, la rueda estaba suelta; if ~ he is right si es que tiene razón

indefensible /ˈɪndɪˈfensəbəl/ *adj* inexcusable

indefinite /ɪnˈdefənət ‖ ɪnˈdefɪnət/ *adj* ⟨1⟩ **(a)** ⟨number/period/outline⟩ indefinido ⟨2⟩ (Ling): ~ article artículo *m* indefinido

indelible /ɪnˈdeləbəl/ *adj* indeleble

indelicate /ɪnˈdeləkət ‖ ɪnˈdelɪkət/ *adj* **(a)** (vulgar) indelicado **(b)** (tactless) indiscreto

indemnify /ɪnˈdemnɪfaɪ ‖ ɪnˈdemnɪfaɪ/ *vt* **-fies, -fying, -fied (a)** (insure) asegurar **(b)** (compensate) indemnizar*

indemnity /ɪnˈdemnətɪ/ *n* (*pl* **-ties**) **(a)** (insurance) indemnidad *f* **(b)** (compensation) indemnización *f*

indent /ɪnˈdent/ *vt* **(a)** ⟨line/paragraph⟩ sangrar **(b)** ⟨surface/edge⟩ marcar*

independence /ˈɪndɪˈpendəns/ *n* independencia *f*

Independence Day *n* día *m* de la Independencia

independent /ˈɪndɪˈpendənt/ *adj* independiente

in-depth /ˈɪnˈdepθ/ *adj* (before *n*) a fondo

indescribable /ˈɪndɪˈskraɪbəbəl/ *adj* indescriptible

indestructible /ˈɪndɪˈstrʌktəbəl/ *adj* indestructible

indeterminate /ˈɪndɪˈtɜːrmənət ‖ ˈɪndɪˈtɜːmɪnət/ *adj* indeterminado

index¹ /ˈɪndeks/ *n* ⟨1⟩ (*pl* **indexes**) **(a)** (in book, journal) índice *m* **(b)** (list) lista *f*; (before *n*) ~ card ficha *f* ⟨2⟩ (*pl* **indexes** *o* **indices**) (Econ, Fin) índice *m* ⟨3⟩ (*pl* **indices**) (Math) índice *m*

index² *vt* ⟨1⟩ (Publ) **(a)** (provide with index) ponerle* un índice a **(b)** (enter in index) incluir* en un índice ⟨2⟩ (Econ, Fin) ⟨prices/wages⟩ indexar

index: ~ finger *n* (dedo *m*) índice *m*; **~-linked** /ˈɪndeksˈlɪŋkt/ *adj* (esp BrE) indexado

India /ˈɪndɪə/ *n* la India

Indian¹ /ˈɪndɪən/ *adj* ⟨1⟩ (of India) indio ⟨2⟩ (of America) indígena, india

Indian² *n* ⟨1⟩ (person from India) indio, -dia *m,f* ⟨2⟩ (American ~) indígena *mf*, indio, -dia *m,f*

Indian: ~ Ocean *n* the ~ Ocean el (Océano) Índico; **~ summer** *n* (in northern hemisphere) ≈ veranillo *m* de San Martín *or* de San Miguel; (in southern hemisphere) ≈ veranillo *m* de San Juan

indicate /ˈɪndəkeɪt ‖ ˈɪndɪkeɪt/ *vt* ⟨1⟩ **(a)** (point out) señalar **(b)** (Auto) indicar* ⟨2⟩ **(a)** (show) ⟨change/condition⟩ ser* indicio de **(b)** (state) señalar

■ ~ *vi* (BrE Auto) indicar*, señalizar*, poner* el intermitente *or* (Col, Méx) las direccionales *or* (Chi) el señalizador

indication /ˈɪndəˈkeɪʃən ‖ ˈɪndɪˈkeɪʃən/ *n* **(a)** (sign, hint) indicio *m* **(b)** (Med) indicación *f*

indicative¹ /ɪnˈdɪkətɪv/ *adj* ⟨1⟩ (revealing) (frml) **to be ~ OF sth** ser* indicio DE algo ⟨2⟩ (Ling) ⟨mood/form⟩ indicativo

indicative² *n* (Ling) indicativo *m*

indicator /ˈɪndəkeɪtər ‖ ˈɪndɪkeɪtə(r)/ *n* ⟨1⟩ **(a)** (pointer) indicador *m* **(b)** (instrument) indicador *m* ⟨2⟩ (Auto) intermitente *m*, direccional *f* (Col, Méx), señalizador *m* (de viraje) (Chi) ⟨3⟩ (sign) indicador *m*

indices /ˈɪndəsiːz ‖ ˈɪndɪsiːz/ *pl of* INDEX¹ 2,3

indict /ɪnˈdaɪt/ *vt* (Law) acusar

indictment /ɪnˈdaɪtmənt/ *n* ⟨1⟩ (Law) acusación *f* ⟨2⟩ (criticism): the report was an ~ of his management el informe censuraba su gestión

indifference /ɪnˈdɪfrəns/ *n* indiferencia *f*

indifferent /ɪnˈdɪfrənt/ *adj* ⟨1⟩ (uninterested) indiferente ⟨2⟩ (mediocre) mediocre

indigenous /ɪnˈdɪdʒənəs/ *adj* ⟨population/language⟩ indígena, autóctono; ⟨species⟩ autóctono

indigestible /ˈɪndaɪˈdʒestəbəl, -də- ‖ ˈɪndɪˈdʒestəbəl/ *adj* (impossible to digest) no digerible; (hard to digest) indigesto

indigestion /ˈɪndaɪˈdʒestʃən, -də- ‖ ˈɪndɪˈdʒestʃən/ *n* indigestión *f*

indignant /ɪnˈdɪɡnənt/ *adj* indignado

indignation /ˈɪndɪɡˈneɪʃən/ *n* indignación *f*

indignity /ɪnˈdɪɡnətɪ/ *n* (*pl* **-ties**) humillación *f*

indigo /ˈɪndɪɡəʊ/ *n* índigo *m*, añil *m*; (before *n*) ⟨ink/sea⟩ color añil *adj inv*

indirect /ˈɪndəˈrekt, -daɪ- ‖ ˈɪndɪˈrekt, -daɪ-/ *adj* ⟨1⟩ **(a)** ⟨route/method⟩ indirecto; ⟨result/benefit⟩ indirecto **(b)** (Ling) ⟨statement/question⟩ indirecto; ~ discourse *o* (BrE) speech estilo *m* indirecto ⟨2⟩ (Fin) ⟨costs/taxes⟩ indirecto

indirectly /ˌɪndə'rektli, -daɪ- ‖ˌɪndɪ'rektli, -daɪ-/ *adv* indirectamente

indiscreet /ˌɪndɪs'kriːt/ *adj* indiscreto

indiscretion /ˌɪndɪs'kreʃən/ *n* indiscreción *f*

indiscriminate /ˌɪndɪs'krɪmənət ‖ˌɪndɪ'skrɪmɪnət/ *adj* indiscriminado

indispensable /ˌɪndɪs'pensəbəl/ *adj* indispensable

indisposed /ˌɪndɪ'spəʊzd/ *adj* (fml) (*pred*) (ill) **to be ~** estar* indispuesto (fml)

indisputable /ˌɪndɪ'spjuːtəbəl/ *adj* ‹*evidence/ proof*› irrefutable; ‹*leader/winner*› indiscutible

indistinct /ˌɪndɪ'stɪŋkt/ *adj* ‹*sound/shape*› poco definido; ‹*speech*› poco claro

indistinguishable /ˌɪndɪ'stɪŋgwɪʃəbəl/ *adj* **~ (FROM sth)** indistinguible (DE algo)

individual¹ /ˌɪndə'vɪdʒuəl ‖ˌɪndɪ'vɪdjʊəl/ *adj* ⒈ (*before n*) (*no comp*) **(a)** (for one person) ‹*portion*› individual; ‹*tuition*› personal **(b)** (single, separate): **you can purchase the whole set or ~ items** se puede comprar el juego o cada pieza por separado **(c)** (particular, personal) ‹*style*› personal ⒉ (distinctive) personal

individual² *n* **(a)** (single person, animal) individuo *m* **(b)** (person) (colloq) individuo, -dua *m,f*

indivisible /ˌɪndə'vɪzəbəl ‖ˌɪndɪ'vɪzəbəl/ *adj* indivisible

indoctrinate /ɪn'dɑːktrəneɪt ‖ɪn'dɒktrɪneɪt/ *vt* adoctrinar

indolent /'ɪndələnt/ *adj* (fml) indolente

Indonesia /ˌɪndə'niːʒə ‖ˌɪndə'niːziə/ *n* Indonesia *f*

Indonesian¹ /ˌɪndə'niːʒən ‖ˌɪndə'niːziən/ *adj* indonesio

Indonesian² *n* **(a)** (person) indonesio, -sia *m,f* **(b)** (language) indonesio *m*

indoor /'ɪndɔːr ‖'ɪndɔː(r)/ *adj* (*before n*) ‹*clothes/shoes*› para estar en casa; ‹*plants*› de interior(es); ‹*swimming pool*› cubierto, techado

indoors /ˌɪn'dɔːrz ‖ˌɪn'dɔːz/ *adv* dentro, adentro (esp AmL)

induce /ɪn'duːs ‖ɪn'djuːs/ *vt* ⒈ (persuade) **to ~ sb to + INF** inducir* a algn A + INF ⒉ (Med) ‹*sleep/labor*› inducir*

inducement /ɪn'duːsmənt ‖ɪn'djuːsmənt/ *n* incentivo *m*

induction /ɪn'dʌkʃən/ *n* ⒈ (introduction) **~ (INTO sth)** iniciación *f* (EN algo); (*before n*) ‹*course/period*› introductorio ⒉ (Med) (of labor) inducción *f*

indulge /ɪn'dʌldʒ/ *vt* ‹*child*› consentir*, mimar; ‹*desire*› satisfacer*; **it doesn't hurt to ~ oneself every now and again** es bueno darse algún gusto de vez en cuando
  ■ **~** *vi* **to ~ IN sth** permitirse algo

indulgence /ɪn'dʌldʒəns/ *n* **(a)** (extravagance): **an occasional cigar is my only ~** un puro de vez en cuando es el único lujo que me permito **(b)** (partaking): **too much ~ in anything is bad** es malo abusar de cualquier placer

indulgent /ɪn'dʌldʒənt/ *adj* indulgente

industrial /ɪn'dʌstriəl/ *adj* ‹*town/production/ engineering*› industrial; **~ dispute** conflicto *m* laboral

industrial estate *n* (BrE) zona *f* industrial, polígono *m* industrial (Esp)

industrialist /ɪn'dʌstriələst ‖ɪn'dʌstriəlɪst/ *n* industrial *mf*

industrialize /ɪn'dʌstriəlaɪz/ *vt* industrializar*

industrial: ~ park *n* (AmE) zona *f* industrial, polígono *m* industrial (Esp); **I~ Revolution** *n* **the I~ Revolution** la Revolución Industrial

industrious /ɪn'dʌstriəs/ *adj* ‹*worker*› trabajador; ‹*student*› aplicado

industry /'ɪndəstri/ *n* (*pl* **-tries**) industria *f*; **the steel ~** la industria siderúrgica; **the tourist ~** el turismo

inebriated /ɪn'iːbrieɪtəd ‖ɪn'iːbrieɪtɪd/ *adj* (fml) ‹*person*› beodo (fml), ebrio (fml); ‹*state*› de embriaguez (fml)

inedible /ɪn'edəbəl/ *adj* (impossible to eat) no comestible; (unpalatable) incomible

ineffective /ˌɪnə'fektɪv ‖ˌɪnɪ'fektɪv/ *adj* ‹*measure*› ineficaz; ‹*attempt*› infructuoso; ‹*person*› incompetente

inefficiency /ˌɪnə'fɪʃənsi ‖ˌɪnɪ'fɪʃənsi/ *n* (of machinery) falta *f* de eficiencia; (of persons, method) ineficiencia *f*

inefficient /ˌɪnə'fɪʃənt ‖ˌɪnɪ'fɪʃənt/ *adj* ineficiente

ineligible /ɪn'elədʒəbəl ‖ɪn'elɪdʒəbəl/ *adj* (*usu pred*) ‹*candidate*› inelegible; **she was ~ to vote** no tenía derecho a votar

inept /ɪ'nept/ *adj* ‹*person*› inepto; ‹*conduct*› torpe

inequality /ˌɪnɪ'kwɑːləti ‖ˌɪnɪ'kwɒləti/ *n* (*pl* **-ties**) desigualdad *f*

inert /ɪ'nɜːrt ‖ɪ'nɜːt/ *adj* inerte

inertia /ɪ'nɜːrʃə ‖ɪ'nɜːʃə/ *n* inercia *f*

inevitable¹ /ɪn'evətəbəl ‖ɪn'evɪtəbəl/ *adj* inevitable

inevitable² *n* **the ~** lo inevitable

inevitably /ɪn'evətəbli ‖ɪn'evɪtəbli/ *adv* inevitablemente

inexact /ˌɪnɪg'zækt/ *adj* inexacto

inexcusable /ˌɪnɪk'skjuːzəbəl/ *adj* imperdonable

inexpensive /ˌɪnɪk'spensɪv/ *adj* económico

inexperience /ˌɪnɪk'spɪriəns ‖ˌɪnɪk'spɪəriəns/ *n* inexperiencia *f*, falta *f* de experiencia

inexperienced /ˌɪnɪk'spɪriənst ‖ˌɪnɪk'spɪəriənst/ *adj* ‹*nurse/pilot*› sin experiencia; ‹*swimmer/driver*› inexperto, novato

inexpert /ɪn'ekspɜːrt ‖ɪn'ekspɜːt/ *adj* inexperto

inexplicable /ˌɪnɪk'splɪkəbəl/ *adj* inexplicable

inextricably /ˌɪnɪk'strɪkəbli/ *adv* inextricablemente

infallibility /ɪnˌfælə'bɪləti/ *n* infalibilidad *f*

infallible /ɪn'fæləbəl/ *adj* infalible

infamous /'ɪnfəməs/ *adj* **(a)** (notorious) de triste fama **(b)** (shameful) infame

infancy /'ɪnfənsi/ *n* primera infancia *f*

infant /'ɪnfənt/ *n* **(a)** (baby) bebé *m*, niño, -ña *m,f*; (*before n*) **~ mortality** mortalidad *f* infantil **(b)** (BrE Educ) niño, -ña *m,f* (*entre cinco y siete años de edad*); (*before n*) **~ school** (in UK) *escuela para niños de entre cinco y siete años de edad*

infantile /'ɪnfəntaɪl/ *adj* pueril, infantil

infantry /ˈɪnfəntri/ n (+ sing or pl vb)
infantería f

infatuated /ɪnˈfætʃueɪtəd ‖ɪnˈfætʃʊeɪtɪd/ adj
to be ~ **WITH sb** estar* encaprichado CON or (Esp
tb) DE algn

infatuation /ɪnˌfætʃuˈeɪʃən ‖ɪnˌfætʃʊˈeɪʃən/ n
encaprichamiento m

infect /ɪnˈfekt/ vt ⟨wound/cut⟩ infectar; ⟨person/
animal⟩ contagiar; **the wound became ~ed** la
herida se infectó

infection /ɪnˈfekʃən/ n **(a)** (disease) infección f
(b) (of wound) infección f; (of person) contagio m

infectious /ɪnˈfekʃəs/ adj ⟨disease⟩ infeccioso,
contagioso; ⟨laughter/enthusiasm⟩ contagioso

infer /ɪnˈfɜː ‖ɪnˈfɜː(r)/ vt -rr- (deduce) to ~ **sth**
(FROM sth) inferir* or deducir* algo (DE algo)

inferior¹ /ɪnˈfɪriər ‖ɪnˈfɪəriə(r)/ adj (no comp)
⟨product⟩ (de calidad) inferior; ⟨workmanship/
rank⟩ inferior

inferior² n inferior mf

inferiority /ɪnˈfɪriˈɔːrəti ‖ɪnˌfɪərɪˈɒrəti/ n
inferioridad f; (before n) ~ **complex** complejo m
de inferioridad

inferno /ɪnˈfɜːnəʊ ‖ɪnˈfɜːnəʊ/ n (pl -noes)
(journ): **the building was a blazing ~** el edificio
estaba totalmente envuelto en llamas

infertile /ɪnˈfɜːrtl ‖ɪnˈfɜːtaɪl/ adj ⟨land⟩ estéril,
infecundo; ⟨woman/man/animal⟩ estéril

infertility /ˈɪnfərˈtɪləti ‖ɪnfəˈtɪləti/ n (Agr)
infecundidad f; (Biol) esterilidad f

infest /ɪnˈfest/ vt infestar

infidelity /ˈɪnfəˈdeləti ‖ɪnfɪˈdeləti/ n (pl -ties)
infidelidad f

infighting /ˈɪnˌfaɪtɪŋ/ n luchas fpl internas

infiltrate /ɪnˈfɪltreɪt ‖ˈɪnfɪltreɪt/ vt infiltrarse
en

infiltrator /ɪnˈfɪltreɪtər ‖ˈɪnfɪltreɪtə(r)/ n
infiltrado, -da m,f

infinite /ˈɪnfənət ‖ˈɪnfɪnət/ adj infinito

infinitesimal /ˈɪnfɪnəˈtesɪml ‖ˌɪnfɪnɪˈtesɪml/
adj infinitesimal

infinitive /ɪnˈfɪnətɪv/ n infinitivo m

infinity /ɪnˈfɪnəti/ n **(a)** (Math) infinito m **(b)**
(endless space) infinito m **(c)** (vast number, quantity)
(liter) (no pl) infinidad f

infirm /ɪnˈfɜːrm ‖ɪnˈfɜːm/ adj (weak) endeble; (ill)
enfermo

infirmary /ɪnˈfɜːrməri ‖ɪnˈfɜːməri/ n (pl -ries)
(used in titles) hospital m

infirmity /ɪnˈfɜːrməti ‖ɪnˈfɜːməti/ n (pl -ties)
dolencia f (frml), padecimiento m

inflame /ɪnˈfleɪm/ vt ⟨person/passion⟩
encender*; ⟨situation⟩ exacerbar

inflamed /ɪnˈfleɪmd/ adj inflamado; **to become**
~ inflamarse

inflammable /ɪnˈflæməbəl/ adj inflamable,
flamable (Méx)

inflammation /ˈɪnfləˈmeɪʃən/ n inflamación f

inflate /ɪnˈfleɪt/ vt (with air, gas) inflar, hinchar
(Esp)

inflation /ɪnˈfleɪʃən/ n inflación f

inflexible /ɪnˈfleksəbəl/ adj ⟨personality/
regulations⟩ inflexible; ⟨material⟩ rígido

inflict /ɪnˈflɪkt/ vt ⟨pain/damage⟩ causar;
⟨punishment⟩ imponer*; **to ~ sth ON sb: the**
suffering which he ~ed on his family el
sufrimiento que le causó a su familia

influence¹ /ˈɪnfluəns/ n influencia f: **to be**
under the ~ of sb/sth estar* bajo la influencia de
algn/algo; **she's a good/bad ~ on him** ejerce
buena/mala influencia sobre él

influence² vt influir* en, influenciar

influential /ˈɪnfluˈentʃəl ‖ɪnfluˈenʃəl/ adj
influyente

influenza /ˈɪnfluˈenzə/ n (Med) gripe f or (Chi tb)
influenza f or (Col, Méx) gripa f

influx /ˈɪnflʌks/ n (of people) afluencia f; (of
goods) entrada f; (of ideas) llegada f

inform /ɪnˈfɔːrm ‖ɪnˈfɔːm/ vt informar; **to keep**
sb ~ed mantener* a algn informado or al
corriente
■ ~ vi **to ~ ON sb** delatar or denunciar a algn

informal /ɪnˈfɔːrməl ‖ɪnˈfɔːməl/ adj informal

informality /ˈɪnfɔːrˈmæləti ‖ɪnfɔːˈmæləti/ n
falta f de ceremonia, informalidad f

informally /ɪnˈfɔːrməli ‖ɪnˈfɔːməli/ adv **(a)**
(casually) ⟨talk/dress⟩ de manera informal **(b)**
(unofficially) ⟨meet/discuss⟩ informalmente

informant /ɪnˈfɔːrmənt ‖ɪnˈfɔːmənt/ n
informante mf

information /ˈɪnfərˈmeɪʃən ‖ɪnfəˈmeɪʃən/ n
información f; **a piece of ~** un dato; (before n) ~
desk información f

information: ~ highway n (Comput)
autopista f de información, infovía f; ~
technology n informática f

informative /ɪnˈfɔːrmətɪv ‖ɪnˈfɔːmətɪv/ adj
⟨article/lecture⟩ instructivo, informativo;
⟨guidebook⟩ lleno de información, informativo

informed /ɪnˈfɔːrmd ‖ɪnˈfɔːmd/ adj ⟨source⟩
bien informado; ⟨criticism/approach⟩ bien
fundado

informer /ɪnˈfɔːrmər ‖ɪnˈfɔːmə(r)/ n
informante mf

infrared /ˈɪnfrəˈred/ adj infrarrojo

infrastructure /ˈɪnfrəˈstrʌktʃər
‖ˈɪnfrəˌstrʌktʃə(r)/ n infraestructura f

infrequent /ɪnˈfriːkwənt/ adj poco frecuente

infringe /ɪnˈfrɪndʒ/ vt ⟨contract⟩ no cumplir
(con); ⟨treaty/rule⟩ infringir*
■ ~ vi **to ~ ON o UPON sth** violar algo

infringement /ɪnˈfrɪndʒmənt/ n (of law)
contravención f, violación f; (of contract)
incumplimiento m; (Sport) falta f; (of rights)
violación f

infuriate /ɪnˈfjʊrieɪt ‖ɪnˈfjʊərieɪt/ vt
enfurecer*

infuriating /ɪnˈfjʊrieɪtɪŋ ‖ɪnˈfjʊərieɪtɪŋ/ adj
exasperante

infuse /ɪnˈfjuːz/ vt ⟨tea/herb⟩ hacer* una
infusión de

infusion /ɪnˈfjuːʒən/ n infusión f

ingenious /ɪnˈdʒiːniəs ‖ɪnˈdʒiːniəs/ adj
ingenioso

ingenuity /ˌɪndʒəˈnuːəti ‖ɪndʒəˈnjuːəti/ n (of
person) ingenio m; (of gadget, idea) lo ingenioso

ingenuous /ɪnˈdʒenjuəs/ adj ingenuo

ingot /ˈɪŋgət/ n lingote m

ingrained /ɪnˈɡreɪnd/ *adj* **(a)** ‹belief/habit› arraigado **(b)** ‹dirt› incrustado

ingratiate /ɪnˈɡreɪʃieɪt/ *v refl* **to ∼ oneself (WITH sb)** congraciarse (CON algn)

ingratitude /ɪnˈɡrætɪtuːd ‖ɪnˈɡrætɪtjuːd/ *n* ingratitud *f*

ingredient /ɪnˈɡriːdiənt/ *n* **(a)** (Culin) ingrediente *m* **(b)** (Pharm) componente *m* **(c)** (element) elemento *m*

ingrowing /ˈɪnˈɡrəʊɪŋ/ *adj* (BrE) ‹toenail› encarnado

ingrown /ˈɪnɡrəʊn/ *adj* ‹toenail› encarnado

inhabit /ɪnˈhæbət ‖ɪnˈhæbɪt/ *vt* habitar (frml), vivir en

inhabitant /ɪnˈhæbətənt ‖ɪnˈhæbɪtənt/ *n* habitante *mf*

inhale /ɪnˈheɪl/ *vi* aspirar

inhaler /ɪnˈheɪlər ‖ɪnˈheɪlə(r)/ *n* inhalador *m*

inherent /ɪnˈhɪrənt, -ˈher- ‖ɪnˈhɪərənt, -ˈher-/ *adj* inherente; **to be ∼ IN sth** ser* inherente A algo

inherit /ɪnˈherət ‖ɪnˈherɪt/ *vt* heredar

inheritance /ɪnˈherətəns ‖ɪnˈherɪtəns/ *n* **(a)** (sth inherited) herencia *f* **(b)** (act) sucesión *f*

inhibit /ɪnˈhɪbət ‖ɪnˈhɪbɪt/ *vt* (frml) inhibir

inhibited /ɪnˈhɪbətəd ‖ɪnˈhɪbɪtɪd/ *adj* inhibido

inhibition /ˌɪnəˈbɪʃən ‖ˌɪnhɪˈbɪʃən/ *n* inhibición *f*

inhospitable /ˌɪnhɑːˈspɪtəbəl ‖ɪnhɒˈspɪtəbəl/ *adj* ‹person› poco hospitalario; ‹climate/region› inhóspito

in-house /ˈɪnhaʊs/ *adj* ‹training› en la empresa (*or* organización *etc*); ‹staff› interno

inhuman /ɪnˈhjuːmən/ *adj* inhumano

inhumane /ˈɪnhjuːˈmeɪn/ *adj* ‹treatment› inhumano; ‹person› cruel

inhumanity /ˈɪnhjuːˈmænəti/ *n* (*pl*-**ties**) **(a)** (cruelty) crueldad *f* **(b)** (cruel act) atrocidad *f*

inimitable /ɪnˈɪmətəbəl ‖ɪˈnɪmɪtəbəl/ *adj* inimitable

initial[1] /ɪˈnɪʃəl/ *adj* inicial

initial[2] *n* inicial *f*

initial[3] *vt*, (BrE) -**ll**- inicialar

initially /ɪˈnɪʃəli/ *adv* inicialmente

initiate /ɪˈnɪʃieɪt/ *vt* **1** (start) (frml) ‹talks› iniciar (frml); ‹reform/plan› poner* en marcha **2** (admit, introduce) **to ∼ sb (INTO sth)** iniciar a algn (EN algo)

initiation /ɪˈnɪʃiˈeɪʃən/ *n* **1** (admission) iniciación *f*; (before *n*) **∼ ceremony** ceremonia *f* iniciática **2** (of plan, talks) inicio *m* (frml)

initiative /ɪˈnɪʃətɪv/ *n* iniciativa *f*; **on one's own ∼** por iniciativa propia; **to take the ∼** tomar la iniciativa

inject /ɪnˈdʒekt/ *vt* ‹drug› inyectar; **to ∼ sth (INTO sth)** ‹capital/resources› inyectarle algo (A algo)

injection /ɪnˈdʒekʃən/ *n* inyección *f*

injunction /ɪnˈdʒʌŋkʃən/ *n* (Law) mandamiento *m* judicial

injure /ˈɪndʒər ‖ˈɪndʒə(r)/ *vt* **(a)** ‹person/feelings› herir* **(b) injured** *past p*: **she gave me an ∼d look** me miró con expresión ofendida; **I am the ∼d party** soy yo quien sufrió el agravio

injurious /ɪnˈdʒʊriəs ‖ɪnˈdʒʊəriəs/ *adj* (frml) perjudicial

injury /ˈɪndʒəri/ *n* (*pl* -**ries**) herida *f*; (before *n*) **∼ time** (BrE Sport) tiempo *m* de descuento

injustice /ɪnˈdʒʌstəs ‖ɪnˈdʒʌstɪs/ *n* injusticia *f*; **to do sb an ∼** cometer una injusticia con algn

ink /ɪŋk/ *n* tinta *f*

inkling /ˈɪŋklɪŋ/ *n*: **I had an ∼ something had gone wrong** tuve el presentimiento *or* (CS, Per tb) el pálpito de que algo había salido mal

inkwell /ˈɪŋkwel/ *n* tintero *m* (*empotrado en un escritorio*)

inlaid[1] /ˈɪnleɪd/ *past & past p of* INLAY[2]

inlaid[2] *adj* ‹design› de marquetería; ‹box/lid› con incrustaciones

inland[1] /ˈɪnlənd/ *adj* (before *n*) ‹town› del interior; ‹sea› interior

inland[2] /ɪnˈlænd/ *adv* tierra adentro

Inland Revenue /ˈɪnlənd/ *n* (in UK) **the ∼ ∼** ≈ Hacienda, ≈ la Dirección General Impositiva (*en RPI*), ≈ Impuestos Internos (*en Chi*)

in-laws /ˈɪnlɔːz/ *pl n* (colloq) (spouse's parents) suegros *mpl*; (spouse's family) parientes *mpl* políticos

inlay[1] /ˈɪnleɪ/ *n* (of wood, metal, ivory) incrustación *f*

inlay[2] /ɪnˈleɪ/ *vt* (*past & past p* **inlaid**) **to ∼ sth WITH sth** hacer* incrustaciones de algo EN algo

inlet /ˈɪnlet/ *n* (in coastline) ensenada *f*, entrada *f*; (of river, sea) brazo *m*

inmate /ˈɪnmeɪt/ *n* (of asylum) interno, -na *m,f*; (of prison) preso, -sa *m,f*; (of hospital) paciente hospitalizado, -da *m,f*

inmost /ˈɪnməʊst/ *adj* ▶ INNERMOST

inn /ɪn/ *n* (tavern) taberna *f*; (hotel) hostal *m*

innards /ˈɪnərdz ‖ˈɪnədz/ *pl n* tripas *fpl* (fam)

innate /ɪˈneɪt/ *adj* innato

inner /ˈɪnər ‖ˈɪnə(r)/ *adj* (before *n*, no comp) **(a)** ‹room/part› interior; **the ∼ city** la zona del centro urbano habitada por familias de escasos ingresos, caracterizada por problemas sociales *etc* **(b)** (of person) ‹life› interior; ‹thoughts› íntimo

innermost /ˈɪnərməʊst ‖ˈɪnəməʊst/ *adj* ‹part/chamber› más recóndito; ‹thoughts› más íntimo

inner tube *n* cámara *f*

inning /ˈɪnɪŋ/ *n* (in baseball) entrada *f*, manga *f*

innings /ˈɪnɪŋz/ *n* (*pl* **∼**) (in cricket) entrada *f*

innkeeper /ˈɪnˌkiːpər ‖ˈɪnˌkiːpə(r)/ *n* posadero, -ra *m,f*

innocence /ˈɪnəsəns/ *n* inocencia *f*

innocent /ˈɪnəsənt/ *adj* inocente

innocuous /ɪˈnɑːkjuəs ‖ɪˈnɒkjuəs/ *adj* ‹drug› inocuo; ‹person/comment› inofensivo

innovation /ˈɪnəˈveɪʃən/ *n* innovación *f*

innovative /ˈɪnəveɪtɪv ‖ˈɪnəvətɪv/ *adj* innovador

innuendo /ˈɪnjuˈendəʊ/ *n* (*pl* -**dos** *or* -**does**) indirecta *f*, insinuación *f*

innumerable /ɪˈnuːmərəbəl ‖ɪˈnjuːmərəbəl/ *adj* innumerable

inoculate /ɪˈnɑːkjəleɪt ‖ɪˈnɒkjʊleɪt/ *vt* inocular

inoculation /ɪˈnɑːkjəˈleɪʃən ‖ɪˌnɒkjʊˈleɪʃən/ *n* inoculación *f*

inoffensive /ˌɪnəˈfensɪv/ adj inofensivo

inordinate /ɪˈnɔːrdnət ‖ɪnˈɔːdɪnət/ adj: an ~ amount of money una cantidad exorbitante de dinero; **they are making ~ demands** lo que piden es excesivo

inpatient /ˈɪnˌpeɪʃənt/ n paciente hospitalizado, -da m,f

input¹ /ˈɪnpʊt/ n **1** **(a)** (of resources) aportación f, aporte m (esp AmL) **(b)** (contribution) aportación f, aporte m (esp AmL) **2** (Comput) entrada f

input² vt (pres p **inputting**; past & past p **input** or **inputted**) ⟨data⟩ entrar

inquest /ˈɪnkwest/ n investigación f

inquire, (BrE) enquire /ɪnˈkwaɪr ‖ɪnˈkwaɪə(r)/ vt preguntar
■ ~ vi preguntar; **to ~ ABOUT sth** informarse ACERCA DE algo

inquiring, (BrE) enquiring /ɪnˈkwaɪrɪŋ ‖ɪnˈkwaɪərɪŋ/ adj (before n) ⟨mind⟩ curioso; ⟨look⟩ inquisitivo

inquiry, (BrE) enquiry /ɪnˈkwaɪri, ˈɪnkwəri ‖ɪnˈkwaɪəri/ n (pl **-ries**) **(a)** (question): **we made inquiries about** o **into his past** hicimos averiguaciones sobre su pasado; **all inquiries to ...** para cualquier información dirigirse a ...; **⑤ inquiries** información **(b)** (investigation) investigación f

inquisition /ˌɪnkwəˈzɪʃən ‖ˌɪnkwɪˈzɪʃən/ n **(a)** (severe questioning) interrogatorio m **(b) the Spanish I~** la (Santa) Inquisición, el Santo Oficio

inquisitive /ɪnˈkwɪzətɪv/ adj ⟨mind⟩ inquisitivo; ⟨person/animal⟩ muy curioso

inroads /ˈɪnrəʊdz/ pl n: **we are making ~ into the Japanese market** estamos haciendo avances en el mercado japonés; **this made substantial ~ into her savings** esto le comió buena parte de los ahorros

INS n (in US) = **Immigration and Naturalization Service**

insane /ɪnˈseɪn/ adj (mad) demente; (foolish) insensato

insanitary /ɪnˈsænəteri ‖ɪnˈsænɪtəri/ adj malsano, insanitorio

insanity /ɪnˈsænəti/ n demencia f

insatiable /ɪnˈseɪʃəbəl/ adj insaciable

inscribe /ɪnˈskraɪb/ vt **to ~ sth (ON sth)** ⟨letters⟩ inscribir* algo (EN algo); ⟨design⟩ grabar algo (EN algo)

inscription /ɪnˈskrɪpʃən/ n inscripción f

insect /ˈɪnsekt/ n insecto m

insecticide /ɪnˈsektəsaɪd ‖ɪnˈsektɪsaɪd/ n insecticida m

insecure /ˌɪnsɪˈkjʊr ‖ˌɪnsɪˈkjʊə(r)/ adj **(a)** (unsafe, exposed) inseguro **(b)** (not firmly fixed) poco seguro **(c)** (not confident) inseguro

insecurity /ˌɪnsɪˈkjʊrəti ‖ˌɪnsɪˈkjʊərəti/ n (pl **-ties**) inseguridad f

insemination /ɪnˌseməˈneɪʃən ‖ɪnˌsemɪˈneɪʃən/ n inseminación f

insensible /ɪnˈsensəbəl/ adj (frml) **(a)** (unconscious) inconsciente **(b)** (without sensation) insensible

insensitive /ɪnˈsensətɪv/ adj ⟨person⟩ insensible; ⟨behavior⟩ falto de sensibilidad

insensitivity /ɪnˈsensəˈtɪvəti/ n falta f de sensibilidad

inseparable /ɪnˈseprəbəl/ adj inseparable

insert /ɪnˈsɜːrt ‖ɪnˈsɜːt/ vt ⟨coin/token⟩ introducir*; ⟨zipper⟩ poner*; ⟨word/paragraph⟩ insertar

insertion /ɪnˈsɜːrʃən ‖ɪnˈsɜːʃən/ n introducción f

inshore¹ /ˈɪnˈʃɔːr ‖ˌɪnˈʃɔː(r)/ adj costero

inshore² adv hacia la costa

inside¹ /ˈɪnˈsaɪd/ n **1** (interior part) interior m; (inner side, surface) parte f de dentro or (esp AmL) de adentro **2 insides** pl (internal organs) (colloq) tripas fpl (fam) **3** inside out adv: **turn it ~ out** ponlo de adentro para fuera; **you've got your socks on ~ out** llevas los calcetines del or al revés

inside² prep **(a)** (within) dentro de; **we did the journey ~ 3 hours** (colloq) hicimos el viaje en menos de 3 horas **(b)** (into): **he followed her ~ the bar** la siguió al interior del bar

inside³ adv **(a)** (within, indoors) dentro, adentro (esp AmL); **come ~** entra, pasa **(b)** (in prison) (colloq) entre rejas (fam), a la sombra (fam)

inside⁴ adj (before n) **(a)** ⟨pages⟩ interior; ⟨pocket⟩ interior, de adentro (esp AmL) **(b) the ~ lane** (Auto) el carril de la derecha; (in UK etc) el carril de la izquierda; (Sport) el carril (AmL) or (Esp) la calle número uno **(c)** (from within group) ⟨information⟩ de dentro, de adentro (esp AmL)

insider /ɪnˈsaɪdər ‖ɪnˈsaɪdə(r)/ n: persona que pertenece a una organización determinada o que tiene acceso a información confidencial

insidious /ɪnˈsɪdiəs/ adj insidioso

insight /ˈɪnsaɪt/ n **(a)** (perceptiveness) perspicacia f **(b)** (comprehension): **to gain an ~ into sth** llegar* a comprender bien algo

insignia /ɪnˈsɪɡniə/ n (pl ~ or ~s) insignia f

insignificant /ˌɪnsɪɡˈnɪfɪkənt/ adj ⟨person/amount⟩ insignificante; ⟨detail⟩ nimio

insincere /ˌɪnsɪnˈsɪr ‖ˌɪnsɪnˈsɪə(r)/ adj ⟨offer⟩ poco sincero; ⟨person/smile⟩ falso

insincerity /ˌɪnsɪnˈserəti/ n falta f de sinceridad

insinuate /ɪnˈsɪnjueɪt/ vt insinuar*

insinuation /ɪnˌsɪnjuˈeɪʃən/ n insinuación f

insipid /ɪnˈsɪpəd ‖ɪnˈsɪpɪd/ adj ⟨food/drink⟩ insípido; ⟨person/novel⟩ insulso

insist /ɪnˈsɪst/ vt **(a)** (demand) **to ~ (THAT)** insistir EN QUE (+ subj) **(b)** (maintain) **to ~ (THAT)** insistir EN QUE
■ ~ vi insistir
■ **insist on** [v + prep + o] **to ~ on -ING** insistir EN + INF/EN QUE (+ subj)

insistence /ɪnˈsɪstəns/ n insistencia f

insistent /ɪnˈsɪstənt/ *adj* **(a)** (persistent) insistente; **to be ~ THAT** insistir EN QUE **(b)** (pressing) ⟨*need*⟩ apremiante

insofar as /ˌɪnsəˈfɑːr ‖ˌɪnsəˈfɑː(r)/ *conj* (fml) en la medida en que

insole /ˈɪnsəʊl/ *n* plantilla *f*

insolence /ˈɪnsələns/ *n* insolencia *f*

insolent /ˈɪnsələnt/ *adj* insolente

insolvent /ɪnˈsɑːlvənt ‖ɪnˈsɒlvənt/ *adj* insolvente

insomnia /ɪnˈsɑːmniə ‖ɪnˈsɒmniə/ *n* insomnio *m*

insomniac /ɪnˈsɑːmniæk ‖ɪnˈsɒmniæk/ *n* insomne *mf*

inspect /ɪnˈspekt/ *vt* **(a)** (look closely at) ⟨*car/ camera*⟩ revisar, examinar; (examine officially) ⟨*school/restaurant/equipment*⟩ inspeccionar **(b)** ⟨*troops*⟩ pasar revista a

inspection /ɪnˈspekʃən/ *n* **(a)** (official examination) inspección *f* **(b)** (of troops) revista *f* **(c)** (scrutiny) examen *m*, revisión *f*

inspector /ɪnˈspektər ‖ɪnˈspektə(r)/ *n* **(a)** (official) inspector, -tora *m,f* **(b)** (police officer) inspector, -tora *m,f*

inspiration /ˌɪnspəˈreɪʃən/ *n* inspiración *f*

inspire /ɪnˈspaɪr ‖ɪnˈspaɪə(r)/ *vt* inspirar; ⟨*hope/courage*⟩ infundir; **what ~d you to do that?** ¿qué te movió *or* te llevó a hacer eso?

inspired /ɪnˈspaɪrd ‖ɪnˈspaɪəd/ *adj* inspirado

inspiring /ɪnˈspaɪrɪŋ ‖ɪnˈspaɪərɪŋ/ *adj* inspirador

instability /ˌɪnstəˈbɪləti/ *n* inestabilidad *f*

install, instal /ɪnˈstɔːl/ *vt* **-ll-** instalar

installation /ˌɪnstəˈleɪʃən/ *n* instalación *f*

installment, (BrE) instalment /ɪnˈstɔːlmənt/ *n* **1** (payment) plazo *m*, cuota *f* (esp AmL); **to buy in** *o* **by ~s** pagar* a plazos, pagar* en cuotas (esp AmL) **2** (of publication) entrega *f*; (of TV, radio serial) episodio *m*

installment plan *n* (AmE) plan *m* de financiación; **to buy sth on an ~ ~** comprar algo a plazos, comprar algo en cuotas (esp AmL)

instance /ˈɪnstəns/ *n* **(a)** (example) ejemplo *m*; **for ~** por ejemplo **(b)** (case) caso *m*; **in this ~** en este caso

instant¹ /ˈɪnstənt/ *adj* instantáneo

instant² *n* **(a)** (precise moment) instante *m* **(b)** (short time) momento *m*

instantaneous /ˌɪnstənˈteɪniəs/ *adj* instantáneo

instantly /ˈɪnstəntli/ *adv* al instante

instant replay *n* repetición *f* (de la jugada)

instead /ɪnˈsted/ *adv*: **I couldn't go, so she went ~** no pude ir, así que fue ella (en vez de mí); **~ of** (*as prep*) en vez de, en lugar de

instep /ˈɪnstep/ *n* (of foot — arch) arco *m* (del pie); (— upper surface) empeine *m*

instigate /ˈɪnstəgeɪt ‖ˈɪnstɪgeɪt/ *vt* ⟨*rebellion/ mutiny*⟩ instigar* a

instigation /ˌɪnstəˈgeɪʃən ‖ˌɪnstɪˈgeɪʃən/ *n* instigación *f*; **it was carried out at the director's ~** se llevó a cabo a instancias del director

instill, instil /ɪnˈstɪl/ *vt* **-ll-**: **to ~ sth IN/INTO sb** ⟨*habit/attitude*⟩ inculcarle* algo A algn; ⟨*courage/fear*⟩ infundirle algo A algn

instinct /ˈɪnstɪŋkt/ *n* instinto *m*

instinctive /ɪnˈstɪŋktɪv/ *adj* instintivo

institute¹ /ˈɪnstətuːt ‖ˈɪnstɪtjuːt/ *vt* (fml) ⟨*search/inquiry*⟩ iniciar; ⟨*proceedings*⟩ entablar

institute² *n* instituto *m*

institution /ˌɪnstəˈtuːʃən ‖ˌɪnstɪˈtjuːʃən/ *n* **1** (established practice) institución *f* **2** **(a)** (organization) organismo *m*; (building) institución *f* **(b)** (hospital, asylum, home) *establecimiento sanitario, penitenciario o de asistencia social*

institutional /ˌɪnstəˈtuːʃnəl ‖ˌɪnstɪˈtjuːʃənl/ *adj* institucional

instruct /ɪnˈstrʌkt/ *vt* **1** (command) **to ~ sb to + INF** ordenar a algn QUE (+ *subj*) **2** (fml) (teach) **to ~ sb IN sth** enseñarle algo a algn

instruction /ɪnˈstrʌkʃən/ *n* instrucción *f*; ⦿ **instructions (for use)** instrucciones; **they were acting on the ~s of the chief of police** cumplían órdenes del jefe de policía

instructive /ɪnˈstrʌktɪv/ *adj* instructivo

instructor /ɪnˈstrʌktər ‖ɪnˈstrʌktə(r)/ *n* **(a)** (teacher) (Mil) instructor, -tora *m,f* **(b)** (in US colleges) profesor, -sora *m,f* auxiliar

instrument /ˈɪnstrəmənt ‖ˈɪnstrʊmənt/ *n* **1** (musical ~) instrumento *m* (musical) **2** **(a)** (piece of equipment) instrumento *m* **(b)**

instruments *pl n* (Aviat) instrumentos *mpl*; (Auto) instrumentación *f*

instrumental /ˌɪnstrəˈmentl ‖ˌɪnstrʊˈmentl̩/ *adj* **1** (serving as a means) **to be ~ IN sth** jugar* un papel decisivo EN algo **2** (Mus) instrumental

instrument panel *n* (Auto) tablero *m* de mandos, salpicadero *m* (Esp); (Aviat) tablero *m* de mandos

insubordination /ˈɪnsəbɔːrdn̩ˈeɪʃən ‖ˌɪnsəbɔːdɪˈneɪʃən/ *n* insubordinación *f*

insubstantial /ˌɪnsəbˈstænʃəl ‖ˌɪnsəbˈstænʃl/ *adj* ⟨*structure/object*⟩ frágil; ⟨*evidence/argument*⟩ inconsistente

insufferable /ɪnˈsʌfrəbəl/ *adj* (fml) ⟨*person/ rudeness*⟩ insufrible; ⟨*heat/noise*⟩ insoportable

insufficient /ˌɪnsəˈfɪʃənt/ *adj* insuficiente

insular /ˈɪnsələr ‖ˈɪnsjʊlə(r)/ *adj* ⟨*mentality*⟩ cerrado; ⟨*person*⟩ estrecho de miras

insulate /ˈɪnsəleɪt ‖ˈɪnsjʊleɪt/ *vt* aislar*

insulation /ˌɪnsəˈleɪʃən ‖ˌɪnsjʊˈleɪʃən/ *n* aislamiento *m*

insulin /ˈɪnsələn ‖ˈɪnsjʊlɪn/ *n* insulina *f*

insult¹ /ɪnˈsʌlt/ *vt* insultar

insult² /ˈɪnsʌlt/ *n* insulto *m*

insulting /ɪnˈsʌltɪŋ/ *adj* insultante

insurance /ɪnˈʃʊrəns ‖ɪnˈʃʊərəns, ɪnˈʃɔːrəns/ *n* seguro *m*; **to take out ~** hacerse* un seguro; (*before n*) **~ company** compañía *f* de seguros

insure /ɪnˈʃʊr ‖ɪnˈʃʊə(r), ɪnˈʃɔː(r)/ *vt* **1** (Fin) asegurar **2** (AmE) ▶ ENSURE

insurer /ɪnˈʃʊrər ‖ɪnˈʃʊərə(r), ɪnˈʃɔːrə(r)/ *n* (company) compañía *f* de seguros; (person) asegurador, -dora *m,f*

insurgent /ɪnˈsɜːrdʒənt ‖ɪnˈsɜːdʒənt/ *adj* (fml) insurgente (fml)

insurmountable /ˌɪnsərˈmaʊntəbəl ‖ˌɪnsəˈmaʊntəbəl/ *adj* (fml) ⟨*difficulty*⟩ insalvable

insurrection /ˌɪnsəˈrekʃən/ *n* (fml) insurrección *f* (fml)

intact /ɪn'tækt/ adj (usu pred) intacto

intake /'ɪnteɪk/ n **1** (of water, air) entrada f; (of calories, protein) consumo m **2** (Tech) (pipe, vent) toma f (de aire, agua etc)

intangible /ɪn'tændʒəbəl/ adj intangible

integral /'ɪntɪgrəl/ adj ‹part/feature› integral

integrate /'ɪntəgreɪt ‖'ɪntɪgreɪt/ vt integrar ■ ∼ vi integrarse

integrated /'ɪntəgreɪtəd ‖'ɪntɪgreɪtɪd/ adj **(a)** ‹system/network› integrado **(b)** (not separate) ‹component/feature› incorporado **(c)** (nonsegregated) no segregacionista

integration /'ɪntə'greɪʃən ‖,ɪntɪ'greɪʃən/ n integración f

integrity /ɪn'tegrəti/ n integridad f

intellect /'ɪntlekt ‖'ɪntəlekt/ n intelecto m

intellectual¹ /'ɪntə'lektʃuəl/ adj intelectual

intellectual² n intelectual mf

intelligence /ɪn'telədʒəns/ n **1** (mental capacity) inteligencia f **2** (Govt, Mil) **(a)** (information) inteligencia f **(b)** (department) servicio m de información

intelligent /ɪn'telədʒənt ‖ɪn'telɪdʒənt/ adj inteligente

intelligible /ɪn'telədʒəbəl ‖ɪn'telɪdʒəbəl/ adj inteligible

intemperate /ɪn'tempərət/ adj ‹climate› inclemente, riguroso

intend /ɪn'tend/ vt: no insult was ∼ed no fue mi intención ofender; **to** ∼ **-ING** pensar* + INF; **to** ∼ **sb/sth to** + INF querer* QUE algn/algo (+ subj)

intense /ɪn'tens/ adj intenso

intensely /ɪn'tensli/ adv (as intensifier) ‹moving› profundamente, sumamente; **I dislike him** ∼ siento una profunda antipatía hacia él

intensify /ɪn'tensəfaɪ ‖ɪn'tensɪfaɪ/ **-fies, -fying, -fied** vt ‹search› intensificar*; ‹efforts› redoblar ■ ∼ vi «pain» agudizarse*; «search» intensificarse*; «fighting» recrudecer*

intensity /ɪn'tensəti/ n intensidad f

intensive /ɪn'tensɪv/ adj intensivo

intensive care n cuidados mpl intensivos, terapia f intensiva (Méx, RPl)

intent¹ /ɪn'tent/ adj **(a)** (determined) (pred) **to be** ∼ **ON sth/-ING** estar* decidido or resuelto A + INF **(b)** (attentive, concentrated) ‹expression› de viva atención; ‹look› penetrante, fijo; **to be** ∼ **ON sth** estar* abstraído EN algo

intent² n propósito m; **to all** ∼**s and purposes** a efectos prácticos

intention /ɪn'tentʃən ‖ɪn'tenʃən/ n intención f; **I have every** ∼ **of going** tengo la firme intención de ir

intentional /ɪn'tentʃnəl ‖ɪn'tenʃənl/ adj ‹destruction› intencional; ‹insult/cruelty› deliberado

intently /ɪn'tentli/ adv ‹listen› atentamente; **he was staring** ∼ **at them** tenía la mirada fija en ellos

inter /ɪn'tɜːr ‖ɪn'tɜː(r)/ vt **-rr-** (frml or liter) inhumar (frml)

interact /'ɪntər'ækt/ vi «people/organizations» relacionarse

interaction /'ɪntər'ækʃən/ n interacción f

interactive /'ɪntər'æktɪv/ adj interactivo

intercede /'ɪntər'siːd ‖,ɪntə'siːd/ vi interceder

intercept /'ɪntər'sept/ vt interceptar; **they were** ∼**ed before they reached the building** les cerraron el paso antes de llegar al edificio

interchange¹ /'ɪntər'tʃeɪndʒ ‖,ɪntə'tʃeɪndʒ/ vt intercambiar

interchange² /'ɪntərtʃeɪndʒ ‖'ɪntətʃeɪndʒ/ n **1** (exchange) intercambio m **2** (on road system) enlace m, intercambiador m (Esp)

interchangeable /'ɪntər'tʃeɪndʒəbəl ‖,ɪntə'tʃeɪndʒəbəl/ adj intercambiable

intercity /'ɪntər'sɪti ‖,ɪntə'sɪti/ adj rápido interurbano

intercom /'ɪntərkɑːm ‖'ɪntəkɒm/ n **(a)** (on plane, ship, in office) interfono m **(b)** (at building entrance) (AmE) portero m eléctrico or (Esp) automático, interfón m (Méx), intercomunicador m (Ven)

intercourse /'ɪntərkɔːrs ‖'ɪntəkɔːs/ n (sexual ∼) coito m (frml), acto m sexual; **to have** ∼ **with sb** tener* relaciones sexuales con algn

interest¹ /'ɪntrəst/ n **1 (a)** (enthusiasm) interés m; **to take (an)** ∼ **IN sth/sb** interesarse POR algo/algn **(b)** (hobby) interés m **2 (a)** (stake) participación f; **he has a number of business** ∼**s abroad** tiene varios negocios en el extranjero **(b)** (advantage) (often pl) interés m; **it was not in our** ∼**(s) to intervene** no nos convenía intervenir **3** (Fin) interés m; (before n) ∼ **rate** tasa f or (esp Esp) tipo m de interés

interest² vt interesar

interested /'ɪntrəstəd ‖'ɪntrəstɪd/ adj interesado; **I am** ∼ **in astronomy** me interesa la astronomía; ∼ **party** parte f interesada

interesting /'ɪntrəstɪŋ/ adj interesante

interface /'ɪntərfeɪs ‖'ɪntəfeɪs/ n (Comput) interface f or m, interfaz f or m, interfase f or m

interfere /'ɪntər'fɪr ‖,ɪntə'fɪə(r)/ vi **1** (get involved) to ∼ (IN sth) entrometerse (EN algo) **2 (a)** (disrupt) to ∼ **WITH sth** afectar (A) algo **(b)** (tamper) to ∼ **WITH sth** tocar* algo

interference /'ɪntər'frəns ‖,ɪntə'fɪərəns/ n **(a)** (interfering) intromisión f **(b)** (Phys, Rad, Telec) interferencia f

interfering /'ɪntər'fɪrɪŋ ‖,ɪntə'fɪərɪŋ/ adj entrometido

interim¹ /'ɪntərəm ‖'ɪntərɪm/ adj (before n) ‹measure› provisional, provisorio (AmS); **an** ∼ **period** un período intermedio

interim² n: **in** o **during the** ∼ en el interín or ínterin

interior¹ /ɪn'tɪriər ‖ɪn'tɪəriə(r)/ n **1 (a)** (of building) interior m **(b)** (Cin) interior m **2 (a)** (Geog) **the** ∼ el interior **(b)** (Govt) **the Ministry/ Department of the I**∼ el Ministerio/Departamento del Interior

interior² adj **1 (a)** (inside) ‹walls› interior **(b)** (mental) interior **2** (inland) del interior

interior: ∼ **decorator** n (painter) pintor, -tora m,f; (designer) interiorista mf, decorador, -dora m,f (de interiores); ∼ **design** n interiorismo m

interjection /'ɪntər'dʒekʃən ‖,ɪntə'dʒekʃən/ n (Ling) interjección f; (exclamation) exclamación f

interloper /'ɪntərləʊpər ‖ 'ɪntələʊpə(r)/ *n* intruso, -sa *m,f*

interlude /'ɪntərluːd ‖ 'ɪntəluːd/ *n* [1] (intervening period) intervalo *m* [2] (a) (Theat) (intermission) entreacto *m* (b) (Mus) interludio *m*

intermediary /'ɪntər'miːdiəri ‖ ,ɪntə'miːdiəri/ *n* (*pl* **-ries**) (frml) intermediario, -ria *m,f*

intermediate /'ɪntər'miːdiət ‖ ,ɪntə'miːdiət/ *adj* ⟨stage/step⟩ intermedio; ⟨size/weight/level⟩ medio; ⟨course⟩ de nivel medio *or* intermedio

intermediate school *n* (in US) (a) (secondary) escuela donde se cursa el primer ciclo de la enseñanza secundaria (b) (primary) escuela donde se cursa segundo ciclo de la enseñanza primaria

interminable /ɪn'tɜːrmənəbəl ‖ ɪn'tɜːmɪnəbəl/ *adj* interminable

intermission /'ɪntər'mɪʃən ‖ ,ɪntə'mɪʃən/ *n* intermedio *m*

intermittent /'ɪntər'mɪtṇt ‖ ,ɪntə'mɪtənt/ *adj* intermitente

intern¹ /ɪn'tɜːrn ‖ ɪn'tɜːn/ *vt* recluir*, confinar

intern² /'ɪntɜːrn ‖ 'ɪntɜːn/ *n* (AmE) (a) (Med) interno, -na *m,f* (b) (Educ) profesor, -sora *m,f* en prácticas

internal /ɪn'tɜːrṇl ‖ ɪn'tɜːnḷ/ *adj* interno

Internal Revenue Service *n* (in US) the ∼ ∼ ∼ ≈ Hacienda, ≈ la Dirección General Impositiva (*en RPl*), ≈ Impuestos Internos (*en Chi*)

international¹ /'ɪntər'næʃṇəl ‖ ,ɪntə'næʃənḷ/ *adj* internacional

international² *n* (Sport) (a) (event) partido *m* internacional (b) (player) internacional *mf*

internationally /'ɪntər'næʃṇəli ‖ ,ɪntə'næʃṇəli/ *adv* (a) ⟨expand/trade⟩ internacionalmente (b) ⟨famous/known⟩ mundialmente

International Monetary Fund *n* the ∼ ∼ ∼ el Fondo Monetario Internacional

Internet /'ɪntərnet ‖ 'ɪntənet/ *n* the ∼ el Internet

Internet service provider /prə'vaɪdər ‖ prə'vaɪdə(r)/ *n* proveedor *m* de servicios Internet

internment /ɪn'tɜːrnmənt ‖ ɪn'tɜːnmənt/ *n* internamiento *m*

interpret /ɪn'tɜːrprət ‖ ɪn'tɜːprɪt/ *vt* interpretar ∎ ∼ *vi* (Ling) (translate) traducir* (*oralmente*), interpretar

interpretation /ɪn'tɜːrprə'teɪʃən ‖ ɪn,tɜːprɪ'teɪʃən/ *n* interpretación *f*

interpreter /ɪn'tɜːrprətər ‖ ɪn'tɜːprɪtə(r)/ *n* intérprete *mf*

interrogate /ɪn'terəgeɪt/ *vt* interrogar*

interrogation /ɪn'terə'geɪʃən/ *n* interrogatorio *m*

interrogation point *n* (AmE frml) signo *m* de interrogación

interrogative /'ɪntə'rɑːgətɪv ‖ ,ɪntə'rɒgətɪv/ *adj* interrogativo

interrupt /'ɪntə'rʌpt/ *vt/i* interrumpir

interruption /'ɪntə'rʌpʃən/ *n* interrupción *f*

intersect /'ɪntər'sekt ‖ ,ɪntə'sekt/ *vi* «roads/paths» cruzarse*

intersection /'ɪntər'sekʃən ‖ ,ɪntə'sekʃən/ *n* (a) (Transp) cruce *m* (b) (Geog, Math) intersección *f*

intersperse /'ɪntər'spɜːrs ‖ ,ɪntə'spɜːs/ *vt* intercalar

interstate (**highway**) /'ɪntərsteɪt ‖ 'ɪntəsteɪt/ *n* (AmE) carretera *f* interestatal

intertwine /'ɪntər'twaɪn ‖ ,ɪntə'twaɪn/ *vi* «fingers/plants» entrelazarse*; «paths/destinies» entrecruzarse* ∎ ∼ *vt* ⟨fingers⟩ entrelazar*

interval /'ɪntərvəl ‖ 'ɪntəvəl/ *n* [1] (time, distance) intervalo *m* [2] (pause) (BrE Cin, Mus) intermedio *m*; (BrE Theat) entreacto *m*; (Sport) descanso *m*, entretiempo *m* (Chi) [3] (Mus) intervalo *m*

intervene /'ɪntər'viːn ‖ ,ɪntə'viːn/ *vi* (a) (interpose oneself) intervenir* (b) **intervening** *pres p*: in the intervening period en el interín *or* ínterin

intervention /'ɪntər'venʃən ‖ ,ɪntə'venʃən/ *n* intervención *f*

interview¹ /'ɪntərvjuː ‖ 'ɪntəvjuː/ *n* entrevista *f*

interview² *vt* entrevistar

interviewee /'ɪntərvjuːˈiː ‖ ,ɪntəvjuːˈiː/ *n* entrevistado, -da *m,f*

interviewer /'ɪntərvjuːər ‖ 'ɪntəvjuːə(r)/ *n* entrevistador, -dora *m,f*

interweave /'ɪntərˈwiːv ‖ ,ɪntəˈwiːv/ *vt* (*past* **-wove** *or* **-weaved**; *past p* **-woven** *or* **-weaved**) entretejer; their lives were interwoven sus vidas estaban inextricablemente unidas

intestate /ɪn'testeɪt/ *adj* intestado

intestine /ɪn'testən ‖ ɪn'testɪn/ *n* (*often pl*) intestino *m*; the small/large ∼ el intestino delgado/grueso

intimacy /'ɪntəməsi ‖ 'ɪntɪməsi/ *n* intimidad *f*

intimate /'ɪntəmət ‖ 'ɪntɪmət/ *adj* ⟨friend/atmosphere⟩ íntimo; ⟨talk⟩ de carácter íntimo; ⟨knowledge⟩ profundo; to be on ∼ terms with sb ser* íntimo de algn

intimation /'ɪntə'meɪʃən ‖ ,ɪntr'meɪʃən/ *n* (sign) indicio *m*; (inkling) presentimiento *m*

intimidate /ɪn'tɪmədeɪt ‖ ɪn'tɪmɪdeɪt/ *vt* intimidar

intimidating /ɪn'tɪmədeɪtɪŋ ‖ ɪn'tɪmɪdeɪtɪŋ/ *adj* intimidante

intimidation /ɪn'tɪmə'deɪʃən ‖ ɪn,tɪmɪ'deɪʃən/ *n* intimidación *f*

into /'ɪntu, *before consonant* 'ɪntə/ *prep* [1] (a) (indicating motion, direction): to walk ∼ a building entrar en *or* (esp AmL) a un edificio; they helped him ∼ the chair lo ayudaron a sentarse en el sillón; she sat staring ∼ space estaba sentada mirando al vacío; to translate sth ∼ Spanish traducir* algo al español (b) (against): she walked ∼ a tree se dio contra un árbol; he drove ∼ the other car chocó con el otro coche [2] (in time, distance): ten minutes ∼ the game a los diez minutos de empezar el partido; they penetrated deep ∼ the jungle entraron en el corazón de la selva [3] (indicating result of action): we split ∼ two groups nos dividimos en dos grupos; roll the dough ∼ a ball haga una bola con la masa [4] (involved in) (colloq) they're ∼ drugs se drogan; at two, children are ∼ everything a los dos años, los niños son muy inquietos

intolerable /ɪn'tɑːlərəbəl ‖m'tɒlərəbəl/ *adj*
intolerable

intolerance /ɪn'tɑːlərəns ‖m'tɒlərəns/ *n*
intolerancia *f*

intolerant /ɪn'tɑːlərənt ‖m'tɒlərənt/ *adj*
intolerante

intonation /ˌɪntə'neɪʃən/ *n* entonación *f*

intone /ɪn'təʊn/ *vt* ‹*psalm/Gloria*› entonar

intoxicated /ɪn'tɑːksəkeɪtəd ‖m'tɒksɪkeɪtɪd/
adj (fml) en estado de embriaguez (fml)

intoxicating /ɪn'tɑːksəkeɪtɪŋ ‖m'tɒksɪkeɪtɪŋ/
adj (fml) ‹*substance*› estupefaciente; ~ **liquor**
bebida *f* alcohólica

intractable /ɪn'træktəbəl/ *adj* (fml) **(a)**
‹*temperament*› obstinado; ‹*child*› incorregible **(b)**
‹*problem/dilemma*› inextricable (fml)

intransigent /ɪn'trænsədʒənt
‖m'trænsɪdʒənt/ *adj* intransigente

intransitive /ɪn'trænsətɪv/ *adj* intransitivo

intrauterine device /ˈɪntrə'juːtərən
‖ˌɪntrə'juːtəram/ *n* dispositivo *m* intrauterino; (in
the shape of a coil) espiral *f*

intravenous /ˌɪntrə'viːnəs/ *adj* intravenoso

intrepid /ɪn'trepəd ‖m'trepɪd/ *adj* intrépido

intricacy /ˈɪntrɪkəsi/ *n* **(a)** (of pattern, embroidery)
lo intrincado **(b)** **intricacies** *pl* (complexities)
complejidades *fpl*

intricate /ˈɪntrɪkət/ *adj* complicado

intrigue¹ /ˈɪntriːɡ/ *n* intriga *f*

intrigue² /ɪn'triːɡ/ *vt* intrigar*

intriguing /ɪn'triːɡɪŋ/ *adj* ‹*problem/text*›
intrigante; ‹*possibility*› fascinante; ‹*person*›
interesante

intrinsic /ɪn'trɪnzɪk/ *adj* intrínseco

introduce /ˈɪntrə'duːs ‖ˌɪntrə'djuːs/ *vt* **1** **(a)**
(acquaint) presentar; **allow me to ~ myself/my**
mother (fml) permítame que me presente/le
presente a mi madre; **to ~ sb** TO **sb** presentarle a
algn A algn **(b)** (initiate) **to ~ sb** TO **sth**
introducir* a algn A algo, iniciar a algn EN algo
(c) (present) ‹*speaker/program*› presentar;
‹*meeting/article*› iniciar **2** (bring in) ‹*subject/*
custom/legislation› introducir*; ‹*product*› lanzar*,
sacar*

introduction /ˈɪntrə'dʌkʃən/ *n* **1** **(a)** (to
person) presentación *f* **(b)** (to activity, experience) ~
TO **sth** introducción *f* A algo **(c)** (of speaker,
performer) presentación *f* **2** (of species, practice,
legislation) introducción *f* **3** (insertion, entry) (fml)
introducción *f* **4** **(a)** (to meeting, lecture)
presentación *f* **(b)** (in book) introducción *f* **(c)**
(Mus) introducción *f* **5** (elementary instruction)
introducción *f*, iniciación *f*

introductory /ˈɪntrə'dʌktəri/ *adj* **(a)** (opening)
‹*notes/remarks*› preliminar; ‹*lecture/chapter*› de
introducción; ‹*offer*› (Busn) de lanzamiento **(b)**
(elementary) ‹*course/lesson*› de introducción

introspective /ˈɪntrə'spektɪv/ *adj*
introspectivo

introvert /ˈɪntrəvɜːrt ‖ˈɪntrəvɜːt/ *n*
introvertido, -da *m,f*

introverted /ˈɪntrəvɜːrtəd ‖ˈɪntrəvɜːtɪd/ *adj*
introvertido

intrude /ɪn'truːd/ *vi* (disturb) importunar;
(interfere) inmiscuirse*; **to ~ on sb's privacy**
inmiscuirse* en la vida privada de algn

intruder /ɪn'truːdər ‖m'truːdə(r)/ *n* intruso, -sa
m,f

intrusion /ɪn'truːʒən/ *n* intrusión *f*

intrusive /ɪn'truːsɪv/ *adj* **(a)** ‹*noise/smell*›
molesto **(b)** ‹*questioning/reporter*› impertinente

intuition /ˈɪntuː'ɪʃən ‖ˌɪntjuː'ɪʃən/ *n* intuición *f*

intuitive /ɪn'tuːətɪv ‖m'tjuːɪtɪv/ *adj* intuitivo

Inuit /ˈɪnuːt ‖ˈɪnjuːɪt/ *n* (*pl* ~ **or** ~**s**) **(a)**
(person) esquimal *mf* **(b)** (Ling) esquimal *m*

inundate /ˈɪnʌndeɪt/ *vt* inundar

invade /ɪn'veɪd/ *vt/i* invadir

invader /ɪn'veɪdər ‖m'veɪdə(r)/ *n* invasor,
-sora *m,f*

invalid¹ /ɪn'væləd ‖m'vælɪd/ *adj* inválido

invalid² /ˈɪnvələd ‖ˈɪnvəliːd, ˈɪnvəlɪd/ *n*
inválido, -da *m,f*

invalidate /ɪn'vælədeɪt ‖m'vælɪdeɪt/ *vt* (fml)
invalidar

invalidity /ˈɪnvə'lɪdəti/ *n* (fml) invalidez *f*

invaluable /ɪn'væljuəbəl/ *adj* inapreciable,
invalorable (AmL)

invariable /ɪn'veriəbəl ‖m'veəriəbəl/ *adj*
invariable

invariably /ɪn'veriəbli ‖m'veəriəbli/ *adv*
invariablemente, siempre

invasion /ɪn'veɪʒən/ *n* invasión *f*

invective /ɪn'vektɪv/ *n* **(a)** (abuse) invectivas
fpl (fml) **(b)** (condemnation) invectiva *f* (fml)

invent /ɪn'vent/ *vt* inventar

invention /ɪn'ventʃən ‖m'venʃən/ *n* **1** **(a)**
(device) invento *m* **(b)** (action) invención *f*
2 (imagination): (powers of) ~ inventiva *f*

inventive /ɪn'ventɪv/ *adj* ingenioso

inventor /ɪn'ventər ‖m'ventə(r)/ *n* inventor,
-tora *m,f*

inventory /ˈɪnvəntɔːri ‖ˈɪnventri/ *n* (*pl* **-ries**)
inventario *m*

inverse /ˈɪnvɜːrs, ˈɪnvɜːrs ‖ˌɪn'vɜːs, ˈɪnvɜːs/ *adj*
(*usu before n*) inverso; **in ~ proportion to sth** en
proporción inversa a algo

inversion /ɪn'vɜːrʒən ‖m'vɜːʃən/ *n* inversión *f*

invert /ɪn'vɜːrt ‖m'vɜːt/ *vt* invertir*

invertebrate /ɪn'vɜːrtəbrət ‖m'vɜːtɪbrət/ *n*
invertebrado, -da *m,f*

inverted commas /ɪn'vɜːrtəd ‖m'vɜːtɪd/ *pl*
n (BrE) comillas *fpl*

invest /ɪn'vest/ *vt* **to ~ sth** (IN **sth**) ‹*money/*
time› invertir* algo (EN algo)
■ ~ *vi* **to ~** (IN **sth**) invertir* (EN algo)

investigate /ɪn'vestəgeɪt ‖m'vestɪgeɪt/ *vt* **(a)**
‹*crime/cause*› investigar*; ‹*complaint/possibility*›
estudiar **(b)** (do research on) hacer* una
investigación sobre
■ ~ *vi* investigar*

investigation /ɪnˌvestəˈgeɪʃən ‖m,vestɪˈgeɪʃən/ n (a) (detailed examination) estudio m (b) (official, scientific) investigación f

investigator /ɪnˈvestəgeɪtər ‖ɪnˈvestɪgeɪtə(r)/ n (a) (private ∼) investigador privado, investigadora privada m,f (b) (official) inspector, -tora m,f

investiture /ɪnˈvestətʃʊr ‖ɪnˈvestɪtʃə(r)/ n investidura f

investment /ɪnˈvestmənt/ n inversión f

investor /ɪnˈvestər ‖ɪnˈvestə(r)/ n inversor, -sora m,f, inversionista mf

inveterate /ɪnˈvetərət/ adj (frml) (usu before n) ⟨thief/liar⟩ empedernido

invigorating /ɪnˈvɪgəreɪtɪŋ/ adj ⟨weather/walk⟩ vigorizante; ⟨environment/change⟩ estimulante

invisible /ɪnˈvɪzəbəl/ adj invisible

invitation /ˌɪnvəˈteɪʃən ‖,ɪnvɪˈteɪʃən/ n invitación f; at the ∼ of invitado por, por invitación de

invite /ɪnˈvaɪt/ vt to ∼ sb (TO sth)/to + INF invitar a algn (A algo)/A + INF or A QUE (+ subj); to ∼ sb in/out invitar a algn a pasar/a salir; his work ∼s comparison with the classics su obra sugiere comparación con los clásicos

inviting /ɪnˈvaɪtɪŋ/ adj ⟨prospect/offer⟩ atractivo

in vitro /ˌɪnˈviːtroʊ/ adj in vitro adj inv

invoice¹ /ˈɪnvɔɪs/ n factura f

invoice² vt to ∼ sb (FOR sth) pasarle A algn factura (POR algo)

invoke /ɪnˈvoʊk/ vt invocar*

involuntary /ɪnˈvɑːlənteri ‖ɪnˈvɒləntri/ adj involuntario

involve /ɪnˈvɑːlv ‖ɪnˈvɒlv/ vt **1** (a) (entail, comprise) suponer*; what exactly does your work ∼? ¿en qué consiste exactamente tu trabajo? (b) (affect, concern): where national security is ∼d ... cuando se trata de la seguridad nacional ...; it's my reputation that's ∼d here es mi reputación lo que está en juego **2** to ∼ sb IN sth/-ING (implicate) implicar* or involucrar a algn EN algo; (allow to participate) darle* participación a algn EN algo **3** involved past p (a) (implicated): I was ∼d in an accident last year el año pasado me vi envuelto en un accidente; several high-ranking officials were ∼d in the affair había varios oficiales de alto rango implicados en el asunto; the people you're ∼d with la gente con la que andas metido (b) to be ∼d IN sth (engrossed) estar* absorto EN algo; (busy) estar* ocupado CON algo (c) (emotionally): she doesn't want to get too ∼d with him no quiere llegar a una relación muy seria con él

involved /ɪnˈvɑːlvd ‖ɪnˈvɒlvd/ adj enrevesado, complicado

involvement /ɪnˈvɑːlvmənt ‖ɪnˈvɒlvmənt/ n (a) n (entanglement) participación f; they deny any ∼ in terrorist attacks niegan estar implicados en ningún ataque terrorista (b) (relationship) relación f (sentimental)

inward¹ /ˈɪnwərd ‖ˈɪnwəd/ adj (a) (toward inside) ⟨curve⟩ hacia adentro (b) (private, mental) ⟨torment/serenity⟩ interior

inward², (BrE also) **inwards** adv (a) (toward inside) ⟨move/bend⟩ hacia adentro; ⟨travel⟩ hacia

el interior (b) (toward mind, spirit): meditation involves looking ∼ la meditación exige introspección

iodine /ˈaɪədaɪn ‖ˈaɪədiːn/ n yodo m

ion /ˈaɪən, ˈaɪɑːn ‖ˈaɪən/ n ión m

iota /aɪˈoʊtə/ n (usu with neg) pizca f, ápice m

IOU n (= **I owe you**) pagaré m

IQ n (= **intelligence quotient**) CI m

IRA n (= **Irish Republican Army**) IRA m

Iran /ɪˈrɑːn, ɪˈræn/ n Irán m

Iranian¹ /ɪˈreɪniən/ adj iraní

Iranian² n iraní mf

Iraq /ɪˈrɑːk, ɪˈræk/ n Irak m

Iraqi¹ /ɪˈrɑːki, ɪˈræki/ adj iraquí

Iraqi² n iraquí mf

irascible /ɪˈræsəbəl/ adj irascible

irate /aɪˈreɪt/ adj airado

ire /aɪr ‖ˈaɪə(r)/ n (liter) ira f, cólera f

Ireland /ˈaɪrlənd ‖ˈaɪələnd/ n (the island) Irlanda f; (the Republic) Irlanda f, (el) Eire

iris /ˈaɪrəs ‖ˈaɪərɪs/ n (Bot) lirio m

Irish¹ /ˈaɪrɪʃ ‖ˈaɪərɪʃ/ adj irlandés; the ∼ Sea el Mar de Irlanda

Irish² n (a) (people) (+ pl vb) the ∼ los irlandeses (b) (language) irlandés m

Irish: ∼**man** /ˈaɪrɪʃmən ‖ˈaɪərɪʃmən/ n (pl -**men** /-mən/) irlandés m; ∼**woman** n irlandesa f

irk /ɜːrk ‖ɜːk/ vt fastidiar, irritar

iron¹ /ˈaɪərn ‖ˈaɪən/ n **1** (a) (metal) hierro m, fierro m (AmL) (b) (in food) hierro m **2** (for clothes) plancha f **3** (golf club) hierro m **4** **irons** pl (fetters) grilletes mpl, grillos mpl

iron² adj (a) (made of iron) de hierro (b) (strong) (before n) ⟨constitution⟩ de hierro; ⟨will/resolve⟩ férreo, de hierro

iron³ vt/i planchar

■ **iron out** [v + o + adv, v + adv + o] ⟨problems⟩ resolver*; ⟨difficulties⟩ allanar

Iron Curtain n the ∼ la cortina de hierro (AmL), el telón de acero (Esp)

ironic /aɪˈrɑːnɪk ‖aɪˈrɒnɪk/ adj irónico

ironically /aɪˈrɑːnɪkli ‖aɪˈrɒnɪkli/ adv irónicamente

ironing /ˈaɪərnɪŋ ‖ˈaɪənɪŋ/ n to do the ∼ planchar

ironing board n tabla f or (Méx) burro m de planchar

ironmonger /ˈaɪərnˌmɑːŋgər ‖ˈaɪənˌmʌŋgə(r)/ n (BrE) ferretero, -ra m,f; at the ∼'s en la ferretería

irony /ˈaɪrəni/ n (pl -**nies**) ironía f

irrational /ɪˈræʃnəl ‖ɪˈræʃənl/ adj irracional

irreconcilable /ɪˈrekənˌsaɪləbəl/ adj irreconciliable

irrefutable /ɪˈrefjətəbəl, ˈɪrɪˈfjuː- ‖,ɪrɪˈfjuːtəbəl/ adj irrefutable

irregular /ɪˈregjələr ‖ɪˈregjʊlə(r)/ adj **1** (in shape, positioning, time) irregular **2** (contrary to rules) inadmisible, contrario a las normas **3** (Ling) irregular

irregularity /ɪˌregjəˈlærəti ‖ɪ,regjʊˈlærəti/ n (pl -**ties**) **1** (in shape, positioning, time) ⋯

irregularidad f **2** (of action) lo inadmisible; **several irregularities** varias contravenciones de las normas

irrelevant /ɪ'reləvənt/ adj ⟨fact/detail⟩ irrelevante; **to be ~ TO sth** no tener* relación or no tener* que ver CON algo

irreparable /ɪ'reprəbəl/ adj irreparable

irreplaceable /ɪrɪ'pleɪsəbəl/ adj irreemplazable

irrepressible /ɪrɪ'presəbəl/ adj ⟨laughter⟩ incontenible; ⟨desire⟩ irreprimible

irresistible /ɪrɪ'zɪstəbəl/ adj irresistible

irrespective /ɪrɪ'spektɪv/ adv ~ OF sth: ~ of what you say independientemente de lo que diga; ~ of age or sex sin distinción de edad o sexo

irresponsible /ɪrɪ'spɑːnsəbəl ‖ ɪrɪ'spɒnsəbəl/ adj irresponsable

irreverent /ɪ'revrənt/ adj irreverente

irreversible /ɪrɪ'vɜːrsəbəl ‖ ɪrɪ'vɜːsəbəl/ adj ⟨decision⟩ irrevocable; ⟨process/event⟩ irreversible

irrigate /'ɪrəgeɪt ‖ 'ɪrɪgeɪt/ vt irrigar*, regar*

irrigation /ɪrə'geɪʃən/ n irrigación f, riego m

irritable /'ɪrətəbəl ‖ 'ɪrɪtəbəl/ adj **1** (bad-tempered) ⟨person/mood⟩ irritable; ⟨reply⟩ irritado **2** (sensitive) ⟨skin/scalp⟩ sensible

irritant /'ɪrətənt ‖ 'ɪrɪtənt/ n (a) (Med) agente m irritante (b) (person, thing) fastidio m

irritate /'ɪrəteɪt ‖ 'ɪrɪteɪt/ vt irritar

irritated /'ɪrəteɪtəd ‖ 'ɪrɪteɪtɪd/ adj **1** ⟨look/frown⟩ de impaciencia; **to be ~ WITH** o AT sth/WITH sb** estar* irritado POR algo/CON algn **2** ⟨skin/hands⟩ irritado

irritating /'ɪrəteɪtɪŋ ‖ 'ɪrɪteɪtɪŋ/ adj irritante

irritation /ɪrə'teɪʃən ‖ ɪrɪ'teɪʃən/ n irritación f

IRS n (in US) = **Internal Revenue Service**

is /ɪz/ 3rd pers sing pres of BE

ISBN n (= **International Standard Book Number**) ISBN m

-ish /ɪʃ/ suff: long~ más bien largo; green~ verdoso; **tennish** a eso de las diez

Islam /'ɪzlɑːm, ɪz'lɑːm/ n el Islam

Islamic /ɪz'læmɪk, ɪz'lɑːmɪk/ adj islámico

Islamist¹ /'ɪzləmɪst/ n islamista mf

Islamist² adj islamista

island /'aɪlənd/ n isla f

islander /'aɪləndər ‖ 'aɪləndə(r)/ n isleño, -ña m,f

isle /aɪl/ n (a) (poet) isla f, ínsula f (liter) (b) (in place names): **the I~ of Wight** la Isla de Wight

Isles of Scilly /'aɪlzəv'sɪli/ pl n **the ~ ~ ~** las islas Scilly or Sorlingas

isn't /'ɪznt/ = **is not**

isolate /'aɪsəleɪt/ vt aislar*

isolated /'aɪsəleɪtəd ‖ 'aɪsəleɪtɪd/ adj aislado

isolation /aɪsə'leɪʃən/ n aislamiento m

ISP n (= **Internet service provider**) ISP m

Israel /'ɪzreɪəl/ n Israel m

Israeli¹ /ɪz'reɪli/ adj israelí

Israeli² n israelí mf

issue¹ /'ɪʃuː ‖ 'ɪʃjuː, ɪsjuː/ n **1** (subject discussed) tema m, cuestión f, asunto m; **to take ~ with sb/sth** discrepar de or con algn/en or de algo **2** (a) (of documents) expedición f; (of library books)

préstamo m; (of tickets) venta f **(b)** (of stamps, shares, bank notes) emisión f **(c)** (of newspaper, magazine) número m

issue² vt (give out) ⟨statement/report⟩ hacer* público; ⟨instructions⟩ dar*; ⟨guidelines⟩ establecer*; ⟨tickets/visas⟩ expedir*; ⟨library books⟩ prestar; ⟨bank notes/stamps/shares⟩ emitir; ⟨summons⟩ dictar; **we can ~ you with the necessary documents** le podemos proporcionar los documentos necesarios

■ ~ vi (fml) **1** (result) **to ~ FROM sth** derivar(se) DE algo (fml) **2** (emerge) salir*; «liquid» fluir*

it /ɪt/ pron **1** (replacing noun — as direct object) lo, la; (— as indirect object) le; (— as subject, after prep) gen not translated; ~'s enormous es enorme; **there's nothing behind ~** no hay nada detrás **2** (introducing person, thing, event): **who is ~?** ¿quién es?; ~'s me soy yo; **I'll see to ~** yo me encargo (de ello); ~'s his attitude that I don't like su actitud es lo que no me gusta; **a little higher up ... that's ~!** un poco más arriba ... ¡ahí está! or ¡eso es!; **one more and that's ~** uno más y ya está or se acabó **3** (in impersonal constructions): ~'s raining está lloviendo; ~'s two o'clock son las dos; ~ says here that ... aquí dice que ...; ~ is known that ... se sabe que ...

Italian¹ /ɪ'tæljən/ adj italiano

Italian² n (a) (person) italiano, -na m,f (b) (language) italiano m

italics /ɪ'tælɪks/ pl n (letra f) cursiva f

Italy /'ɪtli ‖ 'ɪtəli/ n Italia f

itch¹ /ɪtʃ/ vi **1** (a) ⟨scalp/toe⟩ picar* (+ me/te/le etc) **(b)** (be impatient, eager) (colloq) **to be ~ing to + INF:** he was ~ing to tell her estaba que se moría por decírselo (fam) **2** «wool/underwear» (cause irritation) picar*

itch² n (a) (irritation) picor m, picazón f **(b)** (desire) ansia f‡

itchy /'ɪtʃi/ adj **itchier, itchiest** (a) (feeling irritation): **I've got an ~ nose/scalp** me pica la nariz/la cabeza **(b)** (causing irritation) ⟨garment/material⟩ que pica

it'd /'ɪtəd/ (a) = **it had** (b) = **it would**

item /'aɪtəm/ n (a) (article) (Busn) artículo m; (in collection) pieza f; (on agenda) punto m; ~**s of clothing** prendas fpl de vestir **(b)** (in newspaper) artículo m; **news ~** noticia f

itemize /'aɪtəmaɪz/ vt (break down) detallar; (list) hacer* una lista de

itinerant /aɪ'tɪnərənt/ adj (fml) ⟨worker/judge⟩ itinerante (fml); ⟨salesman/musician⟩ ambulante

itinerary /aɪ'tɪnəreri ‖ aɪ'tɪnərəri/ n (pl **-ries**) itinerario m

it'll /'ɪtl/ = **it will**

its /ɪts/ adj (sing) su; (pl) sus

■ **Note** The translation su agrees in number with the noun which it modifies; its is translated by su, sus, depending on what follows: its snout/head su hocico/cabeza; its problems/difficulties sus problemas/dificultades.

it's /ɪts/ (a) = **it is** (b) = **it has**

itself /ɪt'self/ pron (a) (reflexive): **it has earned ~ a reputation** se ha hecho fama; **another problem**

presented ∼ se presentó otro problema **(b)** (emphatic use): **the town ∼ is small** la ciudad en sí *or* propiamente dicha es pequeña
ITV *n* (in UK) (*no art*) = **Independent Television**
IUD *n* (= **intrauterine device**) DIU *m*
I've /aɪv/ = **I have**

ivory /'aɪvəri/ *n* (*pl* **-ries**) **(a)** (material) marfil *m* **(b)** (color) (color *m*) marfil *m*
Ivory Coast *n* Costa *f* de Marfil
ivy /'aɪvi/ *n* hiedra *f*
Ivy League *n* (AmE) **the ∼ ∼** grupo de ocho *universidades prestigiosas de EEUU*

Jj

J, j /dʒeɪ/ *n* J, j *f*
jab¹ /dʒæb/ *vt* **-bb-**: **I ∼bed myself with the needle** me pinché con la aguja, me piqué con la aguja (Méx); **she ∼bed me with her fork** me clavó con el tenedor
jab² *n* **(a)** (prick) pinchazo *m*; (blow) golpe *m*; (with elbow) codazo *m* **(b)** (in boxing) jab *m*, corto *m* **(c)** (injection) (BrE colloq) inyección *f*
jabber /'dʒæbər ‖ 'dʒæbə(r)/ *vi/t* farfullar
jack /dʒæk/ *n* **(a)** (lifting device) gato *m* **(b)** (socket) enchufe *m* hembra **(c)** (in French pack of cards) jota *f*, valet *m*; (in Spanish pack) sota *f*
▪ **jack up** [*v* + *o* + *adv*, *v* + *adv* + *o*] ⟨*car*⟩ levantar (*con el gato*)
jackal /'dʒækəl/ *n* chacal *m*
jackdaw /'dʒækdɔ:/ *n* grajilla *f*
jacket /'dʒækət ‖ 'dʒækɪt/ *n* ⟨1⟩ (Clothing) chaqueta *f*; (sports ∼) americana *f*, saco *m* (sport) (AmL) ⟨2⟩ (of book) sobrecubierta *f*; (of record) (AmE) funda *f*, carátula *f* ⟨3⟩ (of potato) (BrE): **∼ potatoes** papas *fpl* asadas (*con la cáscara*) (AmL), patatas *fpl* asadas (*con la piel*) (Esp)
jack: ∼hammer *n* martillo *m* neumático; **∼-in-the-box** /'dʒækənðə'bɑːks ‖ 'dʒækɪndə,bɒks/ *n* caja *f* de sorpresas (*con muñeco a resorte*); **∼knife** *vi* ⟨*truck*⟩ plegarse*; **∼ of all trades** /'dʒækəv'ɔːltreɪdz/ *n* (*pl* **∼s of all trades**) hombre *m or* mujer *f* orquesta, manitas *mf* (Esp, Méx fam); **∼pot** *n* (in bingo, lottery) bote *m*, pozo *m*; **∼rabbit** *n*: *tipo de liebre de Norteamérica*
Jacuzzi®, jacuzzi /dʒə'kuːzi/ *n* Jacuzzi® *m*
jade /dʒeɪd/ *n* **(a)** (Min) jade *m* **(b)** (color) verde *m* jade
jaded /'dʒeɪdəd ‖ 'dʒeɪdɪd/ *adj* hastiado
jagged /'dʒægəd ‖ 'dʒægɪd/ *adj* ⟨*edge/cut*⟩ irregular; ⟨*rock/cliff*⟩ recortado, con picos
jaguar /'dʒægwɑːr ‖ 'dʒægjʊə(r)/ *n* jaguar *m*
jail¹ /dʒeɪl/ *n* cárcel *f*, prisión *f*; **he went to ∼** lo metieron preso
jail² *vt* encarcelar
jailer, jailor /'dʒeɪlər ‖ 'dʒeɪlə(r)/ *n* carcelero, -ra *m,f*
jailhouse /'dʒeɪlhaʊs/ *n* (AmE) cárcel *f*
jam¹ /dʒæm/ *n* ⟨1⟩ (Culin) mermelada *f*, dulce *m* (RPl) ⟨2⟩ (difficult situation) (colloq) aprieto *m*
jam² **-mm-** *vt* ⟨1⟩ **(a)** (cram) **to ∼ sth INTO sth** meter algo a la fuerza EN algo **(b)** (congest, block) ⟨*road*⟩ atestar; **the switchboard was ∼med with**

calls la centralita estaba saturada de llamadas ⟨2⟩ (wedge firmly): **he ∼med his foot in the door** metió el pie entre la puerta y el marco ⟨3⟩ (Rad) interferir*
■ ∼ *vi* ⟨*brakes*⟩ bloquearse; ⟨*machine*⟩ trancarse*; ⟨*switch/lock*⟩ trabarse; ⟨*gun*⟩ encasquillarse
■ **jam on** [*v* + *o* + *adv*, *v* + *adv* + *o*]: **to ∼ on the brakes** dar* un frenazo
Jamaica /dʒə'meɪkə/ *n* Jamaica *f*
Jamaican /dʒə'meɪkən/ *adj* jamaicano
jamb /dʒæm/ *n* jamba *f*
jam: ∼ jar *n* (BrE) tarro *m or* bote *m* para mermelada; **∼-packed** /'dʒæm'pækt/ *adj* (colloq) repleto, atestado (de gente); **∼ session** *n*: *sesión de un grupo de músicos de jazz o rock que se reúnen para improvisar*
jangle /'dʒæŋgəl/ *vi* hacer* ruido (*metálico*)
janitor /'dʒænətər ‖ 'dʒænɪtə(r)/ *n* conserje *m*
January /'dʒænjueri ‖ 'dʒænjʊəri/ *n* (el) Japón *m*
Japan /dʒə'pæn/ *n* (el) Japón *m*
Japanese¹ /'dʒæpə'niːz/ *adj* japonés
Japanese² *n* (*pl* ∼) **(a)** (language) japonés *m* **(b)** (person) japonés, -nesa *m,f*
jar¹ /dʒɑːr ‖ dʒɑː(r)/ *n* ⟨1⟩ (container) tarro *m*, bote *m* ⟨2⟩ (jolt) sacudida *f*
jar² **-rr-** *vi* **(a)** (clash) desentonar **(b)** (irritate): **it ∼s on my nerves** me crispa los nervios, me enerva
■ ∼ *vt* sacudir
jargon /'dʒɑːrgən ‖ 'dʒɑːgən/ *n* jerga *f*
jarring /'dʒɑːrɪŋ/ *adj* ⟨*sound*⟩ discordante
jasmine /'dʒæzmən ‖ 'dʒæzmɪn/ *n* jazmín *m*
jaundice /'dʒɔːndəs ‖ 'dʒɔːndɪs/ *n* ictericia *f*
jaundiced /'dʒɔːndəst ‖ 'dʒɔːndɪst/ *adj* **(a)** (Med) ⟨*skin/baby*⟩ ictérico **(b)** ⟨*view/opinion*⟩ negativo
jaunt /dʒɔːnt/ *n* excursión *f*
jaunty /'dʒɔːnti/ *adj* **-tier, -tiest** (*usu before n*) ⟨*air*⟩ garboso; ⟨*tune*⟩ alegre
javelin /'dʒævlən ‖ 'dʒævlɪn/ *n* jabalina *f*
jaw /dʒɔː/ *n* **(a)** (of person, animal) mandíbula *f*; (esp of animal) quijada *f*; **his ∼ dropped** se quedó boquiabierto **(b)** **jaws** *pl* fauces *fpl*
jawbone /'dʒɔːbəʊn/ *n* mandíbula *f*, maxilar *m*; (of an animal) quijada *f*
jay /dʒeɪ/ *n* arrendajo *m*

jay: ~**walk** *vi* cruzar* la calzada imprudentemente; ~**walker** *n* peatón *m* imprudente

jazz /dʒæz/ *n* (Mus) jazz *m*
■ **jazz up** [*v + o + adv, v + adv + o*] (colloq) **(a)** ⟨*music*⟩ tocar* con ritmo sincopado **(b)** ⟨*room*⟩ alegrar, darle* vida a

jazzy /'dʒæzi/ *adj* **jazzier, jazziest** ① (flashy) (colloq) llamativo ② (Mus) ⟨*rhythm*⟩ de jazz

jealous /'dʒeləs/ *adj* **(a)** ⟨*husband/wife*⟩ celoso; **to be** ~ estar* celoso, tener* celos **(b)** (envious) envidioso; **to be** ~ **OF sb** tenerle* envidia A algn

jealousy /'dʒeləsi/ *n* (*pl* **-sies**) **(a)** (fear of rivalry) celos *mpl* **(b)** (envy) envidia *f*

jeans /dʒiːnz/ *pl n* vaqueros *mpl*, jeans *mpl*, bluyines *mpl* (Andes)

Jeep®, **jeep** /dʒiːp/ *n* Jeep® *m*

jeer /dʒɪr ‖ dʒɪə(r)/ *vi*: **to** ~ **AT sth/sb** (boo) abuchear (algo/a algn); (mock) burlarse (DE algo/algn)

Jehovah /dʒə'həʊvə/ *n* Jehová

Jehovah's Witness *n* testigo *mf* de Jehová

jell /dʒel/ *vi* ▶ GEL²

Jell-O® /'dʒeləʊ/ *n* (AmE) gelatina *f* (con sabor a frutas)

jelly /'dʒeli/ *n* (*pl* **-lies**) ① (Culin) **(a)** (clear jam) jalea *f* **(b)** (as dessert) (BrE) gelatina *f* (con sabor a frutas) ② (gelatinous substance) gelatina *f*

jellyfish /'dʒeli,fɪʃ/ *n* (*pl* **-fish** *or* **-fishes**) medusa *f*, malagua *f* (Per), aguaviva *f* (RPl), aguamala *f* (Col, Méx)

jeopardize /'dʒepərdaɪz ‖ 'dʒepədaɪz/ *vt* poner* en peligro, hacer* peligrar

jeopardy /'dʒepərdi ‖ 'dʒepədi/ *n*: **in** ~ en peligro

jerk¹ /dʒɜːrk ‖ dʒɜːk/ *vi* «*leg/arm*» hacer* un movimiento brusco; (repeatedly) «*legs/arms*» agitarse; **the train** ~**ed to a stop** el tren se detuvo con una sacudida
■ ~ *vt*: **the impact** ~**ed him forward** el impacto lo propulsó hacia adelante

jerk² *n* ① **(a)** (tug) tirón *m* **(b)** (sudden movement) sacudida *f* ② (contemptible person) (colloq) estúpido, -da *m,f*, pendejo, -ja *m,f* (AmL exc CS fam), gilipollas *mf* (Esp fam), huevón, -ona *m,f* (Andes, Ven fam)

jerky /'dʒɜːrki ‖ 'dʒɜːki/ *adj* **-kier, -kiest** ⟨*speech*⟩ entrecortado; **it was a** ~ **ride** fuimos (*or* fueron *etc*) dando botes por el camino

jerry /'dʒeri/ **: ~-built** *adj* mal construido; ~ **can** *n* bidón *m*

jersey /'dʒɜːrzi ‖ 'dʒɜːzi/ *n* (*pl* **-seys**) ① **(a)** (sports shirt) camiseta *f* **(b)** (Tex) jersey *m* **(c)** (BrE) ▶ SWEATER ② **Jersey** (la isla de) Jersey

Jerusalem /dʒə'ruːsələm/ *n* Jerusalén *m*

jest /dʒest/ *n* (arch) broma *f*, chanza *f* (arc); **in** ~ en broma

jester /'dʒestər ‖ 'dʒestə(r)/ *n* bufón *m*

Jesuit /'dʒeʒuət ‖ 'dʒezjʊɪt/ *n* jesuita *m*

Jesus /'dʒiːzəs/ *n* Jesús; ~ **Christ** Jesucristo

jet¹ /dʒet/ *n* ① (Aviat) avión *m* (con motor a reacción) ② (of water, air, gas) chorro *m* ③ (Min) azabache *m*

jet² *vi* **-tt-** (fly) (colloq) volar*

jet: ~-**black** /'dʒet'blæk/ *adj* (pred ~ **black**) negro azabache *adj inv*; ~ **lag** *n* jet lag *m*, desfase *m* horario

jetsam /'dʒetsəm/ *n* echazón *f*; *see also* FLOTSAM

jet set *n* **the** ~ ~ el jet set (AmL), la jet set (Esp)

jettison /'dʒetəsən ‖ 'dʒetɪsən/ *vt* (Naut) echar por la borda; (Aviat) deshacerse* de

jetty /'dʒeti/ *n* (*pl* **-ties**) embarcadero *m*, malecón *m*

Jew /dʒuː/ *n* judío, -día *m,f*

jewel /'dʒuːəl/ *n* (gem) piedra *f* preciosa; (piece of jewelry) alhaja *f*, joya *f*; (in watch) rubí *m*; (sb, sth wonderful) joya *f*

jeweler, (BrE) **jeweller** /'dʒuːələr ‖ 'dʒuːələ(r)/ *n* joyero, -ra *m,f*; **a** ~**'s** (**shop**) una joyería

jewelry, (BrE) **jewellery** /'dʒuːəlri/ *n* joyas *fpl*, alhajas *fpl*; (before n) ~ **box** joyero *m*; ~ **store** (AmE) joyería *f*

Jewish /'dʒuːɪʃ/ *adj* judío

jibe /dʒaɪb/ *n* pulla *f*

jiffy /'dʒɪfi/ *n* (colloq) (no *pl*) segundo *m*

jig /dʒɪg/ *n* ① (dance) giga *f* ② (Tech) plantilla *f* de guía

jiggle /'dʒɪgəl/ *vt* mover*, sacudir

jigsaw /'dʒɪgsɔː/ *n* ① ~ (**puzzle**) rompecabezas *m*, puzzle *m* ② (saw) sierra *f* de vaivén *or* de puñal

jilt /dʒɪlt/ *vt* dejar plantado

jingle¹ /'dʒɪŋgəl/ *n* ① (sound) (no *pl*) tintineo *m*; (of harness bells) cascabeleo *m*, tintineo *m* ② (Marketing) jingle *m* (publicitario)

jingle² *vi* tintinear

jingoism /'dʒɪŋgəʊɪzəm/ *n* patriotería *f*, jingoísmo *m*

jinx¹ /dʒɪŋks/ *n*: **there's a** ~ **on this project** a este proyecto le han echado una maldición

jinx² *vt* traer* mala suerte a

jitters /'dʒɪtərz ‖ 'dʒɪtəz/ *pl n* (colloq): **he got the** ~ se puso nervioso, le dio el tembleque (fam)

jittery /'dʒɪtəri/ *adj* nervioso

Jnr (BrE) (= **Junior**) (h), Jr.

job /dʒɑːb ‖ dʒɒb/ *n* ① **(a)** (occupation, post) trabajo *m*, empleo *m*; **is he the right person for the** ~? ¿es la persona idónea para el puesto?; (before n) ~ **creation** creación *f* de empleo **(b)** (duty, responsibility): **it's your** ~ **to make the tea** tú eres el encargado de hacer el té; **I'm only doing my** ~ sólo cumplo con mi deber ② **(a)** (task, piece of work) trabajo *m*; (Comput) trabajo *m*; **you're doing a fine** ~ lo estás haciendo muy bien; **a good** ~ (BrE colloq) menos mal; **it's a good** ~ **I did it yesterday** menos mal que lo hice ayer; **to give sth up as a bad** ~ dejar algo por imposible; **to make the best of a bad** ~

apechugar* y hacer* lo que se pueda **(b)** (difficult task) (colloq): **I had a (terrible) ∾ getting that nail out** me dio mucho trabajo sacar ese clavo

job: J∾centre n (in UK) agencia f de colocaciones, oficina f de empleo; **∾ description** n descripción f del puesto; **∾-hunt** vi (usu in -ing form) buscar* trabajo

jobless /'dʒɑːbləs ‖'dʒɒblɪs/ adj (journ) desempleado, en paro (Esp), cesante (Chi)

job: ∾ lot n lote m; **∾share** n puesto m de trabajo compartido (entre dos); **∾ sharing** /'ʃerɪŋ ‖'ʃeərɪŋ/ n sistema en el cual dos personas comparten un puesto de trabajo

jockey /'dʒɑːki ‖'dʒɒki/ n (pl ∾s) jockey mf, jinete mf

Jockey shorts® /'dʒɑːki ‖'dʒɒki/ pl n (AmE) calzoncillos mpl, calzones mpl (Méx), interiores mpl (Col, Ven)

jockstrap /'dʒɑːkstræp ‖'dʒɒkstræp/ n suspensorio m, suspensor m (Per, RPI)

jocular /'dʒɑːkjələr ‖'dʒɒkjʊlə(r)/ adj jocoso

jodhpurs /'dʒɑːdpərz ‖'dʒɒdpəz/ pl n pantalones mpl de montar, breeches mpl (Col, RPI)

jog¹ /dʒɑːg ‖dʒɒg/ **-gg-** vt ‹table› mover*; **∾ged his elbow** le dio en el codo; **to ∾ sb's memory** refrescarle* la memoria a algn
■ ∾ vi **(a)** (run) correr **(b)** (Leisure) hacer* footing or jogging; **to go ∾ging** salir* a hacer footing or jogging

jog² n (no pl) (Leisure): **to go for a ∾** hacer* footing or jogging

jogger /'dʒɑːgər ‖'dʒɒgə(r)/ n: persona que hace footing

jogging /'dʒɑːgɪŋ ‖'dʒɒgɪŋ/ n footing m, jogging m

john /dʒɑːn ‖dʒɒn/ n **1** (toilet) (AmE colloq) baño m, váter m (Esp fam) **2** John Doe (AmE) (Law) persona f inidentificada; (colloq) el típico americano

join¹ /dʒɔɪn/ vt **1** (fasten, link) ‹ropes/wires› unir; (put together) ‹tables› juntar; **to ∾ two things together** unir dos cosas; **to ∾ hands** tomarse or (esp Esp) cogerse* de la mano **2** (meet, keep company with): **we're going for a drink, will you ∾ us?** vamos a tomar algo ¿nos acompañas?; **you go ahead, I'll ∾ you later** ustedes vayan que ya iré yo luego; **may I ∾ you?** ¿le importa si me siento aquí? **3 (a)** (become part of) unirse a, sumarse a; **I ∾ed the line** me puse en la cola **(b)** (become member of) ‹club› hacerse* socio de; ‹union› afiliarse a; ‹army› alistarse en; ‹firm› entrar en or (AmL tb) entrar a
■ ∾ vi **1** to ∾ **(together)** «parts/groups» unirse **2** (merge) «streams» confluir*; «roads» empalmar
■ **join in 1** [v + adv] participar, tomar parte **2** [v + adv + o] ‹celebrations› participar or tomar parte en
■ **join up** [v + adv] **(a)** (enlist) alistarse **(b)** (fit together) «pieces/parts» encajar **(c)** (team up) «people» unirse

join² n juntura f, unión f

joiner /'dʒɔɪnər ‖'dʒɔɪnə(r)/ n carpintero, -ra m,f (de obra)

joint¹ /dʒɔɪnt/ n **1** (Anat) articulación f **2** (Const) (point of joining) unión f, junta f; (in

woodwork) ensambladura f **3** (Culin) trozo m de carne (para asar) **4** (of marijuana) (colloq) porro m (Esp arg), canuto m (Esp arg), toque m (Méx arg), varillo m (Col arg), pito m (Chi arg)

joint² adj (before n) ‹action› conjunto; **∾ owner** copropietario, -ria m,f; **it was a ∾ effort** fue un trabajo realizado en conjunto

joint account n cuenta f conjunta

jointly /'dʒɔɪntli/ adv ‹decide/act› conjuntamente

joint: ∾ stock company n sociedad f por acciones; **∾ venture** n empresa f conjunta

joist /dʒɔɪst/ n viga f

joke¹ /dʒəʊk/ n **(a)** (verbal) chiste m; (directed at sb) broma f; **he can't take a ∾** no sabe aceptar una broma **(b)** (practical ∾) broma f

joke² vi bromear; **you must be joking!** ¡tú debes estar loco!; **I was only joking** lo dije en broma

joker /'dʒəʊkər ‖'dʒəʊkə(r)/ n **1** (cards) comodín m **2** (prankster) bromista mf; (contemptible person) (colloq) tipo, -pa m,f (fam)

jokey /'dʒəʊki/ adj ▶ JOKY

joky /'dʒəʊki/ adj **jokier, jokiest** jocoso

jolly¹ /'dʒɑːli ‖'dʒɒli/ adj **-lier, -liest** ‹person› jovial; ‹laugh/tune› alegre

jolly² adv (BrE colloq) (as intensifier): **you were ∾ lucky!** ¡qué suerte tuviste!; **∾ good!** ¡muy bien!

jolly³ vt **-lies, -lying, -lied** (colloq): **to ∾ sb along** animar a algn

jolt¹ /dʒəʊlt/ vi «train/bus» dar* or pegar* una sacudida; (repeatedly) dar* tumbos
■ ∾ vt: **she ∾ed his arm** le movió el brazo

jolt² n sacudida f

Jordan /'dʒɔːrdn ‖'dʒɔːdn/ n **(a)** (country) Jordania f **(b)** the ∾, the ∾ **River** (AmE), the **River ∾** (BrE) el Jordán

Jordanian /dʒɔːr'deɪmən ‖dʒɔː'deɪmən/ adj jordano

jostle /'dʒɑːsəl ‖'dʒɒsəl/ vt empujar
■ ∾ vi: **people were jostling trying to get out** la gente se empujaba tratando de salir

jot /dʒɑːt ‖dʒɒt/ n (no pl, usu with neg): **it doesn't make a o one ∾ of difference** da exactamente igual
■ **jot down** **-tt-** [v + o + adv, v + adv + o] apuntar or anotar (rápidamente)

journal /'dʒɜːrnl ‖'dʒɜːnl/ n **(a)** (periodical) revista f, publicación f; (newspaper) periódico m **(b)** (diary) (frml) diario m

journalism /'dʒɜːrnlɪzəm ‖'dʒɜːnəlɪzəm/ n periodismo m

journalist /'dʒɜːrnləst ‖'dʒɜːnəlɪst/ n periodista mf

journey /'dʒɜːrni ‖'dʒɜːni/ n (pl **-neys**) viaje m; **to go on o to make a ∾** hacer* un viaje

joust /dʒaʊst/ vi justar

jovial /'dʒəʊviəl/ adj jovial

jowls /dʒaʊlz/ pl n (sometimes sing) parte inferior de los carrillos, que a veces cuelga de la mandíbula

joy /dʒɔɪ/ n **(a)** (emotion) alegría f, dicha f; **to jump for ∾** saltar de alegría **(b)** (source of pleasure): **she's a ∾ to teach** es un verdadero placer or da gusto tenerla como alumna

joyful /'dʒɔɪfəl/ adj ‹event› feliz; ‹dance/news› alegre

joyless /'dʒɔɪləs ‖'dʒɔɪlɪs/ adj ⟨occasion⟩ falto de alegría; ⟨existence⟩ sombrío

joyous /'dʒɔɪəs/ adj ⟨expression⟩ de dicha; ⟨occasion⟩ feliz

joy: ~**rider** n: joven que roba un coche para dar una vuelta; ~**stick** n (Aviat) palanca f de mando; (Electron, Comput) mando m, joystick m

Jr (esp AmE) (= **Junior**) (h), Jr.

jubilant /'dʒuːbələnt ‖'dʒuːbɪlənt/ adj ⟨expression⟩ de júbilo (liter); ⟨speech⟩ exultante (liter); **to be** ~ estar* radiante de alegría

jubilee /'dʒuːbəliː ‖'dʒuːbɪliː/ n: **the Queen's silver** ~ el vigésimo quinto aniversario de la reina

Judaism /'dʒuːdeɪzəm ‖'dʒuːdeɪɪzəm/ n judaísmo m

judge¹ /dʒʌdʒ/ n 1 (Law) juez mf, juez, jueza m,f; (of competition) juez mf; (Sport) juez mf 2 (appraiser): **he's a good** ~ **of character** es muy buen psicólogo; **let me be the** ~ **of that** eso lo decidiré yo

judge² vt 1 (Law) ⟨case/person⟩ juzgar*; ⟨contest⟩ ser* el juez de 2 (a) (estimate) ⟨size/speed⟩ calcular (b) (assess) ⟨situation/position⟩ evaluar*; ⟨person⟩ juzgar* (c) (deem) juzgar* 3 (censure, condemn) juzgar*
■ ~ vi juzgar*; **judging by** a juzgar por

judgment, judgement /'dʒʌdʒmənt/ n 1 (Law) fallo m, sentencia f; (in arbitration) fallo m; **to pass** ~ **on sth/sb** juzgar* algo/a algn 2 (a) (estimation) cálculo m (b) (view) opinión f 3 (sense, discernment): **an error of** ~ una equivocación; **I lent him the money against my better** ~ le presté el dinero sabiendo que era un error

judgmental, judgemental /dʒʌdʒ'mentl/ adj ⟨attitude/assessment⟩ sentencioso

judicial /dʒuː'dɪʃəl/ adj judicial

judiciary /dʒuː'dɪʃieri ‖dʒuː'dɪʃəri/ n (judges) judicatura f; (arm of government) poder m judicial

judicious /dʒuː'dɪʃəs/ adj ⟨decision⟩ acertado; ⟨historian⟩ de criterio

judo /'dʒuːdəʊ/ n judo m

jug /dʒʌg/ n (large) jarra f; (for milk, cream) jarrita f

juggernaut /'dʒʌgənɔːt ‖'dʒʌgənɔːt/ n (BrE) camión m grande

juggle /'dʒʌgəl/ vi hacer* malabarismos
■ ~ vt hacer* malabarismos con

juggler /'dʒʌglər ‖'dʒʌglə(r)/ n malabarista mf

Jugoslavia /ju:gəʊ'slɑːviə, ju:gə'slɑːviə/ etc ▶ YUGOSLAVIA etc

jugular /'dʒʌgjələr ‖'dʒʌgjʊlə(r)/ n (vena f) yugular f

juice /dʒuːs/ n(fruit drink) jugo m, zumo m; (from fruit, meat) jugo m; (Physiol) jugo m

juicer /'dʒuːsər ‖'dʒuːsə(r)/ n exprimidor m (gen eléctrico), juguera f (CS)

juicy /'dʒuːsi/ adj **-cier, -ciest** (a) (Culin) jugoso (b) (colloq) ⟨gossip/details⟩ sabroso (fam)

jukebox /'dʒuːkbɑːks ‖'dʒuːkbɒks/ n máquina f de discos, rocola f (AmL)

July /dʒʊ'laɪ/ n julio m

jumble¹ /'dʒʌmbəl/ vt ~ (up) ⟨cards/pieces⟩ mezclar; **the clothes were all** ~d **up in the drawer** la ropa estaba toda revuelta en el cajón

jumble² n (no pl) (of clothes, papers) revoltijo m; (of facts, data) embrollo m

jumble sale n (BrE) mercadillo de beneficencia donde se venden artículos de segunda mano

jumbo /'dʒʌmbəʊ/ adj (before n) ⟨packet/size⟩ gigante

jumbo (jet) n jumbo m

jump¹ /dʒʌmp/ vi 1 (a) (leap) saltar; **the horse** ~**ed over the gate** el caballo saltó la verja (b) (move quickly): **I** ~**ed out of bed** me levanté (de la cama) de un salto; **they'll** ~ **at the chance** no van a dejar pasar la oportunidad 2 (a) (change, skip) saltar (b) (increase, advance suddenly) subir de un golpe 3 (a) (jerk) saltar (b) (in alarm) sobresaltarse; **you made me** ~! ¡qué susto me diste!
■ ~ vt 1 (leap over) ⟨hurdle⟩ saltar, brincar* (Méx); **to** ~ **rope** (AmE) saltar a la cuerda or (Esp tb) a la comba or (Chi) al cordel, brincar* la reata (Méx) 2 (a) (spring out of) ⟨rails/tracks⟩ salirse* de (b) (disregard) saltarse; **to** ~ **the lights** pasar el semáforo en rojo, pasarse el alto (Méx); **to** ~ **the line** o (BrE) **queue** colarse* 3 (ambush, attack) (colloq) asaltar, atacar*

jump² n 1 (a) (leap) salto m; **I set up with a** ~ me incorporé sobresaltado (b) (fence) valla f 2 (a) (sudden transition) salto m (b) (increase, advance) aumento m

jumper /'dʒʌmpər ‖'dʒʌmpə(r)/ n (a) (dress) (AmE) jumper m or f (AmL), pichi m (Esp) (b) (BrE) ▶ SWEATER

jumper cables pl n (AmE) cables mpl de arranque

jump: ~ **jet** n avión m de despegue vertical; ~ **leads** /liːdz/ pl n (BrE) ▶ JUMPER CABLES; ~ **rope** n (AmE) cuerda f or (Méx) reata f or (Chi) cordel m (de saltar), comba f (Esp); ~**start** vt: hacer arrancar un coche ya sea empujándolo o haciendo un puente; ~ **suit** n mono m, enterito m (RPl)

jumpy /'dʒʌmpi/ adj **-pier, -piest** nervioso

junction /'dʒʌŋkʃən/ n (a) (meeting point — of roads, rails) cruce m; (— of rivers) confluencia f (b) (Elec) empalme m

juncture /'dʒʌŋktʃər ‖'dʒʌŋktʃə(r)/ n coyuntura f; **at this** ~ en este momento

June /dʒuːn/ n junio m

jungle /'dʒʌŋgəl/ n selva f, jungla f

junior¹ /'dʒuːnjər ‖'dʒuːniə(r)/ adj 1 (a) (lower in rank) ⟨official⟩ subalterno; ⟨position⟩ de subalterno (b) (younger) más joven; **James D. Clark J**~ (AmE) James D. Clark, hijo or junior 2 (AmE Educ) (before n) de tercer año

junior² n 1 (a) (younger person): **he is two years my** ~ tiene dos años menos que yo (b) (person of lower rank) subalterno, -na m,f 2 (Educ) (in US) estudiante de tercer año de colegio secundario o universidad; (in UK) alumno de primaria o de los primeros años de secundaria

junior: ~ **college** n (in US) establecimiento universitario donde se estudian los primeros años de la carrera; ~ **high (school)** n (in US) colegio en el que se imparten los dos o tres primeros años de la enseñanza secundaria; ~ **school** n (in UK) escuela f primaria (para niños de 7 a 11 años)

junk /dʒʌŋk/ n 1 (a) (discarded items) trastos mpl (viejos); (before n) ~ **shop** tienda f de viejo

(c) (worthless stuff) (colloq) basura *f* (fam); (*before n*) ~ **mail** propaganda *f* que se recibe por correo ②(boat) junco *m*

junk food *n* comida *f* basura, alimento *m* chatarra (Méx)

junkie /'dʒʌŋki/ *n* (colloq) yonqui *mf* (fam), drogadicto, -ta *m,f*, pichicatero, -ra (CS, Per fam)

junkyard /'dʒʌŋkjɑːrd ‖'dʒʌŋkjɑːd/ *n* depósito *m* de chatarra, deshuesadero *m* (Méx)

junta /'hʊntə ‖'dʒʌntə/ *n* junta *f* militar

Jupiter /'dʒuːpətər ‖'dʒuːpɪtə(r)/ *n* Júpiter *m*

jurisdiction /,dʒʊrəs'dɪkʃən ‖,dʒʊərɪs'dɪkʃən/ *n* jurisdicción *f*

juror /'dʒʊrər ‖'dʒʊərə(r)/ *n* jurado *mf*

jury /'dʒʊri ‖'dʒʊəri/ *n* (*pl* **-ries**) jurado *m*

just¹ /dʒʌst/ *adj* justo

just² *adv* ① **(a)** (in recent past): she's ~ **left** se acaba de ir, recién se fue (AmL) **(b)** (at the moment): I was ~ **about to leave when he called** estaba a punto de salir cuando llamó ②**(a)** (barely) justo; I **arrived** ~ **in time** llegué justo a tiempo; I ~ **missed him** no lo vi por poco *or* por apenas unos minutos **(b)** (a little): ~ **above the knee** justo *or* apenas encima de la rodilla ③**(a)** (only) solo; she was ~ **three when her father died** tenía apenas *or* solo tres años cuando murió su padre; would you like some more? — ~ **a little, please** ¿quieres más? — bueno, un poquito **(b)** (simply): I ~ **stopped by to say hello** pasé para saludarte; that's ~ **gossip** no son más que chismes; ~ **because he's famous doesn't mean he can be rude** (colloq) el hecho de que sea famoso no le da derecho a ser grosero ④**(a)** (exactly, precisely): it's ~ **what I wanted** es justo *or* precisamente *or* exactamente lo que quería; the temperature was ~ **right** la

temperatura era la perfecta **(b)** (equally): **the desserts were** ~ **as good as the rest of the meal** los postres estuvieron tan buenos como el resto de la comida; it's ~ **as well you're leaving** menos mal que te vas ⑤(emphatic use): I ~ **can't understand it** simplemente no lo entiendo; ~ **leave it here** déjelo aquí, déjelo aquí nomás (AmL)

justice /'dʒʌstəs ‖'dʒʌstɪs/ *n* justicia *f*; to do sb/sth ~: the photo doesn't do her ~ la foto no le hace justicia; he couldn't do ~ to the meal no pudo hacerle honor a la comida; she didn't do herself ~ in the exam no rindió a la altura de su capacidad en el examen

Justice of the Peace *n* (*pl* ~**s** ~ ~ ~) juez *mf* de paz, juez, jueza *m,f* de paz

justifiable /'dʒʌstəfaɪəbəl ‖'dʒʌstɪfaɪəbəl/ *adj* justificable

justification /'dʒʌstəfə'keɪʃən ‖,dʒʌstɪfɪ'keɪʃən/ *n* justificación *f*

justified /'dʒʌstəfaɪd ‖'dʒʌstɪfaɪd/ *adj* justificado

justify /'dʒʌstəfaɪ ‖'dʒʌstɪfaɪ/ *vt* **-fies, -fying, -fied** justificar*

jut /dʒʌt/ **-tt-** *vi* sobresalir* ■ **jut out** [*v + adv*] sobresalir*

jute /dʒuːt/ *n* yute *m*

juvenile¹ /'dʒuːvənaɪl, -vənl ‖'dʒuːvənaɪl/ *adj* **(a)** (Law) (*before n*) ‹*court*› de menores; ‹*delinquent*› juvenil **(b)** (childish) (pej) infantil **(c)** ‹*literature*› (AmE) infantil y juvenil

juvenile² *n* (Law) menor *mf*

juxtapose /'dʒʌkstəpəʊz ‖,dʒʌkstə'pəʊz/ *vt* yuxtaponer*

Kk

K, k /keɪ/ *n* K, k *f*

K (Comput) (= **kilobyte**) K

kale /keɪl/ *n* col *f* rizada

kaleidoscope /kə'laɪdəskəʊp/ *n* caleidoscopio *m*

Kampuchea /,kæmpuː'tʃiə/ *n* Kampuchea *f*

kangaroo /'kæŋɡə'ruː/ *n* (*pl* **-roos**) canguro *m*

Kans = **Kansas**

karaoke /'kæri'əʊki/ *n* karaoke *m*

karat *n* (AmE) ▶ CARAT A

karate /kə'rɑːti/ *n* kárate *m*, karate *m* (AmL)

kayak /'kaɪæk/ *n* kayak *m*

Kazakhstan /,kɑːzɑːk'stɑːn/ *n* Kazajstán *m*

kebab /'kəbɑːb ‖kɪ'bæb/ *n* pincho *m*, anticucho *m* (Bol, Chi, Per), brocheta *f* (Esp, Méx)

keel /kiːl/ *n* quilla *f* ■ **keel over** [*v + adv*] **(a)** (capsize) «*ship*» volcar(se)* **(b)** (collapse) (colloq) «*person*» caer* redondo (fam)

keen /kiːn/ *adj* **-er, -est** ① (enthusiastic) ‹*photographer*› entusiasta; ‹*student*› aplicado; he was ~ **to start work** tenía muchas ganas de empezar a trabajar; he's ~ **to take part** tiene mucho interés en participar; to be ~ ON sth/ sb/-ING (BrE): I'm ~ **on golf** me encanta el golf; she's very ~ **on him** le gusta muchísimo; they're ~ **on joining the club** tienen muchas ganas de hacerse socios del club ② **(a)** (sharp) ‹*blade*› afilado, filoso (AmL), filudo (Chi, Per) **(b)** (acute) ‹*hearing*› muy fino; ‹*sight/sense of smell/ intelligence*› agudo **(c)** (intense) ‹*competition*› muy reñido; ‹*interest*› vivo

keep¹ /kiːp/ *n* ① (living) sustento *m* ② *for* ~**s** (colloq) para siempre ③ (in castle, fortress) torre *f* del homenaje

keep² (*past & past p* **kept**) *vt* ① **(a)** (not throw away) ‹*receipt/ticket*› guardar; (not give back) quedarse (con); (not lose) conservar; ~ **the change** quédese (con) el cambio **(b)** (look after, reserve) to ~ **sth** (FOR **sb**) guardar(le) algo (A algn) ···⁖

2 (store) guardar; **I always ∼ a first-aid kit in the car** me gusta tener un botiquín en el coche
3 (reserve for future use) guardar
4 (a) (raise) ⟨*pigs/bees*⟩ criar* (b) (manage, run) ⟨*stall/guesthouse*⟩ tener*
5 (a) (support) mantener* (b) (maintain): **I've kept a note** *o* **record of everything** he tomado nota de todo
6 (a) (cause to remain, continue) mantener*; **try and ∼ it clean** trata de mantenerlo limpio; **the noise kept me awake** el ruido no me dejó dormir (b) (detain): **don't let me ∼ you** no te quiero entretener; **what kept you?** ¿qué te retuvo?; **they kept her in hospital** la dejaron ingresada *or* (CS, Méx tb) internada
7 (adhere to, fulfill) ⟨*promise/vow*⟩ cumplir; ⟨*secret*⟩ guardar

■ **∼** *vi* 1 (remain) mantenerse*; **to ∼ fit** mantenerse* en forma; **to ∼ awake** mantenerse* despierto; **∼ still!** ¡estate quieto!
2 (a) (continue) seguir*; **∼ left** siga por la izquierda; **to ∼ -ING** seguir* + GER; **to ∼ at it** seguir* dandole (fam) (b) (repeatedly): **he ∼s interfering** está continuamente entrometiéndose; **I ∼ forgetting to bring it** nunca me acuerdo de traerlo
3 «*food*» conservarse (fresco)
4 (be in certain state of health) (colloq): **how are you ∼ing?** ¿qué tal estás? (fam)

■ **keep away** [*v* + *adv*] **to ∼ away** (FROM sb/sth) no acercarse* (A algn/algo)

■ **keep back**
I [*v* + *adv*]: **∼ back!** ¡atrás!; **∼ well back from the edge** mantente bien alejado del borde
II [*v* + *o* + *adv*, *v* + *adv* + *o*] 1 (a) ⟨*crowd/floodwaters*⟩ contener* (b) ⟨*tears/sobs*⟩ contener*
2 (not reveal) ⟨*information/facts*⟩ ocultar

■ **keep down** 1 [*v* + *o* + *adv*] (a) (not raise): **∼ your head/voice down** no levantes la cabeza/la voz ⟨*food*⟩ retener*
2 [*v* + *o* + *adv*, *v* + *adv* + *o*] (not allow to increase) ⟨*prices*⟩ mantener* al mismo nivel; ⟨*weeds*⟩ contener*

■ **keep from** [*v* + *o* + *prep* + *o*] 1 (restrain, prevent): **I don't want to ∼ you from your work** no quiero distraerte de tu trabajo; **I managed to ∼ myself from laughing** pude aguantar la risa
2 (not reveal to) ocultar; **he kept vital information from them/us** les/nos ocultó información vital

■ **keep in** [*v* + *o* + *adv*, *v* + *adv* + *o*] (a) (detain): **the teacher kept me in after school** el maestro me hizo quedar después de clase; **he was kept in for observation** lo dejaron ingresado *or* (CS, Méx tb) internado en observación (b) ⟨*anger/feelings*⟩ contener*

■ **keep off** 1 [*v* + *prep* + *o*] (a) (stay away from) ⟨*land/property*⟩ mantenerse* alejado de; **⑤ keep off the grass** prohibido pisar el césped (b) (avoid) ⟨*cigarettes/subject*⟩ evitar
2 [*v* + *o* + *prep* + *o*] **∼ your hands off me!** ¡quítame las manos de encima!

■ **keep on** 1 [*v* + *adv*] (a) (continue) seguir*; **to ∼ on -ING** seguir* + GER (b) (repeatedly): **I ∼ on forgetting to tell him** siempre me olvido de

decírselo; **she kept on interrupting him** lo interrumpía constantemente (c) (talk incessantly): **she ∼s on at me about my weight** me está siempre encima con que estoy muy gordo
2 [*v* + *o* + *adv*, *v* + *adv* + *o*] (continue to employ) no despedir*
3 [*v* + *o* + *adv*] (continue to wear): **∼ your coat on** no te quites el abrigo

■ **keep out** 1 [*v* + *adv*] (not enter): **⑤ keep out** prohibido el paso; **∼ out of the kitchen** no entres en la cocina
2 [*v* + *o* + *adv*, *v* + *adv* + *o*] (prevent from entering, exclude) ⟨*rain/sun*⟩ impedir* que entre

■ **keep out of** [*v* + *adv* + *prep* + *o*] ⟨*danger*⟩ no exponerse* a; ⟨*trouble/argument*⟩ no meterse en

■ **keep to** 1 [*v* + *prep* + *o*] (a) (adhere to, fulfill) ⟨*plan*⟩ ceñirse* a; ⟨*promise*⟩ cumplir (b) (not deviate from) ⟨*path*⟩ seguir* por; ⟨*script*⟩ ceñirse* a (c) (stay on): **∼ to the right** (Auto) mantenga su derecha
2 [*v* + *o* + *prep* + *o*] (not divulge): **to ∼ sth to oneself** guardarse algo
3 [*v* + *prep* + *o*] [*v* + *o* + *prep* + *o*]: **to ∼ (oneself) to oneself** no ser* muy sociable

■ **keep up**
I [*v* + *adv*] 1 (not stop) «*rain/noise*» seguir*, continuar*; **to ∼ up WITH sth** seguir* *or* continuar* CON algo
2 (a) (maintain pace) **to ∼ up WITH sb** seguirle* el ritmo A algn; **he's finding it difficult to ∼ up in class** le está resultando difícil mantenerse al nivel de la clase (b) (remain informed) **to ∼ up WITH sth** mantenerse* al tanto *or* al corriente DE algo
II [*v* + *o* + *adv*, *v* + *adv* + *o*] 1 (maintain at present level) mantener*
2 (continue, not stop) ⟨*payments*⟩ mantenerse* al día con; ⟨*friendship*⟩ mantener*
III [*v* + *o* + *adv*] 1 ⟨*trousers/socks*⟩ sujetar
2 (prevent from sleeping): **I hope we're not ∼ing you up** espero que no te estemos quitando el sueño; **the baby kept me up all night** el niño me tuvo toda la noche en vela

keeper /'kiːpər ‖'kiːpə(r)/ *n* (in zoo) guarda *mf*, cuidador, -dora *m,f*; (in museum) (BrE) conservador, -dora *m,f*

keep-fit /'kiːpˈfɪt/ *n* (BrE) gimnasia *f* (de mantenimiento)

keeping /'kiːpɪŋ/ *n* (a) (conformity): **in ∼ with** ⟨*with law/tradition*⟩ en conformidad con (b) (trust, care): **to leave sth in sb's ∼** dejar algo al cuidado de algn

keepsake /'kiːpseɪk/ *n* recuerdo *m*

keg /keg/ *n* barril *m*

kennel /'kenl/ *n* (a) (AmE) (for boarding) residencia *f* canina; (for breeding) criadero *m* de perros (b) (BrE) (hut) casa *f* del perro

kennels /'kenlz/ *n* (*pl* **∼**) (BrE) (+ *sing vb*) ▶ KENNEL A

Kenya /'kenjə, 'kiː-/ *n* Kenia *f*

Kenyan /'kenjən, 'kiː-/ *adj* keniano

kept /kept/ *past & past p of* KEEP[2]

kerb /kɜːrb ‖kɜːb/ *n* (BrE) ▶ CURB[1] 2

---

kernel /'kɜːrnl̩ ‖'kɜːnl̩/ *n* (of nut, fruit) almendra *f*; (of corn, wheat) grano *m*

kerosene /'kerəsiːn/ *n* queroseno *m*, kerosene *m*

kestrel /'kestrəl/ *n* cernícalo *m*

ketchup /'ketʃəp ‖'ketʃʌp/ *n* salsa *f* de tomate, ketchup *m*, catsup *m*

kettle /'ketl̩/ *n* pava *f or* (Bol, Ur) caldera *f or* (Andes, Méx) tetera *f*

kettledrum /'ketl̩drʌm/ *n* timbal *m*

key¹ /kiː/ *n* (*pl* **∼s**) **1** (for lock) llave *f*; (on can) llave *f*, abridor *m*; (*before n*) ∼ **ring** llavero *m* **2** **(a)** (to puzzle, code etc) clave *f* **(b)** (to map) explicación *f* de los signos convencionales **(c)** (answers) soluciones *fpl* **3** (crucial element) clave *f*; **patience is the** ∼ la paciencia es el factor clave *or* la clave **4** (of typewriter, piano) tecla *f*; (of wind instrument) llave *f* **5** (Mus) tono *m*; **to be off** ∼ no estar* en el tono

key² *adj* ⟨man/question⟩ clave *adj inv*
■ **key in** [*v + o + adv, v + adv + o*] ⟨text/data⟩ teclear

key: **∼board** *n* teclado *m*; **∼hole** *n* ojo *m* de la cerradura; (*before noun*) **∼hole surgery** cirugía *f* no invasiva; **∼note** *n* (Mus) tónica *f*; (central idea) tónica *f*; **∼pad** *n* (Comput, Telec, TV) teclado *m* numérico; **∼word** *n* palabra *f* clave

kg (= **kilo(s)** *o* **kilogram(s)**) Kg.

khaki /'kæki ‖'kɑːki/ *adj* caqui *or* kaki *adj inv*

kibbutz /kɪ'bʊts/ *n* (*pl* **-butzim** /-bʊtsɪm/) kibbutz *m*

kick¹ /kɪk/ *n* **1** (by person) patada *f*, puntapié *m*; (by horse) coz *f* **2** (colloq) (thrill, excitement): **to get a** ∼ **out of doing sth** deleitarse haciendo algo; **just for** ∼**s** nada más que por divertirse

kick² *vi* ⟪person⟫ dar* patadas; ⟪swimmer⟫ patalear; ⟪horse⟫ cocear
■ ∼ *vt* **1** ⟨ball⟩ patear, darle* una patada *or* un puntapié a; ⟨person⟩ pegarle* una patada a **2** (stop) (colloq) ⟨habit⟩ dejar
■ **kick around**, (BrE also) **kick about** (colloq) [*v + o + adv*] **(a)** (treat badly) maltratar **(b)** ⟨idea⟩ estudiar **(c) to** ∼ **a ball around** pelotear
■ **kick down** [*v + o + adv, v + adv + o*] ⟨door⟩ echar abajo (*a patadas*)
■ **kick off** **1** [*v + adv*] **(a)** (in football): **they** ∼ **off at three** el partido empieza a las tres **(b)** (begin) (colloq) ⟪person/meeting⟫ empezar* **2** [*v + adv + o*] (begin) ⟨discussion⟩ iniciar, empezar*
■ **kick out** [*v + o + adv*] echar
■ **kick up** **1** [*v + o + adv, v + adv + o*] ⟨leaves/dust⟩ levantar **2** [*v + adv + o*]: **to** ∼ **up a fuss** *o* **row** armar una bronca (fam); **to** ∼ **up a din** armar un escándalo

kick: **∼off** *n* (Sport) saque *m or* puntapié *m* inicial, patada *f* de inicio; **∼start** *vt* ⟨engine⟩ arrancar* (*con el pedal de arranque*)

kid¹ /kɪd/ *n* **1** (colloq) **(a)** (child) niño, -ña *m,f*, chaval, -vala *m,f* (Esp fam), chavalo, -vala *m,f* (AmC, Méx fam), escuincle, -cla (Méx fam), pibe, -ba *m,f* (RPl fam), cabro, -bra *m,f* (Chi fam) **(b)** (young person) chico, -ca *m,f* **2** **(a)** (goat) cabrito, -ta *m,f*, choto, -ta *m,f* **(b)** (leather) cabritilla *f*

kid² **-dd-** *vi* (colloq) bromear

■ ∼ *vt* **(a)** (tease) **to** ∼ **sb** (ABOUT sth) tomarle el pelo a algn (CON algo) **(b)** (deceive) engañar; **don't** ∼ **yourself!** ¡no te hagas ilusiones!

kidnap /'kɪdnæp/ *vt* **-pp-** *or* (AmE) **-p-** secuestrar, raptar

kidnapper, (AmE also) **kidnaper** /'kɪdnæpər ‖'kɪdnæpə(r)/ *n* secuestrador, -dora *m,f*, raptor, -tora *m,f*

kidnapping, (AmE also) **kidnaping** /'kɪdnæpɪŋ/ *n* secuestro *m*, rapto *m*

kidney /'kɪdni/ *n* (*pl* **-neys**) (Anat, Culin) riñón *m*; (*before n*) ⟨disease/stone⟩ renal; ∼ **machine** riñón *m* artificial

kidney bean *n* frijol *m or* (Esp) judía *f or* (CS) poroto *m* (*con forma de riñón*)

kill¹ /kɪl/ *vt* **1** (cause death of) ⟨person/animal⟩ matar; **she was** ∼**ed in a car crash** se mató *or* murió en un accidente de coche **2** **(a)** (destroy) ⟨hopes⟩ acabar con **(b)** (spoil) ⟨flavor/taste⟩ estropear **(c)** (deaden) ⟨pain⟩ calmar **(d)** (use up): **to** ∼ **time** matar el tiempo
■ ∼ *vi* matar
■ **kill off** [*v + o + adv, v + adv + o*] matar

kill² *n* **(a)** (act): **he went in for the** ∼ entró a matar **(b)** (animal, animals killed) presa *f*

killer /'kɪlər ‖'kɪlə(r)/ *n* (person) asesino, -na *m,f*; (*before n*) ⟨shark⟩ asesino; ⟨disease⟩ mortal

killer whale *n* orca *f*

killing /'kɪlɪŋ/ *n* (of person) asesinato *m*; (of animal) matanza *f*; **to make a** ∼ hacer* un gran negocio, forrarse (fam)

killjoy /'kɪldʒɔɪ/ *n* aguafiestas *mf*

kiln /kɪln/ *n* horno *m*

kilo /'kiːləʊ/ *n* (*pl* **-los**) kilo *m*

kilobyte /'kɪləbaɪt/ *n* kilobyte *m*, kiloocteto *m*

kilogram, (BrE also) **kilogramme** /'kɪləgræm/ *n* kilogramo *m*

kilometer, (BrE) **kilometre** /'kɪləmiːtər ‖kɪ'lɒmɪtə(r), 'kɪləmiːtə(r)/ *n* kilómetro *m*

kilowatt /'kɪləwɑːt ‖'kɪləwɒt/ *n* kilovatio *m*

kilt /kɪlt/ *n* falda *f or* (CS) pollera *f* escocesa

kimono /kə'məʊnəʊ ‖kɪ'məʊnəʊ/ *n* (*pl* **-nos**) kimono *m*, quimono *m*

kin /kɪn/ *n* (+ *pl vb*) familiares *mpl*, parientes *mpl*

kind¹ /kaɪnd/ *n* **1** (sort, type) **(a)** (of things) tipo *m*, clase *f*; **of all** ∼**s** de todo tipo, de toda clase **(b)** (of people) clase *f*, tipo *m* **2** (sth approximating to) especie *f*; **she was overcome by a** ∼ **of yearning** la invadió una especie de añoranza **3** (*in phrases*) **in kind** ⟨pay⟩ en especie; **kind of** (colloq): **he seemed** ∼ **of stupid** parecía como tonto (fam); **of a kind: they served a meal, of a** ∼ sirvieron una especie de comida, si se le puede llamar así; **they're two of a** ∼ son tal para cual

kind² *adj* **-er, -est** ⟨offer⟩ amable; **he's very** ∼ es muy buena persona; **she's always been** ∼ **to me** siempre ha sido muy amable conmigo; **it's very** ∼ **to your skin** no daña la piel; **would you be** ∼ **enough to accompany me?** ¿tendría la amabilidad de acompañarme?

kindergarten /'kɪndər‚gɑːrtn̩ ‖'kɪndəgɑːtn̩/ *n* jardín *m* de infancia *or* de niños

kind-hearted /'kaɪnd'hɑːrtəd ‖‚kaɪnd'hɑːtɪd/ *adj* de buen corazón

k

kindle /'kɪndl/ vt ⟨fire⟩ encender*; ⟨interest⟩ despertar*; ⟨passion⟩ encender*

kindly¹ /'kaɪndli/ adv ① (a) (generously) amablemente (b) (adding polite emphasis) (frml): passengers are ~ requested to ... se ruega a los pasajeros tengan la amabilidad de ... ② (favorably): they didn't take ~ to my suggestions no recibieron demasiado bien mis sugerencias; she doesn't take ~ to being contradicted no le hace ninguna gracia que la contradigan

kindly² adj -lier, -liest bondadoso

kindness /'kaɪndnəs ‖'kaɪndnəs/ n (a) (quality) ~ (TO o TOWARD sb) amabilidad f (PARA CON algn) (b) (act) favor m

kindred /'kɪndrəd ‖'kɪndrɪd/ adj (before n) (similar) similar; ~ spirits almas fpl gemelas

king /kɪŋ/ n rey m

kingdom /'kɪŋdəm/ n reino m; the animal ~ el reino animal

king: ~**fisher** /'kɪŋ,fɪʃər ‖'kɪŋ,fɪʃə(r)/ n martín m pescador; ~**-size**, ~**-sized** /'kɪŋsaɪzd/ adj ⟨cigarette⟩ extralargo; ⟨bed⟩ de matrimonio (extragrande)

kink /kɪŋk/ n (in rope, wire) vuelta f, curva f; (in hair) onda f

kinky /'kɪŋki/ adj -kier, -kiest (colloq) pervertidillo (fam)

kinship /'kɪnʃɪp/ n parentesco m

kiosk /'kiːɑːsk ‖'kiːɒsk/ n (stall) quiosco m

kipper /'kɪpər ‖'kɪpə(r)/ n arenque m salado y ahumado

Kirghizia /kɪr'giːziə ‖kɪə'gɪzɪə/, **Kirghizstan** /,kɪrgɪˈstɑːn ‖kɪəgɪˈstɑːn/ n Kirguizistán m

kiss¹ /kɪs/ vt ⟨person⟩ besar; to ~ sb goodbye/goodnight darle* un beso de despedida/de buenas noches a algn
■ ~ vi besarse

kiss² n beso m; to give sb a ~ darle* un beso a algn; she gave him the ~ of life le hizo (la) respiración artificial

kit /kɪt/ n ① (a) (set of items): first-aid ~ botiquín m de primeros auxilios; tool ~ caja f de herramientas (b) (parts for assembly) kit m ② (a) (personal effects) cosas fpl; (Mil) petate m (b) (Clothing) (esp BrE) gym ~ (Sport) equipo m de gimnasia

kitchen /'kɪtʃən ‖'kɪtʃɪn/ n cocina f

kitchen garden n huerto m

kite /kaɪt/ n cometa f or (RPl tb) barrilete m or (AmC, Méx) papalote m or (Ven) papagayo m or (Chi) volantín m

kitten /'kɪtn/ n gatito, -ta m,f

kitty /'kɪti/ n (pl -ties) (colloq) bote m, fondo m común

kiwi /'kiːwiː/ n (a) (Zool) kiwi m (b) ~ (fruit) kiwi m

kleptomaniac /'kleptə'memiæk/ n cleptómano, -na m,f

klutz /klʌts/ n (AmE colloq) torpe mf, patoso, -sa m,f (Esp fam)

km (= kilometer(s) o (BrE) kilometre(s)) Km.

knack /næk/ n: there's a ~ to making omelettes hacer tortillas tiene su truco or (Méx) su chiste;

I'll never get the ~ of this! ¡nunca le voy a agarrar la onda (AmL fam) or (Esp) coger el tranquillo a esto!

knapsack /'næpsæk/ n mochila f

knave /neɪv/ n (a) (rogue) (arch) truhán m (ant) (b) (in French pack of cards) jota f; (in Spanish pack) sota f

knead /niːd/ vt (Culin) amasar

knee¹ /niː/ n (Anat, Clothing) rodilla f; to be on one's ~s estar* arrodillado; to go o get down on one's ~s ponerse* de rodillas

knee² vt darle* or pegarle* un rodillazo a

knee: ~**cap** n rótula f; ~**-deep** /'niː'diːp/ adj (pred): the water is ~-deep el agua llega hasta la(s) rodilla(s); they were ~-deep in mud estaban con el barro hasta las rodillas; ~**-high** /'niː'haɪ/ adj ⟨sock⟩ largo

kneel /niːl/ vi (past & past p **kneeled** or **knelt**) (get down on one's knees) arrodillarse; (be on one's knees) estar* arrodillado; to ~ down arrodillarse

knee-length /'niːleŋθ/ adj ⟨sock⟩ largo; ⟨skirt⟩ hasta la rodilla; ⟨boot⟩ alto

knelt /nelt/ past & past p of KNEEL

knew /nuː ‖njuː/ past of KNOW

knickerbockers /'nɪkərbɑːkərz ‖'nɪkəbɒkəz/ pl n pantalones mpl bombachos

knickers /'nɪkərz ‖'nɪkəz/ pl n ① ▶ KNICKERBOCKERS ② (BrE) (undergarment) calzones mpl (AmS), bragas fpl (Esp), pantaletas fpl (AmC, Ven), bombacha f (RPl)

knickknack /'nɪknæk/ n chuchería f

knife¹ /naɪf/ n (pl **knives**) cuchillo m; (penknife) navaja f, cortaplumas m or f; (dagger) puñal m

knife² vt acuchillar

knife: ~ edge n filo m (de cuchillo, navaja etc); to be on a ~ edge pender de un hilo; ~**-point** n: he was robbed at ~-point le robaron amenazándolo con un cuchillo

knight¹ /naɪt/ n (a) (Hist) caballero m (b) (holder of title) sir m (c) (in chess) caballo m

knight² vt conceder el título de sir a

knighthood /'naɪthʊd/ n título m de sir

knit /nɪt/ (pres p **knitting**; past & past p **knitted** or **knit**) vt ① (a) ⟨sweater⟩ (by hand) hacer*, tejer; (with machine) tejer, tricotar (Esp) (b) **knitted** o (esp AmE) **knit** past p ⟨jacket/cuffs⟩ de punto, tejido ② (join, unite) ⟨bones⟩ soldar*; a tightly ~ family una familia muy unida
■ ~ vi (by hand) tejer, hacer* punto or calceta (Esp); (with machine) tejer, tricotar (Esp)

knitting /'nɪtɪŋ/ n (a) (piece of work) tejido m, punto m (Esp) (b) (activity): I like ~ me gusta tejer, me gusta hacer* punto or calceta (Esp)

knitting: ~ **machine** n máquina f de tejer, tricotosa f (Esp); ~ **needle** n aguja f de tejer or (Esp) de hacer punto, palillo m (Chi)

knives /naɪvz/ pl of KNIFE¹

knob /nɑːb ‖nɒb/ n (a) (on door) pomo m, perilla f (AmL); (on drawer) tirador m, perilla f (AmL); (on walking stick) puño m; (on radio, TV) botón m (b) (lump) bulto m (c) (small piece) (esp BrE): a ~ of butter un trocito f or una nuez de mantequilla

knobbly /'nɑːbli ‖'nɒbli/ adj -lier, -liest ⟨tree/fingers⟩ nudoso; ⟨knees⟩ huesudo

knock¹ /nɑːk ‖nɒk/ n (sound) golpe m; (blow to head, on door) golpe m

knock² vt **1** (strike, push): **to ~ one's head on/against sth** darse* (un golpe) en la cabeza con/contra algo; **she ~ed the vase off the shelf** tiró el jarrón de la repisa; **they ~ed a large hole in the wall** hicieron un gran boquete en la pared
2 (criticize) (colloq) criticar*
■ ~ vi **(a)** (on door) llamar, golpear (AmL), tocar* (AmL) **(b)** (collide) **to ~ AGAINST/INTO sb/sth** darse* or chocar* CONTRA algn/algo
■ **knock about, knock around** (colloq) [v + o + adv] pegarle* a
■ **knock back** [v + o + adv, v + adv + o] (colloq) ⟨drink⟩ beberse, tomarse
■ **knock down** [v + o + adv, v + adv + o] **1 (a)** (cause to fall) ⟨door/fence⟩ tirar abajo; ⟨obstacle⟩ derribar; **he ran into her and ~ed her down** chocó con ella y la hizo caer **(b)** «vehicle/driver» atropellar **(c)** (demolish) echar abajo
2 (colloq) (reduce) ⟨price/charge⟩ rebajar
■ **knock off** **1** [v + adv] [v + prep + o] (stop work) (colloq): **when do you ~ off (work)?** ¿a qué hora sales del trabajo?, ¿hasta qué hora trabajas?; **let's ~ off for lunch** vamos a parar para comer
2 [v + o + adv, v + adv + o] (stop) (colloq) dejar de; **~ it off, will you!** ¡déjala ya! (fam)
3 [v + o + adv, v + adv + o] (deduct, eliminate) (colloq) rebajar; **I'll ~ off 25% for you** le hago un descuento del 25%
■ **knock out** **1** [v + o + adv, v + adv + o] (make unconscious) dejar sin sentido, hacer* perder el conocimiento; (in boxing) dejar K.O., noquear; **she hit her head and ~ed herself out** se dio un golpe en la cabeza y perdió el conocimiento
2 [v + o + adv, v + adv + o] (of competition) eliminar
■ **knock over** [v + o + adv, v + adv + o] **(a)** (cause to fall) tirar **(b)** «vehicle» atropellar
■ **knock up** [v + o + adv, v + adv + o] (colloq) (assemble hurriedly) improvisar

knocker /ˈnɑːkər ‖ˈnɒkə(r)/ n aldaba f, llamador m

knocking /ˈnɑːkɪŋ ‖ˈnɒkɪŋ/ n **(a)** (noise) (no pl) golpes mpl **(b)** (Auto) golpeteo m, cascabeleo m (AmL)

knock: ~-kneed /ˈnɑːkˈniːd ‖nɒkˈniːd/ adj patizambo; **~-on effect** /ˈnɑːkˈɑːn ‖nɒkˈɒn/ n repercusiones fpl; **~out** n (in boxing) nocaut m, K.O. m (read as: nocaut or (Esp) cao)

knoll /nəʊl/ n loma f, montículo m

knot¹ /nɑːt ‖nɒt/ n **1** (in string, hair, wood) nudo m; (in muscles) nódulo m **2** (measure of speed) nudo m

knot² vt **-tt-** hacer* un nudo en

know¹ /nəʊ/ (past knew; past p known) vt **1 (a)** (have knowledge of, be aware of) saber*; **I don't ~ his name/how old he is** no sé cómo se llama/cuántos años tiene; **it is well ~n that ...** todo el mundo sabe que ...; **to let sb ~ sth** decirle* algo a algn; (warn) avisarle algo a algn; **without our ~ing it** sin saberlo nosotros; **there's no ~ing what he might do** quién sabe qué hará; **I ~ what: let's go skating!** ¡tengo una idea: vayamos a patinar!; **to ~ sth backwards** ⟨part/play⟩

saber* algo al dedillo or al revés y al derecho **(b)** (have skill, ability) **to ~ how to + INF** saber* + INF
2 (be acquainted with) ⟨person/place⟩ conocer*; **how did they get to ~ each other?** ¿cómo se conocieron?; **to get to ~ sth** ⟨subject/job⟩ familiarizarse* con algo
3 (a) (recognize, identify) reconocer*; **to ~ sth/sb BY sth** reconocer* algo/a algn POR algo **(b)** (distinguish) **to ~ sth/sb FROM sth/sb** distinguir* algo/a algn DE algo/algn
■ ~ vi saber*; **how do you ~?** ¿cómo lo sabes?; **I ~!** ¡ya sé!, ¡tengo una idea!; **you never ~** nunca se sabe; **I'm not stupid, you ~!** oye, que no soy tonto ¿eh? or ¿sabes?; **did you ~ about John?** ¿sabías lo de John?; **to get to ~ about sth** enterarse de algo; **she knew of their activities** tenía conocimiento or estaba enterada de sus actividades; **not that I ~ of** que yo sepa, no; **do you ~ of a good carpenter?** ¿conoces a or sabes de algún carpintero bueno?

know² n: **to be in the ~** estar* enterado

know: ~-all n (BrE) ▸ KNOW-IT-ALL; **~how** n know-how m, conocimientos mpl y experiencia

knowing /ˈnəʊɪŋ/ adj ⟨smile⟩ de complicidad; **she gave me a ~ look** me miró dándome a entender que ya lo sabía

knowingly /ˈnəʊɪŋli/ adv **(a)** ⟨smile/nod⟩ de manera cómplice **(b)** (deliberately) ⟨hurt/lie⟩ a sabiendas

know-it-all /ˈnəʊɪtɔːl/ n (colloq) sabelotodo mf (fam)

knowledge /ˈnɑːlɪdʒ ‖ˈnɒlɪdʒ/ n **1** (awareness) conocimiento m; **to the best of my ~** que yo sepa; **it is common ~ that ...** todo el mundo sabe que ... **2** (facts known) saber m; (by particular person) conocimientos mpl

knowledgeable /ˈnɑːlɪdʒəbəl ‖ˈnɒlɪdʒəbəl/ adj (about current affairs) informado; (about given subject) entendido; (in general) culto

known¹ /nəʊn/ past p of KNOW

known² adj ⟨fact⟩ conocido, sabido; **a little-~ artist** un artista poco conocido; **to be ~ AS sth** (have reputation) tener* fama DE algo; **better ~ as ...** más conocido como ...; **for reasons best ~ to herself** por motivos que ella conociera); **he's better ~ for his work in films** se le conoce mejor por su trabajo cinematográfico

knuckle /ˈnʌkəl/ n **(a)** (finger joint) nudillo m **(b)** (of pork) codillo m; (of veal) morcillo m, jarrete m
■ **knuckle down** [v + adv] ponerse* a trabajar en serio
■ **knuckle under** [v + adv] ceder*, pasar por el aro

knuckleduster /ˈnʌkəlˌdʌstər ‖ˈnʌkəlˌdʌstə(r)/ n (BrE) ▸ BRASS KNUCKLES

koala /kəʊˈɑːlə/ n ~ (bear) koala m

kooky /ˈkuːki/ adj **-kier, -kiest** (AmE colloq) chiflado (fam)

Koran /kɔːˈrɑːn/ n the ~ el Corán

Korea /kəˈriːə/ n Corea f

Korean¹ /kəˈriːən/ adj coreano

Korean² n **(a)** (person) coreano, -na m,f **(b)** (language) coreano m

kosher /ˈkəʊʃər ‖ˈkəʊʃə(r)/ adj ⟨food/butcher⟩ kosher adj inv

Kosovo /ˈkɑːsəvəʊ ‖ˈkɒsəvəʊ/ n Kosovo m

k

kowtow /'kaʊtaʊ/ *vi* to ∼ **TO** sb doblar la cerviz ANTE algn

kph (= **kilometers** *o* (BrE) **kilometres per hour**) Km/h.

KS = **Kansas**

kung fu /'kʌŋ'fuː/ *n* kung fu *m*

Kurd /kɜːrd ‖kɜːd/ *n* kurdo, -da *m,f*

Kurdish /'kɜːrdɪʃ ‖'kɜːdɪʃ/ *adj* kurdo

Kuwait /kə'weɪt ‖kʊ'weɪt/ *n* Kuwait *m*

Kuwaiti /kə'weɪti ‖kʊ'weɪti/ *adj* kuwaití

KY, Ky = **Kentucky**

L l

L, l /el/ *n* L, l *f*

l (= **liter(s)** *or* (BrE) **litre(s)**) l.

L (a) (BrE Auto) **◐ L** (= **learner**) L (*conductor en aprendizaje*) (b) (Clothing) (= **large**) G (*talla grande*)

la /lɑː/ *n* (Mus) la *m*

La = **Louisiana**

LA (a) = **Los Angeles** (b) = **Louisiana**

lab /læb/ *n* (colloq) laboratorio *m*

label¹ /'leɪbəl/ *n* etiqueta *f*

label² *vt*, (BrE) **-ll-** (a) ‹*bottle/luggage*› ponerle* una etiqueta a (b) (categorize) to ∼ **sth/sb** (**AS**) **sth** catalogar* algo/a algn DE algo

labor¹, (BrE) **labour** /'leɪbər ‖'leɪbə(r)/ *n* [1] (a) (work) trabajo *m*; (before n) ‹*dispute/laws*› laboral (b) (workers) mano *f* de obra [2] **Labour** (in UK) (Pol) (*no art, + sing or pl vb*) los laboristas, el Partido Laborista [3] (a) (effort) esfuerzos *mpl*, trabajo *m* (b) (task) labor *f*, tarea *f* [4] (Med) parto *m*; **to be in** ∼ estar* de parto; (before n) ∼ **pains** dolores *mpl or* contracciones *fpl* del parto

labor², (BrE) **labour** *vt*: **to** ∼ **a point** insistir excesivamente sobre un punto
■ ∼ *vi* (toil) trabajar; **he** ∼**ed up the hill** subió trabajosamente *or* penosamente la cuesta

laboratory /'læbərətɔːri ‖lə'bɒrətri/ *n* (*pl* **-ries**) laboratorio *m*

Labor Day *n* Día *m* del Trabajo *or* de los trabajadores

labored, (BrE) **laboured** /'leɪbərd ‖'leɪbəd/ *adj* ‹*breathing*› dificultoso, fatigoso; ‹*metaphor/joke*› forzado, torpe

laborer, (BrE) **labourer** /'leɪbərər ‖'leɪbərə(r)/ *n* peón *m*; **farm** ∼ peón *m*, trabajador *m* agrícola

laborious /lə'bɔːriəs/ *adj* ‹*task/process*› laborioso; ‹*style*› farragoso

labor union *n* (AmE) sindicato *m*

labour *etc* (BrE) ▶ LABOR *etc*

labrador /'læbrədɔːr ‖'læbrədɔː(r)/ *n* labrador *m*

labyrinth /'læbərɪnθ/ *n* laberinto *m*

lace¹ /leɪs/ *n* [1] (fabric) encaje *m*; (as border) puntilla *f* [2] (shoe∼) cordón *m* (de zapato), agujeta *f* (Méx), pasador *m* (Per)

lace² *vt* [1] ‹*shoes/boots*› ponerles* los cordones *or* (Méx) las agujetas *or* (Per) los pasadores a [2] (fortify): **he** ∼**d my drink with vodka** me echó un chorro de vodka en la bebida

lacerate /'læsəreɪt/ *vt* lacerar

lack¹ /læk/ *n* ∼ **OF sth** falta *f or* (frml) carencia *f* DE algo

lack² *vt* no tener*, carecer* de (frml); **it** ∼**s originality** le falta *or* no tiene originalidad, carece de originalidad (frml)

lacking /'lækɪŋ/ *adj* (*pred*) (a) (absent): **the necessary resources are** ∼ faltan los recursos necesarios (b) (deficient) **to be** ∼ **IN sth** no tener* algo, carecer DE algo (frml)

lackluster, (BrE) **lacklustre** /'læk,lʌstər ‖'læk,lʌstə(r)/ *adj* (a) ‹*eyes*› apagado; ‹*hair*› opaco (b) (mediocre) ‹*performance/campaign*› deslucido; ‹*candidate*› mediocre

laconic /lə'kɑːnɪk ‖lə'kɒnɪk/ *adj* lacónico

lacquer /'lækər ‖'lækə(r)/ *n* (a) (varnish) laca *f* (b) (hair ∼) laca *f or* fijador *m* (para el pelo)

lad /læd/ *n* muchacho *m*, chaval *m* (Esp fam), pibe *m* (RPI fam), chavo *m* (Méx, Ven fam), chavalo *m* (AmC, Méx fam), cabro *m* (Chi fam)

ladder /'lædər ‖'lædə(r)/ *n* [1] (Const) escalera *f* (de mano) [2] (in stocking, tights) (BrE) carrera *f*

laden /'leɪdn/ *adj* ∼ **WITH sth** cargado DE algo

ladies /'leɪdiz/ *n* (BrE) ▶ LADIES' ROOM

ladies' room /'leɪdiz/ *n* (AmE) baño *m or* (esp Esp) servicio *m* de señoras; **◐ Ladies (Room)** Señoras, Damas

ladle /'leɪdl/ *n* cucharón *m*

lady /'leɪdi/ *n* (*pl* **ladies**) [1] (a) (woman) señora *f*; **ladies and gentlemen** señoras y señores, damas y caballeros (b) (refined woman) señora *f*, dama *f* [2] (noblewoman or wife of a knight) lady *f*

lady: ∼**bug** (AmE), ∼**bird** (BrE) *n* mariquita *f*, catarina *f* (Méx), petaca *f* (Col), chinita *f* (Chi), San Antonio *m* (Ur), vaca *f* de San Antón (Arg); ∼**-in-waiting** /'leɪdiɪn'weɪtɪŋ/ *n* (*pl* **ladies-in-waiting**) dama *f* de honor; ∼**like** *adj* fino

ladyship /'leɪdiʃɪp/ *n*: **Her/Your L**∼ la señora

lag¹ /læg/ *n* (interval) lapso *m*, intervalo *m*; (delay) retraso *m*, demora *f* (esp AmL)

AmC	América Central	Arg	Argentina	Cu	Cuba
AmL	América Latina	Bol	Bolivia	Ec	Ecuador
AmS	América del Sur	Chi	Chile	Esp	España
Andes	Región andina	CS	Cono Sur	Méx	México

Per	Perú
RPI	Río de la Plata
Ur	Uruguay
Ven	Venezuela

lag² **-gg-** *vi* to ~ **(behind)** quedarse atrás; **to ~ behind sb/sth** ir* a la zaga de algn/algo
■ ~ *vt* ‹*pipes*› revestir* con aislantes

lager /'lɑ:gər ‖'lɑ:gə(r)/ *n* cerveza *f* (rubia)

lagoon /lə'gu:n/ *n* laguna *f*

lah /lɑ:/ *n* (BrE Mus) la *m*

laid /leɪd/ *past & past p of* LAY²

laid-back /'leɪd'bæk/ *adj* (colloq) ‹*person*› tranquilo y relajado; ‹*atmosphere*› relajado

lain /leɪn/ *past p of* LIE² II

lair /ler ‖lea(r)/ *n* guarida *f*

lake /leɪk/ *n* lago *m*

Lake District *n* **the ~ ~** el Lake District (*región de lagos al noroeste de Inglaterra*)

lamb /læm/ *n* cordero *m*; (*before n*) ~ **chop** chuleta *f* de cordero

lame¹ /leɪm/ *adj* 1 (in foot, leg) cojo, rengo (AmL); **to go ~** quedarse cojo *or* (AmL tb) rengo 2 (weak) ‹*excuse*› pobre, malo

lame² *vt* lisiar

lament¹ /lə'ment/ *n* lamento *m*

lament² *vt* (a) ‹*misfortune/failure*› lamentar (b) (liter) ‹*death/loss*› llorar

lamentable /'læməntəbəl/ *adj* lamentable

lamp /læmp/ *n* lámpara *f*; (Auto) luz *f*

lamplight /'læmplaɪt/ *n* (of table lamp) luz *f* de (la) lámpara; (of streetlamp) luz *f* de(l) farol

lampoon /læm'pu:n/ *vt* satirizar*

lamp: ~**post** *n* farol *m*; ~**shade** *n* pantalla *f* (*de lámpara*)

lance¹ /læns ‖lɑ:ns/ *n* lanza *f*

lance² *vt* abrir* con lanceta

lancet /'lænsət ‖'lɑ:nsɪt/ *n* lanceta *f*

land¹ /lænd/ *n* 1 (Geog, Agr) tierra *f*; (*before n*) ‹*animal/defenses*› de tierra; ~ **reform** reforma *f* agraria 2 (country, realm) (liter) país *m*; (kingdom) reino *m*

land² *vi* 1 (a) (Aerosp, Aviat) aterrizar*; (on the moon) alunizar* (b) (fall) caer* 2 (arrive, end up) (colloq) ir* a parar (fam) 3 (Naut) ‹*ship*› atracar*; ‹*traveler/troops*› desembarcar*
■ ~ *vt* 1 (a) (from sea) ‹*passengers*› desembarcar*; ‹*cargo*› descargar* (b) (from air) ‹*plane*› hacer* aterrizar; ‹*troops*› desembarcar*; ‹*supplies*› descargar* 2 (fish) sacar* del agua; ‹*contract/job*› conseguir* 3 (burden) (colloq) **to ~ sb WITH sth/sb, to ~ sth/sb ON sb** endilgarle* algo/a algn A algn (fam)

landing /'lændɪŋ/ *n* 1 (a) (Aerosp, Aviat) aterrizaje *m*; (on moon) alunizaje *m*; (*before n*) ~ **strip** pista *f* de aterrizaje (b) (Mil, Naut) desembarco *m* (c) (of cargo) descarga *f*; (of troops) desembarco *m* 2 (on staircase) rellano *m*, descanso *m* (Col, CS)

land: ~**lady** *n* (of rented dwelling) casera *f* (b) (of small hotel) dueña *f* (c) (BrE) (of pub — owner) dueña *f*; (— manager) encargada *f*; ~**locked** /'lændlɑ:kt ‖'lændlɒkt/ *adj* sin salida al mar; ~**lord** *n* (a) (of landed estate) terrateniente *m* (b) (of rented dwelling) casero *m*, dueño *m* (c) (BrE) (of pub — owner) dueño *m*; (— manager) encargado *m*; ~**mark** *n* monumento *m* (or edificio *m* etc) famoso; ~ **mine** *n* mina *f* (de tierra); ~**owner** *n* terrateniente *mf*; ~**scape** /'lændskeɪp/ *n* paisaje *m*; (*before n*) ~**scape gardener** jardinero,

-ra *m,f* paisajista; ~**slide** *n* (a) (Geog) derrumbamiento *m or* desprendimiento *m* de tierras (b) (Pol) victoria *f* aplastante

lane /leɪn/ *n* 1 (in countryside) camino *m*, sendero *m*; (alleyway) callejón *m* 2 (Transp) (a) (for road traffic) carril *m or* (Chi) pista *f or* (RPl) senda *f*; **bus/bicycle ~** carril *m* de autobuses/bicicletas (b) (for ships) ruta *f* 3 (in athletics) carril *m* (AmL), calle *f* (Esp)

language /'læŋgwɪdʒ/ *n* 1 (means of communication, style of speech) lenguaje *m*; **bad ~** palabrotas *fpl* 2 (a) (particular tongue) idioma *m*, lengua *f* (b) (Comput) lenguaje *m*

languid /'læŋgwəd ‖'læŋgwɪd/ *adj* lánguido

languish /'læŋgwɪʃ/ *vi* (liter) languidecer*; (in prison) pudrirse*

lank /læŋk/ *adj* lacio

lanky /'læŋki/ *adj* **-kier, -kiest** desgarbado

lantern /'læntərn ‖'læntən/ *n* farol *m*

Laos /laʊs ‖'lɑːɒs, laʊs/ *n* Laos *m*

lap¹ /læp/ *n* 1 (of body) rodillas *fpl* 2 (a) (Sport) vuelta *f* (b) (stage) etapa *f*

lap² **-pp-** *vt* 1 (Sport) sacarle* una vuelta de ventaja a 2 ‹*water/milk*› beber a lengüetazos
■ ~ *vi* chapalear; **to ~ AGAINST sth** lamer *or* besar algo (liter)
■ **lap up** [v + o + adv, v + adv + o] beber a lengüetazos

lapel /lə'pel/ *n* solapa *f*

Lapland /'læplænd/ *n* Laponia *f*

lapse¹ /læps/ *n* 1 (fault, error) falla *f*, fallo *m* (Esp) 2 (interval) lapso *m*, período *m*

lapse² *vi* 1 (fall, slip): **standards have ~d** el nivel ha decaído; **to ~ into bad habits** adquirir* malos hábitos 2 (a) (cease) ‹*project*› cancelarse; ‹*practice*› perderse* (b) ‹*membership/contract*› caducar*, vencer* 3 ‹*time*› transcurrir

laptop /'læptɑːp ‖'læptɒp/ *n* (~ computer) portátil *m*, laptop *f or* (Esp) *m*

lapwing /'læpwɪŋ/ *n* avefría *f*‡

larceny /'lɑːrsəni ‖'lɑːsəni/ *n* (in US) robo *m*

larch /lɑːrtʃ ‖lɑːtʃ/ *n* alerce *m*

lard /lɑːrd ‖lɑːd/ *n* manteca *f or* (RPl) grasa *f* de cerdo

larder /'lɑːrdər ‖'lɑːdə(r)/ *n* despensa *f*

large¹ /lɑːrdʒ ‖lɑːdʒ/ *adj*
■ **Note** The usual translation of *large*, *grande*, becomes *gran* when it precedes a singular noun.

larger, largest grande; **the ~st collection of stamps in the world** la mayor colección de sellos del mundo

large² *n* **at large** (a) (as a whole) en general; **the public at ~** el público en general (b) (at liberty): **to be at ~** andar* suelto

largely /'lɑːrdʒli ‖'lɑːdʒli/ *adv* en gran parte

lark /lɑːrk ‖lɑːk/ *n* alondra *f*

larva /'lɑːrvə ‖'lɑːvə/ *n* (*pl* **-vae** /-viː/) larva *f*

laryngitis /ˌlærən'dʒaɪtəs ‖ˌlærɪn'dʒaɪtɪs/ *n* laringitis *f*

larynx /'lærɪŋks/ *n* (*pl* **larynxes** *or* **larynges** /lə'rɪndʒiːs/) laringe *f*

laser /'leɪzər ‖'leɪzə(r)/ *n* láser *m*; (*before n*) ~ **beam** rayo *m* láser; ~ **printer** impresora *f* láser

lash¹ /læʃ/ n ⬚1 (eye~) pestaña f ⬚2 (whip) látigo m

lash² vt ⬚1 (a) (whip) ⟨person⟩ azotar; ⟨horse⟩ fustigar* (b) (beat against) azotar ⬚2 (bind) **to ~ sth/sb TO sth** amarrar algo/a algn A algo
■ **lash out** [v + adv (+ prep + o)] atacar*; **to ~ out AT/AGAINST sb** (physically) emprenderla a golpes (or patadas etc) CON algn; (verbally) arremeter CONTRA algn

lass /læs/ n (liter or dial) muchacha f

lasso /ˈlæsəʊ, læˈsuː/ ‖læˈsuː/ n (pl **-sos** or **-soes**) lazo m

last¹ /læst ‖lɑːst/ adj ⬚1 (a) (in series) último; **the ~ door but one** la penúltima puerta; **to be ~** (in race, on arrival) ser* el último (en llegar); **to be ~ to + INF** ser* el último EN + INF (b) (final, ultimate) ⟨chance/day⟩ último; **at the very ~ minute** en el último momento, a última hora (c) (only remaining): **I'm down to my ~ few dollars** solo me quedan unos pocos dólares ⬚2 (previous, most recent) (before n): **~ Tuesday** el martes pasado; **in my ~ letter** en mi última carta ⬚3 (least likely): **that was the ~ thing I expected to hear from you** es lo que menos me esperaba que me dijeras; **that's the ~ thing I'd do!** ¡no se me ocurriría hacer eso!

last² pron ⬚1 (a) (in series) último, -ma m,f; **the ~ to + INF** el último/la última/los últimos/las últimas EN + INF; **the ~ I remember** lo último que recuerdo (b) (only remaining): **the ~ of its kind** el último de su clase; **that's the ~ of the jam** esa es toda la mermelada que queda (c) (in phrases) (liter) **at the last** al final; **to the ~** hasta el último momento ⬚2 (preceding one): **the night before ~** anteanoche, antenoche (AmL); **each hill seemed steeper than the ~** cada colina parecía más empinada que la anterior

last³ adv ⬚1 (a) (at the end): **I went in ~** fui el último en entrar; **our team finished ~** nuestro equipo quedó en último lugar (b) (finally): **~ of all** por último; **and ~ but not least** y por último, pero no por eso menos importante (c) (in phrases) **at last** por fin, al fin; **at long last** por fin, finalmente ⬚2 (most recently): **she was ~ seen a year ago** la última vez que se la vio fue hace un año; **when did you ~ see him?** ¿cuándo fue la última vez que lo viste?

last⁴ vi/t durar

last-ditch /ˈlæstˈdɪtʃ ‖ˈlɑːstˈdɪtʃ/ adj (before n) desesperado

lasting /ˈlæstɪŋ ‖ˈlɑːstɪŋ/ adj duradero

lastly /ˈlæstli ‖ˈlɑːstli/ adv (as linker) por último

last-minute /ˈlæstˈmɪnət ‖ˌlɑːstˈmɪnɪt/ adj (before n) de última hora

latch /lætʃ/ n pasador m, pestillo m; (on lock) seguro m
■ **latch on** [v + adv (+ prep + o)] (understand) (colloq) agarrar or (Esp) coger* la onda; **to ~ on TO sth** entender* algo; (realize) darse* cuenta DE algo

late¹ /leɪt/ adj later, latest ⬚1 (after correct, scheduled time): **the ~ arrival of the train** el retraso en la llegada del tren; **to be ~** «person» llegar* tarde; **the train was an hour ~** el tren llegó con una hora de retraso; **you'll be ~ for work** vas a llegar tarde al trabajo
⬚2 (a) (after usual time): **to have a ~ night**

acostarse* tarde; **Spring is ~ this year** la primavera se ha atrasado este año (b) ⟨chrysanthemum/potatoes⟩ tardío
⬚3 (a) (far on in time): **it's ~** es tarde; **it's getting ~** se está haciendo tarde (b) ⟨before n⟩ ⟨shift/bus⟩ último; **at this ~ stage** a estas alturas; **in ~ April** a finales de abril; **she's in her ~ forties** tiene cerca de cincuenta años
⬚4 (before n) (deceased) difunto (frml); **the ~ John Doe** el difunto John Doe

late² adv **later, latest** ⬚1 (after correct, scheduled time) tarde; **the trains are running 20 minutes ~** los trenes llevan 20 minutos de retraso; **better ~ than never** más vale tarde que nunca ⬚2 (after usual time) ⟨work/sleep⟩ hasta tarde; ⟨mature⟩ tarde ⬚3 (recently): **as ~ as the thirteenth century** aún en el siglo trece; **of ~** últimamente ⬚4 (toward end of period): **~ in the afternoon** a última hora de la tarde; **~ in the year** a finales del año; **~ in her career** hacia el final de su carrera ⬚5 (far on in time) tarde; **don't leave it too ~** no lo dejes para muy tarde; **we stayed up ~** nos quedamos levantados hasta tarde

lately /ˈleɪtli/ adv últimamente

latent /ˈleɪtn̩t/ adj latente

later¹ /ˈleɪtər/ adj posterior

later² adv después, más tarde; **~ that day** más tarde or posteriormente ese día; **not o no ~ than May 14** a más tardar el 14 de mayo; **~ on** más tarde, después; **see you ~!** ¡hasta luego!

lateral /ˈlætərəl/ adj lateral

latest /ˈleɪtəst ‖ˈleɪtɪst/ adj (a) (superl of LATE¹) último (b) (most up to date) (before n) último

latex /ˈleɪteks/ n látex m

lathe /leɪð/ n torno m

lather¹ /ˈlæðər ‖ˈlɑːðə(r), læðə(r)/ n (no pl) espuma

lather² vt enjabonar

Latin¹ /ˈlætn̩ ‖ˈlætɪn/ adj latino

Latin² n (a) (language) latín m (b) (person) latino, -na m,f

Latin America n América f Latina, Latinoamérica f

Latin American¹ adj latinoamericano

Latin American² n latinoamericano, -na m,f

latitude /ˈlætətuːd ‖ˈlætɪtjuːd/ n (a) (Geog) latitud f (b) (freedom to choose) libertad f

latter¹ /ˈlætər ‖ˈlætə(r)/ n (pl ~) **the ~** este, -ta; (pl) estos, -tas

latter² adj (before n) (a) (second of two) segundo, último (b) (later, last): **in the ~ part of the season** hacia el final de la temporada; **in his ~ years** (frml) en sus últimos años

lattice /ˈlætəs ‖ˈlætɪs/ n entramado m, enrejado m

Latvia /ˈlætviə/ n Letonia f

Latvian /ˈlætviən/ adj letón

laugh¹ /læf ‖lɑːf/ n risa f; **; she's a good ~** es muy divertida; **to do/say sth for a ~** hacer*/decir* algo por divertirse; **to have a ~ (about/at sth)** reírse* (de algo)

laugh² vi reír(se)*; **to burst out ~ing** soltar* una carcajada; **to ~ AT sb/sth** reírse* DE algn/algo

■ **laugh off** [v + o + adv, v + adv + o] tomar a broma

laughing /'læfɪŋ ǁ 'lɑːfɪŋ/ adj risueño; **this is no ~ matter** no es motivo de risa

laughingstock /'læfɪŋstɑːk ǁ 'lɑːfɪŋstɒk/ n hazmerreír m; **he made a ~ of his opponent** dejó or puso a su contrincante en ridículo

laughter /'læftər ǁ 'lɑːftə(r)/ n risas fpl

launch¹ /lɔːntʃ/ vt **1 (a)** ‹new vessel› botar; ‹lifeboat› echar al agua **(b)** ‹satellite/missile› lanzar*; ‹attack› emprender **2** ‹product/campaign› lanzar*; ‹company› fundar*

launch² n **1** (motorboat) lancha f (a motor) **2 (a)** (of new vessel) botadura f; (of lifeboat) lanzamiento m (al agua) **(b)** (of rocket, missile) lanzamiento m **3** (of product, campaign) lanzamiento m

launching pad /'lɔːntʃɪŋ/, **launchpad** /'lɔːntʃpæd/ n **(a)** (Aerosp) rampa f de lanzamiento **(b)** (for ideas, career) trampolín m

launder /'lɔːndər ǁ 'lɔːndə(r)/ vt **(a)** (wash and iron) (frml) lavar y planchar **(b)** ‹money› blanquear, lavar (AmL)

launderette /lɔːndə'ret ǁ lɔːn'dret/ n lavandería f automática

Laundromat®, laundromat /'lɔːndrəmæt/ n (AmE) lavandería f automática

laundry /'lɔːndri/ n (pl **-dries**) **(a)** (commercial) lavandería f, lavadero m (RPl); (in home) lavadero m **(b)** (dirty clothes) ropa f sucia or para lavar; (washed clothes) ropa f limpia or lavada; (before n) **~ basket** canasto m or cesto m de la ropa sucia

laurel /'lɔːrəl ǁ 'lɒrəl/ n laurel m

lava /'lɑːvə/ n lava f

lavatory /'lævətɔːri ǁ 'lævətri/ n (pl **-ries**) **(a)** (room in house) (cuarto m de) baño m **(b)** (public) (often pl) baños mpl, servicios mpl (Esp) **(c)** (receptacle) taza f, inodoro m

lavender /'lævəndər ǁ 'lævəndə(r)/ n lavanda f, espliego m

lavish¹ /'lævɪʃ/ adj ‹lifestyle› de derroche; ‹gift/meal› espléndido; ‹production› fastuoso

lavish² vt **to ~ sth ON sb** prodigar(le)* algo A algn

lavishly /'lævɪʃli/ adv ‹give› con esplendidez; ‹decorated/illustrated› magníficamente

law /lɔː/ n **(a)** (rule, principle) ley f **(b)** (collectively): **the ~** la ley; **to break the ~** violar or contravenir* or infringir* la ley; **it is against the ~** es ilegal; **under French ~** según la ley francesa; **to lay down the ~** dar* órdenes **(c)** (as field, discipline) derecho m; (profession) abogacía f; (before n) **~ school** facultad f de Derecho

law: ~-abiding /'lɔːəˌbaɪdɪŋ/ adj respetuoso de la ley; **~ and order** n (+ sing o pl vb) el orden público

lawful /'lɔːfəl/ adj ‹ruler/heir› legítimo; ‹contract› válido, legal; ‹conduct› lícito

lawless /'lɔːləs ǁ 'lɔːlɪs/ adj ‹mob› desmandado; ‹region› anárquico, donde no rige la ley

lawn /lɔːn/ n césped m, pasto m (AmL), grama f (AmC, Ven)

lawnmower /'lɔːnˌməʊər ǁ 'lɔːnˌməʊə(r)/ n máquina f de cortar el césped or (AmL tb) el pasto, cortadora f de césped or (AmL tb) de pasto, cortacésped m (Esp), cortagrama m (AmC, Ven)

lawsuit /'lɔːsuːt/ n juicio m

lawyer /'lɔːjər ǁ 'lɔːjə(r)/ n abogado, -da m,f

lax /læks/ adj ‹discipline/supervision› poco estricto; ‹standards› laxo

laxative /'læksətɪv/ n laxante m

lay¹ /leɪ/ past of LIE² II

lay² (past & past p **laid**) vt **1** (put) poner*; **~ the cloth flat on the table** extiende la tela sobre la mesa

2 (put in position) ‹bricks/carpet› poner*, colocar*; ‹cable/pipes› tender*; ‹mines› sembrar*

3 (prepare) ‹trap› tender*; ‹plans› hacer*; **to ~ the table** poner* la mesa

4 (cause to be): **one blow laid him flat on his back** de un golpe quedó tendido de espaldas en el suelo; **to ~ sb low**: **he was laid low by malaria** estuvo postrado con malaria

5 (Zool): **to ~ eggs** «bird/reptile» poner* huevos; «fish/insects» desovar*
■ **~** vi **1** «hen» poner* huevos
2 (crit) ▶ LIE² II

■ **lay down** [v + o + adv, v + adv + o] **(a)** ‹tools/weapons› dejar (a un lado) **(b)** ‹guidelines/procedure› establecer*

■ **lay off** [v + adv + o, v + o + adv] (AmE) despedir*; (BrE) suspender temporalmente por falta de trabajo

■ **lay on** [v + adv + o, v + o + adv] ‹transport/food› hacerse* cargo de; ‹entertainment› ofrecer*

■ **lay out** [v + o + adv, v + adv + o] **1 (a)** ‹park/garden› diseñar; ‹town› hacer* el trazado de; ‹objects› disponer* **(b)** ‹page› diseñar
2 (spend) gastar; (invest) invertir*
3 (knock unconscious) dejar sin sentido
4 ‹dead body› amortajar

lay³ adj (before n) **(a)** (secular) laico; **~ preacher** predicador, -dora m,f seglar **(b)** (not expert): **the ~ reader** el lector profano en la materia

lay-by /'leɪbaɪ/ n (BrE) área f; de reposo

layer¹ /'leɪər ǁ 'leɪə(r)/ n (of dust, paint, snow) capa f; (of rock, sediment) capa f, estrato m

layer² vt: **I had my hair ~ed** me corté el pelo en or (Esp) a capas, me rebajé el pelo (RPl)

lay: ~man /'leɪmən/ n (pl **-men** /-mən/) (non-expert): **a book written for the ~man** un libro dirigido al gran público; **in ~man's terms** en lenguaje accesible; **~out** n **(a)** (of house) distribución f; (of town, garden) trazado m **(b)** (in magazine, newspaper) diseño m

laze /leɪz/ vi haraganear

lazily /'leɪzəli ǁ 'leɪzɪli/ adv perezosamente

lazy /'leɪzi/ adj **lazier, laziest** perezoso

lazybones /'leɪzibəʊnz/ n (pl **~**) (colloq) haragán, -gana m,f

lb = **pound(s)**

LCD n = **liquid crystal display**

lead¹ n

I /led/ **1** (metal) plomo m; (before n) **~ poisoning** intoxicación f por plomo; (chronic disease) saturnismo m **2** (in pencil) mina f

II /liːd/ **1** (in competition) (no pl): **to be in/take the ~** llevar/tomar la delantera **2** (example, leadership) (no pl) ejemplo m; **to follow sb's ~** seguir* el ejemplo de algn **3** (clue) pista f **4** (for dog) (BrE) correa f **(b)** (Elec) cable m **5 (a)** (main role) papel m principal **(b)** (Mus) solista mf; (before n) ‹guitar/singer› principal

lead² /liːd/ (*past & past p* **led**) *vt* ☐1 (conduct)
⟨*person/animal*⟩ llevar, guiar*; **to ~ sb TO sth/sb**
conducir* *or* llevar a algn A algo/ANTE algn; **to ~
sb away** llevarse a algn; **I was led to believe that**
... me dieron a entender que ...; **he's easily led** se
deja llevar fácilmente
☐2 (head, have charge of) ⟨*discussion*⟩ conducir*;
the expedition was led by Smith la expedición iba
al mando de Smith
☐3 **(a)** (be at front of) ⟨*parade/attack*⟩ encabezar*
(b) (in race, competition) aventajar
☐4 ⟨*life*⟩ llevar
■ **~** *vi* ☐1 **to ~ TO sth** ⟨*road/steps*⟩ llevar *or*
conducir* *or* dar* A algo; ⟨*door*⟩ dar* A algo
☐2 **(a)** (be leader): **you ~,** we'll follow ve delante
or (esp AmL) adelante, que te seguimos **(b)** (in race,
competition) ir* a la cabeza, puntear (AmL); **they are
~ing by three goals** van ganando por tres goles
■ **lead on** ☐1 [*v + adv*]: **~ on!** ¡adelante! (¡te
seguimos!)
☐2 [*v + o + adv*] (raise false hopes) engañar
■ **lead to** [*v + prep + o*] llevar *or* conducir* a

leaded /'ledəd ‖ 'ledɪd/ *adj* ⟨*fuel*⟩ con plomo

leader /'liːdər ‖ 'liːdə(r)/ *n* **(a)** (of group, political
party) líder *mf*; (of expedition) jefe, -fa *m,f*; (of gang)
cabecilla *mf* **(b)** (in race, competition) primero, -ra
m,f; (in league) líder *m*

leadership /'liːdərʃɪp ‖ 'liːdəʃɪp/ *n* **(a)**
(direction, control — of party) liderazgo *m*; (— of
country) conducción *f* **(b)** (quality) autoridad *f*, dotes
fpl de mando **(c)** (leaders) (+ *sing o pl vb*)
dirigentes *mpl*

lead-free /led'friː/ *adj* ⟨*fuel*⟩ sin plomo

leading /'liːdɪŋ/ *adj* (*before n*) **(a)** (principal)
⟨*scientist/playwright*⟩ destacado; ⟨*brand/
company*⟩ líder *adj inv* **(b)** (in front) ⟨*runner/horse/
driver*⟩ que va a la cabeza

leading: **~ lady** *n* (Cin) protagonista *f*; (Theat)
primera actriz *f*; **~ light** *n* estrella *f*

leaf /liːf/ *n* (*pl* **leaves**) ☐1 (of plant) hoja *f*
☐2 (page, sheet) hoja *f*; **to turn (over) a new ~**
reformarse ☐3 (of table) ala *f*₂; (of door, shutter)
hoja *f*
■ **leaf through** [*v + prep + o*] hojear

leaflet /'liːflət ‖ 'liːflɪt/ *n* (Print) folleto *m*; (Pol)
panfleto *m*

leafy /'liːfi/ *adj* **-fier, -fiest** ⟨*boughs*⟩ frondoso;
⟨*lane*⟩ arbolado

league /liːg/ *n* ☐1 (alliance) liga *f*; **to be in ~
(with sb)** estar* aliado (con algn) ☐2 **(a)** (Sport)
liga *f* **(b)** (level, category): **not to be in the same ~
as sb/sth** no estar* a la misma altura que algn/
algo ☐3 (measure of distance) legua *f*

leak¹ /liːk/ *vi* **(a)** ⟨*bucket/tank*⟩ gotear, perder*
(RPI), salirse* (Chi, Méx); ⟨*shoes/tent*⟩ dejar pasar
el agua; ⟨*faucet*⟩ gotear; ⟨*pen*⟩ perder* tinta;
the roof is ~ing hay una gotera/hay goteras en el
techo **(b)** (escape) ⟨*liquid*⟩ escaparse
■ **~** *vt* **(a)** ⟨*liquid/gas*⟩ perder*, botar (AmL exc RPI)
(b) ⟨*information*⟩ filtrar

leak² *n* **(a)** (in bucket, boat, pipe) agujero *m*; (in
roof) gotera *f* **(b)** (escaping liquid, gas) escape *m* **(c)**
(of information) filtración *f*

leakage /'liːkɪdʒ/ *n* escape *m*

leaky /'liːki/ *adj* **-kier, -kiest** agujereado

lean¹ /liːn/ (*past & past p* **leaned** *or* (BrE also)
leant /lent/) *vi* **(a)** (bend, incline): **she ~ed back
in her chair** se echó hacia atrás en la silla; **don't
~ out of the window** no te asomes por la ventana
(b) (support oneself) apoyarse; **to ~ AGAINST sth**
apoyarse CONTRA algo; **to ~ ON sth/sb** apoyarse
EN algo/algn
■ **~** *vt* apoyar

lean² *adj* **(a)** ⟨*person*⟩ delgado; ⟨*animal*⟩ flaco
(b) ⟨*meat*⟩ magro

leant /lent/ (BrE) *past & past p of* LEAN¹

leap¹ /liːp/ *vi/t* (*past & past p* **leaped** *or* (BrE
also) **leapt** /lept/) saltar

leap² *n* salto *m*, brinco *m*; **by ~s and bounds** a
pasos agigantados

leapfrog /'liːpfrɔːg ‖ 'liːpfrɒg/ *n*: **to play ~**
jugar* a la pídola, brincar* al burro (Méx), jugar*
al rango (RPI)

leapt /lept/ (BrE) *past & past p of* LEAP¹

leap year *n* año *m* bisiesto

learn /lɜrn ‖ lɜːn/ (*past & past p* **learned** *or*
(BrE also) **learnt**) *vt* ☐1 **(a)** (gain knowledge of)
aprender; **to ~ to + INF** aprender A + INF **(b)**
(memorize) aprender de memoria ☐2 (become
informed about) enterarse de
■ **~** *vi* ☐1 (gain knowledge) aprender ☐2 (become
informed) **to ~ ABOUT** *o* **OF sth** enterarse DE algo

learned /'lɜrnəd ‖ 'lɜːnɪd/ *adj* docto

learner /'lɜrnər ‖ 'lɜːnə(r)/ *n*: **he's a fast/slow
~** aprende con mucha rapidez/tiene dificultades
de aprendizaje; (*before n*) **~ (driver)** (esp BrE)
persona que está aprendiendo a conducir

learning /'lɜrnɪŋ ‖ 'lɜːnɪŋ/ *n* **(a)** (knowledge)
saber *m*; (education) educación *f*; **a man of ~** un
erudito **(b)** (act) aprendizaje *m*; (*before n*) **~
difficulties** dificultades *fpl* de aprendizaje

learnt /lɜrnt ‖ lɜːnt/ (BrE) *past & past p of*
LEARN

lease¹ /liːs/ *n* ≈ contrato *m* de arrendamiento;
(of real estate) ≈ usufructo *m*

lease² *vt* **(a)** **~ (out)** (grant use of) arrendar*;
⟨*real estate*⟩ dar* en usufructo **(b)** (hold under
lease) arrendar*; ⟨*real estate*⟩ tener* el usufructo
de

leasehold /'liːshəʊld/ *n* arrendamiento *m*

leash /liːʃ/ *n* correa *f*

least¹ /liːst/ *adj* ☐1 (*superl of* LITTLE¹ II): **she
has the ~ money** es quien menos dinero tiene
☐2 (smallest, slightest) más mínimo; **that's the ~ of
my worries** eso es lo que menos me preocupa

least² *pron* ☐1 (*superl of* LITTLE²): **to say the ~**
por no decir más; **it's the ~ I can do** es lo menos
que puedo hacer ☐2 (in adv phrases) **at least** por lo
menos; **in the least** en lo más mínimo

least³ *adv* ①(*superl of* LITTLE³): ~ of all you tú menos que nadie; **when you ~ expect it** cuando menos te lo esperas ②(*before adj, adv*) menos
leather /'leðər ‖ 'leðə(r)/ *n* cuero *m*, piel *f* (Esp, Méx)
leave¹ /liːv/ *n* ①(authorized absence) permiso *m*, licencia *f* (esp AmL); (Mil) licencia *f*; **to be/go on ~** estar*/salir* de permiso *or* (esp AmL) de licencia ②(permission) (frml) permiso *m* ③(departure) (frml): **to take ~ of sb** despedirse* de algn; **have you taken ~ of your senses?** ¿te has vuelto loco?
leave² (*past & past p* **left**) *vt* ①(a) (go away from): **she ~s home at 6** sale de casa a las 6; **I left her reading a book** la dejé leyendo un libro; **to ~ school** terminar el colegio; **she left home at the age of 17** se fue de casa a los 17 años (b) (withdraw from) ⟨*profession/organization/politics*⟩ dejar ②(abandon) dejar; **she left her husband for another man** dejó a su marido por otro (hombre) ③(a) (deposit in specified place) dejar; **to ~ sth FOR sb** dejarle algo A algn (b) (not take — deliberately) dejar; (— inadvertently) olvidarse de, dejarse (c) (not eat) ⟨*food*⟩ dejar ④(allow, cause to remain) dejar; **please ~ the window open** por favor dejen la ventana abierta ⑤(have as aftereffect) ⟨*stain/scar*⟩ dejar ⑥(a) (not attend to) dejar (b) (not disturb) dejar; **~ her to finish on her own** déjala terminar sola ⑦(entrust): **~ it to me!** ¡déjalo por mi cuenta!; **we must ~ nothing to chance** no debemos dejar nada (librado) al azar ⑧(after deduction, elimination): **6 from 10 ~s 4** si a 10 le quitamos 6, quedan 4; **there isn't much time left** no queda mucho tiempo ⑨(bequeath) **to ~ sth TO sb/sth** dejar(le) algo A algn/algo
■ **~** *vi* irse*, marcharse (esp Esp); **the train ~s at 5 o'clock** el tren sale a las 5 en punto
■ **leave behind** [*v + o + adv, v + adv + o*] (a) (not take or bring — deliberately) dejar; (— inadvertently) olvidarse de, dejarse (b) ⟨*worries/cares*⟩ dejar atrás
■ **leave on** [*v + o + adv, v + adv + o*] (a) ⟨*light/machine/television*⟩ dejar encendido *or* (AmL tb) prendido (b) (keep wearing) no quitarse
■ **leave out** ①[*v + o + adv, v + adv + o*] [*v + o + adv (+ prep + o)*] (a) (omit) omitir (b) (exclude) excluir* ②[*v + o + adv*] (a) (leave outside) dejar fuera *or* (esp AmL) afuera (b) (not put away) ⟨*clothes/toys*⟩ no guardar (c) (leave available) dejar preparado
■ **leave over** [*v + o + adv, v + adv + o*] (*usu pass*): **tomorrow we can eat what's left over** mañana podemos comer lo que sobre *or* quede
leaves /liːvz/ *pl of* LEAF
leaving /'liːvɪŋ/ *adj* (*before n*) ⟨*present*⟩ de despedida; **~ party** despedida *f*
Lebanese /ˌlebə'niːz/ *adj* libanés
Lebanon /'lebənɑːn ‖ 'lebənən/ *n* (el) Líbano
lecherous /'letʃərəs/ *adj* libidinoso
lectern /'lektərn ‖ 'lektɜːn/ *n* atril *m*; (in church) facistol *m*
lecture¹ /'lektʃər ‖ 'lektʃə(r)/ *n* (public address) conferencia *f*; (Educ) clase *f*; (*before n*) **~ theater** auditorio *m*
lecture² *vi* (Educ) dar* clase, dictar clase (AmL frml), hacer* clase (Chi)
■ **~** *vt* (scold) sermonear

lecturer /'lektʃərər ‖ 'lektʃərə(r)/ *n* (a) (speaker) conferenciante *mf*, conferencista *mf* (AmL) (b) (esp BrE Educ) profesor universitario, profesora universitaria *m,f*
led /led/ *past & past p of* LEAD²
LED *n* = **light-emitting diode**
ledge /ledʒ/ *n* (a) (on wall) cornisa *f*; (window ~) (exterior) alféizar *m* (de la ventana); (interior) repisa *f* (de la ventana) (b) (on cliff) saliente *m or f*
ledger /'ledʒər ‖ 'ledʒə(r)/ *n* libro *m* de contabilidad
leech /liːtʃ/ *n* sanguijuela *f*
leek /liːk/ *n* puerro *m*
leer /lɪr ‖ lɪə(r)/ *vi* **to ~ AT sb** lanzarle* una mirada lasciva A algn
leeway /'liːweɪ/ *n*: **I am given a lot of ~** me dan mucha libertad de acción; **there isn't much ~ in the budget** el presupuesto tiene poco margen de flexibilidad
left¹ /left/ *past & past p of* LEAVE²
left² *n* ①(a) (left side) izquierda *f*; **on the ~** a la izquierda; **to drive on the ~** manejar *or* (esp Esp) conducir* por la izquierda (b) (left turn): **to make** *o* (BrE) **take a ~** girar a la izquierda (c) (Sport) (hand) izquierda *f* ②(Pol) **the ~** la izquierda
left³ *adj* (*before n*) izquierdo
left⁴ *adv* a *or* hacia la izquierda
left: **~-hand** *adj* (*before n*) de la izquierda; **on the ~-hand side** a mano izquierda; **~-handed** /ˌleft'hændəd ‖ ˌleft'hændɪd/ *adj* ⟨*person*⟩ zurdo; ⟨*tool*⟩ para zurdos; **~-luggage** (office) /ˌleft'lʌgɪdʒ/ *n* (BrE) consigna *f*; **~over** *adj* (*before n*) sobrante; **~overs** /'leftˌəʊvərz ‖ 'leftˌəʊvəz/ *pl n* sobras *fpl*; **~ wing** *n* (a) (Pol) (+ *sing or pl vb*) (ala *f*); (Sport) ala *f*; izquierda *f*; **~-wing** /'leftwɪŋ/ *adj* (Pol) izquierdista; **~-winger** /'leftwɪŋər ‖ 'leftwɪŋə(r)/ *n* (Pol) izquierdista *mf*
leg /leg/ *n* ①(Anat) (of person) pierna *f*; (of animal, bird) pata *f*; **to pull sb's ~** (colloq) tomarle el pelo a algn (fam) ②(a) (Culin) (of lamb, pork) pierna *f*; (of chicken) pata *f*, muslo *m* (b) (Clothing) pierna *f* (c) (of chair, table) pata *f* ③(stage — of competition, race) manga *f*; (— of journey) etapa *f*
legacy /'legəsi/ *n* (*pl* **-cies**) legado *m*
legal /'liːgəl/ *adj* ①(a) (allowed) legal; ⟨*tackle/move*⟩ reglamentario (b) (founded upon law) ⟨*contract/requirement*⟩ legal ②(relating to legal system, profession) (*before n*) jurídico; **we will be forced to take ~ action** nos veremos obligados a poner el asunto en manos de nuestro(s) abogado(s)
legal holiday *n* (AmE) día *m* festivo oficial, feriado *m* oficial (esp AmL)
legalization /ˌliːgələ'zeɪʃən ‖ ˌliːgəlaɪ'zeɪʃən/ *n* legalización *f*
legalize /'liːgəlaɪz/ *vt* legalizar*
legally /'liːgəli/ *adv* legalmente
legal tender *n* moneda *f* de curso legal
legend /'ledʒənd/ *n* leyenda *f*
legendary /'ledʒənderi ‖ 'ledʒəndri/ *adj* legendario
leggings /'legɪŋz/ *pl n* (a) (pants, trousers) leggings *mpl*, mallas *fpl*, calzas *fpl* (RPI) (b) (for lower leg) polainas *fpl*
legible /'ledʒəbəl/ *adj* legible

legion /'liːdʒən/ n legión f

legionnaire /'liːdʒə'neɪr/ n legionario m; ~'s **disease** legionela f

legislate /'ledʒəsleɪt ‖ 'ledʒɪsleɪt/ vi legislar

legislation /ledʒəs'leɪʃən/ n legislación f

legislative /'ledʒəsleɪtɪv ‖ 'ledʒɪslətɪv/ adj (before n) legislativo

legislator /'ledʒəsleɪtər ‖ 'ledʒɪsleɪtə(r)/ n legislador, -dora m,f

legislature /'ledʒəsleɪtʃər ‖ 'ledʒɪsleɪtʃə(r)/ n asamblea f legislativa

legitimate /lɪ'dʒɪtəmət ‖ lɪ'dʒɪtɪmət/ adj legítimo

legitimize /lɪ'dʒɪtəmaɪz/ vt legitimar

legroom /'legruːm, -rʊm/ n espacio m para las piernas

leisure /'liːʒər ‖ 'leʒə(r)/ n tiempo m libre; **read it at your** ~ léalo cuando le venga bien; (before n) ⟨activity⟩ de tiempo libre; ~ **center** (AmE) centro m recreativo; ~ **centre** (BrE) centro m deportivo

leisurely /'liːʒərli ‖ 'leʒəli/ adj lento, pausado; **at a** ~ **pace** sin prisas

lemon /'lemən/ n **(a)** (fruit) limón m, limón m francés (Méx, Ven); (before n) ~ **squeezer** (BrE) exprimelimones m, exprimidor m; ~ **tea** té m con limón **(b)** ~ **(tree)** limonero m **(c)** (color) amarillo m limón; (before n) amarillo limón adj inv

lemonade /lemə'neɪd/ n **(a)** (with fresh lemons) limonada f **(b)** (fizzy drink) (BrE) (bebida f) gaseosa f

lemon cheese, lemon curd n crema f de limón (en conserva)

lend /lend/ vt (past & past p **lent**) prestar; **this** ~**s an air of mystery to the scene** esto le da un aire de misterio a la escena

lender /'lendər ‖ 'lendə(r)/ n (institution) entidad f crediticia; (person) prestamista mf

length /leŋθ/ n **1 (a)** (of line, surface) longitud f; (of sleeve, coat) largo m; **it's 5m in** ~ mide 5 metros de largo; **he traveled the** ~ **and breadth of the country** viajó a lo largo y (a lo) ancho del país; **he'd go to any** ~**s to get what he wants** es capaz de hacer cualquier cosa con tal de obtener lo que se propone **(b)** (of book, list) extensión f **2 (a)** (duration) (of movie, play) duración f; **after a considerable** ~ **of time** después de mucho tiempo **(b) at length** (finally) finalmente; (for a long time) extensamente; (in detail) detenidamente; **to talk at** ~ hablar largo y tendido **3** (section — of wood, pipe) trozo m; (— of river, road) tramo m **4 (a)** (in swimming) largo m **(b)** (in horse, dog racing) cuerpo m; (in rowing) largo m

lengthen /'leŋθən/ vt ⟨skirt/novel⟩ alargar*; ⟨line/visit⟩ alargar*

lengthwise /'leŋθwaɪz/, (esp BrE)
lengthways /-weɪz/ adv a lo largo

lengthy /'leŋθi/ adj **-thier -thiest** (long) largo; (tedious) largo y pesado

lenient /'liːniənt/ adj ⟨attitude/view⟩ indulgente; ⟨sentence⟩ poco severo

lens /lenz/ n (pl **lenses**) **(a)** (Opt) lente f **(b)** (for magnifying) lupa f **(c)** (in spectacles) cristal m **(d)** ▶ CONTACT LENS **(e)** (Phot) lente f

lent /lent/ past & past p of LEND

Lent /lent/ n Cuaresma f

lentil /'lentl/ n lenteja f

Leo /'liːəʊ/ n (pl **-os**) **(a)** (sign) (no art) Leo **(b)** (person) Leo or leo mf

leopard /'lepərd ‖ 'lepəd/ n leopardo m

leotard /'liːətɑːrd ‖ 'liːətɑːd/ n malla f

leper /'lepər ‖ 'lepə(r)/ n leproso, -sa m,f

leprosy /'leprəsi/ n lepra f

lesbian /'lezbiən/ n lesbiana f

lesion /'liːʒən/ n lesión f

less¹ /les/ adj (comp of LITTLE¹ II) menos; ~ **and** ~ **money** cada vez menos dinero

less² pron (comp of LITTLE²) menos; **a sum of** ~ **than $1,000** una suma inferior a los 1.000 dólares

less³ adv (comp of LITTLE³) menos; **the situation is no** ~ **serious than it was** la situación sigue siendo tan grave como antes

-less /ləs ‖ lɪs/ suff sin; **hat**~ sin sombrero

lessen /'lesn/ vt ⟨pain⟩ aliviar; ⟨cost/risk⟩ reducir*
■ ~ vi ⟨noise⟩ disminuir*; ⟨pain⟩ aliviarse; ⟨interest⟩ decrecer*

lesser /'lesər ‖ 'lesə(r)/ adj (before n) menor; **to a** ~ **extent** en menor grado

lesson /'lesn/ n **1** (Educ) **(a)** (class) clase f **(b)** (in textbook) lección f **2** (from experience) lección f; **to learn one's** ~ aprender la lección

lest /lest/ conj (liter) no sea que (+ subj); ~ **we forget** para que no olvidemos

let /let/ (pres p **letting**; past & past p **let**) vt **1** (no pass) **(a)** (allow to) dejar; **he** ~ **his hair grow** se dejó crecer el pelo; ~ **me help you** deja que te ayude; ~ **me see** ¿a ver?; **don't** ~ **me catch you here again!** ¡que no te vuelva a pescar por aquí! **(b)** (cause to, make): ~ **me know if there are any problems** avísame si hay algún problema; **he** ~ **it be known that ...** hizo saber que ... **(c)** to ~ **go** soltar*; ~ **go of my hand!** ¡suéltame la mano!; **to** ~ **oneself go** (enjoy oneself) soltarse*; (neglect oneself) abandonarse **2** (+ adv compl): **to** ~ **sth/sb by** o **past** dejar pasar algo/a algn; **she** ~ **herself into the house** abrió la puerta y entró en la casa **3** [Used to form 1st pers pl imperative] ~'s **go** vamos, vámonos; ~'s **ask Chris** vamos a preguntarle a Chris, preguntémosle a Chris; **don't** ~'s o ~'s **not argue** no discutamos; ~ **us pray** (frml) oremos **4** [Used to form 3rd pers imperative, gen translated by QUE + SUBJ in Spanish] ~ **that be a lesson to you** que te sirva de lección; **just** ~ **them try!** ¡que se atrevan! **5** (rent) (esp BrE) alquilar; **❾ to let** se alquila
■ **let down** [v + o + adv, v + adv + o] **1 (a)** (lower) ⟨rope/bucket⟩ bajar **(b)** (lengthen) ⟨skirt⟩ alargar*; (lower) ⟨hem⟩ bajar, sacar **(c)** ⟨tire/balloon⟩ desinflar **2** (disappoint) fallar; **her spelling** ~**s her down** su ortografía no le hace justicia a su trabajo
■ **let in** [v + o + adv, v + adv + o] dejar entrar
■ **let off**
I 1 (a) [v + o + adv] (forgive, not punish) perdonar; **she was** ~ **off with a reprimand** solo le hicieron una amonestación **(b)** [v + o + adv] [v + o + prep + o] (excuse from) perdonar
2 [v + o + adv] (allow to go) dejar salir

II [*v* + *o* + *adv*, *v* + *adv* + *o*] ⟨*fireworks*⟩ hacer* estallar; ⟨*rocket*/*cracker*⟩ tirar

■ **let on** [*v* + *adv*] [*v* + *adv* + *o*]: **you mustn't ~ on about this to Jim** no le vayas a decir nada de esto a Jim; **don't ~ on (that) you know me!** no digas que me conoces

■ **let out**
I [*v* + *o* + *adv*, *v* + *adv* + *o*] [1] (disclose) ⟨*secret*⟩ revelar
[2] (rent out) (esp BrE) alquilar
[3] (make wider) ⟨*skirt*/*dress*⟩ ensanchar, agrandar
II [*v* + *o* + *adv*, *v* + *adv* + *o*] [*v* + *o* + *adv* (+ *prep* + *o*)] (allow to leave) dejar salir; **someone ~ the air out of my tires** alguien me desinfló los neumáticos
III [*v* + *adv* + *o*] ⟨*scream*/*yell*⟩ soltar*

■ **let up** [*v* + *adv*] «*wind*/*storm*» amainar; «*pressure*/*work*» disminuir*

letdown /'letdaʊn/ *n* decepción *f*

lethal /'liːθəl/ *adj* mortal, letal; ⟨*weapon*⟩ mortífero

lethargic /lə'θɑːrdʒɪk ‖lɪ'θɑːdʒɪk/ *adj* aletargado

let's /lets/ (= **let us**) ▶ LET 3

letter /'letər ‖'letə(r)/ *n* [1] (written message) carta *f* [2] (of alphabet) letra *f*

letter: ~ bomb *n* carta *f* bomba; **~ box** *n* buzón *m*

lettuce /'letəs ‖'letɪs/ *n* lechuga *f*

let-up /'letʌp/ *n* interrupción *f*

leukemia, (esp BrE) **leukaemia** /luː'kiːmiə/ *n* leucemia *f*

level[1] /'levəl/ *n* nivel *m*; **at eye ~** a la altura de los ojos; **a high-~ meeting** una reunión de *or* a alto nivel

level[2] *adj* [1] ⟨*ground*/*surface*⟩ plano, llano; **a ~ spoonful** una cucharada rasa; **to do one's ~ best** hacer* todo lo posible [2] **(a)** (at same height) **to be ~ (WITH sth)** estar* al nivel (DE algo) **(b)** (abreast, equal): **the two teams were ~ at half-time** al medio tiempo los dos equipos iban empatados; **to draw ~ with sb** (in a race) alcanzar* a algn [3] (unemotional, calm) desapasionado

level[3], (BrE) **-ll-** *vt* [1] **(a)** (make flat) ⟨*ground*/*surface*⟩ nivelar **(b)** (raze) ⟨*building*/*town*⟩ arrasar [2] (make equal) igualar [3] (direct) **to ~ sth AT sb/sth** ⟨*weapon*⟩ apuntarle A algn/A algo CON algo; **to ~ an accusation at sb** acusar a algn
■ ~ *vi* (be honest) (colloq) **to ~ WITH sb** ser* franco CON algn

■ **level off** [*v* + *adv*] **(a)** «*aircraft*» nivelarse, enderezarse* **(b)** «*prices*/*growth*/*inflation*» estabilizarse*

level: ~ crossing *n* (BrE) paso *m* a nivel, crucero *m* (Méx); **~-headed** /'levəl'hedəd ‖,levəl'hedɪd/ *adj* sensato

lever[1] /'levər ‖'liːvə(r)/ *n* palanca *f*

lever[2] *vt* (+ *adv compl*): **to ~ sth open** abrir* algo haciendo palanca

levy[1] /'levi/ *vt* **levies, levying, levied (a)** ⟨*tax*/*duty*⟩ (impose) imponer*; (collect) recaudar **(b)** ⟨*fee*/*charge*⟩ cobrar **(c)** ⟨*fine*⟩ imponer*

levy[2] *n* (*pl* **levies**) **(a)** (raising of tax, contributions): **the strike was funded by a ~ on all members** la huelga se financió mediante el cobro de una cuota a todos los miembros **(b)** (tax) impuesto *m*

lewd /luːd ‖ljuːd/ *adj* **-er, -est** lascivo

liability /laɪə'bɪləti/ *n* (*pl* **-ties**) [1] (responsibility) responsabilidad *f* [2] **liabilities** *pl* (debt) (Fin) pasivo *m* [3] (disadvantage) (*no pl*): **she's a positive ~** es un verdadero lastre; **the car turned out to be a ~** el coche terminó dándonos más problemas que otra cosa

liable /'laɪəbəl/ *adj* (*pred*) [1] (responsible) responsable; **to be ~ FOR sth** ser* responsable DE algo [2] (likely): **I'm ~ to forget** es probable que me olvide; **the earlier model was ~ to overheat** el modelo anterior tenía tendencia a recalentarse

liaise /li'eɪz/ *vi* (WITH sb) actuar* de enlace (CON algn); **the departments will ~ closely** los departamentos mantendrán un estrecho contacto

liaison /li'eɪzɑːn ‖li'eɪzɒn/ *n* [1] (coordination) enlace *m* [2] (affair) (liter) affaire *m*

liar /'laɪər ‖'laɪə(r)/ *n* mentiroso, -sa *m,f*

libel[1] /'laɪbəl/ *n* (defamation) difamación *f*; (where a crime is implied) calumnia *f*

libel[2] *vt*, (BrE) **-ll-** (defame) difamar; (where a crime is implied) calumniar

liberal[1] /'lɪbərəl/ *adj* [1] **(a)** (tolerant) ⟨*ideas*⟩ liberal; ⟨*interpretation*⟩ libre **(b) Liberal** (Pol) del Partido Liberal; **L~ Democrat** (in UK) demócrata *mf* liberal [2] (generous) generoso

liberal[2] *n* **(a)** (progressive thinker) liberal *mf* **(b) Liberal** (party member) liberal *mf*

liberalism /'lɪbərəlɪzəm/ *n* liberalismo *m*

liberalize /'lɪbərəlaɪz/ *vt* liberalizar*

liberally /'lɪbərəli/ *adv* **(a)** (generously) generosamente **(b)** (not strictly) libremente

liberate /'lɪbəreɪt/ *vt* liberar

liberation /'lɪbə'reɪʃən/ *n* liberación *f*

Liberia /laɪ'bɪriə ‖laɪ'bɪəriə/ *n* Liberia *f*

Liberian /laɪ'bɪriən ‖laɪ'bɪəriən/ *adj* liberiano

liberty /'lɪbərti ‖'lɪbəti/ *n* (*pl* **-ties**) libertad *f*; **I'm not at ~ to tell you** no se lo puedo decir; **to take the ~ of -ING** (esp BrE) tomarse la libertad DE + INF

Libra /'liːbrə, 'laɪbrə ‖'liːbrə/ *n* **(a)** (sign) (*no art*) Libra **(b)** (person) Libra *or* libra *mf*

librarian /laɪ'breriən ‖laɪ'breəriən/ *n* bibliotecario, -ria *m,f*

library /'laɪbreri ‖'laɪbrəri/ *n* (*pl* **-ries**) biblioteca *f*

libretto /lə'bretəʊ ‖lɪ'bretəʊ/ *n* (*pl* **-tos** *or* **-ti** /-tiː/) libreto *m*

Libya /'lɪbiə/ *n* Libia *f*

Libyan /'lɪbiən/ *adj* libio

lice /laɪs/ *pl of* LOUSE

license[1], (BrE) **licence** /'laɪsns/ *n* [1] **(a)** (permit) permiso *m*; **import**/**export ~** permiso de importación/exportación; (*before n*) **~ number** (AmE Auto) número *m* de matrícula *or* (CS) de patente; **~ plate** matrícula *f*, placa *f* (AmL), patente *f* (CS), chapa *f* (RPl) **(b)** ▶ DRIVER'S LICENSE [2] **(a)** (freedom): **poetic ~** licencia *f* poética **(b)** (excessive freedom) (frml) libertinaje *m*

license[2] /'laɪsns/ *vt* otorgarle* un permiso a

licensed /'laɪsnst/ *adj* ⟨*practitioner*⟩ autorizado para ejercer; ⟨*premises*⟩ (BrE) autorizado para vender bebidas alcohólicas

licentious /laɪ'sentʃəs ‖laɪ'senʃəs/ *adj* licencioso

lichen /'laɪkən, 'lɪtʃən/ *n* liquen *m*

lick /lɪk/ vt lamer; ⟨stamp⟩ pasarle la lengua a

licorice, (BrE) **liquorice** /'lɪkərɪʃ, -ɪs/ n regaliz f, orozuz m

lid /lɪd/ n **1** (of container) tapa f **2** (eye ∼) párpado m

lie¹ /laɪ/ n (untruth) mentira f; **to tell** ∼**s** decir* mentiras, mentir*

lie² vi

I (3rd pers sing pres **lies**; pres p **lying**; past & past p **lied**) (tell untruths) mentir*

II (3rd pers sing pres **lies**; pres p **lying**; past **lay**; past p **lain**) **1** (a) (lie down) echarse, tenderse* (b) (be in lying position) estar* tendido; **I lay awake for hours** estuve horas sin poder dormir (c) (be buried) yacer* (liter); **◉ here lies John Brown** aquí yacen los restos de John Brown **2** (be) «object» estar*; **the snow lay two feet deep** la nieve tenía dos pies de espesor **3** (be located) «building/city» encontrarse*; **a group of islands lying off the west coast** un conjunto de islas situadas cerca de la costa occidental **4** «problem/difference» radicar*; «answer» estar*

∎ **lie down** [v + adv] (a) (adopt lying position) echarse, tenderse* (b) (be lying) estar* tendido

lie detector n detector m de mentiras

lieu /lu: ‖lju:/ n (frml): **in** ∼ **of** en lugar de, en vez de; **time off in** ∼ horas fpl/días mpl libres a cambio

lieutenant /lu:'tenənt ‖lef'tenənt/ n (a) (in navy) teniente mf de navío, teniente mf primero (en Chi) (b) (in other services) teniente mf

life /laɪf/ n (pl **lives**) **1** vida f; **animal/plant** ∼ vida animal/vegetal; **in later** ∼ más tarde or más adelante; **it brings the history of this period to** ∼ hace cobrar vida a este período de la historia; **to bring sb back to** ∼ resucitar a algn; **to come to** ∼ «party» animarse; «puppet» cobrar vida; **he was fighting for his life** se debatía entre la vida y la muerte; **to have the time of one's** ∼ divertirse* como nunca; **run for your lives!** ¡sálvese quien pueda!; **to save sb's** ∼ salvarle la vida a algn; **to be the** ∼ o (esp BrE) **the** ∼ **and soul of the party** ser* el alma de la fiesta; **to live the** ∼ **of Riley** darse* la gran vida; **to take one's** ∼ **in one's hands** jugarse* la vida; (before n) ⟨member/president⟩ vitalicio; **his** ∼ **story** la historia de su vida **2** (duration — of battery) duración f; (— of agreement) vigencia f **3** (imprisonment) (colloq) cadena f perpetua

life: ∼ **assurance** n (BrE) ▶ INSURANCE; ∼ **belt** n (BrE) salvavidas m; ∼**boat** n (on ship) bote m salvavidas, (shore-based) lancha f de salvamento; ∼ **buoy** n salvavidas m; ∼ **cycle** n ciclo m vital; ∼**guard** n salvavidas mf, socorrista mf; ∼ **insurance** n seguro m de vida; ∼ **jacket** n chaleco m salvavidas

lifeless /'laɪfləs ‖'laɪflɪs/ adj (dead) sin vida, inánime (frml), exánime (liter); (unconscious) inerte

life: ∼**like** adj verosímil; ∼**line** n (rope) cuerda

f de salvamento; **his letters were my** ∼**line** sus cartas eran lo único que me mantenía viva; ∼**long** adj (before n): **a** ∼**long friend** un amigo de toda la vida; ∼ **preserver** /prɪ'zɜ:rvər ‖prɪ'zɜ:və(r)/ n (AmE) (a) ▶ LIFE BUOY (b) ▶ LIFE JACKET; ∼ **raft** n balsa f salvavidas; ∼ **ring** n (AmE) salvavidas m; ∼**saver** /'laɪf,seɪvər ‖'laɪf,seɪvə(r)/ n (a) ▶ LIFEGUARD (b) (from bad situation) salvación f; ∼**-saving** adj (before n) que salva vidas; ∼**-size** /'laɪf'saɪz/, ∼**-sized** /-d/ adj (de) tamaño natural; ∼ **span** n (of living creature) vida f; (of project) duración f; (of equipment) vida f útil; ∼**style** n estilo m de vida; ∼**time** n vida f; **the chance of a** ∼**time** la oportunidad de su (or mi etc) vida; (before n) ⟨appointment/post⟩ vitalicio; ∼**time guarantee** garantía f para toda la vida; ∼ **vest** n (AmE) chaleco m salvavidas

lift¹ /lɪft/ n **1** (boost) impulso m **2** (ride): **can I give you a** ∼? ¿quieres que te lleve or (Per fam) jale?, ¿quieres que te dé un aventón (Méx) or (Col fam) una palomita? **3** (elevator) (BrE) ascensor m

lift² vt **1** (raise) levantar **2** (end) ⟨ban/siege⟩ levantar

∎ ∼ vi (a) (rise) «curtain» levantarse (b) (clear) «mist» disiparse

∎ **lift off** [v + adv] «rocket» despegar*

∎ **lift up** [v + o + adv, v + adv + o] levantar

lift-off /'lɪftɔ:f ‖'lɪftɒf/ n (Aerosp) despegue m

ligament /'lɪgəmənt/ n ligamento m

ligature /'lɪgətʃʊr ‖'lɪgətʃə(r)/ n ligadura f

light¹ /laɪt/ n **1** luz f; **by the** ∼ **of the moon** a la luz de la luna; **to come to** ∼ salir* a la luz; **to see the** ∼ abrir* los ojos **2** (a) (source of light) luz f; (lamp) lámpara f; (before n) ∼ **switch** interruptor m (b) (of car, bicycle) luz f (c) (traffic ∼) semáforo m **3** (a) (aspect) (no pl): **to see sth/sb in a good/ bad/new** o **different** ∼ ver* algo/a algn con buenos/malos/otros ojos (b) **in the** ∼ **of** o (AmE also) **in** ∼ **of** (as prep) a la luz de, en vista de **4** (for igniting): **have you got a** ∼? ¿tienes fuego?; **to set** ∼ **to sth** prender fuego a algo

light² adj **-er, -est**

I **1** (not heavy) ligero, liviano (esp AmL); ⟨voice⟩ suave **2** (a) (Meteo) ⟨breeze/wind⟩ suave; ∼ **rain** llovizna f (b) (sparse): **the losses were fairly** ∼ las pérdidas fueron de poca consideración (c) (not strenuous) ⟨work/duties⟩ ligero, liviano (esp AmL) **3** (not serious) ⟨music/comedy/reading⟩ ligero; **to make** ∼ **of sth** quitarle or restarle importancia a algo

II (a) (pale) ⟨green/brown⟩ claro (b) (bright): **it gets** ∼ **very early these days** ahora amanece muy temprano; **it's already** ∼ ya es de día

light³ adv: **to travel** ∼ viajar con el mínimo de equipaje

light⁴ vt **1** (past & past p **lighted** or **lit**) (set alight) encender* **2** (past & past p **lit**) (illuminate) iluminar

∎ ∼ vi (past & past p **lighted** or **lit**) encenderse*

∎ **light up** (past & past p **lit**) **1** [v + adv] (a) «eyes/face» iluminarse (b) «smoker» encender*

---

un cigarrillo (*or* un puro *etc*) **2** [*v* + *o* + *adv*, *v* + *adv* + *o*] (a) ‹*street/square*› iluminar (b) ‹*cigar/pipe*› encender*

light: ~ **bulb** *n* ▶ BULB 2; ~ **cream** *n* (AmE) crema *f* líquida, nata *f* líquida (Esp); ~**-emitting diode** /'daɪəʊd/ *n* diodo *m* emisor de luz

lighten /'laɪtn̩/ *vt* **1** ‹*load/workload*› aligerar; ‹*responsibility/conscience*› descargar* **2** (a) ‹*room*› dar* más luz a; ‹*sky*› iluminar (b) ‹*color/hair*› aclarar
■ ~ *vi* **1** «*load/weight*» hacerse* más ligero *or* (esp AmL) liviano, aligerarse **2** «*sky*» despejarse; «*face*» iluminarse; «*atmosphere*» relajarse

lighter /'laɪtər ‖ 'laɪtə(r)/ *n* (cigarette ~) encendedor *m*, mechero *m* (Esp)

light: ~**-fingered** /'laɪt'fɪŋgərd ‖ ˌlaɪt'fɪŋgəd/ *adj* (colloq): **to be** ~**-fingered** tener* (la) mano larga (fam); ~**-hearted** /'laɪt'hɑːrtəd ‖ ˌlaɪt'hɑːtɪd/ *adj* alegre, desenfadado; ~**house** *n* faro *m*

lighting /'laɪtɪŋ/ *n* iluminación *f*; (on streets) alumbrado *m*

lightly /'laɪtli/ *adv* **1** (a) ‹*touch*› suavemente; ‹*snow*› ligeramente (b) ‹*grill/beat*› ligeramente **2** (a) (frivolously) a la ligera (b) (not severely): **they were let off** ~ los trataron con indulgencia

lightning¹ /'laɪtnɪŋ/ *n*: **a bolt of** ~ un relámpago; **a flash of** ~ un relámpago; **a streak of** ~ un rayo; **like greased** ~ como un relámpago; (*before n*) ~ **conductor** *o* **rod** pararrayos *m*

lightning² *adj* relámpago *adj inv*; **with** ~ **speed** como un rayo

lightweight¹ /'laɪtweɪt/ *adj* ligero, liviano (esp AmL); ‹*writer/performance*› de poco peso

lightweight² *n* (in boxing, wrestling) peso *m* ligero; (minor figure) persona *f* de poco peso

light year *n* año *m* luz

likable /'laɪkəbəl/ *adj* agradable, simpático

like¹ /laɪk/ *vt* **1** (enjoy, be fond of): **I** ~ **tennis** me gusta el tenis; **she** ~**s him, but she doesn't love him** le resulta simpático pero no lo quiere; **do as *o* what you** ~ haz lo que quieras; **I** ~ **dancing** me gusta bailar; **I don't** ~ **to mention it, but ...** no me gusta (tener que) decírtelo pero ...
2 (in requests, wishes) querer*; **we would just** ~ **to say how grateful we are** queríamos decirle lo agradecidos que estamos; **would you** ~ **a cup of tea?** ¿quieres una taza de té?
■ ~ *vi* querer*; **if you** ~ si quieres

like² *n* **1** (sth liked): **her/his** ~**s and dislikes** sus preferencias **2** (similar thing, person) **the** ~: **judges, lawyers and the** ~ jueces, abogados y (otra) gente por el estilo; **I've never heard the** ~ **(of this)** nunca he oído cosa igual

like³ *adj* (dated *or* frml) parecido

like⁴ *prep* **1** (a) (similar to) como; **what's she** ~? ¿cómo es?; **she's very** ~ **her mother** se parece mucho a su madre (b) (typical of): **that's not** ~ **her** es muy raro en ella; **it's just** ~ **you to think of food** ¡típico! *or* ¡cuándo no! ¡tú pensando en comida! **2** (indicating manner): ~ **this/that** así; **to run** ~ **mad** correr como un loco **3** (such as, for example) como

like⁵ *conj* (crit) (a) (as if): **she looks** ~ **she knows**

what she's doing parece que sabe lo que hace; **they stared at him** ~ **he was crazy** se quedaron mirándolo como si estuviera loco (b) (as, in same way) como

-like /laɪk/ *suff*: **prison~** parecido a una prisión; **snake~** ‹*appearance*› (como) de serpiente; ‹*movement*› serpenteante

likeable *adj* ▶ LIKABLE

likelihood /'laɪklihʊd/ *n* probabilidad *f*, posibilidad *f*; **there is every** ~ **that she'll agree** es muy probable que acepte

likely¹ /'laɪkli/ *adj* **-lier, -liest** (a) (probable) ‹*outcome/winner*› probable; **it's more than** ~ **that she's out** lo más seguro es que no esté; **a** ~ **story!** (iro) ¡cuéntame otra! (iró); **it is** ~ **to be a tough match** lo más probable es que sea un partido difícil (b) (promising): **she's the most** ~ **applicant** es la candidata con más posibilidades; **this is a** ~ **place to find a telephone** aquí tiene que haber un teléfono

likely² *adv*: **most** ~ **she'll forget** lo más probable es que se olvide; **not** ~! (colloq) ¡ni hablar! (fam)

liken /'laɪkən/ *vt* **to** ~ **sth/sb TO sth/sb** comparar algo/a algn CON *or* A algo/algn

likeness /'laɪknəs ‖ 'laɪknɪs/ *n* (a) (resemblance) parecido *m* (b) (referring to a portrait): **it's a good** ~ es un buen retrato

likewise /'laɪkwaɪz/ *adv* (a) (in the same way) asimismo (b) (the same): **to do** ~ hacer* lo mismo

liking /'laɪkɪŋ/ *n* (a) (fondness) ~ (**FOR sth**) afición *f* (A algo); **to take a** ~ **to sb/sth** tomarle *or* (esp Esp) cogerle* simpatía a algn/gusto a algo (b) (satisfaction) gusto *m*; **to be to sb's** ~ ser* del gusto de algn

lilac /'laɪlək/ *n* (a) ~ (**bush**) lila *f*, lilo *m*; (*before n*) ~ **flower** lila *f* (b) (color) lila *m*; (*before n*) lila *adj inv*

lilt /lɪlt/ *n* (of song, tune) cadencia *f*; **to speak with a** ~ hablar con un tono cantarín

lilting /'lɪltɪŋ/ *adj* ‹*voice*› cantarín, musical; ‹*melody*› cadencioso

lily /'lɪli/ *n* (*pl* **lilies**) (Bot) liliácea *f*; (white ~) azucena *f*, lirio *m* blanco

lily-of-the-valley /'lɪliəvðə'væli/ *n* (*pl* **lilies-of-the-valley**) lirio *m* de los valles, muguete *m*

limb /lɪm/ *n* (a) (Anat) miembro *m*; **to tear sb** ~ **from** ~ despedazar* a algn (b) (of tree) rama *f* (*principal*); **to go out on a** ~ aventurarse

limber up /'lɪmbər ‖ 'lɪmbə(r)/ [*v* + *adv*] hacer* ejercicios de calentamiento

lime /laɪm/ *n* **1** (calcium oxide) cal *f* **2** (a) (fruit) lima *f* (b) (tree) limero *m*, lima *f* (c) (color) verde *m* lima; (*before n*) verde lima *adj inv* **3** (linden) (BrE) tilo *m*

lime: ~**-green** /'laɪm'griːn/ *adj* (pred ~ **green**) verde lima *adj inv*; ~**light** *n*: **to be in the** ~**light** estar* en primer plano; **to steal the** ~**light** acaparar la atención del público

limerick /'lɪmərɪk/ *n*: *poema humorístico de cinco versos*

limestone /'laɪmstəʊn/ *n* (piedra *f*) caliza *f*

limit¹ /'lɪmət ‖ 'lɪmɪt/ *n* **1** (a) (boundary) límite ⋯⟐

m (b) (furthest extent): **she pushes herself to the ~** se esfuerza al máximo; **that's the ~!** (colloq) ¡es el colmo! (fam) **2** (restriction, maximum) límite *m*

limit² *vt* limitar; **to ~ oneself TO sth/-ING** limitarse A algo/+ INF

limitation /ˌlɪmə'teɪʃən ‖ ˌlɪmɪ'teɪʃən/ *n* limitación *f*

limited /'lɪmətəd ‖ 'lɪmɪtɪd/ *adj* (a) ⟨number/ experience/scope⟩ limitado (b) (AmE Transp) ⟨express/train/bus⟩ semi-directo (c) (Busn) ⟨liability⟩ limitado; **public ~ company** (BrE) sociedad *f* anónima

limitless /'lɪmətləs ‖ 'lɪmɪtlɪs/ *adj* ilimitado, sin límites

limousine /'lɪməziːn, lɪmə'ziːn/ *n* limusina *f*

limp¹ /lɪmp/ *vi* cojear, renguear (AmL)

limp² *n* cojera *f*, renguera *f* (AmL); **she walks with a ~** cojea *or* (AmL tb) renguea

limp³ *adj* ⟨handshake⟩ flojo; ⟨lettuce⟩ mustio; ⟨hair⟩ lacio y sin vida

limpet /'lɪmpət ‖ 'lɪmpɪt/ *n* lapa *f*

linden /'lɪndən/ *n* (AmE) tilo *m*

line¹ /laɪn/ *n* **1** (a) (mark, trace) línea *f*; (Math) recta *f*; **to be on the ~** (colloq) estar* en peligro, peligrar; (before n) **~ drawing** dibujo *m* lineal (b) (on face, palm) línea *f*; (wrinkle) arruga *f* **2** (a) (boundary, border) línea *f*; **the county/state ~** (AmE) (la línea de) la frontera del condado/estado (b) (Sport) línea *f*; (before n) **~ judge** juez *mf* de línea (c) (contour) línea *f* **3** (a) (cable, rope) cuerda *f*; (clothes o washing ~) cuerda (de tender la ropa); (fishing ~) sedal *m*; **power ~** cable *m* eléctrico (b) (Telec) línea *f*; **hold the ~, please** no cuelgue *or* (CS tb) no corte, por favor; **it's a very bad ~** se oye muy mal **4** (Transp) (a) (company, service) línea *f*; **shipping ~** línea de transportes marítimos (b) (Rail) línea *f*; (track) (BrE) vía *f* **5** (a) (path) línea *f*; **it was right in my ~ of vision** me obstruía la visual (b) (attitude, policy) postura *f*, línea *f*; **to take a hard ~ (with sb/on sth)** adoptar una postura *or* línea dura (con algn/ con respecto a algo) (c) (method, style): **~ of inquiry** línea *f* de investigación; **I was thinking of something along the ~s of ...** pensaba en algo del tipo de ... **6** (a) (row) fila *f*; (queue) (AmE) cola *f*; **to wait in ~** (AmE) hacer* cola; **to get in ~** (AmE) ponerse* en la cola; **to cut in ~** (AmE) colarse* (fam), brincarse* *or* saltarse la cola (Méx fam); **in/into ~ with sth**: **the new measures are in ~ with government policy** las nuevas medidas siguen la línea de la política del gobierno; **he needs to be brought into ~** hay que llamarlo al orden (b) (series) serie *f*; **he's the latest in a long ~ of radical leaders** es el último de una larga serie de dirigentes radicales (c) (succession) línea *f*; **he's next in ~ to the throne** es el siguiente en la línea de sucesión al trono **7** (Mil) línea *f* **8** (a) (of text) línea *f*, renglón *m*; (of poem) verso *m*; **to read between the ~s** leer* entre líneas (b) **lines** *pl* (Theat): **to learn one's ~s** aprenderse el papel; **he forgot his ~s** se olvidó de lo que le tocaba decir (c) (note): **to drop sb a ~** escribirle* a algn unas líneas

line² *vt* **1** (a) ⟨skirt/box⟩ forrar (b) (form lining along) cubrir* **2** (border): **the avenue is ~d with trees** la avenida está bordeada de árboles; **crowds ~d the route** cientos de personas estaban alineadas a ambos lados del camino

■ **line up 1** [*v + adv*] (form line, row) ponerse* en fila; (queue up) (AmE) hacer* cola **2** [*v + o + adv*, *v + adv + o*] (a) (form into line) ⟨soldiers/prisoners⟩ poner* en fila (b) (arrange): **we've a busy program ~d up for you** le tenemos preparada una apretada agenda (c) (align) alinear

lineage /'lɪniːdʒ/ *n* linaje *m*

linear /'lɪniər ‖ 'lɪniə(r)/ *adj* lineal

lined /laɪnd/ *adj* (a) ⟨paper⟩ con renglones *or* (Chi) reglones (b) ⟨jacket/boots/curtains⟩ forrado (c) (Tech) revestido (d) ⟨face/skin⟩ arrugado

linen /'lɪnən/ *n* **1** (cloth) hilo *m*, lino *m* **2** (bed ~) ropa *f* blanca *or* de cama; (table ~) mantelerías *fpl*; (before n) **~ basket** canasto *m or* cesto *m* de la ropa sucia

liner /'laɪnər ‖ 'laɪnə(r)/ *n* **1** (ship) buque *m* (de pasaje *or* pasajeros); (ocean ~) transatlántico *m* **2** (a) (lining) forro *m*; (dust)bin ~ (BrE) bolsa *f* de la basura (b) (of record) (AmE) funda *f*, carátula *f*

line: ~**sman** /'laɪnzmən/ *n* (pl **-men** /-mən/) (Sport) juez *m* de línea; ~**up** *n* (a) (Sport) alineación *f*; **the band's original ~up** la integración original del grupo (b) (of suspects) (AmE) rueda *f* de identificación *or* de sospechosos

linger /'lɪŋɡər ‖ 'lɪŋɡə(r)/ *vi* (a) (delay leaving) quedarse (un rato) (b) (on) ⟨aftertaste/smell⟩ persistir; ⟨tradition⟩ perdurar, sobrevivir (c) **lingering** *pres p* persistente, que no desaparece (d) (take one's time): **her eyes ~ed on the child** se quedó largo rato mirando al niño; **they ~ed over their coffee** se entretuvieron tomando el café

lingerie /'lɑːnʒəreɪ ‖ 'lænʒəri/ *n* lencería *f*

linguist /'lɪŋɡwəst ‖ 'lɪŋɡwɪst/ *n* lingüista *mf*

linguistic /lɪŋ'ɡwɪstɪk/ *adj* lingüístico

linguistics /lɪŋ'ɡwɪstɪks/ *n* (+ *sing vb*) lingüística *f*

lining /'laɪnɪŋ/ *n* forro *m*

link¹ /lɪŋk/ *n* **1** (a) (in chain) eslabón *m* (b) ▶ CUFF LINK **2** (a) (connection) conexión *f* (b) (tie, bond) vínculo *m*, lazo *m* (c) (Telec, Transp) conexión *f*, enlace *m*

link² *vt* (a) ⟨components⟩ unir; ⟨terminals⟩ conectar; **to ~ arms** tomarse *or* (esp Esp) cogerse* del brazo (b) ⟨buildings/towns⟩ unir, conectar (c) ⟨facts/events⟩ relacionar

■ **link up 1** [*v + adv*] conectar; ⟨spacecraft⟩ acoplarse **2** [*v + o + adv*, *v + adv + o*] conectar

links /lɪŋks/ *n* (pl **~**) (+ *sing o pl vb*) campo *m* de golf (esp a orillas del mar)

linkup /'lɪŋkʌp/ *n* (a) (connection) conexión *f*; (of spacecraft) acoplamiento *m* (b) (Rad, TV) conexión *f*, enlace *m*

linoleum /lɪ'nəʊliəm/ *n* linóleo *m*

linseed /'lɪnsiːd/ *n* linaza *f*; (before n) **~ oil** aceite *m* de linaza

lint /lɪnt/ *n* hilas *fpl*

lion /'laɪən/ *n* león *m*

lioness /'laɪənəs ‖ 'laɪənes/ *n* leona *f*

lion tamer /'teɪmər ‖ 'teɪmə(r)/ *n* domador, -dora *m,f* de leones

lip /lɪp/ *n* (a) (Anat) labio *m* (b) (of cup, tray) borde *m*

lip: ~ **gloss** n brillo m de labias; ~**read** (past & past p **-read** vi /-red/) leer* los labios; ~ **salve** n bálsamo m labial; ~ **service** n: he just pays ~ **service** to feminism es feminista de los dientes para afuera; ~**stick** n (a) (stick) lápiz m or barra f de labios, lápiz m labial (AmL), pintalabios m (Esp fam) (b) (substance) rouge m

liquefy /'lɪkwəfaɪ ‖'lɪkwɪfaɪ/ **-fies, -fying, -fied** vi licuarse*
■ ~ vt licuar*

liqueur /lɪ'kɜːr ‖lɪ'kjʊə(r)/ n licor m

liquid¹ /'lɪkwəd ‖'lɪkwɪd/ n líquido m

liquid² adj líquido

liquidation /ˌlɪkwə'deɪʃən ‖ˌlɪkwɪ'deɪʃən/ n liquidación f

liquid crystal display n pantalla f de cristal líquido

liquidize /'lɪkwədaɪz ‖'lɪkwɪdaɪz/ vt licuar*

liquidizer /'lɪkwədaɪzər ‖'lɪkwɪdaɪzə(r)/ n (BrE) licuadora f

liquor /'lɪkər ‖'lɪkə(r)/ n alcohol m, bebidas fpl alcohólicas; (before n) ~ **cabinet** (AmE) mueble-bar m

liquorice (BrE) ▶ LICORICE

liquor store n (AmE) ≈ tienda f de vinos y licores, botillería f (Chi)

Lisbon /'lɪzbən/ n Lisboa f

lisp¹ /lɪsp/ n ceceo m

lisp² vi cecear

list¹ /lɪst/ n lista f

list² vt (a) (enumerate) hacer* una lista de; (verbally) enumerar (b) ‹securities/stocks› cotizar*
■ ~ vi (Naut) escorar

listen /'lɪsn̩/ vi escuchar; to ~ TO sth/sb escuchar algo/a algn

listener /'lɪsnər ‖'lɪsnə(r)/ n (a) (Rad) oyente mf, radioyente mf (b) (in conversation): he's a good ~ es una persona que sabe escuchar

listing /'lɪstɪŋ/ n lista f; ~**s magazine** guía f de espectáculos, ≈guía f del ocio (en Esp)

listless /'lɪstləs ‖'lɪstlɪs/ adj (lacking enthusiasm) apático; (lacking energy) lánguido

lit /lɪt/ past & past p of LIGHT⁴

litany /'lɪtəni/ n (pl -nies) letanía f

liter, (BrE) **litre** /'liːtər ‖'liːtə(r)/ n litro m

literacy /'lɪtərəsi/ n alfabetismo m

literal /'lɪtərəl/ adj literal

literally /'lɪtərəli/ adv literalmente; I didn't mean it ~ no lo decía en sentido literal

literary /'lɪtəreri ‖'lɪtərəri/ adj literario

literate /'lɪtərət/ adj alfabetizado

literature /'lɪtərətʃʊr ‖'lɪtərətʃə(r)/ n (a) (art) literatura f (b) (promotional material) folletos mpl

lithe /laɪð/ adj lither, lithest ágil

lithograph /'lɪθəgræf ‖'lɪθəgrɑːf/ n litografía f

Lithuania /ˌlɪθjuˈeɪniə/ n Lituania f

Lithuanian /ˌlɪθjuˈeɪniən/ adj lituano

litigation /ˌlɪtəˈgeɪʃən ‖ˌlɪtɪ'geɪʃən/ n litigio m

litmus /'lɪtməs/: ~ **paper** n papel m (de) tornasol; ~ **test** n (Chem) prueba f de acidez or de tornasol

litre /'liːtər ‖'liːtə(r)/ n (BrE) ▶ LITER

litter¹ /'lɪtər ‖'lɪtə(r)/ n [1] (refuse) basura f [2] (offspring) (Zool) camada f, cría f [3] (for horses, cows) lecho m de paja; (for cats) arena f higiénica

litter² vt: newspapers ~ed the floor el suelo estaba cubierto de papeles; to be ~ed WITH sth estar* lleno DE algo

litter: ~ **bin** n (BrE) papelera f or (AmL tb) papelero m or (Col) caneca f; ~**bug** n: persona que tira basura en lugares públicos; ~ **lout** n (BrE) ▶ ~BUG

little¹ /'lɪtl/ adj
I (comp littler /'lɪtlər ‖'lɪtlə(r)/; superl littlest /'lɪtləst ‖'lɪtlɪst/) (small, young) pequeño, chico (esp AmL); a ~ while un ratito; my ~ sister/brother mi hermanita/hermanito
II (comp less; superl least) (a) (not much) poco; there is very ~ bread left queda muy poco pan (b) a little (some) un poco de

little² pron (comp less; superl least) (a) (not much) poco, -ca; ~ by ~ poco a poco (b) a little (some) un poco, algo

little³ adv (comp less; superl least) poco; ~ did he know that ... lo que menos se imaginaba era que ...; a little (somewhat) un poco; I'm feeling a ~ tired estoy algo or un poco cansado

live¹ /lɪv/ vi vivir; she ~d to be 100 llegó a cumplir 100 años; she had three months to ~ le quedaban tres meses de vida; where do you ~? ¿donde vives?; long ~ the king! ¡viva el rey!; ~ and let ~ (set phrase) vive y deja vivir a los demás
■ ~ vt vivir; she ~s a happy life lleva una vida feliz, vive feliz; to ~ life to the full vivir la vida al máximo
■ **live down** [v + o + adv, v + adv + o]: if they see you wearing that, you'll never ~ it down si te ven con eso no lo van a olvidar nunca
■ **live for** [v + prep + o]: she ~s for her work vive para su trabajo; I've nothing left to ~ for ya no tengo nada por lo que vivir
■ **live off** [v + prep + o] (a) (be supported by) ‹family/friends› vivir a costa de; ‹crime/the land› vivir de (b) (feed on) ‹fruits/seeds› alimentarse de
■ **live on** [1] [v + adv] «memory» seguir* presente; «tradition» seguir* existiendo [2] [v + prep + o] (a) (feed on) alimentarse de (b) (support oneself with): she ~s on $75 a week vive con 75 dólares a la semana
■ **live through** [v + prep + o] ‹war/experience› vivir
■ **live together** [v + adv] (a) (cohabit) vivir juntos (b) (coexist) convivir
■ **live up** [v + o + adv]: to ~ it up (colloq) darse* la gran vida (fam)
■ **live up to** [v + adv + prep + o]: it didn't ~ up to its reputation no estuvo a la altura de su reputación; they ~ up to their name hacen honor a su nombre

live² /laɪv/ adj [1] (alive) vivo [2] (of current interest) ‹issue› candente [3] (Rad, TV): the show was ~ el programa era en directo; the program is recorded before a ~ audience el programa se graba con público en la sala

live³ /laɪv/ adv ‹broadcast› en directo

live-in /'lɪv'ɪn/ adj (before n) ‹staff› residente; ‹nanny/maid› con cama, de planta (Méx), puertas adentro (Chi); she has a ~ lover su amante vive con ella

livelihood /'laɪvlɪhʊd/ n (no pl): farming is their ~ viven de la agricultura; **to earn one's ~** ganarse la vida

lively /'laɪvli/ adj -lier, -liest ‹place/debate› animado; ‹music› alegre; ‹account› vívido

liven up /'laɪvən/ **1** [v + adv] animarse **2** [v + o + adv, v + adv + o] animar

liver /'lɪvər ‖'lɪvə(r)/ n hígado m; (before n) ‹transplant› de hígado; **~ disease** enfermedad f del hígado

lives /laɪvz/ pl of LIFE

livestock /'laɪvstɑːk ‖'laɪvstɒk/ n (+ sing or pl vb) animales mpl (de cría); (cattle) ganado m

livid /'lɪvəd ‖'lɪvɪd/ adj **1** (furious) (colloq) furioso **2** ‹bruise› amoratado; ‹face› lívido

living¹ /'lɪvɪŋ/ n **1** (livelihood) (no pl): **to earn** o **make one's/a ~** ganarse la vida; **to work for a ~** trabajar para vivir; **what does he do for a ~?** ¿en qué trabaja? **2** (style of life) vida f; (before n) ‹space/area› destinado a vivienda; **~ standards** nivel m de vida

living² adj (before n) vivo

living room n sala f (de estar) , living m (esp AmS), salón m (esp Esp)

lizard /'lɪzərd ‖'lɪzəd/ n lagarto m; (wall ~) lagartija f

'll /l/ (a) = **will** (b) = **shall**

llama /'lɑːmə/ n llama f

LLB n = **Bachelor of Laws**

lo /ləʊ/ interj (arch or hum): **~ and behold** ¡y quién lo iba a decir!

load¹ /ləʊd/ n **1** (cargo, burden) carga f; **four ~s of washing** cuatro lavados or (Esp) coladas **2** (often pl) (colloq) (much, many) cantidad f, montón m (fam); **the play is a ~ of rubbish** la obra es una porquería (fam) **3** (Civil Eng) carga f; ❺ **maximum load 15 tons** peso máximo: 15 toneladas

load² vt/i cargar*

■ **load up 1** [v + o + adv, v + adv + o] cargar* **2** [v + adv] cargar*

loaded /'ləʊdəd ‖'ləʊdɪd/ adj (a) ‹vehicle/gun/ camera› cargado (b) (richly provided) (pred) **to be ~ WITH sth** estar* repleto DE algo (c) (weighted) ‹dice› cargado; ‹question› tendencioso

loaf¹ /ləʊf/ n (pl **loaves**): **a ~ (of bread)** un pan; (of French bread) una barra de pan, una flauta (CS); (baked in tin) un pan de molde

loaf² vi (colloq): **to ~ (around** o **about)** holgazanear

loan¹ /ləʊn/ n préstamo m

loan² vt prestar

loath /ləʊθ/ adj (pred) **to be ~ to + INF** resistirse A + INF

loathe /ləʊð/ vt odiar, detestar

loathsome /'ləʊðsəm/ adj repugnante

loaves /ləʊvz/ pl of LOAF¹

lob¹ /lɑːb ‖lɒb/ vt -bb- lanzar* por lo alto

lob² n globo m, lob m

lobby¹ /'lɑːbi ‖'lɒbi/ n (pl **-bies**) **1** (entrance hall) vestíbulo m; (in theater) foyer m **2** (pressure group) grupo m de presión

lobby² -bies, -bying, -bied vt ejercer* presión sobre

■ ~ vi **to ~ FOR sth** ejercer* presión para obtener algo

lobe /ləʊb/ n (ear~) lóbulo m (de la oreja)

lobster /'lɑːbstər ‖'lɒbstə(r)/ n langosta f, bogavante m (Esp)

local¹ /'ləʊkəl/ adj **1** ‹dialect/newspaper› local; ‹council/election› ≈municipal; **a ~ call** una llamada urbana; **he's a ~ man** es de aquí (or de allí) **2** (Med) ‹anesthetic› local; ‹infection› localizado

local² n (a) (inhabitant): **he's not a ~** no es de aquí (or de allí); **the ~s say it's true** los (vecinos) del lugar dicen que es verdad (b) (pub) (BrE colloq): **our ~** el bar de nuestro barrio (or de nuestra zona etc)

locale /ləʊˈkæl ‖ləʊˈkɑːl/ n escenario m

local government n ≈administración f municipal; (before n) ‹elections› ≈municipal

locality /ləʊˈkæləti/ n (pl **-ties**) localidad f

localization /ˌləʊkəlarˈzeɪʃən/ n localización f

localize /'ləʊkəlaɪz/ vt localizar*

locally /'ləʊkəli/ adv ‹live/work› en la zona

locate /'ləʊkeɪt ‖ləʊˈkeɪt/ vt **1** (find) ‹fault/ leak› localizar*, ubicar* (esp AmL) **2** (position) ‹building/business› situar*, ubicar* (esp AmL)

location /ləʊˈkeɪʃən/ n **1** (position) posición f, ubicación f (esp AmL) **2** (Cin) lugar m de filmación; **we were filming on ~ in Italy** estábamos rodando los exteriores en Italia

loch /lɑːk, lɑːx ‖lɒk, lɒx/ n lago m

lock¹ /lɑːk ‖lɒk/ n **1** (device) cerradura f, chapa f (AmL) **2** (on canal) esclusa f **3** (of hair) mechón m

lock² vt ‹door/car› cerrar* (con llave); **to ~ sb in a room** encerrar* a algn en una habitación

■ **lock in** [v + o + adv, v + adv + o] encerrar*

■ **lock out** [v + o + adv, v + adv + o]: **I ~ed myself out (of the house)** me quedé afuera sin llaves

■ **lock up** [v + o + adv, v + adv + o] (a) ‹valuables› guardar bajo llave; ‹person› encerrar* (b) ‹house/shop› cerrar* con llave

locker /'lɑːkər ‖'lɒkə(r)/ n armario m, locker m (AmL); (at bus, railway station) (casilla f de la) consigna f automática

locker room n (esp AmE) vestuario m

locket /'lɑːkət ‖'lɒkɪt/ n relicario m

lock: ~out n cierre m patronal, paro m patronal (AmL); **~smith** n cerrajero, -ra m,f

locomotive /ˌləʊkəˈməʊtɪv/ n locomotora f

locust /'ləʊkəst/ n langosta f

lode /ləʊd/ n veta f, filón m

lodge¹ /lɑːdʒ ‖lɒdʒ/ n **1** (a) (for gatekeeper) (BrE) casa f del guarda (b) (for porter) portería f (c) (on private estate) pabellón m (d) (at resort) (AmE) hotel m **2** (branch, meeting place) logia f

lodge² *vt* [1] ⟨*appeal*⟩ interponer*; ⟨*complaint*⟩ presentar [2] (deposit) depositar
■ ~ *vi* [1] (become stuck): **the bullet had ~d in his spine** la bala se le había alojado en la columna [2] (live as lodger) alojarse, hospedarse

lodger /ˈlɑːdʒər ‖ ˈlɒdʒə(r)/ *n* inquilino, -na *m,f* (*de una habitación en una casa particular*)

lodging /ˈlɑːdʒɪŋ ‖ ˈlɒdʒɪŋ/ *n* **(a)** (accommodations) alojamiento *m* **(b)** **lodgings** *pl* (rented): **to live in ~s** vivir en una habitación alquilada (*or* en una pensión *etc*)

loft /lɔːft ‖ lɒft/ *n* (BrE) desván *m*, altillo *m* (esp AmL), zarzo *m* (Col)

loftily /ˈlɔːftəli ‖ ˈlɒftɪli/ *adv* con altivez, altaneramente

lofty /ˈlɔːfti ‖ ˈlɒfti/ *adj* **-tier, -tiest (a)** (elevated) ⟨*ideals/sentiments*⟩ noble, elevado **(b)** (haughty) altivo, altanero **(c)** (high) (liter) alto, majestuoso (liter)

log¹ /lɔːg ‖ lɒg/ *n* [1] (wood) tronco *m*; (as fuel) leño *m*; **to sleep like a ~** dormir* como un tronco (fam) [2] (record) diario *m* [3] (Math) logaritmo *m*

log² **-gg-** *vt* ⟨*speed/position/time*⟩ registrar, anotar; ⟨*call*⟩ registrar
■ **log in, log on** [*v* + *adv*] (Comput) entrar (al sistema)
■ **log off, log out** [*v* + *adv*] (Comput) salir* (del sistema)

loganberry /ˈlɔːgən‚beri ‖ ˈlɒgənbəri/ *n* (*pl* **-ries**) frambuesa *f* de Logan

logarithm /ˈlɔːgərɪðəm ‖ ˈlɒgərɪðəm/ *n* logaritmo *m*

logbook /ˈlɔːgbʊk ‖ ˈlɒgbʊk/ *n* (register) diario *m*; (Naut) diario *m* de navegación *or* de a bordo; (Aviat) diario *m* de vuelo

loggerheads /ˈlɔːgərhedz ‖ ˈlɒgəhedz/ *pl n*: **they were constantly at ~** siempre estaban en desacuerdo

logic /ˈlɑːdʒɪk ‖ ˈlɒdʒɪk/ *n* lógica *f*

logical /ˈlɑːdʒɪkəl ‖ ˈlɒdʒɪkəl/ *adj* lógico

logistics /ləˈdʒɪstɪks/ *n* **(a)** (Mil) (+ *sing vb*) logística *f* **(b)** (practicalities) (+ *pl vb*) problemas *mpl* logísticos

logo /ˈləʊgəʊ, ˈlɑː- ‖ ˈləʊgəʊ/ *n* (*pl* **logos**) logo *m*

loin /lɔɪn/ *n* **(a)** (meat) lomo *m* **(b)** **loins** *pl* (Anat) (liter) entrañas *fpl* (liter)

loincloth /ˈlɔɪnklɔːθ ‖ ˈlɔɪnklɒθ/ *n* taparrabos *m*

loiter /ˈlɔɪtər ‖ ˈlɔɪtə(r)/ *vi* perder* el tiempo

lollipop /ˈlɑːlipɑːp ‖ ˈlɒlipɒp/ *n* piruleta *f or* (Esp) Chupa Chups®, chupachup(s) *m or* (Andes, Méx) paleta *f or* (RPl) chupetín *m or* (Col) colombina *f or* (Chi, Per) chupete *m*

lolly /ˈlɑːli ‖ ˈlɒli/ *n* (*pl* **-lies**) (BrE) (ice **~**) paleta *f* (helada) *or* (Esp) polo *m or* (RPl) palito *m or* (CS) chupete *m* helado

London /ˈlʌndən/ *n* Londres; (*before n*) londinense

lone /ləʊn/ *adj* solitario; ⟨*explorer/sailor*⟩ en solitario

loneliness /ˈləʊnlinəs ‖ ˈləʊnlinɪs/ *n* soledad *f*

lonely /ˈləʊnli/ *adj* **-lier, -liest (a)** (feeling alone): **to feel ~** sentirse* solo **(b)** (isolated) solitario, aislado

loner /ˈləʊnər ‖ ˈləʊnə(r)/ *n*: **she's a bit of a ~** le gusta estar sola

lonesome /ˈləʊnsəm/ *adj* (esp AmE) ▶ LONELY

long¹ /lɔːŋ ‖ lɒŋ/ *adj* **longer** /ˈlɔːŋgər ‖ ˈlɒŋgə(r)/, **longest** /ˈlɔːŋgəst ‖ ˈlɒŋgɪst/ [1] (in space) ⟨*distance/hair/list*⟩ largo; **how ~ do you want the skirt?** ¿cómo quieres la falda de larga?; **the wall is 200 m ~** el muro mide 200 m de largo; **the book is over 300 pages ~** el libro tiene más de 300 páginas [2] (in time) largo; **two months isn't ~ enough** dos meses no son suficientes; **she's been gone a ~ time** hace tiempo que se fue

long² *adv* **-er, -est** [1] (in time): **how ~ have you been living here?** ¿cuánto hace que vives aquí?; **people live ~er now** ahora la gente vive más (años); **it won't be ~ before they get here** no tardarán en llegar; **not ~ afterwards** poco después; **not ~ ago** no hace mucho [2] **(a)** (*in phrases*) **before long: you'll be an aunt before ~** dentro de poco serás tía; **for long: she wasn't gone for ~** no estuvo fuera mucho tiempo; **no longer, not any longer: I can't stand it any ~er** ya no aguanto más; **they no ~er live here** ya no viven aquí **(b)** **as long as, so long as** (*as conj*) (for the period) mientras ; (providing that) con tal de que (+ *subj*); **for as ~ as I can remember** desde que tengo memoria

long³ *vi* **to ~ to** + INF estar* deseando + INF
■ **long for** [*v* + *prep* + *o*] ⟨*mother/friend*⟩ echar de menos, extrañar (esp AmL); **she ~ed for Friday to arrive** estaba deseando que llegara el viernes

long-distance¹ /ˈlɔːŋˈdɪstəns ‚lɒŋˈdɪstəns/ *adj* ⟨*truck driver*⟩ que hace largos recorridos; ⟨*train*⟩ de largo recorrido; ⟨*race/runner*⟩ de fondo; **a ~ telephone call** una llamada de larga distancia, una conferencia (interurbana) (Esp)

long-distance² *adv* (esp AmE): **to call ~** hacer* una llamada de larga distancia, poner* una conferencia (Esp)

longevity /lɑːnˈdʒevəti ‖ lɒnˈdʒevəti/ *n* (frml) longevidad *f*

long: ~-haired /ˈlɔːŋˈheɪrd ‖ ˌlɒŋˈheəd/ *adj* de pelo largo; **~hand** *n*: **in ~hand** en escritura normal (*no en taquigrafía*); **~-haul** /ˈlɔːŋˈhɔːl ‖ ˌlɒŋˈhɔːl/ *adj* (*before n*) de larga distancia

longing /ˈlɔːŋɪŋ ‖ ˈlɒŋɪŋ/ *n* (nostalgia) añoranza *f*; (desire) vivo deseo *m*

longitude /ˈlɑːndʒətuːd ‖ ˈlɒŋgɪtjuːd, ˈlɒndʒɪtjuːd/ *n* longitud *f*

long: ~ johns /dʒɑːnz ‖ dʒɒnz/ *pl n* calzoncillos *mpl* largos; **~ jump** *n* salto *m* de longitud, salto *m* (en) largo (AmL); **~-lost** /ˈlɔːŋˈlɔːst ‖ ˈlɒŋˈlɒst/ *adj* (*before n*): **she had a ~-lost uncle in Australia** tenía un tío en Australia a quien había perdido de vista hacía mucho tiempo; **~-playing record** /ˈlɔːŋˈpleɪɪŋ ‖ ˈlɒŋ‚pleɪɪŋ/ *n* disco *m* de larga duración; **~-range** /ˈlɔːŋˈreɪndʒ ‖ ˈlɒŋreɪndʒ/ *adj* (*before n*) ⟨*missile*⟩ de largo alcance; ⟨*aircraft*⟩ para vuelos largos; **~-running** /ˈlɔːŋˈrʌnɪŋ ‖ ˈlɒŋˌrʌnɪŋ/ *adj* ⟨*musical/farce*⟩ que lleva tiempo en cartelera; ⟨*feud/controversy*⟩ que viene (or venía *etc*) de largo; **~shoreman** /ˈlɔːŋˈʃɔːrmən ‖ ˈlɒŋˌʃɔːmən/ *n* (*pl* **-men** /-mən/) (AmE) estibador *m*, changador *m* (RPl); **~sighted** /ˈlɔːŋˈsaɪtəd ‖ ˌlɒŋˈsaɪtɪd/ *adj* hipermétrope; **~-sleeved** /ˈlɔːŋˈsliːvd ‖ ˈlɒŋsliːvd/ *adj* de manga larga; **~standing** /ˈlɔːŋˈstændɪŋ

⋯⋰

ǁˌlɒŋˈstændɪŋ/ *adj* antiguo, que viene (*or* venía *etc*) de largo; ~-**suffering** /ˈlɔːŋˈsʌfərɪŋ/ adj sufrido; ~-**term** /ˈlɔːŋˈtɜːrm ǁˈlɒŋtɜːm/ *adj* (*usu before n*) **(a)** (in the future) ⟨*effects/benefits*⟩ a largo plazo **(b)** (for a long period) ⟨*solution*⟩ duradero; ⟨*effects*⟩ prolongado; ⟨*unemployment*⟩ de larga duración; ~ **wave** *n* onda *f* larga; ~-**winded** /ˈlɒŋˈwɪndəd ǁˌlɒŋˈwɪndɪd/ *adj* ⟨*speech/article*⟩ denso, prolijo

loo /luː/ *n* (BrE colloq) baño *m* (esp AmL), váter *m* (Esp fam)

look[1] /lʊk/ *n* ⎡1⎤ (glance) mirada *f*; **to have** *o* **take a ~ at** sth/sb echarle un vistazo a algo/algn ⎡2⎤ (search, examination): **have a ~ for my pipe, will you?** mira a ver si me encuentras la pipa, por favor; **do you mind if I take a ~ around?** ¿le importa si echo un vistazo? ⎡3⎤ **(a)** (expression) cara *f* **(b)** (appearance) aire *m*; **I don't like the ~ of his friend** no me gusta el aspecto *or* (fam) la pinta de su amigo **(c)** (Clothing) moda *f*, look *m* **(d) looks** *pl* (beauty) belleza *f*; **she was attracted by his good ~s** la atrajo lo guapo *or* (AmL tb) lo buen mozo que era

look[2] *vi*
I ⎡1⎤ (see, glance) mirar; **I ~ed around** (behind) me volví a mirar *or* miré hacia atrás; (all around) miré a mi alrededor; **to ~ away** apartar la vista; **to ~ down** (lower eyes) bajar la vista; (from tower, clifftop) mirar hacia abajo; **~ out (of) the window** mira por la ventana; **to ~ up** (raise eyes) levantar la vista; (toward ceiling, sky) mirar hacia arriba; **to ~ on the bright side of sth** ver* el lado bueno *or* positivo de algo ⎡2⎤ (search, investigate) mirar, buscar*
II (seem, appear): **he ~s well** tiene buena cara; **he ~s like his father** se parece a su padre; **I wanted to ~ my best** quería estar lo mejor posible

■ ~ *vt* mirar; **to ~ sb up and down** mirar a algn de arriba (a) abajo; **~ where you're going!** ¡mira por dónde vas!

■ **look after** [*v + prep + o*] **(a)** (care for) ⟨*invalid/child/animal*⟩ cuidar (de); ⟨*guest*⟩ atender* **(b)** (keep watch on) cuidar **(c)** (be responsible for) encargarse* de

■ **look ahead** [*v + adv*] (in space) mirar hacia adelante; (into the future) mirar hacia el futuro

■ **look at** [*v + prep + o*] ⎡1⎤ ⟨*person/picture*⟩ mirar ⎡2⎤ (consider) considerar; **~ at it from my point of view** míralo desde mi punto de vista; **the program ~s at university life** el programa enfoca la vida universitaria ⎡3⎤ (check) ⟨*patient/arm*⟩ examinar; ⟨*car/pump*⟩ revisar

■ **look back** [*v + adv*] **(a)** (in space) mirar (hacia) atrás **(b)** (into the past): **~ing back, it seems foolish** mirándolo ahora, parece una locura; **the program ~s back over the last 20 years** el programa es una retrospectiva de los últimos veinte años

■ **look down on** [*v + adv + prep + o*] mirar por encima del hombro a

■ **look for** [*v + prep + o*] buscar*

■ **look forward to** [*v + adv + prep + o*]: **I'm ~ing forward to my birthday** estoy deseando que llegue mi cumpleaños; **I'm really ~ing forward to the trip** tengo muchas ganas de hacer el viaje; **I ~ forward to hearing from you soon** (Corresp) esperando tener pronto noticias suyas

■ **look into** [*v + prep + o*] ⟨*matter/case*⟩ investigar*; ⟨*possibility*⟩ estudiar

■ **look on** [*v + adv*] mirar

■ **look out** [*v + adv*] **(a)** (be careful) tener* cuidado; **~ out!** ¡cuidado! **(b)** (overlook) **to ~ out on** *o* **over** sth dar* a algo

■ **look out for** [*v + adv + prep + o*]: **~ out for her at the station** fíjate a ver si la ves en la estación; **we were warned to ~ out for thieves** nos advirtieron que tuviéramos cuidado con los ladrones

■ **look over** [*v + o + adv, v + adv + o*] ⟨*work/contract*⟩ revisar; ⟨*building*⟩ inspeccionar

■ **look to** [*v + prep + o*] (rely on): **they are ~ing to you for guidance** esperan que tú los guíes

■ **look up** ⎡1⎤ [*v + o + adv, v + adv + o*] **(a)** ⟨*word*⟩ buscar* (*en el diccionario*) **(b)** ⟨*person*⟩ ir* a ver ⎡2⎤ [*v + adv*] (improve) mejorar

■ **look up to** [*v + adv + prep + o*] admirar

look-alike /ˈlʊkəˌlaɪk/ *n* (colloq) (person) doble *mf*

looking glass /ˈlʊkɪŋˌglæs ǁˈlʊkɪŋˌglɑːs/ *n* (dated) espejo *m*

lookout /ˈlʊkaʊt/ *n* **(a)** (watch) (*no pl*): **to be on the ~ for** sth/sb andar* a la caza de algo/algn **(b)** (person) (Mil) vigía *mf*

loom[1] /luːm/ *n* telar *m*

loom[2] *vi* **(a)** (be imminent) avecinarse **(b)** (look threatening): **the mountain ~ed high above them** la montaña surgió imponente ante ellos; **the problem ~ed large in his mind** el problema dominaba sus pensamientos

■ **loom up** [*v + adv*]: **a figure ~ed up in the darkness** una figura surgió de entre las tinieblas

loop[1] /luːp/ *n* ⎡1⎤ **(a)** (shape) curva *f*; (in river) meandro *m* **(b)** (in string) lazada *f* **(c)** (in sewing) presilla *f* **(d)** (Aviat): **to loop the ~** rizar* el rizo ⎡2⎤ **(a)** (circuit) circuito *m* cerrado **(b)** (Comput) bucle *m*

loop[2] *vt*: **~ the wool** haz una lazada con la lana; **I ~ed the dog's lead over the post** enganché la correa del perro en el poste

■ ~ *vi* «*road*» serpentear

loophole /ˈluːphəʊl/ *n*: **a legal ~** una laguna jurídica (*que se presta a trampas*)

loose[1] /luːs/ *adj* **looser, loosest** ⎡1⎤ **(a)** (not tight) ⟨*garment*⟩ suelto **(b)** (not secure) ⟨*screw/knot*⟩ flojo; ⟨*thread/end*⟩ suelto; ⟨*hair*⟩ suelto; **to be at a ~ end** no tener* nada que hacer **(c)** (separate, not packaged) ⟨*cigarettes*⟩ suelto; ⟨*tea/lentils*⟩ a granel, suelto; **~ change** calderilla *f* ⎡2⎤ (free) (*pred*) suelto; **to let** *o* **set** *o* **turn sb ~** soltar* a algn; **to be on the ~** andar* suelto ⎡3⎤ ⟨*definition*⟩ poco preciso; ⟨*translation*⟩ libre

loose[2] *vt* (liter) **(a)** ⟨*prisoner*⟩ poner* en libertad; ⟨*horse*⟩ soltar* **(b)** ⟨*arrow*⟩ lanzar*; ⟨*violence/wrath*⟩ desatar

loose: ~-**fitting** /ˈluːsˈfɪtɪŋ/ *adj* suelto; ⟨*clothes*⟩ holgado; ~-**leaf** /ˈluːsˈliːf/ *adj* ⟨*binder*⟩ de anillas

loosely /ˈluːsli/ *adv* ⎡1⎤ (not tightly) ⟨*tie/bandage*⟩ sin apretar; **the dress fits ~** el vestido no es entallado ⎡2⎤ (not precisely) ⟨*define*⟩ sin excesivo rigor; ⟨*translate*⟩ libremente; **~ speaking** (indep) (hablando) en términos generales

loosen /ˈluːsn̩/ *vt* **(a)** ⟨*tooth*⟩ aflojar **(b)** ⟨*collar/*

knot/bolt⟩ aflojar, soltar*; **she ~ed her grip on the steering wheel** dejó de apretar con tanta fuerza el volante
■ ~ *vi* «*knot/bolt*» aflojarse

loot¹ /luːt/ *n* **(a)** (*plunder*) botín *m* **(b)** (*money*) (sl) guita *f* (arg), lana *f* (AmL fam), pasta *f* (Esp fam)

loot² *vt/i* saquear

looter /'luːtər ‖ 'luːtə(r)/ *n* saqueador, -dora *m,f*

looting /'luːtɪŋ/ *n* saqueo *m*

lop /lɑːp ‖ lɒp/ *vt* **-pp-** **(a)** ⟨*tree*⟩ podar **(b)** ~ **(off)** ⟨*branch*⟩ cortar

lope /ləʊp/ *vi* «*wolf/dog*» trotar

lopsided /'lɑːp'saɪdəd ‖ ,lɒp'saɪdɪd/ *adj* **(a)** (not straight) torcido, chueco (AmL) **(b)** (asymmetric) ⟨*face/smile*⟩ torcido; ⟨*shape*⟩ asimétrico

lord /lɔːrd ‖ lɔːd/ *n* **1** **(a)** (nobleman) señor *m*, noble *m* **(b)** **Lord** (in UK) lord *m*; **the (House of) L~s** la cámara de los lores **(c)** **my L~** (addressing judge) (BrE) (su) señoría **2** **Lord** (God): **the L~** el Señor; **the L~'s Prayer** el Padrenuestro

lordship /'lɔːrdʃɪp ‖ 'lɔːdʃɪp/ *n*: **His/Your L~** (of or to peers, judges) (su) señoría; (of or to bishops) (su) Ilustrísima

lore /lɔːr ‖ lɔː(r)/ *n*: **French peasant ~** las tradiciones rurales francesas

lorry /'lɔːri ‖ 'lɒri/ *n* (*pl* **-ries**) (BrE) camión *m*; (*before n*) ~ **driver** camionero, -ra *m,f*

lose /luːz/ *vt* (*past & past p* **lost**)
I **1** (mislay) perder*
2 (be deprived of) ⟨*sight/territory/right*⟩ perder*; **to ~ one's voice** quedarse afónico
3 (rid oneself of) ⟨*inhibitions*⟩ perder*; **to ~ weight** adelgazar, perder* peso
4 (cause to lose) costar*; **their hesitation lost them the contract** la falta de decisión les costó *or* les hizo perder el contrato
5 (let pass) ⟨*time/opportunity*⟩ perder*; **my watch ~s three minutes every day** mi reloj (se) atrasa tres minutos por día
II (fail to win) ⟨*game/battle/election*⟩ perder*
■ ~ *vi* **1** **(a)** (be beaten) «*team/contestant/party*» perder*; **they're losing 3-1** van perdiendo 3 a 1; **to ~ TO sb** perder* FRENTE A algn **(b)** **losing** *pres p* ⟨*team/party*⟩ perdedor
2 (suffer losses) perder*
3 «*watch/clock*» atrasar, atrasarse

loser /'luːzər ‖ 'luːzə(r)/ *n* perdedor, -dora *m,f*

loss /lɔːs ‖ lɒs/ *n* pérdida *f*; **to be a dead ~** (colloq): **this typewriter is a dead ~** esta máquina de escribir no sirve para nada *or* (fam) es una porquería; **to be at a ~**: **I was at a ~ for words** no supe qué decir; **to cut one's ~es** cortar por lo sano; (Fin) reducir* las pérdidas

lost¹ /lɔːst ‖ lɒst/ *past & past p of* LOSE

lost² *adj*
I **1** (mislaid, missing) perdido; **to get ~** perderse*, extraviarse* (frml); **get ~!** (sl) ¡vete al diablo! (fam), ¡andá a pasear! (RPl fam) **2** (wasted) ⟨*time*⟩ perdido; ⟨*opportunity*⟩ desperdiciado, perdido; **to be ~ on sb**: **these subtleties are ~ on him** se le escapan estas sutilezas **4** (*pred*) (absorbed) **to be ~ IN sth** estar* ensimismado EN algo; **to be ~ in thought** estar* absorto *or* ensimismado
II (not won) ⟨*battle/election*⟩ perdido

lost: ~ and found /'lɔːstən'faʊnd ‖ ,lɒstən'faʊnd/ *n* (AmE) objetos *mpl* perdidos; **~ property** *n* (esp BrE) objetos *mpl* perdidos

lot /lɑːt ‖ lɒt/ *n* **1** (large number, quantity) **(a)** (*no pl*): **a ~ of wine** mucho vino; **I've seen a ~ of her recently** la he visto mucho últimamente; **what a ~ of books you've got!** ¡cuántos libros tienes! **(b) a ~** (*as adv*) mucho **(c) lots** *pl* (colloq): **how many seats are there left?** — **lots** ¿cuántos asientos quedan? — muchos *or* (fam) montones; **~s of people liked it** a mucha gente le gustó **2** **(a)** (group, mass of things) montón *m*, pila *f* **(b)** (group of people) (colloq): **they're a funny ~** son raros, son gente rara; **come on, you ~!** ¡vamos, ustedes *or* (Esp) vosotros! **(c) the ~** (esp BrE): **they ate the ~** se lo comieron todo (*or* se las comieron todas *etc*)
3 (at auction) lote *m*

loth /ləʊθ/ *adj* ▸ LOATH

lotion /'ləʊʃən/ *n* loción *f*

lottery /'lɑːtəri ‖ 'lɒtəri/ *n* (*pl* **-ries**) lotería *f*

lotus /'ləʊtəs/ *n* (*pl* **~es**) loto *m*

loud¹ /laʊd/ *adj* **-er, -est (a)** ⟨*noise*⟩ fuerte; **he said it in a ~ voice** lo dijo en voz alta **(b)** (vigorous) ⟨*protests*⟩ enérgico **(c)** (ostentatious) ⟨*color*⟩ llamativo, chillón

loud² *adv* **-er, -est** ⟨*speak*⟩ alto; **she laughed (the) ~est of all** fue la que se rio más fuerte

loudly /'laʊdli/ *adv* **(a)** ⟨*shout*⟩ fuerte; ⟨*speak*⟩ alto, en voz alta **(b)** ⟨*complain*⟩ a voz en grito

loud: ~mouth *n* (colloq) gritón, -tona *m,f*; **~speaker** altavoz *m*, altoparlante *m* (AmL)

lounge¹ /laʊndʒ/ *n* (on ship, in hotel) salón *m*; (in house) (BrE) sala *f* (de estar), living *m* (esp AmS), salón *m* (esp Esp)

lounge² *vi*: **to ~ around** *o* **about** no hacer* nada

louse /laʊs/ *n* (*pl* **lice**) (Zool) piojo *m*

lousy /'laʊzi/ *adj* **-sier, -siest** (colloq) ⟨*food/weather*⟩ asqueroso (fam); **a ~ movie** una película malísima

lout /laʊt/ *n* patán *m* (fam), gandalla *m* (Méx fam), jallán *m* (AmC)

louver, (BrE) **louvre** /'luːvər ‖ 'luːvə(r)/ *n* lama *f*, listón *m* (de persiana); (*before n*) ⟨*door/window*⟩ de lamas, tipo persiana

lovable /'lʌvəbəl/ *adj* adorable, amoroso (AmL)

love¹ /lʌv/ *n* **1** **(a)** (emotional attachment) amor *m*; **to fall/be in ~ with sb/sth** enamorarse/estar* enamorado de algn/algo; **to make ~ to sb** hacer* el amor con algn **(b)** (enthusiasm, interest) ~ **OF sth** amor *m* A *or* POR algo **2** **(a)** (greetings, regards): **give my ~ to your parents** (dale) recuerdos a tus padres (de mi parte) **(b)** (in letters) ~ **from John** *o* **~, John** un abrazo, John **3** (person loved) amor *m*; (thing loved) pasión *f* **4** (colloq) (*as form of address*) cariño **5** (in tennis) cero *m*

love² *vt* querer*, amar (liter); **I ~ music/reading** me encanta la música/leer; **I'd ~ a cup of tea** una taza de té me vendría de maravilla

loveable *adj* ▸ LOVABLE

loved one *n* ser *m* querido

loveless /'lʌvləs ‖ 'lʌvlɪs/ *adj* sin amor

lovely *or* /'lʌvli/ *adj* **-lier, liest** ⟨*appearance*⟩ precioso, lindo (esp AmL); ⟨*person/nature*⟩ encantador, amoroso (AmL); ⟨*meal/taste*⟩ (BrE) riquísimo; **the weather was ~** hacía un tiempo buenísimo

lover /'lʌvər ‖'lʌvə(r)/ n ① (partner in love) amante *mf* ② (fan) ~ OF sth amante *mf* DE algo

loving /'lʌvɪŋ/ adj cariñoso; with ~ care con tierno cuidado

lovingly /'lʌvɪŋli/ adv ⟨gaze/whisper⟩ tiernamente; ⟨handwritten/prepared⟩ con amor *or* cariño; ⟨restored⟩ con el mayor cuidado

low¹ /ləʊ/ adj -er, -est ① (in height) bajo; **the dress had a very ~ back** el vestido era muy escotado por la espalda ② (a) (in volume) ⟨voice⟩ bajo; ⟨sound/whisper⟩ débil; **turn the radio down ~** bájale al radio (AmL exc CS), baja la radio (CS, Esp) (b) ⟨key/note/ pitch⟩ grave ③ (in intensity, amount, quality) bajo; ⟨proportion⟩ pequeño; **cook on a ~ flame** *o* **heat** cocinar a fuego lento; **he has a ~ opinion of doctors** no tiene muy buena opinión de los médicos; **a ~ point in his career** un momento bajo en su carrera ④ (in short supply): **stocks are running ~** se están agotando las existencias

low² adv -er, -est ① bajo; **to fly ~** volar* bajo *or* a poca altura ② (in volume, pitch) bajo

low³ n punto *m* más bajo; **relations between the two countries are at an all-time ~** las relaciones entre los dos países nunca han sido peores

low⁴ vi mugir*

low- /'ləʊ/ pref: ~priced de bajo precio; ~income de bajos ingresos

low: ~**alcohol** /'ləʊ'ælkəhɒːl ‖'ləʊˌælkəhɒl/ adj de baja graduación alcohólica; ~**calorie** /'ləʊ'kæləri/ adj bajo en calorías; ~**class** /'ləʊ'klæs ‖,ləʊ'klɑːs/ adj ⟨place⟩ de mala muerte (fam); ⟨clientele⟩ de poca categoría; ~**cut** /'ləʊ'kʌt/ adj escotado; ~**down** n (colloq): **to give sb the ~down (on sth)** poner* a algn al tanto (de algo)

lower¹ /'ləʊər ‖'ləʊə(r)/ adj ① (a) (spatially, numerically) ⟨jaw/lip⟩ inferior; ~ **age limit** edad *f* mínima (b) (in rank, importance) inferior, más bajo (c) ⟨life form⟩ inferior ② (Geog) bajo; **the ~ reaches of the Nile** el curso bajo del Nilo

lower² /'ləʊər ‖'ləʊə(r)/ vt ① ⟨blind/flag⟩ bajar; **he ~ed himself into his chair** se sentó en el sillón ② ⟨temperature/volume/price/voice⟩ bajar ■ v refl **to ~ oneself** rebajarse

lower: ~ **class** n (often pl) clase *f* baja; ~**class** /ˌləʊər'klæs ‖,ləʊə'klɑːs/ adj de clase baja

lowest common denominator /'ləʊəst ‖'ləʊɪst/ n (Math) mínimo común denominador *m*; **a series aimed at the ~ ~ ~ ~** una serie dirigida al público de nivel más bajo

low: ~**fat** /'ləʊ'fæt/ adj de bajo contenido graso; ~**flying** /'ləʊ'flaɪŋ/ adj ⟨aircraft⟩ que vuela bajo; ~**grade** /'ləʊ'greɪd/ adj ⟨oil⟩ de baja calidad; ⟨ore⟩ pobre; ~**key** /'ləʊ'kiː/ adj ⟨speech⟩ mesurado; ⟨ceremony⟩ sencillo; ~**land** /'ləʊlənd/ adj (before n) de las tierras bajas; (in tropical countries) de tierra caliente; ~**lands** /'ləʊləndz/ pl n tierras *fpl* bajas; (in tropical

countries) tierras *fpl* calientes; ~**level** /'ləʊ'levəl/ adj (a) ⟨talks⟩ a bajo nivel (b) ⟨radiation⟩ de baja intensidad (c) (Comput): ~**level language** lenguaje *m* de bajo nivel

lowly /'ləʊli/ adj -lier, -liest humilde

low: ~**lying** /'ləʊ'laɪŋ/ adj bajo; ~**necked** /'ləʊ'nekt/ adj escotado; ~**paid** /'ləʊ'peɪd/ adj mal remunerado; ~**profile** /'ləʊ'prəʊfaɪl/ adj poco prominente; ~**rise** /'ləʊ'raɪz/ adj de poca altura; ~**risk** /'ləʊ'rɪsk/ adj ⟨business⟩ poco arriesgado; ⟨investment⟩ de poco *or* bajo riesgo; ~ **season** n (BrE) temporada *f* baja

loyal /'lɔɪəl/ adj ⟨friend/customer⟩ fiel; **to be ~ TO sth** ⟨to the state/party⟩ ser* leal A algo; ⟨to one's ideals⟩ ser* fiel A algo; **he is ~ to his friends** es un amigo leal *or* fiel

loyalist /'lɔɪələst ‖'lɔɪəlɪst/ n partidario, -ria *m,f* del régimen

loyalty /'lɔɪəlti/ n (pl -ties) lealtad *f*

loyalty card n tarjeta *f* de cliente (que otorga puntos)

lozenge /'lɑːzɪndʒ ‖'lɒzɪndʒ/ n (Med) pastilla *f*

LP n (= **long-playing record**) LP *m*, elepé *m*

L-plate /'elpleɪt/ n (in UK) placa *f* de la L *or* de prácticas (placa que se debe exhibir en el coche cuando se aprende a conducir)

LSD n (= **lysergic acid diethylamide**) LSD *m*

LST (in US) = **Local Standard Time**

Ltd (= **Limited**) Ltda., S.A.

lubricant /'luːbrɪkənt/ n lubricante *m*

lubricate /'luːbrɪkeɪt/ vt lubricar*

lucid /'luːsəd ‖'luːsɪd/ adj lúcido

luck /lʌk/ n suerte *f*; **good ~!** ¡buena suerte!; **a piece** *o* **stroke of ~** un golpe de suerte; **to be down on one's ~** estar* de mala racha; **to push one's ~** desafiar* a la suerte

luckily /'lʌkəli ‖'lʌkɪli/ adv (indep) por suerte

lucky /'lʌki/ adj **luckier, luckiest** ⟨person⟩ con suerte, suertudo (AmL fam); **he's ~ to be alive** tuvo suerte de no matarse; ~ **you!** (colloq) ¡qué suerte (tienes)! (b) (fortuitous): **he had a ~ escape** se salvó de milagro; **it was ~ you were there** fue una suerte que estuvieras ahí (c) (bringing luck): ~ **charm** amuleto *m* (de la suerte); **seven is my ~ number** el siete es mi número de la suerte

lucrative /'luːkrətɪv/ adj lucrativo

ludicrous /'luːdɪkrəs/ adj ridículo

lug /lʌg/ vt -gg- (colloq) arrastrar

luggage /'lʌgɪdʒ/ n equipaje *m*

luggage: ~ **checkroom** n (AmE) consigna *f* (de equipajes); ~ **rack** n (a) (Rail) rejilla *f* (portaequipajes) (b) (Auto) baca *f*, parrilla *f* (Andes)

lugubrious /lʊ'guːbriəs/ adj lúgubre

lukewarm /'luːk'wɔːrm ‖,luːk'wɔːm/ adj (a) ⟨water/milk⟩ tibio (b) ⟨support/reaction⟩ poco entusiasta

lull¹ /lʌl/ vt (a) ⟨baby⟩: **to ~ a baby to sleep**

arrullar a un niño hasta dormirlo **(b)** ⟨*fears*⟩ calmar; ⟨*suspicions*⟩ desvanecer **(c)** (deceive): **we were ~ed into a false sense of security** nos confiamos demasiado

lull² *n* (in activity) período *m* de calma; (in fighting) tregua *f*; (in conversation) pausa *f*

lullaby /'lʌləbaɪ/ *n* (*pl* **-bies**) canción *f* de cuna

lumbago /lʌm'beɪgəʊ/ *n* lumbago *m*

lumber¹ /'lʌmbər ‖'lʌmbə(r)/ *n* **(a)** (timber) (AmE) madera *f* **(b)** (junk) cachivaches *mpl*

lumber² *vt* (colloq) **to ~ sb WITH sth** enjaretarle algo A algn (fam)
∎ ~ *vi* **(a)** (move awkwardly) avanzar* pesadamente **(b) lumbering** *pres p* ⟨*gait*⟩ torpe

lumber: ~jack *n* leñador *m*; **~yard** *n* (AmE) almacén *m* de maderas, barraca *f* (CS)

luminous /'lu:mənəs ‖'lu:mɪnəs/ *adj* luminoso

lump¹ /lʌmp/ *n* [1] (swelling, protuberance) bulto *m*; (as result of knock) chichón *m*; **a ~ in one's throat** un nudo en la garganta [2] (piece — of coal, iron, clay, cheese) trozo *m*, pedazo *m*; (— of sugar) terrón *m*

lump² *vt* **(a)** (put up with) (colloq): **to ~ it** aguantarse (fam); **if you don't like it, (you can) ~ it** si no te gusta, te aguantas **(b)** (place together): **to ~ sth together: you can ~ all those items together under one heading** todo eso puede ir junto bajo el mismo epígrafe; **they can't all be ~ed together as reactionaries** no se puede tachar a todos indiscriminadamente de reaccionarios

lump sum *n* cantidad *f* global (*que se paga o recibe para saldar totalmente una obligación*)

lumpy /'lʌmpi/ *adj* **-pier, -piest (a)** ⟨*sauce*⟩ lleno de grumos **(b)** ⟨*mattress/cushion*⟩ lleno de bultos

lunacy /'lu:nəsi/ *n* (*pl* **-cies**) locura *f*

lunar /'lu:nər ‖'lu:nə(r)/ *adj* lunar

lunatic /'lu:nətɪk/ *n* loco, -ca *m,f*

lunch /lʌntʃ/ *n* almuerzo *m*, comida *f* (esp Esp, Méx); **to have ~** almorzar*, comer (esp Esp, Méx)

lunchbox /'lʌntʃbɑːks ‖'lʌntʃbɒks/ *n* lonchera *f* (AmL), fiambrera *f* (Esp)

luncheon /'lʌntʃən/ *n* (frml) almuerzo *m*

lunchtime /'lʌntʃtaɪm/ *n* hora *f* de almorzar, hora *f* de comer (esp Esp, Méx)

lung /lʌŋ/ *n* (*often pl*) pulmón *m*; (*before n*) **~ cancer** cáncer *m* de pulmón

lunge¹ /lʌndʒ/ *vi* embestir*; **to ~ AT sb/sth** arremeter CONTRA algn/algo

lunge² *n* arremetida *f*

lurch¹ /lɜːrtʃ ‖lɜːtʃ/ *vi* «*vehicle*» dar* bandazos; «*person*» tambalearse

lurch² *n* bandazo *m*; **to leave sb in the ~** (colloq) dejar a algn plantado

lure /lʊr ‖ljʊə(r), lʊə(r)/ *vt* atraer*

lurid /'lʊrəd ‖'lʊərɪd/ *adj* **(a)** (sensational) ⟨*details/imagination*⟩ morboso **(b)** (garish) ⟨*color/ garment*⟩ chillón

lurk /lɜːrk ‖lɜːk/ *vi* merodear

luscious /'lʌʃəs/ *adj* **(a)** ⟨*girl*⟩ seductora **(b)** ⟨*scent/sweetness*⟩ exquisito

lush /lʌʃ/ *adj* **-er, -est** ⟨*vegetation*⟩ exuberante

lust¹ /lʌst/ *n* **(a)** (sexual) lujuria *f* **(b)** (craving) deseo *m*

lust² *vi* **to ~ AFTER sb** desear a algn; **to ~ AFTER sth** codiciar algo

luster, (BrE) **lustre** /'lʌstər ‖'lʌstə(r)/ *n* (liter) lustre *m*

lustful /'lʌstfəl/ *adj* lujurioso

lustre /'lʌstər ‖'lʌstə(r)/ *n* (BrE) ▶ LUSTER

lusty /'lʌsti/ *adj* **-tier, tiest** sano

Luxembourg, Luxemburg /'lʌksəmbɜːrg ‖'lʌksəmbɜːg/ *n* Luxemburgo *m*

luxuriant /lʌg'ʒʊriənt ‖lʌg'zjʊəriənt/ *adj* ⟨*vegetation/growth*⟩ exuberante; ⟨*hair*⟩ hermoso y abundante

luxuriate /lʌg'ʒʊrieɪt ‖lʌg'zjʊərieɪt/ *vi* (revel) **to ~ IN sth** deleitarse CON algo

luxurious /lʌg'ʒʊriəs ‖lʌg'zjʊəriəs/ *adj* lujoso

luxury /'lʌkʃəri/ *n* (*pl* **-ries**) lujo *m*; (*before n*) ⟨*car/hotel*⟩ de lujo

lying¹ /'laɪɪŋ/ *n* mentiras *fpl*

lying² *adj* (*before n*) mentiroso

lymph /lɪmf/ *n* linfa *f*; (*before n*) **~ gland** glándula *f* linfática

lynch /lɪntʃ/ *vt* linchar

lynx /lɪŋks/ *n* (*pl* **~es** *or* **~**) lince *m*

lyre /'laɪr ‖'laɪə(r)/ *n* lira *f*

lyric /'lɪrɪk/ *n* **(a)** (poem) poema *m* lírico **(b) lyrics** *pl n* (Mus) letra *f*

lyrical /'lɪrɪkəl/ *adj* (Lit) lleno de lirismo

M m

M, m /em/ *n* M, m *f*

m (a) (= **million(s)**) m **(b)** (= **meter(s)** *o* (BrE) **metre(s)**) m **(c)** (= **male**) de sexo masculino **(d)** (Ling) (= **masculine**) m

M (a) (Clothing) (= **medium**) M, talla *f* mediana *or* (RPl) talle *m* mediano **(b)** (in UK) (Transp) (= **motorway**) *indicador de autopista*

ma /mɑː/ *n* (colloq) mamá *f*

MA /'em'eɪ/ *n* **(a)** = **Master of Arts (b)** = **Massachusetts**

macabre /mə'kɑːbrə/ *adj* macabro

macaroni /,mækə'rəʊni/ *n* macarrones *mpl*

mace /meɪs/ *n* [1] (Art, Hist, Mil) maza *f* [2] (Culin) macis *f* [3] **Mace**® (tear gas) (AmE) *gas para defensa personal*

Macedonia /,mæsə'dəʊniə/ *n* Macedonia *f*

machete /mə'ʃeti, mə'tʃeti/ *n* machete *m*

machinations /ˌmækəˈneɪʃənz, ˈmæʃ-‖ˌmækɪˈneɪʃənz, ˈmæʃ-/ pl n (liter) maquinaciones fpl

machine /məˈʃiːn/ n máquina f; (washing ∼) lavadora f, máquina f (de lavar), lavarropas m (RPl)

machine gun n ametralladora f

machinery /məˈʃiːnəri/ n (machines) maquinaria f; (working parts) mecanismo m

macho /ˈmɑːtʃəʊ ‖ˈmætʃəʊ/ adj ⟨behavior/attitude⟩ machista; ⟨image⟩ de macho

macintosh n ▶ MACKINTOSH

mackerel /ˈmækrəl/ n (pl ∼ or ∼s) caballa f

mackintosh /ˈmækəntɑːʃ ‖ˈmækɪntɒʃ/ n impermeable m

macro /ˈmækrəʊ/ n (pl **-ros**) (Comput) macro m

mad /mæd/ adj **-dd-** ① (a) (insane) loco; **to go ∼** volverse* loco; **to work/run like ∼** trabajar/correr como un loco (b) ⟨rush⟩ loco; **we made a ∼ dash for the airport** salimos como locos para el aeropuerto (c) ⟨scheme/idea⟩ disparatado ② (angry) (esp AmE) ⟨pred⟩ **to be ∼** (WITH/AT sb) estar* furioso or (esp AmL) enojadísimo or (esp Esp) enfadadísimo (con algn); **to get ∼** ponerse* furioso ③ (very enthusiastic) (colloq) ⟨pred⟩ **to be ∼ ABOUT sb** estar* loco POR algn; **she's ∼ about o on African music** la música africana la vuelve loca

Madagascar /ˌmædəˈɡæskər ‖ˌmædəˈɡæskə(r)/ n Madagascar m

madam /ˈmædəm/ n (as title) señora f

madden /ˈmædn̩/ vt (make angry) enfurecer*; (drive mad) enloquecer*

made¹ /meɪd/ past & past p of MAKE¹

made² adj ⟨pred⟩ (a) (assured of success) **to have it ∼** tener* el éxito asegurado (b) (ideally suited): **they were ∼ for each other** estaban hechos el uno para el otro

Madeira /məˈdɪrə ‖məˈdɪərə/ n Madeira f, Madera f

made-to-measure /ˈmeɪdtəˈmeʒər ‖ˌmeɪdtəˈmeʒə(r)/ adj ⟨pred **made to measure**⟩ hecho a (la) medida

madly /ˈmædli/ adv (a) (frantically) ⟨rush/work⟩ como un loco; ⟨love⟩ locamente (b) (very) (as intensifier): **∼ in love** locamente enamorado

madman /ˈmædmən/ n (pl **-men** /-mən/) loco m

madness /ˈmædnəs ‖ˈmædnɪs/ n locura f

Madrid /məˈdrɪd/ n Madrid m; (before n) madrileño

Mafia /ˈmɑːfiə, ˈmæ- ‖ˈmæfiə/ n Mafia f

magazine /ˌmæɡəˈziːn/ n ① (a) (Publ) revista f; (before n) **∼ rack** revistero m (b) **∼** ⟨program⟩ (Rad, TV) programa m de entrevistas y variedades ② (on gun — compartment) recámara f; (— bullet case) cargador m

maggot /ˈmæɡət/ n gusano m

magic¹ /ˈmædʒɪk/ n magia f

magic² adj (a) ⟨power/potion⟩ mágico; ⟨trick⟩ de magia (b) (enchanting) ⟨moment/beauty⟩ mágico

magical /ˈmædʒɪkəl/ adj mágico

magician /məˈdʒɪʃən/ n (sorcerer) mago m; (conjurer) mago, -ga m,f, prestidigitador, -dora m,f

magistrate /ˈmædʒəstreɪt ‖ˈmædʒɪstreɪt/ n (in UK) juez que conoce de faltas y asuntos civiles de menor importancia

magnanimous /mæɡˈnænəməs ‖mæɡˈnænɪməs/ adj magnánimo

magnesium /mæɡˈniːziəm/ n magnesio m

magnet /ˈmæɡnət ‖ˈmæɡnɪt/ n imán m

magnetic /mæɡˈnetɪk/ adj magnético; ⟨personality⟩ lleno de magnetismo

magnetism /ˈmæɡnətɪzəm ‖ˈmæɡnɪtɪzəm/ n magnetismo m

magnificent /mæɡˈnɪfəsənt ‖mæɡˈnɪfɪsənt/ adj magnífico

magnify /ˈmæɡnəfaɪ ‖ˈmæɡnɪfaɪ/ vt **-fies, -fying, -fied** ⟨image⟩ ampliar*, aumentar de tamaño; ⟨problem/difficulty⟩ exagerar

magnifying glass /ˈmæɡnəfaɪŋ ‖ˈmæɡnɪfaɪŋ/ n lupa f

magnitude /ˈmæɡnətuːd ‖ˈmæɡnɪtjuːd/ n (size) magnitud f; (importance) envergadura f

magpie /ˈmæɡpaɪ/ n urraca f, picaza f

mahogany /məˈhɑːɡəni ‖məˈhɒɡəni/ n caoba f

maid /meɪd/ n ① (a) (servant) sirvienta f, criada f, mucama f (AmL); (parlor/lady's ∼) (primera) doncella f (b) (in hotel) camarera f, mucama f (AmL) (c) (occasional housekeeper) (AmE) señora f de la limpieza, limpiadora f ② (young woman) (arch or liter) doncella f (arc o liter)

maiden¹ /ˈmeɪdn̩/ n (arch or liter) doncella f (arc o liter)

maiden² adj (before n) ⟨flight/speech⟩ inaugural

maiden name n apellido m de soltera

mail¹ /meɪl/ n ① (a) (system) correo m; **by ∼** por correo (b) (letters, parcels) correspondencia f, correo m ② (armor) malla f

mail² vt (esp AmE) ⟨letter/parcel⟩ echar al correo; (drop in mailbox) echar al buzón; **to ∼ sth TO sb** mandarle or enviarle* algo por correo A algn

mail: ∼box n (a) (for receiving mail) (AmE) buzón m, casillero m (Ven) (b) (for sending mail) (AmE) buzón m (de correos) (c) (electronic) buzón m; **∼ carrier** n (AmE) cartero, -ra m,f

mailing list /ˈmeɪlɪŋ/ n (Marketing) banco m or lista f de direcciones

mail: ∼man /ˈmeɪlmæn/ n (pl **-men** /-men/) (AmE) cartero m; **∼ order** n venta f por correo; (before n) **∼-order catalog** catálogo m de venta por correo

maim /meɪm/ vt (cripple) lisiar; (mutilate) mutilar

main¹ /meɪn/ adj (before n, no comp) principal; **the ∼ thing** lo principal; **∼ course** plato m principal or fuerte; **∼ street** calle f principal

main² n (a) (pipe) cañería f or tubería f principal; (cable) cable m principal (b) (supply) **the ∼ o** (BrE) **the ∼s** la red de suministro; **to turn the water/gas off at the ∼ o** (BrE) **the ∼s** cerrar la llave (principal) del agua/del gas

main: ∼frame n unidad f central, computadora f or (Esp tb) ordenador m central; **∼land** /ˈmeɪnlənd, -lænd/ n: **the ∼land** la masa territorial de un país o continente excluyendo sus islas; (before n) **∼land China** (la) China continental; **∼ line** n (Rail) línea f principal

mainly /ˈmeɪnli/ adv principalmente

main: ∼ road n (BrE) carretera f principal;

∼stream adj ⟨culture⟩ establecido; **∼stream politics** la política a nivel de los partidos mayoritarios

maintain /mein'tein/ vt ⊡ (a) ⟨speed/lead⟩ mantener*; ⟨silence⟩ guardar (b) ⟨house/machine⟩ ocuparse del mantenimiento de; ⟨aircraft⟩ mantener* (c) ⟨family/dependents⟩ mantener* ⊡ (claim) mantener*

maintenance /'meintnəns ‖'meintənəns/ n ⊡ (repairs) mantenimiento m ⊡ (money) (BrE Law) pensión f alimenticia

maisonette /'meizn̩'et ‖,meizə'net/ n (BrE) (apartment) dúplex m; (house) vivienda independiente de dos pisos que forma parte de una casa

maize /meiz/ n (a) (plant) maíz m (b) (grains) maíz m, choclo m (CS, Per), elote m (Méx)

majestic /mə'dʒestik/ adj majestuoso

majesty /'mædʒəsti/ n (pl **-ties**) (a) (of appearance, landscape) majestuosidad f (b) (as title) **Her/Your M∼** su Majestad

major¹ /'meidʒər ‖'meidʒə(r)/ adj ⊡ ⟨change/client⟩ muy importante; ⟨setback⟩ serio; ⟨revision⟩ a fondo ⊡ (Mus) mayor

major² n ⊡ (Mil) mayor mf (en AmL), comandante mf (en Esp) ⊡ (AmE Educ) asignatura f principal

major³ vi (AmE Educ) **to ∼ IN sth** especializarse* **EN** algo

Majorca /mə'jɔːrkə ‖mə'jɔːkə, mə'dʒɔːkə/ n Mallorca f

majority /mə'dʒɔːrəti ‖mə'dʒɒrəti/ n (pl **-ties**) (greater number) (+ sing o pl vb) mayoría f; (before n) ⟨decision/party⟩ mayoritario

major league n (Sport) liga f nacional

make¹ /meik/ (past & past p **made**) vt
I ⊡ (create, produce) hacer*; **to ∼ a note of sth** anotar algo; **she made the dress out of an old sheet** se hizo el vestido con una sábana vieja; **it's made of wood** es de madera; see also DIFFERENCE, FUSS¹, MESS 1 etc
⊡ (a) (carry out) ⟨repairs/payment/journey⟩ hacer*; **∼ a left (turn) here** (AmE) dobla a la izquierda aquí (b) ⟨remark/announcement⟩ hacer*
II ⊡ (cause to be): **I'll ∼ you happy** te haré feliz; **that made me sad** eso me entristeció; **the work made me thirsty** el trabajo me dio sed; **what ∼s me angry is …** lo que me da rabia es …; **they've made him supervisor** lo han nombrado supervisor; **if nine o'clock is too early, ∼ it later** si las nueve es muy temprano, podemos reunirnos (or encontrarnos etc) más tarde
⊡ (a) (cause to) hacer*; **whatever made you do it?** ¿por qué lo hiciste? (b) (compel) obligar* a, hacer*; **she was made to apologize** la obligaron a or la hicieron pedir perdón (c) (in phrases) **to make believe: you can't just ∼ believe it never happened** no puedes hacer como si no hubiera sucedido; **to make do (WITH sth)** arreglárselas (CON algo)
III ⊡ (a) (constitute, be) ser*; **it would ∼ a nice change** sería un cambio agradable; **they ∼ a nice couple** hacen buena pareja (b) (amount to) ser*; **five plus five ∼s ten** cinco y or más cinco son diez
⊡ (calculate): **I ∼ it 253** (a mí) me da 253; **what time do you ∼ it?** ¿qué hora tienes?

⊡ (a) (understand): **I could ∼ nothing of the message** no entendí el mensaje; **∼ of that what you will** tú saca tus propias conclusiones (b) (think) **to ∼ sth OF sb/sth: what did you ∼ of him?** ¿qué te pareció?; **I don't know what to ∼ of it** no sé qué pensar
IV ⊡ (a) (gain, earn) ⟨money⟩ hacer* (b) (acquire) ⟨friends⟩ hacer*; **to ∼ a name for oneself** hacerse* un nombre
⊡ (colloq) (manage to attend, reach): **we just made the 3 o'clock train** llegamos justo a tiempo para el tren de las tres; **he'll never ∼ it as a doctor** nunca será un buen médico
⊡ (assure success of): **to ∼ or break sth/sb** ser* el éxito o la ruina de algo/algn
■ **make for** [v + prep + o] ⊡ (head toward) dirigirse* hacia/a
⊡ (encourage, promote) contribuir* a
■ **make out**
I [v + o + adv, v + adv + o] ⊡ (a) (discern) ⟨object/outline⟩ distinguir*; (from a distance) divisar*; ⟨sound⟩ distinguir*; ⟨writing⟩ descifrar (b) (figure out) (colloq) entender*
⊡ (write) ⟨list/invoice/receipt⟩ hacer*; **∼ the check out to P. Jones** haga el cheque pagadero a P. Jones
II (claim, pretend) [v + adv + o]: **she made out it was her own work** dio a entender que lo había hecho ella misma; **you're not as ill as you ∼ out** no estás tan enfermo como pretendes
■ **make up**
I [v + o + adv, v + adv + o] ⊡ ⟨story/excuse⟩ inventar
⊡ (prepare) ⟨prescription/food parcel⟩ preparar; ⟨agenda/list⟩ hacer*
⊡ (a) (complete, add) completar; **she came along to ∼ up the numbers** vino para completar el grupo (b) (compensate for): **I'll take the afternoon off, and ∼ up the time later** me tomaré la tarde libre y ya recuperaré el tiempo más tarde
II [v + adv + o] (constitute) formar; **it is made up of three parts** está compuesto de tres partes
III [v + adv, v + o + adv] (achieve reconciliation) **to ∼ (it) up (WITH sb)** hacer* las paces (CON algn)

make² n marca f

make: ∼-believe n fantasía f; **don't be frightened, it's only ∼-believe** no te asustes, es de mentira; **∼over** n (AmE) maquillaje m; **to have a (cosmetic) ∼over** maquillarse

maker /'meikər ‖'meikə(r)/ n fabricante mf

make: ∼shift adj ⟨repair⟩ provisional, provisorio (AmS); ⟨bed⟩ improvisado; **∼up** n ⊡ (cosmetics) maquillaje m; **to put on one's ∼up** maquillarse, pintarse; (before n) **∼up remover** desmaquillador m; ⊡ (no pl) (of person) carácter m; ⊡ (AmE Educ) examen m de recuperación

making /'meikiŋ/ n (a) (production, creation): **a book about the ∼ of the TV series** un libro que trata de cómo se hizo la serie de televisión; **this is history in the ∼** esto va a pasar a la historia (b) **makings** pl: **you have the ∼s of a good story there** allí tienes material para una buena historia; **she has the ∼s of a great actress** es una gran actriz en ciernes

maladjusted /,mælə'dʒʌstəd ‖,mælə'dʒʌstid/ adj (Psych) inadaptado

maladjustment /,mælə'dʒʌstmənt/ n (Psych) inadaptación f

malaria /məˈleriə ‖məˈleəriə/ n malaria f, paludismo m

Malawi /məˈlɑːwi/ n Malaui m, Malawi m

Malawian /məˈlɑːwiən/ adj malauiano

Malaysia /məˈleɪʒə ‖məˈleɪziə/ n Malaisia f; (continental part) Malasia f

Malaysian¹ /məˈleɪʒən/ adj malaisio; (from continental part) malasio

Malaysian² n malaisio, -sia m,f; (from continental part) malasio, -sia m,f

Maldive Islands /ˈmɔːldiːv, -daɪv/, **Maldives** /-z/ pl n the ~ ~ las (islas) Maldivas

male¹ /meɪl/ adj ‹animal/plant› macho; ‹attitude› masculino; there were several ~ applicants se presentaron varios candidatos varones

male² n (animal) macho m; (person) varón m

malevolent /məˈlevələnt/ adj ‹grin› malévolo; ‹deity› maligno

malformation /ˌmælfɔːrˈmeɪʃən ‖ˌmælfɔːˈmeɪʃən/ n deformación f (esp congénita), malformación f

malfunction¹ /ˈmælˈfʌŋkʃən/ n (a) (defective functioning) mal funcionamiento m (b) (failure) falla f or (Esp) fallo m

malfunction² vi (Med, Tech) fallar, funcionar mal

malice /ˈmæləs ‖ˈmælɪs/ n mala intención f

malicious /məˈlɪʃəs/ adj ‹person/gossip› malicioso; ‹damage› doloso

malignant /məˈlɪgnənt/ adj maligno

malinger /məˈlɪŋgər ‖məˈlɪŋgə(r)/ vi hacerse* el enfermo

mall /mɔːl ‖mæl, mɔːl/ n (a) (for shopping) centro m comercial (b) (avenue) paseo m

mallet /ˈmælət ‖ˈmælɪt/ n mazo m

malnutrition /ˈmælnuːˈtrɪʃən ‖ˌmælnjuːˈtrɪʃən/ n desnutrición f

malpractice /ˈmælˈpræktəs ‖ˌmælˈpræktɪs/ n mala práctica f (en el ejercicio de la profesión)

malt /mɔːlt/ n (a) (grain) malta f (b) ~ (whisky) whisky m de malta

Malta /ˈmɔːltə/ n Malta f

Maltese¹ /ˈmɔːlˈtiːz/ adj maltés

Maltese² n (pl ~) (a) (person) maltés, -tesa m,f (b) (language) maltés m

mamma /ˈmæmə ‖ˈmʌmə/ n ▶ MOMMA

mammal /ˈmæməl/ n mamífero m

mammoth¹ /ˈmæməθ/ n mamut m

mammoth² adj ‹building/cost› gigantesco; ‹task› de titanes

man¹ /mæn/ n (pl men /men/) [1] (a) (adult male) hombre m (b) (husband/boyfriend): her new ~ su nueva pareja (or su nuevo compañero etc); to live together as ~ and wife vivir como marido y mujer (c) (type): he's a local ~ es del lugar; he's a family ~ es un padre de familia

[2] (a) (person) persona f; every ~ for himself (set phrase) sálvese quien pueda (fr hecha) (b) also Man (mankind) (no art) el hombre

[3] men pl: the men (troops) los soldados; (employees) los trabajadores

[4] (in chess) pieza f; (in draughts) ficha f

[5] (as form of address) (colloq): hey, ~! ¡oiga, amigo!, ¡oye, tío (Esp) or (AmL exc CS) mano or (Chi) gallo! (fam), ¡oíme, che! (RPl fam)

man² vt -nn- ‹switchboard› encargarse* de; ‹ship› tripular; soldiers ~ned the barricades había soldados apostados en las barricadas

manacles /ˈmænəkəlz/ pl n (for wrists) esposas fpl; (for legs) grillos mpl

manage /ˈmænɪdʒ/ vt [1] (Busn) ‹company/ bank› dirigir*, administrar, gerenciar (AmL); ‹staff/team› dirigir*; ‹land/finances› administrar

[2] (handle, cope with) ‹children› manejar; ‹household› llevar; she can't ~ the stairs no puede subir la escalera

[3] (achieve): he ~d a smile esbozó una sonrisa forzada; I can't ~ the meeting no puedo ir a la reunión; to ~ to + INF lograr + INF

■ ~ vi [1] (Busn) dirigir*, administrar

[2] (cope): can I help you? — thank you, I can ~ ¿me permite que la ayude? — gracias, yo puedo sola; they have to ~ on $300 a week tienen que arreglarse con 300 dólares a la semana

manageable /ˈmænɪdʒəbəl/ adj ‹child/ animal/hair› dócil; ‹task/goal› posible de alcanzar; ‹size/amount› razonable

management /ˈmænɪdʒmənt/ n [1] (act) (a) (Busn) dirección f, administración f (b) (handling, control) manejo m [2] (managers) (a) (as group) (no art, + sing o pl vb) directivos mpl; senior ~ altos cargos mpl (b) (of particular company) dirección f, gerencia f

manager /ˈmænɪdʒər ‖ˈmænɪdʒə(r)/ n (Busn) (of company, department) director, -tora m,f, gerente mf; (of store, restaurant) gerente mf, encargado, -da m,f; (of estate, fund) administrador, -dora m,f; (of pop group, boxer) manager mf; (Sport) agente mf; (in soccer) entrenador, -dora m,f, director técnico, directora técnica m,f (AmL)

manageress /ˈmænɪdʒərəs ‖ˌmænɪdʒəˈres/ n (esp BrE) encargada f

managerial /ˈmænəˈdʒɪriəl ‖ˌmænɪˈdʒɪəriəl/ adj directivo, gerencial (AmL)

managing director /ˈmænədʒɪŋ ‖ˈmænɪdʒɪŋ/ n (esp BrE) director ejecutivo, directora ejecutiva m,f

mandarin /ˈmændərən ‖ˈmændərɪn/ n ~ (orange) mandarina f

mandate /ˈmændeɪt/ n mandato m

mandatory /ˈmændətɔːri ‖ˈmændətəri/ adj (frml) obligatorio

mane /meɪn/ n (of horse) crin(es) f(pl); (of lion) melena f

maneuver¹, (BrE) **manoeuvre** /məˈnuːvər ‖məˈnuːvə(r)/ n maniobra f

maneuver², (BrE) **manoeuvre** vt: they ~ed the piano up the stairs subieron trabajosamente el piano por la escalera; she ~ed the car out of the garage sacó el coche del garaje maniobrando

■ ~ vi «vehicle/driver» maniobrar, hacer* una

maniobra; **to have room to** ∼ «*driver*» tener* espacio para maniobrar; «*diplomat*» tener* libertad de acción

manger /'meɪndʒər ‖'meɪndʒə(r)/ n pesebre m

mangle¹ /'mæŋgəl/ vt destrozar*

mangle² n rodillo m (escurridor)

mango /'mæŋgəʊ/ n (pl **-goes** or **-gos**) mango m

mangy /'meɪndʒi/ adj **-gier, -giest** ‹cat› sarnoso

man: ∼**handle** vt (move by hand) mover* a pulso; (treat roughly) maltratar; ∼**hole** n registro m, pozo m de inspección; (into sewer) boca f de alcantarilla

manhood /'mænhʊd/ n **(a)** (adulthood) madurez f **(b)** (virility) hombría f

man: ∼**hour** n hora f hombre; ∼**hunt** n persecución f

mania /'meɪniə/ n (pl **-nias**) manía f

maniac /'meɪniæk/ n maniaco, -ca m,f, maníaco, -ca m,f

manic /'mænɪk/ adj ‹behavior› maniaco, maníaco; ‹activity› frenético

manic-depressive /'mænɪkdɪ'presɪv/ n maniacodepresivo, -va m,f

manicure¹ /'mænəkjʊr ‖'mænɪkjʊə(r)/ n manicura f, manicure f (AmL exc RPl)

manicure² vt arreglarle las manos or las uñas a

manifest¹ /'mænəfest ‖'mænɪfest/ v refl (fml) **to** ∼ **itself** «ghost» aparecerse*; «disease/fear» manifestarse*
■ ∼ vt (express) manifestar*

manifest² adj manifiesto

manifestation /'mænəfə'steɪʃən ‖,mænɪfə'steɪʃən/ n manifestación f; (of ghost) aparición f

manifesto /'mænə'festəʊ ‖,mænɪ'festəʊ/ n (pl **-toes** or **-tos**) manifiesto m; (for a specific election) (esp BrE) plataforma f electoral

manifold¹ /'mænəfəʊld ‖'mænɪfəʊld/ adj (frml) múltiples

manifold² n colector m

manipulate /mə'nɪpjəleɪt ‖mə'nɪpjʊleɪt/ vt manipular

manipulative /mə'nɪpjələtɪv ‖mə'nɪpjʊlətɪv/ adj manipulador

mankind /mæn'kaɪnd/ n humanidad f, género m humano

manly /'mænli/ adj **-lier, -liest** ‹physique/ pursuits› varonil, masculino

man-made /'mæn'meɪd/ adj ‹lake› artificial; ‹material› sintético

manna /'mænə/ n maná m

manner /'mænər ‖'mænə(r)/ n **1** (way, fashion) forma f, modo m, manera f; **in a** ∼ **of speaking** en cierto modo **2** (bearing, demeanor) actitud f; **a good telephone** ∼ **is essential** es imprescindible tener buen trato por teléfono **3** (variety) tipo m, suerte f, clase f; **all** ∼ **of things** todo tipo or toda suerte or toda clase de cosas **4 manners** pl (personal conduct) modales mpl, educación f

mannerism /'mænərɪzəm/ n (peculiarity, habit) peculiaridad f; (gesture) gesto m

manoeuvre n/vt/vi (BrE) ▶ MANEUVER¹,²

manor /'mænər ‖'mænə(r)/ n ∼ **(house)** casa f solariega

manpower /'mænpaʊər ‖'mænpaʊə(r)/ n (workers) personal m; (blue-collar) mano f de obra

mansion /'mænʃən/ n mansión f

manslaughter /'mæn,slɔːtər ‖'mæn,slɔːtə(r)/ n homicidio m sin premeditación

mantelpiece /'mæntḷpiːs/ n repisa f de la chimenea

mantle /'mæntḷ/ n **1** (covering) (liter) manto m (liter) **2** (Geol) manto m, sima f

manual¹ /'mænjuəl/ adj manual

manual² n manual m

manufacture¹ /'mænjə'fæktʃər ‖,mænjʊ'fæktʃə(r)/ vt (clothes) fabricar*; ‹clothes› confeccionar; ‹foodstuffs› elaborar

manufacture² n (act) fabricación f; (of clothes) confección f; (of foodstuffs) elaboración f

manufacturer /'mænjə'fæktʃərər ‖,mænjʊ'fæktʃərə(r)/ n fabricante mf

manufacturing /'mænjə'fæktʃərɪŋ ‖,mænjʊ'fæktʃərɪŋ/ adj ‹sector/town› manufacturero; ‹output/capacity› industrial; ∼ **industry** industria f manufacturera

manure /mə'nʊr ‖mə'njʊə(r)/ n estiércol m

manuscript /'mænjəskrɪpt ‖'mænjʊskrɪpt/ n manuscrito m

Manx /mæŋks/ adj manés, de la isla de Man

many¹ /'meni/ adj muchos, -chas; **how** ∼ **plates/cups?** ¿cuántos platos/cuántas tazas?; **I've had as** ∼ **jobs as you** he tenido tantos trabajos como tú; **too** ∼ **problems** demasiados problemas

many² pron muchos, -chas; **how** ∼ **of you smoke?** ¿cuántos/cuántas de ustedes fuman?; **would ten be too** ∼**?** ¿diez serían demasiados?

Maori /'maʊri/ n maorí mf

map¹ /mæp/ n (of country, region) mapa m; (of town, subway, building) plano m

map² **-pp-** vt trazar* el mapa de
■ **map out** [v + o + adv, v + adv + o] ‹itinerary/ holiday› planear

maple /'meɪpəl/ n ∼ **(tree)** arce m; (before n) ∼ **syrup** jarabe m or sirope m de arce

mar /mɑːr ‖mɑː(r)/ vt **-rr-** estropear

marathon /'mærəθɑːn ‖'mærəθən/ n maratón m or f

marauder /mə'rɔːdər ‖mə'rɔːdə(r)/ n (criminal) maleante mf; (prowler) merodeador, -dora m,f

marble /'mɑːrbəl ‖'mɑːbəl/ n **1** (Min) mármol m **2** (Games) canica f or (AmS) bolita f

march¹ /mɑːrtʃ ‖mɑːtʃ/ n **1 (a)** (Mil, Mus) marcha f **(b)** (demonstration) marcha f (de protesta) **2** (of time) paso m; (of science, technology) avance m

march² vi «troops» marchar; **when Saddam** ∼**ed on Kuwait** cuando Saddam invadió Kuwait; **she** ∼**ed into the office** entró con paso firme en or (esp AmL) a la oficina
■ ∼ vt hacer* marchar; **the prisoner was** ∼**ed in** hicieron entrar al prisionero

March /mɑːrtʃ ‖mɑːtʃ/ n marzo m

mare /mer ‖meə(r)/ n yegua f

margarine /'mɑːrdʒərən ‖,mɑːdʒə'riːn/ n margarina f

margin /'mɑːrdʒən ‖'mɑːdʒɪn/ n **1** (on page, typewriter) margen m **2 (a)** (leeway) margen m **(b)** ⋯⊳

(Busn) (of profit) margen *m* (de ganancia) ③ (fringe — of lake) (*often pl*) margen *f*; (— of society) margen *m*

marginal /'mɑːrdʒnəl ‖'mɑːdʒɪnl̩/ *adj* ⟨*difference*⟩ mínimo; ⟨*role*⟩ menor

marginally /'mɑːrdʒnəli ‖'mɑːdʒɪnəli/ *adv* ligeramente

marigold /'mærəgəʊld ‖'mærɪgəʊld/ *n* caléndula *f*, maravilla *f*

marijuana, marihuana /ˌmærə'wɑːnə, -'hwɑː- ‖ˌmæri'wɑːnə/ *n* marihuana *f*

marinade, marinate /'mærəneɪd, -eɪt ‖'mærɪneɪd, -eɪt/ *vt* dejar en adobo

marine¹ /mə'riːn/ *n also* **Marine** (Mil) ≈ infante *m* de marina

marine² *adj* (*before n*) ⟨*biology*⟩ marino; ⟨*engineering*⟩ naval; ⟨*insurance*⟩ marítimo

marital /'mærət ‖'mærɪtl̩/ *adj* ⟨*problems*⟩ matrimonial; ⟨*bliss*⟩ conyugal; ~ **status** estado *m* civil

marjoram /'mɑːrdʒərəm ‖'mɑːdʒərəm/ *n* mejorana *f*

mark¹ /mɑːrk ‖mɑːk/ *n* ① (sign, symbol) marca *f*; (stain) mancha *f*; (imprint) huella *f*; (on body) marca *f*; **as a ~ of respect** en señal de respeto; **to make one's ~** dejar su impronta
② (Educ) nota *f*; (Sport) punto *m*; **to get a good ~** sacar* una buena nota
③ (a) (indicator): **the cost has reached the $100,000 ~** el costo ha llegado a los 100.000 dólares; **to overstep the ~** pasarse de la raya (b) (for race) línea *f* de salida; **on your ~s!** ¡a sus marcas!
④ (target) blanco *m*; **to be wide of the ~**: **his estimate was wide of the ~** erró por mucho en su cálculo
⑤ *also* **Mark** (type, version) modelo *m*
⑥ (Fin) marco *m*

mark² *vt* ① (stain, scar) manchar ② (indicate) señalar, marcar* ③ ⟨*anniversary*⟩ celebrar; ⟨*beginning*⟩ marcar*, señalar ④ ⟨*exam*⟩ (make corrections in) corregir*; (grade) poner(le)* nota a ⑤ (BrE Sport) ⟨*opponent*⟩ marcar*
■ **mark down** [*v + o + adv, v + adv + o*] (a) (Busn) ⟨*goods*⟩ rebajar (b) (BrE Educ) ⟨*person/work*⟩ bajarle la nota a
■ **mark out** [*v + o + adv, v + adv + o*] (a) ⟨*sports ground*⟩ marcar* (b) (select) señalar (c) (distinguish) distinguir*

marked /mɑːrkt ‖mɑːkt/ *adj* ⟨*improvement*⟩ marcado; ⟨*contrast*⟩ acusado

marker /'mɑːrkər ‖'mɑːkə(r)/ *n* (a) (to show position) indicador *m* (b) ~ **(pen)** rotulador *m*

market¹ /'mɑːrkət ‖'mɑːkɪt/ *n* mercado *m*; (street ~) mercado *m or* mercadillo *m or* (CS, Per) feria *f*; **to come on (to) the ~** salir* a la venta; **we put the house on the ~ at $320,000** pusimos la casa en venta en $320.000; (*before n*) ~ **forces** fuerzas *fpl* del mercado ② (Fin) (stock ~) bolsa *f* (de valores); **to corner the ~ (in sth)** hacerse* con el mercado (de algo)

market² *vt* comercializar*

market garden *n* (BrE) huerta *f*

marketing /'mɑːrkətɪŋ ‖'mɑːkɪtɪŋ/ *n* marketing *m*

market: ~**place** *n* (in town) mercado *m*, plaza *f* del mercado; (Busn) mercado *m*; ~ **research** *n* estudio *m or* investigación *f* de mercado

marking /'mɑːrkɪŋ ‖'mɑːkɪŋ/ *n* (a) (on animal, plant) mancha *f* (b) (manmade) marca *f*; road ~s líneas *fpl* de señalización vial

marksman /'mɑːrksmən ‖'mɑːksmən/ *n* (*pl* **-men** /-mən/) tirador *m*

marmalade /'mɑːrməleɪd ‖'mɑːməleɪd/ *n* mermelada *f* (*de cítricos*)

maroon¹ /mə'ruːn/ *adj* granate *adj inv*

maroon² *vt* (*usu pass*) ⟨*castaway*⟩ abandonar (*en una isla desierta*)

marquee /mɑːr'kiː ‖mɑː'kiː/ *n* (a) (canopy) (AmE) marquesina *f* (b) (tent) (BrE) entoldado *m*

marriage /'mærɪdʒ/ *n* ① (a) (act) casamiento *m*, matrimonio *m*; (*before n*) ~ **certificate** certificado *m* de matrimonio (b) (relationship) matrimonio *m*; **her ~ to the poet lasted two years** estuvo dos años casada con el poeta ② (union) (liter) (*no pl*) maridaje *m*, unión *f*

married /'mærid/ *adj* ⟨*man/woman*⟩ casado; **a ~ couple** un matrimonio; **they have been ~ for two years** llevan dos años casados; **to get ~ (to sb)** casarse (con algn)

marrow /'mærəʊ/ *n* ① (bone ~) médula *f* ② ~ **squash** *o* (BrE) ~ (Culin) *tipo de calabaza alargada y de cáscara verde*

marry /'mæri/ **-ries, -rying, -ried** *vt* (a) (get married to) casarse con (b) (perform ceremony) casar (c) (unite, combine) unir
■ ~ *vi* casarse
■ **marry off** [*v + o + adv, v + adv + o*] casar

Mars /mɑːrz ‖mɑːz/ *n* Marte *m*

marsh /mɑːrʃ ‖mɑːʃ/ *n* (*often pl*) pantano *m*; (on coast) marisma *f*

marshal¹ /'mɑːrʃəl ‖'mɑːʃəl/ *n* ① (as title) (Mil) mariscal *m* ② (as title) (AmE) (a) (police chief) jefe, -fa *m,f* de policía (b) (Law) *supervisor de los tribunales de un distrito judicial* ③ (at public gathering) miembro *m* del servicio de vigilancia

marshal² *vt*, (BrE) **-ll-** ⟨*troops/crowd*⟩ reunir*; ⟨*thoughts*⟩ poner* en orden; ⟨*evidence*⟩ reunir*

martial /'mɑːrʃəl ‖'mɑːʃəl/ *adj* marcial

martial: ~ **arts** *pl n* artes *fpl* marciales; ~ **law** *n* ley *f* marcial

martyr /'mɑːrtər ‖'mɑːtə(r)/ *n* mártir *mf*

martyrdom /'mɑːrtərdəm ‖'mɑːtədəm/ *n* martirio *m*

marvel¹ /'mɑːrvəl ‖'mɑːvəl/ *n* maravilla *f*

marvel², (BrE) **-ll-** *vi* **to ~ (AT sth)** maravillarse (DE algo)

marvelous, (BrE) **marvellous** /'mɑːrvləs ‖'mɑːvələs/ *adj* maravilloso

Marxism /'mɑːrksɪzəm ‖'mɑːksɪzəm/ *n* marxismo *m*

Marxist¹ /'mɑːrksəst ‖'mɑːksɪst/ *n* marxista *mf*

Marxist² *adj* marxista

marzipan /'mɑːrzəpɑːn ‖'mɑːzɪpæn, ˌmɑːzɪ'pæn/ *n* mazapán *m*

mascara /mæ'skærə ‖mæ'skɑːrə/ *n* rímel® *m*

mascot /'mæskɑːt ‖'mæskət, -skɒt/ *n* mascota *f*

masculine /'mæskjələn ‖'mæskjʊlɪn/ *adj* masculino

mash¹ /mæʃ/ n(BrE colloq) puré *m* de papas *or* (Esp) de patatas

mash² *vt* hacer* puré de, moler* (Chi, Méx), pisar (RPl, Ven), espichar (Col); **~ed potato(es)** puré *m* de papas *or* (Esp) de patatas

mask¹ /mɑːsk/ n (for disguise, ritual) máscara *f*; (in fencing, ice hockey) careta *f*; (used by doctors) mascarilla *f*, barbijo *m*; (for diving) gafas *fpl* or anteojos *mpl* de bucear; (against dust, fumes) mascarilla *f*

mask² *vt* **(a)** (conceal) ocultar **(b)** (cover) cubrir*

masking tape /'mæskɪŋ ‖'mɑːskɪŋ/ n cinta *f* adhesiva protectora, cinta *f* de enmascarar (Col), tirro *m* (Ven)

masochist /'mæsəkəst ‖'mæsəkɪst/ n masoquista *mf*

mason /'meɪsn/ n **(a)** (Const) albañil *mf*; (stone ~) mampostero *m* **(b)** also **Mason** (Free~) masón *m*, francmasón *m*

masquerade¹ /ˌmæskə'reɪd ‖ˌmɑːskə'reɪd, ˌmæ-/ n mascarada *f*

masquerade² *vi* to ~ **AS** sb hacerse* pasar POR algn

mass¹ /mæs/ n **1** (bulk, body) masa *f*; **her hair was a ~ of curls** tenía la cabeza cubierta de rizos **2 masses** *pl* **(a)** (great quantity) (BrE colloq): **we received ~es of complaints** recibimos montones de quejas (fam) **(b)** the **~es** las masas **3** (Phys) masa *f* **4** also **Mass** (Mus, Relig) misa *f*

mass² *vi* «crowd/clouds» concentrarse

mass³ *adj* (before n) «culture/market» de masas; «hysteria/suicide» colectivo; «protest» masivo; «unemployment» generalizado; **~ meeting** una reunión de todo el personal (or el estudiantado *etc*); **~ transit** (AmE) transporte *m* público

Mass = **Massachusetts**

massacre¹ /'mæsəkər ‖'mæsəkə(r)/ *vt* masacrar

massacre² n matanza *f*, masacre *f*

massage¹ /mə'sɑːʒ ‖'mæsɑːʒ/ *vt* masajear

massage² n masaje *m*

massive /'mæsɪv/ adj «wall» sólido; «support/ task» enorme; «heart attack/overdose» masivo

mass: ~ media *pl* n the **~ media** los medios de comunicación (de masas); **~-produce** /'mæsprə'duːs ‖ˌmæsprə'djuːs/ *vt* fabricar* en serie

mast /mæst ‖mɑːst/ n **(a)** (Naut) mástil *m* **(b)** (flagpole) mástil *m* **(c)** (relay ~) antena *f* repetidora, repetidor *m*

mastectomy /mæ'stektəmi/ n (*pl* **-mies**) mastectomía *f*

master¹ /'mæstər ‖'mɑːstə(r)/ n **1** (of household) señor *m*, amo *m*; (of animal) amo *m*, dueño *m*; (of servant) amo *m*, patrón *m* **2** (expert) **~ OF** sth maestro, -tra *m,f* DE algo **3** (Educ) **(a)** (degree) **~'s (degree)** master *m*, maestría *f*; **M~ of Arts/Science** poseedor de una maestría en Humanidades/Ciencias **(b)** (BrE) (in secondary school) profesor *m* **4** (Naut) capitán *m* **5** (~ copy) (Audio, Comput, Print) original *m*

master² *vt* «technique/subject» llegar* a dominar

master³ *adj* (before n, no comp) **(a)** (expert): **~**

baker/builder maestro *m* panadero/de obras **(b)** (main) «switch/key» maestro **(c)** (original) «tape» original, matriz; **~ plan** plan *m* general

mastermind¹ /'mæstərmaɪnd ‖'mɑːstəmaɪnd/ n cerebro *m*

mastermind² *vt* planear y organizar*

master: ~ of ceremonies n maestro, -tra *m,f* de ceremonias; **~piece** n obra *f* maestra

mastery /'mæstəri ‖'mɑːstəri/ n **(a)** (expertise, skill) maestría *f*; (of language, technique) dominio *m* **(b)** (control) dominio *m*

masturbate /'mæstərbeɪt ‖'mæstəbeɪt/ *vi* masturbarse

mat¹ /mæt/ n (of rushes, straw) estera *f*, esterilla *f*; (door ~) felpudo *m*, tapete *m* (Col, Méx); (table~) (individual) (mantel *m*) individual *m*; (in center of table) salvamanteles *m*, posafuentes *m* (CS)

mat² *adj* (AmE) ▶ MATT

match¹ /mætʃ/ n **1** (for fire) fósforo *m*, cerilla *f* (Esp), cerillo *m* (AmC, Méx) **2** (Sport): **boxing ~** combate *m* de boxeo; **tennis ~** partido *m* de tenis; **football ~** (BrE) partido *m* de fútbol **3** (equal) (no pl): **to be a/no ~ for sb** estar*/no estar* a la altura de algn

match² *vt* **1** (equal) igualar **2 (a)** (correspond to) «description» ajustarse a, corresponder a **(b)** (harmonize with) hacer* juego con **(c)** (make correspond, find equivalent for): **~ the words with the pictures** encuentra la palabra que corresponda a cada dibujo; **to be well ~ed** «competitors» ser* del mismo nivel, ser* muy parejos (esp AmL); «couple» hacer* buena pareja **(d) matching** *pres p* haciendo juego, a juego (Esp)
■ ~ *vi* **(a)** (go together) «clothes/colors» hacer* juego; **a demanding job with a salary to ~** un trabajo que exige mucho con un salario acorde **(b)** (tally) coincidir

match: ~book n (AmE) librito *m* de fósforos or (Esp) de cerillas or (AmC, Méx tb) de cerillos; **~box** n caja *f* de fósforos or (Esp) de cerillas or (AmC, Méx tb) de cerillos; **~maker** n casamentero, -ra *m,f*; **~ point** n punto *m* de partido; **~stick** n **(a)** ▶ MATCH¹ 1 **(b)** (stick) palillo *m*

mate¹ /meɪt/ n **1 (a)** (assistant) ayudante *mf* **(b)** (Naut) oficial *mf* de cubierta; **first ~** primer oficial *m* **2 (a)** (Zool) (male) macho *m*; (female) hembra *f* **(b)** (of person) pareja *f* **3** (BrE colloq) amigo, -ga *m,f*, cuate, -ta *m,f* (Méx fam) **4** (check~) (jaque *m*) mate *m*

mate² *vi* aparearse

material¹ /mə'tɪriəl ‖mə'tɪəriəl/ n **1 (a)** (used in manufacturing etc) material *m* **(b) materials** *pl* (equipment) material *m* **2** (cloth) tela *f*, género *m*, tejido *m* **3 (a)** (for book, show etc) material *m* **(b)** (potential, quality): **this is bestseller ~** este es un bestseller en potencia; **she's champion ~** tiene madera de campeona

material² *adj* material

materialistic /mə'tɪriə'lɪstɪk ‖mə,tɪəriə'lɪstɪk/ adj materialista

materialize /mə'tɪriəlaɪz ‖mə'tɪəriəlaɪz/ *vi* «object/ghost» aparecer*; «hope/idea» hacerse* realidad

maternal /mə'tɜːrnl ‖mə'tɜːnl/ adj **(a)** (motherly) maternal **(b)** (on mother's side) (before n) materno

maternity /mə'tɜ:rnəti IImə'tɜ:nəti/ n maternidad f; (before n) ‹clinic/ward› de obstetricia; ‹dress/clothes› de embarazada, premamá adj inv (Esp); ‹pay/leave› por maternidad; ~ **hospital** maternidad f

math /mæθ/ n (AmE) matemática(s) f(pl)

mathematical /ˈmæθə'mætɪkəl/ adj matemático

mathematician /ˈmæθəmə'tɪʃən/ n matemático, -ca m,f

mathematics /ˈmæθə'mætɪks/ n (+ sing vb) matemática(s) f(pl)

maths /mæθs/ n (BrE) (+ sing vb) matemática(s) f(pl)

matinee, matinée /ˈmætn̩'eɪ IIˈmætɪneɪ/ n (Cin) primera sesión f (de la tarde), matiné(e) f (AmS); (Theat) función f de tarde, matiné(e) f (AmS)

matrices /ˈmeɪtrəsi:z, 'mæt- IIˈmeɪtrɪsi:z/ pl of MATRIX

matriculate /mə'trɪkjəleɪt IImə'trɪkjuleɪt/ vi (frml) matricularse

matrimony /ˈmætrəməʊni IIˈmætrɪməni/ n (frml) matrimonio m

matrix /ˈmeɪtrɪks/ n (pl **matrices** or ~**es**) matriz f

matron /ˈmeɪtrən/ n (a) (dignified woman) matrona f (b) (in prison) (AmE) matrona f (c) (in hospital) (BrE dated) enfermera f jefe or jefa (d) (in school) ≈enfermera f

matt, (AmE also) **matte, mat** /mæt/ adj mate; **a** ~ **finish** un acabado mate

matted /ˈmætəd IIˈmætɪd/ adj enmarañado y apelmazado

matter¹ /ˈmætər IIˈmætə(r)/ n **1** **(a)** (substance) (Phil, Phys) materia f **(b)** (discharge) (Med) pus m, materia f **(c)** (subject ~) temática f, tema m **(d)** (written, printed material): **printed** ~ impresos mpl; **reading** ~ material m de lectura
2 **(a)** (question, affair) asunto m, cuestión f; **it's only a** ~ **of time** solo es cuestión de tiempo; **that's a** ~ **of opinion** eso es discutible **(b)** **matters** pl: **to make** ~**s worse** para colmo (de males); **that didn't help** ~**s** aquello no ayudó a mejorar la situación **(c)** (in phrases) **as a matter of fact: as a** ~ **of fact, I've never been to Spain** la verdad es que nunca he estado en España; **for that matter** en realidad; **no matter** (as interj) no importa; (as conj): **no** ~ **how hard I try** por mucho que me esfuerce
3 (problem, trouble): **what's the** ~? ¿qué pasa?; **what's the** ~ **with Jane?** ¿qué le pasa a Jane?

matter² vi importar

matter-of-fact /ˈmætərəv'fækt/ adj ‹person› práctico; **he explained it in a very** ~ **way** lo explicó con total naturalidad

mattress /ˈmætrəs IIˈmætrɪs/ n colchón m

mature¹ /mə'tʊr IImə'tjʊə(r)/ adj **(a)** (developed) ‹animal/tree› adulto; ‹fruit/artist/ideas› maduro **(b)** (sensible) maduro

mature² vi **(a)** (develop) «plant/animal/person»

desarrollarse; «artist/work» madurar; «wine» añejarse **(b)** (become sensible) madurar **(c)** (Fin) «bond/policy» vencer*

maturity /mə'tʊrəti IImə'tjʊərəti/ n madurez f

maudlin /ˈmɔːdlən IIˈmɔːdlɪn/ adj llorón

maul /mɔːl/ vt atacar* (y herir*)

mausoleum /ˈmɔːsə'li:əm/ n (pl **-ums**) mausoleo m

mauve /məʊv/ adj malva adj inv

maverick /ˈmævərɪk/ n inconformista mf; (Pol) disidente mf

maxim /ˈmæksəm IIˈmæksɪm/ n máxima f

maximize /ˈmæksəmaɪz IIˈmæksɪmaɪz/ vt maximizar*

maximum¹ /ˈmæksəməm IIˈmæksɪməm/ n máximo m

maximum² adj (before n) máximo

may /meɪ/ v mod (past **might**) **1** (asking, granting permission) poder*; ~ **I smoke?** ¿puedo fumar?; ~ **I have your name and address, please?** ¿quiere darme su nombre y dirección, por favor?
2 (indicating probability) [El grado de probabilidad que indica MAY es mayor que el que expresan MIGHT o COULD]: **we** ~ **increase the price** quizás aumentemos el precio; **it** ~ **or** ~ **not be true** puede o no ser cierto
3 (indicating sth is natural): **you** ~ **well ask!** ¡buena pregunta!
4 (conceding): **he** ~ **not be clever, but he's very hard-working** no será inteligente, pero es muy trabajador; **that's as** ~ **be** puede ser

May /meɪ/ n mayo m

Maybe /ˈmeɪbi:/ adv quizá(s), tal vez; ~ **I'll come later** quizá(s) or tal vez venga luego

May: ~ **Day** n el primero de mayo; (in some countries) el día del trabajo; **m**~**fly** n efímera f, cachipolla f

mayhem /ˈmeɪhem/ n caos m

mayonnaise /ˈmeɪə'neɪz, 'meɪəneɪz IIˌmeɪə'neɪz/ n mayonesa f, mahonesa f

mayor /ˈmeɪər IImeə(r)/ n alcalde, -desa m,f, intendente mf (municipal) (RPI)

mayoress /ˈmeɪərəs IIˈmeərəs/ n (BrE) (female mayor) alcaldesa f, intendente f (RPI); (mayor's wife) alcaldesa f

maze /meɪz/ n laberinto m

MB (= **megabyte(s)**) Mb.

MBA n = **Master of Business Administration**

MC n = **master of ceremonies**

Md = **Maryland**

me¹ /mi:, weak form mi/ pron **1** **(a)** (as direct object) me; **she helped** ~ me ayudó; **help** ~ ayúdame **(b)** (as indirect object) me; **he bought** ~ **flowers** me compró flores **(c)** (after prep) mí; **for/behind** ~ para mí/detrás de mí; **come with** ~ ven conmigo; **she's older than** ~ es mayor que yo **2** (emphatic use) yo; **it's** ~ soy yo

me² /mi:/ n (Mus) mi m

ME ⒈ (Geog) = **Maine** ⒉ = **myalgic encephalomyelitis**

meadow /'medəʊ/ n prado m, pradera f

meager, (BrE) **meagre** /'mi:gər ‖'mi:gə(r)/ adj ‹portion/salary› escaso; ‹existence› precario

meal /mi:l/ n ⒈ (Culin) comida f ⒉ (Agr, Culin) harina f (de avena, maíz etc)

mealtime /'mi:ltaɪm/ n hora f de comer

mean¹ /mi:n/ vt (past & past p **meant**)
⒈ (represent, signify) «word/symbol» significar*, querer* decir; **that ~s trouble** eso quiere decir que va a haber problemas; **does the number 0296 ~ anything to you?** ¿el número 0296 te dice algo?; **fame ~s nothing to her** la fama le tiene sin cuidado
⒉ (a) (refer to, intend to say) «person» querer* decir; **what do you ~?** ¿qué quieres decir (con eso)?; **do you know what I ~?** ¿me entiendes?; **I know who you ~** ya sé de quién hablas (b) (be serious about) decir* en serio
⒊ (equal, entail) significar*; **that would ~ repainting the kitchen** eso supondría volver a pintar la cocina
⒋ (a) (intend): **he didn't ~ (you) any harm** no quiso hacerte daño; **to ~ to + INF: I ~ to succeed** mi intención es triunfar; **I ~t to do it but I forgot** tenía toda la intención de hacerlo pero me olvidé (b) **to be ~t to + INF** (supposed, intended): **you weren't ~t to hear that** no pensaron (or pensé etc) que tú estarías escuchando; **I was never ~t to be a teacher** yo no estoy hecho para enseñar

mean² adj ⒈ (miserly) ‹person› tacaño; ‹portion› mezquino ⒉ (a) (unkind, nasty) malo; **it was really ~ of you** fue una maldad (de tu parte) (b) (excellent) (esp AmE sl) genial ⒊ (inferior, humble) (liter) humilde; **that's no ~ feat** no es poca cosa ⒋ (Math) (before n) medio

mean³ n media f, promedio m; see also MEANS

meander /mi'ændər ‖mi'ændə(r)/ vi «river» serpentear; «person» deambular, vagar*

meaning /'mi:nɪŋ/ n significado m

meaningful /'mi:nɪŋfəl/ adj ‹look/experience/relationship› significativo; ‹explanation› con sentido; ‹discussions› positivo

meaningless /'mi:nɪŋləs ‖'mi:nɪŋlɪs/ adj sin sentido

means /mi:nz/ n (pl ~) ⒈ (+ sing vb) (a) (method) medio m; **a ~ to an end** un medio para lograr un fin; **~ of transport** medio de transporte; see also WAYS AND MEANS (b) (in phrases) **by all means** por supuesto, ¡cómo no! (esp AmL); **by no means, or by any means**: **we are by no ~ rich** no somos ricos ni mucho menos; **it's not a perfect film by any ~** de ninguna manera es una película perfecta; **by means of** (as prep) por medio de, mediante
⒉ (frml) (+ pl vb) (wealth) medios mpl (económicos); (income) ingresos mpl

means test n: investigación de los ingresos de una persona para determinar si tiene derecho o no a ciertas prestaciones

meant /ment/ past & past p of MEAN¹

meantime /'mi:ntaɪm/ n: **in the ~** (while sth else happens) mientras tanto, entretanto; (in the intervening period) en el ínterin or interín; **for the ~** por ahora

meanwhile /'mi:nhwaɪl ‖'mi:nwaɪl/ adv mientras tanto, entretanto

measles /'mi:zəlz/ n (+ sing or pl vb) (Med) sarampión m

measure¹ /'meʒər ‖'meʒə(r)/ n ⒈ (a) (system) medida f (b) (unit) medida f (c) (amount) cantidad f; **with a (certain) ~ of success** con cierto éxito ⒉ (device) medida f ⒊ (step) medida f; **to take ~s to + INF** tomar medidas para + INF ⒋ (AmE Mus) compás m

measure² vt ⒈ ‹length/speed/waist› medir*; ‹weight› pesar ⒉ (assess) calcular; **to ~ sth AGAINST sth** comparar algo CON algo
■ ~ vi medir*
■ **measure out** [v + o + adv, v + adv + o] ‹length› medir*; ‹weight› pesar
■ **measure up** [v + adv] estar* a la altura de las circunstancias; **to ~ up TO sth** estar* a la altura DE algo

measurement /'meʒərmənt ‖'meʒəmənt/ n (a) (act) medición f (b) (dimension) medida f

measuring /'meʒərɪŋ/: **~ cup**, (BrE) **~ jug** n jarra f graduada; **~ spoon** n cuchara f de medir

meat /mi:t/ n (a) carne f; (before n) ‹product› cárnico (b) (substance) sustancia f

meat: **~ball** n albóndiga f; **~loaf** n pan m de carne

meaty /'mi:ti/ adj **-tier, -tiest** ‹taste/smell› a carne; ‹soup/stew› con mucha carne

Mecca /'mekə/ n (a) La Meca (b) also **mecca** (center of attraction) meca f

mechanic /mə'kænɪk ‖mɪ'kænɪk/ n mecánico, -ca m,f; see also MECHANICS

mechanical /mə'kænɪkəl ‖mɪ'kænɪkəl/ adj mecánico, maquinal; ‹action/reply› mecánico

mechanics /mə'kænɪks ‖mɪ'kænɪks/ n ⒈ (+ sing vb) (Phys, Mech Eng) mecánica f ⒉ (+ pl vb) **the ~** (practical details) los aspectos prácticos; (mechanical parts) el mecanismo

mechanism /'mekənɪzəm/ n mecanismo m

mechanize /'mekənaɪz/ vt mecanizar*

medal /'medḷ/ n medalla f

medalist, (BrE) **medallist** /'medḷəst ‖'medəlɪst/ n medallista mf; **gold/silver ~** medalla mf de oro/plata

medallion /mə'dæljən/ n medallón m

medallist (BrE) ▶ MEDALIST

meddle /'medḷ/ vi (a) (interfere) **to ~ (IN/WITH sth)** meterse or entrometerse (EN algo) (b) (tamper) **to ~ WITH sth** toquetear algo

media¹ /'mi:diə/ n: **the ~** (+ pl or (crit) sing vb) los medios de comunicación

media² pl of MEDIUM² 1, 2

mediaeval /'mi:di'i:vəl, 'me- ‖,medi'i:vəl/ ▶ MEDIEVAL

median¹ /'mi:diən/ adj (Math) medio

median² n ⒈ (Math) mediana f ⒉ **~ (strip)** (AmE) mediana f, bandejón m (central) (Chi), camellón m (Méx)

mediate /'mi:dieɪt/ vi mediar

mediator /'mi:dieɪtər ‖'mi:dieɪtə(r)/ n mediador, -dora m,f

Medicaid /'medɪkeɪd/ n (in US) organismo y programa estatal de asistencia sanitaria a personas de bajos ingresos

medical¹ /'medɪkəl/ adj ‹care/examination/ insurance› médico; ‹student› de medicina; ~ **school** facultad f de medicina

medical² n revisión f médica

Medicare /'medɪker ‖ 'medɪkeə(r)/ n (in US) organismo y programa estatal de asistencia sanitaria a personas mayores de 65 años

medicated /'medəkeɪtəd ‖ 'medɪkeɪtɪd/ adj medicinal

medication /,medə'keɪʃən ‖ ,medɪ'keɪʃən/ n (a) (substance) medicamento m (b) (drugs) medicación f

medicinal /mə'dɪsnəl ‖ mɪ'dɪsnl̩/ adj medicinal

medicine /'medəsən ‖ 'medsən, 'medəsən/ n **1** (substance) medicamento m, medicina f, remedio m (esp AmL) **2** (science) medicina f

medieval /,mi:di'i:vəl, ,me- ‖ ,medi'i:vəl/ adj medieval, medioeval

mediocre /'mi:di'əʊkər ‖ ,mi:dɪ'əʊkə(r)/ adj mediocre

mediocrity /'mi:di'ɑ:krəti ‖ ,mi:di'ɒkrəti/ n (pl **-ties**) (a) (quality) mediocridad f (b) (person) mediocre mf

meditate /'medəteɪt ‖ 'medɪteɪt/ vi meditar

meditation /,medə'teɪʃən ‖ ,medɪ'teɪʃən/ n meditación f

Mediterranean¹ /'medətə'reɪnɪən ‖ ,medɪtə'reɪnɪən/ adj mediterráneo

Mediterranean² n the ~ (**Sea**) el (mar) Mediterráneo

medium¹ /'mi:diəm/ adj **1** (intermediate) ‹size› mediano **2** (Culin) (a) ‹steak› a punto, término medio (Méx) (b) (as adv): ~ **rare** ‹steak› poco hecho, a la inglesa (Méx); ~ **dry** ‹wine› semi-seco

medium² n **1** (pl **media**) (means, vehicle) medio m **2** (pl **media**) (environment) medio m (ambiente) **3** (middle position) (no pl) punto m medio; **to strike a happy** ~ lograr un término medio **4** (pl **mediums**) (Occult) médium mf

medium: ~**-size** /'mi:diəm'saɪz/, (BrE also) ~**-sized** /-d/ adj ‹book/house› de tamaño mediano; ‹person› de talla media or mediana; ~**-term** /'mi:diəm'tɜ:rm ‖ ,mi:diəm'tɜ:m/ adj (before n) a medio plazo; ~ **wave** n (BrE) (no pl) onda f media

medley /'medli/ n (a) (mixture) mezcla f (b) (Mus) popurrí m

meek /mi:k/ adj **-er, -est** dócil, sumiso

meet¹ /mi:t/ (past & past p **met**) vt **1** (a) (encounter) encontrarse* con (b) (welcome) recibir; (collect on arrival) ir* a buscar; **she ran to** ~ **me** corrió a mi encuentro
2 (make acquaintance of) conocer*; **pleased to** ~ **you** encantado de conocerlo
3 (come up against, experience) encontrar*; **there's more to this than** ~**s the eye** esto es más complicado de lo que parece
4 ‹demands/wishes/debt› satisfacer*; ‹deadline/quota/obligation› cumplir con; ‹requirements› reunir*; ‹cost› hacerse* cargo de
■ ~ vi **1** (a) (encounter each other) encontrarse*; **we arranged to** ~ **at three** quedamos en or (AmL tb) quedamos de encontrarnos a las tres, quedamos a las tres (esp Esp) (b) (hold meeting)

‹‹club›› reunirse*; ‹‹heads of state/ministers›› entrevistarse (c) (make acquaintance) conocerse*; **have you two already met?** ¿ya se conocen?
2 (come into contact): **the vehicles met head on** los vehículos chocaron de frente; **their eyes met** sus miradas se cruzaron
■ **meet up** [v + adv] **to** ~ **up** (WITH sb) encontrarse* (CON algn)
■ **meet with** [v + prep + o] (a) ‹opposition/hostility› ser* recibido con; **she met with an unfortunate accident** le ocurrió un lamentable accidente (b) (meet) (AmE) encontrarse* con

meet² n (a) (AmE Sport) encuentro m (b) (in hunting) partida f (de caza)

meeting /'mi:tɪŋ/ n **1** (assembly) reunión f; **to call/hold a** ~ convocar*/celebrar una reunión; **political** ~ mitin m, mítin m **2** (encounter) encuentro m; (between presidents) entrevista f **3** (BrE Sport) encuentro m

megabyte /'megəbaɪt/ n megabyte m, megaocteto m

megalomaniac /,megələʊ'meɪnɪæk/ n megalómano, -na m,f

megaphone /'megəfəʊn/ n megáfono m

melancholy /'melənkə:li ‖ 'melənkəli/ adj ‹person/mood› melancólico; ‹sound› triste

mellow¹ /'meləʊ/ adj **-er, -est** (a) ‹fruit› maduro; ‹wine› añejo; ‹sound/voice› dulce; ‹light/color› tenue (b) ‹person/mood› apacible

mellow² vt suavizar*
■ ~ vi ‹‹color/voice›› suavizarse*; **he has** ~**ed with age** se le ha suavizado el carácter con los años

melodrama /'melədrɑ:mə/ n melodrama m

melodramatic /'melədrə'mætɪk/ adj melodramático

melody /'melədi/ n (pl **-dies**) melodía f

melon /'melən/ n melón m

melt /melt/ vi ‹‹ice/butter›› derretirse*; ‹‹metal/wax›› fundirse; ‹‹anger›› desaparecer*; **they** ~**ed into the crowd** se perdieron en la muchedumbre
■ ~ vt ‹snow/butter› derretir*; **their cries** ~**ed her heart** su llanto la conmovió
■ **melt away** [v + adv] ‹ice/snow› derretirse*; ‹‹mist/fog›› levantarse; ‹‹fear/suspicion›› disiparse; ‹‹confidence›› desvanecerse*; ‹‹resistance/opposition›› desaparecer*; **they** ~**ed away into the woods** desaparecieron ocultándose en el bosque
■ **melt down** [v + o + adv, v + adv + o] ‹gold/coins› fundir

member /'membər ‖ 'membə(r)/ n **1** (of committee, board) miembro mf; (of club) socio, -cia m,f; ~ **of staff** empleado, -da m,f; **a** ~ **of the audience** un espectador; **the offer is open to any** ~ **of the public** la oferta está abierta al público en general; (before n) ~ **states** países mpl miembros **2** (limb) (arch) miembro m

Member: ~ **of Congress** n (in US) miembro mf del Congreso; ~ **of Parliament** n (in UK etc) diputado, -da m,f, parlamentario, -ria m,f

membership /'membərʃɪp ‖ 'membəʃɪp/ n (a) (being a member): ~ **of the club is restricted to residents** solo los residentes pueden hacerse socios del club; **to apply for** ~ solicitar el ingreso en un club (or partido etc); (before n) ~ **card**

carné *m* de socio **(b)** (members) (+ *sing or pl vb*) socios *mpl* (*or* afiliados *mpl etc*); (number of members) número *m* de socios (*or* afiliados *etc*)

membrane /'membreɪn/ *n* membrana *f*

memento /məˈmentəʊ ‖mɪˈmentəʊ/ *n* (*pl* **-tos** *or* **-toes**) recuerdo *m*

memo /'meməʊ/ *n* (*pl* **-os**) memorándum *m*

memoirs /'memwɑːrz ‖'memwɑːz/ *pl n* memorias *fpl*

memorabilia /ˌmeɱərəˈbɪliə/ *pl n* objetos *mpl* de interés

memorable /'meɱərəbəl/ *adj* memorable

memorandum /ˌmeɱəˈrændəm/ *n* (*pl* **-dums** *or* **-da** /-də/) memorándum *m*

memorial¹ /məˈmɔːriəl/ *n* monumento *m*

memorial² *adj* conmemorativo

Memorial Day *n* (in US) el último lunes de mayo, día en que se recuerda a los caídos en la guerra

memorize /'meɱəraɪz/ *vt* memorizar*

memory /'meɱəri/ *n* (*pl* **-ries**) ⒈ **(a)** (faculty) memoria *f* **(b)** (period): **the worst storm in living** ∼ la peor tormenta que se recuerde ⒉ **(a)** (recollection) recuerdo *m*; **his** ∼ **will live on** su recuerdo permanecerá vivo **(b)** (remembrance) memoria *f*; **in** ∼ **of sb/sth** a la memoria de algn/en conmemoración de algo ⒊ (Comput) memoria *f*

men /men/ *pl of* MAN¹

menace /'menəs ‖'menɪs/ *n* ⒈ **(a)** (threatening quality): **the** ∼ **in his voice** el tono amenazador de su voz **(b)** (threat) amenaza *f* ⒉ (danger) amenaza *f*

menacing /'menəsɪŋ ‖'menɪsɪŋ/ *adj* amenazador

menagerie /məˈnædʒəri/ *n* colección *f* de animales salvajes

mend¹ /mend/ *vt* ⟨*garment*⟩ coser; ⟨*shoe/clock/roof*⟩ arreglar, reparar; **to** ∼ **one's ways** enmendarse*

■ ∼ *vi* (heal) ⟨*injury*⟩ curarse; ⟨*fracture/bone*⟩ soldarse*

mend² *n* remiendo *m*; **to be on the** ∼ (colloq) ir* mejorando

menial /'miːniəl/ *adj* de ínfima importancia

meningitis /ˌmenənˈdʒaɪtəs ‖ˌmenɪnˈdʒaɪtɪs/ *n* meningitis *f*

menopause /'menəpɔːz/ *n* **the** ∼ la menopausia

men's room *n* (AmE) baño *m or* servicios *mpl* de caballeros

menstruate /'menstrueɪt/ *vi* menstruar*

menswear /'menzwer ‖'menzweə(r)/ *n* ropa *f* de caballero

mental /'mentl̩/ *adj* (before n) ⟨*powers/illness*⟩ mental; ⟨*hospital/patient*⟩ psiquiátrico

mental arithmetic *n* cálculos *mpl* mentales

mentality /menˈtæləti/ *n* (*pl* **-ties**) mentalidad *f*

mentally /'mentəli/ *adv* mentalmente; **he's** ∼ **ill/handicapped** es un enfermo mental/un disminuido psíquico

menthol /'menθɔːl ‖'menθɒl/ *n* mentol *m*; (before n) ⟨*cigarettes*⟩ mentolado

mentholated /'menθəleɪtəd ‖'menθəleɪtɪd/ *adj* mentolado

mention¹ /'mentʃən ‖'menʃən/ *vt* mencionar; **I won't** ∼ **any names** no daré nombres; **there's the problem of time, not to** ∼ **the cost** está el problema del tiempo y no digamos ya el costo; **don't** ∼ **it** (on being thanked) no hay de qué, de nada

mention² *n* mención *f*

mentor /'mentɔːr ‖'mentɔː(r)/ *n* (liter) mentor, -tora *m,f* (liter)

menu /'menjuː/ *n* **(a)** (in restaurant) carta *f*, menú *m* (esp AmL) **(b)** (Comput) menú *m*

meow¹ /mi'aʊ/ *n* maullido *m*

meow² *vi* maullar*

MEP *n* (= **Member of the European Parliament**) eurodiputado, -da *m,f*

mercenary /'mɜːrsnəri ‖'mɜːsɪnəri/ *n* (*pl* **-ries**) mercenario, -ria *m,f*

merchandise /'mɜːrtʃəndaɪz ‖'mɜːtʃəndaɪz/ *n* mercancía *f*, mercadería *f* (AmS)

merchant /'mɜːrtʃənt ‖'mɜːtʃənt/ *n* **(a)** (retailer) comerciante *mf* **(b)** (Hist) mercader *m*

merchant marine, (BrE also) **merchant navy** *n* marina *f* mercante

merciful /'mɜːrsɪfəl ‖'mɜːsɪfəl/ *adj* misericordioso

merciless /'mɜːrsɪləs ‖'mɜːsɪlɪs/ *adj* despiadado

mercury /'mɜːrkjəri ‖'mɜːkjʊri/ *n* mercurio *m*

Mercury /'mɜːrkjəri ‖'mɜːkjʊri/ *n* Mercurio *m*

mercy /'mɜːrsi ‖'mɜːsi/ *n* (*pl* **-cies**) **(a)** (clemency) misericordia *f*; **to have** ∼ **(on sb)** tener* misericordia (de algn), apiadarse (de algn); **at the** ∼ **of the elements** a merced de los elementos **(b)** (blessing) bendición *f*; **it's a** ∼ **that** ... (colloq) es una suerte que ...; **let's be thankful for small mercies** (set phrase) seamos positivos, podría haber sido peor

mere /mɪr ‖mɪə(r)/ *adj* (*superl* **merest**) (before n) simple, mero

merely /'mɪrli ‖'mɪəli/ *adv* simplemente

merge /mɜːrdʒ ‖mɜːdʒ/ *vi* ⟨*roads/rivers*⟩ confluir*; ⟨*colors*⟩ fundirse; ⟨*companies*⟩ fusionarse; **he** ∼**d into the crowd** se perdió entre el gentío

■ ∼ *vt* ⟨*companies/organizations*⟩ fusionar; ⟨*colors*⟩ combinar

merger /'mɜːrdʒər ‖'mɜːdʒə(r)/ *n* **(a)** (Busn) fusión *f* **(b)** (of organizations etc) fusión *f*

meringue /məˈræŋ/ *n* merengue *m*

merit¹ /'merət ‖'merɪt/ *n* mérito *m*; **each case is judged on its (own)** ∼**s** se juzga cada caso individualmente

merit² *vt* merecer*

mermaid /'mɜːrmeɪd ‖'mɜːmeɪd/ *n* sirena *f*

merrily /'merəli ‖'merɪli/ *adv* **(a)** (joyfully) alegremente **(b)** (unconcernedly) tranquilamente

merriment /'merɪmənt/ *n* (joy) alegría *f*; (laughter) risas *fpl*

merry /'meri/ *adj* **-rier, -riest** alegre; ∼ **Christmas!** ¡feliz Navidad!, ¡felices Pascuas!

merry-go-round /'merigəʊˌraʊnd/ *n* carrusel *m*, tiovivo *m* (Esp), calesita *f* (Per, RPl)

mesh /meʃ/ *n* malla *f*

mesmerize /'mezməraɪz/ *vt* **(a)** (fascinate) cautivar **(b)** (hypnotize) (dated) hipnotizar*

m

mess /mes/ n **1** (a) (no pl) (untidiness) desorden m; **the bedroom was (in) a** ~ el dormitorio estaba todo desordenado; **my hair is a** ~ (colloq) tengo el pelo hecho un desastre **(b)** (dirt): **what a** ~! ¡qué desastre or (RPl tb) enchastre! (fam); **they made a** ~ **on the carpet** dejaron la alfombra hecha un asco (fam) **2** (no pl) (confused, troubled state): **the country is (in) a complete** ~ la situación del país es caótica; **my life's a** ~ mi vida es un desastre; **to make a** ~ **of sth: you made a real** ~ **of this job** hiciste muy mal este trabajo **3** (Mil): **officers'** ~ casino m or comedor m de oficiales

■ **mess around,** (BrE also) **mess about** (colloq) [v + adv] **(a)** (misbehave) «children» hacer* travesuras **(b)** (interfere): **stop** ~**ing around with my things!** ¡deja mis cosas tranquilas!; **don't** ~ **around with me** no juegues conmigo
■ **mess up** [v + o + adv, v + adv + o] **(a)** (make untidy) desordenar **(b)** (make dirty) ensuciar **(c)** (spoil) «plans» estropear

message /'mesɪdʒ/ n mensaje m; **would you like to leave a** ~? ¿quiere dejar algún recado or (esp AmL) mensaje?, ¿quiere dejar algo dicho? (CS); **to get the** ~ (colloq) entender*, darse* cuenta

messenger /'mesn̩dʒər ‖'mesɪndʒə(r)/ n mensajero, -ra m,f

Messiah /mə'saɪə/ n Mesías m

Messrs /'mesərz ‖'mesəz/ pl of **Mr** Sres.

messy /'mesi/ adj -**sier**, -**siest** **(a)** (untidy) «room» desordenado; «writing» sucio y descuidado, desprolijo (CS) **(b)** (dirty) sucio; **he's a** ~ **eater** no sabe comer **(c)** (unpleasant, confused) «business» turbio

met /met/ past & past p of **MEET**[1]

metabolism /mə'tæbəlɪzəm ‖mə'tæbəlɪzəm/ n metabolismo m

metal /'metl̩/ n (Chem, Metall) metal m; (before n) «box» metálico

metallic /mə'tælɪk/ adj metálico

metamorphosis /ˌmetə'mɔːrfəsəs ‖ˌmetə'mɔːfəsɪs/ n (pl -**phoses** /-fəsiːz/) metamorfosis f

metaphor /'metəfɔːr, -fər ‖'metəfɔː(r), -fə(r)/ n metáfora f

metaphorical /ˌmetə'fɔːrɪkəl ‖ˌmetə'fɒrɪkəl/ adj metafórico

mete /miːt/ ► **METE OUT**

meteor /'miːtiər, -ɔːr ‖'miːtiə(r), -ɔː(r)/ n meteorito m

meteoric /ˌmiːti'ɔːrɪk ‖ˌmiːtɪ'ɒrɪk/ adj «rise/progress» meteórico; ~ **rock** piedra f meteórica

meteorite /'miːtiəraɪt/ n meteorito m

meteorology /ˌmiːtiə'rɑːlədʒi ‖ˌmiːtɪə'rɒlədʒi/ n meteorología f

mete out [v + o + adv, v + adv + o] «fine/punishment» imponer*

meter[1] /'miːtər ‖'miːtə(r)/ n **1 (a)** (measuring device): **gas/electricity/water** ~ contador m or (AmL tb) medidor m de gas/electricidad/agua **(b)** (parking ~) parquímetro m **2** (AmE Mus) compás m **3** (BrE) **metre** (measure) metro m

meter[2] vt medir* (con contador)

methane /'meθeɪn ‖'miːθeɪn/ n metano m

method /'meθəd/ n método m

methodical /mə'θɑːdɪkəl ‖mɪ'θɒdɪkəl/ adj metódico

Methodism /'meθədɪzəm/ n metodismo m

Methodist /'meθədəst ‖'meθədɪst/ n metodista mf

methylated spirit(s) /'meθəleɪtəd ‖'meθəleɪtɪd/ n (+ sing vb) alcohol m desnaturalizado

meticulous /mə'tɪkjələs ‖mə'tɪkjʊləs/ adj meticuloso

metre (BrE) ► **METER**[1] 3

metric /'metrɪk/ adj métrico

metro /'metrəʊ/ n (pl -**ros**) (Rail, Transp) metro m, subterráneo m (RPl)

metropolitan /ˌmetrə'pɑːlətn̩ ‖ˌmetrə'pɒlɪtən/ adj (frml) metropolitano

mettle /'metl̩/ n temple m; **to be on one's** ~ estar* dispuesto a dar lo mejor de sí

mew /mjuː/ vi maullar*

Mexican[1] /'meksɪkən/ adj mexicano, mejicano

Mexican[2] n mexicano, -na m,f, mejicano, -na m,f

Mexico /'meksɪkəʊ/ n México m, Méjico m

Mexico City n (ciudad f de) México m or Méjico m

mezzanine /'mezəniːn/ n **(a)** ~ **(floor)** entresuelo m, mezzanine f or m (AmL) **(b)** (AmE Theat) platea f alta

mi /miː/ n (Mus) mi m

MI = Michigan

miaow /mi'aʊ/ n/vi ► **MEOW**[1,2]

mice /maɪs/ pl of **MOUSE**

Mich = Michigan

microbe /'maɪkrəʊb/ n microbio m

microchip /'maɪkrəʊtʃɪp/ n (micro)chip m, pastilla f de silicio

microcomputer /'maɪkrəʊkəmˌpjuːtər ‖ˌmaɪkrəʊkəm'pjuːtə(r)/ n microcomputadora f (esp AmL), microordenador m (Esp)

microfilm /'maɪkrəʊfɪlm/ n microfilm m, microfilme m

microlight /'maɪkrəʊlaɪt/ n aeroligero m

microphone /'maɪkrəfəʊn/ n micrófono m

microprocessor /'maɪkrəʊˌprɑː'sesər ‖'maɪkrəʊˌprəʊsesə(r)/ n microprocesador m

microscope /'maɪkrəskəʊp/ n microscopio m

microscopic /ˌmaɪkrə'skɑːpɪk ‖ˌmaɪkrə'skɒpɪk/ adj microscópico, al microscopio

microwave /'maɪkrəʊweɪv, 'maɪkrə-/ n ~ **(oven)** (horno m de) microondas m

mid- /mɪd/ *pref*: in ∼**January** a mediados de enero; ∼**morning** a media mañana; **she was in her** ∼**forties** tenía alrededor de 45 años

midair /'mɪd'er ‖‚mɪd'eə(r)/ *n*: **in** ∼ en el aire

midday /'mɪd'deɪ/ *n* mediodía *m*

middle¹ /'mɪdḷ/ *n* **1** (of object, place — center) centro *m*, medio *m*; (— half-way line) mitad *f*; **it stood in the** ∼ **of the room** estaba en el centro *or* en (el) medio de la habitación; **in the** ∼ **of nowhere** quién sabe dónde, en el quinto pino (Esp fam), donde el diablo perdió el poncho (AmS fam) **2** (of period, activity): **in the** ∼ **of the week/January** a mediados de semana/de enero; **it's the** ∼ **of winter** estamos en pleno invierno; **in the** ∼ **of the night** en la mitad de la noche; **I'm in the** ∼ **of a really exciting novel at the moment** en este momento estoy leyendo una novela muy interesante; **I'm in the** ∼ **of cooking dinner** estoy preparando la cena **3** (waist) cintura *f*

middle² *adj* (before *n*): **the** ∼ **house of the three** de las tres, la casa de en medio *or* del medio

middle: ∼**-aged** /'mɪdḷ'eɪdʒd/ *adj* de mediana edad; **M**∼ **Ages** *pl n* the **M**∼ **Ages** la Edad Media; ∼ **class** *n* (often *pl*) clase *f* media; ∼**-class** /'mɪdḷ'klæs ‖‚mɪdḷ'klɑːs/ *adj* de clase media; ∼**-distance** /'mɪdḷ'dɪstəns/ *adj* (before *n*) ⟨running/race⟩ de medio fondo; ∼**-distance runner** mediofondista *mf*; **M**∼ **East** *n* the **M**∼ **East** el Oriente Medio, el Medio Oriente; ∼**man** /'mɪdḷmæn/ *n* (*pl* **-men** /-men/) intermediario *m*; ∼ **management** *n* mandos *mpl* (inter)medios; ∼ **name** *n* segundo nombre *m*; ∼**-of-the-road** /'mɪdḷəvðə'rəʊd/ *adj* ⟨politician/ views⟩ moderado; ⟨artist⟩ del montón; ∼ **school** *n* (in US) *colegio para niños de 12 a 14 años*; (in UK) *colegio para niños de 9 a 13 años*

midge /mɪdʒ/ *n*: *especie de mosquito pequeño*

midget /'mɪdʒət ‖'mɪdʒɪt/ *n* enano, -na *m,f* (*de proporciones normales*)

midnight /'mɪdnaɪt/ *n* medianoche *f*

midst /mɪdst/ *n*: **in the** ∼ **of sth** en medio de algo; **in our** ∼ entre nosotros

midsummer /'mɪd'sʌmər ‖‚mɪd'sʌmə(r)/ *n* pleno verano *m*; **M**∼**'s Day** el solsticio estival *or* vernal; (in the Northern hemisphere) el día de San Juan

midtown /'mɪd'taʊn/ *n* casco *m*, centro *m*; (before *n*) ⟨apartment/hotel⟩ de la periferia del centro

midway /'mɪd'weɪ/ *adv* ⟨stop⟩ a mitad de camino; ∼ **through the morning** a media mañana

midweek¹ /'mɪd'wiːk/ *n*: **around** ∼ a mediados de semana; (before *n*) ⟨concert/flight⟩ de entre semana

midweek² *adv* entre semana

Midwest /'mɪd'west/ *n* the ∼ *la región central de los EEUU*

midwife /'mɪdwaɪf/ *n* (*pl* **-wives**) partera *f*

midwinter /'mɪd'wɪntər ‖‚mɪd'wɪntə(r)/ *n* pleno invierno *m*

might¹ /maɪt/ *v mod* **1** *past of* MAY **2 (a)** (asking permission) (esp BrE) podría (*or* podríamos *etc*); ∼ **I make a suggestion?** si se me permite (hacer) una sugerencia ... **(b)** (in suggestions, expressing annoyance, regret) poder*; **you** ∼ **at least listen** al menos podrías escuchar

3 (indicating possibility) [*La posibilidad que indica* MIGHT *es más remota que la que expresan* MAY *o* COULD]: **somebody** ∼ **have found it** pudiera ser que alguien lo hubiera encontrado; **it** ∼ (**well**) **have been disastrous if the police hadn't arrived** podría haber sido catastrófico si no hubiera llegado la policía **4** (indicating sth is natural): **he rang to apologize — and well he** ∼! llamó para pedir perdón — ¡era lo menos que podía hacer! **5** (conceding): **the house** ∼ **not be big, but ...** la casa no será grande pero ...

might² *n* poder *m*

mighty¹ /'maɪti/ *adj* **-tier, -tiest (a)** (powerful) ⟨empire/ruler⟩ poderoso; ⟨kick/blow⟩ fortísimo **(b)** (imposing) ⟨ocean/river⟩ imponente

mighty² *adv* (colloq) (*as intensifier*) muy

migraine /'maɪgreɪn ‖'miːgreɪn, 'maɪ-/ *n* jaqueca *f*, migraña *f*

migrant¹ /'maɪgrənt/ *n* **(a)** (Zool) (species) especie *f* migratoria; (bird) ave *f*‡ migratoria **(b)** (person) trabajador, -dora *m,f* itinerante

migrant² *adj* **(a)** (Zool) migratorio **(b)** (before *n*) ⟨worker⟩ itinerante; (foreign) extranjero

migrate /'maɪgreɪt ‖maɪ'greɪt/ *vi* emigrar

migration /maɪ'greɪʃən/ *n* migración *f*

mike /maɪk/ *n* (colloq) micro *m* (fam)

milage *n* ▸ MILEAGE

mild /maɪld/ *adj* **-er, -est** **1 (a)** (gentle) ⟨person⟩ afable; ⟨manner/criticism⟩ suave **(b)** (not serious or potent) ⟨attack/form⟩ ligero, leve; ⟨discomfort⟩ ligero **2** ⟨climate⟩ templado; ⟨winter⟩ no muy frío; **it's very** ∼ **today** hoy no hace nada de frío **3** ⟨cheese/tobacco/detergent/ sedative⟩ suave

mildew /'mɪldu ‖'mɪldju:/ *n* (on plants) mildeu *m*, mildiu *m*; (on wall, fabric) moho *m*

mildly /'maɪldli/ *adv* **(a)** (gently) ⟨rebuke⟩ suavemente; **to put it** ∼ por no decir algo peor **(b)** (slightly) ligeramente

mile /maɪl/ *n* milla *f* (*1.609 metros*); **that's** ∼**s away from home** (colloq) eso está lejísimos de aquí; **it sticks** *o* **stands out a** ∼ se ve a la legua

mileage /'maɪlɪdʒ/ *n* **1** (Auto) distancia *f* recorrida (*en millas*), ≈ kilometraje *m* **2** (advantage, profit): **they want to extract maximum** ∼ **from the Pope's visit** quieren explotar al máximo la visita del Papa

mileometer /maɪ'lɑːmətər ‖maɪ'lɒmɪtə(r)/ *n* (BrE) ≈ cuentakilómetros *m*

milestone /'maɪlstəʊn/ *n* (on road) mojón *m*; (significant event) hito *m*, jalón *m*

militant¹ /'mɪlɪtənt/ *adj* militante

militant² *n* militante *mf*

military¹ /'mɪləteri ‖'mɪlɪtri/ *adj* militar; ∼ **academy** (in US) escuela *f* militar; **to do** ∼ **service** hacer* el servicio militar

military² *n* the ∼ los militares

military police *n* policía *f* militar

militia /mə'lɪʃə ‖mɪ'lɪʃə/ *n* (+ *sing or pl vb*) milicia *f*

milk¹ /mɪlk/ *n* **(a)** leche *f*; (before *n*) ⟨production/bottle⟩ de leche; ⟨product⟩ lácteo; ∼ **chocolate** chocolate *m* con leche **(b)** (lotion) (BrE) leche *f*

milk² vt (a) ⟨cow/herd⟩ ordeñar (b) (exploit) explotar

milk: ~**man** /'mɪlkmən/ n (pl **-men** /-mən/) lechero m; ~ **shake** n batido m, (leche f) malteada f (AmL), licuado m con leche (AmL)

milky /'mɪlki/ adj **-kier, -kiest** lechoso; ⟨coffee/tea⟩ con mucha leche

Milky Way n the ~ ~ la Vía Láctea

mill¹ /mɪl/ n **1** (a) (building, machine) molino m (b) (for pepper etc) molinillo m **2** (cotton ~) fábrica f de tejidos de algodón

mill² vt ⟨flour⟩ moler*
■ **mill about, mill around** [v + adv] «crowd» dar* vueltas

millennium /mɪ'leniəm/ n (pl **-niums** or **-nia** /-niə/) milenio m

millennium bug n efecto m dos mil

miller /'mɪlər ‖ 'mɪlə(r)/ n molinero, -ra m,f

milligram /'mɪləgræm ‖ 'mɪlɪgræm/ n miligramo m

millimeter, (BrE) **millimetre** /'mɪlə,mi:tər ‖ 'mɪlimi:tə(r)/ n milímetro m

milliner /'mɪlənər ‖ 'mɪlɪnə(r)/ n sombrerero, -ra m,f de señoras

million /'mɪljən/ n millón m; a ~ people un millón de personas

millionaire /,mɪljə'ner ‖ ,mɪljə'neə(r)/ n millonario, -ria m,f

milometer /maɪ'lɑːmətər ‖ maɪ'lɒmɪtə(r)/ n ▶ MILEOMETER

mime¹ /maɪm/ n (a) (technique) mímica f (b) ~ (artist) mimo mf (c) (performance) pantomima f

mime² vt imitar, hacer* la mímica de
■ ~ vi hacer* la mímica

mimic /'mɪmɪk/ vt **-ck-** imitar

mince¹ /mɪns/ vt ⟨onions⟩ picar* (en trozos menudos); ⟨meat⟩ moler* or (Esp, RPl) picar*; **not to** ~ **(one's) words** no andar(se)* con rodeos
■ ~ vi caminar con afectación

mince² n (BrE) carne f molida or (Esp, RPl) picada

mincemeat /'mɪnsmi:t/ n picadillo de frutos secos, grasa y especias usado en pastelería

mind¹ /maɪnd/ n **1** (a) (Psych) mente f; **to bear** o **keep sth/sb in** ~ tener* algo/a algn en cuenta; **to bring** o **call sth to** ~ recordar(le)* algo (a algn); **to have sth/sb in** ~ tener* algo/a algn en mente; **with that in** ~ pensando en eso; **what's on your** ~? ¿qué es lo que te preocupa?; **that put my** ~ **at rest** con eso me tranquilicé; **put it out of your** ~! ¡no pienses más en eso!; **I can't get him/the thought out of my** ~ no puedo quitármelo de la cabeza; **to read sb's** ~ adivinarle or leerle* el pensamiento a algn (b) (mentality) mentalidad f **2** (attention): **my** ~ **was on other things** tenía la cabeza en otras cosas; **he needs something to take his** ~ **off it** necesita algo que lo distraiga **3** (a) (opinion): **to change one's** ~ cambiar de opinión; **to make up one's** ~ decidirse; **to my** ~ a mi parecer (b) (will, intention): **he has a** ~ **of his own** (he is obstinate) es muy empecinado; (he knows his own mind) sabe muy bien lo que quiere; **I've a good** ~ **to complain to the manager** tengo ganas de ir a quejarme al gerente **4** (mental faculties) juicio m, razón f; **to be/go out of one's** ~ estar*/volverse* loco

mind² vt **1** (look after) ⟨children⟩ cuidar, cuidar de; ⟨seat/place⟩ guardar; ⟨shop/office⟩ atender* **2** (usu in imperative) **(a)** (be careful about): ~ **your head!** ¡ojo or cuidado con la cabeza!; ~ **(that) you don't forget!** procura no olvidarte **(b)** (concern oneself about) preocuparse por; **never** ~ **him!** ¡no le hagas caso! **3** (object to) (usu neg or interrog): **I don't** ~ **the noise** no me molesta or no me importa el ruido; **I don't** ~ **him, but I can't stand her** él no me disgusta, pero a ella no la soporto; **I don't** ~ **what you do** me da igual lo que hagas; **would you** ~ **waiting?** ¿le importaría esperar?
■ ~ vi **1** (in imperative) (concern oneself) **never** ~ no importa, no te preocupes (or no se preocupen etc); **never you** ~! ¡a ti) qué te importa! **2** (object) (usu neg or interrog): **I don't** ~ me da igual; **do you** ~ **if I open the window?** ¿le importa or le molesta si abro la ventana?; **do you** ~ **if I smoke? — yes, I do** ~! ¿te importa si fumo? — ¡sí que me importa!

-minded /'maɪndəd ‖ 'maɪndɪd/ suff: **business**~ con mentalidad para los negocios; **liberal**~ liberal

mindless /'maɪndləs ‖ 'maɪndlɪs/ adj ⟨activity⟩ mecánico; ⟨violence/obedience⟩ ciego

mine¹ /maɪn/ n **1** (Min) mina f; **to be a** ~ **of information** ser* una mina de información **2** (Mil) mina f

mine² pron

■ **Note** The translation mío reflects the gender and number of the noun it is standing for; mine is translated by el mío, la mía, los míos, las mías, depending on what is being referred to.

(sing) mío, mía; (pl) míos, mías; ~ **is here** el mío/la mía está aquí; **a friend of** ~ un amigo mío; **it's a hobby of** ~ es uno de mis hobbies

mine³ vt **1** (Min) ⟨gold/coal⟩ extraer* **2** (Mil) minar

minefield /'maɪnfi:ld/ n campo m minado

miner /'maɪnər ‖ 'maɪnə(r)/ n minero, -ra m,f

mineral /'mɪnərəl/ n mineral m

mineral water n agua f‡ mineral

mingle /'mɪŋgəl/ vi (a) «people» mezclarse; (at a party etc) circular (b) «liquids» mezclarse; «sounds» fundirse
■ ~ vt **to** ~ **sth WITH sth** mezclar algo CON algo

miniature¹ /'mɪnɪtʃʊr ‖ 'mɪnɪtʃə(r)/ n miniatura f

miniature² adj (before n) ⟨portrait⟩ en miniatura; ⟨poodle⟩ enano

minibus /'mɪnɪbʌs/ n microbús m, micro m

minicab /'mɪnɪkæb/ n (BrE) taxi m (que se pide por teléfono)

minim /'mɪnəm ‖ 'mɪnɪm/ n (BrE) blanca f

minimal /'mɪnəməl ‖ 'mɪnɪməl/ adj mínimo

minimize /'mɪnəmaɪz ‖ 'mɪnɪmaɪz/ vt ⟨risk/cost⟩ reducir* (al mínimo)

minimum¹ /'mɪnəməm ‖ 'mɪnɪməm/ n mínimo m

minimum² adj (before n) mínimo

mining /'maɪnɪŋ/ n minería f; (before n) ⟨company/town⟩ minero

miniskirt /'mɪnɪskɜrt ‖ 'mɪnɪskɜ:t/ n minifalda f

minister[1] /'mɪnəstər ‖'mɪnɪstə(r)/ n **1** (Relig) pastor, -tora *m,f* **2** (Pol) ministro, -tra *m,f*, secretario, -ria *m,f* (Méx)

minister[2] *vi* to ~ TO sb cuidar DE algn

ministry /'mɪnəstri ‖'mɪnɪstri/ n (*pl* **-tries**) (Pol) ministerio *m*, secretaría *f* (Méx)

mink /mɪŋk/ n (*pl* ~**s** *or* ~) **(a)** (animal) visón *m* **(b)** (fur) visón *m*

Minn = Minnesota

minor[1] /'maɪnər ‖'maɪnə(r)/ adj **1** (unimportant) ‹poet/work› menor; ‹role› secundario; ‹operation› de poca importancia *or* gravedad **2** (Mus) menor

minor[2] n **1** (Law) menor *mf* (de edad) **2** (AmE Educ) asignatura *f* secundaria

Minorca /mə'nɔːrkə ‖mɪ'nɔːkə/ n Menorca *f*

minority /mə'nɔːrəti ‖maɪ'nɒrɪti/ n (*pl* **-ties**) **(a)** (smaller number) (+ *sing o pl vb*) minoría *f*; ‹before n› ‹group/vote› minoritario **(b)** (in US) (Govt) oposición *f*

minor league n (in US) (Sport) liga *f* menor

minstrel /'mɪnstrəl/ n trovador *m*

mint[1] /mɪnt/ n **1** (Bot, Culin) **(a)** (spear~) menta *f* (verde) **(b)** (pepper~) menta *f*, hierbabuena *f* **(c)** (confection) pastilla *f* de menta **2** (Fin) casa *f* de la moneda

mint[2] *vt* ‹coin› acuñar

mint[3] adj (before n) ‹coin/stamp› sin usar; in ~ condition en perfecto estado

minus[1] /'maɪnəs/ n (*pl* **-nuses** *or* **-nusses**) **(a)** ~ (sign) (signo *m* de) menos *m* **(b)** (disadvantage) (colloq) desventaja *f*

minus[2] adj **(a)** (disadvantageous) (colloq) (before n) on the ~ side, ... un factor negativo es que ... **(b)** (negative) (before n) ‹number› negativo

minus[3] prep **(a)** (Math) menos ▶ FOUR[1] **(b)** (without, missing) (colloq) sin

minuscule /'mɪnəskjuːl/ adj minúsculo

minute[1] /'mɪnət ‖'mɪnɪt/ n **1** **(a)** (unit of time) minuto *m*; (before n) ~ hand minutero *m* **(b)** (short period) minuto *m*, momento *m* **(c)** (instant) minuto *m*; any ~ (now) de un momento a otro **2** **(a)** (memorandum) acta *f* **(b)** (of meeting): the ~s el acta

minute[2] /maɪ'nuːt ‖maɪ'njuːt/ adj ‹amount› mínimo; ‹object› diminuto

miracle /'mɪrɪkəl ‖'mɪrəkəl/ n milagro *m*; (before n) ‹drug/cure› milagroso

miraculous /mə'rækjələs ‖mɪ'rækjʊləs/ adj milagroso

mirage /mə'rɑːʒ ‖'mɪrɑːʒ, mɪ'rɑːʒ/ n espejismo *m*

mirror[1] /'mɪrər ‖'mɪrə(r)/ n espejo *m*; (driving ~) (espejo *m*) retrovisor *m*

mirror[2] *vt* reflejar

mirth /mɜːrθ ‖mɜːθ/ n (liter) regocijo *m* (liter)

misadventure /ˌmɪsəd'ventʃər ‖ˌmɪsəd'ventʃə(r)/ n desventura *f*

misapprehension /mɪsˌæprɪ'hentʃən ‖ˌmɪsæprɪ'henʃən/ n (fml) malentendido *m*

misappropriate /ˌmɪsə'prəʊprɪeɪt/ *vt* malversar

misbehave /ˌmɪsbɪ'heɪv/ *vi* portarse mal

miscalculation /ˌmɪskælkjə'leɪʃən ‖ˌmɪskælkjʊ'leɪʃən/ n error *m* de cálculo

miscarriage /'mɪsˌkærɪdʒ/ n **1** (Med) aborto *m* espontáneo *or* no provocado; **to have a ~** tener* un aborto **2** **a ~ of justice** una injusticia

miscarry /'mɪsˌkæri/ *vi* **-ries, -rying, -ried** **(a)** (Med) abortar (*espontáneamente*), tener* un aborto **(b)** (liter) «*plan*» malograrse (liter)

miscellaneous /ˌmɪsə'leɪnɪəs/ adj ‹collection/ crowd› heterogéneo; ‹assortment› variado

mischance /'mɪs'tʃæns ‖ˌmɪs'tʃɑːns/ n infortunio *m*

mischief /'mɪstʃəf ‖'mɪstʃɪf/ n **(a)** (naughtiness): **to get up to ~** hacer* travesuras **(b)** (trouble, harm) daño *m*; **to make ~** causar daños

mischievous /'mɪstʃəvəs ‖'mɪstʃɪvəs/ adj ‹child› travieso; ‹grin› pícaro

misconception /ˌmɪskən'sepʃən/ n error *m*

misconduct /'mɪs'kɑːndʌkt ‖ˌmɪs'kɒndʌkt/ n (fml) mala conducta *f*

misconstrue /ˌmɪskən'struː/ *vt* (fml) malinterpretar

misdemeanor, (BrE) **misdemeanour** /'mɪsdɪ'miːnər ‖ˌmɪsdɪ'miːnə(r)/ n (Law) delito *m* menor

miser /'maɪzər ‖'maɪzə(r)/ n avaro, -ra *m,f*

miserable /'mɪzərəbəl/ adj **1** **(a)** (in low spirits) abatido **(b)** (depressing) ‹weather› deprimente; ‹prospect› triste **2** **(a)** (mean-spirited) miserable **(b)** (wretched, poor) mísero **(c)** ‹episode/failure› lamentable

miserably /'mɪzərəbli/ adv **(a)** (unhappily) con abatimiento **(b)** ‹fail› de manera lamentable

miserly /'maɪzərli ‖'maɪzəli/ adj mezquino

misery /'mɪzəri/ n sufrimiento *m*; **to make sb's life a ~** amargarle* la vida a algn

misfire /'mɪs'faɪr ‖ˌmɪs'faɪə(r)/ *vi* «*gun/engine/ plan*» fallar

misfit /'mɪsfɪt/ n: **a social ~** un inadaptado social

misfortune /mɪs'fɔːrtʃən ‖ˌmɪs'fɔːtʃən, ˌmɪs'fɔːtʃuːn/ n (fml) desgracia *f*; **to have the ~ to + INF** tener* la desgracia DE + INF

misgiving /mɪs'gɪvɪŋ/ n recelo *m*

misguided /'mɪs'gaɪdəd ‖ˌmɪs'gaɪdɪd/ adj equivocado

mishandle /'mɪs'hændl/ *vt* (deal with ineptly) llevar mal

mishap /'mɪshæp/ n percance *m*

mishear /'mɪs'hɪr ‖ˌmɪs'hɪə(r)/ (*past & past p* **-heard**) *vt/i* entender* mal

misinform /ˌmɪsɪn'fɔːrm ‖ˌmɪsɪn'fɔːm/ *vt* (fml) informar mal, malinformar (CS fml)

misinterpret /ˌmɪsɪn'tɜːrprət ‖ˌmɪsɪn'tɜːprɪt/ *vt* ‹statement/action› interpretar mal; (deliberately) tergiversar

misjudge /'mɪs'dʒʌdʒ/ *vt* **(a)** (judge unfairly) juzgar* mal **(b)** (miscalculate) calcular mal

mislay /'mɪs'leɪ/ *vt* (*past & past p* **-laid**) perder* (*momentáneamente*)

mislead /'mɪs'liːd/ *vt* (*past & past p* **-led**) engañar; ‹court/parliament› inducir* a error

mismanage /'mɪs'mænɪdʒ/ *vt* ‹affair› llevar mal; ‹company› administrar mal

misogynist /mɪ'sɑːdʒənəst ‖mɪ'sɒdʒɪnɪst/ n misógino *m*

misplace /mɪs'pleɪs/ vt perder* (momentáneamente)

misprint /'mɪsprɪnt/ n errata f

misrepresent /ˌmɪsreprɪ'zent/ vt ‹event› deformar; ‹remarks/views› tergiversar

miss¹ /mɪs/ n [1] **Miss** (as title) señorita f; M~ **Jane Smith** la señorita Jane Smith; (in correspondence) Sra Jane Smith [2] (failure to hit) fallo m; **to give sth a ~** (colloq): **I think I'll give swimming a ~ this afternoon** creo que esta tarde no voy a ir a nadar

miss² vt
I [1] (a) (fail to hit): **the bomb ~ed its target** la bomba no cayó en el blanco; **the bullet just ~ed him** la bala le pasó rozando (b) (overlook, fail to notice): **you ~ed three mistakes** se te pasaron (por alto) tres errores; **you can't ~ it** lo va a ver enseguida, no tiene pérdida (Esp) (c) (fail to hear, understand) no oír*; **he's ~ed the point** no ha entendido (d) ‹chance› perder*
[2] (fail to catch) ‹bus/flight› perder*; **sorry, you've just ~ed him** lo siento, acaba de irse
[3] (a) (fail to experience) perderse*; **you didn't ~ much** no te perdiste nada (b) (fail to attend) ‹meeting› faltar a; ‹party/show› perderse*
II (a) (regret absence of) ‹friend/country/activity› echar de menos, extrañar (esp AmL) (b) (notice absence of) echar en falta; **when did you first ~ the necklace?** ¿cuándo echaste en falta el collar?
■ ~ vi «marksman» errar* el tiro, fallar; «bullet» no dar* en el blanco
■ **miss out** [1] [v + o + adv, v + adv + o] ‹line/paragraph› saltarse
[2] [v + adv] **to ~ out ON sth** perderse* algo

Miss = **Mississippi**

misshapen /mɪs'ʃeɪpən/ adj deforme

missile /'mɪsəl ‖ 'mɪsaɪl/ n (Mil) misil m; (sth thrown) proyectil m

missing /'mɪsɪŋ/ adj: **the ~ papers** los papeles que faltan; **~ person** desaparecido, -da m,f; **to be ~** faltar; **to go ~** (BrE) desaparecer*

mission /'mɪʃən/ n misión f

missionary /'mɪʃəneri ‖ 'mɪʃənəri/ n misionero, -ra m,f

misspent /mɪs'spent/ adj (before n) ‹money› malgastado; ‹hours› perdido; **a ~ youth** (set phrase) una juventud disipada

mist /mɪst/ n (a) (Meteo) neblina f; **sea ~** bruma f (b) (condensation) vaho m (c) (spray) vaporización f
■ **mist over** [v + adv] «eyes» empañarse; «glass/mirror» empañarse
■ **mist up** [v + adv] «glass/mirror» empañarse

mistake¹ /mə'steɪk ‖ mɪ'steɪk/ n error m; **to make a ~** cometer un error; **by ~** por equivocación, por error

mistake² vt (past **-took**; past p **-taken**) confundir; **to ~ sth/sb FOR sth/sb** confundir algo/a algn con algo/algn

mistaken /mə'steɪkən ‖ mɪ'steɪkən/ adj ‹impression/idea› equivocado; **unless I'm (very) much ~** si no me equivoco

mistletoe /'mɪsəltəʊ/ n muérdago m

mistook /mɪ'stʊk/ past of MISTAKE²

mistreat /mɪs'triːt/ vt maltratar

mistress /'mɪstrəs ‖ 'mɪstrɪs/ n (a) (of dog) dueña f, ama f‡; (of servant) señora f (b) (lover) amante f

mistrust¹ /mɪs'trʌst/ vt desconfiar* de, recelar de

mistrust² n desconfianza f, recelo m

mistrustful /mɪs'trʌstfəl/ adj desconfiado, receloso

misty /'mɪsti/ adj **-tier, -tiest** ‹day/morning› neblinoso; **it's ~** hay neblina; (it's drizzling) (AmE) está lloviznando

misunderstand /'mɪsʌndər'stænd ‖ ˌmɪs.ʌndə'stænd/ (past & past p **-stood**) vt ‹idea/instructions› entender* or comprender mal; ‹remark/motives› malinterpretar; ‹artist/work› interpretar mal

misunderstanding /'mɪsʌndər'stændɪŋ ‖ ˌmɪs.ʌndə'stændɪŋ/ n malentendido m

misunderstood /'mɪsʌndər'stʊd ‖ ˌmɪs.ʌndə'stʊd/ past & past p of MISUNDERSTAND

misuse¹ /mɪs'juːs/ n (of word) mal uso m; (of power) abuso m; (of funds) malversación f; (of resources) despilfarro m

misuse² /mɪs'juːz/ vt ‹language/tool› utilizar* or emplear mal; ‹resources› despilfarrar; ‹funds› malversar

mite /maɪt/ n (Zool) ácaro m

miter, (BrE) **mitre** /'maɪtər ‖ 'maɪtə(r)/ n mitra f

mitigate /'mɪtəgeɪt ‖ 'mɪtɪgeɪt/ vt (frml) (a) (soften, lessen) mitigar* (frml) (b) **mitigating** pres p ‹factor› atenuante; **mitigating circumstances** (circunstancias fpl) atenuantes fpl or mpl

mitre /'maɪtər ‖ 'maɪtə(r)/ n (BrE) ▶ MITER

mitt /mɪt/ n (a) (mitten) mitón m (b) (in baseball) manopla f, guante m (de béisbol)

mitten /'mɪtn/ n mitón m

mix¹ /mɪks/ n (a) (mixture, ingredients) mezcla f; **cake ~** preparado comercial para hacer pasteles (b) (Audio) mezcla f

mix² vt (a) ‹ingredients/paint› mezclar; ‹cocktail› preparar (b) (Audio) mezclar
■ ~ vi (a) (combine) «substances» mezclarse (b) (go together) «foods/colors» combinar (bien) (c) (socially): **she doesn't ~ well at parties** le cuesta entablar conversación con la gente en una reunión; **to ~ WITH sb** tratarse CON algn
■ **mix up**
I [v + o + adv, v + adv + o] [1] (throw into confusion) desordenar [2] (confuse) confundir
II (usu pass) (a) (involve) **to get ~ed up IN sth** meterse EN algo (b) (confuse): **to get ~ed up** confundirse

mixed /mɪkst/ adj (a) (various) mezclado; **~ spice** mezcla f de especias (b) (male and female) ‹sauna/bathing› mixto (c) (ambivalent) ‹fortunes› desigual; **I have ~ feelings about it** no sé muy bien qué pensar sobre el asunto

mixer /'mɪksər ‖'mɪksə(r)/ n **(a)** (Culin) batidora f **(b)** (Audio, Cin, TV) (person) operador, -dora m,f de sonido; (machine) mezcladora f **(c)** (sociable person) persona f sociable **(d)** (dance) (AmE) baile m **(e)** (drink) refresco m (para mezclar con alcohol)

mixing bowl /'mɪksɪŋ/ n bol m (grande, para mezclar ingredientes)

mixture /'mɪkstʃər ‖'mɪkstʃə(r)/ n mezcla f

mix-up /'mɪksʌp/ n (colloq) lío m (fam)

mm (= **millimeter(s)** o (BrE) **millimetre(s)**) mm.

MN = Minnesota

MO = Missouri

moan¹ /məʊn/ vi **(a)** (make sound) «person/ wind» gemir* **(b)** (complain) (pej) **to ~ (ABOUT sth)** quejarse (DE algo)

moan² n **(a)** (sound) gemido m **(b)** (complaint) (colloq) (no pl) queja f

moat /məʊt/ n foso m

mob¹ /mɑ:b ‖mɒb/ n turba f; (before n) **~ rule** la ley de la calle

mob² vt **-bb-** atacar* en grupo

mobile¹ /'məʊbəl ‖'məʊbaɪl/ adj **(a)** ⟨library/ shop⟩ ambulante **(b)** (able to move): **we try and get the patient ~ as soon as possible** tratamos de que el paciente recupere su movilidad lo más pronto posible

mobile² n móvil m

mobile: ~ home n trailer m (AmL), caravana f fija (Esp); **~ phone** n (teléfono m) celular m (AmL), (teléfono m) móvil m (Esp)

mobilize /'məʊbəlaɪz ‖'məʊbɪlaɪz/ vt movilizar*

mock¹ /mɑ:k ‖mɒk/ vt burlarse de

mock² adj (before n) ⟨examination/interview⟩ de práctica; ⟨anger/outrage⟩ fingido

mockery /'mɑ:kəri ‖'mɒkəri/ n **(a)** (ridicule) burla f **(b)** (travesty) (no pl) farsa f; **to make a ~ of sth** ridiculizar* algo

mocking /'mɑ:kɪŋ ‖'mɒkɪŋ/ adj burlón

mod cons /'mɑ:d'kɑ:nz ‖,mɒd'kɒnz/ pl n (= **modern conveniences**) (BrE colloq & journ) comodidades fpl

mode /məʊd/ n ⓵ **(a)** (means) medio m; (kind) modo m **(b)** (operating method) (Comput, Tech) modalidad f ⓶ (Math) modo m ⓷ (Clothing) moda f

model¹ /'mɑ:dl ‖'mɒdl/ n ⓵ (reproduction) maqueta f, modelo m ⓶ (paragon, example) modelo m ⓷ (design) modelo m ⓸ (person) modelo mf

model², (BrE) **-ll-** vt ⓵ ⟨clay/shape⟩ modelar ⓶ (base): **their education system was ~ed on that of France** su sistema educativo se inspiró en el francés; **to ~ oneself on sb** tomar a algn como modelo ⓷ ⟨garment⟩: **she ~s sportswear** es modelo de ropa sport

model³ adj (before n, no comp) ⓵ (miniature) ⟨railway/village⟩ en miniatura ⓶ (ideal) ⟨citizen/ husband/pupil⟩ modelo adj inv; ⟨answer⟩ tipo adj inv

modem /'məʊdem/ n módem m

moderate¹ /'mɑ:dərət ‖'mɒdərət/ adj moderado

moderate² /'mɑ:dəreɪt ‖'mɒdəreɪt/ vt moderar

moderate³ /'mɑ:dərət ‖'mɒdərət/ n moderado, -da m,f

moderation /'mɑ:də'reɪʃən ‖,mɒdə'reɪʃən/ n moderación f; **drinking is not harmful, in ~** beber no es nocivo, si se hace con moderación

modern /'mɑ:dərn ‖'mɒdṇ/ adj moderno

modernization /,mɑ:dərnə'zeɪʃən ‖,mɒdənaɪ'zeɪʃən/ n modernización f

modernize /'mɑ:dərnaɪz ‖'mɒdənaɪz/ vt modernizar*

modest /'mɑ:dəst ‖'mɒdɪst/ adj **(a)** (not boastful) ⟨person/remark⟩ modesto **(b)** ⟨income/gift⟩ modesto; ⟨improvement/success⟩ moderado **(c)** (chaste) pudoroso

modesty /'mɑ:dəsti ‖'mɒdɪsti/ n **(a)** (absence of conceit) modestia f **(b)** (propriety) recato m, pudor m

modicum /'mɑ:dɪkəm ‖'mɒdɪkəm/ n (no pl) (frml) **a ~ OF sth** un atisbo DE algo (frml), un mínimo DE algo

modification /'mɑ:dəfə'keɪʃən ‖,mɒdɪfɪ'keɪʃən/ n modificación f

modify /'mɑ:dəfaɪ ‖'mɒdɪfaɪ/ vt **-fies, -fying, -fied** modificar*

modular /'mɑ:dʒələr ‖'mɒdjʊlə(r)/ adj ⟨design/ furniture⟩ modular; ⟨degree/course⟩ dividido en módulos

modulate /'mɑ:dʒəleɪt ‖'mɒdjʊleɪt/ vt modular

modulation /'mɑ:dʒə'leɪʃən ‖,mɒdjʊ'leɪʃən/ n modulación f; **frequency ~** frecuencia f modulada

module /'mɑ:dʒu:l ‖'mɒdju:l/ n módulo m

Mohammed /məʊ'hæməd ‖məʊ'hæmɪd/ n Mahoma

moist /mɔɪst/ adj ⟨climate/soil⟩ húmedo; ⟨cake⟩ no seco

moisten /'mɔɪsṇ/ vt humedecer*

moisture /'mɔɪstʃər ‖'mɔɪstʃə(r)/ n humedad f

moisturize /'mɔɪstʃəraɪz/ vt hidratar

moisturizer /'mɔɪstʃəraɪzər ‖'mɔɪstʃəraɪzə(r)/, **moisturizing cream** /'mɔɪstʃəraɪzɪŋ/ n crema f hidratante

molar /'məʊlər ‖'məʊlə(r)/ n muela f

molasses /mə'læsəz ‖mə'læsɪz/ n (+ sing vb) melaza f

mold¹, (BrE) **mould** /məʊld/ n ⓵ **(a)** (hollow vessel) molde m **(b)** (dish) timbal m ⓶ (fungus) moho m

mold², (BrE) **mould** vt ⟨steel/plastic⟩ moldear; ⟨character/attitudes⟩ formar

Moldavia /mɑ:l'deɪvjə ‖mɒl'deɪvɪə/ n Moldavia f

Moldova /mɑ:l'dəʊvə ‖mɒl'dəʊvə/ n Moldova f

moldy, (BrE) **mouldy** /'məʊldi/ adj mohoso; **to become** o (BrE) **go ~** enmohecerse*

mole /məʊl/ n ⓵ (Zool) topo m ⓶ (on skin) lunar m

molecule /'mɑ:lɪkju:l ‖'mɒlɪkju:l/ n molécula f

molest /mə'lest/ vt **(a)** (sexually) abusar (sexualmente) de **(b)** (harass) importunar

mollusk, mollusc /'mɑ:ləsk ‖'mɒləsk/ n molusco m

mollycoddle /'mɑ:lika:dl ‖'mɒlɪkɒdl/ vt (colloq & pej) mimar

m

molt, (BrE) **moult** /məʊlt/ *vi* «*snake*» mudar de piel; «*bird*» mudar de plumas; «*dog/cat*» pelechar, mudar de pelo

molten /'məʊltən/ *adj* ‹*rock/metal*› fundido; ‹*lava*› líquido

mom /mɑːm ‖ mɒm/ *n* (AmE colloq) mamá *f* (fam)

moment /'məʊmənt/ *n* momento *m*; **at the ~** en este momento; **for the ~** de momento; **to have one's ~s** tener* sus (*or* mis *etc*) buenos momentos

momentary /'məʊmənteri ‖ 'məʊməntri/ *adj* ‹*feeling/glimpse*› momentáneo

momentous /məʊ'mentəs/ *adj* ‹*occasion/ decision*› trascendental; ‹*day*› memorable

momentum /məʊ'mentəm/ *n* (*pl* **-ta** /-tə/ *or* **-tums**) **(a)** (Phys) momento *m* **(b)** (speed) velocidad *f*; **to gather ~** ir* adquiriendo velocidad

momma /'mɑːmə ‖ 'mɒmə/ *n* (AmE) (colloq) mamá *f* (fam)

mommy /'mɑːmi ‖ 'mɒmi/ *n* (*pl* **-mies**) (AmE colloq) mami *f* (fam), mamita *f* (fam)

Monaco /'mɑːnəkəʊ, mə'nɑː- ‖ 'mɒnəkəʊ/ *n* Mónaco *m*

monarch /'mɑːnərk ‖ 'mɒnək/ *n* monarca *mf*

monarchist /'mɑːnərkəst ‖ 'mɒnəkɪst/ *n* monárquico, -ca *m,f*

monarchy /'mɑːnərki ‖ 'mɒnəki/ *n* monarquía *f*

monastery /'mɑːnəsteri ‖ 'mɒnəstri/ *n* (*pl* **-ries**) monasterio *m*

Monday /'mʌndeɪ, -di/ *n* **1** (day) lunes *m*; **on ~** el lunes; **next ~** el próximo lunes *or* el lunes que viene; **(on) ~s** los lunes; **the ~ after next** el lunes que viene no, el siguiente; **(***before* ***n***) ~ afternoon/morning** el lunes por la tarde/mañana, la tarde/mañana del lunes **2 Mondays** (*as adv*) los lunes

monetarism /'mɑːnətərɪzəm ‖ 'mʌnɪtərɪzəm/ *n* monetarismo *m*

monetary /'mɑːnəteri ‖ 'mʌnɪtəri/ *adj* monetario

money /'mʌni/ *n* (*pl* **-nies** *or* **-neys**) dinero *m*; (currency) moneda *f*, dinero *m*; **their European operation is making a lot of ~** su operación europea está dando mucho; **to put ~ into sth** invertir* dinero en algo; **~ talks** poderoso caballero es don Dinero

money: ~ **belt** *n* faltriquera *f*; ~**box** *n* alcancía *f* (AmL), hucha *f* (Esp); ~**lender** *n* prestamista *mf*; ~**-making** *adj* lucrativo; ~ **order** *n* ≈ giro *m* postal; ~ **supply** *n* **the ~ supply** la masa monetaria

Mongolia /mɑːn'gəʊliə ‖ mɒŋ'gəʊliə/ *n* Mongolia *f*

Mongolian /mɑːn'gəʊliən ‖ mɒŋ'gəʊliən/ *adj* mongol

mongrel /'mɑːŋgrəl ‖ 'mʌŋgrəl/ *n*: perro *mestizo*, chucho, -cha *m,f* (fam), gozque *m* (Col), quiltro, -tra *m,f* (Chi fam)

monitor¹ /'mɑːnətər ‖ 'mɒnɪtə(r)/ *n* **1** **(a)** (screen) monitor *m* **(b)** (for measuring) monitor *m* **2** (listener) escucha *mf* **3** (Educ) encargado, -da *m,f*, monitor, -tora *m,f* (CS)

monitor² *vt* **(a)** ‹*elections*› observar; ‹*process/ progress*› seguir*; (esp electronically) monitorizar* **(b)** ‹*radio station*› escuchar

monk /mʌŋk/ *n* monje *m*

monkey /'mʌŋki/ *n* mono, -na *m,f*

monkey wrench *n* llave *f* inglesa; **to throw a ~ ~ in the works** *o* **the machinery** (AmE) fastidiarlo todo

mono /'mɑːnəʊ ‖ 'mɒnəʊ/ *n* (Audio) monofonía *f*

monochrome /'mɑːnəkrəʊm ‖ 'mɒnəkrəʊm/ *adj* ‹*picture*› monocromático, monocromo

monogamy /mə'nɑːgəmi ‖ mə'nɒgəmi/ *n* monogamia *f*

monologue, (AmE also) **monolog** /'mɑːnələːg ‖ 'mɒnəlɒg/ *n* monólogo *m*

monopolize /mə'nɑːpəlaɪz ‖ mə'nɒpəlaɪz/ *vt* ‹*market/industry*› monopolizar*; ‹*conversation/ television*› acaparar

monopoly /mə'nɑːpəli ‖ mə'nɒpəli/ *n* (*pl* **-lies**) monopolio *m*

monosyllable /'mɑːnə‚sɪləbəl ‖ 'mɒnəsɪləbəl/ *n* monosílabo *m*

monotone /'mɑːnətəʊn ‖ 'mɒnətəʊn/ *n* tono *m* monocorde

monotonous /mə'nɑːtṇəs ‖ mə'nɒtənəs/ *adj* monótono

monotony /mə'nɑːtṇi ‖ mə'nɒtəni/ *n* monotonía *f*

monsoon /mɑːn'suːn ‖ mɒn'suːn/ *n* monzón *m*

monster /'mɑːnstər ‖ 'mɒnstə(r)/ *n* monstruo *m*

monstrous /'mɑːnstrəs ‖ 'mɒnstrəs/ *adj* **(a)** (huge) gigantesco **(b)** (shocking) monstruoso

Mont = **Montana**

month /mʌnθ/ *n* mes *m*; **$900 a ~** 900 dólares mensuales *or* por mes *or* al mes; **in a ~'s time** dentro de un mes

monthly¹ /'mʌnθli/ *adj* ‹*journal/event*› mensual; ~ **payment** mensualidad *f*, cuota *f* mensual (esp AmL)

monthly² *adv* mensualmente, una vez al *or* por mes

monthly³ *n* (*pl* **-lies**) publicación *f* mensual

monument /'mɑːnjəmənt ‖ 'mɒnjʊmənt/ *n* monumento *m*

monumental /‚mɑːnjə'mentḷ ‖ ‚mɒnjʊ'mentḷ/ *adj* monumental

moo /muː/ *vi* **moos**, **mooing**, **mooed** mugir*

mood /muːd/ *n* **1** **(a)** (state of mind) humor *m*; **to be in a good/bad ~** estar* de buen/de mal humor; **I'm not in the ~** no tengo ganas; **I'm not in the ~ for dancing** no tengo ganas de bailar **(b)** (atmosphere) atmósfera *f* **2** (Ling) modo *m*

moody /'muːdi/ *adj* **-dier, -diest** **(a)** (irritable, sulky) de mal humor; (gloomy) deprimido **(b)** (changeable) ‹*person*› temperamental

moon /muːn/ *n* luna *f*; **once in a blue ~** muy de vez en cuando

moonbeam /'muːnbiːm/ *n* rayo *m* de luna

moonlight¹ /'muːnlaɪt/ *n* luz *f* de la luna

moonlight² *vi* tener* un segundo empleo; **he ~s as a cab driver** trabaja además como taxista

moon: ~**lighting** *n* pluriempleo *m*; ~**lit** *adj* iluminado por la luna

moor¹ /mʊr ‖ mʊə(r), mɔː(r)/ n **(a)** (boggy area) llanura f anegadiza **(b)** (high exposed area) (esp BrE) páramo m; (covered with heather) brezal m

moor² vt amarrar
■ ~ vi echar amarras

mooring /'mʊrɪŋ ‖ 'mʊərɪŋ, 'mɔːrɪŋ/ n **(a)** (place) amarradero m **(b) moorings** pl (ropes) amarras fpl

moose /muːs/ n (pl **moose**) alce m americano or de América

mop¹ /mɑːp ‖ mɒp/ n **(a)** (for floor) trapeador m (AmL), fregona f (Esp) **(b)** ~ **of hair** mata f de pelo

mop² **-pp-** vt ⟨floor/room⟩ limpiar, trapear (AmL), pasarle la fregona a (Esp); **to ~ one's brow** secarse* la frente
■ **mop up** [v + o + adv, v + adv + o] ⟨water⟩ secar*; ⟨mess⟩ limpiar

mope /məʊp/ vi (colloq) estar* deprimido

moped /'məʊped/ n ciclomotor m

moral¹ /'mɔːrəl ‖ 'mɒrəl/ adj moral

moral² n ⨳1⨳ (message) moraleja f ⨳2⨳ **morals** pl (principles) moralidad f

morale /mə'ræl ‖ mə'rɑːl/ n moral f

morality /mə'ræləti/ n (pl **-ties**) moralidad f

morally /'mɔːrəli ‖ 'mɒrəli/ adv moralmente

morbid /'mɔːrbəd ‖ 'mɔːbɪd/ adj morboso

more¹ /mɔːr ‖ mɔː(r)/ adj más; **there'll be no ~ talking** se acabó la charla; **how much ~ flour?** ¿cuánta harina más?; **for ~ information call 387351** para mayor información llamar al 38-73-51; **~ and ~ people** cada vez más gente; **I eat ~ meat than you** yo como más carne que tú

more² pron más; **let's say no ~ about it** no hablemos más del asunto; **the ~ she eats, the thinner she gets** cuanto más come, más adelgaza; **you eat ~ than me** tú comes más que yo

more³ adv más; **you watch television ~ than I do** tú ves más televisión que yo; **~ or less** más o menos; **could you please speak ~ clearly?** ¿podría hacer el favor de hablar más claro?; **~ often** con más frecuencia; **I don't eat meat any ~** ya no como carne

moreover /mɔːr'əʊvər ‖ mɔː'rəʊvə(r)/ adv (frml) (as linker) además

morgue /mɔːrg ‖ mɔːg/ n depósito m de cadáveres, morgue f (AmL)

Mormon /'mɔːrmən ‖ 'mɔːmən/ n mormón, -mona m,f

morning /'mɔːrnɪŋ ‖ 'mɔːnɪŋ/ n ⨳1⨳ (time of day) mañana f; **yesterday/tomorrow ~** ayer/mañana por la mañana or (AmL tb) en la mañana or (RPI tb) a la mañana or de mañana; **we'll do it first thing in the ~** lo haremos por la mañana a primera hora; **(good) ~!** ¡buenos días!, ¡buen día! (RPI) ⨳2⨳ **mornings** (as adv) por las mañanas, en las mañanas (AmL), a la or de mañana (RPI)

morning: **~-after pill** n píldora f del día siguiente; **~ coat** n chaqué m, frac m; **~ sickness** n náuseas fpl (matinales) (del embarazo)

Moroccan /mə'rɑːkən/ adj marroquí

Morocco /mə'rɑːkəʊ/ n Marruecos m

moron /'mɔːrɑːn ‖ 'mɔːrɒn/ n (colloq & pej) imbécil mf, tarado, -da m,f (fam)

morose /mə'rəʊs/ adj taciturno

morphine /'mɔːrfiːn ‖ 'mɔːfiːn/ n morfina f

Morse /mɔːrs ‖ mɔːs/ n morse m; **in ~ (code)** en (código) morse

morsel /'mɔːrsəl ‖ 'mɔːsəl/ n bocado m

mortal¹ /'mɔːrt̬l ‖ 'mɔːtl/ adj **(a)** (subject to death) mortal **(b)** (liter) ⟨blow/injury/sin⟩ mortal

mortal² n mortal mf

mortality /mɔːr'tæləti ‖ mɔː'tæləti/ n **(a)** (death rate) mortalidad f **(b)** (loss of life) mortandad f **(c)** (condition) mortalidad f

mortar /'mɔːrt̬ər ‖ 'mɔːtə(r)/ n ⨳1⨳ (cement) argamasa f, mortero m ⨳2⨳ (weapon) mortero m ⨳3⨳ (bowl) mortero m, molcajete m (Méx)

mortgage¹ /'mɔːrgɪdʒ ‖ 'mɔːgɪdʒ/ n (charge) hipoteca f; (loan) préstamo m hipotecario, hipoteca f; **to take out a ~ on a property** hipotecar* una propiedad

mortgage² vt hipotecar*

mortician /mɔːr'tɪʃən ‖ mɔː'tɪʃən/ n (AmE) (employee) persona que trabaja en una funeraria; (funeral director) director, -tora m,f de pompas fúnebres

mortified /'mɔːrtəfaɪd ‖ 'mɔːtɪfaɪd/ adj: **I was ~** me dio mucha vergüenza, me dio mucha pena (AmL exc CS)

mortuary /'mɔːrtʃueri ‖ 'mɔːtjʊəri/ n (pl **-ries**) depósito m de cadáveres, morgue f (AmL)

mosaic /məʊ'zeɪɪk/ n mosaico m

Moscow /'mɑːskaʊ ‖ 'mɒskəʊ/ n Moscú m

Moslem /'mɑːzləm ‖ 'mɒzləm/ n/adj ▶ MUSLIM¹,²

mosque /mɑːsk ‖ mɒsk/ n mezquita f

mosquito /mə'skiːt̬əʊ ‖ mɒs'kiːtəʊ/ n (pl **-toes** or **-tos**) mosquito m, zancudo m (AmL)

moss /mɔːs ‖ mɒs/ n musgo m

most¹ /məʊst/ adj **(a)** (nearly all) la mayoría de, la mayor parte de; **~ days** casi todos los días **(b)** (as superl) más; **who eats (the) ~ meat in your family?** ¿quién es el que come más carne de tu familia?

most² pron **(a)** (nearly all) la mayoría, la mayor parte; **I read ~ of it** lo leí casi todo **(b)** (as superl): **she ate the ~** fue la que más comió; **at (the) ~** como máximo; **to make the ~ of sth** sacar* el mejor provecho posible de algo **(c)** (people) la mayoría

most³ adv ⨳1⨳ **(a)** (to greatest extent) más; **I enjoyed the last act ~ of all** el último acto fue el que más me gustó **(b)** (before adj, adv) más; **which is the ~ expensive?** ¿cuál es el más caro? ⨳2⨳ (as intensifier): **what happened was ~ interesting** lo que sucedió fue de lo más interesante; **~ likely** muy probablemente ⨳3⨳ (almost) (AmE colloq) casi

mostly /'məʊstli/ adv: **her friends are ~ students** la mayoría de sus amigos son estudiantes; **the land is ~ flat** el terreno es en su mayor parte llano

motel /məʊ'tel/ n motel m

moth /mɔːθ ‖ mɒθ/ n mariposa f de la luz, palomilla f; (clothes ~) polilla f

mother¹ /'mʌðər ‖ 'mʌðə(r)/ n madre f; (before n) ~ **country** madre patria f

mother² vt mimar

motherhood /'mʌðərhʊd ‖ 'mʌðəhʊd/ n maternidad f

Mothering Sunday /'mʌðərɪŋ/ n (BrE) ▶ MOTHER'S DAY

mother: ~-**in-law** n (pl ~**s-in-law**) suegra f; ~**land** n patria f

motherly /'mʌðərli ǁ'mʌðəli/ adj maternal

mother: ~-**of-pearl** /'mʌðərəv'pɜːrl ǁ,mʌðərəv'pɜːl/ n nácar m, madreperla f, concha f nácar (Méx), concha f de perla (Chi); **M**~**'s Day** n el día de la Madre (el segundo domingo de mayo en EEUU y el cuarto domingo de Cuaresma en GB); **M**~ **Superior** n Madre f Superiora; ~-**to-be** /'mʌðərtə'biː ǁ,mʌðətə'biː/ n (pl ~**s-to-be**) futura madre f, futura mamá f; ~ **tongue** n lengua f materna

motif /məʊ'tiːf/ n (a) (theme) tema m (b) (design) motivo m

motion¹ /'məʊʃən/ n ① (a) (movement) movimiento m; **to be in** ~ estar* en movimiento; **to set** o **put sth in** ~ ⟨wheel⟩ poner* algo en movimiento; ⟨project/plan⟩ poner* algo en marcha (b) (action, gesture) gesto m; **to go through the** ~**s**: he went through the ~s of interviewing them los entrevistó por pura fórmula ② (for vote) moción f

motion² vi: she ~ed to her assistant le hizo una señal a su ayudante; they ~ed to us to sit down nos hicieron señas para que nos sentáramos

motionless /'məʊʃənləs ǁ'məʊʃənlɪs/ adj inmóvil

motion picture n película f

motivate /'məʊtəveɪt ǁ'məʊtɪveɪt/ vt motivar

motivation /,məʊtə'veɪʃən ǁ,məʊtɪ'veɪʃən/ n (a) (drive) motivación f (b) (motive) motivo m

motive /'məʊtɪv/ n motivo m

motley /'mɑːtli ǁ'mɒtli/ adj variopinto

motor¹ /'məʊtər ǁ'məʊtə(r)/ n motor m

motor² adj (before n) ① (Auto, Mech Eng) ⟨parts⟩ de automóvil; ⟨mechanic⟩ de automóviles; ~ **show** salón m del automóvil; ~ **vehicle** (vehículo m) automóvil m (frml) ② (Physiol) ⟨neuron/nerve⟩ motor [The feminine of MOTOR is MOTRIZ or MOTORA]

motor: ~**bike** n moto f; ~**boat** n lancha f a motor; ~**car** n (frml) automóvil m (frml); ~**cycle** n motocicleta f; ~**cyclist** n motociclista mf, motorista mf

motoring /'məʊtərɪŋ/ n automovilismo m

motorist /'məʊtərəst ǁ'məʊtərɪst/ n automovilista mf, conductor, -tora m,f

motorway /'məʊtərweɪ ǁ'məʊtəweɪ/ n (BrE) autopista f

mottled /'mɑːtld ǁ'mɒtld/ adj ⟨skin⟩ manchado; ⟨marble⟩ veteado

motto /'mɑːtəʊ ǁ'mɒtəʊ/ n (pl -**toes**) (of family, school) lema m

mould etc (BrE) ▶ MOLD etc

moult vi (BrE) ▶ MOLT

mound /maʊnd/ n (a) (hillock) montículo m (b) (man-made) túmulo m; burial ~ túmulo funerario (c) (heap) montón m

mount¹ /maʊnt/ n ① (mountain) (liter) monte m ② (Equ) montura f ③ (for machine, gun) soporte m; (for picture — surround) paspartú m, maríaluisa f (Méx); (— backing) fondo m; (for slide) marco m; (for stamp) fijasellos m; (for jewel) montura f, engaste m

mount² vt ① (a) ⟨horse⟩ montar, montarse en (b) ⟨platform/throne⟩ subir a ② ⟨gun/picture⟩ montar; ⟨stamp/butterfly⟩ fijar; ⟨gem⟩ engarzar*, montar ③ ⟨attack/offensive⟩ preparar; ⟨campaign/event⟩ organizar*
⬛ ~ vi ① (a) ⟨⟨cost/temperature⟩⟩ subir; ⟨⟨excitement/alarm⟩⟩ crecer* (b) **mounting** pres p ⟨cost/fears/tension⟩ cada vez mayor, creciente ② (climb onto horse) montar
⬛ **mount up** [v + adv] ⟨⟨bills⟩⟩ irse* acumulando

mountain /'maʊntn ǁ'maʊntɪn/ n (Geog) montaña f; (before n) ⟨stream/path⟩ de montaña; ⟨scenery⟩ montañoso; ~ **range** cordillera f; (shorter) sierra f

mountain bike n bicicleta f de montaña

mountaineer /'maʊntn'ɪr ǁ,maʊntɪ'nɪə(r)/ n alpinista mf, andinista mf (AmL)

mountaineering /'maʊntn'ɪrɪŋ ǁ,maʊntɪ'nɪərɪŋ/ n alpinismo m, andinismo m (AmL)

mountainous /'maʊntnəs ǁ'maʊntɪnəs/ adj montañoso

mountaintop /'maʊntn,tɑːp ǁ'maʊntɪn,tɒp/ n cima f or cumbre f (de la montaña)

mounted /'maʊntəd ǁ'maʊntɪd/ adj montado: ~ **police** policía f montada

mourn /mɔːrn ǁmɔːn/ vt ⟨loss/tragedy⟩ llorar
⬛ ~ vi **to** ~ **FOR sb** llorar a algn

mourner /'mɔːrnər ǁ'mɔːnə(r)/ n doliente mf

mournful /'mɔːrnfəl ǁ'mɔːnfəl/ adj ⟨expression/glance⟩ de profunda tristeza; ⟨sigh/cry⟩ lastimero

mourning /'mɔːrnɪŋ ǁ'mɔːnɪŋ/ n (action, period) duelo m, luto m; **to be in** ~ **for sb** estar* de luto por algn

mouse /maʊs/ n (pl **mice**) ① (animal) ratón m, laucha f (CS) ② (Comput) ratón m; (before n) ~ **mat** alfombrilla f para ratón

mousey adj ▶ MOUSY

mousse /muːs/ n (a) (Culin) mousse f or m (b) (for hair) mousse f

moustache n (BrE) ▶ MUSTACHE

mousy /'maʊsi/ adj -**sier**, -**siest** ⟨hair⟩ castaño desvaído adj inv

mouth¹ /maʊθ/ n (pl **mouths** /maʊðz/) ① (of person, animal) boca f; **down in the** ~ alicaído; **to make sb's** ~ **water**: it made my ~ **water** se me hizo agua la boca or (Esp) se me hizo la boca agua ② (of bottle) boca f; (of tunnel, cave) entrada f; (of river) desembocadura f

mouth² /maʊð/ vt (silently): **it's him, she** ~**ed** — es él —me/le dijo articulando para que le leyera los labios

mouthful /'maʊθfʊl/ n (of food) bocado m; (of drink) trago m; (of air) bocanada f

mouth: ~ **organ** n armónica f; ~**piece** n ① (of telephone) micrófono m; (Mus) boquilla f;

AmC	Central America	Arg	Argentina	Cu	Cuba	Per	Peru
AmL	Latin America	Bol	Bolivia	Ec	Ecuador	RPI	River Plate Area
AmS	South America	Chi	Chile	Esp	Spain	Ur	Uruguay
Andes	Andean Region	CS	Southern Cone	Méx	Mexico	Ven	Venezuela

2 (spokesperson) portavoz *mf*; **~-to-~**
/'maʊθtə'maʊθ/ *adj* (*before n*) boca a boca;
~wash *n* enjuague *m* (bucal); **~-watering**
/'maʊθ,wɔ:tərɪŋ/ *adj* delicioso

move¹ /muːv/ *n* **1** (movement) movimiento *m*;
on the ~: *she's always on the ~* siempre está de
un lado para otro **2** (change — of residence)
mudanza *f*, trasteo *m* (Col); (— of premises)
traslado *m* **3** (action, step) paso *m*; (measure)
medida *f*; *what's the next ~?* ¿cuál es el siguiente
paso? **(b)** (in profession, occupation): *it would be a
good career ~* sería un cambio muy provechoso
para mi (*or* su *etc*) carrera profesional **4** (Games)
movimiento *m*; *whose ~ is it?* ¿a quién le toca
mover?

move² *vi* **1** **(a)** (change place): *he ~d nearer
the fire* se acercó al fuego; *to ~ to a new job*
cambiar de trabajo **(b)** (change location, residence)
mudarse
2 (change position) moverse*
3 (proceed, go): *the vehicle began to ~* el
vehículo se puso en marcha; *the police kept the
crowds moving* la policía hacía circular a la
multitud; *the earth ~s around the sun* la Tierra
gira alrededor del sol; *we ~d to one side* nos
apartamos, nos hicimos a un lado
4 (advance, develop): *events ~d rapidly* los
acontecimientos se desarrollaron rápidamente; *to
~ with the times* mantenerse* al día; *to ~ into
the lead* pasar a ocupar el primer lugar
5 (carry oneself) moverse*
6 (go fast) (colloq) correr
7 (take steps, act): *we must ~ now* tenemos que
actuar ahora; *she ~d quickly to scotch rumors*
inmediatamente tomó medidas para acallar los
rumores
■ *~ vt* **1** (transfer, shift position of): *~ your chair a
little* corre un poco la silla; *ask him to ~ the
boxes out of the way* dile que quite las cajas de
en medio; *I can't ~ my leg* no puedo mover la
pierna
2 **(a)** (transport) transportar **(b)** (relocate, transfer)
trasladar **(c)** (change residence, location): *the firm
that ~d us* la compañía que nos hizo la mudanza;
to ~ house (BrE) mudarse de casa
3 **(a)** (arouse emotionally) conmover*; *to ~ sb to
tears* hacer* llorar a algn de la emoción **(b)**
(prompt) *to ~ sb to* + INF: *this ~d her to
remonstrate* esto la indujo a protestar
4 (propose) (Adm, Govt) proponer*
■ **move along** **1** [*v + adv*] **(a)** (go further along)
correrse **(b)** (disperse) circular
2 [*v + o + adv*] (to disperse) hacer* circular
■ **move around,** (BrE also) **move about** [*v +
adv*] **(a)** (walk) andar* **(b)** (change residence)
mudarse (*a menudo*); (change job) cambiar de
trabajo (*a menudo*)
■ **move away** [*v + adv*] **(a)** (move house)
mudarse (*de la ciudad, el barrio etc*) **(b)** ▶ MOVE
OFF
■ **move down** **1** [*v + adv*] bajar
2 [*v + o + adv*] bajar
■ **move in** [*v + adv*] **(a)** (set up home) mudarse (*a
una casa etc*); *to ~ in WITH sb* irse* a vivir CON
algn **(b)** (draw closer) acercarse* **(c)** (go into action)
«*police*» intervenir*; (Mil) atacar*
■ **move off** [*v + adv*] «*procession*» ponerse* en
marcha; «*car*» arrancar*
■ **move on**

I [*v + adv*] **1** (walk further) seguir* adelante;
(continue journey) continuar* el viaje
2 **(a)** (proceed) pasar **(b)** (progress) progresar
II [*v + o + adv*] (cause to disperse) hacer* circular
■ **move out** [*v + adv*] irse* (*de una casa etc*)
■ **move over** [*v + adv*] (make room) correrse
■ **move up** **1** [*v + adv*] **(a)** (rise) subir **(b)** (make
room) correrse
2 [*v + o + adv*] «*picture/shelf*» subir; *they ~d
him up a class* lo pusieron en la clase
inmediatamente superior

movement /'muːvmənt/ *n* **1** **(a)** (motion)
movimiento *m* **(b)** **movements** *pl* (activities,
whereabouts) desplazamientos *mpl*, movimientos
mpl **2** **(a)** (transportation) movimiento *m* **(b)**
(travel) desplazamiento *m* **3** (Art, Pol, Relig)
movimiento *m*

mover /'muːvər ‖'muːvə(r)/ *n* (of furniture,
belongings) (AmE): *a firm of ~s* una compañía de
mudanzas

movie /'muːvi/ *n* (esp AmE) **1** (film) película *f*,
film(e) *m* (period); (before n) «*actor/director*» de
cine **2** **movies** *pl* (esp AmE) *the ~s* el cine

movie camera *n* (esp AmE) filmadora *f or*
(Esp) tomavistas *m*; (large, professional) cámara *f*
cinematográfica

moving /'muːvɪŋ/ *adj* **1** (emotionally) emotivo,
conmovedor **2** (in motion) (before n) ~ **part** pieza *f*
movible **3** (AmE) (before n) «*van/company*» de
mudanzas

mow /məʊ/ *vt* (*past* **mowed**; *past p* **mown** *or*
mowed) «*hay*» segar*; «*lawn*» cortar
■ **mow down** [*v + o + adv*] acribillar

mower /'məʊər ‖'məʊə(r)/ *n* **(a)** (Hort) ▶
LAWNMOWER **(b)** (on farm) segadora *f*

mown /məʊn/ *past p of* MOW

Mozambique /'məʊzəm'biːk ‖,məʊzæm'biːk/
n Mozambique *m*

MP *n* **(a)** (in UK) (Govt) = **Member of
Parliament** **(b)** (= military police) PM *f*

mph = **miles per hour**

Mr /'mɪstər ‖'mɪstə(r)/ (= **Mister**) Sr.

MRI *n* (= **Magnetic Resonance Imaging**)
IRM *f*

Mrs /'mɪsəs ‖'mɪsɪz/ Sra.

Ms /mɪz ‖məz/ ≈ Sra. (*tratamiento que se da a
las mujeres y que no indica su estado civil*)

MS *n* **(a)** *also* **ms** (*pl* **MSS** *or* **mss**)
(= **manuscript**) ms. **(b)** (= **multiple
sclerosis**) E.M. *f* **(c)** (AmE) = **Master of
Science** **(d)** = **Mississippi**

MSc *n* (BrE) = **Master of Science**

MST (in US) = **Mountain Standard Time**

Mt (= **Mount**) *~ Rushmore* el monte Rushmore

MT = **Montana**

much¹ /mʌtʃ/ *adj* mucho, -cha; *how ~ coffee/
milk?* ¿cuánto café/cuánta leche?; *I do as ~ work
as anybody* trabajo tanto como cualquiera; *too ~
coffee* demasiado café

much² *pron* mucho, -cha; *do you see ~ of the
Smiths?* ¿ves mucho a los Smith?; *how ~ does it
cost?* ¿cuánto cuesta?; *I've done as ~ as I can* he
hecho todo lo que he podido; *and as ~ again* otro
tanto; *you've drunk too ~* has bebido
demasiado

much³ *adv* mucho; *I'd very ~ like to meet her* ⋯⟶

me gustaría mucho conocerla; **you deserve the prize just as ~ as I do** te mereces el premio tanto como yo; **so ~ the better** tanto mejor; **you talk too ~** hablas demasiado; **this church is ~ the larger of the two** de las dos iglesias esta es, con mucho, la más grande; **I'm ~ too busy to do it** estoy demasiado ocupada para hacerlo

muck /mʌk/ n (dung) estiércol m; (dirt) mugre f
■ **muck out** [v + o + adv, v + adv + o] limpiar

mucus /'mjuːkəs/ n mucosidad f

mud /mʌd/ n barro m, fango m, lodo m; (before n) ⟨brick/hut⟩ de barro, de adobe

muddle¹ /'mʌdl/ n lío m, follón m (Esp fam); **to be in a ~** ⟨«papers»⟩ estar* (todo) revuelto; ⟨«person»⟩ estar* liado or hecho un lío (fam)

muddle² vt ▶ MUDDLE UP
■ **muddle up** [v + o + adv, v + adv + o] (a) ⟨papers⟩ entreverar (b) (mix up) confundir (c) (bewilder) confundir; **to get ~d up** confundirse

muddled /'mʌdld/ adj confuso; **to get ~** hacerse* un lío (fam)

muddy /'mʌdi/ adj -**dier**, -**diest** ⟨boots/hands/road⟩ lleno or cubierto de barro or de lodo; ⟨water⟩ turbio

mudguard /'mʌdgɑːrd ‖ 'mʌdgɑːd/ n guardabarros m, salpicadera f (Méx), tapabarros m (Chi, Per)

muesli /'mjuːzli, 'muː- ‖ 'mjuːzli/ n (esp BrE) musli m, muesli m

muff¹ /mʌf/ vt (colloq) ⟨shot⟩ errar*; ⟨chance⟩ desperdiciar

muff² n (Clothing) manguito m

muffin /'mʌfən ‖ 'mʌfɪn/ n (AmE) mollete m (bollo dulce hecho con huevos); (BrE) bollo de pan que suele servirse tostado

muffle /'mʌfl/ vt ① ⟨sound⟩ amortiguar* ② ~ (up): **her face was ~d (up) in a scarf** una bufanda casi le tapaba la cara

muffler /'mʌflər ‖ 'mʌflə(r)/ n ① (scarf) bufanda f ② (a) (Mus) sordina f (b) (AmE Auto) silenciador m, mofle m (AmC, Méx)

mug¹ /mʌg/ n ① (cup) taza f (alta y sin platillo), tarro m (Méx, Ven) ② (gullible person) (BrE colloq) idiota mf ③ (face) (sl) cara f, jeta f (arg), careto m (Esp arg)

mug² vt -**gg**- atracar*

mugger /'mʌgər ‖ 'mʌgə(r)/ n atracador, -dora m,f

mugging /'mʌgɪŋ/ n atraco m

muggy /'mʌgi/ adj -**gier**, -**giest** ⟨weather/day⟩ pesado

mug shot n (colloq) foto f (de archivo policial)

Muhammad /məˈhæməd ‖ məˈhæmɪd/ n Mahoma

mulberry /'mʌl,beri ‖ 'mʌlbəri/ n (pl -**ries**) (tree) morera f; (fruit) mora f (de morera)

mule /mjuːl/ n mula f (cruce de burro y yegua); **stubborn as a ~** más terco que una mula

mull /mʌl/ vt (a) (Culin): **~ed wine** ponche caliente de vino y especias (b) (AmE) ▶ MULL OVER
■ **mull over** [v + o + adv, v + adv + o] reflexionar sobre

multicolored, (BrE) **multi-coloured** /'mʌltiˌkʌlərd ‖ ˌmʌltɪˈkʌləd/ adj multicolor

multicultural /ˌmʌltiˈkʌltʃərəl/ adj multicultural

multilevel /ˌmʌltiˈlevl/ adj (AmE) de varias plantas, de varios pisos

multinational¹ /ˌmʌltiˈnæʃnəl ‖ ˌmʌltiˈnæʃənl/ adj multinacional

multinational² n multinacional f

multiple¹ /'mʌltəpəl ‖ 'mʌltɪpəl/ adj (a) (involving many elements) múltiple (b) (many) múltiples

multiple² n múltiplo m

multiple: ~-**choice** /'mʌltəpəl'tʃɔɪs ‖ ˌmʌltɪpəl'tʃɔɪs/ adj de opción múltiple, tipo test; ~ **sclerosis** /sklə'rəʊsəs/ n esclerosis f múltiple

multiplication /'mʌltəplə'keɪʃən ‖ ˌmʌltɪplɪ'keɪʃən/ n multiplicación f

multiply /'mʌltəplaɪ ‖ 'mʌltɪplaɪ/ -**plies**, -**plying**, -**plied** vt (a) (Math) **to ~ sth** (BY sth) multiplicar* algo (POR algo) (b) (increase) multiplicar*
■ ~ vi (a) (Math) multiplicar* (b) (increase, reproduce) multiplicarse*

multipurpose /ˌmʌltiˈpɜːrpəs ‖ ˌmʌltiˈpɜːpəs/ adj ⟨tool/appliance⟩ multiuso adj inv

multistory, (BrE) **multistorey** /ˌmʌltiˈstɔːri/ adj de varias plantas, de varios pisos

multitude /'mʌltətuːd ‖ 'mʌltɪtjuːd/ n (a) (large number) (frml) (no pl) a ~ OF sth: **a ~ of problems** innumerables or múltiples problemas (b) (crowd) (arch or liter) multitud f

mum /mʌm/ n ① (mother) (BrE colloq) mamá f (fam) ② (silence) (colloq): ~'**s the word** ¡punto en boca! (fam); **to keep ~** no decir* ni pío (fam)

mumble /'mʌmbəl/ vi hablar entre dientes
■ ~ vt mascullar

mumbo jumbo /ˈmʌmbəʊˈdʒʌmbəʊ/ n (pej): **religion, he said, was a lot of ~ ~** dijo que la religión no era más que supercherías

mummy /'mʌmi/ n (pl -**mies**) ① (mother) (BrE colloq: esp used by children) mami f (fam), mamita f (fam) ② (Archeol) momia f

mumps /mʌmps/ n paperas fpl

munch /mʌntʃ/ vt/i mascar*

mundane /mʌnˈdeɪn/ adj ⟨existence⟩ prosaico; ⟨activity⟩ rutinario

municipal /mjʊˈnɪsəpəl ‖ mjuˈnɪsɪpəl/ adj (usu before n) municipal

munitions /mjʊˈnɪʃənz ‖ mjuˈnɪʃənz/ pl n municiones fpl

mural /'mjʊərəl ‖ 'mjʊərəl/ n mural m

murder¹ /'mɜːrdər ‖ 'mɜːdə(r)/ n asesinato m; (Law) homicidio m; **to get away with ~: she lets them get away with ~** les permite cualquier cosa

murder² vt (a) (kill) asesinar (b) (ruin) ⟨music/play⟩ destrozar*
■ ~ vi matar

murderer /'mɜːrdərər ‖ 'mɜːdərə(r)/ n asesino, -na m,f

murderous /'mɜːrdərəs ‖ 'mɜːdərəs/ adj ⟨instinct/look⟩ asesino; ⟨individual⟩ de instintos asesinos

murky /'mɜːrki ‖ 'mɜːki/ adj -**kier**, -**kiest** ⟨water⟩ turbio; ⟨green/brown⟩ sucio; ⟨past⟩ turbio

murmur¹ /'mɜːrmər ‖ 'mɜːmə(r)/ n murmullo m

murmur² vt murmurar

muscle /'mʌsəl/ n (a) (Anat) músculo m (b) (power) fuerza f
■ **muscle in** [v + adv] (colloq) meterse por medio (con prepotencia); **a rival company ~d in on their market** una compañía de la competencia se introdujo en su sector del mercado
muscular /'mʌskjələr ‖'mʌskjʊlə(r)/ adj (a) ⟨arms/build⟩ musculoso (b) ⟨strain/contraction⟩ muscular
muscular dystrophy /'dɪstrəfi/ n distrofia f muscular
muse¹ /mjuːz/ vi **to ~ (on** o **upon sth)** cavilar or reflexionar (sobre algo)
muse², Muse n musa f
museum /mjʊ'ziːəm/ n museo m
mush /mʌʃ/ n papilla f, pasta f
mushroom¹ /'mʌʃrʊm, -ruːm/ n hongo m (esp AmL), seta f (esp Esp), callampa f (Chi); (rounded, white) champiñón m
mushroom² vi «town/population» crecer* rápidamente; «companies/buildings» aparecer* como hongos or (Chi) como callampas, multiplicarse*
mushy /'mʌʃi/ adj **mushier, mushiest** ⟨vegetables/fruit⟩ blando
music /'mjuːzɪk/ n (a) (art form) música f; **to face the ~** afrontar las consecuencias (b) (written notes) partitura f, música f
musical¹ /'mjuːzɪkəl/ adj (a) (Mus) (before n) ⟨ability/tradition⟩ musical (b) (musically gifted) con aptitudes para la música (c) (melodious) ⟨voice/laugh⟩ musical
musical² n musical m
musical chairs n (+ sing vb): **to play ~ ~** jugar* a las sillitas
music: ~ box n caja f de música; **~ hall** n (a) (entertainment) music hall m, ≈revista f de variedades (b) (building) teatro m de variedades
musician /mjʊ'zɪʃən/ n músico, -ca m,f
musk /mʌsk/ n almizcle m
musket /'mʌskət ‖'mʌskɪt/ n mosquete m
Muslim¹ /'mʊzləm ‖'mʊzlɪm/ n musulmán, -mana m,f
Muslim² adj musulmán
muslin /'mʌzlən ‖'mʌzlɪn/ n muselina f (de algodón)
muss /mʌs/ vt **~ (up)** (AmE colloq) ⟨room⟩ desordenar; **she ~ed her hair** se despeinó
mussel /'mʌsəl/ n mejillón m
must¹ /mʌst, weak form məst/ v mod
[1] (expressing obligation) tener* que or deber; **it ~ be remembered that ...** hay que recordar que ..., tenemos que or debemos recordar que ...; **she ~ not know that I am here** no debe enterarse de que estoy aquí, que no se entere de que estoy aquí; **I ~ say, everywhere looks very tidy** tengo que reconocer que está todo muy ordenado
[2] (expressing certainty, supposition) deber (de) or (esp AmL) haber* de; **it ~ be six o'clock** deben (de) ser or (esp AmL) han de ser las seis, serán las seis
must² /mʌst/ n (essential thing, activity): **a car is a ~ here** aquí es indispensable tener coche; **this book is a ~** este es un libro que hay que leer
mustache /'mʌstæʃ/, (BrE) **moustache** /mə'staːʃ/ n bigote(s) m(pl); **to grow a ~** dejarse bigote(s) or el bigote

mustard /'mʌstərd ‖'mʌstəd/ n mostaza f
muster /'mʌstər ‖'mʌstə(r)/ vt (a) (Mil) ⟨soldiers⟩ reunir*, llamar a asamblea (b) (succeed in raising) **to ~ (up)** ⟨team/army⟩ lograr formar; **if they can ~ enough support** si logran el apoyo que necesitan
mustn't /'mʌsn̩t/ = **must not**
musty /'mʌsti/ adj **-tier, tiest** que huele a humedad or a moho
mutate /'mjuːteɪt ‖mjuː'teɪt/ vi (a) (Biol, Ling) mutar (b) (change) (frml) sufrir una transformación/transformaciones
mutation /mjuː'teɪʃən/ n (a) (Biol, Ling) mutación f (b) (change) (frml) transformación f
mute /mjuːt/ adj mudo
muted /'mjuːtəd ‖'mjuːtɪd/ adj ⟨sound⟩ sordo; ⟨voice⟩ apagado; ⟨trumpet⟩ con sordina; ⟨shade⟩ apagado; ⟨protest/reaction⟩ débil
mutilate /'mjuːtleɪt ‖'mjuːtɪleɪt/ vt mutilar
mutiny¹ /'mjuːtn̩i ‖'mjuːtɪni/ n (pl **-nies**) (a) (instance) motín m, amotinamiento m (b) (offense) amotinamiento m
mutiny² vi **-nies, -nying, -nied** amotinarse
mutt /mʌt/ n (AmE colloq) (dog) chucho m (fam), gozque m (Col fam), quiltro m (Chi fam), pichicho m (RPl fam)
mutter /'mʌtər ‖'mʌtə(r)/ vi hablar entre dientes
■ **~ vt** mascullar
mutton /'mʌtn̩/ n carne f de ovino (de más de un año), añojo m (Esp), capón m (RPl)
mutual /'mjuːtʃʊəl/ adj (a) (reciprocal) mutuo (b) (shared, common) (before n) ⟨friend/enemy⟩ común
muzzle /'mʌzəl/ n (a) (snout) hocico m (b) (for dog) bozal m (c) (of gun) boca f
my /maɪ/ adj
■ **Note** The translation *mi* agrees in number with the noun which it modifies; *my* is translated by *mi, mis*, according to what follows: *my father/mother* mi padre/ madre; *my books/magazines* mis libros/revistas.

(sing) mi; (pl) mis; **I put ~ hat on** me puse el sombrero; **I broke ~ arm** me rompí el brazo
myalgic encephalomyelitis /maɪˈældʒɪkenˌsefələʊmaɪəˈlaɪtəs ‖maɪˌældʒɪkenˌsefələʊˌmaɪəˈlaɪtɪs/ n encefalomielitis f miálgica
myriad /'mɪriəd/ adj (liter): **the ~ varieties of butterfly** los miles tipos de mariposas
myrrh /mɜːr ‖mɜː(r)/ n mirra f
myself /maɪ'self/ pron (a) (reflexive): **I cut/hurt ~** me corté/lastimé; **I was talking to ~** estaba hablando solo/sola; **I was by ~** estaba solo/sola (b) (emphatic use) yo mismo, yo misma; **I made it ~** lo hice yo mismo/misma (c) (normal self): **I haven't been feeling ~ lately** no me encuentro muy bien últimamente
mysterious /mɪ'stɪriəs ‖mɪ'stɪəriəs/ adj misterioso
mystery /'mɪstəri/ n (pl **-ries**) [1] (a) (puzzle) misterio m (b) (quality) misterio m; (before n) ⟨guest/tour⟩ sorpresa adj inv [2] (Cin, Lit, Theat) película f (or novela f etc) de misterio or de suspenso or (Esp) de suspense

mystical /'mɪstɪkəl/ *adj* místico
mystify /'mɪstəfaɪ ǁ'mɪstɪfaɪ/ *vt* **-fies, -fying, -fied** desconcertar*

myth /mɪθ/ *n* mito *m*
mythology /mɪ'θɑːlədʒi ǁmɪ'θɒlədʒi/ *n* (*pl* **-gies**) mitología *f*

N n

N, n /en/ *n* **(a)** (letter) N, n *f* **(b)** (indeterminate number) (Math) (número *m*) n
'n' /ən/ = **and**
N (= **north**) N
NAACP /'endʌbəl'eɪsi:'pi:/ *n* (in US) = **National Association for the Advancement of Colored People**
nab /næb/ *vt* **-bb-** (colloq) **(a)** (catch) ⟨*person*⟩ pescar* (fam) **(b)** (snatch) agarrar *or* (esp Esp) coger*
nadir /'neɪdɪr ǁ'neɪdɪə(r)/ *n* (Astron) nadir *m*; (lowest point) punto *m* más bajo
nag /næg/ **-gg-** *vt* **(a)** (pester) fastidiar **(b)** (criticize): **he's always ~ging her for being untidy** siempre le está encima con que es desordenada
■ **~** *vi* **1 (a)** (pester) fastidiar **(b)** (criticize) rezongar* **2 nagging** *pres p* ⟨*doubt/worry*⟩ persistente; ⟨*husband/wife*⟩ rezongón (fam)
nail¹ /neɪl/ *n* **1** (Const) clavo *m*; (smaller) puntilla *f*; **to be as hard as ~s** ser* muy duro (de corazón) **2** (Anat) uña *f*; (*before n*) **~ polish** *o* (BrE also) **varnish** esmalte *m* de uñas
nail² *vt* **1** (fix) clavar **2** (colloq) (apprehend) agarrar *or* (esp Esp) coger*
■ **nail down** [*v + o + adv, v + adv + o*], clavar, asegurar con clavos
nail: ~brush *n* cepillo *m* de uñas; **~ clippers** *pl n* cortaúñas *m*; **~ file** *n* lima *f* (de uñas)
naive, naïve /naː'iːv, naɪ'iːv/ *adj* ingenuo
naked /'neɪkəd ǁ'neɪkɪd/ *adj* **(a)** (unclothed) desnudo **(b)** ⟨*sword/blade*⟩ desenvainado; **visible/invisible to the ~ eye** que se puede ver/invisible a simple vista
name¹ /neɪm/ *n* **1** (of person, thing) nombre *m*; (surname) apellido *m*; **what's your ~?** ¿cómo te llamas?, ¿cómo se llama (Ud)?; **my ~ is John Baker** me llamo John Baker; **he knows them all by ~** los conoce a todos por su nombre; **in ~ only** solo de nombre; **mentioning no ~s** sin mencionar a nadie; **to call sb ~s** insultar a algn; (*before n*) **~ tag** etiqueta *f* de identificación **2 (a)** (reputation) fama *f*; **to give sb/sth a bad ~** darle* mala fama a algn/algo **(b)** (person) figura *f*; (company) nombre *m*; **to drop ~s** mencionar a gente importante (*para darse tono*)
name² *vt* **1** (give name to) ⟨*company/town*⟩ ponerle* nombre a; ⟨*boat*⟩ bautizar*; **a man ~d Smith** un hombre llamado Smith; **they ~d her**

after *o* (AmE also) **for Ann's mother** le pusieron el nombre de la madre de Ann **2** (identify, mention): **police have ~d the suspect** la policía ha dado el nombre del sospechoso; **to ~ but a few** por mencionar a unos pocos; **you ~ it, she's done it** ha hecho de todo lo habido y por haber **3** (appoint) nombrar
nameless /'neɪmləs ǁ'neɪmlɪs/ *adj* **1** (not specified) anónimo **2** ⟨*fear/yearning*⟩ indescriptible
namely /'neɪmli/ *adv* (frml) a saber (frml)
namesake /'neɪmseɪk/ *n* tocayo, -ya *m,f*
nanny /'næni/ *n* (*pl* **-nies**) **1** (nursemaid) (esp BrE) niñera *f* **2** (granny) (used to or by children) abuelita *f* (fam) **3 ~ goat** cabra *f*
nap /næp/ *n* sueñecito *m* (fam), sueñito *m* (esp AmL fam); (esp in the afternoon) siesta *f*
nape /neɪp/ *n* nuca *f*
napkin /'næpkɪn/ *n* servilleta *f*
nappy /'næpi/ *n* (*pl* **-pies**) (BrE) pañal *m*
narcotic /nɑːr'kɑːtɪk ǁnɑː'kɒtɪk/ *n* estupefaciente *m*, narcótico *m*
narrate /'næreɪt ǁnə'reɪt/ *vt* **(a)** (Lit frml) ⟨*story/events*⟩ narrar **(b)** ⟨*film/documentary*⟩ hacer* el comentario de
narrative¹ /'nærətɪv/ *adj* narrativo
narrative² *n* **(a)** (story) (frml) narración *f* **(b)** (Lit) (narrated part) narración *f*
narrator /'n: næreɪtər ǁnə'reɪtə(r)/ *n* **(a)** (Lit) narrador, -dora *m,f* **(b)** (Cin, Theat, TV) comentarista *mf*
narrow¹ /'nærəʊ/ *adj* **1 (a)** (not wide) ⟨*path/opening/hips*⟩ estrecho, angosto (esp AmL) **(b)** (slender) ⟨*margin*⟩ escaso; ⟨*win/victory*⟩ conseguido por un escaso margen; **to have a ~ escape** salvarse de milagro **2** (restricted) ⟨*range/view*⟩ limitado; ⟨*attitude/ideas*⟩ cerrado
narrow² *vt* **(a)** (reduce width of) estrechar, angostar (esp AmL) **(b)** (restrict) ⟨*range/field*⟩ restringir*
■ **~** *vi* **(a)** «*road/river/valley*» estrecharse, angostarse (esp AmL) **(b)** «*options/odds*» reducirse*
■ **narrow down** [*v + o + adv, v + adv + o*]: **they've ~ed their investigation down to this area** han restringido su investigación a esta área; **we**

~ed it down to only three candidates fuimos descartando candidatos hasta quedar con solo tres

narrowly /'nærəʊli/ adv por poco

narrow-minded /'nærəʊ'maɪndəd ‖ ,nærəʊ'maɪndɪd/ adj de mentalidad cerrada

NASA /'næsə/ n (in US) (no art) (= **National Aeronautics and Space Administration**) la NASA

nasal /'neɪzəl/ adj (Anat, Ling) nasal; ‹voice/ accent› gangoso, de timbre nasal

nasty /'næsti ‖ 'nɑːsti/ adj **-tier, -tiest** [1] ‹taste/smell/medicine› asqueroso; ‹habit› feo [2] (spiteful) ‹person› malo [3] (a) (severe) ‹cut/ injury/cough› feo; ‹accident› serio; (stronger) horrible (b) (unpleasant) ‹situation/experience› desagradable

nation /'neɪʃn̩/ n nación f

national¹ /'næʃnəl ‖ 'næʃənl̩/ adj nacional

national² n ciudadano, -na m,f

national: N~ Health (Service) n (in UK) the N~ Health (Service) servicio de asistencia sanitaria de la Seguridad Social; **N~ Insurance** n (in UK) Seguridad f Social

nationalism /'næʃnəlɪzəm/ n nacionalismo m

nationalist¹ /'næʃnələst ‖ 'næʃnəlɪst/ adj nacionalista

nationalist² n nacionalista mf

nationality /'næʃə'næləti/ n (pl **-ties**) nacionalidad f; what's your?, what ~ are you? ¿de qué nacionalidad eres?

nationalize /'næʃnəlaɪz/ vt nacionalizar*

nationally /'næʃnəli/ adv a escala nacional

national park n parque m nacional

nationwide¹ /'neɪʃənwaɪd/ adj ‹campaign› a escala nacional; ‹appeal› a toda la nación

nationwide² adv ‹distribute/operate› a escala nacional

native¹ /'neɪtɪv/ adj [1] (a) (of or by birth) ‹country/town› natal; ‹customs› nativo; ‹language› materno; his ~ land su patria, su tierra natal; a ~ speaker of ... un hablante nativo de ... (b) (innate) ‹ability/wit/charm› innato [2] (indigenous) ‹plant/animal› autóctono

native² n (a) (Anthrop) nativo, -va m,f, indígena mf (b) (plant, animal): the dingo is a ~ of Australia el dingo es originario de Australia

Native American n indio americano, india americana m,f

nativity /nə'tɪvəti/ n: The N~ (Relig) la Natividad

NATO /'neɪtəʊ/ n (no art) (= **North Atlantic Treaty Organization**) la OTAN

natural /'nætʃrəl/ adj [1] (as in nature) natural [2] (a) ‹talent/propensity› innato; ‹leader› nato (b) ‹reaction/response› natural; ‹successor› lógico [3] (not forced) ‹warmth/style› natural

natural history n historia f natural

naturalist /'nætʃrələst ‖ 'nætʃrəlɪst/ n naturalista mf

naturalization /,nætʃrələ'zeɪʃən ‖ ,nætʃrələr'zeɪʃən/ n naturalización f

naturalized /'nætʃrəlaɪzd/ adj (a) ‹citizen/ American› naturalizado (b) (Bot, Zool) aclimatado

naturally /'nætʃrəli/ adv [1] (a) (inherently)

‹shy/tidy› por naturaleza (b) (unaffectedly) ‹smile/ behave/speak› con naturalidad [2] (without artifice) ‹form/heal› de manera natural [3] (indep) (of course) naturalmente, por supuesto

nature /'neɪtʃər ‖ 'neɪtʃə(r)/ n [1] (universe, way of things) naturaleza f [2] (a) (of people) carácter m; by ~ por naturaleza (b) (of things, concepts) naturaleza f

nature reserve n reserva f natural

naturist /'neɪtʃərəst ‖ 'neɪtʃərɪst/ n (esp BrE) nudista mf; (before n) ‹beach/camp› nudista

naught /nɔːt/ n (esp AmE) cero m

naughty /'nɔːti/ adj **-tier, -tiest** malo, travieso

nausea /'nɔːsiə, -ziə/ n náusea f

nauseating /'nɔːsieɪtɪŋ, 'nɔːz-/ adj ‹violence/ brutality› repugnante; ‹smell› nauseabundo

nauseous /'nɔːʃəs, 'nɔːziəs ‖ 'nɔːsiəs, nɔːz-/ adj (bilious): to feel ~ sentir* náuseas

nautical /'nɔːtɪkl̩ ‖ 'nɔːtɪkəl/ adj náutico, marítimo; ~ mile milla f marina

naval /'neɪvəl/ adj naval; ‹officer› de marina

nave /neɪv/ n nave f

navel /'neɪvəl/ n ombligo m

navigable /'nævɪgəbəl/ adj navegable

navigate /'nævɪgeɪt/ vi (a) (Aviat, Naut) navegar* (b) (in car) hacer* de copiloto ■ ~ vt (a) (steer) ‹ship/plane› conducir*, llevar (b) (travel across, along) ‹sea/river› navegar* por

navigation /'nævə'geɪʃən ‖ ,nævɪ'geɪʃən/ n navegación f; (in car) dirección f

navigator /'nævəgeɪtər ‖ 'nævɪgeɪtə(r)/ n [1] (crew member) (Naut) oficial m/f de derrota; (Aviat) navegante mf [2] (explorer) navegante m

navy¹ /'neɪvi/ n (pl **navies**) [1] (Mil, Naut) marina f de guerra [2] ~ (**blue**) azul m marino

navy², navy-blue /'neɪvi'bluː/ (pred **navy blue**) adj azul marino adj inv

Nazi¹ /'nɑːtsi/ n nazi mf, nazista mf

Nazi² adj nazi, nazista

NB (= **nota bene**) NB

NBC n (in US) (no art) (= **National Broadcasting Company**) la NBC

NC = **North Carolina**

NCO n = **noncommissioned officer**

ND, N Dak = **North Dakota**

NE (a) (= **northeast**) NE (b) = **Nebraska**

near¹ /nɪr ‖ nɪə(r)/ adj **-er, -est** [1] (a) (in position, time) cercano, próximo (b) ‹relative› cercano [2] (virtual) (before n): there was ~ panic when the alarms sounded casi se produjo el pánico cuando sonaron las alarmas; in a state of ~ exhaustion prácticamente en estado de agotamiento

near² adv **-er, -est** [1] (in position) cerca; from ~ and far de todas partes [2] (nearly) casi

near³ prep **-er, -est** (a) (in position) cerca de; don't go too ~ the fire no te acerques demasiado al fuego (b) (in time): we're getting very ~ Christmas falta muy poco para Navidad (c) (in approximation): I'd say he's ~er 70 than 60 yo diría que está más cerca de los 70 que de los 60

near⁴ vt acercarse* a; the project is ~ing completion el proyecto se está por acabar

near- /nɪr ‖ nɪə(r)/ pref casi

nearby¹ /ˈnɪrbaɪ ‖nɪəˈbaɪ/ *adj* cercano
nearby² *adv* cerca
nearly /ˈnɪrli ‖ˈnɪəli/ *adv* casi; **she very ~ died** por poco *or* casi se muere
nearsighted /ˈnɪrˌsaɪtəd ‖ˌnɪəˈsaɪtɪd/ *adj* miope, corto de vista
neat /niːt/ *adj* **-er, -est** ① (tidy, orderly) ‹appearance› arreglado, cuidado, prolijo (RPl); ‹person› pulcro, prolijo (RPl); ‹garden› muy cuidado ② (good, nice) (AmE colloq) fantástico (fam), padre (Méx fam), chévere (AmL exc CS fam), chulo (Esp fam), encachado (Chi fam) ③ (BrE) ‹brandy/alcohol› solo
neatly /ˈniːtli/ *adv* (a) (tidily): **the papers were ~ organized into piles** los papeles estaban cuidadosamente apilados; **she was ~ dressed** iba bien arreglada (b) (snugly): **the table fits ~ into the alcove** la mesa cabe perfectamente en el hueco (c) ‹explain/evade› hábilmente
Neb, Nebr = **Nebraska**
necessarily /ˈnesəˈserəli ‖ˌnesəˈserɪli/ *adv* forzosamente, necesariamente
necessary /ˈnesəseri ‖ˈnesəsəri/ *adj* necesario
necessitate /nəˈsesɪteɪt ‖nɪˈsesɪteɪt/ *vt* (frml) exigir*
necessity /nəˈsesəti ‖nɪˈsesɪti/ *n* (*pl* **-ties**) ① (imperative need) (*no pl*) necesidad *f*; **~ FOR sth** necesidad DE algo; **out of ~** por necesidad ② (necessary item): **the bare necessities** lo indispensable; **a car is a ~ for me** para mí tener coche es una necesidad
neck /nek/ *n* ① (Anat) (of person) cuello *m*; (of animal) cuello *m*, pescuezo *m*; **they were ~ and ~** iban a la par, iban parejos (esp AmL); **to be up to one's ~ in sth** (colloq): **she's up to her ~ in work** está hasta aquí de trabajo (fam); **they're up to their ~s in debt** deben hasta la camisa (fam) ② (Clothing) cuello *m*, escote *m*; (measurement) cuello *m* ③ (of pork, beef, lamb) (esp BrE) cuello *m* ④ (of bottle, vase) cuello *m*; (of guitar, violin) mástil *m*; **a ~ of land** un istmo
necklace /ˈnekləs ‖ˈneklɪs/ *n* collar *m*
neck: **~line** *n* escote *m*; **~tie** *n* (AmE) corbata *f*
nectar /ˈnektər ‖ˈnektə(r)/ *n* néctar *m*
nectarine /ˈnektəriːn ‖ˈnektərɪn, -riːn/ *n* nectarina *f*, pelón *m* (RPl), durazno *m* pelado (Chi)
née /neɪ/ *adj* de soltera
need¹ /niːd/ *n* ① (requirement, necessity) necesidad *f*; **~ FOR sth/to + INF** necesidad DE algo/DE + INF; **there's no ~ to tell her** no hay ninguna necesidad de decírselo; **if ~ be** si hace falta; **the house is badly in ~ of renovation** a la casa le hacen muchísima falta unos arreglos ② (a) (emergency): **he abandoned them in their hour of ~** los abandonó cuando más falta les hacía (b) (poverty) necesidad *f*; **those in ~** los necesitados
need² *vt* necesitar; **the plants ~ watering** hay que regar las plantas; **to ~ to + INF** tener* QUE + INF
■ **~** *v mod* (*usu with neg or interrog*) (be obliged to): **you ~n't come if you don't want to** no hay necesidad de que vengas si no tienes ganas; **that ~n't mean that …** eso no significa necesariamente que …
needle¹ /ˈniːdl/ *n* (a) (for sewing, on syringe) aguja

f; (on record player) aguja *f*, púa *f* (RPl); (knitting **~**) aguja *f* de tejer *or* (Esp) de hacer punto, palillo *m* (Chi); **to look for a ~ in a haystack** buscar* una aguja en un pajar (b) (on gauge) aguja *f* (c) (Bot) aguja *f*
needle² *vt* pinchar (fam)
needless /ˈniːdləs ‖ˈniːdlɪs/ *adj* innecesario; **~ to say, no one asked me** de más está decir que nadie me preguntó
needlework /ˈniːdlˌwɜːrk ‖ˈniːdlˌwɜːk/ *n* (activity, skill) labores *fpl* de aguja
needn't /ˈniːdn̩t/ = **need not**
needy¹ /ˈniːdi/ *adj* **-dier, -diest** necesitado
needy² *pl n* **the ~** los necesitados
negative¹ /ˈnegətɪv/ *adj* negativo
negative² *n* ① (a) (word, particle) negación *f* (b) (no) negativa *f* ② (Phot) negativo *m*
neglect¹ /nɪˈglekt/ *vt* (a) (leave uncared-for) ‹family/child› desatender*; ‹house/health› descuidar (b) (not carry out) ‹duty/obligations› desatender*; ‹studies/business› descuidar
neglect² *n* (lack of care) abandono *m*; (negligence) negligencia *f*
neglected /nɪˈglektəd ‖nɪˈglektɪd/ *adj* ‹building/garden› abandonado, descuidado; ‹appearance› dejado, abandonado
neglectful /nɪˈglektfəl/ *adj* negligente
negligee /ˈneglɪˈʒeɪ ‖ˈneglɪʒeɪ/ *n* negligé *m*
negligence /ˈneglɪdʒəns/ *n* negligencia *f*
negligent /ˈneglɪdʒənt/ *adj* negligente
negligible /ˈneglɪdʒəbəl/ *adj* insignificante
negotiable /nɪˈgəʊʃəbəl/ *adj* (a) (subject to negotiation) ‹contract/claim/salary› negociable (b) (passable) ‹road› transitable; ‹obstacle› superable
negotiate /nɪˈgəʊʃieɪt/ *vi* negociar
■ **~** *vt* ① (obtain by discussion) ‹contract/treaty› negociar; ‹loan› gestionar ② (pass, deal with) ‹obstacle› sortear; ‹difficulty› superar
negotiation /nɪˈgəʊʃiˈeɪʃən/ *n* (*sometimes pl*) negociación *f*
negotiator /nɪˈgəʊʃieɪtər ‖nɪˈgəʊʃieɪtə(r)/ *n* negociador, -dora *m,f*
Negro /ˈniːgrəʊ/ *n* (*pl* **Negroes**) (often offensive) negro, -gra *m,f*
neigh /neɪ/ *vi* relinchar
neighbor, (BrE) **neighbour** /ˈneɪbər ‖ˈneɪbə(r)/ *n* vecino, -na *m,f*
neighborhood, (BrE) **neighbourhood** /ˈneɪbərhʊd ‖ˈneɪbəhʊd/ *n* (a) (residential area) barrio *m*; (before n) ‹school/policeman› del barrio (b) (inhabitants) vecindario *m* (c) (vicinity) zona *f*; **in the ~** en los alrededores
neighboring, (BrE) **neighbouring** /ˈneɪbərɪŋ/ *adj* ‹country› vecino; **the town and the ~ villages** la ciudad y los pueblos de los alrededores
neither¹ /ˈniːðər, ˈnaɪ- ‖ˈnaɪðə(r), ˈniːð-/ *conj* ① **neither … nor …** ni … ni … ② (nor) tampoco; **I don't want to go — ~ do I** *o* (colloq) **me ~** no quiero ir — yo tampoco *or* ni yo
neither² *adj*: **~ proposal was accepted** no se aceptó ninguna de las (dos) propuestas
neither³ *pron* ninguno, -na
neo- /ˈniːəʊ/ *pref* neo-

neon /'niːɑːn ‖'niːɒn/ n neón m; (before n) ⟨glow/lighting/sign⟩ de neón

Nepal /nə'pɔːl ‖nɪ'pɔːl/ n Nepal m

Nepalese /ˌnepə'liːz/ adj nepalés

nephew /'nefjuː. ‖'nevjuː. 'nef-/ n sobrino m

nepotism /'nepətɪzəm/ n nepotismo m

Neptune /'neptuːn ‖'neptjuːn/ n Neptuno m

nerve /nɜːrv ‖nɜːv/ n ⎡1⎤ (Anat, Bot) nervio m; (before n) ⟨fiber/ending⟩ nervioso ⎡2⎤ **nerves** pl **(a)** (emotional constitution) nervios mpl; **to get on sb's ~s** (colloq) ponerle* los nervios de punta a algn **(b)** (anxiety) nervios mpl ⎡3⎤ **(a)** (resolve) valor m; **to lose one's ~** perder* el valor **(b)** (effrontery) (colloq) (no pl) frescura f (fam); **to have the ~ to + INF** tener* la frescura de + INF (fam)

nerve-racking /'nɜːrvˈrækɪŋ ‖'nɜːvˌrækɪŋ/ adj que destroza los nervios

nervous /'nɜːrvəs ‖'nɜːvəs/ adj ⎡1⎤ (apprehensive, tense) nervioso; **to feel/get ~** estar*/ponerse* nervioso; **to make sb ~** poner* nervioso a algn ⎡2⎤ ⟨system/tissue/tension⟩ nervioso; **she's a ~ wreck** (colloq) es un manojo de nervios

nervously /'nɜːrvəsli ‖'nɜːvəsli/ adv nerviosamente

nest¹ /nest/ n nido m

nest² vi anidar

nest egg n (colloq) ahorros mpl

nestle /'nesəl/ vi (snuggle) acurrucarse*; **the village ~s at the foot of the hill** el pueblo está enclavado al pie de la montaña

net¹ /net/ n ⎡1⎤ red f ⎡2⎤ (Sport) red f ⎡3⎤ (fabric) tela f de visillos; (before n) ~ **curtains** visillos mpl

net² vt -tt- ⎡1⎤ (catch) ⟨butterfly⟩ cazar* (con red); ⟨fish⟩ pescar* (con red) ⎡2⎤ (earn) «company/sale» producir*; **he ~ted $50,000** se embolsó 50.000 dólares limpios (fam)

net³ adj ⟨income/profit⟩ neto; ⟨effect/result⟩ global

netball /'netbɔːl/ n (in UK) deporte similar al baloncesto jugado esp por mujeres

Netherlands /'neðərləndz ‖'neðələndz/ n (+ sing or pl vb) **the ~** los Países Bajos

nett adj (BrE) ▶ NET³

netting /'netɪŋ/ n redes fpl; **wire ~** tela f metálica, tejido m metálico (RPl), anjeo m (Col)

nettle /'netl/ n ortiga f; (stinging ~) ortiga f (romana)

network¹ /'netwɜːrk ‖'netwɜːk/ n **(a)** (system) red f **(b)** (Elec) red f **(c)** (Rad, TV) cadena f; (before n) ~ **television** (in US) emisiones fpl televisivas en cadena

network² vt ⎡1⎤ (BrE Rad, TV) transmitir en cadena ⎡2⎤ (link together) (Comput) interconectar

neuralgia /nʊ'rældʒə ‖njʊə'rældʒə/ n neuralgia f

neurosis /nʊ'rəʊsəs ‖njʊə'rəʊsɪs/ n (pl -roses /-'rəʊsiːz/) neurosis f

neurotic /nʊ'rɑːtɪk ‖njʊə'rɒtɪk/ adj neurótico

neuter¹ /'nuːtər ‖'njuːtə(r)/ adj neutro

neuter² vt castrar

neutral¹ /'nuːtrəl ‖'njuːtrəl/ adj **(a)** (impartial) neutral **(b)** (not bright) ⟨shade/tone⟩ neutro **(c)** (Chem, Elec, Ling) neutro

neutral² n (Auto): **to be in ~** estar* en punto muerto

neutralize /'nuːtrəlaɪz ‖'njuːtrəlaɪz/ vt neutralizar*

neutron /'nuːtrɑːn ‖'njuːtrɒn/ n neutrón m

Nev = Nevada

never /'nevər ‖'nevə(r)/ adv nunca; (more emphatic) jamás; **as ~ before** como nunca; **she said she'd call but she ~ did** dijo que llamaría pero no llamó; **this will ~ do!** ¡esto no puede ser!

never: ~**-ending** /'nevər'endɪŋ/ adj (pred ~ ending) ⟨dispute/saga⟩ interminable; ⟨devotion/ supply⟩ inagotable; ~**theless** /ˌnevərðə'les ‖ˌnevəðə'les/ adv sin embargo, no obstante (frml)

new¹ /nuː ‖njuː/ adj **-er, -est** nuevo; **after the shower I felt like a ~ man** la ducha me dejó como nuevo

new² adv recién

new: **N~ Age** adj New Age, de la Nueva Era; ~**born** /'nuːbɔːrn ‖'njuːbɔːn/ adj recién nacido; ~**comer** /'nuːkʌmər ‖'njuːkʌmə(r)/ n recién llegado, -da m,f; ~**fangled** /'nuːˈfæŋɡəld ‖'njuːˈfæŋɡəld/ adj (before n) (pej) moderno; ~**found** /'nuːfaʊnd ‖'njuːfaʊnd/ adj nuevo, recién descubierto

newlyweds /'nuːliwedz ‖'njuːliwedz/ pl n recién casados mpl

news /nuːz ‖njuːz/ n ⎡1⎤ (fresh information): **a piece of ~** una noticia; **I have (some) good/bad ~** tengo buenas/malas noticias ⎡2⎤ (Journ, Rad, TV) noticias fpl; (before n) ~ **bulletin** boletín m informativo

news: ~**agent** n (BrE) dueño o empleado de una tienda que vende prensa, caramelos etc; ~**caster** n locutor, -tora m,f, presentador, -dora m,f (de un informativo); ~ **flash** n (BrE) información f de última hora; ~ **group** n grupo m de noticias; ~**letter** n boletín m informativo

newspaper /'nuːzˌpeɪpər ‖'njuːsˌpeɪpə(r)/ n periódico m, diario m

news: ~**print** n papel m de prensa; ~**reel** n noticiario m or (AmL tb) noticiero m (cinematográfico), nodo m (Esp); ~**stand** n kiosco m de periódicos

newt /nuːt ‖njuːt/ n tritón m

new: **N~ Year** n Año m Nuevo; **N~ Year's Day** n día m de Año Nuevo; **N~ Year's Eve** n la noche de Fin de Año, la Nochevieja (Esp); **N~ York** /jɔːrk ‖jɔːk/ n Nueva York f; (before n) neoyorquino; **N~ Zealand** /'ziːlənd/ n Nueva Zelanda; (before n) neocelandés

next¹ /nekst/ adj **(a)** (in time — talking about the future) próximo; (— talking about the past) siguiente; **I'll see you ~ Thursday** nos vemos el jueves que viene or el jueves próximo; **the matter was discussed at the ~ meeting** el asunto se trató en la reunión siguiente; **the week after ~** la semana que viene no, la otra or la siguiente **(b)** (in position) siguiente; **take the ~ turning on the right** tome la próxima or la siguiente a la derecha **(c)** (in sequence): **who's ~?** ¿quién sigue?; **you're the ~ to speak** luego te toca a ti hablar

next² adv ⎡1⎤ **(a)** (then) luego, después **(b)** (now): **what shall we do ~?** ¿y ahora qué hacemos?; **what comes ~?** ¿qué sigue (ahora)?; **whatever ~!** ¡adónde vamos (a ir) a parar! ⋯⋗

2 (second): **Tom is the tallest in the class, Bob the ~ tallest** Tom es el más alto de la clase y (a Tom) le sigue Bob; **it's the ~ best thing to champagne** después del champán, es lo mejor que hay

3 **next to (a)** (beside) al lado de; **come and sit ~ to me** ven y siéntate a mi lado **(b)** (compared with) al lado de **(c)** (second): **the ~ to last page** la penúltima página **(d)** (almost, virtually): **I bought it for ~ to nothing** lo compré por poquísimo dinero; **I'll have it ready in ~ to no time** lo termino en un segundo

next: ~ door *adv* al lado; **~ door TO sb/sth** al lado DE algn/algo; **~-door** /'neks'dɔːr ‖'neks'dɔː(r)/ *adj* ⟨before n⟩ de al lado; **~ of kin** *n (pl ~ of kin)* familiar(es) *m(pl)* más cercano(s)

NGO *n* (= **Non-governmental Organization**) ONG *f*

NH = **New Hampshire**

NHS *n* (in UK) = **National Health Service**

nib /nɪb/ *n* plumín *m*, pluma *f*

nibble /'nɪbəl/ *vt* **(a)** (bite) mordisquear **(b)** (eat, pick at) picar*

■ ~ *vi* **(a)** (bite, gnaw) **to ~ AT/ON sth** mordisquear algo **(b)** (eat) picar*

Nicaragua /'nɪkə'rɑːgwə/ *n* Nicaragua *f*

Nicaraguan¹ /'nɪkə'rɑːgwən ‖,nɪkə'rægjʊən/ *adj* nicaragüense

Nicaraguan² *n* nicaragüense *mf*

nice /naɪs/ *adj* **nicer, nicest** **1** **(a)** (kind, amiable) amable; (kind-hearted) bueno; (friendly) simpático; **to be ~ TO sb** ser* amable CON algn **(b)** (attractive, appealing) ⟨place/dress/face⟩ bonito, lindo (esp AmL); ⟨food⟩ bueno, rico; **the soup smells ~** la sopa huele bien **(c)** (enjoyable) ⟨walk/surprise⟩ agradable, lindo (esp AmL)

2 (as intensifier): **I had a ~ hot shower** me di una buena ducha caliente; **her apartment is ~ and sunny** tiene un apartamento muy *or* de lo más soleado

3 (respectable, decent): **he seemed such a ~ boy** parecía tan buen chico; **it isn't a very ~ area** es un barrio bastante feo

nicely /'naɪsli/ *adv* **1** **(a)** (amiably) ⟨treat/smile⟩ amablemente **(b)** (politely, respectably) con buenos modales **2** (attractively) ⟨presented/dressed⟩ bien

niceties /'naɪsətiz/ *pl n* sutilezas *fpl*

niche /nɪtʃ, niːʃ/ *n* nicho *m*, hornacina *f*

nick¹ /nɪk/ *n* (in wood) muesca *f*; (in blade) mella *f*; **did you cut yourself? — it's just a little ~** ¿te cortaste? — es solo un rasguño; **in the ~ of time** justo a tiempo

nick² *vt* **1** (notch) hacer* una muesca en; **I ~ed myself shaving** me corté al afeitarme **2** (steal) (BrE colloq) afanar (arg), volar* (Méx, Ven fam), robar

nickel /'nɪkəl/ **1** *n* (Chem, Metall) níquel *m* **2** (US coin) moneda de cinco centavos

nickname¹ /'nɪkneɪm/ *n* apodo *m*; (relating to personal characteristics) mote *m*

nickname² *vt* apodar

nicotine /'nɪkətiːn/ *n* nicotina *f*

nicotine patch *n* parche *m* de nicotina

niece /niːs/ *n* sobrina *f*

Nigeria /naɪ'dʒɪriə/ *n* Nigeria *f*

Nigerian /naɪ'dʒɪriən/ *adj* nigeriano

niggle /'nɪgəl/ *vt*: **something's niggling him** algo le preocupa

niggling /'nɪglɪŋ/ *adj* ⟨doubt/worry⟩ constante

night /naɪt/ *n* **1** noche *f*; **at ~** por la noche, de noche; **~ and day** día y noche; **last ~** anoche; **the ~ before last** anteanoche, antenoche (AmL); **we stayed (for) the ~** nos quedamos a dormir; **we haven't had a ~ out for ages** hace muchísimo que no salimos por la noche; **good ~** buenas noches; (before n) ⟨flight/patrol⟩ nocturno **2** **nights** (as adv) por las noches

night: ~cap *n* **(a)** (Clothing) gorro *m* de dormir **(b)** (drink) bebida alcohólica o caliente tomada antes de acostarse; **~clothes** *pl n* ropa *f* de dormir; **~club** *n* club *m* nocturno; **~dress** *n* camisón *m*; **~fall** *n* anochecer *m*; **at ~fall** al anochecer; **~gown** *n* camisón *m*

nightingale /'naɪtŋgeɪl ‖'naɪtɪŋgeɪl/ *n* ruiseñor *m*

nightlife /'naɪtlaɪf/ *n* vida *f* nocturna

nightly¹ /'naɪtli/ *adj* diario, de todas las noches

nightly² *adv* todas las noches

nightmare /'naɪtmer ‖'naɪtmeə(r)/ *n* pesadilla *f*

night: ~ school *n* clases *fpl* nocturnas; **~time** *n* noche *f*; **~ watchman** *n* sereno *m*

nil /nɪl/ *n* **(a)** (nothing): **its food value is virtually ~** su valor nutritivo es casi nulo **(b)** (BrE Sport) cero *m*

Nile /naɪl/ *n* **the ~** el Nilo

nimble /'nɪmbəl/ *adj* **-bler** /-blər/, **-blest** /-bləst/ ⟨person/step/mind⟩ ágil; ⟨fingers⟩ diestro

nine¹ /naɪn/ *n* nueve *m*; *see also* FOUR¹

nine² *adj inv*; **~ times out of ten he's late/right** casi siempre llega tarde/tiene razón

ninefold /'naɪnfəʊld/ *adj/adv* ▶ -FOLD

nineteen /'naɪn'tiːn/ *adj/n* diecinueve *adj inv/m*; **to talk ~ to the dozen** hablar (hasta) por los codos *or* como una cotorra (fam); *see also* FOUR¹

nineteenth¹ /'naɪn'tiːnθ/ *adj* decimonoveno

nineteenth² *adv* en decimonoveno lugar

nineteenth³ *n* (Math) diecinueveavo *m*; (part) diecinueveava parte *f*

ninetieth¹ /'naɪntiəθ/ *adj* nonagésimo

ninetieth² *adv* en nonagésimo lugar

ninetieth³ *n* (Math) noventavo *m*; (part) noventava *or* nonagésima parte *f*

nine-to-five /'naɪntə'faɪv/ *adj* ⟨job/worker⟩ de oficina (con horario de nueve a cinco)

ninety /'naɪnti/ *adj/n* noventa *adj inv/m*; *see also* FOUR¹

ninth¹ /naɪnθ/ *adj* noveno

ninth² *adv* en noveno lugar

AmC Central America	Arg Argentina	Cu Cuba	Per Peru
AmL Latin America	Bol Bolivia	Ec Ecuador	RPI River Plate Area
AmS South America	Chi Chile	Esp Spain	Ur Uruguay
Andes Andean Region	CS Southern Cone	Méx Mexico	Ven Venezuela

ninth³ *n* (Math) noveno *m*; (part) novena parte *f*

nip¹ /nɪp/ *n* **(a)** (pinch) pellizco *m*; (bite) mordisco *m* **(b)** (chill): **there's a ~ in the air** hace bastante fresco

nip² *vt* **-pp-** (pinch) pellizcar*; (bite) mordisquear

nipple /'nɪpəl/ *n* **(a)** (on breast — of woman) pezón *m*; (— of man) tetilla *f* **(b)** (on bottle) (AmE) tetina *f*, chupón *m* (Méx)

nippy /'nɪpi/ *adj* **-pier, -piest** (colloq) frío; **it's ~** hace frío

nit /nɪt/ *n* (Zool) liendre *f*

nit: **~pick** *vi* encontrarle* defectos a todo; **~picking** *adj* quisquilloso

nitrate /'naɪtreɪt/ *n* nitrato *m*

nitrogen /'naɪtrədʒən/ *n* nitrógeno *m*

NJ = **New Jersey**

NM, N Mex = **New Mexico**

no¹ /nəʊ/ *adj* ① **(a)** (+ *pl n*): **they have ~ children** no tienen hijos; **the room has ~ windows** la habitación no tiene ninguna ventana *or* no tiene ventanas **(b)** (+ *uncount n*): **there's ~ food left** no queda nada de comida; **there's ~ time for that now** no tenemos tiempo para eso ahora; **I'll be finished in ~ time (at all)** termino enseguida **(c)** (+ *sing count n*): **this cup has ~ handle** esta taza no tiene asa; **~ intelligent person would do that** ninguna persona inteligente haría eso ② (in understatements): **I'm ~ expert, but …** no soy ningún experto, pero …; **she told him what she thought in ~ uncertain terms** le dijo lo que pensaba muy claramente ③ **(a)** (prohibiting, demanding): ❺ **no smoking** prohibido fumar **(b)** (with *-ing form*): **there's ~ pleasing some people** no hay manera de complacer a cierta gente; **there'll be ~ stopping them now** ahora no hay quien los pare

no² *adv* (before adj or adv): **my house is ~ larger than yours** mi casa no es más grande que la tuya; **~ fewer than 200 guests are expected** se espera nada menos que a unos 200 invitados

no³ *interj* no; **to say ~** decir* que no; **have you seen John? — ~, I haven't** ¿has visto a John? — no

no⁴ *n* (*pl* **noes**) no *m*

no⁵ (*pl* **nos**) (= **number**) nº, Nº

Nobel Prize /nəʊ'bel/ *n* **the ~ ~** el Premio Nobel

nobility /nəʊ'bɪləti/ *n* nobleza *f*; **the ~** la nobleza

noble¹ /'nəʊbəl/ *adj* **nobler** /-blər/, **noblest** /-bləst/ noble

noble² *n* noble *mf*

nobleman /'nəʊbəlmən/ *n* (*pl* **-men** /-mən/) noble *m*

nobody¹ /'nəʊˌbɑːdi ‖ 'nəʊbədi/ *pron* nadie

nobody² *n* (*pl* **-dies**): **to be a(~)** ser* un don nadie

nocturnal /nɑːk'tɜːrnḷ ‖ nɒk'tɜːnḷ/ *adj* nocturno

nod¹ /nɑːd ‖ nɒd/ *n*: **he greeted her with a ~** la saludó con un movimiento de cabeza; **to give sb/sth the ~** darle* luz verde a algn/algo

nod² **-dd-** *vt*: **he ~ded his head (in agreement)** asintió con la cabeza

■ **~** *vi*: **she smiled at me and I ~ed to her** me sonrió y la saludé con la cabeza; **they ~ded in assent** asintieron con la cabeza

■ **nod off** [*v + adv*] (colloq) dormirse*

nodule /'nɑːdʒuːl ‖ 'nɒdjuːl/ *n* nódulo *m*

no-fly zone /nəʊ'flaɪ/*n* zona *f* de exclusión aérea

no-good /'nəʊ'gʊd/ *adj* (AmE colloq) maldito (fam)

noise /nɔɪz/ *n* ruido *m*

noisily /'nɔɪzəli ‖ 'nɔɪzɪli/ *adv* ruidosamente

noisy /'nɔɪzi/ *adj* **-sier, -siest** ‹machine/office/street› ruidoso; ‹person/child/party› bullicioso

nomad /'nəʊmæd/ *n* nómada *mf*, nómade *mf* (CS)

no-man's land /'nəʊmænzlænd/ *n* tierra *f* de nadie

nominal /'nɑːmənḷ ‖ 'nɒmɪnḷ/ *adj* **(a)** (in name) nominal **(b)** (token) ‹fee/rent› simbólico

nominate /'nɑːməneɪt ‖ 'nɒmɪneɪt/ *vt* **(a)** (propose) **to ~ sb (FOR sth)** ‹for a post› proponer* *or* (AmL tb) postular a algn (PARA algo) **(b)** (appoint, choose) nombrar; ‹candidate› (AmE Pol) proclamar

nomination /'nɑːmə'neɪʃən ‖ ˌnɒmɪ'neɪʃən/ *n* **(a)** (choice, appointment) nombramiento *m*; (of candidate) (AmE Pol) proclamación *f* **(b)** (proposal) propuesta *f*, postulación *f* (AmL)

nominee /'nɑːmə'niː ‖ ˌnɒmɪ'niː/ *n* **(a)** (person proposed) candidato, -ta *m,f* **(b)** (person appointed) persona *f* nombrada; (candidate) (AmE Pol) candidato, -ta *m,f*

non- /nɑːn ‖ nɒn/ *pref* no; **~swimmers must …** las personas que no saben nadar deben …

nonchalant /'nɑːnʃə'lɑːnt ‖ 'nɒnʃələnt/ *adj* (casual) despreocupado; (indifferent) indiferente

noncommissioned officer /ˌnɑːnkə'mɪʃənd ‖ ˌnɒnkə'mɪʃənd/ *n* ≈suboficial *mf*

noncommittal /ˌnɑːnkə'mɪtḷ ‖ ˌnɒnkə'mɪtḷ/ *adj* ‹reply› evasivo

nondescript /'nɑːndɪ'skrɪpt ‖ 'nɒndɪskrɪpt/ *adj* (not unusual or outstanding) anodino; (dull) insulso

none¹ /nʌn/ *pron* ① (not any, not one) (referring to count *n*) ninguno, ninguna; **I tried to get tickets, but there were ~ left** traté de comprar entradas pero no quedaba ninguna *or* ni una; **~ of us know** *o* **knows her** ninguno de nosotros la conoce ② (no amount or part) (referring to uncount *n*): **did you buy any milk? there's ~ left** ¿compraste leche? no hay más

none² *adv* **(a)** **none the** (not, in no way) (with comp): **I was ~ the wiser after his explanation** su explicación no me aclaró nada **(b)** **none too** (not very) (with adj or adv): **she was ~ too pleased to see me** no le hizo demasiada gracia verme

nonentity /nɑː'nentəti ‖ nɒ'nentəti/ *n* (*pl* **-ties**) persona *f* insignificante

nonetheless /ˌnʌnðə'les/ *adv* ▶ NEVERTHELESS

non-existent /ˌnɑːnɪg'zɪstənt ‖ ˌnɒnɪg'zɪstənt/ *adj* inexistente

nonfiction /'nɑːn'fɪkʃən ‖ 'nɒn'fɪkʃən/ *n* no ficción *f* (ensayos, biografías, obras de divulgación etc)

no-nonsense /'nəʊ'nɑːnsens ‖ ˌnəʊ'nɒnsəns/ *adj* (before *n*) ‹approach/attitude› sensato

n

nonplused, nonplussed /ˌnɑːnˈplʌst
‖ˌnɒnˈplʌst/ *adj* desconcertado

nonprofit /ˈnɑːnˈprɑːfət ‖ˌnɒnˈprɒfɪt/, (BrE)
non-profitmaking /ˈnɑːnˈprɑːfətˌmeɪkɪŋ
‖ˌnɒnˈprɒfɪtmeɪkɪŋ/ *adj* sin fines lucrativos

nonsense /ˈnɑːnsens ‖ˈnɒnsəns/ *n* tonterías
fpl

nonsensical /nɑːnˈsensɪkəl ‖nɒnˈsensɪkəl/
adj disparatado

nonsmoker /ˈnɑːnˈsməʊkər ‖ˌnɒnˈsməʊkə(r)/
n no fumador, -dora *m,f*

nonsmoking /ˈnɑːnˈsməʊkɪŋ ‖ˈnɒnˈsməʊkɪŋ/
adj para no fumadores

nonstick /ˈnɑːnˈstɪk ‖ˌnɒnˈstɪk/ *adj*
antiadherente, de teflón®, de tefal®

nonstop /ˈnɑːnˈstɑːp ‖ˌnɒnˈstɒp/ *adv* **(a)**
⟨*work/talk*⟩ sin parar **(b)** ⟨*sail/fly*⟩ sin hacer
escalas

noodle /ˈnuːdl/ *n* fideo *m*

nook /nʊk/ *n* rincón *m*; **to search every ∼ and
cranny** mirar/buscar* hasta en el último rincón

noon /nuːn/ *n* mediodía *m*; **at ∼** a mediodía

no one *pron* ▶ NOBODY[1]

noose /nuːs/ *n* soga *f*, dogal *m*

noplace /ˈnəʊpleɪs/ *adv* (AmE) ▶ NOWHERE[1] 1

nor /nər, nɔːr ‖nɔː(r)/ *conj* **(a) neither ... nor ...**
▶ NEITHER[1] 1 **(b)** (*usu with neg*) tampoco

norm /nɔːrm ‖nɔːm/ *n* norma *f*

normal /ˈnɔːrməl ‖ˈnɔːməl/ *adj* normal; **when
things get back to ∼** cuando todo vuelva a la
normalidad

normality /nɔːrˈmæləti ‖nɔːˈmæləti/ *n*
normalidad *f*

normally /ˈnɔːrməli ‖ˈnɔːməli/ *adv*
normalmente

north[1] /nɔːrθ ‖nɔːθ/ *n* (point of the compass,
direction) norte *m*; **the ∼, the N∼** (region) el norte

north[2] *adj* (*before n*) norte *adj inv*,
septentrional; ⟨*wind*⟩ norte *adj inv*

north[3] *adv* al norte

north: N∼ America *n* Norteamérica *f*,
América *f* del Norte; **N∼ American** *adj* de
América del Norte, norteamericano; **∼bound**
adj ⟨*traffic/train*⟩ que va (*or* iba *etc*) en dirección
norte

northeast[1], Northeast /ˈnɔːrθˈiːst
‖ˌnɔːθˈiːst/ *n* **the ∼** el nor(d)este *or* Nor(d)este

northeast[2] *adj* nor(d)este *adj inv*, del
nor(d)este, nororiental

northeast[3] *adv* hacia el nor(d)este, en
dirección nor(d)este

northeasterly /ˈnɔːrθˈiːstərli ‖ˌnɔːθˈiːstəli/
adj ⟨*wind*⟩ del nor(d)este

northeastern /ˈnɔːrθˈiːstərn ‖ˌnɔːθˈiːstən/ *adj*
nor(d)este *adj inv*, del nor(d)este, nororiental

northerly /ˈnɔːrðərli ‖ˈnɔːðəli/ *adj* ⟨*wind*⟩ del
norte; ⟨*latitude*⟩ norte *adj inv*; **in a ∼ direction**
hacia el *or* en dirección norte

northern /ˈnɔːrðərn ‖ˈnɔːðən/ *adj* ⟨*region/
country*⟩ del norte, septentrional, norteño,
nortino (Chi, Per); **∼ England** el norte de
Inglaterra; **the ∼ states** (in US) los estados del
norte

Northern Ireland *n* Irlanda *f* del Norte

north: N∼ Sea *n* Mar *m* del Norte; **N∼ Star**
n estrella *f* polar

northward[1] /ˈnɔːrθwərd ‖ˈnɔːθwəd/ *adj*
(*before n*): **in a ∼ direction** en dirección norte,
hacia el norte

northward[2], (BrE) **northwards** /-z/ *adv*
hacia el norte

northwest[1], Northwest /ˈnɔːrθˈwest
‖ˌnɔːθˈwest/ *n* **the ∼** el noroeste *or* Noroeste

northwest[2] *adj* noroeste *adj inv*, del noroeste

northwest[3] *adv* hacia el noroeste, en
dirección noroeste

northwesterly /ˈnɔːrθˈwestərli
‖ˌnɔːθˈwestəli/ *adj* ⟨*wind*⟩ del noroeste

northwestern /ˈnɔːrθˈwestərn ‖ˌnɔːθˈwestən/
adj noroccidental, noroeste *adj inv*, del noroeste

Norway /ˈnɔːrweɪ ‖ˈnɔːweɪ/ *n* Noruega *f*

Norwegian[1] /nɔːrˈwiːdʒən ‖nɔːˈwiːdʒən/ *adj*
noruego

Norwegian[2] *n* **(a)** (person) noruego, -ga *m,f*
(b) (language) noruego *m*

nose[1] /nəʊz/ *n* [1] (of person, animal) nariz *f*; **to
look down one's ∼ at sb** mirar a algn por
encima del hombro; **to poke o stick one's ∼ in**
(colloq) meter las narices en algo (fam); **to turn
one's ∼ up at sth/sb** (colloq) despreciar algo/a
algn [2] (of plane, car) parte *f* delantera, trompa *f*
(RPl)

nose[2] *vi* (rummage, pry) entrometerse; **to ∼
around** *o* **about in sth** husmear en algo

nose: ∼bleed *n* hemorragia *f* nasal (frml); **I've
got a ∼bleed** me sangra la nariz; **∼dive** *vi* **(a)**
(Aviat) ⟨*plane/pilot*⟩ descender* *or* bajar en
picada *or* (Esp) en picado **(b)** (drop sharply)
⟨*prices*⟩ caer* en picada *or* (Esp) en picado

nosey /ˈnəʊzi/ *adj* (BrE) ▶ NOSY

no-smoking /ˈnəʊˈsməʊkɪŋ/ *adj*
⟨*compartment/section*⟩ para no fumadores

nostalgia /nɑːˈstældʒə ‖nɒˈstældʒə/ *n*
nostalgia *f*

nostalgic /nɑːˈstældʒɪk ‖nɒˈstældʒɪk/ *adj*
nostálgico

nostril /ˈnɑːstrəl ‖ˈnɒstrɪl/ *n* ventana *f* de la
nariz

nosy, (BrE also) **nosey** /ˈnəʊzi/ *adj* **nosier,
nosiest** (colloq) ⟨*person*⟩ entrometido, metiche
(AmL fam), metido (AmL fam); ⟨*question*⟩
impertinente

not /nɑːt ‖nɒt/ *adv* **(a)** no; **I asked them ∼ to
tell anyone** les pedí que no se lo dijeran a nadie
(b) not that (*as conj*): **I'm going to London, ∼ that
it's any business of yours** voy a Londres, no es
que a ti te importe, pero ... **(c)** (emphatic) ni; **∼ a
penny more** ni un penique más **(d)** (replacing
clause): **I hope ∼** espero que no; **are you going to
help me or ∼?** ¿me vas a ayudar o no?

notable /ˈnəʊtəbəl/ *adj* ⟨*author/actor*⟩
distinguido; ⟨*success*⟩ señalado; ⟨*improvement/
difference*⟩ notable

notably /ˈnəʊtəbli/ *adv* **(a)** (noticeably)
notablemente **(b)** (in particular) particularmente, en
particular

notch /nɑːtʃ ‖nɒtʃ/ *n* (in wood, metal) muesca *f*;
(on belt) agujero *m*
■ **notch up** [*v* + *adv* + *o*] (colloq) apuntarse

note[1] /nəʊt/ *n* [1] (record, reminder) nota *f*; **to**

make a ~ of sth anotar *or* apuntar algo; **to make ~s** hacer* anotaciones; **to take ~s** tomar apuntes *or* notas; **to compare ~s** cambiar impresiones **2** (message) nota *f*
3 **(a)** (Mus) nota *f* **(b)** (tone): **I detected a ~ of sarcasm in his voice** percibí un tono de sarcasmo en su voz; **the evening ended on a sad ~** la velada terminó con una nota triste
4 (esp BrE) (bank~) billete *m*
5 (attention): **take ~ of what he says** toma nota de *or* presta atención a lo que dice

note² *vt* **(a)** (observe, notice) observar **(b)** (record) ⟨information⟩ apuntar, anotar
■ **note down** [*v + adv + o, v + o + adv*] apuntar

notebook /ˈnəʊtbʊk/ *n* cuaderno *m*

noted /ˈnəʊtəd ‖ ˈnəʊtɪd/ *adj* ⟨historian/surgeon⟩ renombrado, de nota

note: **~pad** *n* bloc *m*; **~paper** *n* papel *m* de carta(s)

nothing /ˈnʌθɪŋ/ *pron* **1** nada; **there's ~ to eat** no hay nada de comer **2** (*in phrases*) **for nothing: she gave it to me for ~** me lo dio gratis; **it was all for ~** todo fue en vano; **if nothing else** al menos, por lo menos; **nothing but: she's caused ~ but trouble** no ha causado (nada) más que problemas; **nothing like: there's ~ like a shower to freshen you up** no hay (nada) como una ducha para refrescarse; **nothing much: ~ much happened** no pasó gran cosa

notice¹ /ˈnəʊtəs ‖ ˈnəʊtɪs/ *n* **1** **(a)** (written sign) letrero *m* **(b)** (item of information) anuncio *m*
2 (attention): **it has come/been brought to my ~ that ...** (frml) ha llegado a mi conocimiento que .../ se me ha señalado que ... (frml); **she took no ~** no hizo caso; **don't take any ~ of him** no le hagas caso
3 **(a)** (notification) aviso *m*; **until further ~** hasta nuevo aviso; **it's impossible to do it at such short ~** es imposible hacerlo a tan corto plazo **(b)** (of termination of employment) preaviso *m*; **I have to give (the company) a month's ~** tengo que dar un mes de preaviso; **to give *o* hand in one's ~** presentar su (*or* mi *etc*) renuncia

notice² *vt* notar; **nobody ~d him put it in his pocket** nadie lo vio ponérselo en el bolsillo
■ ~ *vi* (realize, observe) darse* cuenta

noticeable /ˈnəʊtəsəbəl ‖ ˈnəʊtɪsəbəl/ *adj* perceptible

noticeboard /ˈnəʊtəsbɔːrd ‖ ˈnəʊtɪsbɔːd/ *n* (esp BrE) tablero *m or* (Esp) tablón *m* de anuncios, cartelera *f* (AmL), diario *m* mural (Chi)

notification /ˌnəʊtəfəˈkeɪʃən ‖ ˌnəʊtɪfɪˈkeɪʃən/ *n* notificación *f*

notify /ˈnəʊtəfaɪ ‖ ˈnəʊtɪfaɪ/ *vt* **-fies, -fying, -fied** (inform) informar; (in writing) notificar*; **to ~ sb OR sth** comunicarle* algo A algn

notion /ˈnəʊʃən/ *n* **1** (idea) idea *f* **2** (concept) concepto *m* **3** **notions** *pl* **(a)** (in sewing) artículos *mpl* de mercería **(b)** (AmE): **household/ gift ~s** artículos *mpl* para el hogar/de regalo

notorious /nəʊˈtɔːriəs/ *adj* ⟨thief/womanizer/ gossip⟩ (bien) conocido; ⟨place⟩ de mala fama

notwithstanding¹ /ˈnɑːtwɪθˈstændɪŋ ‖ ˌnɒtwɪθˈstændɪŋ/ *prep* (frml) a pesar de, no obstante (frml)

notwithstanding² *adv* (frml) no obstante (frml)

nougat /ˈnuːɡət ‖ ˈnuːɡɑː, ˈnʌɡət/ *n* ≈turrón *m*

nought /nɔːt/ *n* (esp BrE) cero *m*

noun /naʊn/ *n* sustantivo *m*, nombre *m*

nourish /ˈnɜːrɪʃ ‖ ˈnʌrɪʃ/ *vt* nutrir

nourishing /ˈnɜːrɪʃɪŋ ‖ ˈnʌrɪʃɪŋ/ *adj* nutritivo

nourishment /ˈnɜːrɪʃmənt ‖ ˈnʌrɪʃmənt/ *n* alimento *m*

nouveau riche /ˈnuːvəʊˈriːʃ/ *n* (*pl* **~x ~s** /ˈnuːvəʊˈriːʃ/) (pej) nuevo rico, nueva rica *m,f* (pey)

novel¹ /ˈnɑːvəl ‖ ˈnɒvəl/ *n* novela *f*

novel² *adj* original, novedoso (esp AmL)

novelist /ˈnɑːvələst ‖ ˈnɒvəlɪst/ *n* novelista *mf*

novelty /ˈnɑːvəlti ‖ ˈnɒvəlti/ *n* (*pl* **-ties**) **(a)** (newness): **the ~ will soon wear off** pronto dejará de ser novedad *or* (esp AmL) novedoso **(b)** (new thing, situation) novedad *f*

November /nəʊˈvembər ‖ nəʊˈvembə(r)/ *n* noviembre *m*

novice /ˈnɑːvəs ‖ ˈnɒvɪs/ *n* principiante *mf*, novato, -ta *m,f*

now¹ /naʊ/ *adv* **1** **(a)** (at this time) ahora; **you can come in ~** ya puedes entrar; **any minute ~** en cualquier momento; **~'s your chance** esta es tu oportunidad **(b)** (at that time): **it was ~ time to say goodbye** había llegado el momento de decir adiós **(c)** (nowadays) hoy en día, actualmente **(d)** (*in phrases*) **(every) now and then** *o* **again** de vez en cuando; **for now** por ahora
2 **(a)** (at once, immediately) ahora (mismo); **it's ~ or never!** ¡ahora o nunca! **(b)** (*in phrases*) **just now: he's talking to a client just ~** en este momento está hablando con un cliente; **right now** (immediately) ahora mismo, inmediatamente; (at present) ahora mismo, en este momento
3 **(a)** (showing length of time) ya; **we've been living here for 40 years ~** ya hace 40 años que vivimos aquí **(b)** (*after prep*) **~: between ~ and Friday** de aquí al viernes; **she should be here by ~** ya debería estar aquí; **(up) until** *o* **till ~, up to ~** hasta ahora
4 **(a)** (indicating pause, transition): **~, who's next?** bueno ¿(ahora) a quién le toca? **(b)** (emphasizing command, request, warning, advice): **~ look here!** ¡espera un momento! **(c)** (*in phrases*) **now, now** ¡vamos, vamos!; **now then ...** a ver ...

now² *conj* **~ (that)** ahora que

nowadays /ˈnaʊədeɪz/ *adv* hoy (en) día, actualmente

nowhere¹ /ˈnəʊhwer ‖ ˈnəʊweə(r)/ *adv* **1**: **where did you go last night? — nowhere** ¿adónde fuiste anoche? — a ningún lado *or* a ninguna parte; **she was ~ to be found/seen** no se la encontraba/se la veía por ningún lado *or* por ninguna parte; **to get ~** no conseguir* nada
2 **nowhere near: Warsaw is ~ near Moscow** Varsovia está lejísimos de Moscú; **I'm ~ near finished** me falta mucho para terminar

nowhere² *pron*: **he had ~ to go** no tenía dónde ir; **the car just appeared from ~** el coche apareció de la nada

noxious /ˈnɑːkʃəs ‖ ˈnɒkʃəs/ *adj* (frml) nocivo

nozzle /ˈnɑːzəl ‖ ˈnɒzəl/ *n* (on hose) boca *f*; (on fire extinguisher) boquilla *f*

NSPCC *n* (in UK) (= **National Society for the Prevention of Cruelty to Children**) ≈Asociación *f* de protección a la infancia

nuance /'nu:ɑ:ns ‖'nju:ɑ:ns/ n matiz m

nuclear /'nu:kliər ‖'nju:kliə(r)/ adj nuclear; ~ power energía f nuclear; ~ power station central f nuclear

nuclear: ~ **family** n familia f nuclear; **~-powered** /'nu:kliər'paʊərd ‖'nju:klɪə'paʊəd/ adj nuclear

nucleus /'nu:kliəs ‖'nju:kliəs/ n (pl **-clei** /-kliaɪ/) núcleo m

nude¹ /nu:d ‖nju:d/ n (Art) desnudo m; **in the ~** desnudo

nude² adj desnudo

nudge¹ /nʌdʒ/ vt codear (ligeramente)

nudge² n golpe m (suave) con el codo

nudist /'nu:dəst ‖'nju:dɪst/ n nudista mf; (before n) ⟨beach/camp⟩ nudista

nudity /'nu:dəti ‖'nju:dəti/ n desnudez f

nugget /'nʌgət ‖'nʌgɪt/ n (Min) pepita f

nuisance /'nu:sns ‖'nju:sns/ n (a) (occurrence, thing): **to be a ~** ser* una molestia, ser* un incordio (Esp) (b) (person) pesado, -da m,f, incordio m (Esp fam); **he's always making a ~ of himself** siempre está dando la lata (fam)

null /nʌl/ adj (Law): **to declare sth ~ and void** declarar nulo algo

numb¹ /nʌm/ adj **-er, -est** (with cold) entumecido; **the injection made my gums go ~** la inyección me durmió las encías

numb² vt ⟨cold⟩ entumecer*; ⟨drug⟩ dormir*

number¹ /'nʌmbər ‖'nʌmbə(r)/ n número m; (telephone ~) número de teléfono; **wrong ~** número equivocado; **student ~s** el número de estudiantes; **on a ~ of occasions** en varias ocasiones

number² vt (a) (assign number to) ⟨houses/pages/items⟩ numerar (b) (amount to): **the spectators ~ed 50,000** había (un total de) 50.000 espectadores (c) (count) contar*; **his days are ~ed** tiene los días contados

numberplate /'nʌmbərpleɪt‖'nʌmbəpleɪt/ n (BrE) matrícula f, placa f (AmL), patente f (CS), chapa f (RPl)

numeral /'nu:mərəl ‖'nju:mərəl/ n número m

numerical /nʊ'merɪkəl ‖nju:'merɪkəl/ adj numérico

numerous /'nu:mərəs ‖'nju:mərəs/ adj numeroso

nun /nʌn/ n monja f, religiosa f (frml)

nurse¹ /nɜ:rs ‖nɜ:s/ n (a) (Med) enfermero, -ra m,f (b) (nanny) niñera f

nurse² vt **1** (Med) ⟨patient⟩ atender*; **he ~d her back to health** la atendió hasta que se repuso **2** (cradle) ⟨baby⟩ arrullar **3** (suckle) ⟨baby⟩ amamantar

nursery /'nɜ:rsri ‖'nɜ:səri/ n (pl **-ries**) (a) (day ~) guardería f (b) (room in house) cuarto m or habitación f de los niños (c) (Agr, Hort) vivero m

nursery: ~ **rhyme** n canción f infantil; ~ **school** n jardín m de infancia, jardín m infantil (AmL), kindergarten m (AmL); (preschool) pre-escolar m

nursing /'nɜ:rsɪŋ ‖'nɜ:sɪŋ/ n (a) (profession) enfermería f (b) (care) atención f

nursing home n (for the aged) residencia f de ancianos (con mayor nivel de asistencia médica); (for convalescence) clínica f, casa f de reposo or (Ur) de salud

nurture /'nɜ:rtʃər ‖'nɜ:tʃə(r)/ vt ⟨child/person⟩ criar*; ⟨plant/crop⟩ cuidar; ⟨friendship⟩ cultivar

nut /nʌt/ n **1** (Agr, Bot, Culin) fruto m seco (nuez, almendra, avellana etc) **2** (Tech) tuerca f

nut: ~**case** n (colloq) chiflado, -da m,f (fam); ~**crackers** pl n (BrE) cascanueces m

nutmeg /'nʌtmeg/ n nuez f moscada

nutrient /'nu:triənt ‖'nju:triənt/ n nutriente m

nutrition /nʊ'trɪʃən ‖nju:'trɪʃən/ n nutrición f

nutritious /nʊ'trɪʃəs ‖nju:'trɪʃəs/ adj nutritivo

nuts /nʌts/ adj (colloq) (pred) chiflado (fam)

nutshell /'nʌtʃel/ n cáscara f de nuez; **in a ~** en dos or en pocas palabras

nutty /'nʌti/ adj **-tier, -tiest** **1** ⟨taste⟩ a nueces (or almendras etc) **2** (colloq) (eccentric) ⟨professor⟩ chiflado (fam); ⟨idea⟩ de loco

NVQ n (in UK) = **National Vocational Qualification**

NW (= **northwest**) NO

NY = **New York**

nylon /'naɪlɑ:n ‖'naɪlɒn/ n nylon m

nymph /nɪmf/ n (Myth, Zool) ninfa f

Oo

O, o /əʊ/ n O, o f

oaf /əʊf/ n zoquete mf (fam)

oak /əʊk/ n (a) **~ (tree)** roble m (b) (wood) roble m

OAP n (BrE) = **old age pensioner**

oar /ɔːr ‖ɔː(r)/ n remo m

OAS n (= **Organization of American States**) OEA f

oasis /əʊˈeɪsɪs/ n (pl **oases** /əʊˈeɪsiːz/) oasis m

oat /əʊt/ n (a) (plant) avena f (b) **oats** pl (cereal) avena f, copos mpl de avena

oath /əʊθ/ n (pl **~s** /əʊðz/) (a) (promise) juramento m; **under** o **on ~** (Law) bajo juramento (b) (curse) (liter) juramento m (liter)

oatmeal /ˈəʊtmiːl/ n (Culin) (flour) harina f de avena; (flakes) (AmE) avena f (en copos)

obedience /əˈbiːdɪəns, əʊ-/ n obediencia f

obedient /əˈbiːdɪənt, əʊ-/ adj obediente

obese /əʊˈbiːs/ adj obeso

obesity /əʊˈbiːsəti/ n obesidad f

obey /əˈbeɪ, əʊ-/ vt/i obedecer*

obituary /əˈbɪtʃʊeri ‖əˈbɪtʃʊəri/ n (pl **-ries**) obituario m, nota f necrológica

object¹ /ˈɑːbdʒɪkt ‖ˈɒbdʒɪkt/ n [1] (a) (thing) objeto m (b) **no ~**: money's no **~ for** them el dinero no les preocupa (c) (of actions, feelings) objeto m [2] (aim, purpose) objetivo m [3] (Ling) complemento m

object² /əbˈdʒekt/ vi **to ~ (to** sth) oponerse* (A algo); I **~!** ¡protesto!; **if you don't ~** si no le molesta

■ **~** vt objetar

objection /əbˈdʒekʃən/ n (a) (argument against) objeción f (b) (Law) protesta f; **~!** ¡protesto! (c) (disapproval, dislike): I **have no ~ to** her no tengo nada en contra de ella

objectionable /əbˈdʒekʃnəbəl/ adj ⟨attitude/remark⟩ censurable; ⟨person/tone⟩ desagradable

objective¹ /ɑːbˈdʒektɪv ‖əbˈdʒektɪv/ adj objetivo

objective² n objetivo m

objectively /ɑːbˈdʒektɪvli ‖əbˈdʒektɪvli/ adv objetivamente

obligate /ˈɑːbləgeɪt ‖ˈɒbligeɪt/ vt (esp AmE frml) **to ~ sb to** + INF obligar* a algn A + INF; **to be/feel ~d (to** + INF) estar*/sentirse* obligado (A + INF)

obligation /ˌɑːbləˈgeɪʃən ‖ˌɒbliˈgeɪʃən/ n obligación f; **~ to** + INF obligación DE + INF; I **understand that I am under no ~** entiendo que no contraigo ninguna obligación

obligatory /əˈblɪgətɔːri ‖əˈblɪgətri/ adj obligatorio

oblige /əˈblaɪdʒ/ vt [1] (require, compel) **to ~ sb to** + INF obligar* a algn A + INF; **to be ~d** A + INF estar* obligado A + INF [2] (do favor for): I'd **be much ~d if you could help me** le quedaría muy agradecido si pudiera ayudarme

■ **~** vi: he's **always willing to ~** siempre está dispuesto a hacer un favor

obliging /əˈblaɪdʒɪŋ/ adj atento

oblique /əˈbliːk, əʊ- ‖əˈbliːk/ adj ⟨line/angle⟩ oblicuo; ⟨reply/reference⟩ indirecto

obliterate /əˈblɪtəreɪt/ vt (a) (destroy) arrasar (b) (obscure, erase) borrar

oblivion /əˈblɪvɪən/ n (a) (obscurity) olvido m (b) (unconsciousness) inconsciencia f

oblivious /əˈblɪvɪəs/ adj (pred): she was quite **~ of** o **to her surroundings** estaba totalmente ajena a lo que la rodeaba; **~ of** o **to the danger** (unaware of) ignorante del peligro; (not mindful of) haciendo caso omiso del peligro

oblong¹ /ˈɑːblɔːŋ ‖ˈɒblɒŋ/ adj alargado

oblong² n rectángulo m

obnoxious /ɑːbˈnɑːkʃəs ‖əbˈnɒkʃəs/ adj detestable

oboe /ˈəʊbəʊ/ n oboe m

obscene /ɑːbˈsiːn ‖əbˈsiːn/ adj obsceno

obscenity /ɑːbˈsenəti ‖əbˈsenəti/ n (pl **-ties**) obscenidad f

obscure¹ /əbˈskjʊr ‖əbˈskjʊə(r)/ adj **obscurer, obscurest** (a) (not easily understood) ⟨meaning⟩ oscuro; ⟨message/reference⟩ críptico (b) (little known) ⟨writer/journal⟩ oscuro

obscure² vt ⟨object/beauty/sun⟩ ocultar; ⟨sky⟩ oscurecer*; ⟨issue⟩ impedir* ver claramente

obscurity /əbˈskjʊrəti ‖əbˈskjʊərəti/ n (pl **-ties**) oscuridad f

obsequious /əbˈsiːkwɪəs/ adj servil

observant /əbˈzɜːrvənt ‖əbˈzɜːvənt/ adj observador

observation /ˌɑːbzərˈveɪʃən ‖ˌɒbzəˈveɪʃən/ n (all senses) observación f

observatory /əbˈzɜːrvətɔːri ‖əbˈzɜːvətri/ n (pl **-ries**) observatorio m

observe /əbˈzɜːrv ‖əbˈzɜːv/ vt [1] (watch, notice) observar; ⟨patient⟩ observar [2] (comment) (liter) observar

observer /əbˈzɜːrvər ‖əbˈzɜːvə(r)/ n observador, -dora m,f

obsess /əbˈses/ vt obsesionar

obsessed /əbˈsest/ adj (pred) obsesionado

obsession /əbˈseʃən/ n obsesión f

obsessive /əbˈsesɪv/ adj obsesivo

obsolete /ˈɑːbsəliːt ‖ˈɒbsəliːt/ adj obsoleto

obstacle /ˈɑːbstɪkəl ‖ˈɒbstəkəl/ n obstáculo m

obstetrics /əbˈstetrɪks/ n (+ sing vb) obstetricia f, tocología f

obstinate /ˈɑːbstənət ‖ˈɒbstɪnət/ adj obstinado

obstinately /ˈɑːbstənətli ‖ˈɒbstɪnətli/ adv (stubbornly) obstinadamente; (determinedly) tenazmente

obstruct /əbˈstrʌkt/ vt (a) (block) obstruir* (b) (impede, hinder) ⟨traffic⟩ bloquear (c) (Sport) obstruir*

obstruction /əb'strʌkʃən/ n (a) (in traffic, pipeline) obstrucción f; (Med) obstrucción f, oclusión f (b) (Sport) obstrucción f

obtain /əb'teɪn/ vt conseguir*, obtener* (fml)

obtrusive /əb'truːsɪv/ adj ⟨presence/building⟩ demasiado prominente; ⟨noise⟩ molesto; ⟨smell⟩ penetrante

obtuse /ɑːb'tuːs ‖ɒb'tjuːs/ adj **1** (Math) ⟨angle⟩ obtuso **2** (fml) (stupid) obtuso

obvious /'ɑːbviəs ‖'ɒbviəs/ adj (a) (evident) ⟨answer/advantage/difference⟩ obvio (b) (unmistakable) (before n) ⟨candidate/choice⟩ indiscutible

obviously /'ɑːbviəsli ‖'ɒbviəsli/ adv obviamente; they're ~ not coming está visto que no van a venir; the two ideas are ~ not related es evidente que las dos ideas no tienen relación; ~, I'm sad, but what can I do? (indep) como es lógico estoy triste pero ¿qué puedo hacer?

OCAS (= Organization of Central American States) n ODECA f

occasion /ə'keɪʒən/ n ocasión f

occasional /ə'keɪʒṇəl ‖ə'keɪʒənḷ/ adj ⟨showers/sunny spells⟩ aislado; I like an o the ~ glass of wine de tanto en tanto me gusta tomarme un vaso de vino

occasionally /ə'keɪʒṇəli/ adv de vez en cuando

occult¹ /ə'kʌlt ‖ɒ'kʌlt/ n the ~ las ciencias ocultas

occult² adj ⟨arts/powers⟩ oculto; ⟨ritual⟩ ocultista

occupant /'ɑːkjəpənt ‖'ɒkjʊpənt/ n (of building, room, vehicle) ocupante mf; (tenant) inquilino, -na m,f

occupation /ˌɑːkjə'peɪʃən ‖ˌɒkjʊ'peɪʃən/ n (a) (profession, activity) ocupación f (b) (Mil) ocupación f (c) (of accommodations) ocupación f

occupational /ˌɑːkjə'peɪʃṇəl ‖ˌɒkjʊ'peɪʃənḷ/ adj ⟨training⟩ ocupacional; ⟨disease⟩ profesional; it's an ~ hazard son riesgos de la profesión/del oficio

occupational therapy n terapia f ocupacional

occupier /'ɑːkjəpaɪər ‖'ɒkjʊpaɪə(r)/ n (BrE) ocupante mf

occupy /'ɑːkjəpaɪ ‖'ɒkjʊpaɪ/ vt -pies, -pying, -pied ocupar; to keep sb occupied mantener* a algn ocupado

occur /ə'kɜːr ‖ə'kɜː(r)/ vi -rr- **1** (a) (take place) (fml) «event/incident» tener* lugar (fml); «change» producirse* (fml) (b) (appear, be found) «disease/species» darse*, encontrarse* **2** (come to mind) to ~ TO sb (to (+ INF) ocurrírsele A algn (+ INF)

occurrence /ə'kɜːrəns ‖ə'kʌrəns/ n (a) (event, instance): it is a rare ~ no es algo frecuente (b) (incidence) incidencia f

ocean /'əʊʃən/ n océano m

ocean-going /'əʊʃən,gəʊɪŋ/ adj ⟨vessel⟩ transatlántico

o'clock /ə'klɑːk ‖ə'klɒk/ adv: it's four ~ son las cuatro; it's one ~ es la una; at ten ~ a las diez

octagon /'ɑːktəgɑːn ‖'ɒktəgən/ n octágono m, octógono m

octane /'ɑːkteɪn ‖'ɒkteɪn/ n octano m

octave /'ɑːktɪv ‖'ɒktɪv/ n (Lit, Mus) octava f

October /ɑːk'təʊbər ‖ɒk'təʊbə(r)/ n octubre m

octopus /'ɑːktəpəs ‖'ɒktəpəs/ n (pl **-puses**) pulpo m

odd /ɑːd ‖ɒd/ adj **-er, -est** **1** (strange) raro, extraño **2** (occasional, random) (no comp): she smokes the ~ cigarette se fuma algún or alguno que otro cigarrillo **3** (no comp) (a) (unmatched, single) desparejado, sin pareja; the ~ one out la excepción (b) (Math) ⟨number⟩ impar

oddball /'ɑːdbɔːl ‖'ɒdbɔːl/ n (colloq) bicho m raro (fam)

oddity /'ɑːdəti ‖'ɒdɪti/ n (pl **-ties**) rareza f

odd-job man /'ɑːd'dʒɑːbmæn ‖,ɒd'dʒɒbmæn/ n (pl **-men** /-men/) hombre que hace pequeños trabajos o arreglos

oddly /'ɑːdli ‖'ɒdli/ adv ⟨dress/behave⟩ de una manera rara or extraña

oddment /'ɑːdmənt ‖'ɒdmənt/ n: ~s of fabric o material retazos mpl or (Esp) retales mpl

odds /ɑːdz ‖ɒdz/ pl n **1** (in betting) proporción en que se ofrece pagar una apuesta, que refleja las posibilidades de acierto de la misma **2** (likelihood, chances) probabilidades fpl, posibilidades fpl; the ~ are against her winning tiene pocas probabilidades or posibilidades de ganar; the pilot survived against all (the) ~ aunque parezca increíble, el piloto sobrevivió **3** (variance): those two are always at ~ with each other esos dos siempre están en desacuerdo; that's at ~ with the official version eso no concuerda con la versión oficial

odds and ends /'ɑːdzən'endz ‖,ɒdzən'endz/ pl n (colloq) cosas fpl sueltas; (trinkets) chucherías fpl; (junk) cachivaches mpl

odious /'əʊdiəs/ adj (fml) detestable

odometer /əʊ'dɑːmətər ‖ɒ'dɒmɪtə(r), əʊ-/ n (AmE) cuentarrevoluciones m

odor, (BrE) **odour** /'əʊdər ‖'əʊdə(r)/ n olor m; (pleasant) aroma m

of /ɑːv ‖ɒv, weak form əv/ prep **1** (indicating relationship, material, content) de; it's made ~ wood es de madera; a colleague ~ mine/his un colega mío/suyo **2** (descriptive use): a boy ~ ten un niño de diez años; a woman ~ courage una mujer valiente **3** (a) (partitive use): there were eight ~ us éramos ocho; six ~ them survived seis de ellos sobrevivieron (b) (with superl) de; the wisest ~ men el más sabio de los hombres; most ~ all más que nada **4** (a) (indicating date) de; the sixth ~ October el seis de octubre (b) (indicating time): it's ten (minutes) ~ five (AmE) son las cinco menos diez, son diez para las cinco (AmL exc RPI); Jane, his wife ~ six months ... Jane, con la que lleva/ llevaba casado seis meses ... **5** (on the part of): it was very kind ~ you fue muy amable de su parte **6** (indicating cause): it's a problem ~ their own making es un problema que ellos mismos se han creado; what did he die ~? ¿de qué murió?

off¹ /ɔːf ‖ɒf/ prep **1** (from) de; she picked it up ~ o (crit) ~ of the floor lo recogió del suelo; he bought it ~ a friend (colloq) se lo compró a un amigo

2 (a) (distant from): **3 ft ~ the ground** a 3 pies del suelo; **just ~ the coast of Florida** a poca distancia de la costa de Florida **(b)** (leading from): **it's just ~ Oxford Street** está en una bocacalle de Oxford Street; **the bathroom's ~ the bedroom** el baño da al dormitorio **3** (a) (absent from): **I've been ~ work for a week** hace una semana que no voy a trabajar **(b)** (indicating dislike, abstinence) (BrE): **he's ~ his food** anda sin apetito; **is he ~ drugs now?** ¿ha dejado las drogas?

off² *adv* **1** (a) (removed): **the lid was ~** la tapa no estaba puesta; **20% ~** 20% de descuento **(b) off and on ▶** ON² 2c **2** (indicating departure): **I must be ~** me tengo que ir **3** (distant): **some way ~** a cierta distancia; **my birthday is a long way ~** falta mucho para mi cumpleaños

off³ *adj* **1** (*pred*) (a) (not turned on): **to be ~** «*TV*/*light*» estar* apagado **(b)** (canceled): **the game/wedding is ~** el partido/la boda se ha suspendido; **the deal is ~** ya no hay trato **2** (absent, not on duty) libre; **a day ~** o (AmE also) **an ~ day** un día libre **3** (poor, unsatisfactory) (*before n*) malo; **to have an ~ day** tener* un mal día **4** (Culin) (*pred*) **to be ~** «*meat*/*fish*» estar* malo *or* pasado; «*milk*» estar* cortado; «*butter*/*cheese*» estar* rancio

offal /'ɔːfəl ‖'ɒfəl/ *n* (Culin) despojos *mpl*, achuras *fpl* (RPl), interiores *mpl* (Chi)

off-: **~beat** *adj* poco convencional; **~-chance** *n*: **on the ~-chance** por si acaso; **~-color,** (BrE) **~-colour** /'ɔːfˈkʌlər ‖ˌɒfˈkʌlə(r)/ *adj* (*pred ~* **color**) (a) (unwell) (*pred*): **to feel ~ color** no encontrarse* muy bien **(b)** (risqué) (esp AmE) «*joke*» subido de tono; **~cut** *n* (of leather, fabric, paper, wood) recorte *m*; (of meat) resto *m*

offence /ə'fens/ *n* (BrE) ▶ OFFENSE

offend /ə'fend/ *vt* ofender

■ ~ *vi* (a) (cause displeasure) «*person*/*action*/*remark*» ofender **(b) offending** *pres p*: **he rewrote it omitting the ~ing paragraph** volvió a escribirlo omitiendo el párrafo que había causado controversia **(c)** (Law frml) infringir* la ley (*or* el reglamento *etc*); (criminally) cometer un delito

offender /ə'fendər ‖ə'fendə(r)/ *n* (against regulations) infractor, -tora *m,f*; (criminal) delincuente *mf*; **young ~** menor *mf* (*que ha cometido un delito*)

offense, (BrE) **offence** /ə'fens/ *n* **1** (breach of law, regulations) infracción *f*; (criminal ~) delito *m* **2** (a) (cause of outrage) (*no pl*) atentado *m* **(b)** (resentment, displeasure): **to take ~ at sth** ofenderse *or* sentirse* ofendido por algo **3** (AmE) *also* /'ɑːfens/ (a) (attack) ataque *m* (b) (Sport) (línea *f* de) ataque *m*

offensive¹ /ə'fensɪv/ *adj* **1** «*language*/*gesture*» ofensivo; «*sight*/*smell*» desagradable **2** (a) «*strategy*» ofensivo **(b)** (AmE Sport) «*play*/*tactics*» de ataque

offensive² *n* ofensiva *f*

offer¹ /'ɔːfər ‖'ɒfə(r)/ *vt* **1** (a) (proffer) ofrecer* **(b)** (show willingness) **to ~ to +** INF ofrecerse* a + INF **2** (put forward) «*idea*/*solution*» proponer* **3** (provide) «*reward*» ofrecer*; «*opportunity*» brindar

■ ~ *vi* (show willingness) ofrecerse*

offer² *n* **1** (a) (proposal — of job, money) oferta *f*;

(— of help, mediation) ofrecimiento *m* **(b)** (bid) oferta *f*; **$650 or nearest ~** 650 dólares negociables **2** (bargain, reduced price) oferta *f*; **on ~** (BrE) (at reduced price) de oferta

offering /'ɔːfərɪŋ ‖'ɒfərɪŋ/ *n* ofrenda *f*

offhand¹ /'ɔːfˈhænd ‖ˌɒfˈhænd/ *adj*: **to say sth in a very ~ way** *o* **manner** decir* algo muy a la ligera; **she was very ~ with me** estuvo muy brusca conmigo

offhand² *adv* así de pronto, en este momento

office /'ɑːfəs ‖'ɒfɪs/ *n* **1** (room) oficina *f*, despacho *m*; (building, set of rooms) oficina *f*, oficinas *fpl*; (staff) oficina *f*; (doctor's ~) (AmE) consultorio *m*, consulta *f*; (*before n*) «*work*/*furniture*» de oficina; «*block*/*building*» de oficinas; **during ~ hours** en horas de oficina; **~ worker** oficinista *mf*, empleado, -da *m,f* de oficina **2** (post, position) cargo *m*; **he was in ~ for three years** ocupó el cargo durante tres años

officer /'ɑːfəsər ‖'ɒfɪsə(r)/ *n* (a) (Mil, Naut) oficial *mf* (b) (police ~) policía *mf*, agente *mf* de policía; (*as form of address*) agente

official¹ /ə'fɪʃəl/ *adj* oficial

official² *n* (government ~) funcionario, -ria *m,f* del Estado *or* gobierno; (party/union ~) dirigente *mf* (del partido/sindicato)

officially /ə'fɪʃəli/ *adv* oficialmente

officiate /ə'fɪʃieɪt/ *vi* **to ~ AT sth** «*at mass*/*at a wedding*» oficiar (EN) *or* celebrar algo

officious /ə'fɪʃəs/ *adj* oficioso

offing /'ɔːfɪŋ ‖'ɒfɪŋ/ *n*: **in the ~** en perspectiva

off-: **~ key** *adv*: **to play/sing ~ key** desafinar; **~-licence** *n* (in UK) ≈ tienda *f* de vinos y licores, botillería *f* (Chi); **~ limits** /'lɪmɪts ‖'lɪmɪts/ *adv*: **to go/be ~ limits** entrar/estar* en zona prohibida; **~-line** /'ɔːflaɪn ‖'ɒflaɪn/ *adj* (*pred ~* **line**) «*storage*/*printer*» autónomo; **~-peak** /'piːk/ *adj* (*before noun*) «*travel*/*fare*/*tariffs*» fuera de las horas pico *or* (Esp) punta; (Elec) fuera de (las) horas pico *or* (Esp) punta; **~-putting** /'ɔːfpʊtɪŋ ‖'ɒfpʊtɪŋ/ *adj* (BrE) (disagreeable) desagradable; (discouraging) desmoralizador; **~road** *adj*: **~road vehicle** todoterreno *m*; **~set** /'ɔːfset ‖'ɒfset/ *vt* (*pres* **-sets**; *pres p* **-setting**; *past & past p* **-set**) compensar; **~shoot** *n* (a) (of plant, tree) retoño *m* **(b)** (of company, organization) filial *f*; **~shore** /'ɔːfʃɔːr ‖ˌɒfˈʃɔː(r)/ *adj* «*oilfield*/*pipeline*» submarino; «*exploration*/*drilling*» off-shore *adj inv*; «*company*/*bank account*» ubicado en un paraíso fiscal

offside¹ /ˌɔːfˈsaɪd ‖ˌɒfˈsaɪd/ *adj* (Sport) «*player*» en fuera de juego *or* (AmL tb) de lugar

offside² *adv* (Sport) fuera de juego *or* (AmL tb) de lugar

off-: **~spring** *n* (*pl* **~spring**) (a) (animal) cría *f* **(b)** (hum) (child) hijo, -ja *m,f*, crío, cría *m,f* (fam); (children) prole *f* (fam & hum), críos *mpl* (fam); **~stage** /'ɔːfsteɪdʒ ‖'ɒfsteɪdʒ/ *adv* fuera del escenario; **~-the-peg** /'ɔːfðə'peg ‖'ɒfðə'peg/ *adj* (*pred ~* **the peg**) (esp BrE) ▶ ~-THE-RACK; **~-the-rack** /'ɔːfðə'ræk ‖'ɒfðə'ræk/ *adj* (*pred ~* **the rack**) (AmE) «*suit*» de confección; **~-white** /'ɔːfˈhwaɪt ‖'ɒfˈwaɪt/ *adj* color hueso *adj inv*

often /'ɔːfən, 'ɔːftən ‖ 'ɒfən, 'ɒftən/ *adv* a menudo; **how ~ do you see her?** ¿con qué frecuencia la ves?

ogle /'əʊgəl/ *vt* comerse con los ojos

ogre /'əʊgər ‖ 'əʊgə(r)/ *n* ogro *m*

oh /əʊ/ *interj*: **~, it's you** ah, eres tú; **~ no, not him again!** ¡ay no, es él otra vez!

OH = **Ohio**

oil¹ /ɔɪl/ *n* ① **(a)** (petroleum) petróleo *m*; (*before n*) ~ **refinery** refinería *f* de petróleo; ~ **tanker** (ship) petrolero *m*; (truck) camión *m* cisterna (*para petróleo*) **(b)** (lubricant) aceite *m* **(c)** (fuel ~) fuel-oil *m* ② (Culin) aceite *m* ③ **oils** *pl* (paints): **he paints in ~s** pinta al óleo

oil² *vt* lubricar*, aceitar

oil: ~**can** *n* aceitera *f*; ~**cloth** *n* hule *m*; ~**field** *n* yacimiento *m* petrolífero; ~ **paint** *n* óleo *m*; ~ **painting** *n* óleo *m*; ~ **rig** *n* plataforma *f* petrolífera; (derrick) torre *f* de perforación; ~ **slick** *n* marea *f* negra; ~ **well** *n* pozo *m* petrolero

oily /'ɔɪli/ *adj* **oilier, oiliest** ⟨substance⟩ oleaginoso; ⟨food⟩ aceitoso; ⟨skin/hair⟩ graso (AmL)

ointment /'ɔɪntmənt/ *n* pomada *f*

OK¹, okay /əʊ'keɪ/ *interj* (colloq) ¡bueno!, ¡okey! (esp AmL fam); ¡vale! (Esp fam), ¡vaya (pues)! (AmC)

OK², okay *adj* (all right) (colloq) (*pred*): **how are you? — ~, thanks** ¿qué tal estás? — bien, gracias; **the job's ~, but …** el trabajo no está mal, pero …

OK³, okay *vt* (*pres* **OK's**; *pres p* **OK'ing**; *past & past p* **OK'ed**) (colloq) darle* el visto bueno a

OK⁴, Okla = **Oklahoma**

old /əʊld/ *adj* ① (of certain age): **he's 10 years ~** tiene 10 años; **how ~ are you?** ¿cuántos años tienes?; **she's two years ~er than me** me lleva dos años ② (not young) mayor; (less polite) viejo; ~ *o* ~**er people** los ancianos, las personas mayores *or* de edad; **to get *o* grow ~/~er** envejecer* ③ **(a)** (not new) ⟨clothes/car/custom⟩ viejo; ⟨city/ civilization⟩ antiguo **(b)** (longstanding, familiar) (*before n*) ⟨friend/enemy/rivalry⟩ viejo; ⟨injury/ problem⟩ antiguo ④ (former, previous) (*before n*) antiguo ⑤ (colloq) (*before n*) (*as intensifier*): **just wear any ~ thing** ponte cualquier cosa; **this book is a load of ~ rubbish** este libro es una porquería (fam)

old: ~ **age** *n* vejez *f*; ~ **age pensioner** *n* (BrE) pensionista *mf* (de la tercera edad)

olden /'əʊldən/ *adj* (liter): **in ~ days** *o* **times** antaño (liter)

old: ~**-fashioned** /'əʊld'fæʃənd/ *adj* (outdated) anticuado; (traditional) tradicional; ~ **people's home** *n* residencia *f* de ancianos; ~ **wives' tale** *n* cuento *m* de viejas

olive¹ /'ɑːlɪv ‖ 'ɒlɪv/ *n* **(a)** (Culin) aceituna *f*; (*before n*) ~ **oil** aceite *m* de oliva **(b)** ~ **tree** olivo *m*

olive² *adj* color aceituna *adj inv*; ⟨skin⟩ aceitunado

Olympic /ə'lɪmpɪk/ *adj* olímpico

Olympic Games *pl n* **the ~** los juegos Olímpicos

Olympics /ə'lɪmpɪks/ *pl n* **the ~** las Olimpíadas *or* Olimpiadas

ombudsman /'ɑːmbʊdzmən ‖ 'ɒmbʊdzmən/ *n* (*pl* **-men** /-mən/) defensor *m* del pueblo, ombudsman *m*

omelet, omelette (BrE) /'ɑːmlət ‖ 'ɒmlɪt/ *n* omelette *f or* (Esp) tortilla *f* francesa

omen /'əʊmən/ *n* presagio *m*; **it's a good/bad ~** es un buen/mal augurio

ominous /'ɑːmənəs ‖ 'ɒmɪnəs/ *adj*: **there was an ~ silence** se hizo un silencio que no presagiaba nada bueno; **there are some ~ clouds on the horizon** hay nubes que no auguran nada bueno

omission /əʊ'mɪʃən ‖ ə'mɪʃən/ *n* omisión *f*

omit /əʊ'mɪt ‖ ə'mɪt/ *vt* **-tt-** (leave out) omitir; (accidentally) olvidar incluir

omnibus /'ɑːmnɪbəs ‖ 'ɒmnɪbəs/ *n* (*pl* **-buses**) ① (Publ) antología *f* ② (Transp dated) ómnibus *m* (ant exc en Per y RPI)

omnipotent /ɑːm'nɪpətənt ‖ ɒm'nɪpətənt/ *adj* (frml) omnipotente

omnivorous /ɑːm'nɪvərəs ‖ ɒm'nɪvərəs/ *adj* omnívoro

on¹ /ɑːn ‖ ɒn/ *prep* ① **(a)** (indicating position) en; **put it ~ the table** ponlo en *or* sobre la mesa; ~ **the ground** en el suelo; **he hung it ~ a hook** lo colgó de un gancho **(b)** (belonging to): **the handle ~ the cup** el asa de la taza **(c)** (against): **I hit my head ~ the shelf** me di con la cabeza contra el estante; **he cut his hand ~ the glass** se cortó la mano con el vidrio ② **(a)** (of clothing): **it looks better ~ you than me** te queda mejor a ti que a mí **(b)** (about one's person): **I didn't have any cash ~ me** no llevaba dinero encima ③ (indicating means of transport): **I went ~ the bus** fui en autobús; ~ **a bicycle/horse** en bicicleta/a caballo; ~ **foot** a pie ④ **(a)** (playing instrument) a; **George Smith ~ drums** George Smith a la *or* en la batería **(b)** (Rad, TV): **I heard it ~ the radio** lo oí por la radio; **I was ~ TV last night** anoche salí por televisión; **the play's ~ channel 4** la obra la dan en el canal 4 ⑤ **(a)** (using equipment): **who's ~ the computer?** ¿quién está usando la computadora?; **you've been ~ the phone an hour!** ¡hace una hora que estás hablando por teléfono! **(b)** (contactable via): **call us ~ 800 7777** llámenos al 800 7777 ⑥ (a member of): **she's ~ the committee** está en la comisión; ~ **a team** (AmE) en un equipo ⑦ (indicating time): ~ **Monday** el lunes; ~ **Wednesdays** los miércoles; ~ **-ING** al + INF; ~ **hearing the news** al enterarse de la noticia ⑧ (about, concerning) sobre ⑨ (working on, studying): **we're ~ page 45** vamos por la página 45; **I'm still ~ question 1** todavía estoy con la pregunta número 1

10 (taking, consuming): **she's ~ antibiotics** está tomando antibióticos; **he's ~ heroin** es heroinómano

11 (talking about income, available funds): **I manage ~ less than that** yo me las arreglo con menos de eso

12 (at the expense of): **this round's ~ me** a esta ronda invito yo

13 (in comparison with): **profits are up ~ last year** los beneficios han aumentado respecto al año pasado

on² *adv* **1 (a)** (worn): **she had a blue dress ~** llevaba (puesto) un vestido azul; **I had nothing ~** estaba desnudo **(b)** (in place): **the lid's not ~ properly** la tapa no está bien puesta
2 (indicating progression) **(a)** (in space): **further ~** un poco más allá; **go ~ up; I'll follow in a minute** tú ve subiendo que yo ya voy **(b)** (in time, activity): **from then ~** a partir de ese momento; **from now ~** de ahora en adelante **(c)** on and off, off and on: **we still see each other ~ and off** todavía nos vemos de vez en cuando; **it rained ~ and off** *o* **off and ~ all week** estuvo lloviendo y parando toda la semana

on³ *adj* **1** (*pred*) **(a)** (functioning): **to be ~** «*light/ TV/radio*» estar* encendido, estar* prendido (AmL); «*faucet*» estar* abierto; **the electricity/ water isn't ~ yet** la electricidad/el agua todavía no está conectada **(b)** (on duty): **we work four hours ~, four hours off** trabajamos cuatro horas y tenemos otras cuatro de descanso
2 (*pred*) **(a)** (taking place): **there's a lecture ~ in there** hay una conferencia allí; **while the conference is ~** mientras dure el congreso **(b)** (due to take place): **the party's definitely ~ for Friday** la fiesta es el viernes seguro; **I don't have anything ~ that day** no tengo ningún compromiso ese día **(c)** (being presented): **what's ~ at the Renoir?** (Cin, Rad, Theat, TV) ¿qué dan *or* (Esp tb) ponen en el Renoir?; **the exhibition is still ~** la exposición sigue abierta
3 (indicating agreement, acceptance) (colloq): **you teach me Spanish and I'll teach you French — you're ~!** tú me enseñas español y yo te enseño francés — ¡trato hecho!; **that sort of thing just isn't ~** (esp BrE) ese tipo de cosa no se puede tolerar

once¹ /wʌns/ *adv* **1 (a)** (one time, on one occasion) una vez; **~ a week** una vez por semana **(b)** (formerly): **a health care system which was ~ the pride of the nation** un sistema de asistencia sanitaria que antes era el orgullo de la nación; **~ upon a time there was …** érase una vez …
2 (*in phrases*) **at once: come here at ~!** ¡ven aquí inmediatamente!; **don't all shout at ~** no griten todos al mismo tiempo; **for once** por una vez; **once again** *o* **once more** otra vez; **once (and) for all** de una vez por todas; **(every) once in a while** de vez en cuando; **once or twice** una o dos veces

once² *conj* una vez que; (with verb omitted) una vez

once- /wʌns/ *pref* otrora (liter)

oncoming /'ɑːn,kʌmɪŋ ‖'ɒnkʌmɪŋ/ *adj* (*before n*) «*vehicle*» que viene (*or* venía) en dirección contraria

one¹ /wʌn/ *n* **1 (a)** (number) uno *m*; *see also* FOUR¹ **(b)** (elliptical use): **he's nearly ~** tiene casi un año; **it was interesting in more ways than ~**

fue interesante en más de un sentido/en muchos sentidos **2** (*in phrases*) **as one: they rose as ~** se pusieron de pie todos a la vez; **for one** por lo pronto; **one by one** uno a *or* por uno

one² *adj* **1** (stating number) un, una; **~ button/ pear** un botón/una pera; **~ window looks out over the park** una de las ventanas da al parque
2 (single): **she was the ~ person I trusted** era la única persona en quien confiaba; **there is not ~ shred of evidence** no existe ni la más mínima prueba; **the ~ and only Frank Sinatra** el incomparable Frank Sinatra
3 (unspecified) un, una; **you must come over ~ evening** tienes que venir una noche
4 (with names): **in the name of ~ John Smith/ Sarah Brown** a nombre de un tal John Smith/una tal Sarah Brown

one³ *pron* **1** (thing): **this ~** este/esta; **that ~** ese/ esa; **which ~?** ¿cuál?; **the ~ on the right/left** el/la de la derecha/izquierda; **the ~s on the table** los/ las que están en la mesa; **the blue ~s** los/las azules; **I want the big ~** quiero el/la grande; **~ of the oldest cities in Europe** una de las ciudades más antiguas de Europa
2 (person): **the ~ on the right's my cousin** el/la de la derecha es mi primo/prima; **I'm not ~ to gossip, but …** no me gustan los chismes pero …; **~ after another** *o* **the other** uno tras otro *or* detrás de otro

one⁴ *pron* uno, una; **~ simply never knows** realmente nunca se sabe; **~ another = each other,** ▶ EACH² 2

one: **~-armed** /'wʌn'ɑːrmd ‖'wʌn'ɑːmd/ *adj* manco; **~-man** /'wʌn'mæn/ *adj* (*before n*) «*business*» unipersonal; «*operation*» dirigido por una sola persona; **~-off** /'wʌn'ɔːf ‖'wʌn'ɒf/ *n* (BrE colloq): **this payment is strictly a ~-off** este pago es una excepción; **~ on ~** *adv* (AmE) uno a uno; **~-piece** /'wʌnpiːs/ *adj* «*swimsuit*» entero

onerous /'əʊnərəs/ *adj* «*task*» pesado

one: **~self** /wʌn'self/ *pron* (reflexive) se; (after prep) sí mismo; (emphatic use) uno mismo; **to cut ~self** cortarse; **~-sided** /'wʌn'saɪdəd ‖,wʌn'saɪdɪd/ *adj* «*account/version*» parcial; «*game/contest*» desigual; **~-stop shopping** *n* compras *fpl* en un mismo sitio; **~-time** *adj* antiguo; **~-to-~** /'wʌntə'wʌn/ *adj* «*teaching/ attention*» individualizado; «*discussion*» mano a mano; **on a ~-to-~ basis** de uno a uno

one-upmanship /'wʌn'ʌpmənʃɪp/ *n* (colloq) arte de colocarse siempre en una situación de superioridad con respecto a los demás

one-way /'wʌn'weɪ/ *adj* **(a)** «*street*» de sentido único (b) (for one journey): **~ or round trip?** ¿ida solo o ida y vuelta?, ¿sencillo o redondo? (Méx)

ongoing /'ɑːn,gəʊɪŋ ‖'ɒngəʊɪŋ/ *adj*: **the ~ talks** las conversaciones en curso; **the investigations have been ~ for several months** se están llevando a cabo investigaciones desde hace meses

onion /'ʌnjən/ *n* cebolla *f*

on: **~ line** *adv*: **to edit/work ~ line** (Comput) editar/trabajar en línea; **~-line** /'ɑːn'laɪn ‖,ɒn'laɪn/ *adj* (*pred* **~ line**) (Comput) conectado, en línea; **~-looker** /'ɑːnlʊkər ‖'ɒnlʊkə(r)/ *n* espectador, -dora *m,f*

only¹ /'əʊnli/ *adv* **(a)** (merely, no more than) solo, solamente; **you'll ~ make matters worse** lo único que vas a lograr es empeorar las cosas **(b)**

(exclusively) solo, solamente, únicamente **(c)** (no longer ago than): ~ **last week the very same problem came up** la semana pasada, sin ir más lejos, surgió el mismo problema **(d)** (*in phrases*) **if only: if ~ I were rich!** ¡ojalá fuera rico!; **if ~ I'd known** si lo hubiera sabido; **only just: they've ~ just arrived** ahora mismo acaban de llegar; **will it fit in?** — ~ **just** ¿cabrá? — apenas *or* (fam) justito; **not only ... , but also ...** no solo ... , sino también ...

only² *adj* (*before n*) único; **she's an ~ child** es hija única

only³ *conj* (colloq) pero

-only /'əʊnli/ *suff:* **a men~/women~ session** una sesión solo *or* exclusivamente para hombres/ mujeres

on: ~**set** *n* (of winter, rains) llegada *f;* (of disease) aparición *f;* ~**shore** /'ɑːnʃɔːr ‖'ɒnʃɔː(r)/ *adj* (*adj*) ⟨*wind*⟩ que sopla desde el mar **(b)** (on land) ⟨*oil terminal/location*⟩ en tierra

onslaught /'ɑːnslɔːt ‖'ɒnslɔːt/ *n* ataque *m*

onstage /'ɑːnsteɪdʒ ‖,ɒn'steɪdʒ/ *adv:* **to come ~** salir* a escena

onto /'ɑːntu: ‖'ɒntu:, *before consonant* 'ɑːntə ‖'ɒntə/ *prep* **1** (on): **it fell ~ the table** cayó sobre la mesa; **he climbed ~ the cart** se subió al carro **2** (aware of) (colloq) **the police are ~ her** la policía anda tras ella; **I think we're ~ something big** creo que hemos dado con algo gordo (fam)

onus /'əʊnəs/ *n* (fml) responsabilidad *f;* **the ~ is on him to prove his theory** le corresponde a él probar su teoría

onward¹ /'ɑːnwərd ‖'ɒnwəd/ *adj* (*before n*) hacia adelante

onward², (BrE also) **onwards** /-z/ *adv* (hacia) adelante; **from now ~** de ahora en adelante

ooh /u:/ *interj* ~**, what a beautiful sunset!** ¡ah, qué puesta de sol tan bonita!; ~**, that hurt** ¡ay, eso me dolió!

oops /ʊps ‖u:ps/ *interj* (colloq) ¡uy! (fam)

ooze /u:z/ *vi:* **blood ~d from his wound** le salía sangre de la herida; **to ~ WITH sth: the walls were oozing with damp** las paredes rezumaban humedad
■ ~ *vt:* **the wound ~d pus** la herida (le) supuraba; **he ~s charm** irradia simpatía

opal /'əʊpəl/ *n* ópalo *m*

opaque /əʊ'peɪk/ *adj* opaco

OPEC /'əʊpek/ *n* (*no art*) (= **Organization of Petroleum Exporting Countries**) la OPEC *or* la OPEP

open¹ /'əʊpən/ *adj* **1** (a) (not shut, sealed, fastened) abierto; **he pushed the door ~** abrió la puerta de un empujón **(b)** (not folded) ⟨*flower/ newspaper/book*⟩ abierto
2 (not enclosed) abierto; ~ **prison** cárcel *f* en régimen abierto; **on the ~ seas** en alta mar **3** (a) (not covered) ⟨*carriage*⟩ abierto; ⟨*sewer*⟩ a cielo abierto; **an ~ fire** una chimenea, un hogar **(b)** (exposed, vulnerable) ~ **TO sth** ⟨*to elements/ enemy attack*⟩ expuesto A algo
4 (*pred*) (ready for business) **to be ~** ⟨*shop/ museum*⟩ estar* abierto
5 (unrestricted) ⟨*membership*⟩ abierto al público en general; ⟨*meeting*⟩ a puertas abiertas; ⟨*ticket/ reservation*⟩ abierto
6 (not decided): **let's leave things ~ for the time**

being no descartemos ninguna posibilidad de momento; ~ **verdict** *veredicto que se emite cuando no se puede establecer la causa de la muerte de una persona*
7 (a) (receptive) abierto; **I'm ~ to suggestions** estoy abierto a todo tipo de sugerencias **(b)** (frank, candid): **to be ~ WITH sb** ser* sincero *or* franco CON algn
8 (not concealed) ⟨*resentment/hostility*⟩ abierto

open² *vt* **1** (a) ⟨*door/box/bottle*⟩ abrir*; **to ~ one's mouth/eyes** abrir* la boca/los ojos **(b)** (unfold) ⟨*newspaper/book*⟩ abrir* **2** (clear) ⟨*road/ channel*⟩ abrir* **3** (set up, start) ⟨*shop*⟩ abrir* **4** (begin) ⟨*debate/meeting*⟩ abrir*; ⟨*bidding*⟩ iniciar; ⟨*talks*⟩ entablar
■ ~ *vi* **1** (a) «*door/window/wound*» abrirse* **(b)** (unfold) «*flower/parachute*» abrirse* **2** (give access) **to ~ ONTO/INTO sth** dar* A algo **3** (for business) «*shop/museum*» abrir* **4** (begin) «*play/ book*» comenzar*, empezar*
■ **open up**
I [*v + o + adv, v + adv + o*] abrir*
II [*v + adv*] **1** (become open) abrirse* **2** (become accessible, available) «*country/market*» abrirse* **3** (start up) «*business/factory/store*» abrir*

open³ *n:* **in the ~** (in open space or country) al aire libre; (Mil) al descubierto; **I feel better now it's all out in the ~** me siento mejor ahora que todo el mundo lo sabe

open: ~ **air** *n:* **in the ~ air** al aire libre; ~**-and-shut** /'əʊpənænd'ʃʌt/ *adj:* **an ~-and-shut case** un caso clarísimo; ~ **day** *n* (BrE) *día en que un establecimiento educativo, científico etc puede ser visitado por el público;* ~**-ended** /'əʊpən'endəd ‖,əʊpən'endɪd/ *adj* ⟨*contract/lease*⟩ de duración indefinida; ⟨*discussion*⟩ abierto

opener /'əʊpnər ‖,əʊpnə(r)/ *n* (for bottle) abridor *m*, abrebotellas *m*, destapador *m* (AmL); (for can) abrelatas *m*

open house *n* **1** (*no art*): **to keep ~ ~** tener* las puertas siempre abiertas a todos; **2** (AmE) *día en que un establecimiento educativo, científico etc puede ser visitado por el público*

opening /'əʊpnɪŋ/ *n* **1** (in hedge, fence) abertura *f* **2** (beginning, initial stage) apertura *f* **3** (of exhibition, building) inauguración *f;* (Cin, Theat) estreno *m;* (*before n*) ⟨*speech*⟩ inaugural; ~ **night** noche *f* del estreno **4** (period when open): **hours of ~** (of shop) horario *m* comercial; (of bank, office) horario *m* de atención al público **5** (favorable opportunity) oportunidad *f*

openly /'əʊpənli/ *adv* abiertamente

open: ~**-minded** /'əʊpən'maɪndəd ‖,əʊpən'maɪndɪd/ *adj* ⟨*person*⟩ de actitud abierta; ⟨*approach*⟩ imparcial; ~**-mouthed** /'əʊpən'maʊðd/ *adj* boquiabierto; ~**-plan** /'əʊpən'plæn/ *adj* abierto, de planta abierta; ~ **university** *n* universidad *f* a distancia, universidad *f* abierta (Méx); **the O~ U~** (in UK) *la universidad a distancia del Reino Unido*

opera /'ɑːprə ‖'ɒprə/ *n* (*pl* **-ras**) ópera *f*

operate /'ɑːpəreɪt ‖'ɒpəreɪt/ *vi* **1** «*machine/ mechanism*» funcionar **2** (be applicable) ⟨*rules/ laws*⟩ regir* **3** (pursue one's business) «*company/ airline/gang*» operar **4** (Med) operar, intervenir* (fml); **to ~ ON sb (FOR sth)** operar A algn (DE algo)

■ ~ vt **1** ‹machine/controls› manejar **2** (manage, run) ‹business› llevar; ‹bus service› tener*

operatic /ˌɑːpəˈrætɪk ‖ˌɒpəˈrætɪk/ adj operístico

operating /ˈɑːpəreɪtɪŋ ‖ˈɒpəreɪtɪŋ/ adj (before n) **1** (Busn) ‹profit/loss/costs› de explotación **2** (Med): ~ **room** o (BrE) **theatre** quirófano m, sala f de operaciones; ~ **table** mesa f de operaciones

operation /ˌɑːpəˈreɪʃən ‖ˌɒpəˈreɪʃən/ n **1** (functioning) funcionamiento m; **to be in** ~ «machine» estar* en funcionamiento; «system» regir* **2** (using, running of machine) manejo m **3** (activity, series of activities) operación f **4** (Med) operación f, intervención f quirúrgica (frml)

operative /ˈɑːpərətɪv ‖ˈɒpərətɪv/ adj **to be** ~ «rules/measures» estar* en vigor; **the** ~ **word** la palabra clave

operator /ˈɑːpəreɪtər ‖ˈɒpəreɪtə(r)/ n (a) (Telec) operador, -dora m,f (b) (of equipment) operario, -ria m,f; (Comput) operador, -dora m,f

ophthalmic optician /ɑːpˈθælmɪk, ɑːf- ‖ɒfˈθælmɪk/ n ≈ oculista mf

opinion /əˈpɪnjən/ n opinión f; **what's your** ~? ¿qué opinas?, ¿qué te parece?; **in my** ~ en mi opinión, a mi parecer; **I'd like a second** ~ me gustaría consultarlo con otro especialista

opinionated /əˈpɪnjəneɪtəd ‖əˈpɪnjəˌneɪtɪd/ adj dogmático, aferrado a sus (or tus etc) opiniones

opinion poll n sondeo m or encuesta f de opinión

opium /ˈəʊpiəm/ n opio m

opponent /əˈpəʊnənt/ n (a) (of a regime, policy) opositor, -tora m,f; (in debate) adversario, -ria m,f (b) (Games, Sport) contrincante mf, rival mf

opportune /ˈɑːpərˈtuːn ‖ˈɒpətjuːn/ adj (frml) oportuno

opportunist¹ /ˈɑːpərˈtuːnəst ‖ˌɒpəˈtjuːnɪst/ n oportunista mf

opportunist², opportunistic /-tuːˈnɪstɪk ‖-tjuː-/ adj oportunista

opportunity /ˌɑːpərˈtuːnəti ‖ˌɒpəˈtjuːnəti/ n (pl **-ties**) oportunidad f, ocasión f; ~ **to** + INF/OF -ING oportunidad DE + INF; **there was little** ~ **for sightseeing** hubo poco tiempo para hacer turismo

oppose /əˈpəʊz/ vt (a) (be against) ‹measure/policy/actions› oponerse* a (b) (resist) ‹decision/plan› combatir

opposed /əˈpəʊzd/ adj **1** (against, in disagreement with) (pred) **to be** ~ **TO sth** oponerse* A algo **2** **as opposed to** a diferencia de

opposing /əˈpəʊzɪŋ/ adj (before n) ‹viewpoint/faction/team› contrario; ‹army› enemigo

opposite¹ /ˈɑːpəzət ‖ˈɒpəzɪt/ adj **1** (facing) ‹side/wall/page› de enfrente **2** (contrary) ‹opinions/news› opuesto; **we set off in** ~ **directions** partimos en direcciones opuestas; **it was coming in the** ~ **direction** venía en dirección contraria; **the** ~ **sex** el sexo opuesto

opposite² adv enfrente

opposite³ prep enfrente de, frente a

opposite⁴ n: **the** ~ lo contrario

opposite number n homólogo, -ga m,f

opposition /ˌɑːpəˈzɪʃən ‖ˌɒpəˈzɪʃən/ n

1 (antagonism, resistance) oposición f **2** (+ sing or pl vb) (a) (rivals, competitors) (Busn) competencia f; (Sport) adversarios mpl (b) (Pol) oposición f

oppress /əˈpres/ vt oprimir

oppression /əˈpreʃən/ n (Pol) opresión f; (feeling) agobio m

oppressive /əˈpresɪv/ adj (Pol) opresivo; ‹heat/humidity› agobiante

opt /ɑːpt ‖ɒpt/ vi optar; **to** ~ **FOR sth** optar POR algo; **to** ~ **to** + INF optar POR + INF
■ **opt out** [v + adv] **to** ~ **out** (OF sth) decidir no tomar parte (EN algo); (when already involved) dejar de tomar parte (EN algo)

optical /ˈɑːptɪkəl ‖ˈɒptɪkəl/ adj óptico

optician /ɑːpˈtɪʃən ‖ɒpˈtɪʃən/ n óptico, -ca m,f; (esp in UK) ≈ oculista mf

optics /ˈɑːptɪks ‖ˈɒptɪks/ n (+ sing vb) óptica f

optimism /ˈɑːptəmɪzəm ‖ˈɒptɪmɪzəm/ n optimismo m

optimist /ˈɑːptəməst ‖ˈɒptɪmɪst/ n optimista mf

optimistic /ˌɑːptəˈmɪstɪk ‖ˌɒptɪˈmɪstɪk/ adj optimista

optimum /ˈɑːptəməm ‖ˈɒptɪməm/ adj (before n) óptimo

option /ˈɑːpʃən ‖ˈɒpʃən/ n opción f; (Educ) (asignatura f) optativa f

optional /ˈɑːpʃənl ‖ˈɒpʃənl/ adj ‹accessories/features› opcional; ‹course/subject› optativo

opulence /ˈɑːpjələns ‖ˈɒpjʊləns/ n opulencia f

opulent /ˈɑːpjələnt ‖ˈɒpjʊlənt/ adj opulento

opus /ˈəʊpəs/ n obra f; (Mus) opus m

or /ər, ɔːr ‖ɔː(r)/ conj
■ **Note** The usual translation of or, o, becomes u when it precedes a word beginning with o or ho.

o; **either … or …** ▶ EITHER¹; **five minutes** ~ **so** unos cinco minutos; **do as I say,** ~ **else!** ¡haz lo que digo o vas a ver!

OR = Oregon

oracle /ˈɔːrəkəl ‖ˈɒrəkəl/ n oráculo m

oral¹ /ˈɔːrəl/ adj (usu before n) oral

oral² n (examen m) oral m

orange¹ /ˈɑːrɪndʒ ‖ˈɒrɪndʒ/ n (a) (fruit) naranja f; (before n) ~ **juice** jugo m or (Esp) zumo m de naranja (b) ~ (**tree**) naranjo m (c) (color) naranja m

orange² adj naranja adj inv, de color naranja

orangeade /ˈɑːrɪndʒˈeɪd ‖ˌɒrɪndʒˈeɪd/ n naranjada f

orator /ˈɔːrətər ‖ˈɒrətə(r)/ n orador, -dora m,f

orbit¹ /ˈɔːrbət ‖ˈɔːbɪt/ n órbita f

orbit² vt girar or orbitar alrededor de
■ ~ vi orbitar

orchard /ˈɔːrtʃərd ‖ˈɔːtʃəd/ n huerto m (de árboles frutales)

orchestra /ˈɔːrkəstrə ‖ˈɔːkɪstrə/ n **1** (Mus) orquesta f **2** (AmE Theat) platea f, patio m de butacas

orchestral /ɔːrˈkestrəl ‖ɔːˈkestrəl/ adj ‹music› orquestal; ‹piece› para orquesta

orchestrate /ˈɔːrkəstreɪt ‖ˈɔːkɪstreɪt/ vt orquestar

orchid /ˈɔːrkəd ‖ˈɔːkɪd/ n orquídea f

O

ordain /ɔːˈdeɪn ‖ɔːˈdeɪn/ vt [1] (Relig) ordenar [2] (a) (decree) (frml) to ~ THAT decretar QUE (+ subj) (b) (predestine) predestinar

ordeal /ɔːˈdiːl ‖ɔːˈdiːl/ n terrible experiencia f

order¹ /ˈɔːrdər ‖ˈɔːdə(r)/ n
I [1] (command) orden f; ~ to + INF orden DE + inf [2] (request, goods requested) pedido m; **the books are on ~** los libros están pedidos; **we make them to ~** los hacemos por encargo; **the waiter took my ~** el camarero tomó nota de lo que quería
II [1] (sequence) orden m; **to put sth in(to) ~** poner* algo en orden
[2] (satisfactory condition) orden m; **I'm trying to put my affairs in ~** estoy tratando de poner mis asuntos en orden; **the car was in perfect working ~** el coche funcionaba perfectamente bien [3] (harmony, discipline) orden m; **to keep ~** mantener* el orden
[4] (in phrases) **(a) in order: are her papers in ~?** ¿tiene los papeles en regla?; **an apology would seem to be in ~** parecería que lo indicado sería disculparse **(b)** in order to para **(c)** in order that para que (+ subj) **(d) out of order** (not in sequence) desordenado; (not working) averiado, descompuesto (AmL); **⑤ out of order** no funciona
III [1] (Biol) orden m
[2] (of monks, nuns) orden f

order² vt [1] (a) (command) ordenar; **to ~ sb to + INF** ordenarle a algn QUE (+ subj) **(b)** (Med) mandar [2] (request) pedir*; ⟨goods⟩ encargar* [3] (put in order) ordenar
■ ~ vi (in restaurant): **are you ready to ~?** ¿ya han decidido qué van a tomar?

order book n libro m de pedidos

ordered /ˈɔːrdərd ‖ˈɔːdəd/ adj ordenado

orderly¹ /ˈɔːrdərli ‖ˈɔːdəli/ adj (a) ⟨life/mind⟩ ordenado (b) ⟨crowd⟩ disciplinado

orderly² n (pl -lies) (a) (in hospital) camillero m (b) (Mil) ordenanza m

ordinal (number) /ˈɔːrdn̩əl ‖ˈɔːdɪnəl/ n (número m) ordinal m

ordinarily /ˈɔːrdn̩ˈerəli ‖ˈɔːdənrəli/ adv (a) (usually) normalmente (b) (averagely) medianamente

ordinary¹ /ˈɔːrdn̩eri ‖ˈɔːdənri/ adj (a) (average, normal) normal, corriente (b) (usual) normal

ordinary² n (average): **out of the ~** fuera de lo común

ore /ɔːr ‖ɔː(r)/ n mena f, mineral m metalífero

Ore, Oreg = Oregon

oregano /əˈregənəʊ ‖ˌɒrɪˈɡɑːnəʊ/ n orégano m

organ /ˈɔːrɡən ‖ˈɔːɡən/ n [1] (Anat) órgano m [2] (Mus) órgano m

organic /ɔːrˈɡænɪk ‖ɔːˈɡænɪk/ adj orgánico; ⟨farming⟩ ecológico; ⟨vegetable⟩ biológico, cultivado sin pesticidas ni fertilizantes artificiales

organism /ˈɔːrɡənɪzəm ‖ˈɔːɡənɪzəm/ n organismo m

organization /ˌɔːrɡənəˈzeɪʃən

‖ˌɔːɡənaɪˈzeɪʃən/ n (a) (group) organización f; (before n) ~ **chart** organigrama m (b) (organizing) organización f

organize /ˈɔːrɡənaɪz ‖ˈɔːɡənaɪz/ vt [1] (arrange, set up) organizar* [2] (systematize) ⟨ideas/life⟩ ordenar; **to get oneself ~d** organizarse* [3] (Lab Rels) sindicalizar* (esp AmL), sindicar* (esp Esp)

organized /ˈɔːrɡənaɪzd ‖ˈɔːɡənaɪzd/ adj [1] (methodical) organizado [2] (Lab Rels) sindicalizado (esp AmL), sindicado (esp Esp) [3] ⟨crime⟩ organizado

organizer /ˈɔːrɡənaɪzər ‖ˈɔːɡənaɪzə(r)/ n organizador, -dora m,f

orgasm /ˈɔːrɡæzəm ‖ˈɔːɡæzəm/ n orgasmo m

orgy /ˈɔːrdʒi ‖ˈɔːdʒi/ n (pl **orgies**) orgía f

orient¹, Orient /ˈɔːriənt/ n **the ~** (el) Oriente

orient² vt (esp AmE) orientar

oriental /ˈɔːriˈentl̩/ adj oriental

orientate /ˈɔːrienteɪt/ vt (esp BrE) ▶ ORIENT²

orientation /ˌɔːrienˈteɪʃən/ n (a) (leanings, preference) tendencia f (b) (guidance) orientación f

orienteering /ˌɔːrienˈtɪrɪŋ ‖ˌɔːriənˈtɪərɪŋ/ n orientación f

orifice /ˈɔːrəfəs ‖ˈɒrɪfɪs/ n orificio m

origin /ˈɔːrədʒən ‖ˈɒrɪdʒɪn/ n origen m

original¹ /əˈrɪdʒənl̩/ adj [1] (first) original; **the ~ inhabitants** los primeros habitantes [2] (a) (not copied) original (b) (unusual) original

original² n (document, painting) original m

originality /əˈrɪdʒəˈnæləti/ n originalidad f

originally /əˈrɪdʒənli/ adv (a) (in the beginning) originariamente (b) (unusually) con originalidad

originate /əˈrɪdʒəneɪt ‖əˈrɪdʒɪneɪt/ vi (a) (begin) ⟨custom⟩: ⟨fire⟩ empezar* (b) **to ~ from sth** (develop from) tener* su origen en algo (c) (AmE Transp) salir* de

originator /əˈrɪdʒəneɪtər ‖əˈrɪdʒɪneɪtə(r)/ n creador, -dora m,f

Orkney Islands /ˈɔːrkni ‖ˈɔːkni/, **Orkneys** /-z/ pl n (Islas fpl) Órcadas fpl

ornament /ˈɔːrnəmənt ‖ˈɔːnəmənt/ n adorno m

ornamental /ˈɔːrnəˈmentl̩ ‖ˌɔːnəˈmentl̩/ adj ornamental

ornate /ɔːrˈneɪt ‖ɔːˈneɪt/ adj ornamentado; (pej) recargado

ornithologist /ˌɔːrnəˈθɑːlədʒəst ‖ˌɔːnɪˈθɒlədʒɪst/ n ornitólogo, -ga m,f

ornithology /ˌɔːrnəˈθɑːlədʒi ‖ˌɔːnɪˈθɒlədʒi/ n ornitología f

orphan¹ /ˈɔːrfən ‖ˈɔːfən/ n huérfano, -na m,f

orphan² vt (usu pass): **she was ~ed at the age of two** quedó huérfana a los dos años

orphanage /ˈɔːrfənɪdʒ ‖ˈɔːfənɪdʒ/ n orfanato m

orthodox /ˈɔːrθədɑːks ‖ˈɔːθədɒks/ adj ortodoxo

orthopedic, (BrE) **orthopaedic** /ˈɔːrθəˈpiːdɪk ‖ˌɔːθəˈpiːdɪk/ adj ortopédico

Oscar /ˈɑːskər ‖ˈɒskə(r)/ n oscar m

oscillate /'ɑːsəleɪt ‖ 'ɒsɪleɪt/ *vi* (Elec, Phys) oscilar

ostensible /ɑːs'tensəbəl ‖ ɒ'stensəbəl/ *adj* aparente

ostensibly /ɑːs'tensəbli ‖ ɒ'stensəbli/ *adv* aparentemente

ostentatious /ˌɑːstən'teɪʃəs ‖ ˌɒsten'teɪʃəs/ *adj* ostentoso

osteopath /'ɑːstiəpæθ ‖ 'ɒstiəpæθ/ *n* osteópata *mf*

ostracize /'ɑːstrəsaɪz ‖ 'ɒstrəsaɪz/ *vt* hacerle* el vacío a

ostrich /'ɑːstrɪtʃ ‖ 'ɒstrɪtʃ/ *n* avestruz *m*

other[1] /'ʌðər ‖ 'ʌðə(r)/ *adj* otro, otra; (*pl*) otros, otras; **he doesn't relate easily to ~ people** no se relaciona fácilmente con los demás; **the ~ day** el otro día

other[2] *pron* (*pl* **others**) [1] (a) (different, alternative one or ones) otro, otra; **~s** otros, otras; **I'll think of some excuse or ~** ya me inventaré alguna excusa (u otra); **he was called Richard something or ~** se llamaba Richard no sé cuánto (fam) (b) (the remaining one or ones) otro, otra; **~s** otros, otras; **what do the ~s think?** ¿qué piensan los demás? (c) (additional one or ones) otro, otra; **~s** otros, otras; **answer the first three questions and one ~** conteste las tres primeras preguntas y otra más
[2] **other than** (apart from) aparte de; (different from) distinto (*or* distinta *etc*) de *or* a; **it was none ~ than Bob** no era ni menos que Bob

other[3] *adv*: **somehow or ~** de alguna manera; **somewhere or ~** en algún sitio; **where would you like to live? — anywhere ~ than London** ¿dónde te gustaría vivir? — en cualquier (otro) sitio menos en Londres

otherwise /'ʌðərwaɪz ‖ 'ʌðəwaɪz/ *adv* [1] (if not) (*as linker*) si no [2] (in other respects) por lo demás [3] (a) (in a different way): **he could not have done ~** no podía haber hecho otra cosa; **unless ~ agreed, payments ...** a menos que se convenga otra cosa, los pagos ... (b) (other, different): **there are many problems, legal and ~** hay muchos problemas, legales y de otro tipo

otter /'ɑːtər ‖ 'ɒtə(r)/ *n* nutria *f*

ouch /aʊtʃ/ *interj* (colloq) ¡ay!

ought /ɔːt/ *v mod* **~ to + INF** debería (*or* deberías *etc*) + INF, debiera (*or* debieras *etc*) + INF; **she ~ not to have said that** no debería haber dicho eso

ounce /aʊns/ *n* (a) (unit) onza *f* (*28,35 gramos*) (b) (small quantity) (*no pl*): **if you had an ~ of decency/sense ...** si tuvieras una pizca de vergüenza/sentido común ...

our /aʊr ‖ 'aʊə(r)/ *adj*

■ Note The translation *nuestro* agrees in number and gender with the noun which it modifies; *our* is translated by *nuestro, nuestra, nuestros, nuestras*, according to what follows: *our father/mother* nuestro padre/nuestra madre; *our books/magazines* nuestros libros/nuestras revistas.

(*sing*) nuestro, -tra; (*pl*) nuestros, -tras; **we were washing ~ hair** nos lavábamos el pelo

ours /aʊrz ‖ 'aʊəz/ *pron*

■ Note The translation *nuestro* reflects the gender and

number of the noun it is standing for; *ours* is translated by *el nuestro, la nuestra, los nuestros, las nuestras*, depending on what is being referred to.

(*sing*) nuestro, -tra; (*pl*) nuestros, -tras; **~ is blue** el nuestro/la nuestra es azul; **a friend of ~** un amigo nuestro

ourselves /aʊr'selvz ‖ aʊə'selvz, ɑː-/ *pron* (a) (reflexive): **we behaved ~** nos portamos bien; **we thought only of ~** solo pensamos en nosotros mismos/nosotras mismas; **we were by ~** estábamos solos/solas (b) (emphatic use): **we did it ~** lo hicimos nosotros mismos/nosotras mismas

oust /aʊst/ *vt* ‹*rival/leader*› desbancar*; ‹*government*› derrocar*

out[1] /aʊt/ *adv*
I [1] (a) (outside) fuera, afuera (esp AmL) (b) (not at home, work): **tell him I'm ~** dile que no estoy; **I was ~ most of the day** estuve (a)fuera casi todo el día; **to eat ~** cenar/comer fuera *or* (esp AmL) afuera; **~ and about: you must get ~ and about more** tienes que salir más
[2] (removed): **I'm having my stitches ~ next week** la semana que viene me sacan los puntos
[3] (a) (indicating movement, direction): **~!** ¡fuera!; 🅢 **out** salida; **she went over to the window and looked ~** se acercó a la ventana y miró para afuera (b) (outstretched, projecting): **the dog had its tongue ~** el perro tenía la lengua fuera *or* (esp AmL) afuera
[4] (indicating distance): **~ here in Japan** aquí en Japón; **we live ~ Brampton way** vivimos en la dirección de Brampton
[5] (from hospital, jail): **he's been ~ for a month now** ya hace un mes que salió
[6] (in phrases) out for: **Lewis was ~ for revenge** Lewis quería vengarse; **out to + INF: she's ~ to beat the record** está decidida a batir el récord; **they're only ~ to make money** su único objetivo es hacer dinero; *see also* OUT OF
II [1] (a) (displayed, not put away): **are the plates ~ yet?** ¿están puestos ya los platos? (b) (in blossom) en flor (c) (shining): **when the sun's ~** cuando hay *or* hace sol
[2] (published, produced): **a report ~ today points out that ...** un informe publicado hoy señala que ...; **their new album will be ~ by April** sacarán el nuevo disco para abril

out[2] *adj* [1] (*pred*) (a) (extinguished) **to be ~** ‹*fire/light/pipe*› estar* apagado (b) (unconscious) inconsciente [2] (*pred*) (a) (at an end): **before the month/year is ~** antes de que acabe el mes/año (b) (out of fashion) pasado de moda [3] (Sport) (a) (eliminated) **to be ~** ‹*batter/batsman*› quedar out; ‹*team*› quedar eliminado (b) (outside limit) (*pred*) fuera; **~!** (call) ¡out!

out[3] *prep*: **he looked ~ the window** miró (hacia afuera) por la ventana; *see also* OUT OF 1

out: ~-and-~ /'aʊt'aʊt/ *adj* (*as intensifier*) ‹*villain/liar*› consumado; ‹*radical/feminist*› acérrimo; ‹*defeat/disgrace*› total; **~back** *n* **the ~back** el interior (*zona despoblada de Australia*); **~bid** /'aʊt'bɪd/ *vt* (*pres p* **-bidding**; *past* **-bid**; *past p* **-bid** *or* (AmE also) **-bidden**) **to ~bid sb (FOR sth)** pujar más que algn (POR algo); **~board (motor)** *n* motor *m* fuera de borda, fueraborda *m*; **~break** *n* (of war) estallido *m*; (of hostilities) comienzo *m*; (of cholera, influenza, violence) brote *m*; **~building** *n* edificación *f* anexa; ⋯⟶

~burst n (of emotion) arrebato m; **~cast** n paria mf; **~come** n (result) resultado m; (consequences) consecuencias fpl; **~crop** n afloramiento m; **~cry** n protesta f ⟨enérgica⟩; there was a public **~cry** hubo protestas generalizadas; **~dated** /'aʊt'deɪtəd ‖ ˌaʊt'deɪtɪd/ adj ⟨style/custom⟩ pasado de moda; ⟨idea/theory⟩ anticuado; **~did** /'aʊt'dɪd/ past of ~DO; **~distance** /'aʊt'dɪstəns/ vt dejar atrás; **~do** /'aʊt'duː/ vt (3rd pers sing pres **-does**; past **-did**; past p **-done**) ⟨result/achievement⟩ mejorar; **~door** /'aʊtdɔːr ‖ 'aʊtdɔː(r)/ adj (before n) ⟨clothes⟩ de calle; ⟨plants⟩ de exterior; ⟨swimming pool⟩ descubierto; **~doors** /'aʊt'dɔːrz ‖ ˌaʊt'dɔːz/ adv al aire libre

outer /'aʊtər ‖ 'aʊtə(r)/ adj (before n) exterior; **~ space** el espacio sideral

out: ~fit n (a) (clothes) conjunto m, tenida f (Chi) (b) (equipment) equipo m; **~flow** n (of water) desagüe m, flujo m; **~go** n (AmE) salida f; **~going** adj ① (sociable) sociable; ② ⟨president/administration⟩ saliente; **~goings** pl n (esp BrE) gastos mpl; **~grow** /'aʊt'grəʊ/ vt (past **-grew**; past p **-grown**): he's already **~grown** his new shoes los zapatos nuevos ya le han quedado chicos or (Esp) ya se le han quedado pequeños; she's **~grown** these toys ya está grande para jugar con esos juguetes; **~house** n (a) (building) (BrE) edificación f anexa (b) (outdoor privy) (AmE) excusado m exterior

outing /'aʊtɪŋ/ n excursión f

outlandish /aʊt'lændɪʃ/ adj ⟨clothes⟩ extravagante; ⟨idea/suggestion⟩ descabellado

outlast /'aʊt'læst ‖ ˌaʊt'lɑːst/ vt (a) (last longer than) durar más que (b) (survive) sobrevivir a

outlaw¹ /'aʊtlɔː/ n forajido, -da m,f, bandido, -da m,f

outlaw² vt ⟨activity/product⟩ prohibir*, declarar ilegal; ⟨organization⟩ proscribir*; ⟨person⟩ declarar fuera de la ley

out: ~lay n desembolso m; **~let** n ① (a) (for liquid, gas) salida f (b) (AmE Elec) toma f de corriente, tomacorriente m (AmL); ② (means of expression): she found an **~let** for her feelings encontró una manera de canalizar sus sentimientos; ③ (Busn, Marketing) punto m de venta; **retail ~let** tienda f al por menor

outline¹ /'aʊtlaɪn/ n ① (a) (contour) contorno m (b) (shape) perfil m ② (summary) resumen m; ⟨plan of project, article⟩ esquema m

outline² vt (a) (sketch) ⟨shape⟩ bosquejar; ⟨map⟩ trazar* (b) (summarize) esbozar*

out: ~live /'aʊt'lɪv/ vt sobrevivir a; **~look** n (a) (attitude) punto m de vista (b) (prospects) perspectivas fpl; **~lying** adj (before n) ⟨villages/islands⟩ alejado; ⟨area/hills/suburbs⟩ de la periferia; **~number** /'aʊt'nʌmbər ‖ ˌaʊt'nʌmbə(r)/ vt superar en número a

out of prep ① (from inside): it fell **~ ~** her hand se le cayó de la mano; (come) **~ ~** there! ¡salgan de ahí!; to look **~ ~** the window mirar (hacia afuera) por la ventana

② (outside): I was **~ ~** the room for two minutes estuve dos minutos fuera or (AmL tb) afuera de la habitación

③ (eliminated, excluded): Korea is **~ ~** the tournament Corea ha quedado eliminada; he was left **~ ~** the team no lo incluyeron en el equipo ④ (a) (indicating substance, makeup) de; made **~ ~** steel hecho de acero (b) (indicating motive) por; **~ charity** por caridad

⑤ (from among) de; eight **~ ~** ten people ocho de cada diez personas

⑥ (indicating lack): we're **~ ~** bread nos hemos quedado sin pan

out: ~of-date /'aʊtəv'deɪt/ adj (pred **~ of date**) ⟨ideas/technology⟩ desfasado, perimido (RPl); ⟨ticket/check⟩ caducado, vencido (AmL); ⟨clothes⟩ pasado de moda; **~-of-the-way** /'aʊtəvðə'weɪ/ adj ⟨place⟩ apartado; **~patient** n paciente externo, -na m,f; **~post** n (a) (Mil) avanzada f (b) (settlement) puesto m de avanzada; **~put** n (of factory, writer, artist) producción f; (of worker, machine) rendimiento m; (Comput) salida f; (Elec) salida f

outrage¹ /'aʊtreɪdʒ/ n (a) (cruel act) atrocidad f (b) (scandal) escándalo m (c) (feeling) **~** (AT sth) indignación f (ANTE algo)

outrage² vt (a) (offend) indignar (b) (scandalize) escandalizar*

outrageous /aʊt'reɪdʒəs/ adj (a) (scandalous) ⟨behavior/state of affairs⟩ vergonzoso; ⟨demands/price⟩ escandaloso; how dare you! this is **~**! ¡cómo te atreves! ¡esto es intolerable! (b) (unconventional) ⟨clothes⟩ extravagante

outran /'aʊt'ræn/ past of OUTRUN

outright¹ /'aʊtraɪt/ adj (before n) ⟨refusal/opposition⟩ rotundo; ⟨hostility⟩ declarado; ⟨winner⟩ indiscutido; ⟨lie⟩ descarado

outright² adv (a) (completely) ⟨refuse/reject⟩ rotundamente; ⟨win⟩ indiscutiblemente (b) (directly, frankly) ⟨ask/say⟩ abiertamente (c) (instantly) ⟨kill⟩ en el acto

out: ~run /'aʊt'rʌn/ vt (pres p **-running**; past **-ran**; past p **-run**) dejar atrás; **~set** n: from the **~set** desde el principio; **~shine** /'aʊt'ʃaɪn/ vt (past & past p **-shone**) eclipsar

outside¹ /'aʊt'saɪd/ n (exterior part) exterior m; (surface) parte f de fuera or (esp AmL) de afuera; at the (very) **~** como máximo

outside² adv fuera, afuera (esp AmL); to run **~** salir* corriendo

outside³ prep fuera de; it's just **~** London está en las afueras de Londres; it's **~** my responsibilities no está dentro de mis responsabilidades

outside⁴ adj (before n) (a) (exterior, outward) exterior (b) (outdoor) ⟨toilet⟩ fuera de la vivienda, exterior (c) (outer) exterior; the **~** lane (Auto) el carril de la izquierda; (in UK etc) el carril de la derecha; (Sport) el carril (AmL) or (Esp) la calle número ocho (or seis etc) (d) (external) ⟨interference/pressure⟩ externo

outsider /'aʊt'saɪdər ‖ ˌaʊt'saɪdə(r)/ n (a) (person not belonging) persona f de fuera, afuerano, -na m,f (b) (in competition): he was beaten by an **~** fue derrotado por un desconocido (un competidor que se consideraba tenía pocas probabilidades de ganar)

out: ~size /'aʊt'saɪz/, (esp AmE) **~-sized** /-d/ adj (Clothing) de talla or (RPl) talle gigante; (very large) gigantesco; **~skirts** pl n afueras fpl, alrededores *mpl*; ~**smart** /'aʊt'smɑːrt ‖,aʊt'smɑːt/ *vt* (esp AmE colloq) burlar; ~**source** *vt* externalizar*; ~**spoken** /'aʊt'spəʊkən/ *adj* directo, franco; ~**spread** /'aʊt'spred/ *adj* ⟨*wings*⟩ extendido; ~**standing** /aʊt'stændɪŋ/ *adj* **1** **(a)** (excellent) ⟨*ability/beauty*⟩ extraordinario; ⟨*achievement/performer*⟩ destacado **(b)** (prominent) (*before n*) ⟨*feature*⟩ destacado; **2** ⟨*debt*⟩ pendiente (de pago); ~**stay** /'aʊt'steɪ/ *vt*: **I think we've ~stayed our welcome** creo que nos hemos quedado más de la cuenta; ~**stretched** /'aʊt'stretʃt/ *adj* extendido; ~**strip** /'aʊt'strɪp/ *vt* **-pp-** (run faster than) tomarle la delantera a; (exceed) sobrepasar; ~**vote** /'aʊt'vəʊt/ *vt*: **to be ~voted** perder* la votación

outward¹ /'aʊtwərd ‖'aʊtwəd/ *adj* (*before n*) **(a)** ⟨*appearance*⟩ exterior; ⟨*sign*⟩ externo **(b)** ⟨*journey/flight*⟩ de ida

outward², (BrE also) **outwards** /-z/ *adv* hacia afuera

outwardly /'aʊtwərdli ‖'aʊtwədli/ *adv* en apariencia

out: ~weigh /'aʊt'weɪ/ *vt* ser* mayor que; ~**wit** /'aʊt'wɪt/ *vt* **-tt-** burlar

oval¹ /'əʊvəl/ *n* óvalo *m*

oval² *adj* ovalado, oval

ovary /'əʊvəri/ *n* (*pl* **-ries**) ovario *m*

ovation /əʊ'veɪʃən/ *n* (fml) ovación *f* (fml); **he got a standing ~** los delegados se pusieron de pie para aplaudirlo

oven /'ʌvən/ *n* horno *m*; (*before n*) ~ **glove** guante *m* para el horno

oven: ~proof *adj* refractario; ~**-ready** /'ʌvən'redi/ *adj* listo para el horno

over¹ /'əʊvər ‖'əʊvə(r)/ *adv* **I** **1** **(a)** (across): **come ~ here!** ¡ven aquí!; **look ~ there!** ¡mira allí!; **she called me ~** me llamó (desde el otro lado); **he reached ~ and took the money** se estiró y tomó el dinero **(b)** (overhead) por encima **2** **(a)** (in another place): **she was sitting ~ there** estaba sentada allí; **how long are you ~ (here) for?** ¿cuánto tiempo te vas a quedar (aquí)? **(b)** (on other page, TV station etc): **see ~** véase al dorso; **for the latest news, we go ~ to New York** para las últimas noticias, conectamos ahora con Nueva York **(c)** (Rad, Telec) corto; ~ **and out!** corto y fuera **3** (out of upright position): **to knock sth ~** tirar *or* (AmL exc RPl) botar algo (de un golpe); **to tip sth ~** volcar* algo

II **1** (finished): **the film was ~ by 11 o'clock** la película terminó antes de las 11; **it's all ~ between us** lo nuestro se ha acabado; **to be ~ (and done) with** haber* terminado **2** (remaining): **if you have any material ~** si te sobra tela; **3 into 10 goes 3 and 1 ~** 10 dividido (por) 3 cabe a 3 y sobra 1 **3** **(a)** (*as intensifier*): **twice/ten times ~** dos/diez veces **(b)** (again) (AmE) otra vez; **we had to start ~** tuvimos que volver a empezar **4** (more) más **5** (excessively) demasiado

III (*in phrases*) **1** **all over** (everywhere) por todas partes; **I'm aching all ~** me duele todo (el cuerpo); **that's her all ~** (colloq) eso es típico de ella

2 (all) **over again: to start (all) ~ again** volver* a empezar (desde cero) **3** **over and over** (repeatedly) una y otra vez

over² *prep* **I** **1** (across): **he jumped ~ the fence** saltó (por encima de) la valla; **they built a bridge ~ the river** construyeron un puente sobre el río; **she peered ~ his shoulder** atisbó por encima de su hombro **2** (above) encima de **3** (covering, on): **snow was falling ~ the countryside** nevaba sobre la campiña; **my room looks out ~ the square** mi habitación da a la plaza; **he put a coat on ~ his pajamas** se puso un abrigo encima del pijama; **she hit me ~ the head with her stick** me dio con el bastón en la cabeza **4** **(a)** (through, all around): ~ **an area of 50km²** en un área de 50km²; **I've been ~ the details with her** he repasado los detalles con ella **(b)** (referring to experiences, illnesses): **is she ~ her measles yet?** ¿ya se ha repuesto del sarampión?; **we're ~ the worst now** ya hemos pasado lo peor **5** (during, in the course of): ~ **the past/next few years** en los últimos/próximos años; **we can discuss it ~ lunch** podemos hablarlo mientras comemos **6** (by the medium of) por; ~ **the loudspeaker** por el altavoz **7** (about, on account of): **to cry ~ sth** llorar por algo; **they argued ~ money** discutieron por asuntos de dinero **8** **all over: there are black marks all ~ the floor** hay marcas negras por todo el suelo; **all ~ town** por toda la ciudad

II **1** **(a)** (more than) más de **(b)** **over and above** (in addition to) además de **2** **(a)** (senior to) por encima de **(b)** (indicating superiority) sobre; **to have control ~ sb/sth** tener* control sobre algn/algo

over³ *n* (in cricket) over *m* (*serie de seis lanzamientos*)

over- /'əʊvər ‖'əʊvə(r)/ *pref* **(a)** (excessively) demasiado **(b)** (in deliberate understatement): **she wasn't ~enthusiastic** no demostró mucho entusiasmo que digamos

overact /'əʊvər'ækt/ *vi* sobreactuar*

overall¹ /'əʊvərɔːl/ *adj* (*before n*) ⟨*length*⟩ total; ⟨*result/cost*⟩ global; **the ~ impression** la impresión general

overall² *n*. **1** (protective garment) (esp BrE) bata *f* **2** **overalls** *pl* **(a)** (dungarees) (AmE) overol *m* (AmL), (pantalones *mpl* de) peto *m* (Esp), mameluco *m* (CS) **(b)** (boiler suit) (BrE) overol *m* (AmL), mono *m* (Esp, Méx)

over: ~arm *adv* (esp BrE) por encima de la cabeza; ~**ate** /'əʊvər'et/ *past of* ~**EAT**; ~**awe** /'əʊvər'ɔː/ *vt* intimidar; ~**balance** /'əʊvər'bæləns ‖,əʊvə'bæləns/ *vi* perder* el equilibrio; ~**board** *adv*: **they threw him ~board** lo echaron por la borda; **to go ~board** (colloq — exaggerate) exagerar; (— be excessively enthusiastic, generous) pasarse (fam); ~**came** /'əʊvər'keɪm ‖,əʊvə'keɪm/ *past of* ~**COME**; ~**cast** *adj* ⟨*sky*⟩ cubierto; ⟨*day*⟩ nublado; **it's ~cast** está nublado *or* cubierto; ~**charge** /'əʊvər'tʃɑːdʒ ‖,əʊvə'tʃɑːdʒ/ *vt* **to ~charge sb** (FOR sth) cobrarle más a algn (POR algo); ~**coat** *n* abrigo *m*, sobretodo *m* (esp RPl); ~**come** /'əʊvər'kʌm ‖,əʊvə'kʌm/ (*past* **-came**; *past p* ⋯⟶

-come) *vt* (a) ‹*opponent*› reducir*; ‹*fear*› superar; ‹*inhibitions*› vencer* (b) (overwhelm) invadir; he was ~come by fatigue lo venció la fatiga; to be ~come WITH sth ‹*with guilt/ remorse*› sentirse* abrumado POR algo ■ ~ *vi*: we shall ~come venceremos; ~**crowded** /'əʊvər'kraʊdəd ‖,əʊvə'kraʊdəd/ *adj* abarrotado (de gente); ‹*country*› superpoblado; ~**crowding** /'əʊvər'kraʊdɪŋ ‖,əʊvə'kraʊdɪŋ/ *n*: they complained about the ~crowding on the trains se quejaron de lo aborrotados que iban los trenes; the severe ~crowding in our prisons el hacinamiento en nuestras cárceles; ~**do** /'əʊvər'du: ‖,əʊvə'du:/ *vt* (*3rd pers sing pres* -**does**; *past* -**did**; *past p* -**done**) [1] (exaggerate) exagerar; to ~do it (go too far) írsele la mano a algn; (overexert oneself) exigir* demasiado; [2] (Culin) cocinar demasiado, recocer*; ~**dose** *n* sobredosis *f*; ~**draft** *n* descubierto *m*; ~**draw** /'əʊvər'drɔ:/ *vt* (*past* -**drew**; *past p* -**drawn**) (Fin): I'm ~drawn tengo un descubierto; ~**drive** /'əʊvərdraɪv/ *n* superdirecta *f*; ~**due** /'əʊvər'du:/ *adj*: the book is a month ~due el plazo de devolución del libro venció hace un mes; such measures are long ~due tales medidas deberían haberse adoptado mucho antes; ~**eat** /'əʊvər'i:t/ *vi* (*past* -**ate**; *past p* -**eaten**) comer demasiado; ~**excited** /'əʊvərɪk'saɪtəd/ *adj* sobreexcitado; ~**feed** /'əʊvər'fi:d/ *vt* (*past & past p* -**fed**) sobrealimentar

overflow¹ /'əʊvər'fləʊ ‖,əʊvə'fləʊ/ *vi* ‹*liquid*› derramarse; ‹*bucket/bath/river*› desbordarse; the house is ~ing with junk la casa está hasta el techo de cachivaches

overflow² /'əʊvərfləʊ ‖'əʊvəfləʊ/ *n* (a) (excess): we put a bowl there to catch the ~ pusimos un bol para recoger el líquido que se derramaba (b) (outlet) rebosadero *m*; (*before n*) ~ car park (BrE) aparcamiento *m* disuasorio

over: ~**grown** /'əʊvər'grəʊn ‖,əʊvə'grəʊn/ *adj* (a) ‹*garden*› lleno de maleza (b) (too big) demasiado grande; ~**hand** *adv* (AmE) por encima de la cabeza; ~**hang** /'əʊvər'hæŋ ‖,əʊvə'hæŋ/ (*past & past p* -**hung**) *vt* sobresalir* por encima de ■ ~ *vi* sobresalir*

overhaul¹ /'əʊvər'hɔ:l ‖,əʊvə'hɔ:l/ *vt* revisar

overhaul² /'əʊvərhɔ:l ‖'əʊvəhɔ:l/ *n* revisión *f* (general), overjol *m* (AmC)

overhead¹ /'əʊvər'hed ‖,əʊvə'hed/ *adv*: the sun was directly ~ el sol caía de pleno; a plane flew ~ pasó un avión

overhead² /'əʊvərhed ‖'əʊvəhed/ *adj* ‹*cable*› aéreo; ‹*railway*› elevado

overhead³ /'əʊvərhed ‖'əʊvəhed/ *n* (AmE) gastos *mpl* indirectos

over: ~**heads** /'əʊvərhedz ‖'əʊvəhedz/ *pl n* (BrE) ▶ OVERHEAD³; ~**hear** /'əʊvər'hɪr ‖,əʊvə'hɪə(r)/ *vt* (*past & past p* -**heard**) oír* (*por casualidad*); ~**heat** /'əʊvər'hi:t ‖,əʊvə'hi:t/ *vi* recalentarse*; ~**hung** *past & past p of* OVERHANG; ~**joyed** /'əʊvər'dʒɔɪd ‖,əʊvə'dʒɔɪd/ *adj* encantado; ~**kill** *n* exageración *f*; ~**land**

adj/adv por tierra; ~**lap** /'əʊvər'læp ‖,əʊvə'læp/ *vi* -**pp**- (a) ‹*tiles/planks*› estar* montados unos sobre otros, traslaparse (b) ‹*responsibilities*› coincidir en parte; ~**leaf** /'əʊvər'li:f ‖,əʊvə'li:f/ *adv* al dorso; ~**load** /'əʊvər'ləʊd ‖,əʊvə'ləʊd/ *vt* sobrecargar*; ~**look** /'əʊvər'lʊk ‖,əʊvə'lʊk/ *vt* [1] (a) (not notice) pasar por alto (b) (disregard) disculpar; [2] (have view over): a room ~**looking** the sea una habitación con vista al mar *or* que da al mar

overly /'əʊvərli ‖'əʊvəli/ *adv* demasiado

overnight¹ /'əʊvər'naɪt ‖,əʊvə'naɪt/ *adv* (a) (through the night): to stay ~ quedarse a pasar la noche; there had been a heavy fall of snow ~ durante la noche había nevado mucho; soak the chickpeas ~ ponga los garbanzos en remojo la noche anterior (b) (suddenly) ‹*change/disappear*› de la noche a la mañana

overnight² /'əʊvərnaɪt ‖'əʊvənaɪt/ *adj* (a) (through the night) ‹*journey*› de noche; ‹*stay*› de una noche (b) (sudden) ‹*change/success*› repentino

over: ~**paid** /'əʊvər'peɪd ‖,əʊvə'peɪd/ *adj*: she's ~paid le pagan demasiado ~**pass** *n* paso *m* elevado, paso *m* a desnivel (Méx); ~**population** /,əʊvər,pɒpjə'leɪʃən ‖,əʊvə,pɒpjʊ'leɪʃən/ *n* superpoblación *f*, sobrepoblación *f* (AmL); ~**power** /'əʊvər'paʊər ‖,əʊvə'paʊə(r)/ *vt* (a) (render helpless) dominar (b) (affect greatly) ‹*smell*› marear; ‹*heat*› sofocar*; ‹*emotion*› abrumar; ~**powering** /'əʊvər'paʊrɪŋ ‖,əʊvə'paʊrɪŋ/ *adj* (a) ‹*smell*› muy fuerte; ‹*heat*› aplastante; ‹*desire*› irresistible (b) ‹*personality*› apabullante; ~**priced** /'əʊvər'praɪst ‖,əʊvə'praɪst/ *vt*: it's ~priced es caro para lo que es; ~**ran** /'əʊvər'ræn ‖,əʊvə'ræn/ *past of* ~RUN; ~**rated** /'əʊvər'reɪtəd ‖,əʊvə'reɪtɪd/ *adj* sobrevalorado; ~**reach** /'əʊvər'ri:tʃ ‖,əʊvə'ri:tʃ/ *v refl*: to ~reach oneself intentar hacer demasiado; ~**react** /'əʊvərri'ækt ‖,əʊvəri'ækt/ *vi* reaccionar en forma exagerada; ~**ride** /'əʊvər'raɪd ‖,əʊvə'raɪd/ *vt* (*past* -**rode**; *past p* -**ridden**) ‹*decision/recommendation*› invalidar; ‹*wishes/advice*› hacer* caso omiso de; ~**ripe** /'əʊvər'raɪp ‖,əʊvə'raɪp/ *adj* demasiado maduro; ~**rode** /'əʊvər'rəʊd ‖,əʊvə'rəʊd/ *past of* ~RIDE; ~**rule** /'əʊvər'ru:l ‖,əʊvə'ru:l/ *vt* ‹*decision/ verdict*› anular; ‹*objection*› rechazar*; ~**run** /'əʊvər'rʌn ‖,əʊvə'rʌn/ *vt* (*past* -**ran**; *past p* -**run**) (a) (invade, swarm over) invadir; to be ~run WITH sth estar* plagado DE algo (b) (exceed) exceder; ~**saw** /'əʊvər'sɔ: ‖,əʊvə'sɔ:/ *past of* OVERSEE

overseas¹ /'əʊvər'si:z ‖'əʊvə,si:z/ *adj* (*before n*) ‹*trade*› exterior; ‹*investments/branches*› en el exterior; ‹*student/visitor*› extranjero; ‹*news*› del exterior

overseas² /'əʊvər'si:z ‖,əʊvə'si:z/ *adv* ‹*live*› en el extranjero; ‹*travel/send*› al extranjero

over: ~**see** /'əʊvər'si: ‖,əʊvə'si:/ *vt* (*past* -**saw**; *past p* -**seen**) supervisar; ~**seer** /'əʊvər'sɪr, -'si:ər ‖'əʊvəsi:ə(r)/ *n* capataz *mf*; ~**shadow** /'əʊvər'ʃædəʊ ‖,əʊvə'ʃædəʊ/ *vt*

---

eclipsar; **~shoot** /'əʊvər'ʃuːt ‖,əʊvə'ʃuːt/ *vt* (*past & past p* **-shot**) ⟨*runway*⟩ salirse* de; ⟨*turning*⟩ pasarse de; ⟨*target/budget*⟩ exceder; **~sight** /'əʊvərsaɪt ‖'əʊvəsaɪt/ *n* descuido *m*; **~sleep** /'əʊvər'sliːp ‖,əʊvə'sliːp/ *vi* (*past & past p* **-slept**) quedarse dormido; **~spend** /'əʊvər'spend ‖,əʊvə'spend/ *vi* (*past & past p* **-spent**) gastar más de la cuenta; **~spill** *n* excedente *m* de población; **~staffed** /'əʊvər'stæft ‖,əʊvə'stɑːft/ *adj* con exceso de personal *or* (Esp tb) de plantilla; **~state** /'əʊvər'steɪt ‖,əʊvə'steɪt/ *vt* exagerar; **~stay** /'əʊvər'steɪ ‖,əʊvə'steɪ/ *vt* ▸ OUTSTAY; **~step** /'əʊvər'step ‖,əʊvə'step/ *vt* **-pp-** sobrepasar

overt /əʊ'vɜːrt ‖'əʊvɜːt/ *adj* ⟨*hostility*⟩ declarado; ⟨*criticism*⟩ abierto

over: ~take /'əʊvər'teɪk ‖,əʊvə'teɪk/ (*past* **-took**; *past p* **-taken**) *vt* **(a)** (go past) adelantar, rebasar (Méx) **(b)** (surpass) superar ■ **~** *vi* (BrE) adelantar, rebasar (Méx); **~tax** /'əʊvər'tæks ‖,əʊvə'tæks/ *vt* **(a)** (strain) poner* a prueba **(b)** (Tax) gravar en exceso (*con impuestos*); **~throw** /'əʊvər'θrəʊ ‖,əʊvə'θrəʊ/ *vt* (*past* **-threw**; *past p* **-thrown**) ⟨*government*⟩ derrocar*; **~time** *n* [1] (extra work hours) horas *fpl* extra(s), sobretiempo *m* (Chi, Per); [2] (AmE Sport) prórroga *f*; **~tone** *n* (suggestion, hint) dejo *m*, deje *m* (Esp); **~took** /'əʊvər'tʊk ‖,əʊvə'tʊk/ *past of* ~TAKE

overture /'əʊvərtʃʊr ‖'əʊvətjʊə(r)/ *n* [1] (Mus) obertura *f* [2] **overtures** *pl* (approaches) (frml) intento *m* de acercamiento; (sexual) insinuación *f*

over: ~turn /'əʊvər'tɜːrn ‖,əʊvə'tɜːn/ *vt* **(a)** (tip over) ⟨*table/boat*⟩ darle* la vuelta a, dar* vuelta (CS) **(b)** (depose) ⟨*government*⟩ derrocar* ■ **~** *vi* «*vehicle*» volcar*; **~weight** /'əʊvər'weɪt ‖,əʊvə'weɪt/ *adj* ⟨*person*⟩ demasiado gordo; **I am 10lb ~weight** peso 10 libras de más, tengo un sobrepeso de 10 libras (Chi, Méx)

overwhelm /'əʊvər'hwelm ‖,əʊvə'welm/ *vt* **(a)** (emotionally) abrumar **(b)** (defeat) aplastar **(c)** (swamp): **they've been ~ed with applications/ complaints** han recibido infinidad de solicitudes/ quejas

overwhelming /'əʊvər'hwelmɪŋ ‖,əʊvə'welmɪŋ/ *adj* ⟨*grief*⟩ inconsolable; ⟨*urge*⟩ irresistible; ⟨*anger*⟩ incontenible; ⟨*boredom*⟩ insoportable; ⟨*defeat*⟩ aplastante

overwind /'əʊvər'waɪnd ‖,əʊvə'waɪnd/ *vt* (*past & past p* **-wound** /-waʊnd/) dar* demasiada cuerda a

overwork¹ /'əʊvər'wɜːrk ‖,əʊvə'wɜːk/ *vt* hacer* trabajar demasiado

overwork² *n* agotamiento *m*

ovulate /'ɑːvjəleɪt ‖'ɒvjʊleɪt/ *vi* ovular

ovulation /'ɑːvjə'leɪʃən ‖,ɒvjʊ'leɪʃən/ *n* ovulación *f*

owe /əʊ/ *vt* my/her/your *etc* **~:** to **~** sb sth, **~** sth to sb deberle algo a algn **(b)** (be obliged to give, do) ⟨*explanation/apology/favor*⟩ deber

owing /'əʊɪŋ/ *adj* [1] (*pred*): **the money still ~** el dinero que aún se debe [2] **owing to** (*as prep*) debido a

owl /aʊl/ *n* búho *m*, tecolote *m* (Méx); (barn **~**) lechuza *f*

own¹ /əʊn/ *vt* ⟨*property*⟩ tener*
■ **own up** [*v + adv*]: **no one ~ed up** nadie reconoció tener la culpa; **no one would ~ up to having left the window open** nadie quiso reconocer que había sido quien dejó la ventana abierta

own² *adj* my/her/your *etc* **~:** in our **~** house en nuestra propia casa; **she makes her ~ clothes** se hace la ropa ella misma

own³ *pron* my/her/your *etc* **~:** it isn't a company car, it's her **~** no es un coche de la empresa, es suyo (propio); **she wanted a room of her ~** quería una habitación para ella sola; **on one's ~** solo; **to get one's ~ back** (BrE colloq) desquitarse

owner ?/'əʊnər ‖'əʊnə(r)/ *n* (of house, car) dueño, -ña *m,f*, propietario, -ria *m,f*; (of pet) dueño, -ña *m,f*

ownership /'əʊnərʃɪp ‖'əʊnəʃɪp/ *n* propiedad *f*

own goal *n* autogol *m*, gol *m* en contra (CS)

ox /ɑːks ‖ɒks/ *n* (*pl* **oxen**) buey *m*

oxen /'ɑːksən ‖'ɒksən/ *pl of* ox

oxide /'ɑːksaɪd ‖'ɒksaɪd/ *n* óxido *m*

oxtail /'ɑːksteɪl ‖'ɒksteɪl/ *n* rabo *m* de buey

oxygen /'ɑːksədʒən ‖'ɒksɪdʒən/ *n* oxígeno *m*; (*before n*) **~ mask** (Aviat, Med) mascarilla *f* de oxígeno

oyster /'ɔɪstər ‖'ɔɪstə(r)/ *n* ostra *f*, ostión *m* (Méx)

oz = **ounce(s)**

ozone /'əʊzəʊn/ *n* (Chem) ozono *m*; (*before n*) **the ~ layer** la capa de ozono

● ●

Pp

● ●

P, p /piː/ *n* P, p *f*

p (in UK) (= **penny/pence**) penique(s) *m*(*pl*)

p. (*pl* **pp.**) (= **page**) pág., p.; **pp. 12-48** págs. 12 a 48

pa¹ /pɑː/ *n* (colloq) papá *m*

pa², p.a. /'piː'eɪ/ = **per annum**

PA *n* **(a)** /'piː'eɪ/ **~ (system)** = **public- address system (b)** /piː'eɪ/ (BrE) = **personal assistant (c)** *also* **Pa** = **Pennsylvania**

pace¹ /peɪs/ *n* [1] (stride) paso *m*; **to put sb through her/his ~s** poner* a algn a prueba [2] (speed) (*no pl*) ritmo *m*; **to keep ~ with sb** ···⊱

seguirle* el ritmo lento a algn; **to set the ~**
marcar* la pauta

pace² /peɪs/ *vi:* **to ~ up and down** caminar *or* (esp
Esp) andar de un lado para otro

pace: **~maker** *n* (Sport) liebre *f*; (Med)
marcapasos *m*; **~setter** /'peɪsˌsetə(r)
‖'peɪsˌsetə(r)/ *n* (Sport) liebre *f*; (pioneer) líder *mf*

Pacific /pə'sɪfɪk/ *n* **the ~** (Ocean) el (Océano)
Pacífico

pacifier /'pæsɪfaɪər ‖'pæsɪfaɪə(r)/ *n* (AmE)
chupete *m*, chupón *m* (AmL exc CS), chupo *m*
(Col), chupa *f* (Ven)

pacifism /'pæsəfɪzəm ‖'pæsɪfɪzəm/ *n* pacifismo
m

pacifist /'pæsəfəst ‖'pæsɪfɪst/ *n* pacifista *mf*

pacify /'pæsəfaɪ ‖'pæsɪfaɪ/ *vt* **-fies, -fying,**
-fied **(a)** (calm, satisfy) apaciguar* **(b)** (restore to
peace) pacificar*

pack¹ /pæk/ *n* **1** (bundle, load) fardo *m*;
(rucksack) mochila *f* **2** **(a)** (package) paquete *m*;
(of cigarettes) paquete *m*, cajetilla *f* **(b)** (of cards)
(BrE) baraja *f*, mazo *m* (esp AmL) **3** **(a)** (of wolves)
manada *f*; **a ~ of hounds** (Sport) una jauría **(b)** (in
race) pelotón *m* **4** (of thieves, fools) (pej) partida *f*
(pey); **a ~ of lies** una sarta de mentiras

pack² *vt* **1** **(a)** (Busn) ‹goods/products› (put into
container) envasar; (make packets with) empaquetar;
(for transport) embalar **(b)** (put into suitcase, bag):
have you ~ed your toothbrush? ¿llevas el cepillo
de dientes?; **to ~ one's suitcase** hacer* la maleta
or (RPl) la valija, empacar (AmL); **she takes a ~ed**
lunch to work se lleva el almuerzo *or* (esp Esp,
Méx) la comida al trabajo
  2 **(a)** (press tightly together): **~ the soil** (down)
firmly apisone bien la tierra **(b)** (cram): **the book**
is ~ed with useful information el libro está lleno
de información útil; **we ~ed a lot into a short**
time hicimos un montón de cosas en poco tiempo
fam
  ■ ~ *vi* (fill suitcase) hacer* la(s) maleta(s) *or* (RPl)
la(s) valija(s), empacar* (AmL)
  ■ **pack in** [*v + o + adv, v + adv + o*] **1** (quit)
(colloq) ‹job/course› dejar
  2 (cram in): **we managed to ~ in 50 people**
pudimos meter a 50 personas
  ■ **pack off** [*v + o + adv, v + adv + o*] despachar,
mandar; **she ~ed the children off to school**
mandó a los niños al colegio
  ■ **pack up** **1** [*v + adv*] **(a)** (assemble belongings)
liar* el petate, hacer* su itacate (Méx) **(b)** (stop)
(colloq): **let's ~ up for the day** dejémoslo por hoy
(c) (break down) (colloq) ‹motor/radio› dejar de
funcionar, descomponerse* (esp AmL), tronarse*
(Méx fam)
  2 [*v + o + adv, v + adv + o*] **(a)** ‹tools/
belongings› recoger* **(b)** ▶ PACK IN 1

package /'pækɪdʒ/ *n* paquete *m*

package: **~ holiday** (BrE) ▶ ~ VACATION; **~**
store *n* (AmE) tienda *f* de bebidas alcohólicas; **~**
tour *n* viaje *m* organizado (*en el que se recorren*
diferentes localidades); **~ vacation** *n* (AmE)
vacaciones *fpl* organizadas

packaging /'pækɪdʒɪŋ/ *n* **(a)** (packing)
embalaje *m* **(b)** (wrapping) envoltorio *m* **(c)**
(Marketing) presentación *f*

packed /pækt/ *adj* ‹hall/restaurant› lleno de
gente, repleto

packet /'pækət ‖'pækɪt/ *n* (esp BrE) paquete *m*;
(*before n*) ‹soup/cake mix› de sobre

packing /'pækɪŋ/ *n* **(a)** (of suitcase): **to do one's**
~ hacer* la(s) maleta(s) *or* (RPl) la(s) valija(s),
empacar* (AmL) **(b)** (in factory) embalaje *m*

packing case *n* caja *f* de embalaje

pact /pækt/ *n* pacto *m*

pad¹ /pæd/ *n* **1** (cushioning) almohadilla *f*;
shoulder ~s hombreras *fpl*; **knee ~s** rodilleras
fpl **2** (of paper) bloc *m*

pad² *vt* **-dd-** **1** **(a)** (line) ‹seat/panel› acolchar,
enguatar (Esp) **(b)** **padded** *past p* ‹jacket›
acolchado, enguatado (Esp); ‹bra› con relleno;
‹envelope› acolchado; **~ded cell** celda *f* de
aislamiento **2** **~** (out) ‹essay› rellenar, meter*
paja en (fam)

padding /'pædɪŋ/ *n* (material) relleno *m*, guata *f*
(Esp); (for protection) almohadillas *fpl*

paddle¹ /'pædl/ *n* **1** (oar) zagual *m*, pala *f*
2 (*no pl*): **to go for a ~** ir* a mojarse los pies

paddle² *vi* **1** (wet feet) mojarse los pies (*en la*
orilla) **2** **(a)** (in canoe) remar (*con pala or*
zagual) **(b)** (swim) ‹‹duck/dog›› chapotear
  ■ ~ *vt* ‹boat/canoe› llevar (*remando con pala or*
zagual)

paddling pool /'pædlɪŋ/ *n* (BrE) (in park)
estanque *m*; (inflatable) piscina *f or* (Méx) alberca *f*
inflable (*para niños*)

paddock /'pædək/ *n* prado *m*

paddy /'pædi/ *n* (*pl* **-dies**) **~** (field) arrozal *m*

padlock¹ /'pædlɑːk ‖'pædlɒk/ *n* candado *m*

padlock² *vt* cerrar* con candado

paediatric *etc* (BrE) ▶ PEDIATRIC *etc*

paedophile *n* (BrE) ▶ PEDOPHILE

pagan¹ /'peɪɡən/ *n* pagano, -na *m,f*

pagan² *adj* pagano

page¹ /peɪdʒ/ *n* **1** (of book, newspaper) página *f*;
on ~ four en la página cuatro **2** (attendant) paje
m; (in hotel) botones *m*

page² *vt* (over loudspeaker) llamar por megafonía;
(by beeper) llamar por buscapersonas *or* (Méx) bip
or (Chi) bíper

pageant /'pædʒənt/ *n* **(a)** (show, ceremony)
festividades *fpl* **(b)** (historical show) espectáculo
histórico al aire libre

pageboy /'peɪdʒbɔɪ/ *n* ▶ PAGE¹ 2

pager /'peɪdʒər ‖'peɪdʒə(r)/ *n* buscapersonas *m*,
bip *m* (Méx), bíper *m* (Chi)

paid¹ /peɪd/ *past & past p of* PAY¹

paid² *adj* ‹employment› remunerado; ‹worker›
asalariado; ‹vacation› pagado; ‹leave› con goce de
sueldo

pail /peɪl/ *n* balde *m*, cubo *m* (Esp), cubeta *f*
(Méx)

pain /peɪn/ *n* **1** **(a)** (physical) dolor *m*; **she was**
in great ~ estaba muy dolorida *or* (AmL tb)
adolorida; **to be a ~ in the neck** ser* un pesado
(b) (annoying person or thing) (colloq) lata *f* (fam)
  2 **pains** *pl* (effort): **that's all you get for your ~s**
así te pagan la molestia; **I went to great ~s to**
explain it to them carefully puse mucho esmero
en explicárselo

painful /'peɪnfəl/ *adj* **(a)** (physically) doloroso; **it's**
very ~ duele mucho **(b)** (mentally) ‹task›
desagradable; ‹reminder› doloroso

painfully /'peɪnfəli/ *adv*: she dragged herself ~ along se iba arrastrando con mucho dolor; **she's ~ shy** es tan tímida que da pena

painkiller /'peɪnˌkɪlər ‖'peɪnˌkɪlə(r)/ *n* analgésico *m*

painless /'peɪnləs ‖'peɪnlɪs/ *adj* **(a)** (causing no pain) indoloro; **~ childbirth** parto *m* sin dolor **(b)** (easy, pleasant) (colloq) ⟨*method*⟩ sencillo

painstaking /'peɪnzˌteɪkɪŋ/ *adj* ⟨*research/efforts*⟩ concienzudo; ⟨*person/personality*⟩ meticuloso

paint¹ /peɪnt/ *n* pintura *f*

paint² *vt/i* pintar

paint: ~box *n* caja *f* de acuarelas; **~brush** *n* pincel *m*; (large, for walls) brocha *f*

painter /'peɪntər ‖'peɪntə(r)/ *n* (Art, Const) pintor, -tora *m,f*

painting /'peɪntɪŋ/ *n* **(a)** (picture) cuadro *m*, pintura *f* **(b)** (Art) pintura *f*

paintwork /'peɪntwɜːrk ‖'peɪntwɜːk/ *n* pintura *f*

pair /per ‖peə(r)/ *n* **1** **(a)** (of shoes, socks, gloves) par *m*; **a ~ of trousers** unos pantalones; **a ~ of scissors** unas tijeras **(b)** (in cards) pareja *f*, par *m* **2** (couple) pareja *f*
■ **pair up** [*v + adv*] formar parejas

pajamas, (BrE) **pyjamas** /pə'dʒɑːməz/ *pl n* pijama *m*, piyama *m or f* (AmL)

Pakistan /'pækɪˌstæn ‖,pɑːkɪ'stɑːn, ,pækɪ-/ *n* Pakistán *m*, Paquistán *m*

Pakistani¹ /'pækɪˈstæni ‖,pɑːkɪ'stɑːnɪ, ,pækɪ-/ *adj* pakistaní, paquistaní

Pakistani² *n* pakistaní *mf*, paquistaní *mf*

pal /pæl/ *n* (colloq) amigo *m*, compinche *m* (fam), cuate *m* (Méx fam)

palace /'pæləs ‖'pælɪs/ *n* palacio *m*

palatable /'pælətəbəl/ *adj* agradable

palate /'pælət/ *n* paladar *m*

pale¹ /peɪl/ *adj* **(a)** ⟨*skin/person*⟩ (naturally) blanco; (pallid) pálido **(b)** ⟨*blue/pink*⟩ pálido

pale² *vi* **(a)** «*person*» palidecer* **(b)** (seem minor) **to ~ BESIDE** *o* **BEFORE sb/sth** palidecer* JUNTO A algn/algo

pale³ *n*: **to be beyond the ~** ser* intolerable

Palestine /'pæləstaɪn/ *n* Palestina *f*

Palestinian¹ /'pælə'stɪnɪən/ *adj* palestino

Palestinian² *n* palestino, -na *m,f*

palette /'pælət ‖'pælɪt/ *n* paleta *f*

pall¹ /pɔːl/ *n*: **to cast a ~ on** *o* **over sth** empañar algo

pall² *vi* hacerse* pesado

pallid /'pæləd ‖'pælɪd/ *adj* pálido

palm /pɑːm/ *n* **1** **(a)** **(~ tree)** palmera *f* **(b)** (leaf, branch) palma *f* **2** (Anat) palma *f*
■ **palm off** [*v + o + adv*] **to ~ sth off ON** *o* **ONTO sb** encajarle algo a algn (fam); **to ~ sb off WITH sth** quitarse a algn de encima CON algo

palmistry /'pɑːməstri ‖'pɑːmɪstri/ *n* quiromancia *f*

Palm Sunday *n* Domingo *m* de Ramos

palpable /'pælpəbəl/ *adj* (frml) palmario, palpable

palpitate /'pælpəteɪt ‖'pælpɪteɪt/ *vi* palpitar

palpitation /'pælpə'teɪʃən ‖,pælpɪ'teɪʃən/ *n* (Med) palpitación *f*

paltry /'pɔːltri/ *adj* **-trier -triest** ⟨*sum/amount*⟩ mísero; ⟨*excuse*⟩ malo

pamper /'pæmpər ‖'pæmpə(r)/ *vt* mimar

pamphlet /'pæmflət ‖'pæmflɪt/ *n* (informative) folleto *m*; (political) panfleto *m*

pan¹ /pæn/ *n* **1** (Culin) cacerola *f*; (large, with two handles) olla *f*; (small) cacerola *f*, cazo *m* (Esp); (frying ~) sartén *f* **2** (of toilet) (BrE) taza *f*

pan² *vi* **-nn-** **1** (Min): **to ~ for gold** lavar oro **2** (Cin): **the camera ~s across to the two figures** la cámara recorre hasta enfocar en las dos figuras

panacea /'pænə'siːə/ *n* (frml) panacea *f*

panache /pə'næʃ/ *n* garbo *m*

Panama /'pænəmɑː/ *n* Panamá *m*; (before n) **the ~ Canal** el Canal de Panamá

Panamanian¹ /'pænə'meɪnɪən/ *adj* panameño

Panamanian² *n* panameño, -ña *m,f*

pancake /'pænkeɪk/ *n* (Culin) crep(e) *m*, panqueque *m* (AmL), crepa *f* (Méx), panqué *m* (AmC, Col), panqueca *f* (Ven)

pancreas /'pæŋkrɪəs/ *n* páncreas *m*

panda /'pændə/ *n* (oso, osa *m,f*) panda *mf*

pandemonium /'pændə'məʊnɪəm/ *n* pandemonio *m*, pandemónium *m*

pander /'pændər ‖'pændə(r)/ *vi*: **to ~ to sb's whims** consentirle* los caprichos a algn

pane /peɪn/ *n* (hoja *f* de) vidrio *m*, cristal *m* (Esp)

panel¹ /'pænl/ *n* **1** **(a)** (of door, car body, plane wing) panel *m*; (of garment) pieza *f* **(b)** (instrument ~) tablero *m* (de instrumentos); (control ~) tablero *m* (de control) **2** (in discussion, interview) panel *m or* (Col, Ven) pánel *m*; (in quiz, contest) equipo *m*; (in exam) mesa *f*, comisión *f* (Chi)

panel² *vt*, (BrE) **-ll-** **(a)** ⟨*room/wall*⟩ revestir* con paneles **(b) paneled**, (BrE) **panelled** *past p* ⟨*door*⟩ de paneles

pang /pæŋ/ *n* punzada *f*, **~s of hunger** retorcijones *mpl or* (Esp) retortijones *mpl* de hambre

panhandler /'pænˌhændlər ‖'pænˌhændlə(r)/ *n* (AmE colloq) mendigo *m*

panic¹ /'pænɪk/ *n* (fear, anxiety) pánico *m*; (before n) **~ button** botón *m* de alarma

panic² *vi* **-ck-** dejarse llevar por el pánico; **don't ~!** ¡tranquilo!

panicky /'pæniki/ *adj* ⟨*person*⟩ muy nervioso; ⟨*behavior/decision*⟩ precipitado

panic-stricken /'pænɪkˌstrɪkən/ *adj* aterrorizado

pannier /'pænɪər ‖'pænɪə(r)/ *n* alforja *f*; (on cycle) maletero *m*

panorama /'pænə'ræmə ‖,pænə'rɑːmə/ *n* panorama *m*

panoramic /'pænə'ræmɪk/ *adj* panorámico

pansy /'pænzi/ *n* (*pl* **-sies**) (Bot) pensamiento *m*

pant¹ /pænt/ *vi* jadear

pant² *n* jadeo *m*; *see also* PANTS

pantheon /'pænθiːɑːn ‖'pænθɪən/ *n* panteón *m*

panther /'pænθər ‖'pænθə(r)/ *n* pantera *f*

panties /'pæntiz/ *pl n* calzones *mpl* (AmL), bragas *fpl* (Esp), pantaletas *fpl* (Méx, Ven), bombacha *f* (RPl), calzoneta *f* (AmC)

pantihose /'pæntihəʊz/ *pl n* ▶ PANTYHOSE

pantomime /'pæntəmaɪm/ *n* **(a)** (mime) pantomima *f* **(b)** (in UK) *comedia musical navideña, basada en cuentos de hadas*

pantry /'pæntri/ *n* (*pl* **-tries**) despensa *f*

pants /pænts/ *pl n* **1** (trousers) (AmE) pantalón *m*, pantalones *mpl* **2** (underwear) (BrE) **(a)** (men's) calzoncillos *mpl*, calzones *mpl* (Méx), interiores *mpl* (Col, Ven) **(b)** (women's) ▶ PANTIES

pantsuit /'pæntsuːt/, **pants suit** *n* (AmE) traje *m* pantalón

pantyhose /'pæntihəʊz/ *pl n* (AmE) medias *fpl*, pantimedias *fpl*, medias *fpl* bombacha (RPl) *or* (Col) pantalón *or* (Ven) panty

papa *n* **(a)** /'pɑːpə/ (AmE) papá *m* **(b)** /pə'pɑː/ (BrE dated) padre *m* (ant)

paper¹ /'peɪpər ‖ 'peɪpə(r)/ *n* **1 (a)** (material) papel *m*; (*before n*) ⟨*towel/handkerchief/bag*⟩ de papel **(b)** (wrapper) (esp BrE) envoltorio *m* **2** (newspaper) diario *m*, periódico *m* **3** (for journal) trabajo *m*; (at conference) ponencia *f* **4** (exam ∼) (BrE) examen *m*; (part) parte *f* **5 papers** *pl* (documents) documentos *mpl*

paper² *vt* ⟨*wall/room*⟩ empapelar *or* (Méx tb) tapizar*

paper: ∼**back** *n* libro *m* en rústica *or* (Méx) de pasta blanda; ∼**clip** *n* clip *m*, sujetapapeles *m*; ∼**weight** *n* pisapapeles *m*; ∼**work** *n* papeleo *m* (fam), trabajo *m* administrativo

paprika /pə'priːkə ‖ 'pæprɪkə/ *n* pimentón *m* dulce, paprika *f*

Pap smear, Pap test /pæp/ *n* (AmE) citología *f*, frotis *m*, Papanicolau *m* (AmL)

Papua New Guinea /'pɑːpuə ‖ 'pæpjʊə/ *n* Papua Nueva Guinea *f*

papyrus /pə'paɪrəs/ *n* (*pl* **-ruses** *or* **-ri** /-raɪ/) papiro *m*

par /pɑːr ‖ pɑː(r)/ *n* **1 (a)** (equal level) **on a ∼: the two athletes are on a ∼** los dos atletas son del mismo nivel; **this puts us on a ∼ with workers in other countries** esto nos pone en igualdad de condiciones con los trabajadores de otros países **(b)** (accepted standard): **your work is below** *o* **not up to ∼** tu trabajo no está a la altura de lo que se esperaba; **to feel below** *o* **under∼** no sentirse* del todo bien **2** (in golf) par *m*

parable /'pærəbəl/ *n* parábola *f*

parachute¹ /'pærəʃuːt/ *n* paracaídas *m*

parachute² *vi* saltar en *or* con paracaídas

parachutist /'pærəʃuːtəst ‖ 'pærəʃuːtɪst/ *n* paracaidista *mf*

parade¹ /pə'reɪd/ *n* **(a)** (procession) desfile *m* **(b)** (assembly) (Mil) formación *f*

parade² *vt* **(a)** (display) ⟨*wealth*⟩ hacer* ostentación de **(b)** (march, walk) ⟨*streets*⟩ desfilar por **(c)** (assemble) ⟨*troops*⟩ hacer* formar ■ ∼ *vi* **(a)** (march, walk) desfilar **(b)** (assemble) (Mil) formar

paradise /'pærədaɪs/ *n* **(a)** (heaven) paraíso *m* **(b) Paradise** (Garden of Eden) Paraíso *m* (Terrenal)

paradox /'pærədɑːks ‖ 'pærədɒks/ *n* paradoja *f*

paraffin /'pærəfən ‖ 'pærəfɪn/ *n* **(a)** ∼ **(wax)** parafina *f* **(b)** ∼ **(oil)** (BrE) queroseno *m*, kerosene *m*, parafina *f* (Chi)

paragliding /'pærə,glaɪdɪŋ/ *n* parapente *m*

paragon /'pærəgɑːn ‖ 'pærəgən/ *n*: **a ∼ of virtue** (set phrase) un dechado de virtudes (fr hecha)

paragraph /'pærəgræf/ *n* párrafo *m*

Paraguay /'pærəgwaɪ/ *n* Paraguay *m*

Paraguayan¹ /'pærə'gwaɪən/ *adj* paraguayo

Paraguayan² *n* paraguayo, -ya *m,f*

parallel¹ /'pærələl/ *adj* paralelo

parallel² *n* **1** (Math) (line) paralela *f* **2** (similarity) paralelismo *m*, paralelo *m*; **without ∼** sin parangón

parallel³ *vt* **-l-** *or* (BrE also) **-ll-** (frml) ser* análogo *or* paralelo a

parallel bars *pl n* (barras *fpl*) paralelas *fpl*

Paralympics /,pærə'lɪmpɪks/ *pl n* **the ∼** los Juegos Paralímpicos

paralysis /pə'ræləsəs ‖ pə'ræləsɪs/ *n* (*pl* **-ses** /-siːz/) (Med) parálisis *f*

paralyze /'pærəlaɪz/ *vt* paralizar*

paramedic /'pærə'medɪk/ *n*: *profesional conectado con la medicina, como enfermero, kinesiólogo etc*

parameter /pə'ræmətər/ *n* parámetro *m*

paramilitary /'pærə'mɪləteri ‖ ,pærə'mɪlɪtəri/ *adj* paramilitar

paramount /'pærəmaʊnt/ *adj* (frml) primordial

paranoia /'pærə'nɔɪə/ *n* paranoia *f*

paranoid /'pærənɔɪd/ *adj* paranoico

parapet /'pærəpət ‖ 'pærəpɪt/ *n* parapeto *m*

paraphernalia /'pærəfər'neɪljə ‖ ,pærəfə'neɪljə/ *n* parafernalia *f*

paraphrase /'pærəfreɪz/ *vt* parafrasear

paraplegic /,pærə'pliːdʒɪk/ *n* parapléjico, -ca *m,f*

parasailing /'pærəseɪlɪŋ/ *n* parasailing *m*

parasite /'pærəsaɪt/ *n* parásito *m*

parasol /'pærəsɔːl ‖ 'pærəsɒl/ *n* sombrilla *f*, quitasol *m*

paratrooper /'pærə,truːpər ‖ 'pærə,truːpə(r)/ *n* (Mil) paracaidista *mf* (*del ejército*)

parcel /'pɑːrsəl ‖ 'pɑːsəl/ *n* (BrE) paquete *m*

parched /pɑːrtʃt ‖ pɑːtʃt/ *adj* **(a)** (very dry) reseco **(b)** (very thirsty) (colloq) ⟨*pred*⟩ muerto de sed (fam)

parchment /'pɑːrtʃmənt ‖ 'pɑːtʃmənt/ *n* pergamino *m*

pardon¹ /'pɑːrdn ‖ 'pɑːdn/ *n* **1 (a)** (forgiveness) perdón *m* **(b)** (*as interj*): ∼? *o* (frml) **I beg your ∼?** (requesting repetition) ¿cómo?, ¿mande? (Méx); **I beg your ∼** (apologizing) perdón **2** (Law) indulto *m*

pardon² *vt* **1** (forgive) perdonar; ∼ **me!** (apologizing) ¡perdón!; ∼ **me?** (requesting repetition) (esp AmE) ¿cómo? **2** (Law) ⟨*offender*⟩ indultar

pare /per ‖ peə(r)/ *vt* **(a)** (peel) pelar **(b)** ⟨*nails*⟩ cortar

■ **pare down** [v + o + adv, v + adv + o] reducir*

parent /'perənt ‖'peərənt/ n: **my/his** ∼s mis/sus padres; **the responsibility of being a** ∼ las responsabilidades que conlleva el ser padre/madre; (before n) ∼ **company** sociedad f matriz

parental /pə'rentl/ adj de los padres

parenthesis /pə'renθəsəs ‖pə'renθəsɪs/ n (pl **-theses** /-θəsi:z/) paréntesis m; **in parentheses** entre paréntesis

parenthood /'perənthʊd ‖'peərənthʊd/ n el ser padre/madre

parenting /'perəntɪŋ ‖'peərəntɪŋ/ n crianza f de los hijos

Paris /'pærəs ‖'pærɪs/ n París m

parish /'pærɪʃ/ n 1 (Relig) parroquia f; (before n) ∼ **church** parroquia f, iglesia f parroquial 2 (Govt) distrito m

parishioner /pə'rɪʃənər ‖pə'rɪʃənə(r)/ n feligrés, -gresa m,f (de una parroquia)

Parisian /pə'rɪʒən ‖pə'rɪzɪən/ n parisino, -na m,f, parisiense mf, parisién mf

parity /'pærəti/ n(equality) (fml) igualdad f, paridad f

park¹ /pɑːrk ‖pɑːk/ n parque m; (before n) ∼ **bench** banco m or (Méx) banca f (de plaza)

park² vt ⟨car⟩ estacionar (esp AmL), aparcar* (Esp), parquear (AmL)
■ ∼ vi (Auto) estacionar (esp AmL), aparcar* (Esp), parquear (AmL), estacionarse (Chi, Méx)

parking /'pɑːrkɪŋ ‖'pɑːkɪŋ/ n estacionamiento m (esp AmL), aparcamiento m (Esp); ⊖ **no parking** prohibido estacionar (esp AmL) or (Esp) aparcar or (AmL) parquear; (before n) **a** ∼ **space** un lugar para estacionar (or aparcar etc); ∼ **ticket** multa f (por estacionamiento indebido)

parking: ∼ **garage** n (AmE) estacionamiento m (esp AmL), aparcamiento m (Esp), parking m (Esp); ∼ **lot** n (AmE) estacionamiento m (esp AmL), aparcamiento m (Esp), parking m (Esp), parqueadero m (Col); ∼ **meter** n parquímetro m

Parkinson's Disease /'pɑːrkɪnsənz ‖'pɑːkɪnsənz/ n enfermedad f de Parkinson, Parkinson m

parkway /'pɑːrkweɪ ‖'pɑːkweɪ/ n (AmE) carretera f/avenida f ajardinada

parliament /'pɑːrləmənt ‖'pɑːləmənt/ n (a) (assembly) parlamento m (b) **Parliament** (in UK etc) Parlamento m

parliamentary /ˌpɑːrlə'mentəri ‖ˌpɑːlə'mentri/ adj parlamentario

parlor, (BrE) **parlour** /'pɑːrlər ‖'pɑːlə(r)/ n 1 (dated in BrE) (in house) salón m (esp Esp), sala f (de estar) 2 (for business) (AmE) sala f; **ice-cream** ∼ heladería f

Parmesan (cheese) /'pɑːrməzɑːn ‖'pɑːmɪzæn/ n (queso m) parmesano m

parochial /pə'rəʊkɪəl/ adj (a) (pej) ⟨person/attitude/outlook⟩ provinciano (b) (Relig) parroquial

parody¹ /'pærədi/ n (pl **-dies**) parodia f

parody² vt **-dies, -dying, -died** parodiar

parole /pə'rəʊl/ n libertad f condicional

paroxysm /'pærəksɪzəm/ n (Med) paroxismo m; **the news sent them into** ∼s **of laughter** la noticia los hizo desternillarse de risa

parquet /pɑːr'keɪ ‖'pɑːkeɪ/ n 1 (Const) parqué m, parquet m 2 (AmE Theat) platea f

parrot /'pærət/ n loro m, papagayo m

parry /'pæri/ vt **-ries, -rying, -ried** ⟨blow/thrust⟩ parar; ⟨attack⟩ rechazar*; ⟨question⟩ eludir

parsley /'pɑːrsli ‖'pɑːsli/ n perejil m

parsnip /'pɑːrsnəp ‖'pɑːsnɪp/ n chirivía f, pastinaca f

parson /'pɑːrsn ‖'pɑːsn/ n clérigo m; (vicar) ≈(cura m) párroco m

part¹ /pɑːrt ‖pɑːt/ n 1 (a) (section) parte f (b) (in phrases) **in part** en parte; **for the most part** en su mayor parte; **for my part** por mi parte, por mi lado 2 (component) pieza f; (spare ∼) repuesto m or (Méx) refacción f 3 (a) (in play) papel m (b) (role, share) papel m; **she had** o **played a major** ∼ **in ...** tuvo or desempeñó un papel fundamental en ...; **to take** ∼ **in sth** tomar parte en algo 4 (episode of TV, radio serial) episodio m; (Publ) fascículo m 5 (Mus) (vocal, instrumental line) parte f 6 (in hair) (AmE) raya f, carrera f (Col, Ven), partidura f (Chi) 7 **parts** pl (area): **in/around these** ∼s por aquí; **in foreign** ∼s en el extranjero

part² vt (separate) separar
■ ∼ vi (a) (separate) «lovers» separarse; **they** ∼ed **on bad terms** quedaron disgustados (b) «curtains/lips» (open up) abrirse*
■ **part with** [v + prep + o] desprenderse de

part³ adv en parte

part⁴ adj (before n) ⟨payment⟩ parcial

part exchange n (esp BrE): **in** ∼ ∼ a cuenta or como parte del pago

partial /'pɑːrʃəl ‖'pɑːʃəl/ adj 1 (not complete) parcial 2 (a) (fond) (pred) **to be** ∼ **TO sth** tener* debilidad POR algo (b) (biased) (fml) parcial

partially /'pɑːrʃəli ‖'pɑːʃəli/ adv (a) (partly) parcialmente (b) (with bias) con parcialidad

participant /pər'tɪsəpənt, pɑːr- ‖pɑː'tɪsɪpənt/ n participante mf

participate /pər'tɪsəpeɪt, pɑːr- ‖pɑː'tɪsɪpeɪt/ vi **to** ∼ (IN sth) participar (EN algo)

participation /pərˌtɪsə'peɪʃən, pɑːr- ‖pɑːˌtɪsɪ'peɪʃən/ n participación f

participle /'pɑːrtəsɪpəl ‖'pɑːtɪsɪpəl/ n participio m

particle /'pɑːrtɪkəl ‖'pɑːtɪkəl/ n partícula f

particular¹ /pər'tɪkjələr ‖pə'tɪkjʊlə(r)/ adj 1 (specific, precise): **this** ∼ **one** este en especial; **is there any** ∼ **style you'd prefer?** ¿tiene preferencia por algún estilo determinado?; **for no** ∼ **reason** por nada en especial 2 (special) ⟨interest/concern⟩ especial 3 (fastidious) (pred) **to be** ∼ (ABOUT sth): **she's very** ∼ **about what she eats** es muy especial con la comida

particular² n (a) (detail) (fml) (usu pl) detalle m 2 **in particular** en particular

particularly /pər'tɪkjələrli ‖pə'tɪkjʊləli/ adv (a) (specifically) específicamente (b) (especially) particularmente

p

parting¹ /'pɑːtɪŋ ‖'pɑːtɪŋ/ *n* **1** (separation)
despedida *f* **2** (in hair) (BrE) raya *f*, carrera *f* (Col,
Ven), partidura *f* (Chi)

parting² *adj* (*before n*) ⟨*kiss/words*⟩ de
despedida

partisan¹ /'pɑːtəzən ‖'pɑːtɪzæn/ *n* **(a)**
(guerrilla) partisano, -na *m,f* **(b)** (supporter)
partidario, -ria *m,f*

partisan² *adj* ⟨*crowd/decision*⟩ partidista

partition¹ /pər'tɪʃən, pɑː- ‖pɑː'tɪʃən/ *n* **1**
(a) (screen) tabique *m*; **a glass ∼** una mampara
de vidrio *or* (Esp) de cristal **(b)** (divider) separador
m **2** (of country, territory) división *f*

partition² *vt* **(a)** ⟨*country/territory*⟩ dividir **(b)**
⟨*room*⟩ dividir con un tabique/con una mampara

partly /'pɑːtli ‖'pɑːtli/ *adv* en parte

partner¹ /'pɑːtnər ‖'pɑːtnə(r)/ *n* **(a)** (in an
activity) compañero, -ra *m,f*; (in dancing, tennis)
pareja *f* **(b)** (Busn) socio, -cia *m,f*; **∼s in crime**
cómplices *mpl or fpl* **(c)** (in personal relationship)
pareja *f*, compañero, -ra *m,f*

partner² *vt* bailar (*or* jugar* etc) en pareja con

partnership /'pɑːtnərʃɪp ‖'pɑːtnəʃɪp/ *n* **(a)**
(relationship) asociación *f* **(b)** (Busn) sociedad *f*
(colectiva)

part of speech *n* (*pl* ∼**s** ⟨∼⟩) categoría *f*
gramatical

partridge /'pɑːtrɪdʒ ‖'pɑːtrɪdʒ/ *n* (*pl* ∼**s** *or*
∼) perdiz *f*

part-time¹ /'pɑːtaɪm ‖,pɑːt'taɪm/ *adj* de
medio tiempo (AmL), a tiempo parcial (Esp)

part-time² *adv* de medio tiempo (AmL), a
tiempo parcial (Esp)

party¹ /'pɑːti ‖'pɑːti/ *n* **1** (event) fiesta *f*; **I was
invited to a tea ∼** me invitaron a un té **2** (Pol)
partido *m* **3** (group) grupo *m*; (in hunting) partida *f*
4 (person or body involved) parte *f*; **the guilty/
innocent ∼** el culpable/inocente

party² *vi* (*esp* AmE colloq) (go to parties) ir* a
fiestas; (have fun) divertirse*

party line *n* (Pol) **the ∼ ∼** la línea del partido

pass¹ /pæs ‖pɑːs/ *n* **1** (document, permit) pase *m*;
(ticket) abono *m* **2** (Geog) paso *m*; (narrow)
desfiladero *m* **3** (in test, examination) (BrE)
aprobado *m* **4** (Sport) pase *m* **5** (sexual advance):
to make a ∼ at sb intentar besar a algn

pass² *vt*
I 1 (a) (go by, past) ⟨*shop/house*⟩ pasar por; **I
∼ed him in the street** me crucé con él en la calle
(b) (overtake) pasar, rebasar (Méx)
2 (a) (cross, go beyond) ⟨*limit*⟩ pasar; ⟨*frontier*⟩
pasar, cruzar* **(b)** (surpass) sobrepasar
3 (spend) ⟨*time*⟩ pasar; **to ∼ the time** pasar el
rato
II (a) (convey, hand over) **to ∼ sb sth**, **to ∼ sth TO
sb** pasarle algo a algn **(b)** (Sport) ⟨*ball*⟩ pasar
III (a) (succeed in) ⟨*exam/test*⟩ aprobar*, salvar
(Ur) **(b)** (approve) ⟨*candidate/work*⟩ aprobar* **(c)**
⟨*law/motion*⟩ aprobar*

∼ *vi*
I 1 (move, travel) pasar
2 (a) (go, move past) pasar; **I was just ∼ing**
pasaba por aquí; **they ∼ed on the stairs** se
cruzaron en la escalera **(b)** (overtake) adelantarse,
rebasar (Méx)
3 (a) (elapse) ⟨«*time*»⟩ pasar **(b)** (disappear)
⟨«*feeling/pain*»⟩ pasarse

4 (be transferred) ⟨«*title/estate/crown*»⟩ pasar
5 (decline chance to play) pasar; (*as interj*) ¡paso!
6 (Sport) **to ∼** (**TO sb**) pasar(le) la pelota (*or* el
balón *etc*) (A algn)
II (a) (be acceptable) pasar **(b)** (in an exam)
aprobar

■ **pass away** [*v* + *adv*] (frml & euph) fallecer*
(frml)

■ **pass by 1** [*v* + *adv*] (go past) pasar
2 [*v* + *o* + *adv*] (not affect): **he felt life had ∼ed
him by** sentía que no había vivido

■ **pass down** [*v* + *o* + *adv*, *v* + *adv* + *o*] (*often
pass*) ⟨*heirloom*⟩ pasar; ⟨*story/tradition*⟩
transmitir

■ **pass for** [*v* + *prep* + *o*] pasar por

■ **pass off** [*v* + *o* + *adv*, *v* + *adv* + *o*] (represent
falsely) hacer* pasar; **she ∼ed herself off as a
journalist** se hizo pasar por periodista

■ **pass on 1** [*v* + *adv*] (a) to ∼ on TO sth pasar A algo (b)
⟨*information*⟩ pasar; ⟨*infection*⟩ contagiar
2 [*v* + *adv*] **(a)** to ∼ on TO sth pasar A algo **(b)**
▶ PASS AWAY

■ **pass out 1** [*v* + *adv*] (become unconscious)
desmayarse, perder* el conocimiento
2 [*v* + *o* + *adv*, *v* + *adv* + *o*] (distribute) repartir

■ **pass over 1** [*v* + *adv* + *o*] (omit) ⟨*fact/detail*⟩
pasar por alto
2 [*v* + *o* + *adv*] (disregard for promotion) (*usu pass*)
pasarle por encima a

■ **pass through (a)** [*v* + *adv*] pasar; **we're just
∼ing through** estamos solo de paso **(b)** [*v* + *prep*
+ *o*] ⟨*town/area*⟩ pasar por

■ **pass up** [*v* + *o* + *adv*, *v* + *adv* + *o*] (colloq)
⟨*opportunity*⟩ dejar pasar

passable /'pæsəbəl ‖'pɑːsəbəl/ *adj* **(a)**
(adequate) pasable **(b)** ⟨*road/route*⟩ transitable

passage /'pæsɪdʒ/ *n* **1 (a)** (alleyway) callejón
m, pasaje *m*; (narrow) pasadizo *m* **(b)** (corridor) (esp
BrE) pasillo *m* **(c)** (Anat) conducto *m* **2** (lapse):
the ∼ of time el paso del tiempo **3** (voyage) viaje
m; (fare) pasaje *m* **4** (extract) pasaje *m*

passageway /'pæsɪdʒweɪ/ *n* pasillo *m*

passenger /'pæsɪndʒər ‖'pæsɪndʒə(r)/ *n*
pasajero, -ra *m,f*

passer-by /'pæsər'baɪ ‖,pɑːsə'baɪ/ *n* (*pl*
passers-by) transeúnte *mf*

passing¹ /'pæsɪŋ ‖'pɑːsɪŋ/ *adj* (*before n*)
1 (going past): **she hailed a ∼ taxi** llamó a un taxi
que pasaba **2 (a)** ⟨*fad/fashion*⟩ pasajero;
⟨*glance*⟩ rápido **(b)** (casual): **it was only a ∼
thought** simplemente fue algo que se me ocurrió

passing² *n* **in passing** al pasar, de pasada

passing lane *n* (AmE) carril *m* de
adelantamiento

passion /'pæʃən/ *n* pasión *f*

passionate /'pæʃənət/ *adj* ⟨*love*⟩ apasionado;
⟨*hatred*⟩ mortal; ⟨*admirer*⟩ ardiente; ⟨*speech*⟩
vehemente

passionately /'pæʃənətli/ *adv* ⟨*love*⟩
apasionadamente; ⟨*believe*⟩ fervientemente;
⟨*desire*⟩ ardientemente

passion fruit *n* granadilla *f*, maracuyá *m*,
parchita *f* (Ven)

passive¹ /'pæsɪv/ *adj* pasivo

passive² *n* voz *f* pasiva

pass: ∼ key *n* llave *f* maestra; **P∼over** *n*

Pascua *f* (*judía*); **~port** *n* pasaporte *m*; **~word** *n* **(a)** (secret word or phrase) contraseña *f* **(b)** (Comput) clave *f* de acceso

past¹ /pæst ‖pɑːst/ *adj* 1 **(a)** (former) anterior; ⟨*life*⟩ pasado; (old) antiguo **(b)** (most recent) ⟨*week/ month/year*⟩ último **(c)** (finished, gone) (*pred*): **what's ~ is ~** lo pasado, pasado 2 (Ling): **the ~ tense** el pasado, el pretérito

past² *n* 1 **(a)** (former times) pasado *m*; **steam trains are a thing of the ~** las locomotoras de vapor han pasado a la historia; **in the ~,** **women ...** antes *or* antiguamente las mujeres ...; **that's all in the ~** eso forma parte del pasado **(b)** (of person) pasado *m*; (of place) historia *f* 2 (Ling) pasado *m*, pretérito *m*

past³ *prep* 1 **(a)** (by the side of): **I go ~ their house every morning** paso por (delante de) su casa todas las mañanas; **she walked straight ~ him** pasó de largo por su lado **(b)** (beyond): **it's just ~ the school** queda un poco más allá de la escuela
2 **(a)** (after) (esp BrE): **it's ten ~ six/half ~ two** son las seis y diez/las dos y media; **it was ~ eleven** eran las once pasadas; **it's ~ your bedtime** ya deberías estar acostado **(b)** (older than): **I'm ~ the age/stage when ...** ya he pasado la edad/ superado la etapa en que ...
3 (outside, beyond): **to be ~ -ING: I'm ~ caring** ya no me importa; **I wouldn't put it ~ her** no me extrañaría que lo hiciera; **to be ~ it** (colloq) estar* para el arrastre (fam)

past⁴ *adv* **(a)** (with verbs of motion): **to fly/cycle/ drive ~** pasar volando/en bicicleta/en coche; **he hurried ~** pasó a toda prisa **(b)** (giving time) (esp BrE): **it's twenty-five ~** son y veinticinco

pasta /ˈpɑːstə ‖ˈpæstə/ *n* pasta(s) *f(pl)*

paste /peɪst/ *n* **(a)** (thick mixture) pasta *f* **(b)** (glue) engrudo *m*; (wallpaper **~**) pegamento *m*, cola *f* **(c)** (imitation gem) estrás *m*

pastel /ˈpæstel ‖pæsˈtel/ *n* **(a)** (Art) (crayon) pastel *m* **(b)** (pale shade) tono *m* pastel; (*before n*) ⟨*shades/color*⟩ pastel *adj inv*

pasteurize /ˈpæstʃəraɪz ‖ˈpɑːstʃəraɪz/ *vt* pasteurizar*, pasterizar*

pastille /pæsˈtiːl ‖ˈpæstɪl/ *n* pastilla *f*

pastime /ˈpæstaɪm ‖ˈpɑːstaɪm/ *n* pasatiempo *m*

pastor /ˈpæstər ‖ˈpɑːstə(r)/ *n* pastor, -tora *m,f*

pastoral /ˈpæstərəl ‖ˈpɑːstərəl/ *adj* **(a)** ⟨*painting/scene*⟩ pastoril **(b)** (Relig) ⟨*care/duties*⟩ pastoral

pastry /ˈpeɪstri/ *n* (*pl* **-tries**) **(a)** (substance) masa *f* **(b)** (cake) pastelito *m or* (RPl) masa *f*

pasture¹ /ˈpæstʃər ‖ˈpɑːstʃə(r)/ *n* **(a)** (grazing land) pastos *mpl* **(b)** (grass) pasto *m*, pastura *f*

pasture² *vt* apacentar*, pastar

pasty /ˈpæsti/ *n* (*pl* **-ties**) (esp BrE) empanada *f* (AmL), empanadilla *f* (Esp)

pat¹ /pæt/ *vt* **-tt-** darle* palmaditas a

pat² *n* 1 (tap) palmadita *f*; (touch) toque *m* 2 (of butter) porción *f*

pat³ *adj* (pej) ⟨*answer*⟩ fácil

pat⁴ *adv* (by heart): **to have** *o* **know sth down** (AmE) *o* (BrE) **off ~** saberse* algo al dedillo

patch¹ /pætʃ/ *n* 1 **(a)** (for mending clothes) remiendo *m*, parche *m*; (for reinforcing) refuerzo *m*;

(on knee) rodillera *f*; (on elbow) codera *f* **(b)** (eye **~**) parche *m* (*en el ojo*) 2 **(a)** (area): **she slipped on a ~ of ice/oil** resbaló en el hielo/en una mancha de aceite; **a damp ~** una mancha de humedad; **to go through a bad** *o* **rough** *o* **sticky ~** (BrE) pasar por una mala racha **(b)** (of land): **a ~ of ground** un área de terreno; **a vegetable ~** un huerto **(c)** (territory) (BrE colloq): **my/his ~** mi/su territorio

patch² *vt* remendar*, parchar (esp AmL)
■ **patch up** [*v* + *o* + *adv*, *v* + *adv* + *o*] **(a)** (mend) ⟨*roof/furniture*⟩ hacerle* un arreglo a (*provisionalmente*); ⟨*clothes*⟩ remendar*, parchar (esp AmL); ⟨*hole*⟩ ponerle* un parche a **(b)** (resolve, settle): **I tried to help ~ things up between them** quise ayudar para que hicieran las paces

patchwork /ˈpætʃwɜːrk ‖ˈpætʃwɜːk/ *n* patchwork *m*, labor *f* de retazos *or* (Esp) retales; (*before n*) ⟨*quilt*⟩ de patchwork, de retazos *or* (Esp) retales

patchy /ˈpætʃi/ *adj* **-chier, -chiest** ⟨*paintwork/color*⟩ disparejo; ⟨*coverage*⟩ incompleto; ⟨*description*⟩ fragmentario; ⟨*performance/work*⟩ irregular; **~ fog** zonas *fpl* de niebla

pâté /pɑːˈteɪ ‖ˈpæteɪ/ *n* paté *m*

patent¹ /ˈpætṇt ‖ˈpeɪtṇt, ˈpætṇt/ *n* patente *f*

patent² /ˈpætṇt ‖ˈpeɪtṇt, ˈpætṇt/ *vt* patentar

patent³ *adj* /ˈpeɪtṇt, ˈpæt- ‖ˈpeɪtṇt/ (frml) patente

patent leather /ˈpætṇt ‖ˈpeɪtṇt, ˈpæt-/ *n* charol *m*

patently /ˈpeɪtṇtli, ˈpæt- ‖ˈpeɪtṇtli/ *adv*: **it's ~ clear** *o* **obvious that ...** salta a la vista que ...

paternal /pəˈtɜːrnl ‖pəˈtɜːnl/ *adj* **(a)** (fatherly) ⟨*affection*⟩ paternal; ⟨*pride*⟩ de padre; ⟨*trait/ inheritance*⟩ paterno **(b)** (on father's side) (*before n*) por parte de padre

paternity /pəˈtɜːrnəti ‖pəˈtɜːnəti/ *n* (frml) paternidad *f*

path /pæθ ‖pɑːθ/ *n* **(a)** (track, walkway) sendero *m*, senda *f* **(b)** (of missile) trayectoria *f*; (of the sun) recorrido *m*

pathetic /pəˈθetɪk/ *adj* **(a)** (pitiful) patético **(b)** (feeble) (colloq): **what a ~ excuse!** ¡qué excusa más pobre!; **don't be so ~** no seas tan pusilánime

pathological /ˌpæθəˈlɑːdʒɪkəl ‖ˌpæθəˈlɒdʒɪkəl/ *adj* patológico

pathologist /pəˈθɑːlədʒəst ‖pəˈθɒlədʒɪst/ *n* patólogo, -ga *m,f*

pathology /pəˈθɑːlədʒi ‖pəˈθɒlədʒi/ *n* patología *f*

pathos /ˈpeɪθɑːs ‖ˈpeɪθɒs/ *n* patetismo *m*

pathway /ˈpæθweɪ ‖ˈpɑːθweɪ/ *n* camino *m*, sendero *m*

patience /ˈpeɪʃəns/ *n* **(a)** (quality) paciencia *f* **(b)** (cards) (BrE) solitario *m*

patient¹ /ˈpeɪʃənt/ *adj* paciente; **to be ~ WITH sb** tener* paciencia CON algn

patient² *n* paciente *mf*

patiently /ˈpeɪʃəntli/ *adv* pacientemente

patio /ˈpætiəʊ/ *n* patio *m*

patriot /ˈpeɪtriət ‖ˈpætriət, ˈpeɪ-/ *n* patriota *mf*

patriotic /ˌpeɪtriˈɑːtɪk ‖ˌpætriˈɒtɪk, ˈpeɪ-/ *adj* patriótico

patriotism /'peɪtriətɪzəm ‖ 'pætriətɪzəm, 'peɪ-/ n patriotismo m

patrol¹ /pə'trəʊl/ n **(a)** (act) patrulla f; **to be on ~** estar* patrullando, estar* de patrulla; (before n) ~ **car** coche m patrulla, patrullero m (RPl), auto m patrulla (Chi) **(b)** (group) patrulla f

patrol² vt/i **-ll-** patrullar

patron /'peɪtrən/ n **(a)** (sponsor) patrocinador, -dora m,f; **a ~ of the arts** un mecenas **(b)** (customer) (fml) cliente, -ta m,f

patronize /'peɪtrənaɪz ‖ 'pætrənaɪz/ vt ① (condescend to) tratar con condescendencia ② (frequent) (fml) ⟨shop/hotel⟩ ser* cliente de; ⟨theater/cinema⟩ frecuentar

patronizing /'peɪtrənaɪzɪŋ ‖ 'pætrənaɪzɪŋ/ adj condescendiente

patter¹ /'pætər ‖ 'pætə(r)/ vi golpetear

patter² n ① (of rain) golpeteo m ② (talk): **he has a good sales ~** tiene mucha labia para vender

pattern /'pætərn ‖ 'pætən/ n ① **(a)** (decoration) diseño m, dibujo m; (on fabric) diseño m, estampado m **(b)** (order, arrangement): **it follows the normal ~** sigue las pautas normales; **the murders all seem to follow a ~** todos los asesinatos parecen responder al mismo patrón ② **(a)** (model) modelo m **(b)** (in dressmaking) patrón m, molde m (CS) **(c)** (sample) muestra f

patterned /'pætərnd ‖ 'pætənd/ adj con dibujos; ⟨fabric⟩ estampado

paunch /pɔːntʃ/ n panza f (fam)

pauper /'pɔːpər ‖ 'pɔːpə(r)/ n pobre mf

pause¹ /pɔːz/ n pausa f; **without ~** sin interrupción

pause² vi (in speech) hacer* una pausa; (in movement) detenerse*

pave /peɪv/ vt (with concrete) pavimentar; (with flagstones) enlosar; (with stones) empedrar*

pavement /'peɪvmənt/ n **(a)** (paved area) pavimento m **(b)** (beside road) (BrE) ▶ SIDEWALK

pavilion /pə'vɪljən/ n **(a)** (tent, stand) pabellón m **(b)** (BrE Sport) caseta f

paving /'peɪvɪŋ/ n pavimento m; (of flagstones) enlosado m, (of stones) empedrado m; (before n) ~ **stone** losa f

paw¹ /pɔː/ n pata f

paw² vt ⟨animal⟩ tocar* con la pata; **to ~ the ground** ⟨horse⟩ piafar

pawn¹ /pɔːn/ n **(a)** (in chess) peón m **(b)** (manipulated person) títere m

pawn² vt empeñar

pawnbroker /'pɔːn,brəʊkər ‖ 'pɔːn,brəʊkə(r)/ n prestamista mf

pay¹ /peɪ/ (past & past p **paid**) vt ① **(a)** ⟨tax/rent/sum/debt⟩ pagar*; **how much did you ~ for the painting?** ¿cuánto te costó el cuadro? **(b)** ⟨employee/creditor/tradesperson⟩ pagarle* a; **to ~ sb FOR sth** pagarle* algo a algn ② ⟨respects⟩ presentar; ⟨attention⟩ prestar ■ ~ vi ① **(a)** ⟨person⟩ pagar* **(b)** ⟨work/activity⟩ pagarse*; **teaching doesn't ~ very well** la enseñanza no está muy bien pagada

② (suffer) **to ~ for sth** pagar* algo; **he paid for the mistake with his life** el error le costó la vida
■ ~ v impers convenir*
■ **pay back** [v + o + adv, v + adv + o] ① (repay) ⟨money⟩ devolver*, regresar (AmL exc CS); ⟨loan/mortgage⟩ pagar*; **to ~ sb back** devolverle or (AmL exc CS) regresarle el dinero a algn ② (take revenge on): **I'll ~ you back!** ¡ya me las vas a pagar!
■ **pay in** [v + o + adv, v + adv + o] (BrE) ⟨money⟩ depositar or (Esp) ingresar or (Col) consignar
■ **pay off** ① [v + o + adv, v + adv + o] ⟨debt⟩ cancelar, saldar; ⟨worker⟩ liquidarle el sueldo (or jornal etc) a (al despedirlo) ② [v + adv] (prove worthwhile) valer* la pena, ⟨gamble⟩ resultar
■ **pay out** [v + o + adv, v + adv + o] pagar*
■ **pay up** [v + adv] pagar*

pay² n (of manual worker) paga f, (of employee) sueldo m; **equal ~** igualdad f salarial; (before n) ~ **increase** aumento m salarial

payable /'peɪəbəl/ adj (fml) (pred) pagadero; **the rent becomes ~ on the first of the month** el alquiler vence el primero de mes; **make the check ~ to ...** extienda el cheque a nombre de ...

pay: ~check, (BrE) ~ **cheque** n cheque m del sueldo; (salary) sueldo m; ~**day** n día m de paga

payee /peɪ'iː/ n beneficiario, -ria m,f

payment /'peɪmənt/ n **(a)** (of debt, money, wage) pago m; **he received no ~ for what he did** no recibió remuneración por lo que hizo (fml) **(b)** (installment) plazo m, cuota f (AmL)

pay: ~ phone n teléfono m público, monedero m (público) (Ur); ~**roll** n **(a)** (list) nómina f, planilla f (de sueldos) (AmL), plantilla f (Esp) **(b)** (wages) nómina f; ~ **slip** n nómina f, recibo m del sueldo

PC¹ n ① = **personal computer** ② (in UK) = **police constable**

PC² adj = **politically correct**

PD n (in US) = **Police Department**

PE n = **physical education**

pea /piː/ n arveja f or (Esp) guisante m or (AmC, Méx) chícharo m

peace /piːs/ n ① **(a)** paz f; **in o at ~** en paz; (before n) ⟨proposal/initiative/treaty⟩ de paz; ⟨talks/march/campaign⟩ por la paz; **the ~ movement** el movimiento pacifista; **as a ~ offering** en señal de reconciliación ② (Law): **to keep the ~** mantener* el orden ③ (tranquillity) paz f; **I went to the library for some ~ and quiet** me fui a la biblioteca para poder estar tranquilo; **I turned off the gas for my own ~ of mind** apagué el gas para quedarme tranquilo

peaceful /'piːsfəl/ adj **(a)** (calm, quiet) ⟨place⟩ tranquilo **(b)** (non-violent) ⟨protest⟩ pacífico; **they are a ~ people** son un pueblo amante de la paz

peacefully /'piːsfəli/ adv ⟨sleep⟩ plácidamente; ⟨read/sit⟩ tranquilamente

peace: ~**keeping** adj (before n): ~**keeping forces** fuerzas fpl de paz; ~**maker** n conciliador, -dora m,f; ~**time** n época f de paz

peach /piːtʃ/ n durazno m (esp AmL), melocotón m (Esp); (before n) ~ **tree** duraznero m (esp AmL), melocotonero m (Esp)

peacock /'piːkɑːk ‖'piːkɒk/ n pavo m real

peak¹ /piːk/ n (a) (of mountain) cima f, cumbre f; (mountain) pico m; (of cap) visera f (b) (highest point): **at the** ~ **of her career** en el apogeo de su carrera

peak² adj (before n) (a) (maximum) ‹level/power› máximo; **to be in** ~ **condition** «athlete/horse» estar* en plena forma (b) (busiest): **during** ~ **hours** durante las horas de mayor demanda (or consumo etc); ~ **rate** tarifa f alta

peal /piːl/ n: ~ **of bells** (sound) repique m de campanas; (set) carillón m; ~**s of laughter** carcajadas fpl; **a** ~ **of thunder** un trueno

peanut /'piːnʌt/ n (a) (Agr, Culin) maní m or (Esp) cacahuete m or (Méx) cacahuate m (b) **peanuts** pl (small sum) (colloq) una miseria (fam)

peanut butter n mantequilla f de maní or (Esp) de cacahuete or (Méx) de cacahuate, manteca f de maní (RPl)

pear /per ‖peə(r)/ n pera f; ~ **(tree)** peral m

pearl /pɜːrl ‖pɜːl/ n (a) perla f; ~**s of wisdom** sabias palabras fpl, (iro) joyitas fpl (iró) (b) (mother-of-~) nácar m, madreperla f, concha f nácar (Méx), concha f de perla (Chi)

peasant /'pezn̩t/ n campesino, -na m,f

peat /piːt/ n turba f

pebble /'pebəl/ n guijarro m

pecan /pɪ'kæn ‖'piːkən/ n pacana f, nuez f (Méx)

peck¹ /pek/ n (a) (of bird) picotazo m (b) (kiss) beso m

peck² vt picotear

pecking order /'pekɪŋ/ n jerarquía f

peckish /'pekɪʃ/ adj (esp BrE colloq) (pred) **to be** o **feel** ~ tener* un poco de hambre

peculiar /pɪ'kjuːljər ‖pɪ'kjuːliə(r)/ adj (a) (strange) raro, extraño (b) (particular, exclusive) peculiar, característico

peculiarity /pɪ'kjuːli'jærəti ‖pɪˌkjuːli'ærəti/ n (pl **-ties**) (sth unusual) rasgo m singular; (oddity) rareza f

pedal¹ /'pedl̩/ n pedal m

pedal² vi, (BrE) **-ll-** pedalear

pedal bin n (BrE) cubo m or (Méx) bote m or (CS) tacho m or (Ven) tobo m or (Col) caneca f de la basura (con pedal)

pedantic /pɪ'dæntɪk/ adj pedante

peddle /'pedl̩/ vt vender (en las calles o de puerta en puerta); **to** ~ **drugs** traficar* con drogas

peddler /'pedlər ‖'pedlə(r)/ n vendedor, -dora ambulante m,f; (in former times) buhonero m; **a drug** ~ un traficante de drogas

pedestal /'pedəstl̩ ‖'pedɪstl̩/ n pedestal m

pedestrian¹ /pə'destriən ‖pɪ'destriən/ n peatón, -tona m,f; (before n) ~ **crossing** cruce m peatonal or de peatones; ~ **mall** o (BrE) **precinct** zona f peatonal

pedestrian² adj pedestre

pediatric, (BrE also) **paediatric** /'piːdi'ætrɪk/ adj ‹hospital› pediátrico; ‹specialist› en pediatría

pediatrician, (BrE also) **paediatrician** /'piːdiə'trɪʃən/ n pediatra mf

pedicure /'pedɪkjʊr ‖'pedɪkjʊə(r)/ n: **to have a** ~ arreglarse/hacerse* arreglar los pies

pedigree /'pedəgri ‖'pedɪgriː/ n (a) (ancestry — of animal) pedigrí m; (— of person) linaje m; (before n) ‹bull/dog› de raza (b) (certificate, document) pedigrí m

pedlar /'pedlər ‖'pedlə(r)/ n (BrE) ▶ PEDDLER

pedophile, (BrE) **paedophile** /'piːdəfaɪl/ n pedófilo, -la m,f

pee¹ /piː/ vi (past & past p **peed**) (colloq) hacer* pis or pipí (fam), hacer* del uno (Méx, Per fam & euf)

pee² n (colloq) (no pl) pis m (fam), pipí m (fam)

peek¹ /piːk/ vi ~ **(AT sth/sb)** mirar (algo/a algn) (a hurtadillas), vichar (algo/a algn) (RPl fam)

peek² n **to take** o **have a** ~ **at sth** echar(le) una miradita a algo, vichar algo (RPl fam)

peel¹ /piːl/ vt ‹apple/potato› pelar
■ ~ vi ‹person› pelarse; ‹paint› desconcharse; «wallpaper» despegarse*
■ **peel off** ① [v + adv] «wallpaper/label» despegarse*; ‹paint› desconcharse ② [v + o + adv, v + adv + o] ‹stamp/sticker› despegar*; ‹paint/bark› quitar

peel² n (of potato, apple) piel f, cáscara f (esp AmL); (of orange, lemon) cáscara f

peelings /'piːlɪŋz/ pl n cáscaras fpl, peladuras fpl

peep¹ /piːp/ vi (a) (watch) espiar*, vichar (RPl fam); (look quickly) mirar (a hurtadillas), vichar (RPl fam) (b) (show, stick out) ~ **(out)** asomar
■ ~ vt (colloq): **I** ~**ed the horn** toqué la bocina or el claxon

peep² n ① (quick or furtive look) vistazo m; **to have a** ~ **AT sth** echarle un vistazo A algo ② (of bird) pío m; (of car horn) pitido m

peephole /'piːphəʊl/ n mirilla f

peer¹ /pɪr ‖pɪə(r)/ n ① (a) (equal) par mf (b) (contemporary) coetáneo, -nea m,f ② (lord) (in UK) par m

peer² vi: **to** ~ **AT sth/sb** (with difficulty) mirar algo/a algn con ojos de miope; (closely) mirar algo/a algn detenidamente

peerage /'pɪrɪdʒ ‖'pɪərɪdʒ/ n **the** ~ la nobleza

peer group n grupo m paritario (frml)

peeved /piːvd/ adj ‹expression/look› de fastidio; **to feel** o **feel** ~ estar* molesto

peevish /'piːvɪʃ/ adj ‹remark› desagradable, malhumorado; **to be** ~ estar* fastidioso

peg¹ /peg/ n ① (a) (in ground) estaca f; (on violin, guitar) clavija f; (tent ~) estaquilla f; (on board game) pieza o ficha que encaja en un tablero (b) (clothes-~) (BrE) ▶ CLOTHESPIN ② (hook, hanger) colgador m, perchero m, gancho m

peg² vt **-gg-** (attach, secure) sujetar, asegurar (con estaquillas etc)

pejorative /pɪ'dʒɔːrətɪv ‖pɪ'dʒɒrətɪv/ adj peyorativo

Peking /'piːˈkɪŋ/ n Pekín m

pelican /'pelɪkən/ n pelícano m

pellet /'pelət ‖'pelɪt/ n (a) (of bread, paper) bolita f (b) (ammunition) perdigón m

pelt¹ /pelt/ vt: to ~ sb with tomatoes lanzarle* tomates a algn
■ ~ vi (colloq) ⒈ (rush): they came ~ing down the hill bajaron la cuesta (corriendo) a toda velocidad ⒉ (fall heavily): it was ~ing with rain llovía a cántaros

pelt² n (animal skin) piel f; (stripped) cuero m

pelvis /'pelvəs ‖'pelvɪs/ n (pl **-vises**) pelvis f

pen /pen/ n ⒈ (fountain ~) pluma f estilográfica, pluma f fuente (AmL); (ballpoint ~) bolígrafo m, boli m (Esp fam), birome f (RPl), pluma f atómica (Méx), lápiz m de pasta (Chi); (felt ~) rotulador m ⒉ (Agr) (sheep ~) redil m; (cattle ~) corral m

penal /'piːnl/ adj penal

penalize /'piːnlaɪz ‖'piːnəlaɪz/ vt (a) (punish) ⟨player⟩ sancionar (b) (make punishable, illegal) penalizar*

penalty /'penlti/ n (pl **-ties**) ⒈ (punishment) pena f; (fine) multa f; to pay the ~ pagar* las consecuencias ⒉ (Sport) (in rugby) penalty m; (in US football) castigo m; ~ (**kick**) (in soccer) penalty m, penalti m, penal m (AmL), pénal m (Andes); (before n) ~ **area** (in soccer) área f; de penalty

penance /'penəns/ n (a) (Relig) penitencia f (b) (punishment) (hum) castigo m

pence /pens/ n pl of PENNY 1A

penchant /'pentʃənt ‖'pɒŋʃɒŋ/ n (frml) ~ (**FOR** sth) inclinación f (**POR** algo)

pencil /'pensəl/ n lápiz m; in ~ con lápiz

pencil: ~ **case** n estuche m (para lápices), plumier m (Esp), chuspa f (Col), cartuchera f (RPI); ~ **sharpener** n sacapuntas m, tajalápiz m (Col)

pendant /'pendənt/ n colgante m

pending¹ /'pendɪŋ/ adj (a) (awaiting action) (pred): to be ~ estar* pendiente (b) (imminent) próximo

pending² prep (frml) en espera de

pendulum /'pendʒələm ‖'pendjʊləm/ n (pl **-lums**) péndulo m

penetrate /'penətreɪt ‖'penɪtreɪt/ vt (a) ⟨membrane/defenses⟩ penetrar (en); ⟨armor⟩ atravesar*; ⟨enemy lines⟩ adentrarse en; ⟨territory⟩ penetrar en; ⟨organization⟩ infiltrarse en; ⟨market⟩ introducirse* en (b) «liquid» penetrar (en)
■ ~ vi (a) «arrow/water/light» penetrar (b) (sink in mentally): it took a long time to ~ tardé (or tardó etc) en entenderlo

penetrating /'penətreɪtɪŋ ‖'penɪtreɪtɪŋ/ adj penetrante

penetration /penə'treɪʃən ‖,penɪ'treɪʃən/ n penetración f

pen friend n (esp BrE) ▶ PEN PAL

penguin /'peŋgwən ‖'peŋgwɪn/ n pingüino m

penicillin /penə'sɪlən ‖,penɪ'sɪlɪn/ n penicilina f

peninsula /pə'nɪnsələ ‖pə'nɪnsjʊlə/ n península f

penis /'piːnəs ‖'piːnɪs/ n pene m

penitent /'penətənt ‖'penɪtənt/ adj arrepentido

penitentiary /penə'tentʃəri ‖,penɪ'tenʃəri/ n (pl **-ries**) (AmE) prisión f

penknife /'pennaɪf/ n (pl **-knives**) navaja f

Penn, Penna = Pennsylvania

pen name n seudónimo m

penniless /'peniləs ‖'penɪlɪs/ adj pobre, sin un céntimo

penny /'peni/ n ⒈ (in UK) (a) (pl **pence**) penique m (b) (pl **pennies**) (coin) penique m ⒉ (pl **pennies**) (cent coin) (in US, Canada) (colloq) (moneda f de un) centavo m

penny-pinching /'peni,pɪntʃɪŋ/ adj cicatero (fam)

pen pal /'penpæl/ n (esp AmE) amigo, -ga m,f por correspondencia

pension /'pentʃən ‖'penʃən/ n pensión f; (retirement ~) pensión de jubilación

pensioner /'pentʃənər ‖'penʃənə(r)/ n pensionado, -da m,f, pensionista mf; (retired person) jubilado, -da m,f

pensive /'pensɪv/ adj pensativo

pentagon /'pentəgɑːn ‖'pentəgən/ n (a) (Math) pentágono m (b) (in US) **the Pentagon** el Pentágono

pentathlon /pen'tæθlən/ n pentatlón m

Pentecost /'pentəkɔːst ‖'pentɪkɒst/ n Pentecostés m

penthouse /'penthaʊs/ n penthouse m

pent-up /'pent'ʌp/ adj (pred **pent up**) ⟨emotions⟩ contenido; ⟨energy⟩ acumulado

penultimate /pɪ'nʌltəmət ‖pen'ʌltɪmət/ adj (before n) penúltimo

people¹ /'piːpəl/ n ⒈ (+ pl vb, no art) (a) (in general) gente f; ~ **say that** ... dice que ...; **some** ~ **don't like it** a algunos no les gusta (b) (individuals) personas fpl (c) (specific group): **tall/rich** ~ la gente alta/rica, los altos/ ricos; **young** ~ los jóvenes ⒉ (a) (inhabitants) (+ pl vb): **the** ~ **of this country** la gente de este país; **the country and its** ~ el país y su(s) gente(s) (b) (citizens, nation) (+ pl vb) **the** ~ el pueblo (c) (race) (+ sing vb) pueblo m

people² vt poblar*

pepper¹ /'pepər ‖'pepə(r)/ n ⒈ (spice) pimienta f; **black/white** ~ pimienta negra/blanca ⒉ (capsicum fruit, plant) pimiento m, pimentón m (AmS exc RPl), ají m (RPl); **green** ~ pimiento (or pimentón etc) verde; **red** ~ pimiento (or pimentón etc) rojo or colorado, ají m morrón (RPl)

pepper² vt (intersperse) to ~ sth WITH sth salpicar* algo DE algo

pepper: ~**box** n (AmE) pimentero m; ~**mint** n (a) (plant) menta f; (before n) ⟨tea/oil⟩ de menta; ⟨flavor⟩ a menta (b) (sweet) caramelo m de menta; ~**pot** n (BrE) pimentero m

pep /pep/: ~ **talk** n: he gave them a ~ talk les habló para levantarles la moral/infundirles ánimo; ~ **up: -pp-** [v + o + adv, v + adv + o] (colloq) ⟨person⟩ animar; (physically) darle* energía a

per /pɜːr ‖pɜː(r)/ prep (for each) por; £10 ~ head 10 libras por cabeza; **at $25** ~ **kilo** a 25 dólares el kilo; **30 miles** ~ **hour** 30 millas por hora

per: ~ **annum** /pər'ænəm/ adv al año, por año; ~ **capita** /pər'kæpətə ‖pə'kæpɪtə/ adv per cápita

perceive /pər'siːv ‖pə'siːv/ *vt* **(a)** ⟨*object/ sound*⟩ percibir **(b)** (realize) percatarse de **(c)** (regard) ver*

percent¹, per cent /pər'sent ‖pə'sent/ *n* (*no pl*) porcentaje *m*

percent², per cent *adv* por ciento

percentage /pər'sentɪdʒ ‖pə'sentɪdʒ/ *n* porcentaje *m*

perceptible /pər'septəbəl ‖pə'septəbəl/ *adj* perceptible

perception /pər'sepʃən ‖pə'sepʃən/ *n* **(a)** (faculty) percepción *f* **(b)** (idea) idea *f*; (image) imagen *f* **(c)** (insight) perspicacia *f*

perceptive /pər'septɪv ‖pə'septɪv/ *adj* perspicaz

perch¹ /pɜːrtʃ ‖pɜːtʃ/ *n* **1** (in birdcage) percha *f* **2** (*pl* ~ *or* ~**es**) (fish) perca *f*

perch² *vi* «*bird*» posarse; **he ~ed on the edge of the table** se sentó en el borde de la mesa

percolate /'pɜːrkəleɪt ‖'pɜːkəleɪt/ *vi* **(a)** (filter) filtrarse **(b)** (Culin) «*coffee*» hacerse*

percolator /'pɜːrkəleɪtər ‖'pɜːkəleɪtə(r)/ *n* cafetera *f* eléctrica

percussion /pər'kʌʃən ‖pə'kʌʃən/ *n* percusión *f*

perennial¹ /pə'reniəl/ *adj* **(a)** (Bot) perenne **(b)** (recurring) perenne, perpetuo

perennial² *n* planta *f* perenne *or* vivaz

perfect¹ /'pɜːrfɪkt ‖'pɜːfɪkt/ *adj* **1** (flawless, ideal) perfecto; ⟨*day/opportunity*⟩ ideal; **he speaks ~ French** habla francés perfectamente **2** (complete) (*before n*): **he's a ~ stranger to me** me es totalmente desconocido

perfect² /pər'fekt ‖pə'fekt/ *vt* perfeccionar

perfect³ /'pɜːrfɪkt ‖'pɜːfɪkt/ *n*: **the future/ present ~** el futuro/pretérito perfecto; **the past ~** el pluscuamperfecto

perfection /pər'fekʃən ‖pə'fekʃən/ *n* **(a)** (state, quality) perfección *f* **(b)** (act) perfeccionamiento *m*

perfectionist /pər'fekʃənəst ‖pə'fekʃənɪst/ *n* perfeccionista *mf*

perfectly /'pɜːrfɪktli ‖'pɜːfɪktli/ *adv* **1** **(a)** (exactly) ⟨*round/straight*⟩ totalmente; ⟨*fit/match*⟩ perfectamente **(b)** (faultlessly, ideally) perfectamente **2** (completely, utterly) ⟨*safe/ridiculous*⟩ totalmente; **he knows ~ well that ...** sabe perfectamente que ...

perforate /'pɜːrfəreɪt ‖'pɜːfəreɪt/ *vt* perforar

perforation /'pɜːrfə'reɪʃən ‖,pɜːfə'reɪʃən/ *n* perforación *f*; ~**s** (on sheet of stamps etc) perforado *m*

perform /pər'fɔːrm ‖pə'fɔːm/ *vi* **1** (Mus, Theat) «*actor/comedian*» actuar*; «*singer*» cantar; «*musician*» tocar*; «*dancer*» bailar **2** (work, produce results) «*student/worker*» rendir*, trabajar; «*team/athlete/vehicle*» responder; «*company/stocks*» rendir*
  ■ ~ *vt* **1** (Mus, Theat) ⟨*play*⟩ representar; ⟨*symphony*⟩ tocar* **2** (carry out, fulfill) ⟨*function*⟩ desempeñar; ⟨*role*⟩ desempeñar; ⟨*task*⟩ ejecutar; ⟨*experiment*⟩ realizar*; ⟨*ceremony*⟩ celebrar; ⟨*rites*⟩ practicar*

performance /pər'fɔːrməns ‖pə'fɔːməns/ *n* **1** (Cin, Mus, Theat) **(a)** (session) (Theat) representación *f*, función *f*; (Cin) función *f* **(b)** (of symphony, song) interpretación *f*; (of play)

representación *f* **(c)** (of actor) interpretación *f*; (of pianist, tenor) interpretación *f*; (of entertainer) actuación *f* **2** (of employee) rendimiento *m*, desempeño *m* (AmL); (of student) rendimiento *m*; (of team, athlete) actuación *f*, performance *f* (AmL period); (of machine, vehicle) comportamiento *m*, performance *f* (AmL); (of company) resultados *mpl*

performer /pər'fɔːrmər ‖pə'fɔːmə(r)/ *n* (Theat, Cin) actor, -triz *m,f*; (entertainer) artista *mf*

performing /pər'fɔːrmɪŋ ‖pə'fɔːmɪŋ/ *adj* (*before n*) **(a)** (Mus, Theat): **the ~ arts** las artes interpretativas **(b)** ⟨*seal/dog*⟩ amaestrado

perfume¹ /'pɜːrfjuːm ‖'pɜːfjuːm/ *n* perfume *m*

perfume² /pər'fjuːm ‖'pɜːfjuːm/ *vt* perfumar

perfunctory /pər'fʌŋktəri ‖pə'fʌŋktəri/ *adj* ⟨*inspection/description*⟩ somero; ⟨*greeting*⟩ mecánico

perhaps /pər'hæps ‖pə'hæps/ *adv* quizá(s), tal vez; ~ **they'll come later** tal vez *or* quizá(s) vengan más tarde

peril /'perəl ‖'perɪl, 'perəl/ *n* peligro *m*

perilous /'perələs ‖'perɪləs, 'perələs/ *adj* peligroso

perimeter /pə'rɪmətər ‖pə'rɪmɪtə(r)/ *n* perímetro *m*

period¹ /'pɪriəd ‖'pɪəriəd/ *n* [*the forms* PERÍODO *and* PERIODO *are equally acceptable in Spanish where this translation applies*] **1** **(a)** (interval, length of time) período *m*; (when specifying a time limit) plazo *m*; **for a ~ of five hours/12 months** por un espacio de cinco horas/período de 12 meses **(b)** (epoch) época *f* **2** (menstruation) periodo *m*, regla *f* **3** (in school) hora *f* (*de clase*) **4** (in punctuation) (AmE) punto *m*

period² *adj* ⟨*costume/furniture*⟩ de época

periodic /'pɪri'ɑːdɪk ‖,pɪəri'ɒdɪk/ *adj* periódico

periodical¹ /'pɪri'ɑːdɪkəl ‖,pɪəri'ɒdɪkəl/ *n* publicación *f* periódica

periodical² *adj* ▶ PERIODIC

peripheral /pə'rɪfərəl/ *adj* **(a)** (minor, secondary) secundario **(b)** (Comput) ⟨*device/unit*⟩ periférico

periphery /pə'rɪfəri/ *n* (*pl* -**ries**) (frml) (of city) periferia *f*; (of society) margen *m*

periscope /'perəskəʊp ‖'perɪskəʊp/ *n* periscopio *m*

perish /'perɪʃ/ *vi* **(a)** (die) (liter) perecer* (liter) **(b)** (decay) «*rubber/leather*» deteriorarse; «*foodstuffs*» echarse a perder

perishable /'perɪʃəbəl/ *adj* perecedero

perjure /'pɜːrdʒər ‖'pɜːdʒə(r)/ *v refl* (Law) **to ~ oneself** perjurar(se), cometer perjurio

perjury /'pɜːrdʒəri ‖'pɜːdʒəri/ *n* perjurio *m*

perk /pɜːrk ‖pɜːk/ *n* (colloq) (of job) (beneficio *m*) extra *m*; (particular advantage) ventaja *f*
  ■ **perk up** [*v* + *adv*] ⟨*person*⟩ animarse; «*business/weather*» mejorar

perky /'pɜːrki ‖'pɜːki/ *adj* -**kier**, -**kiest** alegre

perm¹ /pɜːrm ‖pɜːm/ *n* permanente *f or* (Méx) *m*

perm² *vt*: **to have one's hair ~ed** hacerse* la *or* (Méx) un permanente

permanent¹ /'pɜːrmənənt ‖'pɜːmənənt/ *adj* permanente; ⟨*address/job*⟩ fijo, permanente; ⟨*dye/ ink*⟩ indeleble

permanent² *n* (AmE) ▶ PERM¹

permanently /'pɜːrmənəntli ‖'pɜːmənəntli/ *adv* ⟨*work/settle*⟩ permanentemente; ⟨*marked/ disfigured*⟩ para siempre

permeate /'pɜːrmieɪt ‖'pɜːmieɪt/ *vt* «*liquid*» calar; «*smoke/smell*» impregnar

permissible /pər'mɪsəbəl ‖pə'mɪsəbəl/ *adj* (permitted) permisible; (acceptable) tolerable

permission /pər'mɪʃən ‖pə'mɪʃən/ *n* permiso *m*; **she gave me ~** me dio (su) permiso

permissive /pər'mɪsɪv ‖pə'mɪsɪv/ *adj* permisivo

permit[1] /pər'mɪt ‖pə'mɪt/ **-tt-** *vt* permitir; **photography is not ~ted** no se permite tomar fotografías; **to ~ sb to +** INF permitirle a algn que (+ *subj*)
■ **~** *vi*: **weather ~ting** si hace buen tiempo

permit[2] /'pɜːrmɪt ‖'pɜːmɪt/ *n* permiso *m* (*por escrito*); **work/residence ~** permiso de trabajo/de residencia; **gun ~** (AmE) licencia *f* de armas

permutation /,pɜːrmjʊ'teɪʃən ‖,pɜːmjʊ'teɪʃən/ *n* **(a)** (arrangement) variante *f* **(b)** (Math) permutación *f*

peroxide /pər'ɑːksaɪd ‖pə'rɒksaɪd/ *n* peróxido *m*

perpendicular /,pɜːrpən'dɪkjələr ‖,pɜːpən'dɪkjʊlə(r)/ *adj* **(a)** (vertical) ⟨*wall/surface*⟩ perpendicular al horizonte **(b)** (Math) **~ TO sth** perpendicular A algo

perpetrate /'pɜːrpətreɪt ‖'pɜːpɪtreɪt/ *vt* (frml) perpetrar

perpetrator /'pɜːrpətreɪtər ‖'pɜːpɪtreɪtə(r)/ *n* (frml or hum) autor, -tora *m,f* (*de un crimen etc*)

perpetual /pər'petʃuəl ‖pə'petjʊəl/ *adj* eterno, perpetuo

perpetuate /pər'petʃueɪt ‖pə'petjʊeɪt/ *vt* perpetuar*

perplex /pər'pleks ‖pə'pleks/ *vt* dejar perplejo

perplexed /pər'plekst ‖pə'plekst/ *adj* perplejo

per se /'pɜːr'seɪ ‖,pɜː'seɪ/ *adv* en sí, per se

persecute /'pɜːrsɪkjuːt ‖'pɜːsɪkjuːt/ *vt* perseguir*

persecution /,pɜːrsɪ'kjuːʃən ‖,pɜːsɪ'kjuːʃən/ *n* persecución *f*

perseverance /,pɜːrsə'vɪrəns ‖,pɜːsɪ'vɪərəns/ *n* perseverancia *f*

persevere /,pɜːrsə'vɪr ‖,pɜːsɪ'vɪə(r)/ *vi* perseverar

Persia /'pɜːrʒə ‖'pɜːʃə/ *n* Persia *f*

Persian /'pɜːrʒən ‖'pɜːʃən/ *adj* persa; **the ~ Gulf** el Golfo Pérsico

persist /pər'sɪst ‖pə'sɪst/ *vi* persistir; **to ~ IN sth/-**ING: **they ~ed in the belief** *o* **in believing that ...** persistieron en la creencia de que ...

persistence /pər'sɪstəns ‖pə'sɪstəns/ *n* perseverancia *f*

persistent /pər'sɪstənt ‖pə'sɪstənt/ *adj* **(a)** (unceasing) ⟨*demands/warnings*⟩ continuo, constante; ⟨*cough/fog*⟩ persistente; ⟨*rain*⟩ continuo **(b)** (undaunted) ⟨*salesman/suitor*⟩ insistente

person /'pɜːrsn̩ ‖'pɜːsn̩/ *n* **1** (*pl* **people** *o* (frml) **persons**) persona *f*; **Sue's the ~ to ask a** quien hay que preguntarle es a Sue; **in ~** en persona **2** (Ling) (*pl* **persons**) persona *f*

personable /'pɜːrsn̩əbəl ‖'pɜːsn̩əbəl/ *adj* agradable

personal /'pɜːrsn̩l ‖'pɜːsən̩l/ *adj* **1 (a)** (own) ⟨*experience/preference*⟩ personal; ⟨*property*⟩ privado **(b)** (private) personal; **a ~ call** una llamada particular; **don't ask ~ questions** no hagas preguntas indiscretas **(c)** (individual) ⟨*account/loan*⟩ personal **2 (a)** (in person) ⟨*appearance*⟩ en persona **(b)** (physical) ⟨*hygiene*⟩ íntimo; ⟨*appearance*⟩ personal **(c)** (directed against individual): **it's nothing ~, but ...** no tengo nada contra ti (*or* ella *etc*), pero ...

personal: **~ assistant** *n* (Busn) secretario, -ria *m,f* personal; **~ computer** *n* computadora *f or* (Esp tb) ordenador *m* personal

personality /,pɜːrsn̩'æləti ‖,pɜːsə'næləti/ *n* (*pl* **-ties**) personalidad *f*

personally /'pɜːrsn̩əli ‖'pɜːsn̩əli/ *adv* personalmente

personal organizer *n* agenda *f* de uso múltiple, Filofax® *m*

personification /pər'sɑːnəfə'keɪʃən ‖pə,sɒnɪfɪ'keɪʃən/ *n* personificación *f*

personify /pər'sɑːnəfaɪ ‖pə'sɒnɪfaɪ/ *vt* **-fies, -fying, -fied** personificar*

personnel /'pɜːrsn̩'el ‖,pɜːsə'nel/ *n* **(a)** (staff) (+ *pl vb*) personal *m*; (before *n*) **~ manager** jefe *m,f* de personal **(b)** **Personnel** (department) (+ *sing vb*) sección *f* de personal

perspective /pər'spektɪv ‖pə'spektɪv/ *n* perspectiva *f*; **you have to keep things in ~** no tienes que perder de vista la verdadera dimensión de las cosas

Perspex® /'pɜːrspeks ‖'pɜːspeks/ *n* (BrE) acrílico *m*, plexiglás® *m* (Esp)

perspiration /,pɜːrspə'reɪʃən ‖,pɜːspɪ'reɪʃən/ *n* transpiración *f*

perspire /pər'spaɪr ‖pə'spaɪə(r)/ *vi* transpirar

persuade /pər'sweɪd ‖pə'sweɪd/ *vt* ⟨*person*⟩ convencer*, persuadir; **to ~ sb to +** INF convencer* *or* persuadir a algn DE QUE *or* PARA QUE (+ *subj*)

persuasion /pər'sweɪʒən ‖pə'sweɪʒən/ *n* **(a)** (act) persuasión *f* **(b)** (Relig) (frml): **people of all ~s** gente de todas las creencias

persuasive /pər'sweɪsɪv ‖pə'sweɪsɪv/ *adj* ⟨*person/manner*⟩ persuasivo; ⟨*argument*⟩ convincente

pert /pɜːrt ‖pɜːt/ *adj* ⟨*reply*⟩ descarado; ⟨*hat/ dress*⟩ coqueto

pertinent /'pɜːrtn̩ənt ‖'pɜːtɪnənt/ *adj* (frml) pertinente; **to be ~ TO sth** guardar relación CON algo

perturb /pər'tɜːrb ‖pə'tɜːb/ *vt* (*usu pass*) perturbar

Peru /pə'ruː/ *n* (el) Perú *m*

· ·

AmC	América Central	Arg	Argentina	Cu	Cuba
AmL	América Latina	Bol	Bolivia	Ec	Ecuador
AmS	América del Sur	Chi	Chile	Esp	España
Andes	Región andina	CS	Cono Sur	Méx	México

Per	Perú
RPl	Río de la Plata
Ur	Uruguay
Ven	Venezuela

peruse /pə'ruːz/ vt (a) (read through) (frml or hum) leer* detenidamente (b) (examine, study) (frml) examinar

Peruvian¹ /pə'ruːviən/ adj peruano

Peruvian² n peruano, -na m,f

pervade /pər'veɪd ‖ pə'veɪd/ vt ‹idea/mood› dominar; ‹smell› llenar

pervasive /pər'veɪsɪv ‖ pə'veɪsɪv/ adj ‹smell› penetrante; ‹idea/mood› dominante; ‹influence› omnipresente

perverse /pər'vɜːrs ‖ pə'vɜːs/ adj (stubborn) obstinado; (wayward, contrary) retorcido

perversion /pər'vɜːrʒən ‖ pə'vɜːʃən/ n (a) (distortion): a ∼ of justice una deformación de la justicia (b) (Psych) perversión f

pervert¹ /pər'vɜːrt ‖ pə'vɜːt/ vt pervertir*

pervert² /'pɜːrvɜːrt ‖ 'pɜːvɜːt/ n pervertido, -da m,f

peseta /pə'seɪtə/ n peseta f

pesky /'peski/ adj -kier, -kiest (AmE colloq) latoso (fam)

peso /'peɪsəʊ/ n (pl ∼s) peso m

pessimism /'pesəmɪzəm ‖ 'pesɪmɪzəm/ n pesimismo m

pessimist /'pesəməst ‖ 'pesɪmɪst/ n pesimista mf

pessimistic /ˌpesə'mɪstɪk ‖ ˌpesɪ'mɪstɪk/ adj pesimista

pest /pest/ n (a) (Agr, Hort) plaga f (b) (person, thing) (colloq) peste f (fam)

pester /'pestər ‖ 'pestə(r)/ vt molestar

pesticide /'pestəsaɪd ‖ 'pestɪsaɪd/ n pesticida m

pestle /'pesəl/ n mano f de mortero

pet¹ /pet/ n (a) (animal) animal m doméstico or de compañía; (before n) ∼ food comida f para animales; ∼ shop ≈ pajarería f (b) (favorite): he's teacher's ∼ es el niño mimado de la maestra

pet² adj (before n) (a) (kept as pet): his ∼ budgie su periquito (b) (favorite) ‹subject/theory› favorito; my ∼ hate lo que más odio

pet³ -tt- vt ‹animal› acariciar
  ■ ∼ vi acariciarse, manosearse (pey)

petal /'petl/ n pétalo m

peter out /'piːtər/ [v + adv] «supplies» irse* agotando; «conversation» apagarse*

petition /pə'tɪʃən/ n (a) (written document) petición f (b) (Law) demanda f

pet name n apodo m

petrified /'petrɪfaɪd/ adj (a) (terrified) muerto de miedo (b) (Geol) petrificado

petrochemical /ˌpetrəʊ'kemɪkəl/ n producto m petroquímico; (before n) ‹industry/plant› petroquímico

petrol /'petrəl/ n (BrE) gasolina f, bencina f (Andes), nafta f (RPl); (before n) ∼ pump surtidor m; ∼ station estación f de servicio, gasolinera f, bomba f (AmL, Ven), estación f de nafta (RPl), bencinera f (Andes), grifo m (Per)

petroleum /pə'trəʊliəm/ n petróleo m; (before n) ∼ jelly vaselina f

petticoat /'petikəʊt/ n (a) (underskirt) enagua f or (Méx) fondo m (b) (slip) (BrE) combinación f, viso m

petty /'peti/ adj -tier, -tiest (a) (unimportant) ‹details› insignificante, nimio; ∼ thief ladronzuelo, -la m,f (b) (small-minded) mezquino

petty cash n caja f chica, dinero m para gastos menores

petulant /'petʃələnt ‖ 'petjʊlənt/ adj de mal genio

pew /pjuː/ n banco m (de iglesia)

pewter /'pjuːtər ‖ 'pjuːtə(r)/ n peltre m

PG (= **parental guidance**) menores acompañados

PG-13 (in US) mayores de 13 años o menores acompañados

phantom¹ /'fæntəm/ n (liter) fantasma m

phantom² adj (a) (ghostly) (liter) ‹before n› ‹shape› fantasmal; ‹horseman› fantasma adj inv (b) (imaginary) ilusorio

Pharaoh /'ferəʊ ‖ 'feərəʊ/ n faraón m

pharmaceutical /ˌfɑːrmə'suːtɪkəl ‖ ˌfɑːmə'sjuːtɪkəl/ adj farmacéutico

pharmacist /'fɑːrməsəst ‖ 'fɑːməsɪst/ n farmacéutico, -ca m,f, farmaceuta mf (Col, Ven)

pharmacy /'fɑːrməsi ‖ 'fɑːməsi/ n (pl -cies) (a) (discipline) química f farmacéutica, farmacia f (b) (dispensary) farmacia f

phase /feɪz/ n fase f
  ■ **phase out** [v + o + adv, v + adv + o] ‹service› retirar paulatinamente; ‹old model› dejar de producir

PhD n (= **Doctor of Philosophy**) (award) doctorado m; (person) Dr., Dra.

pheasant /'fezn̩t/ n (pl ∼s or ∼) faisán m

phenomena /fɪ'nɑːmənə ‖ fə'nɒmɪnə/ pl of PHENOMENON

phenomenal /fɪ'nɑːmənl̩ ‖ fə'nɒmɪnl̩/ adj (colloq) ‹success/achievement› espectacular; ‹strength› increíble

phenomenon /fɪ'nɑːmənɑːn ‖ fə'nɒmɪnən/ n (pl -mena) fenómeno m

phew /fjuː/ interj (colloq) ¡uf!

philanderer /fə'lændərər ‖ fɪ'lændərə(r)/ n (pej) mujeriego m (pey)

philanthropic /ˌfɪlən'θrɑːpɪk ‖ ˌfɪlən'θrɒpɪk/ adj filantrópico

philanthropist /fə'lænθrəpəst ‖ fɪ'lænθrəpɪst/ n filántropo, -pa m,f

philately /fə'lætl̩i ‖ fɪ'lætəli/ n (frml) filatelia f

Philippine /'fɪləpiːn ‖ 'fɪlɪpiːn/ adj filipino

Philippines /'fɪləpiːnz ‖ 'fɪlɪpiːnz/ pl n the ∼ (las) Filipinas

philistine /'fɪləstiːn, -aɪn ‖ 'fɪlɪstaɪn/ n ignorante mf

philosopher /fə'lɑːsəfər ‖ fɪ'lɒsəfə(r)/ n filósofo, -fa m,f

philosophic /ˌfɪlə'sɑːfɪk ‖ ˌfɪlə'sɒfɪk/, **-ical** /-ɪkəl/ adj filosófico; **to be ∼ ABOUT sth** tomarse algo con filosofía

philosophy /fə'lɑːsəfi ‖ fɪ'lɒsəfi/ n filosofía f

phlegm /flem/ n flema f

phobia /'fəʊbiə/ n fobia f

phoenix /'fiːnɪks/ n Ave f ♯ Fénix, fénix m or f

phone¹ /fəʊn/ n teléfono m; **to be on the ∼** (be speaking) estar* hablando por teléfono; (subscribe) (BrE) tener* teléfono; (before n) ∼ call llamada f (telefónica); ∼ number (número m de) teléfono m

phone² vt ⟨person⟩ llamar (por teléfono), telefonear, hablar (Méx); ⟨place/number⟩ llamar (por teléfono) a
■ **phone up** [v + adv + o, v + o + adv] llamar, telefonear

phone: ~ **book** n (colloq) guía f (telefónica or de teléfonos) or (Col, Méx) directorio m; ~ **booth,** (BrE) ~ **box** n cabina f telefónica; ~**card** n tarjeta f telefónica

phonetics /fə'netɪks/ n (+ sing vb) fonética f

phoney¹, (AmE also) **phony** /'fəʊni/ adj **-nier, -niest** (colloq & pej) falso

phoney², (AmE also) **phony** n (pl **-neys** or **-nies**) (colloq & pej) (person) farsante mf (fam); (thing) falsificación f

phosphate /'fɑːsfeɪt ‖ 'fɒsfeɪt/ n fosfato m

phosphorus /'fɑːsfərəs ‖ 'fɒsfərəs/ n fósforo m

photo /'fəʊtəʊ/ n (pl **-tos**) (colloq) foto f; **to take a ~ (of sb/sth)** sacar(le)* or (Esp tb) hacer(le)* una foto (a algn/algo)

photocopier /'fəʊtəʊ,kɑːpɪər ‖ 'fəʊtəʊ,kɒpiə(r)/ n fotocopiadora f

photocopy¹ /'fəʊtəʊ,kɑːpi ‖ 'fəʊtəʊ,kɒpi/ n (pl **-copies**) fotocopia f

photocopy² vt **-copies, -copying, -copied** fotocopiar

photo: ~ **finish** n foto(-)finish f; **P~fit®** n (BrE): **P~fit** (**picture**) retrato m hablado (AmS) or (Esp) or (Méx) reconstruido

photogenic /ˌfəʊtə'dʒenɪk/ adj fotogénico

photograph¹ /'fəʊtəɡræf ‖ 'fəʊtəɡrɑːf/ n fotografía f, foto f; **to take a ~ (of sb/sth)** sacar(le)* or (Esp tb) hacer(le)* una foto or una fotografía (a algn/algo)

photograph² vt fotografiar*, sacarle* or (Esp tb) hacerle* una foto or una fotografía a

photographer /fə'tɑːɡrəfər ‖ fə'tɒɡrəfə(r)/ n fotógrafo, -fa m,f

photographic /ˌfəʊtə'ɡræfɪk/ adj ⟨copy/ evidence/memory⟩ fotográfico; ⟨shop/equipment⟩ de fotografía

photography /fə'tɑːɡrəfi ‖ fə'tɒɡrəfi/ n fotografía f

photosynthesis /ˌfəʊtəʊ'sɪnθəsəs ‖ ˌfəʊtəʊ'sɪnθəsɪs/ n fotosíntesis f

phrasal verb /ˌfreɪzl̩/ n verbo m con partícula(s)

phrase¹ /freɪz/ n frase f

phrase² vt expresar

phrase book n manual m de conversación, ≈ guía m de bolsillo para el viajero

physical¹ /'fɪzɪkəl/ adj **1** (bodily) físico; ⟨illness⟩ orgánico; ~ **education** educación f física **2** (material) ⟨world⟩ material

physical² n reconocimiento m médico

physically /'fɪzɪkli/ adv ⟨attractive⟩ físicamente; ⟨demanding⟩ desde el punto de vista físico; **it's ~ impossible** es materialmente imposible

physical therapist n (AmE) ▶ PHYSIOTHERAPIST

physical therapy n (AmE) ▶ PHYSIOTHERAPY

physician /fə'zɪʃən ‖ fɪ'zɪʃən/ n (frml) médico, -ca m,f

physicist /'fɪzəsəst ‖ 'fɪzɪsɪst/ n físico, -ca m,f

physics /'fɪzɪks/ n (+ sing vb) física f

physiological /ˌfɪziə'lɑːdʒɪkəl ‖ ˌfɪziə'lɒdʒɪkəl/ adj fisiológico

physiology /ˌfɪzi'ɑːlədʒi ‖ ˌfɪzi'ɒlədʒi/ n fisiología f

physiotherapist /ˌfɪziəʊ'θerəpəst ‖ ˌfɪziəʊ'θerəpɪst/ n fisioterapeuta mf, kinesiólogo, -ga m,f

physiotherapy /ˌfɪziəʊ'θerəpi/ n (discipline) kinesiología f; (treatment) fisioterapia f, kinesiterapia f

physique /fə'ziːk ‖ fɪ'ziːk/ n físico m

pianist /pi'ænəst ‖ 'piənɪst/ n pianista mf

piano /pi'ænəʊ/ n (pl **-os**) piano m

pick¹ /pɪk/ n **1** (a) ▶ PICKAX (b) (ice ~) piolet m (c) (plectrum) púa f, plectro m, uñeta f (CS), uña f (Méx, Ven) **2** (choice) (no pl): **take your ~** elige or escoge el (or los etc) que quieras

pick² vt **1** (a) (choose, select) ⟨number/color⟩ elegir*, escoger*; ⟨team/crew⟩ seleccionar (b) (provoke): **to ~ a fight with sb** meterse con algn **2** (gather) ⟨flower⟩ cortar, coger* (esp Esp); ⟨fruit/ cotton/tea⟩ recoger*, coger* (esp Esp), pizcar* (Méx) **3** (a) (remove matter from): **to ~ one's nose** meterse el dedo en la nariz, hurgarse* la nariz; **don't ~ your spots** no te toques los granitos; **to ~ sb's pocket** robarle la billetera (or las llaves etc) a algn del bolsillo, bolsear a algn (Mex fam), carterear a algn (Chi fam) (b) (open) ⟨lock⟩ abrir* con una ganzúa (or una horquilla etc)
■ ~ vi (a) : **to ~ and choose** ser exigente (b) (take bits): **he was ~ing at his dinner** comía desganado
■ **pick on** [v + prep + o] (colloq) meterse con, agarrársela(s) con (AmL fam)
■ **pick out** [v + o + adv, v + adv + o] **1** (choose, select) elegir*, escoger* **2** (a) (recognize, identify) reconocer* (b) (discern) distinguir*
■ **pick up**
I [v + o + adv, v + adv + o] **1** (gather off floor, ground) recoger*; (take) tomar, agarrar (esp AmL), coger* (esp Esp); (lift up) levantar **2** (learn) ⟨language⟩ aprender; ⟨habit⟩ adquirir, agarrar (esp AmL), coger* (esp Esp) **3** (a) (collect, fetch) recoger* (b) (take on board) ⟨passenger⟩ recoger* (c) (colloq) ⟨man/woman⟩ ligarse* (fam), levantar (AmS fam) **4** (receive) ⟨signal⟩ captar
II [v + adv + o] (gain) ⟨speed⟩ agarrar, coger* (esp Esp)
III [v + o + adv] (a) (revive) reanimar (b) (correct) corregir*
IV [v + adv] (improve) «prices/sales» subir; «economy/business» repuntar; «invalid» mejorar; «weather» mejorar

pickax, (BrE) **pickaxe** /'pɪkæks/ n pico m, piqueta f

picket¹ /'pɪkət ‖ 'pɪkɪt/ n (group) piquete m; (before n) ~ **line** piquete m

picket² vt ⟨factory/workplace⟩ formar un piquete frente a, piquetear (esp AmL)

pickings /'pɪkɪŋz/ pl n (a) (profits) ganancias fpl (b) (food) sobras fpl

pickle¹ /'pɪkəl/ n (a) (dill ~) (AmE) pepinillo m

en vinagre al eneldo **(b)** ~**s** (vegetables) encurtidos *mpl*, pickles *mpl* (CS) **(c)** (relish) (BrE) *condimento a base de encurtidos en una salsa*

pickle² *vt* conservar en vinagre *or* (Chi tb) en escabeche, encurtir

pick: ~**-me-up** *n* (colloq) estimulante *m*; ~**pocket** *n* carterista *mf*, bolsista *mf* (Méx); ~**up** (**truck**) *n* camioneta *f* (de reparto)

picky /ˈpɪki/ *adj* **pickier, pickiest** (colloq) quisquilloso

picnic /ˈpɪknɪk/ *n* picnic *m*; **to go for** *o* **on a** ~ ir* de picnic

pictorial /pɪkˈtɔːriəl/ *adj* ‹representation› pictórico; ‹account/history› en imágenes; ‹magazine› ilustrado

picture¹ /ˈpɪktʃər ‖ˈpɪktʃə(r)/ *n* **1** **(a)** (illustration) ilustración *f*; (drawing) dibujo *m*; (painting) cuadro *m*, pintura *f*; (print) cuadro *m*, lámina *f*; (portrait) retrato *m* **(b)** (photo) foto *f*; **to take a** ~ **of sth/sb** sacarle* *or* (Esp tb) hacerle* una foto a algo/algn **2** (situation) panorama *m*; **to put sb in the** ~ poner* a algn al tanto (de la situación) **3** (idea) idea *f* **4** (TV) imagen *f* **5** (Cin) **(a)** (movie) película *f* **(b)** **pictures** *pl* (cinema) (BrE dated) **the** ~**s** el cine

picture² *vt* imaginarse

picturesque /ˌpɪktʃəˈresk/ *adj* pintoresco

pie /paɪ/ *n* (savory) empanada *f*; (sweet) pastel *m*, pay *m* (AmC, Méx)

piece /piːs/ *n* **1** **(a)** (part of sth broken, torn, cut, divided) pedazo *m*, trozo *m*; **she ripped the letter into** ~**s** rompió la carta en pedacitos; **to come** *o* **fall to** ~**s** hacerse* pedazos; **a** ~ **of land** un terreno, una parcela; **in one** ~ (safe) sano y salvo; (unbroken) intacto; **to go to** ~**s** perder* el control; **to pull sth/sb to** ~**s** destrozar* algo/a algn; **to say one's** ~ dar* su (*or* mi *etc*) opinión **(b)** (component) pieza *f*, parte *f*; **to take sth to** ~**s** desarmar algo **2** (item): **a** ~ **of advice** un consejo; **a** ~ **of furniture** un mueble; **a** ~ **of paper** un papel; **an excellent** ~ **of work** un trabajo excelente; **to give sb a** ~ **of one's mind** cantarle las cuarenta a algn **3** **(a)** (Mus): **a** ~ (**of music**) una pieza (de música) **(b)** (Journ) artículo *m* **4** (coin) moneda *f* **5** (in board games) ficha *f*; (in chess) figura *f* ▪ **piece together** [*v* + *o* + *adv*, *v* + *adv* + *o*] ‹fragments› juntar*; ‹events/facts› reconstruir*

piecemeal¹ /ˈpiːsmiːl/ *adj* poco sistemático

piecemeal² *adv* (gradually) poco a poco; (unsystematically) de manera poco sistemática

piecework /ˈpiːswɜːrk ‖ˈpiːswɜːk/ *n* trabajo *m* a destajo

pier /pɪr ‖pɪə(r)/ *n* **(a)** (landing place) embarcadero *m*, muelle *m* **(b)** (with amusements) *paseo con juegos y atracciones sobre un muelle*

pierce /pɪrs ‖pɪəs/ *vt* **(a)** (make a hole in) agujerear; (go through) atravesar*; **she's had her ears** ~**d** se ha hecho hacer agujeros en las orejas **(b)** ‹sound/light› (liter) rasgar* (liter)

piercing /ˈpɪrsɪŋ ‖ˈpɪəsɪŋ/ *adj* ‹eyes/look› penetrante; ‹scream› desgarrador

piety /ˈpaɪəti/ *n* piedad *f*

pig¹ /pɪg/ *n* **1** (Agr, Zool) cerdo *m*, chancho *m*

(AmL) **2** **(a)** (obnoxious person) (colloq) cerdo, -da *m,f* (fam) **(b)** (glutton) (colloq) glotón, -tona *m,f*, angurriento, -ta *m,f* (CS fam)

pigeon /ˈpɪdʒən ‖ˈpɪdʒɪn, ˈpɪdʒən/ *n* (Zool) paloma *f*; (Culin) pichón *m*

pigeonhole /ˈpɪdʒənhəʊl ‖ˈpɪdʒɪnhəʊl, ˈpɪdʒən-/ *n* **(a)** (on wall, desk) casillero *m* **(b)** (category) casilla *f*

piggy /ˈpɪgi/ *n* (*pl* **-gies**) (used to or by children) cerdito *m*, chanchito *m* (AmL)

piggy: ~**back** *n*: **to give sb a** ~**back** llevar a algn a caballo; ~**bank** *n* alcancía *f* (AmL), hucha *f* (Esp) (*en forma de cerdito*)

pigheaded /ˈpɪgˈhedəd ‖ˌpɪgˈhedɪd/ *adj* terco

piglet /ˈpɪglət ‖ˈpɪglɪt/ *n* cochinillo *m*, lechón *m*, chanchito *m* (AmL)

pigment /ˈpɪgmənt/ *n* pigmento *m*

pigmy /ˈpɪgmi/ *n* ▶ PYGMY

pig: ~**pen** (AmE) ▶ ~STY; ~**sty** *n* pocilga *f*, chiquero *m* (AmL); ~**tail** *n* (bunch) coleta *f*, chape *m* (Chi); (plait) trenza *f*

pike /paɪk/ *n* **(a)** (*pl* ~) (Zool) lucio *m* **(b)** (turn~) (AmE) carretera *f*

pilchard /ˈpɪltʃərd ‖ˈpɪltʃəd/ *n* sardina *f* (*grande*)

pile¹ /paɪl/ *n* **1** (stack, heap) montón *m* **2** (Tex) pelo *m* **3** **piles** *pl* (BrE Med) hemorroides *fpl*, almorranas *fpl*

pile² *vt* amontonar
▪ **pile in** [*v* + *adv*] (colloq) meterse
▪ **pile into** [*v* + *prep* + *o*] (colloq) **(a)** (squeeze into) ‹car› meterse en **(b)** (attack) arremeter contra **(c)** (crash into) ‹vehicle› estrellarse contra
▪ **pile up** **1** [*v* + *adv*] (accumulate) amontonarse **2** [*v* + *o* + *adv*, *v* + *adv* + *o*] (form into pile) apilar

pileup /ˈpaɪlʌp/ *n* choque *m* múltiple

pilfering /ˈpɪlfərɪŋ/ *n* robos *mpl*, hurtos *mpl*

pilgrim /ˈpɪlgrəm ‖ˈpɪlgrɪm/ *n* peregrino, -na *m,f*; (before *n*) **the P**~ **Fathers** *los primeros colonizadores de Nueva Inglaterra*

pilgrimage /ˈpɪlgrəmɪdʒ ‖ˈpɪlgrɪmɪdʒ/ *n* peregrinación *f*

pill /pɪl/ *n* **(a)** (tablet) pastilla *f*, píldora *f* **(b)** (contraceptive) **the P**~ la píldora (anticonceptiva); **to be on the P**~ tomar la píldora

pillage¹ /ˈpɪlɪdʒ/ *n* pillaje *m*

pillage² *vt/i* saquear

pillar /ˈpɪlər ‖ˈpɪlə(r)/ *n* pilar *m*; **he is a** ~ **of the community** es uno de los pilares *or* baluartes de la comunidad

pillar box *n* (BrE) buzón *m*

pillion¹ /ˈpɪljən ‖ˈpɪlɪən/ *n* (Auto) asiento *m* trasero (*de una moto*)

pillion² *adv* ‹ride› en el asiento trasero

pillory /ˈpɪləri/ *n* (*pl* **-ries**) picota *f*

pillow /ˈpɪləʊ/ *n* almohada *f*

pillowcase /ˈpɪləʊkeɪs/, (BrE also) **pillow slip** *n* funda *f*, almohadón *m* (Esp)

pilot¹ /ˈpaɪlət/ *n* **1** (Aerosp, Aviat) piloto *mf* **2** (Naut) práctico *mf* (de puerto) **3** (Rad, TV) programa *m* piloto

pilot² *adj* (before *n*) piloto *adj inv*

pilot³ *vt* **1** (Aviat, Naut) pilotar, pilotear (AmL) **2** (test) poner* a prueba

pilot light *n* piloto *m*

pimple /'pɪmpəl/ n grano m, espinilla f (AmL)

pin¹ /pɪn/ n **1** (for cloth, paper) alfiler m
2 (brooch, badge) (AmE) insignia f **3** **(a)** (on plug)
(BrE Elec) clavija f, borne m **(b)** (peg) (Tech) perno
m

pin² **-nn-** vt **1** (fasten, attach) ‹dress/seam›
prender con alfileres; **I ~ned the papers together**
sujeté los papeles con un alfiler; **she had ~ned**
her hopes on getting a scholarship había
depositado sus esperanzas en conseguir una beca;
they tried to ~ the blame on him trataron de
hacerle cargar con la culpa
2 (hold motionless) inmovilizar*
■ **pin down** [v + o + adv, v + adv + o] **1** (prevent
from moving): **they ~ned him down** (se echaron
sobre él y) lo inmovilizaron
2 **(a)** (define) ‹cause/identity› definir;
something's wrong with me, but I can't ~ it down
algo tengo, pero no sabría decir exactamente qué
(b) (force to state position): **I managed to ~ him**
down to a definite date conseguí que se
comprometiera para una fecha concreta

PIN /pɪn/ n (= **personal identification**
number) PIN m

pinafore /'pɪnəfɔːr ‖'pɪnəfɔː(r)/ n **(a)** ~
(dress) (sleeveless dress) jumper m or (Esp) pichi
m **(b)** (apron) (BrE) delantal m or (esp Méx) mandil
m (con peto) **(c)** (protective overdress) delantal m

pinball /'pɪnbɔːl/ n (before n) ~ **machine** flipper
m

pincer /'pɪnsər ‖'pɪnsə(r)/ n **(a)** (Zool) pinza f
(b) **pincers** pl (tool) tenaza(s) f(pl)

pinch¹ /pɪntʃ/ n **(a)** (act) pellizco m; **in o** (BrE) **at**
a ~ si fuera necesario **(b)** (small quantity) pizca f

pinch² vt **1** «person» pellizcar*; «shoes»
apretar **2** (BrE colloq) (steal) robar

pinched /pɪntʃt/ adj: **faces ~ with grief** caras
transidas de dolor

pincushion /'pɪn,kʊʃən/ n alfiletero m

pine¹ /paɪn/ n **(a)** ~ **(tree)** pino m; (before n)
~ **cone** piña f; ~ **needle** hoja f de pino **(b)** (wood)
(madera f de) pino m

pine² vi estar* triste; **to ~ FOR sth** suspirar POR
algo
■ **pine away** [v + adv] languidecer* de añoranza

pineapple /'paɪn,æpəl/ n piña f or (esp RPl)
ananá f

Ping-Pong®, **ping-pong** /'pɪŋpɑːŋ ‖'pɪŋpɒŋ/
n ping-pong m

pinion /'pɪnjən/ vt ‹person› inmovilizar* (esp
sujetándole los brazos)

pink¹ /pɪŋk/ adj **-er, -est** rosa adj inv, rosado
(AmL); ‹cheeks› sonrosado

pink² n rosa m, rosado m (AmL)

pinking shears /'pɪŋkɪŋ/ pl n tijeras fpl
dentadas

pin money n dinero para gastos personales

pinnacle /'pɪnɪkəl ‖'pɪnəkəl/ n **(a)** (Archit)
pináculo m **(b)** (mountain peak) cumbre f, cima f

pin: ~**point** vt ‹position› localizar* or (AmL tb)
ubicar* con exactitud; **to ~point the causes of**

the problem establecer* con exactitud cuáles son
las causas del problema; ~**prick** n pinchazo m;
~**s and needles** pl n hormigueo m;
~**stripe, ~striped** adj: ~**stripe(d) suit** traje m
oscuro de raya diplomática

pint /paɪnt/ n pinta f (EEUU: 0,47 litros, RU: 0,57
litros)

pinup /'pɪnʌp/ n foto f (de chica atractiva, actor
famoso etc); (person) pin-up mf

pioneer¹ /'paɪə'nɪr ‖,paɪə'nɪə(r)/ n pionero, -ra
m,f

pioneer² vt **(a)** ‹policy› promover*; ‹technique›
ser* el primero (or la primera etc) en aplicar **(b)**
pioneering pres p ‹research› pionero

pious /'paɪəs/ adj piadoso; (sanctimonious) beato

pip /pɪp/ n **1** (seed) pepita f **2** (BrE Rad, Telec)
pitido m

pipe¹ /paɪp/ n **1** (for liquid, gas) caño m **2** (for
tobacco) pipa f **3** (Mus) **(a)** (wind instrument)
caramillo m **(b)** (of organ) tubo m **(c) pipes** pl
gaita f

pipe² vt (transport by pipe) (+ adv compl) llevar
(por tuberías, gasoducto, oleoducto)
■ **pipe down** [v + adv] (colloq) (usu in imperative)
callarse la boca (fam)

piped music /paɪpt/ n música f ambiental,
hilo m musical (fam)

pipe: ~ **dream** n quimera f, sueño m guajiro
(Méx); ~**line** n conducto m, ducto m (Méx); **it's in**
the ~line está proyectado

piper /'paɪpər ‖'paɪpə(r)/ n gaitero, -ra m,f

piping¹ /'paɪpɪŋ/ n cañería f, tubería f

piping² adv (as intensifier): ~ **hot** bien caliente

pique¹ /piːk/ n despecho m

pique² vt: **he was ~d by her lack of interest** se
resintió por su falta de interés

piracy /'paɪrəsi/ n piratería f

pirate /'paɪrət/ n **(a)** (at sea) pirata mf **(b)**
(before n) ‹tape/video/radio station› pirata adj inv

pirouette¹ /'pɪru'et/ n giro m; (in ballet) pirueta
f

pirouette² vi girar

Pisces /'paɪsiːz/ n **(a)** (sign) (no art) Piscis **(b)**
(person) Piscis or piscis mf

piss¹ /pɪs/ n (sl) **(a)** (act) (no pl) meada f (vulg)
(b) (urine) meados mpl (vulg)

piss² vi (sl) mear (vulg)
■ **piss off** (sl) **1** [v + adv] (go away) (BrE): ~ **off!**
¡vete a la mierda! (vulg) **2** [v + o + adv] (anger): **it**
~**es me off** me revienta (fam), me encabrona (Esp,
Méx vulg)

pissed /pɪst/ adj (sl) **(a)** (AmE) (fed up) cabreado
(fam), encabronado (Esp, Méx vulg), choreado (Chi
fam) **(b)** (drunk) (BrE) como una cuba (fam), tomado
(AmL fam)

pistachio /pɪ'stæʃiəʊ/ n ~ **(nut)** pistacho m,
pistache m (Méx)

pistol /'pɪstl/ n pistola f

piston /'pɪstən/ n émbolo m, pistón m

pit¹ /pɪt/ n **1** (hole — in ground) hoyo m; (— for

burying) fosa *f*; (— as trap) trampa *f*; (**inspection**) ∼ (Auto) foso *m or* (RPl) fosa *f* **2** (coalmine) mina *f* (*de carbón*); (quarry) cantera *f* **3** (orchestra ∼) foso *m* orquestal *or* de la orquesta **4** **pits** *pl* (the very worst) (sl) **the ∼s** lo peor que hay (fam) **5** (in fruit) (AmE) hueso *m*, carozo *m* (CS), pepa *f* (Col)

pit² -tt- *vt* ⟨surface/metal⟩ picar*

■ **pit against** [*v + o + prep + o*] enfrentar a; **to ∼ oneself against sb** enfrentarse a algn

pitch¹ /pɪtʃ/ *n* **(a)** (level, degree) (*no pl*) punto *m*, extremo *m* **(b)** (Mus) tono *m* **(c)** (in baseball) lanzamiento *m* **(d)** (Sport) (playing area) (BrE) campo *m*, cancha *f* (AmL) **(e)** (position, site) (BrE) lugar *m*, sitio *m*; (in market, fair) puesto *m* **(f)** (substance) brea *f*

pitch² *vt* **1** (set up) ⟨tent⟩ armar, montar; ⟨camp⟩ montar, hacer* **2** (Sport) ⟨ball⟩ lanzar*, pichear **3** (aim, set, address): **she doesn't know at what level to ∼ her talk** no sabe qué nivel darle a la charla

■ ∼ *vi* **(a)** (fall) (+ *adv compl*) caerse* **(b)** (lurch) ⟨ship/plane⟩ cabecear

■ **pitch in** [*v + adv*] (colloq) arrimar el hombro

pitch-black /ˈpɪtʃˈblæk/, **pitch-dark** /ˈpɪtʃˈdɑːrk ‖ˌpɪtʃˈdɑːk/ *adj* ⟨night⟩ (oscuro) como boca de lobo (fam), muy oscuro; ⟨surface⟩ negro como el azabache

pitched battle /pɪtʃt/ *n* batalla *f* campal

pitcher /ˈpɪtʃər ‖ˈpɪtʃə(r)/ *n* **1** (for pouring) jarra *f*, pichel *m* (AmC); (of clay) (BrE) cántaro *m* **2** (in baseball) lanzador, -dora *m,f*, pitcher *mf*

pitchfork /ˈpɪtʃfɔːrk ‖ˈpɪtʃfɔːk/ *n* horca *f*, horquilla *f*, horqueta *f* (Chi)

pitfall /ˈpɪtfɔːl/ *n* (difficulty) dificultad *f*; (risk) riesgo *m*

pith /pɪθ/ *n* tejido blanco fibroso que recubre el interior de la cáscara de los cítricos

pithy /ˈpɪθi/ *adj* **pithier, pithiest** ⟨remark/ reply⟩ sucinto *or* conciso y expresivo

pitiful /ˈpɪtɪfəl/ *adj* **(a)** (arousing pity) ⟨cry/moan⟩ lastimero; ⟨sight⟩ lastimoso **(b)** (wretched, inadequate) lamentable

pittance /ˈpɪtn̩s/ *n* miseria *f*

pituitary gland /pəˈtuːəteri ‖prˈtjuːɪtəri/ *n* glándula pituitaria *f*

pity¹ /ˈpɪti/ *n* **1** (*no pl*) (cause of regret) lástima *f*, pena *f*; **it's a ∼** (THAT) es una lástima *or* una pena QUE (+ *subj*); **what a ∼!** ¡qué lástima!, ¡que pena! **2** (compassion) piedad *f*; **to take ∼ on sb/ sth** apiadarse de algn/algo

pity² *vt* **pities, pitying, pitied** tenerle* lástima a

pivot /ˈpɪvət/ *vi* (Mech Eng) pivotar; **he ∼ed on his heel** giró sobre sus talones

pixie /ˈpɪksi/ *n* (elf) duendecillo *m*; (fairy) hadita *f*

pizza /ˈpiːtsə/ *n* pizza *f*

pizzeria /ˌpiːtsəˈriːə/ *n* pizzería *f*

placard /ˈplækɑːrd ‖ˈplækɑːd/ *n* letrero *m*; (at demonstration) pancarta *f*

placate /ˈpleɪkeɪt ‖pləˈkeɪt/ *vt* apaciguar*

place¹ /pleɪs/ *n* **1** **(a)** (spot, position, area) lugar *m*, sitio *m*; **to have friends in high ∼s** tener* amigos influyentes; *all over the* ∼ por todas partes; *to fall into* ∼ aclararse **(b)** (specific location) lugar *m*; ∼ **of birth** lugar de nacimiento **(c)** (in

phrases) **in place: to hold sth in ∼** sujetar algo; **out of place: to look out of ∼** ⟪*furniture*⟫ quedar mal; **to feel out of ∼** sentirse* fuera de lugar **2** **(a)** (building, shop, restaurant etc) sitio *m*, lugar *m* **(b)** (home): **my/his ∼** mi/su casa **3** **(a)** (position, role) lugar *m*; **I wouldn't change ∼s with her for anything** no me cambiaría por ella por nada; **nobody can ever take your ∼** nadie podrá jamás ocupar tu lugar **(b)** in place of (*as prep*) en lugar de **(c)** to take place (occur) ocurrir*; ⟪*meeting/concert/wedding*⟫ tener* lugar **4** (seat): **save me a ∼** guárdame un asiento **(b)** (at table) cubierto *m*; **to lay/set a ∼ for sb** poner* un cubierto para algn **5** (in contest, league) puesto *m*; **your social life will have to take second ∼** tu vida social va a tener que pasar a un segundo plano **6** (in book, sequence): **you've made me lose my ∼** me has hecho perder la página (*or* la línea *etc*) por donde iba **7** **(a)** (job) puesto *m* **(b)** (BrE Educ) plaza *f* **(c)** (on team) puesto *m* **8** (in argument) lugar *m*; **in the first/second ∼** en primer/segundo lugar

place² *vt* **1** (put, position) ⟨object⟩ poner*; (carefully, precisely) colocar* **2** (in race): **this victory ∼s her among the top three** este triunfo la sitúa entre las tres primeras **3** **(a)** (find a home, job for) colocar* **(b)** ⟨advertisement⟩ poner*; ⟨phone call⟩ pedir*; **we ∼d an order with Acme Corp** hicimos un pedido a Acme Corp **4** (identify) ⟨tune⟩ identificar*, ubicar* (AmL); **her face is familiar, but I can't quite ∼ her** su cara me resulta conocida pero no sé de dónde *or* (AmL tb) pero no la ubico

placebo /pləˈsiːbəʊ/ *n* (*pl* ∼**s** *or* ∼**es**) placebo *m*

place mat *n* (mantel *m*) individual *m*

placement /ˈpleɪsmənt/ *n* **(a)** (in employment) colocación *f* **(b)** (positioning) colocación *f*, ubicación *f* (esp AmL)

place name *n* topónimo *m*

placenta /pləˈsentə/ *n* (*pl* ∼**s** *or* ∼**e** /-tiː/) placenta *f*

placid /ˈplæsəd ‖ˈplæsɪd/ *adj* plácido

plagiarism /ˈpleɪdʒərɪzəm/ *n* plagio *m*

plagiarize /ˈpleɪdʒəraɪz/ *vt* plagiar

plague¹ /pleɪɡ/ *n* **(a)** (disease) peste *f* **(b)** (horde — of locusts, tourists) plaga *f*

plague² *vt* **(a)** (afflict): **a country ∼d by strikes** un país asolado por constantes huelgas; ∼**d with problems** plagado de problemas **(b)** (pester) acosar

plaice /pleɪs/ *n* (*pl* ∼) platija *f*

plaid /plæd/ *n* (pattern) cuadros *mpl* escoceses; (material) tela *f* escocesa

plain¹ /pleɪn/ *adj* **-er, -est** **1** **(a)** (unadorned) ⟨decor/cooking/language⟩ sencillo; ⟨fabric⟩ liso **(b)** (Culin): ∼ **chocolate** (BrE) chocolate *m* sin leche; ∼ **flour** harina *f* común **2** **(a)** (clear) claro; **the reasons are ∼ to see** las razones saltan a la vista **(b)** (blunt): **the ∼ truth** la pura verdad **3** (not good-looking) feo, poco agraciado

plain² *adv* (as intensifier) totalmente; **that's just ∼ stupid** eso es una completa estupidez

plain³ *n* llanura *f*

p

plain clothes /pl n/: in ∼ de civil or (Esp tb) de paisano

plainly /'pleɪmli/ adv (a) (obviously, visibly) claramente (b) (clearly) ⟨explain⟩ claramente; ⟨remember⟩ perfectamente (c) (bluntly) ⟨speak⟩ claramente (d) ⟨dress⟩ con sencillez

plaintiff /'pleɪntəf ‖ 'pleɪntɪf/ n demandante mf

plaintive /'pleɪntɪv/ adj lastimero

plait¹ /plæt/ n trenza f

plait² vt trenzar*

plan¹ /plæn/ n **1** (a) (diagram, map) plano m (b) (of book, essay) esquema m **2** (arrangement, scheme) plan m; do you have any ∼s for tonight? ¿tienes algún plan para esta noche?

plan² -nn- vt ⟨journey/raid⟩ planear; ⟨garden/house⟩ diseñar; ⟨economy/strategies⟩ planificar*; ⟨essay⟩ hacer* un esquema de; ⟨surprise⟩ preparar; as ∼ned según lo planeado; to ∼ to + INF: where are you ∼ning to spend Christmas? ¿dónde tienes pensado pasar las Navidades?

■ ∼ vi: to ∼ ahead planear las cosas de antemano

■ **plan on** [v + prep + o] (a) (intend) pensar* (b) (expect, count on) contar* con

plane¹ /pleɪn/ n **1** (aircraft) avión m **2** ∼ **(tree)** plátano m **3** (tool) cepillo m de carpintero; (longer) garlopa f **4** (surface) plano m

plane² vt ⟨wood/surface⟩ cepillar

planet /'plænət ‖ 'plænɪt/ n planeta m

planetary /'plænəteri ‖ 'plænɪtəri/ adj (before n) planetario

plank /plæŋk/ n tabla f, tablón m

plankton /'plæŋktən/ n plancton m

planned /plænd/ adj planeado; ∼ **parenthood** (AmE) planificación f familiar

planner /'plænər ‖ 'plænə(r)/ n (a) (of project) planificador, -dora m,f (b) (town ∼) urbanista mf

planning /'plænɪŋ/ n (a) (of project) planificación f (b) (town ∼) urbanismo m; (before n) ∼ **permission** (BrE) permiso m de obras

plant¹ /plænt ‖ plɑːnt/ n **1** (Bot) planta f **2** (a) (factory, installation) planta f (b) (equipment) maquinaria f

plant² vt **1** ⟨flower/trees⟩ plantar; ⟨seeds⟩ sembrar* **2** (place) ⟨bomb⟩ colocar*; ⟨kiss⟩ dar*, plantar (fam); she ∼ed herself right next to me se me plantó justo al lado (fam) **3** ⟨drugs/evidence⟩ colocar*; ⟨agent/informer⟩ infiltrar

plantain /'plæntn̩ ‖ 'plæntɪn/ n plátano m grande (para cocinar), plátano m (Col, Ven), plátano m macho (Méx)

plantation /plæn'teɪʃən ‖ plæn'teɪʃən, plɑːn-/ n plantación f

plaque /plæk/ n **1** (tablet) placa f **2** (Dent) sarro m, placa f (dental)

plasma /'plæzmə/ n plasma m

plaster¹ /'plæstər ‖ 'plɑːstə(r)/ n **1** (a) (Const) (powder, mixture) yeso m; (on walls) revoque m (b) ∼ **(of Paris)** (Art, Med) yeso m, escayola f (Esp); **to have one's leg in** ∼ tener* la pierna enyesada or (Esp) escayolada **2** (sticking ∼) (BrE) ▶ BAND-AID

plaster² vt (Const) ⟨wall/room⟩ revocar*; ⟨cracks⟩ rellenar con yeso

plaster cast n (a) (Med) yeso m or (Esp) escayola f (b) (Art) molde m de yeso, escayola f (Esp)

plastic¹ /'plæstɪk/ n plástico m; (before n) de plástico

plastic² adj **1** (artificial) (pej) ⟨smile/people⟩ de plástico (pey) **2** (a) (malleable) (Tech) plástico, moldeable (b) (Art) plástico

plastic: ∼ **bullet** n bala f de plástico; ∼ **explosive** n explosivo m plástico, goma dos f

Plasticine® /'plæstəsiːn/ n plastilina® f, plasticina® f (CS)

plastic: ∼ **surgeon** n cirujano plástico, cirujana plástica m,f (AmL), especialista mf en cirugía estética or plástica; ∼ **surgery** n cirugía f estética or plástica

plate¹ /pleɪt/ n **1** (a) (dish) plato m (b) (dishes) vajilla f (de plata u oro) **2** (of metal) chapa f; (thin) lámina f; (of glass) placa f **3** (a) (Phot) placa f (b) (Art, Print) plancha f (c) (illustration) ilustración f, lámina f

plate² vt (Metall) to ∼ sth WITH sth recubrir* algo DE algo

plateau /plæ'tə ‖ 'plætə/ n (pl -teaus or -teaux /-z/) meseta f

platform /'plætfɔːrm ‖ 'plætfɔːm/ n (a) (raised structure) plataforma f; (for orator) estrado m, tribuna f (b) (Rail) andén m (c) (Pol) (opportunity to air views) plataforma f, tribuna f

platinum /'plætnəm ‖ 'plætɪnəm/ n platino m

platitude /'plætətuːd ‖ 'plætɪtjuːd/ n lugar m común

platonic /plə'tɑːnɪk ‖ plə'tɒnɪk/ adj platónico

platoon /plə'tuːn/ n (Mil) sección f

platter /'plætər ‖ 'plætə(r)/ n fuente f

platypus /'plætɪpəs/ n (pl ∼**es**) (duck-billed ∼) ornitorrinco m

plausible /'plɔːzəbəl/ adj ⟨argument/story⟩ verosímil; ⟨liar⟩ convincente

play¹ /pleɪ/ n **1** (a) (recreation) juego m (b) (Sport) juego m **2** (interplay) juego m **3** (slack) (Tech) juego m **4** (Theat) obra f (de teatro), pieza f (teatral), comedia f **5** (pun): a ∼ **on words** un juego de palabras, un albur (Méx)

play² vt

I 1 (a) ⟨cards/hopscotch⟩ jugar* a; **to** ∼ **a joke/trick on sb** hacerle* or gastarle una broma/una jugarreta a algn (b) ⟨football/chess⟩ jugar* (AmL exc RPl), jugar* a (Esp, RPl)

2 (a) (compete against) ⟨opponent⟩ jugar* contra (b) ⟨card⟩ tirar, jugar*; ⟨piece⟩ mover* (c) (in particular position) jugar* de

II 1 (Theat) (a) ⟨villain/Hamlet⟩ representar el papel de; **to** ∼ **the innocent** hacerse* el inocente (b) ⟨theater/town⟩ actuar* en

2 (Mus) ⟨instrument/note/piece⟩ tocar*

3 (Audio) ⟨tape/record⟩ poner*

■ ∼ vi

I 1 (amuse oneself) «children» jugar*; **to** ∼ **AT sth** jugar* A algo

2 (Games, Sport) jugar*

II 1 (a) (Theat) «cast» actuar*; «show» ser* representado (b) (pretend): **to** ∼ **dead** hacerse* el muerto; **to** ∼ **hard to get** hacerse* el (or la etc) interesante

2 (Mus) «musician» tocar*; **music was** ∼**ing in the background** se escuchaba una música de fondo

■ **play along 1** [v + adv] (cooperate): **I refuse to**

~ along with him/his schemes me niego a hacerle el juego/a tener nada que ver con sus enjuagues (fam)
[2] [*v* + *o* + *adv*] (deceive, manipulate) manipular
■ **play around** [*v* + *adv*] jugar*, juguetear (fam & pey)
■ **play back** [*v* + *o* + *adv*, *v* + *adv* + *o*] poner* (*una grabación*)
■ **play down** [*v* + *o* + *adv*, *v* + *adv* + *o*] ‹*importance*› minimizar*; ‹*risk/achievement*› quitarle importancia a
■ **play off** [*v* + *o* + *adv*] oponer*; **to ~ sb off against sb**: she ~s her parents off against each other hace pelear a sus padres para lograr sus propósitos
■ **play up** [1] [*v* + *adv*] (BrE) (cause trouble) (colloq) «*child*» dar* guerra (fam); «*car/TV*» no funcionar bien
[2] [*v* + *o* + *adv*] (cause trouble) (BrE colloq) «*child*» darle* guerra a (fam); «*shoulder/back*» darle* problemas a (fam)

play: ~**back** *n* play-back *m*; ~**boy** *n* playboy *m*; ~**-by-~** /'pleɪbaɪ'pleɪ/ *adj* (AmE Sport) (*before n*) jugada a jugada

player /'pleɪər ǁ 'pleɪə(r)/ *n* [1] (Games, Sport) jugador, -dora *m,f* [2] (Mus) músico *m/f*, músico, -ca *m,f*

playful /'pleɪfəl/ *adj* (a) (boisterous) juguetón (b) (not serious) pícaro

playfully /'pleɪfəli/ *adv* (a) (boisterously) juguetonamente (b) (humorously) ‹*remark/slap*› en broma

play: ~**ground** *n* (BrE) patio *m* (de recreo); ~**group** *n*: grupo de actividades lúdico-educativas para niños de edad preescolar

playing /'pleɪŋ/**:** ~ **card** *n* naipe *m*, carta *f*; ~ **field** *n* (BrE) (*often pl*) campo *m* de juego, cancha *f* de deportes (esp AmL)

play: ~**mate** *n* compañero, -ra *m,f* de juegos; ~**off** *n* desempate *m*; ~**pen** *n* corral *m*, parque *m* (Esp); ~**room** *n* cuarto *m* de los juguetes; ~**thing** *n* juguete *m*; ~**time** *n* (*no art*) (BrE) recreo *m*; ~**wright** /'pleɪraɪt/ *n* dramaturgo, -ga *m,f*

plaza /'plæzə ǁ 'plɑːzə/ *n* (a) (square) plaza *f*; (in front of large building) explanada *f* (b) (complex) (AmE) centro *m* comercial

plc, Plc (in UK) (= **public limited company**) ≈ S.A.

plea /pliː/ *n* [1] (appeal) (frml) petición *f*; (in supplication) ruego *m* [2] (Law): **to enter a ~ of guilty/not guilty** declararse culpable/inocente

plead /pliːd/ (*past & past p* **pleaded** *or* (AmE also) **pled**) *vt* alegar*; **she's not coming, she ~ed poverty** no viene, dijo que no tenía dinero
■ ~ *vi* (a) (implore, beg) suplicar*; **to ~ FOR sth** suplicar* algo; **to ~ WITH sb to + INF** suplicarle* a algn QUE (+ *subj*) (b) (Law): **to ~ guilty/not guilty** declararse culpable/inocente

pleasant /'plezənt/ *adj* **-er, -est** agradable; ‹*person*› simpático, agradable

pleasantly /'plezəntli/ *adv* ‹*say/speak*› en tono agradable; ‹*smile*› con simpatía; **I was ~ surprised by the changes** los cambios me causaron una grata sorpresa

pleasantry /'plezəntri/ *n* (*pl* **-ries**) cortesía *f*

please¹ /pliːz/ *interj* por favor; **yes, ~** sí, gracias

please² *vt* (make happy) complacer*; (satisfy) contentar
■ ~ *vi* (a) (satisfy): **we do our best to ~** hacemos todo lo posible por complacer al cliente (*or* a todo el mundo *etc*) (b) (choose) querer*; **do as you ~** haz lo que quieras
■ *v refl* **to ~ oneself**: ~ **yourself** haz lo que quieras

pleased /pliːzd/ *adj* (satisfied) satisfecho; (happy) contento; **I'm very ~ for you!** me alegro mucho por ti; **she was very ~ with herself** estaba muy ufana; **I am ~ to inform you that ...** (frml) tengo el placer de comunicarle que ... (frml); ~ **to meet you** encantado (de conocerlo), mucho gusto

pleasing /'pliːzɪŋ/ *adj* (a) (pleasant) agradable (b) (gratifying) ‹*news*› grato

pleasurable /'pleʒərəbəl/ *adj* placentero

pleasure /'pleʒər ǁ 'pleʒə(r)/ *n* [1] (happiness, satisfaction) placer *m*; **it's a ~ to listen to her** es un placer escucharla; **it gives me great ~ to introduce ...** es un placer para mí presentarles ...; **to take ~ in sth** disfrutar con algo [2] (a) (recreation) placer *m*; **I play just for ~** toco sólo porque me gusta (b) (source of happiness) placer *m*; **Jane is a real ~ to teach** da gusto darle clases a Jane

pleasure boat *n* (steamer) barco *m* de recreo; (small craft) bote *m* de recreo

pleat /pliːt/ *n* pliegue *m*; (wide) tabla *f*

plectrum /'plektrəm/ *n* (*pl* **-trums** *or* **-tra** /-trə/) púa *f*, plectro *m*, uñeta *f* (CS), uña *f* (Méx, Ven)

pled /pled/ (AmE) *past & past p of* PLEAD

pledge¹ /pledʒ/ *vt* ‹*support/funds*› prometer

pledge² *n* (a) (promise) promesa *f*; **to make a ~ to + INF** prometer + INF (b) (of money) cantidad *f* prometida

plentiful /'plentɪfəl/ *adj* abundante

plenty¹ /'plenti/ *n* abundancia *f*

plenty² *pron* [1] (a) (large, sufficient number) muchos, -chas (b) **plenty of** muchos, -chas [2] (a) (large, sufficient quantity) mucho, -cha; **$50 is ~** 50 dólares es más que suficiente (b) **plenty of** mucho, -cha; ~ **of time** tiempo de sobra

plethora /'pleθərə/ *n* (*no pl*) **a ~ OF sth** una plétora DE algo

Plexiglas® /'pleksɪglæs ǁ 'pleksɪglɑːs/ *n* (AmE) acrílico *m*, plexiglás® *m* (Esp)

pliable /'plaɪəbəl/, **pliant** /'plaɪənt/ *adj* ‹*material/substance*› maleable; ‹*person/attitude*› flexible

pliers /'plaɪərz ǁ 'plaɪəz/ *pl n* alicate(s) *m(pl)*, pinza(s) *f(pl)* (Méx, RPl)

plight /plaɪt/ *n* (*no pl*) situación *f* difícil

plimsoll /'plɪmsəl/ *n* (BrE) zapatilla *f* de lona, tenis *m*, playera *f* (Esp)

plinth /plɪnθ/ *n* (of pillar, column) plinto *m*; (of statue) pedestal *m*

plod /plɒd ǁ plɒd/ *vi* **-dd-** (a) (walk) caminar lenta y pesadamente (b) (work): **she's still ~ding away at her thesis** sigue lidiando con la tesis

plonk¹ /plɑːŋk ǁ plɒŋk/ *vt* (BrE colloq) ▶ PLUNK

plonk² *n* (colloq) vino *m* peleón (fam)

plot¹ /plɑːt ‖plɒt/ n **1** (conspiracy) complot m **2** (story) argumento m **3** (piece of land) terreno m, solar m, parcela f

plot² -tt- vt **1** (mark out) ⟨curve/graph⟩ trazar*; ⟨position⟩ determinar **2** (plan) ⟨rebellion/revenge⟩ tramar
■ ~ vi to ~ (AGAINST sb) conspirar (CONTRA algn)

plotter /ˈplɑːtər ‖ˈplɒtə(r)/ n **1** (conspirator) conspirador, -dora m,f **2** (Comput, Tech) trazador m de gráficos

plough etc /plaʊ/ (BrE) ▶ PLOW etc

plow¹, (BrE) **plough** /plaʊ/ n (Agr) arado m

plow², (BrE) **plough** vt arar
■ ~ vi arar la tierra
■ **plow back,** (BrE) **plough back** [v + o + adv, v + adv + o] ⟨profits⟩ reinvertir*
■ **plow into,** (BrE) **plough into** [v + prep + o] ⟨vehicle/wall⟩ estrellarse contra
■ **plow through,** (BrE) **plough through** [v + prep + o] ⟨mud/snow⟩ abrirse* camino a través de; I'm still ~ing through the book todavía estoy tratando de leer el libro, pero me cuesta

plowman, (BrE) **ploughman** /ˈplaʊmən/ n (pl **-men** /-mən/) labrador m

ploy /plɔɪ/ n treta f

pluck¹ /plʌk/ vt (a) ⟨chicken⟩ desplumar; to ~ one's eyebrows depilarse las cejas (b) ⟨fruit/flower⟩ arrancar*; to ~ up (the) courage to + INF armarse de valor para + INF (c) (Mus) ⟨string/guitar⟩ puntear

pluck² n valor m

plucky /ˈplʌki/ adj **pluckier, pluckiest** valiente

plug¹ /plʌg/ n **1** (stopper) tapón m **2** (Elec) (a) (attached to lead) enchufe m; (socket) toma f de corriente, enchufe m, tomacorriente(s) m (AmL) (b) (spark ~) bujía f

plug² -gg- vt **1** ⟨hole/gap⟩ tapar **2** (promote) ⟨record/book⟩ hacerle* propaganda a
■ **plug in 1** [v + o + adv, v + adv + o] enchufar **2** [v + adv] enchufarse

plughole /ˈplʌɡhəʊl/ n (BrE) desagüe m

plum /plʌm/ n ciruela f

plumage /ˈpluːmɪdʒ/ n plumaje m

plumb¹ /plʌm/ adv (colloq) justo

plumb² vt **1** (fathom) ⟨mystery⟩ dilucidar **2** (Naut) sondar, sondear

plumber /ˈplʌmər ‖ˈplʌmə(r)/ n plomero, -ra m,f or (AmC, Esp) fontanero, -ra m,f or (Per) gasfitero, -ra m,f or (Chi) gásfiter mf

plumbing /ˈplʌmɪŋ/ n (pipes) cañerías fpl, tuberías fpl; (installation) instalación f de agua

plume /pluːm/ n pluma f; (cluster of feathers) penacho m

plummet /ˈplʌmət ‖ˈplʌmɪt/ vi caer* en picada or (Esp) en picado

plump /plʌmp/ adj **-er, -est** ⟨person/face⟩ (re)llenito; ⟨chicken/rabbit⟩ gordo
■ **plump for** [v + prep + o] (colloq) decidirse por
■ **plump up** [v + o + adv, v + adv + o] ⟨pillow/cushion⟩ ahuecar*

plunder¹ /ˈplʌndər ‖ˈplʌndə(r)/ vt (a) (steal from) ⟨village⟩ saquear (b) (steal) ⟨treasure/wealth⟩ robar

plunder² n (a) (objects) botín m (b) (action) saqueo m

plunge¹ /plʌndʒ/ vt to ~ sth INTO sth (a) (immerse, thrust) ⟨into liquid⟩ sumergir* algo EN algo; she ~d the knife into his heart le hundió el cuchillo en el corazón (b) (into state, condition) sumir algo/a algn EN algo
■ ~ vi **1** (dive) zambullirse*; (fall) caer* **2** (a) (slope downward steeply) ⟨road/path⟩ descender* bruscamente (b) (drop) ⟨price/temperature/popularity⟩ caer* en picada or (Esp) en picado

plunge² n (in water) zambullida f; **to take the ~** (take a risk) arriesgarse*, jugarse* el todo por todo; (get married) casarse, darse* el paso

plunger /ˈplʌndʒər ‖ˈplʌndʒə(r)/ n (a) (for unblocking drain) desatascador m, chupona f (Esp), destapador m (de caño) (Méx), sopapa f (RPl), sopapo m (Chi), chupa f (Col), goma f (Ven) (b) (in syringe) émbolo m

plunk /plʌŋk/ vt (AmE) poner*, plantificar* (fam)

pluperfect /ˈpluːˈpɜːrfɪkt ‖ˌpluːˈpɜːfɪkt/ n pluscuamperfecto m

plural¹ /ˈplʊrəl ‖ˈplʊərəl/ adj (Ling) en plural

plural² n plural m; **in the ~** en plural

plus¹ /plʌs/ n (pl ~es or ~ses) (a) ~ (sign) (signo m de) más m (b) (advantage, bonus) (colloq) ventaja f

plus² adj (a) (advantageous) (colloq) (before n) ⟨point⟩ positivo (b) (and more) (pred): **children aged 13 ~** niños de 13 años para arriba

plus³ prep más; **~ the fact that ...** aparte de que ...; ▶ FOUR¹

plush /plʌʃ/ adj lujoso

Pluto /ˈpluːtəʊ/ n Plutón m

plutonium /pluːˈtəʊniəm/ n plutonio m

ply¹ /plaɪ/ n (pl **plies**) (a) (of wood) chapa f (b) (of wool, yarn) cabo m; **three-~** wool lana f de tres cabos

ply² plies, plying, plied vt (a) (carry out): to ~ one's trade ejercer* su oficio (b) ⟨oar⟩ mover*; ⟨tools⟩ manejar (c) ⟨ship⟩ ⟨sea⟩ navegar* por
■ ~ vi (frml) ⟨ship/plane/bus⟩ hacer* el trayecto
■ **ply with** [v + o + prep + o]: he kept ~ing me with whiskey estaba constantemente sirviéndome whisky

plywood /ˈplaɪwʊd/ n contrachapado m (tablero en varias capas)

pm (after midday) p.m.; **at 2 ~** a las 2 de la tarde, a las 2 p.m.

PM (BrE) n = **prime minister**

PMS n = **premenstrual syndrome**

PMT n (BrE) = **premenstrual tension**

pneumatic drill /nʊˈmætɪk ‖njuːˈmætɪk/ n martillo m neumático

pneumonia /nʊˈməʊnjə ‖njuːˈməʊnɪə/ n pulmonía f, neumonía f

poach /pəʊtʃ/ vt **1** (Culin) ⟨egg⟩ escalfar; ⟨fish⟩ cocer* a fuego lento **2** (steal) ⟨game⟩ cazar* furtivamente; ⟨staff/ideas⟩ robar
■ ~ vi (hunt game) cazar* furtivamente

poacher /'pəʊtʃər ‖'pəʊtʃə(r)/ n cazador furtivo, cazadora furtiva m,f

PO box n Apdo. postal, Apdo. de correos, C.C. (CS)

pocket¹ /'pɑːkət ‖'pɒkɪt/ n **1 (a)** (in garment) bolsillo m **(b)** (on billiard, snooker, pool table) tronera f **2** (small area) bolsa f; ~s of resistance bolsas fpl de resistencia

pocket² vt **(a)** (put in pocket) meterse en el bolsillo **(b)** (steal, gain) (colloq) embolsarse (fam)

pocket³ adj (before n) de bolsillo

pocket: ~book /'pɑːkətbʊk ‖'pɒkɪtbʊk/ n **(a)** (handbag) (AmE) cartera f or (Esp) bolso m or (Méx) bolsa f **(b)** (wallet) (AmE) cartera f, billetera f **(c)** (paperback) (AmE) libro m en rústica **(d)** (notebook) (BrE) cuaderno m; ~ **money** n (spending money) dinero m para gastos personales; (for children) (BrE) dinero m de bolsillo, ≈ mesada f (AmL), domingo m (Méx), propina f (Per)

pod /pɑːd ‖pɒd/ n (of peas, beans) vaina f

podiatrist /pə'daɪətrəst ‖pə'daɪətrɪst/ n (AmE) pedicuro, -ra m,f, podólogo, -ga, m,f, (frml)

podium /'pəʊdiəm/ n estrado m

poem /'pəʊəm ‖'pəʊɪm/ n poema m

poet /'pəʊət ‖'pəʊɪt/ n poeta mf

poetic /pəʊ'etɪk/ adj poético

poet laureate, Poet Laureate /'lɔːriət ‖'lɒriət/ n (pl ~s ~) poeta laureado, poeta laureada m,f

poetry /'pəʊətri ‖'pəʊɪtri/ n poesía f

poignant /'pɔɪnjənt/ adj ⟨story/moment⟩ conmovedor; ⟨look/plea⟩ patético; ⟨reminder⟩ doloroso

point¹ /pɔɪnt/ n
I 1 (a) (dot) punto m **(b)** (decimal ~) ≈ coma f, punto m decimal (AmL) (the point is used instead of the comma in some Latin American countries)
2 (a) (in space) punto m; the ~s of the compass los puntos cardinales; the ~ of no return we've reached the ~ of no return ahora ya no nos podemos echar atrás **(b)** (on scale) punto m; you're right, up to a ~ hasta cierto punto tienes razón
3 (in time) momento m; at this ~ in time en este momento; to be on the ~ of -ING estar* a punto de + INF
4 (in contest, exam) punto m
II 1 (a) (item, matter) punto m; to bring up o raise a ~ plantear una cuestión; to make a ~ of -ING: I'll make a ~ of watching them closely me encargaré de vigilarlos de cerca **(b)** (argument): yes, that's a ~ sí, ese es un punto interesante; to make a ~: that was a very interesting ~ you made lo que señalaste es muy interesante; all right, you've made your ~! sí, bueno, ya has dicho lo que querías decir; ~ taken de acuerdo **2** (no pl) (central issue, meaning): to come/get to the ~ ir* al grano; she was brief and to the ~ fue breve y concisa; that's beside the ~ eso no tiene nada que ver, eso no viene al caso; the ~ is that ... el hecho es que ...; that's not the ~ no se trata de eso
3 (purpose): what's the ~ of going on? ¿qué

sentido tiene seguir?; there's no ~ o there isn't any ~ (in) feeling sorry for yourself no sirve de nada compadecerse
4 (feature, quality): strong ~ fuerte m; bad ~s defectos mpl; he has many good ~s tiene muchos puntos a su favor
III 1 (a) (sharp end, tip) punta f **(b)** (promontory) (Geog) punta f
2 points pl (BrE Rail) agujas fpl
3 (socket) (BrE) (electrical o power) ~ toma f de corriente, enchufe m, tomacorriente m (AmL)

point² vt (aim, direct) señalar, indicar*; to ~ sth AT sb/sth: he ~ed his finger at me me señaló con el dedo; she ~ed the gun at him le apuntó con la pistola
■ ~ vi **(a)** (with finger, stick etc) señalar; it's rude to ~ es de mala educación señalar con el dedo; to ~ AT/TO sb/sth señalar algo/a algn **(b)** (call attention) to ~ TO sth señalar algo **(c)** (indicate) to ~ TO sth ⟨⟨facts/symptoms⟩⟩ indicar* algo
■ **point out** [v + o + adv, v + adv + o] **1** (on dial, gage) (show) señalar; I'll ~ it/her out to you te lo/la señalaré **2** (make aware of) ⟨problem/advantage⟩ señalar

point: ~ blank adv ⟨shoot⟩ a quemarropa; **~-blank** /'pɔɪnt'blæŋk/ adj: at ~-blank range a quemarropa

pointed /'pɔɪntəd ‖'pɔɪntɪd/ adj **1** (with a point) ⟨stick/leaf⟩ acabado en punta, puntiagudo (Andes); ⟨arch⟩ ojival; ⟨chin/nose⟩ puntiagudo, puntudo (Andes); ⟨shoe⟩ de punta, puntudo (Andes); ⟨hat⟩ de pico **2** (deliberate) ⟨remark/comment⟩ mordaz

pointer /'pɔɪntər ‖'pɔɪntə(r)/ n **1** (on dial, gage) aguja f **2 (a)** (clue, signal) pista f; ~ TO sth indicador m DE algo **(b)** (tip) idea f

pointless /'pɔɪntləs ‖'pɔɪntlɪs/ adj ⟨attempt⟩ vano, inútil; ⟨existence⟩ sin sentido; it's ~ arguing with him no tiene sentido discutir con él

point of view n (pl ~s ~ ~) punto m de vista

poise /pɔɪz/ n **(a)** (bearing) porte m **(b)** (composure) desenvoltura f

poised /pɔɪzd/ adj **1 (a)** (balanced, suspended): ~ in the air suspendido en el aire; they were waiting with pencils ~ esperaban, lápiz en mano **(b)** (ready) listo **2** (self-assured): she is very ~ tiene mucho aplomo

poison¹ /'pɔɪzn̩/ n veneno m

poison² vt **(a)** (with poison) envenenar; (make ill) intoxicar*; ⟨river/soil⟩ contaminar **(b)** (corrupt) ⟨mind/society⟩ corromper; ⟨relationship/ atmosphere⟩ dañar

poisoning /'pɔɪznɪŋ/ n envenenamiento m

poisonous /'pɔɪznəs/ adj venenoso

poison-pen letter /'pɔɪzn̩'pen/ n anónimo m ponzoñoso

poke¹ /pəʊk/ vt **(a)** (jab): to ~ sb's eye out sacarle* un ojo a algn; she ~d him in the ribs le dio en el costado; (with elbow) le dio un codazo en el costado **(b)** (thrust): she ~d her head around the door asomó la cabeza por la puerta; he ~d his finger through the crack metió el dedo por la ranura
■ ~ vi (project) asomar; her feet were poking out of the sheets los pies le asomaban por entre las sábanas; a few shoots were poking up out of the soil unos cuantos brotes asomaban en la tierra ····⫶

■ **poke about, poke around** [v + adv] fisgonear

poke² n golpe m; (with elbow) codazo m

poker /'pəʊkər ‖'pəʊkə(r)/ n **1** (for fire) atizador m **2** (game) póker m, póquer m

poky /'pəʊki/ adj **pokier, pokiest** (colloq) (a) (cramped) diminuto (b) (slow) (AmE) lerdo

Poland /'pəʊlənd/ n Polonia f

polar /'pəʊlər ‖'pəʊlə(r)/ adj polar

polar bear n oso m polar

polarize /'pəʊləraɪz/ vt polarizar*

pole /pəʊl/ n **1** (fixed support) poste m; (flag~) mástil m; (tent ~) palo m **2** (a) (Geog) polo m; **the North/South P~** el Polo Norte/Sur (b) (Phys) polo m

Pole n polaco, -ca m,f

polecat n (a) (of weasel family) turón m (b) (AmE) ▶ SKUNK

polemical /pə'lemɪkəl/ adj polémico

pole: ~star, (BrE) **P~ Star** n estrella f polar; **~-vault** n salto m con garrocha or (Esp) con pértiga

police¹ /pə'liːs/ n (force) (+ sing or pl vb) **the ~** la policía; (before n) ⟨escort/patrol⟩ policial; **~ car** coche m patrulla or de policía; **~ constable** (in UK) agente mf; **~ department** (in US) distrito m policial; **the ~ force** la policía; **~ officer** agente mf, policía mf; **to have a ~ record** estar* fichado or (CS tb) prontuariado

police² vt (keep order in) ⟨streets⟩ patrullar; ⟨region/area⟩ mantener* una fuerza policial en

police: ~ dog n perro m policía; **~man** /pə'liːsmən/ n (pl **-men** /-mən/) policía m, agente m; **~ state** n estado m policía; **~ station** n comisaría f; **~woman** n agente f, policía f, mujer f policía

policy /'pɑːləsi ‖'pɒləsi/ n (pl **-cies**) **1** (a) (Pol) política f (b) (standard practice, plan) (Busn) política f; **it is good/bad ~** es/no es recomendable **2** (insurance ~) (contract) seguro m; (document) póliza f de seguros

policyholder /'pɑːləsiˈhəʊldər ‖'pɒləsiˌhəʊldə(r)/ n asegurado, -da m,f

polio /'pəʊliəʊ/ n polio f

poliomyelitis /'pəʊliəʊˈmaɪəˈlaɪtəs ‖ˌpəʊliəʊˌmaɪəˈlaɪtɪs/ n poliomielitis f

polish¹ /'pɑːlɪʃ ‖'pɒlɪʃ/ n (a) (shoe ~) betún m, pomada f (RPl), pasta f (Chi); (furniture ~) cera f para muebles, lustramuebles m (CS); (metal ~) limpiametales m; (floor ~) (esp BrE) abrillantador m (de suelos); (wax ~) cera f (abrillantadora) (b) (sheen) brillo m (c) (refinement): he lacks ~ tiene que pulir su estilo

polish² vt (a) ⟨floor/table/car/brass⟩ darle* or sacarle* brillo a; ⟨shoes⟩ limpiar, lustrar (esp AmL), bolear (Méx), embolar (Col); ⟨lens/mirror⟩ limpiar; ⟨stone⟩ (by abrasion) pulir (b) (refine) pulir

■ **polish off** [v + o + adv, v + adv + o] (colloq) ⟨food⟩ liquidarse (fam)

Polish¹ /'pəʊlɪʃ/ adj polaco

Polish² n polaco m

polished /'pɑːlɪʃt ‖'pɒlɪʃt/ adj (a) (shiny) ⟨metal/marble⟩ pulido; ⟨wood⟩ brillante, lustrado (esp AmL) (b) (refined) ⟨manners/accent⟩ refinado; ⟨performance/translation⟩ pulido

polite /pə'laɪt/ adj **politer, politest** ⟨manner/

person⟩ cortés; **they were making ~ conversation** conversaban tratando de ser agradables; **it's not ~ to shout** gritar es una falta de educación

politely /pə'laɪtli/ adv ⟨behave⟩ correctamente; ⟨ask/refuse⟩ con buenos modales

politeness /pə'laɪtnəs ‖pə'laɪtnɪs/ n cortesía f

political /pə'lɪtɪkəl/ adj político

politically correct /pə'lɪtɪkli/ adj ⟨term⟩ usado por gente de ideología progresista

politician /'pɑːlɪ'tɪʃən ‖ˌpɒlɪ'tɪʃən/ n político, -ca m,f

politics /'pɑːlətɪks ‖'pɒlɪtɪks/ n **1** (+ sing vb) (science, activity) política f **2** (+ pl vb) (political relations) política f

polka /'pəʊlkə ‖'pɒlkə, 'pəʊlkə/ n polca f, polka f

polka dot /'pəʊkə, pəʊlkə ‖'pɒlkə, 'pəʊlkə/ n lunar m, topo m (Esp)

poll¹ /pəʊl/ n **1** (a) (ballot) votación f (b) (opinion ~) encuesta f or sondeo m (de opinión) **2** **polls** pl (polling stations) to go to the **~s**: to go to the **~s** ir* or acudir a las urnas

poll² vt (Pol) ⟨votes⟩ (obtain) obtener*; (cast) emitir

pollen /'pɑːlən ‖'pɒlən/ n polen m

pollinate /'pɑːləneɪt ‖'pɒləneɪt/ vt polinizar*

polling /'pəʊlɪŋ/ n votación f; (before n) **~ place** o (BrE) **station** centro m electoral

pollutant /pə'luːtŋt/ n (agente m) contaminante m

pollute /pə'luːt/ vt (Ecol) contaminar

pollution /pə'luːʃən/ n contaminación f

polo /'pəʊləʊ/ n polo m

polo: ~ neck n (BrE) (a) (style of neck) cuello m alto (b) ▶ ~ NECK SWEATER; **~ neck sweater** n (BrE) suéter m de cuello alto, polera f (RPl)

poly- /'pɑːli ‖'pɒli/ pref poli-

polyester /'pɑːli'estər ‖ˌpɒli'estə(r)/ n poliéster m

polyethylene /'pɑːli'eθəliːn ‖ˌpɒli'eθəliːn/ n (esp AmE) polietileno m

polygamy /pə'lɪɡəmi/ n poligamia f

Polynesia /'pɑːlə'niːʒə ‖ˌpɒlɪ'niːʒə/ n (la) Polinesia

Polynesian /'pɑːlə'niːʒən ‖ˌpɒlɪ'niːʒən/ adj polinesio

polystyrene /'pɑːli'staɪriːn ‖ˌpɒli'staɪriːn/ n poliestireno m

polythene /'pɑːləθiːn ‖'pɒlɪθiːn/ n (BrE) plástico m, polietileno m (téc)

pomegranate /'pɑːməɡrænət ‖'pɒmɪɡrænɪt/ n granada f

pomp /pɑːmp ‖pɒmp/ n pompa f, fausto m

pompom /'pɑːmpɑːm ‖'pɒmpɒm/ n (on hat) borla f, pompón m

pompous /'pɑːmpəs ‖'pɒmpəs/ adj pomposo

pond /pɑːnd ‖pɒnd/ n (man-made) estanque m; (natural) laguna f

ponder /'pɑːndər ‖'pɒndə(r)/ vt considerar

ponderous /'pɑːndərəs ‖'pɒndərəs/ adj ⟨movement⟩ lento y pesado; ⟨explanation/speech⟩ pesado

pong¹ /pɑːŋ ‖pɒŋ/ n (BrE colloq) peste f (fam)

pong² vi (BrE colloq) apestar (fam)

pontiff /'pɑːntəf ‖'pɒntɪf/ n pontífice m

pony /'pəʊni/ n (pl **ponies**) poni m

ponytail /'pəʊniteɪl/ n cola f de caballo

poodle /'puːdl/ n caniche m

pooh-pooh /puː'puː/ vt (colloq) reírse* de

pool¹ /puːl/ n **1** **(a)** (collection of water) charca f **(b)** (swimming ∼) piscina f, pileta f (RPI), alberca f (esp Méx) **(c)** (puddle) charco m **2** (common reserve of money) fondo m común **3 pools** pl (BrE) ▶ FOOTBALL POOLS **4** (billiards) billar m americano, pool m

pool² vt hacer* un fondo común de

pooped (out) /puːpt/ adj (AmE sl) (pred) reventado (fam)

poor /pɔːr ‖pɔːr, pʊə(r)/ adj **-er, -est** **1** (not wealthy) pobre **2** (unsatisfactory, bad) ‹harvest› pobre, escaso; ‹diet/quality› malo; ‹imitation› burdo **3** (unfortunate) (before n) pobre; **you ∼ thing!** ¡pobrecito!

poorly¹ /'pʊrli ‖'pɔːli, 'pʊəli/ adj (pred) (esp BrE) mal

poorly² adv ‹perform/play› mal

pop¹ /paːp ‖pɒp/ n **1** (noise): **to go ∼** hacer 'pum'; (burst) reventar* **2** (Mus) música f pop **3** (Culin) gaseosa f **4** (father) (AmE colloq) papá m (fam)

pop² -pp- vi **1** «balloon» estallar, reventar(se)*; «cork» saltar; **my ears ∼ped** se me destaparon los oídos **2** (spring) saltar; **his eyes were ∼ping (out of his head)** los ojos se le salían de las órbitas **3** (go casually) (colloq): **to ∼ out** salir* un momento; **he just ∼ped in to say hello** pasó un minuto a saludar
■ **∼** vt **1** (burst) ‹balloon› reventar*, hacer* estallar **2** (put quickly, casually): **she ∼ped her head around the door** asomó la cabeza por la puerta; **∼ it into your pocket** métetelo en el bolsillo
■ **pop up** [v + adv] (colloq) **(a)** (rise) «toast» saltar; **his head ∼ped up from behind the wall** asomó la cabeza por encima del muro **(b)** (appear) aparecer*

pop³ adj **(a)** (popular) ‹sociology/culture› popular; ‹music/singer› (AmE) popular **(b)** (BrE Mus) pop adj inv

popcorn /'paːpkɔːrn ‖'pɒpkɔːn/ n palomitas fpl (de maíz), cabritas fpl (de maíz) (Chi), pororó m (RPI), maíz m pira or tote (Col)

pope /pəʊp/ n papa m

poplar /'paːplər ‖'pɒplə(r)/ n álamo m (blanco)

poppa /'paːpə ‖'pɒpə/ n (AmE) papá m (fam)

poppy /'paːpi ‖'pɒpi/ n (pl **-pies**) amapola f, adormidera f

Popsicle® /'paːpsɪkəl ‖'pɒpsɪkəl/ n (AmE) paleta f (helada) or (Esp) polo m or (RPI) palito m or (CS) chupete m helado

populace /'paːpjələs ‖'pɒpjʊləs/ n (+ sing o pl vb) **the ∼** (common people) el pueblo; (population) la población

popular /'paːpjələr ‖'pɒpjʊlə(r)/ adj **1** **(a)** (well-liked) popular; **she is ∼ with her students** goza de popularidad entre sus alumnos **(b)** ‹resort/restaurant› muy frecuentado; ‹brand/product› popular **2** **(a)** (not highbrow, specialist) ‹music/literature› popular **(b)** (of populace) ‹feeling› popular; ‹rebellion› del pueblo, popular;

by ∼ demand/request a petición or (AmL tb) a pedido del público **(c)** (widespread) ‹belief/notion› generalizado

popularity /ˌpaːpjə'lærəti/ n popularidad f

popularize /'paːpjələraɪz/ vt **(a)** (make popular) popularizar* **(b)** (make accessible) divulgar*

populate /'paːpjəleɪt/ vt ‹popul>eit/ vt poblar*

population /ˌpaːpjə'leɪʃən ‖ˌpɒpjʊ'leɪʃən/ n población f; (before n) **∼ explosion** explosión f demográfica

pop-up /'paːpʌp/ n popup m, ventana f emergente

porcelain /'pɔːrsələn ‖'pɔːsəlɪn/ n porcelana f

porch /pɔːrtʃ ‖pɔːtʃ/ n **(a)** (covered entrance) porche m **(b)** (veranda) (AmE) porche m, galería f

porcupine /'pɔːrkjəpaɪn ‖'pɔːkjʊpaɪn/ n puercoespín m

pore /pɔːr ‖pɔː(r)/ n poro m
■ **pore over** [v + prep + o] estudiar minuciosamente

pork /pɔːrk ‖pɔːk/ n (carne f de) cerdo m, (carne f de) puerco m (Méx), chancho m (Chi, Per), marrano m (Col); (before n) **∼ chop** chuleta f de cerdo (or de chancho etc), costilla f de cerdo (RPI)

pornographic /ˌpɔːrnə'græfɪk ‖ˌpɔːnə'græfɪk/ adj pornográfico

pornography /pɔːr'naːgrəfi ‖pɔː'nɒgrəfi/ n pornografía f

porous /'pɔːrəs/ adj poroso

porpoise /'pɔːrpəs ‖'pɔːpəs/ n marsopa f

porridge /'pɔːrɪdʒ ‖'pɒrɪdʒ/ n avena f (cocida), gachas fpl (de avena) (Esp); (before n) **∼ oats** copos mpl de avena

port¹ /pɔːrt ‖pɔːt/ n **1** (for ships) puerto m; (before n) ‹authority/tax/regulation› portuario **2** (left side) babor m **3** **(a)** (for loading) (Aviat, Naut) porta f **(b)** (Comput) puerto m **4** (Culin) oporto m, vino m de Oporto

port² adj (before n) ‹lights› de babor

portable /'pɔːrtəbəl ‖'pɔːtəbəl/ adj portátil

portcullis /pɔːrt'kʌləs ‖ˌpɔːt'kʌlɪs/ n rastrillo m

portend /pɔːr'tend ‖pɔː'tend/ vt (liter) augurar

portent /'pɔːrtent ‖'pɔːtent/ n augurio m, presagio m

porter /'pɔːrtər ‖'pɔːtə(r)/ n **1** (at station, airport) maletero m, changador m (RPI); (on expedition) porteador m; (in hospital) (BrE) camillero m **2** (in hotel, apartment block) portero m

portfolio /pɔːrt'fəʊliəʊ ‖pɔːt'fəʊliəʊ/ n (pl **-lios**) **1** **(a)** (case) portafolio(s) m **(b)** (samples of work) carpeta f de trabajos **2** (Pol) cartera f

porthole /'pɔːrthəʊl ‖'pɔːthəʊl/ n (Naut) ojo m de buey, portilla f

portion /'pɔːrʃən ‖'pɔːʃən/ n **(a)** (of food) porción f (esp AmL), ración f (esp Esp) **(b)** (share, part) parte f

portrait /'pɔːrtrət, -treɪt ‖'pɔːtrɪt, -treɪt/ n retrato m

portray /pɔːr'treɪ ‖pɔː'treɪ/ vt **(a)** (depict) «picture» representar **(b)** (describe, represent) ‹person/scene› describir*

portrayal /pɔːr'treɪəl ‖pɔː'treɪəl/ n (Art) representación f; (Lit) descripción f; (Theat) interpretación f

Portugal /'pɔːrtʃɪgəl ‖'pɔːtjʊgl/ n Portugal m

p

Portuguese¹ /ˌpɔːrtʃəˈgiːz ‖ˌpɔːrtʃʊˈgiːz/ *adj* portugués

Portuguese² *n* (*pl* ∼) **(a)** (language) portugués *m* **(b)** (person) portugués, -guesa *m,f*

pose¹ /pəʊz/ *vt* ⟨threat⟩ representar; ⟨problem/ question⟩ plantear
■ ∼ *vi* **(a)** (Art, Phot) posar **(b)** (put on an act) hacerse* el interesante **(c)** (pretend to be) **to ∼ AS sb/sth** hacerse* pasar POR algn/algo

pose² *n* **(a)** (position of body) pose *f*, postura *f* **(b)** (assumed manner) pose *f*, afectación *f*

poser /ˈpəʊzər ‖ˈpəʊzə(r)/ *n* **(a)** (question) pregunta *f* difícil; (problem) dilema *m* **(b)** (person) (BrE colloq) ▶ POSEUR

poseur /pəʊˈzɜːr ‖pəʊˈzɜː(r)/ *n*: **he's a real ∼** todo en él es pura pose *or* afectación

posh /pɒʃ ‖pɒʃ/ *adj* **-er, -est** (esp BrE colloq) elegante, pijo (Esp fam), posudo (Col fam), pituco (CS fam), cheto (RPI fam), sifrino (Ven fam), popoff (Méx fam)

position¹ /pəˈzɪʃən/ *n* **1** **(a)** (location) posición *f*, ubicación *f* (esp AmL) **(b)** (Sport) posición *f* **2** **(a)** (posture) posición *f* **(b)** (stance, point of view) postura *f* **3** **(a)** (in league) puesto *m* **(b)** (job, post) (frml) puesto *m* **4** (situation, circumstances) situación *f*; **I'm not in a ∼ to help them** no estoy en condiciones de prestarles ayuda

position² *vt* colocar*, poner*

positive /ˈpɑːzətɪv ‖ˈpɒzətɪv/ *adj* **1** ⟨number/ quantity⟩ positivo; ⟨electrode⟩ positivo; **the test was ∼** (Med) el análisis dio positivo **2** (constructive) ⟨attitude⟩ positivo; ⟨criticism⟩ constructivo **3** (definite): **there is no ∼ evidence** no hay pruebas concluyentes **4** (absolute) (before n) ⟨disgrace/outrage⟩ auténtico **5** (sure) (colloq) (pred): **are you sure? — positive** ¿estás seguro? — segurísimo

positively /ˈpɑːzətɪvli ‖ˈpɒzətɪvli/ *adv* **1** (constructively): **to think ∼** ser* positivo; **they reacted ∼** tuvieron una reacción/respuesta positiva **2** **(a)** (definitely) ⟨prove⟩ de forma concluyente **(b)** (absolutely) ⟨delighted/furious⟩ verdaderamente

posse /ˈpɑːsi ‖ˈpɒsi/ *n* (in US) partida *f* (al mando de un sheriff)

possess /pəˈzes/ *vt* **1** (own) tener*, poseer* (frml) **2** (influence) ⟨anger/fear⟩ apoderarse de; **whatever can gave ∼ed him to say such a thing?** ¿qué lo habrá llevado a decir semejante cosa?

possessed /pəˈzest/ *adj* (pred) **to be ∼ (by the devil)** estar* endemoniado

possession /pəˈzeʃən/ *n* **(a)** (sth owned) bien *m* **(b)** (ownership) posesión *f*; (of arms) tenencia *f*

possessive /pəˈzesɪv/ *adj* posesivo

possessor /pəˈzesər ‖pəˈzesə(r)/ *n* dueño, -ña *m,f*, poseedor, -dora *m,f*

possibility /ˌpɑːsəˈbɪləti ‖ˌpɒsəˈbɪləti/ *n* posibilidad *f*

possible /ˈpɑːsəbəl ‖ˈpɒsəbəl/ *adj* posible; **get here by eight if ∼** llega antes de las ocho, si es posible; **as little as ∼** lo menos posible

possibly /ˈpɑːsəbli ‖ˈpɒsəbli/ *adv* **(a)** (conceivably): **I couldn't ∼ eat any more** me es totalmente imposible comer nada más; **could you ∼ give me a hand with this?** ¿sería tan amable de ayudarme con esto? **(b)** (perhaps) (indep) posiblemente

post¹ /pəʊst/ *n* **1** (pole) poste *m* **2** (mail) (esp BrE) correo *m*; **to send sth by ∼** *o* **through the ∼** mandar *or* enviar* algo por correo; **it's in the ∼** ya ha sido enviado; **the first/second ∼** (delivery) el primer/segundo reparto; (collection) la primera/ segunda recogida **3** (job) puesto *m*

post² *vt* **1** **(a)** (position) ⟨policeman/soldier⟩ apostar **(b)** (send) ⟨employee/diplomat⟩ destinar **2** (mail) (esp BrE) ⟨letter/parcel⟩ echar al correo; (drop in postbox) echar al buzón; **to ∼ sth to sb** mandarle *or* enviarle* algo a algn (por correo)

post- /pəʊst/ *pref* post-, pos-

postage /ˈpəʊstɪdʒ/ *n* franqueo *m*; **∼ and handling** (AmE), **∼ and packing** (BrE) gastos *mpl* de envío

postage: ∼ paid *adv* con franqueo pagado; **∼ stamp** *n* (frml) sello *m* (de correos), estampilla *f* (AmL), timbre *m* (Méx)

postal /ˈpəʊstl̩/ *adj* (before n) postal

postal order *n* (BrE) ≈ giro *m* postal

post: ∼box *n* (BrE) buzón *m*; **∼card** *n* tarjeta *f* postal, postal *f*; **∼code** *n* (BrE) código *m* postal

postdate /ˌpəʊstˈdeɪt/ *vt* ⟨contract/check⟩ posfechar, diferir* (RPI)

poster /ˈpəʊstər ‖ˈpəʊstə(r)/ *n* cartel *m*, póster *m*

posterity /pɑːˈsterəti ‖pɒˈsterəti/ *n* posteridad *f*

postgraduate /ˌpəʊstˈɡrædʒuət/ *n* estudiante *mf* de postgrado; (before n) ⟨student/research⟩ de postgrado

posthumous /ˈpɑːstʃəməs ‖ˈpɒstjʊməs/ *adj* póstumo

posting /ˈpəʊstɪŋ/ *n* destino *m*

postman /ˈpəʊstmən/ *n* (*pl* **-men** /-mən/) (esp BrE) cartero *m*

postmark¹ /ˈpəʊstmɑːrk ‖ˈpəʊstmɑːk/ *n* matasellos *m*

postmark² *vt* matasellar

postmortem /ˈpəʊstˈmɔːrtəm ‖ˌpəʊstˈmɔːtəm/ *n* (esp BrE Med) autopsia *f*

postnatal /ˌpəʊstˈneɪtl̩/ *adj* postnatal

post office *n* oficina *f* de correos, correo *m* (AmL), estafeta *f* de correos (Esp)

postpone /pəʊsˈpəʊn ‖pəˈspəʊn/ *vt* aplazar*, posponer*, postergar* (esp AmL)

postponement /pəʊsˈpəʊnmənt ‖pəˈspəʊnmənt/ *n* aplazamiento *m*, postergación *f* (esp AmL)

postscript /ˈpəʊstskrɪpt/ *n* (to letter) postdata *f*; (to book) epílogo *m*

posture /ˈpɑːstʃər ‖ˈpɒstʃə(r)/ *n* postura *f*

postwar /ˈpəʊstˈwɔːr ‖ˌpəʊstˈwɔː(r)/ *adj* (before n) de la posguerra

posy /'pəʊzi/ *n* (*pl* **posies**) ramillete *m*

pot¹ /pɑːt ‖pɒt/ *n* **1** **(a)** (cooking ∼) olla *f*; ∼**s and pans** cacharros *mpl* (fam), trastes *mpl* (Méx); *to go to* ∼ (colloq) echarse a perder **(b)** (for jam, honey etc) tarro *m*, bote *m* (Esp) **(c)** (tea∼) tetera *f*; (coffee∼) cafetera *f* **(d)** (in pottery) vasija *f* **2** (flower∼) maceta *f*, tiesto *m* (Esp)

pot² *vt* **-tt-** ⟨*plant*⟩ plantar (*en una maceta*)

potash /'pɒtæʃ ‖'pɒtæʃ/ *n* potasa *f*

potassium /pə'tæsiəm/ *n* potasio *m*

potato /pə'teɪtəʊ/ *n* (*pl* **-toes**) papa *f or* (Esp) patata *f*; (*before n*) ∼ **chips** *o* (BrE) **crisps** papas *fpl or* (Esp) patatas *fpl* fritas; ∼ **peeler** pelapapas *m or* (Esp) pelapatatas *m*

potbelly /pɑːt'beli ‖,pɒt'beli /*n* barriga *f* (fam), panza *f* (fam), guata *f* (Chi fam)

potency /'pəʊtnsi/ *n* **(a)** (of drink) lo fuerte **(b)** (sexual ∼) potencia *f* sexual

potent /'pəʊtnt/ *adj* **1** ⟨*drink/drug/medicine*⟩ fuerte **2** (Physiol) potente

potential¹ /pə'tentʃəl ‖pə'tenʃəl/ *n* (capacity) potencial *m*; (possibilities) posibilidades *fpl*

potential² *adj* (*before n*) ⟨*danger*⟩ potencial; ⟨*leader*⟩ en potencia

potentially /pə'tentʃəli ‖pə'tenʃəli/ *adv* potencialmente

pot: ∼**hole** *n* **(a)** (cave) cueva *f* subterránea; (hole) sima *f* **(b)** (in road) bache *m*; ∼**holing** /'pɑːt,həʊlɪŋ ‖'pɒt,həʊlɪŋ/ *n* (BrE) espeleología *f*

potion /'pəʊʃən/ *n* poción *f*, pócima *f*

pot: ∼**luck** /'pɑːt'lʌk ‖,pɒt'lʌk/ *n*: **to take** ∼**luck** conformarse con lo que haya; ∼ **plant** *n* planta *f* (*cultivada en una maceta*), mata *f* (Col, Ven); ∼**shot** *n* (Sport) tiro *m* al azar

potted /'pɑːtəd ‖'pɒtɪd/ *adj* (*before n*) **(a)** ⟨*plant*⟩ en maceta *or* tiesto **(b)** ⟨*account/version*⟩ resumido

potter¹ /'pɑːtər ‖'pɒtə(r)/ *n* alfarero, -ra *m,f*

potter² *vi* (BrE) (+ *adv compl*) ▶ PUTTER²

pottery /'pɑːtəri ‖'pɒtəri/ *n* (*pl* **-ries**) **(a)** (vessels) cerámica *f* **(b)** (workshop) alfarería *f* **(c)** (craft) alfarería *f*

potty¹ /'pɑːti ‖'pɒti/ *n* (*pl* **-ties**) (colloq) orinal *m* (*para niños*) (fam), bacinica *f* (AmL exc RPl), pelela *f* (CS fam); **he's** ∼**-trained** ya no usa pañales

potty² *adj* **-tier, -tiest** (BrE colloq) chiflado (fam)

pouch /paʊtʃ/ *n* **1** **(a)** (small bag) bolsa *f* **(b)** (for correspondence) (AmE) valija *f* **2** (Anat, Zool) bolsa *f*

poultice /'pəʊltəs ‖'pəʊltɪs/ *n* cataplasma *f*

poultry /'pəʊltri/ *n* **(a)** (birds) (+ *pl vb*) aves *fpl* de corral **(b)** (meat) carne *f* de ave

pounce /paʊns/ *vi* saltar; **to** ∼ **ON/UPON sb/sth** abalanzarse* SOBRE algn/algo

pound¹ /paʊnd/ *n* **1** (measure) libra *f* (*454 gramos*) **2** (Fin) libra *f*; (*before n*) **a** ∼ **coin** una moneda de (una) libra **3** (enclosure — for cars) depósito *m*; (— for dogs) perrera *f*

pound² *vt* **(a)** ⟨*corn/spices*⟩ machacar*; ⟨*garlic/chili*⟩ majar **(b)** ⟨*table/door*⟩ aporrear; **the waves** ∼**ed the wall** las olas batían contra el muro
■ ∼ *vi* **(a)** (strike, beat) aporrear **(b)** ⟨*heart*⟩ palpitar; ⟨*sound*⟩ retumbar; **my head is** ∼**ing** tengo la cabeza a punto de reventar

pour /pɔːr ‖pɔː(r)/ *vt* **(a)** (+ *adv compl*) ⟨*liquid*⟩ verter*, echar; ⟨*salt/powder*⟩ echar; **he** ∼**ed the tea down the sink** tiró el té por el fregadero **(b)** ∼ **(out)** (serve) ⟨*drink*⟩ servir*
■ ∼ *vi* (+ *adv compl*) «*blood*» manar; «*water/sweat*» salir*
■ ∼ *v impers* diluviar, llover* a cántaros
■ **pour out 1** [*v* + *o* + *adv, v* + *adv* + *o*] **(a)** ▶ POUR *vt* B **(b)** (emotionally): **he** ∼**ed out his feelings** reveló sus sentimientos; **she** ∼**ed her heart out to him** se desahogó con él **2** [*v* + *adv*] salir*

pouring /'pɔːrɪŋ/ *adj*: **he went out in the** ∼ **rain** salió en medio de una lluvia torrencial

pout /paʊt/ *vi* hacer* un mohín

poverty /'pɑːvərti ‖'pɒvəti/ *n* pobreza *f*

poverty-stricken /'pɑːvərti,strɪkən ‖'pɒvəti,strɪkən/ *adj* pobrísimo

POW *n* = **prisoner of war**

powder¹ /'paʊdər ‖'paʊdə(r)/ *n* **(a)** polvo *m* **(b)** (face ∼) polvo(s) *m(pl)* (de tocador); (*before n*) ∼ **puff** borla *f*, cisne *m* (RPl)

powder² *vt* **1** (cover) empolvar; **to** ∼ **one's nose** retocarse* el maquillaje; (euph) lavarse las manos (euf) **2 powdered** *past p* ⟨*milk/eggs*⟩ en polvo; ∼**ed sugar** (AmE) azúcar *m or f* glas, azúcar *m or f* flor (Chi), azúcar *m or f* impalpable (RPl), azúcar *m or f* en polvo (Col)

powdery /'paʊdəri/ *adj* como polvo

power¹ /'paʊər ‖'paʊə(r)/ *n* **1** **(a)** (control, influence) poder *m*; (of country) poderío *m*, poder *m*; **to be in** ∼ estar* en el poder **(b)** (official authority) poder *m*; **to** ∼ **+ INF** poder PARA + INF **2** **(a)** (nation) potencia *f* **(b)** (person, group): **the** ∼**s that be** los que mandan; **the** ∼**s of darkness** las fuerzas del mal **3** **(a)** (physical strength, force) fuerza *f* **(b)** (of engine, loudspeaker, transmitter) potencia *f* **4** **(a)** (ability, capacity): **I did everything in my** ∼ hice todo lo que estaba en mi(s) mano(s) **(b)** (specific faculty) (*often pl*): **he lost the** ∼ **of speech** perdió el habla; ∼**(s) of concentration** capacidad *f* de concentración **5** **(a)** (Eng, Phys) potencia *f*; (particular source of energy) energía *f* **(b)** (electricity) electricidad *f*; (*before n*) ∼ **lines** cables *mpl* de alta tensión; ∼ **point** (BrE) toma *f* de corriente, enchufe *m*, tomacorriente *m* (AmL) **6** (a lot) (colloq): **to do sb a** ∼ **of good** hacerle* a algn mucho bien

power² *vt*: **the plane is** ∼**ed by four engines** el avión está propulsado por cuatro motores

power: ∼**boat** *n* lancha *f* de motor, lancha *f* motora (Esp); ∼ **cut** *n* apagón *m*

powerful /'paʊərfəl ‖'paʊəfəl/ *adj* **(a)** ⟨*country*⟩ poderoso **(b)** ⟨*shoulders/arms*⟩ fuerte **(c)** ⟨*performance/image*⟩ impactante; ⟨*argument*⟩ poderoso; ⟨*incentive*⟩ poderoso **(d)** ⟨*engine/weapon/drug*⟩ potente; ⟨*smell/current*⟩ fuerte

powerless /'paʊərləs ‖'paʊəlɪs/ *adj* impotente; **they were** ∼ **to prevent it** no pudieron hacer nada para impedirlo

power: ∼ **of attorney** *n* (*pl* ∼**s of attorney**) (Law) poder *m* (notarial); ∼ **plant** *n* (AmE) ▶ ∼ STATION; ∼ **station** *n* central *f* eléctrica, usina *f* eléctrica (AmS)

pp. (= **pages**) págs.

PR¹ n (a) = **public relations** (b) = **proportional representation**

PR² = **Puerto Rico**

practicable /'præktɪkəbəl/ adj factible

practical¹ /'præktɪkəl/ adj (a) práctico; **for all ~ purposes** a efectos prácticos (b) (feasible) factible

practical² n (Educ) práctica f

practicality /ˌpræktɪ'kæləti/ n ☐ (of scheme/ idea) lo práctico ☐ **practicalities** pl aspectos mpl prácticos

practical joke n broma f

practically /'præktɪkli/ adv ☐ (virtually) casi, prácticamente ☐ (in a practical way) ‹consider/ think› con sentido práctico

practice¹ /'præktəs ‖'præktɪs/ n ☐ (training, repetition) práctica f; **he's out of ~** le falta práctica; **piano ~** ejercicios mpl de piano; **~ teaching** o (BrE) **teaching ~** prácticas fpl de magisterio; **~ makes perfect** la práctica hace al maestro ☐ (a) (carrying out, implementing) práctica f; **to put sth into ~** llevar algo a la práctica; **in ~** en la práctica (b) (exercise of profession) ejercicio m ☐ (custom, procedure) costumbre f ☐ (Med) consultorio m

practice², (BrE) **practise** vt ☐ (rehearse) practicar*; ‹song/act› ensayar ☐ «doctor/ lawyer» ejercer* ☐ **practicing** pres p (a) ‹doctor/lawyer› en ejercicio (de su profesión) (b) ‹Catholic› practicante
■ **~** vi ☐ (rehearse, train) practicar* ☐ (professionally) ejercer*

practitioner /præk'tɪʃnər ‖præk'tɪʃnə(r)/ n médico, -ca m,f

pragmatic /præg'mætɪk/ adj pragmático

pragmatism /'prægmətɪzəm/ n pragmatismo m

Prague /prɑːg/ n Praga f

prairie /'preri ‖'preəri/ n pradera f; **the ~(s)** (in US) la Pradera

prairie dog n perro m de las praderas

praise¹ /preɪz/ n (a) (credit, applause) elogios mpl; **to sing sth's/sb's ~s** poner* algo/a algn por las nubes (b) (Relig) alabanza f

praise² vt (a) (compliment) elogiar (b) (Relig) alabar

praiseworthy /'preɪzˌwɜːrði ‖'preɪzˌwɜːði/ adj digno de elogio

pram /præm/ n (BrE) cochecito m

prance /præns ‖prɑːns/ vi (a) «horse» brincar* (b) (pej) «person»: **she ~d into the room wearing her new dress** entró meneándose con el vestido nuevo
■ **prance about** [v + adv] brincar*

prank /præŋk/ n broma f; (of child) travesura f

prat /præt/ n (BrE sl) imbécil mf

prattle /'prætl/ vi «adult» cotorrear (fam); «child» balbucear

prawn /prɔːn/ n (large) langostino m, camarón m (AmL); (medium) camarón m (AmL), gamba f (esp Esp), langostino m (CS); (small) camarón m, quisquilla f (Esp)

pray /preɪ/ vi rezar*, orar (fml)

prayer /prer ‖preə(r)/ n oración f

pre- /priː/ pref (a) (in advance): **~planned** planeado de antemano (b) (before): **a ~dinner drink** una copa antes de cenar

preach /priːtʃ/ vt (a) (Relig) predicar*; ‹sermon› dar* (b) (advocate) ‹doctrine/ideas› preconizar*
■ **~** vi predicar*

preacher /'priːtʃər ‖'priːtʃə(r)/ n (a) (one who preaches) predicador, -dora m,f (b) (minister) (AmE) pastor, -tora m,f

prearrange /ˌpriːə'reɪndʒ/ vt (a) (arrange in advance) concertar* de antemano (b) **prearranged** past p ‹meeting› concertado de antemano; ‹signal/place/time› convenido

precarious /prɪ'kerɪəs ‖prɪ'keərɪəs/ adj precario

precaution /prɪ'kɔːʃən/ n precaución f; **as a ~** por or como precaución

precautionary /prɪ'kɔːʃəneri ‖prɪ'kɔːʃənəri/ adj preventivo

precede /prɪ'siːd/ vt (fml) preceder a
■ **~** vi (a) (come before) preceder (b) **preceding** pres p anterior

precedence /'presədəns/ n precedencia f

precedent /'presədənt/ n precedente m; **to set a ~** (for sth) sentar* precedente (para algo)

precept /'priːsept/ n precepto m

precinct /'priːsɪŋkt/ n ☐ (a) (delimited zone) (BrE): **shopping ~** centro m/zona f comercial (b) (AmE) (police district) distrito m policial; (police station) comisaría f (c) (voting district) (AmE) circunscripción f, distrito m electoral ☐ **precincts** pl (of city) límites mpl; (of cathedral, castle, hospital) recinto m, predio(s) m(pl) (esp AmL)

precious¹ /'preʃəs/ adj ☐ (a) (valuable) ‹jewel/ object› precioso; **~ metal** metal m precioso; **~ stone** piedra f preciosa (b) (dear) querido (c) (iro): **her ~ son** su queridísimo hijo (iró) ☐ (affected) preciosista

precious² adv (colloq) (as intensifier): **~ few** muy pocos; **she's done ~ little to help** bien poco ha hecho para ayudar

precipice /'presəpəs ‖'presɪpɪs/ n precipicio m

precipitate /prɪ'sɪpəteɪt ‖prɪ'sɪpɪteɪt/ vt (fml) precipitar

precipitation /prɪˌsɪpə'teɪʃən ‖prɪˌsɪpɪ'teɪʃən/ n (a) (Meteo) precipitaciones fpl (b) (Chem) precipitación f

precis, précis /'preɪsiː, 'preɪsiː ‖'preɪsiː/ n (pl **~** /-z/) resumen m

precise /prɪ'saɪs/ adj (a) (accurate) ‹calculations/measurements› exacto; ‹description/ instructions› preciso (b) (specific) preciso; **there were about 60, 59 to be ~** había unos 60, 59 para ser exacto or preciso (c) (meticulous) minucioso

precisely /prɪ'saɪsli/ adv (a) (accurately) ‹calculate/measure/describe› con precisión (b) (exactly): **we have ~ one hour** tenemos exactamente una hora; **at two o'clock ~** a las dos en punto; **precisely!** ¡exacto!, ¡justamente!

precision /prɪ'sɪʒən/ n precisión f; (before n) ‹instrument/tool› de precisión

preclude /prɪ'kluːd/ vt (fml) ‹possibility› excluir*

precocious /prɪ'kəʊʃəs/ adj precoz

preconceived /ˈpriːkənˈsiːvd/ adj (before n) preconcebido

preconception /ˈpriːkənˈsepʃən/ n idea f preconcebida

precondition /ˈpriːkənˈdɪʃən/ n condición f previa

precursor /prɪˈkɜːrsər ‖ prɪˈkɜːsə(r)/ n (frml) precursor, -sora m,f

predate /ˈpriːˈdeɪt/ vt (frml) (a) (precede) ser* anterior a (b) ‹document/letter› antedatar (frml)

predator /ˈpredətər ‖ ˈpredətə(r)/ n depredador m, predador m

predatory /ˈpredətɔːri ‖ ˈpredətri/ adj ‹animal› predador, depredador; ‹person› rapaz

predecessor /ˈpredəsesər ‖ ˈpriːdɪsesə(r)/ n predecesor, -sora m,f

predestine /ˈpriːˈdestən ‖ ˌpriːˈdestɪn/ vt predestinar

predetermine /ˈpriːdɪˈtɜːrmən ‖ ˌpriːdɪˈtɜːmɪn/ vt predeterminar

predicament /prɪˈdɪkəmənt/ n aprieto m

predicative /prɪˈdɪkətɪv/ adj predicativo

predict /prɪˈdɪkt/ vt predecir*

predictable /prɪˈdɪktəbəl/ adj ‹result/outcome› previsible; **you're so ~** siempre sales con lo mismo

predictably /prɪˈdɪktəbli/ adv de manera previsible

prediction /prɪˈdɪkʃən/ n (forecast) pronóstico m, predicción f; (prophecy) profecía f

predispose /ˈpriːdɪsˈpəʊz/ vt (frml) predisponer*

predominance /prɪˈdɑːmənəns ‖ prɪˈdɒmɪnəns/ n predominio m

predominant /prɪˈdɑːmənənt ‖ prɪˈdɒmɪnənt/ adj predominante

predominantly /prɪˈdɑːmənəntli ‖ prɪˈdɒmɪnəntli/ adv predominantemente

predominate /prɪˈdɑːməneɪt ‖ prɪˈdɒmɪneɪt/ vi predominar

pre-eminent /ˈpriːˈemənənt ‖ ˈpriːˈemɪnənt/ adj (frml) preeminente

pre-empt /ˈpriːˈempt/ vt ‹attack/move› adelantarse a

pre-emptive /ˈpriːˈemptɪv/ adj ‹strike/attack› preventivo

preen /priːn/ vt ‹feathers› arreglar con el pico ■ v refl **to ~ oneself** «bird» arreglarse las plumas con el pico; «person» acicalarse

pre-exist /ˈpriːɪɡˈzɪst/ vi (frml) (a) preexistir (b) **pre-existing** pres p preexistente

prefab /ˈpriːfæb/ n (colloq) vivienda f prefabricada

prefabricated /ˈpriːˈfæbrɪkeɪtəd ‖ ˌpriːˈfæbrɪkeɪtɪd/ adj prefabricado

preface /ˈprefəs ‖ ˈprefɪs/ n (to book, speech) prefacio m; (to event) prólogo m

prefect /ˈpriːfekt/ n [1] (BrE Educ) alumno encargado de la disciplina, ≈ monitor, -tora m,f [2] (official) prefecto m

prefer /prɪˈfɜːr ‖ prɪˈfɜː(r)/ vt **-rr-** preferir*; **to ~ sth TO sth** preferir* algo A algo; **to ~ to + INF** preferir* + INF

preferable /ˈprefərəbəl/ adj preferible

preferably /ˈprefərəbli/ adv (indep) preferentemente; **I'd like a size 10, ~ in red** quisiera la talla 10, de ser posible en rojo

preference /ˈprefərəns/ n preferencia f; **~ FOR sth** preferencia POR algo

preferential /ˈprefəˈrentʃəl ‖ ˌprefəˈrenʃəl/ adj (before n) preferente, preferencial; **to give ~ treatment to sb** dar* trato preferente or preferencial a algn

prefix /ˈpriːfɪks/ n prefijo m

pregnancy /ˈpreɡnənsi/ n (pl -cies) (of woman) embarazo m; (of animal) preñez f

pregnant /ˈpreɡnənt/ adj [1] ‹woman› embarazada; ‹cow/mare› preñada [2] (liter) (meaningful) ‹pause/silence› elocuente, preñado de significado (liter)

preheat /ˈpriːˈhiːt/ vt precalentar*

prehistoric /ˈpriːhɪˈstɔːrɪk ‖ ˌpriːhɪˈstɒrɪk/ adj prehistórico

prejudge /ˈpriːˈdʒʌdʒ/ vt prejuzgar*

prejudice¹ /ˈpredʒədəs ‖ ˈpredʒʊdɪs/ n prejuicio m

prejudice² vt [1] (influence) predisponer* [2] (harm) ‹case/claim› perjudicar*

prejudiced /ˈpredʒədəst ‖ ˈpredʒʊdɪst/ adj lleno de prejuicios, prejuiciado (AmL)

preliminary¹ /prɪˈlɪməneri ‖ prɪˈlɪmɪnəri/ adj preliminar

preliminary² n (pl -ries) (a) (preamble) prolegómeno m (b) **preliminaries** pl (Sport) etapa f de clasificación previa, preliminares mpl or fpl

prelude /ˈpreljuːd/ n (a) (introduction) **~ (TO sth)** preludio m (DE algo) (b) (Mus) preludio m

premature /ˈpriːməˈtʊr ‖ ˈpremətjʊə(r)/ adj prematuro

prematurely /ˈpriːməˈtʊrli ‖ ˈpremətjʊəli/ adv prematuramente

premeditated /ˈpriːˈmedətətəd ‖ priːˈmedɪteɪtɪd/ adj premeditado

premenstrual /ˈpriːˈmenstruəl/ adj premenstrual; **~ syndrome/tension** síndrome m/ tensión f premenstrual

premier /prɪˈmɪr ‖ ˈpremiə(r)/ n primer ministro, primera ministra m,f, premier mf

premiere¹, première /prɪˈmɪr ‖ ˈpremɪeə(r)/ n estreno m

premiere², première vt ‹play/film› estrenar ■ **~ vi** ‹play/film› estrenarse

premise /ˈpreməs ‖ ˈpremɪs/ n [1] (Phil) premisa f [2] **premises** pl (building, site) local m; **they've moved to new ~s** se han mudado a un nuevo local (or a nuevas oficinas etc); **meals are cooked on the ~s** las comidas se preparan en el mismo establecimiento

premium /ˈpriːmiəm/ n (Fin) (a) (insurance **~**) prima f (de seguro) (b) (surcharge) recargo m; **to be at a ~** (in short supply) escasear; (lit: above par) estar* por encima de la par (c) (bonus) prima f

Premium Bond n (in UK) bono del Estado que permite ganar dinero participando en sorteos mensuales

premonition /ˈpriːməˈnɪʃən, ˈprem-/ n premonición f

prenatal /ˈpriːˈneɪtl/ adj (esp AmE) ▶ ANTENATAL

p

preoccupation /priːˈɑːkjəˈpeɪʃən/ ‖ˌpriːɒkjʊˈpeɪʃən/ n **1** (obsession) obsesión f **2** (concern): my main ~ was not to offend my parents mi mayor preocupación/lo que más me importaba era no ofender a mis padres

preoccupied /priːˈɑːkjəpaɪd ‖ˌpriːˈɒkjʊpaɪd/ adj (absorbed) absorto; (worried) preocupado

preoccupy /priːˈɑːkjəpaɪ ‖ˌpriːˈɒkjʊpaɪ/ vt -pies, -pying, -pied preocupar

prepaid /ˈpriːˈpeɪd/ adj ⟨envelope⟩ con franqueo pagado; ⟨advertisement/insertion⟩ pagado por adelantado

preparation /ˈprepəˈreɪʃən/ n **1** (a) (act) preparación f (b) **preparations** pl (arrangements) preparativos mpl **2** (substance) preparado m

preparatory /prɪˈpærətɔːri ‖prɪˈpærətri/ adj preparatorio

preparatory school n (fml) (a) (in US) colegio secundario privado (b) (in UK) colegio primario privado

prepare /prɪˈper ‖prɪˈpeə(r)/ vt preparar ■ ~ vi to ~ (FOR sth) prepararse (PARA algo)

prepared /prɪˈperd ‖prɪˈpeəd/ adj (a) (ready in advance) ⟨speech/statement⟩ preparado; I wasn't ~ for this no contaba con esto (b) (willing) (pred) to be ~ to + INF estar* dispuesto A + INF

preposition /ˈprepəˈzɪʃən/ n preposición f

prepossessing /ˈpriːpəˈzesɪŋ/ adj (fml) (usu neg) atractivo

preposterous /prɪˈpɑːstərəs ‖prɪˈpɒstərəs/ adj absurdo

prep school /prep/ n ▶ PREPARATORY SCHOOL B

prerequisite /ˈpriːˈrekwəzət ‖ˌpriːˈrekwɪzɪt/ n requisito m esencial

prerogative /prɪˈrɑːgətɪv ‖prɪˈrɒgətɪv/ n prerrogativa f; that's your ~ estás en todo tu derecho

Pres (title) = **President**

Presbyterian[1] /ˈprezbəˈtɪriən ‖ˌprezbɪˈtɪəriən/ n presbiteriano, -na m,f

Presbyterian[2] adj presbiteriano

preschool[1] /ˈpriːˈskuːl/ adj (before n) ⟨child⟩ de edad preescolar; ⟨education⟩ preescolar

preschool[2] n (AmE) jardín m de infancia, kindergarten m (AmL), jardín m de niños (Méx), jardín m de infantes (RPl), jardín m infantil (Chi)

prescribe /prɪˈskraɪb/ vt (a) ⟨drug⟩ recetar; ⟨rest⟩ recomendar* (b) (order) (fml) prescribir* (fml); ~d reading libros mpl de lectura obligatoria

prescription /prɪˈskrɪpʃən/ n receta f; available on ~ only en venta solamente bajo receta

presence /ˈprezns/ n presencia f; to make one's ~ felt hacerse* sentir

presence of mind n presencia f de ánimo

present[1] /prɪˈzent/ vt **1** (a) (give, hand over) to ~ sth TO sb entregarle* algo A algn; to ~ sb

WITH sth obsequiar a algn CON algo (fml), obsequiarle algo A algn (esp AmL fml) (b) (confront): we were ~ed with a very difficult situation nos vimos frente a una situación muy difícil **2** ⟨ticket/passport/account/ideas⟩ presentar **3** (Cin, Theat, Rad, TV) presentar **4** (introduce) (fml) presentar

present[2] /ˈpreznt/ adj **1** (at scene) (pred) to be ~ estar* presente **2** (before n) (a) (current) actual; at the ~ time en este momento (b) (Ling): the ~ tense el presente

present[3] /ˈpreznt/ n **1** (a) (current time): the ~ el presente; at ~ en este momento (b) (Ling) the ~ el presente **2** (gift) regalo m

presentable /prɪˈzentəbəl/ adj presentable

presentation /ˈpriːzenˈteɪʃən, ˈprezənˈteɪʃən ‖ˌprezənˈteɪʃən/ n **1** (of gift, prize) entrega f **2** (a) (of document, bill, proposal) presentación f (b) (display) (Busn) presentación f **3** (manner of presenting) presentación f

present-day /ˈpreznt'deɪ/ adj (before n) actual

presenter /prɪˈzentər ‖prɪˈzentə(r)/ n (BrE) presentador, -dora m,f

presently /ˈprezntli/ adv (a) (now) en este momento (b) (soon afterwards, in past) pronto (c) (soon, in future) poco después

preservation /ˈprezərˈveɪʃən ‖ˌprezəˈveɪʃən/ n conservación f

preservative /prɪˈzɜːrvətɪv ‖prɪˈzɜːvətɪv/ n conservante m

preserve[1] /prɪˈzɜːrv ‖prɪˈzɜːv/ vt (a) ⟨food/specimen⟩ conservar (b) ⟨fruit/vegetables⟩ hacer* conserva de (c) ⟨building/traditions⟩ conservar

preserve[2] n **1** (a) (exclusive privilege, sphere): to be a male ~ ser* terreno exclusivamente masculino (b) (restricted area): game ~ coto m de caza; wildlife ~ (AmE) reserva f de animales **2** (Culin) ⟨jam, jelly⟩ confitura f, mermelada f

preside /prɪˈzaɪd/ vi presidir; to ~ over a meeting presidir una reunión

presidency /ˈprezədənsi ‖ˈprezɪdənsi/ n presidencia f

president /ˈprezədənt ‖ˈprezɪdənt/ n (a) (of state, society) presidente, -ta m,f (b) (of bank, corporation) (esp AmE) director, -tora m,f, presidente, -ta m,f (c) (of university) (AmE) rector, -tora m,f

presidential /ˈprezəˈdentʃəl ‖ˌprezɪˈdenʃəl/ adj (before n) presidencial

press[1] /pres/ n **1** (newspapers, journalists) prensa f; the ~ la prensa; (before n) ~ agency (BrE) agencia f de prensa; ~ photographer reportero gráfico, reportera gráfica m,f; ~ release comunicado m de prensa **2** (a) (printing ~) prensa f, imprenta f; to go to ~ entrar en prensa (b) (publishing house) editorial f **3** (for pressing — grapes, flowers, machine parts) prensa f; (— trousers) prensa f plancha-pantalones

press[2] vt **1** (push) ⟨button/doorbell⟩ apretar*; ⟨pedal/footbrake⟩ pisar **2** (a) (squeeze) apretar*

(a) (in press) ⟨grapes/olives/flowers⟩ prensar **(c)** ⟨disk/album⟩ imprimir* **(d)** ⟨clothes⟩ planchar **3** **(a)** (put pressure on) presionar **(b)** (pursue): to ~ **charges against sb** presentar cargos en contra de algn
■ ~ vi **1** (exert pressure): ~ **firmly** presione con fuerza **2** (urge, pressurize) presionar
■ **press on** [v + adv] **to ~ on** (WITH sth) seguir* adelante (CON algo)

press conference n rueda f de prensa

pressed /prest/ adj ⟨pred⟩: **to be ~ for time** estar* or andar* escaso de tiempo

pressing /'presɪŋ/ adj ⟨engagements/concerns⟩ urgente; ⟨need/desire⟩ apremiante

press: ~ stud n (BrE) broche m or botón m de presión (AmL), cierre m) automático m (Esp); **~-up** n (BrE) flexión f (de brazos or de pecho), fondo m, lagartija f (Méx)

pressure¹ /'preʃər ‖'preʃə(r)/ n presión f; **to put ~ on sth/sb** hacer* presión sobre algo/ presionar a algn; **the ~s of city life** las presiones a las que somete la vida urbana; **I've been under a lot of ~ recently** últimamente he estado muy agobiado

pressure² vt presionar; **to ~ sb to + INF** presionar a algn PARA QUE (+ subj)

pressure: ~ cooker n olla f a presión or (Esp tb) olla f exprés or (Méx) olla f presto; **~ group** n grupo m de presión; **~ pan** n (AmE) ⯈ ~ COOKER

pressurize /'preʃəraɪz/ vt **(a)** (Aerosp, Aviat) presurizar* **(b)** (urge) (BrE) ⯈ PRESSURE²

prestige /pre'stiːʒ/ n prestigio m

prestigious /pre'stɪdʒəs/ adj prestigioso

presumably /prɪ'zuːməbli ‖prɪ'zjuːməbli/ adv (indep): **you've taken the necessary steps, ~** supongo or me imagino que habrás tomado las medidas pertinentes

presume /prɪ'zuːm ‖prɪ'zjuːm/ vt **(a)** (assume) suponer*; **I ~ so** supongo or me imagino que sí **(b)** (dare) **to ~ to + INF** atreverse A + INF

presumption /prɪ'zʌmpʃən/ n **(a)** (boldness) atrevimiento m **(b)** (assumption) suposición f

presumptuous /prɪ'zʌmptʃəs ‖prɪ'zʌmptʃʊəs/ adj impertinente

presuppose /ˌpriːsə'pəʊz/ vt presuponer*

pretence n (BrE) ⯈ PRETENSE

pretend¹ /prɪ'tend/ vt/i fingir*

pretend² adj (used to or by children) ⟨money/gun⟩ de mentira (fam)

pretender /prɪ'tendər ‖prɪ'tendə(r)/ n ~ (TO sth) pretendiente mf (A algo)

pretense, (BrE) **pretence** /'priːtens, prɪ'tens ‖prɪ'tens/ n: **her air of confidence is a ~** ese aire de seguridad suyo es fingido; **let's drop this ~!** ¡vamos a dejarnos de fingir!; **under false ~s** de manera fraudulenta

pretension /prɪ'tentʃən ‖prɪ'tenʃən/ n (often pl) pretensión f

pretentious /prɪ'tentʃəs ‖prɪ'tenʃəs/ adj ⟨person/language/film⟩ pretencioso; ⟨house/decor⟩ presuntuoso

pretext /'priːtekst/ n pretexto m; **on o under the ~ of** con el pretexto de

pretty¹ /'prɪti/ adj **-tier, -tiest** bonito, lindo (AmL)

pretty² adv (rather, quite) bastante; (emphatic) bien

prevail /prɪ'veɪl/ vi **1** (triumph) «justice/common sense» prevalecer*; «enemy» imponerse* **2** (predominate) «attitude/pessimism» preponderar; «situation» reinar

prevailing /prɪ'veɪlɪŋ/ adj (before n) ⟨wind⟩ preponderante; ⟨trend/view⟩ imperante; ⟨uncertainty⟩ reinante

prevalence /'prevələns/ n **(a)** (widespread occurrence) preponderancia f **(b)** (predominance) predominio m

prevalent /'prevələnt/ adj frecuente, corriente; ⟨disease⟩ común

prevaricate /prɪ'værəkeɪt ‖prɪ'værɪkeɪt/ vi **(a)** (not answer directly) andarse* con rodeos **(b)** (lie) (AmE) mentir*

prevent /prɪ'vent/ vt **(a)** (hinder) impedir*; **to ~ sb/sth** (FROM) -ING impedir* QUE algn/algo (+ subj) **(b)** (forestall) ⟨crime/disease/accident⟩ prevenir*, evitar

preventative /prɪ'ventətɪv/ adj ⯈ PREVENTIVE

prevention /prɪ'ventʃən ‖prɪ'venʃən/ n prevención f

preventive /prɪ'ventɪv/ adj preventivo

preview /'priːvjuː/ n **(a)** (advance showing) preestreno m **(b)** (trailer) avance m, trailer m (Esp), sinopsis f (CS)

previous /'priːviəs/ adj (earlier) (before n) ⟨occasion/attempt/page⟩ anterior; ⟨experience/knowledge⟩ previo; **on the ~ day** el día anterior; **I had a ~ engagement** ya tenía un compromiso

previously /'priːviəsli/ adv antes

prewar /ˌpriː'wɔːr ‖ˌpriː'wɔː(r)/ adj de antes de la guerra

prey /preɪ/ n presa f
■ **prey on, prey upon** [v + prep + o] **(a)** ⟨animal⟩ (hunt) cazar*; (feed on) alimentarse de; **it's been ~ing on my mind** me ha estado preocupando **(b)** (exploit) explotar

price¹ /praɪs/ n **1** (cost) precio m; **to go up/down in ~** subir/bajar de precio; **to pay a/the ~ for sth** pagar* algo caro; (before n) ~ **list** lista f de precios; **it's out of my ~ range** cuesta más de lo que puedo pagar **2** (value) (liter) precio m; **one cannot put a ~ on freedom** la libertad no tiene precio

price² vt **(a)** (fix price of) (often pass): **their products are reasonably ~d** sus productos tienen precios razonables; **they have ~d themselves out of the market** han subido tanto los precios que se han quedado sin compradores (or clientes etc) **(b)** (mark price on) ponerle* el precio a

priceless /'praɪsləs ‖'praɪslɪs/ adj inestimable, invalorable (CS)

price tag n etiqueta f (del precio), precio m

pricey, pricy /'praɪsi/ adj **pricier, priciest** (colloq) ⟨item⟩ carito (fam); ⟨store⟩ carero (fam)

prick¹ /prɪk/ vt **1** (pierce, wound) pinchar, picar* (Méx); **that ~ed his conscience** eso hizo que le remordiera la conciencia **2** ~ **up** ⟨ears⟩ «dog» levantar, parar (AmL); **she ~ed up her ears at the mention of France** aguzó el oído or (AmL fam) paró la oreja al oír hablar de Francia
■ ~ vi pinchar

prick² n **(a)** (act) pinchazo m, piquete m (Méx) **(b)** (mark) agujero m

prickle¹ /'prɪkəl/ n (a) (thorn) espina f (b) (sensation) picor m

prickle² vi «wool» picar*; «beard» pinchar, picar* (Méx); «skin/scalp» picar*

prickly /'prɪkli/ adj **-lier, -liest** (a) (with prickles) ⟨plant⟩ espinoso; ⟨animal⟩ con púas (b) (scratchy) ⟨wool⟩ que pica; ⟨beard⟩ que pincha or (Méx) pica

pride¹ /praɪd/ n 1 (a) (self-respect) orgullo m; false ~ vanidad f; she takes great ~ in her work se toma muy en serio su trabajo; to swallow one's ~ tragarse* el orgullo (b) (conceit) orgullo m 2 (source of pride) orgullo m; she is her mother's ~ and joy es el orgullo de su madre 3 (of lions) manada f

pride² v refl to ~ oneself ON sth/-ING enorgullecerse* DE algo/+ INF

priest /pri:st/ n sacerdote m; (parish ~) cura m (párroco), párroco m

priestess /'pri:stəs ‖'pri:stes/ n sacerdotisa f

priesthood /'pri:sthʊd/ n (a) (office) sacerdocio m (b) (clergy) clero m

prig /prɪg/ n mojigato, -ta m,f

prim /prɪm/ adj **-mer, -mest** (a) (prudish) mojigato; (affected) remilgado, repipi (Esp fam); she's so ~ and proper! es tan correcta y formal (b) (neat) cuidado

prima ballerina /'pri:mə/ n primera bailarina f

primaeval adj (BrE) ▶ PRIMEVAL

primarily /praɪ'merəli ‖'praɪmərɪli/ adv fundamentalmente

primary /'praɪmeri ‖'praɪməri/ adj 1 (principal) ⟨purpose/role/aim⟩ primordial 2 (a) (first, basic) ⟨source/energy⟩ primario; ⟨industry⟩ de base (b) ⟨education⟩ primario

primary: ~ color, (BrE) **colour** n color m primario; **~ school** n escuela f (de enseñanza) primaria

primate n 1 /'praɪmeɪt/ (Zool) primate m 2 /'praɪmeɪt, -ət/ (Relig) primado m

prime¹ /praɪm/ adj (no comp) (a) (major) principal (b) (first-rate) ⟨example/location⟩ excelente; ⟨cut⟩ de primera (calidad)

prime² n (best time): to be in one's ~ o in the ~ of life estar* en la flor de la vida

prime³ vt (a) (prepare for painting) ⟨wood/metal⟩ aplicar* una capa de imprimación a; ⟨canvas⟩ preparar (b) ⟨pump/gun⟩ cebar (c) (brief) preparar

prime minister n primer ministro, primera ministra m,f

primer /'praɪmər ‖'praɪmə(r)/ n 1 (a) (paint) imprimación f (b) (explosive) cebo m 2 (textbook) manual m

prime time n horas fpl de máxima audiencia

primeval, (BrE) **primaeval** /praɪ'mi:vəl/ adj primigenio

primitive /'prɪmətɪv ‖'prɪmɪtɪv/ adj primitivo; ⟨urges/instincts⟩ primario

primrose /'prɪmrəʊz/ n primavera f, prímula f

Primus® **(stove)** /'praɪməs/ n hornillo m de queroseno, Primus® m

prince /prɪns/ n príncipe m

princess /'prɪnses ‖'prɪnses/ n princesa f

principal¹ /'prɪnsəpəl/ adj (before n) principal

principal² n (of school) director, -tora m,f; (of university) rector, -tora m,f

principally /'prɪnsəpli/ adv principalmente

principle /'prɪnsəpəl/ n 1 (basic fact, law) principio m; **in ~** en principio 2 (rule of conduct) principio m; **I never borrow money, on ~** nunca pido dinero prestado, por principio; **it is against my ~s** va contra mis principios

print¹ /prɪnt/ n 1 (Print) (a) (lettering) letra f (b) (text): **in ~** ⟨(published⟩ publicado f; (available) a la venta; **out of ~** agotado 2 (a) (Art, Print) grabado m (b) (Phot) copia f 3 (of foot, finger) huella f 4 (fabric) estampado m

print² vt 1 (a) ⟨letter/text/design⟩ imprimir* (b) ⟨fabric⟩ estampar (c) (publish) publicar* (d) **printed** past p impreso 2 (write clearly) escribir* con letra de imprenta 3 (Phot) ⟨negative⟩ imprimir*
■ ~ vi (a) (Print) imprimir* (b) (write without joining the letters) escribir* con letra de imprenta or de molde
■ **print out** [v + adv + o, v + o + adv] imprimir*

printer /'prɪntər ‖'prɪntə(r)/ n (a) (worker) tipógrafo, -fa m,f, impresor, -sora m,f (b) (business) imprenta f (c) (machine) impresora f

printing /'prɪntɪŋ/ n (a) (act, process, result) impresión f (b) (quantity printed) edición f (c) (trade) imprenta f

printing press n imprenta f, prensa f

print: ~out n listado m; **~ run** n tirada f

prior¹ /'praɪər ‖'praɪə(r)/ adj (before n) ⟨knowledge/warning⟩ previo; **I had a ~ engagement** ya tenía un compromiso; **prior to** (as prep) antes de

prior² n prior m

priority /praɪ'ɔ:rəti ‖praɪ'ɒrɪti/ n (pl **-ties**) (a) (precedence) prioridad f; **to have/take ~ (over sth)** tener* prioridad (sobre algo) (b) (important matter, aim): **you have to get your priorities right** tienes que saber decidir qué es lo más importante (c) (in traffic) (BrE) preferencia f

priory /'praɪəri/ n (pl **-ries**) priorato m

prise /praɪz/ vt (BrE) ▶ PRIZE³ 2

prism /'prɪzəm/ n prisma m

prison /'prɪzn/ n prisión f, cárcel f; (before n) ⟨system/reform⟩ carcelario, penitenciario; **~ officer** (BrE) funcionario, -ria m,f de prisiones

prison camp n campo m de prisioneros

prisoner /'prɪznər ‖'prɪznə(r)/ n (a) (captive) prisionero, -ra m,f; **to take sb ~** tomar or (esp Esp) coger* a algn prisionero (b) (in jail) preso, -sa m,f (c) (person arrested) detenido, -da m,f (d) (accused) reo mf, acusado, -da m,f

prisoner of war n (pl **~s ~ ~**) prisionero, -ra m,f de guerra

prissy /'prɪsi/ adj **-sier, -siest** (colloq) remilgado, repipi (Esp fam)

pristine /'prɪsti:n, -taɪn/ adj (frml & liter) inmaculado, prístino (liter)

privacy /'praɪvəsi ‖'prɪvəsi/ n privacidad f

private¹ /'praɪvət ‖'praɪvɪt/ adj 1 (a) (confidential) ⟨conversation/matter⟩ privado; ⟨letter⟩ personal; **in private: she told me ~** me lo dijo confidencialmente; **can we talk in ~?** ¿podemos hablar en privado? 2 (for own use, in own possession) ⟨road/lesson/

secretary⟩ particular; ⟨*income*⟩ personal; ~ **property** propiedad *f* privada; ~ **income** rentas *fpl*

3 **(a)** (not official) ⟨*visit/correspondence*⟩ privado; **their** ~ **life** su vida privada **(b)** (unconnected to the state) ⟨*school*⟩ privado, de pago (Esp); ⟨*ward*⟩ reservado; ⟨*patient*⟩ particular; ~ **enterprise** la empresa privada; **the** ~ **sector** el sector privado **4** **(a)** ⟨*thoughts/doubts*⟩ íntimo; **it's a** ~ **joke** es un chiste que los dos entendemos/entienden **(b)** ⟨*person*⟩ reservado

private[2] *n* soldado *mf* raso

private: ~ **detective** *n* detective *mf* privado; ~ **eye** *n* (esp AmE colloq) sabueso *mf*

privately /ˈpraɪvətli ‖ˈpraɪvɪtli/ *adv* **1** (in private) en privado **2** (not by state): **she had the operation done** ~ (BrE) la operaron en una clínica privada; **this land is** ~ **owned** esta tierra es de particulares

private parts *pl n* (euph & hum) partes *fpl* pudendas (euf & hum)

privation /praɪˈveɪʃən/ *n* (fml) privación *f*

privatization /ˌpraɪvətəˈzeɪʃən ‖ˌpraɪvɪtaɪˈzeɪʃən/ *n* privatización *f*

privatize /ˈpraɪvətaɪz ‖ˈpraɪvɪtaɪz/ *vt* privatizar*

privilege /ˈprɪvəlɪdʒ/ *n* privilegio *m*

privileged /ˈprɪvəlɪdʒd/ *adj* **(a)** (having advantages) ⟨*position*⟩ privilegiado **(b)** (honored) (*pred*) **to be** ~ **to** + INF tener* el privilegio *or* el honor DE + INF

privy /ˈprɪvi/ *adj* (fml) (*pred*) **to be** ~ **TO sth** tener* conocimiento DE algo

prize[1] /praɪz/ *n* premio *m*

prize[2] *adj* (before n) premiado

prize[3] *vt* **1** (value) valorar (mucho) **2** (BrE) **prise**: **to** ~ **information out of sb** arrancarle* información a algn; **he** ~**d the lid off the crate** le arrancó la tapa a la caja haciendo palanca

prize: ~ **money** *n* premio *m* (*en metálico*); ~**winner** *n* ganador, -dora *m,f* (*de un premio*)

pro /prəʊ/ *n* **1** (professional) (colloq) profesional *mf* **2** **pros** *pl* (advantages): **the** ~**s and cons** los pros y los contras

pro- /ˈprəʊ/ *pref* pro(-)

proactive /prəʊˈæktɪv/ *adj* proactivo

probability /ˌprɑːbəˈbɪləti ‖ˌprɒbəˈbɪlɪti/ *n* (*pl* **-ties**) probabilidad *f*

probable /ˈprɑːbəbəl ‖ˈprɒbəbəl/ *adj* probable; ⟨*reason*⟩ posible

probably /ˈprɑːbəbli ‖ˈprɒbəbli/ *adv* (indep) probablemente + *subj*

probation /prəʊˈbeɪʃən ‖prəˈbeɪʃən/ *n* **1** (Law) libertad *f* condicional; **to be on** ~ estar* en libertad condicional **2** (trial period) período *m* de prueba

probationary /ˌprəʊˈbeɪʃəneri ‖prəˈbeɪʃənəri/ *adj* ⟨*period*⟩ de prueba

probe[1] /prəʊb/ *vt* **(a)** (physically) sondar **(b)** (investigate) investigar*; ⟨*mind/subconscious*⟩ explorar
■ ~ *vi* investigar*

probe[2] *n* **(a)** (Med, Elec) sonda *f* **(b)** (investigation) investigación *f*

probing /ˈprəʊbɪŋ/ *adj* ⟨*question*⟩ sagaz; ⟨*study*⟩ a fondo

---

problem /ˈprɑːbləm ‖ˈprɒbləm/ *n* problema *m*; **no** ~! (colloq) ¡no hay problema!; **what's the** ~? ¿qué pasa?; (before n) ⟨*family/child*⟩ difícil

problematic /ˌprɑːbləˈmætɪk ‖ˌprɒbləˈmætɪk/, **-ical** /-ɪkəl/ *adj* problemático

procedure /prəˈsiːdʒər ‖prəˈsiːdʒə(r), prəˈsiːdʒə(r)/ *n* (practice) procedimiento *m*; (step) trámite *m*

proceed /prəʊˈsiːd, prə- ‖prəˈsiːd, prəʊ-/ *vi* **(a)** (move forward) (frml) avanzar* **(b)** (continue) continuar*; **to** ~ **to** + INF: **she** ~**ed to tell us why** pasó a explicarnos por qué **(c)** (act) (frml) proceder **(d)** (progress) marchar

proceedings /prəʊˈsiːdɪŋz, prə- ‖ *pl n* **(a)** (events): ~ **began late** la reunión (*or* el acto *etc*) empezó tarde **(b)** (measures) medidas *fpl*; (Law) juicio *m*

proceeds /ˈprəʊsiːdz/ *pl n*: **the** ~ (from charity sale, function) lo recaudado

process[1] /ˈprɑːses, ˈprəʊ- ‖ˈprəʊses/ *n* **(a)** (series of actions, changes) proceso *m*; **the** ~ **of obtaining a permit** el trámite para obtener un permiso; **I am in the** ~ **of writing to him right now** en este preciso momento le estoy escribiendo **(b)** (method) proceso *m*, procedimiento *m*

process[2] *vt* ⟨*raw materials/waste*⟩ procesar, tratar; ⟨*film*⟩ revelar; ⟨*applications*⟩ dar* curso a; ⟨*order*⟩ tramitar; ⟨*data*⟩ procesar

process cheese (AmE), **processed cheese** /ˈprəʊsest/ (BrE) *n* queso *m* fundido

processing /ˈprɑːsesɪŋ, ˈprəʊ- ‖ˈprəʊsesɪŋ/ *n* **(a)** (of materials, waste) tratamiento *m*, procesamiento *m*; (of film) revelado *m* **(b)** (of an order, an application) tramitación *f* **(c)** (Comput) procesamiento *m*

procession /prəˈseʃən/ *n* desfile *m*; (Relig) procesión *f*; **a funeral** ~ un cortejo fúnebre

processor /ˈprɑːsesər‖ˈprəʊsesə(r)/ *n* **1** (for food) robot *m* de cocina, multiusos *m* **2** (Comput) procesador *m*

proclaim /prəʊˈkleɪm, prə- ‖prəˈkleɪm/ *vt* (frml) ⟨*independence*⟩ proclamar; ⟨*love*⟩ declarar

proclamation /ˈprɑːkləˈmeɪʃən ‖ˌprɒkləˈmeɪʃən/ *n* (frml) proclamación *f*

procrastinate /prəʊˈkræstəneɪt/ *vi* dejar las cosas para más tarde

procreation /ˈprəʊkriˈeɪʃən/ *n* (frml) procreación *f*

procure /prəˈkjʊr ‖prəˈkjʊə(r)/ *vt* (frml) procurar (frml)

prod[1] /prɑːd ‖prɒd/ *vt* **-dd-** (with elbow) darle* un codazo a; (with sth sharp) pinchar

prod[2] *n* (with elbow) codazo *m*; (with sth sharp) pinchazo *m*

prodigal /ˈprɑːdɪgəl ‖ˈprɒdɪgəl/ *adj* pródigo

prodigious /prəˈdɪdʒəs/ *adj* ⟨*amount/cost*⟩ enorme; ⟨*efforts/strength*⟩ prodigioso

prodigy /ˈprɑːdədʒi ‖ˈprɒdɪdʒi/ *n* (*pl* **-gies**) prodigio *m*; **child** ~ niño, -ña *m,f* prodigio

produce[1] /prəˈduːs ‖prəˈdjuːs/ *vt* **1** **(a)** (manufacture, yield) ⟨*cars/cloth*⟩ producir*, fabricar*; ⟨*coal/grain/beef*⟩ producir*; ⟨*fruit*⟩ «*country/region*» producir*; ⟨*tree/bush*⟩ dar*, producir* **(b)** (create, give) ⟨*energy/sound*⟩ producir* **(c)** (cause) ⟨*effect*⟩ surtir, producir* **(d)** (give birth to) ⟨*young*⟩ tener* **2** (show, bring out) ⟨*ticket/* ⋯⟩

p

produce² /'prɑ:du:s ‖'prɒdju:s/ n productos
mpl (alimenticios)

document/evidence› presentar, aportar; ‹*gun/
knife*› sacar* **3** **(a)** (Cin, TV) producir*; (Theat)
‹*play*› poner* en escena; ‹*show*› montar **(b)** (Rad,
Theat) (direct) dirigir*

producer /prə'du:sər ‖prə'dju:sə(r)/ n
1 (manufacturer) fabricante mf **2** **(a)** (Cin, TV,
Theat) productor, -tora m,f **(b)** (Rad, Theat) (director)
director, -tora m,f

product /'prɑ:dəkt ‖'prɒdʌkt/ n producto m

production /prə'dʌkʃən/ n **1** **(a)** (manufacture)
fabricación f **(b)** (output) producción f **2** (showing)
presentación f **3** (staging, version) (Theat, Cin)
producción f **4** **(a)** (act of producing) (Cin, TV)
producción f; (Theat) puesta f en escena **(b)**
(direction) (Rad, Theat) dirección f

production line n cadena f de fabricación

productive /prə'dʌktɪv/ adj ‹*land/factory/
mine*› productivo; ‹*meeting*› fructífero

productively /prə'dʌktɪvli/ adv
productivamente; **I didn't spend my time very** ~
no saqué buen partido del tiempo

productivity /ˌprəʊdʌk'tɪvəti ‖ˌprɒdʌk'tɪvəti/
n productividad f

profane /prə'feɪn/ adj **(a)** (blasphemous)
irreverente **(b)** (secular) profano

profanity /prə'fænəti/ n (pl **-ties**) **(a)**
(blasphemy, vulgarity) irreverencia f **(b)** (swearword)
blasfemia f

profess /prə'fes/ vt **(a)** (claim) (frml) ‹*desire/
belief*› manifestar*; **he** ~**ed to be an expert** se
preciaba de ser un experto **(b)** (Relig) profesar

profession /prə'feʃən/ n **1** **(a)** (occupation)
profesión f; **by** ~ de profesión **(b)** (members) (no
pl): **the medical** ~ el cuerpo médico; **the teaching**
~ la enseñanza **2** (declaration) (frml) profesión f

professional¹ /prə'feʃnəl ‖prə'feʃ(ə)nl/ adj
(before n) ‹*musician/golfer*› profesional; ‹*soldier*›
de carrera; **to take** ~ **advice** asesorarse con un
profesional (or un experto, técnico etc)

professional² n profesional mf; (competent
person) experto, -ta m,f

professionalism /prə'feʃnəlɪzəm
‖prə'feʃ(ə)nl]ɪzəm/ n profesionalidad f

professionally /prə'feʃnəli/ adv **(a)** (as
livelihood) ‹*sing/act*› profesionalmente **(b)** (by
qualified person): **we had the job done** ~ hicimos
hacer el trabajo por un experto (or por un pintor,
albañil etc) **(c)** (in a professional way) con
profesionalidad

professor /prə'fesər ‖prə'fesə(r)/ n (of the
highest academic rank) catedrático, -ca m,f; (any
university teacher) (AmE) profesor universitario,
profesora universitaria m,f

proffer /'prɑ:fər ‖'prɒfə(r)/ vt (frml) ofrecer*

proficiency /prə'fɪʃənsi/ n competencia f

proficient /prə'fɪʃənt/ adj muy competente

profile¹ /'prəʊfaɪl/ n perfil m; **to keep a low** ~
tratar de pasar desapercibido

profile² vt (situation) hacer* un esbozo de; **to** ~
sb's life hacer* una reseña biográfica de algn

profit¹ /'prɑ:fət ‖'prɒfɪt/ n (Busn, Econ)
ganancias fpl, utilidades fpl (AmL); **to sell sth at a**
~ vender algo con ganancia

profit² vi **to** ~ **FROM sth** sacar* provecho DE
algo

profitable /'prɑ:fətəbəl ‖'prɒfɪtəbəl/ adj **(a)**
(Busn) ‹*company/investment/crop*› rentable **(b)**
‹*day/journey*› provechoso

profitably /'prɑ:fətəbli ‖'prɒfɪtəbli/ adv **(a)**
(Busn) ‹*trade/operate*› de manera rentable; ‹*sell*›
con ganancia **(b)** (fruitfully) provechosamente

profiteer /ˌprɑ:fə'tɪr ‖ˌprɒfɪ'tɪə(r)/ n
especulador, -dora m,f

profiteering /ˌprɑ:fə'tɪrɪŋ ‖ˌprɒfɪ'tɪərɪŋ/ n
especulación f

profit-making /'prɑ:fətˌmeɪkɪŋ
‖'prɒfɪtˌmeɪkɪŋ/ adj (profitable) rentable; (which
aims to make a profit) con fines lucrativos

profound /prə'faʊnd/ adj **-er, -est** profundo

profoundly /prə'faʊndli/ adv profundamente

profuse /prə'fju:s/ adj abundante; ‹*bleeding*›
intenso

profusely /prə'fju:sli/ adv ‹*bleed*›
profusamente; ‹*thank*› efusivamente; **he
apologized** ~ se deshizo en disculpas

profusion /prə'fju:ʒən/ n profusión f

prognosis /prɑ:g'nəʊsəs ‖prɒg'nəʊsɪs/ n (pl
-ses /-si:z/) pronóstico m

program¹, (BrE) **programme** /'prəʊgræm/ n
1 **(a)** (schedule, plan) programa m **(b)** (for concert,
performance) programa m **(c)** (esp AmE Educ)
(course) curso m **2** (Rad, TV) programa m
3 **program** (Comput) programa m

program² vt **-mm-** or **-m-** **1** (BrE also)
programme **(a)** (schedule) ‹*activities*›
programar, planear **(b)** (instruct) programar
2 (Comput) programar

programmer, (AmE also) **programer**
/'prəʊgræmər ‖'prəʊgræmə(r)/ n (Comput)
programador, -dora m,f

progress¹ /'prɑ:grəs ‖'prəʊgres/ n
1 (advancement) progreso m; (of situation, events)
desarrollo m; **to make** ~ «*pupil*» adelantar,
hacer* progresos; «*patient*» mejorar **2 in
progress**: **talks are in** ~ **between the two parties**
los dos partidos están manteniendo
conversaciones; **while the examination is in** ~
mientras dure el examen **3** (forward movement)
avance m

progress² /prə'gres/ vi «*work/science/
technology*» progresar; «*patient*» mejorar

progression /prə'greʃən/ n **(a)** (advance)
evolución f **(b)** (Math, Mus) progresión f

progressive /prə'gresɪv/ adj **1** ‹*attitude/
thinker/measure*› progresivo **2** ‹*illness/
deterioration/improvement*› progresivo

prohibit /prəʊ'hɪbɪt ‖prə'hɪbɪt/ vt **(a)** (forbid)
prohibir* **(b)** (prevent) impedir*

prohibition /ˌprəʊə'bɪʃən ‖ˌprəʊhɪ'bɪʃən/ n **(a)**
prohibición f **(b)** **Prohibition** (in US history) (no
art) la Ley seca, la Prohibición

prohibitive /prəʊ'hɪbətɪv ‖prə'hɪbətɪv/ adj
⟨price/cost⟩ prohibitivo

project¹ /'prɑːdʒekt ‖'prɒdʒekt/ n (a) (scheme)
proyecto m (b) (Educ) trabajo m (c) (housing ⁓) (in
US) complejo m de viviendas subvencionadas

project² /prə'dʒekt/ vt ☐ (a) ⟨beam/shadow/
image⟩ proyectar (b) (convey) ⟨personality/image/
voice⟩ proyectar ☐ (frml) ⟨missile⟩ lanzar*
☐ (forecast) pronosticar*; ⟨costs/trends⟩ hacer*
una proyección de; **the ⁓ed figure** la cifra
prevista
■ ⁓ vi (jut out) sobresalir*

projection /prə'dʒekʃən/ n ☐ (of image, slide)
proyección f ☐ (forecast) proyección f, pronóstico
m ☐ (protuberance) saliente f or m

projector /prə'dʒektər ‖prə'dʒektə(r)/ n
proyector m

proletarian /'prəʊlə'teriən ‖,prəʊlə'teəriən/
adj proletario

pro-life adj pro-vida

proliferate /prə'lɪfəreɪt/ vi proliferar

prolific /prə'lɪfɪk/ adj prolífico

prologue, (AmE also) **prolog** /'prəʊlɔːg
‖'prəʊlɒg/ n prólogo m

prolong /prə'lɔːŋ ‖prə'lɒŋ/ vt prolongar*

prom /prɑːm ‖prɒm/ n (a) (ball) (in US) (colloq)
baile m del colegio (or de la facultad etc) (b)
(esplanade) (BrE colloq) ▶ PROMENADE¹

promenade¹ /prɑːmə'neɪd ‖'prɒmənɑːd/ n (at
seaside) (esp BrE) paseo m marítimo, malecón m
(AmL), costanera f (CS)

promenade² vi pasear(se)

prominence /'prɑːmənəns ‖'prɒmɪnəns/ n
(conspicuousness) prominencia f; (eminence,
importance) importancia f

prominent /'prɑːmənənt ‖'prɒmɪnənt/ adj (a)
⟨position⟩ destacado; ⟨role/politician⟩ prominente,
destacado (b) ⟨jaw/nose⟩ prominente

prominently /'prɑːmənəntli ‖'prɒmɪnəntli/
adv: **it was ⁓ displayed** ocupaba un lugar
prominente or destacado; **he figured ⁓ in the
negotiations** desempeñó un papel prominente or
destacado en las negociaciones

promiscuity /'prɑːməs'kjuːəti
‖,prɒmɪ'skjuːəti/ n promiscuidad f

promiscuous /prə'mɪskjuəs/ adj promiscuo

promise¹ /'prɑːməs ‖'prɒmɪs/ n ☐ (pledge)
promesa f ☐ (potential): **his work showed great o a
lot of ⁓** su trabajo prometía mucho

promise² vt/i prometer; **to ⁓ to + INF**
prometer + INF

promising /'prɑːməsɪŋ ‖'prɒmɪsɪŋ/ adj ⟨pupil/
writer/career⟩ prometedor; ⟨future⟩ halagüeño

promote /prə'məʊt/ vt ☐ (a) (raise in rank)
⟨employee⟩ ascender* (b) (AmE Educ) promover*
☐ (a) (encourage) promover*; ⟨growth⟩ estimular
(b) (advocate) promover* ☐ ⟨product/service⟩
promocionar

promoter /prə'məʊtər ‖prə'məʊtə(r)/ n (a)
(Busn) promotor, -tora m,f (b) (Sport) empresario,
-ria m,f

promotion /prə'məʊʃən/ n ☐ (advancement in
rank) ascenso m; **she got a ⁓** la ascendieron ☐
(a) (of research, peace, trade) promoción f (b)
(advocacy) promoción f ☐ (publicity) promoción f

promotional /prə'məʊʃnəl ‖prə'məʊʃənl̩/ adj
de promoción, promocional

prompt¹ /prɑːmpt ‖prɒmpt/ vt ☐ ⟨response/
outcry⟩ provocar*; **to ⁓ sb to + INF** mover* a
algn A + INF ☐ ⟨actor/orator⟩ apuntarle a

prompt² adj **-er, -est** rápido

prompt³ adv (BrE): **at ten o'clock ⁓** a las diez
en punto

prompt⁴ n (a) (reminder) apunte m (b) (Comput)
presto m

prompter /'prɑːmptər ‖'prɒmptə(r)/ n
apuntador, -dora m,f

promptly /'prɑːmptli ‖'prɒmptli/ adv (a) (on
time) puntualmente (b) (speedily) ⟨pay/deliver⟩ sin
demora (c) (instantly) de inmediato

prone /prəʊn/ adj ☐ (liable, disposed) ⟨pred⟩ **to
be ⁓ to sth** ser* propenso A algo; **to be ⁓ to +
INF** ser* propenso a + INF ☐ (face downward)
(tendido) boca abajo

prong /prɔːŋ ‖prɒŋ/ n diente m

pronoun /'prəʊnaʊn/ n pronombre m

pronounce /prə'naʊns/ vt (a) ⟨sound/word/
syllable⟩ pronunciar (b) ⟨judgment/sentence⟩
pronunciar (c) (declare) (frml): **the doctor ⁓d him
dead** el médico dictaminó que estaba muerto

pronounced /prə'naʊnst/ adj pronunciado

pronouncement /prə'naʊnsmənt/ n
declaración f

pronunciation /prə'nʌnsi'eɪʃən/ n
pronunciación f

proof¹ /pruːf/ n ☐ (conclusive evidence) prueba f
☐ (Print) prueba f (de imprenta) ☐ (alcoholic
strength) graduación f alcohólica

proof² adj ⟨pred⟩ **to be ⁓ AGAINST sth** ser* a
prueba DE algo

proof: ⁓read (past & past p **-read** /-red/) vt
corregir ■ ⁓ vi corregir pruebas; **⁓reader** n
corrector, -tora m,f de pruebas

prop¹ /prɑːp ‖prɒp/ n ☐ (holding up roof etc)
puntal m ☐ (Cin, Theat) accesorio m, objeto m de
utilería or (Esp, Méx) del attrezzo

prop² -pp- vt **to ⁓ sth AGAINST sth** apoyar algo
EN or CONTRA algo
■ **prop up** [v + o + adv, v + adv + o] (a) (support)
⟨wall/building⟩ sostener* (b) (lean) apoyar

propaganda /'prɑːpə'gændə ‖prɒpə'gændə/ n
propaganda f

propagate /'prɑːpəgeɪt ‖'prɒpəgeɪt/ vt
propagar*

propel /prə'pel/ vt **-ll-** ⟨plane/ship⟩ propulsar

propeller /prə'pelər ‖prə'pelə(r)/ n hélice f

proper /'prɑːpər ‖'prɒpə(r)/ adj ☐ (before n, no
comp) (correct) ⟨treatment/procedure⟩ apropiado;
⟨pronunciation⟩ correcto ☐ (before n, no comp)
(genuine) ⟨chance⟩ verdadero; ⟨meal⟩ como Dios
manda; ⟨vacation⟩ de verdad ☐ (a) ⟨behavior/
person⟩ correcto (b) (overly decorous) recatado
☐ (in the strict sense) (after n) propiamente
dicho

properly /'prɑːpərli ‖'prɒpəli/ adv (a) ⟨write/
spell/fit⟩ correctamente; ⟨work/concentrate/eat⟩
bien (b) (appropriately) apropiadamente

proper name, proper noun n nombre m
propio

property /'prɑːpərti ‖'prɒpəti/ n (pl **-ties**)
☐ (possessions) propiedad f ☐ (a) (buildings, land) ····ᑉ

propiedades *fpl*, bienes *mpl* raíces (frml); (*before n*) ~ **developer** promotor inmobiliario, promotora inmobiliaria *m,f*; ~ **tax** (in US) impuesto *m* sobre la propiedad inmobiliaria **(b)** (building) inmueble *m* (frml); (piece of land) terreno *m*, solar *m*, parcela *f* **3** (quality) propiedad *f*

prophecy /'prɑːfəsi ‖ 'prɒfəsi/ *n* (*pl* **-cies**) profecía *f*

prophesy /'prɑːfəsaɪ ‖ 'prɒfəsaɪ/ *vt* **-sies, -sying, -sied** predecir*; (Relig) profetizar*

prophet /'prɑːfət ‖ 'prɒfɪt/ *n* profeta, -tisa *m,f*

prophetic /prə'fetɪk/ *adj* profético

proportion /prə'pɔːrʃən ‖ prə'pɔːʃən/ *n* **1** (part) (*no pl*) parte *f* **2** (ratio) proporción *f*; **in equal** ~**s** por partes iguales; **in** ~ **to sth** en proporción a algo **3** (proper relation) proporción *f*; **let's keep things in** ~ no exageremos; **to blow sth up out of all** ~ exagerar algo desmesuradamente **4 proportions** *pl* (size) proporciones *fpl*

proportional /prə'pɔːrʃn̩əl ‖ prə'pɔːʃənl/ *adj* proporcional; ~ **representation** representación *f* proporcional

proportionate /prə'pɔːrʃn̩ət ‖ prə'pɔːʃənət/ *adj* proporcional

proposal /prə'pəʊzəl/ *n* **(a)** (suggestion) propuesta *f* **(b)** (of marriage) proposición *f* matrimonial

propose /prə'pəʊz/ *vt* **1** **(a)** (suggest) proponer*; **to** ~ **-ING/(THAT)** proponer* QUE (+ *subj*) **(b) proposed** *past p*: **the** ~**d cuts** los recortes que se proponen implementar **(c)** (in meeting) ⟨*amendment*⟩ proponer*; ⟨*motion*⟩ presentar **2** (intend) **to** ~ **to** + INF, **to** ~ **-ING** pensar* + INF

■ ~ *vi* **to** ~ **TO sb** proponerle* matrimonio a algn

proposition¹ /ˌprɑːpə'zɪʃən ‖ ˌprɒpə'zɪʃən/ *n* **1** (suggestion) propuesta *f*; (offer) oferta *f* **2** (prospect): **it's not a viable** ~ no es viable

proposition² *vt* hacerle* proposiciones deshonestas a (euf)

proprietary /prə'praɪəteri ‖ prə'praɪətri/ *adj* ⟨*device/software/drug*⟩ de marca registrada

proprietor /prə'praɪətər ‖ prə'praɪətə(r)/ *n* propietario, -ria *m,f*, dueño, -ña *m,f*

propulsion /prə'pʌlʃən/ *n* propulsión *f*

pro rata /ˌprəʊ'rɑːtə/ *adv* a prorrata

prosaic /prəʊ'zeɪɪk/ *adj* prosaico

proscribe /prəʊ'skraɪb ‖ prə'skraɪb/ *vt* proscribir*

prose /prəʊz/ *n* (Lit) prosa *f*

prosecute /'prɑːsɪkjuːt ‖ 'prɒsɪkjuːt/ *vt* (Law) **to** ~ **sb FOR sth** procesar a algn POR algo

■ ~ *vi* iniciar procedimiento criminal; **prosecuting attorney** (in US) fiscal *mf*

prosecution /ˌprɑːsɪ'kjuːʃən ‖ ˌprɒsɪ'kjuːʃən/ *n* (Law) **(a)** (bringing to trial) interposición *f* de una acción judicial **(b)** (prosecuting side) **the** ~ la acusación

prosecutor /'prɑːsɪkjuːtər ‖ 'prɒsɪkjuːtə(r)/ *n* fiscal *mf*; (in private prosecutions) abogado, -da *m,f* de or por la acusación

prospect¹ /'prɑːspekt ‖ 'prɒspekt/ *n* **1** **(a)** (possibility) posibilidad *f*; ~ **OF sth** posibilidades *fpl* DE algo **(b)** (situation envisaged) perspectiva *f* **(c)**

prospects *pl* (chances) perspectivas *fpl*; **a job with no** ~**s** un trabajo sin futuro **2** (potential customer) posible cliente, -ta *m,f*

prospect² /'prɑːspekt ‖ prə'spekt/ *vi* **to** ~ **FOR sth** buscar* algo

prospective /prə'spektɪv/ *adj* (*before n*) ⟨*customer*⟩ posible; ⟨*husband*⟩ futuro

prospector /'prɑːspektər ‖ prə'spektə(r)/ *n* prospector, -tora *m,f*, cateador, -dora *m,f* (AmS)

prospectus /prə'spektəs/ *n* (*pl* ~**es**) (Educ) folleto *m* informativo

prosper /'prɑːspər ‖ 'prɒspə(r)/ *vi* prosperar

prosperity /prɑː'sperəti ‖ prɒ'sperəti/ *n* prosperidad *f*

prosperous /'prɑːspərəs ‖ 'prɒspərəs/ *adj* próspero

prostate (gland) /'prɑːsteɪt ‖ 'prɒsteɪt/ *n* próstata *f*

prostitute¹ /'prɑːstətuːt ‖ 'prɒstɪtjuːt/ *n* prostituta *f*; **male** ~ prostituto *m*

prostitute² *vt* prostituir*; **to** ~ **oneself** prostituirse*

prostitution /ˌprɑːstə'tuːʃən ‖ ˌprɒstɪ'tjuːʃən/ *n* prostitución *f*

prostrate /'prɑːstreɪt ‖ 'prɒstreɪt/ *adj* postrado

protagonist /prəʊ'tægənəst ‖ prə'tægənɪst/ *n* (Lit) protagonista *mf*

protect /prə'tekt/ *vt* proteger*

protection /prə'tekʃən/ *n* protección *f*; (*before n*) ~ **racket** chantaje *m* (*que se practica a propietarios de comercios*)

protectionism /prə'tekʃənɪzəm/ *n* proteccionismo *m*

protective /prə'tektɪv/ *adj* **(a)** ⟨*headgear/ covering*⟩ protector; ⟨*clothing*⟩ de protección **(b)** ⟨*attitude/feelings*⟩ protector

protector /prə'tektər ‖ prə'tektə(r)/ *n* protector, -tora *m,f*

protein /'prəʊtiːn/ *n* proteína *f*

protest¹ /'prəʊtest/ *n* **(a)** (expression of disagreement) protesta *f*; **in** ~ (**against sth**) en señal de protesta (contra algo); **under** ~ bajo protesta **(b)** (complaint) protesta *f* **(c)** (demonstration) manifestación *f* de protesta

protest² /prə'test/ *vi* protestar; **to** ~ **AGAINST/ ABOUT sth** protestar CONTRA/ACERCA DE algo

■ ~ *vt* **1** **(a)** (complain) **to** ~ **THAT** quejarse DE QUE, protestar QUE **(b)** (object to) (AmE) ⟨*decision/ action*⟩ protestar (contra) **2** (assert) ⟨*love*⟩ declarar; ⟨*innocence/loyalty*⟩ hacer* protestas de

Protestant¹ /'prɑːtəstənt ‖ 'prɒtɪstənt/ *n* protestante *mf*

Protestant² *adj* protestante

Protestantism /'prɑːtəstəntɪzəm ‖ 'prɒtɪstəntɪzəm/ *n* protestantismo *m*

protester /prə'testər ‖ prə'testə(r)/ *n* manifestante *mf*

protocol /'prəʊtəkɔːl ‖ 'prəʊtəkɒl/ *n* protocolo *m*

prototype /'prəʊtətaɪp/ *n* prototipo *m*

protracted /prə'træktəd ‖ prə'træktɪd/ *adj* prolongado

protrude /prə'truːd/ *vi* (frml) **(a)** ⟨*nail/ledge*⟩

sobresalir* (b) **protruding** *pres p* ‹*chin*›
prominente; ‹*teeth*› salido; ‹*nail*› que sobresale;
protruding eyes ojos *mpl* saltones

proud /praʊd/ *adj* **-er, -est** (a) (pleased)
‹*parent/winner*› orgulloso; ‹*smile/moment*› de
orgullo; **to be ~ OF sb/sth** estar* orgulloso DE
algn/algo (b) (having self-respect) ‹*nation/race*›
digno (c) (arrogant, haughty) orgulloso

proudly /ˈpraʊdli/ *adv* (a) (with pleasure,
satisfaction) con orgullo (b) (arrogantly)
orgullosamente

prove /pruːv/ (*past* **proved**; *past p* **proved** *or*
proven) *vt* ‹*theory/statement/innocence*› probar*,
demostrar*; ‹*loyalty/courage*› demostrar*
■ *v refl* **to ~ oneself: he was given three months to
~ himself** le dieron tres meses para que
demostrara su valía; **to ~ oneself to be sth**
demostrarse* ser algo
■ **~** *vi* resultar

proven /ˈpruːvən/ *adj* ‹*experience/ability*›
probado; ‹*method*› de probada eficacia

proverb /ˈprɑːvɜːrb ‖ ˈprɒvɜːb/ *n* refrán *m*,
proverbio *m*

proverbial /prəˈvɜːrbiəl ‖ prəˈvɜːbiəl/ *adj*
proverbial

provide /prəˈvaɪd/ *vt* (supply) proporcionar;
‹*accommodation*› dar*; **to ~ sb WITH sth** proveer*
a algn DE algo
■ **provide for** [*v* + *prep* + *o*] (a) (support) ‹*family*›
mantener* (b) (make arrangements for): **I have to ~
for my old age** tengo que asegurarme el bienestar
en la vejez

provided /prəˈvaɪdəd ‖ prəˈvaɪdɪd/ *conj* **~
(that)** siempre que (+ *subj*)

providence /ˈprɑːvədəns ‖ ˈprɒvɪdəns/ *n* (a)
(Relig) providencia *f* (b) (fate, chance): **it was sheer
~ that** ... fue providencial que ...

providing /prəˈvaɪdɪŋ/ *conj* ▶ PROVIDED

province /ˈprɑːvəns ‖ ˈprɒvɪns/ *n*
⊡ (administrative unit) provincia *f* ⊡ (a) (area of
knowledge, activity) terreno *m* (b) (area of responsibility)
competencia *f*

provincial /prəˈvɪntʃəl ‖ prəˈvɪnʃəl/ *adj*
⊡ (Govt) provincial ⊡ (a) ‹*town*› de provincia(s)
(b) (pej) ‹*outlook*› provinciano

provision /prəˈvɪʒən/ *n* ⊡ (of funding) provisión
f; (of food, supplies) suministro *m* ⊡ (preparatory
arrangements) previsiones *fpl* ⊡ (stipulation) (Govt,
Law) disposición *f* ⊡ **provisions** *pl* provisiones
fpl, víveres *mpl*

provisional /prəˈvɪʒnəl ‖ prəˈvɪʒənl̩/ *adj*
provisional, provisorio (AmS)

proviso /prəˈvaɪzəʊ/ *n* (*pl* **-sos**) condición *f*

provocation /ˌprɑːvəˈkeɪʃən ‖ ˌprɒvəˈkeɪʃən/
n provocación *f*

provocative /prəˈvɑːkətɪv ‖ prəˈvɒkətɪv/ *adj*
⊡ (causing trouble) provocador ⊡ (seductive)
provocativo

provoke /prəˈvəʊk/ *vt* ⊡ ‹*person/animal*›
provocar*; **I was ~d into hitting him** tanto me
provocó, que le pegué ⊡ ‹*argument/revolt/
criticism*› provocar*; ‹*discussion/debate*› motivar;
‹*interest/curiosity*› despertar*

prow /praʊ/ *n* proa *f*

prowess /ˈpraʊəs ‖ ˈpraʊɪs/ *n* destreza *f*

prowl /praʊl/ *vi* merodear

proximity /prɑːkˈsɪməti ‖ prɒkˈsɪməti/ *n* (frml)
proximidad *f*

proxy /ˈprɑːksi ‖ ˈprɒksi/ *n* (*pl* **-xies**) (a)
(person) representante *mf* (b) (authorization) poder
m; **by ~** por poder *or* (Esp) por poderes

prude /pruːd/ *n* mojigato, -ta *m,f*

prudence /ˈpruːdn̩s/ *n* prudencia *f*

prudent /ˈpruːdn̩t/ *adj* prudente

prudish /ˈpruːdɪʃ/ *adj* mojigato

prune¹ /pruːn/ *n* ciruela *f* pasa *or* (CS) seca

prune² *vt* (a) (Hort) podar (b) ‹*costs/workforce*›
reducir*

pry /praɪ/ **pries, prying, pried** *vi* curiosear;
to ~ INTO sth entrometerse EN algo
■ **~** *vt* (esp AmE) (+ *adv compl*): **she pried the lid
off** levantó la tapa (haciendo palanca)

PS *n* (postscript) P.D.

psalm /sɑːm/ *n* salmo *m*

pseudonym /ˈsuːdn̩ɪm ‖ ˈsjuːdənɪm/ *n*
(p)seudónimo *m*

PST (in US) = **Pacific Standard Time**

psychiatric /ˌsaɪkiˈætrɪk/ *adj* (p)siquiátrico

psychiatrist /səˈkaɪətrəst ‖ saɪˈkaɪətrɪst/ *n*
(p)siquiatra *mf*

psychiatry /səˈkaɪətri ‖ saɪˈkaɪətri/ *n*
(p)siquiatría *f*

psychic /ˈsaɪkɪk/ *adj* (a) (Occult)
para(p)sicológico (b) (Psych) (p)síquico

psychoanalysis /ˈsaɪkəʊəˈnæləsəs
‖ ˌsaɪkəʊəˈnæləsɪs/ *n* (p)sicoanálisis *m*

psychological /ˌsaɪkəˈlɑːdʒɪkəl
‖ ˌsaɪkəˈlɒdʒɪkəl/ *adj* (p)sicológico

psychologist /saɪˈkɑːlədʒəst ‖ saɪˈkɒlədʒɪst/ *n*
(p)sicólogo, -ga *m,f*

psychology /saɪˈkɑːlədʒi ‖ saɪˈkɒlədʒi/ *n* (*pl*
-gies) (p)sicología *f*

psychopath /ˈsaɪkəpæθ ‖ ˈsaɪkəʊpæθ/ *n*
(p)sicópata *mf*

psychosis /saɪˈkəʊsəs ‖ saɪˈkəʊsɪs/ *n* (*pl* **-ses**
/-siːz/) (p)sicosis *f*

psychosomatic /ˌsaɪkəsəˈmætɪk
‖ ˌsaɪkəʊsəˈmætɪk/ *adj* (p)sicosomático

psychotherapy /ˈsaɪkəʊˈθerəpi/ *n*
(p)sicoterapia *f*

psychotic /saɪˈkɑːtɪk ‖ saɪˈkɒtɪk/ *adj*
(p)sicótico

PTO (= **please turn over**) sigue al dorso

pub /pʌb/ *n* (BrE) ≈ bar *m*; (before n) **to go on a
~ crawl** ir* de bar en bar tomando copas

puberty /ˈpjuːbərti ‖ ˈpjuːbəti/ *n* pubertad *f*

pubic /ˈpjuːbɪk/ *adj* ‹*hair*› púbico, pubiano;
‹*region/bone*› pubiano

public¹ /ˈpʌblɪk/ *adj* público; **it is ~ knowledge**
es de dominio público; **at ~ expense** con fondos
públicos; **the ~ sector** el sector público; **~
speaking** oratoria *f*

public² *n* (+ *sing or pl vb*) (a) (people in general)
the ~ el público (b) (audience) público *m* (c) **in
public** en público

public-address system /ˈpʌblɪkəˈdres/ *n*
(sistema *m* de) megafonía *f*, altoparlantes *mpl*
(AmL)

publican /ˈpʌblɪkən/ *n* (BrE) dueño, -ña *m,f* de
un bar

P

public assistance n (AmE) *ayuda estatal a los sectores más necesitados de la población*; **to be on ~ ~** recibir ayuda estatal

publication /ˌpʌblə'keɪʃən ‖ˌpʌblɪ'keɪʃən/ n publicación f

public: ~ health n salud f or sanidad f pública; **~ holiday** n fiesta f oficial, (día m) feriado m (AmL); **~ house** n (BrE) ≈bar m

publicity /pʌb'lɪsəti/ n publicidad f

publicize /'pʌbləsaɪz ‖'pʌblɪsaɪz/ vt hacer* público

publicly /'pʌblɪkli/ adv (a) públicamente (b) (Govt) ⟨funded/maintained⟩ con fondos públicos

public: ~ relations n relaciones fpl públicas; **~ school** n (in US) escuela f pública; (in UK) colegio m privado; (— boarding school) internado m privado; **~ service** n (communal provision) servicio m público; **~-spirited** /'pʌblɪk'spɪrətəd ‖ˌpʌblɪk'spɪrɪtɪd/ adj solidario; **~ transportation** (AmE), **~ transport** (BrE) n transporte m público

publish /'pʌblɪʃ/ vt (a) ⟨book/newspaper/article⟩ publicar* (b) (make known) hacer* público

publisher /'pʌblɪʃər ‖'pʌblɪʃə(r)/ n (a) (company) editorial f (b) (job title) editor, -tora m,f

publishing /'pʌblɪʃɪŋ/ n mundo m editorial; (before n) **~ house** editorial f

pucker /'pʌkər ‖'pʌkə(r)/ vt fruncir*

pudding /'pʊdɪŋ/ n (a) (baked, steamed) budín m, pudín m (b) (dessert) (BrE) postre m

puddle /'pʌdl̩/ n charco m

Puerto Rican¹ /'pwertə'ri:kən ‖ˌpwɜ:təʊ'ri:kən/ adj portorriqueño, puertorriqueño

Puerto Rican² n portorriqueño, -ña m,f, puertorriqueño, -ña m,f

Puerto Rico /'pwertə'ri:kəʊ ‖ˌpwɜ:təʊ'ri:kəʊ/ n Puerto Rico m

puff¹ /pʌf/ n (a) (of wind, air) ráfaga f; **a ~ of smoke** una nube de humo (b) (action) soplo m; (on cigarette) chupada f, pitada f (AmL), calada f (Esp) (c) (sound) resoplido m

puff² vt (a) (blow) soplar (b) (smoke) ⟨cigarette/cigar/pipe⟩ dar* chupadas or (AmL tb) pitadas or (Esp tb) caladas a
■ **~** vi [1] (a) (blow) soplar (b) (smoke) **to ~ on** o **at sth** ⟨on cigarette/cigar/pipe⟩ dar* chupadas or (AmL tb) pitadas or (Esp tb) caladas a algo [2] (pant) resoplar
■ **puff out** [v + o + adv, v + adv + o] ⟨cheeks⟩ inflar, hinchar (Esp); ⟨feathers⟩ erizar*
■ **puff up** [v + adv] hincharse

puffed /pʌft/ adj ⟨sleeve⟩ abombado

puffed-up /'pʌft'ʌp/ adj (pred **puffed up**) (a) (swollen) hinchado (b) (conceited) engreído

puffin /'pʌfən ‖'pʌfɪn/ n frailecillo m

puff paste, (BrE) **puff pastry** n hojaldre m

puffy /'pʌfi/ adj **-fier, -fiest** hinchado

puke /pju:k/ vi (colloq) vomitar, devolver*

pull¹ /pʊl/ vt [1] (a) (draw) tirar de, jalar (AmL

exc CS); (drag) arrastrar (b) (in specified direction) (+ adv compl): **he was ~ed from the rubble alive** lo sacaron vivo de entre los escombros; **the current ~ed him under** la corriente lo arrastró al fondo [2] (a) (tug) tirar de, jalar (AmL exc CS) (b) (tear, detach): **he ~ed the toy to bits** rompió el juguete [3] (a) ⟨tooth⟩ sacar* (b) ⟨gun⟩ sacar* [4] (colloq) ⟨crowd/audience⟩ atraer* [5] (Med) ⟨muscle/tendon⟩ desgarrarse
■ **~** vi [1] (drag, tug) tirar, jalar (AmL exc CS) [2] «vehicle» (move) (+ adv compl): **to ~ off the road** salir* de la carretera; **to ~ into the station** entrar en la estación
■ **pull apart** [v + o + adv] (a) (separate) separar (b) (pull to pieces) destrozar*, hacer* pedazos
■ **pull away** [v + adv] (a) (free oneself) soltarse* (b) (move off) «train/bus» arrancar*
■ **pull back** [v + adv] (a) (retreat) «troops/enemy» retirarse (b) (withdraw) echarse atrás
■ **pull down** [v + o + adv, v + adv + o] (a) (lower) ⟨blind⟩ bajar (b) (demolish) ⟨building⟩ echar*, tumbar (Méx)
■ **pull in**
I [v + o + adv, v + adv + o] [1] (draw in) ⟨nets/rope⟩ recoger*; ⟨claws⟩ retraer* [2] (attract) ⟨customers⟩ atraer*
II [v + adv] [1] (arrive) «train/bus» llegar* [2] (a) (move over) «ship/car» arrimarse (b) (stop) (BrE) «car/truck» parar
■ **pull off** [v + o + adv, v + adv + o] [1] (remove) ⟨cover/lid⟩ quitar [2] (achieve) (colloq) conseguir*
■ **pull out**
I [v + adv] [1] «vehicle/driver» (a) (depart) arrancar* (b) (enter traffic): **he ~ed out right in front of me** se me metió justo delante [2] (withdraw) ⟨troops/partner⟩ retirarse
II [v + o + adv, v + adv + o] [1] (a) (extract, remove) ⟨tooth/nail/plug⟩ sacar*; ⟨weeds/page⟩ arrancar* (b) (produce) ⟨wallet/gun⟩ sacar* [2] (withdraw) ⟨team/troops⟩ retirar
■ **pull over** (a) [v + adv] «driver/car» hacerse* a un lado; (to stop) acercarse* a la acera (or al arcén etc) y parar (b) [v + o + adv] parar
■ **pull through** [v + adv] (a) (recover) reponerse* (b) (survive) salir* adelante
■ **pull together** [1] [v + adv] (cooperate) trabajar codo con codo [2] [v + o + adv] (control oneself): **to ~ oneself together** calmarse
■ **pull up** [1] [v + o + adv, v + adv + o] (a) (draw up) levantar, subir; **to ~ one's socks up** subirse los calcetines (b) (uproot) ⟨plant⟩ arrancar* [2] [v + o + adv] (reprimand) **to ~ sb up** (**on sth**) regañar or (CS) retar a algn (POR algo) [3] [v + adv] (stop) «car/driver» parar

pull² n [1] (tug) tirón m, jalón m (AmL exc CS) [2] (a) (pulling force) fuerza f (b) (influence) influencia f

pulley /'pʊli/ n (pl **~s**) polea f

pull: ~-out n (a) (withdrawal) retirada f (b) (Journ) suplemento m; **~over**, (AmE also) **~over sweater** n ▶ SWEATER

pulp /pʌlp/ *n* **(a)** (of fruit, vegetable) pulpa *f*, carne *f*; (of wood, paper) pasta *f* (de papel) **(b)** (crushed material) pasta *f*

pulpit /'pʊlpɪt/ *n* púlpito *m*

pulsate /'pʌlseɪt ‖pʌl'seɪt/ *vi* «*heart*» latir; «*light/current*» oscilar

pulse¹ /pʌls/ *n* **1** **(a)** (Physiol) pulso *m*; (*before n*) ~ **rate** número *m* de pulsaciones **(b)** (throbbing) cadencia *f* **(c)** (Phys) pulsación *f* **2** (Agr, Culin) legumbre *f* (*como los garbanzos, las lentejas etc*)

pulse² *vi* latir

pulverize /'pʌlvəraɪz/ *vt* pulverizar*

puma /'puːmə ‖'pjuːmə/ *n* puma *m*, león *m* (Chi, Méx)

pummel /'pʌməl/ *vt*, (BrE) **-ll-** darle* una paliza a

pump¹ /pʌmp/ *n* **1** bomba *f*; (gasoline *o* (BrE) petrol ~) surtidor *m* **2** (AmE Clothing) zapato *m* (de) salón

pump² *vt* **(a)** (supply) bombear; **to** ~ **sth INTO sth** «*water/oil*» bombear algo A algo **(b)** (drain) **to** ~ **sth OUT OF sth** sacar* algo de algo con una bomba; **to** ~ **sb's stomach out** hacerle* un lavado de estómago a algn **(c)** (ask; colloq): **he was** ~**ing me for information** me estaba tratando de (son)sacar información

■ ~ *vi* «*machine/heart*» bombear

■ **pump up** [*v + o + adv, v + adv + o*] (inflate) «*tire*» inflar, hinchar (Esp)

pumpkin /'pʌmpkɪn ‖'pʌmpkɪn/ *n* calabaza *f*, zapallo *m* (CS, Per)

pun /pʌn/ *n* juego *m* de palabras, albur *m* (Méx)

punch¹ /pʌntʃ/ *n* **1** **(a)** (blow) puñetazo *m* **(b)** (vigor) garra *f* (fam), fuerza *f* **2** (for paper) perforadora *f*; (for metal, leather) sacabocados *m* **3** (Culin) **(a)** ponche *m*; (*before n*) ~ **bowl** ponchera *f* **(b)** (in US) refresco *m* de frutas

punch² *vt* **1** (hit) pegarle* a **2** (perforate) «*ticket*» picar*, ponchar (Méx); «*leather/metal*» perforar; **to** ~ **a hole in sth** hacerle* un agujero a algo

■ **punch in** [*v + adv*] (AmE) fichar, marcar* *or* (Méx) checar* tarjeta (*al entrar al trabajo*)

■ **punch out** [*v + adv*] (AmE) fichar, marcar* *or* (Méx) checar* tarjeta (*al salir del trabajo*)

punch: ~**-drunk** *adj* grogui (fam), atontado; ~ **line** *n* remate *m* (*de un chiste*); ~**-up** *n* (BrE colloq) bronca *f* (fam)

punctual /'pʌŋktʃuəl ‖'pʌŋktʃʊəl, 'pʌŋktʃʊəl/ *adj* puntual

punctuality /ˌpʌŋktʃu'æləti ‖ˌpʌŋktʃʊ'ælətɪ, ˌpʌŋktʃʊ'ælətɪ/ *n* puntualidad *f*

punctually /'pʌŋktʃuəli ‖'pʌŋktʃʊəli, 'pʌŋktʃʊəli/ *adv* puntualmente

punctuate /'pʌŋktʃueɪt ‖'pʌŋktʃʊeɪt, 'pʌŋktʃʊeɪt/ *vt* **(a)** «*writing/text*» puntuar* **(b)** (intersperse) salpicar*

punctuation /ˌpʌŋktʃu'eɪʃən ‖ˌpʌŋktʃʊ'eɪʃən, ˌpʌŋktʃʊ'eɪʃən/ *n* puntuación *f*; (*before n*) ~ **mark** signo *m* de puntuación

puncture¹ /'pʌŋktʃər ‖'pʌŋktʃə(r)/ *n* (in tire, ball) pinchazo *m*, pinchadura *f* (AmL), ponchadura *f* (Méx); **we had a** ~ **on the way there** pinchamos por el camino, se nos ponchó una llanta en el camino (Méx)

puncture² *vt* «*tire/ball*» pinchar, ponchar (Méx)

pungent /'pʌndʒənt/ *adj* «*taste/smell*» acre

punish /'pʌnɪʃ/ *vt* castigar*

punishable /'pʌnɪʃəbəl/ *adj* punible; ~ **BY sth** penado CON algo

punishing /'pʌnɪʃɪŋ/ *adj* «*schedule/treatment*» duro; «*pace*» agotador, extenuante

punishment /'pʌnɪʃmənt/ *n* **(a)** (chastisement) castigo *m* **(b)** (rough treatment): **it's taken a lot of** ~ ha sido muy maltratado

punk /pʌŋk/ *n* **1** **(a)** (person) ~ (**rocker**) punk *mf*, punki *mf* **(b)** ~ (**rock**) punk *m* **2** (young hoodlum) (AmE colloq) vándalo, -la *m,f*, gamberro, -rra *m,f* (Esp)

punt¹ /pʊnt/ *n* (Fin) libra *f* (irlandesa)

punt² /pʌnt/ *vi* (in boat): **to go** ~**ing** salir* de paseo en batea

puny /'pjuːni/ *adj* **punier, puniest** (pej) «*person*» enclenque; «*effort*» lastimoso

pup /pʌp/ *n* cría *f*; (of dog) cachorro, -rra *m,f*

pupil /'pjuːpəl ‖'pjuːpɪl/ *n* **1** (Educ) alumno, -na *m,f*, educando, -da *m,f* (frml) **2** (of eye) pupila *f*

puppet /'pʌpət ‖'pʌpɪt/ *n* **1** **(a)** (marionette) marioneta *f*, títere *m* **(b)** (glove puppet) títere *m* **2** (stooge) títere *m*; (*before n*) «*regime/leader*» títere

puppy /'pʌpi/ *n* (*pl* **-pies**) cachorro, -rra *m,f*

purchase¹ /'pɜːrtʃəs ‖'pɜːtʃəs/ *n* (frml) adquisición *f* (frml)

purchase² *vt* (frml) adquirir (frml)

purchaser /'pɜːrtʃəsər ‖'pɜːtʃəsə(r)/ *n* (frml) comprador, -dora *m,f*

pure /pjʊr ‖pjʊə(r)/ *adj* **purer, purest** puro

puree, purée /pjʊ'reɪ ‖'pjʊəreɪ/ *n* puré *m*; **tomato** ~ concentrado *m* de tomate

purely /'pjʊrli ‖'pjʊəli/ *adv* «*decorative*» puramente; ~ **by chance** por pura casualidad

purgatory /'pɜːrgətɔːri ‖'pɜːgətəri/ *n* purgatorio *m*

purge¹ /pɜːrdʒ ‖pɜːdʒ/ *vt* **(a)** (cleanse) purgar* **(b)** (Pol) «*party/government/committee*» hacer* una purga en

purge² *n* (Med, Pol) purga *f*

purify /'pjʊrəfaɪ ‖'pjʊərɪfaɪ/ *vt* **-fies, -fying, -fied** purificar*; «*water*» depurar

purist /'pjʊrəst ‖'pjʊərɪst/ *n* purista *mf*

puritan /'pjʊrətn̩ ‖'pjʊərɪtən/ *n* puritano, -na *m,f*

puritanical /ˌpjʊrə'tænɪkəl ‖ˌpjʊərɪ'tænɪkəl/ *adj* puritano

purity /'pjʊrəti ‖'pjʊərəti/ *n* pureza *f*

purl¹ /pɜːrl ‖pɜːl/ *n* punto *m* (al *or* del) revés

purl² *vt* tejer al *or* del revés

purple¹ /'pɜːrpəl ‖'pɜːpəl/ *adj* (bluish) morado; (reddish) púrpura

purple² *n* (bluish) morado *m*, violeta *m*; (reddish) púrpura *m*

purport /pər'pɔːrt ‖pə'pɔːt/ *vt* (frml) **to** ~ **to +** INF pretender + INF

purpose /'pɜːrpəs ‖'pɜːpəs/ *n* **1** **(a)** (intention, reason) propósito *m*; **for one's own** ~**s** por su (*or* mi *etc*) propio interés; **the machine is good enough for our** ~**s** la máquina sirve para lo que nos proponemos hacer con ella; **on** ~ a propósito **(b)** (use): **to serve a** (useful) ~ servir* de algo **2** (resolution) determinación *f*

p

purposeful /'pɜːrpəsfəl ‖'pɜːpəsfʊl/ adj
⟨person/stride⟩ resuelto; ⟨expression⟩ de
determinación

purposely /'pɜːrpəsli ‖'pɜːpəsli/ adv
⟨facetious/hurtful⟩ deliberadamente; ⟨say/do⟩ a
propósito

purr¹ /pɜːr ‖pɜː(r)/ vi ronronear

purr² n ronroneo m

purse¹ /pɜːrs ‖pɜːs/ n **1** (a) (for money)
monedero m, portamonedas m (b) (funds) fondos
mpl **2** (handbag) (AmE) cartera f or (Esp) bolso m
or (Méx) bolsa f

purse² vt to ~ one's lips fruncir* la boca

purser /'pɜːrsər ‖'pɜːsə(r)/ n sobrecargo mf

pursue /pər'suː ‖pə'sjuː/ vt **1** (chase)
perseguir*; ⟨pleasure/happiness⟩ buscar*
2 ⟨policy/course of action⟩ continuar* con;
⟨research/study⟩ continuar* con; ⟨profession⟩
ejercer*

pursuer /pər'suːər ‖pə'sjuːə(r)/ n perseguidor,
-dora m,f

pursuit /pər'suːt ‖pə'sjuːt/ n **1** (chase)
persecución f; **she set off in ~ of the thief** salió
en persecución del ladrón; **the ~ of happiness** la
búsqueda de la felicidad **2** (pastime) actividad f

pus /pʌs/ n pus m

push¹ /pʊʃ/ n empujoncito m; (violent) empujón
m; **she gave the door a ~** empujó la puerta; **at
the ~ of a button** con solo apretar un botón; **at a
~** (colloq): **at a ~, I could finish it by Friday** si me
apuras, podría terminarlo para el viernes

push² vt **1** (a) ⟨person/car/table⟩ empujar; **I
~ed the door to o shut** cerré la puerta
empujándola (b) (press) ⟨button⟩ apretar* (c)
(force): **to ~ prices up/down** hacer* que suban/
bajen los precios; **I tried to ~ the thought to the
back of my mind** traté de no pensar en ello
2 (put pressure on): **you're ~ing him/yourself too
hard** le/te exiges demasiado; **to be ~ed for time/
money** (colloq) andar* corto de tiempo/de dinero
(fam)
3 (a) (promote) promocionar (b) (sell) (colloq)
⟨drugs⟩ pasar (fam), transar (CS arg)
4 (approach) (colloq) (only in -ing form): **to be
~ing forty** rondar los cuarenta
~ vi **1** (give a push) empujar
2 (apply pressure) presionar

■ **push back** [v + o + adv, v + adv + o] (a) (force
back) ⟨person/object⟩ empujar hacia atrás; ⟨crowd/
army⟩ hacer* retroceder (b) (extend) ⟨limits⟩
ampliar*

■ **push in** [v + adv] colarse* (fam)

■ **push off** [v + adv] (a) (in boat) desatracar* (b)
(leave, go) (colloq) largarse* (fam)

■ **push on** [v + adv] (a) (continue journey) seguir*
el viaje (b) (continue working) seguir* adelante

■ **push through** [v + o + adv, v + adv + o]
⟨legislation⟩ hacer* aprobar

push: ~**bike** n (BrE) bicicleta f; ~**button**
adj (before n) ⟨controls/telephone⟩ de botones;
~**chair** n (BrE) sillita f (de paseo), carreola f
(Méx)

pusher /'pʊʃər ‖'pʊʃə(r)/ n (colloq) camello
mf (arg), jíbaro mf (Col, Ven arg), conecte m,f
(Mex arg)

push: ~**over** n: **to be a ~over** ⟨⟨task/game⟩⟩
ser* pan comido (fam), estar* chupado (Esp fam);

⟨⟨person⟩⟩ ser* un incauto; ~**start** /'pʊʃstɑːrt
‖,pʊʃ'stɑːt/ vt ⟨car⟩ arrancar* empujando; ~**up**
n flexión f (de brazos or de pecho), fondo m,
lagartija f (Méx)

pushy /'pʊʃi/ adj **pushier, pushiest** (colloq)
prepotente

pussy /'pʊsi/ (pl **-sies**), **pussycat** /'pʊsikæt/
n (colloq) minino, -na m,f (fam), gatito, -ta m,f
(fam)

put /pʊt/ (pres p **putting**; past & past p **put**) vt
I **1** (place) poner*; (with care, precision etc)
colocar*; (inside sth) meter; **he ~ it in his mouth** se
lo puso en la boca
2 (a) (thrust): **he ~ his arms around her** la
abrazó; **she ~ her head out of the window** asomó
la cabeza por la ventana (b) (Sport) **to ~ the shot**
lanzar* el peso
3 (a) (rank) poner*; **she ~s herself first** se pone
ella primero; **he ~s his art before everything else**
antepone su arte a todo (b) (in competition, league):
this victory ~s them in o into the lead con esta
victoria pasan a ocupar la delantera
II **1** (cause to be) poner*; **the doctor ~ me on a
diet** el doctor me puso a régimen
2 (make undergo): **to ~ sb TO sth: I don't want to
~ you to any trouble** no quiero causarle ninguna
molestia
III **1** (a) (attribute, assign): **I ~ a high value on
our friendship** valoro mucho nuestra amistad (b)
(impose) **to ~ sth ON sth/sb: to ~ the blame on sb**
echarle la culpa a algb; **it ~ a great strain on
their relationship** eso sometió su relación a una
gran tensión
2 (a) (invest) **to ~ sth INTO sth** ⟨money⟩ invertir*
algo EN algo; **she had ~ a lot of thought into it** lo
había pensado mucho (b) (bet, stake) **to ~ sth
ON sth** ⟨money⟩ apostar* algo A algo (c) (contribute)
to ~ sth TOWARD sth contribuir* CON algoA
algo
IV **1** (present) ⟨views/case⟩ exponer*; ⟨proposal⟩
presentar
2 (write, indicate, mark) poner*
3 (express) decir*; **~ it this way: I wouldn't invite
him again** te digo lo siguiente: no lo volvería a
invitar; **to ~ sth well/badly** expresar algo bien/
mal

■ **put about** [v + o + adv] (colloq) ⟨story/rumor⟩
hacer* correr

■ **put across** [v + o + adv, v + adv + o] ⟨idea/
message⟩ comunicar*

■ **put aside** [v + o + adv, v + adv + o] (a) (lay to
one side) dejar a un lado (b) (reserve) ⟨money⟩
guardar; ⟨goods/time⟩ reservar (c) ⟨differences⟩
dejar de lado

■ **put away** [v + o + adv, v + adv + o] (a) (put in
cupboard, drawer) ⟨dishes/tools/clothes⟩ guardar (b)
(save) ⟨money⟩ guardar, ahorrar (c) (consume)
(colloq) ⟨food/drink⟩ zamparse (fam) (d) (confine)
(colloq) ⟨criminal/lunatic⟩ encerrar* (e) (destroy)
(AmE euph) ⟨animal⟩ sacrificar* (euf)

■ **put back** [v + o + adv, v + adv + o] (a) (replace)
volver* a poner (b) (reset) ⟨clocks⟩ atrasar* (c)
(delay, retard) ⟨project⟩ retrasar (d) (postpone)
posponer*, aplazar*, postergar* (AmL)

■ **put by** [v + o + adv, v + adv + o] ⟨money⟩
ahorrar

■ **put down**
I [v + o + adv, v + adv + o] **1** (a) (set down)

⟨bag/pen⟩ dejar; ⟨telephone⟩ colgar* **(b)** (lay) ⟨tiles/carpet⟩ poner*, colocar* **(c)** (lower) bajar **(d)** ⟨passenger⟩ dejar

2 (a) (suppress) ⟨rebellion⟩ sofocar* **(b)** (destroy) (BrE euph) ⟨animal⟩ sacrificar* (euf)

3 (a) (write down) ⟨thoughts⟩ anotar, escribir*; ⟨name⟩ poner*, escribir* **(b)** (attribute) to ∼ sth down TO sth atribuirle* algo A algo

4 (in part payment) ⟨sum⟩ entregar*; ⟨deposit⟩ dejar

II [v + adv] (belittle) rebajar

■ **put forward** [v + o + adv, v + adv + o] **1 (a)** ⟨theory/plan⟩ presentar; ⟨suggestion⟩ hacer* **(b)** ⟨candidate⟩ proponer*, postular (AmL)

2 (a) ⟨clocks⟩ adelantar **(b)** ⟨trip/meeting⟩ adelantar

■ **put in**

I [v + o + adv, v + adv + o] **1** (install) ⟨central heating/shower unit⟩ poner*, instalar

2 (enter, submit) ⟨claim/request/tender⟩ presentar

3 (invest): how much time can you put in? ¿cuánto tiempo puedes dedicarle?

4 (insert, add) ⟨word/chapter/scene⟩ poner*

II [v + adv] **1** (Naut) hacer* escala

2 (apply) to ∼ in FOR sth solicitar algo

■ **put off**

I [v + o + adv, v + adv + o] **1 (a)** (postpone) ⟨meeting/visit/decision⟩ aplazar*, posponer*, postergar* (AmL); I keep ∼ting off going to the dentist siempre estoy aplazando ir al dentista **(b)** (stall) ⟨visitor/creditor⟩: if Saturday isn't convenient, I can ∼ them off si el sábado no es conveniente, puedo decirles que lo dejen para más adelante

2 (turn off) (BrE) ⟨light⟩ apagar*

II [v + o + adv, v + adv + o] **1** (discourage): the thought of the journey ∼s me off going to see them pensar en el viaje me quita las ganas de ir a visitarlos

2 (distract) distraer*; (disconcert) desconcertar*

■ **put on**

I [v + o + adv, v + adv + o] **1** ⟨jacket/sweater⟩ ponerse*; to put one's clothes on vestirse*, ponerse* la ropa; to ∼ one's shoes on ponerse* los zapatos, calzarse*

2 ⟨light/radio/oven⟩ encender*, prender (AmL); ⟨music⟩ poner*

3 (gain): I've ∼ on four pounds he engordado cuatro libras; to ∼ on weight engordar

4 ⟨exhibition⟩ organizar*; ⟨play/show⟩ presentar

5 (assume) ⟨expression⟩ adoptar; he's just ∼ting it on está haciendo teatro

II [v + o + adv] **1 (a)** (alert) to ∼ sb on TO sb: somebody had ∼ the police on to them alguien había puesto a la policía sobre su pista **(b)** (introduce) to ∼ sb on TO sb: I can ∼ you on to someone who ... puedo ponerte en contacto con una persona que ...

2 (tease) (AmE colloq) tomarle el pelo a (fam)

■ **put out**

I [v + o + adv, v + adv + o] **1 (a)** (put outside) ⟨washing/cat⟩ sacar* **(b)** (set out) disponer* **(c)** (extend) ⟨arm/tongue⟩ sacar* **(d)** (dislocate) dislocarse*, zafarse (Chi, Méx)

2 (a) (extinguish) ⟨fire/light/cigarette⟩ apagar* **(b)** (anesthetize) (colloq) dormir*

3 (offend, inconvenience) molestar

⟨bag/pen⟩ dejar; ...

4 (a) (issue, publish) ⟨statement⟩ publicar* **(b)** (broadcast) transmitir

II [v + adv] (Naut) salir*; to ∼ out to sea hacerse* a la mar

■ **put over (a)** ▶ PUT ACROSS **(b)** (AmE) ▶ PUT OFF I 1A

■ **put past** [v + o + prep + o]: not to ∼ it past sb: I wouldn't ∼ it past her no me extrañaría nada or la creo muy capaz

■ **put through 1** [v + o + prep + o] (make undergo) someter a

2 [v + o + adv, v + adv + o] (Telec): to ∼ sb through (TO sb) pasar or (AmL) comunicar* or (Esp) poner* a algn CON algn

■ **put together** [v + o + adv, v + adv + o] **1 (a)** (assemble) armar; ⟨collection⟩ reunir* **(b)** (create) ⟨team⟩ formar; ⟨magazine⟩ producir*; ⟨meal⟩ preparar; (quickly) improvisar

2 (combine) juntar, reunir*; more than everything else ∼ together más que todo lo demás junto

■ **put up**

I [v + o + adv, v + adv + o] **1 (a)** ⟨hotel⟩ levantar; ⟨tent⟩ armar **(b)** ⟨decorations/curtains/ notice⟩ poner* **(c)** ⟨umbrella⟩ abrir* **(d)** ⟨hand⟩ levantar

2 ⟨price/fare⟩ aumentar

3 ⟨candidate⟩ proponer*, postular (AmL)

4 (in accommodation) alojar; they ∼ us up for the night nos quedamos a dormir en su casa

II [v + adv + o] **(a)** (present): to ∼ up resistance/ a struggle/a fight ofrecer* resistencia **(b)** ⟨money/ capital⟩ poner*

III [v + adv] (stay) quedarse

■ **put up to** [v + o + adv + prep + o]: somebody must have ∼ them up to it alguien debe haberlos empujado a ello

■ **put up with** [v + adv + prep + o] aguantar

put: ∼**-down** n (colloq) desprecio m; ∼ **out** adj (pred) to be ∼ out estar* molesto

putrid /'pjuːtrəd ‖'pjuːtrɪd/ adj putrefacto, pútrido

putt /pʌt/ vi golpear la bola, potear (AmL)
■ ∼ vt golpear

putter¹ /'pʌtər ‖'pʌtə(r)/ n (club) putter m

putter² vi (AmE) (+ adv compl): to ∼ around o about in the garden entretenerse trabajando en el jardín; I've been ∼ing around the house all day me he pasado el día haciendo un poco de esto y un poco de aquello en la casa

putting green /'pʌtɪŋ/ n putting green m

putty /'pʌti/ n masilla f

puzzle¹ /'pʌzəl/ n **(a)** (game,toy) rompecabezas m; (riddle) adivinanza f **(b)** (mystery) misterio m

puzzle² vt: one thing ∼s me hay algo que no entiendo

puzzled /'pʌzəld/ adj ⟨expression/tone⟩ de desconcierto; I'm ∼ about it me tiene perplejo

PVC n PVC m

pygmy /'pɪgmi/ n (pl -mies) **(a)** (Anthrop) also Pygmy pigmeo, -mea m,f **(b)** (Zool) (before n) enano

pyjamas /pə'dʒɑːməz/ n (BrE) ▶ PAJAMAS

pylon /'paɪlɑːn, -lən ‖'paɪlɒn, -lən/ n torre f de alta tensión

pyramid /'pɪrəmɪd/ n pirámide f

pyre /paɪr ‖'paɪə(r)/ n pira f

Pyrenees /ˌpɪrə'niːz ‖ˌpɪrə'niːz/ *pl n* the ~ los Pirineos

Pyrex® /'paɪreks/ *n* pyrex® *m*, arcopal® *m*

python /'paɪθɑːn ‖ 'paɪθən/ *n* (serpiente *f*) pitón *f*

· ·

Qq

· ·

Q, q /kjuː/ *n* Q, q *f*

QC *n* (in UK) (= **Queen's Counsel**) título conferido a ciertos abogados de prestigio

QED (= **quod erat demonstrandum**) Q.E.D. (frml), que es lo que había que demostrar

quack¹ /kwæk/ *vi* graznar

quack² *n* (pej) **1** (charlatan) charlatán, -tana *m,f*; (professing medical skill) (~ doctor) curandero, -ra *m,f* **2** (of duck) graznido *m*

quad /kwɑːd ‖ kwɒd/ *n* (colloq) **1** (quadruplet) cuatrillizo, -za *m,f* **2** (of college) ▶ QUADRANGLE 1

quadrangle /'kwɑːdræŋgəl ‖ 'kwɒdræŋgəl/ *n* **1** (BrE Archit) patio *m* interior **2** (Math) ▶ QUADRILATERAL

quadrant /'kwɑːdrənt ‖ 'kwɒdrənt/ *n* cuadrante *m*

quadrilateral /ˌkwɑːdrə'lætərəl ‖ˌkwɒdrɪ'lætərəl/ *n* cuadrilátero *m*

quadruped /'kwɑːdrəped ‖ 'kwɒdrʊped/ *n* cuadrúpedo *m*

quadruple¹ /kwɑːˈdruːpl̩ ‖ 'kwɒdrʊpl̩/ *adj* cuádruple, cuádruplo

quadruple² /kwɑːˈdruːpl̩ ‖ kwɒ'druːpl̩/ *vi* cuadruplicarse*

quadruplet /kwɑːˈdruːplət ‖ 'kwɒdrʊplət/ *n* cuatrillizo, -za *m,f*

quaff /kwɑːf ‖ kwɒf/ *vt* (hum) beberse, zamparse (fam)

quagmire /'kwægmaɪr, 'kwɑːg- ‖ 'kwɒgmaɪə(r), 'kwæg-/ *n* (a) (bog) lodazal *m*, barrial *m* (AmL) (b) (situation) atolladero *m*

quail¹ /kweɪl/ *vi* temblar*; she ~ed at the idea la idea le daba pavor

quail² *n* (*pl* quails *or* quail) codorniz *f*

quaint /kweɪnt/ *adj* **-er, -est** (a) (charming, picturesque) pintoresco (b) (odd) extraño

quake¹ /kweɪk/ *vi* temblar*

quake² *n* (colloq) (earthquake) terremoto *m*

Quaker /'kweɪkər ‖ 'kweɪkə(r)/ *n* cuáquero, -ra *m,f*

qualification /ˌkwɑːləfə'keɪʃən ‖ˌkwɒlɪfɪ'keɪʃən/ *n* **1** (a) (Educ): she has a teaching ~ tiene título de maestra/profesora; his ~s are very good está muy bien calificado *or* (Esp) cualificado (b) (skill, necessary attribute) requisito *m* **2** (a) (eligibility) derecho *m* (b) (being accepted) clasificación *f* **3** (reservation) reserva *f*

qualified /'kwɑːləfaɪd ‖ 'kwɒlɪfaɪd/ *adj* (a) (trained) titulado; to be ~ to + INF tener* la titulación necesaria PARA + INF (b) (competent) (*pred*) capacitado; to be ~ to + INF estar* capacitado PARA + INF (c) (eligible) (*pred*) to be ~ to + INF reunir* los requisitos necesarios PARA + INF

qualify /'kwɑːləfaɪ ‖ 'kwɒlɪfaɪ/ **-fies, -fying, -fied** *vt* **1** (equip, entitle): this degree qualifies you to practice anywhere in Europe este título te habilita para ejercer en cualquier parte de Europa; their low income qualifies them for some benefits sus bajos ingresos les dan derecho a recibir ciertas prestaciones **2** (a) (limit): I'd like to ~ the statement I made earlier quisiera matizar lo que expresé anteriormente haciendo algunas salvedades (*or* puntualizaciones *etc*) (b) (Ling) calificar*
■ ~ *vi* (a) (gain professional qualification) titularse, recibirse (AmL) (b) (Sport) clasificarse* (c) (be entitled) to ~ (FOR sth) tener* derecho (A algo)

quality /'kwɑːləti ‖ 'kwɒləti/ *n* (*pl* **-ties**) calidad *f*

qualm /kwɑːm/ *n* (*often pl*) (a) (scruple) reparo *m*; to have no ~s about sth no tener* ningún reparo en algo (b) (misgiving) duda *f*

quandary /'kwɑːndri ‖ 'kwɒndri/ *n* (*pl* **-ries**) (*usu sing*) dilema *m*

quango /'kwæŋgəʊ/ *n* (*pl* **-gos**) (BrE) (= **quasi-autonomous non-governmental organization**) organismo *m or* ente *m* semi-autónomo

quantify /'kwɑːntəfaɪ ‖ 'kwɒntɪfaɪ/ *vt* **-fies, -fying, -fied** cuantificar*

quantity /'kwɑːntəti ‖ 'kwɒntəti/ *n* (*pl* **-ties**) cantidad *f*

quantity surveyor *n*: ingeniero o técnico que se ocupa de mediciones y cálculo de materiales

quarantine¹ /'kwɔːrəntiːn ‖ 'kwɒrəntiːn/ *n* cuarentena *f*

quarantine² *vt* poner* en cuarentena

quarrel¹ /'kwɔːrəl ‖ 'kwɒrəl/ *n* (a) (argument) pelea *f*, riña *f*; to have a ~ with sb pelearse con algn (b) (disagreement) discrepancia *f*

quarrel² *vi*, (BrE) **-ll-** (argue) pelearse, discutir

quarrelsome /'kwɔːrəlsəm ‖ 'kwɒrəlsəm/ *adj* peleador, peleón (Esp fam)

· ·

AmC	Central America	Arg	Argentina	Cu	Cuba	Per	Peru
AmL	Latin America	Bol	Bolivia	Ec	Ecuador	RPI	River Plate Area
AmS	South America	Chi	Chile	Esp	Spain	Ur	Uruguay
Andes	Andean Region	CS	Southern Cone	Méx	Mexico	Ven	Venezuela

quarry¹ /'kwɔːri ‖ 'kwɒri/ n (pl **-ries**)
  1 (excavation) cantera f 2 (prey) presa f

quarry² vt **-ries, -rying, -ried** ⟨stone/slate⟩ extraer* (de una cantera); ⟨land/hillside⟩ abrir* una cantera en

quart /kwɔːrt ‖ kwɔːt/ n cuarto m de galón (EEUU: 0,94 litros, RU: 1,14 litros)

quarter /'kwɔːrtər ‖ 'kwɔːtə(r)/ n 1 (fourth part) cuarta parte f, cuarto m; **a ~ of a mile** un cuarto de milla
  2 (US, Canadian coin) moneda f de 25 centavos
  3 **(a)** (in telling time) cuarto m; **a ~ of an hour** un cuarto de hora; **it's a ~ of** o (BrE) **to one** es la una menos cuarto or (AmL exc RPl) un cuarto para la una; **a ~ after** o (BrE) **past one** la una y cuarto **(b)** (three months) trimestre m
  4 **(a)** (district of town) barrio m **(b)** (area) parte f; **at close ~s** de cerca
  5 **quarters** pl (accommodations): **the servants' ~s** las habitaciones de la servidumbre

quarterfinal /'kwɔːrtərfaɪnl̩ ‖ ˌkwɔːtə'faɪnl̩/ n cuarto m de final

quarterly¹ /'kwɔːrtərli ‖ 'kwɔːtəli/ adj trimestral

quarterly² adv trimestralmente

quarter note n (AmE) negra f

quartet /kwɔːr'tet ‖ kwɔː'tet/ n cuarteto m

quartz /kwɔːrts ‖ kwɔːts/ n cuarzo m

quash /'kwɑːʃ ‖ kwɒʃ/ vt **(a)** (Law) ⟨verdict/sentence⟩ anular **(b)** (suppress) ⟨revolt⟩ sofocar*; ⟨protest⟩ acallar

quaver¹ /'kweɪvər ‖ 'kweɪvə(r)/ n **(a)** (in voice) temblor m **(b)** (BrE Mus) corchea f

quaver² vi «voice» (in singing) vibrar; (in speech) temblar*

quay /kiː/ n muelle m

quayside /'kiːsaɪd/ n muelle m

queasy /'kwiːzi/ adj **-sier, -siest** mareado

queen /kwiːn/ n reina f

queen: **~ bee** (Zool) abeja f reina; **~ mother** n reina f madre

queer¹ /kwɪr ‖ kwɪə(r)/ adj 1 (odd) raro, extraño 2 (male homosexual) (colloq & sometimes pej) maricón (fam & pey), gay

queer² n (colloq & sometimes pej) maricón m (fam & pey), gay m

quell /kwel/ vt ⟨revolt⟩ sofocar*; ⟨criticism⟩ acallar

quench /kwentʃ/ vt **(a)** ⟨thirst⟩ quitar, saciar (liter) **(b)** ⟨flames⟩ sofocar*

querulous /'kwerələs ‖ 'kweruləs/ adj quejumbroso

query¹ /'kwɪri ‖ 'kwɪəri/ n (pl **-ries**) (doubt) duda f; (question) pregunta f

query² vt **-ries, -rying, -ried** cuestionar

quest /kwest/ n búsqueda f; **~ FOR sth** búsqueda DE algo

question¹ /'kwestʃən/ n **(a)** (inquiry) pregunta f, **to ask a ~** hacer* una pregunta **(b)** (in quiz, exam) pregunta f **(c)** (issue, problem) cuestión f, asunto m; **the person in ~** la persona en cuestión; **if it's a ~ of money** ... si es cuestión or se trata de dinero ... **(d)** (doubt) duda f; **beyond ~** fuera de duda **(e)** (possibility) posibilidad f; **it is completely out of the ~** es totalmente imposible

question² vt **(a)** ⟨person⟩ hacerle* preguntas a; ⟨suspect/student⟩ interrogar* **(b)** (doubt) ⟨integrity/motives⟩ poner* en duda

questionable /'kwestʃənəbəl/ adj cuestionable

questioner /'kwestʃənər ‖ 'kwestʃənə(r)/ n interrogador, -dora f

questioning¹ /'kwestʃənɪŋ/ adj ⟨expression/voice⟩ inquisidor; ⟨mind⟩ inquisitivo

questioning² n interrogatorio m

question mark n signo m de interrogación

questionnaire /'kwestʃə'ner ‖ ˌkwestʃə'neə(r)/ n cuestionario m

queue¹ /kjuː/ n (BrE) cola f; **to form a ~** hacer* cola; **to jump the ~** colarse* (fam), brincarse* or saltarse la cola (Méx fam)

queue² vi **queues, queueing, queued ~ (up)** (BrE) hacer* cola

quibble¹ /'kwɪbəl/ n objeción f (de poca monta)

quibble² vi hacer* problemas por nimiedades

quick¹ /kwɪk/ adj **quicker, quickest (a)** (speedy) ⟨action/movement⟩ rápido; **I'll be as ~ as I can** volveré (or lo haré etc) lo más rápido que pueda; **that was ~!** ¡qué rapidez! **(b)** (brief) (before n, no comp) ⟨calculation/question⟩ rápido; ⟨nod⟩ breve; **he'd like a ~ word with you** quiere hablar contigo un momento **(c)** (easily roused): **she has a ~ temper** tiene mucho genio **(d)** (prompt): **he's ~ to take offense** se ofende por lo más mínimo

quick² adv **quicker, quickest** rápido, rápidamente

quick³ n **the ~: her nails were bitten to the ~** tenía las uñas en carne viva de mordérselas; **to cut sb to the ~** herir* a algn en lo más vivo

quicken /'kwɪkən/ vt acelerar
  ■ **~** vi acelerarse

quickly /'kwɪkli/ adv **(a)** (speedily) ⟨move/recover⟩ rápidamente, rápido **(b)** (promptly) ⟨understand/reply⟩ pronto

quickness /'kwɪknəs ‖ 'kwɪknɪs/ n rapidez f

quick: **~sand** n (often pl) arenas fpl movedizas; **~-tempered** /'kwɪk'tempərd ‖ ˌkwɪk'tempəd/ adj ⟨person⟩ de genio vivo, irascible; **~-witted** /'kwɪk'wɪtəd ‖ ˌkwɪk'wɪtɪd/ adj agudo

quid /kwɪd/ n (pl **~**) (pound) (BrE colloq) libra f

quiet¹ /'kwaɪət/ adj 1 **(a)** (silent) ⟨street⟩ silencioso; **be ~!** (to one person) ¡cállate!; (to more than one person) ¡cállense! or (Esp tb) ¡callaros or callaos!, ¡silencio!; **I kept ~ about the bill** no dije nada de lo de la factura **(b)** (not loud) ⟨engine⟩ silencioso; **he has a very ~ voice** habla muy bajo **(c)** (not boisterous) ⟨manner⟩ tranquilo; **you're very ~ today** hoy estás muy callada 2 **(a)** (peaceful) tranquilo; **they had a ~ wedding** la boda se celebró en la intimidad **(b)** (not busy) ⟨day⟩ tranquilo

quiet² n **(a)** (silence) silencio m **(b)** (peace, tranquillity) tranquilidad f

quiet³ (AmE) vt **(a)** (silence) ⟨uproar/protests⟩ acallar; ⟨class⟩ hacer* callar **(b)** (calm) ⟨horse/person⟩ tranquilizar*; ⟨fear/suspicion⟩ disipar
  ■ **quiet down** (AmE) ▶ QUIETEN DOWN

quieten /'kwaɪətn̩/ vt (esp BrE) ▶ QUIET³
  ■ **quieten down** 1 [v + o + adv, v + adv + o] ···⟩

⟨person⟩ calmar; ⟨rumors/clamor⟩ acallar **2** [v + adv] «person» calmarse; (with maturity) sentar* la cabeza; «rumors» acallarse

quietly /'kwaɪətli/ adv **1** (silently, not loudly) ⟨move⟩ silenciosamente; ⟨say/speak⟩ en voz baja **2** (a) (peacefully) ⟨sleep/rest⟩ tranquilamente (b) (unobtrusively) ⟨dress/mention/slip away⟩ discretamente

quill /kwɪl/ n pluma f (de oca or ganso)

quilt /kwɪlt/ n edredón m, acolchado m (RPl), cobija f (Méx)

quilted /'kwɪltəd ‖'kwɪltɪd/ adj acolchado, guateado (Esp)

quin /kwɪn/ n (BrE colloq) ▸ QUINTUPLET

quince /kwɪns/ n membrillo m

quint /kwɪnt/ n (AmE colloq) ▸ QUINTUPLET

quintessential /ˌkwɪntə'sentʃəl ‖ˌkwɪntɪ'senʃəl/ adj (usu before n) por excelencia

quintet /kwɪn'tet/ n quinteto m

quintuplet /kwɪn'tuːplət ‖'kwɪntjʊplət/ n quintillizo, -za m,f, quíntuple mf (Chi, Ven)

quip¹ /kwɪp/ n ocurrencia f, salida f

quip² vt -pp- decir* bromeando

quirk /kwɜːrk ‖kwɜːk/ n (a) (of circumstance) singularidad f (b) (of person) rareza f

quit /kwɪt/ (pres p **quitting**; past & past p **quit** or **quitted**) vt (esp AmE) ⟨job/habit⟩ dejar; ⟨contest⟩ abandonar; to ∼ -ING dejar DE + INF ■ ∼ vi (a) (stop) (esp AmE) parar (b) (give in) abandonar (c) (leave): notice to ∼ notificación f de desahucio

quite /kwaɪt/ adv **1** (a) (completely, absolutely) completamente, totalmente; is this what you wanted? — not ∼ ¿es esto lo que buscaba? — no exactamente; there isn't ∼ enough faltan un poquito; there's nothing ∼ like champagne realmente no hay como el champán; ∼ the opposite todo lo contrario (b) (as intensifier): it

makes ∼ a difference hace bastante diferencia; ∼ a few of them muchos de ellos; that was ∼ a game! ¡fue un partidazo! (fam), ¡fue flor de partido! (CS fam) **2** (fairly) (BrE) bastante; it's ∼ warm today hoy hace bastante calor; there were ∼ a few había bastantes, había unos cuantos

quits /kwɪts/ adj to be ∼ estar* en paz or (AmL) a mano; to call it ∼: take the money and call it ∼ toma el dinero y dejémoslo de una vez

quiver¹ /'kwɪvər ‖'kwɪvə(r)/ vi «person/lips» temblar*; «leaves» agitarse

quiver² n **1** (for arrows) carcaj m, aljaba f **2** (movement) temblor m

quiz¹ /kwɪz/ n (pl ∼es) (a) (competition) concurso m; (before n) ∼ show programa m concurso (b) (test) (AmE) prueba f

quiz² vt -zz- (a) (question) ⟨suspect⟩ interrogar* (b) (test) (AmE) ⟨students⟩ poner* or hacer* una prueba a

quizzical /'kwɪzɪkəl/ adj socarrón, burlón

quorum /'kwɔːrəm/ n quórum m

quota /'kwəʊtə/ n (pl ∼s) (EC, Econ) cuota f

quotation /kwəʊ'teɪʃən/ n **1** (passage) cita f **2** (estimate) presupuesto m

quotation marks pl n comillas fpl

quote¹ /kwəʊt/ vt **1** (a) ⟨writer/passage⟩ citar; ⟨reference number⟩ indicar* (b) ⟨example⟩ dar*; ⟨instance⟩ citar **2** (a) (Busn) ⟨price⟩ dar*, ofrecer* (b) (Fin) cotizar* ■ ∼ vi (repeat, recite): he was quoting from the Bible citaba de la Biblia; she said, and I ∼ ... dijo, y lo repito textualmente ..., sus palabras textuales fueron ...

quote² n (colloq) **1** (passage) cita f **2** (estimate) presupuesto m

quotient /'kwəʊʃənt/ n (Math) cociente m

Rr

R, r /ɑːr ‖ɑː(r)/ n R, r f

R (in US) (Cin) (= **restricted**) menores acompañados

rabbi /'ræbaɪ/ n (pl -bis) rabino, -na m,f; (as title) rabí mf

rabbit /'ræbət ‖'ræbɪt/ n (a) (Zool) conejo, -ja m,f (b) (meat) conejo m

rabble /'ræbəl/ n (a) (mob) muchedumbre f (b) (common people) (pej) the ∼ la chusma (pey)

rabid /'ræbəd ‖'ræbɪd/ adj rabioso

rabies /'reɪbiːz/ n rabia f

RAC n (in UK) = **Royal Automobile Club**

raccoon /ræ'kuːn ‖rə'kuːn/ n mapache m

race¹ /reɪs/ n **1** (contest) carrera f **2** (Anthrop) raza f; the human ∼ el género humano; (before n) ∼ relations pl n relaciones fpl raciales

race² vi (a) (rush) (+ adv compl): she ∼d down the hill on her bike bajó la cuesta en bicicleta a

toda velocidad (b) (in competition) correr, competir* (c) «pulse/heart» latir aceleradamente ■ ∼ vt ⟨person⟩ echarle or (RPl) jugarle* una carrera a

race: ∼course n (stadium) hipódromo m; (track) pista f (de carreras); ∼horse n caballo m de carrera(s)

racial /'reɪʃəl/ adj racial

racially /'reɪʃəli/ adv ⟨pure/mixed/motivated/ prejudiced⟩ racialmente

racing¹ /'reɪsɪŋ/ n (a) (horse ∼) carreras fpl de caballos (b) (sport, pastime) carreras fpl

racing² adj (before n) ⟨bicycle/car⟩ de carrera(s)

racism /'reɪsɪzəm/ n racismo m

racist¹ /'reɪsəst ‖'reɪsɪst/ n racista mf

racist² adj racista

rack¹ /ræk/ n **1** (shelf) estante m; (for baggage)

rejilla f; (clothes ∿) perchero m; (drying ∿) tendedero m **2** (for torture) potro m (de tortura); **to go to ∿ and ruin** venirse* abajo

rack² vt (shake): **to be ∿ed with pain** sufrir dolores atroces; **to be ∿ed with guilt** estar* atormentado por el remordimiento

racket /'rækət ‖'rækɪt/ n **1** (Sport) raqueta f **2** (noise) (colloq) jaleo m (fam) **3** (business) (colloq) tinglado m (fam)

racketeer /'rækə'tɪr ‖,rækə'tiə(r)/ n mafioso, -sa m,f

racquet /'rækət ‖'rækɪt/ n ▶ RACKET 1

racy /'reɪsi/ adj **racier, raciest** (a) (lively) animado (b) (risqué) ‹story/joke› subido de tono

radar /'reɪdɑːr ‖'reɪdɑː(r)/ n radar m

radiant /'reɪdiənt/ adj ‹smile/look› radiante; ‹sun/blue› resplandeciente

radiate /'reɪdieɪt/ vt irradiar

radiation /'reɪdi'eɪʃən/ n radiación f; (before n) **∿ sickness** radiotoxemia f

radiator /'reɪdieɪtər ‖'reɪdieɪtə(r)/ n radiador m

radical /'rædɪkəl/ adj radical; ‹writer› de ideas radicales

radically /'rædɪkli/ adv radicalmente

radii /'reɪdiaɪ/ pl of RADIUS

radio¹ /'reɪdiəʊ/ n (pl **-os**) (a) (receiver) radio m (AmL exc CS), radio f (CS, Esp); **I heard it on the ∿** lo oí por el or (CS, Esp) la radio (b) (medium) radio f

radio² (3rd pers sing pres **radios**; pres p **radioing**; past & past p **radioed**) vt ‹person› llamar por radio; ‹message› transmitir por radio

radio: ∿active /'reɪdiəʊ'æktɪv/ adj radiactivo; **∿activity** /'reɪdiəʊæk'tɪvəti/ n radiactividad f; **∿-controlled** /'reɪdiəʊkən'trəʊld/ adj teledirigido

radiographer /'reɪdi'ɑːgrəfər ‖,reɪdi'ɒgrəfə(r)/ n radiógrafo, -fa m,f

radiologist /'reɪdi'ɑːlədʒəst ‖,reɪdi'ɒlədʒɪst/ n radiólogo, -ga m,f

radiotherapy /'reɪdiəʊ'θerəpi/ n radioterapia f

radish /'rædɪʃ/ n rabanito m, rábano m

radius /'reɪdiəs/ n (pl **radiuses** or **radii**) radio m

RAF /'ɑːreɪ'ef/ (in UK) (= **Royal Air Force**) the ∿ la Fuerza Aérea británica

raffle¹ /'ræfəl/ n rifa f

raffle² vt rifar, sortear

raft /ræft ‖rɑːft/ n balsa f

rafter /'ræftər ‖'rɑːftə(r)/ n viga f

rag /ræg/ n **1** (a) (piece of cloth) trapo m (b) **rags** pl (tattered clothes) harapos mpl, andrajos mpl; **dressed in ∿s** harapiento, andrajoso **2** (newspaper) (colloq & pej) periodicucho m (pey)

ragamuffin /'rægə,mʌfən ‖'rægə,mʌfɪn/ n pilluelo, -la m,f

rag doll n muñeca f de trapo

rage¹ /reɪdʒ/ n **1** (a) (violent anger) furia f (b) (fit of fury): **to be in a ∿** estar* furioso **2** (fashion) (colloq): **to be (all) the ∿** hacer* furor

rage² vi (a) «storm/sea» rugir*; «fire» arder

furiosamente (b) «person» rabiar (c) **raging** pres p ‹storm› rugiente; ‹sea› embravecido; ‹headache› enloquecedor; ‹argument› enconado

ragged /'rægəd ‖'rægɪd/ adj ‹clothes/appearance› harapiento, andrajoso; ‹edge› irregular

raid¹ /reɪd/ n (a) (Mil) asalto m (b) (air ∿) bombardeo m aéreo (c) (by thieves) atraco m (d) (by police) redada f, allanamiento m (AmL)

raid² vt (a) (Mil) asaltar (b) ‹bank› asaltar (c) «police» ‹house/building› hacer* una redada en, allanar (AmL)

raider /'reɪdər ‖'reɪdə(r)/ n asaltante mf

rail¹ /reɪl/ n **1** (a) (bar) riel m (b) (hand ∿) pasamanos m (c) (barrier) baranda f **2** (a) (for trains, trams) riel m, raíl m (Esp) (b) (railroad) ferrocarril m; **by ∿** en or por ferrocarril

railing /'reɪlɪŋ/ n (often pl) reja f

rail: ∿road n (AmE) (a) (system) ferrocarril m (b) (track) vía f férrea; **∿way** n (BrE) ▶ ∿ROAD

rain¹ /reɪn/ n lluvia f

rain² v impers llover*; **it's ∿ing** está lloviendo, llueve

rainbow /'reɪnbəʊ/ n arco m iris

rain: ∿coat n impermeable m; **∿drop** n gota f de lluvia; **∿fall** n precipitaciones fpl, lluvia f; **∿ forest** n selva f tropical (húmeda); **∿water** n agua f꞉ de lluvia

rainy /'reɪni/ adj **-nier, -niest** lluvioso

raise¹ /reɪz/ vt

I 1 (a) ‹head/hand› levantar, alzar*; ‹eyebrows› arquear; ‹flag› izar* (b) (make higher) ‹shelf/level› subir **2** (a) (set upright) levantar (b) (erect) ‹monument/building› levantar, erigir* (frml) **3** (a) ‹pressure/temperature› aumentar, elevar; ‹price/salary› subir, aumentar; **to ∿ one's voice** levantar la voz (b) ‹consciousness› aumentar

II 1 (a) ‹money/funds› recaudar (b) ‹army› reclutar **2** ‹fears/doubt› suscitar; **he managed to ∿ a smile** pudo sonreír; **to ∿ the alarm** dar* la alarma **3** ‹subject› sacar*; ‹question› formular; **to ∿ an objection** poner* una objeción **4** (a) ‹family› criar* (b) ‹cattle› dedicarse a la cría de

raise² n (AmE) aumento m or subida f de sueldo

raisin /'reɪzn/ n (uva f) pasa f, pasa f (de uva)

rake¹ /reɪk/ n (tool) rastrillo m

rake² vt rastrillar

rakish /'reɪkɪʃ/ adj (casual, jaunty) desenfadado

rally¹ /'ræli/ n (pl **-lies**) **1** (mass meeting) concentración f; **political ∿** mitin m, mítin m **2** (Auto) rally m **3** (in tennis, badminton) peloteo m

rally² **-lies, -lying, -lied** vi **1** (unite) unirse; (gather) congregarse* **2** (a) (recover) «person» recuperarse, reponerse* (b) (Fin) «currency/price» repuntar, recuperarse

■ ∿ vt **1** ‹support/vote› conseguir* **2** ‹strength/spirits› recobrar

■ **rally round** [v + adv]: **all the neighbors rallied round to help** todos los vecinos se juntaron para ayudar

ram¹ /ræm/ n (Zool) carnero m

ram² **-mm-** vt (a) (force) (+ adv compl): **he ∿med the stake into the ground** hincó la estaca en la tierra; **he ∿med his fist through the door** atravesó la puerta de un puñetazo (b) (crash into) chocar* con; (deliberately) embestir* contra   ⋯⋗

■ **ram home** [*v* + *o* + *adv*, *v* + *adv* + *o*] ⟨*point/ message*⟩ hacer* entender a la fuerza

RAM /ræm/ *n* (Comput) (= **random access memory**) RAM *f*

Ramadan /ˈrɑːmədɑːn ‖ˌræməˈdæn/ *n* Ramadán *m*

ramble¹ /ˈræmbəl/ *n* paseo *m*; (BrE Sport) excursión *f* (*a pie*)

ramble² *vi* (a) (walk) pasear; **to go rambling** (BrE) hacer* excursionismo (b) (in speech, writing) irse* por las ramas

■ **ramble on** [*v* + *adv*] divagar*

rambler /ˈræmblər ‖ˈræmblə(r)/ *n* excursionista *mf*

rambling /ˈræmblɪŋ/ *adj* (a) ⟨*essay/lecture*⟩ que se va por las ramas (b) ⟨*streets*⟩ laberíntico; **a ~ old house** una vieja casona llena de recovecos (c) ⟨*rose*⟩ trepador

ramp /ræmp/ *n* (a) (slope) rampa *f*; **entrance** *o* **on ~** (AmE) vía *f* de acceso; **exit** *o* **off ~** (AmE) vía *f* de salida (b) (on ship, aircraft) (for passengers) escalerilla *f*; (for vehicles) rampa *f* (c) (platform) elevador *m* (d) (hump) (BrE) desnivel *m*

rampage /ˈræmpeɪdʒ/ *n*: **to be/go on the ~** empezar* a arrasarlo todo

rampant /ˈræmpənt/ *adj* ⟨*inflation*⟩ galopante; ⟨*growth*⟩ desenfrenado; ⟨*crime*⟩ endémico

rampart /ˈræmpɑːrt ‖ˈræmpɑːt/ *n* (bank) terraplén *m*; (wall) muralla *f*

ram: ~ raid *n* asalto (*rompiendo el escaparate con un vehículo*); **~-raid** *vt* asaltar (*rompiendo el escaparate con un vehículo*)

ramshackle /ˈræmˌʃækəl/ *adj* destartalado

ran /ræn/ *past of* RUN¹

ranch /ræntʃ ‖rɑːntʃ/ *n*: **cattle ~** finca *f* (ganadera), hacienda *f* (ganadera) (esp AmL), rancho *m* ganadero (Méx), estancia *f* (CS)

rancher /ˈræntʃər ‖ˈrɑːntʃə(r)/ *n* hacendado, -da *m,f*, estanciero, -ra *m,f* (CS), ranchero, -ra *m,f* (Méx); **cattle ~** ganadero, -ra *m,f*

rancid /ˈrænsəd ‖ˈrænsɪd/ *adj* rancio

rancor, (BrE) **rancour** /ˈræŋkər ‖ˈræŋkə(r)/ *n* rencor *m*

rand /rænd/ *n* (*pl* **~**) rand *m*

random /ˈrændəm/ *adj* (a) ⟨*testing/choice*⟩ al azar; ⟨*sample*⟩ aleatorio (b) **at random** (*as adv*) al azar

rang /ræŋ/ *past of* RING²

range¹ /reɪndʒ/ *n* ① (a) (scope) ámbito *m* (b) (Mus) registro *m* (c) (bracket): **within/out of our price ~** dentro de/fuera de nuestras posibilidades ② (a) (variety) gama *f* (b) (selection) línea *f* ③ (a) (of gun, transmitter) alcance *m*; **at close/long ~** de cerca/lejos; **to come/be within ~** ponerse*/estar* a tiro (b) (of vehicle, missile) autonomía *f* ④ (for shooting) campo *m* de tiro ⑤ (chain) cadena *f*; **a mountain ~** una cordillera ⑥ (stove) cocina *f* económica, estufa *f* (Col, Méx)

range² *vi*: **their ages ~ from 12 to 20** tienen entre 12 y 20 años

ranger /ˈreɪndʒər ‖ˈreɪndʒə(r)/ *n* guarda *mf* forestal, guardabosques *mf*

rank¹ /ræŋk/ *n* ① (line) fila *f* ② (status) categoría *f*; (Mil) grado *m*, rango *m* ③ (taxi **~**) (BrE) parada *f* de taxis, sitio *m* (Méx)

rank² *vt*: **he's ~ed fourth** está clasificado cuarto

■ **~** *vi* (a) (be classed) estar*; **it ~s among the best** está entre los mejores (b) (hold rank): **to ~ above/ below sb** estar* por encima/por debajo de algn

rank³ *adj* ① (*before n*) (complete) ⟨*beginner*⟩ absoluto; ⟨*injustice*⟩ flagrante ② ⟨*smell*⟩ fétido

rank and file *n* (Mil) (+ *pl vb*) tropa *f*; **the ~ ~ of the union** las bases del sindicato

rankle /ˈræŋkəl/ *vi* doler*

ransack /ˈrænsæk/ *vt* ⟨*room/drawer*⟩ revolver*; ⟨*house/premises*⟩ (search) registrar (*de arriba a abajo*); (pillage) saquear

ransom /ˈrænsəm/ *n* rescate *m*; **to hold sb to** *o* (AmE also) **for ~** exigir* un rescate por algn

rant /rænt/ *vi* despotricar*

rap¹ /ræp/ *n* ① (blow) golpe *m* ② **to take the ~ for sth** (esp AmE colloq) cargar* con la culpa de algo ③ (a) (chat) (colloq) cháchara *f* (fam) (b) (Mus) rap *m*

rap² **-pp-** *vi* dar* un golpe

■ **~** *vt*: **he ~ped my knuckles** me pegó en los nudillos

rape¹ /reɪp/ *n* ① (a) (sexual violation) violación *f*; (of a minor) estupro *m* (b) (of the countryside) (liter) expoliación *f* (liter) ② (plant) colza *f*

rape² *vt* ⟨*person*⟩ violar

rapid /ˈræpəd ‖ˈræpɪd/ *adj* rápido

rapidly /ˈræpədli ‖ˈræpɪdli/ *adv* rápidamente

rapids /ˈræpədz ‖ˈræpɪdz/ *pl n* rápidos *mpl*

rapist /ˈreɪpəst ‖ˈreɪpɪst/ *n* violador, -dora *m,f*

rapport /ræˈpɔːr ‖ræˈpɔː(r)/ *n* relación *f* de comunicación

rapt /ræpt/ *adj* (liter) ⟨*expression/smile*⟩ embelesado

rapture /ˈræptʃər ‖ˈræptʃə(r)/ *n* éxtasis *m*, arrobamiento *m* (liter)

rapturous /ˈræptʃərəs/ *adj* ⟨*applause/welcome*⟩ calurosísimo

rare /rer ‖reə(r)/ *adj* **rarer** /ˈrerər ‖ˈreərə(r)/, **rarest** /ˈrerəst ‖ˈreərɪst/ ① (a) (uncommon) raro (b) (liter) ⟨*talent/beauty*⟩ excepcional ② (Culin) ⟨*steak*⟩ vuelta y media

rarely /ˈrerli ‖ˈreəli/ *adv* rara vez

raring /ˈrerɪŋ ‖ˈreərɪŋ/ *adj*: **to be ~ to go**: **he's ~ to go** está que ya no se aguanta

rarity /ˈrerəti ‖ˈreərɪti/ *n* (*pl* **-ties**) algo poco común

rascal /ˈræskəl ‖ˈrɑːskəl/ *n* granuja *mf*

rash¹ /ræʃ/ *n* sarpullido *m*

rash² *adj* **-er, -est** precipitado

rasher /ˈræʃər ‖ˈræʃə(r)/ *n* loncha *f*, lonja *f*

rashly /ˈræʃli/ *adv* ⟨*act*⟩ precipitadamente

rasp¹ /ræsp ‖rɑːsp/ *n* escofina *f*

rasp² *vt* ⟨*wood*⟩ raspar, escofinar

raspberry /'ræz,beri ‖'rɑːzbəri/ *n* (*pl* **-ries**) frambuesa *f*

rasping /'ræspɪŋ ‖'rɑːspɪŋ/ *adj* ⟨sound/voice⟩ áspero

Rastafarian /ˌræstə'feriən ‖ˌræstə'feəriən/ *n* rastafari *mf*

rat /ræt/ *n* **(a)** (Zool) rata *f*; (*before n*) ∼ **poison** raticida *m* **(b)** (person) (colloq) rata *f* de alcantarilla (fam)

rate¹ /reɪt/ *n* ⟨1⟩ **(a)** (speed) velocidad; (rhythm) ritmo *m*; **at this** ∼ a este paso; **at any** ∼ (at least) por lo menos; (in any case) en todo caso **(b)** (level, ratio): **birth** ∼ índice *m* de natalidad; **death** ∼ mortalidad *f*; ∼ **of inflation** tasa *f* de inflación; **interest** ∼ tasa *f* or (esp Esp) tipo *m* de interés; ∼ **of exchange** tipo *m* de cambio **(c)** (price, charge) tarifa *f*; **that's the going** ∼ eso es lo que se suele pagar ⟨2⟩ (local tax) (formerly, in UK) (*often pl*) ≈ contribución *f* (municipal *or* inmobiliaria)

rate² *vt* ⟨1⟩ (rank, consider): **I** ∼ **her work very highly** tengo una excelente opinión de su trabajo; **I** ∼ **her as the best woman tennis player** yo la considero la mejor tenista ⟨2⟩ (deserve) merecer*

rather /'rɑːðər ‖'rɑːðə(r)/ *adv* ⟨1⟩ **(a)** (stating preference): **I'd** ∼ **walk than go by bus** prefiero andar a ir en autobús; ∼ **you than me!** ¡menos mal que eres tú y no yo! **(b)** (more precisely): or ∼ o mejor dicho ⟨2⟩ (fairly) bastante; (somewhat) algo

ratification /ˌrætəfə'keɪʃən ‖ˌrætɪfɪ'keɪʃən/ *n* (frml) ratificación *f*

ratify /'rætəfaɪ ‖'rætɪfaɪ/ *vt* **-fies, -fying, -fied** (frml) ratificar*

rating /'reɪtɪŋ/ *n* **(a)** (evaluation): **credit** ∼ clasificación *f* crediticia **(b) ratings** *pl* (Rad, TV) índice *m* de audiencia

ratio /'reɪʃəʊ, -ʃiəʊ ‖'reɪʃiəʊ/ *n* (*pl* **ratios**) proporción *f*, ratio *m* (téc); **in a** ∼ **of two to one** en una proporción de dos a uno

ration¹ /'ræʃən/ *n* **(a)** (allowance) ración *f* **(b) rations** *pl* víveres *mpl*

ration² *vt* racionar

rational /'ræʃnəl ‖'ræʃənl/ *adj* **(a)** (able to reason) ⟨being⟩ racional **(b)** (sane, lucid) **to be** ∼ estar* en su (*or* mi *etc*) sano juicio **(c)** (sensible) ⟨suggestion⟩ razonable

rationale /ˌræʃə'næl ‖ˌræʃə'nɑːl/ *n* (*no pl*) base *f*, razones *fpl*

rationalize /'ræʃnəlaɪz/ *vt* racionalizar*

rationally /'ræʃnəli/ *adv* ⟨think⟩ racionalmente; ⟨behave⟩ con sensatez

rationing /'ræʃənɪŋ/ *n* racionamiento *m*

rat run *n* (Auto) atajo *m* (*para evitar el tráfico de una calle principal en horas punta*)

rattle¹ /'rætl/ *n* ⟨1⟩ (*no pl*) (noise) ruido *m*; (of train, carriage) traqueteo *m* ⟨2⟩ **(baby's)** ∼ sonajero *m*, sonaja *f* (Méx)

rattle² *vi* **(a)** (make noise) «chains/bottles/keys» repiquetear; «window/engine» vibrar **(b)** (move) (+ *adv compl*) traquetear
 ■ ∼ *vt* ⟨keys/chain⟩ hacer* repiquetear; ⟨door/ window⟩ «wind» hacer* vibrar
 ■ **rattle off** [*v* + *o* + *adv, v* + *adv* + *o*] recitar
 ■ **rattle on** [*v* + *adv*] hablar *or* (fam) parlotear sin parar

rattlesnake /'rætlˌsneɪk/ *n* serpiente *f* (de) cascabel, cascabel *f*

raucous /'rɔːkəs/ *adj* (loud) estentóreo; (shrill) estridente

raunchy /'rɔːntʃi/ *adj* **-chier, -chiest** (colloq) ⟨humor⟩ picante; ⟨joke⟩ escabroso

ravage /'rævɪdʒ/ *vt* (plunder) saquear; **a country** ∼**d by war** un país asolado por la guerra

ravages /'rævɪdʒəz ‖'rævɪdʒɪz/ *pl n* estragos *mpl*

rave¹ /reɪv/ *vi* **(a)** (talk deliriously) delirar **(b)** (talk, write enthusiastically): **to** ∼ **about sth** poner* a algo por las nubes **(c)** (talk angrily) despotricar*

rave² *n* (colloq) ⟨1⟩ (*before n*) (full of praise) ∼ **reviews** críticas *fpl* muy favorables ⟨2⟩ (BrE) (party) *fiesta con música acid*

raven /'reɪvən/ *n* cuervo *m*

ravenous /'rævənəs/ *adj* hambriento; **to be** ∼ (colloq) tener* un hambre canina (fam)

ravine /rə'viːn/ *n* barranco *m*, quebrada *f*

raving¹ /'reɪvɪŋ/ *adj* (colloq) (*before n, as intensifier*): **he's a** ∼ **lunatic** está loco de atar (fam); (*as adv*) **he's** ∼ **mad** está como una cabra (fam)

raving² *n* (*often pl*) desvarío *m*

ravish /'rævɪʃ/ *vt* (liter) violar

ravishing /'rævɪʃɪŋ/ *adj* deslumbrante

raw /rɔː/ *adj* ⟨1⟩ **(a)** ⟨meat/vegetables⟩ crudo **(b)** ⟨silk⟩ crudo; ⟨sugar⟩ sin refinar; ⟨sewage⟩ sin tratar ⟨2⟩ (sore): **my fingers were** ∼ tenía los dedos en carne viva ⟨3⟩ (inexperienced) verde (fam); ⟨recruit⟩ novato

raw material *n* materia *f* prima

ray /reɪ/ *n* ⟨1⟩ (beam) rayo *m* ⟨2⟩ (Mus) re *m* ⟨3⟩ (Zool) raya *f*

rayon /'reɪɑːn ‖'reɪɒn/ *n* rayón *m*

raze /reɪz/ *vt*: **to** ∼ **sth (to the ground)** arrasar algo

razor /'reɪzər ‖'reɪzə(r)/ *n* **(a)** (safety ∼) cuchilla *f* or máquina *f* or maquinilla *f* de afeitar, rastrillo *m* (Méx); (*before n*) ∼ **blade** cuchilla *f*, hoja *f* de afeitar **(b)** (electric) máquina *f* or maquinilla *f* de afeitar, máquina *f* de rasurar (esp Méx)

razzmatazz /'ræzməˌtæz/ *n* (colloq) bulla *f*; (publicity) alarde *m* publicitario

Rd = **Road**

re¹ /reɪ/ *n* (Mus) re *m*

re² /riː/ *prep* con relación a, con referencia a

re- /riː/ *pref* re-

RE *n* (BrE) (= **religious education**) religión *f*

reach¹ /riːtʃ/ *n* ⟨1⟩ **(a)** (distance) alcance *m* **(b)** (*in phrases*) **within reach** a mi (*or* tu *etc*) alcance; **out of reach** fuera de su (*or* mi *etc*) alcance ⟨2⟩ (of river) tramo *m*

reach² *vt* ⟨1⟩ **(a)** (with hand) alcanzar* **(b)** (extend to) llegar* a ⟨2⟩ ⟨destination/limit/age⟩ llegar* a; ⟨stage/agreement⟩ llegar* a, alcanzar* ⟨3⟩ (contact) ponerse* en contacto con
 ■ ∼ *vi* **(a)** (extend hand, arm): **he** ∼**ed for his gun** echó mano a la pistola; **she** ∼**ed across the table for the salt** agarró *or* (esp Esp) cogió la sal, que estaba al otro lado de la mesa **(b)** (stretch far enough) alcanzar*; **I can't** ∼! ¡no alcanzo! **(c)** (extend) extenderse*
 ■ **reach out** [*v* + *adv*] alargar* la mano

react /ri'ækt/ *vi* reaccionar

reaction /ri'ækʃən/ *n* reacción *f*

reactionary /ri'ækʃəneri ‖ri'ækʃənri/ adj
(pej) reaccionario (pey)
reactor /ri'æktər ‖ri'æktə(r)/ n (nuclear ∼)
reactor m (nuclear)
read¹ /ri:d/ (past & past p **read** /red/) vt
1 (a) ‹book/map/music/meter› leer* (b) (interpret)
‹sign/mood/situation› interpretar **2** (a) «sign/
notice» decir* (b) (indicate) «thermometer/gauge»
marcar*
■ ∼ vi leer*
■ **read out** [v + o + adv, v + adv + o] leer* (en
voz alta)
■ **read over, read through** [v + o + adv] leer*
(por entero)
■ **read up** [v + adv] **to** ∼ **up** (**ON** sth) estudiar
(algo)
read² /red/ adj: **to be well** ∼ ser* muy leído
readable /'ri:dəbəl/ adj ‹book/style› ameno;
‹writing› legible
reader /'ri:dər ‖'ri:də(r)/ n **1** (person) lector,
-tora m,f; **she's a fast/slow** ∼ lee muy rápido/
lento **2** (Educ, Publ) libro m de lectura
readership /'ri:dərʃɪp ‖'ri:dəʃɪp/ n lectores
mpl; **it has a** ∼ **of over 10 million** tiene una tirada
de 10 millones
readily /'redli ‖'redɪli/ adv (a) (willingly): **she** ∼
agreed accedió de buena gana (b) (easily)
‹understand› fácilmente; **they are** ∼ **available** se
pueden conseguir fácilmente
reading /'ri:dɪŋ/ n **1** (a) (activity, skill) lectura f;
(before n) ‹glasses› para leer; ∼ **list** lista f de
lecturas recomendadas; ∼ **room** sala f de lectura
(b) (event): **poetry** ∼ recital m de poesía **2** (on
dial, gauge) lectura f
readjust /'ri:ə'dʒʌst/ vt reajustar
■ ∼ vi «person» **to** ∼ (**TO** sth) readaptarse (A
algo)
ready¹ /'redi/ adj **-dier, -diest** **1** (a) (having
completed preparations) (pred) **to be** ∼ estar* listo,
estar* pronto (RPl); **to be** ∼ **to** + INF estar* listo
PARA + INF; **to get** ∼ (prepare oneself) prepararse,
aprontarse (CS); (get dressed, made up etc)
arreglarse, aprontarse (CS) (b) (mentally prepared)
(pred) **to be** ∼ **FOR** sth/**to** + INF estar* preparado
PARA algo/PARA + INF **2** (willing) dispuesto
3 (easy, available): ∼ **money** o **cash** dinero m (en
efectivo)
ready² n **at the** ∼ listo
ready³ vt **-dies, -dying, -died** preparar
ready: ∼**-made** /'redi'meɪd/ adj ‹suit› de
confección; ‹soup/sauce› preparado; ∼**-to-wear**
/'reditə'wer ‖,reditə'weə(r)/ adj (before n)
‹clothes› de confección
reaffirm /,ri:ə'fɜ:rm ‖,ri:ə'fɜ:m/ vt reiterar,
reafirmar
real¹ /ri:l, rɪl ‖ri:l, rɪəl/ adj (a) (actual, not
imaginary) real, verdadero (b) (actual, true) (before
n) ‹reason/name› verdadero (c) (genuine, not fake)
‹fur/leather› auténtico; ‹gold› de ley (d) (as
intensifier) auténtico
real² adv (AmE colloq) (as intensifier) muy
real estate n (esp AmE) bienes mpl raíces or
inmuebles, propiedad f inmobiliaria; (before n) ∼
agent ▶ REALTOR
realism /'ri:əlɪzəm/ n realismo m
realist /'ri:əlist ‖'ri:əlɪst/ n realista mf
realistic /'ri:ə'lɪstɪk ‖,rɪə'lɪstɪk/ adj realista

reality /ri'æləti/ n (pl **-ties**) realidad f; **in** ∼
en realidad
realization /'ri:ələ'zeɪʃən ‖,rɪələ'zeɪʃən/ n
1 (understanding) comprensión f **2** (of plan)
realización f
realize /'ri:əlaɪz/ vt **1** (a) (become aware of)
darse* cuenta de, comprender, caer* en la cuenta
de (b) (know, be aware of) saber* **2** (achieve)
‹ambition› hacer* realidad; ‹potential›
desarrollar
■ ∼ vi darse* cuenta
really /'ri:əli ‖'ri:əli, 'rɪəli/ adv (a) (in fact): **I** ∼
did see him! ¡de verdad que lo vi!; **the tomato is**
∼ **a fruit** el tomate en realidad es una fruta (b)
(as intensifier): **it's** ∼ **good/old** es buenísimo/
viejísimo (c) (as interj): (**oh,**) ∼? (expressing
interest) ¿ah sí?; **really?** (expressing surprise) ¿de
verdad?
realm /relm/ n (a) (kingdom) (frml) reino m (b)
(sphere) (often pl) mundo m
realtor /'ri:əltər ‖'rɪəltə(r)/ n (AmE) agente
inmobiliario, -ria m,f
ream /ri:m/ n (Print) resma f
reamer /'ri:mər ‖'ri:mə(r)/ n (AmE)
exprimelimones m, exprimidor m
reap /ri:p/ vt (Agr) cosechar, recoger*; **to** ∼ **the**
benefits of sth cosechar los beneficios de algo
reappear /'ri:ə'pɪr ‖,ri:ə'pɪə(r)/ vi volver* a
aparecer
rear¹ /rɪr ‖rɪə(r)/ n (a) (back part) (no pl) parte f
trasera or de atrás (b) (of column, procession) (no
pl) **the** ∼ la retaguardia (c) (buttocks) (colloq)
trasero m (fam)
rear² adj ‹window/wheel› de atrás, trasero
rear³ vt ‹child/cattle› criar*
■ ∼ vi ∼ (**up**) «horse» encabritarse
rearguard /'rɪrgɑːrd ‖'rɪəgɑːd/ n retaguardia f
rearm /'ri:'ɑːrm ‖,ri:'ɑːm/ vt rearmar
■ ∼ vi rearmarse
rearrange /'ri:ə'reɪndʒ/ vt (a) ‹furniture›
cambiar de lugar (b) (change time of)
‹appointment› cambiar la fecha/la hora de
rear-view mirror /'rɪrvju: ‖'rɪəvju:/ n
(espejo m) retrovisor m
reason¹ /'ri:zn/ n **1** (cause) razón f, motivo m;
∼ **FOR** sth razón or motivo DE algo; **I left it there**
for a ∼ por algo lo dejé ahí **2** (faculty) razón f
3 (good sense): **to listen to** ∼ atender* a razones;
it stands to ∼ es lógico
reason² vt pensar*
■ ∼ vi razonar, discurrir
reasonable /'ri:znəbəl/ adj (a) ‹offer/request/
person› razonable (b) ‹price/sum› razonable,
moderado
reasonably /'ri:znəbli/ adv (a) ‹behave/argue›
razonablemente (b) (fairly): **I'm** ∼ **certain** estoy
casi seguro
reasoning /'ri:znɪŋ/ n razonamiento m
reassemble /'ri:ə'sembəl/ vt (a) ‹people/
group› volver* a reunir, reunir* (b) ‹parts/
engine› reensamblar
■ ∼ vi «meeting/group» volverse* a reunir,
reunirse*
reassurance /'ri:ə'ʃʊrəns ‖,ri:ə'ʃʊərəns,
,ri:ə'ʃɔ:rəns/ n (a) (feeling): **he drew** ∼ **from his**
wife's words lo que le dijo su mujer lo confortó

or lo tranquilizó **(b)** (words, support): **he gave us countless ∼s that ...** nos tranquilizó asegurándonos repetidamente que ...

reassure /ˌriːəˈʃʊr ‖ ˌriːəˈʃʊə(r), ˌriːəˈʃɔː(r)/ *vt* tranquilizar*

reassuring /ˌriːəˈʃʊrɪŋ ‖ ˌriːəˈʃʊərɪŋ, ˌriːəˈʃɔːrɪŋ/ *adj* ⟨voice/manner/answer⟩ tranquilizador; **it's ∼ to know that ...** tranquiliza saber que ...

rebate /ˈriːbeɪt/ *n* (repayment) reembolso *m*; (discount) descuento *m*

rebel¹ /ˈrebəl/ *n* rebelde *mf*

rebel² /rɪˈbel/ *vi* **-ll-** rebelarse, sublevarse

rebellion /rɪˈbeljən/ *n* rebelión *f*

rebellious /rɪˈbeljəs/ *adj* rebelde

rebirth /ˈriːˈbɜːθ ‖ ˌriːˈbɜːθ/ *n* renacimiento *m*

reboot /riːˈbuːt/ *vt* (Comput) reiniciar

rebound¹ /ˈriːbaʊnd/ *n*: **she married him on the ∼** se casó con él por despecho

rebound² /rɪˈbaʊnd/ *vi* «ball» rebotar

rebuff¹ /rɪˈbʌf/ *n*: **to meet with/receive a ∼** ser* rechazado

rebuff² *vt* rechazar*

rebuild /ˈriːˈbɪld/ *vt* (past & past p **rebuilt**) ⟨building/economy⟩ reconstruir*; **he tried to ∼ his life** intentó rehacer su vida

rebuke¹ /rɪˈbjuːk/ *vt* reprender

rebuke² *n* reprimenda *f*

rebut /rɪˈbʌt/ *vt* **-tt-** (fml) rebatir

recall¹ /rɪˈkɔːl, ˈriːkɔːl/ *n* ⓵ (memory) memoria *f*; **to have total ∼** tener* una memoria excelente ⓶ (of goods, ambassador) retirada *f*

recall² /rɪˈkɔːl/ *vt* ⓵ (remember) recordar* ⓶ **(a)** ⟨faulty goods⟩ retirar (del mercado) **(b)** ⟨ambassador⟩ retirar; (temporarily) llamar; ⟨troops⟩ llamar

recant /rɪˈkænt/ *vi* retractarse; (Relig) abjurar

recap¹ /ˈriːkæp/ *n* (colloq) resumen *m*

recap² /riːˈkæp/ **-pp-** *vt* ⓵ (summarize) (colloq) resumir, recapitular ⓶ (AmE Auto) ▶ RETREAD¹
■ **∼** *vi* (colloq) resumir

recapitulate /ˌriːkəˈpɪtʃəleɪt ‖ ˌriːkəˈpɪtjʊleɪt/ *vt/i* (fml) recapitular, resumir

recapture /riːˈkæptʃər ‖ riːˈkæptʃə(r)/ *vt* ⟨convict/animal⟩ capturar; ⟨youth/beauty⟩ recuperar

recede /rɪˈsiːd/ *vi* **(a)** (move back) «tide» retirarse; **to ∼ into the distance** perderse en la distancia **(b)** «danger» alejarse; «prospect» desvanecerse* **(c) receding** *pres p* ⟨chin⟩ hundido; **he has a receding hairline** tiene entradas

receipt /rɪˈsiːt/ *n* **(a)** (paper) recibo *m* **(b)** (act) recibo *m*, recepción *f*

receive /rɪˈsiːv/ *vt* ⓵ **(a)** ⟨letter/award/visit⟩ recibir; ⟨payment⟩ recibir, cobrar, percibir (fml); ⟨stolen goods⟩ comerciar con, reducir* (AmS); ⟨serve/ball⟩ recibir; ⟨injuries⟩ sufrir; ⟨blow⟩ recibir **(b)** (react to) ⟨news/idea⟩ recibir ⓶ (welcome, admit) (fml) ⟨person⟩ recibir, acoger* ⓷ (Rad, TV) ⟨signal⟩ recibir, captar

receiver /rɪˈsiːvər ‖ rɪˈsiːvə(r)/ *n* ⓵ (Telec) auricular *m* ⓶ (Rad, TV) receptor *m* ⓷ (of stolen goods) comerciante *mf* de mercancía robada

receivership /rɪˈsiːvərʃɪp ‖ rɪˈsiːvəʃɪp/ *n* **to go into/be in ∼** ≈ser* declarado/estar* en suspensión *m* or en cesación de pagos

recent /ˈriːsn̩t/ *adj* reciente; **in ∼ years/months** en los últimos años/meses; **in the ∼ past** en los últimos tiempos

recently /ˈriːsn̩tli/ *adv* recientemente; **until quite ∼** hasta hace bien poco

receptacle /rɪˈseptɪkəl/ *n* (fml) recipiente *m*, receptáculo *m*

reception /rɪˈsepʃən/ *n* **(a)** (reaction) (no pl) recibimiento *m*, acogida *f* **(b)** (in hotel, office) (no art) recepción *f*; (before n) **∼ desk** recepción *f* **(c)** (social event) recepción *f* **(d)** (Rad, TV) recepción *f*

receptionist /rɪˈsepʃənəst ‖ rɪˈsepʃənɪst/ *n* recepcionista *mf*

receptive /rɪˈseptɪv/ *adj* receptivo

recess /ˈriːses/ *n* ⓵ **(a)** (of legislative body) receso *m* (AmL), suspensión *f* de actividades (Esp); (of committee etc) intermedio *m* **(b)** (AmE Educ) recreo *m* ⓶ (alcove) hueco *m*, entrada *f*

recession /rɪˈseʃn̩ ‖ rɪˈseʃən/ *n* (Econ) recesión *f*

recharge /ˈriːˈtʃɑːrdʒ ‖ ˌriːˈtʃɑːdʒ/ *vt* volver* a cargar, recargar*

rechargeable /ˈriːˈtʃɑːrdʒəbəl ‖ ˌriːˈtʃɑːdʒəbəl/ *adj* recargable

recipe /ˈresəpi/ *n* receta *f*; (before n) **∼ book** libro *m* de cocina; (personal) cuaderno *m* de recetas (de cocina)

recipient /rɪˈsɪpiənt/ *n* (fml) (of letter) destinatario, -ria *m,f*; (of an organ) (Med) receptor, -tora *m,f*

reciprocal /rɪˈsɪprəkəl/ *adj* recíproco

reciprocate /rɪˈsɪprəkeɪt/ *vt* corresponder a, reciprocar* (AmL)
■ **∼** *vi* corresponder, reciprocar* (AmL)

recital /rɪˈsaɪtl̩/ *n* (Mus) recital *m*

recite /rɪˈsaɪt/ *vt* **(a)** (declaim) ⟨poem⟩ recitar **(b)** (list) ⟨names⟩ enumerar

reckless /ˈrekləs ‖ ˈreklɪs/ *adj* imprudente, temerario

reckon /ˈrekən/ *vt* **(a)** (calculate) calcular **(b)** (consider) considerar **(c)** (think) (colloq) creer*; **what do you ∼?** ¿tú qué opinas?, ¿y a ti qué te parece?
■ **reckon on** [v + prep + o] contar con

reckoning /ˈrekənɪŋ/ *n* cálculos *mpl*

reclaim /rɪˈkleɪm/ *vt* **(a)** (claim back): **I filled in a form to ∼ tax** llené un formulario para que me devolvieran parte de los impuestos; **to ∼ one's luggage** (Aviat) recoger* el equipaje; (at left luggage) (pasar a) retirar el equipaje **(b)** (recover) recuperar; **∼ed land** terreno *m* ganado al mar

recline /rɪˈklaɪn/ *vi* **(a)** (lean back) recostarse*, reclinarse; (rest) apoyarse **(b)** «chair» reclinarse **(c) reclining** *pres p* ⟨chair/seat⟩ reclinable, abatible; ⟨figure⟩ yacente (liter), recostado

recluse /rɪˈkluːs/ *n* ermitaño, -ña *m,f*

reclusive /rɪˈkluːsɪv/ *adj* dado a recluirse

recognition /ˌrekəɡˈnɪʃən/ *n* reconocimiento *m*; **in ∼ of** (fml) en reconocimiento a *or* por (fml)

recognizable /ˈrekəɡnaɪzəbəl/ *adj* reconocible; ⟨difference⟩ apreciable

recognize /ˈrekəɡnaɪz/ *vt* **(a)** ⟨voice/person⟩ reconocer* **(b)** (acknowledge) reconocer*, admitir

recoil[1] /rɪˈkɔɪl/ vi (shrink back) retroceder; **to ~ FROM sth** rehuir* algo

recoil[2] /ˈriːkɔɪl/ n retroceso m

recollect /ˌrekəˈlekt/ vt recordar*

recollection /ˌrekəˈlekʃən/ n recuerdo m

recommend /ˌrekəˈmend/ vt (a) (praise, declare acceptable) recomendar* **(b)** (advise) **to ~ sth/-ING** aconsejar or recomendar* algo/+ INF; **~ed (retail) price** precio m de venta recomendado

recommendation /ˌrekəmenˈdeɪʃən/ n recomendación f

recompense /ˈrekəmpens/ n (frml) recompensa f

reconcile /ˈrekənsaɪl/ vt (a) (enemies) reconciliar (b) (theories/ideals) conciliar (c) **to become ~d TO sth** resignarse A algo

reconciliation /ˌrekənsɪliˈeɪʃən/ n reconciliación f

recondition /ˌriːkənˈdɪʃən/ vt reacondicionar

reconnaissance /rəˈkɑːnəzens, -səns ‖rɪˈkɒnɪsəns/ n (Mil) reconocimiento m

reconnoiter, (BrE) reconnoitre /ˈriːkəˈnɔɪtər, 're- ‖ˌrekəˈnɔɪtə(r)/ vt reconocer*

reconquer /ˈriːˈkɑːŋkər ‖ˌriːˈkɒŋkə(r)/ vt reconquistar

reconsider /ˈriːkənˈsɪdər ‖ˌriːkənˈsɪdə(r)/ vt reconsiderar

reconstruct /ˈriːkənˈstrʌkt/ vt reconstruir*

reconstruction /ˈriːkənˈstrʌkʃən/ n (a) (rebuilding) reconstrucción f (b) (re-creation) reconstitución f

record[1] /ˈrekərd ‖ˈrekɔːd/ n **1 (a)** (document) documento m; (of attendances etc) registro m; (file) archivo m; (minutes) acta f⁑; (note) nota f; **medical ~s** historial m médico; **keep a ~ of your expenses** anote sus gastos; **according to our ~s** según nuestros datos **(b)** (in phrases) **off the record** extraoficialmente; **on record: the hottest summer on ~** el verano más caluroso del que se tienen datos

2 (a) (of performance, behavior): **he has a good academic ~** tiene un buen currículum académico; **our products have an excellent safety ~** nuestros productos son de probada seguridad **(b)** (criminal ~) antecedentes mpl (penales)

3 (highest, lowest, best, worst) récord m, marca f

4 (Audio, Mus) disco m; (before n) **~ store** disquería f, tienda f de discos

record[2] /rɪˈkɔːrd ‖rɪˈkɔːd/ vt **1 (a)** «person» (write down) anotar; (in minutes) hacer* constar **(b)** (register) «instrument» registrar **2** (song/program/album) grabar

record[3] /ˈrekərd ‖ˈrekɔːd/ adj (before n, no comp) récord adj inv

record card n ficha f

recorded /rɪˈkɔːrdəd ‖rɪˈkɔːdɪd/ adj (a) (music) grabado (b) (history) escrito, documentado

recorder /rɪˈkɔːrdər ‖rɪˈkɔːdə(r)/ n (Mus) flauta f dulce

recording /rɪˈkɔːrdɪŋ ‖rɪˈkɔːdɪŋ/ n grabación f

record player n tocadiscos m

recount /rɪˈkaʊnt/ vt narrar, contar*

re-count /ˈriːˈkaʊnt/ vt volver* a contar; (votes) hacer* un segundo escrutinio de, recontar*

recoup /rɪˈkuːp/ vt (costs) recuperar; (losses) resarcirse* de

recourse /ˈriːkɔːrs ‖rɪˈkɔːs/ n **to have ~ to sth/sb** recurrir a algo/algn

recover /rɪˈkʌvər ‖rɪˈkʌvə(r)/ vt (a) (consciousness/strength) recuperar, recobrar; (investment/lead) recuperar (b) (retrieve) rescatar ■ ~ vi (a) «person» reponerse*, restablecerse*, recuperarse (b) «economy» recuperarse, repuntar

recovery /rɪˈkʌvəri/ n (pl **-ries**) **1 (a)** (return to health) recuperación f, restablecimiento m **(b)** (of economy) recuperación f **2** (of stolen goods, missing documents) recuperación f; (retrieval) rescate m

re-create /ˈriːkriˈeɪt/ vt recrear

recreation /ˌrekriˈeɪʃən/ n (a) (leisure) esparcimiento m (b) (in school, prison) (BrE) recreo m

recreational /ˌrekriˈeɪʃnəl ‖ˌrekriˈeɪʃənl/ adj recreativo; **~ drug** droga f recreativa

recrimination /rɪˌkrɪməˈneɪʃən/ n (often pl) recriminación f

recruit[1] /rɪˈkruːt/ n (Mil) recluta mf

recruit[2] vt reclutar; (staff) contratar

recruitment /rɪˈkruːtmənt/ n reclutamiento m

rectangle /ˈrektæŋgəl/ n rectángulo m

rectangular /rekˈtæŋgjələr ‖rekˈtæŋgjʊlə(r)/ adj rectangular

rectify /ˈrektəfaɪ ‖ˈrektɪfaɪ/ vt **-fies, -fying, -fied** rectificar*

rector /ˈrektər ‖ˈrektə(r)/ n (a) (Relig) rector, -tora m,f, ≈párroco m (b) (in US) (Educ) rector, -ra m,f

rectum /ˈrektəm/ n (pl **rectums** or **recta** /ˈrektə/) recto m

recuperate /rɪˈkuːpəreɪt/ vi recuperarse, reponerse*

recuperation /rɪˌkuːpəˈreɪʃən/ n recuperación f, restablecimiento m

recur /rɪˈkɜːr ‖rɪˈkɜː(r)/ vi **-rr- (a)** «phenomenon» volver* a ocurrir or a suceder, repetirse*; «symptom» volver* a presentarse **(b)** **recurring** pres p recurrente

recurrence /rɪˈkɜːrəns ‖rɪˈkʌrəns/ n (of symptoms) reaparición f; (of incident) repetición f

recurrent /rɪˈkɜːrənt ‖rɪˈkʌrənt/ adj recurrente

recycle /ˈriːˈsaɪkəl/ vt reciclar

recycling /ˈriːˈsaɪklɪŋ/ n reciclaje m

red[1] /red/ adj **redder, reddest** (rose/dress) rojo, colorado; (flag/signal) rojo; (meat) rojo; (wine) tinto; **her eyes were ~** tenía los ojos enrojecidos or rojos

red² n rojo m, colorado m; **to see ~** ponerse* hecho una furia *or* un basilisco; **to be in the ~** estar* en números rojos

red: **~ admiral** n vanesa f roja; **~ carpet** n: to roll out the **~ carpet for sb** recibir* a algn con bombos y platillos *or* (Esp) a bombo y platillo; **R~ Cross** n Cruz f Roja

redden /'redn/ vi enrojecerse*

redecorate /ˌriː'dekəreɪt/ vt/i pintar (y empapelar)

redeem /rɪ'diːm/ vt **1** (a) ⟨good name⟩ rescatar (b) ⟨sinners⟩ redimir (c) **redeeming** pres p: **he has no ~ing features** no tiene ningún punto a su favor **2** (from pawnshop) desempeñar

redefine /ˌriːdɪ'faɪn/ vt redefinir

redemption /rɪ'dempʃən/ n (saving) salvación f; (Relig) redención f

redeploy /ˌriːdɪ'plɔɪ/ vt ⟨resources⟩ reorientar; ⟨staff⟩ asignar un nuevo destino a, reubicar* (AmL); ⟨troops⟩ cambiar la disposición de

redevelop /ˌriːdɪ'veləp/ vt reurbanizar*

red: **~-haired** /'red'heɪrd ‖ ˌred'heəd/ adj pelirrojo; **~-handed** /'red'hændəd ‖ ˌred'hændɪd/ adj: **to catch sb ~-handed** agarrar *or* (esp Esp) coger* a algn con las manos en la masa; **~head** n pelirrojo, -ja m,f; **~ herring** n (in detective story) pista f falsa; **~-hot** /'red'hɑːt ‖ ˌred'hɒt/ adj (pred **~ hot**) al rojo vivo

redial /'riː'daɪl ‖ ˌriː'daɪəl/ vi/t, (BrE) **-ll-** volver* a marcar *or* (AmS tb) a discar

redirect /ˌriːdə'rekt, -daɪ- ‖ ˌriːdaɪ'rekt, -də-/ vt (often pass) ⟨mail⟩ enviar* a una nueva dirección; ⟨traffic⟩ desviar*

rediscover /ˌriːdɪ'skʌvər ‖ ˌriːdɪ'skʌvə(r)/ vt redescubrir*, volver* a descubrir

redistribute /ˌriːdɪ'strɪbjət ‖ ˌriːdɪ'strɪbjuːt/ vt redistribuir*

red: **~ light** n luz f roja, semáforo m en rojo, alto m (Méx); **~-light district** n zona f de tolerancia, zona f roja (AmL); **~neck** n (in US) (pej) sureño reaccionario de la clase baja rural

redo /'riː'duː/ vt (3rd pers sing pres **redoes**; past **redid**; past p **redone**) rehacer*, volver* a hacer

redouble /'riː'dʌbəl/ vt ⟨efforts⟩ redoblar

red pepper n (capsicum) ► PEPPER¹ 2

redraft /'riː'dræft ‖ ˌriː'drɑːft/ vt volver* a redactar

redress¹ /rɪ'dres/ n reparación f

redress² vt ⟨wrong⟩ reparar; ⟨imbalance⟩ corregir*

red: **R~ Sea** n the R~ Sea el Mar Rojo; **~ tape** n (bureaucracy) trámites mpl burocráticos, papeleo m (fam)

reduce /rɪ'duːs ‖ rɪ'djuːs/ vt **1** ⟨number/ amount⟩ reducir*; ⟨pressure/speed⟩ disminuir*, reducir*; ⟨price/taxes⟩ reducir*, rebajar; ⟨pain⟩ aliviar; **❸ reduce speed now** disminuya la velocidad **2** (break down, simplify) **to ~ sth TO sth** reducir* algo A algo **3** **to ~ sb to tears** hacer* llorar a algn

reduced /rɪ'duːst ‖ rɪ'djuːst/ adj reducido

reduction /rɪ'dʌkʃən/ n reducción f; (in prices, charges) rebaja f

redundancy /rɪ'dʌndənsi/ n (pl **-cies**) (BrE Lab Rel) despido m, cese m; (before n) **~ money** o **pay** indemnización f (por despido *or* cese)

redundant /rɪ'dʌndənt/ adj (a) (superfluous) superfluo (b) (esp BrE Lab Rel): **she was made ~** la despidieron por reducción de planilla *or* (Esp) de plantilla

reed /riːd/ n (a) (Bot) carrizo m, junco m (b) (Mus) lengüeta f

reeducate /'riː'edʒəkeɪt ‖ ˌriː'edʒʊkeɪt/ vt reeducar*

reef /riːf/ n (Geog) arrecife m; (seen as hazard) escollo m, arrecife m

reek /riːk/ vi (a) (stink) **to ~** (OF sth) apestar *or* heder* (A algo) (b) (have air of) **to ~ OF sth** ⟨of corruption/fraud⟩ oler* A algo

reel¹ /riːl/ n (a) (for wire, thread, tape) carrete m (b) (of film) rollo m, carrete m (esp Esp) (c) (fishing) carrete m, carretel m

reel² vi tambalearse; **my head was ~ing** todo me daba vueltas

■ **reel in** [v + o + adv, v + adv + o] ⟨line⟩ enrollar

■ **reel off** [v + o + adv, v + adv + o] recitar de un tirón

reelect /'riːə'lekt ‖ ˌriːɪ'lekt/ vt reelegir*

reemerge /'riːə'mɜːrdʒ ‖ ˌriːɪ'mɜːdʒ/ vi (a) (reappear) volver* a salir (b) (regain prominence) resurgir*

reenact /'riːə'nækt ‖ ˌriːɪ'nækt/ vt ⟨historical event⟩ recrear; ⟨crime⟩ reconstruir*

reenter /'riː'entər ‖ ˌriː'entə(r)/ vt volver* a entrar en *or* (esp AmL) a

reexamine /'riːɪg'zæmən ‖ ˌriːɪg'zæmɪn/ vt volver* a examinar

ref¹ /ref/ n (colloq) (= **referee**) árbitro, -tra m,f, réferi mf (AmL)

ref² /ref/ (= **reference**) ref.

refectory /rɪ'fektəri/ n (pl **-ries**) comedor m

refer /rɪ'fɜːr ‖ rɪ'fɜː(r)/ **-rr-** vt remitir; **to ~ sb to a specialist** (Med) mandar *or* (AmL) derivar a algn a un especialista

■ **refer to** [v + prep + o] (a) (mention) hacer* referencia a, aludir a (b) (allude to) referirse* a (c) ⟨dictionary/notes⟩ consultar

referee¹ /'refə'riː/ n **1** (a) (Sport) árbitro, -tra m,f, réferi mf (AmL) (b) (in dispute) árbitro -tra m,f **2** (for job candidate) (BrE): **you need two ~s** necesitas el aval de dos personas

referee² vt/i arbitrar

reference /'refrəns, 'refərəns/ n **1** (allusion) alusión f, referencia f; **with ~ to** con referencia *or* relación a **2** (a) (consultation) consulta f; (before n) **~ book/library** obra f/biblioteca f de consulta *or* de referencia (b) (indicator) referencia f; (before n) **~ number** número m de referencia **3** (for job candidate — testimonial) referencia f, informe m; (— person giving testimonial) (AmE): **you need two ~s** necesitas el aval de dos personas

referendum /'refə'rendəm/ n (pl **-dums** or **-da** /-də/) referéndum m, referendo m

refill¹ /'riːfɪl/ n (for pen) repuesto m, recambio m; (for lighter) carga f

refill² /'riː'fɪl/ vt volver* a llenar, rellenar

refine /rɪ'faɪn/ vt (a) ⟨sugar/oil⟩ refinar (b) (improve) ⟨design/style⟩ pulir, perfeccionar

refined /rɪˈfaɪnd/ adj (a) ⟨person/manners⟩ refinado, fino (b) ⟨sugar/oil⟩ refinado

refinement /rɪˈfaɪnmənt/ n (a) (gentility, elegance) refinamiento m, finura f (b) (improvement) mejora f

refinery /rɪˈfaɪnəri/ n (pl -ries) refinería f

reflect /rɪˈflekt/ vt reflejar
■ ~ vi ⒈ (think) to ~ (ON sth) reflexionar or meditar (SOBRE algo) ⒉ ⟨light/heat⟩ reflejarse
■ **reflect on, reflect upon** [v + prep + o] repercutir en; **to ~ badly on sth/sb** perjudicar* algo/a algn

reflection /rɪˈflekʃən/ n ⒈ (a) (Opt, Phys) reflexión f (b) (image) reflejo m; (of situation, feeling) reflejo m ⒉ (a) (contemplation) reflexión f; **on** o **upon ~** ... pensándolo bien ... (b) (comment) observación f

reflector /rɪˈflektər ‖rɪˈflektə(r)/ n (of light, heat) reflector m; (Auto) cataforos m

reflex /ˈriːfleks/ n reflejo m

reflexive /rɪˈfleksɪv/ adj reflexivo

reform¹ /rɪˈfɔːrm ‖rɪˈfɔːm/ n reforma f

reform² vt reformar

reformation /ˌrefərˈmeɪʃən ‖ˌrefəˈmeɪʃən/ n reforma f; **the Reformation** (Relig) la Reforma

reformatory /rɪˈfɔːrmətɔːri ‖rɪˈfɔːmətəri/ n (pl -ries) (in US) reformatorio m

refrain¹ /rɪˈfreɪn/ vi (fml) to ~ (FROM sth/-ING) abstenerse* (DE algo/+ INF)

refrain² n (Lit, Mus) estribillo m

refresh /rɪˈfreʃ/ vt refrescar*

refreshing /rɪˈfreʃɪŋ/ adj ⟨drink/bath⟩ refrescante; ⟨sleep⟩ reparador; ⟨enthusiasm⟩ reconfortante

refreshments /rɪˈfreʃmənts/ pl n refrigerio m

refrigerate /rɪˈfrɪdʒəreɪt/ vt refrigerar

refrigerator /rɪˈfrɪdʒəreɪtər ‖rɪˈfrɪdʒəreɪtə(r)/ n nevera f, refrigerador m, frigorífico m (Esp), heladera f (RPl), refrigeradora f (Col, Per)

refuel /ˈriːˈfjuːəl/, (BrE) **-ll-** vt reabastecer* de combustible
■ ~ vi repostar, reabastecerse* de combustible

refuge /ˈrefjuːdʒ/ n refugio m; **to take ~** refugiarse

refugee /ˌrefjʊˈdʒiː/ n refugiado, -da m,f; (before n) ~ **camp** campamento m de refugiados

refund¹ /rɪˈfʌnd/ vt ⟨expenses/postage⟩ reembolsar

refund² /ˈriːfʌnd/ n reembolso m

refurbish /riːˈfɜːrbɪʃ ‖riːˈfɜːbɪʃ/ vt renovar*, hacer* reformas en; (restore) restaurar

refusal /rɪˈfjuːzəl/ n (of permission, request) denegación f; (of offer) rechazo m; (to do sth) negativa f

refuse¹ /rɪˈfjuːz/ vt ⟨offer/gift⟩ rechazar*, no aceptar, rehusar*; **to ~ to + INF** negarse* A + INF
■ ~ vi negarse*

refuse² /ˈrefjuːs/ n residuos mpl

refute /rɪˈfjuːt/ vt refutar, rebatir

regain /rɪˈgeɪn, ˈriː-/ vt recuperar, recobrar

regal /ˈriːgəl/ adj majestuoso, regio

regalia /rɪˈgeɪljə ‖rɪˈgeɪliə/ pl n ropajes mpl

regard¹ /rɪˈgɑːrd ‖rɪˈgɑːd/ vt ⒈ (a) (consider) considerar; **he is very highly ~ed within the**

profession está muy bien considerado en esa profesión (b) **as regards** en lo que se refiere a, en lo que atañe a ⒉ (look at) (liter) contemplar

regard² n ⒈ (a) (esteem): **to have a high ~ for sb** tener* muy buena opinión de algn, tener* a algn en gran estima (b) (consideration) consideración f ⒉ **regards** pl (greeting) saludos mpl, recuerdos mpl ⒊ (in phrases) **with regard to** (con) respecto a, con relación a, en relación con

regarding /rɪˈgɑːrdɪŋ ‖rɪˈgɑːdɪŋ/ prep (fml) en lo que concierne or respecta a, en lo que se refiere a

regardless /rɪˈgɑːrdləs ‖rɪˈgɑːdlɪs/ adv (a) (in spite of everything): **to carry on ~** seguir* como si no pasara nada or (fam) como si tal cosa (b) **regardless of** (as prep): ~ **of the cost** cueste lo que cueste

regatta /rɪˈgætə/ n regata f

regenerate /rɪˈdʒenəreɪt/ vt (revive) revitalizar*; (Biol) regenerar

regent /ˈriːdʒənt/ n (ruler) regente mf

reggae /ˈregeɪ/ n reggae m

regime, régime /reɪˈʒiːm/ n (a) (rule) régimen m (b) (system) sistema m

regiment /ˈredʒəmənt ‖ˈredʒɪmənt/ n regimiento m

regimental /ˌredʒəˈment ‖ˌredʒɪˈment/ adj (before n) ⟨mascot/band⟩ del regimiento

region /ˈriːdʒən/ n (a) (Anat, Geog) (area) región f, zona f (b) **in the region of** alrededor de

regional /ˈriːdʒən/ adj regional

register¹ /ˈredʒəstər ‖ˈredʒɪstə(r)/ n (a) (record, list) registro m; (in school) lista f; **to take** o **call the ~** (BrE School) pasar lista (b) (Mus) registro m

register² vt ⒈ (record) ⟨death/birth⟩ inscribir*, registrar; ⟨ship/car⟩ matricular ⒉ (Post) mandar certificado or (Méx) registrado ⒊ **registered** past p: (a) (Fin, Adm) ~ed **trademark** marca f registrada; ~ed **nurse** enfermero titulado, enfermera titulada m,f (b) (Post) certificado or (Méx) registrado ⒋ (a) (make known) ⟨complaint⟩ presentar (b) «dial» registrar, marcar*
■ ~ vi ⒈ (enroll) inscribirse*; (Educ) matricularse, inscribirse*; (at a hotel) registrarse ⒉ (show, be revealed) ser* detectado ⒊ (be understood, remembered): **eventually it ~ed who he was** al final caí en la cuenta de quién era

registrar /ˈredʒəstrɑːr ‖ˌredʒɪsˈtrɑː(r), ˈredʒɪstrɑː(r)/ n (a) (Soc Adm) funcionario encargado de llevar los registros de nacimientos, defunciones, etc (b) (in university, college) secretario, -ria m,f de admisiones

registration /ˌredʒəˈstreɪʃən ‖ˌredʒɪsˈtreɪʃən/ n (a) (enrollment) inscripción f, matrícula f; (Educ) inscripción f, matriculación f (b) (BrE Auto) (before n) ~ **number** (número m de) matrícula f

registry /ˈredʒəstri ‖ˈredʒɪstri/ n (pl -tries) registro m; (at university) secretaría f; (at church) ≈ sacristía f

registry office n (in UK) ≈ juzgado m (de paz)

regret¹ /rɪˈgret/ vt **-tt-** arrepentirse* de, lamentar; **we ~ to inform you that ...** lamentamos comunicarle or informarle que ...

regret² n (sadness) pesar m; (remorse) arrepentimiento m

regretful /rɪˈgretfəl/ adj ⟨expression⟩ de pesar

regretfully /rɪˈgretfəli/ adv con pesar; (indep) muy a mi (or nuestro etc) pesar, lamentablemente

regrettable /rɪˈgretəbəl/ adj lamentable

regrettably /rɪˈgretəbli/ adv lamentablemente

regroup /ˈriːˈgruːp/ vi reagruparse

regular¹ /ˈregjələr ‖ˈregjʊlə(r)/ adj **1** (a) ⟨pulse⟩ regular; ⟨breathing⟩ acompasado; **at ~ intervals** (in time) con regularidad; (in space) a intervalos regulares **(b)** ⟨customer/reader⟩ habitual, asiduo; **a ~ income** una fuente regular de ingresos; **on a ~ basis** con regularidad **(c)** (customary) habitual **2** (even, symmetrical) ⟨shape⟩ regular **3** (Ling) ⟨verb/plural⟩ regular **4** (colloq) (as intensifier) verdadero

regular² n cliente mf habitual, asiduo, -dua m,f

regularity /ˈregjəˈlærəti ‖ˌregjʊˈlærəti/ n regularidad f

regularly /ˈregjələrli ‖ˈregjʊləli/ adv con regularidad, regularmente; (frequently) con frecuencia

regulate /ˈregjəleɪt ‖ˈregjʊleɪt/ vt regular

regulation /ˈregjəˈleɪʃən ‖ˌregjʊˈleɪʃən/ n **1** (rule) norma f, regla f; (before n) ⟨dress/haircut⟩ reglamentario **2** (control, adjustment) regulación f

regurgitate /rɪˈgɜːrdʒəteɪt ‖rɪˈgɜːdʒɪteɪt/ vt ⟨food⟩ regurgitar; ⟨information⟩ repetir* mecánicamente

rehabilitate /ˈriːhəˈbɪləteɪt, ˈriːə- ‖ˌriːhəˈbɪlɪteɪt, ˌriːə-/ vt rehabilitar

rehabilitation /ˈriːhəˈbɪləˈteɪʃən, ˈriːə- ‖ˌriːhəˌbɪlɪˈteɪʃən, ˌriːə-/ n rehabilitación f

rehearsal /rɪˈhɜːrsəl ‖rɪˈhɜːsəl/ n ensayo m

rehearse /rɪˈhɜːrs ‖rɪˈhɜːs/ vt/i ensayar

reheat /ˈriːˈhiːt/ vt recalentar*

rehouse /ˈriːˈhaʊz/ vt realojar

reign¹ /reɪn/ n reinado m

reign² vi (a) «monarch» reinar **(b) reigning** pres p ⟨monarch⟩ reinante; ⟨champion⟩ actual

reimburse /ˈriːɪmˈbɜːrs ‖ˌriːɪmˈbɜːs/ vt reembolsar

rein /reɪn/ n (Equ) rienda f; **to give free ~ to sb** darle* carta blanca a algn

reincarnation /ˈriːɪnkɑːrˈneɪʃən ‖ˌriːɪnkɑːˈneɪʃən/ n reencarnación f

reindeer /ˈreɪndɪr ‖ˈreɪndɪə(r)/ n (pl ~) reno m

reinforce /ˈriːɪnˈfɔːrs ‖ˌriːɪnˈfɔːs/ vt reforzar*

reinforcement /ˈriːɪnˈfɔːrsmənt ‖ˌriːɪnˈfɔːsmənt/ n (a) (strengthening) refuerzo m **(b) reinforcements** pl refuerzos mpl

reinstate /ˈriːɪnˈsteɪt/ vt ⟨worker⟩ reintegrar, reincorporar; ⟨official⟩ restituir* en el cargo

reintegrate /ˈriːˈɪntəgreɪt/ vt reintegrar; **they must be ~d into society** es preciso reinsertarlos en la sociedad

reintegration /ˈriːˌɪntəˈgreɪʃən/ n reintegración f; (into society) reinserción f social

reissue /ˈriːˈɪʃuː/ vt ⟨book/record⟩ reeditar; ⟨document⟩ reexpedir*

reiterate /ˈriːˈɪtəreɪt/ vt (fml) reiterar, repetir*

reject¹ /rɪˈdʒekt/ vt rechazar*

reject² /ˈriːdʒekt/ n (flawed product) artículo m (or producto m etc) defectuoso

rejection /rɪˈdʒekʃən/ n rechazo m; (following job application) respuesta f negativa

rejoice /rɪˈdʒɔɪs/ vi alegrarse mucho, regocijarse (liter)

rejoin /ˈriːˈdʒɔɪn/ vt ⟨regiment/team⟩ reincorporarse a; ⟨firm⟩ reincorporarse a, reintegrarse a

rejuvenate /rɪˈdʒuːvəneɪt/ vt rejuvenecer*

rekindle /ˈriːˈkɪndl̩/ vt ⟨fire⟩ reavivar; ⟨desire⟩ reavivar

relapse¹ /ˈriːlæps/ n recaída f

relapse² /rɪˈlæps/ vi recaer*, tener* or sufrir una recaída

relate /rɪˈleɪt/ vt **1** (link) **to ~ sth TO sth** relacionar algo CON algo **2** (tell) (frml) ⟨story⟩ relatar, referir* (liter)
■ ~ vi **1** (a) (be connected with) **to ~ TO sth** estar* relacionado CON algo **(b)** relating to (as prep) relativo a, relacionado con **2** (understand, sympathize with) **to ~ TO sb** sintonizar* CON algn; **to ~ TO sth** identificarse* CON algo

related /rɪˈleɪtɪd ‖rɪˈleɪtɪd/ adj **(a)** (of same family) (pred) **to be ~ (TO sb)** ser* pariente (DE algn), estar* emparentado (CON algn) **(b)** ⟨ideas/questions/subjects⟩ relacionado, afín

relation /rɪˈleɪʃən/ n **1** (relative) pariente mf, pariente, -ta m,f, familiar m **2** (a) (connection) relación f **(b)** in relation to (as prep) en relación con, con relación a **3** relations pl relaciones fpl; **sexual ~s** relaciones sexuales

relationship /rɪˈleɪʃənʃɪp/ n **1** (between people) relación f **2** (between things, events) relación f **3** (kinship) **~ (TO sb)** parentesco m (CON algn)

relative¹ /ˈrelətɪv/ n pariente mf, pariente, -ta m,f, familiar mf

relative² adj **(a)** (comparative): **the ~ merits of** los pros y los contras de **(b)** (not absolute) relativo; **it's all ~** (set phrase) todo es relativo (fr hecha) **(c)** relative to (compared to) en comparación con

relatively /ˈrelətɪvli/ adv relativamente

relax /rɪˈlæks/ vi relajarse
■ ~ vt relajar; **she ~ed her grip** sujetó con menos fuerza

relaxation /ˈriːlækˈseɪʃən/ n (rest) relax m; (recreation) esparcimiento m, distracción f

relaxed /rɪˈlækst/ adj ⟨manner/person⟩ relajado; ⟨atmosphere/party⟩ informal

relaxing /rɪˈlæksɪŋ/ adj relajante

relay¹ /ˈriːleɪ/ n (a) (team) relevo m; **to work in ~s** trabajar en or por relevos **(b) ~ (race)** (Sport) carrera f de relevos or (AmL) de postas

relay² /ˈriːleɪ, rɪˈleɪ/ vt transmitir

release¹ /rɪˈliːs/ vt **1** ⟨prisoner/hostage⟩ poner* en libertad, liberar **2** ⟨information⟩ hacer* público; ⟨record/book⟩ sacar* (a la venta); ⟨movie⟩ estrenar **3** (emit) ⟨gas⟩ despedir* **4** ⟨brake/clutch⟩ soltar*

release² n **1** (from prison, captivity) puesta f en libertad, liberación f **2** (of record) salida f al mercado; (of movie) estreno m; **in o** (BrE) **on general ~** en todos los cines

relegate /ˈreləgeɪt ‖ˈrelɪgeɪt/ vt **(a)** (consign,   ⋯⋙

demote) relegar* **(b)** (BrE Sport) (*usu pass*): **the team was ∼d to the third division** el equipo descendió *or* bajó a tercera división

relent /rɪ'lent/ *vi* ⟨*person*⟩ transigir*, ceder

relentless /rɪ'lentləs ‖rɪ'lentlɪs/ *adj* ⟨*enemy/pursuer*⟩ implacable; ⟨*pursuit*⟩ incesante

relentlessly /rɪ'lentləsli ‖rɪ'lentlɪsli/ *adv* implacablemente

relevance /'reləvəns/ *n* (connection) relación *f*; (importance) relevancia *f*

relevant /'reləvənt/ *adj* ⟨*document/facts*⟩ pertinente, relevante

reliability /rɪˌlaɪə'bɪləti/ *n* (of worker) formalidad *f*, responsabilidad *f*; (of sources) fiabilidad *f*; (of vehicle) fiabilidad *f*

reliable /rɪ'laɪəbəl/ *adj* **(a)** ⟨*information/source*⟩ fidedigno; ⟨*witness*⟩ fiable, confiable (esp AmL) **(b)** ⟨*worker*⟩ responsable, de confianza; ⟨*vehicle*⟩ fiable

reliably /rɪ'laɪəbli/ *adv*: **I am ∼ informed that ...** sé de fuentes fidedignas que ..., sé de buena fuente que ...

reliant /rɪ'laɪənt/ *adj* (*pred*) **to be ∼ on sth/sb** depender DE algo/algn

relic /'relɪk/ *n* reliquia *f*

relief /rɪ'liːf/ *n* ⓵ (from worry, pain) alivio *m*; **it's a ∼ that the rain's stopped at last** menos mal que ha parado de llover ⓶ (aid) ayuda *f*, auxilio *m* (*de emergencia*); **to be on ∼** (AmE) recibir prestaciones de la seguridad social ⓷ (replacement) relevo *m* ⓸ (Art, Geog) relieve *m*

relieve /rɪ'liːv/ *vt* **(a)** ⟨*pain*⟩ calmar, aliviar; ⟨*suffering*⟩ mitigar*, aliviar; ⟨*tension*⟩ aliviar; **to ∼ sb of his/her duties** relevar a algn de su cargo **(b)** ⟨*town/fortress*⟩ liberar **(c)** ⟨*guard/driver*⟩ relevar
■ *v refl* **to ∼ oneself** (euph) orinar

relieved /rɪ'liːvd/ *adj* aliviado; **to feel ∼** sentir* un gran alivio, sentirse* aliviado

religion /rɪ'lɪdʒən/ *n* religión *f*

religious /rɪ'lɪdʒəs/ *adj* religioso

religiously /rɪ'lɪdʒəsli/ *adv* religiosamente

relinquish /rɪ'lɪŋkwɪʃ/ *vt* renunciar a

relish¹ /'relɪʃ/ *vt* ⟨*meal/joke/success*⟩ saborear; **I don't ∼ the prospect of ...** no me entusiasma *or* no me hace ninguna gracia la perspectiva de ...

relish² *n* ⓵ (Culin) salsa o conserva que se come con carnes ⓶ (enjoyment): **with ∼** ⟨*eat/drink*⟩ con gusto, con fruición; ⟨*read/listen to*⟩ con placer, con deleite

relive /'riː'lɪv/ *vt* revivir

relocate /'riːləʊ'keɪt/ *vt* trasladar
■ ∼ *vi* «*company*» trasladarse; «*employee*» mudarse *or* trasladarse de domicilio

reluctance /rɪ'lʌktəns/ *n* renuencia *f* (fml)

reluctant /rɪ'lʌktənt/ *adj* reacio, renuente

reluctantly /rɪ'lʌktəntli/ *adv* a su (*or* mi *etc*) pesar, a regañadientes

rely /rɪ'laɪ/ *vi* **relies, relying, relied (a)** (have confidence) **to ∼ on** *or* **upon sb/sth** contar* CON

algn/algo; **you can ∼ on me** puedes contar conmigo; **she can't be relied (up)on to help** no se puede contar con *or* confiar en que vaya a ayudar **(b)** (be dependent) **to ∼ ON sb/sth FOR sth** depender* DE algn/algo (PARA algo)

remain /rɪ'meɪn/ *vi* ⓵ **(a)** (+ *adj or adv compl*) (continue to be) seguir*, continuar*; **her condition ∼s critical** su estado sigue siendo crítico; **he ∼ed silent** se mantuvo en silencio **(b)** (stay) quedarse, permanecer* (fml); **to ∼ behind** quedarse ⓶ **(a)** (be left) quedar; **what still ∼s to be done?** ¿qué queda por hacer?; **that ∼s to be seen** eso está por verse **(b) remaining** *pres p*: **the ∼ing ten pounds** las diez libras restantes *or* que quedan

remainder /rɪ'meɪndər ‖rɪ'meɪndə(r)/ *n* **the ∼** el resto

remains /rɪ'meɪnz/ *pl n* restos *mpl*; (of meal) sobras *fpl*, restos *mpl*

remake¹ /'riːmeɪk/ *n* nueva versión *f*

remake² /'riː'meɪk/ *vt* (*past & past p* **remade**) volver* a hacer, rehacer*

remand¹ /rɪ'mænd ‖rɪ'maːnd/ *vt*: **to be ∼ed on bail** quedar en libertad bajo fianza; **he was ∼ed in custody** se decretó su prisión preventiva

remand² *n*: **to be on ∼** (in detention) estar* en prisión preventiva

remand centre, remand home *n* (in UK) *centro para menores en prisión preventiva*

remark¹ /rɪ'maːrk ‖rɪ'maːk/ *n* comentario *m*, observación *f*

remark² *vi* **to ∼ on** *o* **upon sth** hacer* un comentario/comentarios ACERCA DE algo
■ ∼ *vt* observar, comentar

remarkable /rɪ'maːrkəbəl ‖rɪ'maːkəbəl/ *adj* ⟨*ability/likeness*⟩ notable; ⟨*achievement*⟩ sorprendente; ⟨*coincidence*⟩ extraordinario; ⟨*person*⟩ excepcional

remarkably /rɪ'maːrkəbli ‖rɪ'maːkəbli/ *adv* **(a)** (surprisingly) sorprendentemente **(b)** (exceptionally) ⟨*stupid*⟩ increíblemente

remarry /'riː'mæri/ *vi* **-ries, -rying, -ried** volver* a casarse

remedial /rɪ'miːdiəl/ *adj* de recuperación

remedy¹ /'remədi/ *n* (*pl* **-dies**) remedio *m*

remedy² *vt* **-dies, -dying, -died** ⟨*mistake/situation*⟩ remediar; ⟨*injustice/evil*⟩ reparar

remember /rɪ'membər ‖rɪ'membə(r)/ *vt* ⓵ (recall) acordarse* de, recordar*; **I ∼ him saying something about ...** me acuerdo de *or* recuerdo que dijo algo de ... ⓶ **(a)** (be mindful of, not forget): **to ∼ to** + INF acordarse* DE + INF **(b)** (commemorate) ⟨*dead*⟩ recordar* **(c)** (send regards): **∼ me to your mother** dale recuerdos *or* saludos a tu madre (de mi parte)
■ ∼ *vi* **(a)** (recall) acordarse*, recordar*; **try to ∼!** ¡haz memoria! **(b)** (be mindful, not forget) no olvidarse

remembrance /rɪ'membrəns/ *n* (liter *or* fml) recuerdo *m*, remembranza *f* (liter); **in ∼ of sth/sb** en memoria de algo/algn; (*before n*) **R∼ Sunday**

AmC	América Central	Arg	Argentina	Cu	Cuba	Per	Perú
AmL	América Latina	Bol	Bolivia	Ec	Ecuador	RPI	Río de la Plata
AmS	América del Sur	Chi	Chile	Esp	España	Ur	Uruguay
Andes	Región andina	CS	Cono Sur	Méx	México	Ven	Venezuela

remind ⋯⟶ repeal ⋯ ⋯

(in UK) *domingo de noviembre en que se conmemora a los caídos en las dos guerras mundiales y otros conflictos*

remind /rɪ'maɪnd/ *vt* recordarle* a; oh, that ~s me ¡ah! por cierto ..., y a propósito ...; **to ~ sb to + INF** recordarle* a algn QUE (+ *subj*); **he ~s me of my grandfather** me recuerda a mi abuelo

reminder /rɪ'maɪndər ‖rɪ'maɪndə(r)/ *n* **(a)** **to serve as a ~ of sth** recordar* algo **(b)** (requesting payment) recordatorio *m* de pago

reminisce /'remə'nɪs ‖,remɪ'nɪs/ *vi* rememorar los viejos tiempos; **to ~ ABOUT sth** rememorar algo

reminiscences /'remə'nɪsnsɪz ‖,remɪ'nɪsnsɪz/ *pl n* recuerdos *mpl*, memorias *fpl*

reminiscent /'remə'nɪsnt ‖,remɪ'nɪsnt/ *adj* (*pred*) **to be ~ OF sb/sth** recordar* a algn/(a) algo

remiss /rɪ'mɪs/ *adj* (fml) (*pred*) negligente

remission /rɪ'mɪʃən/ *n* remisión *f*

remit /rɪ'mɪt/ *vt* **-tt-** (fml) **1** (send) remitir (fml) **2** (Law) ⟨*sentence*⟩ perdonar, condonar (fml)

remnant /'remnənt/ *n* **(a)** (leftover): **a ~ of the past** una reliquia del pasado; **the ~s of a meal** los restos de una comida **(b)** (Tex) retazo *m*, retal *m* (Esp)

remonstrate /rɪ'mɑːnstreɪt, 'remən- ‖'remənstreɪt/ *vi* protestar, quejarse; **to ~ with sb about sth** reprocharle algo a algn

remorse /rɪ'mɔːrs ‖rɪ'mɔːs/ *n* remordimiento *m*

remorseful /rɪ'mɔːrsfəl ‖rɪ'mɔːsfəl/ *adj* arrepentido

remorseless /rɪ'mɔːrsləs ‖rɪ'mɔːslɪs/ *adj* despiadado

remote /rɪ'məʊt/ *adj* **-ter, -test** remoto **remote: ~ control** *n* mando *m* a distancia, control *m* remoto; **~-controlled** /rɪ'məʊtkən'trəʊld/ *adj* (*pred* ~ **controlled**) ⟨*TV/hi-fi*⟩ con mando a distancia *or* con control remoto; ⟨*model/toy*⟩ de control remoto

remotely /rɪ'məʊtli/ *adv* (at all, in the least) (*usu with neg*) remotamente

remould[1] /'riː'məʊld/ *vt* (BrE Auto) ▶ RETREAD[1]

remould[2] /'riː'məʊld/ *n* (BrE Auto) ▶ RETREAD[2]

removable /rɪ'muːvəbəl/ *adj* ⟨*hood/lining*⟩ de quita y pon; ⟨*handle/shelf*⟩ desmontable

removal /rɪ'muːvəl/ *n* **1** (of contents) extracción *f*; (of appendix, tonsils) extirpación *f* **2** (of stain, unwanted hair) eliminación *f* **3** **(a)** (moving, taking away) traslado *m* **(b)** (from house to house) (BrE) mudanza *f*

remove /rɪ'muːv/ *vt* **1** **(a)** (take off) quitar, sacar* **(b)** (take out) ⟨*contents*⟩ sacar*; ⟨*tonsils/appendix*⟩ extirpar (fml); ⟨*bullet*⟩ extraer* (fml) **2** **(a)** (get rid of) ⟨*stain/grease*⟩ quitar; ⟨*unwanted hair*⟩ eliminar **(b)** ⟨*doubt*⟩ disipar; ⟨*threat*⟩ eliminar **3** (take away, move) ⟨*object*⟩ quitar; ⟨*person*⟩ sacar* **4** (dismiss from post, position) destituir*

remover /rɪ'muːvər ‖rɪ'muːvə(r)/ *n* (substance): **makeup ~** desmaquillador *m*; **nail polish** *o* (BrE also) **nail varnish ~** quitaesmalte *m*

remuneration /rɪ'mjuːnə'reɪʃən/ *n* (fml) remuneración *f*

renaissance /'renə'sɑːns ‖rɪ'neɪsəns/ *n* **(a)** **Renaissance** Renacimiento *m* **(b)** (revival) (liter) renacimiento *m*

rename /'riː'neɪm/ *vt* dar* un nuevo nombre a

render /'rendər ‖'rendə(r)/ *vt* **1** (make): **to ~ sth useless** hacer* que algo resulte inútil **2** (give, proffer) (fml) ⟨*thanks*⟩ dar*; ⟨*assistance*⟩ prestar; **for services ~ed** por servicios prestados **3** (translate) traducir*

rendezvous /'rɑːndeɪvuː ‖'rɒndɪvuː, -deɪvuː/ *n* (*pl* ~ /-z/) (meeting) encuentro *m*, cita *f*; (place) lugar *m* señalado para un encuentro *or* una cita

rendition /ren'dɪʃən/ *n* interpretación *f*

renegade /'renɪgeɪd/ *n* renegado, -da *m,f*

renew /rɪ'nuː ‖rɪ'njuː/ *vt* **(a)** ⟨*hope/promise*⟩ renovar*; ⟨*efforts/friendship*⟩ reanudar; ⟨*library book*⟩ renovar* **(b) renewed** *past p* renovado

renewal /rɪ'nuːəl ‖rɪ'njuːəl/ *n* renovación *f*

renounce /rɪ'naʊns/ *vt* **(a)** (cede) (fml) ⟨*claim/title*⟩ renunciar a **(b)** (reject) ⟨*religion*⟩ renunciar a

renovate /'renəveɪt/ *vt* renovar*

renovation /'renə'veɪʃən/ *n* renovación *f*

renown /rɪ'naʊn/ *n* renombre *m*, fama *f*

renowned /rɪ'naʊnd/ *adj* de renombre

rent[1] /rent/ *n* **(a)** (for accommodations, office) alquiler *m*, arrendamiento *m*, arriendo *m*, renta *f* (esp Méx) **(b)** (for boat, suit) (esp AmE) alquiler *m*, arriendo *m* (esp Andes), renta *f* (Méx)

rent[2] *vt* **(a)** (pay for) **to ~ sth** (FROM sb) alquilarle *or* arrendarle* *or* (Méx tb) rentarle algo (A algn) **(b)** ▶ RENT OUT
  ■ **rent out** [*v + o + adv, v + adv + o*] alquilar, arrendar*

rental /'rentl/ *n* **(a)** (act of renting) alquiler *m*, arriendo *m* (esp Andes) **(b)** (charge) alquiler *m*, renta *f* (Méx), arriendo *m* (esp Andes)

renunciation /rɪ'nʌnsi'eɪʃən/ *n* (fml) **(a)** (of faith) rechazo *m* **(b)** (of claim, right, title) renuncia *f*

reopen /'riː'əʊpən ‖,riː'əʊpən/ *vt* ⟨*book/road*⟩ volver* a abrir; ⟨*negotiations/hostilities*⟩ reanudar; ⟨*criminal case*⟩ reabrir*
  ■ ~ *vi* abrir* de nuevo

reorganize /'riː'ɔːrgənaɪz ‖,riː'ɔːgənaɪz/ *vt* reorganizar*

rep /rep/ *n* (sales ~) representante *mf or* agente *mf* (comercial); **a union ~** un/una representante *or* (Esp) un/una enlace sindical

repair[1] /rɪ'per ‖rɪ'peə(r)/ *vt* ⟨*machinery/roof*⟩ arreglar, reparar; ⟨*shoes/clothes*⟩ arreglar

repair[2] *n* arreglo *m*, reparación *f*; **the museum is closed for ~s** el museo está cerrado por obras; **in a good/bad state of ~, in good/bad ~** en buen/mal estado

repairer /rɪ'perər ‖rɪ'peərə(r)/ *n* técnico, -ca *m,f*; **watch ~** (BrE) relojero, -ra *m,f*

repairman /rɪ'permæn ‖rɪ'peəmæn/ *n* (*pl* **-men** /-men/) técnico *m*

repatriate /'riː'peɪtrieɪt ‖,riː'pætrɪeɪt/ *vt* repatriar

repay /'riː'peɪ/ *vt* (*past & past p* **repaid**) **(a)** ⟨*money/loan*⟩ devolver*; ⟨*debt*⟩ pagar*, cancelar **(b)** ⟨*kindness/favor*⟩ pagar*, corresponder a

repayment /'riː'peɪmənt/ *n* **(a)** (act of repaying) pago *m* **(b)** (installment) plazo *m*, cuota *f* (AmL)

repeal[1] /rɪ'piːl/ *vt* (Govt, Law) revocar*

r

repeal² *n* revocación *f*

repeat¹ /rɪ'piːt/ *vt* **1** **(a)** (say again) repetir*
(b) (divulge) contar* **2** (do again) repetir*
■ *v refl* to ~ oneself repetirse*
■ ~ *vi* repetir*

repeat² *n* repetición *f*

repeated /rɪ'piːtəd ‖rɪ'piːtɪd/ *adj* (before *n*)
⟨attempts⟩ repetido, reiterado; ⟨requests⟩
reiterado

repeatedly /rɪ'piːtədli ‖rɪ'piːtɪdli/ *adv*
repetidamente, reiteradamente

repel /rɪ'pel/ *vt* **-ll-** **(a)** ⟨enemy/army⟩ repeler;
⟨attack⟩ repeler, rechazar* **(b)** ⟨insects⟩ repeler,
ahuyentar **(c)** (disgust) repeler, repugnar

repellant /rɪ'pelənt/ *n*: insect ~ repelente *m*
para insectos

repellent /rɪ'pelənt/ *adj* repelente

repent /rɪ'pent/ *vi* arrepentirse*

repentance /rɪ'pentn̩s/ *n* arrepentimiento *m*

repentant /rɪ'pentn̩t/ *adj* arrepentido

repercussions /ˌriːpər'kʌʃənz
‖ˌriːpə'kʌʃənz/ *pl n* repercusiones *fpl*

repertoire /'repərtwɑːr ‖'repətwɑː(r)/ *n*
repertorio *m*

repertory /'repərtɔːri ‖'repətəri/ *n*: to be/act/
work in ~ trabajar en una compañía de
repertorio

repetition /ˌrepə'tɪʃən/ *n* repetición *f*

repetitious /ˌrepə'tɪʃəs/ *adj* repetitivo

repetitive /rɪ'petətɪv/ *adj* repetitivo

repetitive strain injury *n* lesión *f* por
fatiga crónica

rephrase /ˌriː'freɪz/ *vt* expresar de otra
manera

replace /rɪ'pleɪs/ *vt* **1** **(a)** (take the place of)
sustituir*, reemplazar* **(b)** ⟨lost item⟩ reponer*;
⟨broken window/battery⟩ cambiar **2** (put back in
its place) volver* a poner *or* colocar*; ⟨lid⟩ volver*
a poner; ⟨receiver⟩ colgar*

replacement /rɪ'pleɪsmənt/ *n* **(a)** (act)
sustitución *f*, reemplazo *m* **(b)** (person) sustituto,
-ta *m,f* **(c)** (object): **I'll buy you a** ~ te compraré
uno nuevo

replay¹ /ˌriː'pleɪ/ *vt* **(a)** (Sport) ⟨game/match⟩
volver* a jugar, repetir* **(b)** (Audio, Video) volver*
a poner

replay² /'riːpleɪ/ *n* (Sport) repetición *f* (de la
jugada)

replenish /rɪ'plenɪʃ/ *vt* ⟨stock⟩ reponer*

replete /rɪ'pliːt/ *adj* (liter) ~ WITH sth repleto DE
algo

replica /'replɪkə/ *n* (*pl* **-cas**) réplica *f*,
reproducción *f*

reply¹ /rɪ'plaɪ/ *n* (*pl* **replies**) (spoken, written)
respuesta *f*, contestación *f*; in ~ to your letter en
respuesta a su carta

reply² *vi/t* **replies, replying, replied**
responder, contestar

report¹ /rɪ'pɔːrt ‖rɪ'pɔːt/ *n* **1** **(a)** (account)
informe *m*; (piece of news) noticia *f*; (in newspaper)
reportaje *m*, crónica *f* **(b)** (evaluation) informe *m*,
reporte *m* (Méx); medical ~ parte *m* médico;
(school) ~ boletín *m* or (Méx) boleta *f* de
calificaciones **2** (sound) estallido *m*

report² *vt* **1** **(a)** (relate, announce): **several**
people ~ed seeing the tiger varias personas
dijeron haber visto al tigre; **he is** ~ed to be very
rich se dice que es muy rico **(b)** (Journ) «⟨reporter/
media⟩» informar sobre
2 **(a)** (notify) ⟨accident⟩ informar de, dar* parte
de; ⟨crime⟩ denunciar, dar* parte de, reportar
(AmL); to ~ sth TO sb dar* parte DE algo A algn
(b) (denounce) denunciar, reportar (AmL)
■ ~ *vi* **1** (Journ) «⟨reporter⟩» informar
2 (present oneself) presentarse, reportarse (AmL);
to ~ sick dar* parte de enfermo
■ **report back** [*v + adv*] **(a)** (return): to ~ back
(to base) regresar* a la base **(b)** (give report) to ~
back (TO sb) presentar un informe (A algn)

report card *n* (AmE Educ) boletín *m* or (Méx)
boleta *f* de calificaciones

reported speech /rɪ'pɔːrtəd ‖rɪ'pɔːtɪd/ *n*
estilo *m* indirecto

reporter /rɪ'pɔːrtər ‖rɪ'pɔːtə(r)/ *n* periodista
mf, reportero, -tera *m,f*

repose /rɪ'pəʊz/ *n* (liter) reposo *m*

repossess /ˌriːpə'zes/ *vt* ⟨car/house⟩ recuperar
la posesión de (*por falta de pago*)

reprehensible /ˌreprɪ'hensəbəl/ *adj*
reprensible

represent /ˌreprɪ'zent/ *vt* **1** **(a)** (stand for)
representar **(b)** (constitute) representar, constituir*
2 (act as representative for) ⟨client⟩ representar
3 (frml) (describe) presentar

representation /ˌreprɪzen'teɪʃən/ *n*
representación *f*

representative¹ /ˌreprɪ'zentətɪv/ *n* **(a)**
representante *mf* **(b)** (in US) (Govt) representante
mf, diputado, -da *m,f* **(c)** (sales ~) representante
mf or agente *mf* comercial

representative² *adj* representativo

repress /rɪ'pres/ *vt* reprimir

repression /rɪ'preʃən/ *n* represión *f*

repressive /rɪ'presɪv/ *adj* represivo

reprieve¹ /rɪ'priːv/ *n* (Law) indulto *m*

reprieve² *vt* indultar

reprimand¹ /'reprəmænd ‖'reprɪmɑːnd/ *n*
reprimenda *f*

reprimand² *vt* reprender

reprint¹ /'riːprɪnt/ *n* (Publ) reimpresión *f*; (Phot)
copia *f*

reprint² /ˌriː'prɪnt/ *vt* (Publ) reimprimir*

reprisal /rɪ'praɪzəl/ *n* represalia *f*

reproach¹ /rɪ'prəʊtʃ/ *vt* to ~ sb FOR -ING: he
~ed her for not having written to him le reprochó
que no le hubiera escrito

reproach² *n* reproche *m*; above *o* beyond ~
irreprochable, intachable

reproachful /rɪ'prəʊtʃfəl/ *adj* (lleno) de
reproche

reproduce /ˌriːprə'duːs ‖ˌriːprə'djuːs/ *vt*
reproducir*
■ ~ *vi* (Biol) reproducirse*

reproduction /ˌriːprə'dʌkʃən/ *n* reproducción
f

reproductive /ˌriːprə'dʌktɪv/ *adj* reproductor

reproof /rɪ'pruːf/ *n* (frml) reprobación *f*

reprove /rɪ'pruːv/ *vt* (frml) to ~ sb (FOR sth)
reprender *or* (frml) reconvenir* a algn (POR algo)

reptile /'reptl̩, -taɪl ‖'reptaɪl/ *n* reptil *m*

republic /rɪ'pʌblɪk/ n república f

republican¹ /rɪ'pʌblɪkən/ adj **(a)** (of a republic) republicano **(b) Republican** (in US) republicano

republican² n **(a)** (supporter of republic) republicano, -na m,f **(b) Republican** (in US) republicano, -na m,f

repudiate /rɪ'pju:dieɪt/ vt **(a)** (deny) ⟨accusation⟩ rechazar*, negar* **(b)** ⟨violence/ family⟩ repudiar

repugnance /rɪ'pʌgnəns/ n repugnancia f

repugnant /rɪ'pʌgnənt/ adj repugnante

repulse /rɪ'pʌls/ vt repeler, rechazar*

repulsion /rɪ'pʌlʃən/ n (fml) repulsión f

repulsive /rɪ'pʌlsɪv/ adj repulsivo, repugnante

reputable /'repjətəbəl ǁ 'repjʊtəbəl/ adj acreditado (fml), reputado (fml)

reputation /'repjə'teɪʃən ǁ 'repjʊ'teɪʃən/ n reputación f; **good/bad** ～ buena/mala reputación or fama; **a** ～ **FOR** sth fama DE algo

repute /rɪ'pju:t/ n (fml) reputación f, fama f; **of** ～ de renombre

reputed /rɪ'pju:təd ǁ rɪ'pju:tɪd/ adj presunto, supuesto; **she is** ～ **to be the best in the world** está considerada como la mejor del mundo

reputedly /rɪ'pju:tədli ǁ rɪ'pjʊtɪdli/adv (indep) según se dice or cree

request¹ /rɪ'kwest/ n **(a)** (polite demand) petición f, pedido m (esp AmL), solicitud f (fml); ～ **FOR** sth petición (or pedido etc) DE algo **(b)** (for song) petición f, pedido m (esp AmL)

request² vt pedir*, solicitar (fml)

requiem /'rekwiəm/ n réquiem m

require /rɪ'kwaɪr ǁ rɪ'kwaɪə(r)/ vt **1 (a)** (need) necesitar; (call for) ⟨patience/dedication⟩ requerir*, exigir* **(b)** (demand) **to** ～ **sb/sth to + INF** requerir* que algn/algo (+ subj); **I shall do all that is** ～**d of me** haré todo lo que me corresponda **2 required** past p **(a)** ⟨dose/amount⟩ necesario **(b)** (compulsory) ⟨reading/viewing⟩ obligado

requirement /rɪ'kwaɪrmənt ǁ rɪ'kwaɪəmənt/ n **(a)** (usu pl) (need) necesidad f **(b)** (condition) requisito m

requisite /'rekwəzət ǁ 'rekwɪzɪt/ adj (fml) necesario, requerido

requisition /'rekwə'zɪʃən ǁ ,rekwɪ'zɪʃən/ vt requisar

reroute /'ri:'ru:t/ vt desviar*

reschedule /'ri:'skedʒu:l ǁ ,ri:'ʃedju:l/ vt ⟨meeting⟩ cambiar la hora/fecha de

rescind /rɪ'sɪnd/ vt (fml) ⟨contract⟩ rescindir; ⟨order/ruling⟩ revocar*; ⟨law⟩ derogar*

rescue¹ /'reskju:/ n rescate m; **they went to his** ～ acudieron a socorrerlo (liter), fueron or (liter) acudieron en su auxilio

rescue² vt rescatar, salvar

rescuer /'reskjuər ǁ 'reskju:ə(r)/ n salvador, -dora m,f

research¹ /rɪ'sɜ:rtʃ, 'ri:sɜ:rtʃ ǁ rɪ'sɜ:tʃ/ n investigación f; ～ **INTO/ON** sth investigación SOBRE algo

research² vi investigar*

■ ～ vt ⟨causes/problem⟩ investigar*, estudiar; **this article is well** ～**ed** este artículo está bien documentado

researcher /rɪ'sɜ:rtʃər ǁ rɪ'sɜ:tʃə(r)/ n investigador, -dora m,f

resemblance /rɪ'zembləns/ n parecido m, semejanza f; ～ **TO** sb/sth parecido CON algn/algo

resemble /rɪ'zembəl/ vt parecerse* a

resent /rɪ'zent/ vt ⟨person⟩ guardarle rencor a; **he** ～**ed her success** le molestaba que ella tuviera éxito; **I** ～ **having to help him** me molesta tener que ayudarle

resentful /rɪ'zentfəl/ adj ⟨person⟩ resentido, rencoroso; ⟨air/look⟩ de resentimiento

resentment /rɪ'zentmənt/ n resentimiento m, rencor m

reservation /'rezər'veɪʃən ǁ,rezə'veɪʃən/ n **(a)** (booking) reserva f, reservación f (AmL) **(b)** (doubt, qualification) reserva f; **without** ～ sin reservas **(c)** (land) (in US) reserva f, reservación f (AmL)

reserve¹ /rɪ'zɜ:rv ǁ rɪ'zɜ:v/ n **1** (stock) reserva f; **to keep sth in** ～ ⟨money/food⟩ tener* algo reservado **2** (Sport) reserva mf **3 reserves** pl (Mil) reservas fpl **4** (land) coto m, reserva f **5** (self-restraint) reserva f, cautela f

reserve² vt **(a)** (book) ⟨room/table⟩ reservar **(b)** (keep, save) reservar, guardar; **to** ～ **(one's) judgment** reservarse la opinión

reserved /rɪ'zɜ:rvd ǁ rɪ'zɜ:vd/ adj reservado

reservoir /'rezərvwɑ:r ǁ 'rezəvwɑ:(r)/ n embalse m, presa f, represa f (AmS)

reset /'ri:'set/ vt (pres p **resetting**; past & past p **reset**) **(a)** ⟨alarm clock⟩ (volver* a) poner*; ⟨counter/dial⟩ volver* a cero **(b)** (Med) ⟨bone⟩ colocar*

reshuffle /'ri:'ʃʌfəl/ n reorganización f; **cabinet** ～ remodelación f del gabinete

reside /rɪ'zaɪd/ vi (fml) residir (fml)

residence /'rezədəns ǁ 'rezɪdəns/ n **1 (a)** (in a country) residencia f **(b)** (in building) (fml) residencia f; **to take up** ～ instalarse **(c)** ～ **hall** (AmE) residencia f universitaria or de estudiantes, colegio m mayor (Esp) **2** (home) residencia f

resident¹ /'rezədənt ǁ 'rezɪdənt/ n **(a)** (in country) residente mf **(b)** (of district) vecino, -na m,f

resident² adj residente

residential /'rezə'dentʃəl ǁ ,rezɪ'denʃəl/ adj ⟨area/suburb⟩ residencial; ⟨course⟩ con alojamiento para los asistentes

residue /'rezədu: ǁ 'rezɪdju:/ n residuo m

resign /rɪ'zaɪn/ vi renunciar, dimitir; **to** ～ **FROM** sth renunciar A algo, dimitir algo

■ v refl **to** ～ **oneself (TO** sth/-**ING)** resignarse (A algo/+ INF)

resignation /'rezɪg'neɪʃən/ n **1** (from job, position) renuncia f, dimisión f **2** (acceptance, submission) resignación f

resigned /rɪ'zaɪnd/ adj resignado

resilience /rɪ'zɪljəns ǁ rɪ'zɪliəns/ n **(a)** (of person) capacidad f de recuperación, resistencia f **(b)** (of material) elasticidad f

resilient /rɪ'zɪljənt ǁ rɪ'zɪliənt/ adj **(a)** ⟨person⟩ fuerte, con capacidad de recuperación **(b)** ⟨material⟩ elástico

resin /'rezn̩ ǁ 'rezɪn/ n resina f

resist /rɪ'zɪst/ vt resistir; ‹change/plan› oponer* resistencia a; **I can't ~ chocolate** el chocolate me vuelve loco; **to ~ -ING** resistirse a + INF

resistance /rɪ'zɪstəns/ n resistencia f; **the ~** la resistencia

resistant /rɪ'zɪstənt/ adj resistente

resit¹ /'riː'sɪt/ vt (pres p **resitting**; past & past p **resat** /'riː'sæt/) (BrE) ‹examination› volver* a presentarse a

resit² /'riː'sɪt/ n (BrE): **to do a ~** volver* a examinarse

resolute /'rezəluːt/ adj resuelto, decidido

resolution /ˌrezə'luːʃən/ n **(a)** (decision) determinación f, propósito m; **New Year's ~s** buenos propósitos de Año Nuevo **(b)** (in US, passed by legislature) resolución f

resolve¹ /rɪ'zɑːlv ‖rɪ'zɒlv/ n resolución f

resolve² vt **(a)** (clear up) ‹difficulty› resolver*; ‹differences› saldar, resolver **(b)** (decide) **to ~ (to + INF)** resolver* or decidir (+ INF)

resonance /'rezṇəns ‖'rezənəns/ n resonancia f

resonant /'rezṇənt ‖'rezənənt/ adj resonante

resort /rɪ'zɔːrt ‖rɪ'zɔːt/ n **1** (for vacations) centro m turístico or vacacional; **a seaside ~** un centro turístico costero, un balneario (AmL); **a ski ~** una estación de esquí **2** (recourse) recurso m; **as a/the last ~** como último recurso
▪ **resort to** [v + prep + o]: **to ~ to force/violence** recurrir a la fuerza/violencia; **they had to ~ to strike action** no les quedó más remedio que ir a la huelga

resound /rɪ'zaʊnd/ vi retumbar, resonar*

resounding /rɪ'zaʊndɪŋ/ adj (before n) **(a)** ‹cheers/explosion› retumbante, resonante **(b)** ‹success/failure› rotundo

resource /'riːsɔːrs ‖rɪ'zɔːs/ n recurso m; **natural/human ~s** recursos naturales/humanos

resourceful /rɪ'sɔːrsfəl ‖rɪ'sɔːsfəl/ adj de recursos

respect¹ /rɪ'spekt/ n **1 (a)** (esteem) respeto m; **to have ~ for sb** respetar algn **(b)** (consideration) consideración f, respeto m **(c) respects** pl respetos mpl **2 (a)** (way, aspect) sentido m, respecto m; **in this ~** en cuanto a esto, en este sentido **(b) with respect to** (frml) (introducing subject) en lo que concierne a (frml); (in relation to) con respecto a

respect² vt respetar

respectable /rɪ'spektəbəl/ adj **1** (socially acceptable) ‹person/conduct› decente, respetable **2 (a)** (quite large) ‹amount/salary› respetable **(b)** (reasonably good) ‹performance/score› digno, aceptable

respected /rɪ'spektəd ‖rɪ'spektɪd/ adj respetado

respectful /rɪ'spektfəl/ adj respetuoso

respecting /rɪ'spektɪŋ/ prep (frml) en lo que concierne a (frml)

respective /rɪ'spektɪv/ adj (before n) respectivo

respiration /ˌrespə'reɪʃən ‖ˌrespɪ'reɪʃən/ n respiración f

respirator /'respəreɪtər ‖'respɪreɪtə(r)/ n **(a)** (Med) respirador m **(b)** (mask) máscara f de oxígeno

respiratory /'respərətɔːri ‖rɪ'spɪrətəri/ adj respiratorio

respite /'respət ‖'respaɪt/ n (no pl) respiro m, descanso m; **without ~** sin respiro

resplendent /rɪ'splendənt/ adj resplandeciente

respond /rɪ'spɑːnd ‖rɪ'spɒnd/ vi **(a)** (reply) responder, contestar **(b)** (react) responder, reaccionar

response /rɪ'spɑːns ‖rɪ'spɒns/ n **(a)** (reply) respuesta f **(b)** (reaction) respuesta f; (to news) reacción f

responsibility /rɪˌspɑːnsə'bɪləti ‖rɪˌspɒnsə'bɪləti/ n (pl **-ties**) **(a)** (task, duty) responsabilidad f **(b)** (authority, accountability) responsabilidad f; **to take ~ for sth** responsabilizarse* or encargarse* de algo **(c)** (liability, blame) responsabilidad f; **they took full ~ for the disaster** aceptaron ser responsables del desastre

responsible /rɪ'spɑːnsəbəl ‖rɪ'spɒnsəbəl/ adj **(a)** (accountable) (pred) **to be ~ (FOR sth): who's ~?** ¿quién es el responsable?; **a build-up of gas was ~ for the explosion** una acumulación de gas fue la causa de la explosión; **to hold sb ~ for sth** responsabilizar* or hacer* responsable a algn de algo **(b)** (in charge) (pred) **to be ~ FOR sth** ser* responsable DE algo **(c)** (trustworthy) responsable, formal **(d)** (before n) ‹post› de responsabilidad

responsibly /rɪ'spɑːnsəbli ‖rɪ'spɒnsɪbli/ adv con responsabilidad, responsablemente

responsive /rɪ'spɑːnsɪv ‖rɪ'spɒnsɪv/ adj ‹brakes/engine› sensible; ‹person/audience› receptivo

rest¹ /rest/ n
I 1 (a) (break) descanso m; **to have a ~** tomarse un descanso **(b)** (relaxation) descanso m, reposo m; **try to get some ~** trata de descansar un poco **2** (motionlessness) **to come to ~** detenerse* **3** (support) apoyo m **4** (Mus) silencio m
II (remainder) **the ~: the ~ of the money** el resto del dinero; **the ~ of the children** los demás niños

rest² vi **1** (relax) descansar **2 (a)** (be supported) **to ~ ON sth** (Const) descansar or apoyarse EN or SOBRE algo **(b)** (be based, depend) **to ~ ON sth** «argument/theory» descansar SOBRE algo **(c)** (stop) **to ~ ON sth/sb** «eyes/gaze» detenerse* SOBRE algo/algn **3** (be responsibility of) **to ~ WITH sb** «responsibility» recaer* SOBRE algn
▪ **~** vt **1** (relax) descansar **2** (place for support) apoyar
▪ **rest up** [v + adv] (AmE) descansar

rest area n (AmE) área f‡ de reposo

restaurant /'restərɑːnt ‖'restrɒnt/ n restaurante m, restorán m

restaurant car n (BrE) coche-comedor m, vagón m restaurante

AmC Central America	Arg	Argentina	Cu	Cuba	Per	Peru
AmL Latin America	Bol	Bolivia	Ec	Ecuador	RPI	River Plate Area
AmS South America	Chi	Chile	Esp	Spain	Ur	Uruguay
Andes Andean Region	CS	Southern Cone	Méx	Mexico	Ven	Venezuela

restful /'restfəl/ adj tranquilo, apacible

restless /'restləs ‖'restlɪs/ adj ‹person/ manner› inquieto; ‹waves/wind› (liter) agitado

restoration /'restə'reɪʃən/ n [1] (a) (of order, peace) restablecimiento m (b) (to throne, power) restauración f, reinstauración f [2] (of building, painting) restauración f

restore /rɪ'stɔːr ‖rɪ'stɔː(r)/ vt [1] (a) (re-establish) ‹order/peace› restablecer*; ‹confidence/health/energy› devolver*; ‹monarchy/ king› restaurar, reinstaurar (b) (give back) (frml) restituir* (frml) [2] ‹building/painting› restaurar

restrain /rɪ'streɪn/ vt contener*
■ v refl to ~ oneself contenerse*, refrenarse

restrained /rɪ'streɪnd/ adj ‹person/behavior› moderado, comedido; ‹colors/style› sobrio

restraint /rɪ'streɪnt/ n (a) (self-control) compostura f, circunspección f (b) (restriction) limitación f, restricción f

restrict /rɪ'strɪkt/ vt ‹power/freedom/access› restringir*, limitar; ‹imports/movements› restringir*

restricted /rɪ'strɪktəd ‖rɪ'strɪktɪd/ adj (a) ‹number/space› limitado (b) ‹information› confidencial; ~ area (Mil) zona f restringida

restriction /rɪ'strɪkʃən/ n restricción f

restrictive /rɪ'strɪktɪv/ adj restrictivo

rest room n (AmE) baño m, servicio(s) m(pl)

restructure /'riː'strʌktʃər ‖,riː'strʌktʃə(r)/ vt reestructurar

rest stop n (AmE) ▶ REST AREA

result¹ /rɪ'zʌlt/ n [1] (a) (consequence) resultado m; **the company collapsed, with the ~ that ...** la compañía quebró, y como consecuencia ... (b) (of calculation, exam, contest) resultado m [2] **(a) as a result** (as linker) por consiguiente, por ende (frml) **(b) as a result of** (as prep) a raíz de

result² vi: **to ~ in** traer* como consecuencia, resultar en; **it could ~ in his dismissal** podría ocasionar or acarrear su despido

resultant /rɪ'zʌltənt/, **resulting** /rɪ'zʌltɪŋ/ adj (before n) consiguiente, resultante

resume /rɪ'zuːm ‖rɪ'zjuːm/ vt ‹work/journey› reanudar
■ ~ vi «negotiations/work» reanudarse, continuar*

resumé /'rezəmeɪ, 'rezəˈmeɪ ‖'rezjʊmeɪ/ n (a) (summary) resumen m (b) (of career) (AmE) currículum m (vitae), historial m personal

resurgence /rɪ'sɜːrdʒəns ‖rɪ'sɜːdʒəns/ n resurgimiento m, renacer m

resurrect /'rezəˈrekt/ vt desenterrar*, resucitar

resurrection /'rezəˈrekʃən/ n resurrección f

resuscitate /rɪ'sʌsəteɪt ‖rɪ'sʌsɪteɪt/ vt (Med) resucitar

resuscitation /rɪ'sʌsəˈteɪʃən ‖rɪ,sʌsɪˈteɪʃən/ n (Med) resucitación f

retail¹ /'riːteɪl/ vt vender al por menor or al detalle
■ ~ vi venderse al por menor

retail² n venta f al por menor or al detalle; (before n) ~ **price** precio m de venta al público, precio m al por menor

retailer /'riːteɪlər ‖'riːteɪlə(r)/ n minorista mf, detallista mf

retail price index n (BrE) índice m de precios al consumo

retain /rɪ'teɪn/ vt ‹property/money› quedarse con; ‹authority/power› retener*; ‹heat› conservar; ‹moisture/water› retener*; ‹information› retener*

retake¹ /'riːteɪk/ vt (past **retook**; past p **retaken**) (Educ) volver* a presentarse a, volver* a presentar

retake² /'riːteɪk/ n (of exam): **to do a ~** volver* a examinarse

retaliate /rɪ'tælieɪt/ vi (Mil) tomar represalias

retaliation /rɪ'tæliˈeɪʃən/ n represalias fpl

retarded /rɪ'tɑːrdəd ‖rɪ'tɑːdɪd/ adj (sometimes offensive) retrasado

retch /retʃ/ vi hacer* arcadas

retention /rɪ'tentʃən ‖rɪ'tenʃən/ n retención f

retentive /rɪ'tentɪv/ adj ‹memory› retentivo

rethink /'riː'θɪŋk/ vt (past & past p **rethought**) reconsiderar, replantearse

reticence /'retəsəns ‖'retɪsəns/ n reticencia f

reticent /'retəsənt ‖'retɪsənt/ adj reticente

retina /'retnə ‖'retɪnə/ n (pl **-nas** or **-nae** /-niː/) retina f

retinue /'retnuː ‖'retɪnjuː/ n séquito m, comitiva f

retire /rɪ'taɪr ‖rɪ'taɪə(r)/ vi [1] (from occupation) jubilarse, retirarse; «soldier/athlete» retirarse [2] **(a)** (retreat, withdraw) (frml) retirarse **(b)** (go to bed) (frml or hum) retirarse a sus (or mis etc) aposentos (frml o hum)

retired /rɪ'taɪrd ‖rɪ'taɪəd/ adj jubilado, retirado

retirement /rɪ'taɪrmənt ‖rɪ'taɪəmənt/ n (from job) jubilación f, retiro m

retiring /rɪ'taɪrɪŋ ‖rɪ'taɪərɪŋ/ adj (shy) retraído

retort¹ /rɪ'tɔːrt ‖rɪ'tɔːt/ vt replicar* (liter), contestar

retort² n réplica f (liter), contestación f

retrace /'riːtreɪs/ vt **to ~ one's steps** volver* sobre sus (or mis etc) pasos

retract /rɪ'trækt/ vt (a) ‹allegation/statement› retirar (b) ‹undercarriage› replegar*, levantar

retrain /'riːtreɪn/ vi hacer* un curso de reciclaje or recapacitación

retread¹ /'riːtred/ vt (past and past p ~**ed**) ‹tire› recauchutar, recauchar, reencauchar (AmC, Ven)

retread² /'riːtred/ n neumático m recauchutado or recauchado or (AmC, Ven) reencauchado, llanta f vulcanizada (AmL)

retreat¹ /rɪ'triːt/ vi retirarse

retreat² n [1] (Mil) retirada f, repliegue m [2] **(a)** (place) refugio m **(b)** (Relig) retiro m espiritual

retrial /'riː'traɪəl/ n nuevo juicio m

retribution /'retrəˈbjuːʃən ‖,retrɪˈbjuːʃən/ n castigo m

retrieve /rɪ'triːv/ vt ‹object/data› recuperar

retriever /rɪ'triːvər ‖rɪ'triːvə(r)/ n perro m cobrador

retrograde /'retrəgreɪd/ adj retrógrado

retrospect /'retrəspekt/ n: **in ~** mirando hacia atrás, en retrospectiva

retrospective¹ /'retrəˈspektɪv/ adj retrospectivo

r

retrospective² n (exposición f)
retrospectiva f

return¹ /rɪ'tɜːrn ‖ rɪ'tɜːn/ vi **(a)** (to place)
volver*, regresar; **to ~ TO sth** (to former activity,
state) volver* A algo **(b)** (reappear) «symptom»
volver* a aparecer; «doubts/suspicions»
resurgir*
■ ~ vt **1 (a)** (give back) devolver*, regresar (AmL
exc CS), restituir* (frml) **(b)** (reciprocate) «affection»
corresponder a; «blow/favor» devolver*; «greeting»
devolver*, corresponder a; **to ~ sb's call**
devolverle* la llamada a algn **(c)** (Sport) «ball»
devolver* **2** (Law) «verdict» emitir

return² n **1 (a)** (to place) regreso m, vuelta f,
retorno m (frml o liter) **(b)** (reappearance)
reaparición f; **many happy ~s of the day!** ¡que
cumplas muchos más! **2** (to owner) devolución f,
regreso m (AmL) **3** (in phrases) **in ~** (FOR sth) a
cambio (DE algo) **4** (profit) rendimiento m **5** (tax
~) declaración f (de la renta or de impuestos)
6 (ticket) (BrE) boleto m or (Esp) billete m de ida y
vuelta, boleto m de viaje redondo (Méx)

return³ adj (before n) «journey/flight» de vuelta,
de regreso; «ticket/fare» (BrE) de ida y vuelta, de
viaje redondo (Méx)

returnable /rɪ'tɜːrnəbəl ‖ rɪ'tɜːnəbəl/ adj
«deposit» reembolsable, reintegrable; «bottle»
retornable

reunion /riː'juːnjən/ n reunión f, reencuentro
m; **a family ~** una reunión familiar

reunite /'riːjʊ'naɪt/ vt «family/party» volver* a
unir; **to be ~d with sb** reencontrarse* con algn

reusable /riː'juːzəbəl/ adj reutilizable

reuse /'riː'juːz/ vt reutilizar*, volver* a usar

rev¹ /rev/ n revolución f

rev² vt **-vv- ~ (up)** «engine/car» acelerar (sin
desplazarse)

revalue /'riː'væljuː/, (AmE also) **revaluate**
/-juert/ vt «currency» revalorizar*, revaluar* (esp
AmL); «house» reevaluar*, revaluar*

revamp /'riː'væmp/ vt «kitchen/interior»
reformar; (modernize) modernizar*; «image»
cambiar; «organization» modernizar*

reveal /rɪ'viːl/ vt **(a)** (disclose) revelar, develar
(AmL), desvelar (Esp) **(b)** (bring to view) dejar ver

revealing /rɪ'viːlɪŋ/ adj revelador

revel /'revəl/ vi, (BrE) **-ll-** (enjoy greatly) **to ~ IN**
sth deleitarse CON or EN algo

revelation /revə'leɪʃən/ n **(a)** (disclosure)
revelación f **(b)** (Bib): **(the Book of) Revelations** el
Apocalipsis

reveler, (BrE) **reveller** /'revələr ‖ 'revələ(r)/ n
(liter) juerguista mf (fam)

revelry /'revəlri/ n (pl **-ries**) jolgorio m

revenge¹ /rɪ'vendʒ/ n venganza f; **to take ~**
vengarse*, desquitarse

revenge² vt vengar*

revenue /'revənuː ‖ 'revənjuː/ n **(a)** (Tax)
rentas fpl públicas **(b) revenues** pl ingresos
mpl

reverberate /rɪ'vɜːrbəreɪt ‖ rɪ'vɜːbəreɪt/ vi
retumbar

revere /rɪ'vɪr ‖ rɪ'vɪə(r)/ vt (frml) reverenciar
(frml)

reverence /'revərəns/ n reverencia f

Reverend adj (in titles) reverendo

reverent /'revrənt, 'revərənt/ adj reverente

reverie /'revəri/ n ensueño m

reversal /rɪ'vɜːrsəl ‖ rɪ'vɜːsəl/ n **(a)** (inversion)
inversión f **(b)** (of trend, policy) cambio m completo
or total **(c)** (setback) (frml) revés m

reverse¹ /rɪ'vɜːrs ‖ rɪ'vɜːs/ n **1** (of picture,
paper) reverso m, dorso m; (of cloth, garment) revés
m; (of coin) reverso m **2** (no pl) (opposite) **the ~** lo
contrario **3 ~ (gear)** (no art) marcha f atrás,
reversa f (Col, Méx) **4** (setback) (frml) revés m

reverse² vt **(a)** (transpose) «roles/positions»
invertir*; **to ~ the charges** (BrE Telec) llamar a
cobro revertido or (Chi, Méx) por cobrar **(b)** (invert)
«order/process» invertir* **2** (undo, negate) «policy»
cambiar radicalmente; «trend» invertir* el
sentido de; «ruling» revocar* **3** «vehicle»: **she ~d**
her car around the corner dobló la esquina dando
marcha atrás or (Col, Méx) en reversa
■ ~ vi «vehicle/driver» dar* marcha atrás, meter
reversa (Col, Méx)

reverse³ adj (before n) **(a)** (backward, opposite)
«movement/direction/trend» contrario, inverso; **in**
~ order en orden inverso **(b)** (back): **the ~ side**
(of cloth) el revés; (of paper) el reverso, el dorso

reverse-charge call /rɪ'vɜːrs'tʃɑːrdʒ
‖ rɪˌvɜːs'tʃɑːdʒ/ n (BrE) llamada f a cobro
revertido or (Chi, Méx) por cobrar

reversible /rɪ'vɜːrsəbəl ‖ rɪ'vɜːsəbəl/ adj
reversible

reversion /rɪ'vɜːrʒən ‖ rɪ'vɜːʃən/ n (to former
state, practice) vuelta f, reversión f (frml)

revert /rɪ'vɜːrt ‖ rɪ'vɜːt/ vi: **to ~ to** volver* a

review¹ /rɪ'vjuː/ n **1 (a)** (of book, film) crítica
f, reseña f **(b)** (report, summary) resumen m, reseña
f **2 (a)** (reconsideration) revisión f **(b)** (for exam)
(AmE) repaso m

review² vt **1 (a)** (consider) «situation»
examinar, estudiar **(b)** (reconsider) «policy/case»
reconsiderar; «salary» reajustar **2 (a)**
(summarize) «news/events» resumir, reseñar **(b)**
«book/play» hacer* (or escribir* etc) la crítica de,
reseñar **3** (for exam) (AmE) repasar
■ ~ vi (BrE) repasar

revision /rɪ'vɪʒən/ n **1 (a)** (alteration)
modificación f **(b)** (text) edición f corregida **2** (for
exam) (BrE) repaso m

revitalize /'riː'vaɪtəlaɪz/ vt vigorizar*, darle*
vitalidad a; «economy» estimular, reactivar

revival /rɪ'vaɪvəl/ n **(a)** (renewal, upsurge): **a ~ of**
interest in ... un renovado interés por ...;
economic ~ reactivación f económica; **a religious**
~ un renacer or un renacimiento religioso **(b)**
(Med) reanimación f

revive /rɪ'vaɪv/ vt **(a)** (Med) reanimar, resucitar
(b) (revitalize) «economy» reactivar, estimular;
«interest/friendship» hacer* renacer, reavivar **(c)**
«custom/practice» restablecer*
■ ~ vi «trade» reactivarse, repuntar; «hope/
interest» renacer*, resurgir*; «patient»
reanimarse; «plant» revivir

revoke /rɪ'vəʊk/ vt revocar*

revolt¹ /rɪ'vəʊlt/ n revuelta f, sublevación f

revolt² vi sublevarse
■ ~ vt darle* asco a

revolting /rɪˈvəʊltɪŋ/ adj (nauseating) repugnante; (horrible) (colloq) asqueroso, horrible

revolution /ˈrevəˈluːʃən/ n revolución f

revolutionary¹ /ˈrevəˈluːʃəneri ‖ˌrevəˈluːʃənəri/ adj revolucionario

revolutionary² n (pl **-ries**) revolucionario, -ria m,f

revolutionize /ˈrevəˈluːʃənaɪz/ vt revolucionar

revolve /rɪˈvɑːlv ‖rɪˈvɒlv/ vi (a) (rotate) girar (b) **revolving** pres p ⟨chair/door⟩ giratorio

revolver /rɪˈvɑːlvər ‖rɪˈvɒlvə(r)/ n revólver m

revue /rɪˈvjuː/ n revista f

revulsion /rɪˈvʌlʃən/ n repugnancia f, asco m

reward¹ /rɪˈwɔːrd ‖rɪˈwɔːd/ n recompensa f

reward² vt premiar, recompensar

rewarding /rɪˈwɔːrdɪŋ ‖rɪˈwɔːdɪŋ/ adj gratificante

rewind /ˈriːˈwaɪnd/ vt (past & past p **rewound**) rebobinar

rewire /ˈriːˈwaɪr ‖ˌriːˈwaɪə(r)/ vt ⟨house⟩ renovar* la instalación eléctrica de

reword /ˈriːˈwɜːrd ‖ˌriːˈwɜːd/ vt ⟨question⟩ formular de otra manera; ⟨statement⟩ volver* a redactar

rewound /ˈriːˈwaʊnd/ past & past p of REWIND

rewrite /ˈriːˈraɪt/ vt (past **rewrote**; past p **rewritten**) volver* a escribir or redactar

rhapsody /ˈræpsədi/ n (pl **-dies**) rapsodia f

rhetoric /ˈretərɪk/ n retórica f

rhetorical /rɪˈtɔːrɪkəl ‖rɪˈtɒrɪkəl/ adj retórico

rheumatic /ruːˈmætɪk/ adj reumático

rheumatism /ˈruːmətɪzəm/ n reumatismo m

Rhine /raɪn/ n **the** ∼ el Rin

rhino /ˈraɪnəʊ/ n (pl ∼ or ∼**s**) rinoceronte m

rhinoceros /raɪˈnɑːsrəs, -sərəs ‖raɪˈnɒsərəs, -srəs/ n (pl **-oses** or ∼) rinoceronte m

rhubarb /ˈruːbɑːrb ‖ˈruːbɑːb/ n ruibarbo m

rhyme¹ /raɪm/ n (a) (correspondence of sound) rima f (b) (poem) rima f, poema m

rhyme² vi/t rimar

rhythm /ˈrɪðəm/ n ritmo m

rhythmic /ˈrɪðmɪk/, **-mical** /-mɪkəl/ adj rítmico

RI = **Rhode Island**

rib /rɪb/ n (Anat, Culin) costilla f

ribald /ˈrɪbəld/ adj ⟨comments/humor⟩ procaz, picaresco

ribbed /rɪbd/ adj ⟨neck/sleeves⟩ en punto elástico, en canalé, en resorte (AmC, Col, Méx)

ribbon /ˈrɪbən/ n (a) (strip of fabric) cinta f, listón m (Méx) (b) (as insignia, award) galón m (c) (of typewriter, printer etc) cinta f (d) **ribbons** pl (shreds) jirones mpl

ribcage /ˈrɪbkeɪdʒ/ n caja f torácica

rice /raɪs/ n arroz m; (before n) ∼ **pudding** arroz con leche

rice: ∼**field** n arrozal m; ∼ **paper** n papel m de arroz

rich /rɪtʃ/ adj **-er, -est** ① (a) (wealthy) rico (b) (opulent) ⟨banquet⟩ suntuoso; ⟨furnishings⟩ lujoso, suntuoso (c) (abundant) ⟨harvest/supply⟩ abundante; ⟨reward⟩ generoso; ⟨history/

experience⟩ rico ② (a) ⟨food⟩ con alto contenido de grasas, huevos, azúcar etc (b) ⟨soil⟩ rico; ⟨color⟩ cálido e intenso

riches /ˈrɪtʃəz ‖ˈrɪtʃɪz/ pl n riquezas fpl

richness /ˈrɪtʃnəs ‖ˈrɪtʃnɪs/ n riqueza f

rickety /ˈrɪkəti/ adj desvencijado

rickshaw /ˈrɪkʃɔː/ n: calesa oriental de dos ruedas tirada por un hombre

ricochet /ˈrɪkəʃeɪ/ vi **-chets** /-ʃeɪz/, **-cheting** /-ʃeɪɪŋ/, **-cheted** /-ʃeɪd/ **to** ∼ (OFF sth) rebotar (EN algo)

rid /rɪd/ vt (pres p **ridding**; past & past p **rid**): they ∼ **the country of corruption** libraron al país de la corrupción; **to get** ∼ **of** ⟨unwanted object⟩ deshacerse* de; ⟨person, cold⟩ quitarse de encima; ⟨smell⟩ quitar

riddance /ˈrɪdns/ n: **good** ∼! (colloq) ¡adiós y buen viaje! (fam & iró)

ridden /ˈrɪdn/ past p of RIDE¹

riddle¹ /ˈrɪdl/ n (a) (puzzle) adivinanza f, acertijo m (b) (mystery) enigma m, misterio m

riddle² vt (perforate) (often pass) **to be** ∼**d** WITH sth: his body was ∼**d** with bullets lo habían acribillado a balazos; she was ∼**d** with cancer tenía cáncer por todo el cuerpo

ride¹ /raɪd/ (past **rode**; past p **ridden**) vt ① (a) **to** ∼ **a horse** montar a caballo; **to** ∼ **a bicycle/motorbike** montar or (AmL tb) andar* en bicicleta/moto (b) (AmE) ⟨bus/subway/train⟩ ir* en ② (be carried upon) ⟨waves/wind⟩ dejarse llevar por
■ ∼ vi (a) (on horse) montar or (AmL tb) andar* a caballo; **to go riding** ir* a montar or (AmL tb) a andar a caballo (b) (on bicycle, in vehicle) ir*; we rode into town fuimos al centro en bicicleta (or en moto etc)
■ **ride out** [v + o + adv, v + adv + o] aguantar, sobrellevar
■ **ride up** [v + adv] subirse

ride² n (on horse, in vehicle etc): **let's go for a** ∼ **on our bikes/in your car** vamos a dar una vuelta or un paseo en bicicleta/en tu coche; it was a long ∼ fue un viaje largo; **to give sb a** ∼ (esp AmE) llevar a algn en coche, darle* un aventón (Méx) or (Col fam) una palomita a algn; **to take sb for a** ∼ (colloq) tomarle el pelo a algn (fam)

rider /ˈraɪdər ‖ˈraɪdə(r)/ n ① (a) (on horseback) jinete mf; (on bicycle) ciclista mf; (on motorbike) motociclista mf, motorista mf (b) (of subway, bus) (AmE) pasajero, -ra m,f ② (appended statement) cláusula f adicional; (condition) condición f

ridge /rɪdʒ/ n (of hills) cadena f; (hilltop) cresta f

ridicule¹ /ˈrɪdəkjuːl ‖ˈrɪdɪkjuːl/ n burlas fpl

ridicule² vt ridiculizar*, burlarse de

ridiculous /rɪˈdɪkjələs ‖rɪˈdɪkjʊləs/ adj ridículo

riding /ˈraɪdɪŋ/ n equitación f; (before n) ⟨school/lesson⟩ de equitación; ⟨breeches/boots⟩ de montar

rife /raɪf/ adj (pred) extendido; disease is ∼ cunden las enfermedades; corruption is ∼ reina la corrupción

riffraff /ˈrɪfræf/ n (+ sing or pl vb) chusma f

rifle¹ /ˈraɪfəl/ n rifle m, fusil m

rifle² vi **to** ∼ THROUGH sth hojear algo

rift /rɪft/ n **(a)** (in rock) fisura f **(b)** (within party) escisión f; (between people) distanciamiento m; (between countries) ruptura f

rig¹ /rɪg/ n (oil ~) plataforma f petrolífera or petrolera; (derrick) torre f de perforación

rig² **-gg-** vt ‹election/contest› amañar; ‹fight› arreglar

■ **rig out** [v + o + adv, v + adv + o] (colloq) equipar

■ **rig up** [v + o + adv, v + adv + o] (set up) instalar

rigging /'rɪgɪŋ/ n (Naut) jarcia(s) f(pl)

right¹ /raɪt/ adj **1** (correct) ‹answer/interpretation› correcto; **are we going in the ~ direction?** ¿vamos bien?; **did you press the ~ button?** ¿apretaste el botón que debías?; **do you have the ~ change?** ¿tienes el cambio justo?; **do you have the ~ time?** ¿tienes hora (buena)?

2 (not mistaken): **to be ~** «person» tener* razón, estar* en lo cierto; «clock» estar* bien; **you got two answers ~** acertaste dos respuestas; **to be ~ to + INF** hacer* bien en + INF

3 (good, suitable) adecuado, apropiado; **if the price is ~** si está bien de precio; **just ~** perfecto; **the ~ person for the job** la persona indicada para el puesto

4 (just, moral) (pred) **to be ~** ser* justo

5 (pred) (in order): **to put sth ~** arreglar algo

6 (opposite of left) (before n) ‹side/ear/shoe› derecho

right² adv **1** (correctly, well) bien, correctamente; **nothing goes ~ for them** todo les sale mal, nada les sale bien; ▶ SERVE¹ vt 2 **2** **(a)** (all the way, completely): **the road goes ~ along the coast** la carretera bordea toda la costa; **~ from the start** desde el principio **(b)** (directly): **it's ~ in front of you** lo tienes allí delante; **he was ~ here/there** estaba aquí mismo/allí mismo; **~ now** ahora mismo **(c)** (immediately): **~ after lunch** inmediatamente después de comer; **I'll be ~ back** vuelvo enseguida **3** ‹turn/look› a la derecha

right³ n **1** **(a)** (entitlement) derecho m; **~ to sth/+ INF** derecho A algo/+ INF; **the title is his by ~** el título le corresponde a él **(b)** **rights** pl derechos mpl

2 (what is correct): **to know ~ from wrong** saber* distinguir entre el bien y el mal; **to be in the ~** tener* razón, llevar la razón, estar* en lo cierto; **to put** o **set sth to ~s** (esp BrE) arreglar algo **3** **(a)** (opposite the left) derecha f; **on the ~** a la derecha; **to drive on the ~** manejar or (Esp) conducir* por la derecha **(b)** (right turn): **to make** o (BrE) **take a ~** girar a la derecha **(Sport)** (hand) derecha f **4** (Pol) **the ~** la derecha

right⁴ vt **(a)** (set upright) enderezar* **(b)** (redress) reparar; **to ~ a wrong** reparar un daño

right⁵ interj (colloq) ¡bueno!, ¡vale! (Esp fam)

right: **~ angle** n ángulo m recto; **~ away** adv enseguida

righteous /'raɪtʃəs/ adj **(a)** ‹indignation› justificado **(b)** ‹person› recto, honrado

rightful /'raɪtfəl/ adj (before n) ‹owner/heir› legítimo; ‹share/reward› justo

right: **~-hand** /'raɪt'hænd/ adj (before n) de la derecha; **on the ~-hand side** a la derecha, a mano derecha; **~-handed** /'raɪt'hændəd ‖ ,raɪt'hændɪd/ adj ‹person› diestro; **~-hand man** /'raɪt'hænd/ n brazo m derecho

rightly /'raɪtli/ adv **(a)** (correctly, accurately): **if I remember ~** si mal no recuerdo; **I can't ~ say** (colloq) no sabría decir exactamente **(b)** (justly) con toda la razón; **~ or wrongly** justa o injustamente

right: **~ of way** n (precedence in traffic) preferencia f; **~ on** adj (AmE colloq) (pred): **his analysis was ~ on** su análisis era muy acertado or (fam) daba justo en el clavo; **~-on** /'raɪt'ɑːn ‖ ,raɪt'ɒn/ adj (BrE colloq & hum) progre (fam); **~ wing** n **(a)** (Pol) (ala fₜ) derecha f **(b)** (Sport) ala fₜ derecha; **~-wing** /'raɪt'wɪŋ/ adj derechista; **~-winger** /'raɪt,wɪŋər ‖ 'raɪt,wɪŋə(r)/ n (Pol) derechista mf

rigid /'rɪdʒəd ‖ 'rɪdʒɪd/ adj **(a)** (stiff) rígido **(b)** ‹discipline› estricto; ‹person/principles› inflexible

rigmarole /'rɪgmərəʊl/ n (colloq) lío m (fam)

rigor, (BrE) **rigour** /'rɪgər ‖ 'rɪgə(r)/ n rigor m

rigor mortis /'rɪgər'mɔːrtəs ‖ ,rɪgə'mɔːtɪs/ n rigidez f cadavérica; **~ ~ had set in** el cuerpo ya estaba rígido

rigorous /'rɪgərəs/ adj riguroso

rigour n (BrE) ▶ RIGOR

rile /raɪl/ vt (colloq) irritar

rim /rɪm/ n (of cup, bowl) borde m; (of spectacles) montura f, armazón m or f; (of wheel) (Auto) llanta f, rin n (Col, Méx); (of bicycle wheel) aro m

rind /raɪnd/ n (of lemon, orange) cáscara f, corteza f; (of cheese) corteza f; (of bacon) piel f

ring¹ /rɪŋ/ n **1** **(a)** (on finger) anillo m; (woman's) anillo m, sortija f **(b)** (circle) círculo m; **to stand in a ~** hacer* un corro, formar un círculo **(c)** (burner) (BrE) quemador m, hornilla f (AmL exc CS), hornillo m (Esp)

2 **(a)** (in boxing, wrestling) cuadrilátero m, ring m **(b)** (in circus) pista f **(c)** (bull ~) ruedo m

3 (of criminals) red f, banda f

4 **(a)** (sound of bell) (of phone) timbrazo m; **there was a ~ at the door** sonó el timbre de la puerta **(b)** (telephone call) (BrE) (no pl): **to give sb a ~** llamar (por teléfono) a algn

ring² (past **rang**; past p **rung**) vi **1** **(a)** (make sound) sonar* **(b)** (operate bell) «person» tocar* el timbre, llamar al timbre

2 (telephone) (BrE) llamar (por teléfono), telefonear

3 **(a)** (resound) resonar*; **to ~ true** ser* or sonar* convincente **(b)** «ears» zumbar

■ **~** vt **1** **(a)** ‹bell› tocar* **(b)** (telephone) ‹person› (BrE) llamar (por teléfono)

2 (past & past p **ringed**) **(a)** (surround) cercar*, rodear **(b)** (with pen, pencil) marcar* con un círculo

■ **ring back** (BrE) **1** [v + adv] volver* a llamar **2** [v + o + adv] (ring again) volver* a llamar; (return call) llamar

■ **ring off** [v + adv] (BrE) colgar*, cortar (CS)

■ **ring out** [v + adv] «*shot/voice*» oírse*, resonar*; «*bells*» sonar*, resonar*

■ **ring up** $\boxed{1}$ [v + o + adv, v + adv + o] (BrE) ▶ RING² vt 1B

$\boxed{2}$ [v + adv] (BrE) ▶ RING² vi 2

ring binder n archivador m, carpeta f de anillos or (Esp) de anillas

ringing /'rɪŋɪŋ/ n (a) (of bell) repique m, toque m (b) (of doorbell, telephone) timbre m (c) (in ears) zumbido m

ringleader /'rɪŋ,liːdər ‖ 'rɪŋ,liːdə(r)/ n cabecilla mf

ringlet /'rɪŋlət/ n tirabuzón m, rizo m

ring road n (BrE) carretera f de circunvalación

rink /rɪŋk/ n (ice ∼) pista f de hielo; (skating ∼) pista f de patinaje

rinse¹ /rɪns/ vt (a) (wash) ⟨*cutlery/hands*⟩ enjuagar*; ⟨*rice/mushrooms*⟩ lavar (b) (to remove soap) ⟨*clothes/hair*⟩ enjuagar*, aclarar (Esp); ⟨*dishes*⟩ enjuagar*

rinse² n (a) (wash) enjuague m (b) (to remove soap — from clothes) enjuague m, aclarado m (Esp); (— from dishes) enjuague m (c) (tint) tintura f (*no permanente*)

riot¹ /'raɪət/ n (a) (disorder) disturbio m; (mutiny) motín m; **to run ∼** ⟨*fans*⟩ descontrolarse, desmadrarse (fam); **she let her imagination run ∼** dio rienda suelta a su imaginación; (*before n*) ⟨*gear/shield*⟩ antidisturbios adj inv; **the ∼ squad** la brigada antidisturbios (b) (profusion): **a ∼ of color** un derroche or una profusión de color

riot² vi causar disturbios or desórdenes; «*prisoners*» amotinarse

rioter /'raɪətər ‖ 'raɪətə(r)/ n alborotador, -dora m,f

rioting /'raɪətɪŋ/ n disturbios mpl

riotous /'raɪətəs/ adj (a) ⟨*crowd/behavior*⟩ descontrolado, desenfrenado (b) ⟨*occasion*⟩ desenfrenado

rip¹ /rɪp/ **-pp-** vt ⟨*cloth*⟩ rasgar*, romper*; ⟨*skirt/ trousers*⟩ hacerse* un rasgón en; **she ∼ped the letter open** abrió la carta de un rasgón

■ **∼** vi rasgarse*

■ **rip off** [v + o + adv, v + adv + o] $\boxed{1}$ (remove) arrancar* $\boxed{2}$ (sl) (a) (cheat) timar, estafar, tracalear (Méx, Ven fam) (b) (steal) afanar (arg), robar

■ **rip up** [v + o + adv, v + adv + o] romper*, hacer* pedazos

rip² n rasgón m, desgarrón m

RIP (= **rest in peace**) R.I.P.

rip cord n cordón m de apertura

ripe /raɪp/ adj ⟨*fruit*⟩ maduro; ⟨*cheese*⟩ a punto

ripen /'raɪpən/ vi madurar

■ **∼** vt hacer* madurar

rip-off /'rɪpɔːf ‖ 'rɪpɒf/ n (colloq) (con) timo m, estafa f; (theft) robo m; (copy) plagio m

ripple¹ /'rɪpəl/ n (on water) onda f; **a ∼ of applause** un breve aplauso

ripple² vi (a) «*water*» rizarse*; «*wheat/grass*» mecerse* (b) **rippling** pres p ⟨*muscles*⟩ tensado

rise¹ /raɪz/ n $\boxed{1}$ (a) (upward movement — of tide, level) subida f; (— in pitch) elevación f (b) (increase — in prices, interest rates) subida f, aumento m, alza f‡ (frml); (— in pressure, temperature) aumento m,

subida f; (— in number, amount) aumento m (c) (in pay) (BrE) aumento m, incremento m (frml); **a pay ∼** un aumento or (frml) un incremento salarial $\boxed{2}$ (advance) (to fame, power) ascenso m, ascensión f; (of movement, ideology) surgimiento m; **to give ∼ to sth** ⟨*to belief*⟩ dar* origen or lugar a algo; ⟨*to dispute*⟩ ocasionar or causar algo; ⟨*to ideas*⟩ suscitar algo $\boxed{3}$ (slope) subida f, cuesta f

rise² (*past* **rose**; *past p* **risen** /'rɪzn/) vi $\boxed{1}$ (a) (come, go up) subir; «*sun/moon*» salir*; «*river*» crecer*; «*cake*» subir; **to ∼ to the surface** salir* or subir a la superficie (b) (increase) ⟨*price/ temperature/pressure*⟩ subir, aumentar; «*wind*» arreciar; «*wage/amount*» aumentar; «*tension*» crecer*, aumentar (c) «*sound*» (become louder) aumentar de volumen; (become higher) subir de tono (d) (improve) «*standard*» mejorar; **their spirits rose** se les levantó el ánimo, se animaron $\boxed{2}$ (a) (slope upward) ⟨*ground/land*⟩ elevarse (b) (extend upwards) «*building/hill*» levantarse, alzarse* $\boxed{3}$ (a) (stand up) «*person/audience*» (frml) ponerse* de pie, levantarse, pararse (AmL) (b) (out of bed) levantarse $\boxed{4}$ (in rank): **she has ∼n in my estimation** ha ganado en mi estima $\boxed{5}$ (revolt) **to ∼ to (up)** levantarse, alzarse* $\boxed{6}$ (originate) «*river*» (frml) nacer*

■ **rise above** [v + prep + o] ⟨*disability*⟩ sobreponerse* a; ⟨*difficulty*⟩ superar

■ **rise to** [v + prep + o] (respond to): **to ∼ to the challenge** aceptar el reto; **to ∼ to the occasion** estar* a la altura de las circunstancias

rising¹ /'raɪzɪŋ/ n (rebellion) levantamiento m

rising² adj (before n) (a) ⟨*tide/level*⟩ creciente; **the ∼ sun** el sol naciente (b) (increasing) ⟨*number*⟩ creciente; ⟨*temperature*⟩ creciente, en aumento; ⟨*prices/interest rates*⟩ en alza or en aumento (c) (sloping) en pendiente

rising damp n humedad f (*que sube de los cimientos por las paredes*)

risk¹ /rɪsk/ n riesgo m; **those most at ∼ from the disease** los que corren mayor riesgo or peligro de contraer la enfermedad; **at the ∼ of** -ING a riesgo de + INF; **to take a ∼** correr un riesgo; **to take ∼s** arriesgarse, correr riesgos

risk² vt (a) (put in danger) arriesgar*, poner* en peligro (b) (expose oneself to) arriesgarse* a; **to ∼** -ING arriesgarse* A or correr el riesgo DE + INF

risky /'rɪski/ adj **-kier, -kiest** arriesgado, riesgoso (AmL)

risqué /rɪ'skeɪ, 'rɪskeɪ/ adj atrevido, subido de tono

rite /raɪt/ n rito m

ritual¹ /'rɪtʃuəl/ n ritual m

ritual² adj ritual

rival¹ /'raɪvəl/ n rival mf

rival² adj (before n) ⟨*company*⟩ rival, competidor

rival³ vt, (BrE) **-ll-**: **his voice ∼s that of the lead singer** su voz no tiene nada que envidiarle a la del cantante principal

rivalry /'raɪvəlri/ n (pl **-ries**) rivalidad f, competencia f

river /'rɪvər ‖ 'rɪvə(r)/ n río m; (before n) ⟨*traffic/port*⟩ fluvial; ⟨*mouth/basin*⟩ del río

river: **∼bank** n ribera f, margen f (*de un río*); ···❯

∼bed *n* lecho *m* (*de un río*); **R∼ Plate** *n* Río *m* de la Plata; **∼side** *n* ribera *f*, margen *f* (*de un río*); (*before n*) *café* a orillas del río

rivet¹ /'rɪvət ‖'rɪvɪt/ *n* remache *m*, roblón *m*

rivet² *vt* **(a)** (attach) remachar **(b)** (fix) (*usu pass*): my eyes were ∼ed to the screen estaba absorto, con los ojos clavados en la pantalla; their eyes were ∼ed on her no le quitaban los ojos de encima **(c)** (fascinate) (*usu pass*) fascinar

riveting /'rɪvətɪŋ/ *adj* fascinante

Riviera /ˌrɪvi'erə ‖ˌrɪvi'eərə/ *n*: the (French) ∼ la Costa Azul; the Italian ∼ la Riviera

RN *n* (in UK) = **Royal Navy**

RNA *n* (= ribonucleic acid) RNA *m*, ARN *m*

road /rəʊd/ *n* **1** (for vehicles — in town) calle *f*; (— out of town) carretera *f*; (— minor) camino *m*; by ∼ por carretera, por tierra; (*before n*) *accident* de tráfico *or* (AmL tb) de tránsito; ∼ sign señal *f* vial *or* de tráfico *f* en la carretera; ∼ tax impuesto *m* de rodaje

2 (route, way) camino *m*; the economy is on the ∼ to recovery la economía está en vías de recuperación

3 to be on the road «*car*» estar* en circulación; we've been on the ∼ for four days llevamos cuatro días viajando

road: ∼block *n* control *m* (de carretera); ∼ **hog** *n* (colloq) loco, -ca *m,f* del volante; ∼ **hump** *n* badén *m*, tope *m* (Méx), lomo *m* de burro (RPl); **∼map** *n* mapa *m* de carreteras; ∼ **rage** *n* (Auto) agresión *f* (*provocada por el estrés que supone conducir en condiciones difíciles*); **∼side** *n* borde *m* de la carretera/del camino; ∼ **sweeper** *n* (person) barrendero, -ra *m,f*; (machine) barredera *f*, barredora *f*; **∼works** *pl n* (BrE) obras *fpl* (de vialidad); **∼worthy** *adj* **-thier, -thiest** apto para circular

roam /rəʊm/ *vt* vagar* *or* deambular por
■ ∼ *vi* vagar*, errar* (liter)

roar¹ /rɔːr ‖rɔː(r)/ *vi* «*lion/engine*» rugir*; «*sea/wind/fire*» bramar, rugir*; to ∼ with laughter reírse* a carcajadas

roar² *n* (of lion, tiger) rugido *m*; (of person) rugido *m*, bramido *m*; (of thunder) estruendo *m*; (of traffic, engine, guns) estruendo *m*; (of crowd) clamor *m*

roaring /'rɔːrɪŋ/ *adj* (*before n*) *waves* rugiente; *traffic* estruendoso

roast¹ /rəʊst/ *adj* asado; ∼ **beef** rosbif *m*, rosbeef *m*

roast² *n* asado *m* (*al horno*)

roast³ *vt* *meat/potatoes* asar; *coffee beans* tostar*, torrefaccionar; *peanuts* tostar*
■ ∼ *vi* asarse

roasting /'rəʊstɪŋ/ *adj* (colloq): it's absolutely ∼ hace un calor que te asas (fam)

rob /rɑːb ‖rɒb/ *vt* **-bb- (a)** (steal from) *person* robarle a; *bank* asaltar, atracar*, robar **(b)** (deprive) to ∼ sb/sth **of** sth privar a algn/algo DE algo

robber /'rɑːbər ‖'rɒbə(r)/ *n* ladrón, -drona *m,f*; **bank** ∼ atracador, -dora *m,f or* asaltante *mf* de bancos

robbery /'rɑːbəri ‖'rɒbəri/ *n* (*pl* **-ries**) robo *m*, asalto *m*; **bank** ∼ asalto *m or* atraco *m* a un banco

robe /rəʊb/ *n* **(a)** (worn by magistrates) (*often pl*) toga *f* **(b)** (worn in house) bata *f*, salto *m* de cama (CS)

robin /'rɑːbən ‖'rɒbɪn/ *n* (European) petirrojo *m*; (N. American) ceón *m*, tordo *m* norteamericano

robot /'rəʊbɑːt ‖'rəʊbɒt/ *n* robot *m*

robust /rəʊ'bʌst/ *adj* *person/animal* robusto; *health* de hierro; *material* resistente, sólido

rock¹ /rɑːk ‖rɒk/ *n* **1** (substance) roca *f* **2** **(a)** (crag, cliff) peñasco *m*, peñón *m* **(b)** (in sea) roca *f*, escollo *m*; **on the ∼s** *whisky* con hielo; their marriage is on the ∼s su matrimonio anda muy mal **(c)** (boulder) roca *f* **(d)** (stone) (esp AmE) piedra *f* **3** (music) rock *m*

rock² *vt* **(a)** (gently) *cradle* mecer*; *child* acunar **(b)** (violently) sacudir, estremecer*; «*scandal*» convulsionar, conmocionar
■ ∼ *vi* (gently) mecerse*, balancearse

rock: ∼ and roll *n* ▶ ROCK'N'ROLL; **∼bottom** /'rɑːk'bɑːtəm ‖ˌrɒk'bɒtəm/ *n*: to hit/reach ∼bottom tocar* fondo; ∼ **climbing** /'rɑːk'klaɪmɪŋ ‖'rɒk,klaɪmɪŋ/ *n* escalada *f* en roca

rocket¹ /'rɑːkət ‖'rɒkɪt/ *n* **(a)** (spacecraft) cohete *m* espacial **(b)** (missile) cohete *m*, misil *m*; (*before n*) ∼ **launcher** lanzacohetes *m*, lanzamisiles *m*

rocket² *vi* «*price*» dispararse, ponerse* por las nubes

rock: ∼face *n* pared *f* rocosa; **∼hard** /'rɑːk'hɑːrd ‖ˌrɒk'hɑːd/ *adj* (duro) como una piedra

rocking /'rɑːkɪŋ ‖'rɒkɪŋ/**: ∼ chair** *n* mecedora *f*; ∼ **horse** *n* caballito *m* mecedor *or* de balancín

rock'n'roll /'rɑːkən'rəʊl ‖ˌrɒkən'rəʊl/ *n* rocanrol *m*, rock and roll *m*

rocky /'rɑːki ‖'rɒki/ *adj* **rockier, rockiest** **1** *ground* rocoso; *path* pedregoso **2** (unsteady) *period* de incertidumbre; *base* nada sólido, tambaleante

Rocky Mountains *pl n* the ∼ ∼ las Montañas Rocallosas *or* Rocosas

rod /rɑːd ‖rɒd/ *n* **(a)** (bar) varilla *f*, barra *f* **(b)** (fishing ∼) caña *f* (de pescar) **(c)** (for punishment) vara *f*

rode /rəʊd/ *past of* RIDE¹

rodent /'rəʊdṇt/ *n* roedor *m*

rodeo /'rəʊdiəʊ, rə'deɪəʊ/ *n* (*pl* **-os**) rodeo *m*

roe /rəʊ/ *n* **1** (of fish) hueva *f* **2** ∼ **deer** corzo, -za *m,f*

rogue /rəʊg/ *n* pícaro, -ra *m,f*, pillo, -lla *m,f*

roguish /'rəʊgɪʃ/ *adj* pícaro

role, rôle /rəʊl/ *n* **(a)** (Cin, Theat) papel *m* **(b)** (function) papel *m*, rol *m*; (*before n*) ∼ **model** modelo *m* de conducta

role-play /'rəʊlpleɪ/ *n* teatro *m* improvisado; (Psych) psicodrama *m*

roll¹ /rəʊl/ *n* **1** (Culin) (bread) ∼ pancito *m or* (Esp) panecillo *m or* (Méx) bolillo *m* **2** (of paper, wire, fabric) rollo *m*; (of banknotes) fajo *m*; **a** ∼ **of film** un rollo *or* un carrete (de fotos) **3** (sound — of drum) redoble *m*; (— of thunder) retumbo *m* **4** (list) lista *f*; **to call the** ∼ pasar lista

roll² *vi* **1** **(a)** (rotate) «*ball/barrel*» rodar* **(b)** (turn over): the car ∼ed over three times el coche dio tres vueltas de campana; ∼ (over) onto your

back ponte boca arriba, date la vuelta *or* (CS) date vuelta; *to be ~ing in money* o *in it* (colloq) estar* forrado (de oro) (fam) **(c)** (sway) «*ship*» bambolearse

2 (move) (+ *adv compl*): **the car began to ~ down the hill** el coche empezó a deslizarse cuesta abajo; **tears ~ed down his cheeks** las lágrimas le corrían por las mejillas

3 (begin operating) «*camera*» empezar* a rodar **4** (make noise) «*drum*» redoblar; «*thunder*» retumbar

5 rolling *pres p* «*countryside/hills*» ondulado

■ ~ *vt* **1** **(a)** «*ball/barrel*» hacer* rodar; «*dice*» tirar **(b)** *to ~ one's eyes* poner* los ojos en blanco

2 «*cigarette*» liar*; **it ~ed itself into a ball** se hizo un ovillo; *to ~ up one's sleeves* arremangarse **3** «*dough/pastry*» estirar **4** (Ling): *to ~ one's 'r's* hacer* vibrar las erres

■ **roll in** [*v + adv*] (arrive in large quantities) llover*
■ **roll on** [*v + adv*] **(a)** (pass) «*time/months*» pasar **(b)** (arrive) (colloq): *~ on vacation time!* ¡que lleguen pronto las vacaciones!
■ **roll out** [*v + o + adv, v + adv + o*] «*dough/pastry*» estirar
■ **roll up** [*v + adv*] (arrive) (colloq) aparecer*

roll call *n* **(a)** (calling of roll): *~ is 9 a.m.* pasan lista a las nueve de la mañana **(b)** (list) lista *f*

rolled gold /rəʊld/ *n* metal *m* (en)chapado en oro

roller /'rəʊlər ‖'rəʊlə(r)/ *n* **1** (for lawn, in machine, for applying paint) rodillo *m* **2** (for hair) rulo *m* **3** (caster) ruedecita *f*, ruedita *f* (esp AmL) **4** (wave) ola *f* grande

roller: R~blade® *n* patín *m* en línea; *~ blind* *n* persiana *f or* cortina *f* de enrollar; *~ coaster* *n* montaña *f* rusa; *~ skate* *n* patín *m* (de ruedas); *~-skate* /'rəʊlərskeɪt ‖'rəʊləskeɪt/ *vi* patinar (*sobre ruedas*)

rolling pin /'rəʊlɪŋ/ *n* rodillo *m*, rollo *m* pastelero (Esp)

roll-on /'rəʊlɑːn ‖'rəʊlɒn/*adj* (*before n*) «*deodorant*» de bola

ROM /rɑːm ‖rɒm/ *n* (= **read-only memory**) ROM *f*

Roman[1] /'rəʊmən/ *adj* **(a)** (of, from Rome) romano **(b)** **roman** «*numeral*» romano; «*alphabet*» latino

Roman[2] *n* romano, -na *m,f*

Roman Catholic[1] *n* católico, -ca *m,f*

Roman Catholic[2] *adj* católico

romance /rə'mæns, 'rəʊmæns ‖rəʊ'mæns/ *n* **1** **(a)** (affair) romance *m*, idilio *m* **(b)** (feeling) romanticismo *m* **2** (Lit) (love story) novela *f* romántica

Romance /rə'mæns, 'rəʊmæns ‖rəʊ'mæns/ *adj* «*languages*» romance, románico

Romania /rəʊ'meɪniə/ *n* Rumania *f*, Rumanía *f*

Romanian[1] /rəʊ'meɪniən/ *adj* rumano

Romanian[2] *n* **(a)** (language) rumano *m* **(b)** (person) rumano, -na *m,f*

romantic[1] /rəʊ'mæntɪk, rə-/ *adj* romántico

romantic[2] *n* romántico, -ca *m,f*

romanticize /rəʊ'mæntəsaɪz, rə- ‖rəʊ'mæntɪsaɪz/ *vt* idealizar*

Romany /'rɑːməni, 'rəʊ- ‖'rɒməni, 'rəʊ-/ *n* (*pl* **-nies**) **(a)** (person) gitano, -na *m,f* **(b)** (language) romaní *m*

Rome /rəʊm/ *n* Roma *f*

romp[1] /rɑːmp ‖rɒmp/ *n* **(a)** (frolic) retozo *m* **(b)** (sexual) revolcón *m* (fam)

romp[2] *vi* (frolic) retozar*

rompers /'rɑːmpərz ‖'rɒmpəz/ *pl n*, (BrE also) **romper suit** /'rɑːmpər ‖'rɒmpə(r)/ *n* mameluco *m* (AmL), pelele *m* (Esp)

roof[1] /ruːf/ *n* (*pl* ~**s** /ruːfs/) **(a)** (of building) tejado *m*, techo *m* (AmL); (*before n*) *~ garden* terraza *f or* azotea *f* ajardinada **(b)** (of car) techo *m*; (*before n*) *~ rack* baca *f*, portaequipajes *m*, parrilla *f* (AmL) **(c)** the *~ of the mouth* el paladar

roof[2] *vt* techar

roofing /'ruːfɪŋ/ *n* materiales *mpl* para techar

rooftop /'ruːftɑːp ‖'ruːftɒp/ *n* tejado *m*, techo *m* (AmL)

rook /rʊk/ *n* **(a)** (Zool) grajo *m* **(b)** (in chess) torre *f*

rookie /'rʊki/ *n* (colloq) **(a)** (novice) novato, -ta *m,f* **(b)** (military recruit) recluta *m*

room /ruːm, rʊm/ *n* **1** (in house, building) habitación *f*, pieza *f* (esp AmL); (bedroom) habitación *f*, dormitorio *m*, cuarto *m*, pieza *f* (esp AmL), recámara *f* (Méx); (for meeting) sala *f*; (*before n*) *~ temperature* temperatura *f* ambiente **2** (space) espacio *m*, lugar *m*; **there's ~ for improvement** se puede mejorar

room: ~ clerk *n* (AmE) recepcionista *mf*; **~mate** *n* (sharing apartment) compañero, -ra *m,f* de apartamento *or* (Esp) de piso; *~ service* *n* servicio *m* a las habitaciones

roomy /'ruːmi, 'rʊmi/ *adj* **-mier, -miest** amplio

roost /ruːst/ *vi* posarse (*para pasar la noche*)

rooster /'ruːstər ‖'ruːstə(r)/ *n* (esp AmE) gallo *m*

root[1] /ruːt/ *n* **(a)** raíz *f*; *to take ~* «*plant*» echar raíces, arraigar*; «*idea*» arraigarse* **(b)** **roots** *pl* (background) raíces *fpl*

root[2] *vi* **1** «*pig*» hozar* **2** (Bot) echar raíces, arraigar*
■ **root for** [*v + prep + o*] (encourage) animar, alentar; (support) apoyar
■ **root out** [*v + o + adv, v + adv + o*] (remove) arrancar* de raíz, erradicar*

rooted /'ruːtəd ‖'ruːtɪd/ *adj*: **a deeply ~ prejudice** un prejuicio profundamente arraigado; **he stood ~ to the spot** se quedó como clavado donde estaba

rope[1] /rəʊp/ *n* cuerda *f*, soga *f*; (Naut) cabo *m*; *to show sb the ~s*: **Mike will show you the ~s** Mike te enseñará cómo funciona todo

rope[2] *vt* **(a)** (tie) atar, amarrar (AmL exc RPl) (*con una cuerda*) **(b)** (lasso) (AmE) «*steer/cattle*» enlazar* *or* (Méx) lazar* *or* (CS) lacear
■ **rope in** [*v + o + adv, v + adv + o*] (colloq) (*usu pass*) agarrar (fam)

rope ladder *n* escala *f or* escalera *f* de cuerda *or* de soga

ropey, ropy /'rəʊpi/ *adj* **ropier, ropiest** (BrE ···⊹

colloq ⟨wine⟩ malo, chungo (Esp arg); **I feel a bit ∼** me siento bastante mal, estoy bastante pachucho (Esp fam)

rosary /'rəʊzəri/ n (pl **-ries**) rosario m

rose¹ /rəʊz/ past of RISE²

rose² n [1] (Bot) (flower) rosa f; (plant) rosal m; (before n) ∼ **bush** rosal m [2] (on watering can) roseta f

rosé /rəʊ'zeɪ ‖ 'rəʊzeɪ/ n (vino m) rosado m

rose: ∼**bud** n capullo m or pimpollo m de rosa; ∼**hip** n escaramujo m

rosemary /'rəʊz,meri ‖ 'rəʊzməri/ n romero m

rosette /rəʊ'zet/ n escarapela f

roster /'rɑːstər ‖ 'rɒstə(r)/ n (a) (duty) ∼ lista f de turnos (b) (list) lista f

rostrum /'rɑːstrəm ‖ 'rɒstrəm/ n (pl **-trums** or **-tra** /-trə/) (for public speaking) tribuna f, estrado m; (for orchestra conductor) podio m

rosy /'rəʊzi/ adj **rosier, rosiest** ⟨cheeks⟩ sonrosado; ⟨outlook⟩ halagüeño, optimista

rot¹ /rɑːt ‖ rɒt/ n (Biol) podredumbre f, putrefacción f; **the ∼ set in** las cosas empezaron a decaer or a venirse abajo

rot² **-tt-** vi pudrirse*; **to ∼ away** pudrirse* ■ ∼ vt ⟨wood/tree⟩ pudrir*, ⟨teeth⟩ picar*

rota /'rəʊtə/ n (BrE) lista f (de turnos)

rotary /'rəʊtəri/ adj rotatorio, rotativo

rotate /'rəʊteɪt ‖ rəʊ'teɪt/ vi girar, rotar ■ ∼ vt (a) (turn, spin) (hacer*) girar, dar* vueltas a (b) (alternate) ⟨crops⟩ alternar, rotar

rotation /rəʊ'teɪʃən/ n rotación f

rote /rəʊt/ n: **by ∼** de memoria

rotten /'rɑːtn̩ ‖ 'rɒtn̩/ adj (a) (decayed) podrido; ⟨tooth⟩ picado (b) (bad) (colloq) ⟨weather⟩ horrible; ⟨food⟩ pésimo; **to feel ∼** (ill) sentirse* mal or pésimo or (Esp fam) fatal

rotund /rəʊ'tʌnd/ adj (hum & euph) voluminoso

rouble /'ruːbəl/ n (BrE) rublo m

rouge /ruːʒ/ n colorete m

rough¹ /rʌf/ adj **-er, -est** [1] (a) (not smooth) ⟨surface/texture/skin⟩ áspero, rugoso; ⟨cloth⟩ basto; ⟨hands⟩ áspero, basto (b) (uneven) ⟨ground/road⟩ desigual; ⟨terrain⟩ agreste, escabroso (c) ⟨sea⟩ agitado, picado [2] (colloq) (a) (unpleasant, hard) ⟨life⟩ duro (b) (ill): **I feel a bit ∼** no estoy muy bien, me siento bastante mal [3] (not gentle) brusco; ⟨neighborhood⟩ peligroso [4] (a) (crude, unpolished) tosco, rudo; **a ∼ draft** un borrador (b) (approximate) aproximado

rough² adv ⟨sleep⟩ a la intemperie

rough³ vt: **to ∼ it** (colloq) pasar sin comodidades

roughage /'rʌfɪdʒ/ n fibra f (de los alimentos)

rough-and-ready /'rʌfən'redi/ adj improvisado

roughen /'rʌfən/ vt poner* áspero

roughly /'rʌfli/ adv (a) (approximately) aproximadamente (b) (not gently) ⟨play⟩ bruscamente, de manera violenta (c) (crudely) toscamente

roughshod /'rʌfʃɑːd ‖ 'rʌfʃɒd/ adv: **to ride ∼**

over sth: he rides ∼ over other people's feelings no tiene la menor consideración para con los sentimientos de los demás; **to ride ∼ over sb** llevarse por delante a algn

roulette /ruː'let/ n ruleta f

Roumania /ruː'meɪmiə/ etc ▶ ROMANIA etc

round¹ /raʊnd/ adj redondo

round² n [1] (circle) círculo m, redondel m [2] (a) (series) serie f; ∼ **of talks** ronda f de conversaciones (b) (burst): **let's have a ∼ of applause for ...** un aplauso para ... [3] (Sport, Games) (of tournament, quiz) vuelta f; (in boxing, wrestling) round m, asalto m; (in golf) vuelta f, recorrido m; (in showjumping) recorrido m; (in card games) partida f [4] (a) (of visits) (often pl): **the doctor is off making his ∼s** o (BrE) **is on his ∼s** el doctor está haciendo visitas a domicilio or visitando pacientes (b) (of watchman) ronda f; (of postman, milkman) (BrE) recorrido m [5] (of drinks) ronda f, vuelta f [6] (shot) disparo m; (bullet) bala f [7] (of bread) (BrE): **a ∼ of toast** una tostada or (Méx) un pan tostado; **a ∼ of sandwiches** un sándwich [8] (Mus) canon m

round³ vt ⟨corner⟩ doblar ■ **round off** [1] [v + o + adv, v + adv + o] (a) ⟨sharp edge⟩ redondear (b) (end suitably) ⟨day/meal⟩ terminar, rematar (c) ⟨number⟩ redondear [2] [v + adv] concluir*, terminar ■ **round on** [v + prep + o] volverse* contra ■ **round up** [v + o + adv, v + adv + o] ⟨sheep/cattle⟩ rodear; ⟨criminals⟩ hacer* una redada de

round⁴ adv (esp BrE) [1] (a) (in a circle): **we walked all the way ∼** dimos toda la vuelta; **all year ∼** durante todo el año (b) (so as to face in different direction): **she spun ∼** dio media vuelta; see also TURN ROUND (c) (on all sides) alrededor [2] (a) (from one place, person to another): **the curator took us ∼** el conservador nos mostró or nos enseñó el museo (or la colección etc); **a list was handed ∼** se hizo circular una lista (b) **all round** (in every respect) en todos los sentidos; (for everybody) a todos

round⁵ prep (esp BrE) [1] (encircling) alrededor de; **the wall ∼ the garden** el muro que rodea el jardín; ∼ **the corner** a la vuelta (de la esquina) [2] (a) (in the vicinity of) cerca de, en los alrededores de; **she lives ∼ here** vive por aquí (b) (within, through): **he does odd jobs ∼ the house** hace arreglos en la casa; **we had a look ∼ the cathedral** (le) echamos un vistazo a la catedral

round- /'raʊnd/ pref: ∼**faced** de cara redonda; ∼**shouldered** cargado de espaldas, encorvado

roundabout¹ /'raʊndəbaʊt/ n (BrE) (a) ▶ MERRY-GO-ROUND (b) (Transp) rotonda f, glorieta f

roundabout² adj ⟨route⟩ indirecto; **he said it in a very ∼ way** lo dijo con muchos rodeos or circunloquios

rounded /'raʊndəd ‖ 'raʊndɪd/ adj redondeado

rounders /'raʊndərz ‖'raʊndəz/ n (in UK)
(+ sing vb) juego parecido al béisbol

round: ~ **table** n mesa f redonda; ~ **the
clock** adv las 24 horas, día y noche; ~ **trip** n
(a) (there and back) (viaje m de) ida f y vuelta,
viaje m redondo (Méx) (b) (return fare) (AmE) tarifa
f de ida y vuelta or (Méx) de viaje redondo;
(before n) **round-trip ticket** pasaje m or (Esp)
billete m de ida y vuelta, boleto m redondo (Méx);
~**-up** n (a) (of livestock) rodeo m (b) (summary)
resumen m

rouse /raʊz/ vt despertar*

rousing /'raʊzɪŋ/ adj ⟨speech⟩ enardecedor

rout¹ /raʊt/ n derrota f aplastante

rout² vt (defeat) derrotar or vencer* de forma
aplastante; (put to flight) poner* en fuga

route /ruːt, raʊt ‖ruːt/ n (a) (way) camino m,
ruta f; (of bus) ruta f, recorrido m; **air/sea** ~ ruta
aérea/marítima (b) (highway) (AmE) carretera f

routine¹ /ruːˈtiːn/ n [1] (regular pattern) rutina f
[2] (of skater, comedian) número m

routine² adj (a) (usual) ⟨procedure/inquiries⟩ de
rutina (b) (ordinary, dull) rutinario

roving /'rəʊvɪŋ/ adj (before n) errante

row¹ n
I /rəʊ/ [1] (a) (straight line) hilera f; (of people,
seats) fila f (b) (in knitting) vuelta f [2] (succession)
serie f; **four times in a** ~ cuatro veces seguidas
II /raʊ/ (a) (noisy argument) pelea f, riña f; **to have
a** ~ **with sb** pelear or reñir* con algn (b) (about
a public matter) disputa f (c) (noise) (no pl) bulla f
(fam)

row² vt /rəʊ/: **he** ~**ed the boat towards the
shore** remó hacia la orilla
■ ~ vi
I /rəʊ/ remar; **to go** ~**ing** salir* or ir* a remar
II /raʊ/ pelearse, reñir*

rowboat /'rəʊbəʊt/, (BrE) **rowing boat**
/'rəʊɪŋ/ n bote m a remo or de remos

rowdy /'raʊdi/ adj **-dier, -diest** ⟨person⟩
escandaloso, alborotador; (quarrelsome)
pendenciero

row house /'rəʊ/ n (AmE) casa adosada en una
hilera de casas idénticas

rowing /'rəʊɪŋ/ n (Sport) remo m

rowing boat /'rəʊɪŋ/ n (BrE) ▶ ROWBOAT

royal /'rɔɪəl/ adj (a) (monarchic) real (b)
(magnificent) espléndido, regio

royal: ~**-blue** /'rɔɪəl'bluː/ adj (pred ~ blue)
azul real adj inv; **R**~ **Highness** n: **Her/Your
R**~ **Highness** Su/Vuestra Alteza Real

royalist /'rɔɪəlɪst/ adj monárquico

royalty /'rɔɪəlti/ n (pl **-ties**) [1] (status) realeza
f [2] **royalties** npl derechos mpl de autor,
regalías fpl

rpm (= **revolutions per minute**) r.p.m.

RSI n = **repetitive strain injury**

RSPCA n (in UK) (= **Royal Society for the
Prevention of Cruelty to Animals**)
≈ Asociación f protectora de animales

RSVP (please reply) s.r.c., se ruega contestación

rub /rʌb/ **-bb-** vt (a) (with hand, finger) frotar;
(firmly) restregar*; (massage) masajear, friccionar;
to ~ **one's eyes** restregarse* or refregarse* or
(Méx) tallarse los ojos (b) (with a cloth) frotar

■ **rub down** [v + o + adv, v + adv + o] (a)
⟨horse⟩ almohazar* (b) (using sandpaper) lijar

■ **rub in** [v + o + adv, v + adv + o] ⟨cream/lotion⟩
aplicar* frotando

■ **rub off** [v + o + adv, v + adv + o] ⟨dirt/marks⟩
quitar frotando or restregando or refregando;
(from blackboard) (BrE) borrar

■ **rub out** [v + o + adv, v + adv + o] borrar

■ **rub up** [v + o + adv, v + adv + o]: **to** ~ **sb up
the wrong way** caerle* mal a algn

rubber /'rʌbər ‖'rʌbə(r)/ n (a) (substance) goma
f, caucho m, hule m (Méx); (before n) ~ **ring**
flotador m (b) (eraser) (BrE) goma f (de borrar)

rubber: ~ **band** n goma f (elástica), gomita f
(RPl); ~ **bullet** n bala f de goma or caucho; ~
plant n ficus m, gomero m (CS); ~ **stamp** n
(device) sello m; (approval) visto m bueno; ~ **tree**
n árbol m del caucho, hule m (Méx)

rubbery /'rʌbəri/ adj ⟨texture⟩ gomoso;
⟨material⟩ parecido a la goma or al caucho or
(Méx) al hule

rubbish /'rʌbɪʃ/ n (a) (refuse) basura f; (before
n) ~ **bag** bolsa f de la basura; ~ **bin** (BrE) cubo m
or (CS) tacho m or (Méx) bote m or (Col) caneca f
or (Ven) tobo m de la basura (b) (junk) (colloq)
porquerías fpl (fam) (c) (nonsense) (colloq) tonterías
fpl

rubble /'rʌbəl/ n escombros mpl

ruble, (BrE) **rouble** /'ruːbəl/ n rublo m

ruby /'ruːbi/ n (pl **rubies**) rubí m

rucksack /'rʌksæk, 'rʊk-/ n mochila f, morral
m

ructions /'rʌkʃənz/ pl n (colloq) jaleo m (fam)

rudder /'rʌdər ‖'rʌdə(r)/ n timón m

ruddy /'rʌdi/ adj **-dier, -diest** ⟨cheeks⟩
rubicundo

rude /ruːd/ adj (a) (bad-mannered) ⟨person⟩
maleducado, grosero; ⟨remark⟩ grosero,
descortés; **to be** ~ **to sb** ser* grosero con algn
(b) (vulgar) (esp BrE) grosero

rudely /'ruːdli/ adv groseramente

rudeness /'ruːdnəs ‖'ruːdnɪs/ n grosería f,
mala educación f

rudimentary /ˌruːdəˈmentri ‖ˌruːdɪˈmentri/
adj rudimentario

rudiments /'ruːdəmənts ‖'ruːdɪmənts/ pl n
rudimentos mpl, nociones fpl elementales

rue /ruː/ vt lamentar, arrepentirse* de

rueful /'ruːfəl/ adj atribulado, compungido

ruff /rʌf/ n (collar) gorguera f; (on animal, bird)
collar m

ruffian /'rʌfiən/ n rufián m, villano m

ruffle¹ /'rʌfəl/ n (frill) volante m or (RPl) volado
m or (Chi) vuelo m

ruffle² vt (a) ⟨hair⟩ alborotar; ⟨feathers⟩ erizar*;
⟨clothes⟩ arrugar* (b) ⟨person⟩ alterar, contrariar

rug /rʌg/ n (a) (small carpet) alfombra f,
alfombrilla f, tapete m (Col, Méx) (b) (blanket)
manta f de viaje

rugby /'rʌgbi/ n rugby m

rugged /'rʌgəd ‖'rʌgɪd/ adj (a) ⟨rocks/coast⟩
escarpado; ⟨terrain⟩ escabroso (b) ⟨face⟩ de
facciones duras

ruin¹ /'ruːən ‖'ruːɪn/ n (a) (sth ruined) (often pl) ·····>

ruina *f*; **his career was in ~s** su carrera estaba arruinada **(b)** (cause) (*no pl*) ruina *f*, perdición *f* **(c)** (state) ruina *f*

ruin² *vt* **1** (destroy) ⟨*city/building*⟩ destruir*; ⟨*career/plans*⟩ arruinar; ⟨*person*⟩ (financially) arruinar **2** (spoil) ⟨*dress/carpet/toy*⟩ estropear; ⟨*party/surprise*⟩ echar a perder, estropear, arruinar

rule¹ /ruːl/ *n* **1** (regulation, principle) regla *f*, norma *f*; **it's against the ~s** está prohibido; **~s and regulations** reglamento *m*; **to work to ~** (Lab Rel) hacer* huelga de celo **2** **as a ~** por lo general, generalmente **3** (government) gobierno *m*; (of monarch) reinado *m*; **to be under foreign ~** estar* bajo dominio extranjero

rule² *vt* **1** (govern, control) ⟨*country*⟩ gobernar*, administrar; ⟨*person*⟩ dominar **2** (pronounce) dictaminar **3** (draw) ⟨*line*⟩ trazar* con una regla
■ ~ *vi* **1** (govern) gobernar*; «*monarch*» reinar **2** (pronounce) **to ~** (**on** sth) fallar *or* resolver* (EN algo)
■ **rule out** [*v + o + adv, v + adv + o*] ⟨*possibility*⟩ descartar*; ⟨*course of action*⟩ hacer* imposible

ruler /'ruːlər ‖ 'ruːlə(r)/ *n* **1** (leader) gobernante *mf*; (sovereign) soberano, -na *m,f* **2** (measure) regla *f*

ruling¹ /'ruːlɪŋ/ *n* fallo *m*, resolución *f*

ruling² *adj* (*before n*) ⟨*monarch*⟩ reinante; **the ~ classes** las clases dirigentes

rum /rʌm/ *n* ron *m*

Rumania /ruːˈmeɪniə/ *etc* ▶ ROMANIA *etc*

rumble¹ /'rʌmbəl/ *n* (sound) ruido *m* sordo; (of thunder) estruendo *m*; (of stomach) ruido *m* de tripas (fam)

rumble² *vi* «*guns/drums*» hacer* un ruido sordo; «*thunder*» retumbar; **my stomach's rumbling** me suenan las tripas (fam)

ruminate /'ruːmɪneɪt ‖ 'ruːmɪneɪt/ *vi* **(a)** (Zool) rumiar **(b)** (ponder) **to ~ on/about** sth cavilar SOBRE algo, rumiar algo

rummage /'rʌmɪdʒ/ *vi* hurgar*

rumor¹, (BrE) **rumour** /'ruːmər ‖ 'ruːmə(r)/ *n* rumor *m*

rumor², (BrE) **rumour** *vt* (*usu pass*) rumorear; **it is ~ed that ...** se rumorea que ...

rump /rʌmp/ *n* **(a)** (Culin) cadera *f*; (*before n*) **~ steak** filete *m* de cadera, churrasco *m* de cuadril (RPl) **(b)** (bottom) (colloq & hum) traste *m* (fam)

rumpus /'rʌmpəs/ *n* (*pl* **~es**) lío *m*, escándalo *m*

run¹ /rʌn/ (*pres p* **running**; *past* **ran**; *past p* **run**) *vi*

I **1** correr; **he ran downstairs/indoors** bajó/entró corriendo
2 (colloq) (drive) ir* (*en coche*)
3 (Transp): **the trains ~ every half hour** hay trenes cada media hora
4 (flow) «*water/oil*» correr; **she left the water ~ning** dejó la llave abierta (AmL) *or* (Esp) el grifo abierto; **my nose is ~ning** me gotea la nariz
5 (Pol) «*candidate*» presentarse, postularse (AmL)

II (operate, function): **with the engine ~ning** con el motor encendido *or* en marcha *or* (AmL tb) prendido; **it ~s off batteries** funciona con pilas *or* a pila(s)

III **1** (extend) **(a)** (in space): **the streets ~ parallel**

to each other las calles corren paralelas; **the path ~s across the field** el sendero atraviesa el campo **(b)** (*show*) estar* en cartel
2 **(a)** (be, stand): **feelings are ~ning high** los ánimos están caldeados; **inflation is ~ning at 4%** la tasa de inflación es del 4%; **it ~s in the family** es de familia **(b)** (become): **stocks are ~ning low** se están agotando las existencias; *see also* DRY¹ 1c
3 (melt, merge) «*paint/makeup*» correrse; «*color*» desteñir*, despintarse (Méx)
■ ~ *vt*

I **1** ⟨*race/marathon*⟩ correr, tomar parte en **2** **(a)** (push, move) pasar **(b)** (drive) ⟨*person*⟩ (colloq) llevar (*en coche*)
3 **to ~ a bath** preparar un baño
4 **(a)** (extend) ⟨*cable/wire*⟩ tender* **(b)** (pass) (hacer*) pasar

II **1** (operate) ⟨*engine*⟩ hacer* funcionar; ⟨*program*⟩ (Comput) pasar, ejecutar
2 (manage) ⟨*business*⟩ dirigir*, llevar
3 ⟨*course*⟩ organizar*; ⟨*article*⟩ publicar*; ▶ TEMPERATURE B

■ **run about** ▶ RUN AROUND
■ **run across** [*v + prep + o*] **(a)** (meet) ⟨*person*⟩ encontrarse* *or* toparse con **(b)** (find) ⟨*object*⟩ encontrar*
■ **run after** [*v + prep + o*] (pursue) correr detrás de *or* tras; (romantically) andar* detrás de, perseguir*
■ **run along** [*v + adv*] irse*
■ **run around** [*v + adv*] «*children*» corretear
■ **run away** [*v + adv*] huir*, escaparse, fugarse*; (run off) salir* corriendo; **she ran away from home** se escapó de casa
■ **run away with** [*v + adv + prep + o*] **1** **(a)** ⟨*race/contest*⟩ ganar fácilmente **(b)** (take over): **she lets her imagination ~ away with her** se deja llevar por la imaginación
2 (elope with) escaparse *or* fugarse* *or* irse* con
■ **run down**

I [*v + o + adv, v + adv + o*] **1** (disparage) (colloq) criticar*, hablar mal de
2 ⟨*pedestrian*⟩ atropellar

II [*v + adv*] **(a)** «*battery*» (Auto) descargarse* **(b)** «*business/factory*» venirse* abajo **(c)** «*stocks*» agotarse
■ **run in** [*v + o + adv*] (BrE Auto) ⟨*car/engine*⟩ hacer* el rodaje de
■ **run into** [*v + prep + o*] **(a)** ⟨*vehicle*⟩ chocar* con **(b)** ⟨*person/table*⟩ toparse con
■ **run off** **1** [*v + o + adv, v + adv + o*] (produce) ⟨*copies*⟩ tirar*; ⟨*photocopies*⟩ sacar*
2 [*v + adv*] (depart) salir* corriendo
■ **run off with** [*v + adv + prep + o*] ▶ RUN AWAY WITH 2
■ **run out** [*v + adv*] **(a)** (exhaust supplies): **to ~ out OF sth** quedarse SIN algo **(b)** «*money*» acabarse; «*supplies/stock*» acabarse, agotarse; «*lease/policy*» vencer*, caducar*
■ **run over** **1** [*v + o + adv, v + adv + o*] ⟨*pedestrian*⟩ atropellar
2 [*v + prep + o*] (review) ⟨*details/plan*⟩ repasar; (rehearse) ⟨*scene*⟩ ensayar
■ **run through** [*v + prep + o*] ▶ RUN OVER 2
■ **run up** **1** [*v + adv + o*] **(a)** ⟨*total/debts*⟩ ir* acumulando **(b)** ⟨*flag*⟩ izar*
2 [*v + o + adv, v + adv + o*] ⟨*dress*⟩ hacer* (*rápidamente*)

■ **run up against** [v + adv + prep + o]
⟨difficulty/obstacle⟩ toparse or tropezar* con

run² n ⃞1 (on foot): **to go for a ~** salir* a correr;
on the ~: he's on the **~** está prófugo; **after seven
years on the ~** después de estar siete años
huyendo de la justicia; **to make a ~ for it**
escaparse
⃞2 (a) (trip, outing) vuelta f, paseo m (en coche) (b)
(journey): **it's only a short ~** está muy cerca
⃞3 (a) (sequence): **a ~ of good/bad luck** una
racha de buena/mala suerte, una buena/mala
racha (b) (period of time): **in the long ~** a la larga
⃞4 (heavy demand) **~ on sth: there's been a ~ on
these watches** estos relojes han estado muy
solicitados
⃞5 (Cin, Theat) temporada f
⃞6 (track) pista f; **ski ~** pista de esquí
⃞7 (in stocking, knitted garment) carrera f
⃞8 (in baseball, cricket) carrera f
runaway¹ /'rʌnəweɪ/ n fugitivo, -va m,f
runaway² adj ⟨before n⟩ ⟨slave/prisoner⟩
fugitivo
run: ~down n resumen m; **~down**
/'rʌn'daʊn/ adj ⟨pred ~ down⟩ (a) (tired, sickly)
(usu pred) **to be/feel ~ down** estar*/sentirse*
cansado or débil (b) (dilapidated) ⟨district/hotel⟩
venido a menos
rung¹ /rʌŋ/ past p of RING²
rung² n (a) (of ladder, chair) travesaño m (b) (in
career, organization) peldaño m
runner /'rʌnər ‖ 'rʌnə(r)/ n ⃞1 (in race, baseball)
corredor, -dora m,f; (taking messages) mensajero,
-ra m,f ⃞2 (a) (on sled) patín m (b) (for drawer) riel
m, guía f
runner: ~ bean n (esp BrE) habichuela f (Col)
or (Esp) judía f verde or (Chi) poroto m verde or
(RPl) chaucha f or (Ven) vainita f or (Méx) ejote m;
~-up /'rʌnər'ʌp/ n (pl **~s-up**): **to be ~-up**
quedar en segundo lugar or puesto
running¹ /'rʌnɪŋ/ n (a) (exercise): **~ is a good
form of exercise** correr es muy buen ejercicio;
there are five candidates in the ~ for the post hay
cinco candidatos compitiendo or en liza por el
puesto (b) (of machine) funcionamiento m, marcha
f (c) (management) gestión f
running² adj ⟨before n, no comp⟩ ⃞1 (a) **to take
a ~ jump** saltar tomando carrera or (Esp)
carrerilla (b) (continuous) ⟨joke⟩ continuo; **~ water**
agua f⁰ corriente ⃞2 (discharging) ⟨sore⟩ supurante
running³ adv: **the third day ~** el tercer día
consecutivo or seguido
running costs pl n (of car) gastos mpl de
mantenimiento; (of company) costos mpl or (Esp)
costes mpl corrientes
runny /'rʌni/ adj **-nier, -niest** (a) ⟨eyes⟩
lloroso; **I've got a ~ nose** me gotea la nariz (b)
⟨sauce⟩ líquido
run-of-the-mill /'rʌnəvðə'mɪl/ adj ⟨pred **run
of the mill**⟩ ⟨job/car⟩ común or normal y
corriente
runt /rʌnt/ n (Agr) animal más pequeño de una
camada
run: ~-up n (preparatory period) **~-up TO sth**
período m previo A algo; **~way** n (Aviat) pista f;
(at fashion show) (AmE) pasarela f
rupee /'ruːpiː, ruː'piː/ n rupia f
rupture¹ /'rʌptʃər ‖ 'rʌptʃə(r)/ n ruptura f

rupture² vt romper*
rural /'rʊrəl ‖ 'rʊərəl/ adj rural
ruse /ruːs, ruːz ‖ ruːz/ n artimaña f, treta f
rush¹ /rʌʃ/ n ⃞1 (a) (haste) (no pl) prisa f, apuro
m (AmL); **I'm in a ~** tengo prisa, ando or estoy
apurado (AmL) (b) (movement): **a ~ of air** una
ráfaga de aire; **there was a ~ for the exit** todo el
mundo se precipitó hacia la salida ⃞2 (Bot) junco
m
rush² vi (a) (hurry) darse* prisa, apurarse (AmL);
she ~ed through the first course se comió el
primer plato a todo correr or a la carrera (b)
(run) (+ adv compl): **he ~ed in/out** entró/salió
corriendo; **to ~ around ir*** de acá para allá,
correr de un lado para otro (c) (surge, flow): **blood
~ed to his face** (from anger) se le subió la sangre a
la cabeza
■ ~ vt (a) ⟨job⟩ hacer* a todo correr or a la
carrera, hacer* deprisa y corriendo; ⟨person⟩
meterle prisa a, apurar (AmL) (b) (take hastily): **she
was ~ed to hospital** la llevaron rápidamente al
hospital
■ **rush into** [v + prep + o]: **she ~ed into marriage**
se precipitó al casarse; **don't ~ into anything** no
te precipites
rush: ~ hour n hora f pico (AmL), hora f punta
(Esp); **~ job** n (colloq) (urgent) trabajo m urgente;
(hastily done): **it was a ~ job** se hizo a todo correr
or deprisa y corriendo or a la(s) carrera(s)
rusk /rʌsk/ n galleta f (dura, para bebés)
Russia /'rʌʃə/ n Rusia f
Russian¹ /'rʌʃən/ adj ruso
Russian² n (a) (language) ruso m (b) (person)
ruso, -sa m,f
Russian roulette n ruleta f rusa
rust¹ /rʌst/ n óxido m, herrumbre f, orín m
rust² vi oxidarse, herrumbrarse
rustic /'rʌstɪk/ adj rústico
rustle¹ /'rʌsəl/ vi ⟨leaves⟩ susurrar; «paper»
crujir
■ ~ vt ⃞1 «wind» ⟨leaves⟩ hacer* susurrar
⃞2 (steal) ⟨cattle/horses⟩ robar
rustle² n (of leaves) susurro m; (of paper) crujido
m; (of silk) frufrú m
rustler /'rʌslər ‖ 'rʌslə(r)/ n ladrón, -drona m,f
de ganado
rustproof /'rʌstpruːf/ adj ⟨surface/metal⟩
inoxidable; ⟨coating⟩ anticorrosivo, antioxidante
rusty /'rʌsti/ adj **-tier, -tiest** oxidado,
herrumbroso; **to get o** (BrE also) **go ~** oxidarse,
herrumbrarse; **my German is a bit ~** tengo muy
olvidado el alemán
rut /rʌt/ n ⃞1 (groove) surco m, rodada f; **to be in
a ~** estar* anquilosado; **to get into a ~**
anquilosarse ⃞2 (Zool) celo m
rutabaga /'ruːtəbeɪgə ‖ ˌruːtəˈbeɪgə/ n (AmE)
nabo m sueco
ruthless /'ruːθləs ‖ 'ruːθlɪs/ adj ⟨person⟩
despiadado; ⟨persecution⟩ implacable, inexorable
Rwanda /rʊˈændə/ n Ruanda f
Rwandan /rʊˈændən/ adj ruandés
rye /raɪ/ n (a) (plant, grain) centeno m (b) **~
(bread)** pan m de centeno

Ss

S, s /es/ *n* S, s *f*

S (a) (Geog) (= **south**) S **(b)** (Clothing) (= **small**) P

Sabbath /'sæbəθ/ *n* (Jewish) sábado *m*; (Christian) domingo *m*

sabbatical /sə'bætɪkəl/ *n* (year) año *m* sabático; (period) período *m* sabático

saber, (BrE) **sabre** /'seɪbər ‖'seɪbə(r)/ *n* sable *m*

sabotage¹ /'sæbətɑːʒ/ *n* sabotaje *m*

sabotage² *vt* sabotear

saboteur /ˌsæbə'tɜː ‖ˌsæbə'tɜː(r)/ *n* saboteador, -dora *m,f*

sabre *n* (BrE) ▶ SABER

saccharin /'sækərən ‖'sækərɪn/ *n* sacarina *f*

sachet /sæ'ʃeɪ ‖'sæʃeɪ/ *n* (of shampoo, cream) sachet *m*; (of powder, sugar) (BrE) sobrecito *m*

sack¹ /sæk/ *n* **1 (a)** (large bag) saco *m* **(b)** (paper bag) (AmE) bolsa *f* (de papel) **2** (dismissal) (BrE colloq): **to give sb the ~** echar a algn (del trabajo), botar a algn (del trabajo) (AmL fam)

sack² *vt* **1** (dismiss) (BrE colloq) ⟨person/ employee⟩ echar (del trabajo), botar (del trabajo) (AmL fam) **2** (destroy) ⟨town/city⟩ saquear

sacrament /'sækrəmənt/ *n* sacramento *m*

sacred /'seɪkrəd ‖'seɪkrɪd/ *adj* sagrado

sacrifice¹ /'sækrɪfaɪs ‖'sækrɪfaɪs/ *n* **1** (Occult, Relig) **(a)** (practice, act) sacrificio *m* **(b)** (offering) ofrenda *f* **2** (giving up) sacrificio *m*; **to make ~s** sacrificarse*

sacrifice² *vt* sacrificar*

sacrilege /'sækrəlɪdʒ ‖'sækrɪlɪdʒ/ *n* sacrilegio *m*

sad /sæd/ *adj* **-dd-** triste; **~ to say** lamentablemente

sadden /'sædn̩/ *vt* entristecer*

saddle¹ /'sædl̩/ *n* (on horse) silla *f* (de montar); (on bicycle) sillín *m*

saddle² *vt* **(a)** **~ (up)** ⟨horse⟩ ensillar **(b)** (burden) (colloq) **to ~ sb with sth** endilgarle* *or* (esp AmL) encajarle algo A algn

saddle-bag /'sædl̩bæg/ *n* (on horse) alforja *f*; (on bicycle) maletero *m*

sadist /'seɪdəst ‖'seɪdɪst/ *n* sádico, -ca *m,f*

sadly /'sædli/ *adv* **(a)** (sorrowfully) ⟨smile/speak⟩ tristemente, con tristeza **(b)** (regrettably): **you are ~ mistaken** estás totalmente equivocado **(c)** (unfortunately) (indep) lamentablemente

sadness /'sædnəs ‖'sædnɪs/ *n* tristeza *f*

sae, SAE *n* (BrE) (= **stamped, addressed envelope**) ▶ SASE

safari /sə'fɑːri/ *n* safari *m*; (before n) **~ park** safari-park *m*

safe¹ /seɪf/ *adj* **safer, safest** **1** (secure from danger) seguro; ⟨haven/place⟩ seguro; **you are not ~ here** corres peligro aquí; **keep these documents ~** guarda estos documentos en un lugar seguro; **they're ~** están a salvo; **they were found ~ and well** *o* **~ and sound** los encontraron sanos y salvos **2** (not dangerous) ⟨ladder⟩ seguro **3** (not risky) ⟨investment/sex/method⟩ seguro; **to be on the ~ side** por si acaso; *better* **(to be) ~ than sorry** más vale prevenir que curar

safe² *n* caja *f* fuerte, caja *f* de caudales

safe: ~-conduct /'seɪfkɑːndʌkt ‖ˌseɪf'kɒndʌkt/ *n* protección *f*; **~-deposit (box)** /'seɪfdɪ'pɑːzət ‖'seɪfdɪ'pɒzɪt/ *n* caja *f* de seguridad

safeguard¹ /'seɪfgɑːrd ‖'seɪfgɑːd/ *n* salvaguarda *f*

safeguard² *vt* salvaguardar

safe: ~ house *n* piso *m* franco; **~keeping** *n*: **he gave her the watch for ~keeping** le dio el reloj para que lo guardara en lugar seguro *or* (esp Esp frml) para que lo pusiera a buen recaudo

safely /'seɪfli/ *adv* **1 (a)** (without mishap, unharmed): **we got home ~** llegamos a casa sin novedad **(b)** (without danger) sin peligro; **drive ~** conduzca con prudencia *or* cuidado **2** (with certainty) ⟨say/assume⟩ sin temor a equivocarse (*or* equivocarnos *etc*)

safety /'seɪfti/ *n* (*pl* **-ties**)(security, freedom from risk) seguridad *f*; (before n) ⟨device/precautions/ regulations⟩ de seguridad

safety: ~ belt *n* cinturón *m* de seguridad; **~ catch** (on gun) seguro *m*; **~ net** *n* (for acrobats) red *f* de seguridad; (protection) protección *f*; **~ pin** *n* imperdible *m*, gancho *m* (Andes), alfiler *m* de gancho (CS, Ven), gancho *m* de nodriza (Col), seguro *m* (Méx)

saffron /'sæfrən/ *n* azafrán *m*

sag /sæg/ *vi* **-gg- (a)** «beams/ceiling» combarse; «bed» hundirse **(b)** (hang down, droop): **~ging breasts** pechos *mpl* caídos

saga /'sɑːgə/ *n* (Lit) saga *f*; (long story) historia *f*, saga *f*

sage /seɪdʒ/ *n* **1** (Bot, Culin) salvia *f* **2** (wise man) sabio *m*

Sagittarius /ˌsædʒə'teriəs ‖ˌsædʒɪ'teəriəs/ *n* **(a)** (sign) (no art) Sagitario **(b)** (person) Sagitario *or* sagitario *mf*, sagitariano, -na *m,f*

Sahara /sə'hærə ‖sə'hɑːrə/ *n* **the ~** el Sahara *or* (Esp) el Sáhara

said /sed/ *past & past p of* SAY¹

AmC	América Central	Arg	Argentina
AmL	América Latina	Bol	Bolivia
AmS	América del Sur	Chi	Chile
Andes	Región andina	CS	Cono Sur

Cu	Cuba	Per	Perú
Ec	Ecuador	RPI	Río de la Plata
Esp	España	Ur	Uruguay
Méx	México	Ven	Venezuela

sail¹ /seɪl/ n (of ship, boat) vela f; **to set ~** (start journey) zarpar, hacerse* a la mar; «*yacht/galleon*» hacerse* a la vela

sail² vt ‹*boat/ship*› gobernar*

■ ~ vi **(a)** (travel) «*ship/boat*» navegar*; «*person/passenger*» ir* en barco; **to go ~ing** salir a navegar **(b)** (depart) «*person/ship*» zarpar, salir*

■ **sail through** [v + prep + o]: **you'll ~ through the exam** aprobarás el examen con los ojos cerrados

sailboat /'seɪlbəʊt/ n (AmE) velero m, barco m de vela

sailing /'seɪlɪŋ/ n **(a)** (skill) navegación f **(b)** (Sport) vela f

sailing: ~ boat n (BrE) ▶ SAILBOAT; **~ ship** n velero m, barco m de vela

sailor /'seɪlər ‖ 'seɪlə(r)/ n **(a)** (seaman) marinero m **(b)** (Sport) navegante mf

saint /seɪnt/ n

■ Note Although the usual translation for *saint* as a title is *san* for a man or *santa* for a woman, *santo* is used before *Domingo, Tomás, Tomé*, and *Toribio*.

(a) (canonized person) santo, -ta m,f **(b) Saint** /seɪnt ‖ sənt/ (before name) san, santa

sake /seɪk/ n **(a)** (benefit, account): **for my/their ~** por mí/ellos; **for your own ~** por tu propio bien **(b)** (purpose, end): **art for art's ~** el arte por el arte; **for argument's ~** pongamos por caso **(c)** (in interj phrases): **for goodness' o heaven's ~!** ¡por Dios!; **for God's ~!** ¡por el amor de Dios!

salad /'sæləd/ n ensalada f; (before n) **~ bowl** ensaladera f; **~ dressing** aliño m para ensalada

salad cream n (BrE) aliño para ensalada parecido a la mayonesa

salami /sə'lɑːmi/ n (pl **-mis**) salami or (CS) salame m

salary /'sæləri/ n (pl **-ries**) sueldo m

sale /seɪl/ n **1** **(a)** (act of selling) venta f **(b)** (individual transaction) venta f **(c)** (auction) subasta f, remate m (AmL)

2 (in phrases) for sale: ❾ **for sale** se vende; **on sale** (at reduced price) (AmE): **toys are on ~ this week** esta semana los juguetes están rebajados; (offered for sale) (BrE): **on ~ now at leading stores** ya está a la venta en los principales comercios **3** (clearance) liquidación f, (seasonal reductions) rebajas fpl; (before n) ‹*price*› de liquidación **4** **sales** **(a)** pl (volume sold) (sometimes sing) (volumen m de) ventas fpl **(b)** (department) (+ sing o pl vb) ventas (+ sing vb)

saleroom /'seɪlruːm, -rʊm/ n (BrE) ▶ SALESROOM A

sales /seɪlz/: **~clerk** n (AmE) vendedor, -dora m,f, dependiente, -ta m,f, **~man** /'seɪlzmən/ n (pl **-men** /-mən/) (in shop) vendedor m; (representative) representante m, corredor m (RPl); **~room** n (AmE) **(a)** (for auctions) sala f de subastas, sala f de remates (AmL) **(b)** (showroom) salón m de exposición (y ventas); **~ slip** (AmE) recibo m; **~woman** n (in shop) vendedora f; (representative) representante f, corredora f (RPl)

saliva /sə'laɪvə/ n saliva f

sallow /'sæləʊ/ adj **-er, -est** cetrino

salmon /'sæmən/ n (pl ~) salmón m

salon /sæ'lɒn ‖ 'sælɒn/ n (business): **hairdressing ~** peluquería f; **beauty ~** salón m de belleza

saloon /sə'luːn/ n **1** (bar) (AmE) bar m (del Lejano Oeste) **2** **~ (car)** (BrE) sedán m

salt¹ /sɔːlt/ n sal f

salt² vt **(a)** (put salt on) ‹*vegetables/meat*› salar, ponerle* or echarle sal a; ‹*road*› echar sal en **(b) salted** past p salado

salt: ~ cellar n salero m; **~water** adj ‹*lake*› de agua salada; ‹*fish*› de mar, de agua salada

salty /'sɔːlti/ adj **-tier, -tiest** salado

salubrious /sə'luːbriəs/ adj **(a)** (healthy) (frml) saludable, salubre **(b)** (wholesome) (usu neg): **not a very ~ district** un barrio muy poco recomendable

salutary /'sæljətəri ‖ 'sæljʊtri/ adj saludable

salute¹ /sə'luːt/ n **(a)** (gesture) saludo m, venia f (RPl) **(b)** (firing of guns) salva f **(c)** (tribute) homenaje m

salute² vt **(a)** (Mil) ‹*officer*› saludar **(b)** (acknowledge, pay tribute) (frml) ‹*courage/achievement*› rendir* homenaje a

■ ~ vi (Mil) **to ~ (TO sb)** hacerle* el saludo or (RPl) la venia (A algn)

Salvadorean¹, Salvadorian /'sælvə'dɔːriən/ adj salvadoreño

Salvadorean², Salvadorian n salvadoreño, -ña m,f

salvage /'sælvɪdʒ/ vt rescatar

salvation /sæl'veɪʃən/ n salvación f

Salvation Army n Ejército m de Salvación

salve¹ /sæv ‖ sælv/ n (ointment) bálsamo m, ungüento m

salve² vt: **to ~ one's conscience** acallar la voz de su (or mi etc) conciencia

Samaritan /sə'mærətn̩ ‖ sə'mærɪtən/ n (Bib) samaritano, -na m,f; **the good ~** el buen samaritano

same¹ /seɪm/ adj (before n) mismo, misma; **the ~ address/mistake** la misma dirección/el mismo error; **the two boxes are exactly the ~** las dos cajas son exactamente iguales; **that dress is the ~ as mine** ese vestido es igual al mío; **the ~ thing happened to me** a mí me pasó lo mismo; **on that very ~ day** ese mismísimo día

same² pron **(a)** : **the ~** lo mismo; **have a nice vacation! — ~ to you!** ¡felices vacaciones! — ¡igualmente! **(b)** all the same, just the same igual; (as linker) de todas formas or maneras; **it's all the ~ to me/you/them** me/te/les da lo mismo, me/te/les da igual

same³ adv: **the ~** igual

sample¹ /'sæmpəl ‖ 'sɑːmpəl/ n muestra f

sample² vt ‹*food*› degustar

sanatorium /ˌsænə'tɔːriəm/ n (pl **-riums** or **-ria** /-riə/) sanatorio m (para convalecientes)

sanctify /'sæŋktəfaɪ ‖ 'sæŋktɪfaɪ/ vt **-fies, -fying, -fied** santificar*

sanctimonious /ˌsæŋktə'məʊniəs ‖ ˌsæŋktɪ'məʊniəs/ adj (frml) moralista, gazmoño, mojigato

sanction¹ /'sæŋkʃən/ n **1** (authorization) autorización f, sanción f **2** **sanctions** pl (coercive measures) sanciones fpl

sanction² vt ‹*act/initiative*› sancionar (frml), aprobar*; ‹*injustice*› consentir*

sanctity /'sæŋktəti/ n **(a)** (inviolability) inviolabilidad f **(b)** (holiness) santidad f

S

sanctuary /'sæŋktʃueri ‖'sæŋktjuəri/ n (pl -ries) (a) (protection, safety) asilo m, refugio m (b) (place of refuge) santuario m

sand¹ /sænd/ n arena f

sand² vt ~ (down) ⟨wood/furniture⟩ lijar; ⟨floor⟩ pulir

sandal /'sændl/ n sandalia f

sand: ~**bank** n banco m de arena; ~**box** n (AmE) cajón m de arena (en parques y jardines); ~**castle** n castillo m de arena; ~**paper** n papel m de lija; ~**pit** n (BrE) ▶ ~BOX; ~**stone** n arenisca f; ~**storm** n tormenta f de arena

sandwich¹ /'sænwitʃ ‖'sændwidʒ/ n (pl ~es) sándwich m, emparedado m, ≈ bocadillo m (Esp)

sandwich² vt (usu pass): I was ~ed between two fat men estaba apretujado entre dos gordos

sandy /'sændi/ adj -dier, -diest (a) ⟨beach/ path⟩ de arena; ⟨soil⟩ arenoso (b) (in color) ⟨hair⟩ rubio rojizo adj inv

sane /sein/ adj **saner, sanest** (a) (not mad) cuerdo (b) (sensible) sensato

sang /sæŋ/ past of SING

sanitarium /'sænə'teriəm ‖,sænɪ'teəriəm/ n (AmE) ▶ SANATORIUM

sanitary /'sænəteri ‖'sænɪtri/ adj (a) (concerning health) (before n) ⟨conditions/ regulations⟩ sanitario; ⟨inspector⟩ de sanidad (b) (hygienic) higiénico

sanitary napkin, (BrE) **sanitary towel** n compresa f, paño m higiénico

sanitation /'sænə'teɪʃən ‖,sænɪ'teɪʃən/ n (a) (hygiene) condiciones fpl de salubridad (b) (waste disposal system) servicios mpl sanitarios

sanitize /'sænətaɪz ‖'sænɪtaɪz/ vt (a) (disinfect) desinfectar (b) (make inoffensive) (pej) hacer* potable; a ~d version una versión aséptica

sanity /'sænəti/ n (a) (mental health) razón f, cordura f (b) (good sense) sensatez f

sank /sæŋk/ past of SINK¹

Santa Claus /'sæntəklɔ:z/ n Papá Noel, San Nicolás, Santa Claus, Viejo m Pascuero (Chi)

sap¹ /sæp/ n savia f

sap² vt -pp- minar

sapling /'sæpliŋ/ n árbol m joven

sapphire /'sæfaɪr ‖'sæfaɪə(r)/ n zafiro m

sarcasm /'sɑ:rkæzəm/ n sarcasmo m

sarcastic /sɑ:r'kæstɪk/ adj sarcástico

sardine /sɑ:r'di:n ‖sɑ:'di:n/ n sardina f

sardonic /sɑ:r'dɑ:nɪk ‖sɑ:'dɒnɪk/ adj sardónico

sari /'sɑ:ri/ n (pl ~s) sari m

SARS /'sɑ:rz/ n (= Severe Acute Respitory Syndrome) SRAS m, SRAG m

SASE n (AmE) (= self-addressed stamped envelope): I enclose an ~ adjunto sobre franqueado (a mi nombre)

sash /sæʃ/ n **1** (on dress) faja f; (on uniform — around waist) fajín m; (— over shoulder) banda f **2** (of window) marco m

sassy /'sæsi/ adj -sier, -siest (AmE colloq) (a) (impertinent) caradura (fam) (b) (brash) ⟨hat/style⟩ llamativo y atrevido

sat /sæt/ past & past p of SIT

Satan /'seɪtn/ n Satanás

satanic /sə'tænɪk/ adj satánico

satchel /'sætʃəl/ n cartera f (de colegial)

sate /seɪt/ vt (liter) (usu pass) ⟨appetite/lust⟩ saciar (liter)

satellite /'sætlaɪt ‖'sætəlaɪt/ n **1** (a) (Aerosp) satélite m (artificial); (before n) ~ TV televisión f por or vía satélite (b) (Astron) satélite m **2** (dependent body, state) satélite m; (before n) a ~ town una ciudad satélite

satin /'sætn ‖'sætɪn/ n satén m, satín m (AmL)

satire /'sætaɪr ‖'sætaɪə(r)/ n sátira f

satirical /sə'tɪrɪkəl/ adj satírico

satirize /'sætəraɪz/ vt satirizar*

satisfaction /'sætəs'fækʃən ‖,sætɪs'fækʃən/ n satisfacción f

satisfactory /'sætəs'fæktri ‖,sætɪs'fæktəri/ adj satisfactorio

satisfied /'sætəsfaɪd/ adj ⟨expression/customer⟩ satisfecho; ⟨smile⟩ de satisfacción

satisfy /'sætəsfaɪ ‖'sætɪsfaɪ/ vt -fies, -fying, -fied **1** (a) (please) satisfacer* (b) (meet) ⟨requirements⟩ llenar; ⟨demand⟩ satisfacer* **2** (convince) (often pass) to ~ sb OF sth convencer* a algn DE algo

satisfying /'sætəsfaɪŋ ‖'sætɪsfaɪŋ/ adj (a) (pleasing) ⟨result/job⟩ satisfactorio (b) (filling) ⟨meal⟩ que llena

satphone /'sætfəʊn/ n teléfono m satélite

satsuma /sæt'su:mə/ n satsuma f (tipo de mandarina)

saturate /'sætʃəreɪt/ vt **1** (drench) empapar **2** (fill) ⟨market/mind/place⟩ saturar **3** (Chem, Phys) saturar

saturation /'sætʃə'reɪʃən/ n **1** (Busn, Marketing) saturación f **2** (Chem, Phys) saturación f

Saturday /'sætərdeɪ, -di ‖'sætədeɪ, -di/ n sábado m; see also MONDAY

Saturn /'sætərn ‖'sætən/ n Saturno m

sauce /sɔ:s/ n salsa f

saucepan /'sɔ:spæn ‖'sɔ:spən/ n cacerola f, cazo m (Esp); (large) olla f

saucer /'sɔ:sər ‖'sɔ:sə(r)/ n platillo m

saucy /'sɔ:si, 'sɔ:si ‖'sɔ:si/ adj -cier, -ciest insolente, fresco (fam)

Saudi¹ /'saʊdi/ adj saudita, saudí

Saudi² n saudita mf, saudí mf

Saudi Arabia /ə'reɪbiə/ n Arabia f Saudita, Arabia f Saudí

sauna /'sɔ:nə/ n sauna f, sauna m (AmL)

saunter /'sɔ:ntər ‖'sɔ:ntə(r)/ vi pasear; she ~ed in/out entró/salió andando despacio

sausage /'sɔ:sɪdʒ ‖'sɒsɪdʒ/ n (for cooking) salchicha f; (cold, cured) embutido m

sauté /sɔ:'teɪ ‖'səʊteɪ/ vt -tés, -téeing or -téing, -téed or -téd saltear

savage¹ /'sævɪdʒ/ adj (a) (fierce, wild) ⟨beast/ attack⟩ salvaje; ⟨blow⟩ violento (b) (uncivilized) ⟨tribe/people⟩ salvaje

savage² n salvaje mf

savage³ vt atacar* salvajemente a

savagely /'sævɪdʒli/ adv salvajemente

savagery /'sævɪdʒri/ n ferocidad f

save¹ /seɪv/ vt **1** (a) (preserve) ⟨life/person/job⟩ salvar; ⟨possessions⟩ rescatar; **firefighters ~d 20 people** bomberos rescataron a 20 personas (b)

(redeem) ⟨soul/sinner⟩ salvar **2** **(a)** (be economical with) ⟨money/fuel/space/time⟩ ahorrar **(b)** (spare, avoid) ⟨trouble/expense/embarrassment⟩ ahorrar, evitar **3** **(a)** (keep, put aside) guardar; ⟨money⟩ ahorrar; **don't eat it now; ~ it for later** no te lo comas ahora; déjalo para luego; **to ~ one's energy** guardarse las energías **(b)** (Comput) guardar **4** (Sport) ⟨shot/penalty⟩ salvar
■ ~ vi ahorrar
■ **save up** **1** [v + adv] ahorrar **2** [v + o + adv, v + adv + o] ahorrar
save² n parada f
save³ prep (frml) (apart from) ~ **(for)** salvo, excepto
saving¹ /'seɪvɪŋ/ n **(a)** (economy) ahorro m **(b)** **savings** pl ahorros mpl; ⟨before n⟩ **~s account** cuenta f de ahorros
saving² adj ⟨before n⟩ ▶ GRACE 2C
savings /'seɪvɪŋz/: **~ and loan** n **~ ~ ~ (association/company)** (AmE) sociedad f de ahorro y préstamos; **~ bank** n caja f de ahorros
savior, (BrE) **saviour** /'seɪvjər ‖'seɪvjə(r)/ n salvador, -dora m,f
savor¹, (BrE) **savour** /'seɪvər ‖'seɪvə(r)/ vt saborear
savor², (BrE) **savour** n (taste) sabor m; (hint, trace) dejo m
savory, (BrE) **savoury** /'seɪvəri/ adj (tasty) sabroso; (wholesome) (usu with neg) limpio
savour vt/n (BrE) ▶ SAVOR¹,²
savoury /'seɪvəri/ adj (BrE) **(a)** ▶ SAVORY **(b)** (not sweet) salado
saw¹ /'sɔː/ past of SEE
saw² n (manual) sierra f; (— with one handle) serrucho m; (power-driven) sierra f mecánica
saw³ vt (past p **sawed** or (esp BrE) **sawn**) (with handsaw) cortar (con serrucho), serruchar (AmL); (with a larger saw) cortar (con sierra), serrar*, aserrar*
sawdust /'sɔːdʌst/ n serrín m, aserrín m (esp AmL)
sawed-off /'sɔːdˌɔːf ‖'sɔːdˌɒf/, (BrE) **sawn-off** /'sɔːnˌɔːf ‖'sɔːnˌɒf/ adj: ~ **shotgun** escopeta f recortada
sawn /sɔːn/ past p of SAW³
sawn-off adj (BrE) ▶ SAWED-OFF
saxophone /'sæksəfəʊn/ n saxofón m, saxófono m
say¹ /seɪ/ (pres **says** /sez/; past & past p **said** /sed/) vt **1** (utter, express in speech) ⟨word/sentence⟩ decir*; ⟨prayer⟩ rezar*; **I said yes/no** dije que sí/ no; **to ~ sth TO sb** decirle* algo A algn; **why didn't you ~ so before?** haberlo dicho antes; **that's to ~** es decir; **to ~ the least** como mínimo; **what have you got to ~ for yourself?** a ver, explícate; ~ **no more** no me digas más; **you can ~ that again!** ¡y que lo digas!; **it goes without ~ing that ...** huelga decir que ...; **that's easier said than done** del dicho al hecho hay mucho trecho; **no sooner said than done** dicho y hecho; **when all's said and done** al fin y al cabo **2** ⟨watch/dial⟩ marcar*
3 (suppose) (colloq) suponer*; (let's) ~ **that ...** supongamos que ...
4 (allege) decir*; **..., or so he ~s ...,** al menos eso es lo que dice

■ ~ vi decir*; **I'd rather not** ~ prefiero no decirlo; **it's hard to** ~ es difícil decirlo
say² interj (AmE colloq) ¡oye! (fam)
say³ n (no pl) **(a)** (statement of view): **to have one's** ~ dar* su (or mi etc) opinión **(b)** (power): **I have no ~ in the matter** yo no tengo ni voz ni voto en el asunto
saying /'seɪɪŋ/ n refrán m, dicho m
SC = **South Carolina**
scab /skæb/ n **1** (on wound) costra f **2** (strikebreaker) (pej) esquirol mf (pey), carnero, -ra m,f (RPl fam & pey)
scaffold /'skæfəld, -fəʊld/ n (for execution) patíbulo m, cadalso m
scaffolding /'skæfəldɪŋ, -fəʊldɪŋ/ n andamiaje m
scald /skɔːld/ vt escaldar
scale¹ /skeɪl/ n
I **1** (no pl) **(a)** (extent, size) escala f; **on a large/ small** ~ en gran/pequeña escala **(b)** (of map, diagram) escala f; ⟨before n⟩ ⟨model/drawing⟩ a escala **2** (on measuring instrument) escala f **3** (Mus) escala f **4** (for weighing) (usu pl) balanza f, pesa f; **bathroom** ~s una báscula or pesa (de baño)
II **1** (on fish) escama f **2** (deposit in kettle, pipes) sarro m
scale² vt ⟨mountain/wall⟩ escalar; ⟨ladder⟩ subir
■ **scale down** [v + o + adv, v + adv + o] ⟨drawing⟩ reducir* (a escala); ⟨operation⟩ recortar
scallion /'skæljən/ n (AmE) **(a)** (young onion) cebolleta f, cebollino m **(b)** (shallot) chalote m, chalota f
scallop /'skæləp/ n vieira f, ostión m (CS)
scalp¹ /skælp/ n (Anat) cuero m cabelludo
scalp² vt: **to** ~ **sb** arrancarle* la cabellera a algn
scalpel /'skælpəl/ n bisturí m, escalpelo m
scaly /'skeɪli/ adj **-lier, -liest** ⟨skin⟩ escamoso
scamper /'skæmpər ‖'skæmpə(r)/ vi corretear; **she ~ed off** se fue correteando
scampi /'skæmpi/ pl n langostinos mpl (gen rebozados)
scan¹ /skæn/ vt **-nn-** **1** **(a)** ⟨horizon⟩ escudriñar **(b)** ⟨noticeboard/newspaper⟩ recorrer con la vista; ⟨report⟩ echarle un vistazo a **2** (Med) ⟨body/brain⟩ hacer* un escáner de; (with ultrasound scanner) hacer* una ecografía de
scan² n (Med) escáner m; (ultrasound) ecografía f
scandal /'skændl/ n **(a)** (outrage) escándalo m **(b)** (gossip) chismorreo m
scandalize /'skændlaɪz/ vt escandalizar*
scandalous /'skændləs/ adj escandaloso
Scandinavia /ˌskændə'neɪviə ‖ˌskændɪ'neɪviə/ n Escandinavia f
Scandinavian¹ /ˌskændə'neɪviən ‖ˌskændɪ'neɪviən/ adj escandinavo
Scandinavian² n escandinavo, -va m,f
scanner /'skænər ‖'skænə(r)/ n (Med) escáner m, scanner m
scanty /'skænti/ adj **-tier, -tiest** ⟨information⟩ insuficiente; ⟨meal⟩ poco abundante, frugal; ⟨costume⟩ breve
scapegoat /'skeɪpɡəʊt/ n chivo m expiatorio

scar¹ /skɑːr ‖skɑː(r)/ n cicatriz f

scar² vt **-rr-**: his face was badly ~red le quedó una enorme cicatriz en el rostro; she'll be ~red for life (physically) le va a quedar (la) cicatriz; (emotionally) va a quedar marcada

scarce /skers ‖skeəs/ adj escaso; to be ~ escasear

scarcely /'skersli ‖'skeəsli/ adv apenas

scarcity /'skersəti ‖'skeəsəti/ n (pl **-ties**) escasez f

scare¹ /sker ‖skeə(r)/ vt asustar
■ **scare away, scare off** [v + o + adv, v + adv + o] espantar

scare² n (a) (fright, shock) susto m (b) (panic) (Journ): **bomb** ~ amenaza f de bomba

scarecrow /'skerkrəʊ ‖'skeəkrəʊ/ n espantapájaros m

scared /skerd ‖skeəd/ adj asustado; I'm ~ tengo miedo; to be ~ or sth/sb tenerle* miedo A algo/algn

scarf /skɑːrf ‖skɑːf/ n (pl **~s** or **scarves**) (a) (muffler) bufanda f (b) (square) pañuelo m

scarlet /'skɑːrlət ‖'skɑːlət/ adj (rojo) escarlata adj inv

scarlet fever n escarlatina f

scarves /skɑːrvz ‖skɑːvz/ pl of SCARF

scathing /'skeɪðɪŋ/ adj mordaz

scatter /'skætər ‖'skætə(r)/ vt 1 ⟨salt/grit⟩ esparcir*; ⟨seeds⟩ sembrar* (a voleo) 2 (disperse) ⟨crowd/group⟩ dispersar; they are ~ed all over the country están desperdigados por todo el país
■ ~ vi ⟨crowd/light⟩ dispersarse

scatterbrained /'skætər'bremd ‖'skætəbremd/ adj atolondrado, despistado

scattered /'skætərd ‖'skætəd/ adj (before n) ⟨fighting/applause/outbreak⟩ aislado; ⟨community⟩ diseminado; ~ showers chubascos mpl aislados

scavenge /'skævəndʒ ‖'skævɪndʒ/ vi to ~ for sth escarbar or hurgar* en busca de algo

scavenger /'skævəndʒər ‖'skævɪndʒə(r)/ n (a) (animal, bird) carroñero, -ra m,f (b) (person) persona que busca comida etc hurgando en los desperdicios

scenario /sə'neriəʊ, -'næ- ‖sɪ'nɑːriəʊ/ n (pl **-os**) (a) (Cin, TV) guion m (b) (of future) perspectiva f, escenario m (period)

scene /siːn/ n 1 (a) (view, situation) escena f (b) (of incident, crime) escena f; it was the ~ of violent demonstrations fue el escenario de violentas manifestaciones; to appear on the ~ aparecer*; to set the ~ (for sth) situar* la escena (de algo) 2 (in play, book etc) escena f 3 (stage setting) decorado m; behind the ~s entre bastidores 4 (fuss, row) escena f 5 (sphere) ámbito m; it's not my ~ (colloq) no es lo mío

scenery /'siːnəri/ n (a) (surroundings) paisaje m (b) (Theat) escenografía f

scenic /'siːnɪk/ adj pintoresco

scent¹ /sent/ n (a) (fragrance) perfume m (b) (perfume) (BrE) perfume m (c) (trail) rastro m; to put o throw sb off the ~ despistar a algn

scent² vt (a) (sense) ⟨danger/victory⟩ intuir* (b) (perfume) ⟨air/room/skin⟩ perfumar (c) **scented** past p ⟨writing paper⟩ perfumado; ⟨rose⟩ fragante

scepter, (BrE) **sceptre** /'septər ‖'septə(r)/ n cetro m

sceptic etc (BrE) ▶ SKEPTIC etc

sceptre n (BrE) ▶ SCEPTER

schedule¹ /'skedʒuːl ‖'ʃedjuːl/ n 1 (plan) programa m; the flight is due to arrive on ~ el vuelo llegará a la hora prevista; to be ahead of/ behind ~ estar* adelantado/atrasado con respecto al programa 2 (a) (list) (frml) lista f (b) (AmE) (timetable — for transport) horario m; (— for classes) horario m (de clases)

schedule² vt (timetable, plan) (usu pass) programar; the conference is ~d to take place in August la conferencia está planeada para el mes de agosto

scheduled /'skedʒuːld ‖'ʃedjuːld/ adj (before n) (a) (planned) ⟨meeting/visit⟩ previsto, programado (b) ⟨flight/service⟩ regular

scheme¹ /skiːm/ n (plan) plan m; (underhand) ardid m; (plot) confabulación f, conspiración f

scheme² vi intrigar*; (plot) conspirar

scheming¹ /'skiːmɪŋ/ adj intrigante

scheming² n maquinaciones fpl, intrigas fpl

schism /'sɪzəm, 'skɪzəm/ n cisma m

schizophrenia /ˌskɪtsə'friːniə ‖ˌskɪtsə'friːniə/ n esquizofrenia f

schizophrenic /ˌskɪtsə'frenɪk, -'friːnɪk ‖ˌskɪtsəʊ'frenɪk, -'friːnɪk/ adj esquizofrénico

schmaltz /ʃmɔːlts/ n (colloq) sensiblería f

schmaltzy /'ʃmɔːltsi/ adj **-zier, -ziest** (colloq) sensiblero

scholar /'skɑːlər ‖'skɒlə(r)/ n (a) (learned person) erudito, -ta m,f (b) (holder of scholarship) becario, -ria m,f

scholarly /'skɑːlərli ‖'skɒləli/ adj ⟨person⟩ erudito, docto; ⟨attainments⟩ en el campo académico

scholarship /'skɑːlərʃɪp ‖'skɒləʃɪp/ n 1 (grant) beca f 2 (scholarliness) erudición f

school¹ /skuːl/ n 1 (a) (in primary, secondary education) colegio m, escuela f; to go to ~ ir* al colegio or a la escuela; (before n) ⟨uniform/rules⟩ del colegio; ⟨bus⟩ escolar; ~ fees cuotas que se pagan en un colegio particular, colegiatura f (Méx); ~ year año m escolar or lectivo (b) (college, university) (AmE) universidad f (c) (department) facultad f 2 (other training establishment) academia f, escuela f 3 (of fish) cardumen m, banco m; (of dolphins, whales) grupo m

school² vt ⟨person⟩ instruir*; (train) capacitar

school: ~**boy** n colegial m, escolar m; ~**child** n colegial, -giala m,f, escolar mf; ~**girl** n colegiala f, escolar f

schooling /'skuːlɪŋ/ n educación f, estudios mpl

school: ∼-**leaver** /'liːvər ‖'liːvə(r)/ n (BrE) joven mf que termina el colegio; ∼**master** n (BrE frml) (in primary school) maestro m; (in secondary school) profesor m; ∼**mistress** n (BrE frml) (in primary school) maestra; (in secondary school) profesora f; ∼**teacher** n (in primary school) maestro, -tra m,f; (in secondary school) profesor, -sora m,f

science /'saɪəns/ n ciencia f

science fiction n ciencia ficción f

scientific /ˌsaɪən'tɪfɪk/ adj científico

scientist /'saɪəntəst ‖'saɪəntɪst/ n científico, -ca m,f

sci-fi /'saɪfaɪ/ n (colloq) ciencia ficción f

Scillies /'sɪliz/ pl n ▶ ISLES OF SCILLY

scintillating /'sɪntleɪtɪŋ ‖'sɪntɪleɪtɪŋ/ adj ⟨wit/conversation⟩ chispeante

scissors /'sɪzərz ‖'sɪzəz/ n (+ pl vb) tijeras fpl, tijera f

scoff /skɑːf ‖skɒf/ vi to ∼ (AT sb/sth) burlarse (DE algn/algo)
■ ∼ vt (eat greedily) (BrE colloq) engullirse*

scold /skəʊld/ vt reprender, regañar, retar (CS)

scone /skəʊn, skɑːn ‖skɒn, skəʊn/ n (in UK) bollito que se come untado de mantequilla, mermelada etc, scone m (CS), bísquet m (Méx)

scoop /skuːp/ n **1** (a) (for grain, ice cream) pala f (b) (measure — of ice cream) bola f **2** (Journ) primicia f
■ **scoop out** **1** [v + o + adv, v + adv + o] ⟨flour/rice/soil⟩ sacar* ⟨con pala, cuchara etc⟩ **2** [v + adv + o] (hollow) ⟨hole/tunnel⟩ excavar
■ **scoop up** [v + o + adv, v + adv + o] recoger* ⟨con pala, cuchara etc⟩

scooter /'skuːtər ‖'skuːtə(r)/ n (a) (motor ∼) escúter m, Vespa® f (b) (toy) patinete m

scope /skəʊp/ n (of law, regulations) alcance m; (of influence) ámbito m; (of investigation) campo m

scorch /skɔːrtʃ ‖skɔːtʃ/ vt ⟨fabric⟩ chamuscar*; ⟨sun⟩ ⟨plant⟩ quemar, abrasar

score¹ /skɔːr ‖skɔː(r)/ n **1** (a) (in game): the final ∼ el resultado final; what's the ∼? ¿cómo van? (b) (in competition, test etc) puntuación f, puntaje m (AmL) **2** (a) (account): I have no worries on that ∼ en lo que a eso se refiere, no me preocupo; to have a ∼ to settle with sb tener* que arreglar cuentas con algn (b) (situation) (colloq): to know the ∼ saber cómo son las cosas **3** (Mus) (a) (notation) partitura f (b) (music for show, movie) música f **4** (twenty) veintena f; there were ∼s of people there había muchísima gente

score² vt **1** (a) (Sport) ⟨goal⟩ marcar*, anotar(se) (AmL); you ∼ 20 points for that eso te da or (AmL tb) con eso te anotas 20 puntos (b) (in competition, test) ⟨person⟩ sacar* (c) (win) ⟨success⟩ lograr, conseguir* **2** (cut, mark) ⟨surface/paper⟩ marcar*
■ ∼ vi (Sport) marcar*, anotar(se) un tanto (AmL)

scoreboard /'skɔːrbɔːrd ‖'skɔːbɔːd/ n marcador m

scorn¹ /skɔːrn ‖skɔːn/ n desdén m; to pour ∼ on sth desdeñar algo

scorn² vt (reject, despise) desdeñar

scornful /'skɔːrnfəl ‖'skɔːnfəl/ adj desdeñoso; to be ∼ of sth desdeñar algo

Scorpio /'skɔːrpiəʊ ‖'skɔːpiəʊ/ n (pl -os) (a)

(sign) (no art) Escorpio, Escorpión (b) (person) Escorpio or escorpio mf, Escorpión or escorpión mf, escorpio, -na m,f

scorpion /'skɔːrpiən ‖'skɔːpiən/ n escorpión m, alacrán m

Scot /skɑːt ‖skɒt/ n escocés, -cesa m,f

scotch¹ /skɑːtʃ ‖skɒtʃ/ vt ⟨plan/efforts⟩ echar por tierra; ⟨rumors⟩ acallar

scotch², Scotch n whisky m or güisqui m (escocés)

Scotch: ∼ **egg** n: huevo duro envuelto en carne de salchicha y rebozado; ∼ **tape**® n (AmE) cinta f Scotch®, cel(l)o® m (Esp), (cinta f) durex® m (AmL)

scot-free /'skɑːt'friː ‖ˌskɒt'friː/ adj ⟨pred⟩: to get away ∼ quedar impune

Scotland /'skɑːtlənd ‖'skɒtlənd/ n Escocia f

Scots /skɑːts ‖skɒts/ adj ⟨before n⟩ escocés

Scots: ∼**man** /'skɑːtsmən ‖'skɒtsmən/ n (pl -men /-mən/) escocés m; ∼**woman** n escocesa f

Scottish /'skɑːtɪʃ ‖'skɒtɪʃ/ adj escocés

scoundrel /'skaʊndrəl/ n (dated) sinvergüenza mf

scour /skaʊr ‖'skaʊə(r)/ vt **1** (rub hard) fregar* **2** (search thoroughly) registrar

scourge /skɜːrdʒ ‖skɜːdʒ/ n azote m

scouring powder /'skaʊrɪŋ ‖'skaʊərɪŋ/ n polvo m limpiador, limpiador m en polvo, pulidor m (RPl)

scout /skaʊt/ n **1** (person) explorador, -dora m,f **2** also **Scout** (boy ∼) explorador m, (boy) scout m; (girl ∼) exploradora f, (girl) scout f
■ **scout around** [v + adv] to ∼ around (FOR sth) buscar* ⟨algo⟩

scowl¹ /skaʊl/ n ceño m fruncido

scowl² vi fruncir* el ceño; to ∼ AT sb mirar a algn con el ceño fruncido

scrabble /'skræbəl/ vi ⟨dog/chicken⟩ escarbar; he was scrabbling about in the drawers of the desk estaba hurgando en los cajones del escritorio

scraggy /'skrægi/ adj -gier, -giest (a) (scrawny) esmirriado (b) (tough) ⟨meat⟩ duro

scram /skræm/ vi -mm- (colloq): go on, ∼! ¡fuera or largo de aquí! (fam)

scramble¹ /'skræmbəl/ n (no pl) (a) (chaotic rush): barullo m; there was a last-minute ∼ for tickets a último momento hubo una rebatiña para conseguir entradas (b) (difficult climb) subida f difícil

scramble² vi (+ adv compl): we ∼d through the bushes nos abrimos paso con dificultad a través de los arbustos
■ ∼ vt (a) (mix) mezclar (b) ⟨message⟩ codificar*

scrambled egg /'skræmbəld/ n (Culin) huevos mpl revueltos

scrap¹ /skræp/ n **1** (a) (of paper, cloth, leather) pedacito m, trocito m (b) (single bit) ⟨with neg, no pl⟩: it doesn't make a ∼ of difference what you think lo que tú pienses no importa en lo más mínimo **2** scraps pl sobras fpl, sobros mpl (AmC) **3** (reusable waste) chatarra f; ⟨before n⟩ ∼ paper papel m para borrador

scrap² *vt* **-pp- (a)** (abandon) ⟨*idea*⟩ desechar; ⟨*plan*⟩ abandonar **(b)** (throw away) tirar a la basura, botar (AmL exc RPI)

scrapbook /'skræpbʊk/ *n* álbum *m* de recortes

scrape¹ /skreɪp/ *n* (colloq) lío *m* (fam)

scrape² *vt* **1 (a)** (rub against) rozar*; (grate against) rascar* **(b)** (damage, graze) ⟨*paintwork*⟩ rayar; ⟨*knee/elbow*⟩ rasparse, rasguñarse **2 (a)** (clean) ⟨*carrot/potato*⟩ pelar; ⟨*woodwork*⟩ raspar, rascar*; to ~ sth off ⟨*paint/wallpaper*⟩ quitar algo (con una rasqueta/un cuchillo); ~ the mud off your boots quítales el barro a las botas (con un cuchillo, contra una piedra etc) **(b)** ⟨*bowl/pan*⟩ fregar*
■ **scrape through** [*v + adv*] [*v + prep + o*] ⟨*exam*⟩ aprobar* raspando *or* (fam) por los pelos

scraper /'skreɪpər ‖ 'skreɪpə(r)/ *n* (tool) rasqueta *f*, espátula *f*

scrap: ~heap *n*: to throw sth on the ~heap desechar algo; at 50 he found himself on the ~heap a los 50 años se vio sin trabajo y sin perspectivas de futuro; **~yard** *n* chatarrería *f*; (for cars) cementerio *m* de automóviles, desguace *m or* (Méx) deshuesadero *m*

scratch¹ /skrætʃ/ *n* **1** rasguño *m*, arañazo *m*; (on paint, record, furniture) rayón *m* **2** (*in phrases*) from scratch: to start from ~ empezar* desde cero; to be up to ~ (colloq) dar* la talla

scratch² *vt* **(a)** ⟨*paint/record/furniture*⟩ rayar **(b)** (with claws, nails) arañar **(c)** ⟨*name/initials*⟩ marcar* **(d)** (to relieve itch) rascarse*
■ ~ *vi* **(a)** (damage, wound) arañar **(b)** (to relieve itching) rascarse*
■ **scratch out** [*v + o + adv, v + adv + o*] **(a)** (gouge): to ~ sb's eyes out sacarle* los ojos a algn **(b)** (strike out) ⟨*name/sentence*⟩ tachar; (on ticket) rascar*

scratch: ~ card *n* número *m* de la lotería (con sección que se raspa); **~ pad** *n* (AmE) bloc *m* (para borrador o apuntes)

scrawl¹ /skrɔːl/ *n* garabatos *mpl*

scrawl² *vt/i* garabatear

scrawny /'skrɔːni/ *adj* **-nier, -niest** ⟨*person*⟩ escuálido; ⟨*arms/legs*⟩ esquelético

scream¹ /skriːm/ *n* grito *m*, chillido *m*; (louder) alarido *m*

scream² *vi* gritar, chillar; «*baby*» llorar a gritos
■ ~ *vt* ⟨*insult*⟩ gritar, soltar*; ⟨*command*⟩ dar* a voces *or* a gritos

screech¹ /skriːtʃ/ *n* (of terror, pain) alarido *m*; (of joy) chillido *m*; (of brakes) chirrido *m*; (of bird) chillido *m*

screech² *vi* «*person/animal*» chillar; «*brakes/tires*» chirriar*

screen¹ /skriːn/ *n* **1** (folding) biombo *m*; (as partition) mampara *f*; (protective, defensive) cortina *f* **2** (Cin, Comput, Phot, TV) pantalla *f*

screen² *vt* **1 (a)** (conceal) ocultar, tapar **(b)** (protect) proteger* **2** ⟨*TV program*⟩ emitir; ⟨*film*⟩ proyectar **3** (check, examine) ⟨*blood donor*⟩ someter a una revisión (médica); ⟨*applicants*⟩ someter a una investigación de antecedentes
■ **screen off** [*v + o + adv, v + adv + o*] aislar*, separar (con un biombo o una mampara)

screen: ~ door *n* puerta *f* mosquitera;

~play *n* guion *m*; **~ saver** /'seɪvər ‖ 'seɪvə(r)/ *n* (Comput) protector *m* de pantalla, salvapantalla *m*; **~ test** *n* prueba *f* (cinematográfica)

screw¹ /skruː/ *n* (Const, Tech) tornillo *m*; to have a ~ loose (colloq & hum): he's/you've got a ~ loose le/te falta un tornillo (fam & hum)

screw² *vt* (Const, Tech) atornillar; to ~ sth down (securely) atornillar (bien) algo; ~ the lid on tight enrosca bien la tapa
■ **screw up** [*v + o + adv, v + adv + o*] **1** (tighten) ⟨*bolt*⟩ apretar* **2** (crumple) ⟨*letter/paper*⟩ arrugar* **3** (spoil, botch) (sl) fastidiar (fam)

screw: ~ball *n* (eccentric person) (AmE colloq) excéntrico, -ca *mf*, chiflado, -da *m,f* (fam); **~driver** *n* destornillador *m*, desarmador *m* (Méx), desatornillador *m* (AmC, Chi); **~top** *adj* ⟨*bottle*⟩ con tapón de rosca; ⟨*jar*⟩ con tapa de rosca

scribble¹ /'skrɪbəl/ *n* garabato *m*

scribble² *vt* garabatear; to ~ sth down anotar algo rápidamente
■ ~ *vi* garabatear

scrimp /skrɪmp/ *vi*: to ~ ON sth escatimar EN algo; to ~ and save cuidar mucho el dinero

script /skrɪpt/ *n* **1 (a)** (handwriting) letra *f* **(b)** (style of writing) caligrafía *f* **(c)** (alphabet) escritura *f* **2** (text of film, broadcast) guion *m*

scripture /'skrɪptʃər ‖ 'skrɪptʃə(r)/ *n*: the (Holy) S~s las (Sagradas) Escrituras

scriptwriter /'skrɪpt‚raɪtər ‖ 'skrɪpt‚raɪtə(r)/ *n* guionista *mf*

scroll¹ /skrəʊl/ *n* rollo *m*

scroll² *vi* (Comput): to ~ up/down hacer* avanzar/retroceder el texto que aparece en pantalla

scroll bar *n* (Comput) barra *f* de enrollar

scrounge /skraʊndʒ/ (colloq) *vt* to ~ sth FROM/ OFF sb gorronearle *or* gorrearle *or* (RPI) garronearle *or* (Chi) bolsearle algo A algn (fam)
■ ~ *vi* gorronear *or* gorrear *or* (RPI) garronear *or* (Chi) bolsear (fam)

scrub¹ /skrʌb/ *n* **1** (vegetation) matorrales *mpl* **2** (act) (*no pl*): to give sth a good ~ fregar* *or* (Méx) tallar algo bien (con cepillo); (before n) ~ brush (AmE) cepillo *m* de fregar

scrub² *vt* **-bb-** ⟨*floor/table*⟩ fregar*; ⟨*knees/hands*⟩ restregar*

scrubbing brush /'skrʌbɪŋ/ *n* cepillo *m* de fregar

scruff /skrʌf/ *n*: by the ~ of the neck por el pescuezo

scruffy /'skrʌfi/ *adj* **-fier, -fiest** (colloq) ⟨*person*⟩ dejado, desaliñado; a ~-looking building un edificio de aspecto destartalado

scrum /skrʌm/, **scrummage** /'skrʌmɪdʒ/ *n* (in rugby) melé *f* (ordenada), scrum *m*

scrumptious /'skrʌmpʃəs/ *adj* (colloq) ⟨*meal*⟩ para chuparse los dedos (fam)

scruple /'skruːpəl/ *n* (usu pl) escrúpulo *m*

scrupulous /'skruːpjələs ‖ 'skruːpjʊləs/ *adj* escrupuloso

scrupulously /'skruːpjələsli ‖ 'skruːpjʊləsli/ *adv* escrupulosamente; ~ clean impecable

scrutinize /'skruːtḹnaɪz ‖ 'skruːtɪnaɪz/ *vt* ⟨*document*⟩ inspeccionar; ⟨*face*⟩ escudriñar

scrutiny /'skru:tɪni ‖'skru:tɪni/ n (pl **-nies**) examen m

scuba diving /'sku:bə/ n buceo m, submarinismo m

scuff /skʌf/ vt ⟨floor⟩ dejar marcas en; ⟨leather⟩ raspar

scuffle /'skʌfəl/ n refriega f

scullery /'skʌləri/ n (pl **-ries**) habitación anexa a la cocina donde se fregaba, se preparaban las verduras etc

sculpt /skʌlpt/ vt/i esculpir

sculptor /'skʌlptər ‖'skʌlptə(r)/ n escultor, -tora m,f

sculpture¹ /'skʌlptʃər ‖'skʌlptʃə(r)/ n escultura f

sculpture² vt esculpir

scum /skʌm/ n [1] (on liquid) capa f de suciedad [2] (colloq) (people) escoria f; **the ~ of the earth** la escoria de la sociedad

scupper /'skʌpər ‖'skʌpə(r)/ vt (BrE) ⟨ship⟩ hundir; ⟨plan/talks⟩ echar por tierra

scurry /'skɜːri ‖'skʌri/ vi: **he scurried away** o **off** salió disparado; **to ~ around** «mice» corretear

scuttle¹ /'skʌtl/ n (coal ~) cubo m para el carbón

scuttle² vt ⟨ship⟩ hundir; ⟨plans/talks⟩ echar por tierra
■ **~** vi: **the children ~d away** o **off** los niños se escabulleron rápidamente

scythe /saɪð/ n guadaña f

SD, S Dak = South Dakota

SE (= southeast) SE

sea /si:/ n [1] (often pl) (ocean) mar m [The noun MAR is feminine in literary language and in some set idiomatic expressions]; **to go/travel by ~** ir*/ viajar en barco; (before n) ⟨route/transport⟩ marítimo; ⟨battle⟩ naval; **the ~ breeze** la brisa del mar; **~ crossing** travesía f [2] (large mass, quantity) (no pl): **a ~ of faces** una multitud de rostros

sea: ~ anemone n anémona f or ortiga f de mar; **~bed** n the **~bed** el lecho marino; **~ bird** n ave f; **~food** n mariscos mpl, marisco m (Esp); **~front** n paseo m marítimo, malecón m (AmL), costanera f (CS); **~gull** n gaviota f; **~horse** n caballito m de mar

seal¹ /si:l/ n [1] (mark, impression) sello m; **he gave the plan his ~ of approval** dio su aprobación al plan [2] (a) (security device) precinto m (b) (airtight closure) cierre m hermético; (on glass jar) aro m de goma [3] (Zool) foca f

seal² vt [1] (a) ⟨envelope/parcel⟩ cerrar*; (with tape) precintar; (with wax) lacrar; **my lips are ~ed** (set phrase) soy una tumba (b) ⟨jar/container⟩ cerrar* herméticamente; ⟨tomb/door⟩ precintar; ⟨wood⟩ sellar [2] (affix seal to) ⟨document/treaty⟩ sellar [3] (decide, determine) ⟨victory/outcome⟩ decidir; **their fate was ~ed** su destino estaba escrito
■ **seal off** [v + o + adv, v + adv + o] ⟨area/road/ building⟩ acordonar; ⟨exit⟩ cerrar*

sea level n nivel m del mar

sealing wax /'si:lɪŋ/ n lacre m

sea lion n león m marino

seam /si:m/ n [1] (stitching) costura f [2] (of coal, gold) veta f, filón m

seaman /'si:mən/ n (pl **-men** /-mən/) (sailor) marinero m; (officer) marino m

seamy /'si:mi/ adj **-mier, -miest** sórdido

seance /'seɪɑːns/ n sesión f de espiritismo

sear /sɪr ‖sɪə(r)/ vt (a) ⟨flesh⟩ quemar; ⟨meat⟩ (Culin) dorar rápidamente a fuego muy vivo (b) (wither) ⟨heat⟩ secar*, abrasar

search¹ /sɜːrtʃ ‖sɜːtʃ/ vt ⟨building⟩ registrar, esculcar* (AmL exc CS); ⟨person⟩ registrar, cachear, catear (Méx); ⟨luggage⟩ registrar, revisar (AmL), esculcar* (AmL exc CS); ⟨records/files⟩ buscar* en
■ **~** vi buscar*; **to ~ FOR sth/sb** buscar* algo/a algn

search² n (a) (hunt, quest) **~ (FOR sth/sb)** búsqueda f (DE algo/algn) (b) (of building, pockets) registro m, esculque m (Col, Méx); (of records, documents) inspección f (c) (Comput) búsqueda f

search engine n (Comput) buscador m

searching /'sɜːrtʃɪŋ ‖'sɜːtʃɪŋ/ adj ⟨look⟩ inquisitivo; ⟨question⟩ perspicaz

search: ~light n reflector m; **~ party** n partida f de rescate

sea: ~scape /'si:skeɪp/ n marina f; **~shell** n concha f (de mar); **~shore** n orilla f del mar; **~sick** adj mareado; **~sickness** n mareo m (en los viajes por mar); **~side** n costa f, playa f; **we spent two weeks at the ~side** pasamos dos semanas en la costa or en la playa

season¹ /'si:zn/ n [1] (division of year) estación f [2] (for specific activity, event, crop) temporada f [3] (in phrases) **in season** (of female animal) en celo; (of fresh food, game): **cherries are in ~** es época or temporada de cerezas; **out of season** fuera de temporada

season² vt [1] (Culin) condimentar, sazonar; (with salt and pepper) salpimentar* [2] ⟨wood⟩ secar*, curar

seasonal /'si:zn̩əl ‖'si:zənl/ adj ⟨variations/ fluctuations⟩ estacional; ⟨vegetables⟩ del tiempo; ⟨demand⟩ de estación

seasoned /'si:zn̩d/ adj [1] (experienced) ⟨troops/ traveler⟩ avezado, experimentado [2] ⟨food⟩ condimentado, sazonado [3] ⟨wood⟩ seco, curado

seasoning /'si:zn̩ɪŋ/ n (Culin) condimento m, sazón f

season ticket n abono m (de temporada)

seat¹ /si:t/ n [1] (place to sit) asiento m; **please have** o **take a ~** tome asiento, por favor (frml), siéntese, por favor; **there aren't any ~s left** (in cinema) no quedan localidades [2] (of chair) asiento m [3] (a) (Govt) escaño m, banca f (RPl), curul m (Col, Méx) (b) (constituency) (BrE) distrito m electoral [4] (center) sede f; **the ~ of government** la sede del gobierno

seat² vt (a) ⟨child⟩ sentar*; **to remain ~ed** permanecer* sentado (b) (have room for) «auditorium» tener* cabida or capacidad para

seat belt n cinturón m de seguridad

seating /'si:tɪŋ/ n número m de asientos; (before n) **~ capacity** aforo m

sea: ~ urchin n erizo m de mar; **~water** n ⋯⋮

agua *f* de mar, **agua** *f* **salada**; ∼**way** *n* ruta *f* marítima; ∼**weed** *n* alga *f* marina; ∼**worthy** *adj* ⟨*ship*⟩ en condiciones de navegar

secluded /sɪ'kluːdəd ‖sɪ'kluːdɪd/ *adj* ⟨*house/ area*⟩ apartado, aislado; ⟨*life/existence*⟩ solitario

seclusion /sɪ'kluːʒən/ *n* aislamiento *m*

second¹ /'sekənd/ *adj* [1] segundo; ∼ **language** segundo idioma *m*; **our service is** ∼ **to none** nuestro servicio es insuperable [2] (elliptical use): **I leave on the** ∼ **(of the month)** me voy el (día) dos

second² *adv* **(a)** (in position, time, order) en segundo lugar **(b)** (secondly) en segundo lugar **(c)** (with superl): **the** ∼ **highest building** el segundo edificio en altura

second³ *n* [1] (of time) segundo *m*; **it doesn't take a** ∼ no lleva ni un segundo; ⟨*before n*⟩ ∼ **hand** segundero *m* [2] **(a)** ∼ **(gear)** (Auto) ⟨*no art*⟩ segunda *f* **(b)** (in competition): **he finished a good/poor** ∼ quedó en un honroso/deslucido segundo lugar [3] (substandard product) artículo *m* con defectos de fábrica [4] **seconds** *pl* (second helping) (colloq): **to have** ∼**s** repetir*

second⁴ *vt* [1] (support) ⟨*motion/candidate*⟩ secundar [2] /sɪ'kɒnd/ (attach) (BrE) **to** ∼ **sb (to sth)** trasladar a algn temporalmente (A algo)

secondary /'sekəndri ‖'sekəndri/ *adj* [1] **(a)** (subordinate) ⟨*matter*⟩ de interés secundario; ⟨*road*⟩ secundario **(b)** (not primary, original) ⟨*source*⟩ de segunda mano; ⟨*industry*⟩ derivado [2] ⟨*teacher/ pupils*⟩ de enseñanza secundaria

secondary school *n* instituto *m* or colegio *m* de enseñanza secundaria, liceo *m* (CS, Ven)

second: ∼ **best** *n*: **he won't accept** ∼ **best** solo se conforma con lo mejor; ∼ **class** *adv* ⟨*travel/go*⟩ en segunda (clase); ∼**class** /'sekənd'klæs ‖,sekənd'klɑːs/ *adj* ⟨*pred* ∼ **class*) **(a)** (inferior) ⟨*goods/service*⟩ de segunda (clase *or* categoría), de calidad inferior **(b)** (Post): ∼**class mail** (in UK) *servicio regular de correos, que tarda más en llegar a destino que el de primera clase* **(c)** (in UK) (Transp) ⟨*travel/ticket/ compartment*⟩ de segunda (clase)

second-hand¹ /'sekənd'hænd/ *adj* ⟨*pred* **second hand**⟩ ⟨*car/clothes*⟩ de segunda mano, usado; ⟨*bookstore*⟩ de viejo; ⟨*shop*⟩ de artículos de segunda mano; ⟨*information*⟩ de segunda mano

second-hand² *adv*: **to buy sth** ∼ comprar algo de segunda mano

second-in-command /'sekəndɪnkə'mænd ‖,sekəndɪnkə'mɑːnd/ *n* (*pl* **seconds-in-command**) número dos *mf* (*persona directamente por debajo de la autoridad máxima de una organización, departamento etc*)

secondly /'sekəndli/ *adv* (indep) en segundo lugar

second-rate /'sekənd'reɪt/ *adj* mediocre

secrecy /'siːkrəsi/ *n* secreto *m*

secret¹ /'siːkrət ‖'siːkrɪt/ *n* secreto *m*; **in** ∼ en secreto; **to make no** ∼ **of sth** no esconder algo

secret² *adj* secreto

secretarial /'sekrə'teriəl ‖,sekrə'teəriəl/ *adj* ⟨*job*⟩ de oficina, de secretaria/secretario; ⟨*course*⟩ de secretariado

secretary /'sekrətəri ‖'sekrətri/ *n* (*pl* **-ries**) [1] (in office, of committee, of society) secretario, -ria *m,f* [2] (Govt) ministro, -tra *m,f*, secretario, -ria *m,f* (Méx)

Secretary of State *n* (*pl* **Secretaries of State**) (Govt) **(a)** (in US) secretario, -ria *m,f* de Estado (de los Estados Unidos); **(b)** (in UK) ministro, -tra *m,f*, secretario, -ria *m,f* (Méx)

secrete /sɪ'kriːt/ *vt* [1] (Biol, Physiol) segregar*, secretar [2] (hide) (frml) ocultar

secretive /'siːkrətɪv/ *adj* reservado

secret: ∼ **police** *n* policía *f* secreta; ∼ **service** *n* (intelligence service) servicio *m* secreto

sect /sekt/ *n* secta *f*

sectarian /sek'teriən ‖sek'teəriən/ *adj* ⟨*views/ violence*⟩ sectario; ⟨*schooling/school*⟩ confesional

section /'sekʃən/ *n* [1] (of object, newspaper, orchestra) sección *f*; (of machine, piece of furniture) parte *f*; (of road) tramo *m*; (of city, population) sector *m* [2] (department) sección *f* [3] (in geometry, drawing) sección *f*

sector /'sektər ‖'sektə(r)/ *n* sector *m*

secular /'sekjələr ‖'sekjʊlə(r)/ *adj* ⟨*education*⟩ laico; ⟨*society/art*⟩ secular

secure¹ /sɪ'kjʊr ‖sɪ'kjʊə(r)/ *adj* [1] **(a)** (safe) ⟨*fortress/hideaway*⟩ seguro **(b)** (emotionally) ⟨*childhood/home*⟩ estable **(c)** (assured) ⟨*job/ investment*⟩ seguro [2] ⟨*foothold/shelf*⟩ firme; ⟨*foundation*⟩ sólido

secure² *vt* [1] (obtain) ⟨*job/votes/support*⟩ conseguir* [2] (fasten, fix firmly) ⟨*door/shelf*⟩ asegurar

security /sɪ'kjʊrəti ‖sɪ'kjʊərəti/ *n* (*pl* **-ties**) [1] (against crime, espionage etc) seguridad *f*; ⟨*before n*⟩ ∼ **guard** guarda jurado, guarda jurada *m,f* [2] **(a)** (safety, certainty) seguridad *f* **(b)** (protection) seguro *m* [3] (Fin) **(a)** (guarantee) garantía *f* **(b)** **securities** *pl* (Fin) valores *mpl*, títulos *mpl*

Security Council *n* **the (United Nations)** ∼ el Consejo de Seguridad (de las Naciones Unidas)

sedan /sɪ'dæn/ *n* [1] (car) (AmE) sedán *m* [2] ∼ **(chair)** palanquín *m*, silla *f* de manos

sedate¹ /sɪ'deɪt/ *adj* reposado, tranquilo

sedate² *vt* (Med) sedar

sedation /sɪ'deɪʃən/ *n* sedación *f*; **to be under** ∼ estar* bajo el efecto de los sedantes

sedative /'sedətɪv/ *n* sedante *m*

sediment /'sedəmənt ‖'sedɪmənt/ *n* **(a)** (in wine, coffee) poso *m*, asiento *m* **(b)** (Geol) sedimento *m*

seduce /sɪ'duːs ‖sɪ'djuːs/ *vt* seducir*

seduction /sɪ'dʌkʃən/ *n* seducción *f*

seductive /sɪ'dʌktɪv/ *adj* seductor

see /siː/ (*past* **saw**; *past p* **seen**) *vt* [1] (regard, perceive) ver*; **I can't** ∼ **a thing!** ¡no veo nada!; **I saw her cross the street** la vi cruzar la calle; **I**

AmC	América Central	Arg	Argentina	Cu	Cuba	Per	Perú
AmL	América Latina	Bol	Bolivia	Ec	Ecuador	RPI	Río de la Plata
AmS	América del Sur	Chi	Chile	Esp	España	Ur	Uruguay
Andes	Región andina	CS	Cono Sur	Méx	México	Ven	Venezuela

thought I was ~**ing things** pensé que estaba viendo visiones; ~ **page 20** ver página 20; **I don't know what she** ~**s in him** no sé qué es lo que le ve; **anyone can** ~ **she's upset** cualquiera se da cuenta de que está disgustada; **the way I** ~ **it, as I** ~ **it** a mi modo de ver; **can you** ~ **him as a teacher?** ¿te lo imaginas de profesor?; **I'll** ~ **what I can do** veré qué puedo hacer; **that remains to be** ~**n** eso está por verse

2 (understand) ver*; **do you** ~ **what I mean?** ¿entiendes?

3 (ensure) **to** ~ THAT asegurarse DE QUE; ~ **that it doesn't happen again** que no vuelva a suceder

4 (a) (meet, visit) ver*; **I'm** ~**ing him on Tuesday** lo voy a ver el martes **(b)** (go out with) (colloq) salir* con **(c)** (saying goodbye) (colloq): ~ **you!** ¡hasta luego!, ¡hasta la vista!; ~ **you later/soon!** ¡hasta luego/pronto!

5 (a) (consult) ⟨doctor/manager⟩ ver* **(b)** (receive) ver*, atender*; **the doctor will** ~ **you now** el doctor lo verá or lo atenderá ahora

6 (escort, accompany) acompañar; **to** ~ **sb to the door** acompañar a algn a la puerta

■ ~ *vi* ver*; ~ **for yourself!** ¡compruébalo tú mismo!; **as far as I can** ~ por lo que yo veo; **I** ~ (expressing realization) ya veo; (accepting explanation) entiendo; **let's** ~ vamos a ver, veamos; **will it work? — try it and** ~ ¿funcionará? — prueba a ver; ~**ing is believing** ver para creer

■ **see off** [v + adv, v + adv + o] **1** (say goodbye to) despedir*, despedirse* de **2** (get rid of) deshacerse* de

■ **see out** [v + adv, v + adv + o] ⟨person⟩ acompañar (hasta la puerta); **I can** ~ **myself out** no hace falta que me acompañes

■ **see through 1** [v + prep + o] (not be deceived by) calar **2** [v + o + adv] [v + o + prep + o] (last): **make sure this** ~**s you through** con esto te tienes que alcanzar; **$20 should** ~ **me through the week** con 20 dólares me alcanza hasta el fin de semana **3** [v + o + adv] (carry to completion) terminar

■ **see to** [v + prep + o] (attend to) ocuparse de

seed /siːd/ *n* **1** (of plant) semilla *f*; (of orange, grape) (AmE) pepita *f*, semilla *f*; **to go to** ~ estar* en decadencia **2** (Sport) cabeza *mf* de serie, sembrado, -da *m,f* (Méx)

seedless /ˈsiːdləs ‖ˈsiːdlɪs/ *adj* sin pepitas *or* semillas

seedling /ˈsiːdlɪŋ/ *n* planta *f* de semillero

seedy /ˈsiːdi/ *adj* **-dier, -diest** ⟨nightclub/bar⟩ sórdido, de mala muerte (fam), cutre (Esp fam); ⟨appearance⟩ desastrado

seeing /ˈsiːɪŋ/ *conj* (colloq) ~ **(that)** *o* ~ **as** ya que

seek /siːk/ (*past & past p* **sought**) *vt* **(a)** (search for) (frml) ⟨person/object⟩ buscar* **(b)** (try to obtain) ⟨work/companionship⟩ buscar*; ⟨solution/ explanation⟩ tratar de encontrar **(c)** (request) ⟨approval/help⟩ pedir* **(d)** (try to bring about) (frml) ⟨reconciliation⟩ buscar*

■ **seek out** [v + o + adv, v + adv + o] ⟨person⟩ buscar*; ⟨opinion⟩ pedir*

seem /siːm/ *vi* parecer*; **strange as it may** ~ por raro que parezca; **you** ~ **to like you** parece que le caes bien; **so it** ~**s, so it would** ~ eso parece, así parece; **I** ~ **to remember that you ...** creo recordar que tú ...; **it** ~**s to me/him/them**

that ... me/le/les parece que ...; **I can't** ~ **to remember where I put it** no logro acordarme de dónde lo puse

seen /siːn/ *past p of* SEE

seep /siːp/ *vi* «liquid/moisture» filtrarse

seesaw /ˈsiːsɔː/ *n* balancín *m*, subibaja *m*

seethe /siːð/ *vi* **(a)** (be agitated) bullir*; **the town was seething with tourists** la ciudad estaba plagada de turistas **(b)** (be angry) estar* furioso; **I was absolutely seething** me hervía la sangre

see-through /ˈsiːθruː/ *adj* transparente

segment /ˈsegmənt/ *n* **(a)** (Math) (of circle, sphere, line) segmento *m* **(b)** (of citrus fruit) gajo *m*; **(c)** (section) sector *m*

segregate /ˈsegrɪgeɪt/ *vt* ⟨races/sexes⟩ segregar*; ⟨rival groups⟩ mantener* aparte

segregation /ˌsegrɪˈgeɪʃən/ *n* segregación *f*

seize /siːz/ *vt* **1** (grab, snatch) ⟨hand/object⟩ agarrar*; ⟨opportunity⟩ aprovechar; ⟨power⟩ tomar **2** (a) (capture) ⟨town/fortress⟩ tomar*; ⟨person⟩ detener* **(b)** ⟨assets/property⟩ (confiscate) confiscar*; (impound) embargar*; ⟨cargo/ contraband⟩ confiscar*; ⟨drugs/arms⟩ incautar

■ **seize on, seize upon** [v + prep + o] ⟨chance⟩ aprovechar

■ **seize up** [v + adv] «engine» agarrotarse, fundirse (AmL); «muscles» agarrotarse; «traffic» paralizarse*

seizure /ˈsiːʒər ‖ˈsiːʒə(r)/ *n* **1** (of property, contraband) confiscación *f* **2** (Med) ataque *m*

seldom /ˈseldəm/ *adv* rara vez, pocas veces

select[1] /sɪˈlekt/ *vt* ⟨gift/book/wine⟩ elegir*, escoger*; ⟨candidate/team member⟩ seleccionar

select[2] *adj* **(a)** (exclusive) ⟨school⟩ de élite; ⟨district⟩ distinguido **(b)** (choice) ⟨fruit/wine⟩ selecto **(c)** (especially chosen) ⟨group⟩ selecto

selection /sɪˈlekʃən/ *n* **1** (act, thing chosen) selección *f* **2** (Busn) (of chocolates, buttons, spares) surtido *m*; **a wide** ~ **of new and used cars** una amplia gama de coches nuevos y usados

selective /sɪˈlektɪv/ *adj* **(a)** ⟨control/ recruitment⟩ selectivo; ⟨reporting⟩ parcial **(b)** (discriminating): **he's fairly** ~ **about who he mixes with** elige or escoge mucho sus amistades

self /self/ *n* (*pl* **selves**): **she's her old** ~ **again** vuelve a ser la de antes; **you're not your usual cheerful** ~ no estás tan alegre como de costumbre

self- /self/ *pref* **(a)** (concerning the self): ~**doubt** duda *f* de sí mismo **(b)** (with no outside agency) auto; ~**financing** autofinanciado

self: ~**-addressed** /ˌselfəˈdrest/ *adj*: con el nombre y la dirección del remitente; **send a** ~**-addressed envelope to ...:** envíe un sobre con su nombre y dirección a ...; ~**-adhesive** /ˌselfədˈhiːsɪv/ *adj* autoadhesivo; ~**-assured** /ˌselfəˈʃʊrd ‖ˌselfəˈʃʊəd, ˌselfəˈʃɔːd/ *adj* seguro de sí mismo; ~**-catering** /ˌselfˈkeɪtərɪŋ/ *adj* (BrE) ⟨accommodation⟩ equipado con cocina; ~**-centered,** (BrE) ~**-centred** /ˌselfˈsentərd ‖ˌselfˈsentəd/ *adj* egocéntrico; ~**-confessed** /ˌselfkənˈfest/ *adj* (before n) confeso; ~**-confidence** /ˌselfˈkɑːnfədəns ‖ˌselfˈkɒnfɪdəns/ *n* confianza *f* en sí mismo; ~**-confident** /ˌselfˈkɑːnfədənt ‖ˌselfˈkɒnfɪdənt/ *adj* seguro de sí mismo; ~**-conscious** /ˌselfˈkɑːntʃəs ‖ˌselfˈkɒntʃəs/ *adj* **1** (shy,

S

embarrassed) ⟨person/manner⟩ tímido; **to feel ~-conscious** sentirse* cohibido; [2] (unspontaneous, unnatural) (pej) afectado; **~-contained** /selfkən'teɪnd/ adj **(a)** ⟨flat⟩ (BrE) con cocina y cuarto de baño propios **(b)** ⟨person⟩ independiente; **~-control** /'selfkən'trəʊl/ n dominio m de sí mismo; **~-defense,** (BrE) **~-defence** /'selfdɪ'fens/ n **(a)** (Law): **to act in ~-defense** actuar* en defensa propia **(b)** (fighting technique) defensa f personal; **~-destruct** /'selfdɪ'strʌkt/ vi autodestruirse*; **~-destructive** /'selfdɪ'strʌktɪv/ adj autodestructivo; **~-determination** /,selfdɪ,tɜ:rmə'neɪʃən ‖,selfdɪ,tɜ:mɪ'neɪʃən/ n autodeterminación f; **~-discipline** /'self'dɪsəplɪn ‖,self'dɪsɪplɪn/ n autodisciplina f; **~-employed** /'selfɪm'plɔɪd/ adj autónomo; **~-esteem** /'self'sti:m/ n autoestima f; **~-evident** /'self'evədənt ‖,self'evɪdənt/ adj ⟨truth⟩ manifiesto; ⟨conclusion⟩ evidente; **~-explanatory** /'selfɪk'splænətɔ:ri ‖,selfɪk'splænətri/ adj: **the instructions are ~-explanatory** las instrucciones son muy claras; **~-government** /'self'gʌvənmənt ‖,self'gʌvənmənt/ n autogobierno m, autonomía f; **~-help** /'self'help/ n autoayuda f; **~-image** /'self'ɪmɪdʒ/ n imagen f de sí mismo; **~-important** /'selfɪm'pɔ:rtn̩t ‖,selfɪm'pɔ:tn̩t/ adj engreído, presumido; **~-imposed** /'selfɪm'pəʊzd/ adj voluntario, autoimpuesto; **~-indulgent** /'selfɪn'dʌldʒənt/ adj demasiado indulgente consigo mismo; **~-interest** /'self'ɪntrəst ‖,self'ɪntrɪst/ n interés m (personal)

selfish /'selfɪʃ/ adj egoísta

selfishly /'selfɪʃli/ adv egoístamente

selfishness /'selfɪʃnəs ‖'selfɪʃnɪs/ n egoísmo m

self: ~-made /'self'meɪd/ adj (before n) ⟨man/ woman⟩ que ha alcanzado su posición gracias a sus propios esfuerzos; **~-pity** /'self'pɪti/ n autocompasión f; **~-portrait** /'self'pɔ:rtrət ‖,self'pɔ:trɪt/ n autorretrato m; **~-preservation** /'self'prezər'veɪʃən ‖,selfprezə'veɪʃən/ n: **the instinct of ~-preservation** el instinto de conservación; **~-raising** /'self'reɪzɪŋ/ adj (BrE) ▶ ~-RISING; **~-reliant** /'selfrɪ'laɪənt/ adj independiente; **~-respect** /'selfrɪ'spekt/ n dignidad f, amor m propio; **~-respecting** /'selfrɪ'spektɪŋ/ adj (before n): **no ~-respecting editor** would work for them ningún editor que se precie trabajaría para ellos; **~-righteous** /'selfraɪtʃəs/ adj ⟨person⟩ con pretensiones de superioridad moral; **~-rising** /'selfraɪzɪŋ/ adj (AmE) ⟨flour⟩ con polvos de hornear (AmL), con levadura (Esp), leudante (RPl); **~-same** adj (before n) mismísimo; **~-satisfied** /'self'sætsfaɪd ‖,self'sætɪsfaɪd/ adj ufano, satisfecho de sí mismo; ⟨expression/grin⟩ de (auto)suficiencia; **~-service** /'self'sɜ:rvəs ‖,self'sɜ:vɪs/, (esp AmE) **self-serve** /-'sɜ:rv/ adj: **~-service restaurant** autoservicio m, self-service m; **~-sufficiency** /,selfsə'fɪʃənsi/ n independencia f, (Econ) autosuficiencia f; **~-sufficient** /'selfsə'fɪʃənt/ adj ⟨person⟩ independiente; ⟨country⟩ autosuficiente; **~-taught** /'self'tɔ:t/ adj autodidacta, autodidacto

sell /sel/ (past & past p **sold**) vt vender; **to ~ sth TO sb, to ~ sb sth** venderle algo A algn; **to ~ sth FOR sth** vender algo EN or POR algo
■ **~** vi **(a)** «person/company» vender **(b)** (be sold) «product» venderse; **to ~ AT/FOR sth** venderse A/POR algo
■ **sell off** [v + o + adv, v + adv + o] vender; (cheaply) liquidar
■ **sell out** [1] [v + adv + o] (sell all of) ⟨stock⟩ agotar; ⟨article⟩ agotar las existencias de [2] [v + adv] **(a)** (sell all stock) «shop» **to ~ out** (OF sth): **we've** o **we're sold out of umbrellas** los paraguas están agotados, se agotaron los paraguas **(b)** (be sold) «stock/tickets» agotarse **(c)** (be traitor) «leader/artist» venderse

sell-by date /'selbaɪ/ n (BrE) fecha f límite de venta

seller /'selər ‖'selə(r)/ n vendedor, -dora m,f

selling /'selɪŋ/ n ventas fpl; (before n) **~ price** precio m de venta

Sellotape® /'seləteɪp/ n (BrE) ▶ SCOTCH TAPE

sell-out /'selaʊt/ n [1] (performance) éxito m de taquilla [2] (betrayal) capitulación f

selves /selvz/ pl of SELF

semaphore /'seməfɔ:r ‖'seməfɔ:(r)/ n código m de señales

semblance /'sembləns/ n (frml) **~ OF sth** apariencia f DE algo

semen /'si:mən/ n semen m

semester /sə'mestər ‖sɪ'mestə(r)/ n (in US) semestre m (lectivo)

semi- /'semi, 'semaɪ ‖'semi/ pref semi-

semibreve /'semibri:v/ n (BrE) semibreve f, redonda f

semicircle /'semi,sɜ:rkəl ‖'semi,sɜ:kəl/ n semicírculo m

semicolon /'semi'kəʊlən/ n punto y coma m

semiconscious /'semi'kɑ:ntʃəs ‖,semi'kɒnʃəs/ adj semiconsciente

semidetached /'semidɪ'tætʃt/ adj: **a ~ house** una casa pareada or adosada

semifinal /'semi'faɪnl/ n semifinal f

seminar /'semənɑ:r ‖'semɪnɑ:(r)/ n seminario m

semiquaver /'semi,kweɪvər ‖'semi,kweɪvə(r)/ n (BrE) semicorchea f

semiskilled /'semi'skɪld/ adj semicalificado or (Esp) semicualificado

semitone /'semitəʊn/ n semitono m

semitrailer /'semi,treɪlər ‖'semi,treɪlə(r)/ n (AmE) camión m con remolque or (CS tb) con acoplado, tráiler m (Esp), trailer m (Méx)

senate /'senət ‖'senɪt/ n **the Senate** (Govt) el senado or Senado

senator /'senətər ‖'senətə(r)/ n senador, -dora m,f

send /send/ (past & past p **sent**) vt mandar, enviar*; **to ~ sb to prison** mandar a algn a la cárcel; **the blow sent him reeling** el golpe lo dejó tambaleándose; **she sent everything flying** lo hizo saltar todo por los aires; **to ~ sb to sleep** dormir* a algn
■ **send away** [1] [v + o + adv, v + adv + o] **(a)** (dismiss) despachar; **don't ~ me away** no me digas que me vaya **(b)** (send elsewhere) mandar, enviar* [2] [v + adv] ▶ SEND OFF 3

■ **send for** [*v* + *prep* + *o*] **(a)** (ask to come)
‹*doctor/ambulance*› mandar a buscar, mandar
llamar (AmL) **(b)** (order) ‹*catalog/application form*›
pedir*; ‹*books/tapes/clothes*› encargar*
■ **send in** [*v* + *o* + *adv*, *v* + *adv* + *o*] **(a)** ‹*troops*›
enviar*, mandar **(b)** (by post) ‹*entry/coupon/
application*› mandar, enviar* **(c)** (into room)
‹*person*› hacer* pasar; ~ **him in** hágalo pasar
■ **send off** ⓵ [*v* + *o* + *adv*, *v* + *adv* + *o*] (dispatch)
‹*letter/parcel/goods*› despachar, mandar; ‹*person*›
mandar
⓶ [*v* + *o* + *adv*, *v* + *adv* + *o*] (BrE Sport) expulsar
⓷ [*v* + *adv*] **to ~ off FOR sth: I sent off for a
brochure** escribí pidiendo un folleto, mandé pedir
un folleto (AmL)
■ **send on** [*v* + *o* + *adv*, *v* + *adv* + *o*] ‹*luggage*›
enviar* *or* mandar por adelantado; ‹*mail*› hacer*
seguir
■ **send out** [*v* + *o* + *adv*, *v* + *adv* + *o*] **(a)** (emit)
‹*heat*› despedir*, irradiar; ‹*signal/radio waves*›
emitir **(b)** (on errand) mandar **(c)** ‹*invitations*›
mandar, enviar*
■ **send up** [*v* + *o* + *adv*, *v* + *adv* + *o*] ⓵ (to prison)
(AmE) meter preso
⓶ (satirize) (BrE colloq) parodiar

sender /'sendər ‖'sendə(r)/ *n* remitente *mf*

send: ~**-off** *n* (colloq) despedida *f*; ~**-up** *n* (esp
BrE colloq) parodia *f*

Senegal /'senɪ'ɡɔːl/ *n* (el) Senegal

Senegalese /senɪɡə'liːz/ *adj* senegalés

senile /'siːnaɪl/ *adj* senil

senile dementia *n* demencia *f* senil

senior¹ /'siːnjər ‖'siːniə(r)/ *adj* **(a)** (superior in
rank): **a ~ officer in the Army** un oficial de alto
rango del Ejército; **~ lecturer** (BrE) ≈profesor
adjunto, profesora adjunta *m,f*; **she's ~ to him** es
su superior **(b)** (older): **the ~ members of a club**
los socios más antiguos de un club; **Robert King,
S~** (esp AmE) Robert King, padre *or* sénior

senior² *n* ⓵ **(a)** (older person): **he's five years
my ~** me lleva cinco años **(b)** (person of higher
rank) superior *m* **(c)** (AmE) ▶ SENIOR CITIZEN
⓶ (Educ) estudiante *mf* del último año *or* curso

senior: ~ citizen *n* persona *f* de la tercera
edad; **~ high (school)** *n* (in US) *colegio donde
se imparten los tres últimos años de la enseñanza
secundaria*

seniority /siːn'jɔːrəti ‖ˌsiːni'ɒrəti/ *n* **(a)** (in
rank) jerarquía *f* **(b)** (in length of service) antigüedad
f

sensation /sen'seɪʃən/ *n* ⓵ (feeling, impression)
sensación *f* ⓶ **(a)** (furor) sensación *f* **(b)**
(success): **to be a ~** ‹*play/show*› ser* todo un
éxito

sensational /sen'seɪʃnəl ‖sen'seɪʃənl/ *adj* **(a)**
(causing furor) que causa sensación **(b)**
(sensationalist) sensacionalista **(c)** (very good) (colloq)
sensacional (fam)

sensationalist /sen'seɪʃənələst
‖sen'seɪʃənəlɪst/ *adj* sensacionalista

sense¹ /sens/ *n* ⓵ **(a)** (physical faculty) sentido
m; **the ~ of hearing/smell/taste/touch** el (sentido
del) oído/olfato/gusto/tacto **(b) senses** *pl*
(rational state): **to come to one's ~s** entrar en
razón
⓶ **(a)** (impression) (*no pl*) sensación *f* **(b)**

(awareness) sentido *m*; ~ **of direction/humor**
sentido de la orientación/del humor; **I lost all ~
of time** perdí completamente la noción del tiempo
⓷ (common ~) sentido *m* común; **she had the
(good) ~ to leave her phone number** tuvo la
sensatez de dejar su número de teléfono; **I can't
make him see ~** no puedo hacerlo entrar en
razón
⓸ **(a)** (meaning) sentido *m*; **in every ~ of the
word** en todo sentido **(b)** (aspect, way): **in a ~
they're both correct** en cierto modo ambos tienen
razón
⓹ **to make ~ (a)** (be comprehensible) tener*
sentido **(b)** (be sensible): **what he said made a lot
of ~** lo que dijo era muy razonable; *to make ~ of
sth* entender* algo

sense² *vt* **(a)** (be aware of) sentir*, notar **(b)**
(detect) (Tech) detectar

senseless /'sensləs ‖'senslɪs/ *adj* ⓵ (pointless)
‹*act/destruction*› sin sentido ⓶ (unconscious)
inconsciente

sensible /'sensəbəl/ *adj* ‹*person/approach*›
sensato; ‹*decision*› prudente; ‹*clothes/shoes*›
cómodo y práctico

sensitive /'sensətɪv/ *adj* ⓵ **(a)** (emotionally
responsive) ‹*person*› sensible; ‹*performance*› lleno
de sensibilidad **(b)** (touchy) ‹*person*› susceptible
⓶ (physically responsive) ‹*skin/instrument*› sensible
⓷ (requiring tact) ‹*topic/issue*› delicado

sensor /'sensər ‖'sensə(r)/ *n* sensor *m*

sensual /'sentʃuəl ‖'senʃəl/ *adj* sensual

sensuous /'sentʃuəs ‖'sensjuəs/ *adj* sensual

sent /sent/ *past & past p of* SEND

sentence¹ /'sentəns ‖'sentəns/ *n* ⓵ (Ling)
oración *f*, frase *f* ⓶ (Law) (judgment) sentencia *f*;
(punishment) pena *f*; **to pass ~ (on sb)** dictar *or*
pronunciar sentencia (contra algn); **a life ~** una
condena a cadena perpetua

sentence² *vt* **to ~ sb (TO sth)** condenar *or*
sentenciar a algn (A algo)

sentiment /'sentɪmənt/ *n* **(a)** (feeling) sentir *m*,
sentimiento *m* **(b)** (view) opinión *f*; **my ~s exactly**
o **entirely** estoy totalmente de acuerdo

sentimental /sentɪ'mentl/ *adj* sentimental

sentry /'sentri/ *n* (*pl* **-tries**) centinela *m*

Seoul /səʊl/ *n* Seúl *m*

separate¹ /'sepərət/ *adj* **(a)** (individual)
separado **(b)** (physically apart) aparte *adj inv*; ~
FROM sth separado DE algo **(c)** (distinct, different): **it
has three ~ meanings** tiene tres significados
distintos; **answer each question on a ~ sheet of
paper** conteste cada pregunta en una hoja aparte

separate² /'sepəreɪt/ *vt* **(a)** (set apart) separar
(b) (distinguish) distinguir*; **to ~ sth FROM sth**
distinguir* algo DE algo
■ ~ *vi* separarse

separately /'seprətli, 'sepərətli/ *adv* **(a)** (apart)
por separado **(b)** (individually) separadamente

separation /sepə'reɪʃən/ *n* separación *f*

separatism /'seprətɪzəm, 'sepərətɪzəm/ *n*
separatismo *m*

separatist /'sepratəst, 'sepə- ‖'sepərətɪst,
'seprə-/ *n* separatista *mf*; (*before n*) ‹*group/
movement*› separatista

September /sep'tembər ‖sep'tembə(r)/ *n*
septiembre *m*, setiembre *m*

S

septic ···> set

septic /'septɪk/ adj séptico; **to go ~** infectarse

sequel /'siːkwəl/ n **(a)** (Cin, Lit, TV) continuación f **(b)** (later events) secuela f

sequence /'siːkwəns/ n [1] (order): **the police established the ~ of events** la policía estableció cómo se sucedieron los hechos; **it's better to look at the pictures in ~** es mejor ver las fotos en or por orden [2] **(a)** (series) serie f **(b)** (Math, Mus) secuencia f [3] (Cin, TV) secuencia f

sequin /'siːkwən/ n lentejuela f

Serb /sɜːrb ‖sɜːb/ adj/n ▶ SERBIAN[1,2]

Serbia /'sɜːrbiə ‖'sɜːbiə/ n Serbia f, Servia f

Serbian[1] /'sɜːrbiən ‖'sɜːbiən/ adj serbio, servio

Serbian[2] n serbio, -bia m,f, servio, -via m,f

Serbo-Croat /'sɜːrbəʊ'krəʊæt ‖,sɜːbəʊ'krəʊæt/ n serbocroata m

serenade[1] /'serəˈneɪd/ n serenata f

serenade[2] vt darle* (una) serenata a

serene /səˈriːn ‖sɪˈriːn/ adj sereno

sergeant /'sɑːrdʒənt ‖'sɑːdʒənt/ n sargento mf

sergeant major n ≈brigada mf

serial /'sɪriəl ‖'sɪəriəl/ n **(a)** (Rad, TV) serie f, serial m or (CS) serial f **(b)** (Publ): **it was published as a ~** se publicó por entregas

serialize /'sɪriəlaɪz ‖'sɪəriəlaɪz/ vt serializar*

serial: **~ killer** n asesino, -na m,f en serie; **~ number** n número m de serie

series /'sɪriːz ‖'sɪəriːz/ n (pl ~) **(a)** (succession) serie f **(b)** (TV, Rad) serie f, serial m or (CS) f

serious /'sɪriəs ‖'sɪəriəs/ adj [1] **(a)** (in earnest, sincere) serio; **I'm ~** lo digo en serio **(b)** (committed) (before n) (student/worker) dedicado **(c)** (not lightweight) (before n) (newspaper/play/music) serio [2] (grave) (injury/illness) grave; **I have ~ doubts about him** tengo mis serias dudas acerca de él

seriously /'sɪriəsli ‖'sɪəriəsli/ adv [1] **(a)** (not frivolously) seriamente; **to take sth/sb ~** tomar(se) algo/a algn en serio **(b)** (genuinely, sincerely): **you can't ~ mean that** no tú no puedes estar diciendo en serio [2] (gravely) (ill/injured) gravemente

seriousness /'sɪriəsnəs ‖'sɪəriəsnɪs/ n seriedad f; **he said it in all ~** lo dijo muy en serio

sermon /'sɜːrmən ‖'sɜːmən/ n sermón m

serpent /'sɜːrpənt ‖'sɜːpənt/ n (liter) sierpe f (liter)

serrated /'serətəd ‖səˈreɪtɪd/ adj (edge/knife) serrado

serum /'sɪrəm ‖'sɪərəm/ n suero m

servant /'sɜːrvənt ‖'sɜːvənt/ n criado, -da m,f, sirviente, -ta m,f

serve[1] /sɜːrv ‖sɜːv/ vt [1] (work for) (God/country) servir* a
[2] (help, be useful to) servir*; **it ~s no useful purpose** no sirve para nada (útil); **to ~ sb right** (colloq): **it ~s her right!** ¡se lo merece!, ¡le está bien empleado! (Esp)
[3] **(a)** (Culin) (food/drink) servir* **(b)** (in shop) (BrE) atender*
[4] (Law) (summons/notice/order) entregar*
[5] (complete) (apprenticeship) hacer*; (sentence) cumplir
■ **~** vi [1] **(a)** (be servant) (liter) servir* **(b)** (in shop) (BrE) atender* **(c)** (distribute food) servir*
[2] (spend time, do duty): **to ~ in the army** servir* en el ejército
[3] (have effect, function) **to ~ to + INF** servir* PARA + INF
[4] (Sport) sacar*, servir*

serve[2] n servicio m, saque m

server /'sɜːrvər ‖'sɜːvə(r)/ n [1] (Sport) jugador que tiene el saque [2] (Comput) servidor m

service[1] /'sɜːrvəs ‖'sɜːvɪs/ n [1] **(a)** (duty, work) servicio m **(b)** (given by a tool, machine): **you'll get years of ~ from this iron** esta plancha le durará años
[2] (of professional, tradesman, company) servicio m; **we no longer require your ~s** ya no precisamos sus servicios
[3] (assistance) servicio m; **she has done us all a ~** nos ha hecho a todos un favor or servicio; **how can I be of ~ to you?** ¿en qué puedo ayudar or servirlo?
[4] (organization, system) servicio m; **telephone/postal ~** servicio telefónico/postal
[5] (Mil): **the ~s** las fuerzas armadas
[6] (in shop, restaurant) servicio m
[7] (overhaul, maintenance) revisión f, servicio m (AmL), service m (RPl)
[8] (Relig) oficio m religioso
[9] (in tennis) servicio m, saque m
[10] (dinner ~) vajilla f

service[2] vt (car) hacerle* una revisión or (AmL) un servicio a; (machine/appliance) hacerle* el mantenimiento a

service: **~ charge** n **(a)** (in restaurant) servicio m **(b)** (for maintenance — of apartment) gastos mpl comunes or (Esp) de comunidad; (— of office) gastos mpl de mantenimiento; **~ industry** n sector m (de) servicios; **~man** /'sɜːrvəsmən ‖'sɜːvɪsmən/ n (pl **-men** /-mən/) militar m, soldado m; **~ station** n estación f de servicio

serviette /'sɜːrviˈet ‖,sɜːviˈet/ n (BrE) servilleta f

serving /'sɜːrvɪŋ ‖'sɜːvɪŋ/ n porción f, ración f; (before n) **~ dish** fuente f; **~ spoon** cuchara f de servir

session /'seʃən/ n [1] (Adm, Govt, Law) (single meeting) sesión f; **to be in ~** estar* en sesión, estar* sesionando (esp AmL) [2] (period of time) sesión f; **a recording ~** una sesión de grabación

set[1] /set/ n [1] (of tools, golf clubs, pens, keys) juego m; (of books, records) colección f; (of stamps) serie f; **a matching ~ of sheets and pillowcases** un juego de cama [2] (TV) aparato m, televisor m; (Rad) aparato m, receptor m [3] (in tennis, squash) set m [4] **(a)** (Theat) (stage) escenario m; (scenery) decorado m **(b)** (Cin) plató m [5] (in hairdressing) marcado m

set[2] adj [1] (established, prescribed) (wage/price) fijo; **there are no ~ times for visiting** no hay

AmC	Central America	Arg	Argentina	Cu	Cuba	Per	Peru
AmL	Latin America	Bol	Bolivia	Ec	Ecuador	RPl	River Plate Area
AmS	South America	Chi	Chile	Esp	Spain	Ur	Uruguay
Andes	Andean Region	CS	Southern Cone	Méx	Mexico	Ven	Venezuela

horas de visita establecidas; **a ~ phrase** una frase hecha; **we ordered the ~ menu** (BrE) pedimos el menú del día

2 (*pred*) **(a)** (ready, prepared): **to be ~** estar* listo, estar* pronto (RPl) **(b)** (likely, about to) (*journ*) **to be ~ to + INF** llevar camino de + INF **(c)** (determined, resolute): **she's absolutely ~ on that bicycle** está empeñada en que tiene que ser esa bicicleta; **he's dead ~ on going to college** está resuelto a ir a la universidad sea como sea

3 (rigid, inflexible): **to be ~ in one's ways** tener* costumbres muy arraigadas

set³ (*pres p* **setting**; *past & past p* **set**) *vt*

1 (put, place) poner*, colocar*

2 (cause to be, become): **to ~ sb free** poner* en libertad a algn; **to ~ fire to sth, to ~ sth on fire** prenderle fuego a algo

3 (a) (prepare) ⟨*trap*⟩ tender*; ⟨*table*⟩ poner* **(b)** (Med) ⟨*bone*⟩ encajar, componer* (AmL) **(c)** ⟨*hair*⟩ marcar*

4 (adjust) ⟨*oven/alarm clock/watch*⟩ poner*

5 (a) (arrange, agree on) ⟨*date/time*⟩ fijar **(b)** (impose, prescribe) ⟨*target*⟩ establecer* **(c)** (allot) ⟨*task*⟩ asignar; ⟨*homework*⟩ mandar; ⟨*exam/test/ problem*⟩ poner*; ⟨*text*⟩ prescribir* **(d)** (establish) ⟨*precedent*⟩ sentar*; ⟨*record/standard*⟩ establecer*; **to ~ a good example** dar* buen ejemplo

6 (cause to do, start): **she ~ them to work in the garden** los puso a trabajar en el jardín; **to ~ sth going** poner* algo en marcha

7 (*usu pass*) ⟨*book/film*⟩ ambientar; **the novel is ~ in Japan** la novela está ambientada en el Japón

8 (mount, insert) ⟨*gem*⟩ engarzar*, engastar; ⟨*stake*⟩ hincar*, clavar; **the posts are ~ in concrete** los postes están puestos en hormigón

■ **~** *vi* **1** (go down) ⟨*sun/moon*⟩ ponerse*

2 (a) (become solid, rigid) ⟨*jelly*⟩ cuajar(se); ⟨*cement*⟩ fraguar* **(b)** ⟨*bone*⟩ soldarse*

■ **set about** [*v + prep + o*] **(a)** ⟨*task*⟩ (begin) emprender; (tackle) acometer **(b)** **to ~ about -ING** ponerse* a + INF **(c)** (attack) atacar*

■ **set apart** [*v + o + adv*] distinguir*

■ **set aside** [*v + o + adv, v + adv + o*] **(a)** (save, reserve) ⟨*food/goods*⟩ guardar, apartar; ⟨*time*⟩ dejar; ⟨*money*⟩ guardar, ahorrar **(b)** (put to one side, shelve) ⟨*book/project*⟩ dejar (de lado) **(c)** (disregard) ⟨*hostility*⟩ dejar de lado; ⟨*rules/ formality*⟩ prescindir de

■ **set back** [*v + o + adv, v + adv + o*] ⟨*progress*⟩ retrasar, atrasar; ⟨*clock*⟩ atrasar

■ **set in** [*v + adv*] ⟨*infection*⟩ declararse

■ **set off** **1** [*v + adv*] (begin journey) salir*

2 [*v + o + adv, v + adv + o*] **(a)** (activate) ⟨*bomb/ mine*⟩ hacer* explotar; ⟨*alarm*⟩ hacer* sonar; ⟨*firework*⟩ lanzar*, tirar **(b)** (enhance) hacer* resaltar

■ **set out** **1** [*v + adv*] **(a)** (begin journey) salir* **(b)** (begin, intend): **I didn't ~ out with that intention** no empecé con esa intención; **she had failed in what she had ~ out to achieve** no había logrado lo que se había propuesto

2 [*v + o + adv, v + adv + o*] **(a)** ⟨*argument/ theory*⟩ exponer* **(b)** ⟨*goods*⟩ exponer*; ⟨*chess pieces*⟩ colocar*

■ **set to** [*v + adv*] ponerse* a trabajar

■ **set up** [*v + o + adv, v + adv + o*] **1 (a)** (erect, assemble) ⟨*monument*⟩ levantar; ⟨*machine/tent*⟩

montar, armar; **they ~ up camp near the river** acamparon cerca del río **(b)** (arrange, plan) ⟨*meeting*⟩ convocar* a

2 (institute, found) ⟨*committee/commission*⟩ crear; ⟨*inquiry*⟩ abrir*; ⟨*business*⟩ montar

3 (establish): **she ~ herself up as a photographer** se estableció como fotógrafa

4 (colloq) **(a)** (frame) tenderle* una trampa a **(b)** (rig) arreglar

set: ~back *n* revés *m*; **~ square** *n* escuadra *f*; (with two equal sides) cartabón *m*

settee /se'ti:/ *n* sofá *m*

setting /'setɪŋ/ *n* **1** (of dial, switch) posición *f* **2 (a)** (of novel, movie) escenario *m* **(b)** (surroundings) marco *m*, entorno *m* **(c)** (for gem) engarce *m*, engaste *m*, montura *f* **3** (place ~) cubierto *m*

settle /'setl/ *vt* **1 (a)** ⟨*price/terms/time*⟩ acordar*; **it's all been ~d, we're going to Miami** ya está (todo) decidido, nos vamos a Miami; **that ~s it: I never want to see him again** ya no me cabe duda: no lo quiero volver a ver **(b)** (resolve) ⟨*dispute/differences*⟩ resolver*

2 ⟨*bill/account*⟩ pagar*; ⟨*debt*⟩ saldar, liquidar

3 ⟨*country/region*⟩ colonizar*

4 (make comfortable) ⟨*patient/child*⟩ poner* cómodo

5 (make calm) ⟨*child*⟩ calmar; ⟨*doubts*⟩ disipar; ⟨*stomach*⟩ asentar*

■ **~** *vi* **1** (come to live) establecerse*

2 (become calm) ⟨⟨*person*⟩⟩ tranquilizarse*

3 (a) (make oneself comfortable) ponerse* cómodo **(b)** ⟨⟨*bird*⟩⟩ posarse

4 (a) ⟨⟨*dust*⟩⟩ asentarse*; ⟨⟨*snow*⟩⟩ cuajar **(b)** (sink) ⟨⟨*soil/foundations*⟩⟩ asentarse*; ⟨⟨*sediment*⟩⟩ depositarse

5 (a) (pay) saldar la cuenta (*or* la deuda *etc*) **(b)** (Law): **to ~ out of court** resolver* una disputa extrajudicialmente

■ **settle down** **1** [*v + adv*] **(a)** (become calm): **things have ~d down now** las cosas ya se han apaciguado; **~ down please, children** niños, por favor, tranquilos **(b)** (get comfortable): **we ~d down for the night** nos acomodamos para pasar la noche **(c)** (in place, activity): **she's settling down well in her new school** se está adaptando bien a su nueva escuela; **you should get a job and ~ down** deberías conseguir un trabajo y establecerte *or* echar raíces en algún sitio **(d)** (become more responsible) sentar* (la) cabeza

2 [*v + o + adv*] (make calm) calmar, tranquilizar*

■ **settle for** [*v + prep + o*] conformarse con

■ **settle in** [*v + adv*]: **I'll come and see you when you've ~d in** te vendré a ver cuando estés instalado; **she's settling in well in her new job** se está adaptando bien a su nuevo trabajo

■ **settle into** [*v + prep + o*] ⟨*school/job*⟩ adaptarse a; ⟨*routine*⟩ acostumbrarse a

■ **settle on** [*v + prep + o*] ⟨*date/place*⟩ decidirse por

■ **settle up** [*v + adv*] (colloq) arreglar (las) cuentas

settled /'setld/ *adj* **(a)** (established) ⟨*habits/life*⟩ ordenado; ⟨*order*⟩ estable **(b)** ⟨*weather*⟩ estable

settlement /'setlmənt/ *n* **1** (agreement) acuerdo *m*, convenio *m*; **wage ~** (agreement) convenio *m* (laboral), acuerdo *m* salarial; (increase) aumento *m* (salarial) **2 (a)** (of account, bill) pago *m*; (of debt) liquidación *f*, satisfacción *f* **(b)** (payment) pago *m* ③ (of dispute) resolución *f* ④ (village) asentamiento *m*

settler /'setlər ‖ 'setlə(r)/ *n* colono, -na *m,f*

set-up /'setʌp/ *n* (colloq) (situation, arrangement) sistema *f*; (pej) tinglado *m* (fam & pey)

seven /'sevən/ *adj/n* siete *adj inv/m*; *see also* FOUR¹

sevenfold /'sevənfəʊld/ *adj/adv* ▶ -FOLD

seventeen /'sevən'tiːn/ *adj/n* diecisiete *adj inv/m*; *see also* FOUR¹

seventeenth¹ /'sevən'tiːnθ/ *adj* decimoséptimo

seventeenth² *adv* en decimoséptimo lugar

seventeenth³ *n* (Math) diecisieteavo *m*; (part) diecisieteava parte *f*

seventh¹ /'sevənθ/ *adj* séptimo

seventh² *adv* en séptimo lugar

seventh³ *n* (Math) séptimo *m*; (part) séptima parte *f*

seventieth¹ /'sevəntiəθ/ *adj* septuagésimo

seventieth² *adv* en septuagésimo lugar

seventieth³ *n* (Math) setentavo *m*; (part) setentava *or* septuagésima parte *f*

seventy /'sevənti/ *adj/n* setenta *adj inv/m*; *see also* FOUR¹

sever /'sevər ‖ 'sevə(r)/ *vt* **(a)** (cut) ⟨*rope/chain*⟩ cortar; **the saw ~ed his finger** la sierra le cortó *or* le amputó el dedo **(b)** (break off) ⟨*communications*⟩ cortar; ⟨*relations*⟩ romper*

several¹ /'sevrəl/ *adj* varios, -rias

several² *pron* varios, varias

severance /'sevərəns/ *n* **(a)** (of relations, links) ruptura *f* **(b)** (Lab Rel) cese *m*; (before *n*) ~ **pay** indemnización *f* por cese

severe /sə'vɪr ‖ sɪ'vɪə(r)/ *adj* **severer**, **severest** ① **(a)** (strict, harsh) ⟨*punishment/judge*⟩ severo; ⟨*discipline*⟩ riguroso **(b)** (austere) ⟨*style/colors*⟩ austero ② **(a)** (serious, bad) ⟨*illness/injury*⟩ grave; ⟨*pain*⟩ fuerte; ⟨*winter*⟩ severo; ⟨*weather conditions*⟩ muy malo **(b)** (difficult, rigorous) ⟨*conditions*⟩ estricto

severely /sə'vɪrli ‖ sɪ'vɪəli/ *adv* con severidad, severamente

severity /sə'verəti ‖ sɪ'verəti/ *n* severidad *f*; (of illness, injury) gravedad *f*; (of pain) intensidad *f*

sew /səʊ/ (*past* **sewed**; *past p* **sewn** *or* **sewed**) *vt* coser; ⟨*seam/hem*⟩ hacer*; **to ~ sth on** coser algo
■ ~ *vi* coser
■ **sew up** [*v + o + adv, v + adv + o*] coser

sewage /'suːɪdʒ ‖ 'suːɪdʒ, 'sjuːɪdʒ/ *n* aguas *fpl* negras *or* residuales, aguas *fpl* servidas (CS)

sewer /'suːər ‖ 'suːə(r), 'sjuːə(r)/ *n* **(a)** (underground) alcantarilla *f*, cloaca *f* **(b)** (drain) (AmE) boca *f* de (la) alcantarilla, sumidero *m*

sewing /'səʊɪŋ/ *n* costura *f*

sewing machine *n* máquina *f* de coser

sewn /səʊn/ *past p of* SEW

sex /seks/ *n* ① **(a)** (sexual matters) sexo *m*; (before *n*) ~ **education** educación *f* sexual; ~ **symbol** sex symbol *mf* **(b)** (intercourse) relaciones *fpl* sexuales ② **(a)** (gender) sexo *m* **(b)** (men, women collectively) sexo *m*; (before *n*) ~ **discrimination** discriminación *f* sexual

sexism /'seksɪzəm/ *n* sexismo *m*

sexist¹ /'seksəst ‖ 'seksɪst/ *n* sexista *mf*

sexist² *adj* sexista

sextet /seks'tet/ *n* sexteto *m*

sexual /'sekʃuəl/ *adj* sexual

sexuality /sekʃu'æləti/ *n* sexualidad *f*

sexually /'sekʃuəli/ *adv* sexualmente; **a ~ transmitted disease** una enfermedad de transmisión sexual

sexy /'seksi/ *adj* **sexier**, **sexiest** **(a)** (sexually attractive) sexy **(b)** (erotic) ⟨*book/film/talk*⟩ erótico

sh /ʃ/ *interj* ¡sh!

shabby /'ʃæbi/ *adj* **-bier**, **-biest** **(a)** ⟨*carpet/sofa/jacket*⟩ gastado; (threadbare) raído **(b)** (bad, unfair): **what a ~ way to treat him** qué manera más fea de tratarlo

shack /ʃæk/ *n* choza *f*, casucha *f*, rancho *m* (AmL), jacal *m* (Méx), bohío *m* (AmC, Col)

shackles /'ʃækəlz/ *pl n* grilletes *mpl*

shade¹ /ʃeɪd/ *n* ① (dark place) sombra *f*; **in the ~** a la sombra ② (over window) (AmE) persiana *f*, estor *m* (Esp) ③ **(a)** (of color) tono *m* **(b)** (degree of difference, nuance) matiz *m*

shade² *vt* ⟨*eyes/face*⟩ proteger* del sol/de la luz; **her seat was ~d from the sun** su asiento estaba resguardado del sol

shadow¹ /'ʃædəʊ/ *n* sombra *f*; **she was a ~ of her former self** no era ni sombra de lo que había sido; **without a ~ of (a) doubt** sin la más mínima duda

shadow² *vt* seguir* de cerca a

shadowy /'ʃædəʊi/ *adj* **(a)** (indistinct) ⟨*form*⟩ impreciso **(b)** (full of shadows) ⟨*place/forest*⟩ oscuro

shady /'ʃeɪdi/ *adj* **-dier**, **-diest** **(a)** (giving shade) ⟨*place/garden*⟩ sombreado; ⟨*tree*⟩ que da mucha sombra **(b)** (disreputable) (colloq) ⟨*deal/business*⟩ turbio; ⟨*character*⟩ sospechoso

shaft /ʃæft ‖ ʃɑːft/ *n* ① **(a)** (of arrow, spear) asta *f*, astil *m*; (of hammer, ax) mango *m* **(b)** (of light) rayo *m* ② (Mech Eng) eje *m* ③ (of elevator) hueco *m*; (of mine) pozo *m*, tiro *m*

shaggy /'ʃægi/ *adj* **-gier**, **-giest** ⟨*dog*⟩ lanudo, peludo; ⟨*beard/hair*⟩ enmarañado, greñudo

shake¹ /ʃeɪk/ (*past* **shook**; *past p* **shaken**) *vt* ① **(a)** (cause to move, agitate) ⟨*bottle/cocktail*⟩ agitar; ⟨*person/building*⟩ sacudir; ⟨*dice*⟩ agitar, revolver* (AmL); **she shook the sand out of the towel** sacudió la toalla para quitarle la arena; **to ~ hands with sb, to ~ sb's hand** darle* *or* estrecharle la mano a algn; **they shook hands** se dieron la mano; **to ~ one's head** negar* con la cabeza; (meaning yes) (AmE) asentir* con la cabeza **(b)** (brandish) ⟨*sword/stick*⟩ agitar; **to ~ one's fist at sb** amenazar* a algn con el puño ② **(a)** (undermine, impair) ⟨*courage/nerve*⟩ hacer* flaquear; ⟨*faith*⟩ debilitar **(b)** (shock, surprise) ⟨*person*⟩ impresionar
■ ~ *vi* ① (move, tremble) «*earth/hand/voice*» temblar*; **he was shaking with fear/cold/rage** estaba temblando de miedo/frío/rabia ② (shake hands) (colloq): **they shook on it** sellaron el acuerdo con un apretón de manos
■ **shake off** [*v + o + adv, v + adv + o*] ⟨*pursuer/reporter*⟩ deshacerse* de; ⟨*habit*⟩ quitarse; ⟨*cold*⟩ quitarse de encima
■ **shake up** [*v + o + adv, v + adv + o*] ① ⟨*liquid*⟩ agitar

2 (colloq) ⟨*industry/personnel*⟩ reorganizar* totalmente

3 (disturb, shock) (colloq): **he's a bit ∼n up** está un poco alterado

shake² *n* **1** (act) sacudida *f*; (violent) sacudida *f* violenta, sacudón *m* (AmL); **he replied with a ∼ of the head** contestó negando con la cabeza **2** (milk ∼) (AmE) batido *m*, (leche *f*) malteada *f* (AmL), licuado *m* con leche (AmL)

shaken /'ʃeɪkən/ *past p of* SHAKE¹

shaker /'ʃeɪkər ‖'ʃeɪkə(r)/ *n* **(a)** (for cocktails) coctelera *f* **(b)** (for salt) salero *m*; (for pepper) pimentero *m*; (for sugar) azucarero *m* **(c)** (for dice) cubilete *m*, cacho *m* (Andes)

shaky /'ʃeɪki/ *adj* **-kier, -kiest (a)** (trembling) ⟨*hands/voice*⟩ tembloroso; ⟨*writing*⟩ de trazo poco firme **(b)** (unsteady) ⟨*table*⟩ poco firme; ⟨*structure*⟩ tambaleante; ⟨*health*⟩ delicado; ⟨*currency/government*⟩ débil; ⟨*theory/start*⟩ flojo

shale /ʃeɪl/ *n* esquisto *m*, pizarra *f*

shall /ʃæl, *weak forms* ʃl, ʃəl/ *v mod* (*past should*) **1** (*with 1st person*) **(a)** (in statements about the future): **I ∼ be very interested to see what happens** tendré mucho interés en ver qué sucede; **we shan't be able to come** (BrE) no podremos venir **(b)** (making suggestions, asking for assent) [*The present tense is used in this type of question in Spanish*] **∼ I open the window?** ¿abro la ventana?; **∼ we go out tonight?** ¿qué te (*or* le *etc*) parece si salimos esta noche? **2** (*with 2nd and 3rd persons*) (in commands, promises etc): **they ∼ not pass** no pasarán

shallot /ʃə'lɑːt ‖ʃə'lɒt/ *n* chalote *m*, chalota *f*

shallow /'ʃæləʊ/ *adj* **-er, -est (a)** (not deep) ⟨*water/pond/river*⟩ poco profundo; ⟨*dish*⟩ llano, plano; ⟨*breathing*⟩ superficial **(b)** (superficial) ⟨*person*⟩ superficial

shallows /'ʃæləʊz/ *pl n* bajío *m*

sham¹ /ʃæm/ *n* farsa *f*

sham² *adj* (pej) (*no comp*) fingido

sham³ *vt/i* **-mm-** fingir*

shambles /'ʃæmbəlz/ *n* (+ *sing vb*) caos *m*, desquicio *m* (RPl); (fiasco) desastre *m*

shame¹ /ʃeɪm/ *n* **1** (feeling) vergüenza *f*, pena *f* (AmL exc CS); **∼ on you!** ¡qué vergüenza!; **to put sb to ∼**: **she's such a good hostess, she puts me to ∼** es tan buena anfitriona que me hace sentir culpable **2** (pity) (*no pl*) lástima *f*, pena *f*; **what a ∼!** ¡qué lástima!; **it's a ∼ you can't go** es una pena que no puedas ir

shame² *vt* avergonzar*, apenar (AmL exc CS); **they ∼d us into paying** nos hicieron avergonzarnos de tal manera que al final pagamos

shamefaced /'ʃeɪm'feɪst/ *adj* avergonzado

shameful /'ʃeɪmfəl/ *adj* vergonzoso

shameless /'ʃeɪmləs ‖'ʃeɪmlɪs/ *adj* ⟨*lie/exploitation*⟩ descarado; ⟨*liar/cheat*⟩ desvergonzado

shampoo¹ /ʃæm'puː/ *n* (*pl* **-poos**) champú *m*

shampoo² *vt* **-poos, -pooing, -pooed** ⟨*hair*⟩ lavar; ⟨*carpet/upholstery*⟩ limpiar

shan't /ʃænt ‖ʃɑːnt/ = **shall not**

shanty /'ʃænti/ *n* (*pl* **-ties**) **1** (hut) casucha *f*, rancho *m* (AmL), chabola *f* (Esp) **2** (sea ∼) (BrE) canción *f* de marineros

shantytown /'ʃænti.taʊn/ *n* barriada *f* (AmL), chabolas *fpl* (Esp), población *f* callampa (Chi), villa *f* miseria (Arg), ciudad *f* perdida (Méx), cantegril *m* (Ur), ranchos *mpl* (Ven)

shape¹ /ʃeɪp/ *n* **1 (a)** (visible form) forma *f*; **it is triangular in ∼** tiene forma triangular; **in the ∼ of a cross** en forma de cruz; **to take ∼** tomar forma **(b)** (general nature, outline) conformación *f*; **the ∼ of things to come** lo que nos espera **2** (guise): **assistance in the ∼ of food stamps** ayuda consistente en vales canjeables por comida; **I won't tolerate bribery in any ∼ or form** no pienso tolerar sobornos de ningún tipo **3** (condition, order): **she's in pretty good/bad ∼** está bastante bien/mal (de salud); **to keep in ∼** mantenerse* en forma

shape² *vt* **(a)** ⟨*object/material*⟩ darle* forma a **(b)** (influence) ⟨*events*⟩ determinar; ⟨*character/ideas*⟩ formar

■ **∼** *vi* «*project*» tomar forma; «*plan*» desarrollarse

■ **shape up** [*v + adv*] **(a)** ▶ SHAPE² *vi* **(b)** (improve, pull oneself together) entrar en vereda (fam)

-shaped /ʃeɪpt/ *suff*: **L∼/heart∼** con *or* en forma de L/corazón

shapeless /'ʃeɪpləs ‖'ʃeɪplɪs/ *adj* informe, sin forma

shapely /'ʃeɪpli/ *adj* **-lier, -liest** ⟨*figure*⟩ bien modulado, hermoso; ⟨*legs*⟩ torneado

share¹ /ʃer ‖ʃeə(r)/ *n* **1** (portion) parte *f*; **she must take her ∼ of the blame** debe aceptar que tiene parte de la culpa **2** (Busn, Fin) **(a)** (held by partner) (*no pl*) participación *f* **(b)** (held by shareholder) acción *f*

share² *vt* **1 (a)** (use jointly) **to ∼ sth (WITH sb)** compartir algo (CON algn) **(b)** (have in common) ⟨*interest/opinion*⟩ compartir; ⟨*characteristics*⟩ tener* en común **2 (a)** (divide) dividir **(b)** (communicate) ⟨*experience/knowledge*⟩ intercambiar

■ **∼** *vi* **(a)** (use jointly) compartir; **to ∼ and ∼ alike** compartir las cosas **(b)** (have a part) **to ∼ IN sth** compartir algo, participar DE algo

■ **share out** [*v + o + adv, v + adv + o*] repartir, distribuir*

shareholder /'ʃerhəʊldər ‖'ʃeəhəʊldə(r)/ *n* accionista *mf*

shark /ʃɑːrk ‖ʃɑːk/ *n* (Zool) tiburón *m*

sharp¹ /ʃɑːrp ‖ʃɑːp/ *adj* **-er, -est 1 (a)** ⟨*knife/edge/scissors*⟩ afilado, filoso (AmL), filudo (Chi, Per); ⟨*features*⟩ anguloso; ⟨*pencil*⟩ con punta; **it has a ∼ point** es muy puntiagudo **(b)** ⟨*pain*⟩ agudo **(c)** ⟨*wind*⟩ cortante; ⟨*frost*⟩ crudo, fuerte **(d)** ⟨*taste*⟩ ácido **2 (a)** (abrupt, steep) ⟨*bend/angle*⟩ cerrado; ⟨*turn*⟩ brusco; ⟨*rise/fall*⟩ brusco **(b)** (sudden) repentino, súbito **3 (a)** (keen) ⟨*eyesight*⟩ agudo; ⟨*hearing*⟩ fino, agudo **(b)** (acute) ⟨*wit/mind*⟩ agudo **4** (clear, unblurred) ⟨*photo/TV picture*⟩ nítido; ⟨*outline*⟩ definido; ⟨*contrast*⟩ marcado **5** (harsh) ⟨*retort*⟩ cortante; **to have a ∼ tongue** ser* muy mordaz, tener* una lengua muy afilada **6** (clever, shrewd) ⟨*person*⟩ listo, astuto; ⟨*move*⟩ astuto **7** (Mus) (referring to key) sostenido; **C ∼** do *m* sostenido

sharp² *adv* **1** (exactly): **at six o'clock ∼** a las ⋯▶

seis en punto **2** (abruptly): **turn ~ right** gire a la derecha en curva cerrada **3** (Mus) ⟨play⟩ demasiado alto

sharp³ n (Mus) sostenido m

sharpen /ˈʃɑːrpən ‖ˈʃɑːpən/ vt ⟨knife/claws⟩ afilar; ⟨pencil⟩ sacarle* punta a

sharpener /ˈʃɑːrpnər ‖ˈʃɑːpnə(r)/ n (knife ~) afilador m; (pencil ~) sacapuntas m

sharply /ˈʃɑːrpli ‖ˈʃɑːpli/ adv **1** (a) (steeply, abruptly) ⟨drop/fall/increase⟩ bruscamente; ⟨bend⟩ repentinamente **(b)** (suddenly, swiftly) de repente **2** ⟨outlined/defined⟩ claramente, nítidamente **3** (harshly) ⟨answer⟩ con dureza

shat /ʃæt/ past & past p of SHIT²

shatter /ˈʃætər ‖ˈʃætə(r)/ vt ⟨window/plate⟩ hacer* añicos or pedazos; ⟨health/nerves⟩ destrozar*; ⟨confidence/hopes⟩ destruir*; ⟨silence⟩ romper*; **she was ~ed by the news** la noticia la dejó destrozada
■ ~ vi hacer* añicos or pedazos

shave¹ /ʃeɪv/ vt **1** ⟨person⟩ afeitar or (esp Méx) rasurar **2** (touch in passing) rozar*
■ ~ vi «person» afeitarse or (esp Méx) rasurarse

shave² n afeitada f or (esp Méx) rasurada f; **to have a ~** afeitarse or (esp Méx) rasurarse; **a close ~** (colloq): **we won in the end, but it was a pretty close ~** al final ganamos, pero por los pelos or por un pelo (fam)

shaven /ˈʃeɪvən/ adj ⟨head⟩ rapado

shaver /ˈʃeɪvər ‖ˈʃeɪvə(r)/ n (electric ~) máquina f de afeitar, afeitadora f or (esp Méx) rasuradora f

shaving /ˈʃeɪvɪŋ/ n (a) (before n) ⟨cream/soap⟩ de afeitar or (esp Méx) de rasurar; **~ brush** brocha f de afeitar **(b) shavings** pl (pieces) virutas fpl

shawl /ʃɔːl/ n chal m

she /ʃiː, weak form ʃi/ pron ella

■ **Note** Although *ella* is given as the main translation of *she*, it is in practice used only for emphasis, or to avoid ambiguity: *she went to the theater* fue al teatro; *she went to the theater, he went to the cinema* ella fue al teatro y él fue al cine; **she did it** ella lo hizo.

~'s a writer/my sister es escritora/mi hermana; **~ didn't say it, I did** no fue ella quien lo dijo, sino yo

sheaf /ʃiːf/ n (pl **sheaves**) **(a)** (Agr) gavilla f **(b)** (of notes) fajo m; (of arrows) haz m

shear /ʃɪr ‖ʃɪə(r)/ vt (past **sheared**; past p **shorn**) ⟨sheep⟩ esquilar

shears /ʃɪrz ‖ʃɪəz/ pl n (for grass, hedge) tijeras fpl; (for shearing sheep) tijeras fpl de esquilar

sheath /ʃiːθ/ n (pl ~s /ʃiːðz/) (for sword, knife) funda f, vaina f

sheaves /ʃiːvz/ pl of SHEAF

shed¹ /ʃed/ vt (pres p **shedding**; past & past p **shed**) **1 (a)** ⟨tears/blood⟩ derramar **(b)** ⟨leaves/ skin⟩ mudar; ⟨clothing⟩ despojarse de (fml) **2** (send out) ⟨light⟩ emitir

shed² n **(a)** (hut) cabaña f; (garden ~) cobertizo m **(b)** (larger building) nave f

she'd /ʃiːd/ **(a)** = **she would (b)** = **she had**

sheen /ʃiːn/ n brillo m, lustre m

sheep /ʃiːp/ n (pl ~) oveja f

sheepdog /ˈʃiːpdɔːg ‖ˈʃiːpdɒg/ n perro m pastor

sheepish /ˈʃiːpɪʃ/ adj avergonzado

sheepskin /ˈʃiːpskɪn/ n piel f de borrego or de cordero

sheer /ʃɪr ‖ʃɪə(r)/ adj **sheerer, sheerest 1** (pure, absolute) (as intensifier) puro; **the ~ size of the problem** la mera magnitud del problema **2** (vertical) ⟨drop⟩ a pique; ⟨cliff⟩ escarpado **3** (fine) ⟨stockings/fabric⟩ muy fino

sheet /ʃiːt/ n **1** (on bed) sábana f **2** (of paper) hoja f; (of wrapping paper) pliego m, hoja f; (of stamps) pliego m **3 (a)** (of metal) chapa f, plancha f, lámina f; **a ~ of glass** un vidrio **(b)** (of ice) capa f; (before n) **~ lightning** relámpagos mpl difusos

sheet: ~ metal n metal m en planchas or chapas; **~ music** n partituras fpl

sheik, sheikh /ʃiːk ‖ʃeɪk/ n jeque m

shelf /ʃelf/ n (pl **shelves**) **1** (in cupboard, bookcase) estante m, balda f (Esp); **a set of shelves** unos estantes, una estantería **2** (Geol): **continental ~** plataforma f continental

shell¹ /ʃel/ n **1 (a)** (of egg, nut) cáscara f; (of sea mollusk) concha f; (of tortoise, turtle, snail, crustacean) caparazón m or f **(b)** (of building, vehicle) armazón m or f **2** (Mil) proyectil m, obús m

shell² vt **1** (Culin) ⟨peas/nuts/eggs⟩ pelar; ⟨mussel/clam⟩ quitarle la concha a **2** (Mil) ⟨position/troops/city⟩ bombardear

she'll /ʃiːl, weak form ʃɪl/ = **she will**

shell: ~fish n (pl **~fish**) **(a)** (creature) marisco m **(b)** (collectively) mariscos mpl, marisco m (Esp); **~shock** n neurosis f de guerra

shelter¹ /ˈʃeltər ‖ˈʃeltə(r)/ n **1** (building) refugio m **2 (a)** (protection): **to take ~** refugiarse **(b)** (accommodations): **they need food and ~** necesitan alimentos y albergue

shelter² vt **(a)** (protect from weather) resguardar **(b)** ⟨criminal/fugitive⟩ darle* cobijo a
■ ~ vi **to ~ (FROM sth)** refugiarse or resguardarse (DE algo)

sheltered /ˈʃeltərd ‖ˈʃeltəd/ adj ⟨valley/ harbor⟩ abrigado; ⟨life⟩ protegido

shelve /ʃelv/ vt ⟨plan/project⟩ archivar

shelves /ʃelvz/ pl of SHELF

shelving /ˈʃelvɪŋ/ n estantería f

shepherd /ˈʃepərd ‖ˈʃepəd/ n pastor m

sherbet /ˈʃɜːrbət ‖ˈʃɜːbət/ n **(a)** (sorbet) (AmE) sorbete m **(b)** (powder) (BrE) polvos efervescentes con sabor a frutas, sidral® m (Esp)

sheriff /ˈʃerəf ‖ˈʃerɪf/ n (in US) sheriff mf

sherry /ˈʃeri/ n (pl **-ries**) jerez m

she's /ʃiːz, weak form ʃɪz/ **(a)** = **she is (b)** = **she has**

shield¹ /ʃiːld/ n ⓵ (Hist, Mil) escudo m
⓶ (protective cover on machine) revestimiento m

shield² vt to ~ sth/sb (FROM sb/sth) proteger* algo/a algn (DE algn/algo)

shift¹ /ʃɪft/ vt (a) (change position of) ⟨object/ furniture⟩ correr, mover* (b) (transfer): **they tried to ~ the responsibility onto us** trataron de cargarnos la responsabilidad
■ ~ vi ⓵ (change position, direction) «cargo» correrse; «wind» cambiar; **he ~ed uneasily in his chair** se movía intranquilo en la silla; **the focus of attention has ~ed to Europe** el foco de atención ha pasado a Europa ⓶ (change gear) (AmE) cambiar de marcha or de velocidad

shift² n ⓵ (change in position) cambio m ⓶ (work period) turno m; **to work the day/night ~** hacer* el turno de día/de noche; (before n) **~ work** trabajo m por turnos ⓷ (AmE Auto) palanca f de cambio or (Méx) de velocidades

shift key n tecla f de las mayúsculas

shifty /ʃɪfti/ adj -**tier, -tiest** ⟨expression/eyes⟩ furtivo; ⟨appearance⟩ sospechoso

Shiite, Shi'ite¹ /ʃiːaɪt/ n chiíta mf, shií mf

Shiite, Shi'ite² adj chiíta, shií

shilling /ʃɪlɪŋ/ n chelín m

shimmer /ʃɪmər ‖ ʃɪmə(r)/ vi «water/silk» brillar; «lights» titilar; (in water) rielar (liter)

shin /ʃɪn/ n espinilla f, canilla f

shine¹ /ʃaɪn/ n brillo m

shine² (past & past p **shone**) vi (a) (gleam, glow) «star/sun/eyes» brillar; «metal/shoes» relucir*, brillar (b) (excel) **to ~ (AT sth)** destacar(se*) (EN algo)
■ ~ vt (+ adv compl): **to ~ a light on sth** alumbrar algo con una luz

shingle /ʃɪŋgəl/ n guijarros mpl

shingles /ʃɪŋgəlz/ n (Med) (+ sing vb) herpes m, culebrilla f

shining /ʃaɪnɪŋ/ adj ⟨eyes⟩ brillante, luminoso; ⟨hair/metal⟩ brillante, reluciente

shiny /ʃaɪni/ adj -**nier, -niest** ⟨hair/fabric/ shoe⟩ brillante; ⟨coin⟩ reluciente

ship¹ /ʃɪp/ n barco m, buque m

ship² vt -**pp-** (a) (send by sea) enviar* or mandar por barco (b) (send) enviar*, despachar

ship: ~building n construcción f naval; **~load** n cargamento m

shipment /ʃɪpmənt/ n envío m, remesa f

shipping /ʃɪpɪŋ/ n (a) (ships) barcos mpl, embarcaciones fpl (frml); (before n) ⟨lane/route⟩ de navegación (b) (transportation of freight) transporte m

shipshape /ʃɪpʃeɪp/ adj (pred) limpio y ordenado

shipwreck¹ /ʃɪprek/ n naufragio m

shipwreck² vt (usu pass): **to be ~ed** naufragar*

shipyard /ʃɪpjɑːrd/ n astillero m

shirk /ʃɜːrk ‖ ʃɜːk/ vt ⟨task/duty⟩ eludir, rehuir*

shirt /ʃɜːrt ‖ ʃɜːt/ n camisa f

shirtsleeve /ʃɜːrtsliːv ‖ ʃɜːtsliːv/ n manga f de camisa; **in (one's) ~s** en mangas de camisa

shit¹ /ʃɪt/ n (vulg) mierda f (vulg)

shit² vi (pres p **shitting**; past & past p **shit** or **shat**) (vulg) cagar* (vulg)

shit³ interj (vulg) ¡carajo! (vulg), ¡mierda! (vulg)

shiver¹ /ʃɪvər ‖ ʃɪvə(r)/ n escalofrío m; **the scream sent ~s o a ~ down my spine** el grito me produjo escalofríos

shiver² vi (with cold) temblar*; (with fear) temblar*; (with anticipation) estremecerse*

shivery /ʃɪvəri/ adj: **to feel ~** tener* escalofríos

shmaltz, shmalz etc ▶ SCHMALTZ etc

shoal /ʃəʊl/ n ⓵ (of fish) cardumen m, banco m ⓶ (sandbank) bajío m, banco m de arena

shock¹ /ʃɑːk ‖ ʃɒk/ n ⓵ (a) (of impact) choque m; (of earthquake, explosion) sacudida f (b) (electric ~) descarga f (eléctrica) ⓶ (a) (Med) shock m; **to be in (a state of) ~** estar* en estado de shock (b) (distress, surprise) shock m; **to get a ~** llevarse un shock; **the news came as a great ~ to us** la noticia nos conmocionó (c) (scare) susto m; **to get a ~** llevarse un susto ⓷ (bushy mass): **a ~ of hair** una mata de pelo

shock² vt (stun, appal) horrorizar*; (scandalize) escandalizar*

shock absorber /əbsɔːrbər ‖ əbzɔːbə(r)/ n amortiguador m

shocked /ʃɑːkt ‖ ʃɒkt/ adj (a) (appalled) horrorizado (b) (scandalized): **I was ~ to hear that ... me indigné cuando me enteré de que ...**

shocking /ʃɑːkɪŋ ‖ ʃɒkɪŋ/ adj (a) ⟨news/ report⟩ espeluznante (b) ⟨behavior/language⟩ escandaloso

shock wave n (Phys) onda f expansiva

shod /ʃɑːd ‖ ʃɒd/ past & past p of SHOE²

shoddy /ʃɑːdi ‖ ʃɒdi/ adj -**dier, -diest** ⟨goods/workmanship⟩ de muy mala calidad

shoe¹ /ʃuː/ n (a) (Clothing) zapato m; (before n) **~ polish** betún m; **~ repairer** zapatero, -ra m,f (b) (for horse) herradura f (c) (brake ~) zapata f

shoe² vt (pres **shoes**; pres p **shoeing**; past & past p **shod**) ⟨horse⟩ herrar*

shoe: ~brush n cepillo m de los zapatos; **~horn** n calzador m; **~lace** n cordón m (de zapato), agujeta f (Méx), pasador m (Per)

shone /ʃəʊn, ʃɑːn ‖ ʃɒn/ past & past p of SHINE²

shoo¹ /ʃuː/ interj ¡fuera!, ¡úscale! (Méx)

shoo² vt **shoos, shooing, shooed**: **I ~ed the birds off o away** espanté a los pájaros

shook /ʃʊk/ past of SHAKE¹

shoot¹ /ʃuːt/ n ⓵ (Bot) brote m ⓶ (shooting expedition) cacería f ⓷ (Cin) rodaje m

shoot² (past & past p **shot**) vt ⓵ (a) ⟨person/ animal⟩ pegarle* un tiro a; **they shot him dead, they shot him to death** (AmE) lo mataron a tiros/ de un tiro; **to ~ oneself** pegarse* un tiro (b) (hunt) ⟨duck/deer⟩ cazar* ⓶ (fire) ⟨bullet⟩ disparar, tirar; ⟨arrow/missile⟩ lanzar*, arrojar; ⟨glance⟩ lanzar* ⓷ (pass swiftly): **to ~ the rapids** salvar los rápidos ⓸ (Cin) rodar*
■ ~ vi ⓵ (a) (fire weapon) disparar; **to ~ AT sb/sth** dispararle A algn/A algo (b) (hunt) cazar* ⓶ (move swiftly): **she shot past** pasó como una bala (fam); **he shot out of his seat** saltó del asiento ⓷ (Sport) tirar, disparar
■ **shoot down** [v + o + adv, v + adv + o] ⟨plane⟩ derribar, abatir

■ **shoot out** [v + adv] (emerge quickly) salir*
disparado or (fam) como un bólido
■ **shoot up** [v + adv] **(a)** (grow tall) crecer* mucho
(b) (go up quickly) «*prices/temperature*»
dispararse; «*flames*» alzarse*

shoot³ interj (AmE colloq) ¡miércoles! (fam & euf)

shooting /'ʃuːtɪŋ/ n **(a)** (exchange of fire) tiroteo
m, balacera f (AmL); (shots) tiros mpl, disparos
mpl **(b)** (killing) asesinato m

shooting star n estrella f fugaz

shoot-out /'ʃuːtaʊt/ n tiroteo m, balacera f
(AmL), baleo m (Chi)

shop¹ /ʃɑːp ‖ ʃɒp/ n **(a)** (retail outlet) tienda f,
negocio m (CS), comercio m (frml); **to go to the**
∼s ir* de compras **(b)** (business) (colloq): **to talk ∼**
hablar del trabajo

shop² **-pp-** vi hacer* compras; **to go ∼ping** ir*
de compras

shopaholic /ˌʃɑːpə'hɒlɪk ‖ ˌʃɒpə'hɒlɪk/ n
(colloq) persona f adicta a las compras

shop: **∼ assistant** n (BrE) dependiente, -ta
m,f, empleado, -da m,f (de tienda) (AmL),
vendedor, -dora m,f (CS); **∼ floor** n (part of
factory) taller m; (workers) obreros mpl,
trabajadores mpl; (as union members) bases fpl
sindicales; **∼keeper** n comerciante mf, tendero,
-ra m,f; **∼lifter** /'ʃɑːp,lɪftər ‖ 'ʃɒp,lɪftə(r)/ n
ladrón, -drona m,f (que roba en las tiendas);
∼lifting /'ʃɑːp,lɪftɪŋ ‖ 'ʃɒp,lɪftɪŋ/ n hurto m (en
las tiendas)

shopper /'ʃɑːpər ‖ 'ʃɒpə(r)/ n comprador, -dora
m,f

shopping /'ʃɑːpɪŋ ‖ 'ʃɒpɪŋ/ n **(a)** (act): **to do**
the ∼ hacer* la compra or (AmS) las compras,
hacer* el mercado (Col, Ven), hacer* el mandado
(Méx); (before n) «basket» de la compra or (AmS) de
las compras **(b)** (purchases) compras fpl

shopping: **∼ bag** n (given by store) (AmE)
bolsa f (de plástico, papel etc) **(b)** (owned by
customer) (BrE) bolsa f (de la compra or (AmS) de
las compras); **∼ cart** n (AmE) carrito m (de la
compra or (AmS) de las compras); **∼ center,**
(BrE) **∼ centre ▶ ▶** MALL; **∼ list** n lista f de la
compra or (AmS) de las compras or (Col, Ven) del
mercado or (Méx) del mandado; **∼ mall** n (esp
AmE) centro m comercial; **∼ trolley** n (BrE) **(a)**
▶ ▶ CART **(b)** (bag on wheels) carrito m, changuito
m (RPl)

shop: **∼-soiled** adj «goods» deteriorado; **∼**
window n escaparate m, vitrina f (AmL),
aparador m (AmC, Col, Méx); **∼worn** adj (AmE)
«goods» deteriorado

shore /ʃɔːr ‖ ʃɔː(r)/ n **1** **(a)** (of sea, lake) orilla f
(b) (coast) costa f, ribera f **2** (land): **to go on ∼**
bajar a tierra (firme)
■ **shore up** [v + o + adv, v + adv + o] apuntalar

shorn /ʃɔːrn ‖ ʃɔːn/ past & past p of SHEAR

short¹ /ʃɔːrt ‖ ʃɔːt/ adj **-er, -est** **1** (of length,
height, distance) corto; «person» bajo
2 **(a)** (brief) «visit/trip» corto; **the days are**
getting ∼er los días van acortándose; **a ∼ time**
ago hace poco (tiempo); **we call him Rob for ∼** lo
llamamos Rob para abreviar **(b)** **in short** (briefly)
(as linker) en resumen
3 (brusque) «manner» brusco; **she has a ∼ temper**
tiene muy mal genio
4 (inadequate, deficient) escaso; **to be in ∼ supply**

escasear; **we're six people ∼** todavía nos faltan
seis personas; **(to be) ∼ OF sth/sb**: **we're very ∼**
of time estamos muy cortos de tiempo; **they were**
∼ of staff no tenían suficiente personal

short² adv **1** (suddenly, abruptly): **he cut ∼ his**
vacation interrumpió sus vacaciones; **he stopped**
∼ when he saw me se paró en seco cuando me
vio **2** (below target, requirement): **to fall ∼** «shell/
arrow» quedarse corto; **we never went ∼ of food**
nunca nos faltó la comida

short³ n **1** (Cin) cortometraje m, corto m
2 (drink) copa f de bebida alcohólica de las
que se sirven en pequeñas cantidades, como el
whisky o el coñac **3** **shorts** pl **(a)** (short trousers)
shorts mpl, pantalones mpl cortos **(b)** (men's
underwear) (AmE) calzoncillos mpl

short⁴ vi (Elec) hacer* un cortocircuito
■ **short out** (AmE Elec) [v + adv] «fuse»
fundirse; «iron/hairdryer» hacer* (un)
cortocircuito

shortage /'ʃɔːrtɪdʒ ‖ 'ʃɔːtɪdʒ/ n ∼ (OF sth/sb)
falta f or escasez f (DE algo/algn)

short: **∼bread** n galleta dulce de mantequilla;
∼change /'ʃɔːrt'tʃeɪndʒ ‖ ˌʃɔːt'tʃeɪndʒ/ vt (in
shop): **he ∼-changed me** me dio mal el cambio or
(AmL tb) el vuelto; **∼ circuit** n cortocircuito m;
∼circuit /'ʃɔːrt'sɜːrkət ‖ ˌʃɔːt'sɜːkɪt/ vt (Elec)
provocar* un cortocircuito en ■ ∼ vi (Elec)
hacer* (un) cortocircuito; **∼coming** n defecto
m, deficiencia f; **∼crust** (pastry) n (BrE) pasta
f quebradiza (tipo de masa para empanadas,
tartas etc); **∼ cut** n atajo m; **there are no ∼ cuts**
to success no hay fórmulas mágicas para el éxito

shorten /'ʃɔːrtn ‖ 'ʃɔːtn/ vt «skirt/sleeves»
acortar; «text/report» acortar, abreviar

short: **∼fall** n **∼fall** (IN sth): **a ∼fall of 7% in**
revenues un déficit de 7% en los ingresos;
∼haired /'ʃɔːrtherd ‖ ˌʃɔːt'heəd/ adj de pelo
corto; **∼hand** n taquigrafía f; **∼ list** n lista f de
candidatos preseleccionados; **∼-list** vt
preseleccionar; **∼-lived** /'ʃɔːrt'lɪvd ‖ ˌʃɔːt'lɪvd/
adj «success/enthusiasm» efímero; «recovery»
pasajero

shortly /'ʃɔːrtli ‖ 'ʃɔːtli/ adv dentro de poco; **∼**
before/after midnight poco antes/después de la
medianoche

short: **∼sighted** /'ʃɔːrt'saɪtəd ‖ ˌʃɔːt'saɪtɪd/ adj
(a) (esp BrE Med) miope, corto de vista **(b)**
«attitude/policy» corto de miras; **∼sleeved**
/'ʃɔːrt'sliːvd ‖ ˌʃɔːt'sliːvd/ adj de manga corta;
∼staffed /'ʃɔːrt'stæft ‖ ˌʃɔːt'stɑːft/ adj: **they/we**
were ∼staffed les/nos faltaba personal; **∼ story**
n cuento m, relato m breve; **∼tempered**
/'ʃɔːrt'tempərd ‖ ˌʃɔːt'tempəd/ adj de mal genio;
∼term /'ʃɔːrt'tɜːrm ‖ ˌʃɔːt'tɜːm/ adj a corto
plazo; **∼wave** /'ʃɔːrt'weɪv ‖ ˌʃɔːt'weɪv/ n onda f
corta

shot¹ /ʃɑːt ‖ ʃɒt/ past & past p of SHOOT²

shot² n **1** **(a)** (from gun, rifle) disparo m, tiro m;
(from cannon) cañonazo m; **she fired three ∼s**
disparó tres veces; **she was off like a ∼** salió
disparada **(b)** (marksman): **a good/poor ∼** un
buen/mal tirador
2 (colloq) (attempt, try): **it costs $50 a ∼** son 50
dólares por vez; **I'd like another ∼ at it** me
gustaría volver a intentarlo
3 (Phot) foto f; (Cin) toma f
4 (pellets): (lead) ∼ perdigones mpl

5 (used in shotput) bala *f*, peso *m* (Esp)
6 (in soccer) disparo *m*, tiro *m*; (in basketball) tiro *m*, tirada *f*; (in golf, tennis) tiro *m*
7 (injection) inyección *f*

shot: ~**gun** *n* escopeta *f*; ~**put** *n* (event) lanzamiento *m* de bala *or* (Esp) de peso

should¹ /ʃʊd/ *past of* SHALL

should² *v mod* **1** (expressing desirability) debería (*or* deberías *etc*), debiera (*or* debieras *etc*); **you ~ have thought of that before** deberías *or* debieras haber pensado en eso antes
2 (indicating probability, logical expectation) debería (*or* deberías *etc*) (de), debiera (*or* debieras *etc*) (de); **it ~ add up to 100** debería (de) *or* debiera (de) dar 100
3 (*with first person only*) **(a)** (conditional use) (BrE frml): **I ~ like to see her** me gustaría verla **(b)** (venturing a guess) (BrE): **I ~ think she must be over 80** yo diría que debe tener más de 80 **(c)** (expressing indignation): **I ~ think so too!** ¡(no) faltaría más!
4 (subjunctive use) (*with all persons*): **it's natural that he ~ want to go with her** es natural que quiera ir con ella; **if you ~ happen to pass a bookshop …** si pasaras por una librería …

shoulder¹ /'ʃəʊldər ‖'ʃəʊldə(r)/ *n* **1** (Anat, Clothing) hombro *m* **2** (of road) arcén *m*, berma *f* (Andes), acotamiento *m* (Méx), banquina *f* (RPl), hombrillo *m* (Ven)

shoulder² *vt* ⟨*knapsack*⟩ ponerse* *or* echarse al hombro; ⟨*blame/responsibility*⟩ cargar* con

shoulder: ~ **bag** *n* bolso *m or* (CS) cartera *f or* (Méx) bolsa *f* (*con correa larga para colgar del hombro*); ~ **blade** *n* omóplato *m*; ~**-length** /'ʃəʊldərleŋθ ‖ˌʃəʊldəˈleŋθ/ *adj*: ~**-length hair** pelo *m* hasta los hombros; ~ **strap** *n* (of garment) tirante *m or* (CS) bretel *m*; (of bag) correa *f*

shouldn't /'ʃʊdn̩t/ = **should not**

shout¹ /ʃaʊt/ *n* grito *m*

shout² *vi* gritar; **to ~ AT sb** gritarle A algn
■ ~ *vt* gritar
■ **shout out 1** [*v + o + adv, v + adv + o*] ⟨*answer*⟩ gritar **2** [*v + adv*] dar* un grito

shouting /'ʃaʊtɪŋ/ *n* griterío *m*

shove¹ /ʃʌv/ *vt* **(a)** (push roughly) empujar; **they ~d her out of the way** la quitaron de en medio a empellones *or* a empujones **(b)** (put) (colloq) poner*, meter
■ ~ *vi* empujar

shove² *n* empujón *m*, empellón *m*

shovel¹ /'ʃʌvəl/ *n* pala *f*

shovel² *vt*, (BrE) **-ll-** ⟨*coal*⟩ palear; ⟨*snow*⟩ espalar

show¹ /ʃəʊ/ (*past* **showed**; *past p* **shown** *or* **showed**) *vt* **1** **(a)** ⟨*photograph/passport*⟩ mostrar*, enseñar; **to ~ sb sth, to ~ sth TO sb** mostrarle* algo A algn **(b)** ⟨*feelings*⟩ demostrar*; ⟨*interest/enthusiasm*⟩ demostrar*, mostrar*; ⟨*courage*⟩ demostrar* (tener); **could you ~ me the way?** ¿me podría indicar el camino? **(c)** (allow to be seen): **this carpet ~s every mark** en esta alfombra se notan todas las marcas; **he's started to ~ his age** se le han empezado a notar los años
2 (record, register) ⟨*barometer/dial/indicator*⟩ marcar*, señalar, indicar*; ⟨*profit/loss*⟩ arrojar

3 **(a)** (demonstrate) ⟨*truth/importance*⟩ demostrar*; **it just goes to ~ how wrong you can be** eso te demuestra lo equivocado que puedes estar **(b)** (teach) enseñar; **I ~ed her how to do it** le enseñé cómo se hacía
4 (by accompanying) (+ *adv compl*): **he ~ed us to our seats** nos llevó hasta nuestros asientos; **to ~ sb in** hacer* pasar a algn; **to ~ sb out** acompañar a algn a la puerta
5 **(a)** (screen) ⟨*movie*⟩ dar*, pasar, poner* (Esp); ⟨*program*⟩ dar*, poner* (Esp); ⟨*slides*⟩ pasar **(b)** (exhibit) ⟨*paintings/sculpture*⟩ exponer*; ⟨*horse/dog*⟩ presentar
■ ~ *vi* **1** (be visible) «*dirt/stain*» verse*; «*emotion/scar*» notarse; **your petticoat is ~ing** se te ve la enagua
2 (be screened) (Cin): **it's ~ing at the Trocadero** la están dando el Trocadero, la ponen en el Trocadero (Esp)
■ *v refl* **to ~ oneself (a)** (become visible) «*person*» asomarse **(b)** (prove to be) demostrar* ser; (turn out to be) resultar ser
■ **show off 1** [*v + adv*] lucirse*; **stop ~ing off** déjate de hacer tonterías
2 [*v + o + adv, v + adv + o*] **(a)** (display for admiration) ⟨*car/girlfriend*⟩ lucir*, presumir de (Esp); ⟨*wealth/knowledge*⟩ presumir de **(b)** (display to advantage) ⟨*beauty/complexion*⟩ hacer* resaltar
■ **show up 1** [*v + o + adv, v + adv + o*] **(a)** (reveal) ⟨*mistake/deception*⟩ poner* de manifiesto (frml) **(b)** (embarrass) ⟨*parents/friends*⟩ hacer* quedar mal
2 [*v + adv*] **(a)** (be visible) «*imperfection*» notarse **(b)** (arrive) (colloq) aparecer* (fam)

show² *n* **1** (exhibition) (Art) exposición *f*; **to be on ~** estar* expuesto; **to put sth on ~** exponer* algo
2 **(a)** (stage production) espectáculo *m*; **to steal the ~** robarse el espectáculo **(b)** (on television, radio) programa *m*
3 (*no pl*) **(a)** (display) muestra *f*, demostración *f*; **a ~ of force** un despliegue de fuerza **(b)** (outward appearance): **I made a ~ of enthusiasm** fingí estar entusiasmado; **their plush office is simply for ~** su elegante oficina es solo para darse tono
4 (colloq) (*no pl*) (activity, organization) asunto *m*; **to run the ~** llevar la voz cantante (fam)

show: ~ **business** (colloq) *n* mundo *m* del espectáculo; ~**case** *n* **(a)** (cabinet) vitrina *f* **(b)** (for products, ideologies) escaparate *m*; ~**down** *n* enfrentamiento *m*

shower¹ /'ʃaʊər ‖'ʃaʊə(r)/ *n* **1** (in bathroom) ducha *f*, regadera *f* (Méx); **to take** *o* (BrE) **have a ~** ducharse; (*before n*) ~ **cap** gorro *m* de ducha **2** (Meteo) chaparrón *m*, chubasco *m* **3** (party) (AmE) *fiesta en la que los invitados obsequian a la homenajeada con motivo de su próxima boda, el nacimiento de su niño etc*

shower² *vt* (spray) regar*; **to ~ sb WITH sth** tirarle algo A algn **(b)** (bestow lavishly) **to ~ sb WITH sth:** **he ~ed her with gifts** la llenó de regalos; **the country ~ed him with honors** el país lo colmó de honores
■ ~ *vi* **(a)** (wash) ducharse **(b)** (be sprayed) «*water/ leaves/stones*» caer*; «*letters/congratulations/ protests*» llover*

show jumping /ˌdʒʌmpɪŋ/ *n* concursos *mpl* hípicos

shown /ʃəʊn/ *past p of* SHOW¹

show: ~-off n (colloq) fanfarrón, -rrona m,f, fantasma mf (Esp fam); ~room n (often pl) salón m de exposición (y ventas)

showy /'ʃəʊi/ adj **showier, showiest (a)** (gaudy) llamativo **(b)** (attractive) vistoso

shrank /ʃræŋk/ past of SHRINK

shrapnel /'ʃræpnl/ n metralla f

shred¹ /ʃred/ n (of paper, fabric) tira f, trozo m; **not a (single)** ~ **of evidence** ni una (sola) prueba; **not a** ~ **of truth** ni pizca de verdad; **to be in** ~s «clothes/fabric» estar* hecho jirones or tiras; «argument/reputation» estar* destrozado

shred² vt **-dd-** cortar en tiras; «documents» destruir*, triturar

shredder /'ʃredər ‖ 'ʃredə(r)/ n (for paper) trituradora f; (for vegetables) cortadora f

shrew /ʃruː/ n (Zool) musaraña f

shrewd /ʃruːd/ adj **-er, -est** «person» astuto; «move/investment/assessment» hábil

shriek¹ /ʃriːk/ n (of delight, terror) grito m, chillido m; (of pain) grito m, alarido m; **we could hear** ~s **of laughter** oíamos risotadas

shriek² vi/t gritar, chillar

shrift /ʃrɪft/ n: **to give sth short** ~ «idea/ suggestion» desestimar algo de plano; **to give sb short** ~ echar a algn con cajas destempladas

shrill /ʃrɪl/ adj **-er, -est** «whistle/laugh» agudo, estridente; «voice» agudo, chillón

shrimp /ʃrɪmp/ n (pl ~ or BrE also) ~s) (large) (AmE) langostino m; (medium) camarón m (AmL), gamba f (esp Esp); (small) (BrE) camarón m, quisquilla f (Esp)

shrine /ʃraɪn/ n (holy place) santuario m; (in out-of-the-way place) ermita f

shrink /ʃrɪŋk/ (past **shrank** or **shrunk**; past p **shrunk** or **shrunken**) vi **1** (diminish in size) «clothes/fabric» encoger(se)*; «meat» achicarse*; «wood» contraerse*; «area/amount» reducirse* **2** (recoil) retroceder; **to** ~ **back** o **away from sth/sb** echarse atrás or retroceder ante algo/algn

■ ~ vt «clothes/fabric» encoger*

shrinkage /'ʃrɪŋkɪdʒ/ n (of clothes, fabric) encogimiento m; (of wood, metal) contracción f

shrivel /'ʃrɪvəl/, (BrE) **-ll-** ~ (**up**) vi «leaf/ plant» marchitarse, secarse*; «fruit/vegetables» resecarse* y arrugarse*; «skin» ajarse

■ vt «leaf/plant» secar*, marchitar

shroud¹ /ʃraʊd/ n mortaja f

shroud² vt envolver*; **a case** ~ed **in mystery** (journ) un caso envuelto en un velo de misterio

Shrove Tuesday /ʃrəʊv/ n martes m de Carnaval

shrub /ʃrʌb/ n arbusto m, mata f

shrubbery /'ʃrʌbəri/ n arbustos mpl, matas fpl

shrug¹ /ʃrʌg/ n: **with a** ~ (of her shoulders) encogiéndose de hombros

shrug² **-gg-** vi encogerse* de hombros

■ ~ vt: **to** ~ **one's shoulders** encogerse* de hombros

■ **shrug off** [v + o + adv, v + adv + o] «misfortune/disappointment» superar; «criticism» hacer* caso omiso de

shrunk /ʃrʌŋk/ past & past p of SHRINK

shrunken¹ /'ʃrʌŋkən/ past p of SHRINK

shrunken² adj «body» consumido

shudder¹ /'ʃʌdər ‖ 'ʃʌdə(r)/ vi **(a)** «person» estremecerse* **(b)** «bus/train/plane» dar* sacudidas; **to** ~ **to a halt** pararse abruptamente

shudder² n **(a)** (of person) estremecimiento m **(b)** (of vehicle, engine) sacudida f

shuffle /'ʃʌfl/ vt **1** **to** ~ **one's feet** arrastrar los pies **2** «cards/papers» barajar

■ ~ vi caminar or andar* arrastrando los pies

shun /ʃʌn/ vt **-nn-** «person/society» rechazar*, rehuir*; «publicity/limelight» evitar, rehuir*

shunt /ʃʌnt/ vt (Rail) cambiar de vía

shush¹ /ʃʊʃ/ vt acallar

shush² interj: ~! ¡chitón!, ¡silencio!

shut¹ /ʃʌt/ (pres p **shutting**; past & past p **shut**) vt **1** **(a)** «window/book/eyes» cerrar* **(b)** «store/business» cerrar* **2** (confine) **to** ~ **sb IN sth** encerrar* a algn EN algo; **he** ~ **himself in his room** se encerró en su cuarto

■ ~ vi **1** «door/window» cerrar(se)* **2** (esp BrE) (cease business — for day) cerrar*; (— permanently) cerrar* (sus puertas)

■ **shut down** **1** [v + adv] «factory/business» cerrar*; «machinery» apagarse* **2** [v + o + adv, v + adv + o] «factory/business» cerrar*; «machinery» apagar*

■ **shut in** [v + o + adv, v + adv + o] encerrar*

■ **shut off** [v + o + adv, v + adv + o] **(a)** «water/ electricity» cortar; «engine» apagar* **(b)** (isolate) (often pass) «place/person» aislar*

■ **shut out** [v + o + adv, v + adv + o] **(a)** «person/ animal» dejar (a)fuera; «light/heat» no dejar entrar; **to** ~ **oneself out** encerrarse* (a)fuera (b) (AmE Sport) «team/pitcher» ganarle a (sin conceder ni un gol o carrera etc)

■ **shut up** **1** [v + o + adv, v + adv + o] **(a)** (close) «house/office» cerrar* **(b)** (confine) «dog» encerrar* **2** [v + o + adv] (silence) (colloq) hacer* callar **3** [v + adv] **(a)** (close business) cerrar* **(b)** (stop talking) (colloq) callarse

shut² adj (pred) cerrado

shutdown /'ʃʌtdaʊn/ n (of hospital, college) cierre m; (of power) corte m; (of services) paralización f

shutter /'ʃʌtər ‖ 'ʃʌtə(r)/ n **1** (on window) postigo m **2** (Phot) obturador m

shuttle¹ /'ʃʌtl/ n **1** (in loom, sewing machine) lanzadera f **2** **(a)** (Aviat) puente m aéreo; (bus, train service) servicio m (regular) de enlace **(b)** (space ~) transbordador m or lanzadera f espacial

shuttle² vi: **to** ~ **back and forth** ir* y venir*

■ ~ vt «passengers» transportar, llevar

---

shuttlecock /'ʃʌt‖kɑːk ‖'ʃʌt‖kɒk/ n volante m, plumilla f, rehilete m, gallito m (Col, Méx)

shy¹ /ʃaɪ/ adj **shyer, shyest** ⟨person⟩ tímido; ⟨animal⟩ huraño

shy² vi **shies, shying, shied** «horse» respingar*

shyly /'ʃaɪli/ adv tímidamente, con timidez

shyness /'ʃaɪnəs ‖'ʃaɪnɪs/ n timidez f

Siamese /'saɪə'miːz/ n (pl ~) ~ **(cat)** gato m siamés

Siamese twins pl n (hermanos) siameses mpl, (hermanas) siamesas fpl

sibling /'sɪblɪŋ/ n (frml) (brother) hermano m; (sister) hermana f

sick /sɪk/ adj **-er, -est** [1] (ill) enfermo; **to be off** ~ estar* ausente por enfermedad [2] (nauseated) (pred): **to feel** ~ (dizzy, unwell) estar* mareado; (about to vomit) tener* ganas de vomitar; **to be** ~ vomitar; **he makes me** ~ me da asco [3] **(a)** (disturbed, sickened) (pred): **to be** ~ **with fear/worry** estar* muerto de miedo/preocupación **(b)** (weary, fed up) **to be** ~ **OF sth/-ING** estar* harto DE algo/+ INF; **I'm** ~ **and tired of hearing that** estoy absolutamente harto de oír eso [4] (gruesome) ⟨person/mind⟩ morboso; ⟨humor/joke⟩ de muy mal gusto

sick: ~ **bay** n enfermería f; ~**bed** n (liter) lecho m de enfermo (liter)

sicken /'sɪkən/ vt dar* rabia, enfermar (AmL); (stronger) asquear
■ ~ vi (BrE) **to be** ~**ing FOR sth** estar* incubando algo

sickening /'sɪkənɪŋ/ adj **(a)** (appalling): **it's** ~, **isn't it?** da mucha rabia ¿no?; (stronger) da asco ¿no? **(b)** ⟨smell/sight⟩ nauseabundo

sickle /'sɪkəl/ n hoz f

sick leave n permiso m or (Esp) baja f or (RPl) licencia f por enfermedad

sickly¹ /'sɪkli/ adj **-lier, -liest (a)** ⟨complexion/child⟩ enfermizo **(b)** ⟨taste/smell⟩ empalagoso **(c)** ⟨color⟩ horrible, asqueroso

sickly² adv: ~ **sweet** demasiado empalagoso

sickness /'sɪknəs ‖'sɪknɪs/ n **(a)** (disease) (liter) enfermedad f **(b)** (nausea) náuseas fpl; (vomiting) vómitos mpl

sick pay n salario que se percibe mientras se está con permiso por enfermedad

side¹ /saɪd/ n [1] (surface — of cube, record, coin, piece of paper) lado m, cara f; (— of building, cupboard) lado m, costado m; (— of mountain, hill) ladera f, falda f
[2] (boundary, edge): **they were playing by the** ~ **of the pool** estaban jugando junto a or al lado de la piscina
[3] **(a)** (of person) costado m; (of animal) ijada f, ijar m; **Roy stood at her** ~ Roy estaba a su lado; **they sat** ~ **by** ~ estaban sentados uno junto al otro **(b)** (Culin) **a** ~ **of beef** media res f
[4] (contrasted area, part, half) lado m; **from** ~ **to** ~ de un lado al otro; **on the** ~: **he repairs cars on the** ~ arregla coches como trabajo extra
[5] **(a)** (faction): **to take** ~**s** tomar partido; **whose** ~ **are you on?** ¿tú de parte de quién estás? **(b)** (Sport) equipo m
[6] (area, aspect) lado m, aspecto m; **you must**

listen to both ~**s of the story** hay que oír las dos versiones; **it's a little on the short** ~ es un poco corto
■ **side with** [v + prep + o] ponerse* de parte de

side² adj (before n, no comp) **(a)** ⟨door/entrance/ wall⟩ lateral; **a** ~ **street** una calle lateral, una lateral **(b)** (incidental, secondary) ⟨issue⟩ secundario **(c)** (Culin): ~ **dish** acompañamiento m; **a** ~ **salad** una ensalada (como acompañamiento)

side: ~**board** n [1] (piece of furniture) aparador m, seibó m (Ven); [2] ~**boards** pl (BrE) ▶ ~BURNS; ~**burns** pl n patillas fpl; ~**car** n sidecar m; ~ **effect** n (of drug, treatment) efecto m secundario; (incidental result) consecuencia f indirecta; ~**kick** n (colloq) adlátere mf; ~**line** n [1] (Sport) línea f de banda; [2] (subsidiary activity) actividad f suplementaria; ~**long** adj (before n) ⟨glance⟩ de reojo, de soslayo; ~**saddle** adv a mujeriegas (con las dos piernas hacia el mismo lado); ~**show** n (at fair) puesto m; ~**step** vt -**pp**- ⟨blow/opponent⟩ esquivar; ⟨problem/ question⟩ eludir; ~**track** vt **(a)** (from subject) hacer* desviar del tema **(b)** (from purpose): **sorry, I got** ~**tracked** perdón, me entretuve haciendo otra cosa; ~**walk** n (AmE) acera f, banqueta f (Méx), andén m (AmC, Col), vereda f (CS, Per)

sideways¹ /'saɪdweɪz/ adv **(a)** ⟨glance⟩ de reojo, de soslayo; ⟨walk⟩ de lado, de costado **(b)** (with side part forward) de lado

sideways² adj ⟨look⟩ de reojo, de soslayo; ⟨movement⟩ lateral, de lado

siding /'saɪdɪŋ/ n (Rail) apartadero m

sidle /'saɪdl/ vi **to** ~ **up to sb** acercársele* sigilosamente a algn

siege /siːdʒ/ n sitio m; **the city was under** ~ la ciudad estaba sitiada

Sierra Leone /si'erəli'əʊn/ n Sierra Leona f

siesta /si'estə/ n siesta f; **to have a** ~ dormir* or echarse una siesta

sieve¹ /sɪv/ n (Culin) (for flour etc) tamiz m, cedazo m, cernidor m

sieve² vt ⟨flour⟩ (BrE) tamizar*, cernir*, cerner*

sift /sɪft/ vt **(a)** ⟨sugar/flour⟩ tamizar*, cernir*, cerner*; (sprinkle) espolvorear **(b)** ⟨facts/evidence⟩ pasar por el tamiz or la criba

sigh¹ /saɪ/ vi suspirar*; **he** ~**ed with relief/ contentment** suspiró aliviado/satisfecho

sigh² n suspiro m; **she breathed** o **heaved a** ~ **of relief** dio un suspiro de alivio

sight¹ /saɪt/ n [1] (eye ~) vista f
[2] (range of vision): **to come into** ~ aparecer*; **to lose** ~ **of sth/sb** perder* algo/a algn de vista; **the finishing line was now in** ~ ya se veía la meta; **she watched until they were out of** ~ los siguió con la mirada hasta que los perdió de vista
[3] (act of seeing, view) (no pl): **at first** ~ a primera vista; **it was love at first** ~ fue amor a primera vista; **to catch** ~ **of sth/sb** ver* algo/a algn; (in distance) avistar algo/a algn; **to know sb by** ~ conocer* a algn de vista; **to play at** o **by** ~ (Mus) tocar* a primera vista; **I can't stand the** ~ **of him** (colloq) no lo puedo ver (fam)
[4] **(a)** (thing seen): **the sparrow is a familiar** ~ **in our gardens** el gorrión se ve con frecuencia en nuestros jardines; **it's not a pretty** ~ (colloq) no es ⋯➤

muy agradable de ver **(b) sights** pl (famous places): **to see the ∼s** visitar los lugares de interés

⑤ **(a)** (of gun) mira f **(b) sights** pl (ambition): **to have sth in one's ∼s** tener* la mira puesta en algo

sight² vt ‹land/ship› divisar; ‹person/animal› ver*

sighted /'saɪtəd ‖'saɪtɪd/ adj vidente; **he's partially ∼** tiene visión parcial

sight: ∼read /'saɪtˌriːd/ (past & past p **-read** /-red/) vt/i repentizar*; **∼seeing** /'saɪtˌsiːɪŋ/ n: **to go ∼seeing** ir* a visitar los lugares de interés; **∼seer** /'saɪtˌsiːər/ n turista mf, visitante mf

sign¹ /saɪn/ n ① **(a)** (indication) señal f, indicio m; **it's a ∼ of the times** es un indicio de los tiempos que corren **(b)** (omen) presagio m ② (gesture) seña f, señal f ③ **(a)** (notice, board) letrero m, cartel m; (in demonstration) pancarta f **(b)** (road ∼) señal f (vial) ④ **(a)** (symbol) símbolo m; (Math) signo m **(b)** (Astrol) signo m

sign² vt **(a)** (write signature on) firmar **(b)** (hire) ‹actor› contratar; ‹player› fichar
■ **∼** vi firmar
■ **sign for** [v + prep + o] ‹goods/parcel› firmar el recibo de
■ **sign on** [v + adv] **(a)** (enlist) «recruit» alistarse, enlistarse (AmC, Col, Ven) **(b)** (in UK) (Soc Adm) anotarse para recibir el seguro de desempleo, apuntarse al paro (Esp)
■ **sign up** ① [v + adv] (for a course) inscribirse*, matricularse; (to join the army) alistarse, enlistarse (AmC, Col, Ven) ② [v + o + adv, v + adv + o] ‹soldiers› reclutar; ‹player› fichar

signal¹ /'sɪgnḷ/ n señal f

signal², (BrE) **-ll-** vt señalar
■ **∼** vi **(a)** (gesture) **to ∼ (to sb)** hacer(le)* señas/ una seña (a algn) **(b)** (Auto) señalizar*, poner* el intermitente or (Col, Méx) la direccional or (CS) el señalizador

signature /'sɪgnətʃʊr ‖'sɪgnətʃə(r)/ n ① (written name) firma f ② (Mus): **time ∼** compás m, tiempo m

signature tune n (BrE) sintonía f (del programa), cortina f musical (CS)

significance /sɪg'nɪfɪkəns/ n importancia f

significant /sɪg'nɪfɪkənt/ adj **(a)** (important) importante **(b)** (meaningful) ‹look/smile› expresivo; ‹fact/remark› significativo

significantly /sɪg'nɪfɪkəntli/ adv considerablemente

signify /'sɪgnəfaɪ ‖'sɪgnɪfaɪ/ vt **-fies, -fying, -fied** significar*

signing /'saɪnɪŋ/ n **(a)** (act of signing) firma f **(b)** (Sport) fichaje m

sign language n lenguaje m gestual

signpost¹ /'saɪnpəʊst/ n señal f, poste m indicador

signpost² vt (BrE Auto) ‹way/route› señalizar*

Sikh¹ /siːk/ n sij mf

Sikh² adj sij adj inv

silage /'saɪlɪdʒ/ n ensilaje m, ensilado m (forraje fermentado en silos)

silence¹ /'saɪləns/ n silencio m; **in ∼** en silencio

silence² vt ‹cries/voice› acallar; ‹child/animal› hacer* callar; ‹opposition/criticism› silenciar

silencer /'saɪlənsər ‖'saɪlənsə(r)/ n **(a)** (on gun) silenciador m **(b)** (on car) (BrE) silenciador m, mofle m (AmC, Méx)

silent /'saɪlənt/ adj **(a)** (noiseless, still) ‹night/ forest› silencioso **(b)** (not speaking) ‹gesture/ protest› mudo; **the 'h' is ∼** la hache es muda; **a ∼ movie** una película muda

silently /'saɪləntli/ adv **(a)** (noiselessly) ‹creep/ glide/enter› silenciosamente **(b)** (without speaking) ‹pray/stand/listen› en silencio, calladamente

silent partner n socio, -cia m,f capitalista

silhouette /ˌsɪlu'et/ n silueta f

silicon /'sɪləkən ‖'sɪlɪkən/ n silicio m; (before n) **∼ chip** (Comput) pastilla f de silicio

silk /sɪlk/ n seda f

silky /'sɪlki/ **-kier, -kiest** adj ‹fabric/fur› sedoso

sill /sɪl/ n (window∼) alféizar m, antepecho m

silly /'sɪli/ adj **-lier, -liest** ‹person/idea/ mistake› tonto; ‹name/hat› ridículo

silo /'saɪləʊ/ n (pl **-los**) silo m

silt /sɪlt/ n cieno m, limo m

silver¹ /'sɪlvər ‖'sɪlvə(r)/ n ① (metal) plata f ② **(a)** (household items) platería f, plata f **(b)** (coins) monedas fpl (de plata, aluminio etc)

silver² adj **(a)** (made of silver) de plata **(b)** (in color) plateado **(c)** (representing 25 years) (before n): **∼ jubilee** el vigésimo quinto aniversario; **∼ wedding** (BrE) bodas fpl de plata

silver: ∼ foil n (BrE Culin) papel m de aluminio or de plata; **∼-plate** /'sɪlvər'pleɪt ‖ˌsɪlvə'pleɪt/ vt dar*(le) un baño de plata a, platear; **∼smith** n platero, -ra m,f, orfebre mf; **∼ware** /'sɪlvərwer ‖'sɪlvəweə(r)/ n platería f, plata f

similar /'sɪmələr ‖'sɪmɪlə(r)/ adj similar, parecido, semejante; **to be ∼ to sth** parecerse* A algo

similarity /ˌsɪmə'lærəti ‖ˌsɪmɪ'lærəti/ n (pl **-ties**) **(a)** (likeness — between things) similitud f, parecido m, semejanza f; (— between persons) parecido m **(b)** (common feature) semejanza f, similitud f

similarly /'sɪmələrli ‖'sɪmɪləli/ adv **(a)** (in a similar way) de modo parecido or similar **(b)** (equally) igualmente **(c)** (as linker) asimismo

simile /'sɪməli ‖'sɪmɪli/ n símil m

simmer /'sɪmər ‖'sɪmə(r)/ vt/i hervir* a fuego lento

simple /'sɪmpəl/ adj **simpler** /-plər/, **simplest** /-pləst/ ① (uncomplicated) ‹task/ problem› sencillo, simple ② (plain, unpretentious) ‹dress/food› sencillo, simple ③ **(a)** (unsophisticated, humble) simple **(b)** (backward) simple

simplicity /sɪm'plɪsəti/ n simplicidad f, sencillez f

simplify /'sɪmpləfaɪ ‖'sɪmplɪfaɪ/ vt **-fies, -fying, -fied** simplificar*

simplistic /sɪm'plɪstɪk/ adj simplista

simply /'sɪmpli/ adv ① (only, merely) simplemente, sencillamente ② (plainly) con sencillez, sencillamente **(b)** (in simple language) simplemente, sencillamente

simulate /'sɪmjəleɪt ‖'sɪmjʊleɪt/ vt simular

simultaneous /'saɪməl'teɪniəs
‖ˌsɪməl'teɪniəs/ *adj* simultáneo

simultaneously /'saɪməl'teɪniəsli
‖ˌsɪməl'teɪniəsli/ *adv* simultáneamente, a la vez

sin¹ /sɪn/ *n* pecado *m*

sin² *vi* **-nn-** pecar*

since¹ /sɪns/ *conj* **1** (in time) desde que; ~
coming to London desde que vino (*or* vine *etc*) a
Londres **2** (introducing a reason) ya que; ~ you
can't go, can I have your ticket? ya que no puedes
ir ¿me das tu entrada?

since² *prep* desde; they've worked there ~ 1970
han trabajado allí desde 1970; how long is it ~
your operation? ¿cuánto (tiempo) hace de tu
operación?

since³ *adv* desde entonces; she has lived here
ever ~ desde entonces que vive aquí

sincere /sɪn'sɪr ‖sɪn'sɪə(r)/, **sincerer,
sincerest** *adj* sincero

sincerely /sɪn'sɪrli ‖sɪn'sɪəli/ *adv*
sinceramente; ~ (yours) *o* (BrE) yours ~ (in letters)
(saluda) a usted atentamente

sincerity /sɪn'serəti/ *n* sinceridad *f*

sinew /'sɪnjuː/ *n* tendón *m*; (in meat) nervio *m*

sinful /'sɪnfəl/ *adj* ⟨person⟩ pecador; ⟨act⟩
pecaminoso

sing /sɪŋ/ (*past* sang; *past p* sung) *vt/i* cantar
■ **sing along** [*v* + *adv*] to ~ along (WITH sb)
cantar (CON algn)

Singapore /'sɪŋgə'pɔːr ‖ˌsɪŋə'pɔː(r)/ *n*
Singapur *m*

singe /sɪndʒ/ *vt* **singes, singeing, singed**
chamuscar*

singer /'sɪŋər ‖'sɪŋə(r)/ *n* cantante *mf*

singing /'sɪŋɪŋ/ *n* canto *m*; (before n) a good ~
voice una buena voz (para el canto)

single¹ /'sɪŋgəl/ *adj* **1** (just one) (before n) solo;
the largest ~ shareholder el mayor accionista
individual; every ~ day todos los días sin
excepción; (with neg) not a ~ house was left
standing no quedó ni una sola casa en pie
2 (before n) (a) (for one person) ⟨room⟩ individual;
⟨bed/sheet⟩ individual, de una plaza (AmL) (b) (not
double): in ~ file en fila india (c) (BrE Transp)
⟨fare/ticket⟩ de ida, sencillo
3 (unmarried) soltero
■ **single out** [*v* + *o* + *adv*, *v* + *adv* + *o*]: to ~ sb
out (select) escoger* a algn en particular; (identify)
señalar a algn en particular; she was ~d out for
criticism/praise se la criticó/elogió a ella en
particular

single² *n* **1** (Mus) single *m*, (disco *m*) sencillo
m **2** (ticket) (BrE) boleto *m* or (Esp) billete *m* de
ida

single: ~-breasted /'sɪŋgəl'brestəd
‖ˌsɪŋgəl'brestɪd/ *adj* de una fila de botones,
derecho (AmL); ~ cream *n* (BrE) crema *f*
líquida, nata *f* líquida (Esp); ~-handed
/'sɪŋgəl'hændəd ‖ˌsɪŋgəl'hændɪd/ *adv* sin (la)
ayuda de nadie; ~ market *n* mercado *m* único;
~-minded /'sɪŋgəl'maɪndəd ‖ˌsɪŋgəl'maɪndɪd/
adj decidido, resuelto; ~ parent *n*: he's/she's a
~ parent es un padre/una madre que cría a su(s)
hijo(s) sin pareja

singles /'sɪŋgəlz/ *pl n* (Sport) individuales *mpl*,
singles *mpl* (AmL)

singsong /'sɪŋsɔːŋ ‖'sɪŋsɒŋ/ *adj* ⟨voice/accent⟩
cantarín

singular¹ /'sɪŋgjələr ‖'sɪŋgjolə(r)/ *adj* singular

singular² *n* singular *m*; in the ~ en singular

sinister /'sɪnɪstər ‖'sɪnɪstə(r)/ *adj* siniestro

sink¹ /sɪŋk/ (*past* sank; *past p* sunk) *vi*
1 (a) ⟨ship/stone⟩ hundirse (b) (subside) to ~
(INTO sth) ⟨building/foundations⟩ hundirse (EN
algo); he sank back into the chair se arrellanó en
el sillón
2 (fall, drop) ⟨water/level⟩ descender*, bajar;
⟨price/value⟩ caer* a pique; ⟨attendance/
output⟩ decaer*; my heart sank se me cayó el
alma a los pies
3 (degenerate) degradarse; I'd never ~ so low
nunca caería tan bajo
■ ~ *vt* **1** ⟨ship⟩ hundir
2 (bury, hide) ⟨pipe/cable⟩ enterrar*
3 (a) (drive in): the dog sank its teeth into my
thigh el perro me clavó los dientes en el muslo
(b) (excavate) ⟨shaft⟩ abrir*; ⟨well⟩ perforar
■ **sink in** [*v* + *adv*] (colloq): it finally sank in that
... finalmente nos dimos cuenta de que ...

sink² *n* (a) (in kitchen) fregadero *m*, lavaplatos *m*
(Andes) (b) (washbasin) (AmE) lavabo *m*, lavamanos
m, lavatorio *m* (CS), pileta *f* (RPl)

sinner /'sɪnər ‖'sɪnə(r)/ *n* pecador, -dora *m,f*

sinus /'saɪnəs/ *n* (*pl* **-nuses**) seno *m*

sip¹ /sɪp/ *vt* **-pp-** sorber, beber *or* tomar a
sorbos

sip² *n* sorbo *m*

siphon /'saɪfən/ *n* sifón *m*
■ **siphon off** [*v* + *o* + *adv*, *v* + *adv* + *o*] ⟨liquid/
fuel⟩ sacar* con sifón; ⟨money⟩ desviar*

sir /sɜːr ‖sɜː(r)/ *n* **1** (a) (as form of address — to
male customer) señor, caballero; (— to male teacher)
(BrE) profesor, señor (b) (Corresp): Dear Sir De mi
mayor consideración:, Muy señor mío: **2** **Sir** (as
title) sir *m*

siren /'saɪrən/ *n* sirena *f*

sirloin /'sɜːrlɔɪn ‖'sɜːlɔɪn/ *n preciado corte de
carne vacuna del cuarto trasero*

sirup *n* (AmE) ▶ SYRUP

sister /'sɪstər ‖'sɪstə(r)/ *n* **1** (sibling) hermana *f*;
(before n) ⟨company⟩ afiliado; ~ ship buque *m*
gemelo **2** (a) (nun) hermana *f*, monja *f* (b)
(nurse) (BrE) enfermera *f* jefe *or* jefa (a cargo de
una o más salas)

sisterhood /'sɪstərhʊd ‖'sɪstəhʊd/ *n* (a)
(association of women) asociación *f* de mujeres (b)
(Relig) congregación *f* (c) (sisterly relationship)
solidaridad *f* (entre mujeres)

sister-in-law /'sɪstərənlɔː ‖'sɪstərɪnlɔː/ *n* (*pl*
sisters-in-law) cuñada *f*

sisterly /'sɪstərli ‖'sɪstəli/ *adj* (propio) de
hermana

sit /sɪt/ (*pres p* **sitting**; *past & past p* **sat**) *vi*
1 (a) (sit down) sentarse* (b) (be seated) estar*
sentado
2 (be in session) ⟨committee/court⟩ reunirse* en
sesión, sesionar (esp AmL)
3 sitting *pres p* ⟨figure⟩ sentado
■ ~ *vt* **1** (cause to be seated) ⟨person⟩ sentar*;
⟨object⟩ poner*, colocar* (en posición vertical)
2 (BrE Educ): to ~ an exam hacer* *or* dar* *or*
(CS) rendir* *or* (Méx) tomar un examen,
examinarse   ⋯⋗

S

■ **sit around** [v + adv]: he ∼s around all day doing nothing se pasa el día sentado sin hacer nada

■ **sit back** [v + adv] (colloq) recostarse*

■ **sit down** [v + adv] sentarse*

■ **sit in** [v + adv] **to ∼ in on a class** asistir a una clase como oyente (or observador etc)

■ **sit out** [v + o + adv, v + adv + o] **(a)** (wait until end of) ⟨siege⟩ aguantar; **to ∼ it out** aguantarse **(b)** (not participate in) ⟨dance⟩ no bailar; ⟨game⟩ no tomar parte en

■ **sit up** [v + adv] **(a)** (in upright position) «person/patient» incorporarse; «dog» sentarse* sobre las patas traseras; **that should make them ∼ up and take notice** eso debería alertarlos **(b)** (with straight back) ponerse* derecho, enderezarse* **(c)** (not go to bed): **we sat up talking** nos quedamos (levantados) conversando

sitcom /'sɪtkɑːm ‖ 'sɪtkɒm/ n (colloq) ▸ SITUATION COMEDY

site /saɪt/ n **(a)** (location) emplazamiento m (fml); (piece of land) terreno m, solar m **(b)** (building ∼) obra f **(c)** (archeological ∼) yacimiento m (arqueológico) **(d)** (camp∼) camping m

sit-in /'sɪtɪn/ n (demonstration) sentada f, sitin m (Méx); (strike) encierro m, ocupación f or toma f (del lugar de trabajo)

sitting /'sɪtɪŋ/ n **(a)** (for meal etc) turno m; **I watched three movies in a single ∼** vi tres películas de una sentada (fam) **(b)** (of committee, parliament) sesión f

sitting: ∼ **duck** n (colloq) presa f fácil, blanco m seguro; ∼ **room** n (BrE) sala f de estar, living m (esp AmL), salón m (esp Esp)

situate /'sɪtʃueɪt ‖ 'sɪtjoeɪt/ vt (locate) (often pass) ⟨building/town⟩ situar*, ubicar* (esp AmL)

situation /ˌsɪtʃu'eɪʃən ‖ ˌsɪtjo'eɪʃən/ n **1** (circumstances, position) situación f **2** (job) (fml) empleo m; **➍ situations vacant** ofertas de empleo

situation comedy n comedia f (acerca de situaciones de la vida diaria)

sit-up /'sɪtʌp/ n (ejercicio m) abdominal m (levantando el torso del suelo)

six¹ /sɪks/ n seis m; **it's ∼ of one and half a dozen of the other** (colloq) (it makes no difference) da lo mismo; (both parties are to blame) los dos tienen parte de la culpa; see also FOUR¹

six² adj seis adj inv

sixteen /ˌsɪks'tiːn/ adj/n dieciséis adj inv/m; see also FOUR¹

sixteenth¹ /ˌsɪks'tiːnθ/ adj decimosexto

sixteenth² adv en decimosexto lugar

sixteenth³ n dieciseisavo m; (part) dieciseisava parte f

sixteenth note n (AmE) semicorchea f

sixth¹ /sɪksθ/ adj sexto

sixth² adv en sexto lugar

sixth³ n (Math) sexto m; (part) sexta parte f, sexto m

sixth: ∼ **form** n (in UK) los dos últimos años de la enseñanza secundaria; ∼ **sense** n sexto sentido m

sixtieth¹ /'sɪkstiəθ/ adj sexagésimo

sixtieth² adv en sexagésimo lugar

sixtieth³ n (Math) sesentavo m; (part) sesentava or sexagésima parte f

sixty /'sɪksti/ adj/n sesenta adj inv/m; see also FOUR¹

sizable /'saɪzəbəl/ adj ⟨fortune⟩ considerable; ⟨property⟩ de proporciones considerables

size /saɪz/ n **1** (dimensions) tamaño m; (of problem, task) magnitud f; **what ∼ is it?** ¿de qué tamaño es?; **to cut sb down to ∼** poner* a algn en su sitio, bajarle los humos a algn (fam) **2** (of clothes) talla f or (RPI) talle m; (of shoes, gloves) número m; **what ∼ do you take?** ¿qué talla or (RPI) talle tiene or usa?; **I take (a) ∼ 10 in shoes** calzo or (Esp tb) gasto el número 10

■ **size up** [v + o + adv, v + adv + o] (colloq) ⟨problem⟩ evaluar*; **she ∼d him up immediately** enseguida lo caló

sizeable adj ▸ SIZABLE

sizzle /'sɪzəl/ vi chisporrotear

skate¹ /skeɪt/ n **1** (ice ∼) patín m (para patinaje sobre hielo); (roller ∼) patín m (de ruedas) **2** (pl ∼ or ∼s) (Culin, Zool) raya f

skate² vi patinar

skate: ∼**board** n monopatín m or (CS, Méx, Ven) patineta f; ∼**boarding** n deporte m del monopatín or (CS, Méx, Ven) de la patineta

skater /'skeɪtər ‖ 'skeɪtə(r)/ n patinador, -dora m,f

skating /'skeɪtɪŋ/ n (ice ∼) patinaje m sobre hielo; (roller ∼) patinaje m sobre ruedas; (before n) ∼ **rink** pista f de patinaje

skeleton /'skelətn ‖ 'skelɪtn/ n **(a)** (Anat) esqueleto m **(b)** (of building, vehicle) armazón m or f

skeleton key n llave f maestra

skeptic, (BrE) **sceptic** /'skeptɪk/ n escéptico, -ca m,f

skeptical, (BrE) **sceptical** /'skeptɪkəl/ adj ⟨person/attitude⟩ escéptico

skepticism, (BrE) **scepticism** /'skeptɪsɪzəm/ n escepticismo m

sketch¹ /sketʃ/ n **1** (drawing) bosquejo m, esbozo m **2** (Theat, TV) sketch m, apunte m

sketch² vt hacer* un bosquejo de, bosquejar ■ ∼ vi hacer* bosquejos o bocetos

sketch: ∼**book** n cuaderno m de bocetos; ∼**pad** n bloc m de dibujo

sketchy /'sketʃi/ adj **-chier, -chiest** ⟨account/treatment⟩ muy superficial; ⟨knowledge⟩ muy básico

skewer /'skjuːər ‖ 'skjuːə(r)/ n pincho m, brocheta f

ski¹ /skiː/ n esquí m

ski² vi **skis, skiing, skied** esquiar*; **to go ∼ing** ir* a esquiar

skid¹ /skɪd/ n (Auto) patinazo m, patinada f (AmL)

skid² vi **-dd-** «*car/plane/wheels*» patinar; «*person*» resbalarse; «*object*» deslizarse*

skier /'skiːər ‖ 'skiːə(r)/ n esquiador, -dora m,f

skiing /'skiːɪŋ/ n esquí m

skilful adj (BrE) ▶ SKILLFUL

skilift /'skiːlɪft/ n telesquí m

skill /skɪl/ n **(a)** (ability) habilidad f; **technical** ~ destreza f **(b)** (technique): **typing is a very useful** ~ **to have** saber escribir a máquina es muy útil; **social** ~s don m de gente

skilled /skɪld/ adj ‹*negotiator*› hábil; ‹*pilot*› diestro; ‹*worker/labor*› calificado or (Esp) cualificado; ‹*work*› de especialista

skillful, (BrE) **skilful** /'skɪlfəl/ adj ‹*liar/play*› hábil; ‹*surgeon/mechanic*› diestro; (at sewing, craftwork) habilidoso

skim /skɪm/ **-mm-** vt ① (Culin) ‹*milk*› descremar, desnatar (Esp); ‹*soup*› espumar ② **(a)** ‹*water/treetops*› pasar casi rozando **(b)** (throw): **to** ~ **stones** hacer* cabrillas ③ (read quickly) leer* por encima
  ■ ~ vi ① (glide): **the speedboat** ~**med over the sea** la lancha apenas rozaba la superficie del mar ② (read quickly) leer* por encima

skim milk, (BrE) **skimmed milk** /skɪmd/ n leche f descremada or (Esp b) desnatada

skimp /skɪmp/ vi (colloq) **to** ~ **(on** sth**)** escatimar (algo)

skimpy /'skɪmpi/ adj **-pier, -piest** ‹*meal/ portion*› mezquino, pobre; ‹*funds*› escaso; ‹*nightdress/bikini*› brevísimo

skin¹ /skɪn/ n **(a)** (of person) piel f; (esp of face; in terms of quality, condition) cutis m, piel f; (in terms of color) tez f, piel f; **to have a thick/thin** ~ ser* insensible/muy sensible a las críticas **(b)** (of animal, bird, fish) piel f **(c)** (of tomatoes, plums, sausage) piel f; (of potatoes, bananas) piel f, cáscara f **(d)** (on milk, custard) nata f; (on paint) capa f dura

skin² vt **-nn-** ‹*animal*› despellejar, desollar*

skin: ~**deep** /'skɪn'diːp/ adj (pred) superficial; ~**dive** /'skɪndaɪv/ vi hacer* submarinismo, bucear; **to go** ~**diving** ir* a hacer submarinismo, ir* a bucear; ~**diver** n buzo m, submarinista mf; ~**diving** n submarinismo m, buceo m; ~**head** n cabeza mf rapada

skinny /'skɪni/ adj **-nier, -niest** flaco, flacucho (fam)

skintight /'skɪntaɪt/ adj muy ceñido, muy ajustado

skip¹ /skɪp/ n ① (jump) brinco m, saltito m ② (BrE) (container) contenedor m (*para escombros, basura etc*)

skip² **-pp-** vi **(a)** (move lightly and quickly) brincar, dar* saltitos **(b)** (with rope) (BrE) ▶ vt 2
  ■ ~ vt ① **(a)** (omit) ‹*page/chapter*› saltarse **(b)** (not attend) ‹*class/meeting*› faltar a ② (jump) (AmE): **to** ~ **rope** saltar a la cuerda or (Esp tb) a la comba

skipper /'skɪpər ‖ 'skɪpə(r)/ n (colloq) **(a)** (of boat) patrón, -trona m,f, capitán, -tana m,f; (of plane) capitán, -tana m,f **(b)** (Sport) (coach) entrenador, -dora m,f; (captain) capitán, -tana m,f

skip rope, (BrE) **skipping rope** /'skɪpɪŋ/ n ▶ JUMP ROPE

skirmish /'skɜːrmɪʃ ‖ 'skɜːmɪʃ/ n escaramuza f

skirt¹ /skɜːrt ‖ skɜːt/ n falda f, pollera f (CS)

skirt² vt **(a)** (run alongside) bordear **(b)** ▶ SKIRT AROUND
  ■ **skirt around,** (BrE also) **skirt round** [v + prep + o] **(a)** ‹*mountain/lake*› bordear **(b)** ‹*issue/ problem*› eludir

skittle /'skɪtl/ n bolo m

skittles /'skɪtl̩z/ n (+ sing vb) bolos mpl

skive off /skaɪv/ [v + adv] (BrE colloq) **(a)** (disappear) escurrir el bulto (fam), escaparse, pirarse (Esp fam) **(b)** (stay away — from school) hacer* novillos (fam); (— from work) no ir* a trabajar, capear (Chi) or (Col) capar trabajo (fam)

skulk /skʌlk/ vi: **I saw him** ~**ing in the background** lo vi al fondo, tratando de pasar desapercibido; **to** ~ **around** merodear

skull /skʌl/ n cráneo m

skullcap /'skʌlkæp/ n casquete m; (Relig) solideo m

skunk /skʌŋk/ n mofeta f, zorrillo m (AmL), zorrino m (CS), mapurite m (AmC, Ven)

sky /skaɪ/ n (pl **skies**) cielo m

sky: ~**diving** n paracaidismo m (*en la modalidad de caída libre*); ~**high** /'skaɪ'haɪ/ adj: **prices are** ~**high** los precios están por las nubes; ~**lark** n alondra f; ~**light** n tragaluz m, claraboya f; ~**line** n **(a)** (horizon) línea f (del horizonte **(b)** (of city): **the Manhattan** ~**line** los edificios de Manhattan recortados contra el horizonte; ~**scraper** n rascacielos m

slab /slæb/ n (of stone) losa f; (of concrete) bloque m; (of wood) tabla f; (of cake, bread) pedazo m, trozo m (*grueso*)

slack¹ /slæk/ adj **-er, -est** ① (loose) ‹*rope/ cable*› flojo ② (lax, negligent) ‹*student*› poco aplicado; ‹*piece of work*› flojo ③ (not busy) ‹*period*› de poca actividad

slack² n: **there's too much** ~ **in the rope** la cuerda está demasiado floja; **to take up the** ~ **in** sth tensar algo

slack³ vi (colloq) haraganear, flojear (fam)

slacken /'slækən/ vi **(a)** (become looser) «*rope/ wire*» aflojarse **(b)** (diminish) ▶ SLACKEN OFF 1
  ■ ~ vt **(a)** (loosen) ▶ SLACKEN OFF 2 **(b)** (reduce) ‹*speed*› reducir*; ‹*pace*› aflojar
  ■ **slacken off** ① [v + adv] «*wind*» amainar, aflojar; «*student*» aflojar el ritmo de trabajo; «*speed/rate*» decaer*, disminuir* ② [v + o + adv, v + adv + o] ‹*rope/wire*› aflojar

slacks /slæks/ n pantalones mpl (de sport)

slag /slæg/ n (Metall) escoria f; (Min) escombro m, escoria f; (before n) ~ **heap** escorial m, escombrera f

slain /sleɪn/ past p of SLAY

slake /sleɪk/ vt (liter) ‹*thirst*› saciar

slalom /'slɑːləm/ n slalom m

slam /slæm/ **-mm-** vt ① **(a)** (close violently): **to** ~ **the door** dar* un portazo **(b)** (put with force): **he** ~**med the book down on the table** tiró el libro sobre la mesa ② (criticize) (journ) atacar* violentamente
  ■ ~ vi «*door*» cerrarse* de un portazo

slander¹ /'slændər ‖ 'slɑːndə(r)/ n calumnia f, difamación f

slander² vt calumniar, difamar

S

slang /slæŋ/ n argot m

slant¹ /slænt ‖slɑːnt/ n **1** (slope) inclinación f; (of roof, floor) pendiente f **2** (point of view) enfoque m; (bias) sesgo m

slant² vi (a) inclinarse (b) **slanting** pres p inclinado; ‹eyes› rasgado

slap¹ /slæp/ vt **-pp-** **1** (hit): to ~ sb (on face) pegarle* or darle* una bofetada or (AmL tb) una cachetada a algn; (on arm, leg) pegarle* or darle* una palmada a algn **2** (a) (put with force) (b) (put, apply carelessly): he ~ped some paint on it le dio una mano de pintura rápidamente; she ~ped on some makeup se maquilló de cualquier manera

slap² n (on face) bofetada f, cachetada f (AmL); (on back, leg) palmada f

slap: ~**dash** adj ‹work› chapucero (fam); ~**stick** n bufonadas fpl; (before n) ~**stick comedy** astracanada f

slash¹ /slæʃ/ n **1** (cut — on body) cuchillada f, tajo m; (— in tire, cloth) raja f, corte m **2** (oblique) barra f (oblicua)

slash² vt **1** ‹person/face› acuchillar, tajear (AmL); ‹tires/coat› rajar; he ~ed his wrists se cortó las venas **2** (reduce) ‹prices/taxes› rebajar drásticamente

slat /slæt/ n (of wood) listón m, tablilla f; (of other material) tira f

slate¹ /sleɪt/ n pizarra f

slate² vt **1** ‹roof› empizarrar **2** (criticize) ‹book/film/writer› poner* por los suelos

slaughter¹ /ˈslɔːtər ‖ˈslɔːtə(r)/ n (of animals) matanza f; (massacre) matanza f, carnicería f

slaughter² vt ‹animal› matar, carnear (CS); ‹people› matar salvajemente

slaughterhouse /ˈslɔːtərhaʊs ‖ˈslɔːtəhaʊs/ n matadero m

Slav /slɑːv/ n eslavo, -va m,f

slave¹ /sleɪv/ n esclavo, -va m,f

slave² vi (colloq): I've been slaving away all day he estado trabajando como un negro todo el día (fam)

slave: ~ **driver** n (colloq) negrero, -ra m,f (fam); ~ **labor**, (BrE) ~ **labour** n el trabajo de los esclavos

slaver /ˈslævər ‖ˈslævə(r)/ vi babear

slavery /ˈsleɪvəri/ n esclavitud f

slaw /slɔː/ n (AmE) ensalada de repollo, zanahoria y cebolla con mayonesa

slay /sleɪ/ vt (past **slew**; past p **slain**) (liter or journ) dar* muerte a

sleazy /ˈsliːzi/ adj **-zier, -ziest** ‹district/bar› sórdido; ‹character/type› de mala pinta

sled¹ /sled/ n (AmE) trineo m

sled² vi **-dd-** (AmE) ir* en trineo

sledge /sledʒ/ n/vi ▶ SLED¹,²

sledgehammer /ˈsledʒhæmər ‖ˈsledʒˌhæmə(r)/ n mazo m, almádena f

sleek /sliːk/ adj **-er, -est** (a) (glossy) ‹hair/fur› lacio y brillante (b) (well-groomed) acicalado

sleep¹ /sliːp/ n **1** sueño m; to go to ~ dormirse*; my foot has gone to ~ se me ha dormido el pie; the cat had to be put to ~ (euph) hubo que sacrificar al gato (euf); to talk in one's ~ hablar dormido **2** (in eyes) lagañas fpl, legañas fpl

sleep² (past & past p **slept**) vi dormir*
■ ~ vt: the hotel ~s 200 guests el hotel tiene 200 camas
■ **sleep around** [v + adv] (colloq & pej) acostarse* con cualquiera
■ **sleep in** [v + adv] (a) (sleep late) dormir* hasta tarde (b) «servant/nurse» vivir en (la) casa (or hospital etc)
■ **sleep on** [v + prep + o] ‹decision/problem› consultar con la almohada
■ **sleep through** [v + prep + o]: he slept through the alarm clock no oyó el despertador y siguió durmiendo; she slept through the whole film durmió durante toda la película
■ **sleep together** [v + adv] (euph) tener* relaciones (sexuales)
■ **sleep with** [v + prep + o] (euph) acostarse* con (euf)

sleeper /ˈsliːpər ‖ˈsliːpə(r)/ n **1** (person): to be a heavy/light ~ tener* el sueño pesado/ligero **2** (Rail) (a) (berth) litera f (b) (train) tren m con coches camas or (CS) coches dormitorio **3** (on track) (Rail) durmiente m or (Esp) traviesa f

sleeping /ˈsliːpɪŋ/: ~ **bag** n saco m de dormir; ~ **car** n (Rail) coche m cama, coche m dormitorio (CS); ~ **partner** n (BrE) socio, -cia m,f capitalista; ~ **pill**, ~ **tablet** (BrE) n somnífero m

sleepless /ˈsliːpləs ‖ˈsliːplɪs/ adj: to have a ~ night pasar la noche en blanco

sleepwalk /ˈsliːpwɔːk/ vi caminar dormido

sleepy /ˈsliːpi/ adj **-pier, -piest** ‹expression› adormilado, somnoliento; to be/feel ~ tener* sueño

sleet /sliːt/ n aguanieve f

sleeve /sliːv/ n (a) (of garment) manga f; to have sth up one's ~ (colloq) tener* algo planeado (b) (of record) (BrE) funda f, carátula f

sleeveless /ˈsliːvləs ‖ˈsliːvlɪs/ adj sin mangas

sleigh /sleɪ/ n trineo m

sleight of hand /slaɪt/ n prestidigitación f

slender /ˈslendər ‖ˈslendə(r)/ adj **-derer, -derest** (a) ‹person/figure› delgado, esbelto; ‹waist/neck› fino, delgado (b) ‹means› escaso; ‹majority› estrecho

slept /slept/ past & past p of SLEEP²

sleuth /sluːθ/ n sabueso mf

slew /sluː/ past of SLAY

slice¹ /slaɪs/ n (piece — of bread, cheese) rebanada f; (— of cake) trozo m; (— of lemon, cucumber) rodaja f; (— of meat) tajada f; (— of ham) loncha f, lonja f; (— of melon) raja f

slice² vt ‹bread› cortar (en rebanadas); ‹meat› cortar (en tajadas); ‹cake› cortar (en trozos); ‹lemon/cucumber› cortar (en rodajas); ‹ham› cortar (en lonchas)

slick¹ /slɪk/ adj **-er, -est** **1** (a) ‹book/program› ingenioso pero insustancial (b) ‹person› (glib) de mucha labia; (clever) hábil; ‹reply› fácil (c) ‹performance/production› muy logrado or pulido **2** (slippery) (AmE) ‹surface› resbaladizo

slick² n (oil ~) marea f negra

slide¹ /slaɪd/ (past & past p **slid** /slɪd/) vi deslizarse*

■ ~ *vt* (+ *adv compl*): **she slid the book across the table to him** le pasó el libro deslizándolo por la mesa; **to ~ the bolt back** correr el cerrojo

slide² *n* **1** (in playground) tobogán *m* **2** (action — accidental) resbalón *m*, resbalada *f*; (— deliberate) deslizamiento *m* **3** (a) (Phot) diapositiva *f*; (*before n*) ~ **projector** proyector *m* de diapositivas **(b)** (for microscope — glass plate) portaobjetos *m*; (— specimen) muestra *f* **4** (for hair) (BrE) ▶ BARRETTE

slide rule *n* regla *f* de cálculo

sliding /'slaɪdɪŋ/: ~ **door** puerta *f* corrediza; ~ **scale** *n* escala *f* móvil

slight¹ /slaɪt/ *adj* **-er, -est** **1** (a) ⟨*improvement/accent*⟩ ligero, leve; **she has a ~ temperature** tiene un poco de fiebre; **I haven't the ~est idea** no tengo (ni) la menor idea; **he's not the ~est bit interested** no le interesa en lo más mínimo **(b)** (minimal) ⟨*chance/hope*⟩ escaso **2** (slim) delgado, menudo

slight² *vt* (frml) desairar

slight³ *n* (frml) desaire *m*

slightly /'slaɪtli/ *adv* ligeramente

slim¹ /slɪm/ *adj* **-mm-** ⟨*person/figure*⟩ esbelto, delgado; ⟨*waist*⟩ fino; ⟨*chance*⟩ escaso; ⟨*majority*⟩ estrecho

slim² *vi* **-mm-** **(a)** (become slimmer) adelgazar*, bajar de peso **(b)** (BrE) (diet) hacer* régimen

slime /slaɪm/ *n* (thin mud) limo *m*, cieno *m*; (of snail, slug etc) baba *f*

slimmer /'slɪmər ‖ 'slɪmə(r)/ *n* (BrE) persona que está a régimen

slimy /'slaɪmi/ *adj* **-mier, -miest** **(a)** ⟨*substance/surface*⟩ viscoso **(b)** ⟨*person*⟩ excesivamente obsequioso, falso

sling¹ /slɪŋ/ *n* **(a)** (Med) cabestrillo *m* **(b)** (for carrying a baby) canguro *m* **(c)** (for lifting) eslinga *f*

sling² *vt* (*past & past p* **slung**) (colloq) tirar, lanzar*, aventar* (Col, Méx, Per)

slink /slɪŋk/ *vi* (*past & past p* **slunk**) (+ *adv compl*): **to ~ off** *o* **away** escabullirse*

slip¹ /slɪp/ *n* **1** (slide) resbalón *m*, resbalada *f* (AmL); **to give sb the ~** (colloq) lograr zafarse de algn **2** (mistake) error *m*; **a ~ of the tongue/pen** un lapsus (linguae/cálami) **3** **a ~ of paper** un papelito, un papel **4** (undergarment) (full-length) combinación *f*; (half-length) enagua *f*, fondo *m* (Méx)

slip² **-pp-** *vi* **1** (a) (slide, shift position) ⟨*person*⟩ resbalar(se); ⟨*clutch*⟩ patinar; **it just ~ped out of my hands** se me resbaló de las manos **(b)** ⟨*standards/service*⟩ decaer*

2 (a) (move unobtrusively) (+ *adv compl*): **he ~ped out the back door** se deslizó por la puerta trasera; **we managed to ~ past the guards** logramos pasar sin que nos vieran las guardias **(b)** (escape, be lost): **to let ~ an opportunity** dejar escapar una oportunidad; **to ~ through one's fingers** escapársele a algn de las manos; **I didn't mean to say that: it just ~ped out** no quería decirlo, pero se me escapó

■ ~ *vt* **1 (a)** (put unobtrusively) (+ *adv compl*) poner*, meter, deslizar*; **she ~ped a coin into his hand** le pasó disimuladamente una moneda **(b)** (pass) **to ~ sth TO sb** pasarle algo A algn con disimulo

2 *to ~ sb's mind*: **it ~ped my mind** me olvidé, se me olvidó

■ **slip away** ⟪*person/opportunity*⟫ escabullirse*; ⟪*hours/time*⟫ pasar

■ **slip in** [*v + o + adv*, *v + adv + o*] ⟨*comment/reference*⟩ incluir*

■ **slip off** **1** [*v + o + adv*, *v + adv + o*] ⟨*clothes/shoes*⟩ quitarse **2** [*v + adv*] escabullirse*

■ **slip on** [*v + o + adv*, *v + adv + o*] ⟨*clothes/shoes*⟩ ponerse*

■ **slip up** [*v + adv*] equivocarse*

slipped disc /slɪpt/ *n* hernia *f* de disco

slipper /'slɪpər ‖ 'slɪpə(r)/ *n* zapatilla *f*, pantufla *f* (esp AmL)

slippery /'slɪpəri/ *adj* **(a)** ⟨*surface/soap*⟩ resbaladizo, resbaloso (AmL) **(b)** ⟨*person*⟩ (elusive) escurridizo; (untrustworthy) que no es de fiar

slip: ~-**road** *n* (BrE) vía *f* de acceso; ~-**up** *n* error *m*

slit¹ /slɪt/ *n* (opening) rendija *f*; (cut) raja *f*

slit² *vt* (*pres p* **slitting**; *past & past p* **slit**) cortar, rajar (Méx); **to ~ sb's throat** degollar a algn

slither /'slɪðər ‖ 'slɪðə(r)/ *vi* ⟪*snake*⟫ deslizarse*

sliver /'slɪvər ‖ 'slɪvə(r)/ *n* **(a)** (of glass, wood) astilla *f* **(b)** (thin slice) tajada *f* (*or* rodaja *f etc*) fina; *see also* SLICE

slob /slɑːb ‖ slɒb/ *n* (colloq) vago, -ga *m,f* (fam)

slobber /'slɑːbər ‖ 'slɒbə(r)/ *vi* babear

slog /slɑːg ‖ slɒg/ *n* (colloq) (*no pl*): **we've got a long ~ ahead of us** tenemos un largo y arduo camino por delante

■ **slog away**: **-gg-** [*v + adv*] (BrE colloq) sudar tinta (fam), trabajar duro (esp AmL)

slogan /'sləʊgən/ *n* (Busn) slogan *m*, eslogan *m*; (Pol) lema *m*, consigna *f*

slop /slɑːp ‖ slɒp/ *vi* **-pp-** (colloq) (spill) derramarse, volcarse*

slope¹ /sləʊp/ *n* **(a)** (sloping ground) cuesta *f*, pendiente *f*, barranca *f* (RPl) **(b)** (of mountain) ladera *f*, falda *f* **(c)** (for skiing) pista *f* de esquí, cancha *f* de esquí (CS)

slope² *vi*: **to ~ down** ⟪*hill/road*⟫ tener* un declive; **her handwriting ~s backward/forward** tiene la letra inclinada hacia atrás/adelante

sloping /'sləʊpɪŋ/ *adj* ⟨*field/floor*⟩ en declive; ⟨*roof/handwriting*⟩ inclinado

sloppy /'slɑːpi ‖ 'slɒpi/ *adj* **-pier, -piest** **1** (careless) ⟨*manners/work*⟩ descuidado; ⟨*presentation*⟩ descuidado, desprolijo (CS) **2** ⟨*kiss*⟩ baboso

slosh /slɑːʃ ‖ slɒʃ/ *vt* (splash) echar

■ ~ *vi* **to ~ around** *o* **about** ⟪*person*⟫ chapotear; ⟪*liquid*⟫ agitarse haciendo ruido

slot¹ /slɑːt ‖ slɒt/ *n* **1** (opening, groove) ranura *f* **2** (Rad, TV) espacio *m*

slot² **-tt-** *vt* (insert) **to ~ sth INTO sth** encajar algo EN algo

■ **slot in** **1** [*v + adv*] ⟨*shelf/part*⟩ encajar **2** [*v + o + adv*, *v + adv + o*] ⟨*component*⟩ hacer* encajar

sloth /sləʊθ/ *n* (Zool) perezoso *m*

slot machine *n* **(a)** (vending machine) distribuidor *m* automático, máquina *f* expendedora **(b)** (for gambling) máquina *f* tragamonedas *or* (Esp tb) tragaperras

slouch /slaʊtʃ/ *vi* (a) (droop shoulders) encorvarse; **don't ~!** ¡ponte derecho! (b) (walk) (+ *adv compl*): **he ~ed out of the room** salió de la habitación arrastrando los pies

Slovak /ˈsləʊvæk/ *n* (a) (person) eslovaco, -ca *m,f* (b) (language) eslovaco *m*

Slovakia /sləʊˈvɑːkiə ‖ sləʊˈvækiə/ *n* Eslovaquia *f*

Slovene /ˈsləʊviːn/ *n* (a) (person) esloveno, -na *m,f* (b) (language) esloveno *m*

Slovenia /sləʊˈviːnjə/ *n* Eslovenia *f*

slovenly /ˈslʌvənli/ *adj* **-lier, -liest** ⟨work⟩ descuidado; ⟨person⟩ desaliñado

slow¹ /sləʊ/ *adj* **-er, -est** [1] ⟨speed/rate/ reactions⟩ lento; **to be ~ to + INF** tardar EN + INF [2] (a) (not lively) ⟨novel/plot⟩ lento (b) (stupid) (euph) poco despierto (euf) [3] (of clock, watch) (*pred*): **my watch is five minutes ~** mi reloj está cinco minutos atrasado

slow² *vi*: **the train ~ed to a stop** el tren fue disminuyendo la velocidad hasta detenerse
■ **~** *vt*: **bad weather ~ed their progress** el mal tiempo los retrasó
■ **slow down** [1] [*v* + *adv*] (a) (go more slowly) «*runner*» aflojar el paso; «*vehicle/driver*» reducir* la velocidad; «*speaker*» hablar más despacio (b) (be less active) (colloq) tomarse las cosas con más calma [2] [*v* + *o* + *adv, v* + *adv* + *o*] (a) ⟨*process*⟩ hacer* más lento (b) ⟨*vehicle/ engine*⟩ reducir* la velocidad de
■ **slow up** ▶ SLOW DOWN

slow³ *adv* lentamente, despacio

slowly /ˈsləʊli/ *adv* lentamente, despacio

slow motion *n* cámara *f* lenta; **in ~ ~** en *or* (Esp) a cámara lenta

sludge /slʌdʒ/ *n* lodo *m*, fango *m*

slug /slʌg/ *n* (Zool) babosa *f*

sluggish /ˈslʌgɪʃ/ *adj* (a) (slow-moving) lento; ⟨stream/river⟩ de aguas mansas (b) ⟨growth⟩ lento

sluice /sluːs/ *n* (a) (channel) canal *m*, conducto *m* (de esclusa) (b) (sluicegate) compuerta *f*

sluicegate /ˈsluːsgeɪt/ *n* compuerta *f* (de esclusa)

slum /slʌm/ *n* (a) (poor urban area) (*often pl*) barrio *m* bajo, barriada *f* (AmL exc CS), barrio *m* de conventillos (CS) (b) (filthy place) (colloq & pej) pocilga *f*

slumber¹ /ˈslʌmbər ‖ ˈslʌmbə(r)/ *n* (liter) (*often pl*) sueño *m*

slumber² *vi* (liter) dormir*

slump¹ /slʌmp/ *n* (a) (economic depression) depresión *f* (b) (in prices, sales) caída *f or* baja *f* repentina; (in attendance, interest) disminución *f*

slump² *vi* [1] (collapse) (+ *adv compl*) desplomarse; **they found her ~ed over her desk** la encontraron desplomada sobre su escritorio [2] «*prices/output/sales*» caer* *or* bajar repentinamente

slung /slʌŋ/ *past & past p of* SLING²

slunk /slʌŋk/ *past & past p of* SLINK

slur¹ /slɜːr ‖ slɜː(r)/ *n* [1] (insult): **a racist ~** un comentario racista; **to cast a ~ on sb** injuriar a algn [2] (Mus) ligado *m*

slur² *vt* **-rr-** [1] (pronounce unclearly): **to ~ one's words** arrastrar las palabras [2] (Mus) ligar*

slurp /slɜːrp ‖ slɜːp/ *vt* sorber (*haciendo ruido*)

slurred /slɜːrd ‖ slɜːd/ *adj*: **her speech was ~** arrastraba las palabras

slush /slʌʃ/ *n* (a) (snow) nieve *f* fangosa *or* medio derretida (b) (sentimental trash) sensiblería *f*

sly /slaɪ/ *adj* **-er, -est** ⟨person⟩ astuto; ⟨look/ grin⟩ malicioso; **on the ~** a hurtadillas

smack¹ /smæk/ *n* manotazo *m*, palmada *f* (AmL)

smack² *vt* (a) (slap) ⟨child⟩ pegarle* a (*con la mano*) (b) **to ~ one's lips** relamerse
■ **~** *vi* **to ~ OF sth** oler* A algo

smack³ *adv* (colloq): **~ in the middle** justo en el medio; **he went ~ into a tree** se dio contra un árbol

small¹ /smɔːl/ *adj* **-er, -est** pequeño, chico (esp AmL); ⟨sum/price⟩ módico, reducido; ⟨mistake/problem⟩ pequeño, de poca importancia; **to feel ~** sentirse* insignificante

small² *n* **the ~ of the back** región baja de la espalda, que corresponde al segmento dorsal de la columna vertebral

small: **~ ad** *n* (BrE) anuncio *m* (clasificado), aviso *m* (clasificado) (AmL); **~ change** *n* cambio *m*, (dinero *m*) suelto *m*, sencillo *m* (AmL), feria *f* (Méx fam); **~ hours** *pl n* **the ~ hours (of the morning)** la madrugada; **~-minded** /ˈsmɔːlˈmaɪndəd ‖ ˌsmɔːlˈmaɪndɪd/ *adj* cerrado, de miras estrechas; **~pox** /ˈsmɔːlpɑːks ‖ ˈsmɔːlpɒks/ *n* viruela *f*; **~ print** *n* (BrE) **the ~ print** la letra pequeña *or* menuda, la letra chica (esp AmL); **~ talk** *n* charla *f* sobre temas triviales; **~-time** /ˈsmɔːlˈtaɪm/ *adj* de poca monta; **~-town** /ˈsmɔːlˈtaʊn/ *adj* pueblerino

smart¹ /smɑːrt ‖ smɑːt/ *adj* **-er, -est** [1] (esp BrE) (neat, stylish) ⟨appearance/dress/hotel/ neighborhood⟩ elegante [2] (clever, shrewd) ⟨child⟩ listo; ⟨answer⟩ inteligente [3] (a) (brisk, prompt) ⟨pace⟩ rápido (b) (forceful) ⟨blow/tap⟩ seco, fuerte

smart² *vi* «*eyes/wound*» escocer*

smarten up /ˈsmɑːrtən ‖ ˈsmɑːtən/ (a) [*v* + *o* + *adv, v* + *adv* + *o*] ⟨house/town⟩ arreglar (b) [*v* + *adv*] ⟨person⟩ mejorar su (*or* mi etc) aspecto

smash¹ /smæʃ/ *n* [1] (a) (sound) estrépito *m*, estruendo *m* (b) (collision) (BrE) choque *m* [2] (a) (blow) golpe *m* (b) (Sport) smash *m*, remate *m*, remache *m* [3] (success) (colloq) exitazo *m* (fam)

smash² *vt* [1] (break) ⟨furniture⟩ romper*; ⟨car⟩ destrozar*; ⟨glass⟩ romper*; (into small pieces) hacer* añicos [2] (destroy) ⟨rebellion⟩ aplastar; ⟨drug racket/spy ring⟩ acabar con [3] (Sport) rematar, remachar
■ **~** *vi* (shatter) hacerse* pedazos
■ **smash up** [*v* + *o* + *adv*] (colloq) destrozar*

smash: **~ hit** *n* (colloq) exitazo *m* (fam); **~up** *n* (colloq) choque *m* violento

smattering /'smætərɪŋ/ n (no pl) nociones fpl

smear¹ /smɪr ‖smɪə(r)/ n **1** (stain) mancha f
2 (slander, slur) calumnia f; (before n) ~ **campaign**
campaña f difamatoria **3** (Med) ~ (**test**)
citología f, frotis m cervical, Papanicolau m (AmL)

smear² vt **1** to ~ sth **ON(TO)/OVER** sth ⟨paint/
grease⟩ embadurnar algo de algo; ⟨butter⟩ untar
algo con algo **2** (slander, libel) difamar
■ ~ vi «ink/lipstick» correrse

smell¹ /smel/ n (a) (odor) olor m (b) (sense of
smell) olfato m

smell² (past & past p **smelled** or (BrE also)
smelt) vt (a) (sense) oler*; **we could** ~ **gas/
burning** olía a gas/quemado; **to** ~ **danger** olfatear
el peligro (b) (sniff at) «person» oler*; «animal»
olfatear
■ ~ vi oler*; **to** ~ **OF** sth oler* A algo

smelling salts /'smelɪŋ/ pl n sales fpl
(aromáticas)

smelly /'smeli/ adj **-lier, -liest** que huele mal

smelt¹ /smelt/ (BrE) past & past p of SMELL²

smelt² vt fundir

smile¹ /smaɪl/ n sonrisa f

smile² vi sonreír*; **to** ~ **AT** sb sonreírle* A algn

smirk¹ /smɜːrk ‖smɜːk/ n sonrisita f (de
suficiencia, de complicidad, etc)

smirk² vi sonreírse* (con suficiencia,
complicidad etc)

smith /smɪθ/ n herrero, -ra m,f

smithereens /ˌsmɪðəˈriːnz/ pl n: **to smash** sth
to ~ hacer* algo pedazos or añicos

smock /smɑːk ‖smɒk/ n (a) (of fisherman, artist)
blusón m, bata f (b) (dress) vestido m amplio

smog /smɑːg ‖smɒg/ n smog m

smoke¹ /sməʊk/ n humo m; **to go up in** ~
«books/papers» quemarse; «hopes» esfumarse;
«ambitions/plans» quedar en agua de borrajas

smoke² vi **1** «person» fumar **2** (give off
smoke) echar humo
■ ~ vt **1** ⟨cigarettes/tobacco⟩ fumar; **he** ~**s a pipe**
fuma en pipa **2** (cure) ⟨fish/cheese⟩ ahumar*

smoke-bomb /'sməʊkbɑːm ‖'sməʊkbɒm/ n
bomba f de humo

smoked /sməʊkt/ adj ahumado

smoke detector n detector m de humo

smokeless /'sməʊkləs ‖'sməʊklɪs/ adj ⟨fuel⟩
que arde sin humo; ~ **zone** (in UK) zona donde
está prohibido usar combustibles que produzcan
humo

smoker /'sməʊkər ‖'sməʊkə(r)/ n fumador,
-dora m,f; **he's a heavy** ~**fuma mucho**

smoke: ~**screen** n cortina f de humo; ~
signal n señal f de humo

smoking /'sməʊkɪŋ/ n 🅢 **no smoking**
prohibido fumar; **to give up** ~ dejar de fumar

smoking: ~ **car** n (AmE) vagón m or (Chi, Méx)
carro m de fumadores; ~ **compartment** n
compartimento m de fumadores

smoky /'sməʊki/ adj **-kier, -kiest** ⟨fire/
chimney⟩ que echa humo; ⟨room⟩ lleno de humo;
⟨atmosphere⟩ cargado de humo

smolder, (BrE) **smoulder** /'sməʊldər
‖'sməʊldə(r)/ vi «fire» arder (sin llama); «eyes»
arder

smooth¹ /smuːð/ adj **-er, -est** **1** (a)

⟨texture/stone⟩ liso, suave; ⟨skin⟩ suave, terso;
⟨sea⟩ tranquilo (b) (of consistency) ⟨sauce⟩ sin
grumos (c) (of taste) ⟨wine⟩ suave **2** (a) (of
movement) ⟨take-off⟩ suave; ⟨flight⟩ cómodo (b)
(trouble-free) ⟨journey⟩ sin complicaciones **3** (a)
(easy, polished) ⟨performance⟩ fluido (b) (glib, suave)
(pej) poco sincero, falso; **he's a** ~ **talker** tiene
mucha labia

smooth² vt (a) ⟨dress/sheets/hair⟩ alisar,
arreglar (b) (polish) pulir
■ **smooth out** [v + o + adv, v + adv + o] (a)
⟨sheets/creases⟩ alisar (b) ⟨difficulties/problems⟩
allanar
■ **smooth over** [v + o + adv, v + adv + o]
⟨differences⟩ dejar de lado

smoothly /'smuːðli/ adv **1** (a) (of movement)
⟨take off/drive⟩ suavemente (b) (without problems)
sin problemas **2** (glibly, suavely) (pej) ⟨talk⟩ con
mucha labia

smother /'smʌðər ‖'smʌðə(r)/ vt (a) (stifle)
⟨person⟩ asfixiar, ahogar*; ⟨flames⟩ sofocar* (b)
(suppress) ⟨yawn/giggle⟩ reprimir (c) (cover
profusely): **she** ~**ed him with kisses** lo cubrió de
besos

smoulder vi (BrE) ▶ SMOLDER

smudge¹ /smʌdʒ/ n mancha f

smudge² vt correr; (deliberately) difuminar

smug /smʌg/ adj **-gg-** ⟨expression⟩ de
suficiencia, petulante; ⟨person⟩ pagado de sí
mismo, petulante

smuggle /'smʌgəl/ vt ⟨tobacco/drugs⟩
contrabandear, pasar de contrabando; **I** ~**d her
into my room** la hice entrar a mi habitación a
escondidas

smuggler /'smʌglər ‖'smʌglə(r)/ n
contrabandista mf

smuggling /'smʌglɪŋ/ n contrabando m

snack /snæk/ n tentempié m; **to have a** ~
comer algo ligero or (esp AmL) liviano, tomar(se)
un tentempié

snack bar n bar m, cafetería f

snag¹ /snæg/ n (a) (difficulty) inconveniente m,
pega f (Esp fam) (b) (in fabric, stocking) enganchón m

snag² vt **-gg-** enganchar

snail /sneɪl/ n caracol m; **at a** ~**'s pace** a paso
de tortuga

snake /sneɪk/ n culebra f, serpiente f;
(poisonous) víbora f

snake: ~**bite** n mordedura f de serpiente; ~
charmer /'tʃɑːrmər ‖'tʃɑːmə(r)/ n encantador,
-dora m,f de serpientes

snap¹ /snæp/ n **1** (sound) chasquido m **2** ~
(**fastener**) (AmE) (on clothes) broche m or botón
m de presión (AmL), (cierre m) automático m
(Esp) **3** (photo) (colloq) foto f, instantánea f
4 (Meteo): **a cold** ~ una ola de frío

snap² **-pp-** vt **1** (a) (break) partir (b) (cause to
make sharp sound): **she** ~**ped the lid/book shut**
cerró la tapa/el libro de un golpe; ▶ FINGER¹
2 (utter sharply) decir* bruscamente
3 (photograph) ⟨person/thing⟩ sacarle* una foto a
■ ~ vi **1** (bite) **to** ~ **AT** sth intentar morder algo
2 (a) (break) «twigs/branch» romperse*,
quebrarse* (esp AmL); «elastic» romperse* (b)
(click): **to** ~ **shut** cerrarse* (con un clic)
3 (speak sharply) hablar con brusquedad   ⋯⟡

4 (move quickly): **to ~ out of it** (of depression) animarse; (of lethargy, inertia) espabilarse
■ **snap up** [v + o + adv, v + adv + o] ‹offer› no dejar escapar

snap³ adj ‹decision› precipitado, repentino

snappy /'snæpi/ adj **-pier, -piest** (a) ‹person› irascible; ‹retort› brusco (b) ‹pace› (colloq) ágil

snapshot /'snæpʃɑːt ‖'snæpʃɒt/ n foto f, instantánea f

snare¹ /sner ‖sneə(r)/ n trampa f

snare² vt atrapar

snarl¹ /snɑːrl ‖snɑːl/ n gruñido m

snarl² vi/t gruñir*
■ **snarl up** [v + adv + o] (usu pass) ‹ball of wool› enmarañar, enredar; ‹traffic› atascar*

snatch¹ /snætʃ/ vt **1** (a) (grab) **to ~ sth FROM sb** arrebatarle algo A algn; **she ~ed the letter out of my hand** me arrancó la carta de las manos (b) (steal) (colloq & journ) robar (arrebatando) (c) (kidnap) (journ) secuestrar, raptar **2** (take hurriedly) ‹opportunity› no dejar pasar

snatch² n **1** (robbery) (BrE journ) robo m **2** (a) (fragment) fragmento m (b) (brief spell) rato m; **to sleep in ~es** dormir* (de) a ratos

sneak /sniːk/ (past & past p **sneaked** or (AmE also) **snuck**) vt (a) (smuggle) (+ adv compl): **he ~ed the files out of the office** sacó los archivos de la oficina a escondidas; **she tried to ~ him in without paying** trató de colarlo sin pagar (b) (take furtively): **to ~ a look at sth/sb** mirar algo/a algn con disimulo
■ ~ vi (+ adv compl): **to ~ in** entrar a hurtadillas; **to ~ away** escabullirse*
■ **sneak up** [v + adv] **to ~ up** (ON sb) acercarse* sigilosamente (A algn)

sneakers /'sniːkərz ‖'sniːkəz/ pl n zapatillas fpl (de deporte), tenis mpl, playeras fpl (Esp)

sneak: ~ preview n (Cin, TV) preestreno m; **~ thief** n ratero, -ra m,f

sneaky /'sniːki/ adj **-kier, -kiest** (colloq) ‹person› artero, taimado; ‹behavior› solapado

sneer¹ /snɪr ‖snɪə(r)/ vi adoptar un aire despectivo; (with facial expression) hacer* una mueca de desprecio

sneer² n expresión f desdeñosa

sneeze¹ /sniːz/ vi estornudar

sneeze² n estornudo m

snide /snaɪd/ adj insidioso

sniff /snɪf/ vt (a) (smell) «person» oler*; «animal» olfatear (b) ‹glue› inhalar, esnifar
■ ~ vi «animal» husmear, olfatear; «person» sorberse la nariz

sniffer dog /'snɪfər ‖'snɪfə(r)/ n (BrE) perro m rastreador

sniffle /'snɪfəl/ vi (due to cold) sorberse la nariz; (when crying) gimotear

snigger¹ /'snɪgər ‖'snɪgə(r)/ n risilla f, risita f

snigger² vi reírse* (por lo bajo)

snip¹ /snɪp/ n (act) tijeretazo m; (sound) tijereteo m

snip² vt **-pp-** cortar (con tijera)

sniper /'snaɪpər ‖'snaɪpə(r)/ n francotirador, -dora m,f

snippet /'snɪpət ‖'snɪpɪt/ n (of conversation) trozo m; **~s of information** (algunos) datos aislados

snivel /'snɪvəl/ vi, (BrE) **-ll-** lloriquear

snob /snɑːb ‖snɒb/ n (e)snob mf

snobbery /'snɑːbəri ‖'snɒbəri/ n (e)snobismo m

snobbish /'snɑːbɪʃ ‖'snɒbɪʃ/ adj (e)snob

snooker /'snʊkər ‖'snuːkə(r)/ n snooker m (modalidad de billar que se juega con 15 bolas rojas y 6 de otro color)

snoop /snuːp/ vi (colloq) husmear, fisgonear

snooper /'snuːpər ‖'snuːpə(r)/ n (colloq) fisgón, -gona m,f

snooze¹ /snuːz/ vi (colloq) dormitar

snooze² n (colloq) sueñecito m (fam), sueñito m (esp AmL fam); **to have a ~** echar una cabezada (fam)

snore¹ /snɔːr ‖snɔː(r)/ vi roncar*

snore² n ronquido m

snoring /'snɔːrɪŋ/ n ronquidos mpl

snorkel /'snɔːrkəl ‖'snɔːkəl/ n esnórkel m

snort¹ /snɔːrt ‖snɔːt/ vi bufar, resoplar
■ ~ vt (utter) bramar, gruñir*

snort² n bufido m, resoplido m

snout /snaʊt/ n hocico m, morro m

snow¹ /snəʊ/ n (a) nieve f (b) (snowfall) nevada f

snow² v impers nevar*
■ **snow in** [v + o + adv]: **to be ~ed in** estar* aislado por la nieve
■ **snow under** [v + o + adv]: **I'm ~ed under with work** estoy agobiada or desbordada de trabajo

snowball¹ /'snəʊbɔːl/ n (Meteo) bola f de nieve

snowball² vi «problems» agravarse

snow: ~board n snowboard m; **~boarding** n snowboard m; **~bound** adj bloqueado por la nieve; **~drift** n: nieve acumulada durante una ventisca; **~drop** n campanilla f de invierno; **~fall** n nevada f; **~flake** n copo m de nieve; **~man** /'snəʊmæn/ n (pl **-men** /-men/) muñeco m de nieve; **~plow**, (BrE) **~plough** n quitanieves m; **~shoe** n raqueta f; **~storm** n tormenta f de nieve

snowy /'snəʊi/ adj **snowier, snowiest** nevoso

snub¹ /snʌb/ vt **-bb-** (a) ‹person› desairar; (ignore) ignorar; (treat coldly) tratar fríamente (CS) (b) (reject) ‹offer› desdeñar, rechazar*

snub² n desaire m

snub³ adj ‹nose› respingón, respingado (AmL)

snub-nosed /'snʌbˈnəʊzd/ adj de nariz respingona or (AmL tb) respingada

snuck /snək/ (AmE colloq) past & past p of SNEAK

snuff /snʌf/ n rapé m
■ **snuff out** [v + o + adv, v + adv + o] ‹candle› apagar*

snuffbox /'snʌfbɑːks ‖'snʌfbɒks/ n caja f de rapé

snug /snʌg/ adj (a) (cosy) cómodo y acogedor (b) (close-fitting) ceñido, ajustado

snuggle /'snʌgəl/ vi acurrucarse*; **he ~d up against her** se le arrimó

so¹ /səʊ/ adv **1** (a) (very) tan; **she's ~ tall** es tan alta; **he did it ~ quickly** lo hizo tan rápido; **thank you ~ much** muchísimas gracias (b) so much/many (as adj) tanto, -ta/tantos, -tas; **~ ~**

much space/food tanto espacio/tanta comida; ~ **many things** tantas cosas **(c) so much** *(as pronoun)* tanto; **he eats ~ much** come tanto **2 or so** más o menos

3 (with clauses of result or purpose) ~ ... **(that)** tan ... que; **he was ~ rude (that) she slapped him** fue tan grosero, que le dio una bofetada

4 (a) (thus, in this way): **the street was ~ named because ...** se le puso ese nombre a la calle porque ...; **hold the bat like ~** agarra el bate así **(b)** (as stated) así; **that is ~** (frml) así es; **if ~, they're lying** si es así *or* de ser así, están mintiendo **(c) and so on** (and so forth) etcétera (etcétera)

5 *(replacing clause, phrase, word)*: **I expect ~** me imagino que sí; **I got a bit dirty — ~ I see** me ensucié un poco — sí, ya veo; **I told you ~** ¿no te lo dije?

6 *(with v aux)* **(a)** (also, equally): **Peter agrees and ~ does Bill** Peter está de acuerdo y Bill también **(b)** (indeed): **you promised — ~ I did!** lo prometiste — ¡es verdad! *or* ¡tienes razón!

7 (a) (indicating pause or transition) bueno; **~ here we are again** bueno, aquí estamos otra vez **(b)** (querying, eliciting information): **~ now what do we do?** ¿y ahora qué hacemos? **(c)** (summarizing, concluding) así que; **~ now you know** así que ya sabes **(d)** (expressing surprised reaction) así que, conque; **~ that's what he's after!** ¡así que *or* conque eso es lo que quiere! **(e)** (challenging): **~ what?** ¿y qué?

so² conj 1 *(in clauses of purpose or result)* **(a)** so (that) (expressing purpose) para que (+ *subj*); (expressing result) así que *or* de manera que (+ *indic*); **she said it slowly, ~ (that) we'd all understand** lo dijo despacio, para que todos entendiéramos; **she said it slowly, ~ (that) we all understood** lo dijo despacio, así que *or* de manera que todos entendimos **(b) so as to + INF** para + INF **2** (therefore, consequently) así que, de manera que

so³ *n* (Mus) sol *m*

soak /səʊk/ *vt* **(a)** ⟨*lentils/clothes*⟩ (immerse) poner* en *or* a remojo; (leave immersed) dejar en *or* a remojo **(b)** (drench) empapar; **to be ~ed up (to the skin)** estar* empapado, estar* calado hasta los huesos

■ ~ *vi* **(a)** (lie in liquid): **to leave sth to ~** dejar algo en *or* a remojo **(b)** (penetrate) (+ *adv compl*): **to ~ into/through sth** calar algo

■ **soak up** [*v + o + adv, v + adv + o*] ⟨*liquid/ information*⟩ absorber; ⟨*sun*⟩ empaparse de

soaking /ˈsəʊkɪŋ/ *adj* empapado; (*as adv*) **it's ~ wet** está empapado

so-and-so /ˈsəʊənsəʊ/ *n* (colloq) (unspecified person) (*no art*) fulano, -na *m,f*

soap /səʊp/ *n* **1** jabón *m*; (*before n*) **~ dish** jabonera *f* **2** ▶ SOAP OPERA

soap: ~flakes *pl n* jabón *m* en escamas; **~ opera** *n* (TV) telenovela *f*, culebrón *m*; (Rad) radionovela *f*, comedia *f* (AmL); **~ powder** *n* (BrE) jabón *m* en polvo, detergente *m* (en polvo); **~suds** *pl n* espuma *f* (*de jabón*)

soapy /ˈsəʊpi/ *adj* **-pier, -piest (a)** ⟨*water*⟩ jabonoso; ⟨*cloth/hands*⟩ enjabonado **(b)** ⟨*smell/ taste*⟩ a jabón

soar /sɔːr ‖ sɔː(r)/ *vi* **1 (a)** (fly) «*bird/glider*» planear **(b)** (rise) «*bird/kite*» elevarse; «*prices/ costs*» dispararse; «*hopes*» aumentar;

«*popularity*» aumentar **(c)** (tower) «*skyscraper/ mountain*» alzarse* **2 soaring** *pres p* ⟨*inflation*⟩ galopante, de ritmo vertiginoso; ⟨*popularity*⟩ en alza; **caused by ~ temperatures** causado por una subida vertiginosa de las temperaturas

sob¹ /sɑːb ‖ sɒb/ *vi* **-bb-** sollozar*

sob² *n* sollozo *m*

sober /ˈsəʊbər ‖ ˈsəʊbə(r)/ *adj* **1** (not drunk) sobrio **2 (a)** (serious) ⟨*expression*⟩ grave; ⟨*young man*⟩ serio; ⟨*occasion*⟩ formal **(b)** (subdued) ⟨*dress/ colors*⟩ sobrio

■ **sober up 1** [*v + adv*]: **he's ~ed up now** ya está sobrio **2** [*v + o + adv, v + adv + o*] despejar

sobriety /səʊˈbraɪəti, sə- ‖ səˈbraɪəti/ *n* seriedad *f*, sensatez *f*; *(before n)* ~ **test** (AmE) prueba *f* del alcohol *or* de la alcoholemia

so-called /ˈsəʊˈkɔːld/ *adj* (*usu before n*) **(a)** (commonly named) (así) llamado **(b)** (indicating skeptical attitude) ⟨*expert*⟩ supuesto, presunto

soccer /ˈsɑːkər ‖ ˈsɒkə(r)/ *n* fútbol *m or* (AmC, Méx) futbol *m*

sociable /ˈsəʊʃəbəl/ *adj* sociable

social /ˈsəʊʃəl/ *adj* social; **he has no ~ graces** no sabe cómo comportarse; **~ life** vida *f* social

social democrat *n* socialdemócrata *mf*

socialism /ˈsəʊʃəlɪzəm/ *n* socialismo *m*

socialist¹, Socialist /ˈsəʊʃələst ‖ ˈsəʊʃəlɪst/ *adj* socialista

socialist², Socialist *n* socialista *mf*

socialize /ˈsəʊʃəlaɪz/ *vi* alternar; (at party) circular

socially /ˈsəʊʃəli/ *adv* **(a)** (relating to the community) ⟨*divisive/useful*⟩ socialmente; (*indep*) desde el punto de vista social **(b)** (in social situations): **it's not ~ acceptable** está mal visto, no se considera correcto

social: ~ science *n* ciencia *f* social; **~ security** *n* (BrE) seguridad *f* social; **~ service** *n* **(a)** (welfare work) (AmE) asistencia *f or* trabajo *m* social **(b)** (in UK) servicio *m* social; **~ work** *n* asistencia *f* social; **~ worker** *n* (Soc Adm) asistente, -ta *m,f* social, trabajador, -dora *m,f* social (Méx), visitador, -dora *m,f* social (Chi)

society /səˈsaɪəti/ *n* (*pl* **-ties**) **1 (a)** (community) sociedad *f*; **in polite ~** entre la gente educada **(b)** (fashionable elite) (alta) sociedad *f* **2** (association, club) sociedad *f*

sociologist /ˌsəʊsiˈɑːlədʒəst, -ʃi- ‖ ˌsəʊsiˈɒlədʒɪst, -ʃi-/ *n* sociólogo, -ga *m,f*

sociology /ˌsəʊsiˈɑːlədʒi, -ʃi- ‖ ˌsəʊsiˈɒlədʒi, -ʃi-/ *n* sociología *f*

sociopath /ˈsəʊsiəpæθ, -ʃi-/ *n* (p)sicópata *mf*

sock /sɑːk ‖ sɒk/ *n* calcetín *m*, media *f* (AmL)

socket /ˈsɑːkət ‖ ˈsɒkɪt/ *n* **(a)** (Anat) (of eye) cuenca *f*, órbita *f*; (of joint) fosa *f*, hueco *m* **(b)** (Elec) (for plug) enchufe *m*, toma *f* de corriente, tomacorriente *m* (AmL) **(c)** (Tech) encaje *m*

sod /sɑːd ‖ sɒd/ *n* **1** (piece of turf) tepe *m*, champa *f* (Andes) **2** (BrE vulg) (obnoxious person) cabrón, -brona *m,f* (vulg)

soda /ˈsəʊdə/ *n* **1 (a)** (soda water) soda *f*, agua *f* ‡ de seltz (b) (flavored) (AmE) refresco *m*, fresco *m* (AmL) **(c)** (ice-cream soda) (AmE) ice-cream soda *m* (AmL) (*refresco con helado*) **2** (Chem) soda *f*, sosa *f*

soda: ~ **pop** n (AmE) refresco m; ~ **water** n soda f, agua f‡ de seltz

sodden /'sɑ:dn̩ ‖'sɒdn̩/ adj empapado

sodium /'səʊdiəm/ n sodio m

sodium bicarbonate n bicarbonato m sódico or de sodio

sofa /'səʊfə/ n sofá m

soft /sɔ:ft ‖sɒft/ adj **-er, -est** ① (a) (not hard) blando; ⟨metal⟩ maleable; **to go** ~ ablandarse (b) (smooth) ⟨fur/fabric/skin⟩ suave ② (mild, subdued) ⟨light/color/music⟩ suave ③ (lenient) blando, indulgente ④ ⟨drugs/pornography⟩ blando ⑤ (Chem) ⟨water⟩ blando

soft: ~**ball** n softball m (especie de béisbol que se juega con pelota blanda); ~ **drink** n refresco m (bebida no alcohólica)

soften /'sɔ:fən ‖'sɒfən/ vt (a) ⟨butter/leather⟩ ablandar; ⟨skin⟩ suavizar*; ⟨light/color⟩ suavizar*; ⟨contours⟩ difuminar (b) (mitigate) ⟨effect⟩ atenuar*, mitigar*; **to** ~ **the blow** suavizar* el golpe (c) ⟨water⟩ ablandar, descalcificar*

■ ~ vi (a) «butter/leather» ablandarse; «skin» suavizarse* (b) (become gentler) ablandarse; (become more moderate) volverse* menos intransigente

■ **soften up** [v + o + adv, v + adv + o] ablandar

softener /'sɔ:fn̩ər ‖'sɒfn̩ə(r)/ n (a) (for water) descalcificador m (b) (for fabric) suavizante m

softly /'sɔ:ftli ‖'sɒftli/ adv (a) (gently) ⟨touch⟩ suavemente (b) (quietly) ⟨speak⟩ bajito

soft: ~**-spoken** /'sɔ:ft'spəʊkən ‖,sɒft'spəʊkən/ adj de voz suave; ~ **top** n (AmE) (car) descapotable m, convertible m (AmL); (roof) capota f; ~**ware** /'sɔ:ftweər ‖'sɒftweə(r)/ n software m

soggy /'sɑ:gi ‖'sɒgi/ adj **-gier, -giest** ⟨ground/grass⟩ empapado; ⟨vegetables⟩ pasado

soh /səʊ/ n (Mus) sol m

soil¹ /sɔɪl/ n (a) (earth) tierra f (b) (filth, dirt) (AmE) suciedad f

soil² vt ensuciar

soiled /sɔɪld/ adj ⟨linen⟩ sucio; ⟨goods⟩ dañado

sol /səʊl ‖sɒl/ n (Mus) sol m

solace /'sɑ:ləs ‖'sɒlɪs/ n (liter) consuelo m

solar /'səʊlər ‖'səʊlə(r)/ adj solar

solar system n the ~ ~ el sistema solar

sold /səʊld/ past & past p of SELL

solder /'sɑ:dər ‖'səʊldə(r)/ vt soldar*

soldier /'səʊldʒər ‖'səʊldʒə(r)/ n soldado mf; (officer) militar mf

■ **soldier on** [v + adv] (BrE colloq) seguir* al pie del cañón

sole¹ /səʊl/ n ① (of foot) planta f; (of shoe) suela f ② (fish) (pl ~ or ~**s**) lenguado m

sole² adj (before n) (a) (only) único (b) (exclusive) ⟨rights⟩ exclusivo

sole³ vt (usu pass): **to have one's shoes** ~**d and heeled** hacerles* poner suelas y tacones or (CS, Per) tacos a los zapatos

solely /'səʊlli/ adv (a) (wholly) únicamente, exclusivamente (b) (only, simply) solo, solamente, únicamente

solemn /'sɑ:ləm ‖'sɒləm/ adj (a) (serious, formal) ⟨occasion/silence⟩ solemne (b) (grave) ⟨person⟩ serio; ⟨face⟩ solemne

sol-fa /'səʊl'fɑ: ‖'sɒl'fɑ:/ n solfa f

solicit /sə'lɪsət ‖sə'lɪsɪt/ vt (frml) ⟨information/help⟩ solicitar (frml)

■ ~ vi «prostitute» ejercer la prostitución callejera (abordando a posibles clientes)

solicitor /sə'lɪsətər ‖sə'lɪsɪtə(r)/ n (a) (in US and in UK) abogado responsable de los asuntos legales de un municipio o de un departamento gubernamental (b) (in UK) abogado, -da m,f (que prepara causas legales y desempeña también funciones de notario)

solid¹ /'sɑ:led ‖'sɒlɪd/ adj **-er, -est** ① (a) (not liquid or gaseous) sólido (b) (not hollow) ⟨rubber ball/tire⟩ macizo ② (a) (unbroken) ⟨line/row⟩ continuo, ininterrumpido (b) (continuous) (colloq) ⟨month/year⟩ seguido ③ (a) (physically sturdy) ⟨furniture/house⟩ sólido; ⟨meal⟩ consistente (b) (substantial) ⟨reason⟩ sólido ④ (pure) ⟨metal/wood⟩ macizo, puro; ⟨rock⟩ vivo

solid² n ① (Chem, Phys) sólido m ② **solids** pl (food) alimentos mpl sólidos

solid³ adv: **to be packed/jammed** ~ estar* lleno hasta el tope or hasta los topes

solidarity /ˌsɑ:lə'dærəti ‖ˌsɒlɪ'dærəti/ n solidaridad f

solidify /sə'lɪdəfaɪ/ vi **-fies, -fying, -fied** solidificarse*

solidly /'sɑ:lədli ‖'sɒlɪdli/ adv (a) (sturdily) ⟨fixed/grounded⟩ firmemente; ⟨made⟩ sólidamente (b) (unanimously) unánimemente

solitaire /'sɑ:lə,ter ‖'sɒlɪ,teə(r)/ n ① ~ (diamond) solitario m ② (Games) solitario m

solitary /'sɑ:ləteri ‖'sɒlɪtəri/ adj (a) (alone) ⟨person/life/place⟩ solitario (b) (single) (before n) solo

solitary confinement n incomunicación f; he's in ~ ~ lo han incomunicado

solitude /'sɑ:lətu:d ‖'sɒlɪtju:d/ n soledad f

solo¹ /'səʊləʊ/ n (pl **-los**) solo m

solo² adj (a) (Mus) ⟨violin/voices⟩ solista; ⟨album⟩ en solitario (b) ⟨flight⟩ en solitario

solo³ adv en solitario

soloist /'səʊləʊəst ‖'səʊləʊɪst/ n solista mf

so long interj (colloq) hasta luego, hasta la vista

solstice /'sɑ:lstəs ‖'sɒlstɪs/ n solsticio m

soluble /'sɑ:ljəbəl ‖'sɒljʊbəl/ adj soluble

solution /sə'lu:ʃən/ n solución f

solve /sɑ:lv ‖sɒlv/ vt ⟨mystery/equation⟩ resolver*; ⟨crossword puzzle⟩ sacar*; ⟨crime⟩ esclarecer*; ⟨riddle⟩ encontrar* la solución a

solvent¹ /'sɑ:lvənt ‖'sɒlvənt/ adj solvente

solvent² n disolvente m, solvente m

Somali /sə'mɑ:li/ adj somalí

Somalia /sə'mɑ:liə/ n Somalia f

somber, (BrE) **sombre** /'sɑːmbər ‖'sɒmbə(r)/ *adj* **(a)** (dark) sombrío **(b)** (melancholy) ⟨*mood/ thought*⟩ sombrío; ⟨*music*⟩ lúgubre

some¹ /sʌm, *weak form* səm/ *adj* **⒈ (a)** (unstated number or type) (+ *pl n*) unos, unas; **there were ~ children in the park** había unos niños en el parque; **would you like ~ cherries?** ¿quieres (unas) cerezas? **(b)** (unstated quantity or type) (+ *uncount n*): **~ paint fell on my head** me cayó (un poco de) pintura en la cabeza; **would you like ~ coffee?** ¿quieres café? **⒉** (a, one) (+ *sing count noun*) algún, -guna; **~ day I'll get my revenge** ya me vengaré algún día **⒊** (particular, not all) (+ *pl n*) algunos, -nas; **I like ~ modern artists** algunos artistas modernos me gustan; **in ~ ways** en cierto modo **⒋ (a)** (not many, a few) ⟨*lemons/apples*⟩ algunos, -nas **(b)** (not much, a little) ⟨*meat/rice*⟩ un poco de **⒌ (a)** (several, many): **she's been bedridden for ~ years now** hace algunos años que está postrada en cama **(b)** (large amount of): **we've known each other for quite ~ time now** ya hace mucho (tiempo) que nos conocemos **⒍** (colloq) **(a)** (expressing appreciation): **that's ~ car you've got!** ¡vaya coche que tienes! **(b)** (stressing remarkable, ridiculous nature): **that was ~ exam!** ¡vaya examen! **(c)** (expressing irony): **~ friend you are!** ¡qué buen amigo eres! (iró)

some² *pron* **⒈ (a)** (a number of things or people) algunos, -nas **(b)** (an amount): **there's no salt left; we'll have to buy ~** no queda sal; vamos a tener que comprar; **the coffee's ready: would you like ~?** el café está listo: ¿quieres? **⒉** (certain people) algunos, -nas; **~ say that ...** algunos dicen que ...

some³ *adv* (approximately) unos, unas, alrededor de

somebody¹ /'sʌm,bɑːdi ‖'sʌmbədi/ *pron* alguien; **~'s coming** viene alguien; **who was it? — John ~** ¿quién era? — John algo *or* John no sé cuánto (fam)

somebody² *n* (*no pl*): **to be ~** ser* alguien

somehow /'sʌmhaʊ/ *adv* **(a)** (by some means) de algún modo, de alguna manera; **~ or other** de algún modo u otro **(b)** (in some way, for some reason): **it isn't the same, ~** no sé por qué, pero no es lo mismo

someone /'sʌmwʌn/ *pron* ▶ SOMEBODY¹

someplace /'sʌmpleɪs/ *adv* (AmE) ▶ SOMEWHERE¹ 1

somersault¹ /'sʌmərsɔːlt ‖'sʌməsɒlt, -sɔːlt/ *n* (on ground) voltereta *f*, vuelta *f* (de) carnero (CS); (in air) (salto *m*) mortal *m*

somersault² *vi* (on ground) hacer* volteretas, dar* vueltas (de) carnero (CS); (in air) dar* un (salto) mortal

something /'sʌmθɪŋ/ *pron* **⒈** algo; **have ~ to eat/drink** come/bebe algo; **it's not ~ to be proud of** no es como para estar orgulloso; **that was ~ I hadn't expected** eso no me lo esperaba; **is it ~ I said?** ¿qué pasa? ¿qué he dicho? **⒉ (a)** (in vague statements or approximations): **she's 30 ~** tiene treinta y pico años (fam); **he said it was because of the traffic or ~** dijo que era por el tráfico *o* qué sé yo **(b)** (something like: **~ like 200 spectators** alrededor de *or* unos 200 espectadores **(c)** something of (rather): **she's ~ of an eccentric** es algo excéntrica; **it came as ~ of a surprise** me (*or* nos *etc*) sorprendió un poco

⒊ (sth special): **it was quite ~ for him to reach that position** era todo un logro que él alcanzara esa posición

sometime¹ /'sʌmtaɪm/ *adv* (at unspecified time): **I'll get around to it ~** ya lo haré en algún momento; **we'll have to finish it ~ or another** algún día habrá que terminarlo; **~ next week** un día de la semana que viene

sometime² *adj* (*before n*) (fml) ex, antiguo

sometimes /'sʌmtaɪmz/ *adv* a veces, algunas veces

someway /'sʌmweɪ/ *adv* (AmE) ▶ SOMEHOW

somewhat /'sʌmhwɑːt ‖'sʌmwɒt/ *adv* algo, un tanto

somewhere¹ /'sʌmhwer ‖'sʌmweə(r)/ *adv* **⒈** (in, at a place) en algún lado *or* sitio *or* lugar; (to a place) a algún lado *or* sitio *or* lugar; **to get ~** avanzar*, adelantar **⒉** (in approximations): **~ around $10,000** cerca de *or* alrededor de 10.000 dólares

somewhere² *pron*: **will there be ~ open?** ¿habrá algo (*or* algún sitio *etc*) abierto?; **she's found ~ to live** ha encontrado casa (*or* habitación *etc*)

son /sʌn/ *n* hijo *m*

sonata /sə'nɑːtə/ *n* (*pl* **-tas**) (Mus) sonata *f*

song /sɔːŋ ‖sɒŋ/ *n* **(a)** (piece) canción *f* **(b)** (of bird) canto *m*

song: **~bird** *n* pájaro *m* cantor; **~writer** *n* compositor, -tora *m,f* (de canciones)

sonic /'sɑːnɪk ‖'sɒnɪk/ *adj* sónico

son-in-law /'sʌnɪnlɔː/ *n* (*pl* **sons-in-law**) yerno *m*, hijo *m* político

sonnet /'sɑːnət ‖'sɒnɪt/ *n* soneto *m*

son of a bitch *n* (*pl* **sons of bitches**) (esp AmE sl) hijo *m* de puta, hijo *m* de la chingada (Méx vulg)

soon /suːn/ *adv* **-er, -est** **⒈** (shortly, after a while) pronto, dentro de poco; **~ afterward** poco después; **it'll ~ be spring** ya falta poco para (que empiece) la primavera; **~er or later** tarde o temprano **⒉ (a)** (early, quickly) pronto; **how ~ can you be here?** ¿cuándo puedes llegar?, ¿qué tan pronto puedes llegar? (AmL); **I finished ~er than I expected** terminé antes de lo que esperaba; **not a minute too ~** no antes de tiempo; **to speak too ~** hablar antes de tiempo; **as ~ as possible** lo antes posible, cuanto antes; **the ~er the better** cuanto antes mejor **(b)** (*as conj*): **as ~ as** en cuanto, tan pronto como; **as ~ as you've finished, you can go** en cuanto hayas terminado *or* tan pronto como hayas terminado, te puedes ir; **no ~er had we set out than it began to rain** apenas nos habíamos puesto en camino cuando empezó a llover; **no ~er said than done** dicho y hecho **⒊** (*in phrases*) as soon ... (as): **I'd just as ~ stay at home (as go out)** no me importaría quedarme en casa, tanto me da quedarme en casa (como salir)

soot /sʊt/ *n* hollín *m*

soothe /suːð/ *vt* ⟨*person/nerves*⟩ calmar; ⟨*pain/ cough*⟩ aliviar

soothing /'suːðɪŋ/ *adj* **(a)** ⟨*voice/words*⟩ tranquilizador; ⟨*music/bath*⟩ relajante **(b)** ⟨*ointment/syrup*⟩ balsámico; ⟨*medicine*⟩ calmante

sophisticated /səˈfɪstəkeɪtəd ‖ səˈfɪstɪkeɪtɪd/ *adj* (a) ⟨appearance/person⟩ sofisticado (b) ⟨machine/technique⟩ complejo, altamente desarrollado

sophomore /ˈsɑːfəmɔːr ‖ ˈsɒfəmɔː(r)/ *n* (AmE) estudiante *mf* de segundo curso (*en una universidad o colegio secundario estadounidense*)

sopping[1] /ˈsɑːpɪŋ ‖ ˈsɒpɪŋ/ *adj* empapado

sopping[2] *adv* (as intensifier) ∼ **wet** (of people) calado hasta los huesos; (of clothes) chorreando

soprano[1] /səˈprænəʊ ‖ səˈprɑːnəʊ/ *n* (*pl* **-nos**) soprano *mf*

soprano[2] *adj* ⟨voice/recorder⟩ soprano; ⟨part/ role⟩ de soprano

sorbet /ˈsɔːrbeɪ, ˈsɔːrbət ‖ ˈsɔːbeɪ/ *n* sorbete *m*

sorcerer /ˈsɔːrsərər ‖ ˈsɔːsərə(r)/ *n* (liter) hechicero *m*, brujo *m*

sordid /ˈsɔːrdəd ‖ ˈsɔːdɪd/ *adj* (a) (base) ⟨method/ deal⟩ vergonzoso (b) (squalid) ⟨hotel/conditions⟩ sórdido

sore[1] /sɔːr ‖ sɔː(r)/ *adj* **sorer** /ˈsɔːrər ‖ ˈsɔːrə(r)/, **sorest** /ˈsɔːrəst ‖ ˈsɔːrɪst/ (a) (painful) ⟨finger/foot⟩ dolorido; ⟨eye⟩ irritado; ⟨lips⟩ reseco; **she has a** ∼ **throat** le duele la garganta; **a** ∼ **point/subject** un punto/tema delicado (b) (angry) (AmE colloq) **to be** ∼ **AT** *o* **WITH sb** estar* picado con algn (fam)

sore[2] *n* llaga *f*, úlcera *f*

sorority /səˈrɔːrəti ‖ səˈrɒrəti/ *n* (*pl* **-ties**) (in US) hermandad *f* femenina de estudiantes (*en universidades norteamericanas*)

sorrow /ˈsɑːrəʊ ‖ ˈsɒrəʊ/ *n* pesar *m*, pena *f*

sorrowful /ˈsɑːrəʊfəl ‖ ˈsɒrəʊfəl/ *adj* afligido, triste

sorry /ˈsɑːri ‖ ˈsɒri/ *adj* **-rier, -riest** [1] (*pred*) (a) (grieved, sad): **I'm** ∼ lo siento; **I'm very** ∼, **but I can't help you** lo siento mucho, pero no te puedo ayudar; **to feel** *o* **be** ∼ **FOR sb**: **I feel so** ∼ **for you/him** te/lo compadezco; **to feel** ∼ **for oneself** lamentarse de su (*or* tu *etc*) suerte; **I'm** ∼ **to have to tell you that** ... siento tener que decirte que ...; **to be** ∼ **(THAT)** sentir* QUE (+ *subj*) (b) (apologetic, repentant): **to say** ∼ pedir* perdón, disculparse; **I'm** ∼, **I didn't mean to** ... perdóname *or* lo siento *or* disculpa, no fue mi intención ...; **I'm very sorry, but I can't help you** lo siento mucho, pero no te puedo ayudar; **to be** ∼ **ABOUT sth** arrepentirse* DE algo; **I'm** ∼ **I didn't make it to your party** siento no haber podido ir a tu fiesta [2] (*as interj*) perdón, lo siento [3] (pitiful, miserable) (*before n*) ⟨tale⟩ lamentable; **he was a** ∼ **sight** tenía un aspecto lamentable

sort[1] /sɔːrt ‖ sɔːt/ *n* [1] (kind, type) tipo *m*, clase *f*; **what** ∼ **of car is it?** ¿qué tipo *or* clase de coche es?; **she's not the** ∼ **to let you down** no es de las que te fallan; **a** ∼ **of** *o* ∼ **of a** una especie de; **I didn't say anything of the** ∼ no dije nada semejante [2] (*in phrases*) sort of (colloq): **it's** ∼ **of sad to think of him all alone** da como pena pensar que está solo (fam); **do you want to go? — well,** ∼ **of** ¿quieres ir? — bueno, en cierto modo sí

sort[2] *vt* (a) (classify) ⟨papers/letters⟩ clasificar* (b) (mend) arreglar

■ **sort out** [v + o + adv, v + adv + o] [1] (a) (put in order) ⟨books/photos/desk/room⟩ ordenar; ⟨finances⟩ organizar* (b) (separate out) separar

[2] (a) (arrange) (BrE) ⟨date⟩ fijar; ⟨deal⟩ llegar* a (b) (resolve) ⟨problem/dispute⟩ solucionar; ⟨misunderstanding⟩ aclarar

■ **sort through** [v + prep + o] ⟨papers/files⟩ revisar

SOS *n* S.O.S. *m*

so-so /ˈsəʊsəʊ/ *adj* (colloq) así así (fam)

soufflé /suːˈfleɪ ‖ ˈsuːfleɪ/ *n* suflé *m*

sought /sɔːt/ *past & past p of* SEEK

sought-after /ˈsɔːtæftər ‖ ˈsɔːtˌɑːftə(r)/ *adj* ⟨pred **sought after**⟩ ⟨product⟩ solicitado, en demanda; ⟨prize⟩ codiciado; ⟨area⟩ en demanda

soul /səʊl/ *n* [1] (Relig) alma *f*‡ [2] (person): **I won't tell a** ∼ no se lo diré a nadie; **poor old** ∼! ¡pobrecilla!, ¡pobrecita! [3] ∼ **(music)** soul *m*

soul-destroying /ˈsəʊldɪˈstrɔɪŋ/ *adj* desmoralizador

soulful /ˈsəʊlfəl/ *adj* enternecedor, conmovedor

soul: ∼**mate** *n* alma *f*‡ gemela; ∼**-searching** /ˈsəʊlˈsɜːrtʃɪŋ ‖ ˈsəʊlˌsɜːtʃɪŋ/ *n* introspección *f*

sound[1] /saʊnd/ *n* [1] (noise) sonido *m*; (unpleasant, disturbing) ruido *m*; (*before n*) **the** ∼ **barrier** la barrera del sonido; ∼ **effects** efectos *mpl* sonoros [2] (impression conveyed) (colloq) (*no pl*): **I don't like the** ∼ **of that at all** eso no me huele nada bien; **by** *o* **from the** ∼ **of it, everything's going very well** parece que *or* por lo visto todo marcha muy bien

sound[2] *vi* [1] (a) (give impression) sonar*; **you** ∼ **as if** *o* **as though you could do with a rest** me da la impresión de que no te vendría mal un descanso; **that** ∼**s like Susan now** esa debe (de) ser Susan (b) (seem) parecer*; **how does that** ∼ **to you?** ¿qué te parece?; **it** ∼**s as if** *o* **as though you had a great time** parece que lo pasaste fenomenal [2] (make noise, resound) «bell/alarm» sonar*

■ ∼ *vt* ⟨trumpet/horn⟩ tocar*, hacer* sonar

■ **sound out** [v + o + adv, v + adv + o] tantear, sondear

sound[3] *adj* **-er, -est** [1] (a) (healthy) sano; **being of** ∼ **mind** (estando) en pleno uso de sus facultades (b) (in good condition) ⟨basis/foundation⟩ sólido, firme; ⟨timber⟩ en buenas condiciones [2] (valid) ⟨reasoning/knowledge⟩ sólido; ⟨advice/ decision⟩ sensato

sound[4] *adv* **-er, -est**: ∼ **asleep** profundamente dormido

sound bite *n* (Journ, Pol) frase *f* corta (*que suena bien en los titulares y en los discursos*)

soundly /ˈsaʊndli/ *adv* [1] ⟨sleep⟩ profundamente [2] (solidly, validly) sólidamente

soundproof[1] /ˈsaʊndpruːf/ *adj* insonorizado

soundproof[2] *vt* insonorizar*

sound: ∼ **system** *n* equipo *m* de sonido; ∼**track** *n* banda *f* sonora

soup /suːp/ *n* sopa *f*; **clear** ∼ caldo *m*, consomé *m*

sour[1] /saʊər ‖ saʊə(r)/ *adj* **sourer, sourest** (a) (sharp, acid) ácido, agrio (b) (spoiled) ⟨milk⟩ agrio, cortado (c) (bad-tempered, disagreeable) agrio, avinagrado

sour[2] *vt* ⟨relationship/occasion⟩ amargar*

source /sɔːrs ‖ sɔːs/ *n* [1] (origin, supply) fuente *f*;

(of river) nacimiento *m*; **~ of income** fuente de
ingresos **2** (providing information) **(a)** (person) (journ)
fuente *f* **(b)** (text, document) fuente *f*
sourdough /'saʊərdəʊ ‖'saʊədəʊ/ *n* (AmE)
masa *f* fermentada (*para hacer pan*)
south¹ /saʊθ/ *n* (point of the compass, direction) sur
m; **the ~, the S~** (region) el sur
south² *adj* (before *n*) sur *adj inv*, meridional;
⟨wind⟩ del sur
south³ *adv* al sur
South Africa *n* Sudáfrica *f*, Suráfrica *f*
South African *adj* sudafricano, surafricano
South America *n* América *f* del Sur *or* del
Sud, Sudamérica *f*, Suramérica *f*
South American¹ *adj* sudamericano,
suramericano
South American² *n* sudamericano, -na *m,f*,
suramericano, -na *m,f*
southbound /'saʊθbaʊnd/ *adj* ⟨traffic/train⟩
que va (*or* iba *etc*) hacia el sur *or* en dirección
sur
southeast¹, Southeast /'saʊθ'i:st/ *n* **the ~**
el sudeste *or* Sudeste, el sureste *or* Sureste
southeast² *adj* sudeste *adj inv*, sureste *adj
inv*, del sudeste *or* sureste, sudoriental
southeast³ *adv* hacia el sudeste *or* sureste,
en dirección sudeste *or* sureste
south: ~easterly /'saʊθ'i:stərli ‖,saʊθ'i:stəli/
adj ⟨wind⟩ del sudeste *or* sureste; **~eastern**
/'saʊθ'i:stərn ‖,saʊθ'i:stən/ *adj* sudeste *adj inv*,
sureste *adj inv*, del sudeste *or* sureste,
sudoriental
southerly /'sʌðərli ‖'sʌðəli/ *adj* ⟨wind⟩ del
sur; ⟨latitude⟩ sur *adj inv*; **in a ~ direction** hacia
el sur, en dirección sur
southern /'sʌðərn ‖'sʌðən/ *adj* ⟨region⟩ del
sur, meridional, sur *adj inv*; ⟨country⟩ del sur,
meridional; **~ Italy** el sur de Italia; **the ~ states**
(in US) los estados del sur
southward¹ /'saʊθwərd ‖'saʊθwəd/ *adj*
(before *n*): **in a ~ direction** hacia el sur, en
dirección sur
southward², (BrE also) **southwards** /-z/ *adv*
hacia el sur
southwest¹, Southwest /'saʊθ'west/ *n* **the
~** el sudoeste *or* Sudoeste, el suroeste *or*
Suroeste
southwest² *adj* sudoeste *adj inv*, suroeste *adj
inv*, del sudoeste *or* suroeste
southwest³ *adv* hacia el sudoeste *or* suroeste,
en dirección sudoeste *or* suroeste
south: ~westerly /'saʊθ'westərli
‖,saʊθ'westəli/ *adj* ⟨wind⟩ del sudoeste *or*
suroeste; **~western** /'saʊθ'westərn
‖,saʊθ'westən/ *adj* sudoccidental, sudoeste *adj
inv*, suroeste *adj inv*, del sudoeste *or* suroeste
souvenir /'su:vənɪr ‖,su:və'nɪə(r)/ *n* recuerdo
m, souvenir *m*
sovereign¹ /'sɑːvrən ‖'sɒvrɪn/ *n* **1** (monarch)
soberano, -na *m,f* **2** (coin) soberano *m*, libra *f* (de
oro)
sovereign² *adj* soberano
sovereignty /'sɑːvrənti ‖'sɒvrənti/ *n*
soberanía *f*
Soviet /'səʊviet, 'sɑːviət ‖'səʊviət/ *adj* (Hist)
soviético

Soviet Union *n* (Hist) **the ~** la Unión
Soviética
sow¹ /səʊ/ *vt/i* (past **sowed**; *past p* **sowed** *or*
sown) sembrar*
sow² /saʊ/ *n* cerda *f*, puerca *f*
sown /səʊn/ *past p of* sow¹
soy /sɔɪ/, (BrE) **soya** /'sɔɪə/ *n* soya *f* (AmL), soja *f*
(Esp)
soy: ~ bean, (BrE) **soya bean** *n* soya *f* (AmL),
soja *f* (Esp); **~ sauce** *n* salsa *f* de soya (AmL) *or*
(Esp) soja
spa /spɑː/ *n* **(a)** (resort) balneario *m* **(b)** (spring)
manantial *m* (*de agua mineral*) **(c)** (health club)
(AmE) gimnasio *m*
space¹ /speɪs/ *n* **1** **(a)** (Phys) espacio *m* **(b)**
(Aerosp) espacio *m*; (before *n*) ⟨station/program⟩
espacial **2** **(a)** (room) espacio *m*, lugar *m* **(b)**
(empty area) espacio *m*; **let's clear a ~ for it first**
hagámosle (un) sitio primero **3** (of time) (*no pl*)
espacio *m*; **in the ~ of one hour** en el espacio *or*
lapso de una hora **4** (Print) espacio *m*
space² *vt* **~ (out)** espaciar
space: ~-age *adj* ⟨technology⟩ futurista,
espacial; **~craft** *n* (*pl* **~craft**) nave *f* espacial;
~man /'speɪsmæn/ *n* (*pl* **-men** /-men/)
astronauta *m*, cosmonauta *m*; **~ship** *n* nave *f*
espacial, astronave *f*
spacing /'speɪsɪŋ/ *n* (Print) espaciado *m*
spacious /'speɪʃəs/ *adj* ⟨house/room⟩ amplio,
espacioso; ⟨park⟩ grande, extenso
spade /speɪd/ *n* **1** (tool) pala *f*; **to call a ~ a ~**
llamar al pan, pan y al vino, vino **2** (Games)
spades *pl* (suit) (+ *sing or pl vb*) picas *fpl*
spaghetti /spə'geti/ *n* espaguetis *mpl*,
spaghetti *mpl*
Spain /speɪn/ *n* España *f*
span¹ /spæn/ *n* **(a)** (of hand) palmo *m*; (of wing)
envergadura *f*; (of bridge, arch) luz *f* **(b)** (part of
bridge) arco *m* **(c)** (of time) lapso *m*; ▶ LIFE SPAN
span² *vt* **-nn-** **(a)** (extend over) abarcar* **(b)**
(cross) ⟨bridge⟩ ⟨river⟩ extenderse* sobre
Spaniard /'spænjərd ‖'spænjəd/ *n* español,
-ñola *m,f*
spaniel /'spænjəl/ *n* spaniel *m*
Spanish¹ /'spænɪʃ/ *adj* español; ⟨language⟩
castellano, español
Spanish² *n* **(a)** (language) castellano *m*, español
m **(b)** (people) (+ *pl vb*) **the ~** los españoles
Spanish omelet, (BrE) **Spanish
omelette** *n* tortilla *f* de papas *or* (Esp) patatas,
tortilla *f* española
spank /spæŋk/ *vt* pegarle* a (*en las nalgas*)
spanner /'spænər ‖'spænə(r)/ *n* (BrE) (adjustable
~) llave *f* inglesa; (box **~**) llave *f* de tubo; **to
throw a ~ in the works** fastidiarlo todo
spar¹ /spɑːr ‖spɑː(r)/ *n* (Naut) palo *m*
spar² *vi* **-rr-** (in boxing) entrenarse; (argue)
discutir
spare¹ /sper ‖speə(r)/ *adj* **(a)** (not in use)
⟨umbrella/pen⟩ de más; **have you got any ~
paper?** ¿tienes un poco de papel que no te haga
falta? **(b)** (before *n*) ⟨key/cartridge⟩ de repuesto
(c) (free) libre; **if you've got a ~ minute** si tienes
un minuto (libre)
spare² *n*: **I'll take a ~ just in case** llevaré uno
de repuesto por si acaso

S

spare³ vt ⟦1⟧ **(a)** (do without): can you ∼ your dictionary for a moment? ¿me permites el diccionario un momento, si no lo necesitas?; **if you can ∼ the time** si tienes or dispones de tiempo **(b)** (give) **to ∼ (sb) sth: can you ∼ me a pound?** ¿tienes una libra que me prestes/des?; **can you ∼ me a few minutes?** ¿tienes unos minutos? **(c)** to spare (as adj): **there's food to ∼** hay comida de sobra; **have you got a few minutes to ∼?** ¿tienes unos minutos?
⟦2⟧ **(a)** (keep from using, stint) (usu neg): **to ∼ no effort** no escatimar esfuerzos; **to ∼ no expense** no reparar en gastos **(b)** (save, relieve) **to ∼ sb sth** ⟨trouble/embarrassment⟩ ahorrarle algo a algn **(c)** (show mercy, consideration toward) perdonar

spare: ∼ **part** n repuesto m or (Méx) refacción f; ∼ **room** n cuarto m de huéspedes or (Esp) de los invitados, recámara f de visitas (Méx); ∼ **time** n tiempo m libre; ∼ **tire,** (BrE) ∼ **tyre** n rueda f de repuesto or (Esp tb) de recambio, llanta f de refacción (Méx)

sparingly /'speɪrɪŋli ‖ 'speərɪŋli/ adv ⟨use⟩ con moderación

spark¹ /spɑːrk ‖ spɑːk/ n chispa f

spark² vt, (BrE also) **spark off** ⟨rioting/revolution⟩ hacer* estallar; ⟨interest⟩ suscitar; ⟨criticism⟩ provocar*

sparking plug /'spɑːrkɪŋ ‖ 'spɑːkɪŋ/ n (BrE) ▶ SPARK PLUG

sparkle¹ /'spɑːrkəl ‖ 'spɑːkəl/ vi ⟨gem/glass⟩ centellear, destellar, brillar; ⟨eyes⟩ brillar

sparkle² n **(a)** (no pl) (of gem, glass) destello m, brillo m; (of eyes) brillo m **(b)** (animation) chispa f, brillo m

sparkler /'spɑːrklər ‖ 'spɑːklə(r)/ n (firework) luz f de Bengala, bengala f

sparkling /'spɑːrklɪŋ ‖ 'spɑːklɪŋ/ adj **(a)** (shining) ⟨gems/stars⟩ centelleante; ⟨eyes⟩ chispeante **(b)** ⟨wit/conversation⟩ chispeante **(c)** (effervescent) ⟨wine⟩ espumoso

spark plug n bujía f, chispero m (AmC)

sparrow /'spærəʊ/ n gorrión m

sparse /spɑːrs ‖ spɑːs/ adj ⟨population/vegetation/furniture⟩ escaso; ⟨beard/hair⟩ ralo

sparsely /'spɑːrsli ‖ 'spɑːsli/ adv: **the area was ∼ populated** la zona estaba escasamente poblada; **the room is ∼ furnished** la habitación tiene pocos muebles

spartan /'spɑːrtn̩ ‖ 'spɑːtn̩/ adj espartano

spasm /'spæzəm/ n espasmo m

spasmodic /spæz'mɑːdɪk ‖ spæz'mɒdɪk/ adj **(a)** ⟨growth/activity⟩ irregular **(b)** (Med) ⟨pain/cough⟩ espasmódico

spat /spæt/ past & past p of SPIT²

spate /speɪt/ n racha f, serie f; **to be in (full) ∼** (BrE) ⟨river⟩ estar* crecido

spatial /'speɪʃəl/ adj (before n) espacial

spatter /'spætər ‖ 'spætə(r)/ vt/i salpicar*

spatula /'spætʃələ ‖ 'spætjʊlə/ n **(a)** (Culin) (for turning, serving) pala f (de servir); (for scraping out bowls) espátula f **(b)** (Pharm, Med) espátula f

spawn¹ /spɔːn/ n (of fish) hueva(s) f(pl); (of frogs) huevas fpl

spawn² vt (journ) generar, producir*
■ ∼ vi «frogs/fish» desovar

SPCA n (in US) (= **Society for the Prevention of Cruelty to Animals**) ≈ Asociación f protectora de animales

SPCC n (in US) (= **Society for the Prevention of Cruelty to Children**) ≈ Asociación f de protección a la infancia

speak /spiːk/ (past **spoke**; past p **spoken**) vi ⟦1⟧ **(a)** (say sth) hablar; **to ∼ TO** o (esp AmE) **WITH sb** hablar CON algn, hablarle A algn; **they are not ∼ing** (to each other) no se hablan; **to ∼ OF sth/sb/-ING** hablar DE algo/algn/+ INF; **so to ∼** por así decirlo **(b)** (on telephone): **hello, Barbara Mason ∼ing ...** buenas tardes, habla or (Esp tb) soy Barbara Mason; **could I ∼ to Mrs Hodges, please? — ∼ing!** ¿podría hablar con la Sra. Hodges, por favor? — con ella (habla) or (Esp tb) soy yo
⟦2⟧ (make speech) hablar; **to ∼ ON** o **ABOUT sth** hablar ACERCA DE or SOBRE algo
■ ∼ vt **(a)** (say, declare): **nobody spoke a word** nadie dijo nada; **to ∼ one's mind** hablar claro; **to ∼ the truth** decir* la verdad **(b)** ⟨language⟩ hablar
■ **speak for** [v + prep + o] hablar por; **we'd love to meet him — ∼ for yourself!** nos encantaría conocerlo — ¡eso lo dirás por ti!; **the facts ∼ for themselves** los hechos son elocuentes
■ **speak out** [v + adv]: **to ∼ out AGAINST sth** denunciar algo
■ **speak up** [v + adv] **(a)** (speak loudly, clearly) hablar más fuerte or más alto **(b)** (speak boldly) decir* lo que se piensa; **to ∼ up FOR sb** defender* a algn

speaker /'spiːkər ‖ 'spiːkə(r)/ n ⟦1⟧ **(a)** (in public) orador, -dora m,f **(b)** (of language) hablante mf **(c)** (Govt) presidente, -ta m,f ⟦2⟧ (Audio) **(a)** (loudspeaker) altavoz m, (alto)parlante m (AmS) **(b)** (of hi-fi) baf(f)le m, parlante m (AmS)

speaking /'spiːkɪŋ/ n (before n): **a good ∼ voice** una voz muy clara (or potente etc); **to be on ∼ terms with sb** estar* en buenas relaciones con algn

-speaking /ˌspiːkɪŋ/ suff -hablante, -parlante; **Spanish∼** hispanohablante, hispanoparlante; **French∼** francófono; **English∼** de habla inglesa

spear¹ /spɪr ‖ spɪə(r)/ n **(a)** (weapon) lanza f **(b)** (for fishing) arpón m

spear² vt ⟨fish⟩ arponear

spear: ∼**head** vt (Mil) encabezar*; ∼**mint** n menta f verde

spec /spek/ n: **on ∼** (colloq) por si acaso

special /'speʃəl/ adj **(a)** (exceptional) (before n) ⟨favor/request⟩ especial **(b)** (for specific purpose) (before n) ⟨arrangements/fund⟩ especial **(c)** (particular, individual) especial, particular; **children with ∼ needs** (Educ) niños que requieren una atención diferenciada

AmC Central America	Arg Argentina	Cu Cuba	Per Peru
AmL Latin America	Bol Bolivia	Ec Ecuador	RPI River Plate Area
AmS South America	Chi Chile	Esp Spain	Ur Uruguay
Andes Andean Region	CS Southern Cone	Méx Mexico	Ven Venezuela

special: ~ delivery n correo m exprés or expreso; **~ effects** pl n efectos mpl especiales

specialist /'speʃələst ‖'speʃəlɪst/ n especialista mf; (before n) ⟨knowledge/shop⟩ especializado

speciality /'speʃi'æləti/ n (pl **-ties**) (BrE) ▶ SPECIALTY[1]

specialize /'speʃəlaɪz/ vi to ~ (IN sth) especializarse* (EN algo)

specialized /'speʃəlaɪzd/ adj especializado

specially /'speʃəli/ adv (a) (specifically) especialmente, expresamente (b) (especially) ⟨long/difficult⟩ particularmente

specialty[1] /'speʃəlti/ n (pl **-ties**) especialidad f

specialty[2] adj (AmE) (before n: no comp) ⟨merchandise/store⟩ especializado

species /'spi:ʃi:z/ n (pl ~) especie f

specific /spɪ'sɪfɪk ‖spə'sɪfɪk/ adj (a) (particular, individual) específico; ⟨example⟩ concreto (b) (exact, precise) preciso

specifically /spɪ'sɪfɪkli/ adv (a) ⟨state/mention⟩ explícitamente (b) ⟨built/designed⟩ específicamente

specification /'spesəfə'keɪʃən ‖,spesɪfɪ'keɪʃən/ n (often pl) especificación f

specify /'spesəfaɪ ‖'spesɪfaɪ/ vt **-fies, -fying, -fied** especificar*

specimen /'spesəmən ‖'spesɪmən/ n (a) (sample — of rock, plant, tissue) muestra f, espécimen m; (— of blood, urine) muestra f; (— of work, handwriting) muestra f (b) (individual example) ejemplar m, espécimen m

speck /spek/ n (of dust) mota f; (in distance) punto m; (dirt stain) manchita f

speckle /'spekəl/vt (usu pass) motear; **a ~d hen** una gallina pinta or (RPl) bataraza

spectacle /'spektəkəl ‖'spektəkəl/ n [1] (show, sight) espectáculo m [2] **spectacles** pl gafas fpl, anteojos mpl (esp AmL), lentes mpl (esp AmL)

spectacular /spek'tækjələr ‖spek'tækjʊlə(r)/ adj espectacular

spectator /'spekteɪtər ‖spek'teɪtə(r)/ n espectador, -dora m,f

specter, (BrE) **spectre** /'spektər ‖'spektə(r)/ n (liter) espectro m

spectra /'spektrə/ pl of SPECTRUM

spectre /'spektər/ n (BrE) ▶ SPECTER

spectrum /'spektrəm/ n (pl **-tra**) [1] (Opt, Phys) espectro m [2] (range) espectro m, gama f; **the political ~** el espectro político

speculate /'spekjəleɪt ‖'spekjʊleɪt/ vi [1] (Fin) especular [2] (guess, conjecture) to ~ (ON o ABOUT sth) hacer* conjeturas or especular (SOBRE algo)

speculation /'spekjə'leɪʃən ‖,spekjʊ'leɪʃən/ n especulación f

speculative /'spekjələtɪv/ adj especulativo

sped /sped/ past & past p of SPEED[2] vi A

speech /spi:tʃ/ n [1] (a) (act, faculty) habla f‡ (b) (manner of speaking) forma f de hablar (c) (language, dialect) habla f‡ [2] (a) (oration) discurso m; **to make a ~** dar* un discurso (b) (Theat) parlamento m

speechless /'spi:tʃləs ‖'spi:tʃlɪs/ adj: **she was ~ with rage** enmudeció de rabia; **I'm ~!** no sé qué decir

speech therapy n foniatría f, logopedia f

speed[1] /spi:d/ n [1] (a) (rate of movement, progress) velocidad f (b) (relative quickness) rapidez f [2] (Phot): **film ~** sensibilidad f de la película; **shutter ~** tiempo m de exposición [3] (gear) velocidad f, marcha f [4] (amphetamine) (sl) anfetas fpl (fam)

speed[2] vi (a) (past & past p **sped**) (go, pass quickly) (+ adv compl): **to ~ off** o **away** alejarse a toda velocidad; **he sped by** o **past in his new sports car** nos pasó a toda velocidad con su nuevo coche deportivo; **the hours sped by** las horas pasaron volando (b) (past & past p **speeded**) (drive too fast) ir* a velocidad excesiva ■ ~ vt (past & past p **speeded**) (hasten) acelerar ■ **speed up** (past & past p **speeded**) [1] [v + adv] (a) (move faster) ⟨⟨vehicle/driver⟩⟩ acelerar; ⟨⟨walker⟩⟩ apretar* el paso (b) ⟨⟨process/production⟩⟩ acelerarse [2] [v + o + adv, v + adv + o] (a) ⟨vehicle⟩ acelerar (b) ⟨work/production⟩ acelerar

speed: ~boat n (lancha f) motora f; **~ bump** n badén m, guardia m tumbado (Esp), tope m (Méx), policía m acostado (Col), lomo m de burro (RPl), baden m (Chi); **~ camera** n cámara f de control de velocidad; **~ dating** n cita f flash, speed dating m; **~ limit** n velocidad f máxima, límite m de velocidad

speedometer /spɪ'dɑ:mətər ‖spiː'dɒmɪtə(r)/ n velocímetro m, indicador m de velocidad

speedway /'spi:dweɪ/ n (a) (sport) carreras fpl de motocicletas (b) (AmE Transp) autopista f

speedy /'spi:di/ adj **-dier, -diest** ⟨reply/delivery⟩ rápido; ⟨solution⟩ pronto, rápido

spell[1] /spel/ n [1] (magic ~) encanto m, hechizo m, encantamiento m; **evil ~** maleficio m; **to cast a ~ over** o **to put a ~ on sth/sb** hechizar* or embrujar algo/a algn [2] (a) (of weather) período m (b) (of work, activity) período m, temporada f; **a bad ~** una mala racha

spell[2] (past & past p **spelled** or (BrE also) **spelt**) vt [1] (write) escribir*; (orally) deletrear; **how do you ~ Zimbabwe?** ¿cómo se escribe Zimbabwe?; **could you ~ it for me?** ¿me lo deletrea? [2] (mean) significar*; (foretell) anunciar ■ ~ vi: **he can't ~** tiene mala ortografía ■ **spell out** [v + o + adv, v + adv + o] (a) ⟨word⟩ deletrear (b) (explain) explicar* en detalle

spell: ~binding adj ⟨speech/film⟩ fascinante; **~bound** adj embelesado, maravillado; **~checker** n (Comput) corrector m ortográfico

spelling /'spelɪŋ/ n (a) (system, ability) ortografía f; **to be good/bad at ~** tener* buena/mala ortografía; (before n) ~ **mistake** falta f de ortografía, error m ortográfico (b) (of a word) grafía f, ortografía f

spelt /spelt/ (BrE) past & past p of SPELL[2]

spelunking /spɪ'lʌŋkɪŋ/ n (AmE) espeleología f

spend /spend/ vt (past & past p **spent**) [1] (a) ⟨money⟩ gastar (b) (expend) **to ~ sth** (ON sth) dedicarle* algo A algo; **don't ~ too long on each question** no le dediquen mucho tiempo a cada pregunta [2] (pass) ⟨period of time⟩ pasar [3] (exhaust) agotar

S

spending /'spendɪŋ/ n gastos mpl; **public** ∼ el gasto público; (before n) ∼ **power** poder m adquisitivo

spending money n dinero m para gastos personales

spendthrift /'spendθrɪft/ n despilfarrador, -dora m,f

spent /spent/ past & past p of SPEND

sperm /spɜːrm ‖spɜːm/ n (pl ∼ or ∼s) (a) (seminal liquid) esperma m or f (b) (gamete) espermatozoide m, espermatozoo m

spew /spjuː/ vi (a) «water» salir* a borbotones (b) (vomit) (BrE sl) vomitar, lanzar* (fam) ∎ ∼ vt ‹lava/flames› arrojar

sphere /sfɪr ‖sfɪə(r)/ n esfera f

spherical /'sfɪrɪkəl ‖'sferɪkəl/ adj esférico

Sphinx /sfɪŋks/ n the ∼ la Esfinge

spice¹ /spaɪs/ n (a) (seasoning) especia f (b) (zest, interest) sabor m

spice² vt (Culin) (often pass) condimentar, sazonar* (b) (add excitement to): **to** ∼ **up a story** darle* más sabor a un relato

spick-and-span /ˌspɪkən'spæn/ adj colloq (pred) limpio y ordenado

spicy /'spaɪsi/ adj -cier, -ciest (a) ‹sauce/food› (with spices) con muchas especias; (hot, peppery) picante (b) (racy) ‹story/account› sabroso; (with sexual connotations) picante

spider /'spaɪdər ‖'spaɪdə(r)/ n araña f

spike¹ /spaɪk/ n ① (pointed object) punta f, púa f, pincho m or (Arg) pinche m; (on track shoes) clavo m or (Chi, Ven) púa f or (Col) carramplón m ② **spikes** pl (running shoes) zapatillas fpl de clavos or (Chi, Ven) de púas or (Col) con carramplones, picos mpl (Méx)

spike² vt ① (pierce) pinchar, clavar ② (add sth to) (colloq): **they** ∼**d his lemonade with vodka** le echaron vodka en la limonada

spiky /'spaɪki/ adj -kier, -kiest (a) (having spikes) con puntas or púas or pinchos (b) (sharp, pointed) puntiagudo, puntudo (Col, CS) (c) ‹hair› de punta

spill /spɪl/ (past & past p spilled or spilt /spɪlt/) vt ‹liquid› derramar, verter*; (knock over) volcar* ∎ ∼ vi «liquid» derramarse; **people** ∼**ed (out) into the streets** la gente se volcó or se echó a las calles ∎ **spill over** [v + adv] «container» desbordarse; «liquid» rebosar; «fighting/conflict» extenderse*

spillage /'spɪlɪdʒ/ n vertido m, derrame m

spilt /spɪlt/ past & past p of SPILL

spin¹ /spɪn/ n ① (on ball) (Sport) efecto m, chanfle m (AmL) ② (a) (of aircraft) barrena f (b) (Auto) trompo m ③ (ride) (colloq): **to go for a** ∼ ir* a dar un paseo en coche (or en moto etc), ir* a dar un garbeo (Esp fam)

spin² (pres p **spinning**; past & past p **spun**) vt ① ‹wheel/top› hacer* girar ② (a) ‹wool/cotton› hilar (b) ‹web› tejer ∎ ∼ vi ① (a) (rotate) «wheel/top» girar; **my head is** ∼**ning** la cabeza me da vueltas (b) «washing machine» centrifugar* (c) (move rapidly) (+ adv compl): **the car spun out of control** el coche giró fuera de control ② (Tex) hilar

spin out [v + o + adv, v + adv + o] ‹money› estirar; ‹vacation/story› alargar*, prolongar*

spina bifida /ˌspaɪnə'bɪfədə ‖ˌspaɪnə'bɪfɪdə/ n espina f bífida

spinach /'spɪnɪtʃ ‖'spɪnɪdʒ, -ɪtʃ/ n (Bot) espinaca f, (Culin) espinaca(s) f(pl)

spinal /'spaɪnl/ adj de la columna vertebral

spinal: ∼ **column** n columna f vertebral; ∼ **cord** n médula f espinal

spindle /'spɪndl/ n (a) (Mech Eng) eje m (b) (Tex) huso m

spindly /'spɪndli/ adj -dlier, -dliest ‹legs› largo y flaco; ‹plant› alto y débil

spin: ∼ **doctor** n (esp Pol) portavoz mf (contratado para dar a la prensa, TV, etc, una interpretación favorable de los hechos); ∼ **drier** n centrifugadora f (de ropa); ∼-**dry** /'spɪn'draɪ/ vt -**dries, -drying, -dried** centrifugar*; ∼ **dryer** n ▶ ⟶ DRIER

spine /spaɪn/ n ① (a) (Anat) columna f (vertebral) (b) (of book) lomo m ② (on animal) púa f; (on plant) espina f

spine-chilling /'spaɪnˌtʃɪlɪŋ/ adj espeluznante

spineless /'spaɪnləs ‖'spaɪnlɪs/ adj (a) (cowardly, weak) débil, sin carácter (b) (Zool) invertebrado

spinning /'spɪnɪŋ/ n (Tex) hilado m

spinning wheel n rueca f

spin-off /'spɪnɔːf ‖'spɪnɒf/ n (product) producto m derivado; (result) resultado m indirecto

spinster /'spɪnstər ‖'spɪnstə(r)/ n soltera f

spiral¹ /'spaɪrəl ‖'spaɪərəl/ n (a) (shape, movement) espiral f (b) (of smoke) voluta f, espiral f

spiral² adj ‹shape› de espiral, acaracolado; ∼ **staircase** escalera f de caracol

spiral³ vi, (BrE) -ll- «unemployment» escalar; «prices» dispararse

spire /spaɪr ‖'spaɪə(r)/ n aguja f, chapitel m

spirit /'spɪrət ‖'spɪrɪt/ n ① (a) (life force, soul) espíritu m (b) (Occult) espíritu m ② (vigor, courage) espíritu m, temple m; **to break sb's** ∼ quebrantarle el espíritu a algn ③ (mental attitude, mood) (no pl) espíritu m; **the party/Christmas** ∼ el espíritu festivo/navideño ④ **spirits** pl (emotional state): **to be in good** ∼**s** estar* animado; **keep your** ∼**s up** ¡arriba ese ánimo! ⑤ **spirits** pl (alcohol) bebidas fpl alcohólicas (de alta graduación), licores mpl

spirited /'spɪrətəd ‖'spɪrɪtɪd/ adj ‹horse/child› brioso; ‹reply› enérgico; ‹defense› ardiente

spirit level n nivel m (de burbuja or de aire)

spiritual¹ /'spɪrɪtʃuəl ‖'spɪrɪtjuəl/ adj espiritual

spiritual² n (negro ∼) espiritual m (negro)

spiritualism /'spɪrɪtʃuəlɪzəm ‖'spɪrɪtjuəlɪzəm/ n (Occult) espiritismo m; (Phil) espiritualismo m

spit¹ /spɪt/ n ① (saliva) saliva f ② (for roasting) asador m (en forma de varilla), espetón m

spit² vi (pres p **spitting**; past & past p **spat** or (AmE esp) **spit**) (a) ‹person/animal› escupir; **to** ∼ **AT sb** escupirle A algn; ▶ IMAGE (b) «fire/fat» chisporrotear (c) «cat» bufar ∎ ∼ vt (past & past p **spat**) ‹food/blood› escupir

■ ~ *v impers* (colloq): **it's** ~**ting** caen algunas gotas (de lluvia), está chispeando (fam)

■ **spit out** [*v* + *o* + *adv*, *v* + *adv* + *o*] escupir

spite¹ /spaɪt/ *n* **1** (malice) maldad *f*; (resentment) rencor *m*, resentimiento *m* **2** **in spite of** (*as prep*) a pesar de

spite² *vt* molestar, fastidiar

spiteful /'spaɪtfəl/ *adj* ⟨remark⟩ malicioso; ⟨person⟩ malo; (resentful) rencoroso

spittle /'spɪtl/ *n* baba *f*

splash¹ /splæʃ/ *n* **1** (a) (spray) salpicadura *f* (b) (sound): **we heard a** ~ oímos el ruido de algo al caer al agua (c) (paddle, swim) (*no pl*) chapuzón *m* **2** (a) (of milk, paint) (*no pl*) **a** ~ un poco (b) (mark, patch) salpicadura *f*, manchón *m*

splash² *vt* salpicar*; **to** ~ **sth/sb WITH sth** salpicar* algo/a algn DE algo

■ ~ *vi* (a) ⟨water/paint⟩ salpicar* (b) ⟨person/animal⟩ chapotear

■ **splash out** (BrE colloq) [*v* + *adv*] darse* un lujo; **to** ~ **out ON sth** gastar(se) un dineral EN algo (fam)

splashguard /'splæʃɡɑːrd ‖'splæʃɡɑːd/ *n* (AmE) guardabarros *m*, salpicadera *f* (Méx), tapabarros *m* (Chi, Per)

splatter /'splætər ‖'splætə(r)/ *vt/i* ▶ SPATTER

splay /spleɪ/ *vt* ~ (**out**) ⟨fingers⟩ abrir*, separar; **to** ~ **one's legs** abrirse* de piernas

spleen /spliːn/ *n* (Anat) bazo *m*

splendid /'splendəd ‖'splendɪd/ *adj* (a) (very good) ⟨idea/opportunity/meal⟩ espléndido (b) (imposing) ⟨clothes/building⟩ magnífico; ⟨ceremony⟩ lleno de esplendor

splendor, (BrE) **splendour** /'splendər ‖'splendə(r)/ *n* esplendor *m*

splice /splaɪs/ *vt* ~ (**together**) ⟨ropes⟩ coser; ⟨tape/film⟩ unir

splint /splɪnt/ *n* tablilla *f*

splinter¹ /'splɪntər ‖'splɪntə(r)/ *n* (of wood) astilla *f*; (of glass, bone, metal) esquirla *f*, astilla *f*; (*before n*) ~ **group** grupo *m* escindido

splinter² *vi* (a) (break into pieces) ⟨wood/bone⟩ astillarse (b) ⟨political party/society⟩ escindirse

■ ~ *vt* ⟨wood/bone⟩ astillar

split¹ /splɪt/ *n* **1** (a) (in garment, cloth — in seam) descosido *m*; (— part of design) abertura *f*, raja *f* (b) (in wood, glass) rajadura *f*, grieta *f* **2** (a) (Pol) escisión *f*; (Relig) cisma *m*, escisión *f* (b) (breakup) ruptura *f*, separación *f* **3** **splits** *pl*: **to do the** ~**s** abrirse* completamente de piernas, hacer* el spagat (Esp)

split² *adj* **1** (damaged) ⟨wood⟩ rajado, partido; ⟨lip⟩ partido **2** (a) (divided): ~ **personality** doble personalidad *f*; ~ **shift** horario *m* (de trabajo) partido (b) (in factions) dividido

split³ (*pres p* **splitting**; *past & past p* **split**) *vt* **1** (a) (break) ⟨wood/stone⟩ partir; **to** ~ **the atom** fisionar el átomo (b) (burst) ⟨pants/trousers⟩ reventar* (c) (divide into factions) ⟨nation/church⟩ dividir

2 (divide, share) ⟨cost/food⟩ dividir

■ ~ *vi* **1** (crack, burst) ⟨wood/rock⟩ partirse, rajarse; ⟨leather/seam⟩ abrirse*, romperse*; **I've got a** ~**ting headache** tengo un dolor de cabeza espantoso

2 ⟨political party/church⟩ dividirse, escindirse **3** (leave) (sl) abrirse* (arg), largarse* (fam)

■ **split away, split off** [*v* + *adv*] **to** ~ **away** *o* **off FROM sth** escindirse *or* separarse DE algo

■ **split up** **1** [*v* + *adv*] ⟨couple/band⟩ separarse; ⟨crowd⟩ dispersarse

2 [*v* + *o* + *adv*, *v* + *adv* + *o*] ⟨wrestlers/boxers⟩ separar; ⟨lovers⟩ hacer* que se separen; ~ **them up into groups** divídelos en grupos

split: ~ **end** *n* (of hair): **I've got** ~ **ends** tengo las puntas abiertas *or* (CS) florecidas, tengo horquillas (Col) *or* (Méx) orzuela *or* (Ven) horquetillas; ~**-level** /'splɪt'levəl/ *adj* ⟨apartment⟩ en dos niveles; ~ **second** *n* fracción *f* de segundo; (*before n*) ~**-second timing** sincronización *f* perfecta

splutter /'splʌtər ‖'splʌtə(r)/ *vi* (a) ⟨fire/fat⟩ chisporrotear; ⟨engine⟩ resoplar (b) ⟨person⟩ resoplar; (in anger, embarrassment etc) farfullar

spoil /spɔɪl/ (*past & past p* **spoiled** *or* (BrE also) **spoilt**) *vt* **1** ⟨party/surprise⟩ echar a perder, estropear; **I don't want to** ~ **your fun but ...** no les quiero aguar la fiesta pero ...; **it will** ~ **your appetite** te quitará el apetito **2** (overindulge) ⟨child⟩ consentir*, malcriar*; **to be** ~**ed for choice** tener* mucho de donde elegir

■ ~ *vi* **1** ⟨food/meal⟩ echarse a perder, estropearse **2** (be eager) (colloq): **to be** ~**ing for a fight** estar* *or* andar* buscando pelea

spoiled /spɔɪld/, (BrE also) **spoilt** /spɔɪlt/ *adj* mimado

spoils /spɔɪlz/ *pl n* botín *m*

spoilsport /'spɔɪlspɔːrt ‖'spɔɪlspɔːt/ *n* (colloq) aguafiestas *mf* (fam)

spoilt¹ /spɔɪlt/ (BrE) *past & past p of* SPOIL

spoilt² *adj* (BrE) ▶ SPOILED

spoke¹ /spəʊk/ *n* rayo *m* (de una rueda)

spoke² *past of* SPEAK

spoken¹ /'spəʊkən/ *past p of* SPEAK

spoken² *adj* (*before n*) hablado, oral

spokesman /'spəʊksmən/ *n* (*pl* **-men** /-mən/) portavoz *m*, vocero *m* (esp AmL)

spokesperson /'spəʊks,pɜːrsn̩ ‖'spəʊks,pɜːsn̩/ *n* portavoz *mf*, vocero, -ra *m,f* (esp AmL)

spokeswoman /'spəʊks,wʊmən/ (*pl* **-women**) *n* portavoz *f*, vocera *f* (esp AmL)

sponge¹ /spʌndʒ/ *n* **1** (a) (Zool) esponja *f* (b) (for bath) esponja *f* **2** (Culin) ~ (**cake**) bizcocho *m*, bizcochuelo *m* (CS)

sponge² *vt* pasar una esponja por

■ ~ *vi*: **he lives by sponging on** *o* **off his relatives** vive a costillas de sus parientes

sponsor¹ /'spɑːnsər ‖'spɒnsə(r)/ *n* (a) (of program, show, sporting event) patrocinador, -dora *m,f*, espónsor *mf*; (for the arts) mecenas *mf* (b) (for membership): **you need two members to act as** ~**s** te tienen que presentar dos socios (c) (of bill, motion) proponente *mf*

sponsor² *vt* (a) ⟨event/festival⟩ patrocinar; ⟨research/expedition⟩ subvencionar (b) ⟨applicant/application⟩ apoyar (c) ⟨bill/motion⟩ (present) presentar, proponer*; (support) apoyar

sponsorship /'spɑːnsərʃɪp ‖'spɒnsəʃɪp/ *n* patrocinio *m*; (of the arts) mecenazgo *m*

spontaneous /spɑːn'teɪniəs ‖spɒn'teɪniəs/ *adj* espontáneo

S

spontaneously /spɑːn'teɪnɪəsli ‖spɒn'teɪnɪəsli/ *adv* espontáneamente

spoof /spuːf/ *n* (colloq) parodia *f*, burla *f*

spooky /'spuːki/ *adj* **-kier, -kiest** (colloq) espeluznante

spool /spuːl/ *n* carrete *m*, carretel *m* (AmL)

spoon /spuːn/ *n* cuchara *f*; (small) cucharita *f*

spoonfeed /'spuːnfiːd/ *vt* (*past & past p* **-fed**) ‹*baby*› darle* de comer en la boca a; **she ~s her students** se lo da todo mascado a sus alumnos

spoonful /'spuːnfʊl/ *n* (*pl* **~s** *or* **spoonsful**) cucharada *f*; (small) cucharadita *f*

sporadic /spə'rædɪk/ *adj* esporádico

sport¹ /spɔːrt ‖spɔːt/ *n* **1** deporte *m* **2** (person): **to be a good ~** (to be sporting) tener* espíritu deportivo; (to be understanding) ser* comprensivo

sport² *vt* ‹*clothes/hairstyle*› lucir*

sport³ *adj* (AmE) **(a)** (Sport) ‹*equipment*› de deportes **(b)** (casual) ‹*clothes*› sport *adj inv*, de sport

sporting /'spɔːrtɪŋ ‖'spɔːtɪŋ/ *adj* **1** (fair) ‹*spirit*› deportivo; **it's very ~ of you** es muy amable de tu parte **2** (*no comp*) (relating to sport) ‹*press/interests*› deportivo

sports /spɔːrts ‖spɔːts/ *adj* **(a)** (Sport) (page/program) de deportes; **~ complex** polideportivo *m* **(b)** (casual) ‹*clothes/shirt*› sport *adj inv*

sports: ~ car *n* coche *m* deportivo, carro *m* sport (AmL exc CS), auto *m* sport *or* deportivo (CS); **~man** /'spɔːrtsmən ‖'spɔːtsmən/ *n* (*pl* **-men** /-mən/) deportista *m*

sportsmanship /'spɔːrtsmənʃɪp ‖'spɔːtsmənʃɪp/ *n* espíritu *m* deportivo

sportswoman /'spɔːrtswʊmən ‖'spɔːtswʊmən/ *n* deportista *f*

sporty /'spɔːrti ‖'spɔːti/ *adj* **-tier, -tiest** **(a)** ‹*person*› deportista **(b)** (Auto) deportivo

spot¹ /spɑːt ‖spɒt/ *n* **1** **(a)** (dot — on material) lunar *m*, mota *f*; (— on animal's skin) mancha *f* **(b)** (blemish, stain) mancha *f* **(c)** (pimple) (BrE) grano *m*, espinilla *f* (AmL)
2 **(a)** (location, place) lugar *m*, sitio *m*; **on the ~**: **he had to decide on the ~** tuvo que decidir en ese mismo momento; **they were killed on the ~** los mataron allí mismo; **on-the-~ fine** *multa que se paga en el acto* **(b)** (difficult situation): **to be in a** (tight) **~** estar* en apuros
3 **(a)** (drop) gota *f* **(b)** (small amount) (BrE colloq) (*no pl*): **do you fancy a ~ of supper?** ¿quieres cenar algo?

spot² *vt* **-tt-** **1** ‹*error*› descubrir*; ‹*bargain*› encontrar*; **he ~ted her in the crowd** la vio *or* (AmL tb) la ubicó entre el gentío **2** (mark) (*usu pass*) manchar

spot check *n*: *control o inspección realizada al azar*

spotless /'spɑːtləs ‖'spɒtlɪs/ *adj* ‹*clothes*› impecable; ‹*house*› limpísimo; ‹*reputation/record*› intachable

spotlight /'spɑːtlaɪt ‖'spɒtlaɪt/ *n* (in theater) foco *m*; (on building) reflector *m*

spotted /'spɑːtəd ‖'spɒtɪd/ *adj* ‹*tie/material*› de *or* a lunares *or* motas

spotty /'spɑːti ‖'spɒti/ *adj* **-tier, -tiest** (BrE) ‹*skin*› lleno de granos; ‹*youth*› con la cara llena de granos

spouse /spaʊs/ *n* (fml *or* hum) cónyuge *mf* (fml)

spout¹ /spaʊt/ *n* **(a)** (of teapot, kettle) pico *m*, pitorro *m* (Esp) **(b)** (pipe — on gutter) canalón *m*; (— on fountain, gargoyle) caño *m* **(c)** (jet) chorro *m*

spout² *vt* ‹*oil/liquid*› arrojar *or* expulsar chorros de
■ **~** *vi* «*liquid*» salir* a chorros; «*whale*» expulsar chorros de agua

sprain¹ /spreɪn/ *n* esguince *m*, distensión *f*

sprain² *vt* hacerse* un esguince en, distenderse*

sprang /spræŋ/ *past of* SPRING¹

sprawl¹ /sprɔːl/ *vi* «*person*» sentarse* (*or* tumbarse *etc*) de forma poco elegante

sprawl² *n* (of built-up area) expansión *f*

spray¹ /spreɪ/ *vt* **(a)** ‹*liquid*› pulverizar*, aplicar* con atomizador; ‹*paint*› aplicar* con pistola pulverizadora **(b)** ‹*plants*› rociar* (con atomizador)

spray² *n* **1** **(a)** (fine drops) rocío *m* **(b)** (liquid in spray form) espray *m*; (before *n*) ‹*deodorant/polish*› en aerosol, en espray, en atomizador **(c)** (implement) rociador *m* **2** (bunch) ramillete *m*

spread¹ /spred/ (*past & past p* **spread**) *vt* **1** (extend) ‹*arms/legs*› extender*; ‹*map/sails/wings*› desplegar*; **you can ~ the cost over five years** se puede pagar el costo a lo largo de cinco años
2 **(a)** ‹*paint/glue*› extender*; ‹*seeds/sand*› esparcir*; **to ~ butter on a piece of toast** untar una tostada con mantequilla **(b)** ‹*knowledge/news*› difundir; ‹*influence*› extender*; ‹*rumor*› hacer* correr; ‹*disease*› propagar*; ‹*fear*› sembrar*; ‹*ideas/culture*› diseminar
■ **~** *vi* **1** «*disease*» propagarse*; «*liquid/fire*» extenderse*; «*ideas/culture*» diseminarse; «*panic/fear*» cundir; «*influence/revolt*» extenderse*
2 (extend in space, time) extenderse*
3 «*paint*» extenderse*; «*butter*» untarse
■ **spread out** [*v + adv*] **(a)** (move apart) «*troops*» desplegarse* **(b)** (extend) extenderse*

spread² *n* **1** (diffusion — of disease) propagación *f*; (— of ideas) difusión *f*, diseminación *f*; (— of fire) propagación *f* **2** (of wings, sails) envergadura *f* **3** (Culin) **(a)** (meal) (colloq) festín *m*, banquete *m* **(b)** (paste) *pasta para extender sobre pan, tostadas etc* **4** (Journ, Print): **it was advertised in a full-page ~** venía anunciado a plana entera

spread: ~-eagled /'spred'iːgəld/ *adj* con los brazos y piernas abiertos; **~sheet** *n* hoja *f* de cálculo; (before *n*) **~sheet program** hoja *f* electrónica

spree /spriː/ *n*: **to go on a shopping ~** ir* de expedición a las tiendas

---

sprig /sprɪg/ n ramito m

sprightly /'spraɪtli/ adj **-lier, -liest** ⟨person⟩ lleno de brío; ⟨walk/step⟩ ágil

spring¹ /sprɪŋ/ (past **sprang** or (esp AmE) **sprung**; past p **sprung**) vi **1** (leap) saltar; **to ~ into action** entrar en acción **2** (a) (liter) «stream» surgir*, nacer*; «shoots» brotar **(b) to ~ FROM sth** «ideas/doubts» surgir* DE algo; «problem» provenir* DE algo

■ ~ vt **(a)** (produce suddenly): **to ~ a surprise on sb** darle* una sorpresa a algn **(b) to ~ a leak** empezar* a hacer agua

■ **spring up** [v + adv] «stores/housing estates» surgir*; «plant» brotar; «wind» levantarse

spring² n **1** (season) primavera f; **in (the) ~** en primavera; (before n) ⟨weather/showers⟩ primaveral **2** (Geog) manantial m, fuente f **3** (jump) salto m, brinco m **4 (a)** (in watch, toy) resorte m; (in mattress) muelle m, resorte m (AmL) **(b)** (elasticity) (no pl) elasticidad f

spring: **~board** n trampolín m; **~clean** /'sprɪŋ'kliːn/ vi hacer* limpieza general; **~cleaning** /'sprɪŋ'kliːnɪŋ/ n (no pl) limpieza f general; **~ onion** n (BrE) cebolleta f, cebollino m; **~time** n primavera f

springy /'sprɪŋi/ adj **-gier, -giest** ⟨mattress/ grass⟩ mullido; ⟨floor⟩ elástico

sprinkle /'sprɪŋkəl/ vt **(a)** (scatter) **to ~ sth ON sth: to ~ water on the plants** rociar* las plantas con agua; **to ~ sugar on sth** espolvorear algo con azúcar **(b)** (cover) **to ~ sth WITH sth: ~ the board with flour** espolvoree la tabla con harina

sprinkler /'sprɪŋklər ‖'sprɪŋklə(r)/ n **(a)** (garden ~) aspersor m **(b)** (for firefighting) (usu pl) rociador m; (before n) **~ system** sistema m de rociadores

sprint¹ /sprɪnt/ n **(a)** (fast run) (e)sprint m **(b)** (short race) (Sport) carrera f corta

sprint² vi **(a)** (Sport) (e)sprintar **(b)** (run fast): I **~ed after him** salí corriendo tras él a toda velocidad

sprout¹ /spraʊt/ vt ⟨leaves/shoots⟩ echar

■ ~ vi «plant» echar retoños, retoñar*; «leaf» brotar, salir*; «seeds» germinar

sprout² n **(a)** (Brussels ~) col f or (AmS) repollito m de Bruselas **(b)** (shoot) brote m

spruce¹ /spruːs/ n (tree) picea f, abeto m falso

spruce² adj **sprucer, sprucest** ⟨appearance⟩ cuidado, acicalado; ⟨garden⟩ cuidado, arreglado

■ **spruce up** [v + o + adv, v + adv + o] ⟨garden/ room⟩ arreglar

sprung /sprʌŋ/ past p & (esp AmE) past of SPRING¹

spry /spraɪ/ adj **-er, -est** lleno de vida, dinámico

spud /spʌd/ n (colloq) papa f or (Esp) patata f

spun¹ /spʌn/ past & past p of SPIN²

spun² adj ⟨silk/cotton⟩ hilado

spur¹ /spɜːr ‖spɜː(r)/ n **(a)** (Equ) espuela f; **on the ~ of the moment** sin pensarlo **(b)** (stimulus) acicate m

spur² vt **-rr- (a)** (Equ) ⟨horse⟩ espolear **(b)** ~ **(on)** ⟨person/team⟩ estimular

spurious /'spjʊriəs ‖'spjʊəriəs/ adj ⟨document⟩ falso, espurio; ⟨argument⟩ falaz, espurio

spurn /spɜːrn ‖spɜːn/ vt desdeñar, rechazar*

spurt¹ /spɜːrt ‖spɜːt/ n **(a)** (of speed, activity) racha f; **to put on a ~** acelerar **(b)** (jet) chorro m

spurt² vi «liquid/steam» salir* a chorros

spy¹ /spaɪ/ n (pl **spies**) espía mf; (before n) ⟨story⟩ de espías, de espionaje; **~ ring** red f de espionaje

spy² **spies, spying, spied** vi espiar*; **to ~ ON sb** espiar* a algn

■ ~ vt descubrir*, ver*

sq adj (= square): **220 ~ m** 220 m²

Sq (= **Square**) Pza.

squabble /'skwɑːbəl ‖'skwɒbəl/ vi pelear(se), reñir*

squad /skwɑːd ‖skwɒd/ n **(a)** (Mil) pelotón m; (of workmen) cuadrilla f **(b)** (of policemen) brigada f; **drug ~** brigada f antidroga **(c)** (Sport) equipo m

squad car n (AmE) coche m or (AmL tb) auto m patrulla, patrullero m (CS, Per)

squadron /'skwɑːdrən ‖'skwɒdrən/ n (Mil, Aviat) escuadrón m; (Naut) escuadra f

squalid /'skwɑːləd ‖'skwɒlɪd/ adj **(a)** (dirty) ⟨existence/house⟩ miserable **(b)** (sordid) ⟨story/ business⟩ sórdido

squall /skwɔːl/ n borrasca f, turbión m

squalor /'skwɑːlər ‖'skwɒlə(r)/ n miseria f

squander /'skwɑːndər ‖'skwɒndə(r)/ vt ⟨money⟩ despilfarrar; ⟨opportunity⟩ desaprovechar

square¹ /skwer ‖skweə(r)/ n **1 (a)** (shape) cuadrado m; (in fabric design) cuadro m **(b)** (on chessboard) casilla f, escaque m; (in crossword) casilla f; **to go back to ~** volver* a empezar desde cero **2** (in town, city) plaza f **3** (Math) cuadrado m

square² adj **squarer, squarest 1 (a)** ⟨box/table/block⟩ cuadrado; **the room is 15 feet ~** la habitación mide 15 (pies) por 15 (pies) **(b)** (having right angles) ⟨corner/edges⟩ en ángulo recto **(c)** ⟨face⟩ cuadrado; ⟨jaw⟩ angular **2** (Math) (before n) ⟨yard/mile⟩ cuadrado **3 (a)** (fair, honest): **he'll give you a ~ deal** no te va a engañar **(b)** (large and wholesome) (before n) ⟨meal⟩ decente

square³ vt **1** (make square) ⟨angle/side⟩ cuadrar **2** (Math) elevar al cuadrado **3 (a)** (settle, make even) ⟨debts/accounts⟩ pagar*, saldar **(b)** (reconcile) ⟨facts/principles⟩ conciliar

■ ~ vi «ideas/arguments» concordar*

■ **square up** [v + adv] (settle debts) (colloq) **to ~ up (WITH sb)** arreglar cuentas (CON algn)

square root n raíz f cuadrada

squash¹ /skwɑːʃ ‖skwɒʃ/ n **1** (Sport) squash m **2** (drink) (BrE) refresco a base de extractos; **orange ~** naranjada f **3** (Bot, Culin) nombre genérico de varios tipos de calabaza y zapallo

squash² vt **1 (a)** (crush) ⟨fruit/insect⟩ aplastar **(b)** (squeeze): **to ~ sth/sb in** meter algo/a algn (apretando) **2** (suppress, silence) (colloq) ⟨protests/ rumors⟩ acallar

■ ~ vi (+ adv compl): **we all ~ed into his study** nos metimos todos en su despacho

squashy /'skwɑːʃi ‖'skwɒʃi/ adj **-shier, -shiest** ⟨fruit⟩ blando; ⟨ground⟩ húmedo y mullido

squat¹ /skwɑ:t ‖skwɒt/ *vi* **-tt-** ① (crouch) agacharse, ponerse* en cuclillas ② (in building, on land) *ocupar un inmueble ajeno sin autorización*

squat² *adj* **-tt-** ⟨person⟩ rechoncho y bajo; ⟨building/church⟩ achaparrado

squatter /'skwɒːtər ‖'skwɒtə(r)/ *n* (in building) ocupante *mf* ilegal, ocupa *or* okupa *mf* (Esp), paracaidista *mf* (Méx)

squawk¹ /skwɔːk/ *n* (of bird) graznido *m*

squawk² *vi* «bird» graznar; «person» chillar

squeak¹ /skwiːk/ *n* (of animal, person) chillido *m*; (of hinge) chirrido *m*; (of shoes) crujido *m*

squeak² *vi* «animal/person» chillar; «hinge» chirriar*; «shoes» crujir

squeaky /'skwiːki/ *adj* **-kier, kiest** ⟨hinge/ pen⟩ chirriante; ⟨voice⟩ chillón, de pito

squeal¹ /skwiːl/ *vi* (a) (make noise) «person/ animal» chillar; «brakes/tires» chirriar* (b) (inform) (colloq) cantar (fam), chivarse (Esp fam), sapear (Ven fam)

squeal² *n* (of animal) chillido *m*; (of person) grito *m*, chillido *m*; (of brakes, tires) chirrido *m*

squeamish /'skwiːmɪʃ/ *adj* impresionable, aprensivo

squeeze¹ /skwiːz/ *n* ① (a) (application of pressure) apretón *m*; **he gave her hand a ~** le dio un apretón de manos (b) (restrictions): **a credit ~** una restricción crediticia (c) (hug) apretón *m* ② (confined, restricted condition) (colloq) (*no pl*): **it will be a (tight) ~** vamos (*or* van *etc*) a estar apretados

squeeze² *vt* (a) (press) ⟨tube/pimple⟩ apretar*, espichar (Col); ⟨lemon⟩ exprimir; **to ~ a cloth (out)** retorcer* un trapo (b) (extract) ⟨liquid/juice⟩ extraer*, sacar*; **he tried to ~ more money out of them** trató de sacarles más dinero (c) (force, fit) meter; **I can ~ you in tomorrow morning** le puedo hacer un huequito mañana por la mañana ■ **~** *vi*: **he ~d in through the hole** se metió por el agujero

squelch /skweltʃ/ *vi* «shoes/hooves» hacer* un ruido como de succión

squid /skwɪd/ *n* (*pl* **~**) calamar *m*

squiggle /'skwɪgəl/ *n* garabato *m*

squint¹ /skwɪnt/ *n* bizquera *f*, estrabismo *m*

squint² *vi* (a) (attempting to see) entrecerrar* los ojos (b) (be cross-eyed) bizquear, torcer* la vista

squire /skwaɪr ‖'skwaɪə(r)/ *n* (a) (Hist, Mil) escudero *m* (b) (in UK: landowner) señor *m*

squirm /skwɜːrm ‖skwɜːm/ *vi* retorcerse*; **she ~ed with embarrassment** le dio mucha vergüenza, no sabía dónde meterse de la vergüenza

squirrel /skwɜːrl ‖'skwɪrəl/ *n* ardilla *f*

squirt¹ /skwɜːrt ‖skwɜːt/ *n* ① (stream) chorrito *m* ② (person) (colloq) mequetrefe *m* (fam)

squirt² *vt* ⟨liquid⟩ echar un chorro de ■ **~** *vi* «liquid» salir* a chorros

Sr (= **Senior**) Sr.

Sri Lanka /sriː'lɑːŋkə, ʃriː- ‖srɪ'læŋkə, ʃrɪ-/ *n* Sri Lanka *m*

St (a) (= **Saint**) S(an), Sta.; **~ Thomas** Sto. Tomás (b) (= **Street**) c/

stab¹ /stæb/ *n* (a) (with knife) puñalada *f*,

cuchillada *f*; **to have a ~ at sth** intentar algo (b) (sudden sensation): **a ~ of pain** una punzada de dolor

stab² *vt* **-bb-** apuñalar, acuchillar; **he had been ~bed to death** había muerto apuñalado *or* acuchillado

stabbing¹ /'stæbɪŋ/ *n* apuñalamiento *m*

stabbing² *adj* ⟨pain/sensation⟩ punzante

stability /stə'bɪləti/ *n* estabilidad *f*

stabilize /'steɪbəlaɪz/ *vt* estabilizar* ■ **~** *vi* estabilizarse*

stable¹ /'steɪbəl/ *adj* **-bler, -blest** (a) (firm, steady) estable (b) (Psych) equilibrado

stable² *n* (*often pl*) (for horses) caballeriza *f*, cuadra *f*; (for other livestock) establo *m*

staccato /stə'kɑːtəʊ/ *adj* (Mus) staccato

stack¹ /stæk/ *n* (a) (pile) montón *m*, pila *f* (b) (many, much) (colloq) (*often pl*) montón *m* (fam), pila *f* (AmS fam)

stack² *vt* **~** (up) amontonar, apilar

stadium /'steɪdiəm/ *n* (*pl* **-diums** *or* **-dia** /-diə/) estadio *m*

staff¹ /stæf ‖stɑːf/ *n* ① (a) (as group) (+ *sing o pl vb*) personal *m*; **the teaching ~** el personal docente; **a member of ~** un empleado (b) (as individuals) (BrE) (*pl* **~**) (*pl vb*) empleados *mpl* ② (*pl* **staffs** *or* **staves** /steɪvz/) (stick) bastón *m*; (of bishop) báculo *m*, cayado *m* ③ (Mus) ▶ STAVE 2

staff² *vt* proveer* de personal

staffroom /'stæfruːm, -rʊm ‖'stɑːfruːm, -rʊm/ *n* (BrE) sala *f* de profesores

stag /stæg/ *n* ciervo *m*, venado *m*

stage¹ /steɪdʒ/ *n* ① (a) (platform) tablado *m*; (in theater) escenario *m*; (before n) **~ door** entrada *f* de artistas (b) (medium, profession) **the ~** el teatro; (before n) **~ name** nombre *m* artístico ② (in development, activity) fase *f*, etapa *f*; **at some ~** en algún momento

stage² *vt* ① (a) (event) organizar*, montar; ⟨strike/demonstration⟩ hacer*; ⟨attack⟩ llevar a cabo; ⟨coup⟩ dar* (b) (engineer, arrange) arreglar, orquestar ② (Theat) ⟨play⟩ poner* en escena

stage-: ~coach *n* diligencia *f*, **~ fright** *n* miedo *m* a salir a escena; **~hand** *n* tramoyista *mf*, **~manage** *vt* ⟨event⟩ orquestar, arreglar; **~ manager** *n* director, -tora *m,f* de escena

stagger /'stægər ‖'stægə(r)/ *vi* tambalearse ■ **~** *vt* ① (amaze) dejar estupefacto ② ⟨shifts/ payments⟩ escalonar

staggering /'stægərɪŋ/ *adj* asombroso

stagnant /'stægnənt/ *adj* estancado

stagnate /'stægneɪt ‖stæg'neɪt/ *vi* «water/ economy» estancarse*; «person» anquilosarse

stag: ~ night *n* (for men only) ▶ **~ PARTY A; ~ party** *n* (a) (before wedding) despedida *f* de soltero (b) (all-male celebration) fiesta *f* para hombres, noche *f* de cuates (Méx)

staid /steɪd/ *adj* **-er, -est** serio, formal; ⟨clothes⟩ serio, sobrio; (pej) aburrido

stain¹ /steɪn/ *n* (a) (dirty mark) mancha *f* (b) (dye) tintura *f*, tinte *m* (c) (on character) mancha *f*

stain² *vt* (a) ⟨clothes/skin⟩ manchar (b) (dye) ⟨wood⟩ teñir* ■ **~** *vi* manchar

stained glass /steind/ n vidrio m or cristal m de colores; (before n) ~ ~ **window** vitral m, vidriera f (de colores)

stainless steel /'steɪnləs ‖'steɪnlɪs/ n acero m inoxidable

stain remover n quitamanchas m

stair /ster ‖steə(r)/ n **(a) stairs** pl (flight of stairs, stairway) escalera(s) f(pl) **(b)** (single step) escalón m, peldaño m

stair: ~**case,** ~**way** n escalera(s) f(pl); ~**well** n caja f or hueco m or (Méx) cubo m de la escalera

stake¹ /steɪk/ n **1** (pole) estaca f **2 (a)** (bet) apuesta f; **to be at** ~ estar* en juego **(b)** (interest): **to have a** ~ **in a company** tener* participación or intereses en una compañía

stake² vt **1** (risk) ⟨money/reputation⟩ jugarse* **2 (a)** (mark with stakes) marcar* con estacas, estacar*; **the government was quick to** ~ **its claim** el gobierno se apresuró a reclamar su parte **(b)** ⟨tree/plant⟩ arrodrigar*

stalactite /stə'læktaɪt ‖'stæləktaɪt/ n estalactita f

stalagmite /stə'lægmaɪt ‖'stæləgmaɪt/ n estalagmita f

stale /steɪl/ adj **staler, stalest** ⟨bread⟩ no fresco; ⟨butter/cheese⟩ rancio; ⟨beer⟩ pasado; ⟨air⟩ viciado; ⟨joke⟩ añejo, viejo; ⟨ideas⟩ trasnochado

stalemate /'steɪlmeɪt/ n (in chess) tablas fpl (por ahogar al rey); **to be at a** ~ estar* en un punto muerto

stalk¹ /stɔːk/ n (of plant) tallo m; (of leaf, flower) pedúnculo m, tallo m; (of fruit) rabillo m

stalk² vt acechar
■ ~ vi: **to** ~ **off** irse* ofendido/indignado

stall¹ /stɔːl/ n **1** (in market) puesto m, tenderete m **2 stalls** pl (in theater, movie house) (BrE) platea f, patio m de butacas **3** (in stable) compartimiento m

stall² vi **1** ⟨engine/car⟩ pararse, calarse (Esp), atascarse* (Méx) **2** (play for time) (colloq): **quit** ~**ing** no andes con rodeos or con evasivas
■ ~ vt **1** ⟨engine/car⟩ parar, calar (Esp), atascar* (Méx) **2** (delay) (colloq) entretener*

stallion /'stæljən/ n semental m

stalwart /'stɔːlwərt ‖'stɔːlwət/ adj ⟨supporter⟩ incondicional, fiel

stamina /'stæmənə ‖'stæmɪnə/ n resistencia f

stammer¹ /'stæmər ‖'stæmə(r)/ n tartamudeo m

stammer² vi tartamudear

stamp¹ /stæmp/ n **1** (postage ~) sello m, estampilla f (AmL), timbre m (Méx); (before n) ~ **collecting** filatelia f; ~ **collector** coleccionista mf de sellos (or estampillas etc), filatelista mf **2 (a)** (instrument) sello m **(b)** (printed mark) sello m **3** (character) impronta f; **she left her** ~ **on the institute** dejó su impronta en el instituto

stamp² vt **1** (with foot) ⟨ground⟩ dar* una patada en; **to** ~ **one's foot** dar* una patada en el suelo

2 ⟨letter/parcel⟩ franquear, ponerle* sellos (or estampillas etc) a, estampillar (AmL), timbrar (Méx); **a** ~**ed addressed envelope** un sobre franqueado or (AmL tb) estampillado or (Méx) timbrado con su dirección

3 (a) ⟨passport/ticket⟩ sellar **(b)** ⟨coin⟩ acuñar
■ ~ vi «person» dar* patadas en el suelo; «horse» piafar; **he** ~**ed on the spider** le dio un pisotón a la araña
■ **stamp out** [v + o + adv, v + adv + o] **(a)** ⟨fire⟩ apagar* (con los pies) **(b)** (suppress) ⟨resistance⟩ aplastar; ⟨rebellion⟩ sofocar*; ⟨crime⟩ erradicar*

stampede¹ /stæm'piːd/ n estampida f

stampede² vi salir* en estampida

stance /stæns ‖stɑːns/ n postura f

stand¹ /stænd/ n **1 (a)** (position) lugar m **(b)** (attitude) postura f **(c)** (resistance) resistencia f; **to make a** ~ **against sth** oponer* resistencia a algo **2 (a)** (base) pie m, base f **(b)** (for coats, hats) perchero m **3** (at fair, exhibition) stand m, caseta f; **newspaper** ~ puesto m de periódicos; **a hot-dog** ~ (esp AmE) un puesto de perritos calientes **4** (for spectators) (often pl) tribuna f **5** (witness box) (AmE) estrado m

stand² (past & past p **stood**) vi **1 (a)** (be, remain upright) «person» estar* de pie, estar* parado (AmL) **(b)** (rise) levantarse, ponerse* de pie, pararse (AmL); **her hair stood on end** se le pusieron los pelos de punta, se le pararon los pelos (AmL); see also STAND UP

2 (move, take up position) ponerse*, pararse (AmL); ~ **over there** ponte or (AmL tb) párate allí; **to** ~ **aside** hacerse* a un lado; **to** ~ **on one's head** pararse de cabeza (AmL), hacer el pino (Esp)

3 (a) (be situated, located): **a church stood here long ago** hace mucho tiempo aquí había una iglesia; **I won't** ~ **in your way** no seré yo quien te lo impida **(b)** (hold position): **where do you** ~ **on this issue?** ¿cuál es tu posición en cuanto a este problema?; **you never know where you** ~ **with him** con él uno nunca sabe a qué atenerse **(c)** (be mounted, fixed): **a hut** ~**ing on wooden piles** una choza construida sobre pilotes de madera

4 (a) (stop, remain still) «person»: **they stood and stared** se quedaron mirando; **time stood still** el tiempo se detuvo **(b)** (Culin) «batter/water»: **leave to** ~ dejar reposar **(c)** (survive, last): **the tower is still** ~**ing** la torre sigue en pie

5 (remain unchanged, valid) «law/agreement» seguir* vigente; **the offer still** ~**s** la oferta sigue en pie

6 (a) (be currently): **as things** ~ tal (y) como están las cosas **(b)** (be likely to): **to** ~ **to** + INF: **he** ~**s to lose a fortune** puede llegar a perder una fortuna; **what does she** ~ **to gain out of this?** ¿qué es lo que puede ganar con esto?

7 (for office, election) (BrE) presentarse (como candidato)
■ ~ vt **1** (place) poner*; (carefully, precisely) colocar* **2 (a)** (tolerate, bear) (with CAN, CAN'T, WON'T) ⟨pain/noise⟩ aguantar, soportar; **I can't** ~ **him** no lo aguanto or soporto; **I can't** ~ **it any longer!** ¡no puedo más!; **she can't** ~ **being interrupted** no soporta que la interrumpan **(b)** (withstand) ⟨heat/strain⟩ soportar
■ **stand back** [v + adv] (move away) **to** ~ **back** (FROM sth) apartarse (DE algo)
■ **stand by 1** [v + adv] **(a)** (remain uninvolved) mantenerse* al margen; **people just stood by and did nothing** la gente estaba allí mirando sin hacer nada **(b)** (be at readiness) «army/troops» estar* en estado de alerta
2 [v + prep + o] **(a)** ⟨promise⟩ mantener*; ⟨decision⟩ atenerse* a **(b)** (support) ⟨friend⟩ apoyar ····❖

S

■ **stand down** [v + adv] (relinquish position) retirarse; (resign) renunciar, dimitir

■ **stand for** [v + prep + o] **(a)** (represent) «initials/symbol» significar*; **CTI ~s for ...** CTI son las siglas de ...; **he has betrayed everything he once stood for** ha traicionado todo aquello con lo que solía identificar **(b)** (put up with) (usu with neg) consentir*

■ **stand in** [v + adv] **to ~ in FOR sb** sustituir* a algn

■ **stand out** [v + adv] **(a)** (project) **to ~ out (FROM sth)** sobresalir* (DE algo) **(b)** (be conspicuous, contrast) sobresalir*, destacar(se)*; «color» resaltar

■ **stand up** ①[v + adv] **(a)** (get up) ponerse* de pie, levantarse, pararse (AmL) **(b)** (be, remain standing): **~ up straight** ponte derecho **(c)** (endure, withstand wear) resistir; **to ~ up TO sth** «to cold/pressure» resistir or soportar algo; see also **STAND UP TO**

②[v + o + adv] **(a)** (set upright) poner* de pie, levantar **(b)** (not keep appointment with) (colloq) dejar plantado a (fam)

■ **stand up for** [v + adv + prep + o] defender*; **I can ~ up for myself** me puedo defender solo

■ **stand up to** [v + adv + prep + o] «person/threats» hacerle* frente a; see also **STAND UP 1C**

standard¹ /'stændərd ‖'stændəd/ n ① **(a)** (level) nivel m; (quality) calidad f; **~ of living** nivel m or estándar m de vida **(b)** (norm): **she sets very high ~s** exige un estándar or nivel muy alto; **the product was below ~** el producto no era de la calidad requerida **(c)** (official measure) estándar m ② **(a)** (yardstick) criterio m, parámetro m **(b) standards** pl (moral principles) principios mpl ③ (flag, emblem) estandarte m

standard² adj ① (normal) «size» estándar adj inv, normal; «model» (Auto) estándar adj inv, de serie; «procedure» habitual; «reaction» típico; **~ rate** tarifa f normal ② (officially established) «weight/measure» estándar adj inv, oficial; **~ time** hora f oficial

standardization /ˌstændərdə'zeɪʃən ‖ˌstædədə'zeɪʃən/ n estandarización f

standardize /'stændərdaɪz ‖'stændədaɪz/ vt estandarizar*

standard lamp n (BrE) lámpara f de pie

standby¹ /'stændbaɪ/ n (pl -bys) **(a)** (thing one can turn to): **frozen meals are a useful ~** las comidas congeladas son muy socorridas **(b)** (state of readiness): **to be on ~** «police/squadron» estar* en estado de alerta **(c)** (Aviat) stand-by m

standby² adj (before n) **(a)** (ready for emergency) de emergencia; **to be on ~ duty** estar* de guardia **(b)** (Aviat) «passenger/ticket/fare» stand-by adj inv

stand-in /'stændɪn/ n suplente mf; (Cin) doble mf

standing¹ /'stændɪŋ/ n **(a)** (position) posición f; (prestige) prestigio m **(b)** (duration): **friends of more than 20 years' ~** amigos desde hace más de 20 años

standing² adj (before n, no comp) **(a)** (permanent) permanente; **~ charge** cuota f fija; (for utilities) cuota f abono; **it's a ~ joke that he never pays for a single drink** tiene fama de no invitar nunca a una copa **(b)** (upright, not seated) «passenger» de pie, parado (AmL)

standing order n **(a)** (with bank) (BrE) orden f permanente de pago **(b)** (with supplier) pedido m fijo

stand: **~off** n (AmE) **(a)** (tie, draw) empate m **(b)** (deadlock) callejón m sin salida; **~point** n punto m de vista; **~still** n (no pl): **to be at a ~still** «traffic» estar* paralizado; **to come to a ~still** «vehicle» parar; «city/factory» quedar paralizado

stank /stæŋk/ past of **STINK²**

staple¹ /'steɪpəl/ n ① (for fastening paper, cloth etc) grapa f, ganchito m, corchete m (Chi) ② **(a)** (basic food) alimento m básico **(b)** (principal product) producto m principal

staple² adj «food/ingredient» básico; «industry» principal; **rice is their ~ diet** se alimentan principalmente a base de arroz

staple³ vt grapar, engrapar (AmL), corchetear (Chi)

stapler /'steɪplər ‖'steɪplə(r)/ n grapadora f, engrapadora f (AmL), corchetera f (Chi)

star¹ /stɑːr ‖stɑː(r)/ n ① (in sky) estrella f; (Astrol, Astron) astro m; (before n) **~ sign** signo m del zodíaco ② (symbol) estrella f; (asterisk) asterisco m; **a four-~ hotel** un hotel de cuatro estrellas; **four-~ petrol** (BrE) gasolina f or (RPl) nafta f súper, bencina f especial (Andes) ③ (celebrity) estrella f

star² -rr- vt: **the famous film which ~red Bogart and Bergman** la famosa película que tuvo como protagonistas a Bogart y Bergman; **'2005', ~ring Mike Kirnon** '2005', con (la actuación estelar de) Mike Kirnon

■ **~** vi: **to ~ in a film** protagonizar* una película

starboard¹ /'stɑːrbərd ‖'stɑːbəd/ n estribor m

starboard² adj (before n) de estribor

starch /stɑːrtʃ ‖stɑːtʃ/ n **(a)** (in food, for clothes) almidón m **(b)** (starchy food) fécula f, almidón m

starchy /'stɑːrtʃi ‖'stɑːtʃi/ adj **-chier, -chiest** «diet» a base de féculas or almidones

stardom /'stɑːrdəm ‖'stɑːdəm/ n estrellato m

stare¹ /ster ‖steə(r)/ vi mirar (fijamente); **to ~ AT sth/sb** mirar algo/a algn fijamente

stare² n mirada f (fija)

starfish /'stɑːrfɪʃ ‖'stɑːfɪʃ/ n (pl -fish) estrella f de mar

stark¹ /stɑːrk ‖stɑːk/ adj **-er, -est** «landscape» agreste; «truth» escueto; «realism» descarnado

stark² adv: **~ naked** completamente desnudo

starlet /'stɑːrlət ‖'stɑːlət/ n starlet(te) f (joven actriz que aspira al estrellato)

starling /'stɑːrlɪŋ ‖'stɑːlɪŋ/ n estornino m

starry /'stɑːri/ adj **-rier, -riest** estrellado

starry-eyed /ˌstɑːri'aɪd/ adj **(a)** (full of illusions) «person» iluso, soñador **(b)** (dreamy): **she gazed at him all ~** lo miraba arrobada

star: S∼s and Stripes n the S∼s and Stripes la bandera de las barras y las estrellas;
∼**-spangled** /ˈstɑːr.spæŋɡəld ‖ˈstɑːˌspæŋɡəld/ adj (liter) ⟨sky/heavens⟩ tachonado de estrellas (liter); **S∼-Spangled Banner** n the S∼ Spangled Banner el himno de las barras y las estrellas (himno nacional de EEUU)

start¹ /stɑːrt ‖stɑːt/ n **1** (a) (beginning) principio m, comienzo m; **from** ∼ **to finish** del principio al fin; **to make a** ∼ **(ON sth)** empezar* (algo); **to make an early** ∼ empezar* temprano; (on a journey) salir* temprano **(b) for a** ∼ (as linker) para empezar **2** (Sport) **(a)** (of race) salida f **(b)** (lead, advantage) ventaja f **3** (jump): **to give sb a** ∼ darle* or pegarle* un susto a algn; **I woke up with a** ∼ me desperté sobresaltado

start² vt **1** (begin) empezar*, comenzar*; **I** ∼ **work at eight** empiezo a trabajar a las ocho; **to** ∼ **-ING, to** ∼ **to + INF** empezar* A + INF
2 (cause to begin) ⟨race⟩ dar* comienzo a, largar* (CS, Méx); ⟨fire/epidemic⟩ provocar*; ⟨argument/fight⟩ empezar*; ⟨war⟩ «incident» desencadenar
3 (establish) ⟨business⟩ abrir*; ⟨organization⟩ fundar
4 (cause to operate) ⟨engine/dishwasher⟩ encender*, prender (AmL); ⟨car⟩ arrancar*
■ ∼ vi
I 1 (a) (begin) empezar*, comenzar*; **to get** ∼ed empezar*, comenzar*; **to** ∼ **BY -ING** empezar* POR + INF; ∼**ing (from) next January** a partir del próximo mes de enero **(b) to** ∼ **with** (as linker) primero, para empezar
2 (originate) empezar*, originarse
3 (set out) (+ adv compl): **to** ∼ **back** emprender el regreso; **we** ∼ **from the hotel at six** salimos del hotel a las seis
4 (begin to operate) «car» arrancar*
II (move suddenly) dar* un respingo; (be frightened) asustarse, sobresaltarse
■ **start off 1** [v + adv] **(a)** ▶ START OUT A **(b)** (begin moving) arrancar* **(c)** (begin) empezar*
2 [v + o + adv, v + adv + o] (begin) ⟨discussion/concert⟩ empezar*
3 [v + o + adv] (get sb started): **I'll do the first one, just to** ∼ **you off** yo haré el primero, para ayudarte a empezar
■ **start out** [v + adv] **(a)** (set out) salir* **(b)** (in life, career) empezar* **(c)** (begin) **to** ∼ **out (BY) -ING: we** ∼**ed out (by) thinking it would be easy** empezamos pensando que sería fácil
■ **start over** (AmE) [v + adv] [v + o + adv] volver* a empezar
■ **start up 1** [v + adv] **(a)** ▶ START vi I 4 **(b)** (begin business) empezar*
2 [v + o + adv, v + adv + o] ⟨engine/car/machinery⟩ arrancar*, poner* en marcha **(b)** ⟨business⟩ montar **(c)** ⟨conversation⟩ entablar; ⟨discussion⟩ empezar*

starter /ˈstɑːrtər ‖ˈstɑːtə(r)/ n **1** (Culin) entrada f, primer plato m, entrante m (Esp) **2** (Auto) (∼ motor) motor m de arranque

starting /ˈstɑːrtɪŋ/**:** ∼ **line** n línea f de salida; ∼ **point** n ∼ point (FOR sth) punto m de partida (DE/PARA algo)

startle /ˈstɑːrt̬l ‖ˈstɑːtl/ vt sobresaltar, asustar

startling /ˈstɑːrtlɪŋ ‖ˈstɑːtlɪŋ/ adj **(a)** (surprising) asombroso; ⟨similarity/coincidence⟩ extraordinario **(b)** (alarming) ⟨report/increase⟩ alarmante

starvation /stɑːrˈveɪʃən ‖stɑːˈveɪʃən/ n hambre f, inanición f

starve /stɑːrv ‖stɑːv/ vt **(a)** (deny food) privar de comida a; **I'm** ∼**d** (AmE colloq) me muero de hambre **(b)** (deprive) **to** ∼ **sth/sb OF sth** privar algo/a algn DE algo
■ ∼ vi (die) morirse* de hambre or de inanición; (feel hungry) pasar hambre; **I'm starving** (BrE colloq) me muero de hambre

starving /ˈstɑːrvɪŋ ‖ˈstɑːvɪŋ/ adj hambriento, famélico

stash /stæʃ/ vt ∼ (away) (colloq) (hide) esconder; (save) ir* ahorrando

state¹ /steɪt/ n
I 1 (a) (nation) estado m; (before n) ∼ **visit** visita f oficial **(b)** (division of country) estado m; **the S∼s** los Estados Unidos
2 (Govt) estado m; (before n) (esp BrE) ⟨control/funding⟩ estatal; ∼ **school** escuela f pública or estatal
3 (pomp): **to lie in** ∼ yacer* en capilla ardiente
II (condition) estado m; ∼ **of war/emergency** estado de guerra/emergencia; ∼ **of mind** estado de ánimo; **I was in no (fit)** ∼ **to make a decision** no estaba en condiciones de tomar una decisión; **the kitchen is in a** ∼ (colloq) la cocina está hecha un asco (fam)

state² vt «person» ⟨facts/case⟩ exponer*; ⟨problem⟩ plantear; ⟨name/address⟩ (in writing) escribir*; (orally) decir*; «law/document» establecer*; **he** ∼**d that he had seen her there earlier** afirmó haberla visto antes allí

State Department n (in US) **the** ∼ ∼ el Departamento de Estado de los EEUU, ≈ el Ministerio de Asuntos Exteriores or de Relaciones Exteriores

stately /ˈsteɪtli/ adj **-lier, -liest** majestuoso

stately home n (in UK) casa f solariega

statement /ˈsteɪtmənt/ n **1** (a) (declaration) declaración f, afirmación f; **official** ∼ comunicado m oficial **(b)** (to police, in court) declaración f
2 (bank ∼) estado m or extracto m de cuenta

state: ∼**-of-the-art** /ˈsteɪtəvðiˈɑːrt ‖ˌsteɪtəvðiˈɑːt/ adj último modelo adj inv;
S∼side, ∼**side** adv (AmE colloq) en/a/hacia los Estados Unidos

statesman /ˈsteɪtsmən/ n (pl **-men** /-mən/) estadista m, hombre m de estado

static¹ /ˈstætɪk/ adj **1** ⟨situation⟩ estacionario **2** ⟨electricity⟩ estático

static² n **(a)** (electricity) electricidad f estática **(b)** (interference) estática f

station¹ /ˈsteɪʃən/ n **1** (a) (Rail) estación f **(b)** (bus ∼) estación f or terminal f de autobuses
2 (place of operations) **research** ∼ centro m de investigación; see also FIRE STATION, POLICE STATION etc **3** (TV) canal m; (Rad) emisora f or (AmL tb) estación f (de radio)

station² vt **(a)** (position) ⟨sentries⟩ apostar* **(b)** (post) (usu pass) ⟨personnel⟩ destinar; ⟨fleet/troops⟩ emplazar*

stationary /ˈsteɪʃəneri ‖ˈsteɪʃənəri/ adj ⟨object/vehicle⟩ estacionario

stationery /ˈsteɪʃəneri ‖ˈsteɪʃənəri/ n **(a)** (writing materials) artículos mpl de papelería or de escritorio **(b)** (writing paper) papel m y sobres mpl de carta

S

station: ~ **house** n (AmE) **(a)** (police station) comisaría f **(b)** ▶ FIRE STATION; ~**master** n jefe, -fa m,f de estación; ~ **wagon** n (AmE) ranchera f, (coche m) familiar m, camioneta f (AmL)

statistic /stə'tɪstɪk/ n estadística f; **the** ~**s show that ...** las estadísticas demuestran que ...

statistical /stə'tɪstɪkəl/ adj estadístico

statistics /stə'tɪstɪks/ n (+ sing vb) estadística f

statue /'stætʃuː/ ‖'stætjuː, 'stætʃuː/ n estatua f

stature /'stætʃər ‖'stætʃə(r)/ n **(a)** (status) talla f **(b)** (height) (frml) estatura f, talla f

status /'stætəs ‖'steɪtəs/ n (pl **-tuses**) **(a)** (category, situation): **the group has no official** ~ el grupo no está oficialmente reconocido como tal; **financial** ~ situación f económica **(b)** (social ~) posición f social, estatus m **(c)** (kudos) estatus m; (before n) ~ **symbol** símbolo m de estatus

status quo /kwəʊ/ n statu quo m

statute /'stætʃuːt ‖'stætjuːt, 'stætʃuːt/ n ley f

statutory /'stætʃuːtɔːri ‖'stætʃʊtəri, 'stætʃuːtəri/ adj (right/obligation) legal; (penalty) establecido por la ley

staunch /stɔːntʃ/ adj **-er, -est** (supporter) incondicional; (Protestant) acérrimo

stave /steɪv/ n ⓵ (of barrel, hull) duela f ⓶ (Mus) pentagrama m

■ **stave off** [v + o + adv, v + adv + o] (defeat/disaster) evitar; (danger) conjurar

staves (a) pl of STAFF[1] 2 **(b)** pl of STAVE

stay[1] /steɪ/ vi ⓵ **(a)** (in specified place, position) quedarse; ~ **there** quédate ahí; **to** ~ **put** quedarse **(b)** (in specified state): ~ **still** quédate quieto; **we** ~**ed friends** seguimos siendo amigos ⓶ **(a)** (remain, not leave) quedarse **(b)** (reside temporarily) quedarse; (in a hotel etc) hospedarse, alojarse, quedarse; **he's** ~**ing with us over Easter** va a pasar la Semana Santa con nosotros

■ **stay away** [v + adv] **to** ~ **away FROM sth/sb** no acercarse* A algo/algn

■ **stay in** [v + adv] (remain in position) quedarse en su sitio; (remain indoors) quedarse en casa

■ **stay on** [v + adv] **(a)** (remain in position) «hat/top» quedarse en su sitio **(b)** (at school, in job) quedarse

■ **stay out** [v + adv] **(a)** (not come home): **to** ~ **out late** quedarse fuera hasta tarde; **he usually** ~**s out late** normalmente no vuelve hasta tarde **(b)** (out of doors) quedarse fuera

■ **stay out of** [v + adv + prep + o] **(a)** (avoid) (trouble) no meterse en; ~ **out of the sun** quédate a la sombra **(b)** (not get involved in) (argument) no meterse en

■ **stay up** [v + adv] **(a)** (not fall or sink) «tent/pole» sostenerse* **(b)** (not go to bed) quedarse levantado

stay[2] n ⓵ (time) estadía f (AmL), estancia f (Esp, Méx); **during her** ~ **in hospital** mientras estuvo en el hospital ⓶ (Law): ~ **of execution** suspensión f del cumplimiento de la sentencia

staying power /'steɪɪŋ/ n resistencia f, aguante m

stead /sted/ n: **in sb's** ~ (liter) en lugar de algn; **to stand sb in good** ~ resultarle muy útil a algn

steadfast /'stedfæst ‖'stedfɑːst/ adj (liter) (refusal) firme, categórico; (resolve) inquebrantable

steadily /'stedli ‖'stedɪli/ adv **(a)** (constantly, gradually) (breathe/beat/work) regularmente **(b)** (incessantly) (rain/work) sin cesar, sin parar **(c)** (not shaking) (gaze) fijamente; (walk) con paso seguro

steady[1] /'stedi/ adj **-dier, -diest** ⓵ (not shaky) (gaze) fijo; (chair/table/ladder) firme, seguro; **with a** ~ **hand** con pulso firme; **hold the camera** ~ no muevas la cámara ⓶ **(a)** (constant) (rain/speed/pace) constante; (flow/stream) continuo **(b)** (regular) (before n) (job) fijo; (income) regular; ~ **boyfriend** novio m; ~ **girlfriend** novia f **(c)** (dependable) (person/worker) serio, formal

steady[2] vt **-dies, -dying, -died (a)** (make stable) (table/ladder) (by holding) sujetar (para que no se mueva) **(b)** (make calm) calmar, tranquilizar*

steak /steɪk/ n **(a)** bistec m, filete m, churrasco m (CS), bife m (RPl, Bol) **(b)** (cut) carne f para filete (or bistec etc)

steal /stiːl/ (past **stole**; past p **stolen**) vt ⓵ (object/idea) robar; **to** ~ **sth FROM sb** robarle algo A algn; **to** ~ **a glance at sth/sb** (liter) echar una mirada furtiva a algo/algn ⓶ **stolen** past p (money/property) robado

■ ~ vi ⓵ robar ⓶ (go stealthily) (+ adv compl): **to** ~ **away** o **off** escabullirse*; **they stole into the room** entraron en la habitación a hurtadillas

stealth /stelθ/ n sigilo m

stealthy /'stelθi/ adj **-thier, -thiest** (movement/departure) furtivo; (footsteps) sigiloso

steam[1] /stiːm/ n vapor m; **to let off** ~ desahogarse*; **to run out of** ~ perder* ímpetu

steam[2] vt (Culin) (vegetables/rice) cocinar or cocer* al vapor; (pudding) cocinar or cocer* al baño (de) María

■ ~ vi (give off steam) echar vapor; «hot food» humear

■ **steam up** [v + adv] «window/glass» empañarse

steam: ~**boat** n vapor m, barco m de or a vapor; ~ **engine** n **(a)** (Mech Eng) motor m de or a vapor **(b)** (esp BrE Rail) locomotora f or máquina f de or a vapor

steamer /'stiːmər ‖'stiːmə(r)/ n ⓵ (Naut) vapor m, buque m or barco m de or a vapor ⓶ (cooking vessel) vaporera f

steam: ~**roller** n apisonadora f, aplanadora f (AmL); ~**ship** n ▶ STEAMER 1

steamy /'stiːmi/ adj **-mier, -miest** (room/atmosphere) lleno de vapor; (window/glass) empañado

steel[1] /stiːl/ n (Metall) acero m

steel[2] v refl **to** ~ **oneself FOR sth/to** + INF armarse de valor PARA algo/PARA + INF

steel wool n lana f de acero, virulana® f (Arg), fibra f metálica (Méx)

steely /'stiːli/ adj **-lier, -liest** (gaze/expression) duro; (determination) férreo

steep[1] /stiːp/ adj **-er, -est** ⓵ **(a)** (slope) empinado; (drop) brusco; (descent) en picada or (Esp) en picado **(b)** (large) (increase/decline) considerable ⓶ (colloq) (prices) alto, excesivo

steep² vt (to soften, clean) remojar; (to flavor) macerar

steeple /'sti:pəl/ n aguja f, campanario m

steeple: ~**chase** n carrera f de obstáculos; ~**jack** n: *persona que repara chimeneas, torres etc*

steeply /'sti:pli/ adv (a) ⟨slope/rise/fall⟩ abruptamente (b) ⟨increase/decline⟩ considerablemente

steer¹ /stɪr ‖'stɪə(r)/ n (a) (castrated bull) buey m (b) (young bull) novillo m

steer² vt (a) ⟨vehicle/plane⟩ dirigir*, conducir*; ⟨ship⟩ gobernar* (b) (guide) llevar, conducir*
■ ~ vi (Naut) estar* or ir* al timón; (Auto) ir* al volante; **to ~ clear of sth/sb** evitar algo/a algn

steering /'stɪrɪŋ ‖'stɪərɪŋ/ n dirección f

steering wheel n (Auto) volante m

stem¹ /stem/ n [1] (of plant) tallo m; (of leaf) peciolo m, pecíolo m; (of fruit) pedúnculo m [2] (of glass) pie m

stem² **-mm-** vt ⟨flow/bleeding⟩ contener*; ⟨outbreak/decline⟩ detener*
■ ~ vi **to ~ FROM sth** provenir* DE algo

stench /stentʃ/ n fetidez f

stencil¹ /'stensəl ‖'stensɪl/ n (a) (for lettering, decoration) plantilla f, troquel m (b) (for duplicating) stencil m, cliché m (Esp)

stencil² vt, (BrE) **-ll-** ⟨design/pattern⟩ escribir, dibujar o pintar utilizando una plantilla

stenographer /stə'nɑ:grəfər ‖ste'nɒgrəfə(r)/ n (esp AmE) taquígrafo, -fa m,f, estenógrafo, -fa m,f

stenography /stə'nɑ:grəfi ‖ste'nɒgrəfi/ n (AmE) taquigrafía f, estenografía f

step¹ /step/ n [1] (footstep, pace) paso m; **to take a ~** formal dar* un paso adelante; **to watch one's ~** andarse* con cuidado [2] (a) (of dance) paso m (b) (in marching, walking) paso m; **to be in/out of ~** llevar/no llevar el paso [3] (measure) medida f; **to take ~s (to + INF)** tomar medidas (PARA + INF) [4] (on stair) escalón m, peldaño m; (on ladder) travesaño m, escalón m [5] (AmE Mus): **whole ~** tono m; **half ~** semitono m

step² **-pp-** vi: would you ~ **inside/outside for a moment?** ¿quiere pasar/salir un momento?; **to ~ off a plane** bajarse de un avión; **to ~ IN/ON sth** pisar algo
■ **step aside** [v + adv] hacerse* a un lado
■ **step back** [v + adv] (a) (move back) dar* un paso atrás (b) (become detached) **to ~ back (FROM sth)** distanciarse (DE algo)
■ **step down** [v + adv] (a) (get down) bajar (b) (resign) renunciar, dimitir
■ **step forward** [v + adv] (a) (move forward) dar* un paso adelante (b) (present oneself) ofrecerse*
■ **step in** [v + adv] intervenir*
■ **step up** [v + o + adv, v + adv + o] ⟨production/campaign⟩ intensificar*; ⟨efforts/security/attacks⟩ redoblar

step: ~**brother** n hermanastro m; ~ **by** ~ adv (one stage at a time) paso a paso; (gradually) poco a poco; ~**by-**~ /'stepbar'step/ adj ⟨instructions⟩ detallado, paso a paso; ~**child** n (son) hijastro m; (daughter) hijastra f; ~**daughter** n hijastra f; ~**father** n padrastro m; ~**ladder** n escalera f de mano or de tijera; ~**mother** n madrastra f

stepping-stone /'stepɪŋstəʊn/ n: cada una de las piedras que se colocan para cruzar un arroyo, un pantano etc; **a ~ to success** un peldaño en el camino del éxito

step: ~**sister** n hermanastra f; ~**son** n hijastro m

stereo¹ /'steriəʊ/ n (pl **-os**) (a) (player) estéreo m (b) (sound) estéreo m

stereo² adj estéreo adj inv

stereotype¹ /'steriətaɪp/ n estereotipo m

stereotype² vt catalogar*, estereotipar

sterile /'sterəl ‖'steraɪl/ adj estéril

sterility /stə'rɪləti/ n esterilidad f

sterilize /'sterəlaɪz/ vt esterilizar*

sterling¹ /'stɜːrlɪŋ ‖'stɜːlɪŋ/ n la libra (esterlina)

sterling² adj: **the pound ~** la libra esterlina

stern¹ /stɜːrn ‖stɜːn/ n popa f

stern² adj **-er, -est** severo

steroid /'stɪrɔɪd, 'ste- ‖'stɪərɔɪd, 'ste-/ n esteroide m

stethoscope /'steθəskəʊp/ n estetoscopio m

stevedore /'sti:vədɔːr ‖'sti:vədɔː(r)/ n estibador, -dora m,f

stew¹ /stu: ‖stju:/ n estofado m, guiso m

stew² vt ⟨meat⟩ estofar, guisar; ⟨fruit⟩ hacer* compota de

steward /'stu:ərd ‖'stju:əd/ n [1] (a) (on ship) camarero m (b) (on plane) auxiliar (m) de vuelo, sobrecargo (m), aeromozo (m) (AmL) [2] (a) (manager of estate) administrador, -dora m,f (b) (at public gatherings) (BrE) persona encargada de supervisar al público en manifestaciones

stewardess /'stu:ərdəs ‖'stju:ədes/ n (a) (on ship) camarera f (b) (on plane) auxiliar f de vuelo, azafata f, sobrecargo f, aeromoza f (AmL)

stick¹ /stɪk/ n [1] (of wood) palo m, vara f; (twig) ramita f; (for fire) astilla f [2] (a) (walking ~) bastón m (b) (hockey ~) palo m [3] (of celery, rhubarb) rama f, penca f; (of dynamite) cartucho m; (of rock, candy) palo m; **a ~ of chalk** una tiza; **a ~ of chewing gum** un chicle [4] **sticks** pl **the ~s** (colloq): **to live out in the ~s** vivir en la Cochinchina or (Esp tb) en las Batuecas

stick² (past & past p **stuck**) vt [1] (attach, glue) pegar*
[2] (a) (thrust) ⟨needle/knife/sword⟩ clavar (b) (impale) **to ~ sth ON sth** clavar algo EN algo [3] (put, place) (colloq) poner* [4] (tolerate) (esp BrE colloq) aguantar, soportar
■ ~ vi [1] (adhere) «glue» pegar*; «food» pegarse*; **to ~ TO sth** pegarse* or (frml) adherirse* A algo; **the two pages have stuck together** las dos páginas se han pegado; **the song stuck in my mind** la canción se me quedó grabada [2] (become jammed) atascarse*; *see also* STUCK²
■ **stick at** [v + prep + o] (colloq) seguir* con; ~ **at it** sigue así
■ **stick by** [v + prep + o] ⟨friend⟩ no abandonar; ⟨promise⟩ mantener* en pie
■ **stick out** [1] [v + adv] (a) (protrude) sobresalir* (b) (be obvious) resaltar; **he really ~s out in a crowd** uno enseguida lo nota en un grupo de gente [2] [v + o + adv, v + adv + o] (stretch out) (colloq) ⟨hand⟩ extender*; ⟨tongue⟩ sacar*
■ **stick to** [v + prep + o] (a) (hold to) ⟨road/path⟩ ⋯⟶

seguir* por; ⟨*principles*⟩ mantener*; ⟨*rules*⟩
ceñirse* a, atenerse* a; **I'll ~ to my original plan**
seguiré con mi plan original **(b)** (not digress from)
⟨*subject/facts*⟩ ceñirse* a **(c)** (restrict oneself to)
limitarse a
■ **stick together** [*v* + *adv*] no separarse; (support
each other) mantenerse* unidos
■ **stick up** **1** [*v* + *o* + *adv*, *v* + *adv* + *o*] **(a)** (on
wall) ⟨*notice*⟩ colocar*, poner* **(b)** (raise) ⟨*hand*⟩
levantar
2 [*v* + *adv*] (project): **something was ~ing up out
of the ground** algo sobresalía del suelo; **her hair
was ~ing up** tenía el pelo de punta, tenía el pelo
parado (AmL)
■ **stick up for** [*v* + *adv* + *prep* + *o*] ⟨*person*⟩
sacar* la cara por, defender*; **to ~ up for oneself**
hacerse* valer

sticker /'stɪkər ‖'stɪkə(r)/ *n* (label) etiqueta *f*;
(with slogan etc) pegatina *f*, adhesivo *m*

sticking plaster /'stɪkɪŋ/ *n* (BrE) **(a)**
(individual strip) curita® *f* (AmL), tirita® *f* (Esp) **(b)**
(tape) esparadrapo *m*, cinta *f* adhesiva

stick: ~ insect *n* insecto *m* palo;
~-in-the-mud *n* (colloq): **don't be such a
~-in-the-mud** no seas tan rutinario e inflexible

stickler /'stɪklər ‖'stɪklə(r)/ *n*: **he's a ~ for
discipline** insiste mucho en la disciplina

stick: ~-on *adj* adhesivo; **~ shift** *n* (AmE) **(a)**
(lever) palanca *f* de cambio(s) *or* (Méx) de
velocidades **(b)** (car) coche *m* (de transmisión)
estándar *or* manual; **~up** *n* (colloq) atraco *m*,
asalto *m*

sticky /'stɪki/ *adj* **stickier, stickiest** **1** **(a)**
⟨*label*⟩ engomado, autoadhesivo; ⟨*surface*⟩
pegajoso **(b)** ⟨*weather*⟩ bochornoso **2** (difficult)
(colloq) ⟨*problem/issue*⟩ peliagudo; ⟨*situation*⟩
violento

stiff¹ /stɪf/ *adj* **-er, -est** **1** **(a)** ⟨*collar/bristles*⟩
duro; ⟨*fabric*⟩ tieso, duro; ⟨*corpse*⟩ rígido;
⟨*muscles*⟩ entumecido, agarrotado; **to have a ~
neck** tener* tortícolis; **I'm ~ after that walk** estoy
dolorido *or* (esp AmL) adolorido despues de la
caminata **(b)** ⟨*paste/dough*⟩ consistente; ⟨*egg
white*⟩ firme **2** ⟨*test/climb*⟩ difícil, duro;
⟨*resistance*⟩ férreo; ⟨*penalty*⟩ fuerte; ⟨*breeze/
drink*⟩ fuerte **3** ⟨*person/manner*⟩ estirado; ⟨*bow/
smile*⟩ forzado

stiff² *adv* (colloq): **I'm frozen ~** estoy helado
hasta los huesos (fam); **we were bored ~** nos
aburrimos como ostras (fam); **scared ~** muerto de
miedo

stiffen /'stɪfən/ *vt* **(a)** (with starch) almidonar;
(with fabric underneath) armar **(b)** ~ **(up)** ⟨*resolve*⟩
fortalecer*
■ ~ *vi* **(a)** ~ **(up)** (become rigid) «*person/muscles/
joint*» agarrotarse **(b)** (become firm) endurecerse*
(c) (in manner, reaction) ponerse* tenso

stiffly /'stɪfli/ *adv* **(a)** ⟨*walk/move*⟩ rígidamente,
con rigidez **(b)** ⟨*greet*⟩ fríamente; ⟨*bow*⟩ con fría
formalidad

stifle /'staɪfəl/ *vt* **1** (suffocate) (often pass)
⟨*person*⟩ sofocar* **2** (suppress) ⟨*flames*⟩ sofocar*;
⟨*yawn/anger*⟩ contener*; ⟨*noise*⟩ ahogar*

stifling /'staɪflɪŋ/ *adj* ⟨*heat*⟩ sofocante

stigma /'stɪgmə/ *n* (*pl* **-mas**) estigma *m*

stile /staɪl/ *n*: *escalones que permiten pasar por
encima de una cerca*

stiletto /stɪ'letəʊ/ *n* (*pl* **-tos** *or* **-toes**) ~
(heel) tacón *m* de aguja, taco *m* aguja *or* alfiler
(CS)

still¹ /stɪl/ *adv*

■ **Note** Spanish has two words for *still*: *todavía* and
aún. Both can go at the beginning or end of the
sentence: *I still haven't seen him* todavía *or* aún no lo
he visto *or* no lo he visto todavía *or* aún. The
distinction in English between *he hasn't arrived yet*
and *he still hasn't arrived* is not expressed verbally in
Spanish. Both can be translated by *todavía* or *aún no
ha llegado*, or *no ha llegado todavía* or *aún*. The
degree of intensity, surprise, or annoyance is often
expressed by intonation. Note that the verb *seguir* can
be used to express continuation: *I still don't
understand why* sigo sin entender por qué; *he's still
looking for a job* sigue buscando trabajo.

1 (even now, even then) todavía, aún; **there's ~
plenty left** todavía *or* aún queda mucho; **are we ~
friends?** ¿seguimos siendo amigos?
2 (*as intensifier*) aún, todavía; **the risk is greater
~** el riesgo es aún *or* todavía mayor
3 (*as linker*): **they say it's safe, but I'm ~ scared**
dicen que no hay peligro pero igual *or* aun así
tengo miedo; **~, it could have been worse** de
todos modos, podría haber sido peor

still² *adj* **(a)** (motionless) ⟨*lake/air*⟩ en calma,
quieto, tranquilo; **sit/stand ~** quédate quieto; **her
heart stood ~ for a moment** el corazón se le paró
un momento **(b)** ⟨*drink*⟩ sin gas, no efervescente

still³ *n* **1** (Cin, Phot) fotograma *m* **2** (distillery)
destilería *f*; (distilling apparatus) alambique *m*

still: ~born /'stɪl'bɔːrn ‖'stɪlbɔːn/ *adj* nacido
muerto; **~ life** *n* (*pl* ~ **lifes**) naturaleza *f*
muerta

stilt /stɪlt/ *n* zanco *m*

stilted /'stɪltəd ‖'stɪltɪd/ *adj* **(a)** ⟨*conversation/
manner*⟩ forzado **(b)** ⟨*language/writing*⟩
rebuscado; ⟨*acting*⟩ acartonado

stimulate /'stɪmjələrt ‖'stɪmjʊleɪt/ *vt*
estimular

stimulating /'stɪmjələrtɪŋ ‖'stɪmjʊleɪtɪŋ/ *adj*
estimulante

stimulation /stɪmjə'leɪʃən ‖,stɪmjʊ'leɪʃən/ *n*
estímulo *m*

stimulus /'stɪmjələs ‖'stɪmjʊləs/ *n* (*pl* **-li**
/-laɪ/) estímulo *m*

sting¹ /stɪŋ/ *n* **1** **(a)** (of bee, wasp) aguijón *m*
(b) (action, wound) picadura *f* **2** (*no pl*) (pain)
escozor *m*, ardor *m* (CS)

sting² (*past* & *past p* **stung**) *vt* **1** « *bee/
nettle*» picar* **2** (cause pain) hacer* escocer,
hacer* arder (CS)

■ ~ *vi* [1] «*insect/nettle*» picar* [2] (hurt physically) «*ointment*» hacer* escocer, hacer* arder (CS); «*cut*» escocer*, arder (CS)

stinging nettle /'stɪŋɪŋ/ *n* ortiga *f*

stingy /'stɪndʒi/ *adj* **-gier -giest** ‹*person*› tacaño; ‹*portion*› mezquino

stink¹ /stɪŋk/ *n* **(a)** (bad smell) hediondez *f*, mal olor *m*, peste *f* (fam) **(b)** (fuss) (colloq) escándalo *m*, lío *m* (fam), follón *m* (Esp fam); **to make** *o* **kick up a** ~ armar un lío (*or* un escándalo *etc*)

stink² *vi* (*past* **stank** *or* **stunk**; *past p* **stunk**) «*person/place/breath*» apestar; **the whole business** ~**s** (colloq) todo el asunto da asco

stink bomb *n* bomba *f* fétida

stinking /'stɪŋkɪŋ/ *adj* (before *n*) hediondo, fétido, apestoso; **I've got a** ~ **cold** (colloq) tengo un resfriado espantoso

stint¹ /stɪnt/ *n* **(a)** (fixed amount, share): **I've done my** ~ **for today** hoy ya he hecho mi parte **(b)** (period) período *m*; **he did a five-year** ~ **in the army** pasó (un período de) cinco años en el ejército

stint² *vi* **to** ~ **on sth** escatimar algo

stipulate /'stɪpjəleɪt/ *vi* ‹*stipjʊleɪt*› *vt* estipular

stipulation /ˌstɪpjəˈleɪʃən/ ‹ˌstɪpjʊˈleɪʃən/ *n* condición *f*, estipulación *f*

stir¹ /stɜːr/ ‹stɜː(r)/ *n* **(a)** (action) **to give sth a** ~ revolver* *or* (Esp) remover* algo **(b)** (excitement) revuelo *m*, conmoción *f*

stir² **-rr-** *vt* [1] (mix) ‹*liquid/mixture*› revolver*, remover* (Esp) [2] **(a)** (move slightly) agitar, mover* **(b)** (get moving) (colloq) mover* **(c)** (waken) despertar* [3] **(a)** (arouse) ‹*imagination*› estimular **(b)** (move, affect) conmover* **(c)** (provoke, incite) **to** ~ **sb into action** empujar *or* incitar a algn a la acción

■ ~ *vi* **(a)** (change position) moverse*, agitarse **(b)** (venture out) moverse*, salir* **(c)** (wake up) despertarse*; (get up) levantarse

■ **stir up** [*v* + *o* + *adv*, *v* + *adv* + *o*] ‹*mud/waters*› revolver*, remover* (Esp); ‹*hatred/unrest/revolt*› provocar*; ‹*discontent*› promover*; **to** ~ **up trouble** armar lío (fam)

stir-fry /'stɜːr'fraɪ/ ‹'stɜː'fraɪ/ *vt* **-fries, -frying, -fried** *freír en poco aceite y revolviendo constantemente*

stirring /'stɜːrɪŋ/ *adj* conmovedor

stirrup /'stɜrəp/ ‹'stɪrəp/ *n* estribo *m*

stitch¹ /stɪtʃ/ *n* [1] **(a)** (in sewing) puntada *f* **(b)** (in knitting) punto *m* **(c)** (Med) punto *m* [2] (pain) (*no pl*) punzada *f* *or* (CS) puntada *f* (en el costado), flato *m* (Esp)

stitch² *vt* **(a)** (sew) coser **(b)** (embroider) bordar **(c)** (Med) suturar

stoat /stəʊt/ *n* armiño *m*

stock¹ /staːk/ ‹stɒk/ *n* [1] **(a)** (supply) (*often pl*) reserva *f* **(b)** (of shop, business) existencias *fpl*, estoc *m*; **we're out of** ~ las verdes se han agotado; **to take** ~ **of sth** hacer* un balance de algo
[2] (Fin) **(a)** (shares) acciones *fpl*, valores *mpl*; (government securities) bonos *mpl* *or* papel *m* del Estado **(b)** ~**s and bonds** *o* (BrE) ~**s and shares** acciones *fpl*
[3] (livestock) ganado *m*
[4] (descent) linaje *m*, estirpe *f*
[5] (Culin) caldo *m*

[6] **stocks** *pl* (Hist) **the** ~**s** el cepo
[7] (Am Theat) repertorio *m*

stock² *vt* [1] (Busn) vender [2] (fill) ‹*store*› surtir, abastecer*; ‹*larder/freezer*› llenar

■ **stock up** [*v* + *adv*] abastecerse*; (Busn) hacer* un estoc; **we'd better** ~ **up on coffee before it goes up** más vale que compremos bastante café antes de que suba

stock³ *adj* (before *n*) ‹*size*› estándar *adj inv*; ‹*model*› de serie

stock: ~**broker** *n* corredor, -dora *m,f* de valores *or* de Bolsa, agente *mf* de Bolsa; ~ **company** *n* (AmE) **(a)** (Fin) sociedad *f* anónima **(b)** (Theat) compañía *f* de repertorio; ~ **cube** *n* cubito *m* de caldo; ~ **exchange** *n* bolsa *f* (de valores), Bolsa *f*; ~**holder** *n* accionista *mf*

Stockholm /'staːkhəʊlm/ ‹'stɒkhəʊm/ *n* Estocolmo

stocking /'staːkɪŋ/ ‹'stɒkɪŋ/ *n* media *f*

stock-in-trade /'staːkɪn'treɪd/ ‹ˌstɒkɪn'treɪd/ *n* especialidad *f*

stockist /'staːkəst/ ‹'stɒkɪst/ *n* (BrE) proveedor, -dora *m,f*, distribuidor, -dora *m,f*

stock market *n* mercado *m* de valores, mercado *m* (bursátil)

stockpile¹ /'staːkpaɪl/ ‹'stɒkpaɪl/ *n* reservas *fpl*

stockpile² *vt* almacenar

stock: ~**room** *n* almacén *m*, depósito *m*, bodega *f* (Méx); ~**still** /'staːk'stɪl/ ‹stɒk'stɪl/ *adj* inmóvil; ~**taking** /'staːkˌteɪkɪŋ/ ‹'stɒkˌteɪkɪŋ/ *n* (esp BrE Busn): **⑤ closed for stocktaking** cerrado por inventario

stocky /'staːki/ ‹'stɒki/ *adj* **stockier, stockiest** bajo y fornido

stockyard /'staːkjɑːrd/ ‹'stɒkjɑːd/ *n* (AmE) corral *m*

stodgy /'staːdʒi/ ‹'stɒdʒi/ *adj* **-dgier, -dgiest** (BrE) ‹*food*› feculento, pesado

stoical /'stəʊɪkəl/ *adj* estoico

stoke /stəʊk/ *vt* echarle carbón (*or* leña *etc*) a

stole¹ /stəʊl/ *past of* STEAL

stole² *n* estola *f*

stolen /'stəʊlən/ *past p of* STEAL

stolid /'staːləd/ ‹'stɒlɪd/ *adj* impasible

stomach¹ /'stʌmək/ *n* **(a)** (organ) estómago *m*; **on an empty** ~ con el estómago vacío, en ayunas **(b)** (belly) barriga *f* (fam), panza *f* (fam)

stomach² *vt* (*usu neg*) ‹*insults/insolence/person*› soportar, aguantar

stomach: ~**ache** *n* dolor *m* de estómago; (in lower abdomen) dolor *m* de barriga *or* (frml) de vientre; ~ **pump** *n* bomba *f* estomacal

stomp /staːmp/ ‹stɒmp/ *vi* (+ *adv compl*): **to** ~ **in/out** entrar/salir* pisando fuerte

stone¹ /stəʊn/ *n* [1] (substance, piece) piedra *f* [2] **(a)** (gem) piedra *f* **(b)** (in kidney) cálculo *m*, piedra *f* **(c)** (of fruit) hueso *m*, cuesco *m* [3] (*pl* *or* ~**s**) (in UK) *unidad de peso equivalente a 14 libras o 6,35kg*

stone² *vt* apedrear, lapidar

stone: S~ **Age** *n* Edad *f* de Piedra; ~**-cold** /'stəʊn'kəʊld/ *adj* (colloq) helado

stoned /stəʊnd/ *adj* (colloq) (*usu pred*) (from ···⋮

drugs) volado, pacheco (Méx), colocado (Esp fam); **to get** ~ volarse*, ponerse* pacheco (Méx), colocarse* (Esp fam)

stone: ~**deaf** /'stəʊn'def/ *adj* (colloq) sordo como una tapia (fam); ~**mason** *n* picapedrero *m*, cantero *m*; ~**wall** /'stəʊn'wɔːl/ *vi* (be evasive) andarse* con evasivas; (be obstructive) utilizar* tácticas obstruccionistas

stony /'stəʊni/ *adj* **-nier, -niest** 1 ⟨ground/path⟩ pedregoso 2 ⟨look/person⟩ frío, glacial; ⟨silence⟩ sepulcral

stood /stʊd/ *past & past p of* STAND²

stool /stuːl/ *n* taburete *m*, banco *m*

stoop¹ /stuːp/ *vi* 1 (have a stoop): he ~s a little es un poco cargado de espaldas *or* encorvado 2 (bend over) agacharse 3 (demean oneself): how could he ~ so low? ¿cómo pudo llegar tan bajo?; **to** ~ **TO sth** rebajarse A algo

stoop² *n* (*no pl*): she walks with a ~ camina encorvada

stop¹ /staːp ‖ stɒp/ *n* 1 (halt): **to come to a** ~ «vehicle/aircraft» detenerse*; «production/conversation» interrumpirse; **to put a** ~ **to sth** ⟨to mischief/malpractice⟩ poner* fin a algo 2 **(a)** (break on journey) parada *f* **(b)** (stopping place) parada *f*, paradero *m* (AmL exc RPl)

stop² **-pp-** *vt* 1 **(a)** (halt) ⟨taxi/bus⟩ parar; ⟨person⟩ parar, detener* **(b)** (switch off) ⟨machine/engine⟩ parar
2 **(a)** (bring to an end, interrupt) ⟨decline/inflation⟩ detener*, parar; ⟨discussion/abuse⟩ poner* fin a, acabar con; ~ **that noise!** ¡deja de hacer ruido! **(b)** (cease): ~ **what you're doing and listen to me** deja lo que estás haciendo y escúchame; ~ **it!** ¡basta ya!; **to** ~ **-ING** dejar DE + INF
3 (prevent): **what's stopping you?** ¿qué te lo impide?; **I had to tell him, I couldn't** ~ **myself** tuve que decírselo, no pude contenerme; **to** ~ **sb (FROM) -ING** (esp BrE) impedirle* a algn + INF, impedir* QUE algn (+ *subj*); **to** ~ **sth happening** impedir* que ocurra algo
4 (cancel, withhold) ⟨subscription⟩ cancelar; ⟨payment⟩ suspender
5 (block) ⟨hole⟩ tapar; ⟨gap⟩ rellenar
6 (parry) ⟨blow/punch⟩ parar, detener*
■ ~ *vi* 1 **(a)** (halt) «vehicle/driver» parar, detenerse*; ~ **or I'll shoot!** ¡alto o disparo! **(b)** (interrupt journey) «train/bus» parar **(c)** (cease operating) «watch/clock/machine» pararse
2 **(a)** (cease): **the rain has** ~**ped** ha dejado *or* parado de llover, ya no llueve; **the pain/bleeding has** ~**ped** ya no le (*or* me *etc*) duele/sale sangre **(b)** (interrupt activity) parar; **I didn't** ~ **to think** no me detuve a pensar
3 (colloq) (stay) quedarse
■ **stop by** [*v* + *adv*] [*v* + *prep* + *o*]: **I** ~**ped by** (at) **the store for some milk** pasé por la tienda para comprar leche
■ **stop off** [*v* + *adv*]: **I** ~**ped off at home to change** pasé por casa para cambiarme; **we** ~**ped off in San Juan for a few hours** paramos unas horas en San Juan
■ **stop over** [*v* + *adv*] **(a)** (overnight) hacer* noche **(b)** (Aviat) «plane» hacer* escala
■ **stop up** [*v* + *o* + *adv*, *v* + *adv* + *o*] (fill) ⟨hole/crack⟩ tapar, rellenar

stop: ~**gap** *n* recurso *m* provisional *or* (AmS tb) provisorio; ~**over** *n* (break in journey) parada *f*; (Aviat) escala *f*

stoppage /'staːpɪdʒ ‖ 'stɒpɪdʒ/ *n* 1 **(a)** (in play, production) interrupción *f* **(b)** (strike) huelga *f*, paro *m* (AmL) **(c)** (cancellation) suspensión *f* 2 (blockage) obstrucción *f*

stopper /'staːpər ‖ 'stɒpə(r)/ *n* tapón *m*

stopping train /'staːpɪŋ ‖ 'stɒpɪŋ/ *n* (BrE) tren con parada en todas las estaciones

stop: ~ **press** *n* noticias *fpl* de última hora; ~**watch** *n* cronómetro *m*

storage /'stɔːrɪdʒ/ *n* **(a)** (of goods) depósito *m*, almacenaje *m*, almacenaje *m*; (before *n*) ~ **space** lugar *m* *or* espacio *m* para guardar cosas **(b)** (Comput) almacenamiento *m*

store¹ /stɔːr ‖ stɔː(r)/ *n* 1 **(a)** (stock, supply) reserva *f*, provisión *f*; **in** ~: **there's a surprise in** ~ **for her** la espera una sorpresa; **who knows what the future has in** ~? ¿quién sabe lo que nos deparará el futuro?; **to set great/little** ~ **by sth** dar* mucho/poco valor a algo **(b)** **stores** *pl* (Mil, Naut) pertrechos *mpl* 2 (warehouse, storage place) (often *pl*) almacén *m*, depósito *m*, bodega *f* (Méx) 3 **(a)** (shop) (esp AmE) tienda *f* **(b)** (department ~) grandes almacenes *mpl*, tienda *f*

store² *vt* **(a)** (keep) ⟨food/drink/supplies⟩ guardar; (Busn) almacenar; ⟨information⟩ almacenar; ⟨electricity⟩ acumular **(b)** (Comput) ⟨data/program⟩ almacenar
■ **store up** [*v* + *o* + *adv*, *v* + *adv* + *o*] **(a)** ⟨supplies⟩ almacenar **(b)** ⟨resentment⟩ ir* acumulando

store: ~**house** *n* **(a)** (warehouse) almacén *m*, depósito *m*, bodega *f* (Méx) **(b)** (source) mina *f*; ~**keeper** *n* tendero, -ra *m,f*, ~**room** *n* almacén *m*, depósito *m*, bodega *f* (Méx); (for food) despensa *f*

storey /'stɔːri/ *n* (BrE) ▶ STORY II

stork /stɔːrk ‖ stɔːk/ *n* cigüeña *f*

storm¹ /stɔːrm ‖ stɔːm/ *n* 1 (Meteo) tormenta *f*; **a** ~ **at sea** una tempestad; **to take sth by** ~ ⟨city/fortress⟩ tomar algo por asalto; **she took New York's audiences by** ~ cautivó al público neoyorquino 2 (of protest) ola *f*, tempestad *f*

storm² *vi* 1 (move violently) (+ *adv compl*): **she** ~**ed into the office** irrumpió en la oficina
2 (express anger) despotricar*, vociferar
■ ~ *vt* ⟨city/fortress⟩ tomar por asalto; ⟨house⟩ irrumpir en

stormy /'stɔːrmi ‖ 'stɔːmi/ *adj* **-mier, -miest** **(a)** (Meteo) tormentoso; ⟨sea⟩ tempestuoso **(b)** (turbulent) ⟨relationship⟩ tempestuoso

story /'stɔːri/ *n* (*pl* **-ries**)
I 1 **(a)** (account) historia *f*, relato *m*; (genre) cuento *m*; **to cut a long** ~ **short** en pocas palabras **(b)** (anecdote) anécdota *f* 2 (plot) argumento *m*, trama *f* 3 (Journ) artículo *m*
4 (lie) (colloq) cuento *m* (fam), mentira *f*
II **(a)** **storey** (of building) piso *m*, planta *f*

story: ~**book** *n* libro *m* de cuentos; ~ **line** *n* argumento *m*; ~**teller** *n* narrador, -dora *m,f*

stout¹ /staʊt/ *adj* **-er, -est** ⟨person/figure⟩ robusto, corpulento; ⟨door⟩ sólido

stout² *n* cerveza *f* negra

stove /stəʊv/ *n* **(a)** (for cooking) cocina *f*, estufa *f* (Col, Méx) **(b)** (for warmth) estufa *f*

stow /stəʊ/ *vt* (put away) guardar, poner*; (hide) esconder; (Naut) estibar
■ **stow away** [*v + adv*] viajar de polizón

stowaway /'stəʊə,weɪ/ *n* polizón *mf*

straddle /'strædl/ *vt* ⟨*horse*⟩ sentarse* a horcajadas sobre; **he ∼d the chair** se sentó a caballo *or* a horcajadas en la silla

straggle /'strægəl/ *vi* [1] (spread untidily) «*plant*» crecer* desordenadamente [2] (lag behind, fall away) rezagarse*

straggler /'stræglər ‖'stræglə(r)/ *n* rezagado, -da *m,f*

straggly /'strægli/ *adj* **-glier, -gliest** ⟨*hair*⟩ desordenado, desgreñado; ⟨*beard*⟩ descuidado

straight¹ /streɪt/ *adj* **-er, -est** [1] **(a)** (not curved or wavy) recto; ⟨*hair*⟩ lacio, liso **(b)** (level, upright, vertical) (*pred*) **to be ∼** estar* derecho; **is my tie ∼?** ¿tengo la corbata derecha *or* bien puesta?
[2] (in order) (*pred*): **I have to put my room ∼** tengo que ordenar mi cuarto; **let's get this ∼** a ver si nos entendemos; **to set the record ∼** dejar las cosas en claro
[3] **(a)** (direct, clear) ⟨*denial/refusal*⟩ rotundo, categórico **(b)** (unmixed) ⟨*gin/vodka*⟩ solo
[4] (honest, frank) ⟨*question*⟩ directo; ⟨*answer*⟩ claro
[5] (successive): **he won in ∼ sets** (Sport) ganó sin conceder *or* sin perder ningún set; **she's had five ∼ wins** ha ganado cinco veces seguidas
[6] **(a)** (serious) ⟨*play/actor*⟩ dramático, serio **(b)** (conventional) (colloq) convencional **(c)** (heterosexual) (colloq) heterosexual

straight² *adv* [1] **(a)** (in a straight line) ⟨*walk*⟩ en línea recta; **she looked ∼ ahead** miró al frente; **the truck was coming ∼ at me** el camión venía derecho hacia mí; **he made ∼ for the bar** se fue derecho al bar; **keep ∼ on until you come to the lights** sigue derecho hasta llegar al semáforo **(b)** (erect) ⟨*sit/stand*⟩ derecho; **sit up ∼** ponte derecho
[2] **(a)** (directly) directamente; **I came ∼ home from work** vine directamente *or* derecho a casa después del trabajo **(b)** (immediately): **∼ after dinner** inmediatamente después de cenar; **I'll bring it ∼ back** enseguida lo devuelvo; **I'll come ∼ to the point** iré derecho al grano; **∼ away** ▶ STRAIGHTAWAY
[3] (colloq) (frankly) con franqueza; **she told him ∼ out** se lo dijo sin rodeos
[4] (clearly) ⟨*see/think*⟩ con claridad

straight: ∼ and narrow *n* **the ∼ and narrow** el buen camino, el camino recto; **∼away** /'streɪtə'weɪ/, **∼ away** *adv* enseguida, inmediatamente

straighten /'streɪtn/ *vt* **(a)** ⟨*nail/wire/picture*⟩ enderezar*; ⟨*hair*⟩ alisar; **he ∼ed his tie** se enderezó la corbata **(b)** (tidy) ⟨*room/papers*⟩ arreglar, ordenar
■ **straighten out** [*v + o + adv, v + adv + o*] ⟨*confusion/misunderstanding*⟩ aclarar; ⟨*problem*⟩ resolver*
■ **straighten up** [1] [*v + o + adv, v + adv + o*] (tidy) ⟨*room/papers*⟩ ordenar, arreglar; ⟨*bed*⟩ arreglar [2] [*v + adv*] (stand up straight) ponerse* derecho

straight: ∼faced /'streɪt'feɪst/ *adj*: **he said it completely ∼faced** lo dijo muy serio; **∼forward** /'streɪt'fɔ:rwərd ‖,streɪt'fɔ:wəd/ *adj* **(a)** (honest,

frank) ⟨*person/answer*⟩ franco **(b)** (uncomplicated) ⟨*problem/question*⟩ sencillo; **∼jacket** *n* ▶ STRAITJACKET

strain¹ /streɪn/ *n* [1] (tension) tensión *f*; (pressure) presión *f*; **it puts ∼ on the spine** ejerce presión sobre la columna vertebral; **the incident put a ∼ on Franco-German relations** las relaciones franco-alemanas se volvieron tirantes a raíz del incidente [2] (Med) (resulting from wrench, twist) torcedura *f*; (on a muscle) esguince *m* [3] **strains** *pl* (tune): **the ∼s of** el sonido de; **to the ∼s of the violin** al son del violín [4] **(a)** (type — of plant) variedad *f*; (— of virus) cepa *f*; (— of animal) raza *f* **(b)** (streak) (*no pl*) veta *f*

strain² *vt* [1] (exert): **to ∼ one's eyes/voice** forzar* la vista/voz; **he ∼ed every muscle to lift the weight** usó todas sus fuerzas para levantar el peso [2] **(a)** (overburden) ⟨*beam/support*⟩ ejercer* demasiada presión sobre **(b)** (injure): **to ∼ one's back** hacerse* daño en la espalda; **to ∼ a muscle** hacerse* un esguince **(c)** (overtax, stretch) ⟨*relations*⟩ someter a demasiada tensión; ⟨*patience*⟩ poner* a prueba [3] (filter) filtrar; (Culin) colar*; ⟨*vegetables/rice*⟩ escurrir
■ ∼ *vi*: **to ∼ AT sth** tirar de algo; **to ∼ to + INF** hacer* un gran esfuerzo PARA + INF

strained /streɪnd/ *adj* [1] (tense) ⟨*relations/atmosphere*⟩ tenso, tirante; ⟨*expression*⟩ tenso, crispado; ⟨*voice*⟩ forzado [2] (Med) **a ∼ muscle** un esguince

strainer /'streɪnər ‖'streɪnə(r)/ *n* (Culin) colador *m*

strait /streɪt/ *n* [1] (Geog) (often *pl*) estrecho *m* [2] **straits** *pl* (difficulties, difficult position): **to be in dire ∼s** estar* en grandes apuros

strait: ∼jacket *n* camisa *f* de fuerza, chaleco *m* de fuerza (CS); **∼laced** /'streɪt'leɪst/ *adj* puritano

strand¹ /strænd/ *n* (of rope, string) ramal *m*; (of thread, wool) hebra *f*; (of wire) filamento *m*; **a ∼ of hair** un pelo

strand² *vt* (usu pass): **to be ∼ed** «*ship*» quedar encallado; «*whale*» quedar varado; **they left me ∼ed** me abandonaron a mi suerte, me dejaron tirado *or* (AmL exc RPI) botado (fam)

strange /streɪndʒ/ *adj* **stranger, strangest** [1] (odd) raro, extraño; **it is ∼ (THAT)** es raro QUE (+ *subj*) [2] **(a)** (unfamiliar, unaccustomed) ⟨*faces/handwriting*⟩ desconocido **(b)** (alien) (liter): **in a ∼ land** en tierras extrañas

strangely /'streɪndʒli/ *adv* ⟨*behave/act*⟩ de una manera rara *or* extraña; **∼ enough** (*indep*) aunque parezca mentira

stranger /'streɪndʒər ‖'streɪndʒə(r)/ *n* desconocido, -da *m,f*; (from another place) forastero, -ra *m,f*; **I'm a ∼ here myself** yo tampoco soy de aquí

strangle /'stræŋgəl/ *vt* **(a)** ⟨*person*⟩ estrangular **(b)** **strangled** *past p* ⟨*cry/voice*⟩ ahogado

stranglehold /'stræŋgəlhəʊld/ *n* **(a)** (Sport) llave *f* al cuello **(b)** (absolute control) poder *m*, dominio *m*

strap¹ /stræp/ *n* **(a)** (of leather) correa *f*; (of canvas) asa *f*; **(b)** (shoulder ∼) tirante *m*, bretel *m* (CS)

strap² *vt* **-pp-** (tie) atar *or* sujetar con una correa, amarrar con una correa (AmL exc RPI)

S

strapless /'stræpləs ‖'stræplɪs/ *adj* sin tirantes, sin breteles (CS)

strapping /'stræpɪŋ/ *adj* robusto, fornido

Strasbourg /'strɑːsbʊrg ‖'stræzbɜːg/ *n* Estrasburgo *m*

strata /'streɪtə, 'strætə ‖'strɑːtə, 'streɪtə/ *pl of* STRATUM

stratagem /'strætədʒəm/ *n* estratagema *f*

strategic /strə'tiːdʒɪk/ *adj* estratégico

strategy /'strætədʒi/ *n* (*pl* **-gies**) estrategia *f*

stratify /'strætɪfaɪ ‖'strætɪfaɪ/ *vt* **-fies, -fying, -fied** (*usu pass*) estratificar*

stratum /'streɪtəm, 'stræ- ‖'strɑːtəm, 'streɪ-/ *n* (*pl* **-ta**) estrato *m*

straw /strɔː/ *n* (a) (material, single stem) paja *f*; **to be the last** o **final ~** ser* el colmo; **to clutch** o **grasp at ~s** aferrarse desesperadamente a una esperanza (b) (for drinking) pajita *f*, paja *f*, caña *f* (Esp), pitillo *m* (Col), popote *m* (Méx)

strawberry /'strɔːˌberi ‖'strɔːbəri/ *n* (*pl* **-ries**) fresa *f*, frutilla *f* (Bol, CS); (large) fresón *m*

stray¹ /streɪ/ *vi* (a) (wander away) apartarse, alejarse; (get lost) extraviarse*, perderse* (b) (digress) apartarse, desviarse*

stray² *adj* (a) ⟨dog⟩ (ownerless) callejero; (lost) perdido; ⟨sheep⟩ descarriado (b) (random, scattered) ⟨bullet⟩ perdido; ⟨hair⟩ suelto

stray³ *n* (ownerless animal) perro *m*/gato *m* callejero; (lost animal) perro *m*/gato *m* perdido

streak¹ /striːk/ *n* **1** (a) (line, band) lista *f*, raya *f*; (in hair) reflejo *m*, mechón *m*; (in marble) veta *f*; (of ore) veta *f*, filón *m* (b) (in personality) veta *f* **2** (spell) racha *f*; **to be on a winning ~** tener* una buena racha

streak² *vi* (+ *adv compl*): **to ~ past** pasar como una centella

■ **~** *vt*: **tears ~ed her face** tenía el rostro surcado de lágrimas; **to have one's hair ~ed** hacerse* mechas *or* reflejos *or* (RPl) claritos *or* (Méx) luces *or* (Chi) visos (en el pelo)

streaky /'striːki/ *adj* **-kier, -kiest** (a) (uneven) ⟨paint⟩ no uniforme, disparejo (AmL) (b) (BrE Culin): **~ bacon** tocino *m or* (Esp) bacon *m or* (RPl) panceta *f*

stream¹ /striːm/ *n* **1** (a) (small river) arroyo *m*, riachuelo *m* (b) (current) corriente *f* **2** (flow): **a thin ~ of water** un chorrito de agua; **a ~ of abuse** una sarta de insultos; **there is a continuous ~ of traffic** pasan vehículos continuamente

stream² *vi* **1** (flow) (+ *adv compl*): **blood ~ed from the wound** salía *or* manaba mucha sangre de la herida; **tears were ~ing down her cheeks** lloraba a lágrima viva; **the sunlight was ~ing in through the window** el sol entraba a raudales por la ventana; **I've got a ~ing cold** tengo un resfriado muy fuerte **2** (wave) ⟨⟨flag/hair⟩⟩ ondear

■ **~** *vt* (BrE Educ) dividir (*a los alumnos*) en grupos *según su aptitud para una asignatura*

streamer /'striːmər ‖'striːmə(r)/ *n* (a) (banner) banderín *m* (b) (of paper) serpentina *f*

stream: ~line *vt* ⟨car/plane⟩ hacer* más aerodinámico el diseño de, aerodinamizar*; ⟨organization/production⟩ racionalizar*; **~lined** *adj* ⟨car/plane⟩ aerodinámico; ⟨methods/ production⟩ racionalizado

street /striːt/ *n* calle *f*; **it's on** o (BrE) **in Elm S~** queda en la calle Elm; (*before n*) ⟨musician/ theater⟩ callejero; **~ corner** esquina *f*; **~ map** o **plan** plano *m* de la ciudad, callejero *m* (Esp); **~ market** mercado *m* al aire libre, feria *f* (CS)

street: ~car *n* (AmE) tranvía *m*; **~ cleaner** *n* (AmE) barrendero, -ra *m,f*; **~ lamp** *n* farol *m*; **~ level** *n*: **at ~ level** a nivel de la calle; **~ light** *n* ▶ **~** LAMP; **~ sweeper** *n* (person) barrendero, -ra *m,f*; (machine) (máquina *f*) barredora *f*

strength /streŋθ/ *n* **1** (of persons) (a) (physical energy) fuerza(s) *f(pl)*; (health) fortaleza *f* física; **to get one's ~ back** recobrar las fuerzas (b) (emotional, mental) fortaleza *f* **2** (of economy, currency) solidez *f* **3** (a) (of materials) resistencia *f*; (of wind, current) fuerza *f*; (of drug, solution) concentración *f*; (of alcoholic drink) graduación *f* (b) (of sound, light) potencia *f*; (of emotions) intensidad *f* (c) (of argument, evidence) lo convincente; (of protests) lo enérgico **4** (strong point) virtud *f*, punto *m* fuerte **5** (force in numbers): **their fans were there in ~** sus hinchas estaban allí en bloque *or* en masa

strengthen /'streŋθən/ *vt* ⟨muscle/limb⟩ fortalecer*; ⟨wall/furniture/glass⟩ reforzar*; ⟨support⟩ aumentar

■ **~** *vi* ⟨⟨limb/muscle⟩⟩ fortalecerse*; ⟨⟨opposition/ support⟩⟩ aumentar

strenuous /'strenjuəs/ *adj* (a) ⟨activity⟩ agotador (b) ⟨denial⟩ vigoroso; ⟨opposition⟩ tenaz

stress¹ /stres/ *n* **1** (a) (tension) tensión *f*; (Med) estrés *m*, tensión *f*; **she's under a lot of ~** está sometida a muchas presiones (b) (Phys, Tech) tensión *f* **2** (a) (emphasis) énfasis *m*, hincapié *m* (b) (Ling, Lit) acento *m* (tónico)

stress² *vt* (a) (emphasize) poner* énfasis *or* hacer* hincapié en, enfatizar* (b) (Ling) acentuar*

stressful /'stresfəl/ *adj* ⟨life/job⟩ estresante

stretch¹ /stretʃ/ *vt* ⟨arm/leg⟩ estirar, extender*; ⟨wing⟩ extender*, desplegar* **2** ⟨sheet/canvas⟩ extender* **3** (eke out) ⟨money/resources⟩ estirar **4** (a) (make demands on) exigirle* a; **she's not being ~ed at school** en el colegio no le exigen de acuerdo a su capacidad (b) (strain): **our resources are ~ed to the limit** nuestros recursos están empleados al máximo **5** ⟨truth/meaning⟩ forzar*; ⟨rules⟩ apartarse un poco de

■ **~** *vi* **1** ⟨⟨person⟩⟩ estirarse; (when sleepy) desperezarse*

⠂⠂

AmC Central America	Arg Argentina	Cu Cuba	Per Peru
AmL Latin America	Bol Bolivia	Ec Ecuador	RPl River Plate Area
AmS South America	Chi Chile	Esp Spain	Ur Uruguay
Andes Andean Region	CS Southern Cone	Méx Mexico	Ven Venezuela

2 (a) (reach, extend) «*sea/influence/power*» extenderse* (b) (in time): to ~ over a period alargarse* *or* prolongarse* durante un período
3 (a) (be elastic) «*elastic/rope*» estirarse (b) (become loose, longer) «*garment*» estirarse
4 (be enough) «*money/resources/supply*» alcanzar*, llegar*
■ *v refl* to ~ oneself (physically) estirarse; (when sleepy) desperezarse*
■ **stretch out** 1 [*v + o + adv, v + adv + o*] (extend) estirar
2 [*v + adv*] (a) (lie full length) tenderse* (b) (extend — in space) extenderse*; (— in time) alargarse*

stretch² *n* 1 (act of stretching) (*no pl*): to have a ~ estirarse; (when sleepy) desperezarse* 2 (a) (expanse — of road, river) tramo *m*, trecho *m* (b) (period) período *m*; at a ~ (without a break) sin parar 3 (elasticity) elasticidad *f*

stretch³ *adj* (*before n, no comp*) ⟨*fabric/pants*⟩ elástico; ~ limo (colloq) limusina *f* (*grande*)

stretcher /'stretʃər ‖'stretʃə(r)/ *n* (Med) camilla *f*

stretch marks *pl n* estrías *fpl*

stretchy /'stretʃi/ *adj* **-chier, -chiest** elástico

strew /struː/ *vt* (*past* **strewn** /struːn/ *past p* **strewn** *or* **strewed** /-d/) ⟨*gravel/seeds*⟩ esparcir*; ⟨*objects*⟩ (untidily) desparramar

stricken /'strɪkən/ *adj* (a) (afflicted) ~ WITH sth: a country ~ with famine un país asolado por el hambre; I was suddenly ~ with remorse de pronto me empezó a remorder la conciencia (b) ⟨*vessel*⟩ siniestrado (fml), dañado; ⟨*area*⟩ damnificado, afectado

strict /strɪkt/ *adj* **-er, -est** (a) (severe) estricto, severo (b) (rigorous) ⟨*vegetarian*⟩ estricto, riguroso (c) (exact) (*before n*) estricto, riguroso; in the ~ sense of the word en el sentido estricto *or* riguroso de la palabra (d) (completo) (*before n*) absoluto; in ~est secrecy en el más absoluto secreto

strictly /'strɪktli/ *adv* (a) (severely) con severidad, severamente, rigurosamente (b) (rigorously): smoking is ~ prohibited fumar está terminantemente prohibido; ~ (speaking) (*indep*) en rigor, en sentido estricto (c) (exactly) totalmente; that's not ~ true eso no es totalmente cierto (d) (exclusively) exclusivamente; this is ~ between ourselves que quede entre nosotros

stride¹ /straɪd/ *vi* (*past* **strode**; *past p* **stridden** /'strɪdn/) (+ *adv compl*): he strode across the room cruzó la habitación a grandes zancadas

stride² *n* zancada *f*, tranco *m*; to take sth in one's ~ tomarse algo con calma

strident /'straɪdnt/ *adj* estridente

strife /straɪf/ *n* (journ *or* frml) conflictos *mpl*; (armed) luchas *fpl*

strike¹ /straɪk/ (*past & past p* **struck**) *vt*
1 (a) (hit) ⟨*person*⟩ pegarle* a, golpear; ⟨*blow*⟩ dar*, pegar*; ⟨*key*⟩ pulsar (b) (collide with, fall on) «*vehicle*» chocar* *or* dar* contra; «*stone/ball*» pegar* *or* dar* contra; «*lightning/bullet*» alcanzar*; I struck my head on the beam me di (un golpe) en la cabeza contra la viga; he was struck by lightning le cayó un rayo
2 (a) (cause to become): to be struck blind/dumb

quedarse ciego/mudo; to ~ sb dead matar a algn (b) (introduce): to ~ fear into sb infundirle miedo a algn
3 (a) (occur to) ocurrírsele (+ *me/te/le etc*); it ~s me (that) ... me da la impresión de que ..., se me ocurre que ... (b) (impress) parecerle* a; it ~s me as odd me parece raro; I was struck by his changed appearance me llamó la atención lo cambiado que estaba
4 ⟨*oil/gold*⟩ encontrar*, dar* con
5 ⟨*match/light*⟩ encender*
6 (a) (Mus) ⟨*note*⟩ dar* (b) «*clock*» dar*; the clock struck five el reloj dio las cinco
7 (enter into, arrive at): to ~ a deal llegar* a un acuerdo, cerrar* un trato; to ~ a balance between ... encontrar* el justo equilibrio entre ...
8 (adopt) ⟨*pose/attitude*⟩ adoptar
9 (delete) suprimir; his name was struck off the register se borró su nombre del registro; *see also* STRIKE OFF
■ ~ *vi* 1 (hit) «*person*» golpear; «*lightning*» caer*
2 (a) (attack) atacar* (b) (happen suddenly) «*illness/misfortune*» sobrevenir*; «*disaster*» ocurrir
3 (withdraw labor) hacer* huelga, declararse en huelga *or* (esp AmL) en paro
4 «*clock*» dar* la hora
■ **strike back** [*v + adv*] (Mil) contraatacar*; he struck back at his critics devolvió el golpe a sus detractores
■ **strike down** [*v + o + adv, v + adv + o*] (liter): she was struck down with cholera fue abatida por el cólera (liter)
■ **strike off** [*v + o + adv, v + adv + o*] (a) (delete) tachar (b) (disqualify) (BrE) ⟨*doctor/lawyer*⟩ prohibirle* el ejercicio de la profesión a
■ **strike out**
I [*v + adv*] to ~ out (AT sb/sth) arremeter (CONTRA algn/algo)
II [*v + o + adv, v + adv + o*] (remove from list) tachar
■ **strike up** 1 [*v + adv + o*] (a) (begin) ⟨*conversation*⟩ entablar; ⟨*friendship*⟩ trabar, entablar (b) (start to play) ⟨*tune*⟩ empezar* a tocar
2 [*v + adv*] «*band*» empezar* a tocar

strike² *n* 1 (stoppage) huelga *f*, paro *m* (esp AmL); to be on ~ estar* en *or* de huelga, estar* en *or* de paro (esp AmL); to come out *o* go (out) on ~ ir* a la huelga, declararse en huelga, ir* al paro (esp AmL), declararse en paro (esp AmL); hunger ~ huelga de hambre 2 (find) descubrimiento *m* 3 (attack) ataque *m*

strikebreaker /'straɪk,breɪkər ‖'straɪk,breɪkə(r)/ *n* rompehuelgas *mf*

striker /'straɪkər ‖'straɪkə(r)/ *n* 1 (Lab Rel) huelguista *mf* 2 (in soccer) artillero, -ra *m,f*, ariete *mf*

striking /'straɪkɪŋ/ *adj* ⟨*resemblance/similarity*⟩ sorprendente, asombroso; ⟨*color*⟩ llamativo; a ~ woman una mujer muy atractiva

string¹ /strɪŋ/ *n* 1 (a) (cord, length of cord) cordel *m*, bramante *m* (Esp), mecate *m* (AmC, Méx, Ven), pita *f* (Andes), cáñamo *m* (Andes), piolín *m* (RPl) (b) (on apron) cinta *f*; (on puppet) hilo *m*; no ~s attached sin compromisos, sin condiciones
2 (a) (on instrument) cuerda *f* (b) (on racket) cuerda *f* (c) **strings** *pl* (Mus) cuerdas *fpl*
3 (a) (set — of pearls, beads) sarta *f*, hilo *m*; (— of ┅⫶

onions, garlic) ristra *f* **(b)** (series — of people)
sucesión *f*; (— of vehicles) fila *f*; (— of events) serie
f; (— of curses, complaints, lies) sarta *f*

string² (*past & past p* **strung**) *vt* **1** (suspend)
colgar* **2** ⟨*guitar/racket/bow*⟩ encordar*,
ponerle* (las) cuerdas a; ⟨*beads/pearls*⟩ ensartar,
enhebrar
▪ **string along** (colloq) [*v* + *o* + *adv*] (mislead)
tomarle el pelo a (fam) ⟨*dando esperanzas falsas*⟩
▪ **string together** [*v* + *o* + *adv*, *v* + *adv* + *o*]
⟨*thoughts*⟩ coordinar, hilar; **she could barely ~ a**
sentence together apenas podía hilar una frase

string bean *n* ▶ RUNNER BEAN

stringed /strɪŋd/ *adj* ⟨*instrument*⟩ de cuerda

stringent /'strɪndʒənt/ *adj* riguroso, estricto

strip¹ /strɪp/ **-pp-** *vt* **1** **(a)** (remove covering from)
⟨*bed*⟩ deshacer*, quitar la ropa de; ⟨*wood/*
furniture⟩ quitarle la pintura (*or* el barniz *etc*) a,
decapar; **to ~ sb (naked)** desnudar a algn **(b)**
(remove contents from) ⟨*room/house*⟩ vaciar*
2 (Auto, Tech) **~ (down)** desmontar
▪ **~** *vi* desnudarse, desvestirse*
▪ **strip off** [*v* + *o* + *adv*, *v* + *adv* + *o*] ⟨*wallpaper/*
paint⟩ quitar; ⟨*leaves*⟩ arrancar*

strip² *n* **1** (of leather, cloth, paper) tira *f*; (of metal)
tira *f*, cinta *f*; (of land) franja *f* **2** (BrE Sport) (*no*
pl) equipo *m*

strip cartoon *n* (BrE) historieta *f*, tira *f*
cómica

stripe /straɪp/ *n* raya *f*, lista *f*

striped /straɪpt/ *adj* a *or* de rayas, rayado,
listado

strip: ~ lighting *n* (BrE) luz *f* fluorescente;
~-search /'strɪp'sɜːrtʃ ‖ 'strɪp,sɜːtʃ/ *vt* hacer*
desnudar y registrar

strive /straɪv/ *vi* (*past* **strove** *or* **strived**;
past p **striven** /'strɪvən/) **to ~ FOR** *o* **AFTER** sth
luchar *or* esforzarse* por alcanzar algo; **to ~ to +**
INF esforzarse* POR + INF

strobe (light) /strəʊb/ *n* luz *f* estroboscópica

strode /strəʊd/ *past of* STRIDE¹

stroke¹ /strəʊk/ *n* **1** (Sport) **(a)** (in ball games)
golpe *m* **(b)** (in swimming — movement) brazada *f*;
(— style) estilo *m* **(c)** (in rowing — movement) palada
f, remada *f*
2 **(a)** (blow) golpe *m* **(b)** (of clock) campanada *f*
3 **(a)** (of thin brush) pincelada *f*; (of thick brush)
brochazo *m*; (of pen, pencil) trazo *m* **(b)** (oblique,
slash) barra *f*, diagonal *f*
4 **(a)** (action, feat) golpe *m*; **not to do a ~ of work**
no hacer* absolutamente nada **(b)** (instance): **a ~**
of luck un golpe de suerte
5 (Med) ataque *m* de apoplejía, derrame *m*
cerebral
6 (caress) caricia *f*

stroke² *vt* acariciar

stroll¹ /strəʊl/ *vi* pasear(se), dar* un paseo

stroll² *n* paseo *m*; **to have** *o* **go for a ~** dar* un
paseo

stroller /'strəʊlər ‖ 'strəʊlə(r)/ *n* **1** (person)
paseante *mf* **2** (pushchair) (esp AmE) sillita *f* (de
paseo), cochecito *m*, carreola *f* (Méx)

strong¹ /strɔːŋ ‖ strɒŋ/ *adj* **stronger**
/'strɔːŋgər ‖ 'strɒŋgə(r)/, **strongest** /'strɔːŋgəst
‖ 'strɒŋgɪst/ **1** **(a)** (physically powerful) ⟨*person/*

arm⟩ fuerte **(b)** (healthy, sound) ⟨*heart/lungs*⟩
fuerte, sano; ⟨*constitution*⟩ robusto **(c)** (firm)
⟨*character/leader*⟩ fuerte
2 **(a)** (solid) ⟨*material/construction*⟩ fuerte **(b)**
(powerful) ⟨*army/economy*⟩ fuerte **(c)** ⟨*current/*
wind⟩ fuerte
3 **(a)** (deeply held) ⟨*views/faith/support*⟩ firme **(b)**
(forceful) ⟨*protest*⟩ enérgico; ⟨*argument/evidence*⟩
de peso
4 (definite) **(a)** ⟨*tendency/resemblance*⟩ marcado; ⟨*candidate*⟩ con muchas posibilidades **(b)**
⟨*features*⟩ marcado
5 (good) ⟨*team*⟩ fuerte; ⟨*cast*⟩ sólido; **~ point**
punto *m* fuerte; **she's a ~ swimmer** es una buena
nadadora
6 **(a)** (concentrated) ⟨*color/light*⟩ fuerte, intenso;
⟨*tea/coffee*⟩ cargado; ⟨*solution*⟩ concentrado **(b)**
(pungent) ⟨*smell/flavor*⟩ fuerte **(c)** (unacceptable)
⟨*language*⟩ fuerte
7 (in number) (*no comp*): **an army ten thousand ~**
un ejército de diez mil hombres

strong² *adv*: **to be going ~** «*car/machine*»
marchar bien; «*organization*» ir* *or* marchar
viento en popa; **he's still going ~** «*old person*»
sigue (estando) en plena forma

strong: ~box *n* caja *f* fuerte *or* de caudales;
~hold *n* (fortress) fortaleza *f*, bastión *m*; (center of
support) bastión *m*, baluarte *m*

strongly /'strɔːŋli ‖ 'strɒŋli/ *adv* **1** **(a)**
(powerfully) fuerte, con fuerza **(b)** (sturdily) ⟨*made/*
welded⟩ sólidamente **2** **(a)** (deeply, ardently)
totalmente; **it's something I feel very ~ about** es
algo que me parece sumamente importante **(b)**
(forcefully) ⟨*protest/criticize*⟩ enérgicamente; **I ~**
advise you not to sell te recomiendo con
insistencia que no vendas

strong: ~ room *n* cámara *f* acorazada;
~-willed /'strɔːŋ'wɪld ‖ ,strɒŋ'wɪld/ *adj*
(determined) tenaz; (obstinate) terco, tozudo

strove /strəʊv/ *past of* STRIVE

struck /strʌk/ *past & past p of* STRIKE¹

structural /'strʌktʃərəl/ *adj* estructural

structure¹ /'strʌktʃər ‖ 'strʌktʃə(r)/ *n* **(a)**
(composition, organization) estructura *f* **(b)** (thing
constructed) construcción *f*

structure² *vt* estructurar

struggle¹ /'strʌgəl/ *n* **(a)** (against opponent)
lucha *f*; (physical) refriega *f*; **to put up a ~** luchar,
oponer* resistencia **(b)** (against difficulties) lucha *f*;
it's a ~ to make ends meet cuesta mucho llegar a
fin de mes

struggle² *vi* **1** **(a)** (thrash around) forcejear **(b)**
(contend, strive) luchar; **she had to ~ to support**
her family tuvo que luchar para mantener a su
familia; **to ~** (AGAINST/WITH sth) luchar (CONTRA
algo); **to ~ FOR** sth luchar POR algo **(c)** (be in
difficulties) pasar apuros **2** (move with difficulty) (+
adv compl): **he ~d up the hill** subió penosamente
la cuesta; **he ~d to his feet** se levantó con gran
dificultad

strum /strʌm/ *vt* **-mm-** ⟨*guitar/tune*⟩ rasguear

strung /strʌŋ/ *past & past p of* STRING²

strut¹ /strʌt/ *vi* **-tt-** (+ *adv compl*): **to ~ around**
o **about** pavonearse

strut² *n* (Const) tornapunta *f*, puntal *m*

stub¹ /stʌb/ *n* **(a)** (of candle, pencil) cabo *m*; (of cigarette) colilla *f*, pucho *m* (AmL fam) **(b)** (of check) talón *m* (AmL), matriz *f* (Esp); (of ticket) contraseña *f*, resguardo *m* (Esp)

stub² -bb- *vt*: to ~ one's toe darse* en el dedo (*del pie*)

■ **stub out** [*v + o + adv, v + adv + o*] ‹*cigarette*› apagar*

stubble /'stʌbəl/ *n* **(a)** (Agr) rastrojo *m* **(b)** (of beard): **he had three days'** ~ **on his chin** tenía una barba de tres días

stubborn /'stʌbərn ‖'stʌbən/ *adj* **(a)** ‹*person/ nature*› (obstinate) terco, testarudo; (resolute) tenaz, tesonero; ‹*refusal/insistence*› pertinaz **(b)** ‹*cold/ weeds*› pertinaz, persistente; ‹*stain*› rebelde

stuck¹ /stʌk/ *past & past p of* STICK²

stuck² *adj* (*pred*) **(a)** (unable to move): **the drawer is** ~ el cajón se ha atascado; **the door is** ~ la puerta se ha atrancado; **she's** ~ **at home with the kids all day** está todo el día metida en la casa con los niños **(b)** (at a loss) atascado; **I got** ~ **on the second question** me quedé atascado en la segunda pregunta **(c)** (burdened) (colloq): **I was** ~ **with the bill** me tocó pagar la cuenta, me cargaron el muerto (fam); **I got** ~ **with Bob all evening** tuve que aguantar a Bob toda la noche

stuck-up /'stʌk'ʌp/ *adj* (colloq) estirado (fam)

stud¹ /stʌd/ *n* **1** **(a)** (nail, knob) tachuela *f* **(b)** (earring) arete *m or* (Esp) pendiente *m* (*en forma de bolita*) **(c)** (for collar, shirtfront) gemelo *m* (*para cuello o pechera de camisa*) **2** (male animal) semental *m*

stud² *vt* -dd- (*usu pass*) (with studs) tachonar; **the sky was** ~ded **with stars** el cielo estaba tachonado de estrellas (liter)

student /'stu:dnt ‖'stju:dnt/ *n* (at university) estudiante *mf*; (at school) (esp AmE) alumno, -na *m,f*; **a medical** ~ un/una estudiante de medicina; (*before n*) ~ **driver** (AmE) *persona que está aprendiendo a conducir*; ~ **nurse** estudiante *mf* de enfermería

student union *n* (association) asociación *f* de estudiantes; (building) *centro estudiantil en el campus*

studio /'stu:diəʊ ‖'stju:diəʊ/ *n* **(a)** (Art, Mus, Phot) estudio *m* **(b)** (Cin, Rad, TV) estudio *m* **(c)** ~ (**apartment** *o* (BrE also) **flat**) estudio *m*

studious /'stu:diəs ‖'stju:diəs/ *adj* estudioso, aplicado

study¹ /'stʌdi/ *n* (*pl* -dies) **1** (act, process of learning) estudio *m* **2** **studies** *pl* **(a)** (work of student) estudios *mpl* **(b)** (academic discipline): **business studies** empresariado *m or* (Esp) empresariales *fpl*; **social studies** *estudios vinculados a las relaciones sociales que comprenden cursos de historia, sociología y otras asignaturas afines* **3** (room) estudio *m* **4** (investigation, examination) estudio *m* **5** (Art, Liter, Mus) estudio *m*

study² -dies, -dying, -died *vt* **(a)** (at school, university) estudiar **(b)** (investigate, research into) estudiar **(c)** (examine, scrutinize) estudiar

■ ~ *vi* estudiar; **she's** ~**ing to be a doctor/lawyer** estudia medicina/derecho

stuff¹ /stʌf/ *n* **1** (colloq) **(a)** (substance, matter): **what's this** ~ **called?** ¿cómo se llama esto *or* (fam) esta cosa? **(b)** (miscellaneous items) cosas *fpl*; (personal items) cosas *fpl*, bártulos *mpl*; (junk,

rubbish) cachivaches *mpl*; **and** ~ **like that** y cosas de esas; **what sort of** ~ **does he write?** ¿qué tipo de cosa(s) escribe? **2** (nonsense, excuse) (colloq): **surely you don't believe all that** ~ **he tells you?** tú no te creerás todo lo que te cuenta ¿no?

stuff² *vt* **1** **(a)** (fill) ‹*quilt/mattress/toy*› rellenar; ‹*hole*› tapar; **the drawer was** ~ed **with clothes** el cajón estaba atiborrado de ropa; **to** ~ **oneself/ one's face** (colloq) darse* un atracón (fam), ponerse* morado *or* ciego (Esp fam) **(b)** (Culin) rellenar **(c)** (in taxidermy) disecar* **2** **(a)** (thrust) **to** ~ **sth** INTO **sth** meter algo EN algo **(b)** (put) (colloq) poner*

stuffed /stʌft/ *adj* **(a)** (in taxidermy) disecado; (toy) de peluche **(b)** ‹*pepper/tomatoes*› relleno

stuffing /'stʌfɪŋ/ *n* relleno *m*

stuffy /'stʌfi/ *adj* -fier, -fiest **1** **(a)** ‹*air*› viciado; **it's** ~ **in here** está muy cargado el ambiente **(b)** ‹*nose*› tapado **2** (staid) (colloq) ‹*person*› acartonado, estirado (fam); ‹*organization*› convencional

stumble /'stʌmbəl/ *vi* **(a)** (trip) tropezar*, dar* un traspié **(b)** (in speech) atrancarse*; **he** ~d **over the long words** se atrancaba la lengua con las palabras largas

■ **stumble across** ▶ STUMBLE ON

■ **stumble on, stumble upon** [*v + prep + o*] dar* con, encontrar*

stumbling block /'stʌmblɪŋ/ *n* escollo *m*

stump¹ /stʌmp/ *n* (of tree) tocón *m*, cepa *f*; (of limb) muñón *m*; (of pencil, candle) cabo *m*

stump² *vt* (colloq) (*often pass*): **the problem has me** ~ed el problema me tiene perplejo; **to be** ~ed **for an answer** no saber qué contestar

stun /stʌn/ *vt* -nn- **(a)** (make unconscious) dejar sin sentido; (daze) aturdir **(b)** (amaze) dejar atónito *or* (fam) helado; (shock) dejar anonadado

stung /stʌŋ/ *past & past p of* STING²

stunk /stʌŋk/ *past p of* STINK²

stunned /stʌnd/ *adj* **(a)** (unconscious) sin sentido; (dazed) aturdido **(b)** (shocked, amazed) ‹*expression*› de asombro; **he was** ~ **when they told me** se quedó atónito *or* (fam) helado cuando se lo dijeron

stunning /'stʌnɪŋ/ *adj* ‹*success/performance*› sensacional; ‹*person/dress*› despampanante

stunt¹ /stʌnt/ *n* **1** (feat of daring) proeza *f*; **she does all her own** ~s (Cin, TV) hace todas las escenas peligrosas ella misma; (*before n*) ~ **man/ woman** especialista *mf* **2** (hoax, trick) truco *m*, maniobra *f*; (publicity ~) ardid *m* publicitario

stunt² *vt* detener*, atrofiar

stunted /'stʌntəd ‖'stʌntɪd/ *adj* ‹*growth/ development*› atrofiado; ‹*tree/body*› raquítico

stupefy /'stu:pəfaɪ ‖'stju:pɪfaɪ/ *vt* -fies, -fying, -fied (*usu pass*) dejar estupefacto

stupendous /stu:'pendəs ‖stju:'pendəs/ *adj* (colloq) ‹*effort/strength*› tremendo; ‹*success*› formidable

stupid /'stu:pəd ‖'stju:pɪd/ *adj* (foolish) tonto (fam); (unintelligent) estúpido

stupidity /stu:'pɪdəti ‖stju:'pɪdəti/ *n* estupidez *f*, tontería *f*

stupor /'stu:pər ‖'stju:pə(r)/ *n* (Med) estupor *m*; (lethargy) aletargamiento *m*; **in a drunken** ~ en un sopor etílico (frml *o* hum)

S

sturdy /'stɜːrdi ‖'stɜːdi/ *adj* **-dier, -diest** ‹*build/legs/figure*› robusto, macizo; ‹*furniture/ bicycle*› sólido y resistente

stutter¹ /'stʌtər ‖'stʌtə(r)/ *n* tartamudeo *m*

stutter² *vi* tartamudear
■ ~ *vt* balbucear, decir* tartamudeando

St Valentine's Day ▶ VALENTINE'S DAY

sty /staɪ/ *n* (*pl* **sties**) (a) (pig~) pocilga *f*, chiquero *m* (AmL) (b) ▶ STYE

stye /staɪ/ *n* (*pl* **sties** *or* **styes**) orzuelo *m*

style /staɪl/ *n* [1] (a) (manner of acting) estilo *m*; **telling lies is not my** ~ decir mentiras no va conmigo (b) (Art, Lit, Mus) estilo *m* [2] (elegance) estilo *m*; **to live/travel in** ~ vivir/viajar a lo grande [3] (a) (type, model) diseño *m*, modelo *m* (b) (fashion) moda *f*; **to be in** ~ estar* de moda (c) (hair ~) peinado *m*

-style /staɪl/ *suff*: **American**~ al estilo americano, a la americana

stylish /'staɪlɪʃ/ *adj* ‹*furniture/clothes/decor*› con mucho estilo; ‹*person*› con clase or estilo, estiloso (AmL fam); ‹*resort/restaurant*› elegante

stylist /'staɪləst ‖'staɪlɪst/ *n* (hair ~) estilista *mf*

stylistic /star'lɪstɪk/ *adj* estilístico

stylized /'staɪlaɪzd/ *adj* estilizado

stylus /'staɪləs/ *n* (*pl* **-li** *or* **-luses**) aguja *f*, púa *f* (RPI)

Styrofoam® /'staɪrəfəʊm/ *n* (AmE) espuma *f* de poliestireno

suave /swɑːv/ *adj* **suaver, suavest** ‹*voice*› engolado; ‹*man*› elegante y desenvuelto

sub /sʌb/ *n* (colloq) (a) (substitute) suplente *mf*, sustituto, -ta *m,f* (b) (submarine) submarino *m* (c) **subs** *pl* (subscription) cuota *f*

subconscious¹ /ˌsʌb'kɑːntʃəs ‖ˌsʌb'kɒnʃəs/ *adj* subconsciente

subconscious² *n* **the** ~ el subconsciente

subcontract /ˌsʌb'kɑːntrækt ‖ˌsʌbkən'trækt/ *vt* subcontratar

subcontractor /ˌsʌb'kɑːntræktər ‖ˌsʌbkən'træktə(r)/ *n* subcontratista *mf*

subdivide /ˌsʌbdə'vaɪd ‖ˌsʌbdɪ'vaɪd/ *vt* subdividir

subdivision /'sʌbdə,vɪʒən ‖ˌsʌbdɪ'vɪʒən/ *n* subdivisión *f*

subdue /səb'duː ‖səb'djuː/ *vt* (a) (bring under control) ‹*person*› someter, dominar (b) (vanquish) (liter) sojuzgar* (liter)

subdued /səb'duːd ‖səb'djuːd/ *adj* ‹*lighting/ color*› tenue, apagado; ‹*person/atmosphere*› apagado

subheading /'sʌb,hedɪŋ/ *n* subtítulo *m*

subject¹ /'sʌbdʒɪkt/ *n* [1] (topic) tema *m*; **to change the** ~ cambiar de tema [2] (discipline) asignatura *f*, materia *f* (esp AmL), ramo *m* (Chi) [3] (Pol) súbdito, -ta *m,f* [4] (Ling) sujeto *m*

subject² /'sʌbdʒɪkt/ *adj* [1] (owing obedience) ‹*people/nation*› sometido [2] (a) (liable, prone) **to be** ~ **TO sth** ‹*to change/delay*› estar* sujeto A algo,

ser* susceptible DE algo; ‹*to flooding*› estar* expuesto A algo (b) (conditional upon) **to be** ~ **TO sth** estar* sujeto A algo

subject³ /səb'dʒekt/ *vt* **to** ~ **sth/sb TO sth** someter algo/a algn A algo

subject index *n* índice *m* de materias

subjective /səb'dʒektɪv/ *adj* subjetivo

subject matter *n* (theme) tema *m*; (content) contenido *m*

subjugate /'sʌbdʒəgeɪt ‖'sʌbdʒʊgeɪt/ *vt* subyugar*

subjunctive¹ /səb'dʒʌŋktɪv/ *n* subjuntivo *m*

subjunctive² *adj* subjuntivo

sublet /'sʌb'let/ *vt/i* (*pres p* **-letting**; *past & past p* **-let**) subarrendar*

sublime /sə'blaɪm/ *adj* sublime

submachine gun /'sʌbmə'ʃiːn/ *n* metralleta *f*

submarine /'sʌbmə'riːn/ *n* submarino *m*

submerge /səb'mɜːrdʒ ‖səb'mɜːdʒ/ *vt* (a) (cover, flood) sumergir* (b) (plunge) **to** ~ **sth IN sth** sumergir* algo EN algo
■ ~ *vi* sumergirse*

submission /səb'mɪʃən/ *n* [1] (surrender) sumisión *f* [2] (plan, proposal) propuesta *f*

submissive /səb'mɪsɪv/ *adj* sumiso

submit /səb'mɪt/ **-tt-** *vt* [1] ‹*claim/report/ application*› presentar [2] (subject) **to** ~ **sb TO sth** someter a algn A algo [3] (contend) sostener*
■ ~ *vi* rendirse*

subnormal /'sʌb'nɔːrməl ‖ˌsʌb'nɔːməl/ *adj* por debajo de lo normal; ‹*person*› retrasado, subnormal

subordinate¹ /sə'bɔːrdnət ‖sə'bɔːdɪnət/ *adj* subordinado

subordinate² *n* subordinado, -da *m,f*

subscribe /səb'skraɪb/ *vi* [1] (buy) **to** ~ (**TO sth**) ‹*to magazine/newspaper*› suscribirse* (A algo) [2] (support) **to** ~ **TO sth** suscribir* algo (frml); **I** ~ **to the view that ...** yo soy de la opinión de que ...

subscriber /səb'skraɪbər ‖səb'skraɪbə(r)/ *n* (to paper, magazine) suscriptor, -tora *m,f*

subscription /səb'skrɪpʃən/ *n* (a) (to magazine) suscripción *f*; (for theatrical events) abono *m* (b) (membership fees) (BrE) cuota *f*

subsequent /'sʌbsɪkwənt/ *adj* (*before n*) posterior, subsiguiente

subsequently /'sʌbsɪkwəntli/ *adv* posteriormente

subservient /səb'sɜːrviənt ‖səb'sɜːviənt/ *adj* servil

subside /səb'saɪd/ *vi* [1] «*land/road/ foundations*» hundirse [2] (abate) «*storm/wind*» amainar; «*floods/swelling*» decrecer*, bajar; «*excitement*» decaer*; «*anger*» calmarse, pasarse

subsidence /səb'saɪdn̩s, 'sʌbsədn̩s ‖səb'saɪdn̩s, 'sʌbsɪdəns/ *n* hundimiento *m*

subsidiary¹ /səb'sɪdieri ‖səb'sɪdiəri/ *adj*
⟨*role*/*interest*⟩ secundario; ∼ **subject** materia *f*
complementaria

subsidiary² *n* (*pl* **-ries**) (Busn) filial *f*

subsidize /'sʌbsədaɪz ‖'sʌbsɪdaɪz/ *vt*
subvencionar, subsidiar (AmL)

subsidy /'sʌbsədi ‖'sʌbsɪdi/ *n* (*pl* **-dies**)
subvención *f*, subsidio *m*

subsist /səb'sɪst/ *vi* subsistir

subsistence /səb'sɪstəns/ *n* subsistencia *f*;
(*before n*) ⟨*farming*⟩ de subsistencia; ∼ **wage**
sueldo *m* de hambre; **to live at** ∼ **level** vivir con
lo justo para subsistir

substance /'sʌbstəns/ *n* ⑴ (type of matter)
sustancia *f* ⑵ **(a)** (solid quality, content) sustancia *f*;
(of book) enjundia *f*, sustancia *f* **(b)** (foundation)
fundamento *m* **(c)** in ∼ en lo esencial

substandard /'sʌb'stændərd ‖,sʌb'stændəd/
adj ⟨*goods*/*clothes*⟩ de calidad inferior

substantial /səb'stæntʃəl ‖səb'stænʃəl/ *adj*
⑴ **(a)** ⟨*amount*/*income*/*loan*⟩ considerable,
importante **(b)** ⟨*changes*/*difference*⟩ sustancial;
⟨*contribution*⟩ importante ⑵ **(a)** (sturdy, solid)
⟨*furniture*/*building*⟩ sólido **(b)** (nourishing, filling)
⟨*meal*⟩ sustancioso

substantiate /səb'stæntʃieɪt ‖səb'stænʃieɪt/
vt ⟨*rumors*/*story*/*statement*⟩ confirmar,
corroborar; **can you** ∼ **these accusations?** ¿puede
probar estas acusaciones?

substation /'sʌbsteɪʃən/ *n* (AmE) estafeta *f* de
correos

substitute¹ /'sʌbstətu:t ‖'sʌbstɪtju:t/ *n* **(a)**
(thing) ∼ (**FOR** sth) sucedáneo *m* (**DE** algo); **sugar**
∼ sucedáneo *m* del azúcar; **there's no** ∼ **for**
experience nada puede sustituir a la experiencia
(b) (person) sustituto, -ta *m*,*f*, reemplazo *m*,
suplente *mf*

substitute² *vt* sustituir*, reemplazar*

substitute teacher *n* (AmE) (profesor,
-sora *m*,*f*) suplente *mf*

substitution /'sʌbstə'tu:ʃən ‖,sʌbstɪ'tju:ʃən/
n sustitución *f*

subterfuge /'sʌbtərfju:dʒ ‖'sʌbtəfju:dʒ/ *n*
subterfugio *m*

subterranean /'sʌbtə'reɪniən/ *adj*
subterráneo

subtitle¹ /'sʌb,taɪtl/ *n* subtítulo *m*

subtitle² *vt* (*usu pass*) subtitular

subtle /'sʌtl/ *adj* **subtler** /'sʌtlər ‖'sʌtlə(r)/,
subtlest /'sʌtləst ‖'sʌtlɪst/ *adj* **(a)** (delicate, elusive)
⟨*fragrance*⟩ sutil **(b)** (not obvious) ⟨*difference*/
distinction/*hint*⟩ sutil; ⟨*change*⟩ imperceptible **(c)**
(tactful) (colloq) delicado

subtlety /'sʌtlti/ *n* (*pl* **-ties**) **(a)** (delicacy,
elusiveness) sutileza *f* **(b)** (tact, finesse) delicadeza *f*;
to lack ∼ ser* poco delicado

subtly /'sʌtli/ *adv* **(a)** (delicately, elusively)
sutilmente **(b)** (tactfully) con delicadeza

subtotal /'sʌbtəʊtl/ *n* subtotal *m*, total *m*
parcial

subtract /səb'trækt/ *vt* to ∼ sth (**FROM** sth)
restar algo (**DE** algo)

subtraction /səb'trækʃən/ *n* resta *f*,
sustracción *f* (frml)

suburb /'sʌbɜːrb ‖'sʌbɜːb/ *n* barrio *m* or (Méx)

colonia *f* residencial de las afueras; **the** ∼**s** los
barrios periféricos *or* de las afueras (de la
ciudad)

suburban /sə'bɜːrbən ‖sə'bɜːbən/ *adj* ⟨*area*⟩
suburbano; ⟨*shopping mall*⟩ de las afueras

suburbia /sə'bɜːrbiə ‖sə'bɜːbiə/ *n* zonas
residenciales de las afueras de una ciudad

subversive /səb'vɜːrsɪv ‖səb'vɜːsɪv/ *adj*
subversivo

subway /'sʌbweɪ/ *n* ⑴ (AmE Rail) metro *m*,
subterráneo *m* (RPl) ⑵ (BrE) (for pedestrians) pasaje
m subterráneo

succeed /sək'siːd/ *vi* ⑴ (have success) ⟨*plan*⟩
dar* resultado, surtir efecto; **she tried to**
persuade him, but did not ∼ intentó convencerlo
pero no lo consiguió; **he's** ∼**ed in all that he's**
done ha tenido éxito en todo lo que ha hecho; **to**
∼ **in life** triunfar en la vida; **he finally** ∼**ed in**
passing the exam al final logró aprobar el
examen ⑵ **to** ∼ (**TO** sth): **he** ∼**ed to the throne**
subió al trono; **to** ∼ **to a title** heredar un título
∎ ∼ *vt* suceder; **who** ∼**ed him?** ¿quién lo sucedió?

succeeding /sək'siːdɪŋ/ *adj* (*before n*)
subsiguiente

success /sək'ses/ *n* éxito *m*; **to be a** ∼ ser* un
éxito; **without** ∼ sin (ningún) éxito

successful /sək'sesfəl/ *adj* ⟨*person*⟩ de éxito,
exitoso (AmL); **the** ∼ **applicant for the job** el
candidato que obtenga el puesto; **to be** ∼ **in life**
triunfar en la vida

successfully /sək'sesfəli/ *adv*
satisfactoriamente

succession /sək'seʃən/ *n* ⑴ **(a)** (act of
following) sucesión *f*; **for 6 years in** ∼ durante seis
años consecutivos; **in rapid** ∼ uno tras otro **(b)**
(series) sucesión *f* ⑵ (to office, rank) sucesión *f*

successive /sək'sesɪv/ *adj* (*before n*)
consecutivo

successor /sək'sesər ‖sək'sesə(r)/ *n* sucesor,
-sora *m*,*f*

succinct /sək'sɪŋkt/ *adj* sucinto, conciso

succulent /'sʌkjələnt ‖'sʌkjʊlənt/ *adj*
suculento

succumb /sə'kʌm/ *vi* to ∼ (**TO** sth) sucumbir
(A algo)

such¹ /sʌtʃ/ *adj* ⑴ **(a)** (emphasizing degree, extent)
tal (+ *noun*); tan (+ *adj*); **I woke up with** ∼ **a**
headache me levanté con tal dolor de cabeza ...;
I've got ∼ **a lot of work to do** tengo tanto
(trabajo) que hacer; **I've never heard** ∼ **nonsense**
nunca he oído semejante estupidez **(b)** (*with*
clauses of result or purpose) **such** ... (**that**) tal/tan
... que **(c)** (*in comparisons*) **such** ... **as** tan ...
como

⑵ **(a)** (of this, that kind) tal; ∼ **children are known**
as ... a dichos *or* a tales niños se los conoce como
...; **there's no** ∼ **thing as the perfect crime** el
crimen perfecto no existe; **I said no** ∼ **thing!** ¡yo
no dije tal cosa! **(b)** (unspecified) tal; **the letter tells**
you to go to ∼ **a house on** ∼ **a date** la carta te
dice que vayas a tal casa en tal fecha

such² *pron* ⑴ **(a)** (of the indicated kind) tal; ∼
were her last words tales fueron sus últimas
palabras **(b)** such as como; **many modern**
inventions, ∼ **as radar** ... muchos inventos
modernos, (tales) como el radar ... **(c)** as such
como tal/tales ⑵ (indicating lack of quantity, quality): ····❖

the evidence, ∼ as it is, seems to ... las pocas pruebas que hay parecen ... **3** (of such a kind, extent, degree) **such that** tal ... que

such: ∼**-and-**∼ *adj* tal (o cual); **we were told to get** ∼**-and-**∼ **a book** nos dijeron que compráramos tal (o cual) libro; ∼**like** *pron* (colloq) (of things) cosas por el estilo; (of people) gente por el estilo

suck /sʌk/ *vt* **(a)** «*person*» ‹*thumb/candy*› chupar; ‹*liquid*› (through a straw) sorber; «*vacuum cleaner*» aspirar; «*pump*» succionar, aspirar; «*insect*» ‹*blood/nectar*› chupar **(b)** (pull, draw) (+ *adv compl*) arrastrar; **she was** ∼**ed under by the current** la corriente se la tragó

  ∎ ∼ **in** **1** «*person*» chupar; **to** ∼ **AT/ON sth** chupar algo **2** (be objectionable) (AmE sl): **the movie really** ∼**s** la película es una mierda (vulg)

  ∎ **suck in** [*v + o + adv, v + adv + o*] ‹*air/breath*› tomar

sucker /ˈsʌkər ‖ˈsʌkə(r)/ *n* **1** (colloq) (fool) (pej) imbécil *mf*; **to be a** ∼ **for punishment** ser* un masoquista **2** (suction device — on animal, plant) ventosa *f*; (— made of rubber) (BrE) ventosa *f* **3** (Bot) (shoot) chupón *m*, mamón *m*

suckle /ˈsʌkəl/ *vt* amamantar, darle* de mamar a

  ∎ ∼ *vi* mamar

suction /ˈsʌkʃən/ *n* succión *f*; (before n) ∼ **cup** ventosa *f*

Sudan /suːˈdɑːn/ *n* (**the**) ∼ (el) Sudán

Sudanese /ˌsuːdn̩ˈiːz ‖ˌsuːdəˈniːz/ *adj* sudanés

sudden /ˈsʌdn̩/ *adj* **(a)** (rushed) repentino, súbito; (unexpected) imprevisto, inesperado; **all of a** ∼ de repente, de pronto **(b)** (abrupt) ‹*movement*› brusco

suddenly /ˈsʌdn̩li/ *adv* **(a)** (unexpectedly) de repente, de pronto **(b)** (abruptly) bruscamente

suds /sʌdz/ *pl n* espuma *f* de jabón

sue /su: ‖su:, sju:/ *vt* **to** ∼ **sb (FOR sth)** demandar a algn (POR algo)

  ∎ ∼ *vi* (Law) entablar una demanda, poner* pleito (Esp)

suede /sweɪd/ *n* ante *m*, gamuza *f*

suet /ˈsuːət ‖ˈsuːɪt, ˈsjuːɪt/ *n* sebo *m*, grasa *f* de pella

suffer /ˈsʌfər ‖ˈsʌfə(r)/ *vt* **(a)** (undergo) ‹*injury/ damage/loss*› sufrir; ‹*pain*› padecer*, sufrir **(b)** (endure) aguantar, tolerar

  ∎ ∼ *vi* **(a)** (experience pain, difficulty) sufrir **(b)** (be affected, deteriorate) «*health/eyesight*» resentirse*; «*business/relationship*» verse* afectado, resentirse* **(c)** (be afflicted) **to** ∼ **FROM sth** sufrir *or* (frml) padecer* DE algo

sufferer /ˈsʌfərər ‖ˈsʌfərə(r)/ *n* ∼**s from arthritis, arthritis** ∼**s** quienes sufren de artritis, los artríticos

suffering /ˈsʌfərɪŋ/ *n* sufrimiento *m*

suffice /səˈfaɪs/ *vi* (frml) bastar, ser* suficiente

sufficient /səˈfɪʃənt/ *adj* suficiente, bastante

sufficiently /səˈfɪʃəntli/ *adv* lo suficientemente

suffix /ˈsʌfɪks/ *n* sufijo *m*

suffocate /ˈsʌfəkeɪt/ *vt* asfixiar, ahogar*

  ∎ ∼ *vi* asfixiarse, ahogarse*

suffocating /ˈsʌfəkeɪtɪŋ/ *adj* ‹*smoke/routine*› asfixiante; ‹*heat*› sofocante

suffocation /ˌsʌfəˈkeɪʃən/ *n* asfixia *f*

suffrage /ˈsʌfrɪdʒ/ *n* sufragio *m*

sugar /ˈʃʊgər ‖ˈʃʊgə(r)/ *n* azúcar *m or f*; (before n) ∼ **bowl** azucarero *m*, azucarera *f* (esp AmL); ∼ **cube** *o* **lump** terrón *m* de azúcar

sugar: ∼ **beet** *n* remolacha *f* azucarera *or* (Méx) betabel *m* blanco; ∼ **cane** *n* caña *f* de azúcar

sugary /ˈʃʊgəri/ *adj* **(a)** ‹*drink/taste*› dulce, azucarado **(b)** ‹*tones/smile*› meloso, almibarado

suggest /səgˈdʒest ‖səˈdʒest/ *vt* **1** **(a)** (propose) sugerir*; **to** ∼ **sth TO sb** sugerirle* algo A algn; **to** ∼ **-ING** sugerir* + INF, sugerir* QUE (+ *subj*); **to** ∼ **TO sb THAT** sugerirle* a algn QUE (+ *subj*) **(b)** (offer for consideration): **can you** ∼ **a possible source for this rumor?** ¿se le ocurre quién puede haber empezado este rumor? **(c)** (imply, insinuate) insinuar*; **are you** ∼**ing (that) my son is a thief?** ¿insinúa usted que mi hijo es un ladrón? **2** (indicate, point to) indicar* **3** (evoke, bring to mind) sugerir*

suggestion /səgˈdʒestʃən ‖səˈdʒestʃən/ *n* **1** **(a)** (proposal) sugerencia *f*; **to make a** ∼ hacer* una sugerencia; **have you any** ∼**s for speeding up the process?** ¿se le ocurre algo para acelerar el proceso? **(b)** (explanation, theory) teoría *f* **(c)** (insinuation) insinuación *f* **2** (indication, hint) indicio *m* **3** (Psych) sugestión *f*

suggestive /səgˈdʒestɪv ‖səˈdʒestɪv/ *adj* **1** ‹*gesture/laugh*› insinuante, provocativo **2** (*pred*) **to be** ∼ **OF sth** **(a)** (indicative) parecer* indicar algo **(b)** (reminiscent) hacer* pensar EN algo, evocar* algo

suicidal /ˌsuːəˈsaɪdl̩ ‖ˌsuːɪˈsaɪdl̩, ˌsjuː-/ *adj* suicida

suicide /ˈsuːəsaɪd ‖ˈsuːɪsaɪd, ˈsjuː-/ *n* (act) suicidio *m*; **to commit** ∼ suicidarse; (before n) ‹*attempt/pact*› de suicidio; ‹*mission/bombing*› suicida; ∼ **note** carta *f* de despedida de un suicida

suit¹ /suːt ‖suːt, sjuːt/ *n* **1** (Clothing) (male) traje *m*, terno (AmS); (female) traje *m* (de chaqueta), traje *m* sastre **2** (Law) juicio *m*, pleito *m* **3** (in cards) palo *m*; **to follow** ∼ seguir* su (*or* nuestro *etc*) ejemplo

suit² *vt* **1** (be convenient to, please) venirle* bien a, convenirle* a; **to** ∼ **oneself** hacer* lo que uno quiere; ∼ **yourself!** ¡haz lo que quieras! **2** **(a)** (be appropriate, good for): **the job doesn't** ∼ **him** el trabajo no es para él *or* no le va **(b)** (look good on) «*hairstyle/dress*» quedarle *or* (esp Esp) irle* bien a; *see also* SUITED **3** (adapt) **to** ∼ **sth TO sth/sb** adaptar algo A algo/algn

suitable /ˈsuːtəbl̩ ‖ˈsuːtəbl̩, ˈsjuː-/ *adj* **(a)** (appropriate) apropiado, adecuado; (**to be**) ∼ **FOR sb/sth/-ING** (ser*) apropiado *or* adecuado PARA algn/algo/+ INF **(b)** (acceptable, proper) apropiado **(c)** (convenient) conveniente

suitably /ˈsuːtəbli ‖ˈsuːtəbli, ˈsjuː-/ *adv* ‹*qualified*› adecuadamente; ‹*dressed/equipped*› apropiadamente

suitcase /ˈsuːtkeɪs ‖ˈsuːtkeɪs, ˈsjuː-/ *n* maleta *f*, valija *f* (RPl), petaca *f* (Méx)

suite /swiːt/ *n* **(a)** (of rooms) suite *f* **(b)** (of furniture) juego *m* **(c)** (Mus) suite *f*

suited /ˈsuːtəd ‖ˈsuːtɪd, ˈsjuː-/ *adj* (*pred*) **to be** ∼ **TO sth** «*thing*» ser* apropiado *or* adecuado PARA algo; **I'm not ∼ to this type of work** no sirvo para este tipo de trabajo; **they are very well ∼ (to each other)** están hechos el uno para el otro

suitor /'suːtər ‖'suːtə(r), 'sjuː-/ n (dated) pretendiente m

sulfur, (BrE) **sulphur** /'sʌlfər ‖'sʌlfə(r)/ n azufre m

sulk /sʌlk/ vi enfurruñarse

sulky /'sʌlki/ adj **-kier, -kiest** ⟨child⟩ con tendencia a enfurruñarse; ⟨look/reply⟩ malhumorado

sullen /'sʌlən/ adj hosco, huraño

sultan /'sʌltn̩/ n sultán m

sultana /sʌl'tænə ‖sʌl'tɑːnə/ n (Culin) pasa f sultana or de Esmirna

sultry /'sʌltri/ adj **-trier, -triest** (a) ⟨climate/day⟩ bochornoso (b) ⟨voice/smile/person⟩ seductor

sum /sʌm/ n **1** (calculation — in general) cuenta f; (— addition) suma f, adición f (frml) **2** (total, aggregate) suma f, total m **3** (of money) suma f or cantidad f (de dinero)

■ **sum up**: **-mm-** **1** [v + o + adv, v + adv + o] **(a)** (summarize) ⟨discussion/report⟩ resumir **(b)** (assess) ⟨person⟩ catalogar*; **she quickly ∼med up the situation** enseguida se hizo una composición de lugar **2** [v + adv] **(a)** (summarize) recapitular; **to ∼ up** (as linker) resumiendo, en resumen **(b)** (Law) recapitular

summarize /'sʌməraɪz/ vt resumir

summary¹ /'sʌməri/ n (pl **-ries**) resumen m

summary² adj ⟨dismissal⟩ inmediato; ⟨trial/judgment⟩ sumario

summer /'sʌmər ‖'sʌmə(r)/ n verano m; **in (the) ∼** en (el) verano; (before n) ⟨weather/clothes/vacation⟩ de verano; **∼ camp** (in US) colonia f de vacaciones

summer: ∼house n cenador m; **∼ school** n (in US) clases fpl de verano (gen de repaso); (in UK) curso m de verano; **∼time** n verano m, estío m (liter); **∼ time** n (BrE) horario m de verano

summery /'sʌməri/ adj veraniego, de verano

summing-up /'sʌmɪŋ'ʌp/ n (pl **summings-up**) recapitulación f

summit /'sʌmət ‖'sʌmɪt/ n **1** (of mountain, career) cumbre f, cima f **2** **∼ (conference)** (conferencia f) cumbre f

summon /'sʌmən/ vt **(a)** (send for) ⟨servant/waiter⟩ llamar, mandar llamar (AmL); ⟨police/doctor⟩ llamar; ⟨help/reinforcements⟩ pedir*; ⟨meeting/parliament⟩ convocar* **(b)** (Law) ⟨witness/defendant⟩ citar, emplazar* **(c)** ▶ SUMMON UP

■ **summon up** [v + adv + o] **(a)** (gather) **he ∼ed up the courage to ask her** se armó de valor para preguntárselo; **I couldn't even ∼ up the strength to get up the stairs** ni siquiera pude reunir fuerzas para subir la escalera **(b)** (call up) ⟨thoughts/memories⟩ evocar*

summons¹ /'sʌmənz/ n (pl **-monses**) **(a)** (Law) citación f, citatorio m (Méx) **(b)** (for help etc) llamamiento m, llamado m (AmL)

summons² vt (Law) citar, emplazar*

sumptuous /'sʌmptʃuəs ‖'sʌmptjuəs/ adj ⟨fabric/color⟩ suntuoso; ⟨mansion/decor⟩ lujoso

sun¹ /sʌn/ n sol m; **under the ∼: I've tried everything under the ∼** he probado de todo

sun² v refl **-nn-**: **to ∼ oneself** tomar el sol or (CS tb) tomar sol, asolearse (AmL)

sun: ∼bathe vi tomar el sol or (CS tb) tomar sol, asolearse (AmL); **∼beam** n rayo m de sol; **∼bed** n cama f solar; **∼block** n filtro m solar; **∼burn** n quemadura f de sol; **∼burned** /'sʌnbɜːrnd ‖'sʌnbɜːnd/, (BrE also) **∼burnt** /'sʌnbɜːrnt ‖'sʌnbɜːnt/ adj **(a)** (painfully) quemado por el sol **(b)** (brown) bronceado, tostado, quemado (AmL), moreno (Esp), asoleado (Méx)

sundae /'sʌndeɪ/ n sundae m (helado con fruta, crema, jarabe etc)

Sunday /'sʌndeɪ, '-di/ n domingo m; (before n) **∼ school** sesiones dominicales de catequesis para niños; see also MONDAY

sun: ∼dial n reloj m de sol; **∼down** n (no art) puesta f de(l) sol; **∼dress** n vestido m de tirantes, solera f (CS)

sundries /'sʌndriz/ pl n **(a)** (goods) artículos mpl diversos **(b)** (expenses) gastos mpl varios

sundry¹ /'sʌndri/ adj varios, diversos

sundry² pron: **all and ∼** todos sin excepción, todo el mundo

sunflower /'sʌnflaʊr ‖'sʌnflaʊə(r)/ n girasol m; (before n) **∼ oil** aceite m de girasol; **∼ seed** semilla f de girasol, pipa f (Esp)

sung /sʌŋ/ past p of SING

sunglasses /'sʌn,glæsəz/ pl n gafas fpl or (esp AmL) lentes mpl or anteojos mpl de sol

sunk¹ /sʌŋk/ past p of SINK¹

sunk² adj (pred) **(a)** (in trouble) (colloq) **to be ∼** estar* perdido **(b)** (immersed) **to be ∼ in sth** ⟨in depression/gloom⟩ estar* sumido EN algo (liter)

sunken /'sʌŋkən/ adj **(a)** (before n) ⟨ship/treasure⟩ hundido, sumergido **(b)** (before n) ⟨garden/patio⟩ a nivel más bajo **(c)** (hollow) ⟨eyes/cheeks⟩ hundido

sun: ∼ lamp n lámpara f de rayos ultravioletas; **∼light** n sol m, luz f del sol; **∼lit** adj soleado

Sunni¹ /'sʊni‖'sʌni/ n suní mf, sunita mf

Sunni² adj suní, sunita

sunny /'sʌni/ adj **-nier, -niest** **(a)** ⟨day⟩ de sol; ⟨room/garden⟩ soleado; **it's ∼ today** hoy hace sol **(b)** (good-humored) alegre

sun: ∼rise n salida f del sol; **∼roof** n techo m corredizo; **∼screen** n filtro m solar; **∼set** n puesta f de(l) sol; **at ∼set** al atardecer, a la caída de la tarde; **∼shine** n sol m; **∼spot** n **(a)** (Astron) mancha f solar **(b)** (resort) (colloq) lugar de veraneo con mucho sol; **∼stroke** n insolación f; **∼tan** n bronceado m, moreno m (Esp); **to get a ∼tan** broncearse, tostarse*, quemarse (AmL); (before n) ⟨lotion⟩ bronceador; **∼trap** n: lugar muy soleado y resguardado

super /'suːpər ‖'suːpə(r)/ adj (colloq) genial (fam), súper adj inv (fam)

superb /suˈpɜːrb ‖suːˈpɜːb/ adj magnífico, espléndido

superbug /'suːpərbʌg ‖'suːpəbʌg/ n microbio m multiresistente

supercilious /ˌsuːpərˈsɪliəs/ adj desdeñoso

superficial /ˌsuːpərˈfɪʃəl/ adj superficial

superfluous /suːˈpɜːrfluəs/ adj superfluo

S

superglue¹ /'su:pərglu: ‖'su:pəglu:/ *n* cola *f* de contacto, superglue *m* (Esp)

superglue² *vt* pegar* con cola de contacto, pegar* con superglue (Esp)

superhighway /'su:pər'haɪweɪ ‖'su:pə,haɪweɪ/ *n* (a) (AmE Auto) autopista *f* (b) (Comput): **the information** ∼ autopista *f* de la información, infovía *f*

superhuman /'su:pər'hju:mən ‖,su:pə'hju:mən/ *adj* sobrehumano

superimpose /'su:pərɪm'pəʊz/ *vt* superponer*

superintend /'su:pərɪn'tend/ *vt* supervisar

superintendent /'su:pərɪn'tendənt/ *n* (a) (person in charge — of maintenance, hostel, swimming pool) encargado, -da *m,f*; (— of building) (AmE) portero, -ra *m,f*; (— of institution) director, -tora *m,f* (b) (police officer) (in US) superintendente *mf* (*jefe de un departamento de policía*); (in UK) comisario, -ria *m,f* de policía

superior¹ /sʊ'pɪriər ‖su:'pɪəriə(r)/ *adj* **1** (a) (better) **to be** ∼ (**TO sth/sb**) ser* superior (**A** algo/algn), ser* mejor (**QUE** algo/algn) (b) (above average) ⟨*workmanship/writer*⟩ de gran calidad **2** (arrogant) ⟨*tone/smile*⟩ de superioridad; **he's so** ∼ se da unos aires de superioridad **3** ⟨*rank*⟩ superior; **his** ∼ **officer** su superior

superior² *n* superior *m*

superiority /sʊ'pɪri'ɔːrəti ‖su:,pɪəri'ɒrəti/ *n* superioridad *f*

superlative¹ /sʊ'pɜːrlətɪv ‖su:'pɜːlətɪv/ *adj* inigualable, excepcional

superlative² *n* superlativo *m*

superman /'su:pərmæn ‖'su:pəmæn/ *n* (*pl* **-men** /-men/) superhombre *m*

supermarket /'su:pər,mɑːrkət ‖'su:pə,mɑːkɪt/ *n* supermercado *m*, autoservicio *m*

supernatural /'su:pər'nætʃərəl ‖,su:pə'nætʃərəl/ *adj* sobrenatural

superpower /'su:pərpaʊər ‖'su:pəpaʊə(r)/ *n* superpotencia *f*

supersede /'su:pər'si:d ‖,su:pə'si:d/ *vt* (*often pass*) reemplazar*, sustituir*

supersonic /'su:pər'sɑːnɪk ‖,su:pə'sɒnɪk/ *adj* supersónico

superstar /'su:pərstɑːr ‖'su:pəstɑː(r)/ *n* superestrella *f*, gran estrella *f*

superstition /'su:pər'stɪʃən ‖,su:pə'stɪʃən/ *n* superstición *f*

superstitious /'su:pər'stɪʃəs ‖,su:pə'stɪʃəs/ *adj* supersticioso

superstore /'su:pərstɔːr ‖'su:pəstɔː(r)/ *n* (BrE) hipermercado *m*

supervise /'su:pərvaɪz ‖'su:pəvaɪz/ *vt* (a) ⟨*project/staff*⟩ supervisar (b) (watch over) vigilar

supervision /'su:pər'vɪʒən ‖,su:pə'vɪʒən/ *n* supervisión *f*

supervisor /'su:pərvaɪzər ‖'su:pəvaɪzə(r)/ *n* supervisor, -sora *m,f*

supper /'sʌpər ‖'sʌpə(r)/ *n* cena *f* (*ligera*), comida *f* (*ligera*) (esp AmL); **to have** ∼ cenar, comer (esp AmL)

supplant /sə'plænt ‖sə'plɑːnt/ *vt* sustituir*, reemplazar*

supple /'sʌpəl/ *adj* **-pler** /-plər ‖-plə(r)/, **-plest** /-pləst ‖-plɪst/ ⟨*body/fingers*⟩ ágil; ⟨*leather*⟩ fino y flexible, suave

supplement¹ /'sʌpləmənt ‖'sʌplɪmənt/ *n* **1** (addition to diet, income) complemento *m* **2** (a) (additional part published separately) suplemento *m* (b) (section of newspaper — separate) suplemento *m*; (— inserted) separata *f*

supplement² /'sʌpləmənt ‖ 'sʌplɪment/ *vt* ⟨*diet/income*⟩ complementar; ⟨*report*⟩ completar

supplementary /'sʌplə'mentəri ‖,sʌplɪ'mentəri/ *adj* suplementario

supplier /sə'plaɪər ‖sə'plaɪə(r)/ *n* (Busn) proveedor, -dora *m,f*, abastecedor, -dora *m,f*

supply¹ /sə'plaɪ/ *n* (*pl* **-plies**) **1** (provision) suministro *m*; **the water/electricity** ∼ el suministro de agua/electricidad; **the law of** ∼ **and demand** la ley de la oferta y la demanda **2** (stock, store): **food supplies are running low** se están agotando las provisiones *or* los víveres *or* (Mil) los pertrechos; **we only have a month's** ∼ **of coal left** solo nos queda carbón para un mes; (Busn) las existencias de carbón solo van a durar un mes; **to be in short** ∼ escasear

supply² *vt* **-plies, -plying, -plied** **1** (a) (provide, furnish) ⟨*electricity/gas*⟩ suministrar; ⟨*goods*⟩ suministrar, abastecer* *or* proveer* de; ⟨*evidence/information*⟩ proporcionar, facilitar (b) ⟨*retailer/manufacturer*⟩ abastecer*; **to** ∼ **sb WITH sth** ⟨*with equipment*⟩ proveer* a algn DE algo; (Busn) abastecer* a algn DE algo, suministrarle algo A algn; ⟨*with information*⟩ facilitarle *or* proporcionarle algo A algn **2** (meet) (frml) ⟨*demand/need*⟩ satisfacer*

support¹ /sə'pɔːrt ‖sə'pɔːt/ *vt* **1** (hold up) ⟨*bridge/structure*⟩ sostener*; **the chair couldn't** ∼ **his weight** la silla no pudo aguantar *or* resistir su peso **2** (a) (maintain, sustain) ⟨*family*⟩ mantener*; **to** ∼ **oneself** ganarse la vida (b) (Comput) admitir **3** (a) (back) ⟨*cause/motion*⟩ apoyar; **what team do you** ∼? ¿de qué equipo eres (hincha)? (b) (back up) apoyar **4** (corroborate) ⟨*theory*⟩ respaldar, confirmar

support² *n* **1** (a) (of structure) soporte *m* (b) (physical): **to lean on sb for** ∼ apoyarse en algn (para sostenerse) **2** (a) (financial) ayuda *f* (económica), apoyo *m* (económico) (b) (person) sostén *m* **3** (backing, encouragement) apoyo *m* **4** (Mil) apoyo *m*, refuerzo *m* **5** **in support of** (*as prep*) en apoyo de

support band *n* grupo *m* telonero

supporter /sə'pɔːrtər ‖sə'pɔːtə(r)/ *n* (a) (adherent) partidario, -ria *m,f* (b) (Sport) hincha *mf*

supporting /sə'pɔːrtɪŋ ‖sə'pɔːtɪŋ/ *adj* (*before n*) ‹*role/actor*› secundario; ~ **act** número *m* telonero

supportive /sə'pɔːrtɪv ‖sə'pɔːtɪv/ *adj*: she's been very ~ me (*or* lo *etc*) ha apoyado mucho

suppose /sə'pəʊz/ *vt* **1 (a)** (assume, imagine) suponer*, imaginarse; ~ **he phones and you're not in** ¿y si llama y tú no estás?; **I ~ so** supongo *or* me imagino que sí; **I ~ not** supongo que no *or* no creo **(b)** (believe, think) creer*; **what do you ~ he'll do?** ¿tú qué crees que hará?
2 to be supposed to + INF (a) (indicating obligation, expectation): **I'm ~d to start work at nine** se supone que tengo que empezar a trabajar a las nueve; **aren't you ~d to be at home?** ¿tú no tendrías que estar en casa? **(b)** (indicating intention): **what's that ~d to be?** ¿y eso qué se supone que es?; **what's that ~d to mean?** ¿y qué quieres (*or* quieren *etc*) decir con eso, (si se puede saber)? **(c)** (indicating general opinion): **it's ~d to be a very interesting book** dicen que es un libro muy interesante

supposing /sə'pəʊzɪŋ/ *conj* **(a)** (expressing hypothesis) suponiendo que; ~ **she agrees, will they let us go?** suponiendo que ella esté de acuerdo ¿nos dejarán ir? **(b)** (introducing suggestion) ¿y si … ?

supposition /ˌsʌpə'zɪʃən/ *n* suposición *f*

suppress /sə'pres/ *vt* **(a)** ‹*anger/laughter*› contener*; ‹*feelings*› reprimir **(b)** ‹*facts/evidence/truth*› ocultar **(c)** ‹*revolt*› sofocar*; ‹*organization*› suprimir

suppression /sə'preʃən/ *n* **(a)** (of feelings) represión *f* **(b)** (of evidence) ocultación *f* **(c)** (of revolt) represión *f*

supremacy /sə'preməsi ‖suː'preməsi, sjuː-/ *n* supremacía *f*

supreme /suː'priːm ‖suː'priːm, sjuː-/ *adj* supremo

Supreme Court *n* the ~ ~ el Tribunal Supremo *or* (esp AmL) la Corte Suprema (de Justicia)

surcharge /'sɜːrtʃɑːrdʒ ‖'sɜːtʃɑːdʒ/ *n* recargo *m*

sure¹ /ʃʊr ‖ʃʊə(r), ʃɔː(r)/ *adj* **surer, surest**
1 (convinced) (*pred*) seguro; **to be ~ ABOUT sth** estar* seguro DE algo; **I'm not ~ I agree with you** no sé si estoy de acuerdo contigo; **I'm not ~ who/why/what …** no sé muy bien quién/por qué/qué …; **to be ~ OF sth/sb** estar* seguro DE algo/algn; **I want to be ~ of getting there on time** quiero asegurarme de que voy a llegar a tiempo; **to be ~ of oneself** (convinced one is right) estar* seguro; (self-confident) ser* seguro de sí mismo
2 (certain): **one thing is ~:** he's lying lo que está claro *or* lo que es seguro es que está mintiendo; **it's ~ to rain** seguro que llueve; **to make ~ of sth** asegurarse de algo; **make ~ (that) you're not late** no vayas a llegar tarde
3 (accurate, reliable) ‹*remedy/method*› seguro; ‹*judgment/aim*› certero; ‹*indication*› claro; ‹*ground*› seguro
4 (*in phrases*) **for sure: we don't know anything for ~** no sabemos nada seguro *or* con seguridad; **we'll win for ~** seguro que ganamos; **to be sure** (admittedly) (*indep*) por cierto

sure² *adv* **1** (colloq) (*as intensifier*): **she ~ is clever, she's ~ clever** ¡qué lista es!, ¡sí será lista!;

do you like it? — I ~ do! ¿te gusta? — ¡ya lo creo!
2 (of course) por supuesto, claro **3** **sure enough** efectivamente, en efecto

sure: ~**fire** *adj* (*before n*) ‹*method*› segurísimo, infalible; ~**footed** /'ʃʊr'fʊtəd ‖ˌʃʊə'fʊtɪd, ˌʃɔː'fʊtɪd/ *adj* ‹*goat/cat*› de pie firme

surely /'ʃʊrli ‖'ʃʊəli, 'ʃɔːli/ *adv* **1 (a)** (expressing conviction): ~ **the real problem is …** el verdadero problema, digo yo *or* me parece a mí, es …; ~ **she doesn't mean that!** ¡no puede ser que lo diga en serio! **(b)** (expressing uncertainty): **he must be mistaken, ~?** tiene que estar equivocado ¿no? **(c)** (expressing disbelief): ~ **you don't believe that!** ¡no te creerás eso!; ~ **not!** ¡no es posible! *or* ¡no puede ser! **2** (undoubtedly, certainly) seguramente, sin duda **3** (gladly, willingly) por supuesto, desde luego

surf¹ /sɜːrf ‖sɜːf/ *n* **(a)** (waves) olas *fpl* (rompientes); (swell) oleaje *m* **(b)** (foam) espuma *f*

surf² *vi* hacer* surf *or* surfing
■ ~ *vt* (Comput) explorar, navegar* en

surface¹ /'sɜːrfəs ‖'sɜːfəs/ *n* **1 (a)** (of solid, land) superficie *f*; (*before n*) ‹*wound/mark*› superficial **(b)** (of liquid, sea) superficie *f* **(c)** **on the surface** (superficially) en apariencia **2** (Math) ~ (**area**) superficie *f*, área *f*‡

surface² *vi* «*diver/submarine*» salir* a la superficie; «*problems/difficulties*» aflorar, aparecer*
■ ~ *vt* ‹*road*› revestir*, recubrir*; (with asphalt) asfaltar

surfboard /'sɜːrfbɔːrd ‖'sɜːfbɔːd/ *n* tabla *f* de surf *or* de surfing

surfeit /'sɜːrfət ‖'sɜːfɪt/ *n* (liter) **a ~ OF sth** un exceso *or* (liter) una plétora DE algo

surfer /'sɜːrfər ‖'sɜːfə(r)/ *n* surfista *mf*

surfing /'sɜːrfɪŋ ‖'sɜːfɪŋ/ *n* surf *m*, surfing *m*

surge¹ /sɜːrdʒ ‖sɜːdʒ/ *n* (in demand, sales) aumento *m*; **a ~ of people** una oleada de gente; **we felt a new ~ of hope** sentimos renacer nuestras esperanzas

surge² *vi* «*wave*» levantarse; «*sea*» hincharse; **the crowd ~d out through the gates** la gente salió en tropel por las puertas; **anger/hatred ~d up inside her** la ira/el odio la invadió; **to ~ ahead of sb** adelantársele a algn

surgeon /'sɜːrdʒən ‖'sɜːdʒən/ *n* cirujano, -na *m,f*

surgery /'sɜːrdʒəri ‖'sɜːdʒəri/ *n* (*pl* **-ries**) **1** (science) cirugía *f* **2** (BrE) **(a)** (room) consultorio *m*, consulta *f* **(b)** (consultation period of doctor) consulta *f*; (*before n*) ‹*times/hours*› de consulta

surgical /'sɜːrdʒɪkəl ‖'sɜːdʒɪkəl/ *adj* ‹*instruments/treatment*› quirúrgico; ‹*stocking/appliance*› ortopédico

surgical spirit *n* (BrE) alcohol *m* (*de 90°*)

surly /'sɜːrli ‖'sɜːli/ *adj* **-lier, -liest** hosco

surmise /sər'maɪz ‖sə'maɪz/ *vt* (frml) conjeturar (frml)

surmount /sər'maʊnt ‖sə'maʊnt/ *vt* superar

surname /'sɜːrneɪm ‖'sɜːneɪm/ *n* apellido *m*

surpass /sər'pæs ‖sə'pɑːs/ *vt* superar

surplus¹ /'sɜːrpləs ‖'sɜːpləs/ *n* (*pl* ~**es**) (of produce, stock) excedente *m*; (of funds) superávit *m*

surplus² adj ⟨goods/stocks⟩ excedente

surprise¹ /sə'praɪz/ n sorpresa f; **to my ~** para mi sorpresa; **to take sb by ~** sorprender a algn, pillar or (esp Esp) coger* a algn desprevenido; (before n) ⟨gift/visit/attack⟩ sorpresa adj inv

surprise² vt (a) (astonish) sorprender (b) (catch unawares) sorprender, pillar or agarrar or (esp Esp) coger* desprevenido

surprised /sə'praɪzd/ adj ⟨look⟩ sorprendido, de sorpresa; **I was so ~** me quedé tan sorprendido; **I'm ~ about** o **at that** eso me sorprende mucho; **I'm ~ (THAT)** ... me sorprende or me extraña QUE ... (+ subj)

surprising /sə'praɪzɪŋ/ adj sorprendente

surprisingly /sə'praɪzɪŋli/ adv (a) ⟨quiet/near/good⟩ sorprendentemente (b) (indep): **~, she feels no resentment** no está resentida, lo cual es sorprendente

surreal /sə'riːəl/ adj surrealista

surrealism /sə'riːəlɪzəm/ n surrealismo m

surrealist /sə'riːəlɪst ‖sə'riːəlɪst/ n surrealista mf; (before n) ⟨painter/poem⟩ surrealista

surrender¹ /sə'rendər ‖sə'rendə(r)/ vt (a) (Mil) rendir*, entregar* (b) (fml) ⟨document/ticket⟩ entregar* (c) (relinquish) ⟨right/claim⟩ renunciar a ■ ~ vi rendirse*; **to ~ TO sb** entregarse* A algn

surrender² n (a) (capitulation) rendición f, capitulación f (b) (fml) (no pl) (of passport, document) entrega f

surreptitious /ˌsʌrəp'tɪʃəs/ adj furtivo, subrepticio

surrogate¹ /'sʌrəgət/ n (fml) sustituto m

surrogate² adj ⟨material⟩ sucedáneo; **~ mother** madre f suplente or de alquiler

surround¹ /sə'raʊnd/ vt (a) (encircle) ⟨place/person⟩ rodear; **the house is ~ed by trees** la casa está rodeada de árboles (b) (Mil) rodear, cercar*

surround² n marco m

surrounding /sə'raʊndɪŋ/ adj (before n) ⟨countryside/area⟩ de alrededor

surroundings /sə'raʊndɪŋz/ pl n (a) (of town, village) alrededores mpl (b) (environment) ambiente m

surveillance /sər'veɪləns ‖sə'veɪləns/ n vigilancia f

survey¹ /'sɜːrveɪ ‖'sɜːveɪ/ n ① (a) (of land) inspección f, reconocimiento m; (for mapping) medición f (b) (of building) inspección f, peritaje m, peritación f; (written report) informe m del perito, peritaje m, peritación f ② (overall view) visión f general ③ (investigation) estudio m; (poll) encuesta f, sondeo m

survey² /sər'veɪ ‖sə'veɪ/ vt ① (a) ⟨land/region⟩ (measure) medir*; (inspect) inspeccionar, reconocer* (b) ⟨building⟩ inspeccionar, llevar a cabo un peritaje de ② (a) (look at) contemplar, mirar (b) (view, consider) ⟨situation/plan/prospects⟩ examinar, analizar* ③ (question) ⟨group⟩ encuestar, hacer* un sondeo de

surveyor /sər'veɪər ‖sə'veɪə(r)/ n (a) (of land) agrimensor, -sora m,f; topógrafo, -fa m,f (b) (of building) perito, -ta m,f

survival /sər'vaɪvəl ‖sə'vaɪvəl/ n (continued existence) sobrevivencia f, supervivencia f

survive /sər'vaɪv ‖sə'vaɪv/ vi sobrevivir; **her last surviving descendant** su último descendiente vivo; **I can just ~ on $100 a week** con 100 dólares semanales apenas me alcanza para vivir ■ ~ vt ① ⟨accident/crash⟩ salir* con vida de; ⟨war/earthquake⟩ sobrevivir a; ⟨experience⟩ superar ② (outlive) ⟨person⟩ sobrevivir

survivor /sər'vaɪvər ‖sə'vaɪvə(r)/ n superviviente mf, sobreviviente mf

susceptible /sə'septəbəl/ adj **~ TO sth** ⟨to colds/infections⟩ propenso A algo; **he's ~ to a bit of flattery** se le puede persuadir halagándolo

suspect¹ /sə'spekt/ vt ① (a) (believe guilty) ⟨person⟩ sospechar de; **we ~ him of lying** sospechamos que miente (b) (doubt, mistrust) ⟨sincerity/probity⟩ dudar de, tener* dudas acerca de ② (a) (believe to exist): **they ~ nothing** no sospechan nada; **arson is not ~ed** no existen sospechas de que el incendio haya sido provocado (b) **suspected** past p: **a ~ed fracture** una posible fractura; **the ~ed murderer** el presunto asesino ③ (think probable) **to ~ (THAT)** imaginarse QUE

suspect² /'sʌspekt/ n sospechoso, -sa m,f

suspect³ /'sʌspekt/ adj ⟨package/behavior⟩ sospechoso; ⟨document/evidence⟩ de dudosa autenticidad

suspend /sə'spend/ vt ① ⟨payment/work⟩ suspender ② (debar, ban) suspender; ⟨student⟩ expulsar temporariamente, suspender (AmL) ③ (hang) (often pass) suspender

suspended sentence n: pena de prisión que no se cumple a menos que el delincuente reincida

suspenders /sə'spendərz ‖sə'spendəz/ pl n (sometimes sing) ① (braces) (AmE) tirantes mpl or (RPl) tiradores mpl or (Chi) suspensores mpl or (Col) cargaderas fpl ② (for stockings, socks) (BrE) ligas fpl

suspense /sə'spens/ n (in literary work, movie) suspenso m or (Esp) suspense m; **to keep sb in ~** mantener* a algn sobre ascuas

suspension /sə'spenʃən/ n ① (cessation) suspensión f ② (banning, withdrawal) suspensión f; (of student) expulsión f temporaria, suspensión f (AmL) ③ (hanging, being hung) suspensión f ④ (Auto) suspensión f

suspension: ~ bridge n puente m colgante; **~ points** pl n (AmE) puntos mpl suspensivos

suspicion /sə'spɪʃən/ n (belief) sospecha f; (mistrust) desconfianza f, recelo m; **he's under ~** está bajo sospecha

suspicious /sə'spɪʃəs/ adj (a) (mistrustful) desconfiado, suspicaz; **to be ~ OF/ABOUT sb/sth** desconfiar* DE algn/algo (b) (arousing suspicion) ⟨actions/movements⟩ sospechoso

suspiciously /sə'spɪʃəsli/ adv (a) (mistrustfully) ⟨regard/watch⟩ con desconfianza, con recelo (b) (arousing suspicion) ⟨act⟩ sospechosamente

sustain /sə'steɪn/ vt (a) ⟨life⟩ preservar, sustentar; ⟨hope/interest⟩ mantener*; ⟨pretense/conversation⟩ mantener*; ⟨effort⟩ sostener* (b) (suffer) ⟨injury/loss/defeat⟩ sufrir

sustainable /sə'steɪnəbəl/ adj sostenible

sustained /sə'steɪnd/ adj ⟨efforts⟩ sostenido

sustenance /'sʌstənəns/ n alimento m, sustento m

SW (= **southwest**) SO

swab¹ /swɑːb ‖ swɒb/ n (a) (of cotton, gauze) hisopo m húmedo (b) (specimen) muestra f, frotis m

swab² vt **-bb-** to ~ (**down**) ‹deck› lavar, limpiar

swagger /'swægər ‖ 'swægə(r)/ vi caminar or andar* con aire arrogante

Swahili /swɑːˈhiːli ‖ swəˈhiːli/ n swahili m, suajili m

swallow¹ /'swɑːləʊ ‖ 'swɒləʊ/ n [1] (Zool) golondrina f [2] (gulp) trago m

swallow² vt [1] ‹food/drink› tragar* [2] ‹insult/taunts› tragarse* (fam); that's a bit hard to ~ eso no hay quien se lo trague (fam) [3] ▶ SWALLOW UP
■ ~ vi tragar*
■ **swallow up** [v + o + adv, v + adv + o] (a) (use up) ‹money/time› consumir, tragarse* (fam), comerse (fam) (b) (cause to disappear) tragarse*

swam /swæm/ past of SWIM¹

swamp¹ /swɑːmp ‖ swɒmp/ n pantano m, ciénaga f; (of sea water) marisma f, ciénaga f

swamp² vt (a) (with water) ‹land› anegar*, inundar (b) (overwhelm) ‹often pass›: they were ~ed by offers of help los abrumaron con ofertas de ayuda; I'm absolutely ~ed with work estoy inundada de trabajo

swan /swɑːn ‖ swɒn/ n cisne m

swanky /'swæŋki/ adj **-kier, -kiest** (colloq) (a) (boastful) (pej) ‹person› fanfarrón (fam) (b) (classy) chic adj inv, pijo (Esp fam), pituco (CS fam), posudo (Col fam), popoff adj inv (Méx fam)

swap¹ /swɑːp ‖ swɒp/ n (colloq) cambio m, trueque m

swap² vt **-pp-** ‹possessions/ideas› intercambiar; to ~ sth FOR sth cambiar algo POR algo

swarm¹ /swɔːrm ‖ swɔːm/ n enjambre m

swarm² vi ‹‹bees›› enjambrar; the flies ~ed around the meat las moscas revoloteaban alrededor de la carne; the beaches were ~ing with tourists las playas eran un hormiguero de turistas

swarthy /'swɔːrði ‖ 'swɔːði/ adj **-thier, -thiest** moreno

swastika /'swɑːstɪkə ‖ 'swɒstɪkə/ n svástica f, esvástica f, suástica f, cruz f gamada

swat /swɑːt ‖ swɒt/ vt **-tt-** ‹insect› matar (con matamoscas, periódico etc)

sway¹ /sweɪ/ n to hold ~ ‹‹ideas›› prevalecer*; ‹‹leader›› ejercer* dominio

sway² vi ‹‹branch/tree›› balancearse; (gently) mecerse*; ‹‹tower/building›› bambolearse
■ ~ vt [1] (influence) ‹person/crowd› influir* en [2] (move) ‹hips› menear, bambolear

swear /swer ‖ sweə(r)/ (past **swore**; past p **sworn**) vt ‹allegiance/fidelity/revenge› jurar; I could have sworn I left it there hubiera jurado que lo dejé ahí
■ ~ vi (a) (vow) jurar; but I couldn't ~ to it pero no podría jurarlo (b) (curse) decir* palabrotas, soltar* tacos (Esp fam), mentar* madres (Méx fam); to ~ AT sb insultar a algn (usando palabrotas)
■ **swear by** [v + prep + o] ‹gadget› ser* un entusiasta de; ‹remedy› tenerle* una fe ciega a
■ **swear in** [v + o + adv, v + adv + o] ‹jury/witness/president› tomarle juramento a, juramentar

swearword /'swerwɜːrd ‖ 'sweəwɜːd/ n palabrota f, mala palabra f, taco m (Esp)

sweat¹ /swet/ n (perspiration) sudor m, transpiración f; I broke out in a cold ~ me vino un sudor frío

sweat² vi (past & past p **sweated** or (AmE also) **sweat**) sudar, transpirar

sweater /'swetər ‖ 'swetə(r)/ n suéter m, pulóver m, jersey m (Esp), chompa f (Per)

sweat: ~**shirt** n sudadera f, camiseta f gruesa; ~**shop** n: fábrica donde se explota a los trabajadores; ~**suit** n (AmE) equipo m (de deportes), chándal m (Esp), pants mpl (Méx)

sweaty /'sweti/ adj **-tier, -tiest** sudado, transpirado

swede /swiːd/ n (esp BrE) nabo m sueco

Swede /swiːd/ n sueco, -ca m,f

Sweden /'swiːdn/ n Suecia f

Swedish¹ /'swiːdɪʃ/ adj sueco

Swedish² n (a) (language) sueco m (b) (people) (+ pl vb) the ~ los suecos

sweep¹ /swiːp/ n [1] (a) (movement): with a ~ of his arm con un amplio movimiento del brazo (b) (curve — of road, river) curva f (c) (range) (no pl) alcance m, extensión f [2] (chimney ~) deshollinador, -dora m,f

sweep² (past & pp **swept**) vt [1] (a) (clean) ‹floor/path› barrer; ‹chimney› deshollinar (b) (remove) ‹leaves/dirt› barrer; ‹mines› barrer; to ~ sth under the rug o (BrE) carpet correr un velo sobre algo
[2] (touch lightly, brush) ‹surface› rozar*
[3] (a) (pass over, across) ‹‹storm›› azotar, barrer; the epidemic is ~ing the country la epidemia se extiende como un reguero de pólvora por el país (b) (remove by force) ‹‹sea/tide›› arrastrar
[4] (a) (scan) recorrer (b) (search) ‹area› peinar
■ ~ vi [1] (+ adv compl) (move proudly): she swept into the room entró majestuosamente en la habitación
[2] (+ adv compl) (a) (spread): fire swept through the hotel el fuego se propagó por todo el hotel (b) (extend): the path ~s down to the road el sendero baja describiendo una curva hasta la carretera
■ **sweep aside** [v + o + adv, v + adv + o] ‹object› apartar; ‹opposition/doubts› desechar
■ **sweep away** [v + o + adv, v + adv + o] (a) (carry away) ‹‹flood/storm›› arrastrar (b) (abolish) erradicar*
■ **sweep up** [1] [v + adv] (clear up) barrer, limpiar
[2] [v + o + adv, v + adv + o] (a) (clear up) ‹dust/leaves› barrer y recoger* (b) (gather up) ‹belongings/bags› recoger*

sweeper /'swiːpər ‖ 'swiːpə(r)/ n (a) (road~) barrendero, -ra m,f, barredor, -dora m,f (Per) (b) (carpet ~) cepillo m mecánico

sweeping /'swiːpɪŋ/ adj (a) ‹movement› amplio; ‹gesture› dramático, histriónico (b) (indiscriminate) (pej): that's rather a ~ statement, isn't it? ¿no estás generalizando demasiado? (c) (far-reaching) ‹reforms/changes› radical; ‹powers› amplio

sweet¹ /swiːt/ adj **-er, -est** [1] ‹taste› dulce [2] ‹wine/sherry› dulce [3] (fresh, wholesome) ‹smell› agradable [4] (a) (pleasant, gratifying) ‹sounds/voice/music› dulce, melodioso (b) (kind, lovable) ‹nature/ ⋯✦

temper/smile) dulce; **she's a very ~ person** es un encanto (de persona); **it was very ~ of her to offer** fue un detalle que se ofreciese **(c)** (attractive) ⟨*baby/puppy*⟩ rico (fam), mono (fam), amoroso (AmL fam)

sweet² *n* ⎣1⎦ (item of confectionery) (BrE) caramelo *m or* (AmL exc RPl) dulce *m* ⎣2⎦ (dessert) (BrE) postre *m* ⎣3⎦ **sweets** *pl* (sugary food) (AmE) dulces *mpl*

sweet: ~-and-sour /'swiːtn̩'saʊr ‖,swiːtn̩'saʊə(r)/ *adj* (*before n*) agridulce; **~corn** *n* maíz *m* tierno, elote *m* (Méx), choclo *m* (AmS), jojoto *m* (Ven)

sweeten /'swiːtn̩/ *vt* **(a)** ⟨*drink/dish*⟩ endulzar* **(b)** ⟨*air/breath*⟩ refrescar*

sweetener /'swiːtn̩ər ‖ 'swiːtn̩ə(r)/ *n* (Culin) endulzante *m*; (artificial) edulcorante *m*

sweet: ~heart /'swiːthɑːrt ‖ 'swiːthɑːt/ *n* **(a)** (lover, darling) novio, -via *m,f*, enamorado, -da *m,f* **(b)** (colloq) (*as form of address*) (mi) amor; **~ potato** *n* boniato *m*, batata *f*, camote *m* (Andes, Méx); **~shop** *n* (BrE) tienda *f* de golosinas; **~-talk** *vt* (colloq) engatusar (fam), camelar (Esp fam)

swell¹ /swel/ (*past p* **swollen** *or* (AmE esp) **swelled**) *vi* ⎣1⎦ «*wood/sails/ankles*» hincharse; «*river/stream*» crecer*, subir ⎣2⎦ (increase) «*population/crowd*» crecer*, aumentar
■ **~** *vt* ⎣1⎦ (increase in size) ⟨*body/joint/features*⟩ hinchar; ⟨*sails*⟩ hinchar; ⟨*river*⟩ hacer* crecer *or* subir ⎣2⎦ (increase in number, volume) ⟨*population/ total/funds*⟩ aumentar
■ **swell up** [*v + adv*] hincharse

swell² *n* **(a)** (of sea) oleaje *m* **(b)** (surge, movement) oleada *f*

swell³ *adj* (fine, excellent) (AmE colloq) fenomenal (fam), bárbaro *m*

swelling /'swelɪŋ/ *n* hinchazón *f*

sweltering /'sweltərɪŋ/ *adj* sofocante

swept /swept/ *past & past p of* SWEEP²

swerve /swɜːrv ‖ swɜːv/ *vi* «*vehicle/driver/ horse*» virar bruscamente

swift¹ /swɪft/ *adj* **-er, -est** ⟨*runner/movement/ animal*⟩ veloz, rápido; ⟨*reply/reaction/denial*⟩ rápido

swift² *n* vencejo *m*

swiftly /'swɪftli/ *adv* (rapidly) rápidamente, con rapidez; (promptly) con prontitud *or* rapidez

swig¹ /swɪg/ *n* (colloq) trago *m*

swig² *vt* **-gg-** (colloq) tomar, beber

swill¹ /swɪl/ *n* comida *f* para cerdos

swill² *vt* ⎣1⎦ (wash, rinse) **~ sth out** ⟨*cups/pans*⟩ lavar/enjuagar* algo ⎣2⎦ (drink) (colloq & pej) ⟨*beer*⟩ tomar *or* beber (*a grandes tragos*)

swim¹ /swɪm/ (*pres p* **swimming**; *past* **swam**; *past p* **swum**) *vi* ⎣1⎦ «*person/animal/ fish*» nadar; **to go ~ming** ir* a nadar; **he swam across the river** cruzó el río nadando *or* a nado ⎣2⎦ (be immersed, overflowing) (*usu in -ing form*) **to ~**

IN sth nadar *or* flotar **EN** algo ⎣3⎦ (of blurred, confused perceptions) dar* vueltas; **my head was ~ming** la cabeza me daba vueltas
■ **~** *vt* ⟨*length*⟩ nadar, hacer*; ⟨*river*⟩ cruzar* a nado

swim² *n*: **to go for a ~** ir* a nadar; **to have a ~** nadar, bañarse, darse* un baño

swimmer /'swɪmər ‖ 'swɪmə(r)/ *n* nadador, -dora *m,f*

swimming /'swɪmɪŋ/ *n* natación *f*; (*before n*) **~ cap** gorro *m or* gorra *f* (de baño)

swimming: ~ bath *n*, **~ baths** *pl n* (BrE) piscina *f* cubierta, alberca *f* techada (Méx), pileta *f* cubierta (RPl); **~ costume** *n* (BrE) ▶ SWIMSUIT; **~ pool** *n* piscina *f*, alberca *f* (Méx), pileta *f* (RPl); **~ trunks** *pl n* ▶ TRUNK 4

swimsuit /'swɪmsuːt ‖ 'swɪmsuːt, -sjuːt/ *n* traje *m* de baño, bañador *m* (Esp), malla *f* (de baño) (RPl)

swindle¹ /'swɪndl̩/ *n* estafa *f*, timo *m* (fam)

swindle² *vt* estafar, timar

swindler /'swɪndlər ‖ 'swɪndlə(r)/ *n* estafador, -dora *m,f*, timador, -dora *m,f*

swine /swaɪn/ *n* **(a)** (*pl* **~**) (pig, hog) cerdo *m* **(b)** (*pl* **~s**) (contemptible person) (colloq) cerdo, -da *m,f* (fam), canalla *mf*

swing¹ /swɪŋ/ (*past & past p* **swung**) *vi* ⎣1⎦ (hang, dangle) balancearse; (on a swing) columpiarse *or* (RPl) hamacarse*; «*pendulum*» oscilar ⎣2⎦ **(a)** (move on pivot) mecerse*; **the door swung open/shut** la puerta se abrió/se cerró **(b)** (turn) girar *or* doblar (*describiendo una curva*); **the ball swung away** la pelota salió desviada ⎣3⎦ (shift, change) «*opinion/mood*» cambiar, oscilar
■ **~** *vt* ⎣1⎦ (move to and fro) ⟨*arms/legs*⟩ balancear; ⟨*object on rope*⟩ hacer* oscilar; **to ~ one's hips** contonearse, contonear *or* menear las caderas ⎣2⎦ (wave, brandish) ⟨*club/hammer*⟩ blandir ⎣3⎦ (shift) ⟨*vote*⟩ inclinar
■ **swing around,** (BrE also) **swing round** ⎣1⎦ [*v + adv*] «*vehicle*» dar* un viraje, girar *or* virar (en redondo); **she swung around to face me** giró sobre sus talones para darme la cara ⎣2⎦ [*v + o + adv*] ⟨*car/boat*⟩ hacer* girar en redondo

swing² *n* ⎣1⎦ **(a)** (movement) oscilación *f*, vaivén *m* **(b)** (blow, stroke) golpe *m*; (in golf, boxing) swing *m*; **to take a ~ at sb/sth** intentar darle a algn/ algo ⎣2⎦ **(a)** (shift) cambio *m*; **a ~ in public opinion** un cambio en la opinión pública **(b)** (Pol) viraje *m* ⎣3⎦ **(a)** (rhythm, vitality): **to be in full ~** estar* en pleno desarrollo; **the party was in full ~** la fiesta estaba ya muy animada; **to get into the ~ of sth** agarrarle el ritmo *or* (Esp) cogerle* el tranquillo a algo **(b)** (Mus) swing *m* ⎣4⎦ (Leisure) columpio *m or* (RPl) hamaca *f*

swing: ~ bin *n* cubo *m or* (CS) tacho *m or* (Méx) bote *m or* (Col) caneca *f or* (Ven) tobo *m* de la basura (*con tapa de vaivén*); **~ bridge** *n* puente *m* giratorio; **~ door** *n* puerta *f* (de) vaivén

swinging door /'swɪŋɪŋ/ n (AmE) ▶ SWING
DOOR

swipe¹ /swaɪp/ n (colloq) golpe m

swipe² vt (colloq) [1] (hit) darle* (un golpe) a
[2] (steal) afanarse (arg), volarse* (Méx fam)

swipe card n tarjeta f de plástico con banda
magnética

swirl¹ /swɜːrl ‖ swɜːl/ n (of water, dust, people)
remolino m; (of smoke) voluta f, espiral f

swirl² vi «water/dust/paper» arremolinarse;
«dancers/skirts» girar

swish /swɪʃ/ n (a) (of cane) silbido m (b) (of
water) rumor m, susurro m (c) (of skirt) frufrú m

Swiss¹ /swɪs/ adj suizo

Swiss² n (pl ~) suizo, -za m,f

switch¹ /swɪtʃ/ vt [1] (a) (change) cambiar de;
to ~ channels cambiar de canal; my appointment
has been ~ed to Tuesday me cambiaron la cita
al martes (b) (exchange) «suitcases/roles»
intercambiar
[2] (shunt) (AmE Rail) cambiar de vía
■ ~ vi cambiar; I ~ed to Channel Four cambié al
Canal Cuatro; we've ~ed from electricity to gas
hemos empezado a usar gas en lugar de
electricidad
■ **switch off** [1] [v + o + adv, v + adv + o] «light/
TV/heating» apagar*; «gas/electricity/water»
cortar, desconectar
[2] [v + adv] «light/machine/heating» apagarse*
■ **switch on** [1] [v + o + adv, v + adv + o] (esp
BrE) «light/heating/television» encender*, prender
(AmL)
[2] [v + adv] «light/heating/machine»
encenderse*, prenderse (AmL)
■ **switch over** [v + adv] (a) (change) to ~ over
TO sth cambiar A algo (b) (change channels)
cambiar de canal (c) (exchange positions, roles)
cambiar

switch² n [1] (a) (Elec) interruptor m, llave f
(de encendido/de la luz) (b) (AmE Rail) agujas fpl
[2] (exchange) intercambio m, trueque m

switchboard n centralita f, conmutador m
(AmL); (before n) ~ **operator** telefonista mf

Switzerland /'swɪtsərlənd ‖ 'swɪtsələnd/ n
Suiza f

swivel /'swɪvəl/, (BrE) **-ll-** vi girar
■ ~ vt hacer* girar

swivel chair n silla f giratoria

swollen¹ /'swəʊlən/ past p of SWELL¹

swollen² adj «ankle/knee/joints» hinchado;
«gland» inflamado; ~ **with pride** hinchado de
orgullo; **the river was** ~ el río iba crecido

swoon /swuːn/ vi (a) (show rapture) to ~ (OVER
sb) derretirse* (POR algn) (b) (faint) (arch or liter)
desvanecerse*

swoop¹ /swuːp/ vi «bird of prey» abatirse;
«police» llevar a cabo una redada

swoop² n (of bird, aircraft) descenso m en picada
or (Esp) en picado; (by police) redada f; **in one fell
~** de una sola vez, de un tirón (fam)

swop /swɒp ‖ swɒp/ vt/n ▶ SWAP¹,²

sword /sɔːrd ‖ sɔːd/ n espada f

sword: ~**fish** n (pl ~**fish** or ~**fishes**) pez m
espada; ~**sman** /'sɔːrdzmən ‖ 'sɔːdzmən/ n (pl
-men /-mən/) espadachín m, espada m

swore /swɔːr ‖ swɔː(r)/ past of SWEAR

sworn¹ /swɔːrn ‖ swɔːn/ past p of SWEAR

sworn² adj (before n) [1] «enemy» declarado,
acérrimo [2] «statement» jurado

swot¹ /swɑːt ‖ swɒt/ n (BrE colloq & pej) matado,
-da m,f or (Col) pilo, -la m,f or (Chi) mateo, -tea
m,f or (Per) chancón, -cona m,f or (RPl) traga mf
or (Esp) empollón, -llona m,f (fam & pey)

swot² vi **-tt-** (BrE colloq) estudiar como loco
(fam), empollar (Esp fam), matearse (Chi fam),
chancar* (Per arg), tragar* (RPl fam)

swum /swʌm/ past p of SWIM¹

swung /swʌŋ/ past & past p of SWING¹

sycamore /'sɪkəmɔːr ‖ 'sɪkəmɔː(r)/ n ~
(maple) plátano m (falso), sicómoro m,
sicomoro m

sycophantic /ˌsɪkə'fæntɪk/ adj adulador

syllable /'sɪləbəl/ n sílaba f

syllabus /'sɪləbəs/ n (pl **-buses**) plan m de
estudios; (of a particular subject) programa m

symbol /'sɪmbəl/ n símbolo m

symbolic /sɪm'bɑːlɪk ‖ sɪm'bɒlɪk/ adj
simbólico; **to be** ~ **OF sth** simbolizar* algo

symbolism /'sɪmbəlɪzəm/ n simbolismo m

symbolize /'sɪmbəlaɪz/ vt simbolizar*

symmetrical /sə'metrɪkəl ‖ sɪ'metrɪkəl/ adj
simétrico

symmetry /'sɪmətri/ n simetría f

sympathetic /ˌsɪmpə'θetɪk/ adj
[1] (understanding) comprensivo; **he was most** ~ **to**
o **toward me when my wife died** me dio todo su
apoyo y comprensión cuando murió mi mujer
[2] (approving) «response/view» favorable;
«audience» bien dispuesto, receptivo

sympathetically /ˌsɪmpə'θetɪkli/ adv (a)
(with understanding) «listen/consider/respond» con
comprensión (b) (showing pity) con compasión

sympathize /'sɪmpəθaɪz/ vi (a) (commiserate): I
~ **with him** lo compadezco (b) (understand) to ~
(WITH sth/sb) comprender or entender* (algo/a
algn)

sympathizer /'sɪmpəθaɪzər ‖ 'sɪmpəθaɪzə(r)/ n
simpatizante mf, partidario, -ria m,f

sympathy /'sɪmpəθi/ n (pl **-thies**) [1] (a)
(pity) compasión f, lástima f (b) (condolences)
(often pl): **you have my deepest** ~ lo acompaño
en el sentimiento (fr hecha), mi más sentido
pésame (fr hecha) [2] (a) (support, approval): **to come
out in** ~ **with sb** (Lab Rel) declararse en huelga en
solidaridad con algn (b) **sympathies** pl (loyalty,
leanings) simpatías fpl

symphony /'sɪmfəni/ n (pl **-nies**) sinfonía f;
(before n) ~ **orchestra** orquesta f sinfónica

symptom /'sɪmptəm/ n síntoma m

symptomatic /ˌsɪmptə'mætɪk/ adj ~ (OF sth)
sintomático (DE algo)

synagogue /'sɪnəgɑːg ‖ 'sɪnəgɒg/ n sinagoga f

synchronize /'sɪŋkrənaɪz/ vt sincronizar*

syndicate /'sɪndəkət ‖ 'sɪndɪkət/ n (a) (group,
cartel) agrupación f; **a crime** ~ una organización
mafiosa (b) (in US) (Journ, TV) agencia f de
distribución periodística

syndrome /'sɪndrəʊm/ n síndrome m

synonymous /sə'nɑːnəməs ‖ sɪ'nɒnɪməs/ adj
«terms/phrases» sinónimo; «ideas» análogo; **to be**
~ **WITH sth** ser* sinónimo DE algo

S

synopsis /sə'nɑ:psəs ‖sɪ'nɒpsɪs/ *n* (*pl* **-opses** /-siːz/) sinopsis *f*

syntax /'sɪntæks/ *n* sintaxis *f*

synthesis /'sɪnθəsəs ‖'sɪnθəsɪs/ *n* (*pl* **-theses** /-θəsiːz/) síntesis *f*

synthesize /'sɪnθəsaɪz/ *vt* sintetizar*

synthesizer /'sɪnθəsaɪzər ‖'sɪnθəsaɪzə(r)/ *n* sintetizador *m*

synthetic[1] /sɪn'θetɪk/ *adj* sintético

synthetic[2] *n* fibra *f* sintética, tejido *m* sintético

syphilis /'sɪfələs ‖'sɪfɪlɪs/ *n* sífilis *f*

syphon *n*/*vt* /'saɪfən/ ▶ SIPHON

Syria /'sɪriə/ *n* Siria *f*

Syrian /'sɪriən/ *adj* sirio

syringe /sə'rɪndʒ ‖sɪ'rɪndʒ/ *n* jeringa *f*, jeringuilla *f*

syrup /'sɜːrəp, 'sɪ- ‖'sɪrəp/ *n* **(a)** (Culin) (sugar solution) almíbar *m*; (with other ingredients) jarabe *m*, sirope *m* **(b)** (medicine) jarabe *m*

system /'sɪstəm/ *n* **1** (ordered structure) sistema *m*, método *m* **2** **(a)** (technical, mechanical) sistema *m* **(b)** (Comput) sistema *m* **3** (Anat, Physiol): **the digestive** ~ el aparato digestivo; **the nervous** ~ el sistema nervioso; **to get sth out of one's** ~ desahogarse* **4** (establishment, status quo): **the** ~ el sistema

systematic /ˌsɪstə'mætɪk/ *adj* sistemático

systematically /ˌsɪstə'mætɪkli/ *adv* sistemáticamente

systems analyst *n* analista *mf* de sistemas

Tt

T, t /tiː/ *n* T, t *f*

tab /tæb/ *n* **1** **(a)** (flap) lengüeta *f* **(b)** (label on clothing) etiqueta *f* **2** (account, bill) (colloq) cuenta *f*; **to keep** ~**s on sth/sb** tener* algo/a algn controlado **3** (on typewriter, word processor) tabulador *m*

tabby /'tæbi/ (*pl* **-bies**), **tabby cat** *n* gato atigrado, gata atigrada *m,f*

tab key *n* tecla *f* de tabulación

table /'teɪbəl/ *n* **1** (piece of furniture) mesa *f*; (*before n*) ~ **football** (BrE) futbolín *m*, taca-taca *m* (Chi), metegol *m* (Arg), futbolito *m* (Ur); ~ **mat** (mantelito *m*) individual *m* **2** (list) tabla *f*; **multiplication** *o* (used by children) **times** ~**s** tablas de multiplicar

table: ~**cloth** *n* mantel *m*; ~**spoon** *n* (utensil) cuchara *f* grande *or* de servir; (measure) cucharada *f* (grande)

tablet /'tæblət ‖'tæblɪt/ *n* **(a)** (pill) pastilla *f*, comprimido *m* **(b)** (commemorative, of stone) lápida *f*

table tennis *n* ping-pong *m*, tenis *m* de mesa

tabloid /'tæblɔɪd/ *n* tabloide *m* (*formato de periódicos utilizado por la prensa popular*)

taboo /tə'buː/ *adj* tabú *adj inv*

tabulate /'tæbjəleɪt ‖'tæbjʊleɪt/ *vt* tabular

tacit /'tæsət ‖'tæsɪt/ *adj* tácito

taciturn /'tæsətɜːrn ‖'tæsɪtɜːn/ *adj* taciturno

tack[1] /tæk/ *n* **(a)** (nail) tachuela *f* **(b)** (Naut) bordada *f* **(c)** (stitch) (BrE) puntada *f*; (seam) hilván *m* **(d)** (Equ) arreos *mpl*, aperos *mpl* (AmL)

tack[2] *vt* **1** (nail) ⟨carpet⟩ ~ **down** clavar con tachuelas **2** (stitch) (BrE) hilvanar

■ ~ *vi* (Naut) dar* bordadas

■ **tack on** [*v* + *o* + *adv, v* + *adv* + *o*] agregar*, añadir

tackle[1] /'tækəl/ *n* **1** (equipment): **sports** ~ equipo *m* de deporte; **fishing** ~ aparejo *m* or

avíos *mpl* de pesca **2** (Sport) (in rugby, US football) placaje *m*, tacle *m* (AmL); (in soccer) entrada *f* fuerte **3** (Naut) aparejo *m*, polea *f*

tackle[2] *vt* **1** **(a)** (come to grips with) ⟨problem⟩ enfrentar, abordar; ⟨subject⟩ tratar; ⟨task⟩ abordar **(b)** (confront) ⟨intruder/colleague⟩ enfrentar, enfrentarse con **2** (Sport) (in rugby, US football) placar*, taclear (AmL); (in soccer) entrarle a

tacky /'tæki/ *adj* **tackier, tackiest** **1** (cheap, tawdry) chabacano, hortera (Esp fam), naco (Méx fam), lobo (Col fam), rasca (Chi fam), mersa (RPl fam) **2** (sticky) pegajoso

tact /tækt/ *n* tacto *m*

tactful /'tæktfəl/ *adj* ⟨person⟩ de mucho tacto; ⟨question/reply⟩ diplomático

tactfully /'tæktfəli/ *adv* con mucho tacto

tactic /'tæktɪk/ *n* táctica *f*

tactical /'tæktɪkəl/ *adj* táctico

tactics /'tæktɪks/ *n* (Mil) (+ *sing or pl vb*) táctica *f*

tactless /'tæktləs ‖'tæktlɪs/ *adj* poco diplomático

tadpole /'tædpəʊl/ *n* renacuajo *m*

Tadzhikistan /tɑːˌdʒɪkɪ'stɑːn// *n* Tayiquistán *m*

taffeta /'tæfətə ‖'tæfɪtə/ *n* tafetán *m*

taffy /'tæfi/ *n* (AmE) caramelo *m* masticable

tag /tæg/ *n* **1** (label) etiqueta *f* (atada) **2** (Ling) coletilla *f*; (*before n*) ~ **question** coletilla interrogativa

■ **tag on** **-gg-** [*v* + *o* + *adv, v* + *adv* + *o*] agregar*, añadir

Tahiti /tə'hiːti/ *n* Tahití *m*

tail[1] /teɪl/ *n* **(a)** (of horse, fish, bird) cola *f*; (of dog, pig) rabo *m*, cola *f* **(b)** (of plane, kite) cola *f*; (of shirt, coat) faldón *m*; *see also* TAILS 1

tail[2] *vt* (follow) ⟨suspect⟩ seguir*

■ **tail off** [*v* + *adv*] **(a)** ⟨demand⟩ disminuir*, mermar **(b)** ⟨sound/words⟩ apagarse*

tail: ~**back** n (BrE) caravana f, cola f (debido a un embotellamiento); ~**coat** n frac m; ~ **end** n: the ~ **end** (of film, concert) el final, los últimos minutos; (of procession) la cola; ~**light** n luz f trasera

tailor[1] /ˈteɪlər ‖ ˈteɪlə(r)/ n sastre m

tailor[2] vt [1] (Clothing) (a) (make) confeccionar (b) **tailored** past p (before n) (fitted) entallado; (lined, structured etc) armado [2] (adapt) adaptar

tailor-made /ˈteɪlərˈmeɪd ‖ ˌteɪləˈmeɪd/ adj (a) ⟨suit⟩ hecho a (la) medida (b) ⟨product/plan⟩ a la medida de sus (or nuestras etc) necesidades

tailpipe /ˈteɪlpaɪp/ n (AmE Auto) tubo m or (RPl) caño m de escape

tails /teɪlz/ n [1] (tailcoat) (+ pl vb) frac m [2] (on coin) (+ sing vb) cruz f, sello m (Andes, Ven), sol m (Méx), ceca f (Arg)

taint /teɪnt/ vt (a) ⟨meat/water⟩ contaminar (b) ⟨name/reputation⟩ mancillar (liter), deshonrar

Taiwan /ˈtaɪˈwɑːn/ n Taiwan m

take[1] /teɪk/ (past **took**; past p **taken**) vt
I (carry, lead, drive) llevar; ~ **an umbrella** lleva un paraguas
II [1] (a) ⟨train/plane/bus/taxi/elevator⟩ tomar, coger* (esp Esp) (b) ⟨road/turning⟩ tomar, agarrar (esp AmL), coger* (esp Esp); ~ **a left** (turn) (BrE) dobla a la izquierda (c) ⟨bend⟩ tomar, coger* (esp Esp); ⟨fence⟩ saltar
[2] (a) (grasp, seize) tomar, agarrar (esp AmL), coger* (esp Esp); ⟨opportunity⟩ aprovechar; **she took the knife from him** le quitó el cuchillo (b) (take charge of): **may I ~ your coat?** ¿me permite el abrigo? (c) (occupy): ~ **a seat** siéntese, tome asiento (frml); **this chair is ~n** esta silla está ocupada
[3] (remove, steal) ⟨wallet/purse⟩ llevarse
[4] **to be ~n ill** caer* enfermo
[5] (a) (capture) ⟨town/position⟩ tomar; ⟨pawn/piece⟩ comer (b) (win) ⟨prize/title⟩ llevarse, hacerse* con; ⟨game/set⟩ ganar (c) (receive as profit) hacer*, sacar*
[6] ⟨medicine/drugs⟩ tomar; **I don't ~ sugar in my coffee** no le pongo azúcar al café
[7] (a) (buy, order) llevar(se); **I'll ~ this pair** (me) llevo este par (b) (rent) alquilar, coger* (esp Esp)
III [1] (of time) «job/task» llevar; «process» tardar; «person/letter» tardar, demorar(se) (AmL); **the flight ~s two hours** el vuelo dura dos horas; **it took me a long time to do it** me llevó mucho tiempo hacerlo
[2] (need): **it ~s courage to do a thing like that** hay que tener or hace falta valor para hacer algo así; **it took four men to lift it** se necesitaron cuatro hombres para levantarlo
[3] (a) (wear): **what size shoes do you ~?** ¿qué número calzas?; **she ~s a 14** usa la talla or (RPl) el talle 14 (b) (Ling) construirse* con, regir*
IV [1] (accept) ⟨money/bribes/job⟩ aceptar; **do you ~ checks?** ¿aceptan cheques?; ~ **it from me** hazme caso
[2] (a) (hold, accommodate): **it ~s/will ~ 42 liters** tiene una capacidad de 42 litros; **we can ~ up to 50 passengers** tenemos cabida para un máximo de 50 pasajeros (b) ⟨patients/pupils⟩ admitir, tomar
[3] (a) (withstand, suffer) ⟨strain/weight⟩ aguantar; ⟨beating⟩ recibir (b) (tolerate, endure) aguantar; **he**

can't ~ a joke no sabe aceptar una broma (c) (bear): **she's ~n it very badly/well** lo lleva muy mal/bien; see also HEART 2, 3
[4] (a) (understand, interpret) tomarse; **don't ~ it personally** no te lo tomes como algo personal; **I ~ it you didn't like him much** por lo que veo no te cayó muy bien (b) (consider) (in imperative) mirar; ~ **Japan, for example** mira el caso del Japón, por ejemplo
V [1] ⟨steps/measures⟩ tomar; ⟨exercise⟩ hacer*; **to ~ a step forward** dar* un paso adelante
[2] (Educ) (a) (teach) (BrE) darle* clase a (b) (learn) ⟨subject⟩ estudiar, hacer*; ⟨course⟩ hacer*; **to ~ an exam** examinarse or dar* or (CS) rendir* or (Méx) tomar un examen, examinarse (Esp)
[3] (a) (record) ⟨measurements/temperature⟩ tomar (b) (write down) ⟨notes⟩ tomar
[4] (adopt): **he ~s the view that ...** opina que ..., es de la opinión de que ...; see also LIKING A, OFFENSE 2B, SHAPE[1] 1A etc
■ ~ vi (a) «cutting» prender (b) «dye» agarrar (esp AmL), coger* (esp Esp)
■ **take aback** [v + o + adv] (usu pass) sorprender
■ **take after** [v + prep + o] salir* a, parecerse* a; **he ~s after his father** salió a su padre, se parece a su padre
■ **take along** [v + o + adv, v + adv + o] llevar
■ **take apart** [v + o + adv] (a) (dismantle) desmontar (b) (show weakness of) ⟨argument⟩ desbaratar
■ **take around,** (BrE) **take round** [v + o + prep + o] ⟨house/estate⟩ mostrar*, enseñar (esp Esp)
■ **take aside** [v + o + adv] llevar aparte or a un lado
■ **take away**
I [v + o + adv, v + adv + o] (a) (carry, lead away) ⟨person/object⟩ llevarse (b) (remove, confiscate) ⟨possession⟩ quitar; **to ~ sth away FROM sb** quitarle algo a algn (c) (erase, obliterate): **this will ~ the pain away** con esto se te pasará el dolor; **this will ~ the taste away** esto te quitará el sabor de la boca
II [v + adv + o] (BrE) ⟨food⟩ llevar
■ **take back** [1] [v + o + adv, v + adv + o] (a) (return) devolver* (b) (repossess) llevarse or (accept back): **she wouldn't ~ back the money she'd lent me** no quiso que le devolviera el dinero que me había prestado (d) (withdraw, retract) ⟨statement⟩ retirar
[2] [v + o + adv] (in time): **it ~s me back to my childhood** me transporta a mi niñez
■ **take down** [v + o + adv, v + adv + o] (a) ⟨decorations/notice⟩ quitar (b) (dismantle) desmontar (c) ⟨name/address⟩ apuntar, anotar
■ **take home** [v + adv + o]: **she ~s home less than £600** su sueldo neto or líquido es de menos de 600 libras
■ **take in**
I [v + o + adv, v + adv + o] [1] (move indoors) meter (dentro), entrar (esp AmS)
[2] (give home to) ⟨orphan⟩ recoger*; ⟨lodger⟩ alojar
[3] (grasp) ⟨information⟩ asimilar
[4] (make narrower) ⟨dress/waist⟩ meterle or tomarle a
II [v + o + adv] (deceive) engañar
III [v + adv + o] (a) (include) ⟨areas/topics⟩ incluir*, abarcar* (b) (visit) visitar, incluir* (en el recorrido)

■ **take off**

I [v + o + adv, v + adv + o] [v + o + prep + o] ① (detach, remove) quitar, sacar*; **to ~ off one's clothes** quitarse or (esp AmL) sacarse* la ropa ② **(a)** (cut off) cortar **(b)** (deduct) descontar* ③ (have free): **she's ~n the morning off (from) work** se ha tomado la mañana libre

II [v + adv] **(a)** «aircraft/pilot» despegar*, decolar (AmL); «flight» salir* **(b)** (succeed) «career» tomar vuelo **(c)** (depart) largarse* (fam), irse*

III [v + o + adv] [v + o + prep + o] ① (remove) quitar, sacar* (esp AmL); **~ your hands off me!** ¡quítame las manos de encima! ② (take away from) (colloq) quitar, sacar* (CS)

■ **take on** ① [v + o + adv, v + adv + o] **(a)** (employ) «staff» contratar, tomar (esp AmL) **(b)** (undertake) «work» encargarse* de, hacerse* cargo de; «responsibility» asumir **(c)** (tackle) «opponent» enfrentarse a ② [v + adv + o] (acquire) «expression» adoptar; «appearance» adquirir*

■ **take out**

I [v + o + adv, v + adv + o] ① **(a)** (remove physically) sacar*; **to ~ it out of sb** «fight/race» dejar a algn rendido **(b)** (exclude) eliminar **(c)** (transport) sacar* **(d)** (AmE) «food» llevar ② (withdraw) «money» sacar* ③ (produce) «gun/wallet» sacar*

II [v + o + adv, v + adv + o] **(a)** (extract) «tooth/appendix» sacar* **(b)** (obtain) «insurance/permit» sacar*

III [v + o + adv] (accompany, conduct): **he'd like to ~ her out** le gustaría invitarla a salir; **she took me out to dinner** me invitó a cenar

■ **take out on** [v + o + adv + prep + o]: **to ~ it out on sb** desquitarse con algn

■ **take over** ① [v + adv] **(a)** (assume control) «political party» asumir el poder; **he will ~ over as managing director** asumirá el cargo de director ejecutivo; **to ~ over FROM sb** sustituir* a algn; (in shift work) relevar a algn **(b)** (seize control) hacerse* con el poder ② [v + o + adv, v + adv + o] «responsibility/role» asumir; «job» hacerse* cargo de; «company» absorber

■ **take round** (BrE) ▶ TAKE AROUND

■ **take to** [v + prep + o] **(a)** (develop liking for): **she took to teaching immediately** enseguida le tomó gusto a la enseñanza; **I didn't ~ to him** no me cayó muy bien **(b)** (form habit of): **to ~ to drink** darse* a la bebida; **to ~ to -ING** darle* a algn POR + INF

■ **take up**

I [v + o + adv, v + adv + o] ① **(a)** (pick up) tomar **(b)** (accept) «offer/challenge» aceptar **(c)** (adopt) «cause» hacer* suyo (or mío etc) **(d)** (begin): **he's ~n up pottery** ha empezado a hacer cerámica ② (lift) «carpet/floorboards» levantar ③ **(a)** (continue) «story» seguir*, continuar*; «conversation» reanudar **(b)** «issue/point» tratar; (pursue) volver* a ④ (shorten) «skirt» acortar; «hem» subir

II [v + adv + o] ① (use up) «time» llevar; «space» ocupar ② (move into) «position» tomar

■ **take up on** [v + o + adv + prep + o] **(a)** (take person at word): **I may well ~ you up on that** a lo mejor te tomo la palabra or te acepto el ofrecimiento **(b)** (challenge): **I must ~ you up on that** sobre eso discrepo con usted

take² n (Cin) toma f

takeaway¹ /'teɪkəweɪ/ adj (BrE) «meal/pizza» para llevar; «restaurant» de comida para llevar

takeaway² n (BrE) **(a)** (restaurant) restaurante m de comida para llevar **(b)** (meal) comida f preparada

take-home pay /'teɪkhəʊm/ n sueldo m neto

taken¹ /'teɪkən/ past p of TAKE¹

taken² adj (pred) **to be ~ WITH sth/sb: I was quite ~ with him** me cayó muy bien; **they were very ~ with the house** quedaron encantados con la casa

takeoff /'teɪkɔːf ‖'teɪkɒf/ n **(a)** (Aviat) despegue m, decolaje m (AmL) **(b)** (imitation) (colloq) parodia f

takeout¹ /'teɪkaʊt/ adj (AmE) «meal» para llevar; «restaurant» de comida para llevar

takeout² n (AmE) comida f preparada

takeover /'teɪkəʊvər ‖'teɪkəʊvə(r)/ n **(a)** (Govt) toma f del poder **(b)** (Busn) absorción f, adquisición f (de una empresa por otra); (before n) **~ bid** oferta f pública de adquisición or de compra, OPA f

takings /'teɪkɪŋz/ n pl (BrE Busn) recaudación f; (at box office) taquilla f, entrada f

talc /tælk/ n polvos mpl de talco, talco m (AmL)

talcum powder /'tælkəm/ n polvos mpl de talco

tale /teɪl/ n cuento m, relato m; **to tell ~s** contar* chismes or cuentos

talent /'tælənt/ n **(a)** (aptitude, skill) talento m **(b)** (talented people) gente f con talento

talented /'tæləntəd ‖'tæləntɪd/ adj talentoso, de talento

talisman /'tæləsmən ‖'tælɪzmən/ n (pl ~s) talismán m

talk¹ /tɔːk/ vi ① (speak) hablar; (converse) hablar, platicar* (esp AmC, Méx); **to ~ ABOUT sb/ sth** hablar DE algn/algo; **to ~ OF sth/-ING** hablar DE algo/DE + INF; **to ~ TO sb** hablar CON algn; **he was ~ing to Jane** estaba hablando con Jane; **are you ~ing to me ?** ¿me hablas a mí?; **we ~ ing to each other** no nos hablamos; **to ~ WITH sb** hablar CON algn ② (a) (have discussion) hablar; **we need to ~** tenemos que hablar; **to ~ ABOUT sth** discutir algo **(b)** (give talk) **to ~ ABOUT/ON sth** hablar DE/ SOBRE algo

■ ~ vt ① (speak) (colloq): **to ~ business** hablar de negocios; **don't ~ nonsense!** ¡no digas tonterías! ② (argue, persuade) **to ~ sb INTO/OUT OF sth/-ING** convencer* a algn DE QUE/DE QUE NO (+ subj)

■ **talk down to** [v + adv + prep + o] hablarle en tono condescendiente a

■ **talk over** [*v* + *o* + *adv*, *v* + *adv* + *o*] discutir

talk² *n* ▢1 **(a)** (conversation) conversación *f*; **I had a long ∼ with him** estuve hablando *or* (AmC, Méx tb) platicando un rato largo con él **(b)** (lecture) charla *f* **(c)** **talks** *pl* (negotiations) conversaciones *fpl* ▢2 (words) (colloq & pej) palabrería *f* (fam & pey)

talkative /'tɔːkətɪv/ *adj* conversador, hablador

talker /'tɔːkər ‖'tɔːkə(r)/ *n* hablador, -dora *m,f*

talking /'tɔːkɪŋ/: **∼ point** *n* tema *m* de conversación; **∼-to** *n* (*pl* **-tos**) (colloq): **to give sb a good ∼-to** leerle* la cartilla a algn (fam)

talk show *n* programa *m* de entrevistas

tall /tɔːl/ *adj* **-er, -est** alto; **how ∼ are you?** ¿cuánto mides?; **he's nearly 6 feet ∼** mide casi 6 pies

tall story, tall tale *n* cuento *m* chino (fam)

tally¹ /'tæli/ *n* (*pl* **-lies**) cuenta *f*

tally² *vi* **-lies, -lying, -lied** coincidir, cuadrar

Talmud /'tælmʊd/ *n* **the ∼** el Talmud

talon /'tælən/ *n* garra *f*

tambourine /tæmbə'riːn/ *n* pandereta *f*

tame¹ /teɪm/ *adj* **tamer, tamest (a)** ⟨*animal*⟩ (by nature) manso, dócil; (tamed) domado, domesticado **(b)** (unexciting) ⟨*show/story*⟩ insulso, insípido

tame² *vt* ⟨*wild animal*⟩ domar; ⟨*stray*⟩ domesticar*

Tamil /'tæməl ‖'tæmɪl/ *n* **(a)** (person) tamil *mf*, tamul *mf* **(b)** (language) tamul *m*

tamper with /'tæmpər ‖'tæmpə(r)/ *v* + *o* + *adv*, *v* + *adv* + *o* ⟨*engine/controls*⟩ tocar*; ⟨*figures*⟩ alterar

tampon /'tæmpɑːn ‖'tæmpɒn/ *n* tampón *m*

tan¹ /tæn/ **-nn-** *vt* ▢1 ⟨*leather/hide*⟩ curtir ▢2 ⟨*sun*⟩ ⟨*body/skin*⟩ broncear, tostar*
■ **∼** *vi* broncearse, quemarse (AmL)

tan² *n* (on skin) bronceado *m*, moreno *m* (esp Esp)

tan³ *adj* habano

tandem /'tændəm/ *n* tándem *m*

tang /tæŋ/ *n* (strong taste) sabor *m* fuerte; (sharp taste) acidez *f*; (smell) olor *m* penetrante

tangent /'tændʒənt/ *n* tangente *f*; **to go o fly off at o on a ∼** irse* por las ramas

tangerine /tændʒə'riːn/ *n* mandarina *f*, tangerina *f*

tangible /'tændʒəbəl/ *adj* tangible

tangle¹ /'tæŋɡəl/ *vt* enredar, enmarañar; **to get ∼d (up)** enredarse
■ **tangle up** [*v* + *o* + *adv*, *v* + *adv* + *o*] enredar, enmarañar

tangle² *n* (of threads, hair) enredo *m*, maraña *f*, embrollo *m*; (of weeds) maraña *f*

tangled /'tæŋɡəld/ *adj* enredado

tango /'tæŋɡəʊ/ *n* (*pl* **-gos**) tango *m*

tank /tæŋk/ *n* ▢1 (for liquid, gas) depósito *m*, tanque *m*; (on trucks, rail wagons) cisterna *f*; (Auto) tanque *m*, depósito *m* ▢2 (Mil) tanque *m*, carro *m* de combate

tankard /'tæŋkərd ‖'tæŋkəd/ *n* jarra *f*

tanker /'tæŋkər ‖'tæŋkə(r)/ *n* **(a)** (ship) buque *m* cisterna *or* tanque **(b)** (truck) camión *m* cisterna

tanned /tænd/ *adj* bronceado, moreno

Tannoy® /'tænɔɪ/ *n* (BrE) sistema *m* de megafonía

tantalizing /'tæntlaɪzɪŋ ‖'tæntəlaɪzɪŋ/ *adj* tentador

tantamount /'tæntəmaʊnt/ *adj* **to be ∼ TO sth** equivaler* A algo

tantrum /'tæntrəm/ *n* berrinche *m*, rabieta *f*; **Jack had o threw a ∼** a Jack le dio un berrinche, Jack hizo un berrinche (Méx)

Tanzania /tænzə'niːə/ *n* Tanzania *f*, Tanzanía *f*

Tanzanian /tænzə'niːən/ *adj* tanzano

tap¹ /tæp/ *n* ▢1 **(a)** (for water) (BrE) llave *f or* (Esp) grifo *m or* (RPl) canilla *f or* (Per) caño *m or* (AmC) paja *f or* (AmC, Ven) chorro *m* ▢2 (gas ∼) llave *f* del gas **(c)** (on barrel) espita *f* ▢2 (light blow) toque *m*, golpecito *m* ▢3 ▶ TAP DANCING

tap² **-pp-** *vt* ▢1 (strike lightly) dar* un toque *or* golpecito en ▢2 ⟨*tree*⟩ sangrar **(b)** ⟨*resources/reserves*⟩ explotar ▢3 ⟨*telephone*⟩ intervenir*, pinchar (fam); ⟨*conversation*⟩ interceptar
■ **∼** *vi* **(a)** (strike lightly) **to ∼ AT/ON sth** dar* toques *or* golpecitos EN algo **(b)** (make tapping sound) dar* golpecitos, tamborilear

tap dancing *n* claqué *m*

tape¹ /teɪp/ *n* ▢1 **(a)** (of paper, cloth) cinta *f* **(b)** (adhesive) cinta *f* adhesiva; (Med) esparadrapo *m*; *see also* MASKING TAPE, SCOTCH TAPE® *etc* **(c)** (Sport) cinta *f* de llegada **(d)** ▶ TAPE MEASURE ▢2 (Audio, Comput, Video) cinta *f*

tape² *vt* (record) grabar

tape: ∼ deck *n* platina *f*, pletina *f*; **∼ measure** *n* cinta *f* métrica, metro *m*

taper *vi* afilarse, estrecharse
■ **∼** *vt* afilar, estrechar
■ **taper off** [*v* + *adv*] **(a)** ⟨*enthusiasm*⟩ decaer*; ⟨*demand/sales*⟩ disminuir* **(b)** ▶ TAPER *vi*

tape: ∼-record /'teɪprɪ'kɔːrd ‖'teɪprɪkɔːd/ *vt* grabar; **∼ recorder** *n* grabador *m*, grabadora *f*; (for cassette format) grabador *m*, grabadora *f*, casete *m* (Esp)

tapestry /'tæpəstri/ *n* (*pl* **-tries**) **(a)** (wall hanging) tapiz *m* **(b)** (art form) tapicería *f*

tapeworm /'teɪpwɜːrm ‖'teɪpwɜːm/ *n* (lombriz *f*) solitaria *f*, tenia *f*

tar¹ /tɑːr ‖tɑː(r)/ *n* alquitrán *m*

tar² *vt* **-rr-** ⟨*road/fence*⟩ alquitranar; ⟨*roof*⟩ impermeabilizar* (con alquitrán)

target¹ /'tɑːrɡət ‖'tɑːɡɪt/ *n* ▢1 **(a)** (thing aimed at) blanco *m*; (Mil) objetivo *m*; (board) (Sport) diana *f* **(b)** (of criticism) blanco *m* ▢2 (objective, goal) objetivo *m*; **to be on ∼** ir* de acuerdo a lo previsto (*or* al plan de trabajo *etc*); (before *n*) ⟨*date/figure*⟩ fijado; ⟨*market*⟩ objetivo *adj inv*

target² *vt* **(a)** (select as target): **the company is ∼ing the small investor** la empresa está intentando captar al pequeño inversor **(b)** (direct) ⟨*advertising*⟩ dirigir*; **to ∼ benefits at those most in need** concentrar la ayuda a los más necesitados

target practice *n* prácticas *fpl* del tiro

tariff /'tærəf ‖'tærɪf/ *n* ▢1 **(a)** (price list) (BrE) tarifa *f* ▢2 (Tax) arancel *m* (aduanero)

tarmac /'tɑːrmæk ‖'tɑːmæk/ *n* **(a) tarmac®** (AmE) (tar mixture) asfalto *m* **(b)** (surface — in airport, racetrack) pista *f*; (— on road) asfalto *m*

Tarmac® *n* (BrE) ▶ TARMAC A

tarnish /'tɑːrnɪʃ ‖'tɑːnɪʃ/ *vt* **(a)** ⟨*silver*⟩ deslustrar **(b)** ⟨*reputation/name*⟩ empañar

tarot card /'tærəʊ/ *n* carta *f* de tarot

tarpaulin /tɑːr'pɔːlən ‖tɑː'pɔːlɪn/ *n* **(a)** (sheet) lona *f* **(b)** (material) lona *f* impermeabilizada

tarragon /'tærəgən/ *n* estragón *m*

tart¹ /tɑːrt ‖tɑːt/ *n* **1** (Culin) (large) tarta *f*; (individual) tartaleta *f* **2** (promiscuous woman) (colloq) fulana *f* (fam), puta *f* (vulg)

tart² *adj* **(a)** ⟨*taste/apple*⟩ ácido, agrio **(b)** ⟨*remark*⟩ cortante, áspero

tartan /'tɑːrtn ‖'tɑːtn/ *n* **(a)** (cloth) tela *f* escocesa *or* de cuadros escoceses **(b)** (pattern) tartán *m*

tartar /'tɑːrtər ‖'tɑːtə(r)/ *n* (Dent) sarro *m*

task /tæsk ‖tɑːsk/ *n* tarea *f*; **to take sb to ~** llamarle la atención *or* leerle* la cartilla a algn

tassel /'tæsəl/ *n* borla *f*

taste¹ /teɪst/ *n* **1** **(a)** (flavor) sabor *m*, gusto *m* **(b)** (sense) gusto *m* **2** (*no pl*) (sample, small amount): **can I have a ~ of your ice cream?** ¿me dejas probar tu helado?; **we got a ~ of what was to come** fue un anticipo de lo que nos esperaba **3** (liking) gusto *m*; **to be to one's ~** ser* de su (*or* mi *etc*) gusto **4** (judgment) gusto *m*; **in good/bad ~** de buen/mal gusto

taste² *vt* **(a)** (test flavor of) ⟨*food/wine*⟩ probar* **(b)** (test quality of) ⟨*food*⟩ degustar; ⟨*wine*⟩ catar **(c)** (perceive flavor): **you can ~ the sherry in it** se nota el jerez, le siento gusto a jerez (AmL) **(d)** (experience) ⟨*freedom*⟩ conocer*
■ **~** *vi* saber*; **to ~ of** *or* **sth** saber* A algo

taste bud *n* papila *f* gustativa

tasteful /'teɪstfəl/ *adj* de buen gusto

tastefully /'teɪstfəli/ *adv* con (buen) gusto

tasteless /'teɪstləs ‖'teɪstlɪs/ *adj* **(a)** (flavorless) insípido, soso, desabrido **(b)** (in bad taste) de mal gusto

tasty /'teɪsti/ *adj* **-tier, -tiest** sabroso, apetitoso

tattered /'tætərd ‖'tætəd/ *adj* ⟨*clothes*⟩ hecho jirones; ⟨*pride/image*⟩ destrozado

tatters /'tætərz ‖'tætəz/ *pl n*: **to be in ~** «*clothes*» estar* hecho jirones

tattoo¹ /tæ'tuː/ *n* (*pl* **-toos**) **1** (picture) tatuaje *m* **2** (display) *espectáculo militar con música*

tattoo² *vt* **-toos, -tooing, -tooed** tatuar*

tatty /'tæti/ *adj* **-tier, -tiest** (BrE colloq) ⟨*clothes/shoes*⟩ gastado, estropeado; ⟨*furniture*⟩ estropeado

taught /tɔːt/ *past & past p of* TEACH

taunt¹ /tɔːnt/ *vt* provocar* mediante burlas

taunt² *n* (insult) insulto *m*; (jibe) pulla *f*

Taurus /'tɔːrəs/ *n* **(a)** (sign) (*no art*) Tauro **(b)** (person) Tauro *or* tauro *mf*, taurino -na *m,f*

taut /tɔːt/ *adj* ⟨*rope/sail*⟩ tenso, tirante; ⟨*skin*⟩ tirante

tavern /'tævərn ‖'tævən/ *n* taberna *f*

tawdry /'tɔːdri/ *adj* **-drier, -driest** ⟨*jewelry/ decorations*⟩ de oropel; ⟨*decor*⟩ de mal gusto

tawny /'tɔːni/ *adj* **-nier, -niest** leonado, pardo rojizo *adj inv*

tawny owl *n* cárabo *m*, antillo *m*

tax¹ /tæks/ *n* (individual charge) impuesto *m*, tributo *m*; (in general) impuestos *mpl*; (before *n*) **the ~ year** (in UK) el año *or* ejercicio fiscal

tax² *vt* **1** ⟨*company/goods/earnings*⟩ gravar; **we're being ~ed too highly** nos están cobrando demasiado en impuestos **2** (strain) ⟨*resources/ health*⟩ poner* a prueba

taxable /'tæksəbəl/ *adj* ⟨*goods*⟩ sujeto a impuestos; **~ income** ingresos *mpl* gravables, ≈ base *f* imponible

taxation /tæk'seɪʃən/ *n* (taxes) impuestos *mpl*, cargas *fpl* fiscales; (system) sistema *m or* régimen *m* tributario *or* fiscal

tax: ~ collector *n* recaudador, -dora *m,f* de impuestos; **~ evasion** *n* evasión *f* fiscal *or* de impuestos; (large scale) fraude *m* fiscal; **~-free** /'tæks'friː/ *adj* libre de impuestos; **~ haven** *n* paraíso *m* fiscal

taxi¹ /'tæksi/ *n* (*pl* **~s**) taxi *m*; (before *n*) **~ driver** taxista *mf*

taxi² *vi* **taxies, taxiing** *or* **taxying, taxied** (Aviat) rodar* por la pista de despegue/de aterrizaje, carretear (AmL)

taxidermy /'tæksədɜːrmi ‖'tæksɪˌdɜːmi/ *n* taxidermia *f*

taxing /'tæksɪŋ/ *adj* ⟨*problem*⟩ difícil, complicado; ⟨*job*⟩ (mentally) que exige mucho

tax: ~man /'tæksmæn/ (*pl* **-men** /-men/) *n* (colloq) **the ~man** Hacienda *f*, el fisco; **~payer** /'peɪər ‖'peɪə(r)/ *n* contribuyente *mf*; **~ return** *n* declaración *f* de la renta *or* (esp AmL) de impuestos

TB *n* = **tuberculosis**

tbs, tbsp = **tablespoon(s)**

te /tiː/ *n* (BrE Mus) si *m*

tea /tiː/ *n* **1** (drink, leaves, plant) té *m* **2** (meal) **(a)** (in the afternoon) té *m*, merienda *f* **(b)** (evening) (BrE) cena *f*, comida *f* (AmL)

tea bag *n* bolsita *f* de té

teach /tiːtʃ/ (*past & past p* **taught**) *vt* ⟨*subject*⟩ dar* clases de, enseñar; ⟨*course*⟩ dar*, impartir (fml); **to ~ sb to + INF** enseñarle a algn a + INF; **who ~es you?** ¿quien te da clase?; **to ~ school** (AmE) dar* clase(s) en un colegio
■ **~** *vi* dar* clase(s)

teacher /'tiːtʃər ‖'tiːtʃə(r)/ *n* profesor, -sora *m,f*, docente *mf* (fml), enseñante *mf* (period); (primary school **~**) maestro, -tra *m,f*

teacher: ~s college *n* (AmE) (for primary education) escuela *f* normal; (for secondary education) instituto *m* de profesorado; **~ training** *n* formación *f* pedagógica *or* de profesorado; (before *n*) **~ training college** (BrE) ▶ **~s COLLEGE**

tea chest *n* caja *f* de embalaje (*utilizada en mudanzas*)

teaching /'tiːtʃɪŋ/ *n* **1** (profession) enseñanza *f*, docencia *f* **2** (doctrine) (*often pl*) enseñanza *f*

teaching practice *n* (BrE) práctica *f* docente

tea: ~ cloth *n* (BrE) ▶ **TEA TOWEL**; **~ cozy**, (BrE) **~ cosy** *n* cubretetera *m*; **~cup** *n* taza *f* de té

teak /tiːk/ *n* (madera *f* de) teca *f*

tealeaf /'tiːliːf/ *n* (*pl* **-leaves**) hoja *f* de té

team /tiːm/ n **(a)** (of players, workers) equipo m; (before n) it was a ~ effort fue un trabajo de equipo **(b)** (of horses) tiro m; (of oxen) yunta f

team: ~**mate** n compañero, -ra m,f de equipo; ~ **spirit** n espíritu m de equipo

teamster /ˈtiːmstər ‖ ˈtiːmstə(r)/ n (AmE) camionero, -ra m,f

teamwork /ˈtiːmwɜːrk ‖ ˈtiːmwɜːk/ n trabajo m or labor f de equipo

tea: ~ **party** n té m; ~**pot** n tetera f

tear[1] n [1] /tɪr ‖ tɪə(r)/ lágrima f; to be in ~s estar* llorando [2] /ter ‖ teə(r)/ rotura f; (rip, slash) desgarrón m, rasgón m; see also WEAR[1] 1B

tear[2] /ter ‖ teə(r)/ (past **tore**; past p **torn**) vt **(a)** ⟨cloth/paper⟩ romper*, rasgar*; I **tore open the letter** abrí la carta (rasgando el sobre); **to ~ sth to pieces** o **shreds** ⟨cloth/paper⟩ hacer* algo pedazos; ⟨play/essay⟩ hacer* algo pedazos or trizas or (fam) polvo; ⟨argument⟩ echar algo por tierra **(b)** (divide) (usu pass) dividir; **he was torn between … and …** se debatía entre … y … **(c)** (remove forcibly) **to ~ sth FROM sth** arrancar* algo DE algo

■ ~ vi [1] ⟨cloth/paper⟩ romperse*, rasgarse* [2] (rush) (+ adv compl): **to ~ along** ir* a toda velocidad

■ **tear apart** [v + o + adv] desgarrar

■ **tear down** [v + o + adv, v + adv + o] tirar abajo

■ **tear off** [v + o + adv, v + adv + o] arrancar*

■ **tear out** [v + o + adv, v + adv + o] arrancar*

■ **tear up** [v + o + adv, v + adv + o] romper*

teardrop /ˈtɪrdrɑːp ‖ ˈtɪədrɒp/ n lágrima f

tearful /ˈtɪrfl ‖ ˈtɪəfl/ adj ⟨look/expression⟩ lloroso; ⟨farewell⟩ triste, emotivo

tear gas /ˈtɪrgæs ‖ ˈtɪəgæs/ n gas m lacrimógeno

tearoom /ˈtiːruːm, -rʊm/ n salón m de té

tease /tiːz/ vt tomarle el pelo a (fam); (cruelly) burlarse or reírse de

tea: ~ **service**, ~ **set** n juego m de té; ~**shop** n (esp BrE) ▶ TEAROOM; ~**spoon** n **(a)** (spoon) cucharita f, cucharilla f **(b)** (quantity) cucharadita f; ~ **strainer** n colador m (pequeño)

teat /tiːt/ n **(a)** (Zool) tetilla f **(b)** (of feeding bottle) (BrE) ▶ NIPPLE B

tea: ~**time** n (of afternoon snack) la hora del té, ≈ la hora de merendar; (of evening meal) (BrE) la hora de cenar or (AmL tb) de comer; ~ **towel** n (BrE) paño m or trapo m de cocina

technical /ˈteknɪkl/ adj técnico

technical college n (in UK) escuela f politécnica, ≈ instituto m de formación profesional (en Esp)

technicality /ˌteknɪˈkæləti/ n (pl **-ties**) (detail) detalle m técnico

technically /ˈteknɪkli/ adv técnicamente; (indep) desde el punto de vista técnico

technician /tekˈnɪʃən/ n técnico mf, técnico, -ca m,f

technique /tekˈniːk/ n técnica f

technological /ˌteknəˈlɑːdʒɪkəl ‖ ˌteknəˈlɒdʒɪkəl/ adj tecnológico

technology /tekˈnɑːlədʒi ‖ tekˈnɒlədʒi/ n (pl **-gies**) tecnología f

teddy bear /ˈtedi/ n osito m de peluche

tedious /ˈtiːdiəs/ adj tedioso

tedium /ˈtiːdiəm/ n tedio m

teem /tiːm/ vi **to ~ WITH sth**: **the forest is ~ing with birds** el bosque está repleto de pájaros; **the streets were ~ing with people** las calles hervían de gente

teenage /ˈtiːneɪdʒ/ adj ⟨girl/boy⟩ adolescente; ⟨fashions⟩ juvenil, para adolescentes

teenager /ˈtiːneɪdʒər ‖ ˈtiːneɪdʒə(r)/ n adolescente mf

teens /tiːnz/ pl n adolescencia f

tee shirt /tiː/ n ▶ T-SHIRT

teeter /ˈtiːtər ‖ ˈtiːtə(r)/ vi ⟨person⟩ tambalearse

teeth /tiːθ/ pl of TOOTH

teethe /tiːð/ vi: **she's teething** le están saliendo los dientes

teething troubles /ˈtiːðɪŋ/ pl n problemas mpl iniciales

teetotal /ˈtiːˈtəʊtl/ adj abstemio

teetotaler, (BrE) **teetotaller** /ˈtiːˈtəʊtlər ‖ ˈtiːˈtəʊtlə(r)/ n abstemio, -mia m,f

TEFL /ˈtefl/ n (BrE) (= **teaching English as a foreign language**) enseñanza del inglés como lengua extranjera

tel (= **telephone number**) Tel., fono (CS)

telebanking /ˈteliˌbæŋkɪŋ/ n telebanca f

telecommunications /ˈtelikəˌmjuːnəˈkeɪʃənz ‖ ˌtelikəˌmjuːnɪˈkeɪʃənz/ n telecomunicaciones fpl

telegram /ˈtelɪɡræm ‖ ˈtelɪɡræm/ n telegrama m

telegraph /ˈtelɪɡræf ‖ ˈtelɪɡrɑːf/ n **(a)** (method) telégrafo m; (before n) ⟨wire/cable⟩ telegráfico; ~ **pole** poste m telegráfico **(b)** (message) telegrama m, despacho m telegráfico

telemarketing /ˈteliˌmɑːrkətɪŋ ‖ ˈteliˌmɑːkɪtɪŋ/ n telemarketing m, teletienda f

telepathic /ˌteləˈpæθɪk ‖ ˌtelɪˈpæθɪk/ adj ⟨message⟩ telepático; ⟨person⟩ con telepatía, telépata

telepathy /təˈlepəθi/ n telepatía f

telephone[1] /ˈteləfəʊn ‖ ˈtelɪfəʊn/ n teléfono m; (before n) ⟨message/line⟩ telefónico; ~ **number** (número m de) teléfono m; ~ **operator** telefonista mf; see also PHONE[1]

telephone[2] vt telefonear, llamar por teléfono a

telephone: ~ **booth**, (BrE) ~ **box** n cabina f telefónica or de teléfonos; ~ **directory** n guía f telefónica or de teléfonos; ~ **exchange** n central f telefónica or de teléfonos

telephonist /təˈlefənəst ‖ təˈlefənɪst/ n (BrE) telefonista mf

telesales /ˈteliseɪlz/ pl n televentas fpl

telescope /ˈteləskəʊp ‖ ˈtelɪskəʊp/ n telescopio m

telescopic /ˌteləˈskɑːpɪk ‖ ˌtelɪˈskɒpɪk/ adj telescópico

teleshopping /ˈteliˌʃɑːpɪŋ ‖ ˈteliˌʃɒpɪŋ/ n compra(s) f(pl) por teléfono

teletext /ˈtelitekst/ n teletex(to) m, videotex(to) m

televise /ˈteləvaɪz ‖ ˈtelɪvaɪz/ vt televisar

television /'teləvɪʒən ‖'telɪvɪʒən/ n **(a)** (medium, industry) televisión f; on ~ en or por (la) televisión; (before n) ~ **licence** (in UK) impuesto y licencia que debe obtenerse para poder usar un receptor de televisión **(b)** ~ (**set**) televisor m

telex /'teleks/ n télex m

tell /tel/ (past & past p **told**) vt [1] (inform, reveal) decir*; he was told that … le dijeron que …; could you ~ me the way to the station? ¿me podría decir cómo se llega a la estación? [2] (recount, relate) ⟨joke/story⟩ contar*; she's told me all about you me ha hablado mucho de ti; ~ us about Lima cuéntanos cómo es Lima (or qué tal se fue en Lima etc) [3] (instruct, warn) decir*; to ~ sb to + INF decirle* a algn QUE (+ subj) [4] **(a)** (ascertain, know): I could ~ from her voice that … noté por la voz que …; to ~ the time decir la hora **(b)** (distinguish) to ~ sth/sb (FROM sth/sb) distinguir* algo/a algn (DE algo/algn); I can't ~ the difference yo no veo or no noto ninguna diferencia [5]: all told en total
■ ~ vi [1] (reveal): promise you won't ~? ¿prometes que no se lo vas a contar or decir a nadie?; to ~ ON sb (TO sb) (colloq) acusar a algn (A or CON algn) [2] (know) saber*; you never can ~ nunca se sabe [3] (count, have an effect): her age is beginning to ~ se le está empezando a notar la edad
■ **tell apart** [v + o + adv] distinguir*
■ **tell off** [v + o + adv, v + adv + o] (colloq) regañar, reñir* (esp Esp), retar (CS), resondrar (Per), rezongar* (AmC, Ur)

teller /'telər ‖'telə(r)/ n (in bank) cajero, -ra m,f

telling /'telɪŋ/ adj ⟨sign/remark⟩ revelador

telltale¹ /'telteɪl/ adj (before n) revelador

telltale² n (person) (colloq) soplón, -plona m,f (fam), acusete mf (fam)

temp /temp/ n empleado, -da m,f eventual or temporal

temper¹ /'tempər ‖'tempə(r)/ n **(a)** (no pl) (mood) humor m; (temperament, disposition) carácter m, genio m; to have a bad ~ tener* mal genio **(b)** (rage): to be in a ~ estar* furioso or hecho una furia **(c)** (composure): to lose one's ~ perder* los estribos

temper² vt **(a)** (moderate) ⟨criticism⟩ atenuar* **(b)** (Metall) templar

temperament /'temprəmənt/ n temperamento m

temperamental /ˌtemprə'mentl̩/ adj ⟨person⟩ temperamental

temperance /'tempərəns/ n **(a)** (moderation) (fml) templanza f (fml), moderación f **(b)** (alcohol avoidance) abstinencia f de bebidas; (before n) ⟨movement⟩ antialcohólico

temperate /'tempərət/ adj templado

temperature /'temprətʃər ‖'temprətʃə(r)/ n **(a)** (Phys) temperatura f **(b)** (Med) (reading on thermometer) temperatura f; (abnormally high reading)

fiebre f, temperatura f (CS); to have o run a ~ tener* fiebre or (CS) temperatura; to take sb's ~ tomarle la temperatura a algn

tempest /'tempəst ‖'tempɪst/ n (liter) tempestad f (liter)

tempestuous /tem'pestʃuəs ‖tem'pestjuəs/ adj **(a)** ⟨relationship⟩ tempestuoso **(b)** ⟨sea⟩ (liter) tempestuoso (liter)

temple /'tempəl/ n [1] (Relig) templo m [2] (Anat) sien f

tempo /'tempəʊ/ n (pl **-pos** or **-pi** /-pi/) ritmo m; (Mus) tempo m

temporal /'tempərəl/ adj temporal

temporarily /ˌtempə'rerəli ‖'tempərərɪli/ adv temporalmente, temporariamente (AmL)

temporary /'tempəreri ‖'temprəri/ adj ⟨accommodation/arrangement⟩ temporal, provisional; ⟨job/work/worker⟩ eventual, temporal

tempt /tempt/ vt (often pass) tentar*

temptation /temp'teɪʃən/ n tentación f

tempting /'temptɪŋ/ adj tentador

ten¹ /ten/ n diez m; see also FOUR¹

ten² adj diez adj inv

tenable /'tenəbəl/ adj defendible

tenacious /tə'neɪʃəs ‖tɪ'neɪʃəs/ adj tenaz

tenacity /tə'næsəti ‖tɪ'næsəti/ n tenacidad f

tenancy /'tenənsi/ n (pl **-cies**) (holding, possession) tenencia f

tenant /'tenənt/ n inquilino, -na m,f, arrendatario, -ria m,f

tend /tend/ vi [1] (have tendency, be inclined) tender*; to ~ to + INF tender* A + INF [2] (attend) to ~ TO sth/sb ocuparse DE algo/algn
■ ~ vt ⟨sheep⟩ cuidar (de), ocuparse de; ⟨victims⟩ cuidar (de), atender*; ⟨garden/grave⟩ ocuparse de

tendency /'tendənsi/ n (pl **-cies**) tendencia f; (Med) propensión f, tendencia f

tender¹ /'tendər ‖'tendə(r)/ adj **(a)** (sensitive) ⟨spot⟩ sensible; ⟨age⟩ tierno **(b)** ⟨meat⟩ tierno **(c)** (loving) tierno

tender² n **(a)** (Busn) (offer) propuesta f, oferta f **(b)** (legal ~) moneda f de curso legal

tender³ vt (frml) ⟨resignation⟩ presentar, ofrecer*

tenderize /'tendəraɪz/ vt ⟨meat⟩ ablandar

tenderly /'tendərli ‖'tendəli/ adv tiernamente, con ternura

tendon /'tendən/ n tendón m

tendril /'tendrəl ‖'tendrɪl/ n zarcillo m

tenet /'tenət ‖'tenɪt/ n principio m

tenfold /'tenfəʊld/ adj/adv ▶ -FOLD

Tenn = Tennessee

tennis /'tenəs ‖'tenɪs/ n tenis m; (before n) ~ court cancha f or (Esp) pista f de tenis; ~ player tenista mf; ~ racket raqueta f de tenis

tenor¹ /'tenər ‖'tenə(r)/ n [1] (Mus) tenor m [2] (frml) (sense) tenor m

AmC	América Central	Arg	Argentina	Cu	Cuba	Per	Perú
AmL	América Latina	Bol	Bolivia	Ec	Ecuador	RPI	Río de la Plata
AmS	América del Sur	Chi	Chile	Esp	España	Ur	Uruguay
Andes	Región andina	CS	Cono Sur	Méx	México	Ven	Venezuela

tenor² adj (before n) ⟨voice⟩ de tenor; ⟨saxophone⟩ tenor

ten: ~**pin bowling** n (BrE) ▶ ~PINS; ~**pins** n (+ sing vb) (AmE) bolos mpl, bowling m

tense¹ /tens/ adj (a) ⟨situation/person⟩ tenso (b) (taut) tenso, tirante

tense² vt ⟨muscles⟩ poner* tenso, tensar
■ **tense up** [v + adv] (colloq) ponerse* tenso

tense³ n (Ling) tiempo m

tension /'tenʃən ‖ 'tenʃən/ n ⏺ (a) (of situation) tensión f, tirantez f (b) (felt by person) tensión f (c) (between two parties) conflicto m ⏹ (tautness) tensión f ⏹ (Elec) tensión f

tent /tent/ n tienda f (de campaña), carpa f (AmL)

tentacle /'tentɪkəl ‖ 'tentəkəl/ n tentáculo m

tentative /'tentətɪv/ adj (a) ⟨plan⟩ provisional, provisorio (AmS); ⟨offer⟩ tentativo (b) ⟨person⟩ indeciso

tenterhooks /'tentərhʊks ‖ 'tentəhʊks/ pl n: to be on ~ estar* en or sobre ascuas

tenth¹ /tenθ/ adj décimo

tenth² adv en décimo lugar

tenth³ n (Math) décimo m; (part) décima parte f

tenuous /'tenjuəs/ adj ⟨claim⟩ poco fundado; ⟨link⟩ indirecto

tenure /'tenjər ‖ 'tenjə(r)/ n (a) (of property, land) tenencia f (b) (period of office) ejercicio m, ocupación f

tepid /'tepəd ‖ 'tepɪd/ adj tibio

term¹ /tɜːrm ‖ tɜːm/ n
I ⏺ (word) término m ⏹ (a) (period) período m, periodo m; ~ **of** o (AmE also) **in office** mandato m; **in the short/long** ~ a corto/largo plazo (b) (Educ) trimestre m
II terms pl ⏺ (conditions) condiciones fpl; **to come to** ~**s with sth** aceptar algo ⏹ (relations): **to be on good/bad** ~**s with sb** estar* en buenas/malas relaciones con algn ⏹ (a) (sense): **in financial** ~**s** desde el punto de vista financiero; **in real** ~**s** en términos reales (b) **in terms of: in** ~ **of efficiency** en cuanto a eficiencia

term² vt calificar* de

terminal¹ /'tɜːrmənl ‖ 'tɜːmɪnl/ adj ⟨illness⟩ terminal; ⟨patient⟩ (en fase) terminal, desahuciado

terminal² n (a) (Transp) (at airport) terminal f; **bus** ~ terminal f de autobuses (b) (Comput) terminal m (c) (Elec) terminal m

terminally /'tɜːrmənəli ‖ 'tɜːmɪnəli/ adv: **he's** ~ **ill** está en fase terminal, está desahuciado

terminate /'tɜːrmənert ‖ 'tɜːmɪnert/ vt (frml) ⟨relationship⟩ poner* fin a; ⟨contract⟩ poner* término a; ⟨employee⟩ (AmE) despedir*, cesar (frml or period); ⟨pregnancy⟩ interrumpir
■ ~ vi «lease/relationship» terminarse; **this train** ~**s here** este es el final del recorrido de este tren

termination /ˌtɜːrmə'nerʃən ‖ ˌtɜːmɪ'nerʃən/ n (a) (of contract) (frml) terminación f (b) (Med): ~ **of pregnancy** interrupción f del embarazo

terminology /ˌtɜːrmə'nɑːlədʒi ‖ ˌtɜːmɪ'nɒlədʒi/ n (pl -**gies**) terminología f

terminus /'tɜːrmənəs ‖ 'tɜːmɪnəs/ n (pl -**nuses** or -**ni** /-niː, -naɪ ‖ -naɪ/) (of buses) terminal f, (of trains) estación f terminal

termite /'tɜːrmaɪt ‖ 'tɜːmaɪt/ n termita f

terrace /'terəs ‖ 'terəs, 'terɪs/ n (a) (patio) terraza f (b) (balcony) (AmE) terraza f (c) (on hillside) terraza f (d) (row of houses) (BrE) hilera de casas adosadas

terraced /'terəst ‖ 'terəst, 'terɪst/ adj (a) ⟨hillside/slope⟩ en terrazas or bancales (b) ⟨house⟩ (BrE) adosado (en una hilera de casas uniformes)

terrain /te'rem/ n terreno m

terrestrial /tə'restriəl/ adj terrestre

terrible /'terəbəl/ adj espantoso, atroz

terribly /'terəbli/ adv ⟨suffer⟩ terriblemente; ⟨sing/act⟩ terriblemente mal

terrier /'teriər ‖ 'teriə(r)/ n terrier mf

terrific /tə'rɪfɪk/ adj (a) (enormous) (colloq) tremendo, increíble; ⟨argument⟩ espantoso (b) (very good) (colloq) estupendo, genial (fam)

terrified /'terəfaɪd ‖ 'terɪfaɪd/ adj ⟨crowd⟩ aterrorizado, aterrado; **to be** ~ **of sth/sb** tenerle* terror or pánico a algo/algn

terrify /'terəfaɪ ‖ 'terɪfaɪ/ vt -**fies, -fying, -fied** aterrorizar*

terrifying /'terəfaɪŋ ‖ 'terɪfaɪŋ/ adj aterrador

territorial /ˌterə'tɔːriəl ‖ ˌterɪ'tɔːriəl/ adj territorial

territory /'terətɔːri ‖ 'terɪtəri, -tri/ n (pl -**ries**) territorio m

terror /'terər ‖ 'terə(r)/ n terror m; **they fled in** ~ huyeron aterrorizados or despavoridos

terrorism /'terərɪzəm/ n terrorismo m

terrorist /'terərəst ‖ 'terərɪst/ n terrorista mf

terrorize /'terəraɪz/ vt aterrorizar*, tener* atemorizado

terse /tɜːrs ‖ tɜːs/ adj seco, lacónico

test¹ /test/ n (a) (Educ) prueba f; (multiple-choice type) test m (b) (of machine, drug) prueba f; (before n) ⟨run/flight⟩ experimental, de prueba (c) (of blood, urine) análisis m; (for hearing, eyes) examen m

test² vt (a) ⟨student/class⟩ examinar, hacerle* una prueba a; ⟨knowledge/skill⟩ evaluar* (b) ⟨product⟩ probar*, poner* a prueba (c) ⟨friendship/endurance⟩ poner* a prueba (d) ⟨blood/urine⟩ analizar*; ⟨sight/hearing⟩ examinar; ⟨hypothesis⟩ comprobar*

testament /'testəmənt/ n ⏺ (will) testamento m ⏹ **Testament** (Bib): **the Old/New T**~ el Antiguo/Nuevo Testamento

test: ~ **case** n: caso que sienta jurisprudencia; ~ **drive** n (Auto) prueba f de circulación en carretera

testicle /'testɪkəl/ n testículo m

testify /'testəfaɪ ‖ 'testɪfaɪ/ vi -**fies, -fying, -fied** (Law frml) prestar declaración, testificar*; **to** ~ **TO sth** declarar or testificar* algo

testimonial /ˌtestə'məʊniəl ‖ ˌtestɪ'məʊniəl/ n recomendación f

testimony /'testəməʊni ‖ 'testɪməni/ n (pl -**nies**) (Law) declaración f, testimonio m

testing¹ /'testɪŋ/ n pruebas fpl

testing² adj duro, arduo

test: ~ **match** n (Sport) partido m internacional; ~ **paper** n (Educ) examen m, prueba f; ~ **pilot** n piloto mf de pruebas; ~ **tube** n probeta f, tubo m de ensayo; (before n) ~**-tube baby** niño, -ña m,f probeta

tetanus /'tetnəs/ n tétano(s) m
tether¹ /'teðər ‖'teðə(r)/ n soga f
tether² vt atar, amarrar
Tex = **Texas**
text¹ /tekst/ n texto m
text² vt: **to ~ sb** mandar un mensaje de texto a algn
textbook /'tekstbʊk/ n libro m de texto
textile /'tekstaɪl/ n textil m
textual /'tekstʃuəl ‖'tekstjuəl/ adj textual
texture /'tekstʃər ‖'tekstʃə(r)/ n textura f
Thai¹ /taɪ/ adj tailandés
Thai² n (a) (person) tailandés, -desa m,f (b) (language) tailandés m
Thailand /'taɪlænd/ n Tailandia f
Thames /temz/ n **the ~** el Támesis
than¹ /ðæn, weak form ðən/ conj **(a)** (in comparisons) que; (with quantity) de; **I'm feeling better ~ I was** me siento mejor que antes; **more ~ $25** más de 25 dólares; **the situation is worse ~ we thought** la situación es peor de lo que pensábamos **(b)** (with alternatives): **I'd rather walk ~ go by bus** prefiero ir a pie a tomar el autobús **(c)** (when) cuando; **no sooner had I sat down ~ the bell rang** apenas me había sentado cuando sonó el timbre
than² prep (in comparisons) que; (with quantity) de
thank /θæŋk/ vt **to ~ sb (FOR sth)** darle* las gracias a algn (POR algo), agradecerle* (algo) a algn; **~ God/heaven(s)** menos mal, gracias a Dios; see also THANK YOU
thankful /'θæŋkfəl/ adj ‹look/smile› de agradecimiento, agradecido
thankfully /'θæŋkfəli/ adv (indep) menos mal, gracias a Dios
thankless /'θæŋkləs ‖'θæŋklɪs/ adj ingrato
thanks /θæŋks/ n **(a)** (expression of gratitude) agradecimiento m **(b)** (as interj) **~!** ¡gracias!; **~ very much** o **a lot!** ¡muchas gracias!; **many ~** muchas gracias **(c)** thanks to gracias a
Thanksgiving (Day) /'θæŋks'gɪvɪŋ/ n (in US) el día de Acción de Gracias
thank you interj ¡gracias!; **~ ~ very much** muchas gracias; **to say ~ ~** dar* las gracias; **~ for coming/your help** gracias por venir/tu ayuda
that¹ /ðæt/ pron **1** (pl **those**) (demonstrative) ese, esa; (neuter) eso; **those** esos, esas; (to refer to sth more distant or to the remote past) aquel, aquélla; (neuter) aquello; **those** aquellos, aquellas; **~'s wonderful!** ¡es maravilloso!; **those who have been less fortunate** los que no han tenido tanta suerte **2** (in phrases) **at that** (moreover) además; (thereupon): **at ~ they all burst out laughing** al oír (or ver etc) eso, todos se echaron a reír; **that is** es decir; **that's it:** **~'s it for today** eso es todo por hoy; **now lift your left arm: ~'s it!** ahora levanta el brazo izquierdo ¡eso es! or ¡ahí está!; **~'s it: I've had enough!** ¡se acabó! ¡ya no aguanto más! **3** /ðət, strong form ðæt/ (relative) que; **it wasn't Helen (~) you saw** no fue a Helen a quien viste, no fue a Helen que viste (AmL)
that² /ðæt/ adj (pl **those**) ese, esa; **those** esos, esas; (to refer to sth more distant, to the remote past) aquel, aquella; **those** aquellos, aquellas

that³ /ðət, strong form ðæt/ conj que; **she said (~) ... dijo que ...; the news ~ our team had won** la noticia de que nuestro equipo había ganado
that⁴ /ðæt/ adv tan; **he can't be all ~ stupid** no es posible que sea tan tonto
thatched /θætʃt/ adj ‹roof› de paja (or de juncos etc)or (AmS) de quincha; ‹cottage› con el tejado de paja (or de juncos etc), quinchado (AmS)
thaw¹ /θɔː/ vi «snow/ice» derretirse*, fundirse; «frozen food» descongelarse; «relations» hacerse* más cordial
■ **~** vt ‹frozen food› descongelar
thaw² n (Meteo, Pol) deshielo m
the¹ /before vowel ði, ðɪ; before consonant ðə, strong form ðiː/ def art **1** (sing) el, la; (pl) los, las **2** **(a)** (with names): **Henry ~ First** Enrique primero; **~ Smiths** los Smith **(b)** (in abstractions, generalizations) (+ sing vb): **~ impossible** lo imposible; **~ young** los jóvenes **3** (per): **they sell it by ~ square foot** lo venden por pie cuadrado; **I get paid by ~ hour** me pagan por hora
the² /before vowel ði; before consonant ðə/ adv (+ comp) (as conj) cuanto; **~ more you have, ~ more you want** cuanto más tienes, más quieres; **~ sooner, ~ better** cuanto antes, mejor
theater, (BrE) **theatre** /'θiːətər ‖'θɪətə(r)/ n **1** **(a)** (building) teatro m **(b)** (theatrical world) **the ~** el teatro **(c)** (movie ~) (AmE) cine m
theatrical /θi'ætrɪkəl/ adj teatral
theft /θeft/ n robo m
their /ðer ‖ðeə/ adj

■ **Note** The translation su agrees in number with the noun which it modifies; their is translated by su, sus, depending on what follows: their father/mother su padre/madre; their books/magazines sus libros/ revistas.

(a) (sing) su; (pl) sus; **he cut off ~ heads** les cortó la cabeza **(b)** (belonging to indefinite person) (sing) su; (pl) sus; **whoever called didn't leave ~ number** la persona que ha llamado no dejó su teléfono
theirs /ðerz ‖ðeəz/ pron

■ **Note** The translation suyo reflects the gender and number of the noun it is standing for; theirs is translated by el suyo, la suya, los suyos, las suyas, depending on what is being referred to.

(sing) suyo, -ya; (pl) suyos, -yas; **~ is blue** el suyo/la suya or el/la de ellos es azul; **a friend of ~** un amigo suyo or de ellos
them /ðem, weak form ðəm/ pron **1** **(a)** (as direct object) los, las; (referring to people) los or (Esp tb) les, las; **where did you buy ~?** ¿dónde los/las compraste?; **he has two sons, do you know ~?** tiene dos hijos ¿los or (Esp tb) les conoces? **(b)** (as indirect object) les; (with direct object pronoun present) se; **I lent ~ some money** les presté dinero **(c)** (after preposition) ellos, ellas **2** (emphatic use) ellos, ellas; **that'll be ~** deben de ser ellos **3** (indefinite person): **if anyone calls, tell ~ that ...** si llama alguien, dile que ...
theme /θiːm/ n tema m; (before n) **~ park** parque m temático; **~ song** tema m musical; (of TV program) (AmE) música f de un programa
themselves /ðəm'selvz/ pron **(a)** (reflexive): **they bought ~ a new car** se compraron otro coche; **they only think of ~** solo piensan en sí

mismos; **they were by ~** estaban solos/solas **(b)** (emphatic) ellos mismos, ellas mismas **(c)** (normal selves): **the children aren't ~** los niños no son los de siempre **(d)** (indefinite person or persons): **if anyone's interested they can find out for ~** si a alguien le interesa, puede averiguarlo por sí mismo

then¹ /ðen/ *adv* **1 (a)** (at that time) entonces **(b)** (in those days) en aquel entonces **2** *(after prep)*: **by ~** para entonces; **from ~ on** a partir de ese momento, desde entonces; **(up) until** *o* **till ~** hasta entonces **3 (a)** (next, afterward) después, luego **(b)** (in those circumstances) entonces **(c)** (besides, in addition) además **4** (in that case) entonces; **you do it, ~!** ¡hazlo tú, entonces! **5 then again** (*as linker*) también

then² *adj* (*before n*) entonces; **the ~ leader** el entonces líder

theologian /ˈθɪəˈləʊdʒən/ *n* teólogo, -ga *m,f*

theological /ˈθɪəˈlɑːdʒɪkəl ‖ˌθɪəˈlɒdʒɪkəl/ *adj* teológico

theology /θɪˈɑːlədʒi ‖θɪˈɒlədʒi/ *n* (*pl* **-gies**) teología *f*

theorem /ˈθɪərəm/ *n* teorema *m*

theoretical /ˈθɪəˈretɪkəl/ *adj* teórico

theorize /ˈθɪəraɪz/ *vi* especular, teorizar*

theory /ˈθɪəri/ *n* (*pl* **-ries**) teoría *f*

therapeutic /ˈθerəˈpjuːtɪk/ *adj* terapéutico

therapist /ˈθerəpəst ‖ˈθerəpɪst/ *n* terapeuta *mf*

therapy /ˈθerəpi/ *n* (*pl* **-pies**) terapia *f*

there¹ /ðer ‖ðeə(r)/ *adv* **1 (a)** (close to person being addressed) ahí; (further away) allí, ahí (esp AmL); (less precise, further) allá; **up/down ~** ahí arriba/abajo **(b)** **there and then** *(decide)* en ese mismo momento; **they mended it for me ~ and then** me lo arreglaron en el acto **2** (calling attention to sth): **~ you are** (giving sth) aquí tiene; **~ go my chances of promotion!** ¡adiós ascenso! **3** (present): **all his friends were ~** estaban todos sus amigos; **is Tony ~?** ¿está Tony?; **who's ~?** (at the door) ¿quién es?; (in the dark) ¿quién anda ahí? **4** (*as interj*) **~!** that's the last of the boxes ¡listo! esa es la última caja; **~, ~, don't cry!** vamos, no llores

there² /ðer, *weak form* ðər ‖ðeə(r), *weak form* ðə(r)/ *pron*: **there is/are** hay; **there was** había/hubo; **there will be** habrá

there: ~about /ˈðerəbaʊt ‖ˈðeərəbaʊt/ *adv* (AmE) ▶ **~ABOUTS**; **~abouts** /ˈðerəbaʊts ‖ˈðeərəbaʊts/ *adv* **(a)** (near that figure, time) por ahí **(b)** (in that vicinity) por allí; **~after** /ˈðerˈæftər ‖ˈðeərˈɑːftə(r)/ *adv* (frml) a partir de entonces; **~by** /ˈðerˈbaɪ ‖ˈðeəˈbaɪ, ˈðeəbaɪ/ *adv* (frml) de ese modo, así; **~fore** /ˈðerfɔːr ‖ˈðeəfɔː(r)/ *adv* por lo tanto, por consiguiente

there's /ðerz, *weak form* ðərz ‖ðeəz, *weak form* ðəz/ **(a)** = **there is (b)** = **there has**

thermal /ˈθɜːrməl ‖ˈθɜːməl/ *adj* **(a)** *(stream/bath)* termal **(b)** *(underwear/glove)* térmico

thermometer /θərˈmɑːmətər ‖θəˈmɒmɪtə(r)/ *n* termómetro *m*

Thermos® **(flask)** /ˈθɜːrməs ‖ˈθɜːməs/, (AmE also) **thermos** **(bottle)** *n* termo *m*

thermostat /ˈθɜːrməstæt ‖ˈθɜːməstæt/ *n* termostato *m*

thesaurus /θɪˈsɔːrəs/ *n* (*pl* **-ruses** *or* **-ri** /-raɪ/) diccionario *m* ideológico *or* de ideas afines, tesauro *m*

these /ðiːz/ *pl of* THIS¹,²

thesis /ˈθiːsəs ‖ˈθiːsɪs/ *n* (*pl* **-ses** /-siːz/) tesis *f*; (shorter) tesina *f*

they /ðeɪ/ *pron*

■ **Note** Although *ellos* and *ellas* are given as translations of *they*, they are in practice used only for emphasis, or to avoid ambiguity: *they went to the theater* fueron al teatro; *they did it* ellos *or* ellas lo hicieron.

(a) (*pl of* he, she, it) ellos, ellas **(b)** (indefinite person or persons): **~'ve dug up the road** han levantado la calle

they'd /ðeɪd/ **(a)** = **they would (b)** = **they had**

they'll /ðeɪl/ = **they will**

they're /ðer, *weak form* ðər ‖ðeə(r), *weak form* ðə(r)/ = **they are**

they've /ðeɪv/ = **they have**

thick /θɪk/ *adj* **-er, -est** **1 (a)** *(layer/book/sweater)* grueso, gordo (fam); *(line)* grueso; **it's 5cm ~** tiene 5cm de espesor *or* de grosor **(b)** *(sauce/paint)* espeso **(c)** *(fog/smoke)* espeso, denso; *(fur)* tupido; *(beard/eyebrows)* poblado; **through ~ and thin** tanto en las duras como en las maduras **2** (colloq) (stupid) burro (fam), corto (fam)

thicken /ˈθɪkən/ *vt* *(sauce/paint)* espesar
■ **~** *vi* *(sauce/paint)* espesar(se); *(fog)* hacerse* más espeso *or* denso

thicket /ˈθɪkət ‖ˈθɪkɪt/ *n* matorral *m*

thickly /ˈθɪkli/ *adv* **(a)** (in a thick layer): **spread the jam ~** pon una capa gruesa de mermelada **(b)** (densely) *(populated)* densamente

thickness /ˈθɪknəs ‖ˈθɪknɪs/ *n* (of fabric, wire) grosor *m*; (of paper, wood, wall) espesor *m*, grosor *m*

thick: ~set /ˈθɪkˈset/ *adj* fornido; **~-skinned** /ˈθɪkˈskɪnd/ *adj* insensible

thief /θiːf/ *n* (*pl* **thieves** /θiːvz/) ladrón, -drona *m,f*

thigh /θaɪ/ *n* muslo *m*

thimble /ˈθɪmbəl/ *n* dedal *m*

thin¹ /θɪn/ *adj* **-nn-** **1 (a)** *(layer/slice)* delgado, fino **(b)** *(person)* delgado, flaco; *(waist)* delgado **2 (a)** *(soup/sauce)* claro, poco espeso **(b)** *(hair)* ralo

thin² *vt* **-nn-** *(paint)* diluir*, rebajar; *(sauce)* aclarar, hacer* menos espeso
■ **~** *vi*: **his hair is ~ning** está perdiendo pelo

thing /θɪŋ/ *n* **1** (physical object) cosa *f* **2** (non-material) cosa *f*; **the same ~ happened to me** a mí me pasó lo mismo; **it's a good ~ (that)** ... menos mal que ...; **the last ~ I expected** lo que menos me imaginaba; **he hadn't done a ~** no había hecho absolutamente nada; **it's just one of those ~s** son cosas que pasan **3** (affair, matter) asunto *m*; **I'm fed up with the whole ~** estoy harto del asunto **4** **the thing (a)** (that which, what) lo que **(b)** (what is needed): **I've got just the ~** tengo exactamente lo que necesitas *or* lo que te hace falta **(c)** (crucial point, factor): **the ~ is, ...** resulta que *or* el caso es que *or* lo que pasa es que ... **5** **things** *pl* **(a)** (belongings, equipment) cosas *fpl* ⋯▷

(b) (matters, the situation) cosas *fpl*; **if ~s don't improve** si las cosas no mejoran; **how's ~s?** (colloq) ¿qué tal? (fam)

⑥ (person, creature): **you poor ~!** ¡pobrecito!; **you lucky ~!** ¡qué suerte tienes!

⑦ (preference, fad) (colloq): **it's not my ~** no es lo mío

⑧ (in expressions of time): **first ~ (in the morning)** a primera hora (de la mañana)

thingamabob /'θɪŋəmɑbɑ:b ‖'θɪŋəməbɒb/, **thingamajig** /-dʒɪg/ *n* (colloq) cosa *f*, chisme *m* (Esp, Méx fam), coso *m* (AmS fam), vaina *f* (Col, Per, Ven fam)

think /θɪŋk/ (*past & past p* **thought**) *vi* ① (use one's mind) pensar*; **to ~ ABOUT sth** pensar* EN algo; (consider) pensar* algo; **to ~ OF sth/sb** pensar* EN algo/algn; **I hadn't thought of that** no se me había ocurrido eso

② (intend, plan) **to ~ OF -ING** pensar* + INF

③ **(a)** (find, come up with): **can you ~ of anything better?** ¿se te ocurre algo mejor? **(b)** (remember) **to ~ OF sth** acordarse* DE algo; **I can't ~ of his name** no me puedo acordar de su nombre

④ (have opinion): **to ~ highly of sb** tener* muy buena opinión de algn; **he ~s a lot of you** te aprecia mucho

■ **~** *vt* ① (reflect, ponder) pensar*; **~ what that would cost** piensa en lo que costaría; **that's wrong, I thought to myself** eso está mal — pensé para mí *or* para mis adentros; **I didn't ~ to look there** no se me ocurrió mirar allí

② **(a)** (suppose, imagine, expect) pensar*; **I thought you knew** pensé que lo sabías; **I can't ~ why he refused** no me explico por qué se negó **(b)** (indicating intention): **we thought we'd eat out tonight** esta noche tenemos pensado salir a cenar

③ (believe) creer*; **I ~ so** creo que sí *or* me parece que sí; **I don't think so** creo que no *or* me parece que no; **I thought as much** ya me parecía *or* ya me lo imaginaba

■ **think ahead** [*v + adv*]: **you have to ~ ahead** hay que ser previsor

■ **think back** [*v + adv*] (reflect) recordar*; **~ back** haz memoria; **to ~ back TO sth** recordar* algo, acordarse* DE algo

■ **think out** [*v + o + adv, v + adv + o*] pensar *or* planear cuidadosamente; **a well thought-out proposal** una propuesta bien elaborada

■ **think over** [*v + o + adv*] pensar*

■ **think through** [*v + o + adv, v + adv + o*] ‹*project*› planear detenidamente; ‹*idea*› considerar detenidamente

■ **think up** [*v + o + adv, v + adv + o*] ‹*excuse*› inventar; ‹*slogan*› idear

thinker /'θɪŋkər ‖'θɪŋkə(r)/ *n* pensador, -dora *m,f*

thinking /'θɪŋkɪŋ/ *n* ideas *fpl*, pensamiento *m*; **to my (way of) ~** a mi modo de ver, en mi opinión; **good ~!** ¡buena idea!

think tank *n* gabinete *m* estratégico

thinly /'θɪnli/ *adv* **(a)** ‹*slice*› en rebanadas finas **(b)** (sparsely): **~ populated** poco poblado

thinner /'θɪnər ‖'θɪnə(r)/ *n* disolvente *m*, diluyente *m*

third[1] /θɜːrd ‖θɜːd/ *adj* tercero

■ **Note** The usual translation of *third*, *tercero*, becomes *tercer* when it precedes a masculine singular noun.

third[2] *adv* **(a)** (in position, time, order) en tercer lugar **(b)** (thirdly) en tercer lugar **(c)** (*with superl*): **the ~ highest mountain** la tercera montaña en altura

third[3] *n* ① **(a)** (Math) tercio *m* **(b)** (part) tercera parte *f*, tercio *m* **(c)** (Mus) tercera *f* ② **~ (gear)** (Auto) (*no art*) tercera *f*

third-class /'θɜːrd'klæs ‖,θɜːd'klɑːs/ *adj* (*pred* **~ class**) **(a)** (inferior) de tercera **(b)** ‹*mail*› (in US) de franqueo económico

thirdly /'θɜːrdli ‖'θɜːdli/ *adv* (*indep*) en tercer lugar

third: ~ party insurance *n* seguro *m* contra terceros; **T~ World** *n* **the T~ World** el Tercer Mundo; (*before n*) ‹*nation*› tercermundista

thirst /θɜːrst ‖θɜːst/ *n* sed *f*

thirsty /'θɜːrsti ‖'θɜːsti/ *adj* **-tier, -tiest** ‹*person/animal*› que tiene sed; **to be ~** tener* sed

thirteen /'θɜːr'tiːn ‖,θɜː'tiːn/ *adj/n* trece *adj inv/m*; *see also* FOUR[1]

thirteenth[1] /'θɜːr'tiːnθ ‖,θɜː'tiːnθ/ *adj* decimotercero; (before masculine singular nouns) decimotercer

thirteenth[2] *adv* en decimotercer lugar

thirteenth[3] *n* (Math) treceavo *m*; (part) treceava parte *f*

thirtieth[1] /'θɜːrtiəθ ‖'θɜːtiəθ/ *adj* trigésimo

thirtieth[2] *adv* en trigésimo lugar

thirtieth[3] *n* (Math) treintavo *m*; (part) treintava *or* trigésima parte *f*

thirty /'θɜːrti ‖'θɜːti/ *adj/n* treinta *adj inv/m*; *see also* FOUR[1]

this[1] /ðɪs/ *pron* (*pl* **these**) este, -ta; (*neuter*) esto; these estos, -tas; **what is ~?** ¿qué es esto?; **~ is John** (on photo) este es John; (introducing) te presento a John; **is ~ where you work?** ¿aquí es donde trabajas?; **~ is Jack Smith** (on telephone) habla Jack Smith, soy Jack Smith

this[2] *adj* (*pl* **these**) este, -ta; (*pl*) estos, -tas; **look at ~ tree/house** mira este árbol/esta casa; **I like these ones** me gustan estos/estas

this[3] *adv*: **it's ~ big** es así de grande; **now we've come ~ far ...** ya que hemos venido hasta aquí ...

thistle /'θɪsəl/ *n* cardo *m*

thong /θɔːŋ ‖θɒŋ/ *n* **(a)** (leather strip) correa *f* **(b)** (sandal) (AmE) chancla *f*, chancleta *f*

thorn /θɔːrn ‖θɔːn/ *n* espina *f*

thorny /'θɔːrni ‖'θɔːni/ *adj* **-nier, -niest** ‹*plant*› espinoso; ‹*problem/issue*› espinoso, peliagudo

thorough /'θɜːroʊ ‖'θʌrə/ *adj* ‹*person*› concienzudo, cuidadoso; ‹*search/investigation*› riguroso

thoroughbred /'θɜːrəbred ‖'θʌrəbred/ *adj* ‹horse› de pura sangre, de raza

thoroughfare /'θərə'fer ‖'θʌrəfeə(r)/ *n* **(a)** (street) (liter) calle *f*, vía *f* **(b)** (public road) vía *f* pública

thoroughly /'θɜːrəʊli ‖'θʌrəli/ *adv* **(a)** ‹wash/clean› a fondo, a conciencia; ‹research› rigurosamente; ‹examine› minuciosamente **(b)** (completely) ‹understand› perfectamente; **we ~ enjoyed ourselves** nos divertimos muchísimo

those /ðəʊz/ *pl of* THAT¹,²

though¹ /ðəʊ/ *conj* aunque

though² *adv*: **it's easy, ~, to understand their feelings** sin embargo, es fácil comprender sus sentimientos; **the course is difficult; it's interesting, ~** el curso es difícil, pero es interesante

thought¹ /θɔːt/ *past & past p of* THINK¹

thought² *n* ☐1 **(a)** (intellectual activity) pensamiento *m* **(b)** (deliberation): **after much ~** tras mucho pensarlo ☐2 **(a)** (reflection) pensamiento *m*; **what are your ~s on the matter?** ¿tú qué opinas al respecto?; **on second ~(s)** pensándolo bien **(b)** (idea) idea *f*; **I've just had a ~** se me acaba de ocurrir una idea; **the ~ never even entered my head** ni se me pasó por la cabeza

thoughtful /'θɔːtfəl/ *adj* **(a)** (kind) atento, amable; (considerate) considerado **(b)** (pensive) pensativo, meditabundo

thoughtfully /'θɔːtfəli/ *adv* pensativamente

thoughtless /'θɔːtləs ‖'θɔːtlɪs/ *adj* desconsiderado

thought-provoking /'θɔːtprə,vəʊkɪŋ/ *adj* que hace pensar *or* reflexionar

thousand /'θaʊzn̩d/ *n* mil *m*

thousandth¹ /'θaʊzəndθ/ *adj* milésimo

thousandth² *adv* en milésimo lugar

thousandth³ *n* (Math) milésimo *m*; (part) milésima parte *f*

thrash /θræʃ/ *vt* golpear; (as punishment) azotar; darle* una paliza a
■ ~ *vi*: ~ **(around** *o* **about)** revolverse*, retorcerse*; (in mud, water) revolcarse*
■ **thrash out** [*v + o + adv, v + adv + o*] ‹problem› discutir, tratar de resolver

thrashing /'θræʃɪŋ/ *n* paliza *f*, zurra *f*

thread¹ /θred/ *n* **(a)** (filament) hilo *m*; (of plot, conversation) hilo *m* **(b)** (of screw) rosca *f*, filete *m*

thread² *vt* ‹needle› enhebrar; ‹bead› ensartar

threadbare /'θredber ‖'θredbeə(r)/ *adj* gastado, raído

threat /θret/ *n* amenaza *f*; **to be under ~** ‹‹way of life›› verse* amenazado; ‹‹factory›› estar* bajo amenaza de cierre

threaten /'θretn̩/ *vt* **(a)** ‹person/stability› amenazar*; **to ~ sb WITH sth** amenazar* a algn CON algo **(b)** (give warning of) ‹action/violence› amenazar* con
■ ~ *vi* amenazar*

threatening /'θretnɪŋ/ *adj* amenazador

three /θriː/ *adj/n* tres *adj inv/m*; *see also* FOUR¹

three-: **~-dimensional** /'θriːdə'mentʃn̩əl, -daɪ- ‖,θriːdaɪ'menʃən̩l, -dɪ-/ *adj* tridimensional; **~fold** *adj/adv* ▶ -FOLD; **~-piece** /'θriː'piːs/ *adj*

(before *n*): **~-piece suit** traje *m* con chaleco, terno *m*; **~-piece suite** juego *m* de living (de sofá y dos sillones) (AmL), tresillo *m* (Esp)

three-quarters¹ /'θriː'kwɔːrtərz ‖,θriː'kwɔːtəz/ *pron* las tres cuartas partes

three-quarters² *adv*: **it's ~ full** contiene el 75% *or* las tres cuartas partes de su capacidad

threshold /'θreʃhəʊld/ *n* **(a)** (doorway) umbral *m*; **to be on the ~ of sth** estar* en el umbral *or* a las puertas de algo **(b)** (of pain) umbral *m*

threw /θruː/ *past of* THROW¹

thrift /θrɪft/ *n* economía *f*, ahorro *m*; (before *n*) **~ shop** (esp AmE) tienda que vende artículos de segunda mano con fines benéficos

thrifty /'θrɪfti/ *adj* **-tier, -tiest** económico, ahorrativo

thrill¹ /θrɪl/ *n* (excitement) emoción *f*; **it was a real ~** fue verdaderamente emocionante

thrill² *vt* emocionar

thrilled /θrɪld/ *adj* (pred) **to be ~ (ABOUT/WITH sth)** estar* contentísimo *or* (fam) chocho (CON algo); **to be ~ to + INF: she was really ~ to meet him** le encantó *or* (Esp tb) le hizo muchísima ilusión conocerlo

thriller /'θrɪlər ‖'θrɪlə(r)/ *n* novela *f*/película *f* de misterio *or* de suspenso *or* (Esp) de suspense

thrilling /'θrɪlɪŋ/ *adj* emocionante

thrive /θraɪv/ *vi* (*past* **thrived** *or* (liter) **throve**; *past p* **thrived**) ‹‹business/town›› prosperar; ‹‹plant›› crecer* con fuerza

thriving /'θraɪvɪŋ/ *adj* (before *n*) ‹business/town› próspero

throat /θrəʊt/ *n* garganta *f*; (neck) cuello *m*

throb /θrɑːb ‖θrɒb/ *vi* **-bb-** **(a)** ‹‹heart/pulse›› latir con fuerza; ‹‹engine›› vibrar **(b)** (with pain): **his leg was ~bing** tenía un dolor punzante en la pierna

throes /θrəʊz/ *pl n* (death ~) agonía *f*; **to be in one's death ~** agonizar*, estar agonizando

thrombosis /θrɑːm'bəʊsəs ‖θrɒm'bəʊsɪs/ *n* (*pl* **-ses** /-siːz/) trombosis *f*

throne /θrəʊn/ *n* trono *m*

throng /θrɔːŋ ‖θrɒŋ/ *n* muchedumbre *f*

throttle¹ /'θrɑːtl̩ ‖'θrɒtl̩/ *vt* ahogar*, estrangular

throttle² *n* **(a)** (Auto) acelerador *m* (que se acciona con la mano) **(b)** (pedal) acelerador *m*

through¹ /θruː/ *prep* ☐1 **(a)** (from one side to the other) por; **it went right ~ the wall** atravesó la pared de lado a lado; **to hear sb ~ sth** oír* algo a través de algo; **we drove ~ Munich** atravesamos Munich (en coche) **(b)** (past, beyond) **to be ~ sth** haber* pasado algo
☐2 **(a)** (in time): **we worked ~ the night** trabajamos durante toda la noche; **half-way ~ his speech** en medio de su discurso; **~ the centuries** a través de los siglos **(b)** (until and including) (AmE): **Tuesday ~ Thursday** de martes a jueves; **October ~ December** desde octubre hasta diciembre inclusive
☐3 (by): **she spoke ~ an interpreter** habló a través de un intérprete; **I heard about it ~ a friend** me enteré a través de *or* por un amigo

through² *adv* ☐1 (from one side to the other): **it sped ~ without stopping** pasó a toda velocidad sin parar; **the red paint shows ~** se nota la ···᠅

pintura roja que hay debajo; *see also* GET, PULL,
PUT *etc* THROUGH **2** (completely): **wet** ~ mojado
hasta los huesos

through³ *adj* **1** (Transp) (*before n*) ⟨*train/route*⟩
directo; ~ **traffic** tráfico *m* de paso; **🅢 no through
road** calle sin salida **2** (finished) (colloq) ⟨*pred*⟩: **to
be** ~ **WITH** sb/sth haber* terminado CON algn/
algo

throughout¹ /θruː'aʊt/ *prep* **1** (all over): ~
Europe en toda Europa **2** (in time): ~ **the
weekend** (durante) todo el fin de semana; ~ **his
career** a lo largo de toda su carrera

throughout² *adv* **(a)** ⟨*decorated/carpeted*⟩
totalmente **(b)** (in time) desde el principio hasta el
fin

throughway /'θruːweɪ/ *n* (AmE) autopista *f*

throve /θrəʊv/ *past of* THRIVE

throw¹ /θrəʊ/ (*past* **threw**; *past p* **thrown**) *vt*
1 (a) ⟨*ball/stone*⟩ tirar, aventar* (Col, Méx, Per);
⟨*grenade/javelin*⟩ lanzar* **(b)** ⟨*dice*⟩ echar, tirar
2 (send, propel) (+ *adv compl*): **to** ~ **sb into jail**
meter a algn preso *or* en la cárcel; **to** ~ **oneself
into a task** meterse de lleno en una tarea
3 «*horse*» ⟨*rider*⟩ desmontar, tirar
4 (disconcert) desconcertar*
5 (have, hold) ⟨*party*⟩ hacer*, dar*

■ **throw away** [*v + o + adv, v + adv + o*] **(a)**
(discard) ⟨*can/paper*⟩ tirar (a la basura), botar (a
la basura) (AmL exc RPl) **(b)** (waste) ⟨*money*⟩ tirar,
botar (AmL exc RPl)

■ **throw back** [*v + o + adv, v + adv + o*] **(a)**
⟨*ball*⟩ devolver* **(b)** (pull back) ⟨*curtains*⟩
(des)correr; ⟨*bedclothes*⟩ echar atrás

■ **throw off** [*v + o + adv, v + adv + o*] **(a)**
⟨*jacket/hat*⟩ quitarse (*rápidamente*) **(b)** ⟨*illness/
habit*⟩ quitarse; ⟨*pursuer*⟩ despistar

■ **throw out** [*v + o + adv, v + adv + o*] **(a)**
(discard) tirar (a la basura), botar (a la basura)
(AmL exc RPl) **(b)** ⟨*bill/proposal*⟩ rechazar **(c)**
⟨*person*⟩ echar

■ **throw together** [*v + o + adv, v + adv + o*]
⟨*meal/plan*⟩ improvisar

■ **throw up**
I [*v + adv + o*] **1** (raise) ⟨*hands*⟩ levantar *or*
alzar* (*rápidamente*)
2 (bring to light) ⟨*facts*⟩ revelar (la existencia de)
II [*v + adv*] (vomit) (colloq) devolver*, arrojar

throw² *n* **1** (a) (of ball) tiro *m*; (of javelin, discus)
lanzamiento *m* **(b)** (of dice) tirada *f*, lance *m*
2 (AmE) **(a)** (bedspread) cubrecama *m* **(b)** (shawl)
chal (*m*), echarpe (*m*)

thrown /θrəʊn/ *past p of* THROW¹

thrush /θrʌʃ/ *n* **1** (bird) tordo *m*, zorzal *m*
2 (Med) aftas *fpl*

thrust¹ /θrʌst/ *vt* (*past & past p* **thrust**) (push)
empujar; (push out) sacar*; **to** ~ **out one's chest**
sacar* pecho; **she** ~ **the book at me** me tendió el
libro bruscamente; **he** ~ **his hands into his
pockets** se metió las manos en los bolsillos; **to** ~
sth INTO sth ⟨*knife/sword*⟩ clavar algo EN algo

thrust² *n* **1 (a)** (with sword) estocada *f* **(b)**
(push) empujón *m* **(c)** (attack, advance) ofensiva *f*
2 (impetus) empuje *m*, fuerza *f*

thruway /'θruːweɪ/ *n* (AmE) autopista *f*

thud /θʌd/ *n* ruido *m* sordo

thug /θʌg/ *n* matón *m*

thumb¹ /θʌm/ *n* pulgar *m*

thumb² *vt* **: I** ~**ed a lift home** me fui a casa a
dedo (fam)

thumbtack /'θʌmtæk/ *n* (AmE) tachuela *f*,
chinche *m* (Andes), chinche *f* (AmC, Méx, RPl),
chincheta *f* (Esp)

thump¹ /θʌmp/ *n* (sound, blow) golpazo *m*

thump² *vt* golpear

thunder¹ /'θʌndər ‖ 'θʌndə(r)/ *n* **(a)** (Meteo)
truenos *mpl* **(b)** (*no pl*) (sound — of traffic)
estruendo *m*

thunder² *vi* (move loudly): **the train** ~**ed through
the station** el tren pasó por la estación con gran
estruendo

■ ~ *vt* (shout): **get out! he** ~**ed** —¡fuera de aquí! —
bramó *or* rugió

thunder: ~bolt *n* rayo *m*; ~**storm** *n*
tormenta *f* eléctrica

thundery /'θʌndəri/ *adj* tormentoso

Thursday /'θɜːzdeɪ, -di ‖ 'θɜːzdeɪ, -di/ *n* jueves
m; see also MONDAY

thus /ðʌs/ *adv* **1** (in this way) (frml) así, de este
modo **2** (consequently) (*as linker*) por lo tanto, por
consiguiente (frml)

thwart /θwɔːrt ‖ θwɔːt/ *vt* ⟨*plan/attempt*⟩
frustrar

thyme /taɪm/ *n* tomillo *m*

thyroid (gland) /'θaɪrɔɪd/ *n* tiroides *f*,
glándula *f* tiroidea

ti /tiː/ *n* (Mus) si *m*

tiara /tiˈɑːrə/ *n* diadema *f*

Tibet /tɪ'bet/ *n* el Tíbet

Tibetan¹ /tɪ'betn̩/ *adj* tibetano

Tibetan² *n* **(a)** (person) tibetano, -na *m,f* **(b)**
(language) tibetano *m*

tic /tɪk/ *n* tic *m*

tick¹ /tɪk/ *n* **1** (sound) tic *m* **2** (Zool) garrapata
f **3** (mark) (BrE) marca *f*, tic *m*, palomita *f* (Méx),
visto *m* (Esp)

tick² *vi* ⟨*clock/watch*⟩ hacer* tictac

■ ~ *vt* (BrE) marcar* (*con un visto or una palomita
etc*)

■ **tick over** [*v + adv*] «*engine*» marchar al
ralentí

ticket /'tɪkət ‖ 'tɪkɪt/ *n* **1** (for bus, train) boleto *m*
or (Esp) billete *m*; (for plane) pasaje *m or* (Esp)
billete *m*; (for theater, museum) entrada *f*; (for
baggage, coat) ticket *m*; (*before n*) ~ **collector**
revisor, -sora *m,f*, ~ **office** (Transp) mostrador *m*
(*or* ventanilla *f etc*) de venta de pasajes (*or*
billetes *etc*); (Theat) taquilla *f*, boletería *f* (AmL)
2 (label) etiqueta *f*

tickle /'tɪkəl/ *vt* hacerle* cosquillas a

■ ~ *vi* «*wool/beard*» picar*

ticklish /'tɪklɪʃ/ *adj*: **to be** ~ tener* cosquillas,
ser* cosquilloso *or* (Méx) cosquilludo

tidal /'taɪdl̩/ *adj* con régimen de marea

tidal wave *n* maremoto *m*

tidbit /'tɪdbɪt/ *n* (AmE) ▶ TITBIT

tide /taɪd/ *n* **1** (Geog) marea *f*; **the** ~ **is in/out** la
marea está alta/baja; **high/low** ~ marea alta/baja
2 (movement) corriente *f*; (of violence) oleada *f*

■ **tide over** [*v + o + adv*]: **this should** ~ **us over
until next month** nos arreglaremos con esto hasta
el próximo mes

tidily /'taɪdl̩i ‖ 'taɪdɪli/ *adv* ordenadamente,
prolijamente (RPl)

tidiness /'taɪdɪnəs ‖'taɪdɪnɪs/ n orden m, prolijidad f (RPl)

tidy¹ /'taɪdi/ adj **tidier, tidiest** ordenado, prolijo (RPl)

tidy² tidies, tidying, tidied vt arreglar, ordenar
- ■ **tidy up** ☐ [v + o + adv, v + adv + o] ‹room/desk› ordenar, arreglar; ‹toys› ordenar, recoger* ☐ [v + adv] ordenar

tie¹ /taɪ/ n ☐ (Clothing) corbata f ☐ (a) (bond) lazo m, vínculo m (b) (obligation, constraint) atadura f; **family ~s** obligaciones fpl familiares ☐ (Sport) (equal score) empate m

tie² ties, tying, tied vt ☐ (a) (make) ‹knot/bow› hacer* (b) (fasten) atar, amarrar (AmL exc RPl) ☐ (restrict) ‹person› atar ☐ (Games, Sport) ‹game› empatar
- ■ ~ vi ☐ (fasten) atarse ☐ (draw) «teams» empatar
- ■ **tie in** [v + adv] **to ~ in** (WITH sth) concordar* or cuadrar (CON algo)
- ■ **tie up** [v + o + adv, v + adv + o] (a) ‹parcel/animal› atar, amarrar (AmL exc RPl) (b) **to be ~d up** (busy) estar* ocupado (c) **to be ~d up WITH sth** (connected) estar* ligado A or relacionado CON algo

tie: ~break n ▶ ~BREAKER A; **~breaker** n (a) (in tennis) muerte f súbita (b) (in quiz game) pregunta f de desempate; **~pin** n alfiler m de corbata

tier /tɪr ‖tɪə(r)/ n (a) (layer) hilera f superpuesta (b) (of cake) piso m (c) (in hierarchy) escalón m

tiger /'taɪgər ‖'taɪgə(r)/ n (pl **~s** or ~) tigre m

tight¹ /taɪt/ adj **-er, -est** ☐ (a) (fitting closely) ‹dress/skirt› ajustado, ceñido; (if uncomfortable) apretado (b) ‹knot› apretado (c) (stiff) ‹screw/lid› apretado, duro (d) ‹schedule› apretado; ‹budget› limitado ☐ (strict) ‹security/control› estricto ☐ (taut) ‹cord/thread› tirante, tenso ☐ (colloq) (a) (mean) ▶ TIGHTFISTED (b) (drunk) (pred) borracho, como una cuba (fam)

tight² adv: **hold ~!** ¡agárrate bien or fuerte!; **screw the lid on ~** aprieta bien el tapón; **sleep ~!** ¡que duermas bien!

tighten /'taɪtn/ vt (a) ‹nut/bolt/knot› apretar*; ‹rope› tensar; **to ~ one's belt** apretarse* el cinturón (b) ‹regulations› hacer* más estricto or rígido
- ■ **tighten up** [v + o + adv, v + adv + o] ‹laws/rules› hacer* más estricto; **to ~ up security** reforzar* las medidas de seguridad

tight: ~fisted /'taɪt'fɪstəd ‖,taɪt'fɪstɪd/ adj (colloq) agarrado (fam), amarrete (AmS fam); **~fitting** /'taɪt'fɪtɪŋ/ adj ‹jeans› ajustado, ceñido

tightly /'taɪtli/ adv ‹hold/grip› fuerte; **~ fastened** fuertemente atado

tightrope /'taɪtrəʊp/ n cuerda f floja; (before n) **~ walker** funámbulo, -la m,f, equilibrista mf

tights /taɪts/ pl n (a) (for ballet etc) malla(s) f(pl), leotardo(s) m(pl) (b) (BrE) ▶ PANTYHOSE

tile¹ /taɪl/ n (a) (for floor) baldosa f, losa f; (for wall) azulejo m (b) (for roof) teja f

tile² vt ‹floor› embaldosar; ‹wall› revestir* de azulejos, azulejar, alicatar (Esp); ‹roof› tejar

till¹ /tɪl/ conj/prep ▶ UNTIL¹,²

till² n caja f (registradora)

till³ vt cultivar, labrar

tiller /'tɪlər ‖'tɪlə(r)/ n (Naut) caña f or barra f del timón

tilt¹ /tɪlt/ vt inclinar
- ■ ~ vi inclinarse

tilt² n inclinación f

timber /'tɪmbər ‖'tɪmbə(r)/ n (a) (material) madera f (para construcción) (b) (trees) árboles mpl (madereros) (c) (beam) viga f, madero m

time¹ /taɪm/ n

I ☐ (past, present, future) tiempo m; **at this point o moment in ~** en este momento, en el momento presente; (before n) ‹travel› en el tiempo; **~ machine** máquina f del tiempo

☐ (time available, necessary for sth) tiempo m; **to make ~ for sth** hacer(se)* or encontrar* tiempo para algo; **just take your ~** tómate todo el tiempo que necesites or quieras

☐ (no pl) (period — of days, months, years) tiempo m; (— of hours) rato m; **that was a long ~ ago** eso fue hace mucho (tiempo); **in an hour's/ten years' ~** dentro de una hora/diez años; **for the ~ being** por el momento, de momento

☐ (in phrases) **all the ~** (constantly) constantemente; (the whole period) todo el tiempo; **in time** (early enough) a tiempo; (eventually) con el tiempo; **in good time** con tiempo; **in no time (at all)** rapidísimo, en un abrir y cerrar de ojos

☐ (with respect to work): **to take o** (BrE also) **have ~ off** tomarse tiempo libre

☐ (epoch, age) (often pl) época f, tiempo m; **in former ~s** antiguamente; **in ~s to come** en el futuro, en tiempos venideros; **to be behind the ~s** ser* anticuado, estar* desfasado

II ☐ (a) (by clock) hora f; **what ~ is it?** o **what's the ~?** ¿qué hora es? (b) (of event) hora f; **we have to arrange a ~ for the next meeting** tenemos que fijar una fecha y hora para la próxima reunión; **it's ~ you left** o **you were leaving** es hora de que te vayas

☐ (point in time): **at this ~ of (the) year** en esta época del año; **at this ~ of night** a estas horas de la noche; **at all ~s** siempre; **it'll be dark by the ~ we get there** (para) cuando lleguemos ya estará oscuro

☐ (instance, occasion) vez f; **let's try one more ~** probemos otra vez or una vez más; **nine ~s out of ten** en el noventa por ciento de los casos

☐ (in phrases) **about time: it's about ~ someone told him** ya es hora or ya va siendo hora de que alguien se lo diga; **about ~ (too)!** ¡ya era hora!; **at a time: four at a ~** de cuatro en cuatro, de a cuatro (AmL); **I can only do one thing at a ~** solo puedo hacer una cosa a la or por vez; **at the same time** (simultaneously) al mismo tiempo; (however) (as linker) al mismo tiempo, de todas formas; **at times** a veces; **every o each time** (as conj) (whenever) cada vez; **from time to time** de vez en cuando; **on time** (on schedule): **the buses never run on ~** los autobuses casi nunca pasan a su hora or puntualmente; **she's never on ~** nunca llega temprano, siempre llega tarde

☐ (experience): **to have a good/bad/hard ~** pasarlo bien/mal/muy mal; **have fun ~!** ¡que te diviertas (or que se diviertan etc)!, ¡que lo pases (or pasen etc) bien!

☐ (Mus) compás m; (before n) **~ signature** llave f de tiempo

☐ **times** pl (Math): **it's four ~s bigger** es cuatro veces más grande

time² *vt* (Sport) cronometrar; **I've ~d how long it takes me** he calculado cuánto tiempo me lleva

time: ~ **bomb** *n* bomba *f* de tiempo *or* de relojería; ~**-consuming** /kən'su:mɪŋ ‖kən'sju:mɪŋ/ *adj* que lleva mucho tiempo; ~**keeper** *n* (a) (Sport) cronometrador, -dora *m,f* (b) (worker) (BrE): **to be a good/bad ~keeper** ser* puntual/impuntual

timeless /'taɪmləs ‖'taɪmlɪs/ *adj* (liter) eterno

time limit *n* plazo *m*

timely /'taɪmli/ *adj* **-lier, -liest** oportuno

timer /'taɪmər ‖'taɪmə(r)/ *n* temporizador *m*; (of oven, video etc) reloj *m* (automático)

times /taɪmz/ *prep*: **3 ~ 4 is 12** 3 (multiplicado) por 4 son 12; ▸ FOUR¹

time: ~**saving** *adj* que ahorra tiempo; ~**scale** *n* escala *f* de tiempo; ~**share** *n* (property) multipropiedad *f*; ~**sheet** *n* hoja *f* de asistencia; ~**table** *n* (a) (Transp) horario *m* (b) (esp BrE Educ) horario *m* (c) (schedule, programme) agenda *f*

timid /'tɪməd ‖'tɪmɪd/ *adj* tímido; ⟨animal⟩ huraño

timidly /'tɪmədli ‖'tɪmɪdli/ *adv* tímidamente, con timidez

timing /'taɪmɪŋ/ *n* (choice of time): **the ~ of the action was disastrous** la acción fue de lo más inoportuna; **that was good ~: we've just arrived** calculaste muy bien el tiempo: acabamos de llegar

tin /tɪn/ *n* **1** (a) (metal) estaño *m* (b) (tinplate) (hoja)lata *f*; (before n) ⟨soldier⟩ de plomo **2** (can) (esp BrE) lata *f or* (Esp tb) bote *m* (de conservas, bebidas etc)

tinfoil /'tɪnfɔɪl/ *n* (made of tin) papel *m* de estaño; (made of aluminium) papel *m* de aluminio

tinge¹ /tɪndʒ/ *n* (a) (of color) tinte *m*, matiz *m* (b) (hint, trace) dejo *m*, matiz *m*

tinge² *vt* (*usu pass*) (color) **to be ~d WITH sth** estar* matizado DE algo

tingle /'tɪŋgəl/ *vi*: **it makes your skin ~** te hace sentir un cosquilleo *or* hormigueo en la piel

tingling /'tɪŋglɪŋ/ *n* cosquilleo *m*, hormigueo *m*

tinker /'tɪŋkər ‖'tɪŋkə(r)/ *vi* **to ~ WITH sth** hacerle* pequeños ajustes A algo; (pej) juguetear CON algo

tinkle *vi* «*bell/glass*» tintinear

tinned /tɪnd/ *adj* (BrE) enlatado, en *or* de lata

tin: ~ **opener** *n* (BrE) abrelatas *m*; ~**plate** *n* hojalata *f*

tint¹ /tɪnt/ *n* (a) (of color) tinte *m*, matiz *m*; (color) tono *m* (b) (for hair) tintura *f*, tinte *m*

tint² *vt* teñir*

tinted /'tɪntəd ‖'tɪntɪd/ *adj* ⟨glass⟩ coloreado; ⟨lenses⟩ con un tinte; ⟨hair⟩ teñido

tiny /'taɪni/ *adj* **tinier, tiniest** minúsculo, diminuto

tip¹ /tɪp/ *n* **1** (end, extremity) punta *f*; (of stick, umbrella) contera *f*, regatón *m*; (filter ~) filtro *m*; **to be standing on the ~s of one's toes** estar* de puntillas *or* (CS) en puntas de pie; **on the ~ of one's tongue** en la punta de la lengua **2** (helpful hint) consejo *m* (práctico) **3** (gratuity) propina *f* **4** (BrE) (rubbish dump) vertedero *m* (de basuras)

tip² **-pp-** *vt* **1** (give gratuity to) darle* (una) propina a **2** (a) (tilt) inclinar (b) (pour, throw) tirar

■ **tip off** [*v + o + adv, v + adv + o*] ⟨police/criminal⟩ avisar(le a), darle* el dato a (CS), darle* un chivatazo a (Esp fam)

■ **tip over** **1** [*v + o + adv, v + adv + o*] volcar* **2** [*v + adv*] caerse*

tipped /tɪpt/ *adj* ⟨cigarette⟩ con filtro

tiptoe¹ /'tɪptəʊ/ *vi* **-toes, -toeing, -toed** caminar *or* (esp Esp) andar* de puntillas

tiptoe² *n*: **on ~** de puntillas

tiptop /'tɪp'tɑːp ‖,tɪp'tɒp/ *adj* de primera, excelente; **in ~ condition** en excelente estado

tirade /taɪ'reɪd/ *n* diatriba *f*

tire¹ /taɪr ‖'taɪə(r)/ *vt* cansar

■ ~ *vi* (a) (become weary) cansarse (b) (become bored) **to ~ OF sth/sb/-ING** cansarse DE algo/algn/+ INF

■ **tire out** [*v + o + adv, v + adv + o*] agotar

tire², (BrE) **tyre** /taɪr ‖'taɪə(r)/ *n* neumático *m*, llanta *f* (AmL)

tired /taɪrd ‖'taɪəd/ *adj* (a) (weary) cansado; **to get ~** cansarse (b) (fed up) **to be ~ OF sth/sb/-ING** estar* cansado DE algo/algn /+ INF

tiredness /'taɪrdnəs ‖'taɪədnɪs/ *n* cansancio *m*

tireless /'taɪrləs ‖'taɪəlɪs/ *adj* ⟨person⟩ infatigable, incansable; ⟨patience/efforts⟩ inagotable

tiresome /'taɪrsəm ‖'taɪəsəm/ *adj* ⟨person⟩ pesado; ⟨task⟩ tedioso

tiring /'taɪrɪŋ ‖'taɪərɪŋ/ *adj* cansador (AmS), cansado (AmC, Esp, Méx)

tissue /'tɪʃu: ‖'tɪʃu:, 'tɪsju:/ *n* **1** (Anat, Bot) tejido *m* **2** (a) (paper handkerchief) pañuelo *m* de papel, Kleenex® *m* (b) (~ paper) papel *m* de seda

tit /tɪt/ *n* **1** (Zool) paro *m* **2** (sl) (breast) teta *f* (fam)

titbit /'tɪtbɪt/ *n* (a) (of food) exquisitez *f* (b) (of gossip) chisme *m*

tit for tat /tæt /*n*: **it was ~ ~ ~** fue ojo por ojo, diente por diente

title /'taɪtl̩/ *n* **1** (of creative work) título *m* **2** (a) (status) tratamiento *m* (como Sr, Sra, Dr etc) (b) (noble rank) título *m* (nobiliario *or* de nobleza) (c) (Sport) título *m* **3** (Law) (right of ownership) derecho *m*

title: ~ **deed** *n* (*usu pl*) título *m* de propiedad; ~**holder** *n* campeón, -peona *m,f*, ~ **page** *n* portada *f*, carátula *f*

titter /'tɪtər ‖'tɪtə(r)/ *vi* reírse* disimuladamente

tittle-tattle /'tɪtl̩,tætl̩/ *n* (colloq) chismes *mpl*

titular /'tɪtʃələr ‖'tɪtjʊlə(r)/ *adj* nominal

T-junction /'ti:,dʒʌŋkʃən/ *n* (BrE) cruce *m* (en forma de T)

AmC	América Central	Arg	Argentina	Cu	Cuba
AmL	América Latina	Bol	Bolivia	Ec	Ecuador
AmS	América del Sur	Chi	Chile	Esp	España
Andes	Región andina	CS	Cono Sur	Méx	México

Per	Perú
RPI	Río de la Plata
Ur	Uruguay
Ven	Venezuela

TN = Tennessee

to¹ /tuː, *weak form* tə/ *prep* **1** **(a)** (indicating destination) a; **you can wear it ~ the wedding** puedes ponértelo para la boda **(b)** (indicating direction) hacia; **move a little ~ the right** córrete un poco hacia la derecha **(c)** (indicating position) a; **~ the left/right of sth** a la izquierda/derecha de algo **2** **(a)** (as far as) hasta; **she can count ~ 10** sabe contar hasta 10 **(b)** (until) hasta; **I can't stay ~ the end** no puedo quedarme hasta el final; *see also* FROM 5

3 **(a)** (showing indirect object): **give it ~ me** dámelo; **I gave it ~ Rachel** se lo di a Rachel; **what did you say ~ him/them?** ¿qué le/les dijiste?; **I was talking ~ myself** estaba hablando solo **(b)** (in dedications): **~ Paul with love from Jane** para Paul, con cariño de Jane

4 (indicating proportion, relation): **how many ounces are there ~ the pound?** ¿cuántas onzas hay en una libra?; **Barcelona won by two goals ~ one** Barcelona ganó por dos (goles) a uno; **there's a 10 ~ 1 chance of …** hay una probabilidad de uno en 10 de …

5 (producing): **~ my horror …** para mi horror …

6 (indicating belonging) de; **the key ~ the front door** la llave de la puerta principal

7 (telling time) (BrE): **ten ~ three** las tres menos diez, diez para las tres (AmL exc RPl)

to² /tə/ (*in infinitives*) **1** **(a)** **~ sing/fear/leave** cantar/temer/partir **(b)** (in order to) para; **I do it ~ save money** lo hago para ahorrar dinero **2** (*after adj or n*): **it's easy ~ do** es fácil de hacer; **you're too young ~ drink wine** eres demasiado joven para beber vino; **she was the first ~ arrive** fue la primera en llegar; **she has a lot ~ do** tiene mucho que hacer

to³ /tuː/ *adv* (shut): **I pulled the door ~** cerré la puerta

toad /təʊd/ *n* sapo *m*

toadstool /'təʊdstuːl/ *n* hongo *m* (*no comestible*)

to and fro /frəʊ/ *adv* de un lado a otro

toast¹ /təʊst/ *n* **1** (bread) tostadas *fpl*, pan *m* tostado; **a piece of ~** una tostada *or* (Chi, Méx) un pan tostado; (*before n*) **~ rack** portatostadas *m* **2** (tribute) brindis *m*; **we drank a ~ to him** brindamos por él

toast² *vt* **1** (Culin) tostar* **2** (drink tribute to) ⟨*person/success*⟩ brindar por

toaster /'təʊstər ‖ 'təʊstə(r)/ *n* tostadora *f* (eléctrica), tostador *m*

tobacco /tə'bækəʊ/ *n* (*pl* **-cos** *or* **-coes**) tabaco *m*

tobacconist /tə'bækənəst ‖ tə'bækənɪst/ *n*: *expendedor de tabaco, cigarrillos y artículos para el fumador,* ≈ estanquero, -ra *m,f* (*en Esp*); **~'s** (shop) tabaquería *f*, tienda *f* de artículos para fumador, ≈ estanco *m* (*en Esp*)

-to-be /tə'biː/ *suff*: **father~/husband~** futuro padre/esposo

toboggan /tə'bɑːgən ‖ tə'bɒgən/ *n* trineo *m*, tobogán *m*

today¹ /tə'deɪ/ *adv* **(a)** (this day) hoy **(b)** (nowadays) hoy (en) día, actualmente

today² *n* (*no art*) **(a)** (this day) hoy *adv*; **(as) from ~** a partir de hoy *or* del día de hoy **(b)** (present age) hoy *adv*, hoy (en) día

toddler /'tɑːdlər ‖ 'tɒdlə(r)/ *n* niño pequeño, niña pequeña *m,f* (*entre un año y dos años y medio de edad*)

to-do /tə'duː/ *n* (colloq) (*no pl*) lío *m*, jaleo *m*

toe¹ /təʊ/ *n* dedo *m* (*del pie*); **big ~** dedo *m* gordo (del pie); **to be on one's ~s** estar* *or* mantenerse* alerta

toe² *vt*: **to ~ the line** acatar la disciplina

toenail *n* uña *f* (*del pie*)

toffee /'tɑːfi ‖ 'tɒfi/ *n* toffee *m* (*golosina hecha con azúcar y mantequilla*)

toffee-nosed /'tɑːfiˌnəʊzd ‖ 'tɒfiˌnəʊzd/ *adj* (BrE colloq) estirado (fam)

tofu /'təʊfuː/ *n* tofu *m*, queso *m* de soya (AmL) *or* (Esp) soja

toga /'təʊgə/ *n* toga *f*

together /tə'geðər ‖ tə'geðə(r)/ *adv* **(a)** : **they went ~** fueron juntos/juntas; **we left them alone ~** los dejamos solos a los dos; **all ~ now!** ¡todos (juntos *or* a la vez)! **(b)** **together with** junto con

toil¹ /tɔɪl/ *n* (liter) trabajo *m* duro

toil² *vi* (liter) trabajar duro

toilet /'tɔɪlət ‖ 'tɔɪlɪt/ *n* **1** (room) baño *m* (esp AmL), servicio *m* (esp Esp), váter *m* (Esp); (bowl) water *m* *or* (Esp) váter *m*, inodoro *m*; (*before n*) **~ paper** papel *m* higiénico; **~ roll** rollo *m* de papel higiénico **2** (washing and dressing) (*before n*) **~ soap** jabón *m* de tocador; **~ water** agua *fₓ* de colonia

toiletries /'tɔɪlətriz ‖ 'tɔɪlɪtriz/ *pl n* artículos *mpl* de tocador *or* de perfumería

token¹ /'təʊkən/ *n* **1** (expression, indication): **a small ~ of gratitude** un pequeño obsequio como muestra *or* prueba de agradecimiento; **as a ~ of respect** en señal de respeto; **by the same ~** de igual modo **2** **(a)** (coin) ficha *f* **(b)** (voucher) (BrE) vale *m*; (given as present) vale *m*, cheque-regalo *m*

token² *adj* (*before n, no comp*) ⟨*fine/gesture*⟩ simbólico

told /təʊld/ *past & past p of* TELL

tolerable /'tɑːlərəbəl ‖ 'tɒlərəbəl/ *adj* **(a)** (endurable) tolerable **(b)** (passable) pasable

tolerance /'tɑːlərəns ‖ 'tɒlərəns/ *n* tolerancia *f*

tolerant /'tɑːlərənt ‖ 'tɒlərənt/ *adj* tolerante

tolerate /'tɑːləreɪt ‖ 'tɒləreɪt/ *vt* **(a)** ⟨*attitude/behavior*⟩ tolerar **(b)** ⟨*person/pain/noise*⟩ soportar, aguantar

toleration /ˌtɑːlə'reɪʃən ‖ ˌtɒlə'reɪʃən/ *n* tolerancia *f*

toll¹ /təʊl/ *n* **(a)** (Transp) peaje *m*, cuota *f* (Méx); (*before n*) **~ call** (AmE) llamada *f* interurbana, conferencia *f* (Esp); **~ road** carretera *f* de peaje *or* (Méx) de cuota **(b)** (cost, damage): **the climate took a ~ on his health** el clima le afectó la salud

toll² *vi* tocar*, doblar

toll: **~booth** *n* cabina *f* de peaje; **~bridge** *n* puente *m* de peaje *or* (Méx) de cuota; **~-free** /'təʊl'friː/ *adj* (AmE) gratuito

tomato /tə'meɪtəʊ ‖ tə'mɑːtəʊ/ *n* (*pl* **-toes**) tomate *m* *or* (Méx) jitomate *m*

tomb /tuːm/ *n* tumba *f*, sepulcro *m*

tomboy /'tɑːmbɔɪ ‖ 'tɒmbɔɪ/ *n* niña *f* poco femenina, machona *f* (RPl), machetona *f* (Méx), varonera *f* (Arg)

tombstone /'tuːmstəʊn/ *n* lápida *f*

tomcat /'tɑːmkæt ‖'tɒmkæt/ *n* gato *m* (macho)

tome /təʊm/ *n* (hum) libro *m*, librote *m*

tomorrow¹ /təˈmɔːrəʊ, təˈmɑːrəʊ ‖təˈmɒrəʊ/ *adv* mañana; ~ **morning** mañana por la mañana, mañana en la mañana (AmL); **the day after** ~ pasado mañana

tomorrow² *n* (*no art*) **(a)** (day after today) mañana *adv* **(b)** (future) mañana *m*

tom-tom /'tɑːmtɑːm ‖'tɒmtɒm/ *n* tam-tam *m*

ton /tʌn/ *n* **1** (unit of weight) tonelada *f* (*EEUU: 907kg., RU: 1.016kg.*); **this suitcase weighs a** ~ (colloq) esta maleta pesa una tonelada (fam) **2** (large amount) (colloq) (*usually pl*): ~**s of people/ work** montones *mpl* de gente/trabajo (fam)

tone¹ /təʊn/ *n* **1** **(a)** (quality of sound, voice) tono *m* **(b) tones** *pl* (sound) sonido *m*; (voice) voz *f* **(c)** (Telec) señal *f* (sonora) **2** (shade) tono *m*, tonalidad *f* **3** **(a)** (mood, style) tono *m* **(b)** (standard, level) nivel *m* **4** (Mus) (interval) tono *m*

tone² *vt* ⟨muscles/skin⟩ tonificar*
■ **tone down** [*v + o + adv, v + adv + o*] ⟨language⟩ moderar; ⟨color⟩ atenuar*

tone-deaf /'təʊn'def/ *adj*: **to be** ~ no tener* oído (musical)

tongs /tɑːŋz, tɔːŋz ‖tɒŋz/ *pl n* tenacillas *fpl*

tongue /tʌŋ/ *n* **(a)** (Anat) lengua *f*; **to say sth** ~ **in cheek** decir* algo medio burlándose *or* medio en broma **(b)** (language) lengua *f*

tongue: ~**-tied** /taɪd/ *adj* tímido, cohibido; ~ **twister** *n* trabalenguas *m*

tonic /'tɑːnɪk ‖'tɒnɪk/ *n* **(a)** (pick-me-up) tónico *m* **(b)** ~ **(water)** (agua *f* ‡) tónica *f*

tonight¹ /təˈnaɪt/ *adv* esta noche

tonight² *n* (*no art*) esta noche *f*

tonne /tʌn/ *n* tonelada *f* (métrica)

tonsil /'tɑːnsəl ‖'tɒnsəl/ *n* amígdala *f*

tonsillitis /ˌtɑːnsəˈlaɪtəs ‖ˌtɒnsɪˈlaɪtɪs/ *n* amigdalitis *f*

too /tuː/ *adv* **1** (excessively) demasiado; **there were** ~ **many people/cars** había demasiada gente/demasiados coches; **that's** ~ **difficult for her to understand** es demasiado difícil para que lo entienda **2** (as well) también **3** (very) muy; **I'm not** ~ **sure** no estoy muy seguro

took /tʊk/ *past of* TAKE¹

tool /tuːl/ *n* (instrument) instrumento *m*; (workman's etc) herramienta *f*; **garden** ~**s** herramientas *fpl or* utensilios *mpl* de jardinería

tool: ~**bar** *n* (Comput) barra *f* de herramientas; ~**box** *n* caja *f* de herramientas; ~**kit** *n* juego *m* de herramientas; ~**shed** *n* cobertizo *m* (*para herramientas*)

toot¹ /tuːt/ *n* bocinazo *m*

toot² *vi* «driver» tocar* la bocina *or* el claxon, pitar
■ ~ *vt* ⟨car horn⟩ tocar*

tooth /tuːθ/ *n* (*pl* **teeth**) **(a)** (of person, animal) diente *m*; (molar) muela *f*; **front teeth** dientes *mpl* de adelante; **back teeth** muelas *fpl*; **to grit one's teeth** aguantarse; (lit) apretar* los dientes; **to have a sweet** ~ ser* goloso; **to lie through one's teeth** mentir* descaradamente; (*before n*) ~ **decay** caries *f* dental **(b)** (of zip, saw, gear) diente *m*; (of comb) púa *f*, diente *m*

tooth: ~**ache** *n* dolor *m* de muelas; ~**brush** *n* cepillo *m* de dientes; ~**paste** *n* dentífrico *m*,

pasta *f* dentífrica *or* de dientes; ~**pick** *n* palillo *m* (de dientes), escarbadientes *m*, mondadientes *m*

top¹ /tɑːp ‖tɒp/ *n* **1** **(a)** (highest part) parte *f* superior *or* de arriba; (of mountain) cima *f*, cumbre *f*; (of tree) copa *f*; (of page) parte *f* superior; **from** ~ **to bottom** de arriba abajo; **at the** ~ **of one's voice** a voz en cuello *or* en grito, a grito pelado (fam) **(b)** (BrE) (of road) final *m* **2** (highest rank, position): **she came** ~ **of the class** sacó la mejor nota de la clase; **at the** ~ **of the league** (Dep) a la cabeza de la liga **3** **(table)** ~ tablero *m* **4** (Clothing): **a blue** ~ una blusa (*or* un suéter *or* un top *etc*) azul **5** **on top** (*as adv*) encima, arriba; **to come out on** ~ salir* ganando **6** **on top of** (*as prep*) encima de; **and on** ~ **of it all** *o* **on** ~ **of all that, ...** y encima *or* para colmo, ... **7** (of jar, box) tapa *f*, tapón *m* (Esp); (of pen) capuchón *m*; **to blow one's** ~ (colloq) explotar (fam) **8** (spinning ~) trompo *m*, peonza *f*

top² *adj* (*before n*) **1** **(a)** ⟨layer/shelf⟩ de arriba, superior; ⟨note⟩ más alto; **on the** ~ **floor** en el último piso; **the** ~ **left-hand corner of the page** la esquina superior izquierda de la página **(b)** ⟨speed/temperature⟩ máximo, tope **2** **(a)** (best): **to be** ~ **quality** ser* de primera calidad; **the service is** ~ **class** el servicio es de primera **(b)** (in ranked order): **our** ~ **priority** nuestra prioridad absoluta **(c)** (leading, senior) ⟨scientists/chefs⟩ más destacado; **the** ~ **jobs** los mejores puestos

top³ **-pp-** *vt* **1** (exceed, surpass) superar*; **to** ~ **it all** para coronarlo, para colmo **2** (cover) ~**ped with cheese** con queso por encima
■ **top up** [*v + o + adv, v + adv + o*] ⟨glass⟩ llenar; ⟨battery, SIM card⟩ cargar*; ⟨income⟩ suplementar

topaz /'təʊpæz/ *n* topacio *m*

top: ~ **hat** *n* sombrero *m* de copa; ~**-heavy** /'tɑːp'hevi ‖'tɒp'hevi/ *adj* ⟨structure⟩ inestable (*por ser muy pesado en su parte superior*)

topic /'tɑːpɪk ‖'tɒpɪk/ *n* tema *m*

topical /'tɑːpɪkəl ‖'tɒpɪkəl/ *adj* de interés actual, de actualidad

topless /'tɑːpləs ‖'tɒplɪs/ *adj* topless

top-level /'tɑːp'levəl ‖'tɒp'levəl/ *adj* (*before n*) ⟨talks⟩ de alto nivel

topography /təˈpɑːgrəfi ‖təˈpɒgrəfi/ *n* topografía *f*

topping /'tɑːpɪŋ/ *n*: **ice-cream with chocolate** ~ helado con (salsa de) chocolate por encima

topple /'tɑːpəl ‖'tɒpəl/ *vi* caerse*
■ ~ *vt* **(a)** ⟨government/dictator⟩ derrocar*, derribar **(b)** (overturn) volcar*

top: ~**-ranking** /'tɑːp'ræŋkɪŋ ‖ˌtɒp'ræŋkɪŋ/ *adj* (*before n*) de alto nivel; ~**-secret** /'tɑːp'siːkrət ‖ˌtɒp'siːkrɪt/ *adj* (*pred* ~ **secret**) secreto, reservado; ~**soil** *n* capa *f* superior del suelo; ~**-up card** *n* tarjeta *f* de prepago

topsy-turvy /'tɑːpsi'tɜːrvi/ *adj* (colloq) ⟨room⟩ desordenado, patas (para) arriba (fam)

Torah /'tɔːrə/ *n* **the** ~ la *or* el Torá

torch /tɔːrtʃ ‖ tɔːtʃ/ n **(a)** (flame) antorcha f, tea f **(b)** (electric) (BrE) linterna f

torchlight /'tɔːrtʃlaɪt ‖ 'tɔːtʃlaɪt/ n: **by ~ a** la luz de la(s) antorcha(s); (before n) ⟨procession⟩ con antorchas

tore /tɔːr ‖ tɔː(r)/ past of TEAR²

torment¹ /'tɔːrment ‖ 'tɔːment/ n tormento m

torment² /tɔːr'ment ‖ tɔː'ment/ vt atormentar, torturar; (tease) martirizar*

torn /tɔːrn ‖ tɔːn/ past p of TEAR²

tornado /tɔːr'neɪdəʊ ‖ tɔː'neɪdəʊ/ n (pl **-does** or **-dos**) tornado m

torpedo¹ /tɔːr'piːdəʊ ‖ tɔː'piːdəʊ/ n (pl **-does**) (Mil) torpedo m

torpedo² vt **-does, -doing, -doed** torpedear

torpor /'tɔːrpər ‖ 'tɔːpə(r)/ n (frml) letargo m, sopor m

torrent /'tɔːrənt ‖ 'tɒrənt/ n torrente m

torrential /tɔː'rentʃəl ‖ tə'renʃəl/ adj torrencial

torrid /'tɔːrəd ‖ 'tɒrɪd/ adj ⟨heat⟩ tórrido; ⟨affair⟩ apasionado

torso /'tɔːrsəʊ ‖ 'tɔːsəʊ/ n (pl **-sos**) torso m

tortoise /'tɔːrtəs ‖ 'tɔːtəs/ n tortuga f

tortoiseshell¹ /'tɔːrtəʃel, -təsʃəl ‖ 'tɔːtəsʃel, 'tɔːtəʃəl/ n (material) carey m, concha f

tortoiseshell² adj (color) de color carey; ⟨cat⟩ pardo

tortuous /'tɔːrtʃʊəs ‖ 'tɔːtjʊəs/ adj tortuoso, sinuoso

torture¹ /'tɔːrtʃər ‖ 'tɔːtʃə(r)/ n tortura f

torture² vt ⟨person/animal⟩ torturar; **she was ~d by doubts** las dudas la atormentaban

Tory /'tɔːri/ n (pl **Tories**) (in UK) tory mf

toss¹ /tɔːs ‖ tɒs/ n **(a)** (throw) lanzamiento m; **with a ~ of his head** con un movimiento brusco de la cabeza **(b)** (of coin): **to win/lose the ~** ganar/perder* jugándoselo a cara o cruz (or sello etc)

toss² vt **(a)** (throw) ⟨ball⟩ tirar, lanzar*, aventar* (Col, Méx, Per); ⟨pancake⟩ darle* la vuelta a (lanzándolo al aire); **let's ~ a coin** echémoslo a cara o cruz or (Andes, Ven) a cara o sello or (Arg) a cara o ceca or (Méx) a águila o sol **(b)** (agitate) ⟨boat⟩ sacudir, zarandear **(c)** ⟨salad⟩ mezclar
■ **~ vi** ⟨boat⟩ dar* bandazos; **to ~ and turn** dar* vueltas (en la cama)

tot /tɑːt ‖ tɒt/ n **(a)** (young child) pequeño, -ña m,f, chiquito, -ta m,f (esp AmL) **(b)** (of alcohol) copita f
■ **tot up: -tt-** [v + o + adv, v + adv + o] (colloq) sumar

total¹ /'təʊtl/ adj total; ⟨failure⟩ rotundo

total² n total m

total³ vt, (BrE) **-ll- (a)** (amount to) ascender* or elevarse a un total de **(b)** (add up) totalizar*

totalitarian /təʊ'tælə'teriən ‖ ˌtəʊtælɪ'teəriən/ adj totalitario

totally /'təʊtli ‖ 'təʊtəli/ adv totalmente, completamente

tote /təʊt/ vt (esp AmE colloq) ⟨weapons⟩ llevar

totem pole /'təʊtəm/ n tótem m

totter /'tɑːtər ‖ 'tɒtə(r)/ vi tambalearse

touch¹ /tʌtʃ/ n ① **(a)** (sense) tacto m **(b)** (physical contact): **at the ~ of a button** con solo tocar un botón ② (small amount, degree — of humor, irony) dejo m, toque m; (— of paint) toque m; (— of salt) pizca f ③ (detail) detalle m; **to add o put the final o finishing ~es to sth** darle* los últimos toques a algo ④ (communication): **to get/keep o stay in ~ with sb** ponerse*/mantenerse* en contacto con algn; **I lost ~ with her** perdí el contacto con ella

touch² vt ① **(a)** (be in physical contact with) tocar*; **my feet don't ~ the bottom** (of pool) no hago pie, no toco fondo **(b)** (brush, graze) rozar*, tocar* ② **(a)** (affect, concern) afectar **(b)** (move emotionally): **he was ~ed by her kindness** su amabilidad lo enterneció or le llegó al alma; **I was very ~ed** me emocioné
■ **~ vi (a)** (with finger, hand) tocar* **(b)** ⟨hands⟩ rozarse*; ⟨wires⟩ tocarse*
■ **touch down** [v + adv] (on land) aterrizar*, tomar tierra; (on moon) alunizar*
■ **touch on** [v + prep + o] ⟨subject⟩ tocar*, mencionar
■ **touch up** [v + o + adv, v + adv + o] ⟨photograph/painting⟩ retocar*

touch: ~-and-go /tʌtʃən'gəʊ/ adj: **I passed the exam, but it was ~-and-go** aprobé el examen, pero por poco; **how is the patient? — it's ~-and-go at the moment** ¿cómo está el paciente? — en situación crítica; **~down** n (on land) aterrizaje m; (on moon) alunizaje m

touching /'tʌtʃɪŋ/ adj enternecedor, conmovedor

touch: ~line n línea f de banda; **~-type** vi mecanografiar* al tacto

touchy /'tʌtʃi/ adj **-chier, -chiest** ⟨person⟩ susceptible; ⟨subject⟩ delicado

tough /tʌf/ adj **-er, -est** ① **(a)** (strong, hard-wearing) ⟨fabric/clothing⟩ resistente, fuerte **(b)** ⟨meat⟩ duro ② ⟨person⟩ **(a)** (resilient) fuerte **(b)** (aggressive, violent) bravucón ③ **(a)** (strict) ⟨boss/teacher⟩ severo; ⟨policy/discipline⟩ duro **(b)** ⟨exam/decision⟩ difícil

toughen /'tʌfən/ ~ (up) vt **(a)** ⟨muscles⟩ endurecer*; ⟨material⟩ hacer* más fuerte or resistente **(b)** ⟨person⟩ hacer* más fuerte

toupee /tuːˈpeɪ ‖ 'tuːpeɪ/ n peluquín m, tupé m

tour¹ /tʊr ‖ tʊə(r), tɔː(r)/ n **(a)** (by bus, car) viaje m, gira f; (of castle, museum) visita f; (of town) visita f turística, recorrido m turístico; (before n) **~ guide** guía mf de turismo or (Méx) de turistas **(b)** (official visit) (to country, region) gira f, viaje m; (of factory, hospital) visita f; (Mus, Sport, Theat) gira f, tournée f; **to be/go on ~** estar*/ir* de gira

tour² vt **(a)** ⟨country/area⟩ recorrer, viajar por **(b)** (visit officially) visitar **(c)** (Mus, Sport, Theat) ir* de gira or hacer* una gira por

tourism /'tʊrɪzəm ‖ 'tʊərɪzəm, 'tɔːr-/ n turismo m

tourist /'tʊrəst ‖ 'tʊərɪst, 'tɔːr-/ n turista mf; (before n) **~ guide** (book) guía f turística; (person) guía mf de turismo or (Méx) de turistas; **the ~ industry** el turismo, la industria del turismo; **~ office** oficina f de (información y) turismo

tournament /'tʊrnəmənt ‖ 'tɔːnəmənt/ n torneo m

tourniquet /'tʊrnɪkət ‖ 'tʊənɪkeɪ/ n torniquete m

tousled /'taʊzəld/ adj despeinado, alborotado

tout /taʊt/ *vi*: to ~ for customers andar* a la
caza de clientes

tow¹ /təʊ/ *n* remolque *m*; to give sb a ~
remolcar* a algn

tow² *vt* remolcar*, llevar a remolque; they ~ed
the car away se llevaron el coche a remolque

toward /tɔːrd ‖ təˈwɔːd/, (esp BrE) **towards**
/tɔːrdz ‖ təˈwɔːdz/ *prep* **1** (in the direction of) hacia
2 (as contribution): she gave us $100 ~ it nos dio
100 dólares como contribución **3** (regarding) para
con, hacia; your attitude ~ them tu actitud para
con *or* hacia ellos

towel¹ /ˈtaʊəl/ *n* toalla *f*; (before *n*) ~ bar *o*
(BrE) rail toallero *m* (*de barra*)

towel² *vt*, (BrE) **-ll-** secar* con toalla

toweling, (BrE) **towelling** /ˈtaʊəlɪŋ/ *n* (tela *f*
de) toalla *f*, felpa *f*

tower /ˈtaʊər ‖ ˈtaʊə(r)/ *n* torre *f*
■ **tower above, tower over** [*v* + *prep* + *o*]
⟨building⟩ descollar* sobre; ⟨person⟩ destacar*
sobre

tower block *n* (BrE) (residential) edificio *m or*
bloque *m* de apartamentos *or* (AmL tb) de
departamentos *or* (Esp tb) de pisos, torre *f*

towering /ˈtaʊərɪŋ/ *adj* (before *n*) **(a)**
⟨building⟩ altísimo **(b)** ⟨genius⟩ destacado

town /taʊn/ *n* (in general) ciudad *f*; (smaller)
pueblo *m*, población *f*; to go to ~ on sth tirar la
casa por la ventana; (before *n*) ~ center *o* (BrE)
centre centro *m* de la ciudad

town: ~ **clerk** *n* (in US) *funcionario encargado
de llevar los registros de nacimientos, defunciones
etc*; ~ **council** *n* (in UK) ayuntamiento *m*,
municipio *m*, municipalidad *f*; ~ **crier** /ˈkraɪər
‖ ˈkraɪə(r)/ *n* pregonero *m*; ~ **hall** *n*
ayuntamiento *m*, municipio *m*; ~ **planner** *n*
urbanista *mf*; ~ **planning** *n* urbanismo *m*

township /ˈtaʊnʃɪp/ *n* **(a)** (in US) (Govt)
municipio *m*, municipalidad *m*, ayuntamiento *m*
(b) (in South Africa) distrito *m* segregado

tow: ~**path** *n* camino *m* de sirga; ~**rope** *n*
(Naut) sirga *f*; (Auto) cuerda *f or* cable *m* de
remolque; ~ **truck** *n* grúa *f*

toxic /ˈtɑːksɪk ‖ ˈtɒksɪk/ *adj* tóxico

toxin /ˈtɑːksən ‖ ˈtɒksɪn/ *n* toxina *f*

toy¹ /tɔɪ/ *n* juguete *m*
■ **toy with** [*v* + *prep* + *o*] ⟨pen/food⟩ juguetear
con; ⟨idea/possibility⟩ darle* vueltas a

toy² *adj* **(a)** ⟨car/gun⟩ de juguete **(b)** (miniature)
enano

toyshop /ˈtɔɪʃɑːp ‖ ˈtɔɪʃɒp/ *n* juguetería *f*

trace¹ /treɪs/ *n* **(a)** (indication) señal *f*, indicio *m*,
rastro *m* **(b)** (small amount): ~s of poison rastros
de veneno

trace² *vt* **1** **(a)** ⟨criminal/witness⟩ localizar*,
ubicar* (AmL) **(b)** ⟨fault/malfunction⟩ descubrir*
2 **(a)** (on tracing paper) calcar* **(b)** ⟨line/outline⟩
trazar*

tracing paper /ˈtreɪsɪŋ/ *n* papel *m* de calco
or de calcar

track¹ /træk/ *n* **1** (mark) pista *f*, huellas *fpl*; to

throw sb off the ~ despistar a algn; to keep/lose
~ of the conversation seguir*/perder* el hilo de
la conversación; I lost all ~ of the time no me di
cuenta de la hora
2 **(a)** (road, path) camino *m*, sendero *m* **(b)** to be
on the right/wrong ~ estar* bien/mal
encaminado, ir* por buen/mal camino
3 (race ~) pista *f*; (before *n*) ~ events atletismo
m en pista
4 (track events) (AmE) atletismo *m* en pista
5 (Rail) **(a)** (way) vía *f* (férrea) **(b)** (rails etc) vías
fpl
6 (song, piece of music) tema *m*, pieza *f*

track² *vt* seguirle* la pista a, rastrear
■ **track down** [*v* + *o* + *adv*, *v* + *adv* + *o*]
⟨criminal/lost object⟩ localizar*

trackball /ˈtrækbɔːl/ *n* (Comput) ratón *m* de bola

tracker /ˈtrækər ‖ ˈtrækə(r)/ *n* rastreador,
-dora *m,f*; (before *n*) ~ dog perro *m* rastreador

tracking /ˈtrækɪŋ/ *n* (AmE Educ) *división del
alumnado en grupos de acuerdo al nivel
académico*

track: ~ **record** *n* historial *m*, antecedentes
mpl; ~**suit** *n* equipo *m* (de deportes), chándal *m*
(Esp), pants *mpl* (Méx), buzo *m* (Chi, Per), sudadera
f (Col)

tract /trækt/ *n* **1** (of land, sea) extensión *f*
2 (Anat) tracto *m* **3** (short treatise) tratado *m*
breve

traction /ˈtrækʃən/ *n* **(a)** (Mech Eng, Med)
tracción *f* **(b)** (grip) agarre *m*, adherencia *f*

tractor /ˈtræktər ‖ ˈtræktə(r)/ *n* (Agr) tractor *m*

trade¹ /treɪd/ *n* **(a)** (buying, selling) comercio *m*
(b) (business, industry) industria *f* **(c)** (skilled
occupation) oficio *m* **(d)** (people in particular trade): the
~ el gremio

trade² *vi* (buy, sell) comerciar
■ ~ *vt* ⟨blows/insults⟩ intercambiar; to ~ sth FOR
sth cambiar *or* canjear algo POR algo
■ **trade in** [*v* + *o* + *adv*, *v* + *adv* + *o*] entregar*
como parte del pago

trade: ~**mark** *n* **(a)** (symbol, name) marca *f* (de
fábrica) **(b)** (distinctive characteristic) sello *m*
característico; ~ **name** *n* nombre *m* comercial

trader /ˈtreɪdər ‖ ˈtreɪdə(r)/ *n* comerciante *mf*

trade: ~ **secret** *n* secreto *m* comercial;
~**sman** /ˈtreɪdzmən/ *n* (*pl* **-men** /-mən/) **(a)**
(shopkeeper) (dated) comerciante *m*, tendero *m* **(b)**
(deliveryman) proveedor *m*; ~ **union** *n* sindicato
m, gremio *m* (CS, Per); (before *n*) ⟨leader⟩ sindical,
sindicalista, gremial (AmL)

trading /ˈtreɪdɪŋ/ *n* **(a)** (in goods) comercio *m*,
actividad *f or* movimiento *m* comercial **(b)** (on
stock exchange) contratación *f*, operaciones *fpl*
(bursátiles)

tradition /trəˈdɪʃən/ *n* tradición *f*

traditional /trəˈdɪʃnəl ‖ trəˈdɪʃənl/ *adj*
tradicional

traffic /ˈtræfɪk/ *n* **1** (vehicles) tráfico *m*,

circulación *f*, tránsito *m* (esp AmL) **2** (goods, people transported) tránsito *m* **3** (trafficking) tráfico *m*

■ **traffic in**: -ck- [*v + prep + o*] traficar* en

traffic: ~ **calming** /'kɑːmɪŋ/ *n* (*before n*): ~ **calming measures** medidas *fpl* para reducir la velocidad del tráfico; ~ **circle** *n* (AmE) rotonda *f*, glorieta *f*; ~ **island** *n* isla *f* peatonal; ~ **jam** *n* embotellamiento *m*, atasco *m*

trafficker /'træfɪkər ‖'træfɪkə(r)/ *n* traficante *mf*

traffic: ~ **light** *n* (*often pl*) semáforo *m*; ~ **warden** *n* (in UK) *persona que controla el estacionamiento de vehículos en las ciudades*

tragedy /'trædʒədi/ *n* (*pl* **-dies**) tragedia *f*

tragic /'trædʒɪk/ *adj* trágico

tragicomedy /ˌtrædʒɪ'kɑːmədi ‖ˌtrædʒɪ'kɒmədi/ *n* tragicomedia *f*

trail¹ /treɪl/ *n* (a) (left by animal, person) huellas *fpl*, rastro *m*; **to be on the ~ of sb/sth** seguir* la pista de algn/algo, seguirle* la pista a algn/algo (b) (path) sendero *m*, senda *f*

trail² *vt* **1** (drag) arrastrar **2** (follow) seguir* la pista de, seguirle* la pista a, rastrear

■ ~ *vi* **1** (drag) arrastrar **2** (lag behind) ir* a la zaga **3** «*plant*» trepar

■ **trail away, trail off** [*v + adv*] irse* apagando

trailer /'treɪlər ‖'treɪlə(r)/ *n* **1** (a) (for boats, equipment) remolque *m* (b) (house ~) (AmE) caravana *f*, tráiler *m* (AmL), casa *f* rodante (CS, Ven), cámper *f* (Chi, Méx), rulot *f* (Esp) **2** (Cin, TV) avance(s) *m*(*pl*) or (Esp tb) tráiler *m* or (CS) sinopsis *f*

train¹ /treɪn/ *n* **1** (Rail) tren *m*; (*before n*) ~ **driver** (BrE) maquinista *mf*; ~ **set** ferrocarril *m* de juguete **2** (a) (of servants) séquito *m* (b) (of events) serie *f*; **to lose one's ~ of thought** perder* el hilo (de las ideas) **3** (of dress, robe) cola *f*

train² *vt* **1** (a) (instruct) ‹*athlete*› entrenar; ‹*soldier*› adiestrar; ‹*animal*› (to perform tricks etc) amaestrar, adiestrar; ‹*employee*› capacitar; ‹*teacher*› formar (b) ‹*voice/ear*› educar* (c) ‹*plant*› guiar* **2** (aim) **to ~ sth ON sth/sb** ‹*gun*› apuntarle A algo/algn con algo

■ ~ *vi* (a) «*nurse/musician*» estudiar (b) (Sport) entrenar(se)

trained /treɪnd/ *adj* (a) ‹*worker*› calificado (esp AmL), cualificado (Esp); ‹*teacher*› titulado, diplomado; **a highly ~ army** un ejército muy bien adiestrado (b) ‹*dog*› entrenado (c) ‹*voice*› educado

trainee /treɪ'niː/ *n* (a) (in a trade) aprendiz, -diza *m,f*; (*before n*) ~ **manager** *empleado que está haciendo prácticas de gerencia* (b) (AmE Mil) recluta *mf*

trainer /'treɪnər ‖'treɪnə(r)/ *n* **1** (of athletes) entrenador, -dora *m,f*; (of performing animals) amaestrador, -dora *m,f*, adiestrador, -dora *m,f* **2** (training shoe) (BrE colloq) zapatilla *f* de deporte, tenis *m*

training /'treɪnɪŋ/ *n* (a) (instruction) capacitación *f* (b) (Sport) entrenamiento *m*

traipse /treɪps/ *vi* (colloq) (+ *adv compl*): **I ~d all over town** me pateé (fam) toda la ciudad

trait /treɪt/ *n* rasgo *m*

traitor /'treɪtər ‖'treɪtə(r)/ *n* traidor, -dora *m,f*

tram /træm/ *n* (BrE Transp) tranvía *m*

tramp¹ /træmp/ *vi* (+ *adv compl*) **to ~ (along)** caminar *or* marchar (pesadamente)

tramp² *n* vagabundo, -da *m,f*

trample /'træmpəl/ *vt* pisotear; **they were ~d to death** murieron aplastados

■ ~ *vi* **to ~ ON sth** pisotear algo

trampoline /'træmpəliːn/ *n* trampolín *m*, cama *f* elástica

trance /træns ‖trɑːns/ *n* trance *m*

tranquil /'træŋkwəl ‖'træŋkwɪl/ *adj* tranquilo

tranquility, (BrE) **tranquillity** /træŋ'kwɪləti/ *n* (of place, atmosphere) paz *f*, tranquilidad *f*; (of person) calma *f*, serenidad *f*

tranquilize, (BrE) **tranquillize** /'træŋkwəlaɪz ‖'træŋkwɪlaɪz/ *vt* sedar, dar* un sedante a

tranquilizer, (BrE) **tranquillizer** /'træŋkwəlaɪzər ‖'træŋkwɪlaɪzə(r)/ *n* sedante *m*, tranquilizante *m*

transaction /trænz'ækʃən/ *n* transacción *f*, operación *f*

transatlantic /'trænzət'læntɪk/ *adj* transatlántico

transcend /træn'send/ *vt* (frml) (a) (go beyond) ‹*boundaries*› ir* más allá de, trascender* (b) (overcome) superar

transcribe /træn'skraɪb/ *vt* transcribir*

transcript /'trænskrɪpt/ *n* transcripción *f*

transcription /træn'skrɪpʃən/ *n* transcripción *f*

transfer¹ /træns'fɜːr ‖træns'fɜː(r)/ *vt* -**rr**- (a) ‹*funds/account*› transferir* (b) ‹*property/right*› transferir*, traspasar, transmitir (c) ‹*call*› pasar (d) ‹*employee/prisoner*› trasladar; ‹*player*› (esp BrE) traspasar

transfer² /'trænsfɜːr ‖'trænsfɜː(r)/ *n* **1** (a) (Fin, Law) transferencia *f* (b) (of employee) traslado *m*; (of player) (esp BrE) traspaso *m* (c) (of passengers) transbordo *m* **2** (design) calcomanía *f*

transferable /træns'fɜːrəbəl/ *adj* transferible; **not ~** intransferible

transferal /træns'fɜːrəl/ *n* (AmE) ▶ TRANSFER² 1 A, B

transfix /træns'fɪks/ *vt* (*usu pass*) paralizar*

transform /træns'fɔːrm ‖træns'fɔːm/ *vt* transformar

transformation /'trænsfər'meɪʃən ‖ˌtrænsfə'meɪʃən/ *n* transformación *f*

transformer /træns'fɔːrmər ‖træns'fɔːmə(r)/ *n* transformador *m*

transfusion /træns'fjuːʒən/ *n* transfusión *f*

transgress /træns'gres ‖trænz'gres/ *vt* (frml) (a) ‹*law*› transgredir (frml) (b) (go beyond) exceder, sobrepasar

■ ~ *vi* pecar*

transient /'trænziənt, 'trænʃənt ‖'trænziənt/ *adj* pasajero, fugaz

transistor /træn'zɪstər, -'sɪstər ‖træn'zɪstə(r), -'sɪstə(r)/ *n* (a) (Electron) transistor *m* (b) (~ radio) (esp BrE) transistor *m*, radio *f* or (AmL exc CS) radio *m* a transistores

transit /'trænsət, -zət ‖'trænzɪt, -sɪt/ *n* tránsito *m*; **passengers in ~** pasajeros *mpl* en or de tránsito; **it was lost in ~** se perdió en el viaje

transition /træn'zɪʃən/ *n* transición *f*

transitional /træn'zɪʃnəl ‖træn'zɪʃənl/ *adj* ⟨*stage/period*⟩ de transición

transitive /'trænsətɪv/ *adj* transitivo

translate /træns'leɪt/ *vt/i* traducir*

translation /træns'leɪʃən/ *n* traducción *f*

translator /træns'leɪtər ‖træns'leɪtə(r)/ *n* traductor, -tora *m,f*

transmission /trænz'mɪʃən/ *n* transmisión *f*

transmit /trænz'mɪt/ *vt* **-tt-** transmitir

transmitter /'trænzmɪtər ‖trænz'mɪtə(r)/ *n* transmisor *m*

transparency /træns'pærənsi/ *n* (*pl* **-cies**) (Phot) transparencia *f*, diapositiva *f*

transparent /træns'pærənt/ *adj* transparente

transpire /træn'spaɪr ‖træn'spaɪə(r)/ *vi* **1** (a) (become apparent): **it** ~**d that ...** resultó que ... (b) (happen) ocurrir, suceder **2** (Biol, Bot) transpirar

transplant¹ /træns'plænt ‖træns'plɑːnt/ *vt* (Hort, Med) trasplantar

transplant² /'trænsplænt ‖'trænsplɑːnt/ *n* (Med) trasplante *m*

transport¹ /'trænspɔːrt ‖'trænspɔːt/ *n* transporte *m*

transport² /træns'pɔːrt ‖træns'pɔːt/ *vt* transportar

transportation /ˌtrænspər'teɪʃən ‖ˌtrænspɔː'teɪʃən/ *n* transporte *m*

transpose /træns'pəʊz/ *vt* trasponer*, transponer*

transvestite /trænz'vestaɪt/ *n* travestido *m*, travestí *m*, travesti *m*

trap¹ /træp/ *n* trampa *f*

trap² *vt* **-pp-** (a) ⟨*animal*⟩ cazar* (con trampa) (b) (cut off, catch) (*often pass*) atrapar; **he was** ~**ped in the car** quedó atrapado en el coche

trapdoor, trap door /træp'dɔːr ‖'træpdɔː(r)/ trampilla *f*

trapeze /træ'piːz, trə- ‖trə'piːz/ *n* trapecio *m*

trapper /'træpər ‖'træpə(r)/ *n* trampero, -ra *m,f*

trappings /'træpɪŋz/ *pl n* (a) (paraphernalia): **all the** ~ **of success** los símbolos del éxito (b) (of horse) arreos *mpl*, jaeces *mpl*

trash¹ /træʃ/ *n* (a) (refuse) (AmE) basura *f*; (*before n*) ~ **bag** bolsa *f* de la basura; ~ **can** cubo *m or* (CS, Per) tacho *m or* (Méx) bote *m or* (Col) caneca *f or* (Ven) tobo *m* de la basura (b) (worthless stuff) basura *f* (c) (worthless people) (AmE colloq) escoria *f*

trash² *vt* (AmE) (a) (dispose of) botar (a la basura) (AmL exc RPl), tirar (a la basura) (Esp, RPl) (b) (criticize) (colloq) ⟨*movie/book*⟩ poner* por los suelos *or* por el suelo; ⟨*person*⟩ despellejar (fam)

trashman /'træʃmæn/ *n* (*pl* **-men** /-men/) (AmE) basurero *m*

trashy /'træʃi/ *adj* **-shier, -shiest** ⟨*souvenir*⟩ barato, de porquería (fam); ⟨*movie/magazine*⟩ malo

trauma /'trɔːmə/ *n* (*pl* **-mas**) trauma *m*

traumatic /trɔː'mætɪk/ *adj* traumático, traumatizante

travel¹ /'trævəl/, (BrE) **-ll-** *vi* **1** (make journey) viajar **2** (move, go) «*vehicle*» desplazarse*, ir*; «*light/waves*» propagarse*

■ ~ *vt* ⟨*country/world*⟩ viajar por, recorrer; ⟨*road/ distance*⟩ recorrer

travel² *n* (*before n*) ⟨*company/brochure*⟩ de viajes

travel: ~ **agency** *n* agencia *f* de viajes; ~ **agent** *n* agente *mf* de viajes; ~ **agent's** agencia *f* de viajes

traveler, (BrE) **-ll-** /'trævlər ‖'trævlə(r)/ *n* (a) viajero, -ra *m,f* (b) (itinerant person) (BrE) *persona que ha adoptado el estilo de vida errante de los gitanos*

traveler's check, (BrE) **traveller's cheque** *n* cheque *m* de viaje *or* de viajero

traveling¹, (BrE) **-ll-** /'trævlɪŋ/ *n* (*before n*) ~ **expenses** gastos *mpl* de viaje

traveling², (BrE) **-ll-** *adj* (a) ⟨*clothes/ companion*⟩ de viaje (b) (itinerant) ambulante; ~ **salesman** viajante *m*

travel: ~**sick** /'trævəlsɪk/ *adj* (BrE) mareado; **to get** ~ marearse; ~ **sickness** *n* (BrE) mareo *m*; (*before n*) ⟨*pills*⟩ para el mareo

trawl /trɔːl/ *vi* hacer* pesca de arrastre

trawler /'trɔːlər ‖'trɔːlə(r)/ *n* barca *f* pesquera (*utilizada para hacer pesca de arrastre*), bou *m*

tray /treɪ/ *n* bandeja *f*

treacherous /'tretʃərəs/ *adj* ⟨*person*⟩ traicionero, traidor; ⟨*sea/current*⟩ traicionero

treachery /'tretʃəri/ *n* (*pl* **-ries**) traición *f*

treacle /'triːkəl/ *n* (esp BrE) melaza *f*

tread¹ /tred/ (*past* **trod**; *past p* **trodden** *or* **trod**) *vi* pisar; **to** ~ **in sth** pisar algo; **to** ~ **carefully** *o* **warily** andarse* con cuidado *or* con pie(s) de plomo

■ ~ *vt*: **she trod the earth down** apisonó la tierra; **to** ~ **grapes** pisar uvas; **to** ~ **water** flotar (*en posición vertical*)

■ **tread on** [*v* + *prep* + *o*] (esp BrE) pisar

tread² *n* **1** (step, footfall) paso *m*; (steps) pasos *mpl* **2** (on tire) banda *f* de rodamiento

treadle /'tredl/ *n* pedal *m*

treason /'triːzn/ *n* traición *f*

treasure¹ /'treʒər ‖'treʒə(r)/ *n* (a) (hoard of wealth) tesoros *mpl* (b) (sth valuable, prized) tesoro *m*; (*before n*) ~ **hunt** (Games) búsqueda *f* del tesoro

treasure² *vt* (a) (value greatly): **thank you for the book, I shall always** ~ **it** gracias por el libro, lo guardaré como algo muy especial (b) **treasured** *adj* ⟨*possession*⟩ preciado

treasurer /'treʒərər ‖'treʒərə(r)/ *n* tesorero, -ra *m,f*

treasury /'treʒəri/ *n* (*pl* **-ries**) (a) (public funds) erario *m*, tesoro *m* (b) **the Treasury** *o* **the treasury** el fisco, la hacienda pública, el tesoro (público); **Department of the T**~ (in US) Departamento del Tesoro (*de los Estados Unidos*), ≈ministerio *m* de Hacienda

treat¹ /triːt/ *vt* (a) (+ *adv compl*) ⟨*person/ animal*⟩ tratar; **you seem to** ~ **this whole thing as a joke** pareces tomarte a broma todo esto (b) (process) tratar (c) (deal with) (fml) ⟨*subject*⟩ tratar (d) (Med) ⟨*patient/disease*⟩ tratar (e) (entertain): **I'm** ~**ing you** te invito yo; **I** ~**ed myself to a new dress** me di el gusto de comprarme un vestido nuevo

treat² *n* gusto *m*; **I bought myself an ice cream as ₀ for a** ~ me compré un helado para darme (un) gusto

treatise /'tri:təs ‖'tri:tɪs, -ɪz/ *n* tratado *m*

treatment /'tri:tmənt/ *n* **(a)** (of person, animal, object) trato *m*; (of subject) tratamiento *m* **(b)** (of waste) tratamiento *m* **(c)** (Med) tratamiento *m*

treaty /'tri:ti/ *n* (*pl* **-ties**) tratado *m*

treble¹ /'trebəl/ *n* **(a)** (singer) tiple *mf*; (voice) voz *f* de tiple **(b)** (Audio) agudos *mpl*

treble² *vt* triplicar*
■ ~ *vi* triplicarse*

treble³ *adj* [1] (threefold) triple [2] (*before n*) (Mus) de tiple *or* soprano

treble clef *n* clave *f* de sol

tree /tri:/ *n* árbol *m*; (*before n*) ~ **trunk** tronco *m*

tree: ~**-lined** *adj* (*before n*) bordeado de árboles, arbolado; ~**top** *n* copa *f* de árbol

trek¹ /trek/ *n* (hike) caminata *f*; **it's quite a** ~ **to the shops** hay un buen paseo hasta llegar a las tiendas

trek² *vi* **-kk-** caminar; **to go** ~**king** hacer* senderismo

trellis /'treləs ‖'trelɪs/ *n* enrejado *m*, espaldera *f*

tremble /'trembəl/ *vi* temblar*

tremendous /trɪ'mendəs/ *adj* **(a)** (great, huge) tremendo **(b)** (very good) formidable

tremendously /trɪ'mendəsli/ *adv* tremendamente

tremor /'tremər ‖'tremə(r)/ *n* **(a)** (quiver) temblor *m* **(b)** (earth ~) temblor *m* (de tierra), seísmo *m*, sismo *m* (AmL)

trench /trentʃ/ *n* zanja *f*; (Mil) trinchera *f*

trench coat *n* trinchera *f*

trend /trend/ *n* **(a)** (pattern, tendency) tendencia *f* **(b)** (fashion) moda *f*

trendy /'trendi/ *adj* **-dier, -diest** moderno

trepidation /ˌtrepə'deɪʃən ‖ˌtrepɪ'deɪʃən/ *n* (frml) (fear) temor *m* (frml); (anxiety) inquietud *f*

trespass /'trespəs/ *vi* (Law) entrar sin autorización en propiedad ajena

trespasser /'trespəsər ‖'trespəsə(r)/ *n* intruso, -sa *m,f*; ❸ **trespassers will be prosecuted** ≈ prohibido el paso

tress /tres/ *n* (liter) **(a)** (lock of hair) mechón *m* **(b)** **tresses** *pl* (hair) cabellera *f* (liter), cabellos *mpl*

trestle /'tresəl/ *n* caballete *m*

trial¹ /'traɪəl/ *n* [1] (Law) **(a)** (court hearing) proceso *m*, juicio *m* **(b)** (judgment) juicio *m*; **a fair** ~ un juicio imparcial; **to be on** ~ **for murder** estar* siendo procesado por asesinato [2] (test) prueba *f*; **clinical** ~ ensayo *m* clínico; **on** ~ **a** prueba; **by** ~ **and error** por ensayo y error [3] (trouble): ~**s and tribulations** tribulaciones *fpl* [4] (Sport) (*usu pl*) prueba *f* de selección

trial² *adj* (*period/flight*) de prueba; ~ **offer** oferta *f* especial (*para promover un producto nuevo*); ~ **run** prueba *f*

triangle /'traɪˌæŋgəl/ *n* (Math, Mus) triángulo *m*

triangular /traɪ'æŋgjələr ‖traɪ'æŋgjʊlə(r)/ *adj* triangular

tribal /'traɪbəl/ *adj* tribal

tribe /traɪb/ *n* tribu *f*

tribesman /'traɪbzmən/ *n* (*pl* **-men** /-mən/) miembro *m* de una tribu

tribunal /traɪ'bju:nl/ *n* (court) tribunal *m*

tributary /'trɪbjətəri ‖'trɪbjʊtəri/ *n* (*pl* **-ries**) afluente *m*, río *m* tributario

tribute /'trɪbju:t/ *n* [1] (acknowledgment) homenaje *m*, tributo *m* (AmL); **to pay** ~ **to sb/sth** rendir* homenaje *or* (AmL tb) tributo a algn/algo [2] (payment) tributo *m*

triceps /'traɪseps/ *n* (*pl* ~) tríceps *m*

trick¹ /trɪk/ *n* [1] **(a)** (ruse) trampa *f*, ardid *m*; (*before n*) ~ **photography** trucaje *m*; **a** ~ **question** una pregunta con trampa **(b)** (prank, joke) broma *f*, jugarreta *f* [2] (feat, skilful act) truco *m*; **to do card** ~**s** hacer* trucos con las cartas [3] (in card games) baza *f*

trick² *vt* engañar

trickle¹ /'trɪkəl/ *vi* (+ *adv compl*) **(a)** «*liquid*»: **sweat** ~**d down his forehead** le corrían gotas de sudor por la frente **(b)** (arrive, go): **letters are still trickling in** todavía se está recibiendo alguna que otra carta

trickle² *n* hilo *m*

trickster /'trɪkstər ‖'trɪkstə(r)/ *n* embaucador, -dora *m,f*

tricky /'trɪki/ *adj* **trickier, trickiest** **(a)** (difficult) (*task/problem*) difícil, peliagudo, que tiene sus bemoles **(b)** (sensitive) (*matter/problem*) delicado

tricycle /'traɪsɪkəl/ *n* triciclo *m*

trifle /'traɪfəl/ *n* [1] **(a)** (trivial thing) nimiedad *f* **(b)** (small amount) (*no pl*) insignificancia *f* [2] (Culin) postre de bizcocho, jerez, crema y frutas
■ **trifle with** [*v* + *prep* + *o*] jugar* con

trifling /'traɪflɪŋ/ *adj* insignificante, sin importancia

trigger¹ /'trɪgər ‖'trɪgə(r)/ *n* gatillo *m*

trigger² *vt* ~ (**off**) (*reaction/response*) provocar*

trill /trɪl/ *n* **(a)** (in music, of birdsong) trino *m* **(b)** (Ling) vibración *f*

trilogy /'trɪlədʒi/ *n* (*pl* **-gies**) trilogía *f*

trim¹ /trɪm/ *adj* **-mm-** **(a)** (slim) esbelto, estilizado **(b)** (neat) (*uniform/suit*) elegante

trim² *n* [1] (good condition): **to be in** (**good**) ~ estar* en buen estado *or* en buenas condiciones [2] (cut) recorte *m*

trim³ *vt* **-mm-** [1] (cut) recortar [2] (decorate): ~**med with velvet** con adornos de terciopelo; (round edge) ribeteado de terciopelo

trimester /traɪ'mestər ‖traɪ'mestə(r)/ *n* (AmE) trimestre *m*

trimming /'trɪmɪŋ/ *n* [1] (on clothes) adorno *m*; (along edges) ribete *m* [2] **trimmings** *pl* (offcuts) recortes *mpl*

Trinidad /'trɪnɪdæd ‖'trɪnɪdæd/ *n* Trinidad *f*; ~ **and Tobago** Trinidad y Tobago

Trinity /'trɪnəti/ *n* **the** (**Holy**) ~ la (Santísima) Trinidad

trinket /'trɪŋkət ‖'trɪŋkɪt/ *n* chuchería *f*, baratija *f*

trio /'tri:əʊ/ *n* trío *m*

trip¹ /trɪp/ *n* [1] (journey) viaje *m*; (excursion) excursión *f*; (outing) salida *f*; **she's going on a** ~ ···⊹·

to Japan se va de viaje al Japón; **a** ～ **to the zoo**
una visita al zoológico **2** (stumble, fall) tropezón
m, traspié *m*
trip² **-pp-** *vi* tropezar*
■ ～ *vt* ～ **(up)** hacerle* una zancadilla a
■ **trip over** [*v* + *adv*] tropezar* y caerse*
tripe /traɪp/ *n* **(a)** (Culin) mondongo *m* (AmS),
callos *mpl* (Esp), pancita *f* (Méx) **(b)** (nonsense)
(colloq) paparruchas *fpl* (fam)
triple¹ /ˈtrɪpəl/ *adj* triple
triple² *adv*: ～ **the amount** el triple
triple³ *vt* triplicar*
■ ～ *vi* triplicarse*
triple jump *n* triple salto *m* (de longitud)
triplet /ˈtrɪplət ‖ˈtrɪplɪt/ *n* trillizo, -za *m,f*
triplicate /ˈtrɪpləkət ‖ˈtrɪplɪkət/ *n*: **in** ～ por
triplicado
tripod /ˈtraɪpɑːd ‖ˈtraɪpɒd/ *n* trípode *m*
trite /traɪt/ *adj* **triter, tritest** trillado
triumph¹ /ˈtraɪəmf ‖ˈtraɪʌmf/ *n* triunfo *m*
triumph² *vi* triunfar
triumphal /traɪˈʌmfəl/ *adj* triunfal
triumphant /traɪˈʌmfənt/ *adj* ‹troops/team›
triunfador; ‹moment/entry› triunfal; ‹smile› de
triunfo, triunfal
trivia /ˈtrɪviə/ *pl n* trivialidades *fpl*, nimiedades
fpl
trivial /ˈtrɪviəl/ *adj* ‹events/concerns› trivial;
‹sum/details› insignificante, nimio
triviality /ˌtrɪviˈæləti/ *n* (*pl* **-ties**) trivialidad *f*
trivialize /ˈtrɪviəlaɪz/ *vt* trivializar*
trod /trɑːd ‖trɒd/ *past and past p of* TREAD¹
trodden /ˈtrɑːdn̩ ‖ˈtrɒdn̩/ *past p of* TREAD¹
trolley /ˈtrɑːli ‖ˈtrɒli/ *n* **1 (a)** (～ bus) trolebús
m **(b)** (～ car) (AmE) tranvía *m* **2** (BrE) (for food,
drink) carrito *m*, mesa *f* rodante; (at airport, in
supermarket, in hospital) carrito *m*
trombone /trɑːmˈbəʊn ‖trɒmˈbəʊn/ *n*
trombón *m*
troop¹ /truːp/ *n* **1** (unit) compañía *f*; (of cavalry)
escuadrón *m* **2 troops** *pl*: **our** ～**s** nuestras
tropas; **500** ～**s** 500 soldados
troop² *vi* (+ *adv compl*): **to** ～ **in/out** entrar/
salir* en tropel *or* en masa
trooper /ˈtruːpər ‖ˈtruːpə(r)/ *n* **(a)** (cavalryman)
soldado *m* de caballería **(b)** (state police officer)
(AmE) agente *mf*
trophy /ˈtrəʊfi/ *n* (*pl* **-phies**) trofeo *m*
tropic /ˈtrɑːpɪk ‖ˈtrɒpɪk/ *n* **(a)** (line) trópico *m*;
the T～ of Cancer/Capricorn el trópico de Cáncer/
Capricornio **(b) tropics** *pl* (area) **the** ～**s** el
trópico
tropical /ˈtrɑːpɪkəl ‖ˈtrɒpɪkəl/ *adj* tropical
trot¹ /trɑːt ‖trɒt/ *n* (*no pl*) trote *m*; **on the** ～
(BrE colloq): **four nights on the** ～ cuatro noches
seguidas
trot² **-tt-** *vi* trotar
■ **trot out** [*v* + *o* + *adv*, *v* + *adv* + *o*] ‹excuses/
clichés› salir* con; ‹facts› recitar de memoria

trouble¹ /ˈtrʌbəl/ *n* **1** (problems, difficulties)
problemas *mpl*; (particular problem) problema *m*; **to
get into** ～ meterse en problemas *or* en líos; **to
have** ～ **with sb/sth** tener* problemas con algn/
algo; **what's the** ～? ¿qué pasa?
2 (effort) molestia *f*; **I don't want to put you to
any** ～ no quiero ocasionarle ninguna molestia;
to go to the ～ **of doing sth, to take the** ～ **to do
sth** molestarse en hacer algo
3 (strife, unrest) (*often pl*): **the** ～**s in Northern
Ireland** los disturbios de Irlanda del Norte; **to
look for** ～ buscar* camorra; (*before n*) ～ **spot**
punto *m* conflictivo
trouble² *vt* **(a)** (worry) preocupar **(b)** (bother)
molestar; **I'm sorry to** ～ **you** perdone *or* disculpe
la molestia
troubled /ˈtrʌbəld/ *adj* **(a)** ‹person›
preocupado, atribulado; ‹look› de preocupación
(b) (strife-torn) (journ) aquejado de problemas
trouble: ～**maker** *n* alborotador, -dora *m,f*;
～**shooter** /ˈʃuːtər ‖ˈʃuːtə(r)/ *n* (within company)
persona que se envía a resolver problemas, crisis
etc; (mediator) mediador, -dora *m,f*
troublesome /ˈtrʌbəlsəm/ *adj* problemático
trough /trɔːf ‖trɒf/ *n* **1** (for water) abrevadero
m, bebedero *m*; (for feed) comedero *m* **2** (Geog)
hoya *f*, depresión *f*
troupe /truːp/ *n* (Theat) compañía *f* teatral; (in
circus) troupe *f*
trousers /ˈtraʊzərz ‖ˈtraʊzəz/ *pl n* pantalón *m*,
pantalones *mpl*; **a pair of** ～ un pantalón, unos
pantalones, un par de pantalones
trouser suit *n* (BrE) traje *m* pantalón, traje *m*
de chaqueta y pantalón
trousseau /ˈtruːsəʊ/ *n* (*pl* **-x** *or* **-s** /-z/) ajuar
m
trout /traʊt/ *n* (*pl* **trout** *or* Zool **trouts**) trucha
f
trowel /ˈtraʊəl/ *n* (Const) paleta *f*, llana *f*; (for
gardening) desplantador *m*, palita *f*
truancy /ˈtruːənsi/ *n* ausentismo *m or* (Esp)
absentismo *m* escolar
truant /ˈtruːənt/ *n*: **to play** ～ faltar a clase,
hacer* novillos *or* (Méx) irse* de pinta *or* (RPl)
hacerse* la rata *or* la rabona *or* (Per) la vaca *or*
(Chi) hacer* la cimarra *or* (Col) capar clase (fam)
truce /truːs/ *n* tregua *f*
truck /trʌk/ *n* **1 (a)** (vehicle) camión *m*; (*before
n*) ～ **driver** camionero, -ra *m,f* **(b)** (BrE Rail)
furgón *m*, vagón *m* **2** (vegetables, fruit) (AmE)
productos *mpl* de la huerta; (*before n*) ～ **farm**
huerta *f*
trucker /ˈtrʌkər ‖ˈtrʌkə(r)/ *n* (AmE) camionero,
-ra *m,f*, transportista *mf*
trucking /ˈtrʌkɪŋ/ *n* (AmE) transporte *m* por
carretera
truculent /ˈtrʌkjələnt ‖ˈtrʌkjʊlənt/ *adj*
malhumorado y agresivo
trudge /trʌdʒ/ *vi* caminar con dificultad
true¹ /truː/ *adj* **truer, truest** **1 (a)** (consistent
with fact, reality) ‹story› verídico; **to be** ～ ser*

cierto, ser* verdad; **to come ~** hacerse* realidad; **to hold ~** ser* válido **(b)** (accurate) (*before n*) ⟨*account*⟩ verídico **2** (real, actual, genuine) (*before n*) ⟨*purpose/courage*⟩ verdadero; ⟨*friend*⟩ auténtico, de verdad; **~ north** el norte geográfico; **it's ~ love** es amor de verdad **3** (faithful) fiel; **~ TO sth/sb** fiel A algo/algn **4** (Tech) (*pred*): **to be ~** «*wall*» estar* a plomo; «*beam*» estar* a nivel

true² *n*: **to be out of ~** no estar* a plomo

true: ~-life /ˈtruːˈlaɪf/ *adj* (journ) (*before n*) ⟨*story*⟩ verídico; **~-to-life** /ˈtruːtəˈlaɪf/ *adj* (*pred* **~ to life**) ⟨*novel/film*⟩ realista; ⟨*situation*⟩ verosímil

truffle /ˈtrʌfəl/ *n* trufa *f*

truly /ˈtruːli/ *adv* verdaderamente, realmente; ⟨*grateful*⟩ sinceramente, verdaderamente; **yours ~** (Corresp) cordiales saludos

trump /trʌmp/ *n* **(a) ~ (card)** (Games) triunfo *m*; (resource, weapon) baza *f* **(b) trumps** *pl* (suit) triunfo *m*

trumped-up /ˈtrʌmptˈʌp/ *adj* (*before n*) falso, fabricado

trumpet /ˈtrʌmpət/ ‖/ˈtrʌmpɪt/ *n* trompeta *f*

trumpeter /ˈtrʌmpətər/ ‖/ˈtrʌmpɪtə(r)/ *n* trompetista *mf*, trompeta *mf*

truncheon /ˈtrʌntʃən/ *n* (esp BrE) porra *f*, cachiporra *f*

trunk /trʌŋk/ *n* **1 (a)** (of tree) tronco *m* **(b)** (torso) tronco *m* **2** (of elephant) trompa *f* **3 (a)** (box) baúl *m* **(b)** (of car) (AmE) maletero *m* **4 trunks** *pl* (Clothing) traje *m* de baño *or* (Esp tb) bañador *m* (*de hombre*)

truss /trʌs/ *vt* atar

■ **truss up** [*v + o + adv, v + adv + o*] atar

trust¹ /trʌst/ *n* **1 (a)** (confidence, faith) confianza *f* **(b)** (responsibility): **a position of ~** un puesto de confianza *or* responsabilidad **2** (Fin) **(a)** (money, property) fondo *m* de inversiones **(b)** (institution) fundación *f* **(c)** (custody) (Law) fideicomiso *m*

trust² *vt* **1** (have confidence in) ⟨*person*⟩ confiar* en, tener* confianza en; (in negative sentences) fiarse* de; **he can't be ~ed** no es de fiar; **to ~ sb WITH sth** confiarle* algo A algn **2** (hope, assume) (frml) esperar

■ **~** *vi* **to ~ IN sb/sth** confiar* *or* tener* confianza EN algn/algo

trusted /ˈtrʌstəd/ ‖/ˈtrʌstɪd/ *adj* (*before n*) leal, de confianza

trustee /trʌsˈtiː/ *n* **(a)** (of money, property) fideicomisario, -ria *m,f*, fiduciario, -ria *m,f* **(b)** (of institution) miembro *m* del consejo de administración

trust fund *n* fondo *m* fiduciario *or* de fideicomiso

trusting /ˈtrʌstɪŋ/ *adj* confiado

trustworthy /ˈtrʌstˌwɜːrθi/ ‖/ˈtrʌstˌwɜːði/ *adj* ⟨*colleague/child*⟩ digno de confianza; ⟨*account/witness*⟩ fidedigno

truth /truːθ/ *n* (*pl* **~s** /truːðz/) **(a)** verdad *f*; (of account, story) veracidad *f* **(b)** (fact) verdad *f*

truthful /ˈtruːθfəl/ *adj* ⟨*person*⟩ que dice la verdad, veraz; ⟨*answer*⟩ veraz

try¹ /traɪ/ *n* (*pl* **tries**) **1** (attempt) intento *m*, tentativa *f* **2** (in rugby) ensayo *m*

try² **tries, trying, tried** *vt* **1 (a)** (attempt) intentar; **to ~ to + INF** tratar DE + INF, intentar +

INF; **~ not to forget** procura no olvidarte **(b)** (attempt to operate): **he tried all the windows** probó a abrir todas las ventanas

2 (a) ⟨*product/technique/food*⟩ probar*; **~ some** pruébalo, prueba un poquito **(b)** (have recourse to): **I'll ~ his work number** voy a probar a llamarlo al trabajo

3 (test, strain) ⟨*courage/patience*⟩ poner* a prueba **4 to ~ one's luck at sth** probar* suerte con algo **5** (Law) ⟨*person*⟩ procesar, juzgar*; **to ~ sb FOR sth** juzgar* a algn POR algo

■ **~** *vi* (make attempt) intentar, probar; (make effort) esforzarse*; **you must ~ harder** tienes que esforzarte más

■ **try on** [*v + o + adv, v + adv + o*] probarse*

■ **try out** [*v + o + adv, v + adv + o*] ⟨*product/method*⟩ probar*; ⟨*employee/player*⟩ probar*, poner* a prueba; **to ~ sth out ON sb** probar* algo CON algn

trying /ˈtraɪɪŋ/ *adj* ⟨*day/experience*⟩ duro

tsar /zɑːr ‖zɑː(r)/ *n* zar *m*

T-shirt /ˈtiːʃɜːrt ‖/ˈtiːʃɜːt/ *n* camiseta *f*

tsp = teaspoon(s)

tub /tʌb/ *n* **(a)** (for holding liquids) cuba *f*; (for washing clothes) tina *f* **(b)** (bath~) bañera *f*, tina *f* (AmL) **(c)** (for ice cream) envase *m* (*gen de plástico*), tarrina *f* (Esp)

tuba /ˈtuːbə ‖/ˈtjuːbə/ *n* tuba *f*

tubby /ˈtʌbi/ *adj* **-bier, -biest** (colloq) rechoncho (fam)

tube /tuːb ‖tjuːb/ *n* **1** (pipe, container) tubo *m* **2** (television) (esp AmE colloq): **the ~** la tele (fam) **3** (BrE Transp colloq): **the ~** el metro, el subte (Arg)

tuber /ˈtuːbər ‖/ˈtjuːbə(r)/ *n* (Bot) tubérculo *m*

tuberculosis /tʊˈbɜːrkjəˈləʊsəs ‖tjʊˌbɜːkjʊˈləʊsɪs/ *n* tuberculosis *f*

tubing /ˈtuːbɪŋ ‖/ˈtjuːbɪŋ/ *n* tubería *f*

tubular /ˈtuːbjələr ‖/ˈtjuːbjʊlə(r)/ *adj* tubular

TUC *n* (in UK) **= Trades Union Congress**

tuck¹ /tʌk/ *n* (fold, pleat) jareta *f*, alforza *f* (CS)

tuck² *vt* meter; **he ~ed the blanket under the mattress** metió bien la manta debajo del colchón

■ **tuck in 1** [*v + adv*] (eat) (colloq) ponerse* a comer, atacar* (fam) **2** [*v + o + adv, v + adv + o*] **(a)** ⟨*sheet*⟩ meter; **~ your shirt in** métete la camisa por dentro (de los pantalones) **(b)** ⟨*child*⟩ arropar

■ **tuck up** [*v + o + adv*] **to ~ sb up (in bed)** arropar a algn (en la cama)

tuckered out /ˈtʌkərd ‖/ˈtʌkəd/ *adj* (AmE colloq) (*pred*) molido (fam), hecho polvo (fam)

Tuesday /ˈtuːzdeɪ, -di ‖/ˈtjuːzdeɪ, -di/ *n* martes *m*; *see also* MONDAY

tuft /tʌft/ *n* **(a)** (of hair) mechón *m*; (on top of head) copete *m* **(b)** (of grass) mata *f*

tug¹ /tʌg/ **-gg-** *vt* tirar de, jalar (de) (AmL exc CS)

■ **~** *vi* **to ~ AT sth** tirar DE algo, jalar (DE) algo (AmL exc CS)

tug² *n* **1** (pull) tirón *m*, jalón *m* (AmL exc CS) **2** (Naut) remolcador *m*

tug of war *n*: juego de tira *y afloja con una cuerda*

tuition /tʊˈɪʃən ‖tjuːˈɪʃən/ *n* **(a)** (instruction) (frml) **~ (IN sth)** clases *fpl* (DE algo); **private ~** clases *fpl* particulares **(b)** (fees) matrícula *f*

t

tulip /'tu:ləp ‖'tju:lɪp/ n tulipán m

tumble¹ /'tʌmbl/ n (fall) caída f

tumble² vi **1** (fall) caerse* **2** (roll, turn) «acrobat» dar* volteretas

tumble: ~**down** adj (before n) en ruinas; ~ **dryer** /'tʌmbəl'draɪər ‖'tʌmbəlˌdraɪə(r)/ n secadora f

tumbler /'tʌmblər ‖'tʌmblə(r)/ n (glass) vaso m (de lados rectos)

tummy /'tʌmi/ n (pl **-mies**) (used to or by children) barriga f (fam), pancita f (fam), tripita f (fam)

tumor, (BrE) **tumour** /'tu:mər ‖'tju:mə(r)/ n tumor m

tumult /'tu:mʌlt ‖'tju:mʌlt/ n tumulto m

tumultuous /tʊ'mʌltʃuəs ‖tjʊ'mʌltjʊəs/ adj «applause» apoteósico; «protest» tumultuoso

tuna /'tu:nə ‖'tju:nə/ n (pl ~ or ~s) atún m

tundra /'tʌndrə/ n tundra f

tune¹ /tu:n ‖tju:n/ n **(a)** (melody) melodía f; (piece) canción f, tonada f; to change one's ~ cambiar de parecer **(b)** (correct pitch): to be in/out of ~ estar* afinado/desafinado

tune² vt **(a)** (Mus) afinar **(b)** (Auto) poner* a punto, afinar **(c)** (Rad, TV) sintonizar*
■ **tune in** [v + adv] to ~ in **TO** sth sintonizar* (CON) algo

tuneful /'tu:nfəl ‖'tju:nfəl/ adj melódico

tuner /'tu:nər ‖'tju:nə(r)/ n **(a)** (piano ~) (Mus) afinador, -dora m,f de pianos **(b)** (Rad) sintonizador m

tunic /'tu:nɪk ‖'tju:nɪk/ n **(a)** (of military uniform) guerrera f **(b)** (in ancient Rome) túnica f

tuning fork /'tu:nɪŋ ‖'tju:nɪŋ/ n diapasón m

Tunisia /tu:'ni:ʒə ‖tju:'nɪziə/ n Túnez m

Tunisian /tu:'ni:ʒən ‖tju:'nɪziən/ adj tunecino

tunnel¹ /'tʌnl/ n túnel m; (in mine) galería f, socavón m

tunnel², (BrE) vi **-ll-** abrir* or hacer* un túnel

turban /'tɜːrbən ‖'tɜːbən/ n turbante m

turbid /'tɜːrbəd ‖'tɜːbɪd/ adj turbio

turbine /'tɜːrbən, -baɪn ‖'tɜːbaɪn/ n turbina f

turbo /'tɜːrbəʊ ‖'tɜːbəʊ/ n turbocompresor m, turbo m

turbulence /'tɜːrbjələns ‖'tɜːbjʊləns/ n turbulencia f

turbulent /'tɜːrbjələnt ‖'tɜːbjʊlənt/ adj turbulento

tureen /tjʊ'ri:n, tə- ‖tjʊə'ri:n/ n sopera f

turf¹ /tɜːrf ‖tɜːf/ n (pl ~s or **turves**) **(a)** (grass) césped m **(b)** (square of grass) (esp BrE) tepe m

turf² vt «garden» encespedar, colocar* tepes en

turgid /'tɜːrdʒəd ‖'tɜːdʒɪd/ adj «prose» ampuloso

Turk /tɜːrk ‖tɜːk/ n turco, -ca m,f

turkey /'tɜːrki ‖'tɜːki/ n (pl ~s) pavo m, guajolote m (Méx)

Turkey /'tɜːrki ‖'tɜːki/ n Turquía f

Turkish¹ /'tɜːrkɪʃ ‖'tɜːkɪʃ/ adj turco

Turkish² n turco m

Turkish: ~ **bath** n baño m turco; ~ **delight** n delicia f turca (dulce gelatinoso recubierto de azúcar)

Turkmenistan /ˌtɜːrkmenɪ'stɑːn ‖ˌtɜːkmenɪ'stɑːn/ n Turkmenistán m

turmeric /'tɜːrmərɪk ‖'tɜːmərɪk/ n cúrcuma f

turmoil /'tɜːrmɔɪl ‖'tɜːmɔɪl/ n confusión f

turn¹ /tɜːrn ‖tɜːn/ n **1** **(a)** (rotation) vuelta f; the meat was done to a ~ la carne estaba hecha a la perfección, la carne estaba en su punto justo **(b)** (change of direction) vuelta f, giro m **(c)** (bend) curva f **(d)** (change, alteration): this dramatic ~ of events este dramático giro de los acontecimientos; to take a ~ for the better empezar* a mejorar; to take a ~ for the worse empeorar, ponerse* peor; the ~ of the century el final del siglo (y el principio del siguiente)
2 (place in sequence): whose ~ is it? ¿a quién le toca?; I think it's my ~ creo que me toca (el turno) a mí; to take ~s o to take it in ~(s) turnarse
3 (service): to do sb a good ~ hacerle* un favor a algn
4 (bout of illness): he had a funny ~ le dio un ataque (or un mareo etc)

turn² vt **1** (rotate) «knob/wheel/key» (hacer*) girar
2 (change position, direction of) «head» volver*, voltear (AmL exc RPl); she ~ed her back on them les volvió or les dio la espalda, les volteó la espalda (AmL exc RPl); the nurse ~ed her onto her side la enfermera la puso de lado;
3 (reverse) «mattress/omelette» darle* la vuelta a, voltear (AmL exc CS), dar* vuelta (CS); «page» pasar, volver*, dar* vuelta (CS)
4 **(a)** (go around) «corner» dar* la vuelta a, dar* vuelta (CS) **(b)** (pass): she's just ~ed 16 acaba de cumplir (los) 16
5 (change, transform) volver*; to ~ sth **TO/INTO** sth transformar or convertir* algo **EN** algo
6 (shape — on lathe) tornear; (— on potter's wheel) hacer*
■ ~ vi **1** (rotate) «handle/wheel» girar, dar* vuelta(s)
2 (to face in different direction) «person» volverse*, darse* la vuelta, voltearse (AmL exc CS), darse* vuelta (CS); «car» dar* la vuelta, dar* vuelta (CS); he ~ed onto his side se volvió or se puso de lado **(b)** (change course, direction): to ~ into a side street meterse en una calle lateral; to ~ left/right girar or doblar or torcer* a la izquierda/ derecha **(c)** (curve) «road/river» torcer*
3 **(a)** (focus on): to ~ to another subject pasar a otro tema; his mind ~ed to thoughts of escape se puso a pensar en escaparse **(b)** (have recourse to): to ~ to sb (for protection, advice) recurrir a algn; to ~ to drink darse* a la bebida
4 **(a)** (become): his face ~ed red se le puso la cara colorada; her hair had ~ed gray había encanecido **(b)** (be transformed) to ~ **INTO/TO** sth convertirse* **EN** algo **(c)** (change) «luck/ weather/tide» cambiar **(d)** (go sour) «milk» agriarse*
5 (when reading): ~ to page 19 vayan a la página 19
■ **turn against** [v + o + prep + o]: she ~ed them against me los puso en mi contra
■ **turn around,** (BrE also) **turn round** **1** [v + adv] darse* la vuelta, volverse*, voltearse (AmL exc CS), darse* vuelta (CS)
2 [v + o + adv] darle* la vuelta a, voltear (AmL exc CS), dar* vuelta (CS)

■ **turn aside** [v + adv] darse* la vuelta, voltearse (AmL exc CS), darse* vuelta (CS)

■ **turn away** [1] [v + adv] apartarse

  [2] [v + o + adv, v + adv + o] (a) ⟨head/face⟩ volver*, voltear (AmL exc RPl), dar* vuelta (CS); he ~ed his eyes away apartó la mirada (b) (send away) ⟨business⟩ no aceptar; the doorman ~ed them away el portero no los dejó entrar

■ **turn back** [1] [v + adv] (go back) volver*, regresar

  [2] [v + o + adv, v + adv + o]: he was ~ed back at the border en la frontera lo hicieron regresar

■ **turn down** [v + o + adv, v + adv + o] (a) (fold back) doblar (b) (diminish) ⟨heating/volume/ temperature⟩ bajar (c) (reject) ⟨offer/candidate⟩ rechazar*

■ **turn in** [1] [v + adv] (go to bed) (colloq) acostarse*

  [2] [v + o + adv, v + adv + o] (hand in, over) entregar*

■ **turn off** [1] [v + o + adv, v + adv + o] ⟨light/ radio/heating⟩ apagar*; ⟨faucet⟩ cerrar*; ⟨water⟩ cortar

  [2] [v + adv] (a) (from road) doblar (b) (switch off) apagarse*

■ **turn on** [1] [v + o + adv, v + adv + o] (a) ⟨light/television/oven⟩ encender*, prender (AmL); ⟨faucet⟩ abrir* (b) (excite) (colloq) gustar; (sexually) excitar

  [2] [v + prep + o] (attack) atacar*

■ **turn out** [1] [v + o + adv, v + adv + o] (a) (switch off) ⟨light⟩ apagar* (b) (empty) ⟨pockets/ cupboard⟩ vaciar*

  [2] [v + adv + o] (produce) sacar*

  [3] [v + o + adv, v + adv + o] (force to leave) echar

  [4] [v + adv] (a) (attend): several thousand ~ed out to welcome the Pope varios miles de personas acudieron or fueron/vinieron a recibir al Papa (b) (result, prove): everything ~ed out well todo salió bien

■ **turn over** [1] [v + o + adv] (a) (flip, reverse) darle* la vuelta a, voltear (AmL exc CS), darle* vuelta (CS); ⟨soil⟩ remover*; ⟨idea⟩ darle* vueltas a (b) (Auto) ⟨engine⟩ hacer* funcionar

  [2] [v + o + adv, v + adv + o] (hand over) entregar*

  [3] [v + adv + o] ⟨page⟩ pasar, volver*, dar* vuelta (CS)

  [4] [v + adv] (onto other side) darse* la vuelta, darse* vuelta (CS); ⟨car⟩ volcarse*

■ **turn round** (esp BrE) ▶ TURN AROUND

■ **turn up** [1] [v + o + adv, v + adv + o] (a) ⟨collar⟩ levantarse, subirse (b) (shorten) ⟨trousers⟩ acortar; ⟨hem⟩ subir (c) (increase) ⟨oven/volume⟩ subir; ⟨radio⟩ subir el volumen de

  [2] [v + adv] (colloq) (a) (be found) «sth lost» aparecer* (b) (arrive) (BrE) llegar*; she didn't ~ up no apareció

turn: ~**about,** ~**around** n giro m, cambio m; ~**coat** n renegado, -da m,f

turned-up /'tɜːrnd'ʌp ‖ 'tɜːnd'ʌp/ adj ⟨nose⟩ respingón, respingado (AmL)

turning /'tɜːrnɪŋ ‖ 'tɜːnɪŋ/ n (in town) bocacalle f; we've missed the ~ nos hemos pasado la calle (or carretera etc)

turning point n momento m decisivo or crucial

turnip /'tɜːrnəp ‖ 'tɜːnɪp/ n nabo m

turn: ~**out** n (at election) número m de votantes; (at public spectacle) número m de asistentes;

~**over** n [1] (a) (volume of business, sales) facturación f (b) (of stock) rotación f (c) (of staff) movimiento m [2] (Culin) empanada f (esp AmL), empanadilla f (esp Esp); ~**pike** n (AmE) autopista f de peaje or (Méx) de cuota; ~ **signal** n (AmE) intermitente m direccional f (Col, Méx), señalizador m (de viraje) (Chi); ~**stile** n torniquete m; ~**table** n (Audio) (platter) plato m; (deck) platina f, tornamesa f or m (AmL); ~**up** n (a) (hem) dobladillo m (b) (on trousers) (BrE) vuelta f or (RPl) botamanga f or (Chi) bastilla f or (Méx) valenciana f

turpentine /'tɜːrpəntaɪn ‖ 'tɜːpəntaɪn/ n aguarrás m, trementina f

turquoise /'tɜːrkwɔɪz ‖ 'tɜːkwɔɪz/ adj (azul) turquesa adj inv

turret /'tɜːrət ‖ 'tʌrɪt/ n torrecilla f

turtle /'tɜːrtl ‖ 'tɜːtl/ n (a) (marine reptile) tortuga f marina or de mar (b) (AmE) (tortoise) tortuga f

turtleneck /'tɜːrtlnek ‖ 'tɜːtlnek/ n (a) ~ (collar) cuello m alto (b) ~ (sweater) suéter m de cuello vuelto

turves /tɜːrvz ‖ tɜːvz/ pl of TURF[1]

tusk /tʌsk/ n colmillo m

tussle /'tʌsəl/ n pelea f, lucha f

tut /tʌt/ or **-tt-** chasquear la lengua

tutor /'tuːtər ‖ 'tjuːtə(r)/ n profesor, -sora m,f particular

tutorial /tuːˈtɔːriəl ‖ tjuːˈtɔːriəl/ n: clase individual o con un pequeño número de estudiantes

tutu /'tuːtuː/ n (pl ~s) tutú m

tuxedo /tʌkˈsiːdəʊ/ n (pl **-dos** or **-does**) (AmE) esmoquin m, smoking m

TV n (= **television**) televisión f, tele f (fam), TV f

twang /twæŋ/ n (of guitar) tañido m; (of voice, accent): his voice has a nasal ~ tiene la voz gangosa

tweak /twiːk/ vt pellizcar* (retorciendo)

twee /twiː/ adj (BrE) cursi

tweed /twiːd/ n (Tex) tweed m

tweet /twiːt/ vi piar*, gorjear

tweezers /'twiːzərz ‖ 'twiːzəz/ pl n pinza(s) f(pl)

twelfth[1] /twelfθ/ adj duodécimo

twelfth[2] adv en duodécimo lugar

twelfth[3] n (Math) doceavo m; (part) doceava parte f

Twelfth Night n Noche f de Reyes

twelve /twelv/ adj/n doce adj inv/m; ~ (o'clock) midnight/noon las doce de la noche/del mediodía; see also FOUR[1]

twentieth[1] /'twentiəθ/ adj vigésimo

twentieth[2] adv en vigésimo lugar

twentieth[3] n (Math) veinteavo m; (part) veinteava or vigésima parte f

twenty /'twenti/ adj/n veinte adj inv/m; see also FOUR[1]

twenty-first[1] /'twenti'fɜːrst ‖ ,twenti'fɜːst/ adj vigesimoprimero

twenty-first[2] adv en vigesimoprimer lugar

twice /twaɪs/ adv dos veces; ~ a year dos veces por año; to think ~ pensarlo* dos veces; ~ three is six dos por tres es (igual a) seis; I've got ~ as many as you yo tengo el doble que tú

twiddle /'twɪdl/ vt (hacer*) girar   ⋯⟫

■ ~ *vi* **to** ~ **with** sth juguetear CON algo

twig /twɪg/ *n* ramita *f*

twilight /'twaɪlaɪt/ *n* **(a)** (dusk) crepúsculo *m* **(b)** (half-light) penumbra *f* **(c)** (period of decline) (liter) crepúsculo *m* (liter)

twin¹ /twɪn/ *n* mellizo, -za *m,f*, gemelo, -la *m,f* (esp Esp); **identical** ~**s** gemelos idénticos *or* (téc) univitelinos, gemelos (AmL)

twin² *adj* **(a)** ‹brother/sister› mellizo, gemelo (esp Esp) **(b)** (paired): ~ **beds** camas *fpl* gemelas

twin³ *vt* **-nn-** (BrE) (*usu pass*) **to be** ~**ned with** sth estar* hermanado CON algo

twine¹ /twaɪn/ *n* cordel *m*, bramante *m* (Esp), cáñamo *m* (Andes), mecate *m* (AmC, Méx, Ven)

twine² *vi* **to** ~ **around** sth enroscarse* ALREDEDOR DE algo

twinge /twɪndʒ/ *n* (of pain) punzada *f*, puntada *f* (CS); (of remorse) puntada *f*

twinkle¹ /'twɪŋkəl/ *n* **(a)** (of lights, stars) centelleo *m*, titilar *m* **(b)** (in eye) brillo *m*

twinkle² *vi* **(a)** ‹‹light/star›› titilar, centellear **(b)** ‹‹eyes›› brillar

twinkling /'twɪŋklɪŋ/ *n*: **in the** ~ **of an eye** en un abrir y cerrar de ojos

twirl /twɜːrl ‖ twɜːl/ *vt* ‹cane/baton› (hacer*) girar

■ ~ *vi* ‹‹baton›› girar; **to** ~ **around** girar

twist¹ /twɪst/ *vt* **1** **(a)** (screw, coil) retorcer*; **to** ~ sth **around** sth enrollar *or* enroscar* algo ALREDEDOR DE algo **(b)** (turn) ‹handle/knob› girar **2** **(a)** (distort) retorcer* **(b)** (sprain) torcer* **(c)** (alter, pervert) ‹words› tergiversar; ‹meaning› torcer*

■ ~ *vi* **(a)** (wind, coil) ‹‹rope/wire›› enrollarse, enroscarse*; ‹‹road/river›› serpentear **(b)** (turn, rotate) girar

twist² *n* **1** **(a)** (bend — in wire, rope) vuelta *f*, onda *f*; (— in road) recodo *m*, vuelta *f* **(b)** (turning movement) giro *m* **(c)** **a** ~ **of lemon** una rodajita de limón ‹retorcida› **2** (in story, events) giro *m* inesperado **3** (dance) twist *m*

twisted /'twɪstɪd ‖ 'twɪstɪd/ *adj* retorcido

twister /'twɪstər ‖ 'twɪstə(r)/ *n* (AmE colloq) tornado *m*

twit /twɪt/ *n* (BrE colloq) imbécil *mf*

twitch¹ /twɪtʃ/ *vi* ‹tail/nose› moverse*

twitch² *n* tic *m*

twitter /'twɪtər ‖ 'twɪtə(r)/ *vi* **(a)** ‹‹birds›› gorjear **(b)** ‹‹person›› parlotear, cotorrear (fam)

two¹ /tuː/ *n* dos *m*; ~ **by** ~ (liter) de dos en dos, de a dos (AmL); **to put** ~ **and** ~ **together** atar cabos; *see also* FOUR¹

two² *adj* dos *adj inv*

two: ~**-bit** *adj* (AmE) (*before n*) (colloq) de tres al cuarto (fam); ~**-dimensional** /'tuː.də'mentʃnəl, -daɪ- ‖,tuː.dɪ'menʃən̩l, -daɪ-/ *adj* bidimensional; ~**-edged** /'tuː'edʒd/ *adj* de doble filo; ~**-faced** /'tuː'feɪst/ *adj* (colloq) falso, doble (Andes, Ven fam); ~**fold** *adj/adv* ▶ -FOLD; ~**pence** /'tʌpəns/ *n* dos peniques *mpl*; ~**-piece** *adj* ‹swimsuit› de dos piezas; ~**-piece suit** traje *m or* (Col) vestido *m* de dos piezas, ambo *m* (CS); ~**-seater** /'tuː'siːtər ‖,tuː'siːtə(r)/ *n* biplaza

twosome /'tuːsəm/ *n* (pair) pareja *f*

two: ~**-time** *vt* (colloq) (be unfaithful to) ponerle* *or* meterle los cuernos a (fam); (double-cross) engañar; ~**-tone** *adj* de dos tonos; ~**-way** /'tuː'weɪ/ *adj* ‹traffic/street› de doble sentido *or* dirección; ‹agreement› bilateral; ~**-way radio** aparato *m* emisor y receptor

TX = **Texas**

tycoon /taɪ'kuːn/ *n* magnate *mf*

tympani /'tɪmpəni/ *pl n* timbales *mpl*

type¹ /taɪp/ *n* **1** **(a)** (sort, kind) tipo *m*; **it's a** ~ **of ...** (in descriptions, definitions) es una especie de ... **(b)** (typical example) tipo *m*, ejemplo *m* típico; (stereotype) estereotipo *m* **2** (Print) (characters) tipo *m* (de imprenta)

type² *vt/i* escribir* a máquina, tipear (AmS)

type: ~**cast** *vt* (*past & past p* **-cast**) ‹actor› encasillar (en cierto tipo de papel); ~**face** *n* tipo *m* (de imprenta), (tipo *m* de) caracteres *mpl*, (tipo *m* de) letra *f*; ~**script** *n* texto *m* mecanografiado, manuscrito *m* (de una obra, novela etc); ~**set** *vt* (*pres p* **-setting**; *past & past p* **-set**) componer*; ~**setter** /'taɪpsetər ‖ 'taɪpsetə(r)/ *n* (person) cajista *mf*, componedor, -dora *m,f*; ~**write** (*past* **-wrote**; *past p* **-written**) *vt* (*usu pass*) escribir* a máquina, mecanografiar*; ~**writer** *n* máquina *f* de escribir

typhoid (fever) /'taɪfɔɪd/ *n* (fiebre *f*) tifoidea

7**typhoon** /'taɪ'fuːn/ *n* tifón *m*

typical /'tɪpɪkəl/ *adj* típico

typically /'tɪpɪkli/ *adv* típicamente

typify /'tɪpəfaɪ ‖ 'tɪpɪfaɪ/ *vt* **-fies, -fying, -fied** tipificar*

typing /'taɪpɪŋ/ *n* mecanografía *f*; (before n) ‹error› de máquina; ‹lesson› de mecanografía

typist /'taɪpəst ‖ 'taɪpɪst/ *n* mecanógrafo, -fa *m,f*, dactilógrafo, -fa *m,f*

typography /taɪ'pɒ:grəfi ‖ taɪ'pɒgrəfi/ *n* tipografía *f*

tyrannical /tə'rænɪkəl ‖ tɪ'rænɪkəl/ *adj* tiránico

tyranny /'tɪrəni/ *n* tiranía *f*

tyrant /'taɪrənt/ *n* tirano, -na *m,f*

tyre /taɪr ‖ 'taɪə(r)/ *n* (BrE) ▶ TIRE²

U u

U, u /ju:/ *n* U, u *f*

U (in UK) (Cin) (= **universal**) apta para todo público (AmL), todos los públicos (Esp)

U, u /ju:/ *n* U, u *f*

ubiquitous /ju:ˈbɪkwətəs ‖ju:ˈbɪkwɪtəs/ *adj* omnipresente (frml), ubicuo (liter)

udder /ˈʌdər ‖ˈʌdə(r)/ *n* ubre *f*

UFO *n* (= **unidentified flying object**) ovni *m*, OVNI *m*

Uganda /ju:ˈɡændə/ *n* Uganda *f*

Ugandan /ju:ˈɡændən/ *adj* ugandés

ugly /ˈʌɡli/ *adj* **uglier, ugliest** feo

UHT *adj* (BrE) (= **ultra high temperature**) UHT, UAT (AmL), uperizado (Esp)

UK *n* (= **United Kingdom**) RU *m*

Ukraine /ju:ˈkreɪn/ *n* Ucrania *f*

Ukrainian¹ /ju:ˈkreɪniən/ *adj* ucraniano, ucranio

Ukrainian² *n* **(a)** (person) ucraniano, -na *m,f*, ucranio, -nia *m,f* **(b)** (language) ucraniano *m*, ucranio *m*

ulcer /ˈʌlsər ‖ˈʌlsə(r)/ *n* (internal) úlcera *f*; (external) llaga *f*; **a mouth ~** una llaga en la boca

ulterior /ʌlˈtɪriər ‖ʌlˈtɪəriə(r)/ *adj* oculto; **~ motive** segunda intención *f*, motivo *m* oculto

ultimata /ˈʌltəˈmeɪtə ‖ˌʌltɪˈmeɪtə/ *pl of* ULTIMATUM

ultimate¹ /ˈʌltəmət ‖ˈʌltɪmət/ *adj* **1** (eventual) ⟨aim/destination⟩ final **2** **(a)** (utmost, supreme) ⟨sacrifice⟩ máximo **(b)** (most sophisticated) (journ): **the ~ sound system** lo último en sistemas de sonido, el no va más en sistemas de sonido (fam)

ultimate² *n*: **the ~ in sth** lo último en algo, el no va más en algo (fam)

ultimately /ˈʌltəmətli ‖ˈʌltɪmətli/ *adv* **(a)** (finally) en última instancia **(b)** (in the long run) a la larga

ultimatum /ˈʌltəˈmeɪtəm ‖ˌʌltɪˈmeɪtəm/ *n* (*pl* **-tums** *or* **-ta**) ultimátum *m*

ultra- /ˈʌltrə/ *pref* ultra-, super- (fam)

ultrasonic /ˈʌltrəˈsɑːnɪk ‖ˌʌltrəˈsɒnɪk/ *adj* ultrasónico

ultrasound /ˈʌltrəsaʊnd/ *n* **(a)** (Phys) ultrasonido *m* **(b)** (Med) ecografía *f*

ultraviolet /ˈʌltrəˈvaɪələt/ *adj* ultravioleta *adj inv*

umbilical cord /əmˈbɪlɪkəl ‖ʌmˈbɪlɪkəl/ *n* cordón *m* umbilical

umbrage /ˈʌmbrɪdʒ/ *n*: **to take ~** (AT sth) ofenderse *or* sentirse* agraviado (POR algo)

umbrella /ʌmˈbrelə/ *n* (*pl* **-las**) paraguas *m*

umpire /ˈʌmpaɪr ‖ˈʌmpaɪə(r)/ *n* árbitro, -tra *m,f*, (in baseball) umpire *mf*

umpteen /ˈʌmpˈtiːn/ *adj* (colloq) tropecientos (fam), miles *or* un millón de

umpteenth /ˈʌmpˈtiːnθ/ *adj* (colloq) enésimo; **for the ~ time** por enésima vez

un- /ʌn/ *pref* in-, des-, no, sin, poco; *see individual words*

UN *n* (= **United Nations**) ONU *f*

unable /ʌnˈeɪbəl/ *adj* (pred) **to be ~ to + INF** no poder* + INF

unabridged /ˈʌnəˈbrɪdʒd/ *adj* íntegro

unacceptable /ˈʌnəkˈseptəbəl/ *adj* ⟨conduct/ standard⟩ inaceptable, inadmisible; ⟨terms/ conditions⟩ inadmisible

unaccompanied /ˈʌnəˈkʌmpənid/ *adj* **(a)** ⟨luggage⟩ no acompañado; ⟨person⟩ solo **(b)** (Mus) ⟨singing⟩ sin acompañamiento; ⟨instrument⟩ solo

unaccounted for /ˈʌnəˈkaʊntəd ‖ˌʌnəˈkaʊntɪd/ *adj* (pred): **the rest of the money is ~ ~** no se han dado explicaciones sobre qué sucedió con el resto del dinero; **the others are still ~ ~** los otros siguen su aparecer

unaccustomed /ˈʌnəˈkʌstəmd/ *adj* **(a)** (unusual) desacostumbrado, poco habitual **(b)** (unused) **to be ~ TO sth/-ING** no estar* acostumbrado A algo/+ INF

unadventurous /ˈʌnədˈventʃərəs/ *adj* poco atrevido *or* audaz

unaffected /ˈʌnəˈfektəd ‖ˌʌnəˈfektɪd/ *adj* **(a)** (sincere, natural) ⟨person⟩ natural, sencillo **(b)** (not damaged, hurt) no afectado

unaided /ʌnˈeɪdəd ‖ʌnˈeɪdɪd/ *adj* sin ayuda

unambitious /ˈʌnæmˈbɪʃəs/ *adj* poco ambicioso

unanimous /ju:ˈnænəməs ‖ju:ˈnænɪməs/ *adj* unánime

unanimously /ju:ˈnænəməsli ‖ju:ˈnænɪməsli/ *adv* ⟨vote/state⟩ unánimemente; ⟨elect⟩ por unanimidad

unanswered /ʌnˈænsərd ‖ʌnˈɑːnsəd/ *adj* ⟨question/letter⟩ sin contestar

unappetizing /ʌnˈæpətaɪzɪŋ/ *adj* ⟨dish/smell⟩ poco apetitoso; ⟨prospect⟩ poco apetecible

unappreciative /ˈʌnəˈpriːʃətɪv/ *adj* ⟨person⟩ ingrato, desagradecido

unapproachable /ˈʌnəˈprəʊtʃəbəl/ *adj* ⟨person⟩ inabordable, poco accesible *or* asequible

unarmed /ʌnˈɑːrmd ‖ʌnˈɑːmd/ *adj* ⟨person⟩ desarmado; ⟨combat⟩ sin armas

unassisted /ˈʌnəˈsɪstəd ‖ˌʌnəˈsɪstɪd/ *adj* sin ayuda

unassuming /ˈʌnəˈsuːmɪŋ ‖ˌʌnəˈsjuːmɪŋ/ *adj* sencillo, sin pretensiones

unattached /ˈʌnəˈtætʃt/ *adj* **(a)** (not affiliated) independiente **(b)** (not married) sin ataduras

unattended /ˈʌnəˈtendəd ‖ˌʌnəˈtendɪd/ *adj* (usu pred) **(a)** (unwatched, unsupervised): **to leave sb ~** dejar a algn solo; **don't leave your luggage ~** vigile su equipaje en todo momento **(b)** (not dealt with) desatendido

unattractive /ˈʌnəˈtræktɪv/ *adj* poco atractivo

u

unauthorized /ˌʌnˈɔ:θəraɪzd/ *adj* no autorizado

unavailable /ˌʌnəˈveɪləbəl/ *adj*: that number is ~ ese número está desconectado (*or* averiado *etc*); he is ~ for comment no desea hacer ningún comentario

unavoidable /ˌʌnəˈvɔɪdəbəl/ *adj* inevitable

unavoidably /ˌʌnəˈvɔɪdəbli/ *adv*: I was ~ delayed no pude evitar llegar retrasado

unaware /ˌʌnəˈwer ‖ˌʌnəˈweə(r)/ *adj* (a) (not conscious) (*pred*) to be ~ OF sth no ser* consciente DE algo (b) (naive): politically ~ sin conciencia política

unawares /ˌʌnəˈwerz ‖ˌʌnəˈweəz/ *adv*: to catch *o* take sb ~ agarrar *or* (esp Esp) coger* a algn desprevenido

unbalanced /ˌʌnˈbælənst/ *adj* (a) ⟨diet/composition⟩ desequilibrado (b) (mentally) desequilibrado, trastornado

unbearable /ˌʌnˈberəbəl ‖ˌʌnˈbeərəbəl/ *adj* insoportable, inaguantable

unbeatable /ˌʌnˈbi:təbəl/ *adj* ⟨team⟩ invencible; ⟨quality/value⟩ insuperable; ⟨price⟩ imbatible

unbeaten /ˌʌnˈbi:tn̩/ *adj* ⟨champion/army⟩ invicto; ⟨record⟩ insuperado

unbeknown /ˌʌnbɪˈnəʊn/, **unbeknownst** /-ˈnəʊnst/ *adv* (liter): ~ to me/her sin saberlo yo/ella

unbelievable /ˌʌnbəˈli:vəbəl ‖ˌʌnbɪˈli:vəbəl/ *adj* increíble

unbelievably /ˌʌnbəˈli:vəbli ‖ˌʌnbɪˈli:vəbli/ *adv* increíblemente

unbelieving /ˌʌnbəˈli:vɪŋ ‖ˌʌnbɪˈli:vɪŋ/ *adj* ⟨smile/look⟩ de incredulidad

unbending /ˌʌnˈbendɪŋ/ *adj* ⟨person/attitude⟩ inflexible; ⟨determination⟩ firme

unbiased /ˌʌnˈbaɪəst/ *adj* imparcial, objetivo

unblock /ˌʌnˈblɒ:k ‖ˌʌnˈblɒk/ *vt* desatascar*, destapar (AmL)

unbolt /ˌʌnˈbəʊlt/ *vt* ⟨gate/door⟩ descorrer el pestillo *or* cerrojo de

unborn /ˌʌnˈbɔ:rn ‖ˌʌnˈbɔ:n/ *adj* ⟨child⟩ que todavía no ha nacido

unbreakable /ˌʌnˈbreɪkəbəl/ *adj* irrompible

unbridled /ˌʌnˈbraɪdl̩d/ *adj* desenfrenado

unbroken /ˌʌnˈbrəʊkən/ *adj* intacto, en perfecto estado; ⟨silence/run⟩ ininterrumpido

unbuckle /ˌʌnˈbʌkəl/ *vt* desabrochar

unbutton /ˌʌnˈbʌtn̩/ *vt* desabotonar, desabrochar

uncalled-for /ˌʌnˈkɔ:ldfɔ:r ‖ˌʌnˈkɔ:ldfɔ:(r)/ *adj* ⟨criticism/remark⟩ fuera de lugar

uncanny /ˌʌnˈkæni/ *adj* raro, extraño

uncaring /ˌʌnˈkerɪŋ ‖ˌʌnˈkeərɪŋ/ *adj* indiferente

unceremonious /ˌʌnˈserəˈməʊniəs ‖ˌʌnˌserɪˈməʊniəs/ *adj* brusco, poco ceremonioso

uncertain /ˌʌnˈsɜ:rtn̩ ‖ˌʌnˈsɜ:tn̩/ *adj* **1** (a) (unsure) (*pred*) to be ~ ABOUT/OF sth no estar* seguro DE algo (b) (hesitant) vacilante **2** ⟨prospects/future⟩ incierto **3** (vague): in no ~ terms muy claramente, inequívocamente

uncertainty /ˌʌnˈsɜ:rtn̩ti ‖ˌʌnˈsɜ:tn̩ti/ *n* incertidumbre *f*

unchanged /ˌʌnˈtʃeɪndʒd/ *adj* (*usu pred*): she was quite ~ no había cambiado para nada; the ceremony has remained ~ for centuries la ceremonia se ha celebrado de la misma forma durante siglos

uncharacteristic /ˌʌnˈkærəktəˈrɪstɪk/ *adj* desacostumbrado, inusitado

uncharitable /ˌʌnˈtʃærətəbəl ‖ˌʌnˈtʃærɪtəbəl/ *adj* ⟨act/remark⟩ poco caritativo

unchecked /ˌʌnˈtʃekt/ *adj* libre, sin obstáculos

uncivilized /ˌʌnˈsɪvəlaɪzd ‖ˌʌnˈsɪvɪlaɪzd/ *adj* incivilizado

uncle /ˈʌŋkəl/ *n* tío *m*

unclean /ˌʌnˈkli:n/ *adj* impuro

unclear /ˌʌnˈklɪr ‖ˌʌnˈklɪə(r)/ *adj* poco claro, confuso; he was ~ about his reasons for doing it no dio una explicación muy clara de sus motivos

uncoil /ˌʌnˈkɔɪl/ *vi* desenroscarse*

uncomfortable /ˌʌnˈkʌmfərtəbəl ‖ˌʌnˈkʌmftəbəl/ *adj* incómodo

uncommon /ˌʌnˈkɑ:mən ‖ˌʌnˈkɒmən/ *adj* poco común *or* frecuente

uncommunicative /ˌʌnkəˈmju:nəkeɪtɪv ‖ˌʌnkəˈmju:nɪkətɪv/ *adj* poco comunicativo

uncomplaining /ˌʌnkəmˈpleɪnɪŋ/ *adj* resignado

uncomplicated /ˌʌnˈkɑ:mpləkeɪtəd ‖ˌʌnˈkɒmplɪkeɪtɪd/ *adj* sin complicaciones; ⟨character/style⟩ poco complicado

uncompromising /ˌʌnˈkɑ:mprəmaɪzɪŋ ‖ˌʌnˈkɒmprəmaɪzɪŋ/ *adj* inflexible, intransigente

unconcerned /ˌʌnkənˈsɜ:rnd ‖ˌʌnkənˈsɜ:nd/ *adj* indiferente

unconditional /ˌʌnkənˈdɪʃn̩əl ‖ˌʌnkənˈdɪʃənl̩/ *adj* incondicional

unconnected /ˌʌnkəˈnektəd ‖ˌʌnkəˈnektɪd/ *adj* (unrelated) sin conexión; these incidents are completely ~ estos incidentes no guardan ninguna relación (entre sí)

unconscious[1] /ˌʌnˈkɑ:ntʃəs ‖ˌʌnˈkɒnʃəs/ *adj* **1** (Med) inconsciente **2** (unaware) (*pred*) to be ~ OF sth no ser* consciente DE algo **3** (Psych) inconsciente

unconscious[2] *n* the ~ el inconsciente

unconsciously /ˌʌnˈkɑ:ntʃəsli ‖ˌʌnˈkɒnʃəsli/ *adv* inconscientemente

uncontested /ˌʌnkənˈtestəd ‖ˌʌnkənˈtestɪd/ *adj* ⟨will⟩ no impugnado; ⟨leader⟩ indiscutible

uncontrollable /ˌʌnkənˈtrəʊləbəl/ *adj* ⟨trembling⟩ incontrolable; ⟨urge⟩ irresistible, irrefrenable; ⟨laughter⟩ incontenible

uncontrolled /ˌʌnkənˈtrəʊld/ *adj* incontrolado

unconventional /ˌʌnkənˈventʃn̩əl ‖ˌʌnkənˈvenʃənl̩/ *adj* poco convencional

unconvinced /ˌʌnkənˈvɪnst/ *adj*: I'm still ~ aún no estoy muy convencida

unconvincing /ˌʌnkənˈvɪnsɪŋ/ *adj* poco convincente

uncoordinated /ˌʌnkəʊˈɔ:rdn̩eɪtəd ‖ˌʌnkəʊˈɔ:dmeɪtɪd/ *adj* ⟨person⟩ falto de coordinación; ⟨movements⟩ no coordinado

uncork /ˌʌnˈkɔ:rk ‖ˌʌnˈkɔ:k/ *vt* descorchar

uncorroborated /ˈʌnkəˈrɑːbəreɪtəd ‖ˌʌnkəˈrɒbəreɪtɪd/ *adj* no confirmado, no corroborado

uncouth /ʌnˈkuːθ/ *adj* zafio, burdo

uncover /ʌnˈkʌvər ‖ʌnˈkʌvə(r)/ *vt* (a) (remove covering of) destapar (b) (expose) ⟨*scandal/plot*⟩ revelar, sacar* a la luz

unctuous /ˈʌŋktʃuəs ‖ˈʌŋktjuəs/ *adj* empalagoso

uncultivated /ʌnˈkʌltəveɪtəd ‖ʌnˈkʌltɪveɪtɪd/ *adj* ⟨*land/mind*⟩ sin cultivar

uncurl /ʌnˈkɜːrl ‖ʌnˈkɜːl/ *vt* desenrollar
■ ~ *vi* «*snake*» desenroscarse*

uncut /ʌnˈkʌt/ *adj* (a) ⟨*grass/hedge*⟩ sin cortar (b) ⟨*diamond/gem*⟩ sin tallar, en bruto; ⟨*stone/marble*⟩ sin labrar [2] (unabridged) íntegro, completo

undamaged /ʌnˈdæmɪdʒd/ *adj* intacto

undaunted /ʌnˈdɔːntəd ‖ʌnˈdɔːntɪd/ *adj* impertérrito

undecided /ʌndɪˈsaɪdəd ‖ʌndɪˈsaɪdɪd/ *adj* (a) (wavering) (*usu pred*) indeciso (b) ⟨*matter*⟩ pendiente, no resuelto

undefeated /ʌndɪˈfiːtəd ‖ʌndɪˈfiːtɪd/ *adj* invicto

undemanding /ʌndɪˈmændɪŋ ‖ʌndɪˈmɑːndɪŋ/ *adj* ⟨*job*⟩ cómodo, que exige poco; ⟨*person*⟩ poco exigente

undeniable /ʌndɪˈnaɪəbəl/ *adj* innegable

undeniably /ʌndɪˈnaɪəbli/ *adv* sin lugar a dudas

under¹ /ˈʌndər ‖ˈʌndə(r)/ *prep* (a) (beneath) debajo de, abajo de (AmL) (b) (less than) menos de (c) ⟨*name/heading*⟩ bajo (d) ⟨*government/authority*⟩ bajo; **he has 20 people ~ him** tiene 20 personas a su mando (e) (according to) según

under² *adv* [1] (less) menos; **it will cost $10 or ~** costará 10 dólares como mucho [2] (under water): **they pushed him ~** lo empujaron debajo del agua

under- /ˈʌndər/ *pref* (a) (below, lower): **the ~mentioned** los abajo mencionados (b) (less than proper): **they are ~represented on the committee** no tienen la representación que les corresponde en la comisión (c) (of lesser rank) sub-; **~manager** subgerente *m*

under: **~age** /ˈʌndərˈeɪdʒ/ *adj* (*before n*) ⟨*person*⟩ menor de edad; **~arm** *adj* (*before n*) (Sport) sin levantar el brazo por encima del hombro; **~carriage** *n* tren *m* de aterrizaje; **~charge** /ˈʌndərˈtʃɑːrdʒ ‖ˌʌndəˈtʃɑːdʒ/ *vt* cobrarle de menos a; **~coat**, (AmE also) **~coating** *n* [1] (a) (paint) pintura *f* base (b) (coating) primera mano *f* de pintura; [2] (AmE Auto) tratamiento *m* anticorrosivo del chasis; **~cover** /ˈʌndərˈkʌvər ‖ˌʌndəˈkʌvə(r)/ *adj* secreto; **~current** *n* (a) (of discontent) trasfondo *m*, corriente *f* subyacente (b) (of water) contracorriente *f*; **~cut** /ˈʌndərˈkʌt ‖ˌʌndəˈkʌt/ *vt* (*pres p* **-cutting**; *past & past p* **-cut**) ⟨*competitor*⟩ vender más barato que; **~developed** /ˌʌndərdɪˈveləpt ‖ˌʌndədɪˈveləpt/ *adj* poco desarrollado; ⟨*nation*⟩ subdesarrollado; **~done** /ˈʌndərˈdʌn ‖ˌʌndəˈdʌn/ *adj* ⟨*meat*⟩ poco cocido, poco hecho (Esp); **~estimate** /ˈʌndərˈestəmeɪt ‖ˌʌndərˈestɪmeɪt/ *vt* (a) (guess too low): **they ~estimated the cost** calcularon el costo en menos de lo que correspondía (b)

(underrate) subestimar; **~fed** /ˈʌndərˈfed ‖ˌʌndəˈfed/ *adj* subalimentado; **~foot** /ˈʌndərˈfut ‖ˌʌndəˈfut/ *adv* debajo de los pies; **~go** /ˈʌndərˈgəu ‖ˌʌndəˈgəu/ *vt* (*3rd pers sing pres* **-goes**; *pres p* **-going**; *past* **-went**; *past p* **-gone**) ⟨*change/hardship*⟩ sufrir; **he is ~going treatment** está en tratamiento; **~graduate** /ˈʌndərˈgrædʒuət ‖ˌʌndəˈgrædʒuət/ *n* estudiante universitario, -ria *m,f* (de licenciatura); (*before n*) ⟨*course/student*⟩ universitario

underground¹ /ˈʌndərgraund ‖ˈʌndəgraund/ *adj* (*before n*) subterráneo; ⟨*organization*⟩ clandestino

underground² /ˈʌndərˈgraund ‖ˌʌndəˈgraund/ *adv* bajo tierra

underground³ /ˈʌndərˈgraund ‖ˌʌndəˈgraund/ *n* [1] *also* **Underground** (BrE Transp) metro *m*, subterráneo *m* (RPl) [2] (secret organization) movimiento *m* clandestino

under: **~growth** *n* maleza *f*, monte *m* bajo; **~hand** /ˈʌndərˈhænd ‖ˌʌndəˈhænd/, **~handed** /ˈʌndərˈhændəd ‖ˌʌndəˈhændɪd/ *adj* ⟨*person*⟩ solapado; ⟨*method/dealings*⟩ poco limpio; **~lie** /ˈʌndərˈlaɪ ‖ˌʌndəˈlaɪ/ *vt* (*3rd pers sing pres* **-lies**; *pres p* **-lying**; *past* **-lay**; *past p* **-lain**) subyacer* a; **~line** *vt* subrayar; **~lying** /ˈʌndərˈlaɪɪŋ ‖ˌʌndəˈlaɪɪŋ/ *adj* (*before n*) subyacente; **~manned** /ˈʌndərˈmænd ‖ˌʌndəˈmænd/ *adj* ⟨*factory*⟩ con personal *or* con mano de obra insuficiente; **~mine** /ˈʌndərˈmaɪn ‖ˌʌndəˈmaɪn/ *vt* ⟨*health/strength*⟩ minar; ⟨*authority*⟩ quitar

underneath¹ /ˈʌndərˈniːθ ‖ˌʌndəˈniːθ/ *prep* debajo de, abajo de (AmL)

underneath² *adv* debajo, abajo; ⟨*dig/crawl*⟩ por debajo, por abajo

under: **~nourished** /ˈʌndərˈnɜːrɪʃt ‖ˌʌndəˈnʌrɪʃt/ *adj* desnutrido; **~paid** /ˈʌndərˈpeɪd ‖ˌʌndəˈpeɪd/ *adj* mal pagado; **~pants** *pl n* calzoncillos *mpl*, calzones *mpl* (Méx); **~pass** *n* (for traffic) paso *m* inferior; pedestrian **~pass** pasaje *m* subterráneo; **~privileged** /ˈʌndərˈprɪvəlɪdʒd ‖ˌʌndəˈprɪvəlɪdʒd/ *adj* desfavorecido; **~rate** /ˈʌndərˈreɪt ‖ˌʌndəˈreɪt/ *vt* (a) ⟨*ability/opponent*⟩ subestimar (b) ⟨*rated past p* ⟨*writer/play*⟩ no debidamente apreciado *or* valorado; **~secretary** /ˈʌndərˈsekrəteri ‖ˌʌndəˈsekrətri/ *n* subsecretario, -ria *m,f*; **~sell** *vt* (*past & past p* **-sold**) ⟨*competitor*⟩ vender más barato que; **~shirt** *n* (AmE) camiseta *f* (interior); **~shorts** *pl n* (AmE) calzoncillos *mpl* (en forma de pantalón corto); **~side** *n* parte *f* inferior *or* de abajo; **~skirt** *n* enagua(s) *f(pl)*, viso *m*, fondo *m* (Méx); **~sold** /ˈʌndərˈsəuld ‖ˌʌndəˈsəuld/ *past and past p of* UNDERSELL; **~staffed** /ˈʌndərˈstæft ‖ˌʌndəˈstɑːft/ *adj*: **to be ~staffed** estar* muy escaso *or* falto de personal

understand /ˈʌndərˈstænd ‖ˌʌndəˈstænd/ (*past & past p* **-stood**) *vt* [1] (a) (grasp meaning of) entender* (b) (sympathize, empathize with) comprender, entender* [2] (believe, infer): **I ~ you play tennis** tengo entendido que juega al tenis
■ ~ *vi* entender*, comprender

understandable /ˈʌndərˈstændəbəl ‖ˌʌndəˈstændəbəl/ *adj* comprensible

understanding¹ /ˈʌndərˈstændɪŋ ‖ˌʌndəˈstændɪŋ/ *n* [1] (a) (grasp) entendimiento ⋯⇨

m **(b)** (interpretation) interpretación *f* **(c)** (sympathy) comprensión *f* **2** (agreement, arrangement) acuerdo *m*; **we had an ~ that ...** habíamos convenido que ... **3 on the ~ that** bien entendido que

understanding² *adj* comprensivo

understatement /'ʌndər'steɪtmənt ‖ˌʌndəstɛɪtmənt/ *n*: **to say it wasn't well attended is an ~** decir que no estuvo muy concurrido es quedarse corto

understood¹ /'ʌndər'stʊd ‖ˌʌndəstʊd/ *past & past p of* UNDERSTAND

understood² *adj* (assumed): **expenses will be paid, that's ~** se sobreentiende que nos (*or* les *etc*) pagarán los gastos

under: **~study** *n* suplente *mf*, sobresaliente *mf*; **~take** /'ʌndər'teɪk ‖ˌʌndə'teɪk/ *vt* (*past* **-took**; *past p* **-taken**) **(a)** ⟨responsibility⟩ asumir; ⟨obligation⟩ contraer*; ⟨task⟩ emprender **(b) to ~take to +** INF comprometerse A + INF; **~taker** /'ʌndər'teɪkər ‖ˌʌndəˌteɪkə(r)/ *n* ▶ MORTICIAN; **~taking** /'ʌndər'teɪkɪŋ ‖ˌʌndə'teɪkɪŋ/ *n* **(a)** (task) empresa *f*, tarea *f* **(b)** (promise) promesa *f*; **~tone** *n* **(a)** (low voice): **to speak in an ~tone** hablar en voz baja **(b)** (hint) trasfondo *m*; **~took** /'ʌndər'tʊk ‖ˌʌndə'tʊk/ *past of* ~TAKE; **~value** /'ʌndər'vælju: ‖ˌʌndə'vælju:/ *vt* ⟨goods⟩ subvalorar; ⟨person/ skill⟩ subvalorar

underwater¹ /'ʌndər'wɔːtər ‖ˌʌndə'wɔːtə(r)/ *adj* submarino

underwater² *adv* debajo del agua

under: **~wear** *n* ropa *f* interior; **~weight** /'ʌndər'weɪt ‖ˌʌndə'weɪt/ *adj* ⟨person/baby⟩ de peso más bajo que el normal; **~went** /'ʌndər'went ‖ˌʌndə'went/ *past of* UNDERGO; **~world** *n* **(a)** (Myth) **the U~world** el infierno, el averno (liter) **(b)** (criminals): **the ~world** el hampa, los bajos fondos; **~write** /'ʌndər'raɪt ‖ˌʌndə'raɪt/ *vt* (*past* **-wrote**; *past p* **-written**) **(a)** (in insurance) asegurar **(b)** (guarantee financially) ⟨project/venture⟩ financiar

undeserving /'ʌndɪ'zɜːrvɪŋ ‖ˌʌndɪ'zɜːvɪŋ/ *adj* ⟨person⟩ de poco mérito; ⟨cause⟩ poco meritorio

undesirable /'ʌndɪ'zaɪrəbəl ‖ˌʌndɪ'zaɪərəbəl/ *adj* ⟨consequence⟩ no deseado; ⟨person⟩ indeseable

undeveloped /'ʌndɪ'veləpt/ *adj* ⟨resources/ region⟩ sin explotar

undid /'ʌn'dɪd/ *past of* UNDO

undignified /'ʌn'dɪgnəfaɪd ‖ʌn'dɪgnɪfaɪd/ *adj* **(a)** (lacking modesty) indecoroso **(b)** (inappropriate to status) poco digno

undisciplined /'ʌn'dɪsəplənd ‖ʌn'dɪsɪplɪnd/ *adj* indisciplinado

undiscovered /'ʌndɪs'kʌvərd ‖ˌʌndɪs'kʌvəd/ *adj* (not found) no descubierto; (unknown) desconocido

undisguised /'ʌndɪs'gaɪzd/ *adj* manifiesto, abierto

undisputed /'ʌndɪ'spjuːtəd ‖ˌʌndɪ'spjuːtɪd/ *adj* ⟨champion/leader⟩ indiscutido; ⟨facts⟩ innegable

undivided /'ʌndɪ'vaɪdəd ‖ˌʌndɪ'vaɪdɪd/ *adj*: **you have my ~ attention** tienes toda mi atención

undo /'ʌn'duː/ *vt* (*3rd pers sing pres* **-does**; *pres p* **-doing**; *past* **-did**; *past p* **-done**) ⟨button/ jacket⟩ desabrochar; ⟨zipper⟩ abrir*; ⟨knot/parcel⟩ desatar, deshacer*; ⟨shoelaces⟩ desatar, desamarrar (AmL exc RPl)

undone /'ʌn'dʌn/ *adj* (pred) **(a)** (unfastened) desatado, desamarrado (AmL exc RPl) **(b)** (not started) sin empezar; (unfinished) sin terminar

undoubtedly /ʌn'daʊtədli ‖ʌn'daʊtɪdli/ *adv* indudablemente, sin duda

undress /'ʌn'dres/ *vt* desvestir*, desnudar; **to get ~ed** desvestirse*, desnudarse

undue /'ʌn'duː ‖ʌn'djuː/ *adj* (before *n*) excesivo, demasiado

unduly /'ʌn'duːli ‖ʌn'djuːli/ *adv* excesivamente, demasiado

unearth /'ʌn'ɜːrθ ‖ʌn'ɜːθ/ *vt* **(a)** ⟨remains⟩ desenterrar* **(b)** ⟨fact/document⟩ descubrir*

unearthly /'ʌn'ɜːrθli ‖ʌn'ɜːθli/ *adj* **-lier, -liest** sobrenatural; **at this ~ hour** a estas horas (intempestivas)

unease /'ʌn'iːz/ *n* (nervousness) inquietud *f*; (tension, discontent) malestar *m*

uneasy /'ʌn'iːzi/ *adj* **-sier, -siest (a)** (anxious, troubled) inquieto, preocupado **(b)** (awkward, constrained) ⟨laugh/silence⟩ incómodo, molesto

uneconomical /'ʌn'ekə'nɑːmɪkḷ, -'iːkə- ‖ʌnˌiːkə'nɒmɪkəl, -,ek-/ *adj* poco económico

uneducated /'ʌn'edʒəkeɪtəd ‖ʌn'edʒʊkeɪtɪd/ *adj* sin educación, inculto

unemotional /'ʌnɪ'məʊʃṇəl ‖ˌʌnɪ'məʊʃənḷ/ *adj* ⟨person⟩ indiferente; ⟨account/report⟩ objetivo

unemployable /'ʌnɪm'plɔɪəbəl/ *adj* inempleable

unemployed /'ʌnɪm'plɔɪd/ *adj* ⟨person⟩ desempleado, parado (Esp), en paro (Esp), cesante (Chi)

unemployment /'ʌnɪm'plɔɪmənt/ *n* (being out of work) desempleo *m*, paro *m* (Esp), cesantía *f* (Chi); (before *n*) **~ benefit** o (AmE also) **compensation** subsidio *m* de desempleo, paro *m* (Esp), subsidio *m* de cesantía (Chi)

unending /'ʌn'endɪŋ/ *adj* interminable, sin fin

unenthusiastic /'ʌnɪn'θuːzi'æstɪk ‖ˌʌnɪnθjuːzi'æstɪk/ *adj* poco entusiasta

unenviable /'ʌn'enviəbəl/ *adj* nada envidiable

unequal /'ʌn'iːkwəl/ *adj* desigual

UNESCO /juː'neskəʊ/ *n* (no art) (= **United Nations Educational, Scientific and Cultural Organization**) la UNESCO

unethical /ʌn'eθɪkəl/ *adj* inmoral, poco ético

uneven /'ʌn'iːvən/ *adj* **1 (a)** (not straight) torcido **(b)** (not level) ⟨surface⟩ desigual, irregular, disparejo (AmL); ⟨ground⟩ desnivelado, desigual, disparejo (AmL) **2** ⟨color/paint⟩ poco uniforme, disparejo (AmL) **3** (unequal) ⟨widths/lengths/ contest⟩ desigual

---

AmC	América Central	Arg	Argentina
AmL	América Latina	Bol	Bolivia
AmS	América del Sur	Chi	Chile
Andes	Región andina	CS	Cono Sur

Cu	Cuba	Per	Perú
Ec	Ecuador	RPl	Río de la Plata
Esp	España	Ur	Uruguay
Méx	México	Ven	Venezuela

uneventful /ˈʌnɪˈventfəl/ adj ‹journey› sin incidentes; ‹day› tranquilo; ‹life› sin acontecimientos de nota

unexciting /ˈʌnɪkˈsaɪtɪŋ/ adj ‹prospect/job› poco estimulante; ‹food› insulso, poco apetitoso

unexpected /ˈʌnɪkˈspektəd ‖ˌʌnɪkˈspektɪd/ adj ‹reaction/visitor› inesperado; ‹result/delay› imprevisto

unexpectedly /ˈʌnɪkˈspektədli ‖ˌʌnɪkˈspektɪdli/ adv ‹arrive› de improviso; ‹happen› de forma imprevista

unexploded /ˈʌnɪkˈspləʊdəd/ adj sin detonar

unexplored /ˈʌnɪkˈsplɔːrd ‖ˌʌnɪksˈplɔːd/ adj inexplorado

unfailing /ʌnˈfeɪlɪŋ/ adj ‹optimism› indefectible, a toda prueba; ‹interest/support› constante

unfair /ˈʌnˈfer ‖ʌnˈfeə(r)/ adj ‹treatment/ decision› injusto; ‹competition› desleal; ‹dismissal› improcedente, injustificado; **it was ~ of him to blame you** fue injusto que te echara la culpa a ti

unfairly /ˈʌnˈferli ‖ʌnˈfeəli/ adj injustamente

unfaithful /ˈʌnˈfeɪθfəl/ adj ‹spouse/lover› infiel; ‹follower› desleal

unfamiliar /ˈʌnfəˈmɪljər ‖ˌʌnfəˈmɪliə(r)/ adj ‹face/surroundings› desconocido, nuevo

unfashionable /ʌnˈfæʃnəbəl/ adj fuera de moda

unfasten /ʌnˈfæsn̩ ‖ʌnˈfɑːsn̩/ vt ‹seat belt/ button› desabrochar; ‹knot› deshacer*, desatar

unfavorable, (BrE) **unfavourable** /ʌnˈfeɪvrəbəl/ adj desfavorable

unfinished /ʌnˈfɪnɪʃt/ adj sin terminar, inacabado

unfit /ʌnˈfɪt/ adj (a) (unsuitable) ‹mother› inepto, incapaz; **he was ~ for the job** no estaba capacitado para el trabajo; **~ for human consumption** no apto para el consumo (b) (physically): **I'm ~** no estoy en forma, estoy fuera de forma

unflagging /ʌnˈflægɪŋ/ adj ‹energy/ enthusiasm› inagotable; ‹interest› sostenido

unflattering /ʌnˈflætərɪŋ/ adj ‹remark/ description› poco halagüeño; ‹dress› poco favorecedor

unfold /ʌnˈfəʊld/ vt ‹tablecloth/map› desdoblar, extender*; ‹wings› desplegar*
■ ~ vi (a) «flower/leaf» abrirse*; «wings» desplegarse* (b) «story/events» desarrollarse; «scene» extenderse*

unforeseen /ˈʌnfɔːrˈsiːn ‖ˌʌnfɔːˈsiːn/ adj imprevisto

unforgettable /ˈʌnfərˈgetəbəl ‖ˌʌnfəˈgetəbəl/ adj inolvidable

unforgivable /ˈʌnfərˈgɪvəbəl ‖ˌʌnfəˈgɪvəbəl/ adj imperdonable

unfortunate /ʌnˈfɔːrtʃnət ‖ʌnˈfɔːtʃənət/ adj desafortunado; **he has been very ~** ha tenido muy mala suerte

unfortunately /ʌnˈfɔːrtʃnətli ‖ʌnˈfɔːtʃənətli/ adv (indep) lamentablemente, desafortunadamente; (stronger) desgraciadamente, por desgracia

unfounded /ʌnˈfaʊndəd ‖ʌnˈfaʊndɪd/ adj infundado

unfriendly /ʌnˈfrendli/ adj -lier, -liest poco amistoso; (stronger) antipático

unfulfilled /ˈʌnfʊlˈfɪld/ adj ‹ambition/hope› frustrado; ‹prophecy› no cumplido

unfurl /ˈʌnˈfɜːrl ‖ʌnˈfɜːl/ vt desplegar*

unfurnished /ˈʌnˈfɜːrnɪʃt ‖ʌnˈfɜːnɪʃt/ adj sin amueblar

ungainly /ʌnˈgeɪnli/ adj desgarbado

ungracious /ʌnˈgreɪʃəs/ adj descortés

ungrateful /ʌnˈgreɪtfəl/ adj desagradecido, ingrato, malagradecido

unguarded /ˈʌnˈgɑːrdəd ‖ʌnˈgɑːdɪd/ adj (incautious): **in an ~ moment** en un momento de descuido

unhappily /ʌnˈhæpəli ‖ʌnˈhæpɪli/ adv (a) ‹sigh› tristemente, con tristeza (b) (unfortunately) (indep) lamentablemente

unhappiness /ʌnˈhæpinəs ‖ʌnˈhæpɪnɪs/ n infelicidad f; (stronger) desdicha f; (sadness) tristeza f

unhappy /ʌnˈhæpi/ adj -pier, -piest (a) (sad) ‹childhood› infeliz; (stronger) desgraciado, desdichado (b) (worried) (pred): **I was ~ about the children being left alone** me preocupaba or inquietaba que los niños se quedaran solos (c) (discontented) (pred) **to be ~ ABOUT sth** no estar* contento con algo

unharmed /ˈʌnˈhɑːrmd ‖ʌnˈhɑːmd/ adj: **he escaped ~** salió or resultó ileso

unhealthy /ʌnˈhelθi/ adj -thier, -thiest (a) ‹person› de mala salud; ‹complexion› enfermizo; ‹climate› poco saludable, insalubre, malsano (b) ‹interest/obsession› malsano

unheard of /ˈʌnˈhɜːrdɑːv ‖ʌnˈhɜːdɒv/ adj insólito

unhelpful /ʌnˈhelpfəl/ adj ‹assistant/secretary› poco servicial; **he was most ~** no se mostró nada dispuesto a ayudar

unhinge /ʌnˈhɪndʒ/ vt ‹person/mind› trastornar

unhurt /ˈʌnˈhɜːrt ‖ʌnˈhɜːt/ adj ileso; **to escape ~** salir* or resultar ileso

unhygienic /ˈʌnhaɪˈdʒiːnɪk/ adj antihigiénico

UNICEF /ˈjuːnɪsef/ n (no art) (= **United Nations International Children's Emergency Fund**) UNICEF m or f

unicorn /ˈjuːnəkɔːrn ‖ˈjuːnɪkɔːn/ n unicornio m

unidentified /ˈʌnaɪˈdentəfaɪd ‖ˌʌnaɪˈdentɪfaɪd/ adj no identificado; **~ flying object** objeto m volador or (Esp) volante no identificado

unification /ˈjuːnəfəˈkeɪʃən ‖ˌjuːnɪfɪˈkeɪʃən/ n unificación f

uniform¹ /ˈjuːnəfɔːrm ‖ˈjuːnɪfɔːm/ n uniforme m

uniform² adj ‹color/length› uniforme; ‹temperature/speed› constante

uniformity /ˈjuːnəˈfɔːrməti ‖ˌjuːnɪˈfɔːməti/ n uniformidad f

unify /ˈjuːnəfaɪ ‖ˈjuːnɪfaɪ/ vt -fies, -fying, -fied unir

unilateral /ˈjuːnɪˈlætərəl/ adj unilateral

unimaginable /ˈʌnəˈmædʒənəbəl ‖ˌʌnɪˈmædʒɪnəbəl/ adj inimaginable

unimaginative /ˈʌnəˈmædʒənətɪv
‖ˌʌnɪˈmædʒɪnətɪv/ *adj* ⟨*person*⟩ poco imaginativo; ⟨*story/design*⟩ falto de imaginación

unimportant /ˈʌnɪmˈpɔːrtn̩t ‖ˌʌnɪmˈpɔːtn̩t/ *adj* ⟨*matter/detail*⟩ sin importancia

uninhabited /ˈʌnɪnˈhæbətəd ‖ˌʌnɪnˈhæbɪtɪd/ *adj* ⟨*house*⟩ deshabitado; ⟨*region/island*⟩ despoblado

uninhibited /ˈʌnɪnˈhɪbətəd ‖ˌʌnɪnˈhɪbɪtɪd/ *adj* desinhibido, desenfadado

unintelligent /ˈʌnɪnˈteləʒənt ‖ˌʌnɪnˈtelɪdʒənt/ *adj* poco inteligente

unintelligible /ˈʌnɪnˈteləʒəbəl ‖ˌʌnɪnˈtelɪdʒəbəl/ *adj* ininteligible

unintentional /ˈʌnɪnˈtentʃn̩əl ‖ˌʌnɪnˈtenʃənl̩/ *adj* involuntario, no deliberado

unintentionally /ˈʌnɪnˈtentʃn̩əli ‖ˌʌnɪnˈtenʃn̩əli/ *adv* involuntariamente, sin querer

uninterested /ˈʌnˈɪntrəstəd ‖ʌnˈɪntrestɪd/ *adj* indiferente

uninteresting /ˈʌnˈɪntrəstɪŋ/ *adj* ⟨*topic*⟩ sin interés; ⟨*person*⟩ poco interesante

uninvited /ˈʌnɪnˈvaɪtəd ‖ˌʌnɪnˈvaɪtɪd/ *adj*: **they came ~** vinieron sin que nadie los invitara

uninviting /ˈʌnɪnˈvaɪtɪŋ/ *adj* ⟨*appearance*⟩ poco atractivo; ⟨*food*⟩ poco apetitoso

union /ˈjuːnjən/ *n* **1** (act, state) unión *f* **2** (Lab Rel) sindicato *m*, gremio *m* (CS, Per); (*before n*) ⟨*official/movement*⟩ sindical, gremial (CS, Per); **~ card** carné *m* de afiliado **3** (at college, university) asociación *f* or federación *f* de estudiantes

unionize /ˈjuːnjənaɪz / *vt* sindicalizar* (esp AmL), sindicar* (esp Esp)

Union Jack *n* bandera *f* del Reino Unido

unique /jʊˈniːk/ *adj* (*no comp*) único

unisex /ˈjuːnəseks ‖ˈjuːnɪseks/ *adj* unisex *adj inv*

unison /ˈjuːnəsən ‖ˈjuːnɪsən/ *n*: **in ~** al unísono

unit /ˈjuːnət ‖ˈjuːnɪt/ *n* **1** (a) (item) (Busn) unidad *f* (b) (of furniture) módulo *m* **2** (group) (Mil) unidad *f* **3** (of measurement) unidad *f* **4** (Educ) (in course) módulo *m*

unite /jʊˈnaɪt ‖juːˈnaɪt/ *vt* unir
■ ~ *vi* unirse

united /jʊˈnaɪtəd ‖juːˈnaɪtɪd/ *adj* unido

united: U~ Arab Emirates /ˈemɪrəts ‖ˈemɪrəts/ *pl n* **the U~ Arab Emirates** los Emiratos Árabes Unidos; **U~ Kingdom** *n* **the U~ Kingdom** el Reino Unido; **U~ Nations (Organization)** *n* (+ *sing o pl vb*) **the U~ Nations (organization)** (la Organización de) las Naciones Unidas; **U~ States** *n* (*usu* + *sing vb*) **the U~ States** los Estados Unidos; **U~ States of America** *n* (*usu* + *sing vb*) **the U~ States of America** los Estados Unidos de América

unity /ˈjuːnəti/ *n* (*pl* **-ties**) unidad *f*

universal /ˈjuːnəˈvɜːrsəl ‖juːnɪˈvɜːsəl/ *adj* (a) (general) general (b) (worldwide) universal (c) (all-purpose, versatile) ⟨*adaptor*⟩ universal

universally /ˈjuːnəˈvɜːrsəli ‖juːnɪˈvɜːsəli/ *adv* ⟨*known/admired*⟩ mundialmente, universalmente

universe /ˈjuːnəvɜːrs ‖ˈjuːnɪvɜːs/ *n* universo *m*

university /ˈjuːnəˈvɜːrsəti ‖juːnɪˈvɜːsəti/ *n* (*pl* **-ties**) universidad *f*; (*before n*) ⟨*town/life*⟩ universitario

unjust /ˈʌnˈdʒʌst/ *adj* injusto

unjustified /ˈʌnˈdʒʌstəfaɪd ‖ʌnˈdʒʌstɪfaɪd/ *adj* injustificado

unkempt /ˈʌnˈkempt/ *adj* (frml) ⟨*appearance*⟩ descuidado, desarreglado; ⟨*hair*⟩ despeinado

unkind /ˈʌnˈkaɪnd/ *adj* **-er, -est** (unpleasant) poco amable; (cruel) cruel, malo; ⟨*remark*⟩ hiriente

unknown¹ /ˈʌnˈnəʊn/ *adj* desconocido

unknown² *n* (a) (phenomenon) **the ~** lo desconocido (b) (person) desconocida, -da *m,f*

unknown³ *adv*: **~ to her** sin ella saberlo

unlawful /ˈʌnˈlɔːfəl/ *adj* ⟨*conduct*⟩ ilegal; ⟨*possession*⟩ ilícito

unleaded /ˈʌnˈledəd ‖ʌnˈledɪd/ *adj* sin plomo

unleash /ˈʌnˈliːʃ/ *vt* ⟨*dog*⟩ soltar*, desatar; ⟨*anger/imagination*⟩ dar(le)* rienda suelta a; ⟨*war*⟩ desencadenar

unless /ʌnˈles, ən-/ *conj* a no ser que (+ *subj*), a menos que (+ *subj*)

unlike /ˈʌnˈlaɪk/ *prep* (a) (not similar to) diferente *or* distinto de (b) (untypical of): **it's ~ you to be so optimistic** tú no sueles ser tan optimista (c) (in contrast to) a diferencia de

unlikely /ˈʌnˈlaɪkli/ *adj* **-lier, liest** (a) (improbable) ⟨*outcome/victory*⟩ improbable, poco probable (b) (far-fetched) ⟨*story/explanation*⟩ inverosímil (c) (odd, unexpected) insólito

unlimited /ˈʌnˈlɪmətəd ‖ʌnˈlɪmɪtɪd/ *adj* ilimitado

unlined /ˈʌnˈlaɪnd/ *adj* (a) ⟨*paper*⟩ sin pautar (b) ⟨*dress/jacket*⟩ sin forro

unlisted /ˈʌnˈlɪstəd ‖ʌnˈlɪstɪd/ *adj* (AmE Telec) que no figura en la guía telefónica

unlit /ˈʌnˈlɪt/ *adj* ⟨*road*⟩ sin luz, sin alumbrado

unload /ˈʌnˈləʊd/ *vt/i* descargar*

unlock /ˈʌnˈlɑːk ‖ʌnˈlɒk/ *vt* abrir* (algo que está cerrado con llave)

unlucky /ˈʌnˈlʌki/ *adj* **unluckier, unluckiest** ⟨*person*⟩ sin suerte, desafortunado; ⟨*day*⟩ funesto, de mala suerte; ⟨*object*⟩ que trae mala suerte; **to be ~** tener* mala suerte

unmanageable /ˈʌnˈmænɪdʒəbəl/ *adj* ⟨*child/horse*⟩ rebelde; ⟨*hair*⟩ rebelde

unmanned /ˈʌnˈmænd/ *adj* ⟨*vehicle/rocket*⟩ sin tripulación; ⟨*space flight*⟩ no tripulado

unmarried /ˈʌnˈmærid/ *adj* soltero

unmask /ˈʌnˈmæsk ‖ʌnˈmɑːsk/ *vt* desenmascarar

unmentionable /ˈʌnˈmentʃn̩əbəl ‖ʌnˈmenʃənəbəl/ *adj* inmencionable, innombrable

unmistakable /ˈʌnmɪˈsteɪkəbəl ‖ˌʌnmɪˈsteɪkəbəl/ *adj* inconfundible; ⟨*proof*⟩ inequívoco

unnamed /ˈʌnˈneɪmd/ *adj* no identificado

unnatural /ˈʌnˈnætʃərəl/ *adj* (a) (unusual) poco natural *or* normal (b) (awkward, affected) ⟨*smile*⟩ poco natural (c) (against nature) (frml) antinatural

unnecessarily /ˈʌnnesəˈserəli ‖ˌʌnnesəˈserɪli, ˌʌnˈnesəserɪli/ *adv* innecesariamente

unnecessary /ʌnˈnesəseri ‖ʌnˈnesəsəri/ *adj* innecesario

unnerve /ʌnˈnɜːrv ‖ʌnˈnɜːv/ *vt* poner* nervioso, turbar (liter)

unnerving /ʌnˈnɜːrvɪŋ ‖ʌnˈnɜːvɪŋ/ *adj* desconcertante, que pone nervioso

unnoticed /ʌnˈnəʊtəst ‖ʌnˈnəʊtɪst/ *adj* (*pred*): **to go ~** pasar desapercibido *or* inadvertido

unobtainable /ʌnəbˈteɪnəbəl/ *adj* imposible de conseguir

unobtrusive /ʌnəbˈtruːsɪv/ *adj* discreto

unoccupied /ʌnˈɑːkjəpaɪd ‖ʌnˈɒkjʊpaɪd/ *adj* (a) ⟨*seat/toilet*⟩ desocupado, libre; ⟨*house*⟩ deshabitado, desocupado (b) (Mil) no ocupado

unofficial /ʌnəˈfɪʃəl/ *adj* no oficial

unofficially /ʌnəˈfɪʃəli/ *adv* extraoficialmente

unopened /ʌnˈəʊpənd/ *adj* sin abrir

unopposed /ʌnəˈpəʊzd/ *adj* sin oposición

unoriginal /ʌnəˈrɪdʒənl/ *adj* poco original, sin originalidad

unorthodox /ʌnˈɔːrθədɑːks ‖ʌnˈɔːθədɒks/ *adj* poco ortodoxo

unpack /ʌnˈpæk/ *vt* ⟨*bags*⟩ sacar* las cosas de, desempacar* (AmL); ⟨*suitcase*⟩ deshacer*, desempacar* (AmL)
■ ~ *vi* deshacer* las maletas, desempacar* (AmL)

unpaid /ʌnˈpeɪd/ *adj* ⟨*work*⟩ no retribuido, no remunerado; ⟨*leave*⟩ sin sueldo; ⟨*debt*⟩ pendiente, no liquidado

unpalatable /ʌnˈpælətəbəl/ *adj* (a) ⟨*food/drink*⟩ de sabor desagradable (b) ⟨*fact/truth*⟩ desagradable, difícil de digerir

unparalleled /ʌnˈpærəleld/ *adj* ⟨*success/achievement*⟩ sin paralelo, sin parangón; ⟨*disaster*⟩ sin precedentes; ⟨*beauty*⟩ incomparable

unperturbed /ʌnpərˈtɜːrbd ‖ʌnpəˈtɜːbd/ *adj* impasible, impertérrito; **she carried on ~** siguió sin inmutarse

unpleasant /ʌnˈpleznt/ *adj* desagradable

unplug /ʌnˈplʌg/ *vt* **-gg-** desenchufar, desconectar

unpopular /ʌnˈpɑːpjələr ‖ʌnˈpɒpjʊlə(r)/ *adj* impopular; **he is ~ with everybody** le cae muy mal a todo el mundo

unprecedented /ʌnˈpresədentəd ‖ʌnˈpresɪdentɪd/ *adj* ⟨*success/hostility*⟩ sin precedentes; ⟨*decision*⟩ inaudito

unpredictable /ʌnprɪˈdɪktəbəl/ *adj* ⟨*result/weather*⟩ imprevisible; **she's very ~** nunca se sabe cómo va a reaccionar

unprepared /ʌnprɪˈperd ‖ʌnprɪˈpeəd/ *adj* (a) (not ready) (*pred*) **to be ~** no estar* preparado (b) (not expecting) (*pred*) **to be ~ FOR sth** no esperar algo

unprepossessing /ʌnpriːpəˈzesɪŋ/ *adj* poco atractivo

unprincipled /ʌnˈprɪnsəpəld/ *adj* sin escrúpulos *or* principios

unproductive /ʌnprəˈdʌktɪv/ *adj* ⟨*meeting*⟩ infructuoso

unprofessional /ʌnprəˈfeʃnəl ‖ʌnprəˈfeʃənl/ *adj* poco profesional

unprofitable /ʌnˈprɑːfətəbəl ‖ʌnˈprɒfɪtəbəl/ *adj* no rentable

unprotected /ʌnprəˈtektəd ‖ʌnprəˈtektɪd/ *adj* sin protección; ⟨*sex*⟩ sin el uso de preservativos

unproven /ʌnˈpruːvən/ *adj* ⟨*theory*⟩ (que está) por demostrar *or* probar

unpublished /ʌnˈpʌblɪʃt/ *adj* inédito, no publicado

unpunished /ʌnˈpʌnɪʃt/ *adj*: **to go ~** ⟨*person*⟩ quedar sin castigo; ⟨*crime*⟩ quedar impune

unqualified /ʌnˈkwɑːləfaɪd ‖ʌnˈkwɒlɪfaɪd/ *adj* **1** (complete, total) ⟨*approval*⟩ incondicional; ⟨*disaster*⟩ absoluto; ⟨*success/failure*⟩ rotundo **2** (without qualifications) ⟨*teacher/nurse*⟩ sin titulación *or* título, no titulado; ⟨*staff*⟩ no calificado *or* (Esp) cualificado

unquestionable /ʌnˈkwestʃənəbəl/ *adj* ⟨*sincerity/loyalty*⟩ incuestionable, innegable

unquestioning /ʌnˈkwestʃənɪŋ/ *adj* ⟨*obedience/faith*⟩ ciego; ⟨*loyalty*⟩ incondicional

unravel /ʌnˈrævəl/ *vt*, (BrE) **-ll-** (a) ⟨*threads/string*⟩ desenredar (b) ⟨*mystery*⟩ desentrañar

unreadable /ʌnˈriːdəbəl/ *adj* (a) ⟨*handwriting*⟩ ilegible (b) ⟨*novel*⟩ muy difícil de leer

unrealistic /ʌnriːəˈlɪstɪk ‖ʌnrɪəˈlɪstɪk/ *adj* ⟨*expectations*⟩ poco realista; **it's ~ to expect that** no es realista esperar eso

unreasonable /ʌnˈriːznəbəl/ *adj* ⟨*person*⟩ poco razonable, irrazonable; ⟨*demand/price*⟩ excesivo, poco razonable

unrecognizable /ʌnˈrekəgnaɪzəbəl/ *adj* irreconocible

unrefined /ʌnrɪˈfaɪnd/ *adj* ⟨*flour/sugar*⟩ sin refinar, no refinado; ⟨*gold*⟩ en estado bruto; ⟨*person*⟩ poco refinado; **~ oil** crudo *m*

unrelated /ʌnrɪˈleɪtəd ‖ʌnrɪˈleɪtɪd/ *adj* ⟨*facts/events*⟩ no relacionados (entre sí)

unreliable /ʌnrɪˈlaɪəbəl/ *adj* ⟨*person*⟩ informal; ⟨*information*⟩ poco fidedigno; ⟨*weather*⟩ variable

unrepeatable /ʌnrɪˈpiːtəbəl/ *adj* irrepetible

unrepentant /ʌnrɪˈpentnt/ *adj* impenitente

unreported /ʌnrɪˈpɔːrtəd ‖ʌnrɪˈpɔːtɪd/ *adj* ⟨*crime*⟩ no denunciado

unrepresentative /ʌnreprəˈzentətɪv/ *adj* poco representativo

unrequited /ʌnrɪˈkwaɪtəd ‖ʌnrɪˈkwaɪtɪd/ *adj* ⟨*love*⟩ no correspondido

unresolved /ʌnrɪˈzɑːlvd ‖ʌnrɪˈzɒlvd/ *adj* no resuelto

unresponsive /ʌnrɪˈspɑːnsɪv ‖ʌnrɪˈspɒnsɪv/ *adj* ⟨*audience/expression*⟩ indiferente; ⟨*pupil*⟩ que no responde

unrest /ʌnˈrest/ *n* (Pol) descontento *m*, malestar *m*; (active) disturbios *mpl*

unrestricted /ʌnrɪˈstrɪktəd ‖ʌnrɪˈstrɪktɪd/ *adj* ilimitado

unrewarded /ʌnrɪˈwɔːrdəd ‖ʌnrɪˈwɔːdɪd/ *adj* no recompensado

unripe /ʌnˈraɪp/ *adj* verde, que no está maduro

unrivaled, (BrE) **unrivalled** /ʌnˈraɪvəld/ *adj* incomparable, inigualable

unroll /ʌnˈrəʊl/ *vt* desenrollar

unruffled /ʌnˈrʌfəld/ *adj* (a) (undisturbed) ⟨*manner*⟩ sereno (b) (smooth) liso

unruly /ʌnˈruːli/ *adj* **-lier, -liest** ⟨class⟩ indisciplinado, difícil de controlar; ⟨conduct⟩ rebelde; ⟨child⟩ revoltoso

unsafe /ʌnˈseɪf/ *adj* inseguro

unsaid /ʌnˈsed/ *adj*: **to leave sth ~** callar(se) algo, no decir* algo

unsalted /ʌnˈsɔːltəd ‖ ʌnˈsɔːltɪd/ *adj* sin sal

unsatisfactory /ʌnˈsætəsˈfæktri ‖ ˌʌnsætɪsˈfæktəri/ *adj* insatisfactorio; ⟨explanation⟩ poco convincente

unsatisfying /ʌnˈsætəsfaɪŋ ‖ ʌnˈsætɪsfaɪŋ/ *adj* ⟨meal⟩ que no llena *or* satisface; ⟨job⟩ poco gratificante; ⟨ending⟩ decepcionante

unsavory, (BrE) **unsavoury** /ʌnˈseɪvəri/ *adj* desagradable

unscathed /ʌnˈskeɪðd/ *adj* (*pred*) (unhurt) ileso; (of reputation etc) indemne

unscented /ʌnˈsentəd ‖ ʌnˈsentɪd/ *adj* sin perfume

unscheduled /ʌnˈskedʒuːld ‖ ʌnˈʃedjuːld/ *adj* no programado, no previsto

unscientific /ʌnˈsaɪənˈtɪfɪk/ *adj* falto de rigor científico

unscrew /ʌnˈskruː/ *vt* ⟨screw/panel⟩ destornillar, desatornillar; ⟨lid⟩ desenroscar*

unscrupulous /ʌnˈskruːpjələs ‖ ʌnˈskruːpjʊləs/ *adj* inescrupuloso

unseat /ʌnˈsiːt/ *vt* **(a)** ⟨rider⟩ desmontar **(b)** ⟨government⟩ derribar

unseen /ʌnˈsiːn/ *adj* **(a)** (invisible) ⟨danger/obstacle⟩ oculto **(b)** (unnoticed) sin ser visto

unselfish /ʌnˈselfɪʃ/ *adj* ⟨person⟩ nada egoísta; ⟨act⟩ desinteresado

unsentimental /ʌnˈsentəˈmentl̩ ‖ ˌʌnsentɪˈmentl̩/ *adj* ⟨person/outlook⟩ poco sentimental

unsettle /ʌnˈsetl̩/ *vt* ⟨plans⟩ alterar; ⟨situation⟩ desestabilizar*; **the question clearly ~d him** la pregunta lo desconcertó visiblemente

unsettled /ʌnˈsetl̩d/ *adj* **1** **(a)** (troubled) ⟨period⟩ agitado; ⟨childhood⟩ poco estable **(b)** ⟨weather⟩ inestable **2** (undecided) ⟨issue/dispute⟩ pendiente (de resolución), sin resolver; ⟨future⟩ incierto

unsettling /ʌnˈsetl̩ɪŋ/ *adj* inquietante; ⟨effect⟩ desestabilizador

unshakable, unshakeable /ʌnˈʃeɪkəbəl/ *adj* inquebrantable

unshaven /ʌnˈʃeɪvən/ *adj* sin afeitar, sin rasurar (esp Méx)

unsightly /ʌnˈsaɪtli/ *adj* **-lier, -liest** feo, antiestético

unsigned /ʌnˈsaɪnd/ *adj* sin firmar

unskilled /ʌnˈskɪld/ *adj* ⟨worker⟩ no calificado *or* (Esp) cualificado; ⟨work⟩ no especializado

unsociable /ʌnˈsəʊʃəbəl/ *adj* insociable, poco sociable

unsold /ʌnˈsəʊld/ *adj* no vendido

unsolicited /ʌnsəˈlɪsətəd ‖ ˌʌnsəˈlɪsɪtɪd/ *adj* que no se ha pedido *or* solicitado

unsolved /ʌnˈsɒlvd ‖ ʌnˈsɒlvd/ *adj* no resuelto

unsophisticated /ʌnsəˈfɪstəkeɪtəd ‖ ˌʌnsəˈfɪstɪkeɪtɪd/ *adj* ⟨person⟩ sencillo; ⟨tastes/technology⟩ simple, poco sofisticado

unspeakable /ʌnˈspiːkəbəl/ *adj* ⟨evil⟩ incalificable, atroz; ⟨joy⟩ indescriptible

unspecified /ʌnˈspesəfaɪd ‖ ʌnˈspesɪfaɪd/ *adj* no especificado

unspoiled /ʌnˈspɔɪld/, (BrE also) **unspoilt** /ʌnˈspɔɪlt/ *adj* ⟨countryside⟩ que conserva su belleza natural

unspoken /ʌnˈspəʊkən/ *adj* ⟨agreement⟩ tácito; ⟨wish⟩ no expresado

unstable /ʌnˈsteɪbəl/ *adj* inestable; ⟨prices⟩ variable

unsteadily /ʌnˈstedl̩i ‖ ʌnˈstedɪli/ *adv* de modo inseguro *or* vacilante

unsteady /ʌnˈstedi/ *adj* ⟨chair/ladder⟩ inestable, poco firme; ⟨walk/step⟩ vacilante, inseguro

unstick /ʌnˈstɪk/ *vt* (*past & past p* **unstuck**) despegar*, quitar

unstuck /ʌnˈstʌk/ *adj* despegado; **to come ~** despegarse*

unsuccessful /ʌnsəkˈsesfəl/ *adj* ⟨attempt⟩ infructuoso, fallido; **they were ~ in their attempt** fracasaron en su intento

unsuccessfully /ʌnsəkˈsesfəli/ *adv* en vano, sin éxito

unsuitable /ʌnˈsuːtəbəl/ *adj* ⟨clothing⟩ poco apropiado *or* adecuado; ⟨candidate⟩ poco idóneo; ⟨time⟩ inconveniente

unsuited /ʌnˈsuːtəd ‖ ʌnˈsuːtɪd/ *adj* (*pred*) **she is ~ to this work** no sirve para este trabajo; **they are completely ~** son totalmente incompatibles

unsure /ʌnˈʃʊr ‖ ʌnˈʃʊə(r), ʌnˈʃɔː(r)/ *adj* inseguro, indeciso; **to be ~ of oneself** estar* *or* sentirse* inseguro de sí mismo

unsurpassed /ʌnsərˈpæst ‖ ˌʌnsəˈpɑːst/ *adj* ⟨beauty/mastery⟩ sin igual, sin par (liter)

unsuspecting /ʌnsəˈspektɪŋ/ *adj* desprevenido; **to be ~** no sospechar nada

unsweetened /ʌnˈswiːtn̩d/ *adj* (without sugar) sin azúcar; (without sweeteners) sin edulcorantes

unsympathetic /ʌnˈsɪmpəˈθetɪk/ *adj* **(a)** (showing no sympathy) ⟨person/attitude⟩ indiferente, poco comprensivo **(b)** (unfavorable) ⟨account⟩ adverso, desfavorable; **she was ~ to our cause** no veía nuestra causa con simpatía

unsystematic /ʌnˈsɪstəˈmætɪk/ *adj* poco sistemático

untamed /ʌnˈteɪmd/ *adj* ⟨animal⟩ sin domar; ⟨wilderness/forests⟩ virgen, agreste

untangle /ʌnˈtæŋgəl/ *vt* desenredar, desenmarañar; ⟨mystery⟩ desentrañar

untapped /ʌnˈtæpt/ *adj* sin explotar

untenable /ʌnˈtenəbəl/ *adj* (frml) insostenible

untended /ʌnˈtendəd ‖ ʌnˈtendɪd/ *adj* ⟨garden⟩ descuidado; ⟨patient⟩ desatendido

u

AmC	Central America	Arg	Argentina	Cu	Cuba
AmL	Latin America	Bol	Bolivia	Ec	Ecuador
AmS	South America	Chi	Chile	Esp	Spain
Andes	Andean Region	CS	Southern Cone	Méx	Mexico

Per	Peru
RPI	River Plate Area
Ur	Uruguay
Ven	Venezuela

unthinkable ⸱⸱⸱⟶ up ⸱⸱⸱

unthinkable /ʌnˈθɪŋkəbəl/ adj inconcebible, inimaginable

untidy /ʌnˈtaɪdi/ adj **-dier, -diest** ⟨room/desk/ person⟩ desordenado; ⟨appearance⟩ descuidado, desprolijo (RPl); ⟨writing/schoolwork⟩ descuidado, desprolijo (RPl)

untie /ʌnˈtaɪ/ vt **unties, untying, untied** ⟨knot⟩ desatar; ⟨shoelaces⟩ desatar, desamarrar (AmL exc RPl); ⟨animal⟩ soltar*, desatar, desamarrar (AmL exc RPl)

until¹ /ʌnˈtɪl, ənˈtɪl/ conj hasta que

■ **Note** When used as a conjunction in positive sentences expressing the future, until is translated by hasta que + subjunctive: we'll stay here until Carol comes back nos quedaremos aquí hasta que llegue Carol. In negative sentences no is used optionally before the verb: he won't be satisfied until they give him his money back no estará satisfecho hasta que (no) le devuelvan su dinero.

---

until² prep hasta

untimely /ʌnˈtaɪmli/ adj (a) ⟨death/end⟩ prematuro (b) ⟨arrival⟩ inoportuno, intempestivo

untold /ʌnˈtəʊld/ adj (before n) ⟨wealth/sums⟩ incalculable; ⟨misery/pleasures⟩ indecible, inenarrable

untouched /ʌnˈtʌtʃt/ adj (a) (not handled) intacto, sin tocar; **he left his food ~** no probó la comida (b) (safe, unharmed) intacto

untoward /ʌnˈtɔːrd, ˌʌntəˈwɔːrd ‖ ˌʌntəˈwɔːd/ adj (frml) perjudicial, adverso; **I hope nothing ~ has happened** espero que no haya pasado nada (que haya que lamentar)

untrained /ʌnˈtreɪnd/ adj falto de formación or capacitación; ⟨teacher⟩ sin título; **to the ~ eye/ ear ...** para el (ojo/oído de) quien no es experto ...

untreated /ʌnˈtriːtəd ‖ ʌnˈtriːtɪd/ adj ⟨sewage/ waste⟩ sin tratar or procesar

untried /ʌnˈtraɪd/ adj (a) (not tested) ⟨method⟩ no probado (b) (Law) ⟨case⟩ no sometido a juicio

untroubled /ʌnˈtrʌbəld/ adj tranquilo

untrue /ʌnˈtruː/ adj falso; **it is ~ (to say) that ...** es falso or no es cierto que ...

untrustworthy /ʌnˈtrʌstˌwɜːrði ‖ ʌnˈtrʌstˌwɜːði/ adj ⟨person⟩ de poca confianza; ⟨source⟩ no fidedigno

untruthful /ʌnˈtruːθfəl/ adj ⟨account/answer⟩ falso; ⟨person⟩ falso, mentiroso

unusual /ʌnˈjuːʒuəl/ adj poco corriente or común, fuera de lo corriente or común, inusual; **with ~ frankness** con inusitada or insólita franqueza; **did you notice anything ~ about him?** ¿le notaste algo raro or fuera de lo normal?

unusually /ʌnˈjuːʒuəli/ adv excepcionalmente, inusitadamente; **she was ~ talkative** estaba más conversadora que de costumbre

unveil /ʌnˈveɪl/ vt descubrir*, develar (AmL)

unwanted /ʌnˈwɒntəd ‖ ʌnˈwɒntɪd/ adj ⟨pregnancy/child⟩ no deseado; ⟨object⟩ superfluo

unwarranted /ʌnˈwɔːrəntəd ‖ ʌnˈwɒrəntɪd/ adj injustificado

unwavering /ʌnˈweɪvərɪŋ/ adj ⟨loyalty/belief⟩ inquebrantable; ⟨determination⟩ férreo

unwelcome /ʌnˈwelkəm/ adj ⟨visit⟩ inoportuno; ⟨guest⟩ inoportuno, poco grato; ⟨news⟩ poco grato

unwell /ʌnˈwel/ adj mal

unwholesome /ʌnˈhəʊlsəm/ adj ⟨diet/ climate⟩ poco sano or saludable; ⟨smell/person⟩ desagradable

unwieldy /ʌnˈwiːldi/ adj **-dier, -diest** pesado y difícil de manejar

unwilling /ʌnˈwɪlɪŋ/ adj mal dispuesto; **to be ~ to + INF** no querer* + INF, no estar* dispuesto a + INF

unwillingly /ʌnˈwɪlɪŋli/ adv de mala gana, a regañadientes

unwind /ʌnˈwaɪnd/ (past & past p **unwound** /ʌnˈwaʊnd/) vt desenrollar
■ **~** vi (colloq) relajarse

unwise /ʌnˈwaɪz/ adj poco prudente or sensato; **it would be ~ of you to do that** hacer eso no sería sensato

unwitting /ʌnˈwɪtɪŋ/ adj involuntario

unwittingly /ʌnˈwɪtɪŋli/ adv sin ser consciente (de ello), sin darse* cuenta

unworthy /ʌnˈwɜːrði ‖ ʌnˈwɜːði/ adj **-thier, -thiest** indigno; **to be ~ to + INF** no ser* digno DE + INF

unwound /ʌnˈwaʊnd/ past & past p of UNWIND

unwrap /ʌnˈræp/ vt **-pp-** desenvolver*

unwritten /ʌnˈrɪtn/ adj ⟨rule⟩ no escrito; ⟨agreement⟩ verbal, de palabra

unyielding /ʌnˈjiːldɪŋ/ adj ⟨person⟩ inflexible; ⟨opposition⟩ implacable

up¹ /ʌp/ adv
I **1** (in upward direction): **~ a bit ... left a bit** un poco más arriba ... un poco a la izquierda; **we saw them on the way ~** los vimos cuando subíamos; **from the waist ~** desde la cintura para arriba
2 (a) (of position) arriba; **~ here/there** aquí/allí arriba; **300ft ~** a una altura de 300 pies (b) (upstairs, on upper floor): **I'll be ~ in a minute** subiré en un minuto (c) (raised): **with the blinds ~** con las persianas levantadas or subidas; **face ~** boca arriba
3 (a) (upright): **the nurse helped him ~** la enfermera lo ayudó a sentarse (b) (out of bed): **they're not ~ yet** todavía no se han levantado
4 (of numbers, intensity): **she had the volume ~ high** tenía el volumen muy alto; **from $25/the age of 11 ~** a partir de 25 dólares/los 11 años
5 (at or to another place): **the path ~ to the house** el sendero hasta la casa
6 (in position, erected): **is the tent ~?** ¿ya han armado la tienda or (AmL) la carpa?; **the shelves are ~** los estantes están colocados or puestos
7 (going on) (colloq): **what's ~ with you?** ¿a ti qué te pasa?; **what's ~?** (what's the matter?) ¿qué pasa?; (as greeting) (AmE) ¿qué hay? (colloq)
8 (finished): **your time is ~** se te ha acabado el tiempo
9 (Sport) (ahead in competition): **they're two goals ~** van ganando por dos goles; **to be one ~ on sb** tener* una ventaja sobre algn
II (in phrases) **1 up against (a)** (next to) contra **(b)** (confronted by): **you don't know what you're ~ against** no sabes a lo que te enfrentas
2 up and down (a) (vertically): **to jump ~ and down** dar* saltos; **to look sb ~ and down** mirar a algn de arriba abajo **(b)** (back and forth) de arriba abajo

⸱⸱⟶

3 **up till** o **until** hasta

III **up to** **1** (as far as, as much as) hasta; ∼ **to here/now** hasta aquí/ahora

2 **(a)** (equal to): **it isn't** ∼ **to the usual standard** no es del alto nivel al que estamos acostumbrados; ► COME UP TO B **(b)** (capable of): **she's not** ∼ **to the job** no tiene las condiciones necesarias para el trabajo; **I'm not** ∼ **to going out** no me siente con fuerzas (como) para salir **3** (depending on): **that's** ∼ **to you** eso depende de ti; **it's not** ∼ **to me to decide** no me corresponde a mí decidir

4 **to be** ∼ **to sth** (colloq): **they're** ∼ **to something** (planning) están tramando algo, se traen algo entre manos; (doing) están haciendo algo; **what have you been** ∼ **to lately?** ¿en qué has andado últimamente?

up² prep **1** **(a)** (in upward direction): **to go** ∼ **the stairs/hill** subir la escalera/colina **(b)** (at higher level): **80ft** ∼ **the cliff** a 80 pies del pie del acantilado **2** **(a)** (along): **to go** ∼ **the river** ir* por el río; **she walked** ∼ **and down the room** iba de un lado a otro de la habitación **(b)** (further along): **it's just** ∼ **the road** está un poco más allá or adelante

up³ n: ∼**s and downs** (of life) vicisitudes fpl; (of marriage) altibajos mpl

up: ∼**-and-coming** /ˈʌpənˈkʌmɪŋ/ adj (before n): **an** ∼**-and-coming actor** un actor que promete; ∼**beat** adj (colloq) optimista; ∼**braid** /ʌpˈbreɪd/ vt (frml) reprender, reconvenir* (frml); ∼**bringing** /ˈʌpˌbrɪŋɪŋ/ n (no pl) educación f; ∼**coming** /ˈʌpˈkʌmɪŋ/ adj (before n) próximo, que se acerca

update¹ /ʌpˈdeɪt/ vt poner* al día

update² /ˈʌpdeɪt/ n: **to give sb an** ∼ **on sth** poner* a algn al corriente or al tanto de algo

up: ∼**end** /ʌpˈend/ vt poner* vertical, parar (AmL); ∼**front** /ˈʌpˈfrʌnt/ adv por adelantado; ∼**grade** vt **(a)** ⟨employee⟩ elevar de categoría; ⟨job⟩ elevar la categoría de **(b)** (improve) ⟨facilities⟩ mejorar

upheaval /ʌpˈhiːvəl/ n trastorno m; (social, political) agitación f

up: ∼**held** /ʌpˈheld/ past & past p of ∼HOLD; ∼**hill** /ˈʌpˈhɪl/ adv cuesta arriba, en subida; ∼**hold** /ʌpˈhəʊld/ vt (past & past p ∼**held**) **(a)** ⟨tradition⟩ conservar; ⟨principle⟩ mantener* **(b)** (Law) ⟨decision/verdict⟩ confirmar

upholster /ʌpˈhəʊlstər ‖ʌpˈhəʊlstə(r)/ vt tapizar*

upholstery /ʌpˈhəʊlstəri/ n **(a)** (stuffing, springs) relleno m; (covers) tapizado m **(b)** (craft, trade) tapicería f

up: ∼**keep** n (running, maintenance) mantenimiento m; (costs) gastos mpl de mantenimiento; ∼**lift** /ʌpˈlɪft/ vt elevar; ∼**lifting** /ʌpˈlɪftɪŋ/ adj (spiritually) que eleva el espíritu; (emotionally) que levanta el ánimo; ∼**load** /ʌpˈləʊd/ vt (Comput) cargar*, subir

upmarket¹ /ˈʌpˈmɑːrkət ‖ʌpˈmɑːkɪt/ adj de categoría, para gente pudiente

upmarket² adv: **to go** ∼ subir de categoría

upon /əˈpɑːn ‖əˈpɒn/ prep (frml) **(a)** (on) sobre; ∼ -ING al + INF **(b)** (indicating large numbers): **thousands** ∼ **thousands** miles y miles

upper /ˈʌpər ‖ˈʌpə(r)/ adj (before n) **1** **(a)**

(spatially, numerically) superior; ⟨lip⟩ superior, de arriba **(b)** (in rank, importance) superior, más elevado **2** (Geog) alto; **the U**∼ **Danube** el alto Danubio

upper: ∼ **class** n clase f alta; ∼**-class** /ˈʌpərˈklæs ‖ˌʌpəˈklɑːs/ adj de clase alta; ∼**most** adj más alto

upright /ˈʌpraɪt/ adj **(a)** ⟨post/position⟩ vertical; **to place/stand sth** ∼ colocar*/poner* algo de pie or vertical **(b)** ⟨citizen⟩ recto

up: ∼**rising** n levantamiento m, alzamiento m; ∼**river** /ˈʌpˈrɪvər ‖ʌpˈrɪvə(r)/ adv río arriba; ∼**roar** n (noise, chaos) tumulto m, alboroto m; (outcry) protesta f airada; ∼**root** /ʌpˈruːt/ vt ⟨plant⟩ arrancar* de raíz, desarraigar* (téc); ⟨person⟩ desarraigar*

upset¹ /ʌpˈset/ adj **1** (unhappy, hurt) disgustado; (distressed) alterado; (offended) ofendido; (disappointed) desilusionado **2** (Med): **I have an** ∼ **stomach** estoy or ando mal del estómago, estoy descompuesto (del estómago) (esp AmL)

upset² /ʌpˈset/ vt (pres p **upsetting**; past & past p **upset**) **1** (hurt) disgustar; (distress) alterar, afectar; (offend) ofender **2** (make ill): **it** ∼**s my stomach** me cae mal, me sienta mal (al estómago) (esp AmL) **3** ⟨plans/calculations⟩ desbaratar, trastornar

upset³ /ˈʌpset/ n **1** **(a)** (upheaval) trastorno m **(b)** (emotional trouble) disgusto m **2** (Med): **to have a stomach** ∼ estar* mal or (esp AmL) descompuesto del estómago

upshot /ˈʌpʃɑːt ‖ˈʌpʃɒt/ n: **the** ∼ **of it all is that** ... lo que resulta de todo esto es que ...

upside down /ˈʌpsaɪd/ adj al revés (con la parte de arriba abajo); **to turn sth** ∼ ∼ poner* algo boca abajo; ⟨theory/world⟩ revolucionar algo

upstage /ˈʌpˈsteɪdʒ/ vt eclipsar

upstairs /ˈʌpˈsterz ‖ˈʌpˈsteəz/ adv arriba; **to go** ∼ subir

up: ∼**start** n advenedizo, -za m,f; ∼**state** /ˈʌpˈsteɪt/ adv (AmE): **he lives** ∼**state** vive en el norte del estado (fuera de la capital); ∼**stream** /ˈʌpˈstriːm/ adv río or corriente arriba; ∼**surge** n ⟨of/in violence⟩ recrudecimiento m; ⟨in demand⟩ aumento m; ∼**take** n: **to be quick on the** ∼**take** agarrar or (esp Esp) coger* las cosas al vuelo; ∼**tight** /ˈʌpˈtaɪt/ adj (colloq) nervioso, tenso; ∼**-to-date** /ˈʌptəˈdeɪt/ adj (pred ∼ **to date**) al día, actualizado

uptown¹ /ˈʌpˈtaʊn/ adj (AmE) que va hacia el norte/hacia el distrito residencial (de la ciudad)

uptown² adv (AmE): **they live/went** ∼ viven en/ fueron hacia el norte/hacia el distrito residencial de la ciudad

up: ∼**turn** n (in demand, production) repunte m, mejora f; ∼**turned** /ˈʌpˈtɜːrnd ‖ˈʌpˈtɜːnd/ adj ⟨nose⟩ respingón, respingado (AmL); ⟨table⟩ boca abajo, patas arriba; ⟨car/crate⟩ volcado

upward¹ /ˈʌpwərd ‖ˈʌpwəd/ adj (before n) ⟨direction⟩ hacia arriba; ⟨movement⟩ ascendente; ⟨tendency⟩ al alza

upward², (esp BrE) **upwards** /-z/ adv ⟨climb/ look⟩ hacia arriba; **face** ∼ boca arriba

upwardly mobile /ˈʌpwərdli ‖ˈʌpwədli/ adj de movilidad social ascendente

uranium /jʊˈreɪniəm/ n uranio m

Uranus /ˈjʊərənəs, jʊəˈreɪnəs/ n Urano m

urban /'ɜːrbən ‖'ɜːbən/ adj urbano

urbane /ɜːr'beɪn ‖ɜː'beɪn/ adj (frml) fino y cortés, urbano (frml)

urchin /'ɜːrtʃən ‖'ɜːtʃɪn/ n golfillo, -lla m,f, pilluelo, -la m,f

Urdu /'ʊrduː ‖'ʊədu:/ n urdu m

urge¹ /ɜːrdʒ ‖ɜːdʒ/ n (wish, whim) ganas fpl; (creative, sexual) impulso m

urge² vt instar (frml); (entreat) pedir* con insistencia; **to ~ sb to + INF** instar a algn A QUE (+ subj) (frml), pedirle* A algn con insistencia QUE (+ subj)
■ **urge on** [v + o + adv] animar, alentar*; ⟨horse⟩ espolear

urgency /'ɜːrdʒənsi ‖'ɜːdʒənsi/ n urgencia f

urgent /'ɜːrdʒənt ‖'ɜːdʒənt/ adj ⟨matter/case⟩ urgente; ⟨tone⟩ apremiante

urgently /'ɜːrdʒəntli ‖'ɜːdʒəntli/ adv urgentemente, con urgencia

urinal /'jʊərənl ‖jʊə'raɪn|/ n (place) urinario m; (receptacle) orinal m

urinate /'jʊərəneɪt ‖'jʊərɪneɪt/ vi (frml) orinar

urine /'jʊrən ‖'jʊərɪn/ n orina f

urn /ɜːrn ‖ɜːn/ n (a) (vase) urna f (b) (for ashes) urna f funeraria (c) (for tea, coffee) recipiente grande para hacer o mantener caliente té, café etc

Uruguay /'jʊərəgwaɪ ‖'jʊərəgwaɪ/ n Uruguay m

Uruguayan¹ /'jʊərə'gwaɪən ‖ˌjʊərə'gwaɪən/ adj uruguayo

Uruguayan² n uruguayo, -ya m,f

us /ʌs, weak form əs/ pron **1** (a) (as direct object) nos; **they helped ~** nos ayudaron (b) (as indirect object) nos; **he gave ~ the book** nos dio el libro; **he gave it to ~** nos lo dio (c) (after preposition) nosotros, -tras; **there were four of ~** éramos cuatro **2** (emphatic use) nosotros, -tras; **it was ~** fuimos nosotros

US n (+ sing vb) EEUU, EE UU, EE.UU.

USA n (a) (= United States of America) EEUU, EE UU, EE.UU. (b) (= United States Army) ejército m estadounidense or de los EEUU

usable, useable /'juːzəbəl/ adj utilizable

USAF n (= United States Air Force) la Fuerza Aérea de los EEUU

usage /'juːsɪdʒ/ n (Ling) uso m

use¹ /juːs/ n **1** (of machine, substance, method, word) uso m, empleo m, utilización f; **to be in ~** «machine» estar* funcionando or en funcionamiento; «word» emplearse, usarse; **to make ~ of sth** usar algo, hacer* uso de algo; **to put sth to good ~** hacer* buen uso de algo **2** (application, function) uso m **3** (usefulness): **to be of ~ to sb** serle* útil or de utilidad a algn, servirle* a algn; **these scissors aren't much ~** estas tijeras no sirven para nada; **it's no ~** es inútil, no hay manera, no hay caso (AmL); **what's the ~ (of -ING)?** ¿de qué sirve (+ INF)?, ¿qué sentido tiene (+ INF)? **4** (right to use): **to have the ~ of sb's car** poder* usar el coche de algn

use² /juːz/ vt **1** (a) (for task, purpose) usar; **to ~ sth AS sth** usar algo DE or COMO algo (b) (avail oneself of) ⟨service/facilities⟩ utilizar*, usar, hacer*

uso de; **may I ~ your phone?** ¿puedo hacer una llamada or llamar por teléfono?; **may I ~ your toilet?** ¿puedo pasar or ir al baño? **2** (do with) (colloq): **I could ~ a drink** no me vendría mal un trago **3** (consume) ⟨food/fuel⟩ consumir, usar **4** (manipulate, exploit) (pej) utilizar*, usar (esp AmL)
■ ~ v mod /juːs/ (in neg, interrog sentences): **I didn't ~ to visit them very often** no solía visitarlos muy a menudo; **where did you ~ to live?** ¿dónde vivías?; see also USED²
■ **use up** [v + o + adv, v + adv + o] ⟨supplies/strength⟩ agotar, consumir; ⟨leftovers⟩ usar

useable adj ▶ USABLE

used¹ adj **1** /juːzd/ ⟨needle/stamp/car⟩ usado **2** /juːst/ (accustomed) (pred) **to be ~ TO sth/-ING** estar* acostumbrado A algo/+ INF; **to get ~ TO sth/-ING** acostumbrarse A algo/+ INF

used² /juːst/ v mod (indicating former state, habit) (only in past) **~ to (+ INF)**: **there ~ to be** (antes) había; **I ~ to work in that shop** (antes) trabajaba en esa tienda; see also USE² v mod

useful /'juːsfəl/ adj útil; **to come in ~** (BrE) ser* útil, venir* bien

useless /'juːsləs ‖'juːslɪs/ adj (a) (ineffective) inútil; **these scissors are ~** estas tijeras no sirven para nada (b) (not capable) (colloq) ⟨person⟩ inútil, negado (fam)

user /'juːzər ‖'juːzə(r)/ n usuario, -ria m,f; **drug ~** consumidor, -dora m,f de drogas

user-friendly /'juːzər'frendli ‖ˌjuːzə'frendli/ adj fácil de usar or de utilizar

usher¹ /'ʌʃər ‖'ʌʃə(r)/ n (a) (Cin, Theat) acomodador, -dora m,f (b) (at wedding) persona allegada a los novios que se encarga de recibir y sentar a los invitados en la iglesia

usher² vt: **to ~ sb to her/his seat** conducir* a algn hasta su asiento; **he ~ed her into the room** la hizo pasar a la habitación
■ **usher in** [v + o + adv, v + adv + o] ⟨person⟩ hacer* pasar; ⟨new era⟩ marcar* el comienzo de

usherette /ˌʌʃə'ret/ n acomodadora f

USN n = United States Navy

USS = United States ship

USSR n (= Union of Soviet Socialist Republics) URSS f

usual /'juːʒuəl/ adj ⟨method/response⟩ acostumbrado, habitual, usual; ⟨time/place⟩ de siempre, de costumbre; ⟨clothes⟩ de costumbre; **as ~** como de costumbre

usually /'juːʒuəli/ adv normalmente, usualmente; **what do you ~ do in the evenings?** ¿qué sueles hacer por las noches?

usurp /jʊ'sɜːrp ‖ju:'zɜːp/ vt (frml) usurpar

UT = Utah

utensil /juː'tensəl ‖ju:'tensɪl/ n utensilio m

uterus /'juːtərəs/ n (pl -teri /-təraɪ/ or -teruses) útero m, matriz f

utility /juː'tɪləti/ n (pl -ties) (public service ~) empresa f de servicio público

utility room n: cuarto para lavar y planchar

utilize /'juːtlaɪz ‖'juːtɪlaɪz/ vt (frml) utilizar*

utmost¹ /'ʌtməʊst/ adj (before n) mayor, sumo; **with the ~ care** con el mayor cuidado, con sumo cuidado; **of the ~ importance** de suma importancia

u

utmost² *n*: to do one's ∼ (**to** + INF) esforzarse* al máximo *or* hacer* todo lo posible (PARA + INF)

utopia, Utopia /juːˈtəʊpɪə/ *n* (*pl* **-as**) utopía *f*

utter¹ /ˈʌtər ‖ ˈʌtə(r)/ *adj* (*as intensifier*) completo, total

utter² *vt* ⟨*word*⟩ decir*, pronunciar; ⟨*cry*⟩ dar*

utterly /ˈʌtərli ‖ ˈʌtəli/ *adv* (*as intensifier*) completamente, totalmente

U-turn /ˈjuːˈtɜːrn ‖ ˈjuːtɜːn/ *n* cambio *m* de sentido; **to make** (AmE) *o* (BrE) **do a** ∼ cambiar de sentido

Uzbekistan /ˈʊzbekɪˈstɑːn/ *n* Uzbekistán *m*

· ·

Vv

· ·

V, v /viː/ *n* V, v *f*

v ①▸ vs ② (*pl* **vv**) (Bib, Lit) = **verse** ③ (colloq) (= **very**) muy

V (Elec) (= **volt(s)**) V (*read as: voltio(s)*)

VA *n* = **Virginia**

vacancy /ˈveɪkənsi/ *n* (*pl* **-cies**) (a) (job) vacante *f*; ⑤ **vacancies** ofertas de trabajo (b) (in hotel) habitación *f* libre

vacant /ˈveɪkənt/ *adj* ① (a) ⟨*building/ premises*⟩ desocupado (b) ⟨*post*⟩ vacante (c) ⟨*room*⟩ disponible, libre; ⟨*seat/space*⟩ libre ② (blank) ⟨*look/expression*⟩ ausente

vacate /ˈveɪkeɪt ‖ vəˈkeɪt, vəˈ-/ *vt* (fml) ⟨*building*⟩ desocupar, desalojar; ⟨*seat/room*⟩ dejar libre; ⟨*job/post*⟩ abandonar, dejar

vacation¹ /veɪˈkeɪʃər *n* (esp AmE) (from work) vacaciones *fpl*, licencia *f* (Col, Méx, RPl); (from studies) vacaciones *fpl*; **to go/be on** ∼ irse*/estar* de vacaciones

vacation² *vi* (AmE) pasar las vacaciones, vacacionar (Méx)

vacationer /veɪˈkeɪʃər ‖ vəˈkeɪʃənə(r)/, **vacationist** /-ʃənəst ‖ -ʃənɪst/ *n* (AmE) turista *mf*; (in summer) veraneante *mf*

vaccinate /ˈvæksənərt ‖ ˈvæksmeɪt/ *vt* vacunar

vaccination /ˌvæksəˈneɪʃən ‖ ˌvæksɪˈneɪʃən/ *n* vacunación *f*

vaccine /vækˈsiːn ‖ ˈvæksiːn/ *n* vacuna *f*

vacillate /ˈvæsəleɪt/ *vi* (hesitate) vacilar; (sway) oscilar

vacuum¹ /ˈvækjuəm, -juːm/ *n* vacío *m*; (*before n*) ∼ **pump** bomba *f* neumática

vacuum² *vi* pasar la aspiradora, aspirar (AmL)

vacuum: ∼ **bottle** *n* (AmE) termo *m*; ∼ **cleaner** *n* aspiradora *f*, ∼ **flask** *n* termo *m*

vagabond /ˈvæɡəbɒnd ‖ ˈvæɡəbɒnd/ *n* vagabundo, -da *m,f*

vagina /vəˈdʒaɪnə/ *n* vagina *f*

vagrant /ˈveɪɡrənt/ *n* vagabundo, -da *m,f*

vague /veɪɡ/ *adj* **vaguer, vaguest** (a) (imprecise, unclear) ⟨*term/wording/concept*⟩

imprecise, vago (b) (indistinct) ⟨*outline*⟩ borroso (c) (absentminded) ⟨*expression*⟩ distraído; ⟨*person*⟩ distraído, despistado

vaguely /ˈveɪɡli/ *adv* (a) (in imprecise, unclear way) ⟨*explain/remember*⟩ vagamente; ⟨*answer/define*⟩ con vaguedad *or* imprecisión; ⟨*suspicious/ ridiculous*⟩ ligeramente; **he looks** ∼ **like his father** tiene un ligero parecido con *or* a su padre (b) (absentmindedly) distraídamente

vain /veɪn/ *adj* **-er, -est** ① (self-admiring) vanidoso ② (before n, no comp) (a) ⟨*attempt*⟩ vano; ⟨*hope/belief*⟩ vano (b) ⟨*promise/words*⟩ vano (c) **in vain** en vano, vanamente

vainly /ˈveɪnli/ *adv* (uselessly) en vano, vanamente

valentine /ˈvæləntaɪn/ *n* (a) (card) tarjeta de tono humorístico y/o amoroso que se envía anónimamente el día de San Valentín (b) also **Valentine** (person) enamorado, -da *m,f*

Valentine's Day /ˈvæləntaɪmz/ *n* el día de San Valentín, el día de los enamorados

valet /ˈvælət, ˈvæleɪ ‖ ˈvæleɪ, ˈvælɪt/ *n* (a) (servant) ayuda *m* de cámara (b) (in hotel) mozo *m* de hotel

valiant /ˈvæljənt/ *adj* ⟨*hero/deed*⟩ valiente, valeroso; ⟨*attempt*⟩ valeroso

valid /ˈvæləd ‖ ˈvælɪd/ *adj* válido

validate /ˈvælədeɪt/ *vt* (a) (fml) ⟨*theory*⟩ dar* validez a, validar (frml) (b) (Law) ⟨*contract/document*⟩ validar

valley /ˈvæli/ *n* (*pl* **-leys**) valle *m*

valor, (BrE) **valour** /ˈvælər ‖ ˈvælə(r)/ *n* (fml *o* liter) valor *m*, valentía *f*

valuable /ˈvæljuəbəl/ *adj* valioso; ⟨*time*⟩ precioso

valuables /ˈvæljuəbəlz/ *pl n* objetos *mpl* de valor

valuation /ˌvæljuˈeɪʃən/ *n* valoración *f*, tasación *f*, avalúo *m* (AmL)

value¹ /ˈvæljuː/ *n* ① (worth) valor *m* ② **values** (standards) valores *mpl*

value² *vt* (a) (Fin) ⟨*assets/property*⟩ tasar, valorar, avaluar* (AmL) (b) (regard highly) ⟨*friendship/advice*⟩ valorar, apreciar; ⟨*freedom/ privacy*⟩ valorar

· ·

AmC	América Central	Arg	Argentina	Cu	Cuba	Per	Perú
AmL	América Latina	Bol	Bolivia	Ec	Ecuador	RPl	Río de la Plata
AmS	América del Sur	Chi	Chile	Esp	España	Ur	Uruguay
Andes	Región andina	CS	Cono Sur	Méx	México	Ven	Venezuela

value-added tax /ˈvælju:ˈædəd ‖ˌvælju:ˈædɪd/ n impuesto m al valor agregado or (Esp) sobre el valor añadido

valve /vælv/ n válvula f; (on musical instrument) pistón m

vampire /ˈvæmpaɪr ‖ˈvæmpaɪə(r)/ n vampiro m

van /væn/ n (a) (Auto) furgoneta f, camioneta f (b) (BrE Rail) furgón m

vandal /ˈvændl/ n vándalo m

vandalism /ˈvændlɪzəm/ n vandalismo m

vandalize /ˈvændlaɪz/ vt destrozar*

vanguard /ˈvænɡɑːrd ‖ˈvænɡɑːd/ n vanguardia f

vanilla /vəˈnɪlə/ n vainilla f

vanish /ˈvænɪʃ/ vi desaparecer*

vanity /ˈvænəti/ n (pl **-ties**) (a) (about appearance) vanidad f (b) (pride) orgullo m, vanidad f

vanity case n neceser m

vanquish /ˈvæŋkwɪʃ/ vt (liter) vencer*

vantage point /ˈvæntɪdʒ ‖ˈvɑːntɪdʒ/ n posición f ventajosa; (for view) mirador m

vapor, (BrE) **vapour** /ˈveɪpər ‖ˈveɪpə(r)/ n (on glass) vaho m; (steam) vapor m

vaporize /ˈveɪpəraɪz/ vi evaporarse, vaporizarse*

vapour n (BrE) ▶ VAPOR

variable /ˈveəriəbəl ‖ˈveəriəbəl/ adj variable

variance /ˈveriəns ‖ˈveəriəns/ n: to be at ∼ with sth no estar* de acuerdo con algo, discrepar de algo

variant /ˈveriənt ‖ˈveəriənt/ n variante f

variation /ˌveriˈeɪʃən ‖ˌveəriˈeɪʃən/ n variación f

varicose veins /ˈværəkəʊs ‖ˈværɪkəʊs/ pl n varices fpl, várices fpl (esp AmL)

varied /ˈverid ‖ˈveərid/ adj variado

variegated /ˈverɪɡeɪtəd ‖ˈveərɪɡeɪtɪd/ adj abigarrado, multicolor

variety /vəˈraɪəti/ n (pl **-ties**) (a) (diversity) variedad f, diversidad f (b) (assortment) ∼ oʀ sth: it comes in a ∼ of shades viene en varios colores (c) (sort) clase f

variety show n espectáculo m de variedades

various /ˈveriəs ‖ˈveəriəs/ adj (a) (several) (before n, no comp) varios (b) (different, diverse) diferentes, diversos

varnish¹ /ˈvɑːrnɪʃ ‖ˈvɑːnɪʃ/ n barniz m; (for nails) (BrE) esmalte m

varnish² vt barnizar*; to ∼ one's nails (BrE) pintarse las uñas

vary /ˈveri ‖ˈveəri/, **varies, varying, varied** vi (a) (change, fluctuate) variar*; the temperature varies between ... la temperatura oscila entre ... (b) (differ) «standards/prices» variar*
■ ∼ vt variar*; ⟨diet⟩ dar* variedad a

vase /veɪs, veɪz ‖vɑːz/ n (for flowers) florero m; (ornament) jarrón m

vasectomy /vəˈsektəmi/ n (pl **-mies**) vasectomía f

Vaseline® /ˈvæsəliːn/ n vaselina f

vast /væst ‖vɑːst/ adj ⟨size/wealth⟩ inmenso, enorme; ⟨area⟩ vasto, extenso; ⟨knowledge⟩ vasto

vastly /ˈvæstli ‖ˈvɑːstli/ adv infinitamente

vat /væt/ n cuba f, tanque m

VAT n (= **value-added tax**) IVA m

Vatican /ˈvætɪkən/ n the ∼ el Vaticano

Vatican City n Ciudad f del Vaticano

vault¹ /vɔːlt/ n ⟦1⟧ (a) (strongroom) cámara f acorazada, bóveda f de seguridad (AmL) (b) (crypt) cripta f ⟦2⟧ (Archit) bóveda f

vault² vi/t saltar (apoyándose en algo)

VCR n = **videocassette recorder**

VD n = **venereal disease**

VDT n (esp AmE) = **visual display terminal**

VDU n = **visual display unit**

've /əv/ = **have**

veal /viːl/ n ternera f (de animal muy joven y de carne pálida)

VE-Day /ˈviːˈiːdeɪ/ n: día de la victoria aliada en Europa en la segunda guerra mundial

veer /vɪr ‖vɪə(r)/ vi «vehicle/horse» dar* un viraje, virar; «wind» cambiar de dirección; the road ∼s to the left el camino tuerce or se desvía hacia la izquierda

vegan /ˈviːɡən/ n vegetariano estricto, vegetariana estricta m,f

vegetable /ˈvedʒtəbəl/ n (a) (Culin) verdura f; fresh/frozen/canned ∼s verdura fresca/congelada/enlatada (b) (plant) vegetal m; (before n) ⟨oil/fats⟩ vegetal

vegetarian¹ /ˈvedʒəˈteriən ‖ˌvedʒɪˈteəriən/ n vegetariano, -na m,f

vegetarian² adj vegetariano

vegetate /ˈvedʒəteɪt ‖ˈvedʒɪteɪt/ vi vegetar

vegetation /ˌvedʒəˈteɪʃən ‖ˌvedʒɪˈteɪʃən/ n vegetación f

vehement /ˈviːəmənt/ adj vehemente

vehemently /ˈviːəməntli/ adv con vehemencia, vehementemente

vehicle /ˈviːəkəl/ n vehículo m

veil¹ /veɪl/ n velo m

veil² vt (cover with a veil): to ∼ one's face taparse or cubrirse* con un velo, velarse (liter)

veiled /veɪld/ adj ⟨threat/insult⟩ velado

vein /veɪn/ n ⟦1⟧ (Anat, Bot, Zool) vena f ⟦2⟧ (a) (of ore, mineral) veta f, filón m, vena f (b) (in marble) veta f ⟦3⟧ (no pl) (mood, style) vena f

velocity /vəˈlɑːsəti ‖vəˈlɒsəti/ n (pl **-ties**) velocidad f

velvet /ˈvelvət ‖ˈvelvɪt/ n terciopelo m

vendetta /venˈdetə/ n vendetta f

vending machine /ˈvendɪŋ/ n máquina f expendedora

vendor /ˈvendər ‖ˈvendə(r)/ n (Busn, Law) vendedor, -dora m,f

veneer /vəˈnɪr ‖vɪˈnɪə(r)/ n (of wood, gold) enchapado m, chapa f

venerate /ˈvenəreɪt/ vt venerar, reverenciar

venereal disease /vəˈnɪriəl ‖vəˈnɪəriəl/ n enfermedad f venérea

Venetian blind /vəˈniːʃən/ n persiana f veneciana or de lamas

Venezuela /ˈvenəˈzweɪlə ‖ˌvenɪˈzweɪlə/ n Venezuela f

Venezuelan¹ /ˈvenəˈzweɪlən ‖ˌvenɪˈzweɪlən/ adj venezolano

Venezuelan² n venezolano, -na m,f

vengeance /'vendʒəns/ n venganza f; **with a** ~ (colloq) de verdad or con ganas

vengeful /'vendʒfəl/ adj vengativo

venison /'venəsən ‖'venɪsən/ n (carne f de) venado m

venom /'venəm/ n **(a)** (Zool) veneno m **(b)** (malice) ponzoña f, veneno m

venomous /'venəməs/ adj ⟨snake/spider⟩ venenoso; ⟨look/words⟩ ponzoñoso

vent¹ /vent/ n **(a)** (in building, tunnel) (conducto m de) ventilación f; (in chimney, furnace) tiro m **(b)** (air ~) (shaft) respiradero m; (grille) rejilla f de ventilación

vent² vt descargar*; **she** ~**ed her anger on the children** descargó su ira sobre los niños

ventilate /'ventɪleɪt ‖'ventɪleɪt/ vt ventilar

ventilation /'ventɪ'eɪʃən ‖ˌventɪ'leɪʃən/ n ventilación f; (system) sistema m de ventilación

ventilator /'ventɪleɪtər ‖'ventɪleɪtə(r)/ n (Med) respirador m (artificial)

ventriloquist /ven'trɪləkwəst ‖ven'trɪləkwɪst/ n ventrílocuo, -cua m,f

venture¹ /'ventʃər ‖'ventʃə(r)/ n (Busn) empresa f

venture² vi atreverse; **to** ~ **out** (atreverse a) salir*
■ ~ vt ⟨opinion/guess⟩ aventurar

venue /'venjuː/ n (for concert) lugar m de actuación; (for conference, Olympics) sede f

Venus /'viːnəs/ n Venus m

veranda, verandah /vəˈrændə/ n galería f

verb /vɜːrb ‖vɜːb/ n verbo m

verbal /'vɜːrbəl ‖'vɜːbəl/ adj verbal

verbatim /vərˈbeɪtəm ‖vɜːˈbeɪtɪm/ adv al pie de la letra

verbose /vərˈbəʊs ‖vɜːˈbəʊs/ adj ampuloso, verboso

verdict /'vɜːrdɪkt ‖'vɜːdɪkt/ n **(a)** (Law) veredicto m **(b)** (opinion) opinión f

verge /vɜːrdʒ ‖vɜːdʒ/ n ① **(a)** (border) (BrE) borde m **(b) to be on the** ~ **of tears** estar* al borde de las lágrimas; **to be on the** ~ **of** -ING estar* a punto de + INF ② (of road) (BrE) arcén m
■ **verge on** [v + prep + o] rayar en

verification /ˌverəfəˈkeɪʃən ‖ˌverɪfɪˈkeɪʃən/ n **(a)** (confirmation) confirmación f **(b)** (checking) verificación f

verify /'verəfaɪ ‖'verɪfaɪ/ vt **-fies, -fying, -fied (a)** (confirm) confirmar **(b)** (check) ⟨fact/ statement⟩ verificar*

veritable /'verətəbəl ‖'verɪtəbəl/ adj (frml or hum) auténtico, verdadero

vermin /'vɜːrmən ‖'vɜːmɪn/ n (pl ~) (animals) alimañas fpl; (insects) bichos mpl

vernacular /vərˈnækjələr ‖vəˈnækjʊlə(r)/ n (native language) lengua f vernácula; (local speech) habla f‡ local

verruca /vəˈruːkə/ n verruga f

versatile /'vɜːrsət̬l ‖'vɜːsətaɪl/ adj ⟨person⟩ polifacético, versátil; ⟨tool⟩ versátil; ⟨mind⟩ flexible

versatility /ˌvɜːrsəˈtɪləti ‖ˌvɜːsəˈtɪləti/ n versatilidad f

verse /vɜːrs ‖vɜːs/ n ① (poetry) verso m ② **(a)** (short poem) verso m, rima f **(b)** (stanza) estrofa f **(c)** (in Bible) versículo m

versed /vɜːrst ‖vɜːst/ adj (pred): **to be well** ~ **in sth ser*** muy versado en algo

version /'vɜːrʒən ‖'vɜːʃən/ n versión f

versus /'vɜːrsəs ‖'vɜːsəs/ prep (Law) contra; (Sport) contra, versus

vertebra /'vɜːrtəbrə ‖'vɜːtəbrə/ n (pl **-bras** or **-brae** /-breɪ/) vértebra f

vertebrate /'vɜːrtəbrət ‖'vɜːtɪbrət/ n vertebrado m

vertical /'vɜːrtɪkəl ‖'vɜːtɪkəl/ adj vertical

vertigo /'vɜːrtɪgəʊ ‖'vɜːtɪgəʊ/ n vértigo m

verve /vɜːrv ‖vɜːv/ n brío m

very¹ /'veri/ adv **(a)** (extremely) muy; **she's** ~ **tall** es muy alta; (more emphatic) es altísima; **it was** ~ **hot** hacía mucho calor **(b)** (in phrases) very much ⟨like/enjoy⟩ mucho; **thank you** ~ **much** muchas gracias **(c)** (emphatic): **the** ~ **next day** precisamente al día siguiente; **at the** ~ **least** como mínimo

very² adj (before n) **(a)** (exact, precise) mismo; **for that** ~ **reason** por esa misma razón, por eso mismo **(b)** (actual) mismo; **its** ~ **existence is threatened** su misma existencia se halla amenazada **(c)** (mere, sheer) solo, mero; **the** ~ **mention of her name** la sola or mera mención de su nombre

vespers /'vespərz ‖'vespəz/ pl n vísperas fpl

vessel /'vesəl/ n ① (Naut frml) navío m (frml), nave f (liter) ② (receptacle) (frml) recipiente m; (drinking ~) vasija f ③ (Anat, Bot) vaso m

vest /vest/ n **(a)** (waistcoat) (AmE) chaleco m **(b)** (undergarment) (BrE) camiseta f

vested interest /'vestəd ‖'vestɪd/ n **to have a** ~ ~ **in** -ING/sth tener* gran interés en + INF/ algo

vestige /'vestɪdʒ/ n vestigio m

vestry /'vestri/ n (pl **-tries**) sacristía f

vet¹ /vet/ n ① (veterinarian) veterinario, -ria m,f ② (veteran) (AmE colloq) veterano, -na m,f

vet² vt **-tt-** ⟨applicant⟩ someter a investigación; ⟨application⟩ examinar

veteran /'vetərən/ n **(a)** (of war) veterano, -na m,f de guerra **(b)** (experienced person) veterano, -na m,f

veteran: ~ **car** n (BrE) coche m antiguo (fabricado antes de 1919); **V**~**s Day** /'vetərənz/ n (in US) día m del Armisticio

veterinarian /ˌvetərəˈneriən ‖ˌvetərɪˈneəriən/ n (AmE) médico veterinario, médica veterinaria m,f

veterinary /'vetərəneri ‖'vetrɪnəri/ adj veterinario; ~ **surgeon** (BrE frml) médico veterinario, médica veterinaria m,f

veto¹ /'viːtəʊ/ n (pl **vetoes**) veto m

veto² vt **vetoes, vetoing, vetoed** vetar

vex /veks/ vt **(a)** (annoy) irritar, sacar* de quicio **(b)** (worry, puzzle) desconcertar*

vexed /vekst/ adj (a) (annoyed) ⟨expression/tone⟩ irritado; **to be** ~ estar* enojado (esp AmL), estar* enfadado (esp Esp) **(b)** (worried, puzzled) desconcertado

VHF (= **very high frequency**) VHF

973

via ⋯**⟩ violin** ⋯

via /'vaɪə, 'vi:ə ‖'vaɪə/ *prep* **(a)** (by way of) vía **(b)** (by means of) a través de

viable /'vaɪəbəl/ *adj* viable

viaduct /'vaɪədʌkt/ *n* viaducto *m*

vibrant /'vaɪbrənt/ *adj* **(a)** ⟨color⟩ vibrante; ⟨atmosphere⟩ efervescente **(b)** (resonant) ⟨voice⟩ vibrante

vibrate /'vaɪbreɪt ‖vaɪ'breɪt/ *vi* vibrar

vibration /vaɪ'breɪʃən/ *n* vibración *f*

vicar /'vɪkər ‖'vɪkə(r)/ *n* párroco *m*

vicarage /'vɪkərɪdʒ/ *n* vicaría *f*, casa *f* del párroco

vicarious /vɪ'keriəs ‖vɪ'keəriəs/ *adj* indirecto

vice /vaɪs/ *n* **1** (wickedness) vicio *m* **2** (BrE) ▶ VISE

vice- /'vaɪs/ *pref* vice-

vice: ~ **president** *n* vicepresidente, -ta *m,f*; ~ **versa** /'vaɪsi'vɜ:rsə, 'vaɪs'vɜ:rsə ‖,vaɪsi'vɜ:sə, ,vaɪs'vɜ:sə/ *adv* viceversa

vicinity /vɪ'sɪnəti/ *n* (fml) inmediaciones *fpl*

vicious /'vɪʃəs/ *adj* **(a)** (savage, violent) ⟨dog⟩ fiero; ⟨criminal⟩ despiadado; ⟨attack⟩ feroz, salvaje; ⟨crime⟩ atroz **(b)** (malicious) ⟨rumor⟩ malicioso

vicious circle *n* círculo *m* vicioso

viciously /'vɪʃəsli/ *adv* brutalmente, ferozmente

victim /'vɪktəm ‖'vɪktɪm/ *n* víctima *f*; the flood ~s los damnificados por las inundaciones

victimize /'vɪktəmaɪz ‖'vɪktɪmaɪz/ *vt* victimizar*

victor /'vɪktər ‖'vɪktə(r)/ *n* vencedor, -dora *m,f*

Victorian /vɪk'tɔ:riən/ *adj* victoriano

victorious /vɪk'tɔ:riəs/ *adj* ⟨army⟩ victorioso; ⟨team⟩ vencedor

victory /'vɪktəri/ *n* (*pl* **-ries**) victoria *f*, triunfo *m*; (Mil) victoria *f*

video[1] /'vɪdiəʊ/ *n* (*pl* **videos**) video *m or* (Esp) vídeo *m*; (before *n*) ~ **camera** videocámara *f*; ~ **recorder** aparato *m* de video *or* (Esp) vídeo

video[2] *vt* **videoes, videoing, videoed** grabar

video: ~**cassette** /'vɪdiəʊkə'set/ *n* videocasete *m*; (before *n*) ~**cassette recorder** magnetoscopio *m*, video *m or* (Esp) vídeo *m*; ~ **game** *n* videojuego *m*

Vienna /vi'enə/ *n* Viena *f*

Vietnam /'vi:et'nɑ:m, -næm ‖vjet'næm/ *n* Vietnam *m*

Vietnamese[1] /vi'etnə'mi:z ‖,vjetnə'mi:z/ *adj* vietnamita

Vietnamese[2] *n* (*pl* ~) **(a)** (person) vietnamita *mf* **(b)** (language) vietnamita *m*

view[1] /vju:/ *n* **1** **(a)** (sight) vista *f*; in full ~ of sb a la vista de algn **(b)** (range of vision): we had a good ~ of the stage veíamos muy bien el escenario **2** (scene, vista) vista *f* **3** (opinion, attitude) opinión *f*, parecer *m*; in my ~ en mi opinión, a mi modo de ver **4** (plan, intention): with a ~ to -ING con vistas A + INF **5** (in phrases) in view of en vista de; on view: to be on ~ (to the public) exponerse* (al público)

view[2] *vt* **(a)** ⟨sights/scene⟩ ver*, mirar **(b)** (inspect) ⟨property⟩ ver* **(c)** (regard) ver*, considerar

viewer /'vju:ər ‖'vju:ə(r)/ *n* **(a)** (person) telespectador, -dora *m,f*, televidente *mf* **(b)** (for slides) visionadora *f*

view: ~**finder** /'vju:faɪndər ‖'vju:,faɪndə(r)/ *n* visor *m*; ~**point** *n* punto *m* de vista

vigil /'vɪdʒəl ‖'vɪdʒɪl/ *n* **(a)** (watch) (liter *or* journ) vela *f*; to keep a ~ over sth velar sobre algo **(b)** (Relig) vigilia *f*

vigilance /'vɪdʒələns ‖'vɪdʒɪləns/ *n* vigilancia *f*

vigilant /'vɪdʒələnt ‖'vɪdʒɪlənt/ *adj* alerta, vigilante

vigilante /'vɪdʒə'lænti ‖,vɪdʒɪ'lænti/ *n* vigilante, -ta *m,f*

vigor, (BrE) **vigour** /'vɪgər ‖'vɪgə(r)/ *n* vigor *m*

vigorous /'vɪgərəs/ *adj* enérgico; ⟨growth⟩ vigoroso

vigorously /'vɪgərəsli/ *adv* enérgicamente; ⟨deny⟩ rotundamente

vigour *n* (BrE) ▶ VIGOR

Viking /'vaɪkɪŋ/ *n* vikingo, -ga *m,f*

vile /vaɪl/ *adj* **viler, vilest (a)** (despicable) (liter) vil (liter) **(b)** (colloq) ⟨taste/food⟩ vomitivo (fam), asqueroso; ⟨color/weather⟩ horrible

villa /'vɪlə/ *n* **(a)** (Hist) villa *f* **(b)** (holiday house) chalet *m*

village /'vɪlɪdʒ/ *n* (large) pueblo *m*; (small) aldea *f*

villager /'vɪlədʒər ‖'vɪlɪdʒə(r)/ *n* (of large village) vecino, -na *m,f or* habitante *mf* del pueblo; (of small village) aldeano, -na *m,f*

villain /'vɪlən/ *n* **(a)** (in fiction) villano, -na *m,f* **(b)** (criminal) (BrE sl) maleante *mf*

vinaigrette /vɪnɪ'gret/ *n* vinagreta *f*

vindicate /'vɪndəkeɪt ‖'vɪndɪkeɪt/ *vt* (fml) (justify) ⟨action⟩ justificar*; ⟨assertion⟩ confirmar; ⟨right⟩ reivindicar*

vindictive /vɪn'dɪktɪv/ *adj* vengativo

vine /vaɪn/ *n* (grape~) (on ground) vid *f*; (climbing) parra *f*

vinegar /'vɪnɪgər ‖'vɪnɪgə(r)/ *n* vinagre *m*

vineyard /'vɪnjərd, -jɑ:rd ‖'vɪnjəd, -jɑ:d/ *n* viñedo *m*, viña *f*

vintage[1] /'vɪntɪdʒ/ *n* **(a)** (wine, year) cosecha *f* **(b)** (harvest, season) vendimia *f*

vintage[2] *adj* (before *n*, no comp) **(a)** ⟨wine⟩ añejo **(b)** (outstanding) ⟨year/performance⟩ excelente

vintage car *n* (esp BrE) coche *m* antiguo (fabricado entre 1919 y 1930)

vinyl /'vaɪnl/ *n* vinilo *m*

viola /vi'əʊlə/ *n* (Mus) viola *f*

violate /'vaɪəleɪt/ *vt* **1** ⟨agreement/rights⟩ violar; ⟨ban⟩ desobedecer* **2** ⟨shrine/grave⟩ profanar

violation /vaɪə'leɪʃən/ *n* violación *f*

violence /'vaɪələns/ *n* violencia *f*

violent /'vaɪələnt/ *adj* **(a)** ⟨person/behavior⟩ violento **(b)** (strong, forceful) ⟨storm/explosion⟩ violento, fuerte; he has a ~ temper tiene muy mal genio

violently /'vaɪələntli/ *adv* violentamente

violet /'vaɪələt/ *n* **(a)** (Bot) violeta *f* **(b)** (color) violeta *m*; (before *n*) violeta *adj inv*

violin /vaɪə'lɪn/ *n* violín *m*

violinist /ˈvaɪəˈlɪnəst ‖ˌvaɪəˈlɪnɪst/ n violinista mf

VIP n (colloq) (= **very important person**) VIP mf

viper /ˈvaɪpər ‖ˈvaɪpə(r)/ n víbora f

virgin[1] /ˈvɜːrdʒən ‖ˈvɜːdʒɪn/ n virgen f

virgin[2] adj ⟨forest⟩ virgen; ⟨snow⟩ intacto

virginity /vərˈdʒɪnəti ‖vəˈdʒɪnɪti/ n virginidad f; **to lose one's ~** perder* la virginidad

Virgo /ˈvɜːrɡəʊ ‖ˈvɜːɡəʊ/ n (pl **-gos**) (a) (sign) (no art) Virgo (b) (person) Virgo or virgo mf

virile /ˈvɪrəl ‖ˈvɪraɪl/ adj viril

virtual /ˈvɜːrtʃuəl ‖ˈvɜːtʃʊəl, ˈvɜːtʃuəl/ adj (before n) 1 (near total): **traffic is at a ~ standstill** el tráfico está prácticamente paralizado 2 (Comput, Opt) virtual

virtually /ˈvɜːrtʃuəli ‖ˈvɜːtjuəli, ˈvɜːtʃuəli/ adv prácticamente, casi

virtue /ˈvɜːrtʃuː ‖ˈvɜːtjuː, ˈvɜːtʃuː/ n (a) (moral excellence) virtud f (b) (advantage) ventaja f (c) **by virtue of** (as prep) en virtud de

virtuoso /ˈvɜːrtʃuˈəʊsəʊ ‖ˌvɜːtjʊˈəʊsəʊ, ˌvɜːtʃʊˈəʊsəʊ/ n (pl **-sos** or **-si** /-siː/) virtuoso, -sa m,f

virtuous /ˈvɜːrtʃuəs ‖ˈvɜːtjʊəs, ˈvɜːtʃʊəs/ adj virtuoso

virulent /ˈvɪrələnt, ˈvɪrjə- ‖ˈvɪrʊlənt, ˈvɪrjʊ-/ adj virulento

virus /ˈvaɪrəs ‖ˈvaɪərəs/ n (pl **~es**) (Med, Comput) virus m

virus checker n (Comput) programa m antivirus

visa /ˈviːzə/ n (pl **-s**) visado m, visa f (AmL)

vis-à-vis /ˈviːzəˈviː ‖ˌviːzɑːˈviː/ prep con respecto a, respecto de

viscose /ˈvɪskəʊs/ n viscosilla f

viscount /ˈvaɪkaʊnt/ n vizconde m

viscous /ˈvɪskəs/ adj viscoso

vise, (BrE) **vice** /vaɪs/ n torno m or tornillo m de banco

visibility /ˈvɪzəˈbɪləti/ n visibilidad f

visible /ˈvɪzəbəl/ adj visible; ⟨sign/improvement⟩ evidente

visibly /ˈvɪzəbli/ adv visiblemente

vision /ˈvɪʒən/ n 1 (a) (faculty of sight) visión f, vista f (b) (visibility) visibilidad f 2 (imagination, foresight) visión f (de futuro) 3 (dreamlike revelation) visión f

visionary /ˈvɪʒəneri ‖ˈvɪʒənri/ n (pl **-ries**) visionario, -ria m,f

visit[1] /ˈvɪzət ‖ˈvɪzɪt/ n visita f; **to pay a ~ to sb** hacerle* una visita a algn

visit[2] vt visitar
■ ~ vi hacer* una visita; (stay) estar* de visita

visitor /ˈvɪzətər ‖ˈvɪzɪtə(r)/ n (to museum, town etc) visitante mf; (to person's home) visita f

visitor center n (AmE) centro m de informaciones

visor /ˈvaɪzər ‖ˈvaɪzə(r)/ n visera f

vista /ˈvɪstə/ n vista f

visual /ˈvɪʒuəl/ adj visual; **~ display unit** pantalla f, monitor m

visualize /ˈvɪʒuəlaɪz/ vt (a) (picture mentally) imaginarse, visualizar* (b) (expect) prever*

vital /ˈvaɪtl̩/ adj (a) (essential) esencial, fundamental (b) ⟨factor/issue⟩ decisivo, de vital importancia (c) ⟨organ/function⟩ vital

vitality /vaɪˈtæləti/ n vitalidad f

vitamin /ˈvaɪtəmɪn ‖ˈvɪtəmɪn, ˈvaɪt-/ n vitamina f; (before n) **~ pill** o **tablet** vitamina f

vivacious /vəˈveɪʃəs ‖vɪˈveɪʃəs/ adj vivaz

vivid /ˈvɪvəd ‖ˈvɪvɪd/ adj (a) ⟨color⟩ vivo (b) ⟨account/dream⟩ vívido (c) ⟨imagination⟩ rico

vividly /ˈvɪvədli ‖ˈvɪvɪdli/ adv (a) ⟨colored⟩ vistosamente (b) ⟨describe⟩ vívidamente, gráficamente

vivisection /ˈvɪvəˈsekʃən ‖ˌvɪvɪˈsekʃən/ n vivisección f

vixen /ˈvɪksən/ n (Zool) zorra f, raposa f

viz /vɪz/ adv a saber

VJ-Day /ˈviːˈdʒeɪdeɪ/ n: día de la victoria aliada sobre el Japón

V-neck /ˈviːnek/, (BrE also) **V-necked** /ˈviːnekt/ adj de escote or cuello en pico, de escote en V

vocabulary /vəʊˈkæbjəleri ‖vəʊˈkæbjʊləri/ n (pl **-ries**) vocabulario m

vocal /ˈvəʊkəl/ adj vocal

vocal cords pl n cuerdas fpl vocales

vocalist /ˈvəʊkələst ‖ˈvəʊkəlɪst/ n cantante mf

vocation /vəʊˈkeɪʃən/ n vocación f

vodka /ˈvɑːdkə ‖ˈvɒdkə/ n vodka m

vogue /vəʊɡ/ n moda f

voice[1] /vɔɪs/ n voz f

voice[2] vt expresar

voice: ~ mail n correo m de voz, mensajería f de voz; **~ message** n mensaje m de voz

void[1] /vɔɪd/ n vacío m

void[2] adj 1 (liter) (pred) **to be ~ of sth** estar* desprovisto de algo 2 (Law) nulo, inválido

vol (pl **vols**) (= **volume**) vol., t.

volatile /ˈvɑːlət̬l̩ ‖ˈvɒlətaɪl/ adj (a) (Chem) volátil (b) ⟨person/personality⟩ imprevisible (c) ⟨situation⟩ volátil

volcanic /vɑːlˈkænɪk ‖vɒlˈkænɪk/ adj volcánico

volcano /vɑːlˈkeɪnəʊ ‖vɒlˈkeɪnəʊ/ n (pl **-noes** or **-nos**) volcán m

volition /vəʊˈlɪʃən ‖vəˈlɪʃən/ n (fml) volición f (fml); **of one's own ~** por voluntad propia, (de) motu proprio

volley[1] /ˈvɑːli ‖ˈvɒli/ n 1 (of shots) descarga f (cerrada) 2 (Sport) volea f

volley[2] vt/i volear

volleyball /ˈvɑːlibɔːl ‖ˈvɒlibɔːl/ n vóleibol m, balonvolea m

volt /vəʊlt/ n voltio m

voltage /ˈvəʊltɪdʒ/ n voltaje m

AmC	Central America	Arg	Argentina	Cu	Cuba	Per	Peru
AmL	Latin America	Bol	Bolivia	Ec	Ecuador	RPI	River Plate Area
AmS	South America	Chi	Chile	Esp	Spain	Ur	Uruguay
Andes	Andean Region	CS	Southern Cone	Méx	Mexico	Ven	Venezuela

volume /'vɑːljuːm ‖'vɒljuːm/ n **1** (Phys) (of a body) volumen m; (of container) capacidad f **2** (amount) cantidad f, volumen m; (of business, trade) volumen m **3** (of sound) volumen m **4** (book) tomo m, volumen m

voluminous /və'luːmənəs ‖və'luːmɪnəs/ adj **(a)** ⟨blouse/skirt⟩ amplísimo **(b)** ⟨correspondence⟩ voluminoso

voluntarily /'vɑːlən'terəli ‖'vɒləntrɪli/ adv voluntariamente, por voluntad propia

voluntary /'vɑːlənteri ‖'vɒləntri/ adj **1** (unforced) voluntario; ~ **redundancy** (BrE) baja f incentivada **2** (unpaid) ⟨work⟩ voluntario; ⟨organization⟩ de beneficencia

volunteer¹ /'vɑːlən'tɪr ‖,vɒlən'tɪər/ n voluntario, -ria m,f

volunteer² vt ofrecer*
■ ~ vi ofrecerse*; **to ~ to + INF** ofrecerse* A + INF

voluptuous /və'lʌptʃuəs/ adj voluptuoso

vomit¹ /'vɑːmət ‖'vɒmɪt/ vi/t vomitar

vomit² n vómito m

voodoo /'vuːduː/ n vudú m

voracious /vɔː'reɪʃəs ‖və'reɪʃəs/ adj voraz

vote¹ /vəʊt/ n **1** **(a)** (ballot cast) voto m **(b)** (right to vote) **the ~** el sufragio, el derecho de or al voto **2** (act) votación f; **to take a ~ on sth** someter algo a votación

vote² vi votar; **to ~ FOR sb** votar POR or A algn; **to ~ ON sth** someter algo a votación; **to ~ FOR/ AGAINST sth** votar A FAVOR DE/EN CONTRA DE algo

■ ~ vt **1** **(a)** (support, choose) votar por, votar **(b)** (elect) elegir* por votación **2** (decide) **to ~ to + INF** votar POR + INF
■ **vote in** [v + o + adv, v + adv + o] elegir* (por votación)

voter /'vəʊtər ‖'vəʊtə(r)/ n votante mf

voting /'vəʊtɪŋ/ n votación f

vouch /vaʊtʃ/ vi **to ~ FOR sb** responder POR algn

voucher /'vaʊtʃər ‖'vaʊtʃə(r)/ n (cash substitute) vale m

vow¹ /vaʊ/ n voto m, promesa f

vow² vt jurar, hacer* voto de (frml)

vowel /'vaʊəl/ n vocal f

voyage /'vɔɪɪdʒ/ n viaje m; (overseas) travesía f

voyager /'vɔɪədʒər ‖'vɔɪɪdʒə(r)/ n (liter) viajero, -ra m,f; (by sea) navegante mf

voyeur /vwɑː'jɜːr, 'vɔɪ- ‖vwɑː'jɜː(r), 'vɔɪ-/ n voyeur mf

vs = versus

VT, Vt = Vermont

vulgar /'vʌlgər ‖'vʌlgə(r)/ adj **(a)** (coarse) ⟨person/remark⟩ grosero, ordinario, vulgar **(b)** (tasteless) de mal gusto, ordinario

vulgarity /vʌl'gærəti/ n **(a)** (coarseness) ordinariez f, grosería f, vulgaridad f **(b)** (tastelessness) mal gusto m, chabacanería f

vulnerable /'vʌlnərəbəl/ adj vulnerable

vulture /'vʌltʃər ‖'vʌltʃə(r)/ n buitre m; (turkey ~) gallinazo m, zopilote m (AmC, Méx)

vv = verses

Ww

W, w /'dʌbəljuː/ n W, w f

W (a) (Elec) (= **watt(s)**) W **(b)** (Geog) (= **west**) O

WA = Washington

wad /wɑːd ‖wɒd/ n (roll, bundle — of bills, notes) fajo m; (— of papers) montón m, tambache m (Méx); (— tied together) lío m

waddle /'wɑːdl̩ ‖'wɒdl̩/ vi «person» caminar or andar* como un pato; «duck» caminar balanceándose

wade /weɪd/ vi caminar (por el agua, barro etc)
■ **wade through** [v + prep + o] (colloq) leerse* (algo difícil, largo, aburrido etc)

wader /'weɪdər ‖'weɪdə(r)/ n **(a)** (Zool) ave f‡ zancuda **(b)** **waders** pl (Clothing) botas fpl de pescador

wading pool /'weɪdɪŋ/ n (AmE) piscina f or (Méx) alberca f inflable (para niños)

wafer /'weɪfər ‖'weɪfə(r)/ n **(a)** (Culin) galleta f de barquillo, oblea f **(b)** (Relig) hostia f

wafer-thin /'weɪfər'θɪn ‖,weɪfə'θɪn/ adj finísimo

waffle¹ /'wɑːfəl ‖'wɒfəl/ n **1** (Culin) wafle m (AmL), gofre m (Esp) **2** (nonsense) (BrE pej) palabrería f; (in essay, exam) paja f (fam)

waffle² vi (esp BrE) hablar sin decir nada; (in essay, exam) meter paja (fam), payar (RPl)

waft /wɑːft ‖'wɒft/ vi (+ adv compl): **the smell of coffee that ~ed from the kitchen** el olor a café que venía de la cocina

wag /wæg/ -**gg**- vt ⟨tail⟩ menear
■ ~ vi «tail» menearse, moverse*

wage¹ /weɪdʒ/ n (rate of pay) sueldo m; **wages** (actual money) sueldo m, paga f

wage² vt: **to ~ war** hacer* la guerra

wager¹ /'weɪdʒər ‖'weɪdʒə(r)/ n apuesta f

wager² vt apostar*

waggon n (BrE) ▶ WAGON

wagon /'wægən/ n **1** (drawn by animals) carro m; (covered) carromato m **2** **(a)** (delivery truck) (AmE) furgoneta f or camioneta f de reparto **(b)** (BrE Rail) vagón m de mercancías

waif /weɪf/ n (liter) persona o animal sin hogar

wail¹ /weɪl/ vi «person» llorar; «siren/ bagpipes» gemir*; «wind» aullar*

wail² n gemido m

waist /weɪst/ n (of body) cintura f; (of garment) talle m

waist: ~**band** n pretina f, cinturilla f; ~**coat** n (esp BrE) chaleco m; ~**line** n (of garment) talle m; (of body) cintura f

wait¹ /weɪt/ vi **1** esperar; **we'll have to** ~ **and see** habrá que esperar a ver qué pasa; **I can't** ~ **to see his face** me muero de ganas de ver la cara que pone; **to** ~ **FOR sth/sb** esperar algo/a algn; **to** ~ **FOR sb/sth to** + INF esperar (A) QUE algn/algo (+ subj) **2** (serve) **to** ~ **ON sb** atender* a algn
■ ~ vt **1** (await) esperar; **you have to** ~ **your turn** tienes que esperar (a) que te toque **2** (serve): **to** ~ **table** (AmE) servir* a la mesa
■ **wait up** [v + adv] (not go to bed) **to** ~ **up (FOR sb)** esperar (A algn) levantado

wait² n (no pl) espera f; **to lie in** ~ **for sb/sth** estar* al acecho de algn/algo

waiter /'weɪtər ‖'weɪtə(r)/ n camarero m, mesero m (AmL), mozo m (Col, CS), mesonero m (Ven)

waiting /'weɪtɪŋ/: ~ **list** n lista f de espera; ~ **room** n sala f de espera

waitress /'weɪtrəs ‖'weɪtrɪs/ n camarera f, mesera f (AmL), moza f (Col, CS), mesonera f (Ven)

waive /weɪv/ vt (frml) **(a)** (not apply) ⟨rule⟩ no aplicar*; ⟨condition⟩ no exigir* **(b)** (renounce) ⟨right/privilege⟩ renunciar a

wake¹ /weɪk/ (past **woke**; past p **woken**) vt despertar*; see also WAKE UP 1
■ ~ vi despertar*, despertarse*
■ **wake up 1** [v + o + adv, v + adv + o] despertar* **2** [v + adv] (become awake) despertarse*; ~ **up!** ¡despiértate!; (pay attention) ¡espabílate!, ¡despabílate!; **to** ~ **up TO sth** ⟨to danger/fact⟩ darse* cuenta DE algo

wake² n **1** (of ship) estela f; **the hurricane left a trail of destruction in its** ~ el huracán dejó una estela de destrucción a su paso **2** (for dead person) velatorio m

Wales /weɪlz/ n (el país de) Gales

walk¹ /wɔːk/ vi **1** (go by foot) caminar, andar* (esp Esp); (in a leisurely way) pasear; **he** ~**ed down/up the steps** bajó/subió los peldaños; **to** ~ **in/out** entrar/salir*; **to** ~ **up to sb** acercarse* a algn **2** (not use bus, car, etc) ir* a pie
■ ~ vt **1** (go along) ⟨hills/path⟩ recorrer **2 (a)** (take for walk) ⟨dog⟩ pasear, sacar* a pasear **(b)** (accompany) acompañar
■ **walk away** [v + adv] alejarse
■ **walk into** [v + prep + o] **(a)** (enter) ⟨room/building⟩ entrar en, entrar a (AmL) **(b)** (fall into) ⟨trap⟩ caer* en **(c)** (collide with) darse* contra
■ **walk off 1** [v + adv] (go away) irse*, marcharse (esp Esp) **2** [v + o + adv, v + adv + o]: **we went out to** ~ **off our lunch** salimos a dar un paseo para bajar la comida
■ **walk out** [v + adv] (Lab Rel) abandonar el trabajo (como medida reivindicatoria)
■ **walk out on** [v + adv + prep + o] ⟨lover/family⟩ dejar, abandonar
■ **walk over** [v + prep + o] (colloq): **don't let him** ~ **all over you** no te dejes pisotear (por él)

walk² n **1** (leisurely) paseo m; (long) caminata f; **to go for a** ~ ir* a pasear or a dar un paseo, ir* a caminar (esp AmL); **it's five minutes' o a**

five-minute ~ **from here** está a cinco minutos de aquí a pie **2** (path) (esp AmE) camino m **3** (gait) manera f de caminar or andar; see also WALK OF LIFE

walker /'wɔːkər ‖'wɔːkə(r)/ n **(a)** (sb that walks): **to be a fast/slow** ~ caminar or andar* rápido/despacio **(b)** (hiker) excursionista mf

walkie-talkie /'wɔːki'tɔːki/ n walkie-talkie m

walk-in /'wɔːkɪn/ adj: ~ **closet** vestidor m

walking¹ /'wɔːkɪŋ/ n: **I do a lot of** ~ yo camino or ando mucho; (before n) ⟨tour⟩ a pie; **is it within** ~ **distance?** ¿se puede ir a pie?

walking² adj: **she's a** ~ **encyclopedia** (hum) es una enciclopedia ambulante (hum); **he's a** ~ **miracle** vive de milagro

walking stick n bastón m

Walkman® /'wɔːkmən/ n (pl **-mans** /-mənz/) walkman® m

walk: ~ **of life** n: **people from all** ~**s of life** gente de todas las profesiones y condiciones sociales; ~**on** n (before n) ~**on part** (Theat) papel m de figurante; (Cin) papel m de extra; ~**out** n (from talks, meeting) retirada f en señal de protesta; (strike) abandono del trabajo como medida reivindicatoria; ~**over** n (victory by default) walkover m (victoria por la no comparecencia del contrincante); (easy victory) (colloq) paseo m (fam); ~**way** n (bridge) puente m, pasarela f; (passageway) pasillo m; (path) sendero m

wall /wɔːl/ n **1 (a)** (freestanding) muro m; (of castle, city) muralla f; **garden** ~ tapia f, muro m **(b)** (barrier) barrera f; **a** ~ **of fire** una barrera de fuego **2** (of building, room) pared f, muralla f (Chi); (before n) ~ **chart** gráfico m mural; ~ **painting** mural m **3** (of stomach, artery) pared f
■ **wall off** [v + o + adv, v + adv + o] separar con un muro or una pared or una tapia
■ **wall up** [v + o + adv, v + adv + o] ⟨doorway/window⟩ tapiar; ⟨person/body⟩ emparedar

walled /wɔːld/ adj ⟨city⟩ amurallado; ⟨garden⟩ tapiado

wallet /'wɑːlət ‖'wɒlɪt/ n **(a)** (for money) cartera f, billetera f **(b)** (folder) carpeta f

wallflower /'wɔːlflaʊr ‖'wɔːlflaʊə(r)/ n **1** (Bot) alhelí m **2** (person) (colloq): **she was always a** ~ nunca la sacaban a bailar, siempre planchaba (Bol, CS fam), siempre comía pavo (Col fam)

wallop /'wɑːləp ‖'wɒləp/ vt (colloq) darle* una paliza a

wallow /'wɑːləʊ ‖'wɒləʊ/ vi **(a)** (bathe) «animal» revolcarse* **(b)** (delight): **to** ~ **in self-pity** regodearse en la autocompasión

wall: ~**paper** n papel m pintado, tapiz m de empapelar (Méx, Ven); **W**~ **Street** n Wall Street (centro financiero de los EEUU); ~**to-**~ **carpet** /'wɔːltə'wɔːl/ n alfombra f de pared a pared, moqueta f (Esp), moquette f (RPl)

walnut /'wɔːlnʌt/ n **(a)** (nut) nuez f, nuez f de Castilla (Méx) **(b)** ~ **(tree)** nogal m **(c)** (wood) nogal m

walrus /'wɔːlrəs/ n (pl **-es** or ~) morsa f

waltz¹ /wɔːls, wɔːlts/ n vals m

waltz² vi valsar, valsear

wan /wɑːn ‖wɒn/ adj **(a)** (pallid) ⟨face/complexion⟩ pálido **(b)** ⟨smile⟩ lánguido

wand /wɑːnd ‖wɒnd/ *n* (of sorcerer, conjurer) varita *f* mágica

wander¹ /ˈwɑːndər ‖ˈwɒndə(r)/ *vi* **(a)** (+ *adv compl*) (walk — in a leisurely way) pasear; (— aimlessly) deambular, vagar* **(b)** (stray): **don't let the children ~ away from the car** no dejes que los niños se alejen del coche; **don't let your mind ~!** ¡no te distraigas!

wander² *n* (esp BrE) (*no pl*) vuelta *f*, paseo *m*

wanderer /ˈwɑːndərər ‖ˈwɒndərə(r)/ *n* trotamundos *mf*

wanderings /ˈwɑːndərɪŋz ‖ˈwɒndərɪŋz/ *pl n* correrías *fpl*

wanderlust /ˈwɑːndərlʌst ‖ˈwɒndəlʌst/ *n* ansias *fpl* de conocer mundo

wane¹ /weɪn/ *vi* **(a)** «*moon*» menguar* **(b)** «*interest/popularity*» decaer*, disminuir* **(c)** **waning** *pres p* «*moon*» menguante; «*interest/popularity/influence*» decreciente

wane² *n*: **to be on the ~** «*moon*» estar* menguando; «*popularity*» estar* decayendo *or* disminuyendo

wangle /ˈwæŋɡəl/ *vt* (colloq) agenciarse (fam)

want¹ /wɑːnt ‖wɒnt/ *vt* **1** **(a)** (require, desire) querer*; **to ~ to** + INF querer* + INF; **to ~ sb/sth to** + INF querer* QUE algn/algo (+ *subj*) **(b)** «*police*» buscar*; **Ⓢ wanted** se busca **(c)** (as price for sth) pedir* **(d)** «*person*» (sexually) desear **2** (need) necesitar; **Ⓢ gardener wanted** se necesita *or* se precisa jardinero; **you ~ to see a doctor** tienes que ver a un médico

■ **~** *vi* (lack) (frml) (*usu with neg*): **you/they will ~ for nothing** no te/les faltará nada

want² *n* **1** (requirement, need) necesidad *f* **2** (lack, absence) falta *f*, carencia *f* (frml); **for ~ of sth** a falta de algo; **for ~ of a better word** por así decirlo **3** (destitution, penury) miseria *f*

wanted /ˈwɑːntəd ‖ˈwɒntɪd/ *adj* «*criminal/terrorist*» buscado (por la policía); *see also* WANT¹ 1B

wanton /ˈwɑːntn̩ ‖ˈwɒntən/ *adj* **(a)** (willful) sin sentido, gratuito **(b)** (licentious) licencioso

war /wɔːr ‖wɔː(r)/ *n* guerra *f*; **to be at ~ with sb/sth** estar* en guerra con algn/algo; **the ~ on crime** la lucha contra la delincuencia; (*before n*) **~ memorial** monumento *m* a los caídos

warble /ˈwɔːrbəl ‖ˈwɔːbəl/ *vi* trinar, gorjear

ward /wɔːrd ‖wɔːd/ *n* **1** (in hospital) sala *f* **2** (person) pupilo, -la *m,f*

■ **ward off** [*v* + *adv* + *o*] «*attack*» rechazar*; «*blow*» desviar*; «*danger*» conjurar; «*illness*» protegerse* contra

warden /ˈwɔːrdn̩ ‖ˈwɔːdn̩/ *n* (of castle, museum) guardián, -diana *m,f*; (of hostel, home) encargado, -da *m,f*; (of university, college) rector, -tora *m,f*; (church~) coadjutor *m*; (fire ~) (AmE) encargado, -da *m,f* de la lucha contra incendios; (game ~) guardabosque(s) *mf*; (of prison) (AmE) director, -tora *m,f* (*de una cárcel*)

warder /ˈwɔːrdər ‖ˈwɔːdə(r)/ *n* (BrE) celador, -dora *m,f* (*de una cárcel*)

wardrobe /ˈwɔːrdroʊb ‖ˈwɔːdrəʊb/ *n* **(a)** (clothes cupboard) armario *m*, ropero *m* (esp AmL) **(b)** (set of clothes) guardarropa *m*, vestuario *m*

warehouse /ˈwerhaʊs ‖ˈweəhaʊs/ *n* depósito *m*, almacén *m*, bodega *f* (Chi, Col, Méx)

wares /werz ‖weəz/ *pl n* mercancía(s) *f(pl)*, mercadería(s) *f(pl)* (AmS)

war: **~fare** *n* guerra *f*; **~head** *n* cabeza *f*, ojiva *f*

warily /ˈwerəli ‖ˈweərɪli/ *adv* con cautela, cautelosamente

warlike /ˈwɔːrlaɪk ‖ˈwɔːlaɪk/ *adj* guerrero

warm¹ /wɔːrm ‖wɔːm/ *adj* **-er, -est** **1** «*water/day*» tibio, templado; «*climate/wind*» cálido; **the ~est room in the house** la habitación más caliente de la casa; **I'm lovely and ~ now** estoy muy calentito ahora; **~ clothes** ropa *f* de abrigo *or* (RPl, Ven tb) abrigada *or* (Andes, Méx tb) abrigadora; **to get ~** «*person*» entrar en calor, calentarse*; «*room*» calentarse* **2** **(a)** (affectionate, cordial) «*person*» cariñoso; «*welcome*» caluroso **(b)** «*color/atmosphere*» cálido **3** (fresh) «*scent/trail*» reciente, fresco

warm² *vt* calentar*

■ **~** *vi* **(a)** (become hotter) calentarse* **(b)** (become affectionate) **to ~ TO** *o* **TOWARD sb: we soon ~ed to** *o* **toward her** pronto se ganó nuestra simpatía

■ **warm over** [*v* + *o* + *adv, v* + *adv* + *o*] (AmE Culin) calentar*

■ **warm up** **1** [*v* + *adv*] **(a)** (become warmer) «*place/food*» calentarse*; «*person*» entrar en calor **(b)** «*engine/apparatus*» calentarse* **(c)** (become lively) «*party/match*» animarse **(d)** (for action) «*athlete*» hacer* ejercicios de calentamiento **2** [*v* + *o* + *adv, v* + *adv* + *o*] **(a)** (heat) «*food/place*» calentar* **(b)** «*engine/apparatus*» calentar* **(c)** (make lively) animar

warm: **~-blooded** /ˈwɔːrmˈblʌdəd ‖ˌwɔːmˈblʌdɪd/ *adj* (Zool) de sangre caliente; **~-hearted** /ˈwɔːrmˈhɑːrtəd ‖ˌwɔːmˈhɑːtɪd/ *adj* afectuoso

warmly /ˈwɔːrmli ‖ˈwɔːmli/ *adv* «*congratulate/welcome*» calurosamente; «*smile*» afectuosamente

warmth /wɔːrmθ ‖wɔːmθ/ *n* **(a)** (heat) calor *m* **(b)** (of welcome) lo caluroso **(c)** (of color, atmosphere) calidez *f*

warm-up /ˈwɔːrmʌp ‖ˈwɔːmʌp/ *n* (exercise) ejercicio *m* de calentamiento; (practice) (pre)calentamiento *m*

warn /wɔːrn ‖wɔːn/ *vt* **(a)** (admonish) advertir*; **we had been ~ed not to go** nos habían advertido que no fuéramos **(b)** (inform, advise) avisar, advertir*; **we were ~ed against swimming in the river** nos advirtieron que era peligroso nadar en el río

warning /ˈwɔːrnɪŋ ‖ˈwɔːnɪŋ/ *n* **(a)** (advice, threat) advertencia *f* **(b)** (prior notice) aviso *m*; **they arrived without ~** llegaron sin avisar *or* sin previo aviso

warp /wɔːrp ‖wɔːp/ *vt* «*wood/metal*» alabear

warped /wɔːrpt ‖wɔːpt/ *adj* «*timber/metal*» alabeado; «*record*» combado; «*mind/sense of humor*» retorcido

warplane /ˈwɔːrpleɪn ‖ˈwɔːpleɪn/ *n* avión *m* de combate

warrant¹ /ˈwɔːrənt ‖ˈwɒrənt/ *n* (written authorization) (Law) orden *f* judicial; (search ~) orden *f* de registro *or* (AmL tb) de allanamiento; **to have a ~ for sb's arrest** tener* una orden de arresto contra algn

warrant² *vt* **1** (justify) justificar* **2** (guarantee) (*often pass*) garantizar*

W

warranty /'wɒ:rənti ‖'wɔrənti/ n (pl **-ties**) garantía f

warren /'wɒ:rən ‖'wɔrən/ n (Zool) madriguera f (de conejos), conejera f

warring /'wɒːrɪŋ/ adj (before n) ‹countries/ tribes› en guerra; ‹factions› enfrentado

warrior /'wɒːrjər ‖'wɔriə(r)/ n guerrero, -ra m,f

Warsaw /'wɒːrsɔː ‖'wɔːsɔː/ n Varsovia f

warship /'wɒːrˌʃɪp ‖'wɔːʃɪp/ n buque m de guerra

wart /wɒːrt ‖wɔːt/ n verruga f

war: ~**time** n: in ~time en tiempo de guerra; ~**torn** adj devastado por la guerra

wary /'weri ‖'weəri/ adj **warier, wariest** cauteloso; to be ~ OF sb/sth no fiarse* DE algn/ algo

was /wɑːz, weak form wəz ‖wɒz, weak form wəz/ past of BE

wash[1] /wɒːʃ ‖wɒʃ/ n [1] (a) (act): to have a ~ lavarse; I'll give the car a ~ voy a lavar el coche, voy a darle una lavada al coche (AmL) (b) (in washing machine) lavado m; your shirt is in the ~ tu camisa está lavándose [2] (left by boat, plane) estela f

wash[2] vt [1] (clean) ‹shirt/car/fruit› lavar; ‹floor› fregar*, lavar (esp AmL); to ~ one's face/hair lavarse la cara/la cabeza or el pelo; to ~ the dishes fregar* or lavar los platos [2] (carry away) (+ adv compl): the body had been ~ed ashore by the tide la corriente había arrastrado el cuerpo hasta la orilla; see also WASH AWAY, WASH UP

■ ~ vi (a) (clean oneself) lavarse (b) (do dishes) lavar, fregar* (c) (do laundry) «washing machine/ person» lavar (la ropa), hacer* la colada (Esp)

■ **wash away** [v + o + adv, v + adv + o] (a) (carry away) llevarse (b) (cleanse) ‹dirt› quitar (lavando)

■ **wash down** [v + o + adv, v + adv + o] (a) (clean) ‹paintwork/wall› lavar (b) (accompany) (colloq): a plate of pasta ~ed down with the local wine un plato de pasta acompañado del vino de la región

■ **wash out** [1] [v + o + adv, v + adv + o] ‹sink/ cloth› (clean) lavar; (rinse) enjuagar* [2] [v + adv] (disappear): the stain will ~ out la mancha saldrá or se quitará al lavarlo

■ **wash up** [1] [v + adv] (a) (wash oneself) (AmE) lavarse (b) (wash dishes) (BrE) lavar los platos, fregar* (los platos) [2] [v + o + adv, v + adv + o] (a) (deposit) (usu pass) to be ~ed up «body/wreckage» ser* traído por la corriente (b) ‹dishes› (BrE) lavar, fregar*

Wash = Washington

washable /'wɒːʃəbəl ‖'wɒʃəbəl/ adj lavable

wash: ~**basin** n (BrE) ▶ ~**BOWL**; ~**bowl** n (AmE) (a) (in modern bathroom) lavabo m, lavamanos m, lavatorio m (CS), pileta f (RPI) (b) (bowl) palangana f, jofaina f, lavatorio m (Chi, Per); ~**cloth** n (AmE) toallita f (para lavarse), ≈manopla f

washed-out /wɒːʃt'aʊt ‖ˌwɒʃt'aʊt/ adj (pred **washed out**) (a) ‹fabric› descolorido; ‹color› pálido, lavado (RPI fam) (b) (exhausted) rendido

washer /'wɒːʃər ‖'wɒʃə(r)/ n [1] (Tech) (ring) arandela f; (— on faucet) arandela f, junta f, suela f universal, cuerito m (CS fam), empaque m (Col, Ven) [2] ▶ WASHING MACHINE

washing /'wɒːʃɪŋ ‖'wɒʃɪŋ/ n (a) (laundry — dirty) ropa f para lavar; (— clean) ropa f lavada; to do the ~ lavar la ropa, hacer* la colada (Esp) (b) (act) lavado m

washing: ~ **line** n (BrE) cuerda f para tender la ropa; ~ **machine** n máquina f de lavar, lavadora f, lavarropas m (RPI); ~ **powder** n (esp BrE) jabón m en polvo, detergente m; ~-**up** /'wɒːʃɪŋ'ʌp ‖ˌwɒʃɪŋ'ʌp/ n (BrE): to do the ~-up lavar los platos, fregar* (los platos); (before n) ~-up liquid lavavajillas m

wash: ~**out** n (failure) (colloq) desastre m (fam); ~**room** n baño(s) m(pl), servicios mpl (esp Esp)

wasn't /'wɑːznt ‖'wɒznt/ = **was not**

wasp /wɑːsp ‖wɒsp/ n avispa f

WASP /wɑːsp ‖wɒsp/ n (esp AmE) (= **white Anglo-Saxon Protestant**) persona de la clase privilegiada de los EEUU, blanca, anglosajona y protestante

waspish /'wɑːspɪʃ ‖'wɒspɪʃ/ adj sardónico

wastage /'weɪstɪdʒ/ n: there is too much ~ of raw material se desperdicia demasiada materia prima; natural ~ (of workforce) bajas fpl vegetativas

waste[1] /weɪst/ n [1] (of fuel, materials) desperdicio m; a ~ of time una pérdida de tiempo; it's a ~ of money es tirar el dinero; to go to ~ «talent» desperdiciarse; «food» echarse a perder [2] (a) (refuse) residuos mpl (b) (surplus matter) material m sobrante [3] **wastes** (pl): the deserted ~s of Antarctica las desiertas inmensidades de la Antártida

waste[2] vt [1] ‹talents/efforts› desperdiciar; ‹money/electricity› despilfarrar; ‹food› tirar; ‹time› perder*; ‹space› desaprovechar [2] **wasted** past p (a) (misused, futile) ‹time/ money› perdido; ‹opportunity/space› desperdiciado; ‹effort› inútil (b) (shrunken) ‹body› debilitado; ‹limb› atrofiado

■ **waste away** [v + adv] «person/body» consumirse; «muscle» atrofiarse

waste[3] adj [1] ‹ground› (barren) yermo; (not cultivated) baldío; to lay ~ (to) sth arrasar algo [2] ‹material/matter› de desecho

waste: ~**basket** n (esp AmE) ▶ WASTE-PAPER BASKET; ~ **disposal unit** n triturador m or trituradora f de desperdicios

wasteful /'weɪstfəl/ adj ‹person› despilfarrador; ‹method› poco económico

waste: ~**land** n (often pl) (barren land) páramo m, tierra f yerma or baldía; (uncultivated land) erial m; ~ **paper** n papel m sobrante; ~-**paper basket, ~-paper bin** /'weɪst'peɪpər ‖ˌweɪst'peɪpə(r)/ n papelera f, papelero m (CS); ~ **pipe** n tubo m de desagüe

---

AmC América Central	Arg Argentina	Cu Cuba	Per Perú
AmL América Latina	Bol Bolivia	Ec Ecuador	RPI Río de la Plata
AmS América del Sur	Chi Chile	Esp España	Ur Uruguay
Andes Región andina	CS Cono Sur	Méx México	Ven Venezuela

watch¹ /wɑːtʃ ‖ wɒtʃ/ n **1** (timepiece) reloj m (de pulsera/de bolsillo); (before n) ~ **band** o (BrE) **strap** correa f de reloj **2** (observation) vigilancia f; **to keep** ~ hacer* guardia **3** (a) (period of time) guardia f (b) (individual) guardia mf; (group) guardia f

watch² vt **1** ‹person/expression› observar; ‹movie/game› mirar; **to** ~ **television** ver* televisión; **we** ~**ed the sun go down** miramos la puesta de sol
2 (a) (keep under observation) ‹suspect/house› vigilar (b) (look after) ‹luggage/children› cuidar (c) (pay attention to) mirar (con atención) **3** (be careful of) ‹diet/weight› vigilar, tener* cuidado con; ~ **it!** (colloq) ¡cuidado!
■ ~ vi (look on) mirar
■ **watch out** [v + adv] **(a)** (be careful) tener* cuidado; ~ **out!** ¡(ten) cuidado!, ¡ojo! (fam), ¡abusado! (Méx fam) **(b)** (look carefully) estarse* atento; ~ **out for spelling mistakes** estáte atento por si hay faltas de ortografía
■ **watch over** [v + prep + o] ‹patient/child› cuidar (de); ‹safety/interests› velar por

watchdog /'wɑːtʃdɔːg ‖ 'wɒtʃdɒg/ n (dog) perro m guardián; (group) organismo m de control

watchful /'wɑːtʃfəl ‖ 'wɒtʃfəl/ adj vigilante

watch: ~**maker** n relojero, -ra m,f; ~**man** /'wɑːtʃmən ‖ 'wɒtʃmən/ n (pl -**men** /-mən/) vigilante m; ~**tower** n atalaya f, torre f de vigilancia

water¹ /'wɔːtər ‖ 'wɔːtə(r)/ n **1** agua f‡; **to be/lie under** ~ estar*/quedar inundado; **high/low** ~ marea f alta/baja; **to pass** ~ (frml & euph) orinar, hacer* aguas menores (euph); **to hold** ~ tenerse* en pie; (before n) ‹bird/plant› acuático; ~ **sports** deportes mpl acuáticos **2** **waters** pl (of sea, river) aguas fpl

water² vi: **her eyes began to** ~ empezaron a llorarle los ojos; **his mouth** ~**ed** se le hizo agua la boca (AmL), se le hizo la boca agua (Esp)
■ ~ vt ‹plant/garden/land› regar*; ‹livestock› dar* de beber a
■ **water down** [v + o + adv, v + adv + o] ‹liquid/mixture› diluir*; ‹wine/beer› aguar

water: ~ **bed** n cama f de agua; ~ **bottle** n cantimplora f; ~**color**, (BrE) ~**colour** n acuarela f; ~**cress** n berro m; ~**fall** n cascada f, salto m de agua; (large) catarata f; ~**front** n (beside lake, river) zona de una ciudad que bordea un lago o río; (docks) (esp AmE) muelles mpl

watering can /'wɔːtərɪŋ/ n regadera f

water: ~ **lily** n nenúfar m; ~**logged** /'wɔːtərlɔːgd ‖ 'wɔːtəlɒgd/ adj ‹land/soil› anegado, inundado; ‹shoes› empapado; ~**mark** n filigrana f; ~**melon** n sandía f; ~ **mill** n molino m de agua; ~ **parting** n (AmE) ▸ WATERSHED A

waterproof¹ /'wɔːtərpruːf ‖ 'wɔːtəpruːf/ adj ‹fabric› impermeable; ‹mascara› a prueba de agua; ‹watch› sumergible

waterproof² n (esp BrE) prenda f impermeable

waterproof³ vt impermeabilizar*

water: ~-**resistant** adj impermeabilizado, hidrófugo; ~**shed** n (Geog) (a) (divide) (línea f) divisoria f de aguas (b) (drainage basin) (AmE) cuenca f; ~-**ski** vi -**skis**, -**skiing**, -**skied** hacer* esquí acuático; ~-**skiing** n esquí m acuático; ~ **table** n nivel m freático; ~**tight**

adj ‹seal/container› hermético; ‹boat› estanco; ‹argument› irrebatible, sin fisuras; ‹alibi› a toda prueba; ~**way** n (river) vía f fluvial; (canal) vía f or canal m navegable; ~ **wheel** n (for driving machinery) rueda f hidráulica; (for raising water) noria f; ~ **wings** pl n flotadores mpl (que se colocan en los brazos)

watery /'wɔːtəri/ adj **(a)** (of, like water) acuoso **(b)** ‹beer/gravy› aguado **(c)** ‹eyes› lloroso

watt /wɑːt ‖ wɒt/ n vatio m

wave¹ /weɪv/ n **1** (a) (of water) ola f (b) (in hair) onda f (c) (Phys) onda f **2** (surge, movement) oleada f **3** (gesture): **she gave them a** ~ les hizo adiós/los saludó con la mano

wave² vt **1** (a) (shake, swing) ‹handkerchief/flag› agitar; **to** ~ **sth around** agitar algo; **she** ~**d goodbye to him** le hizo adiós con la mano **(b)** (direct) (+ adv compl): **the policeman** ~**d us on** el policía nos hizo señas para or de que siguiéramos adelante
2 (curl) ‹hair› marcar*, ondular
■ ~ vi **1** (signal): **he** ~**d when he saw us** nos saludó con la mano al vernos; **to** ~ **AT** o **TO sb** (to say goodbye) hacerle* adiós A algn con la mano; (in greeting) saludar a algn con la mano
2 (sway, flutter) «corn/trees» agitarse; «flag» ondear
■ **wave aside** [v + o + adv, v + adv + o] **(a)** (with hand): **he** ~**d me aside** me hizo señas para que me hiciera a un lado **(b)** ‹arguments/attempts› rechazar*

wave: ~**band** n banda f de frecuencia; ~**length** n longitud f de onda

waver /'weɪvər ‖ 'weɪvə(r)/ vi **1** (falter) «person» flaquear; «faith» tambalearse **2** (be indecisive) titubear

wavy /'weɪvi/ adj **wavier, waviest** ondulado

wax¹ /wæks/ n **1** n cera f; (ear~) cera f (de los oídos), cerumen m; (sealing ~) lacre m

wax² vt **(a)** (treat with wax) ‹floor/table/skis› encerar **(b)** (to remove hair) depilar con cera
■ ~ vi «moon» crecer*; **his popularity** ~**ed and waned** su popularidad sufrió muchos altibajos

waxworks /'wækswɜːrks ‖ 'wækswɜːks/ n (pl ~**works**) (+ sing or pl vb) museo m de cera

way¹ /weɪ/ n
I 1 (a) (route) camino m; **the** ~ **back** el camino de vuelta; **the** ~ **in/out** la entrada/salida; **it's difficult to find one's** ~ **around this town** es difícil orientarse en esta ciudad; **can you find your** ~ **there by yourself?** ¿sabes ir solo?; **I can drop the package off on my** ~ de paso puedo dejar el paquete; **which** ~ **did you come?** ¿por dónde viniste?; **which** ~ **did he go?** ¿por dónde fue?; (following sb) ¿por dónde se fue?; **could you tell me the** ~ **to the city center?** ¿me podría decir por dónde se va al centro (de la ciudad)?; **on my** ~ **to work** de camino al trabajo; **the doctor is on her** ~ la doctora ya va para allí/viene para aquí; **I'll tell you on the** ~ te lo cuento por el camino; **I don't know the** ~ **up/down** no sé por dónde se sube/se baja; **to lead the** ~ ir* delante; **to lose one's** ~ perderse*; **there is no** ~ **around it** no hay otra solución; **to go out of one's** ~ (make a detour) desviarse* del camino; (make special effort): **they went out of their** ~ **to be helpful** se desvivieron por ayudar **(b)** (road, path) camino m, senda f

W

2 (passage, space): **to be/get in the** ∼ estorbar; **to stand in the** ∼: **they stood in our** ∼ nos impidieron el paso; **I couldn't see it, she was standing in my** ∼ no podía verlo, ella me tapaba (la vista); **I won't stand in your** ∼ no seré yo quien te lo impida; **(get) out of the** ∼! ¡hazte a un lado!; **to move sth out of the** ∼ quitar algo de en medio; **to keep out of sb's** ∼ rehuir* a algn
3 (direction): **it's that** ∼ es en esa dirección, es por ahí; **this** ∼! ¡por aquí!; **we didn't know which** ∼ **to go** no sabíamos por dónde ir; **this** ∼ **and that** de un lado a otro; **we're both going the same** ∼ vamos para el mismo lado; **look the other** ∼! ¡mira para otro lado!; **whichever** ∼ **you look at it, it's a disaster** es un desastre, lo mires por donde lo mires; **the other** ∼ **around** al revés; **which** ∼ **up should it be?** ¿cuál es la parte de arriba?; **to split sth three** ∼s dividir algo en tres partes; **every which** ∼ (AmE) para todos lados; **to go sb's** ∼: **are you going my** ∼? ¿vas en mi misma dirección?; **the decision went our** ∼ se decidió en nuestro favor; ∼ **to go!** (AmE colloq) ¡así se hace!
4 (distance) (no pl): **there's only a short** ∼ **to go now** ya falta poco para llegar; **it's a long** ∼ **from here to Rio** Río queda muy lejos de aquí; **he's come a long** ∼ ha venido de muy lejos; **we've come a long** ∼ **since those days** hemos evolucionado mucho desde entonces; **a little goes a long** ∼ un poco cunde or (AmL tb) rinde mucho; **we had to walk all the** ∼ **up** tuvimos que subir a pie hasta arriba
II **1** (method, means) forma f, manera f, modo m; **there's no** ∼ **of crossing the border without a passport** es imposible cruzar la frontera sin pasaporte; **it doesn't matter to me one** ∼ **or the other** me da igual una cosa u otra; **all right, we'll do it your** ∼ muy bien, lo haremos a tu manera; **to do sth the hard/easy** ∼ hacer* algo de manera difícil/fácil; **to have it both** ∼s quererlo* todo, querer* la chancha y los cinco reales or los veinte (RPl fam); **you can't have it both** ∼s tienes que elegir entre una cosa u otra
2 (manner) manera f, modo m, forma f; **in a subtle** ∼ de manera or modo or forma sutil; **he's in a bad** ∼ está muy mal; **that's the** ∼ **it goes** así son las cosas, así es la vida; **it looks that** ∼ or **eso parece**; **this** ∼ **it's better for everyone** así es mejor para todos; **the** ∼ **I see it** tal y como yo lo veo; **to have a** ∼ **with ...**: **to have a** ∼ **with children/animals** saber* cómo tratar a los niños/tener* mano con los animales; **to have a** ∼ **with words** tener* mucha facilidad de palabra
3 (a) (custom, characteristic): **the** ∼s **of our people** las costumbres de nuestro pueblo; **he has a** ∼ **of making people feel at ease** sabe hacer que la gente se sienta cómoda; **to be set in one's** ∼s estar* muy acostumbrado a hacer las cosas de cierta manera **(b)** (wish, will): **to get/have one's (own)** ∼ salirse* con la suya (or mía etc)
4 (feature, respect) sentido m, aspecto m; **in a** ∼, **it's like losing an old friend** de alguna manera or en cierta forma es como perder a un viejo amigo; **our product is in no** ∼ **inferior to theirs** nuestro producto no es de ninguna manera inferior al suyo
III (in phrases) **1** **by the way** (indep) a propósito, por cierto
2 **by way of** (as prep) (a) (via) vía, pasando por **(b)** (to serve as) a modo or manera de

3 **in the way of** (as regards) (as prep): **don't expect too much in the** ∼ **of help** en cuanto a ayuda, no esperes mucho
4 **no way** (colloq): **no** ∼ **is he going to do it** de ninguna manera lo va a hacer (fam); **no** ∼! ¡ni hablar! (fam)
5 **to give way (a)** (break, collapse) «ice/rope/cable» romperse*; «floor» hundirse **(b)** (succumb, give in) **to give** ∼ **to sth** «to threats/blackmail» ceder A or ANTE algo **(c)** (BrE Transp) **to give** ∼ (TO sb/sth) ceder el paso (A algn/algo) **(d)** (be replaced, superseded by) **to give** ∼ **to sth** dejar or dar* paso A algo
6 **under way**: **to get under** ∼ ponerse* en marcha; **an investigation is under** ∼ se está llevando a cabo una investigación

way² adv (colloq): ∼ **back in February** allá por febrero; ∼ **behind** muy por detrás; **they were** ∼ **out in their calculations** se equivocaron en mucho en los cálculos; ∼ **past midnight** mucho después de la medianoche; ∼ **and away** (as intensifier) (AmE) con mucho, lejos (AmL fam)

way: ∼**lay** /'werleɪ/ vt (past & past p ∼**laid**) abordar; ∼**-out** /'weraʊt/ adj (pred ∼ **out**) (colloq) ultramoderno, estrambótico (fam); ∼ **and means** pl n ∼s **and means** (OF -ING) métodos mpl (DE + INF)

we /wiː, weak form wɪ/ pron
■ Note Although pron nosotros and nosotras are given as translations of we, in practice they are used only for emphasis: we went to the theater fuimos al teatro; we did it nosotros or nosotras lo hicimos.

nosotros, -tras; ∼ **English** nosotros los ingleses

weak /wiːk/ adj -er, -est **1** (a) «person/muscles/economy» débil; «structure» poco sólido, endeble; «handshake» flojo; **to have a** ∼ **heart** sufrir del corazón; **to grow** ∼ debilitarse **(b)** (ineffectual) «character/leader» débil **2** (a) (not competent) «student/performance» flojo **(b)** (not convincing) «argument/excuse» poco convincente **3** (diluted) «coffee/tea» poco cargado; «beer» suave; «solution» diluido

weaken /'wiːkən/ vt debilitar
■ ∼ vi «person/animal» (physically) debilitarse; «resolve» flaquear; «power» debilitarse; (relent) ceder

weakling /'wiːklɪŋ/ n alfeñique m

weakly /'wiːkli/ adv «say» con voz débil; **he struggled** ∼ **and then gave in** se rindió sin apenas oponer resistencia

weakness /'wiːknəs ‖'wiːknɪs/ n **1** (a) (of body, defenses) debilidad f; (of structure, material) falta f de solidez, endeblez f; (of argument) pobreza f **(b)** (ineffectualness) falta f de carácter **2** (a) (weak point — in structure, policy) punto m débil; (— in character) flaqueza f, punto m débil **(b)** (liking) debilidad f; **to have a** ∼ **for sth** tener* debilidad por algo

weak-willed /'wiːk'wɪld/ adj «person» de poca (fuerza de) voluntad; **to be** ∼ tener* poca fuerza de voluntad

weal /wiːl/ n verdugón m (de un golpe dado con una cuerda, correa etc)

wealth /welθ/ n **1** riqueza f **2** (large quantity): **a** ∼ **of sth** abundancia f de algo

wealthy /'welθi/ adj -thier, -thiest «person/family» adinerado, rico; «nation/area» rico

wean /wi:n/ *vt* ⟨baby/young⟩ destetar; **to ~ sb OFF sth: we ~ed him off drugs** conseguimos que dejara las drogas, conseguimos desengancharle de las drogas (Esp)

weapon /'wepən/ *n* arma *f*‡; **~s of mass destruction** armas de destrucción masiva

weaponry /'wepənri/ *n* armamento *m*

wear¹ /wer ‖ weə(r)/ *n* **1 (a)** (use): **I've had a lot of ~ out of these shoes** les he dado mucho uso a estos zapatos; **carpets that stand hard ~** alfombras que resisten el uso constante **(b)** (damage) desgaste *m*; **~ and tear** uso *m* or desgaste natural **2 (a)** (wearing of clothes): **clothes for evening ~** ropa para la noche **(b)** (clothing) ropa *f*; **children's ~** ropa de niños

wear² (*past* **wore**; *past p* **worn**) *vt* **1 (a)** (at specific moment) ⟨clothes/jewelry/watch/makeup⟩ llevar; ⟨glasses⟩ llevar (puesto), usar; ⟨green/black⟩ de; **what perfume are you ~ing?** ¿qué perfume llevas? **(b)** (usually) ⟨clothes⟩ usar, ponerse*, ⟨glasses⟩ llevar, usar; ⟨makeup/perfume/earrings⟩ usar; **he ~s size 44 shoes** calza (el) 44; **she ~s her hair in a ponytail** se peina con cola de caballo

2 (through use): **the step had been worn smooth** el peldaño se había alisado con el uso; **she's worn holes in the soles** se le han agujereado las suelas

■ **~** *vi* **1** (through use) ⟨collar/carpet/brakes⟩ gastarse; **to ~ thin** (lit: through use) ⟨cloth/metal⟩ gastarse; ⟨joke⟩ perder* la gracia

2 (last) (+ *adv compl*) durar; **to ~ well** ⟨cloth/clothes⟩ durar mucho; ⟨person⟩ conservarse bien

■ **wear away** **1** [*v + o + adv, v + adv + o*] (erode) ⟨rock⟩ desgastar; ⟨pattern/inscription⟩ borrar

2 [*v + adv*] (become eroded) ⟨rock⟩ desgastarse; ⟨inscription⟩ borrarse

■ **wear down** **1** [*v + o + adv, v + adv + o*] **(a)** (by friction) ⟨heel/pencil⟩ gastar **(b)** (weaken) ⟨resistance⟩ menoscabar; ⟨person⟩ agotar

2 [*v + adv*] ⟨heel/tread⟩ gastarse

■ **wear off** [*v + adv*] **(a)** (be removed) ⟨paint⟩ quitarse **(b)** (disappear) ⟨distress/numbness⟩ pasarse

■ **wear on** [*v + adv*] ⟨winter/years⟩ pasar (lentamente); ⟨meeting/drought⟩ continuar*

■ **wear out** **1** [*v + o + adv, v + adv + o*] **(a)** (through use) ⟨shoes/carpet/batteries⟩ gastar **(b)** (exhaust) ⟨person⟩ agotar

2 [*v + adv*] (through use) ⟨shoes/towel/batteries⟩ gastarse

■ **wear through** [*v + adv*] (get hole in) ⟨soles/cloth⟩ agujerearse

wearily /'wɪrəli ‖ 'wɪərɪli/ *adv* ⟨walk/move⟩ cansinamente; **he sighed ~** suspiró cansado

weary¹ /'wɪri ‖ 'wɪərɪ/ *adj* **-rier, -riest** ⟨person/legs⟩ cansado; ⟨sigh⟩ de cansancio; **to be ~ OF sth/-ING** estar* cansado DE algo/+ INF

weary² *vt* **-ries, -rying, -ried (a)** (tire) cansar **(b)** (annoy) hartar, cansar

weasel /'wi:zəl/ *n* (Zool) comadreja *f*

weather¹ /'weðər ‖ 'weðə(r)/ *n* tiempo *m*; **what's the ~ like?** ¿cómo está el tiempo?, ¿qué tiempo hace?; **you can't go out in this ~** no puedes salir con este tiempo; (*before n*) ⟨map/chart⟩ meteorológico; **~ forecast** pronóstico *m* del tiempo

weather² *vt* **(a)** (wear) ⟨rocks⟩ erosionar; ⟨surface⟩ desgastar; ⟨skin/face⟩ curtir **(b)** ⟨wood⟩ secar*

■ **~** *vi* ⟨rock⟩ erosionarse; ⟨surface⟩ desgastarse

weather: **~beaten** *adj* ⟨face/sailor⟩ curtido; ⟨walls/rocks⟩ azotado por los elementos; **~cock** *n* veleta *f*

weathered /'weðərd ‖ 'weðəd/ *adj* ⟨rocks/brick/stone⟩ erosionado (*por la acción de los elementos*); ⟨wood⟩ curado

weather: **~man** /'weðərmæn ‖ 'weðəmæn/ *n* (*pl* **-men** /-men/) hombre que transmite el pronóstico del tiempo por radio o televisión; **~proof** *adj* impermeable; **~ vane** /veɪn/ *n* veleta *f*

weave /wi:v/ *vt* (*past* **wove**; *past p* **woven**) **(a)** ⟨cloth/mat⟩ tejer (*en telar*); ⟨basket/web⟩ tejer; ⟨story/plot⟩ tejer **(b)** (thread together) ⟨threads/branches/straw⟩ entretejer

■ **~** *vi* **1** (*past* **wove**; *past p* **woven**) (make cloth, baskets) tejer **2** (*past* **wove** *or* **weaved**; *past p* **woven** *or* **weaved**) ⟨road⟩ serpentear; ⟨person⟩ zigzaguear

weaver /'wi:vər ‖ 'wi:və(r)/ *n* tejedor, -dora *m,f*

weaving /'wi:vɪŋ/ *n* (of cloth) tejido *m*

web /web/ *n* **(a)** (spider's ~) telaraña *f*; **a ~ of intrigue** una red de intriga **(b)** (Comput): **World Wide ~** telaraña *f* mundial

webbed /webd/ *adj* palmeado

web: **W~ page** *n* (Comput) página *f* web; **W~ site** *n* (Comput) sitio *m* web

wed /wed/ *vt* (*past & past p* **wedded** *or* **wed**) (marry) (dated *or* journ) ⟨man/woman⟩ casarse con

we'd /wi:d/ **(a)** = **we had (b)** = **we would**

wedding /'wedɪŋ/ *n* **(a)** (ceremony) boda *f*, casamiento *m*, matrimonio *m* (AmS exc RPl); **to have a church/civil** (AmE) *o* (BrE) **registry-office ~** casarse por la iglesia *or* (RPl) por iglesia/por lo civil *or* (Per, RPl, Ven) por civil *or* (Chi, Méx) por el civil; (*before n*) **~ dress** vestido *m* or traje *m* de novia; **~ ring** alianza *f*, anillo *m* de boda, argolla *f* (de matrimonio) (Chi) **(b)** (anniversary): **silver/golden ~** bodas *fpl* de plata/oro

wedge¹ /wedʒ/ *n* **(a)** (for securing) cuña *f* **(b)** (for splitting) cuña *f* **(c)** (shape): **a ~ of cake** un trozo grande de pastel

wedge² *vt* **(a)** (secure): **to ~ a door open** ponerle* una cuña a una puerta para que no se cierre **(b)** (squeeze) meter (*a presión*)

Wednesday /'wenzdeɪ, -di/ *n* miércoles *m; see also* MONDAY

wee¹ /wi:/ *adj* (small) (esp Scot, IrE) pequeño, chico (esp AmL); **in the ~ small hours** *o* (AmE also) **the ~ hours** a las altas horas de la madrugada

wee² *n* (BrE colloq): **to have** *o* **do a ~** hacer* pis *or* pipí (fam), hacer* del uno (Méx, Per fam)

weed¹ /wi:d/ *n* **(a)** (Hort) hierbajo *m*, mala hierba *f*, yuyo *m* (RPl), maleza *f* (AmL) **(b)** (aquatic growth) algas *fpl*

weed² *vt* deshierbar, desherbar*, desmalezar* (AmL), sacar* los yuyos de (RPl)

■ **weed out** [*v + o + adv, v + adv + o*] **(a)** (Hort) quitar **(b)** ⟨errors/items⟩ eliminar; ⟨applicants⟩ eliminar

weedkiller /'wi:d̩kɪlər ‖ 'wi:d̩kɪlə(r)/ *n* herbicida *m*

weedy /'wi:di/ adj **-dier, -diest (a)** (lanky)
(AmE) larguirucho (fam) **(b)** (feeble, puny) (BrE
colloq) enclenque

week /wi:k/ n **(a)** (7 days) semana f; **once a ~**
una vez por semana or a la semana; **we get paid
by the ~** nos pagan semanalmente; **(on) Tuesday
~ o** (BrE also) **a ~ on Tuesday** el martes que
viene no, el otro; **she arrived a ~ (ago) yesterday**
ayer hizo una semana que llegó **(b)** (working days):
I never go out in o during the ~ nunca salgo los
días de semana

week: ~day n día m de semana; **~end**
/'wi:kend ‖wi:k'end/ n fin m de semana; **what
are you doing on o** (BrE) **at the ~?** ¿qué vas a
hacer el fin de semana?

weekly¹ /'wi:kli/ adj semanal

weekly² adv semanalmente; **we get paid ~** nos
pagan por semana

weekly³ n (pl **weeklies**) semanario m

weep /wi:p/ vi (past & past p **wept**) [1] (cry)
llorar [2] (exude liquid) «wound/eye» supurar

weeping willow /'wi:pɪŋ/ n sauce m llorón

weepy /'wi:pi/ adj **-pier, -piest** (colloq) [1] **(a)**
«person»: **to feel ~** tener* ganas de llorar **(b)**
«film/play» que hace llorar, cebollento (Chi fam)
[2] «eye» lloroso

weigh /weɪ/ vt [1] «person/load/food» pesar; **to
~ oneself** pesarse
[2] (consider) «factors/arguments/evidence» sopesar;
to ~ one's words medir* sus (or mis etc)
palabras
■ **~ vi** (measure in weight) «person/load/food»
pesar; **how much or what do you ~?** ¿cuánto
pésas?; **your inexperience will ~ against you** tu
falta de experiencia será un factor en tu contra
■ **weigh down** [v + o + adv, v + adv + o] **(a)**
(impose weight on): **the bag was ~ing me down** la
bolsa me pesaba mucho; **trees ~ed down with
fruit** árboles cargados de fruta **(b)** (depress)
abrumar **(c)** ▶ WEIGH DOWN
■ **weigh on** [v + prep + o]: **it still ~ed heavily on
her conscience** todavía sentía un gran cargo de
conciencia; **it's been ~ing heavily on my mind** me
ha estado preocupando
■ **weigh out** [v + o + adv, v + adv + o] pesar
■ **weigh up** [v + o + adv, v + adv + o] «situation»
considerar; «pros and cons» sopesar; «person»
evaluar*

weight¹ /weɪt/ n [1] (mass, heaviness) peso m;
the bag is 5kg in ~ la bolsa pesa 5kg; **you
mustn't lift heavy ~s** no debe levantar cosas
pesadas; **that has taken a ~ off my mind** eso me
ha sacado un peso de encima; **to pull one's ~:**
John isn't pulling his ~ John no trabaja como
debería [2] (importance, value) peso m [3] **(a)** (unit)
peso m; **~s and measures** pesos y medidas **(b)**
(for scales, clocks) pesa f **(c)** (Sport) pesa f; **(before
n) ~ training** entrenamiento m con pesas

weight² vt (make heavier) darle* peso a; «fishing
net» lastrar

■ **weight down** [v + o + adv, v + adv + o] **(a)**
«tarpaulin/papers» sujetar con algo pesado **(b)**
«body» (to make it sink) ponerle* un lastre a

weightless /'weɪtləs ‖'weɪtlɪs/ adj ingrávido

weight: ~lifter /'weɪt,lɪftər ‖'weɪt,lɪftə(r)/ n
levantador, -dora m,f de pesas, pesista mf (Andes),
halterófilo, -la m,f; **~lifting** /'weɪt,lɪftɪŋ/ n
levantamiento m de pesas, halterofilia f

weighty /'weɪti/ adj **-tier, -tiest** «argument»
de peso; «matter» importante

weir /wɪr ‖wɪə(r)/ n presa f

weird /wɪrd ‖wɪəd/ adj **-er, -est (a)** (strange)
(colloq) raro, extraño **(b)** (unearthly) «apparition/
figure» misterioso

welcome¹ /'welkəm/ interj bienvenido

welcome² adj **(a)** (gladly received) «guest»
bienvenido; «change/news» grato **(b)** (freely
permitted): **you're ~ to use the phone** el teléfono
está a tu disposición; **you're ~ to these books**
puedes llevarte estos libros, si quieres **(c)**
(responding to thanks): **you're ~!** ¡de nada!, ¡no hay
de qué!

welcome³ vt (greet) darle* la bienvenida a;
(receive): **we would ~ any advice you can give us**
le agradeceríamos cualquier consejo que pudiera
darnos

welcome⁴ n bienvenida f

welcoming /'welkəmɪŋ/ adj **(a)** «ceremony/
delegation» de bienvenida **(b)** «smile/hug»
acogedor; **the little bar looked very ~** el barcito
parecía muy acogedor

weld /weld/ vt/i soldar*

welfare /'welfer ‖'welfeə(r)/ n [1] (well-being)
bienestar m [2] (Soc Adm) **(a)** (assistance)
asistencia f social **(b)** (payment) (AmE)
prestaciones fpl sociales

welfare state n estado m de bienestar

well¹ /wel/ adv (comp **better**; superl **best**)
[1] (to high standard, satisfactorily) «sing/write/work»
bien; **he's doing very ~** le van muy bien las
cosas; **~ done!** ¡así se hace!, ¡muy bien!; **to go ~**
«performance/operation» salir* bien
[2] (thoroughly) «wash/dry/know» bien; **it was ~
worth the effort** realmente valió la pena; **~ and
truly** (colloq): **he was ~ and truly drunk** estaba
pero bien borracho
[3] **(a)** (considerably) (no comp) bastante; **until ~
into the next century** hasta bien entrado el siglo
que viene **(b)** (with justification): **you may ~ ask!**
¡muy buena pregunta!; **she couldn't very ~ deny
it** ¿cómo iba a negarlo?
[4] (advantageously) «marry» bien; **to do ~ to + INF**
hacer* bien en + INF, deber + INF; **to do ~ out of
sth** salir* bien parado de algo
[5] (in phrases) **(a)** as well (in addition) también **(b)**
as well as (in addition to) además de **(c)** may/might
as well: **now you've told him, you may o might as
~ give it to him!** ahora que se lo has dicho dáselo
¿total?

well² adj (comp **better**; superl **best**)
[1] (healthy) bien; **how are you? — I'm very ~,
thank you** ¿cómo estás? — muy bien, gracias; **get**

~ soon! ¡que te mejores! **2** (pleasing, satisfactory) bien; **it's all very ~ for him to talk, but ...** él podrá decir todo lo que quiera pero ... **3** **as well: it would be as ~ to keep this quiet** mejor no decir nada de esto; **it's just as ~ I've got some money with me** menos mal que llevo dinero encima

well³ *interj* **1** **(a)** (introducing/continuing topic, sentence) bueno, bien **(b)** (expressing hesitation): **do you like it? — well ...** ¿te gusta? — pues *or* (esp AmL) este ... **2** **(a)** (expressing surprise): **~, ~, ~! look who's here!** ¡vaya, vaya! ¡mira quién está aquí! **(b)** (expressing indignation) bueno **(c)** (dismissively) ¡bah! **(d)** (expressing resignation) bueno **3** (expressing expectation): **~? who won?** bueno ¿y quién ganó?

well⁴ *n* (for water, oil, gas) pozo *m*
■ **well up** [*v + adv*] «*water*» brotar, manar; **tears ~ed up in his eyes** los ojos se le llenaron de lágrimas

well- /'wel/ *pref* bien

we'll /wiːl/ = **we will**

well: ~-balanced /'wel'bælənst/ *adj* (*pred* **~ balanced**) «*person*» equilibrado; «*diet*» equilibrado, balanceado; **~-behaved** /'welbɪ'hervd/ *adj* (*pred* **~ behaved**) «*child*» que se porta bien, bueno; «*dog*» obediente; **~-being** /'wel'biːɪŋ/ *n* bienestar *m*; **~-disposed** /'weldɪ'spəʊzd/ *adj* (*pred* **~ disposed**) dispuesto a colaborar (*or* ayudar *etc*); **~-done** /'wel'dʌn/ *adj* (*pred* **~ done**) (Culin) bien cocido *or* (Esp) muy hecho; **~-dressed** /'wel'drest/ *adj* (*pred* **~ dressed**) bien vestido; **~-educated** /'wel'edʒəkeɪtəd ‖ˌwel'edjʊkeɪtɪd/ *adj* (*pred* **~ educated**) culto; **~-founded** /'wel'faʊndəd ‖ˌwel'faʊndɪd/ *adj* (*pred* **~ founded**) bien fundado; **~-groomed** /'wel'gruːmd/ *adj* (*pred* **~ groomed**) «*person*» bien arreglado; «*hair*» bien peinado; «*horse/ garden*» bien cuidado; **~-informed** /'welɪn'fɔːrmd ‖ˌwelɪn'fɔːmd/ *adj* bien informado

wellington (boot) /'welɪŋtən/ *n* **(a)** (short boot) (AmE) botín *m*, bota *f* (*corta*) **(b)** (gumboot) (BrE) bota *f* de goma *or* de agua *or* de lluvia, catiusca *f* (Esp)

well: ~-kept /'wel'kept/ *adj* (*pred* **~ kept**) **(a)** «*house/lawns*» bien cuidado **(b)** «*secret*» bien guardado; **~-known** /'wel'nəʊn/ *adj* (*pred* **~ known**) «*person*» conocido, famoso; **it is ~ known that ...** es bien sabido que ...; **~-mannered** /'wel'mænərd ‖'wel'mænəd/ *adj* (*pred* **~ mannered**) de buenos modales, educado; **~-meaning** /'wel'miːnɪŋ/ *adj* (*pred* **~ meaning**) «*person*» bienintencionado; **he's ~ meaning, but ...** lo hace con la mejor intención, pero ...; **~-off** /'wel'ɔːf ‖ˌwel'ɒf/ *adj* (*pred* **~ off**) adinerado; **~-read** /'wel'red/ *adj* (*pred* **~ read**) culto; **~-to-do** /'weltə'duː/ *adj* «*businessman/family*» adinerado; **~-wisher** /'wel,wɪʃər ‖'wel,wɪʃə(r)/ *n*: **she received lots of cards from ~-wishers** recibió muchas tarjetas en que le deseaban una pronta recuperación (*or* mucha felicidad *etc*); **~-worn** /'wel'wɔːrn ‖ˌwel'wɔːn/ *adj* (*pred* **~ worn**) «*coat/carpet*» muy gastado; «*phrase*» muy trillado

Welsh¹ /welʃ/ *adj* galés

Welsh² *n* **(a)** (language) galés *m* **(b)** (people) (+ *pl vb*) **the ~** los galeses

Welshman /'welʃmən/ *n* (*pl* **-men** /-mən/) galés *m*

welt /welt/ *n* (weal) verdugón *m*

went /went/ *past of* GO¹

wept /wept/ *past & past p of* WEEP

were /wɜːr ‖wɜː(r)/, *weak form* wər ‖wə(r)/ **(a)** *2nd pers sing past ind of* BE **(b)** *1st, 2nd & 3rd pers pl past ind of* BE **(c)** *subjunctive of* BE

we're /wɪr ‖wɪə(r)/ = **we are**

weren't /wɜːrnt ‖wɜːnt/ = **were not**

west¹ /west/ *n* **1** (point of the compass, direction) oeste *m*; **the ~, the W~** (region) el oeste **2** **the West** (the Occident) (el) Occidente *m*; (Pol, Hist) el Oeste

west² *adj* (*before n*) oeste *adj inv*, occidental; «*wind*» del oeste

west³ *adv* al oeste

westbound /'westbaʊnd/ *adj* que va (*or* iba *etc*) hacia el *or* en dirección oeste

westerly /'westərli ‖'westəli/ *adj* «*wind*» del oeste; **in a ~ direction** hacia el oeste, en dirección oeste

western¹ /'westərn ‖'westən/ *adj* **(a)** (Geog) oeste *adj inv*, del oeste, occidental; **the ~ areas of the country** las zonas oeste *or* occidentales del país **(b)** (occidental) (Geog, Pol) occidental

western² *n* western *m*, película *f* (*or* novela *f etc*) del Oeste *or* de vaqueros

Westerner, westerner /'westərnər ‖'westənə(r)/ *n* occidental *mf*

westernized /'westərnaɪzd ‖'westənaɪzd/ *adj* occidentalizado

west: W~ Indian *adj* antillano; (in UK) afroantillano; **W~ Indies** /'ɪndɪz/ *pl n* **the W~ Indies** las Antillas

westward¹ /'westwərd ‖'westwəd/ *adj* (*before n*): **in a ~ direction** hacia el oeste, en dirección oeste

westward², (BrE) **westwards** /-z/ *adv* hacia el oeste

wet¹ /wet/ *adj* **-tt-** **(a)** (moist) «*floor/grass/ clothes*» mojado; (damp) húmedo; «*concrete/plaster*» blando; ❺ **wet paint** pintura fresca *or* (Esp tb) ojo, pinta; **to get ~** mojarse **(b)** (rainy) «*weather/day*» lluvioso

wet² *vt* (*pres p* **wetting**; *past & past p* **wet** *or* **wetted**) mojar; (dampen) humedecer*; **to ~ the bed** mojar la cama; **to ~ oneself** orinarse, hacerse* pipí (encima) (fam)

wet: ~ blanket *n* (colloq) aguafiestas *mf* (fam); **~ suit** *n* traje *m* de neoprene *or* de neopreno

we've /wiːv/ = **we have**

whack¹ /hwæk ‖wæk/ *n* (blow) golpe *m*; (sound) ¡zas!

whack² *vt* golpear, aporrear; «*person*» pegarle* a

whale /hweɪl ‖weɪl/ *n* **1** (*pl* **~s** *or* **~**) (Zool) ballena *f* **2** (colloq) (*as intensifier*): **we had a ~ of a time** lo pasamos bomba *or* genial (fam)

wharf /hwɔːrf ‖wɔːf/ *n* (*pl* **wharves** /hwɔːrvz ‖wɔːvz/) muelle *m*, embarcadero *m*

what¹ /hwɑːt ‖wɒt/ *pron* **1** (in questions) qué; **~'s that?** ¿qué es eso?; **~'s the problem?** ¿cuál es el problema?; **~'s 'I don't understand' in Russian?** ¿cómo se dice 'no entiendo' en ruso? **2** (*in phrases*) **or what?** (colloq) ¿o qué?; **so what?** ⋯⋙

W

¿y qué?; **what about: but ~ about the children?** y los niños ¿qué?; **you know Julie's boyfriend? — yes, ~ about him?** ¿conoces al novio de Julie? — sí ¿por qué?; **what … for: ~'s this button for?** ¿para qué es este botón?; **~ are you complaining for?** ¿por qué te quejas?; **what if: ~ if she finds out?** ¿y si se entera?; **what's-her/-his-name** (colloq): **go and ask ~'s-her-name next door** ve y pregúntale a la de al lado ¿cómo se llama? **3** (a) (in indirect speech) qué; **she knows ~ to do** ella sabe qué hacer; **I still don't know ~'s ~ in the office** aún no sé cómo funcionan las cosas en la oficina; **(I'll) tell you ~,** … mira, … **(b)** (relative use) lo que; **they did ~ they could** hicieron lo que pudieron

what² *adj* **1 (a)** (in questions) qué; **~ color are the walls?** ¿de qué color son las paredes? **(b)** (in indirect speech) qué; **she didn't know ~ color to choose** no sabía qué color elegir **2** (in exclamations) qué; **~ a surprise!** ¡qué sorpresa!; **~ a lot of people!** ¡cuánta gente!

whatever¹ /hwɑ:ˈtevər ‖ hwɒtˈevə(r)/ *pron* **1** (in questions, exclamations) qué; **~ is she doing?** ¿qué (es lo que) está haciendo? **2 (a)** (no matter what): **~ you do, don't laugh!** hagas lo que hagas ¡no te vayas a reír!; **he talked about percentiles, ~ they are** habló de percentiles, que no tengo ni idea de qué son **(b)** (all that): **they let him do ~ he likes** lo dejan hacer todo lo que quiere; **~ you say** lo que tú digas, como quieras

whatever² *adj* **(a)** (no matter what): **don't give up, ~ doubts you may have** no renuncies, tengas las dudas que tengas; **all people, of ~ race or creed** todos, cualquiera sea su raza o credo **(b)** (any): **~ changes are necessary** los cambios que sean necesarios

whatever³ *adv* (as intensifier): **none/nothing ~** ninguno/nada en absoluto

wheat /hwi:t ‖ wi:t/ *n* trigo *m*

wheatgerm /ˈhwi:tdʒɜ:rm ‖ ˈwi:tdʒɜ:m/ *n* germen *m* de trigo

wheedle /ˈhwi:dl̩ ‖ ˈwi:dl̩/ *vt* **to ~ sth OUT OF sb** sonsacarle* algo a algn

wheel¹ /hwi:l ‖ wi:l/ *n* **1 (a)** (of vehicle) rueda *f* **(b)** (potter's ~) torno *m* **2** (steering **~ —** of car) volante *m*; **(— of ship)** timón *m*; **at the ~** (of car) al volante; (of ship) al timón

wheel² *vt* ‹bicycle/wheelchair› empujar; ‹person› llevar (en silla de ruedas etc)
■ **~** *vi* **(a)** (turn suddenly) **~ (around** o (BrE) **round)** «person» girar sobre sus (or mis etc) talones **(b)** (circle) dar* vueltas; «birds» revolotear

wheel: ~barrow *n* carretilla *f*; **~chair** *n* silla *f* de ruedas; **~ clamp** *n* cepo *m*

wheeling and dealing /ˈhwi:lmənˈdi:lm ‖ ˌwi:lmənˈdi:lm/ *n* (colloq) tejemanejes *mpl* (fam)

wheeze /hwi:z ‖ wi:z/ *vi* «person» respirar con dificultad (produciendo un sonido sibilante como los asmáticos); «machine» resollar*

when¹ /hwen ‖ wen/ *adv*

■ **Note** When used as a conjunction in sentences expressing the future, *when* is translated by *cuando* + subjunctive: *we'll speak to Carol when she gets back* hablaremos con Carol cuando vuelva.

1 (in questions, indirect questions) cuándo; **that was ~ I realized that …** fue entonces cuando *or* (esp AmL tb) que me di cuenta de que …; **say ~!** di

cuándo **2** (as relative): **the year ~ we got married** el año en que nos casamos; **in December, ~ we were on holiday** en diciembre, cuando estábamos de vacaciones

when² *conj* **1 (a)** (temporal sense) cuando; **I'll ask him ~ I see him** se lo preguntaré cuando lo vea **(b)** (if) si, cuando **2 (a)** (since, considering that) si, cuando **(b)** (although) cuando; **he said he was 18 ~ in fact he's only 15** dijo que tenía 18 años cuando en realidad solo tiene 15

when³ *pron* cuándo; **~ do you have to be in London by?** ¿para cuándo tienes que estar en Londres?

whenever /hwenˈevər ‖ wenˈevə(r)/ *conj* **(a)** (every time that) siempre que; **~ I hear that song I think of Spain** siempre que *or* cada vez que escucho esa canción, me acuerdo de España **(b)** (at whatever time): **we'll go ~ you're ready** saldremos cuando estés listo

where¹ /hwer ‖ weə(r)/ *adv* dónde; (indicating direction) adónde, dónde; **~'s Lewes?** ¿dónde está Lewes?; **~ are you taking me?** ¿(a)dónde me llevan?; **~ are you from?** ¿de dónde eres?

where² *conj* **(a)** donde; (indicating direction) adonde, donde **(b)** (in cases where) cuando; **~ appropriate** cuando *or* allí donde sea apropiado

whereabouts¹ /ˈhwerəˈbaʊts ‖ ˌweərəˈbaʊts/ *adv*: **~ in Austria do you live?** ¿en qué parte de Austria vives?

whereabouts² /ˈhwerəbaʊts ‖ ˈweərəbaʊts/ *n* (+ *sing* or *pl vb*) paradero *m*

whereas /hwerˈæz ‖ ˌweərˈæz/ *conj* mientras que

whereby /hwerˈbaɪ ‖ weəˈbaɪ/ *pron* (frml): **a system ~ payments are made automatically** un sistema por *or* según el cual los pagos se efectúan automáticamente

wherever¹ /hwerˈevər ‖ weərˈevə(r)/ *adv* **(a)** (in questions) dónde **(b)** (no matter where) (colloq) en cualquier parte *or* lado

wherever² *conj*: **you can use your card ~ you see this sign** puede usar su tarjeta (en cualquier establecimiento) donde vea este símbolo; **~ he goes, I'll go too** vaya donde vaya, yo iré tambien; **you can sit ~ you like** puedes sentarte donde quieras

wherewithal /ˈhwerwɪðɔ:l ‖ ˈweəwɪðɔ:l/ *n* **the ~** los medios; **we don't have the ~ to do this** no tenemos los recursos para hacer esto

whet /hwet ‖ wet/ *vt* -**tt**- ‹interest/curiosity› estimular; **the walk ~ted our appetites** la caminata nos abrió el apetito

whether /ˈhweðər ‖ ˈweðə(r)/ *conj*: **tell me ~ you need us or not** o *— ~* or not you need us dime si nos necesitas o no; **I doubt ~ he knew** dudo que lo supiera; **~ you like it or not** te guste o no te guste

whey /hwer ‖ wer/ *n* suero *m* (de la leche)

which¹ /hwɪtʃ ‖ wɪtʃ/ *pron* **1 (a)** (in questions) (sing) cuál; (pl) cuáles **(b)** (in indirect use) cuál; **I can never remember ~ is ~** nunca recuerdo cuál es cuál **2** (as relative): **the parcel ~ arrived this morning** el paquete que llegó esta mañana; **the newspaper in ~ the article appeared** el diario en el que *or* en el cual apareció el artículo

which² *adj* **1** (in questions) (sing) qué, cuál; (pl)

qué, cuáles **2** (as relative): **we arrived at two, by ~ time they had gone** llegamos a las dos y para entonces ya se habían ido; **in ~ case** en cuyo caso

whichever¹ /hwɪtʃ'evər ‖ wɪtʃ'evə(r)/ *pron* **(a)** (no matter which): **there are several options, but ~ you choose …** hay varias opciones, pero elijas la que elijas *or* cualquiera que elijas … **(b)** (the one, ones that): **buy ~ is cheaper** compra el que sea más barato

whichever² *adj* **(a)** (no matter which): **~ party is in power** sea cual sea *or* cualquiera que sea el partido que esté en el poder **(b)** (any that): **you can write about ~ subject you know best** puedes escribir sobre el tema que mejor conozcas, sea cual sea *or* fuere

while¹ /hwaɪl ‖ waɪl/ *conj* **1** (in time) mientras; **they don't drink ~ on duty** no beben cuando están de guardia **2** (though) aunque **3** (whereas) mientras que

■ **while away** [*v + adv + o, v + o + adv*]: **we had a game of chess to ~ away the time** jugamos una partida de ajedrez para pasar el rato

while² *n*: **wait a ~** (a few days, weeks) espera un tiempo; (a few minutes, hours) espera un rato; (a very short period) espera un ratito *or* un momentito; **it's been a good ~ since we had any rain** hace bastante (tiempo) que no llueve; **he was here a little ~ ago** hace un ratito estaba aquí; **(every) once in a ~** de vez en cuando

whilst /hwaɪlst ‖ waɪlst/ *conj* (BrE) ▶ WHILE¹

whim /hwɪm ‖ wɪm/ *n* capricho *m*

whimper¹ /'hwɪmpər ‖ 'wɪmpə(r)/ *vi* gimotear

whimper² *n* quejido *m*

whimsical /'hwɪmzɪkəl ‖ 'wɪmzɪkəl/ *adj* ⟨person⟩ caprichoso; ⟨mood⟩ voluble

whine¹ /hwaɪn ‖ waɪn/ *vi* **(a)** ⟨dog⟩ aullar*; ⟨person⟩ gemir*; ⟨child⟩ lloriquear **(b)** (complain) (pej) quejarse

whine² *n* (of dog) aullido *m*; (of person) quejido *m*; (of engine) chirrido *m*; (of bullet) silbido *m*

whinny /'hwɪni ‖ 'wɪni/ *vi* (*3rd pers sing pres* **whinnies**; *pres & past p* **whinnying**; *past & past p* **whinnied**) ⟨horse⟩ relinchar

whip¹ /hwɪp ‖ wɪp/ *n* (in horse riding) fusta *f*, fuete *m* (AmL exc CS); (of tamer) látigo *m*; (for punishment) azote *m*

whip² **-pp-** *vt* **1** **(a)** (lash) ⟨horse⟩ pegarle* a (con la fusta), fustigar*; ⟨person⟩ azotar; ⟨child⟩ darle* una paliza a **(b)** (beat) ⟨egg whites⟩ batir; ⟨cream⟩ batir *or* (Esp) montar; **~ped cream** crema *f* batida *or* (Esp) nata *f* montada **2** (take quickly) (+ *adv compl*): **she ~ped out her notebook** sacó rápidamente la libreta

■ **whip up** [*v + o + adv, v + adv + o*] **1** **(a)** (arouse) ⟨trouble/unrest⟩ provocar*; ⟨hatred⟩ fomentar; ⟨support⟩ conseguir* **(b)** (incite) ⟨crowd⟩ incitar **(c)** ⟨wind⟩ ⟨sea/waves⟩ agitar; ⟨dust⟩ levantar **2** **(a)** (beat, whisk) ⟨egg whites⟩ batir; ⟨cream⟩ batir, montar (Esp) **(b)** (prepare hurriedly) (colloq) ⟨meal⟩ improvisar

whip: **~lash injury** *n* (Med) traumatismo *m* cervical; **~round** *n* (BrE colloq) colecta *f*, vaca *f* (AmL fam)

whir, (BrE) **whirr** /hwɜːr ‖ wɜː(r)/ *vi* **-rr-** ⟨machine/propellers⟩ runrunear, zumbar

whirl¹ /hwɜːrl ‖ wɜːl/ *vi* **(a)** (spin) ⟨person⟩ girar, dar* vueltas; ⟨leaves/dust⟩ arremolinarse **(b)** (move fast) (+ *adv compl*): **he ~ed around** se dio media vuelta rápidamente

■ **~** *vt* (+ *adv compl*) hacer* girar

whirl² *n* (turn) giro *m*, vuelta *f*; (of dust) remolino *m*; **my head was in a ~** la cabeza me daba vueltas

whirl: **~pool** *n* vorágine *f*, remolino *m*; **~wind** *n* torbellino *m*; (before *n*) **a ~wind romance** un idilio arrollador

whirr /hwɜːr ‖ wɜː(r)/ *vi* (BrE) ▶ WHIR

whisk¹ /hwɪsk ‖ wɪsk/ *vt* **1** (Culin) batir **2** (convey quickly) (+ *adv compl*): **she was ~ed off to a meeting** se la llevaron a una reunión a toda prisa; **he ~ed away the plates** retiró los platos rápidamente

whisk² *n* (Culin) batidor *m*

whisker /'hwɪskər ‖ 'wɪskə(r)/ *n* **1** **(a)** (single hair) pelo *m* (de la barba) **(b)** (narrow margin) (no *pl*) pelo *m* **2** **whiskers** *pl* (of animal) bigotes *mpl*

whiskey /'hwɪski ‖ 'wɪski/ *n* (*pl* **-keys**) whisky *m*, güisqui *m* (*esp americano o irlandés*)

whisky /'hwɪski ‖ 'wɪski/ *n* (*pl* **-kies**) whisky *m*, güisqui *m* (*esp escocés*)

whisper¹ /'hwɪspər ‖ 'wɪspə(r)/ *vi* **(a)** ⟨person⟩ cuchichear **(b)** (liter) ⟨wind/leaves⟩ susurrar (liter)

■ **~** *vt* ⟨remark/words⟩ susurrar

whisper² *n* **(a)** (soft voice) susurro *m*; **yes, he said in a ~** —sí —susurró **(b)** (rumor) rumor *m*

whistle¹ /'hwɪsəl ‖ 'wɪsəl/ *vi* ⟨person/kettle/wind⟩ silbar; (loudly) chiflar; ⟨referee⟩ pitar; ⟨train⟩ pitar

■ **~** *vt* ⟨tune⟩ silbar

whistle² *n* **(a)** (instrument) silbato *m*, pito *m* **(b)** (sound — made with mouth) silbido *m*; (loud) chiflido *m*; (— made by referee's whistle) silbato *m*, pitido *m*; (— of kettle, wind, bullet) silbido *m*

white¹ /hwaɪt ‖ waɪt/ *adj* **-er, -est (a)** ⟨paint/cat/bread/wine/chocolate⟩ blanco; ⟨coffee/tea⟩ con leche; **she had a ~ wedding** se casó de blanco; **he went ~** se puso blanco **(b)** (Caucasian) blanco

white² *n* **1** (color) blanco *m* **2** *also* **White** (person) blanco, -ca *m,f* **3** **(a)** (of egg) clara *f* **(b)** (of eye) blanco *m*

white: **~bait** *n* morralla *f*, chanquetes *mpl* (Esp), cornalitos *mpl* (Arg), majuga *f* (Ur); **~collar** /'hwaɪt'kɑːlər ‖ ,waɪt'kɒlə(r)/ *adj* ⟨worker/job⟩ no manual; (clerical) de oficina; **~ elephant** *n* (building, project) elefante *m* blanco; (object) objeto superfluo; **~ gasoline, ~ gas** *n* (AmE) gasolina *f or* (Andes) bencina *f or* (RPl) nafta *f* sin plomo; **~hot** /'hwaɪt'hɑːt ‖ ,waɪt'hɒt/ *adj* ⟨metal⟩ al rojo blanco; **W~ House** *n* the **W~ House** la Casa Blanca; **~ lie** *n* mentira *f* piadosa

whiten /'hwaɪtn̩ ‖ 'waɪtn̩/ *vt* blanquear

white: **~ sauce** *n* salsa *f* blanca *or* bechamel; **~ spirit** *n* (BrE) espíritu *m* de petróleo (*usado como sustituto del aguarrás*)

whitewash¹ /'hwaɪtwɑːʃ ‖ 'waɪtwɒʃ/ *n* **1** (Const) cal *f* **2** (defeat) (colloq) paliza *f* (fam)

whitewash² *vt* ⟨wall/building⟩ blanquear, encalar, enjalbegar*

whiting /'hwaɪtɪŋ ‖ 'waɪtɪŋ/ *n* (*pl* **~s** *or* **~**) pescadilla *f*

Whitsun /'hwɪtsən ‖'wɪtsən/ n (esp BrE) Pentecostés f

whittle /'hwɪtḷ ‖'wɪtḷ/ vt tallar

■ **whittle away** [v + o + adv, v + adv + o] ⟨funds/resources⟩ ir* mermando; ⟨influence⟩ ir* reduciendo; ⟨rights⟩ ir* menoscabando

■ **whittle down** [v + o + adv, v + adv + o] ⟨expenses⟩ recortar; ⟨applicants⟩ reducir* el numero de

whiz, whizz /hwɪz ‖wɪz/ vi **-zz-** (+ adv compl): **to ~ by** ⟪bullet/arrow/car⟫ pasar zumbando; **I ~zed through my homework** hice los deberes zumbando or a toda velocidad

whiz kid, whizz kid n (colloq) lince m (fam)

who /hu:/ pron ❶ **(a)** (in questions) (sing) quién; (pl) quiénes; **~ are you writing to?** ¿a quién le estás escribiendo? **(b)** (in indirect questions) quién; **I don't know ~ you're talking about** no sé de quién estás hablando ❷ (as relative): **the boy ~ won the prize** el chico que ganó el premio; **there are blankets for those ~ want them** hay mantas para quienes quieran

WHO n (= **World Health Organization**) OMS f

who'd /hu:d/ **(a)** = **who had (b)** = **who would**

whodunit, whodunnit /'hu:'dʌnət ‖,hu:'dʌnɪt/ n (colloq) novela f policíaca

whoever /hu:'evər ‖hu:'evə(r)/ pron **(a)** (no matter who): **she's not coming in here, ~ she is** aquí no entra, quien quiera que sea; **~ you ask** se lo preguntes a quien se lo preguntes **(b)** (the one, ones who): **~ did this must be insane** quienquiera que haya hecho esto debe (de) estar loco; **I'll invite ~ I like** voy a invitar a quien (se) me dé la gana **(c)** (in questions) quién

whole¹ /həʊl/ adj ❶ (entire) (before n, no comp): **there's a ~ bottle left** queda una botella entera; **the ~ truth** toda la verdad; **I'm fed up with the ~ affair** estoy harto del asunto ❷ (pred) (in one piece) entero

whole² n **(a)** (integral unit) todo m; **the ~ of sth:** **a threat to the ~ of mankind** una amenaza para toda la humanidad **(b)** (in phrases) **as a whole:** **this will affect Europe as a ~** esto va a afectar a Europa en su totalidad; **on the whole** (indep) en general

wholehearted /'həʊl'hɑːrtəd ‖,həʊl'hɑːtɪd/ adj ⟨approval⟩ sin reservas; ⟨support⟩ incondicional

wholeheartedly /'həʊl'hɑːrtədli ‖,həʊl'hɑːtɪdli/ adv ⟨approve/support⟩ sin reservas

whole: **~meal** adj (BrE) integral; **~ note** n (AmE) semibreve f, redonda f

wholesale¹ /'həʊlseɪl/ adj **(a)** (Busn) (before n) al por mayor **(b)** ⟨destruction/slaughter⟩ sistemático

wholesale² adv **(a)** (Busn) ⟨buy/sell⟩ al por mayor **(b)** (on a large scale) de modo general

wholesaler /'həʊlseɪlər ‖'həʊlseɪlə(r)/ n mayorista mf

wholesome /'həʊlsəm/ adj **(a)** (healthy) ⟨food/ climate⟩ sano **(b)** (morally good) ⟨image⟩ de persona sana

wholewheat /'həʊlhwiːt ‖'həʊlwiːt/ adj integral

who'll /hu:l/ = **who will**

wholly /'həʊlli/ adv totalmente

whom /hu:m/ pron (frml) **(a)** (in questions): **~ did you visit?** ¿a quién visitaste? **(b)** (as relative): **the cousin ~ I mentioned earlier** el primo que or a quien mencioné antes; **the girls, both of ~ could dance** las chicas, que ambas sabían bailar

whooping cough /'hu:pɪŋ/ n tos f convulsa or convulsiva

whoops /hwʊps ‖wʊps/ interj ¡ay!, ¡epa! (AmS fam), ¡híjole! (Méx fam)

whore /hɔːr ‖hɔː(r)/ n (pej) puta f (vulg & pey)

who's /hu:z/ **(a)** = **who is (b)** = **who has**

whose¹ /hu:z/ pron (sing) de quién; (pl) de quiénes

whose² adj **(a)** (in questions) (sing) de quién; (pl) de quiénes **(b)** (as relative) (sing) cuyo; (pl) cuyos

who've /hu:v/ = **who have**

why¹ /hwaɪ ‖waɪ/ adv por qué; **~ not?** ¿por qué no?; **~ don't you apply for the post?** ¿por qué no solicitas el puesto?; **this is ~ the attempt failed** fue por esto que el intento fracasó; **the reason ~ he couldn't attend** la razón por la cual no pudo asistir

why² interj ¡vaya!

why³ n porqué m

WI = **Wisconsin**

wick /wɪk/ n mecha f

wicked /'wɪkəd ‖'wɪkɪd/ adj **-er, -est (a)** (evil) ⟨person⟩ malvado, malo; ⟨thought⟩ malo; ⟨lie⟩ infame **(b)** (vicious) ⟨blow⟩ malintencionado **(c)** (mischievous) ⟨grin/laugh⟩ travieso

wicker /'wɪkər ‖'wɪkə(r)/ n mimbre m

wickerwork /'wɪkərwɜːrk ‖'wɪkəwɜːk/ n **(a)** (articles) artículos mpl de mimbre **(b)** ▶ WICKER

wicket /'wɪkət ‖'wɪkɪt/ n ❶ (in cricket) (stumps and bails) palos mpl ❷ (window) (AmE) ventanilla f

wide¹ /waɪd/ adj **wider, widest** ❶ (in dimension) ⟨river/feet/trousers⟩ ancho; ⟨gap⟩ grande; ⟨desert/ocean⟩ vasto; **it's two meters ~** tiene or mide dos metros de ancho ❷ (in extent, range) ⟨experience/powers/area⟩ amplio; **a ~ variety of things** una gran variedad de cosas ❸ (off target) ⟨ball/shot⟩ desviado; **~ of sth** lejos DE algo; ▶ MARK¹ 4

wide² adv **wider, widest** **~ apart: with your feet ~ apart** con los pies bien separados; **~ awake: to be ~ awake** estar* completamente espabilado or despierto; **open ~!** abra bien la boca; **you left the door ~ open** dejaste la puerta abierta de par en par

wide-angle lens /'waɪd'æŋɡəl/ n granangular m

widely /'waɪdli/ adv **(a)** (extensively): **she is very**

AmC	América Central	Arg	Argentina	Cu	Cuba	Per	Perú
AmL	América Latina	Bol	Bolivia	Ec	Ecuador	RPI	Río de la Plata
AmS	América del Sur	Chi	Chile	Esp	España	Ur	Uruguay
Andes	Región andina	CS	Cono Sur	Méx	México	Ven	Venezuela

~ traveled ha viajado mucho; it was ~ publicized se le dio mucha publicidad (b) (commonly): a ~ held view una opinión muy extendida (c) (to a large degree) ⟨vary⟩ mucho

widen /'waɪdn̩/ vt ⟨road/entrance⟩ ensanchar; ⟨range/debate/scope⟩ ampliar*

■ ~ vi «road/tunnel» ensancharse

wide: ~-ranging /'waɪdreɪndʒɪŋ/ adj ⟨powers/ curriculum⟩ amplio; ⟨interests⟩ variado; ⟨effects⟩ de gran alcance; **~-screen** /'waɪdskriːn/ adj para pantalla ancha; **~spread** adj ⟨custom/ belief⟩ extendido

widget /'wɪdʒət ‖'wɪdʒɪt/ n (colloq) aparato m, artilugio m, chisme m (Esp fam)

widow¹ /'wɪdəʊ/ n viuda f

widow² vt: to be ~ed enviudar, quedar viudo

widower /'wɪdəʊər ‖'wɪdəʊə(r)/ n viudo m

width /wɪdθ/ n (a) (measurement) ancho m, anchura f; what ~ is the cloth? ¿qué ancho tiene la tela? (b) (in swimming pool) ancho m

wield /wiːld/ vt ⟨sword⟩ blandir*; ⟨power/ authority⟩ ejercer*

wife /waɪf/ n (pl **wives**) esposa f, mujer f

wig /wɪg/ n peluca f

wiggle /'wɪgəl/ vt ⟨toes⟩ mover*; ⟨hips⟩ contonear

wild¹ /waɪld/ adj **-er, -est** 1 (a) ⟨animal⟩ salvaje; ⟨plant/flower⟩ silvestre; ⟨vegetation⟩ agreste (b) (uncivilized) ⟨tribe⟩ salvaje (c) (desolate) ⟨country⟩ agreste

2 (a) (unruly) ⟨party/lifestyle⟩ desenfrenado (b) (random, uncontrolled) ⟨attempt⟩ desesperado; a ~ guess una conjetura hecha totalmente al azar (c) ⟨allegation/exaggeration⟩ absurdo

3 (a) (violent) (liter) ⟨sea/waters⟩ embravecido, proceloso (liter); ⟨wind⟩ fuertísimo, furioso (liter) (b) (frantic) ⟨excitement/dancing⟩ desenfrenado; ⟨shouting⟩ desaforado; ⟨appearance/stare⟩ de loco; her perfume was driving him ~ su perfume lo estaba enloqueciendo (c) (enthusiastic) (colloq) (pred) to be ~ ABOUT sth: I'm not ~ about the idea la idea no me enloquece (d) (angry) (colloq) (pred): it makes me ~ me saca de quicio

wild² adv: these flowers grow ~ estas flores son silvestres; to run ~: these kids have been allowed to run ~ a estos niños los han criado como salvajes; the garden has run ~ la maleza ha invadido el jardín

wild³ n the ~: an opportunity to observe these animals in the ~ una oportunidad de observar estos animales en libertad

wild: ~ boar n jabalí m; **~ card** n (Comput) comodín m; **~cat** /'waɪldkæt/ n (pl **~cats** or **~cat**) (European) gato m montés; (bobcat) (esp AmE) lince m

wilderness /'wɪldərnəs ‖'wɪldənɪs/ n (a) (wasteland) páramo m; (jungle) jungla f (b) (undeveloped land) (AmE) parque m natural

wild: ~fire n (AmE) fuego m arrasador; to spread like ~fire (also BrE) extenderse* como un reguero de pólvora; **~goose chase** /'waɪld'guːs/ n: I'm not going into town again on another ~goose chase no pienso ir otra vez al centro a perder el tiempo para nada; **~life** n fauna f y flora f

wildly /'waɪldli/ adv 1 (a) (frantically) ⟨kick/

struggle/rush⟩ como (un) loco (b) (violently) ⟨rage/ blow⟩ con furia 2 (a) (in undisciplined fashion) ⟨live⟩ desordenadamente (b) (haphazardly, randomly) ⟨shoot/guess⟩ a lo loco 3 (extremely): ~ funny comiquísimo; ~ inaccurate estimates cálculos absolutamente errados

Wild West n the ~ ~ el Lejano Oeste; (before n) ⟨adventure/story⟩ del oeste

wiles /waɪlz/ pl n artimañas fpl

wilful adj (BrE) ▶ WILLFUL

will¹ /wɪl/ v mod

■ Note When translating will into Spanish, the future tense is not always the first option. Ir + a + infinitive is common in Latin American countries. For examples, see the entry below.

⟨past **would**⟩ ['LL es la contracción de WILL, WON'T de WILL NOT y 'LL'VE de WILL HAVE]

1 (talking about the future): he'll come on Friday vendrá el viernes, va a venir el viernes; he said he would come on Friday dijo que vendría or iba a venir el viernes; at the end of this month, he'll have been working here for a year este fin de mes hará un año que trabaja aquí; I won't let you down no te fallaré

2 (a) (expressing willingness): ~ o would you do me a favor? ¿quieres hacerme un favor?; she won't tell us what happened no nos quiere decir qué pasó (b) (in orders, invitations): be quiet, ~ you! cállate, ¿quieres?; ~ you have a drink? ¿quieres tomar algo?

3 (expressing conjecture): won't they be having lunch now? ¿no estarán comiendo ahora?; that would have been in 1947 eso debe (de) haber sido en 1947

4 (a) (indicating habit, characteristic): I'll watch anything on television yo soy capaz de mirar cualquier cosa en la televisión; he'd get drunk every Saturday se emborrachaba todos los sábados (b) (indicating capability): this door won't shut esta puerta no cierra or no quiere cerrar

■ ~ vt (past & past p **willed**) 1 (a) (urge, try to cause): I was ~ing her to get the answer right estaba deseando con todas mis fuerzas que diera la respuesta correcta (b) (desire, ordain) (frml) «God» disponer*, querer*

2 (bequeath) legar*

will² n 1 (a) (faculty) voluntad f (b) (willpower) voluntad f; to lose the ~ to live perder* las ansias de vivir (c) (desire, intention) voluntad f; patients may come and go at ~ los pacientes pueden entrar y salir a voluntad; ▶ FREE WILL

2 (testament) testamento m

willful, (BrE) **wilful** /'wɪlfəl/ adj 1 (deliberate) ⟨misconduct/neglect⟩ intencionado; ⟨damage⟩ causado con premeditación 2 (obstinate) ⟨person⟩ terco

willing /'wɪlɪŋ/ adj (a) (eager, compliant) (before n) ⟨servant/worker⟩ servicial (b) (inclined) (pred) to be ~ to + INF estar* dispuesto A + INF

willingly /'wɪlɪŋli/ adv (gladly) con gusto; (readily, freely) por voluntad propia

willingness /'wɪlɪŋnəs ‖'wɪlɪŋnɪs/ n buena voluntad f, buena disposición f

willow /'wɪləʊ/ n sauce m

willpower /'wɪlpaʊər ‖'wɪlpaʊə(r)/ n (fuerza f de) voluntad f

W

willy-nilly /ˈwɪlɪˈnɪlɪ/ adv (a) (haphazardly) de cualquier manera (b) (like it or not) sea como sea

wilt /wɪlt/ vi «plant/flower» ponerse* mustio, marchitarse

wily /ˈwaɪlɪ/ adj **wilier, wiliest** astuto

win¹ /wɪn/ (pres p **winning**; past & past p **won**) vt ⊡ (gain) ⟨prize/title⟩ ganar; ⟨support⟩ conseguir*; ⟨fame/recognition/affection⟩ ganarse; ⟨scholarship/promotion/contract⟩ conseguir* ⊡ (be victorious in) ⟨war/race/bet/election⟩ ganar

■ ~ vi ganar

■ **win over,** (BrE also) **win round** [v + o + adv, v + adv + o] conquistarse a

win² n victoria f, triunfo m

wince /wɪns/ vi hacer* un gesto de dolor; (shudder) estremecerse*

winch¹ /wɪntʃ/ n cabrestante m, torno m

winch² vt: levantar con un torno o cabrestante

wind¹ /wɪnd/ n ⊡ (Meteo) viento m; **to get ~ of sth** enterarse de algo; (before n) ~ **power** energía f eólica ⊡ (in bowels) gases mpl ⊡ (breath) aliento m ⊡ (Mus): **the ~** los instrumentos de viento; (before n) ~ **instrument** instrumento m de viento

wind² vt

I /wɪnd/ (a) «exertion» dejar sin aliento; «blow» cortarle la respiración a (b) ⟨baby⟩ sacarle* el aire a (fam)

II /waɪnd/ (past & past p **wound** /waʊnd/) ⊡ (coil) ⟨yarn/wool⟩ ovillar; **to ~ sth AROUND** o (esp BrE) **ROUND sth** enroscar* algo ALREDEDOR DE algo; **to ~ sth into a ball** hacer* un ovillo con algo; **to ~ the film on** (hacer*) correr la película ⊡ (a) (turn) ⟨handle⟩ hacer* girar, darle* vueltas a; ⟨clock/watch⟩ darle* cuerda a (b) (hoist, pull) levantar

■ ~ vi /waɪnd/ (past & past p **wound** /waʊnd/) (a) «river/road» serpentear (b) **winding** pres p ⟨river/road⟩ sinuoso, serpenteante

■ **wind down** ⊡ [v + o + adv, v + adv + o] ⟨window⟩ (Auto) bajar; ⟨production/trade⟩ reducir* paulatinamente ⊡ [v + adv] (colloq) relajarse

■ **wind up** ⊡ [v + o + adv, v + adv + o] (a) (tighten spring) ⟨watch/toy⟩ darle* cuerda a (b) (bring to conclusion) ⟨meeting/speech⟩ cerrar* (c) (close down) ⟨company⟩ cerrar*, liquidar ⊡ [v + o + adv] (colloq) (make angry) torear, darle* manija a (RPl fam); (tease) tomarle el pelo a (fam) ⊡ [v + adv] (a) (end up, find oneself) (colloq) terminar, acabar (b) (conclude) «speaker» concluir*, terminar

wind /wɪnd/: ~**fall** n (a) (fruit) fruta caída del árbol (b) (unexpected benefit): **the $100 prize was a nice little ~fall** el premio de 100 dólares le (or me etc) cayó como llovido del cielo; ~**mill** n molino m de viento

window /ˈwɪndəʊ/ n ⊡ (a) (of building) ventana f; (of car) ventanilla f; (of shop) vitrina f (AmL), vidriera f (AmL), escaparate m (esp Esp); **to fly/go out (of) the ~** «plans» venirse* abajo, desbaratarse; «hopes» desvanecerse* (b) (sales counter) ventanilla f ⊡ (Comput) ventana f, recuadro m

window: ~ **box** n jardinera f, ~ **cleaner** n (product) limpiacristales m, limpiavidrios m (esp AmL); (person) limpiacristales mf, limpiavidrios mf (esp AmL); ~ **dressing** n (in shop) vitrinismo m (AmL), vidrierismo m (AmL), escaparatismo m

(esp Esp); ~ **ledge** n alféizar m or repisa f de la ventana; ~**pane** n vidrio m or (Esp) cristal m (de una ventana); ~ **seat** n (in train, plane) asiento m junto a la ventanilla; ~-**shop** vi -**pp**-: **to go ~-shopping** ir* a mirar vitrinas or vidrieras or (esp Esp) escaparates; ~**sill** n alféizar m or repisa f de la ventana

wind /wɪnd/: ~**pipe** n tráquea f; ~**screen** n (BrE) ▶ ~SHIELD; ~**shield** n (AmE) parabrisas m; (before n) ~**shield wiper** limpiaparabrisas m, limpiador m (Méx); ~**surfer** n (person) tablista mf, surfista mf; (board) tabla f de windsurf; ~**surfing** n windsurf m, windsurfing m, surf m a vela; ~**swept** adj ⟨beach/plain⟩ azotado por el viento; ⟨person⟩ despeinado; ⟨hair⟩ alborotado

windy /ˈwɪndɪ/ adj -**dier, -diest** ⟨day/weather⟩ ventoso, de viento; **it's ~** hace viento

wine /waɪn/ n (a) (beverage) vino m; (before n) ~ **cellar** bodega f; ~ **list** carta f de vinos; ~ **rack** botellero m; ~ **waiter** sommelier m, sumiller m (b) (color) rojo m granate; (before n) rojo granate adj inv

wine: ~ **and dine** vt agasajar (con una comida); ~ **bar** n bar m (especializado en vinos); ~ **glass** n copa f de vino; ~**growing** n viticultura f; (before n) ⟨area/region⟩ vinícola; ⟨country⟩ productor de vino; ~**tasting** /ˈwaɪn,teɪstɪŋ/ n (a) (act, skill) cata f or catadura f de vinos (b) (event) degustación f de vinos

wing /wɪŋ/ n ⊡ (Zool) ala f; ⊡ (Aviat) ala f; ⊡ (BrE Auto) guardabarros m or (Méx) salpicadera f or (Chi, Per) tapabarros m ⊡ (Pol) ala f; ⊡ (of building) ala f; ⊡ **wings** pl (Theat) **the ~s** los bastidores

wingspan /ˈwɪŋspæn/ n envergadura f

wink¹ /wɪŋk/ n guiño m, guiñada f; **to give sb a ~** guiñarle el ojo a algn; **not to get a ~ of sleep** no pegar* (el or un) ojo

wink² vi (a) «person» guiñar el ojo (b) (flash) «light» parpadear

winner /ˈwɪnər ‖ ˈwɪnə(r)/ n ganador, -dora m,f

winning /ˈwɪnɪŋ/ adj (a) (victorious) (before n) ⟨candidate/team⟩ ganador; ⟨goal/shot⟩ de la victoria (b) (appealing) ⟨smile/personality⟩ encantador

winning post n (poste m de) llegada f

winnings /ˈwɪnɪŋz/ pl n ganancias fpl (obtenidas en el juego)

winter /ˈwɪntər ‖ ˈwɪntə(r)/ n invierno m; **in (the) ~** en invierno; (before n) ⟨weather⟩ invernal; ~ **sports** deportes mpl de invierno

wintertime /ˈwɪntərtaɪm ‖ ˈwɪntətaɪm/ n invierno m

wintry /ˈwɪntrɪ/ adj -**trier, -triest** invernal

wipe¹ /waɪp/ n (a) (action): **give the table a ~ with a damp cloth** pásale un trapo húmedo a la mesa (b) (cloth) toallita f

wipe² vt ⟨floor/table⟩ limpiar, pasarle un trapo a; ⟨dishes⟩ secar*; ~ **your nose** límpiate la nariz

■ ~ vi (dry dishes) secar*

■ **wipe away** [v + o + adv, v + adv + o] ⟨tears⟩ secar*; ⟨memory⟩ borrar

■ **wipe off** [v + o + adv, v + adv + o] (a) (remove) ⟨mud/oil⟩ limpiar (b) (erase) ⟨recording⟩ borrar

■ **wipe out** [v + o + adv, v + adv + o] (a) (clean) limpiar, pasarle un trapo a (b) (destroy, eradicate)

⟨species/population⟩ exterminar; ⟨resistance⟩ acabar con; ⟨disease⟩ erradicar*; ⟨army⟩ aniquilar **(c)** (erase) ⟨writing/memory⟩ borrar
■ **wipe up** [υ + o + adv, υ + adv + o] limpiar
wire¹ /waɪr ‖ 'waɪə(r)/ n **1 (a)** (metal strand) alambre m; (before n) ~ **fence** alambrada f, alambrado m (AmL) **(b)** (fencing, mesh) alambrada f, alambrado m (AmL) **(c)** (finishing line) (AmE): the ~ la línea de llegada, la meta **2 (a)** (Elec, Telec) cable m **(b)** (telegram) (colloq) telegrama m
wire² vt (Elec): to be ~d to sth estar* conectado a algo
wire: ~ **cutters** /'kʌtərz ‖ 'kʌtəz/ pl n cortaalambres m, pinzas fpl de corte (Méx); (large) cizalla(s) f(pl); ~**less** adj ⟨technology/ communications⟩ inalámbrico; ~**walker** n (AmE) equilibrista mf, funámbulo, -la m,f; ~ **wool** n ▶ STEEL WOOL
wiring /'waɪrɪŋ ‖ 'waɪərɪŋ/ n (Elec) cableado m, instalación f eléctrica
wiry /'waɪri ‖ 'waɪəri/ adj **wirier, wiriest (a)** ⟨person⟩ enjuto y nervudo **(b)** ⟨hair⟩ áspero =
Wis = Wisconsin
wisdom /'wɪzdəm/ n sabiduría f
wisdom tooth n muela f del juicio
wise /waɪz/ adj **wiser, wisest (a)** (prudent) ⟨person⟩ prudente; ⟨choice/decision⟩ acertado **(b)** (learned, experienced) sabio; to be none the ~r. I'm none the ~r sigo sin entender **(c)** (aware) (colloq) to be ~ TO sth/sb: I'm ~ to him/his tricks lo conozco muy bien/le conozco las mañas
■ **wise up** (colloq) [υ + adv] (d)espabilarse, avivarse (AmL fam), apiolarse (RPl fam)
-wise /waɪz/ suff **(a)** (with reference to): price~/ weather~ en lo que respecta al precio/tiempo **(b)** (in particular way): length~ a lo largo
wisecrack n broma f, chiste m
wisely /'waɪzli/ adv sabiamente
wish¹ /wɪʃ/ n **(a)** (desire) deseo m; to make a ~ pedir* un deseo; they got married against my ~es se casaron en contra de mi voluntad **(b)**
wishes pl (greetings): give your mother my best ~es dale a tu madre muchos recuerdos de mi parte, cariños a tu madre (AmL); best ~es, Jack saludos or un abrazo de Jack
wish² vt **(a)** (desire fervently) desear; to ~ sth ON sb desearle algo a algn; I ~ I were rich ¡ojalá fuera rico!; she ~ed she hadn't told him lamentó habérselo dicho; I ~ you wouldn't say things like that me disgusta mucho que digas esas cosas **(b)** (want) desear (frml) **(c)** (want for sb) desear; ~ me luck! ¡deséame suerte!; to ~ sb good night darle* las buenas noches a algn
■ ~ vi **(a)** (make magic wish) pedir* un deseo **(b)** (want, desire): if you ~ como quieras
wishful thinking /'wɪʃfəl/ n: are you sure or is it just ~ ~? ¿lo sabes a ciencia cierta o es simplemente lo que tú querrías?
wisp /wɪsp/ n (of smoke) voluta f; (of hair) mechón m
wispy /'wɪspi/ adj **-pier, -piest** ⟨cloud⟩ tenue; ⟨hair⟩ ralo
wistful /'wɪstfəl/ adj ⟨smile/thought⟩ nostálgico
wit /wɪt/ n **1** (often pl) (intelligence) inteligencia f; (ingenuity) ingenio m; to be at one's ~s' end estar* desesperado **2** (humor) ingenio m
witch /wɪtʃ/ n bruja f

witch: ~**craft** n brujería f, hechicería f; ~ **doctor** n hechicero m, brujo m
with /wɪð, wɪθ/ prep
■ **Note** When the translation con is followed by the pronouns mí, ti, and si, it combines with them to form conmigo, contigo, and consigo: come with me ven conmigo; take it with you llévalo contigo; he had his dog with him tenía el perro consigo.

1 (a) (in the company of) con; she went ~ him/ them/me/you fue con él/con ellos/conmigo/ contigo **(b)** (member, employee, client etc of): I've been banking ~ them for years hace años que tengo cuenta en ese banco
2 (in descriptions): the shirt is black ~ white stripes la camisa es negra a or con rayas blancas; the man ~ the beard el hombre de barba; a tall woman ~ long hair una mujer alta con el pelo largo or de pelo largo; he is married, ~ three children está casado y tiene tres hijos
3 (a) (indicating manner) con; the proposal was greeted ~ derision la propuesta fue recibida con burlas **(b)** (by means of, using) con; she ate it ~ her fingers lo comió con la mano **(c)** (as a result of): trembling ~ fright temblando de miedo
withdraw /wɪð'drɔː/ (past -drew; past p -drawn) vt **1 (a)** (recall, remove) ⟨troops/ representative⟩ retirar; ⟨hand/arm⟩ retirar; ⟨coin/ note⟩ retirar de la circulación; ⟨product⟩ retirar de la venta **(b)** ⟨money/cash⟩ retirar, sacar* **2 (a)** (cancel, discontinue) ⟨support/funding⟩ retirar; ⟨permission⟩ cancelar; they threatened to ~ their labor amenazaron con ir a la huelga **(b)** (rescind) ⟨application/charges⟩ retirar; ⟨demand⟩ renunciar a **(c)** (retract) ⟨statement/allegation⟩ retirar
■ ~ vi **(a)** «troops/competitor/candidate» retirarse **(b)** (socially) recluirse*; (psychologically) retraerse*
withdrawal /wɪð'drɔːəl/ n **1** (of troops, team, representative) retirada f; (of coinage) retirada f de la circulación; (of product) retirada f de la venta **2** (of support, funding) retirada f, retiro m (AmL); (of application, nomination, competitor) retirada f **3** (Psych) retraimiento m **4** (of cash) retirada f, retiro m (AmL) **5** (from drugs) abandono m; (before n) ~ **symptoms** síndrome m de abstinencia
withdrawn¹ /wɪð'drɔːn/ past p of WITHDRAW
withdrawn² adj retraído
withdrew /wɪð'druː/ past of WITHDRAW
wither /'wɪðər ‖ 'wɪðə(r)/ vi «plant/flower» marchitarse; «limb» atrofiarse
withered /'wɪðərd ‖ 'wɪðəd/ adj ⟨plant/flower⟩ marchito, mustio; ⟨limb⟩ atrofiado
withering /'wɪðərɪŋ/ adj **(a)** ⟨heat⟩ abrasador **(b)** ⟨look⟩ fulminante
withhold /wɪð'həʊld ‖ wɪð'həʊld/ vt (past & past p -held) ⟨payment/funds⟩ retener*; ⟨truth⟩ ocultar; ⟨consent⟩ negar*; ⟨information⟩ no revelar
within¹ /wɪð'ɪn/ prep **1** (inside) dentro de; ~ a radius of 20 miles en un radio de 20 millas **2** (indicating nearness) a; we were ~ 150m of the summit estábamos a 150m de la cumbre **3** (in less than): ~ the time allotted dentro del tiempo establecido; they'll be here ~ an hour estarán aquí en menos de una hora
within² adv (arch or liter) dentro

W

without /wɪð'aʊt/ prep sin; **do it ~ cheating** hazlo sin hacer trampas

withstand /wɪð'stænd/ vt (past & past p **-stood**) ⟨attack⟩ resistir; ⟨heat/pain⟩ soportar

witness¹ /'wɪtnəs ‖'wɪtnɪs/ n **1** (person) testigo mf; (before n) **~ stand** o (BrE) **box** estrado m **2** (testimony, evidence) **to be ~ TO sth** ser* testimonio DE algo

witness² vt (a) (observe) ⟨change/event⟩ ser* testigo de; (crime/accident) presenciar (b) (authenticate) (Law) ⟨signature⟩ atestiguar*; ⟨will⟩ atestiguar* la firma de

witticism /'wɪtəsɪzəm ‖'wɪtɪsɪzəm/ n agudeza f; (in conversation) salida f

witty /'wɪti/ adj **-tier, -tiest** ⟨person⟩ ingenioso; (funny) gracioso; ⟨answer/remark⟩ ingenioso

wives /waɪvz/ pl of WIFE

wizard /'wɪzərd ‖'wɪzəd/ n mago m, brujo m

wizened /'wɪznd/ adj (wrinkled) arrugado; (withered) marchito

wk = **week**

WMD n (= **weapons of mass destruction**) ADM fpl

wobble /'wɑːbəl ‖'wɒbəl/ vi (a) (tremble) «jelly» temblar* (b) (sway, waver) «cyclist» bambolearse; «wheel» bailar; «chair» tambalearse

wobbly /'wɑːbli ‖'wɒbli/ adj **-blier, -bliest** (a) ⟨voice⟩ tembloroso (b) ⟨wheel/tooth⟩ flojo; ⟨table/chair⟩ poco firme, que se tambalea; **my legs are ~** me tiemblan las piernas

woe /wəʊ/ n (a) (sorrow) congoja f (liter), aflicción f; **~ betide you if you lose it!** ¡pobre de ti or ay de ti si lo pierdes! (b) **woes** pl (afflictions) males mpl

woeful /'wəʊfəl/ adj (a) (deplorable) ⟨neglect/ ignorance⟩ lamentable (b) (sorrowful) (liter) ⟨person⟩ acongojado (liter); ⟨expression⟩ desconsolado

woke /wəʊk/ past of WAKE¹

woken /'wəʊkən/ past p of WAKE¹

wolf¹ /wʊlf/ n (pl **wolves**) (Zool) lobo m

wolf² vt **~ (down)** devorar(se)

wolves /wʊlvz/ pl of WOLF¹

woman /'wʊmən/ n (pl **women**) mujer f; (before n) **a ~ lawyer** una abogada; **a ~ friend of mine** una amiga mía

womanizer /'wʊmənaɪzər/ n mujeriego m

womanly /'wʊmənli/ adj femenino

womb /wuːm/ n útero m, matriz f

women /'wɪmɪn/ pl of WOMAN

women's room n (AmE) baño m or (Esp) servicios mpl de damas or señoras

won /wʌn/ past & past p of WIN¹

wonder¹ /'wʌndər ‖'wʌndə(r)/ n **1** (awe, curiosity) asombro m **2** (marvel, miracle) maravilla f; **no ~ you feel tired!** ¡no me extraña que estés cansado!

wonder² vi (a) (ponder, speculate): **why do you ask? — oh, I was just ~ing** ¿por qué preguntas?

— por nada (b) (marvel, be surprised) maravillarse; **I ~ at your patience** me maravilla la paciencia que tienes

■ **~** vt (a) (ask oneself) preguntarse; **I ~ if** o **whether he'll be there** me pregunto si estará (b) (be amazed): **I ~ (that) she didn't fire you on the spot** me sorprende que no te haya echado inmediatamente

wonder³ adj (before n) ⟨drug/cure⟩ milagroso

wonderful /'wʌndərfəl ‖'wʌndəfəl/ adj maravilloso

wonderfully /'wʌndərfli ‖'wʌndəfəli/ adv maravillosamente, de maravilla

wont /wɑːnt ‖wəʊnt/ n (liter or hum) costumbre f; **as is her ~** como tiene por costumbre

won't /wəʊnt/ = **will not**

woo /wuː/ vt ⟨woman⟩ cortejar; ⟨customers/ investors⟩ atraer*; ⟨voters⟩ buscar* el apoyo de

wood /wʊd/ n **1** (material) madera f; (firewood) leña f **2** (wooded area) (often pl) bosque m **3** (in golf) palo m de madera

wooded /'wʊdəd ‖'wʊdɪd/ adj boscoso

wooden /'wʊdn/ adj (a) (made of wood) de madera; **~ leg** pata f de palo (fam) (b) (stiff) ⟨expression⟩ rígido; ⟨performance⟩ acartonado

wood: ~land /'wʊdlənd/ n (often pl) bosque m; **~louse** n (pl **-lice**) cochinilla f, chanchito m (Andes, CS fam); **~pecker** /'wʊdˌpekər ‖'wʊdˌpekə(r)/ n pájaro m carpintero, pico m (barreno or carpintero); **~ pigeon** n paloma f torcaz; **~pile** n (AmE) montón m de leña; **~shed** n leñera f; **~wind** /'wʊdwɪnd/ n (pl **~wind** or **~winds**) **the ~wind(s)** los instrumentos de viento de madera; **~work** n (a) (wooden fittings) carpintería f (b) (BrE) ▶ **~WORKING; ~working** n (AmE) (carpentry) carpintería f; (cabinet making) ebanistería f; (craftwork) artesanía f en madera; **~worm** n (pl **~worm**) (a) (larva) carcoma f (b) (infestation): **the table's full of ~worm** la mesa está llena de carcoma or está toda carcomida

woody /'wʊdi/ adj **-dier, -diest** leñoso

woof n /wʊf/ (colloq) ladrido m; **~ ~!** ¡guau guau!

wool /wʊl/ n lana f

woolen, (BrE) **woollen** /'wʊlən/ adj de lana

woolens, (BrE) **woollens** /'wʊlənz/ pl n (Clothes) prendas fpl de lana

wooly, (BrE) **woolly** /'wʊli/ adj **-lier, -liest** (a) ⟨hat/sweater⟩ de lana (b) (unclear) ⟨thinking/ argument⟩ vago, impreciso

word¹ /wɜːrd ‖wɜːd/ n **1** (term, expression) palabra f; **what's the German ~ for 'dog'?** ¿cómo se dice 'perro' en alemán?; **in other ~s** (introducing a reformulation) es decir; **to be lost for ~s** no encontrar* palabras **2** (thing said) palabra f, **a ~ of advice** un consejo; **I can't hear a ~ you're saying** no te oigo nada; **I don't believe a ~ of it** no me lo creo; **by ~ of mouth: the news spread by ~ of mouth** la noticia se fue transmitiendo de boca en boca; **the last ~:**

W

to have the last ~ tener* la última palabra; **the last ~ in computers** la última palabra en computadoras; **to eat one's ~s: I was forced to eat my ~s** me tuve que tragar lo que había dicho; **to have a ~ with sb about sth** hablar con algn de *or* sobre algo; **to have ~s with sb** tener* unas palabras con algn; ▶ MINCE¹

3 (assurance) (*no pl*) palabra *f*; **to keep/give one's ~** cumplir/dar* su (*or* mi *etc*) palabra; **you can take my ~ for it** te lo aseguro; **to take sb at her/his ~** tomarle la palabra a algn

4 (a) (news, message): **there is still no ~ of survivors** todavía no se sabe si hay supervivientes; **~ has it that ...** corre la noticia *or* el rumor de que ... **(b)** (instruction): **if you need a hand just say the ~** si quieres que te ayude no tienes más que pedirlo; **to give the ~ (to + INF)** dar* la orden (de + INF)

5 words *pl* **(a)** (lyrics) letra *f* **(b)** (Theat): **he forgot his ~s** se le olvidó lo que tenía que decir

word² *vt* ⟨document/letter⟩ redactar; ⟨question⟩ formular

word for word *adv* ⟨repeat/copy⟩ palabra por palabra; ⟨translate⟩ literalmente

wording /'wɜːrdɪŋ ‖'wɜːdɪŋ/ *n* (of paragraph, letter) redacción *f*; (of question) formulación *f*

word: ~ processing *n* tratamiento *m or* procesamiento *m* de textos; **~ processor** /'prɑːsesər, 'prəʊ- ‖'prəʊsesə(r)/ *n* procesador *m* de textos

wordy /'wɜːrdi ‖'wɜːdi/ *adj* **-dier, -diest** verboso

wore /wɔːr ‖wɔː(r)/ *past of* WEAR²

work¹ /wɜːrk ‖wɜːk/ *n* **1** (labor, tasks) trabajo *m*; **she put a lot of ~ into it** puso mucho esfuerzo en ello; **it's hard ~ digging** cavar es muy duro

2 (employment) trabajo *m*; **to go to ~** ir* a trabajar *or* al trabajo

3 (*in phrases*) **at work: he's at ~** está en el trabajo, está en la oficina (*or* la fábrica *etc*); **they were hard at ~** estaban muy ocupados trabajando; **off work: she was off ~ for a month after the accident** después del accidente estuvo un mes sin trabajar; **he took a day off ~** se tomó un día libre; **out of work: to be out of ~** estar* sin trabajo *or* desocupado *or* desempleado *or* (Chi tb) cesante, estar* parado (Esp); (*before n*) **out-of-work** desocupado, desempleado, parado (Esp), cesante (Chi)

4 (a) (product, single item) obra *f*; **a ~ of art** una obra de arte **(b)** (output) trabajo *m*; **a piece of ~** un trabajo; **it was the ~ of a professional** era obra de un profesional; *see also* WORKS

work² *vi* **1** ⟨person⟩ trabajar; **I ~ as a receptionist** trabajo de recepcionista; **to ~ hard** trabajar mucho *or* duro; **to ~ FOR sb** trabajar PARA algn; **to ~ in oils** pintar al óleo, trabajar con óleos; **he's ~ing on his car** está arreglando el coche; **scientists are ~ing on a cure** los científicos están intentando encontrar una cura; **to ~ UNDER sb** trabajar bajo la dirección de algn

2 (a) (operate, function) ⟨machine/system⟩ funcionar; ⟨drug/person⟩ actuar*; **it ~s both ways: you have to make an effort too, you know: it ~s both ways** tú también tienes que hacer el esfuerzo, ¿sabes? funciona igual *or* (esp AmL)

parejo para los dos **(b)** (have required effect) ⟨drug/plan/method⟩ surtir efecto; **try it, it might ~** pruébalo, quizás resulte

■ ~ *vt* **1 (a)** (force to work) hacer* trabajar; **to ~ oneself to death** matarse trabajando **(b)** (exploit) ⟨land/soil⟩ trabajar; ⟨mine⟩ explotar **(c)** ⟨nightclubs/casinos⟩ trabajar en **(d)** (pay for by working): **he ~ed his passage to Australia** se costeó el pasaje a Australia trabajando en el barco

2 (cause to operate): **do you know how to ~ the machine?** ¿sabes manejar la máquina?; **this lever ~s the sprinkler system** esta palanca acciona el sistema de riego

3 (a) (move gradually, manipulate) (+ *adv compl*): **~ the brush into the corners** mete bien el cepillo en los rincones; **to ~ one's way: we ~ed our way toward the exit** nos abrimos camino hacia la salida; **she ~ed her way to the top of her profession** trabajó hasta llegar a la cima de su profesión **(b)** (shape, fashion) ⟨clay/metal⟩ trabajar; ⟨dough⟩ sobar

4 (a) (*past & past p* **worked** *or* **wrought**) (bring about) ⟨miracle⟩ hacer*; *see also* WROUGHT **(b)** (arrange) (colloq) arreglar

■ **work off** [*v + o + adv, v + adv + o*] **(a)** (get rid of): **you can ~ off a few kilos in the gym** puede rebajar algunos kilos en el gimnasio **(b)** ⟨debt⟩ amortizar*, pagar* (*trabajando*)

■ **work out**

I [*v + adv*] **1 (a)** (turn out) salir*, resultar; **it ~s out at $75 a head** sale (a) 75 dólares por cabeza **(b)** (be successful) ⟨plan⟩ salir* bien

2 (train, exercise) (Sport) hacer* ejercicio

II [*v + o + adv, v + adv + o*] **1 (a)** (solve) ⟨sum⟩ hacer*; ⟨riddle/puzzle⟩ resolver* **(b)** (find, calculate) ⟨percentage/probability⟩ calcular; **have you ~ed out the answer?** ¿lo has resuelto? **(c)** (understand) entender*

2 (devise, determine) ⟨solution/procedure⟩ idear; ⟨plan⟩ elaborar

■ **work up** [*v + o + adv, v + adv + o*] **(a)** (stimulate): **they had ~ed up an appetite** se les había abierto el apetito; **I couldn't ~ up much enthusiasm** no me entusiasmaba demasiado **(b)** (excite, arouse): **she gets very ~ed up about it** se pone como loca; **they had been ~ed up into a frenzy** los habían puesto frenéticos, los habían exaltado

workable /'wɜːrkəbəl ‖'wɜːkəbəl/ *adj* ⟨arrangement/solution⟩ factible

work: ~bench *n* banco *m* de trabajo; **~day** *n* **(a)** (part of day) jornada *f* laboral **(b)** (weekday) día *m* hábil *or* laborable *or* laboral *or* de trabajo

worker /'wɜːrkər ‖'wɜːkə(r)/ *n* **(a)** trabajador, -dora *m,f*; **he's a good/slow ~** trabaja bien/ lentamente **(b)** (ant, bee) obrera *f*

work: ~ experience *n* experiencia *f* laboral; **~ force** *n* (of nation) población *f* activa; (of company) personal *m*, plantilla *f* (Esp)

working /'wɜːrkɪŋ ‖'wɜːkɪŋ/ *adj* (*before n*) **1 (a)** ⟨mother/parent⟩ que trabaja; **~ population** población *f* activa **(b)** ⟨hours/conditions⟩ de trabajo; **we have a good ~ relationship** trabajamos muy bien juntos **2 (a)** (capable of operating): **it's in perfect ~ order** funciona perfectamente **(b)** (suitable for working with) ⟨hypothesis⟩ de trabajo; **I have a ~ knowledge of Russian** tengo conocimientos básicos de ruso

W

working: ~ class n (sometimes pl) the ~ class(es) la clase obrera or trabajadora; **~class** /'wɜːrkɪŋˈklæs ‖,wɜːkɪŋˈklɑːs/ adj ⟨person⟩ de clase obrera or trabajadora; ⟨area⟩ obrero; **~ day** n (a) (weekday) día m hábil or laborable or laboral or de trabajo (b) ▶ WORKDAY A; **~ party** n equipo m de trabajo

workings /'wɜːrkɪŋz ‖'wɜːkɪŋz/ pl n (of machine) funcionamiento m

work: ~load n (volumen m de) trabajo m; **~man** /'wɜːrkmən ‖'wɜːkmən/ n (pl **-men** /-mən/) obrero m

workmanlike /'wɜːrkmənlaɪk ‖'wɜːkmənlaɪk/ adj eficiente, profesional

workmanship /'wɜːrkmənʃɪp ‖'wɜːkmənʃɪp/ n (of craftsman) trabajo m; (of object) factura f

work: ~out n sesión f de ejercicios or gimnasia; **~place** n lugar m de trabajo

works /wɜːrks ‖wɜːks/ n **1** (actions) (liter) (+ pl vb) obras fpl **2** (engineering operations) (+ pl vb) obras fpl; **road ~** obras viales **3** (factory) (+ sing or pl vb) fábrica f **4** (mechanism) (+ pl vb) mecanismo m

work: ~shop n taller m; **~station** n (Comput) terminal m de trabajo; **~surface** n (a) (area) superficie f de trabajo (b) ▶ ~TOP; **~top** n encimera f, mesada f (RPl)

world /wɜːrld ‖wɜːld/ n **1** (earth) mundo m; the longest bridge in the ~ el puente más largo del mundo; to see the ~ ver* mundo; (it's a) small ~! el mundo es un pañuelo, ¡qué pequeño or (AmL) chico es el mundo!; to be out of this ~ ⟨food/music⟩ ser* increíble; to have the best of both ~s tener* todas las ventajas; (before n) ⟨economy/peace⟩ mundial; ⟨politics/trade⟩ internacional

2 (a) (people generally) mundo m; what is the ~ coming to? ¿adónde vamos a ir a parar? (b) (society): they've gone up in the ~ han prosperado mucho (or hecho fortuna etc); a woman/man of the ~ una mujer/un hombre de mundo **3** (specific period, group) mundo m; the art ~ el mundo del arte **4** (as intensifier): we are ~s apart no tenemos nada que ver; it did her a ~ of good le hizo la mar de bien; he thinks the ~ of her tiene un altísimo concepto de ella; to have all the time in the ~ tener* todo el tiempo del mundo; without a care in the ~ sin ninguna preocupación **5** (Relig): this/the other ~ este/el otro mundo

world: W~ Bank n the W~ Bank el Banco Mundial; **~ champion** n campeón, -peona m,f mundial; **W~ Cup** n the W~ Cup el Mundial, la Copa del Mundo; **~famous** /'wɜːrldˈfeɪməs ‖,wɜːldˈfeɪməs/ adj mundialmente famoso

worldly /'wɜːrldli ‖'wɜːldli/ adj (a) ⟨goods⟩ material; ⟨desires⟩ mundano (b) ⟨person⟩ de mucho mundo; ⟨manner/charm⟩ sofisticado

worldly-wise /'wɜːrldliˈwaɪz ‖,wɜːldliˈwaɪz/ adj de mucho mundo

world: ~ record n récord m or marca f mundial; **W~ Series** n (in US baseball) the W~ Series la Serie Mundial, el campeonato mundial de béisbol; **W~ War** n guerra f mundial; the First/Second W~ War, W~ War I/II la primera/ segunda Guerra Mundial

worldwide¹ /'wɜːrldˈwaɪd ‖,wɜːldˈwaɪd/ adj mundial

worldwide² adv ⟨travel⟩ por todo el mundo

World Wide Web n telaraña f mundial

worm¹ /wɜːrm ‖wɜːm/ n (a) (earth~) gusano m, lombriz f (de tierra) (b) (maggot) gusano m (c) **worms** pl (Med) lombrices fpl

worm² vt (Vet Sci) ⟨dog/cat⟩ desparasitar

worn¹ /wɔːrn ‖wɔːn/ past p of WEAR²

worn² adj ⟨tire/clothes⟩ gastado; ⟨carpet⟩ raído; ⟨flagstones/steps⟩ desgastado

worn-out /'wɔːrnˈaʊt ‖,wɔːnˈaʊt/ adj (pred **worn out**) (a) ⟨shoes/clothes⟩ muy gastado (b) (exhausted) rendido

worried /'wɜːrid ‖'wʌrid/ adj ⟨look/voice⟩ de preocupación; ⟨person⟩ preocupado; to get ~ preocuparse, inquietarse; to be ~ ABOUT sb/sth estar* preocupado POR algn/algo

worrier /'wɜːriər ‖'wʌriə(r)/ n: she's such a ~ se preocupa or se angustia tanto por todo

worry¹ /'wɜːri ‖'wʌri/ n (pl **-ries**) preocupación f

worry² **-ries, -rying, -ried** vt **1** (trouble) preocupar, inquietar **2** «dog» ⟨sheep⟩ acosar ■ ~ vi preocuparse, inquietarse; to ~ ABOUT sth/ sb preocuparse POR algo/algn

worrying /'wɜːriɪŋ ‖'wʌriɪŋ/ adj inquietante, preocupante

worse¹ /wɜːrs ‖wɜːs/ adj (comp of BAD¹) peor; to get ~ empeorar; (sicker) ponerse* peor; things are getting ~ and ~ las cosas van de mal en peor; to make things ~, it started snowing por si fuera poco, empezó a nevar

worse² adv (comp of BADLY) peor

worse³ n the ~ el (or la etc) peor; a change for the ~ un cambio para mal

worsen /'wɜːrsn̩ ‖'wɜːsn̩/ vi/t empeorar

worse-off /'wɜːrsˈɒf ‖,wɜːsˈɒf/ adj (pred **worse off**) (a) (financially) en peor posición económica (b) (emotionally, physically) (pred) peor

worship¹ /'wɜːrʃəp ‖'wɜːʃɪp/ n **1** (Relig) culto m, adoración f **2** **Worship** (as title): Your/His W~ (of magistrate) Su Señoría; (of mayor) el señor alcalde

worship² vt, (BrE) **-pp-** ⟨God⟩ adorar; ⟨success/ wealth⟩ rendir* culto a; ⟨hero⟩ idolatrar

worshipper /'wɜːrʃəpər ‖'wɜːʃɪpə(r)/ n (Relig) fiel m

worst¹ /wɜːrst ‖wɜːst/ adj (superl of BAD¹) peor; he's the ~ student in the class es el peor alumno de la clase; ~ of all lo peor de todo

worst² adv (superl of BADLY): she did (the) ~ (of all) in both exams le fue peor que a nadie en los dos exámenes

worst³ n **1** the ~ (a) (+ sing vb) lo peor; his sister brings out the ~ in him cuando está con su hermana está peor que nunca; if (the) ~ comes to (the) ~ en el peor de los casos (b) (+ pl vb) los peores **2** (a) at worst en el peor de los casos (b) at her/his/its worst: I'm at my ~ in the morning la mañana es mi peor momento del día; this is racism at its ~ esto es racismo de la peor especie

worth¹ /wɜːrθ ‖wɜːθ/ adj (pred) (a) (equal in value to) to be ~ valer*; it cost 300 dólares, but it was ~ the money costó $300, pero valió la pena; goods ~ £5,000 were stolen robaron mercancías por valor de 5.000 libras; this is my opinion, for what it's ~ esta es mi opinión, si es que a alguien le interesa **(b)** (worthy of): **it's ~ a try** vale la pena intentarlo; **that's ~ knowing** es bueno saberlo; **don't argue with them, it isn't ~ it** no discutas con ellos, no vale *or* no merece la pena

worth² *n* **(a)** (equivalent): **$2,000 dollars' ~ of furniture** muebles por valor de 2.000 dólares; **I've had my money's ~ out of this car** le he sacado mucho jugo a este coche (fam) **(b)** (of thing) valor *m*; (of person) valía *f*

worthless /'wɜːrθləs ‖ 'wɜːθlɪs/ *adj* ‹object› sin ningún valor; ‹person› despreciable; **to be ~** no tener* ningún valor, no valer* nada

worthwhile /'wɜːrθ'hwaɪl ‖ wɜːθ'waɪl/ *adj* ‹enterprise/project› que vale la pena

worthy /'wɜːrði ‖ 'wɜːði/ *adj* **-thier, -thiest** **1** (appropriate, equal) ‹opponent/successor› digno; **to be ~ OF sth/sb** ser* digno DE algo/algn **2** (good, estimable) ‹person› respetable; **a ~ cause** una buena causa

would /wʊd/ *v mod*

■ Note When *would* + a verb in English is used to form the conditional tense, it is translated by the conditional tense in Spanish. When *would* + a verb in English is used to express habitual activity in the past, it is translated by the imperfect tense in Spanish. For examples of both, see the entry below.

['D *es la contracción de* WOULD, WOULDN'T *de* WOULD NOT *y* 'D'VE *de* WOULD HAVE] **1** *past of* WILL¹

2 (in conditional sentences): **I ~ if I could** lo haría si pudiera; **if I had known, I ~n't have come** si lo hubiera sabido no habría *or* no hubiera venido **3** (expressing wishes): **I wish you'd stop pestering me!** ¡deja de fastidiarme por Dios! **4** (in requests, invitations): **~ you type this for me please?** ¿me haría el favor de pasar esto a máquina?; **~ you like to come with us? — I'd love to** ¿quieres venir con nosotros? — me encantaría

would-be /'wʊdbi/ *adj* (before n): **a ~ star/ poet** un aspirante a estrella/poeta

wouldn't /'wʊdn̩t/ = **would not**

would've /'wʊdəv/ = **would have**

wound¹ /wuːnd/ *n* herida *f*

wound² /wuːnd/ *vt/i* herir*

wound³ /waʊnd/ *past & past p of* WIND² *vt* II, *vi*

wounded /'wuːndəd ‖ 'wuːndɪd/ *adj* ‹soldier/ animal/pride› herido; ‹look/tone› dolido

wove /wəʊv/ *past of* WEAVE

woven /'wəʊvən/ *past p of* WEAVE

WP *n* **(a)** = **word processor (b)** = **word processing**

wpm (= **words per minute**) palabras por minuto

wrangle¹ /'ræŋɡəl/ *vi* discutir, reñir*

wrangle² *n* altercado *m*, riña *f*

wrap¹ /ræp/ **-pp-** *vt* **(a)** (cover) ‹parcel/gift› envolver* **(b)** (wind, entwine): **she ~ped a shawl about her** se envolvió en un chal

■ **wrap up** **1** [*v + o + adv, v + adv + o*] **(a)** ▶ WRAP¹ *vt* A **(b)** (complete) (colloq) ‹order/sale› conseguir*; ‹deal› cerrar* **(c)** (conclude) (colloq) ‹meeting› dar* H **(d)** (engross) (colloq) **to be ~ped up IN sth: she's totally ~ped up in her work** no piensa más que en su trabajo, vive para su trabajo **2** [*v + adv*] (dress warmly) abrigarse*

wrap² *n* **(a)** (shawl) chal *m*, pañoleta *f* **(b)** (robe) (AmE) bata *f*, salto *m* de cama (CS)

wraparound /'ræpə,raʊnd/ *adj* ‹skirt/dress› cruzado

wrapper /'ræpər ‖ 'ræpə(r)/ *n* envoltorio *m*, envoltura *f*

wrapping /'ræpɪŋ/ *n* envoltorio *m*, envoltura *f*

wrapping paper *n* (plain) papel *m* de envolver; (decorative) papel *m* de regalo

wrath /ræθ ‖ rɒθ/ *n* (liter) cólera *f*, ira *f*

wreak /riːk/ *vt* (liter) ‹destruction/chaos› sembrar* (liter); **to ~ havoc** causar estragos

wreath /riːθ/ *n* corona *f*

wreck¹ /rek/ *n* **1** (ship) restos *mpl* del naufragio; (vehicle) restos *mpl* del avión (*or* tren *etc*) siniestrado **2** (sth, sb ruined): **the attack left him a physical ~** el ataque lo dejó hecho una ruina; **he's a nervous ~** tiene los nervios destrozados

wreck² *vt* **(a)** ‹ship› provocar* el naufragio de; ‹train› hacer* descarrilar; ‹car› destrozar* **(b)** (damage) destrozar* **(c)** (demolish) (AmE) ‹house/ building› demoler* **(d)** (spoil, ruin) ‹plans/chances› echar por tierra; ‹marriage/happiness› destrozar*

wreckage /'rekɪdʒ/ *n* (of plane, car, ship) restos *mpl*; (of house) ruinas *fpl*

wrecker /'rekər ‖ 'rekə(r)/ *n* (AmE) **(a)** (demolition worker) obrero *m* de demolición *or* derribo **(b)** (car dismantler) desguazador *m or* (Méx) deshuesador *m*

wren /ren/ *n* (Zool) carrizo *m*

wrench¹ /rentʃ/ *vt* **(a)** (pull) arrancar*; **to ~ oneself away** soltarse* de un tirón *or* (AmL exc CS) de un jalón **(b)** (sprain) ‹muscle› desgarrarse; ‹joint› dislocarse*

wrench² *n* **1** **(a)** (twist, pull) tirón *m*, jalón *m* (AmL exc CS) **(b)** (emotional pain) dolor *m* (causado por una separación) **2** (adjustable ~) llave *f* inglesa; *see also* MONKEY WRENCH

wrest /rest/ *vt* **to ~ sth FROM sb** arrancarle* algo A algn

wrestle /'resəl/ *vi* **(a)** (Sport) luchar **(b)** (grapple) **to ~ WITH sb** forcejear CON algn; **to ~ WITH sth** batallar CON algo

wrestler /'reslər ‖ 'reslə(r)/ *n* luchador, -dora *m,f*

wrestling /'reslɪŋ/ *n* lucha *f*

wretch /retʃ/ *n* (liter) **(a)** (unfortunate person) desdichado, -da *m,f*, infeliz *mf* **(b)** (despicable person) desgraciado, -da *m,f*

wretched /'retʃəd ‖ 'retʃɪd/ *adj* **(a)** (abject, pitiable) ‹existence/creature› desdichado **(b)** (very bad) (colloq) ‹weather› horrible; **to feel ~** sentirse* muy mal

wriggle /'rɪɡəl/ *vi* (move) retorcerse*; **the children ~d in their seats** los niños se movían inquietos en sus asientos

■ **wriggle out of** [*v + adv + prep + o*] ‹dress/ jeans› quitarse (con dificultad); **don't try to ~ out of it!** ¡no trates de escabullirte!

wring /rɪŋ/ (*past & past p* **wrung**) *vt* **1** **(a)** ‹cloth/garment› escurrir, retorcer* **(b)** **to ~ sth FROM/OUT OF sb** ‹confession/information› arrancarle* algo A algn **2** ‹neck› retorcer*

⋯⊕

W

■ **wring out** [v + o + adv, v + adv + o] **1** ⟨cloth/ swimsuit⟩ retorcer*, escurrir **2** ⟨water⟩ escurrir; ⟨truth/money⟩ sacar*

wrinkle¹ /ˈrɪŋkəl/ n arruga f

wrinkle² vi «skin/garment» arrugarse*

wrinkled /ˈrɪŋkəld/ adj arrugado

wrinkly /ˈrɪŋkli/ adj **-klier, -kliest** (colloq) arrugado

wrist /rɪst/ n (Anat) muñeca f

wrist: ~**band** n (bracelet) pulsera f; (strap) correa f; (sweatband) muñequera f; ~**watch** n reloj m (de) pulsera

writ /rɪt/ n (Law) orden f or mandato m judicial

write /raɪt/ (past **wrote**; past p **written**) vt **(a)** (put in writing) escribir*; **I wrote him a letter** le escribí una carta; **to** ~ **sb a check** o (BrE) **cheque** extenderle or hacerle* un cheque a algn **(b)** (write letter to) (AmE) escribirle* a
■ ~ vi escribir*; **to** ~ **TO sb** escribirle* A algn
■ **write back** [v + adv] **to** ~ **back (TO sb)** contestar(le A algn)
■ **write down** [v + o + adv, v + adv + o] anotar
■ **write off** **1** [v + adv] **to** ~ **off FOR sth: she wrote off for a form** escribió pidiendo que le mandaran un formulario
2 [v + o + adv, v + adv + o] **(a)** (consider beyond repair) ⟨vehicle⟩ declarar siniestro total **(b)** (damage beyond repair) (BrE) destrozar* **(c)** ⟨marriage/ project⟩ dar* por perdido **(d)** ⟨debt⟩ cancelar
■ **write out** [v + o + adv, v + adv + o] **(a)** (write fully, copy) escribir* **(b)** (complete, fill out) ⟨prescription⟩ escribir*; ⟨check/receipt⟩ hacer*, extender* (frml)
■ **write up** [v + o + adv, v + adv + o] ⟨report/ notes⟩ pasar en or (Esp) a limpio; ⟨experiment⟩ redactar un informe sobre

write-off /ˈraɪtɔːf ‖ˈraɪtɒf/ n: **the car was a** ~ el coche fue declarado un siniestro total

write-protected /ˈraɪtprəˈtektəd/ adj (Comput) protegido contra escritura

writer /ˈraɪtər ‖ˈraɪtə(r)/ n (author) escritor, -tora m,f; **the** ~ **of the letter** el autor de la carta; ~'**s cramp** calambre m (que da por escribir mucho)

write-up /ˈraɪtʌp/ n (colloq) (review) crítica f, reseña f; (report) artículo m

writhe /raɪð/ vi «snake» retorcerse*

writing /ˈraɪtɪŋ/ n **(a)** (script) escritura f **(b)** (written material): **the** ~'**s rather blurred** la letra está algo borrosa; **in** ~ por escrito; (before n) ~ **desk** escritorio m; ~ **pad** bloc m; ~ **paper** papel m de carta **(c)** (BrE) (handwriting) letra f **(d)** (act of composing): ~ **takes up a lot of my time** paso mucho tiempo escribiendo **(e)** (written composition) literatura f **(f) writings** pl: **the** ~**s of Swift** la obra de Swift

written¹ /ˈrɪtn̩/ past p of WRITE

written² adj ⟨examination/language⟩ escrito; ~ **permission** permiso m por escrito

wrong¹ /rɔːŋ ‖rɒŋ/ adj **1** **(a)** (incorrect, inappropriate) ⟨answer⟩ equivocado, incorrecto; **you've given me the** ~ **change** se ha equivocado al darme el cambio; **we've taken the** ~ **bus** nos hemos equivocado de autobús; **he went in the** ~ **direction** tomó or (esp Esp) cogió para dónde no debía; **I did it the** ~ **way** lo hice mal; **this is the** ~ **time to mention the subject** este no es (el) momento oportuno para mencionar el tema; **she always says the** ~ **thing** siempre dice lo que no debe; **the picture is the** ~ **way up** el cuadro está al revés; **you've got your T-shirt on the** ~ **way round** llevas la camiseta al or del revés; **I'm the** ~ **person to ask** no soy la persona indicada para contestar esa pregunta **(b)** (mistaken) (pred) **to be** ~ estar* equivocado; **I was** ~ **about her** la había juzgado mal
2 (morally): **stealing is** ~ robar está mal; **you were** ~ **to shout at her like that** no debiste haberle gritado así, estuviste mal en gritarle así; **I haven't done anything** ~ no he hecho nada malo; **what's** ~ **with that?** ¿qué hay de malo en eso?
3 (amiss) (pred): **what's** ~? ¿qué pasa?; **there's something** ~ **with her/with the lock** algo le pasa/ algo le pasa a la cerradura; **there's nothing** ~ **with your heart** su corazón está perfectamente bien

wrong² adv ⟨answer⟩ mal, incorrectamente; **I did it all** ~ lo hice todo mal; **to go** ~ «machinery» estropearse, descomponerse* (AmL); «plans» salir* mal, fallar

wrong³ n **(a)** (immoral action) mal m; (injustice) injusticia f; **in her eyes he can do no** ~ para ella, es incapaz de hacer nada malo; **to be in the** ~ estar* equivocado **(b)** (Law) agravio m

wrong⁴ vt (frml): **she had been** ~**ed by her family** su familia había sido muy injusta con ella

wrong: ~**doer** /ˈrɔːŋˌduːər ‖ˈrɒŋˌduːə(r)/ n malhechor, -chora m,f; ~**doing** n: **she was punished for her** ~ la castigaron por sus fechorías

wrongful /ˈrɔːŋfəl ‖ˈrɒŋfəl/ adj ⟨accusation/ punishment⟩ injusto

wrongly /ˈrɔːŋli ‖ˈrɒŋli/ adv ⟨spell/pronounce⟩ mal, incorrectamente; ⟨believe/assume⟩ equivocadamente; ⟨accuse⟩ injustamente

wrote /rəʊt/ past of WRITE

wrought /rɔːt/ (past & past p of WORK² vt 4A) (frml or liter): **the devastation** ~ **by the war** los estragos causados por la guerra

wrought iron n hierro m forjado

wrung /rʌŋ/ past & past p of WRING

wry /raɪ/ adj **wrier, wriest** ⟨smile/laugh/joke⟩ irónico; **to make a** ~ **face** torcer* el gesto

WV, W Va = **West Virginia**

WWW n (= World Wide Web) WWW

WY, Wyo = **Wyoming**

X, x /eks/ n (a) (letter) X, x f (b) (Cin) (in US) prohibida para menores de 18 años
xenophobia /ˌzenəˈfəʊbiə/ n xenofobia f
xenophobic /ˌzenəˈfəʊbɪk/ adj xenófobo
xerox /ˈzɪrɑːks, ˈze- ‖ˈzɪərɒks/ vt fotocopiar, xerografiar*
XL = **extra large**
Xmas /ˈkrɪsməs, ˈeksməs/ n Navidad f

X-rated /ˈeksˈreɪtəd ‖ˌeksˈreɪtɪd/ adj (BrE) ⟨film⟩ solo para adultos, clasificado X (Esp)
X-ray¹, x-ray /ˈeksreɪ/ n (a) (ray) rayo m X (b) (photograph) radiografía f; **I had a chest ~** me hicieron or me sacaron una radiografía de tórax
X-ray², x-ray vt hacer* or sacar* una radiografía de
xylophone /ˈzaɪləfəʊn/ n xilofón m, xilófono m

Yy

Y, y /waɪ/ n Y, y f
yacht /jɑːt ‖jɒt/ n (a) (sailing boat — large) velero m, yate m; (— small) balandro m; (before n) ~ **club** club m náutico; **~ race** regata f (b) (pleasure cruiser) yate m
yachting /ˈjɑːtɪŋ ‖ˈjɒtɪŋ/ n navegación f a vela
yak /jæk/ n yac m, yak m
yam /jæm/ n (a) (plant, vegetable) ñame m (b) (AmE) ▶ SWEET POTATO
yank /jæŋk/ vt tirar de, jalar de (AmL exc CS)
Yank /jæŋk/ n (BrE colloq & often pej) ▶ YANKEE c
Yankee /ˈjæŋki/ n (a) (Hist) yanqui mf (b) (sb from Northern US) (AmE colloq) norteño, -ña m,f (c) (US citizen) (colloq: in BrE often pej) yanqui mf (fam & pey), gringo, -ga m,f (fam & pey)
yap¹ /jæp/ vi **-pp-** ladrar (con ladridos agudos)
yap² n ladrido m (agudo)
yard /jɑːrd ‖jɑːd/ n 1 (a) (of school, prison) patio m (b) (of house) (BrE) patio m; (garden) (AmE) jardín m (c) (stock~) corral m 2 (boat~, ship~) astillero m 3 (measure) yarda f (0,91m)
yardstick /ˈjɑːrdstɪk ‖ˈjɑːdstɪk/ n criterio m
yarn /jɑːrn ‖jɑːn/ n 1 (Tex) hilo m 2 (tale) (colloq) historia f
yawn¹ /jɔːn/ vi bostezar*
yawn² n bostezo m
yawning /ˈjɔːnɪŋ/ adj (before n) enorme
yd (pl **yd** or **yds**) = **yard**
yeah /jeə/ interj (colloq) sí
year /jɪr ‖jɪə(r)/ n 1 (period of time) año m; **all (the) ~ round** todo el año; **by the ~ 2000** para el año 2000; **over the ~s I've grown accustomed to it** con el tiempo or con los años me he ido acostumbrando; **~ after ~/~ in, ~ out** año tras año; **I'm 12 ~s old** tengo doce años 2 **years** pl (a long time): **I haven't seen him for ~s** hace años que no lo veo; **~s ago, there was a church here** años atrás, aquí había una iglesia 3 (Educ) curso m, año m

-year /jɪr ‖jɪə(r)/ suff: **a third~ student** un estudiante de tercer año or de tercero
yearly¹ /ˈjɪrli ‖ˈjɪəli/ adj anual; **on a ~ basis** cada año
yearly² adv cada año; **twice ~** dos veces al or por año
yearn /jɜːrn ‖jɜːn/ vi **to ~ to +** INF anhelar + INF; **to ~ FOR sth** añorar algo
yearning /ˈjɜːrnɪŋ ‖ˈjɜːnɪŋ/ n ~ **FOR sth/to +** INF anhelo m or ansia f; DE algo/+ INF
-year-old /jər ˈəʊld ‖jɪər ˈəʊld/ suff: **a thirty-two~ woman** una mujer de treinta y dos años; **a six~** un niño/una niña de seis años
yeast /jiːst/ n levadura f
yell¹ /jel/ vi/t gritar
yell² n grito m
yellow¹ /ˈjeləʊ/ adj amarillo; ⟨hair⟩ muy rubio or (Méx) güero or (Col) mono or (Ven) catire; ⟨traffic light⟩ (AmE) amarillo, ámbar adj inv
yellow² n (a) (color) amarillo m (b) (signal) (AmE) luz f amarilla
yellow³ vi ponerse* amarillo
yellow: ~ **fever** n fiebre f amarilla; ~ **pages,** (BrE) ~ **Pages**® pl n páginas fpl amarillas
yelp¹ /jelp/ vi dar* un gañido or aullido
yelp² n gañido m, aullido m
Yemen /ˈjemən/ n Yemen m
yen /jen/ n 1 (longing) (colloq) (no pl) **to have a ~ to +** INF morirse* de ganas DE + INF (fam) 2 (pl ~) (Fin) yen m
yes¹ /jes/ interj sí; **are you ready? — ~, I am** ¿estás listo? — sí; **you didn't tell me — ~, I did!** no me lo dijiste — ¡sí que te lo dije!
yes² n (pl **~es**) sí m
yes-man /ˈjesmæn/ n (pl **-men** /-men/) (pej): **he's a ~** es de los que dicen amén a todo
yesterday¹ /ˈjestərdeɪ, -di ‖ˈjestədeɪ, -di/ adv ⋯⟶

ayer; ~ **morning** ayer por la mañana, ayer en la mañana (AmL), ayer a la mañana *or* de mañana (RPl)

yesterday² *n*: ~ **was a busy day** ayer fue un día de mucha actividad; **the day before** ~ anteayer

yet¹ /jet/ *adv* [1] **(a)** (up to this or that time, till now) (*with neg*) todavía, aún; **I haven't eaten** o (AmE also) **I didn't eat** ~ todavía *or* aún no he comido, todavía no comí (RPl); **as** ~ aún, todavía **(b)** (now, so soon) (*with neg*) todavía **(c)** (thus far) (*after superl*) **it's his best book** ~ es el mejor libro que ha escrito hasta ahora
[2] (by now, already) (*with interrog*) ya; **has she decided** o (AmE also) **did she decide** ~? ¿ya se ha decidido?, ¿ya se decidió? (AmL)
[3] (still) todavía, aún
[4] (eventually, in spite of everything): **we may win** ~ todavía podemos ganar
[5] (*as intensifier*) **(a)** (even) (*with comp*) aún, todavía; **the story becomes** ~ **more complicated** el cuento se complica aún *or* todavía más **(b)** (in addition, besides): ~ **more problems** más problemas aún; **we had to go back** ~ **again** tuvimos que volver otra vez más (aún)
[6] (but, nevertheless) (*as linker*) sin embargo

yet² *conj* pero

yew /juː/ *n* tejo *m*

Yiddish /ˈjɪdɪʃ/ *n* yídish *m*, yiddish *m*

yield¹ /jiːld/ *vt* [1] (surrender) ⟨*position/territory*⟩ ceder; **to** ~ **one's right of way** (AmE Transp) ceder el paso [2] ⟨*crop/fruit/mineral/oil*⟩ producir*; ⟨*results*⟩ dar*
■ ~ *vi* [1] **(a)** (give way) ceder **(b)** (give priority): ⑤ **yield** (AmE) ceda el paso [2] «*ground/ice*» ceder

yield² *n* rendimiento *m*

YMCA *n* (= **Young Men's Christian Association**) YMCA *f*, Asociación *f* Cristiana de Jóvenes

yodel /ˈjəʊdl/ *vi*, (BrE) **-ll-** cantar al estilo tirolés

yoga /ˈjəʊɡə/ *n* yoga *m*

yoghurt, yoghourt, yogurt /ˈjəʊɡərt ‖ˈjɒɡət/ *n* yogur *m*, yoghourt *m*

yoke¹ /jəʊk/ *n* **(a)** (for oxen, horses) yugo *m* **(b)** (burden, bondage) yugo *m*

yoke² *vt* ⟨*oxen*⟩ uncir*

yokel /ˈjəʊkəl/ *n* (pej or hum) pueblerino, -na *m,f or* (Méx) indio, -dia *m,f or* (Col) montañero, -ra *m,f or* (RPl) pajuerano, -na *m,f or* (Chi) huaso, -sa *m,f* (pey o hum)

yolk /jəʊk/ *n* yema *f* (de huevo)

yonder /ˈjɑːndər ‖ˈjɒndə(r)/ *adv* (poet *or* dial) allá

you /juː/ *pron* [1] (sing) **(a)** (as subject — familiar) tú, vos (AmC, RPl); (— formal) usted; ~ **liar!** ¡mentiroso! **(b)** (as direct object — familiar) te; (— formal, masculine) lo, le (Esp); (— formal, feminine) la **(c)** (as indirect object — familiar) te; (— formal) le; (— with direct object pronoun present) se; **I told** ~ te dije/ le dije; **I gave it to** ~ te lo di/se lo di **(d)** (after prep — familiar) ti, vos (AmC, RPl); (— formal) usted
[2] (pl) **(a)** (as subject, after preposition — familiar) ustedes (AmL), vosotros, -tras (Esp); (— formal) ustedes; **be quiet,** ~ **two** ustedes dos: ¡cállense!, vosotros dos: ¡callaos! (Esp) **(b)** (as direct object — familiar) los, las (AmL), os (Esp); (— formal, masculine)

los, les (Esp); (— formal, feminine) las **(c)** (as indirect object — familiar) les (AmL), os (Esp); (— formal) les; (— with direct object pronoun present) se; **I gave** ~ **the book** les *or* (Esp tb) os di el libro; **I gave it to** ~ se *or* (Esp tb) os lo di
[3] (one) **(a)** (as subject): ~ **can't do that here** aquí no se puede hacer eso, aquí uno no puede hacer eso, no puedes hacer eso aquí (Esp) **(b)** (as direct object): **people stop** ~ **in the street and ask for money** la gente lo para a uno en la calle y le pide dinero, la gente te para en la calle y te pide dinero (Esp) **(c)** (as indirect object): **they can cause** ~ **a lot of trouble** le pueden a uno crear muchos problemas, te pueden crear muchos problemas (Esp)

you'd /juːd/ **(a)** = **you had (b)** = **you would**

you'll /juːl/ = **you will**

young¹ /jʌŋ/ *adj* **younger** /ˈjʌŋɡər ‖ˈjʌŋɡə(r)/, **youngest** /ˈjʌŋɡəst ‖ˈjʌŋɡɪst/ **(a)** ⟨*animal/ person*⟩ joven; **I have a** ~**er brother** tengo un hermano menor; **she is four years** ~**er than me** tiene cuatro años menos que yo; **a** ~ **man/woman** un/una joven; **a** ~ **lady** una señorita, una chica joven; ~ **people** la gente joven, los jóvenes, la juventud; **to marry** ~ casarse joven **(b)** ⟨*appearance/manner/complexion*⟩ juvenil

young² *pl n* (animals) crías *fpl*

youngster /ˈjʌŋstər ‖ˈjʌŋstə(r)/ *n* chico, -ca *m,f*

your /jʊr, *weak form* jər ‖jɔː(r), *weak form* jʊə(r)/ *adj*
■ **Note** The translations *tu* and *su* agree in number with the noun which they modify; they appear as *tu, tus, su, sus,* depending on what follows: *your father/ mother* tu padre/madre *or* su padre/madre; *your books/magazines* tus libros/revistas *or* sus libros/ revistas. The translation *vuestro* agrees in number and gender with the noun which it modifies; it appears as *vuestro, vuestra, vuestros, vuestras,* depending on what follows: *your father/mother* vuestro padre/ vuestra madre; *your books/magazines* vuestros libros/ vuestras revistas.

(a) (belonging to one person) (*sing, familiar*) tu; (*pl, familiar*) tus; (*sing, formal*) su; (*pl, formal*) sus; **wash** ~ **hands** lávate/lávese las manos **(b)** (belonging to more than one person) (*sing, familiar*) su (AmL), vuestro, -tra (Esp); (*pl, familiar*) sus (AmL), vuestros, -tras (Esp); (*sing, formal*) su; (*pl, formal*) sus; **put** ~ **shoes on** pónganse *or* (Esp) pone(r)os los zapatos **(c)** (one's): **if** ~ **name begins with A** ... si tu/su nombre empieza con A ...; **you have to take** ~ **shoes off in a mosque** hay que quitarse los zapatos en una mezquita

you're /jʊər ‖jʊə(r), jɔː(r)/ = **you are**

yours /jʊrz ‖jɔːz/ *pron*
■ **Note** The three translations of *yours* reflects the gender and number of the noun they are standing for; *yours* is translated by *tuyo, tuya, tuyos, tuyas, suyo, suya, suyos, suyas, vuestro, vuestra, vuestros, vuestras,* depending on the meaning being translated, and what is being referred to.

(a) (belonging to one person) (*sing, familiar*) tuyo, -ya; (*pl, familiar*) tuyos, -yas; (*sing, formal*) suyo, -ya; (*pl, formal*) suyos, -yas; ~ **is here** el tuyo/la tuya/el suyo/la suya está aquí; **a friend of** ~ un amigo tuyo/suyo **(b)** (belonging to more than one person) (*sing, formal*) suyo, -ya; (*pl, formal*) suyos, -yas; (*sing, familiar*) suyo, -ya (AmL), vuestro, -tra (Esp); (*pl, familiar*) suyos, -yas (AmL), vuestros, -tras (Esp); **~ are here, children** los suyos *or* los de ustedes están aquí, niños (AmL), los vuestros están aquí, niños (Esp); **is he a friend of ~?** ¿es amigo de ustedes *or* suyo *or* (Esp) vuestro? **(c)** (Corresp): **~, Daniel** un abrazo, Daniel

yourself /jər'self ‖ jɔː'self/ *pron* **(a)** (reflexive): **describe ~** (formal) descríbase; (familiar) descríbete; **stop thinking about ~** (formal) deje de pensar en sí mismo; (familiar) deja de pensar en ti mismo; **by ~** solo/sola **(b)** (emphatic use) (formal) usted mismo, usted misma; (familiar) tú mismo, tú misma; **you're a musician ~, I hear** usted también es *or* (*familiar*) tú también eres músico, tengo entendido **(c)** (normal self): **just be ~** compórtate con naturalidad; **you're not ~ today** hoy no eres el/la de siempre **(d)** (oneself) uno mismo, una misma

yourselves /jər'selvz ‖ jɔː'selvz/ *pron* **(a)** (reflexive): **behave ~!** ¡pórtense bien! (AmL), ¡porta(r)os bien! (Esp); **by ~** solos/solas **(b)** (emphatic use) (formal) ustedes mismos/mismas; (familiar) ustedes mismos/mismas *or* (Esp) vosotros mismos/vosotras mismas **(c)** (normal selves): **just be ~** compórtense *or* (Esp) comporta(r)os con naturalidad

youth /juːθ/ *n* (*pl* **youths** /juːðz/) **[1]** (early life) juventud *f* **[2]** (young people) (+ *sing or pl vb*) juventud *f*; (*before n*) ‹*movement/orchestra*› juvenil; **~ club** club *m* de jóvenes **[3]** (young man) (frml) joven *m*

youthful /'juːθfəl/ *adj* ‹*enthusiasm/manner*› juvenil; ‹*folly/ignorance*› de juventud

youth hostel *n* albergue *m* juvenil *or* de la juventud

you've /juːv/ = **you have**

yowl /jaʊl/ *vi* ‹*person*› dar* alaridos; «*dog*» aullar*; «*cat*» maullar*

yo-yo /'jəʊjəʊ/ *n* yo-yo *m*

yr (*pl* **yrs**) = **year**

Yugoslav /'juːgəʊ'slɑːv ‖ 'juːgəslɑːv/ *adj*/*n* ▶ YUGOSLAVIAN[1,2]

Yugoslavia /'juːgəʊ'slɑːviə ‖ 'jʊgə'slɑːviə/ *n* (Hist) Yugoslavia *f*

Yugoslavian[1] /'juːgəʊ'slɑːviən ‖ 'jʊgə'slɑːviən/ *adj* (Hist) yugoslavo

Yugoslavian[2] *n* (Hist) yugoslavo, -va *m,f*

yuppie, yuppy /'jʌpi/ *n* (*pl* **-pies**) (colloq) yuppy *mf* (fam)

YWCA *n* (= **Young Women's Christian Association**) YWCA *f*, Asociación *f* de Jóvenes Cristianas

---

Zz

Z, z /ziː ‖ zed/ *n* Z, z *f*

Zaire /zɑːir ‖ zɑːˈiə(r)/ *n* Zaire *m*

Zairean /zɑːˈiriən ‖ zɑːˈiəriən/ *adj* zaireño

Zambia /'zæmbiə/ *n* Zambia *f*

Zambian /'zæmbiən ‖ 'zæmbiən/ *adj* zambiano

zany /'zeini/ *adj* **zanier, zaniest** (colloq) ‹*person*› chiflado (fam); ‹*adventure*› loco

zap /zæp/ *vt* **-pp-** **(a)** (defeat, blast) (colloq) liquidar (fam) **(b)** (Comput) eliminar, borrar

zeal /ziːl/ *n* (Pol, Relig) fervor *m*, celo *m*

zealot /'zelət/ *n* (fanatic) fanático, -ca *m,f*

zealous /'zeləs/ *adj* ‹*follower*› ferviente; ‹*worker*› que pone gran celo en su trabajo

zebra /'ziːbrə ‖ 'zebrə, ziː-/ *n* (*pl* **-bras** *or* **-bra**) cebra *f*

zebra crossing *n* (BrE) paso *m* de cebra

zee /ziː/, (BrE) **zed** /zed/ *n* zeta *f*

zenith /'ziːnəθ ‖ 'zenɪθ/ *n* (Astron) cenit *m*, zenit *m*; **at the ~ of her popularity** en el cenit *or* el apogeo de su popularidad

zero[1] /'zɪrəʊ, 'ziː- ‖ 'zɪərəʊ/ *n* (*pl* **zeros** *or* **zeroes**) cero *m*; **the temperature fell below ~** la temperatura bajó de los cero grados; (*before n*) **~ hour** hora *f* cero

zero[2] *adj* cero *adj inv*; **~ degrees centigrade** cero grados centígrados

zest /zest/ *n* entusiasmo *m*

zigzag[1] /'zɪgzæg/ *n* zigzag *m*

zigzag[2] *vi* **-gg-** zigzaguear

zilch /zɪltʃ/ *n* (sl) nada de nada

Zimbabwe /zɪm'bɑːbwi, -wei/ *n* Zimbabwe *m*, Zimbabue *m*

Zimbabwean /zɪm'bɑːbwiən/ *adj* zimbabuense, de Zimbabwe

zinc /zɪŋk/ *n* cinc *m*, zinc *m*

Zionism /'zaɪənɪzəm/ *n* sionismo *m*

Zionist /'zaɪənəst ‖ 'zaɪənɪst/ *adj* sionista

zip[1] /zɪp/ *n* **[1]** (vigor) (colloq) garra *f* (fam) **[2]** (fastener) (BrE) ▶ ZIPPER[1]

zip[2] **-pp-** *vt* ‹*pocket/bag*› cerrar* la cremallera (*or* el cierre *etc*) de
■ **~** *vi* **[1]** (with zipper): **the suitcase ~s open/shut** la maleta se abre/cierra con cremallera (*or* cierre *etc*) **[2]** (move fast) (colloq): **we ~ped through the work** (nos) despachamos el trabajo en un santiamén (fam)
■ **zip up** [*v* + *o* + *adv*, *v* + *adv* + *o*] ‹*bag*› cerrar*

zip: **~ code** *n* (AmE) código *m* postal; **~ fastener** *n* (BrE) ▶ ZIPPER[1]; **~-on** *adj* (*before n*) ‹*hood/lining*› que se puede quitar, desmontable

zipper[1] /'zɪpər ‖ 'zɪpə(r)/ *n* (AmE) cremallera *f*, cierre *m* (AmL), zíper *m* (AmC, Méx, Ven), cierre *m* relámpago (RPl) *or* (Chi) eclair

zipper[2] *vt* (AmE) ▶ ZIP[2] *vt*

zodiac /'zəʊdiæk/ *n* **the ~** el zodíaco *or* zodiaco

zombie /'zɑːmbi ‖ 'zɒmbi/ *n* zombie *mf*

zone /zəʊn/ n **(a)** (area) zona f; **time** ~ huso m horario **(b)** (AmE) distrito m

zoo /zuː/ n (pl **zoos**) zoológico m, zoo m (esp Esp)

zoologist /zəʊˈɑːlədʒəst ‖ zəʊˈɒlədʒɪst, zuː/ n zoólogo, -ga m,f

zoology /zəʊˈɑːlədʒi ‖ zəʊˈɒlədʒi, zuː/ n zoología f

zoom¹ /zuːm/ n ⊡ (sound) (no pl) zumbido m ⊡ ~ (**lens**) (Cin, Phot, TV) teleobjetivo m, zoom m

zoom² vi (move fast) (colloq) (+ adv compl): **to** ~ **along/past** ir*/pasar zumbando (fam)
■ **zoom in** [v + adv] **to** ~ **in** (ON sth/sb) hacer* un zoom in (SOBRE algo/algn) (acercar rápidamente una imagen usando un teleobjetivo)

zucchini /zʊˈkiːni/ n (pl ~ or ~s) (AmE) calabacín m, calabacita f (Méx), zapallito m (largo or italiano) (CS)

Zulu¹ /ˈzuːluː/ adj zulú

Zulu² n **(a)** (person) zulú mf **(b)** (language) zulú m

Contents

Glossary of grammatical terms

Abbreviation A shortened form of a word or phrase: **Mr = Sr.**

Absolute use The use of a transitive verb without an expressed object, as in: **I didn't** *realize*

Active In the active form the subject of the verb performs the action: **Pedro** *kisses* **Ana = Pedro** *besa* **a Ana**

Adjective A word describing a noun: **a** *red* **pencil = un lápiz** *rojo*; *my* **house =** *mi* **casa**

Adverb A word that describes or changes the meaning of a verb, an adjective, or another adverb: **he ran** *quickly* **= corrió** *rápidamente*; *very* **pretty =** *muy* **bonito; she sings** *very* **badly = canta** *muy* **mal**

Apocope The omission of the final sound of a word, as in Spanish **algún** (alguno), **tan** (tanto)

Article The definite article, **the = el/la/los/las**, and indefinite article, **a/an = un/una**

Attributive An adjective or noun is attributive when it is used directly before a noun: **a** *good* **wine = un** *buen* **vino;** *business* **hours = horas** *de oficina*

Auxiliary verb A verb used with another verb to form compound tenses, as English **be, do,** and **have: I** *have* **eaten =** *he* **comido; he** *was* **sleeping =** *estaba* **durmiendo**

Cardinal number A whole number representing a quantity: **one/two/three = uno/dos/tres**

Clause A self-contained section of a sentence that contains a subject and a verb

Collective noun A noun that is singular in form but refers to a group of individual persons or things, e.g. **royalty, government**

Collocate A word that regularly occurs with another; in Spanish, **libro** is a typical collocate of the verb **leer.**

Comparative The form of an adjective or adverb that makes it "more": **smaller = más pequeño; better = mejor**

Compound An adjective, noun, or verb formed from two or more separate words: **self-confident (self + confident) = seguro de sí mismo; airmail (air + mail) = correo aéreo; outdo (out + do) = superar**

Conditional tense A tense of a verb that expresses what might happen if something else occurred: **he would go = iría**

Conjugation Variation of the form of a verb to show tense, person, mood, etc

Conjunction A word used to join clauses together: **and = y; because = porque**

Countable noun A noun that can form a plural and, in the singular, can be used with the indefinite article, e.g. **a book, two books**

Consonant All the letters of the alphabet other than **a, e, i, o, u**

Definite article: the **= el/la/los/las**

Demonstrative adjective An adjective indicating the person or thing referred to: *this* **table =** *esta* **mesa**

Demonstrative pronoun A pronoun indicating the person or thing referred to: *this* **is my sister =** *ésta* **es mi hermana**

Direct object The noun or pronoun directly affected by the verb: **I bought** *a book* **= compré** *un libro*

Direct speech A speaker's actual words or the use of these in writing: **he said:** *be quiet!* **= dijo:** *¡cállense!*

Elliptical Having a word or words omitted, especially where the sense can be guessed from the context

Ending Letters added to the stem of a word to show a change in function

Feminine One of the genders in Spanish, applied to nouns, pronouns, adjectives, and articles: **la casa blanca = the white house; ella = she**

Future tense The tense of a verb that refers to something that will happen in the future: **he** *will arrive* **late =** *llegará* **tarde**

Gender Spanish nouns, pronouns, adjectives, and articles almost all fall into two genders, masculine and feminine; in addition, Spanish uses the neuter pronouns **esto, eso,** and **aquello,** and the neuter article **lo**

Gerund The part of a verb used in Spanish to form continuous tenses: **muriendo = dying; cantando = singing**

Imperative A form of a verb that expresses a command: **come here! = ¡ven aquí!**

Imperfect tense The tense of a verb that refers to an uncompleted or a habitual action in the past: **the children** *were playing* **= los niños** *jugaban*; **I** *went/used to go* **there every Monday =** *iba* **allí todos los lunes**

Impersonal verb A verb in English used only with **it: it is raining = está lloviendo**

Indefinite article: **a/an = un/una**

Indefinite pronoun A pronoun that does not identify a specific person or object: **one, something**

Indicative form The form of a verb used when making a statement of fact or asking questions of fact in various tenses: **I'm not hungry = no tengo hambre**

Indirect object The noun or pronoun indirectly affected by the verb, at which the direct object is aimed: **I wrote a letter *to my mother* = *le* escribí una carta *a mi madre***

Indirect speech A report of what someone has said which does not reproduce the exact words: **she said that they had gone out = dijo que habían salido; he told me to be quiet = me dijo que me callara**

Infinitive The basic form of a verb: **to sing = cantar**

Inflect To change the ending or form of a word to show its tense or its grammatical relation to other words: **gone** and **went** are inflected forms of **to go**

Interjection A sound, word, or remark expressing a strong feeling such as anger, fear, or joy, or attracting attention: **¡ouch! = ¡ay!; good heavens! = ¡Dios mío!**

Interrogative An adjective, adverb, or pronoun that asks a question: **what? = ¿qué?; how much? = ¿cuánto?; who? = ¿quién?**

Intransitive verb A verb that does not have a direct object: **he died suddenly = murió repentinamente**

Invariable noun A noun that has the same form in the plural as the singular: **sheep, species**

Irregular verb A verb that does not follow one of the set patterns and has its own individual forms, e.g. English **to be**, Spanish **ser**

Masculine One of the genders in Spanish applied to nouns, pronouns, adjectives, and articles: **el perro negro = the black dog; él = he**

Modal verb A verb that is used with another verb to express necessity or possibility, e.g. **might, should, will**

Mood A category of verb use, expressing fact (indicative), command (imperative), or wish or conditionality (subjunctive)

Negative expressing refusal or denial

Neuter One of the genders in Spanish, used only in the pronouns **esto, eso**, and **aquello**, and the article **lo**

Noun A word that names a person or a thing

Number The state of being either singular or plural

Object The word or words naming the person or thing acted upon by a verb or preposition: **John studies *geography* = John estudia *geografía***

Ordinal number A number that shows a person's or thing's position in a series: **first = primero**

Part of speech A grammatical term for the function of a word; noun, verb, adjective, etc, are parts of speech.

Passive In the passive form the subject of the verb experiences the action rather than performs it – common in English, but not in Spanish: **Ana *is kissed by* Pedro = Ana *es besada por* Pedro**

Past participle The part of a verb used to form past tenses: **she had *gone* = había *ido***

Perfect tense The tense of the verb that refers to an event that has taken place in a period of time that includes the present: **I have eaten = he comido**

Person Any of the three groups of personal pronouns and forms taken by verbs; the **first person** (e.g. **I/yo**) refers to the person(s) speaking, the **second person** (e.g. **you/tú**) refers to the person(s) spoken to; the **third person** (e.g. **he/él**) refers to the persons spoken about

Personal pronoun A pronoun that refers to a person or thing: **I/he/she = yo/él/ella**

Phrasal verb A verb in English combined with a preposition or an adverb to have a particular meaning: **run away = huir; go past = pasar**

Phrase A self-contained section of a sentence that does not contain a full verb

Pluperfect tense The tense of a verb that refers to something that happened before a particular point in the past: **he had left = había salido**

Plural Of nouns etc, referring to more than one: **the houses = las casas**

Possessive adjective An adjective that shows possession, belonging to someone or something: **my/your = mi/tu**

Possessive pronoun A pronoun that shows possession, belonging to someone or something: **mine/yours = mío/tuyo**

Postpositive Placed after the word to which it relates, such as "in stock" in the phrase **items in stock**

Predicative An adjective is predicative when it comes after a verb such as **be** or **become**: **she is beautiful = es hermosa**

Prefix A letter or group of letters added to the beginning of a word to change its meaning: ***im*possible = *im*posible, *un*lucky = *desa*fortunado**

Preposition A word that stands in front of a noun or pronoun, relating it to the rest of the sentence: **with = con; without = sin**

Present participle The part of a verb that in English ends in –ing, and is used in forming continuous tenses: **doing = haciendo**

Present tense The tense of a verb that refers to something happening now: **I *open* the door = *abro* la puerta**

Preterite tense A simple tense referring to a completed action in the past: **I *did* it yesterday = lo *hice* ayer**

Pronominal verb A Spanish verb conjugated using the pronouns **me, te, se, nos,** and **os,** in which the pronoun refers to the subject of the verb: **(yo) me equivoqué = I was wrong.** A subgroup of these verbs are **Reflexive verbs**

Pronoun A word that stands instead of a noun: **he/she = él/ella; someone = alguien; mine = el mío/la mía**

Proper noun A name of a person, place, institution, etc, written with an initial capital letter. **Spain, the Atlantic, London, Juan, Madrid** are all proper nouns.

Reflexive pronoun A pronoun that refers back to the subject of the clause in which it is used: **myself = me; themselves = se**

Reflexive verb A verb whose object is the same as its subject; in Spanish, it is used with a reflexive pronoun: **he washed himself = se lavó**

Regular verb A verb that follows a set pattern in its different forms

Relative pronoun A pronoun that introduces a subordinate clause, relating to a person or thing mentioned in the main clause: **the man *who* visited us = el hombre *que* nos visitó**

Reported speech Another name for **Indirect speech**

Sentence A sequence of words, with a subject and a verb, that can stand on its own to make a statement, ask a question, or give a command

Singular Of nouns etc, referring to just one: **the house = la casa**

Stem The part of a word to which endings are added: **care** is the stem of **careful** and **careless**; in Spanish **cuidado** is the stem of **cuidadoso.**

Subject In a clause or sentence, the noun or pronoun that causes the action of the verb: *John* **studies geography =** *John* **estudia geografía**

Subjunctive A verb form that is used to express wishes or conditionality: **long *live* the King! = ¡*viva* el Rey!; if it *was* or *were* possible = si *fuera* posible**

Subordinate clause A clause which adds information to the main clause of a sentence but cannot be used as a sentence by itself, e.g. **she answered the phone *when it rang***

Suffix A letter or group of letters joined to the end of a word to make another word, e.g. **quick*ly* = rápida*mente***

Superlative The form of an adjective or adverb that makes it "most": **the smallest = la más pequeña; the best = el mejor**

Syllable A division of a word that contains a vowel sound that is pronounced as a single unit: **bala** has two syllables, *ba-la*

Tense The form of a verb that tells when the action takes place: present, future, imperfect, perfect, pluperfect are all tenses.

Transitive verb A verb that is used with a direct object: **she *read* the book = *leyó* el libro**

Uncountable noun A noun that cannot form a plural in ordinary usage and is not used with the indefinite article: **china, luggage**

Verb A word or group of words that describes an action: **the children *are playing* = los niños *están jugando***

Vowel One of the following letters: **a, e, i, o, u**

Spanish verb tables

1 Guide to Verb Tables

Every Spanish verb entry in the dictionary is cross-referred to one of the conjugation models shown in the following tables. The reference is given in square brackets immediately after the headword.

All the simple tenses are shown for **hablar** [A1], **meter** [E1], and **partir** [I1], the conjugation models for regular **-ar**, **-er**, and **-ir** verbs. For other verbs only the irregular tenses are given.

Compound tenses are not listed in the tables. The perfect tenses are formed with the relevant tense of the auxiliary **haber** and the past participle:

- Le *he hablado* de ti
- Lamento que *se haya ofendido*
- El profesor nos *había visto*
- Cuando *hubo terminado* de hablar, ...

- Para entonces ya *habremos terminado*
- Si lo *hubiera sabido, habría llamado*

The continuous tenses are formed with the relevant tense of the auxiliary **estar** and the present participle:

- *Estoy estudiando* el problema
- Cuando llegó, *estábamos cerrando*
- *Estuvieron esperando* mucho tiempo
- ¿*Han estado hablando* de mí?

Other verbs such as **andar**, **ir**, and **venir** can also be used as auxiliaries to express different nuances of meaning:

- *Andaba diciendo* que ...
- A medida que lo *fui conociendo*...
- ¿Por qué no *te vas vistiendo*?
- Hace mucho tiempo que te lo *vengo diciendo*

2 Verbs ending in -ar

A1 hablar

gerundio (gerund)	participio pasado (past participle)	indicativo (indicative)			
hablando	hablado	*presente (present)*	*imperfecto (imperfect)*	*pretérito indefinido (past simple)*	*futuro (future)*
		hablo	hablaba	hablé	hablaré
		hablas	hablabas	hablaste	hablarás
		habla	hablaba	habló	hablará
		hablamos	hablábamos	hablamos	hablaremos
		habláis	hablabais	hablasteis	hablaréis
		hablan	hablaban	hablaron	hablarán

condicional (conditional)	subjuntivo (subjunctive)			imperativo (imperative)
	presente (present)	*imperfecto (imperfect)*	*futuro (future)*	
hablaría	hable	hablara*	hablare	
hablarías	hables	hablaras	hablares	habla
hablaría	hable	hablara	hablare	hable
hablaríamos	hablemos	habláramos	habláremos	hablemos
hablaríais	habléis	hablarais	hablareis	hablad
hablarían	hablen	hablaran	hablaren	hablen

* all **-ar** verbs have an alternative form in which **-ara** is replaced by **-ase**, e.g. hablase, hablases, hablase, hablásemos, hablaseis, hablasen

Spanish verb tables

. . . .

2 Verbs ending in -ar continued

A2 sacar

indicativo pretérito indefinido	subjuntivo presente	imperativo
saqué	saque	
sacaste	saques	saca
sacó	saque	saque
sacamos	saquemos	saquemos
sacasteis	saquéis	sacad
sacaron	saquen	saquen

A3 pagar

indicativo pretérito indefinido	subjuntivo presente	imperativo
pagué	pague	
pagaste	pagues	paga
pagó	pague	pague
pagamos	paguemos	paguemos
pagasteis	paguéis	pagad
pagaron	paguen	paguen

A4 cazar

indicativo pretérito indefinido	subjuntivo presente	imperativo
cacé	cace	
cazaste	caces	caza
cazó	cace	cace
cazamos	cacemos	cacemos
cazasteis	cacéis	cazad
cazaron	cacen	cacen

A5 pensar

indicativo presente	pretérito indefinido	subjuntivo presente	imperativo
pienso	pensé, etc	piense	
piensas		pienses	piensa
piensa		piense	piense
pensamos		pensemos	pensemos
pensáis		penséis	pensad
piensan		piensen	piensen

A6 empezar

indicativo presente	pretérito indefinido	subjuntivo presente	imperativo
empiezo	empecé	empiece	
empiezas	empezaste	empieces	empieza
empieza	empezó	empiece	empiece
empezamos	empezamos	empecemos	empecemos
empezáis	empezasteis	empecéis	empezad
empiezan	empezaron	empiecen	empiecen

A7 regar

indicativo presente	pretérito indefinido	subjuntivo presente	imperativo
riego	regué	riegue	
riegas	regaste	riegues	riega
riega	regó	riegue	riegue
regamos	regamos	reguemos	reguemos
regáis	regasteis	reguéis	regad
riegan	regaron	rieguen	rieguen

A8 rogar

indicativo presente	pretérito indefinido	subjuntivo presente	imperativo
ruego	rogué	ruegue	
ruegas	rogaste	ruegues	ruega
ruega	rogó	ruegue	ruegue
rogamos	rogamos	roguemos	roguemos
rogáis	rogasteis	roguéis	rogad
ruegan	rogaron	rueguen	rueguen

A9 volcar

indicativo presente	pretérito indefinido	subjuntivo presente	imperativo
vuelco	volqué	vuelque	
vuelcas	volcaste	vuelques	vuelca
vuelca	volcó	vuelque	vuelque
volcamos	volcamos	volquemos	volquemos
volcáis	volcasteis	volquéis	volcad
vuelcan	volcaron	vuelquen	vuelquen

A10 contar

indicativo presente	pretérito indefinido	subjuntivo presente	imperativo
cuento	conté, etc	cuente	
cuentas		cuentes	cuenta
cuenta		cuente	cuente
contamos		contemos	contemos
contáis		contéis	contad
cuentan		cuenten	cuenten

A11 forzar

indicativo presente	pretérito indefinido	subjuntivo presente	imperativo
fuerzo	forcé	fuerce	
fuerzas	forzaste	fuerces	fuerza
fuerza	forzó	fuerce	fuerce
forzamos	forzamos	forcemos	forcemos
forzáis	forzasteis	forcéis	forzad
fuerzan	forzaron	fuercen	fuercen

2 Verbs ending in -ar continued

A12 degollar

indicativo presente	pretérito indefinido	subjuntivo presente	imperativo
degüello	degollé, etc	degüelle	
degüellas		degüelles	degüella
degüella		degüelle	degüelle
degollamos		degollemos	degollemos
degolláis		degolléis	degollad
degüellan		degüellen	degüellen

A13 avergonzar

indicativo presente	pretérito indefinido	subjuntivo presente	imperativo
avergüenzo	avergoncé	avergüence	
avergüenzas	avergonzaste	avergüences	avergüenza
avergüenza	avergonzó	avergüence	avergüence
avergonzamos	avergonzamos	avergoncemos	avergoncemos
avergonzáis	avergonzasteis	avergoncéis	avergonzad
avergüenzan	avergonzaron	avergüencen	avergüencen

A14 desosar

indicativo presente	pretérito indefinido	subjuntivo presente	imperativo
deshueso	desosé, etc	deshuese	
deshuesas		deshueses	deshuesa
deshuesa		deshuese	deshuese
desosamos		desosemos	desosemos
desosáis		desoséis	desosad
deshuesan		deshuesen	deshuesen

A15 jugar

indicativo presente	pretérito indefinido	subjuntivo presente	imperativo
juego	jugué	juegue	
juegas	jugaste	juegues	juega
juega	jugó	juegue	juegue
jugamos	jugamos	juguemos	juguemos
jugáis	jugasteis	juguéis	jugad
juegan	jugaron	jueguen	jueguen

A16 averiguar

indicativo pretérito indefinido	subjuntivo presente	imperativo
averigüé	averigüe	
averiguaste	averigües	averigua
averiguó	averigüe	averigüe
averiguamos	averigüemos	averigüemos
averiguasteis	averigüéis	averiguad
averiguaron	averigüen	averigüen

A17 vaciar

indicativo presente	pretérito indefinido	subjuntivo presente	imperativo
vacío	vacié, etc	vacíe	
vacías		vacíes	vacía
vacía		vacíe	vacíe
vaciamos		vaciemos	vaciemos
vaciáis		vaciéis	vaciad
vacían		vacíen	vacíen

A18 actuar

indicativo presente	pretérito indefinido	subjuntivo presente	imperativo
actúo	actué, etc	actúe	
actúas		actúes	actúa
actúa		actúe	actúe
actuamos		actuemos	actuemos
actuáis		actuéis	actuad
actúan		actúen	actúen

A19 aislar

indicativo presente	pretérito indefinido	subjuntivo presente	imperativo
aíslo	aislé, etc	aísle	
aíslas		aísles	aísla
aísla		aísle	aísle
aislamos		aislemos	aislemos
aisláis		aisléis	aislad
aíslan		aíslen	aíslen

A20 ahincar

indicativo presente	pretérito indefinido	subjuntivo presente	imperativo
ahínco	ahinqué	ahínque	
ahíncas	ahincaste	ahínques	ahínca
ahínca	ahincó	ahínque	ahínque
ahincamos	ahincamos	ahinquemos	ahinquemos
ahincáis	ahincasteis	ahinquéis	ahincad
ahíncan	ahincaron	ahínquen	ahínquen

A21 arcaizar

indicativo presente	pretérito indefinido	subjuntivo presente	imperativo
arcaízo	arcaicé	arcaíce	
arcaízas	arcaizaste	arcaíces	arcaíza
arcaíza	arcaizó	arcaíce	arcaíce
arcaizamos	arcaizamos	arcaicemos	arcaicemos
arcaizáis	arcaizasteis	arcaicéis	arcaizad
arcaízan	arcaizaron	arcaícen	arcaícen

Spanish verb tables

. . . .

2 Verbs ending in -ar continued

A22 cabrahigar

indicativo		subjuntivo	imperativo
presente	*pretérito indefinido*	*presente*	
cabrahígo	cabrahigué	cabrahígue	
cabrahígas	cabrahigaste	cabrahígues	cabrahíga
cabrahíga	cabrahigó	cabrahígue	cabrahígue
cabrahigamos	cabrahigamos	cabrahiguemos	cabrahiguemos
cabrahigáis	cabrahigasteis	cabrahiguéis	cabrahigad
cabrahígan	cabrahigaron	cabrahíguen	cabrahíguen

A23 aunar

indicativo		subjuntivo	imperativo
presente	*pretérito indefinido*	*presente*	
aúno	auné, etc	aúne	
aúnas		aúnes	aúna
aúna		aúne	aúne
aunamos		aunemos	aunemos
aunáis		aunéis	aunad
aúnan		aúnen	aúnen

A24 andar

indicativo	subjuntivo
pretérito indefinido	*imperfecto*
anduve	anduviera
anduviste	anduvieras
anduvo	anduviera
anduvimos	anduviéramos
anduvisteis	anduvierais
anduvieron	anduvieran

A25 dar

indicativo		subjuntivo	
presente	*pretérito indefinido*	*presente*	*imperfecto*
doy	di	dé	diera
das	diste	des	dieras
da	dio	dé	diera
damos	dimos	demos	diéramos
dais	disteis	deis	dierais
dan	dieron	den	dieran

A26 errar

indicativo	subjuntivo	imperativo
presente	*presente*	
yerro	yerre	
yerras	yerres	yerra
yerra	yerre	yerre
erramos	erremos	erremos
erráis	erréis	errad
yerran	yerren	yerren

A27 estar

gerundio	participio pasado	indicativo			
		presente	*imperfecto*	*pretérito indefinido*	*futuro*
estando	estado	estoy	estaba	estuve	estaré
		estás	estabas	estuviste	estarás
		está	estaba	estuvo	estará
		estamos	estábamos	estuvimos	estaremos
		estáis	estabais	estuvisteis	estaréis
		están	estaban	estuvieron	estarán

condicional	subjuntivo		imperativo
	presente	*imperfecto*	
estaría	esté	estuviera	
estarías	estés	estuvieras	está
estaría	esté	estuviera	esté
estaríamos	estemos	estuviéramos	estemos
estaríais	estéis	estuvierais	estad
estarían	estén	estuvieran	estén

· ·

3 Verbs ending in -er

E1 meter

gerundio (gerund)	participio pasado (past participle)	indicativo (indicative)			
		presente (present)	imperfecto (imperfect)	pretérito indefinido (past simple)	futuro (future)
metiendo	metido	meto	metía	metí	meteré
		metes	metías	metiste	meterás
		mete	metía	metió	meterá
		metemos	metíamos	metimos	meteremos
		metéis	metíais	metisteis	meteréis
		meten	metían	metieron	meterán

condicional (conditional)	subjuntivo (subjunctive)			imperativo (imperative)
	presente (present)	imperfecto (imperfect)	futuro (future)	
metería	meta	metiera*	metiere	
meterías	metas	metieras	metieres	mete
metería	meta	metiera	metiere	meta
meteríamos	metamos	metiéramos	metiéremos	metamos
meteríais	metáis	metierais	metiereis	meted
meterían	metan	metieran	metieren	metan

* all –er verbs have an alternative form in which –era is replaced by –ese, e.g. metiese, metieses, metiese, metiésemos, metieseis, metiesen

E2 vencer

indicativo		subjuntivo	imperativo
presente	pretérito indefinido	presente	
venzo	vencí, etc	venza	
vences		venzas	vence
vence		venza	venza
vencemos		venzamos	venzamos
vencéis		venzáis	venced
vencen		venzan	venzan

E3 conocer

indicativo		subjuntivo	imperativo
presente	pretérito indefinido	presente	
conozco	conocí, etc	conozca	
conoces		conozcas	conoce
conoce		conozca	conozca
conocemos		conozcamos	conozcamos
conocéis		conozcáis	conoced
conocen		conozcan	conozcan

Spanish verb tables

3 Verbs ending in -er continued

E4 placer

indicativo		subjuntivo			imperativo
presente	pretérito indefinido	presente	imperfecto	futuro	
plazco	plací	plazca	placiera	placiere	
places	placiste	plazcas	placieras	placieres	place
place	plació[1]	plazca[3]	placiera[4]	placiere[5]	plazca
placemos	placimos	plazcamos	placiéramos	placiéremos	plazcamos
placéis	placisteis	plazcáis	placierais	placiereis	placed
placen	placieron[2]	plazcan	placieran	placieren	plazcan

alternative forms, applicable only to the verb 'placer':
[1]plugo; [2]pluguieron; [3]plega or plegue; [4]pluguiera or pluguiese; [5]pluguiere.

E5 yacer

indicativo		subjuntivo	imperativo
presente	pretérito indefinido	presente	
yazco[1]	yací, etc	yazca[2]	
yaces		yazcas	yace[3]
yace		yazca	yazca
yacemos		yazcamos	yazcamos
yacéis		yazcáis	yaced
yacen		yazcan	yazcan

[1]alternative forms: yazgo or yago; [2]alternative conjugations: yazga, yazgas, etc or yaga, yagas, etc.
[3]alternative conjugations: yaz, yazga or yaga, yazgamos or yagamos, yaced, yazgan or yagan.

E6 coger

indicativo		subjuntivo	imperativo
presente	pretérito indefinido	presente	
cojo	cogí, etc	coja	
coges		cojas	coge
coge		coja	coja
cogemos		cojamos	cojamos
cogéis		cojáis	coged
cogen		cojan	cojan

E7 atañer

gerundio	indicativo	subjuntivo
	pretérito indefinido	imperfecto
atañendo	atañí	atañera
	atañiste	atañeras
	atañó	atañera
	atañimos	atañéramos
	atañisteis	atañerais
	atañeron	atañeran

E8 entender

indicativo		subjuntivo	imperativo
presente	pretérito indefinido	presente	
entiendo	entendí	entienda	
entiendes	entendiste	entiendas	entiende
entiende	entendió	entienda	entienda
entendemos	entendimos	entendamos	entendamos
entendéis	entendisteis	entendáis	entended
entienden	entendieron	entiendan	entiendan

E9 mover

indicativo		subjuntivo	imperativo
presente	pretérito indefinido	presente	
muevo	moví, etc	mueva	
mueves		muevas	mueve
mueve		mueva	mueva
movemos		movamos	movamos
movéis		mováis	moved
mueven		muevan	muevan

Spanish verb tables

. . . .

3 Verbs ending in -er continued

E10 torcer

indicativo presente	pretérito indefinido	subjuntivo presente	imperativo
tuerzo	torcí, etc	tuerza	
tuerces		tuerzas	tuerce
tuerce		tuerza	tuerza
torcemos		torzamos	torzamos
torcéis		torzáis	torced
tuercen		tuerzan	tuerzan

E11 volver

participio pasado	indicativo presente	pretérito indefinido	subjuntivo presente	imperativo
vuelto	vuelvo	volví, etc	vuelva	
	vuelves		vuelvas	vuelve
	vuelve		vuelva	vuelva
	volvemos		volvamos	volvamos
	volvéis		volváis	volved
	vuelven		vuelvan	vuelvan

E12 oler

indicativo presente	pretérito indefinido	subjuntivo presente	imperativo
huelo	olí, etc	huela	
hueles		huelas	huele
huele		huela	huela
olemos		olamos	olamos
oléis		oláis	oled
huelen		huelan	huelan

E13 leer

gerundio	indicativo pretérito indefinido	subjuntivo imperfecto
leyendo	leí	leyera
	leíste	leyeras
	leyó	leyera
	leímos	leyéramos
	leísteis	leyerais
	leyeron	leyeran

E14 proveer

participio pasado	indicativo pretérito indefinido	subjuntivo imperfecto
provisto	proveí	proveyera
	proveíste	proveyeras
	proveyó	proveyera
	proveímos	proveyéramos
	proveísteis	proveyerais
	proveyeron	proveyeran

Spanish verb tables

3 Verbs ending in -er continued

E15 caber

indicativo				condicional	subjuntivo		imperativo
presente	imperfecto	pretérito indefinido	futuro		presente	imperfecto	
quepo	cabía	cupe	cabré	cabría	quepa	cupiera	
cabes	cabías	cupiste	cabrás	cabrías	quepas	cupieras	cabe
cabe	cabía	cupo	cabrá	cabría	quepa	cupiera	quepa
cabemos	cabíamos	cupimos	cabremos	cabríamos	quepamos	cupiéramos	quepamos
cabéis	cabíais	cupisteis	cabréis	cabríais	quepáis	cupierais	cabed
caben	cabían	cupieron	cabrán	cabrían	quepan	cupieran	quepan

E16 caer

gerundio	participio pasado	indicativo			subjuntivo		imperativo
		presente	imperfecto	pretérito indefinido	presente	imperfecto	
cayendo	caído	caigo	caía	caí	caiga	cayera	
		caes	caías	caíste	caigas	cayeras	cae
		cae	caía	cayó	caiga	cayera	caiga
		caemos	caíamos	caímos	caigamos	cayéramos	caigamos
		caéis	caíais	caísteis	caigáis	cayerais	caed
		caen	caían	cayeron	caigan	cayeran	caigan

E17 haber

indicativo				condicional	subjuntivo		imperativo
presente	imperfecto	pretérito indefinido	futuro		presente	imperfecto	
he	había	hube	habré	habría	haya	hubiera	
has	habías	hubiste	habrás	habrías	hayas	hubieras	he
ha	había	hubo	habrá	habría	haya	hubiera	haya
hemos	habíamos	hubimos	habremos	habríamos	hayamos	hubiéramos	hayamos
habéis	habíais	hubisteis	habréis	habríais	hayáis	hubierais	habed
han	habían	hubieron	habrán	habrían	hayan	hubieran	hayan

E18 hacer

participio pasado	indicativo			condicional	subjuntivo		imperativo
	presente	pretérito indefinido	futuro		presente	imperfecto	
hecho	hago	hice	haré	haría	haga	hiciera	
	haces	hiciste	harás	harías	hagas	hicieras	haz
	hace	hizo	hará	haría	haga	hiciera	haga
	hacemos	hicimos	haremos	haríamos	hagamos	hiciéramos	hagamos
	hacéis	hicisteis	haréis	haríais	hagáis	hicierais	haced
	hacen	hicieron	harán	harían	hagan	hicieran	hagan

3 Verbs ending in -er continued

E19 rehacer

participio pasado	indicativo			condicional	subjuntivo		imperativo
	presente	pretérito indefinido	futuro		presente	imperfecto	
rehecho	rehago	rehíce	reharé	reharía	rehaga	rehiciera	
	rehaces	rehiciste	reharás	reharías	rehagas	rehicieras	rehaz
	rehace	rehízo	rehará	reharía	rehaga	rehiciera	rehaga
	rehacemos	rehicimos	reharemos	reharíamos	rehagamos	rehiciéramos	rehagamos
	rehacéis	rehicisteis	reharéis	reharíais	rehagáis	rehicierais	rehaced
	rehacen	rehicieron	reharán	reharían	rehagan	rehicieran	rehagan

E20 satisfacer

indicativo			condicional	subjuntivo		imperativo
presente	pretérito indefinido	futuro		presente	imperfecto	
satisfago	satisfice	satisfaré	satisfaría	satisfaga	satisficiera	
satisfaces	satisficiste	satisfarás	satisfarías	satisfagas	satisficieras	satisfaz[1]
satisface	satisfizo	satisfará	satisfaría	satisfaga	satisficiera	satisfaga
satisfacemos	satisficimos	satisfaremos	satisfaríamos	satisfagamos	satisficiéramos	satisfagamos
satisfacéis	satisficisteis	satisfaréis	satisfaríais	satisfagáis	satisficierais	satisfaced
satisfacen	satisficieron	satisfarán	satisfarían	satisfagan	satisficieran	satisfagan

[1]alternative form: satisface

E21 poder

gerundio	participio pasado
pudiendo	podido

indicativo			condicional	subjuntivo		imperativo
presente	pretérito indefinido	futuro		presente	imperfecto	
puedo	pude	podré	podría	pueda	pudiera	
puedes	pudiste	podrás	podrías	puedas	pudieras	puede
puede	pudo	podrá	podría	pueda	pudiera	pueda
podemos	pudimos	podremos	podríamos	podamos	pudiéramos	podamos
podéis	pudisteis	podréis	podríais	podáis	pudierais	poded
pueden	pudieron	podrán	podrían	puedan	pudieran	puedan

E22 poner

participio pasado	indicativo			condicional	subjuntivo		imperativo
	presente	pretérito indefinido	futuro		presente	imperfecto	
puesto	pongo	puse	pondré	pondría	ponga	pusiera	
	pones	pusiste	pondrás	pondrías	pongas	pusieras	pon
	pone	puso	pondrá	pondría	ponga	pusiera	ponga
	ponemos	pusimos	pondremos	pondríamos	pongamos	pusiéramos	pongamos
	ponéis	pusisteis	pondréis	pondríais	pongáis	pusierais	poned
	ponen	pusieron	pondrán	pondrían	pongan	pusieran	pongan

3 Verbs ending in -er continued

E23 traer

gerundio	participio pasado	indicativo		subjuntivo		imperativo
		presente	*pretérito indefinido*	*presente*	*imperfecto*	
trayendo	traído	traigo	traje	traiga	trajera	
		traes	trajiste	traigas	trajeras	trae
		trae	trajo	traiga	trajera	traiga
		traemos	trajimos	traigamos	trajéramos	traigamos
		traéis	trajisteis	traigáis	trajerais	traed
		traen	trajeron	traigan	trajeran	traigan

E24 querer

indicativo				condicional	subjuntivo		imperativo
presente	*imperfecto*	*pretérito indefinido*	*futuro*		*presente*	*imperfecto*	
quiero	quería	quise	querré	querría	quiera	quisiera	
quieres	querías	quisiste	querrás	querrías	quieras	quisieras	quiere
quiere	quería	quiso	querrá	querría	quiera	quisiera	quiera
queremos	queríamos	quisimos	querremos	querríamos	queramos	quisiéramos	queramos
queréis	queríais	quisisteis	querréis	querríais	queráis	quisierais	quered
quieren	querían	quisieron	querrán	querrían	quieran	quisieran	quieran

E25 saber

indicativo			condicional	subjuntivo		imperativo
presente	*pretérito indefinido*	*futuro*		*presente*	*imperfecto*	
sé	supe	sabré	sabría	sepa	supiera	
sabes	supiste	sabrás	sabrías	sepas	supieras	sabe
sabe	supo	sabrá	sabría	sepa	supiera	sepa
sabemos	supimos	sabremos	sabríamos	sepamos	supiéramos	sepamos
sabéis	supisteis	sabréis	sabríais	sepáis	supierais	sabed
saben	supieron	sabrán	sabrían	sepan	supieran	sepan

E26 ser

gerundio	participio pasado	indicativo			
		presente	*imperfecto*	*pretérito indefinido*	*futuro*
siendo	sido	soy	era	fui	seré
		eres	eras	fuiste	serás
		es	era	fue	será
		somos	éramos	fuimos	seremos
		sois	erais	fuisteis	seréis
		son	eran	fueron	serán

condicional	subjuntivo			imperativo
	presente	*imperfecto*	*futuro*	
sería	sea	fuera	fuere	
serías	seas	fueras	fueres	sé
sería	sea	fuera	fuere	sea
seríamos	seamos	fuéramos	fuéremos	seamos
seríais	seáis	fuerais	fuereis	sed
serían	sean	fueran	fueren	sean

· ·

3 Verbs ending in -er continued

E27 tener

indicativo			condicional	subjuntivo		imperativo
presente	pretérito indefinido	futuro		presente	imperfecto	
tengo	tuve	tendré	tendría	tenga	tuviera	
tienes	tuviste	tendrás	tendrías	tengas	tuvieras	ten
tiene	tuvo	tendrá	tendría	tenga	tuviera	tenga
tenemos	tuvimos	tendremos	tendríamos	tengamos	tuviéramos	tengamos
tenéis	tuvisteis	tendréis	tendríais	tengáis	tuvierais	tened
tienen	tuvieron	tendrán	tendrían	tengan	tuvieran	tengan

E28 valer

indicativo			condicional	subjuntivo		imperativo
presente	pretérito indefinido	futuro		presente	imperfecto	
valgo	valí	valdré	valdría	valga	valiera	
vales	valiste	valdrás	valdrías	valgas	valieras	vale
vale	valió	valdrá	valdría	valga	valiera	valga
valemos	valimos	valdremos	valdríamos	valgamos	valiéramos	valgamos
valéis	valisteis	valdréis	valdríais	valgáis	valierais	valed
valen	valieron	valdrán	valdrían	valgan	valieran	valgan

E29 ver

participio pasado	indicativo			subjuntivo	imperativo
	presente	imperfecto	pretérito indefinido	presente	
visto	veo	veía	vi	vea	
	ves	veías	viste	veas	ve
	ve	veía	vio	vea	vea
	vemos	veíamos	vimos	veamos	veamos
	veis	veíais	visteis	veáis	ved
	ven	veían	vieron	vean	vean

E30 romper

participio pasado

roto

E31 verter

gerundio	indicativo		subjuntivo	imperativo
	presente	pretérito indefinido	imperfecto	
vertiendo[1]	vierto	vertí	vertiera[4]	
	viertes	vertiste	vertieras	vierte
	vierte	vertió[2]	vertiera	vierta
	vertemos	vertimos	vertiéramos	vertamos
	vertéis	vertisteis	vertierais	verted
	vierten	vertieron[3]	vertieran	viertan

alternative forms: [1]virtiendo; [2]virtió; [3]virtieron; [4]virtiera, virtieras, etc.

4 Verbs ending in -ir

I1 partir

gerundio (gerund)	participio pasado (past participle)	indicativo (indicative)			
partiendo	partido	*presente (present)*	*imperfecto (imperfect)*	*pretérito indefinido (past simple)*	*futuro (future)*
		parto	partía	partí	partiré
		partes	partías	partiste	partirás
		parte	partía	partió	partirá
		partimos	partíamos	partimos	partiremos
		partís	partíais	partisteis	partiréis
		parten	partían	partieron	partirán

condicional (conditional)	subjuntivo (subjunctive)			imperativo (imperative)
	presente (present)	*imperfecto (imperfect)*	*futuro (future)*	
partiría	parta	partiera*	partiere	
partirías	partas	partieras	partieres	parte
partiría	parta	partiera	partiere	parta
partiríamos	partamos	partiéramos	partiéremos	partamos
partiríais	partáis	partierais	partiereis	partid
partirían	partan	partieran	partieren	partan

* all **-ir** verbs have an alternative form in which **-era** is replaced by **-ese**, e.g. partiese, partieses, partiese, partiésemos, partieseis, partiesen

I2 distinguir

indicativo		subjuntivo	imperativo
presente	*pretérito indefinido*	*presente*	
distingo	distinguí,	distinga	
distingues	etc	distingas	distingue
distingue		distinga	distinga
distinguimos		distingamos	distingamos
distinguís		distingáis	distinguid
distinguen		distingan	distingan

I3 delinquir

indicativo		subjuntivo	imperativo
presente	*pretérito indefinido*	*presente*	
delinco	delinquí,	delinca	
delinques	etc	delincas	delinque
delinque		delinca	delinca
delinquimos		delincamos	delincamos
delinquís		delincáis	delinquid
delinquen		delincan	delincan

I4 zurcir

indicativo		subjuntivo	imperativo
presente	*pretérito indefinido*	*presente*	
zurzo	zurcí, etc	zurza	
zurces		zurzas	zurce
zurce		zurza	zurza
zurcimos		zurzamos	zurzamos
zurcís		zurzáis	zurcid
zurcen		zurzan	zurzan

I5 lucir

indicativo		subjuntivo	imperativo
presente	*pretérito indefinido*	*presente*	
luzco	lucí, etc	luzca	
luces		luzcas	luce
luce		luzca	luzca
lucimos		luzcamos	luzcamos
lucís		luzcáis	lucid
lucen		luzcan	luzcan

4 Verbs ending in -ir continued

I6 reducir

indicativo presente	pretérito indefinido	subjuntivo presente	imperfecto	imperativo
reduzco	reduje	reduzca	redujera	
reduces	redujiste	reduzcas	redujeras	reduce
reduce	redujo	reduzca	redujera	reduzca
reducimos	redujimos	reduzcamos	redujéramos	reduzcamos
reducís	redujisteis	reduzcáis	redujerais	reducid
reducen	redujeron	reduzcan	redujeran	reduzcan

I7 dirigir

indicativo presente	pretérito indefinido	subjuntivo presente	imperativo
dirijo	dirigí, etc	dirija	
diriges		dirijas	dirige
dirige		dirija	dirija
dirigimos		dirijamos	dirijamos
dirigís		dirijáis	dirigid
dirigen		dirijan	dirijan

I8 regir

indicativo presente	pretérito indefinido	subjuntivo presente	imperativo
rijo	regí, etc	rija	
riges		rijas	rige
rige		rija	rija
regimos		rijamos	rijamos
regís		rijáis	regid
rigen		rijan	rijan

I9 gruñir

gerundio	indicativo pretérito indefinido	subjuntivo imperfecto
gruñendo	gruñí	gruñera
	gruñiste	gruñeras
	gruñó	gruñera
	gruñimos	gruñéramos
	gruñisteis	gruñerais
	gruñeron	gruñeran

I10 asir

indicativo presente	pretérito indefinido	subjuntivo presente	imperativo
asgo	así, etc	asga	
ases		asgas	ase
ase		asga	asga
asimos		asgamos	asgamos
asís		asgáis	asid
asen		asgan	asgan

I11 sentir

gerundio	participio pasado	indicativo presente	pretérito indefinido	subjuntivo presente	imperfecto	imperativo
sintiendo	sentido	siento	sentí	sienta	sintiera	
		sientes	sentiste	sientas	sintieras	siente
		siente	sintió	sienta	sintiera	sienta
		sentimos	sentimos	sintamos	sintiéramos	sintamos
		sentís	sentisteis	sintáis	sintierais	sentid
		sienten	sintieron	sientan	sintieran	sientan

I12 concernir

indicativo presente	pretérito indefinido	subjuntivo presente	imperativo
concierno	concerní, etc	concierna	
conciernes		conciernas	concierne
concierne		concierna	concierna
concernimos		concernamos	concernamos
concernís		concernáis	concernid
conciernen		conciernan	conciernan

I13 adquirir

indicativo presente	pretérito indefinido	subjuntivo presente	imperativo
adquiero	adquirí, etc	adquiera	
adquieres		adquieras	adquiere
adquiere		adquiera	adquiera
adquirimos		adquiramos	adquiramos
adquirís		adquiráis	adquirid
adquieren		adquieran	adquieran

4 Verbs ending in -ir continued

I14 pedir

gerundio	participio pasado	indicativo		subjuntivo		imperativo
		presente	pretérito indefinido	presente	imperfecto	
pidiendo	pedido	pido	pedí	pida	pidiera	
		pides	pediste	pidas	pidieras	pide
		pide	pidió	pida	pidiera	pida
		pedimos	pedimos	pidamos	pidiéramos	pidamos
		pedís	pedisteis	pidáis	pidierais	pedid
		piden	pidieron	pidan	pidieran	pidan

I15 ceñir

gerundio	participio pasado	indicativo			subjuntivo		imperativo
		presente	imperfecto	pretérito indefinido	presente	imperfecto	
ciñendo	ceñido	ciño	ceñía	ceñí	ciña	ciñera	
		ciñes	ceñías	ceñiste	ciñas	ciñeras	ciñe
		ciñe	ceñía	ciñó	ciña	ciñera	ciña
		ceñimos	ceñíamos	ceñimos	ciñamos	ciñéramos	ciñamos
		ceñís	ceñíais	ceñisteis	ciñáis	ciñerais	ceñid
		ciñen	ceñían	ciñeron	ciñan	ciñeran	ciñan

I16 dormir

gerundio	participio pasado	indicativo		subjuntivo		imperativo
		presente	pretérito indefinido	presente	imperfecto	
durmiendo	dormido	duermo	dormí	duerma	durmiera	
		duermes	dormiste	duermas	durmieras	duerme
		duerme	durmió	duerma	durmiera	duerma
		dormimos	dormimos	durmamos	durmiéramos	durmamos
		dormís	dormisteis	durmáis	durmierais	dormid
		duermen	durmieron	duerman	durmieran	duerman

I17 embaír

gerundio	indicativo pretérito indefinido	subjuntivo imperfecto
embayendo	embaí	embayera
	embaíste	embayeras
	embayó	embayera
	embaímos	embayéramos
	embaísteis	embayerais
	embayeron	embayeran

4 Verbs ending in -ir continued

I18 reír

gerundio	participio pasado
riendo	reído

indicativo				condicional	subjuntivo		imperativo
presente	imperfecto	pretérito indefinido	futuro		presente	imperfecto	
río	reía	reí	reiré	reiría	ría	riera	
ríes	reías	reíste	reirás	reirías	rías	rieras	ríe
ríe	reía	rio	reirá	reiría	ría	riera	ría
reímos	reíamos	reímos	reiremos	reiríamos	riamos	riéramos	riamos
reís	reíais	reísteis	reiréis	reiríais	riáis	rierais	reíd
ríen	reían	rieron	reirán	reirían	rían	rieran	rían

I19 argüir

gerundio	participio pasado	indicativo			subjuntivo		imperativo
		presente	imperfecto	pretérito indefinido	presente	imperfecto	
arguyendo	argüido	arguyo	argüía, etc	argüí	arguya	arguyera	
		arguyes		argüiste	arguyas	arguyeras	arguye
		arguye		arguyó	arguya	arguyera	arguya
		argüimos		argüimos	arguyamos	arguyéramos	arguyamos
		argüís		argüisteis	arguyáis	arguyerais	argüid
		arguyen		arguyeron	arguyan	arguyeran	arguyan

I20 huir

gerundio	participio pasado	indicativo			subjuntivo		imperativo
		presente	imperfecto	pretérito indefinido	presente	imperfecto	
huyendo	huido	huyo	huía, etc	huí	huya	huyera	
		huyes		huiste	huyas	huyeras	huye
		huye		huyó	huya	huyera	huya
		huimos		huimos	huyamos	huyéramos	huyamos
		huís		huisteis	huyáis	huyerais	huid
		huyen		huyeron	huyan	huyeran	huyan

I21 rehuir

indicativo		subjuntivo	imperativo
presente	pretérito indefinido	presente	
rehúyo	rehuí, etc	rehúya	
rehúyes		rehúyas	rehúye
rehúye		rehúya	rehúya
rehuimos		rehuyamos	rehuyamos
rehuís		rehuyáis	rehuid
rehúyen		rehúyan	rehúyan

I22 prohibir

indicativo		subjuntivo	imperativo
presente	pretérito indefinido	presente	
prohíbo	prohibí, etc	prohíba	
prohíbes		prohíbas	prohíbe
prohíbe		prohíba	prohíba
prohibimos		prohibamos	prohibamos
prohibís		prohibáis	prohibid
prohíben		prohíban	prohíban

4 Verbs ending in -ir continued

I23 reunir

indicativo		subjuntivo	imperativo
presente	pretérito indefinido	presente	
reúno	reuní, etc	reúna	
reúnes		reúnas	reúne
reúne		reúna	reúna
reunimos		reunamos	reunamos
reunís		reunáis	reunid
reúnen		reúnan	reúnan

I24 decir

gerundio	participio pasado
diciendo	dicho

indicativo				condicional	subjuntivo		imperativo
presente	imperfecto	pretérito indefinido	futuro		presente	imperfecto	
digo	decía	dije	diré	diría	diga	dijera	
dices	decías	dijiste	dirás	dirías	digas	dijeras	di
dice	decía	dijo	dirá	diría	diga	dijera	diga
decimos	decíamos	dijimos	diremos	diríamos	digamos	dijéramos	digamos
decís	decíais	dijisteis	diréis	diríais	digáis	dijerais	decid
dicen	decían	dijeron	dirán	dirían	digan	dijeran	digan

I25 bendecir

gerundio	participio pasado
bendiciendo	bendecido

indicativo			condicional	subjuntivo		imperativo
presente	pretérito indefinido	futuro		presente	imperfecto	
bendigo	bendije	bendeciré	bendeciría	bendiga	bendijera	
bendices	bendijiste	bendecirás	bendecirías	bendigas	bendijeras	bendice
bendice	bendijo	bendecirá	bendeciría	bendiga	bendijera	bendiga
bendecimos	bendijimos	bendeciremos	bendeciríamos	bendigamos	bendijéramos	bendigamos
bendecís	bendijisteis	bendeciréis	bendeciríais	bendigáis	bendijerais	bendecid
bendicen	bendijeron	bendecirán	bendecirían	bendigan	bendijeran	bendigan

I26 erguir

gerundio	indicativo		subjuntivo		imperativo
	presente	pretérito indefinido	presente	imperfecto	
irguiendo	yergo[1]	erguí	yerga[2]	irguiera	
	yergues	erguiste	yergas	irguieras	yergue[3]
	yergue	irguió	yerga	irguiera	yerga
	erguimos	erguimos	yergamos	irguiéramos	yergamos
	erguís	erguisteis	yergáis	irguierais	erguid
	yerguen	irguieron	yergan	irguieran	yergan

[1]alternative conjugation: irgo, irgues, irgue, erguimos, erguís, irguen; [2]alternative conjugation: irga, irgas, irga, irgamos, irgáis, irgan; [3]alternative conjugation: irgue, irga, irgamos, erguid, irgan.

4 Verbs ending in -ir continued

I27 ir

gerundio	participio pasado	indicativo			
		presente	*imperfecto*	*pretérito indefinido*	*futuro*
yendo	ido	voy	iba	fui	iré
		vas	ibas	fuiste	irás
		va	iba	fue	irá
		vamos	íbamos	fuimos	iremos
		vais	ibais	fuisteis	iréis
		van	iban	fueron	irán

condicional	subjuntivo			imperativo
	presente	*imperfecto*	*futuro*	
iría	vaya	fuera	fuere	
irías	vayas	fueras	fueres	ve
iría	vaya	fuera	fuere	vaya
iríamos	vayamos	fuéramos	fuéremos	vayamos
iríais	vayáis	fuerais	fuereis	id
irían	vayan	fueran	fueren	vayan

I28 oír

gerundio	participio pasado
oyendo	oído

indicativo				condicional	subjuntivo		imperativo
presente	*imperfecto*	*pretérito indefinido*	*futuro*		*presente*	*imperfecto*	
oigo	oía	oí	oiré	oiría	oiga	oyera	
oyes	oías	oíste	oirás	oirías	oigas	oyeras	oye
oye	oía	oyó	oirá	oiría	oiga	oyera	oiga
oímos	oíamos	oímos	oiremos	oiríamos	oigamos	oyéramos	oigamos
oís	oíais	oísteis	oiréis	oiríais	oigáis	oyerais	oíd
oyen	oían	oyeron	oirán	oirían	oigan	oyeran	oigan

I29 salir

indicativo			condicional	subjuntivo		imperativo
presente	*pretérito indefinido*	*futuro*		*presente*	*imperfecto*	
salgo	salí, etc	saldré	saldría	salga	saliera	
sales		saldrás	saldrías	salgas	salieras	sal
sale		saldrá	saldría	salga	saliera	salga
salimos		saldremos	saldríamos	salgamos	saliéramos	salgamos
salís		saldréis	saldríais	salgáis	salierais	salid
salen		saldrán	saldrían	salgan	salieran	salgan

I30 seguir

indicativo		subjuntivo		imperativo
presente	*pretérito indefinido*	*presente*	*imperfecto*	
sigo	seguí	siga	siguiera	
sigues	seguiste	sigas	siguieras	sigue
sigue	siguió	siga	siguiera	siga
seguimos	seguimos	sigamos	siguiéramos	sigamos
seguís	seguisteis	sigáis	siguierais	seguid
siguen	siguieron	sigan	siguieran	sigan

. . . .

4 Verbs ending in -ir continued

I31 venir

| gerundio | indicativo | | | condicional | subjuntivo | | imperativo |
	presente	pretérito indefinido	futuro		presente	imperfecto	
viniendo	vengo	vine	vendré	vendría	venga	viniera	
	vienes	viniste	vendrás	vendrías	vengas	vinieras	ven
	viene	vino	vendrá	vendría	venga	viniera	venga
	venimos	vinimos	vendremos	vendríamos	vengamos	viniéramos	vengamos
	venís	vinisteis	vendréis	vendríais	vengáis	vinierais	venid
	vienen	vinieron	vendrán	vendrían	vengan	vinieran	vengan

I32 abolir

This is a regular verb but in the present indicative it is only used in the first and second person plural.

I33 abrir

participio pasado

abierto

I34 escribir

participio pasado

escrito

I35 freír

| gerundio | participio pasado | indicativo | | subjuntivo | | imperativo |
		presente	pretérito indefinido	presente	imperfecto	
friendo	frito	frío	freí	fría	friera	
		fríes	freíste	frías	frieras	fríe
		fríe	frió	fría	friera	fría
		freímos	freímos	friamos	friéramos	friamos
		freís	freísteis	friáis	frierais	freíd
		fríen	frieron	frían	frieran	frían

I36 imprimir

participio pasado

impreso

I37 morir

| gerundio | participio pasado | indicativo | | subjuntivo | |
		presente	pretérito indefinido	presente	imperfecto
muriendo	muerto	muero	morí	muera	muriera
		mueres	moriste	mueras	murieras
		muere	murió	muera	muriera
		morimos	morimos	muramos	muriéramos
		morís	moristeis	muráis	murierais
		mueren	murieron	mueran	murieran

I38 pudrir

infinitivo	participio pasado
pudrir, podrir	podrido

All other forms are regular and are derived from the infinitive pudrir e.g. pudro, pudres, etc.

Summary of Spanish grammar

1 Nouns

All Spanish nouns are either masculine or feminine in gender, including nouns referring to objects or ideas. For this reason every Spanish noun mentioned in both sides of the dictionary is accompanied by gender information, shown in italics, *m* for masculine and *f* for feminine. Some nouns can be both masculine and feminine and this is indicated by the abbreviation *mf*, e.g. **belga** *mf* Belgian. Some nouns vary in gender according to region, e.g. **radio** (= radio) is masculine in most of Latin America and feminine in Spain. This information is also given in both sides of the dictionary. The following general rules will help to determine the gender of many nouns:

The following nouns are masculine:

■ Male humans and male animals: **el hombre** *man*, **el muchacho** *boy*, **el toro** *bull*, **el león** *lion*, **el gallo** *cockerel*

■ Nouns ending in -**o**: **el libro** *book*, **el rollo** *roll*, **el bolígrafo** *ball-point pen*. Exceptions: **la mano** *hand*, **la foto** *photo*, **la moto** *motor-bike*

■ Nouns ending in -**aje**: **el viaje** *journey*, **el equipaje** *luggage*

■ Nouns ending in a stressed vowel (i.e. an accented vowel): **el tisú** *tissue*, **el menú** *menu*, **el sofá** *sofa*

■ Days of the week and months: **el lunes** *Monday*, **los domingos** *Sundays*, **un diciembre frío** *a cold December*

The following nouns are feminine:

■ Female humans and female animals: **la mujer** *woman*, **la actriz** *actress*, **la vaca** *cow*, **la gallina** *chicken*

■ Nouns ending in -**a** (but see 'Gender problems' below for words ending in -**ma**): **la casa** *house*, **la comida** *meal*, **la camiseta** *tee-shirt*. Exceptions: **el día** *day*, **el mapa** *map*, **el planeta** *planet*, **el tranvía** *tramway*

■ Nouns ending in -**ción**: **la nación** *nation*, **la calefacción** *heating*, **la elección** *election*

■ Nouns ending in -**dad**, -**tad**, -**tud**, or -**is**; **la ciudad** *city*, **la libertad** *liberty*, **la actitud** *attitude*, **la crisis** *crisis*, **la apendicitis** *appendicitis*. Exceptions: **el análisis** *analysis*, **el tenis** *tennis*

Gender problems

■ Some common nouns ending in -**ma** are masculine, e.g. **el programa** *programme*, **el diagrama** *diagram*, **el clima** *climate*, **el problema** *problem*

- Some nouns change their meaning according to their gender: **el corte** *cut*, but **la corte** *court* (i.e. the royal court), **el margen** *margin*, but **la margen** *river-bank*, **el orden** *order*, *sequence*, but **la orden** *order*, *command*

Plurals of nouns

The plural indicates more than one of a thing, and, as in English, it usually ends in **-s** in Spanish. The two most important ways of making Spanish plurals are:

- If a noun ends in a vowel (**a, e, i, o**, or **u**), add **-s**: **la casa-las casas** *house-houses*, **el hombre-los hombres** *man-men*, **el taxi-los taxis** *taxi-taxis*, **el tisú-los tisús** *tissue-tissues*.

- If a noun ends in a consonant (any letter except a vowel), add **-es**: **el corredor-los corredores** *runner-runners*, **el español-los españoles** *Spaniard-Spaniards*, **el inglés-los ingleses** *English person-English people*. Note: If the last consonant of a singular noun is **z**, the plural ends in **-ces**; **la voz-las voces** *voice-voices*.

Exception: If the singular already ends in **-s** and the last vowel in the word does not have an accent, the plural is the same as the singular: **el martes-los martes** *Tuesday-Tuesdays*, **la crisis-las crisis** *crisis-crises*.

2 Adjectives

2.1 Simple adjectives

Spanish adjectives are different from English ones in two ways:

- They usually come after the noun: **un libro interesante** *an interesting book*, **el pan blanco** *white bread*, **las camisas azules** *blue shirts*. But some, like **grande** *big* or **pequeño** *small*, often come before the noun: **un gran escritor** *a great writer*, **un pequeño problema** *a small problem*.

- They agree with the noun or pronoun they describe. This means that if the noun is plural the adjective in Spanish must also be plural, and if the noun is feminine the adjective must also be feminine, if it has a variant feminine form

un hombre delgado	**una mujer delgada**	**un coche nuevo**	**una camisa nueva**
a thin man	*a thin woman*	*a new car*	*a new shirt*
hombres delgados	**mujeres delgadas**	**tres coches nuevos**	**camisas nuevas**
thin men	*thin women*	*three new cars*	*new shirts*

· ·

The following adjectives agree in both number and gender:

- Adjectives that end in **-o**. Add **-s** for the plural, change the **-o** to **-a** for the feminine: **el pañuelo blanco-los pañuelos blancos** *white handkerchief-white handkerchiefs*, **la bandera blanca-las banderas blancas** *white flag-white flags*.

- Adjectives that end in **-és**. Add **-a** for the feminine, and **-es** for the masculine plural. Note that the accent is no longer required, because the ending changes the stress pattern. **El vino francés-los vinos franceses** *French wine-French wines*, **la bebida francesa-las bebidas francesas** *French drink-French drinks*. Exceptions: **cortés** *polite* and **descortés** *impolite*. These have no separate feminine form, and the plural is **corteses/descorteses**.

- Most adjectives ending in **-n**. Add **-a** for the feminine, and **-es** for the masculine plural: **alemán-alemana-alemanes-alemanas** *German*. Exception: **marrón** (masculine and feminine) *brown*, plural **marrones** (masculine and feminine.)

- **Español-española-españoles-españolas** *Spanish*, **andaluz-andaluza-andaluces-andaluzas** *Andalusian*.

All adjectives ending in **-dor** add **-a** to show the feminine: **tranquilizador-tranquilizadora-tranquilizadores-tranquilizadoras** *soothing*.

The rest do not have a separate feminine form. Those ending in a vowel (usually **-e**) simply add **-s** for the plural; those ending in anything else add **-es**. If the singular ends in **-z**, the plural ends in **-ces**:

Singular masculine & fem.	Plural masculine & fem.	Meaning
grande	grandes	*big*
difícil	difíciles	*difficult*
superior	superiores	*superior/higher*
feroz	feroces	*ferocious*

2.2 Shortened adjectives

A few adjectives have a short form used immediately before a noun. The most important are:

		Short form	When used
grande	*big*	gran	before all singular nouns
cualquiera	*any*	cualquier	before all singular nouns
bueno	*good*	buen	before singular masculine nouns
malo	*bad*	mal	before singular masculine nouns
primero	*first*	primer	before singular masculine nouns
tercero	*third*	tercer	before singular masculine nouns

Compare **un buen libro** *a good book* and **una buena respuesta** *a good answer*.

Summary of Spanish grammar

2.3 Comparison of adjectives

The comparative form of the adjective (the -er form in English as in: *large, larger*) is expressed in Spanish by putting **más** *more*, or **menos** *less* in front of the adjective: **Luis es más/menos alto que ella** *Luis is taller/less tall than her*.

To indicate the superlative form of the adjective (in English: *most...* or *least...* of three or more things), put **el más/el menos** (or **la más/la menos**, **los más/los menos**, **las más/las menos**, according to gender) before the adjective:

pero ella es la más alta de todos *but she is the tallest of all.*

Note: the following two very common exceptions:

		singular	plural	
bueno/buen	*good*	**mejor**	**mejores**	*better/best*
malo/mal	bad	**peor**	**peores**	*worse/worst*

Example:

San Miguel es una de las mejores cervezas españolas
San Miguel is one of the best Spanish beers.

3 The definite and indefinite articles: el & la, un & una

These words vary in Spanish according to whether their noun is masculine or feminine, singular or plural:

	Singular	Plural	English equivalent
MASCULINE	**el**	**los**	the
FEMININE	**la**	**las**	

	Singular	Plural	
MASCULINE	**un**	**unos**	a *or* an
FEMININE	**una**	**unas**	

They are used in more or less the same way as their English equivalents:

el hombre compró una camisa y la mujer compró unos zapatos y un sombrero
the man bought a shirt, and the woman bought a pair of shoes and a hat.

Unos/unas means *some*, a *few* before plural nouns: **unos euros** *a few euros*, **unas muchachas** *some girls*. They mean *a pair of* before things that come in pairs like shoes or gloves (**unos guantes** = *a pair of gloves*).

But note the following points

- Always use **el** and **un** before nouns that begin with **a-** or **ha-** when the **a** is stressed, even though these words may be feminine: **el agua** *water*, **el/un arma** *weapon*, **el hambre** *hunger*. These are all feminine nouns and their adjectives take feminine endings; their plurals are **las aguas**, **las armas**, etc.

- **De** + **el** (*of the*) is shortened to **del**: **el coche del profesor** *the teacher's car*. **A** + **el** (*to the*) is shortened to **al**: **doy el libro al profesor** *I give the book to the teacher*.

- Spanish uses the definite article for nouns that refer to things in general: *doctors say apples are good for children* means doctors, apples, and children in general. In Spanish this is: **los médicos dicen que las manzanas son buenas para los niños**. In the same way *el* **amor** = *love*, *la* **libertad** = *freedom*, *la* **justicia** = *justice*.

- The indefinite article **un/una** is not used in Spanish before professions or occupations: **es profesora** = *she is* a *teacher*, **soy estudiante** = *I am* a *student*.

4 Demonstratives

Demonstrative adjectives and pronouns are used to point out people and things. In Spanish the words for *this* and *that*, *this one* and *that one* must agree in number and gender with the following noun. Note that in Spanish there are two words for *that*, **ese/esa**, **aquel/aquella**. **aquel/aquella** refers to something distant or relatively distant from the speaker:

	Singular	Plural	
MASCULINE	**este**	**estos**	*this/these* **or** *this one/these ones*
FEMININE	**esta**	**estas**	
MASCULINE	**ese**	**esos**	*that/those* **or** *that one/those ones*
FEMININE	**esa**	**esas**	
MASCULINE	**aquel**	**aquellos**	*that/those over there* **or** *that one/*
FEMININE	**aquella**	**aquellas**	*those ones over there*

- When these words are used as pronouns, i.e. to mean *this one* or *that one*, they are usually written with an accent. **¿ves estos dos coches? éste es amarillo y ése es rojo** *do you see these two cars? this one is yellow and that one is red*. However, the Spanish *Real Academia de la Lengua* (Royal Academy of the (Spanish) Language) has ruled that these accents are no longer necessary, so follow your course book or your teacher's advice on this point.

- When these words do not refer to any noun in particular, a genderless form must be used, **esto**, **eso**, or **aquello**: **esto es terrible** *this is terrible*, **no quiero hablar de eso** *I don't want to talk about that*. (**éste es terrible** means *this one is terrible* and would refer to something masculine. **no quiero hablar de ésa** means *I don't want to talk about that girl/woman* or some other feminine noun.)

Summary of Spanish grammar

• •

5 Possessives

5.1 Possessive Adjectives

In Spanish the possessive adjectives (= my, your, his, her, our, their) agree in number with the thing possessed, not with the person that possesses it. Examples: **mi mano** *my hand* and **mis manos** *my hands*, **tu libro** *your book* and **tus libros** *your books*. Only **nuestro** and **vuestro** have special feminine forms: **nuestra casa** *our house*, **vuestras amigas** *your female friends*. Note: Spanish has no separate words for *his*, *her*, or *their*: **su/sus** cover all these meanings:

Singular	Plural	
mi	mis	*my*
tu	tus	*your* (when speaking to a friend or relative)
su	sus	*his/her/their/your* (use **su** for *your* when using the **usted** form)
nuestro	nuestros	*our* (before masculine nouns)
nuestra	nuestras	*our* (before feminine nouns)
vuestro	vuestros	*your* (before masculine nouns)
vuestra	vuestras	*your* (before feminine nouns)

■ **Vuestro** is used in Spain when speaking to more than one friend or relative. Latin Americans never use **vuestro** and always use **su** for *your* when speaking to more than one person.

■ Spanish does not use these words with parts of the body or clothes.
levanta la mano *put up your hand*   **ponte la camisa** *put on your shirt*.

5.2 Possessive Pronouns

In Spanish the possessive pronouns (= mine, your, his, hers, ours, theirs) agree in gender and number with the noun that they refer to:

MASC.	**mío**	**míos**	*mine*
FEM.	**mía**	**mías**	
MASC.	**tuyo**	**tuyos**	*yours* (familiar form)
FEM.	**tuya**	**tuyas**	
MASC.	**suyo**	**suyos**	*his/hers/theirs/yours* (polite form)
FEM.	**suya**	**suyas**	
MASC.	**nuestro**	**nuestros**	*ours*
FEM.	**nuestra**	**nuestras**	
MASC.	**vuestro**	**vuestros**	*yours*
FEM.	**vuestra**	**vuestras**	

■ **Vuestro** is used in Spain when speaking informally to more than one person. Latin Americans never use **vuestro** and always use **su** for *your* when speaking to more than one person.

■ Examples: **este abrigo es mío/tuyo** *this coat is mine/yours*, **estas llaves son suyas** *these keys are his/hers/yours/theirs*, **esta dirección es nuestra** *this address is ours*. After a preposition (see page 1031) the article **el** or **la** must be used: **no vamos en tu coche**, **vamos en *el* mío** *we're not going in your car, we're going in mine*.

• •

6 Personal pronouns

6.1 Me, you, it, us etc

Personal pronouns replace nouns, as in *'John saw Jill and John spoke to Jill'*.
We normally say: *John saw Jill and he spoke to her*. *He* and *her* are the
personal pronouns. The most important Spanish personal pronouns are the
ones used to translate *me, him, her, us, them* in sentences like *John saw me,
Anne bought it, Jenny met them*. These are the 'direct object pronouns' and
they stand for the person or thing to whom something is done or happens:

me *me*	**nos** *us*
te *you* (familiar form)	**os** *you* (familiar form)
lo *him*, *you* (male polite form), or *it*	**los** *them* (masculine), or *you* (male polite form)
la *her*, *you* (female polite form), or *it*	**las** *them* (feminine), or *you* (female polite form)

- Note: in Spain, **le** is used for *him/you* (male) instead of **lo**, but **lo** must be
used for *it* when it refers to a masculine thing like a book (**el libro**). Latin
Americans use only **lo**. Both forms are considered correct, so follow your
teacher or course book on this point.

- **Os** is not used in Latin America. Latin Americans say **los** for males, **las**
for females.

- Personal pronouns come directly before verbs: **me ve** *he/she sees me*, **los
veo** *I see them*. However, they are joined to the end of infinitives, gerunds,
and imperatives (see below): **quiero verla** *I want to see her*, **estoy
haciéndolo** *I'm doing it*, **cómpralo** *buy it*.

6.2 To me, to you, to him, etc

The same forms as above are used: **me da cien euros** *he gives 100 euros to
me*, **te manda una carta** *he sends a letter to you*, **nos dicen todo** *they tell
everything to us*. These forms are the 'indirect object pronouns'.

Note: There are two indirect object forms, **le** and **les**. **Le** means *to him, to her*,
or *to you* (speaking formally). **Les** means *to them* and also *to you* when
speaking formally: *le* dije *I said to him* or *to her* or *to you* (one person), **les
dije** *I said to them* or *to you* (two or more people).

6.3 Order of pronouns

These pronouns can be combined, but the order is indirect object first, then
direct object, i.e.

me or **te** or **nos** or **os** first   then **lo**, **la**, **los**, or **las**

Examples: **me lo dan** *they give it to me*, **te lo dicen** *they say it to you*, **nos los
mandan** *they send them to us*.

- The rule of two L's. It is an important rule of Spanish that when **le** or **les**
is followed by **lo**, **la**, **los**, or **las**, the **le** or **les** becomes **se**. In other words,
two pronouns beginning with L can never stand side-by-side: **se lo doy**
I give it to him/to her/to you, not 'le lo doy'.

• •

6.4 Subject pronouns

The equivalents of *I, you, he, she, we, they* exist in Spanish, but are not often used, because they are explicit in verb endings: **hablo** already means *I speak*, **vas** means *you go*, **compramos** means *we buy*. In nearly all situations the use of the personal pronouns as in, **yo hablo, tú vas, nosotros compramos**, is to be avoided, because they are unnecessary. But they are needed sometimes, and their forms are as follows:

yo *I*	**nosotros** (males) *we*,
	nosotras (females) *we*
tú *you* (familiar form)	**vosotros** (to two or more males) *you*,
	vosotras (two or more females) *you*
usted *you* (formal form)	**ustedes** *you* (formal form)
él *he*	**ellos** *they* (males)
ella *she*	**ellas** *they* (females)

■ These words are used: (a) to contrast one person with another: **yo trabajo en casa y ella va a la oficina** *I work at home and she goes to the office.* (b) when there is no following verb: —**¿quién lo hizo?** —**Yo** *'Who did it?'* *'I did.'*

■ **Vosotros** and **vosotras** are not used in Latin America, where they always say **ustedes** to two or more persons.

■ **Tú** (note the accent) and **vosotros** or **vosotras** are the familiar forms used for people you know well (and anyone of your own age group if you are young), relatives, animals, and children. Nowadays Spaniards use them more and more even to complete strangers as a way of being friendly, but you must use **usted, ustedes** to people you do not know well, strangers, officials, policemen, etc.

■ **Usted** and **ustedes** are followed by third-person verb forms (i.e. the forms used for *he* and *they*): **usted habla** = *you speak*, **ustedes hablan** *you* (more than one) *speak*.

6.5 *mí* and *ti*

These are forms meaning *me* and *you* (familiar form) that are used after certain prepositions, e.g. after **de** *of/about*, **contra** *against*, **para** *for*, **por** *because of/on behalf of*, **sin** *without*: **hablamos de ti** *we're talking about you*, **esto es para mí** *this is for me*.

Note: When **con** + **mí** or **con** + **ti** are used together, the words **conmigo** *with me*, and **contigo** *with you* (familiar form) must be used: **Miguel va conmigo** *Miguel is going with me*.

• •

7 Hay: There is; there are

There is and *there are* are both **hay** in Spanish: **hay lobos en España** *there are wolves in Spain*, **no hay pan** *there is no bread*.

There was and *there were* are **había** (never habían): **había lobos en Inglaterra** *there were* (or *there used to be*) *wolves in England*. For completed events in the past Spanish uses **hubo**: **hubo una explosión/un accidente** *there was an explosion/accident*. *There will be* is **habrá**.

8 Ser & estar: to be

Spanish has two important verbs for the English *to be*: **ser** and **estar**. Both are irregular and their forms are given on pages 1012 and 1006 respectively.

8.1 Ser

Generally **ser** is used to convey the idea of inherent qualities and is used in the following situations: When stating the origin of someone or something:

Es de California.	*He's* or *She's* or *It's from California.*
Es americano.	*He's American.*

When stating the material from which something is made:

Es de plata.	*It's made of silver.*

When stating ownership:

Son de Alfonso.	*They belong to Alfonso.*

When describing someone's characteristics:

Es un señor muy simpático.	*He's a very nice man.*
Es muy aburrido.	*He's very boring.*

When stating one's occupation:

Es abogada.	*She's a lawyer.*
Es aduanero.	*He's a customs officer.*

When expressing identity:

Soy Juan Muñoz.	*I'm Juan Muñoz.*
¿Es usted la Señora Sánchez?	*Are you Mrs Sánchez?*

8.2 Estar

As a general rule **estar** is used in the following circumstances:
To indicate location:

Está en la esquina.	*It's on the corner.*
Están en el jardín.	*They're in the garden.*
Está de viaje.	*She's away on a trip.*

To indicate the condition or state something or someone is in:

Las sábanas estaban sucias.	*The sheets were dirty.*
Estaba enferma.	*She was ill.*
Estoy aburrido.	*I'm bored.*
Está enamorado de ella.	*He's in love with her.*
Estaba furiosa.	*She was furious.*
Estoy de muy buen humor.	*I'm in a very good mood.*

8.3 Exceptions and anomalies

Ser is used with the following adjectives: **rico** *rich, wealthy*; **pobre** *poor*;
feliz *happy*; **desgraciado** *unfortunate*.

Son muy ricos.	*They are very wealthy.*
Somos felices.	*We are happy.*

Marital status. Both verbs can be used in this context. **Ser** is used in formal
contexts regarding marital status:

¿Es usted casado o soltero?	*Are you married or single?*
Está casado con mi prima.	*He's married to my cousin.*
Mis padres están divorciados.	*My parents are divorced.*

Ser is used when specifying where an event takes place:

¿Dónde es la fiesta?	*Where is the party?*
La reunión es a las diez.	*The meeting is at ten.*

Ser is used when telling the time:

Es la una.	*It's one o'clock.*
Son las tres.	*It's three o'clock.*

Estar is used with **muerto** *dead* and **vivo** *alive*:

Ya estaba muerta.	*She was already dead.*
Aún está vivo.	*He's still alive.*

9 Question words: how, what, which, when etc

These are written with an accent:

¿cómo? *how?*	**¿cuánto?** *how much?, how many?*	**¿qué?** *what?*
¿cuál? *which?*	**¿de quién?** *whose?*	**¿quién?** *who?*
¿cuándo? *when?*	**¿por qué?** *why?*	

¿Cuál? and **¿quién?** become **¿cuáles?** and **¿quiénes?** when they refer to
more than one thing or person: **¿quiénes son?** *who are they?*, **¿cuáles
quieres?** *which ones do you want?* **¿Cuánto?** agrees in number and gender
with what it refers to: **¿cuánto dinero?** *how much money?*, **¿cuántos
clavos?** *how many nails?*, **¿cuántas chicas?** *how many girls?*

- ■ Note: the accented form is used in indirect questions, i.e. when there is no
  question mark in the sentence: **no sé cuál prefiero** *I don't know which I
  prefer*.

- ■ Note: the meaning of these words changes when no accent is used: **como**
  = *as* or *like* (**habla como un niño** = *he talks like a little boy*), **porque** (one
  word) = *because*, **que** = *that* as in **dice que está enfermo** *he says that he is
  ill*.

Summary of Spanish grammar

10 Prepositions

These are words placed before nouns and pronouns to link them to the meaning of the rest of the sentence. In general they are used in more or less the same way as their English equivalents except that:

■ **a** basically means *to*, not *at*, which is usually **en** in Spanish: **en la estación** = *in the station* or *at the station. At the bus-stop* is **en la parada de autobús**, *at the traffic-lights* is **en el semáforo**. A means *at* only when movement is involved, as in **tiró una flecha *al* blanco** *he fired an arrow at the target*.

■ **personal a**: The use of **a** before personal objects of verbs is very important in Spanish. Note carefully the difference between these two sentences: **vi tu casa** *I saw your house*, and **vi *a* tu madre** *I saw your mother*. The **a** is necessary in the second example because the thing seen was a human being. So: **no conozco *a* María** *I don't know María* and **admiro *al* profesor** *I admire the teacher*, but **no conozco la ciudad** *I don't know the city*.

■ **para** and **por**: **para** means *for*, as in **este dinero es para ti** *this money is for you*. **Por** means, among other things, *because of*: **lo hago por amor, no por dinero** *I do it for love not for money* (it really means *because of love, because of money*), **lo hice para ti** = *I made it for you*, **lo hice por ti** = *I did it because of you*. **Para** and **por** have many shades of meaning, which are exemplified at their entries in the Spanish-English section of the dictionary.

11 Verbs

Transitive and intransitive verbs

Verbs may be transitive, i.e. they take a direct object, or they may be intransitive, i.e. they do not take a direct object. In the sentence: *he kicks the ball, kicks* is the transitive verb, and the direct object is *ball*. In the sentence: *he is sleeping*, the verb *is sleeping* is intransitive as there is no object. Spanish verbs are also transitive and intransitive and this is information is shown by the abbreviations *vt* for 'verb transitive' and *vi* for 'verb intransitive'. It is important not to use transitive verbs intransitively and vice versa.

Reflexive verbs

These are verbs which have a personal pronoun object which is the same as the subject of the verb, e.g. *I shave myself*. Reflexive verbs are very common in Spanish and are listed in the dictionary with the infinitive followed by **se**, e.g. **lavarse** = *to wash oneself*. Note that in the third person, singular and plural, all genders, the reflexive pronoun is **se**. The following are the most important uses of reflexive verbs in Spanish

- If more than one human or animal is performing the action, it often shows that they are doing the action to one another: **se escriben mucho** *they write to one another a lot*.

- Sometimes the reflexive form is the only form used, as in **me atrevo** *I dare*, or **te arrepientes** *you regret* (having done something).

- If no human agent is involved, then the verb often has to be understood as a 'passive', as the translation shows: **este libro se publicó en Argentina** *this book was published in Argentina*, **se dijeron muchas cosas en la reunión** *many things were said in the meeting*.

- The reflexive form of many verbs alters or intensifies the meaning of the basic verb: **ir** = *to go*, **irse** = *to go away*; **caer** = *to fall*, **caerse** = *to fall over*.

12 Tenses of verbs

12.1 The present tense

English has two ways of describing present actions: compare *I smoke*, which describes a habit, and *I'm smoking*, which shows that you are smoking right now. Spanish is very similar in this respect: **fumo** = *I smoke*, **estoy fumando** = *I am smoking* (right now). However, the second of these forms is used less than in English and the simple form, **fumo**, can be used for both meanings:

—¿Qué haces? —Fumo	*'What are you doing?' 'I'm smoking'*
Hablan mucho	*They talk a lot* or *They are talking a lot*
Vamos al cine	*We go to the movies* or *We're going to the movies*

See 12.6 for the use of the present tense with a future meaning.

12.2 The past tenses

In English there are several different verb forms that can be used to describe events that happened in the past. Compare *I did it*, *I have done it*, *I was doing it*, and *I had done it*. Spanish also has several ways of describing past events:

(a) The past simple tense (also referred to as the 'pretérito indefinido' in the verb tables): **hablé** *I spoke*, **llegaron** *they arrived*, **compraste** *you bought*.

(b) The imperfect tense (also referred to as the 'imperfecto' in the verb tables): **hablaba** *I was speaking* or *I used to speak*, **llegaban** *they were arriving* or *they used to arrive*, **comprabas** *you were buying* or *you used to buy*.

(c) The perfect tense: **he hablado** *I have spoken*, **han llegado** *they have arrived*, **has comprado** *you have bought*.

(d) The pluperfect tense: **había hablado** *I had spoken*, **habían llegado** *they had arrived*, **habías comprado** *you had bought*.

• •

The two commonest past tenses in Spanish are the past simple and the imperfect.

12.3 The past simple and the imperfect tenses compared

The past simple is used to describe actions that took place *once* or a *specific number* of times in the past:

Ayer compré una nueva impresora	*Yesterday I bought a new printer*
Ganó la lotería	*He/She won the lottery*
Fue presidente durante tres años	*He was President for three years*
Estuve enfermo hace tres meses	*I was ill three months ago*

The imperfect is used to describe actions, events or processes that were not yet finished at the time we are talking about:

Miguel fumaba demasiado	*Miguel was smoking too much/* *Miguel used to smoke too much*
Mi hermana iba mucho a la disco	*My sister used to go/was going to the disco a lot*
Roberto era alto y moreno	*Roberto was tall and dark*

If an event happened once or a specific number of times the past simple tense is used, regardless of how long it went on for: **los dinosaurios reinaron sobre la tierra durante millones de años** *dinosaurs reigned on earth for millions of years* (it only happened once), **ocurrió más de mil veces** *it happened more than a thousand times* (but it happened a specific number of times). The imperfect must be used when an event is described that was interrupted by another event: **yo dormía cuando empezó la tormenta** *I was sleeping when the storm started.*

12.4 The perfect tense

This tense is formed in Spanish with the present tense of **haber**, and the past participle of the verb, which in Spanish usually ends with **-ado**, **-ido**, or **-isto**, see verb tables pages 1003–1020. As a rule, whenever you say '*I have been*', '*she has done*', '*we have seen*', etc. in English, you use the parallel tense in Spanish: **he sido, ha hecho, hemos visto.**

Nunca he bebido vodka	*I have never drunk vodka*
He estado tres veces en Chicago	*I've been in Chicago three times*
¿Has visto La guerra de las galaxias?	*Have you seen Star Wars?*

Many Latin Americans replace this tense by the past simple tense described earlier: **nunca bebí vodka, estuve tres veces en Chicago, ¿viste La guerra de las galaxias?** If your teacher is Latin American, imitate him or her on this point.

Note: If you study Peninsular Spanish you will notice a big difference between English and Spanish: the latter often uses the perfect tense for any event that has happened since midnight: **esta mañana me he duchado, he desayunado, he cogido el metro y he llegado aquí a las nueve** *this morning I had a shower, I had breakfast, I took the metro, and I got here at nine o'clock.*

. . . .

12.5 The pluperfect tense

This is almost exactly equivalent to the English tense formed with *had*:
I had seen, they had eaten, **había visto, habían comido**. It is used in both
languages to show that an event finished before another past event
happened: **mamá ya se había ido cuando llegué a casa** *mother had
already gone when I got home*, **yo iba a mandarles una tarjeta, pero mi
hermano ya lo había hecho** *I was going to send them a card, but my brother
had already done it*.

12.6 The future

There are several ways in English and Spanish of talking about future
events:

(a) *We're going to arrive tomorrow*   **Vamos a llegar mañana**
(ir + infinitive)

(b) *We are arriving tomorrow*   **Llegamos mañana**
(present tense)

(c) *We will arrive tomorrow*   **Llegaremos mañana**
(future tense)

The first two are more or less the same in both languages. Model (c) involves
learning the forms of the future tense, see **hablar** [A1], **meter** [E1] and
partir [I1] in the verb tables, and is normally used where English uses *will*.
It is used above all in promises and forecasts as in **te pagaré el dinero
mañana** *I will pay you the money tomorrow*, and **el viernes hará buen
tiempo** *the weather will be fine on Friday*.

12.7 The conditional tense

This tense, whose forms are given in the Spanish verb tables at **hablar** [A1],
meter [E1] and **partir** [I1], is used to talk of an event that *would* happen:
estarías más guapa con el pelo recogido *you would be more attractive with
your hair up*, **en ese caso te costaría menos** *in that case it would cost you
less*.

12.8 The imperative

The imperative is used to give orders or to ask someone to do something.
The forms of the verb used vary:

■ When addressing one person using the familiar form of *you*, the
imperative is formed by dropping the -**s** from the **tú** form of the present
tense: **das** = *you give*, so *give* is **da**; similarly **hablas** > **habla** *speak*,
comes > **come** *eat*. There are eight important exceptions:

decir *to say* **di**	**poner** *to put* **pon**	**tener** *to have* **ten**
hacer *to make* **haz**	**salir** *to go out* **sal**	**venir** *to come* **ven**
ir *to go* **ve**	**ser** *to be* **sé**	

- When addressing one person formally the **usted** form is used, which is the same as the *present subjunctive* form for *he/she*. To speak formally to more than one person the **ustedes** form is used, which is the *they* form of the present subjunctive. These forms are given in the Spanish verb tables, beginning on page 1003. Examples: ¡**venga!** *come!*, ¡**conteste!** *answer!*, ¡**vengan!** (plural) *come!*, ¡**contesten!** *answer!* (plural)

- In Spain, when talking informally to more than one person, the **vosotros** form of the imperative is used. This is formed by replacing the **-r** of the infinitive form (the form by which verbs are listed in dictionaries) by **-d**. There are no important exceptions: ¡**venid!** *come!*, ¡**contestad!** *answer!*, ¡**dad!** *give!* This form is never used in Latin America, where the formal **ustedes** form is used instead.

- To tell someone not to do something, the present subjunctive of the verb is used: ¡**no vengas!** (**tú**), ¡**no venga!** (**usted**), ¡**no vengan!** (**ustedes**), ¡**no vengáis!** (**vosotros**). These all mean *don't come!*, but the form varies in Spanish according to whether you are speaking to one or more people and whether you are using the informal or formal options.

- If we need to add pronouns, for example to translate *give it to her*, *sell me them*, these are added to the end of the imperative. In these examples **lo** and **los** refer to a masculine noun like **libro**, **libros** *book(s)*. Note the accents:

familiar to 1 person	formal to to 1 person	to 2 + people	to 2+ people: (familiar Spain)	
dámelo	**démelo**	**dénmelo**	**dádmelo**	= *give it to me*
mándanoslos	**mándenoslos**	**mándennoslos**	**mandádnoslos**	= *send them to us*

But if the order is negative (i.e. it has **no** in front of it), the pronouns come before the present subjunctive of the verb:

no me lo des	**no me lo dé**	**no me lo den**	**no me lo deis**	= *don't give it to*
me				

. . . .

13 The gerund (-ando, -iendo forms of verbs)

This form of the Spanish verb always ends in **-ando** or **-iendo** and it never changes. It is used:

- With the verb **estar** to stress the fact that an action is actually going on right now, or was in the middle of happening: **estoy comiendo** *I'm eating* (right now), **estabas durmiendo** *you were* (in the middle of) *sleeping*. It is never used for actions in the future: **voy a Madrid mañana** *I'm going to Madrid tomorrow*.

- To show that another action happens at the same time as the main action: **entré silbando** *I went in whistling*, **María salió llorando de la clase** *María came out of the classroom crying*.

14 The subjunctive

The subjunctive is very important in Spanish. The forms of the present subjunctive are given in the Spanish verb tables, beginning on page 1003. The present subjunctive is used:

- To give negative orders, i.e. to tell someone *not* to do something: see section 12.8 on the imperative.

- In a sentence consisting of a present-tense *negative verb* + **que** + *another verb*, the second verb is in the subjunctive: compare **creo que está enferma** *I think that she is ill* and **no creo que esté enferma** *I don't think that she is ill*.

- After the present tense of verbs **querer** *want* or **esperar** *hope* + **que**: **quiero que vengas a mi casa** *I want you to come to my house*, **espero que ganes** *I hope you win*. But if the person doing the wanting is the same person that is going to perform the action of the second verb, the infinitive (-**r** form) must be used for the second verb: **quiero ir a mi casa** *I want to go to my house*, **espero ganar** *I hope I'll win/I hope to win*.

- After emotional reactions followed by **que**: **es una pena que no trabajes más** *it's a shame that you don't work more*, **estoy muy contento de que no haya llovido** *I'm very pleased that it hasn't rained* (**haya** is the present subjunctive of **haber**).

- After certain words, when the action following them still has not happened. The most important of these are **cuando** *when*, **en cuanto** or **apenas** *as soon as*: **te daré el dinero cuando llegues** *I'll give you the money when you arrive*, **te llamaré apenas encuentre mi agenda** *I'll ring you as soon as I find my diary*.

- Always after these words: **antes de que** *before*, **para que** *in order to*, **sin que** *without*, **con tal de que** *provided that*: **llegaremos antes de que salga el tren** *we'll arrive before the train leaves*, **te doy el dinero con tal de que me lo devuelvas** *I'll give you the money provided that you give it back to me*.

Índice

Resumen de la gramática inglesa

Glosario de términos gramaticales

Abreviatura Representación de una palabra de una manera más corta por una o varias de sus letras: **Sr.** = **Mr**

Acento Mayor énfasis al pronunciar una determinada sílaba dentro de una palabra y representación gráfica (tilde) de dicho énfasis: *casa; café*

Adjetivo Palabra que califica o determina a un sustantivo: **un lápiz *rojo*** = **a *red* pencil, *mi* casa** = ***my* house**

Adverbio Palabra que modifica a un verbo, a un adjetivo o a otro adverbio: **corrió *rápidamente*** = **he ran *quickly*; *muy* bonito** = ***very* pretty; canta *muy* mal** = **she sings *very* badly**

Agente El que ejecuta la acción del verbo: *el perro* ladra = *the dog* barks; fue descubierta por *Colón* = it was discovered by *Columbus*

Aguda Tratándose de palabras, que llevan el acento en la última sílaba: infor*mar*, re*vés*

Apócope Pérdida o supresión de uno o más sonidos al final de una palabra: **algún** (alguno), **tan** (tanto)

Artículo Palabra que va antepuesta al sustantivo e indica su género y su número

Artículo definido Es el que se antepone a un sustantivo que ya nos es conocido: **el/la/los/las** = **the**

Artículo indefinido Es el que se antepone a un sustantivo que no conocemos de antemano: **un/una** = **a/an**

Aumentativo Palabra formada con un sufijo que indica aumento: **grand*ote*; cabez*azo*; simpl*ón***

Cardinal Tratándose de números, que expresan la cantidad entera de elementos de un conjunto: **ocho/nueve/diez** = **eight/nine/ten**

Comparativo Adjetivo, adverbio o conjunción que expresa una comparación. De superioridad: **más ... (que)** = **more ... (than)**. De inferioridad: **menos ... (que)** = **less ... (than)**. De igualdad: **tan/tanto ... como** = **as ... as**

Complemento directo Ver **Objeto directo**

Complemento indirecto Ver **Objeto indirecto**

Complemento circunstancial Completa el significado de un verbo, expresando una circunstancia de la acción: **compré un libro** *ayer* = **I bought a book** *yesterday*

Condicional Tiempo verbal que expresa una acción como posible si algo ocurre: **iría** = **he/she/it would go; comeríamos** = **we would eat**

Concordancia Correspondencia del género y el número de un adjetivo con los de un sustantivo y del número y la persona del verbo con el sujeto de una oración: **gato negro; los niños españoles; mi marido y yo hablamos inglés; Pedro y Juan ganaron**

Conjugación Serie ordenada de las formas que toma un verbo para expresar modo, tiempo, número y persona y cada uno de los tres tipos de verbos en que se dividen, según la terminación del infinitivo: **-ar, -er, -ir**

Conjunción Palabra que une dos oraciones o dos elementos de una oración: **y** = **and; porque** = **because**

Contracción Unión de dos palabras en una sola: **al** (a + el); **del** (de + el)

Demostrativo Tratándose de adjetivos y pronombres, que muestran o señalan algo o a alguien: *esta* mesa = *this* table; *ésta* es mi hermana = *this* is my sister

Diéresis Signo que indica que debe pronunciarse la vocal 'u' de las sílabas 'güe' y 'güi': ci**güe**ña; pin**güi**no

Diminutivo Palabra que se forma con un sufijo que indica menor tamaño, poca importancia o valor afectivo: **perr*ito*; doctorc*illo*; abuel*ita***

Esdrújula Palabra que lleva el acento (tilde) en la antepenúltima sílaba: *trá*fico

Estilo directo El que consiste en narrar lo que se ha dicho citando textualmente las palabras del hablante: **me dijo: ¡cállate!** = **he said: be quiet!**

Estilo indirecto El que consiste en narrar lo que se ha dicho sin citar textualmente las palabras del hablante: **me dijo que me callara** = **he told me to be quiet**

Femenino Género que se aplica a los seres del sexo femenino y el que se atribuye a las cosas por la terminación (-a) o por el uso: **la mujer; la perra; la página; la cruz**

Frase Unidad dentro de una oración, que tiene sentido y que no tiene verbo

Futuro Tiempo verbal que sitúa la acción en un momento futuro: **llegará tarde** = **he will arrive late**

Género Una de las tres categorías gramaticales de los sustantivos, adjetivos, artículos y pronombres: masculino, femenino y neutro

Gentilicio Expresa el lugar de origen o la nacionalidad: **londinense** = **Londoner; español** = **Spanish**

Gerundio Forma verbal que presenta la acción en proceso de ejecución. En español acaba en -ando o -iendo: habl*ando*; com*iendo* y en inglés en -ing: speak*ing*

Grave Tratándose de palabras, que llevan el acento en la penúltima sílaba: *exa*men; *dé*bil

Imperativo Modo verbal que expresa una orden, un mandato o una petición: ¡ven aquí! = come here!

Imperfecto Tiempo verbal que indica una acción pasada sin que se dé idea de su comienzo o final o una acción pasada habitual: los niños jugaban = the children were playing; iba allí todos los lunes = I used to go/I went there every Monday

Indicativo Modo verbal en el que la acción del verbo se considera como un hecho sin aportar otro tipo de matices: no tengo hambre = I'm not hungry

Infinitivo Forma no personal del verbo que se construye añadiendo la terminación -ar, -er, -ir, a la raíz: cant*ar* = to sing

Interjección Palabra o expresión exclamativa que expresa una impresión repentina de sorpresa, dolor, alegría, ira etc. o que sirve para llamar la atención: ¡caramba! = good heavens!; ¡ay! = ouch!

Interrogativo Adjetivo, adverbio o pronombre que pregunta algo o acerca de alguien: ¿qué? = what?; ¿cuánto? = how much?; ¿quién? = who?

Locución Combinación fija de dos o más palabras cuyo sentido no es el resultado de la suma de los significados de sus miembros. Equivale con frecuencia a un adjetivo, un adverbio o una preposición: de balde = for free

Masculino Género que se aplica a los seres del sexo masculino y el que se atribuye a las cosas por su terminación (-o) o por el uso: el hombre; el perro; el pelo; el árbol

Modo Conjunto de determinadas formas de un verbo que manifiesta la actitud del hablante respecto de lo que está diciendo, diferente según se trate del modo indicativo, modo subjuntivo o modo imperativo.

Negativo Que contiene un adverbio de negación

Neutro El género del español, que no es ni masculino ni femenino: *eso* es *lo* bueno de *esto* = that's the good thing about this

Nombre Ver **Sustantivo**

Nombre propio Es el que se aplica a una persona, lugar, institución, etc., y se escribe con mayúscula: Juan, España, London

No numerable Se aplica a los sustantivos que no se pueden contar y que por lo tanto no se usan en plural: tristeza = sadness; solidaridad = solidarity

Numerable Se aplica a los sustantivos que se pueden contar, o sea, que se pueden usar en singular o en plural: una, dos, tres casas etc. = one, two, three houses etc

Número Indica si un elemento es singular o plural

Objeto Palabra o conjunto de palabras que designa a la persona, el animal o la cosa sobre la que recae la acción del verbo

Objeto directo Es aquel sobre el que recae directamente la acción del verbo: compré *un libro* = I bought *a book*

Objeto indirecto Es aquel sobre el que recae indirectamente la acción del verbo: le escribí una carta *a mi madre* = I wrote a letter *to my mother*

Oración Conjunto de palabras que tiene un sentido gramatical completo, con sujeto y predicado y que se puede comprender sin necesidad de otras explicaciones o referencias.

Oración subordinada es la que depende de la principal, a la que completa o determina: quiero *que estudies* = I want you to study

Ordinal Tratándose de números, que indican el orden o la colocación en una serie, como primero = first; quinto = fifth; undécimo = eleventh

Parte de la oración Cada uno de los términos gramaticales con los que se designa la función que una palabra desempeña en una oración: sustantivo, verbo, adjetivo, etc., son todos partes de la oración

Participio pasado Parte del verbo que se utiliza para formar tiempos compuestos, expresando una acción acabada, Se utiliza también como adjetivo: he terminado = I have finished; un producto terminado = a finished product

Pasiva Ver **Voz pasiva**

Pasiva refleja Oración con significado pasivo que se forma con el pronombre 'se' y el verbo en tercera persona en voz activa y sin agente expreso: se construyeron muchas casas = many houses were built

Persona Cualquiera de los tres grupos de pronombres personales y de las formas verbales que designan al individuo que habla o primera persona (p.ej. yo/I); al individuo al que se habla o segunda persona (p.ej. tú o Ud/you); al individuo del cual se habla o tercera persona (p.ej. él o ella/he o she)

Plural Número de los sustantivos, adjetivos etc., cuando se refieren a más de una cosa o persona: las casas = the houses

Posesivo Tratándose de pronombres (p.ej. mío/tuyo = mine/yours) o de adjetivos (p.ej. mi/tu = my/your), que indican pertenencia o posesión

Glosario de términos gramaticales

Predicado Parte de la oración que dice algo del sujeto y cuyo núcleo es el verbo: **Ana** *estudia mucho* = **Ana** *studies a lot*

Prefijo Letra o grupo de letras que se antepone a una palabra y que modifica su sentido: *i*legible; *ante*sala

Preposición Palabra invariable que establece una relación entre otras dos palabras en una oración: **con** = **with; sin** = **without**

Presente Tiempo verbal que indica que algo sucede en el momento en que se habla

Pretérito Tiempo verbal que indica que la acción ya ha ocurrido o pertenece al pasado.

Pretérito imperfecto ver **Imperfecto**

Pretérito indefinido Tiempo simple que indica una acción pasada completa y acabada: **se despertó** = **he woke up**

Pretérito perfecto Tiempo compuesto que indica que una acción, comenzada en el pasado, dura hasta el presente o tiene efectos todavía o bien que sucedió inmediatamente antes del momento presente: **he aprendido mucho/ha salido** = **I have learnt a lot/he has gone out**

Pretérito pluscuamperfecto Tiempo compuesto que indica una acción pasada y terminada, anterior a otra también pasada: **se había marchado** = **he had left**

Pronombre Palabra que sustituye o determina a un sustantivo o nombre: p.ej. **él/ella** = **he/she; alguien** = **someone; el mío/la mía** = **mine**

Pronombre personal Es el que se refiere a una persona o a una cosa: p.ej. **yo/tú/usted** etc.= **I/you** etc; **me/te** = **me/you** etc.

Pronombre reflexivo Es el que representa al sujeto y es parte de un verbo pronominal: **me/te/se/nos/os/se**

Pronombre relativo Es el que representa en una oración subordinada a una persona o a una cosa mencionada en la principal: **el hombre** *que* **nos visitó** = **the man** *who* **visited us**

Raíz Parte de una palabra que es común a todas las de la misma familia: *com-* es la raíz de *com*eré y *com*ida

Singular Número de los sustantivos, adjetivos etc., al referirse a una sola persona o cosa

Sintagma Sección, dentro de una oración, que constituye una unidad aislable

Sobresdrújula Tratándose de palabras, que llevan el acento en la sílaba anterior a la antepenúltima: *tíramelo*

Subjuntivo Modo verbal que expresa idea de duda, posibilidad, deseo etc., y que se usa especialmente en oraciones subordinadas: **espero que** *venga* = **I hope he will come; si** *fuera* **posible** = **if it** *was* **o** *were* **possible**

Sufijo Letra o grupo de letras que se añade a una palabra o a su raíz para formar otra palabra: caf*etera*; frut*ería*; cas*ita*

Sujeto Palabra o conjunto de palabras que disigna a la persona, el animal o la cosa que realiza la acción del verbo: *Inés* **estudia geografía** = *Inés* **studies geography;** *el mío* **corre más rápido** = *mine* **runs faster**

Superlativo Grado máximo de significación de un adjetivo o de un adverbio: **la casa más pequeña de la calle** = **the smallest house in the street; muchísimo** = **very much**

Sustantivo Palabra que nombra a las personas o a las cosas: **silla** = **chair**

Sustantivo colectivo Es el que en singular se refiere a un conjunto, p.ej: **ejército, rebaño**

Sustantivo compuesto Es el que está formado de dos palabras, p.ej: **aeropuerto (aero + puerto)** = **airport**

Terminación Letra o letras que siguen a la raíz de un vocablo para formar tiempos verbales, el plural de los sustantivos, etc.

Verbo Palabra o conjunto de palabra que describe una acción o un estado: **Los niños están jugando** = **the children are playing**

Verbo auxiliar Es el que se une a otro para formar los tiempos compuestos o para expresar distintos matices, p.ej.: **haber, estar, poder:** *he* **comido** = **I** *have* **eaten**

Verbo impersonal Es el que no admite sujeto, p.ej.: **llover: está lloviendo** = **it is raining**

Verbo intransitivo Es el que no tiene complemento u objeto directo: **murió repentinamente** = **he died suddenly**

Verbo irregular Es el que no sigue un modelo sistemático, sino que tiene su propias formas individuales de conjugación

Verbo pronominal Es el que se conjuga en todas sus formas con los pronombres **me/te/se/os/se**, p.ej. **equivocarse**

Verbo reflexivo Es el verbo pronominal que expresa una acción que es realizada y recibida por su propio sujeto: **se lavó** = **he washed himself**

Verbo recíproco Es el verbo pronominal cuya acción se intercambia entre dos o más sujetos y recae sobre todos ellos, p.ej. **besarse: Pedro y Ana se besaron** = **Pedro and Ana kissed each other**

Verbo regular Es aquél cuya conjugación se ajusta a la de los verbos que se toman como modelo

Voz activa Indica que el sujeto del verbo es el agente de la acción: **Pedro** *besa* **a Ana** = **Pedro** *kisses* **Ana**

Voz pasiva Indica que el sujeto recibe la acción del verbo y el agente se introduce por la preposición "por", no es muy usual en español: **Ana** *es besada* **por Pedro**

Los verbos irregulares ingleses

Las formas irregulares que solo se usan en algunas acepciones se indican con un asterisco (e.g. *abode).

La información completa acerca del uso, la pronunciación, etc., de cada verbo se encontrará en el artículo correspondiente.

infinitive/ infinitivo	past tense/ pretérito	past participle/ participio pasado	infinitive/ infinitivo	past tense/ pretérito	past participle/ participio pasado
abide	abided, *abode	abided, *abode	deal	dealt	dealt
arise	arose	arisen	dig	dug	dug
awake	awoke	awoken	dive	dived, (AmE also) dove	dived
be	was/were	been			
bear	bore	borne	do	did	done
beat	beat	beaten	draw	drew	drawn
become	became	become	dream	dreamed, (BrE also) dreamt	dreamed, (BrE also) dreamt
befall	befell	befallen			
beget	begot, (arch) begat	begotten			
begin	began	begun	drink	drank	drunk
behold	beheld	beheld	drive	drove	driven
bend	bent	bent	dwell	dwelt, dwelled	dwelt, dwelled
beseech	beseeched, besought	beseeched, besought	eat	ate	eaten
			fall	fell	fallen
beset	beset	beset	feed	fed	fed
bet	bet	bet	feel	felt	felt
bid	*bade, bid	*bidden, bid	fight	fought	fought
bind	bound	bound	find	found	found
bite	bit	bitten	flee	fled	fled
bleed	bled	bled	fling	flung	flung
bless	blessed	blessed, (arch) blest	floodlight	floodlit	floodlit
			fly	flew	flown
blow	blew	blown, *blowed	forbid	forbade, forbad	forbidden
break	broke	broken	forecast	forecast, forecasted	forecast, forecasted
breed	bred	bred			
bring	brought	brought	foresee	foresaw	foreseen
broadcast	broadcast	broadcast	foretell	foretold	foretold
browbeat	browbeat	browbeaten	forget	forgot	forgotten
build	built	built	forgive	forgave	forgiven
burn	burned, burnt	burned, burnt	forsake	forsook	forsaken
bust	busted, (BrE also) bust	busted, (BrE also) bust	freeze	froze	frozen
			get	got	got, (AmE also) gotten
buy	bought	bought	give	gave	given
cast	cast	cast	go	went	gone
catch	caught	caught	grind	ground	ground
choose	chose	chosen	grow	grew	grown
cling	clung	clung	hang	*hung, *hanged	*hung, *hanged
come	came	come	have	had	had
cost	*cost, *costed	*cost, *costed	hear	heard	heard
creep	crept	crept	hew	hewed	hewn, hewed
crow	crowed	crowed	hide	hid	hidden, (arch) hid
cut	cut	cut			

Los verbos irregulares ingleses

infinitive/ infinitivo	past tense/ pretérito	past participle/ participio pasado	infinitive/ infinitivo	past tense/ pretérito	past participle/ participio pasado
hit	hit	hit	outshine	outshone	outshone
hold	held	held	overbid	overbid	overbid
hurt	hurt	hurt	overcome	overcame	overcome
inlay	inlaid	inlaid	overdo	overdid	overdone
input	input, inputted	input, inputted	overdraw	overdrew	overdrawn
interweave	interwove, interweaved	interwoven, interweaved	overeat	overate	overeaten
			overfly	overflew	overflown
keep	kept	kept	overhang	overhung	overhung
kneel	kneeled, knelt	kneeled, knelt	overhear	overheard	overheard
knit	knitted, *knit	knitted, *knit	overlay	overlaid	overlaid
know	knew	known	overlie	overlay	overlain
lay	laid	laid	overpay	overpaid	overpaid
lead	led	led	override	overrode	overridden
lean	leaned, (BrE also) leant	leaned, (BrE also) leant	overrun	overran	overrun
			oversee	oversaw	overseen
			overshoot	overshot	overshot
leap	leaped, (BrE also) leapt	leaped, (BrE also) leapt	oversleep	overslept	overslept
			overtake	overtook	overtaken
			overthrow	overthrew	overthrown
learn	learned, (BrE also) learnt	learned, (BrE also) learnt	partake	partook	partaken
			pay	paid	paid
leave	left	left	plead	pleaded, (AmE also) pled	pleaded, (AmE also) pled
lend	lent	lent			
let	let	let	prove	proved	proved, proven
lie (yacer etc)	lay	lain	put	put	put
light	lighted, lit	lighted, lit	quit	quit, quitted	quit, quitted
lose	lost	lost	read /riːd/	read /red/	read /red/
make	made	made	rend	rent	rent
mean	meant	meant	rid	rid	rid
meet	met	met	ride	rode	ridden
miscast	miscast	miscast	ring	rang	rung
misdeal	misdealt	misdealt	rise	rose	risen
mishear	misheard	misheard	run	ran	run
mishit	mishit	mishit	saw	sawed	sawed, (esp BrE) sawn
mislay	mislaid	mislaid			
mislead	misled	misled	say	said	said
misread /ˈmɪsˈriːd/	misread /ˈmɪsˈred/	misread /ˈmɪsˈred/	see	saw	seen
			seek	sought	sought
misspell	misspelled, (BrE also) misspelt	misspelled, (BrE also) misspelt	sell	sold	sold
			send	sent	sent
			set	set	set
misspend	misspent	misspent	sew	sewed	sewn, sewed
mistake	mistook	mistaken	shake	shook	shaken
misunderstand	misunderstood	misunderstood	shear	sheared	*shorn, *sheared
mow	mowed	mown, mowed			
outbid	outbid	outbid, (AmE also) outbidden	shed	shed	shed
			shine	*shone, *shined	*shone, *shined
			shit	shit, shat	shit, shat
outdo	outdid	outdone	shoe	shod	shod
outfight	outfought	outfought	shoot	shot	shot
outgrow	outgrew	outgrown	show	showed	shown, showed
output	output, outputted	output, outputted	shrink	shrank, shrunk	shrunk, shrunken
outrun	outran	outrun	shut	shut	shut
outsell	outsold	outsold	sing	sang	sung
			sink	sank	sunk

Los verbos irregulares ingleses

infinitive/ _infinitivo_	past tense/ _pretérito_	past participle/ _participio pasado_	infinitive/ _infinitivo_	past tense/ _pretérito_	past participle/ _participio pasado_
sit	sat	sat	swim	swam	swum
slay	slew	slain	swing	swung	swung
sleep	slept	slept	take	took	taken
slide	slid	slid	teach	taught	taught
sling	slung	slung	tear	tore	torn
slink	slunk	slunk	tell	told	told
slit	slit	slit	think	thought	thought
smell	smelled, (BrE also) smelt	smelled, (BrE also) smelt	thrive	thrived, (liter) throve	thrived, (arch) thriven
sow	sowed	sowed, sown	throw	threw	thrown
speak	spoke	spoken	thrust	thrust	thrust
speed	*sped, *speeded	*sped, *speeded	tread	trod	trodden, trod
spell	spelled, (BrE also) spelt	spelled, (BrE also) spelt	typecast	typecast	typecast
			typeset	typeset	typeset
spend	spent	spent	typewrite	typewrote	typewritten
spill	spilled, spilt	spilled, spilt	undercut	undercut	undercut
spin	spun, (arch) span	spun	undergo	underwent	undergone
			underlie	underlay	underlain
spit	spat, (esp AmE) spit	spat, (esp AmE) spit	undersell	undersold	undersold
			understand	understood	understood
split	split	split	undertake	undertook	undertaken
spoil	spoiled, (BrE also) spoilt	spoiled, (BrE also) spoilt	undo	undid	undone
			unstick	unstuck	unstuck
spread	spread	spread	unwind	unwound	unwound
spring	sprang, (AmE also) sprung	sprung	uphold	upheld	upheld
			upset	upset	upset
stand	stood	stood	wake	woke	woken
steal	stole	stolen	waylay	waylaid	waylaid
stick	stuck	stuck	wear	wore	worn
sting	stung	stung	weave	wove, *weaved	woven, *weaved
stink	stank, stunk	stunk	wed	wedded, wed	wedded, wed
strew	strewed	strewn, strewed	weep	wept	wept
stride	strode	stridden	wet	wet, wetted	wet, wetted
strike	struck	struck	win	won	won
string	strung	strung	wind	wound	wound
strive	strove	striven	(dar cuerda, etc.)		
sublet	sublet	sublet	withdraw	withdrew	withdrawn
swear	swore	sworn	withhold	withheld	withheld
sweat	sweated, (AmE also) sweat	sweated, (AmE also) sweat	withstand	withstood	withstood
			work	worked, *wrought	worked, *wrought
sweep	swept	swept	wring	wrung	wrung
swell	swelled	swollen, (esp AmE) swelled	write	wrote	written

Resumen de la gramática inglesa

1 El artículo

1.1 El artículo indeterminado

El artículo indeterminado es **a** si la palabra que sigue empieza con una consonante. Nótese que el sonido de la *u* inicial de *union* no es vocálico (/ju:/).

a ball una pelota   **a girl** una niña   **a union** una unión

Es *an* delante de una vocal o de *h* muda:

an apple una manzana   **an hour** una hora

Nótese el uso del artículo en los siguientes casos:

con profesiones

She is a doctor. Es médico.   **He is an engineer.** Es ingeniero.

después de una preposición:

She works as a tour guide.   **Anna has gone out without an umbrella.**
Trabaja de guía turística.   Ana ha salido sin paraguas.

con sentido genérico:

A hare is larger than a rabbit.
La liebre es más grande que el conejo.

1.2 El artículo determinado

El artículo determinado es *the*, tanto para el singular como para el plural:

the cat   **the cats**   **the frog**   **the frogs**
el gato   los gatos   la rana   las ranas

El artículo determinado no se usa por lo general en los siguientes casos:

con instituciones:

I don't go to church.   **He's starting school next week.**
No voy a la iglesia.   Empieza el colegio la próxima semana.

Cuando se hace referencia al edificio, el sustantivo va acompañado del artículo: **Turn right at the school** (= Al llegar al colegio, gire a la derecha).

con los nombres de las comidas:

Breakfast is at 8.30.   **Dinner is ready!**
El desayuno es a las 8.30.   ¡La cena está lista!

para referirse a cosas abstractas:

Hatred is a destructive force.   **The book is on English grammar.**
El odio es una fuerza destructora.   Es un libro de gramática inglesa.

delante de las estaciones del año:

Spring is here!   **It's like winter today.**
¡Ha llegado la primavera!   Hoy hace de invierno.

con los nombres de calles, parques, etc.:

a concert in Central Park   **I work in Bath Street**
un concierto en Central Park   Trabajo en la calle Bath

• •

Los nombres de ríos y océanos y nombres geográficos plurales van acompañados por regla general del artículo determinado:

the Thames	**the Pacific**	**the Alps**
el Támesis	el Pacífico	los Alpes

• •

2 El plural

El plural de los sustantivos se indica por lo general añadiendo una -s al final de la palabra:

dog, dogs (= perros)   **tape, tapes** (= cintas)

-es se añade a las palabras que terminan en -s, -x, -ch o -sh:

dress, dresses (= vestidos)   **box, boxes** (= cajas)
hatch, hatches (= cubiertas)   **splash, splashes** (= salpicaduras)

Los nombres que terminan en consonante + y: **baby, babies** (= bebés)
Los nombres que terminan en vocal + y: **volley, volleys** (= voleas)
Los nombres que terminan en -o a veces añaden -s, a veces -es:

potato, potatoes (= patatas)   **hero, heroes** (= héroes)
tomato, tomatoes (= tomates)   **zero, zeros** (= ceros)

El plural de los nombres que terminan en -f(e) es de dos tipos:

life, lives (= vidas)   **dwarf, dwarfs/dwarves** (= enanos)   **roof, roofs/rooves** (= tejados)

Plurales irregulares frecuentes:

child, children (= niños)	**foot, feet** (= pies)	**man, men** (= hombres)
mouse, mice (= ratones)	**tooth, teeth** (= dientes)	**woman, women** (= mujeres)

• •

3 El femenino

El inglés tiene un número relativamente bajo de palabras con forma femenina. Algunos ejemplos de sustantivos femeninos son: **actress** (= actriz); **widow** (= viuda); **heiress** (= heredera). Pero normalmente el sustantivo no especifica el género: **cousin** (= primo o prima); **friend** (= amigo o amiga); **doctor** (= médico o médica). Si es necesario especificar el sexo de la persona a la que nos estamos refiriendo, hay que decir por ejemplo, **a male student** (= un estudiante), **a woman doctor** (= una médica).

• •

4 El genitivo sajón

Las reglas de uso del genitivo son las siguientes:

-'s se añade a los nombres que están en singular:

the boy's book (= el libro del niño)

• •

el apóstrofo solo (') se añade a los nombres que están en plural y terminan en
-*s*:

the boys' room (= la habitación de los niños)
the boys' books (= los libros de los niños)

Si el plural de un nombre no termina en -*s*, el genitivo se forma añadiendo -'*s*:

the children's toys (= los juguetes de los niños)

Los nombres propios que terminan en -s, pueden formar el genitivo de las
dos maneras -'*s* y *s*':

Keats's poetry o **Keats' poetry** (= la poesía de Keats).

El genitivo se usa sobre todo con nombres de personas, animales
(especialmente domésticos) y países: **Andrew's house** (= la casa de
Andrew), **the lion's den** (= la guarida del león), **America's foreign policy**
(= la política exterior de Estados Unidos).

Debe tenerse en cuenta los siguientes usos del genitivo:

We're going to Anne's. Vamos a casa de Anne.
I got it at the baker's/the chemist's. Lo compré en la panadería/farmacia.

En inglés coloquial es frecuente el uso del "genitivo doble":

He's a friend of my brother's. Es un amigo de mi hermano.

• •

5 El adjetivo

Los adjetivos ingleses tienen sólo una forma, no concuerdan ni en género ni
en número con el sustantivo al que modifican:

an old man   **three old women**
un anciano   tres ancianas

5.1 Posición del adjetivo

El adjetivo generalmente va delante del sustantivo: **a long story** (= una
historia larga) o después del verbo: **this story is long** (= esta historia es
larga).

Algunos adjetivos sólo pueden preceder al sustantivo que modifican y no
constituir el predicado de una oración. Estos adjetivos van precedidos por el
indicador (*before n*), véanse **adoptive**, **laico -ca**.

5.2 Grados del adjetivo

Hay tres grados de intensidad: el grado positivo, el comparativo y el
superlativo.

Los adjetivos de una sílaba forman el comparativo añadiendo -(*e*)*r* y el
superlativo añadiendo -(*e*)*st*:

dull aburrido   **duller** más aburrido   **dullest** el más aburrido
big grande   **bigger** más grande   **biggest** el más grande
nice amable   **nicer** más amable   **nicest** el más amable

Nótese que si el adjetivo termina en consonante sencilla, se dobla la

• •

consonante final.

Los adjetivos de tres sílabas forman el comparativo usando **more** y el superlativo usando **most**:

generous generoso   **more generous**   **most generous**

Lo dicho se aplica también a algunos adjetivos de dos sílabas, p. ej. **useful** útil.

Sin embargo, no existe una regla para los adjetivos de dos sílabas, aunque se suele añadir *-er*, *-est* para formar el comparativo y superlativo respectivamente de los adjetivos que terminan en *-y, -le, -ow, -er*.

Ejemplos:

pretty bonito   **prettier**   **prettiest**

(Nótese que la *-y* se sustituye por *-ie-*)

narrow estrecho   **narrower**   **narrowest**
curious curioso   **more curious**   **most curious**

Para el gerundio y el participio pasado, se usa **more/most**:

boring aburrido   **more boring**   **most boring**
bored aburrido   **more bored**   **most bored**

Most se puede usar como sinónimo de "very" (= muy): **That was a most interesting story** (= Esa fue una historia muy interesante).

Algunos adjetivos de uso frecuente tienen comparativos y superlativos irregulares:

bad malo	**worse** peor	**worst** pésimo, el peor
good bueno	**better** mejor	**best** óptimo, el mejor
little poco	**less** menos	**least** el menos
many/much mucho	**more** más	**most** el más
far lejos	**farther/further**	**farthest/furthest**
old[1] viejo	**elder**	**eldest** (se usa sólo para personas)

[1]La forma regular (*old, older, oldest* = viejo, más viejo, el más viejo) se usa tanto para personas como para cosas.

Las comparaciones de inferioridad se forman usando **less/least**:

expensive caro   **less expensive** menos caro   **least expensive** el menos caro

5.3 Los adjetivos posesivos

Los adjetivos posesivos son:

my mi, mis, mío, mía, míos, mías   **our** nuestro, nuestra, nuestros, nuestras
your tu, tus, tuyo, tuya, tuyos, tuyas   **your** vuestro, vuestra, vuestros, vuestras
his, her, its su, sus, suyo, suya, suyos, suyas   **their** su, sus, suyo, suya, suyos, suyas

Concuerdan con el poseedor y no con la cosa poseída:

his mother su madre (= la madre del niño)
her mother su madre (= la madre de la niña)
their mother su madre (= la madre de los niños, o de las niñas, o de los niños y de las niñas)

Tienen la misma forma para los nombres en singular y en plural:

my cat mi gato   **my boots** mis botas

··

6 El adverbio

Muchos adverbios se forman añadiendo el sufijo *-ly* al adjetivo: **sad, sadly** triste, tristemente; **brave, bravely** valiente, valientemente; **careful, carefully** cuidado, cuidadosamente

Los adverbios pueden modificar los adjetivos:

> **The job was *extremely* dangerous.** El trabajo era muy peligroso.

los verbos:

> **He finished *quickly*.** Terminó enseguida.

u otros adverbios:

> ***very* quickly** muy rápido

Nótese que se producen algunos cambios ortográficos y fonéticos: **ready, readily** listo, fácilmente; **true, truly** verdadero, verdaderamente; **due, duly** debido, debidamente; **whole, wholly** entero, enteramente.

Algunos adverbios comunes tienen la misma forma que el adjetivo correspondiente; por ejemplo **back** atrás, **early** pronto, **far** lejos, **fast** rápidamente, **left** a la izquierda, **little** poco, **more** más, **much** mucho, **only** solamente, **right** correctamente, a la derecha, **still** todavía, **straight** en línea recta, directamente, **well** bien, **wrong** incorrectamente, mal.
Ejemplos:

a wrong answer (adjetivo) una respuesta incorrecta	**He did it wrong.** (adverbio) Lo hizo mal
an early summer un verano temprano	**Summer has arrived early.** El verano ha llegado pronto.
a straight road una carretera recta	**He came straight to the point.** Fue directamente al grano.

···

7 Los pronombres

7.1 Los pronombres personales

Sujeto	Complemento
I yo	**me** me
you tú, usted	**you** te
he él	**him** le
she ella	**her** la, le
one uno, una	**one** uno, una
it ello	**it** lo
we nosotros, nosotras	**us** nos
you vosotros, vosotras, ustedes	**you** os
they ellos, ellas	**them** los, las, les

Nótese que el pronombre personal sujeto **I** siempre se escribe con mayúscula.

El pronombre nunca se puede omitir en inglés cuando tiene función de sujeto, por consiguiente, la traducción del español de *voy* es **I go**, de *vamos* **we go**.

• •

Los pronombres complemento se usan como complemento directo:

Mary loves *him*. Mary lo quiere.

como complemento indirecto:

John gave it to *me*. John me lo dio (a mí).

y después de una preposición:

The book is from *her*. El libro es de su parte.

7.1.1 Otros usos de los pronombres personales

he y **she**

Estos pronombres se usan para referirse a animales, sobre todo a los domésticos:

Poor Whiskers, we had to take him to the vet's.
Pobrecito Whiskers, tuvimos que llevarlo al veterinario.

it

Se usa en construcciones impersonales:

It's sunny.   **It's hard to know what to do.**   **It looks as though they were right.**
Hace sol.   Es difícil saber qué hacer.   Parece que tenían razón.

En expresiones de tiempo y de distancia en el espacio:

It's five o'clock.   **It's January the sixth.**   **How far is it to Edinburgh?**
Son las cinco.   Es el seis de enero.   ¿A qué distancia está Edimburgo?

Nótese que *it's* es la contracción de *it is*, y por consiguiente sigue el modelo de otras contracciones como: *he's, she's, isn't, wasn't* etc. No debe confundirse con el pronombre posesivo *its*, que sigue el modelo de los otros posesivos: *his, hers, ours, yours, theirs*.

you

Para referirse a una persona, el inglés no distingue entre el pronombre *tú* y el pronombre de cortesía *usted*, ambos se traducen por *you*.

You se usa a menudo en sentido genérico, para referirse a la gente en general:

You never know.   **You can't buy cars like that any more.**
Nunca se sabe.   Ya no se pueden comprar coches así.

they

Se usa para referirse a una persona o a un grupo de personas desconocidas, especialmente dotados de cierto poder, autoridad o habilidad:

They don't make cars like that any more.   **You'll have to get them to repair it.**
Ya no fabrican coches así.   Tendrás que decirles que lo arreglen.

They will have to find the murderer first.
Primero tendrán que encontrar al asesino.

En lugar de *he* o *she* (él o ella):

The person appointed will be answerable to the director. They (= he/she) **will be responsible for ...**
La persona que nombren tendrá que rendir cuentas al director. Será responsable de ...

Para referirse a los pronombres indefinidos *somebody, someone* alguien; *anybody, anyone* alguien; *everybody, everyone* todos; *nobody, no one* nadie:

If anyone has seen my pen, will they please tell me.

• •

Si alguien ha visto mi pluma, por favor que me lo diga.

one

One equivale al pronombre genérico *you*, pero es más formal:

One needs to get a clearer picture of what one wants.
Uno necesita tener una idea más clara de lo que quiere.

7.2 Pronombres reflexivos

myself me	**ourselves** nos
yourself te	**yourselves** os
himself, herself, itself, oneself se	**themselves** se

Los pronombres reflexivos tienen varias funciones, ejemplos:

He burned himself badly. (complemento directo)
Se quemó gravemente.

I always buy myself a Christmas present. (complemento indirecto)
Siempre me compro un regalo de Navidad.

She talks to herself. (después de preposición)
Habla sola, habla consigo misma.

Do it yourself. (enfático)
Hazlo tú mismo.

7.3 Pronombres posesivos

mine el mío, la mía, los míos, las mías
yours el tuyo, la tuya, los tuyos, las tuyas
his, hers, its el suyo, la suya, los suyos, las suyas
ours el nuestro, la nuestra, los nuestros, las nuestras
yours el vuestro, la vuestra, los vuestros, las vuestras
theirs el suyo, la suya, los suyos, las suyas

Los pronombres posesivos concuerdan con el poseedor y no con la cosa poseída:

Whose book is this? – It's hers. ¿De quién es este libro? – Es suyo/Es de ella.

Whose shoes are these? – They are hers. ¿De quién son estos zapatos? – Son suyos/Son de ella.

Whose car is that? – It's theirs. ¿De quién es ese coche? – Es suyo/Es de ellos.

• •

8 Los adjetivos y los pronombres interrogativos

who quién, quiénes	**which** cuál, cuáles, qué
whom a quién, a quiénes	**whose** de quién, de quiénes
what qué	

who se usa para personas como sujeto: **Who is it?** ¿Quién es?

whom se usa para personas como complemento:

To whom did you send the letter?   **Whom did you see?**
¿A quién enviaste la carta?   ¿A quién viste?

Whom se considera muy formal y se suele sustituir por **who**:

Who did you send the letter to?   **Who did you see?**
¿A quién enviaste la carta?   ¿A quién viste?

whose es la forma genitiva de *who*:

∙∙

Whose are these?
¿De quién/de quiénes son éstos?

Whose socks are these?
¿De quién son estos calcetines?

which puede referirse a personas o a cosas. Se usa como sujeto:

Which of you are going?
¿Cuál *or* quién de ustedes va a ir?

Which is bigger?
¿Cuál es más grande?

y como complemento:

Which of the singers/pictures do you prefer?
De los cuadros/cantantes ¿cuál prefieres?/¿Qué cantante/cuadro prefieres?

Which dress should I wear?
¿Qué vestido me pongo?

what se usa sólo para cosas. Puede desempeñar la función de sujeto:

What is this?
¿Qué es esto?

What type of bird is that?
¿Qué clase de pájaro es ése?

y de complemento:

What are you going to do?
¿Qué vas a hacer?

What sort of books do you like?
¿Qué tipo de libros te gustan?

∙∙

9 Los pronombres relativos

Los pronombres relativos hacen referencia normalmente a un antecedente.
En **She phoned the man who had contacted her** (= Llamó por teléfono al
señor que la había llamado), el pronombre relativo *who* (= que) se refiere a
the man (= al señor).

antecedente	sujeto	complemento
PERSONA	**who/that** que, quien	**whom/who/that** que, quien
COSA	**which/that** que	**which/that** que

9.1 Who, that

9.1.1 Para personas: con función de sujeto

who es el pronombre relativo que se usa generalmente en este caso; también
se puede usar *that*:

There is a prize for the student who/that gets the highest marks.
Hay un premio para el estudiante que saque las mejores notas.

9.1.2 Para personas: con función de complemento

The man who/that/whom she met that night was a spy.
El hombre que conoció aquella noche era un espía.

Whom se considera muy formal y se suele sustituir por **who** o **that**.

El pronombre relativo se suele omitir cuando tiene función de complemento:

The man (who/that) **she met last night was a spy.**
El hombre que conoció ayer por la noche era un espía.

9.2 Which, that

9.2.1 Para cosas: con función de sujeto

The book, which is on the table, was a present.
El libro que está encima de la mesa fue un regalo.

John gave me the book which/that is on the table.
John me regaló el libro que está encima de la mesa.

9.2.2 Para cosas: con función de complemento

His latest film, which we went to see last week, is excellent.
Su última película, que fuimos a ver la semana pasada, es fenomenal.

The film, which/that we went to see last week, is excellent.
La película que fuimos a ver la semana pasada es fenomenal.

Nótese que en el último ejemplo también se puede omitir el pronombre relativo:

The film (which/that) **we went to see last week was excellent.**

9.3 Whose

Whose es la forma genitiva:

This is the boy whose dog has been killed.
Este es el niño al que le mataron el perro.

Nótese que *who's* es la contracción de *who is*, y no debe confundirse con el pronombre relativo *whose*.

10 Los adjetivos y los pronombres indefinidos

10.1 Some, any

Como adjetivos, se usan con sustantivos plurales o no contables:

Take some boxes.	**Have some butter.**
Coge unas cajas.	Toma mantequilla.
Do you have any nails?	**Have you any jam?**
¿Tienes clavos?	¿Tienes mermelada?

Como pronombres, sustituyen a los sustantivos plurales o no contables:

We haven't got any. No tenemos.

10.2 Some

Some (adjetivo y pronombre) se usa en: Frases afirmativas:

He bought some.	**He bought some jam.**	**He bought some screws.**
Compró algunos/algunas.	Compró mermelada.	Compró tornillos.

Preguntas cuando se espera una respuesta afirmativa:

Can you lend me some money? ¿Puedes prestarme dinero?

Para ofrecer o solicitar algo:

Would you like some?	**Could you buy some onions for me?**
¿Quieres?	¿Podrías comprarme cebollas?

10.3 Any

Any (adjetivo y pronombre) se usa en: Frases negativas:

I haven't got any brothers or sisters. No tengo hermanos.

Preguntas:

Do you have any bananas?	**Do you have any sugar?**
¿Tiene plátanos?	¿Tienes azúcar?

Los compuestos con *any* y *some* se usan de forma similar. Ejemplos:

I saw something very strange today. Hoy he visto algo muy extraño.	**I met someone who knows you.** Me encontré con alguien que te conoce.
We didn't see anything interesting. No vimos nada interesante.	**Did you meet anyone you knew?** ¿Te encontraste con alguien conocido?

11 El verbo

11.1 El infinitivo constituye la raíz o forma básica del verbo. La forma completa del infinitivo incluye también *to*: *to live* vivir, *to die* morir, etc. Los verbos irregulares más comunes se dan en la página 1041–1043. Los verbos regulares se conjugan de la forma siguiente:

Infinitivo	want	love¹	stop²	prefer³
GERUNDIO/ PARTICIPIO PRESENTE	wanting	loving	stopping	preferring
PRETÉRITO/ PARTICIPIO PASADO	wanted	loved	stopped	preferred

1 Infinitivos que terminan en -*e*
2 Infinitivos de una sílaba que terminan en vocal + consonante sencilla
3 Infinitivos que terminan en vocal con acento tónico + consonante sencilla

El gerundio se usa con función nominal:

I don't like swimming. No me gusta la natación.	**Dancing is fun.** Bailar es divertido.

11.2 Los tiempos verbales

11.2.1 Presente

Los verbos *to be* y *to have*:

to be ser *o* estar	**to have** tener
I am soy *o* estoy	**I have** tengo
you are eres *o* estás	**you have** tienes
he/she/it is es *o* está	**he/she/it has** tiene
we are somos *o* estamos	**we have** tenemos
you are sois *o* estáis	**you have** tenéis
they are son *o* están	**they have** tienen

Para formar el presente de los demás verbos se utiliza el infinitivo sin *to* para todas las personas excepto para la tercera persona del singular que se forma añadiendo al infinitivo sin *to* la desinencia -*s*:

to want (= querer): I want, you want, he/she/it wants, we want, you want, they want
to love (= amar): I love, you love, he/she/it loves, we love, you love, they love

La tercera persona del singular del presente de los verbos terminados en -*ch*, -*sh*, -*x* o -*ss* se forma añadiendo al infinitivo sin *to* la desinencia -*es*:

to watch mirar: **he/she/it watches**	**to kiss** besar: **he/she/it kisses**
to wish desear: **he/she/it wishes**	**to fix** arreglar: **he/she/it fixes**
to witness ser testigo de: **he/she/it witnesses**	

El presente se usa para expresar algo que es siempre cierto o que sucede regularmente y para enunciar hechos:

. . . .

He takes the 8 o'clock train to work.   **I work in publishing.**
Coge el tren de las 8 para ir al trabajo.   Trabajo en una casa editorial.

11.2.2 Pretérito

Tiene la misma forma para todas las personas, tanto para el singular como para el plural:

I/you/he/she/it/we/you/they wanted

Se usa para referirse a hechos que tuvieron lugar en el pasado, a menudo va acompañado de expresiones adverbiales que especifican un momento o una fecha concretos:

He flew to America last week. La semana pasada se fue a América en avión.

11.2.3 Pretérito perfecto

Se forma con el presente del verbo *to have* (= haber) y el participio pasado del verbo que se conjuga:

I/you have loved, he/she/it has loved, we/you/they have loved

Se usa para referirse a acciones pasadas o acontecimientos que tienen alguna relación con el momento presente. Se puede ver la diferencia entre el pretérito perfecto y el pretérito comparando las frases siguientes:

Have you seen Peter this morning?
¿Has visto a Peter esta mañana? (es aún por la mañana)
Did you see Peter this morning?
¿Viste a Peter por la mañana? (es por la tarde o noche)

Obsérvese el uso siguiente del pretérito perfecto y del pretérito:

I have lived in Glasgow for three years.
Vivo en Glasgow desde hace tres años.
I lived in Glasgow for three years.
Viví en Glasgow durante tres años. (y ahora no)

11.2.4 Pretérito pluscuamperfecto

Se forma con el pasado del verbo *to have* (= haber) y el participio pasado del verbo que se conjuga:

I/you/he/she/it/we/you/they had wanted

Se usa para referirse a acciones o acontecimientos pasados cuya terminación es anterior a la de otra acción también pasada y completa:

She had already left home when I arrived. Cuando llegué, ya había salido de casa.

11.2.5 Las formas perifrásticas

Las formas perifrásticas se forman con el verbo *to be* (= ser), en el tiempo y la persona requeridos, y el gerundio del verbo que se conjuga.

Presente continuo

I am singing estoy cantando, you are singing, etc.

Se usa para referirse a algo que está sucediendo en el momento de hablar o a algo que está en proceso, aunque no esté sucediendo precisamente cuando se habla:

What are you doing? – I'm trying to fix the television.
¿Qué estás haciendo? – Estoy tratando de arreglar la televisión.

He always interrupts when I'm reading to the children.
Siempre me interrumpe cuando estoy leyendo a los niños.

Pasado continuo

I was singing estaba cantando, **you were singing**, etc.

Se usa para referirse a acciones que se desarrollaban en un determinado momento en el pasado:

He rushed into my office while I was talking to the manager.
Entró a toda prisa en mi despacho mientras yo estaba hablando con el director.

Los otros tiempos verbales también tienen formas continuas: *I have been living*; *I had been living*; *I will be living*

Obsérvese el uso siguiente del pretérito perfecto en la forma continua:

I have been living in Glasgow for three years. Llevo tres años viviendo en Glasgow.

11.2.6 El futuro

En inglés hay varias formas de expresar el futuro.

11.2.6.1 Will/shall

Will se puede utilizar con todas las personas; *shall* sólo se utiliza con la primera persona del singular y del plural:

I will/shall go iré	**we will/shall go** iremos
you will go irás	**you will go** iréis
he/she/it will go irá	**they will go** irán

Will y las formas negativas *will not* y *shall not* se pueden contraer:

You'll be angry.	**We won't/shan't stay long.**
Te enfadarás.	No estaremos mucho tiempo.

11.2.6.2 Going to

Esta forma se suele usar para expresar una intención o para predecir algo que va a ocurrir:

I'm going to go to Richmond tomorrow. Mañana voy a Richmond.

Going to es intercambiable con *will*:

The boss is going to be/will be furious when he hears.
El jefe se va a poner furioso cuando se entere.

11.2.6.3 El Presente

Se puede usar para expresar algo que ocurrirá en un momento determinado:

When does term end? ¿Cuándo termina el trimestre?

Se usa de forma parecida a *going to* para expresar una intención:

I'm spending Christmas in Paris. Pasaré las Navidades en París.

11.3 El imperativo

Se forma con el infinitivo sin *to*. El imperativo se usa para dar órdenes:

Be quiet! ¡Cállate!   **Shut the door!** ¡Cierra la puerta!

La forma negativa se hace con *don't*:

Don't forget to phone Alan! ¡No os olvidéis de llamar a Alan!

Let's se usa con la primera persona del plural para formular propuestas:

Let's go. Vamos.	**Don't let's go.** No vamos.	**Let's not go.** No vamos.

Resumen de la gramática inglesa

. . . .

12 La forma interrogativa

12.1 La forma interrogativa de las oraciones en presente y en pasado simple necesitan utilizar el verbo *to do*, y tiene que concordar con el sujeto de la oración:

Do you live here?	**Did you live here?**
¿Vives aquí?	¿Viviste aquí?

Si la oración tiene un verbo auxiliar (*have, be*) o modal, la forma interrogativa se hace invirtiendo el verbo y el sujeto:

Are they going to get married?	**Have they seen us?**	**Can John come at eight?**
¿Se van a casar?	¿Nos han visto?	¿John puede venir a las ocho?

Con los pronombres interrogativos, las formas son las siguientes:

Who came?	**Who fed the cat?**
¿Quién vino?	¿Quién le dio de comer al gato?
What have they done to you?	**What shall we write about?**
¿Qué te han hecho?	¿Sobre qué vamos a escribir?

12.2 Las coletillas interrrogativas

Se trata de preguntas cortas, que se añaden al final de una oración para solicitar confirmación de lo que se ha dicho. Si la oración es afirmativa, va seguida de una coletilla interrogativa negativa:

You smoke, don't you?
Fumas ¿no?

Nótese el auxiliar *don't* que sustituye en la coletilla interrogativa al verbo **smoke**.

Si la oración es negativa, va seguida de una coletilla interrogativa afirmativa:

You don't smoke, do you?	**She doesn't mind, does she?**
No fumas ¿verdad?	No le importa ¿verdad?

Si la oración tiene un verbo auxiliar o modal, es éste el que se repite en la coletilla:

You aren't going, are you?	**You will come, won't you?**
No vas a ir ¿verdad?	Vendrás/Vas a venir ¿no?
You shouldn't say that, should you?	
No deberías decir eso ¿verdad?	

12.3 Las respuestas cortas

En las respuestas cortas, no es necesario repetir la forma completa del verbo principal; se puede simplemente repetir el verbo auxiliar (*be, have, do*) o modal que aparece en la pregunta:

Do you like fish? – Yes, I do./No, I don't.	**Can you drive? – Yes, I can./No, I can't.**
¿Te gusta el pescado? – Sí./No.	¿Sabes conducir? – Sí./No.

. . . .

13 Las oraciones negativas

Las oraciones negativas se forman con el verbo auxiliar *do* concordando con

• •

el sujeto + *not*. Las contracciones son *don't* y *doesn't* para el presente y *didn't* para el pasado:

> **They do not/don't understand English.**　　　**We did not/didn't go anywhere yesterday.**
> No entienden el inglés.　　　　　　　　　　　Ayer no fuimos a ninguna parte.

• •

14 Los verbos auxiliares modales

can, **could**; **may**, **might**; **shall**, **should**; **will**, **would**; **must**; **ought**

Los verbos modales son invariables: **I can**, **you can**, **he can**, etc.

Los verbos modales forman las interrogaciones invirtiendo el orden del sujeto y del verbo: **Can I go now?** (= ¿Puedo ir ahora?).

La contracción de *will* y *shall* es *'ll*:

I'll be going (= Iré).

La contracción de *would* es *'d*: **I'd like a cup of tea** (= Me gustaría tomar un té.)

Los verbos modales en la forma negativa utilizan *not* (*would not*, *might not*, etc.). Es especial la forma negativa de **can**: **cannot**.

Las contracciones negativas son: **can't**, **couldn't**; **mightn't**; **shan't**, **shouldn't**; **won't**, **wouldn't**; **mustn't**; **oughtn't**. (*Mayn't* no es muy frecuente).

14.1 can

Sus significados incluyen: autorización:

> **Can I leave the table?**　　　　　　　　**I can have another sweet, daddy said so.**
> ¿Puedo levantarme de la mesa?　　　　　　Puedo tomar otro caramelo, lo dijo papá.

aptitud:

> **He can count to a hundred.**　　　　　　**Can he drive?**
> Sabe contar hasta cien.　　　　　　　　　¿Sabe conducir?

posibilidad:

> **Accidents can happen.**
> Puede haber accidentes.

peticiones:

> **Can you open the door for me please?**
> ¿Me puedes abrir la puerta, por favor?

14.1.1 could

Could es el pasado de *can*. Sus significados incluyen: autorizaciones, aptitudes, posibilidades, peticiones, expresadas en el pasado:

> **Daddy said I could have another sweet.**
> Papá dijo que podía tomar otro caramelo.
> **By the time he was three, he could count to a hundred.**
> A los tres años ya sabía contar hasta cien.
> **She asked if he could open the door for her.**
> Preguntó si le podía abrir la puerta.

• •

peticiones formales en el presente:

> **Could I leave a message please?** ¿Podría dejar un recado, por favor?

posibilidad expresada en el presente:

> **I don't know where John is; I suppose he could be at Anne's.**
> No se dónde está John; supongo que estará en casa de Anne.

indignación/reproche:

> **You could have warned me!**
> ¡Podías haberme avisado!

14.2 may

Sus significados incluyen: autorizaciones y peticiones formales:

> **May I use your telephone please?**
> ¿Puedo usar su teléfono, por favor?
>
> **You may not leave the examination hall until I give the sign.**
> No pueden salir del aula de examen hasta que les haga la seña.

posibilidad:

> **We may get an extra day's holiday.**   **They may have left.**
> Puede que tengamos un día más de vacaciones.   Puede que se hayan ido.

14.2.1 might

Sus significados incluyen: posibilidad:

> **We might get a pay rise.**
> A lo mejor nos suben el sueldo. (es poco probable)

Se usa también en pasado:

> **He was afraid he might have missed the train.**
> Temía que quizá había perdido el tren.

(*Might* se diferencia de *may* en que a menudo la posibilidad que expresa es más remota que la que expresa *may*.)

autorizaciones y peticiones formales:

> **Do you think I might have another whisky?**
> ¿Crees que podría tomar otro whisky?

indignación/reproche:

> **You might have phoned!**
> ¡Podías haber llamado!

14.3 shall

Para ver cómo se expresa el futuro con *shall*, véase 11.2.6.1. *Shall* se puede usar para expresar: peticiones o consejos:

> **Where shall we put the shopping?**
> ¿Dónde ponemos la compra?

propuestas o sugerencias:

> **Shall we meet outside the station?**
> ¿Qué te parece si nos vemos en la entrada de la estación?

14.3.1 should

Should es el pasado de *shall*; y también se utiliza para expresar:

Numbers / Números

zero	0	cero		
one (first)	1	uno (primero)		
two (second)	2	dos (segundo)		
three (third)	3	tres (tercero)		
four (fourth)	4	cuatro (cuarto)		
five (fifth)	5	cinco (quinto)		
six (sixth)	6	seis (sexto)		
seven (seventh)	7	siete (séptimo)		
eight (eighth)	8	ocho (octavo)		
nine (ninth)	9	nueve (noveno)		
ten (tenth)	10	diez (décimo)		
eleven (eleventh)	11	once (undécimo)		
twelve (twelfth)	12	doce (duodécimo)		
thirteen (thirteenth)	13	trece (decimotercero)		
fourteen (fourteenth)	14	catorce (decimocuarto)		
fifteen (fifteenth)	15	quince (decimoquinto)		
sixteen (sixteenth)	16	dieciséis (decimosexto)		
seventeen (seventeenth)	17	diecisiete (decimoséptimo)		
eighteen (eighteenth)	18	dieciocho (decimoctavo)		
nineteen (nineteenth)	19	diecinueve (decimonoveno)		
twenty (twentieth)	20	veinte (vigésimo)		
twenty-one (twenty-first)	21	veintiuno (vigésimo primero)		
twenty-two (twenty-second)	22	veintidós (vigésimo segundo)		
twenty-three (twenty-third)	23	veintitrés (vigésimo tercero)		
twenty-four (twenty-fourth)	24	veinticuatro (vigésimo cuarto)		
twenty-five (twenty-fifth)	25	veinticinco (vigésimo quinto)		
thirty (thirtieth)	30	treinta (trigésimo)		
thirty-one (thirty-first)	31	treinta y uno (trigésimo primero)		
forty (fortieth)	40	cuarenta (cuadragésimo)		
fifty (fiftieth)	50	cincuenta (quincuagésimo)		
sixty (sixtieth)	60	sesenta (sexagésimo)		
seventy (seventieth)	70	setenta (septuagésimo)		
eighty (eightieth)	80	ochenta (octogésimo)		
ninety (ninetieth)	90	noventa (nonagésimo)		
a/one hundred (hundredth)	100	cien (centésimo)		
two hundred (two hundredth)	200	doscientos (ducentésimo)		
three hundred (three hundredth)	300	trescientos (tricentésimo)		
five hundred (five hundredth)	500	quinientos (quingentésimo)		
seven hundred (seven hundredth)	700	setecientos (septingentésimo)		
nine hundred (nine hundredth)	900	novecientos (noningentésimo)		
a/one thousand (thousandth)	1000	mil (milésimo)		
a/one million (millionth)	1,000,000	un millón (millonésimo)		